AN EXHAUSTIVE CONCORDANCE

OF THE
BOOK OF MORMON
DOCTRINE AND COVENANTS
AND
PEARL OF GREAT PRICE

Compiled by
R. GARY SHAPIRO

Hawkes Publishing Inc.
3775 South 500 West
(P.O. Box 15711)
Salt Lake City, Utah 84115
Phone (801) 262-5555

Copyright 1977
Hawkes Publishing Inc.
All Rights Reserved

ISBN 0-89036-085-5

Typesetting by R. Gary Shapiro

Lithographed in the United States of America
PUBLISHERS PRESS
Salt Lake City, Utah

PREFACE

The concordance lists alphabetically all words exactly as they appear in the sacred text. The various forms of the same word are given separately. There follows, for all but eighty-nine words, an individual context entry for each occurrence of a word with its location in the scriptures. The references are given by book, chapter, and verse in the order in which they appear in the triple combination.

The indexed word in each context entry is abbreviated to its initial letter, followed by a period (.). All capitalization, punctuation, and italics found in the original text are otherwise preserved in the individual context entries.

The title page and thirty chapter headings from the Book of Mormon are included in this work because they are translations from the plates and not modern compositions. The headings included for this reason are: 1Ne 1; 2Ne 1; Jac 1; En; Jar; Om; WM; Mos 1, 9, 23; Al 1, 5, 7, 9, 17, 21, 36, 38, 39, 45; He 1, 7, 13; 3Ne 1, 11; 4Ne; Mrm 1; Eth 1; Mro 1, 9.

Also included are the Official Declaration, the explanations of the Facsimiles of the Book of Abraham, and the Articles of Faith.

By placing the following eighty-nine words in a separate appendix, the size of the concordance is reduced 60%, while providing full reference information for 99% of the 7800 words in the triple combination: a, all, also, am, an, and, are, art, as, at, be, been, but, by, came, can, come, did, do, even, for, from, had, has, hath, have, he, him, his, I, if, in, into, is, it, let, me, my, no, not, now, O, of, on, one, or, our, out, shall, shalt, should, so, that, the, thee, their, them, then, there, these, they, things, this, those, thou, thus, thy, to, unto, up, upon, us, verily, was, we, were, what, when, wherefore, which, who, whom, will, with, would, ye, yea, you, your.

The appendix cites, without context entries, every occurrence of the above eighty-nine words. An index of numbers that appear in the sacred text as digits instead of words is included at the back of the appendix.

The concept of a concordance originated among Bible scholars during the thirteenth century. The preparation of concordances, however, was tedious and time consuming. Five hundred monks, for instance, helped with the first concordance of the Latin Vulgate. Dr. James Strong's *Exhaustive Concordance* of the King James translation was first issued in 1894 after a hundred men had worked on it for thirty years.

The present work is a concordance of approximately the same amount of scripture as the Old Testament. Using conventional methods, its compilation could conceivably have taken twenty years. With the use of today's computer technology, however, the work was completed in four years.

I am grateful to my sister Gloria, my devoted wife Deborah, and many others who have helped in countless ways to make this work possible.

R. Gary Shapiro

ABBREVIATIONS

T Pg	Title page
1Ne	First Nephi
2Ne	Second Nephi
Jac	Jacob
En	Enos
Jar	Jarom
Om	Omni
WM	Words of Mormon
Mos	Mosiah
Al	Alma
He	Helaman
3Ne	Third Nephi
4Ne	Fourth Nephi
Mrm	Mormon
Eth	Ether
Mro	Moroni
DC	Doctrine and Covenants
OD	Official Declaration
Mses	Moses
Abr	Abraham
Fac	Facsimile
JS	Joseph Smith
AoF	Articles of Faith
Hd	Heading

AN EXHAUSTIVE CONCORDANCE

A: *see in the APPENDIX.*

AARON: *see also JOHNSON, Aaron.*
their names were Ammon, and A.,	Mos	27:34
A. thy son should be our king		29: 2
A. had gone up to the land of		29: 3
A. take upon him the kingdom;		29: 3
the city which was called A.	Al	8:13
for behold, thy brother A., and		20: 2
An account of the preaching of A.,		21:hd
behold A. took his journey towards		21: 1
A. came to the city of Jerusalem,		21: 4
as A. entered into one of their		21: 5
Now A. said unto him:		21: 7
Now A. began to open the scriptures		21: 9
A. and a certain number of his		21:13
account of A. and his brethren;		22: 1
And A. said unto the king:		22: 4
And A. answered him and said		22: 7
And now when A. heard this,		22: 8
And A. said unto him:		22:10
when A. saw that the king would		22:12
A. did expound unto him the		22:13
A. did expound all these things		22:14
after A. had expounded these things		22:15
But A. said unto him:		22:16
when A. had said these words,		22:17
O God, A. hath told me that		22:18
also A. and his brethren standing		22:19
durst not lay their hands on A.		22:20
might slay A. and his brethren.		22:21
when A. saw the determination of		22:22
because of A. and his brethren.		22:24
they were pacified towards A.		22:25
that A. and his brethren should		22:26
the account of Ammon and A.,		22:35
Ammon, or A., or Omner, or Himni,		23: 1
A. and his brethren went forth		23: 4
the king consulted with A. and		23:16
the words which A. and his		25: 6
Ammon, and A., and Omner, and		25:17
his brother A. rebuked him,		26:10
and also the joy of A., of Omner,		27:19
with Ammon and A., and his		27:25
Therefore he took Ammon, and A.,		31: 6
yea, Ammon, and A., and Omner,		31:32
city of Moroni and the city of A.,		50:14
joining the borders of A. and		50:14
had a king, and his name was A.;	Mrm	2: 9
Amnigaddah was the son of A.	Eth	1:15
A. was a descendant of Heth,		1:16
And Heth begat A., and Aaron		10:31
A. dwelt in captivity all his days;		10:31
as have fled to the army of A.	Mro	9:17
gift, which is the gift of A.;	DC	8: 6
this gift of A. to be with you.		8: 7
I confer the Priesthood of A.,		13: 1
be called and ordained even as A.;		27: 8
I shall give unto him, even as A.,		28: 3
they be literal descendants of A.		68:15
be literal descendants of A.		68:16
firstborn among the sons of A.		68:16
and the firstborn of A.		68:18
when no literal descendant of A.		68:19
And a literal descendant of A.,		68:20
a priesthood also upon A. and		84:18
to continue with the house of A.		84:27
confirmed upon A. and his sons.		84:30
also the sons of A. shall offer an		84:31
the sons of Moses and of A. shall		84:32
the sons of Moses and of A.		84:34
is called the Priesthood of A.,		107:13
conferred upon A. and his seed,	DC	107:13
be a literal descendant of A.		107:16
descendant of A. can be found,		107:17
a literal descendant of A.;		107:69
is a literal descendant of A.		107:70
not a literal descendant of A.,		107:73
a literal descendant of A. has		107:76
over the Priesthood of A.		107:87
of my Father, as was A.,		132:59
I confer the Priesthood of A.,	JS	2:69

AARONIC
the Melchizedek and A.	DC	107: 1
the A. or Levitical Priesthood.		107: 6
of the lesser, or A. Priesthood,		107:20
He said this A. Priesthood had	JS	2:70
ordained him to the A. Priesthood,		2:71

ABANDON
Therefore they did a. their design	He	4:19
and a. myself to destruction	JS	2:16

ABANDONED
a. their design in marching into	Al	52: 2
he a. his designs and returned		52:17

ABASE
Let him therefore a. himself	DC	124:114

ABASED
that exalteth himself shall be a.,	DC	101:42
as thou hast a. thyself thou		112: 3

ABASETH
that a. himself shall be exalted.	DC	101:42

ABASING
while others were a. themselves,	Al	4:13

ABATED
And the famine a.;	Abr	2: 5

ABEL
if he would murder his brother A.	He	6:27
And from Enoch to A., who	DC	84:16
conceived and bare his brother A.	Mses	5:17
A. hearkened unto the voice of		5:17
And A. was a keeper of sheep,		5:17
A. he also brought of the		5:20
the Lord had respect unto A.,		5:20
Lord, neither to A., his brother,		5:26
thy brother A. into thine hands.		5:29
Cain talked with A., his brother.		5:32
Cain rose up against A.,		5:32
Where is A., thy brother?		5:34
his brother A., for the sake of		5:50
me another seed, instead of A.,		6: 2
like unto his brother A.		6: 3

ABHOR
teach them to a. such wickedness	Al	37:29

ABHORRENCE
upon sin save it were with a.;	Al	13:12
with the greatest a.;		27:28

ABHORREST
the land that thou a. shall be	2Ne	17:16

ABHORRETH
to him whom the nation a.,	1Ne	21: 7
Behold, my soul a. sin,	2Ne	9:49

ABIDE

ABIDE
a. upon him in the form of a dove.	1Ne	11:27
were obliged to a. by the laws	Al	1: 1
this people must a. by the law.		1:14
go with them, and a. with them,		17: 9
who may a. the day of his coming,	3Ne	24: 2
of the Lord did not a. in us;	Mrm	2:26
may be and a. in you forever.	Eth	12:41
be, and a. with you forever.	Mro	9:26
of my coming, if he a. in me,	DC	35:18
shall a. the day of my coming;		35:21
not purified shall not a. the day.		38: 8
he be taken, if he a. in me.		43: 3
the fire, but shall a. the day.		45:57
you may a. the day of his coming,		61:39
man a. the presence of God,		67:12
to a. the presence of God now,		67:13
that it may a. in your hearts,		88: 3
who is not able to a. the law of		88:22
cannot a. a celestial glory.		88:22
he who cannot a. the law of a		88:23
cannot a. a terrestrial glory.		88:23
he who cannot a. the law of a		88:24
cannot a. a telestial glory;		88:24
he must a. a kingdom which is		88:24
shall a. the power by which it is		88:26
and willeth to a. in sin,		88:35
who a. not in those conditions		88:39
A. ye in the liberty wherewith		88:86
as he continueth to a. in me		97: 4
you will a. in my covenant,		98:14
if ye will not a. in my covenant		98:15
before me, and a. in my word,		112:22
found worthy to a. among you.		119: 5
can a. the day of his coming,		128:24
and if ye a. not that covenant,		132: 4
shall a. the law which was		132: 5
must and shall a. the law,		132: 6
these angels did not a. my law;		132:17
and if ye a. in my covenant,		132:19
except ye a. my law ye cannot		132:21
neither do they a. in my law.		132:25
a. and cleave unto my servant		132:54
will not a. this commandment		132:54
if she a. not in my law.		132:54
will not a. this commandment,		132:55
who receive and a. in my law.		132:64
shalt a. in me, and I in you;	Mses	6:34
it is given to a. in you;		6:61
for a season a. upon my face?		7:48

ABIDETH
the truth a. forever and ever.	DC	1:39
a. forever with the priesthood		84:18
a. the law of a celestial kingdom,		88:25
a. not by law, but seeketh to		88:35
in sin, and altogether a. in sin,		88:35
truth a. and hath no end;		88:66
Parley P. Pratt, for he a. in me.		97: 3
he that a. not this law can		132:27

ABILITY
step forward and use their a. in	DC	134: 8

ABINADI
among them whose name was A.;	Mos	11:20
when A. had spoken these words		11:26
the words which A. had spoken		11:27
Who is a., that I and my people		11:27
command you to bring A. hither,		11:28
hearts against the words of A.,		11:29
A. came among them in disguise,		12: 1
A., go and prophesy unto this my		12: 1
many things did A. prophesy		12: 8
that A. should be cast into prison;		12:17
And now A. said unto them:		12:25
But now A. said unto them:		12:33
Now A. said unto them,		12:37
after A. had spoken these words		13: 5
after A. had made an end of these		13:25
And now A. said unto them:		15: 1
after A. had spoken these words		16: 1
when A. had finished these sayings,		17: 1
the words which A. had spoken,	Mos	17: 2
which A. had testified against them;		17: 2
he would not be angry with A.,		17: 2
all the words which A. had spoken.		17: 4
should surround A. and take him;		17: 5
A., we have found an accusation		17: 7
Now A. said unto him:		17: 9
when A. had said these words,		17:20
began to teach the words of A.		18: 1
the words of A. fulfilled, which		20:21
did mourn for the death of A.;		21:30
which had been spoken by A.		21:30
they teach them the words of A.;		24: 5
he that believed the words of A.		24: 9
the words alone of my servant A.		26:15
delivered by the mouth of A.?	Al	5:11
words of A. were brought to pass,		25: 9
And now A. was the first that		25:11
fulfilling of all the words of A.,	Mrm	1:19

ABINADOM
I, A., am the son of Chemish.	Om	1:10
I am Amaleki, the son of A.		1:12

ABISH
women, whose name was A.,	Al	19:16

ABLE
the Lord is a. to deliver us,	1Ne	4: 3
the Lord is a. to do all things		7:12
the Lord was a. to make them known		11: 1
more than we are a. to bear.		16: 1
I am a. to do mine own work;	2Ne	27:20
I am a. to do mine own work.		27:21
a. to speak and the world was,	Jac	4: 9
why not a. to command the earth,		4: 9
God was a. to preserve our records,	En	1:15
is a. to interpret the language	Mos	8:11
men that were a. to bear arms,		10: 9
not a. to withstand his blows,	Al	1: 9
as many as were a. to take up		53:16
as many as were a. to use a		55:10
language, we are not a. to write.	3Ne	5:18
art a. to show forth great power,	Eth	3: 5
whoso was not a. to pay taxes		10: 6
no power shall be a. to take it	DC	8: 8
be a. to withstand the evil day,		27:15
that ye may be a. to stand.		27:15
a. to quench all the fiery darts of		27:17
For I am a. to make you holy,		60: 7
he that is a., let him return it		60:11
a. to go up to the land of Zion		61:16
a. to cast the soul down to hell.		63: 4
that which he is a. to bear,		64:20
a. to abide the presence of God		67:13
may be a. to bear his presence		76:118
you yourselves are not a. to fill.		84:107
shall the body be a. to stand?		84:109
who is not a. to abide the law of		88:22
and shall not be a. to stand.		88:89
as fast as ye are a. to receive		111:11
not a. to build a house unto me.		124:30
without being a. to decide		130:16
of a.-bodied and expert men,		136: 7
I have not been a. to learn who		OD
so as to be a. to speak,	JS	2:18
to be a. to endure all things.	AoF	13

ABLE-BODIED: *see ABLE and BODIED.*

ABLOM
to a place which was called A.,	Eth	9: 3

ABOARD
got a. of their vessels or barges,	Eth	6: 4

ABODE
present time in your places of a.,	DC	48: 1
him, and a. in my law;		132:37
of heaven, and a. upon him.	Mses	6:26
Behold mine a. forever.		7:21
And there shall be mine a.,		7:64

ABOLISH   3   ABOUNDING

ABOLISH
And the idols he shall utterly a.   2Ne 12:18

ABOLISHED
my righteousness shall not be a.   2Ne 8: 6

ABOLISHMENT
of the desolation and utter a.   DC 84:114

ABOMINABLE
a church which is most a.	1Ne	13: 5
this great and a. church;		13: 6
this great and a. church.		13: 8
foundation of a great and a. church,		13:26
most a. above all other churches,		13:26
the great and a. church,		13:28
kept back by that a. church,		13:32
kept back by that a. church,		13:34
that great and a. church,		14: 3
that great and a. church,		14: 9
poured out upon the great and a.		14:15
harlots, which is the great and a.		14:17
the blood of that great and a.		22:13
great and a. church, shall tumble		22:14
to that great and a. church,	2 Ne	6:12
out of thy grave like an a. branch,		24:19
that great and a. church,		28:18
which sin appeareth very a.	Jac	2: 5
yea, and a. unto God.		2: 5
that such things are a. unto him		2:21
which thing was a. before me,		2:24
was a. in the sight of the Lord.	Mos	11: 2
were a. in the sight of the Lord		23: 9
most a. above all sins save	Al	39: 5
of the wicked and a. traditions	He	15: 7
those wicked and a. robbers.	3Ne	3:11
secret, and a. combinations,		5: 6
which combination is most a. and	Eth	8:18
And the great and a. church,	DC	29:21

ABOMINATION
wickedness and a. before him.	1Ne	14: 4
rid you from this iniquity and a.	Jac	2:16
whoredoms are an a. before me;		2:28
waxed strong in iniquity and a.;	Al	13:17
an a. in the sight of the Lord;		39: 5
a. which was among them;	He	4:11
a. which has come among you;		7:25
and a. of their fathers,	4Ne	1:39
of their wickedness and a.	Mrm	3:11
this great a. of the Lamanites,	Mro	9: 9
whose delight is in so much a.		9:13
the desolation of a. in the	DC	84:117
the desolation of a. which		88:85
see the a. of desolation,	JS	1:12
shall the a. of desolation,		1:32
were an a. in his sight;		2:19

ABOMINATIONS
for I have seen thine a.!	1Ne	1:13
their wickedness and their a.;		1:19
idleness and all manner of a.		12:23
church, which is the mother of a.,		14: 9
church, which is the mother of a.;		14:10
because of the wickedness and a.		14:12
mother of a. did gather		14:13
belonged to the mother of a.,		14:16
darkness, and of murders, and of a.	2Ne	10:15
their doings were doings of a.		25: 2
iniquity and all manner of a.		27: 1
wickedness and a. of the people.		27: 8
of pride, and wickedness, and a.,		28:14
of their wickedness and a.		28:17
concerning your wickedness and a.,	Jac	2:10
because of the wickedness and a.		2:31
and the a. of his people.	Mos	3: 7
view of their own guilt and a.,		3:25
because of our iniquities and a.		7:20
them of their wickedness and a.,		7:26
for I have seen their a.,		11:20
them in their iniquities and a.		12: 1
because of their iniquities and a.		12: 7
may discover the a. of this people		12: 8
the iniquities and a. of his people;	Mos	28:15
Noah, his wickedness and his a.,		29:18
wickedness and a. of his people.		29:18
such a. should come upon you.		29:24
Yea, all his iniquities and a.,		29:36
of their wickedness and their a.;	Al	4: 3
strong in wickedness and their		21: 3
and all their wickedness and a.,		37:21
work secret murders and a.;		37:22
and their wickedness and a.		37:23
their secret works and their a.;		37:25
to light all their secrets and a.,		37:25
their secret a. have been		37:26
their agreements in their secret a.;		37:27
and their murders and their a.		37:29
wickedness and a. and murders;		37:29
of their wickedness and a.		37:29
their whoredoms, and their a.,		50:21
and a. of the Nephites,	He	1:hd
and all manner of a.		3:14
their wickedness and their a.,		6:24
the works of darkness and a.		6:28
and grow in wickedness and a.,		6:34
of your wickedness and a.!		7:27
know of the wickedness and a.		9:23
because of the wickedness and a.		13:14
for the wickedness and a. which		13:15
because of the wickedness and a.		13:16
of their wickedness and their a.		13:17
wax strong in wickedness and a.;	3Ne	2: 3
forsake all their sins, and their a.,		5: 3
unto their wickedness and a.;		7:15
because of their iniquity and a.		9: 2
hide their iniquities and their a.		9: 5
to hide their wickedness and a.		9: 7
to hide their wickedness and a.		9: 8
their wickedness and their a.		9:10
wickedness and a. might be hid		9:11
of their wickedness and their a.		9:12
and whoredoms, and of secret a.;		16:10
whoredoms, and of your secret a.,		30: 2
from all your wickedness and a.,		30: 2
of all the wickedness and a.;	Mrm	2:18
of their wickedness and a.,		2:18
wickedness and a. has been		2:18
of their wickedness and their a.		2:27
whoredoms, and all manner of a.;		8:31
do ye build up your secret a.		8:40
with his whoredoms and a.	Eth	10: 7
their secret society and wicked a.		11:22
and a. had prepared a way for		14:25
their sins, and wickedness, and a.	Mro	9:15
of their iniquities and their a.	DC	3:18
and full of wickedness and a.;		10:21
as I live, for a. shall not reign.		29:21
their a. shall be made manifest		35: 7
because of wickedness and a.;		45:12
have seen a. in the church		50: 4
great church, the mother of a.,		88:94
is kindled against their a.		97:24
band and of all their secret a.,		117:11
your follies, and by all your a.,		124:48
these a. were had from Cain;	Mses	5:25
and their works were a.,		5:52
in their own a. have they		6:28

ABOUND
if iniquity shall a. cursed	2Ne	1: 7
doth a. most plentifully.	Jac	2:12
they did a. in the grace of God.	Mos	27: 5
will always a. in good works.	Al	7:24
wax cold, and iniquity shall a.	DC	45:27
in me; otherwise ye could not a.		88:50
and if it be in you it shall a.		88:66
if these things a. in them		107:31
let thy love a. unto all men,		112:11
And because iniquity shall a.,	JS	1:10
because iniquity shall a.,		1:30

ABOUNDING
always a. in good works,	Mos	5:15
always a. in good works,	Eth	12: 4

ABOUT

ABOUT

my brethren were a. to return	1 Ne	3:14
gird on his armor a. my loins.		4:19
the sword girded a. my loins.		4:21
was a. to flee from before me		4:30
as I cast my eyes round a.,		8:13
they did cast their eyes a.		8:25
I also cast my eyes round a.,		8:26
Lord can bring a. great things.		16:29
I was a. to build a ship,		17:17
at this day a. to be destroyed;		17:43
and were a. to worship me,		17:55
we were a. to be swallowed up		18:15
a. to be brought down to lie low		18:18
they were a. to be swallowed up		18:20
Lift up thine eyes round a.		21:18
in bringing a. his covenants		22:11
I am encircled a. eternally	2 Ne	1:15
to bring a. his eternal purposes		2:15
I am encompassed a., because of		4:18
compass yourselves a. with sparks,		7:11
concerning the regions round a.;		25: 6
have camped against them round a.,		26:15
to bring a. the restoration of		30: 8
I will prune it, and dig a. it,	Jac	5: 4
he pruned it, and digged a. it,		5: 5
should be digged a., and pruned,		5:11
Let us prune it, and dig a. it,		5:27
and I have digged a. it,		5:47
and dig a. the trees,		5:63
dig a. them, and prune them,		5:64
and pruned it, and dug a. it,		5:76
know that thou goest a. much,		7: 6
as he was a. to give up the ghost,		7:21
went a. among the people of Nephi,	En	1:19
wandering a. in the wilderness		1:20
a short skin girdle a. their loins		1:20
I am a. to lie down in my grave;	Om	1:30
a. to deliver up the record	WM	1: 1
they pitched their tents round a.,	Mos	2: 5
their tents round a. the temple,		2: 6
and am a. to yield up this mortal		2:26
I am a. to go down to my grave,		2:28
that he cast his eyes round a.		4: 1
a. four hundred and seventy-six		6: 4
and the land round a.		7:21
I set guards round a. the land,		10: 2
my spies out round a. the land		10: 7
a leathern girdle a. their loins.		10: 8
look over all the land round a.		11:12
vineyards round a. in the land;		11:15
sent guards round a. the land		11:17
Lord bringeth a. the restoration		15:24
king Noah was a. to release him,		17:11
and went a. privately among		18: 1
a. two hundred and four souls;		18:16
a. four hundred and fifty souls.		18:35
that he was a. to overpower him,		19: 5
and was a. to get upon the tower		19: 6
cast his eyes round a. towards		19: 6
so much concerned a. his people		19: 8
people as he was a. his own life;		19: 8
were a. to take the priests also		19:21
they were a. to return to the land		19:22
set guards round a. the land,		19:28
borders of the land round a.		21: 2
should watch the land round a.,		21:20
went round a. the land of Shilom		22:11
while tilling the land round a.,		23:25
guards round a. the land of Helam,		23:37
throughout the land round a.		27: 2
going a. to destroy the church		27:10
did go a. secretly with the sons		27:10
going a. rebelling against God,		27:11
round a. through all the land,		27:32
he keepeth his guards a. him;		29:22
had gone a. among the people,	Al	1: 3
which was girded a. their loins,		3: 5
armor, which was girded a. them,		3: 5
a. three thousand five hundred		4: 5
encircled a. by the bands of death,		5: 7
of hell which encircled them a.,		5: 9
a. to set my back towards this		8:24

was a. to deliver up the kingdom,	Al	10:19
were heard by the people round a.;		12: 2
encircle you a. with his chains,		12: 6
thing which I was a. to explain.		12:22
encircled a. by the pains of hell.		14: 6
questioned them a. many words;		14:18
all the region round a. Sidom,		15:14
in all the region round a.,		16:15
Encircle the flocks round a. that		17:33
therefore he was a. to return out		18:12
they were a. to take his body and		19: 1
contended with many a. the word.		21:11
Middoni unto the regions round a.		21:13
and in all the land round a.		21:21
were in all the regions round a.,		22:27
and round a. on the borders of		22:27
round a. on the wilderness side;		22:29
Nephi, and the wilderness round a.		22:34
in all the land round a.,		24: 1
to bring a. this great work.		26: 3
were encircled a. with everlasting		26:15
are encircled a. with the matchless		26:15
and we were a. to turn back,		26:27
set round a. the land of Jershon,		28: 1
the borders round a. the land of		28: 1
Why do ye go a. perverting the		30:22
many travels round a. the land		30:32
and he doth carry you a.,		30:42
And yet do ye go a., leading		30:45
and went a. from house to house		30:56
did go a. from house to house,		30:58
which they knew nothing a.		31:22
he turned him a., his face		32: 6
by merely casting a. your eyes		33:21
ye would not cast a. your eyes,		33:21
then cast a. your eyes and begin		33:22
to bring a. the bowels of mercy,		34:15
and bringeth a. means unto men		34:15
brought a. the great and eternal		34:16
plan of redemption be brought a.		34:31
For I went a. with the sons of		36: 6
encircled a. by the everlasting		36:18
to bring a. his great and eternal		37: 7
and bringeth a. the salvation of		37: 7
this bringeth a. the restoration		40:22
could not be brought a., only on		42:13
of mercy could not be brought a.		42:15
to bring a. the plan of mercy,		42:15
thus God bringeth a. his great		42:26
thus cometh a. the salvation		42:26
which was girded a. their loins;		43:20
round a. in the wilderness,		43:22
round a. in the wilderness,		43:24
Moroni placed spies round a.,		43:28
and encircled the Lamanites a.		43:35
turned them a. and began to		43:36
they were a. to shrink and flee		43:48
armies of Moroni encircled them a.,		43:52
encircled a. by the Nephites,		43:53
they were all a. to be destroyed,		44:19
girded on his armor a. his loins;		46:13
their armor girded a. their loins,		46:21
banks of earth round a.		48: 8
walls of stone to encircle them a.,		48: 8
round a. their cities and the		48: 8
yea, all round a. the land.		48: 8
had cast up dirt around a.		49: 2
a ridge of earth round a. them,		49: 4
city in all the land round a.;		49:13
which had been dug round a.,		49:18
were a. fifty who were wounded,		49:24
heaps of earth round a. all		50: 1
of a man, round a. the cities.		50: 2
built upon the timbers round a.;		50: 3
round a. every city in all the land.		50: 6
and in the land round a.		50: 9
But he kept his men round a.,		52: 6
by casting up walls round a.		52: 6
and strengthen the cities round a.,		52:10
a ditch round a. the land,		53: 3
the city of Bountiful round a.		53: 4
a. to take their weapons of war,		53:14
they were a. to break the oath		53:14

ABOUT ABOVE

round a. the city Gid.	Al	55:25	driven a. as chaff before the wind.	Mrm	5:16
to encircle them a. by night,		55:29	behold, they are led a. by Satan,		5:18
were a. to break the covenant		56: 7	as a vessel is tossed a. upon the		5:18
that we kept spies out round a.,		56:22	around a. the hill Cumorah;		6: 4
were a. to fall into the hands of		56:50	be encompassed a. by the floods.	Eth	3: 2
Lamanites had turned them a.,		56:53	encompassed a. by many waters		6: 7
and from the land round a.,		57: 6	number a. twenty and two souls;		6:16
we did camp round a. the city		57: 9	he was a. to put him to death,		7:18
were a. to enter the city by night.		57:10	they were a. to slay him also;		8: 6
as they were a. to overpower us.		57:18	and in all the countries round a.		9:35
of our army were a. to give way		57:20	And I was a. to write more,		13:13
a. to perish for the want of food.		58: 7	saw that he was a. to fall		15: 7
sent out their spies round a. us		58:14	were a. to flee for their lives;		15:28
a. to fall upon us with the sword,		58:18	marvelous work is a. to come forth	DC	4: 1
people, in all the land round a.		59: 2	marvelous work is a. to come forth		6: 1
and from the land round a.,		59: 6	marvelous work is a. to come forth		11: 1
were a. to perish with hunger,		60: 9	marvelous work is a. to come forth		12: 1
there are thousands round a.		60:22	marvelous work is a. to come forth		14: 1
in number a. four thousand who		62:17	may bring a. my righteous purposes		17: 4
round a. in the borders of the		62:34	bring a. my righteous purposes		17: 9
encircled a. in the borders by		62:34	run a. longer as a blind guide?		19:40
a. to flatter away those people	He	1: 7	your loins girt a. with truth,		27:16
as he was a. to do this, behold,		1: 8	and in the regions round a.		30: 4
a. to go forth against all the land.		1:22	and in that region round a.,		30:10
would attack the cities round a.		1:26	go forth into the regions round a.,		44: 3
parts round a. by the borders.		1:26	in those regions round a.,		48: 3
an army round a. to head them		1:28	in the regions round a. them;		52:39
and in all the regions round a.,		3:31	in all the regions round a.,		57: 6
land of Zarahemla and round a.		5:19	gospel in the regions round a.;		58:46
were encircled a. as if by fire,		5:23	in those regions round a. where		66: 5
encircled a. with a pillar of fire,		5:24	world in the regions round a.,		71: 2
were a. to tumble to the earth;		5:27	churches in the regions round a.,		73: 1
were a. to tumble to the earth;		5:31	preach in the regions round a.		73: 4
as if it were a. to divide asunder.		5:33	glory of the Lord shone round a.		76:19
he turned him a., and behold,		5:36	encompasseth them round a.		76:29
that when they cast their eyes a.,		5:43	and mine angels round a. you,		84:88
saw that they were encircled a.,		5:43	also should travel round a. and		84:112
yea, they were encircled a.;		5:44	all things are round a. him;		88:41
there were a. three hundred souls		5:49	and is round a. all things;		88:41
all the regions round a.		5:50	place, in the regions round a.;		100:3
great cities which are round a.,		7:22	be opened in the regions round a.		100:3
multitudes who were scattered a.		10:12	wet watchmen round a. them,		101:45
were a. to perish by famine,		11: 7	may overlook the land round a.,		101:45
was a. to return to his own land.		13: 2	and built a hedge round a.,		101:46
which are in the land round a.,		13:16	and built the hedge round a.,		101:53
encircled a. by the angels of		13:37	in the region round a. the land		101:70
he did go a. spreading rumors		16:22	and the counties round a.,		101:71
who were a. to be destroyed	3Ne	1:11	can stay in the region round a.,		105:20
Satan did go a., leading away		2: 3	who dwell in the regions round a.		105:23
a. to be smitten down by it,		2:19	the adjoining counties round a.		105:28
should be built round a. them,		3:14	and the regions round a.;		106:1
be placed as guards round a.		3:14	and thy glory be round a. them,		109:22
girded a. after the manner of		4: 7	judgements thou art a. to send,		109:38
had a lamb-skin a. their loins,		4: 7	not yourselves a. your debts,		111:5
lay siege round a. the people of		4:16	Concern not yourselves a. Zion,		111:6
were a. to perish with hunger.		4:20	and in the regions round a.;		111:7
carried a. by the temptations of		6:17	stakes in the regions round a.,		115:18
which was a. to be administered		6:29	had been hanged a. their necks,		121:22
as if it was a. to divide		8: 6	I am a. to call upon them to		124:6
for a. the space of three hours;		8:19	I am a. to restore many things		127:8
in a. the space of three hours		8:19	I am a. to give unto you;		132:3
round a. the temple which was		11: 1	unto the regions round a.		133:9
conversing a. this Jesus Christ,		11: 2	a. five o'clock p.m., by an		135:1
they cast their eyes round a.,		11: 3	In a. four years after my	JS	2: 3
he cast his eyes round a. on		15: 1	words and a contest a. opinions.		2: 6
any parts of that land round a.		16: 1	that it was a. to be fulfilled.		2:40
he looked round a. again on		17: 1	with me a. the plates,		2:42
he cast his eyes round a. again		17: 5	a. my father's family,		2:61
upon the ground round a. him,		17:12	father's family, and a. myself.		2:61
and encircled those little ones a.,		17:24			
they were encircled a. with fire;		17:24	ABOVE		
a. two thousand and four hundred		17:25	a. that of the sun at noon-day.	1Ne	1: 9
encircled a. as if it were by fire;		19:14	choice a. all other lands.		2:20
things shall be a. to take place		21: 1	a. all that I ever before tasted.		8:11
Behold, I was a. to write them,		26:11	desirable a. all other fruit.		8:12
I was a. to write the names of		28:25	desirable a. all other fruit.		8:15
in all the lands round a.	4Ne	1: 1	in the air, high a. the earth.		8:26
And a. the time that Ammaron	Mrm	1: 2	yea, even a. all.		11: 6
(I being a. ten years of age,		1: 2	the tree which is precious a. all.		11: 9
when ye are a. twenty and four		1: 3	fair a. all other virgins.		11:15
for the space of a. four years,		1:12	the most desirable a. all things.		11:22
shall be a. to prepare to return		3:17	abominable a. all other churches,		13: 5
were a. to overthrow the land,		4:23	abominable a. all other churches;		13:26
that the Father may bring a.,		5:14			

ABOVE

a. all other nations,	1 Ne 13:30
choice a. all other lands,	13:30
mine afflictions were great a. all,	15: 5
desirable a. all other fruits;	15:36
which is choice a. all other lands;	2 Ne 1: 5
God unto me, a. all other lands	10:19
shall be exalted a. the hills,	12: 2
A. it stood the seraphim;	16: 2
depths, or in the heights a.	17:11
my throne a. the stars of God;	24:13
I will ascend a. the heights	24:14
that I rule in the heavens a.	29: 7
was choice unto me a. all other	Jac 5:43
most precious a. all other fruit.	5:61
in it a. that of the world.	En 1:26
distinguished a. all the people	Mos 1:11
spirit may join the choirs a.	2:28
and in earth, who is God a. all.	5:15
which were a. all the other seats,	11:11
likeness of any thing in heaven a.	12:36
of things which are in heaven a.,	13:12
not esteem one flesh a. another,	23: 7
shall not think himself a. another;	23: 7
not esteeming himself a. his	Al 1:26
Minon, a. the land of Zarahemla,	2:24
been favored a. every other nation,	9:20
not be tempted a. that which ye	13:28
Lamoni said: Is it a. the earth?	18:31
which was high a. the head,	31:13
is sweet a. all that is sweet,	32:42
is white a. all that is white,	32:42
and pure a. all that is pure;	32:42
most abominable a. all sins	39: 5
it were a. the cloud of darkness,	He 5:29
might be lifted up one a. another;	6:17
both a. the earth and beneath,	14:21
both a. the earth and beneath.	14:22
was a. all the wickedness of	3 Ne 9: 9
of their hearts a. all nations,	16:10
a. all the people of the whole	16:10
shall make them mighty a. all,	20:27
praises with the choirs a.,	Mrm 7: 7
which is choice a. all the earth?	Eth 1:38
is choice a. all the lands of	1:42
was choice a. all other lands,	2: 7
is choice a. all other lands;	2:10
a land choice a. all other lands.	2:15
whether it was a. the water or	6:10
abominable and wicked a. all,	8:18
combinations shall get a. you,	8:23
was choice a. all other lands;	9:20
that was choice a. all lands,	10:28
a choice land a. all other lands,	13: 2
dear and precious a. all things,	Mro 9: 9
it is sacred and cometh from a.	DC 6:10
which I give unto you are a. all	18:45
and white a. all other whiteness;	20: 6
shall be greater signs in heaven a.	29:14
shown forth in the heavens a.,	45:40
possess that which is a. another,	49:20
lurketh beneath, and not from a.	58:33
blessed even a. measure,	58:61
crowned with blessings from a.,	59: 4
the Lord, rule in the heavens a.,	60: 4
Behold, I am from a.,	63:59
which cometh from a. is sacred,	63:64
tempted a. that which he is able	64:20
righteous cometh down from a.	67: 9
hands of the a. named Presidency.	68:14
may stand independent a. all	78:14
hath brought down Zion from a.	84:100
a. all things, and in all things,	88:41
a. all things, clothe yourselves	88:125
in the ground or a. the ground.	89:16
most precious, things that are a.,	101:34
The a.-named councilors were	102: 4
appointing the a.-named councilors	102: 5
of the a.-named councilors,	102: 6
one of the a.-named councilors,	102: 8
according to the form a. written.	102:13
a. the brightness of the sun;	110: 3
them in love a. many others,	112:11
and a. all, if the very jaws	122: 7
The a. offices I have given unto	DC 124:143
believes the a. statement and	128: 4
then shall they be a. all,	132:20
which were a. the firmament,	Mses 2: 7
which may fly a. the earth	2:20
shalt be cursed a. all cattle,	4:20
a. every beast of the field;	4:20
which are in the heavens a.,	6:63
earth, both a. and beneath:	6:63
I will bless thee a. measure,	Abr 2: 9
is a. or greater than that upon	3: 5
because it standeth a. the earth	3: 5
shall be another fact a. them,	3: 8
time of one planet a. another,	3: 9
and there be one a. the other,	3:16
be greater things a. them;	3:16
be two things, one a. the other,	3:17
and the moon be a. the earth,	3:17
planet or a star may exist a. it;	3:17
for I rule in the heavens a.,	3:21
waters which were a. the expanse;	4: 7
that they may fly a. the earth	4:20
The a. translation is given	Fac 2:12
characters a. his head.	3: 2
as written a. the hand.	3: 4
the characters a. his hand.	3: 5
a. the brightness of the sun,	JS 2:16
standing a. me in the air,	2:17
the Personages who stood a. me	2:18
the a.-mentioned twenty-first of	2:29
arms also, a little a. the wrist;	2:31
his legs a little a. the ankles.	2:31
of it was visible a. the ground,	2:51

ABOVE-MENTIONED: see ABOVE and MENTIONED.

ABOVE-NAMED: see ABOVE and NAMED.

ABRAHAM

come unto the God of A.,	1 Ne 6: 4
the Lord made to our father A.,	15:18
yea, even A., Isaac, and Jacob;	17:40
the God of A., and of Isaac,	19:10
unto A., saying: In thy seed	22: 9
Look unto A., your father,	2 Ne 8: 2
saith the Lord, who redeemed A.,	27:33
and that I covenanted with A.	29:14
even as it was accounted unto A.	Jac 4: 5
the God of A., and Isaac, and	Mos 7:19
the God of A. and Isaac and	23:23
with A., with Isaac, and with	Al 5:24
to sit down with A., Isaac, and	7:25
to whom A. paid tithes;	13:15
even our father A. paid tithes	13:15
the Lord God, the God of A.,	29:11
except it was the God of A.,	36: 2
to sit down with A., and Isaac,	He 3:30
his days even to the days of A.	8:16
behold, A. saw of his coming,	8:17
A. not only knew of these things,	8:18
were many before the days of A.	8:18
that even since the days of A.	8:19
May the God of A., and the God	3 Ne 4:30
with your fathers, saying unto A.:	20:25
covenant which he made with A.,	20:27
covenant which he made unto A.	Mrm 5:20
the God of A., and the God of	9:11
God made with their father, A.	Eth 13:11
and Isaac, and A., your fathers,	DC 27:10
also lived in the days of A.,	84:13
A. received the priesthood from	84:14
and of Aaron and the seed of A.,	84:34
and Jacob, and Isaac, and A.,	98:32
chastened and tried, even as A.,	101: 4
of Israel, and of the seed of A.,	103:17
didst give to A., their father.	109:64
dispensation of the gospel of A.,	110:12
with A. at his right hand,	124:19
I said unto A. concerning the	124:58
servants A., Isaac, and Jacob,	132: 1
A. received all things,	132:29
A. received promises concerning	132:30

ABRAHAM — ABUSED

as touching A. and his seed,	DC 132:30
yours also, because ye are of A.,	132:31
the promise was made unto A.;	132:31
and do the works of A.;	132:32
Father, which he made unto A.	132:33
God commanded A., and	132:34
gave Hagar to A. to wife.	132:34
Was A., therefore, under	132:35
A. was commanded to offer his	132:36
A., however, did not refuse,	132:36
A. received concubines, and	132:37
my Father, with A. your father.	132:49
as I accepted the offering of A.	132:50
to prove you all, as I did A.,	132:51
as I was with A., thy father,	132:57
administered unto A. according	132:65
commanded A. to take Hagar	132:65
with A., Isaac, and Jacob,	133:55
the God of A. and of Isaac	136:21
from the days of Adam to A.,	136:37
from A. to Moses, from Moses	136:37
I, A., saw that it was needful	Abr 1: 1
A., Abraham, behold, my name is	1:16
A., behold, my name is Jehovah,	1:16
up his hand against thee, A.,	1:17
I, A., took Sarai to wife,	2: 2
A., get thee out of thy country,	2: 3
I, A., and Lot, my brother's	2: 6
I, A., departed as the Lord had	2:14
I, A., was sixty and two years	2:14
I, A., built an altar in the land	2:17
I A., arose from the place of	2:20
And I, A., journeyed, going	2:21
I, A., concluded to go down into	2:21
I, A., told Sarai, my wife,	2:25
And I, A., had the Urim and	3: 1
Now, A., these two facts exist,	3: 6
I, A., talked with the Lord,	3:11
A., I show these things unto	3:15
the Lord had shown unto me, A.,	3:22
A., thou art one of them;	3:23
I, A., saw that it was after	5:13
A. fastened upon an altar.	Fac 1: 2
offer up A. as a sacrifice.	1: 3
A. in Egypt.	1:10
revealed from God to A.,	2: 2
Seth, Noah, Melchizedek, A.,	2: 3
Holy Ghost unto A.,	2: 7
A. sitting upon Pharaoh's	3: 1
Signifies A. in Egypt	3: 3
referring to A., as given in	3: 3
A. is reasoning upon the	3: 6

ABRIDGED
a. the record of my father	1Ne 1:17

ABRIDGING
a. the account of the people of	Mro 1: 1

ABRIDGMENT
Wherefore, it is an a.	TPg
An a. taken from the Book of	TPg
a. of the record of my father,	1Ne 1:17
an a. from the plates of Nephi,	WM 1: 3
therefore I write a small a.,	Mrm 5: 9
or an a. of the account of Nephi.	DC 10:44

ABROAD
which sheddeth itself a.	1Ne 11:22
a., who are of my people,	21: 1
and began to scatter a.	Mos 27: 6
and they were scattered a. upon	28:17
even to them that are scattered a.	Al 13:22
should be scattered a. and slain,	25:12
were slain and scattered a.	28: 2
the saying went a. in the church	45:19
was a proclamation sent a.	He 9: 9
be smitten and scattered a.,	15:12
scattered a. upon all the face of	3Ne 5:24
was noised a. among the people	19: 2
was noised a. concerning Jesus;	19: 3
scattered a. upon the face of	20:13
from going a. unto the world	DC 45:72
from going a. unto the world	DC 45:72
which have gone a. in the earth	50: 1
Satan is a. in the land,	52:14
servants who are a. in the earth	69: 5
at home, things which are a.;	88:79
The high priests, when a.,	102:24
This council of high priests a. is	102:28
or located high priests a.	102:29
or traveling high priests a.,	102:30
concerning my churches a.	105: 8
have spread lying reports a.,	109:29
send it a. among all nations,	112: 1
a. among all nations.	112:16
scattered a. in all the world;	115: 3
of the earth scattered a.	124: 3
those who are scattered a.,	124:35
different stakes scattered a.;	124:134
you to send my word a.,	126: 3
and declared these things a.,	Mses 5:53
the saying a. in the land:	6:36
the saying a. among the people,	6:54
at home, and sometimes a.,	JS 2:55

ABSENCE
while in the a. of Moroni	Al 53: 8
in the a. of the elder or priest.	DC 20:56
the long a. of your spirits	45:17
in case of the a. of one or both	102:11

ABSENT
act in the place of a. councilors.	DC 102: 7
and in case he himself is a.,	102:11

ABSTAIN
forbiddeth to a. from meats,	DC 49:18

ABUNDANCE
honey in a., and provisions	1Ne 18: 6
wherefore, we were blessed in a.	18:24
and we did reap again in a.	2Ne 5:11
ores, which were in great a.	5:15
for the a. of milk they shall give	17:22
and made wine in a.;	Mos 11:15
testified of their iniquity in a.	26: 9
having a. of all things whatsoever	Al 1:29
and a. of flocks and herds,	1:29
and also a. of grain, and of gold,	1:29
and a. of silk and fine-twined	1:29
They did raise grain in a.,	He 6:12
did they lay up in store in a.,	4Ne 1:46
and that he might have in a.	DC 49:19
which a. is multiplied unto them	70:13
the a. of the manifestations of	70:14
sufficient, yea, even an a.,	101:75
of the a. which I have made,	104:18
blossom, and to bring forth in a.?	117: 7

ABUNDANT
according to thy a. mercy	Al 18:41

ABUNDANTLY
you have obtained more a.	Jac 2:13
out his Spirit more a. upon you?	Mos 18:10
if he have more a. he should	18:27
he should impart more a.;	18:27
and began to raise grain more a.,	21:16
labor a. with their hands.	Al 24:18
we have labored a. to build	32: 5
them who shall have more a.	Eth 12:35
wanted more a. among them	DC 61:32
Yea, even more a.,	70:13
it shall be given more a.,	71: 6
Let the waters bring forth a.	Mses 2:20
the waters brought forth a.	2:21
the waters to bring forth a.	Abr 4:20
waters were to bring forth a.	4:21

ABUSE
where personal a. is inflicted or	DC 134:11

ABUSED
that ye have ever a. his laws?	Mrm 9: 3

ABUSES / ACCORDING

ABUSES
and a. put upon them by — DC 123: 1

ABYSS
I was in the darkest a.; — Mos 27:29
yea, even in the darkest a., — Al 26: 3

ACCEPT
who would a. of the kingdom. — Mos 28:10
I will a. none of your sacrifices — 3Ne 9:19
did not a. the offering of peace, — DC 98:35
and will a. their offering; — 105:19
O Lord, to a. of this house, — 109: 4
a. the dedication of this house — 109:78
I will not a. it at their hands. — 115:15
a. it at the hands of my people. — 115:16
which I a. if he continue, — 124:17
but to a. of their offerings. — 124:49
and I will a. of his offerings, — 124:75
Will I a. of an offering, saith — 132: 9
a. his declaration concerning — OD
for his offering thou didst a. — Mses 5:38

ACCEPTABLE
In an a. time have I heard — 1Ne 21: 8
for none is a. before God, — Mro 7:44
Wherefore his writing is not a. — DC 63:56
rendereth every man a., — 72:17
offer an a. offering and sacrifice — 84:31
proclaim the a. year of the Lord, — 93:51
Your prayers are a. before me; — 124: 2
and cannot be a. to me, only — 124:30
baptisms shall be a. unto me. — 124:31
dead shall not be a. unto me; — 124:32
dead cannot be a. unto me; — 124:33
not a. unto me, saith the Lord. — 124:35
your washings be a. unto me, — 124:37
offer unto me an a. offering, — 124:104
for your offering is a. to me. — 126:1
but offered an a. sacrifice, — Mses 6: 3

ACCEPTANCE
thine honor and to thy divine a.; — DC 109:10

ACCEPTATION
a house, worthy of all a., — DC 124:23
which shall be worthy of all a. — 128:24

ACCEPTED
the same is a. of me if he — DC 52:15
Otherwise he shall not be a. — 72:18
whose offering I have a., — 96: 6
they are a. of me. — 97: 8
Lord, have a. of her offering; — 97:27
were then asked whether they a. — 102: 4
they all answered that they a. — 102: 4
behold, I have a. this house, — 110: 7
I a. the offerings of those whom — 124:51
I a. the offering of Abraham — 132:50
doest well, thou shalt be a. — Mses 5:23

ACCESS
have free a. to their houses, — Al 23: 2

ACCLAMATIONS
throne, with a. of praise, — DC 109:79

ACCOMPANYING
the testimony a. their decision, — DC 102:26
the evidences and statements a. it. — 102:33

ACCOMPLISH
way for them that they may a. — 1Ne 3: 7
power whereby they could a. — 5: 8
he prepareth a way to a. — 9: 6
means whereby they can a. — 17: 3
canst not a. so great a work. — 17:19
that he might a. his designs — Al 47:16
that he should a. his design; — He 2: 9
thou mayest a. the thing which — DC 5:34
Satan shall a. his evil design — 10:14
they shall not a. their evil designs — 10:31
be patient until you shall a. it. — 11:19
and a. the things which I have — 38:40

thing he needeth to a. the work — DC 43:13
that ye may a. this work — 45:72
to a. the residue of the work — 58:58
you may a. the commandments — 78:13
a. all things pertaining to Zion. — 105:37
a. the work that my servant — 124:79

ACCOMPLISHED
in the wilderness until we have a. — 1Ne 3:15
having a. his designs thus far, — Al 48: 2
he had a. his design, — 48: 3
that we soon a. our desire; — 57: 8
thus we had a. our designs — 57:12
have a. the work of translation. — DC 10:34
a. and finished the will of him — 19: 2
until ye have a. the thing which — 45:72
spoken of in this chapter to be a.? — 77:10
They are to be a. in the — 77:10
When are the things to be a., — 77:13
They are to be a. after the — 77:13
And until this be a., let not — 109:40
until I had a. by them what — JS 2:60

ACCOMPLISHING
hindered in a. those things — DC 90:27

ACCOMPLISHMENT
to the a. of his designs. — Al 43: 7

ACCORD
we should be led with one a. — 1Ne 10:13
they did cry out with one a., — 3Ne 11:16
all the multitude, with one a., — 17: 9
belong to you all with one a. — DC 104:62
might a. with the other; — 128:12
may a. one with another — 128:13

ACCORDANCE
So, in a. with this, — JS 2:14

ACCORDING
a. to the account of Nephi; — 1Ne 1:hd
I make it a. to my knowledge. — 1: 3
a. to the words of the prophets. — 2:13
a. to the law of Moses, — 4:15
a. to his commandments. — 4:17
all things a. to his will, — 7:12
a. to my faith which is in thee, — 7:17
a. to the multitude of his — 8: 8
a. to the own due time — 10: 3
a. to the word of the angel; — 12:19
bear record a. to the truth — 13:24
a. to the truth which is in God. — 13:25
a. to the plainness which is — 13:29
must come a. to the words — 13:41
a. to the captivity of the devil, — 14: 4
also a. to the justice of God, — 14: 4
a. to the captivity of the devil, — 14: 7
a. to the truth which is in the — 14:26
a. to the word of the angel. — 14:27
a. to the truth; — 16: 2
a. to the faith and diligence and — 16:28
a. to the faith and diligence which — 16:29
a. to the directions which — 16:30
a. to his will and pleasure. — 16:38
a. to the law of Moses; — 17:22
a. to the power of God — 17:29
a. to his word he did destroy — 17:31
a. to his word he did lead — 17:31
a. to his word he did do all things — 17:31
a. to the word which he — 17:54
a. to the word of the Lord, — 18: 4
a. to that which the Lord had — 18: 6
every one a. to his age; — 18: 6
a. to that which I have spoken; — 19: 5
which is in me, a. to the flesh, — 19: 6
a. to the words of the angel — 19: 8
a. to the words of the angel, — 19:10
a. to the words of Zenock, — 19:10
a. to the words of Neum, — 19:10
a. to the words of Zenos, — 19:10
a. to the words of the prophet — 19:16
a. to things which are spiritual, — 22: 1

ACCORDING

a. to the spirit and not the flesh?	1 Ne	22: 1	a. as the good shall grow,	Jac	5:66
children of men a. to the flesh		22: 2	a. to the strength thereof.		5:73
it cometh unto men a. to the flesh		22:18	a. to the commandments of		5:74
a. to the words of the prophet.		22:23	that I have done a. to my will;		5:75
must come a. to the flesh.		22:27	a. to that which I have spoken.		5:76
a. to the workings of the Spirit	2 Ne	1: 6	And a. to the power of justice,		6:10
a. to the commandments which		1: 7	a. to the power of the devil.		7: 4
a. to the will and captivity		1:18	a. to the best of my knowledge,		7:26
a. to that which is in God,		1:26	a. to their diligence in keeping	En	1:10
down his life a. to the flesh,		2: 8	thy brethren a. as I have said;		1:10
a. to the truth and holiness		2:10	grant unto thee a. to thy desires,		1:12
a. to the things which I have		2:17	a. to the covenant which he had		1:17
a. to that which is written,		2:17	unto them a. to their faith;		1:18
a. to the will of God,		2:21	a. to the truth which is in Christ.		1:26
a. to the commandments which		2:21	a. to the commandment of	Jar	1: 1
a. to the commandments which		2:26	a. to their faith.		1: 4
men are free a. to the flesh;		2:27	a. to the word of God,		1:10
a. to the captivity and power		2:27	a. to the writings of the kings,		1:14
a. to the will of his Holy Spirit;		2:28	a. to the commandments of		1:15
a. to the will of the flesh		2:29	a. to the commandments of	Om	1: 3
a. to the words of the prophet.		2:30	a. to the commandments of		1: 9
a. to the simpleness of their		3:20	a. to the generations;		1:11
a. to the words which I have		3:25	a. as the Lord had commanded		1:13
a. to the feelings of his heart		4:12	a. to his memory,		1:18
speak unto them, a. to his word;		4:14	a. to his judgments,		1:22
a. to the law of Moses.		5:10	a. to the workings of the Spirit	WM	1: 7
a. to that which is written.		5:12	in me to do a. to his will.		1: 7
a. to that which was in my		5:18	I make it a. to the knowledge		1: 9
a. to the commandments of		5:19	a. to the word of God		1:11
a. to the words of the angel		6: 9	they punished a. to their crimes;		1:15
a. to the words of the prophet,		6:14	been punished a. to their crimes;		1:16
a. to the holy judgment of God.		9:15	a. to the promises which the	Mos	1: 7
a. to the plainness of the truth		9:47	a. to the heed and diligence		1:16
be destroyed, a. to the flesh,		9:53	a. to the law of Moses.		2: 3
unto us a. to the flesh;		10: 2	every man a. to his family,		2: 5
a. to his will and pleasure.		10:22	and do a. to your own will,		2:21
if they speak not a. to this word,		18:20	only a. to the words which I		3:22
a. to the joy in harvest,		19: 3	every man a. to his works,		3:24
a. to the slaughter of Midian		20:26	a. to the words which king		4: 3
a. to the word which he hath		25: 3	every man a. to that which		4:13
a. to the spirit which is in me;		25: 4	every man a. to that which		4:26
a. to the plainness which hath		25: 4	temporally, a. to their wants.		4:26
a. to all that which Isaiah		25: 6	a. as he doth agree,		4:28
a. to my plainness;		25: 7	every one, a. to their families,		6: 3
a. to their iniquities;		25: 9	a. to that which his father had		6: 7
and a. to my prophecy		25:10	a. to his own will and pleasure,		7:33
a. to the words of the prophets,		25:19	every man a. to his age.		10: 9
a. to the words of the prophets,		25:19	of him a. to their works		16:10
a. to the will and pleasure of		25:22	a. to their own carnal wills		16:12
a. to the words which are written.		25:22	baptized him a. to the first,		18:15
we write a. to our prophecies,		25:26	every one a. to that which he		18:27
children of men a. to their faith.		26:13	a. to their needs and their wants.		18:29
a. to the combinations of		26:22	they should do a. to their desires.		21: 6
a. to the will of God,		27:13	a. to the desires of their enemies.		21:13
save it be a. to their faith.		27:23	I will go a. to thy command		22: 7
a. as the Spirit hath constrained		28: 1	a. as it was delivered to him		25:21
and judged a. to their works,		28:23	judge them a. to their crimes.		26:11
a. to mine own pleasure.		29: 9	judge a. to the sins which he		26:29
every man a. to their works,		29:11	a. to the commandments of God.		26:33
a. to that which is written.		29:11	a. to the word of the Lord.		26:34
a. to the plainness of my		31: 2	the word of God, a. to his sins,		26:39
a. to their language,		31: 3	be answered a. to their faith,		27:14
a. to the flesh he humbleth		31: 7	go and do a. to their request.		28: 8
into the water, a. to his word,		31:13	a. to the commandments of God,		28:11
a. to the commandments of		31:18	judge this people a. to our law;		29:11
a. to the plainness of the truth;		33: 5	a. to the commandments of God.		29:11
a. to the reigns of the kings.	Jac	1: 9	people a. to his commandments,		29:13
a. to the reigns of the kings;		1:11	have I punished a. to the law		29:15
a. to the reigns of the kings.		1:14	ye may be judged a. to the laws		29:25
a. to the responsibility which		2: 2	not judge you a. to the law		29:28
admonish you a. to your crimes,		2: 9	a. to the voice of the people.		29:29
a. to the strict commands of		2:10	to judge them a. to the law		29:39
truth a. to the plainness of		2:11	to judge them a. to the law;		29:41
a. to his will and pleasure?		4: 9	*a. to the record of Alma,*	Al	1:hd
resurrection, a. to the power of		4:11	judged a. to the crimes which		1:10
a. to the scriptures,		4:16	to die, a. to the law which has		1:14
nourished it a. to his word.		5: 5	to preach a. to their belief;		1:17
a. to the word of the Lord		5:10	every man a. to his strength.		1:26
and nourish it, a. to my words.		5:12	man a. to that which he had,		1:27
a. to his will and pleasure		5:14	a. to that which he had done,		1:33
every sort a. to its number.		5:31	who was executed a. to the law		2: 1
a. to that which I have said.		5:57	they knew that a. to their law		2: 3
a. to the strength of the good		5:65	every man a. to his mind,		2: 5

ACCORDING

captains, a. to their numbers. Al	2:13
a. to the mark which was set	3: 6
their rewards a. to their works,	3:26
a. to the spirit which they listed	3:26
this a. to the words of the spirit	3:27
let it be a. to the truth.	3:27
a. to their own will and pleasure.	4: 8
come a. to the spirit of prophecy;	4:13
a. to the will and power and	4:14
a. to the voice of the people,	4:16
a. to the laws which had been	4:16
a. to the wickedness and the	4:16
a. to the spirit of revelation	4:20
a. to the holy order of God,	5:hd
a. to his own record, saying:	5: 2
And a. to his faith there was	5:12
judged a. to the deeds which	5:15
a. to the commandments of God.	5:43
a. to the holy order of God,	5:44
a. to the spirit of prophecy	5:47
a. to the order of God,	6: 1
a. to the revelation of the truth	6: 8
a. to the spirit of prophecy	6: 8
a. to the testimony of Jesus	6: 8
a. to his own record.	7:hd
a. to the Spirit of God which	7: 5
things which are a. to his word.	7: 8
with mercy, a. to the flesh,	7:12
know a. to the flesh how to succor	7:12
people a. to their infirmities.	7:12
suffereth a. to the flesh that	7:13
a. to the power of his deliverance;	7:13
a. to the testimony of the Holy	7:16
a. to the Spirit which testifieth	7:26
a. to your faith and good works,	7:27
a. as he had before done in the	8: 1
a. to the holy order of God,	8: 4
a. to your tradition;	8:11
a. to the spirit of revelation and	8:24
a. to the spirit and power which	8:32
a. to the record of Alma.	9:hd
a. to the fierce anger of the Lord.	9:18
unto them, a. to their desires,	9:20
a. to that which they have been	9:28
a. to the power and deliverance	9:28
a. to the power and captivation	9:28
a. to the words which he spake.	10:11
a. to the spirit of prophecy	10:12
might be judged a. to the law,	10:13
prison, a. to the crime which	10:13
are spoken, a. to their truth?	10:25
they got gain a. to their employ.	10:32
wages a. to the time which	11: 1
judged the man a. to the law	11: 2
for his wages a. to his time	11: 3
is a. to the law which was given.	11: 3
of their silver, a. to their value.	11: 3
a. to the minds and the	11: 4
number, a. to their reckoning.	11: 4
their wages a. to their employ,	11:18
money a. to the suits which	11:20
it be a. to the Spirit of the Lord,	11:20
be judged a. to their works.	11:22
to be judged a. to their works,	11:41
a. to the power of his captivity.	11:44
a. to the spirit of prophecy.	12: 6
to be judged a. to their works?	12: 7
only a. to the portion of his word	12: 8
a. to the heed and diligence which	12: 9
to be judged a. to our works.	12: 9
a. to the power and captivity	12:12
subjected them a. to his will.	12:17
redeemed a. to God's justice;	12:17
a. to the word of God;	12:18
a. to their faith and repentance	12:22
a. to their wills and pleasures,	12:30
a. to the supreme goodness of	12:31
a. to his word in the last	12:32
therefore, a. to his word,	12:36
is prepared a. to his word.	12:36
a. to the foreknowledge of God,	12:37
with, and a. to, a preparatory	13: 3
a. to his foreknowledge of all	13: 3
	13: 7

a. to the holy order of God, Al	13:18
a. to that which they have spoken	13:26
a. to the spirit of prophecy	13:26
a. to the hardness of their	14:11
a. to the will of the Lord.	14:13
this people a. to your words.	14:24
give us strength a. to our faith	14:26
them power, a. to their faith	14:28
Yea, I believe a. to thy words.	15: 9
and heal him a. to his faith	15:10
a. to the record of Alma	17:hd
a. to the word and power of	17:17
a. to their several stations,	17:18
a. to his will and pleasure.	17:20
a. to the custom of the Lamanites.	17:25
slay him a. to their pleasure,	17:35
of an hour, a. to their time,	18:14
a. to my faith and desires	18:35
a. to thy abundant mercy	18:41
a. as the queen had desired	19: 7
shall be a. as thou hast said.	19: 9
arose, a. to the words of Ammon;	19:12
poured out a. to his prayers	19:14
be unto him a. to thy faith	19:23
the old king a. to his desire,	20:24
he may do a. to his own desires	20:24
their God a. to their desires,	21:22
might flee, a. to their desires.	22:34
the word a. to their desires,	23: 3
a. to the spirit of revelation and	23: 6
a. as he had suffered.	25:11
a. as their brethren had,	25:14
unto them a. to their prayers,	25:17
a. to the desires of their enemies.	27: 3
a. to the promises of the Lord,	28:11
a. to the promises of the Lord,	28:12
unto men a. to their desire,	29: 4
unto men a. to their wills,	29: 4
him it is given a. to his desires,	29: 5
a. to that which is just and true.	29: 8
may be done a. to my words,	29:17
of God, a. to the law of Moses;	30: 3
be judged a. to their crimes.	30:11
a. to the management of the	30:17
prospered a. to his genius,	30:17
conquered a. to his strength;	30:17
brought down a. to thy words.	30:23
and a. to your own desires;	30:27
do yoke them a. to their desires,	30:28
they did not do a. to their words,	30:28
only a. to law for our time.	30:33
struck dumb, a. to my words;	30:49
a. to the words of Alma.	30:50
statutes, a. to the law of Moses.	31: 9
was a. to the prayer of Alma;	31:38
be unto every man a. to his work.	32:20
only a. to that which is true	32:24
judgment day, a. to their works.	33:22
for a. to the great plan of the	34: 9
unto them a. to their wants.	35: 9
unto them a. to his own record.	35:16
Now this is a. to his word.	36:30
this people, a. as I have done,	37: 2
a. to that which the Lord doth	37:16
a. to the power of God,	37:28
them a. to their faith in God;	37:40
a. to the words which have been	40:15
and be judged a. to their works.	40:21
a. to the power and resurrection	41: 1
be judged a. to their works;	41: 3
a. to his desires of happiness,	41: 5
or good a. to his desires of good;	41: 5
to evil a. to his desires of evil;	41: 5
forever, a. to the word of God,	42: 2
Therefore, a. to justice,	42:13
to be judged a. to their works,	42:23
works, a. to the law and justice.	42:23
unto him a. to his deeds.	42:27
a. to the restoration of God.	42:28
unto you even a. to my words.	42:31
a. to the spirit of prophecy and	43: 2
worship God a. to their desires.	43: 9
placed his army a. to his desire,	43:33

ACCORDING

a. to the record of Helaman,	Al 45:hd
a. to the spirit of revelation	45:10
that he did a. to his desires,	46:32
he had power a. to his will with	46:34
a. to the commandments of	47: 8
for war, a. to their danger;	48:15
massacre them a. to their pleasure.	49: 7
thus it was a. to his desires.	49:15
a. to their pleasure and their	50: 5
Bountiful, a. to their pleasure.	50:11
to justice a. to their crime.	50:39
a. to the voice of the people.	51:16
a. to the power of their armies.	52:13
a. to their oath they would have	53:11
prisoners a. to your request,	54:20
give unto him a. to my words;	55: 3
You may do a. to your desires.	55:12
was a. to the design of Moroni.	55:16
the city Gid, a. to his desires,	55:26
a. to their faith it was done unto	57:21
a. to the goodness of God, and to	57:25
not strong, a. to our numbers,	58:15
a. to the fulfilling of his word.	60:16
it is a. to his commandments	60:28
a. the covenant which I have	60:34
a. to the Spirit of God, which is	61:15
a. to the faith which is in us.	61:17
a. to the desire of Pahoran,	62: 3
their trial, a. to the law,	62: 9
were executed a. to the law;	62: 9
speedily executed a. to the law.	62:10
was granted a. to their desires.	62:28
did bless them, a. to his word,	62:51
a. to the records of Helaman,	He 1:hd
a. to the records of his sons,	1:hd
a. to the record of Helaman	1:hd
a. to the voice of the people,	1: 8
a. to the voice of the people,	1:13
and it was a. to his right.	1:13
not frightened a. to his desire,	1:27
might be executed a. to the law.	2:10
to get gain, a. to their desire.	6: 8
not a. to the laws of their	6:24
a. to the laws of their wickedness,	6:24
a. as he can get hold upon	6:30
to rule and do a. to their wills,	7: 5
and do a. to their own wills	7: 5
condemned a. to the crime	8: 1
a. to the words of Jeremiah.	8:20
God come, a. to his prophecy?	8:20
ran and came a. as ye desired,	9:15
dead, a. to the words of Nephi.	9:15
a. as Nephi had said unto them.	9:37
a. to the words he did deny;	9:37
a. to the words he did confess.	9:37
done unto thee a. to thy word,	10: 5
a. to the wickedness of this	10: 6
a. to the words of Nephi.	11: 5
a. to the words which had been	11: 9
may be done a. to my words,	11:13
bless them a. to thy words	11:16
a. to his word the earth goeth	12:15
grace for grace, a. to their works.	12:24
of God, a. to the law of Moses.	13: 1
a. to the law of Moses.	15: 5
this is a. to the prophecy,	15:13
a. to the record of Helaman	16:25
a. as they had been spoken;	3Ne 1:15
a. to its proper order;	1:19
a. to the words of the prophets.	1:20
did appear, a. to the word.	1:21
a. to the words of the prophecy	1:26
a. to the words of Lachoneus.	3:16
themselves up a. to their wishes.	4:16
a. to the words of the prophets;	5: 2
a. to that which had been	5: 2
and punished a. to the law.	5: 5
a. to the record of Nephi,	5:10
that I, a. to the will of God,	5:14
be fulfilled a. to their faith,	5:14
which, a. to our language,	5:18
prospered them a. to his word.	5:22
lands, a. to their numbers,	6: 3
laws a. to equity and justice.	3Ne 6: 4
by ranks, a. to their riches	6:12
unto death, not a. to the law.	6:25
a. to the law which had been	6:26
were to be tried a. to the law.	6:27
be administered a. to the law.	6:29
tribes, every man a. to his family	7: 2
every one a. to his tribe;	7:11
tribes, every man a. to his family,	7:14
established a. to the minds of	7:14
a. to our record, and we know	8: 1
a. as I have commanded you	11:28
a. to the words which he spake.	23: 3
a. to the time and the will of	23: 4
did prophesy a. to thy words,	23:10
written a. as he commanded.	23:13
a. to the mercy, and the justice,	26: 5
a. to the words which Jesus	26: 8
a. to the power of the Father	27:15
be judged a. to their works.	27:15
a. to the judgment which I shall	27:27
a. to the will of the Father,	28: 7
a. to the record which hath been	28:18
blessed, a. to the word of Jesus.	28:23
would a. to the words of Christ,	28:33
unto the Gentiles a. to his word,	29: 1
a. to the word of Christ!	29: 7
a. to that which he hath sworn.	29: 8
of Nephi, a. to his record.	4Ne 1:hd
blessed a. to the multitude of	1:11
to kill Jesus, a. to his word.	1:31
a. to the prophecies and the	1:49
gone a. to the word of Ammaron,	Mrm 2:17
a. to the words of Ammaron.	2:17
a. to the love of God which was	3:12
a. to the manifestations of the	3:16
shall be judged a. to your works	3:18
a. to the words of the Lord,	4:12
a. to the commandment of the	5:13
be judged a. to your works;	6:21
a. to his justice and mercy.	6:22
a. to that which he hath	7:10
unto light, a. to the word of God;	8:16
a. to his works shall his wages be;	8:19
this record a. to our knowledge,	9:32
a. to our manner of speech.	9:32
a. to the prayers of all the	9:36
be answered a. to their faith;	9:37
a. to the word of the Lord the	Eth 1:33
a. to that which had been spoken	1:39
a. to the instructions of the	2:16
a. as thou hast directed me.	2:18
a. as the Lord had commanded.	2:21
may receive a. to our desires.	3: 2
a. to the commandment of the	4: 5
commanded me, a. to my memory;	5: 1
of Shule a. to his desires.	7:22
a. to that which he desired.	9:10
a. to the commandment of the	9:29
children of men a. to their faith;	12:29
a. to the will of the Lord.	Mro 1: 4
a. to the gifts and callings of	3: 4
a. to the commandments of	4: 1
a. to of his command,	7:30
a. to the power thereof;	7:32
saved, a. to the words of Christ,	7:38
faith in him a. to the promise.	7:41
a. to the knowledge which I have	9: 7
a. to the faith of the children of	10: 7
man severally, a. as he will.	10:17
only a. to the unbelief of the	10:19
a. to the words of Christ;	10:26
unto every man a. to his work,	DC 1:10
to every man a. to the measure	1:10
work, a. to my commandments,	6: 9
both have a. to your desires,	7: 8
a. to your faith shall it be done	8:11
a. to that which you desired	9: 1
a. to their faith in their prayers;	10:47
a. to their faith in their prayers	10:52
work, a. to my commandments,	11: 9
behold, a. to your desires,	11:17
yea, even a. to your faith	11:17

ACCORDING

added a. to that which is just	DC 11:23
you a. to my commandments.	15: 5
you a. to my commandments.	16: 5
a. to that which I have	18: 7
a. to that which is written;	18:29
a. to the words which are written.	18:30
a. to the power of the Holy Ghost	18:32
a. to the callings and gifts of	18:32
judging every man a. to his works	19: 3
this a. to the grace of our Lord	20: 4
power a. to the will of the father;	20:24
and a. to the revelations of John,	20:35
a. to the scriptures;	20:41
a. to the commandments and	20:45
a. to the gifts and callings of God	20:60
do a. to that which is written.	24:14
amite them a. to your words,	24:16
shall do even a. to this pattern.	24:19
a. as it shall be given thee by	25: 7
I will, a. to their faith.	25: 9
a. to the covenants of the in prayer a. to my command,	28:14
a. as it is spoken by the mouth	29: 6
I will, a. to mine own pleasure,	29:21
in me to do a. as it is written.	29:48
a. to the office wherewith I have	29:50
a. to the commandment	38:23
and receive a. to his wants.	42: 2
a. to that which I have said.	42:33
he that doeth a. to these things	42:55
a. to the laws of the land;	42:60
a. to the laws of the land.	42:79
a. to the law of God.	42:79
a. to the laws of man;	42:81
may be done a. to my law	44: 4
a. as the Lord will, suiting his	44: 6
a. to the conditions of the	46:15
asketh a. to the will of God;	46:15
every man a. to his family,	46:30
family, a. to his circumstances,	48: 6
church, a. to the laws and	48: 6
not a. to that which he has	48: 6
a. to that which shall be taught	49: 4
a. to the holy commandment,	49: 4
of man, a. to his creation	49:13
unto you, a. as ye have asked	49:17
be organized a. to my laws;	50: 1
equal a. to his family,	51: 2
a. to his circumstances and	51: 3
a. to the laws and covenants of	51: 3
a. to the laws of the land.	51: 4
a. to the wants of this people.	51: 6
a. as they shall agree;	51: 8
themselves a. to my laws.	51:11
are heirs a. to the covenant.	51:15
a. to the revelations and truths	52: 2
fruits, even a. to this pattern,	52:17
a. to men's faith it shall be done	52:18
of sins, a. to my word,	52:20
a. to commandments which	53: 3
a. to your labor in my vineyard.	53: 4
a. to that which they do;	53: 6
For a. to that which they do	56:12
a. to my commandments,	56:13
a. to the laws of the kingdom	57: 1
a. to the counsel of his own	58:18
moneys a. as the law directs.	58:20
a. to the knowledge which they	58:36
a. to my commandments,	58:56
this is a. to the law and	59: 1
them a. to their judgments	59:22
to do a. to judgment and	61:22
even a. to the pattern which	62: 8
let him do a. to wisdom.	63:21
reward thee a. to thy deeds.	63:44
a. to the will of the Lord	64:11
minister even a. to the first;	64:29
forgiven, a. to the covenants	68:14
a. to the laws of the kingdom	68:24
a. to that portion of Spirit and	70: 8
a. to the law every man that	71: 1
truth a. to the revelations	72:15
this a. to the commandment	75: 4
	76:51
judged a. to men in the flesh;	DC 76:73
be judged a. to their works,	76:111
receive a. to his own works,	76:111
a. to the laws of the Lord.	82:15
a. to his wants and his needs,	82:17
a. to the laws of my church,	82:21
a. to the laws of the land.	83: 3
a. to the Holy Priesthood	84: 6
a. to the oath and covenant	84:39
but to do a. to that which	84:57
A. to the election of grace,	84:99
lawful heirs, a. to the flesh,	86: 9
a. as his lord had commanded	88:60
a. to the decree which God hath	88:61
and a. to his own will.	88:68
judged a. to men in the flesh.	88:99
a. to the pattern given in the	88:141
forgiven thee, a. to thy petition,	90: 1
truth, a. to the commandments;	93:42
even a. to the prayer of faith;	93:52
a. to the pattern which I have	94: 2
a. to the pattern which shall be	94: 5
a. to the order of the priesthood,	94: 6
a. to the pattern which shall be	94: 6
a. to the pattern in all things	94:12
a. to the commandment, which I,	94:15
divided into lots, a. to wisdom,	96: 3
visit her a. to all her works,	97:26
rewardest him a. to his works	98:31
a. to mine everlasting gospel,	101:22
a. to the parable of the wheat and	101:65
a. as his work shall be;	101:65
a. to the laws and constitution of	101:77
a. to just and holy principles;	101:77
a. to the moral agency which I	101:78
a. to the law of heaven,	102: 4
a. to the grace of God	102: 4
a. to the dignity of his office	102:10
a. to the foregoing pattern,	102:12
a. to the form above written.	102:13
speak a. to equity and justice.	102:16
a. to the understanding which	102:19
a. to the former pattern written,	102:27
a. to the law of my gospel,	104:18
a. to the counsel of the order,	104:21
a. as my servant Gazelam	104:26
a. to the counsel of the order,	104:36
a. to that which shall be	104:81
a. to my commandments,	104:86
a. to the union required by the	105: 4
and justice for us a. to law,	105:25
a. to the laws of consecration	105:29
a. to the voice of the Spirit	105:40
a. to the covenants and	107:63
before him a. to the laws,	107:72
a. to the laws of the church.	107:79
a. to truth and righteousness.	107:84
is given a. to the covenants.	107:85
a. to the covenants.	107:89
it is a. to the vision showing	107:93
done a. to thy commandment.	109: 3
organized a. to thy laws,	109:15
a. to that which thou hast	109:41
every man a. as his work shall be.	112:34
a. to the pattern which I will	115:14
not a. to the pattern which I	115:15
a. to the pattern which I shall	115:16
a. as his works shall be.	121:25
A. to that which was ordained in	121:32
a. to the contract which he	124:115
in the books, a. to their works.	128: 6
in the books, a. to their works;	128: 7
be judged, a. to their own works,	128: 8
a. to the ordinance which God	128: 8
a. to the records which they	128: 8
a. to the decrees of the great	128: 9
a. to the planet on which they	130: 4
marry a wife a. to my word,	132:26
a. to mine appointment,	132:26
a. to the promises, and sit	132:37
given unto you a. to my word.	132:40
by word and a. to my law,	132:48
a. to my law and by my word,	132:59

ACCORDING 13 ACCOUNTED

a. to my commandment,	DC 132:63
unto him a. to my word;	132:65
unto Abraham a. to the law	132:65
upon them a. to his goodness,	133:52
and a. to his loving kindness,	133:52
this a. to the mind and will of	133:61
a. to the nature of the offense;	134: 8
punished a. to their criminality	134: 8
a. to the rules and regulations of	134:10
a. to the dividend of their	136: 8
made even a. to my word.	Mses 2:16
and made a. to my word.	3: 7
be unto thee a. to his desire.	5:23
would do a. to his commands.	5:30
a. to the pattern given by	6:46
hath all power a. to wisdom,	6:61
fled, even a. to his command;	7:13
a. to the appointment of God	Abr 1: 4
a. to its times and seasons in	3: 4
a. to the time appointed unto	3: 4
a. to the reckoning of Kolob.	3: 4
A. to all that which they had	5: 5
a. to the celestial time,	Fac 2: 1
a. to the measurement of this	2: 1
elect's sake, a. to the covenant,	JS 1:20
the elect a. to the covenant.	1:22
a. to the prophecy of Moses,	1:55
When, a. to arrangements,	2:60
a. to the dictates of our own	AoF 11

ACCORDINGLY

a. the people were gathered	Eth 6:20
the decision shall be altered a.	DC 102:21
and should be punished a.;	134: 5
A. a famine prevailed	Abr 1:30
A., as I had been commanded,	JS 2:54
I a. took it out of my pocket	2:65
and a. he had come to make	2:66
A. we went and were baptized.	2:71

ACCOUNT

An A. Written by THE HAND	TPg
An a. of Lehi and his wife	1Ne 1:hd
The a. of their sufferings.	1:hd
according to the a. of Nephi;	1:hd
I, Nephi, do not make a full a.	1:16
I shall not make a full a..	1:16
a. of my proceedings, in my days.	1:17
I make an a. of mine own life.	1:17
an a. of the creation of the world,	5:11
a. of all the things of my father,	6: 3
a. of the history of my people;	9: 2
I make a full a. of my people	9: 2
an a. engraven of the ministry	9: 3
an a. of the reign of the kings,	9: 4
give an a. upon these plates	10: 1
to proceed with mine a.,	10: 1
other plates, which gives an a.,	19: 4
a greater a. of the wars	19: 4
an a. of my making these plates	19: 5
An a. of the death of Lehi.	2Ne 1:hd
gave an a. of one Coriantumr,	Om 1:21
this small a. of the prophets,	WM 1: 3
An a. of his people, from	Mos 9:hd
and an a. of their baptism	21:35
An a. of Alma and the people	23:hd
he also read the a. of Alma	25: 6
give an a. of their proceedings	28: 9
it gave an a. of the people who	28:17
Now this a. did cause the people	28:18
this a. shall be written hereafter;	28:19
which are written in this a.	28:19
The a. of Alma, who was	Al 1:hd
An a. of the reign of the	1:hd
And also an a. of a war	1:hd
on a. of their exceeding faith	13: 3
on a. of their faith,	13: 4
on a. of the hardness of their	13: 4
on a. of their exceeding faith	13:10
on a. of his wickedness,	15: 3
An a. of the sons of Mosiah,	17:hd
on a. of a remarkable vision	19:16
An a. of the preaching of Aaron,	21:hd
we will return to the a. of Aaron	22: 1

again to the a. of Ammon and	Al 22:35
on a. of their fear to take up	27:23
on a. of their many murders	27:23
And this is the a. of Ammon	28: 8
And this is the a. of the wars	28: 9
an a. shall be given of their wars	35:13
an a. of his commandments,	35:16
on a. of their wickedness and	37:29
I return to an a. of the wars	43: 3
a. of the people of Nephi,	45:hd
on a. of some intrigue amongst	53: 8
thus ended the a. of Alma,	63:hd
An a. of the Nephites.	He 1:hd
An a. of their conversion.	1:hd
An a. of the righteousness of	1:hd
the a. which I have written.	2:14
the a. of the Lamanites and of	3:14
now I return again to mine a.;	3:17
but true a. was given by Nephi.	3Ne 5: 9
and proceed to give my a. of	5:19
an a. of his ministry shall	10:19
an a. of all the marvelous works	28:33
An a. of the people of Nephi,	4Ne 1:hd
a full a. of all the wickedness	Mrm 2:18
a full a. of their wickedness and	2:18
daring not to give a full a. of	5: 9
an a. of those ancient inhabitants	Eth 1: 1
I take mine a. from the twenty	1: 2
an a. from that time even to	1: 3
that he may get the full a.	1: 4
But behold, I give not the full a.,	1: 5
but a part of the a. I give,	1: 5
on this wise do I give the a.	1: 6
not make a full a. of these things	3:17
is there not an a. concerning	8: 9
the a. of the people of Jared,	Mro 1: 1
an a. of those things that you	DC 10:38
a more particular a. was given	10:39
the a. which is engraven upon	10:40
of the people in this a.	10:40
an abridgment of the a. of Nephi.	10:44
let him a. it of God;	50:34
which a. the fulness ye have not	63:21
an a. of this stewardship	70: 4
render an a. of his stewardship,	72: 3
an a. of their stewardship	72: 5
To take an a. of the elders	72:11
an a. shall be taken and	72:13
give an a. of his stewardship	72:16
shall give an a. unto the bishop	72:19
That every man may give an a.	104:12
But only an a. of this earth,	Mses 1:35
an a. of the vision which I had	JS 2:21
related the a. of the vision he	2:24
giving an a. of the former	2:34
I refer to his own a. of the	2:63

ACCOUNTABILITY

have arrived at the years of a.	DC 18:42
arrived unto the years of a.	20:71

ACCOUNTABLE

baptism unto those who are a.	Mro 8:10
begin to become a. before me;	DC 29:47
shall be made a. unto me,	42:32
may be a. for his own sins	101:78
should make every man a.,	104:13
he holds men a. for their acts	134: 1

ACCOUNTED

wherein is he to be a. of?	2Ne 12:22
even as it was a. unto Abraham	Jac 4: 5
a. of God worthy to receive.	DC 50:34
transgresses and is not a. worthy	51: 4
transgress and is not a. worthy	51: 5
is a. worthy to inherit the	72: 4
and be a. as wise stewards.	72:22
not be a. as a wise steward.	72:26
they are a. as a light thing,	90: 5
they are a. as equal with thee	90: 6
it shall be a. unto you as	98:24
are a. as the salt of the earth	101:39
be a. unto them for stock in	124:122
was a. unto him for righteousness.	132:36

ACCOUNTED 14 ACTS

ACCOUNTED
was a. unto him for righteousness, DC 132:37
and shall be a. thy seed, Abr 2:10

ACCOUNTS
the a. which have been given by 3Ne 5:16
the a. of their stewardships DC 69: 5
his a. approved in all things. 72:19

ACCURATE
qualified for taking a. minutes; DC 128: 3

ACCURSED
Let it be a., because of the He 12:18
behold, it shall be a. 12:18
Be thou a., that no man shall 12:19
thou shalt be a. forever— 12:20
word of the Lord, let him be a.; Eth 4: 8
deny these things, let him be a.; 4: 8
they shall be a., and shall DC 124:71

ACCUSATION
have found an a. against thee, Mos 17: 7
Not with railing a., that ye DC 50:33

ACCUSATIONS
with all manner of false a.; DC 122: 6

ACCUSE
that thereby I might a. you; Mos 2:15
might have wherewith to a. him; 12:19
and began to a. him, saying: 17:12
foremost to a. Amulek and Alma, Al 10:31
that they might a. him to death— He 9:19

ACCUSED
have a. him that he sought power 2Ne 1:25
who are a. of their brethren; Mos 26:11
the things whereof they were a., Al 10:12
The a., in all cases, has DC 102:15
to stand up in behalf of the a., 102:17
the accuser and the a. shall have 102:18
accuser and a. have spoken, 102:19
If thou art a. with all manner 122: 6

ACCUSER
the a. and the accused shall have DC 102:18
a. and accused have spoken, 102:19

ACCUSING
a. them of leading away the Al 30:31

ACKNOWLEDGE
he was caused, or rather did a., Al 1:15
and a. to our everlasting shame 12:15
a. your unworthiness before God 38:14
a. your faults and that wrong 39:13
Now tell us, and a. thy fault; He 9:20
a. the agreement which thou hast 9:20
and a. unto me the things that DC 5:28
Therefore, verily I a. him 81: 3
to a. that the kingdom of Zion is 105:32
a. that thou hast sanctified it, 109:13

ACKNOWLEDGED
and they were a. by the people; Al 1: 1
it has been a. by this people; 1:14
a. king throughout all the land, 47:35
a. presidents by the voice DC 102: 3
a. in his administration by the 102: 9

ACKNOWLEDGETH
the Christ, but a. that he is. Mro 10: 6

ACKNOWLEDGMENTS
with your offering and a., DC 124: 1
an acceptable offering, and a., 124:104

ACQUAINT
to a. him concerning the affairs of Al 58: 4

ACQUAINTANCE
form a. with men in this DC 111: 3

ACQUAINTED
of sorrows, and a. with grief; Mos 14: 3
the most a. with the strength of Al 48: 5
become a. with our secret works, 3Ne 3: 7
a. with the elder or priest, DC 20:84
is not a. with my voice, 84:52
become a. with all good books, 90:15
is a. with my native cheery JS 2:28

ACQUIRED
and I have also a. much riches Al 10: 4

ACRES
ten a. of vineyard shall yield 2Ne 15:10

ACROSS
even a. the many waters 1Ne 13:29
a. the river Laman. 16:12
carry thy people a. these waters. 17: 8
of the Lord a. the great waters, Om 1:16
a. that everlasting gulf of He 3:29
shall go forth a. this raging deep Eth 3: 3
bringing them a. the great deep 7:27
fathers brought a. the great deep? 8: 9
Jared and his brother a. the deep; 10: 2

ACT
neither to a. nor to be acted upon; 2Ne 2:13
both things to a. and things to be 2:14
man that he should a. for himself save 2:16
to a. for themselves and not to be 2:26
ye are free to a. for yourselves— 10:23
placing themselves in a state to a., Al 12:31
to a. according to their wills 12:31
even in the very a. of perishing 24:23
permitted to a. for yourselves; He 14:30
that ye may know how to a. and DC 43: 8
to a. upon the points of my law 43: 8
to a. in all holiness before me— 43: 9
let them a. upon this land 51:17
power, to move, to a., etc. 77: 4
how you may a. before me, 82: 9
has placed, it to a. for itself, 93:30
may bring to pass my strange a., 95: 4
how to a. concerning this matter, 96: 1
every man may a. in doctrine 101:78
proceed to bring to pass my a. 101:95
my act, my strange a., 101:95
a. in that office according to 102: 4
power to a. without seven of 102: 6
and capable to a. in the place of 102: 7
to a. in the name of the church. 102: 8
convenes to a. upon any case, 102:13
that you may know how to a. 103: 1
to a. in the name of the Lord, 107:34
they shall a. in the same office. 107:75
to a. in the office of bishop 107:76
to a. in the office in which he 107:99
by their own free will and a., 124:69
That he may a. in concert also 124:95
for how to a. I did not know, JS 2:12
in the a. of calling upon God, 2:30

ACTED
neither to act nor to be a. upon; 2Ne 2:13
to act and things to be a. upon. 2:14
and not to be a. upon, save it be 2:26
a. under the direction of Peter, JS 2:72

ACTING
a. no hypocrisy and no deception 2Ne 31:13
a. in the authority which I DC 68: 8

ACTIVE
a. in getting up and promoting JS 2: 6
who was very a. in the 2:21

ACTIVITY
and also for strength and a.; Al 53:20

ACTS
their secret a. shall be revealed, DC 1: 3

ACTS 15 ADDED

and reveal the secret a. of men,	DC 88:108	unto A., I, the Lord God, said:	Mses 4:23
and reveal the secret a. of man,	88:109	A. called his wife's name Eve,	4:26
men accountable for their a.	134: 1	Unto A., and also unto his wife,	4:27
also the third chapter of A.,	JS 2:40	A. began to till the earth,	5: 1
		A. knew his wife, and she bare	5: 2
ACTUAL		the sons and daughters of A.	5: 3
were a. descendants of Laman	Al 24:29	And A. and Eve, his wife,	5: 4
to any man by a. revelation,	DC 128: 9	And A. was obedient unto the	5: 5
to the power of some a. being	JS 2:16	of the Lord appeared unto A.,	5: 6
		And A. said unto him:	5: 6
ACTUALLY		the Holy Ghost fell upon A.,	5: 9
I had a. seen a light, and in	JS 2:25	A. blessed God and was filled,	5:10
I have a. seen a vision,	2:25	A. and Eve blessed the name	5:12
deny what I have a. seen:	2:25	And A. and Eve, his wife,	5:16
		And A. knew Eve, his wife,	5:16
ADAH		A. and his wife mourned before	5:27
the name of one being A., and	Mses 5:44	reveal it unto the sons of A.;	5:49
And A. bare Jabal; he was	5:45	things were confirmed unto A.	5:59
unto his wives, A. and Zillah:	5:47	A. hearkened unto the voice of	6: 1
		And A. knew his wife again,	6: 2
ADAM		A. glorified the name of God;	6: 2
and also of A. and Eve,	1Ne 5:11	recorded, in the language of A.,	6: 5
after A. and Eve had partaken	2Ne 2:19	Now this prophecy A. spake,	6: 8
if A. had not transgressed	2:22	book of the generations of A.,	6: 8
A. fell that men might be;	2:25	and called their name A.,	6: 9
who belong to the family of A.	9:21	A. lived one hundred and	6:10
fallen by the transgression of A.,	Mos 3:11	And the days of A., after he	6:11
as in A., or by nature, they fall,	3:16	all the days that A. lived	6:12
and has been from the fall of A.,	3:19	genealogy of the sons of A.,	6:22
could deny that A. should fall	3:26	I gave unto their father, A.	6:28
which ever were since the fall of A.,	4: 7	first of all we know, even A.	6:45
back until the creation of A.	28:17	Because that A. fell, we are;	6:48
A. did fall by the partaking of	Al 12:22	he called upon our father A.	6:51
if it had been possible for A. to	12:23	father A. spake unto the Lord,	6:53
and also the creation of A.	18:36	And the Lord said unto A.:	6:53
began from the creation of A.,	22:12	the Lord spake unto A., saying:	6:55
scriptures from the creation of A.,	22:13	for, in the language of A.,	6:57
from the days of A. down to the	40:18	the Lord had spoken with A.,	6:64
if A. had put forth his hand	42: 5	that A. cried unto the Lord,	6:64
by the fall of A.	He 14:16	father A. taught these things,	7: 1
the whole human family of A.;	Mrm 3:20	people which were the sons of A.;	7:22
Behold he created A., and by	9:12	mixture of all the seed of A.	7:22
and by A. came the fall of man.	9:12	on the first man, who is A.,	Abr 1: 3
of the world, and also of A.,	Eth 1: 3	reign, even in the reign of A.,	1:26
transpired from the days of A.	1: 4	appointed unto A. his reckoning.	5:13
the curse of A. is taken from	Mro 8: 8	a deep sleep to fall upon A.;	5:15
from the creation of A. even	10: 3	And A. said: This was bone	5:17
And also with Michael, or A.,	DC 27:11	and brought them unto A.	5:20
A., your father, whom I created.	29:34	whatsoever A. called every	5:20
A., being tempted of the devil—	29:36	A. gave names to all cattle,	5:21
behold, the devil was before A.,	29:36	for A., there was found an	5:21
that the devil tempted A., and	29:40	as revealed to A. in the	Fac 2: 3
unto A. and unto his seed,	29:42		
by the hand of his father A.,	84:16	**ADAM-ONDI-AHMAN**	
was instituted in the days of A.,	107:41	established the foundations of A.;	DC 78:15
From A. to Seth, who was	107:42	righteous, into the valley of A.,	107:53
was ordained by A. at the age	107:42	A., because, said he, it is the	116: 1
four months, by the hand of A.	107:44	on the mountains of A.,	117: 8
he met A. in journeying to	107:45	come up to the land of A.,	117:11
ordained by the hand of A.,	107:46		
ordained under the hand of A.,	107:47	**ADAM'S**	
ordained under the hand of A.;	107:48	previous to his (A.) death,	DC 107:42
sixty-five and A. blessed him.	107:48	and not for A. transgression.	AoF 2
ordained under the hand of A.	107:50		
previous to the death of A.,	107:53	**ADAPTED**	
and they rose up and blessed A.,	107:54	a. to the capacity of the weak	DC 89: 3
administered comfort unto A.,	107:55		
And A. stood up in the midst of	107:56	**ADD**	
the place where A. shall come	116: 1	do a. to their numbers daily.	He 15: 6
or the land where A. dwelt,	117: 8	can a. one cubit unto his stature?	3Ne 13:27
revealed from the days of A.	128:18		
from Michael or A. down to	128:21	**ADDED**	
the days of A. to Abraham,	136:37	was a. to his church.	Mos 18:17
of all men have I called A.,	Mses 1:34	and what a. more to his joy,	Al 17: 2
that they should come unto A.,	3:19	these things shall be a. unto you.	3Ne 13:33
whatsoever A. called every	3:19	then shall all things be a. thereto.	DC 11:22
A. gave names to all cattle,	3:20	be a. according to that which	11:23
as for A., there was not found	3:20	glory shall be a. to the kingdom	43:10
a deep sleep to fall upon A.;	3:21	this earth shall be a. unto him,	78:19
And A. said: This I know now	3:23	necessary shall be a. thereunto;	106: 3
A. and his wife went to hide	4:14	first estate shall be a. upon;	Abr 3:26
the Lord God, called unto A.,	4:15	have glory a. upon their heads	3:26
I, the Lord God, said unto A.:	4:17	and a. a caution to me,	JS 2:46

ADDING 16 ADMONITIONS

ADDING
neither a. to, nor diminishing	DC	20:35

ADDITION
and also an a. to our army,	Al	57: 6
daily an a. to their numbers,	He	11:25
And in a. to your testimony,	DC	5:11
in a. to the covenants and		68:13
in a. to the law which has		72: 9
in a. to the laws of the kingdom,		72:24
in a. to the laws of the church		83: 1
in a. to the church laws		107:59
In a. to these, he quoted the	JS	2:40

ADDITIONAL
a. light is shown upon the case,	DC	102:21
in case no a. light is given,		102:22
I have had a few a. views		128: 2

ADDRESS
to a. you in my language;	Al	7: 1

ADDRESSED
to have a. them from the stand	DC	127:10
the Personage who a. me said	JS	2:19

ADHERE
should a. to the word of God,	Al	60:34

ADIEU
may read my words. Brethren, a.	Jac	7:27

ADJOINING
in the a. counties round about.	DC	105:28
own place, but in the a. counties;		106: 2

ADJOURNED
After prayer the conference a.	DC	102:34

ADMINISTER
and a. relief to the sick	Jac	2:19
ye will a. of your substance unto	Mos	4:16
to a. the law at their times of	Al	10:14
did a. unto him in his tribulations,		15:18
or rather he did a. unto them,		17:18
insist that ye shall a. unto me;		22: 3
they did a. unto them according		35: 9
a. poison by degrees to Lehonti		47:18
a. of their wine to the Nephites,		55:30
did a. death unto all those who		57:19
except ye do a. unto our relief,		60:30
did a. that which was sacred unto	4Ne	1:27
Akish did a. unto them the oaths	Eth	8:15
to a. these oaths unto the people,		8:16
did a. that which was good unto		9:23
And to a. bread and wine—	DC	20:40
baptize, and a. the sacrament,		20:46
to baptize, a. the sacrament,		20:58
the elder or priest shall a. it;		20:76
this manner shall he a. it—		20:76
and a. to their relief that		38:35
to a. to those who have not,		42:33
to a. to the poor and the needy,		42:34
the needy and a. to their relief,		44: 6
appointed to a. spiritual things,		70:12
to a. in temporal things;		70:12
and to a. to their wants,		72:11
to a. the everlasting gospel;		77:11
if any man shall a. poison		84:71
to a. to their wants by		84:112
world, to a. in spiritual things.		107: 8
are to a. in spiritual things,		107:12
and to a. in outward ordinances,		107:20
may a. blessings upon the heads		124:21
a. unto him deadly poison;		124:98
she believe and a. unto him,		132:64
a. unto him according to my		132:65
as will a. the law in equity		134: 3
be ordained to a. the same;	Abr	1: 2
a. in the ordinances thereof.	AoF	5

ADMINISTERED
day when justice shall be a.	2Ne	9:46
a. unto them before his departure;	Al	17:18
he also a. unto them,		19:33
among them and a. unto them.		22:25
that no poison should be a.		55:32
and a. by the devil,	3Ne	6:28
to be a. according to the law.		6:29
Akish a. it unto his kindred	Eth	8:17
a. oaths after the manner of the		10:33
they a. it according to the	Mro	4: 1
ways that these gifts are a.;		10: 8
be a. in the following manner	DC	20:72
is to be a. by the president,		88:140
the Lord a. comfort unto Adam,		107:55
name alone salvation can be a.		109: 4
a. unto Abraham according to		132:65
was a. unto Cain by Satan;	Mses	5:49

ADMINISTERETH
a. the gospel and holdeth the	DC	84:19

ADMINISTERING
and a. to their relief,	Mos	4:26
a. the flesh and blood of Christ	Mro	4: 1
The manner of a. the wine—		5: 1
The manner of a. the wine—	DC	20:78
a. the gospel and the things of		72:14
receive it of the a. of angels		76:88
in a. spiritual things,		107:10
power in a. outward ordinances.		107:14
preaching and a. the gospel,		107:38
the a. of ordinances and		107:67
is in a. all temporal things;		107:68
in making laws and a. them,		134: 1
his own brother, in a. death,	Mses	6:15

ADMINISTRATION
to know the differences of a.,	DC	46:15
As also through your a. the		90: 7
through your a. they may		90: 9
through their a. the word		90: 9
by the a. of the Comforter,		90:11
and acknowledged in his a. by		102: 9
whether any a. is from God.		129: 9

ADMIT
thereof would only a. one person.	Al	31:13
Yea, I a. it may be termed a		40:15
as your circumstances will a.	DC	104:53
as the circumstances may a. of.		127: 1

ADMITTED
where they could be a.	Al	21:16

ADMITTING
concerning the a. their brethren,	Al	27:21

ADMONISH
a. you according to your crimes,	Jac	2: 9
And they did a. their brethren;	Mos	26:39
A. him in his faults, and also	DC	6:19
A. them sharply for my name's		112:12

ADMONISHED
And they were a. continually	Om	1:13
should be a. by the church.	Mos	26: 6
and they were also a., every one		26:39
be a. in all your high—mindedness	DC	90:17
let them be a. for all their sins,		112:12

ADMONISHING
a. him with the words of God.	Al	1: 7

ADMONITION
nurture and a. of the Lord—	En	1: 1
and also receive a. of him.	DC	6:19
that we follow the a. of Paul—	AoF	13

ADMONITIONS
because of the a. of the Lord.	2Ne	4:13

ADOPTED

ADOPTED
and they a. the old plans, and — Eth 10:33

ADORN
a. them with all manner of — 4Ne 1:41
Why do ye a. yourselves with — Mrm 8:39

ADORNED
be a. as a bride for that day — DC 109:74

ADORNING
and the a. of your churches, — Mrm 8:37

ADULTERERS
against the a., and against — 3Ne 24: 5
There were among you a. — DC 63:14
who are liars, and sorcerers, and a., — 76:103

ADULTERESSES
among you adulterers and a.; — DC 63:14

ADULTEROUS
become a wicked and an a. people, — Mos 1:13

ADULTERY
or plunder, or steal, or commit a.; — Mos 2:13
Thou shalt not commit a. — 13:22
murdering, committing a., and — Al 16:18

ADULTERY
nor to steal, nor to commit a., — Al 23: 3
and if he committed a. he was — 30:10
lying, stealing, committing a., — He 4:12
might the more easily commit a., — 7: 5
that thou shalt not commit a., — 3Ne 12:27
committed a. already in his heart. — 12:28
causeth her to commit a.; — 12:32
who is divorced committeth a. — 12:32
Thou shalt not commit a.; — DC 42:24
and he that committeth a., — 42:24
But he that has committed a. — 42:25
for the sake of a., — 42:75
man or woman shall commit a., — 42:80
not steal; neither commit a., — 59: 6
shall commit a. in their hearts, — 63:16
Commit not a.— — 66:10
as ye have asked concerning a., — 132:41
she hath committed a. and — 132:41
she has committed a. — 132:42
and hath committed a. — 132:43
if she hath not committed a., — 132:44
that hath not committed a. — 132:44
he cannot commit a. for they — 132:61
for he cannot commit a. with — 132:61
he cannot commit a., — 132:62
she has committed a., — 132:63

ADVANCE
to a. the cause, which ye have — DC 78: 4

ADVANTAGE
take the a. of one because of — 2Ne 28: 8
did obtain much a. over them; — Om 1:24
did gain a. over the Lamanites. — Al 51:31
they might gain a. over them — 52:19
the a. which they had retaken. — 55:27
Moronihah great a. over them, — He 1:25
did gain some a. of the robbers, — 3Ne 2:17
this was an a. to the Nephites; — 4:18
to gain a. over the Lamanites. — Mrm 6: 4
take no a. of your weakness; — Eth 12:26
you may have a. of the world, — DC 63:27
he will have so much the a. in — 130:19

ADVANTAGES
did gain many a. over them. — 3Ne 2:18

ADVERSARIES
up the a. of Rezin against him, — 2Ne 19:11
the a. of Judah shall be cut off; — 21:13
contend warmly with their a., — Al 1:22
shall be lifted up upon thine a., — 3Ne 20:17
shall be lifted up upon their a., — 21:13
make thy name known to thine a., — DC 133:42

AFFECTIONS

ADVERSARY
the fiery darts of the a. — 1Ne 15:24
Who is mine a.? Let him come — 2Ne 7: 8
Now this was a plan of thine a., — Al 12: 5
that this was a snare of the a., — 12: 6
Agree with thine a. quickly while — 3Ne 12:25
all the fiery darts of the a.; — DC 3: 8
which has given the a. power; — 50: 7
the a. spreadeth his dominions, — 82: 5
saying: Avenge me of mine a. — 101:83
as though the a. was aware, — JS 2:20

ADVERSITY
thine a. and thine afflictions — DC 121: 7

ADVICE
the words and a. of your brother, — DC 30: 5
my a. to the Latter-day Saints — OD

ADVOCATE
am your a. with the Father; — DC 29: 5
am their a. with the Father, — 32: 3
who is the a. with the Father, — 45: 3
even Jesus Christ, your a., — 62: 1
I am your a. with the Father. — 110: 4

ADVOCATETH
wherefore he a. the cause of — Mro 7:28

AFAR
when he had driven them a. off, — Al 17:39
Hearken ye people from a.; — DC 1: 1
shall stand a. off and tremble. — 45:74
hearts and give ear from a.; — 63: 1
of my church who are a. off, — 70: 1
enemy while he was yet a. off; — 101:54
strangers may come from a. — 124:23
let all my saints come from a. — 124:25
the nations which are a. off; — 133: 8
their eyes cannot see a. off; — Mses 6:27
that they fled and stood a. off — 7:14
of the land, also, stood a. off; — 7:15

AFFAIRS
all the a. of the kingdom. — Mos 1:15
changed the a. of the kingdom. — 11: 4
regulate all the a. of the church; — 26:37
in the a. of the church, — 26:37
newly arrange the a. of this people, — 29:11
all the a. of the church. — 29:42
establish the a. of the church; — Al 1:28
thus were the a. of the people — 46: 7
management of a. among the — 49:11
settle the a. of their contentions — 51:12
stating the a. of the people in — 56: 1
concerning the a. of our people. — 58: 4
and manage the a. of this war. — 60: 1
which a. were settled in the — He 3: 1
thus were the a. of the people. — 16: 8
in the a. of the people, — 16:12
were the a. of the people of Nephi. — 3Ne 7:13
thus were the a. of the people. — 4Ne 1:40
a. of the property of this church. — DC 38:36
the a. of the storehouse — 78: 3
To manage the a. of the poor, — 82:12
a. of the church and the school; — 90:13
a. of this church and kingdom. — 90:16
regulate all the a. of the same — 107:33
regulating all the a. of the same — 107:34
in the a. of the church, — 107:36
in the a. of the church, — 107:37
concerning the a. of my church — 112:27
I have left my a. with agents — 127: 1

AFFECTED
of country seemed a. by it, — JS 2: 5

AFFECTION
behold, they are without a., — Mses 7:33

AFFECTIONATE
in a proper and a. manner — JS 2:28

AFFECTIONS
let the a. of thy heart be placed — Al 37:36

AFFIDAVITS / AFFLICTIONS

AFFIDAVITS
to take statements and a.; DC 123: 4

AFFIRM
I continued to a. that I had JS 2:27

AFFIXED
of the punishment which is a., 2Ne 2:10
which punishment that is a. is 2:10
of the happiness which is a. 2:10
a. opposite to the plan of Al 42:16
there was a punishment a., 42:18
law given, and a punishment a., 42:22
the penalty which is a. unto DC 82: 4
a broad seal a. to "Mormonism" 135: 7

AFFLICT
destroy my peace and a. my soul? 2Ne 4:27
into the hand of them that a. thee; 8:23
I will a. thy seed by the hand of 10:18
did more grievously a. by the way of 19: 1
they did a. the king sorely with Mos 21: 6
did persecute them, and a. them Al 1:20
by the Great Spirit to a. them 19:27
that he should a. others, to 30:51
a. the people with his whoredoms Eth 10: 7

AFFLICTED
a. with all manner of diseases, 1Ne 11:31
having been a. with my brethren 16:21
will have mercy upon his a. 21:13
that we may not be a. more 2Ne 5: 3
that they shall be smitten and a. 6:10
many shall be a. in the flesh, 6:11
now this, thou a., and drunken, 8:21
lightly a. the land of Zebulun, 19: 1
relief to the sick and the a. Jac 2:19
you which have a. your neighbor, 2:20
and ye are smitten and a. Mos 7:32
a. by the hand of their enemies. 11:21
should be oppressed and a.? 13:35
stricken, smitten of God, and a. 14: 4
He was oppressed, and he was a., 14: 7
be a. with all manner of diseases 17:16
needy, and the sick, and the a.; Al 1:27
himself being a. with a wound 3:22
But the people were a., yea, 4: 2
a. for the loss of their brethren, 4: 2
and those who were sick and a. 4:12
ye are a. and cast out— 32:24
and visit not the sick and a., 34:28
were a. with hunger and thirst, 37:42
but were a. and smitten, He 4:13
thus were the Lamanites a. also, 3Ne 1:30
Israel to be smitten, and to be a., 16: 9
or that are a. in any manner? 17: 7
forth with their sick and their a., 17: 9
that were a. in any manner; 17: 9
O thou a., tossed with tempest, 22:11
the needy, the sick and the a. Mrm 8:37
sick and the a. to pass by you, 8:39
be you a. in all his afflictions, DC 30: 6
the needy, the sick and the a., 52:40
and for this evil they were a. 64: 8
wherewith you have been a. 98: 3
your brethren who have been a., 101: 1
wherewith they have been a., 101: 2
the redemption of mine a. people— 105: 1
to the poor and a. among them, 105: 3
been greatly oppressed and a. 109:48
needy, and a. ones of the earth; 109:55
with all their sick and a. ones, 109:72
In all their afflictions he was a. 133:53
they deliver you up to be a., JS 1: 7

AFFLICTION
and we have suffered much a., 1Ne 16:35
and wade through much a. 17: 1
chosen thee in the furnace of a. 20:10
And is not this, our a., great? Mos 7:23
upon my people such great a.? 11:27
cause of much a. to the church; Al 1:23
the cause of much a. to Alma, 4: 7
through much a. and sorrow. 7: 5
their children from famine and a., 53: 7
their God in this their time of a. 55:31
the cause of sore a. among us; 61: 4
and bloodsheds, and famine, and a., 62:39
and to wade through much a. He 3:34
Be patient in a. DC 66: 9
and this is the cause of your a. 93:42
with sore a., with pestilence, 97:26
the a. to come upon them, 101: 2
to bring a. upon you. 104:81
this yoke of a. that has been 109:47
suffer this people to bear this a., 109:49
Joseph Smith, in the hour of a.; 124:16
turn away their hearts from a.; 124:76
with a great a. by the death of JS 2:56

AFFLICTIONS
and a. in the wilderness. 1Ne 1:hd
1: 1
and having seen many a. 15: 5
overcome because of my a., 15: 5
mine a. were great above all, 16:20
and a. in the wilderness; 16:35
we had suffered many a. 17: 6
than to have suffered these a. 17:20
because of mine a. 18:16
the a. of their mother; 18:19
notwithstanding our a., 2Ne 1: 5
suffered a. and much sorrow, 2: 1
consecrate thine a. for thy gain. 2: 2
in the wilderness of mine a.; 3: 1
out of the wilderness of mine a., 3: 3
through mine a. in the wilderness; 4:20
strength slacken, because of mine a.? 4:26
my strength because of mine a. 4:29
he will console you in your a., Jac 3: 1
smitten with famine and sore a. Mos 1:17
they are smitten with sore a.? 7:28
grieved for the a. of my people, 8: 7
smitten with famine and sore a.; 9: 3
will I deliver them out of their a.; 11:25
smite this my people with sore a., 12: 4
the a. of the Nephites were great, 21: 5
with the king because of their a.; 21: 6
deliver them out of their a. 21:14
so great were their a. that they 24:10
Lord came to them in their a., 24:13
do visit my people in their a. 24:14
and his brethren, and all their a., 25: 6
suffering all manner of a., 26:38
And so great were their a. that Al 4: 3
and suffering all manner of a., 4:13
a. of the humble followers of God, 4:15
by the cause of so much a. 7: 5
a. and temptations of every kind; 7:11
suffer these great a., O Lord? 14:26
for thy had many a.; 17: 5
patient in long-suffering and a., 17:11
when he saw the a. of those 17:30
hunger, thirst, and all kinds of a.; 20:29
not suffer their a. on every hand, 22:34
suffered much loss and so many a., 25: 6
and bear with patience thine a., 26:27
we have suffered all manner of a., 26:30
their sorrows, and their a., 28: 8
may suffer with patience these a. 31:31
that they may bear their a. 31:33
should suffer no manner of a., 31:38
their a. had truly humbled them 32: 6
didst hear me because of mine a. 33:11
will cry unto thee in all mine a., 33:11
should do, because of your a.; 34: 3
ye bear with all manner of a.; 34:40
patience, and bear with those a., 34:41
shall one day rest from all your a. 34:41
surely did deliver them in their a. 36: 2
and their troubles, and their a., 36: 3
yea, and in all manner of a.; 36:27

AFFLICTIONS 19 AFTER

and your troubles, and your a.,	Al 38: 5	at any time shall I give it a.	1Ne 6: 1
the many a. and tribulations	53:13	a. my father, Lehi, had made an	7: 1
brethren wade through their a.,	53:15	a. they had done praying	7:21
a. and our tribulations for them,	56: 7	a. I and my brethren and all	7:22
suffered great a. of every kind.	56:16	a. I had traveled for the space	8: 8
all manner of a. of every kind.	60: 3	a. I had prayed unto the Lord	8: 9
should suffer all manner of a.,	60:17	a. they had partaken of the fruit	8:25
I do not joy in your great a.,	61: 2	a. they had tasted of the fruit	8:28
are those who joy in your a.,	61: 3	a. they did enter into that	8:33
very many exceedingly sore a.	62:37	a. my father had spoken all	8:36
were softened because of their a.,	62:41	a. he had preached unto them,	8:38
prisons, and from all manner of a.	62:50	Nephi, a. mine own name;	9: 2
chasten his people with many a.,	He 12: 3	a. my father had made an end	10: 2
many a. which they shall have,	15:12	a. they should be destroyed,	10: 3
the people in a state of many a.;	3Ne 2:19	a. they should be brought back	10: 3
persecution and all manner of a.,	6:13	a. he had baptized the Messiah	10:10
could deliver them from their a.	Mrm 5: 1	a. my father had spoken	10:11
lifted thee up out of thine a.,	DC 24: 1	a. they had slain the Messiah,	10:11
Be patient in a., for thou shalt	24: 8	and a. he had been slain	10:11
thy husband, in his a.,	25: 5	a. the house of Israel should be	10:14
And be you afflicted in all his a.,	30: 6	a. the Gentiles had received	10:14
many a. because of your family;	31: 2	a. this manner of language	10:15
Be patient in a., revile not	31: 9	a. I, Nephi, having heard all	10:17
all his a. and persecutions—	109:68	a. I had desired to know	11: 1
thine a. shall be but a small	121: 7	a. thou hast beheld the tree	11: 7
In all their a. he was afflicted.	133:53	a. ye have witnessed him	11: 7
in the midst of our a. we	JS 2:61	a. I had seen the tree,	11: 9
		a. the manner of the flesh.	11:18
AFFORDED		a. she had been carried away	11:19
all of which a. strongholds for	Al 51:27	a. he had said these words,	11:24
made to the laws, and relief a.	DC 134:11	a. he was baptized, I beheld	11:27
		a. he was slain I saw	11:34
AFFRIGHTED		a. the manner of wars	12: 3
saw this they were a.;	Al 52: 2	a. I saw these things, I saw	12: 5
they were a. exceedingly,	62:24	a. they had dwindled in unbelief	12:23
arose and were a., and fled;	DC 101:51	And a. they go forth	13:26
		a. the book hath gone forth	13:28
AFLOAT		a. these plain and precious things	13:29
libelous publications that are a.;	DC 123: 4	a. it goeth forth unto all the	13:29
		a. I have visited the remnant	13:34
AFOREMENTIONED		a. I have visited them	13:34
the a. Mr. Martin Harris came	JS 2:63	a. the Gentiles do stumble	13:34
		a. thy seed shall be destroyed,	13:35
AFRAID		a. it had come forth unto them	13:39
neither be ye a. of their revilings.	2Ne 8: 7	a. he has manifested himself	13:42
that thou shouldst be a. of man,	8:12	a. I, Nephi, had been carried	15: 1
fear ye their fear, nor be a.	18:12	a. I had received strength	15: 6
be not a. of the Assyrian;	20:24	a. the Messiah shall be manifested	15:13
Ramath is a.;	20:29	until a. they are scattered	15:17
I will trust, and not be a.;	22: 2	and a. they were restored	15:20
And they shall be a.;	23: 8	a. the death of the temporal	15:31
would he be a. he would die	Al 42:19	a. I, Nephi, had made an end	16: 1
men would not be a. to sin.	42:20	a. we had slain food for our	16:14
a. of the armies of the Nephites	43:21	a. we had traveled for the	16:17
they were exceedingly a.;	47: 2	a. I did break my bow, behold,	16:18
they were exceedingly a., lest	58:24	a. we had traveled for the space	16:33
Lamanites were exceedingly a.,	He 4: 3	a. all these sufferings we must	16:35
And all nations shall be a.	DC 45:75	a. he has led us away, he has	16:38
be not a. of your enemies,	98:14	a. this manner did my brother	16:38
Let no man be a. to lay	103:27	a. they were chastened by the voice	16:39
and I was a., because I beheld	Mses 4:16	a. I, Nephi, had been in the land	17: 7
first looked upon him, I was a.;	JS 2:32	a. the manner which I shall show	17: 8
		a. the manner which thou hast	17: 9
AFTER		and a. I had made a bellows,	17:11
a. the record of the Jews.	1Ne 1:hd	a. ye have arrived in the promised	17:14
a. this manner was the language	1:15	a. this manner of language did	17:22
a. I have abridged the record	1:17	a. they had crossed the river	17:32
a. the Lord had shown so many	1:18	a. they were bitten he prepared	17:41
a. he hath been commanded	3:18	a. all these things, the time has	17:43
a. this manner of language	3:21	a. what manner I should work	18: 1
a. we had gathered these things	3:23	a. the manner which was learned	18: 2
he did lust a. it, insomuch	3:25	a. the manner of men; but	18: 2
a. the angel had spoken	3:30	a. the manner which the Lord	18: 2
a. the angel had departed,	3:31	it was not a. the manner of men.	18: 2
a. they had hid themselves,	4: 5	a. I had finished the ship,	18: 4
a. I had smitten off his head	4:19	a. we had prepared all things,	18: 6
a. I had done this, I went	4:20	a. we had all gone down into	18: 8
I called a. them, and they did	4:29	a. we had been driven forth	18: 9
a. we had come down into the	5: 1	a. they had bound me insomuch	18:12
a. this manner of language	5: 3	a. we had been driven back	18:15
a. this manner of language	5: 6	a. they had loosed me, behold,	18:21
a. this manner of language	5: 8	a. I had prayed the winds did	18:21
a. they had given thanks	5:10	a. we had sailed for the space	18:23

AFTER 20 AFTER

a. I had made these plates	1Ne 19: 3	a. there had been false prophets,	WM 1:16
what they should do a. I was	19: 4	and a. there having been much	1:16
a. this manner has the prophet	19:24	a. king Benjamin had made an	Mos 1: 9
a. thou hast lost the first,	21:20	a. king Benjamin had made an	1:15
a. I, Nephi, had read these	22: 1	a. Mosiah had done as his father	2: 1
a. they shall be nursed by the	22: 6	a. ye have known and have been	2:36
a. all the house of Israel have been	22: 7	and even a. all this they shall	3: 9
a. our seed is scattered the Lord	22: 8	a. they had spoken these words	4: 3
a. I, Nephi, had made an end of	2Ne 1: 1	a. having finished speaking	6: 1
a. they have received so great	1:10	a. king Mosiah had had continual	7: 1
a. he had created our first parents,	2:15	a. Limhi had heard the words of	7:14
a. Adam and Eve had partaken of	2:19	image a. which man was created	7:27
they were a. they were created;	2:22	was created a. the image of God,	7:27
his name shall be called a. me;	3:15	a. king Limhi had made an end	8: 1
a. the name of his father.	3:15	a. he had done all this,	8: 4
a. many generations have gone by	3:20	a. many days' wandering in the	9: 4
a. this manner did my father	3:22	a. we had dwelt in the land for	9:11
a. my father had made an end of	4: 3	a. they had crossed the sea,	10:13
a. my father had made an end of	4: 8	a. having told all these things	10:19
a. he had made an end of speaking	4:11	a. the desires of his own heart.	11: 2
a. my father, Lehi, had spoken	4:12	a. the space of two years	12: 1
not many days a. his death,	4:13	a. Abinadi had spoken these	13: 5
a. we had journeyed for the space	5: 7	what you do with me, a. this,	13:10
a. the manner of it did make	5:14	a. Abinadi had made an end of	13:25
construct it a. the manner of the	5:16	And a. all this, after working	15: 6
lived a. the manner of happiness.	5:27	a. working many mighty miracles	15: 6
a. the manner of his holy order,	6: 2	a. Abinadi had spoken these	16: 1
and a. he should manifest himself	6: 9	and sent his servants a. him	17: 3
a. they have hardened their hearts	6:10	And a. three days,	17: 6
a. they are driven to and fro,	6:11	a. many days there were a	18: 7
ye that follow a. righteousness.	8: 1	a. Alma had said these words,	18:14
a. ye are reconciled unto God,	10:24	a. this manner he did baptize	18:16
the lambs feed a. their manner,	15:17	And Gideon pursued a. him	19: 6
thee, a. the manner of Egypt.	20:24	a. they had ended the ceremony,	19:24
lift if up a. the manner of Egypt.	20:26	a. many days the Lamanites	21: 2
not judge a. the sight of his eyes,	21: 3	And a. being many days in	22:13
reprove a. the hearing of his ears.	21: 3	And a. they had pursued them	22:16
a. the manner of the things of the	25: 5	Nevertheless, a. much tribulation,	23:10
a. the manner of the Jews;	25: 6	a. the people of king Limhi,	23:30
a. my father left Jerusalem;	25:10	a. Alma had shown them the way	23:37
a. he is laid in a sepulchre	25:13	called a. the name of his father;	24: 3
a. the Messiah hath risen	25:14	a. they had been in the wilderness	24:25
a. they have been scattered,	25:16	a. Alma had taught the people	25:17
a. they had been bitten by	25:20	a. the manner he did his brethren	25:18
we are saved, a. all we can do.	25:23	and remained so ever a.,	26: 4
And a. the law is fulfilled	25:27	a. he had poured out his whole	26:14
a. Christ shall have risen	26: 1	being called Alma, a. his father;	27: 8
a. the Messiah shall come	26: 3	a. the manner of his iniquities.	27: 8
A. my seed and the seed of my	26:15	a. they had fasted and prayed	27:23
a. the Lord God shall have camped	26:15	a. wandering through much	27:28
a. they shall have been brought	26:15	a. the sons of Mosiah had done	28: 1
shall teach a. this manner,	28: 9	a. having translated and	28:11
a. the book of which I have spoken	30: 3	a. the manner of old times.	28:16
a. this manner doth the Lord God	31: 3	Now a. Mosiah had finished	28:17
a. he was baptized with water	31: 8	a. king Mosiah had done these	28:20
a. ye have repented of your sins,	31:14	away a part of this people a. him,	29: 7
and a. this should deny me,	31:14	laws a. the manner of his own	29:23
a. ye have gotten into this	31:19	a. king Mosiah had sent these	29:37
a. ye have entered in by the way.	32: 1	a. the manner of his preaching.	Al 1: 6
a. ye had received the Holy Ghost	32: 2	being a. the order of the man that	2: 1
a. I have spoken these words,	32: 4	drawn away much people a. him;	2: 2
a. he shall manifest himself unto	32: 6	a. the persuasions of Amlici;	2: 3
a. the death of Nephi;	Jac 2: 1	called a. that Gideon who was slain	2:20
a. ye have obtained a hope in	2:19	a. having buried those who had	3: 1
a. having rejected the sure	4:17	A. they had finished burying their	3: 1
a. many days it began to put	5: 6	a. the manner of the Lamanites;	3: 4
a. that the end soon cometh.	6: 2	not many days a. the battle	3:20
a. ye have been nourished by	6: 7	And behold, a. that, they were	5: 5
a. so many have spoken	6: 8	a shepherd hath called a. you	5:37
a. some years had passed away,	7: 1	and is still calling a. you,	5:37
a. this manner did Sherem	7: 7	called to speak a. this manner,	5:44
a. I, Enos, had heard these words,	En 1:11	the order a. which I am called,	5:49
a. I had prayed and labored	1:12	do walk a. the holy order of God,	5:54
And a. this manner do I write	1:23	good shepherd doth call a. you;	5:60
And a. this manner did they teach	Jar 1:11	a. Alma had made an end of	6: 1
a. the manner of wars,	1:13	called a. the man who was slain	6: 7
a. he had led them out of the land	Om 1: 6	a. wading through much affliction	7: 5
And a. this manner we keep	1: 9	walk a. the holy order of God,	7:22
a. they were taught in the	1:18	a. which ye have been received.	7:22
years a. the coming of Christ	WM 1: 2	a. having taught the people of	8: 1
a. I had made an abridgment	1: 3	a. the name of him who first	8: 7
a. Amaleki had delivered up these	1:10	a. Alma had received his message	8:18
a. there had been false Christs,	1:15	a. he had eaten and was filled	8:23

a. having had so much light	Al	9:19
a. having been such a highly		9:20
a. having been favored above		9:20
a. having had all things made		9:20
a. having been delivered of God		9:22
out of bondage time a. time,		9:22
a. all this, I never have known		10: 5
a. the manner of the Jews who		11: 4
a. the manner of the Jews;		11: 4
a. the resurrection of the dead.		12:24
and a. death, they must come to		12:27
a. God had appointed that		12:28
a. having made known unto		12:32
ordained priests, a. his holy order,		13: 1
was a. the order of his Son,		13: 1
a. the order of his Son,		13: 2
a. which they were ordained—		13: 3
being a. the order of his Son,		13: 7
were ordained a. this manner—		13: 8
forever, a. the order of the Son,		13: 9
they were called a. this holy order,		13:11
a. being sanctified by the Holy		13:12
a high priest a. this same order		13:14
were given a. this manner,		13:16
a. he had made an end of		14: 1
A. what ye have seen, will ye		14:14
a. the order and faith of Nehor,		14:16
a. they had thus suffered for		14:23
a. Alma having established the		15:17
a. many days their dead bodies		16:11
built a. the manner of the Jews.		16:13
unto them a. his resurrection.		16:20
a. the church had been established		16:21
from them, a. having blessed them		17:18
called a. the sons of Ishmael,		17:19
a. he had been in the service of		17:26
was created a. the image of God,		18:34
a. he had said all these things,		18:40
a. the manner of the Lamanites,		18:43
a. two days and two nights they		19: 1
calling it a. the land of their		21: 1
a. the order of the Nehors;		21: 4
a. the order of the Nehors.		21: 4
a. he departed from the land of		22: 1
created man a. his own image,		22:12
a. Aaron had expounded these		22:15
I, a. having said this, return		22:35
were a. the order of the Nehors.		24:28
that a. a people have been once		24:30
And a. that, they had many		25: 3
a. having suffered much loss and		25: 6
a. their many struggles to destroy		27: 1
by that name ever a.		27:26
a. the people of Ammon were		28: 1
a. the people of Ammon were		30: 1
a. the Lamanites were driven out		30: 1
a. they had buried their dead,		30: 2
and also a. the days of fasting,		30: 2
a. this manner did he preach,		30:12
a. the foolish traditions of your		30:27
a. the silly traditions of their		30:31
all gone astray a. an unknown God.		30:53
a. the manner of Korihor.		30:58
that a. the end of Korihor,		31: 1
did worship a. a manner which		31:12
a. the foolish traditions of our		31:17
a. Alma and his brethren and		31:19
a. the tradition of their brethren,		31:22
a. the people had all offered up		31:23
offered up thanks a. this manner,		31:23
offer up thanks a. their manner.		31:23
And a. that they did separate		31:37
a. much labor among them,		32: 2
a. ye have tasted this light		32:35
a. Alma had spoken these words,		33: 1
a. Alma had spoken these words		34: 1
a. ye have done all these things,		34:28
a. ye have received so many		34:30
for a. this day of life, which is		34:33
a. Amulek had made an end of		35: 1
a. they had preached the word		35: 2
a. the more popular part of the		35: 3
a. they had found out the minds		35: 6
a. having been instruments in the	Al	35:14
work a. the manner of so curious		37:39
Lamanites, a. the harlot Isabel.		39: 3
a. the lusts of your eyes,		39: 9
again a. those wicked harlots.		39:11
Seek not a. riches nor the		39:14
or as a. the time of his coming?		39:19
until a. the coming of Christ.		40: 2
die a. the resurrection of Christ.		40:19
it be at his resurrection of a.,		40:21
a. the Lord God sent our first		42: 2
a. to follow a. their own will.		42: 7
a. the holy order of God		43: 2
and a. they had entered into a		44:20
a. Alma had said these things		45:15
a. Helaman and his brethren		45:23
a. the servants of the king.		47:28
saw an army pursuing a. them,		47:29
army which pursued a. them		47:30
having pursued a. them in vain;		47:30
not long a. their dissensions		47:36
to battle a. the manner of the		49: 8
fortified a. the manner of the		51:27
a. this manner were they driven.		51:32
a. the Lamanites had finished		53: 3
exceeding stronghold ever a.;		53: 5
to carry on a. his death.		54: 5
march in a straight course a. us;		56:37
from their support a. this manner,		57:11
a. they had surrendered		57:14
that a. the Lamanites had fled,		57:24
a. we had thus taken care of our		57:28
the Lamanites did follow a. us		58:19
a. having traveled much in the		58:23
a. Moroni had received and		59: 1
a. Moroni had sent his epistle		61: 1
a. they had taken them, they		62:16
a. he had obtained possession of		62:30
a. Moroni had fortified those		62:42
called a. the name of his father.		63:11
a. Moronihah had established	He	2: 1
passed a. there had been great		3:17
walk a. the ways of his father,		3:20
a. they had been cast into prison		5:22
was a. the son of Zedekiah;		6:10
even a. the order of his Son;		8:18
a. the pride of your hearts;		13:27
walk a. the pride of your eyes,		13:27
shall ever a. be found in seams		14:22
a. the manner of his instruction.	3Ne	3:26
a. the manner of robbers;		4: 7
called a. the land of Mormon,		5:12
them a. their transgression.		5:12
of the land until a. their death.		6:23
a. he had been stoned and		7:19
And a. these sayings there was		10: 1
a. the people had heard these		10: 8
soon a. the ascension of Christ		10:18
them a. his ascension into heaven.		11:12
And a. this manner shall ye baptize		11:27
and a. that ye are baptized		12: 1
a. that ye have seen me and		12: 1
and thirst a. righteousness, for		12: 6
on a woman, to lust a. her,		12:28
A. this manner therefore pray ye:		13: 9
write these sayings a. I am gone,		16: 4
I say unto you, that a. all this,		16: 9
And a. this manner do they bear		17:16
a. the blessing which they shall		20:15
a. they have scattered my		20:15
Samuel and those that follow a.,		20:24
And a. that ye were blessed		20:27
a. he had expounded all the		23: 6
a. they were written he		24: 1
a. that he did show himself unto		26:13
a. he had ascended into heaven—		26:15
a. having healed all their sick,		26:15
a. that I had been lifted up		27:14
a. that I am gone to the Father?		28: 1
a. we have lived unto the age of		28: 2
a. that ye are seventy and two		28: 3
walk any more a. the performances	4Ne	1:12
did walk a. the commandments		1:12

AFTER 22 AFTER

a. three hundred and five years	4Ne	1:47	a. repenting, and humbling himself	DC	20: 6
a. the manner of the learning of	Mrm	1: 2	a. his own image and in his own		20:18
a. this tenth year had passed		3: 4	a. he came in the meridian of		20:26
a. I had delivered them,		3:15	as those who should come a.,		20:27
they are written a. this manner,		5:12	a. they are received by baptism.		20:68
a. they have been driven and		5:20	and a. this manner shall he		20:76
a. the great and tremendous		8: 2	a. thou hast sowed thy fields		24: 3
being called a. the mighty hunter)	Eth	2: 1	until a. you shall go to the west		26: 1
a. the manner of barges		2:16	this place until a. the conference;		28:10
built barges a. the manner which		2:16	upon a woman to lust a. her		42:23
built a. a manner that they were		2:17	a. they are laid before the bishop		42:32
ye are created a. mine own image?		3:15	a. that he has received these		42:32
the beginning a. mine own image.		3:15	a. this first consecration,		42:33
created a. the body of my spirit;		3:16	earnestly seeking a. the kingdom,		46: 6
a. the manner and in the likeness		3:17	but a. your brethren come from		48: 5
until a. that he should be lifted		4: 1	And a. you have done journeying,		54: 9
until a. Christ should show		4: 1	a. thou hast been baptized		55: 1
And a. Christ truly had showed		4: 2	a. I have commanded and		56: 3
And now, a. that, they have all		4: 3	shall follow a. much tribulation.		58: 3
a. the Lord had prepared the		6: 2	a. much tribulation come the		58: 4
a. that they had numbered them,		6:21	And a. that cometh the day of		58:11
drew away many people a. him.		7: 4	and a. that let them return		58:46
a. he had armed them with		7: 9	a. that let my servants Sidney		58:58
more part of the people a. them.		9:11	and a. thou hast come up unto the		60:14
a. that he had anointed Emer		9:15	mattereth not, unto me, a. a little,		61:22
a. he had anointed Coriantum		9:22	a. they leave the canal they shall		61:24
a. the space of many years,		10: 9	who have sought a. signs and		63:12
a. that he had established		10:10	looketh on a woman to lust a. her,		63:16
a. the death of his father, for		10:15	the dead and shall not die a.,		63:49
a. he had obtained unto himself		10:16	a. the manner of the Lord,		63:53
and a. he had seen many days		10:17	Sidney Gilbert, a. a few weeks,		64:18
oaths a. the manner of the ancients,		10:33	And a. that day, I, the Lord,		64:22
a. the manner by which he		11:21	a. today cometh the burning—		64:24
until a. the trial of your faith.		12: 6	a. the manner of the Lord—		64:24
a. he had risen from the dead;		12: 7	neither a. the carnal mind.		67:12
until a. they had faith in him;		12: 7	a. that it is expedient to continue		73: 4
called a. the holy order of God.		12:10	a. the many testimonies which		76:22
not himself until a. their faith.		12:12	Spirit a. having received it,		76:35
and also those who were a.		12:16	a. the sufferings of his wrath.		76:38
the promise until a. their faith.		12:17	a. the Father has revealed him.		76:43
miracles until a. their faith;		12:18	a. the manner of his burial,		76:51
And a. the brother of Jared had		12:21	a. the order of Melchizedek,		76:57
thou workest a. men have faith.		12:30	was a. the order of Enoch,		76:57
for a. they had faith, and did		12:31	was a. the order of the Only		76:57
that a. the waters had receded		13: 2	a. the opening of the seventh seal,		77:13
a. it should be destroyed it		13: 5	to the Jews a. they are gathered		77:15
now, a. the space of two years,		14: 3	a. that, they have claim		83: 5
and a. the death of Shared,		14: 3	is a. the holiest order of God.		84:18
that Shiz pursued a. Coriantumr,		14:17	covenant a. he hath received it,		84:41
clothed a. the manner of war—		15:15	searching a. the poor to		84:112
and a. they had retired to		15:16	a. receiving their inheritances.		85: 2
a. he had smitten off the head of		15:31	And a. they have fallen asleep		86: 3
a. that he had struggled for breath,		15:31	a. the gathering of the wheat,		86: 7
a. having made an end of	Mro	1: 1	a. many days, slaves shall rise up		87: 4
a. ye have done this ye shall		2: 2	a. it hath filled the measure of its		88:19
A. they had prayed unto the		3: 2	a. your testimony cometh wrath		88:88
a. this manner did they ordain		3: 4	a. your testimony cometh the		88:89
a. they had been received unto		6: 4	immediately a. shall the curtain		88:95
a. the manner of the workings		6: 9	scroll is unfolded a. it is rolled up,		88:95
for a. this manner did he speak		7: 1	a. this another angel shall sound,		88:99
a. this manner doth the devil		7:17	when any shall come in a. him,		88:132
a. that he came men also were		7:26	a. partaking of bread and wine,		88:141
a. this manner bringeth to pass		7:32	not a. the manner of the world,		95:13
a. my calling to the ministry.		8: 1	live a. the manner of the world;		95:13
For immediately a. I had learned		8: 7	a. the manner which I shall		95:14
a. this manner did the Holy		8: 9	if a. thine enemy has come		98:39
of the Lord a. this manner,		8:16	a. a few years, if thou desirest		99: 7
a. rejecting so great a knowledge,		8:29	of necessity they feel a. me.		101: 8
thirst a. blood and revenge		9: 5	a. ye had planted the vineyard		101:53
a. depriving them of that which		9: 9	a. many days all things were		101:62
And a. they had done this thing,		9:10	who call themselves a. my name,		101:75
and a. they have done this,		9:10	who call themselves a. my name;		101:97
a. I have spoken a few words		10: 2	appointed a. the same manner		102:10
and a. the image of his own God,	DC	1:16	a. the evidence is examined,		102:16
a. the manner of their language,		1:24	a. the evidences are heard		102:18
a. having received the record of the		1:29	A. the evidences are heard,		102:19
a. the dictates of his own will		3: 4	a. hearing the evidences and		102:20
dealt with you a. this manner.		9: 6	And if, a. a careful re-hearing,		102:21
a. that you have obtained faith,		17: 3	a. the manner of the foregoing,		102:24
a. that you have received this,		18:43	a. examining the appeal and		102:33
a. that you have received this,		18:46	A. prayer the conference adjourned.		102:34
A. it was truly manifested		20: 5	who call themselves a. my name		103: 4

AFTER 23 AGAIN

For a. much tribulation,	DC 103:12
promised a. your tribulations,	103:13
own lands a. these testimonies,	103:24
upon him, and his seed a. him;	104:22
for him and his seed a. him;	104:24
upon him and his seed a. him.	104:25
for them and their seed a. them.	104:32
them and their seed a. them,	104:33
unto him and his seed a. him.	104:37
upon him and his seed a. him,	104:40
his agent, and his seed a. him.	104:41
upon him and his seed a. him,	104:42
A. you are organized, you shall	104:48
brethren, a. they are organized,	104:48
and a. they are purchased that	105:29
a. these lands are purchased.	105:30
fulfilled a. her redemption.	105:34
have power a. many days to	105:37
a. the Order of the Son of God.	107: 3
that priesthood a. Melchizedek,	107: 4
a. the order of Melchizedek,	107: 9
High priests a. the order of	107:10
a. the order of Melchizedek,	107:29
a. the order of Melchizedek,	107:71
a. the order of Melchizedek,	107:73
a. the order of Melchizedek,	107:76
a. this decision it shall be had	107:80
A. this vision closed, the heavens	110:11
A. this, Elias appeared, and	110:12
all generations a. us should be	110:12
A. this vision had closed, another	110:13
day a. day let thy warning	112: 5
And a. their temptations,	112:13
I, the Lord, will feel a. them,	112:13
And a. that, those who have	119: 4
nor their posterity a. them	121:21
shall inquire a. thy name,	122: 1
open the mouth wide a. thee,	122: 7
is a. the similitude of a palace.	124: 2
a. you have had sufficient time	124:33
a. this time, your baptisms for	124:35
head of his posterity a. him.	124:57
Joseph and his seed a. him	124:59
and for his generation a. him,	124:69
and for his generation a. him,	124:74
and his generation a. him,	124:77
himself and his seed a. him,	124:81
himself and his seed a. him,	124:82
and for his generation a. him,	124:117
a. the order of Melchizedek,	124:123
is a. the order of mine Only	124:123
and a. that to send my word to	124:128
in and a. the resurrection from	132: 7
not remain a. men are dead,	132:13
in nor a. the resurrection,	132:13
if it be a. the first resurrection,	132:19
a. ye have received my new	132:27
a. she is espoused, shall be with	132:63
a. their pain shall be sanctified	133:35
both shot a. they were dead,	135: 1
a. Hyrum had made ready to	135: 4
Thou art a. the similitude of	Mses 1:16
tree yielding fruit, a. his kind,	2:11
herb yielding seed a. his kind,	2:12
should be in itself, a. his kind;	2:12
forth abundantly, a. his kind,	2:21
every winged fowl a. his kind,	2:21
the living creature a. his kind,	2:24
beasts of the earth a. their kind,	2:24
beasts of the earth a. their kind,	2:25
and cattle a. their kind,	2:25
upon the earth a. his kind;	2:25
our image, a. our likeness,	2:26
drawn away many a. him,)	4: 6
a. I, the Lord God, had driven	5: 1
And a. many days an angel	5: 6
a. the name of his son, Enoch,	5:42
Satan, a. the manner of Cain,	5:49
own likeness, a. his own image,	6:10
a. he had begotten Seth,	6:11
Seth lived, a. he begat Enos,	6:14
which he called a. his own son,	6:17
Enos lived, a. he begat Cainan,	6:18
lived a. he bagat Mahalaleel	6:19
lived, a. he begat Jared, eight	Mses 6:20
Jared lived, a. he bagat Enoch,	6:21
a. the order of him who was	6:67
a. that Zion was taken up into	7:23
cross, a. the manner of men;	7:55
lived, a. he bagat Lamech,	8: 6
Lamech lived, a. he begat Noah,	8:10
ordained Noah a. his own order,	8:19
a. that they had heard him,	8:21
a. the manner of the Egyptians.	Abr 1: 9
a. the manner of the Egyptians.	1:11
a. the form of a bedstead,	1:13
it was a. the manner of the	1:25
a. the priest of Elkenah was	1:29
posterity that shall come a. me.	1:31
also my father followed a. me,	2: 4
will give unto thy seed a. thee	2: 6
blessing unto thy seed a. thee,	2: 9
shall be called a. thy name,	2:10
thee, and in thy seed a. thee	2:11
a. the Lord had withdrawn	2:12
a. the manner of the Lord,	3: 4
a. his manner of reckoning,	3: 4
a. the reckoning of the Lord's	3: 9
thee, and thy seed a. thee,	3:14
they shall exist a., for they	3:18
that day, many followed a. him.	3:28
And the earth, a. it was formed,	4: 2
yielding fruit, a. his kind, and	4:11
seed, yielding seed a. his kind;	4:12
same in itself, a. his kind;	4:12
forth abundantly a. their kind;	4:21
every winged fowl a. their kind.	4:21
the living creature a. his kind,	4:24
beasts of the earth a. their kind;	4:24
forth the beasts a. their kind,	4:25
and cattle a. their kind,	4:25
upon the earth a. its kind;	4:25
our image, a. our likeness,	4:26
that it was a. the Lord's time,	5:13
which was a. the time of Kolob;	5:13
a. that he was glorified and	JS 1: 1
a. the tribulation of those days	1:21
a. the tribulation of those days,	1:33
a. the tribulation of those days,	1:36
and put all inquirers a. truth	2: 1
a. my father's arrival in	2: 3
a. our removal to Manchester,	2: 5
A. I had retired to the place	2:15
few days a. I had this vision,	2:21
a. I had retired to my bed for	2:29
A. telling me these things,	2:36
A. this communication, I saw	2:43
A. this third visit, he again	2:47
a. the heavenly messenger had	2:47
shortly a. arose from my bed,	2:48
A. I went to live with him,	2:56
to cease digging a. it.	2:56
Immediately a. my marriage,	2:58
immediately a. my arrival there	2:62
them to me a. his return,	2:63
Two days a. the arrival of Mr.	2:67
a. which I laid my hands upon	2:71
water a. we had been baptized,	2:73
we seek a. these things.	AoF 13

AFTERWARD

but a. he said within himself:	DC 101:84
and a. that which is spiritual.	128:14
forty-two years a. he begat	Mses 8:12
who a. settled her sons in it;	Abr 1:24

AFTERWARDS

a. did more grievously afflict	2Ne 19: 1
and also there were many a.,	Al 13:19
in the flesh, but a. received it.	DC 76:74
showing forth a. an increase	121:43
and a. remain in the flesh	Mses 1: 5
that a. he should baptize me.	JS 2:70
and a. he baptized me—	2:71
a. he laid his hands on me and	2:71

AGAIN

we went up a. unto the house	1Ne 3:23

AGAIN 24 AGAIN

ye shall go up to Jerusalem a.,	1 Ne	3:29	natural fruit a. in the vineyard;	Jac	5:73
Laman and Lemuel a. began		3:31	had become a. the natural fruit;		5:74
Let us go up a. unto		4: 1	unto me a. the natural fruit		5:75
And the Spirit said unto me a.:		4:11	evil fruit shall a. come into my		5:77
the Spirit said unto me a.:		4:12	set his hand a. the second time		6: 2
And a., I knew that the Lord had		4:17	love of God was restored a. among		7:23
bring them down a. unto us		5: 5	Lord came into my mind a., saying:	En	1:10
the Lord spake unto him a., saying		7: 1	they returned a. to the land of	Om	1:28
should a. return unto the land		7: 2	journey a. into the wilderness.		1:29
I, Nephi, did a., with my brethren,		7: 3	once a. come to the knowledge of	WM	1: 8
and I spake unto them a.		7:18	once a. be a delightsome people.		1: 8
they were angry with me a.,		7:19	And a. my brethren, I would	Mos	3: 1
did a. travel on our journey		7:21	king Benjamin a. opened his mouth		4: 4
they should return a., yea, even		10: 3	I would a. call your attention,		4: 4
they should possess a. the land		10: 3	And a., believe that ye must		4:10
should be gathered together a.;		10:14	And a. I say unto you as I have		4:11
I looked and beheld the virgin a.,		11:20	And a., I say unto the poor,		4:24
And the angel said unto me a.:		11:26	And a., it is expedient that he		4:27
the angel spake unto me a.,		11:30	And a., doth a man ride an ass		5:14
and I beheld the heavens open a.,		11:30	And a., it came to pass that		6: 3
And he spake unto me a.,		11:31	were a. brought before the king,		7: 8
the angel spake unto me a.,		11:32	and rising a. he said: O king,		7:12
spake unto me a., saying:		11:35	And a., that same God has		7:20
spake unto me a., saying:		11:36	And a., he saith: If my people		7:30
shall be remembered a. among		15:16	And a. he saith: If my people		7:31
neither should they be scattered a.		15:20	And a., they have brought swords,		8:11
they did speak unto me a.,		15:21	And I say unto thee a.:		8:12
and we did pitch our tents a.;		16:13	and started a. on our journey		9: 3
did return a. to our families		16:14	I went a. with four of my men		9: 5
go forth a. in the wilderness,		16:14	we a. began to establish the		10: 1
that we might a. rest ourselves		16:17	we a. began to possess the land		10: 1
had hardened their hearts a.,		16:22	should come up a. to war		10: 1
we did a. take our journey,		16:33	not come upon us a. unawares		10: 2
we did pitch our tents a.,		16:33	And a., that they were wronged		10:13
they were desirous to return a.		16:36	And a., they were wroth with him		10:15
the Lord did bless us a. with food,		16:39	And a., they were wroth with him		10:16
we did a. take our journey		17: 1	did drive them a. out of our land;		10:20
Stretch forh thine hand a.		17:53	we returned a. to our own land,		10:21
they did humble themselves a.		18: 4	a. began to tend their flocks,		10:21
we sailed a. towards the		18:22	And a., he saith that thou shalt		12:11
a.: Hearken, O ye house of Israel,		21: 1	And a., he saith thou shalt be		12:12
to bring Jacob a. to him—		21: 5	when the Lord shall bring a. Zion;		12:22
shall a. in thine ears say:		21:20	And a. he said unto them:		12:29
bring them a. out of captivity,		22:12	And a., because I have spoken		13: 4
lest he shall suffer a.;	2 Ne	1:25	And a.: Thou shalt not bow		13:13
taketh it a. by the power of		2: 8	And a., how beautiful upon the		15:16
Do not anger a. because of		4:29	And a., how beautiful upon the		15:17
we did reap a. in abundance.		5:11	when the Lord shall bring a. Zion.		15:29
I speak unto you a.; for I am		6: 3	should a. be brought before him.		17: 6
unto me that they should return a.		6: 9	And a., Alma took another,		18:15
they shall be gathered together a.		6:11	not bury himself a. in the water.		18:15
set himself a. the second time		6:14	And a. Alma commanded that		18:27
thou shalt no more drink it a.		8:22	to dwell in the land a. in peace.		21: 1
the body is restored to itself a.,		9:13	began a. to be stirred up		21: 2
now I, Jacob, speak unto you a.,		10: 1	gathered themselves together a.,		21: 7
the Lord spake a. unto Ahaz,		17:10	and they went a. to battle,		21:11
The Lord spake also unto me a.,		18: 5	but they were driven back a.,		21:11
shall no more a. stay upon him		20:20	they went a. even the third time,		21:12
set his hand a. the second time		21:11	returned a. to the city of Nephi		21:12
they shall return a., and possess		25:11	Limhi was a. filled with joy in		21:28
shall be restored a. to the land		25:11	of the Lord came unto them a.,		24:16
Jerusalem shall be destroyed a.;		25:14	until they returned a.		25: 5
set his hand a. the second time		25:17	until the time they returned a.		25: 6
a., the Lord God hath commanded		26:32	And a., when they thought of		25: 9
God will deliver a. the book		27:19	And a., when they thought of		25:10
then shalt thou seal up the book a.,		27:22	And a., when they thought upon		25:11
And a. it shall come to pass		27:24	the spirit of Alma was a. troubled;		26:13
set my hand a. the second time		29: 1	and they began a. to have peace		26:37
and sealed up a. unto the Lord,		30: 3	to be much peace a. in the land;		27: 6
And a., it showeth unto the		31: 9	Nevertheless he cried a., saying:		27:13
For behold, a. I say unto you		32: 5	And a., the angel said:		27:14
said a. unto his servant:	Jac	5:24	fell a. to the earth,		27:18
we may labor a. in the vineyard.		5:29	and people, must be born a.;		27:25
may preserve a. good fruit thereof		5:33	Mosiah sent a. among the people;		29: 4
we will nourish a. the trees of		5:58	turn a. to his pride and vain things		29: 9
branches a. into their mother tree,		5:60	they all returned a. diligently	Al	1:26
may bring forth a. good fruit,		5:60	began to have continual peace a.,		1:28
may have joy in the fruit of		5:60	he contended a. with Amlici;		2:31
bring forth a. the natural fruit		5:61	return a. to the Amlicites,		3:13
that all may be nourished once a.		5:63	And a.: I will set a mark		3:15
I graft in a. into the natural tree;		5:67	And a.: I will set a mark		3:16
thus will I bring them together a.,		5:68	And a., I say he that departeth		3:17

AGAIN 25 AGAIN

And then they returned a. and	Al 3:24
and a. the Lord did deliver them	5: 5
And a. I ask, were the bands	5: 9
And a. I say unto you, is there	5:30
they must repent and be born a.	5:49
And a. I say unto you, the Spirit	5:52
are established a. in the way of	7: 4
ye must repent, and be born a.;	7:14
are not born a. ye cannot inherit	7:14
and preach a. unto the people	8:16
I should turn a. and prophesy	8:25
And a., I, Alma, having been	9: 1
and preach a. unto this people,	9: 1
And a. it is said that: Inasmuch	9:13
And a., I know that the things	10:10
And a., he has reviled against	10:29
Now Zeezrom said unto him a.:	11:30
And Zeezrom said a.:	11:32
And Zeezrom said a.:	11:34
Now Amulek saith a. unto him:	11:36
And I say unto you a. that he	11:37
Now Zeezrom saith a. unto him:	11:38
reunited a. in its perfect form;	11:43
began a. to be astonished,	11:46
And a., my brethren, I would	13: 1
ye preach a. unto this people,	14:14
smote them a. upon their cheeks,	14:15
and he smote them a.,	14:17
but came a. on the morrow;	14:20
also smote them a. on their cheeks.	14:20
ye stand a. and judge this people,	14:20
before them, and smote them a.,	14:24
did not come a. to war against	16:12
that they should meet a. at the	17:13
together a. to the place of water.	17:32
men a. stood to scatter their flocks;	17:33
Ammon said unto him a.:	18:15
these words, he marveled a.,	18:18
And Ammon said unto him a.:	18:28
on the morrow he shall rise a.;	19: 8
and he sunk a. with joy;	19:13
to marvel a. among themselves	19:24
a. may rob us of our property.	20:13
And a., it is expedient that	20:18
went forth a. to declare the word,	21:15
return a. to the account of	22:35
if we should stain our swords a.	24:13
they never would use weapons a.	24:18
and they would not take them a.,	24:25
returned a. to their own land;	25:13
of God we have been delivered a.	26:29
returned a. to the land of Nephi.	27: 1
they began a. to destroy them.	27: 2
a. refused to take their arms,	27: 3
and he fell a. to the earth.	27:17
returned a. to their land.	28: 3
ye deny a. that there is a God,	30:39
therefore if thou shalt deny a.,	30:47
a. lead away the hearts of this	30:55
all converted a. unto the Lord;	30:58
his heart a. began to sicken	31: 1
And a. we thank thee, O God,	31:18
never speaking of their God a.	31:23
together a. to the holy stand,	31:23
in bringing them a. unto thee	31:34
these, our brethren, a. unto thee.	31:35
And a., O God, when I did	33: 6
he shall rise a. from the dead,	33:22
Yea, and a. I say unto you,	36:21
limbs did receive their strength a.,	36:23
to lead away your heart a.	39:11
behold, a. it hath been spoken,	40:16
is to bring back a. evil for evil,	41:13
have mercy restored unto you a.;	41:14
have justice restored unto you a.;	41:14
judgment restored unto you a.	41:14
have good rewarded unto you a.	41:14
send out shall return unto you a.,	41:15
Lamanites did flee a. before them,	43:42
met a. by the armies of Moroni.	43:42
And a., the Lord has said that:	43:47
and come not a. to war against	44: 6
will not return a. against us	44:11
never would come to war a.	Al 44:19
work of death should cease a.	44:20
the Lord had a. delivered them	45: 1
And Alma said a.: Believest	45: 4
And Alma said unto him a.:	45: 6
forth to establish the church a.	45:22
began to have peace a.	46:37
gather themselves together a.	47: 1
Amalickiah sent a. the second	47:11
and he sent a. the third time.	47:11
and he sent a. the fourth time	47:12
they were frightened a., and fled	47:29
would a. become an easy prey	49: 3
they were a. disappointed,	49:17
had a. stirred up the hearts of the	51: 9
And he returned a. privily to	51:35
he might take a. by stratagem	52:10
a. to the city Bountiful,	52:17
and take a. the city of Mulek.	52:19
so I may expect you will do it a.	54: 8
began a. to be victorious,	55:28
that a., when the light of	56:41
and came a. upon the rear of	56:53
a. delivered out of the hands of	57:35
retreat into the wilderness a.,	58:24
he began a. to lay a plan that he	59: 4
he wrote a. to the governor of	60: 1
they were a. frightened and fled	62:31
take upon him a. to preach unto	62:44
a regulation should be made a.	62:44
did establish a. the church of God,	62:46
began to prosper a. in the land,	62:48
exceeding strong a. in the land.	62:48
a. to the land northward.	63: 7
they were stirred up a. to anger	63:14
back a. to their own lands,	63:15
And they came down a. that they	He 1:15
of the city of Zarahemla a.,	1:33
had established a. peace	2: 1
began to be a contention a.	2: 1
now I return a. to mine account;	3:17
walls of the prison trembled a.,	5:31
behold the voice came a., saying:	5:32
the earth shook a., and the walls	5:32
a. the third time the voice came,	5:33
and the walls did tremble a.,	5:33
to grow exceedingly wicked a.	6:16
returned a. unto the land of	7: 3
began a. to speak unto them,	8:10
he cried a. unto the Lord, saying:	11: 9
try a. if they will serve thee?	11:16
began to prosper a. in the land,	11:20
they did go forth a. against this	11:30
a. obliged to return out of the	11:31
up a. in remembrance of the	11:34
began a. to forget the Lord	11:36
were ripening a. for destruction.	11:37
should return a., and prophesy	13: 3
shall find them a. no more,	13:18
a., another sign I give unto you,	14:14
upon them a. a spiritual death,	14:18
are cut off a. as to things	14:18
he shall rise a. from the dead.	14:20
a. to the knowledge of the truth—	15:11
never would a. have dwindled	15:15
they shall return a. unto me,	15:16
the sun did rise in the morning a.,	3Ne 1:19
the people began a. to have peace	1:23
of the hearts of the people a.,	2: 2
of the Nephites did return a.	4:15
robbers did not come a. to battle;	4:15
neither did they come a. in	4:15
rejoice and cry a. with one voice,	4:30
a. bring a remnant of the seed	5:23
a. to prosper and to wax great;	6: 4
and would not turn and revile a.,	6:13
life, and have taken it up a.;	9:22
came a voice a. unto the people,	10: 3
And a., how oft would I have	10: 5
they began to weep and howl a.	10: 8
earth did cleave together a.,	10:10
that a. they heard the voice,	11: 4
And a. the third time they did	11: 5

AGAIN 26 AGAIN

their eyes up a. towards heaven;	3Ne	11: 8
I am a. ascended into heaven.		11:21
And a. the Lord called others,		11:22
come forth a. out of the water.		11:26
And a. I say unto you, ye must		11:37
And a. I say unto you, ye must		11:38
And a., more blessed are they		12: 2
And a., blessed are all they that		12: 4
And a. it is written, thou shalt		12:33
he turned a. to the multitude,		14: 1
did open his mouth unto them a.,		14: 1
it shall be measured to you a.		14: 2
and turn a. and rend you.		14: 6
I say unto you a. that the other		15:20
when the Lord shall bring a. Zion.		16:18
he looked round about a. on		17: 1
morrow, and I come unto you a.		17: 3
he cast his eyes round about a.		17: 5
he had done this he wept a.;		17:22
he turned a. unto the multitude		18:17
his eyes a. upon the disciples		18:26
he ascended a. into heaven.		18:39
they knelt a. and prayed to the		19: 8
kneel down a. upon the earth,		19:16
And he turned from them a.,		19:27
he prayed a. unto the Father,		19:27
he came a. unto his disciples;		19:30
and he did smile upon them a.;		19:30
he went a. a little way off		19:31
he came a. to the disciples,		19:35
he brake bread a. and blessed it,		20: 3
give unto them a. the land of		20:29
Father gather them together a.,		20:33
Awake, awake a., and put on		20:36
shall Jerusalem be inhabited a.		20:46
establish a. among them my Zion;		21: 1
words he said unto them a.,		23: 6
be brought a. unto this people,		26: 8
And Jesus a. showed himself		27: 2
And a., ye shall not have pain		28: 9
did a. minister upon the face of		28:16
that they did build cities a.	4Ne	1: 7
did they cause to be built a.		1: 8
there began to be Lamanites a.		1:20
And a., there was another		1:29
people of Jesus did not smite a.		1:34
began a. to build up the secret		1:42
come a. unto the remnant of		1:49
hold them, nor retain them a.	Mrm	1:18
began to be a war a. between		2: 1
a. become a righteous people.		2:12
sorrow did return unto me a.,		2:15
people of Nephi a. were hunted		2:20
they began to come upon us a.		2:22
armies, and did meet them a.,		2:26
until we had a. taken possession		2:27
did not come to battle a. until		3: 1
and build up a. my church,		3: 2
preparing to come a. to battle		3: 4
return to their own lands a.		3: 7
did come down a. to battle.		3: 8
And we did beat them a., and did		3: 8
the Nephites were driven back a.		4: 2
did a. boast of their strength;		4: 8
took possession a. of the city		4: 8
the Lamanites came a. upon		4:10
they did beat a. the Lamanites,		4:15
not come a. against the Nephites		4:16
they fled a. from before them,		4:20
they had come a. the second time.		4:20
were a. sacrificed unto idols.		4:21
that the Nephites did a. flee		4:22
me command a. of their armies,		5: 1
that they came against us a.,		5: 4
did come a. against us to battle,		5: 6
that we did a. take to flight,		5: 7
take them not a., save it be		7: 4
of the Father he hath risen a.,		7: 5
rashly shall be judged rashly a.;		8:19
that smiteth shall be smitten a.,		8:19
And A. I speak unto you who		9: 7
Cry a. unto the Lord, and it	Eth	1:36
Jared spake a. unto his brother,	Eth	1:38
came a. unto the brother of Jared,		2:14
he cried a. unto the Lord, saying:		2:22
I will bring you up a. out of		2:24
and cried a. unto the Lord,		3: 1
hide them up a. in the earth.		4: 3
he did bring them forth a. upon		6: 7
he gave battle a. unto Shule,		7:17
began to prosper a. in the land.		7:26
Omer was restored a. to the		9:13
began a. to take the curse from		9:16
had spread a. over all the face		9:26
began a. to be an exceeding great		9:26
the secret plans a. of old,		9:26
came prophets in the land a.,		9:28
the people began to revive a.,		9:35
to buile up a. a broken people.		10: 1
brought peace a. unto his father.		10: 3
the people began a. to spread over		10: 4
began to be war a. in the land,		10: 8
sought a. to destroy the kingdom.		10:33
prophesied a. unto the people;		11:12
and did obtain the kingdom a.		11:16
And a., I remember that thou		12:33
that thou mightest take it a.		12:33
it should be built up a., a holy		13: 5
but it should be built up a.,		13: 5
hid a. in the cavity of the rock.		13:22
and did obtain the kingdom a.		13:24
Shared gave him battle a. upon		13:29
back a. to the valley of Gilgal.		13:29
gave Shared battle a. in the valley		13:30
he did not go to battle a. for		13:31
they fled a. to the wilderness of		14:14
Coriantumr fled a. before the		14:16
came forth, but were driven a.;		14:29
were driven a. the second time.		14:29
they came a. the third time,		14:29
fled a. before the people of Shiz.		15: 7
Coriantumr was wounded a.,		15: 9
morrow they did go a. to battle,		15:17
when the night came a. they did		15:17
wrote a. an epistle unto Shiz,		15:18
would not come a. to battle.		15:18
wherefore they went a. to battle.		15:19
they slept a. upon their swords.		15:22
on the morrow they fought a.;		15:23
on the morrow they fought a.,		15:24
they fought a. with the sword.		15:29
And a., my beloved brethren,	Mro	7:40
And a., behold I say unto you		7:43
I will write unto you a. if I		8:27
unto you, or shall meet you a.		8:30
I write unto you a. that ye may		9: 1
And a., my son, there are many		9:16
And a., I exhort you, my brethren,		10: 8
And a., to another, that he may		10:12
And a., to another, that he may		10:13
And a., to another, the beholding		10:14
And a., to another, all kinds of		10:15
And a., to another, the		10:16
And a. I would exhort you that		10:30
And a., if ye by the grace of		10:33
spirit and body shall a. reunite,		10:34
And a., verily I say unto you,	DC	1:34
and art a. called to the work;		3:10
And now, a., I speak unto		5:23
even until I command thee a.;		5:30
then thou mayest translate a.		5:30
and did commence a. to write		9: 1
it is now restored unto you a.;		10: 3
in asking to translate it over a.		10:15
he will also give him power a.;		10:16
if God giveth him power a.,		10:17
or if he translates a.,		10:17
shall not translate a. those words		10:30
never be taken a. from the earth,		13: 1
Levi to offer a. an offering		13: 1
he hath risen a. from the dead,		18:12
A., it is written *eternal damnation*;		19: 7
I command you a. to repent,		19:20
And a., I command thee that		19:25

AGAIN

And a., I command thee that	DC 19:26	And a., inasmuch as there is	DC 58:54
And a., I command thee that	19:28	a. I say unto you, let them take	61:21
a. in the vanities of the world;	20: 5	come not a. upon the waters,	61:23
died, and rose a. the third day;	20:23	And a., verily I say unto you,	61:30
And a., by way of commandment	20:37	And a., verily I say unto you,	63:57
come forth a. out of the water.	20:74	And a., I say unto you,	64:20
And a., thou shalt take thy	28:11	And a., verily I say unto you	67:10
And a., verily, verily, I say unto	29:12	And a., no bishop or high priest	68:22
And a., verily, verily, I say unto	29:22	And a., inasmuch as parents	68:25
men a. begin to deny their God,	29:22	And a., let my servants who	72:20
and a., first temporal, and secondly	29:32	it is expedient to translate a.;	73: 3
And, a., I say unto you, that	29:49	forgive him and say unto him a.,	75: 8
And a., I say unto you that	37: 2	And a., verily thus saith the	75:13
And a., a commandment I give	37: 3	And a., verily I say unto my	75:14
a. I will stand upon it.	38:17	And a., I say unto my servant	75:15
ye shall possess it a. in eternity,	38:20	And a., I say unto my servant	75:17
And a. I say unto you, let	38:25	And a., thus saith the Lord unto	75:23
And a., I say unto you that	38:28	And a., verily I say unto you,	75:28
And a., I say unto you, I give	38:40	but straightway shut it up a.;	76:47
And a., it shall come to pass that	39:23	And a. we bear record	76:50
And a., it is meet that my	41: 7	And a., we saw the terrestrial	76:71
And a., it is meet that my	41: 8	And a., we saw the glory of	76:81
And a., I have called my servant	41: 9	go a. into the eastern countries,	79: 1
A. I say unto you, hearken and	42: 2	will crown him a. with sheaves.	79: 3
And a., I say unto you, that my	42:10	And a., I say unto you,	82: 8
A. I say unto you, that it shall	42:11	And a., the offices of elder and	84:29
And a., the elders, priests and	42:12	And a., the offices of teacher and	84:30
And a., I say, thou shalt not	42:19	apostles I say unto you a.,	84:64
But if he doeth it a., he shall	42:26	And a. I say unto you,	84:77
And a., if there shall be	42:33	return not a. unto that man.	84:92
shall not receive a. that which	42:37	Wo, I say a., unto that house,	84:95
And a., thou shalt not be proud	42:40	The Lord hath brought a. Zion;	84:99
And a., it shall come to pass that	42:48	And a., verily, verily, I say	84:103
And a., I say unto you, that ye	42:76	And a., verily I say unto you,	88:25
And a. every person who	42:78	die, it shall be quickened a.,	88:26
And a., I say unto you, that if ye	43:13	die, they also shall rise a.,	88:27
A. I say, hearken ye elders of	43:15	shall return a. to their own place,	88:32
and sleep until I shall call a.	43:18	And a., verily I say unto you,	88:34
Yea, and a., when the lightnings	43:22	And a., verily I say unto you,	88:42
And a., the Lord shall utter his	43:23	And a., verily I say unto you,	88:62
and when he is loosed a. he shall	43:31	when I shall send you a. to	88:80
And a. I say, hearken unto	45: 2	And a., another trump shall	88:100
But they shall be gathered a.;	45:25	they live not a. until the thousand	88:101
And a. I say unto you,	46: 5	a. until the end of the	88:101
And a. I say unto you,	46: 6	And a., another angel shall	88:105
And a., verily I say unto you,	46:10	And a., another angel shall	88:106
And a., to some it is given	46:15	first angel a. sound his trump	88:108
And a., it is given by the Holy	46:16	And a., the order of the house	88:127
And a., verily I say unto you,	46:17	And a., the ordinance of washing	88:140
And a., to some it is given to	46:19	And, a., strong drinks are not	89: 7
And a., to some is given the	46:21	And a., tobacco is not for	89: 8
And a., it is given to some to	46:24	And a., hot drinks are not for	89: 9
And a., I say unto you,	46:31	And a., verily I say unto you,	89:10
A., verily I say unto you that	47: 2	And a., verily I say unto thy	90: 6
And a., I say unto you that it	47: 3	And a., verily I say unto you	90:28
And a., verily I say unto you,	49:15	And a., I say unto you my	92: 2
And a., verily I say unto you,	49:22	men became a., in their infant	93:38
And a., he that receiveth the	50:19	And a., verily I say unto you,	94: 1
And a., verily I say unto you,	50:25	And a., verily I say unto you,	94:10
let them pay unto this church a.	51:11	And a. let it be divided into lots,	96: 3
And a., let the bishop appoint	51:13	And a. verily I say unto you,	96: 6
And a., verily I say unto you,	52: 7	my name's sake shall find it a.,	98:13
And a., I will give unto you a	52:14	And a., the hearts of the Jews	98:17
And a., he that trembleth	52:17	And a. I say unto you,	98:22
And a., he that is overcome	52:18	And a., if your enemy shall	98:25
And a., verily I say unto you,	52:22	And a., if he shall smite you	98:26
And a., let my servant Isaac	52:23	And a., this is the law that I	98:33
And a., let my servants Edward	52:24	And a., verily I say unto you,	98:39
And a., I say unto you,	52:35	A., verily I say unto you,	101:63
And a., verily I say unto you,	52:38	And a. I say unto you,	101:76
And a., let my servants Joseph	52:41	And a., I say unto you,	101:96
And a., verily I say unto you,	53: 5	life for my sake shall find it a.	103:27
And a., I would that ye should	53: 7	And a., let my servant	104:24
And a., be patient in tribulation	54:10	And a., let my servant	104:27
And a., you shall be ordained	55: 4	And a., let my servant	104:34
And a., verily I say unto you,	55: 5	And a., let my servant	104:39
And a., let my servant Joseph	55: 6	And a., let my servant	104:43
And a., verily I say unto you,	56: 8	And a., a commandment I	104:54
the Lord, will pay it unto him a.	56:12	And a., there shall be another	104:67
be rewarded a. according to that	56:12	And a., verily I say unto you,	104:78
And a., verily I say unto you,	57: 8	And a. I say unto you,	105:38
And a., verily I say unto you,	57:11	And a., verily I say unto you,	106: 4
and it shall not be given a.	58:16	And a., verily I say unto you,	106: 6

A., verily, I say unto you,	DC	107:78
And a., verily I say unto you,		107:85
A., the duty of the president		107:89
And a., the duty of the President		107:91
the heavens were a. opened unto		110:11
And a., I say unto you,		112:21
of priesthood to bring a. Zion,		113: 8
And a., verily I say unto you,		115:17
send a. the snows upon the earth.		117: 1
And a., I say unto you,		117:12
when he falls he shall rise a.,		117:13
And a., verily I say unto you,		117:16
hail thee a. with warm hearts		121: 9
And a., we would suggest for		123: 1
And a., I will visit and soften		124: 9
And a., verily I say unto you,		124:12
And a., verily I say unto you,		124:15
A., let my servant John C. Bennett		124:16
And a., I say unto you that it		124:18
And a., verily I say unto you,		124:20
And a., verily I say unto you,		124:25
restore a. that which was lost		124:28
And a., verily I say unto you,		124:37
And a., verily I say unto you,		124:55
I command you a. to build a		124:55
And a., verily I say unto you,		124:70
And a., verily I say unto you,		124:91
And a., verily I say unto you,		124:103
he shall lift up his voice a. on		124:104
And a., verily I say unto you,		124:111
And a., verily I say unto you,		124:115
And a., verily I say unto you,		124:119
And a., verily I say unto you,		124:121
And a., I say unto you, I give		124:131
And a., I give unto you		124:133
And a., I say unto you,		124:137
And a., I give unto you		124:138
And a., I say unto you,		124:141
And a., I say unto you,		124:142
were a. in the pursuit of me;		127: 1
then I will return to you a.		127: 1
And a., verily thus saith the Lord:		127: 4
And a., I give unto you a word		127: 5
And a., let all the records be		127: 9
And a., for the precedent,		128:10
And a., in connection with this		128:17
And a., what do we hear?		128:20
And a., the voice of God in the		128:21
And a., I say how glorious is		128:23
And a., verily I say unto you,		132:18
And a., verily I say unto you,		132:19
And a., verily I say,		132:47
And a., verily I say unto you,		132:48
And a., verily I say, let mine		132:56
And a., I say, let not my		132:57
And a., as pertaining to		132:61
And a., verily, verily, I say		132:64
Yea, verily I say unto you a.,		133: 7
When I called a. there was none		133:67
thou shalt deliver it to him a.		136:26
a. receive his natural strength	Mses	1:10
And a. Moses said:		1:18
of God, he beheld his glory a.,		1:25
they shall be had a. among		1:41
And a., I, God, said:		2: 6
a. in the flesh I shall see God.		5:10
And she a. conceived and bare		5:17
And Adam knew his wife a.,		6: 2
born a. into the kingdom of		6:59
a. the Lord said unto me:		7: 6
And a. Enoch wept and cried		7:58
not come a. upon the earth?		7:59
wilt not come a. on the earth.		7:59
turned a. unto his idolatry,	Abr	2: 5
called a. upon the name of		2:20
he should come a. on the earth,	JS	1: 1
shall be sent a. upon Israel.		1:18
and a., after the tribulation of		1:21
And a., because iniquity shall		1:30
And a., this Gospel of the		1:31
And a. shall the abomination of		1:32
I reflected on it a. and		2:12
reflected on it again and a.,		2:12
He a. forbade me to join with	JS	2:20
When I came to myself a.,		2:20
And a., he quoted the fifth verse		2:38
Al, he told me, that when I got		2:42
I knew the place a. when I		2:42
until the room was a. left dark,		2:43
my room was a. beginning to		2:44
heavenly messenger was a. by		2:44
a. related the very same things		2:45
he a. ascended as he had done		2:45
a. I beheld the same messenger		2:46
or repeat over a. to me		2:46
he a. ascended into heaven as		2:47
I was a. left to ponder on		2:47
He then a. related unto me all		2:49
was a. informed that the time		2:53
never be taken a. from the earth		2:69
do offer a. an offering unto the		2:69
And a., so soon as I had		2:73

AGAINST

Nephi's brethren rebel a. him.	1Ne	1:hd
many things a. their father,		2:11
did murmur a. their father.		2:12
they durst not utter a. him;		2:14
I did not rebel a. him		2:16
brethren shall rebel a. thee,		2:21
day that they shall rebel a. me,		2:23
except they shall rebel a. me also.		2:23
if it so be that they rebel a. me,		2:24
had complained a. my father,		5: 2
my mother complained a. my		5: 3
and their families, did rebel a. us;		7: 6
against us; yea, a. me, Nephi,		7: 6
thing that they had done a. me.		7:20
fight a. the apostles of the Lamb;		11:34
to fight a. the twelve apostles		11:35
shall fight a. the twelve apostles		11:36
to battle, one a. the other;		12: 2
a. the seed of my brethren;		12:15
brethren did contend a. my seed,		12:19
land also, to battle a. them.		13:17
together a. them to battle.		13:18
hearts a. the Lamb of God,		14: 2
hearts a. the Lamb of God.		14: 6
to fight a. the Lamb of God.		14:13
spoken hard things a. the wicked,		16: 2
Thou speakest hard things a. us.		16: 3
began to murmur a. the Lord		16:20
they did murmur a. the Lord.		16:20
complaining a. the Lord their		16:22
his murmuring a. the Lord,		16:25
they did murmur a. my father,		16:35
they did murmur a. my father,		16:36
my father, and also a. me;		16:36
they began to murmur a. me,		17:17
my brethren did complain a. me,		17:18
murmur and complain a. us.		17:22
reviled a. Moses and against		17:30
and a. the true and living God.		17:30
did curse the land a. them,		17:35
yea, he did curse it a. them		17:35
they did revile a. Moses and		17:42
against Moses, and also a. God;		17:42
murmur no more a. their father;		17:49
and could not contend a. me;		17:52
I did not murmur a. the Lord		18:16
a. anyone that should speak for me;		18:17
hearts a. the Holy One of Israel,		19:15
make haste a. thy destroyers;		21:17
a. him will they harden their		22: 5
nation which shall war a. thee,		22:14
shall be turned one a. another,		22:14
all that fight a. Zion shall		22:14
hearts a. the Holy One of Israel.		22:18
who fight a. Zion shall be cut off.		22:19
Nephi's brethren rebel a. him.	2Ne	1:hd
Rebel no more a. your brother,		1:24
their anger did increase a. me,		5: 2
Yea, they did murmur a. me,		5: 3
words which they murmured a. me.		5: 4
had hardened their hearts a. him,		5:21
their necks a. the Holy One		6:10

AGAINST

repent and fight not a. Zion,	2Ne	6:12
they that fight a. Zion and the		6:13
transgressing a. the Holy God,		9:39
I have spoken hard things a. you;		9:40
if ye do, ye will revile a. the truth;		9:40
the words of truth are hard a. all		9:40
necks a. him, that he be crucified.		10: 5
this land a. all other nations.		10:12
that fighteth a. Zion shall perish,		10:13
he that raiseth up a king a. me		10:14
he that fighteth a. Zion, both Jew		10:16
who are not for me are a. me,		10:16
shall not lift up sword a. nation,		12: 4
himself proudly a. the ancient,		13: 5
and the base a. the honorable.		13: 5
doings have been a. the Lord,		13: 8
countenance doth witness a. them,		13: 9
of the Lord kindled a. his people,		15:25
stretched forth his hand a. them,		15:25
that day they shall roar a. them		15:30
toward Jerusalem to war a. it,		17: 1
but could not prevail a. it.		17: 1
taken evil counsel a. thee, saying:		17: 5
Let us go up a. Judah		17: 6
the adversaries of Rezin a. him,		19:11
they together shall be a. Judah.		19:21
send him a. a hypocritical nation,		20: 6
and a. the people of my wrath		20: 6
as boast itself a. him that heweth		20:15
the saw magnify itself a. him that		20:15
shake itself a. them that lift if up,		20:15
lift up his staff a. thee,		20:24
shall shake his hand a. the mount		20:32
I will stir up the Medes a. them,		23:17
proverb a. the king of Babylon,		24: 4
no feller is come up a. us.		24: 8
For I will rise up a. them,		24:22
wo unto them that fight a. God		25:14
need not harden their hearts a. him		25:27
shall stand as a testimony a. you;		25:28
God from the ground a. them.		26: 3
Lord shall be kindled a. them,		26: 6
God shall have camped a. them		26:15
shall have laid siege a. them		26:15
and raised forts a. them;		26:15
the nations that fight a. Zion,		27: 3
nations be that fight a. Mount Zion.		27: 3
shall cry from the ground a. them.		28:10
and revile a. that which is good,		28:16
up to anger a. that which is good.		28:20
unto them that fight a. my word		29:14
against my word and a. my people,		29:14
their hearts a. the Holy Spirit,		33: 2
And it speaketh harshly a. sin,		33: 5
brought a. you at the judgment		33:15
all men not to rebel a. God,	Jac	1: 8
unto me a. the men of my people,		2:32
hearts ascend up to God a. you.		2:35
which cometh down a. you,		2:35
revile no more a. them because		3: 9
shall ye revile a. them because		3: 9
warning them a. fornication and		3:12
lay up fruit thereof a. the season,		5:13
I shall lay up a. the season,		5:18
of the fruit thereof a. the season,		5:19
and lay it up a. the season,		5:20
and lay it up a. the season,		5:23
canst lay it up a. the season.		5:27
I must lay up fruit a. the season,		5:29
laid up unto myself a. the season		5:31
laid up fruit thereof a. the season,		5:46
a. the time which will soon come.		5:71
unto mine own self a. the season,		5:76
did Sherem contend a. me.		7: 7
they had an eternal hatred a. us,		7:24
of Nephi did fortify a. them		7:25
they came many times a. us,	Jar	1: 7
they did not prosper a. us.		1: 9
to battle a. his people.	WM	1:13
and he did stand a. them;		1:13
they did contend a. their enemies,		1:14
did contend a. the Lamanites		1:14
out in open rebellion a. God;	Mos	2:37
knoweth that he rebelleth a. God!		3:12
a bright testimony a. this people,		3:24
for father fought a. father,		9: 2
and brother a. brother, until		9: 2
did go forth a. the Lamanites		9:16
forth to battle a. the Lamanites;		9:17
did go forth a. the Lamanites,		9:18
a. the time the Lamanites should		10: 1
up again to war a. my people.		10: 1
up in rebellion a. my people;		10: 6
come up to battle a. my people.		10: 6
that I might guard a. them,		10: 7
to go to battle a. the Lamanites;		10: 9
go up to battle a. the Lamanites;		10:10
go up to battle a. the Lamanites.		10:10
hardened their hearts a. the Lord.		10:14
king Noah sent his armies a. them,		11:18
their fifty could stand a. thousands		11:19
hearts a. the words of Abinadi,		11:29
his heart a. the word of the Lord,		11:29
their hearts a. my words;		12: 1
Abinadi prophesy a. this people.		12: 8
me to prophesy a. this people,		12:29
even a great evil a. this people?		12:29
bear false witness a. thy neighbor.		13:23
none such that rebel a. him		15:26
have wilfully rebelled a. God,		15:26
ways of sin and rebellion a. God,		16: 5
Abinadi had testified a. them;		17: 2
have found an accusation a. thee,		17: 7
shall stand as a testimony a. you.		17:10
also stand as a testimony a. you		17:10
lifted up their voices a. him,		17:12
was stirred up in anger a. him,		17:12
what have you a. being baptized		18:10
the people to rebellion a. him;		18:33
out threatenings a. the king,		19: 3
to come up to war a. my people?		20:14
to come up to war a. thy people.		20:15
already preparing to come a. us;		20:19
fulfilled, which he prophesied a. us—		20:21
up in anger a. the Nephites,		21: 2
desirous to go a. them to battle.		21: 6
and went forth a. the Lamanites		21: 7
to anger a. the Lamanites;		21:11
many sins and iniquities a. God;		21:30
were many witnesses a. them;		26: 9
whosoever transgresseth a. me,		26:29
forgive their trespasses a. me.		26:30
were going about rebelling a. God,		27:11
whosoever doth rebel a. him		29:23
will send his armies a. them to war,		29:23
bearing down a. the church;	Al	1: 3
whether it were for or a. Amlici,		2: 5
of the people came a. Amlici,		2: 7
hearts of those who were a. him;		2: 8
a. those who were not in his favor.		2: 8
take up arms a. their brethren;		2:10
them to war a. their brethren.		2:14
a. the Amlicites to battle.		2:16
might guard himself a. them,		2:21
their rebellion a. their brethren,		3: 6
that fighteth a. thee and thy seed.		3:16
come out in open rebellion a. God;		3:18
at this time a. the Lamanites.		3:22
up a numerous army a. them;		3:23
down in pure testimony a. them.		4:19
will these things testify a. you?		5:22
what have ye to say a. this?		5:58
if ye speak a. it, it matters not,		5:58
to testify a. them concerning		8:25
that if ye will rebel a. him that		9:24
hardened a. the word of God,		9:30
I went on rebelling a. God,		10: 6
they might find witness a. them,		10:13
make appear or witness a. them.		10:13
anger he will come out a. you;		10:23
revile a. our laws which are just,		10:24
have I testified a. your law?		10:26
that I have spoken a. your law;		10:26
people cried out a. him, saying:		10:28

for he hath spoken a. our law.	Al 10:28	them to come to battle a. them;	Al 46:30
says that he has not spoken a. it.	10:28	to anger a. the people of Nephi,	47: 1
he has reviled a. our lawyers,	10:29	to go to battle a. the Nephites.	47: 1
remember these things a. him.	10:30	to go to battle a. the Nephites	47: 2
which were brought a. him,	11: 2	subjected to go a. the Nephites.	47: 6
stir up the people a. Alma and	11:20	to go a. the Nephites to battle.	47:21
that thou mightest set them a. us,	12: 4	does not this testify a. them?	47:34
hardened our hearts a. the word,	12:13	a. the people of Nephi	48: 1
and had reviled a. their law	14: 2	their towers, a. the Nephites.	48: 1
also a. their lawyers and judges.	14: 2	inspire their hearts a. the Nephites,	48: 2
so plainly a. their wickedness,	14: 3	to go to battle a. the Nephites.	48: 3
forth and witnessed a. them—	14: 5	themselves a. their enemies,	48:14
that they had reviled a. the law,	14: 5	sword except it were a. an enemy,	48:14
the people testify a. Alma and	14: 5	themselves a. their enemies,	48:16
shall stand as a witness a. them,	14:11	take up arms a. the Lamanites,	48:23
and cry mightily a. them	14:11	for them to come a. the Nephites.	49:12
again to war a. the Nephites	16:12	themselves a. the Lamanites.	49:20
might not be hardened a. the word,	16:17	his people a. the Lamanites;	50: 1
did preach a. all lyings,	16:18	a. the coming of their enemies,	50: 6
their arms as were lifted a. him,	17:38	took up arms a. their brethren,	50:26
a. those who sought to slay him,	18: 2	a. the people of the Nephites,	51: 9
did not fight a. God any more,	23: 7	come to battle a. the Nephites.	51:10
neither a. any of their brethren.	23: 7	coming down to battle a. them,	51:13
to anger a. their brethren.	24: 1	soul was filled with anger a. them.	51:14
became exceeding sore a. them,	24: 2	should go a. those king-men,	51:17
they began to rebel a. their king,	24: 2	armies did march forth a. them;	51:18
a. the people of Anti-Nephi-Lehi.	24: 2	to fight a. the men of Moroni	51:18
for war a. the people of God.	24: 4	for war a. the Lamanites,	51:22
themselves a. the Lamanites.	24: 5	to go a. the city of Nephihah	51:25
take up arms a. their brethren;	24: 6	to defend himself a. them,	52: 6
that they were coming a. them	24:21	and behold, I go a. them,	52:11
been racked with hatred a. us,	26: 9	marched forth a. the Nephites	52:12
Let us take up arms a. them,	26:25	with his army a. the Lamanites;	52:17
take up arms a. their brethren,	26:34	to come out a. them to battle;	52:19
had gone to war a. the Nephites	27: 1	did march forth a. Teancum,	52:23
people in anger a. their brethren,	27: 2	the Lamanites coming out a. him	52:23
sins we have committed a. them.	27: 6	with his army coming a. them,	52:28
which we have committed a. them.	27: 8	with exceeding fury a. Moroni.	52:33
It is a. the law of our brethren,	27: 9	a. the breastwork of timbers;	53: 4
to anger a. their brethren	27:12	to guard a. the Lamanites,	53: 7
take up arms a. their brethren	27:23	taking up arms a. their brethren;	53:11
take up arms a. their brethren;	27:28	themselves a. their enemies,	53:16
unto the people a. the prophecies	30: 6	ye have waged a. my people,	54: 5
was no law a. a man's belief;	30: 7	thy brother hath waged a. them,	54: 5
was no law a. a man's belief;	30:11	fought a. the people of the Lord,	54: 8
do ye speak a. all the prophecies	30:22	I will come a. you with my armies;	54:12
that he would revile even a. God,	30:29	and I will come a. you, and I will	54:12
revile a. the priests and teachers,	30:31	threatenings a. me and my people;	54:19
ye deny a. all these witnesses?	30:45	a war a. the people of Nephi.	55: 1
a. the power of your enemies.	34:22	go a. the Nephites to battle.	55:10
Yea, cry unto him a. the devil,	34:23	us to go a. the Nephites.	55:11
no more a. the Holy Ghost,	34:38	weapons of war a. their brethren	56: 6
a. those who do cast you out	34:40	not come a. the city of Judea,	56:18
out many threatenings a. them.	35: 9	of Lamoni, or a. us, to battle.	56:18
anger a. the people of Ammon,	35:10	down a. the city of Zarahemla;	56:25
them up also to anger a. them.	35:10	their army and marched a. us.	56:35
for war a. the people of Ammon,	35:11	and we could not stand a. them,	56:40
Ammon, and also a. the Nephites.	35:11	that we should come a. them,	56:43
that I had rebelled a. my God,	36:13	will ye go a. them to battle?	56:44
hatred a. sin and iniquity.	37:32	thousand a. these Lamanites	56:49
Now this is what I have a. thee;	39: 2	to go a. the city of Antiparah,	57: 3
a. the light and knowledge of	39: 6	did rise up in rebellion a. us.	57:32
testimony a. you at the last day.	39: 8	forth a. us from time to time,	58: 6
one more offense a. your God	41: 9	all our might a. the Lamanites,	58:13
if there was no law given a. sin	42:20	out to battle a. us and kill us,	58:15
to anger a. the Nephites;	43: 8	to come out a. us to battle.	58:15
to withstand a. the Lamanites,	43:13	preparations to come out a. us,	58:16
durst not come a. the Nephites	43:22	a. the time that the Lamanites	58:17
themselves a. the Lamanites.	43:23	with their numerous army a. us.	58:18
to battle a. the Lamanites,	43:26	to go a. the Lamanites to battle,	59: 5
they were prepared a. the time of	43:26	forth a. the people of Nephihah,	59: 7
to stand a. the Lamanites	43:50	and send forth a. the Lamanites,	60: 2
not come out to battle a. you	44: 2	and gone forth a. our enemies,	60:16
for which ye have come a. us;	44: 2	of taking up their swords a. us,	60:16
and come not again to war a. us.	44: 6	a. them in the strength of the Lord,	60:16
not return again a. us to war.	44:11	other power can operate a. them—	60:25
powerfully a. the Nephites.	44:16	in judgment a. the Lamanites,	60:32
come to war again a. them.	44:19	ye shall go up to battle a. them.	60:33
they shall sin a. so great light	45:12	have risen up in rebellion a. me,	61: 3
together a. their brethren.	46: 1	have risen up in rebellion a. us	61: 7
were wroth a. their brethren	46: 3	durst not come out a. us to battle.	61: 7
to stand a. Amalickiah and	46:28	and take the sword a. us.	61:11
the Lamanites to anger a. them,	46:30	go speedily a. those dissenters,	61:17

AGAINST

yea, we will go forth a. them	Al	61:18
just in us to go a. our brethren.		61:19
you that ye should go a. them.		61:20
had rebelled a. their country		62: 2
and went forth a. the city,		62: 7
country, but would fight a. it,		62: 9
the land a. the Lamanites.		62:13
weapons of war a. the Nephites.		62:16
should come out to battle a. them,		62:19
they durst not come out a. them;		62:19
should march forth a. them,		62:25
that Moroni was coming a. them,		62:31
at that time a. the Nephites.		62:38
again to anger a. the Nephites.		63:14
war a. the people of Moronihah,		63:15
or a. the army of Moronihah,		63:15
up in rebellion a. their brethren.	He	1: 7
pitch battle a. the Nephites.		1:15
could stand a. the Lamanites,		1:16
to battle a. the Nephites.		1:17
did smite him a. the wall,		1:21
about to go forth a. all the land.		1:22
Lamanites to war a. the Nephites;		4: 3
up to anger a. the Nephites;		4: 4
down a. the Nephites to battle,		4: 5
they did fortify a. the Lamanites,		4: 7
provoked him to anger a. you.		7:18
false witness a. your neighbor,		7:21
to withstand a. your enemies.		7:22
sinned a. that great knowledge		7:24
and they cried out a. him,		8: 1
hearest him revile a. this people		8: 2
this people and a. our law?		8: 2
lest they should cry out a. them.		8: 4
suffer this man to revile a. us?		8: 5
up the people to anger a. Nephi,		8: 7
and rebelled a. your holy God;		8:25
wrath a. the day of judgment.		8:25
did cry out a. Nephi, saying:		9:16
which they had spoken a. Nephi,		9:18
therefore they did revile a. him,		10:15
they were divided a. themselves		10:18
forth again a. this band of robbers,		11:30
should not declare wars a. them;		12: 2
hearts of their brethren a. them,		13: 8
will harden their hearts a. me,		13:12
is already kindled a. you;		13:30
and because it was hard a. you,		14:10
will not lift their swords a. them,		15: 9
the people a. that which was good		16:22
and a. that which should come·		16:22
should take up arms a. them.	3Ne	2:11
arms a. those Gadianton robbers,		2:12
come forth a. the people of Nephi;		2:18
can stand a. so many brave men		3: 3
if they should come down a. you		3: 4
my armies shall come down a. you,		3: 8
for strength a. the time that		3:12
should come down a. them.		3:12
out of the wilderness a. them.		3:17
for if we should go up a. them		3:21
and we will not go a. them,		3:21
wait till they shall come a. us;		3:21
defend themselves a. their enemies.		3:22
themselves a. their enemies;		3:25
come down a. them to battle.		3:25
in open battle a. the Nephites;		4: 4
go up to battle a. the Nephites,		4: 5
go up to battle a. the Nephites.		4: 6
threatenings a. their brethren		5: 5
they did wilfully rebel a. God.		6:18
a. these judges who had		6:25
to combine a. all righteousness.		6:28
a. the people of the Lord,		6:29
were divided one a. another;		7: 2
given his voice a. the prophets		7:10
should not trespass a. another,		7:14
come any more unto me a. them.		9: 5
up any more unto me a. them.		9: 7
up any more unto me a. them.		9: 8
up unto me any more a. them.		9: 9
unto me from the ground a. them.		9:11
men with anger, one a. another:		11:30
hell shall not prevail a. them.	3Ne	11:39
all manner of evil a. you falsely,		12:11
thy brother hath aught a. thee—		12:23
Gentiles shall sin a. my gospel,		16:10
shall harden their hearts a. me		20:28
surely gather together a. thee,		22:15
shall gather together a. thee		22:15
No weapon that is formed a. thee		22:17
tongue that shall rise a. thee		22:17
swift witness a. the sorcerers,		24: 5
sorcerers, and a. the adulterers,		24: 5
adulterers, and a. false swearers,		24: 5
a. those that oppress the hireling		24: 5
words have been stout a. me,		24:13
What have we spoken a. thee?		24:13
rebel a. the gospel of Christ;	4Ne	1:38
wilfully rebelled a. their God;	Mrm	1:16
of Nephites, a. the Lamanites;		2: 2
defent ourselves a. the Lamanites.		2: 4
came a. us with an army of		2: 9
in open rebellion a. their God,		2:15
did stand with boldness a. them.		2:24
a. an army of fifty thousand.		2:25
did go forth a. the Lamanites		2:27
their arms a. the time of battle.		3: 1
harden their hearts a. the Lord		3: 3
to come again to battle a. us.		3: 4
fortify a. them with all our force.		3: 6
of Desolation to battle a. us;		3: 7
go up to battle a. their enemies.		3:10
refused to go up a. mine enemies;		3:16
to battle a. the Lamanites,		4: 1
to come a. the city Teancum.		4: 6
did come a. the city Teancum,		4: 7
forward a. the city Teancum,		4:14
they did go a. the Lamanites		4:15
not come again a. the Nephites		4:16
did come down a. the Nephites		4:17
come down a. the city Desolation;		4:19
they did stand a. the Lamanites		4:20
the Lamanites did come a. us		5: 3
that they came a. us again,		5: 4
did come again a. us to battle,		5: 6
we did stand a. them boldly;		5: 6
come out in justice a. you—		5:24
that they came to battle a. us,		6: 8
strifes a. the work of the Lord,		8:21
a. the covenant people of the Lord		8:21
stand a. the works of God?		9:26
rise up a. the almighty power of		9:26
I prepare you a. these things;	Eth	2:25
you a. the waves of the sea,		2:25
contend a. the word of the Lord,		4: 8
stand as a testimony a. the world		5: 4
he rebelled a. his father, and went		7: 4
that Noah rebelled a. Shule,		7:15
people did revile a. the prophets,		7:24
a. all those who did revile		7:24
who did revile a. the prophets.		7:24
And Jared rebelled a. his father,		8: 2
name was Shez, did rebel a. him;		10: 3
did rise up in rebellion a. him;		10: 8
did rise up in rebellion a. him,		10:14
make war a. the king of the land,		10:15
to battle a. the king, Amgid,		10:32
Now Com did fight a. them much;		10:34
he did not prevail a. them.		10:34
of Shiblom rebelled a. him,		11: 4
would execute judgment a. them		11:20
fighting a. Coriantumr that they		13:18
he went a. him with his armies		13:27
Shared fought a. him for the		13:28
of Lib did come a. Coriantumr		14:16
to anger a. the people of Shiz;		15: 6
a. the people of Coriantumr;		15: 6
forth one a. another to battle;		15:15
and fighteth a. him continually,	Mro	7:12
stand a. you at the judgment-seat		8:21
not out soon a. the Lamanites.		8:27
they tremble and anger a. me;		9: 4
they harden their hearts a. it;		9: 4
his hand in judgment a. us?		9:14
you a. all the fiery darts of the	DC	3: 8

AGAINST 32 AGE

mine anger is kindled a. them.	DC	5: 8
they harden their hearts a. them;		5:18
let earth and hell combine a. you,		6:34
iniquity a. that which is good;		10:20
their hearts to anger a. this work.		10:24
designs in lying a. those words.		10:31
to stir them up to anger a. you,		10:32
same is not of me, but is a. me;		10:68
of hell shall not prevail a. them.		10:69
of hell shall not prevail a. you;		17: 8
of hell shall not prevail a. you.		18: 5
Contend a. no church, save it be		18:20
in me, reviling not a. revilers.		19:30
of hell shall not prevail a. you;		21: 6
and a. poisonous serpents,		24:13
and a. deadly poisons;		24:13
the dust of your feet a. them		24:15
in all things a. the day when		29: 8
that they shall not utter a. me;		29:19
for he rebelled a. me, saying,		29:36
prepare them a. the time when		31: 8
revile not a. those that revile.		31: 9
nothing shall prevail a. them.		32: 3
of hell shall not prevail a. you.		33:13
a. the time that my servant		37: 3
word shall be established a. him		42:80
shall lift up their hands a. him		42:81
will harden their hearts a. me,		45:33
up the sword, one a. another,		45:33
take his sword a. his neighbor		45:68
not go up to battle a. Zion,		45:70
you shall proclaim a. that spirit		50:32
is kingled a. the rebellious,		56: 1
or a. none is his wrath kindled,		59:21
mine anger is kindled a. them.		60: 2
a. those who receive thee not,		60:15
as a testimony a. them		60:15
voices unto God a. that people,		61:31
is kindled a. their wickedness,		61:31
anger is kindled a. the wicked		63: 2
their hearts to anger a. you,		63:28
have sought occasion a. him		64: 6
sought occasion a. one another		64: 8
their strong reasons a. the Lord.		71: 8
weapon that is formed a. you		71: 9
any man lift his voice a. you		71:10
as a testimony a. them.		75:20
rebelled a. the Only Begotten		76:25
the devil, who rebelled a. God,		76:28
who sins a. the greater light		82: 3
a. the inhabitants of the earth;		82: 6
soul that sins a. this covenant,		82:21
and hardeneth his heart a. it,		82:21
his anger was kindled a. them,		84:24
for their rebellion a. you		84:76
a. the day of vengeance and		85: 3
divided a. the Northern States		87: 3
defend themselves a. other nations;		87: 3
shall rise up a. their masters,		87: 4
come up to battle a. Michael		88:113
For ye have sinned a.		95: 1
is kindled a. their abominations		97:24
of hell shall not prevail a. you.		98:22
patiently and revile not a. them,		98:23
you revile not a. your enemy,		98:25
shall stand a. your enemy if		98:27
go out unto battle a. any nation,		98:33
should proclaim war a. them,		98:34
out to battle a. that nation,		98:36
as a testimony a. thine enemy—		98:39
he has trespassed a. thee,		98:40
And if he trespass a. thee		98:41
And if he trespass a. thee		98:42
And if he trespass a. thee		98:43
But if he trespass a. thee		98:44
he has trespassed a. thee,		98:44
before the Lord a. them.		98:48
the way for a testimony a. them.		99: 4
they have committed a. me,		99: 5
as they gather together a. you,		101:58
sore and grievous sin a. me		101:98
against me, and a. my people,		101:98
to prevail a. mine enemies		103: 6
the world shall prevail a. them.		103: 8
as mine enemies come a. you		103:24
brought before me a. them,	DC	103:24
no weapon formed a. them shall		109:25
if any people shall rise a. this		109:27
thine anger be kindled a. them;		109:27
a. thy servant or servants,		109:29
and slanders a. thy people.		109:30
prepared a. the day of burning.		109:46
stiffen not their necks a. me,		112:13
rebel not a. my servant Joseph;		112:15
and have blasphemed a. me		112:26
anger be kindled a. our enemies;		121: 5
thy friends do not contend a. thee,		121:10
the heel a. mine anointed,		121:16
swear falsely a. my servants,		121:18
murder, and testify a. them,		121:23
himself, to kick a. the pricks,		121:38
the saints, and to fight a. God.		121:38
and hell shall rage a. thee;		122: 1
shall never be turned a. thee		122: 3
surge conspire a. thee;		122: 7
of their prosecutions a. me;		127: 1
of hell shall not prevail a. it.		128:10
blasphemy a. the Holy Ghost,		132:27
did he sin a. me save in the case		132:39
she has trespassed a. me;		132:56
bringing offenders a. good laws		134: 8
ears of the Lord a. this people.		136: 8
crieth from the ground a. them.		136:36
that Satan rebelled a. me,	Mses	4: 3
Cain rose up a. Abel, his brother,		5:32
and they rebelled a. him,		5:53
hand was a. his own brother,		6:15
fierce anger is kindled a. them;		6:27
voice, testifying a. their works;		6:37
array a. the people of Shum,		7: 7
enemies came to battle a. them;		7:13
all people that fought a. God;		7:15
indignation is kindled a. them;		7:34
fierce anger is kindled a. them.		7:34
is kindled a. the sons of men,		8:15
hath lifted up his hand a. thee,	Abr	1:17
which he had determined a. me,		1:30
for nation shall rise a. nation,	JS	1:29
nation, and kingdom a. kingdom;		1:29
a. its character as a Church		2: 1
priest contending a. priest,		2: 6
priest, and convert a. convert;		2: 6
most decided a. the Baptists		2: 9
of darkness combine a. me?		2:20
and persecution that arose a. me,		2:20
a great deal of prejudice a. me		2:22
excite the public mind a. me,		2:22
all manner of evil a. me		2:25

AGATES

I will make thy windows of a.,	3Ne	22:12

AGE

every one according to his a.;	1Ne	18: 6
in the thirtieth year of his a.,	Mos	6: 4
every man according to his a.		10: 9
and I, even I, in my old a.,		10:10
were many who died with old a.;	Al	46:41
we have lived unto the a. of man,	3Ne	28: 2
(I being about ten years of a.,	Mrm	1: 2
when ye are of that a. go to		1: 3
And I, being fifteen years of a.		1:15
he had begat Kib in his old a.	Eth	7: 3
Kib begat Shule in his old a.,		7: 7
sons and daughters in his old a.		7:26
in his old a. he begat Emer;		9:14
to wife, in his old a., a young maid,		9:24
did live to an exceeding old a.;		10: 4
did live to an exceeding great a.,		10:13
and in his old a. he begat Levi;		10:14
and he did live to a good old a.,		10:16
And he lived to a good old a.,		11: 4
in this a. and generation,	DC	20:11
to him to die at the a. of man.		63:50
maintenance until they are of a.		83: 4
life shall be as the a. of a tree;		101:30
they that are of middle a. also		101:55
at the a. of sixty-nine years,		107:42
from him only by his a.		107:43

AGE

AGE
at the a. of one hundred and — DC 107:44
in the fortieth year of his a.; — 107:45
he was bowed down with a., — 107:56
son, although but six years of a., — 122: 6
From a. to age shall their — 135: 6
age to a. shall their names go — 135: 6
in the 27th year of his a.), — JS 2: 4
fourteen and fifteen years of a., — 2:22
little over fourteen years of a., — 2:23

AGED
yea, I say unto you the a., — Al 5:49
the aged, and also the middle a., — 5:49
mine a. servant, Joseph Smith, Sen., — DC 90:20
especially mine a. servant Joseph — 90:25
young men and the middle a.— — 103:22
my young men, and middle-a., — 105:16
my a. servant Joseph Smith, Sen., — 124:19

AGENCY
away from me because of their a.; — DC 29:36
to his a. in the land of Zion; — 64:18
Behold, here is the a. of man, — 93:31
the moral a. which I have given — 101:78
sought to destroy the a. of man, — Mses 4: 3
gave I unto man his a.; — 7:32

AGENT
he should be an a. unto himself; — DC 29:35
a. appointed unto this people, — 51: 8
through the bishop or the a., — 51:12
also to be an a. unto this church — 53: 4
to be an a. unto the church, — 57: 6
Let the bishop and the a. make — 57:15
let there be an a. appointed — 58:49
the bishop, of himself or the a., — 58:51
the bishop or the a. of the church. — 58:55
return it by the way of the a.; — 60:11
let him be ordained as an a. — 63:45
neither the a. who keepeth the — 70:11
He should also employ an a. to — 84:113
search diligently to obtain an a., — 90:22
him and his a., and his seed after — 104:41

AGENTS
could not be a. unto themselves; — DC 29:39
they are a. unto themselves. — 58:28
Wherefore, as ye are a., — 64:29
to be a. unto themselves. — 104:17
with a. and clerks who will — 127: 1
or by the means of their own a., — 128: 8
they are a. unto themselves, — Mses 6:56

AGES
days of old, and for a. to come, — DC 76: 7
the church in all a. of the world, — 107: 8
in all a. of the world, whenever — 128: 9

AGGRAVATING
most a. and distressing manner — Al 27:29

AGHAST
and to stand a. and pale, — DC 123:10

AGONY
he did exclaim in the a. of his soul: — He 7: 6

AGOSH
until he came to the plains of A. — Eth 14:15
he had come to the plains of A. — 14:16

AGREE
borroweth, according as he doth a., — Mos 4:28
A. with thine adversary quickly — 3Ne 12:25
thus they did a. with Akish. — Eth 8:15
Therefore they will not a., — DC 10:18
together to a. upon my word; — 41: 2
again according as they shall a.; — 51:11
with him, as you shall a. — 61:12

AGREEABLE
a. to the laws of our country, — DC 20: 1

AIR

a. to the holy scriptures— — DC 20:69
a. to my commandments, — 42:32
a. to his law, which he has — 85: 3
a. to the commandment — 92: 1
a. to the covenants and — 107:12
a. to the covenants and — 107:20
a. to the institution of heaven; — 107:33
a. to the revelation which says: — 107:58
a. to the commandment which — 107:77

AGREED
he hath a. to maintain the city — Al 61: 8
Nephi must have a. with some one — He 9:16
ye say that I have a. with a man — 9:23
ye say that I have a. with a man — 9:24
a. with thee, in the which ye — 9:27
be a. as touching all things — DC 27:18
have asked it of me and are a. — 29:33
are a. as touching this one thing, — 42: 3
are a. as touching the church, — 50: 1
as shall be a. by this — 104:53
must be a. to its decisions, — 107:27
shall be a. among themselves, — 124:121

AGREEING
principle a. precisely with the — DC 128: 7

AGREEMENT
the a. which thou hast made — He 9:20
they had come to an a. that — 3Ne 7:14

AGREEMENTS
a. in their secret abominations; — Al 37:27

AGRIPPA
his defense before King A., — JS 2:24

AHA
he had two sons, Lehi and A.)— — Al 16: 5

AHAH
And Ethem was the son of A. — Eth 1: 9
And A. was the son of Seth. — 1:10
A., his son, did obtain the — 11:10
being a descendant of A., did — 11:11

AHASHDAH
my servant A. [Newel K. Whitney] — DC 78: 9
my servants Alam and A. — 82:11
servant A. [Newel K. Whitney] — 96: 2
servant A. [Newel K. Whitney] — 104:39
servant A. [Newel K. Whitney] — 104:40
my servant A. [N. K. Whitney] — 104:41

AHMAN
Redeemer, even the Son A., — DC 78:20
mine apostles, saith Son A., — 95:17

AHAZ
in the days of A. the son of — 2Ne 17: 1
Go forth now to meet A., — 17: 3
the Lord spake again unto A., — 17:10
But A. said: I will not ask, — 17:12
in the year that king A. died — 24:28

AIATH
He is come to A., — 2Ne 20:28

AID
By this timely a. was I enabled — JS 2:62

AIR
it stood as it were in the a., — 1Ne 8:26
of the field and the fowls of the a., — 2Ne 2:15
and the vultures of the a., — Mos 12: 2
and also the vultures of the a.; — Al 2:38
part of his garment in the a., — 46:19
Behold the fowls of the a., for — 3Ne 13:26
snares and catch fowls of the a.; — Eth 2: 2
it is the a. which is in them; — 2:19
when thou shalt suffer for a. — 2:20
unstop the hole and receive a. — 2:20

AIR 34 ALMA

AIR (cont.)
they did rend the a. exceedingly.	Eth	15:16
did rend the a. with their cries,		15:17
forth triumphant through the a.,	Mro	10:34
the fowls of the a. shall devour	DC	29:20
and beasts, the fowls of the a.,		29:24
field and the fowls of the a.,		49:19
field and the fowls of the a.,		59:16
and of the fowls of the a.;		77: 2
beasts and of the fowls of the a.,		89:12
and over the fowl of the a.,	Mses	2:26
and over the fowl of the a.,		2:28
and to every fowl of the a.,		2:30
in the water, neither in the a.;		3: 5
field, and every fowl of the a.;		3:19
and to the fowl of the a.,		3:20
things, and the fowls of the a.;		8:26
and over the fowl of the a.,	Abr	4:26
and over the fowl of the a.,		4:28
and to every fowl of the a.,		4:30
and every fowl of the a.,		5:20
all cattle, to the fowl of the a.,		5:21
standing above me in the a.	JS	2:17
my bedside, standing in the a.,		2:30

AKISH
let my father send for A.,	Eth	8:10
now Omer was a friend to A.;		8:11
when Jared had sent for A.,		8:11
A. gathered in unto the house of		8:13
the assistance which A. desired		8:14
whatsoever thing A. made known		8:14
thus they did agree with A.		8:15
A. did administer unto them		8:15
Jared put it into the heart of A.;		8:17
wherefore, A. administered it		8:17
the secret combinations of A.		9: 1
he gave unto A. his daughter		9: 4
that A. sought the life of his		9: 5
and A. reigned in his stead.		9: 6
A. began to be jealous of his son,		9: 7
that A. begat other sons, and		9:10
the people of A. were desirous		9:11
as A. was desirous for power;		9:11
sons of A. did offer them money,		9:11
war between the sons of A. and		9:12
between the sons of Akish and A.,		9:12
him to the wilderness of A.		14: 3
him in the wilderness of A.;		14: 4
fled again to the wilderness of A.		14:14

ALAM
my servants A. and Ahashdah	DC	82:11

ALARM
just at this moment of great a.,	JS	2:16

ALARMING
a. to the people of the church,	Al	2: 3

ALBANY
New York, also to the city of A.,	DC	84:114

ALE: see BAURAK ALE.

ALERT
for the enemy is on the a.,	DC	127:11
and multitudes were on the a.	JS	2:60

ALIKE
and all are a. unto God,	2Ne	26:33
enjoy his rights and privileges a.,	Mos	29:32
all children are a. unto me;	Mro	8:17
they are all a. and partakers of		8:17
they are a. brutal, sparing none,		9:19
and be a. among this people,	DC	51: 9
receive a., that ye may be one,		51: 9

ALIVE
and we are made a. in Christ	2Ne	25:25
the roots, that they are a.	Jac	5:34
whithersoever I would are yet a.;		5:54
God this day that I am yet a.,	Mos	7:12
land of Zarahemla are yet a.		7:14

AIR (cont.)
none other have they spared a.	Al	56:12
of the people who were spared a.	3Ne	10:10
I mean them who are now a.		27:31
But little children are a. in Christ,	Mro	8:12
for they are all a. in him		8:19
all little children are a. in Christ,		8:22
ye may know that I am yet a.;		9: 1
are upon the earth, who are a.,	DC	88:96
which maketh a. all things;	Mses	6:61
but they will save her a.;	Abr	2:23

ALL: see in the APPENDIX.

ALLEGE
a. that plural marriages are still	DC	OD
parties a. that the marriage was		OD

ALLEGED
of this a. occurrence	DC	OD

ALLIANCE
he hath joined an a. with him;	Al	61: 8
in the which a. he hath agreed to		61: 8

ALLOTTED
the Lord hath a. unto me.	Al	29: 3

ALLOTTETH
he a. unto men according to	Al	29: 4

ALLOW
as their circumstances shall a.,	DC	107:98
a. all men the same privilege,	AoF	11

ALLOWANCE
sin with the least degree of a.	Al	45:16
sin with the least degree of a.;	DC	1:31

ALLOWED
a. to continue the work of	JS	2:75

ALLOWING
a. human beings to be held in	DC	134:12

ALL-POWERFUL: see ALL and POWERFUL.

ALL-SEARCHING: see ALL and SEARCHING.

ALL-WISE: see ALL and WISE.

ALMA
among them whose name was A.,	Mos	17: 2
caused that A. should be cast out		17: 3
A., who had fled from the servants		18: 1
and A. resorted thither,		18: 5
to hear the words of A.		18: 7
A. took Helam, he being one of		18:12
after A. had said these words,		18:14
both A. and Helam were buried in		18:14
A. took another, and went forth		18:15
A., having authority from God,		18:18
A. commanded that the people of		18:27
A. was stirring up the people		18:33
A. and the people of the Lord		18:34
and also for the departure of A.		21:30
desirous to become even as A.		21:34
A. and the people of the Lord,		23:hd
A., having been warned of the		23: 1
that A. should be their king,		23: 6
Thus did A. teach his people,		23:15
now, A. was their high priest,		23:16
the brethren of A. fled from		23:26
A. went forth and stood among		23:27
A. and his brethren went forth		23:29
possessed by A. and his brethren.		23:35
promised unto A. and his brethren,		23:36
after A. had shown them the way		23:37
over A. and his brethren.		23:37
to exercise authority over A.		24: 8
For Amulon knew A., that he		24: 9

ALMA 35 ALMA

And A. and his people did not	Mos 24:12	after A. had made an end of	Al 6: 1
burdens which were laid upon A.	24:15	A. had made these regulations	6: 7
And he said unto A.:	24:17	A. went and began to declare the	6: 8
A. and his people in the night-time	24:18	*The words of A. which he*	7:hd
A. and his people departed into	24:20	A. returned from the land of	8: 1
and they called the valley A.,	24:20	that A. departed from thence and	8: 3
in the valley of A. they poured	24:21	when A. had come to the city of	8: 8
And now the Lord said unto A.:	24:23	hearken unto the words of A.	8: 9
he also read the account of A.	25: 6	A. labored much in the spirit,	8:10
his power in delivering A.	25:10	we know that thou art A.;	8:11
desired that A. should also speak	25:14	while A. was thus weighed down	8:14
And A. did speak unto them,	25:15	Blessed art thou, A.; therefore,	8:15
after A. had taught the people	25:17	after A. had received his message	8:18
A. did go forth into the water	25:18	bread and meat and set before A.	8:21
of their belief on the words of A.	25:18	A. ate bread and was filled;	8:22
king Mosiah granted unto A. that	25:19	I am A., and am the high	8:23
to him by the mouth of A.	25:21	And A. tarried many days with	8:27
A., who was the high priest.	26: 7	And the word came to A.,	8:29
Mosiah had given A. the authority	26: 8	A. went forth, and also Amulek,	8:30
A. did not know concerning them;	26: 9	*The words of A., and also the*	9:hd
A. was troubled in his spirit,	26:10	*according to the record of A.*	9:hd
But king Mosiah said unto A.:	26:12	A., having been commanded of	9: 1
the spirit of A. was again troubled;	26:13	when I, A., had spoken these words,	9:31
Blessed art thou, A., and blessed	26:15	this A. hath dwelt at my house.	10:10
when A. had heard these words	26:33	to accuse Amulek and A.,	10:31
A. went and judged those that had	26:34	stir up the people against A. and	11:20
A. did regulate all the affairs of	26:37	Now A., seeing that the words	12: 1
did A. and his fellow laborers do	26:38	words that A. spake unto Zeezrom	12: 2
and they did complain to A.	27: 1	when A. had spoken these words,	12: 7
A. laid the case before their king,	27: 1	A. and Amulek had a knowledge	12: 7
and also one of the sons of A.	27: 8	And he said unto A.:	12: 8
being called A., after his father;	27: 8	And now A. began to expound	12: 9
A., arise and stand forth,	27:13	when A. had made an end of	12:19
his servant, A., who is thy father;	27:14	Now A. said unto him:	12:22
I say unto thee, A., go thy way,	27:16	when A. had said these words	13:21
which the angel spake unto A.,	27:17	And A. spake many more words	13:31
A. and those that were with him	27:18	might destroy A. and Amulek;	14: 2
astonishment of A. was so great	27:19	for they were angry with A.,	14: 2
he would open the mouth of A.,	27:22	also angry with A. and Amulek;	14: 3
the limbs of A. received their	27:23	testify against A. and Amulek.	14: 5
A. began from this time forward	27:32	been spoken by A. and Amulek;	14: 7
and those who were with A. at	27:32	that they took A. and Amulek,	14: 9
and conferred them upon A.,	28:20	was pained; and he said unto A.:	14:10
upon Alma, who was the son of A.;	28:20	But A. said unto him:	14:11
A. was appointed to be the first	29:42	Now Amulek said unto A.:	14:12
A. did walk in the ways of the	29:43	And A. said: Be it according	14:13
A. was the first and chief judge.	29:44	and stood before A. and Amulek,	14:14
and thus ended the days of A.,	29:47	that A. and Amulek answered	14:17
THE BOOK OF A.	Al 1:hd	where A. and Amulek were bound	14:23
THE SON OF A.	1:hd	power of God was upon A. and	14:25
The account of A., who was	1:hd	And A. cried, saying:	14:26
the son of A. the first,	1:hd	who smote upon A. and Amulek,	14:27
according to the record of A.,	1:hd	And A. and Amulek came forth	14:28
the first year of the reign of A.	1: 2	save it were A. and Amulek,	14:28
brought before A., to be judged	1:10	when they saw A. and Amulek	14:29
that he stood before A. and	1:11	fled from the presence of A. and	14:29
But A. said unto him:	1:12	flee from the presence of A. and	14:29
second year of the reign of A.,	1:23	A. and Amulek were commanded	15: 1
Now A., being the chief judge and	2:16	they believed in the words of A.	15: 1
A. could pursue the Amlicites no	2:20	he supposed that A. and Amulek	15: 3
And A. sent spies to follow	2:21	A. and Amulek were in the land	15: 4
A. fought with Amlici	2:29	A. said unto him, taking him by	15: 6
A., being a man of God,	2:30	And A. said: If thou believest	15: 8
when A. had said these words he	2:31	then A. cried unto the Lord,	15:10
fled back from before A. and	2:32	when A. had said these words,	15:11
his guards to contend with A.	2:32	And A. baptized Zeezrom	15:12
A., with his guards, contended	2:33	And A. established a church in	15:13
A. himself being afflicted with a	3:22	ascribing all the power of A. and	15:15
were baptized by the hand of A.,	4: 4	A. and Amulek, Amulek having	15:16
by the hand of his father A.	4: 4	after A. having established the	15:17
the cause of much affliction to A.,	4: 7	A. having seen all these things,	15:18
whom A. had consecrated to be	4: 7	knowing that A. was high priest	16: 5
A. saw the wickedness of the	4:11	A. inquired of the Lord	16: 6
A., having seen the afflictions of	4:15	A. returned and said unto them:	16: 6
A. did not grant unto him the	4:18	And A. and Amulek went forth	16:13
A. delivered up the judgment-seat	4:20	thus did A. and Amulek go forth,	16:15
The words which A., the High Priest	5:hd	*according to the record of A.*	17:hd
A. began to deliver the word of	5: 1	as A. was journeying from the	17: 1
I, A., having been consecrated by	5: 3	sons of Mosiah were with A. at	17: 2
consecrated by my father, A.,	5: 3	A. did rejoice exceedingly to	17: 2
did not my father A. believe in	5:11	that he and his brethren met A.,	27:16
and my father A. believe them?	5:11	the joy of A. in meeting his	27:19
now I, A., do command you in	5:61	A. conducted his brethren back	27:20

ALMA 36 ALONE

A. with him, into the wilderness,	Al	27:25
And A. also related unto them		27:25
he might be brought before A.,		30:29
before A. and the chief judge,		30:30
great swelling words before A.,		30:31
Now A. said unto him:		30:32
And then A. said unto him:		30:37
Now A. said unto him:		30:39
And now Korihor said unto A.:		30:43
But A. said unto him:		30:44
that A. said unto him:		30:46
Now A. said unto him:		30:49
when A. had said these words,		30:50
according to the words of A.		30:50
that A. should show forth his sign?		30:51
that A. should pray unto God,		30:54
But A. said unto him:		30:55
A. having received tidings that		31: 1
the cause of great sorrow to A.		31: 2
A. thought it was expedient that		31: 5
A. and his brethren went into		31:11
which A. and his brethren had		31:12
after A. and his brethren and his		31:19
when A. saw this his heart was		31:24
when A. had said these words,		31:36
according to the prayer of A.;		31:38
as A. was teaching and speaking		32: 4
And they came unto A.;		32: 5
And now when A. heard this,		32: 6
after A. had spoken these words,		33: 1
And A. said unto them:		33: 2
And now A. said unto them:		33:12
after A. had spoken these words		34: 1
spoken by A. and his brethren		35: 6
A. and his brethren did minister		35: 7
And A., and Ammon, and their		35:14
the two sons of A. returned		35:14
A., being grieved for the iniquity		35:15
The commandments of A. to		36:hd
The commandments of A. to		38:hd
The commandments of A. to		39:hd
the sons of A. did go forth		43: 1
A., also, himself, could not rest,		43: 1
knowing of the prophecies of A.,		43:23
word of the Lord came unto A.,		43:24
A. informed the messengers of		43:24
And thus ended the record of A.,		44:24
A. came unto his son Helaman		45: 2
And A. said again: Believest		45: 4
And A. said unto him again:		45: 6
Then A. said unto him:		45: 8
after A. had said these things		45:15
when A. had said these words		45:17
And when A. had done this		45:18
has also received A. in the spirit,		45:19
yea, and also A. and his sons,		48:18
he had refused A. to take		50:38
esteemed by A. and his fathers		50:38
A. had conferred them upon		50:38
I am Helaman, the son of A.		58:41
delivered unto Helaman by A.		63: 1
which had been commanded by A.		63:12
thus ended the account of A.,		63:17
remember the prophecies of A.,	He	4:21
who was taught unto you by A.,		5:41
which A. commanded his son		6:25
who was the son of A.,	3Ne	1:hd
who was the son of A.,		1:hd
land in which A. did establish		5:12
the faith of A. and Amulek that	Eth	12:13

ALMIGHTY

are thy works, O Lord God A.!	1Ne	1:14
by the power of his a. word		17:46
In the name of the A. God, I		17:48
thy judgments, O Lord God A.—	2Ne	9:46
as a destruction from the A.		23: 6
saith the Lord God A.,		28:15
of the piercing eye of the A. God.	Jac	2:10
except it be the Lord the A. God.	Mos	11:23
having authority from the A. God,		18:13
and the sword of his a. wrath,	Al	54: 6
the Lord God, who is the A.:	He	10:11
the name of the Lord God A.	3Ne	4:32

will rise up against the a. power	Mrm	9:26
And it is by my a. power that	DC	19:14
humble you with my a. power;		19:20
the A. God gave his Only		20:21
to reign with a. power		20:24
suffer the wrath of A. God,		76:106
of the wrath of A. God.		76:107
For, I, the A., have laid my		84:96
with you saith the Lord A.,		84:118
chastening hand of an A. God,		87: 6
of the wrath of A. God.		88:106
O Lord God A., hear us in		109:77
O Lord God A., maker of		121: 4
to hinder the A. from pouring		121:33
Behold, I am the Lord God A.,	Mses	1: 3
I, the A., have chosen thee,		1:25
and the End, the A. God;		2: 1
for the judgments of the A. God,		7:66
me with the vision of the A.,	Abr	1:15
and supplication to A. God	JS	2:29
privilege of worshiping A. God	AoF	11

ALMON: see BABBITT, Almon.

ALMOST

forth mine hand a. all the day	Jac	5:47
witnessed a. all the destruction	WM	1: 1
being as numerous a., as it were,	Al	2:27
were a. all the seed of Amulon		25: 4
my soul, a. as it were, fleeth at		26:20
brought death a. at every stroke.		43:37
a. the entire destruction of	He	2:13
possession of a. all their lands.		4:13
and also a. all of our fathers,		8:22
a. all the lawyers and the high	3Ne	6:27
as numerous a., as it were	Mrm	1: 7
and disposition of a. all men,	DC	121:39
against me, a. in my infancy?	JS	2:20
when a. immediately after the		2:47

ALMS

ye should do a. unto the poor;	3Ne	13: 1
that ye do not your a. before men		13: 1
when ye shall do your a. do not		13: 2
But when thou doest a. let not		13: 3
That thine a. may be in secret;		13: 4
the a. of your prayers have	DC	88: 2
thine a. have come up as a		112: 1

ALONE

family into the wilderness a.;	1Ne	7: 1
hath not spoken of our seed a.,		15:18
Behold, I was left a.;		21:21
I called him a., and blessed him.	2Ne	8: 2
the Lord a. shall be exalted		12:11
the Lord a. shall be exalted		12:17
a. in the midst of the earth!		15: 8
be a. in his appointed times.		24:31
behold, we are not witnesses a.	Jac	4:13
doth not come by the law a.;	Mos	13:28
faith in the words a. of my servant		26:15
faith in the words a. which thou		26:16
every man a., according to the	Al	17:17
upon the mercies of the world a.		26:28
not joy in my own success a.,		29:14
not written that Zenos a. spake		33:15
the Nephites were compelled, a.,		43:13
brethren if they would let us a.;		56:46
Let this man a., for he is a	He	10: 1
went their ways, leaving Nephi a.,	Mrm	8: 3
I even remain a. to write the		8: 5
and ore I have none, for I am a.	Mro	6: 4
relying a. upon the merits of	DC	15: 3
knoweth save me and thee a.—		16: 3
knoweth save me and thee a.—		28:11
between him and thee a., and tell		42:88
between him or her and thee a.;		76:107
trodden the wine-press a.,		82:23
Leave judgment a. with me,		84:92
go away from him a.		88:106
and trodden the wine-press a.,		109: 4
in whose name a. salvation can		124:102
servant Hyrum, and for them a.;		133:50
I have trodden the wine-press a.,		

ALONE / ALTAR / ALWAYS

ALONE
good that the man should be a.;	Mses	3:18
that the man should be a.,	Abr	5:14
around me, and finding myself a.,	JS	2:15

ALONG
river of water; and it ran a.,	1Ne	8:13
extended a. the bank of the river,		8:19
which came a. by the rod of iron,		8:20
thus bordering a. by the seashore.	Al	22:28
and leadeth them a. until he	DC	10:26
for I will lead you a.		78:18
who was laboring a. with me,	JS	2:48

ALOOF
still I kept myself a. from all	JS	2: 8

ALOUD
they all cried a. with one voice,	Mos	4: 2
forth into singing, and cry a.,	3Ne	22: 1
and thy saints shout a. for joy.	DC	109:80
let my servant William cry a.		124:101
and all ye valleys cry a.		128:23

ALPHA
I am A. and Omega, the	3Ne	9:18
I am A. and Omega, Christ	DC	19: 1
even A. and Omega, the		35: 1
the Great I AM, A. and Omega,		38: 1
that I am A. and Omega,		45: 7
the Lord, even A. and Omega,		54: 1
everlasting, even A. and Omega,		61: 1
I am A. and Omega, even Jesus		63:60
Behold, I am A. and Omega,		68:35
even A. and Omega, your Lord		75: 1
the words of A. and Omega,		81: 7
I am A. and Omega,		84:120
I am A. and Omega.		112:34
Behold, I am A. and Omega.		132:66

ALPHEUS: see CUTLER, Alpheus.

ALPHUS
or in other words, A.;	DC	95:17

ALREADY
there are many who are a. lost	1Ne	22: 4
have a. gone forth among them.	2Ne	3:11
and we had a. had wars		5:34
of those who are a. wounded,	Jac	2: 9
him to come as though he a. was.	Jar	1:11
even as though he had a. come	Mos	3:13
as though they have a. come,		16: 6
they are a. preparing to come		20:19
our flocks are scattered a.	Al	17:28
I have had great joy in thee a.,		38: 3
whom thou hast a. destroyed.	He	11:11
anger of the Lord is a. kindled		13:30
desolation is a. come upon you,		13:32
had been given was a. at hand.	3Ne	1:16
had been given was a. at hand;		1:18
things which had come to pass a.		5: 2
adultery a. in his heart.		12:28
hath a. commenced unto the		21: 7
is a. beginning to be fulfilled.		29: 1
Spirit of the Lord hath a. ceased	Mrm	5:16
slain by the sword a. nearly two	Eth	15: 2
the field is white a. to harvest;	DC	4: 4
the field is white a. to harvest;		6: 3
the field is white a. to harvest;		11: 3
the field is white a. to harvest;		12: 3
the field is white a. to harvest;		14: 3
to come who has a. come.		19:27
which is white a. to be burned.		31: 4
the field is white a. to harvest;		33: 3
the field is white a. to harvest;		33: 7
for even now a. summer is nigh.		35:16
even now a. in store sufficient,		101:75
a. come into the borders of	Abr	2:18
had a. come into the land of		2:18
which had a. manifested itself	JS	2:74

ALSO: see in the APPENDIX.

ALTAR
he built an a. of stones,	1Ne	2: 7
with the tongs from off the a.,	2Ne	16: 6
to worship God before the a.,	Al	15:17
were brought before the a. of God,		17: 4
under the a. that John saw,	DC	135: 7
to offer up upon the a. which	Abr	1: 8
the a. which stood by the hill		1:10
priest had offered upon this a.		1:11
they were killed upon this a.,		1:11
those virgins upon this a.;		1:12
may have a knowledge of this a.,		1:12
broke down the a. of Elkenah,		1:20
an a. in the land of Jershon,		2:17
arose from the place of the a.		2:20
built another a. unto the Lord,		2:20
Abraham fastened upon an a.	Fac	1: 2
The a. for sacrifice by the		1: 4
offered sacrifice upon an a.,		2: 2

ALTER
behold, Pahoran would not a.	Al	51: 3
into their hearts to a. the words	DC	10:10

ALTERATION
little a. in the affairs of the	He	16:12

ALTERED
but they a. their reckoning and	Al	11: 4
Moroni had a. the management		49:11
points of the law should be a.		51: 2
alter nor suffer the law to be a.;		51: 3
desirous that the law should be a.		51: 4
a. in a manner to overthrow		51: 5
a. and trampled under their feet	He	4:22
handed down and a. by us,	Mrm	9:32
Hebrew hath been a. by us also;		9:33
because they have a. the words,	DC	10:11
with us, and we have a. them;		10:17
behold, they have a. these words,		10:29
those who have a. my words.		10:42
decision shall be a. accordingly.		102:21

ALTERING
concerning the a. of the law.	Al	51: 3

ALTHOUGH
a. he should preach unto us that	Al	9: 2
a. a man shall declare it unto	3Ne	21: 9
a. he shall be marred because		21:10
a. a man may have many revelations	DC	3: 4
A. men set at naught the counsels		3: 7
a. a man should be baptized		22: 2
redeemed, a. she is chastened		100:13
a. their influence shall cast thee		122: 4
son, a. but six years of age,		122: 6
A., the days will come, that	JS	1:35

ALTOGETHER
Are not my princes a. kings?	2Ne	20: 8
a. for my name's glory.	DC	19: 7
yea, even a., or two by two,		62: 5
and a. turneth therefrom,		84:41
in sin, and a. abideth in sin,		88:35
not hearken a. unto the precepts		103: 4
Spirit hath not a. withdrawn	Mses	1:15

ALVIN
my brothers, A. (who died	JS	2: 4
death of my eldest brother, A.		2:56

ALWAYS
to keep his commandments a.	1Ne	15:25
of the Lord will not a. strive with	2Ne	26:11
ye must pray a., and not faint;		32: 9
commandments a. before our eyes,	Mos	1: 5
and a. retain in remembrance,		4:11
if ye do this ye shall a. rejoice,		4:12
and a. retain a remission of		4:12
the name written a. in your hearts,		5:12
a. abounding in good works,		5:15
ye could a. have just men to be		23: 8
the judgments of God are a. just,		29:12

ALWAYS 38 AMALICKIAHITES

judgments of man are not a. just.	Mos	29:12
if this could a. be the case		29:13
that ye should a. have kings to		29:13
a. returning thanks unto God	Al	7:23
ye will a. abound in good works.		7:24
the love of God a. in your hearts,		13:29
had a. attended the Nephites,		19:27
a. remembered the captivity of		29:12
have a. retained in remembrance		36:29
ye do a. remember your riches,	He	13:22
this shall ye a. observe to do,	3Ne	18: 6
that ye do a. remember me.		18: 7
And if ye do a. remember me		18: 7
And this shall ye a. do to those		18:11
that ye do a. remember me.		18:11
And if ye do a. remember me		18:11
if ye shall a. do these things		18:12
ye must watch and pray a.,		18:15
ye must watch and pray a. lest		18:18
Therefore ye must a. pray unto		18:19
unto the Father, a. in my name,		18:21
Lord would not a. suffer them to	Mrm	2:13
Spirit will not a. strive with man;	Eth	2:15
shall a. cry unto him from		8:22
a. abounding in good works,		12: 4
and a. remember him, and keep	Mro	4: 3
that they may a. have his Spirit		4: 3
that they do a. remember him,		5: 2
mindful of you a. in my prayers,		8: 3
Spirit shall not a. strive with	DC	1:33
Pray a., that you may come off		10: 5
cannot a. judge the righteous,		10:37
cannot a. tell the wicked from		10:37
Pray a., and I will pour out		19:38
the church take heed and pray a.,		20:33
is to watch over the church a.,		20:53
assisted a., in all his duties		20:57
thy Son, and a. remember him		20:77
that they may a. have his Spirit		20:77
that they do a. remember him,		20:79
Pray a., lest you enter into		31:12
shall pray a. that I may unfold		32: 4
be faithful, praying a.,		33:17
it a. has been given to the		46: 2
a. remembering for what they		46: 8
that ye should a. remember,		46:10
and a. retain in your minds		46:10
Pray a. that you enter		61:39
and lo, I am with the faithful a.		62: 9
Praying a. that they faint not;		75:11
belong a. unto the Presidency		81: 2
in prayer a., vocally and in thy		81: 3
Pray a., that ye may not faint,		88:126
pray a., and be believing,		90:24
pray a. lest that wicked one		93:49
concerned at home, and pray a.,		93:50
seek the face of the Lord a.,		101:38
for men ought a. to pray		101:81
but men do not a. do my will.		103:31
are a. commanded to build		124:39
this power has a. been given.		128: 9
of his seed should a. be found	Mses	7:52
shall not a. strive with man,		8:17

AM: *see in the APPENDIX.*

AMALEKI
I am A., the son of Abinadom.	Om	1:12
I, A., was born in the days of		1:23
And I, A., had a brother,		1:30
Benjamin, of whom A. spake,	WM	1: 3
after A. had delivered up these		1:10
and their names were A., Helem,	Mos	7: 6

AMALEKITE
behold there arose an A.	Al	21: 5

AMALEKITES
the Lamanites and the A. and	Al	21: 2
but the A. and the Amulonites		21: 3
first began to preach to the A.		21: 4
the A. and the Amulonites were		21: 4
in every synagogue of the A.,		21:16
the A. say that there is a God,	Al	22: 7
And the A. were not converted,		23:14
the A. and the Amulonites and		24: 1
were stirred up by the A. and		24: 1
brethren were A. and Amulonites,		24:28
there were none who were A.		24:29
the A., because of their loss, were		27: 2
hold on the hearts of the A.,		27:12
as the A. were of a more wicked		43: 6
they were all A. and Zoramites.		43: 6
who were A. and Zoramites,		43:13
it were the Zoramites and the A.:		43:20
by the Zoramites and the A.,		43:44

AMALICKIAH
and his name was A.	Al	46: 3
And A. was desirous to be a		46: 4
been led by the flatteries of A.,		46: 5
led away by A. to dissensions,		46: 6
the flattering words of A.,		46: 7
we see that A., because he		46:10
he was angry with A.		46:11
to stand against A. and those		46:28
when A. saw that the people		46:29
to cut off the people of A.,		46:30
back, and put A. to death;		46:30
this he knew that A. would do		46:30
to cut off the course of A. in		46:31
and headed the armies of A.		46:32
A. fled with a small number of		46:33
we will return in our record to A.		47: 1
he gave A. the command of		47: 3
behold, this was the desire of A.;		47: 4
A. sent again the second time,		47:11
when A. found that he could not		47:12
come down with his guards to A.,		47:13
A. desired him to come down with		47:13
make him (A.) a second leader		47:13
and surrounded the men of A.,		47:14
plead with A. that he would		47:15
the very thing which A. desired.		47:15
was the thing that A. desired,		47:16
A. caused that one of his		47:18
the Lamanites appointed A. to be		47:19
A. marched with his armies		47:20
he supposed that A. had fulfilled		47:21
A. had gathered together so great		47:21
A. caused that his servants		47:22
servants of A. raised a cry,		47:25
A. commanded that his armies		47:27
A. pretended to be wroth,		47:27
thus A., by his fraud, gained		47:30
for A. had sent an embassy to		47:32
she sent unto A., desiring him		47:33
A. took the same servant that		47:34
A. sought the favor of the queen,		47:35
as soon as A. had obtained		48: 1
while A. had thus been obtaining		48: 7
if king A. had come down out		49:10
A. did not come down himself		49:11
inform their king, A., who was		49:25
A. had again stirred up the hearts		51: 9
A. had gathered together a		51:11
even A. did himself come down,		51:12
therefore A. did drive them,		51:23
A. took possession of the city,		51:23
A. would not suffer the Lamanites		51:25
obtained, by the cunning of A.,		51:27
that he headed A. also, as he was		51:30
A. did pitch his tents in the		51:32
and went into the camp of A.;		51:33
thus endeth the days of A.		51:37
they found A. was dead in his		52: 1
the brother of A. was appointed		52: 3
Ammoron, the brother of king A.,		52: 3
I am the brother of A. whom		54:16
king who was murdered by A.		55: 5
Ammoron, and A. his brother,		62:35

AMALICKIAHITES
dissented, who were called A.	Al	46:28
more numerous than the A.—		46:29
A. that would not enter into a		46:35
the Lamanites, or the A., were		49: 9

AMALICKIAH'S

AMALICKIAH'S
it was not A. intention to give — Al 47: 8

AMARON
conferred them upon my son A. — Om 1: 3
And now I, A., write the — 1: 4

AMASA: see *LYMAN, Amasa.*

AMAZED
they shall be a. one at another; — 2Ne 23: 8
ye shall all be a., and wonder, — He 14: 7

AMAZEMENT
words fill you with wonder and a., — Mos 13: 8
were struck with wonder and a. — 25: 7
struck with such great fear and a. — Al 36:11
they were struck dumb with a. — He 5:25

AMBASSADOR
an a. for the religion of Jesus — DC 135: 7

AMBER
of pure gold, in color like a. — DC 110: 2

AMBITION
to gratify our pride, our vain a., — DC 121:37

AMEN
And thus it is. A. — 1Ne 9: 6
And thus it is. A. — 14:30
spake unto my brethren. A. — 15:36
And thus it is. A. — 22:31
welfare of your souls. A. — 2Ne 2:30
the words of thy dying father. A. — 3:25
and mine everlasting God. A. — 4:35
the remainder of my words. A. — 9:54
praise him through grace divine. A. — 10:25
which is one God, without end. A. — 31:21
and I must obey. A. — 33:15
with awful dread and fear. A. — Jac 6:13
the mansions of my Father. A. — En 1:27
hath the Lord commanded me. A. — Mos 3:27
who is God above all. A. — 5:15
may the Lord bless my people. A. — 10:22
is the very Eternal Father. A. — 16:15
And thus it is written. A. — Al 6: 8
And thus I have spoken. A. — 7:27
And thus it is. A. — 13: 9
unto my God forever. A. — 26:37
even as I have spoken. A. — 29:17
a chosen and a holy people. A. — 31:18
all this can ye do if ye will. A. — 33:23
according to my words. A. — 42:31
And thus it is. A. — He 12:26
so shall it be. A. — 3Ne 5:26
and of the Holy Ghost. A. — 11:25
and the glory, forever. A. — 13:13
in the day of judgment. A. — Mrm 7:10
on the name of Jesus Christ. A. — 9:37
I that hath spoken it. A. — Eth 4:19
before God at the last day. A. — 5: 6
abide in you forever. A. — 12:41
saved in the kingdom of God. A. — 15:34
on his name to the end. A. — Mro 3: 3
his Spirit to be with them. A. — 4: 3
his Spirit to be with them. A. — 5: 2
even as he is pure. A. — 7:48
or shall meet you again. A. — 8:30
abide with you forever. A. — 9:26
of both quick and dead. A. — 10:34
abideth forever and ever. A. — DC 1:39
they might be saved. A. — 3:20
shall be opened unto you. A. — 4: 7
lifted up at the last day. A. — 5:35
the kingdom of heaven. A. — 6:37
from the beginning. A. — 8:12
lifted up at the last day. A. — 9:14
your Lord and your God. A. — 10:70
that believe on my name. A. — 11:30
and then you are called. A. — 12: 9
great shall be your reward. A. — 14:11
kingdom of my Father. A. — 15: 6

kingdom of my Father. A. — DC 16: 6
unto the children of men. A. — 17: 9
have spoken it. A. — 18:47
come unto me thy Savior. A. — 19:41
both now and forever. A. — 20: 4
today, and forever. A. — 20:12
glory forever and ever. A. — 20:16
and eternal, without end. A. — 20:28
name, both now and ever. A. — 20:36
and of the Holy Ghost. A. — 20:73
his Spirit to be with them. A. — 20:77
his Spirit to be with them. A. — 20:79
lo, lo! to the Jews also. A. — 21:12
not to counsel your God. A. — 22: 4
henceforth and forever. A. — 23: 2
because of thy family. A. — 23: 3
preach before the world. A. — 23: 4
henceforth and forever. A. — 23: 5
reward of the laborer. A. — 23: 7
according to this pattern. A. — 24:19
this is my voice unto all. A. — 25:16
shall receive by faith. A. — 26: 2
where I am ye shall be also. A. — 27:18
with the sound of rejoicing. A. — 28:16
unto you at this time. A. — 29:50
the regions round about. A. — 30: 4
blessed unto eternal life. A. — 30: 8
can do, for I am with you. A. — 30:11
by the will of the Father. A. — 31:13
and I will bless them. A. — 32: 5
Even so. A. — 33:18
Even so. A. — 34:12
Even so. A. — 35:27
Even so. A. — 36: 8
Even so. A. — 37: 4
Even so. A. — 38:42
Even so. A. — 39:24
as seemeth me good. A. — 40: 3
Even so. A. — 41:12
Even so. A. — 42:10
Even so. A. — 42:69
Even so. A. — 43:35
which ye have received. A. — 44: 6
Even so. A. — 45:75
Even so. A. — 46:33
Even so. A. — 47: 4
Even so. A. — 48: 6
Even so. A. — 49:28
Even so. A. — 50:46
Even so. A. — 51:20
Even so. S. — 52:44
Even so. A. — 53: 7
Even so. A. — 54:10
even as I will. A. — 55: 6
Even so. A. — 56:20
Even so. A. — 57:16
the Son of Man cometh. A. — 58:65
and the spirit beareth record. A. — 59:24
Even so. A. — 60:17
Even so. A. — 61:39
Even so. A. — 62: 9
a greater condemnation. A. — 63:66
The Lord hath spoken it. A. — 64:43
glory, forever and ever. A. — 65: 6
even Jesus Christ. A. — 66:13
servant Joseph Smith, Jun. A. — 67:14
seal them up unto eternal life. A. — 68:12
and I come quickly. A. — 68:35
forever and ever. A. — 69: 8
Even so. A. — 70:18
Even so. A. — 71:11
Even so. A. — 72: 8
an end of my sayings. A. — 72:23
This is also an ensample. A. — 72:26
Even so. A. — 73: 6
Even so. A. — 75:12
Even so. A. — 75:22
Even so. A. — 75:36
dominion forever and ever. A. — 76:119
shall inherit all things. A. — 78:22
Lord, even Jesus Christ. A. — 79: 4
even Jesus Christ. A. — 80: 5
even Jesus Christ. A. — 81: 7

AMEN 40 AMMON

Even so, A.	DC 82:24
as also the poor. A.	83: 6
Forever and ever. A.	84:102
the beginning and the end. A.	84:120
The Lord hath said it. A.	86:11
quickly, saith the Lord. A.	87: 8
and receive you unto myself. A.	88:126
forever and ever. A.	88:133
saying a., in token of the same.	88:135
testimony concerning me. A.	88:141
and not slay them. A.	89:21
I the Lord have spoken it. A.	90:37
that it should be translated. A.	91: 6
you shall be blessed forever. A.	92: 2
for the salvation of Zion. A.	93:53
no more at this time. A.	94:17
Jesus Christ your Lord. A.	95:17
Even so. A.	96: 5
Even so. A.	96: 9
saith the Lord your God. A.	97:28
the Lord against them. A.	98:48
until thou be taken. A.	99: 8
Even so. A.	100:17
Even so. A.	101:101
Even so. A.	103:40
Even so. A.	104:86
Even so. A.	105:41
of my Father. Even so. A.	106: 8
worthy to stand. Even so. A.	107:100
and deliver you forever. A.	108: 8
aloud for joy. A., and Amen.	109:80
aloud for joy. Amen and A.	109:80
of my people. Even so. A.	110:10
are able to receive them. A.	111:11
I am Alpha and Omega. A.	112:34
and receive their bishopric. A.	114: 2
and ministry. Even so. A.	115:19
saith the Lord. Even so. A.	117:16
the stakes of Zion. Even so. A.	119: 7
saith the Lord. Even so. A.	120: 1
A. to the priesthood or the	121:37
all his sins, saith the Lord. A.	124:76
hereafter. Even so. A.	124:102
be well with him. Even so. A.	124:110
may be exalted. Even so. A.	124:114
forever and ever. Even so. A.	124:118
Lord your God. Even so. A.	124:120
in that house. Even so. A.	124:122
Lord your God. Even so. A.	124:145
henceforth and forever. A.	126: 3
I am Alpha and Omega. A.	132:66
your God hath spoken it. A.	133:74
that blood on the earth. A.	135: 7
So no more at present. A.	136:42
at present. Amen and A.	136:42
that believe. Even so. A.)	Mses 1:42
to them that believe. A.)	4:32
thereof; and thus it was. A.	5:59
may all become my sons. A.	6:68
so let it be. A.	Fac 2:11

AMENABLE
and that men are a. to him,	DC 134: 4

AMERICAN
upon this [the A.] continent;	AoF 10

AMGID
to battle against the king, A.,	Eth 10:32
Com gained power over A.,	10:32

AMIDST
for a. all my anxieties I had	JS 2:14

AMINADAB
Now the man's name was A.	He 5:39
And A. said unto them:	5:39
And A. said unto them:	5:41

AMINADI
who was a descendant of A.;	Al 10: 2
the same A. who interpreted	10: 2
A. was a descendant of Nephi,	10: 3

AMISS
God will give me, if I ask not a.;	2Ne 4:35
for ye cannot go a.	DC 80: 3

AMLICI
a certain man, being called A.,	Al 2: 1
this A. had, by his cunning, drawn	2: 2
to establish A. to be king	2: 2
after the persuasions of A.;	2: 3
possible that A. should gain the	2: 4
whether it were for or against A.,	2: 5
of the people came against A.,	2: 7
but A. did stir up those who	2: 8
did consecrate A. to be their king.	2: 9
when A. was made king over them	2:10
people of A. were distinguished	2:11
distinguished by the name of A.,	2:11
that A. did arm his men with	2:14
Alma fought with A.	2:29
he contended again with A.;	2:31
that he slew A. with the sword.	2:31

AMLICITES
name of Amlici, being called A.;	Al 2:11
aware of the intent of the A.,	2:12
were prepared to meet the A.	2:13
the A. came upon the hill	2:15
armies, against the A. to battle.	2:16
And they began to slay the A.	2:17
the A. did contend with the	2:17
Nephites did fall before the A.	2:17
Nephites, that they slew the A.	2:18
the Nephites did pursue the A.	2:19
that there were slain of the A.	2:19
when Alma could pursue the A.	2:20
to follow the remnant of the A.,	2:21
out to watch the camp of the A.	2:22
man to watch the camp of the A.	2:22
we followed the camp of the A.	2:24
behold, the A. have joined them.	2:24
the Lamanites and the A.,	2:27
and the A. did fall before them.	2:28
with the Lamanites and the A.	2:34
and the A. began to flee before	2:35
and the A. who had been slain	3: 3
the A. were distinguished from	3: 4
will return again to the A.,	3:13
Now the A. knew not that	3:18
by the Lamanites and the A.,	3:20
where the first army met the A.	3:20

AMMAH
Muloki and A. are in prison.	Al 20: 2
and also A. and his brethren.	21:11

AMMARON
his brother, A., did keep the	4Ne 1:47
A., being constrained by the	1:48
thus is the end of the record of A.	1:49
that A. hid up the records unto	Mrm 1: 2
and A. said unto me:	1: 2
things which A. commanded me.	1: 5
A. had deposited the records	2:17
according to the word of A.,	2:17
according to the words of A.	2:17
records which A. had hid up	4:23

AMMON
children of A. shall obey them.	2Ne 21:14
having with them one A.,	Mos 7: 3
A. took three of his brethren,	7: 6
when A. saw that he was	7:12
For I am A., and an a	7:13
Limhi had heard the words of A.,	7:14
no more bind A. nor his brethren,	7:16
he caused that A. should stand	8: 2
should be brought before A.,	8: 5
as soon as A. had read the record,	8: 6
A. told him that he could not.	8: 6
Now A. said unto him:	8:13
A. said that a seer is a revelator	8:16
when A. had made an end of	8:19

AMMON

that A. and his brethren came	Mos	21:22
discovered A. and his brethren;		21:23
sent, previous to the coming of A.,		21:25
days before the coming of A.		21:26
in learning from the mouth of A.		21:28
and A. also did rejoice.		21:28
A. and his brethren were filled		21:29
And now since the coming of A.,		21:32
A. declined doing this thing,		21:33
the study of A. and his people,		21:36
A. and king Limhi began to consult		22: 1
being led by A. and his brethren.		22:11
their names were A., and Aaron,		27:34
A. being the chief among them,	Al	17:18
A. went to the land of Ishmael,		17:19
as A. entered the land of Ishmael,		17:20
A. was carried before the king		17:21
And the king inquired of A. if		17:22
And A. said unto him:		17:23
was much pleased with A.,		17:24
A. should take one of his daughters		17:24
But A. said unto him:		17:25
Therefore A. became a servant		17:25
as A. and the servants of the king		17:27
and scattered the flocks of A.		17:27
when A. saw this his heart was		17:29
these were the thoughts of A.,		17:30
and they did follow A., and they		17:32
but A. said unto his brethren:		17:33
did as A. commanded them,		17:34
Therefore they did not fear A.,		17:35
But A. stood forth and said forth		17:36
that lifted his club to smite A.,		17:37
smitten off by the sword of A.,		17:39
learned of the faithfulness of A.		18: 2
that A. was preparing his horses		18:10
because of the faithfulness of A.,		18:10
A. had made ready the horses		18:12
A. turned himself unto the king,		18:14
that A. said unto him again:		18:15
A., being filled with the Spirit		18:16
A. could discern his thoughts;		18:18
A. answered and said unto him:		18:19
Now A. being wise, yet harmless,		18:22
And A. began to speak unto him		18:24
And then A. said:		18:26
And A. said: This is God.		18:28
And A. said unto him again:		18:28
And A. said unto him:		18:30
And A. said: Yea, and		18:32
A. said unto him: I am a man;		18:34
Now when A. had said these words,		18:36
having heard of the fame of A.,		19: 2
A. did as he was commanded,		19: 3
Now this was what A. desired,		19: 6
And A. said unto her:		19: 9
And A. said unto her:		19:10
A. had appointed that he should		19:11
according to the words of A.;		19:12
A. seeing the Spirit of the Lord		19:14
concerning the great power of A.		19:15
A. lay prostrate upon the earth,		19:17
and they also saw A.,		19:18
for they were angry with A.		19:21
been slain with the sword of A.,		19:22
being exceeding angry with A.,		19:22
that he might let it fall upon A.,		19:22
we see that A. could not be slain,		19:23
who lifted the sword to slay A.,		19:24
that A. was the Great Spirit,		19:25
A. was sent by the Great Spirit		19:27
heard from the mouth of A.;		19:31
when A. arose he also		19:33
that A. should go with him to		20: 1
voice of the Lord came to A.		20: 2
when A. had heard this, he said		20: 3
Now Lamoni said unto A.:		20: 4
And A. said unto him:		20: 5
And he said unto A.:		20: 7
as A. and Lamoni were journeying		20: 8
should slay A. with the sword.		20:14
I will not slay A., neither will I		20:15
may release the brethren of A.,		20:15
But A. stood forth and said unto	Al	20:17
when A. had said these words		20:19
forth his hand to slay A.		20:20
But A. withstood his blows,		20:20
king saw that A. could slay him,		20:21
he began to plead with A.		20:21
But A. raised his sword,		20:22
Now when A. saw that he had		20:24
when A. had said these words,		20:25
A. had no desire to destroy him,		20:26
that A. and Lamoni proceeded on		20:28
brethren of A. were brought forth		20:28
when A. did meet them he was		20:29
were delivered by Lamoni and A.		20:30
when A. and his brethren separated		21: 1
by the hand of Lamoni and A.,		21:14
A. and Lamoni returned from the		21:18
suffer that A. should serve him,		21:19
A. did preach unto the people of		21:23
as A. was thus teaching the		22: 1
O king, we are the brethren of A.,		22: 2
of the words of thy brother A.;		22: 3
also, what is this that A. said—		22: 6
the account of A. and Aaron,		22:35
should not lay their hands on A.,		23: 1
through the preaching of A.		23: 6
Now when A. and his brethren		24: 5
there A. met all his brethren;		24: 5
A., and Aaron, and Omner, and		25:17
the words of A. to his brethren		26: 1
when A. had said these words,		26:10
A., I fear that thy joy doth carry		26:10
But A. said unto him:		26:11
when A. and his brethren saw this		27: 4
when A. and his brethren saw this		27: 4
And A. said: I will go and		27: 7
But A. said unto him:		27: 9
A. went and inquired of the Lord,		27:11
A. went and told the king all		27:13
that A. said unto them		27:15
as A. was going forth into the land,		27:16
the joy of A. was so great		27:17
that when A. had heard this,		27:25
conversion, with A. and Aaron,		27:25
by the Nephites the people of A.;		27:26
after the people of A. were		28: 1
account of A. and his brethren,		28: 8
that after the people of A. were		30: 1
things among the people of A.,		30:19
and carried him before A., who		30:20
Therefore he took A., and Aaron		31: 6
A., and Aaron, and Omner, and		31:32
angry with the people of A.		35: 8
sent over unto the people of A.		35: 8
the people of A. did not fear		35: 9
anger against the people of A.,		35:10
for war against the people of A.,		35:11
the people of A. departed out of		35:13
Alma, and A., and their brethren,		35:14
A. and his brethren could not		37: 9
were called the people of A.—		43:11
the people of A. did give unto		43:13
and joined the people of A.		47:29
Behold, he was a man like unto A.,		48:18
and A. and his brethren		49:30
say concerning the people of A.,		53:10
but by A. and his brethren,		53:10
love which A. and his brethren		53:11
whom A. brought down out of		56: 3
those sons of the people of A.,		58:39
to dwell with the people of A.,		62:17
desirous to join the people of A.		62:27
did join the people of A.,		62:29
were many of the people of A.,	He	3:12
that same prison in which A. and		5:21
the faith of A. and his brethren	Eth	12:15

AMMONIHAH

to a city which was called A.	Al	8: 6
thus it was with the land of A.		8: 7
Alma had come to the city of A.		8: 8
of the people of the city of A.;		8: 9
who were in the city of A.,		8:14

AMMONIHAH 42 AMONG

thou return to the city of A.,	Al	8:16
speedily to the land of A.		8:16
is on the south of the city of A.		8:18
who were in the land of A.		9:hd
who were in the city of A.,		9: 1
who were in the land of A.,		10: 1
chief judge over the land of A.		14:23
departed out of the land of A.,		15: 1
that were in the land of A.,		15:15
which were in the land of A.,		15:16
even into the city of A.,		16: 2
who were in the city of A.,		16: 3
the people of A. were destroyed;		16: 9
go in to possess the land of A.		16:11
who were in the land of A.,		25: 2
towards the land of A.		49: 1
the city of A. had been rebuilt.		49: 3
the Nephites at the city of A.;		49:10
the Nephites at the city of A.,		49:11
the strength of the city A.		49:14
be frightened at the city A.;		49:15
Zeezrom, in the city of A.;	He	5:10

AMMONIHAHITES
yea, every living soul of the A.	Al	16: 9

AMMONITES
joined them to my stripling A.,	Al	56:57
besides sixty of the sons of the A.		57: 6

AMMORON
and his name was A.,	Al	52: 3
thus king A., the brother of king		52: 3
the king (A.) had departed out of		52:12
A. sent unto Moroni desiring		54: 1
and sent it by the servant of A.,		54: 4
the words which he wrote unto A.,		54: 4
Behold, A., I have written unto		54: 5
A., when he had received this		54:15
I am A., the king of the		54:16
I am A., and a descendant of		54:23
A. had a perfect knowledge of his		55: 1
he knew that A. knew that it was		55: 1
not exchange prisoners with A.		55: 2
as A. would not grant unto me		55: 3
compelled by the orders of A.		56:18
commanded by A. to maintain		56:20
that I received an epistle from A.,		57: 1
And A. refused mine epistle,		57: 3
A. had sent to their support		57:17
by the command of A. they		59: 7
A., the king of the Lamanites,		62:33
was exceedingly angry with A.,		62:35
A., and Amalickiah his brother,		62:35
Tubaloth, who was the son of A.,	He	1:16

AMNIGADDAH
Coriantum was the son of A.	Eth	1:14
And A. was the son of Aaron.		1:15
and he begat A., and		10:31
A. also dwelt in captivity all		10:31

AMNIHU
Amlicites came upon the hill A.,	Al	2:15

AMNOR
called Zeram, and A., and	Al	2:22
an a. of silver, an ezrom of silver,		11: 6
an a. of silver was as great as		11:11

AMONG
he went forth a. the people,	1Ne	1:18
had been out by night a. them,		4:22
his works a. the children of men;		9: 6
up a. the Jews—even a Messiah,		10: 4
one a. you whom ye know not;		10: 8
should be preached a. the Jews,		10:11
forth a. the children of men;		11:24
they cast him out from a. them.		11:28
forth a. the children of men.		11:31
with the sword a. my people.		12: 2
and rumors of wars a. them;		12:21
a. the nations of the Gentiles		13: 4
beheld a man a. the Gentiles,		13:12
and it was carried forth a. them.	1Ne	13:20
seed, which are a. thy brethren.		13:30
thou hast seen a. the Gentiles,		13:40
shall be numbered a. the seed		14: 2
numbered a. the house of Israel;		14: 2
work a. the children of men;		14: 7
a. all nations, kindreds, tongues,		14:11
a. all the nations of the Gentiles,		14:13
rumors of wars a. all the nations		14:15
rumors of wars a. all the nations		14:16
again a. the house of Israel;		15:16
sent fiery flying serpents a. them;		17:41
miracles a. the children of men,		17:51
and be hated a. all nations.		19:14
in other lands, a. people of old.		19:22
who a. them hath declared these		20:14
and also a. all nations.		22: 3
shall be scattered a. all nations		22: 5
a mighty nation a. the Gentiles,		22: 7
a marvelous work a. the Gentiles,		22: 8
for they shall war a. themselves,		22:13
be cut off from a. the people.		22:20
built up a. the children of men,		22:22
a. them which are in the flesh—		22:22
and great visitations a. them;	2Ne	1:12
save it shall be iniquity a. them,		1:31
highly a. the fruit of thy loins.		3: 7
have already gone forth a. them.		3:11
peace a. the fruit of thy loins,		3:12
shall commence a. all my people,		3:13
shall rise up one mighty a. them,		3:24
Who is a. you that feareth the		7:10
a. all the sons she hath brought		8:18
that it should be a. them;		9: 5
should come a. the Jews,		10: 3
a. those who are the more wicked		10: 3
be wrought a. other nations		10: 4
be scattered a. all nations.		10: 6
numbered a. the house of Israel.		10:18
who shall be numbered a. thy seed,		10:19
he shall judge a. the nations,		12: 4
that is written a. the living		14: 3
be weary nor stumble a. them.		15:26
And many a. them shall stumble		18:15
seal the law a. my disciples.		18:16
send a. his fat ones, leanness,		20:16
declare his doings a. the people,		22: 4
of prophesying a. the Jews.		25: 1
hath come to pass a. the Jews,		25: 6
hath been destroyed a. the Jews		25: 9
shall be scattered a. all nations;		25:15
a wonder a. the children of men.		25:17
and contentions a. my people.		26: 2
wonders, a. the children of men		26:13
which shall be done a. them,		26:17
good a. the children of men;		26:33
have been a. the children of men,		27:11
not a. the children of men save		27:23
a marvelous work a. this people,		27:26
the poor a. men shall rejoice		27:30
do a marvelous work a. them,		29: 1
Christ shall be declared a. them;		30: 5
which was had a. their fathers.		30: 5
shall not pass away a. them, save		30: 6
commence his work a. all nations,		30: 8
a great division a. the people,		30:10
work a. the children of men.		31: 3
which were taught a. my people;		33: 1
labored diligently a. our people,	Jac	1: 7
there shall not any man a. you		2:27
away the righteous out from a. you.		3: 4
whoredoms committed a. them.		3: 5
there came a man a. the people		7: 1
began to preach a. the people,		7: 2
was restored again a. the people;		7:23
went about a. the people of Nephi,	En	1:19
exceeding many prophets a. us.		1:22
should be done a. this people,	Jar	1: 3
there are many a. us who have		1: 4
a. the people of Zarahemla;	Om	1:14
he caused a contention a. them;		1:28
I searched a. the records which	WM	1: 3
of contentions a. his own people.		1:12

and teachers a. the people,	WM	1:16
prophets who were a. his people—		1:16
a. all the people who belonged to	Mos	1: 1
all this land a. all this people,		1:10
sent forth a. those that were not		2: 8
shall arise contentions a. you,		2:32
there are not any a. you, except		2:34
a. the children of men		3: 5
a. all the children of men,		3:13
he had already come a. them.		3:13
down a. the children of men.		4: 2
whosoever a. you borroweth of		4:28
he sent a. them, desiring to		5: 1
that he shall feed a. his flocks,		5:14
even so shall it be a. you if		5:14
no contention a. all his people		6: 7
a proclamation a. all his people,		7:17
there arose contentions a. them,		7:25
they did shed blood a. themselves.		7:25
down a. the children of men,		7:27
in a land a. many waters,		8: 8
sent as a spy a. the Lamanites		9: 1
that which was good a. them		9: 1
a man a. them whose name was		11:20
and he went forth a. them,		11:20
raise contentions a. my people;		11:28
that Abinadi came a. them.		12: 1
and began to prophesy a. them,		12: 1
I will send forth hail a. them,		12: 6
down a. the children of men,		13:34
down a. the children of men,		15: 1
miracles a. the children of men,		15: 6
one a. them whose name was		17: 2
should be cast out from a. them,		17: 3
down a. the children of men;		17: 8
about privately a. the people,		18: 1
a movement a. the people,		18:32
a division a. the remainder of		19: 2
be a great contention a. them.		19: 3
a man a. them whose name was		19: 4
a. those that were taken captive,		19:16
to establish peace a. his people.		19:27
a. the number of their dead;		20:12
has fallen a. their dead,		20:13
I will search a. my people and		20:16
a search to be made a. his people.		20:16
and lamentation a. the people		21: 9
proclamation a. all this people		22: 6
be no contention a. them.		23:15
went forth and stood a. them,		23:27
to be taught a. all the people		24: 4
it were a. their own brethren.		24: 7
a. those who were called Nephites.		25:12
of the dissensions a. the brethren		26: 5
a church a. this people;		26:17
not be numbered a. my people,		26:32
a. the people of the church;		26:35
a. the people of the church,		26:36
be no persecutions a. them,		27: 3
should be an equality a. all men;		27: 3
numbered a. the unbelievers;		27: 8
of Alma was numbered a. them,		27: 8
much dissension a. the people;		27: 9
and a. all the people who were		27:35
sons go up a. the Lamanites		28: 6
the word a. the Lamanites;		28: 9
all the land, a. all the people,		29: 1
Mosiah sent again a. the people;		29: 4
word sent he a. the people.		29: 4
would rise contentions a. you.		29: 7
wars and contentions a. you,		29: 7
all cases a. the children of men,		29:20
sendeth them forth a. his people,		29:23
especially a. this my people;		29:32
these things forth a. the people		29:37
a. all the people who were called		29:44
and contententions a. the people.	Al	1:hd
had gone about a. the people,		1: 3
has been introduced a. this people.		1:12
to be enforced a. this people		1:12
done much good a. this people;		1:13
there was a strict law a. the people		1:21
be no persecution a. themselves.		1:21
there were many a. them who	Al	1:22
no more a. the people		1:24
withdrew themselves from a. them.		1:24
was much peace a. the people		1:33
to be a contention a. the people;		2: 1
had begun to be a. their people.		4: 7
great contentions a. the people,		4: 9
great inequality a. the people,		4:12
for lamentations a. the people,		4:13
was a. the elders of the church,		4:16
might go forth a. his people,		4:19
or a. the people of Nephi,		4:19
which were a. his people,		4:19
is there one a. you who is not		5:29
is there one a. you that doth make		5:30
forth a. all the children of men.		5:50
a. the names of the righteous,		5:57
For what shepherd is there a. you		5:59
no ravenous wolf to enter a. you		5:60
a. those of the righteous.		6: 3
and cometh a. his people.		7: 7
not say that he will come a. us		7: 8
the word of God a. all this people,		8:24
and also Amulek, a. the people,		8:30
than one man a. his people,		9: 6
a. all those who know me;		10: 4
there were some a. them who		10:13
I will come down a. my people,		10:21
out the righteous from a. you		10:23
there was one a. them whose name		10:31
one of the most expert a. them,		10:31
much business to do a. the people.		10:31
be cast out from a. the people		11: 2
who was a chief ruler a. them,		12:20
glad tidings a. all his people,		13:22
should send his Son a. the people,		14: 5
he had caused a. the people		14: 6
and cast him out from a. them,		14: 7
a. all the people of the Nephites.		16:15
there was no inequality a. them;		16:16
which should be taught a. them		16:16
who did go forth a. the people		16:18
fourteen years a. the Lamanites,		17: 4
Go forth a. the Lamanites, thy		17:11
and went forth a. them,		17:17
Ammon being the chief a. them,		17:18
in the land a. the Lamanites,		17:22
the Lamanites, or a. his people.		17:22
I desire to dwell a. this people		17:23
that he was set a. other servants		17:25
a practice of plunder a. them.		18: 7
any servant a. all my servants		18:10
such great faith a. all the people		19:10
much mourning a. the Nephites,		19:14
or a. all the people of God		19:14
what had happened a. them,		19:17
began to murmur a. themselves;		19:19
to marvel again a. themselves		19:24
there were many a. them who		19:25
to be exceeding sharp a. them.		19:28
which was a. the multitude		19:28
the contention a. his people,		19:31
there were many a. them who		19:32
did establish a church a. them.		19:35
did commence a. the Lamanites;		19:36
and a disturbance a. them;		22:22
to be great murmurings a. them		22:24
the king stood forth a. them		22:25
a proclamation a. all his people,		23: 1
Yea, he sent a decree a. them,		23: 2
a. the Lamanites, to preach and		23: 4
teach the word of God a. them;		23: 4
not one soul a. all the people		24: 6
not a wicked man slain a. them;		24:27
a. those who joined the people of		24:29
a. the Lamanites who were slain		25: 4
they had had a. the Lamanites,		25:17
has not, even a. the Nephites.		26:33
a. those whom they so dearly		27: 4
and a. those who had so dearly		27: 4
should be any slaves a. them;		27: 9
a. their brethren, the Lamanites.		27:20
it did cause great joy a. them.		27:26

AMONG 44 AMONG

they were a. the people of Nephi,	Al	27:27
numbered a. the people who		27:27
had been known a. all the people		28: 2
slaughter a. the people of Nephi;		28: 3
a. all the people of Nephi—		28: 4
was heard a. all of them,		28: 5
and contentions a. the Nephites,		28: 9
death and destruction a. men,		28:14
did establish his church a. them;		29:13
things a. the people of Ammon,		30:19
as he went forth a. the people,		30:59
a. a people who had separated		30:59
to know of iniquity a. his people;		31: 2
went with him a. the Zoramites,		31: 7
wickedness a. the children of men?		31:26
iniquity shall be a. this people?		31:30
such wickedness a. this people		31:30
that after much labor a. them,		32: 2
success a. the poor class of people;		32: 2
who was the foremost a. them		32: 5
that there are some a. you		32:25
before your dissension from a. us.		34: 2
shall come a. the children of men,		34: 8
contentions which were a. them;		35:15
a. all the people in every city;		35:15
came a. them to declare unto them		37:30
a. the people of the Zoramites.		38: 3
work of destruction a. his people;		38: 7
a. the people of the Zoramites.		39: 2
a. the borders of the Lamanites,		39: 3
did go forth a. the people,		43: 1
a man fell a. the Nephites,		43:38
work of death a. the Lamanites.		43:38
the great destruction a. them,		43:39
should cease again a. the people.		44:20
numbered a. the people of Nephi,		45:13
numbered a. the people of Nephi.		45:13
be numbered a. the Lamanites,		45:14
Helaman went forth a. the people		45:20
which had been a. the people,		45:21
should be declared a. them,		45:21
arose a dissension a. them,		45:23
take place a. the children of men.		46: 9
he went forth a. the people,		46:19
of liberty a. the Nephites.		46:36
of Nephi a. the Lamanites,		47: 1
all his land, a. all his people,		47: 1
had gone forth a. them they were		47: 2
the custom a. the Lamanites,		47:17
a. all the people of the Lamanites,		47:35
and contentions a. themselves,		48:20
known a. the children of Lehi.		49: 8
of affairs a. the Nephites,		49:11
was continual peace a. them,		49:30
forth to preach a. the people.		49:30
which were a. themselves,		50:21
time a. the people of Nephi,		50:23
been peace a. the people of Nephi		50:25
which took place a. them		50:25
a. the people of Nephi,		50:32
a contention a. the people		51: 2
thus was the division a. them,		51: 6
a. the brethren of Pahoran		51: 7
to be a. the people of Nephi;		51: 9
and dissensions a. the people;		51:16
contentions a. his own people,		51:22
and intrigue a. themselves		53: 9
a. all the prisoners of Moroni,		54: 3
yea, I will seek death a. them		55: 3
search should be made a. his men		55: 4
a descendant of Laman a. them.		55: 4
should be administered a. them;		55:32
should be taken from a. the dead,		57:24
neither was there one soul a. them		57:25
been the slaughter a. our people;		60: 5
which broke out a. ourselves;		60:16
much bloodshed a. ourselves;		60:16
we were contending a. ourselves,		60:16
much bloodshed a. ourselves;		60:16
if there be any a. you that has		60:27
I will stir up insurrections a. you,		60:27
the cause of sore affliction a. us;		61: 4
Zarahemla, a. their own people,	Al	62:11
of iniquity a. the people of Nephi;		62:40
established a. the people of Nephi.		62:42
forth a. the children of men		63:12
a. the people of the Nephites.	He	1: 1
judgment-seat a. the brethren,		1: 2
three divisions a. the people.		1: 4
not known a. the people of Nephi,		1:12
did mingle themselves a. the people,		1:12
a dissenter from a. the Nephites;		1:15
a. the number who were slain		1:30
contention again a. the people		2: 1
and authority a. the people;		2: 5
contention a. the people of Nephi		3: 1
little dissensions a. the people,		3: 1
no contention a. the people		3: 2
dissensions, a. the people of Nephi.		3:17
a. the people of the Nephites,		3:22
also a contention a. the people,		4: 1
slaughter which was a. them,		4:11
abomination which was a. them;		4:11
a. those also who professed to		4:11
of Nephi, a. the Lamanites—		4:12
a. all the people of Nephi,		5:14
a. all the people of Nephi who		5:16
of Zarahemla, a. the Lamanites.		5:16
one a. them who was a Nephite		5:35
which did come a. them.		6: 2
had been established a. them.		6: 3
whether a. the Nephites or		6: 7
whether it were a. the Lamanites		6: 8
Lamanites or a. the Nephites,		6: 8
were many, even a. the Nephites,		6:18
a. the more wicked part of the		6:18
that there were robbers a. them		6:20
a. the more wicked part of them,		6:37
destroyed from a. the Lamanites.		6:37
a. the people who were in the		7: 2
that he could not stay a. them,		7: 3
which has come a. you;		7:25
raised contentions a. them;		8: 7
should ye dispute a. yourselves,		8:12
certain men who were a. them		9: 1
and they said a. themselves,		9: 1
the cry of murder a. them;		9: 6
therefore they said a. themselves:		9: 8
that they inquired a. the people,		9:12
abominations which are a. you.		9:23
there were some a. the people,		9:40
arose a division a. the people,		10: 1
ye have power a. this people.		10: 7
or sent it forth a. all the people.		10:17
a. all the people of Nephi.		11: 1
a. all the people of Nephi.		11: 5
even a. the Lamanites as well as		11: 6
as well as a. the Nephites,		11: 6
a. the people of Nephi,		11:27
a. the people of the Lamanites.		11:27
cast out the righteous from a. you,		13:14
if a prophet come a. you and		13:26
if a man shall come a. you and		13:27
if a man shall come a. you and		13:27
have cast me out from a. you.		14:10
unbelief a. the children of men—		14:28
and be numbered a. his sheep.		15:13
which I have done a. them;		15:17
working miracles a. the people,		16: 4
to prophesy a. his own people.		16: 7
heard of more a. the Nephites;		16: 8
have guessed right, a. so many;		16:16
contend a. themselves, saying:		16:17
not a. us, but in a land which is		16:20
wrought a. the people of the Lord,		16:23
miracles wrought a. the people.	3Ne	1: 4
lyings sent forth a. the people,		1:22
Nephi went forth a. the people,		1:23
do much slaughter a. the people.		1:27
much sorrow a. the Lamanites;		1:29
which was sent a. them;		2:10
were numbered a. the Nephites;		2:14
were numbered a. the Nephites,		2:16
a proclamation a. all the people,		3:13
were numbered a. the Nephites,		3:14

AMONG 45 AMONG

the chiefest a. all the captains	3Ne 3:18
the custom a. all the Nephites	3:19
was a great prophet a. them,	3:19
a. all the people of Lehi since	4:11
of provisions a. the robbers—	4:19
which had been made a. them,	4:24
a. all the people of the Nephites	5: 1
what was done a. so many people	5: 8
establish the church a. the people,	5:12
which was established a. them	5:12
to declare his word a. his people,	5:13
some disputings a. the people;	6:10
were a. a few of the Lamanites	6:14
sent forth, standing a. the people	6:20
there was no man a. them save	7: 4
there were no wars as yet a. them;	7: 5
but few righteous men a. them.	7: 7
did cast them out from a. them.	7:14
forth a. them in that same year,	7:16
do some miracles a. the people.	7:22
and disputations a. the people,	8: 4
and weeping a. all the people	8:23
a. all the inhabitants of the	9: 1
were none righteous a. them,	9:11
the saints whom I sent a. them	9:11
had been prophesied a. them	11:12
Nephi was a. the multitude)	11:18
shall be no disputations a. you.	11:22
shall be no disputations a. you,	11:28
shall there be disputations a. you	11:28
whom I have chosen from a. you	12: 1
some a. them who marveled,	15: 2
ye were separated from a. them	15:19
and ye are numbered a. those	15:24
shall be numbered a. my sheep,	16: 3
have been cast out from a. them,	16: 8
to be cast out from a. them,	16: 9
a hiss and a by-word a. them—	16: 9
fulness of my gospel from a. them.	16:10
shall be numbered a. my people,	16:13
to go through a. them,	16:14
they shall go through a. them,	16:15
Have ye any that are sick a. you?	17: 7
shall one be ordained a. you,	18: 5
whoso a. you shall do more or less	18:13
And as I have prayed a. you	18:16
a. my people who do repent	18:16
not cast him out from a. you,	18:30
not be numbered a. my people,	18:31
which have been a. you.	18:34
if ye have no disputations a. you.	18:34
was noised abroad a. the people	19: 2
have I never seen a. all the Jews;	19:35
of Jacob, go forth a. them;	20:16
and ye shall be a. them as a lion	20:16
lion a. the beasts of the forest,	20:16
young lion a. the flocks of sheep,	20:16
be cut off from a. the people.	20:23
establish again a. them my Zion;	21: 1
which shall be wrought a. you	21: 5
be numbered a. my people,	21: 6
and a marvelous work a. them;	21: 9
there shall be a. them those who	21: 9
be cut off from a. my people	21:11
of Jacob shall be a. the Gentiles,	21:12
lion a. the beasts of the forest,	21:12
young lion a. the flocks of sheep,	21:12
I cut off from a. my people,	21:20
establish my church a. them,	21:22
a. this remnant of Jacob,	21:22
of heaven come down a. them;	21:25
a. the remnant of this people.	21:26
a. all the dispersed of my people,	21:26
a. all the dispersed of my people,	21:27
with the Father, a. all nations,	21:28
done all manner of cures a. them,	26:15
all things common a. them,	26:19
are disputations a. the people	27: 3
forth a. all the people of Nephi,	28:23
they will be a. the Gentiles,	28:27
They will also be a. the Jews,	28:28
a. the Gentiles shall there be	28:32
he hath chosen and sent a. them;	28:34
sayings coming forth a. you,	3Ne 29: 4
and disputations a. them,	4Ne 1: 2
had all things common a. them;	1: 3
they work a. the children of man;	1: 5
no contention a. all the people,	1:13
miracles wrought a. the disciples	1:13
a. all the people who had been	1:16
there began to be a. them those	1:24
no more common a. them.	1:25
which were wrought a. them.	1:29
doing might miracles a. them.	1:30
they did come forth from a. them,	1:33
a great division a. the people.	1:35
a. them there were those who	1:36
(a. whom were the three disciples	1:37
the war began to be a. them	Mrm 1:10
But I did remain a. them,	1:17
who were a. the Lamanites,	1:18
especially a. the people of Nephi.	2:11
which ye shall have a. you;	3:21
carnage which was a. the people,	4:11
a. all the children of Lehi,	4:12
even a. all the house of Israel,	4:12
the Lord, as was a. this people.	4:12
I did go forth a. the Nephites,	5: 1
be counted as naught a. them—	5: 9
which hath been a. the Lamanites,	5:15
shall go forth a. you as a lion,	5:24
(a. whom was my son Moroni)	6:11
by the power of God a. them.	7: 9
numbered a. the people of the	7:10
things shall come forth a. you.	8:34
miracles a. the children of men	9:20
characters which are called a. us	9:32
transpired a. the children of men	Eth 1: 3
that time, is had a. the Jews—	1: 3
a. the children of the land,	2:10
Choose ye out from a. our sons	6:24
a. whom were twenty and three	7: 2
a. the sons of Corihor there was	7:14
came prophets a. the people,	7:23
a. whom were Esrom and	8: 4
that they are had a. all people,	8:20
and they are had a. the Lamanites.	8:20
see these things come a. you	8:24
combination which shall be a. you;	8:24
be a great destruction a. them,	11: 6
withdrew from a. the people.	11:13
arose a rebellion a. the people,	11:15
a mighty man a. them in iniquity,	11:15
no faith a. the children of men	12:12
God can do no miracle a. them;	12:12
great a miracle a. the Lamanites.	12:15
a. the mansions of thy Father,	12:32
a. the remnant of the seed of	13:10
was cast out from a. the people	13:15
be a great war a. the people,	13:15
any other man a. all the people.	14:10
destruction a. the armies of Shiz	14:27
exceedingly fierce a. themselves;	Mro 1: 2
a. the people of the church of	6: 4
should be no iniquity a. them;	6: 7
numbered a. the people of Christ.	6: 7
the way a. the children of men,	7:31
a. the people of his church.	7:39
should disputations rise a. you.	8: 4
have been disputations a. you	8: 5
should be removed from a. you;	8: 6
of God shall be done away a. you,	10:24
be none that doeth good a. you,	10:25
be one a. you that doeth good,	10:25
be cut off from a. the people;	DC 1:14
come forth a. the children of men.	4: 1
testimony a. this generation,	5:14
a. the inhabitants of the earth,	5:19
a greater work yet a. men than	7: 5
will establish my church a. them.	10:53
come forth a. the children of men.	11: 1
gone forth a. the children of men,	11:22
come forth a. the children of men,	11:22
come forth a. the children of men.	12: 1
work a. the children of men,	18:44
and a. every people that thou	19:29
shall be a record kept a. you;	21: 1

AMONG

Reference	Citation	Reference	Citation
your family, and a. your friends,	DC 23: 6	and dwelt a. the sons of men.	DC 93: 4
such as is not known a. men.	24:12	in the flesh, and dwelt a. us.	93:11
except it is made new a. you;	27: 4	who have been ordained a. you,	95: 5
church to be established a. them;	28: 8	place which is named a. you,	96: 2
thy journey a. the Lamanites.	28:14	determined in council a. you.	96: 3
and wailing a. the hosts of men;	29:15	upon the house named a. you,	96: 9
my church a. the Lamanites;	30: 6	all a. them who know their	97: 8
the wilderness a. the Lamanites.	32: 2	and covetous desires a. them;	101: 6
in the land, even a. the Gentiles,	35: 7	began to say a. themselves:	101:47
gospel a. the nations—	36: 5	long time, saying a. themselves:	101:48
the earth, a. the children of men,	38:11	also a. all my servants,	101:55
what man a. you having twelve	38:26	a. hypocrites, and unbelievers;	101:90
shall go forth a. all nations,	38:33	that the innocent a. you may not	104: 7
that certain men a. them shall	38:34	that the guilty a. you may not	104: 7
go ye out from a. the wicked.	38:42	if any man a. you, of the order,	104:10
not known a. the children of men,	39:15	one a. you to keep the treasury,	104:61
shall be cast out from a. you;	41: 5	no man a. you shall call it his	104:62
embrace my gospel a. the Gentiles	42:39	if any man a. you obtain	104:69
And whosoever a. you are sick,	42:43	let not any a. you say that it	104:70
that whatever persons a. you,	42:74	that any man a. you say to the	104:72
not cast them out from a. you;	42:74	the poor and afflicted a. them;	105: 3
shall be cast out from a. you.	42:75	from a. those who are ordained	107:21
ye receive none such a. you	42:76	a. the elders of the church.	107:72
if any persons a. you shall kill	42:79	a. the inhabitants of Zion,	107:74
the iniquity which is a. you;	43:11	to travel a. all nations,	107:98
lest ye be found a. the wicked.	43:19	from a. all these, thy servants,	109:58
and scattered a. all nations.	45:19	send it abroad a. all nations,	112: 1
be scattered a. all nations;	45:24	a. the children of men.	112: 6
a light shall break forth a. them	45:28	the path lieth a. the mountains,	112: 7
but a. the wicked, men shall	45:32	and a. many nations.	112: 7
shall come to pass a. the wicked,	45:68	abroad a. all nations—	112:16
it shall be said a. the wicked:	45:70	First a. those among you,	112:26
gathered out from a. all nations,	45:71	a. you, saith the Lord, who have	112:26
shall be any a. you professing	46:27	condition a. the gentiles.	113:10
that ye go a. this people,	49:11	those a. you who deny my	114: 2
there are hypocrites a. you,	50: 7	found worthy to abide a. you.	119: 5
he that is weak a. you	50:16	art in perils a. false brethren;	122: 5
may chase darkness from a. you;	50:25	thou art in perils a. robbers;	122: 5
go forth a. the churches	50:37	many yet on the earth a. all sects,	123:12
and be alike a. this people,	51: 9	of the oppressor a. hypocrites,	124: 8
and a. the armies of the earth;	60: 4	Galland be appointed a. you,	124:79
a. the congregations of the	60: 8	shall be agreed a. themselves,	124:121
a. the congregations of the	60:13	sociality which exists a. us here	130: 2
a. the congregations of the	60:14	will exist a. us there,	130: 2
he that is faithful a. you shall	61: 6	a. other things, the promises.	132:34
more abundantly a. them than	61:32	upon all the ungodly a. you.	133: 2
than a. the congregations of the	61:32	ye out from a. the nations,	133: 7
a. the congregations of the	61:33	the cry go forth a. all people,	133:10
a. the congregations of the	62: 5	who are a. the Gentiles flee	133:12
the faithful a. you should be	62: 6	Go ye out from a. the nations,	133:14
if any a. you desire to ride	62: 7	shall be heard a. all people;	133:21
those a. you who seek signs,	63: 8	things might be known a. you,	133:36
those a. you who have sought	63:12	be cut off from a. the people.	133:63
There were a. you adulterers	63:14	no man a. you received me,	133:66
because these things are a. you.	63:19	their tendency to evil a. men,	134: 6
will be foolish virgins a. the wise;	63:54	be classed a. the martyrs of	135: 6
those a. you who have sinned;	64: 3	of honest men a. all nations;	135: 7
wonderful works a. the people.	65: 4	not had a. the children of men.	Mses 1:23
the least that is a. them,	67: 6	again a. the children of men—	1:41
that is the most wise a. you;	67: 6	a. as many as shall believe.	1:41
if there be any a. you that	67: 7	known a. the children of men.	1:42
firstborn a. the sons of Aaron;	68:16	Satan came a. them, saying:	5:13
for there are idlers a. them;	68:31	spread a. all the sons of men.	5:52
be done away from a. them;	68:32	And it was a. the sons of men,	5:53
a. all the Jews who believed not	74: 2	a. the daughters of men these	5:53
a great contention a. the people	74: 3	came not a. the sons of men,	5:54
should be done away a. them.	74: 5	prevail a. all the sons of men.	5:55
for it was had a. the Jews;	74: 6	had great dominion a. men,	6:15
living, and a. thy brethren.	81: 3	in the land, a. the people;	6:26
there are those a. you who have	82: 2	in the land, a. the people,	6:37
a. the children of Israel until	84:27	a wild man hath come a. us.	6:38
let no man a. you, for	84:86	we have written a. us,	6:46
if any man a. you be strong in	84:106	come a. the children of men,	6:49
about and a. all the churches,	84:112	saying abroad a. the people,	6:54
appointed them a. unbelievers,	85: 9	were despised a. all people.	7: 8
an inheritance a. the saints of	85:11	wars and bloodshed a. them;	7:16
the wheat from a. the tares,	86: 7	there was no poor a. them.	7:18
a. the Gentiles for the last time,	88:84	and had not place a. them.	7:22
a. those who are to remain	88:102	a. all the workmanship of	7:36
Appoint a. yourselves a teacher,	88:122	wickedness as a. thy brethren.	7:36
shall not have place a. you;	88:134	always be found a. all nations,	7:52
ye shall not receive any a. you	88:138	shall be a. the children of men,	7:61
wine or strong drink a. you,	89: 5	tribulations a. the wicked;	7:66

as was had a. the Chaldeans,	Abr	1:13	
thy name great a. all nations,		2: 9	
a. all these there were many of		3:22	
stood a. those that were spirits,		3:23	
there stood one a. them that		3:24	
Gods took counsel a. themselves		4:26	
the Gods said a. themselves:		5: 2	
counseled a. themselves to form;		5: 3	
they counseled a. themselves		5: 3	
be cut off from a. the people;	JS	1:55	
became general a. all the sects		2: 5	
a. the different denominations,		2: 8	
a. professors of religion,		2:22	
common a. all the sects—		2:22	
for good and evil a. all nations,		2:33	
and evil spoken of a. all people.		2:33	
be cut off from a. the people,"		2:40	

AMONGST

and shall go forth a. men,	Mos	3: 5	
power he did sling stones a. them;	Al	17:36	
his children are also come a. us		20:13	
a. all his people who were in all		22:27	
Go a. thy brethren, the Lamanites,		26:27	
come, and been forth a. them;		26:28	
and as he went forth a. them,		30:59	
their peace a. themselves,		48:21	
of some intrigue a. the Nephites,		53: 8	
which caused dissensions a. them.		53: 8	
of iniquity a. themselves,		53: 9	
nay, not a. all the Nephites.		56:45	
bend of Gadianton from a. them	He	11:10	
that which ever hath been a. us,	Mrm	5:15	
God a. the trees of the garden.	Mses	4:14	
and division a. the people,	JS	2: 5	

AMORON

which I have received from A.,	Mro	9: 7	

AMOS: see also DAVIES, Amos.

his son A. kept it in his stead;	4Ne	1:19	
it came to pass that A. died also,		1:21	
and his son A. kept the record		1:21	
A. died; and his brother,		1:47	

AMOUNT

to the a. of one half of our corn,	Mos	7:22	
the a. of a seon of gold was twice	Al	11: 8	
to the a. of five thousand and		63: 4	
a. of damages which they have	DC	123: 2	
in proportion to the a. of stock		124:68	

AMOZ

word that Isaiah, the son of A.,	2Ne	12: 1	
Isaiah the son of A. did see.		23: 1	

AMPLY

has need may be a. supplied	DC	42:33	

AMULEK

and the man was called A.;	Al	8:21	
he blessed A. and his house,		8:22	
he said unto A.: I am Alma,		8:23	
now, A., because thou hast fed me		8:26	
Alma tarried many days with A.		8:27	
and also say unto my servant A.,		8:29	
and also A., among the people,		8:30	
and also the words of A.,		9:hd	
I should take A. and go forth		9: 1	
A. went and stood forth, and began		9:34	
words of A. are not all written,		9:34	
the words which A. preached unto		10: 1	
I am A.; I am the son of		10: 2	
A., return to thine own house,		10: 7	
when A. had spoken these words		10:12	
that they began to question A.,		10:16	
A. could know of their designs.		10:17	
people were more angry with A.,		10:24	
But A. stretched forth his hand,		10:25	
when A. had spoken these words		10:28	
foremost to accuse A. and Alma,		10:31	
the people against Alma and A.		11:20	
this Zeezrom began to question A.,		11:21	

therefore, he said unto A.:	Al	11:21	
And A. said unto him:		11:22	
Now A. said: O thou child of hell,		11:23	
And A. said: Yea there is a		11:27	
A. answered and said unto him:		11:34	
Now A. saith again unto him:		11:36	
And A. said unto him:		11:39	
when A. had finished these words		11:46	
And thus ended the words of A.,		11:46	
A. had silenced Zeezrom,		12: 1	
A. had caught him in his lying		12: 1	
and to establish the words of A.,		12: 1	
beyond that which A. had done.		12: 1	
and A. had a knowledge of him,		12: 7	
which A. hath spoken concerning		12: 8	
A. hath spoken plainly concerning		12:12	
which has been spoken of by A.,		12:24	
they might destroy Alma and A.;		14: 2	
that A. had lied unto them,		14: 2	
were also angry with Alma and A.;		14: 3	
testify against Alma and A.		14: 5	
had been spoken by Alma and A.;		14: 7	
that they took Alma and A.,		14: 9	
And when A. saw the pains of		14:10	
Now A. said unto Alma:		14:12	
and stood before Alma and A.,		14:14	
and A. answered him nothing;		14:17	
and A. were bound with cords.		14:23	
of God was upon Alma and A.,		14:25	
who smote upon Alma and A.,		14:27	
And Alma and A. came forth		14:28	
save it were Alma and A.,		14:28	
saw Alma and A. coming forth		14:29	
from the presence of Alma and A.		14:29	
from the presence of Alma and A.		14:29	
Alma and A. were commanded		15: 1	
that Alma and A. were no more;		15: 3	
heard that Alma and A. were		15: 4	
all the power of Alma and A. to		15:15	
Alma and A., Amulek having		15:16	
A. having forsaken all his gold,		15:16	
he took A. and came over to		15:18	
And Alma and A. went forth		16:13	
thus did Alma and A. go forth,		16:15	
and also A. and Zeezrom, who		31: 6	
and also A. and Zeezrom and		31:32	
A. arose and began to teach them,		34: 1	
after A. had made an end of		35: 1	
also the words which A. spake	He	5:10	
unto you by Alma and A.,		5:41	
it was the faith of Alma and A.	Eth	12:13	

AMULON

in a place which they called A.;	Mos	23:31	
begun to possess the land of A.		23:31	
the leader of those priests was A.		23:32	
A. did plead with the Lamanites,		23:33	
compassion on A. and his brethren,		23:34	
And A. and his brethren did join		23:35	
granted unto A. that he should		23:39	
A. did gain favor in the eyes of		24: 1	
of Shilom, and in the land of A.		24: 1	
teachers of the brethren of A.		24: 4	
did the brethren of A. teach them		24: 5	
A. began to exercise authority		24: 8	
For A. knew Alma, that he had		24: 9	
A. commanded them that they		24:11	
those who were the children of A.		25:12	
and the people of A. had built	Al	21: 2	
who were in the land of A.,		24: 1	
were almost all the seed of A.		25: 4	
remnant of the children of A.		25: 7	
began to hunt the seed of A.		25: 8	

AMULONITES

and the A. were still harder;	Al	21: 3	
the A. were after the order of		21: 4	
neither were any of the A.;		23:14	
the A. and the Lamanites who		24: 1	
and by the A. to anger against		24: 1	
brethren were Amalekites and A.,		24:28	
who were Amalekites or A.,		24:29	

ANARCHY

ANARCHY
supplanted by a. and terror; DC 134: 6

ANATHOTH
heard unto Laish, O poor A. 2Ne 20:30

ANCHOR
upon the waves, without sail or a., Mrm 5:18
maketh an a. to the souls of men, Eth 12: 4

ANCIENT
awake as in the a. days. 2Ne 8: 9
and the prudent, and the a.; 13: 2
himself proudly against the a., 13: 5
The a., he is the head; 19:15
the Jews, mine a. covenant people. 29: 4
the Jews, mine a. covenant people? 29: 5
all records that are of a. date; Mos 8:13
which are laid down by a. priests, Al 30:23
that those a. prophecies are true. 30:24
and they are of a. date and they 3Ne 3: 9
a. and long dispersed covenant Mrm 8:15
account of those a. inhabitants Eth 1: 1
of old records, which are a., DC 8: 1
from all those a. records 8:11
the prince of all, the a. of days; 27:11
like as it was in a. days, 58:17
mine apostles, in a. days, built 84:108
mine a. prophets and apostles. 98:32
they, the church, in a. days, 107: 4
the more a. inhabitants and 111: 9
the A. of Days shall sit, 116: 1
the Lord's anointed in a. times, 135: 3
the Savior to the a. inhabitants; JS 2:34
"seers" in a. or former times; 2:35

ANCIENTLY
of three presidents were a., DC 107:29

ANCIENTS
with the a. of his people 2Ne 13:14
had sworn by the oath of the a., Eth 9: 5
oaths after the manner of the a., 10:33
the law that I gave unto mine a., DC 98:33

AND: *see in the APPENDIX.*

ANEW
there were many cities built a., 3Ne 6: 7

ANGEL
behold, an a. of the Lord came 1Ne 3:29
And after the a. had spoken 3:30
And after the a. had departed, 3:31
an a. hath spoken unto you; 4: 3
ye have seen an a. of the Lord? 7:10
and an a. came down and stood 11:14
the a. spake unto me, saying: 11:19
And the a. said unto me: 11:21
And the a. said unto me again: 11:26
the a. spake unto me again, 11:30
and the a. spake and showed 11:31
the a. spake unto me again, 11:32
called by the a. of the Lord. 11:34
a. of the Lord spake unto me 11:35
a. of the Lord spake unto me 11:36
the a. said unto me: Look, and 12: 1
And the a. spake unto me, 12: 8
the a. said unto me: Look! 12:11
And the a. said unto me! These 12:11
And the a. said unto me: 12:14
And the a. spake unto me, 12:16
And while the a. spake these words, 12:19
according to the word of the a.; 12:19
And the a. said unto me: 12:22
the a. spake unto me, saying: Look! 13: 1
And the a. said unto me: 13: 2
And the a. said unto me: 13: 5
And the a. spake unto me, 13: 8
the a. said unto me: Behold 13:11
And the a. said unto me: 13:21
And the a. of the Lord said 13:24
the a. of the Lord spake unto me, 13:34

ANGEL

And the a. spake unto me, 1Ne 13:40
the a. spake unto me, Nephi, 14: 5
when the a. had spoken these 14: 8
the a. spake unto me, saying: 14:16
the a. spake unto me, saying: 14:18
And the a. said unto me: 14:20
according to the word of the a. 14:27
a. of the Lord did make them known 14:29
which the a. said unto me was 15:29
Ye have seen an a., and he spake 17:45
according to the words of the a., 19: 8
according to the words of the a., 19:10
needs suppose that an a. of God, 2Ne 2:17
according to the words of the a. 6: 9
to and fro, for thus saith the a., 6:11
subject to that a. who fell 9: 8
nigh unto an a. of light, 9: 9
the a. spake unto me that 10: 3
also the word of the a. of God, 25:19
unto me by an a. from God. Mos 3: 2
unto him by the a. of the Lord, 4: 1
spoken by the mouth of the a., 4:11
as has been spoken by the a., 5: 5
the a. of the Lord appeared unto 27:11
And again, the a. said: 27:14
the last words which the a. spake 27:17
they had beheld an a. of the Lord; 27:18
the a. appeared unto them, 27:32
an a. of the Lord appeared Al 8:14
message from the a. of the Lord 8:18
the man whom an a. said in a vision: 8:20
the Lord has sent his a. to visit 9:25
this is the voice of the a., 9:29
an a. of the Lord appeared 10: 7
I obeyed the voice of the a., 10: 8
man whom the a. said unto me: 10: 8
And the a. said unto he is a 10: 9
it was said by an a. of God. 10: 9
even so has he sent his a. to 10:10
An a. hath made them known 11:31
the time the a. first appeared 17: 2
Hast thou seen an a.? 21: 5
O that I were an a., and could 29: 1
should I desire that I were an a., 29: 7
unto me in the form of an a., 30:53
by the mouth of his holy a., 36: 5
God sent his holy a. to stop 36: 6
and stood up, and beheld the a. 36: 8
And the a. spake more things 36:11
sent his a. to declare unto me 38: 7
I have seen an a. face to face, 38: 7
for the Lord to send his a. to 39:19
made known unto me by an a., 40:11
an a. of the Lord hath declared it He 13: 7
Lord commanded me, by his a., 14: 9
thus hath the a. spoken unto me; 14:26
And the a. said unto me that 14:28
for they thought it was an a. 3Ne 11: 8
flaming fire and a ministering a.; DC 7: 6
ministered unto him by an holy a. 20: 6
an a. shall sound his trump, 45:45
the a. shall sound his trumpet. 49:23
a. of God who was in authority 76:25
the a. ascending from the east, 77: 9
the a. ascending from the east is 77: 9
was ordained by the a. of God 84:28
another a. shall sound his trump, 88:94
of the trump of the a. of God. 88:98
after this another a. shall sound, 88:99
fifth trump, which is the fifth a. 88:103
another a. shall sound his trump, 88:105
his trump, which is the sixth a., 88:105
another a. shall sound his trump, 88:106
trump, which is the seventh a., 88:106
first a. again sound his trump 88:108
the second a. sound his trump, 88:109
And so on, until the seventh a. 88:110
And Michael, the seventh a., 88:112
the destroying a. shall pass by 89:21
Mine a. shall go up before you, 103:19
Moroni, an a. from heaven, 128:20
he appeared as an a. of light! 128:20
If he be an a. he will do so, 129: 5
be the devil as an a. of light, 129: 8

ANGEL 49 ANGER

sent forth the a. crying through	DC 133:17
I have sent forth mine a.	133:36
the a. of his presence saved	133:53
an a. of the Lord appeared	Mses 5: 6
then the a. spake, saying:	5: 7
the a. of his presence stood by	Abr 1:15
send thine a. to deliver me	2:13
sent his a. to deliver thee	3:20
The A. of the Lord.	Fac 1: 1
an a. of God had revealed it	JS 2:64

ANGEL'S
a. time, prophet's time, and	DC 130: 4

ANGELS
numberless concourses of a.	1Ne 1: 8
and I saw a. descending upon	11:30
that a. have ministered unto him.	16:38
and a. came down and ministered	2Ne 4:24
become devils, a. to a devil,	9: 9
filthy are the devil and his a.;	9:16
can ye speak with the tongue of a.,	31:13
yea, even with the tongue of a.,	31:14
could speak with the tongue of a.?	32: 2
could ye speak with the tongue of a.	32: 2
A. speak by the power of the	32: 3
may not become a. to the devil,	Jac 3:11
for I truly had seen a.,	7: 5
and the ministering of a.	7:17
and in the ministering of a.,	Om 1:25
prepared for the devil and his a.	Mos 26:27
having conversed with a.,	Al 9:21
this people, by the voice of his a.:	10:20
cry, by the voice of his a. that:	10:21
sent a. to converse with them,	12:29
the Lord, by the mouth of a.,	13:22
a. are declaring it unto many	13:24
unto us by the mouth of a.,	13:25
holy men, by the mouth of a.,	13:26
God dwells and all his holy a.	18:30
that they had seen a. and had	19:34
Why do not a. appear unto us?	21: 5
mercy he doth visit us by his a.,	24:14
treated as though they were a.	27: 4
he imparteth his word by a.	32:23
with numberless concourses of a.	36:22
he hath sent his a. to declare	He 5:11
even as the faces of a.	5:36
do converse with the a. of God.	5:39
a. came down out of heaven	5:48
in the presence of mine a.,	10: 6
the a. of him who hath sought to	13:37
a. did appear unto men, wise men,	16:14
having been visited by a. and	3Ne 7:15
therefore having seen a., and	7:15
a. did minister unto him daily.	7:18
devil laugheth, and his a. rejoice,	9: 2
saw a. descending out of heaven	17:24
the a. did minister unto them.	17:24
a. did come down out of heaven	19:14
while the a. were ministering	19:15
rejoiceth, and also all the holy a.,	27:30
And they are as the a. of God,	28:30
no, not one; neither do his a.;	Mro 7:17
he sent a. to minister unto the	7:22
by the ministering of a., and	7:25
neither have a. ceased to	7:29
Or have a. ceased to appear	7:36
it is by faith that a. appear	7:37
to another, the beholding of a.	10:14
keys of the ministering of a.,	DC 13: 1
others by the ministering of a.,	20:10
of God or the ministering of a.	20:35
sent mine a. to commit unto you;	27:16
prepared for the devil and his a.	29:28
thus came the devil and his a.;	29:37
should send forth a. to declare	29:42
a. are waiting the great command	38:12
my word like unto a. of God.	42: 6
and by the ministering of a.,	43:25
Glory; with all the holy a.;	45:44
neither the a. in heaven,	49: 7
heaven for the a. to look upon;	62: 3
mine a. to pluck out the wicked	DC 63:54
neither the ministering of a.;	67:13
And saw the holy a.,	76:21
with the devil and his a.	76:33
with the devil and his a.—	76:36
with the devil and his a.	76:44
an innumerable company of a.,	76:67
of the administering of a.	76:88
to understand by the four a.,	77: 8
four a. sent forth from God,	77: 8
he crieth unto the four a.	77: 9
the a. to whom is given power	77:11
of the trumpets of the seven a.	77:12
the key of the ministering of a.	84:26
mine a. charge concerning you.	84:42
and mine a. round about you	84:88
the a. are crying unto the Lord	86: 5
and the a. rejoice over you;	88: 2
a. shall fly through the midst of	88:92
a. be crowned with the glory of	88:107
and the a. rejoice over them.	90:34
Mine a. shall go up before you,	103:20
keys of the ministering of a.,	107:20
thine a. have charge over them;	109:22
were pointed to by the a.,	121:27
duty that we owe to God, to a.,	123: 7
of Raphael, and of divers a.,	128:21
A., who are resurrected	129: 1
there are no a. who minister	130: 5
The a. do not reside on a	130: 6
are appointed a. in heaven,	132:16
a. are ministering servants,	132:16
these a. did not abide my law;	132:17
a. of God forever and ever.	132:17
the a. and the gods are appointed	132:18
and they shall pass by the a.,	132:19
the a. are subject unto them.	132:20
and are not a. but are gods.	132:37
I did call upon by mine a.,	136:37
declared by holy a. sent forth	Mses 5:58
a. descending out of heaven;	7:25
laughed, and his a. rejoiced.	7:26
a. descending out of heaven,	7:27
and all the holy a. with him.	JS 1: 1
shall send his a. before him	1:37
not the a. of God in heaven,	1:40
now as ministering of a.,	2:65
keys of the ministering of a.,	2:69

ANGER
Laman stir up their hearts to a.	1Ne 16:38
they did turn away their a., and	16:39
sake will I defer mine a.,	20: 9
and that which ye call a. was	2Ne 1:26
Do not a. again because of	4:29
because of the a. of my brethren.	5: 1
behold, their a. did increase	5: 2
is the a. of the Lord kindled	15:25
his a. is not turned away,	15:25
for the fierce a. of Rezin	17: 4
his a. is not turned away,	19:12
his a. is not turned away,	19:17
his a. is not turned away,	19:21
his a. is not turned away,	20: 4
the rod of mine a., and the staff	20: 5
indignation shall cease, and mine a.	20:25
thine a. is turned away,	22: 1
mine a. is not upon them that	23: 3
both with wrath and fierce a.,	23: 9
in the day of his fierce a.	23:13
he that ruled the nations in a.,	24: 6
the fire of the a. of the Lord	26: 6
and they be stirred up to a.,	28:19
to a. against that which is good.	28:20
God, to provoke him to a.,	Jac 1: 8
I will visit them in mine a.	Mos 11:20
he might stir up my people to a.	11:28
I will visit them in my a.,	12: 1
in my fierce a. will I visit them	12: 1
and amazement, and with a.	13: 8
was stirred up in a. against him,	17:12
in my a. I did cause my people	20:15
up in a. against the Nephites,	21: 2

ANGER

to a. against the Lamanites;	Mos 21:11
to a. against those who were not	Al 2: 8
I will visit this people in mine a.;	8:29
will not turn my fierce a. away.	8:29
yea, he will visit you in his a.,	9:12
and in his fierce a. he will not	9:12
to the fierce a. of the Lord.	9:18
but in his fierce a. he will	10:23
fall at this time, in thine a.,	20:17
to a. against their brethren.	24: 1
should be stirred up to a.;	25: 8
began to stir up the people in a.	27: 2
do stir up the Lamanites to a.	27:12
thou didst visit them in thine a.	33:10
did stir up the Zoramites to a.	35:10
and to stir them up also to a.	35:10
to stir up the Lamanites to a.	43: 8
did smite in their fierce a.	43:44
and the a. of the Lamanites,	43:48
remainder of his soldiers to a.,	44:16
the Lamanites to a. against them,	46:30
to a. against the people of Nephi,	47: 1
minds, and stirred them up to a.,	48: 3
his soul was filled with a.	51:14
Behold, I am in my a., and also	54:13
Teancum in his a. did go forth	62:36
they were stirred up again to a.	63:14
he did stir them up to a.,	He 1:17
to a. against the Nephites;	4: 4
had not been stirred up to a.,	6:17
he will visit them in his a.,	7:hd
ye have provoked him to a.	7:18
did stir up the people to a.	8: 7
wilt thou turn away thine a.,	11:11
let thine a. be appeased in	11:11
wilt thou turn away thine a.,	11:12
thine anger, yea, thy fierce a.,	11:12
wilt thou turn away thine a.,	11:16
the Lord did turn away his a.	11:17
being stirred up to a. by them,	11:24
I will visit them in my fierce a.,	13:10
I will turn away mine a.,	13:11
the a. of the Lord is already	13:30
not turn away thine a. from us?	13:37
the a. of the Lord be turned away	13:39
of men to contend with a.,	3Ne 11:29
stir up the hearts of men with a.	11:30
Lamanites with exceeding great a.,	Mrm 4:15
will turn away his a. from them	Eth 1:36
turn away thine a. from this thy	3: 3
and they did meet in great a.,	13:27
to a. against the people of Shiz;	15: 6
to a. against the people of	15: 6
came they were drunken with a.,	15:22
to a. one with another.	Mro 9: 3
they tremble and a. against me;	9: 4
so exceedingly do they a. that	9: 5
the a. of the Lord is kindled,	DC 1:13
mine a. is kindled against them.	5: 8
he stirreth up their hearts to a.	10:24
stir them up to a. against you,	10:32
and by my wrath, and by my a.,	19:15
mine a. is kindled against the	56: 1
mine a. is kindled against them.	60: 2
have decreed in mine a.	61: 5
today mine a. is turned away.	61:20
whose a. is kindled against their	61:31
whose a. is kindled against the	63: 2
may not be stirred up unto a.	63:27
their hearts to a. against you,	63:28
the a. of God kindleth against	82: 6
his a. was kindled against them,	84:24
displeasure, and in his fierce a.,	101:90
that thine a. be kindled against	109:27
send upon them in thine a.,	109:30
may thine a. be kindled,	109:52
Let thine a. be kindled against	121: 5
tread upon them in mine a.,	133:51
fierce a. is kindled against them;	Mses 6:27
fierce a. is kindled against them.	7:34
for behold mine a. is kindled	8:15

ANGOLA

we did come to the city of A.,	Mrm 2: 4

ANGRY

they were a. with him: yea, even	1Ne 1:20
Laban was a., and thrust him out	3:13
Laman was a. with me and also	3:28
brethren, they were a. with me.	7:16
they were a. with me again,	7:19
my brethren were a. with me	16:18
they were a. with me, and were	17:48
lest the Lord should be a. with us,	18:10
they were a. with me, saying:	18:10
say that he hath been a. with you;	2Ne 1:26
sons of Ishmael were a. with me	4:13
why am I a. because of mine	4:27
though thou wast a. with me	22: 1
all those who tremble, and are a.	28:28
no man will be a. at the words	33: 5
that they were a. with him.	Mos 12: 9
you the truth ye are a. with me.	13: 4
he would not be a. with Abinadi,	17: 2
and they were a. with the king,	19:20
were a. with the people of Limhi,	20: 6
should turn to be a. and draw away	29: 7
people they were a. with me,	Al 9:32
were more a. with Amulek,	10:24
for they were a. with Alma,	14: 2
also a. with Alma and Amulek;	14: 3
were a. because of the slain of	17:36
for they were a. with Ammon	19:21
exceeding a. with Ammon,	19:22
his father was a. with him,	20:13
he was a. with him, and he drew	20:16
they were a. with him,	21:10
she was a. with them,	22:19
those Lamanites were more a.	25: 1
of their loss were exceeding a.	27: 2
and wast a. with mine enemies,	33:10
Thou art a., O Lord, with this	33:16
they were a. because of the word,	35: 3
a. with the people of Ammon	35: 8
a. with us because of our religion.	44: 2
and he was a. with Moroni,	44:12
And now Moroni was a.,	44:17
he was a. with Amalickiah.	46:11
exceedingly a. with his people,	49:26
a. with one of his maid servants,	50:30
were a. with him, and desired that	51: 4
had received this epistle, was a.;	54:15
was more a., because he knew	55: 1
was a. with the government,	59:13
I am not a., but do rejoice in the	61: 9
exceedingly a. with Ammoron,	62:35
unto death, therefore they were a.,	He 1: 9
they were a., and they cried out	8: 1
those judges were a. with him	8: 4
ye are a. with me, and seek to	9:24
ye are a. with him, and cast	13:26
ye are a. with me and do seek	14:10
words of Samuel were a. with him;	16: 2
the people who were exceeding a.	3Ne 6:21
those who were a. were chiefly	6:21
those who were lawyers were a.	6:21
that they were a. with him,	7:18
were a. with him because of	7:20
whosoever is a. with his brother	12:22
the Nephites being a. because	Mrm 4:15
do not be a. with thy servant	Eth 3: 2
Shule was a. with his brother;	7: 8
they were exceedingly a. because	8: 5
was a. with his father because	9: 8
was exceedingly a. with Shared,	13:27
was a. with you yesterday,	DC 61:20
and with whom God is a.	63:11
Lord, am a. with the wicked;	63:32
a. with him who was my	64:15
and shall become exceedingly a.,	87: 5
stars shall become exceedingly a.,	88:87
Lamech, being a., slew him,	Mses 5:50
and was a. with the wicked,	5:56
I am a. with this people, and	6:27
And the second was a.,	Abr 3:28

ANGUISH

Behold, my soul is rent with a.	1Ne 17:47
trouble, and darkness, dimness of a.	2Ne 18:22

ANGUISH — ANOTHER

ANGUISH (cont.)
the pain, and the a. of my soul	2 Ne	26: 7
breast with guilt, and pain, and a.,	Mos	2:38
so great shall be his a. for the		3: 7
cried out in the a. of his soul,		19: 7
they were filled with pain and a.		25:11
they suffered much a. of soul		28: 4
much tribulation and a. of soul,	Al	8:14
bitter pain and a. of soul;		38: 8
And my soul was rent with a.,	Mrm	6:16
and indignation, wailing, and a.,	DC	124:52

ANI-ANTI
village which was called A.,	Al	21:11

ANIMAL
whatsoever beast or a. or fowl	Eth	6: 4
and all manner of wild a.,	1 Ne	18:25
herds, and a. of every kind.	2 Ne	5:11
manner of wild a. of every kind,	Al	22:31
also many other kinds of a.	Eth	9:18
covered with a. of the forest.		10:19
all wild a. that run or creep	DC	89:14
and barley for all useful a.,		89:17

ANKLES
also mine a. were much swollen,	1 Ne	18:15
his legs, a little above the a.	JS	2:31

ANNOUNCE
we a. the martyrdom of Joseph	DC	135: 1

ANNOYER
and an a. of his kingdom;	JS	2:20

ANNUAL
Sun in their a. revolutions.	Fac	2: 5

ANNUALLY
one-tenth of all their interest a.;	DC	119: 4

ANNULLED
heaven, and could not be a.,	DC	128: 9

ANOINT
when thou fastest, a. thy head,	3 Ne	13:17
a. one of their sons to be a king	Eth	6:22
they did a. him to be their king.		10:10
A. thine eyes with clay, and	Mses	6:35

ANOINTED
he a. a man to be a king and a	Jac	1: 9
and Orihah was a. to be king	Eth	6:27
Jared was a. king over the people,		9: 4
he a. Emer to be king to reign		9:14
after that he had a. Emer to		9:15
and he a. Coriantum to reign		9:21
after he had a. Coriantum to		9:22
whom he a. king in his stead.		10:16
a., and ordained under the hands	DC	68:20
lookest upon the face of thine A.		109:53
let these, thine a. ones,		109:80
up the heel against mine a.,		121:16
have chosen him and a. him,		124:76
be appointed, ordained, and a.,		124:91
of promise, of him who is a.,		132: 7
through the medium of mine a.,		132: 7
through him whom I have a.		132:18
of promise, by him who is a.,		132:19
the Lord's a. in ancient times,		135: 3

ANOINTING
destroyed because of the a.	2 Ne	20:27
they may claim their a. if	DC	68:21
Let the a. of thy ministers be		109:35
this a. have I put upon his		124:57
unto her by the holy a.,		132:41

ANOINTINGS
your a., and you washings,	DC	124:39

ANOTHER
brethren did consult one with a.	1 Ne	3:10
as a man speaketh with a.	1 Ne	11:11
they were disputing one with a.		15: 2
down from one generation to a.,		19: 4
another, or from one prophet to a.,		19: 4
I will not give my glory unto a.		20:11
shall be turned one against a.		22:14
as one generation passeth to a.	2 Ne	1:12
be oppressed, every one by a.,		13: 5
And one cried unto a., and said:		16: 3
they shall be amazed one at a.;		23: 8
forward any more for a. Messiah,		25:16
should not contend one with a.;		26:32
shall deliver these words unto a.;		27: 9
and deliver them to a., that he may		27:15
they shall contend one with a.;		28: 4
priests shall contend one with a.,		28: 4
remember one nation like unto a.?		29: 8
unto one nation like unto a.		29: 8
not suppose that I cannot speak a.;		29: 9
some in one and some in a.,	Jac	5:14
have planted a. branch of the tree		5:23
and behold a. branch also,		5:24
family being separate one from a.	Mos	2: 5
ye should make slaves one of a.,		2:13
ye to labor to serve one a.?		2:18
should live in peace one with a.—		2:20
you from one moment to a.—		2:21
not have a mind to injure one a.,		4:13
and fight and quarrel one with a.,		4:14
ye will teach them to love one a.,		4:15
one another, and to serve one a.		4:15
substance that ye have one to a.		4:21
my people to anger one with a.,		11:28
And again, Alma took a.,		18:15
be no contention one with a.,		18:21
unity and in love one towards a.		18:21
imparting to one a.		18:29
not esteem one flesh above a.,		23: 7
shall not think himself above a.;		23: 7
a people friendly one with a.;		24: 5
that they might write one to a.		24: 6
and began to trade one with a.		24: 7
and he went from one body to a.,		25:15
forgive one a. your trespasses;		26:31
might become friendly to one a.,		28: 2
down from one generation to a.,		28:20
should be a. appointed in his stead,		29: 7
we have any right to destroy a.		29: 8
the word of God, one with a.,	Al	1:20
smite one a. with their fists.		1:22
wonderful contentions one with a.		2: 5
did contend mightily, one with		2:29
was a. army of the Lamanites		3:20
to be scornful, one towards a.		4: 8
from one piece of iniquity to a.,		4:11
that ye are better one than a.;		5:54
hath given to a., to reign		7: 2
he entered the city by a. way,		8:18
Now if a man owed a.,		11: 2
and departed one from a.,		17:13
themselves one from a.,		17:17
the Lord has called him a. way;		22: 4
from one house of worship to a.,		23: 4
and to place a. in his stead,		24:20
separate themselves one from a.,		31:37
which will atone for the sins of a.,		34:11
down from one generation to a.,		37: 4
wrote a. epistle unto Moroni,		54:15
should march forward by a. way		58:26
from one generation to a.;		63:13
down from one generation to a.	He	3:16
And even from one city to a.,		5:16
they did fellowship one with a.		6: 3
and did rejoice one with a.,		6: 3
have free intercourse one with a.,		6: 8
might be lifted up one above a.;		6:17
protect and preserve one a.		6:21
I will show unto you a. sign,		9:25
to slay one a. with the sword.		10:18
again, a. sign I give unto you,		14:14
said unto you concerning a. sign,		14:20
unto themselves a. leader,	3 Ne	4:17

enter into a covenant one with a.,	3Ne	6:28
they did covenant one with a.		6:30
were divided one against a.;		7: 2
separate one from a. into tribes,		7: 2
would not go to war one with a.;		7:14
should not trespass against a.,		7:14
And in a. place they were heard		8:25
and wondering one with a.,		11: 1
showing one to a. the great and		11: 1
were thus conversing one with a.,		11: 3
their mouths, even one to a.,		11: 8
contend with anger, one with a.		11:29
men with anger, one against a.;		11:30
I give unto you a. commandment,		18:27
spake often one to a., and the		24:16
and did minister one to a.;		26:19
man dealing justly, one with a.		26:19
man did deal justly one with a.	4Ne	1: 2
was a. church which denied		1:29
exceeding wicked one like unto a.		1:45
Lamanites are at war one with a.:	Mrm	8: 8
and sell and traffic one with a.,	Eth	10:22
that there arose a. mighty man;		11:17
send or bring forth a. people		11:21
even as a man telleth a. in mine		12:39
been spoken concerning a. people		13:21
forth one against a. to battle;		15:15
to speak one with a. concerning	Mro	6: 5
continually to anger one with a.		9: 3
lost their love, one towards a.;		9: 5
And to a., that he may teach		10:10
And to a., exceeding great faith;		10:11
and to a., the gifts of healing		10:11
to a., that he may work mighty		10:12
to a., that he may prophesy		10:13
to a., the beholding of angels		10:14
to a., all kinds of tongues;		10:15
to a., the interpretation of		10:16
for you have a. gift, which is	DC	8: 6
supposeth that a. lieth to deceive,		10:28
you can read them one to a.;		18:35
appoint one then 7 in his stead.		28: 7
if not, a. will I plant in his stead.		35:18
teach one a. according to the		38:23
a. shall be appointed in his		42:10
to appoint a. in his stead.		43: 4
not be left one stone upon a.		45:20
take up the sword, one against a.,		45:33
they will kill one a.		45:33
shall not be at war one with a.		45:69
and to some is given a.,		46:12
To a. is given the word of		46:18
to a. is given the interpretation		46:25
I have appointed to a. office.		47: 3
possess that which is above a.,		49:20
as a man reasoneth one with a.		50:11
understand one a., and both		50:22
given unto that of a. church.		51:10
if a. church would receive money		51:11
and he shall make a.;		63:56
sought occasion against one a.		64: 8
and forgave not one a.		64: 8
that ye ought to forgive one a.;		64: 9
as one star differs from a. star		76:98
so differs one from a. in glory		76:98
some of one and some of a.—		76:100
as you have forgiven one a.		82: 1
send upon you a. Comforter,		88: 3
must inherit a. kingdom,		88:21
shall teach one a. the doctrine of		88:77
a. angel shall sound his trump,		88:94
after this a. angel shall sound,		88:99
again, a. trump shall sound,		88:100
And a. trump shall sound,		88:102
And a. trump shall sound,		88:103
a. angel shall sound his trump,		88:105
a. angel shall sound his trump,		88:106
teach one a. words of wisdom;		88:118
See that ye love one a.;		88:123
learn to impart one to a. as		88:123
cease to find fault one with a.;		88:124
for a salutation to one a.		88:136
shall the oracles be given to a.,		90: 4

ye have covenanted one with a.	DC	90:24
were at variance one with a.		101:50
should be in bondage one to a.		101:79
build, and a. shall not inherit it;		101:101
shall be a. treasury prepared,		104:67
a. shall be appointed in his stead.		104:77
their duty, edifying one a.,		107:85
teach one a. words of wisdom;		109: 7
a. great and glorious vision burst		110:13
a. may be appointed unto the		124:130
a. may be appointed unto		124:132
and a. book was opened, which		128: 6
and a. book was opened, which		128: 7
they may accord one with a.—		128:13
give you a. quotation of Paul,		128:16
continue the subject a. time.		128:25
diligence and obedience than a.,		130:19
for I gave them unto a., saith		132:39
and if she be with a. man,		132:41
and she be with a. man,		132:42
her husband be with a. woman,		132:43
virgin, and desire to espouse a.,		132:61
espoused, shall be with a. man,		132:63
and speak often one to a.		133: 6
and a. proscribed in its spiritual		134: 9
all your pledges one with a.;		136:20
Cease to contend one with a.,		136:23
cease to speak evil one of a.		136:23
words tend to edifying one a.		136:24
even so shall a. come;	Mses	1:38
raise up a. like unto thee;		1:41
God hath appointed me a. seed,		6: 2
I have given unto you a. law		6:56
as a man talketh one with a.,		7: 4
that they should love one a.,		7:33
obtain a. place of residence;	Abr	1: 1
built a. altar unto the Lord,		2:20
shall be a. fact above them,		3: 8
a. planet whose reckoning of		3: 8
the time of one planet above a.,		3: 9
as one man talketh with a.;		3:11
a. more intelligent than they;		3:19
And a. answered and said:		3:27
one stone upon a. that shall not	JS	1: 3
and shall betray one a.;		1: 8
to one party and some to a.,		2: 6
all their good feelings one for a.,		2: 6
as usual at the end of a. year		2:59
ANOTHER'S		
willing to bear one a. burdens,	Mos	18: 8
not build upon a. foundation,	DC	52:33
neither journey in a. track.		52:33
ANSWER		
to a. the ends of the law,	2Ne	2: 7
to a. the ends of the atonement—		2:10
called, yea, there was none to a.		7: 2
What shall then a. the		24:32
that I can a. a clear conscience	Mos	2:15
I a. you, Nay.		2:25
that they should a. the questions		7: 8
our cries and did a. our prayers;		9:18
my prayers, and did a. my prayers,		23:10
willingness to a. for his own sins.		29:38
and to a. their prayers.	Al	9:26
Will ye a. me a few questions		11:21
Will ye a. the questions which		11:21
not a. the words of this people?		14:19
Behold, I a. for you;		26: 3
might a. the end of its creation;	DC	49:16
shall a. this question yourselves;		50:16
shall a. the debt unto the bishop		72:14
A. It is the earth, in its		77: 1
A. They are figurative		77: 2
A. They are limited to four		77: 3
A. Their eyes are a		77: 4
A. We are to understand that		77: 5
A. We are to understand that		77: 6
A. We are to understand that		77: 7
A. We are to understand that		77: 8
A. We are to understand that		77: 9
A. They are to be accomplished		77:10

ANSWER		53	ANTUM	

A. We are to understand that	DC	77:11	Professor A. stated that the	JS 2:64
A. We are to understand that		77:12	when Mr. A. called me back	2:64
A. They are to be accomplished		77:13	what Professor A. had said	2:65
A. We are to understand		77:14		
A. They are two prophets that		77:15	ANTI-CHRIST	
to a. them in the day of their		101: 7	he was a., for he began to	Al 30: 6
and a. us from heaven, thy		109:77	this a., whose name was Korihor,	30:12
a. these petitions, and accept		109:78		
and give thee a. to thy prayers.		112:10	ANTI-NEPHI-LEHI	
in a. to them I say unto you,		124: 2	taken upon them the name of A.,	Al 24: 1
I will a. judgment, wrath,		124:52	arms against the people of A.	24: 2
a. the ordinance just the same		128: 4	his son, and he called his name A.	24: 3
is only to a. the will of God,		128: 5	and also with his brother A.,	24: 5
to a. to the likeness of the dead,		128:12	of destroying the people of A.	24:20
In a. to the question—		130: 4	attempt to slay the people of A.	25: 1
I a., Yes.		130: 5	who were the people of A.	25:13
will a. thee as touching this		132: 2	their brethren, the people of A.;	27: 2
this shall be the a. of the Lord		133:65	who were the people of A.	27:21
there was none of you to a.;		133:67	he returned to the people of A.,	27:25
unto me in a. to my prayers,	Abr	2:19	who were the people of A.,	43:11

ANSWERED
And I a. him, saying: Yea, it is	1Ne	11:22	ANTI-NEPHI-LEHIES	
can the ends of the law be a.	2Ne	2: 7	that they called their names A.;	Al 23:17
a. upon the heads of your parents.		4: 6	ANTIOMNO	
heard my cry and a. my prayer.	Jac	7:22	whose name is A., is a friend unto	Al 20: 4
heard his prayers and a. them,	Mos	10:13		
but he a. them boldly,		12:19	ANTION	
And they a. and said that		12:32	an a. of gold is equal to three	Al 11:19
prayers of his servants might be a.		27:14		
that their prayers may be a.,		27:16	ANTIONAH	
shall be a. upon their own heads.		29:30	But there was one A., who was	Al 12:20
a. upon the heads of their kings.		29:31		
And he a., No.	Al	11:29	ANTIONUM	
Amulek a. and said unto him:		11:34	in a land which they called A.,	Al 31: 3
Alma and Amulek a. him nothing;		14:17	they came into the land of A.,	43: 5
but they a. them nothing.		14:18	together in the land of A.,	43:15
but they a. nothing.		14:19	departed out of the land of A.	43:22
And he a. and said:		15: 7	and A., and Shiblom, and Shem,	Mrm 6:14
And they a. the king, and said:		18: 3		
And the king a. him not		18:14	ANTIPARAH	
But the king a. him not.		18:15	of Cumeni, and the city of A.	Al 56:14
Ammon a. and said unto him:		18:19	to march near the city of A.,	56:31
the king a. him, and said:		18:23	and came near the city A.	56:33
And he a., and said unto him:		18:25	in the city A. were stationed	56:34
unto him, he a. him, saying:		20:19	would deliver up the city of A.	57: 1
Aaron a. him and said unto him:		22: 7	sufficient to take the city of A.	57: 2
And Korihor a. him, Yea.		30:36	to go against the city of A.	57: 3
And he a., Nay.		30:38	people of A. did leave the city,	57: 4
And they a. and said:	He	9:12	the city of A. fell into our hands.	57: 4
his disciples a. him and said:	3Ne	23:10		
prayers may be a. according to	Mrm	9:37	ANTIPAS	
And he a.: Nay; Lord, show	Eth	3:10	of the mount which was called A.,	Al 47: 7
And he a.: Yea, Lord, I know		3:12	which was near the mount A.	47: 9
he hath a. the ends of the law,	Mor	7:28	secret embassy into the mount A.,	47:10
and it shall be a. with a blessing	DC	25:12		
they are to be a. upon your souls		41:12	ANTIPUS	
to be a. upon the heads of		56: 4	assist A., whom ye had appointed	Al 56: 9
to which they all a. that they		102: 4	to the army of A., in which	56:10
shall be a. upon their heads;		133:41	which strength A. did rejoice	56:10
to be a. by man to his Maker.		134: 6	I found A. and his men	56:15
cannot be a. upon the heads	Mses	6:54	that A. had received a greater	56:18
one a. like unto the Son of Man:	Abr	3:27	A. ordered that I should march	56:30
And another a. and said:		3:27	A. did march forth with a part of	56:33
And Jesus a., and said unto	JS	1: 5	the army of A. pursuing them,	56:37
I was a. that I must join none		2:19	before A. should overtake them,	56:37
I a. that an angel of God had		2:64	A., beholding our danger,	56:38
			neither did A. overtake them;	56:38
ANSWERETH			they were overtaken by A.	56:43
a. all things, for an inheritance,	DC	72:17	should overpower the army of A.	56:46
			the armies of A. had overtaken	56:49
ANSWERING			The army of A. being weary,	56:50
a. the sins of the people upon our	Jac	1:19	For A. had fallen by the sword,	56:51
a. to the Hebrew word,	Fac	1:12	the men of A., being confused	56:51
a. to the measuring of the		2: 4	when the people of A. saw that	56:53
			people of Nephi, the people of A.,	56:54
ANSWERS			men who were not slain of A.,	56:57
A. to the Hebrew word	Fac	2: 4		
			ANTIQUITIES	
ANTHEMS			stones, and with all your a.;	DC 124:26
Let the dead speak forth a.	DC 128:22		all who have knowledge of a.,	124:26

ANTHON, Charles			ANTUM	
to Professor A., a gentleman	JS	2:64	go to the land A., unto a hill	Mrm 1: 3

ANXIETIES

ANXIETIES
amidst all my a. I had never	JS	2:14

ANXIETY
this hath been the a. of my soul	2Ne	1:16
Yea, mine a. is great for you;		6: 3
because of faith and great a.,	Jac	1: 5
with much more desire and a. for		2: 3
the great a. of his people;	Mos	28:12
with great a. even unto pain,	Al	13:27
await with great a. for the word—	3Ne	3: 3

ANXIOUS
a. that every man should have an	Mos	29:38
awaited with a. expectation	DC	121:27

ANXIOUSLY
be a. engaged in a good cause,	DC	58:27

ANY
Never at a. time have I shed the	1Ne	4:10
they be dimmed a. more by time.		5:19
neither at a. time shall I give it		6: 1
cannot a. unclean thing enter		15:34
there was not a. thing done		17:31
swords, lest by a. means the people	2Ne	5:14
neither shall they learn war a. more.		12: 4
is there a. end of their treasures;		12: 7
is there a. end of their chariots.		12: 7
hath a. of them been destroyed		25: 9
and look not forward a. more for		25:16
need not look forward a. more for		25:18
for there should not a. come, save		25:18
sufficient to teach a. man the right		25:28
doth he cry unto a., saying:		26:25
hath he commanded a. that		26:26
Hath he commanded a. that		26:27
hath the Lord commanded a. that		26:28
there cannot be a. more Bible.		29: 3
must not perform a. thing unto		32: 9
lest by a. means he should swear	Jac	1: 7
there shall not a. man among you		2:27
if I do not, by a. means, get		4:18
and by a. means be destroyed,	En	1:13
nor silver nor a. manner of riches	Mos	2:12
commit a. manner of wickedness,		2:13
do merit a. thanks from you,		2:19
there are not a. among you, except		2:34
nor a. other way nor means		3:17
neither are there a. conditions		4: 8
of a. one that can translate?		8:12
lest by a. means my people		9:11
make unto thee a. graven image,		12:36
or a. likeness of any thing in		12:36
of a. thing in heaven above,		12:36
make unto thee a. graven image,		13:12
or a. likeness of things which are		13:12
thou shalt not do a. work,		13:18
could not a. man be saved except		13:32
neither was a. deceit in his		14: 9
listened to my words in a. degree,		22: 4
had not a. such thing happened		26:10
not a. unbeliever persecute		27: 2
persecute a. of those who belonged		27: 2
that a. human soul should perish;		28: 3
that a. soul should endure endless		28: 3
was not a. of his sons who would		28:10
neither were a. of the sons of		29: 3
have a. right to destroy another		29: 8
nor a. manner of iniquity;		29:14
as long as a. of our posterity		29:32
him more than a. other man;		29:40
could have no power on a. man	Al	1:17
that there should not a. man,		1:21
teacher a. better than the learner;		1:26
not send away a. who were naked,		1:30
durst not commit a. wickedness		1:33
how will a. of you feel, if ye shall		5:22
that a. man could slay them;		8:31
without a. respect of persons,		16:14
has not been a. servant among		18:10
him or a. of those who had fallen;		19:24
that thou knowest a. such thing.	Al	21: 8
should be in a. part of their land		23: 1
commit a. manner of wickedness.		23: 3
did not fight against God a. more,		23: 7
against a. of their brethren.		23: 7
were a. of the Amulonites;		23:14
make a. preparations for war;		24: 6
without meeting a. resistance,		24:22
that there should be a. slaves		27: 9
death with a. degree of terror		27:28
not make a. reply to his words;		30:29
neither a. of my brethren,		30:33
never open thy mouth a. more,		30:47
not deceive this people a. more.		30:47
a. more than faith is a perfect		32:26
behold it will not get a. root;		32:38
neither of a. manner of fowl;		34:10
Now there is not a. man that can		34:11
if ye do not a. of these things,		34:28
harden not your hearts a. longer;		34:31
not of a. worthiness of myself.		36: 5
there cannot a. man work after		37:39
be led away be a. vain or foolish		39:11
not prepared with a. such thing;		43:20
lest by a. means of part of the		43:25
a. one to the yoke of bondage.		44: 2
should have a. more strength;		46:30
so long as there were a. who		48:25
by a. other way save by the		49:18
to enter the fort by a. other way,		49:19
not a. known by the appellation		51:21
they had not taken a. cities save		52: 4
shall have a. more power than		55: 2
not a. more than sufficient for		57:15
lest by a. means the judgments		58: 9
if there be a. among you that		60:27
not resolve upon a. stratagem		62:35
lest by a. means they should sin;	He	15: 9
lest by a. means those things	3Ne	1: 7
there should be a. more signs or		2: 3
that they should not spare a.		4:13
have a. effect upon the Nephites,		4:18
have power to condemn a. one		6:22
a. man should be put to death		6:24
a. man who could do a miracle		8: 1
there could not be a. light at all;		8:21
there was not a. light seen,		8:22
shall not come a. more unto me		9: 5
not come up a. more unto me		9: 7
not come up a. more unto me		9: 8
not come up unto me a. more		9: 9
lest at a. time he shall get thee,		12:25
And if a. man will sue thee at		12:40
not at a. time hath the Father		15:14
at a. time hath the Father		15:15
not at a. time hear my voice—		15:23
neither in a. parts of that land		16: 1
have I at a. time manifested		16: 2
Have ye a. that are sick among		17: 7
Have ye a. that are lame, or		17: 7
that are afflicted in a. manner?		17: 7
that were afflicted in a. manner;		17: 9
can there be written by a. man,		17:17
not forbid a. man from coming		18:22
shall not suffer a. one knowingly		18:28
so marred, than a. man,		20:44
of thy widowhood a. more.		22: 4
should not a. man write them.		26:16
ye need not a. longer spurn at		29: 4
and ye need not a. longer hiss,		29: 8
nor a. of the remnant of the		29: 8
they did not walk a. more after	4Ne	1:12
nor a. manner of lasciviousness;		1:16
nor a. manner of -ites;		1:17
Holy Ghost did not come upon a.,	Mrm	1:14
get possession of a. of our lands;		3: 6
not suffer their cries a. longer.		8:41
if they drink a. deadly thing		9:24
but thou shalt not sin a. more,	Eth	2:15
not gain power a. more over Shule		7:29
neither at a. time hath any		12:18
hath a. wrought miracles until		12:18

more than a. other man among	Eth	14:10
not to have written a. more;	Mro	1: 4
did they receive a. unto baptism		6: 2
faith there cannot be a. hope.		7:42
I cannot a. longer enforce my		9:18
a. more concerning this matter.	DC	5:29
not thy gift known unto a.		6:12
ordained to a. office in this church,		20:65
A. member of the church of Christ		20:80
if a. have been expelled from		20:83
may be signed by a. elder or		20:84
if thou art led at a. time by the		28: 4
appointed unto a. of this church		28:12
never at a. time have I declared		29:29
and not at a. time have I given		29:34
neither a. man, nor the children of		29:34
should translate a. more until		37: 1
shall not be given to a. one to go		42:11
neighbor, nor do him a. harm.		42:27
the church, or a. individuals of it,		42:33
if ye shall find that a. persons have		42:75
if a. persons among you shall kill		42:79
And if a. man or woman shall		42:80
or she do a. manner of iniquity,		42:87
And if a. one offend openly,		42:91
If a. shall offend in secret,		42:92
of a. that shall come before you		43: 5
to know a. further concerning		45:60
never to cast a. one out from		46: 3
a. one who belongeth to the		46: 4
nevertheless, if a. have trespassed,		46: 4
ye shall not cast a. out of your		46: 5
be a. that are not of the church,		46: 6
be a. among you professing		46:27
if a. among you desire to ride		62: 7
or if a. shall commit adultery		63:16
will not hold a. guilty that		64:22
spare a. that remain in Babylon.		64:24
it is not said at a. time that		64:28
if there be a. among you that		67: 7
seen God at a. time in the flesh,		67:11
Neither can a. natural man abide		67:12
if at a. time they can prove their		68:21
tried or condemned for a. crime,		68:22
Zion, or in a. of her stakes		68:25
of Zion, or in a. of her stakes		68:26
hereafter appoint unto a. man.		70: 9
if a. man lift his voice against		71:10
there a. who can stay his hand.		76: 3
second death shall have a. power;		76:37
neither a. man except those		76:48
will not lay a. sin to your charge;		82: 7
if a. man shall administer		84:71
a. man that shall go and preach		84:80
if a. man shall give unto any of		84:105
unto a. of you a coat, or a suit,		84:105
if a. man among you be strong		84:106
be found on a. of the records		85: 4
and a. man who hath seen any		88:47
a. or the least of these hath		88:47
over the saints a. more at all.		88:114
they shall not a. more see death.		88:116
when a. shall come in after him,		88:132
ye shall not receive a. among you		88:138
as a. man drinketh wine		89: 5
not suffer a. unclean thing to		94: 8
come into it a. unclean thing,		94: 9
do not suffer a. unclean thing to		97:15
out unto battle against a. nation,		98:33
if a. nation, tongue, or people		98:34
brought a. more as a testimony		98:48
there be a. other place appointed		101:20
whatsoever a. man shall ask,		101:27
have power to tempt a. man.		101:28
that a. man should be in bondage		101:79
whenever a. vacancy shall occur		102: 8
of a. one of the above-named		102: 8
convenes to act upon a. case,		102:13
not spoken, or a. one of them,		102:20
a. additional light is shown upon		102:21
determine whether a. such case,		102:33
a. man belonging to the order		104: 5
that if a. man among you,	DC	104:10
if a. man shall take of the		104:18
call it his own, or a. part of it,		104:62
out of the treasury by a. one,		104:64
if a. man among you obtain		104:69
let not a. among you say that it		104:70
be called his, nor a. part of it.		104:70
shall not a. part of it be used,		104:71
that a. man among you say to		104:72
a. decision of these quorums is		107:32
the gospel, instead of a. others.		107:38
in a. branch of the church where		107:74
There is not a. person		107:81
people transgress, a. of them,		109:21
if a. people shall rise against		109:27
a. nation whithersoever ye shall		112:21
at a. time from the beginning		112:31
get in debt a. more for the		115:13
a. degree of unrighteousness,		121:37
shall not suffer a. pollution to		124:24
to a. of the sons of men to do		124:49
from a. one man for stock in		124:64
dollars stock from a. one man.		124:65
from a. one man in that house.		124:66
permitted to receive a. man,		124:67
receive a. stock in that house.		124:68
if a. pay stock into their hands		124:69
receive a. stock into their hands,		124:70
a. portion of their stock to		124:70
that stock to a. other purpose,		124:70
appropriate a. portion of that		124:71
be mocked in a. of these things.		124:71
neither can a. other man,		124:72
When a. of you are baptized		127: 6
if there be a. present, who can		128: 3
can at a. time when called upon		128: 3
to a. man by actual revelation,		128: 9
or a. set of men, this power		128: 9
whether a. administration is		129: 9
not be a. sooner than that time.		130:17
when we obtain a. blessing from		130:21
they are not bound by a. law when		132:15
he or she shall commit a. sin		132:26
you give a. one on earth,		132:48
if a. man espouse a virgin,		132:61
if a. man have a wife, who		132:64
neither hath a. eye seen, O God,		133:45
that a. religious society has		134:10
to inflict a. physical punishment		134:10
than a. other man that ever		135: 3
They were innocent of a. crime,		135: 7
be rejected by a. court on earth,		135: 7
if a. man shall seek to build up		136:19
permitting a. person to enter		OD
forty or a. other number of		OD
Temples or in a. other place		OD
when a. Elder of the Church has		OD
to convey a. such teaching,		OD
a. marriage forbidden by the		OD
Show them not unto a. except	Mses	1:42
was more subtle than a. beast		4: 5
listened not a. more to the		5:26
lest a. finding him should kill		5:40
have a. right to give at	Fac	2:12
if a. man shall say unto you,	JS	1:21
for another, if they ever had a.,		2: 6
to come to a. certain conclusion		2: 8
If a. one of them be right,		2:10
If a. of you lack wisdom, let		2:11
Never did a. passage of scripture		2:12
if a. person needed wisdom from		2:12
never before felt in a. being—		2:16
to join with a. of them;		2:20
would never be a. more of them.		2:21
duty to join with a. of them		2:26
to join a. of the religious sects		2:28
of a. great or malignant sins.		2:28
a. one who recollects my youth,		2:28
that a. earthly thing could be		2:31
not show them to a. person;		2:42
influenced by a. other motive		2:46
of a. in the neighborhood.		2:51

ANY / APPEALED

or through a. neglect of mine,	JS 2:59
more so than a. he had before	2:64

ANYONE
a. that should speak for me:	1Ne 18:17

ANYTHING: *see also ANY and THING.*
not write a. upon plates save it	1Ne 19: 6
is not a. save he knows it.	2Ne 9:20
He doeth not a. save it be	26:24
upon a. save it be upon plates	Jac 4: 2
nor a. that is thy neighbor's	Mos 13:24
a. contrary to the will of the king	23:39
them a. concerning the Lord	24: 5
a. contrary to that which is right;	29:26
filthiness or a. which is unclean	Al 7:21
know a. concerning the Lord;	17:35
could not merit a. of himself;	22:14
know of a. which is to come.	30:13
not receive a. for our labors in	30:34
or a. else which had happened	31: 5
without a. wherewith to steer	Mrm 5:18
could not withhold a. from him,	Eth 3:26
not withhold a. from his sight;	12:21
neither shall a. be appointed	DC 28:12
without faith shall not a. be	35:11
But he that doeth not a. until	58:29
nor kill, nor do a. like unto it.	59: 6
a. that is not expedient for you,	88:65
a. remain that is not finished.	115:12
and you will not feel a.;	129: 8
if he do a. in my name,	132:59
not formed a. but the earth;	Abr 4: 2
to take a. out of his house;	JS 1:14
a whiteness beyond a. earthly	2:31
was quite unconscious of a.	2:48
If there is a. virtuous, lovely,	AoF 13

ANYWHERE
portion of that stock a. else,	DC 124:71
which they appropriate a. else,	124:71

APART
were set a. for the high priests,	Mos 11:11
set a. that they should gather	18:25
a day set a. by the unbelievers,	3Ne 1: 9
and set a. for that purpose.	DC 42:31
other bishops to be set a.	68:14
is called and set a. and ordained	68:19
shall be set a. for this ministry	68:22
provided he is called and set a.	107:17
be set a. unto the ministering	107:71
be set a. unto this ministry,	107:74

APOCRYPHA
unto you concerning the A.—	DC 91: 1
that the A. should be translated.	91: 3

APOLLOS
and of A. and of Cephas.	DC 76:99

APOSTATE
persecutor of the church, the a.,	DC 86: 3

APOSTATES
and also of the a. who apostatize	DC 85: 2

APOSTATIZE
and also of the apostates who a.	DC 85: 2

APOSTATIZED
or that are found to have a.,	DC 85:11

APOSTLE
this a. of the Lamb shall write	1Ne 14:24
the a. of the Lamb of God	14:25
the a. of the Lamb was John,	14:27
even as unto Paul mine a.,	DC 18: 9
ordained an a. of Jesus Christ,	20: 2
of God, an a. of Jesus Christ,	20: 3
An a. is an elder, and it is	20:38
a prophet, an a. of Jesus Christ,	21: 1
by you, Oliver Cowdery mine a.;	21:10
like unto mine a. of old,	DC 49:11
the a. wrote unto the church,	74: 5

APOSTLES
against the a. of the Lamb;	1Ne 11:34
against the twelve a. of the Lamb.	11:35
against the twelve a. of the Lamb.	11:36
thou rememberest the twelve a.	12: 9
the twelve a. bear record;	13:24
by the hand of the twelve a.	13:26
and of the twelve a. of the Lamb	13:39
are of the twelve a. of the Lamb,	13:40
in the records of the twelve a.	13:41
Behold one of the twelve a.	14:20
wrought by the hands of the a.	Mrm 9:18
the prophets and a. have written,	Eth 12:41
ye give it, for thus do mine a.	Mro 2: 2
the words of the prophets and a.,	DC 1:14
you to know even as mine a.	19: 8
and confirmed you to be a.	27:12
which was spoken by mine a.	29:10
mine a., the Twelve which were	29:12
of the hands, even as the a. of old.	35: 6
the prophets and a. have written,	52: 9
than the prophets and a.,	52:36
which was shown unto mine a.	63:21
preached the a. unto the world	63:52
who are not a. and prophets	64:39
written by the prophets and a.	66: 2
in the days of the a. the	74: 2
And as I said unto mine a.,	84:63
unto you, for you are mine a.,	84:63
as I said unto mine a. I say	84:64
this is the way that mine a.,	84:108
a. were the sowers of the seed;	86: 2
mine a. to prune my vineyard	95: 4
even as mine a. at Jerusalem.	95: 9
me for the school of mine a.,	95:17
all mine ancient prophets and a.	98:32
council composed of the twelve a.,	102:30
are called to be the Twelve A.,	107:23
witnesses or A. just named.	107:26
traveling high council, mine a.,	124:139
the holy a., with Abraham,	133:55
the direction of the Twelve A.	136: 3
from Moses to Jesus and his a.,	136:37
from Jesus and his a. to Joseph	136:37
things had ceased with the a.,	JS 2:21
a., prophets, pastors, teachers,	AoF 6

APPAREL
The changeable suits of a.,	2Ne 13:22
and wear our own a.;	14: 1
of the costliness of your a.,	Jac 2:13
and to wear very costly a.,	Al 1: 6
they did not wear costly a.,	1:27
and strife; wearing costly a.;	1:32
they began to wear very costly a.	4: 6
in the wearing of costly a.	5:53
their costly a., and their ringlets,	31:28
of the coarseness of their a.—	32: 2
ye will clothe him with costly a.;	He 13:28
such as the wearing of costly a.,	4Ne 1:24
unto the wearing of very fine a.,	Mrm 8:36
your substance, and your fine a.,	8:37
known, clothed in his glorious a.,	DC 133:46
Lord shall be red in his a.,	133:48

APPEAL
we might a. unto our brethren to	Mos 8: 7
(for you must a. unto the Lord	Al 37:16
hold your peace; a. unto my Spirit;	DC 11:18
they may a. to the high council	102:27
of the former there can be an a.;	102:31
after examining the a. and the	102:33
can be no a. from their decision.	107:32
men should a. to the civil law	134:11
where immediate a. cannot	134:11
question by an a. to the Bible.	JS 2:12

APPEALED
and also he has a. unto Moses,	Al 34: 7
and a. unto him for assistance;	50:27

APPEALED 57 APPOINTED

any such case, as may be a., DC 102:33

APPEAR
a. before the judgment-seat of	2Ne	9:15
the Son of righteousness shall a.		26: 9
crime which they could make a.	Al	10:13
that he would a. unto them		16:20
Why do not angels a. unto us?		21: 5
a. unto man as if it was day.	He	14: 3
many saints shall a. unto many.		14:25
And angels did a. unto men,		16:14
the Son of God must shortly a.;	3Ne	1:17
also that a new star did a.,		1:21
they may a. unto men to fast.		13:16
That thou a. not unto men to fast,		13:18
and should a. unto many,		23: 9
saints did arise and a. unto many		23:11
even as I a. unto thee to be in	Eth	3:16
I a. unto my people in the flesh.		3:16
have angels ceased to a. unto the	Mro	7:36
it is by faith that angels a. and		7:37
when he shall a. we shall be		7:48
For when the Lord shall a.	DC	45:74
there shall a. a great sign		88:93
I will a. unto my servants,		110: 8
that is the only way he can a.—		129: 6
When the Savior shall a. we		130: 1
who shall a. unto many that		133:36
a. the sign of the Son of Man	JS	1:36
to a. so exceedingly white		2:31

APPEARANCE
I may shake at the a. of sin?	2Ne	4:31
of the a. of the Lamanites.	Mos	23:26
terrible was the a. of the armies	3Ne	4: 7
the a. of the army of Giddianhi,		4: 8
in that verse, is a personal a.;	DC	130: 3
heavenly light had made its a.	JS	2:43

APPEARED
the angel of the Lord a. unto them;	Mos	27:11
the time the angel a. unto them,		27:32
an angel of the Lord a. unto him,	Al	8:14
an angel of the Lord a. unto me		10: 7
at the time the angel first a. unto		17: 2
for he a. unto me in the form of		30:53
an angel that had a. unto them.	3Ne	11: 8
And the Lord a. unto them,	DC	107:54
and Moses a. before us,		110:11
After this, Elias a.,		110:12
when he a. as an angel of light!		128:20
who hath a. unto some and		133:36
language which a. to convey		OD
angel of the Lord a. unto Adam,	Mses	5: 6
and the Lord a. unto me,	Abr	2: 6
And the Lord a. unto me in		2:19
It no sooner a. than I found	JS	2:17
a personage a. at my bedside,		2:30

APPEARETH
which sin a. very abominable	Jac	2: 5
it a. unto man that the sun	He	12:15
and who shall stand when he a.?	3Ne	24: 2
and who can stand when he a.?	DC	128:24

APPEARING
them at the time of his first a.;	Mro	2: 3
The a. of the Father and the	DC	130: 3
or to some previous a.,		130:16
a light a. in my room,	JS	2:30

APPEARS
for it a. that the house of Israel, 1Ne 22: 3

APPEASE
to a. the demands of justice, Al 42:15

APPEASED
let thine anger be a. in the He 11:11

APPELLATION
known by the a. of king-men; Al 51:21

APPENDAGE
it is an a. to the greater, DC 107:14

APPENDAGES
necessary a. belonging unto	DC	84:29
necessary a. belonging to the		84:30
are a. to this priesthood.		107: 5

APPETITE
and his soul hath a.; 2Ne 27: 3

APPLIED
Ye have not a. your hearts to	Mos	12:27
he a. unto those whom he had	Eth	9: 5

APPLY
a. the atoning blood of Christ	Mos	4: 2
is thy gift; a. unto it,	DC	8: 4

APPOINT
let us a. judges, to judge this	Mos	29:11
we will a. wise men to be judges,		29:11
did a. judges to rule over them,		29:41
did a. priests and teachers	Al	45:22
to a. the second leader to be		47:17
he did a. men to speak unto the		48: 1
thus he did a. chief captains of		48: 5
a. Coriantumr to be their leader,	He	1:17
Lachoneus did a. chief captains	3Ne	3:17
to a. for their chief captains		3:19
And every tribe did a. a chief or		7: 3
conferences shall direct or a.;	DC	20:61
elders shall a. from time to time;		20:82
I shall a. unto them another		28: 7
a. unto man the days of his		29:43
as he shall a. or has appointed		42:31
to a. another in his stead.		43: 4
a. ye my servant Joseph Smith,		43:12
such as God shall a. and ordain		46:27
a. unto this people their portions,		51: 3
he shall a. a man his portion,		51: 4
a. a storehouse unto this church;		51:13
a. whom you will to be your		54: 7
place I shall a. unto him,		57:13
a. him that is the most wise		67: 6
appointed or shall hereafter a.		70: 9
and a. every man his portion.		78:21
A. among yourselves a teacher,		88:122
whom ye shall a. and ordain		95:14
which I will a. unto them,		101:21
a. them their portion among		101:90
power to a. other high priests,		102: 7
to a. one of their own number		102:25
a. every man his stewardship;		104:11
a. one among you to keep the		104:61
Joseph shall a. unto them;		105:21
whatsoever he shall a. unto		105:22
which thou didst a. a Zion		109:51
We ask thee to a. unto Zion		109:59
a. the portion of the oppressor		124: 8
a. one of them to be a president		124:62
I a. unto him that he may be		124:94
unto the places which I shall a.		125: 2
And will I a. unto you,		132:11
And a. presidents, and captains		136:15
and shall a. him his portion	JS	1:54

APPOINTED
none shall be alone in his a. times.	2Ne	24:31
was a. to be their king.	Om	1:19
a. just men to be their teachers,	Mos	2: 4
and he a. unto them a law,		3:14
had a. priests to teach the people,		6: 3
be a. teachers over his people,		24: 1
of the Lamanites had a. kings		24: 2
And he a. teachers of the		24: 4
be another a. in his stead,		29: 7
if he should be a. in his stead.		29: 8
a. to be the first chief judge,		29:42
And there were a. captains,	Al	2:13
he also a. rulers and leaders		2:14
and he was a. chief judge;		4:17

APPOINTED 58 APPOINTED

were hired or a. by the people	Al	10:14
who were a. to be judges,		11: 1
a. unto men that they must die;		12:27
after God had a. that		12:28
whereof he had a. unto them;		12:28
he that had been a. chief captain		16: 5
feast a. at the land of Nephi,		18: 9
had a. that he should rise.		19:11
a time a. that all shall come		40: 4
knoweth the time which is a.		40: 4
a time a. that all shall rise from		40: 5
the time a. for the resurrection?		40: 7
than one time a. for men to rise		40: 8
there is a time a. unto men		40: 9
times which are a. unto man.		40:10
the time which is a. of God		40:21
it was a. unto man to die—		42: 6
Zerahemnah a. chief captains		43: 6
a. to be the chief captain over		43:16
a. chief captain over the armies		43:17
had a. priests and teachers over		45:23
who was a. by the chief judges		46:34
they had a. a man to be a king		47: 6
a. Amalickiah to be their leader		47:19
he a. them to be chief captains		48: 5
had a. Lehi to be chief captain		49:16
the son of Nephihah was a. to		50:39
was a. chief judge and governor		50:39
was a. king over the people;		52: 3
was a. to reign in his stead.		52: 3
Moroni a. Laman and caused		55: 7
Antipus, whom ye had a. a leader		56: 9
band who was a. to guard them		57:29
been a. to gather together men,		60: 2
whom ye have a. your governors		60:33
they have a. a king over them,		61: 8
a. by the voice of the people to be	He	1: 5
Pacumeni was a., according to		1:13
was a. to fill the judgment-seat,		2: 2
been a. by the people in his stead,		6:15
armies of the Nephites was a.,	3Ne	3:18
to the place which had been a.		3:22
the land which was the		3:23
they had a. unto themselves		4:17
those who had been a. leaders,		6: 6
people of Nephi a. me that	Mrm	2: 1
a. to receive commandments	DC	28: 2
a. to preside over the conference		28:10
have not been a. unto him,		28:12
be a. unto any of this church		28:12
have I a. to be his counselor		30: 7
which I have a. unto him		32: 2
wherewith I have a. you;		38:23
man among them shall be a.,		38:34
a. by the voice of the church;		38:34
a. by the voice of the church,		41: 9
as it shall be a. unto him		41:10
whereunto I have a. him.		42:10
another shall be a. in his stead.		42:10
as he shall appoint or has a.		42:31
shall be a. by the high council		42:34
and is not a. unto death,		42:48
shall be given as I have a.,		42:56
are a. to assist the bishop		42:71
him whom I have a. unto you		43: 2
there is none other a. unto you		43: 3
shall be a. unto this gift		43: 4
through him whom I have a.		43: 7
of my church, whom I have a.:		43:15
shall hereafter be a. unto you.		45:65
shall be a. unto him to keep		47: 3
I have a. to another office.		47: 3
there are to be certain men a.,		48: 5
be a. to purchase the lands,		48: 6
as is a. to him by the presidency		48: 6
unto the place which I have a.		49:25
is a. to be the greatest,		50:26
as ye are a. to the head,		50:30
which I have a. unto them—		50:38
be a. unto this people.		51: 7
an agent a. unto this people,		51: 8
a. by the voice of the church.		51:12
shall be a. by the bishop,		53: 4
whereunto I have a. you.	DC	54: 2
to the land which I have a.		56: 7
he shall be a. still to go to		56: 9
which is the land which I have a.		57: 1
office to which I have a. him,		57: 6
office to which I have a. him,		57: 7
whom he has a. to assist him.		57: 7
have a. unto him his mission		58:14
is a. to be a judge in Israel,		58:17
and those whom he has a.		58:24
have a. to keep my storehouse;		58:24
office to which I have a. him,		58:40
as it shall be a. unto them		58:44
are not a. to stay in this land,		58:46
a. by the voice of the church,		58:49
the work which I have a.		58:58
is a day a. unto you to rest		59:10
a. a way for the journeying of		61:24
whom I have a. to receive.		63:40
it is a. to him to die at the age		63:50
office to which I have a. him		63:56
through the means I have a.,		64: 5
whose mission is a. unto them		68: 2
be a. by the First Presidency		68:15
inasmuch as they are a. to labor,		68:30
I the Lord have a. them,		70: 3
Wherefore, I have a. unto them,		70: 5
even as I the Lord have a.		70: 9
he who is a. in a stewardship		70:11
He who is a. to administer		70:12
are a. to a stewardship		70:12
for a bishop to be a. unto you,		72: 2
bishop who shall be a. of me		72: 5
who shall be a. and ordained		72: 8
who are a. as stewards over		72:20
that are a. by the Holy Spirit		72:24
which the Lord had a. unto us,		76:15
are a. to minister for them,		76:88
are a. to be ministering spirits		76:88
hath a. Michael your prince.		78:16
office which I have a. unto you,		81: 3
office which I have a. unto you;		81: 5
a. to be an everlasting order		82:20
is a. by the finger of the Lord,		84: 3
consecrated spot as I have a.—		84:31
be a. to watch over the church,		84:111
the Lord's clerk, whom he has a.,		85: 1
who was called of God and a.,		85: 8
be a. them among unbelievers,		85: 9
He that is a. to be president,		88:128
which I have a. unto them,		94:15
there is none other place a.		101:20
than that which I have a.;		101:20
shall there be any other place a.		101:20
than that which I have a.,		101:20
only whom I have a. to tarry;		101:55
unto the places which I have a.		101:67
a. to be the land of Zion,		101:70
And let honorable men be a.,		101:73
I have a. unto my people,		101:96
Let not that which I have a.		101:97
which I have a. unto them,		101:99
council was a. by revelation		102: 2
their regularly a. successors		102: 6
council, is a. by revelation,		102: 9
a. after the same manner that he		102:10
manner that he himself was a.		102:10
those who are a. to assist him,		102:11
to be difficult, four shall be a.;		102:14
shall more than six be a. to		102:14
the councilors a. to speak		102:16
councilors who are a. to speak		102:18
of the stewardship which is a.		104:12
a. unto him the place where he		104:20
[Martin Harris] have a. unto him,		104:24
their stewardship which shall be a.		104:30
the stewardship which I have a.		104:32
the stewardship which I have a.		104:37
have a. unto him the houses		104:39
I have a. unto my servant		104:40
stewardship which I have a.		104:41
a. unto him the lot which is		104:43
the stewardship which I have a.		104:44

APPOINTED   59   ARISE

your stewardship which I have a.	DC 104:54
a. unto you to be stewards	104:57
the stewardship which I have a.	104:63
a treasurer a. to keep the	104:67
the properties which I have a.	104:68
another shall be a. in his stead.	104:77
are a. to lead my people,	105: 7
[mine elders], whom I have a.	105:27
Warren A. Cowdery should be a.	106: 1
a. of or from among those who	107:21
a. and ordained to that office,	107:22
severally as they are a.,	107:63
be a. of the High Priesthood	107:65
as there are other bishops a.	107:75
the office in which he is a.,	107:99
counsel of him whom I have a.	108: 1
this one which thou hast a.,	109:59
who are a. with you to be	112:30
are and shall be a. hereafter;	115: 1
places should be a. for stakes	115:18
let men be a. to supply	118: 1
be a. to fill the places of those	118: 6
is a time a. for every man,	121:25
all the a. days, months, and	121:31
perhaps a committee can be a.	123: 4
corner-stone I have a. for Zion.	124:23
which shall be a. unto it	124:24
which I have a. for refuge,	124:36
my servants whom I have a.	124:45
of these men whom I have a.,	124:46
servant Isaac Galland be a.	124:79
let my servant William be a.,	124:91
was a. unto him by his father,	124:91
city which I have a. unto you,	124:109
hands of those whom I have a.	124:111
be a. unto the same calling.	124:130
be a. unto the same priesthood	124:132
shall be a. standing presidents	124:134
the stakes which I have a.,	125: 4
which I have a. unto you,	127: 4
a recorder a. in each ward	128: 3
which was a. for that blessing,	132: 5
whom I have a. on the earth	132: 7
have a. unto my servant Joseph	132: 7
that which I have not a.?	132:10
but are a. angels in heaven,	132:16
anointed and a. unto this power,	132:18
angels and the gods are a.,	132:18
whom I have a. this power	132:19
I have not a. unto her by	132:41
my servants that have been a.	136:16
God hath a. me another seed,	Mses 6: 2
according to the time a. unto	Abr 3: 4
not a. unto Adam his reckoning.	5:13

APPOINTING
in a. the above-named councilors	DC 102: 5

APPOINTMENT
stakes, the places of thine a.,	DC 109:39
officially notified of their a.	118: 6
at the end of this a. your	124:32
these things at the end of the a.	124:32
a. of those men by the church.	128: 4
according to mine a.,	132:26
thee, my servant Joseph, an a.,	132:40
I sought for mine a. unto	Abr 1: 4
according to the a. of God	1: 4

APPOINTMENTS
send them before you to make a.,	DC 84:107
to prepare the way, and to fill a.	84:107
whether they accepted their a.,	102: 4
that they accepted their a.,	102: 4

APPRISED
the people of the Lord were a. of	Mos 18:34

APPROACH
attempt to a. near the walls of	Al 50: 5

APPROACHING
Lamanites were seen a. towards	Al 49: 1
and I found that day was a.,	JS 2:47

APPROPRIATE
a. any portion of that stock	DC 124:70
if they do a. any portion of	124:71
which they a. anywhere else,	124:71

APPROVE
a. of those names which I have	DC 124:144

APPROVED
his accounts a. in all things.	DC 72:19
themselves a. in all things,	72:22
and shows himself not a. shall	107:100

APRIL
of the month which is called A.—	DC 20: 1
of the month which is called A.	21: 3
the twenty-sixth day of A. next,	118: 5
On the 5th day of A., 1829,	JS 2:66
(being the 7th of A.)	2:67

APRONS
and made themselves a.	Mses 4:13

ARABIAN
neither shall the A. pitch tent	2Ne 23:20

ARABIC
Chaldaic, Assyriac, and A.;	JS 2:64

ARCHANGEL
Michael mine a. shall sound	DC 29:26
the seventh angel, even the a.,	88:112
Michael, the prince, the a.	107:54
the voice of Michael, the a.;	128:21

ARCHEANTUS
and A. has fallen by the sword,	Mro 9: 2

ARCHIVES
in the a. of my holy temple,	DC 127: 9

ARE: *see in the APPENDIX.*

ARIGHT
not in the least a. before him;	He 7: 4
that he has testified a. unto us	8: 8

ARISE
A., and get thee into the mountain.	1Ne 17: 7
we should a. and go down into the	18: 5
Kings shall see and a., princes also	21: 7
Awake! and a. from the dust,	2Ne 1:14
a. from the dust, my sons,	1:21
of obscurity, and a. from the dust.	1:23
a., sit down, O Jerusalem;	8:25
lest there shall a. contentions	Mos 2:32
Alma, a. and stand forth,	27:13
a. and persecute those that did	Al 1:21
A., for I will grant unto you your	22: 3
the voice said unto me: a.	36: 8
behold, there shall a new star a.,	He 14: 5
A. and come forth unto me,	3Ne 11:14
him that he should a.	11:20
unto them, and bade them a.	17:19
that they should a. and stand	20: 2
a., sit down, O Jerusalem;	20:37
who should a. from the dead,	23: 9
many saints did a. and appear	23:11
shall the Son of Righteousness a.	25: 2
A., why hast thou fallen?	Eth 3: 7

ARISE / ARMIES

ARISE
a. from the dust, O Jerusalem;	Mro 10:31
A. and be baptized, and wash	DC 39:10
Ye saints a. and live;	43:18
Zion must a. and put on her	82:14
a. early that your bodies and	88:124
let the teacher a., and, with	88:132
will the Lord a. and come forth	101:89
which might a. in the church,	102: 2
And a. up and be more careful	108: 3
A. and gird up your loins,	112:14
A. and shine forth, that thy	115: 5
Let them awake, and a.,	117: 2
let him a. and come up and	124:103
It may probably a. through	130:13
Awake and a. and go forth to	133:10
A., and take Lot with thee;	Abr 2: 6
And many false prophets shall a.,	JS 1: 9
there shall also a. false Christs,	1:22

ARISETH
when he a. to shake terribly	2Ne 12:19
when he a. to shake terribly	12:21

ARK
tight like unto the a. of Noah;	Eth 6: 7
his hand to steady the a. of God,	DC 85: 8
saw that Noah built an a.;	Mses 7:43
that Noah entered into the a.	JS 1:42

ARM
I did a. myself with a bow	1Ne 16:23
his a. shall come upon the	20:14
unless he shall make bare his a.	22:10
will proceed to make bare his a.	22:11
not put my trust in the a. of flesh;	2Ne 4:34
putteth his trust in the a. of flesh.	4:34
trust in man or maketh flesh his a.	4:34
and mine a. shall judge the people.	8: 5
and on mine a. shall they trust.	8: 5
Put on strength, O a. of the Lord;	8: 9
every man the flesh of his own a.—	19:20
trust in man, or maketh flesh his a.,	28:31
lengthen out mine a. unto them	28:32
for mine a. is lengthened out	28:32
by the power of mine a.,	Jac 2:25
while his a. of mercy is extended	6: 5
so be by the power of his holy a.,	En 1:13
were led by the power of his a.,	Om 1:13
with the strength of his own a.,	WM 1:13
if he had not extended his a.	Mos 1:14
I did a. them with bows,	9:16
hath made bare his holy a.	12:24
is the a. of the Lord revealed?	14: 1
hath made bare his holy a.	15:31
extending the a. of mercy	29:20
did a. themselves with swords,	Al 2:12
that Amlici did a. his men	2:14
to flee by the strength of his a.	17:37
his a. is extended to all people	19:36
and also smote his a. that he	20:20
merciful a. which he extended	29:10
breastplates and with a.-shields,	43:19
breastplates, and their a.-shields,	43:38
a. my women and children,	54:12
men, and a. them with swords,	60: 2
mine a. of mercy is extended	3Ne 9:14
Lord hath made bare his holy a.	16:20
Father hath made bare his holy a.	20:35
Lib did smite upon his a. that	Eth 14:12
a. of the Lord shall be revealed;	DC 1:14
neither trust in the a. of flesh.-	1:19
he would have extended his a.	3: 8
for mine a. is over all the earth.	15: 2
for mine a. is over all the earth.	16: 2
whose a. of mercy hath atoned	29: 1
and mine a. is not shortened;	35: 8
And their a. shall be my arm,	35:14
And their arm shall be my a.,	35:14
the a. of the Lord shall fall,	45:45
Then shall the a. of the Lord fall	45:47
mine a. and mine indignation,	56: 1
the a. of the Lord shall be revealed	90:10
and with a stretched-out a.	103:17
make bare thine a., O Lord,	DC 109:51
stretch forth his puny a. to stop	121:33
forth the power of his mighty a.	123: 6
and for his a. to be revealed.	123:17
he shall make bare his holy a.	133: 3
my a. was not shortened at all	133:67
and my a. is stretched out in	136:22

ARMED
they were a. with righteousness	1Ne 14:14
a. with bows, and with arrows,	Mos 10: 8
his people were a. with swords,	Al 43:18
were not a. with breastplates,	43:21
together, and a. themselves,	46:31
insomuch that they were all a.;	55:16
had a. all those prisoners;	55:17
for he had a. those prisoners	55:20
their prisoners were a. within.	55:22
and a. them with swords,	He 1:14
and after he had a. them with	Eth 7: 9
men women and children being a.	15:15
this house a. with thy power,	DC 109:22
five o'clock p.m., by an a. mob—	135: 1

ARMIES
the a. of Pharaoh did follow	1Ne 4: 2
who were the a. of Pharaoh.	17:27
fortify against them with their a.,	Jac 7:25
the a. of the Lamanites came	WM 1:13
gathered together his a.,	1:13
Noah sent his a. against them,	Mos 11:18
they sent their a. forth;	20: 7
that the a. of king Noah would	23: 1
before the a. of king Noah.	23: 1
Now the a. of the Lamanites,	23:30
he will send his a. against them	29:23
yea, at the head of his a.,	Al 2:16
the a. of the Lamanites had come	16: 2
over the a. of the Nephites,	16: 5
the river Sidon, with their a.,	16: 7
upon the a. of the Lamanites,	16: 8
I would guard thee with my a.;	18:21
with their guards and their a.,	22:33
But they took their a. and went	25: 2
we will set our a. between the	27:23
from their enemies with our a.,	27:24
us that we may maintain our a.	27:24
and the a. of the Nephites were	28: 1
the a. of the Lamanites had	28: 1
for the a. of the Nephites,	35:13
with the a. of the Lamanites and	35:13
and the a. of the Zoramites;	35:13
they gathered together their a. in	43: 4
substance to support their a.;	43:13
as the a. of the Lamanites had	43:15
a. of the Nephites were prepared	43:15
of all the a. of the Nephites—	43:16
over the a. of the Nephites.	43:17
when the a. of the Lamanites	43:19
afraid of the a. of the Nephites	43:21
the a. of Moroni would know	43:22
the a. of the Nephites should go	43:23
the a. of the Lamanites were	43:24
And Lehi retained his a. upon	43:40
met again by the a. of Moroni.	43:42
the a. of Moroni encircled them	43:52
the a. of Moroni on the west of	43:53
And the a. of the Nephites,	44:23
the chief commander of the a.	46:11
that he should take his a.,	46:31
headed the a. of Amalickiah.	46:32
with the a. of the Nephites,	46:34
with the a. of the Lamanites,	47: 8
surrounded by the a. of Lehonti.	47:14
Amalickiah marched with his a.	47:20
that his a. should march forth	47:27
the city Nephi with his a.,	47:31
to be chief captains over his a.	48: 5
the a. of the Nephites,	48: 8
round about to enclose his a.,	48: 8
a. of the Lamanites were seen	49: 1
they brought up their a.	49:17
Lamanites brought up their a.	49:21

ARMIES

might obtain a pass to their a.,	Al 49:22
that his a. should commence	50: 1
that his a. should go forth into	50: 7
he also placed a. on the south,	50:10
secure their a. and their people	50:10
Thus Moroni, with his a.,	50:12
did prepare himself and his a.	51:10
Now his a. were not so great as	51:11
the a. did march forth against	51:18
a. should stand in readiness,	51:36
according to the power of their a.	52:13
a. to protect the south and the	52:15
that he would come out with his a.	52:20
a. of the Lamanites did march	52:23
a. of the Lamanites coming out	52:23
of the a. of the Lamanites,	53: 6
and providing food for their a.	53: 7
that the a. of the Lamanites,	53: 8
repent and withdraw your a.	54: 6
with your a. to your own lands.	54: 7
our a. shall come upon you	54:10
will come against you with my a.;	54:12
will come upon you with my a.	54:16
the a. of the Lamanites.	55:21
the a. of Antipus had overtaken	56:49
from the a. of the Lamanites,	56:57
we did meet the spies of our a.,	57:30
a. of the Lamanites are marching	57:31
a. of the Lamanites did arrive	58:29
the a. of the Lamanites did flee	58:30
our a. are small to maintain so	58:32
the weakness of our a.,	58:37
or the a. of Helaman, insomuch	59: 3
their a. were so numerous that	59: 8
unto our a. sufficient strength	60: 5
might have sent a. unto them,	60: 8
also men to strengthen our a.?	60:19
to strengthen and fortify our a.,	60:25
a. into the land of Zarahemla,	62: 7
to the a. of Lehi and Teancum.	62:13
did not camp with their a.	62:22
the a. of Moroni were within	62:24
reduce the a. of the Lamanites	62:30
And the a. of the Lamanites	62:33
did encamp with their a. round	62:34
yielded up the command of his a.	62:43
he did gather together his a.,	He 1:17
to gather together their a.	1:19
their strong a. should maintain	1:26
and the a. of Moronihah were	4: 6
stationed their a. to defend	4: 7
did succeed with his a. in	4: 9
all his a. in maintaining	4:19
upon the a. of the Egyptians	8:11
the whole a. of the Nephites,	11:32
my a. shall come down against	3Ne 3: 8
And he caused that a., both of	3:14
over all the a. of the Nephites,	3:17
the great commander of the a. of	3:18
will gather all our a. together,	3:21
a. of robbers had prepared for	4: 1
gave commandment unto his a.	4: 6
of the a. of Giddianhi,	4: 7
that the a. of the Nephites,	4: 8
when the a. of Giddianhi saw	4: 9
because of the terror of their a.	4: 9
when the a. of Giddianhi did	4:10
that his a. should pursue them	4:13
a. of the Nephites did return	4:15
night, and falling upon their a.,	4:21
out his a. in the night-time,	4:24
did place his a. in the way of	4:24
met by the a. of the Nephites	4:25
leader, or the leader of their a.	Mrm 2: 1
that they did frighten my a.;	2: 3
we did pursue them with our a.,	2:26
And there we did place our a.,	3: 6
stop the a. of the Lamanites,	3: 6
go up with their a. to battle	4: 1
the a. of the Nephites were	4: 2
the a. of the Nephites went up	4: 4
me command again of their a.,	5: 1

ARMS

behold the a. of the Lamanites	Mrm 6: 7
he went against him with his a.	Eth 13:27
began to flock together in a.,	14:19
destruction among the a. of Shiz	14:27
before the a. of Coriantumr;	14:27
Coriantumr did gather his a.	14:28
a trumpet unto the a. of Shiz	14:28
pursue the a. of Coriantumr;	14:31
the a. of Coriantumr did press	15:10
press upon the a. of Shiz that	15:10
the a. of the Lamanites are	Mro 9:17
among the a. of the earth;	DC 60: 4
he may gather together his a.	88:111
shall gather together his a.,	88:112
devil shall gather together his a.;	88:113
against Michael and his a.	88:113
the devil and his a. shall be cast	88:114
hold the a. of Israel guiltless	105:30
of all the a. of the nations of	117: 6

ARMING

a. them, and preparing for war	Al 51: 9

ARMOR

did gird on his a. about my loins.	1Ne 4:19
put on the a. of righteousness.	2Ne 1:23
put on their a., and went forth	Mos 21: 7
and also their a., which was girded	Al 3: 5
the Nephites because of their a.	43:21
girded on his a. about his loins;	46:13
their a. girded about their loins,	46:21
and they should be strong with a.,	3Ne 3:26
of Giddianhi, because of their a.,	4: 7
and take upon you my whole a.,	DC 27:15

ARMS

again, bearing a child in her a.	1Ne 11:20
shall bring thy sons in their a.,	21:22
have been carried in their a.,	22: 6
and being carried in their a.	22: 8
eternally in the a. of his love.	2Ne 1:15
shall bring thy sons in their a.,	6: 6
sought by the power of their a.	Jac 7:24
all my old men that could bear a.,	Mos 10: 9
men that were able to bear a.,	10: 9
rest their bodies and their a.	11:11
the a. of mercy were extended	16:12
the a. of mercy were extended	16:12
to meet my people, without a.;	20:24
without a. to meet the Lamanites.	20:25
of Limhi, that they were without a.,	20:26
take up a. against their brethren;	Al 2:10
the a. of mercy are extended	5:33
smote off their a. with his sword;	17:37
by smiting their a. with the edge	17:37
as many of their a. as were	17:38
bearing the a. which had been	17:39
and smote off the a. of others,	18:16
smote off the a. of my brethren	18:20
took up a. against the people of	24: 2
take up a. against their brethren;	24: 6
whose a. were lifted to slay them.	24:25
let us take up a. against them,	26:25
take up a. against their brethren;	26:34
again refused to take their a.,	27: 3
of their fear to take up a.	27:23
prevailed upon to take up a.	27:28
them in the a. of safety,	34:16
and they have taken up a. to	35:14
and they would not take up a.,	43:11
did smite off many of their a.,	43:44
God, who has strengthened our a.	44: 5
go forth and compel them to a.	47: 5
to Onidah, to the place of a.	47: 5
they were sorry to take up a.	48:23
people of Morianton took up a.	50:26
and they refused to take up a.,	51:13
that they would not take up a.	51:13
or they should take up a. and	51:17
and to take up a. in defence of	51:20
had been kept from taking up a.	53:11
and were desirous to take up a.	53:13

ARMS 62 AROSE

many as were able to take up a.,	Al	53:16
behold, if ye will lay down your a.,		54:18
flocking to us daily, to their a.,		61: 6
whosoever would not take up a.		62: 9
take up a. against them.	3Ne	2:11
to take up a. against those		2:12
at this time stand in their a.,		3: 3
preparing their lands and their a.	Mrm	3: 1
been clasped in the a. of Jesus.		5:11
with open a. to receive you!		6:17
encircle thee in the a. of my love,	DC	6:20
wept and stretched forth his a.,	Mses	7:41
and his a. also, a little above	JS	2:31

ARM-SHIELDS: see ARM and SHIELDS.

ARMY

our a. might come upon them	Mos	9: 1
number of our a. was destroyed		9: 2
he sent his a. to destroy them.		18:33
of the coming of the king's a.;		18:34
the a. of the king returned,		19: 1
the a. of the Lamanites were		19: 6
sent an a. into the wilderness		22:15
an a. of the Lamanites was in		23:25
was another a. of the Lamanites	Al	3:20
the first a. met the Amlicites.		3:20
was an a. sent to drive them out		3:21
a numerous a. against them;		3:23
a sufficient a. to drive them out		16: 3
Now the a. of Zerahemnah		43:20
leaving a part of his a. in the		43:25
took the remaining part of his a.		43:25
that his a. should be		43:27
he divided his a. and brought a		43:31
And thus having placed his a.		43:33
a part of the a. of Moroni		43:34
the a. which was concealed on the		43:35
and led his a. forth and		43:35
to contend with the a. of Lehi.		43:36
Moroni and his a. met the		43:41
he took his a. and marched out		46:31
of his a. which was obedient		47: 3
they discovered the a. coming,		47: 5
caused his a. to pitch their tents		47: 9
down with his a. in the night-time,		47:13
second leader over the whole a.		47:13
gathered together so great an a.		47:21
saw an a. pursuing after them,		47:29
the a. which pursued after them		47:30
he had pursued them with his a.,		47:32
Moroni had stationed an a. by		49: 2
of Nephi, at the head of his a.,		49:10
lest the a. of Moroni should		50:28
Therefore Moroni sent an a., with		50:33
the a. which was sent by Moroni,		50:35
slay Morianton and defeat his a.,		50:35
together a wonderfully great a.,		51:11
that his a. should go against		51:17
forth with his numerous a.		51:30
and retreated with all their a.		52: 2
of men to strengthen his a.		52: 7
march forth with his a. against		52:17
might receive strength to his a.		52:17
Moroni did arrive with his a. at		52:18
to the a. of the Lamanites,		52:20
would not come out with his a.		52:20
and Moroni and his a., by night,		52:22
part of his a. who were with		52:24
city Mulek with a part of his a.,		52:26
were met by Lehi and a small a.,		52:27
had beheld Lehi with his a.		52:28
had been in their rear with his a.;		52:29
should meet Moroni and his a.		52:30
for the strengthening of his a.		54: 2
they did join the a. of Moroni,		55:24
were a great strength to his a.		55:24
sons) to the a. of Antipus,		56:10
his a. had been reduced by the		56:10
a greater strength to his a.,		56:18
perhaps destroyed our little a.;		56:19
pass by us with their whole a.,		56:24
march forth with a part of his a.,		56:33
had gone forth with my little a.,	Al	56:33
strongest a. of the Lamanites;		56:34
they came forth with their a.		56:35
powerful a. of the Lamanites;		56:36
when they saw the a. of Antipus		56:37
did speed the march of his a.		56:38
overpower the a. of Antipus.		56:46
The a. of Antipus being weary,		56:50
whole a. of the Lamanites halted		56:52
and also an addition to our a.,		57: 6
a. which was placed to protect		57: 7
and also a numerous a. of men.		57:17
of our a. were about to give way		57:20
also the foes of our whole a.,		57:25
was astonishing to our whole a.,		57:26
more numerous than was our a.		58: 2
by an a. of two thousand men		58: 8
number and the strength of our a.		58:14
with the remainder of my a.,		58:17
with their numerous a. against us.		58:18
when the a. had passed by,		58:20
did suffer their whole a., save		58:22
that they had driven their whole a.		58:25
and joined the a. of Moroni.		59: 8
the chief captain over the a.		61: 2
over the remainder of his a.,		62: 3
also an a. of six thousand men		62:12
that an a. of six thousand men,		62:13
did camp with their a.		62:20
now Moroni returned to his a.,		62:21
did strengthen the a. of Moroni		62:30
and fled before the a. of Moroni.		62:31
Moroni and his a. did pursue		62:32
came down with a numerous a.		63:15
or against the a. of Moronihah,		63:15
an innumerable a. of men,	He	1:14
march forth with his whole a.		1:20
did march forth with a large a.,		1:23
sent forth Lehi with an a.		1:28
a numerous a. of the Lamanites,		4: 8
by an a. of the Lamanites		5:21
they sent an a. of strong men		11:28
of the a. of Giddianhi,	3Ne	4: 8
head of an a. of the Nephites,	Mrm	2: 2
an a. of forty and four thousand.		2: 9
that I beat him with my a.		2: 9
with an a. of thirty thousand		2:25
against an a. of fifty thousand.		2:25
a fresh a. of the Lamanites did		4: 2
he had gathered together an a.	Eth	7: 5
that they did raise an a. and		8: 5
they had slain the a. of Jared		8: 6
together an a. of outcasts,		10: 9
part of the a. of Coriantumr,		14: 5
Coriantumr dwelt with his a. in		14: 7
receive great strength to his a.		14: 7
received great strength to his a.,		14: 8
the a. of Coriantumr did press		14:12
smite the a. of Coriantumr,		14:14
the a. of the brother of Lib.		14:16
can stand before the a. of Shiz?		14:18
of them fled to the a. of Shiz,		14:20
fled to the a. of Coriantumr.		14:20
the a. of Coriantumr did pitch		15:11
together to the a. of Coriantumr;		15:13
gathered together to the a. of Shiz.		15:13
every one to the a. which he		15:15
the a. of Zenephi has carried	Mro	9:16
the a. which is with me is weak;		9:17
have fled to the a. of Aaron		9:17
terrible as an a. with banners.	DC	5:14
until the a. of Israel becomes		105:26
let my a. become very great,		105:31
terrible as an a. with banners;		109:73
those who have gone into the a.,		136: 8

AROSE

there a. a mist of darkness;	1Ne	8:23
my father a. in the morning,		16:10
I a. and went up into the		17: 7
there a. a great storm, yea, a great		18:13
there a. contentions among them,	Mos	7:25
they a. and came forth out of		18:14

AROSE

he a., according to the words of	Al	19:12
as he a., he stretched forth his		19:12
she a. and stood upon her feet,		19:29
he a. and stood upon his feet.		19:30
when Ammon a. he also		19:33
behold there a. an Amalekite		21: 5
Amulek a. and began to teach		34: 1
And I a. and stood up, and		36: 8
that there a. a dissension		45:23
therefore there a. a warm dispute		51: 4
when Nephi a. he beheld the	He	7:12
there a. a division among the		10: 1
there a. a great storm, such an	3Ne	8: 5
And Nephi a. and went forth,		11:19
And he a. and stood before him.		11:20
praying unto the Father, he a.;		17:18
And they a. from the earth,		17:20
they a. and ministered unto		19: 7
they a. up and stood upon their		20: 2
there a. a people who were	4Ne	1:36
that there a. a rebellion among	Eth	11:15
there a. a mighty man among		11:15
there a. another mighty man;		11:17
there a. up Shared, and he also		13:23
there a. the brother of Shared		14: 3
behold, Shiz a., and also his men,		15:28
that there a. a great contention	DC	74: 3
contentions a. in the school of		95:10
nobleman a. and were affrighted,		101:51
the saints a., and were crowned	Mses	7:56
I, Abraham, a. from the place of	Abr	2:20
persecution that a. against me,	JS	2:20
I shortly after a. from my bed,		2:48
Hence a. the very prevalent		2:56

AROUND

encircle me a. in the robe of thy	2Ne	4:33
will travel a. the land of Shilom.	Mos	22: 8
some a. the borders of Noah,	Al	16: 3
all a. us are elected to be cast		31:17
welfare of those who are a. you.		34:27
they had cast up dirt a. about		49: 2
the work of death a. you?		60: 7
pitch our tents a. about the hill	Mrm	6: 4
shining seraphs a. thy throne,	DC	109:79
and thine enemies prowl a. thee		122: 6
having looked a. me, and finding	JS	2:15
Thick darkness gathered a. me,		2:15
as immediately a. his person.		2:32
gather immediately a. the person		2:43
left dark, except just a. him;		2:43
the edge all a. was covered		2:51

AROUSE

a. the faculties of your soul;	Jac	3:11
will awake and a. your faculties,	Al	32:27
my words did a. them somewhat	Mrm	2:24

ARPAD

Is not Hamath as A.?	2Ne	20: 9

ARRAIGNED

be a. before the bar of Christ	Al	11:44

ARRANGE

newly a. the affairs of this people,	Mos	29:11
a. their temporal concerns,	DC	63:38
to a. by lot the inheritances of		85: 7

ARRANGEMENTS

When, according to a., the	JS	2:60

ARRAY

go forth in battle a. against	Mses	7: 7

ARRAYED

was not a. like one of these.	3Ne	13:29
are not a. like one of these.	DC	84:82

ARRIVAL

after my father's a. in Palmyra,	JS	2: 3
immediately after my a. there		2:62
after the a. of Mr. Cowdery		2:67

ARRIVE

we did a. at the promised land;	1Ne	18:23
Moroni did a. with his army at	Al	52:18
provisions a. for our support,		56:29
At length their provisions did a.,		57:10
did a. in season to check them,		57:18
we did a. in time that we might		57:34
that we did a. before them at the		58:27
Lamanites did a. near the city,		58:29
until they a. at Cincinnati.;	DC	61:30

ARRIVED

After ye have a. in the promised	1Ne	17:14
had a. in the promised land,	Mos	10:15
having a. in the borders of		21:26
a. in the land of Zarahemla,		22:13
a. in the land of Zarahemla;		24:25
a. in the borders of the land of	Al	17:13
had a. in the land of Middoni;		20:30
when I a. at the city of Judea;		56:15
because of this time which has a.,	He	13:24
a. at the years of accountability.	DC	18:42
a. unto the years of accountability		20:71
place the instant that I a. there.	JS	2:50
not yet a., neither would it,		2:53
the time a. for obtaining the		2:59
between the time I a. at the		2:62

ARROGANCY

the a. of the proud to cease,	2Ne	23:11

ARROW

out of a straight stick, an a.;	1Ne	16:23
arm myself with a bow and an a.,		16:23
yea, the sharp pointed a.	Jar	1: 8
with the bow, and with the a.	Mrm	6: 9

ARROWS

we did take our bows and our a.,	1Ne	16:14
our bows and our a. and our stones		16:15
Whose a. shall be sharp,	2Ne	15:28
With a. and with bows shall men		17:24
arm them with bows, and with a.,	Mos	9:16
men armed with bows, and with a.,		10: 8
and with bows, and with a.,	Al	2:12
and their bows, and with a.,		3: 5
and their bows, and their a.,		17: 7
their bows and their a.,		43:20
to shield them from the a. and		49: 2
fought with stones and with a.		49: 2
not cast their a.		49: 4
by casting over stones and a.		49:19
swept off by the stones and a.		49:22
exposed to the a. of the Lamanites		49:24
and the a. of the Lamanites		50: 4
and with bows, and with a.,	He	1:14
and also many shot a. at him		16: 2
their stones neither with their a.		16: 2
him with their stones and their a.,		16: 6
him with our stones and our a.;		16: 6

ART (noun)

things of every kind and a.;	He	12: 2
the magic a., and the witchcraft	Mrm	2:10

ART (verb): *see in the APPENDIX.*

ARTICLES

ye shall remember the church a.	DC	33:14
the covenants and church a.		42:13

ARTIFICER

cunning a., and the eloquent	2Ne	13: 3
an instructor of every a. in	Mses	5:46

ARTS

many things by his cunning a.,	1Ne	16:38
in all the a. and cunning of	Al	10:15
the mysterious a. of the evil one,	He	16:21
in all the a. of war and all the	Eth	13:16

AS: *see in the APPENDIX.*

ASA: *see DODDS, Asa.*

ASCEND 64 ASK

ASCEND
shall forever a. up unto thee,	2Ne 4:35
I will a. into heaven,	24:13
I will a. above the heights	24:14
a. up to God from the ground	26: 3
a. up to God against you.	Jac 2:35
to a. up in thine ears,	DC 109:49
Enoch beheld the Son of Man a.	Mses 7:59

ASCENDED
Having a. into heaven,	Mos 15: 9
when I am again a. into heaven.	3Ne 11:21
taught before I a. to my Father;	15: 1
from them, and a. into heaven.	18:39
that he a. again into heaven.	18:39
when Jesus had a. into heaven,	19: 1
after he had a. into heaven-	26:15
and had a. unto the Father-	26:15
because Christ hath a. into	Mro 7:27
And a. into heaven, to sit down	DC 20:24
He that a. up on high,	88: 6
he a. till he entirely disappeared,	JS 2:43
a. as he had done before.	2:45
again a. into heaven as before,	2:47
a. from me for the third time,	2:47

ASCENDETH
fire, which a. up unto God	1Ne 15:30
whose flame a. up forever	2Ne 9:16
whose smoke a. up forever	Jac 6:10
whose flame a. up forever	Mos 2:38
whose smoke a. up forever	3:27
whose flame a. up forever	Al 12:17

ASCENDING
the angel a. from the east,	DC 77: 9
angel a. from the east is	77: 9

ASCENSION
resurrection and a. into heaven.	Mos 18: 2
of Christ and his a. into heaven.	Al 40:20
soon after the a. of Christ into	3Ne 10:18
them after his a. into heaven.	11:12

ASCERTAIN
or do a. it by revelation from	DC 68:21
a. who of the twelve shall	102:12
to a. who should speak first,	102:34

ASCRIBE
And we do justly a. it to the	Al 57:26

ASCRIBED
and might, be a. to our God;	DC 84:102

ASCRIBING
a. all the power of Alma and	Al 15:15

ASHAMED
eyes about as if they were a.	1Ne 8:25
they were a., because of those	8:28
shall be not a. that wait for me.	21:23
for they shall not be a.	2Ne 6: 7
people of the Lord shall not be a.	6:13
and I know that I shall not be a.	7: 7
Jacob shall not now be a.,	27:33
being a. to return to the city	Mos 20: 3
be a. to take upon them the	Al 46:21
Fear not, for thou shalt not be a.;	3Ne 22: 4
Why are ye a. to take upon	Mrm 8:38
do this that we may not be a.	DC 10:19
will I be a. to own	29:27
openly, that he or she may be a.	42:91
Be not a., neither confounded;	90:17
be a. of the Nicolaitane band	117:11
and his wife, and were not a.	Mses 3:25
and his wife, and were not a.	Abr 5:19

ASHERY
the lot on which the Shule [a.] is	DC 104:39

ASHES
they repent in sackcloth and a.,	Mos 11:25
they shall be a. under the soles	3Ne 25: 3

ASHLEY, Major N.
I say unto my servant A.,	DC 75:17

ASIDE
turn their hearts a., rejecting signs	1Ne 19:13
because they turn their hearts a.,	19:14
they no more turn a. their hearts	19:15
counsel of God, for they set if a.,	2Ne 9:28
remember him, and lay a. our sins,	10:20
and turn a. the just for a	27:32
that turn a. the just for a	28:16
yea, can ye lay a. these things,	Al 5:53
fear not, and lay a. every sin,	7:15
neither would they turn a. to the	24:23
neither must ye lay a. your faith,	32:36
plan of redemption, (laying it a.)	42:11
laying a. the commandments of	He 7: 4
and that turn a. the stranger,	3Ne 24: 5
lay a. the things of this world,	DC 25:10
lay a. all his hard speeches;	124:116

ASK
and a. me in faith, believing that	1Ne 15:11
God will give me, if I a. not amiss;	2Ne 4:35
A. thee a sign of the Lord thy	17:11
a. it either in the depths, or in	17:11
But Ahaz said: I will not a.,	17:12
And now, I would a. of you,	31: 6
I would a. if all is done?	31:19
ye a. not, neither do ye knock;	32: 4
thing ye shall a. in faith,	En 1:15
And now I a., can ye say aught	Mos 2:25
and a. in sincerity of heart	4:10
whatsoever ye a. that is right,	4:21
questions which he should a. them.	7: 8
now I a. of you, my brethren,	Al 5: 8
And again I a., were the bands	5: 9
And now I a. of you on what	5:10
And now behold, I a. of you,	5:14
now I a. of you, my brethren,	5:22
I would a., can ye feel so now?	5:26
questions which I shall a. you?	11:21
unto thee whatsoever thou wilt a.,	20:23
And now, I a., what great	26: 2
And moreover, I a., do ye	32:11
Now I a., is this faith?	32:18
I would a. if ye have read the	33:14
not a. that which is contrary to	He 10: 5
ye have need of before ye a. him.	3Ne 13: 8
A., and it shall be given unto you;	14: 7
who, if his son a. bread, will give	14: 9
Or if he a. a fish, will he give	14:10
good things to them that a. him?	14:11
not a. the Father in my name,	16: 4
a. of the Father in my name,	17: 3
a. him to tarry a little longer	17: 5
shall a. the Father in my name,	18:20
shall a. the Father in my name	27:28
a., and ye shall receive;	27:29
I would a. of you, have all these	Mrm 9:15
whatsoever he shall a. the Father	9:21
and a. the Father in the name of	9:27
a. not, that ye may consume it	9:28
a. with a firmness unshaken,	9:28
a. thee in the name of thy Son,	Mro 4: 3
a. thee, in the name of thy Son,	5: 2
Whatsoever thing ye shall a. the	7:26
exhort you that ye would a. God,	10: 4
if ye shall a. with a sincere	10: 4
A. and ye shall receive; knock	DC 4: 7
if you will a. of me you shall	6: 5
For if you shall a. what you will,	7: 1
of whatsoever things you shall a.	8: 1
whatsoever you shall a. me	8: 9
therefore a. in faith.	8:10
do not a. for that which you	8:10
A. that you may know the	8:11
no thought save it was to a. me.	9: 7
you must a. me if it be right,	9: 8
therefore they will not a. of me.	10:21
if you will a. of me you shall	11: 5
if you will a. of me you shall	12: 5
if you will a. of me you shall	14: 5
shall a. the Father in my name,	14: 8

ASK   65   ASSEMBLED

A. the Father in my name,	DC	18:18
we a. thee in the name of thy son,		20:77
we a. thee in the name of thy son,		20:79
things whatsoever ye a. of me,		27:18
Whatsoever ye shall a. in faith,		29: 6
shall a. it in my name,		35: 9
Thou shalt a., and my		42:56
If thou shalt a., thou shalt		42:61
Thou shalt a., and it shall be		42:62
let him a., of me and I will give		42:68
in all things to a. of God,		46: 7
be benefited that seek or that a. of me,		46: 9
of me, that a. and not for a sign		46: 9
a. and ye shall receive;		49:26
I the Lord a. you this question—		50:13
ye shall a. whatsoever you will		50:29
be given you what you shall a.;		50:30
a. of the Father in the name of		50:31
sins before me and a. forgiveness,		64: 7
A., and ye shall receive; knock,		66: 9
Let them a. and they shall		75:27
a. and ye shall receive; knock,		88:63
whatsoever ye a. the Father in		88:64
if ye a. anything that is not		88:65
whatsoever any man shall a.,		101:27
a. and ye shall receive; but		103:31
a. and ye shall receive; pray		103:35
now we a. thee, Holy Father,		109: 4
we a. thee, O Lord, to accept		109: 4
we a. thee to assist us,		109:10
And we a. thee, Holy Father,		109:22
We a. thee, Holy Father, to		109:24
We a. thee, Holy Father, to		109:29
We a. thee, Holy Father, to		109:47
We a. thee to appoint unto		109:59
We therefore a. thee to have		109:62
whereby he may a. and receive,		124:95
he may a. and receive blessings;		124:97
A. him to shake hands with		129: 7
when you a. him to shake		129: 8
A. what ye will, and it shall be		132:40
and whatsoever ye shall a.,	Mses	6:52
I a. thee, O Lord, in the name		7:50
a. in the name of thine Only		7:59
I a. thee if thou wilt not come		7:59
let him a. of God, that giveth to	JS	2:11
directs, that is, a. of God.		2:13
the determination to "a. of God,"		2:13
my determination to a. of God,		2:14
lacked wisdom might a. of God,		2:26

ASKED

again upon their cheeks, and a.:	Al	14:15
Now, as you have a.,	DC	6: 6
Now, as you have a.,		11: 6
Now, as you have a.,		12: 6
because ye have a. it of me		29:33
have a. the Father in my name,		42: 3
As ye have a. of me concerning		45:16
as ye have a. and are agreed		50: 1
a. whether they accepted		102: 4
they have a. it at my hands.		124:73
have a. concerning adultery,		132:41
I a. the personages who stood	JS	2:18
a. me how the young man found		2:64

ASKETH

will give liberally to him that a.	2Ne	4:35
Give to him that a. thee,	3Ne	12:42
For every one that a., receiveth;		14: 8
for he that a., receiveth;		27:29
he that a. in Spirit	DC	46:28
He that a. in the Spirit asketh		46:30
a. according to the will of God;		46:30
wherefore it is done even as he a.		46:30

ASKING

a. for whatsoever things ye stand	Al	7:23
in a. to translate it over again.	DC	10:15
a. all things in his name,	Mses	6:52

ASLEEP

when they are drunken and a.	Mos	22: 7

and behold, his men were a.,	Al	51:35
entrance; and they were all a.		62:21
shall see me, and shall not be a.,	DC	35:21
And after they have fallen a.		86: 3
vineyard, and not have fallen a.,		101:53

ASP

shall play on the hole of the a.,	2Ne	21: 8
shall play on the hole of the a.,		30:14

ASPIRE

and a. to the honors of men,	DC	121:35

ASPIRETH

he a. to establish his counsel	DC	124:84

ASS

both the cow and the ox, and the a.	1Ne	18:25
doth a man take an a. which	Mos	5:14
be driven before like a dumb a.		12: 5
nor his ox, nor his a.,		13:24
them as they would a dumb a.—		21: 3

ASSASSINATION

or three days previous to his a.,	DC	135: 4

ASSAULTS

unlawful a. and encroachments	DC	134:11

ASSEMBLE

All ye, a. yourselves, and hear;	1Ne	20:14
shall a. the outcasts of Israel,	2Ne	21:12
ye should a. yourselves together,	Mos	2:27
ye should a. yourselves together		2:28
ye should a. yourselves together,		2:29
to a. themselves together.		18:25
they did a. themselves together		25:21
should a. themselves together;		27:22
they did a. themselves together	Al	2: 6
began to a. themselves together		15:17
began to a. themselves together		19:18
we do a. ourselves together		21: 6
should a. themselves together.		21:20
they may a. themselves together		22: 7
should a. themselves together,		22:22
they did a. themselves together		53:16
no time to a. themselves together	He	1:24
a. themselves together to mourn		9:10
that they should a. together at	DC	37: 3
as my people shall a. themselves		39:15
ye shall a. yourselves together		41: 2
that they a. themselves together.		44: 2
a. ye yourselves together		45:64
a. yourselves together to refoice		52:42
a. yourselves together;		58:46
A. yourselves upon the land of		62: 4
that they should a. themselves		63:24
that you a. yourselves together,		88:74
where the living are wont to a.,		128:13

ASSEMBLED

that have a. yourselves together,	Mos	2: 9
people of Nephi were a. together,		25: 4
were a. together in large bodies,		25:15
that they a. themselves together		29:39
the people a. themselves together	Al	2: 5
all the people were a. together,		24:17
had a. themselves together again		31:23
have a. yourselves together	DC	42: 1
ye have a. yourselves together		42: 3
when ye are a. together ye		43: 8
and shall be a. together unto		49:25
who have a. yourselves together,		57: 1
who are a. upon this spot,		61: 2
be a. upon the land of Zion.		63:36
who have a. yourselves together,		67: 1
who have a. yourselves together,		72: 1
who have a. yourselves together;		78: 1
who have a. yourselves together		88: 1
high priests, a. in Kirtland,		89: 1
a. at the house of Joseph Smith,		102: 1
who have a. yourselves together		105: 1
in General Conference a.,		OD

ASSEMBLIES

ASSEMBLIES
and upon her a., a cloud — 2Ne 14: 5
and your solemn a., — DC 124:39
Call your solemn a., — 133: 6

ASSEMBLING
they were a. themselves together — Mos 18:32
deprived of the privilege of a. — Al 6: 5
in a. yourselves together — DC 89: 5

ASSEMBLY
hear the word of God in one a.; — Mos 25:20
or in every a. of the Lamanites — Al 21:16
to the general a. and church of — DC 76:67
and call a solemn a., — 88:70
my friends, call your solemn a., — 88:117
you should call your solemn a., — 95: 7
commune with the general a. — 107:19
be brought before a general a. — 107:32
the solemn a. shall be called — 108: 4
call your solemn a., as I have — 109: 6
in calling our solemn a., — 109:10

ASSENT
and a. unto my death, — DC 132:27

ASSERT
continuing to a. that I had seen — JS 2:58

ASSES
And they also had horses, and a., — Eth 9:19

ASSIST
to a. us that we may maintain — Al 27:24
that he might a. Teancum with — 52:15
city of Judea, to a. Antipus, — 56: 9
that we might a. our brethren — 57:34
to a. him in preserving that part — 62:12
And they shall a. my people, — 3Ne 21:23
then shall they a. my people — 21:24
that I would no more a. them; — Mrm 5: 1
shall a. to bring forth this work; — Eth 5: 2
and a. to bring forth my work, — DC 6: 9
shall you a. in bringing to light, — 6:27
that you may a. to translate, — 9: 2
and a. to bring forth my work, — 11: 9
you may a. in bringing to light — 11:19
no one can a. in this work — 12: 8
and thou art called to a.; — 14:11
a. the elder if occasion requires. — 20:52
shalt a. to settle all these things, — 28:14
are appointed to a. the bishop — 42:71
and a. you, my servant Joseph, — 47: 1
to a. my servant Oliver Cowdery — 55: 4
whom he has appointed to a. him. — 57: 7
servant Oliver Cowdery a. him, — 57:13
to a. in supporting the families — 75:24
a. in bringing forth my word — 96: 8
who are appointed to a. him, — 102:11
twelve, to a. as counselors; — 107:79
Father, we ask thee to a. us, — 109:10
Let him a. my servant Joseph, — 124:107
a. my servant Joseph, — 124:107
to a. us on our journey. — JS 2:61

ASSISTANCE
with the a. of the holy prophets — WM 1:16
the a. of his cunning servants, — Al 47:35
and appealed unto him for a.; — 50:27
of two thousand men to our a.; — 58: 8
all the a. which we did receive — 58: 8
do not send more men to our a.; — 58:36
to the a. of the people to maintain — 59: 9
Behold, I wait for a. from you; — 60:30
from the a. which Akish desired — Eth 8:14
by the a. of his counselors, — DC 58:18
that he receive counsel and a. — 69: 4
claim for a. upon the bishop — 72:20
the Seventy, when they need a., — 107:38
by the a. of his counselors, — 107:72

ASSISTANT
over the council without an a.; — DC 102:11

ASTONISHED

ASSISTED
a. always, in all his duties — DC 20:57
be a. by two other presidents, — 102:10
be a. by twelve counselors of — 107:82

ASSISTING
with thy grace a. them: — DC 109:44

ASSOCIATE
A. yourselves, O ye people, — 2Ne 18: 9

ASSOCIATED
a. with jovial company, etc., — JS 2:28

ASSOCIATES
or in those of my a., — DC OD

ASSOCIATIONS
performances, connections, a., — DC 132: 7

ASSURANCE
because of the a. of protection — Al 50:12
and a. wherewith he may stand; — DC 106: 8
stand still, with the utmost a., — 123:17

ASSURANCES
with a. that he would deliver us; — DC 58:11

ASSURE
let me a. you that these are — DC 128:15

ASSURED
I am a. that if ye had known — Mos 7:13

ASSUREDLY
And a., as the Lord liveth, — 2Ne 9:16
For a. as the Lord liveth — 27:31
I can a. tell thee, O king, — Mos 8:13
And a. it was great, for they — Al 17:14
behold, a. as thou livest, O king, — 22: 8
a. as the Lord liveth, — DC 8: 1
And this ye shall know a.— — 43: 3
heard and most a. believe, — 52:36
he knows and most a. believes. — 58:59

ASSYRIA
departed from Judah, the king of A. — 2Ne 17:17
for the bee that is in the land of A. — 17:18
beyond the river, by the king of A., — 17:20
be taken away before the king of A. — 18: 4
the king of A. and all his glory; — 18: 7
the stout heart of the king of A., — 20:12
people which shall be left, from A., — 21:11
people which shall be left, from A., — 21:16
which goeth toward the east of A. — Mses 3:14

ASSYRIAC
were Egyptian, Chaldaic, A., and — JS 2:64

ASSYRIAN
O A., the rod of mine anger, — 2Ne 20: 5
be not afraid of the A.; — 20:24
I will bring the A. in my land, — 24:25

ASTONISH
confound, and a., and to bring to — DC 109:29

ASTONISHED
they were a. exceedingly; — Jac 7:21
being greatly a., and struck — Al 2:23
the people began to be a., seeing — 10:12
the people began again to be a., — 11:46
the people began to be more a.; — 12:19
Zeezrom was a. at the words — 14: 6
they began to be a. at his power; — 17:36
insomuch that they began to be a., — 17:37
he was a. exceedingly, and said: — 18: 2
he was more a., because of — 18:10
he was a. exceedingly, and said: — 20:26
For the king was greatly a. at — 20:27
they were a. beyond all measure. — 31:19
Lamanites were a. exceedingly, — 49: 5

ASTONISHED

a. at their manner of preparation	Al	49: 9
were a. exceedingly and struck		58:29
the teachers were themselves a.	He	3:25
when they saw this they were a.		9: 4
a. insomuch that we fell to the		9:14
he shall make as if he were a.;		9:30
and the people began to be a.	3Ne	1:15
exceedingly a. that they fell		1:17
less a. at a sign or a wonder		2: 1
this epistle he was exceedingly a.,		3:11
As many were a. at thee—		20:44

ASTONISHING

their preservation was a. to	Al	57:26
such an a. influence over me	JS	2:15

ASTONISHMENT

to his great a. he beheld	1Ne	16:10
their questions, yea, to their a.;	Mos	12:19
And so great was their a., that		27:12
to the earth, for great was their a.;		27:18
the a. of Alma was so great that		27:19
and to our great a.,	Al	2:24
to the great a. of all the people;		15:11
behold, to his a., he met with		17: 1
to their a., they beheld the king,		19:18
to his a., his father was angry		20:13
to their a. they found that		31:12
behold, to their uttermost a.,		49: 8
But behold, to their a.,		49:14
to our great a., and also the foes		57:25
great a. of the Lamanites,	He	5:19
to their a. they saw those		9: 7
we were recovered from our a.,		9:14
great was the a. of the people	3Ne	10: 2
and I lay overwhelmed in a. at	JS	2:46

ASTRAY

for ye have all gone a.,	2Ne	12: 5
they have all gone a. save it be		28:14
All we, like sheep, have gone a.;	Mos	14: 6
to lead a. the people of the Lord,		27:10
nevertheless have gone a.,	Al	5:37
yea, they had all gone a.;		13:17
all gone a. after an unknown God.		30:53
gone far a. because of this thing.		41: 1
created them, have they gone a.,	Mses	6:28

ASTRONOMY

upon the principles of A.,	Fac	3: 6

ASUNDER

shake as if it were to divide a.	1Ne	17:45
as though it would part a.	Mos	27:18
shall divide a. all the cunning	He	3:29
as if it were about to divide a.		5:33
and thither, to the dividing a.,		12: 8
as if it was about to divide a.	3Ne	8: 6
dividing a. of both joints and	DC	6: 2
dividing a. of both joints and		11: 2
dividing a. of both joints and		12: 2
the dividing a. of both joints and		14: 2
the dividing a. of the joints and		33: 1
but they shall be cut a.,		85: 9
And shall cut him a., and shall	JS	1:54

AT: see in the APPENDIX.

ATE

Alma a. bread and was filled;	Al	8:22
they a. and slept, and prepared	Eth	15:26

ATHIRST

that were hungry, or that were a.,	Al	1:30
hungry, and those who were a.,		4:12
shall not go hungry, neither a.	DC	84:80

ATONE

death of Christ a. for their sins,	Al	22:14
and die to a. for their sins;		33:22
a. for the sins of the world;		34: 8
will a. for the sins of another.		34:11
to a. for the sins of the world.		36:17

ATONED

of mercy hath a. for your sins;	DC	29: 1
hath a. for original guilt,	Mses	6:54

ATONEMENT

to answer the ends of the a.—	2Ne	2:10
it must needs be an infinite a.—		9: 7
save it should be an infinite a.		9: 7
upon them, because of the a.;		9:25
the a. satisfieth the demands of		9:26
death by the power of the a.,		10:25
Christ, the Son of God, and the a.,		25:16
through the a. of Christ,	Jac	4:11
speak of the a. of Christ,		4:12
if there should be no a. made		7:12
through the a. of his blood.	Mos	3:15
through the a. of Christ the Lord,		3:19
the a. which has been prepared		4: 6
the a. which was prepared		4: 7
and were it not for the a.,		13:28
the a. of the Only Begotten Son,	Al	13: 5
and the a. of his blood.		21: 9
be shed for the a. of our sins.		24:13
that there could be no a.		30:17
that an a. should be made;		34: 9
there must be an a. made,		34: 9
perish except it be through the a.		34: 9
which is short of an infinite a.		34:12
except an a. should be made;		42:15
mercy cometh because of the a.;		42:23
and the a. bringeth to pass the		42:23
hope through the a. of Christ	Mro	7:41
setteth at naught the a. of him		8:20
through the a. of Jesus Christ;	DC	74: 7
who wrought out this perfect a.		76:69
that through the A. of Christ,	AoF	3

ATONETH

his blood a. for the sins of those	Mos	3:11
blood of Christ a. for their sins.		3:16
God himself a. for the sins of	Al	42:15

ATONING

through the a. blood of Christ,	Mos	3:18
and apply the a. blood of Christ		4: 2
the a. blood of Jesus Christ,	He	5: 9

ATTACK

an a. upon the weaker part of	Al	43:24
captains durst not a. the Nephites		49:11
sworn with an oath to a. the city;		49:17
attempt to a. them in their forts.		52: 5
an a. upon the city of Mulek,		52:16
an a. upon the city of Mulek,		52:17
make an a. upon the Lamanites.		53: 5
to a. the city Moriantron,		55:33
to make an a. upon them in		56:21
make an a. upon our other cities		56:22
and a. them in their strongholds.		58: 2
to a. that great city Zarahemla.	He	1:18
would a. the cities round about		1:26

ATTACKED

caused the Lamanites to have a.	Al	49:10
were a. by the Lamanites.		59: 5

ATTAIN

a. to a perfect knowledge of him,	Jac	4:12
as to a. to the knowledge of		4:12
is it that ye can a. unto faith,	Mro	7:40
principle of intelligence we a.	DC	130:18
ye cannot a. to this glory.		132:21
we never could a. to previously,	JS	2:74

ATTAINMENTS

celebrated for his literary a.	JS	2:64

ATTEMPT

a. to address you in my language;	Al	7: 1
they did no more a. to slay the		25: 1
all such as should a. to climb up		49:19
who should a. to come into		49:20
did a. to destroy the Nephites		49:23

ATTEMPT

a. to approach near the walls of — Al 50: 5
a. to attack them in their forts. — 52: 5
he did no more **a.** a battle with — 53: 7
Lamanites **a.** to encircle them — 55:29
a. to administer of their wine to — 55:30
for ye shall **a.** to flee and there — He 15: 2
that whoso should **a.** to pass — Eth 9:33
and was shot dead in the **a.**, — DC 135: 1
to the woods to make the **a.** — JS 2:14
that I had made such an **a.**, — 2:44
made the **a.** to pray vocally. — 2:14
I made an **a.** to take them out, — 2:53

ATTEMPTED

and **a.** to lay their hands on him; — Mos 13: 2
which they **a.** many times; — Al 57: 9
as many times as they **a.** this — 57: 9

ATTEMPTING

while **a.** to speak unto you; — Mos 2:30
a. to offer up Abraham as — Fac 1: 3
in **a.** to work as at other times, — JS 2:48
in **a.** to cross the fence out — 2:48

ATTEMPTS

these **a.** they were swept off — Al 49:22
in these **a.** they did lose — 55:29

ATTEND

and **a.** to all family duties. — DC 20:47
and **a.** to all family duties. — 20:51
to **a.** the several conferences held — 20:81
A. to thy calling and thou shalt — 24: 9
And you shall **a.** to the ministry — 30: 4
a. to the words of wisdom which — 50: 1
and my grace shall **a.** you, — 88:78

ATTENDED

the circumstances which **a.** them — Al 17: 5
had always **a.** the Nephites, — 19:27
These should then be **a.** to — DC 123:14
shall be **a.** with cursings and — 124:120
being **a.** with certificates over — 128: 4
have **a.** to the ordinances in — 128: 8
I **a.** their several meetings — JS 2: 8

ATTENDING

and all the **a.** witnesses, — DC 128: 4

ATTENTION

my brethren, I would call your **a.**, — Mos 3: 1
people, I would again call your **a.**, — 4: 4
attract the **a.** of the great ones — JS 2:23

ATTITUDE

angels in the **a.** of singing — 1Ne 1: 8
they were in the **a.** of mocking — 8:27
thus they were in this **a.** when the — Al 24:21
in the **a.** of singing and praising — 36:22
in the **a.** as if talking or lifting — He 5:36

ATTRACT

to **a.** the attention of the great — JS 2:23

ATTRIBUTED

and **a.** the carrying away of — Mos 20:23

AUDIENCE

throne, giving **a.** to his people. — Eth 9: 5

AUGHT

can ye say **a.** of yourselves? — Mos 2:25
thy brother hath **a.** against thee— — 3Ne 12:23

AUSTERE

an **a.** and a blood-thirsty man — Mos 9: 2

AUTHOR

it is he who is the **a.** of all sin. — He 6:30
a. is Gadianton and the evil one — 8:28
a. and the finisher of their faith. — Mro 6: 4

AUTHORITATIVE

as **a.** and binding." — DC OD

AUTHORITIES

the general **a.** of the church — DC 102:32
All other **a.** or offices in the — 107: 5
when there are no higher **a.** — 107:22
the spiritual **a.** of the church; — 107:32
concerning those kings and **a.**, — 124: 5
the **a.** which I have called to — 124:118

AUTHORITY

And the Holy Ghost giveth **a.** — 1Ne 10:22
he sought power and **a.** over you; — 2Ne 1:25
hath not sought for power nor **a.** — 1:25
with power and with **a.**; — WM 1:17
with power and **a.** from God; — Mos 13: 6
having **a.** from the Almighty God, — 18:13
by the power and **a.** of God — 18:17
Alma, having **a.** from God, — 18:18
with power and **a.** from God. — 18:26
and exercise **a.** over them; — 21: 3
that had **a.** from God. — 21:33
none received **a.** to preach — 23:17
began to exercise **a.** over Alma — 24: 8
yet he exercised **a.** over them, — 24: 9
Alma the **a.** over the church. — 26: 8
of the power and **a.** of God, — 27:14
having power and **a.** from God — Al 5: 3
that sendeth no more **a.** than one — 9: 6
and the judge executed **a.**, — 11: 2
as though he had **a.** to — 11:35
as though I had **a.** to command — 11:36
taught with power and **a.** of God. — 17: 3
usurped the power and **a.** over — 25: 5
usurp power and **a.** over them, — 30:23
and to exercise **a.** over them. — 46:34
power and **a.** over the people. — 51: 8
subjecting the Nephites to our **a.** — 54:20
desire of power and **a.** which — 60:16
are seeking for power and **a.**, — 60:17
ye yourselves are seeking for **a.**, — 60:18
desires to usurp power and **a.** — 60:27
not fear your power and **a.** — 60:28
power and **a.** among the people; — He 2: 5
with such great power and **a.**, — 5:18
for they had power and **a.**, — 5:18
exceedingly great power and **a.**, — 6: 5
the power and **a.** of the land; — 7: 4
having great power and **a.** — 11:18
them to seek for power, and **a.**, — 3Ne 6:15
with power and with great **a.** — 7:17
Having **a.** given me of Jesus — 11:25
received power and **a.** to baptize, — 12: 1
they did exercise power and **a.** — 4Ne 1:30
if I have no **a.** for these things, — Eth 5: 6
shall know that I have **a.** when — 5: 6
boldness, having **a.** from God; — Mro 8:16
and **a.** which cometh from God; — 8:28
Behold, this is mine **a.**, — DC 1: 6
and the **a.** of my servants, — 1: 6
have **a.** to baptize, — 20:58
a. from Jesus Christ to baptize, — 20:73
power and **a.** unto the church. — 28: 3
ordained by some one who has **a.**, — 42:11
that he has **a.** and has been — 42:11
and use it in vain, having not **a.** — 63:62
acting in the **a.** which I have — 68: 8
the keys or **a.** of the same. — 68:17
a. to officiate in all the lesser — 68:19
in **a.** in the presence of God, — 76:25
and the **a.** of the priesthood, — 84:21
and are in **a.** over you— — 101:76
a. over all the offices in the — 107: 8
holds the keys or **a.** of the same. — 107:15
has **a.** to officiate in all the — 107:17
The power and **a.** of the higher, — 107:18
The power and **a.** of the lesser, — 107:20
equal in **a.** and power to the — 107:24
equal in **a.** to that of the Twelve — 107:26
equal in **a.** in the affairs of the — 107:36

AUTHORITY 69 AWAY

AUTHORITY
equal in a. in the affairs of the	DC 107:37
put on the a. of the priesthood,	113: 8
priesthood or the a. of that man.	121:37
as soon as they get a little a.,	121:39
shall seek counsel, and a., and	122: 2
open up the a. of my kingdom	124:128
whatsoever those men did in a.,	128: 9
a. to try men on the right of	134:10
clothed with power and a.;	Fac 2: 3
by those who are in a. to preach	AoF 5

AUTHORIZE
a. him to perform the duties of	DC 20:64

AUTHORIZED
not legally a. to officiate in	DC 68:20
recommended and a. by you,	112:21
we consider him fully a.	OD

AUTHORS
designed by the a. thereof	JS 2: 1

AVAILETH
the law of Moses a. nothing except	Mos 3:15
is vain, and a. you nothing,	Al 34:28
unto such baptism a. nothing—	Mro 8:22
times it a. him nothing,	DC 22: 2

AVAILS
the a. of the sacred things shall	DC 104:64
the a. of the sacred things in	104:65

AVENGE
I will a. his blood upon you,	Al 54:16
been waged to a. their wrongs,	54:24
freedom, and to a. our wrongs.	61: 6
ye do this, I will a. their wrongs.	3Ne 3:10
a. themselves of the blood of	Mrm 3: 9
a. themselves of the blood of	3:14
and yet he a. them not.	Eth 8:22
for he had sworn to a. himself	14:24
I the Lord, will a. thee of	DC 98:45
a. me of mine enemies, that by	101:58
A. me of mine adversary.	101:83
widow troubleth me I will a. her,	101:84
ye shall a. me of mine enemies.	103:25
thy sword a. us of our wrongs.	121: 5

AVENGED
to be a. of their enemies.	DC 87: 7
until they had a. themselves on	98:37
If Cain shall be a. sevenfold,	Mses 5:48

AVENGES
till he a. that blood on the earth.	DC 135: 7

AVENGETH
he a. the blood of the saints	Mrm 8:41

AVENGING
a. the wrongs of those that had	3Ne 3:11
even in a. me of mine enemies,	DC 103:26
and a. me of mine enemies	105:30

AVOID
to a. the too frequent repetition	DC 107: 4

AWAIT
everlasting destruction did a. them.	Al 5: 7
which at this time doth a. you,	He 9:22
a. you because of your iniquities,	14:11
do a. with great anxiety for the	3Ne 3: 3
did they a. to receive them.	Mrm 6: 7
destructions a. the wicked.	DC 34: 9
that great things a. you;	45:62
utter abolishment which a. them	84:114
a. patiently and diligently for	124:88

AWAITED
a. with anxious expectation	DC 121:27

AWAITETH
heavy destruction a. this people,	He 13: 6

AWAITS
that awful hell that a. to receive	Al 54: 7
abomination which a. the wicked,	DC 88:85

AWAKE
O that ye would a.;	2Ne 1:13
a. from a deep sleep,	1:13
A.! and arise from the dust,	1:14
A., my sons; put on the armor	1:23
A., my soul! No longer droop	4:28
A., awake! Put on strength,	8: 9
Awake, a.! Put on strength,	8: 9
a. as in the ancient days.	8: 9
A., awake, stand up, O Jerusalem,	8:17
Awake, a., stand up, O Jerusalem,	8:17
A., awake put on thy strength,	8:24
Awake, a., put on thy strength,	8:24
should a. you to an awful reality	9:47
may a. from the slumber of death;	Jac 3:11
ye should a. to a remembrance of	Mos 2:40
And he said unto me: A.;	3: 2
A., and hear the words which I	3: 3
if ye will a. and arouse your	Al 32:27
that he did not a. his servants.	51:34
the king did a. his servant before	62:36
A., awake again, and put on thy	3Ne 20:36
a. again, and put on thy strength,	20:36
ye shall a. to a sense of your	Eth 8:24
And a., and arise from the dust,	Mro 10:31
and then shall all the dead a.,	DC 29:26
Let them a., and arise, and	117: 2
A., O kings of the earth!	124:11
A. and arise and go forth to	133:10

AWAKEN
do a. his immortal soul to	Mos 2:38
that I might a. you to a sense of	Al 7:22

AWAKENED
has a. you to a sense of your	Mos 4: 5
we were a. to a remembrance of	9:17
for the Lamanites have a.	24:23
a. to a remembrance of their duty.	Al 4: 3
he a. them out of a deep sleep,	5: 7
lest the Lamanites had a.	51:36
But had they a. the Lamanites,	55:18
shall be a. by the power of God	Mrm 9:13

AWAKETH
but he a. and his soul is empty;	2Ne 27: 3
but he a. and behold he is faint,	27: 3

AWARE
a. of the intent of the Amlicites,	Al 2:12
Gidgiddoni being a. of their design,	3Ne 4:24
let him be a. lest he shall be in	Mrm 8:17
if thou art not a. thou wilt fall.	DC 3: 3
Behold, ere he is a., he is left	121:38
in an hour that he is not a. of,	JS 1:53
as though the adversary was a.,	2:20

AWAY
he was carried a. in a vision,	1Ne 1: 8
carried a. captive into Babylon,	1:13
his life, that they might take it a.	1:20
they seek to take a. thy life.	2: 1
to take a. the life of my father.	2:13
sought to take a. mine own life;	4:11
he also had taken a. our property.	4:11
had sought to take a. their lives	4:28
to take a. the life of my father,	7:14
they sought to take a. my life,	7:16
cease striving to take a. my life.	7:19
they fell a. into forbidden paths	8:28
many as heeded them, had fallen a.	8:34
carried a. captive into Babylon,	10: 3
take a. the sins of the world.	10:10
I was caught a. in the Spirit	11: 1
she was carried a. in the Spirit;	11:19
had been carried a. in the Spirit	11:19
they were carried a. in the Spirit	11:29
beheld many generations pass a.,	12: 3
beheld three generations pass a.	12:11

AWAY

who passed a. in righteousness.	1Ne 12:12
leadeth them a. into broad roads,	12:17
I saw many generations pass a.	12:21
they have taken a. from the gospel	13:26
of the Lord have they taken a.	13:26
plain and precious things taken a.	13:28
and precious things were taken a.	13:29
taken a. out of the gospel	13:29
things which have been taken a.	13:40
taking a. of their stumbling blocks—	14: 1
lead a. the souls of men down to	14: 3
while I was carried a. in the spirit;	14:30
had been carried a. in the spirit,	15: 1
to lead them a. to destruction.	15:24
that he may lead us a. into some	16:38
and after he has led us a., he has	16:38
they did turn a. their anger,	16:39
like unto our father, led a. by the	17:20
led us a. because we would hearken	17:22
Israel, would have been led a. out	17:23
And he leadeth a. the righteous	17:38
shall be led a. into captivity.	17:43
sought to take a. his life;	17:44
sought to take a. his life;	17:44
the earth that it shall pass a.;	17:46
swallowed thee up shall be far a.	21:19
of the mighty shall be taken a.,	21:25
of all the tribes have been led a.;	22: 4
know that they have been led a.	22: 4
And since they have been led a.,	22: 5
nor to take a. the land of their	2Ne 1: 9
will take a. from them the lands	1:11
they are carried a. captive down	1:13
ye sought to take a. his life;	1:24
I take a. my first blessing, yea,	1:29
all things must have vanished a.	2:13
hath my body been carried a. upon	4:25
and my flesh waste a.,	4:26
they did seek to take a. my life.	5: 2
they did seek to take a. my life.	5: 4
they sought to take a. my life.	5:19
And thirty years had passed a.	5:28
that forty years had passed a.,	5:34
been slain and carried a. captive.	6: 8
of the mighty shall be taken a.,	6:17
Have I put thee a., or have I cast	7: 1
To whom have I put thee a., or	7: 1
is your mother put a.	7: 1
rebellious, neither turned a. back.	7: 5
heavens shall vanish a. like smoke,	8: 6
sorrow and mourning shall flee a.	8:11
our flesh must waste a. and die;	9: 4
eternal word, which cannot pass a.,	9:16
shall go a. into everlasting fire;	9:16
save they shall cast these things a.,	9:42
brethren, turn a. from your sins;	9:45
the Lord God has led a. from	10:22
doth take a. from Jerusalem,	13: 1
the Lord will take a. the bravery	13:18
thy name to take a. our reproach.	14: 1
shall have washed a. the filth	14: 4
I will take a. the hedge thereof,	15: 5
and take a. the righteousness of the	15:23
because they have cast a. the law	15:24
his anger is not turned a.,	15:25
and shall carry a. safe,	15:29
and thine iniquity is taken a.,	16: 7
Lord have removed men far a.,	16:12
spoil of Samaria shall be taken a.	18: 4
his anger is not turned a.,	19:12
his anger is not turned a.,	19:17
his anger is not turned a.,	19:21
To turn a. the needy from	20: 2
and to take a. the right from	20: 2
his anger is not turned a.,	20: 4
his burden shall be taken a.	20:27
thine anger is turned a.,	22: 1
carried a. captive into Babylon.	25:10
they have been carried a.	25:11
when the law ought to be done a.	25:27
many generations shall pass a.,	26: 2
and whirlwinds shall carry them a.,	26: 5
generations shall have passed a.,	26: 9
generation shall have passed a.	26: 9
when these things have passed a.	2Ne 26:10
shall be as chaff that passeth a.—	26:18
lull them a. into carnal security,	28:21
and leadeth them a. carefully	28:21
behold, others he flattereth a.,	28:22
from them shall be taken a.	28:30
of Israel, which I have led a.,	29:12
many generations shall not pass a.	30: 6
take a. the sins of the world.	31: 4
they cast many things a. which are	33: 2
fifty and five years had passed a.	Jac 1: 1
not lead a. captive the daughters	2:33
God will lead a. the righteous out	3: 4
must perish and vanish a.;	4: 2
God hath taken a. his plainness	4:14
which are beginning to wither a.,	5: 7
I take a. many of these young	5: 8
a long time passed a.,	5:15
a long time had passed a.,	5:29
branch that withered a. and died.	5:40
whose branch hath withered a.,	5:43
branch that it hath withered a.	5:45
ye shall clear a. the branches which	5:65
ye shall not clear a. the bad	5:65
shall clear a. the bad according	5:66
and thus will I sweep a. the bad	5:66
And the bad shall be cast a.,	5:69
be plucked off and to be cast a.;	5:73
until the bad had been cast a.	5:74
and the bad is cast a.,	5:75
and the bad will I cast a.	5:77
ye must go a. into that lake of	6:10
after some years had passed a.,	7: 1
lead a. the hearts of the people,	7: 3
that he did lead a. many hearts;	7: 3
ye have led a. much of this people	7: 7
that the time passed a. with us,	7:26
and also our lives passed a. like as	7:26
wherefore, my guilt was swept a.	En 1: 6
And many years pass a. before he	1: 8
and nine years had passed a. from	1:25
two hundred years had passed a.,	Jar 1: 5
swept them a. out of our lands,	1: 7
and eight years had passed a.—	1:13
and six years had passed a.,	Om 1: 3
eighty and two years had passed a.,	1: 3
and twenty years had passed a.,	1: 5
king of Judah, was carried a.	1:15
a. unto the Lamanites,	WM 1:16
drive him a., and cast him out.	Mos 5:14
a. on the south of the land of	9:14
and sought to take a. his life;	11:26
A. with this fellow, and slay him;	13: 1
did carry a. the daughters of	20:15
the carrying a. of their daughters	20:23
stealing a. the hearts of the people;	27: 9
and draw a. a part of this people	29: 7
lead a. the people of the church;	Al 1: 7
not send a. any who were naked,	1:30
drawn a. much people after him;	2: 2
those who had not been drawn a.	2: 3
a. beyond the borders of the land;	2:36
to be led a. by the Lamanites	3:10
to take a. the sins of the world,	5:48
taketh a. the sins of the world,	7:14
will not turn my fierce anger a.	8:29
that the earth should pass a.?	9: 2
that the earth should pass a.	9: 2
fierce anger he will not turn a.	9:12
sought to put them a. privily.	14: 3
who had been carried a. captive	16: 4
a. up beyond the borders of	16: 6
marched a. beyond the borders	16: 7
a. to the land of Manti,	17: 1
thereby they might drive a. many	18: 7
was being cast a. from his mind,	19: 6
and he was carried a. in God—	19: 6
was a. joining the borders of	21: 1
and I will give a. all my sins	22:18
unto the Lord never did fall a.	23: 6
taken a. the guilt from our hearts,	24:10
to take them a. from our hearts,	24:11
that he would take a. our stain.—	24:11
God hath taken a. our stains,	24:12

AWAY

get our stains taken a. from us,	Al	24:15
let us hide them a. that they		24:15
we will hide a. our swords,		24:16
rather than take a. from a		24:18
and then have fallen a. into sin		24:30
doth carry thee a. unto boasting.		26:10
yea, and my joy is carried a.,		26:35
my soul is carried a., even to the		29:16
which lead you a. into a belief		30:16
leading a. the hearts of many,		30:18
yea, leading a. many women,		30:18
And thus ye lead a. this people		30:27
leading a. the people after the		30:31
leading a. the hearts of this		30:45
again lead a. the hearts of this		30:55
led a. after the foolish traditions		31:17
he did not lead them a. after		31:22
their hearts were not stolen a.		31:22
not good therefore it is cast a.		32:32
it hath no root it withers a.,		32:38
hast turned thy judgments a.		33:11
hast turned a. thy judgments		33:13
and none shall have passed a.		34:13
if ye turn a. the needy, and		34:28
be led a. by the temptation of		34:39
led them a. unto destruction;		36:14
taken a. from you by the power		37:15
did steal a. the hearts of many;		39: 4
Suffer not yourself to be led a.		39:11
the devil to lead a. your heart		39:11
lest they lead a. the hearts of		39:12
ye lead a. the hearts of no more		39:13
to take a. the sins of the world;		39:15
a. by the head of the river Sidon,		43:22
generation shall not all pass a.		45:12
they were led a. by Amalickiah		46: 6
and to be led a. by the evil one.		46: 8
he led a. the hearts of many		46:10
draw a. a part of their forces		52:13
thus leading a. the Lamanites		52:24
lead a. the most powerful army of		56:36
not many days had passed a.		57:12
we could not decoy them a.		58: 1
to be led a. into the wilderness.		58:22
and ye have drawn a. the forces		58:35
also carrying them a. captive,		60:17
to take a. the judgment-seat		61: 4
led a. the hearts of many people,		61: 4
when they had sent them a.		62:18
about to flatter a. those people	He	1: 7
a. into the land of Nephi,		4:12
eternal, and which fadeth not a.;		5: 8
fourth year did pass a. in peace.		6:13
passed a. the sixty and fifth year		6:14
marvel because ye are given a.		7:15
given a. to the enticing of him		7:16
is seeking to hurl a. your souls		7:16
our possession, shall be taken a.		7:22
by the Spirit and conveyed a.		10:16
he turn a. from us this famine,		11: 8
swept a. the band of Gadianton		11:10
wilt thou turn a. thine anger,		11:11
wilt thou turn a. thine anger,		11:12
wilt thou turn a. thine anger,		11:16
the Lord did turn a. his anger		11:17
and did carry a. others captive		11:33
four hundred years pass not a.		13: 5
take a. my word from them,		13: 8
hundred years shall not pass a.		13: 9
I will turn a. mine anger,		13:11
they have slipped a. from us,		13:35
not turn a. thine anger from us?		13:37
anger of the Lord be turned a.		13:39
that they went a. unto Nephi		16: 3
and bind him, and a. with him.		16: 6
and first year had passed a.	3Ne	1: 1
jot or tittle should not pass a.		1:25
and second year did pass a.,		1:26
year did also pass a. in peace,		1:27
were led a. by some who were		1:29
thus passed a. the ninety		2: 1
lead a. and deceive the hearts		2: 2
lead them a. to believe that s		2: 2
leading a. the hearts of the people,	3Ne	2: 3
thus did pass a. the ninety and		2: 4
an hundred years had passed a.		2: 5
and nine years had passed a.		2: 6
And nine years had passed a.		2: 7
nine years had passed a.		2: 8
thus passed a. the tenth year		2:10
year also passed a. in iniquity.		2:10
this thirteenth year had passed a.		2:13
who have dissented a. from you		3:10
dissenting a. unto those wicked		3:11
eighteenth year did pass a.		4: 4
this nineteenth year did pass a.,		4:15
and second year passed a.,		5: 7
twenty and five years passed a.		5: 7
sixth and seventh years passed a.,		6: 4
thus passed a. the twenty and		6: 9
Satan did lead a. the hearts of		6:16
thus six years had not passed a.		7: 8
thirty and first year did pass a.,		7:21
Thus passed a. the thirty and		7:23
more part of the year did pass a.		7:26
and third year had passed a.;		8: 2
carried a. in the whirlwind;		8:16
know that they were carried a.		8:16
burnt offerings shall be done a.,		9:19
thus did the three days pass a.		10: 9
the tumultuous noises did pass a.		10: 9
not carried a. in the whirlwind;		10:13
such things should be done a.		11:30
nor one tittle hath not passed a.		12:18
whosoever shall put a. his wife,		12:31
whosoever shall put a. his wife,		12:32
at the law and take a. thy coat,		12:40
borrow of thee turn thou not a.		12:42
Old things are done a., and all		12:47
that old things had passed a.,		15: 2
that old things had passed a.,		15: 3
that old things have passed a.,		15: 7
hath led a. out of the land.		15:15
and ye be led a. captive by him		18:15
that none of you should go a.,		18:25
in turning a. every one of you		20:26
and whoredoms, shall be done a.		21:19
hath led a. out of Jerusalem.		21:26
gone a. from mine ordinances,		24: 7
and the earth should pass a.,		26: 3
they are led a. captive by him		27:32
thirty and fourth year passed a.,	4Ne	1: 1
and seventh year passed a. also,		1: 4
thirty and eighth year pass a.,		1: 6
forth and nine years had passed a.,		1: 6
and nine years had passed a.		1: 6
seventy and first year passed a.		1:14
and ninth year had passed a.;		1:14
an hundred years had passed a.,		1:14
of that generation had passed a.		1:14
and ten years had passed a.;		1:18
from Christ had passed a.,		1:18
hundred years had passed a.;		1:22
generation had all passed a.		1:22
and ten years had passed a.		1:27
and thirty years had passed a.		1:34
and four years had passed a.		1:40
hundred and fifty years pass a.,		1:41
hundred years had passed a.,		1:45
and five years had passed a.,		1:47
and twenty years had passed a.,		1:48
the Lord did take a. his beloved	Mrm	1:13
beloved disciples were taken a.		1:16
and six years had passed a.		2: 2
and thirty years had passed a.		2: 9
and four years had passed a.		2:15
and ninth year had passed a.		2:28
ten years more had passed a.		3: 1
this tenth year had passed a.,		3: 4
and sixth year had passed a.,		4:10
seventy and nine years passed a.		5: 5
and four years had passed a.,		6: 5
four hundred years have passed a.		8: 6
said that miracles are done a.;		8:26
and say that they are done a.,		9: 7
be that he will turn a. his anger	Eth	1:36

AWAY 72 AWOKE

turn a. thine anger from this thy	Eth	3: 3
inhabitants thereof shall pass a.,		4: 9
Corihor drew a. many people		7: 4
whom he had drawn a. with him;		7: 9
and drew a. Cohor his brother,		7:15
and carried him a. captive into		7:17
carry a. his father into captivity,		8: 3
leading them a. by fair promises		8:17
things that evil may be done a.,		8:26
they drew a. the more part of		9:11
seen many days he did pass a.,		10:17
that Kish passed a. also,		10:18
kingdom was taken a. from him.		10:30
that Com drew a. the half of		10:32
and take a. their talent, yea,		12:35
when the earth shall pass a.		13: 8
old save the old have passed a.,		13: 9
was carried a. as though he		14:30
circumcision is done a. in me.	Mro	8: 8
only a few years have passed a.,		9:12
the Lamanites did not carry a.,		9:16
army of Zenephi has carried a.		9:16
and twenty years have passed a.		10: 1
spiritual, never will be done a.,		10:19
shall be done. among you,		10:24
shall do these things a. and die,		10:26
the heavens and the earth pass a.,	DC	1:38
my word shall not pass a.,		1:38
are consumed a. and utterly		5:19
will take a. the things which		5:31
to take it a. out of your hands,		8: 8
taken a. this privilege from you.		9: 5
to take a. the things wherewith		10: 7
thus he flattereth them a.		10:29
have I caused to be done a.		22: 1
shall be consumed and pass a.,		29:23
all old things shall pass a.,		29:24
before the earth shall pass a.,		29:26
the hosts of heaven turned he a.		29:36
in eternity, no more to pass a.		38:20
and wash a. your sins,		39:10
having put a. their companions		42:74
and the earth shall pass a.		43:32
the wicked shall go a. into		43:33
of Jews shall not pass a. until		45:21
and the earth shall pass a.;		45:22
shall not pass a. until all shall		45:23
heaven and the earth pass a.,		56:11
these words shall not pass a.,		56:11
it shall be taken a., even that		60: 3
shalt not idle a. thy time,		60:13
today mine anger is turned a.		61:20
many have turned a. from my		63:13
whom have turned a. from you,		63:14
and old things shall pass a.,		63:49
of Zion, and shall be sent a.,		64:35
turned a. from your iniquities,		66: 1
must be done a. from among		68:32
law of Moses should be done a.		74: 5
the tradition might be done a.,		74: 6
go a. into the lake of fire and		76:36
a. everlasting punishment,		76:44
their hearts a. from the truth,		78:10
shall not all pass a. until an		84: 5
you not, go a. from him alone		84:92
cast a. your idle thoughts and		88:69
be cast a. into their own place,		88:114
cometh and taketh a. light		93:39
diligently to take a. incumbrances		96: 9
turn a. all wrath and indignation		98:22
indignation shall be turned a.;		98:47
be taken a. out of their minds		104:81
and be swept a. by the hail,		109:30
that they may be wasted a.,		109:52
wilt turn a. thy wrath when		109:53
and swept a. as with a flood;		109:70
their prospects shall melt a. as		121:11
or which he hath taken a.,		124:28
convey the stock a. out of their		124:69
and turn a. their hearts from		124:76
shall go a. into outer darkness,		133:73
many worlds that have passed a.	Mses	1:35
And as one earth shall pass a.,		1:38

had drawn a. many after him,)	Mses	4: 6
he was caught a. by the Spirit		6:64
sought Noah to take a. his life;		8:18
endeavored to take a. my life	Abr	1: 7
me up and take a. my life,		1:15
a. from thy father's house,		1:16
turned their hearts a. from me,		1:17
my son, to take a. thy life.		1:17
was led a. by their idolatry;		1:27
against me, to take a. my life.		1:30
to take thee a. out of Haran,		2: 6
are taken a. by a whirlwind,		2: 7
a.from my father's house,		2:17
shall not pass a. until all I	JS	1:34
heaven and earth shall pass a.;		1:35
yet my words shall not pass a.,		1:35
came, and took them all a.;		1:43

AWFUL

in that a. state of blindness,	1Ne	13:32
an a. gulf, which separated		15:28
a representation of that a. hell,		15:29
even that a. hell of which I gave		15:35
and shake off the a. chains	2Ne	1:13
from the grasp of this a. monster;		9:10
from that a. monster the devil,		9:19
delivered from that a. monster,		9:26
probation, for a. is his state!		9:27
ye may not shrink with a. fear;		9:46
may not remember your a. guilt		9:46
I am a prey to his a. misery.		9:46
should awake you to an a. reality		9:47
grasps them with his a. chains,		28:22
the a. consequences of them.	Jac	3:12
to stand with shame and a. guilt		6: 9
the wicked with a. dread and fear.		6:13
fear lest my case shall be a.;		7:19
the a. situation of those that	Mos	2:40
to an a. view of their own guilt		3:25
that ye were not in the a. dilemma	Al	7: 3
then will our state be a., for then		12:13
in this a. state we shall not dare		12:14
How can we witness this a. scene?		14:10
who has saved me from an a. hell!		19:29
our a., sinful, and polluted state?		26:17
consign us to an a. destruction,		26:19
murders and their a. wickedness.		27:23
to pass an a. scene of bloodshed.		28:10
ye are brought to that a. crisis,		34:34
a state of a., fearful looking for		40:14
behold, an a. death cometh upon		40:26
tell you concerning that a. hell		54: 7
of unbelief and a. wickedness;	He	4:25
a. solemn fear came upon them.		5:28
their plans of a. wickedness,		6:30
that they were in an a. state,		6:40
a state of such a. wickedness,		7: 4
were in a state of a. wickedness.	3Ne	6:17
an a. scene of blood and carnage	Mrm	5: 8
with that a. fear of death which		6: 7
in your a. state of wickedness,	Eth	4:15
to a sense of your a. situation,		8:24
and a. is the state of man,	Mro	7:38
For a. is the wickedness to		8:15
it is a. wickedness to deny the		8:19
victims to their a. brutality.		9:17

AWFULNESS

remember the a. in transgressing	2Ne	9:39
and also the a. of yielding		9:39

AWKWARDNESS

because of the a. of our hands.	Eth	12:24

AWOKE

unto me: Awake; and I a.,	Mos	3: 2
and they a. unto God.	Al	5: 7
before they a. at the dawn		47:14
he a. them and told them all		51:35
when the Lamanites a. on the		52: 1
when the Lamanites a. in the		55:22
when the Lamanites a. and saw		62:24

AX

AX
Shall the a. boast itself against 2Ne 20:15
bow, and in the cimeter, and the a. En 1:20
Behold, the a. is laid at the root Al 5:52
with the arrow, and with the a., Mrm 6: 9
The a. is laid at the root of DC 97: 7

BABBITT, Almon
And with my servant B., DC 124:84

BABBLINGS
in idolatry or idleness, and in b., Al 1:32

BABES
and b. shall rule over them. 2Ne 13: 4
even b. did open their mouths 3Ne 26:16
shall be revealed unto b. DC 128:18

BABYLON
be carried away captive into B. 1Ne 1:13
be carried away captive into B. 10: 3
and he will do his pleasure on B., 20:14
Go ye forth of B., flee ye 20:20
The burden of B., 2Ne 23: 1
And B., the glory of kingdoms, 23:19
proverb against the king of B., 24: 4
and cut off from B. the name, 24:22
carried away captive into B. 25:10
also B. shall be destroyed; 25:15
carried away captive into B. Om 1:15
old, and shall perish in B. DC 1:16
B. the great which shall fall. 1:16
except desolations upon B., 35:11
not spare any that remain in B. 64:24
the apostate, the whore, even B., 86: 3
Go ye out from B. 133: 5
Go ye out of B.; gather ye 133: 7
the nations, even from B., 133:14
wickedness, which is spiritual B. 133:14

BACK
be brought b. out of captivity; 1Ne 10: 3
be brought b. out of captivity 10: 3
kept b. by that abominable 13:32
kept b. by that abominable 13:34
were driven b. upon the waters 18:13
we had been driven b., 18:14
after we had been driven b. 18:15
neither turned away b. 2Ne 7: 5
I gave my b. to the smiter, 7: 6
and who shall turn it b.? 24:27
their journey, but were driven b., Mos 1:17
and they were driven b., 11:18
they drove them b. for a time; 11:18
them b. to the land of Nephi, 19:15
did beat them, and drove them b., 21: 8
but they were driven b. again, 21:11
Behold the b. pass, through the 22: 6
through the b. wall, on the back 22: 6
on the b. side of the city. 22: 6
b. to the building of the great 28:17
b. until the creation of Adam. 28:17
the king of the Lamanites fled b. Al 2:32
until he slew and drove them b. 2:33
to set my b. towards this land 8:24
and bring them b. unto the place 17:31
and we were about to turn b.; 26:27
b. to the land of Zarahemla, 27:20
to bring b. again evil for evil, 41:13
b. man into the prescence or God; 42:23
to take them and bring them b., 46:30
b. into the land of Zarahemla. 46:33
driven b. from time to time, 49:21
people of Morianton brought b. 50:36
b. into the land Bountiful; 53: 3
march b. to the city of Judea. 56:57
driven b. to the city of Manti. 57:22
even b. by the same way which 58:24
were beaten and driven b. again 63:15
to retreat b. towards the land He 1:29
retreat b. into the mountains, 11:25
b. even into their own lands. 11:29
unto the earth—Thou shalt go b., He 12:14
to his word the earth goeth b., 12:15
b. into the presence of the Lord. 14:17
drive them b. out of their lands 3Ne 2:17
did fall b. from before them. 4:12
Nephites were driven b. again Mrm 4: 2
and driven b. by the Nephites. 4: 8
they were driven b. that they 5: 3
brought b. into the presence of 9:13
brought b. into my presence; Eth 3:13
b. again to the valley of Gilgal 13:29
had been kept b. because of DC 6:26
laden with sheaves upon your b., 31: 5
Let not your minds turn b.; 67:14
which was sealed on the b. with 77: 6
let him not look b. lest sudden 133:15
it shall be driven b. into the 133:23
be turned b. into their own place, 133:24
the chronology running b. from Abr 1:28
return b. to take his clothes; JS 1:15
I found myself lying on my b., 2:20
when Mr. Anthon called me b., 2:64

BACKBITING
lying, b., nor evil speaking. DC 20:54

BACKS
have burdens lashed upon their b.; Mos 12: 5
put heavy burdens upon their b., 21: 3
you cannot feel them upon your b., 24:14
turning their b. upon the needy Al 4:12
turning your b. upon the poor, 5:55
turn their b. upon the poor He 6:39
with sheaves upon your b., DC 33: 9

BACKWARD
Go forward and not b. DC 128:22

BAD
nor misery, neither good nor b. 2Ne 2:11
because of b. examples 2:35
there are all kinds of b. fruit; 5:32
away the b. thereof all at once, 5:65
shall clear away the b. according 5:66
the good shall overcome the b., 5:66
the b. be hewn down and cast into 5:66
and thus will I sweep away the b. 5:66
and the b. shall be cast away, 5:69
until the b. had been cast away 5:74
and the b. is cast away, 5:75
good and the b. to be gathered; 5:77
and the b. will I cast away 5:77
good or whether they were b., Al 3:26
be a good spirit or a b. one. 3:26
for some good end, or b., as DC 127: 2
things, whether it be good or b. 127: 2
and b. feeling ensued JS 2: 6

BADE
and b. him that he should read. 1Ne 1:11
b. him that he should follow me. 4:25
and b. me follow him. 8: 6
he b. them to keep the 8:38
unto them, and b. them arise. 3Ne 17:19

BAINBRIDGE
of Squire Tarbill, in South B., JS 2:58

BAKER, Jesse
Samuel Williams, and B., DC 124:137

BALDNESS
instead of well set hair, b.; 2Ne 13:24

BALDWIN, Wheeler
Let my servants B. and William DC 52:31

BALL
round b. of curious workmanship; 1Ne 16:10
within the b. were two spindles; 16:10
follow the directions of the b., 16:16
Look upon the b., and behold 16:26

BALL 74 BAPTISM

which were written upon the b.,	1Ne 16:27
the pointers which were in the b.,	16:28
which were given upon the b.	16:30
and also the b., or compass,	2Ne 5:12
and the b. or director, which led	Mos 1:16
fathers call a b., or director—	Al 37:38

BALLOT
then proceeded to cast lots or b.,	DC 102:34

BALLS
and both received four b.	DC 135: 1
a savage manner with four b.,	135: 2

BAND
a b. of Christians remain to	Al 46:13
my little b. of two thousand.	57: 6
b. of two thousand and sixty	57:19
b. who was appointed to guard	57:29
and Kishkumen and his a.,	He 1:12
and he was upheld by his b.,	2: 3
leader of the b. of Kishkumen.	2: 4
those who belonged to his b.	2: 5
which had been laid by this b.	2: 6
all those who belonged to his b.	2: 8
to take this b. of robbers and	2:10
that his b. should follow him.	2:11
were a b. who had been formed	6:18
Nephites, of Gadianton's b.	6:18
those who did belong to his b.,	6:22
those who belonged to their b.	6:24
the b. of robbers of Gadianton;	6:37
insomuch that this b. of robbers	6:37
yea, to that secret b. which was	7:25
to the secret b. of Gadianton,	8: 1
both belonged to your secret b.,	8:28
it was this secret b. of robbers	11: 2
swept away the b. of Gadianton	11:10
an exceeding great b. of robbers;	11:26
to search out this b. of robbers,	11:28
again against this b. of robbers,	11:30
governor of this b. of robbers;	3Ne 3: 1
of the b. who were desirous to	6: 3
bacame a king over this wicked b.;	7:10
he being the king of the b.,	7:12
from this eternal b. of death,	Mrm 9:13
every man with his b. fighting	Eth 13:25
ashamed of the Nicolaitane b.	DC 117:11
an iron yoke, it is a strong b.;	123: 8

BANDS
these b. with which I am bound.	1Ne 7:17
the b. were loosed from off my	7:18
the b. which were upon my wrist,	18:15
loose thyself from the b. of thy	2Ne 8:25
and the head-b., and tablets,	13:20
and their b. were loosed;	Mos 7: 8
that I should have worn these b.	7:13
God breaketh the b. of death,	15: 8
having broken the b. of death,	15: 9
the b. of death shall be broken,	15:20
who has broken the b. of death.	15:23
or have broken the b. of death	16: 7
bound with the b. of iniquity.	23:12
Christ from the b. of death.	Al 4:14
about by the b. of death,	5: 7
were the b. of death broken,	5: 9
loosed from the b. of death,	5:10
he may loose the b. of death	7:12
bound in b. and cast into prison.	8:31
the loosing of the b. of death;	11:41
loose the b. of this temporal death,	11:42
deliver yourselves from these b.,	14:24
and they were loosed from their b.;	14:28
that his b. should be loosed;	17:24
that he breaketh the b. of death,	22:14
out of the city by our small b.	58: 1
unite with those b. of robbers,	He 6:21
Loose thyself from the b. of thy	3Ne 20:37
her b. are made strong,	DC 88:94
from the b. of her neck;	113: 9
The b. of her neck are the	113:10
and immediately unloosed my b.;	Abr 1:15

BANEEMY
and B. [mine elders],	DC 105:27

BANISHED
Oh, thought I, that I could be b.	Al 36:15

BANK
along the b. of the river,	1Ne 8:19
the ground, or rather the b.,	Al 2:34
slain upon the b. of the river	3: 3
near the b. of the river Sidon,	43:27
upon the b. of the river Sidon	43:40
upon the b. by the river Sidon.	43:51
because of the highness of the b.	49:18
upon the inner b. of the ditch;	53: 4

BANKS
and go over all his b.	2Ne 18: 7
throwing up b. of earth round	Al 48: 8
to dig down their b. of earth	49:22
by pulling down the b. of earth,	49:22
on the b. of the Susquehanna,	DC 128:20

BANNER
Lift ye up a b. upon the	2Ne 23: 2
blood on the b. of liberty,	DC 135: 7

BANNERS
and terrible as an army with b.	DC 5:14
and that her b. may be terrible	105:31
and terrible as an army with b.;	109:73

BAPTISM
out of the waters of b.	1Ne 20: 1
the name of Christ, by b.—	2Ne 31:13
then cometh the b. of fire	31:13
by the b. of water,	31:14
and have received the b. of fire	31:14
is repentance and b. by water;	31:17
having one faith and one b.,	Mos 18:21
an account of their b. shall be	21:35
by going into the waters of b.	Al 7:15
And now I speak concerning b.	Mro 6: 1
did they receive any unto b.	6: 2
none were received unto b. save	6: 3
they had been received unto b.,	6: 4
the b. of your little children.	8: 5
repentance and b. unto those	8:10
need no repentance, neither b.	8:11
b. is unto repentance to the	8:11
children have died without b.!	8:12
could not be saved without b.,	8:13
that little children need b.	8:14
saveth one child because of b.,	8:15
perish because he hath no b.	8:15
saith that little children need b.	8:20
unto such b. availeth nothing—	8:22
first fruits of repentance is b.;	8:25
b. cometh by faith unto the	8:25
gospel of repentance, and of b.	DC 13: 1
and remission of sins by b.	19:31
concerning the manner of b.—)	20:37
be received by b. into his church.	20:37
b. of fire and the Holy Ghost,	20:41
after they are received by b.—)	20:68
B. is to be administered in the	20:72
presented himself or herself for b.,	20:73
b. of fire and of the Holy Ghost.	33:11
repentance and b. by water,	39: 6
b. of fire and the Holy Ghost,	39: 6
remission of sins by way of b.	55: 2
b. and the gift of the Holy Ghost	68:25
the gospel of repentance and of b.,	84:27
the b. of repentance for the	107:20
relation to the b. for your dead.	127: 5
subject of b. for the dead,	127:10
of the b. for the dead,	128: 1
The ordinance of b. by water,	128:12
ordinance of b. for the dead,	128:12
relation to the b. for the dead,	128:16
namely, the b. for the dead;	128:17
It is the b. for the dead.	128:18
b. for the remission of the sins,	JS 2:68

BAPTISM 75 BAPTIZED

and of b. by immersion for the	JS 2:69
third, B. by immersion for the	AoF 4

BAPTISMAL

For a b. font there is not	DC 124:29
the b. font was instituted as	128:13

BAPTISMS

your b. shall be acceptable	DC 124:31
your b. for your dead shall not	124:32
your b. for your dead cannot	124:33
your b. for the dead, by those	124:35
places for your b. for your dead.	124:36
and your b. for the dead,	124:39
him be eye-witness of your b.;	127: 6

BAPTIST

and some for the B.	JS 2: 5
same that is called John the B.	2:72

BAPTISTS

most decided against the B.	2: 9
the B. and Methodists in their	2: 9

BAPTIZE

my father said he should b.	1Ne 10: 9
and he also said he should b.	10: 9
that he should b. the Messiah	10: 9
that should b. the Lamb of God,	2Ne 31: 9
I b. thee, having authority	Mos 18:13
after this manner he did b. every	18:16
into the water and did b. them;	25:18
he did b. them after the manner	25:18
as many as he did b. did belong	25:18
and he did b. his brethren in	Al 5: 3
might b. them unto repentance.	8:10
to b. unto the Lord whosoever	15:13
they did b. unto repentance	48:19
him will I b. with fire and	3Ne 9:20
power that ye shall b. this people	11:21
gave unto them power to b.	11:22
On this wise shall ye b.;	11:22
on this wise shall ye b. them—	11:23
in my name shall ye b. them.	11:23
I b. you in the name of the	11:25
after this manner shall ye b. it	11:27
commanded you thus shall ye b.	11:28
power and authority to b.,	12: 1
they may b. you with water;	12: 1
behold, I will b. you with fire	12: 1
out of the water and began to b.	19:12
to b. and to teach as many as	26:17
ye should b. little children.	Mro 8: 9
who are ordained of me to b.	DC 18:29
and it is his calling to b.;	20:38
to teach, expound, exhort, b.,	20:42
teach, expound, exhort, and b.,	20:46
teach, expound, exhort, and b.,	20:50
have authority to b.,	20:58
authority from Jesus Christ to b.,	20:73
I b. you in the name of	20:73
b. by water unto repentance,	35: 5
thou shalt b. by water,	35: 6
many as ye shall b. with water,	39:23
nor b. them contrary to the will	134:12
b. in the name of the Father,	Mses 7:11
I should b. Oliver Cowdery,	JS 2:70
that afterwards he should b. me.	2:70

BAPTIZED

after he had b. the Messiah	1Ne 10:10
that he had b. the Lamb of God,	10:10
went forth and was b. of him;	11:27
of him; and after he was b.,	11:27
and be b. in his name,	2Ne 9:23
and be b. in his name,	9:24
have need to be b. by water,	31: 5
to be b., yea, even by water!	31: 5
righteousness in being b. by water?	31: 6
after he was b. with water	31: 8
be b. in the name of my Beloved	31:11
He that is b. in my name,	31:12
what have you against being b.	Mos 18:10
and b. him according to the first,	Mos 18:15
were b. in the waters of Mormon,	18:16
whosoever was b. by the power	18:17
his people were desirous to be b.;	21:33
They were dewirous to be b. as	21:35
was desirous that he might be b.;	25:17
desirous that he might be b. also.	25:17
And they would not be b.;	26: 4
and blessed are they who were b.	26:15
whosoever is b. shall be baptized	26:22
shall be b. unto repentance.	26:22
many were b. in the waters of	Al 4: 4
were b. by the hand of Alma,	4: 4
to the church of God and were b.	4: 5
and be b. unto repentance,	5:62
were b. unto repentance,	6: 2
come and be b. unto repentance,	7:14
were b. throughout all the land;	8: 5
who will be b. unto repentance,	9:27
Alma b. Zeezrom unto the Lord;	15:12
whosoever were desirous to be b.	15:13
about Sidom, and were b.	15:14
as many as did believe were b.;	19:35
b. without stubbornness of heart,	32:16
being b. unto repentance,	49:30
be b. unto the Lord their God.	62:45
and were b. unto repentance.	He 3:24
and were b. unto repentance,	5:17
round about b. unto repentance,	5:19
they might be b. unto the Lord.	16: 1
went away unto Nephi to be b.	16: 3
went forth unto him to be b.,	16: 5
who were not b. with water.	3Ne 7:24
them whould be b. with water,	7:25
that were b. unto repentance;	7:26
were b. with fire and with the	9:20
desireth to be b. in my name,	11:23
whoso believeth in me, and is a.,	11:33
and is not b., shall be damned.	11:34
child, and be b. in my name,	11:37
repent, and be b. in my name,	11:38
after that ye are b. with water,	12: 1
ye shall believe in me and be b.,	12: 1
the depths of humility and be b.,	12: 2
believe and be b. in my name.	18: 5
repent and are b. in my name;	18:11
repent and are b. in my name.	18:16
and is b. in my name,	18:30
down into the water and was b.	19:11
And he b. all those whom	19:12
when they were all b. and had	19:13
unto me and be b. in my name	21: 6
and repenteth and is b.,	23: 5
were b. in the name of Jesus	26:17
were b. in the name of Jesus	26:21
that whoso repenteth and is b.	27:16
unto me and be b. in my name,	27:20
as many as were b. did receive	28:18
and be b. in my name,	30: 2
were b. in the name of Jesus;	4Ne 1: 1
come unto me, and be ye b.,	Mrm 3: 2
and be b. in the name of Jesus,	7: 8
are b., first with water, then	7:10
he that believeth and is b. shall	9:23
that ye are not b. unworthily;	9:29
and be b. in my name;	Eth 4:18
and is b. shall be saved;	4:18
that they were b. with fire and	12:14
priests, and teachers were b.;	Mro 6: 1
they were not b. save they	6: 1
unto me, and be b. in my name,	7:34
they must repent and be b.,	8:10
b. by the hands of my servant	DC 18: 7
repent and are b. in my name,	18:22
You must repent and be b.,	18:41
all men must repent and be b.,	18:42
and be b. in his holy name,	20:25
God, and desire to be b.,	20:37
those who are b. into the church,	20:41
be b. an hundred times it	22: 2
Yea, repent and be b.,	33:11
yea, be b. even by water,	33:11
Arise, and be b., and wash	39:10

BAPTIZED 76 BATTLE

BAPTIZED
Repent and be b. in the name of	DC 49:13
hast been b. by water,	55: 1
he that believeth and is b. shall	68: 9
b. for the remission of their sins	68:27
b. after the manner of his burial,	76:51
For he was b. while he was yet	84:28
b. by water for the remission of	84:64
are not b. in water in my name,	84:74
he that believeth and is b. shall	112:29
and is not b., shall be damned.	112:29
b. for those who are dead—	124:29
of you are b. for your dead,	127: 6
do which are b. for the dead,	128:16
are they then b. for the dead?	128:16
and be b., even in water,	Mses 6:52
repent and be b. in water?	6:53
And thus he was b., and	6:65
Thou art b. with fire, and with	6:66
be b. in the name of Jesus	8:24
commanded us to go and be b.,	JS 2:70
we went and were b.	2:71
I b. him first, and afterwards	2:71
and afterwards he b. me—	2:71
hand of this messenger, and b.	2:72
the water after we had been b.,	2:73
No sooner had I b. Oliver	2:73
soon as I had been b. by him,	2:73
and our having been b.,	2:74

BAPTIZING
receiving many, and b. many.	Mos 26:37
b. and uniting to the church of	He 3:26
Nephi was b., and prophesying,	16: 4
b. unto repentance, in the which	3Ne 1:23
were b. in the name of Jesus,	27: 1
b. them, and as many as were	28:18
Go forth b. with water,	DC 39:20
shall go forth b. with water,	42: 7
b. by water, and the laying on	52:10
b. in the name of the Father,	68: 8
ordinance of b. for the dead	124:33

BAR
stand face to face before his b.;	2Ne 33:11
against you at the judgment b.;	33:15
awful guilt before the b. of God?	Jac 6: 9
before the pleasing b. of God,	6:13
which b. striketh the wicked with	6:13
to stand before the b. of God,	Mos 16:10
shall stand before the b. of God,	Al 5:22
before the b. of Christ the Son,	11:44
brought before the b. of God,	12:12
all shall stand before his b.,	Mrm 9:13
ye shall see me at the b. of God;	Mro 10:27
pleasing b. of the great Jehovah,	10:34

BARBAROUS
massacred by the b. cruelty of	Al 48:24

BARE
unless he shall make b. his arm	1Ne 22:10
will proceed to make b. his arm	22:11
and unto Sarah, she that b. you;	2Ne 8: 2
and she conceived and b. a son.	18: 3
b. unto him sons and daughters,	Mos 5: 2
and she conceived and b. Cain,	5:16
conceived and b. his brother Abel.	5:17
and she conceived and b. Enoch	5:42
Adah b. Jabal; he was the father	5:45
Zillah, she also b. Tubal Cain,	5:46
she b. a son, and he called his	6: 2
Lord hath made b. his holy arm	12:24
Lord hath made b. his holy arm	15:31
and their b. heads were exposed	Al 44:18
Lord hath made b. his holy arm	3Ne 16:20
the multitude b. record of it,	17:21
but the disciples b. record that	18:37
Father hath made b. his holy arm	20:35
make b. thine arm, O Lord,	DC 109:51
he shall make b. his holy arm	133: 3
His head and neck were also b.	JS 2:31

BARGES
and did build b., in which they	Eth 2: 6
b. which ye have hitherto built.	2:16
built b. after the manner which	2:16
I have made the b. according	2:18
got aboard of their vessels or b.,	6: 4

BARLEY
one half of our corn, and our b.,	Mos 7:22
of corn, and of wheat, and of b.,	9: 9
and either for a measure of b.,	Al 11: 7
a shiblon for half a measure of b.	11:15
and b. for all useful animals,	DC 89:17

BARNS
do they reap nor gather into b.;	3Ne 13:26
raiment, or for houses, or for b.,	DC 59:17
and their b. shall perish,	121:20

BARREN
it is because your ground is b.,	Al 32:39
Sing, O b., thou that didst	3Ne 22: 1
in the b. deserts there shall	DC 133:29
land shall be b. and unfruitful,	Mses 7: 7

BARRENNESS
the b. thereof shall go forth	Mses 7: 8

BARS
trouble, and into b. and walls,	DC 122: 4

BASE
and the b. against the honorable.	2Ne 13: 5

BASENESS
the b. of the traditions of their	Al 17: 9

BASHAN
upon all the oaks of B.;	2Ne 12:13

BASKET
Their b. shall not be full,	DC 121:20

BASSET, Heman
which was bestowed upon B.	DC 52:37

BATH
of vineyard shall yield one b.,	2Ne 15:10

BATHE
did b. his feet with their tears.	3Ne 17:10

BATHED
his sword is b. in heaven	DC 1:13
the moon shall be b. in blood;	88:87

BATS
to the moles and to the b.;	2Ne 12:20

BATTLE
gathered together to b.,	1Ne 12: 2
were gathered together to b.	12:15
also, to b. against them.	13:17
together against them to b.	13:18
For every b. of the warrior is	2Ne 19: 5
mustereth the hosts of the b.	23: 4
against us, the Nephites, to b.	Jar 1: 7
to b. against his people.	WM 1:13
forth against the Lamanites to b.	Mos 9:16
forth to b. against the Lamanites;	9:17
come up to b. against my people.	10: 6
to go to b. against the Lamanites;	10: 9
go up to b. against the Lamanites;	10:10
go up to b. against the Lamanites.	10:10
up in the strength of the Lord to b.	10:10
to go to b. with their might,	10:19
that the b. became exceeding sore,	20:10
desirous to go against them to b.	21: 6
and they went again to b., but	21:11
against the Amlicites to b.	Al 2:16

BATTLE — BEAR

not many days after the b.	Al	3:20
not go up to b. at this time		3:22
they having waxed strong in b.,		9:22
thus there was a tremendous b.;		28: 2
to b. against the Lamanites,		43:26
not come out to b. against you		44: 2
and cause them to come to b.		46:30
go to b. against the Nephites.		47: 1
go to b. against the Nephites Antipas, in preparation to b.		47: 2
give them b. according to the		47: 7
to go against the Nephites to b.		47: 8
to go to b. against the Nephites.		47:21
to b. after the manner of the		48: 3
did not come down himself to b.		49: 8
they would march thither to b.;		49:11
a b. commenced between them,		49:15
come to b. against the Nephites.		50:35
coming down to b. against them,		51:10
leaders who were not slain in b.		51:13
receive the Lamanites to b.		51:19
city of Nephihah to b.,		51:24
was ready to give them b. on		51:25
to come out against them to b.;		52: 1
led the Lamanites forth to b.		52:19
attempt a b. with the Lamanites		52:33
I will give you b. even until		53: 7
go against the Nephites to b.		54:12
of Judea, or against us, to b.		55:10
will ye go against them to b.?		56:18
a terrible b. had commenced.		56:44
wage a b. with the army which		56:49
could not come to b. with them,		57: 7
should come out to b. against us		58: 6
to come out against us to b.		58:15
Lamanites should come out to b.		58:15
go against the Lamanites to b.,		58:17
shall go up to b. against them.		59: 5
not come out against us to b.		60:33
that they did come to b.		61: 7
come out to b. against them,		62: 7
did not come to b. in that day.		62:19
pitch b. against the Nephites.		62:19
to b. against the Nephites.	He	1:15
Bountiful, and gave unto them b.,		1:17
and did give unto them b.,		1:29
became an exceedingly bloody b.;		1:30
down against the Nephites to b.,		1:30
day we have sought them for b.		4: 5
proved them in the field of b.,		13:34
your noble spirit in the field of b.	3Ne	3: 4
come down against them to b.		3: 5
of robbers had prepared for b.,		3:25
in open b. against the Nephites;		4: 1
go up to b. against the Nephites,		4: 4
go up to b. against the Nephites.		4: 5
that they did come up to b.;		4: 6
day that they did come up to b.;		4: 7
the b. commenced in this the		4: 7
and terrible was the b. thereof,		4:11
robbers did not come again to b.;		4:11
they did not come up to b.,		4:15
the Lamanites did not come to b.		4:16
their arms against the time of b.	Mrm	3: 1
to come again to b. against us.		3: 1
Desolation to b. against us;		3: 4
they did come down again to b.		3: 7
go up to b. against their enemies,		3: 8
had led them many times to b.,		3:10
go up unto their enemies to b.		3:12
to b. against the Lamanites,		3:14
and they had a sore b.		4: 1
again upon the Nephites to b.;		4: 2
an exceedingly sore b. fought		4:10
did come again against us to b.,		4:19
and there we could give them b.		5: 6
that they came to b. against us,		6: 2
and tremendous b. at Cumorah,		6: 8
My father hath been slain in b.,		8: 2
gave b. unto his brother Corihor,		8: 5
he gave b. unto Shule the king,	Eth	7: 9
he gave b. again unto Shule,		7:16
people should give b. unto Shule,		7:17
		7:21
he gave b. unto his father,	Eth	8: 3
an army and gave b. unto Jared.		8: 5
did give b. unto him by night.		8: 5
and gave b. unto the people;		10: 9
he went to b. against the king,		10:32
iniquity, and gave b. unto Moron,		11:15
gave b. unto them who sought to		13:16
he also gave b. unto Coriantumr;		13:23
against him with his armies to b.;		13:27
the b. became exceeding sore.		13:27
Shared gave him b. again upon		13:29
Coriantumr gave Shared b. again		13:30
did not go to b. again for the		13:31
he gave b. unto Coriantumr,		14: 3
of Shared did give b. unto him		14: 4
the b. became exceeding sore,		14: 4
of Moron, and gave b. unto Lib.		14:11
Lib gave b. unto him upon the		14:13
of Agosh he gave b. unto Lib,		14:16
the b. became exceeding sore,		14:16
gave b. unto Shiz for the space of		14:26
of Shiz to invite them forth to b.		14:28
the b. became exceeding sore.		14:29
people of Shiz did give b. unto		15: 6
the morrow they did come to b.		15: 8
fought an exceedingly sore b.,		15: 9
forth one against another to b.;		15:15
morrow they did go again to b.,		15:17
he would not come again to b.,		15:18
they went again to b.		15:19
a sore b. with the Lamanites,	Mro	9: 2
not go up to b. against Zion,	DC	45:70
to b. against Michael and his		88:113
the b. of the great God;		88:114
they should not go out unto b.		98:33
justify them in going out to b.		98:36
as thou didst in the day of b.,		109:28
go forth in b. array against	Mses	7: 7
enemies came to b. against		7:13

BATTLES

had many b. with the Nephites,	Al	25: 3
in the more part of all his b.;		53: 2
in this same year a number of b.,	Mrm	1:11
For Michael shall fight their b.,	DC	88:115
the Lord would fight their b.,		98:37
battles, and their children's b.,		98:37
hands to fight the b. of Zion;		105:14
I will fight your b.		105:14

BAURAK ALE

B. [Joseph Smith, Jun.]	DC	103:21
B. [Joseph Smith, Jun.]		103:22
B. [Joseph Smith, Jun.]		103:35
B. [Joseph Smith, Jun.]		105:16
B. [Joseph Smith, Jun.]		105:27

BDELLIUM

was b. and the onyx stone.	Mses	3:12

BE: see in the APPENDIX.

BEACH

on the b. by the seashore,	Al	51:32

BEAM

considerest not the b. that is	3Ne	14: 3
behold, a b. is in thine own eye?		14: 4
cast the b. out of thine own eye;		14: 5

BEAR

b. record that he had baptized	1Ne	10:10
b. record that it is the Son of God.		11: 7
and I saw and b. record.		11:32
I saw and b. record, that the		11:36
And I also saw and b. record		12: 7
the twelve apostles b. record;		13:24
b. record according to the truth		13:24
I, Nephi, heard and b. record		14:27
I b. record that I saw the things		14:29
more than we are able to b.		16: 1
did b. children in the wilderness.		17: 1
b. their journeyings without		17: 2

BEAR 78 BEASTS

sorrow did thy mother b. thee.	2Ne 3: 1	this people to b. this affliction,	DC 109:49
shall conceive, and shall b. a son,	17:14	to b. testimony of thy name;	109:56
And the cow and the b. shall feed;	21: 7	to b. testimony of my name	112: 1
to b. testimony of his word unto	27:13	shalt b. record of my name,	112: 4
And the cow and the b. shall feed;	30:13	b. glad tidings unto all the world.	114: 1
and b. the shame of the world;	Jac 1: 8	and b. record of my name.	118: 4
sprung forth and begun to b. fruit.	5:17	b. him up as on eagles' wings;	124:18
And I b. record that the people	En 1:20	they should b. it with them	124:38
all my old men that could b. arms,	Mos 10: 9	b. record of the things which	124:96
men that were able to b. arms,	10: 9	b. his proportion of their wages,	124:122
Thou shalt not b. false witness	13:23	to b. record of my name in	124:139
for he shall b. their iniquities.	14:11	to b. record of the book!	128:20
willing to b. one another's burdens	24:15	they may b. the souls of men;	132:63
who are willing to b. my name;	26:18	Be ye clean that b. the vessels	133: 5
they could not b. that any human	28: 3	b. an equal proportion,	136: 8
that every man might b. his patt.	29:34	that will not b. chastisement	136:31
above that which ye can b.,	Al 13:28	ye can not yet b. my glory;	136:37
b. with patience thine afflictions,	26:27	is greater than I can b.	Mses 5:38
I may b. with mine infirmities.	31:30	and made to b. record of me,	6:63
that they may b. their afflictions	31:33	all things b. record of me.	6:63
b. with all manner of afflictions;	34:40	to b. testimony of mine Only	7:62
and b. with those afflictions,	34:41	our wives b. unto us children,	8:21
b. all these things with patience	38: 4	to b. my name in a strange land	Abr 2: 6
could not b. that their brethren	48:25	they shall b. this ministry and	2: 9
and b. false witness against your	He 7:21		
did he not b. record that the	8:14	BEARD	
of a surety and did b. record,	3Ne 11:15	it shall also consume the b.	2Ne 17:20
and I b. record of the Father,	11:32		
and I b. record that the Father	11:32	BEARER	
I b. record of it from the Father;	11:35	be as when a standard-b. fainteth.	2Ne 20:18
will the Father b. record of me,	11:35		
will the Father b. record of me,	11:36	BEARETH	
Holy Ghost will b. record unto	11:36	of whom the Holy Ghost b. record,	1Ne 12:18
and the multitude did b. record	17:15	and the Father b. record of me,	3Ne 11:32
this manner do they b. record:	17:16	the Holy Ghost b. record of the	11:32
did see and hear and b. record;	17:25	the Holy Ghost b. record of the	28:11
therefore they did not b. record;	18:37	the Holy Ghost, which b. record	Eth 12:41
disciples saw and did b. record	18:39	b. all things, believeth all	Mro 7:45
did witness it, and did b. record;	19:14	and the Spirit b. record,	DC 1:39
did hear and do b. record;	19:33	which b. record of the Father	20:27
be ye clean that b. the vessels of	20:41	and b. record of the Father	42:17
barren, thou that didst not b;	22: 1	and the Spirit b. record.	59:24
and he shall know and b. record.	Eth 4:11	which b. record of the Father	Mses 1:24
and the Holy Ghost b. record—	5: 4	which b. record of the Father	5: 9
they may b. testimony of him.	Mro 7:31	which b. record of the Father	7:11
how hard to b. you know not.	DC 19:15		
For they cannot b. meat now,	19:22	BEARING	
heard and b. witness to the words	20:16	again, b. a child in her arms.	1Ne 11:20
and b. the keys of your ministry	27:12	b. the beasts which I had slain;	16:32
that b. the vessels of the Lord.	38:42	b. down against the church;	Al 1: 3
thou shalt b. their infirmities.	42:52	b. down in pure testimony	4:19
and ye cannot b. all things now;	50:40	b. the arms which had been	17:39
to b. testimony of the things	58: 6	b. these tidings unto the	DC 1: 8
b. testimony of the truth in all	58:47	church of Christ, b. my name.—	21:11
except he b. record by the way,	58:59	b. my name before the world,	24:10
that ye might b. record;	61: 4	in b. record of the land upon	58: 7
you may return to b. record,	62: 5	b. record of the things which	58:63
that which he is able to b.	64:20	we heard the voice b. record	76:23
b. testimony in every place,	66: 7	in b. testimony to all the world	84:61
if ye do not b. record that	67: 8	in b. record unto all things	100: 8
and ye shall b. record of me,	68: 6	in b. record of thy name,	109:31
as the Father shall b. record,	68:12	given you every herb b. seed,	Mses 2:29
b. record, and prepare the way	71: 4	b. testimony of the Father and	7:27
Of whom we b. record;	76:14	every herb b. seed that shall	Abr 4:29
the record which we b. is the	76:14		
we saw also, and b. record.	76:25	BEAST	
and to b. the sins of the world,	76:41	a sacrifice of man, neither of b.,	Al 34:10
And again we b. record—	76:50	and whatsoever b. or animal	Eth 6: 4
may be able to b. his presence	76:118	as also the spirit of the b.,	DC 77: 2
ye cannot b. all things now;	78:18	And to every b. of the earth,	Mses 2:30
round about you, to b. you up.	84:88	formed every b. of the field,	3:19
and b. testimony of it unto	84:92	and to every b. of the field;	3:20
that b. the keys of the kingdom	90: 2	subtle than any b. of the field	4: 5
money to b. her expenses,	90:28	and above every b. of the field;	4:20
b. record that I beheld his glory,	93:11	both man and b., and the	8:26
And I, John, b. record, and lo,	93:15	And to every b. of the earth,	Abr 4:30
And I, John, b. record that he	93:16	formed every b. of the field,	5:20
ye b. it patiently and revile not	98:23	to every b. of the field;	5:21
But if ye b. it not patiently,	98:24		
your enemy, and b. it patiently,	98:25	BEASTS	
third time, and ye b. it patiently,	98:26	to be devoured by wild b.	1Ne 7:16
they may b. exceedingly great	109:23	did slay wild b., insomuch that	16:31

BEASTS 79 BECAME

bearing the b. which I had slain;	1Ne	16:32
of the skins of b.;		17:11
that there were b. in the forests		18:25
the b. of the field and the fowls	2Ne	2:15
in the wilderness for b. of prey.		5:24
But wild b. of the desert shall		23:21
And the wild b. of the islands shall		23:22
I went to hunt b. in the forests;	En	1: 3
feeding upon b. of prey,		1:20
and would drink the blood of b.	Jar	1: 6
with bones of men, and of b.,	Mos	8: 8
devoured by the b. of the forest.		8:21
and the dogs, yea, and the wild b.,		12: 2
which is run over by the b.		12:11
is driven by wild and ferocious b.		17:17
by times or at seasons, by wild b.		18: 4
infested by wild and ravenous b.	Al	2:37
and were devoured by those b.		2:38
were mangled by dogs and wild b.		16:10
is driven and slain by wild b.;		25:12
become meat for dogs and wild b.	He	7:19
there were no wild b. nor game	3Ne	4: 2
lion among the b. of the forest,		20:16
lion among the b. of the forest,		21:12
they cast into a den of wild b.;		28:22
did play with the b. as a child		28:22
cast them into dens of wild b.,	4Ne	1:33
they did play with the wild b.		1:33
neither wild b. nor poisonous	Mrm	8:24
did follow the course of the b.,	Eth	9:34
with which they did work their b.		10:26
their flesh like unto wild b.,	Mro	9:10
the b. of the forest and the	DC	29:20
both men and b., the fowls		29:24
the b. of the field and the fowls		49:19
the b. of the field and the fowls		59:16
to understand by the four b.,		77: 2
happiness of man, and of b.,		77: 2
Are the four b. limited to		77: 3
beasts limited to individual b.,		77: 3
limited to four individual b.,		77: 3
and wings which the b. had?		77: 4
flesh also of b. and of the fowls		89:12
for the use of man and of b.,		89:14
but for the b. of the field,		89:14
swine, and for all b. of the field,		89:17
of man, or of the b. of the field,		101:24
of man, and the enmity of b.,		101:26
and the b. of the mountains?		117: 6
b. of the earth after their kind,	Mses	2:24
b. of the earth after their kind,		2:25
dominion over all the b. of		5: 1
b. of the earth after their kind;	Abr	4:24
forth the b. after their kind,		4:25

BEAT

b. their swords into plow-shares,	2Ne	12: 4
Ye b. my people to pieces,		13:15
God will b. us with a few stripes,		28: 8
that the Lamanites did b.,	Mos	21: 8
fell upon her and b. her much.	Al	50:30
they who did b. the Lamanites;		57:22
mighty storm shall b. upon you,	He	5:12
behold, the Nephites did b. them,	3Ne	4:12
and the winds b. upon them.		11:40
blew, and b. upon that house;		14:25
blew, and b. upon that house;		14:27
winds blow, and b. upon them,		18:13
shalt b. in pieces many people;		20:19
Nephites did b. the Lamanites	Mrm	1:11
that I b. him with my army		2: 9
them again, and did b. them;		2:26
that in that year we did b. them,		3: 7
And we did b. them again,		3: 8
did b. again the Lamanites,		4:15
which they did b. the Nephites.		4:19
the Lamanites did not b. them		4:20
in which Shule did b. them	Eth	7:21
he did b. him, insomuch that		13:23
in the fourth year, did b. Shared,		13:24
that Coriantumr b. him,		13:28
behold, he did b. Coriantumr,		13:29
he b. Shared and slew him.		13:30
which Coriantumr did b. him		14: 3
armies of Shiz that they b. them,	Eth	15:10
descend, and b. upon their house,	DC	90: 5

BEATEN

not be b. down by the storm	Al	26: 6
were b. and driven back again		63:15

BEAUTIFUL

A virgin, most b. and fair	1Ne	11:15
and b., like unto my people before		13:15
how b. upon the mountains shall		13:37
put on thy b. garments,	2Ne	8:24
shall the branch of the Lord be b.		14: 2
How b. upon the mountains are	Mos	12:21
And O how b. upon the mountains		15:15
again, how b. upon the mountains		15:16
again, how b. upon the mountains		15:17
For O how b. upon the mountains		15:18
how b. are they to the eyes of them		18:30
even a very b. and pleasant land,		23: 4
put on thy b. garments, O	3Ne	20:36
how b. upon the mountains are		20:40
him an exceedingly b. throne;	Eth	10: 6
yea, and put on thy b. garments,	Mro	10:31
arise and put on her b. garments.	DC	82:14
behold, this is b., that he may		88:130
How b. upon the mountains are		128:19
the morning of a b., clear day,	JS	2:14

BEAUTY

b. thereof was far beyond, yea,	1Ne	11: 8
beyond, yea, exceeding of all b.;		11: 8
burning instead of b.	2Ne	13:24
the b. of the Chaldees' excellency,		23:19
there is no b. that we should desire	Mos	14: 2
charmed with the b. of their women.		19:14
and their b. the beauty of the	DC	42:40
b. of the work of thine own		42:40
For Zion must increase in b.,		82:14

BECAME

they b. a dark, and loathsome, and	1Ne	12:23
wherefore, he b. a devil,	2Ne	2:17
state b. a state of probation,		2:21
and because man b. fallen they		9: 6
and b. the devil, to rise no more.		9: 8
and they b. like unto one body;	Jac	5:74
they b. as yet, conquerors of		7:25
that they b. wild, and ferocious,	En	1:20
b. exceeding rich in gold,	Jar	1: 8
Yea, and they also b. idolatrous,	Mos	11: 7
and therefore he b. a wine-bibber,		11:15
thus they b. the children of God.		18:22
that the battle b. exceeding sore,		20:10
people, and b. his subjects.		22:13
they b. more numerous.		26: 5
it b. expedient that those who		26: 6
by the unbelievers b. so great that		27: 1
they b. a large and wealthy people.		27: 7
he b. a very wicked and an		27: 8
And he b. a great hinderment		27: 9
was so great that he b. dumb,		27:19
yea, and he b. weak, even that		27:19
and b. exceedingly anxious		29:38
they b. more still, and durst not	Al	1:33
b. a lost and fallen people.		12:22
life b. a probationary state;		12:24
and b. high priests of God;		13:10
the church b. general throughout		16:15
who also b. Lamanites.		17:19
b. a servant to king Lamoni.		17:25
and they b. a righteous people,		19:35
For they b. a righteous people;		23: 7
their hatred b. exceeding sore		24: 2
and man b. lost forever,		42: 6
forever, yea, they b. fallen man.		42: 6
they b. subjects to follow after		42: 7
b. a state for them to prepare;		42:10
it b. a preparatory state.		42:10
the Zoramites b. Lamanites;		43: 4
the Lamanites b. frightened,		43:39
it b. expedient that the word of		45:21
they b. more hardened and		47:36
and they b. exceedingly rich;		50:18

BECAME 80 BECAUSE

city b. an exceeding stronghold	Al	53: 5
b. now at this period of time		53:19
it b. expedient that we should		57:11
it b. expedient for us, that we		57:15
it b. a very serious matter to		57:16
it b. expedient that we should		58: 3
it b. expedient that we should		58: 3
Pahoran they b. exceeding strong,		62: 6
thus it b. expedient that this		62:10
it b. expedient for Shiblon		63:11
b. an exceedingly bloody battle;	He	1:30
he b. the leader of the band		2: 4
b. exceeding expert in the working		3: 7
it b. impossible for the Nephites		4:19
that they b. exceeding rich,		6: 9
the sword but b. sore by famine.		11: 5
they b. an exceeding great band		11:26
they b. robbers of Gadianton.		11:26
earth and b. as if they were dead,	3Ne	1:16
that they soon b. converted		1:25
that they b. for themselves,		1:29
that it b. expedient that all the		2:11
and their skin b. white like unto		2:15
daughters b. exceedingly fair,		2:16
game b. scarce in the wilderness—		4:20
it b. the desire of the people of		4:22
thus there b. a great inequality		6:14
b. tribes and leaders of tribes.		7: 3
their tribes b. exceeding great.		7: 4
therefore he b. a king over this		7:10
city there b. a great mountain.		8:10
many smooth places b. rough.		8:13
of the whole earth b. deformed,		8:17
and b. an exceedingly fair and	4Ne	1:10
b. exceedingly more numerous		1:40
and they b. slippery, because	Mrm	1:18
and they b. exceedingly rich.	Eth	6:28
and they b. exceeding fair;		7: 4
until he b. exceeding old;		7: 7
b. mighty as to the strength of		7: 8
he b. a king over that part of		7:16
Jared b. exceeding sorrowful		8: 7
that they b. exceeding rich—		9:16
and the war b. exceeding sore,		10: 9
the people b. exceeding rich under		10:12
also himself b. a great hunter.		10:19
it b. a choice land above all		13: 2
the battle b. exceeding sore.		13:27
the battle b. exceeding sore,		14: 4
the battle b. exceeding sore,		14:16
the people b. troubled by day		14:23
the battle b. exceeding sore.		14:29
and b. as if he had no life.		15:32
and your mind b. darkened.	DC	10: 2
man b. sensual and devilish,		20:20
and b. fallen man.		20:20
he b. subject to the will of		29:40
he b. spiritually dead,		29:41
wherein they b. unholy.		74: 4
b. again, in their infant state,		93:38
they b. very slothful, and they		101:50
it b. a law of earth and in		128: 9
and man b. a living soul,	Mses	3: 7
And it b. also a living soul.		3: 9
parted, and b. into four heads.		3:10
And he b. Satan, yea, even the		4: 4
that it b. pleasant to the eyes,		4:12
wherein he b. Master Mahan,		5:49
b. living souls in the land		6: 9
and so b. of dust a living soul,		6:59
b. quickened in the inner man.		6:65
I b. a rightful heir, a High	Abr	1: 2
for the famine b. very grievous.		2:21
of life, and man b. a living soul.		5: 7
parted and b. into four heads.		5:10
b. general among all the sects	JS	2: 5
my mind b. somewhat partial		2: 8
The persecution b. more bitter		2:60
b. so intolerable that I was		2:61

BECAUSE

b. he prophesieth unto the people	1Ne	1:hd
b. of the things which he saw and		1: 6
b. thou art merciful, thou wilt not	1Ne	1:14
b. of the things which he had		1:15
b. of the things which he testified		1:19
hath chosen, b. of their faith,		1:20
b. of the things which thou hast		2: 1
and b. thou hast been faithful		2: 1
spake b. of the stiffneckedness		2:11
b. he was a visionary man,		2:11
b. of the foolish imaginations		2:11
b. they knew not the dealings of		2:12
b. of the hardness of their hearts		2:18
art thou, Nephi, b. of thy faith,		2:19
b. thou hast not murmured.		3: 6
b. of the commandments of the Lord.		3:16
b. of the wickedness of the people.		3:17
and this b. of your iniquities?		3:29
for she truly had mourned b. of us.		5: 1
sorrowful, b. of their wickedness,		7:20
b. of the thing which I have seen,		8: 3
rejoice in the Lord b. of Nephi		8: 3
I fear exceedingly b. of you;		8: 4
b. of those that were scoffing		8:28
b. of these things which he saw		8:36
Nephi, b. thou believest in the Son		11: 6
tumble to the earth, b. of the quaking		12: 4
fallen b. of the great and terrible		12: 5
b. of their faith in the Lamb		12:10
b. of their faith in him.		12:11
b. of the pride of my seed,		12:19
b. of the many plain and precious		13:29
b. of these things which are taken		13:29
b. of the plain and most precious		13:32
b. of the most plain and precious		13:34
numbers were few b. of the wickedness		14:12
small, b. of the wickedness of the		14:12
b. of the hardness of their hearts,		15: 4
b. of the things which I had seen,		15: 4
b. of the great wickedness of the		15: 4
I was overcome b. of my afflictions,		15: 5
b. of the destructions of my people,		15: 5
b. of the hardness of your hearts?		15:10
cast out b. of that justice		15:35
would not murmur b. of the truth,		16: 3
with me b. of the loss of my bow,		16:18
fatigued, b. of their journeying,		16:19
b. of their sufferings and afflictions		16:20
brethren b. of the loss of my bow,		16:21
b. they had hardened their hearts		16:22
humbled themselves b. of my word;		16:24
chastened b. of his murmuring		16:25
b. of the loss of their father,		16:35
and b. of their afflictions in the		16:35
murmur against my father, b. he had		16:35
Bountiful, b. of its much fruit		17: 5
Bountiful, b. of its much fruit.		17: 6
b. of the hardness of their hearts;		17:19
b. we would hearken unto his words;		17:22
straitened them b. of their iniquity.		17:41
b. of the simpleness of the way,		17:41
soul is rent with anguish b. of you,		17:47
smite us b. of our iniquity,		18:10
the Lord b. of mine afflictions.		18:16
much grief b. of their children,		18:17
b. of their grief and much sorrow,		18:18
b. of the afflictions of their mother;		18:19
excuse myself b. of other men,		19: 6
b. of the weakness which is in me,		19: 6
the world, b. of their iniquity, shall		19: 9
b. of his loving kindness and his		19: 9
b. of their righteousness, unto their		19:11
b. of the groanings of the earth,		19:12
b. they crucify the God of Israel,		19:13
And b. they turn their hearts aside,		19:14
b. I knew that thou art obstinate		20: 4
b. of the wickedness of the pastors		21: 1
b. of the Lord that is faithful.		21: 7
b. of the Holy One of Israel;		22: 5
b. of the righteousness of his people,		22:26
it shall be b. of iniquity;	2Ne	1: 7
with gladness b. of you,		1:21
suffered much sorrow b. of you.		1:24
fear and tremble b. of you,		1:25
murmured b. he hath been plain		1:26

BECAUSE 81 BECAUSE

b. thou hast been faithful	2Ne	1:31
b. of the rudeness of thy brethren.		2: 1
b. of the righteousness of thy		2: 3
b. of the intercession for all,		2:10
b. he had fallen from heaven,		2:18
lost, b. of the transgression of		2:21
And b. that they are redeemed		2:26
b. of their faith their words		3:21
b. of this covenant thou art		3:23
b. of my blessing the Lord God		4: 7
b. of the admonitions of the Lord.		4:13
heart sorroweth b. of my flesh;		4:17
soul grieveth b. of mine iniquities.		4:17
b. of the temptations and the sins		4:18
heart groaneth b. of my sins,		4:19
slacken, b. of mine afflictions?		4:26
yield to sin, b. of my flesh?		4:27
Why am I angry b. of mine enemy?		4:27
anger again b. of mine enemies.		4:29
my strength b. of mine afflictions.		4:29
b. that my heart is broken		4:32
b. of the anger of my brethren.		5: 1
we have had much trial b. of him;		5: 3
afflicted more b. of his words,		5: 3
a sore cursing, b. of their iniquity.		5:21
And b. of their cursing which		5:24
b. ye are of the house of Israel.		6: 5
b. of the prayers of the faithful;		6:11
stink b. the waters are dried up,		7: 2
and they die b. of thirst.		7: 2
b. of the fury of the oppressor,		8:13
b. of the blessings which the Lord		9: 3
and b. man became fallen they		9: 6
b. of the way of deliverance		9:11
upon them, b. of the atonement;		9:25
b. they are rich they despise		9:30
puffed up b. of their learning,		9:42
and b. of his greatness,		9:53
perish in the flesh b. of unbelief,		10: 2
But b. of priestcrafts and		10: 5
Wherefore, b. of their iniquities,		10: 6
b. they be replenished from the		12: 6
b. their tongues and their doings		13: 8
B. the daughters of Zion are		13:16
b. they have no knowledge;		15:13
b. they have cast away the law		15:24
b. I am a man of unclean lips;		16: 5
B. Syria, Ephraim and the son of		17: 5
b. all the land shall become briers		17:24
b. there is no light in them.		18:20
destroyed b. of the anointing.		20:27
b. thou hast destroyed thy land		24:20
b. the rod of him that smote thee		24:29
for b. the words of Isaiah are not		25: 4
among the Jews b. of iniquity,		25: 9
b. of the spirit which is in me.		25:11
reject him, b. of their iniquities,		25:12
alive in Christ b. of our faith;		25:25
b. of the commandments.		25:25
b. they cast out the prophets,		26: 3
b. they yield unto the devil		26:10
b. of the greatness of their		26:20
covered b. of your iniquity.		27: 5
b. of the things which are sealed		27: 8
b. of the glory of the world		27:16
advantage of one b. of his words,		28: 8
B. of pride, and because of		28:12
and b. of false teachers.		28:12
b. of pride they are puffed up.		28:12
b. of their fine sanctuaries;		28:13
b. of their fine clothing;		28:13
b. in their pride they are puffed up.		28:13
b. of pride, and wickedness,		28:14
b. they are taught by the precepts		28:14
b. of the truth of God!		28:28
b. my words shall hiss forth—		29: 3
b. that ye shall receive more		29: 8
b. that I have spoken one word		29: 9
b. that ye have a Bible ye need		29:10
b. of the words which have been		30: 1
it will be b. ye ask not,		32: 4
to mourn b. of the unbelief,		32: 7
my pillow by night, b. of them;	2Ne	33: 3
b. I mean them from whence I		33: 8
b. of faith and great anxiety,	Jac	1: 5
b. of the strict commandment		2: 9
b. some of you have obtained more		2:13
b. of the costliness of your		2:13
b. ye suppose that ye are better		2:13
b. ye were proud in your hearts,		2:20
rejoice exceedingly b. of you.		2:22
b. of your grosser crimes.		2:23
b. of the things which were		2:23
b. of the wickedness and		2:31
b. of their tenderness,		2:33
b. of your bad examples before		2:35
b. of the strictness of the word		2:35
whom ye hate b. of their filthiness		3: 5
b. of this observance, in keeping		3: 6
b. of the iniquity of their fathers;		3: 7
b. of the darkness of their skins;		3: 9
against them b. of their filthiness;		3: 9
filthiness came b. of their fathers.		3: 9
b. of the example that ye have		3:10
that ye may, b. of your filthiness,		3:10
b. of the difficulty of engraving		4: 1
Wherefore, b. of their blindness,		4:14
understand, b. they desired it.		4:14
b. they desired it God hath done		4:14
stumble b. of my overanxiety		4:18
b. of the much strength of the		5:18
b. thou didst graft in the branches		5:34
and b. of their much strength		5:36
b. that the wild branches have		5:37
b. that it hath brought forth		5:37
and b. I plucked not the branches		5:45
b. the branches have overcome		5:48
take strength b. of their goodness;		5:59
b. of the change of the branches,		5:59
And b. that I have preserved		5:60
for b. ye have been diligent		5:75
b. of the fruit of my vineyard.		5:75
b. thou art of the devil.		7:14
b. I have thus lied unto God		7:19
B. of thy faith in Christ,	En	1: 8
to thy desires, b. of thy faith.		1:12
b. of the hardness of their hearts,	Jar	1: 3
b. the Lord had sent the people	Om	1:14
b. of the prophecies of the coming	WM	1: 4
b. of the stiffneckedness of the		1:17
b. of the traditions of their fathers,	Mos	1: 5
b. we have them before our eyes.		1: 6
b. they have been a diligent		1:11
b. of the greatness of the multitude;		2: 8
b. I said unto you that I had spent		2:16
fall b. of his partaking of the		3:26
b. of the exceeding faith which		4: 3
deny the beggar, b. ye have not;		4:24
I give not b. I have not, but		4:24
b. of the Spirit of the Lord		5: 2
b. of the covenant which ye have		5: 7
it is b. of our iniquities		7:20
spilt in vain, and all b. of iniquity.		7:24
And b. he said unto them that		7:27
And now, b. he said this,		7:28
b. of the iniquities of their fathers,		10:12
b. that Nephi was more faithful		10:13
b. they understood not the dealings		10:14
b. they hardened their hearts		10:14
b. they said that he had taken		10:15
b. he departed into the wilderness		10:16
b. they were deceived by the vain		11: 7
b. of this great victory they were		11:19
b. of the wickedness of their king		11:19
b. of their iniquities, shall be		12: 2
will I do b. of their iniquities		12: 7
and this b. of thine iniquities.		12:12
and b. I have told you the truth		13: 4
b. I have spoken the word of God		13: 4
b. I tell you the truth concerning		13: 7
b. of the hardness of their hearts;		13:32
b. he had done no evil,		14: 9
b. he hath poured out his soul		14:12
And b. he dwelleth in flesh		15: 2

b. he was conceived by the power	Mos	15: 3
and the Son, b. of the flesh;		15: 3
b. they would not hearken unto		16: 2
b. they believe in the salvation of		17:15
of diseases b. of your iniquities.		17:16
b. he would not deny the		17:20
b. their wives and their children		19:24
b. thy people did carry away the		20:15
b. we would not hearken unto		20:21
not slay them, b. of the oath		21: 3
the king b. of their afflictions;		21: 6
their cry b. of their iniquities;		21:15
b. of the greatness of their number		21:17
b. so many of their brethren had		21:29
frightened b. of the appearance of		23:26
not destroy them, b. of their wives.		23:34
b. he led their way in the		24:20
b. he had been merciful unto		24:21
b. the kingdom had been conferred		25:13
b. of their belief on the words of		25:18
b. there were so many people that		25:20
b. of their unbelief they could not		26: 3
but b. of the dissensions among		26: 5
b. of thy exceeding faith in the words		26:15
b. of their exceeding faith in the		26:16
b. thou hast established a		26:17
b. thou hast inquired of me		26:19
b. I was like to be cast off.		27:27
b. of their iniquities,		28: 4
b. of the great anxiety of his		28:12
b. all men are not just it is not		29:16
and also b. of their iniquities		29:18
b. of their sincere repentance,		29:19
b. they did humble themselves		29:20
b. they cried mightily unto him		29:20
b. of the liberty which had been		29:39
b. Gideon withstood him with	Al	1: 9
and this b. of their humility;		1:20
b. they were not proud in their		1:20
b. they did impart the word of		1:20
b. of the steadiness of the church		1:29
b. of the greatness of their		3: 1
b. of their transgression and		3: 6
upon them b. of their wickedness		4: 3
b. of their exceeding riches,		4: 6
b. of their many flocks and herds,		4: 6
great joy b. of the resurrection		4:14
b. your faith is strong concerning		7:17
b. of the exceeding diligence		7:26
that b. we are not of thy church		8:12
b. of the wickedness of the people		8:14
b. thou hast fed me and taken		8:26
it is b. of the traditions of		9:16
wroth with me b. I said unto them		9:31
And also b. I said unto them		9:32
b. of the sins of this people,		10: 7
b. it was said by an angel of God.		10: 9
b. they received their wages		11:20
b. I said he shall not save his		11:36
this b. of our being wanderers in		13:23
b. of the plainness of his words		14: 2
b. they had testified so plainly		14: 3
b. they were of thy faith.		14:15
b. they believed in the words of		15: 1
had been slain b. of his iniquity.		15: 3
sore b. of his iniquities;		15: 5
not destroy, b. of its greatness.		16: 9
b. of the traditions of their		17:15
b. their flocks were scattered by		17:28
b. of the fear of being slain.		17:29
b. of the slain of their brethren,		17:36
this people, b. of their murders?		18: 2
b. of his expertness and		18: 3
b. their brethren had scattered		18: 6
b. they had had their flocks		18: 6
b. of the faithfulness of Ammon,		18:10
Is it b. thou hast heard that I		18:16
b. of thy exceeding faith;		19:10
b. of their iniquities and their		19:14
b. he had suffered that the		19:19
b. he slew his servants who had		19:20
b. of the number which he had		19:21
afflict them b. of their iniquities;		19:27
began to rejoice b. of his life.	Al	20:25
B. this is all that thou hast		20:26
b. of being bound with strong		20:29
b. of the generosity and		22: 3
b. of transgression, man had		22:12
b. of the commandment of		22:24
b. of Aaron and his brethren.		22:24
b. he loveth our souls as well as		24:14
b. they had slain their brethren;		25: 1
by fire b. of their belief—		25: 5
by fire b. of his belief in God;		25:11
this b. of the power of his word		26:13
b. of their love towards their		26:31
b. of their love towards their		26:32
b. of their love and of their hatred		26:34
the Amalekites, b. of their loss,		27: 2
b. of the many murders and sins		27: 6
came b. of their sore repentance		27:23
b. they have reason to fear,		28:11
b. of sin and transgression,		28:13
b. of death and destruction		28:14
joy b. of the light of Christ		28:14
b. of the success of my brethren,		29:14
b. of the greatness of their		30: 2
b. of the traditions of your		30:16
B. I do not teach the foolish		30:23
b. I do not teach this people to		30:23
b. of the transgression of a parent.		30:25
child is not guilty b. of its parents.		30:25
b. of the hardness of your heart,		30:46
b. they were pleasing unto the		30:53
b. of the iniquity of the people.		31: 1
b. of the separation of the		31: 2
b. of the iniquity of this people.		31:31
b. of the iniquities of this people.		31:33
and this b. he prayed in faith.		31:38
b. of the coarseness of their		32: 2
b. of their poverty as to the		32: 4
of all men b. of their poverty,		32: 5
b. of our exceeding poverty;		32: 5
for it is b. that ye are cast out,		32:12
b. of your exceeding poverty,		32:12
b. ye are compelled to be humble		32:13
b. ye were compelled to be		32:14
themselves b. of the word?		32:14
b. of their exceeding poverty.		32:15
b. ye are afflicted and cast out—		32:24
b. ye have tried the experiment,		32:33
and this b. ye know, for ye		32:34
unto you, Yea, b. it is light;		32:35
light, is good, b. it is discernible,		32:35
b. it hath no root it withers away,		32:38
is not b. the seed was not good,		32:39
neither is it b. the fruit thereof		32:39
it is b. your ground is barren,		32:39
b. of your diligence and your		32:42
b. ye are cast out of your		33: 2
hear me b. of mine afflictions		33:11
it is b. of thy Son that thou hast		33:11
away from me, b. of thy Son.		33:11
thy judgments b. of thy Son.		33:13
b. they will not understand thy		33:16
upon them b. of thy Son.		33:16
and b. the people would not		33:17
b. of the hardness of their hearts.		33:20
b. they did not believe that it		33:20
should do, b. of your afflictions,		34: 3
b. the Lord hath said he dwelleth		34:36
b. of your exceeding poverty,		34:40
they were angry b. of the word,		35: 3
b. of the strictness of the word,		35:15
For b. of the word which he		36:26
b. those miracles were worked by		37:41
thirst, b. of their transgressions.		37:42
b. of the easiness of the way;		37:46
b. of your steadiness and your		38: 2
b. of thy faithfulness and thy		38: 3
b. the Lord was with thee;		38: 4
this b. of their own iniquity,		40:13
gone far astray b. of this thing.		41: 1
b. it has been spoken concerning		41:10
b. of his own disobedience;		42:12
cometh b. of the atonement;		42:23

BECAUSE 83 BECAUSE

the least point b. of your sins,	Al 42:30	
Nephites b. of their armor,	43:21	
b. of the great destruction	43:39	
angry with us b. of our religion.	44: 2	
b. of our religion and our faith	44: 3	
b. of the stubbornness of	44:17	
numbered b. of the greatness of	44:21	
b. the Lord had again delivered	45: 1	
b. they shall dwindle in unbelief	45:12	
b. they shall sin against so	45:12	
b. of iniquity, this prophecy shall	45:14	
b. of their wars with the	45:21	
b. of their exceeding great riches;	45:24	
b. of their deliverance by the	46: 7	
b. he was a man of cunning	46:10	
b. of their belief in Christ who	46:15	
b. we take upon us the name of	46:18	
b. of that part of his seed	46:25	
b. of the excellent qualities of	46:40	
wroth b. of their disobedience;	47: 3	
reverence him b. of his greatness.	47:22	
b. of the greatness of the number	48: 4	
themselves b. of their words,	48:20	
b. they did not delight in	48:23	
b. the Lamanites had destroyed	49: 3	
b. of the iniquity of the people,	49: 3	
b. of the wisdom of the Nephites	49: 5	
b. of the greatness of their	49: 6	
b. of the highness of the bank	49:18	
b. he had not obtained his desire	49:26	
this b. Moroni had kept the	49:27	
b. of his matchless power in	49:28	
b. of their heed and diligence	49:30	
b. of the assurance of protection	50:12	
b. of the many thousands who	51:11	
b. of the stubbornness of those	51:14	
b. of their much fatigue,	51:33	
b. of the smallness of his	52:23	
were wearied b. of their march,	52:28	
wearied b. of their long march.	52:31	
b. it was easy to guard them	53: 5	
thus b. of iniquity amongst	53: 9	
b. of dissensions and intrigue	53: 9	
b. of their oath that had been	53:11	
b. he knew that Ammoron had a	55: 1	
b. of the fulfilling the oath	56: 8	
b. their forces had slain a vast	56:10	
b. of their long march in so	56:50	
leaders, b. of their weariness,	56:51	
b. of the fall of their leaders,	56:51	
fainted b. of the loss of blood;	57:25	
b. of their exceeding faith in that	57:26	
b. of their rebellion we did cause	57:33	
b. of the goodness of God in	57:36	
b. of their retreats and their	58: 6	
b. the Lamanites did suffer their	58:22	
were weary b. of their march;	58:25	
b. of this our march in the	58:27	
rejoiced b. of the welfare,	59: 1	
b. of the wickedness of the	59:11	
b. of the wickedness of the	59:12	
b. of the success of the	59:12	
b. of their indifference	59:13	
b. of their great desires which	60: 9	
b. of your exceeding great	60: 9	
b. of the exceeding goodness of	60:11	
b. so many of your brethren have	60:12	
it is b. of their wickedness?	60:12	
are lost b. they are slain;	60:13	
b. of their exceeding slothfulness,	60:14	
this b. of the great wickedness	60:17	
b. ye are in the heart of our	60:19	
this b. of their exceeding faith,	60:26	
it is b. of your iniquity that we	60:28	
b. of the faithfulness of Pahoran,	62: 1	
b. of the iniquity of those who	62: 2	
b. of those who had rebelled	62: 2	
b. of the greatness of the march;	62:35	
b. of the prayers of the righteous,	62:40	
b. of the exceeding great length of	62:41	
b. of the exceeding great length of	62:41	
softened b. of their afflictions,	62:41	
b. of so many wars and	62:44	

b. of so much contention and	He 1:18	
b. of the many inhabitants who	3: 5	
but b. of the greatness of the	3: 6	
b. of their yielding their hearts	3:35	
b. of their exceeding great riches	3:36	
b. of the pride of their hearts,	4:12	
b. of their exceeding riches,	4:12	
b. of their oppression to the poor,	4:12	
b. of this their great wickedness,	4:13	
the people b. of their iniquity,	4:14	
b. of the greatness of the	4:20	
And b. of their iniquity	4:23	
b. the Spirit of the Lord doth not	4:24	
weak, b. of their transgression,	4:26	
weary b. of their iniquity;	5: 4	
from their sins b. of repentance;	5:11	
b. of the rock upon which ye are	5:12	
b. of the cloud of darkness which	5:34	
b. of the fear which did come	5:34	
b. of your faith in my	5:47	
b. of the greatness of the	5:50	
b. of their firmness and their	6: 1	
joy b. of the conversion of	6: 3	
yea, b. of the church of God,	6: 3	
b. of the wickedness and the	6:35	
b. of their easiness and	6:36	
b. of their righteousness;	7: 5	
unpunished b. of their money;	7: 5	
b. of this the wickedness of	7: 9	
b. I have got upon my tower	7:14	
b. of the exceeding sorrow of my	7:14	
which is b. of your iniquities!	7:14	
And b. of my mourning and	7:15	
marvel b. ye are given away	7:15	
It is b. you have hardened	7:18	
b. of that great abomination	7:25	
b. of that pride which ye have	7:26	
b. of your exceeding great riches!	7:26	
b. of your wickedness and	7:27	
b. it is not of myself that I	7:29	
b. the Lord God has made them	7:29	
b. he spake plainly unto them	8: 4	
compelled b. of their fear,	8:10	
b. he testified of these things.	8:22	
b. of that which is to come.	8:23	
ripening, b. of your murders	8:26	
b. of the great destruction which	9:22	
b. I have testified unto you that	9:23	
And b. I have done this, ye say	9:24	
b. I showed unto you this sign	9:24	
B. of this fear and this paleness	9:34	
believed b. of the testimony of	9:39	
cast down b. of the wickedness	10: 3	
b. thou hast done this with such	10: 5	
b. of this their humility wilt	11:11	
repented, b. of the famine and	11:15	
b. of the exceeding greatness of	11:31	
the people b. of their iniquity,	11:34	
and this b. of their ease,	12: 2	
b. of the iniquity of him who	12:18	
B. of thine iniquities, thou shalt	12:20	
B. of thine iniquities thou shalt	12:21	
B. of the hardness of the hearts	13: 8	
b. of those who are righteous	13:12	
b. of the wickedness and	13:14	
b. of the wickedness and	13:16	
b. of the people's sake who are	13:17	
b. of their wickedness and their	13:17	
b. of the great curse of the land,	13:18	
b. of the curse of the land.	13:19	
b. they have set their hearts upon	13:20	
b. they have set their hearts upon	13:20	
b. they will not hide them up	13:20	
ye are cursed b. of your riches,	13:21	
b. ye have set your hearts upon	13:21	
and this b. of your iniquities.	13:23	
b. of this time which has arrived,	13:24	
b. he testifieth that your deeds	13:26	
b. he speaketh flattering words	13:28	
the land b. of your iniquity.	13:30	
b. of the curse of the land.	13:35	
And now, b. I am a Lamanite,	14:10	
and b. it was hard against you,	14:10	

BECAUSE

await you b. of your iniquities,	He	14:11
chastened them b. he loveth them.		15: 3
b. their deeds have been evil		15: 4
this b. of the iniquity of the		15: 4
this b. of their faith in Christ.		15: 9
b. of their steadfastness when		15:10
b. of their firmness when they		15:10
b. of the traditions of their fathers,		15:15
saith the Lord, b. of their unbelief		15:17
b. of the power of the devil which		16: 6
b. of their faith in the tradition	3Ne	1:11
of the Father b. of me,		1:14
and of the Son b. of my flesh,		1:14
b. there was no darkness when		1:15
to fear b. of their iniquity		1:18
b. of the sign which had been		1:19
b. of the signs which did come		1:26
b. there were many dissenters of		1:28
b. of the wickedness of the		1:30
utter destruction b. of this war,		2:13
b. of the wickedness of the people		2:18
and this b. of their iniquity.		2:19
great praise b. of your firmness,		3: 2
b. of the many wrongs which ye		3: 4
b. of your firmness in that which		3: 5
b. of your wickedness in		3:10
b. of the boldness of Giddianhi		3:11
b. of the great curse which was		3:24
sorrowful b. of their enemy.		3:26
of Giddianhi, b. of their armor,		4: 7
b. of their being dyed in blood.		4: 7
a loud voice, b. of their joy,		4: 9
b. of the terror of their armies.		4: 9
weary b. of his much fighting		4:14
b. of their much provision		4:18
B. of the scantiness of provisions		4:19
b. of the great destruction		4:22
weakness b. of the want of food,		4:24
seek to slay them b. of power		4:29
b. of the great goodness of God		4:33
it was b. of their repentance and		4:33
b. of the many signs which		5: 2
b. of the things which had come		5: 2
b. of their exceeding great riches,		6:10
ignorant b. of their poverty		6:12
great learning b. of their riches		6:12
angry b. of those who testified		6:21
b. they did yield themselves		7: 5
b. of the secret combination of		7: 6
b. he had greater power than		7:18
angry with him b. of his power;		7:20
changed, b. of the tempest and		8:12
deformed b. of the tempests,		8:17
no light, b. of the darkness,		8:21
b. of the darkness and the		8:23
b. of the slain of the fair sons		9: 2
it is b. of their iniquity and		9: 2
burned with fire b. of their sins		9: 9
b. of their secret murders and		9: 9
b. of their wickedness in		9:10
b. they did cast them all out,		9:11
b. of their wickedness and their		9:12
spared b. ye were more righteous		9:13
b. of their faith in me at		9:20
b. of the loss of their kindred		10: 8
b. they testified of these things.		10:15
b. they testified particularly		10:16
b. that ye shall testify that ye		12: 2
b. thou canst not make one hair		12:36
B. strait is the gate and narrow		14:14
b. I said unto you that old		15: 7
b. of stiffneckedness and		15:18
among them b. of their iniquity		15:19
therefore it is b. of their iniquity		15:19
and it is b. of their iniquity that		15:20
of the earth b. of their unbelief,		16: 4
b. of their belief in me,		16: 6
Behold, b. of their belief in,		16: 7
and b. of the unbelief of you,		16: 7
b. of the mercies of the Father		16: 9
troubled b. of the wickedness		17:14
Blessed are ye b. of your faith.		17:20
b. of the disputations which		18:34
b. it is expedient that I	3Ne	18:35
and it is b. of their belief in me		19:20
b. they believe in me;		19:22
in me b. thou hearest them,		19:22
pray unto me b. I am with them.		19:22
have chosen, b. of their faith,		19:28
b. of their faith that they may		19:29
miracles, b. of their unbelief.		19:35
this b. ye are the children of		20:26
in belief b. of iniquity;		21: 5
he shall be marred b. of them.		21:10
and dispute b. of this thing?		27: 4
it is b. of their works that they		27:12
Father, b. my Father sent me.		27:13
b. of the justice of the Father.		27:17
in my blood, b. of their faith,		27:19
even unto fulness, b. of you,		27:30
b. of you and this generation;		27:30
b. of the fourth generation		27:32
b. ye desired this thing of me;		28: 3
b. of the thing which ye have		28: 9
the children of men, b. of me.		28:11
b. of the commandment which		28:16
b. of the convincing power of		28:29
b. of the love of God which did	4Ne	1:15
b. of their prosperity in Christ.		1:23
forbidden b. of unworthiness.		1:27
exceedingly b. of iniquity,		1:28
b. of the power of Satan who		1:28
b. of their humility and their		1:29
b. of the many miracles which		1:29
it was b. of the wickedness and		1:39
b. of their exceeding riches,		1:43
b. of the iniquity of the people.	Mrm	1:13
b. of their wickedness and		1:14
b. of their iniquity.		1:16
b. of the hardness of their hearts;		1:17
b. of the hardness of their hearts		1:17
b. the Lord had cursed the land,		1:18
all the land b. of these things,		2:11
b. of the goodness of God;		2:13
b. the Lord would not always		2:13
wo is me b. of their wickedness;		2:19
sorrow b. of their wickedness,		2:19
b. of this the great calamity of		2:27
b. of their wickedness and their		2:27
b. of this great thing which my		3: 3
b. of their wickedness and		3:11
b. of the hardness of their hearts.		3:12
b. this people repented not		3:15
b. the armies of the Nephites		4: 4
this b. their number did exceed		4:13
b. the Lamanites had sacrificed		4:15
b. of the greatness of their		4:17
b. of the commandment which I		5: 9
b. of the wickedness of this		5: 9
b. it is known of God that		5:12
and this b. of their unbelief		5:15
b. of the greatness of their		6: 8
b. of the slain of my people,		6:16
b. of the imperfections which		8:12
b. of the commandment of the		8:14
b. of the power of his word.		8:24
b. of secret combinations and		8:27
b. of the pride of your hearts.		8:36
b. of the praise of the world?		8:38
b. of the fall of man came Jesus		9:12
and b. of Jesus Christ came the		9:12
b. of the redemption of man,		9:13
b. the death of Christ bringeth		9:13
b. that they dwindle in unbelief,		9:20
Condemn me not b. of mine		9:31
father, b. of his imperfection,		9:31
b. this long time ye have cried	Eth	1:43
b. he remembered not to call		2:14
Shelem, b. of its exceeding height,		3: 1
b. of his weakness before thee;		3: 2
b. of the fall our fathers have		3: 2
smitten us b. of our iniquity,		3: 3
B. of thy faith thou hast seen		3: 9
B. thou knowest these things		3:13
b. of the many great works		3:18
b. of the knowledge of this man		3:19

BECAUSE

b. of my Spirit he shall know	Eth	4:11
which is hid up b. of unbelief.		4:13
come unto you, b. of unbelief.		4:14
b. of the mountain waves which		6: 6
b. of the multitude of his tender		6:12
b. of the thing which Shule had		7:10
b. the people did repent of their		7:26
b. of his cunning words, until he		8: 2
angry b. of the doings of Jared		8: 5
b. of the loss of the kingdom,		8: 7
b. of this secret combination		8:24
b. of the blood of them who		8:24
b. of the secret combinations		9: 1
b. of that which his father had		9: 8
fast b. of the dearth,		9:30
b. of his exceeding riches,		10: 3
b. of his many whoredoms;		10:11
b. of their wicked combinations;		11: 7
b. of that secret combination		11:15
b. of their secret society and		11:22
b. of the Spirit of the Lord which		12: 2
b. they saw them not.		12: 5
dispute not b. ye see not,		12: 6
b. of the faith of men he has		12: 8
b. of his word which he had		12:20
b. of the promise which the		12:21
b. of our weakness in writing;		12:23
b. of the Holy Ghost which thou		12:23
b. of the awkwardness of our		12:24
b. of the placing of our words;		12:25
b. of our weakness, that thou		12:35
b. thou hast seen thy weakness		12:37
b. of my weakness in writing.		12:40
b. of the iniquity of the people,		14: 1
b. of secret combinations.		14: 8
b. of the scent thereof.		14:23
b. of their hatred they put to	Mro	1: 2
b. of the gift of his calling unto		7: 2
b. of your peaceable walk with		7: 4
b. Christ hath ascended into		7:27
b. he hath done this, my beloved		7:29
for it is b. of unbelief,		7:37
in Christ b. of your meekness;		7:39
and this b. of your faith in him		7:41
saveth one child b. of baptism,		8:15
perish b. he hath no baptism.		8:15
all alive in him b. of his mercy.		8:19
b. of meekness and lowliness of		8:26
b. of the hardness of their		9:10
b. of the wilfulness of their		9:23
despair cometh b. of iniquity.		10:22
you, it shall be b. of unbelief.		10:24
but b. of transgression,	DC	3: 9
b. of the iniquity of their fathers,		3:18
b. of their iniquities and their		3:18
b. I foresee the lying in wait		5:32
blessed art thou b. of thy gift.		6:10
unto thee b. of thy desires;		6:20
b. of the wickedness of the		6:26
been hidden b. of iniquity.		6:27
b. thou desirest this thou shalt		7: 3
b. you did not translate		9: 1
it is b. that you did not continue		9: 5
b. you delivered up those writings		10: 1
b. you have delivered the		10: 8
b. they have altered the words,		10:11
b. their deeds are evil;		10:21
b. he supposeth that another lieth		10:28
b. Satan saith unto them:		10:29
b. I show unto you wisdom,		10:34
b. the account which is		10:40
b. of their dissensions.		10:48
and it is b. he had faith.		17: 5
b. of the thing which you,		18: 1
to tremble b. of pain,		19:18
it is b. of your dead works		22: 3
and this b. of thy family.		23: 3
b. of the things which thou hast		25: 4
b. of the wickedness of the world,		29:17
b. ye have asked it of me		29:33
from me b. of their agency;		29:36
b. he yielded unto temptation.		29:40
b. of his transgression,	DC	29:41
b. they repent not;		29:44
b. of your faith in my work.		31: 1
afflictions b. of your family;		31: 2
instances b. of priestcrafts,		33: 4
b. you have believed;		34: 4
b. you are called of me to preach		34: 5
and this b. of the enemy		37: 1
not b. of your iniquity,		38:14
things b. of your prayers;		38:30
b. of pride and the cares of the		39: 9
this b. his heart is pure		41:11
found it not b. of wickedness		45:12
b. of the precepts of men.		45:29
they weep b. of their iniquities;		45:53
b. they persecuted their king.		45:53
b. of the terror of the Lord,		45:75
b. he reasoneth as a man;		50:12
b. you seek to counsel in your		56:14
b. of the fear of man.		60: 2
b. these things are among you.		63:19
not b. ye forgive not,		64:13
earth shall tremble b. of her,		64:43
shall fear b. of her terrible ones.		64:43
sin, b. they come not unto me.		84:50
been darkened b. of unbelief,		84:54
b. you have treated lightly the		84:54
b. they were not willing to enjoy		88:32
b. you cannot see him —		88:66
my voice, b. my voice is Spirit;		88:66
Father b. he gave me of his fulness,		93: 4
Son b. I was in the world		93: 4
b. the world was made by him,		93: 9
b. he received not of the fulness		93:14
b. that which was from the		93:31
b. of the tradition of their		93:39
no sorrow b. there is no death.		101:29
yet b. this widow troubleth me		101:84
b. they did not hearken		103: 4
b. I, the Lord, have promised		104: 7
b. Melchizedek was such a		107: 2
b. it was conferred upon Aaron		107:13
b. it is an appendage to the		107:14
B. the promise is, if these things		107:31
B. he (Seth) was a perfect man,		107:43
b. you have obeyed my voice		108: 1
b. of their transgressions,		109:38
b. of their grievous burdens,		109:48
smitten b. of their transgression,		109:65
earth slumber, b. of thy speech.		112: 5
b., said he, it is the place		116: 1
b. their hearts are corrupted,		121:13
b. they are the servants of sin,		121:17
b. they have offended my little		121:19
B. their hearts are set so much		121:35
b. of thy righteousness;		122: 4
b. they know not where to find		123:12
b. of the integrity of his heart,		124:15
b. he loveth that which is		124:15
b. of the integrity of his heart;		124:20
b. they pollute mine holy		124:46
b. of the sickness of the land.		124:87
b. it is contrary to the order		129: 7
b. they are not joined by me,		132:18
b. the angels and the gods are		132:18
be gods, b. they have no end;		132:20
to everlasting, b. they continue;		132:20
b. all things are subject unto		132:20
be gods, b. they have all power,		132:20
b. ye receive me not in the		132:22
b. they receive me not, neither		132:25
also, b. ye are of Abraham,		132:31
B. this was the law;		132:34
B. they were given unto him,		132:37
b. they did none other things		132:37
b. she did not believe and		132:65
b. thou hast seen thy weakness,		135: 5
marveled b. of his death;		136:39
b. of wickedness it is not had	Mses	1:23
b. that in it I had rested from		3: 3
b. she was taken out of man.		3:23
b. that Satan rebelled against		4: 3

BECAUSE 86 BECOME

b. I beheld that I was naked,	Mses	4:16
B. thou hast done this thou		4:20
B. thou hast hearkened unto the		4:23
b. she was the mother of all		4:26
b. of my transgression my eyes		5:10
b. of Cain and his brethren,		5:27
b. of my brother's flocks.		5:38
slay me, b. of mine iniquities,		5:39
b. that Lamech had spoken		5:53
b. of secret works, seeking for		6:15
men were offended b. of him.		6:37
B. that Adam fell, we are;		6:48
b. they were of one heart and		7:18
b. of the wickedness of my		7:48
b. of the ground which the Lord		8: 9
offered up b. of their virtue;	Abr	1:11
this b. they have turned their		1:17
tormented b. of the famine,		1:30
b. we had already come into		2:18
my soul shall live b. of thee.		2:25
Kolob, b. it is near unto me,		3: 3
b. it standeth above the earth,		3: 5
b. it is nearest unto me.		3:16
b. they had not formed		4: 2
b. that on the seventh time		5: 3
b. she was taken out of man;		5:17
And b. iniquity shall abound,	JS	1:10
again, b. iniquity shall abound,		1:30
b. I continued to affirm that I		2:27

BECKONED

I b. unto them; and I also did say	1 Ne	8:15

BECOME

food b. sweet, that ye cook it not;	1 Ne	17:12
they have b. wicked, yea, nearly		17:43
b. a hiss and a by word, and be hated		19:14
those who are built up to b. popular		22:23
and b. miserable forever.	2 Ne	2: 5
and had b. miserable forever,		2:18
they have b. free forever,		2:26
they had b. like unto a flint;		5:21
they did b. an idle people,		5:24
b. subject unto man in the flesh,		9: 5
all men might b. subject unto him.		9: 5
b. subject to that angel who fell		9: 8
must have b. like unto him,		9: 9
and we b. devils, angels to a devil,		9: 9
and all men b. incorruptible,		9:13
insomuch as they have b. immortal,		9:15
they shall b. a righteous branch		9:53
queens shall b. nursing mothers;		10: 9
the land shall b. briers and thorns.		17:24
he also has b. my salvation.		22: 2
Art thou also b. weak as we?		24:10
Art thou b. like unto us?		24:10
the law hath b. dead unto us,		25:25
they have b. corrupted.		28:11
their churches have b. corrupted,		28:12
shall also b. a delightsome people.		30: 7
they shall b. a blessed people.	Jac	3: 6
may not b. angels to the devil,		3:11
this stone shall b. the great,		4:16
it may b. the head of their corner?		4:17
and it will soon b. ripened,		5:37
natural branches had b. corrupt		5:39
and they had all b. corrupt.		5:39
were these, had b. corrupted.		5:42
fruit have also b. corrupted;		5:42
trees thereof have b. corrupted,		5:46
b. like unto the wild olive-tree,		5:46
thy vineyard have b. corrupted?		5:48
natural tree which had b. wild,		5:55
trees, which also had b. wild.		5:55
natural trees which had b. wild,		5:56
had b. again the natural fruit;		5:74
they had b. exceeding numerous.	Om	1:17
their language had b. corrupted;		1:17
might b. men of understanding;	Mos	1: 2
and b. a wicked and an adulterous		1:13
b. weak like unto their brethren;		1:13
and b. victims to their hatred,		1:14
and b. as little children,		3:18

born of him and have b. his sons	Mos	5: 7
he might not b. burdensome		6: 7
b. even as Alma and his brethren,		21:34
And thus they b. new creatures;		27:26
might b. friendly to one another,		28: 2
and teacher ought to b. popular;	Al	1: 3
b. far more wealthy than those		1:31
to b. subjects to the devil?		5:20
Thus they b. high priests		13: 9
until it did b. exceeding sore,		15: 3
and our swords have b. bright,		24:12
they b. more hardened,		24:30
that thou shalt b. dumb,		30:47
it will b. a tree, springing up in		33:23
have b. subjected to the spirit of		34:35
that ye may not b. his subjects		34:39
lest ye b. sinners like unto them;		34:40
b. extinct both soul and body,		36:15
that the man had b. as God,		42: 3
as they had b. carnal, sensual,		42:10
that ye may b. extinct.		44: 7
people of Nephi shall b. extinct—		45:11
and shall b. like unto them,		45:14
even until they shall b. extinct.		45:14
again b. an easy prey for them.		49: 3
b. strong, yea, even to exceed		49:14
had b. an exceeding stronghold.		55:33
and authority shall b. extinct.		60:27
of Ammon and b. a free people.		62:27
many had b. hardened, because		62:41
b. expedient that a regulation		62:44
that their laws had b. corrupted,	He	4:22
they had b. a wicked people,		4:22
they saw that they had b. weak,		4:24
yea, thus had they b. weak,		4:26
for the laws had b. corrupted.		5: 2
Nephi had b. weary because of		5: 4
and the Lamanites had b.,		6: 1
Nephites who had b. hardened		6: 2
and thus they did b. rich.		6:11
they had b. exceedingly wicked;		6:31
b. meat for dogs and wild beasts.		7:19
thou cast down and b. smooth,		10: 9
that they have b. extinct,		11;10
are broken up, and b. smooth,		12:10
your riches, that they b. slippery,		13:31
they would not have b. slippery		13:33
and all things are b. slippery,		13:36
valleys which shall b. mountains,		14:23
and many cities shall b. desolate.		14:24
robbers had b. so numerous,	3 Ne	2:11
Lamanites who had b. converted		2:12
which had b. exceedingly sore.		2:13
and did b. exceedingly sore;		2:17
b. acquainted with our secret		3: 7
b. our brethren that ye may be		3: 7
until ye shall b. extinct.		3: 8
it hath b. expedient that I,		5:14
people had nearly all b. wicked,		7: 7
b. sufficiently strong to contend		7:12
given to b. the sons of God;		9:17
your dwellings shall b. desolate		10: 7
repent, and b. as a little child,		11:37
and b. as a little child,		11:38
and all things have b. new.		12:47
and that all things had b. new.		15: 2
and that all things had b. new.		15: 3
and to b. hated by them,		16: 9
and to b. a hiss and a by-word		16: 9
b. like unto the son of perdition,		29: 7
they had b. exceeding rich,	4 Ne	1:23
b. vain like unto their brethren,		1:43
b. exceeding wicked		1:45
had b. covered with buildings,	Mrm	1: 7
would again b. a righteous people.		2:12
therefore we had b. weak		2:26
and shall b. a dark, a filthy,		5:15
soon b. incorruptible bodies;		6:21
and churches b. defiled and be		8:28
have b. polluted because of		8:36
natures have b. evil continually;	Eth	3: 2
they shall b. my sons and my		3:14
and b. clean before the Lord.		4: 6

BECOME   87   BEFORE

they may b. sanctified in me, Eth 4: 7
had b. exceeding numerous. 7:11
they had b. exceeding strong, 9:16
should b. as heaps of earth 11: 6
weak things b. strong unto them. 12:27
and b. a holy city of the Lord; 13: 5
and all things have b. new. 13: 9
to b. a prey to the worms of 14:22
faith, they b. the sons of God. Mro 7:26
ye may b. the sons of God; 7:48
have b. strong in their perversion; 9:19
things shall b. subject unto him, 9:26
that ye b. holy, without spot. 10:33
and b. as other men, DC 3:11
also all that had b. Lamanites 10:48
power to b. the sons of God, 11:30
and all things shall b. new, 29:24
to b. accountable before me; 29:47
my vineyard has b. corrupted 33: 4
shall b. even as Nephi of old, 33: 8
believe might b. the sons of God. 34: 3
they may b. the sons of God, 35: 2
lest ye b. as the Nephites of old. 38:39
gave I power to b. my sons; 39: 4
power to b. my sons. 39: 4
my gospel, and b. sanctified, 39:18
have power to b. my sons; 42:52
ye shall b. instructed in the law of 43: 9
and to b. the sons of God; 45: 8
rough places to b. smooth— 49:23
b. truly humble before me 54: 3
has b. void and of none effect. 54: 4
away, and all things b. new, 63:49
shall grow up until they b. old; 63:51
they b. heirs according to the 70: 8
b. subject to the law of Moses, 74: 3
b. blinded and understand not 78:10
unto you, ye b. transgressors; 82: 4
to b. the common property of 82:18
They b. the sons of Moses 84:34
that ye b. even as my friends 84:77
that he may b. strong also. 84:106
and shall b. exceedingly angry, 87: 5
seeketh to b. a law unto itself, 88:35
your minds b. single to God, 88:68
stars shall b. exceedingly angry, 88:87
that it may b. a sanctuary, 88:137
b. acquainted with all good 90:15
b. a member of the order, 96: 8
b. very glorious, very great, 97:18
and all things shall b. new, 101:25
let my army b. very great, 105:31
that it may b. fair as the sun, 105:31
let us b. subject unto her laws. 105:32
may b. a great mountain and fill 109:72
all flesh has b. corrupt before 112:23
if fierce winds b. thine enemy; 122: 7
has b. a second nature to him; 127: 2
will b. a Urim and Thummim to 130:10
the islands shall b. one land; 133:23
Their enemies shall b. a prey 133:28
little one b. a strong nation, 133:58
the man is b. as one of us to Mses 4:28
and men have b. carnal, sensual, 6:49
and thus may all b. my sons. 6:68
believed and b. the sons of God, 7: 1
wickedness of men had b. great 8:22
had b. very friendly to me, JS 2:75

BECOMES
thus their state b. worse than Al 24:30
the army fo Israel b. very great. DC 105:26
it b. necessary to have other 107:74
she then b. the transgressor; 132:65

BECOMETH
and our faith b. unshaken, Jac 4: 6
b. an enemy to all righteousness; Mos 2:37
b. a saint through the atonement 3:19
and b. as a child, submissive, 3:19
he b. a great benefit to his fellow 8:18
the same b. a child of the devil, Al 5:41
what b. of the souls of men 40: 7

what b. of the souls of men Al 40: 9
and b. expedient that he dieth, He 14:15
it b. every man who hath been DC 88:81
as b. saints, to the poor and 105: 3

BECOMING
thus b. the Father and Son— Mos 15: 3
the flesh b. subject to the Spirit, 15: 5
flesh b. subject even unto death, 15: 7
b. carnal, sensual, devilish, 16: 3
of God, b. his sons and daughters, 27:25
whole b. spiritual and immortal, Al 11:45
b. as Gods, knowing good from 12:31
b. humble, meek, submissive, 13:28
b. wicked, and wild, and ferocious, He 3:16
yea, even b. Lamanites. 3:16

BED
and he cast himself upon his b., 1Ne 1: 7
they found him upon his b., sick, Al 15: 5
his wife, and laid him upon a b.; 18:43
laid upon his b. for the space of 19: 5
she watched over the b. of her 19:11
retire to thy b. early, that ye DC 88:124
retired to my b. for the night, JS 2:29
shortly after arose from my b., 2:48

BEDS
down, yea, even upon their sick-b. 1Ne 18:17

BEDSIDE
personage appeared at my b., JS 2:30
messenger was again by my b. 2:44
the same messenger at my b., 2:46

BEDSTEAD
was made after the form of a b., Abr 1:13

BEE
the b. that is in the land of Assyria. 2Ne 17:18
by interpretation, is a honey b.; Eth 2: 3

BEEN: *see in the APPENDIX.*

BEES
did carry with them swarms of b., Eth 2: 3

BEFALL
all things which shall b. us He 8: 8
which are soon to b. the nations. DC 101:98
should b. his posterity unto 107:56
even what shall b. them in 124: 5

BEFALLEN
All things which have b. them JS 1:19

BEFORE
and dwelt upon a rock b. him; 1Ne 1: 6
came and stood b. my father, 1:11
their frames did shake b. him. 2:14
did flee b. the servants of Laban, 3:26
came and stood b. them, and he 3:29
he had fallen to the earth b. me, 4: 7
they fled from b. my presence; 4:28
was about to flee from b. me 4:30
and I stood b. my brethren, 7:18
they did bow down b. me, and 7:20
and he came and stood b. me. 8: 5
above all that I ever b. tasted. 8:11
who should come b. the Messiah, 10: 7
b. the judgment-seat of God; 10:21
which I never had b. seen, 11: 1
which I never had b. set my foot. 11: 1
he had gone from b. my presence. 11:12
came down and stood b. me; 11:14
should prepare the way b. him. 11:27
in the Spirit from b. my face, 11:29
they were scattered b. the Gentiles 13:14
unto my people b. they were slain. 13:15
did humble themselves b. the Lord; 13:16
wickedness and abomination b. him. 14: 4
did humble themselves b. the Lord. 15:20
to stand b. God, to be judged 15:33

BEFORE

ye might walk uprightly b. God,	1 Ne 16: 3
did humble themselves b. the Lord;	16: 5
did humble themselves b. the Lord,	16:32
I will prepare the way b. you,	17:13
b. they came out of Jerusalem	17:20
their Redeemer, going b. them,	17:30
as naught b. the power of God,	17:48
lest they should wither b. me,	17:52
they shall not wither b. thee,	17:53
they did not wither b. me;	17:54
And they fell down b. me,	17:55
themselves again b. the Lord.	18: 4
were driven forth b. the wind	18: 8
had been driven forth b. the wind	18: 9
transpired b. I made these plates	19: 2
b. it came to pass I showed them	20: 5
b. the day when thou heardest them	20: 7
cut off nor destroyed from b. me.	20:19
thy walls are continually b. me.	21:16
sought that which was evil b. God.	2 Ne 2:17
of Lemuel to be brought b. him.	4: 8
and also my father, b. his death;	4:14
causing of them to quake b. me.	4:22
bold in mighty prayer b. him;	4:24
hell be shut continually b. me,	4:32
gates of thy righteousness b. me,	4:32
for mine escape b. mine enemies!	4:33
thou make my path straight b. me!	4:33
thou wouldst clear my way b. me,	4:33
angel who fell from b. the presence	9: 8
must appear b. the judgment-seat	9:15
that all might stand b. him	9:22
lieth in a straight course b. him.	9:41
consider themselves fools b. God,	9:42
and I shake them b. you;	9:44
I stand with brightness b. him,	9:44
For b. the child shall know	17:16
b. the riches of Damascus	18: 4
away b. the king of Assyria.	18: 4
they joy b. thee according to	19: 3
Syrians b. and the Philistines behind;	19:12
dashed to pieces b. their eyes;	23:16
which he did raise up b. them,	25:20
wherefore ye must bow down b. him,	25:29
b. the presence of the Lord;	26: 7
must stand b. the throne of God,	28:23
he humbleth himself b. the Father,	31: 7
he having set the example b. them.	31: 9
and no deception b. God,	31:13
shall stand face to face b. his bar;	33:11
b. the presence of my Maker,	Jac 2: 6
b. your wives and your children,	2: 7
and chaste and delicate b. God,	2: 7
But b. ye seek for riches,	2:18
thing which be abominable b. me,	2:24
are an abomination b. me;	2:28
wherefore, ye have known them b.;	2:34
of your bad examples b. them;	2:35
that are filthy this day b. God;	3: 3
with them b. the throne of God.	3: 8
that ye have set b. them;	3:10
many hundred years b. his coming;	4: 4
holy prophets which were b. us.	4: 4
b. he manifesteth himself in the	4:11
awful guilt b. the bar of God?	6: 9
you b. the pleasing bar of God,	6:13
unto the people b. I shall die.	7:16
the wrestle which I had b. God,	En 1: 2
b. I received a remission of my	1: 2
and I kneeled down b. my Maker,	1: 4
thou hast never b. heard nor seen.	1: 8
b. he shall manifest himself	1: 8
and shall stand b. him;	1:27
to be a just man b. the Lord,	Om 1:25
always b. our eyes,	Mos 1: 5
we have them b. our eyes.	1: 6
he had Mosiah brought b. him;	1:10
clear conscience b. God this day.	2:15
with a clear conscience b. God,	2:27
and behold he stood b. me.	3: 2
shall be found blameless b. God,	3:21
and humble yourselves b. God;	4:10
I say unto you as I have said b.,	4:11
ye may walk guiltless b. God—	Mos 4:26
were again brought b. the king,	7: 8
and they stood b. the king,	7: 8
and bowed himself b. the king;	7:12
I am very thankful b. God	7:12
as a stumbling block b. them.	7:29
stand up b. the multitude,	8: 2
should be brought b. Ammon,	8: 5
a breastwork to be built b. them,	11:11
shall be driven b. like a dumb ass.	12: 5
carried him bound b. the king,	12: 9
we have brought a man b. thee	12: 9
he should be brought b. them.	12:18
and you ought to tremble b. God.	12:30
shalt have no other God b. me.	12:35
grow up b. him as a tender plant,	14: 2
as a sheep b. her shearers is dumb	14: 7
as a sheep b. the shearer is dumb,	15: 6
that have died b. Christ came,	15:24
and fear, and tremble b. God,	15:26
and shall confess b. God that his	16: 1
to stand b. the bar of God,	16:10
But he fled from b. them	17: 4
should again be brought b. him.	17: 6
as a witness b. him that ye have	18:10
they did walk uprightly b. God,	18:29
they should flee b. the Lamanites,	19: 9
and he himself did go b. them,	19: 9
and flee b. the Lamanites.	19:11
and they fled b. them.	19:21
king himself went b. his people;	20: 7
to drive the Lamanites b. them;	20:11
and brought him b. Limhi,	20:13
we have brought him b. you;	20:13
did bow himself down b. them,	20:25
days b. the coming of Ammon.	21:26
went forth and stood b. the king,	22: 3
b. the armies of king Noah.	23: 1
and was driven out b. the king,	24: 9
Thou shalt go b. this people,	24:17
they were brought b. the priests,	26: 7
the priests brought them b. Alma,	26: 7
thing happened b. in the church;	26:10
should be brought b. the king.	26:10
whom we have brought b. thee,	26:11
we have brought them b. thee,	26:11
come forth and shall stand b. me.	26:25
if he confess his sins b. thee	26:29
walking circumspectly b. God,	26:37
Alma laid the case b. their king,	27: 1
can ye not also behold me b. you?	27:15
even until he was laid b. his father.	27:19
and every tongue confess b. him.	27:31
did humble themselves b. him;	29:20
reigned in righteousness b. him;	29:22
walking uprightly b. God,	Al 1: 1
there was a man brought b. him	1: 2
and was brought b. Alma, to be	1:10
he stood b. Alma and pleaded	1:11
they were laid b. the judges.	2: 6
did fall b. the Amlicites.	2:17
that they began to flee b. them.	2:18
and they are fleeing b. them	2:25
the Amlicites did fall b. them.	2:28
fled back from b. Alma and sent	2:32
Amlicites began to flee b. them,	2:35
And they fled b. the Nephites	2:36
to stand b. God to be judged	5:15
brought b. the tribunal of God	5:18
shall stand b. the bar of God,	5:22
yourselves blameless b. God?	5:27
and humble themselves b. God—	6: 3
had humbled yourselves b. God,	7: 3
that ye were blameless b. him,	7: 3
ye may walk blameless b. him,	7:22
according as he had b. done	8: 1
bread and meat and set b. Alma.	8:21
b. he began to preach unto the	8:27
earth long b. this period of time,	9:11
crimes of the people b. the judges.	10:14
brought b. them to be judged.	11: 1
man should be brought b. him;	11: 2
which were brought b. them;	11:20

BEFORE 89 BEFORE

hast lied b. God unto me.	Al	11:25
from the dead and stand b. God,		11:41
shall be brought to stand b. God,		11:43
arraigned b. the bar of Christ		11:44
are brought to stand b. God		12: 8
being brought b. the bar of God,		12:12
must come forth and stand b. him		12:15
and their righteousness b. God,		13:10
pure and spotless b. God,		13:12
should humble yourselves b. God,		13:13
Now, there were many b. him,		13:19
the scriptures are b. you;		13:20
humble yourselves b. the Lord,		13:28
and took them b. the chief judge		14: 4
this was done b. the chief judge		14: 5
these men are spotless b. God.		14: 7
and stood b. Alma and Amulek,		14:14
the judge stood b. them, and said:		14:19
the chief judge stood b. them,		14:24
to humble themselves b. God,		15:17
to worship God b. the altar,		15:17
b. the Nephites could raise a		16: 3
were brought b. the altar of God,		17: 4
and confess their sins b. him.		17: 4
unto them b. his departure;		17:18
and carry them b. the king;		17:20
Ammon was carried b. the king		17:21
and began to flee b. him;		17:37
and laid b. him the records and		18:36
they who had stood b. the king		19:15
and bowed himself b. the king,		22: 2
laying the fall of man b. him,		22:13
if thou wilt bow down b. God,		22:16
and will bow down b. God,		22:16
the king did bow down b. the Lord,		22:17
Therefore we shall fall b. them.		22:20
to repent sufficiently b. God		24:11
to stand b. him to be judged,		24:15
prostrated themselves b. them		24:21
b. they would take the sword or		27:29
and evil have come b. all men;		29: 5
and carried him b. Ammon,		30:20
and carried b. the high priest,		30:21
he might be brought b. Alma,		30:29
when he was brought b. Alma		30:30
in great swelling words b. Alma,		30:31
The scriptures are laid b. thee,		30:44
to know, b. they will believe.		32:16
that all men shall stand b. him,		33:22
b. your dissension from among		34: 2
And now, as I said unto you b.,		34:33
your salvation with fear b. God,		34:37
may sift you as chaff b. the wind.		37:15
they repent b. they are fully ripe.		37:31
unworthiness b. God at all times.		38:14
of the soul, b. the resurrection,		40:15
b. the resurrection of those who		40:19
and be brought to stand b. God,		40:21
Lamanites did flee again b. them,		43:42
Lamanites began to flee b. them;		43:50
withdrew from b. them into		44:12
b. the swords of the Nephites;		44:18
b. this great iniquity shall come.		45:12
to walk uprightly b. God.		45:24
words of Jacob, b. his death,		46:24
b. they awoke at the dawn of		47:14
bowed themselves b. the king,		47:22
armies b. the place of entrance,		49:21
with perfect uprightness b. God.		50:37
driving the Nephites b. them		51:28
b. Lehi should overtake them;		52:28
b. the Lamanites had retreated		52:31
not give way b. the Lamanites.		52:34
and to walk uprightly b. him,		53:21
to pass that we did flee b. them,		56:36
b. Antipus should overtake them,		56:37
that b. the dawn of the morning,		56:39
and we did flee b. them.		56:41
not pursue us far b. they halted;		56:42
to give way b. the Lamanites.		56:51
a little b. they were to receive		57: 8
b. the Lamanites began to lose		57:12
were firm b. the Lamanites,		57:19
to give way b. the Lamanites,	Al	57:20
did arrive b. them at the city of		58:27
were obliged to flee b. them;		59: 8
have driven me out b. them,		61: 5
that they were fleeing b. him,		62:25
and fled b. the army of Moroni.		62:31
did awake his servant b. he died,		62:36
did humble themselves b. God,		62:41
themselves exceedingly b. him.		62:49
he did walk uprightly b. God;		63: 2
b. his death upon the son of		63:11
b. the death of Shiblon.		63:13
b. *the coming of Christ*,	He	1:hd
judge, did flee b. Coriantumr,		1:21
the Nephites had fled b. them,		1:22
b. they should come to the land		1:28
b. they came to the land		1:29
who had b. inherited the land.		3: 5
who had b. inhabited the land.		3: 6
and driven b. the Lamanites,		4:13
in truth and uprightness b. him.		6:34
not in the least aright b. him;		7: 4
many b. the days of Abraham		8:18
thousand years b. his coming,		8:18
and brought b. the multitude,		9:19
had some years b. gone over		11:24
b. I will cause that they shall be		13: 9
they shall flee b. their enemies;		13:20
that in the night b. he cometh		14: 3
shall be the night b. he is born.		14: 4
do walk circumspectly b. God,		15: 5
more circumspectly b. God.		16:10
b. this thirteenth year had passed	3Ne	2:13
they did fall back from b. them		4:12
given by those who were b. me,		5:16
things which have been b. me.		5:19
humble and penitent b. God.		6:13
and brought up b. the judge		6:26
witness and a testimony b. God,		7:25
b. this great and terrible day,		8:24
b. this great and terrible day,		8:25
abominations from b. my face,		9: 5
abominations from b. my face,		9: 7
abominations from b. my face,		9: 8
destroy them from b. my face.		9: 9
might be hid from b. my face,		9:11
and bowed himself b. the Lord		11:19
And he arose and stood b. him.		11:20
the prophets who were b. you.		12:12
light so shine b. this people,		12:16
have the commandments b. you,		12:19
and it is also written b. you,		12:21
that ye do not your alms b. men		13: 1
do not sound a trumpet b. you,		13: 2
ye have need of b. ye ask him.		13: 8
cast ye your pearls b. swine,		14: 6
b. I ascended to my Father;		15: 1
neither hath the ear heard, b.,		17:16
immediately, b. it was yet dark,		19: 2
written, ye have them b. you,		20:11
for the Lord will go b. you,		20:42
for I will go b. them, saith		21:29
the records, and laid them b. him,		23: 8
he shall prepare the way b. me,		24: 1
her fruit b. the time in the fields,		24:11
mournfully b. the Lord of Hosts?		24:14
written b. him for them that		24:16
b. the coming of the great and		25: 5
and tongues shall stand b. God,		26: 4
who was b. the world began.		26: 5
up by the Father, to stand b. me,		27:14
I hold guiltless b. my Father		27:16
spotless b. me at the last day.		27:20
b. that I was lifted up by the		28: 6
b. the great and coming day		28:31
b. the judgment-seat of Christ;		28:31
by them, b. that judgment day.		28:32
my army that he fled b. me.	Mrm	2: 9
and their sorrow b. the Lord,		2:12
begin to flee b. the Lamanites;		2:16
b. it was possible to stop them		2:16
has been b. mine eyes ever since		2:18
stand boldly b. the Lamanites		2:23

BEFORE

not flee from b. the Lamanites,	Mrm	2:24
that we did stand b. them with		2:25
that they did flee from b. us.		2:25
to swear b. the heavens that		3: 9
b. the judgment-seat of Christ,		3:20
b. the judgment-seat of Christ.		3:22
even as a dew b. the sun.		4:18
they fled again from b. them,		4:20
did again flee from b. them,		4:22
the country which lay b. us,		5: 4
b. them such an awful scene of		5: 8
as was laid b. mine eyes;		5: 8
driven about as chaff b. the wind.		5:16
as chaff is driven b. the wind,		5:18
ye stand b. the power of God,		5:22
and humble yourselves b. him,		5:24
march forth b. the Lamanites.		6: 1
b. the judgment-seat of Christ		6:21
fathers who have gone b. you.		6:21
b. this great destruction had		6:22
to stand b. his judgment-seat.		7: 6
that is found guiltless b. him		7: 7
which shall be set b. you,		7: 8
saints who have gone b. me,		8:23
should mourn b. the Lord,		8:40
orphans to mourn b. the Lord,		8:40
stand b. the Lamb of God—		9: 2
of your filthiness b. him,		9: 4
to see your nakedness b. God,		9: 5
and all shall stand b. his bar,		9:13
with fear and trembling b. him.		9:27
them who have written b. him;		9:31
I will go b. thee into a land	Eth	1:42
that the Lord did go b. them,		2: 5
because of his weakness b. thee;		3: 2
that we are unworthy b. thee;		3: 2
of Jared fell down b. the Lord,		3: 6
b. me with such exceeding faith		3: 9
he had said unto him in times b.,		3:26
and become clean b. the Lord.		4: 6
stand b. God at the last day.		5: 6
the waves of the sea b. the wind.		6: 5
were driven forth b. the wind.		6: 8
humble themselves b. the Lord,		6:12
shed tears of joy b. the Lord,		6:12
b. they came to the promised		6:16
to walk humbly b. the Lord;		6:17
b. we go down to our graves.		6:19
b. they went down to their graves.		6:21
did walk humbly b. the Lord,		6:30
am fair, and I will dance b. him,		8:10
daughter of Jared danced b. him		8:11
flee b. the poisonous serpents,		9:31
themselves sufficiently b. the Lord		9:35
which was wicked b. the Lord.		11:14
even those who were b. Christ		12:16
strong, even b. Christ came,		12:19
that humble themselves b. me;		12:27
they humble themselves b. me,		12:27
b. the judgment-seat of Christ,		12:38
fled from b. them and hid again		13:22
with him as he fled b. Lib		14:15
b. the army of the brother of Lib.		14:16
can stand b. the army of Shiz?		14:18
he sweepeth the earth b. him!		14:18
b. the armies of Coriantumr;		14:27
off the inhabitants b. them,		14:27
fled again b. the people of Shiz.		15: 7
caused them to flee b. them;		15:10
did condemn them b. the elders,	Mro	6: 7
he is counted evil b. God.		7: 8
for none is acceptable b. God,		7:44
it is solemn mockery b. God,		8: 9
But it is mockery b. God,		8:23
abominations from b. thy face!		9:15
meet you b. the pleasing bar of		10:34
world, and b. kings and rulers.	DC	1:23
b. the coming of the great and		2: 1
promises which were made b. God,		3:13
blameless b. God at the last day.		4: 2
and walk more uprightly b. me,		5:21
humble himself sufficiently b. me;		5:24
but if he will bow down b. me,	DC	5:24
which he has b. covenanted		5:27
and shalt prophesy b. nations,		7: 3
than what he has b. done.		7: 5
you have my gospel b. you,		18:17
that which is written b. you;		18:30
you must walk uprightly b. me		18:31
b. the world as well as in secret.		19:28
and conduct thyself wisely b. me?		19:41
means which were b. prepared,		20: 8
as many as were b. he came,		20:26
who humble themselves b. God,		20:37
and witness b. the church that		20:37
shall manifest b. the church,		20:69
church, and also b. the elders,		20:69
walking in holiness b. the Lord.		20:69
unto the elders b. the church,		20:70
years of accountability b. God,		20:71
walking in all holiness b. me;		21: 1
powers of darkness from b. you,		21: 6
the church, and b. the world,		21:12
world, yea, b. the Gentiles;		21:12
church, and also b. the world,		23: 2
called to preach b. the world.		23: 4
b. the world as well as in secret,		23: 6
bearing my name b. the world,		24:10
walk in the paths of virtue b. me,		25: 2
b. thou shalt take thy journey		28:14
and humble themselves b. me,		29: 2
b. this great day shall come		29:14
b. the earth shall pass away,		29:26
ashamed to own b. the Father;		29:27
behold, the devil was b. Adam,		29:36
to become accountable b. me;		29:47
the church, and b. the world,		30: 4
b. that great day shall come,		34: 9
to prepare the way b. me,		35: 4
b. Elijah which should come,		35: 4
as shall come b. my servants		36: 5
heaven, b. the world was made;		38: 1
things are present b. mine eyes;		38: 2
pleaded b. the Father for them.		38: 4
all flesh is corrupted b. me;		38:11
some of you are guilty b. me,		38:14
the poor have complained b. me,		38:16
virtue and holiness b. me.		38:24
thine heart is now right b. me		39: 8
be with thee and go b. thy face.		39:12
preparing the way b. my face		39:20
James Covill was right b. me,		40: 1
and have all things right b. me.		41: 3
or the pearls to be cast b. swine.		41: 6
because his heart is pure b. me,		41:11
and they are pure b. me;		41:12
shall be laid b. the bishop		42:31
after they are laid b. the bishop		42:32
be done in cleanliness b. me.		42:41
purposes, as b. mentioned;		42:71
if they shall testify b. you		42:74
tried b. two elders of the church,		42:80
shall lay the case b. the church,		42:81
cases which shall come b. you.		42:83
and that not b. the world.		42:89
shall be chastened b. many.		42:90
of any that shall come b. you		43: 5
ordained as I have told you b.,		43: 7
to act in all holiness b. me—		43: 9
sanctify yourselves b. me;		43:11
and uphold him b. me by		43:12
unto myself a pure people b. me.		43:14
they come b. me in judgment.		43:33
is pleading your cause b. him—		45: 3
to be a messenger b. my face		45: 9
face to prepare the way b. me.		45: 9
I stood b. them in the flesh,		45:16
And b. the day of the Lord shall		45:42
b. the arm of the Lord shall fall,		45:45
which are held b. the world.		46: 3
walking uprightly b. me,		46: 7
virtue and holiness b. me		46:33
for they are not right b. me		49: 2
creation b. the world was made.		49:17

BEFORE

b. the great day of the Lord	DC 49:24	he will humble himself b. me.	DC 106: 7
I will go b. you and be your	49:27	B. his day it was called	107: 3
truth and righteousness b. me.	50: 9	brought b. a general assembly	107:32
become truly humble b. me	54: 3	was b. his face continually;	107:49
if they are contrite b. me,	55: 3	as it shall be laid b. him	107:72
may receive instruction b. me	55: 4	b. the Presidency of the High	107:78
may go, that are contrite b. me,	56: 7	no more b. the Lord;	107:80
all things may be right b. me,	57:13	b. the common council of the	107:82
this, which I tell you b., that	58: 5	and in solemnity b. him,	107:84
b. the bishop of the church.	58:35	who walk uprightly b. thee,	109: 1
not sufficiently meek b. me.	58:41	have been innocent b. thee	109:31
faithful and diligent b. me.	59: 4	Therefore we plead b. thee	109:32
thy brethren, and b. the Lord.	59:12	their souls are precious b. thee;	109:43
and they shall be spotless b. me.	61:34	come up in testimony b. thee,	109:49
have humbled yourselves b. me,	61:37	people may not fail b. thee	109:52
unto you, as I have said b.,	63:16	may give way b. the truth,	109:56
an inheritance b. the Lord,	63:49	Lord, we have spoken b. thee,	109:60
who confess their sins b. me	64: 7	oppression, and rejoice b. thee.	109:67
condemned b. the Lord;	64: 9	breastwork of the pulpit, b. us;	110: 2
ye shall bring b. the church,	64:12	you are clean b. me;	110: 5
desires have come up b. me.	67: 1	and Moses appeared b. us,	110:11
which are lying b. you.	67: 4	stood b. us, and said:	110:13
and humble yourselves b. me,	67:10	b. the great and dreadful day	110:14
it be b. the First Presidency	68:22	come up as a memorial b. me,	112: 1
guilty b. this Presidency,	68:23	be of good cheer b. my face;	112: 4
to walk uprightly b. the Lord.	68:28	and be ye faithful b. me	112:12
in remembrance b. the Lord.	68:30	shall humble themselves b. me,	112:22
not his prayers b. the Lord	68:33	become corrupt b. my face.	112:23
remembrance b. the judge of	68:33	But purify your hearts b. me;	112:28
as b. has been commanded;	72:11	sanctify him b. the people;	115:19
things b. the bishop in Zion.	72:15	b. I, the Lord, send again	117: 1
b. them the wisdom of the wise	76: 9	their covetous desires, b. me,	117: 4
beginning b. the world was,	76:13	all his littleness of soul b. me,	117:11
are sanctified b. his throne,	76:21	b. thine heart shall be softened	121: 3
b. the worlds were made.	76:39	melteth b. the burning rays of	121:11
B. whose throne all things bow	76:93	they have not sinned b. me,	121:16
and purify themselves b. him;	76:116	other gods b. this world was,	121:32
way b. the time of his coming.	77:12	b. we can fully and completely	123: 6
seal, b. the coming of Christ.	77:13	b. he can send forth the power	123: 6
which you have presented b. me,	78: 2	prayers are acceptable b. me;	124: 2
all things b. he taketh you;	78:20	that which is right b. me,	124:15
how you may act b. me,	82: 9	confessing me b. the world;	124:18
Lord b. the face of his people,	84:28	b. the foundation of the world,	124:33
speak them b. the world;	84:73	been hid from b. the world was.	124:38
for I will go b. your face.	84:88	b. the foundation of the world,	124:41
b. you to make appointments,	84:107	which you practise b. me,	124:48
goeth b. the face of him who	88:40	let him be humble b. me,	124:97
and all things are b. him,	88:41	and humble himself b. me.	124:103
your hands and your feet b. me,	88:74	be a spokesman b. my face.	124:104
prayer upon his knees b. God,	88:131	even as I have b. said unto you.	124:107
cometh in and is faithful b. me.	88:135	to prepare a way b. my face.	124:139
offer up your sacraments b. him.	89: 5	b. the foundation of the world	127: 2
b. the eyes of the people.	90:23	righteous men that were b. you.	127: 4
overcomes and is clean b. me.	90:36	in my letter b. I left my place,	128: 1
beginning, b. the world was;	93: 7	a record of a truth b. the Lord.	128: 2
infant state, innocent b. God.	93:38	b. the foundation of the world,	128: 5
stand rebuked b. the Lord;	93:47	*small and great, stand b. God*;	128: 6
and stand rebuked b. my face;	95: 2	b. the foundation of the world,	128: 8
and is justifiable b. me.	98: 5	subject that is lying b. us,	128:11
all flesh be consumed b. me.	98:17	*b. the coming of the great and*	128:17
brought into judgment b. me,	98:28	hath ordained, b. the world was,	128:22
these testimonies b. the Lord;	98:35	are continually b. the Lord.	130: 7
God, for justification b. me.	98:38	b. the foundations of this world,	130:20
these testimonies b. the Lord;	98:44	b. the foundation of the world,	132: 5
as a testimony b. the Lord	98:48	unto you, b. the world was?	132:11
not be confounded b. men;	100: 5	my father b. the world was.	132:28
shall cease from b. my face.	101:26	are virtuous and pure b. me;	132:52
all things be prepared b. you.	101:68	b. the foundation of the world,	132:63
all things be prepared b. you,	101:69	all things be prepared b. you;	133:15
all things prepared b. you.	101:72	in the days b. it was divided.	133:24
to speak b. the council	102:16	in remembrance b. the Lord;	133:26
in its true light b. the council;	102:16	in holiness b. the Lord,	133:35
for themselves b. the council,	102:18	the prophets who were b. him;	133:54
Mine angel shall go up b. you,	103:19	and they who were b. him;	133:54
Mine angels shall go up b. you,	103:20	and they who were b. him;	133:54
which ye have brought b. me	103:24	sanctifieth himself b. the Lord	133:62
as he will be humble b. me.	104:23	*b. the judgment-seat of Christ,*	135: 5
and it is manifest the council	104:74	they had often been proved b.,	135: 7
shall humble yourselves b. me,	104:79	b. Moses did again receive his	Mses 1:10
which I have laid b. you,	104:86	I was transfigured b. him.	1:11
continue in humility b. me.	105:12	I were strengthened b. him.	1:14
prayerful, and humble b. me,	105:23	field b. it was in the earth,	3: 5
and let it be sanctified b. me,	105:31	herb of the field b. it grew.	3: 5

BEFORE 92 BEGAN

b. they were naturally upon the	Mses	3: 5
all things were b. created;		3: 7
he came b. me, saying—		4: 1
for thou wast also b. the world.		5:24
walked in holiness b. the Lord.		5:26
his wife mourned b. the Lord,		5:27
b. the foundation of the world.		5:57
to the earth, b. the Lord,		6:31
spake b. the Lord, saying:		6:31
mountains shall flee b. you,		6:34
men b. they were in the flesh.		6:51
Lord, and he stood b. my face,		7: 4
nations of the earth were b. him;		7:23
mercy shall go b. thy face		7:31
chosen hath plead b. my face.		7:39
b. that day the heavens shall		7:61
b. that day he saw great		7:66
they came up b. him, saying:		8:21
The earth was corrupt b. God,		8:28
end of all flesh is come b. me,		8:30
b. the foundations of the earth	Abr	1: 3
stood b. the gods of Elkenah,		1:13
they multiplied b. mine eyes,		3:12
unto thee b. ye go into Egypt,		3:15
they existed b., they shall have		3:18
organized b. the world was;		3:22
chosen b. thou wast born.		3:23
b. it was in the earth,		5: 5
herb of the field b. it grew;		5: 5
standing b. the gods of Elkenah,	Fac	1: 4
was not b. sent upon Israel,	JS	1:18
Behold, I have told you b.;		1:24
And, as I said b., after the		1:36
shall send his angels b. him		1:37
days which were b. the flood;		1:42
power as I had never b. felt		2:16
in the b. mentioned religious		2:21
his defense b. King Agrippa,		2:24
my state and standing b. him;		2:29
b. *the coming of the great and*		2:38
b. this heavenly light had		2:43
ascended as he had done b.		2:45
to me the same things as b.;		2:46
ascended into heaven as b.,		2:47
surrounded by light as b.		2:49
more bitter and sever than b.,		2:60
more so than any he had b. seen		2:64
nor ever b. had thought of.		2:74

BEFOREHAND

not knowing b. the things which	1Ne	4: 6
these things known unto us b.,	Al	24:14
should be known so long b.		39:17
been made known unto them b.,	He	16: 5
Neither take ye thought b.	DC	84:85

BEFRIENDING

in b. that law which is the	DC	98: 6

BEGAN

and b. to prophesy and to declare	1Ne	1:18
we b. to be exceeding sorrowful,		3:14
since the world b., even down unto		3:20
and Lemuel again b. to murmur,		3:31
he b. to tremble, and was about		4:30
b. to prophesy concerning his seed—		5:17
I b. to pray unto the Lord that he		8: 8
I b. to be desirous that my family		8:12
And as there b. to be wars and		14:16
and also my father b. to murmur		16:20
it b. to be exceedingly difficult,		16:21
they b. to bear their journeyings		17: 2
they b. to murmur against me,		17:17
that I b. to be sorrowful		17:19
wives b. to make themselves merry,		18: 9
they b. to dance, and to sing,		18: 9
I, Nephi, b. to fear exceedingly		18:10
I Nephi, b. to speak to them		18:10
and they b. to be frightened		18:13
tempest b. to be exceeding sore.		18:14
my brethren b. to see that the		18:15
and we b. to plant seeds;		18:24

And we b. to raise flocks,	2Ne	5:11
we b. to prosper exceedingly,		5:13
Now Nephi b. to be old,	Jac	1: 9
b. to grow hard in their hearts,		1:15
they also b. to search much gold		1:16
b. to be lifted up somewhat in		1:16
which now b. to be numerous,		3:13
and waxed old, and b. to decay.		5: 3
that his olive-tree b. to decay;		5: 4
after many days it b. to put forth		5: 6
the main top thereof b. to perish.		5: 6
there b. to be the natural fruit		5:73
the natural branches b. to grow		5:73
wild branches b. to be plucked		5:73
b. to preach among the people,		7: 2
that I, Jacob, b. to be old;		7:26
I b. to feel a desire for the	En	1: 9
my faith b. to be unshaken		1:11
I b. to be old,		1:25
and b. to fortify our cities,	Jar	1: 7
that I b. to be old;	Om	1:25
he b. to speak to his people	Mos	2: 8
and b. to speak unto them,		4: 4
And Mosiah b. to reign in his		6: 4
And he b. to reign in the		6: 4
And we b. to build buildings,		9: 8
And we b. to till the ground,		9: 9
king Laman b. to grow uneasy,		9:11
king Laman b. to stir up his people		9:13
therefore there b. to be wars		9:13
upon them and b. to slay them,		9:14
again b. to establish the kingdom		10: 1
again b. to possess the land in peace.		10: 1
his son b. to reign in his stead.		10: 6
And he b. to stir his people up		10: 6
they b. to prepare for war,		10: 6
again b. to tend their flocks,		10:21
Noah b. to reign in his stead;		11: 1
the Lamanites b. to come in upon		11:16
the Lamanites b. to destroy them,		11:17
and b. to prophesy, saying:		11:20
and b. to prophesy among them,		12: 1
And they b. to question him,		12:19
ever since the world b.—		13:33
ever since the world b.?		15:13
ever since the world b.,		15:26
he b. to plead with the king		17: 2
and b. to accuse him, saying:		17:12
when the flames b. to scorch him,		17:14
b. to teach the words of Abinadi—		18: 1
there b. to be a division among		19: 2
part b. to breathe out threatenings		19: 3
there b. to be a great contention		19: 3
and b. to slay them.		19:10
Limhi b. to establish the kingdom		19:27
of Limhi b. to fall upon them		20: 9
and b. to slay them.		20: 9
b. to drive the Lamanites before		20:11
and b. to dwell in the land again		21: 1
Lamanites b. again to be stirred		21: 2
they b. to come into the borders		21: 2
and b. to put heavy burdens upon		21: 3
the people b. to murmur with		21: 6
and they b. to be desirous to go		21: 6
and b. to soften the hearts of		21:15
that they b. to ease their burdens;		21:15
they b. to prosper by degrees in		21:16
b. to raise grain more abundantly,		21:16
b. to consult with the people		22: 1
and b. to till the ground,		23: 5
and b. to build buildings;		23: 5
they b. to prosper exceedingly		23:19
and b. to cry unto the Lord		23:28
the language of Nephi b. to be		24: 4
Lamanites b. to increase in riches,		24: 7
and b. to trade one with another		24: 7
and b. to be a cunning and a wise		24: 7
Amulon b. to exercise authority		24: 8
and b. to persecute him,		24: 8
they b. to cry mightily to God.		24:10
and they b. again to have peace		26:37
that the church b. to murmur,		27: 1
And there b. to be much peace again		27: 6

BEGAN

people b. to be very numerous,	Mos 27: 6	And he b. to cry unto the Lord,	Al	18:41
and b. to scatter abroad upon	27: 6	and b. to pour out his soul in		19:14
they b. to fast, and to pray	27:22	they also b. to cry unto God,		19:15
he stood up and b. to speak	27:23	they b. to assemble themselves		19:18
Alma b. from this time forward	27:32	b. to murmur among themselves;		19:19
that they b. to support him	Al 1: 5	and they b. to marvel again		19:24
he b. to be lifted up in the	1: 6	b. to be exceeding sharp among		19:28
even b. to establish a church	1: 6	went forth and b. to rebuke them,		19:31
b. to contend with him sharply,	1: 7	he b. to plead with Ammon		20:21
his sword and b. to smite him.	1: 9	the king b. to rejoice because of		20:25
b. to persecute those that did	1;19	b. to preach to the Amalekites.		21: 4
among them who b. to be proud,	1:22	he b. to preach to them in their		21: 4
b. to contend warmly with their	1:22	and b. to contend with him,		21: 5
b. to have continual peace again,	1:28	Aaron b. to open.the scriptures		21: 9
they b. to be exceeding rich,	1:29	as he b. to expound these things		21:10
there b. to be a contention	2: 1	with him, and b. to mock him;		21:10
they b. to be very powerful;	2: 2	that the Lord b. to bless them,		21:17
they b. to endeavor to establish	2: 2	his heart b. to rejoice, and he		22: 8
there they b. to make war	2:15	he b. from the creation of Adam,		22:12
And they b. to slay the Amlicites	2:17	she also b. to fear exceedingly,		22:21
that they b. to flee before them.	2:18	greatly marveled, and b. to fear.		22:23
Amlicites b. to flee before them,	2:35	and b. to minister unto them.		22:23
they b. to mark themselves in	3:18	there b. to be great murmurings		22:24
b. to establish peace in the land,	3:24	thus they b. to have great success.		23: 4
they b. to establish the church	4: 4	they b. to be a very industrious		23:18
of the church b. to wax proud,	4: 6	they b. to rebel against their king,		24: 2
b. to wear very costly apparel.	4: 6	b. to make preparations for war		24: 4
b. to be lifted up in the pride of	4: 8	and b. to call on the name of		24:21
that they b. to be scornful,	4: 8	Lamanites b. to fall upon them,		24:21
and they b. to persecute those that	4: 8	b. to slay them with the sword.		24:21
there b. to be great contentions	4: 9	b. to be stirred up in		25: 6
and thus the church b. to fail	4:10	b. to disbelieve the traditions of		25: 6
b. to lead those who were	4:11	and there b. to be contention in		25: 8
b. to be very sorrowful;	4:15	Lamanites b. to hunt the seed		25: 8
Alma b. to deliver the word of	5: 1	his brethren and b. to slay them;		25: 8
he b. to establish a church in	5: 3	b. to be a righteous people;		25:14
we b. to establish the church	5: 5	rejoice as we, since the world b.;		26:35
they b. to establish the order of	6: 4	b. to stir up the people in anger		27: 2
and b. to declare the word of God	6: 8	they b. again to destroy them.		27: 2
have been ever since the world b.,	7:25	there b. to be continual peace		30: 2
And he b. to teach the people	8: 4	he b. to preach unto the peopled		30: 6
and he b. to teach the people	8: 4	b. to preach unto the people that		30:12
he b. to preach the word of God	8: 8	and b. to preach unto them also;		30:21
he b. to preach unto the people.	8:27	his heart again b. to sicken		31: 1
went forth and b. to preach	8:32	and b. to preach the word of God		32: 1
as I b. to preach unto them,	9: 1	they b. to have success among		32: 2
b. to contend with me, saying:	9: 1	and b. to teach them, saying:		34: 1
b. to preach unto them also.	9:34	b. to mix with the Lamanites		35:10
the people b. to be astonished,	10:12	b. to make preparations for war		35:11
that they b. to question Amulek,	10:16	of the people b. to wax hard,		35:15
as they b. to question him,	10:17	they b. to be offended because of		35:15
Zeezrom b. to question Amulek,	11:21	people b. to work in darkness,		37:22
people b. again to be astonished,	11:46	and b. to cross the river Sidon,		43:35
also Zeezrom b. to tremble.	11:46	b. to contend with the army of		43:36
and seeing that he b. to tremble	12: 1	even until they b. to flee		43:39
and b. to speak unto him,	12: 1	b. to fall upon them and to slay		43:41
Zeezrom b. to tremble more	12: 7	And they b. to stand against		43:50
Zeezrom b. to inquire of them	12: 8	Lamanites b. to flee before them;		43:50
Alma b. to expound these things	12: 9	that they b. to slay them;		44:14
people b. to be more astonished;	12:19	and they b. to be swept down,		44:18
And they b. from that time forth	12:30	they b. to have peace again in		46:37
and b. to repent, and to search	14: 1	he b. to inspire the hearts of the		48: 1
his soul b. to be harrowed up	14: 6	b. to contend with the Nephites,		49:21
he b. to be encircled about by	14: 6	they b. to dig down their banks		49:22
that he b. to cry unto the people,	14: 7	Nephites b. the foundation of		50:13
And he b. to plead for them	14: 7	also b. a foundation for a city		50:14
people saw this, they b. to flee,	14:26	they also b. in that same year		50:15
he b. to be scorched with a	15: 3	there b. to be a warm contention		50:26
his heart b. to take courage;	15: 4	there b. to be a contention among		51: 2
upon his feet, and b. to walk;	15:11	he b. to retreat down by the		52:23
b. from that time forth to preach	15:12	Lamanites saw that he b. to flee,		52:24
b. to humble themselves before	15:17	that the Nephites b. again to be		55:28
and b. to assemble themselves	15:17	they b. to be fearful, and began		56:29
and b. to slay the people	16: 2	fearful, and b. to sally forth,		56:29
of the king b. to murmur,	17:28	the Lamanites b. to grow uneasy		56:30
And they b. to weep exceedingly,	17:28	b. to give way before the		56:51
and b. to cast stones at them	17:36	courage, and b. to pursue them;		56:52
that they b. to be astonished	17:36	b. to slay them exceedingly,		56:52
that they b. to be astonished,	17:37	b. to make preparations to go		57: 3
and b. to flee before him;	17:37	b. to lose all hopes of succor;		57:12
Lamoni b. to fear exceedingly,	18: 5	b. to make preparations to		58:15
Ammon b. to speak unto him	18:24	b. to retreat into the wilderness		58:24
b. at the creation of the world,	18:36	he b. again to lay a plan that he		59: 4

BEGAN — 94 — BEGAN

sorrowful, and b. to doubt,	Al	59:11
people of Nephi b. to prosper		62:48
b. to multiply and to wax		62:48
they b. to grow exceeding rich.		62:48
b. to be a serious difficulty	He	1: 1
b. to be a serious contention		1: 2
that they b. to retreat back		1:29
there b. to be a contention		2: 1
they b. to cover the face of		3: 8
they b. to grow up unto the Lord.		3:21
and contentions b. to cease,		3:22
pride which b. to enter into		3:33
Nephi b. to reign in his stead.		3:37
b. to remember the prophecies		4:21
they b. to disbelieve in the		4:23
and b. to speak unto them,		5:26
b. to grow exceedingly wicked		6:16
they b. to set their hearts upon		6:17
they b. to seek to get gain		6:17
b. to commit secret murders,		6:17
b. to grow exceedingly in the		6:34
b. to withdraw from the Nephites,		6:35
b. to pour out his Spirit upon		6:36
he b. again to speak unto them,		8:10
b. to question him in divers ways		9:19
b. to declare unto them the word		10:12
there b. to be contentions,		10:18
and b. to slay one another		10:18
they b. to remember the Lord		11: 7
b. to remember the words of		11: 7
the people b. to plead with their		11: 8
people of Nephi b. to prosper		11:20
b. to build up their waste places,		11:20
and b. to multiply and spread,		11:20
and seventh year b. in peace;		11:21
there b. to be much strife.		11:23
they b. again to forget the Lord		11:36
b. to wax strong in iniquity.		11:36
and b. to preach unto the people.		13: 2
b. to preach and to prophesy		16: 7
people b. to be more hardened		16:12
prophets b. to be fulfilled.		16:13
the scriptures b. to be fulfilled.		16:14
people b. to harden their hearts,		16:15
and b. to depend upon their own		16:15
b. to reason and to contend		16:17
b. to be fulfilled more fully;	3Ne	1: 4
there b. to be greater signs		1: 4
there were some who b. to say		1: 5
b. to rejoice over their brethren,		1: 6
believed b. to be very sorrowful,		1: 7
people b. to be astonished		1:15
they b. to know that the Son		1:17
they b. to fear because of their		1:18
there b. to be lyings sent forth		1:22
the people b. again to have peace		1:23
were a few that b. to preach,		1:24
b. to increase in great degree,		1:28
and b. to wax strong in years,		1:29
b. to decrease as to their faith		1:30
people b. to forget those signs		2: 1
b. to be less and less astonished		2: 1
they b. to be hard in their hearts,		2: 1
b. to disbelieve all which they had		2: 1
b. to wax strong in wickedness		2: 3
b. to reckon their time from		2: 8
b. to be wars and contentions		2:11
b. to come down and to sally		4: 1
b. to take possession of the		4: 1
b. to take possession of all the		4: 1
b. to shout with a loud voice,		4: 9
when the robbers b. their march,		4:25
And they b. again to prosper		6: 4
there b. to be some disputings		6:10
people b. to be distinguished by		6:12
the church b. to be broken up;		6:14
And there b. to be men inspired		6:20
b. to testify, boldly, repentance		7:16
b. to look with great earnestness		8: 3
there b. to be great doubtings		8: 4
they b. to weep and howl again		10: 8
of the water and b. to baptize.		19:12
And behold, they b. to pray;		19:18
who was before the world b.	3Ne	26: 5
b. from that time forth to		26:17
there b. to be Lamanites again	4Ne	1:20
there b. to be among them		1:24
they b. to be divided into		1:26
they b. to build up churches		1:26
b. to deny the true church of		1:26
b. again to build up the secret		1:42
b. to be proud in their hearts,		1:43
the disciples b. to sorrow for		1:44
I b. to be learned somewhat	Mrm	1: 2
there b. to be a war between		1: 8
the war b. to be among them		1:10
b. to hide up their treasures in		1:18
b. to be a war again between		2: 1
and they b. to retreat towards		2: 3
that the Nephites b. to repent		2:10
and b. to cry even as had been		2:10
Thus there b. to be a mourning		2:11
they b. to come upon us again.		2:22
they b. to boast in their own		3: 9
b. to swear before the heavens		3: 9
that they b. to be smitten;		4: 4
but b. to be swept off by them		4:18
I, Mormon, b. to be old;		6: 6
and b. to till the earth.	Eth	6:13
therefore they b. to be many.		6:16
b. to spread upon the face of		6:18
brother of Jared b. to be old,		6:19
And he b. to reign, and the		6:28
and the people b. to prosper;		6:28
he b. to reign in the stead of		7:10
b. to prosper again in the land.		7:26
Akish b. to be jealous of his son,		9: 7
there b. to be a war between		9:12
that Omer b. to be old;		9:14
the Lord b. again to take the		9:16
there b. again to be an exceeding		9:26
Heth b. to embrace the secret		9:26
there b. to be a great dearth		9:30
inhabitants b. to be destroyed		9:30
that their flocks b. to flee		9:31
b. to repent of their iniquities		9:34
the people b. to revive again,		9:35
there b. to be fruit in the north		9:35
Shez b. to build up again a		10: 1
the people b. again to spread over		10: 4
and there b. to be war again		10: 8
there b. to be robbers in the		10:33
b. to be an exceeding great war		11: 4
b. to be wars and contentions		11: 7
b. to repent of their iniquity;		11: 8
b. to prophesy unto the people,		12: 2
there b. to be a great war among		13:15
there b. to be a war upon all		13:25
there b. to be a great curse upon		14: 1
people b. to flock together in		14:19
the people b. to be frightened,		14:27
b. to flee before the armies of		14:27
he b. to remember the words		15: 1
and he b. to sorrow in his heart;		15: 2
He b. to repent of the evil		15: 3
he b. to remember the words		15: 3
men b. to exercise faith in	Mro	7:25
when you b. to translate,	DC	9: 5
holy prophets since the world b.,		27: 6
holy prophets since the world b.		86:10
and b. to build a tower.		101:46
b. to say among themselves:		101:47
Moses b. to fear exceedingly;	Mses	1:20
and as he b. to fear, he saw		1:20
And now Satan b. to tremble,		1:21
Adam b. to till the earth,		5: 1
they b. to multiply and to		5: 2
b. to divide two and two in		5: 3
b. to prophesy concerning all		5:10
men b. from that time forth to		5:13
b. to reveal it unto the sons		5:49
b. to spread among all the sons		5:52
works of darkness b. to prevail		5:55
Gospel b. to be preached,		5:58
then b. these men to call upon		6: 4
forth Enoch b. to prophesy,		7: 2

BEGAN

these men b. to multiply on	Mses	8:14
when the converts b. to file off,	JS	2: 6
b. to offer up the desire of my		2:15
and he b. to write for me.		2:67
we b. to have the scriptures		2:74

BEGAT

now, my father had b. two sons	1Ne	18: 7
also b. sons and daughters.	Eth	6:15
they also b. sons and daughters		6:16
he b. sons and daughters;		7: 2
yea, he b. thirty and one,		7: 2
he also b. Kib in his old age.		7: 3
and Kib b. Corihor.		7: 3
and he b. sons and daughters,		7: 4
Kib b. Shule in his old age,		7: 7
also b. many sons and daughters.		7:12
Shule b. sons and daughters in		7:26
came to pass that he b. Omer,		8: 1
And Omer b. Jared; and Jared		8: 1
and Jared b. sons and daughters.		8: 1
that he b. sons and daughters		8: 4
that Akish b. other sons,		9:10
in his old age he b. Emer;		9:14
he b. many sons and daughters;		9:21
and he b. Coriantum, and he		9:21
and b. sons and daughters;		9:24
came to pass that he b. Com,		9:25
and nine years, and he b. Heth;		9:25
also b. other sons and daughters.		9:25
and he b. sons and daughters.		10: 2
and he b. Riplakish.		10: 4
great age, and then he b. Kim;		10:13
he b. sons and daughters in		10:14
and in his old age he b. Levi;		10:14
and b. sons and daughters,		10:16
and he also b. Corom, whom he		10:16
he b. many sons and daughters,		10:17
and b. sons and daughters;		10:29
and he also b. Hearthom.		10:29
And he b. Heth, and Heth		10:31
Heth b. Aaron, and Aaron		10:31
and he b. Amnigaddah, and		10:31
and he b. Coriantum, and		10:31
and he b. Com.		10:31
good old age, and b. Shiblom;		11: 4
all his days; and he b. Moron.		11:14
and he b. Coriantor.		11:18
Coriantor b. Ether, and he died,		11:23
also b. sons and daughters.	Mses	5: 3
also b. many sons and daughters.		5:42
And Irad b. Mahujael,		5:43
And Mahujael b. Methusael,		5:43
And Methusael b. Lamech.		5:43
b. a son in his own likeness,		6:10
b. many sons and daughters;		6:11
and b. Enos, and prophesied		6:13
And Seth lived, after he b. Enos,		6:14
and b. many sons and daughters.		6:14
ninety years, and b. Cainan.		6:17
Enos lived, after he b. Cainan,		6:18
and b. many sons and daughters.		6:18
years, and b. Mahalaleel;		6:19
lived after he b. Mahalaleel		6:19
and b. sons and daughters.		6:19
sixty-five years, and b. Jared;		6:20
lived, after he b. Jared,		6:20
and b. sons and daughters.		6:20
sixty-two years, and b. Enoch;		6:21
Jared lived, after he b. Enoch,		6:21
and b. sons and daughters.		6:21
years, and b. Methuselah.		6:25
years, and b. Lamech;		8: 5
lived, after he b. Lamech,		8: 6
and b. sons and daughters;		8: 6
eighty-two years, and b. a son,		8: 8
Lamech lived, after he b. Noah,		8:10
and b. sons and daughters.		8:10
years old, and b. Japheth.		8:12
years afterward he b. Shem		8:12
hundred years old he b. Ham.		8:12

BEGET

he shall b. glory and honor to	DC	124:18

BEGGAR

the b. putteth up his petition to	Mos	4:16
I mean all you who deny the b.,		4:24

BEGGARS

For behold, are we not all b.?	Mos	4:19

BEGGED

suffered that ye have b. in vain?	Mos	4:20

BEGGING

b. for a remission of your sins.	Mos	4:20
house to house b. for his food.	Al	30:56
to house, b. food for his support.		30:58
nor his seed be found b. bread.	DC	124:90

BEGIN

sons of Ishmael did b. to murmur	1Ne	16:20
we did b. to till the earth,		18:24
scales of darkness shall b. to fall	2Ne	30: 6
shall b. to believe in Christ;		30: 7
they shall b. to gather in		30: 7
This people b. to wax in iniquity;	Jac	2:23
b. at the last that they may be		5:63
And as they b. to grow ye shall		5:65
and we did b. to multiply	Mos	9: 9
Lord did b. to pour out his Spirit	Al	19:36
will b. to swell within your breasts;		32:28
will b. to say within yourselves—		32:28
doth b. to be enlightened,		32:34
your mind doth b. to expand.		32:34
should b. to exercise their faith.		33: 1
b. to believe in the Son of God,		33:22
ye may b. to exercise your faith		34:17
ye b. to call upon his holy name,		34:17
and they did b. to slay them		59: 7
and b. to be up and doing,		60:24
and did b. to labor exceedingly,		62:29
did repent they did b. to prosper.	He	4:15
all did b. to cry unto the voice of		5:42
did b. to dwindle in unbelief,		6:34
they did b. to keep his statutes		6:34
ought to b. to howl and mourn,		9:22
shall b. to know these things—	3Ne	21: 7
my heart did b. to rejoice	Mrm	2:12
the Nephites did b. to flee		2:16
and b. as in times of old,		9:27
men again b. to deny their God,	DC	29:22
they b. to become accountable		29:47
You shall b. to preach from		31: 4
light shall b. to break forth,		45:36
when they b. to shoot forth,		45:37
then shall ye b. to be gathered		48: 8
brethren in Zion b. to repent,		90:34
b. to prevail against mine		103: 6
may b. to be redeemed;		109:62
bondage may b. to be broken off		109:63
b. to return to the lands which		109:64
And upon my house shall it b.,		112:25
b. to exercise unrighteous		121:39
so when they b. to grow up,	Mses	6:55
b. to smite his fellow-servants,	JS	1:52
b. to gather immediately around		2:43

BEGINNETH

beholdest that it b. to perish;	Jac	5:37
for it b. to enlarge my soul;	Al	32:28
b. to enlighten my understanding,		32:28
yea, it b. to be delicious to me.		32:28
and sprouteth, and b. to grow.		32:30
and sprouteth, and b. to grow.		32:30
and sprouteth, and b. to grow,		32:33
behold, as the tree b. to grow,		32:37
nourish the tree as it b. to grow,		32:41
and as it b. to swell even so		33:23

BEGINNING

(b. at the eldest) Laman, Lemuel,	1Ne	1:hd
he did search them from the b.		5:10
a record of the Jews from the b.,		5:12
of the holy prophets, from the b.,		5:13
knoweth all things from the b.;		9: 6
from the b. of the world until		12:18

BEGINNING 96 BEGOTTEN

the same course as in the b.;	1Ne	16:33	all nations, b. at this place.	DC	87: 2
the former things from the b.;		20: 3	B. at the first, and so on unto		88:59
from the b. declared to thee;		20: 5	b. at the high priests, even down		88:127
now, and not from the b.,		20: 7	glory, that he was in the b.,		93: 7
not spoken in secret; from the b.,		20:16	in the b. the Word was, for he		93: 8
the commandments from the b.,	2Ne	1:10	I was in the b. with the Father,		93:21
anxiety of my soul from the b.		1:16	also in the b. with the Father		93:23
even from the b. down,		9: 2	one who was a liar from the b.		93:25
from the b. of the world,		11: 4	was also in the b. with God.		93:29
from the b. of the world to the		27: 7	that which was from the b. is		93:31
how that ye are b. to labor in sin,	Jac	2: 5	man was innocent in the b.;		93:38
branches which are b. to wither		5: 7	preparing a b. and foundation		94: 1
precious unto him from the b.		5:74	of Kirtland, b. at my house.		94: 1
even like as it was in the b.		5:75	the first day, the b. and the end.		95: 7
has created you from the b.,	Mos	2:21	the b. of the gathering of my		101:70
Creator of all things from the b.;		3: 8	this is the b. of the stewardship		104:32
which man was created in the b.;		7:27	this is the b. of the stewardship		104:37
were prepared from the b.,		28:14	this is the b. of the stewardship		104:44
our creator a liar from the b.,	Al	5:25	this is the b. of the blessing		110:10
that he is a liar from the b.,		5:25	from the b. of the creation;		112:31
For as I said unto you from the b.,		7:18	let there be a b. of this work,		115: 9
from the b. of their transgressions		9:14	let the b. be made on the		115:10
destruction of this people is b. to		10:27	shall be the b. of the tithing		119: 3
he is the b. and the end, the first		11:39	for the b. of the revelations		124:39
without b. of days or end of		13: 7	is now b. to usher in,		128:18
priesthood, is without b. or end.—		13: 8	to the b. of the millennium		130:16
without b. of days or end of		13: 9	from the b. of creation until		132:38
they all created from the b.		18:32	For since the b. of the world		133:45
man in the b. was created after		18:34	b. of days or end of years;	Mses	1: 3
ways of a transgressor from the b.?		26:24	I am the B. and the End,		2: 1
our forefathers, even from the b.—		37: 3	in the b. I created the heaven,		2: 1
courage, no, not even from the b.		43:43	was with me from the b.:		2:26
who in the b., were Lamanites;		53:10	the same which was from the b.,		4: 1
b. at the city Bountiful;	He	5:14	and Chosen from the b.,		4: 2
from the b. of man even down to		6:29	of the Father from the b.,		5: 9
b. at the more wicked part of		6:38	to be preached, from the b.,		5:58
Creator of all things from the b.;		14:12	Priesthood, which was in the b.,		6: 7
was with the Father from the b.	3Ne	9:15	forth in the b. of the world,		6:30
and Omega, the b. and the end.		9:18	b. of days or end of years,		6:67
Father in all things from the b.		11:11	it would not be a b. to the		7:30
all things, even from the b. until		26: 3	of God, even as it was in the b.		8:16
is already b. to be fulfilled.		29: 1	fathers, from the b. of time,	Abr	1: 3
as their fathers, from the b.,	4Ne	1:38	yea, even from the b.,		1: 3
fathers, even as it was in the b.		1:39	them in the figures at the b.,		1:14
children of Nephi from the b.		1:39	to the b. of the creation,		1:28
men were created in the b. after	Eth	3:15	of the b. of the creation,		1:31
who was a murderer from the b.		8:15	I know the end from the b.;		2: 8
from the b. of man.		8:19	than the other, have no b.;		3:18
to commit murder from the b.;		8:25	thine eyes have seen from the b.;		3:21
and cast them out from the b.		8:25	I came down in the b. in		3:21
all things, from the b. of man;		13: 2	And they went down at the b.,		4: 1
trampled upon from the b.	DC	3:15	this was the first, or the b.,		4: 5
in this the b. of the rising up		5:14	since the b. of their kingdom	JS	1:18
that spake unto you from the b.		8:12	only the b. of the sorrows		1:19
I am he, the b. and the end,		19: 1	was again b. to get lighted,		2:44
but all those from the b.,		20:26			
even that which was from the b.		22: 1	BEGINS		
which is the b. of my work;		29:32	and it b. to put forth leaves,	JS	1:38
my works have no end, neither b.;		29:33			
prepared for them from the b.;		29:38	BEGOTTEN		
and Omega, the b. and the end,		35: 1	Who hath b. me these, seeing	1Ne	21:21
and Omega, the b. and the end,		38: 1	the Only B. of the Father,	2Ne	25:12
and Omega, the b. and the end,		45: 7	of God and his Only B. Son.	Jac	4: 5
of my church from the b.,		46: 2	of Christ, his Only B. Son,		4:11
that which was from the b.		49: 9	he hath spiritually b. you;	Mos	5: 7
to come, the b. and the end;		49:12	the Only B. of the Father,	Al	5:48
Omega, the b. and the end,		54: 1	of the Only B. of the Father,		9:26
and Omega, the b. and the end.		61: 1	through mine Only B. Son;		12:33
in the b. blessed the waters;		61:14	through mine Only B. Son,		12:34
Lord, in the b. cursed the land,		61:17	atonement of the Only B. Son,		13: 5
have been such even from the b.;		63: 8	the Only B. of the Father,		13: 9
things which were from the b.		76:13	God gave his Only B. Son,	DC	20:21
of the Father, even from the b.;		76:13	on the name of mine Only B. Son.		29:42
the b. of the seventh thousand		77:12	the world through mine Only B.;		29:46
the b. of the seventh thousand		77:12	have sent mine Only B. Son		49: 5
b. of days or end of life.		78:16	Father, through his Only B. Son,		76:13
be built, at the temple lot,		84: 4	he is the Only B. of the Father—		76:23
the saints, b. at this place,		84: 4	b. sons and daughters unto God.		76:24
b. of days or end of years.		84:17	rebelled against the Only B. Son		76:25
the b. and the end. Amen.		84:120	the Only B. Son of the Father,		76:35
is b. to bring forth the word,		86: 4	the order of the Only B. Son.		76:57
b. at the rebellion of South		87: 1	of the Only B. of the Father,		93:11

BEGOTTEN 97 BEHELD

BEGOTTEN
who are b. through me	DC 93:22
the order of mine Only B. Son.	124:123
the similitude of mine Only B.;	Mses 1: 6
mine Only B. is and shall be	1: 6
in the similitude of his Only B.;	1:13
the similitude of mine Only B.	1:16
in the name of mine Only B.,	1:17
I am the Only B., worship me.	1:19
In the name of the Only B.,	1:21
which is mine Only B. Son,	1:32
them, which is mine Only B.	1:33
by mine Only B. I created	2: 1
I, God, said unto mine Only B.,	2:26
in the image of mine Only B.	2:27
God, said unto mine Only B.,	3:18
in the name of mine Only B.,	4: 1
by the power of mine Only B.,	4: 3
God, said unto mine Only B.	4:28
the Only B. of the Father,	5: 7
I am the Only B. of the Father	5: 9
nor believe on his Only B. Son,	5:57
of Adam, after he had b. Seth,	6:11
the name of mine Only B. Son,	6:52
the name of his Only B. is	6:57
even the blood of mine Only B.;	6:59
the blood of mine Only B.,	6:62
in the name of thine Only B.,	7:50
ask in the name of thine Only B.;	7:59
bear testimony of mine Only B.;	7:62

BEGUILE
that did b. our first parents,	Mos 16: 3
and he sought also to b. Eve,	Mses 4: 6

BEGUILED
being who b. our first parents,	2Ne 9: 9
liar who b. our first parents,	Eth 8:25
The serpent b. me, and I did	Mses 4:19

BEGUN
you have b. to search for gold,	Jac 2:12
sprung forth and b. to bear fruit.	5:17
they had b. to possess the land of	Mos 23:31
and had b. to till the ground.	23:31
b. to be among their people.	Al 4: 7
as ye have b. to teach the word	38:10
b. to settle the affairs of their	51:12
had b. his march towards the land	52:15
the church had b. to dwindle;	He 4:23
of translation as you have b.	DC 10: 3

BEHALF
all his heart, in b. of his people.	1Ne 1: 5
in b. of the people of Limhi.	Mos 20:25
in b. of the welfare of the souls	Al 6: 6
to his God in b. of his people,	3Ne 1:11
they were in b. of their brethren.	Mrm 8:24
prayers were also in b. of him	8:25
let fall the sword in their b.,	DC 35:14
indignation in b. of my people;	101:10
to stand up in b. of the accused,	102:17
of thy testimony in their b.?	109:49
in b. of those, thy brethren,	112: 1

BEHAVE
the child shall b. himself proudly	2Ne 13: 5

BEHAVIOR
I was greatly surprised at his b.;	JS 2:21

BEHELD
he b. that his luster was above	1Ne 1: 9
I b. a man, and he had fallen to	4: 7
I b. his sword, and I drew it forth	4: 9
he b. the garments and also the sword	4:21
servant of Laban b. my brethren	4:30
he b. that they did contain the	5:11
as I followed him I b. myself	8: 7
I b. a large and spacious field.	8: 9
I b. a tree, whose fruit was	8:10
I b. that it was most sweet, above	8:11
I b. that the fruit thereof was white,	8:11
I b. a river of water; and it ran	1Ne 8:13
I b. your mother, Sariah, and	8:14
I b. a rod of iron, and it extended	8:19
I also b. a straight and narrow path,	8:20
I b. others pressing forward, and	8:24
and b., on the other side of the river	8:26
after thou hast b. the tree which	11: 7
I looked and b. a tree; and it	11: 8
I b. that he was in the form	11:11
and b. the great city of Jerusalem,	11:13
And I b. the city of Nazareth;	11:13
I b. a virgin, and she was	11:13
I b. that she was carried away in	11:19
I looked and b. the virgin again,	11:20
I b. the Son of God going forth	11:24
I b. that the rod of iron, which	11:25
I also b. that the tree of life	11:25
I looked and b. the Redeemer of	11:27
I also b. the prophet who should	11:27
after he was baptized, I b. the heavens	11:27
And I b. that he went forth	11:28
I b. that they cast him out	11:28
And I also b. twelve others	11:29
I b. the heavens open again,	11:30
and b. the Lamb of God going forth	11:31
I b. multitudes of people who were	11:31
I looked and b. the Lamb of God,	11:32
I b. that they were in a large	11:35
I looked and b. the land of promise;	12: 1
I b. multitudes of people, yea,	12: 1
I b. multitudes gathered together	12: 2
I b. wars, and rumors of wars,	12: 2
I b. many generations pass away,	12: 3
I b. many cities, yea, even	12: 3
I looked, and b. three generations	12:11
and b. the people of my seed	12:15
I b. and saw that the seed of my	12:19
I b. that the seed of my brethren	12:19
I b., and saw the people of the seed	12:20
I b., after they had dwindled in	12:23
and b. many nations and kingdoms.	13: 1
I b. this great and abominable	13: 6
I looked and b. many waters;	13:10
and b. a man among the Gentiles,	13:12
and I b. the Spirit of God,	13:12
I b. the Spirit of God, that it	13:13
I b. many multitudes of the Gentiles	13:14
and I b. the wrath of God,	13:14
And I b. the Spirit of the Lord,	13:15
I b. that they were white, and	13:15
I, Nephi, b. that the Gentiles	13:16
I b. that their mother Gentiles	13:17
I b. that the power of God was	13:18
And I, Nephi, b. that the Gentiles	13:19
I, Nephi, b. that they did prosper	13:20
I b. a book, and it was carried	13:20
And I, Nephi, b. it; and he said	13:23
Thou hast b. that the book	13:24
I b. the remnant of the seed	13:38
I b. other books, which came forth	13:39
Thou hast b. that if the Gentiles	14: 5
and b. the whore of all the earth,	14:11
I b. the church of the Lamb of God,	14:12
I b. the church of the Lamb,	14:12
I b. that the great mother of	14:13
I, Nephi, b. the power of the Lamb	14:14
I b. that the wrath of God was	14:15
I looked and b. a man, and he	14:19
written in the book which thou b.	14:23
I b. my brethren, and they were	15: 2
my people, for I had b. their fall.	15: 5
he b. not the filthiness of the	15:27
he b. upon the ground a round ball	16:10
my father b. the things which were	16:27
I, Nephi, b. the pointers which were	16:28
they b. that I had obtained food,	16:32
we b. the sea, which we called	17: 5
my brethren b. that it was good,	18: 4
I have b. his glory, and I am	2Ne 1:15
hast b. that in the fulness of time	2: 3
hast b. in thy youth his glory;	2: 4
mine eyes have b. great things,	4:25

BEHELD 98 BEHOLD

hath b. the things of the Jews,	2Ne	25: 5
I have b. that many generations		26: 2
and b. the tree in the which the	Jac	5:17
And he b. that it was good;		5:17
and he b. the first that it had		5:20
and he b. also that it was good.		5:20
they b. that the fruit of the		5:39
for when they b. those that had	Mos	25: 8
they had b. an angel of the Lord;		27:18
and b. with great sorrow that	Al	4: 8
he b. that Amulek had caught		12: 1
he b. that Ammon could discern		18:18
they b. the king, and the queen,		19:18
b. that the man had fallen dead,		19:24
and his brethren had never b.;		31:12
and he b. with great joy;		32: 6
he b. that their afflictions had		32: 6
cried unto those whom he b.,		32: 7
b. that the great question which		34: 5
ye also b. that my brother has		34: 6
and stood up, and b. the angel.		36: 8
b. Lehi with his army coming		52:28
b. that they were surrounded by		55:22
and b. that it was not a voice of	He	5:30
he b. that they did lift their eyes		5:36
to some being whom they b.		5:36
he b. the multitudes of people		7:12
I have b. how thou hast with		10: 4
such an one as ye never have b.;		14: 5
and b. they were in tears,	3Ne	17: 5
we also b. the ten thousand of	Mrm	6:12
they had b. with an eye of faith,	Eth	12:19
had b. the finger of the Lord,		12:21
he b. that the people who were		15:13
b. that the words of the Lord		15:33
we b. the glory of the Son,	DC	76:20
And we b., and lo, he is fallen!		76:27
we b. Satan, that old serpent,		76:28
bear record that I b. his glory,		93:11
b. the world upon which he was	Mses	1: 8
Moses b. the world and the		1: 8
mine own eyes have b. God;		1:11
natural eyes could not have b.;		1:11
and I b. his face, for I was		1:11
of Moses, that he b. him not.		1:22
of God, he b. this glory again,		1:25
cast his eyes and b. the earth,		1:27
he b. also the inhabitants		1:28
not a soul which he b. not;		1:28
he b. many lands; and each land		1:29
because I b. that I was naked,		4:16
he b. the spirits that God had		6:36
he b. also things which were		6:36
by the sea east, I b. a vision;		6:42
I b. the heavens open,		7: 3
I b. in the valley of Shum,		7: 5
I b. the people of Canaan,		7: 6
and I b. the land of Sharon,		7: 9
and he b., and lo, Zion, in		7:21
Enoch also b. the residue of		7:22
Enoch b., and lo, all the		7:23
And he b. Satan; and he had		7:26
Enoch b. angels descending out		7:27
b. all the families of the earth;		7:45
b. the Son of Man lifted up on		7:55
Enoch b. the Son of Man ascend		7:59
a fact that I had b. a vision.	JS	2:24
again I b. the same messenger		2:46
b. the same messenger standing		2:49

BEHELDEST

And thou b. that I also cut	Jac	5:44
And thou b. that a part thereof		5:45

BEHIND

obliged to leave b. our property,	1Ne	3:26
and the Philistines b.	2Ne	19:12
they shall leave a record b. them,	Mos	12: 8
not a whit b. him as to things	He	11:19
are to remain b. this season;	DC	136: 9

BEHOLD

B., I make an abridgment of the	1Ne	1:17
b. he went forth among the people,	1Ne	1:18
b., I, Nephi, will show unto you		1:20
For b., it came to pass that		2: 1
b., they seek to take away thy life.		2: 1
b. they did murmur in many things		2:11
b. he did visit me, and did soften		2:16
b., Laman and Lemuel would not		2:18
For b., in that day that they		2:23
B. I have dreamed a dream, in		3: 2
For b., Laban hath the record of		3: 3
And now, b. thy brothers murmur,		3: 5
but b. I have not required it		3: 5
And b., it came to pass that		3:13
B. thou art a robber, and I will		3:13
But b. I said unto them that:		3:15
for b. he left gold and silver,		3:16
For b., they have refected the		3:18
b., he would also perish. Wherefore,		3:18
And b., it is wisdom in God		3:19
b., an angel of the Lord came		3:29
B. ye shall go up to Jerusalem		3:29
B., he is a mighty man, and he can		3:31
b. he is mightier than all the earth,		4: 1
Now b. ye know that this is true;		4: 3
B. the Lord hath delivered him		4:11
B. the Lord slayeth the wicked		4:13
b., I saw the servant of Laban		4:20
b., he was filled with joy, and		5: 1
B. thou hast led us forth from		5: 2
b., I have obtained a land of		5: 5
b. their joy was full, and my		5: 7
b. Laman and Lemuel, and two of the		7: 6
B. ye are mine elder brethren,		7: 8
b., the Spirit of the Lord ceaseth		7:14
b., they have rejected the prophets,		7:14
Now b., I say unto you that		7:15
b., they were exceeding wroth,		7:16
b., the bands were loosed from off		7:18
but b., one of the daughters of		7:19
B., I have dreamed a dream; or,		8: 2
b., because of the thing which I		8: 3
But b., Laman and Lemuel, I fear		8: 4
b., me thought I saw in my dream,		8: 4
I looked to b. from whence it came;		8:14
b., he saw other multitudes		8:30
b. they are not the plates upon		9: 2
for b., he hath all power unto		9: 6
For b., it came to pass after my		10: 2
he should b. and bear record		10:10
unto me: B., what desirest thou?		11: 2
to b. the things which my father		11: 3
thou shalt b. the things which		11: 6
And b. this thing shall be		11: 7
b. a man descending out of		11: 7
I b. thou hast shown unto me the		11: 9
B., the virgin whom thou seest		11:18
B. the Lamb of God, yea, even		11:21
b. the condescension of God!		11:26
B. the world and the wisdom		11:35
b. the house of Israel hath		11:35
b. thy seed, and also the seed		12: 1
b., I saw multitudes who had		12: 5
B. the twelve disciples of the Lamb,		12: 8
B. they are they who shall		12: 9
b., they are righteous forever;		12:10
B. thy seed, and also the seed		12:14
B. the fountain of filthy water		12:16
B. these shall dwindle in unbelief.		12:22
I b. many nations and kingdoms.		13: 2
B. the foundation of a church		13: 5
B. the gold, and the silver, and the		13: 8
B. the wrath of God is upon		13:11
B. it proceedeth out of the mouth		13:23
b., they have taken away from the		13:26
B., saith the Lamb of God,		13:34
b., saith the Lamb: I will manifest		13:35
b., these things shall be hid up,		13:35
For b., this is according to the		14: 4
b. that great and abominable		14: 9
B. there are save two churches		14:10
B., the wrath of God is upon		14:16
b., thou seest all these things—		14:16
B. one of the twelve apostles		14:20

B., he shall see and write	1 Ne 14:21	B., my soul delighteth in	2 Ne	4:16
b., they are written in the book	14:23	B., he hath heard my cry by day,		4:23
b., the things which this apostle	14:24	B., my voice shall forever ascend		4:35
b., the remainder shalt thou see.	14:24	B., it came to pass that		5: 1
b., I, Nephi, am forbidden that I	14:28	But b., their anger did increase		5: 2
B., we cannot understand the	15: 7	For b., we will not have him to		5: 3
B., I said unto them: How	15:10	And b., the words of the Lord had		5:19
B., I say unto you, that the	15:12	b., they were cut off from his		5:20
b. are we not broken off from the	15:12	b., they had hardened their hearts		5:21
B., I say unto you, Yea; they	15:16	B., my beloved brethren,		6: 2
b., I say unto you, the kingdom	15:34	b. ye know that I have spoken		6: 2
b. they said unto me: Thou hast	16: 1	And now, b., I would speak		6: 4
b., I did break my bow, which	16:18	B., I will lift up mine hand		6: 6
b., my brethren were angry with	16:18	b., the Lord has shown me that		6: 8
b. the things which are written.	16:26	b., the judgments of the Holy One		6:10
B., let us slay our father, and also	16:37	for b., if it so be that they shall		6:12
b., we know that he lies unto us;	16:38	And b., according to the words of		6:14
B., these many years we have	17:21	B., for your iniquities have ye		7: 1
B., I say unto you, Nay.	17:33	B., at my rebuke I dry up the		7: 2
B., the Lord esteemeth all flesh in	17:35	b., all they shall wax old		7: 9
But b., this people had rejected	17:35	B. all ye that kindle fire,		7:11
B., the Lord hath created the earth	17:36	B., who art thou, that thou		8:12
B., he loved our fathers, and he	17:40	unto Zion: B., thou art my people.		8:16
B., my soul is rent with anguish	17:47	b., I have taken out of thine hand		8:22
B., I am full of the Spirit of God,	17:47	B., my beloved brethren, I speak		9: 3
b., my brethren and the sons of	18: 9	b., if the flesh should rise no more		9: 8
b. they were angry with me,	18:10	But, b., the righteous, the saints of		9:18
b. they had swollen exceedingly;	18:15	for b., he suffereth the pains of		9:21
b., they did breathe out much	18:17	And b., their treasure shall perish		9:30
b., I took the compass, and it	18:21	and b. his face, and remain in		9:38
b., I proceed according to that	19: 5	B., the way for man is narrow,		9:41
b. he cometh, according to the words	19: 8	B., I take off my garments,		9:44
b., I have workings in the spirit,	19:20	b., my brethren, is it expedient		9:47
B., I have declared the former	20: 3	B., if ye were holy I would speak		9:48
shouldest say – B. I knew them.	20: 7	B., my soul abhorreth sin,		9:49
For, b., I have refined thee,	20:10	B., my beloved brethren, remember		9:52
b., these shall come from far;	21:12	And b. how great the covenants		9:53
But, b., Zion hath said: The Lord	21:14	For b., the promises which we have		10: 2
B., I have graven thee upon the	21:16	But b., thus saith the Lord God:		10: 7
up thine eyes round about and b.;	21:18	But b., this land, said God, shall		10:10
B., I was left alone; these, where	21:21	For b., the Lord God has led away		10:22
B., I will lift up mine hand to the	21:22	now b., the Lord remembereth		10:22
B., are they to be understood	22: 1	B., my soul delighteth in		11: 4
B. they were manifest unto the	22: 2	b., the Lord, the Lord of Hosts,		13: 1
b., there are many who are already	22: 4	for judgment, and b., oppression;		15: 7
b. these things of which are spoken	22: 6	for righteousness, but b., a cry.		15: 7
For b., saith the prophet, the	22:15	and b., they shall come with speed		15:26
B., my brethren, I say unto you,	22:18	b., darkness and sorrow,		15:30
b., the righteous shall not perish;	22:19	B., a virgin shall conceive,		17:14
And now b., I, Nephi, say unto you	22:27	For b., the child shall not have		18: 4
b., all nations, kindreds, tongues,	22:28	therefore, b., the Lord bringeth up		18: 7
For, b., said he, I have been	2 Ne 1: 4	B., I and the children whom the		18:18
And b., it is wisdom that	1: 8	and b. trouble, and darkness,		18:22
for b., many nations would	1: 8	B., the Lord, the Lord of Hosts shall		20:33
But b., when the time cometh	1:10	B., God is my salvation;		22: 2
b., I say, if the day shall come	1:10	B., the day of the Lord cometh,		23: 9
b., the judgments of him that is	1:10	B., I will stir up the Medes		23:17
But b., the Lord hath redeemed	1:15	For b., Isaiah spake many things		25: 1
b., this hath been the anxiety	1:16	b., my soul delighteth in plainness		25: 4
But b., his will be done;	1:19	But b., I, Nephi, have not taught		25: 6
for b., ye have accused him that he	1:25	but b., I, of myself, have dwelt at		25: 6
but b., his sharpness was	1:26	But b., I proceed with mine own		25: 7
But b., it was not he, but it	1:27	But, b., they shall have wars,		25:12
b., if ye will hearken unto	1:28	b., they will reject him,		25:12
B., thou art the servant of Laban;	1:30	B., they will crucify him;		25:13
And b., in thy childhood	2: 1	And b. it shall come to pass		25:14
B., he offereth himself a sacrifice	2: 7	B., Jerusalem shall be destroyed		25:14
And now, b., if Adam had not	2:22	yea, b. I say unto you,		25:20
But b., all things have been done	2:24	And now b., my people,		25:28
For b., thou art the fruit of	3: 4	And now b., I say unto you		25:29
B., that seer will the Lord bless;	3:14	For b., I say unto you that		26: 2
B., I am sure of the fulfilling	3:14	But b., the righteous that hearken		26: 8
And I, b., I will give unto him	3:18	b., they are they which shall		26: 8
And now, b., my son Joseph,	3:22	But b., I prophesy unto you		26:14
B., thou art little;	3:25	For b., my beloved brethren,		26:23
For b., he truly prophesied	4: 2	B., doth he cry unto any, saying:		26:25
B., my sons, and my daughters,	4: 3	B., I say unto you, Nay;		26:25
But b., my sons and my daughters,	4: 5	B., hath he commanded any that		26:26
for b., I know that if ye are	4: 5	B., I say unto you, Nay.		26:26
b., I leave my blessing upon you,	4: 6	B. I say unto you, Nay;		26:27
B., my sons and my daughters,	4: 9	B., hath the Lord commanded any		26:28
b. I leave unto you the same	4: 9	B. I say unto you, Nay;		26:28
b., he spake unto the sons of	4:10	for, b., priestcrafts are that men		26:29

B., the Lord hath forbidden this	2Ne	26:30
But, b. in the last days,		27: 1
yea, b. all the nations of the Gentiles		27: 1
b., they will be drunken with		27: 1
and b. he eateth but he awaketh		27: 3
b. he drinketh but he awaketh		27: 3
he awaketh and b. he is faint,		27: 3
For b., all ye that doeth iniquity,		27: 4
For b., the Lord hath poured out		27: 5
For b., ye have closed your eyes,		27: 5
And b. the book shall be sealed;		27: 7
for b., they reveal all things from		27:10
the eyes of none shall b. it save		27:12
three witnesses shall b. it,		27:12
But b., it shall come to pass that		27:15
For b., I am God; and I am a God		27:23
But b., I will show unto them,		27:27
But b., saith the Lord of Hosts:		27:28
And now, b., my brethren, I have		28: 1
B., I, I am the Lord's;		28: 3
for b. there is no God today,		28: 5
B., hearken ye unto my precept;		28: 6
b., if the inhabitants of the earth		28:17
But b., that great and abominable		28:18
For b., at that day shall he		28:20
And b., others he flattereth away,		28:22
b., he that is built upon the rock		28:28
For b., thus saith the Lord God:		28:30
But b., there shall be many—		29: 1
But b., I will return all these		29: 5
For b., I shall speak unto the		29:12
And now b., my beloved brethren,		30: 1
For b., except ye shall keep the		30: 1
For b., I say unto you that		30: 2
b., then shall ye receive the		31:13
But, b., my beloved brethren,		31:14
B., I say unto you, Nay;		31:19
b., thus saith the Father:		31:20
And now b., my beloved brethren,		31:21
And now, b., this is the doctrine		31:21
And now, b., my beloved brethren,		32: 1
But, b., why do ye ponder these		32: 1
for b., the words of Christ will		32: 3
For b., again I say unto you that		32: 5
B., this is the doctrine of Christ,		32: 6
But b., I say unto you that		32: 9
But b., there are many that		33: 2
But b., for none of these can I		33: 9
b., I bid you an everlasting		33:14
For b., it came to pass	Jac	1: 1
b., as yet, ye have been obedient		2: 4
But b., hearken ye unto me,		2: 5
b., as I inquired of the Lord,		2:11
And now b., my brethren,		2:12
B., I say unto you, Nay.		2:14
For b., thus saith the Lord:		2:23
B., David and Solomon truly had		2:24
For b., I, the Lord, have seen		2:31
And now b., my brethren,		2:34
B., ye have done greater iniquities		2:35
b., I, Jacob, would speak unto you		3: 1
B., the Lamanites your brethren,		3: 5
B., their husbands love their wives,		3: 7
Now b., it came to pass that		4: 1
B., they believed in Christ and		4: 5
B., great and marvelous are the		4: 8
For b., by the power of his		4: 9
For b., ye yourselves know		4:10
B., my brethren, he that		4:13
But b., we are not witnesses alone		4:13
But b., the Jews were a stiffnecked		4:14
But b., according to the scriptures,		4:16
B., my beloved brethren, I will		4:18
B., my brethren, do ye not		5: 1
For b., thus saith the Lord,		5: 3
but b., the main top thereof		5: 6
And b., saith the Lord of		5: 8
B., look here; behold the tree.		5:16
Behold, look here; b. the tree.		5:16
B., the branches of the wild tree		5:18
And now b., I shall lay up much		5:18
and b. if the natural branches of		5:19
B. these; and he beheld the		5:20
for b., said he, this long time	Jac	5:20
For b., it was the poorest spot		5:21
b. I have planted another branch		5:23
But, b. the tree.		5:23
and b. another branch also,		5:24
b. that I have nourished it also,		5:24
Look hither and b. the last.		5:25
B., this have I planted in a good		5:25
b., I have nourished this tree like		5:25
But b., the servant said unto him:		5:27
For b., the time draweth near,		5:29
b. all sorts of fruit did cumber		5:30
B., this long time have we nourished		5:31
But b., this time it hath brought		5:32
And b., there are all kinds of		5:32
B., because thou didst graft in		5:34
But b., the wild branches have		5:37
and b. if the natural branches have		5:38
B., I knew that all the fruit of		5:42
And b. this last, whose branch		5:43
b., they have overcome the good		5:45
And now, b., notwithstanding		5:46
But, b., they have become like		5:46
b. they grew faster than the		5:48
B., I say, is not this the cause		5:48
But, b., the servant said unto		5:50
And, b., the roots of the natural		5:54
for b. the end draweth nigh,		5:62
for b., only this once will I		5:69
For b., this is the last time that		5:71
B., for this last time have we		5:75
b. ye shall have joy with me		5:75
For b., for a long time will		5:76
And now, b., my brethren,		6: 1
b., this is my prophecy—		6: 1
For b., after ye have been		6: 7
B., will ye reject these words?		6: 8
And now b., I, Sherem, declare		7: 7
But b., the Lord God poured in		7: 8
B., I say unto you that		7:11
B., it came to pass that	En	1: 1
B., I went to hunt beasts		1: 3
b., the voice of the Lord came into		1:10
now b., this was the desire which		1:13
Now b., I, Jarom, write a few	Jar	1: 1
B., it is expedient that		1: 3
And now, b., two hundred years		1: 5
But b., my brethren, ye can		1:14
for b., upon them the records		1:14
B., it came to pass that	Om	1: 1
b., I of myself am a wicked man.		1: 2
B., it came to pass that		1: 5
for b., I saw the last which he		1: 9
B., I Abinadom, am the son of		1:10
B., it came to pass that		1:10
And b., the record of this people		1:11
B., I am Amaleki, the son of		1:12
B., I will speak unto you		1:12
for b., he being warned of the		1:12
B., it came to pass that		1:15
B., I, Jacob, was born of the		1:23
And b., I have seen, in the days		1:24
But b., the Nephites did obtain		1:24
b. I have witnessed almost all	WM	1: 1
But b., I shall take these		1: 6
But b., king Benjamin gathered		1:13
b., it came to pass that king		1:16
For b., king Benjamin was a holy		1:17
And b., also the plates of Nephi,	Mos	1: 6
B., I say unto you that		2:16
And b., I tell you these things		2:17
B., ye have called me your king;		2:18
And b. aiso, if I, whom ye call		2:19
And b., all that he requires of		2:22
but b., it belongeth to him who		2:25
And ye b. that I am old,		2:26
For b., there is a wo pronounced		2:33
And b., also, they spake that		2:35
For b., they are blessed in all		2:41
for b., I have things to tell		3: 1
and b. he stood before me.		3: 2
for b., I am come to declare		3: 3
For b.. the time cometh,		3: 5

BEHOLD

for b., blood cometh from every	Mos	3: 7	B., this is the first time that	Al 1:12
and b., he standeth to judge the		3:10	And b., thou are not only guilty	1:12
and b., all these things are done		3:10	B., we followed the camp of	2:24
For b., and also his blood atoneth		3:11	b., the Amlicites have joined them;	2:24
for b., as in Adam, or by nature,		3:16	And b., as they were crossing	2:27
For b. he judgeth, and his		3:18	and b. their bones are in the	3: 3
And b., when that time cometh,		3:21	B., the Lamanites have I cursed,	3:14
b. they had fallen to the earth,		4: 1	B., I say unto you that he	5: 3
For b., if the knowledge of		4: 5	And b., I say unto you, they	5: 4
And b., I say unto you that		4:12	And b., after that, they were	5: 5
For b., are we not all beggars?		4:19	And now b., I say unto you,	5: 6
And b., even at this time, they have		4:20	B., he changed their hearts;	5: 7
for b., this day he hath spiritually		5: 7	B., they were in the midst of	5: 7
And b., they met the king of		7: 7	B., I say unto you Nay,	5: 8
B., I am Limhi, the son of		7: 9	B., I can tell you—	5:11
For b., we are in bondage to		7:15	B. I say unto you that this is	5:12
And now, b., our brethren will		7:15	And b., he preached the word	5:13
for b., the time is at hand,		7:18	And b., they were faithful until	5:13
and b., it is because of our		7:20	And now of you, I ask	5:14
And b., we at this time do pay		7:22	for b., your works have been	5:16
Now b., how great reason we have		7:23	B., what will these things testify	5:22
for b. how many of our brethren		7:24	B. will they not testify that	5:23
But b., they would not hearken unto		7:25	B., my brethren, do ye suppose	5:24
For b., the Lord hath said:		7:29	And now b., I say unto you,	5:26
And now, b., the promise of		7:32	B., are ye stripped of pride?	5:28
And b., also, they have brought		8:10	B. ye must prepare quickly;	5:28
And b., the king of the people who		8:14	B., I say, is there one among you	5:29
And b., to our great sorrow and		9:19	B., he sendeth an invitation	5:33
For b., he did not keep the		11: 2	For b., the time is at hand	5:36
B., thus saith the Lord,		11:20	B., I say unto you, that	5:38
b., I will deliver them into		11:21	b., ye are not the sheep of the	5:38
B., we have brought a man before		12: 9	B., I say unto you, that the devil	5:39
now, O king, b., we are guiltless,		12:14	B., I say unto you, whosoever	5:39
And b., we are strong,		12:15	for b., I have spoken unto you	5:43
B., here is the man,		12:16	B., I testify unto you that I	5:45
But b., I say unto you, that		13:31	B., I say unto you they are	5:46
For b., did not Moses prophesy		13:33	B., I have fasted and prayed	5:46
B., I say unto you, that when		15:10	And b., it is he that cometh	5:48
B. I say unto you, that whosoever		15:11	B. the glory of the King of all	5:50
And b., I say unto you, this is		15:18	B., the ax is laid at the root of	5:52
But b., the bands of death shall		15:20	B., and remember, the Holy One	5:52
But b., and fear, and tremble		15:26	and b., their names shall be	5:57
and b., they would have been		16: 4	And b., if a wolf enter his flock	5:59
B., even as ye have done		17:15	B. my beloved brethren,	7: 1
B., here are the waters of Mormon		18: 8	And b., I have come having	7: 3
But b., it came to pass that		18:32	for b., my joy cometh over them	7: 5
And now b., the forces of the		19: 2	And b., I trust that ye are not	7: 6
and b., the army of the Lamanites		19: 6	For b., I say unto you there be	7: 7
B., here is the king of the		20:13	and b., there is one thing which	7: 7
and b., we have brought him		20:13	for b., the time is not far	7: 7
B., my people have not broken		20:14	B., I do not say that he will	7: 8
And now, b., and tell the king		20:19	for b., the Spirit hath not said	7: 8
for b. they are already preparing		20:19	But b., the Spirit hath said this	7: 9
and b. also there are but few		20:19	for b., the kingdom of heaven is	7: 9
And b., they come with their		20:20	And b., he shall be born of	7:10
B. the back pass, through the		22: 6	now b., this is the testimony	7:13
B., it is not expedient that		23: 7	B., I say unto you, yea,	7:17
For b., I will show unto you		23:23	B., we know that thou art Alma;	8:11
For b., it came to pass that		23:25	b. an angel of the Lord appeared	8:14
b. an army of the Lamanites was		23:25	B., I am he that delivered it	8:15
And b., they had found those		23:31	And b., I am sent to command	8:16
B., here are many whom we have		26:11	For b., they do study at this	8:17
B., I judge them not; therefore		26:12	And b., I have been called to	8:24
For b., this is my church;		26:22	But b., I have been commanded	8:25
For b., in my name are they		26:24	but b., they did not.	9: 7
b., the angel of the Lord appeared		27:11	B., O ye wicked and perverse	9: 8
B., the Lord hath heard me		27:14	B., now I say unto you that	9:12
And now b., can ye dispute		27:15	But b., this is not all—	9:12
For b., doth not my voice shake		27:15	B., do ye not remember the	9:13
can ye not also b. me before you?		27:15	But b., I say unto you that	9:18
b. I am born of the Spirit.		27:24	And now b. I say unto you,	9:23
now I b. the marvelous light		27:29	For b., the promises of the Lord	9:24
b., it gave an account of the people		28:17	And b., he cometh to redeem	9:27
for b., it is expedient that all		28:19	Now b., this is the voice of	9:29
B., O ye my people, of my		29: 5	b., the people were wroth with me	9:31
b. I fear there would rise		29: 7	And b., I am also a man of no	10: 4
For b., how much iniquity doth		29:17	and b., I have many kindreds	10: 4
B. what great destruction did		29:18	but b., I mistake, for I have	10: 5
But b., he did deliver them		29:20	b. an angel of the Lord appeared	10: 7
And b., now I say unto you,		29:21	And b. it was this same man	10: 8
For b., he has his friends in		29:22	for b. I say unto you, that as	10:10
And now b. I say unto you,		29:24	For b., he hath blessed mine	10:11
For b. I say unto you,		29:31	For b., have I testified against	10:26

BEHOLD 102 BEHOLD

And now b., I say unto you,	Al 10:27	B., thousands of them do rejoice,	Al	26: 4
B., here are six onties of silver,	11:22	B., the field was ripe, and blessed		26: 5
B. these six onties which are	11:25	b. the number of your sheaves!		26: 5
And now b., for this great evil	11:25	But b., they are in the hands of		26: 7
B. thou hast lied, for thou sayest	11:36	but b., my joy is full, yea,		26:11
for b., the day cometh that all	11:41	yea, b., many mighty miracles we		26:12
Now, b., I have spoken unto you	11:45	B., how many thousands of		26:13
for b., he knows all thy thoughts,	12: 3	but b., he has brought them		26:15
And b. I say unto you all	12: 6	B., who can glory too much in		26:16
And now b., I say unto you	12:16	B., I say unto you, I cannot say		26:16
And now b., I say unto you	12:23	B., we went forth even in wrath		26:18
And now b., if it were possible	12:26	B., he did not exercise his justice		26:20
But b., it was not so;	12:27	And now b., my brethren,		26:21
b., then he saw that it was	12:28	But b., my beloved brethren,		26:26
who caused men to b. of his glory.	12:29	b., the Lord comforted us,		26:27
b., I swear in my wrath that he	12:35	And now b., we have come,		26:28
my brethren, b. I say unto you,	12:36	Now b., we can look forth and		26:31
And b., they did repent;	13:18	For b., they had rather sacrifice		26:32
B., the scriptures are before	13:20	And now b. I say unto you,		26:33
For b., angels are declaring it	13:24	B., I say unto you, Nay,		26:33
B., I am guilty, and these men	14: 7	For b., they would take up arms		26:34
for b. the Lord receiveth them	14:11	But b. how many of these		26:34
B., perhaps they will burn us also.	14:12	B., the Nephites will destroy us,		27: 6
But, b., our work is not	14:13	B., I and my brethren will go		27:15
B., ye see that ye had not	14:15	and b., this was a joyful		27:16
and b., there they found all the	15: 1	B., this is joy which none		27:18
For b., the armies of the	16: 2	but b. their joy was not that		27:19
B., the Lamanites will cross the	16: 6	B., we will give up the land of		27:22
And b. there shall ye meet them,	16: 6	And b., we will set our armies		27:23
But b., in one day it was	16:10	And now b., this will we do unto		27:24
b., to his astonishment, he met	17: 1	b. the armies of the Lamanites		28: 1
b., a certain number of the	17:27	But b., I am a man, and do sin		29: 3
B., our flocks are scattered	17:28	For b., the Lord doth grant unto		29: 8
But b., every man that lifted his	17:37	And b., when I see many of my		29:10
B., is not this the Great Spirit	18: 2	B., they have labored exceedingly,		29:15
B., he is feeding thy horses.	18: 9	B., now it came to pass that after		30: 1
b., is it this that causeth thy	18:16	B., these things which ye call		30:14
B., I am a man, and am thy	18:17	b., they are foolish traditions of		30:14
b., I have seen my Redeemer;	19:13	B., ye cannot know of things which		30:15
and b., he was a Nephite.	19:18	But b., it is the effect of a		30:16
to smite him, b., he fell dead.	19:22	But b. they were more wise than		30:20
and b. he arose and stood upon	19:30	B., I say they are in bondage.		30:24
And b., many did declare unto	19:34	B., I say that ye do not know		30:24
for b., the king will seek thy life;	20: 2	B., I say that a child is not		30:25
for b., thy brother Aaron,	20: 2	But b., I say that ye do not		30:26
B., my brother and brethren are	20: 3	for b. I have labored even		30:32
But b., I will go with thee to the	20: 4	For b., I say unto you, I know		30:39
And b., the father of Lamoni	20: 9	But, b., I have all things as a		30:41
b., to his astonishment,	20:13	B., I know that thou believest,		30:42
B., he robbed our fathers;	20:13	B., I am grieved because of the		30:46
B., thou shalt not slay thy son;	20:17	But b., it is better that thy soul		30:47
for b., he has repented of his sins;	20:17	b. God shall smite thee, that thou		30:47
B., I will smite thee except thou	20:22	B., he has showed unto you a		30:51
b., I will grant unto you that	20:26	But b., the devil hath deceived		30:53
for b. they were naked, and their	20:29	b., he was run upon and		30:59
b. Aaron took his journey	21: 1	b., to their astonishment they		31:12
b. there arose an Amalekite and	21: 5	For b., every man did go forth		31:20
B. are not this people as good	21: 5	to b. such gross wickedness		31:26
B., we have built sanctuaries,	21: 6	B., O God, they cry unto thee,		31:27
B., O king, we are the brethren of	22: 2	B., O God, they cry unto thee		31:27
B., the Spirit of the Lord has	22: 4	B., O my God, their costly		31:28
B., this is the thing which	22: 5	and b., their hearts are set upon		31:28
there is a God, b. I will believe.	22: 7	B., O Lord, their souls are precious,		31:35
B., assuredly as thou livest, O king,	22: 8	And b., as he clapped his hands		31:36
B., said he, I will give up all that	22:15	for b., they were cast out of the		32: 2
when b. one of them is mightier	22:20	B., what shall these my brethren		32: 5
B., now it came to pass that	23: 1	and b., what shall we do?		32: 5
And b., I thank my great God	24: 8	I b. that ye are lowly in heart;		32: 8
And b., I also thank my God,	24: 9	B. thy brother hath said, what		32: 9
And now b., my brethren,	24:11	B. I say unto you, do ye suppose		32:10
B., I say unto you, Nay,	24:13	B., I say unto you, Nay;		32:18
And now b., since it has been as	24:15	B., I say unto you, that it is		32:20
b., we will hide away our swords,	24:16	And now, b., I say unto you,		32:22
b., we shall go to our God	24:16	But b., if ye will awake and arouse		32:27
And b., now it came to pass that	25: 1	b., if it be a true seed,		32:28
And b. they are hunted at this	25: 9	b. it will begin to swell within		32:28
and now b., these words were	25:12	Now b., would not this increase		32:29
And now b., Ammon, and Aaron,	25:17	But b., as the seed swelleth,		32:30
b. I say unto you, how great	26: 1	for b. it swelleth, and sprouteth,		32:30
B., I answer for you; for our	26: 3	And now, b., are ye sure that		32:31
but b., how many of them are	26: 3	it groweth not, b. it is not good,		32:32
to b. the marvelous light of God!	26: 3	And now, b., because ye have		32:33

And now, b., is your knowledge	Al 32:34	but b., I give it as my opinion,	Al 40:20
and now b., after ye have	32:35	But b., an awful death cometh	40:26
B. I say unto you, Nay;	32:36	for b., some have wrested the	41: 1
And b., as the tree beginneth to	32:37	But b., I will explain it unto thee.	41: 1
And now b., if ye nourish it with	32:37	B., it is requisite and just,	41: 2
b. it will not get any root;	32:38	for b., they are their own judges,	41: 7
and b. it shall be a tree	32:41	And now b., my son, do not	41: 9
b., by and by ye shall pluck the	32:42	B., I say unto you, wickedness	41:10
B., ye have said that ye could	33: 2	And now b., is the meaning of	41:12
But b., I say unto you, if ye	33: 2	Now b., my son, I will explain	42: 2
B., if ye do, ye must believe what	33:13	For b., after the Lord God sent	42: 2
for, b. he said: Thou hast	33:13	For b., if Adam had put forth	42: 5
Now b., my brethren, I would ask	33:14	But b., it was appointed unto man	42: 6
For b., he said: Thou art angry,	33:16	Now b., it was not expedient	42: 8
But b., this is not all;	33:18	For b., justice exerciseth all	42:24
B., he was spoken of by Moses;	33:19	b., evil shall be done unto him,	42:28
and b. a type was raised up in	33:19	For b., it came to pass that the	43: 4
would ye not b. quickly, or would	33:21	For b., his designs were to stir up	43: 8
And b., it will become a tree,	33:23	b., the armies of the Nephites	43:15
And now, b., I will testify unto	34: 8	B., now it came to pass that	43:22
B., I say unto you, that I do	34: 8	for b., on the east were the men	43:52
b. will our law, which is just,	34:11	B., Zerahemnah, that we do not	44: 1
And b., this is the whole meaning	34:14	B., we have not come out to	44: 2
now b., my beloved brethren,	34:28	ye b. that the Lord is with us;	44: 3
b., your prayer is vain,	34:28	ye b. that he has delivered you	44: 3
for b., now is the time and the day	34:31	b., ye are in our hands, and I will	44: 7
For b., this life is the time for	34:32	B., here are our weapons of war;	44: 8
yea, b. the day of this life is the	34:32	B., we are not of your faith;	44: 9
b., if we do not improve our time	34:33	B., it is your breastplates and	44: 9
For b., if ye have procrastinated	34:35	B., we will end the conflict.	44:10
b., ye have become subjected to	34:35	b., one of Moroni's soldiers smote	44:12
for b., he rewardeth you no	34:39	But b., their naked skins and	44:18
b., thou art in thy youth,	36: 3	yea, b. they were pierced and	44:18
Now, b., I say unto you, if I	36: 5	B., now it came to pass that the	45: 1
but b., God sent his holy angel	36: 6	But b., I have somewhat to	45: 9
And b., he spake unto us, as it	36: 7	B., I perceive that this very people,	45:10
But b., the voice said unto me:	36: 8	b., the time very soon cometh	45:13
b., I remembered also to have	36:17	B., this we know, that he was a	45:19
And now, b., when I thought	36:19	But b., the scriptures saith	45:19
what marvelous light I did b.;	36:20	For b., because of their wars	45:21
But b., my limbs did receive their	36:23	And now b., they were exceeding	46: 2
Yea, and now b., O my son,	36:25	B., whosoever will maintain this	46:20
b., many have been born of God,	36:26	b., the people came running	46:21
But b., my son, this is not all;	36:30	B., we are a remnant of the seed	46:23
B., it has been prophesied by	37: 4	b., let us remember to keep the	46:23
And now b., if they are kept	37: 5	for b., he saw that a part of the	46:24
but b. I say unto you, that	37: 6	Now b., this giveth my soul	46:25
for b., they have enlarged the	37: 8	Now b., this was the language	46:26
And now b., I tell you by the	37:15	b., he had taken those who went	47: 1
b., these things which are sacred	37:15	Now b., this was the desire of	47: 4
b., no power of earth or hell can	37:16	but b., this was his intention to	47: 8
And now b., one purpose hath	37:19	And b., it came to pass that he	47: 9
For b., the Lord saw that his	37:22	But b., as the king came out to	47:22
For b., there is a curse upon	37:28	b. he stabbed the king to the	47:24
For b., they murdered all the	37:30	B., the servants of the king have	47:26
And b., there cannot any man	37:39	b., come and see.	47:26
And b., it was prepared to show	37:39	b., the very powers of hell would	48:17
they should go, b., it was done;	37:40	B., he was a man like unto Ammon,	48:18
For b., it is as easy to give heed	37:44	Now b., Helaman and his brethren	48:19
But b., the Lord in his great mercy	38: 7	And b., the city had been rebuilt,	49: 2
But b., I did cry unto him and	38: 8	for b., they fought with stones	49: 2
B., he is the life and the light of	38: 9	B., I said that the city of	49: 3
B., he is the word of truth and	38: 9	But b., how great was their	49: 4
for b., have ye not observed the	39: 1	for b., the Nephites had dug up a	49: 4
B., has he not set a good example	39: 1	But b., to their uttermost	49: 8
For b., if ye deny the Holy Ghost	39: 6	for b., he did care not for the	49:10
b., this is a sin which is	39: 6	But b., Amalickiah did not come	49:11
But b., ye cannot hide your crimes	39: 8	And b., his chief captains durst	49:11
for b., thou art in thy youth,	39:10	But b., to their astonishment,	49:14
B., O my son, how great iniquity	39:11	And now b., this was wisdom	49:15
for b., you cannot carry them	39:14	And b., Moroni had appointed	49:16
B. I say unto you, that it is he	39:15	And now b. it came to pass,	49:17
B., you marvel why these things	39:17	Now b., the Lamanites could	49:18
B., I say unto you, is not a soul	39:17	but b., they were driven back	49:21
B., I say unto you, that there is	40: 2	but b., in these attmpts they	49:22
B., he bringeth to pass the	40: 3	we can b. that his words are	50:19
But b., my son, the resurrection is	40: 3	But b. there never was a	50:23
B., there is a time appointed	40: 4	For b., the people who possessed	50:26
B., it has been made known unto	40:11	But b., the people who possessed	50:27
for b., they have no part nor	40:13	for b. they were not in the wrong.	50:27
for b., they chose evil works rather	40:13	And b., they would have carried	50:30
And b., again it hath been spoken,	40:16	but b., Morianton being a man	50:30
B., I say unto you, Nay;	40:18	Now b., the people who were	50:32

BEHOLD   104   BEHOLD

B., it came to pass that the	Al	50:39	b., those two thousand and sixty	Al	57:20
Now b., his name was Pahoran.		50:40	now b., it was these my sons,		57:22
for b., there were a part of the		51: 2	b., we did inquire of Gid		57:28
But b., Pahoran would not alter		51: 3	B., we did start to go down to		57:30
But b., this was a critical time		51: 9	B., the armies of the Lamanites		57:31
for b., Amalickiah had again		51: 9	and b., they will fall upon them,		57:31
But b., we shall see that his		51:10	And b., when they had fled and		57:34
for b., this had been hitherto		51:16	and b.. we did arrive in time		57:34
B., it came to pass that while		51:22	And b., we are again delivered		57:35
b., the Lamanites had come into		51:22	for b., it is he that has delivered		57:35
But b. he met with a		51:31	And b., now it came to pass that		58: 1
and b., sleep had overpowered		51:33	but b., there was no way that		58: 1
and b., his men were asleep,		51:35	For b., they remembered that		58: 1
b., when the Lamanites awoke		52: 1	But b., this did profit us but		58: 5
b., they found Amalickiah was		52: 1	b., I caused that Gid, with a		58:16
but b., the Lamanites are upon us		52:11	b., I remained, with the remainder		58:17
and b., I go against them,		52:11	And b., it was night and they		58:25
But b., it came to pass in the		52:15	b., on the morrow we were beyond		58:27
But b., Jacob, who was a Zoramite,		52:20	But b., they have carried with		58:30
b., Moroni commanded that a		52:24	But b., our armies are small to		58:32
And now b., when the chief		52:28	But b., we trust in our God who		58:33
But b., Moroni and his men were		52:34	B., we do not know but what ye		58:35
b. we will forbear shedding your		52:37	b., we fear that there is some		58:36
But b., there were many that		52:39	But, b., it mattereth not—		58:37
Now b., this Lehi was a man who		53: 2	B., this is the twenty and ninth		58:38
And now b., I have somewhat		53:10	But b., they have received many		58:40
But b., as they were about to		53:14	And now, b., I close mine epistle.		58:41
compelled to b. their brethren		53:15	b., the people of Nephihah,		59: 5
But b., it came to pass they		53:16	B., I direct mine epistle to		60: 1
Now b., there were two thousand		53:18	For b., I have somewhat to		60: 2
And now b., as they never had		53:19	for b., ye yourselves know that		60: 2
but b., this was not all—		53:20	And now b., I say unto you that		60: 3
B., Ammoron, I have written unto		54: 5	But b., were this all we had		60: 4
B., I would tell you somewhat		54: 6	But b., great has been the		60: 5
And now b., we are prepared		54: 9	And now b., we desire to know		60: 6
b. ye will pull down the wrath		54: 9	But b., this is not all—		60: 9
But b., it supposeth me that		54:11	but b., ye have neglected them		60:10
And b., if you do not this,		54:12	B., could ye suppose that ye		60:11
B., I am in my anger, and also		54:13	B., if ye have supposed this ye		60:11
But b., if ye seek to destroy us		54:13	b. it is to your condemnation;		60:12
B., I will avenge his blood upon		54:16	but b., they do enter into the		60:13
For b., your fathers did wrong		54:17	And now b., I say unto you,		60:14
And now b., if ye will lay down		54:18	But b., now the Lamanites are		60:17
b., ye have breathed out many		54:19	ye sit still and b. these things?		60:23
b., we fear not your threatenings.		54:19	B., I say unto you, Nay.		60:23
b., we know not such a being;		54:21	b. it will be expedient that we		60:24
b. will he not send you there to		54:22	b. I will leave a part of my		60:25
But b. these things matter not.		54:22	b. I will stir up insurrections		60:27
And b. now, I am a bold		54:24	Yea, b. I do not fear your power		60:28
b., this war hath been waged		54:24	B. it is time, yea, the time is		60:29
B., I will not exchange prisoners		55: 2	B., I wait for assistance from you;		60:30
B., I know the place where the		55: 3	b., I come unto you, even in the		60:30
b., I will give unto him according		55: 3	For b., the Lord will not suffer		60:31
and b., they saw him coming		55: 8	B., can you suppose that the		60:32
Fear not; b., I am a Lamanite.		55: 8	B., the Lord saith unto me:		60:33
B., we have escaped from the		55: 8	And now b., I, Moroni, am		60:34
b. we have taken of their wine		55: 8	And b., if you will not do this I—		60:35
b. they were drunken and the		55:18	for b., God will not suffer that		60:35
But b., this was not the desire		55:19	B., I am Moroni, your chief		60:36
Now b. this was done in the		55:22	B., now it came to pass that soon		61: 1
Now b., this was the desire of		55:24	B., I say unto you, Moroni,		61: 2
But b., the Nephites were not		55:31	But b., there are those who do		61: 3
for b., the Lamanites had, by		55:33	And b., they have driven me out		61: 5
b., my beloved brother, I have		56: 2	And b., I have sent a proclamation		61: 6
B., two thousand of the sons of		56: 3	and b., they are flocking to us		61: 6
But b., here is one thing in		56: 9	And now, b., we will resist		61:10
For b., in the twenty and sixth		56: 9	But b. he doth not command us		61:13
for b., his army had been reduced		56:10	B. I have sent a few provisions		61:16
but b., we were disappointed in		56:23	And b., Pachus was slain and		62: 8
But b., it was night; therefore		56:38	For b., the Nephites and the		62:35
b., the Lamanites were pursuing		56:39	But b., the king did awake his		62:36
B., we know not but they have		56:43	for b., he had been a man who		62:37
b. our God is with us, and he		56:46	But b., he was dead, and had gone		62:37
And now b., the armies of		56:49	But b., because of the exceeding		62:41
b., I numbered those young men		56:55	And b., there were many of the		63: 6
But b., to my great joy, there		56:56	Now b., all those engravings		63:12
And now b., we were strong, yea,		57: 6	And now b., it came to pass	He	1: 1
And now b., I will show unto		57: 8	For b., Pahoran had died,		1: 2
For b., they would break out in		57:14	But b., Paanchi, and that part of		1: 7
And now b., we did not inquire		57:17	b., he was taken and was tried		1: 8
for b., the Lamanites were		57:17	and b., they sent forth one		1: 9
For b., Ammoron had sent to		57:17	but b., so speedy was the flight		1:10
But b., my little band of two		57:19	And now b., Pacumeni was		1:13

BEHOLD 105 BEHOLD

But b., this march of Coriantumr	He 1:25	and do ye not b. that the seed of	He	8:21
For b., Moronihah had supposed	1:26	But b., this is not all—		8:21
But b., the Lamanites were not	1:27	And b., he is God, and he is with		8:23
And now, b., the Lamanites	1:31	But b., ye have rejected the		8:25
b. there was no one to fill the	2: 1	Yea, b. it is now even at your		8:27
But b., Kishkumen, who had	2: 3	and b., your judge is murdered,		8:27
b. one of the servants of	2: 6	And b., they both belong to your		8:28
but b., the servant of Helaman,	2: 9	B., now it came to pass that when		9: 1
But b., when Gadianton had	2:11	B., now we will know of a surety		9: 2
And b., in the end of this book	2:13	We do not believe that he		9: 2
B. I do not mean the end of	2:14	and b., the chief judge had fallen		9: 3
But b., a hundredth part of	3:14	And now b., when they saw this		9: 4
But b., there are many books	3:15	And b. the people did gather		9: 7
but b., the Lamanites were	4: 3	and b., to their astonishment		9: 7
But b., Moronihah did preach	4:14	now b., the people knew nothing		9: 8
For b., they saw that the strength	4:26	and b. they were the five who		9:13
b., Nephi delivered up the	5: 1	and b. the judges inquired of		9:13
B., my sons, I desire that ye	5: 6	b. they cast us into prison.		9:14
B., I have given unto you the	5: 6	and b. he was dead, according		9:15
b. I have somewhat more to desire	5: 8	B., we know that this Nephi must		9:16
b., they went forth into the prison	5:22	And now b., we will detect this		9:17
for b., it is God that has shown	5:26	B. here is money; and also we		9:20
And b., when they had said these	5:27	B. ye say that I have agreed with		9:23
but b. they did not fall.	5:27	But b., I say unto you, that this		9:23
And b., they that were in the	5:27	now b., I will show unto you		9:25
but b., it was a still voice of	5:30	B. I say unto you: go to		9:26
b. the earth shook exceedingly,	5:31	b., he shall say unto you, Nay.		9:28
and b. the cloud of darkness,	5:31	And b., he shall deny unto you;		9:30
And b. the voice came again,	5:32	But b., ye shall examine him,		9:31
and b., he saw through the cloud	5:36	b., we know that thou art guilty.		9:34
and b., they did shine exceedingly	5:36	And b., the words which he had		9:37
And b., there was power given	5:37	B., he is a god, for except he		9:41
and they did b. the faces of	5:37	For b., he has told us the		9:41
B., what do all these things mean,	5:38	b., a voice came unto him saying:		10: 3
b., they saw that they were	5:43	b., I will bless thee forever;		10: 5
And b., the Holy Spirit of	5:45	B., thou art Nephi, and I am God.		10: 6
to b. from whence the voice came;	5:48	B., I declare it unto thee in the		10: 6
and b., they saw the heavens	5:48	B., I give unto you power		10: 7
For b., there were many of the	6: 2	And b., if ye shall say that God		10:10
And b., there was peace in the	6: 7	And now b., I command you,		10:11
And b., there was all manner of	6:11	And b., now it came to pass that		10:12
B. their women did toil and spin,	6:13	Now b., notwithstanding that		10:13
b. Cezoram was murdered by an	6:15	b., they did still harden their		10:15
For b., the Lord had blessed	6:17	But b., the power of God was		10:16
And now b., those murderers	6:18	B., we know that thou art a man of		11: 8
But b., they were more numerous	6:18	Lord, b. this people repenteth,		11:10
and b., they were not found.	6:19	And b., the people did rejoice and		11:18
But b., Satan did stir up the	6:21	And b., Lehi, his brother, was not		11:19
Now b., it is these secret oaths	6:25	Now b., these robbers did make		11:27
Now b., those secret oaths and	6:26	But b., it came to pass that in		11:29
but b., they were put into the	6:26	And thus we can b. how false,		12: 1
And b., it is he who is the author	6:30	B., they do not desire that the		12: 6
And b., he doth carry on his	6:30	For b., the dust of the earth		12: 8
And now b., he had got great	6:31	Yea, b. at his voice do the hills		12: 9
B., now it came to pass in the	7: 1	yea, and b., this is so;		12:15
But b., I am consigned that	7: 9	And b., also, if he say unto the		12:16
And B., now it came to pass	7:10	B., if he say unto this mountain—		12:17
B., why have ye gathered	7:13	be buried up—b. it is done.		12:17
And b., instead of gathering you,	7:19	b., if a man hide up a treasure		12:18
b., he shall scatter you forth	7:19	b., it shall be accursed.		12:18
But b., it is to get gain, to be	7:21	b., no man getteth it henceforth		12:19
b., this great city, and also all	7:22	And b., if the Lord shall say		12:20
for b., the Lord will not grant	7:22	But b., the voice of the Lord		13: 3
For b., thus saith the Lord;	7:23	B., I, Samuel, a Lamanite,		13: 5
I would that ye should b.,	7:23	and b. he hath put it into my		13: 5
For b., they are more righteous	7:24	And b., an angel of the Lord hath		13: 7
B. now, I do not say that these	7:29	And b., I was sent unto you to		13: 7
but b., I know that these things	7:29	but b. ye would not receive me.		13: 7
b., there were men who were	8: 1	to b. your utter destruction;		13:10
For b., Nephi had spoken unto	8: 3	for b., it is because of those		13:12
For b. he doth condemn all	8: 5	But b., if it were not for the		13:13
for b., we are powerful, and our	8: 6	b., I would cause that fire should		13:13
Yea, b., all the judgments will	8: 8	But b., it is for the righteous'		13:14
And b. they are many, and he	8: 8	But b., the time cometh, saith the		13:14
b., if he had not been a prophet	8: 9	And b., a curse shall come upon		13:17
B., my brethren, have ye not	8:11	B. ye, the people of this great		13:21
And now b., if God gave unto	8:12	for b., he saith that ye are cursed		13:21
But, b., ye not only deny my	8:13	B. ye are worse than they;		13:26
b., Moses did not only testify of	8:16	But b., if a man shall come		13:27
Yea, and b., Abraham saw of his	8:17	Yea, b., the anger of the Lord is		13:30
Yea, and b. I say unto you,	8:18	b., he hath cursed the land		13:30
yea, b., the prophet Zenos did	8:19	And b., the time cometh that he		13:31
And b., also Zenock, and also	8:20	for b., our riches are gone		13:33

BEHOLD

B., we lay a tool here and on	He	13:34
and b., our swords are taken from		13:34
for b. the land is cursed, and		13:36
B., we are surrounded by demons,		13:37
B., our iniquities are great.		13:37
But b., your days of probation		13:38
And b., he said unto them:		14: 2
B., I give unto you a sign;		14: 2
and b., then cometh the Son of		14: 2
And b., this will I give unto you		14: 3
for b., there shall be great lights		14: 3
And b., there shall a new star		14: 5
And b. this is not all,		14: 6
And b., thus hath the Lord		14: 9
And b., again, another sign I give		14:14
For b., he surely must die that		14:15
Yea, b., this death bringeth		14:16
But b., the resurrection of		14:17
But b., as I said unto you		14:20
b., in that day that he shall		14:20
And b., there shall be great		14:23
And b., thus hath the angel spoken		14:26
for b., ye are free; ye are		14:30
for b., God hath given unto you		14:30
b., I declare unto you that except		15: 1
for b., they have been a chosen		15: 3
But b. my brethren, the		15: 4
But b., salvation hath come		15: 4
I would that ye should b. that		15: 5
And b., ye do know of yourselves,		15: 7
for b. they will suffer themselves		15: 9
b., the Lord shall bless them		15:10
For b., had the mighty works been		15:15
And now b., saith the Lord,		15:17
For b., Nephi was baptizing,		16: 4
for b. he hath a devil;		16: 6
b., he did cast himself down		16: 7
And b., he was never heard of		16: 8
but b., we know that all these		16:16
But b., we know that this is a		16:20
b., the prophecies of the prophets	3Ne	1: 4
B. the time is past, and the		1: 6
But b., they did watch		1: 8
and b., the voice of the Lord		1:12
for b., the time is at hand,		1:13
B., I come unto my own,		1:14
And b., the time is at hand,		1:14
for b., at the going down of		1:15
for b., they had many children		1:29
b., I write this epistle unto you,		3: 2
And b., I swear unto you,		3: 8
And b., I am Giddianhi;		3: 9
Now b., this Lachoneus,		3:12
But b., there were no wild beasts		4: 2
and b., great and terrible was		4: 7
b., the Nephites did beat them,		4:12
but b., this was an advantage		4:18
for b., they had nothing save it		4:19
And now b., there was not a		5: 1
But b. there are records which		5: 9
And b., I do make the record		5:11
And b., I am called Mormon,		5:12
B., I am a disciple of Jesus Christ,		5:13
Now b., this was contrary to		6:24
Now b., I will show unto you		7: 1
Now b., there was no man among		7: 4
for b., it was a just man who		8: 1
But b., there was a more great		8:12
for b., the whole face of the		8:12
And b., the rocks were rent		8:18
for b., they did last for about		8:19
and then b., there was darkness		8:19
B., that great city Zarahemla		9: 3
And b., that great city Moroni		9: 4
And b., that great city Moronihah		9: 5
And b., the city of Gilgal have		9: 6
And b., the city of Gadiandi,		9: 8
And b., that great city Jacobugath,		9: 9
And b., the city of Laman,		9:10
B., mine arm of mercy is extended		9:14
B., I am Jesus Christ the Son		9:15
for b., by me redemption		9:17
B., I have come unto the world		9:21
B., for such I have laid down	3Ne	9:22
And now b., it came to pass that		10: 1
b., they began to weep and howl		10: 8
see and b. if all these deaths		10:14
B., I say unto you, Yea, many		10:15
B., our father Jacob also testified		10:17
And b., are not we a remnant of		10:17
b., I will show unto you that		10:18
And b., the third time they did		11: 6
B. my Beloved Son, in whom I		11: 7
and b., they saw a man		11: 8
B., I am Jesus Christ, whom the		11:10
And b., I am the light and the		11:11
B., ye shall go down and stand		11:23
And now b., these are the words		11:24
for b., verily I say unto you,		11:27
B., this is not my doctrine,		11:30
B., verily, verily, I say unto you,		11:31
and b., he stretched forth his hand		12: 1
b., I will baptize you with fire		12: 1
B., do men light a candle and		12:15
And b., I have given you the law		12:19
B. ye have the commandments		12:19
B., it is written by them of old		12:27
B., I give unto you a		12:29
And b., it is written, an eye for		12:38
And b. it is written also,		12:43
But b. I say unto you, love your		12:44
For b., ye are they whom I have		13:25
B. the fowls of the air, for they		13:26
and b., a beam is in thine own		14: 4
B., ye have heard the things		15: 1
B., I say unto you that the law		15: 4
B., I am he that gave the law,		15: 5
B.. I do not destroy the		15: 6
For b., the covenant which I		15: 8
B., I am the law, and the light.		15: 9
B., I have given unto you the		15:10
And b., this is the land of your		15:13
But b., ye have both heard my		15:24
B., because of their belief in me,		16: 7
b., saith the Father, I will bring		16:10
b. they shall be numbered among		16:13
B., now it came to pass that when		17: 1
B., my time is at hand.		17: 1
B., my bowels are filled with		17: 6
b. he prayed unto the Father,		17:15
And now b., my joy is full.		17:20
B. your little ones.		17:23
as they looked to b. they cast		17:24
B. there shall one be ordained		18: 5
B. I am the light; I have set		18:16
B., verily, verily, I say unto you,		18:18
b. it shall be given unto you.		18:20
And b., ye shall meet together		18:22
B. I am the light which ye		18:24
B. ye see that I have prayed		18:24
B. verily, verily, I say unto you,		18:27
now b., this is the commandment		18:28
for b. I know my sheep, and		18:31
b., Nephi and his brother whom		19: 4
And b., the multitude was so		19: 5
and b., they did cause that the		19: 6
b., they knelt again and prayed		19: 8
And b., they were encircled		19:14
b., Jesus came and stood in the		19:15
And b., they began to pray;		19:18
and b., they did still continue,		19:24
and b. they were as white as the		19:25
and b. the whiteness thereof did		19:25
b. they did pray steadfastly,		19:30
b. they were white, even as Jesus.		19:30
b., they were filled with the		20: 9
B. now I finish the		20:10
b. they are written, ye have		20:11
And b., I am he who doeth it.		20:19
And b., this people will I establish		20:22
B., I am he of whom Moses spake,		20:23
And b., ye are the children of		20:25
B., my servant shall deal		20:43
And b., this is the thing which I		21: 2
But b., the life of my servant		21:10
B., I will lay thy stones with		22:11
B.. they shall surely gather		22:15

B., I have created the smith that	3Ne 22:16	And b., it is the hand of the	Mrm 8: 8
And now, b., I say unto you,	23: 1	And b. also, the Lamanites are	8: 8
B., other scriptures I would that	23: 6	And now, b., I say no more	8: 9
B., I will send my messenger,	24: 1	But b., my father and I have	8:11
b., he shall come, saith the	24: 1	B., I am Moroni; and were it	8:12
For b., the day cometh that shall	25: 1	B., I make an end of speaking	8:13
B., I will send you Elijah the	25: 5	But b., we know no fault;	8:17
But b. the plates of Nephi do	26: 7	For b., the same that judgeth	8:19
B., I was about to write them,	26:11	B. what the scripture says—	8:20
I would that ye should b. that	26:13	B., I cannot write them.	8:23
B., it came to pass on the morrow	26:16	Yea, b. I say unto you,	8:23
B. I have given unto you my	27:13	And b., their prayers were also	8:25
b., him will I hold guiltless	27:16	B., look ye unto the	8:33
For b., out of the books which	27:25	for b., the time cometh at that	8:33
And b., all things are written by	27:26	B., the Lord hath shown unto	8:34
And now, b., my joy is great,	27:30	B., I speak unto you as if ye were	8:35
B., I would that ye should	27:31	But b., Jesus Christ hath shown	8:35
But b., it sorroweth me because	27:32	For b., ye do love money,	8:37
B., I know your thoughts, and ye	28: 6	B., the sword of vengeance	8:41
shall live to b. all the doings of	28: 7	B., will ye believe in the day of	9: 2
And b., the heavens were opened,	28:13	b., when the Lord shall come,	9: 2
they could b. the things of God.	28:15	or can ye b. the Lamb of God?	9: 3
b. they did play with the beasts	28:22	b., I say unto you that ye would	9: 4
B., I was about to write the	28:25	For b., when ye shall be brought	9: 5
But b., I have seen them, and	28:26	B. I say unto you, he that	9: 8
And b. they will be among the	28:27	But b., I will show unto you	9:11
And now b., as I spake concerning	28:36	B. he created Adam, and by	9:12
But b., since I wrote, I have	28:37	B. I say unto you, Nay;	9:15
And now b., I say unto you that	29: 1	B., are not the things that God	9:16
for b., the Lord will remember	29: 3	And b., I say unto you he	9:19
and b., at that day, if ye shall	29: 4	B., I say unto you that whoso	9:21
for b., the Lord remembereth	29: 8	For b., thus said Jesus Christ,	9:22
for, b. he commandeth me that	30: 1	And now, b., who can stand	9:26
b. the disciples of Jesus had	4Ne 1: 1	B., all ye who are despisers of	9:26
And now b., it came to pass	1:10	B., I speak unto you as though	9:30
And b., ye shall take the plates	Mrm 1: 4	And now b., we have written this	9:32
for b. they had wilfully	1:16	b., ye would have had no	9:33
But b., the land was filled with	2: 8	And b., these things which we	9:36
And b., I withstood him with	2: 9	But b., I give not the full	Eth 1: 5
And b., all this was done, and	2: 9	we can b. the decrees of God	2: 9
for b. no man could keep that	2:10	For b., this is a land which is	2:10
But b. this my joy was vain,	2:13	B., this is a choice land,	2:12
And b. I had gone according to	2:17	for b., it came to pass that the	2:13
for b., a continual scene of	2:18	And b., O Lord, in them	2:19
sufficient to b. the ways of man.	2:18	B., thou shalt make a hole in	2:20
But b., we did go forth against	2:27	b., ye shall stop the hole, that	2:20
And b., I had employed my	3: 1	O Lord, b. I have done even	2:22
And b. they did harden their	3: 3	and b. there is no light in them.	2:22
B., I had led them,	3:12	B., O Lord, wilt thou suffer that	2:22
b. the voice of the Lord came	3:14	For b., ye cannot have windows,	2:23
b., they shall be cut off from	3:15	For b., ye shall be as a whale	2:24
Yea, b., I write unto all the ends	3:18	And b., I prepare you against	2:25
But, b., the judgments of God	4: 5	Now b., O Lord, and do not be	3: 2
But b., I was without hope,	5: 2	B., O Lord, thou hast smitten us	3: 3
but b., they were driven back	5: 3	but b. these things which I have	3: 3
And now b., I, Mormon,	5: 8	B., O Lord, thou canst do this.	3: 5
And now b., this I speak unto	5:10	b., the Lord stretched forth his	3: 6
and b., they shall come forth	5:13	b., the Lord showed himself unto	3:13
And b., they shall go unto the	5:14	B., I am he who was prepared	3:14
For b.. the Spirit of the Lord	5:16	B., I am Jesus Christ.	3:14
But now b., they are led about	5:18	B., this body, which ye now	3:16
And b., the Lord hath reserved	5:19	this body, which ye now b., is	3:16
But b., it shall come to pass	5:20	B., thou shalt not suffer these	3:21
b., then will the Lord remember	5:20	B., when ye shall come unto me	3:22
b., I, Mormon, began to be old;	6: 6	And b., these two stones will	3:23
b. the armies of the Lamanites	6: 7	For b., the language which ye	3:24
did b. on the morrow, when the	6:11	B., I have written upon these	4: 4
And b., the ten thousand of	6:13	For b., I am the Father, I am	4:12
B., if ye had not done this,	6:18	B., when ye shall rend that veil	4:15
But b., ye are fallen, and I mourn	6:18	And b. it is I that hath spoken	4:19
But b., ye are gone, and my	6:20	And b., ye may be privileged	5: 2
But b., ye are gone, and the	6:22	and b., they did give light unto	6: 2
And now, b., I would speak	7: 1	And now b., this was grievous	6:23
For b., this is written for the	7: 9	B., is there not an account	8: 9
B. I, Moroni, do finish the record	8: 1	and b., I am fair, and I will	8:10
B., I have but few things to write,	8: 1	b., they shall be destroyed;	8:22
b., the Nephites who had escaped	8: 2	Therefore, b., it came to pass	9: 1
But b., they are gone, and I fulfil	8: 3	b., they did overthrow the	9: 1
B., my father hath made this	8: 5	b. the kingdom was taken away	10:30
And b., I would write it also	8: 5	B. it was by faith that they of	12:10
B., four hundred years have passed	8: 6	B., it was the faith of Alma and	12:13
And b., the Lamanites have	8: 7	B., it was the faith of Nephi and	12:14

B., it was the faith of Ammon	Eth 12:15
And b., we have seen in this	12:20
B., thou hast not made us	12:24
we write we b. our weakness,	12:25
B., I will show unto the Gentiles	12:28
For b., they rejected all the	13: 2
B., Ether saw the days of Christ,	13: 4
and b., he did beat Coriantumr,	13:29
b., upon the morrow, he could not	14: 1
b., there arose the brother of	14: 3
B., he sweepeth the earth before	14:18
Ether did b. all the doings of	15:13
And b., the Spirit of the Lord	15:19
but b., Shiz arose, and also his	15:28
b. Shiz had fainted with the	15:29
For b., their wars are	Mro 1: 2
B., they took the cup, and said:	5: 1
B., elders, priests, and teachers	6: 1
For b., God hath said a man being	7: 6
For b., it is not counted unto him	7: 7
For b., if a man being evil giveth	7: 8
For b., a bitter fountain cannot	7:11
But b., that which is of God	7:13
For b., my brethren, it is given	7:15
For b., the Spirit of Christ is	7:16
For b., God knowing all things,	7:22
b., he sent angels to minister	7:22
And b., there were divers ways	7:24
b., it shall be done unto you.	7:26
B. I say unto you, Nay;	7:29
For b., they are subject unto	7:30
B. I say unto you, Nay;	7:37
But b., my beloved brethren,	7:39
B. I say unto you that ye shall	7:41
And again, b. I say unto you	7:43
B., I came into the world not to	8: 8
B. I say unto you that this thing	8:10
B., baptism is unto repentance to	8:11
B. I say unto you, that he	8:14
B., I speak with boldness,	8:16
For b. that all little children	8:22
B., my son, this thing ought not	8:24
B., my son, I will write unto	8:27
B., the pride of this nation, or	8:27
But b., I fear lest the Spirit hath	8:28
For b., I have had a sore battle	9: 2
And now b., my son, I fear lest	9: 3
B., I am laboring with them	9: 4
b., the Lamanites have many	9: 7
For b., many of the daughters of	9: 9
B., my heart cries: Wo unto	9:15
b., the army of Zenephi has	9:16
B., I am but a man, and I have	9:18
B., thou knowest the wickedness	9:20
B., my son, I cannot recommend	9:21
But b., my son, I recommend	9:22
B., I would exhort you that	10: 3
For b., to one is given by the	10: 9
And b., they shall proceed forth	10:28
B., this is mine authority,	DC 1: 6
B., I am God and have spoken	1:24
For b., and lo, the Lord is	1:39
B., I will reveal unto you the	2: 1
B., you have been entrusted	3: 5
And b., how oft you have transgressed	3: 6
For b., you should not have	3: 7
B., thou art Joseph and thou	3: 9
Now b., a marvelous work is	4: 1
For b., the field is white already	4: 4
B., I say unto you, that as my	5: 1
And now, b., this shall you say	5: 2
B., if they will not believe my	5: 7
B., verily I say unto you,	5: 9
may b. and view these things	5:13
And b., whosoever believeth	5:16
B., I tell you these things,	5:20
b., I grant unto you eternal	5:22
B., I say unto him, he exalts	5:24
B., I have seen the things	5:25
and b., he is condemned.	5:27
b., I say unto him, he shall	5:28
B., I say into thee. Joseph,	5:30
b., thou shalt have no more gift	5:31
B., I am God; give heed unto	DC 6: 2
B., the field is white already	6: 3
b., I say unto you, keep my	6: 6
and b., the mysteries of God	6: 7
b., he that hath eternal life is	6: 7
B., thou hast a gift, and	6:10
and b., as often as thou hast	6:14
B., thou knowest that thou hast	6:15
B., thou art Oliver, and I	6:20
B., I am Jesus Christ, the Son of	6:21
now, b., you have received	6:24
b., I grant unto you a gift,	6:25
now, b., I give unto you	6:28
b., there will I be in the midst	6:32
B., I do not condemn you;	6:35
B. the wounds which pierced my	6:37
b., I will tell you in your mind	8: 2
b., this is the spirit of revelation;	8: 3
b., this is the spirit by which	8: 3
b., it has told you many things.	8: 6
B., there is no other power,	8: 7
B., it is I that have spoken it;	8:12
B., I say unto you, my son,	9: 1
b., other records have I,	9: 2
B., the work which you are	9: 4
b., it is because that you did not	9: 5
B., you have not understood;	9: 7
b., I say unto you, that you must	9: 8
B., it was expedient when you	9:11
do you not b. that I have	9:12
Now, b., I say unto you,	10: 1
B., they have sought to destroy	10: 6
b., wicked men have taken them	10: 8
b., Satan hath put it into their	10:10
And b., I say unto you	10:11
b., he has put it into their	10:15
then, b., they say and think	10:16
b., we have the same with us,	10:17
destroy; b., this is no harm.	10:25
b., they have altered these	10:29
B., I say unto you that you	10:30
b., they shall not accomplish	10:31
b., if you should bring forth	10:31
And, b., they will publish this	10:32
But b., here is wisdom,	10:34
B., I do not say that you shall	10:36
And b., you shall publish it as	10:42
B., they have only got a part,	10:44
B., there are many things	10:45
b., all the remainder of this	10:46
b., according to their faith	10:52
B., I do not bring it to destroy	10:52
B., I am Jesus Christ, the Son	10:57
b., they shall not deny that	10:62
b., I will gather them as a hen	10:65
B., this is my doctrine—	10:67
B., whosoever is of my church,	10:69
B., I am God, give heed to	11: 2
B., the field is white already	11: 3
b., I say unto you, keep my	11: 6
b., the mysteries of God shall	11: 7
b.. he that hath eternal life is	11: 7
B., thou hast a gift, or thou	11:10
b., it is I that have spoken,	11:11
B., I am the light which	11:11
B., I command you that you	11:15
b., according to your desires,	11:17
B., this is your work,	11:20
B. thou art Hyrum, my son;	11:23
B., I speak unto all who have	11:27
B., I am Jesus Christ, the Son	11:28
B., I am God, give heed to	12: 2
B., the field is white already	12: 3
b., I say unto you, keep my	12: 6
B., I speak unto you, and also	12: 7
B., I am the light and the life	12: 9
B., I am God; give heed to	14: 2
B., the field is white already	14: 3
B., I am Jesus Christ, the Son	14: 9
b., thou art David and thou art	14:11
For b., I speak unto you with	15: 2
B., blessed are you for this	15: 5
now, b., I say unto you,	15: 6

BEHOLD 109 BEHOLD

For b., I speak unto you with	DC	16: 2
B., blessed are you for this		16: 5
now, b., I say unto you,		16: 6
B., I say unto you, that you		17: 1
b., because of the thing which		18: 1
b., I have manifested unto		18: 2
b., I give unto you a		18: 3
B., the world is ripening in		18: 6
for, b., I command all men		18: 9
b., the Lord your Redeemer		18:11
B., you have my gospel before		18:17
B., Jesus Christ is the name		18:23
b., there are others who are		18:26
B. my grace is sufficient for you;		18:31
b., you are they who are		18:32
b., I give unto you, Oliver		18:37
B., I, Jesus Christ, your Lord		18:47
b., the mystery of godliness		19:10
For, b., I am endless,		19:10
For, b., I, God, have suffered		19:16
B., this is a great and the last		19:32
B., canst thou read this		19:39
B., there shall be a record		21: 1
For, b., I will bless all those		21: 9
B., I say unto you, that all		22: 1
B., I speak unto you, Oliver,		23: 1
B., thou art blessed, and art		23: 1
B., I speak unto you, Hyrum,		23: 3
B., I speak a few words unto you		23: 4
B., I speak a few words unto you,		23: 5
B., I manifest unto you,		23: 6
b., it is your duty to unite with		23: 7
B., thou wast called and		24: 1
B., I will smite them		24:16
B., thy sins are forgiven		25: 3
B., I say unto you that you shall		26: 1
For, b., I say unto you,		27: 2
B., this is wisdom in me;		27: 5
B., I say unto thee, Oliver,		28: 1
B., verily, verily, I say unto thee,		28: 2
b., I say unto you that you shall		28: 8
B., I say unto you that it is not		28: 9
B., I say unto you that it shall		29: 9
b., these things have not been		28:12
B., verily, verily, I say unto you,		29: 3
But, b., I say unto you that		29:14
b., my blood shall not cleanse		29:17
b., verily I say unto you,		29:26
b., I say unto you, never at any		29:29
B., I gave unto him that he		29:35
b., the devil was before Adam,		29:36
b., there is a place prepared		29:38
But, b., I say unto you, that I,		29:42
But b., I say unto you,		29:46
B., I say unto you, David,		30: 1
B., I say unto you, Peter		30: 5
B., I say unto you, my servant		30: 9
B., you have had many		31: 2
B. verily I say unto you,		31: 6
B., I say unto you that you		31:10
b., I say unto him that as		32: 1
B., I say unto you, my servants		33: 1
b., the field is white already		33: 3
B., verily, verily, I say unto you,		33:12
b., verily, verily, I say unto you,		33:18
hearken and hear and b. what		34: 1
b., verily, verily, I say unto you,		34: 7
b., I am with you until I		34:11
B., verily, verily, I say unto my		35: 3
B. thou wast sent forth,		35: 4
b., it shall be given unto him		35:23
B., I come quickly. Even so.		35:27
B., I say unto you my servant		36: 1
B., I say unto you that it is		37: 1
b., they pray unto me in much		37: 2
B., here is wisdom, and let every		37: 4
b., the residue of the wicked have		38: 5
b., verily, verily, I say unto you		38: 7
B., the kingdom is yours,		38: 9
b., the enemy is combined.		38:12
and b. it is my footstool,		38:17
B., this I have given unto you		38:27
b., I say unto you, my servant		39: 7
b., I have bestowed great	DC	39: 8
b., the days of thy deliverance		39:10
B., verily, verily, I say unto thee,		39:14
B., verily, verily, I say unto you,		39:16
B., I come quickly. Even so.		39:24
B., verily I say unto,		40: 1
b. I give unto you a		41: 2
b., I come quickly, and ye		41: 4
B., verily I say unto you,		42: 4
b., the Comforter knoweth all		42:17
B., I speak unto the church.		42:18
b., thou wilt remember the		42:30
b., it shall come to pass that		42:63
B., thou shalt observe all these		42:65
B., verily I say unto you,		42:74
b., verily, verily, I say unto you,		43: 2
now, b., I give unto you a		43: 8
b., the great day of the Lord is		43:17
B., the day has come, when the		43:26
B., verily I say unto you,		43:27
B., I am Jesus Christ,		43:34
B., thus saith the Lord unto you		44: 1
B., I say unto you, that ye must		44: 6
b. the sufferings and death of him		45: 4
b. the blood of thy Son which		45: 4
now ye b. this temple which		45:18
Ye look and b. the fig-trees,		45:37
And they shall b. blood and fire		45:41
look for me, and, b., I will come;		45:44
as you now b. me and know		45:46
And now, b., I say unto you,		45:60
but, b., I say unto you, they		45:63
B., it is expedient in me that		47: 1
for b., verily I say unto you,		49: 1
B., I say unto you, that		49: 2
For, b., the beasts of the field		49:19
B., I say unto you, go forth		49:26
B., I will go before you and		49:27
B., I am Jesus Christ, and I		49:28
B., verily I say unto you, that		50: 2
B., I, the Lord, have looked		50: 4
B., verily I say unto you,		50: 7
but b. such shall be reclaimed;		50: 7
B. ye shall answer this question		50:16
if you b. a spirit manifested		50:31
And b., verily I say unto you,		50:36
B., ye are little children and		50:40
B., this shall be an example		51:18
B., thus saith the Lord unto		52: 1
And b., he that is faithful		52:13
B., this commandment is given		52:21
But, b., I, the Lord, will hasten		52:43
B., I am Jesus Christ, the Son		52:44
B., I say unto you, my servant		53: 1
B., I, the Lord, who was		53: 2
B., these are the first ordinances		53: 6
B., thus saith the Lord, even		54: 1
B., verily, verily, I say unto you,		54: 2
b., I say unto you, seek ye		54: 9
and, b., I come quickly,		54:10
B., thus saith the Lord unto you,		55: 1
b., mine anger is kindled against		56: 1
B., I, the Lord, command;		56: 3
b., I revoke the commandment		56: 6
b., I, the Lord, will pay it unto		56:12
B., thus saith the Lord unto		56:14
for b., your sins have come up		56:14
For b., the Lord shall come,		56:19
B., the place which is now called		57: 3
B., this is wisdom, that they		57: 5
b. here is wisdom, and whoso		57: 9
b. here is wisdom—		57:12
cannot b. with your natural eyes,		58: 3
B., verily I say unto you, for		58: 6
B., I, the Lord, have spoken it.		58:12
B. his mission is given unto him,		58:16
B., the laws which ye have		58:23
B., here is wisdom.		58:23
For b., it is not meet that I		58:26
B., he who has repented of		58:42
b., he will confess them and		58:43
For, b., they shall push the		58:45
For, b., verily I say unto you,		58:52

B., here is wisdom.	DC 58:53
b. the Son of Man cometh.	58:65
B., blessed, saith the Lord, are	59: 1
B., this is according to the law	59:22
B., thus saith the Lord unto the	60: 1
B., it pleaseth me, that you	60: 1
B., they have been sent to	60:13
B., this is sufficient for you,	60:16
B., and hearken unto the voice	61: 1
B., verily thus saith the Lord	61: 2
b., there are many dangers	61: 4
And now, b., for your good I	61:13
B., I, the Lord, in the beginning	61:14
B., I, the Lord, have appointed	61:24
and b., this is the way—	61:24
And b., this commandment	61:26
B., and hearken, O ye elders of	62: 1
B., I, the Lord, have brought	62: 6
B., the kingdom is yours.	62: 9
And b., and lo, I am with the	62: 9
B., I, the Lord, utter my voice,	63: 5
b., faith cometh not by signs,	63: 9
b., I, the Lord, say unto you	63:19
b. I will make it known unto	63:22
And now, b., this is the will	63:24
B., the land of Zion—	63:25
by purchase, b. you are blessed;	63:30
And b., this is not yet,	63:35
B., I, the Lord, will give unto	63:41
B., these things are in his own	63:44
B., this is my will, obtaining	63:46
now b., verily I say unto you,	63:55
b. he standeth no longer in	63:56
B., I am from above, and my	63:59
B., I am Alpha and Omega,	63:60
For b., verily I say, that many	63:62
B., thus saith the Lord your God	64: 1
B., I, the Lord, was angry with	64:15
b., he hath sinned, and Satan	64:17
B., now it is called today until	64:23
B., it is said in my laws, or	64:27
But b., it is not said at any	64:28
And b., I, the Lord, declare unto	64:31
B., the Lord requireth the heart	64:34
B., I, the Lord, have made my	64:37
b., I say unto you that Zion	64:41
B., thus saith the Lord unto my	66: 1
B., verily I say unto you, that	66: 5
B. and hearken, O ye elders of	67: 1
B. and lo, mine eyes are upon	67: 2
b., verily I say unto you there	67: 3
b., and lo, this is an ensample	68: 2
B., this is the promise of the	68: 5
B., I am Alpha and Omega,	68:35
B., and hearken, O ye inhabitants	70: 1
B., this is what the Lord	70: 9
And b., none are exempt from	70:10
B., I, the Lord, am merciful	70:18
B., thus saith the Lord unto you	71: 1
Now, b. this is wisdom;	71: 5
b., this shall be an ensample	72:23
b., it shall be made known unto	73: 2
B., I say unto you that it is my	75: 3
B., this is the will of the Lord	75:12
b., and lo, I am with them also,	75:14
B., I say unto you, that it is	75:24
and b. and lo, these are they	76:71
B., these are they who died	76:72
But b., and lo, we saw the glory	76:109
b., this is Elias, who, as it is	77:14
and b., and lo, it must needs	78: 3
B., this is the preparation	78:13
B., this is the will of him who	80: 5
B., and lo, these are the words	81: 7
B., here is wisdom also in me	82:16
they might b. the face of God;	84:23
B., I send you out to prove	84:79
B.. I send you out to reprove	84:87
B., this is the way that mine	84:108
And b., the high priests should	84:111
B., verily I say, the field was	86: 2
b. he soweth the tares;	86: 3
But b., in the last days, even	86: 4
B., verily I say unto you,	DC 86: 5
b. and lo, the tares are bound	86: 7
For b., the Southern States	87: 3
for b., it cometh quickly;	87: 8
B., this is pleasing unto your	88: 2
B., he rejoices not in that which	88:33
B., all these are kingdoms,	88:47
B., I will liken these kingdoms	88:51
b. the joy of my countenance.	88:52
B., that which you hear is	88:66
B., and lo, I will take care	88:72
B., I will hasten my work	88:73
B., I sent you out to testify	88:81
B., and lo, the bridegroom	88:92
b., she is the tares of the earth;	88:94
B., and lo, I will come quickly,	88:126
b., this is beautiful, that he	88:130
B., verily, I say unto you,	88:136
B., verily, thus saith the Lord	89: 4
among you, b. it is not good,	89: 5
And, b., this should be wine,	89: 6
b., and lo, they shall turn	90: 9
And b., verily I say unto you,	90:32
B., I say unto you that	90:34
B., here is the agency of men,	93:31
And b., it must be done	94: 2
But b., verily I say unto you,	95: 5
B., I say unto you,	96: 1
For b., verily I say unto you,	96: 5
B., I say unto you,	97: 3
B.. this is the tithing and	97:12
And now, b., if Zion do these	97:18
For b., and lo, vengeance	97:22
B., I, the Lord, am not well	98:19
B., this is the law I gave	98:32
B., this is an ensample unto all	98:38
B., thus saith the Lord unto	99: 1
And b., and lo, I come quickly	99: 5
B., and lo, I have much people	100: 3
for b., and lo, I am with you	100:12
B., I say unto you there were	101: 6
And, b., there is none other	101:20
B., it is my will that all they	101:22
b., it is thenceforth good for	101:40
B., here is wisdom concerning	101:41
Now, b., the nobleman,	101:52
And b., the watchman upon the	101:54
b., I will give unto you a	103: 1
B. they shall, for I have	103: 6
B., this is the blessing which I	103:13
B., I say unto you,	103:15
B. this is my will; ask and ye	103:31
and b. this is the way that I.	104:16
"b., I will bless, and multiply"	104:31
For b., I have reserved an	104:45
B., all these properties are	104:55
b. it is my will that you shall	104:78
b., I will soften the hearts of	104:80
b., I will give you the victory.	104:82
b., if you proceed to do the	104:86
B., I say unto you,	105: 2
But b., they have not learned	105: 3
B., he will deliver them in	105: 8
For b., I have prepared a	105:12
For b., I do not require at	105:14
B., the destroyer I have sent	105:15
B., I have commanded my	105:16
And b., I will give unto you	105:25
Now, b., I say unto you,	105:26
b., and lo, I am with you	105:41
B., here is wisdom; yea, to be	107:92
B., this is the promise of the	108: 5
And b., and lo, I am with you	108: 8
B., your sins are forgiven you;	110: 5
b., I have accepted this house,	110: 7
B., the time has fully come,	110:14
B., I, the Lord, will feel after	112:13
B., vengeance cometh speedily	112:24
b. how great is your calling.	112:33
B., thus saith the Lord:	113: 4
B., thus saith the Lord,	113: 6
For b., I will be with him,	115:19
b., verily I say unto him that	117:12

BEHOLD — BEING

b., verily I say unto you, it shall	DC 119: 6
b. from the eternal heavens	121: 2
B., mine eyes see and know all	121:24
B., there are many called, but	121:34
b., the heavens withdraw	121:37
B., ere he is aware, he is left	121:38
For, b., I am about to call upon	124: 6
b., at the end of this appointment	124:32
b., verily I say unto you, they	124:45
b., it behooveth me to require	124:49
B., verily I say unto you let,	124:62
b., he aspireth to establish his	124:84
B., I say unto you, I have	124:102
b., I, the Lord your God, will	124:104
B., it is not my will that he	124:109
b., his priesthood no man taketh	124:130
for b., and lo, I shall triumph	127: 2
B., my prayer to God is that	127:12
B., I will send you Elijah	128:17
and b. what is that subject?	128:18
B., thy God reigneth!	128:19
B., the great day of the Lord is	128:24
B., and lo, I am the Lord thy	132: 2
b., I reveal unto you a new	132: 4
B., mine house is a house of	132: 8
B., I have seen your sacrifices,	132:50
and b., and lo, I am with him,	132:57
B., I am Alpha and Omega.	132:66
And b., and lo, this shall be	133: 9
b. and lo, the Bridegroom	133:10
For b., the Lord God hath sent	133:17
For b., he shall stand upon	133:20
B., this is the blessing of the	133:34
For, b., the day cometh that	133:64
B., at my rebuke I dry up the	133:68
B., and lo, there are none to	133:71
B. the Lord your God hath	133:74
but ye shall b. it if ye are	136:37
B., I am the Lord God Almighty,	Mses 1: 3
And, b., thou art my son;	1: 4
no man can b. all my works,	1: 5
except he b. all my glory;	1: 5
no man can b. all my glory,	1: 5
And now, b., this one thing	1: 7
b., Satan came tempting him,	1:12
For b., I am a son of God,	1:13
b., I could not look upon God,	1:14
of it which he did not b.,	1:27
And b., the glory of the Lord	1:31
For b., there are many worlds	1:35
For b., this is my work and	1:39
b., I will raise up another like	1:41
B., I reveal unto you concerning	2: 1
B., I have given you every herb	2:29
b., all things which I had made	2:31
And now, b., I say unto you,	3: 4
and man could b. it.	3: 9
B., here am I, send me, I will	4: 1
But, b., my Beloved Son, which	4: 2
B., the man is become as one of	4:28
But b., Cain hearkened not,	5:16
B. thou hast driven me out	5:39
B. my Spirit is upon you,	6:34
we go yonder to b. the seer,	6:38
B., he laid it, an host of men	6:44
B. Satan hath come among the	6:49
B. I have forgiven thee thy	6:53
And now, b., I say unto you:	6:62
b., all things have their likeness.	6:63
B., thou art one in me, a son	6:68
B., our father Adam taught	7: 1
B. the people of Canaan, which	7: 7
For b., the Lord shall curse the	7: 8
B. mine abode forever.	7:21
b., the power of Satan was upon	7:24
B. these thy brethren; they are	7:32
b., they are without affection,	7:33
B., I am God; Man of Holiness	7:35
But b., their sins shall be upon	7:37
But b., these which thine eyes	7:38
and b., I will shut them up;	7:38
And b., Enoch saw the day of	7:47
and b., Zion is with me.	7:47
for b. mine anger is kindled	Mses 8:15
B., we are the sons of God;	8:21
and, b., it was corrupt,	8:29
and b. I will destroy all flesh	8:30
b., I lifted up my voice unto	Abr 1:15
b.. my name is Jehovah,	1:16
B., I will lead thee by my hand,	1:18
B., Potiphar's Hill was in the	1:20
and b., they are taken away	2: 7
b., Sarai, thy wife, is a very	2:22
b. thine eyes see it;	3: 6
b., I will show you all these.	3:12
B., we will give them every herb	4:29
b., we will give them life,	4:30
and b., they shall be very	4:31
B., these things I have spoken	JS 1:21
B., I speak these things unto	1:23
B., I have told you before;	1:24
B., he is in the desert;	1:25
B., he is in the secret chambers;	1:25
B., wheresoever the carcass is,	1:27
B. I speak for mine elect's	1:29
For b., the day cometh that shall	2:37
B., I will reveal unto you the	2:38
indeed did I b. the plates,	2:52
BEHOLDEST	
unto me: Nephi, what b. thou?	1Ne 11:14
twelve ministers whom thou b.	12:10
said unto me: What b. thou?	13: 2
The book that thou b. is a record	13:23
thou b. that the Gentiles who have	13:30
blindness, which thou b. they are	13:32
thou b. that it hath brought forth	Jac 5:22
thou b. that they are yet good.	5:34
thou b. that it beginneth to perish;	5:37
thou b. that I have done according	5:75
And why b. thou the mote that	3Ne 14: 3
And now thou b., O Lord, that	DC 109: 3
of the tree which thou b. in the	Mses 4: 9
BEHOLDING	
that by b. this scent it would	Al 19:17
Antipus, b. our danger, did	56:38
and b. the greatness of their	62:19
be kept from b. within the veil;	Eth 3:19
to another, the b. of angels and	Mro 10:14
BEHOOVETH	
for it b. the great Creator that he	2Ne 9: 5
for thus it b. our God,	10: 3
yea, it b. him and becometh	He 14:15
For thus it b. the Father that	3Ne 21: 6
it b. me that he should	DC 21:10
it b. me that ye should part.	61: 9
it b. me to require that work	124:49
BEING	
b. called, (beginning at the eldest)	1Ne 1:hd
b. overcome with the Spirit	1: 7
b. thus overcome with the Spirit,	1: 8
Laman and Lemuel, b. the eldest,	2:12
power, b. filled with the Spirit,	2:14
I, Nephi, b. exceeding young,	2:16
b. large in stature, and also	2:16
b. grieved because of the hardness	2:18
I, Nephi, b. a man large in stature,	4:31
b. grieved for the hardness of	7: 8
b. brought down into captivity,	14: 7
they b. hard in their hearts,	15: 3
b. a natural branch of the olive-	15:16
b. much fatigued, because of their	16:19
b. interpreted, is many waters.	17: 5
women have toiled, b. big with	17:20
notwithstanding they b. led,	17:30
my parents b. stricken in years,	18:17
Jacob and Joseph also, b. young,	18:19
their b. nourished by the Gentiles	22: 8
and b. carried in their arms	22: 8
b. the first that should rise.	2Ne 2: 8
one b. sweet and the other bitter.	2:15
b. an instrument in the hands of	3:24

BEING

that b. who beguiled our first	2Ne	9: 9	b. troubled no more for a time	Al	3:24
righteousness, b. clothed with purity,		9:14	b. filled with great joy because		4:14
if the Lamb of God, he b. holy,		31: 5	of b. high priest over the church,		4:18
we, b. unholy, to be baptized,		31: 5	b. loosed from the bands of		5:10
all righteousness in b. baptized		31: 6	can ye think of b. saved when		5:20
But notwithstanding he b. holy,		31: 7	b. dead unto all good works.		5:42
the one b. is as precious in his	Jac	2:21	b. called after the man who was		6: 7
if God b. able to speak and the		4: 9	she b. a virgin, a precious and		7:10
of a b. which ye say shall come		7: 7	b. temperate in all things;		7:23
b. kept on the other plates of		7:26	b. diligent in keeping the		7:23
we b. a lonesome and a solemn		7:26	b. weighed down with sorrow,		8:14
And thus b. prepared to meet	Jar	1: 9	them from b. destroyed,		9:10
kept them from b. destroyed		1:12	he b. one of the most expert		10:31
b. commanded by my father,	Om	1: 1	the existence of a Supreme B.		11:22
he b. warned of the Lord		1:12	and b. raised from this mortality		12:12
denied the b. of their Creator;		1:17	b. brought before the bar of God,		12:12
their leader b. a strong and		1:28	or b. placed in a state to act		12:31
I, Mormon, b. about to deliver up	WM	1: 1	penalty thereof b. a second death,		12:32
every family b. separate	Mos	2: 5	(this b. the plan of redemption		12:33
the multitude b. so great that		2: 7	b. called and prepared from the		13: 3
he b. an enemy to all		4:14	b. left to choose good or evil;		13: 3
all depend upon the same B.,		4:19	b. prepared from the foundation		13: 5
he b. a strong and mighty man,		7: 3	b. in and through the atonement		13: 5
he b. over-zealous to inherit		7:21	b. called by this holy calling,		13: 6
b. deceived by the cunning		7:21	b. after the order of his Son,		13: 7
B. grieved for the afflictions of		8: 7	b. without beginning of days or		13: 7
but he b. an austere and a		9: 2	b. prepared from eternity to		13: 7
I b. over-zealous to inherit		9: 3	b. called with a holy calling,		13: 8
now I, b. old, did confer the		10:22	b. sanctified by the Holy Ghost,		13:12
b. the Father and the Son—		15: 2	b. pure and spotless before		13:12
Son to the Father, b. one God,		15: 5	it b. a type of his order, or		13:16
will of the Son b. swallowed up in		15: 7	or it b. his order,		13:16
b. filled with compassion towards		15: 9	b. wanderers in a strange land;		13:23
b. redeemed by the Lord.		15:24	b. very low with a burning		15: 5
b. an enemy to God;		16: 5	he b. rejected by those who were		15:16
b. delivered up to the devil,		16:11	b. preached in its purity in all		16:21
they b. warned of their iniquities		16:12	Ammon b. the chief among them,		17:18
he also b. a descendant of Nephi.		17: 2	land b. called after the sons of		17:19
he b. concealed for many days		17: 4	because of the fear of b. slain.		17:29
b. in the borders of the land		18: 4	it b. a practice of plunder		18: 7
there b. near the water a		18: 5	b. interpreted, powerful or		18:13
have you against b. baptized		18:10	b. filled with the Spirit of God,		18:16
took Helam, he b. one of the first,		18:12	Ammon b. wise, yet harmless,		18:22
rejoicing, b. filled with the Spirit.		18:14	veil of unbelief was b. cast away		19: 6
and he b. a strong man		19: 4	b. overpowered by the Spirit.		19:13
he himself b. a just men.		19:17	b. exceeding angry with		19:22
also Limhi, b. the son of the king,		19:26	b. filled with joy, speaking		19:30
b. ashamed to return to the city		20: 3	thy son, he b. an innocent man,		20:18
he b. the king's captain,		20:17	of b. bound with strong cords.		20:29
for the Lamanites b. so numerous,		22: 2	it b. so far northward that		22:30
b. led by Ammon and his		22:11	b. the place of their first landing.		22:30
b. many days in the wilderness		22:13	it b. the wilderness which is		22:31
he b. the founder of their church.		23:16	there b. a small neck of land		22:32
b. called after the name of his		24: 3	it b. in their view a testimony		24:18
bodies, b. called churches;		25:21	and he is a merciful B.,		26:35
there b. many churches		25:22	offend some unknown b., who		30:28
b. little children at the time he		26: 1	a b. who never has been seen		30:28
b. persecuted by all those who		26:38	b. led by a man whose name was		30:59
b. commanded of God to pray		26:39	b. interpreted, is the holy stand.		31:21
b. called Alma, after his father;		27: 8	b. esteemed as filthiness;		32: 3
b. redeemed of God,		27:25	b. compelled to be humble;		32:16
b. greatly persecuted by those who		27:32	b. brought to know the word,		32:16
b. smitten by many of them.		27:32	b. the intent of this last sacrifice,		34:15
he b. also the high priest,		29:42	do cast out, (it b. of no worth)		34:29
died, b. eighty and two years old,		29:45	b. a very wicked man,		35: 8
b. sixty and three years old;		29:46	b. grieved for the iniquity of his		35:15
b. stricken with many years,	Al	1: 9	is, b. interpreted, a compass;		37:38
b. lifted up in the pride of		1:32	b. led captive by the will of the		40:13
a certain man, b. called Amlici,		2: 1	b. cut off from the presence of		42:11
he b. a very cunning man,		2: 1	their number b. so much greater		43:21
he b. after the order of the man		2: 1	they b. shielded from the more		43:38
he, b. a wicked man, would		2: 4	vital parts of the body b. shielded		43:38
of Amlici, b. called Amlicites;		2:11	proud, b. lifted up in their hearts,		45:24
Now Alma, b. the chief judge and		2:16	Moroni b. a man who was		46:34
b. called after that Gideon		2:20	b. a very subtle man to do evil		47: 6
his people from b. destroyed.		2:21	b. fixed in their minds with a		47: 6
haste, b. greatly astonished,		2:23	they b. the most acquainted with		48: 5
b. as numerous almost, as it were,		2:27	And b. thus prepared they		49: 7
the Nephites b. strengthened by		2:28	b. baptized unto repentance,		49:30
that Alma, b. a man of God,		2:30	b. a man of much passion,		50:35
b. exercised with much faith,		2:30	(b. inspired by his wickedness		50:35
himself b. afflicted with a wound		3:22	b. repulsed by Teancum and his		51:31

BEING / BELIEVE

Jacob, b. their leader, being also	Al	52:33
their leader, b. also a Zoramite,		52:33
Moroni b. in their course of		52:34
of them, b. much confused,		52:36
behold, we know not such a b.;		54:21
The army of Antipus b. weary,		56:50
b. confused because of the fall		56:51
we, instead of b. Lamanites,		57:10
the Lamanites b. cut off from		57:11
thus b. exceeding numerous,		59: 7
b. determined to overthrow the		62:14
he b. an exceedingly curious man,		63: 5
b. called after the name of his		63:11
Coriantumr, b. a mighty man,	He	1:16
there b. but little timber upon		3: 7
it b. a day's journey for a		4: 7
to some b. whom they beheld.		5:36
by that same b. who did entice		6:26
same b. who did plot with Cain,		6:27
that same b. who put it into		6:28
same b. who led on the people		6:28
that same b. who put it into		6:29
(Jeremiah b. that same prophet		8:20
he b. stabbed by his brother		9: 6
b. much cast down because of the		10: 3
b. stirred up to anger by them,		11:24
b. cut off from the presence of		14:16
such a b. as a Christ shall come;		16:18
b. a descendant of Nephi who	3Ne	1:hd
and the Nephites b. in one body,		4: 4
because of their b. dyed in blood.		4: 7
b. weary because of his much		4:14
Gidgiddoni b. aware of their		4:24
Mormon, b. called after the land		5:12
he b. the king of the band,		7:12
seen angels, and b. eye-witness,		7:15
also b. eye-witness to their		7:15
b. grieved for the hardness of		7:16
notwithstanding it b. a small		11: 3
If ye then, b. evil, know how		14:11
b. on a parallel, the one on the		26: 5
b. constrained by the Holy Ghost,	4Ne	1:48
(I b. about ten years of age,	Mrm	1: 2
I, Mormon, b. a descendant of		1: 5
that I b., eleven years old,		1: 6
And I, b. fifteen years of age		1:15
b. somewhat of a sober mind,		1:15
notwithstanding I b. young,		2: 1
the Nephites b. angry because		4:15
upon that b. who created them.		5: 2
b. led in the front by me.		6:11
b. left by the hands of those		6:15
to dwell with that holy B.		9: 3
b. redeemed and loosed from		9:13
and yet be an unchangeable B.?		9:19
b. handed down and altered by		9:32
b. a large and mighty man,	Eth	1:34
b. called after the mighty hunter)		2: 1
b. directed continually by the hand		2: 6
vessels b. tight like unto a dish,		6: 7
of Jared b. exceeding expert,		8: 8
b. an hundred and two years old.		9:24
(he b. a descendant of		10: 9
b. a descendant of Ahah,		11:11
works, b. led to glorify God.		12: 4
b. armed with weapons of war,		15:15
b. clothed after the manner of		15:15
a man b. evil cannot do that	Mro	7: 6
if a man b. evil giveth a gift,		7: 8
a man b. evil cannot do that		7:10
a man b. a servant of the devil		7:11
b. from everlasting to		7:22
God, neither a changeable b.;		8:18
b. temperate in all things,	DC	12: 8
b. one thousand eight hundred		20: 1
it b. regularly organized and		20: 1
the only b. whom they should		20:19
b. confirmed by the laying on of		20:68
or b. overtaken in a fault, shall		20:80
B. inspired of the Holy Ghost		21: 2
This b. an ordinance unto you,		21:11
he b. the first unto you,		21:11
b. united in prayer according to		29: 6

b. clothed with robes of	DC	29:12
b. tempted of the devil—		29:36
live, and move, and have a b.		45: 1
b. brought up in subjection to		74: 4
b. sanctified through the		74: 7
b. in the Spirit on the sixteenth		76:11
b. buried in the water in his		76:51
is written of as b. typical.		76:70
b. in the likeness of that which		77: 2
b. filled with the Holy Ghost		84:27
b. quickened in him and by him.		88:49
b. meted out as a just measure		98:24
over such council for the time b.		102:25
B. driven and smitten by the		103: 2
his eyes in hell, b. in torment.		104:18
of their b. driven out		104:51
b. broken through transgression,		104:52
to the name of the Supreme B.,		107: 4
The Twelve b. sent out,		107:35
b. full of the Holy Ghost,		107:56
b. sent down from heaven unto		112:32
b. kept workways with the wind		123:16
b. attended with certificates over		128: 4
b. in likeness of the dead.		128:12
without b. able to decide		130:16
b. placed for the protection of		134: 6
human laws b. instituted for		134: 6
are still b. solemnized		OD
b. filled with the Holy Ghost,	Mses	1:24
the name of one b. Adah,		5:44
Lamech, b. angry, slew him,		5:50
b. declared by holy angels sent		5:58
b. only evil continually.		8:22
b. first discovered by a woman,	Abr	1:23
Pharaoh, b. a righteous man,		1:26
Pharaoh b. of that lineage by		1:27
it b. one thousand years		3: 4
one b. more intelligent than		3:19
b. now the eighth year since	JS	2: 2
to the power of some actual b.		2:16
had never before felt in any b.—		2:16
and b. of very tender years,		2:28
much opposed to our b. married.		2:58
b. the second day of May,		2:60
b. very poor, and the		2:61
my father b. one of those who		2:66
(b. the 7th of April)		2:67
Our minds b. now enlightened,		2:74
threatened with b. mobbed,		2:75
We believe in b. subject to kings,	AoF	12
We believe in b. honest, true,		13

BEINGS

in the service of your fellow b.	Mos	2:17
a great benefit to his fellow b.		8:18
of b. in their destined order or	DC	77: 3
greatest good unto thy fellow b.,		81: 4
All b. who abide not in those		88:39
two kinds of b. in heaven,		129: 1
allowing human b. to be held		134:12

BELIEF

their b. on the words of Alma.	Mos	25:18
to preach according to their b.;	Al	1:17
no power on any man for his b.		1:17
by fire because of their b.—		25: 5
by fire because of his b. in God;		25:11
was no law against a man's b.;		30: 7
was no law against a man's b.		30:11
a b. of things which are not so.		30:16
bind them down to a b. of Christ,		31:17
because of their b. in Christ		46:15
because of their b. in me,	3Ne	16: 6
because of their b. in me,		16: 7
it is because of their b. in me		19:20
humility and their b. in Christ;	4Ne	1:29
exercise of their religious b.;	DC	134: 7

BELIEVE

Neither did they b. that Jerusalem,	1Ne	2:13
that I did b. all the words which		2:16
I b. all the words of my father.		11: 5
not b. that I could build a ship;		17:18

neither would they b. that I was	1Ne 17:18	will repent and b. on his name.	Al	19:36
Do ye b. that our fathers, who	17:23	b. that God will save all men.		21: 6
persuade them to b. in the Lord	19:23	do not b. that thou knowest		21: 8
they that b. in him shall be saved.	2Ne 2: 9	not b. in these foolish traditions.		21: 8
cometh when they shall b. in him;	6:14	do not b. that thou knowest		21: 8
none will he destroy that b. in him.	6:14	neither do we b. that thy		21: 8
And they that b. not in him shall	6:15	there is a God, behold I will b.		22: 7
if they will not repent and b. in	9:24	I b. that the Great Spirit		22:11
cometh that they shall b. in me,	10: 7	and I will b. thy words.		22:11
If ye will not b. surely ye shall	17: 9	the king would b. his words,		22:12
all those who shall b. on his name	25:13	whosoever would b. on his name.		22:13
as many as will b. on his name,	25:14	brought to b. in the traditions		23: 5
shall be persuaded to b. in Christ,	25:16	to b. and to know the truth,		24:19
come that they shall b. in Christ,	25:16	and to b. in the Lord,		25: 6
that they should b. these things.	25:16	will repent and b. on his name.		26:35
also our brethren, to b. in Christ,	25:23	but if he did not b. in him		30: 9
notwithstanding we b. in Christ,	25:24	and have brought them to b.,		30:28
the right way is to b. in Christ	25:28	I do not b. that there is a God;		30:48
the right way is to b. in Christ	25:29	ye show me a sign, I will not b.		30:48
himself unto all those who b. in him,	26:13	we b. that thou art God,		31:15
b. it not; for this day he is not	28: 6	and we b. that thou art holy,		31:15
them that repent and b. in his Son,	30: 2	Holy God, we b. that thou hast		31:16
shall b. the words which are written;	30: 3	we do not b. in the tradition of		31:16
also shall begin to b. in Christ;	30: 7	we b. that thou hast elected us to		31:16
as many as shall b. in Christ	30: 7	away to b. in things to come,		31:22
and persuadeth them to b. in him,	33: 4	to know, before they will b.		32:16
unto these words and b. in Christ;	33:10	of a surety; then we shall b.		32:17
and if ye b. not in these words	33:10	he hath no cause to b., for he		32:18
not in these words b. in Christ.	33:10	or only hath cause to b.,		32:19
And if ye shall b. in Christ	33:10	unto all who b. on his name;		32:22
in Christ ye will b. in these words,	33:10	the first place, that ye should b.,		32:22
that all men would b. in Christ,	Jac 1: 8	I verily b. that there are some		32:25
unto the Messiah, and b. in him	Jar 1:11	ye can no more than desire to b.,		32:27
and b. in prophesying,	Om 1:25	even until ye b. in a manner that		32:27
or even do not b. them when	Mos 1: 5	they should b. in one God,		33: 1
b. that Christ should come,	3:13	Do ye b. those scriptures which		33:12
and b. that salvation was,	3:18	ye must b. what Zenos said;		33:13
for we b. in Jesus Christ,	4: 2	not b. that it would heal them.		33:20
B. in God; believe that he is,	4: 9	and begin to b. in the Son of God,		33:22
b. that he is, and that he created	4: 9	those who shall b. on his name;		34:15
b. that he has all wisdom,	4: 9	if they had faith to b. that God		37:40
b. that men doth not comprehend	4: 9	they would not b. in my words.		39:11
b. that ye must repent of your sins	4:10	we do not b. that it is God that		44: 9
now, if you b. all these things	4:10	we b. that it is your cunning		44: 9
we b. all the words which thou	5: 2	said unto him: Yea, I b.		45: 3
because they b. in the salvation	17:15	Yea, I b. all the words which		45: 5
And many did b. his words.	18: 3	they had been taught to b.—		57:26
as many as did b. him did go	18: 4	b. on the name of Jesus Christ,	He	3:28
they did not b. the tradition of	26: 1	willingness to b. in his words.		6:36
They did not b. what had been	26: 2	come down to b. in their works		6:38
neither did they b. concerning	26: 2	we do not b. that he hath;		9: 2
shall b. in my name;	26:22	do not b. that he is a prophet;		9: 2
for many shall b. on their words,	28: 7	then will we b. that the other		9: 2
that many did b. on his words,	Al 1: 5	those who shall b. on his name.		14: 2
and b. in incorrect traditions	3: 8	shall b. on the Son of God,		14: 8
would not b. in the tradition of	3:11	that ye might b. on his name.		14:12
persecute those that did not b.	4: 8	And if ye b. on his name ye		14:13
Alma b. in the words which	5:11	that they might b. that these signs		14:28
and my father Alma b. them?	5:11	whosoever will b. might be saved,		14:29
do you b. these things?	7:17	and that whosoever will not b.,		14:29
yea, I know that ye b. them;	7:17	are led to b. the holy scriptures,		15: 7
that I know that ye b. them	7:17	when they do b. in that		15:10
not b. in such foolish traditions.	8:11	in that thing which they do b.,		15:10
b. the testimony of one man,	9: 2	not b. in the words of Samuel		16: 2
We will not b. thy words if	9: 4	more who did b. on his words,		16: 3
will be brought to b. in his word,	9:17	to the intent that they might b.;		16: 5
of those who b. on his name;	11:40	not b. in the words of Samuel;		16: 6
many of them did b. on his words,	14: 1	that we should b. in some great		16:20
taught to b. in the word of God	14: 8	the intent that they might not b.	3Ne	1:22
b. that the Lord will destroy	14:24	more part of the people did b.,		1:22
Yea, I b. all the words that thou	15: 7	lead them away to b. that the		2: 2
Yea, I b. according to thy words.	15: 9	did not b. that there should be		2: 3
did not b. in the repentance of	15:15	that which ye b. to be right,		3: 5
lead them to b. in my words.	17:29	many as shall b. on my name,		9:17
we do not b. that a man has	18: 3	to repent and b. in me.		11:32
Yea, I will b. all thy words.	18:23	shall b. in me and be baptized,		12: 1
I b. that he created all things	18:29	who shall b. in your words		12: 2
I b. all these things which	18:33	who shall b. in your words,		12: 2
I b. that it shall be according	19: 9	that ye shall b. in me,		12:19
all mankind who b. on his name.	19:13	unto all those who shall b.		18: 5
to b. in the power of God,	19:17	them that shall b. in their words.		19:21
many that did b. in their words;	19:35	because they b. in me;		19:22
many as did b. were baptized;	19:35	thou seest that they b. in me		19:22

BELIEVE 115 BELIEVED

who shall b. on their words,	3Ne	19:23	We b. that all religious	DC	134:10
that they may b. in me,		19:23	do not b. that any religious		134:10
them who shall b. on their words,		19:28	We b. that men should appeal to		134:11
And they shall b. in me,		20:31	we b. that all men are justified		134:11
those who will not b. it,		21: 9	We b. it just to preach the gospel		134:12
will not b. in my words,		21:11	we do not b. it right to interfere		134:12
that they shall b. these things		26: 9	we b. to be unlawful and unjust,		134:12
they will not b. these things,		26:10	among as many as shall b.	Mses	1:41
as would b. in their preaching;		28:18	unto any except them that b.		1:42
that they should not b.,	4Ne	1:38	you, except to them that b.		4:32
may b. the gospel of Jesus Christ,	Mrm	3:21	B. it not; and they believed it		5:13
may more fully b. his gospel,		5:15	nor b. on his Only Begotten Son,		5:57
and b. in Jesus Christ, that he		7: 5	hearken unto my voice, and b.,		6:52
the intent that ye may b. that;		7: 9	B. and repent of your sins		8:24
and if ye b. that ye will believe		7: 9	is Christ, or there, b. him not;	JS	1:21
believe that ye will b. this also;		7: 9	the secret chambers; b. it not;		1:25
and if ye b. this ye will know		7: 9	make him think or b. otherwise.		2:24
if it so be that ye b. in Christ,		7:10	nor do I b. that any earthly		2:31
those who do not b. in Christ.		9: 1	We b. in God, the Eternal	AoF	1
b. in the day of your visitation—		9: 2	We b. that men will be punished		2
signs shall follow them that b.—		9:24	We b. that through the Atonement		3
whosoever shall b. in my name,		9:25	We b. that the first principles		4
they who shall b. on my name;	Eth	3:14	We b. that a man must be called		5
if he would b. in him that he		3:26	We b. in the same organization		6
he that will not b. my words		4:12	We b. in the gift of tongues,		7
my words will not b. me—		4:12	We b. the Bible to be the word		8
he that will not b. me will not		4:12	also b. the Book of Mormon to		8
not b. the Father who sent me.		4:12	We b. all that God has revealed,		9
unto me, and b. in my gospel,		4:18	we b. that He will yet reveal		9
follow them that b. in my name.		4:18	We b. in the literal gathering		10
exhorting the people to b. in God		12: 3	We b. in being subject to kings,		12
the people, which they did not b.,		12: 5	We b. in being honest, true,		13
and to persuade to b. in Christ,	Mro	7:16	we b. all things, we hope all		13
do evil, and b. not in Christ,		7:17			
that they may b. the gospel	DC	3:20	BELIEVED		
if they will not b. my words,		5: 7	to pass that he b. in my words.	1Ne	2:17
they would not b. you,		5: 7	those who b. in the warnings	2Ne	5: 6
that they will not b. my words.		10:32	they who have b. in the Holy One		9:18
whosoever should b. in this gospel		10:50	Behold, they b. in Christ	Jac	4: 5
to them that b. on my name. Amen.		11:30	and said that I b. the scriptures;		7:19
that they may b. the gospel,		19:27	if they b. the words which	Mos	5: 1
That as many as would b.		20:25	Who hath b. our report,		14: 1
who should b. in the gifts and		20:27	and b. that the Lord would		15:11
b. on the name of Jesus Christ,		20:29	those that have b. in their words,		15:22
and they shall b. on his words,		21: 9	he b. the words which Abinadi had		17: 2
even as many as would b.;		29:43	as many as b. him went		18: 6
And they that b. not unto		29:44	together that b. on his word,		18: 7
the day cometh that they will b.		31: 2	he that b. the words of Abinadi		24: 9
even as many as will b. in me,		33: 6	to those who b. on his word,	Al	1: 7
as many as would b. might		34: 3	but b. those records which were		3:11
as many as will b. on my name,		35: 2	who b. in the commandments		3:11
all those who b. on my name.		35: 8	they b. that it was the judgments		4: 3
inasmuch as ye b. on my name		42: 1	who b. in the words which		14: 7
not faith to be healed, but b.,		42:43	whosoever b. or had been taught		14: 8
do these things, but b. in me,		42:52	they b. in the words of Alma.		15: 1
brethren that b. on my name,		45: 5	they b. in a Great Spirit		18: 5
is given to b. on their words,		46:14	that the king b. all his words.		18:40
B. on the name of the Lord Jesus,		49:12	as many as heard his words b.,		19:31
heard and most assuredly b.,		52:36	few b. on the words which		21:12
signs following them that b.		58:64	so sure as many as b.,		23: 6
but signs follow those that b.		63: 9	as b. in their preaching,		23: 6
if ye b. me, ye will labor while		64:25	all those that b. in these things.		25: 7
of as many as b. on my name.		66: 1	if he b. in God it was his		30: 9
Ye endeavored to b. that ye		67: 3	I verily b. that they were true;		30:53
verily b., and know to be true.		80: 4	had b. in the words of Korihor		30:57
shall follow them that b.—		84:65	who b. in the flattering words		46: 7
they who b. not on your words,		84:74	for they had not b. the words	He	9: 4
Gentiles, as many as will b.:		90: 8	But now, when they saw they b.,		9: 5
b. in the Messiah, and be		109:67	who b. on the words of Nephi;		9:39
I b. the coming of the Son of		130:17	who b. because of the testimony		9:39
then shall she b. and administer		132:64	as many as b. on his word		16: 1
not b. and administer unto him		132:65	as many as b. on the words of		16: 5
We b. that governments were		134: 1	the people who b. began to be	3Ne	1: 7
We b. that no government can		134: 2	those who b. in those traditions		1: 9
We b. that all governments		134: 3	who had not b. the words of		1:16
We b. that religion is instituted		134: 4	those who b. in the words of		1:16
we do not b. that human law		134: 4	Jesus Christ, in whom they b.		7:21
We b. that all men are bound to		134: 5	never has man b. in me as thou	Eth	3:15
We b. that every man should be		134: 6	the people b. not the words of		9:29
We b. that rulers, states,		134: 7	they first b. in the Son of God.		12:18
we do not b. that they have		134: 7	Not only those who b.	DC	20:26
We b. that the commission of		134: 8	who b. in the words of the holy		20:26
We do not b. it just to mingle		134: 9	are you because you have b.;		34: 4

BELIEVED — BELONGED

BELIEVED
as have b. in my name,	DC	38: 4
them that b. on my name		45: 8
Jews who b. not the gospel of		74: 2
b. not the gospel of Christ,		74: 4
and b. on his name and were		76:51
ye b. not my servants, and when		133:71
and they b. it not, and they	Mses	5:13
And as many as b. in the Son,		5:15
and as many as b. not and		5:15
many have b. and become the		7: 1
and many have b. not, and		7: 1
were but few who b. him;	JS	2:24

BELIEVER
a b. should not be united to	DC	74: 5
a b. in the Book of Mormon,		124:119

BELIEVERS
were all the true b. of Christ,	Al	46:14
those who were true b. in Christ		46:15
they were true b. in Christ;	4Ne	1:36
the true b. in Christ,		1:37

BELIEVES
he knows and most assuredly b.	DC	58:59
verily b. the above statement		128: 4

BELIEVEST
B. thou that thy father saw the tree	1Ne	11: 4
because thou b. in the Son of the		11: 6
B. thou the scriptures?	Jac	7:10
B. thou that there is no God?	Al	11:24
B. thou in the power of Christ		15: 6
If thou b. in the redemption of		15: 8
B. thou that there is a God?		18:24
B. thou that there is a Great		18:26
B. thou that this Great Spirit,		18:28
B. thou this? And she said		19: 9
B. thou that the Son of God		21: 7
B. thou that there is a God?		22: 7
B. thou this?		22:10
b. thou that we deceive this		30:35
B. thou that there is a God?		30:37
B. thou that these things are true?		30:41
Behold, I know that thou b.,		30:42
B. thou the words which I spake		45: 2
B. thou in Jesus Christ, who shall		45: 4
B. thou the words which I shall	Eth	3:11

BELIEVETH
unto him that b. unto the end	Mos	26:23
who steadfastly b. on his name.	Al	5:48
every man that b. on his name		12:15
he that b. in the word of God,		32:16
than he that only b.,		32:19
whoso b. in me, and is baptized	3Ne	11:33
And whoso b. not in me,		11:34
and whoso b. in me believeth		11:35
in me b. in the Father also;		11:35
unto you that whoso b. in Christ,	Mrm	9:21
And he that b. and is baptized		9:23
he that b. not shall be damned;		9:23
And he that b. not my words	Eth	4:10
my words b. not my disciples;		4:10
But he that b. these things		4:11
he that b. and is baptized shall		4:18
that b. not shall be damned;		4:18
whoso b. in God might with		12: 4
b. all things, hopeth all things,	Mro	7:45
whosoever b. on my words,	DC	5:16
he that b. and is baptized shall		68: 9
he that b. not shall be		68: 9
he that b. shall be blest with		68:10
soul who b. on your words,		84:64
he that b. and is baptized shall		112:29
he that b. not, and is not		112:29

BELIEVING
b. that the Lord was able to make	1Ne	11: 1
in faith, b. that ye shall receive,		15:11
b. that ye shall receive	En	1:15
in faith, b. that ye shall receive,	Mos	4:21
b. in the tradition of their	Mos	10:12
B. that they were driven out of		10:12
b. that ye shall receive,	Al	22:16
and b. that they must keep those		25:15
firmly b. that their souls were		46:39
were the most b. part of them,	He	16:15
is right, b. that ye shall receive,	3Ne	18:20
Doubt not, but be b., and begin	Mrm	9:27
in faith b. that ye shall receive,	Mro	7:26
b. that you shall receive a	DC	8: 1
b. in the power of Jesus Christ,		11:10
in faith b. in me that you		11:14
in my name, in faith b.,		14: 8
in faith b. that you shall receive,		18:18
pray always, and be b.,		90:24

BELLIES
whose b. are not satisfied,	DC	56:17

BELLOWS
a b. wherewith to blow the fire,	1Ne	17:11
after I had made a b., that I might		17:11

BELLY
strong drinks are not for the b.,	DC	89: 7
for the body, neither for the b.,		89: 8
drinks are not for the body or b.		89: 9
upon thy b. shalt thou go,	Mses	4:20

BELONG
who b. to the kingdom of the devil	1Ne	22:23
who b. to the family of Adam.	2Ne	9:21
they which b. to it must needs be		28:19
doth not b. to you but to God,	Mos	4:22
did b. to the church of God;		25:18
did not b. to the church of God.		26:38
whom the kingdom doth rightly b.		29: 6
to whom the kingdom doth b.,		29: 7
did not b. to the church of God	Al	1:19
did b. to the church of God,		1:19
that did not b. to the church,		1:21
who did not b. to their church.		1:31
who did not b. to their church		1:32
did not b. to. the church of God.		4: 9
who did not b. to the church;		4:10
you that b. to this church,		5: 6
unto you that b. to the church;		5:62
who do not b. to the church		5:62
did not b. to the church		6: 2
whosoever did b. to the church		6: 3
who did not b. to the church.		46:14
those who did b. to the church		46:15
the government doth rightly b.,		54:18
to b. to the church of God—	He	3:33
to b. to the church of God.		4:11
by those who did b. to his band,		6:22
they both b. to your secret band,		8:28
Lamanites, did b. to the church;		11:21
whatsoever did b. unto them.	3Ne	6: 1
who did not b. to the church.		28:19
them who b. not to their churches.	Mrm	8:28
of the church to which they b.,	DC	20:63
which b. to the children of		41: 6
to b. to the church.		51: 4
worthy to b. to the church,		51: 5
who b. to the church of		70:10
b. always unto the Presidency		81: 2
those who b. to the church,		83: 1
who do not b. to your families;		90:25
properties which b. to the order		104: 1
for it shall b. to you all		104:62
first seventy to whom they b.,		107:95
who b. not unto the Twelve,		107:98
those who do b. or have		130: 5
adultery, for they b. to him,		132:62
which b. to the same order as	Abr	3: 3
which b. to the same order as		3: 9

BELONGED
b. to the mother of abominations,	1Ne	14:16
people who b. to king Benjamin,	Mos	1: 1
those who b. to the church of God.		27: 2

BELONGED

who b. to the church of God,	Al 1: 7
flocks which b. to the king,	19:21
who b. to the church of God,	46:14
when it rightly b. unto them.	54:17
unto those who b. to his band	He 2: 5
of all those who b. to his band	2: 8
once b. to the church of God	5:35
of those who b. to their band	6:24
also b. to the secret band	8: 1
who b. to the seven churches,	DC 77: 5
do belong or have b. to it.	130: 5

BELONGETH

whoso b. not to the church of the	1Ne 14:10
b. to that great church, which is	14:10
it b. to him who created you.	Mos 2:25
to God, to whom also your life b.;	4:22
an ass which b. to his neighbor,	5:14
whosoever b. to my church	DC 10:55
who b. to this church of Christ,	42:78
any one who b. to the church	46: 4
that which b. to this people	51:10
which b. to the priesthood.	84:39
this ordinance b. to my house,	124:30
of baptizing for the dead b.,	124:33
with that that b. unto him	132:61

BELONGING

not any man, b. to the church,	Al 1:21
b. unto the high priesthood.	DC 84:29
b. to the lesser priesthood,	84:30
as any man b. to the order	104: 5
not any person b. to the church	107:81
officers b. to my Priesthood,	124:123
b. to the everlasting gospel,	128:17
the right b. to the fathers.	Abr 1: 2
a slave b. to the prince.	Fac 3: 6

BELONGS

it b. unto us, who are the elder	2Ne 5: 3
b. to the whole human family	Mrm 3:20
let that which b. to this people	DC 51: 7
b. to all mankind, and is	98: 5
b. to the literal descendants of	107:40
whom rightly b. the priesthood,	113: 6

BELOVED

Behold, my b. brethren,	2Ne 6: 2
And now, my b. brethren,	9: 1
Behold, my b. brethren,	9: 3
O, my b. brethren,	9:39
O, my b. brethren,	9:40
O then, my b. brethren,	9:41
O, my b. brethren,	9:44
O, my b. brethren,	9:45
Behold, my b. brethren,	9:52
unto you again, my b. brethren,	10: 1
Wherefore, my b. brethren,	10:18
And now, my b. brethren,	10:20
Wherefore, my b. brethren,	10:24
will I sing to my well-b. a song	15: 1
well-beloved a song of my b.,	15: 1
My well-b. hath a vineyard	15: 1
my children, and my b. brethren;	26: 1
For behold, my b. brethren,	26:23
And now behold, my b. brethren,	30: 1
And now, my b. brethren,	30:18
unto you, my b. brethren.	31: 1
I would ask of you, my b. brethren,	31: 6
Wherefore, my b. brethren,	31:10
in the name of my B. Son.	31:11
Wherefore, my b. brethren,	31:13
But, behold, my b. brethren,	31:14
Yea, the words of my B. are true	31:15
And now, my b. brethren,	31:16
And now, my b. brethren,	31:19
And now, behold, my b. brethren,	31:21
And now, behold, my b. brethren,	32: 1
And now, my b. brethren,	32: 8
And now, my b. brethren,	33:10
And now, my b. brethren,	33:13
Now, my b. brethren, I, Jacob,	Jac 2: 2
children, and also our b. brethren,	4: 2
our b. brethren and our children	Jac 4: 3
Wherefore, b. brethren, be	4:11
And now, b., marvel not that I	4:12
And now, my b., how is it possible	4:17
Behold, my b. brethren, I will	4:18
Wherefore, my b. brethren, I	6: 5
O then, my b. brethren, repent	6:11
And now, my b. brethren,	Om 1:26
for he was b. by his people.	Mos 23: 6
to preach unto my b. brethren,	Al 5:49
Yea, my b. brethren,	5:50
And now my b. brethren,	5:53
Behold my b. brethren,	7: 1
And now my b. brethren,	7:17
And now my b. brethren,	7:22
And now my b. brethren,	7:26
And now, my b. brethren,	9:30
brethren, and ye ought to be b.,	9:30
I thank my God, my b. people,	24: 7
Now, my best b. brethren,	24:12
these our dearly b. brethren, who	26: 9
who have so dearly b. us,	26: 9
But behold, my b. brethren,	26:26
those whom they so dearly b.,	27: 4
those who had so dearly b. them—	27: 4
were a zealous and b. people,	27:30
And now, my b. brethren,	32:24
desired of my b. brother that he	34: 3
now behold, my b. brethren,	34:28
And now, my b. brethren,	34:37
And now my b. brethren,	34:40
they were b. by each other,	53: 2
also b. by all the people of Nephi.	53: 2
My dearly b. brother, Moroni,	56: 2
behold, my b. brother, I have	56: 2
my b. brother Moroni, that never	56:45
now, my b. brother, Moroni,	58:41
And now, my b. brethren—	60:10
brethren-for ye ought to be b.;	60:10
Therefore, my b. brother, Moroni,	61:14
mine epistle to my b. brother,	61:21
of your faith in my Well B.,	He 5:47
And now, my b. brethren, behold,	15: 1
Behold my B. Son, in whom I	3Ne 11: 7
repent and come unto my B. Son,	21:20
the thing which John, my b.,	28: 6
did take away his b. disciples,	Mrm 1:13
the b. disciples were taken away	1:16
bring about, through his most B.,	5:14
speak unto you, my b. brethren,	Mro 7: 2
take heed, my b. brethren, that	7:14
Wherefore, my b. brethren,	7:27
he hath done this, my b. brethren,	7:29
And now, my b. brethren, if this	7:35
But behold, my b. brethren,	7:39
And again, my b. brethren,	7:40
Wherefore, my b. brethren, if	7:46
Wherefore, my b. brethren, pray	7:48
My b. son, Moroni, I rejoice	8: 2
wherefore, my b. son, I know that	8: 9
My b. son, I write unto you again	9: 1
And now, my b. son,	9: 6
O my b. son, how can a people	9:11
would exhort you, my b. brethren,	10:18
would exhort you, my b. brethren,	10:19
John, my b., what desirest thou?	DC 7: 1
my b. has desired that he	7: 5
saying: This is my b. Son.	93:15
Therefore, dearly b. brethren,	123:17
Dear and well-b. brother,	126: 1
dearly b. brethren and sisters,	128:15
But, behold, my B. Son,	Mses 4: 2
which was my B. and Chosen	4: 2
This is My B. Son.	JS 2:17

BELOW

thy servants shall dwell here b.	Al 31:26
he descended b. all things,	DC 88: 6
hath descended b. them all.	122: 8

BENEATH

and look upon the earth b.;	2Ne 8: 6
Hell from b. is moved for thee	24: 9

BENEATH — BESTOWED

BENEATH
heavens above and in the earth b.;	2Ne 29: 7	king B. again opened his mouth	Mos 4: 4
or things which are in the earth b.	Mos 12:36	when king B. had thus spoken	5: 1
or which are in the earth b.,	13:12	which king B. desired of them;	5: 6
and shrink b. the glance of	27:31	king B. thought it was expedient,	6: 1
earth did tremble b. our feet;	Al 36: 7	when king B. had made an end	6: 3
are both above the earth and b.,	He 14:21	king B. lived three years and he	6: 5
yea, both above the earth and b.	14:22	words which king B. had taught	8: 3
heaven above and in the earth b.;	DC 29:14	understand the words of king B.,	26: 1
above, and in the earth b.	45:40	would do even as my father B. did	29:13
for their reward lurketh b.,	58:33	the words which king B. spake	He 5: 9
above, and my power lieth b.	63:59	come to the reign of king B.,	DC 10:41
creatures b. the celestial world;	78:14		
hath brought up Zion from b.	84:100	BENNETT, John C.	
are above, and things that are b.,	101:34	let my servant B. help you	DC 124:16
the earth, both above and b.:	Mses 6:63		
above, and in the earth b.,	Abr 3:21	BENSON, Ezra T.	
		Let my servants B. and	DC 136:12

BENEFIT
save it be for the b. of the world;	2Ne 26:24	BENT	
for the intent of the b. of	Jar 1: 2	be sharp, and all their bows b.,	2Ne 15:28
a great b. to his fellow beings.	Mos 8:18	and b. their course towards the	Mos 22:11
thou wilt for the b. of man;	Eth 3: 4		
for the public b. of the church,	DC 42:35	BENT, Samuel	
for the b. of those who love me	46: 9	Namely, B., Henry G Sherwood,	DC 124:132
the b. of the children of God.	46:26		
for the b. and the use of man,	59:18	BESEECH	
for their b. while they remain,	70:15	I b. of you in words of soberness	Jac 6: 5
funds which shall b. the church	72:21	I b. of you that ye do not	Al 34:33
for the b. of the saints of	82:13	I b. of thee that thou wilt hear	36: 3
for the b. of managing the	82:17	Wherefore, I b. of you, brethren,	Mro 7:19
for the b. of the church of the	82:18	O Jehovah, we b. thee,	DC 109:42
or make use of it for their b.,	84:103		
for the b. of the council of	89: 1	BESET	
Spirit shall obtain b. therefrom;	91: 5	sins which do so easily b. me.	2Ne 4:18
for the b. of those who seek	96: 3	sin, which easily doth b. you,	Al 7:15
is necessary to b. mine order,	96: 4		
for the b. of my church,	104: 1	BESIDE	
for the b. of the Ozondah	104:40	and b. him there is no Savior.	DC 76: 1
for you, for the b. of Zion,	111: 2	but there is no God b. me,	Mses 1: 6
in due time for the b. of Zion,	111: 2		
for the b. of my people.	117:14	BESIDES	
of God for the b. of man;	134: 1	b. him to whom the book shall	2Ne 27:12
the b. of the children of men;	135: 3	b. sixty of the sons of the	Al 57: 6
for the b. of my posterity that	Abr 1:31	shall have other witness b. him	Mrm 3:21
		are to choose other seventy b.	DC 107:95
BENEFITED		other stakes b. this one which	109:59
all may be b. that seek or that	DC 46: 9	any eye seen, O God, b. thee,	133:45
not by the Spirit cannot be b.	91: 6		
large ship is b. very much by	123:16	BESOM	
		it with the b. of destruction,	2Ne 24:23
BENEFITS			
yea, the b. thereof.	DC 70: 5	BESOUGHT	
the b. shall be consecrated unto	70: 8	and b. them that they would	Al 15: 5
		he b. that Alma should pray	30:54
BENEVOLENT			
true, chaste, b., virtuous,	AoF 13	BESPEAKETH	
		that b. the power of God.	DC 60: 4
BENIGHTED			
and b. dominion of Sheol—	DC 121: 4	BEST	
		to the b. of my knowledge,	Jac 7:26
BENJAMIN		Now, my b. beloved brethren,	Al 24:12
B., his son, reigneth in his stead.	Om 1:23	to be the next b. place for them to	49:12
have seen, in the days of king B.,	1:24	as may be thought b. or decided	DC 42:72
king B. did drive them out of	1:24	seek ye earnestly the b. gifts,	46: 8
knowing king B. to be a just	1:25	seek ye out of the b. books	88:118
down to the reign of this king B.,	WM 1: 3	seek ye out of the b. books	109: 7
down to the reign of this king B.,	1: 3	wisdom out of the b. books,	109:14
plates into the hands of king B.,	1:10	b. calculated to secure the public	134: 5
until the days of king B.	1:10	the b. blood of the nineteenth	135: 6
were handed down from king B.,	1:11		
And now, concerning this king B.—	1:12	BESTEAD	
behold, king B. gathered together	1:13	shall pass through it hardly b.	2Ne 18:21
king B., with the assistance of	1:16		
behold, king B. was a holy man,	1:17	BESTIR	
king B., by laboring with all	1:18	except ye do b. yourselves in the	Al 60:29
people who belonged to king B.,	Mos 1: 1		
king B. had continual peace	1: 1	BESTOW	
did king B. teach his sons,	1: 8	God shall b. upon your children.	2Ne 9: 3
after king B. had made an end	1: 9	which he doth b. upon you.	Al 34:38
after king B. had made an end	1:15	Shule did b. great favors upon	Eth 7:22
which king B. should speak	2: 1	will b. the gift of the Holy Ghost	DC 33:15
which king B. should speak	2: 6		
king B. could not teach them	2: 7	BESTOWED	
when king B. had made an end	4: 1	great blessings has he b. upon us?	Al 26: 2
words which king B. had spoken	4: 3		

BESTOWED

which hath been b. upon us,	Al	26: 3
which thou hast b. upon them		33:16
which he b. upon his people;		48:12
father b. upon him the kingdom;	Eth	7:10
b. upon all who are true followers	Mro	7:48
the first gift that I b. upon you;	DC	5: 4
b. great blessings upon thy head;		39: 8
was b. upon Heman Basset		52:37
has been b. upon Ziba Peterson		58:60
if a gift is b. upon him,		88:33
grace of God b. upon them.		102: 4
b. upon them his last blessing.		107:53
all that he has b. upon them		133:52

BESTOWS

God b. on those who love him,	DC	76:116
b. upon the head of the church.		107:92

BETHABARA

father said he should baptize in B.,	1Ne	10: 9

BETHEL

a mountain on the east of B.,	Abr	2:20
B. on the west, and Hai on		2:20

BETIMES

Reproving b. with sharpness,	DC	121:43

BETOOK

I b. myself to prayer and	JS	2:29

BETRAY

and shall b. one another;	JS	1: 8

BETTER

It is b. that one man should perish	1Ne	4:13
have been b. that they had died		17:20
we have been led to a b. land,	2Ne	10:20
it would have been b. for you that		31:14
suppose that ye are b. than they.	Jac	2:13
how much b. are you than they,		3: 7
am no b. than ye yourselves are;	Mos	2:26
it is b. that we be slaves to the		7:15
it b. that we should be in bondage		20:22
is b. that man should be judged		29:12
was no b. than the hearer,	Al	1:26
teacher any b. than the learner;		1:26
that ye are b. one than another;		5:54
b. that he should fall than thee,		20:17
it is b. that thy soul should be		30:47
into a b. land of promise.		37:45
that we are b. than our brethren;		38:14
were inspired by a b. cause,		43:45
it shall be b. for the Lamanites	He	7:23
shall be b. for them than for you		15:14
it is b. that ye should deny	3Ne	12:30
Are ye not much b. than they?		13:26
And it would be b. for them if		28:35
with surety hope for a b. world,	Eth	12: 4
I judge b. things of you, for I	Mro	7:39
and seek for the things of a b.	DC	25:10
more than two witnesses it is b.		42:80
b. for him that he had been		54: 5
b. for them never to have been		76:32
It had been b. for them that		121:22

BETWEEN

I saw wars b. the Nephites and	En	1:24
b. my people, the Nephites, and	Om	1:10
b. the Nephites and the		1:24
disturbance b. the Lamanites and	Mos	21:22
a war b. the Nephites and the	Al	1:hd
b. the heavens and the earth,		1:15
b. the land northward and the		22:32
b. the land Jershon and the land		27:23
also the wars b. the Nephites and		28: 9
a space b. the time of death and		40: 9
b. death and the resurrection—		40:11
b. death and the resurrection of		40:21
the wars b. the Nephites and		43: 3
the line b. the Nephites and		50:11
b. the land of Zarahemla and the		50:11
b. the city of Moroni and the		50:14

to be a warm contention b.	Al	50:26
a battle commenced b. them,		50:35
b. them and the people of Lehi;		50:36
peace b. the people of Lehi and		51: 1
upon the plains b. the two cities.		52:20
war b. them and the Lamanites,		62:35
the war b. the Nephites and the		62:41
peace b. the Nephites and the	He	2: 1
the war b. the robbers and	3Ne	2:17
b. the land Bountiful and the		3:23
discern b. the righteous and		24:18
b. him that serveth God and		24:18
to be a war b. the Nephites,	Mrm	1: 8
this war was b. the Nephites, and		1: 8
a war again b. the Nephites and		2: 1
b. the sons of Akish and Akish,	Eth	9:12
b. him and thee alone,	DC	28:11
b. him or her and thee alone;		42:88
directly b. Jew and Gentile;		57: 4
counsel b. themselves and me.		58:25
let God judge b. me and thee,		64:11
b. the righteous and the wicked,		101:95
distinction b. the high council or		102:30
The difference b. this quorum		124:140
b. the fathers and the children,		128:18
b. Harmony, Susquehanna		128:20
and nations, b. man and man;		134: 6
can judge b. thee and God;	Mses	1:15
can judge b. him and thee.		1:18
enmity b. thee and the woman,		4:21
b. thy seed and her seed;		4:21
b. fourteen and fifteen years	JS	2:22
b. the time I had the vision and		2:28
b. the time I arrived at the		2:62

BETWIXT

judge, I pray you, b. me and my	2Ne	15: 3
standing b. them and justice;	Mos	15: 9
a war b. the Lamanites and	Al	35:13
a space b. the time of death and		40: 6
are b. Sherrizah and me;	Mro	9:17

BEWARE

b. lest there shall arise	Mos	2:32
B. of false prophets, who come	3Ne	14:15
let him b. lest he commandeth	Mrm	8:18
But b. of pride, lest thou	DC	23: 1
of meekness, and b. of pride.		25:14
b. of pride, lest ye become as		38:39
b. how you hold them, for they		41:12
b. lest ye are deceived;		46: 8
let every man b. lest he do that		50: 9
let my servant Lyman Wight b.,		52:12
Let such b. and repent		63:15
let all men b. how they take		63:61
b. from henceforth, and refrain		82: 2
to b. concerning yourselves,		84:43
b. how they hold them lest		90: 5

BEYOND

baptize in Bethabara, b. Jordan;	1Ne	10: 9
far b., yea, exceeding of all beauty;		11: 8
by them b. the river,	2Ne	17:20
the Red Sea b. Jordan in Galilee		19: 1
came by looking b. the mark,	Jac	4:14
as many as go b. this day must	WM	1: 4
desirous b. measure to know	Mos	28:12
yea, exceedingly, b. measure.		29:40
away b. the borders of the land;	Al	2:36
and to explain things b., or to		12: 1
b. that which Amulek had done.		12: 1
b. the borders of the land of		16: 6
away b. the borders of Manti		16: 7
were astonished b. all measure.		31:19
carry us b. this vale of sorrow		37:45
as if we were going to the city b.,		56:31
we were b. the Lamanites,		58:27
astonished b. measure.	He	3:25
up b. that which is good		7:26
on their march b. the robbers,	3Ne	4:25
b. the description of that which	Mrm	5:15
stop b. the sea in the wilderness,	Eth	2: 7
might express b. his language;	DC	67: 5
themselves b. their bounds.		88:90

b. anything earthly I had ever JS 2:31
was glorious b. description, 2:32

BIBBER
therefore he became a wine b., Mos 11:15

BIBLE
the gentiles shall say: A B.! 2Ne 29: 3
A Bible! A B.! We have got a 29: 3
A Bible! We have got a B., 29: 3
and there cannot be any more B. 29: 3
O fools, they shall have a B.; 29: 4
thank they the Jews for the B. 29: 4
Thou fool, that shall say: A B., 29: 6
A Bible, we have got a B., 29: 6
and we need no more B. 29: 6
a B. save it were by the Jews? 29: 6
because that ye have a B. ye need 29:10
in the B. and the Book of DC 42:12
by an appeal to the B. JS 2:12
the B. to be the word of God AoF 8

BIBLES
from the way it reads in our B. JS 2:36

BID
I b. you an everlasting farewell, 2Ne 33:14
Finally, I b. you farewell, until I Jac 6:13
and to the reader I b. farewell, 7:27
And now I, Moroni, b. farewell Eth 12:38
And now I b. unto all, farewell. Mro 10:34
b. farewell unto the Gentiles; DC 135: 5

BIDDEN
I was b. that I should not write 2Ne 4:25
and they were b. to go forth He 5:49

BIDDING
b. them to be of good comfort: Mos 27:23

BIG
have toiled, being b. with child; 1Ne 17:20

BILL
b. of your mother's divorcement? 2Ne 7: 1

BILLINGS, Titus
Let my servant B., who has DC 63:39

BILLOWING
if the b. surge conspire against DC 122: 7

BIND
and they did b. me with cords, 1Ne 7:16
take me and b. me with cords, 18:11
and b. them on even as a bride. 21:18
chains which b. the children of 2Ne 1:13
chains of him that would b. you 9:45
B. up the testimony, seal the law 18:16
they should no more b. Ammon Mos 7:16
of death which b. his people; Al 7:12
doth b. you down to destruction, 7:15
to b. all the Nephites who 17:20
hands on them to b. them, 23: 2
to b. themselves down under the 30:23
b. them down to a belief of Christ, 31:17
Take this fellow and b. him, He 16: 6
therefore take him and b. him, 16: 6
b. yourselves to act in all holiness DC 43: 9
b. yourselves by this covenant, 82:15
to b. up the law and seal up the 88:84
the law, and b. up the testimony, 109:46
whatsoever he shall b. on earth 124:93
whatsoever you b. on earth, may 127: 7
whatsoever you b. on earth shall 128: 8
whatsoever thou shalt b. on earth 128:10
whatsoever you b. on earth, 132:46
to b. the consciences of men, 134: 4
as to b. my tongue so that JS 2:15

BINDETH
and tortureth them and b. them 1Ne 13: 5
until he b. them with his 2Ne 26:22

BINDING
is the sealing and b. power, DC 128:14
as authoritative and b." OD

BINDS
liberty which b. us to our lands Al 44: 5
which records or b. on earth DC 128: 9
on earth and b. in heaven. 128: 9

BIRTH
signs given unto my people of his b. 2Ne 26: 3
who was a Nephite by b., Al 49:25
of kings were those of high b., 51: 8
who were Lamanites by b., He 3:12
who was a Nephite by b., 5:35
blood of the Canaanites by b. Abr 1:21

BISHOP
b., high councilor, and high priest, DC 20:67
ordained a b. unto the church, 41: 9
laid before the b. of my church 42:31
laid before the b. of my church, 42:32
to be consecrated unto the b., 42:33
and the b. and his council; 42:34
to assist the b. as counselors 42:71
which is consecrated to the b., 42:71
decided by the counselors and b. 42:72
the b., also, shall receive his 42:73
that the b. be present also. 42:82
And unto the b. of the church, 46:27
and the b. of the church, 48: 6
has consecrated unto the b. for 51: 5
done through the b. or the agent, 51:12
let the b. appoint a storehouse 51:13
be kept in the hands of the b. 51:13
shall be appointed by the b., 53: 4
Let the b. and the agent make 57:15
before the b. of the church. 58:35
be put into the hands of the b., 58:51
the b. or the agent of the church. 58:55
And even the b., who is a judge, 64:40
may officiate in the office of b. 68:19
no b. or high priest who shall 68:22
neither the b., neither the agent 70:11
a b. to be appointed unto you, 72: 2
their stewardship unto the b., 72: 5
over unto the b. in Zion. 72: 6
the duty of the b. shall be 72: 7
the duty of the b. who has 72: 9
handed over to the b. of Zion, 72:13
the debt unto the b. in Zion; 72:14
things before the b. in Zion. 72:15
of his stewardship unto the b. 72:16
certificate from the judge or b. 72:17
unto the b. in Zion, rendereth 72:17
be accepted of the b. of Zion. 72:18
unto the b. of the church in 72:19
claim for assistance upon the b. 72:20
up unto the b. a certificate 72:25
or a certificate from the b.; 72:25
the offices of elder and b. are 84:29
send it up unto the b. in Zion, 84:104
or unto the b. in Ohio, 84:104
And the b., Newel K. Whitney, 84:112
let the b. go unto the city of 84:114
inheritances legally from the b.; 85: 1
let the b. search diligently to 90:22
from the hand of the b.; 90:30
the b. also, and others have 90:35
Whitney also, a b. of my church, 93:50
up kindly unto the b. of Zion. 99: 6
may officiate in the office of b. 107:17
the office of a b. is not equal 107:68
for the office of a b. is in 107:68
a b. must be chosen from the 107:69
This is the duty of the b. who is not 107:73
the office of b. independently, 107:76
the b. or judges, 107:78
This president is to be a b.; 107:88
and be a b. unto my people, 117:11
be put into the hands of the b. 119: 1
of the b. and his council, 120: 1

BISHOPRIC — BLESS

BISHOPRIC
have a legal right to the b.,	DC 68:16
all things pertaining to the b.	82:12
The b. is the presidency of	107:15
their stead and receive their b.	114: 2
upon his head the office of a b.,	124:21
to preside over the b.;	124:141
a knowledge of said b. is given	124:141

BISHOP'S
the church or the b. council	DC 102: 2

BISHOPS
the presiding elders, traveling b.,	DC 20:66
other b. to be set apart unto	68:14
bishop or b. in all things—	72:20
to have other b. or judges in	107:74
inasmuch as there are other b.	107:75

BITTEN
after they were b. he prepared	1Ne 17:41
been b. by the poisonous serpents,	2Ne 25:20

BITTER
one being sweet and the other b.	2Ne 2:15
that put b. for sweet, and sweet	15:20
bitter for sweet, and sweet for b.!	15:20
branches whose fruit is most b.,	Jac 5:52
it be those which are most b.;	5:57
which bring forth b. fruit,	5:65
and so b. as were my pains.	Al 36:21
in the most b. pain and anguish	38: 8
they drink the dregs of a b. cup.	40:26
have drunk out of that b. cup	3Ne 11:11
For behold, a b. fountain cannot	Mro 7:11
fountain bring forth b. water;	7:11
I might not drink the b. cup,	DC 19:18
if they never should have b.	29:39
unto them, for their death is b.	42:47
and they taste the b., that they	Mses 6:55
and create a b. persecution;	JS 2:22
of the most b. persecution	2:23
The persecution became more b.	2:60

BITTERN
for the b., and pools of water?	2Ne 24:23

BITTERNESS
redeemed from the gall of b.	Mos 27:29
on me, who am in the gall of b.,	Al 36:18
are in the gall of b. and in	41:11
for they are in the gall of b. and	Mrm 8:31
is in the gall of b. and in the	Mro 8:14
to fear, he saw the b. of hell.	Mses 1:20
he had b. of soul, and wept	7:44

BLACK
b. and white, bond and free,	2Ne 26:33
not make one hair b. or white;	3Ne 12:36
by an armed mob-painted b.—	DC 135: 1
for the seed of Cain were b.,	Mses 7:22

BLACKENING
Which dark and b. deeds are	DC 123:10

BLACKEST
in falsehood of the b. dye,	DC 127: 1

BLACKNESS
a skin of b. to come upon them.	2Ne 5:21
I clothe the heavens with b.,	7: 3
if the heavens gather b.,	DC 122: 7
I clothe the heavens with b.,	133:69
there was a b. came upon all	Mses 7: 8

BLADE
I saw that the b. there of was of	1Ne 4: 9
the b. is springing up and is	DC 86: 4
tares while the b. is yet tender	86: 6

BLADES
the b. thereof were cankered with	Mos 8:11

BLAMELESS
that I might be found b.,	Mos 2:27
none shall be found b. before God,	3:21
no more b. in the sight of God,	3:22
yourselves b. before God?	Al 5:27
that ye were b. before him,	7: 3
ye may walk b. before him,	7:22
knoweth not good from evil is b.;	29: 5
b. before God at the last day.	DC 4: 2
without spot and b.—	38:31
the commandments of God b.,	88:133

BLASPHEME
profaned not; neither did they b.	Jar 1: 5
yea, he went on to b.	Al 30:30
b. my name upon the lands	DC 105:15

BLASPHEMED
b. against me in the midst of	DC 112:26

BLASPHEMIES
whatever, and all manner of b.,	DC 132:26

BLASPHEMY
declare unto you that this is b.;	Jac 7: 7
The b. against the Holy Ghost,	DC 132:27

BLASTED
their hope shall be b.,	DC 121:11

BLED
have fought and b. out their lives	Al 60: 9
fought much and b. much.	Eth 13:19

BLEED
and to b. at every pore,	DC 19:18
the sword, yea, wounded and b.?	Al 60:22

BLESS
Lord did b. us again with food,	1Ne 16:39
and b. it unto our fathers? yea, he	17:35
did b. it unto our fathers unto	17:35
may the Lord b. thee forever,	2Ne 3: 3
Behold, that seer will the Lord b.;	3:14
he doth b. you and prosper you.	Mos 2:22
he doth immediately b. you;	2:24
And may the Lord b. my people.	10:22
and I will b. thee, and	Al 3:17
And may the Lord b. you,	7:25
he shall b. thee and thy house;	10: 7
that the Lord began to b. them,	21:17
of all men, b. their souls forever.	28: 8
And may the Lord b. your soul,	38:15
that the Lord God may b. them.	46:20
that the Lord did b. them,	62:51
behold, I will b. thee forever;	He 10: 5
thou canst b. them according to	11:16
doth b. and prosper those who put	12: 1
the Lord shall b. them and prolong	15:10
I have reason to b. my God	3Ne 5:20
b. them that curse you, do good	12:44
he shall break bread and b. it	18: 5
to b. you in turning away every	20:26
did break bread oft, and b. it,	26:13
will b. the church for my sake.	27: 7
the Lord did b. them in all	4Ne 1:18
to light, him will the Lord b.	Mrm 8:14
and may he b. them forever,	9:37
there will I b. thee and thy seed,	Eth 1:43
to b. and sanctify this bread to	Mro 4: 3
to b. and sanctify this wine to	5: 2
and b. them in his name.	DC 20:70
to b. and sanctify this bread	20:77
to b. and sanctify this wine	20:79
I will b. all those who labor in	21: 9
will b. them both spiritually and	24: 3
I will b. you and your family,	31: 2
trifle not, and I will b. them.	32: 5
whom I delight to b. with	41: 1
and by so doing I will b. him,	49: 4
am merciful and will b. them,	70:18
and will b. him, and also thee,	81: 3

BLESS 122 BLESSED

will b. him with a multiplicity of	DC 97: 5	b. are ye, for ye did thrust in	Al	26: 5
And I will b. her with blessings,	97:28	B. be the name of our God;		26: 8
I will b., and multiply blessings	104:31	Yea, b. is the name of my God,		26:36
I am with you to b. you	108: 8	I say, b. be the name of my God,		26:36
b. him with a multiplicity of	124:13	and b. are this people in this		27:12
that I may b. you, and crown	124:55	and if so, b. are ye.		32: 8
b. him with a multiplicity of	124:90	to be humble b. are ye;		32:13
whomsoever you b. I will	132:47	to be humble ye were b.,		32:14
you bless I will b.,	132:47	that they are more b. who		32:14
I will b. him and multiply him	132:55	to the end, the same shall be b.—		32:15
I, the Lord thy God, will b. her,	132:56	much more b. than they who		32:15
not b. the children of Noah?	Mses 7:49	b. are they who humble		32:16
I will b. thee above measure,	Abr 2: 9	b. is he that believeth in the		32:16
will b. them through thy name;	2:10	b. is he that endureth to the end.		38: 2
and shall rise up and b. thee,	2:10	B. art thou; and the Lord shall		45: 8
And I will b. them that bless	2:11	he b. him, and also his other sons;		45:15
I will bless them that b. thee,	2:11	and he also b. the earth for the		45:15
We will b. them, and cause	4:22	these words he b. the church,		45:17
We will b. them.	4:28	B. art thou and thy children;		50:20
		and they shall be b.,		50:20
BLESSED		And b. is the name of our God;		57:35
B. art thou Lehi, because of the	1Ne 2: 1	the Lord had b. them so long	He	6:17
B. art thou Nephi, because of	2:19	B. art thou, Nephi, for those		10: 4
that I had been b. of the Lord.	3: 8	b. are they who will repent		12:23
b. art thou, Nephi, because thou	11: 6	b. are they who will repent		13:11
And b. are they who shall seek	13:37	But b. are they who will repent,		13:13
a b. people upon the promised land	14: 2	things with which he hath b. you,		13:22
all the kindreds of the earth be b.	15:18	B. be the name of the Lord God	3Ne	4:32
I, Nephi, had been b. of the Lord	16: 8	he hath b. the house of Jacob,		5:21
we were b. in abundance.	18:24	hath b. them and prospered		5:22
tongue and people shall be b.	19:17	b. are those who come unto me.		9:14
all the kindreds of the earth be b.	22: 9	B. be the name of the Most		11:17
cannot be b. unless he shall make	22:10	B. are ye if ye shall give heed		12: 1
righteous it shall be b. forever.	2Ne 1: 7	b. are ye if ye shall believe in		12: 1
be b. upon the face of this land,	1: 9	more b. are they who shall		12: 2
thy seed shall be b. with his seed,	1:31	b. are they who shall believe		12: 2
Wherefore, thy soul shall be b.,	2: 3	b. are the poor in spirit who		12: 3
thou art b. even as they	2: 4	b. are all they that mourn,		12: 4
because of this covenant thou art b.;	3:23	And b. are the meek, for they		12: 5
And now, b. art thou, Joseph.	3:25	b. are all they who do hunger		12: 6
in the end thy seed shall be b.	4: 9	And b. are the merciful, for		12: 7
B. art thou, and thy seed;	4:11	And b. are all the pure in heart,		12: 8
thou shalt be b. in all thy days.	4:11	And b. are all the peacemakers,		12: 9
And b. are the Gentiles,	6:12	And b. are all they who are		12:10
I called him alone, and b. him.	8: 2	And b. are ye when men shall		12:11
Gentiles shall be b. upon the land.	10:10	b. are the Gentiles, because of		16: 6
Gentiles shall be b. and numbered	10:18	B. are ye because of your faith.		17:20
b. are those who hearken unto my	28:30	children, one by one, and b. them,		17:21
they shall become a b. people.	Jac 3: 6	of the bread and brake and b. it;		18: 3
And b. art thou; for because	5:75	as I have broken bread and b. it		18: 6
b. are they who have labored	6: 3	B. are ye for this thing which		18:10
and b. be the name of my God	En 1: 1	always do these things b. are ye,		18:12
and thou shalt be b.	1: 5	b. are ye if ye shall keep my		18:14
Come unto me, ye b.,	1:27	and your children may be b.		18:21
that ye may be b., prospered, and	Mos 2:36	And b. are ye if ye have no		18:34
the b. and happy state of those	2:41	Jesus b. them as they did pray		19:25
For behold, they are b. in all	2:41	he brake bread again and b. it,		20: 3
I say unto you they are b.;	3:16	the kindreds of the earth be b.		20:25
the Lord b. the sabbath day,	13:19	And after that ye were b.		20:27
yea, and how b. are they,	18:30	the kindreds of the earth be b.—		20:27
and they were b., and prospered	25:24	And all nations shall call you b.,		24:12
B. art thou, Alma, and blessed	26:15	if ye do these things b. are ye,		27:22
and b. are they who were	26:15	B. are ye because ye desired		28: 3
Thou art b. because of thy	26:15	Therefore, more b. are ye, for ye		28: 7
And b. are they because of	26:16	b. in the kingdom of my father.		28: 8
And b. art thou because thou	26:17	of that generation were b.,		28:23
Yea, b. is this people who are	26:18	b. according to the multitude	4Ne	1:11
the transgressor, thou art b.	26:19	And how b. were they!		1:18
And how b. are they!	27:37	they were b. and prospered until		1:18
Come unto me ye b., for behold,	Al 5:16	then are ye b. with your fathers	Mrm	6:21
And b. be the name of God,	7: 4	And b. be he that shall bring		8:16
B. art thou, Alma? therefore,	8:15	b. is he that is found faithful	Eth	4:19
he b. Amulek and his house,	8:22	a people more b. than were they,		10:28
and taken me in, thou art b.;	8:26	he was b. in all the remainder		11: 3
behold, he hath b. mine house,	10:11	b. are they who dwell therein,		13:10
he hath b. me, and my women,	10:11	inhabitants thereof, b. are they,		13:11
yea, even all my kindred hath he b.,	10:11	strong, and b. from on high,	DC	1:28
after having b. them according	17:18	and you shall be b.		6: 9
B. art thou because of thy	19:10	b. art thou because of thy gift.		6:10
B. be the name of God, and	19:12	b. art thou for what thou hast		6:14
name of God, and b. art thou.	19:12	b. are ye for they can do no		6:29
O b. Jesus, who has saved me	19:29	b. are ye, for you shall dwell		6:30
O b. God, have mercy on this	19:29	b. are they, and then shall ye		6:31
and we know that they are b.,	24:22	b. art thou, for it shall deliver		8: 4

BLESSED 123 BLESSINGS

and you shall be b.	DC	11: 9
shall be b. both spiritually and		14:11
b. are you for this thing,		15: 5
b. are you for this thing,		16: 5
shall be b. unto eternal life;		18: 8
b. be the name of the Lord God!		19:37
Behold, thou art b., and art		23: 1
shall be b. unto eternal life.		30: 8
b. are you because of your faith		31: 1
b. are you because you have		34: 4
more b. are you because you		34: 5
Thou art b., for thou shalt		35: 4
in weakness have I b. him;		35:17
you are b. and your sins are		36: 1
b. be the name of the most		36: 3
b., not because of your		38:14
b. be the name of the Most		39:19
have slept in peace b. are you;		45:46
blessing ye are b. with.		46:32
b. are they who are faithful and		50: 5
b. are you who are now hearing		50:36
kept and b. with much fruit.		52:34
b. are they who have kept		54: 6
b. are the poor who are pure in		56:18
b. is he that keepeth my		58: 2
b. even above measure,		58:61
Behold, b., saith the Lord, are		59: 1
b. are they whose feet stand		59: 3
in the beginning b. the waters;		61:14
so in the last days have I b. it,		61:17
Nevertheless, ye are b., for the		62: 3
by purchase, behold you are b.;		63:30
and b. are the dead that die in		63:49
hath kept the faith, b. is he;		63:50
B. are you, inasmuch as you		66: 1
b. are you for receiving mine		66: 2
Abraham, and was b. of him—		84:13
b. are ye inasmuch as you		84:60
b. are ye if ye continue in my		86:11
thou art b. from henceforth		90: 2
you shall be b. forever.		92: 2
b. are such, for they shall obtain;		97: 2
b. are they, for they shall obtain		99: 3
be b. with a multiplicity of		104: 2
b. is my servant Warren,		106: 7
b. by him three years previous		107:42
Adam, who also b. him.		107:46
of Adam, who also b. him.		107:47
was sixty-five and Adam b. him.		107:48
and they rose up and b. Adam,		107:54
you shall be b. with		108: 3
generations after us should be b.		110:12
be b. with the blessings of my		117:10
b. is my servant Hyrum Smith;		124:15
b. and holy is he, for he is mine.		124:19
the kindred of the earth be b.		124:58
and be b. of him, to go with		124:79
and they shall be greatly b.		124:79
whoever he blesses shall be b.,		124:93
in all faithfulness, ye are b.;		136:11
you shall be b. in your flocks,		136:11
B. be the name of my God, for	Mses	1:15
B. art thou, Moses, for I, the		1:25
And I, God, b. the, saying:		2:22
And I, God, b. them, and said		2:28
I, God, b. the seventh day,		3: 3
Adam b. God and was filled,		5:10
B. be the name of God, for		5:10
and Eve b. the name of God,		5:12
and the Lord b. them;		6: 4
created he them, and b. them,		6: 9
And the Lord b. the land,		7:17
were b. upon the mountains,		7:17
Zion have I b., but the residue		7:20
B. is he through whose seed		7:53
b. are they of whom I have		7:53
Noah, his father, who b. him	Abr	1:26
the families of the earth be b.,		2:11
B. is he who cometh in the	JS	1: 1
B. is that servant whom his		1:50

BLESSES
whoever he b. shall be blessed,	DC	124:93

BLESSING
I leave unto you a b.,	2Ne	1:28
yea, even my first b.		1:28
I take away my first b.,		1:29
even my b., and it shall rest upon		1:29
save I should leave a b. upon you;		4: 5
behold, I leave my b. upon you,		4: 6
Wherefore, because of my b.		4: 7
I leave unto you the same b.		4: 9
a b. unto them from the hand of		30: 6
be a b. unto me and my house.	Al	8:20
the b. of the Lord shall rest upon		10: 7
the b. of the Lord hath rested		10:11
the b. which hath been bestowed		26: 3
the b. of God upon the land,		45:16
which b. God had sent upon the		46:10
the b. which they shall receive,	3Ne	20:15
which b. upon the Gentiles shall		20:27
and pour you out a b. that there		24:10
did leave a b. upon this land	DC	10:50
and great shall be your b.—		19:38
in my vineyard with a mighty b.,		21: 9
them a cursing instead of a b.		24: 4
them a cursing instead of a b.		24: 6
leave a cursing instead of a b.		24:15
and it shall be answered with a b.		25:12
a b. so great as you never have		39:10
a b. such as is not known		39:15
whatsoever b. ye are blessed		46:32
and they receive not the b.		58:32
he shall receive this b., if he		62: 7
the b. which was offered unto		67: 3
leave your b. upon that house.		75:19
shall ordain him unto this b.,		96: 9
be my seal and b. upon you—		101:61
commandment, cometh the.b.		103:12
the b. which I have promised		103:13
And this stewardship and b.,		104:22
a b. upon him, and his seed		104:22
a b. unto him and his seed		104:37
a b. upon him and his seed		104:40
a b. upon him, and upon his,		104:44
shall be ordained unto this b.		104:61
obtain this b. by your diligence		104:79
b. to be poured out upon them,		105:12
I have prepared a b. and an		105:18
bestowed upon them his last b.		107:53
the b. which shall be poured out		110:10
his b. shall also be put upon		124:57
by b. and also by right;		124:91
be crowned with the same b.,		124:95
we obtain any b. from God,		130:21
will have a b. at my hands		132: 5
which was appointed for that b.,		132: 5
the b. of the everlasting God		133:34
the richer b. upon the head		133:34
a b. unto thy seed after thee,	Abr	2: 9

BLESSINGS
so great were the b. of the Lord	1Ne	17: 2
great b. from the hand of the Lord	2Ne	1:10
the b. which the Lord God shall		9: 3
who have received so many b.	Al	9:23
the Lord pouring out his b.		16:21
granted unto us such great b.?		26: 1
what great b. has he bestowed		26: 2
and b. which he doth bestow		34:38
for the b. of liberty to rest		46:13
for the many privileges and b.		48:12
and the b. of God upon them,		60:25
the b. which were poured out	He	3:25
great b. poured out upon their	3Ne	10:18
from whence their b. come.	Mrm	5:10
the Lord hath reserved their b.,		5:19
the Lord did pour out his b. upon	Eth	9:20
the b. which I give unto you are	DC	18:45
and the manifestations of my b.		21: 8
great b. upon thy head;		39: 8
bless with the greatest of all b.,		41: 1
much tribulation come the b.		58: 4
crowned with b. from above,		59: 4
the b. of the kingdom are yours.		61:37
for a manifestation of my b.		70:15

BLESSINGS 124 BLOOD

how great b. the Father hath	DC 78:17	b. by the craftiness of men.	DC 76:75
and the b. thereof are yours,	78:18	become b. and understand not	78:10
my b. continue with you.	82:23	b. by the subtle craftiness of	123:12
a partaker of the b. of	96: 7		
him with a multiplicity of b.,	97: 5	**BLINDETH**	
And I will bless her with b.,	97:28	of the devil, which b. the eyes,	1Ne 12:17
multiplicity of b. upon her,	97:28		
with a multiplicity of b.;	104: 2	**BLINDNESS**	
as a steward over earthly b.,	104:13	remain in that awful state of b.,	1Ne 13:32
I will multiply b. upon him,	104:23	and the b. of their minds unto	14: 7
I will multiply b. upon him	104:25	adversary overpower them unto b.,	15:24
and multiply b. upon them.	104:31	because of their b., which	Jac 4:14
I will multiply b. upon them	104:33	which b. came by looking beyond	4:14
even a multiplicity of b.	104:33	and the b. of their minds,	Jar 1: 3
I will multiply b. upon him.	104:35	and b. of their minds,	Al 13: 4
a multiplicity of b. upon him.	104:38	concerning the b. of the minds,	14: 6
I will multiply b. upon him	104:42	and the b. of their minds—	3Ne 7:16
even a multiplicity of b.	104:42	hardness of heart, and b. of mind,	Eth 4:15
I will multiply b. upon the	104:46	and the b. of their minds that	15:19
even a multiplicity of b.	104:46	are unbelief and b. of heart,	DC 58:15
the spiritual b. of the church—	107:18		
not entitled to the same b.	107:29	**BLISS**	
and b. upon the church,	107:67	a straight course to eternal b.,	Al 37:44
blessed with exceeding great b.	108: 3		
the b. which thou hast ordained	109:21	**BLOCK**	
b. which shall be poured out,	110: 9	not place a stumbling b. in my	2Ne 4:33
with the b. of my people.	117:10	the greatness of their stumbling b.,	26:20
the b. of my people be on him	117:15	doings shall be as a stumbling b.	Mos 7:29
b. constantly from under thy	122: 2	a great stumbling-b. to those	Al 4:10
him with a multiplicity of b.;	124:13		
and will crown him with b.	124:17	**BLOCKS**	
b. upon the heads of the poor	124:21	taking away of their stumbling b.—	1Ne 14: 1
For instead of b., ye, by your	124:48		
him with a multiplicity of b.,	124:90	**BLOOD**	
the keys of the patriarchal b.	124:92	time have I shed the b. of man.	1Ne 4:10
he may ask and receive b.;	124:97	garments are made white in his b.	12:10
with cursings and not b.,	124:120	These are made white in the b. of	12:11
the sealing b. of my church,	124:124	shall be drunken with their own b.	21:26
which all b. are predicated—	130:20	the b. of that great and abominable	22:13
visited with b. and not cursings,	132:48	shall be drunken with their own b.	22:13
for the b. of the fathers,	Abr 1: 2	b., and fire, and vapor of smoke	22:18
with the b. of the earth,	1:26	shall be drunken with their own b.	2Ne 6:18
and with the b. of wisdom,	1:26	before him, and am rid of your b.	9:44
with the b. of the Gospel,	2:11	have purged the b. of Jerusalem	14: 4
which are the b. of salvation,	2:11	noise, and garments rolled in b.;	19: 5
great and glorious b. from	JS 2:73	the cry of the b. of the saints	26: 3
		the b. of the saints shall cry	28:10
BLEST		their b. might not come upon	Jac 1:19
be b. with signs following,	DC 68:10	their b. would come upon our	1:19
they shall not be b., because	124:46	and a b.-thirsty people,	En 1:20
		and would drink the b. of beasts.	Jar 1: 6
BLEW		your b. should not come upon me,	Mos 2:27
floods came, and the winds b.,	3Ne 14:25	rid my garments of your b.,	2:28
floods came, and the winds b.,	14:27	b. cometh from every pore,	3: 7
		his b. atoneth for the sins of	3:11
BLIND		through the atonement of his b.	3:15
and so b. in your minds, that ye	1Ne 7: 8	the b. of Christ atoneth for	3:16
b. the eyes and harden the hearts	13:27	through the atoning b. of Christ,	3:18
Wo unto the b. that will not see;	2Ne 9:32	apply the atoning b. of Christ	4: 2
the b. shall see out of obscurity	27:29	their b. has been spilt in vain,	7:24
the b. to receive their sight,	Mos 3: 5	did shed b. among themselves.	7:25
and how b. and impenetrable are	8:20	and take upon him flesh and b.,	7:27
power over you, to b. your eyes,	Al 10:25	an austere and a b.-thirsty man	9: 2
ye b., and ye stiffnecked people,	He 9:21	by the shedding of much b.;	9: 2
led by foolish and b. guides?	13:29	ferocious, and a b.-thirsty people,	10:12
their hearts, and b. in their minds,	3Ne 2: 1	did boast, and did delight in b.,	11:19
that he did b. their eyes and	2: 2	of the b. of their brethren,	11:19
Have ye any that are lame, or b.,	17: 7	slay me ye will shed innocent b.,	17:10
and their lame, and with their b.,	17: 9	to the shedding of so much b.	20:22
and opened the eyes of their b.	26:15	be the cause of shedding much b.	29: 7
the b. to receive their sight,	4Ne 1: 5	and the shedding of much b.	29:21
run about longer as a b. guide?	DC 19:40	delighted in the shedding of b.;	29:40
the b. to receive their sight,	35: 9	shed the b. of a righteous man,	Al 1:13
poor, the lame, and the b.,	58:11	his b. would come upon us for	1:13
shall open the eyes of the b.,	84:69	through the b. of him of whom it	5:21
and to b. their minds, that they	121:12	your garments stained with b.	5:22
to deceive and to b. men, and	Mses 4: 4	white through the b. of Christ,	5:27
		through the b. of the Lamb.	13:11
BLINDED		and the b. of the innocent shall	14:11
their hearts and b. their minds,	1Ne 17:30	his b. would cry from the ground	20:18
the eyes of the people were b.;	Mos 11:29	that I should shed innocent b.;	20:19
Lamanites and b. their minds,	Al 48: 3	and the atonement of his b.	21: 9

BLOOD 125 BLOODSHED

with the b. of our brethren.	Al	24:12
with the b. of our **brethren**;		24:13
bright through the b. of the Son		24:13
swords in the b. of our brethren		24:15
used for the shedding of men's b.,		24:17
for the shedding of man's b.;		24:18
than shed the b. of their brethren		24:18
belight in the shedding of b.;		26:24
shedding the b. of their brethren		27:28
that can sacrifice his own b.		34:11
a stop to the shedding of b.;		34:13
white through the b. of the Lamb.		34:36
b. of those whom they murdered		37:30
be the shedding of innocent b.		39: 5
their swords and the loss of b.,		43:38
they should stop shedding their b.		43:54
not desire to be men of b.		44: 1
might shed your b. for power;		44: 2
and we will seek not your b.,		44: 6
spill your b. upon the ground,		44:11
religion, even to the loss of his b.		48:13
even to the shedding of b. if it		48:14
not in the shedding of b. but in		48:16
not delight in the shedding of b.;		48:23
over the b. of the Nephites,		48:25
care not for the b. of his people.		49:10
oath that he would drink his b.;		49:27
sworn to drink the b. of Moroni.		51: 9
who professed the b. of nobility;		51:21
had taken by the shedding of b.;		52: 4
cities save they had lost much b.		52: 4
we will forbear shedding your b.		52:37
they never would shed b. more;		53:11
yea, and it shall be b. for blood,		54:12
yea, and it shall be blood for b.,		54:12
I will avenge his b. upon you,		54:16
against their brethren to shed b.		56: 6
by the shedding of the b. of so		56:13
attempted this their b. was spilt.		57: 9
fainted because of the loss of b.;		57:25
Manti without the shedding of b.		58:28
the b. of thousands shall come		60:10
shed the b. of the Lamanites		61:10
shed the b. of our brethren		61:11
the atoning b. of Jesus Christ,	He	5: 9
murdered, and he lieth in his b.;		8:27
to the earth, and did lie in his b.		9: 3
b. upon the skirts of his cloak.		9:31
From whence cometh this b.?		9:32
that it is the b. of your brother?		9:32
without the shedding of b.,	3Ne	3:10
loins, and they were dyed in b.,		4: 7
because of their being dyed in b.		4: 7
that the b. of the prophets and		9: 5
that the b. of the prophets and		9: 7
that the b. of the prophets and		9: 8
that the b. of the prophets and		9: 9
that the b. of the prophets and		9:11
me no more the shedding of b.;		9:19
not shed the b. of the saints,		10:12
do it in remembrance of my b.,		18:11
of my flesh and b. unworthily,		18:28
my flesh and b. unworthily		18:29
eat and drink of my flesh and b.		18:29
unto him of my flesh and b.		18:30
drinketh of my b. to his soul;		20: 8
washed their garments in my b.,		27:19
b. and carnage spread throughout	Mrm	2: 8
of the b. of their brethren who		3: 9
of the b. of their brethren,		3:14
scene of the b. and carnage		4:11
delighted in the shedding of b.		4:11
awful scene of b. and carnage		5: 8
and bones, and b. lay upon the		6:15
no more in the shedding of b.		7: 4
when the b. of saints shall cry		8:27
also the b. of their fathers and		8:40
he avangeth the b. of the saints		8:41
cleansed by the b. of the Lamb,		9: 6
garments of the b. of our brethren,		9:35
of a man, like unto flesh and b.	Eth	3: 6
that the Lord had flesh and b.		3: 8
shall take upon me flesh and b.;		3: 9
he will that man should shed b.,	Eth	8:19
suffer that the b. of his saints,		8:22
because of the b. of them who		8:24
cause the shedding of much b.;		11:10
are not spotted with your b.		12:38
through the b. of the Lamb;		13:10
washed in the b. of the Lamb;		13:11
face of the land were shedding b.,		13:31
from the shedding of b. to the		14:22
of blood to the shedding of b.,		14:22
of the b. of his brother,		14:24
Coriantumr, having lost his b.,		14:30
he fainted with the loss of b.		15: 9
they fainted with the loss of b.		15:27
had fainted with the loss of b.		15:29
the flesh and b. of Christ unto	Mro	4: 1
of the b. of thy Son,		5: 2
they thirst after b. and revenge		9: 5
seeking for b. and revenge.		9:23
the shedding of the b. of Christ,		10:33
of the flesh and b. of Christ—	DC	20:40
remembrance of the b. of thy Son,		20:79
and my b. which was shed for		27: 2
the moon shall be turned into b.,		29:14
my b. shall not cleanse them if		29:17
and the moon be turned into b.,		34: 9
of the b. which I have spilt,		38: 4
b. of thy Son which was shed,		45: 4
the b. of him whom thou gavest		45: 4
And they shall behold b., and fire,		45:41
and the moon be turned into b.,		45:42
be unto man that sheddeth b.		49:21
save it be by the shedding of b.		58:53
and to the shedding of b.		63:28
but by purchase or by b.,		63:29
if by b., as you are forbidden		63:31
as you are forbidden to shed b.,		63:31
are not of the b. of Ephraim,		64:36
the shedding of his own b.		76:69
and of the b. of the saints,		87: 7
the b. of this wicked generation;		88:75
from the b. of this generation.		88:85
the moon shall be bathed in b.;		88:87
saints of God that shed their b.—		88:94
from the b. of this generation;		88:138
the land by the shedding of b.		101:80
and cleanse them from their b.		109:42
their b. come up in testimony		109:49
lest the b. of this generation be		112:33
wolves for the b. of the lamb;		122: 6
whereby to shed innocent b.,		132:19
whereby to shed innocent b.,		132:19
wherein they shed innocent b.,		132:26
wherein ye shed innocent b.,		132:27
their b. have I sprinkled upon		133:51
and his works with his own b.;		135: 3
HE WAS MURDERED IN COLD B."—		135: 4
are not spotted with your b.		135: 5
best b. of the nineteenth century		135: 6
their *innocent b.* on the floor of		135: 7
innocent b. on the escutcheon		135: 7
their *innocent b.* on the banner		135: 7
and their *innocent b.*, with the		135: 7
the innocent b. of all the martyrs		135: 7
avenges that b. on the earth.		135: 7
and they have shed innocent b.,		136:36
seal his testimony with his b.,		136:39
thy brother's b. cries unto me	Mses	5:35
to receive thy brother's b.		5:36
by water, and b., and the spirit,		6:59
and be cleansed by b., even the		6:59
the b. of mine Only Begotten;		6:59
and by the b. ye are sanctified;		6:60
the b. of mine Only Begotten,		6:62
and they hate their own b.;		7:33
the b. of the Righteous be shed,		7:45
signifies king by royal b.	Abr	1:20
of the b. of the Canaanites		1:21
the b. of the Canaanites was		1:22
BLOODSHED		
famines, pestilences, and b. shall	2Ne	10: 6
they delighted in wars and b.,	Jac	7:24

BLOODSHED — BODIES

BLOODSHED
seasons of serious war and b.	Om	1: 3
a serious war and much b.		1:24
wars, and contentions and, b.,	Mos	29:36
to pass an awful scene of b.	Al	28:10
with their brethren, even unto b.		43:14
your families even unto b.		43:47
pestilences, yea, famines and b.,		45:11
a man that did not delight in b.;		48:11
the matter, but not unto b.		51: 4
did not delight in murder of b.,		55:19
so much b. among ourselves;		60:16
so much b. among ourselves;		60:16
resist wickedness even unto b.		61:10
cause of so much war and b..		62:35
insomuch that there was much b.	He	4: 1
up to anger, to wars, nor to b.;		6:17
four years, that there was no b.	Mrm	1:12
of the children of men unto b.		4: 5
round of murder and b.;		8: 8
the scene of b. and carnage,	Eth	14:21
thus, with the sword and by b.	DC	87: 6
lay down their weapons of b.,		109:66
will cause much b. previous to		130:12
thenceforth came wars and b.;	Mses	6:15
were wars and b. among them;		7:16

BLOODSHEDS
there shall be b., and great	2Ne	1:12
and by earthquakes, and by b.,		6:15
yea for the wars, and the b.,	Al	35:15
thus they had had wars, and b.,		62:39

BLOOD-THIRSTY: see BLOOD and THIRSTY.

BLOODY
became an exceedingly b. battle;	He	1:30

BLOSSOM
Lamanites shall b. as the rose.	DC	49:24
solitary places to bud and to b.,		117: 7

BLOSSOMS
and their b. shall go up as dust;	2Ne	15:24
shalt be as the b. of a thistle,	Mos	12:12

BLOT
might b. out their transgressions	Al	7:13

BLOTTED
a name that never shall be b. out,	Mos	1:12
that never should be b. out, except		5:11
that the name be not b. out of		5:11
and their names were b. out.		26:36
and their names were b. out,	Al	1:24
their names shall be b. out,		5:57
and their names were b. out,		6: 3
their names were b. out, and	Mro	6: 7
that their names may be b. out	DC	20:83
and shall not be b. out.		98:27
shall not be b. out until he		98:44
let them be b. out forever.		109:34

BLOW
bellows wherewith to b. the fire,	1Ne	17:11
have wherewith to b. the fire,		17:11
floods, come, and the winds b.,	3Ne	18:13
a furious wind b. upon the face	Eth	6: 5
did never cease to b. towards		6: 8
storms descend, and the winds b.,	DC	90: 5

BLOWETH
if the wind b., it is driven forth	Mos	12:12
that b. the coals in the fire,	3Ne	22:16

BLOWN
that the storm is fully b. over,	DC	127: 1

BLOWS
not able to withstand his b.,	Al	1: 9
their adversaries, even unto b.;		1:22
for he did withstand their b. by		17:37
But Ammon withstood his b.,		20:20
the heavy b. of the Nephites		43:37

BOARD
to b. with a Mr. Isaac Hale,	JS	2:57
to b. for a season at his house,		2:66

BOARDING
And it shall be for a house for b.,	DC	124:23
as pertaining to my b. house		124:56
to build for the b. of strangers,		124:56
to build a house for b.,		124:111

BOAST
Shall the ax b. itself against	2Ne	20:15
done these things that I might b.,	Mos	2:15
your service, I do not desire to b.,		2:16
therefore, of what have ye to b.?		2:24
they did b. in their own strength,		11:19
and thus they did b.,		11:19
I do not b. in my own strength,	Al	26:11
therefore I will not b. of myself,		26:12
but I will b. of my God,		26:12
is boasting, even so will I b.;		26:36
do not b. in your own wisdom,		38:11
do these things that ye may b.,	He	5: 8
yea, how quick to b., and do all		12: 5
to b. in their own strength,	Mrm	3: 9
did again b. of their strength;		4: 8
not b. themselves of these things,	DC	84:73
neither b. of faith nor of		105:24

BOASTED
and b. in his own wisdom.	DC	3:13

BOASTING
doth carry thee away unto b.	Al	26:10
away, even unto b. in my God;		26:35
Now if this is b., even so will		26:36
were lifted up unto great b.,		31:25
go on unto b. in thy strength		39: 2
do swell with great pride, unto b.,	He	13:22
neither with b. nor rejoicing,	DC	50:33

BOASTINGS
their b. in their own strength,	He	4:13
lifted up unto pride and b.	3Ne	6:10

BOASTS
if he b. in his own strength,	DC	3: 4

BOAZ
and they came to the city B.;	Mrm	4:20

BODIED
of able-b. and expert men,	DC	136: 7

BODIES
in our b. we shall see God.	2Ne	9: 4
must deliver up its captive b.,		9:12
and the b. and the spirits of men		9:12
that they might rest their b.	Mos	11:11
were gathered together in two b.		25: 4
were assembled together in large b.,		25:15
themselves together in different b.,		25:21
themselves together in b.		29:39
or against Amlici, in separate b.,	Al	2: 5
the b. of the Lamanites who had		2:34
spirits uniting with their b.,		11:45
when the b. of those who had		14:14
their dead b. were heaped up		16:11
And the b. of many thousands		28:11
while the b. of many thousands		28:11
spirit which doth possess your b.		34:34
the souls and the b. of those		40:19
the souls and the b. are reunited,		40:20
the wounds of death in your b.,		44: 7
with their dead and wounded b.		49:22
covered with large b. of water,		50:29
save it were in small b.;	He	1:24
they came to large b. of water		3: 4
be separated into twelve b.	3Ne	19: 5
a change wrought upon their b.,		28:37
a change wrought upon their b.,		28:38
and these b. which are now	Mrm	6:21
soon become incorruptible b.;		6:21

BODIES

covered with the b. of the dead.	Eth 14:21
leaving the b. of both men,	14:22
torturing their b. even unto	Mro 9:10
of your spirits from your b.	DC 45:17
they whose b. are celestial,	76:70
they are b. terrestrial,	76:78
and not b. celestial,	76:78
unto the renewing of their b.	84:33
That b. who are of the celestial	88:20
even ye shall receive your b.,	88:28
by which your b. are quickened.	88:28
your whole b. shall be filled with	88:67
your b. and your minds may	88:124
but for the washing of your b.	89: 7
having b. of flesh and bones.—	129: 1
when our b. are purified	131: 8

BODY

put them upon mine own b.;	1Ne 4:19
Messiah shall be manifested in b.	15:13
torment of the b. in the days of	15:31
after the death of the temporal b.,	15:31
which were done by the temporal b.	15:32
worth, both to the b. and soul,	19: 7
destruction of both soul and b.	2Ne 1:22
if it should be one b. it must	2:11
hath my b. been carried away upon	4:25
thou hast laid thy b. as the ground	8:23
in the b. he shall show himself	9: 5
which I call the death of the b.,	9:10
deliver up the b. of the righteous;	9:13
the spirit and the b. is restored	9:13
fruitful field, both soul and b.;	20:18
they became like unto one b.;	Jac 5:74
with all the might of his b.	WM 1:18
of infirmities in b. and mind;	Mos 2:11
temptations, and pain of b.,	3: 7
I mean the life of the mortal b.—	4: 6
you are dead as to the mortal b.	18:13
kept together in a b. as much as	21:18
he went from one b. to another,	25:15
mortal b. raised in immortality,	Al 5:15
have been done in the mortal b.?	5:15
spirit and the b. shall be reuinited	11:43
frame, as it is now, or in the b.,	11:44
the death of the mortal b.	11:45
resurrection of the mortal b.	11:45
that this mortal b. is raised to	11:45
is raised to an immortal b.,	11:45
much, both in b. and in mind,	17: 5
his b. and lay it in a sepulchre,	19: 1
lost both its b. in a strange land;	26:36
the separation of it from the b.,	29:16
have power to possess your b.	34:34
become extinct both soul and b.,	36:15
are departed from this mortal b.,	40:11
reuniting of the soul with the b.,	40:18
and the resurrection of the b.,	40:21
be reunited, both soul and b.,	40:21
soul shall be restored to the b.,	40:23
and the b. to the soul;	40:23
joint shall be restored to its b.;	40:23
should be restored to its b.,	41: 2
every part of the b. should be	41: 2
the more vital parts of the b.	43:38
the more vital parts of the b.	43:38
were gathered together in one b.	43:51
yea, a b. of their strongest men,	49:20
and they were depressed in b.	56:16
yea, a b. run upon our swords,	57:33
leaving a large b. of men in the	62:14
march with a large b. of men	62:14
they took a large b. of men of	62:15
one b. in the land of Moroni.	62:33
dwell in one land, and in one b.,	3Ne 3:25
and they were in one b.	4: 3
and the Nephites being in one b.,	4: 4
Showing his b. unto them,	10:19
The light of the b. is the eye;	13:22
thy whole b. shall be full of light.	13:22
b. shall be full of darkness.	13:23
your b., what ye shall put on.	13:25
and the b. than raiment?	13:25
do in remembrance of my b.,	18: 7
eateth of my b. to his soul:	3Ne 20: 8
And whether they were in the b.	28:15
were in the body or out of the b.,	28:15
changed from this b. of flesh	28:15
get them together in one b.	Mrm 2: 7
this b., which ye now behold,	Eth 3:16
behold, is the b. of my spirit;	3:16
after the b. of my spirit;	3:16
in the likeness of the same b.	3:17
remembrance of the b. of thy Son,	Mro 4: 3
showing his b. unto our fathers,	9:25
spirit and b. shall again reunite,	10:34
and to suffer both b. and spirit—	DC 19:18
in remembrance of the b. of	20:77
my b. which was laid down for	27: 2
to strengthen the b. and to	59:19
neither in b., limb, nor joint;	84:80
shall the b. be able to stand?	84:109
the b. hath need of every member,	84:110
the spirit and the b. are the soul	88:15
shall rise again, a spiritual b.	88:27
spirit shall receive the same b.	88:28
body which was a natural b.;	88:28
that b. which is filled with light	88:67
again, tobacco is not for the b.,	89: 8
hot drinks are not for the b. or	89: 9
Therefore, care not for the b.,	101:37
neither the life of the b.;	101:37
High Priests, chosen by the b.,	107:22
The Father has a b. of flesh and	130:22
has not a b. of flesh and bones,	130:22
In the image of his own b.,	Mses 6: 9
seed, or the seed of the b.)	Abr 2:11
the b. which they had formed.	5: 8

BOIL

which causeth the waters to b.	DC 133:41

BOLD

have I waxed b. in mighty prayer	2Ne 4:24
so b. as to come near the walls	Mos 7:10
now, I am a b. Lamanite;	Al 54:24
to some to be a very b. doctrine	DC 128: 9

BOLDLY

manifesting b. concerning your	2Ne 1:26
but he answered them b.,	Mos 12:19
yea, I did b. testify unto them	Al 9: 7
Thou mayest speak b., and tell	18:20
the prophet Zenos did testify b.;	He 8:19
preaching and testifying b. of	3Ne 6:20
they did testify b. of his death	6:20
to Christ who testified b.,	6:23
began to testify, b., repentance	7:16
stand b. before the Lamanites	Mrm 2:23
and we did stand against them b.;	5: 6
I speak it b.; God hath	Mro 8:21

BOLDNESS

I must use so much b. of speech	Jac 2: 7
I will endeavor to speak with b.;	Mos 7:12
pleaded for himself with much b.	Al 1:11
with b. to declare unto them,	9: 7
began to speak unto him with b.,	18:24
they durst not look up with b.,	30:27
Use b., but not overbearance;	38:12
because of the b. of Giddianhi	3Ne 3:11
had stood and fought with b.,	4:14
did stand with b. against them.	Mrm 2:24
the Lamanites with exceeding b.,	4:20
Behold, I speak with b., having	Mro 8:16

BOND

both b. and free, both male and	2Ne 10:16
b. and free, male and female;	26:33
old and young, both b. and free;	Al 1:30
old and young, both b. and free;	5:49
not rich and poor, b. and free,	11:44
old and young, both b. and free,	4Ne 1: 3
that every b. may be broken	DC 43:20
a b. or everlasting covenant	44: 5
together by a b. and covenant	78:11
yourselves with the b. of charity,	82:11
	88:125

the b. of perfectness and peace.	DC 88:125	delivered this once out of your b.	DC 104:83
to interfere with b.-servants,	134:12	enough to deliver yourself from b.,	104:84
		the yoke of b. may begin to	109:63
BONDAGE		they might bring them into b.	121:18
would have been led out of b.,	1Ne 17:24	shalt deliver my people from b.,	Mses 1:26
that he should lead them out of b.?	17:24		
the children of Israel were in b.;	17:25	**BONDS**	
they should be brought out of b.	17:25	the power of God out of these b.;	Mos 23:13
led out of Egypt, out of b.,	19:10	and also from the b. of iniquity,	23:13
from thy fear, and from the hard b.	2Ne 24: 3	of bitterness and b. of iniquity.	27:29
we are in b. to the Lamanites,	Mos 7:15	and from b., and from death;	Al 36:27
will deliver us out of our b.,	7:15	For I know that thou wast in b.;	38: 4
that he has brought us into b.	7:20	and in the b. of iniquity;	41:11
into subjection or into b.	7:22	them from death, and from b.,	62:50
wondereth that they are in b.,	7:28	and in the b. of iniquity.	Mrm 8:31
deliver you out of b.	7:33	and in the b. of iniquity,	Mro 8:14
brethren to deliver us out of b.	8: 7	strength, whether in b. or free;	DC 24:11
to bring my people into b.,	9:10	in the b. of heavenly things,	78: 5
and bring them into b.	9:11	grace of God in the b. of love,	88:133
desirous to bring us into b.,	9:12	All covenants, contracts, b.,	132: 7
they shall be brought into b.;	11:21		
they shall be brought into b.;	11:23	**BOND-SERVANTS**: see BOND and	
shall be brought into b.,	12: 2	SERVANTS.	
we shall not come into b.	12:15		
out of the house of b.	12:34	**BONE**	
that we should be in b.	20:22	I know now is b. of my bones,	Mses 3:23
themselves to the yoke of b.,	21:13	This was b. of my bones,	Abr 5:17
to deliver them out of b.	21:15		
of the Lamanites and from b.	21:36	**BONES**	
deliver themselves out of b.;	22: 1	their b. lay scattered in the land	Om 1:22
to deliver themselves out of b.,	22: 2	which was covered with b. of men,	Mos 8: 8
to deliver themselves out of b.	22: 2	which was covered with dry b.;	21:26
deliver this people out of b.	22: 4	people whose b. they had found;	21:27
and have been in b. to him	23:12	and their b. have been found,	Al 2:38
that they were brought into b.,	23:23	their b. are in the depths of the	3: 3
and deliver them out of b.	24:13	of whose b. we have spoken,	22:30
even while you are in b.;	24:14	their flesh, and b., and blood	Mrm 6:15
I will deliver you out of b.	24:16	b. should become as heaps of	Eth 11: 6
and deliver this people out of b.	24:17	flesh shall fall from off their b.,	DC 29:19
had delivered them out of b.;	24:21	maketh my b. to quake while	85: 6
for they were in b.,	24:21	navel and marrow to their b.;	89:18
had been delivered out of b.	25: 8	having bodies of flesh and b.—	129: 1
of the Lamanites and of b.,	25:10	*spirit hath not flesh and b.,*	129: 2
had been delivered out of b.,	25:16	has a body of flesh and b.	130:22
for they were in b.,	27:16	has not a body of flesh and b.,	130:22
they were brought into b.	29:18	I know now is bone of my b.,	Mses 3:23
must unavoidably remain in b.	29:19	This was bone of my b.,	Abr 5:17
he did deliver them out of b.;	29:20		
delivered from all manner of b.	29:40	**BONNETS**	
the people of Limhi out of b.	Al 1: 8	The b. and the ornaments	2Ne 13:20
they were brought into b. by	5: 5		
did deliver them out of b. by	5: 5	**BONUM**	
having been brought out of b.	9:22	and the *summum b.* of the whole	DC 128:11
Lord did deliver them out of b.,	29:11		
did deliver them out of b.	29:11	**BOOK**	
did deliver them out of b.	29:12	THE B.OF MORMON	T Pg
Behold, I say they are in b.	30:24	taken from the B. of Ether also,	T Pg
down, even as it were in b.,	30:27	THE FIRST B. OF NEPHI	1Ne 1:hd
they were in b., and none could	36: 2	and gave unto him a b.,	1:11
he has delivered them out of b.	36:28	things which he read in the b.,	1:19
delivered them out of b. and	36:29	which I do not write in this b.;	10:15
by bringing them into b.	43: 8	expedient for me in mine other b.	10:15
them and bring them into b.	43:29	I beheld a b., and it was carried	13:20
yea, their freedom from b.	43:48	thou the meaning of the b.?	13:21
and their freedom from b.	43:49	The b. that thou beholdest is a	13:23
to bring any one to the yoke of b.,	44: 2	the b. proceeded forth from the mouth	13:24
see who shall be brought into b.	44: 7	after the b. hath gone forth	13:28
and to bring them into b.	48: 4	things taken away from the b.,	13:28
brethren from b. and slavery;	48:11	is the b. of the Lamb of God.	13:28
their brethren to the yoke of b.,	49: 7	have been taken out of the b.,	13:29
subjected them to the yoke ot b.	49:26	also the b. of the Lamb of God,	13:38
have been consigned to b.,	50:22	behold they are written in the b.	14:23
for their freedom from b.	51:21	the b. proceeded out of the mouth	14:23
and themselves from b.	53:17	were written in the b. of Moses;	19:23
ourselves to the yoke of b.	61:12	THE SECOND B. OF NEPHI	2Ne 1:hd
they might not come into b.	62: 5	hearken unto the words of the b.	3:23
possess it shall be free from b.,	Eth 2:12	be written and sealed up in a b.,	26:17
Release thy self from b.	DC 19:35	forth unto you the words of a b.,	27: 6
from your bodies to be a b.,	45:17	And behold the b. shall be sealed;	27: 7
and under the b. of sin.	84:49	in the b. shall be a revelation	27: 7
they are under the b. of sin,	84:50	the b. shall be kept from them.	27: 7
is under the b. of sin.	84:51	But the b. shall be delivered unto	27: 9
should be in b. one to another.	101:79	shall deliver the words of the b.,	27: 9
be led out of b. by power,	103:17	neither shall he deliver the b.	27:10

BOOK 129 BORDERS

For the b. shall be sealed	2Ne	27:10
shall be kept in the b. until		27:10
the words of the b. which were sealed		27:11
the b. shall be delivered unto		27:12
the b. shall be hid from the eyes		27:12
to whom the b. shall be delivered;		27:12
shall testify to the truth of the b.		27:12
to bring forth the words of the b.;		27:14
to whom he shall deliver the b.:		27:15
Bring hither the b., and I will read		27:15
I cannot bring the b., for it is		27:17
Lord God will deliver again the b.		27:19
then shalt thou seal up the b. again,		27:22
the deaf hear the words of the b.,		27:29
which shall be written out of the b.		28: 2
after the b. of which I have spoken		30: 3
THE B. OF JACOB	Jac	1:hd
THE B. OF ENOS	En	1:hd
THE B. OF JAROM	Jar	1:hd
THE B. OF OMNI	Om	1:hd
are few, in the b. of my father.		1: 4
in the same b. with my brother;		1: 9
THE B. OF MOSIAH	Mos	1:hd
which are not written in this b.		1: 8
of them have I written in this b.,		8: 1
THE B. OF ALMA	Al	1:hd
shall be written in the b. of life,		5:58
his words are written in this b.		9:34
which are not written in this b.		13:31
THE B. OF HELAMAN	He	1:hd
is called the b. of Helaman,		1:hd
in the end of this b. ye shall see		2:13
the end of the b. of Helaman,		2:14
mean the end of the b. of Nephi,		2:14
thus ended the b. of Helaman,		16:25
THE B. OF NEPHI	3Ne	1:hd
cannot all be written in this b.;		5: 8
yea, this b. cannot contain even		5: 8
they are not written in this b.		7:17
and a b. of remembrance was		24:16
cannot be written in this b.		26: 6
THE B. OF NEPHI	4Ne	1:hd
also written in the b. of Nephi,		1:21
book of Nephi, which is this b.		1:21
THE B. OF MORMON	Mrm	1:hd
and call it the B. of Mormon.		1: 1
THE B. OF ETHER	Eth	1:hd
which is called the b. of Ether.		1: 2
THE B. OF MORONI	Mro	1:hd
the b. of my commandments,	DC	1: 6
power of God, the B. of Mormon.		1:29
And he has translated the b.,		17: 6
printing of the B. of Mormon,		19:26
to translate the B. of Mormon;		20: 8
from the prophecy of his b.		20:35
whole church may be kept in a b.		20:82
to write the B. of Mormon,		24: 1
you to reveal the B. of Mormon,		27: 5
the B. of Mormon and the holy		33:16
the Bible and the B. of Mormon,		42:12
of the B. of Commandments,		67: 6
by the b. which John saw,		77: 6
the little b. which was eaten by		77:14
even the B. of Mormon and the		84:57
in the b. of the law of God,		85: 5
in the b. of the law of God;		85: 7
written in the b. of remembrance		85: 9
written in the b. of the law,		85:11
in the b. of the names of the		88: 2
of me in the volume of the b.		99: 5
written in the b. of Enoch,		107:57
believer in the B. of Mormon,		124:119
the b. of Doctrine and Covenants.		124:141
record on the general church b.,		128: 4
is done on the general church b.,		128: 4
same on the general church b.		128: 4
and another b. was opened,		128: 6
opened, which is the b. of life;		128: 6
and another b. was opened,		128: 7
which was the b. of life;		128: 7
And the b. which was the		128: 7
book which was the b. of life		128: 7
the b. to be revealed.		128:20

to bear record of the b.!	DC	128:20
a b. containing the records of		128:24
in the Lamb's B. of Life,		132:19
To seal the testimony of this b.		135: 1
book and the B. of Mormon,		135: 1
brought forth the B. of Mormon,		135: 3
b. of Doctrine and Covanants,		135: 3
of Ether in the B. of Mormon		135: 4
the B. of Mormon, and this		135: 6
b. of Doctrine and Covenants		135: 6
the b. which thou shalt write,	Mses	1:41
a b. of remembrance was kept,		6: 5
was the b. of the generations		6: 8
a b. of remembrance we		6:46
first facsimile of this b.)	Fac	3: 3
He said there was a b. deposited,	JS	2:34
purpose of translating the b.		2:35
'I cannot read a sealed b.'		2:65
translate the B. of Mormon,		2:67
also believe the B. of Mormon to	AoF	8
BOOKS		
did contain the five b. of Moses,	1Ne	5:11
beheld other b., which came forth		13:39
for out of the b. which shall be	2Ne	29:11
many b. and many records	He	3:15
out of the b. which have been	3Ne	27:25
out of the b. which shall be		27:26
and writing b. for schools	DC	55: 4
seek ye out of the best b.		88:118
acquainted with all good b.,		90:15
seek ye out of the best b.		109: 7
of wisdom out of the best b.,		109:14
and the b. were opened;		128: 6
which were written in the b.,		128: 6
that the b. were opened,		128: 7
which were written in the b.,		128: 7
the b. spoken of must be the		128: 7
the b. which contained the record		128: 7
out of the b. shall your dead		128: 8
verse as it reads in our b.,	JS	2:36
BOOTH, Ezra		
servant B. take their journey,	DC	52:23
him who was my servant B.,		64:15
BORDERED		
And it b. upon the land which	Al	22:30
also b. upon the wilderness south,		31: 3
BORDERING		
which was b. even to the sea,	Al	22:27
thus b. along by the seashore.		22:28
the land b. on the wilderness,		22:29
nearly b. upon the seashore,		31: 3
every tract b. by the prairies,	DC	57: 5
BORDERS		
down by the b. near the shore	1Ne	2: 5
the b. which are nearer the Red Sea;		2: 5
in the b. near the mouth thereof.		2: 8
in the b. near the Red Sea.		16:14
I have moved the b. of the people,	2Ne	20:13
being in the b. of the land	Mos	18: 4
were done in the b. of the land,		18:31
were within the b. of the land.		19: 6
to come into the b. of the land		21: 2
arrived in the b. of the land		21:26
was in the b. of the land.		23:25
away beyond the b. of the land;	Al	2:36
out of the b. of their land.		3:23
which was in the b. of Nephi;		5: 3
by the b. of the wilderness.		8: 3
throughout all the b. of the land		8: 5
into the b. of the land,		16: 2
some around the b. of Noah,		16: 3
the b. of the land of Manti.		16: 6
away beyond the b. of Manti		16: 7
b. of the land of the Lamanites,		17:13
b. of the land of the Lamanites,		21: 1
away joining the b. of Mormon.		21: 1
about on the b. of the seashore,		22:27
the b. of the wilderness which was		22:27

BORDERS 130 BOSOMS

through the b. of Manti,	Al	22:27
in the b. by the seashore,		22:28
the b. of the land of Zarahemla,		25: 2
came over near the b. of the land.		27:14
yea, in all the b. round about		28: 1
among the b. of the Lamanites,		39: 3
Lamanites in the b. of Jershon,		43:18
Nephites in the b. of Jershon;		43:22
into the b. of the land Manti.		43:32
cities and the b. of their lands;		48: 8
an army by the b. of the city,		49: 2
even to the b. by the seashore,		50: 9
in the b. of their possessions,		50:10
the b. of Aaron and Moroni;		50:14
north by the b. of the seashore.		50:15
joined upon the b. of Lehi;		50:25
were on the b. by the seashore.		50:25
the b. of the land Desolation,		50:34
coming into the b. of the land,		51:14
was in the b. by the seashore.		51:22
on the east b. by the seashore.		51:26
to the b. of the land Bountiful,		51:28
the b. of the land Bountiful;		51:32
b. on the beach by the seashore,		51:32
b. of the land by the west sea;		52:11
on the b. by the west sea.		52:12
on the b. by the east sea,		52:13
south and the west b. of the land,		52:15
the b. of the land on the south		53:22
beyond, in the b. by the seashore.		56:31
in the b. by the wilderness		58:14
about in the b. of the land		60:22
was in the b. by the seashore.		62:25
upon the b. by the seashore,		62:32
the b. of the land of Moroni,		62:34
b. by the wilderness on the south,		62:34
b. by the wilderness on the east.		62:34
the b. of the land Bountiful,		63: 5
the cities round about in the b.	He	1:26
parts round about by the b.		1:26
as far as the b. of the wilderness,	3Ne	4:13
to the b. of the wilderness,		4:13
and all thy b. of pleasant stones.		22:12
them in the b. of Zarahemla,	Mrm	1:10
in the b. west by the seashore.		2: 6
to a city which was in the b.,		3: 5
lay in the b. by the seashore;		4: 3
fled to the b. upon the seashore.	Eth	14:12
even to the b. of the seashore,		14:26
and enlarge thy b. forever,	Mro	10:31
on the b. of the Red Sea.	DC	17: 1
on the b. by the Lamanites.		28: 9
unto the b. of the Lamanites.		54: 8
her b. must be enlarged;		82:14
until the b. of Zion are enlarged		107:74
that the b. of my people may		133: 9
into the b. of the land of	Abr	2:18

BORE
beheld the tree which b. the fruit	1Ne	11: 7
and he b. the sins of many,	Mos	14:12
b. with patience the persecution	Al	1:25
which the Nephites b. for them,		53:13
voice out of the heavens b. record	DC	76:40
And John saw and b. record of		93: 6
And he b. record, saying:		93: 7
John b. record of me, saying:		93:26
and they b. him children;		132:37
redeemed them, and b. them,		133:53
of this thing Moses b. record;	Mses	1:23
Enoch b. record of it, saying:		7:28

BORN
having been b. of goodly parents,	1Ne	1: 1
thou art my first-b. in the days		2: 1
my first-b. in the wilderness,	2Ne	2:11
speak unto you, Joseph, my last-b.		3: 1
Thou wast b. in the wilderness		3: 1
And now, Joseph, my last-b.,		3: 3
sons and daughters of my first-b.,		4: 3
For unto us a child is b.,		19: 6
the first-b. of the poor shall feed,		24:30

b. in tribulation, in a wilderness,	Jac	7:26
was b. in the days of Mosiah;	Om	1:23
therefore, ye are b. of him	Mos	5: 7
behold I am b. of the Spirit.		27:24
must be b. again; yea, born of God,		27:25
must be born again; yea, b. of God,		27:25
and I am b. of God.		27:28
ye spiritually been b. of God?	Al	5:14
must repent and be b. again.		5:49
he shall be b. of Mary,		7:10
must repent, and be b. again;		7:14
if ye are not b. again ye cannot		7:14
come forth, and be b. of a woman,		19:13
I do that I may be b. of God,		22:15
if I had not been b. of God		36: 5
that I had been b. of God.		36:23
they might also be b. of God,		36:24
many have been b. of God,		36:26
for if I had not been b. of God		38: 6
shall be the night before he is b.	He	14: 4
day that the Lord should be b.,	3Ne	1:19
for them if they had not been b.		28:35
and they shall be b. of me,	DC	5:16
for them never to have been b.;		76:32
And unto Enoch was b. Irad,	Mses	5:43
And to him also was b. a son,		6: 3
were b. into the world by water,		6:59
b. again into the kingdom		6:59
thus he was b. of the Spirit,		6:65
daughters were b. unto them,		8:14
chosen before thou wast b.	Abr	3:23
I was b. in the year of our	JS	2: 3

BORNE
have b. children in the wilderness	1Ne	17:20
tasks, which were grievous to be b.;		17:25
which was grievous to be b.—	Mos	2:14
a tax which is grievous to be b.		7:15
is not this grievous to be b.?		7:23
Surely he has b. our griefs,		14: 4
are they whose sins he has b.:		15:12
which was grievous to be b.;	Eth	10: 5
you have testified and b. record	DC	5: 1
the testimony which ye have b.		62: 3

BORROW
from him that would b. of thee	3Ne	12:42
would not b. neither would he lend;	Eth	14: 2
to b. its light from Kolob	Fac	2: 5

BORROWED
restore that which thou hast b.;	DC	136:25

BORROWEST
thou b. of thy neighbor,	DC	136:25

BORROWETH
whosoever among you b. of his	Mos	4:28
should return the thing that he b.,		4:28

BOSOM
cause that your b. shall burn	DC	9: 8
even as they are in mine own b.,		35:20
of Enoch into mine own b.;		38: 4
unto the b. of the church.		38:38
was in the b. of the Father,		76:13
was in the b. of the Father,		76:25
was in the b. of the Father		76:39
who is in the b. of eternity,		88:13
in whose b. it is decreed that		88:17
Jesus Christ, the Son of thy b.,		109: 4
from the b. of thy wife,		122: 6
even in the b. of the Father,	Mses	7:24
art there, and thy b. is there;		7:30
hast taken Zion to thine own b.,		7:31
I am in the b. of the Father,		7:47
will receive them into our b.,		7:63
received it up into his own b.;		7:69
so that I could see into his b.	JS	2:31

BOSOMS
treasure up wisdom in your b.,	DC	38:30

BOSTON

BOSTON
and also to the city of B.,	DC 84:114

BOTH
which he had b. seen and heard.	1Ne	1:18
b. of grain of every kind, and also		8: 1
b. old and young, both male and		8:27
and young, b. male and female;		8:27
they b. shall be established in one;		13:41
b. unto the Jews and also unto		13:42
b. temporally and spiritually,		14: 7
things b. temporal and spiritual;		15:32
b. the cow and the ox, and the ass		18:25
b. of gold, and of silver, and of		18:25
great worth, b. to the body and soul,		19: 7
things b. temporal and spiritual;		22: 3
destruction of b. soul and body.	2Ne	1:22
b. the heavens and the earth,		2:14
b. things to act and things to be		2:14
much good, b. in word and in deed,		3:24
b. by fire, and by tempest,		6:15
b. men, women, and children,		9:21
b. Jew and Gentile, both bond and		10:16
b. bond and free, both male and		10:16
b. male and female, shall perish;		10:16
be forsaken of b. her kings.		17:16
offense to b. the houses of Israel,		18:14
fruitful field, b. soul and body;		20:18
b. with wrath and fierce anger,		23: 9
alike unto God, b. Jew and Gentile.		26:33
b. those who shall come upon this		27: 1
b. in the east and in the west,		29:11
b. old and young, the first and the	Jac	5:63
of Israel, b. roots and branches;		6: 4
b. in heaven and in earth;		7:14
things, b. temporal and spiritual;	Mos	2:41
b. in heaven and in earth;		4: 9
b. in heaven and in earth;		4: 9
for b. food and raiment, and for		4:19
b. spiritually and temporally,		4:26
b. Alma and Helam were buried in		18:14
b. temporally and spiritually		18:29
b. old and young, both bond and	Al	1:30
b. bond and free, both male and		1:30
b. male and female, whether out		1:30
b. old and young, both bond and		5:49
old and young, b. bond and free;		5:49
need, b. spiritual and temporal;		7:23
b. limb and joint shall be restored		11:43
b. old and young, both bond and		11:44
b. bond and free, both male and		11:44
b. male and female, both the		11:44
b. the wicked and the righteous;		11:44
b. the just and the unjust,		12: 8
much, b. in body and in mind,		17: 5
things b. in heaven and in earth.		22:10
b. morning, mid-day, and evening.		34:21
become extinct b. soul and body,		36:15
be reunited, b. soul and body,		40:21
b. temporally and spiritually		42: 7
of death commenced on b. sides,		43:37
even on b. sides of the river,		43:52
b. on the Nephites and on the		44:21
b. on the north and on the south—		46:17
b. of which were on the borders		50:25
on b. hands with exceeding fury;		52:35
were many slain on b. sides;		52:35
who had been slain on b. sides.		52:40
b. men, women, and children,	He	1:27
b. of wood and of cement.		3:11
b. the Lamanites and the		6: 9
b. in the land south and in		6: 9
of Gold in b. these lands,		6:11
b. in the north and in the south;		6:12
b. in the north and in the south.		6:12
b. things in heaven, and all		8:24
b. belong to your secret band,		8:28
b. on the northward and on the		11:20
b. the Nephites and the		11:21
b. as to things temporal and		14:16
b. above the earth and beneath,		14:21
b. above the earth and beneath.		14:22
b. of the Nephites and also of		16:15
b. of the Father and of the	3Ne	1:14
b. in the land north and in the	3Ne	1:17
b. the Nephites and the		2:11
armies, b. of the Nephites and		3:14
b. which were in the land south		4: 1
b. in their front and in their rear.		4:25
b. on the north and on the		6: 2
b. on the land northward and		6: 2
ye have b. heard my voice, and		15:24
b. they who had been healed and		17:10
b. saw and heard Jesus speak;		17:17
whom they b. saw and heard.		20: 9
b. treadeth down and teareth in		20:16
b. treadeth down and teareth in		21:12
unto them, b. great and small.		26: 1
b. saw and heard these children;		26:16
which they had b. heard and seen,		27: 1
b. Nephites and Lamanites,	4Ne	1: 2
b. to pray and to hear the word		1:12
b. the people of Nephi and the		1:45
which I have b. seen and heard,	Mrm	2: 8
b. on the part of the Nephites		2:15
b. temporally and spiritually;		4: 9
thousands slain on b. sides		4: 9
both sides b. the nephites and the		4:11
b. of the nephites and of the		4:14
prisoners b. women and children,		4:22
b. in towns and villages.		9:13
come forth b. small and great,	Eth	1:41
b. male and female, of every kind;		10:12
b. in buildings, and in gold and		10:25
b. to plow and to sow, to reap		14:17
slay b. women and children,		14:22
b. men, women, and children		14:31
on b. sides was so great that		15:15
b. men women and children being	Mro	10:34
Judge of b. quick and dead.	DC	1: 8
seal b. on earth and in heaven,		6: 2
asunder of b. joints and marrow;		7: 8
ye shall b. have according to		7: 8
for ye b. joy in that which ye		11: 2
asunder of b. joints and marrow;		12: 2
asunder of b. joints and marrow;		14: 2
asunder of b. joints and marrow;		14: 8
which you shall b. hear and see,		14:11
be blessed b. spiritually and		18: 6
b. the Gentiles and also the		18:26
b. unto Gentile and unto Jew;		19:18
and to suffer b. body and spirit—		20: 4
be all glory, b. now and forever.		20:36
his holy name, b. now and ever amen.		24: 3
will bless them b. spiritually and		24:12
of a trump, b. day and night.		27:13
b. which are in heaven, and which		29:13
shall sound b. long and loud,		29:24
b. men and beasts, the fowls of		29:31
things b. spiritual and temporal—		34: 6
of a trump, b. long and loud,		38:40
b. elder, priest, teacher, and also		42:67
b. here and in the New Jerusalem.		43:18
shall sound b. long and loud,		43:20
b. old and young, both bond and		43:20
old and young, b. bond and free,		50:22
b. are edified and rejoice together.		50:27
b. in heaven and on the earth,		51:13
b. in money and in meat,		52:32
b. be ordained, and also take		57:16
the residue of b. elders and		59:18
b. to please the eye and to		63:37
declare b. by word and by		71: 7
b. in public and in private;		72: 3
b. in time and in eternity.		78: 3
b. in this place and in the land		82:12
b. in the land of Zion and in		88:79
b. in heaven and in the earth,		88:85
b. in this world and in the world		88:94
his trump b. long and loud,		88:104
b. in heaven and in earth,		93:17
b. in heaven and on earth,		101:24
b. of man, or of the beasts of		102:11
the absence of one or b. of those		102:11
his stead, b. or either of them.		109:52
wasted away, b. root and branch,		123: 2
b. of character and personal		

b. in Missouri and this state,	DC 127: 1	they are not b. by any law when	DC 132:15
b. as well for the dead as for	128:11	be eternally b. in the heavens;	132:46
b. as well for time and for all	132: 7	testimony and b. up the law,	133:72
b. in the world and out of the	132:30	all men are b. to sustain and	134: 5
b. in making laws and	134: 1	and are b. to enact laws for	134: 7
b. to be answered by man to	134: 6	the enemy which held me b.	JS 2:17
they were b. shot after they	135: 1		
and b. received four balls.	135: 1	**BOUNDARIES**	
And they were b. naked, the man	Mses 3:25	in the western b. of the State	DC 84: 3
the eyes of them b. were opened,	4:13	the b. of the everlasting hills	133:31
b. things which are temporal,	6:63		
earth, b. above and beneath:	6:63	**BOUNDS**	
b. man and beast, and the	8:26	certain b. also and conditions.	DC 88:38
And they were b. naked,	Abr 5:19	themselves beyond their b.	88:90
b. to myself and the Church,	JS 2: 1	b. of this church government,	102: 8
feelings of b. the priests and	2: 6	if there be b. set to the heavens	121:30
of b. reason and sophistry	2: 9	their b. are set, they cannot pass.	122: 9
he had b. seen a light and	2:24		
b. religious and irreligious,	2:27	**BOUNTIFUL**	
b. good and evil spoken of	2:33	*They call the place B.*	1Ne 1:hd
what I had b. seen and heard.	2:46	to the land which we called B.,	17: 5
respecting b. the characters and	2:65	called the place B., because	17: 6
		Nephi, had been in the land of B.	17: 7
BOTTOM		to the land which they called B.	Al 22:29
the b. thereof was tight like unto	Eth 2:17	on the southward was called B.,	22:31
in the top, and also in the b.;	2:20	on the line B. and the land	22:32
In the b. of the box were laid	JS 2:52	had inhabited the land B.,	22:33
		which joins the land B.,	27:22
BOUGH		on the south of the land B.;	27:22
shall lop the b. with terror;	2Ne 20:33	was northward of the land B.,	50:11
		people who were in the land B.,	50:32
BOUGHT		to the borders of the land B.,	51:28
Let there be a craft made, or b.,	DC 60: 5	take possession of the land B.,	51:30
I have b. it with money.	101:56	in the borders of the land B.;	51:32
land which I have b. with money	103:22	he should fortify the land B.,	52: 9
		his march towards the land B.,	52:15
BOUND		returned again to the city B.,	52:17
these bands with which I am b.	1Ne 7:17	with his army at the land of B.,	52:18
after they had b. me insomuch	18:12	they came near the city B.,	52:27
awful chains by which ye are b.,	2Ne 1:13	been left to protect the city B.	52:27
the chains with which ye are b.,	1:23	brethren forth into the land B.	52:39
and were taken, and were b.,	Mos 7: 7	marched back into the land B.;	53: 3
carried him b. before the king,	12: 9	about the land, or the city, B.	53: 3
they b. him and cast him into	17: 5	the city of B. round about	53: 4
that they took him and b. him,	17:13	should be taken to the city B.;	55:26
took him and b. up his wounds,	20:13	on the borders of the land B.,	63: 5
and b., and cast into prison.	21:23	even towards the city of B.;	He 1:23
ye were b. with the bands of	23:12	should come to the land B.	1:28
until they were b. in bands and	Al 8:31	before they came to the land B.,	1:29
b. down by the chains of hell,	13:30	land which was near the land B.,	4: 5
and b. them with strong cords,	14: 4	driven even into the land of B.;	4: 6
and Amulek, as they were b.;	14:14	Nephi, beginning at the city B.,	5:14
thus they were b. with strong cords,	14:22	of Zarahemla and the land B.,	3Ne 3:23
and Amulek were b. with cords.	14:23	land B. and the land Desolation.	3:23
the cords with which they were b.;	14:26	*gathered together in the land B.,*	11:hd
Lamanites took him and b. him,	17:20	temple which was in the land B.;	11: 1
of being b. with strong cords.	20:29		
prison, and b. with strong cords,	20:30	**BOUNTIFULLY**	
taken and b. with strong cords,	26:29	things were taught unto you b.	Al 34: 2
that are b. down under a foolish	30:13		
for they took him, and b. him,	30:20	**BOUNTY**	
for he was taken and b.	30:21	with the matchless b. of his love;	Al 26:15
they caused that he should be b.;	30:29		
their swords were taken and b.,	52:39	**BOW**	
and b. them and cast them into	He 9: 9	they did b. down before me,	1Ne 7:20
Nephi should be taken and b.	9:19	behold, I did break my b.,	16:18
covenants by which ye are b.;	DC 35:24	and after I did break my b.,	16:18
For Satan shall be b.,	43:31	because of the loss of my b.,	16:18
And Satan shall be b., that he	45:55	because of the loss of my b.,	16:21
I, the Lord, am b. when ye	82:10	did make out of wood a b.,	16:23
be b. together by a bond and	82:11	I did arm myself with a b.	16:23
And Satan is b. and time is	84:100	they shall b. down to thee with their	21:23
lo, the tares are b. in bundles,	86: 7	they shall b. down to thee with	2Ne 6: 7
earth; she is b. in bundles;	88:94	B. down, that we may go over—	8:23
and Satan shall be b.,	88:110	Without me they shall b. down	20: 4
the tares shall be b. in bundles,	101:66	ye must b. down before him,	25:29
covenant with which ye are b.,	104: 5	and their skill was in the b.	En 1:20
be b. as a united order to your	104:47	shalt not b. down thyself unto	Mos 13:13
not b. only up to this hour	104:53	did b. himself down before them,	20:25
on earth shall be b. in heaven;	124:93	Yea, every knee shall b.,	27:31
on earth may be b. in heaven;	127: 7	fastened into the two rims of a b.	28:13
on earth shall be b. in heaven,	128: 8	if thou wilt b. down before God,	Al 22:16
on earth shall be b. in heaven;	128:10	and will b. down before God,	22:16

BOW   133   BRANCHES

king did b. down before the Lord,	Al	22:17
people to b. down to dumb idols,		31: 1
his b. into the hands of Moroni,		44: 8
were whole, b. down at his feet,	3Ne	17:10
with the b., and with the arrow,	Mrm	6: 9
if he will b. down before me,	DC	5:24
of the earth shall b. to it;		49:10
all things b. in humble		76:93
These all shall b. the knee,		76:110
and every knee shall b.,		88:104
been made to b. down with grief,		123: 7
would not b. down to worship	Abr	1:11

BOWED

haughtiness of men shall be b.	2Ne	12:11
loftiness of man shall be b.		12:17
and b. himself before the king;	Mos	7:12
and b. himself before the king,	Al	22: 2
and he b. himself to the earth,		46:13
and b. themselves before the king,		47:22
Nephi had b. himself upon the	He	7:10
b. himself down upon the earth,	3Ne	1:11
and b. himself before the Lord		11:19
and b. himself to the earth,		19:19
and b. himself to the earth;		19:27
they b. themselves down upon	Eth	6:12
servant Warren b. to my scepter,	DC	106: 6
he was b. down with age, being		107:56
he b. himself to the earth,	Mses	6:31

BOWELS

the offspring of thy b. like the	1Ne	20:19
from the b. of my mother hath		21: 1
heaven, having the b. of mercy;	Mos	15: 9
his b. may be filled with mercy,	Al	7:12
b. of mercy are over all the earth.		26:37
to bring about the b. of mercy,		34:15
my b. are filled with compassion	3Ne	17: 6
my b. are filled with mercy.		17: 7
truth is established in her b.;	DC	84:101
his b. shall be a fountain of		85: 7
my b. are filled with compassion		101: 9
thy b. be moved with compassion		121: 3
thy b. moved with compassion		121: 4
Let thy b. also be full of charity		121:45
his b. yearned; and all eternity	Mses	7:41
a voice from the b. thereof,		7:48

BOWETH

the mean man b. not down,	2Ne	12: 9

BOWS

did take our b. and our arrows,	1Ne	16:14
their b. having lost their springs,		16:21
and all their b. bent,	2Ne	15:28
With arrows and with b.		17:24
Their b. shall also dash the		23:18
arm them with b., and with arrows,	Mos	9:16
armed with b., and with arrows,		10: 8
and with cimeters, and with b.,	Al	2:12
and their b., and their arrows,		3: 5
and their b., and their arrows,		17: 7
their b. and their arrows,		43:20
and with cimeters and with b.,	He	1:14
were two stones in silver b.—	JS	2:35

BOX

bring the b.-tree, and the fir-tree,	DC	124:26
plates, deposited in a stone b.	JS	2:51
The b. in which they lay was		2:52
In the bottom of the b. were		2:52
two stones crossways of the b.,		2:52

BOX TREE: *see BOX and TREE*.

BOY

though I was an obscure b.,	JS	2:22
to make a b. of no consequence		2:22
it was that an obscure b.,		2:23

BRACELETS

and the b., and the mufflers;	2Ne	13:19
and their ringlets, and their b.,	Al	31:28

BRAKE

he took of the bread and b.	3Ne	18: 3
he b. bread again and blessed it,		20: 3

BRANCH

a b. of the house of Israel?	1Ne	15:12
a natural b. of the olive-tree,		15:16
a b. who have been broken off;		19:24
would rise up a righteous b. unto	2Ne	3: 5
a b. which was to be broken off,		3: 5
they shall become a righteous b.		9:53
this righteous b. of which I have		10: 1
the b. of the Lord be beautiful		14: 2
head and tail, b. and rush		19:14
a b. shall grow out of his roots.		21: 1
like an abominable b.		24:19
raise up unto me a righteous b.	Jac	2:25
this tree, or this b. of the tree?		5:21
planted another b. of the tree also;		5:23
and behold another b. also,		5:24
that the b. had withered away		5:40
whose b. hath withered away,		5:43
they have overcome the good b.		5:45
as a b. be grafted into the	Al	16:17
are a b. of the tree of Israel,		26:36
leave them neither root nor b.	3Ne	25: 1
a b. of the house of Jacob;	DC	10:60
organized b. of the same,		20:65
where there is no b. of the church		20:66
in any b. of the church where		107:74
wasted away, both root and b.,		109:52
leave them neither root nor b.		133:64
leave them neither root nor b.	JS	2:37

BRANCHES

an olive-tree, whose b. should	1Ne	10:12
the natural b. of the olive-tree,		10:14
the natural b. of the olive-tree,		15: 7
grafting in of the natural b.		15:13
shoot forth young and tender b.,	Jac	5: 4
a little, young and tender b.;		5: 6
the b. from a wild olive-tree,		5: 7
we will pluck off those main b.		5: 7
of these young and tender b.,		5: 8
take these young and tender b.,		5: 8
the b. of the wild olive-tree,		5: 9
the b. of the wild olive-tree.		5:10
the natural b. of the tree;		5:13
b. of the tame olive-tree		5:14
wild olive b. had been grafted;		5:17
behold, the b. of the wild tree		5:18
the wild b. have brought forth		5:18
if we had not grafted in these b.,		5:18
if the natural b. of the tree		5:19
hid the natural b. of the tree,		5:20
Pluck off the b. that have not		5:26
natural b. had been broken off,		5:30
wild b. had been grafted in;		5:30
the b. of the wild olive-tree		5:34
from the wild b., good fruit.		5:36
behold, the wild b. have grown		5:37
wild b. have overcome the roots		5:37
if the natural b. have also brought		5:38
the fruit of the natural b. had		5:39
I plucked not the b. thereof		5:45
the b. thereof overcome the roots		5:48
the b. have overcome the roots		5:48
take of the b. of these which		5:52
those b. whose fruit is most		5:52
and graft in the natural b. of		5:52
the roots of the natural b. of		5:54
take of the b. of this tree,		5:54
them the b. of their mother tree,		5:54
Pluck not the wild b. from the		5:57
we will trim up the b. thereof;		5:58
trees those b. which are ripened,		5:58
because of the change of the b.,		5:59
I have preserved the natural b.		5:60
I have grafted in the natural b.		5:60
and the b. of the first fruit—		5:60
Graft in the b.;		5:63
ye shall clear away the b. which		5:65
And the b. of the natural tree		5:67

BRANCHES

And the b. of the natural tree	Jac 5:68
into the natural b. of the tree;	5:68
the natural b. began to grow	5:73
wild b. began to be plucked off	5:73
of Israel, both roots and b.;	6: 4
extensive b. of my church,	DC 72:23
in all large b. of the church,	107:39
When its b. are yet tender,	JS 1:38

BRANDS

two tails of these smoking fire-b.,	2Ne 17: 4

BRASS

are engraven upon plates of b.	1Ne 3: 3
engraven upon the plates of b.,	3:12
engraven upon the plates of b.,	3:24
engraven upon the plates of b.	4:16
which were upon the plates of b.,	4:24
that we took the plates of b.	4:38
engraven upon the plates of b.,	5:10
also found upon the plates of b.	5:14
plates of b. should go forth unto	5:18
plates of b. should never perish;	5:19
which are upon the plates of b.,	13:23
and it was of fine b.	16:10
written upon the plates of b.	19:21
engraven upon the plates of b.,	19:22
is an iron sinew, and thy brow b.;	20: 4
engraven upon the plates of b.,	22: 1
written upon the plates of b.	22:30
written upon the plates of b.	2Ne 4: 2
engraven upon the plates of b.	4:15
engraven upon the plates of b.;	5:12
and of copper, and of b.,	5:15
also in iron and copper, and b.	Jar 1: 8
the plates of b. which contained	Om 1:14
were engraven on the plates of b.,	Mos 1: 3
were engraven on the plates of b.,	1:16
they are of b. and of copper,	8:10
were engraven on the plates of b.,	10:16
and of their b. and their iron;	11: 3
of silver, and of iron, and of b.,	11: 8
fine wood, and of copper, and of b.	11:10
were engraven on the plates of b.,	28:11
he took the plates of b.,	28:20
And these plates of b., which	Al 37: 3
concerning the plates of b.,	3Ne 1: 2
not written upon the plates of b.	10:17
and I will make thy hoofs b.	20:19
gold, and silver, and iron, and b.,	Eth 10:23
with copper, and with b., and	DC 124:27
of every artificer in b. and iron.	Mses 5:46

BRAVE

stand against so many b. men	3Ne 3: 3

BRAVERY

the b. of their tinkling ornaments,	2Ne 13:18
and they do it for a token of b.	Mro 9:10

BRAZEN

as he lifted up the b. serpent	He 8:14

BREACH

let us make a b. therein for us,	2Ne 17: 6
and the b. of the general peace,	DC 134: 8

BREAD

nor that his b. should fail.	2Ne 8:14
and the staff, the whole staff of b.,	13: 1
there is neither b. nor clothing;	13: 7
We will eat our own b.,	14: 1
of the b. and the waters of life	Al 5:34
he brought forth b. and meat	8:21
Alma ate b. and was filled;	8:22
if his son ask b., will give him	3Ne 14: 9
bring forth some b. and wine	18: 1
they were gone for b. and wine,	18: 2
had come with b. and wine,	18: 3
he took of the b. and brake	18: 3
he shall break b. and bless it	18: 5
as I have broken b. and blessed	18: 6
he brake b. again and blessed it,	20: 3
that they should break b.,	3Ne 20: 4
Now, there had been no b.,	20: 6
truly gave unto them b. to eat,	20: 7
He that eateth this b. eateth of	20: 8
did break b. oft, and bless it,	26:13
to bless and sanctify this b. to	Mro 4: 3
oft to partake of b. and wine,	6: 6
to administer b. and wine—	DC 20:40
often to partake of b. and wine	20:75
to bless and sanctify this b.	20:77
shall not eat the b. nor wear the	42:42
after partaking of b. and wine.	88:141
nor his seed be found begging b.	124:90
of thy face shalt thou eat b.,	Mses 4:25
to eat his b. by the sweat of	5: 1

BREADTH

shall fill the b. of thy land.	2Ne 18: 8

BREAK

behold, I did b. my bow, which	1Ne 16:18
after I did b. my bow, behold,	16:18
b. forth into singing, O mountains;	21:13
I will b. down the wall thereof,	2Ne 15: 5
they b. forth into singing.	24: 7
B. forth into joy; sing together	Mos 12:23
B. forth into joy, sing together	15:30
ye b. the oath which ye made unto	20:14
and they would not b. it—	Al 43:11
which we know that we shall b.,	44: 8
they were about to b. the oath	53:14
were about to b. the covenant	56: 7
they should b. this covenant	56: 8
would b. out in great numbers,	57:14
they did b. forth, all as one,	3Ne 4:31
and thieves b. through and steal;	13:19
do not b. through nor steal.	13:20
B. forth into joy, sing together,	16:19
he shall b. bread and bless it	18: 5
them that they should b. bread,	20: 4
Then shall they b. forth into joy—	20:34
b. forth into singing, and cry	22: 1
thou shalt b. forth on the right	22: 3
did b. bread oft, and bless it,	26:13
thieves can b. through and steal.	27:32
monster of the sea could b. them,	Eth 6:10
b. down the mighty and strong	DC 1:19
deny this he will b. the covenant	5:27
as they b. not my laws	42:52
light shall b. forth among them	45:28
light shall begin to b. forth,	45:36
Let no man b. the laws of	58:21
to b. the laws of the land.	58:21
which he cannot b., neither can	84:40
b. down the walls of mine enemies;	101:57
shall b. the covenant with which	104: 5
B. it off, O Lord; break it off from	109:33
b. it off from the necks of thy	109:33
b. off, O Lord, this yoke of	109:47
the earth b. forth into singing.	128:22
shall b. down the mountains,	133:22

BREAKETH

thus God b. the bands of death,	Mos 15: 8
that he b. the bands of death,	Al 22:14
whosoever b. this commandment	3Ne 18:25
he who b. it shall lose his	DC 78:12
whoso b. this covenant after he	84:41
That which b. a law,	88:35

BREAKING

was thus b. down the wars	Al 51:22
enemy from b. down the hedge	DC 101:54

BREAST

and doth fill his b. with guilt,	Mos 2:38
wicked spirit rooted out of my b.,	Al 22:15
swollen with sorrow within his b.;	He 7: 6

BREASTPLATE

on his head-plate, and his b.,	Al 46:13
plates, and also of the b.,	DC 17: 1
having on the b. of righteousness,	27:16

BREASTPLATE 135 BRETHREN

these stones, fastened to a b.,	JS	2:35
neither the b. with the Urim		2:42
and Thummim, and the b.,		2:52
and Thummim, and the b.		2:59

BREASTPLATES
have brought b., which are large,	Mos	8:10
had prepared his people with b.	Al	43:19
But they were not armed with b.,		43:21
their b., and their arm-shields,		43:38
they did pierce many of their b.,		43:44
it is your b. and your shields		44: 9
with shields, and with b.;		49: 6
by their shields, and their b.,		49:24
with head-plates, and with b.,	He	1:14
having shields, and b., and	Eth	15:15

BREASTS
will begin to swell within you b.;	Al	32:28
fills the b. of all the wicked,	Mrm	6: 7

BREASTWORK
and he caused a b. to be built	Mos	11:11
should build a b. of timbers	Al	53: 4
ditch against the b. of timbers;		53: 4
upon the b. of the pulpit,	DC	110: 2

BREATH
to that God who gave them b.,	2Ne	9:26
whose b. is in his nostrils;		12:22
with the b. of his lips shall he		21: 4
with the b. of his lips shall he		30: 9
by lending you b., that ye may	Mos	2:21
after he had struggled for b.,	Eth	15:31
into his nostrils the b. of life;	Mses	3: 7
into them the b. of life,		3:19
into his nostrils the b. of life,	Abr	5: 7
would know to his latest b.,	JS	2:24

BREATHE
did b. out much threatenings	1Ne	18:17
began to b. out threatenings	Mos	19: 3
he that shall b. out wrath and	Mrm	8:21
for in them we cannot b., save	Eth	2:19

BREATHED
And he b. out many threatenings	Al	35: 9
have b. out many threatenings		54:19
b. into his nostrils the breath of	Mses	3: 7
b. into them the breath of life,		3:19
and b. into his nostrils the	Abr	5: 7

BREATHING
b. out threatenings against	3Ne	5: 5

BRETHREN
Nephi taketh his b. and	1Ne	1:hd
Nehpi's b. rebel against him.		1:hd
inasmuch as thy b. shall rebel		2:21
a ruler and a teacher over thy b.		2:22
thou and thy b. shall return to		3: 2
I, Nephi, and by b. took our		3: 9
I and my b. did consult one with		3:10
and my b. were about to return		3:14
did I persuade my b., that		3:21
I spake unto my b., saying:		4: 1
the plates of brass, to my elder b.,		4:24
spake of the b. of the church,		4:26
as I went forth unto my b.,		4:27
servant of Laban beheld my b.		4:30
and had perished with my b.		5: 4
that I, Nephi, and my b., should		7: 2
did again, with my b., go forth		7: 3
Behold ye are mine elder b.,		7: 8
had spoken these words unto my b.,		7:16
me from the hands of my b.;		7:17
and I stood before my b., and		7:18
of Ishmael, did plead with my b.,		7:19
And after I and my b. and all		7:22
of my father, and also of my b.		10: 1
he spake unto my b. concerning the		10:11
prophesy and speak unto my b.,		10:15
and also the seed of thy b.		12: 1
and also the seed of thy b.		12:14

against the seed of my b.;	1Ne	12:15
saw that the seed of my b.		12:19
I beheld that the seed of my b.		12:19
people of the seed of my b.		12:20
Gentiles from the seed of my b.		13:10
is upon the seed of thy b.		13:11
separated from the seed of my b.		13:12
even unto the seed of my b.,		13:12
it was upon the seed of my b.;		13:14
thy seed, which are among thy b.		13:30
shall destroy the seed of thy b.		13:31
and also the seed of thy b.,		13:35
remnant of the seed of my b.,		13:38
remnant of the seed of my b.		13:38
remnant of the seed of my b.,		13:39
I beheld my b., and they were		15: 2
I spake unto my b., desiring		15: 6
did speak many words unto my b.,		15:20
And thus I spake unto my b.		15:36
an end of speaking to my b.,		16: 1
And now my b., if ye were		16: 3
I, Nephi, did exhort my b.,		16: 4
my b. took of the daughters of		16: 7
my b. were angry with me		16:18
having been afflicted with my b.		16:21
Nephi, did speak much unto my b.,		16:22
my b. and the sons of Ishmael		16:27
our teacher, who are his elder b.		16:37
exhort my b. to faithfulness		17:15
my b. saw that I was about to build		17:17
my b. did complain against me,		17:18
did my b. murmur and complain		17:22
said many things unto my b.,		17:52
thine hand again unto thy b.		17:53
forth my hand unto my b.,		17:54
my b. beheld that it was good,		18: 4
by b. and the sons of Ishmael		18: 9
my b. began to see that the		18:15
and the iniquity of my b.,		18:18
soften the hearts of my b.		18:19
did teach my b. these things;		19:22
your b. from whom ye have		19:24
my b. came unto me and said		22: 1
our b. who are of the house		22: 6
I would, my b., that ye should		22:10
Behold, my b., I say unto you,		22:18
Wherefore, my b., I would that		22:30
Nephi's b. rebel against him.	2Ne	1:hd
made an end of teaching my b.,		1: 1
because of the rudeness of thy b.		2: 1
inheritance of thy seed with thy b.,		3: 2
for the fruit of thy loins, his b.,		3: 7
even repentance unto their b.,		3:20
out of my mouth unto their b.		3:21
and unto the seed of thy b.		3:24
because of the anger of my b.		5: 1
unto us, who are the elder b.,		5: 3
Jacob and Joseph, my younger b.,		5: 6
had been fulfilled unto my b.,		5:19
wars and contentions with our b.		5:34
Behold, my beloved b.,		6: 2
And now, my beloved b.,		9: 1
Behold, my beloved b.,		9: 3
O, my beloved b.,		9:39
O, my beloved b.,		9:40
O then, my beloved b.,		9:41
O, my beloved b.,		9:44
O, my beloved b.,		9:45
But behold, my b.,		9:47
Come, my b., every one		9:50
Behold, my beloved b.,		9:52
And now, my b.,		9:54
speak unto you again, my beloved b.,		10: 1
Wherefore, my beloved b.,		10:18
And now, my beloved b.,		10:20
they are inhabited also by our b.		10:21
Wherefore, my beloved b.,		10:24
And now, my b.,		25:20
also our b., to believe in Christ,		25:23
my children, and my beloved b.;		26: 1
and the seed of my b. shall have		26:15
For behold, my beloved b.,		26:23
And now, behold, my b.,		28: 1
And now behold, my beloved b.,		30: 1

BRETHREN

And now, my beloved b.,	2Ne	30:18
unto you, my beloved b.		31: 1
I would ask of you, my beloved b.,		31: 6
Wherefore, my beloved b.,		31:10
Wherefore, my beloved b.,		31:13
But, behold, my beloved b.,		31:14
And now, my beloved b.,		31:16
And now, my beloved b.,		31:19
now, behold, my beloved b.,		31:21
now behold, my beloved b.,		32: 1
And now my beloved b.,		32: 8
And now my beloved b.,		33:10
And now my beloved b.,		33:13
words of his preaching unto his b.	Jac	1:hd
Now, my beloved b., I, Jacob,		2: 2
And now behold, my b.,		2:12
abundantly than that of your b.		2:13
and persecute your b. because		2:13
And now, my b., do ye		2:14
Think of your b. like unto		2:17
And now, my b., I have spoken		2:20
Wherefore, my b., hear me,		2:27
And now behold, my b.,		2:34
than the Lamanites, our b.		2:35
Behold, the Lamanites your b.,		3: 5
O my b., I fear that unless ye		3: 8
O my b., hearken unto my word;		3:11
children, and also our beloved b.,		4: 2
our beloved b. and our children		4: 3
wherefore, b., despise not the		4: 8
Wherefore, b., seek not to counsel		4:10
Wherefore, beloved b., be		4:11
Behold, my b., he that		4:13
Behold, my beloved b., I will		4:18
Behold, my b., do ye not		5: 1
And now, behold, my b.,		6: 1
Wherefore, my beloved b.,		6: 5
O then, my beloved b., repent		6:11
eternal hatred against us, their b.		7:24
and hated of our b.,		7:26
that many of my b. may read		7:27
B., adieu.		7:27
welfare of my b., the Nephites;	En	1: 9
I will visit thy b. according to		1:10
I will visit thy b. according as		1:10
for my b., the Lamanites.		1:11
of our b. the Lamanites,	Jar	1: 2
But behold, my b., ye can go to		1:14
in the defence of my b.	Om	1:10
And now, my beloved b.,		1:26
they will be choice unto my b.	WM	1: 6
to God is concerning my b.,		1: 8
and their b. shall be judged at		1:11
like unto our b., the Lamanites,	Mos	1: 5
become weak like unto their b.;		1:13
My b., all ye that have assembled		2: 9
Yet, my b., I have not done		2:15
I say unto you, my b., that		2:20
And now, my b., I would that		2:31
And now, I say unto you, my b.,		2:36
And again my b., I would call		3: 1
My friends and my b., my kindred		4: 4
to inquire concerning their b.		7: 2
Ammon took three of his b.,		7: 6
to inquire concerning our b.,		7:13
my b. who were in the land of		7:14
our b. will deliver us out of		7:15
no more had Ammon nor his b.,		7:16
and bring their b. into the city,		7:16
many of our b. have been slain,		7:24
their b. who were in the land of		8: 1
that had happened unto their b.		8: 2
that we might appeal unto our b.		8: 7
I contended with my b.		9: 2
the place where our b. were slain,		9: 4
seventy-nine of our b. were slain.		9:19
in the wilderness by their b.,		10:12
And his b. were wroth with him		10:14
shedding of the blood of their b.,		11:19
and the brothers for their b.		21: 9
Ammon and his b. came into		21:22
discovered Ammon and his b.;		21:23
but that they were his b.,		21:24
Ammon and his b. were filled	Mos	21:29
many of their b. had been slain;		21:29
become even as Alma and his b.,		21:34
with our b., the Lamanites.		22: 3
being led by Ammon and his b.		22:11
the b. of Alma fled from their		23:26
And Alma and his b. went forth		23:29
to plead with their b., that		23:33
compassion on Amulon and his b.,		23:34
And Amulon and his b. did join		23:35
was possessed by Alma and his b.		23:35
promised unto Alma and his b.,		23:36
over Alma and his b.		23:37
granted unto him and his b.		24: 1
teachers of the b. of Amulon		24: 4
did the b. of Amulon teach them		24: 5
it were among their own b.		24: 7
authority over Alma and his b.,		24: 8
were laid upon Alma and his b.)		24:15
the account of Alma and his b.,		25: 6
when they thought of their b.		25: 9
in delivering Alma and his b.		25:10
the Lamanites, who were their b.,		25:11
children of Amulon and his b.,		25:12
the people of Limhi and his b.,		25:16
after the manner he did his b.		25:18
of the dissensions among the b.		26: 5
who are accused of their b.;		26:11
And they did admonish their b.;		26:39
to their b., the Lamanites—		28: 1
O ye my people, or my b.,		29: 5
take up arms against their b.;	Al	2:10
lead them to war against their b.		2:14
are upon our b. in that land;		2:25
their rebellion against their b.,		3: 6
their b. sought to destroy them,		3: 7
from the seed of their b.,		3: 8
mingleth his seed with thy b.,		3:15
afflicted for the loss of their b.,		4: 2
and he did baptize his b.		5: 3
behold, I say unto you, my b.,		5: 6
And now I ask of you, my b.,		5: 8
of you, my b. of the church,		5:14
And now I ask of you, my b.,		5:22
Behold, my b., do ye suppose		5:24
behold, I say unto you, my b.,		5:26
And now, my b., I would that		5:43
to preach unto my beloved b.,		5:49
Yea, my beloved b., I say unto		5:50
And now my beloved b., I say		5:53
in the persecution of your b.,		5:54
And now, my b., what have ye		5:58
Behold my beloved b.,		7: 1
dilemma that our b. were in		7: 3
had for the b. at Zarahemla,		7: 5
much unbelief as were your b.;		7: 6
And now my beloved b., do you		7:17
state of dilemma like your b.,		7:18
And now my beloved b., I have		7:22
And now my beloved b., I have		7:26
by the hands of their own b.?		9:10
And now, my beloved b.,		9:30
beloved brethren, for ye are my b.,		9:30
into Egypt by the hands of his b.		10: 3
And now, by b., behold I say		12:36
And now, my b., seeing we		12:37
And again, my b., I would		13: 1
had as great privilege as their b.		13: 4
the same standing with their b.;		13: 5
And now, my b., I would		13:13
And now, my b., I wish from		13:27
wilderness in search of their b.,		16: 5
will deliver unto thee thy b.		16: 6
b. who had been taken captive		16: 8
And they were brought by their b.		16: 8
exceedingly to see his b.;		17: 2
were still his b. in the Lord;		17: 2
their b., the Lamanites, to the		17: 9
among the Lamanites, thy b.,		17:11
will slay us, as he has our b.		17:28
whom he termed to be his b.		17:30
By b., be of good cheer and let		17:31
but Ammon said unto his b.:		17:33

BRETHREN

in the destruction of their b.;	Al 17:35	of their love towards their b.	Al 26:31
because of the slain of their b.,	17:36	of their love towards their b.	26:32
not slay you as I did your b.	18: 4	take up arms against their b.;	26:34
their b. had scattered their flocks	18: 6	Now my b., we see that God is	26:37
and slew seven of their b. with	18:16	people in anger against their b.,	27: 2
and smote off the arms of my b.	18:20	when Ammon and his b. saw this	27: 4
upon the Lamanites, his b., who	19:14	when Ammon and his b. saw this	27: 4
for what he had done for his b.;	19:14	to our b. the Nephites,	27: 5
which he had slain of their b.	19:21	go down unto our b., will ye go?	27: 7
destroyed so many of their b.,	19:27	we will go down unto our b.,	27: 8
my brother and b. are in prison	20: 3	It is against the law of our b.,	27: 9
he will cast thy b. out of prison.	20: 4	rely upon the mercies of our b.	27: 9
thee that thy b. were in prison?	20: 4	to anger against their b.	27:12
Go and deliver thy b., for	20: 5	I and my b. will go forth into	27:15
he will cast thy b. out of prison.	20: 7	we will try the hearts of our b.,	27:15
I may release the b. of Ammon,	20:15	that he and his b. met Alma,	27:16
my b. may be cast out of prison.	20:22	the joy of Alma in meeting his b.	27:19
that I would release thy b.,	20:26	Alma conducted his b. back to	27:20
thy b. may be cast out of prison,	20:27	among their b., the Lamanites.	27:20
thy b. may come unto me,	20:27	concerning the admitting their b.,	27:21
the b. of Ammon were brought	20:28	which we will give unto our b.	27:22
Aaron, and Muloki, and their b.,	21:hd	that we may protect our b.	27:23
when Ammon and his b. separated	21: 1	and this we do for our b.,	27:23
and also Ammah and his b.	21:11	to take up arms against their b.	27:23
and a certain number of his b.	21:13	this will we do unto our b.,	27:24
account of Aaron and his b.;	22: 1	Ammon and Aaron, and his b.	27:25
the king's palace, with his b.,	22: 2	shedding the blood of their b.	27:28
O king, we are the b. of Ammon,	22: 2	to take up arms agains their b.;	27:28
and also Aaron and his b.	22:19	could be inflicted by their b.,	27:29
their hands on Aaron and his b.;	22:20	had followed their b. into	28: 1
might slay Aaron and his b.	22:21	account of Ammon and his b.,	28: 8
because of Aaron and his b.	22:24	the reception and safety of the b.	28: 8
that Aaron and his b. should	22:26	many of my b. truly penitent,	29:10
Omner and Himni, and their b.	22:35	because of the success of my b.,	29:14
or Himni, nor either of their b.	23: 1	of the success of these my b.	29:16
convinced that they were all b.,	23: 3	may God grant unto these, my b.,	29:17
Aaron and his b. went forth	23: 4	neither have any of my b., save	30:33
preaching of Ammon and his b.,	23: 6	rejoicings in the joy of our b.?	30:34
neither against any of their b.	23: 7	the testimony of all these thy b.,	30:44
be distinguished from their b.;	23:16	Alma and his b. went into	31:11
to anger against their b.	24: 1	Alma and his b. had never beheld;	31:12
when Ammon and his b. and	24: 5	hast separated us from our b.,	31:16
Lamanites to destroy their b.,	24: 5	believe in the tradition of our b.,	31:16
there Ammon met all his b.;	24: 5	the foolish traditions of our b.,	31:17
take up arms against their b.	24: 6	Alma and his b. and his sons had	31:19
sent these our b., the Nephites,	24: 7	after the tradition of their b.,	31:22
a correspondence with these b.,	24: 8	and many of them are our b.,	31:35
And now behold, my b.,	24:11	that we may bring these, our b.,	31:35
Now, my best beloved b.,	24:12	esteemed by their b. as dross;	32: 3
no more with the blood of our b.	24:12	what shall these my b. do,	32: 5
stained with the blood of our b.;	24:13	that ye are despised of your b.	32:12
our swords in the blood of our b.	24:15	And now, my beloved b.,	32:24
And now, my b., if our	24:16	Then, my b., ye shall reap the	32:43
if our b. seek to destroy us,	24:16	Now behold, my b., I would ask	33:14
and if our b. destroy us,	24:16	And now, my b., ye see that a	33:17
than shed the blood of their b.	24:18	O my b., if ye could be healed	33:21
their b., the Lamanites, made	24:20	And now, my b., I desire that	33:23
that their b. would not flee	24:23	My b., I think that it is impossible	34: 2
of their b. who had fallen	24:24	may God grant unto you, my b.,	34:17
they came down even as their b.,	24:25	now behold, my beloved b.,	34:28
who slew so many of their b.	24:28	And now, my b., I would that,	34:30
they had slain their b.;	25: 1	And now, my beloved b.,	34:37
the seed of Amulon and his b.,	25: 4	Yea, and I also exhort you, my b.,	34:39
Aaron and his b. had preached	25: 6	And now my beloved b., I would	34:40
their b. should be stirred up	25: 8	Yea, and the rest of the b.,	35: 2
the seed of Amulon and his b.	25: 8	been spoken by Alma and his b.	35: 6
according as their b. had,	25:14	Alma and his b. did minister	35: 7
Himni, and their b. did rejoice	25:17	Alma, and Ammon, and their b.,	35:14
the words of Ammon to his b.	26: 1	which were heard by my b.,	36:11
My brothers and my b., behold	26: 1	Ammon and his b. could not	37: 9
for our b., the Lamanites, were	26: 3	thousands of our stiffnecked b.,	37:10
these our dearly beloved b.,	26: 9	unto them the works of their b.,	37:23
how many thousands of our b.	26:13	that we are better than our b.;	38:14
our b. from the chains of hell.	26:14	remember of b. in mercy—	38:14
And now behold, my b., what	26:21	you are merciful unto your b.;	41:14
bring these our b. to repentance.	26:22	the Lamanites towards their b.,	43:11
Now do ye remember, my b., that	26:23	to contend with their b.,	43:14
b. in the land of Zarahemla,	26:23	their intention to destroy their b.,	43:29
unto our b., the Lamanites,	26:23	Helaman and his b. went forth	45:22
Now my b., ye remember that	26:24	after Helaman and his b. had	45:23
But behold, my beloved b., we	26:26	the words of Helaman and his b.;	45:23
with the intent to destroy our b.,	26:26	the words of Helaman and his b.	46: 1
amongst thy b., the Lamanites,	26:27	gathered together against their b.	46: 1

BRETHREN

were wroth against their b.	Al	46: 3
preaching of Helaman and his b.,		46: 6
of liberty to rest upon his b.,		46:13
our b. in the land northward,		46:22
whose coat was rent by his b.		46:23
garments shall be rent by our b.,		46:23
them to fall in with their b.,		47:15
freedom of his country, and his b.		48:11
Helaman and his b. were no less		48:19
to contend with their b.,		48:21
of their b. out of this world		48:23
of those who were once their b.,		48:24
their b. should rejoice over		48:25
subject their b. to the yoke of		49: 7
and Ammon and his b.,		49:30
wicked b. have been consigned		50:22
took up arms against their b.,		50:26
among the b. of Pahoran and		51: 7
themselves like unto their b.,		51:21
to march with their b. forth		52:39
but by Ammon and his b.,		53:10
taking up arms against their b.;		53:11
fallen into the hands of their b.,		53:11
Ammon and his b. had had		53:11
of Helaman and his b.		53:14
b. wade through their afflictions,		53:15
your fathers did wrong their b.,		54:17
weapons of war against their b.		56: 6
we would not slay our b. if		56:46
who had come to join their b.,		57: 6
of our b. who were slain.		57:26
assist our b. in preserving		57:34
fall into the hands of their b.		59:11
murdering thousands of your b.—		60: 7
And now, my beloved b.—		60:10
of your b. have been killed		60:12
great neglect towards their b.,		60:14
not shed the blood of our b.		61:11
just in us to go against our b.		61:19
Helaman and his b. went forth,		62:45
the judgment-seat among the b.,	He	1: 2
up in rebellion against their b.		1: 7
persecution of many of their b.		3:34
and smiting their humble b.		4:12
like unto their b., the Lamanites,		4:24
in which Ammon and his b. were		5:21
joy in the righteousness of his b.		7: 8
of this the wickedness of my b.		7: 9
that ye should behold, my b.,		7:23
Behold, my b., have ye not		8:11
and many of their b. who knew		11:23
commenced a war with their b.		11:24
hearts of their b. against them.		13: 8
remember, remember, my b.,		14:30
And now, my beloved b., behold,		15: 1
But behold my b., the Lamanites		15: 4
bring the remainder of their b. to		15: 6
the restoration of our b.,		15:11
have been extended to our b.,		15:12
began to rejoice over their b.,	3Ne	1: 6
unite with their b., the Nephites,		2:12
become our b. that ye may be		3: 7
but our b. and partners of all our		3: 7
threatenings against their b.		5: 5
would our b. have been spared,		8:24
tell it unto your b. at Jerusalem.		15:14
done unto your b. at Jerusalem,		17: 8
raise up unto you of your b.,		20:23
become unto you like unto their b.,	4Ne	1:43
become weak like unto our b.	Mrm	2:26
their b. who had been slain by		3: 9
of the blood of their b.,		3:14
they were in behalf of their b.		8:24
garments of the blood of our b.,		9:35
have desired concerning our b.,		9:36
bring Jared and his b. forth	Eth	2:13
for his b. who were with him.		2:15
thee and thy b. of their sins;		2:15
did go to work, and also his b.,		2:16
his b. and many of the people.		7:15
the faith of Ammon and his b.		12:15
things should come unto their b.		12:22
also unto my b. whom I love,		12:38
may be of worth unto my b.,	Mro	1: 4
speak unto you, my beloved b.;		7: 2
And now my b., I judge		7: 4
take heed, my beloved b., that		7:14
For behold, my b., it is given		7:15
And now, my b., seeing that		7:18
Wherefore, I beseech of you, b.,		7:19
And now, my b., how is it		7:20
Wherefore, my beloved b., have		7:27
he hath done, this my beloved b.,		7:29
And now, my beloved b., if this		7:35
But behold, my beloved b.,		7:39
And again, my beloved b.,		7:40
Wherefore, my beloved b., if		7:46
Wherefore, my beloved b., pray		7:48
many of our b. have dissented		9:24
write unto my b., the Lamanites;		10: 1
And again, I exhort you, my b.,		10: 8
would exhort you, my beloved b.,		10:18
would exhort you, my beloved b.,		10:19
destroy their b. the Nephites,	DC	3:18
unto their b. the Lamanites,		10:48
spare these my b. that believe		45: 5
the God of Enoch, and his b.,		45:11
shall impart to the eastern b.;		48: 2
after your b. come from the		48: 5
if your b. desire to escape		54: 3
with his own hands, with the b.,		58:60
confessing thy sins unto thy b.,		59:12
forewarn your b. concerning		61:18
you shall give unto all your b.		61:26
for the congregations of thier b.,		61:32
as your b. are willing to open		75:25
of the living, and among thy b.		81: 3
your b. in Zion for their		84:76
salute his brother or b. with		88:132
Art thou a brother or b.?		88:133
is a brother, or if they be b.,		88:135
prayers of thy b. have come		90: 1
again, verily I say unto thy b.,		90: 6
say unto your b. in Zion,		90:32
your b. in Zion begin to repent,		90:34
your b. in the land of Zion,		97: 1
and your b. of my church,		98: 6
Thy b., my servants Orson Hyde		100:14
concerning your b. who have		101: 1
and redemption of your b.,		103: 1
I have decreed that your b.		103:11
and the tribulations of your b.—		103:13
and the redemption of your b.,		103:13
return to the land of their b.,		103:30
order to your b. of Zion,		104:47
And your b., after they are		104:48
as a united order with your b.,		104:53
strengthen your b. in all your		108: 7
Let the hearts of your b. rejoice,		110: 6
in behalf of those, thy b., who		112: 1
thy prayers concerning thy b.		112:11
pray for thy b. of the Twelve.		112:12
voice of your b., the Twelve,		112:21
thou art in perils among false b.;		122: 5
thy father and mother and b.		122: 6
You know, b., that a very large		123:16
beloved b., let us cheerfully do		123:17
of your b. who have been		124:54
dearly beloved b. and sisters,		128:15
B., shall we not go on in so		128:22
Courage, b.; and on, on to the		128:22
B., I have many things to say		128:25
also unto my b. whom I love,		135: 5
Thy b. have rejected you and		136:34
because of Cain and his b.	Mses	5:27
swear thy b. by their heads,		5:29
with his wife and many of his b.		5:41
and ye are my b., and why		6:43
Behold these thy b.;		7:32
And unto thy b. have I said,		7:33
wickedness as among thy b.		7:36
and wept over his b., and said		7:44

BRICKS

The b. are fallen down,	2Ne	19:10

BRIDE 139 BRING

BRIDE
and blind them on even as a b.	1Ne 21:18
be adorned as a b. for that day	DC 109:74

BRIDEGROOM
ready at the coming of the B.—	DC 33:17
Lamb, make ready for the B.	65: 3
Behold, shall be for the B. cometh;	88:92
go forth to meet the B.;	133:10
the B. cometh; go ye out to meet	133:10
for the coming of the B.;	133:19

BRIDLE
see that ye b. all your passions,	Al 38:12

BRIERS
there shall come up b. and thorns;	2Ne 15: 6
which shall be for b. and thorns.	17:23
the land shall become b. and thorns.	17:24
thither the fear of b. and thorns;	17:25
it shall devour the b. and thorns,	19:18
shall devour his thorns and his b.	20:17

BRIGHAM: see also YOUNG, Brigham.
my servant B., it is no more	DC 126: 1

BRIGHT
a b. testimony against this people,	Mos 3:24
a b. recollection of all our guilt.	Al 11:43
and our swords have become b.,	24:12
they can no more be washed b.	24:13
and our swords are made b.,	24:15
away that they may be kept b.,	24:15
earth, that they may be kept b.,	24:16
with those b., shining seraphs	DC 109:79
the light, for it was b.;	Abr 4: 4
not so very b. as immediately	JS 2:32

BRIGHTER
and that light groweth b.	DC 50:24
groweth brighter and b.	50:24

BRIGHTNESS
their b. did exceed that of the	1Ne 1:10
the b. thereof was like unto	15:30
like unto the b. of a flaming fire,	15:30
and that I stand with b. before	2Ne 9:44
having a perfect b. of hope,	31:20
kept they must retain their b.;	Al 37: 5
yea, and they will retain their b.;	37: 5
by the b. of my coming.	DC 5:19
clothed in the b. of his glory,	65: 5
shone above the b. of the sun;	110: 3
above the b. of the sun,	JS 2:16
whose b. and glory defy all	2:17

BRILLIANT
so exceedingly white and b.	JS 2:31

BRIM
yea, my heart is b. with joy,	Al 26:11

BRIMSTONE
is as a lake of fire and b.,	2Ne 9:16
and that lake of fire and b.,	9:19
and the lake of fire and b.,	9:26
even a lake of fire and b.,	28:23
into that lake of fire and b.	Jac 3:11
into that lake of fire and b.,	6:10
which lake of fire and b. is	6:10
is as a lake of fire and b.,	Mos 3:27
shall be as a lake of fire and b.,	Al 12:17
cast into a lake of fire and b.?	14:14
which burneth with fire and b.,	DC 63:17
away into the lake of fire and b.,	76:36

BRING
the records, and b. them down	1Ne 3: 4
to b. forth his righteous purposes.	4:13
and b. them down again unto us	5: 5
b. down Ishmael and his family	7: 2
b. them down into captivity.	13: 9
I will b. forth unto them,	13:34
shall seek to b. forth my Zion	13:37
Lord can b. about great things.	16:29
I did b. you out of the land	1Ne 17:14
he did b. them out of the land	17:40
to b. Jacob again to him	21: 5
shall b. thy sons in their arms,	21:22
will b. them again out of captivity,	22:12
unto him whom he shall b.	2Ne 1: 7
b. out of the land of Jerusalem	1: 9
he will b. other nations unto	1:11
cometh to b. salvation unto men.	2: 3
he may b. to pass the resurrection	2: 8
to b. about his eternal purposes	2:15
captivate, to b. you down to hell,	2:29
give power to b. forth my word	3:11
which the Lord shall b. forth	3:15
shall b. my people unto salvation.	3:15
shall b. thy sons in their arms,	6: 6
that it should b. forth grapes,	15: 2
that it should b. forth grapes	15: 4
The Lord shall b. upon thee,	17:17
and b. them to their place;	24: 2
That I will b. the Assyrian	24:25
he shall b. forth his words unto	25:18
God shall b. these things forth	26:14
God shall b. forth unto you the	27: 6
will proceed to b. forth the words	27:14
B. hither the book, and I will read	27:15
I cannot b. the book, for it is	27:17
for I will b. them forth in mine	27:21
and I b. forth my word unto	29: 7
to b. about the restoration of	30: 8
b. your children unto destruction,	Jac 3:10
and b. them hither unto me;	5: 7
perhaps it may b. forth good fruit	5:27
long as it shall b. forth evil fruit.	5:35
that they b. forth no good fruit;	5:46
they may b. forth good fruit	5:54
may b. forth again good fruit;	5:60
b. forth again the natural fruit,	5:61
and b. forth the natural fruit,	5:64
which b. forth bitter fruit,	5:65
thus will I b. them together again,	5:68
they shall b. forth the natural fruit,	5:68
will ye b. forth evil fruit,	6: 7
will b. you to stand with shame	6: 9
their transgressions will I b. down	En 1:10
that he would b. them forth unto	1:16
we may not b. upon ourselves a	Mos 5: 5
and b. their brethren into the city,	7:16
to b. my people into bondage,	9:10
and b. them into bondage.	9:11
desirous to b. us into bondage,	9:12
that shall b. upon my people such	11:27
you to b. Abinadi hither,	11:28
B. him hither that we may question	12:18
when the Lord shall b. again Zion;	12:22
should b. to pass the resurrection	13:35
when the Lord shall b. again Zion.	15:29
not slay him, but b. him hither	20:14
might b. them to the knowledge of	28: 2
b. the same curse upon his seed.	Al 3: 9
b. upon himself his own	3:19
b. forth of righteousness,	5:35
they do b. forth works which are	5:54
he will b. you into his fold,	5:60
and b. forth a son, yea, even	7:10
ye ought to b. forth works which	9:30
and to b. down the wrath of God	10:18
he might b. you into subjection	12: 6
shall b. to pass the resurrection	12:25
b. forth fruit meet for repentance,	13:13
not b. down his wrath upon you,	13:30
to b., if it were possible, their	17: 9
might b. them unto repentance;	17:16
they might b. them to know of	17:16
b. them back unto the place of	17:31
God to b. about this great work.	26: 3
to b. thousands of souls to	26:22
to b. these our brethren to	26:22
that ye can b. the Lamanites to	26:24
to b. some soul to repentance;	29: 9
b. men on to unequal grounds.	30: 7
God could b. this upon me;	30:52
we may b. these, our brethren,	31:35
up, and b. forth fruit unto us.	32:37
and grow up and b. forth fruit.	32:37

BRING 140 BRINGETH

for the tree to b. forth fruit	Al 32:43	
shall b. to pass the resurrection,	33:22	
And thus he shall b. salvation	34:15	
to b. about the bowels of mercy,	34:15	
and b. fruit unto repentance.	34:30	
might b. souls unto repentance;	36:24	
I might b. them to taste of the	36:24	
to b. about his great and eternal	37: 7	
I will b. forth out of darkness	37:25	
will b. to light all their secrets	37:25	
director did b. our fathers	37:45	
is to b. back again evil for evil,	41:13	
to b. about the plan of mercy,	42:15	
shall b. you down unto repentance.	42:29	
let it b. you down to the dust in	42:30	
mayest b. souls unto repentance,	42:31	
might b. them into subjection	43: 7	
and b. them into bondage that	43:29	
desire to b. any one to the yoke of	44: 2	
until we b. it upon us by our own	46:18	
to take them and b. them back,	46:30	
he would b. his guards with him.	47:12	
should b. witnesses with him	47:33	
and to b. them into bondage.	48: 4	
works did b. forth unto them,	50:12	
and to b. the wicked to justice	50:39	
If ye will b. forth your weapons	52:37	
not b. upon him injustice,	55:19	
and thus b. them up in the rear	56:23	
to b. a stratagem into effect	56:30	
the Lord did b. Mulek into	He 6:10	
upon this man and b. him forth,	8: 1	
that she may b. forth her fruit,	11:13	
that it did b. forth her fruit in	11:17	
it did b. forth her grain in	11:17	
he did b. glad tidings to my soul.	13: 7	
to b. to pass the resurrection of	14:15	
they b. upon themselves their	14:29	
b. the remainder of their brethren	15: 6	
b. a remnant of the seed of	3Ne 5:23	
b. redemption unto the world,	9:21	
A good tree cannot b. forth evil	14:18	
a corrupt tree b. forth good fruit.	14:18	
them also I must b., and they	15:17	
them also I must b., and they	15:21	
I will b. the fulness of my gospel	16:10	
I will b. my gospel unto them.	16:11	
the Lord shall b. again Zion.	16:18	
sick among you? B. them hither.	17: 7	
B. them hither and I will heal	17: 7	
b. forth some bread and wine	18: 1	
to b. forth unto the Gentiles,	21:11	
b. them forth unto the Gentiles,	21:11	
B. forth the record which ye	23: 7	
B. ye all the tithes into the	24:10	
b. the souls of men unto me,	28: 9	
shall b. out of them unto Jesus	28:29	
wickedness will not b. them forth	Mrm 5:12	
that the father may b. about,	5:14	
sorrows cannot b. your return.	6:20	
and whoso shall b. it to light,	8:14	
have power to b. it to light	8:15	
that shall b. this thing to light;	8:16	
suffer to b. these things forth.	8:25	
b. damnation upon your souls?	8:33	
b. down the fulness of the wrath	Eth 2:11	
the Lord did b. Jared and	2:13	
I will b. you up again out of	2:24	
shall assist to b. forth this work;	5: 2	
he did b. them forth again upon	6: 7	
if ye will b. unto me the head	8:10	
if ye will b. unto me the head	8:12	
he did b. him into captivity;	10:14	
or b. forth another people to	11:21	
he did b. him into captivity.	13:23	
cannot b. forth good water;	Mro 7:11	
fountain b. forth bitter water;	7:11	
to b. it forth out of obscurity	DC 1:30	
b. forth and establish the cause of	6: 6	
and assist to b. forth my work,	6: 9	
b. many to the knowledge of	6:11	
shall b. to light this ministry;	6:28	
and b. souls unto thee.	7: 2	

that he might b. souls unto me,	DC 7: 4	
and b. your soul to destruction.	8: 4	
should b. forth the same words	10:31	
would b. to the knowledge of	10:40	
I b. this part of my gospel	10:52	
not b. it to destroy that which	10:52	
b. to light their marvelous works,	10:61	
will also b. to light my gospel	10:62	
b. to light the true points of	10:62	
b. forth and establish the cause of	11: 6	
and assist to b. forth my work,	11: 9	
b. forth and establish the cause of	12: 6	
b. forth and establish this work;	12: 7	
b. forth and establish my Zion.	14: 6	
b. forth the fulness of my	14:10	
that you may b. souls unto me,	15: 6	
that you may b. souls unto me,	16: 6	
b. about my righteous purposes	17: 4	
b. about my righteous purposes	17: 9	
he might b. all men unto him,	18:12	
b., save it be one soul unto me,	18:15	
should b. many souls unto me!	18:16	
is to b. them unto the elders	20:70	
to b. to pass the gathering of	29: 7	
b. to pass even your destruction	38:13	
and to b. forth Zion,	39:13	
I will b. them to judgment.	50: 6	
shall b. forth fruits of praise	52:17	
let them b. their families to this	58:25	
b. to pass much righteousness;	58:27	
it shall b. forth in its strength.	59: 3	
ye shall b. before the church,	64:12	
b. forth their strong reasons	71: 8	
whom he shall b. with him,	76:63	
to b. as many as will come to	77:11	
That they may b. forth fruit	84:58	
beginning to b. forth the word,	86: 4	
for you, to b. to pass my work,	90:26	
b. up your children in light and	93:40	
may b. to pass my strange act,	95: 4	
I shall b. them unto judgment.	97: 2	
b. forth as a very fruitful tree	97: 9	
b. these testimonies before the	98:35	
b. these testimonies before the	98:44	
proceed to b. to pass my act,	101:95	
inasmuch as they b. forth fruit	101:100	
power to b. evil upon you.	104:10	
minds to b. affliction upon you.	104:81	
to b. to shame and confusion,	109:29	
b. again Zion, and the redemption	113: 8	
bud and to blossom, and to b. forth	117: 7	
they are willing to b. upon others,	121:13	
might b. them into bondage and	121:18	
b. the box-tree, and the fir-tree,	124:26	
by your own works, b. cursings,	124:48	
that b. glad tidings of good things,	128:19	
shall b. forth their rich treasures	133:30	
to b. them forth for the salvation	135: 6	
heavens, to b. forth my work.	136:37	
to b. to pass the immortality	Mses 1:39	
Let the earth b. forth grass,	2:11	
Let the waters b. forth	2:20	
Let the earth b. forth the	2:24	
thou shalt b. forth children,	4:22	
thistles shall it b. forth to thee,	4:24	
the earth to b. forth grass;	Abr 4:11	
the earth to b. forth grass	4:12	
the herb to b. forth herb from	4:12	
the earth to b. forth the tree	4:12	
b. forth the same in itself,	4:12	
b. forth abundantly the moving	4:20	
might b. forth great whales,	4:21	
to b. forth abundantly after	4:21	
b. forth the living creature	4:24	
to b. forth the beasts after	4:25	
if I would b. the plates to him	JS 2:65	
I was forbidden to b. them.	2:65	

BRINGETH

b. them down into captivity.	1Ne 13: 5	
Behold, the Lord b. up upon them	2Ne 18: 7	
which b. immediate destruction.	Mos 7:31	
feet of him that b. good tidings;	12:21	

BRINGETH 141 BROKEN

that b. good tidings of good;	Mos	12:21
feet of him that b. good tidings,		15:18
he b. to pass the resurrection		15:20
Lord b. about the restoration of		15:24
whosoever b. forth not good	Al	5:36
if a man b. forth good works		5:41
whosoever b. forth evil works,		5:41
that b. not forth good fruit		5:52
b. forth fruit meet for repentance.		12:15
and b. forth good works and		26:22
for every seed b. forth unto its		32:31
and b. about means unto men		34:15
b. about the salvation of many		37: 7
he b. to pass the resurrection of		40: 3
this b. about the restoration of		40:22
b. to pass the resurrection of the		42:23
b. back men into the presence		42:23
thus God b. about his great and		42:26
b. unto the power of the	He	5:11
death b. to pass the resurrection,		14:16
b. them back into the presence of		14:17
it b. to pass the condition of		14:18
repentance b. a change of heart		15: 7
good tree b. forth good fruit;	3Ne	14:17
a corrupt tree b. forth evil fruit.		14:17
that b. not forth good fruit		14:19
that b. good tidings unto them,		20:40
that b. good tidings unto them		20:40
that b. forth an instrument for		22:16
he b. to pass the resurrection of	Mrm	7: 6
b. to pass the resurrection,		9:13
b. to pass a redemption		9:13
it b. to pass the destruction of	Eth	8:25
hope and charity b. unto me—		12:28
b. to pass the scripture which		13:12
manner b. to pass the Father,	Mro	7:32
b. remission of sins;		8:25
remission of sins b. meekness,		8:26
but b. salvation to his soul;	DC	4: 4
if he b. forth the same words,		10:17
that which b. joy that which		42:61
that which b. life eternal.		42:61
and b. not forth fruits,		52:18
confusion, which b. pestilence.		63:24
it b. a snare upon your souls.		90:17
that b. not forth good fruit		97: 7
the fall, which fall b. death,	Mses	6:59

BRINGING

in b. about his covenants and his	1Ne	22:11
in b. them out of the land of	2Ne	1: 1
in b. us forth into the land of		1:24
the b. of them out of darkness		3: 5
the b. of them to the knowledge		3: 7
to the b. forth my word		3:11
and b. them to the knowledge		3:12
unto the b. to pass much		3:24
in b. forth salvation unto		29: 4
of b. this people into subjection	Mos	7:22
in b. so many of you to a knowledge		23:10
in b. many to the knowledge of		27:36
thus b. on the destruction of	Al	4:11
in b. many to the knowledge of		17: 4
the means of b. many souls down		30:47
b. them again unto thee in Christ.		31:34
of b. many of the Zoramites to		35:14
the means of b. many thousands		37:10
by b. them into bondage.		43: 8
were continually b. new forces		55:34
the b. down many of them into	He	6: 5
a means of b. down the people		6:25
b. glad tidings unto the people	3Ne	1:26
means of b. salvation unto them.		18:32
was b. a curse upon the land,	Eth	7:23
in b. them across the great deep		7:27
in b. Jared and his brother		10: 2
shall you assist in b. to light,	DC	6:27
assist in b. to light those		11:19
keys of the b. to pass the restoration		27: 6
the b. forth of the revelations		84:104
the purpose of b. forth my word		96: 4
may assist in b. forth my word		96: 8
b. to light all the hidden things		123:13

ability in b. offenders against	DC	134: 8
the time for b. them forth	JS	2:53

BRITAIN

even the nation of Great B.,	DC	87: 3

BROAD

leadeth them away into b. roads,	1Ne	12:17
is the gate, and b. is the way,	3Ne	14:13
b. the way which leads to death,		27:33
B. is the gate, and wide the	DC	132:25
a b. seal affixed to "Mormonism"		135: 7
Heaven, which is b. as eternity;	Mses	7:53

BROKE

they b. the cords with which they	Al	14:26
the earth, and it b. by the hilt;		44:12
remainder of them b. through		57:33
been for the war which b. out		60:16
waves which b. upon them,	Eth	6: 6
b. down the door of the prison		7:18
Wherefore he b. my covenant,	DC	40: 3
by night, and b. down the hedge;		101:51
and b. down the olive-trees.		101:51
the Lord b. down the altar	Abr	1:20

BROKEN

whose branches should be b. off	1Ne	10:12
the earth, that they were b. up;		12: 4
behold are we not b. off from		15:12
and smooth places shall be b. up.		17:46
a branch who have been b. off;		19:24
from whom ye have been b. off;		19:24
all ye that are b. off and are		21: 1
all ye that are b. off, that are		21: 1
a b. heart and a contrite spirit;	2Ne	2: 7
a branch which was to be b. off,		3: 5
my heart is b. and my spirit is		4:32
all them who have been b. off,		10:22
nor the latchet of their shoes be b.;		15:27
shall Ephraim be b. that it be		17: 8
and ye shall be b. in pieces;		18: 9
and ye shall be b. in pieces;		18: 9
and ye shall be b. in pieces.		18: 9
shall stumble and fall, and be b.,		18:15
hast b. the yoke of his burden,		19: 4
hath b. the staff of the wicked,		24: 5
rod of him that smote thee is b.;		24:29
pure in heart, and the b. heart,	Jac	2:10
Ye have b. the hearts of your		2:35
natural branches had been b. off,		5:30
having b. the bands of death,	Mos	15: 9
the bands of death shall be b.,		15:20
who has b. the bands of death.		15:23
or have b. the bands of death		16: 7
my people have not b. the oath		20:14
I have b. the oath because		20:15
were the bands of death b.,	Al	5: 9
of his voice they are b. up,	He	12:10
is one solid mass, shall be b. up;		14:21
in b. fragments upon the face of		14:22
many highways shall be b. up,		14:24
the church began to be b. up;	3Ne	6:14
church was b. up in all the land		6:14
And the highways were b. up,		8:13
were b. up upon the face of the		8:18
were found in b. fragments,		8:18
a b. heart and a contrite spirit.		9:20
a b. heart and a contrite spirit,		9:20
a b. heart and a contrite spirit.		12:19
as I have b. bread and blessed it		18: 6
with b. hearts and contrite spirits,	Mrm	2:14
a b. heart and a contrite spirit,	Eth	4:15
to build up again a b. people.		10: 1
a b. heart and a contrite spirit,	Mro	6: 2
and under the curse of a b. law,		8:24
b. mine everlasting covenant;	DC	1:15
has b. the most sacred promises		3:13
b. hearts and contrite spirits,		20:37
and a deed which cannot be b.		42:30
that every bond may be b.		44: 5
they made unto me has been b.,		54: 4
and the commandment is b.		56: 3
men, whose hearts are not b.,		56:17

BROKEN — 142 — BROTHER

BROKEN

in heart, whose hearts are b.,	DC	56:18
a b. heart and a contrite spirit.		59: 8
covenant that cannot be b.		78:11
covenant that cannot be b.		82:11
their hearts are honest, and are b.,		97: 8
olive-trees may not be b. down		101:45
have b. the covenant through		104: 4
being b. through transgression,		104:52
ye have made unto me are b.;		104:55
suffer his house to be b. up.		104:86
b. off from the house of David;		109:63
their prejudices may be b. up		109:70
he hath b. his vow and hath		132:43
innocent and hath not b. her vow,		132:44
with the b. faith of the State as		135: 7
his house to have been b. up,	JS	1:47

BROODING

b. upon the face of the waters.	Abr	4: 2

BROOKS

And ye rivers, and b., and rills,	DC	128:23

BROOME

B. county, on the Susquehanna	DC	128:20

BROTHER

smite your younger b. with a rod?	1Ne	3:29
that I, your younger b., should		7: 8
our father, and also our b. Nephi,		16:37
after this manner did my b.		16:38
Our b. is a fool, for he thinketh		17:17
yea, and our b. is like unto him.		17:22
I am thy b., yea, even thy		17:55
yea, even thy younger b.;		17:55
will not that our younger b. shall		18:10
Rebel no more against your b.,	2Ne	1:24
dwell safely with thy b., Nephi;		2: 3
hearken unto the words of thy b.,		3:25
inherit the land like unto thy b.		4:11
thou shalt be even like unto thy b.,		4:11
younger b. thinks to rule over us;		5: 3
and Sam, mine elder b. and his		5: 6
Jacob, the b. of Nephi,		6: 1
consecrated by my b. Nephi,		6: 2
words which my b. has desired		6: 4
And my b., Jacob, also has seen		11: 3
a man shall take hold of his b.		13: 6
no man shall spare his b.		19:19
of the words of my b. Jacob.		31: 1
THE B. OF NEPHI	Jac	1:hd
commandment of my b. Nephi.		1: 8
For I, Jacob, and my b. Joseph		1:18
Jacob, the b. of Nephi, spake		2: 1
B. Jacob, I have sought much		7: 6
my b. Nephi had commanded me,		7:27
the plates unto my b. Chemish.	Om	1: 8
in the same book with my b.;		1: 9
And I, Amaleki, had a b.,		1:30
and b. against brother,	Mos	9: 2
against him, until the greater		9: 2
that doth make a mock of his b.,	Al	5:30
whose b. had been slain with the		19:22
thy b. Aaron, and his son Muloki		20: 2
my b. and brethren are in		20: 3
the words of thy b. Ammon;		22: 3
also with his b. Anti-Nephi-Lehi,		24: 5
rather than take away from a b.		24:18
his b. Aaron rebuked, him saying:		26:10
sons, and the daughter for the b.,		28: 5
yea, the b. for the father;		28: 5
Behold thy b. hath said, what		32: 9
desired of my beloved b. that he		34: 3
that my b. has proved unto you,		34: 6
My b. has called upon the words		34: 7
is just, take the life of his b.?		34:11
than what I said unto thy b.;		39: 1
observed the steadiness of thy b.,		39: 1
heed unto my words as did thy b.,		39: 2
the b. of Amalickiah was		52: 3
the b. of king Amalickiah, was		52: 3
concerning the death of his b.,		52:12
rather which thy b. hath waged		54: 5
as thou and thy b. have been.	Al	54: 7
I am the b. of Amalickiah whom		54:16
my b. whom ye have murdered,		54:22
My dearly beloved b., Moroni,		56: 2
behold, my beloved b., I have		56: 2
unto you, my beloved b. Moroni,		56:45
now, my beloved b., Moroni,		58:41
my beloved b., Moroni, let us		61:14
mine epistle to my beloved b.,		61:21
Ammoron, and Amalickiah his b.,		62:35
Lord his God; and also did his b.		63: 2
in the stead of his b. Pahoran;	He	1:13
and his b. Lehi also, all the		5: 4
that they might distinguish a b.		6:22
wickedness his b. should do		6:22
should not be injured by his b.,		6:22
if he would murder his b. Abel		6:27
he hath been murdered by his b.,		8:27
he being stabbed by his b.		9: 6
who is the b. of Seezoram,		9:26
Seezoram, who is your b.?		9:27
Have ye murdered your b.?		9:29
that it is the blood of your b.?		9:32
Lehi, his b., was not a whit		11:19
even his b., did he raise from the	3Ne	7:19
whosoever is angry with his b.		12:22
shall say to his b., Raca,		12:22
thy b. hath aught against thee—		12:23
Go thy way unto thy b., and first		12:24
and first be reconciled to thy b.,		12:24
Or how wilt thou say to thy b.:		14: 4
Nephi and his b. whom he had		19: 4
Mathoni, and Mathonihah, his b.,		19: 4
his b., Ammaron, did keep the	4Ne	1:47
Jared came forth with his b.	Eth	1:33
the b. of Jared being a large		1:34
Jared, his b., said unto him:		1:34
the b. of Jared did cry unto		1:35
and his b. were not confounded.		1:35
Then Jared said unto his b.:		1:36
the b. of Jared did cry unto the		1:37
Jared spake again unto his b.,		1:38
the b. of Jared did cry unto the		1:39
the Lord did hear the b. of Jared,		1:40
also Jared thy b. and his family;		1:41
thy seed, and of the seed of thy b.,		1:43
to pass that Jared and his b.,		2: 1
the friends of Jared and his b.		2: 1
and talked with the b. of Jared;		2: 4
b. of Jared saw him not.		2: 4
his wrath unto the b. of Jared,		2: 8
came again unto the b. of Jared,		2:14
Lord talk with the b. of Jared,		2:14
the b. of Jared repented of the		2:15
the b. of Jared did go to work,		2:16
the b. of Jared cried unto the		2:18
Lord said unto the b. of Jared:		2:20
that the b. of Jared did so,		2:21
Lord said unto the b. of Jared:		2:23
to pass that the b. of Jared,		3: 1
when the b. of Jared had said		3: 6
off the eyes of the b. of Jared,		3: 6
the b. of Jared fell down before		3: 6
that the b. of Jared had fallen to		3: 7
the Lord said unto the b. of Jared:		3:21
he showed unto the b. of Jared		3:25
commanded the b. of Jared to		4: 1
things which the b. of Jared saw;		4: 4
manifest unto the b. of Jared.		4: 4
even as the b. of Jared did,		4: 7
things which the b. of Jared saw,		4: 7
the record of Jared and his b.		6: 1
which the b. of Jared had carried		6: 2
the b. of Jared came down out of		6: 2
the b. of Jared did sing praises		6: 9
the b. of Jared also begat sons		6:15
the friends of Jared and his b.		6:16
the b. of Jared began to be old,		6:19
the daughters of the b. of Jared		6:20
the b. of Jared said unto them:		6:23
But Jared said unto his b.:		6:24
the firstborn of the b. of Jared;		6:25
that Jared died, and his b. also.		6:29

BROTHER

the saying of the b. of Jared	Eth 7: 5
that Shule was angry with his b.;	7: 8
gave battle unto his b. Corihor,	7: 9
and drew away Cohor his b.,	7:15
of the doings of Jared their b.,	8: 5
b. of him that suffered death,	9: 8
his father had done unto his b.	9: 8
Jared and his b. across the deep;	10: 2
his b. did rise up in rebellion	10:14
the b. of Shiblom rebelled	11: 4
the b. of Shiblom caused that	11: 5
a descendant of the b. of Jared.	11:17
one of these was the b. of Jared;	12:20
from the sight of the b. of Jared,	12:20
after the b. of Jared had beheld	12:21
the b. of Jared had obtained by	12:21
writing like unto the b. of Jared,	12:24
the b. of Jared said unto the	12:30
there arose the b. of Shared and	14: 3
the b. of Shared did give battle	14: 4
the b. of Shared did march forth	14: 5
the b. of Shared, whose name was	14: 8
the b. of Lib did come against	14:16
before the army of the b. of Lib.	14:16
the b. of Lib was called Shiz.	14:17
of the blood of his b., who	14:24
and for thy b. James;	DC 7: 7
were given to the b. of Jared	17: 1
thy b. Oliver shall continue in	24:10
shalt take thy b., Hiram Page,	28:11
journey with your b. Oliver;	30: 5
the words and advice of your b.,	30: 5
except it is his b., Joseph Smith,	30: 7
be at your b. Philip Burroughs',	30:10
esteem his b. as himself,	38:24
esteem his b. as himself.	38:25
thou shalt receive of thy b.	42:54
if thy b. or sister offend thee,	42:88
if thy b. or sister offend many,	42:90
for he that forgiveth not his b.	64: 9
slain by the conspiracy of his b.,	84:16
salute his b. or brethren with	88:132
Art thou a b. or brethren?	88:133
to be your friend and b.	88:133
faithful before me, and is a b.,	88:135
well-beloved b., Brigham Young,	126: 1
blood; and so has his b. Hyrum.	135: 3
conceived and bare his b. Abel,	Mses 5:17
Lord, neither to Abel, his b.,	5:26
I will deliver thy b. Abel into	5:29
Cain talked with Abel, his b.	5:32
Cain rose up against Abel, his b.,	5:32
flocks of my b. falleth	5:33
Where is Abel, thy b.?	5:34
not like unto Cain, his b. Abel,	5:50
they knew every man his b.	5:51
like unto his b. Abel.	6: 3
hand was against his own b.	6:15
that Haran, my b., died;	Abr 2: 1
Nehor, my b., took Milcah	2: 2
by the death of my eldest b.,	JS 2:56

BROTHERLY

b. kindness, godliness, charity,	DC 4: 6
patience, godliness, b. kindness, and	107:30

BROTHER'S

the mote that is in thy b. eye,	3Ne 14: 3
to cast the mote out of thy b. eye.	14: 5
shalt not take thy b. garment;	DC 42:54
covet not that which is thy b.	136:20
Am I my b. keeper?	Mses 5:34
The voice of thy b. blood	5:35
to receive thy b. blood	5:36
because of my b. flocks.	5:38
and his b. name was Jubal,	5:45
and I took Lot, my b. son,	Abr 2: 4
Abraham, and Lot, my b. son,	2: 6
and Lot, my b. son, and all	2:15

BROTHERS

mother, Sariah, and my elder b.,	1Ne 2: 5
against him like unto my b.	2:16
thou and thy b. should go unto	3: 4
thy b. murmur, saying it is a	3: 5
words unto us, their younger b.,	3:28
and the b. for their brethren.	Mos 21: 9
My b. and my brethren, behold	Al 26: 1
to counsel with your elder b. in	39:10
in need to be nourished by your b.	39:10
they chose all the b. of Pagag,	Eth 6:26
of fathers and mothers, b. and	DC 132:55
my b., Alvin (who died	JS 2: 4
my b. Hyrum and Samuel	2: 7

BROTHERS'

of his b. daughters to wife,	Mses 5:28

BROUGHT

even be b. back out of captivity;	1Ne 10: 3
should be b. back out of captivity	10: 3
thou shalt be b. into judgment.	10:20
no more b. down into captivity;	14: 2
being b. down into captivity,	14: 7
must be b. to stand before God,	15:33
b. down into the depths of sorrow.	16:25
because he had b. them out of	16:35
they should be b. out of bondage.	17:25
whatsoever thing we had b. with	18: 6
by what power they had been b.	18: 9
they were b. down, yea, even	18:17
they were b. near even to be	18:18
about to be b. down to lie low	18:18
b. from the land of Jerusalem,	18:24
I have b. him, and he shall	20:15
And who hath b. up these?	21:21
shall be b. out of obscurity	22:12
who must be b. low in the dust;	22:23
be b. by the hand of the Lord.	2Ne 1: 6
be b. down into captivity;	1: 7
been b. by his infinite goodness	1:10
be b. down with grief and sorrow	1:21
b. out of the land of Jerusalem,	1:30
righteousness could not be b. to	2:11
they have b. forth children;	2:20
have b. out of the wilderness	3: 3
b. up in the way ye should go	4: 5
of Lemuel to be b. before him.	4: 8
I, Nephi, had also b. the records	5:12
the sons she hath b. forth;	8:18
the sons she hath b. up.	8:18
and he shall be b. low.	12:12
and it b. forth wild grapes.	15: 2
it b. forth wild grapes.	15: 4
the mean man shall be b. down,	15:15
Thy pomp is b. down to the	24:11
thou shalt be b. down to hell,	24:15
that b. Israel up out of the land	25:20
they shall have been b. down	26:15
the terrible one is b. to naught,	27:31
ye are not b. into the light,	32: 4
b. against you at the judgment bar;	33:15
when ye shall be b. with them	Jac 3: 8
hath b. forth much strength;	5:18
branches have b. forth tame fruit.	5:18
the tree thereof hath b. forth;	5:18
not b. forth much fruit also,	5:19
that it had b. forth much fruit;	5:20
and it hath b. forth much fruit.	5:20
that it hath b. forth much fruit.	5:22
and it hath b. forth much fruit;	5:23
and it hath b. forth fruit.	5:24
the tree hath b. forth tame fruit,	5:25
the tree hath b. forth wild fruit;	5:25
that have not b. forth good fruit,	5:26
it hath b. forth much fruit,	5:32
they have hitherto b. forth,	5:36
it hath b. forth much evil fruit;	5:37
hath b. forth so much evil fruit	5:37
have also b. forth evil fruit.	5:38
tree which b. forth good fruit,	5:40
have once b. forth good fruit	5:42
part thereof b. forth good fruit,	5:45
part thereof b. forth wild fruit;	5:45
and b. other servants;	5:70

BROUGHT 144 BROUGHT

b. unto me again the natural fruit,	Jac	5:75
that it might be b. forth	En	1:13
they might be b. unto salvation—		1:13
were b. by the hand of the Lord	Om	1:16
they had b. no records with		1:17
was a large stone b. unto him		1:20
he had Mosiah b. before him;	Mos	1:10
b. out of the land of Jerusalem;		1:11
who had b. them out of the land		2: 4
The man has b. upon himself his		4:17
has b. us to this great knowledge,		5: 4
that you may be b. to heaven,		5:15
were again b. before the king,		7: 8
Zeniff b. up out of that land.		7:13
who b. the children of Israel out		7:19
same God has b. our fathers out		7:20
that he has b. us into bondage.		7:20
which b. down the wrath of God		7:28
should be b. before Ammon,		8: 5
they have b. twenty-four plates		8: 9
also, they have b. breastplates,		8:10
again, they have b. swords,		8:11
that I have b. this my people up		10:18
they shall be b. into bondage;		11:21
they shall be b. into bondage;		11:23
shall be b. into bondage,		12: 2
we have b. a man before thee who		12: 9
he should be b. before them.		12:18
who hath b. thee out of the land of		12:34
he is b. as a lamb to the		14: 7
have b. good tidings of good,		15:14
be b. to stand before the bar of		16:10
he should again be b. before him.		17: 6
which was to be b. to pass through		18: 2
and b. him before Limhi,		20:13
we have b. him before you;		20:13
And they b. him.		20:14
they b. a record with them,		21:27
and have been b. into iniquity		23:12
that they were b. into bondage,		23:23
and also b. with them the wives		23:38
they were b. before the priests,		26: 7
the priests b. them before Alma,		26: 7
they should be b. before the king.		26:10
whom we have b. before thee,		26:11
we have b. them before thee,		26:11
b. himself under condemnation.		26:31
b. to the knowledge of the truth;		27:14
be b. to rejoice in the Lord		28: 2
they were b. into bondage.		29:18
b. before him to be judged,	Al	1: 2
was b. before Alma, to be judged		1:10
b. out of the land of Jerusalem,		3:11
b. upon themselves the curse;		3:19
they were b. into bondage by		5: 5
we were b. into this land,		5: 5
b. before the tribunal of God		5:18
have been b. into this church,		5:54
b. to sit down with Abraham,		7:25
and he b. forth bread and meat		8:21
Lehi, was b. out of Jerusalem by		9: 9
will be b. to believe in his word,		9:17
having been b. out of bondage		9:22
were b. before them to be judged.		11: 1
man should be b. before him;		11: 2
which were b. against him,		11: 2
suits which were b. before them;		11:20
shall be b. to stand before God,		11:43
shall be b. and be arraigned		11:44
and are b. to stand before God		12: 8
being b. before the bar of God,		12:12
they b. their wives and children		14: 8
they also b. forth their records		14: 8
they were b. by their brethren to		16: 8
were b. before the altar of God,		17: 4
b. to a knowledge of that which		18:34
The king hath b. this evil upon		19:20
were b. forth out of prison.		20:28
they b. many to the knowledge of		21:17
b. our fathers out of the land of		22: 9
b. to the knowledge of the Lord,		23: 5
b. to believe in the traditions		23: 5
b. to the knowledge of the truth,		23: 6
shall be b. to stand before him	Al	24:15
these Lamanites were b. to believe		24:19
b. to the knowledge of the truth;		24:27
words of Abinadi were b. to pass,		25: 9
b. to behold the marvelous light		26: 3
have been b. into the fold of God.		26: 4
are b. to sing redeeming love,		26:13
b. them into his everlasting		26:15
b. us over that everlasting gulf		26:20
b. to pass the destruction of		28:10
b. to pass an awful scene of		28:10
and have b. forth much fruit;		29:15
be b. down according to thy words.		30:23
and have b. them to believe, by		30:28
that he might be b. before Alma,		30:29
when he was b. before Alma		30:30
until I have b. this great curse		30:53
ye are b. to a lowliness of heart;		32:12
are necessarily b. to be humble.		32:12
without being b. to know the		32:16
is b. about the great and eternal		34:16
plan of redemption be b. about		34:31
ye are b. to that awful crisis,		34:34
as many as were b. to repentance		35:14
b. to stand in the presence of		36:15
has b. our fathers out of Egypt,		36:28
he has also b. our fathers out		36:29
are great things b. to pass;		37: 6
and b. them to the knowledge of		37: 8
words b. them unto repentance;		37: 9
they b. them to the knowledge of		37: 9
have been b. out of darkness		37:26
ye b. upon the Zoramites;		39:11
and be b. to stand before God,		40:21
fall had b. upon all mankind		42: 9
which man had b. upon himself		42:12
redemption could not be b. about,		42:13
plan of mercy could not be b. about		42:15
which b. remorse of conscience		42:18
b. a part over into the valley,		43:31
b. death almost at every stroke.		43:37
see who shall be b. into bondage.		44: 7
therefore, they b. up their armies.		49:17
Lamanites b. up their armies		49:21
which b. upon them their wars		50:21
the people of Morianton b. back.		50:36
they were b. down to humble		51:21
been b. down into the land of		53:10
were b. down into the land of		53:12
had b. an epistle to Moroni.		54: 4
pressed and b. out of Jerusalem.		54:23
of their wine and b. with us.		55: 8
and they b. them forth and cast		55:23
men whom Ammon b. down		56: 3
little force which I b. with me,		56:17
was b. unto us many provisions		56:27
plenty of provisions b. unto us.		57: 6
b. it forth from the beginning of	He	6:29
desired that they should be b.;		9:13
and they were b., and behold		9:13
and b. before the multitude,		9:19
he was b. to prove that he		9:38
he has b. unto our knowledge		9:41
men might be b. unto repentance		12:24
b. into the presence of the Lord.		14:15
b. down unto this second death.		14:19
b. to the knowledge of the truth,		15: 7
be b. to the true knowledge,		15:13
b. to a knowledge of their error	3Ne	1:25
that he b. our fathers out of		5:20
whom he b. out of that land)		5:20
taken and b. up before the judge		6:26
had b. so great iniquity upon		7: 9
who were b. unto repentance		7:24
father Lehi b. out of Jerusalem?		10:17
may be b. in, or may be		16: 4
be b. to a knowledge of me,		16: 4
as they were b. forth unto him.		17: 9
their little children should be b.		17:11
So they b. their little children		17:12
they had all been b. unto him.		17:12
that when they had all been b.,		17:13
wine, b. by the disciples,		20: 6
be b. to the knowledge of the		20:13

And then shall be b. to pass	3Ne	20:36
Nephi had b. forth the records,		23: 8
may be b. again unto this people,		26: 8
hath b. to pass the redemption	Mrm	7: 7
shall be b. out of darkness		8:16
it shall be b. out of the earth,		8:16
b. to stand before the Lamb		9: 2
shall be b. to see your nakedness		9: 5
are b. back into the presence of		9:13
are b. back into my presence;	Eth	3:13
which b. to pass the saying of		7: 5
they would be b. into captivity.		7: 5
prison and b. out their father,		7:18
people were b. unto repentance.		7:25
fathers b. across the great deep?		8: 9
b. peace again unto his father.		10: 3
and Seth was b. into captivity,		11: 9
by which he b. their fathers.		11:21
as Joseph b. his father down		13: 7
the Lord b. a remnant of the		13: 7
save they b. forth fruit meet	Mro	6: 1
should be b. under condemnation;		9: 6
and I am b. forth triumphant		10:34
b. the children of Israel through	DC	8: 3
soul that you have b. unto me		18:16
the Lord, have b. you together		62: 6
being b. up in subjection to		74: 4
b. forth by the resurrection of		76:39
have b. the whole church under		84:55
The Lord hath b. again Zion;		84:99
Which was b. to pass by the faith		84:99
hath b. down Zion from above.		84:100
hath b. up Zion from beneath.		84:100
and b. forth her strength;		84:101
is b. to pass the resurrection		88:14
and are b. under condemnation		90: 5
may not be b. into disrepute		90:23
that he be not b. into judgment		98:28
be b. any more as a testimony		98:48
which ye have b. before me		103:24
is b. to pass unto you through		103:36
this cannot be b. to pass until		105:11
be b. thus far for a trial of		105:19
b. before a general assembly of		107:32
their works may be b. to naught,		109:30
many high ones shall be b. low,		112: 8
with whom we shall be b. to stand,		123: 7
b. judgment upon all people;		133:50
has b. forth the Book of Mormon,		135: 3
has b. forth the revelations and		135: 3
And the earth b. forth grass,	Mses	2:12
waters b. forth abundantly,		2:21
and b. her unto the man.		3:22
Cain b. of the fruit of the		5:19
Abel he also b. of the firstlings		5:20
have b. upon themselves death;		6:29
an host of men hath he b. in		6:44
was b. forth out of the water.		6:64
and b. her unto the man.	Abr	5:16
and b. them unto Adam to see		5:20

BROW

an iron sinew, and thy b. brass;	1Ne	20: 4
bread by the sweat of his b.,	Mses	5: 1

BRUISE

Yet it pleased the Lord to b. him;	Mos	14:10
and he shall b. thy head,	Mses	4:21
and thou shalt b. his heel.		4:21

BRUISED

he was b. for our iniquities;	Mos	14: 5

BRUISES

an herb for b. and all sick cattle,	DC	89: 8

BRUNSON, Seymour

Stanton and my servant B.;	DC	75:33
B. I have taken unto myself;		124:132

BRUTAL

they are alike b. sparing none,	Mro	9:19
shot after they were dead, in a b.	DC	135: 1

BRUTALITY

fallen victims to their awful b.	Mro	9:17

BUCKLER

will be their shield and their b.;	DC	35:14

BUCKLERS

and with shields, and with b.,	3Ne	3:26

BUD

solitary places to b. and to	DC	117: 7

BUFFETINGS

over to the b. of Satan	DC	78:12
over to the b. of Satan		82:21
cannot escape the b. of Satan		104: 9
him over unto the b. of Satan;		104:10
delivered unto the b. of Satan		132:26

BUILD

that I was about to b. a ship,	1Ne	17:17
thinketh that he can b. a ship;		17:17
believe that I could b. a ship;		17:18
me that I should b. a ship.		17:49
me, that I should b. a ship?		17:51
did I b. the ship after the manner		18: 2
but I did b. it after the manner		18: 2
teach my people to b. buildings,	2Ne	5:15
And I, Nephi, did b. a temple;		5:16
we will b. with hewn stones;		19:10
stone upon which they might b.	Jac	4:15
upon which the Jews can b.		4:16
can ever b. upon it,		4:17
And we began to b. buildings,	Mos	9: 8
and began to b. buildings;		23: 5
that they should b. sanctuaries,	Al	22: 7
to b. with our own hands;		32: 5
to b. many cities on the north,		50:15
b. a breastwork of timbers upon		53: 4
to b. with their own hands.		53: 5
they did b. houses of cement,	He	3: 7
have timber to b. their houses,		3: 9
that they might b. many cities,		3:11
ye must b. your foundation;		5:12
a foundation whereon if men b.		5:12
b. a tower sufficiently high that		6:28
b. up unto themselves idols		6:31
did b. them up and support them,		6:38
to b. up their waste places,		11:20
there b. up another,	3Ne	7:12
they may b. a city, which shall		21:23
that they did b. cities again	4Ne	1: 7
they began to b. up churches		1:26
to b. up many churches		1:34
continue to b. up churches		1:41
to b. up the secret oaths and		1:42
and b. up again my church,	Mrm	3: 2
why do ye b. up your secret		8:40
and did b. barges, in which they	Eth	2: 6
Go to work and b., after the		2:16
of Noah did b. up his kingdom		7:19
and did b. many mighty cities,		9:23
to b. up again a broken people.		10: 1
did b. up a righteous kingdom;		10: 2
his father did b. up many cities		10: 4
did b. many spacious buildings.		10: 5
and he did b. many prisons,		10: 6
b. up a holy city unto the Lord,		13: 8
have received but to b. it up.	DC	10:52
I say this to b. up my church,		10:54
b. up churches unto themselves		10:56
b. up the kingdom of the devil—		10:56
but they shall b. it up,		10:62
B. upon my rock, which is		11:24
if you shall b. up my church,		18: 5
b. it up unto the most holy faith.		21: 2
power to b. up my church		30: 6
this rock I will b. my church;		33:13
and to b. up my church,		39:13
ye shall b. up my church in		42: 8
or to b. up my church,		42:11
repent, b. up churches unto me.		45:64
not b. upon another's foundation,		52:33

BUILD   146   BUILT

And let them b. up churches,	DC 58:48
sent forth to b. up my church.	84:32
a committee to b. mine houses,	94:15
that you should b. a house,	95: 8
will that you should b. a house.	95:11
you shall have power to b. it.	95:11
I design to b. mine holy house.	96: 2
my people b. a house unto me	97:15
b. up the waste places of Zion—	101:18
and b. a tower, that one may	101:45
and began to b. a tower.	101:46
may b. them up unto my name	101:64
They shall b., and another shall	101:101
b. up the waste places of Zion.	103:11
b. up the church, and regulate	107:33
to b. a house to thy name in	109: 2
thou didst command us to b.	109: 4
of our substance to b. a house to	109: 5
to b. a holy city to thy name,	109:58
I command you to b. a house unto	115: 8
let my people labor diligently to b.	115:10
if my people b. it not according	115:15
if my people do b. it according	115:16
b. a house unto my name, such	124:22
b. a house to my name, for the	124:27
wherein ye are not able to b. a	124:30
saints, to b. a house unto me;	124:31
unto you a sufficient time to b.	124:31
have had sufficient time to b. a	124:33
that he should b. a tabernacle,	124:38
b. a house in the land of promise,	124:38
to b. unto my holy name.	124:39
ye shall b. it on the place where	124:43
which I have chosen for you to b.	124:43
if you b. a house unto my name,	124:47
whom I commanded to b. up a	124:51
command you again to b. a house	124:55
to b. for the boarding of strangers,	124:56
I, the Lord, will b. up Kirtland,	124:83
whom I have appointed to b.	124:111
b. a house for my servant Joseph,	124:115
when you b. it unto my name,	124:145
and b. up cities unto my name,	125: 2
b. up a city unto my name upon	125: 3
and upon this rock I will b. my	128:10
man shall seek to b. up himself,	136:19

BUILDED
And he b. a city, and he	Mses 5:42

BUILDETH
confoundeth them, and b. a ship.	1Ne 1:hd
and whoso b. upon this	3Ne 11:39
upon this b. upon my rock,	11:39
he b. upon a sandy foundation,	11:40
whoso b. it up seeketh to	Eth 8:25
He that b. upon this rock shall	DC 50:44
Who b. up at his own will and	63: 4

BUILDING
when they were b. a tower	TPg
a great and spacious b.;	1Ne 8:26
that great and spacious b.	8:31
enter into that strange b.	8:33
they did enter into that b.	8:33
a large and spacious b.,	11:35
building, like unto the b.	11:35
the great and spacious b.	11:36
the large and spacious b.,	12:18
b. large cities and villages	Mos 27: 6
back to the b. of the great tower,	28:17
b. walls of stone to encircle them	Al 48: 8
shipping and their b. of ships,	He 3:14
and their b. of temples, and of	3:14
and b. houses of worship,	DC 42:35
b. up of the New Jerusalem	42:35
b. of a house for the presidency,	94: 3
for the b. of a house unto me,	94:10
the b. of mine house;	95: 3
reserved for the b. of my houses,	104:34
the b. up of the city of my saints,	104:36
the lot and b. on which the	104:39

laid off for the b. of my house,	DC 104:43
purpose of b. up my church	104:59
b. up the church and regulating	107:34
the b. of a house unto my name;	115:13
on the b.-spot of my house, saith	118: 5
For the b. of mine house, and	119: 2
where you have contemplated b.	124:43
quorum for the purpose of b. that	124:62
stock for the b. of that house.	124:63
stock into their hands for the b.	124:72
their labors which they do in b.	124:121
than that of b. his kingdom;	JS 2:46

BUILDINGS
I did teach my people to build b.,	2Ne 5:15
and b. shall fall upon them	26: 5
fine workmanship of wood, in b.,	Jar 1: 8
ruins of b. of every kind,	Mos 8: 8
And we began to build b.,	9: 8
many elegant and spacious b.;	11: 8
he caused many b. to be built	11:13
and began to build b.;	23: 5
and all manner of their b.	He 3: 9
b. thereof had fallen to the earth,	3Ne 8:14
had become covered with b.,	Mrm 1: 7
he did build many spacious b.	Eth 10: 5
in b., and in gold and silver,	10:12
the b. of the temple,	JS 1: 2

BUILDING-SPOT: *see BUILDING and SPOT.*

BUILT
he b. an altar of stones,	1Ne 2: 7
b. up among the children of men,	22:22
which are b. up to get gain,	22:23
b. up to get power over the	22:23
who are b. up to become popular	22:23
not b. of so many precious things;	2Ne 5:16
b. like unto Solomon's temple.	5:16
and b. a tower in the midst of it,	15: 2
they have b. up many churches;	26:20
there are many churches b. up	26:21
the churches which are b. up,	28: 3
say that hath b. up churches,	28: 3
he that is b. upon the rock	28:28
he that is b. upon a sandy	28:28
king Noah b. many elegant and	Mos 11: 8
he also b. him a spacious palace,	11: 9
he caused a breastwork to be b.	11:11
he b. a tower near the temple;	11:12
he caused many buildings to be b.	11:13
he caused a great tower to be b.	11:13
and he b. winepresses,	11:15
they b. a city, which they called	23:20
there having been a city b.,	Al 6: 7
b. after the manner of the Jews.	16:13
of Amulon had b. a great city,	21: 2
for they had b. synagogues	21: 4
we have b. sanctuaries, and we	21: 6
there should be synagogues b.	21:20
Zoramites had b. synagogues,	31:12
a place b. up in the center of	31:13
or had b. forts of security,	49:13
works of timbers b. up to the	50: 2
should be a frame of pickets b.	50: 3
places of security to be b.	50: 4
he had also b. a stronghold to	53: 6
b. him an exceedingly large	63: 5
this man b. other ships.	63: 7
of the rock upon which ye are b.,	He 5:12
that fortifications should be b.	3Ne 3:14
there were many cities b. anew,	6: 7
and is not b. upon my rock;	11:40
who b. his house upon a rock—	14:24
who b. his house upon the sand—	14:26
for ye are b. upon my rock.	18:12
these are not b. upon my rock,	18:13
are b. upon a sandy foundation;	18:13
that they are b. upon my gospel.	27: 8
that ye are b. upon my gospel;	27: 9
the church is b. upon my gospel	27:10
if it be not b. upon my gospel,	27:11

BUILT 147 BURNED

and is b. upon the works of men,	3Ne	27:11
Zarahemla did they cause to be b.	4Ne	1: 8
churches b. up that shall say:	Mrm	8:32
why have ye b. up churches unto		8:33
barges which ye have hitherto b.	Eth	2:16
b. barges after the manner		2:16
the manner which they had b.,		2:16
they were b. after a manner that		2:17
are b. up to get power and gain—		8:23
also upon those who b. it up.		8:24
for it is b. up by the devil,		8:25
Morianton b. up many cities,		10:12
they b. a great city by the narrow		10:20
was b. up to get power and gain;		11:15
it should be b. up again,		13: 5
but it should be b. up again,		13: 5
be b. unto the house of Israel.		13: 5
a New Jerusalem should be b.		13: 6
the house of Joseph shall be b.		13: 8
synagogue which they had b. for	Mro	7: 1
for if ye are b. upon my rock,	DC	6:34
church to be b. up unto me,		22: 3
which shall be b. up on the earth.		27: 4
where the city Zion shall be b.,		28: 9
yea, upon this rock ye are b.,		33:13
should have a house b.,		41: 7
the New Jerusalem shall be b.		42:62
have b. the city of Jerusalem in		77:15
Which city shall be b., beginning		84: 3
shall be b. by the gathering of		84: 4
house shall be b. unto the Lord,		84: 5
house shall be b. unto the Lord		84:31
b. up my church unto me.		84:108
that it shall be b. fifty-five by		94: 4
two houses are not to be b. until		94:16
let the house be b., not after		95:13
let it be b. after the manner		95:14
a house should be b. unto me		97:10
Yea, let it be b. speedily,		97:11
that there may be a house b.		97:12
and b. a hedge round about,		101:46
and b. the hedge round about,		101:53
b. the tower also, and set a		101:53
countries, when they are b. up,		101:74
the heavens, and b. the earth,		104:14
Zion cannot be b. up unless it is		105: 5
b. unto my name in the land of		105:33
which we have b. unto thy name;		109:78
with their might, b. this house		110: 6
let a house be b. unto my name		115:14
Far West should be b. up speedily		115:17
healthful habitation if it be b. unto		124:24
in a house which you have b.		124:37
this house be b. unto my name,		124:40
the place whereon it shall be b.		124:42
let it be b. unto my name, and let		124:56
he b. a city that was called	Mses	7:19
saw that Noah b. an ark;		7:43
the altar which was b. in the	Abr	1: 8
b. an altar in the land of		2:17
which I had b. unto the Lord,		2:20
there I b. another altar unto		2:20
he had b. unto the Lord.	Fac	2: 2
that Zion will be b. upon this	AoF	10

BULL
as a wild b. in a net,	2Ne	8:20

BUNDLES
lo, the tares are bound in b.,	DC	86: 7
the earth; she is bound in b.;		88:94
the tares shall be bound in b.,		101:66

BURDEN
hast broken the yoke of his b.,	2Ne	19: 4
his b. shall be taken away		20:27
The b. of Babylon,		23: 1
his b. depart from off their		24:25
that king Ahaz died was this b.		24:28
but that the b. should come upon	Mos	29:34
did ease the b. of the people,	Eth	10:10
on them have I laid the b.	DC	112:18

BURDENED
and to be driven to and fro, and b.,	Mos	21:13

BURDENETH
Wherefore, it b. my soul	Jac	2: 9

BURDENS
have b. lashed upon their backs;	Mos	12: 5
willing to bear one another's b.,		18: 8
put heavy b. upon their backs,		21: 3
that they began to ease their b.;		21:15
I will also ease the b. which		24:14
the b. which were laid upon Alma		24:15
that they could bear up their b.		24:15
unto them, and eased their b.,		24:21
that your b. may be light,	Al	33:23
because of their grievous b.	DC	109:48

BURDENSOME
not become b. to his people,	Mos	6: 7

BURIAL
not be joined with them in b.,	2Ne	24:20
his death or b. we know not of.	Al	45:18
concerning his death and b.		45:19
at the b. of the great chief judge	He	9:10
also gathered together at the b.		9:11
liberated on the day of the b.		9:18
Coriantumr should receive a b.	Eth	13:21
after the manner of his b.,	DC	76:51

BURIED
Ishmael died, and was b.	1Ne	16:34
to be b. in a sepulchre,		19:10
he died, and was b.	2Ne	4:12
and Helam was b. in the water;	Mos	18:14
b. those who had been slain—	Al	3: 1
they b. their weapons of peace,		24:19
or they b. the weapons of war,		24:19
have b. their weapons of war		26:32
their dead were b. by the people		30: 1
after they had b. their dead,		30: 2
are b. in the depths of the sea,		44:22
or b. by the hand of the Lord,		45:19
and had b. our dead and also		57:28
upon that city, that it be b. up—	He	12:17
they have b. their weapons of war,		15: 9
been b. up in that great city	3Ne	8:25
b. up in the depths of the earth;		9: 6
b. up in the depths of the earth,		9: 8
not sunk and b. up in the earth;		10:13
b. in the depths of the sea,	Eth	6: 6
when they were b. in the deep		6: 7
b. in the water in his name,	DC	76:51

BURLINGTON
also unto the inhabitants of B.,	DC	124:88

BURN
shall b. and shall devour his	2Ne	20:17
the day that cometh shall b.		26: 4
cast into the fire and b. them,	Jac	5: 9
perhaps they will b. us also.	Al	14:12
therefore they b. us not.		14:13
and did cause their hearts to b.	3Ne	11: 3
cometh that shall b. as an oven;		25: 1
day that cometh shall b. them up,		25: 1
and he did b. the cities.	Eth	14:17
your bosom shall b. within you;	DC	9: 8
and I will b. them up,		29: 9
and I will b. them up, for I am		64:24
cometh that shall b. as an oven,		133:64
day that cometh shall b. them up,		133:64
will b. up the dry trees to purify		135: 6
cometh that shall b. as an oven,	JS	2:37
do wickedly shall b. as stubble;		2:37
they that come shall b. them,		2:37

BURNED
that they were b. with fire;	1Ne	12: 4
day cometh that they must be b.		22:15
into the fire that they may be b.	Jac	5: 7
into the fire that they should be b.		5:47

BURNED

will I cause to be b. with fire.	Jac	5:77
the world shall be b. with fire.		6: 3
be b. and destroyed by fire.	Al	14: 8
for fear lest they should be b.	He	5:23
Nephi and Lehi were not b.;		5:23
the midst of fire and were not b.		5:23
of fire, and that it b. them not,		5:24
were sunk, and many were b.,	3Ne	8:14
b. in that great city Zarahemla.		8:24
great city Zarahemla have I b.		9: 3
have I caused to be b. with fire		9: 9
I did cause them to be b.,		9: 9
have I caused to be b. with fire,		9:10
and they were not b. by fire,		10:13
where there had been cities b.	4Ne	1: 7
and cities were b. with fire;	Mrm	5: 5
which is white already to be b.	DC	31: 4
the tares that they may be b.;		38:12
shall not be b. at his coming.		64:23
and the field remaineth to be b.		86: 7
therefore, she is ready to be b.		88:94
may be b. with unquenchable fire.		101:66

BURNETH

wickedness b. as the fire;	2Ne	19:18
which b. with fire and brimstone,	DC	63:17
be as the melting fire that b.,		133:41

BURNETT, Stephen

Eames and my servant B.;	DC	75:35
Lord unto you my servant B.:		80: 1

BURNING

b. instead of beauty.	2Ne	13:24
and by the spirit of b.		14: 4
shall be with b. and fuel of fire.		19: 5
under his glory he shall kindle a b.		20:16
a burning like the b. of a fire.		20:16
me out of an everlasting b.,	Mos	27:28
sick at Sidom, with a b. fever,	Al	15: 3
to be scorched with a b. heat.		15: 3
being very low with a b. fever;		15: 5
your lamps trimmed and b.,	DC	33:17
For after today cometh the b.—		64:24
the day of vengeance and b.,		85: 3
be prepared against the day of b.		109:46
a day of wrath, a day of b.,		112:24
frost melteth before the b. rays		121:11
unto me out of the b. bush,	Mses	1:17

BURNT

offer sacrifice and b. offerings	1Ne	5: 9
offer sacrifice and b. offerings		7:22
offer sacrifice and b. offerings	Mos	2: 3
sacrifices and your b. offerings	3Ne	9:19
sacrifices and b. offerings.		9:19

BURR: *see RIGGS BURR.*

BURROUGHS', Philip

labor shall be at your brother B.	DC	30:10

BURST

strength that I may b. these bands	1Ne	7:17
great and glorious vision b. upon	DC	110:13

BURTHEN

Nephites relieved from a great b.;	Al	62:29

BURTHENS

But the word of God b. me	Jac	2:23

BURY

did help to b. their dead.	Mos	9:19
not b. himself again in the water.		18:15
rise again; therefore b. him not.	Al	19: 8
will b. them deep in the earth,		24:16
did b. them up deep in the earth.		24:17
did also b. their weapons of war,		25:14
to go forth and b. their dead,		53: 1
there was none left to b. the dead,	Eth	14:22
neither shalt thou b. thy talent	DC	60:13

BURYING

they had finished b. their dead	Al	3: 1
for the purpose of b. their dead.		19: 1
had finished b. their dead and		53: 3

BUSH

unto me out of the burning b.,	Mses	1:17

BUSHEL

a candle and put it under a b.?	3Ne	12:15

BUSHES

upon all thorns, and upon all b.	2Ne	17:19

BUSINESS

to do your b. by the voice of	Mos	29:26
having had much b. that I could	Al	7: 1
much b. to do among the people.		10:31
whatever church b. is necessary	DC	20:62
be employed in doing this b.		51:14
shall return upon his b., and to		64:18
will of the Lord is the Lord's b.		64:29
this is their b. in the church		70: 5
his secular b. as he shall direct.		84:113
shall be your b. and mission		90:16
do their b. in their own name,		104:49
do your b. in your own name,		104:50
church laws respecting church b.—		107:59
to do the b. of the church, to sit		107:72
most important b. of the church,		107:78
he settle up all his b. as soon		114: 1
let them settle up their b. speedily		117: 1
to all those with whom I have b.,		127: 1
clerks who will transact all b.		127: 1
at all times, and to do all the b.		128: 3

BUT: *see in the APPENDIX.*

BUTTER

B. and honey shall he eat,	2Ne	17:15
he shall eat b.;		17:22
for b. and honey shall every one		17:22

BUTTERFIELD, Josiah

Joseph Young, B., Daniel Miles	DC	124:138

BUY

he that hath no money, come b.	2Ne	9:50
yea, come b. wine and milk		9:50
b. milk and honey, without money		26:25
one with another, to b. and to sell,	He	6: 8
and they did b. and sell and	Eth	10:22
let them b. for the present time	DC	48: 3
disciples are enabled to b. lands.		57: 5
to b. land in all the regions		57: 6
may obtain money to b. lands		57: 8
may b. lands and gather together		101:74

BY: *see in the APPENDIX.*

BY-WORD: *see BY and WORD.*

CAESAR

render unto C. the things which	DC	63:26

CAESAR'S

Caesar the things which are C.	DC	63:26

CAHOON, Reynolds

Let my servants C. and	DC	52:30
only let my servant C., and		61:35
Hyrum Smith and my servant C.;		75:32
my servants C. and Jared Carter		94:14

CAIN

same being who did plot with C.,	He	6:27
plot with C. and his followers		6:27
been handed down even from C.,	Eth	8:15
unto me as the offerings of C.,	DC	124:75
and she conceived and bare B.,	Mses	5:16
C. hearkened not, saying:		5:16
but C. was a tiller of the ground.		5:17
C. loved Satan more than God.		5:18

CAIN 149 CALL

C. brought of the fruit of the	Mses 5:19	go to, and c. servants, that we	Jac	5:61
But unto C., and to his offering,	5:21	that which ye c. the gospel,		7: 6
And C. was very wroth, and his	5:21	and if I, whom ye c. your king,	Mos	2:18
And the Lord said unto C.:	5:22	also, if I, whom ye c. your king,		2:19
abominations were had from C.;	5:25	even I, whom ye c. your king,		2:26
C. was wroth, and listened not	5:26	I would c. your attention,		3: 1
because of C. and his brethren.	5:27	I would again c. your attention,		4: 4
C. took one of his brothers'	5:28	name by which he shall c. you.		5:12
And Satan said unto C.:	5:29	and did c. upon me for protection.		9:15
And Satan sware unto C. that he	5:30	they would not c. upon the Lord		26: 4
And C. said: Truly I am	5:31	the good shepherd doth c. you;	Al	5:38
C. was called Master Mahan,	5:31	in his own name he doth c. you,		5:38
And C. went into the field,	5:32	good shepherd doth c. after you;		5:60
C. talked with Abel, his brother.	5:32	to c. their lands, and their cities,		8: 7
C. rose up against Abel,	5:32	unto all who c. on his name.		9:17
And C. gloried in that which	5:33	that time forth to c. on his name;		12:30
And the Lord said unto C.:	5:34	But God did c. on men, in the		12:33
And C. said unto the Lord:	5:38	the Lord, and c. on his holy name,		13:28
I the Lord set a mark upon C.,	5:40	to c. on his name and confess		17: 4
And C. was shut out from the	5:41	did c. on the name of the Lord,		19:16
And C. knew his wife,	5:42	and c. on his name in faith,		22:16
C. shall be avenged sevenfold,	5:48	they should go and c. the people,		22:21
Satan, after the manner of C.,	5:49	to c. on the name of the Lord;		24:21
administered unto C. by Satan;	5:49	the great c. of diligence of men		28:14
slew him, not like unto C.,	5:50	things which ye c. prophecies,		30:14
from the days of C., there was	5:51	they did c. the day of the Lord;		31:12
instead of Abel, whom C. slew.	6: 2	ye begin to c. upon his holy name,		34:17
save it was the seed of C.,	7:22	thing which our fathers c. a ball,		37:38
for the seed of C. were black,	7:22	c. upon his holy name.	He	3:27
		or that which ye do c. so.	3Ne	3: 2
CAINAN		shall c. on the name of their God		4:30
called upon C. in the wilderness	DC 107:45	a man whom they did c. Jacob;		7: 9
called Seth, Enos, C., Mahalaleel,	107:53	And they did c. him their king;		7:10
lived ninety years, and begat C.	Mses 6:17	may c. on the Father in my name.		21:27
son, whom he had named B.	6:17	all nations shall c. you blessed,		24:12
Enos lived, after he begat C.,	6:18	now we c. the proud happy;		24:15
And C. lived seventy years,	6:19	whereby we shall c. this church;		27: 3
C. lived after he begat Mahalaleel	6:19	shall c. the church in my name;		27: 7
all the days of C. were nine	6:19	c. upon the Father in my name		27: 7
came out from the land of C.,	6:41	ye shall c. whatsoever things ye		27: 9
journeyed from the land of C.,	6:42	call whatsoever things ye do c.,		27: 9
		if ye c. upon the Father, for		27: 9
CAINHANNOCH		and c. it the Book of Mormon.	Mrm	1: 1
write speedily to C. [New York]	DC 104:81	to c. upon the name of the Lord.	Eth	2:14
		did c. upon the name of the Lord		2:15
CALAMITY		that we must c. upon thee,		3: 2
this the great c. of my people,	Mrm 2:27	c. upon the Father in my name,		4:15
the c. of the house of Israel;	5:11	Ye shall c. on the Father in my	Mro	2: 2
was great c. in all the land,	Eth 11: 6	is to c. men unto repentance,		7:31
the c. which should come upon	DC 1:17	not to c. the righteous but		8: 8
And c. shall cover the mocker,	45:50	whom I shall c. and ordain,	DC	5:11
deliver thy people from the c. of	109:46	and c. them to his holy work		20:11
now cometh the day of their b.,	136:35	c. upon the Father in solemn		20:76
		c. upon me in mighty prayer.		29: 2
CALCULATED		c. laborers into my vineyard.		33: 3
c. to secure the public interest;	DC 134: 5	I c. upon the weak things of		35:13
		c. on the holy prophets to prove		35:23
CALEB		in Ohio c. upon me in much faith,		39:16
received it under the hand of C.;	DC 84: 7	c. faithful laborers into my		39:17
C. received it under the hand of	84: 8	and sleep until I shall c. again.		43:18
		C. upon the nations to repent,		43:20
CALF		and c. upon you to repent,		43:21
and the c. and the young lion	2Ne 21: 6	c. upon the inhabitants of the		43:28
and the c., and the young lion,	30:12	which ye c. the house of God,		45:18
a golden c. for the worship of my	DC 124:84	c. upon the inhabitants to repent,		45:64
		and c. upon the rich, the high		58:47
CALL		that c. yourselves the people of		63: 1
They c. the place Bountiful.	1Ne 1:hd	c. upon his holy name,		65: 4
did c. the name of the place Shazer.	16:13	C. upon the Lord, that his		65: 5
we did c. it the promised land.	18:23	C. upon the inhabitants of the		71: 4
they c. themselves of the holy city,	20: 2	c. upon them to meet you both		71: 7
I c. unto them and they stand up	20:13	Ye c. upon my name for		82: 4
that which ye c. anger	2Ne 1:26	henceforth I shall c. you friends,		84:77
c. the name of the place Nephi;	5: 8	States will c. on other nations,		87: 3
wherefore, we did c. it Nephi.	5: 8	shall also c. upon other nations,		87: 3
c. themselves the people of Nephi.	5: 9	c. upon me while I am near—		88:62
which I c. the death of the body,	9:10	and c. a solemn assembly,		88:70
Wo unto them that c. evil good,	15:20	c. on the Lord and ponder the		88:71
and shall c. his name Immanuel.	17:14	of the Lord shall c. them,		88:85
C. his name, Maher-shalal-hash-baz.	18: 3	friends, c. your solemn assembly,		88:117
Praise the Lord, c. upon his name,	22: 4	I will c. you friends, for you		93:45
but I shall c. them Lamanites	Jac 1:14	should c. your solemn assembly,		95: 7
I shall c. Nephites, or the people of	1:14	c. upon the name of the Lord,		100:17

CALL 150 CALLED

all they who c. on my name,	DC 101:22	the voice by which ye shall be c.,	Mos	5:12
who c. themselves after my name,	101:75	not the name by which ye are c.		5:14
who c. themselves after my name;	101:97	the things are c. interpreters,		8:13
and c. upon the twelve councilors	102:19	look in them, the same is c. seer.		8:13
power to c. and organize a council	102:24	he shall be c. the Son of God,		15: 2
be sufficient to c. such council.	102:28	of Christ-for so shall he be c.		15:21
to c. such a council or not.	102:29	having never c. upon the Lord		16:12
who c. themselves after my name	103: 4	to a place which was c. Mormon,		18: 4
among you shall c. it his own,	104:62	Mormon (for thus were they c.)		18: 8
faithful and c. upon my name,	104:82	and to be c. his people,		18: 8
of the traveling high council to c.	107:38	they were c. the church of God,		18:17
power to c. other high priests,	107:79	and they c. the land Helam.		23:19
saying-C. your solemn assembly,	109: 6	which they c. the city of Helam.		23:20
God should c. in the last days,	113: 8	in a place which they c. Amulon;		23:31
promise which shall c. him forth	123: 6	Laman, being c. after the name of		24: 3
I am about to c. upon them to	124: 6	therefore he was c. king Laman.		24: 3
C. ye, therefore, upon them with	124: 7	and they c. the valley Alma,		24:20
who c. themselves by my name	125: 2	no longer be c. by the names of		25:12
bad, as you may choose to c. it.	127: 2	might be c. the children of Nephi		25:12
C. your solemn assemblies, and	133: 6	among those who were c. Nephites.		25:12
every man c. upon the name of	133: 6	different bodies, being c. churches;		25:21
c. upon all nations, first upon the	133: 8	they were c. the people of God.		25:24
sorrowful, c. on the Lord thy God	136:29	for in my name shall they be c.;		26:18
I did c. upon by mine angels,	136:37	behold, in my name are they c.;		26:24
C. upon God in the name of mine	Mses 1:17	being c. Alma, after his father;		27: 8
I sill not cease to c. upon God,	1:18	has these things is c. seer,		28:16
to see what he would c. them;	3:19	which ye are c. to consider—		29: 5
and c. upon God in the name of	5: 8	people who were c. the Nephites;		29:44
ceased not to c. upon God.	5:16	a certain man, being c. Amlici,	Al	2: 1
c. upon the name of the Lord,	6: 4	of Amlici, being c. Amlicites,		2:11
to c. upon all the people,	7:12	the remainder were c. Nephites,		2:11
c. upon the children of Noah;	7:51	being c. after that Gideon who		2:20
to see what he would c. them;	Abr 5:20	c. Zeram, and Amnor, and Manti,		2:22
as they were pleased to c. it,	JS 2: 6	which was c. Hermounts;		2:37
all my powers to c. upon God	2:16	was c. under that head,		3:10
messenger, should c. for them,	2:59	were c. the Nephites, or the		3:11
he would c. for them.	2:60	shall no more be c. thy seed;		3:17
		whomsoever shall be c. thy seed,		3:17
CALLED		was c. the land of Mormon;		5: 3
being c., (beginning at the eldest)	1Ne 1:hd	if ye were c. to die at this time,		5:27
he c. the name of the river,	2: 8	a shepherd hath c. after you		5:37
I c. after them, and they did	4:29	to the name by which ye are c.,		5:38
they are c. the plates of Nephi,	9: 2	am c. to speak after this manner,		5:44
also are c. the plates of Nephi.	9: 2	is the order after which I am c.,		5:49
the twelve c. by the angel	11:34	which was c. the city of Gideon,		6: 7
in the valley which he c. Lemuel.	16: 6	in the valley that was c. Gideon,		6: 7
in the place which was c. Nahom.	16:34	c. after the man who was slain		6: 7
the land which we c. Bountiful,	17: 5	holy order by which he was c.		6: 8
the sea, which we c. Irreantum,	17: 5	by which he had been c.;		8: 4
we c. the place Bountiful, because	17: 6	city which was c. Ammonihah.		8: 6
the elder was c. Jacob and the	18: 7	the city which was c. Aaron.		8:13
who are c. by the name of Israel,	20: 1	and the man was c. Amulek;		8:21
wast c. a transgressor from the	20: 8	I have been c. to preach the word		8:24
O Jacob, and Israel my c.,	20:12	who are c. the people of Nephi,		9:19
yea, I have c. him to declare,	20:15	for I was c. many times and		10: 6
Lord hath c. me from the womb;	21: 1	which is c. a temporal death;		11:42
his name shall be c. after me;	2Ne 3:15	being c. and prepared from		13: 3
he c. the children of Laman,	4: 3	are c. with a holy calling,		13: 3
who were now c. Lamanites	5:14	have been c. to this holy calling		13: 4
those who were c. my people.	5:14	being c. by this holy calling,		13: 6
I, Jacob, having been c. of God,	6: 2	being c. with a holy calling,		13: 8
when I c., yea, there was none	7: 2	they were c. after this holy order,		13:11
I c. him alone, and blessed him.	8: 2	he was c. the prince of peace,		13:18
only let us be c. by thy name	14: 1	it was c. Desolation of Nehors;		16:11
shall be c. holy, every one that	14: 3	c. after the sons of Ishmael,		17:19
his name shall be c., Wonderful,	19: 6	which was c. the water of Sebus,		17:26
I have also c. my mighty ones,	23: 3	and I am c. by his Holy Spirit		18:34
which are c. the people of Nephi.	Jac 1: 2	c. by the Lamanites, Jerusalem,		21: 1
c. by the people, second Nephi,	1:11	city, which was c. Jerusalem.		21: 2
thus they were c. by the people,	1:11	village which was c. Ani-Anti,		21:11
they were c. Nephites, Jacobites,	1:13	the Spirit of the Lord has c. him		22: 4
plates are c. the plates of Jacob,	3:14	land which they c. Bountiful.		22:29
he c. up his servants, and said	5:75	land which they c. Desolation,		22:30
which is c. the land of Zarahemla.	Om 1:13	northward was c. Desolation,		22:31
were c. the people of Zarahemla.	1:14	southward was c. Bountiful,		22:31
and he c. their names Mosiah,	Mos 1: 2	that they c. their names		23:17
Behold, ye have c. me your king;	2:18	and they were c. by this name		23:17
And he shall be c. Jesus Christ,	3: 8	and were no more c. Lamanites.		23:17
and his mother shall be c. Mary.	3: 8	he c. his name Anti-Nephi-Lehi.		24: 3
shall be c. the children of Christ,	5: 7	they were c. by the Nephites		27:26
know the name by which he is c.;	5: 9	the work to which I have been c.?		29: 6
shall be c. by the name of Christ.	5: 9	and that same God hath c. me by		29:13
must be c. by some other name;	5:10	and c. themselves Zoramites,		30:59

CALLED

land which they c. Antionum,	Al	31: 3
was c. by them Rameumptom,		31:21
has c. upon the words of Zenos,		34: 7
or our fathers c. it Liahona,		37:38
ministry unto which ye were c.,		39:16
happiness, which is c. paradise,		40:12
are c. of God to preach the word		42:31
of God by which they were c.		43: 2
were c. the people of Ammon—		43:11
be c. the disciples of the Lord;		45:14
(and he c. it the title of liberty)		46:13
c. by those who did not belong to		46:14
or Christians as they were c.,		46:15
who were c. Amalickiahites.		46:28
the place which was c. Onidah,		47: 5
the mount which was c. Antipas,		47: 7
which was c. by their enemies		48:10
c. the name of the city Moroni;		50:13
and they c. the name of the city,		50:14
manner which they c. Lehi,		50:15
were c. king-men, for they were		51: 5
the men who were c. king-men		51:13
they c. themselves Nephites.		53:16
they are worthy to be c. sons)		56:10
as I had ever c. them my sons		56:46
Helaman, who was c. Helaman,		63:11
c. after the name of his father.		63:11
c. the book of Helaman,	He	1:hd
the land it was c. desolate.		3: 6
are no more c. the Nephites,		3:16
the land south was c. Lehi		6:10
the land north was c. Mulek,		6:10
they were c. Gadianton's robbers		6:18
were c. by the order of God;		8:18
places which are now c. valleys		14:23
who are c. the people of Nephi		15: 3
Nephites, and were c. Nephites.	3Ne	2:16
people who were c. Nephites,		3:24
were c. the plates of Nephi.		5:10
And behold, I am c. Mormon,		5:12
c. after the land of Mormon,		5:12
I have been c. of him to declare		5:13
who had been c. Lamanites,		10:18
And again the Lord c. others,		11:22
and to those who had been c.,		12: 1
number of them who had been c.,		12: 1
shall be c. the children of God.		12: 9
shall be c. the New Jerusalem.		21:23
of the whole earth shall he be c.		22: 5
For the Lord hath c. thee as		22: 6
were c. the church of Christ.		26:21
For by this name shall ye be c.		27: 5
save it be c. in my name?		27: 8
a church be c. in Moses: name		27: 8
if it be c. in the name of a man		27: 8
but if it be c. in my name then		27: 8
ministry, wherein thou hast c. us,		28: 2
who were c. the Nephites,	4Ne	1:36
were c. by the Lamanites—		1:36
were c. Nephites, and Jacobites,		1:37
c. Lamanites, and Lemuelites,		1:38
who were c. the people of Nephi		1:43
a hill which shall be c. Shim;	Mrm	1: 2
Ishmaelites were c. Lamanites,		1: 9
the land which was c. Shem.		2:20
a hill which was c. Cumorah,		6: 2
characters which are c. among		9:32
which is c. the Book of Ether.	Eth	1: 2
being c. after the mighty hunter)		2: 1
they c. the name of the place		2:13
which they c. the mount Shelem,		3: 1
they were c. Jacom, and Gilgah,		6:14
land which is c. Desolation		7: 6
a son who was c. Nimrod;		7:22
to a place which was c. Ablom,		9: 3
c. by the Nephites Zarahemla.		9:31
c. after the holy order of God.		12:10
the brother of Lib was c. Shiz.		14:17
in a place which was c. Ogath.		15:10
And he c. them by name, saying:	Mro	2: 2
were c. the elders of the church,		3: 1
and hath c. you to his ministry,		8: 2
c. upon my servant Joseph Smith,	DC	1:17

151

CALLED

and art again c. to the work;	DC	3:10
serve God ye are c. to the work;		4: 3
reap, the same is c. of God.		6: 4
the work which you are c. to do		9: 4
the work wherewith I have c. you,		9:14
reap, the same is c. of God.		11: 4
need not suppose that you are c.		11:15
called to preach until you are c.		11:15
reap, the same is c. of God.		12: 4
your might, and then you are c.		12: 9
reap, the same is c. of God.		14: 4
and thou art c. to assist;		14:11
c. him unto mine own purpose,		18: 8
c. even with that same calling		18: 9
calling with which he was c.		18: 9
you are c. to cry repentance unto		18:14
shall they be c. at the last day;		18:24
the name by which they are c.,		18:25
who are c. to declare my gospel,		18:26
are c. to go into all the world		18:28
the month which is c. April.—		20: 1
Joseph Smith, Jun., who was c.		20: 2
Oliver Cowdery, who was also c.		20: 3
church that a vote may be c.		20:66
The person who is c. of God		20:73
and in it thou shalt be c. a seer,		21: 1
of the month which is c. April.		21: 3
art not as yet c. to preach		23: 4
wast c. and chosen to write the		24: 1
art c. to prune my vineyard		24:19
elect lady, whom I have c.		25: 3
c. and ordained even as Aaron;		27: 8
c. to bring to pass the gathering		29: 7
whereunto you have been c.;		30: 2
are c. to lift up your voices		33: 2
c. forth out of the wilderness.		33: 5
c. of me to preach my gospel—		34: 5
are c. to preach my gospel		36: 1
art c. to labor in my vineyard,		39:13
not c. to go into the eastern		39:14
thou art c. to go to the Ohio.		39:14
of my church whom I have c.,		41: 2
c. my servant Edward Partridge;		41: 9
two or more, shall be c.,		42:44
I c. upon you by the mouth of		43:25
church should be c. together,		44: 1
voice while it is c. today,		45: 6
be c. the New Jerusalem,		45:66
unto it, and it shall be c. Zion.		45:67
until he is c. to further duties.		47: 1
whom he hath c. and chosen		52: 1
you have c. upon me that it		53: 1
thou art c. and chosen;		55: 1
which is now c. Independence		57: 3
let a conference meeting be c.;		58:58
the place which is c. St. Louis.		60: 5
now it is c. today until the		64:23
ye will labor while it is c. today.		64:25
c. by his ordination to proclaim		68: 1
provided he is c. and set apart		68:19
families of those who are c.		75:24
And was c. Perdition, for the		76:26
will of him who hath c. you,		80: 5
calling wherewith you are c.,		81: 1
and also many whom I have c.		84:32
the faithful who are c. of God,		84:86
was c. of God and appointed,		85: 8
of Great Britain, as it is c.,		87: 3
calling whereunto I have c. you,		88:80
serpent, who is c. the devil,		88:110
those who are c. to the		88:127
ye are c. to do this by prayer		88:137
who are or can be c. saints.		89: 3
c. you also to preside over Zion		90:32
thus he was c. the Son of God,		93:14
I c. you servants for the World's		93:46
among you, whom I have c.		95: 5
those who are c. to the work		97:13
thou art c. to go into the		99: 1
and they shall be c. stakes,		101:21
are c. to lay down their lives		101:35
c. unto mine everlasting gospel,		101:39
are c. to be the savor of men;		101:40

CALLED

c. upon his servants, and said	DC	101:52
be c. on the most difficult cases		102:28
can only be c. in question by the		102:32
shall be c. the United Order of		104:48
shall be c. the United Order of		104:48
c. the sacred treasury of the Lord;		104:66
for it shall not be c. his,		104:70
is c. the Melchizedek Priesthood		107: 2
day it was c. *the Holy Priesthood*.		107: 3
ancient days, c. that priesthood		107: 4
is c. the Priesthood of Aaron,		107:13
Why it is c. the lesser priesthood		107:14
provided he is c. and set apart		107:17
are c. to be the twelve Apostles,		107:23
The Seventy are also c. to preach		107:25
c. upon Cainan in the wilderness		107:45
to the death of Adam, he c.		107:53
c. him Michael, the prince,		107:54
he shall be c. President of the		107:65
the solemn assembly shall be c.		108: 4
in Zion, for thus it shall be c.,		115: 3
my church be c. in the last days,		115: 4
and it shall be c. most holy,		115: 7
many c., but few are chosen.		121:34
many are c., but few are chosen.		121:40
If thou art c. to pass through		122: 5
that you are now c. immediately		124: 2
that house be c. Nauvoo House;		124:60
c. to lay the foundation of Zion;		124:118
which I am c. to pass through,		127: 2
when c. upon certify to the same,		128: 3
c. of my father, as was Aaron,		132:59
When I c. again there was none		133:67
ye obeyed not my voice when I c.		133:71
when he c. unto me out of the	Mses	1:17
strength, and c. upon God,		1:21
and each land was c. earth,		1:29
that Moses c. upon God,		1:30
of all men have I c. Adam,		1:34
And I, God, c. the light Day;		2: 5
and the darkness, I c. Night;		2: 5
God, c. the firmament Heaven;		2: 8
I, God, c. the dry land Earth;		2:10
of the waters, c. I the Sea;		2:10
c. the name of the first Pison,		3:11
second river was c. Gihon;		3:13
Adam c. every living creature,		3:19
she shall be c. Woman,		3:23
the Lord God, c. unto Adam,		4:15
Adam c. his wife's name Eve,		4:26
c. the first of all women,		4:26
c. upon the name of the Lord,		5: 4
the Lord God c. upon men		5:14
thou shalt be c. Perdition;		5:24
Cain was c. Master Mahan,		5:31
he c. the name of the city after		5:42
of Tubal Cain was c. Naamah.		5:46
and c. upon his sons to repent.		6: 1
and he c. his name Seth.		6: 2
son, and he c. his name Enos.		6: 5
unto as many as c. upon God		6: 5
them, and c. their name Adam,		6: 9
image, and c. his name Seth.		6:10
the land, which was c. Shulon,		6:17
which he c. after his own son,		6:17
c. upon all men, everywhere,		6:23
he c. upon our father Adam		6:51
the Lord c. his people ZION,		7:18
was c. the City of Holiness,		7:19
he c. unto the Lord, saying:		7:59
be c. Zion, a New Jerusalem.		7:62
And he c. his name Noah,		8: 9
they were c. the sons of God.		8:13
Noah c. upon the children of men		8:20
and he hath c. upon me;		8:26
by the hill c. Potiphar's Hill,	Abr	1:10
is c. by the Chaldeans		1:14
shall be c. after thy name,		2:10
and c. on the Lord devoutly,		2:18
c. again upon the name of		2:20
the Gods c. the light Day,		4: 5
the darkness they c. Night.		4: 5
until morning they c. night;		4: 5

152

until the evening they c. day;	Abr	4: 5
which they c. day and night.		4: 5
And the Gods c. the expanse,		4: 8
morning that they c. night;		4: 8
evening that they c. day;		4: 8
that they c. night and day.		4: 8
the morning they c. night;		4:13
until the evening they c. day;		4:13
morning that they c. night;		4:23
until evening that they c. day;		4:23
until morning they c. night;		4:31
until evening that they c. day;		4:31
now she shall be c. Woman,		5:17
Adam c. every living creature,		5:20
which is c. by the Egyptians	Fac	2: 1
c. by the Egyptians Oliblish,		2: 2
Is c. in Egyptian		2: 5
my mind was c. up to serious	JS	2: 8
by one who was c. of God		2:28
He c. me by name, and said unto		2:33
is c. the Urim and Thummim—		2:35
the messenger c. for them,		2:60
when Mr. Anthon c. me back,		2:64
that is c. John the Baptist in		2:72
I should be c. the first Elder		2:72
that a man must be c. of God,	AoF	5

CALLETH

unto me, and c. on my name,	DC	93: 1
the Lord; for he c. upon all men,		133:16

CALLING

been diligent in the office of my c.;	Jac	2: 3
c. on the name of the Lord daily,	Mos	4:11
ye have been c. on his name,		4:20
should be found c. upon God		24:11
and is still c. after you,	Al	5:37
are called with a holy c., yea,		13: 3
yea, with that holy c. which was		13: 3
have been called to this holy c.		13: 4
this holy c. being prepared from		13: 5
being called by this holy c.,		13: 6
being called with a holy c.,		13: 8
which c., and ordinance, and		13: 8
c. it after the land of their		21: 1
hath called me by a holy c.,		29:13
ye shall say, c. them by name,	3Ne	11:24
c. him their Lord and their God.		19:18
without c. upon that Being	Mrm	5: 2
of the gift of his c. unto me,	Mro	7: 2
soon after my c. to the ministry.		8: 1
c. with which he was called.	DC	18: 9
and it is his c. to baptize;		20:38
to perform the duties of his c.,		20:64
say, c. him or her by name:		20:73
Make known thy c. unto		23: 2
and thy c. is to exhortation,		23: 3
and thy c. is to exhortation,		23: 4
thy c. also is to exhortation,		23: 5
in c. upon God in my name,		24: 5
for this is not thy c.		24: 9
Attend to thy c. and thou shalt		24: 9
the office of thy c. shall be for		25: 5
for unto him is his c., that		25: 9
this c. and commandment		36: 4
this c. and commandment,		36: 5
your sins, c. on my name,		39:10
your c. and election in the		53: 1
C. on the name of the Lord		75:10
c. wherewith you are called,		81: 1
and the magnifying their c.,		84:33
office, and labor in his own c.;		84:109
to magnify the c. whereunto		88:80
I will ordain you unto this c.,		100: 9
There has been a day of c.,		105:35
time to this high and holy c.,		106: 3
church in the duties of their c.		107:23
church in the duties of their c.		107:25
c. us thy friends, saying-Call		109: 6
in c. our solemn assembly,		109:10
behold how great is your c.		112:33
up and stand in the office of his c.,		124:103
be appointed unto the same c.		124:130

CALLING

be ordained unto this c. in	DC 124:132
this is the office of their b.,	124:135
C. upon the name of the Lord	133:40
and c. upon the Lord his God,	136:32
Nevertheless, c. upon God,	Mses 1:20
And c. upon the name of God,	1:25
spake unto me, c. me by name	JS 2:17
in the act of c. upon God,	2:30
unto me, c. me by name.	2:49
praying and c. upon the Lord	2:68

CALLINGS

to the gifts and c. of God	Mro 3: 4
to the c. and gifts of God	DC 18:32
in the gifts and c. of God	20:27
gifts and c. of God unto him;	20:60
in your several c., unto the	84:117
their several c. and offices;	97:13

CALLS

fill the several c. for preaching	DC 107:38

CALM

and there was a great c.	1Ne 18:21
I am c. as a summer's morning;	DC 135: 4

CALMLY

Hyrum was shot first and fell c.,	DC 135: 1

CALNO

Is not C. as Carchemish?	2Ne 20: 9

CALVES: *see also* WILSON, Calves.

must be led up as c. of the stall,	1Ne 22:24
and grow up as c. in the stall.	3Ne 25: 2

CAME: *see in the APPENDIX.*

CAMENIHAH

and C. and Moronihah	Mrm 6:14

CAMP

the secret pass on the left of the c.	Mos 22: 7
to watch the c. of the Amlicites	Al 2:22
to watch the c. of the Amlicites.	2:22
into the c. of the Nephites	2:23
followed the c. of the Amlicites,	2:24
wilderness to watch their c.;	43:23
when the c. of the Lamanites	43:28
mount, nearly to Lehonti's c.;	47:12
they took their c., and moved	48: 6
and took their b. and marched	49:12
of Lehi fled to the c. of Moroni,	50:27
had fled to the c. of Moroni.	50:28
came over to the c. of Moroni,	50:31
sent an army, with their c.,	50:33
returned to the c. of Moroni,	50:35
went into the c. of Amalickiah;	51:33
again privily to his own c.,	51:35
therefore we did c. for the night.	56:38
we did c. round about the city	57: 9
watch the c. of the Lamanites.	57:30
did c. with their army.	62:20
did not c. with their armies.	62:22
into the c. of the Lamanites,	62:36
they returned to their c.	Eth 14:31
the saints of the c. of the Lord,	DC 61:29
concerning the C. of Israel in	136: 1

CAMPED

God shall have c. against them	2Ne 26:15

CAMPS

surround those men in their c.	Al 47:13
had returned unto their c.,	Mrm 6:11
weary, and retired to their c.;	Eth 15:16
after they had retired to their c.	15:16

CAN: *see in the APPENDIX.*

CANAAN

and I beheld the people of C.,	Mses 7: 6
Behold the people of C.,	7: 7

CANNOT

the people of C. shall divide	Mses 7: 7
dwell there but the people of C.;	7: 7
upon all the children of C.,	7: 8
save it were the people of C.,	7:12
to go into the land of C.;	Abr 2: 4
in the way to the land of C.,	2:15
to come to the land of C.	2:16

CANAANITES

partaker of the blood of the C.	Abr 1:21
blood of the C. was preserved	1:22
borders of the land of the C.,	2:18

CANAL

waters, save it be upon the c.,	DC 61:23
to journey, save upon the c.	61:23
that after they leave the c.	61:24

CANCELED

will see that all my debts are c.	DC 127: 1

CANDLE

do men light a c. and put it	3Ne 12:15

CANDLES

neither c., neither torches;	3Ne 8:21

CANDLESTICK

but on a c., and it giveth light	3Ne 12:15

CANKER

yourselves for that which will c.,	Mrm 8:38
your riches will c. your souls;	DC 56:16

CANKERED

blades thereof were c. with rust;	Mos 8:11

CANNOT

c. be written upon these plates,	1Ne 6: 3
c. be written upon these plates.	9: 1
unto him, or they c. be saved.	13:40
we c. understand the words	15: 7
c. dwell in the kingdom of God;	15:33
c. any unclean thing enter into	15:34
much that we c. write them all,	17: 6
how is it that he c. instruct me,	17:51
c. be blessed unless he shall make	22:10
he c. be loosed for the space of	22:26
I c. go down to my grave save I	2Ne 4: 5
shortened at all that it c. redeem,	7: 2
eternal word, which c. pass away,	9:16
or they c. be saved in the kingdom	9:23
for he c. be deceived,	9:41
your labor for that which c. satisfy.	9:51
as Sodom, and they c. hide it.	13: 9
have spoken plainly that ye c. err.	25:20
unto you, that ye c. misunderstand.	25:28
I c. bring the book, for it is	27:17
the learned say: I c. read it.	27:18
and there c. be any more Bible.	29: 3
suppose that I c. speak another;	29: 9
I c. write but a few things,	31: 1
he c. be saved.	31:16
if ye c. understand them it will	32: 4
And now I, Nephi, c. say more;	32: 7
And now I, Nephi, c. write all	33: 1
c. be written upon these plates;	Jac 3:13
I c. write but a little of my words,	4: 1
things which they c. understand,	4:14
for justice c. be denied,	6:10
for he c. tell of things to come.	7: 7
I c. write the hundredth part of	WM 1: 5
Ye c. say that ye are even as	Mos 2:25
I c. tell you all the things whereby	4:29
so many that I c. number them.	4:29
for he c. deny himself;	15:27
for he c. deny justice	15:27
you c. feel them upon your backs,	24:14
ye c. dethrone an iniquitous king	29:21
iniquities which c. be enumerated—	29:36
at that day that ye c. be saved;	Al 5:21
ye c. suppose that such can	5:25
he must repent or he c. be saved!	5:31

CANNOT

unto you plainly that ye c. err,	Al 5:43	I c. any longer enforce my	Mro 9:18
yea, a fire which c. be consumed,	5:52	tongue c. tell, neither can it	9:19
ye c. inherit the kingdom of	7:14	I c. recommend them unto God	9:21
he c. walk in crooked paths;	7:20	they c. be saved in the kingdom	10:26
many things which c. be written,	8:1	the Lord c. look upon sin with	DC 1:31
that he c. save them in their sins;	11:37	purposes of God c. be frustrated,	3:1
for I c. deny his word, and he	11:37	upon my rock, they c. prevail.	6:34
ye c. be saved in your sins.	11:37	you c. write that which is sacred	9:9
But this c. be; we must	12:15	c. always judge the righteous,	10:37
they c. be redeemed according	12:18	c. always tell the wicked	10:37
and they c. die, seeing there	12:18	which c. be hid in darkness;	14:9
understand, that we c. err;	13:23	c. have place in the kingdom of	18:25
he c. be slain by the enemies of	18:3	c. be saved in the kingdom of	18:46
for we know he c. be slain.	18:3	For they c. bear meat now,	19:22
the storm c. penetrate to them;	26:6	c. be saved in the kingdom of	20:29
I c. say the smallest part which	26:16	c. enter in at the strait gate	22:2
ye c. know of things which ye do	30:15	where I am you c. come.	25:15
ye c. know that there shall be a	30:15	for where I am they c. come,	29:29
that I am dumb, for I c. speak;	30:52	they c. be redeemed from their	29:44
that we c. worship our God.	32:9	Wherefore, they c. sin,	29:47
that ye c. worship God save	32:10	your midst and ye c. see me;	38:7
Ye c. know of their surety at first	32:26	that have farms that c. be sold,	38:37
ye c. have the fruit thereof.	32:39	but I c. deny my word.	39:16
ye suppose that ye c. worship God,	33:2	a deed which c. be broken.	42:30
Ye c. say while we are brought	34:34	they c. be taken from the church,	42:32
Nay, ye c. say this; for that	34:34	wherefore we c. stand.	45:70
there c. any man work after the	37:39	why is it that ye c. understand	50:21
ye c. hide your crimes from God;	39:8	that you c. understand,	50:31
you c. carry them with you.	39:14	and ye c. bear all things now;	50:40
Ye c. suppose that this is what it	40:17	Ye c. behold with your natural	58:3
Mind, which ye c. understand—	42:1	promise the faithful and c. lie.	62:6
that ye c. destroy this our faith.	44:3	if ye c. make one like unto it,	67:8
Now I c. recall the words which	44:11	that c. be impeached,	68:23
the Lord c. look upon sin with	45:16	they c. come, worlds without	76:112
therefore I c. come unto you.	52:11	ye c. be equal in obtaining	78:6
whatsoever evil we c. resist with	61:14	covenant that c. be broken.	78:11
c. be contained in this work.	He 3:14	ye c. bear all things now;	78:18
whereon if men build they c. fall.	5:12	for ye c. go amiss.	80:3
that ye c. lay your hands on us	5:26	covenant that c. be broken	82:11
words which c. be uttered by man;	5:33	of my Father, which he c. break,	84:40
Nephi speak which c. be written;	8:3	place c. go ye shall send,	84:62
c. deny them except ye shall lie,	8:24	ye c. see it now, yet a little	84:119
do iniquity, and he c. be saved;	12:22	c. abide a celestial glory.	88:22
slippery, that ye c. hold them;	13:31	he who c. abide the law of a	88:23
of your poverty ye c. retain them.	13:31	c. abide a terrestrial glory.	88:23
slippery, and we c. hold them.	13:36	he who c. abide the law of a	88:24
more things which c. be written.	14:1	c. abide a telestial glory;	88:24
they shall be heavy and c. flee;	15:2	in sin, c. be sanctified by law,	88:35
we c. hit him with our stones and	16:6	because you c. see him—	88:66
marvelous works c. come to pass,	16:16	by the Spirit, c. be benefited.	91:6
we c. witness with our own eyes	16:20	man c. receive a fulness of joy.	93:34
mystery which we c. understand,	16:21	and surely Zion c. fall,	97:19
c. all be written in this book;	3Ne 5:8	but deny me, c. be sanctified.	101:5
c. contain even a hundredth part	5:8	c. have power to act without	102:6
and all of them c. be written,	7:17	the decision of the latter there c.	102:31
city that is set on a hill c. be hid.	12:14	if you c. obtain five hundred,	103:32
ye c. serve God and Mammon.	13:24	if ye c. obtain three hundred,	103:33
good tree c. bring forth evil fruit,	14:18	you c. escape my wrath	104:8
ye c. understand all my words	17:2	ye c. escape the buffetings of	104:9
which he prayed c. be written,	17:15	Zion c. be built up unless it is by	105:5
tongue c. speak the words which	19:32	I c. receive her unto myself.	105:5
prayed that they c. be written,	19:34	this c. be brought to pass until	105:11
c. be written in this book even	26:6	And those that c. stay, who	105:21
my sorrows c. bring your return.	Mrm 6:20	he c. hold the keys of that	107:70
repentance, or ye c. be saved.	7:3	if it c. be otherwise, that the	109:52
Behold, I c. write them.	8:23	and my servant Hyrum, c. come;	112:17
for in them we c. breathe, save	Eth 2:19	powers of heaven c. be controlled	121:36
For behold, ye c. have windows,	2:23	their bounds are set, they c. pass.	122:9
ye c. cross this great deep save	2:25	belongeth to my house, and c.	124:30
a language that they c. be read.	3:22	your baptisms for your dead c.	124:33
even that we c. write them;	12:25	am God, and c. be mocked in	124:71
or he c. receive an inheritance	12:32	my servant Joseph c. pay over	124:72
they c. inherit that place which	12:34	serpent c. lay hold upon his	124:99
evil c. do that which is good;	Mro 7:6	that c. be lightly passed over,	128:15
evil c. do that which is good;	7:10	without us c. be made perfect—	128:15
c. bring forth good water;	7:11	For we without them c. be made	128:18
of the devil c. follow Christ;	7:11	if he does not, he c. obtain it.	131:3
he c. be a servant of the devil.	7:11	he c. have an increase.	131:4
faith there c. be any hope.	7:42	We c. see it; but when our bodies	131:8
that he c. have faith and hope,	7:43	therefore, they c. be enlarged	132:17
Little children c. repent;	8:19	out of the world it c. be received	132:18
no condemnation, c. repent;	8:22	there, by whom they c. pass;	132:18

CANNOT 155 CAPTIVITY

c., therefore, inherit my glory;	DC 132:18	their chief c. came forward and	Al	49:13
abide my law ye c. attain to this	132:21	their chief c. had sworn with an		49:17
if ye enter not into my law ye c.	132:33	the c. of the Lamanites brought		49:21
he c. commit adultery for they are	132:61	their chief c. were all slain;		49:23
he c. commit adultery with that	132:61	their chief c. were all slain		49:25
this law, he c. commit adultery,	132:62	chief c. held a council of war—		52:19
where immediate appeal c. be	134:11	the chief c. of the Lamanites		52:28
fame and name that c. be slain.	135: 3	their chief c., all those who		52:38
that c. be rejected by any court	135: 7	their chief c. demanded their		55:23
gospel that all the world c. impeach;	135: 7	all of whom are chief c.,		56:12
they c. be numbered unto man;	Mses 1:37	the chief c. of the Lamanites		58:25
so my words c. return void,	4:30	was the case with all his chief c.		59:12
and their eyes c. see afar off;	6:27	they cried unto their c., saying:	He	16: 6
we know them, and c. deny,	6:45	Lachoneus did appoint chief c.	3Ne	3:17
c. be answered upon the heads	6:54	the chiefest among all the c.		3:18
writings that c. be revealed	Fac 2: 8	to appoint for their chief c.,		3:19
which I c. write at this time.	JS 2:20	organized with c. of hundreds,	DC	136: 3
which c. be mentioned here.	2:41	hundreds, c. of fifties,		136: 3
'I c. read a sealed book.'	2:65	of fifties, and c. of tens,		136: 3
		Let each company, with their c.		136: 7
CANST		presidents, and c. of hundreds,		136:15
c. not accomplish so great a work.	1Ne 17:19			
thou c. lay it up against the season.	Jac 5:27	CAPTIVATE		
I said unto thee: C. thou translate?	Mos 8:11	spirit of the devil power to c.,	2Ne	2:29
of Christ thou c. be healed.	Al 15: 8			
of the Lord thou c. do all things.	20: 4	CAPTIVATION		
thou c. bless them according to	He 11:16	the power and c. of the devil.	Al	9:28
c. thou not turn away thine	13:37			
thou c. not make one hair black	3Ne 12:36	CAPTIVE		
Behold, O Lord, thou c. do this.	Eth 3: 5	carried away c. into Babylon.	1Ne	1:13
a God of truth, and c. not lie.	3:12	carried away c. into Babylon,		10: 3
c. thou read this without rejoicing	DC 19:39	and am desolate, a c., and		21:21
c. thou run about longer as a	19:40	they are carried away c. down to	2Ne	1:13
c. thou be humble and meek,	19:41	who was carried c. into Egypt.		3: 4
c. not repay then go straightway	136:25	been slain and carried away c.		6: 8
How is it that thou c. weep,	Mses 7:29	or the lawful c. delivered?		6:16
how is it thou c. weep?	7:31	The c. exile hasteneth,		8:14
if thou c. count the number of	Abr 3:14	thy neck, O c. daughter of Zion.		8:25
		hell must deliver up its c. spirits,		9:12
CAN'T		must deliver up its c. bodies,		9:12
father, why c. you stay with us?	DC 122: 6	are carried away c. into Babylon.		25:10
		and to liberate the c.,	Jac	2:19
CAPABLE		not lead away c. the daughters		2:33
if ye were c. of hearkening	Al 54: 7	carried away c. into Babylon.	Om	1:15
are not c. of committing sin;	Mro 8: 8	or be taken c. by our enemies,	Mos	12:15
and c. of committing sin;	8:10	among those that were taken c.,		19:16
before God, and is c. of repentance.	DC 20:71	they are taken c. by the devil,	Al	12:11
is man c. to make them know,	76:116	others c. into the wilderness.		16: 3
they may consider worthy and c.	102: 7	away c. into the wilderness.		16: 4
		been taken c. by the Lamanites.		16: 5
CAPACITY		been taken c. by the Lamanites.		16: 6
adapted to the c. of the weak	DC 89: 3	been taken c. by the Lamanites,		16: 8
		been lost that were taken c.		16: 8
CAPITAL		led c. by the will of the devil.		40:13
and had taken the c. city which	He 1:27	and also carrying them away c.,		60:17
the most c. parts of the land,	1:27	and did carry away others c.	He	11:33
		and ye be led away c. by him.	3Ne	18:15
CAPTAIN		neck, O c. daughter of Zion.		20:37
The c. of fifty,	2Ne 13: 3	for they are led away c. by him		27:32
he being the king's c.,	Mos 20:17	king dwelt, and took him c.,	Eth	7: 5
chief c. over the armies of the	Al 16: 5	king, and carried him away c.		7:17
chief c. over the Nephites—	43:16	and to lead them c. at his will,	Mses	4: 4
the chief c. took the command of	43:16			
when he was appointed chief c.	43:17	CAPTIVES		
who was their chief c., or their	43:44	or the lawful c. delivered?	1Ne	21:24
appointed Lehi to be chief c.	49:16	even the c. of the mighty		21:25
Now Gid was the chief c. over	57:29	the c. of the mighty shall be	2Ne	6:17
I am Moroni, your chief c.	60:36	and they shall take them c. unto		24: 2
the chief c. over the army.	61: 2	unto whom they were c.;		24: 2
		their lives, and took them c.	Mos	19:15
CAPTAINS				
And there were appointed c.,	Al 2:13	CAPTIVITY		
appointed captains, and higher c.,	2:13	out of c., on dry ground,	1Ne	4: 2
higher captains, and chief c.,	2:13	And they were also led out of c.		5:15
with his people, yea, with his c.,	2:16	be brought back out of c.;		10: 3
with his captains, and chief c.,	2:16	be brought back out of c.		10: 3
Zerahamnah appointed chief c.	43: 6	bringeth them down into c.		13: 5
who were their chief c. and	43:44	and bring them down into c.		13: 9
appoint chief c. of the Zoramites,	48: 5	they went forth out of c.,		13:13
to be chief c. over his armies.	48: 5	who had gone forth out of c.		13:16
the chief c. of the Lamanites	49: 5	Gentiles that had gone out of c.		13:19
his chief c. durst not attack	49:11	which have gone forth out of c.,		13:29

CAPTIVITY 156 CARRIED

who have gone forth out of c.,	1Ne 13:30	down with grief, sorrow, and c.,	DC 123: 7
be no more brought down into c.;	14: 2	shall be entrusted unto his c.,	124:113
according to the c. of the devil,	14: 4	take especial c. of your family	126: 3
their being brought down into c.,	14: 7		
according to the c. of the devil,	14: 7	CAREFUL	
who shall be led away into c.	17:43	that ye shall be watchful and c.,	DC 42:76
will bring them again out of c.,	22:12	And if, after a c. re-hearing,	102:21
never be brought down into c.;	2Ne 1: 7	And arise up and be more c.	108: 3
to the will and c. of the devil.	1:18		
ye may not come down into c.;	1:21	CAREFULLY	
or to choose c. and death,	2:27	leadeth them away c. down to	2Ne 28:21
the c. and power of the devil;	2:27	hear his words c. and distinctly,	DC 88:129
and out of c. unto freedom.	3: 5	but c. gather together, as much	105:24
my people are gone into c.,	15:13		
remember the c. of thy fathers	Mos 27:16	CARELESSLY	
I say unto you, they were in c.,	Al 5: 5	that if I should let them go c.,	JS 2:59
the c. of your fathers?	5: 6		
according to the power of his c.	12: 6	CARES	
to the power and c. of Satan,	12:17	of pride and the c. of the world.	DC 39: 9
or to retain them in c., or to	17:20	and the c. of the world caused	40: 2
remember the c. of my fathers;	29:11		
remembered the c. of my fathers;	29:12	CARLOS: see DON CARLOS and SMITH,	
the c. of our fathers;	36: 2	DON C.	
them out of bondage and c.	36:28		
them out of bondage and c.,	36:29	CARMEL	
retained in remembrance their c.;	36:29	As the dews of C., so shall the	DC 128:19
as I have done, their c.	36:29		
forgotten the c. of our fathers?	60:20	CARNAGE	
from bondage, and from c.,	Eth 2:12	did spread so much death and c.	3Ne 2:11
Surely this thing leadeth into c.	6:23	there was blood and c. spread	Mrm 2: 8
that they would be brought into c.	7: 5	scene of the blood and c.	4:11
to pass that Kib dwelt in c.,	7: 7	an awful scene of blood and c.	5: 8
old age, while he was yet in c.	7: 7	the scene of bloodshed and c.,	Eth 14:21
did carry away his father into c.,	8: 3		
and did make him serve in c.;	8: 3	CARNAL	
he was in c. the half of his days.	8: 4	lull them into c. security,	2Ne 28:21
which he did bring him into c.;	10:14	themselves in their own c. state,	Mos 4: 2
did remain in c. all his days;	10:14	For they are c. and devilish,	16: 3
begat sons and daughters in c.,	10:14	becoming c., sensual, devilish,	16: 3
Levi did serve in c. after the	10:15	persists in his own c. nature,	16: 5
And he served many years in c.,	10:30	according to their own c. wills	16:12
Heth lived in c. all his days.	10:31	even in their c. and sinful state;	26: 4
Aaron dwelt in c. all his days;	10:31	from their c. and fallen state,	27:25
and Amnigaddah also dwelt in c.	10:31	their c. state and also the plan	Al 22:13
and Coriantum dwelt in c.	10:31	were pleasing unto the c. mind;	30:53
and Seth was brought into c.,	11: 9	not of the c. mind but of God.	36: 4
and did dwell in c. all his days.	11: 9	or I would say, in a c. state,	41:11
Moron dwelt in c. all the	11:18	evil for evil, or c. for carnal,	41:13
Coriantor dwelt in c. all his	11:19	evil for evil, or carnal for c.,	41:13
having escaped the c. all his days.	11:23	as they had become c., sensual,	42:10
year he did bring him into c.	13:23	of his own will and c. desires,	DC 3: 4
		temporal, neither c. nor sensual.	29:35
CARBUNCLES		not with the c. neither natural	67:10
of agates, and thy gates of c.,	3Ne 22:12	neither after the c. mind.	67:12
		the law of c. commandments,	84:27
CARCASS		to be c., sensual, and devilish.	Mses 5:13
as a c. trodden under feet.	2Ne 24:19	men have become c., sensual,	6:49
Behold, wheresoever the c. is,	JS 1:27		
		CARNALLY	
CARCASSES		to be c.-minded is death,	2Ne 9:39
their c. were torn in the midst of	2Ne 15:25		
the c. were mangled by dogs	Al 16:10	CARNALLY-MINDED: see CARNALLY and	
did devour the c. of them	Eth 9:34	MINDED.	
CARCHEMISH		CAROLINA	
Is not Calno as C.?	2Ne 20: 9	at the rebellion of South C.,	DC 87: 1
		will be in South C.	130:12
CARE			
notwithstanding all the c. which	Jac 5:46	CARRIAGES	
Let us nourish it with great c.,	Al 32:37	he hath laid up his c.	2Ne 20:28
if ye nourish it with much c.	32:37		
take c. of these sacred things,	37:47	CARRIED	
all their troubles and from all c.,	40:12	hs was c. away in a vision,	1Ne 1: 8
great c. over the church,	46: 6	be c. away captive into Babylon.	1:13
c. not for the blood of his people.	49:10	be c. away captive into Babylon,	10: 3
it was his first c. to put an end	51:16	she was c. away in the Spirit;	11:19
taken c. of our wounded men,	57:28	had been c. away in the Spirit	11:19
have c. for the house of Israel,	Mrm 5:10	they were c. away in the Spirit	11:29
shall be entrusted to his c.	DC 12: 8	and it was c. forth among them.	13:20
who has the c. thereof,	63:39	while I was c. away in the spirit;	14:30
and must be spoken with c.,	63:64	had been c. away in the spirit,	15: 1
lo, I will take c. of your flocks,	88:72	even to be c. out of this time	18:18
c. not for the body, neither the	101:37	mountains which shall be c. up.	19:11
but c. for the soul, and for the	101:37	shall be c. upon their shoulders.	21:22

CARRIED 157 CASE

have been c. in their arms,	1 Ne 22: 6	
have been c. upon their shoulders,	22: 6	
being c. in their arms and upon	22: 8	
they are c. away captive down	2 Ne 1:13	
who was c. captive into Egypt.	3: 4	
Joseph, who was c. into Egypt.	4: 1	
hath my body been c. away upon	4:25	
shall be c. upon their shoulders.	6: 6	
been slain and c. away captive.	6: 8	
are c. away captive into Babylon.	25:10	
they have been c. away	25:11	
c. away captive into Babylon.	Om 1:15	
and c. him bound before the king,	Mos 12: 9	
our griefs, and c. our sorrows;	14: 4	
and c. them back to the land of	19:15	
and c. them into the wilderness;	20: 5	
they c. into the wilderness.	20: 5	
and c. off their grain	21:21	
and c. helpless, even until he was	27:19	
they c. him upon the top of the	Al 1:15	
and c. them forth to the place of	14: 9	
who had been c. away captive	16: 4	
Ammon was c. before the king	17:21	
they were c. in unto the king	17:39	
and c. him in unto his wife,	18:43	
and he was c. away in God—	19: 6	
yea, and my joy is c. away,	26:35	
my brethren my soul is c. away,	29:16	
and c. him before Ammon,	30:20	
should be c. out of the land.	30:21	
and c. before the high priest,	30:21	
have c. this plan into effect,	50:30	
have c. with them many women	58:30	
and c. off by the Lamanites.	58:31	
be c. about by the temptations	3 Ne 6:17	
earth was c. up upon the city	8:10	
were c. away in the whirlwind;	8:16	
know that they were c. away.	8:16	
not c. away in the whirlwind;	10:13	
c. by my father into the land	Mrm 1: 6	
had c. up into the mount,	Eth 6: 2	
and c. him away captive into	7:17	
c. away as though he were dead.	14:30	
army of Zenephi has c. away,	Mro 9:16	
c. up unto the council of the	DC 107:78	
and c. them all the days of old.	133:53	
was c. down into the water,	Mses 6:64	

CARRIETH

Holy Ghost c. it unto the	2 Ne 33: 1	

CARRY

I should c. the engravings which	1 Ne 4:24	
we should c. them with us, as we	5:22	
whatsoever things we should c.	16:11	
we might c. into the wilderness.	16:11	
c. thy people across these waters.	17: 8	
and shall c. away safe,	2 Ne 15:29	
and whirlwinds shall c. them away,	26: 5	
and they shall c. them forth unto	30: 3	
did c. away the daughters of my	Mos 20:15	
things, which they could c.,	22:12	
and c. them before the king;	Al 17:20	
the enemy listeth to c. them.	26: 6	
doth c. thee away unto boasting.	26:10	
and he doth c. you about,	30:42	
c. us beyond this vale of sorrow	37:45	
you cannot c. them with you.	39:14	
did c. on the work of death	43:38	
ye are still determined to c. on	54: 5	
to c. forth provisions unto the	63:10	
c. on the secret work of murder	He 2: 4	
still c. on the work of darkness,	6:29	
doth c. on his works of darkness	6:30	
did c. on this work of destruction	11: 2	
and did c. away others captive	11:33	
he desired to c. them,	3 Ne 6:17	
c. us forth into a land which is	Eth 1:38	
in which they did c. with them	2: 2	
did also c. with them deseret,	2: 3	
did c. with them swarms of bees,	2: 3	
he did c. them in his hands upon	3: 1	
that they should c. with them	6: 4	
he did c. away his father into	8: 3	
the Lamanites did not c. away,	Mro 9:16	

c. these sayings unto the land of	DC 68:32	
shall c. unto the land of	69: 1	
Let them c. up unto the bishop	72:25	

CARRYING

in c. them forth to the lands of	2 Ne 10: 8	
the c. away of their daughters	Mos 20:23	
as if we were c. provisions to	Al 56:30	
also c. them away captive,	60:17	

CART

as it were with a c. rope;	2 Ne 15:18	

CARTER, Gideon

Smith and my servant C.;	DC 75:34	

CARTER, Jared

let C. be ordained a priest,	DC 52:38	
that my servant C. should go	79: 1	
heart be glad, my servant C.,	79: 4	
servants Reynolds Cahoon and C.	94:14	
Martin Harris, John S. Carter, C.,	102: 3	
9, C.; 10, Joseph Smith, Sen.;	102:34	

CARTER, John S.

C., Jared Carter, Oliver Cowdery,	DC 102: 3	
4, Luke Johnson; 5, C.;	102:34	

CARTER, Simeon

Solomon Hancock and C. also	DC 52:27	
let my servant C. and my	75:30	

CARTER, William

Wheeler Baldwin and C. also	DC 52:31	

CARTHAGE

and also unto the inhabitants of C.,	DC 124:88	
were shot in C. jail, on the 27th of	135: 1	
went to C. to deliver himself up	135: 4	
innocent blood on the floor of C.	135: 7	

CASE

fear lest my c. shall be awful;	Jac 7:19	
Alma laid the c. before their king,	Mos 27: 1	
unless this be the c., they must	27:27	
if this could always be the c.	29:13	
that this should be the c.	Al 7: 8	
unto you that if this be the c.,	9:23	
Therefore, if this is the c.,	19: 5	
me to know that this is the c.—	40: 5	
O, my son, this is not the c.;	41:13	
in this c. the Lamanites did	43:43	
this be the c. that ye will do it,	54:11	
the c. with all his chief captains.	59:12	
ye shall in no c. enter into the	3 Ne 12:20	
if this be the c. that these things	Mro 7:35	
of men if this be the c.;	10:25	
And if this be the c.,	DC 5:29	
And if this be the c.,	5:30	
of heart that this is the c.,	42:74	
lay the c. before the church,	42:81	
as the c. might require.	102: 1	
in c. of the absence of one or	102:11	
in c. he himself is absent,	102:11	
convenes to act upon any c.,	102:13	
in no c. shall more than six be	102:14	
the council are to present the c.,	102:16	
are appointed to speak on the c.	102:18	
which he shall have of the c.,	102:19	
the c. shall have a re-hearing.	102:20	
light is shown upon the c.,	102:21	
in c. no additional light is given,	102:22	
In c. of difficulty respecting	102:23	
make the c. clear to the minds of	102:23	
c. shall there be conducted,	102:27	
and no common or ordinary c.	102:28	
in c. of transgression.	102:32	
determine whether any such c.,	102:33	
But in c. of transgression,	104:76	
in c. the treasurer is found an	104:77	
Unless this is the c., their decisions	107:29	
in c. their decision of these	107:32	
except in a c. where a President	107:76	
otherwise, as the c. may require,	127: 1	
is sufficient to know, in this c.,	128:18	

CASE 158 CAST

save in the c. of Uriah and his	DC	132:39	hewn down and c. into the fire	Al 5:56
One c. has been reported, in which		OD	he should be c. out of their city,	8:13
but in this c., in relation	Fac	1:12	but they c. me out and I was	8:24
			in bands and c. into prison.	8:31
CASES			and also they are c. into prison,	9:hd
in all c. save it were in sickness,	Mos	27: 5	that they might c. me into prison.	9:32
all c. among the children of men,		29:20	that time and c. me into prison.	9:33
would fight in all c. to protect	Al	53:17	might be slain or c. into prison,	10:13
And thus ye shall do in all c.	DC	42:83	if ye will c. out the righteous	10:23
shall know the spirits in all c.		52:19	be c. out from among the people	11: 2
The accused, in all c., has a		102:15	to revile us and to c. us out—	12: 4
In all c. the accuser and the		102:18	and c. off your sins,	13:27
most difficult c. of church matters;		102:28	c. him out from among them,	14: 7
the most difficult c. of the church,		107:78	and they c. them out, and sent	14: 7
			sent men to c. stones at them.	14: 7
CAST			they should be c. into the fire,	14: 8
they are not c. off forever—	T. Pg.		and c. them into the fire also,	14: 8
and he c. himself upon his bed,	1Ne	1: 7	those who had been c. into the fire	14:14
whom they had c. out, and stoned,		1:20	records which were c. in with them,	14:14
we c. lots-who of us should go		3:11	be c. into a lake of fire and	14:14
Jeremiah have they c. into		7:14	who had been c. into the fire;	14:15
as I c. my eyes round about,		8:13	the officers to be c. into prison.	14:17
I c. mine eyes towards the head		8:17	had been c. into prison three days,	14:18
they did c. their eyes about as if		8:25	who had been c. out and stoned,	15: 1
I also c. my eyes round about,		8:26	or to c. them into prison,	17:20
c. off from the presence of the Lord.		8:36	or to c. them out of his land,	17:20
merciful to them, and not c. them		8:37	and began to c. stones at them	17:36
wherefore, ye must be c. off		10:21	veil of unbelief was being c. away	19: 6
they c. him out from among them.		11:28	will c. thy brethren out of prison.	20: 4
the unclean spirits were c. out.		11:31	will c. thy brethren out of prison.	20: 7
they must be c. off also,		15:33	may be c. out of prison.	20:22
c. out because of that justice		15:35	may be c. out of prison,	20:24
fear lest ye shall be c. off forever.		17:47	may be c. out of prison,	20:27
c. with sorrow into a watery grave.		18:18	and they had c. them out,	20:30
or have I c. thee off forever?	2Ne	7: 1	were taken and c. into prison,	20:30
save they shall c. these things		9:42	were taken and c. into prison,	21:13
for we are not c. off;		10:20	those who were c. into prison	21:14
a man shall c. his idols of silver,		12:20	ye shall be c. off at the last day?	22: 6
because they have c. away the		15:24	may not be c. off at the last day?	22:15
in them when they c. their leaves;		16:13	them, or to c. them into prison;	23: 2
thou art c. out of thy grave		24:19	c. them out of their synagogues,	23: 2
if they would c. their eyes unto		25:20	should they c. stones at them,	23: 2
ye shall in nowise be c. out.		25:29	we have been c. out, and mocked,	26:29
because they c. out the prophets,		26: 3	strong cords, and c. into prison;	26:29
as will not repent shall be c. off;		30: 2	he was c. out, and went about	30:56
they c. many things away which		33: 2	c. by thy wrath down to hell;	31:17
to be c. into that lake of fire	Jac	3:11	were c. out of the synagogues	32: 2
and we will c. them into the fire		5: 7	have c. us out of our synagogues	32: 5
I will c. into the fire and burn		5: 9	they have c. us out because of	32: 5
and c. them into the fire.		5:26	we are c. out of our synagogues,	32: 9
that it may be c. into the fire,		5:37	ye are c. out of your synagogues,	32:12
hewn down and c. into the fire.		5:42	it is because that ye are c. out,	32:12
thereof and c. them into the fire,		5:45	ye are afflicted and c. out—	32:24
hewn down and c. into the fire;		5:46	do not c. it out by your unbelief,	32:28
and c. them into the fire that		5:47	not good, therefore it is c. away.	32:32
and c. them into the fire,		5:49	ye pluck it up and c. it out.	32:38
and c. them into the fire.		5:58	are c. out of your synagogues.	33: 2
hewn down and c. into the fire,		5:66	heard me when I have been c. out	33:10
And the bad shall be c. away,		5:69	ye would not c. about your eyes,	33:21
plucked off and to be c. away;		5:73	then c. about your eyes and begin	33:22
until the bad had been c. away		5:74	dross, which the refiners do c. out,	34:29
and the bad is c. away,		5:75	against those who do c. you out	34:40
and the bad will I c. away into		5:77	brethren were c. out of the land;	35: 6
be c. out into their own place!		6: 3	c. out of their land all those who	35: 8
hewn down and c. into the fire?		6: 7	they did not c. them out, but	35: 9
wanderers, c. out from Jerusalem,		7:26	be c. out of his presence.	38: 1
And he shall c. out devils,	Mos	3: 6	be c. out into outer darkness;	40:13
he c. his eyes round about		4: 1	they are c. out, and consigned	40:26
drive him away, and c. him out.		5:14	c. their dead into the waters of	44:22
Abinadi should be c. into prison;		12:17	they c. their garments at the feet	46:22
mocked, and scourged, and c. out,		15: 5	he may c. us at the feet of our	46:22
then shall the wicked be c. out,		16: 2	have c. our garments at thy feet	46:22
Alma should be c. out from among		17: 3	and we be c. into prison, or be	46:23
bound him and c. him into prison.		17: 5	had c. up dirt around about	49: 2
the king c. his eyes round about		19: 6	could not c. their stones and	49: 4
and bound, and c. into prison.		21:23	c. stones from the top thereof,	50: 5
if thou wilt of thyself be c. off.		27:16	were taken and c. into prison,	51:19
be the case, they must be c. off;		27:27	they c. up dirt out of the ditch	53: 4
because I was like to be c. off.		27:27	in weapons of war unto	55:16
that they should be c. off forever.		28: 4	and c. them at the feet of the	55:23
to c. in their voices concerning		29:39	been taken and c. into prison;	62: 9
to c. in their voices concerning	Al	2: 6	he did c. a javelin at him,	62:36
were c. into the waters of Sidon;		3: 3	taken, and were c. into prison,	He 1:22
but they shall be c. out		5:25	Lamanites and c. into prison;	5:21
hewn down and c. into the fire—		5:35	c. by the servants of Limhi.	5:21
hewn down and c. into the fire,		5:52		

CAST

been c. into prison many days	He	5:22
when they c. their eyes about,		5:43
they c. up their eyes as if to		5:48
them and c. them into prison.		9: 9
taken and were c. into prison.		9: 9
whom we have c. into prison.		9:12
behold they c. us into prison.		9:14
being much c. down because of		10: 3
Be thou c. down and become		10: 9
they might c. him into prison.		10:15
take him to c. him into prison,		10:16
are some who shall be c. out,		12:25
be c. off from the presence of		12:25
and they did c. him out,		13: 2
when ye shall c. out the righteous		13:14
that ye do c. out the prophets,		13:24
mock them, and c. stones, at them,		13:24
stoned them, and c. them out.		13:25
angry with him, and c. him out		13:26
stoned them, and c. them out.		13:33
have c. me out from among you.		14:10
hewn down and c. into the fire;		14:18
hewn down and c. into the fire;		14:18
c. stones at him upon the wall,		16: 2
c. himself down from the wall,		16: 7
did c. their prisoners into prison,	3Ne	5: 4
there were many highways c. up,		6: 8
c. them out from among them.		7:14
c. out devils and unclean spirits;		7:19
as many as had devils c. out		7:22
the prophets, and c. them out;		8:25
because they did c. them all out,		9:11
they c. their eyes round about,		11: 3
c. their eyes up again towards		11: 8
to be c. out and to be trodden		12:13
and thou shalt be c. into prison.		12:25
that ye should be c. into hell.		12:30
and tomorrow is c. into the oven,		13:30
first c. the beam out of thine		14: 5
to c. the mote out of thy brother's		14: 5
c. ye your pearls before swine,		14: 6
hewn down, and c. into the fire.		14:19
in thy name have c. out devils,		14:22
he c. his eyes round about on		15: 1
been c. out from among them,		16: 8
to be c. out from among them,		16: 9
good for nothing but to be c. out,		16:15
he c. his eyes round about again		17: 5
they c. their eyes towards heaven,		17:24
and shall not c. them out;		18:23
not c. him out from among you,		18:30
shall not c. him out of your		18:32
c. his eyes upon them and said:		23: 8
your vine c. her fruit before		24:11
hewn down and c. into the fire,		27:11
hewn down and c. into the fire,		27:17
they were c. into the fire by		28:19
they were c. down into the earth;		28:20
they were c. into a furnace		28:21
twice were they c. into a den of		28:22
they did c. them into prison;	4Ne	1:30
c. them into furnaces of fire,		1:32
c. them into dens of wild beasts,		1:33
their dead were c. into the sea.	Mrm	3: 8
hewn down and c. into the fire;		8:21
my name shall they c. out devils;		9:24
ye will in nowise be c. out.		9:29
c. them out from the beginning.	Eth	8:25
prophets, but they c. them out;		9:29
some of them they c. into pits		9:29
unto taxes he did c. into prison;		10: 6
pay taxes he did c. into prison;		10: 6
did c. up mighty heaps of earth		10:23
as naught, and c. him out;		13:13
c. out from among the people		13:15
c. your mind upon the night	DC	6:22
be c. down by devouring fire,		29:21
c. out from the Garden of Eden,		29:41
in faith, they shall c. out devils;		35: 9
shall be c. out from among you;		41: 5
the pearls to be c. before swine.		41: 6
will not repent shall be c. out.		42:20
will not repent shall be c. out.		42:21

he repents not he shall be c. out.	DC	42:23
repenteth not, shall be c. out.		42:24
forgiven, but shall be c. out.		42:26
repenteth not shall be c. out.		42:28
shall be c. out of the church,		42:37
c. them out from among you;		42:74
shall be c. out from among you.		42:75
hewn down and c. into the fire.		45:50
hewn down and c. into the fire,		45:57
to c. any one out from your		46: 3
to c. any one who belongeth to		46: 4
ye shall not c. any out of your		46: 5
ye shall not c. them out.		46: 6
able to c. the soul down to hell.		63: 4
c. them into unquenchable fire.		63:54
they who are c. down to hell		76:106
or to c. down to the regions of		77: 8
be c. into the Lord's storehouse,		82:18
my name they shall c. out devils;		84:67
the old and c. it unto the poor,		84:105
c. away your idle thoughts and		88:69
c. themselves down as a fig		88:87
be c. away into their own place,		88:114
be hewn down and c. into the fire.		97: 7
c. out from the land of their		101: 1
I will not utterly c. them off;		101: 9
be c. out and trodden under		101:40
councilors to c. lots by numbers,		102:12
proceeded to c. lots or ballot,		102:34
to be c. out and trodden under		103:10
shall be c. into the treasury		104:68
him c. them into the treasury;		104:69
influence shall c. thee into trouble,		122: 4
if thou shouldst be c. into the pit,		122: 7
if thou be c. into the deep;		122: 7
heal the sick, he shall c. out devils,		124:98
an highway shall be c. up in the		133:27
Moses c. his eyes and beheld	Mses	1:27
caused that he should be c. down;		4: 3
was despised, and c. out,		5:54

CASTETH

for perfect love c. out all fear.	Mro	8:16

CASTING

the c. of it into that hell	1Ne	14: 3
by merely c. about your eyes	Al	33:21
by c. over stones and arrows		49:19
by c. up walls round about		52: 6
wickedness in c. out the prophets,	3Ne	9:10
in c. before them such an awful	Mrm	5: 8
except c. out devils,	DC	24:13
c. off the dust of your feet		24:15

CATCH

they might c. them in their words,	Al	10:13
snares to c. the holy ones of God.		10:17
he has laid to c. this people,		12: 6
they might c. us in their snare;		56:43
snares and c. fowls of the air;	Eth	2: 2
Deceive and lie in wait to c.,	DC	10:25
they may c. a man in a lie,		10:25
c. themselves in their own snare.		10:26

CATHERINE

Sophronia, C., and Lucy.	JS	2: 4

CATTLE

and the treading of lesser c.	2Ne	17:25
of all manner of c. of every kind,	En	1:21
nor thy maid-servant, nor thy c.,	Mos	13:18
and their c., and all their flocks,	3Ne	3:22
provisions, and horses and c.,		4: 4
his herds, his horses and his c.,		6: 1
And also all manner of c.,	Eth	9:18
an herb for bruises and all sick c.,	DC	89: 8
in houses, or in lands, or in c.,		104:68
c., and creeping things, and	Mses	2:24
and c. after their kind,		2:25
of the air, and over the c.,		2:26
And Adam gave names to all c.,		3:20
shalt be cursed above all c.,		4:20
and they were keepers of c.;		5:45

CATTLE   160   CAUSE

c. and creeping things,	Abr 4:24	now, for this c. thou shalt be put	Mos 17: 8
and c. after their kind,	4:25	seed shall c. that many shall suffer	17:15
and over the c., and over all	4:26	What c. have ye to come up to	20:14
Adam gave names to all c.,	5:21	I did c. my people to come up to	20:15
		did c. that all the people should	22: 1
CAUGHT		and c. that his children should	24: 8
c. hold of the end of the rod	1Ne 8:24	did c. them to commit many sins;	26: 6
c. hold of the end of the rod	8:30	and c. it to tremble as though it	27:18
I was c. away in the Spirit of	11: 1	did c. them to quake and tremble.	28: 3
I myself was c. in a snare,	Mos 23: 9	this account did c. the people of	28:18
Amulek had c. him in his lying	Al 12: 1	c. which ye are called to consider—	29: 5
And thus he was c. with guile.	18:23	which would c. wars and contentions	29: 7
my mind c. hold upon this thought,	36:18	the c. of shedding much blood	29: 7
they were c. up into heaven,	3Ne 28:13	would c. him and also this people	29: 9
who were c. up into the heavens,	28:36	wicked king c. to be committed,	29:17
they have c. you in the words	DC 10:13	ye can c. that they may be judged	29:28
and ye shall be c. up,	27:18	ye shall c. that a small number of	29:29
fail and they are c. in snares;	61:18	and it was a c. of much affliction	Al 1:23
to be c. up unto the church	76:102	c. of much trial with the church.	1:23
and be c. up to meet him.	88:96	Now this did c. much joy in	2: 8
also shall be c. up to meet him	88:97	that every soul had c. to mourn;	4: 3
are first c. up to meet him;	88:98	the c. of much affliction to Alma,	4: 7
of an eye, and shall be c. up,	101:31	was a great c. for lamentations	4:13
we shall be c. up in the cloud to	109:75	the c. of their being loosed from	5:10
when Moses was c. up into an	Mses 1: 1	the same have c. to wail and	5:36
was c. away by the Spirit of	6:64	by the c. of so much afflictions	7: 5
c. up by the powers of heaven	7:27	for thou hast great c. to rejoice;	8:15
		And now for this c., that ye	9:25
CAULS		mightest have c. to destroy me.	11:25
c., and round tires like the moon;	2Ne 13:18	multitudes to know the c. of it;	14:29
		this was the c. for which	17:16
CAUSE		and for this c. they stood to	17:35
Laban into my hands for this c.—	1Ne 4:17	the c. of so much mourning	19:14
should tarry with us for this c.,	4:36	it would c. them to believe in	19:17
the c. of their disputations.	15: 6	be the c. of this great power,	19:24
for the very c. that he shall be	15:17	the c. of his tarrying in his own	20:12
which did c. the earth to shake	17:45	they did c. the Lamanites that	21: 3
he can c. the earth that it shall	17:46	thou that we have c. to repent?	21: 6
he can c. the rough places to be	17:46	the c. why he has not come up	22: 3
c. to inherit the desolate heritages;	21: 8	they had been the c. of his fall,	22:19
he will c. them to be scattered	2Ne 1:11	had seen the c. of the king's fall,	22:20
did c. my people to be industrious,	5:17	c. many to be put to death,	25:12
God did c. a skin of blackness	5:21	it did c. great joy among them,	27:26
c. that they shall be loathsome	5:22	for this c. I withstood the truth,	30:53
for this c. the prophet has	6:12	the c. of great sorrow to Alma	31: 2
God pleadeth the c. of his people;	8:22	therefore, for this c., Alma and	31:11
Wherefore, for this c.,	10:15	he hath no c. to believe, for he	32:18
they who lead thee c. thee to err	13:12	or only hath c. to believe,	32:19
of this people c. them to err;	19:16	God could c. that those spindles	37:40
c. it to be heard unto Laish,	20:30	were inspired by a better c.,	43:45
moon shall not c. her light to shine.	23:10	for this c. were the Nephites	43:47
I will c. the arrogancy of the proud	23:11	this is the very c. for which ye	44: 2
Wherefore, for this c. hath	25:21	for this c. we know nothing	45:19
built up which c. envyings,	26:21	wicked man can c. to take place	46: 9
Lord God shall c. a great division	30:10	that the c. of the Christians,	46:16
for, for this c. have they been	31:17	concerning the justice of the c.	46:29
and he will plead your c.,	Jac 3: 1	and c. them to come to battle	46:30
and for this c. it is sanctified	4: 5	to support the c. of freedom,	46:35
is not this the c. that the trees	5:48	to remove the c. of diseases,	46:40
then will I c. the good and the	5:77	their enemies the c. of Christians.	48:10
vineyard will I c. to be burned	5:77	a c. to have been lamented)	50:30
save it be for the c. of iniquity;	En 1:10	and maintain the c. of God	50:39
which doth c. him to shrink from	Mos 2:38	to maintain the c. of freedom.	51: 7
which doth c. them to shrink from	3:25	a c. of all their destruction.	51:16
the same hath great c. to repent;	4:18	and support the c. of liberty.	51:17
shalt c. thy neighbor to commit sin	4:28	he did c. the death of the king	51:34
king Mosiah did c. his people that	6: 7	to c. the Lamanites to come	52:19
to know the c. whereby ye were	7:10	did c. the Lamanites to labor	53: 4
for this c. have I suffered that	7:11	to c. the Lamanites to labor,	53: 5
I will c. that my people shall	7:14	for this c. they were brought	53:12
know the c. of their destruction.	8:12	our religion and the c. of our God.	54:10
I did c. that the men should	10: 4	then will I c. that my people	54:18
I did c. that the women should	10: 5	knew that it was not a just ac.	55: 1
For this very c. has Laman,	10:18	for this c. he might not bring	55:19
did c. his people to commit sin,	11: 2	that he did c. the Lamanites,	55:25
I will c. that they shall howl	12: 4	for which c. we have to mourn.	56:10
I will c. that they shall have	12: 5	died in the c. of their country	56:11
and c. this people to commit sin,	12:29	for this c. did the Lamanites	56:56
the Lord has c. to send me	12:29	did c. that our swords should	57:33
and they shall have c. to howl,	16: 2	c. of these our embarrassments,	58: 9
which was the c. of their fall;	16: 3	the c. why they did not send	58: 9
c. of all mankind becoming carnal,	16: 3	did c. us that we should hope	58:11
c. that he should be put to death.	17: 1	and the c. of our liberty.	58:12

CAUSE — CAUSED

we do not know the c. that	Al	58:34
should c. men to be gathered		59: 3
the c. of this exceeding great		60: 6
the c. of your thoughtless state.		60: 6
true to the c. of our freedom,		60:16
the c. of so much bloodshed		60:16
do not c. food to be sent unto us,		60:19
to defend the c. of my country,		60:28
people in the c. of our freedom.		60:30
for the c. of your love of glory		60:32
the c. of this great iniquity;		61: 4
will be the c. of sore affliction		61: 4
and in the c. of our Redeemer		61:14
freedom and c. of his country.		62: 1
not true to the c. of freedom.		62:11
he did c. that his men should		62:25
the c. of this great and lasting war		62:35
the c. of so much war and		62:35
did c. them to repent of their		62:45
did also c. the people to contend;	He	1: 3
they did c. three divisions among		1: 4
c. that they should march down		1:17
did c. some little dissensions		3: 1
did c. the more humble part of		3:34
the c. of so great mourning		7:11
for this c. wo shall come unto		7:22
and c. that this famine may cease		11:12
c. that it may be done according		11:13
they did c. great fear to come		11:32
he will c. that it shall be so.		12:21
for this c., that men might be		12:22
will c. that they shall be smitten;		13: 9
c. that fire should come down		13:13
For this c. hath the Lord God		13:23
should be no c. for unbelief		14:28
shall have great c. to mourn in		15: 2
but I will c. that in the day of		15:16
to c. us that we should believe in		16:20
which did c. much sorrow unto	3Ne	1:28
was also a c. of much sorrow		1:29
did c. that his people should cry		3:12
they did c. fear to come upon		3:16
did c. that they should gather		3:24
did c. that they should make		3:26
c. them to yield themselves up		4:16
that did c. that this siege should		4:17
may c. to be felled to the earth		4:29
c. the word of God to be preached		5: 4
the c. of this iniquity of the		6:15
they did c. a great contention		7: 7
I did c. them to be burned,		9: 9
that it did not c. to quake;		11: 3
and did c. their hearts to burn.		11: 3
saving for the c. of fornication,		12:32
c. that they should be separated		19: 5
c. that the multitude should		19: 6
for this c. that the Gentiles, if		21: 6
c. him to bring forth unto the		21:11
for this c. have I been lifted up;		27:15
for this c. he fulfilleth the		27:18
for this c. ye shall have fulness		28:10
he will c. that it shall soon		29: 4
and c. the lame to walk,	4Ne	1: 5
Zarahemla did they c. to be built		1: 8
I did c. my people that they	Mrm	3: 5
for this c. I write unto you,		3:20
could they c. the earth to shake;		8:24
did they c. prisons to tumble to		8:24
c. that widows should mourn		8:40
I will c. in my own due time	Eth	3:24
for this c. did king Mosiah keep		4: 1
c. you to remain in your awful		4:15
by this c. the people were brought		7:25
the Lord did c. the serpents that		9:33
he did c. that they should labor		10: 6
he did c. to be put to death.		10: 6
he did c. to be refined in prison,		10: 7
he did c. to be wrought in prison.		10: 7
did c. the shedding of much blood;		11:10
he advocateth the c. of the	Mro	7:28
for this c., that thy days may be	DC	5:33
Yea, for this c. I have said:		5:34
and establish the c. of Zion;		6: 6
for this c. the Lord said unto	DC	7: 4
can c. this gift of Aaron to be		8: 7
c. that your bosom shall burn		9: 8
shall c. you to forget the thing		9: 9
for this c. I said that he is a		10: 7
And for this c. have I said:		10:53
and c. to tremble and shake		10:56
and establish the c. of Zion.		11: 6
and establish the c. of Zion.		12: 6
and c. the heavens to shake for		21: 6
inspired to move the c. of Zion		21: 7
will c. that he shall mourn for		21: 8
that he can say enough in my c.;		24:10
c. my church to be established		28: 8
c. maggots to come in upon them;		29:18
ever open your mouth in my c.,		30:11
c. the blind to receive their		35: 9
I will c. the heavens to shake		35:24
will I c. the wicked to be kept,		38: 6
for this c. I gave unto you the		38:32
for the c. of fornication,		42:74
is pleading your c. before him—		45: 3
for this c. you shall take your		55: 5
for this c. I have sent you—		58: 6
for this c. I have sent you		58:14
anxiously engaged in a good c.,		58:27
for this c. preached the apostles		63:52
occasion against him without c.;		64: 6
this c. ye shall do these things.		64:14
for this c. have I spoken these		64:19
for this c. the apostle wrote		74: 5
my church, to advance the c.,		78: 4
c. groanings in the midst of her,		88:89
this is the c. of your affliction.		93:42
for this c. I gave unto you a		95: 7
will c. them to bring forth as		97: 9
layeth down his life in my c.,		98:13
what is the c. of this great evil?		101:52
c. of thy people may not fail		109:52
c. that the remnants of Jacob,		109:65
c. the mountains to flow down at		109:74
for this c. I commanded Moses		124:38
for this c. have I accepted the		124:51
to plead the c. of the poor and		124:75
support the c. of the poor,		124:89
as they pursue me without a c.,		127: 1
for what c. it seems mysterious,		127: 2
we not go on in so great a c.?		128:22
will c. much bloodshed previous		130:12
this c., that men might be made		133:57
this c. these commandments were		133:60
to c. them to be dissatisfied with		134:12
for this c. I know that man is	Mses	1:10
for this c., to keep the		6:42
will I c. to sweep the earth		7:62
I c. the wind and the fire to	Abr	2: 7
to c. to divide the light from		4:17
c. them to be fruitful and		4:22
c. the fowl to multiply in		4:22
We will c. them to be fruitful		4:28
was the c. of great persecution,	JS	2:22
often the c. of great sorrow		2:23

CAUSED

I c. that they should hide	1Ne	4: 5
he c. the waters to flow out of		20:21
he c. the sons and daughters of	2Ne	4: 8
c. the cursing to come upon them,		5:21
things have I c. to be written,		11: 1
I have not c. more to be written.		29:10
c. that it should be digged about,	Jac	5:11
which c. wars and contentions;		7:26
those which they c. to be written.	Jar	1:14
Mosiah c. that they should be	Om	1:18
he c. a contention among them;		1:28
he c. that they should be taught	Mos	1: 2
he c. a tower to be erected,		2: 7
he c. that the words which he		2: 8
he spake and c. to be written,		2: 9
and has c. that ye should rejoice,		2:20
have c. that ye should assemble		2:27
have c. that ye should assemble		2:28
have c. that ye should assemble		2:29

CAUSED

has c. that your hearts should	Mos	4:20
has c. that your mouths should		4:20
have c. that my guards should		7:11
but c. that they should go to		7:16
c. that they should walk through		7:19
he c. that Ammon should stand		8: 2
and c. that they should return		8: 4
c. that the plates which contained		8: 5
I c. that forty and three of		8: 7
I c. that there should be weapons		10: 1
I c. that the women and children		10: 9
I also c. that all my old men		10: 9
he also c. that his workmen		11:10
he c. a breastwork to be built		11:11
he c. many buildings to be built		11:13
he c. a great tower to be built		11:13
king Noah c. that Abinadi should		12:17
would not have c. me to come		13:26
c. that Alma should be cast out		17: 3
the king c. that his guards should		17: 5
he c. that he should again be		17: 6
c. that their fair daughters should		19:13
and c. that he should suffer,		19:20
he c. a search to be made among		20:16
he c. that his people should		21:20
had c. such a great destruction		21:20
he c. that they should be taken,		21:23
c. that they should be put to death.		21:23
had c. the people to commit		21:30
c. that his people should gather		22:10
which c. me sore repentance;		23: 9
the Lord c. a deep sleep to come		24:19
Mosiah c. that all the people		25: 1
Mosiah did read, and c. to be read,		25: 5
c. that they should be brought		26:10
which c. the earth to shake		27:11
he c. that a multitude should be		27:21
he c. that the priests should		27:22
translated and c. to be written		28:11
c. by the iniquities of their kings;		29:31
was c., or rather did acknowledge,	Al	1:15
he c. that his people should pitch		2:20
and c. that he should be cast out		8:13
that c. them to remain in their		9:16
who c. men to behold of his glory.		12:29
which he had c. among the		14: 6
they c. that they should be cast		14: 8
was c. by the great tribulations		15: 3
and c. that his bands should be		17:24
he c. them to flee by the		17:37
king Lamoni c. that his servants		18: 1
c. the multitude to be gathered		19:28
he c. that his servants should		20: 6
But he c. that there should be		21:20
and he c. that his people, or the		21:20
he c. that Aaron and his brethren		22:26
c. that many of the Lamanites		25: 5
c. that they should be put to		25: 7
c. that many of their brethren		25: 8
c. that he should suffer death		25: 9
he c. that he should be carried		30:21
they c. that he should be bound;		30:29
he c. that his sons should be		35:16
he c. that all the people in that		43:26
Moroni c. that his army should be		43:27
Moroni c. that the work of death		44:20
he c. to be put to death;		46:35
he c. the title of liberty to be		46:36
he c. his army to pitch their		47: 9
Amalickiah c. that one of his		47:18
Amalickiah c. that his servants		47:22
would have c. the Lamanites		49:10
he c. that his armies should		50: 1
c. that there should be timbers,		50: 2
he c. that upon those works of		50: 3
he c. towers to be erected that		50: 4
he c. places of security to be		50: 4
Moroni c. that his armies should		50: 7
he c. that the inhabitants who		50: 9
c. them to erect fortifications		50:10
which c. much rejoicing among		51: 7
was c. by the labors and heat		51:33

CAUSETH

he c. that his armies should	Al	51:36
he c. that Teancum should take		52:22
c. that they should commence		53: 3
he c. that they should build a		53: 4
which they had c. them to build		53: 5
which c. dissensions amongst		53: 8
c. him to wage a war against		55: 1
c. that a search should be made		55: 4
Moroni c. that Laman and a		55: 6
and c. that a small number		55: 7
he c. the men who were with him		55:21
c. that all the prisoners should		55:24
he c. that his prisoners should		55:26
c. that their wounds should be		57:24
which c. them to take courage;		57:32
I c. that Gid, with a small		58:16
I c. that my men, those who were		58:18
I c. that my men should not		58:26
who c. so much bloodshed		60:16
fathers that has c. their hatred,		60:32
c. that provisions should be sent,		62:12
c. that an army of six thousand		62:13
they c. them to enter into a		62:16
c. that they should prepare in		62:21
Moroni c. that his men should		62:22
c. that their strong armies should	He	1:26
c. that the Lamanites who had		1:33
he c. that his band should		2:11
c. that Nephi should be taken		9:19
c. that rain should fall upon the		11:17
c. that a curse should come upon		13:23
which I have c. to be spoken by	3Ne	1:13
he c. that fortifications should		3:14
he c. that armies, both of the		3:14
Moroni have I c. to be sunk		9: 4
of Gilgal have I c. to be sunk,		9: 6
waters have I c. to come up in		9: 7
all these have I c. to be sunk,		9: 8
have I c. to be burned with fire		9: 9
have I c. to be burned with fire,		9:10
have I c. to come upon this land,		9:12
I have c. my people who are		16: 9
which I have c. to be written	Eth	4:16
the Lord c. stones to shine in		6: 3
the Lord God c. that there should		6: 5
c. by the fierceness of the wind.		6: 6
c. that his people should give		7:21
they have c. the destruction of		8:21
hath c. man to commit murder		8:25
c. that all the prophets who		11: 5
that c. the prison to tumble to		12:13
they c. them to flee before them;		15:10
I have c. you that you should	DC	5: 3
which you have c. to be written,		10:10
translated and c. to be written;		10:11
Which suffering c. myself,		19:18
have I c. to be done away		22: 1
have c. this last covenant		22: 3
c. that he should be cast out		29:41
c. him to reject the word.		40: 2
Now this c. us to marvel,		76:18
which the Lord in his wrath c.		84:27
I c. darkness to come up upon	Mses	2: 2
had not c. it to rain upon		3: 5
c. a river to go out of Eden		3:10
c. a deep sleep to fall upon		3:21
c. that he should be cast down;		4: 3
God the famine to wax sore	Abr	2: 1
or c. it to be divided, from		4: 4
c. them to divide the day from		4:14
the Gods had not c. it to rain		5: 5
the Gods c. a deep sleep to		5:15
difficulties c. by the contests	JS	2:11
It c. me serious reflection then,		2:23

CAUSES

that c. such joy in their hearts?	Al	30:35

CAUSETH

and c. me to shrink with shame	Jac	2: 6
which c. such exceeding great joy	Mos	4:11
he c. to be destroyed;		29:23

CAUSETH — CELESTIAL

CAUSETH
it this that c. thy marvelings?	Al 18:16
c. her to commit adultery;	3Ne 12:32
c. them to catch themselves	DC 10:26
Which c. silence to reign,	38:12
fire which c. the waters to boil.	133:41

CAUSING
the c. of them to quake before me.	2Ne 4:22
c. the lame to walk,	Mos 3: 5
c. much dissension among	27: 9
c. that this people be	Al 10:19
c. them to lift up their heads in	30:18
c. them that they should suffer	60:17
c. them that they should do	3Ne 2: 3

CAUTION
added a c. to me, telling me	JS 2:46

CAUTIOUS
thus c. that no poison should	Al 55:32

CAVES
and into the c. of the earth,	2Ne 12:19

CAVITY
ourselves in the c. of rock.	1Ne 3:27
hid himself in the c. of a rock	Eth 13:13
as he dwelt in the c. of a rock	13:14
Ether dwelt in the c. of rock,	13:18
hid again in the c. of the rock.	13:22

CEASE
did c. to flee from my presence.	1Ne 4:29
our fears did c. concerning him.	4:37
c. striving to take away my life.	7:19
he did c. speaking unto them.	8:38
of the Lord, did c. to work.	18:12
the winds did c., and the storm	18:21
and the storm did c., and the	18:21
C. ye from man, whose breath is	2Ne 12:22
and the indignation shall c.,	20:25
the arrogancy of the proud to c.,	23:11
if so, God would c. to be God.	Al 42:13
and God would c. to be God.	42:22
If so, God would c. to be God.	42:25
the work of death should c. again	44:20
their wars never did c. for the	48:22
wars and contentions began to c.,	He 3:22
the Lord did c. to preserve them	4:25
destruction did c. by the sword	11: 5
this famine may c. in this land.	11:12
pestilence of the sword might c.;	11:14
quakings of the earth did c.—	3Ne 8:19
did c. lamenting and howling for	10: 2
the earth did c. to tremble,	10: 9
and the rocks did c. to rend,	10: 9
the dreadful groanings did c.,	10: 9
who were spared alive did c.;	10:10
they did not c. to pray.	19:26
that they should c. to pray,	20: 1
not c. to pray in their hearts.	20: 1
miracles and of healing did c.	Mrm 1:13
if so he would c. to be God;	9:19
the wind did never c. to blow	Eth 6: 8
they did not c. to praise the Lord.	6: 9
did not c. to pursue Coriantumr;	14:24
for if we should c. to labor,	Mro 9: 6
c. to come up into the ears of	DC 87: 7
c. from all your light speeches,	88:121
c. to be covetous; learn to impart	88:123
C. to be idle; cease to be unclean;	88:124
Cease to be idle; c. to be unclean;	88:124
c. to find fault one with another;	88:124
c. to sleep longer than is needful;	88:124
let them c. wearying me concerning	90:33
shall c. from before my face.	101:26
shall never c. to prevail until	103: 7
that they may c. to spoil,	109:50
bloodshed, and c. their rebellions.	109:66
let the tongue of the slanderer c.	112: 9
work, and c. not their diligence,	124:49
c. to fear concerning his family,	124:87

c. to do evil, and lay aside all his	DC 124:116
be continued on and not c.;	127: 4
C. to contend one with another;	136:23
c. to speak evil one of another.	136:23
C. drunkenness;	136:24
my words, for they never c.	Mses 1: 4
I will not c. to call upon God,	1:18
to c. digging after it.	JS 2:56

CEASED
How hath the oppressor c.,	2Ne 24: 4
ceased, the golden city c.!	24: 4
then those marvelous works c.,	Al 37:41
the Lord hath already c. to strive	Mrm 5:16
not c. to be a God of miracles.	9:15
God c. to be a God of miracles	9:19
and the wars c. not;	Eth 13:22
of the Lord had c. striving	15:19
have miracles c. because Christ	Mro 7:27
brethren, have miracles c.?	7:29
have angels c. to minister unto	7:29
has the day of miracles c.?	7:35
have angels c. to appear unto	7:36
if these things have c. wo be	7:37
wherefore, if these things have c.,	7:38
ceased, then has faith c. also;	7:38
lest the Spirit hath c. striving	8:28
of the Lord hath c. striving with	9: 4
c. not to call upon God.	Mses 5:16
things had c. with the apostles,	JS 2:21

CEASELESS
sing c. praises with the choirs	Mrm 7: 7

CEASETH
the Spirit of the Lord c. soon	1Ne 7:14
when the Spirit c. to strive with	2Ne 26:11
But God c. not to be God	Al 42:23
and he c. not to be God,	Mrm 9:19
why he c. to do miracles	9:20

CEASING
of God to pray without c.,	Mos 26:39
prayeth continually without c.—	Al 26:22
I have labored without c., that I	36:24
they did still continue, without c.,	3Ne 19:24
did pray steadfastly, without c.,	19:30

CEDARS
upon all the c. of Lebanon,	2Ne 12:13
we will change them into c.	19:10
and also the c. of Lebanon,	24: 8

CELEBRATED
c. for his literary attainments.	JS 2:64

CELESTIAL
are they whose bodies are c.,	DC 76:70
terrestrial, and not bodies c.,	76:78
the ministration of the c.	76:87
thus we saw the glory of the c.,	76:92
And the glory of the c. is one,	76:96
unto you a place in the c. world,	78: 7
creatures beneath the c. world;	78:14
even them of the c. world.	88: 2
the glory of the c. kingdom;	88: 4
be prepared for the c. glory;	88:18
bodies who are of the c. kingdom	88:20
to abide the law of a c. kingdom	88:22
cannot abide a c. glory.	88:22
abideth the law of a c. kingdom,	88:25
They who are of a c. spirit	88:28
by a portion of the c. glory	88:29
and be crowned with c. glory,	101:65
by the law of the c. kingdom;	105: 4
of the law of the c. kingdom;	105: 5
who come into the c. kingdom,	130:11
c. glory there are three heavens	131: 1
nearest to the c., or the	Fac 2: 1
according to c. time,	2: 1
c. time signifies one day to	2: 1
near to the c. or the	2: 2

CEMENT

CEMENT
expert in the working of c.;	He	3: 7
they did build houses of c.,		3: 7
in tents, and in houses of c.,		3: 9
cities, both of wood and of c.		3:11
together in some kind of c.	JS	2:52

CENSURED
your epistle you have c. me,	Al	61: 9

CENTER
it cutteth them to the very c.	1Ne	16: 2
up in the c. of their synagogue,	Al	31:13
was in the c. of the land,	He	1:24
through the c. of the land		1:25
not come into the c. of the land,		1:26
had come into the c. of the land,		1:27
rock, even to the very c.		12:12
ourselves in the c. of our lands,	3Ne	3:21
them that did hear to the c.,		11: 3
to tremble and shake to the c.	DC	10:56
Independence is the c. place;		57: 3

CENTER PLACE: *see CENTER and PLACE.*

CENTURY
best blood of the nineteenth c.	DC	135: 6

CEPHAS
Paul, and of Apollos, and of C.	DC	76:99

CEREMONY
after they had ended the c.,	Mos	19:24
to learn who performed the c.;	DC	OD

CERTAIN
concerning a c. number who went	Om	1:27
a c. man, being called Amlici,	Al	2: 1
for a c. number of years, even		16: 1
a c. number of the Lamanites,		17:27
he slew a c. number of them		17:36
a c. number of his brethren		21:13
sent c. men unto him, desiring		43:23
there were c. men passing by	He	7:11
c. men who were among them		9: 1
a c. number of the dissenters		11:24
also a c. number who were real		11:24
c. men among them shall be	DC	38:34
there are to be c. men appointed,		48: 5
there are c. bounds also and		88:38
A c. nobleman had a spot of		101:44
to come to any c. conclusion	JS	2: 8
we on a c. day went into the		2:68

CERTAINLY
ye c. will be a child of Christ.	Mro	7:19

CERTAINTY
know the c. of all things	DC	100:11

CERTIFICATE
take a c. from him at the time,	DC	20:64
which c., when presented to		20:64
which c. may be signed by		20:84
A c. from the judge or		72:17
a c. from three elders of the		72:25
or a c. from the bishop;		72:25
He gave me a c., certifying to	JS	2:64
I took the c. and put it into		2:64
said to me, 'Let me see that c.'		2:65

CERTIFICATES
with c. over their own signatures,	DC	128: 4
c. and all the attending witnesses,		128: 4

CERTIFY
this matter, which I now c.	DC	128: 2
when called upon c. to the same,		128: 3

CERTIFYING
c. that they are regular	DC	20:84
c. in his record that he saw		128: 3
c. that the record they have		128: 4
c. to the people of Palmyra	JS	2:64

164

CEZORAM
to a man whose name was C.	He	5: 1
C. was murdered by an unknown		6:15
murder the chief judge C.,		6:19

CHAFF
and the flame consumeth the c.,	2Ne	15:24
shall be as c. that passeth away—		26:18
they shall reap the c. thereof	Mos	7:30
that he may sift you as c.	Al	37:15
about as c. before the wind.	Mrm	5:16
as c. is driven before the wind,		5:18
desireth to sift him as c.	DC	52:12

CHAIN
c. you down to everlasting	Al	12: 6
he had a great c. in his hand,	Mses	7:26

CHAINED
be c. down to an everlasting	Al	12:17

CHAINS
awful c. by which ye are bound,	2Ne	1:13
which are the c. which bind		1:13
the c. with which ye are bound,		1:23
the c. of him that would bind you		9:45
The c. and the bracelets,		13:19
grasp them with his everlasting c.,		28:19
he grasps them with his awful c.,		28:22
of death, and the c. of hell,	Al	5: 7
the c. of hell which encircled		5: 9
yea, and also the c. of hell?		5:10
encircle you about with his c.,		12: 6
what is meant by the c. of hell.		12:11
bound down by the c. of hell,		13:30
our brethren from the c. of hell.		26:14
by the everlasting c. of death.		36:18
have I kept in c. of darkness	DC	38: 5
are the very handcuffs, and c.,		123: 8
reserved in c. of darkness	Mses	7:57

CHALDAIC
Egyptian, C., Assyriac, and Arabic;	JS	2:64

CHALDEA
which was built in the land of C.,	Abr	1: 8
was in the land of Ur, of C.		1:20
there was great mourning in C.,		1:20
concerning the land of C.,		1:29
throughout all the land of C.,		1:30
to wife when I was in Ur, in C.,		2:15

CHALDEAN
in the C. signifies Egypt,	Abr	1:23

CHALDEANS
his arm shall come upon the C.	1Ne	20:14
flee ye from the C., with a		20:20
In the land of the C.,	Abr	1: 1
as was had among the C.,		1:13
called by the C. Rahleenos,		1:14

CHALDEES
in the land of Ur, of the C.	Abr	2: 1
I left the land of Ur, of the C.,		2: 4
given unto me in Ur of the C.;		3: 1

CHALDEES'
the beauty of the C. excellency	2Ne	23:19

CHAMBER
the c. of old Father Whitmer,	DC	128:21

CHAMBERS
thing which is had in secret c.,	DC	38:13
the enemy in the secret c.		38:28
Behold, he is in the secret c.;	JS	1:25

CHANCE
a c. for the enemy of God to	Mos	27: 9
every man should have an equal c.		29:38
that there was no possible c. that	Al	12:21
have an equal c. to fight;		49:22

CHANCE   165   CHARITY

no c. for the robbers to plunder	3Ne	4: 4
unto them a c. for repentance.	Mrm	3: 3
a c. to loan money by hundreds,	DC	104:84

CHANCES
riches and their c. for learning,	3Ne	6:12

CHANGE
we will c. them into cedars.	2Ne	19:10
because of the c. of the branches,	Jac	5:59
has wrought a mighty c. in us,	Mos	5: 2
mighty c. wrought in his heart.	Al	5:12
c. was also wrought in their hearts,		5:13
this mighty c. in your hearts?		5:14
have experienced a c. of heart,		5:26
repentance bringeth a c. of heart	He	15: 7
the great and marvelous c.	3Ne	11: 1
For I am the Lord, I c. not;		24: 6
a c. wrought upon their bodies,		28:37
a c. wrought upon their bodies,		28:38
this c. was not equal to that		28:39
was a c. wrought upon them,		28:39
were to receive a greater c.,		28:40
that wrought the c. upon the	Eth	12:14
to c. the times and seasons,	DC	121:12
but let him c. their habitation,		124:108

CHANGEABLE
The c. suits of apparel,	2Ne	13:22
partial God, and also a c. God,	Mro	8:12
partial God, neither a c. being;		8:18

CHANGED
c. from time to time, according to	1Ne	16:29
your hearts are c. through faith	Mos	5: 7
had c. the affairs of the kingdom.		11: 4
c. from their carnal and fallen		27:25
Behold, he c. their hearts;	Al	5: 7
be c. from this mortal to an		12:20
countenance of the king was c.;		18:12
that their hearts had been c.;		19:33
whole face of the land was c.	3Ne	8:12
be c. in the twinkling of an eye		28: 8
c. from this body of flesh into		28:15
c. in the twinkling of an eye,	DC	43:32
c. in the twinkling of an eye.		63:51
be c. in the twinkling of an eye,		101:31

CHANGERS
overthrow the money c. in mine	DC	117:16

CHANGETH
I say unto you he c. not;	Mrm	9:19

CHANGING
variableness neither shadow of c.?	Mrm	9: 9
in whom there is shadow of c.?		9:10

CHANNELS
he shall come up over all his c.,	2Ne	18: 7

CHAPTER
any further concerning this c.,	DC	45:60
verse of the fifth c. of John,		76:15
spoken of by John, 4th c.,		77: 1
angels, spoken of in the 7th c.		77: 8
Revelation 7th c. and 2nd verse?		77: 9
the things spoken of in this c.		77:10
in the 8th c. of Revelation?		77:12
in the 9th c. of Revelation?		77:13
in the 10th c. of Revelation?		77:14
the eleventh c. of Revelation?		77:15
recorded in the second c. and		85:12
in the thirteenth c. of John's		88:141
of the 11th c. of Isaiah.		113: 1
verse of the 11th c. of Isaiah,		113: 3
in the 10th verse of the 11th c.		113: 5
the command in Isaiah, 52nd c.,		113: 7
Malachi says, last c., verses 5th		128:17
close of the twelfth c. of Ether,		135: 4
first c. and fifth verse,	JS	2:11
part of the third c. of Malachi;		2:36
last c. of the same prophecy,		2:36
the eleventh c. of Isaiah,	JS	2:40
quoted also the third c. of Acts,		2:40
quoted the second c. of Joel,		2:41

CHARACTER
both of c. and personal injuries,	DC	123: 2
his knowledge of the general c.		128: 4
right of property or c. infringed,		134:11
against its c. as a Church	JS	2: 1
a c. of sufficient importance		2:23
c. which ought to be maintained		2:28

CHARACTERS
c. which are called among us	Mrm	9:32
in the c. above his head.	Fac	3: 2
by the c. above his hand.		3: 5
copying the c. off the plates.	JS	2:62
got the c. which I had drawn		2:63
relative to him and the c.,		2:63
presented the c. which had		2:64
and he said they were true c.		2:64
that they were true c.,		2:64
respecting both the c. and		2:65

CHARGE
give him a c. to take the spoil,	2Ne	20: 6
c. concerning all the affairs of the	Mos	1:15
c. concerning the records		1:16
and lay not this thing to their c.		20:17
c. concerning all the affairs of the		29:42
give unto them every one his c.,	Al	35:16
gave them c. over our prisoners		57:16
the c. of Lehi and Teancum;		61:15
giving c. unto his son Nephi,	3Ne	1: 2
who had the c. of the records,		2: 9
will not lay any sin to your c.;	DC	82: 7
mine angels c. concerning you.		84:42
also employ an agent to take c.		84:113
take c. of the place which is		96: 2
thine angels have c. over them;		109:22
c. thee with transgression, as		121:10
they who do c. thee with		121:11
them up to me with this c.:	JS	2:59
in his c. until this day,		2:60

CHARGES
all the c. concerning the kingdom,	Mos	6: 3
declare that these c. are false.	DC	OD
such strict c. to keep them safe,	JS	2:60

CHARIOT
wind and the fire to be my c.;	Abr	2: 7

CHARIOTS
is there any end of their c.	2Ne	12: 7
should prepare his horses and c.,	Al	18: 9
preparing his horses and his c.		18:10
ready the horses and the c.		18:12
ready his horses and his c.		20: 6
taken their horses, and their c.,	3Ne	3:22
and I will destroy thy c.;		21:14
horses, or upon mules, or in c.,	DC	62: 7

CHARITABLE
if ye do not remember to be c.,	Al	34:29

CHARITY
that all men should have c.,	2Ne	26:30
which c. is love.		26:30
except they should have c.		26:30
if they should have c. they would		26:30
I have c. for my people,		33: 7
I have c. for the Jew—		33: 8
I also have c. for the Gentiles.		33: 9
that ye have faith, hope, and c.,	Al	7:24
faith, hope and c. bringeth unto	Eth	12:28
had for the children of men is c.;		12:34
except men shall have c. they		12:34
that if the Gentiles have not c.,		12:35
grace, that they might have c.		12:36
they have not c. it mattereth		12:37
concerning faith, hope, and c.;	Mro	7: 1
he must needs have c.;		7:44

CHARITY

if he have not c. he is nothing;	Mro	7:44
wherefore he must needs have c.		7:44
And c. suffereth long, and is		7:45
ye have not c., ye are nothing,		7:46
are nothing, for c. never faileth.		7:46
Wherefore, cleave unto c.,		7:46
But c. is the pure love of Christ,		7:47
hath neither faith, hope, nor c.;		8:14
And I am filled with c.,		8:17
be hope there must also be c.		10:20
And except ye have c. ye can		10:21
faith, hope, c. and love,	DC	4: 5
godliness, c., humility, diligence.		4: 6
patience, faith, hope and c.		6:19
having faith, hope, and c.,		12: 8
have not faith, hope, and c.,		18:19
yourselves with the bond of c.,		88:125
brotherly kindness and c.;		107:30
Let thy bowels also be full of c.		121:45
and clothe himself with c.;		124:116
grace, that they might have c.		135: 5
If they have not c. it mattereth not		135: 5

CHARLES: see ANTHON, Charles and RICH, Charles C.

CHARMED
c. with the beauty of their women. Mos 19:14

CHARTA: see MAGNA CHARTA.

CHARTERS
mine holy ordinances, and c., DC 124:46

CHASE
c. darkness from among you; DC 50:25

CHASED
And it shall be as the c. roe, 2Ne 23:14

CHASTE
and c. and delicate before God,	Jac	2: 7
honest, true, c., benevolent,	AoF	13

CHASTEN
and did c. them exceedingly;	1Ne	16:39
the Lord seeth fit to c. his people;	Mos	23:21
except the Lord doth c. his people	He	12: 3
c. him for the murmurings of	DC	75: 7
and c. her until she overcomes		90:36
and whom I love I also c.		95: 1
I, the Lord, will c. them		98:21

CHASTENED
c. because of his murmuring	1Ne	16:25
c. by the voice of the Lord		16:39
loved, and also hath he c. them;	He	15: 3
c. them because he loveth them.		15: 3
c. him because he remembered	Eth	2:14
as they sinned they might be c.,	DC	1:27
shall be c. before many.		42:90
until he is sufficiently c. for		58:60
you were c. for all your sins,		61: 8
they were afflicted and sorely c.		64: 8
hath need to be c.,		93:50
Wherefore, ye must needs be c.		95: 2
I sent them forth to be c.		95:10
those that must needs be c.		97: 6
redeemed, although she is c.		100:13
they must needs be c. and tried,		101: 4
therefore they must needs be c.—		101:41
might be c. for a little season		103: 4
be c. until they learn obedience,		105: 6

CHASTENING
c. hand of an Almighty God,	DC	87: 6
all those who will not endure c.,		101: 5

CHASTISEMENT
the c. of our peace was upon him;	Mos	14: 5
with the c. I prepare a way	DC	95: 1
with a sore and grievous c.,		103: 4
will not bear c. is not worthy		136:31

CHASTITY
delight in the c. of women.	Jac	2:28
which is c. and virtue—	Mro	9: 9

CHEATETH
thus the devil c. their souls, 2Ne 28:21

CHECK
seeing a great c., yea, seeing	Al	15:17
arrive in season to c. them,		57:18

CHECKED
c. as to the pride of their hearts, Al 15:17

CHEEK
and shall be smitten on the c.;	Mos	12: 2
humble brethren upon the c.,	He	4:12
shall smite thee on thy right c.,	3Ne	12:39

CHEEKS
my c. to them that plucked off	2Ne	7: 6
they would smite them on their c.,	Mos	21: 3
with his hand upon their c.,	Al	14:14
smote them again upon their c.,		14:15
also smote them again on their c.		14:20
spit upon, and smote upon our c.;		26:29

CHEER
Therefore, c. up your hearts,	2Ne	10:23
My brethren, be of good c. and let	Al	17:31
up your head and be of good c.;	3Ne	1:13
I say unto all, be of good c.,	DC	61:36
be of good c., and do not fear,		68: 6
nevertheless, be of good c.,		78:18
Let thy heart be of good c.		112: 4

CHEERFUL
c. hearts and countenances,	DC	59:15
heart and a c. countenance.—		59:15

CHEERFULLY
and they did submit c.	Mos	24:15
let us c. do all things that lie in	DC	123:17

CHEERY
with my native c. temperament. JS 2:28

CHEMISH
the plates unto my brother C.	Om	1: 8
I, C., write what few things I write,		1: 9
I, Abinadom, am the son of C.		1:10

CHENANGO
who lived in C. county,	JS	2:56
South Bainbridge, C. county,		2:58

CHERUBIM
placed c. and a flaming sword	Al	12:21
c., and a flaming sword which		42: 2
placed c. and the flaming sword,		42: 3
c. and a flaming sword,	Mses	4:31

CHICKENS
as a hen gathereth her c. under	3Ne	10: 4
as a hen gathereth her c. under		10: 5
as a hen gathereth her c., and ye		10: 5
as a hen gathereth her c. under		10: 6
as a hen gathereth her c. if they	DC	10:65
as a hen gathereth her c. under		29: 2
as a hen gathereth her c. under		43:24

CHIEF

even all the c. ones of the earth;	2Ne	24: 9
appointed to be the first c. judge,	Mos	29:42
Alma was the first and c. judge.		29:44
and C. Judge over the people	Al	1:hd
of Alma, the first and c. Judge.		1:hd
higher captains, and c. captains,		2:13
Now Alma, being the c. judge and		2:16
with his captains, and c. captains,		2:16
and he was appointed c. judge;		4:17
art not the c. judge over us.		8:12

CHIEF 167 CHILDREN

who was a c. ruler among them,	Al	12:20
before the c. judge of the land.		14: 4
before the c. judge of the land.		14: 5
the c. judge of the land came and		14:14
the c. judge over the land of		14:23
the c. judge stood before them,		14:24
the c. judge, and the lawyers,		14:27
had been appointed c. captain		16: 5
being the c. among them,		17:18
they went and told the c. judge		27:20
the c. judge sent a proclamation		27:21
also the c. judge over the land.		30:21
the c. judge saw the hardness of		30:29
before Alma, and the c. judge		30:29
before Alma and the c. judge,		30:30
now when the c. judge saw this,		30:51
was sent forth by the c. judge		30:57
and the c. ruler of the Zoramites,		35: 8
Zerahemnah appointed c. captains		43: 6
appointed to be the c. captain		43:16
the c. captain took the command		43:16
when he was appointed c. captain		43:17
their c. captains and leaders,		43:44
who was their c. captain, or		43:44
their c. leader and commander;		43:44
which is the scalp of your c.,		44:14
the c. commander of the armies		46:11
was appointed by the c. judges		46:34
if their c. leader was killed,		47:17
leader to be their c. leader.		47:17
leader and their c. commander.		47:19
of Nephi, which was the c. city.		47:20
c. captains of the Zoramites,		48: 5
to be c. captains over his armies.		48: 5
the c. captains of the Lamanites		49: 5
his c. captains durst not attack		49:11
their c. captains came forward		49:13
appointed Lehi to be c. captain		49:16
their c. captains had sworn with		49:17
their c. captains were all slain;		49:23
their c. captains were all slain		49:25
Nephihah, the second c. judge,		50:37
appointed c. judge and governor		50:39
concerning the c. judge Pahoran;		51: 2
he should no longer be c. judge		51: 4
Pahoran should remani c. judge		51: 6
concerning the c. judge, Pahoran.		51:12
were so wroth with the c. judge,		51:13
and many of the c. captains		52:19
the c. captains of the Lamanites		52:28
their c. captains, all those who		52:38
their c. captains demanded their		55:23
all of whom are c. captains,		56:12
Gid was the c. captain over the		57:29
the c. captains of the Lamanites		58:25
the case with all his c. captains.		59:12
is the c. judge and the governor		60: 1
I am Moroni, your c. captain.		60:36
his epistle unto the c. governor,		61: 1
from Pahoran, the c. governor.		61: 1
am the c. governor of this land,		61: 2
the c. captain over the army.		61: 2
and their c. judges were chosen.		62:47
to be c. judge and a governor	He	1: 5
to be a c. judge and a governor		1:13
Pacumeni, who was the c. judge,		1:21
murder the c. judge Cezoram,		6:19
which led to the c. market,		7:10
said concerning the c. judge		9: 2
the c. judge had fallen to the		9: 3
spoken concerning the c. judge.		9: 4
the burial of the great c. judge		9:10
inquire concerning the c. judge		9:12
murder Seezoram, our c. judge.		9:23
true murderer of our c. judge.		9:41
the death of the c. judge,		10:13
to plead with their c. judges		11: 8
that Lachoneus was the c. judge	3Ne	1: 1
and c. governor of the land,		3: 2
did appoint c. captains over		3:17
appoint for their c. captains,		3:19
as also was the c. judge.		3:19
angry were chiefly the c. judges,		6:21

murder the c. judge of the land.	3Ne	7: 1
And every tribe did appoint a c.		7: 3
CHIEFEST		
the c. among all the captains	3Ne	3:18
he was one of the c. who had		7:10
CHIEFLY		
been kept c. by the Nephites.	He	3:15
angry were c. the chief judges,	3Ne	6:21
CHIEFS		
minds of those who were their c.	3Ne	7:14
CHILD		
bearing a c. in her arms.	1Ne	11:20
have toiled, being big with c.;		17:20
can a woman forget her sucking c.,		21:15
the c. shall behave himself proudly	2Ne	13: 5
before the c. shall know to refuse		17:16
the c. shall not have knowledge to		18: 4
For unto us a c. is born,		19: 6
few, that a c. may write them.		20:19
and a little c. shall lead them.		21: 6
And the sucking c. shall play		21: 8
and the weaned c. shall put his		21: 8
and a little c. shall lead them.		30:12
And the sucking c. shall play		30:14
and the weaned c. shall put his		30:14
and becometh as a c., submissive,	Mos	3:19
as a c. doth submit to his father.		3:19
is a liar and a c. of the devil,	Al	5:39
becometh a c. of the devil,		5:41
that this man is a c. of the devil,		10:28
O thou c. of hell, why tempt ye		11:23
that a c. is not guilty because of		30:25
now a woman nor a c. among all		54: 3
me that thou art a c. of hell;		54:11
wo unto them which are with c.,	He	15: 2
cometh unto me as a little c.,	3Ne	9:22
repent, and become as a little c.,		11:37
and become as a little c.,		11:38
that didst not travail with c.;		22: 1
as a c. with a suckling lamb,		28:22
even as a c. with a lamb;	4Ne	1:33
perceive that thou art a sober c.,	Mrm	1: 2
ye certainly will be a c. of Christ.	Mro	7:19
in the name of his Holy C.,		8: 3
suppose that God save one c.		8:15
who receiveth you as a little c.,	DC	99: 3
Even the thank-offering of a c.	Abr	1:10
wo unto them that are with c.,	JS	1:16
CHILDHOOD		
And behold, in thy c. thou hast	2Ne	2: 1
while he was yet in his c.,	DC	84:28
CHILDISHNESS		
by the c. of their fathers;	Al	31:16
CHILDREN		
prophesied and spake unto his c.,	1Ne	1:16
commandments unto the c. of men,		3: 7
that we may preserve unto our c.		3:19
of the Lord unto our c.		5:21
not of worth unto the c. of		6: 6
to his will, for the c. of men,		7:12
works among the c. of men;		9: 6
himself unto the c. of men.		10:17
I know that he loveth his c.;		11:17
in the hearts of the c. of men;		11:22
going forth among the c. of men;		11:24
descending upon the c. of men,		11:30
going forth among the c. of men.		11:31
the hearts of the c. of men,		12:17
the pride of the c. of men.		12:18
the hearts of the c. of men.		13:27
understanding of the c. of men,		13:29
founded by the devil and his c.,		14: 3
work among the c. of men;		14: 7
wickedness of the c. of men.		15: 4
in body unto the c. of men,		15:13
did bear c. in the wilderness.		17: 1
give plenty of suck for their c.,		17: 2

CHILDREN

if it so be that the c. of men	1Ne	17: 3
have borne c. in the wilderness		17:20
fathers, who were the c. of Israel,		17:23
c. of Israel were in bondage;		17:25
that the c. of Israel might		17:29
driving out of the c. of the land,		17:32
the c. of this land, who were in		17:33
created him c. that they should		17:36
miracles among the c. of men,		17:51
ship, with our wives and our c.		18: 6
much grief because of their c.,		18:17
tears and prayers, and also my c.,		18:19
duffering towards the c. of men.		19: 9
Thy c. shall make haste against		21:17
The c. whom thou shalt have,		21:20
seeing I have lost my c., and am		21:21
and I will save thy c.		21:25
shall come upon the c. of the		22: 2
c. have been carried in their arms,		22: 6
the hearts of the c. of men;		22:15
out upon all the c. of men;		22:16
built up among the c. of men,		22:22
And he gathereth his c. from the		22:25
unto me, and to my c. forever,	2Ne	1: 5
chains which bind the c. of men,		1:13
intercession for all the c. of men;		2: 9
they have brought forth c.;		2:20
the days of the c. of men		2:21
gave unto the c. of men.		2:21
they would have had no c.;		2:23
may redeem the c. of men		2:26
he called the c. of Laman,		4: 3
learning and the profit of my c.		4:15
condescension unto the c. of men		4:26
their hatred towards me and my c.		5:14
which he has made unto his c.;		6:12
God shall bestow upon your c.		9: 3
stirreth up the c. of men		9: 9
both men, women, and c.,		9:21
condescensions unto the c. of men;		9:53
that many of our c. shall perish		10: 2
and our c. shall be restored,		10: 2
have made unto the c. of men,		10:15
have made unto the c. of men,		10:17
send them forth unto all my c.,		11: 2
send their words forth unto my c.		11: 3
themselves in the c. of strangers.		12: 6
I will give c. unto them		13: 4
c. are their oppressors,		13:12
the c. whom the Lord hath given		18:18
the c. of Ammon shall obey them.		21:14
Their c. also shall be dashed		23:16
their eyes shall not spare c.		23:18
Prepare slaughter for his c.		24:21
have not taught my c. after the		25: 6
mention unto my c. concerning		25: 6
unto my c., according to all		25: 6
of worth unto the c. of men,		25: 8
a wonder among the c. of men.		25:17
to write, to persuade our c.,		25:23
that our c. may know to what		25:26
our c. may know the deadness		25:27
my c., and my beloved brethren;		26: 1
wonders, among the c. of men		26:13
things forth unto the c. of men.		26:14
is good among the c. of men;		26:33
it be plain unto the c. of men;		26:33
be revealed unto the c. of men		27:11
have been among the c. of men,		27:11
of his word unto the c. of men;		27:13
I will show unto the c. of men		27:21
all things unto the c. of men.		27:22
not among the c. of men save		27:23
I will show unto the c. of men		27:28
But when he seeth his c.,		27:34
great worth unto the c. of men,		28: 2
in the hearts of the c. of men,		28:20
I will give unto the c. of men		28:30
have made unto the c. of men,		29: 1
my word unto the c. of men,		29: 7
made known unto the c. of men.		30:16
revealed unto the c. of men		30:18
the hearts of the c. of men		30:18
work among the c. of men.	2Ne	31: 3
showeth unto the c. of men		31: 7
showeth unto the c. of men		31: 9
he said unto the c. of men:		31:10
unto the hearts of the c. of men.		33: 1
while the c. of Israel were in the	Jac	1: 7
before your wives and your c.,		2: 7
lost the confidence of your c.,		2:35
and their wives love their c.;		3: 7
ye shall remember your c.,		3:10
bring your c. unto destruction,		3:10
which will give our c., and also		4: 2
our beloved brethren and our c.		4: 3
condescensions unto the c. of men,		4: 7
manifest unto the c. of men,	Jar	1: 4
to have taught them to his c.,	Mos	1: 4
and teach them to his c.,		1: 4
they could teach them to their c.,		1: 4
except it be your little c. that		2:34
ye young men, and you little c.		2:40
from heaven among the c. of men,		3: 5
in the hearts of the c. of men.		3: 6
might come unto the c. of men		3: 9
might come upon the c. of men.		3:10
prophets among all the c. of men,		3:13
were possible that little c. could sin		3:16
can come unto the c. of men,		3:17
and become as little c.,		3:18
before God, except it be little c.,		3:21
come down among the c. of men.		4: 2
suffering towards the c. of men,		4: 6
And ye will not suffer your c. that		4:14
shall be called the c. of Christ,		5: 7
except it were little c.,		6: 2
who brought the c. of Israel out		7:19
come down among the c. of men		7:27
such mysteries to the c. of men.		8:19
understandings of the c. of men;		8:20
tale to their wives and their c.		9: 2
the women and c. of my people		10: 9
thus they have taught their c.		10:17
hatred towards the c. of Nephi.		10:17
been a resort for the c. of Nephi		11:13
of the fathers upon the c.,		13:13
given to the c. of Israel,		13:29
come down among the c. of men,		13:34
come down among the c. of men,		15: 1
miracles among the c. of men,		15: 6
intercession for the c. of men—		15: 8
compassion towards the c. of men;		15: 9
little c. also have eternal life.		15:25
come down among the c. of men;		17: 8
thus they became the c. of God.		18:22
with their women and their c.		19: 9
leave their wives and their c.,		19:11
left their wives and their c.		19:12
with their wives and their c.		19:13
if their wives and their c. were		19:19
to their wives and their c.;		19:22
wives and their c. were not slain;		19:24
return to their wives and their c.		20: 3
for their wives, and for their c.;		20:11
of the widows and their c.,		21:17
to take their women and c.,		22: 2
depart with our women and our c.,		22: 8
and their wives, and their c.		23:28
the wives and the c. of the guards		23:38
and cause that his c. should		24: 8
children should persecute their c.		24: 8
their women and all their c. that		24:22
not so many of the c. of Nephi.		25: 2
those who were the c. of Amulon		25:12
might be called the c. of Nephi		25:12
being little c. at the time he spake		26: 1
in all cases among the c. of men,		29:20
their wives, and their c.,	Al	2:25
our wives, and our c. be slain.		2:25
and their wives, and their c.		3: 1
women and c. had been slain		3: 2
c. of the kingdom of the devil.		5:25
forth among all the c. of men.		5:50
the c. of God were commanded		6: 6
your women and your c.,		7:27

CHILDREN

me, and my women, and my c.,	Al 10:11
doth grant unto the c. of men,	12: 9
he is merciful unto the c. of men,	12:15
these commandments unto his c.;	13: 1
unto the c. of men,	13: 6
the hearts of the c. of men	13:24
their wives and c. together,	14: 8
the pains of the women and c.	14:10
unto their wives and c.,	15: 2
the minds of the c. of men,	16:16
down upon all the c. of men;	18:32
who is one of the c. of a liar?	20:10
and now his c. are also come	20:13
souls as well as he loveth our c.;	24:14
remnant of the c. of Amulon	25: 7
towards the c. of men?	26:16
he may destroy the c. of God.	30:42
devil will not support his c.	30:60
hast elected us to be thy holy c.;	31:16
wickedness among the c. of men?	31:26
little c. do have words given	32:23
thou art merciful unto thy c.	33: 8
shall come among the c. of men,	34: 8
their wives, and c., and their lands.	35:14
I had murdered many of his c.	36:14
Command thy c. to do good,	39:12
may prepare the minds of their c.	39:16
people as well as unto their c.?	39:18
tidings unto us as unto our c.,	39:19
and their wives, and their c.,	43: 9
liberties, their wives and their c.,	43:45
we owe to our wives and our c.,	44: 5
we shall break, and also our c.;	44: 8
quick the c. of men do forget	46: 8
take place among the c. of men.	46: 9
our wives, and our c.—	46:12
lands, their wives, and their c.,	48:10
over the hearts of the c. of men.	48:17
their c. should be massacred	48:24
known among the c. of Lehi.	49: 8
his words unto the c. of men;	50:19
Blessed art thou and thy c.;	50:20
women and their c. from famine	53: 7
had taken many women and c.,	54: 3
a man and his wife and his c.,	54:11
I will arm my women and my c.,	54:12
and all those of their c.,	55:17
also for their wives and their c.	56:28
and our wives, and our c.,	58:12
with them many women and c.	58:30
women and our c. are returning	58:31
yea, our women and our c.,	60:17
with their wives and their c.,	63: 4
and also many women and c.;	63: 6
sent forth among the c. of men	63:12
both men, women, and c.	He 1:27
upon the hearts of the c. of men.	6:30
no justice unto the c. of men;	7: 4
their women and their c.	11:33
of the hearts of the c. of men;	12: 1
do good are the c. of men;	12: 4
the nothingness of the c. of men;	12: 7
unbelief among the c. of men	14:28
known unto the c. of men	3Ne 1:14
had many c. and did grow up	1:29
and their women and their c.,	2:12
together their women, and their c.,	3:13
insomuch as the c. of Lehi have	5:22
and our c. have been spared,	8:25
shall be called the c. of God.	12: 9
the c. of your Father who is	12:45
to give good gifts unto your c.,	14:11
little c. should be brought.	17:11
So they brought their little c.	17:12
took their little c., one by one,	17:21
consist of men, women, and c.	17:25
and your c. may be blessed.	18:21
did take his wife and his c.	19: 1
ye are the c. of the prophets;	20:25
ye are the c. of the covenant—	20:26
more are the c. of the desolate	22: 1
than the c. of the married wife,	22: 1
all thy c. shall be taught of the	3Ne 22:13
great shall be the peace of thy c.	22:13
the heart of the fathers to the c.,	25: 6
heart of the c. to their fathers,	25: 6
teach and minister unto the c.	26:14
both saw and heard these c.;	26:16
hath given unto the c. of men.	27:18
the Father unto the c. of men,	28: 7
Holy Ghost unto the c. of men,	28:11
hath made with the c. of Israel,	29: 1
coming unto the c. of Israel.	29: 2
work among the c. of men;	4Ne 1: 5
were in one, the c. of Christ,	1:17
they did teach their c. that	1:38
taught to hate the c. of God,	1:39
taught to hate the c. of Nephi	1:39
for their wives, and their c.,	Mrm 2:23
up the hearts of the c. of men	4: 5
among all the c. of Lehi,	4:12
prisoners both women and c.,	4:14
their women and their c.,	4:15
their c. were again sacrificed	4:21
with their wives and their c.,	6: 7
miracles among the c. of men	9:20
Who will despise the c. of Christ?	9:26
transpired among the c. of men	Eth 1: 3
among the c. of the land,	2:10
due time unto the c. of men.	3:27
show them unto the c. of men.	3:28
to come unto the c. of men	4: 1
light unto men, women, and c.,	6: 3
upon the hearts of the c. of men,	8:26
he had no c. even until he was	9:23
no faith among the c. of men God	12:12
workest unto the c. of men	12:29
prepare a place for the c. of men.	12:33
had for the c. of men is charity;	12:34
own life and of his wives and c.	14: 2
he did slay both women and c.,	14:17
of both men, women, and c.	14:22
the loss of men, women and c.	14:31
and also their wives and their c.	15: 2
with their wives and their c.—	15:15
men women and c. being armed	15:15
walk with the c. of men.	Mro 7: 4
to minister unto the c. of men,	7:22
things unto the c. of men,	7:24
he hath upon the c. of men?	7:27
the cause of the c. of men;	7:28
to minister unto the c. of men.	7:29
hath made unto the c. of men,	7:31
the way among the c. of men,	7:31
hath made unto the c. of men.	7:32
to appear unto the c. of men?	7:36
wo be unto the c. of men,	7:37
the baptism of your little c.	8: 5
wherefore, little c. are whole,	8: 8
that ye should baptize little c.	8: 9
themselves as their little c.,	8:10
all be saved with their little c.	8:10
little c. need no repentance,	8:11
But little c. are alive in Christ,	8:12
c. have died without baptism!	8:12
if little c. could not be saved	8:13
that little c. need baptism	8:14
all c. are alike unto me;	8:17
love little c. with a perfect love;	8:17
Little c. cannot repent;	8:19
saith that little c. need baptism	8:20
all little c. are alive in Christ,	8:22
there were men, women, and c.	9: 7
fathers of those women and c.	9: 8
the c. upon the flesh of their	9: 8
our women and our c. upon	9:19
hath been unto the c. of men,	10: 3
to the faith of the c. of men,	10: 7
the unbelief of the c. of men.	10:19
wo be unto the c. of men if	10:25
plant in the hearts of the c.	DC 2: 2
the hearts of the c. shall turn	2: 2
come forth among the c. of men.	4: 1
my words unto the c. of men.	5: 6

CHILDREN

come forth unto the c. of men.	DC	6: 1
brought the c. of Israel through		8: 3
come forth among the c. of men.		11: 1
gone forth among the c. of men,		11:22
come forth among the c. of men,		11:22
shall grant unto the c. of men		11:22
come forth among the c. of men.		12: 1
come forth unto the c. of men.		14: 1
purposes unto the c. of men		17: 4
purposes unto the c. of men.		17: 9
that the c. of men are stirred		18: 6
expedient unto the c. of men.		18:18
and c. who have arrived at		18:42
work among the c. of men,		18:44
the hearts of the c. of men,		19: 7
preparations unto the c. of men.		19:19
of the church of Christ having c.		20:70
hearts of the fathers to the c.,		27: 9
hearts of the c. to the fathers,		27: 9
man, nor the c. of men;		29:34
should tempt the c. of men,		29:39
that little c. are redeemed		29:46
unto Satan to tempt little c.,		29:47
shown forth unto the c. of men;		35:10
earth, among the c. of men,		38:11
inheritance of your c. forever,		38:20
not known among the c. of men,		39:15
to the c. of the kingdom		41: 6
but to teach the c. of men		43:15
the hearts of the c. of men.		45:55
and their c. shall grow up		45:58
conditions of the c. of men.		46:15
the benefit of the c. of God.		46:26
Behold, ye are little c. and		50:40
Fear not, little c., for you		50:41
c. also may receive instruction		55: 4
heritage of God unto his c.;		58:17
inheritance for the c. of God.		58:51
the disciples and the c. of men		58:52
do like unto the c. of Israel,		61:25
be of good cheer little c.;		61:36
c. shall grow up until they		63:51
the hearts of the c. of men.		64:22
sent forth unto the c. of men,		66: 2
as parents have c. in Zion,		68:25
their c. shall be baptized for		68:27
also teach their c. to pray,		68:28
their c. are also growing up		68:31
else were your c. unclean,		74: 1
his c. should be circumcised		74: 3
the c., being brought up in		74: 4
their c. might remain without		74: 6
saith that little c. are unholy;		74: 6
But little c. are holy,		74: 7
ye are little c., and ye have		78:17
concerning women and c.,		83: 1
All c. have claim upon		83: 4
the c. of Israel in the wilderness,		84:23
among the c. of Israel until		84:27
resteth upon the c. of Zion,		84:56
poured out upon the c. of Zion.		84:58
the c. of the kingdom pollute		84:59
the names of the c. written		85: 5
of their fathers, and of their c.,		85: 7
as unto the c. of the priest,		85:12
by them, as the c. of Israel,		89:21
disobedience, from the c. of men,		93:39
bring up your c. in light and		93:40
have not taught your c. light		93:42
concerning his c.;		93:44
forth my word to the c. of men.		96: 4
go forth unto the c. of men		96: 5
the hearts of the c. of men		96: 5
my word unto the c. of men.		96: 8
hearts of the c. to their fathers,		98:16
hearts of the fathers to the c.;		98:16
your children's c. unto the third		98:28
come upon you or your c.,		98:29
your children's c. unto the third		98:29
also thy c. and thy children's		98:30
thy children's c. unto the third		98:30
And upon his c., and upon		98:46
and upon his children's c.		98:46
But if the c. shall repent,	DC	98:47
repent, or the children's c.,		98:47
go until your c. are provided for,		99: 6
her c. are scattered.		101:17
inheritances, they and their c.,		101:18
wisdom concerning the c. of Zion,		101:41
what shall I liken the c. of Zion?		101:81
will I liken the c. of Zion.		101:85
as Moses led the c. of Israel.		103:16
For ye are the c. of Israel,		103:17
and establish the c. of Zion		103:35
have given unto the c. of men		104:17
that you may be the c. of light,		106: 5
be administered to the c. of men,		109: 4
a great love for the c. of Jacob,		109:61
have mercy upon the c. of Jacob,		109:62
c. of Judah may begin to return		109:64
O Lord, upon his wife and c.,		109:69
hearts of the fathers to the c.,		110:15
c. to the fathers, lest the whole		110:15
my name among the c. of men.		112: 6
and are the c. of disobedience		121:17
upon the souls of the c. of men,		121:37
to ourselves, to our wives and c.,		123: 7
lies, upon the hearts of the c.,		123: 7
not only to our own wives and c.,		123: 9
to the salvation of the c. of men,		128:11
the heart of the fathers to the c.,		128:17
the heart of the c. to their fathers,		128:17
between the fathers and the c.,		128:18
and they bore him c.;		132:37
houses and lands, wives and c.,		132:55
treasures unto the c. of Ephraim,		133:30
even the c. of Ephraim.		133:32
for the benefit of the c. of men;		135: 3
am he who led the c. of Israel		136:22
all the c. of men which are,	Mses	1: 8
not had among the c. of men.		1:23
the c. of men shall esteem		1:41
again among the c. of men—		1:41
known among the c. of men.		1:42
had created all the c. of men;		3: 5
sorrow thou shalt bring forth c.,		4:22
their c. were taught to read		6: 6
was kept of the c. of God.		6: 8
the c. of men were numerous		6:15
taught unto the c. of men.		6:23
come among the c. of men,		6:49
shall come unto the c. of men,		6:52
upon the heads of the c.,		6:54
thy c. are conceived in sin,		6:55
Wherefore teach it unto your c.,		6:57
these things freely unto your c.,		6:58
upon all the c. of Canaan,		7: 8
all the doings of the c. of men;		7:41
of the wickedness of my c.		7:48
thou not bless the c. of noah?		7:49
would call upon the c. of Noah;		7:51
concerning the c. of Noah;		7:60
shall be among the c. of men,		7:61
his Gospel unto the c. of men,		8:19
Noah called upon the c. of men		8:20
And our wives bear unto us c.,		8:21
in offering up their c. unto	Abr	1: 7
men, women, and c.		1: 8
shall plant in the hearts of the c.	JS	2:39
the hearts of the c. shall turn		2:39
generation of the c. of men.		2:73

CHILDREN'S

your c. children unto the third	DC	98:28
your c. children unto the third		98:29
thy c. children unto the third		98:30
battles, and their c. battles,		98:37
battles, and their c. children's,		98:37
battles, and their children's c.,		98:37
and upon his c. children		98:46
shall repent, or the c. children,		98:47

CHOICE

which is c. above all other lands.	1Ne	2:20
And now, if ye have c., go up		7:15
which is c. above all other lands,		13:30

CHOICE / CHRIST

CHOICE (cont.)

more c. than they if they had	1Ne 17:34
which is c. above all other lands;	2Ne 1: 5
be a c. and a favored people	1:19
c. seer unto the fruit of my loins.	3: 6
A c. seer will I raise up	3: 7
for it is a c. land, saith God	10:19
even that which was c. unto me	Jac 5:43
record, for they are c. unto me;	WM 1: 6
they will be c. unto my brethren.	1: 6
which is c. above all the earth?	Eth 1:38
c. above all the lands of the earth.	1:42
was c. above all other lands,	2: 7
which is c. above all other lands;	2:10
Behold, this is a c. land,	2:12
a land c. above all other lands.	2:15
was c. above all other lands;	9:20
land that was c. above all lands,	10:28
a c. land above all other lands,	13: 2
a great number of our c. men.	Mro 9: 2
had a spot of land, very c.;	DC 101:44
upon this very c. piece of land,	101:44

CHOICEST

planted it with the c. vine,	2Ne 15: 2

CHOIRS

spirit may join the c. above	Mos 2:28
praises with the c. above,	Mrm 7: 7

CHOKE

the tares c. the wheat and drive	DC 86: 3

CHOOSE

And they are free to c. liberty	2Ne 2:27
or to c. captivity and death,	2:27
and c. eternal life, according to	2:28
And not c. eternal death,	2:29
to c. the way of everlasting	10:23
and to c. the good.	17:15
refuse the evil and c. the good,	17:16
and will yet c. Israel,	24: 1
and c. works of darkness	26:10
c. you by the voice of this people,	Mos 29:25
of the people doth c. iniquity,	29:27
this people should c. iniquity,	Al 10:19
being left to c. good or evil;	13: 3
C. ye this day, whom ye will serve.	30: 8
ye c. darkness rather than light?	He 13:29
that ye might c. life or death;	14:31
C. ye out from among our sons	Eth 6:24
and let every man c. for himself	DC 37: 4
whom he has chosen or will c.	107:72
these seven presidents are to c.	107:95
they may travel also if they c.,	124:135
or bad, as you may c. to call it.	127: 2
c. out a sufficient number of	136: 7
thou mayest c. for thyself,	Mses 3:17
C. ye this day, to serve the	6:33
should c. me, their Father;	7:33

CHOOSING

God they c. to repent and work	Al 13:10
time has come for a day of c.;	DC 105:35

CHOSE

Wherefore, I c. these things,	WM 1: 5
they c. evil works rather than	Al 40:13
they who c. evil were more	He 5: 2
than they who c. good,	5: 2
whom Jesus c. to be his disciples	Mrm 3:18
whom Jesus c. in this land;	3:19
the other twelve whom Jesus c.	3:19
they c. even the firstborn of the	Eth 6:25
c. all the brothers of Pagag,	6:26
took them wives, even as they c.	Mses 8:14

CHOSEN

over all those whom he hath c.,	1Ne 1:20
Lord hath c. him to be a ruler	3:29
they were ordained of God, and c.	12: 7
c. to minister unto thy seed.	12: 8
c. thee in the furnace of affliction.	20:10
and I have c. the good part,	2Ne 2:30
yet I have been c. by this people,	Mos 2:11
yea, a c. man of God,	7:26
virgin, a precious and c. vessel,	Al 7:10
man, who is a c. man of God;	10: 7
therefore they having c. good,	13: 3
who had been c. for the work,	16:15
we are a c. and a holy people.	31:18
God that they were c. of him,	31:22
for we are a c. people unto thee,	31:28
A c. land, and the land of	46:17
who have been c. by this people	60: 1
and their chief judges were c.	62:47
to be a great man, c. of God,	He 9:16
have been a c. people of the Lord;	15: 3
whom I have c. from among you	3Ne 12: 1
upon the twelve whom he had c.,	13:25
c. to minister unto this people.	13:25
those twelve whom he had c.:	15:11
the disciples whom he had c.,	18:26
the disciples whom he had c.,	18:36
disciples whom Jesus had c.—	19: 4
all those whom Jesus had c.	19:12
unto these whom I have c.;	19:20
I have c. them out of the world.	19:20
purified those whom I have c.,	19:28
the disciples whom Jesus had c.	26:17
also to them whom he hath c.	28:34
those whom the Lord hath c.,	28:36
of Jesus, whom he had c.,	4Ne 1:14
a c. land of the Lord;	Eth 13: 2
the twelve whom he had c.,	Mro 2: 1
unto the c. vessels of the Lord,	7:31
my disciples, whom I have c.	DC 1: 4
c. to do the work of the Lord,	3: 9
and thou art still c.,	3:10
you that are c. in this thing,	19: 9
c. to write the Book of Mormon,	24: 1
that ye are c. out of the world	29: 4
and those whom he has c.,	51: 3
and c. in these last days,	52: 1
all the elders whom I have c.	52:21
thou art called and c.;	55: 1
called but few of them are c.	95: 5
They who are not c. have	95: 6
endow those whom I have c.	95: 8
c. to be a standing council	102: 3
let those be c. that are worthy.	105:35
of the Spirit, those that are c.;	105:36
High Priests, c. by the body,	107:22
literal descendants of the c. seed,	107:40
should be the c. of the Lord,	107:42
a bishop must be c. from the	107:69
whom he has c. or will choose	107:72
c. out of the number of the	107:93
of mine elders shom I have c.	108: 4
who were c. to bear testimony	112: 1
feet be shod also, for thou art c.,	112: 7
thou art the man whom I have c.	112:16
many called, but few are c.	121:34
And why are they not c.?	121:34
many are called, but few are c.	121:40
messengers, yea, c. messengers,	124:26
that is the spot which I have c.	124:43
I have c. him and anointed him.	124:76
the Almighty, have c. thee,	Mses 1:25
bondage, even Israel my c.	1:26
and C. from the beginning,	4: 2
that which I have c. hath	7:39
my C. shall return unto me,	7:39
thou wast c. before thou	Abr 3:23

CHRIST

JESUS is the C., the ETERNAL	T Pg
at the judgment-seat of C.	T Pg
it must needs be expedient that C.—	2Ne 10: 3
shall believe in me, that I am C.,	10: 7
the truth of the coming of C.;	11: 4
save C. should come all men must	11: 6
For if there be no C. there be	11: 7
But there is a God, and he is C.,	11: 7
be persuaded to believe in C.,	25:16
that they shall believe in C.,	25:16
his name shall be Jesus C.,	25:19

CHRIST

save it be this Jesus C.,	2Ne 25:20	through the atoning blood of C.,	Mos	3:18
our brethren, to believe in C.,	25:23	the atonement of C. the Lord,		3:19
notwithstanding we believe in C.,	25:24	apply the atoning blood of C.		4: 2
forward with steadfastness unto C.,	25:24	for we believe in Jesus C.,		4: 2
and we are made alive in C.	25:25	faith which they had in Jesus C.		4: 3
And we talk of C., we rejoice	25:26	shall be called the children of C.,		5: 7
we rejoice in C., we preach	25:26	take upon you the name of C.,		5: 8
we preach of C., we prophesy	25:26	shall be called by the name of C.		5: 9
we prophesy of C., and we write	25:26	take upon him the name of C.		5:10
unto that life which is in C.,	25:27	that C., the Lord God Omnipotent,		5:15
after the law is fulfilled in C.,	25:27	taken upon them the name of C.		6: 2
the right way is to believe in C.	25:28	come, yea, even the coming of C.		7:26
the right way is to believe in C.,	25:29	C. was the God, the Father of all		7:27
and C. is the Holy One of Israel;	25:29	even until the resurrection of C.–		15:21
after C. shall have risen from	26: 1	they have eternal life through C.,		15:23
but look forward unto C.	26: 8	that have died before C. came,		15:24
that Jesus is the very C.,	26:12	if C. had not come into the world,		16: 6
also that Jesus is the C.,	26:12	if C. had not risen from the dead,		16: 7
shall be read by the power of C.;	27:11	of death is swallowed up in C.		16: 8
are the humble followers of C.;	28:14	in and through C. ye can be saved?		16:13
And the gospel of Jesus C. shall	30: 5	cometh through C. the Lord,		16:15
to the knowledge of Jesus C.,	30: 5	and sufferings, and death of C.,		18: 2
shall begin to believe in C.;	30: 7	through the redemption of C.,		18:13
as many as shall believe in C.	30: 7	of God, or the church of C.,		18:17
speak concerning the doctrine of C.;	31: 2	take upon them the name of C.,		25:23
to take upon you the name of C.,	31:13	concerning the coming of C.		26: 2
save it were by the word of C.	31:19	taken upon them the name of C.	Al	1:19
forward with a steadfastness in C.,	31:20	and deliverance of Jesus C.		4:14
feasting upon the word of C.,	31:20	white through the blood of C.,		5:27
this is the doctrine of C.,	31:21	call you, which is the name of C.;		5:38
they speak the words of C.	32: 3	of God, which is in C. Jesus;		5:44
feast upon the words of C.;	32: 3	I know that Jesus C. shall come,		5:48
behold, the words of C. will tell	32: 3	to the testimony of Jesus C.,		6: 8
Behold, this is the doctrine of C.,	32: 6	and deliverance of Jesus C.;		9:28
unto the Father in the name of C.,	32: 9	the death of C. shall loose the		11:42
and great faith in C. that I shall	33: 7	before the bar of C. the Son,		11:44
they shall be reconciled unto C.,	33: 9	to our faith which is in C.,		14:26
and believe in C.;	33:10	to their faith which was in C.		14:28
not in these words believe in C.,	33:10	the power of C. unto salvation?		15: 6
And if ye shall believe in C.	33:10	believest in the redemption of C		15: 8
for they are the words of C.,	33:10	to his faith which is in C.		15:10
if they are not the words of C.,	33:11	concerning the coming of C.,		18:39
judge ye–for c. will show	33:11	concerning the coming of C.,		21: 9
pray the Father in the name of C.	33:12	the death and sufferings of C.,		21: 9
to overthrow the doctrine of C.	Jac 1:hd	through C., for all whosoever		22:13
wherefore, we knew of C.	1: 6	the sufferings and death of C.		22:14
persuade them to come unto C.,	1: 7	look forward to the coming of C.,		25:15
that all men would believe in C.,	1: 8	to strengthen their faith in C.;		25:16
ye have obtained a hope in C.	2:19	they were firm in the faith of C.,		27:27
may know that we knew of C.,	4: 4	views of C. and the resurrection;		27:28
Behold, they believed in C. and	4: 5	by the victory of C. over it.		27:28
him through the atonement of C.,	4:11	joy because of the light of C.		28:14
the resurrection which is in C.,	4:11	concerning the coming of C.		30: 6
the first-fruits of C. unto God,	4:11	that there should be no C.		30:12
speak of the atonement of C.,	4:12	Why do ye look for a C.?		30:13
have been spoken concerning C.,	6: 8	know that there shall be a C.		30:15
and deny the good word of C.,	6: 8	people that there shall be no C.,		30:22
the resurrection, which is in C.,	6: 9	And ye also say that C. shall come.		30:26
them that there should be no C.	7: 2	know that there shall be a C.		30:26
might overthrow the doctrine of C.	7: 2	a God, and also deny the C.?		30:39
faith in C. who should come,	7: 3	and also that C. shall come.		30:39
the gospel, or the doctrine of C.	7: 6	no God, or that C. cometh not?		30:40
Deniest thou the C. who should	7: 9	unto us that there shall be no C.		31:16
If there should be a c., I would	7: 9	bind them down to a belief of C.,		31:17
but I know that there is no C.,	7: 9	them that there shall be no C.		31:29
for they truly testify of C.	7:11	wilt thou comfort my soul in C.		31:31
have spoken concerning this C.	7:11	thou comfort their souls in C.		31:32
and also, that C. shall come,	7:14	them again unto thee in C.		31:34
taught them, and confessed the C.,	7:17	swallowed up in the joy of C.		31:38
lied unto God; for I denied the C.,	7:19	concerning the coming of C.,		34: 2
Because of thy faith in C.,	En 1: 8	or whether there shall be no C.		34: 5
shall receive in the name of C.,	1:15	the word is in C. unto salvation.		34: 6
to the truth which is in C.	1:26	I do know that C. shall come		34: 8
that ye should come unto C.,	Om 1:26	no more deny the coming of C.;		34:37
years after the coming of C.	WM 1: 2	take upon you the name of C.;		34:38
and somewhat concerning C.,	1: 2	the coming of one Jesus C., a		36:17
prophecies of the coming of C.;	1: 4	in Jesus C. their Redeemer.		37: 9
yea, the redemption of C.;	1: 8	and faith on the Lord Jesus C.;		37:33
And he shall be called Jesus C.,	Mos 3: 8	their faith on the Lord Jesus C.		37:33
and faith on the Lord Jesus C.	3:12	to give heed to the word of C.,		37:44
believe that C. should come,	3:13	the words of C., if we follow		37:45
blood of C. atoneth for their sins.	3:16	unto the Lord Jesus C. for mercy,		38: 8
in and through the name of C.,	3:17	be saved only in and through C.		38: 9

CHRIST

concerning the coming of C.	Al 39:15
until after the coming of C.	40: 2
down to the resurrection of C.	40:16
down to the resurrection of C.	40:18
die after the resurrection of C.	40:19
cometh at the resurrection of C.;	40:20
at the resurrection of C., and	40:20
power and resurrection of C.,	41: 2
our religion and our faith in C.	44: 3
Believest thou in Jesus C.,	45: 4
Jesus C. shall manifest himself	45:10
were all the true believers of C.,	46:14
who were true believers in C.	46:15
upon them, gladly, the name of C.,	46:15
their belief in C. who should come.	46:15
we take upon us the name of C.,	46:18
take upon them the name of C.,	46:21
not stand fast in the faith of C.	46:27
redeemed by the Lord Jesus C.;	46:39
those who died in the faith of C.	46:41
who was firm in the faith of C.,	48:13
before the coming of C.,	He 1:hd
down to the coming of C.	1:hd
down to the coming of C.,	1:hd
believe on the name of Jesus C.,	3:28
lead the man of C. in a straight	3:29
and firmer in the faith of C.,	3:35
atoning blood of Jesus C.,	5: 9
who is C., the Son of God	5:12
until ye shall have faith in C.,	5:41
have testified of the coming of C.,	8:22
and faith on the Lord Jesus C.,	13: 6
know of the coming of Jesus C.,	14:12
resurrection of C. redeemeth	14:17
this because of their faith in C.	15: 9
that the C. must shortly come—	16: 4
such a being as a C. shall come;	16:18
the doctrine of C. was a foolish	3Ne 2: 7
given, or from the coming of C.;	2: 8
year from the coming of C.,	3: 1
expedient that C. had come,	5: 2
I am a disciple of Jesus C.,	5:13
God and my Savior Jesus C.,	5:20
who is Jesus C., the Son of God;	5:26
the resurrection of C.;	6:20
of the things pertaining to C.	6:23
concerning the ministry of C.,	7:15
faith on the Lord Jesus C.	7:16
his faith on the Lord Jesus c.	7:18
God, which was in Jesus C.,	7:21
I am Jesus C. the Son of God.	9:15
unto the Lord Jesus C.,	10:10
these things at the coming of C.,	10:15
soon after the ascension of C.	10:18
Jesus C. did show himself unto	11:hd
conversing about this Jesus C.,	11: 2
Behold, I am Jesus C., whom the	11:10
that C. should show himself unto	11:12
authority given me of Jesus C.,	11:25
believe in me, that I am Jesus C.,	20:31
in my words, who am Jesus C.	21:11
and the holiness which is in C.,	26: 5
were called the church of C.	26:21
take upon you the name of C.,	27: 5
and did preach the gospel of C.	28:23
united unto the church of C.,	28:23
before the judgment-seat of C.;	28:31
of all the marvelous works of C.,	28:33
according to the words of C.,	28:33
until the judgment day of C.;	28:40
shall deny the C. and his works!	29: 5
no miracle wrought by Jesus C.;	29: 7
according to the word of C.!	29: 7
and hear the words of Jesus C.,	30: 1
THE DISCIPLES OF JESUS C.	4Ne 1:hd
had formed a church of C.	1: 1
were in one, the children of C.,	1:17
the first generation from C.	1:18
years from the coming of C.)	1:21
because of their prosperity in C.	1:23
to deny the true church of C.	1:26
which professed to know the C.,	1:27
church which denied the C.;	1:29
persecute the true church of C.,	4Ne 1:29
humility and their belief in C.;	1:29
they were true believers in C.;	1:36
the true believers in C.,	1:37
and the true worshipers of C.,	1:37
rebel against the gospel of C.;	1:38
year from the coming of C.	1:48
years from the coming of C.,	Mrm 3: 4
our Lord and Savior Jesus C.,	3:14
before the judgment-seat of C.,	3:20
believe the gospel of Jesus C.,	3:21
the very C. and the very God.	3:21
before the judgment-seat of C.	3:22
persuaded that Jesus is the C.,	5:14
and they are without C. and God	5:16
they had C. for their shepherd;	5:17
before the judgment-seat of C.	6:21
and believe in Jesus C.,	7: 5
lay hold upon the gospel of C.,	7: 8
if it so be that ye believe in C.,	7:10
Jesus C. hath shown you unto	8:35
take upon you the name of C.?	8:38
those who do not believe in C.	9: 1
Then will ye longer deny the C.,	9: 3
and the holiness of Jesus C.,	9: 5
knoweth not the gospel of C.;	9: 8
of the fall of man came Jesus C.,	9:12
because of Jesus C. came the	9:12
of man, which came by Jesus C.,	9:13
the death of C. bringeth to pass	9:13
who shall say that Jesus C. did	9:18
whoso believeth in C., doubting	9:21
ask the Father in the name of C.	9:21
For behold, thus said Jesus C.,	9:22
will despise the children of C.?	9:26
the sacrament of C. unworthily;	9:29
do it in the name of Jesus C.,	9:29
restoration to the knowledge of C.,	9:36
may the Lord Jesus C. grant	9:37
faith on the name of Jesus C.	9:37
of the land, who is Jesus C.,	Eth 2:12
Behold, I am Jesus C.	3:14
until after C. should show	4: 1
after C. truly had showed himself	4: 2
have rejected the gospel of C.;	4: 3
saith Jesus C., the Son of God,	4: 7
no greater things, saith Jesus C.;	4: 8
by faith that C. showed himself	12: 7
even those who were before C.	12:16
strong, even before C. came,	12:19
me, yea, even Jesus C.	12:22
before the judgment-seat of C.,	12:38
and also the Lord Jesus C.,	12:41
Behold, Ether saw the days of C.,	13: 4
Nephite that will not deny the C.	Mro 1: 2
Moroni, will not deny the C.;	1: 3
The words of C., which he	2: 1
Now C. spake these words unto	2: 3
the Father in the name of C.,	3: 2
In the name of Jesus C. I	3: 3
remission of sins through Jesus C.,	3: 3
the flesh and blood of C. unto	4: 1
to the commandments of C.;	4: 1
the Father in the name of C.,	4: 2
the name of thy Son, Jesus C.,	4: 3
the name of thy Son, Jesus C.,	5: 2
took upon them the name of C.,	6: 3
the people of the church of C.;	6: 4
alone upon the merits of C.,	6: 4
numbered among the people of C.	6: 7
Father, and our Lord Jesus C.,	7: 2
the peaceable followers of C.,	7: 3
of the devil cannot follow C.;	7:11
if he follow C. he cannot be a	7:11
the Spirit of C. is given to	7:16
and to persuade to believe in C.,	7:16
by the power and gift of C.;	7:16
evil, and believe not in C.,	7:17
which light is the light of C.,	7:18
diligently in the light of C.	7:19
ye certainly will be a child of C.	7:19
concerning the coming of C.;	7:22
in C. there should come every	7:22

CHRIST

that C. should come.	Mro	7:23
which are good cometh of C.;		7:24
began to exercise faith in C.;		7:25
it was until the coming of C.		7:25
as sure as C. liveth he spake		7:26
because C. hath ascended into		7:27
by declaring the word of C.		7:31
of men may have faith in C.,		7:32
And C. hath said:		7:33
according to the words of C.,		7:38
I judge that ye have faith in C.		7:39
through the atonement of C.		7:41
Holy Ghost that Jesus is the C.,		7:44
charity is the pure love of C.,		7:47
followers of his Son, Jesus C.;		7:48
your Lord Jesus C. hath been		8: 2
Listen to the words of C., your		8: 8
little children are alive in C.,		8:12
denieth the mercies of C.,		8:20
at the judgment-seat of C.		8:21
little children are alive in C.,		8:22
denying the mercies of C.,		8:23
I trust in C. that thou wilt be		9:22
My son, be faithful in C.;		9:25
but may C. lift thee up,		9:25
and our Lord Jesus C., who		9:26
was given of the coming of C.		10: 1
Father, in the name of C.,		10: 4
real intent, having faith in C.,		10: 4
that is good denieth the C.,		10: 6
gifts come by the Spirit of C.;		10:17
Every good gift cometh of C.		10:18
C. truly said unto our fathers:		10:23
according to the words of C.;		10:26
that ye would come unto C.,		10:30
come unto C., and be perfected		10:32
grace ye may be perfect in C.;		10:32
grace of God ye are perfect in C.,		10:32
the grace of God are perfect in C.,		10:33
then are ye sanctified in C.		10:33
the shedding of the blood of C.,		10:33
rely upon the merits of Jesus C.,	DC	3:20
Behold, I am Jesus C., the Son		6:21
Behold, I am Jesus C., the Son		10:57
in the power of Jesus C.,		11:10
Behold, I am Jesus C., the Son		11:28
Behold, I am Jesus C., the Son		14: 9
listen to the words of Jesus C.,		15: 1
listen to the words of Jesus C.,		16: 1
I, Jesus C., your Lord and		17: 9
Take upon you the name of C.,		18:21
in my name, which is Jesus C.,		18:22
Jesus C. is the name which is		18:23
I, Jesus C., your Lord and		18:33
in the name of Jesus C.;		18:41
I, Jesus C., your Lord and		18:47
Alpha and Omega, C. the Lord;		19: 1
I am Jesus C.;		19:24
The rise of the Church of C.		20: 1
of our Lord and Savior Jesus C.		20: 1
ordained an apostle of Jesus C.,		20: 2
of God, an apostle of Jesus C.,		20: 3
our Lord and Savior Jesus C.,		20: 4
fulness of the gospel of Jesus C.		20: 9
believe on the name of Jesus C.,		20:29
our Lord and Savior Jesus C.		20:30
our Lord and Savior Jesus C.		20:31
them the name of Jesus C.,		20:37
have received of the Spirit of C.		20:37
members of the church of C.—		20:38
of the flesh and blood of C.—		20:40
and invite all to come unto C.		20:59
composing this church of C.		20:61
concerning the church of C.		20:68
member of the church of C.		20:70
them in the name of Jesus C.,		20:70
received into the church of C.		20:71
has the authority from Jesus C.		20:73
been commissioned of Jesus C.		20:73
the name of thy Son, Jesus C.,		20:77
the name of thy Son, Jesus C.,		20:79
member of the church of C.		20:80
composing the church of C.,		20:81
a prophet, an apostle of Jesus C.,	DC	21: 1
the grace of your Lord Jesus C.,		21: 1
an elder unto this church of C.,		21:11
Listen to the voice of Jesus C.,		27: 1
Listen to the voice of Jesus C.,		29: 1
but of me, even Jesus C.,		31:13
even Jesus C. your redeemer;		34: 1
I am Jesus C., the Son		35: 2
I am Jesus C., the Son		36: 8
even Jesus C., the Great I AM,		38: 1
in my name for, I am C.,		38: 4
the Great I AM, even Jesus C.—		39: 1
even Jesus C. the Son of		42: 1
belongeth to this church of C.,		42:78
I am Jesus C., the Savior of		43:34
that C. delayeth his coming		45:26
Jesus C. is the Son of God,		46:13
be done in the name of C.,		46:31
in the name of Jesus C.,		49:13
Behold, I am Jesus C.,		49:28
through Jesus C., his Son.		50:27
I say unto you, I am Jesus C.,		51:20
I am Jesus C., the Son of God,		52:44
in the name of Jesus C.,		55: 2
in the name of Jesus C.		59: 5
the Lord your God, even Jesus C.,		62: 1
Alpha and Omega, even Jesus C.		63:60
your Redeemer, even Jesus C.		66:13
record of me, even Jesus C.,		68: 6
faith in C. the Son of the living		68:25
not the gospel of Jesus C.		74: 2
believed not the gospel of C.,		74: 4
the atonement of Jesus C.;		74: 7
of the gospel of Jesus C.,		76:14
kingdom of our God and his C.—		76:28
testimony of the gospel of C.		76:50
are Christ's, and C. is God's.		76:59
presence of God and his C.		76:62
God and C. are the judge of		76:68
received not the gospel of C.,		76:82
the Lord, even C. the Lamb,		76:85
some of C. and some of John,		76:100
when C. shall have subdued all		76:106
but where God and C. dwell		76:112
before the coming of C.		77:13
saith your Lord, even Jesus C.		79: 4
your Redeemer, even Jesus C.		80: 5
Alpha and Omega, even Jesus C.		81: 7
A revelation of Jesus C. unto his		84: 1
Spirit, even the Spirit of Jesus C.		84:45
from the world with C. in God—		86: 9
through Jesus C. his Son—		88: 5
This is the light of C.		88: 7
unto you, even the law of C.,		88:21
in the name of the Lord Jesus C.,		88:133
for the revelation of Jesus C.		90:11
even Jesus C. your Lord.		95:17
high council of the church of C.,		102: 1
high council of the church of C.,		102:12
kingdom of our God and his C.;		105:32
witnesses of the name of C. in		107:23
of the gospel of Jesus C.,		107:35
church of C. in the land of Zion,		107:59
Father, in the name of Jesus C.,		109: 4
thus saith the Lord: It is C.		113: 2
is a servant in the hands of C.,		113: 4
Church of Jesus C. of Latter-Day		115: 3
even The Church of Jesus C. of		115: 4
for the gospel of Jesus C.		121:29
seer of the church of Jesus C.		127:12
by the revelation of Jesus C.		128: 8
Church of Jesus C. of Latter-Day		128:21
and Jesus C., whom he hath sent.		132:24
were with C. in his resurrection,		133:55
meet before the judgment seat of C.,		135: 5
religion of Jesus C., that will		135: 7
Church of Jesus C. of Latter-Day		136: 2
Church of Jesus C. of Latter-Day		OD
President of the Church of Jesus C.		OD
President of the Church of Jesus C.		OD
and truth, which is Jesus C.,	Mses	6:52
Son of Man, even Jesus C.		6:57
Begotten, even Jesus C.,		7:50

CHRIST 175 CHURCH

in the name of Jesus C.,	Mses	8:24
my name, saying— I am C.—	JS	1: 6
say unto , you Lo, here is C.,		1:21
of the Church of Jesus C. of		2: 1
said that that prophet was C.;		2:40
and in His Son, Jesus C., and	AoF	1
through the Atonement of C.,		3
Faith in the Lord Jesus C.;		4
that C. will reign personally		10

CHRISTIANS
should a band of C. remain	Al	46:13
gladly, the name of Christ, or C.		46:15
prayed that the cause of the C.,		46:16
by their enemies the cause of C.		48:10

CHRIST'S
for C. sake, and for the sake of	Jac	1: 4
afflictions, for C. sake, who	Al	4:13
all are theirs and they are C.,	DC	76:59
They are C., the first fruits,		88:98
redemption of those who are C.		88:99
and this earth will be C.		130: 9

CHRISTS
after there had been false C.,	WM	1:15
there shall also arise false C.,	JS	1:22

CHRONOLOGY
delineate the c. running back	Abr	1:28

CHURCH
spake of the brethren of the c.,	1Ne	4:26
the foundation of a great c.		13: 4
a c. which is most abominable		13: 5
this great and abominable c.;		13: 6
this great and abominable c.		13: 8
of a great and abominable c.,		13:26
of the great and abominable c.,		13:28
kept back by that abominable c.,		13:32
kept back by that abominable c.,		13:34
by that great and abominable c.,		14: 3
that great and abominable c.,		14: 9
one is the c. of the Lamb of God,		14:10
the other is the c. of the devil;		14:10
to the c. of the Lamb of God		14:10
great c., which is the mother of		14:10
beheld the c. of the Lamb of God,		14:12
beheld that the c. of the Lamb,		14:12
the saints of the c. of the Lamb,		14:14
the great and abominable c.,		14:15
the great and abominable c.		14:17
that great and abominable c.,		22:13
that great and abominable c.,		22:14
that great and abominable c.	2Ne	6:12
shall be restored to the true c.		9: 2
God and the people of his c.		25:14
that great and abominable c.		28:18
they were called the c. of God,	Mos	18:17
or the c. of Christ,		18:17
of God was added to his c.		18:17
people of the c. should impart of		18:27
who had formed a c. of God		21:30
form themselves into a c.,		21:34
he being the founder of their c.		23:16
did belong to the c. of God;		25:18
priests and teachers over every c.		25:19
every c. having their priests and		25:21
churches they were all one c.,		25:22
yea, even the c. of God;		25:22
neither would they join the c.		26: 4
who were in the c., and did cause		26: 6
committed sin, that were in the c.,		26: 6
should be admonished by the c.		26: 6
Alma the authority over the c.		26: 8
thing happened before in the c.;		26:10
a c. among this people;		26:17
him shall ye receive into the c.,		26:21
For behold, this is my c.;		26:22
shall ye not receive into my c.,		26:28
might judge the people of that c.		26:33
among the people of the c.;		26:35
among the people of the c.,		26:36
regulate all the affairs of the c.;	Mos	26:37
exceedingly in the affairs of the c.,		26:37
laborers do who were over the c.,		26:38
did not belong to the c. of God.		26:38
which were inflicted on the c.		27: 1
that the c. began to murmur,		27: 1
who belonged to the c. of God.		27: 2
the prosperity of the c. of God;		27: 9
about to destroy the c. of God,		27:10
seeking to destroy the c.,		27:10
persecutest thou the c. of God?		27:13
This is my c., and I will establish		27:13
seek to destroy the c. no more,		27:16
much consolation to the c.,		27:33
which they had done to the c.,		27:35
concerning all the affairs of the c.		29:42
who was the founder of their c.		29:47
the High Priest over the C.	Al	1:hd
bearing down against the c.;		1: 3
and even began to establish a c.		1: 6
who belonged to the c. of God,		1: 7
lead away the people of the c.;		1: 7
taken by the people of the c.		1:10
did not belong to the c. of God		1:19
did belong to the c. of God,		1:19
law among the people of the c.		1:21
any man, belonging to the c.,		1:21
that did not belong to the c.,		1:21
of much affliction to the c.;		1:23
cause of much trial with the c.		1:23
establish the affairs of the c.;		1:28
of the steadiness of the c.		1:29
whether out of the c. or in		1:30
out of the church or in the c.,		1:30
who did not belong to their c.		1:31
who did not belong to their c.		1:32
alarming to the people of the c.,		2: 3
rights and privileges of the c.;		2: 4
intent to destroy the c. of God.		2: 4
to establish the c. more fully;		4: 4
were joined to the c. of God;		4: 4
priest over the people of the c..		4: 4
themselves to the c. of God		4: 5
the people of the c. began to		4: 6
priests, and elders over the c.;		4: 7
the people of the c. began to be		4: 8
among the people of the c.;		4: 9
did not belong to the c. of God.		4: 9
and the wickedness of the c. was		4:10
who did not belong to the c.;		4:10
the c. began to fail in its progress.		4:10
saw the wickedness of the c.,		4:11
the example of the c. began to		4:11
was among the elders of the c.,		4:16
of being high priest over the c.		4:18
the people in the c. which was		5: 2
a high priest over the c. of God,		5: 3
to establish a c. in the land		5: 3
began to establish the c. of God		5: 5
you that belong to this c.,		5: 6
ask of you, my brethren of the c.,		5:14
have been brought into this c.,		5:54
unto you that belong to the c.;		5:62
who do not belong to the c.		5:62
unto the people of the c.,		6: 1
to preside and watch over the c.		6: 1
did not belong to the c. who		6: 2
and were received into the c.		6: 2
whosoever did belong to the c.		6: 3
to establish the order of the c.		6: 4
yea, from the c. which was in		6: 7
word of God unto the c. which		6: 8
established the order of the c.		8: 1
thou art high priest over the c.		8:11
and we are not of thy c., and we		8:11
because we are not of thy c.		8:12
high priest over the c. of God		8:23
Alma established a c. in the land		15:13
established the c. at Sidom,		15:17
was high priest over the c.,		16: 5
establishment of the c. became		16:15
after the c. had been established		16:21

CHURCH

did establish a c. among them.	Al	19:35	polluted the holy c. of God?	Mrm 8:38
established a c. in that land,		20: 1	were called the elders of the c.,	Mro 3: 1
threatenings to destroy his c.		26:18	blood of Christ unto the c.;	4: 1
people who were of the c. of God.		27:27	they did kneel down with the c.,	4: 2
a c. also established in the land		28: 1	witnessed unto the c. that they	6: 2
and by this did establish his c.;		29:11	the people of the c. of Christ;	6: 4
that same God did establish his c.		29:13	the c. did meet together oft,	6: 5
I have performed in the c.,		30:33	and three witnesses of the c.	6: 7
anything for our labors in the c.,		30:34	were conducted by the c.	6: 9
it profit us to labor in the c.		30:34	unto you that are of the c.,	7: 3
Himni he did leave in the c.		31: 6	among the people of his c.	7:39
the performances of the c.,		31:10	Hearken, O ye people of my c.,	DC 1: 1
to destroy the c. of God;		36: 6	to lay the foundation of this c.,	1:30
no more to destroy the c. of God.		36: 9	the only true and living c.	1:30
more to destroy the c. of God—		36:11	unto the c. collectively	1:30
and their liberty, and their c.,		43:30	the coming forth of my c.	5:14
their rites of worship and their c.		43:45	establish my c. among them.	10:53
rites of worship, and by our c.,		44: 5	not say this to destroy my c.,	10:54
he blessed the c., yea, all those		45:17	I say this to build up my c.;	10:54
the saying went abroad in the c.		45:19	whosoever belongeth to my c.	10:55
be made throughout the c.		45:21	unto me, the same is my c.	10:67
forth to extablish the c. again		45:22	therefore he is not of my c.	10:68
exceeding great care over the c.,		46: 6	whosoever is of my c.,	10:69
were high priests over the c.		46: 6	endureth of my c. to the end,	10:69
many in the c. who believed in		46: 7	my word, my rock, my c.,	11:16
they dissented even from the c.;		46: 7	the foundation of my c.,	18: 4
seek to destroy the c. of God,		46:10	if you shall build up my c.,	18: 5
who belonged to the c. of God,		46:14	Contend against no c.	18:20
who did not belong to the c.		46:14	save it be the c. of the devil.	18:20
belong to the c. were faithful,—		46:15	The rise of the C. of Christ	20: 1
also maintain order in the c.;		46:38	to be the first elder of this c.;	20: 2
peace and rejoicing in the c.		46:38	to be the second elder of this c.,	20: 3
and had dissented from their c.,		48:24	and we, the elders of the c.,	20:16
great prosperity in the c.		49:30	Therefore let the c. take heed	20:33
in the great privilege of our c.,		61:14	of commandment to the c.	20:37
should be made again in the c.		62:44	and witness before the c. that	20:37
did establish again the c. of God.		62:46	received by baptism into his c.	20:37
little pride which was in the c.,	He	3: 1	members of the c. of Christ—	20:38
great prosperity in the c.,		3:24	who are baptized into the c.,	20:41
did join themselves unto the c.		3:24	baptize, and watch over the c.;	20:42
was the prosperity of the c.,		3:25	And to confirm the c. by the	20:43
and uniting to the c. of God,		3:26	to watch over the c. always,	20:53
began to enter into the c.—		3:33	there is no iniquity in the c.,	20:54
not into the c. of God, but		3:33	that the c. meet together often,	20:55
to belong to the c. of God—		3:33	in all his duties in the c.,	20:57
were many dissensions in the c.,		4: 1	several elders composing this c.	20:61
to belong to the c. of God.		4:11	whatever c. business is necessary	20:62
the c. had begun to dwindle;		4:23	by vote of the c. to which they	20:63
once belonged to the c. of God		5:35	ordained to any office in this c.,	20:65
the people of the c. did have		6: 3	without the vote of that c.;	20:65
yea, because of the c. of God,		6: 3	where there is no branch of the c.	20:66
the c. did spread throughout the		11:21	all things concerning the c.	20:68
Lamanites, did belong to the c.;		11:21	shall manifest before the c.,	20:69
and the privileges of their c.	3Ne	2:12	Every member of the c.	20:70
did establish the c. among the		5:12	unto the elders before the c.,	20:70
first c. which was established		5:12	can be received into the c.	20:71
the c. began to be broken up;		6:14	that the c. meet together often	20:75
the c. was broken up in all the		6:14	he shall kneel with the c.	20:76
it unto the people of my c.,		18: 5	member of the c. of Christ	20:80
even so shall ye pray in my c.,		18:16	composing the c. of Christ,	20:81
I will establish my c. among		21:22	held by the elders of the c.,	20:81
were called the c. of Christ.		26:21	uniting themselves with the c.	20:82
whereby we shall call this c.;		27: 3	all the names of the whole c.	20:82
ye shall call the c. in my name;		27: 7	have been expelled from the c.,	20:83
he will bless the c. for my sake.		27: 7	out of the general c. record	20:83
And how be it my c. save it		27: 8	members removing from the c.	20:84
is a c. be called in Moses'		27: 8	to a c. where they are not known,	20:84
Moses' name then it be Moses' c.;		27: 8	the teachers or deacons of the c.	20:84
then it be the c. of a man;		27: 8	an elder of the c. through	21: 1
in my name then it is my c.,		27: 8	Which c. was organized and	21: 3
call upon the Father, for the c.,		27: 9	Wherefore, meaning the c., thou	21: 4
the c. is built upon my gospel		27:10	an elder unto this c. of Christ,	21:11
things that ye must do in my c.;		27:21	the first preacher of this c.	21:12
uniting as many to the c. as		28:18	of this church unto the c.,	21:12
who did not belong to the c.		28:19	this c. to be built up unto me,	22: 3
united unto the c. of Christ,		28:23	known thy calling unto the c.,	23: 2
had formed a c. of Christ	4Ne	1: 1	to strengthen the c. continually.	23: 3
who had revolted from the c.		1:20	thy duty is unto the c.	23: 3
to deny the true c. of Christ.		1:26	and to strengthen the c.;	23: 4
And this c. did multiply		1:28	and to strengthen the c.;	23: 5
another c. which denied the		1:29	duty to unite with the true c.,	23: 7
persecute the true c. of Christ,		1:29	the c. which is in Colesville,	24: 3
and build up again my c.,	Mrm	3: 2	all scriptures unto the c.	24: 5

CHURCH

the world, and also to the c.	DC 24:10
for the c. shall give unto thee	24:18
scriptures, and to exhort the c.,	25: 7
shall support thee in the c.;	25: 9
unto me, to be had in my c.	25:11
confirming the c. at Colesville,	26: 1
by common consent in the c.,	26: 2
thou shalt be heard by the c.	28: 1
and revelations in this c.	28: 2
and authority unto the c.	28: 3
of commandment unto the c.,	28: 4
and at the head of the c.;	28: 6
cause my c. to be established	28: 8
appointed unto any of this c.	28:12
contrary to the c. covenants.	28:12
by common consent in the c.,	28:13
to the covenants of the c.,	28:14
the great and abominable c.,	29:21
attend to the ministry in the c.,	30: 4
power to build up my c.	30: 6
counselor over him in the c.,	30: 7
church, concerning c. matters,	30: 7
be one with you in my c.	31: 2
will establish a c. by your hand;	31: 7
shall be a physician unto the c.,	31:10
that this c. have I established	33: 5
upon this rock I will build my c.;	33:13
ye shall remember the c. articles	33:14
you shall confirm in my c.,	33:15
given unto the elders of my c.,	36: 7
and have stranthened up the c.	37: 2
commandment I give unto the c.,	37: 3
unto the c. in these parts	38:34
appointed by the voice of the c.;	38:34
affairs of the property of this c.	38:36
unto the bosom of the c.	38:38
vineyard, and to build up my c.,	39:13
Hearken, O ye elders of my c.	41: 2
may know how to govern my c.	41: 3
appointed by the voice of the c.,	41: 9
ordained a bishop unto the c.,	41: 9
time in the labors of the c.;	41: 9
Hearken, O ye elders of my c.,	42: 1
ye shall build up my c.	42: 8
or to build up my c.,	42:11
and it is known to the c. that	42:11
ordained by the heads of the c.	42:12
priests and teachers of this c.	42:13
the covenants and c. articles	42:18
behold, I speak unto the c.	42:31
laid before the bishop of my c.	42:32
laid before the bishop of my c.,	42:32
of the properties of my c.,	42:32
they cannot be taken from the c.,	42:32
properties in the hands of the c.,	42:33
by the high council of the c.,	42:34
for the public benefit of the c.,	42:35
shall be cast out of the c.,	42:37
the poor and needy of my c.,	42:37
And the elders of the c.,	42:44
to be my law to govern my c.;	42:59
hereafter receive c. covenants,	42:67
keys of the c. have been given.	42:69
for all his services in the c.	42:73
person who belongeth to this c.	42:78
and covenants of the c.	42:78
tried before two elders of the c.,	42:80
by two witnesses of the c.,	42:80
shall lay the case before the c.,	42:81
the c. shall lift up their hands	42:81
him or her up unto the c.,	42:89
that the c. may not speak	42:92
O hearken, ye elders of my c.,	43: 1
for a law unto my c.,	43: 2
how to act and direct my c.,	43: 8
instructed in the law of my c.,	43: 9
I say, hearken ye elders of my c.,	43:15
that the elders of my c. should	44: 1
Hearken, O ye people of my c.,	45: 1
Hearken, O ye people of my c.,	45: 6
together ye elders of my c.,	45:64
Hearken, O ye people of my c.;	46: 1
given to the elders of my c.	46: 2

177

CHURCH

any one who belongeth to the c.	DC 46: 4
those who are not of the c.	46: 5
be any that are not of the c.,	46: 6
are, that are given unto the c.	46:10
And unto the bishop of the c.,	46:27
ordain to watch over the c.	46:27
and to be elders unto the c.,	46:27
unto him to keep the c. record	47: 3
and the bishop of the c.	48: 6
hands of the elders of the c.	49:14
Hearken, O ye elders of my c.,	50: 1
are agreed as touching the c.,	50: 1
seen abominations in the c.	50: 4
who are cut off from my c.,	50: 8
unto the elders of his c.,	50:10
and this inheritance in the c.,	51: 4
worthy by the voice of the c.,	51: 4
laws and covenants of the c.,	51: 4
church, to belong to the c.	51: 4
worthy to belong to the c.,	51: 5
the poor and needy of my c.;	51: 5
given unto that of another c.	51:10
if another c. would receive	51:11
receive money of this c.,	51:11
let them pay unto this c.	51:11
by the voice of the c.	51:12
appoint a storehouse unto this c.;	51:13
a recomment from the c.	52:41
calling and election in the c.,	53: 1
also to be an agent unto this c.	53: 4
to be an elder unto this c.,	55: 1
books for schools in this c.,	55: 4
shall be cut off out of my c.,	56:10
Hearken, O ye elders of my c.,	57: 1
to be an agent unto the c.,	57: 6
as a printer unto the c.	57:11
Hearken, O ye elders of my c.,	58: 1
hand are the laws of the c.,	58:23
be an example unto the c.,	58:35
before the bishop of the c.	58:35
residue of the elders of my c.,	58:44
appointed by the voice of the c.,	58:49
unto the c. in Ohio,	58:49
bishop or the agent of the c.	58:55
counseled by the elders of the c.	58:56
stand as a member in the c.,	58:60
residue of the elders of this c.,	58:61
Lord unto the elders of his c.,	60: 1
unto you, O ye elders of my c.,	61: 2
hearken, O ye elders of my c.,	62: 1
let the c. repent of their sins,	63:63
unto you, O ye elders of my c.,	64: 1
ye shall bring before the c.,	64:12
until the residue of the c.,	64:26
made my c. in these last days	64:37
hearken, O ye elders of my c.,	67: 1
all the faithful elders of my c.—	68: 7
to be set apart unto the c.,	68:14
First Presidency of the c.;	68:22
and commandments of the c.	68:24
and know concerning my c.;	69: 3
and from c. to church, that	69: 7
from church to c., that he may	69: 7
be for the good of the c.,	69: 8
ye people of my c. who are	70: 1
business in the c. of God,	70: 5
give these things unto the c.,	70: 6
to the c. of the living God;	70:10
round about, and in the c. also,	71: 2
are the high priests of my c.,	72: 1
unto the c. in this part of	72: 2
the elders of the c. in this	72: 5
has been ordained unto the c.	72: 9
to receive the funds of the c.	72:10
to the good of the c.,	72:12
of the kingdom unto the c.,	72:14
Thus it cometh out of the c.,	72:15
unto the bishop of the c. in	72:19
be recommended by the c.	72:19
the literary concerns of my c.	72:20
which shall benefit the c. in	72:21
extensive branches of my c.,	72:23
the members of the c.—	72:24

CHURCH 178 CHURCH

from three elders of the c.,	DC 72:25	offices in the c. are appendages	DC 107: 5
the apostle wrote unto the c.,	74: 5	over all the offices in the c.	107: 8
unto you, O ye elders of my c.,	75:23	ovviciate in all the offices in the c.	107: 9
the duty of the c. to assist in	75:24	and commandments of the c.;	107:12
support of the c. for them,	75:26	in all these offices of the c.	107:12
and let him labor in the c.	75:28	the spiritual blessings of the c.—	107:18
shall not have place in the c.,	75:29	assembly and c. of the Firstborn,	107:19
are the c. of the Firstborn.	76:54	faith and prayer of the c.,	107:22
assembly and c. of Enoch,	76:67	of the Presidency of the C.	107:22
of the c. of the Firstborn	76:71	from other officers in the c. in	107:23
are the c. of the Firstborn;	76:94	from other officers in the c. in	107:25
unto the c. of the Firstborn,	76:102	the spiritual authorities of the c.;	107:32
to the c. of the Firstborn.	77:11	of the Presidency of the C.,	107:33
the high priesthood of my c.,	78: 1	build up the c., and regulate	107:33
and order unto my c.,	78: 4	building up the c. and regulating	107:34
office and standing in the c.,	78:12	authority in the affairs of the c.,	107:36
the c. may stand independent	78:14	authority in the affairs of the c.,	107:37
are the c. of the Firstborn,	78:21	in all large branches of the c.,	107:39
to be a high priest in my c.,	81: 1	all the other officers of the c.,	107:58
of the c. of the living God,	82:18	the c. of Christ in the land of Zion,	107:59
property of the whole c.—	82:18	in addition to the c. laws	107:59
according to the laws of my c.,	82:21	church laws respecting c. business—	107:59
addition to the laws of the c.	83: 1	and commandments of the c.	107:63
those who belong to the c.,	83: 1	of the High Priesthood of the C.;	107:65
shall have fellowship in the c.	83: 2	the High Priesthood of the C.	107:66
not have fellowship in the c.;	83: 3	and blessings upon the c.,	107:67
they have claim upon the c.,	83: 5	to do the business of the c.,	107:72
by the consecrations of the c.:	83: 6	among the elders of the c.	107:72
of the Lord concerning his c.,	84: 2	or in any branch of the c. where	107:74
continueth in the c. of God	84:17	most important business of the c.,	107:78
sent forth to build up my c.	84:32	the most difficult cases of the c.,	107:78
the c. and kingdom, and the elect	84:34	up unto the council of the c.,	107:78
the whole c. under condemnation.	84:55	according to the laws of the c.	107:79
who are called of God in the c.	84:86	highest council of the c. of God,	107:80
in ancient days, built up my c.	84:108	and person belonging to the c.	107:81
appointed to watch over the c.,	84:111	from this council of the c.	107:81
standing ministers unto the c.	84:111	the common council of the c.,	107:82
a general c. record of all things	85: 1	is to preside over the whole c.,	107:91
of the records or history of the c.	85: 4	bestows upon the head of the c.	107:92
to have been cut off from the c.,	85:11	Whereas other officers of the c.,	107:98
the great persecutor of the c.,	86: 3	and responsible offices in the c.	107:98
drive the c. into the wilderness.	86: 3	all the presidents of thy c.,	109:71
that of the c. of the Firstborn,	88: 5	Remember all thy c., O Lord,	109:72
That great c., the mother of	88:94	That thy c. may come forth out	109:73
even for all the officers of the c.,	88:127	c., to put upon it thy name.	109:79
called to the ministry in the c.,	88:127	concerning the affairs of my c.	112:27
or presiding elder of the c.	88:140	the high council of my c. in Zion,	115: 3
and the c., and also the saints	89: 1	C. of Jesus Christ of Latter-Day	115: 3
yea, even unto the c.	90: 4	For thus shall my c. be called	115: 4
preside over the affairs of the c.	90:13	C. of Jesus Christ of Latter-Day	115: 4
the affairs of this c. and kingdom.	90:16	of the First Presidency of my C.,	117:13
and are the c. of the Firstborn.	93:22	of the bishop of my c. in Zion,	119: 1
Whitney also, a bishop of my c.,	93:50	debts of the Presidency of my C.	119: 2
pertaining to the c. and kingdom.	94: 3	the First Presidency of my C.,	120: 1
the school, and of the c. in Zion.	97: 5	ye shall be rejected as a c.,	124:32
and your brethren of my c.,	98: 6	reveal unto my c. things which	124:41
who are in the c. at Kirtland;	98:19	that of the presidency of my C.;	124:84
to the sanctification of the c.	100:15	and a revelator unto my c.,	124:94
high council of the c. of Christ,	102: 1	hold the sealing blessings of my c.,	124:124
which might arise in the c.,	102: 2	a presiding elder over all my c.,	124:125
could not be settled by the c.	102: 2	the oracles for the whole c.	124:126
a standing council for the c.,	102: 3	quorum of high priests of my c.,	124:136
voted in the name and for the c.	102: 5	to be standing ministers to my c.,	124:137
the bounds of this c. government,	102: 8	prophet and seer of the C. of	127:12
to act in the name of the c.	102: 8	the general c. recorder can enter	128: 4
The president of the c., who is	102: 9	record on the general c. book,	128: 4
by the voice of the c.	102: 9	of those men by the c.	128: 4
preside over the council of the c.;	102:10	is done on the general c. book,	128: 4
high council of the c. of Christ	102:12	the same on the general c. book.	128: 4
the First Presidency of the C.	102:26	upon this rock I will build my c.;	128:10
the First Presidency of the C.,	102:27	tribulations of this C. of Jesus	128:21
most difficult cases of c. matters;	102:28	therefore, as a c. and a people,	128:24
the general authorities of the c.	102:32	Hearken, O ye people of my c.,	133: 1
the First Presidency of the C.,	102:33	together, O ye people of my c.,	133: 3
order for the benefit of my c.,	104: 1	Send forth the elders of my c.	133: 8
up my c. and kingdom	104:59	Listen, ye elders of my c.	133:16
speaking concerning the c.	105: 2	Doctrine and Covenants of the c.,	135: 6
who are the first elders of my c.,	105: 7	people of the C. of Jesus Christ	136: 2
the first elders of my c. should	105:33	hearken, O ye people of my c.,	136:41
presiding high priest over my c.,	106: 1	leaders of the c. have taught,	OD
witness and a light unto the c.	106: 8	as President of the C. of	OD
in the c., two priesthoods,	107: 1	the C. over which I preside.	OD
they, the c., in ancient days,	107: 4	in my teachings to the C.	OD

CHURCH

when any elder of the C. has	DC	OD
President of the C. of Jesus		OD
as the President of the C. of		OD
as a C. in General Conference		OD
of the C. of Jesus Christ of	JS	2: 1
against its character as a C.		2: 1
both to myself and the C.,		2: 1
events in relation to this C.,		2: 2
the organization of the said C.		2: 2
four of them joined that c.,		2: 7
called the first Elder of the C.,		2:72
concerning the rise of this C.,		2:73
connected with the C.,		2:73
that existed in the Primitive C.,	AoF	6

CHURCHES

abominable above all other c.,	1Ne	13: 5
abominable above all other c.;		13:26
there are save two c. only;		14:10
c. which are built up to get gain,		22:23
they have built up many c.;	2Ne	26:20
there are many c. built up		26:21
that the c. which are built up,		28: 3
built up c., and not unto the Lord—		28: 3
their c. have become corrupted,		28:12
and their c. are lifted up;		28:12
that he might establish c.	Mos	25:19
different bodies, being called c.;		25:21
there being many c. they were		25:22
preached in all the c. except		25:22
were seven c. in the land of		25:23
they did join the c. of God;		25:23
command throughout all the c.		27: 3
establishing c., and consecrating	Al	23: 4
all the land, over all the c.		45:22
priests and teachers over the c.		45:23
build up c. unto themselves	4Ne	1:26
there were many c. in the land;		1:27
c. which professed to know		1:27
to build up many c.,		1:34
build up c. unto themselves,		1:41
and c. become defiled and be	Mrm	8:28
when leaders of c. and teachers		8:28
of them who belong to their c.		8:28
be c. built up that shall say:		8:32
why have ye built up c. unto		8:33
your c., yea, even every one,		8:36
and the adorning of your c.,		8:37
but build up c. unto themselves	DC	10:56
be the duty of the several c.,		20:81
the hands and confirming the c.		24: 9
build up c. unto me.		45:64
go forth among the c. and		50:37
in other places, in all c.		51:18
the elders watch over the c.,		52:39
And let them build up c.,		58:48
be presented unto all the c.		58:51
until they return to the c. from		60: 8
all this for the good for the c.;		60: 9
now speedily visit the c.,		63:46
by the church or c.,		72:19
and in exhortation to the c.		73: 1
who belonged to the seven c.,		77: 5
about and among all the c.,		84:112
And set in order the c.,		90:15
in me concerning all the c.,		101:63
I give unto all the c.,		101:67
let all the c. gather together		101:72
the c. in the eastern countries,		101:74
were the c., who call themselves		101:75
let all the c. send up wise men		103:23
in preparing the c. to keep the		103:29
speak concerning my c. abroad—		105: 8
earth, and all people, and the c.,		109:55
laid the burden of all the c.		112:18
other is to preside over the c.		124:140

CIMETER

skill was in the bow, and in the c.,	En	1:20
the sword or c. to smite them.	Al	27:29
delivered up his sword and his c.		44: 8

CIMETERS

with swords, and with c.,	Mos	9:16
with swords, and with c.,		10: 8
with swords, and with c.,	Al	2:12
armed with swords, and with c.,		43:18
only their swords and their c.,		43:20
with their their swords and their c.,		43:37
with sword, and with c.,		60: 2
and with c. and with bows,	He	1:14

CINCINNATI

take their journey for C.;	DC	60: 6
wicked until they arrive at C.;		61:30

CIRCULATING

employed in c. falsehoods	JS	2:61

CIRCULATION

which have been put in c. by	JS	2: 1

CIRCUMCISED

that his children should be c.	DC	74: 3

CIRCUMCISION

the law of c. is done away	Mro	8: 8
the law of c. was had among	DC	74: 2
people concerning the law of c.,		74: 3
might remain without c.;		74: 6

CIRCUMSPECTLY

walking c. before God,	Mos	26:37
they do walk c. before God,	He	15: 5
walking more c. before God.		16:10

CIRCUMSTANCES

And thus, in their prosperous c.,	Al	1:30
minds and the c. of the people,		11: 4
the c. which attended them in		17: 5
in whatsoever c. they might.		32:25
And in these prosperous c.		50:17
the Nephites in those dangerous c.		52:14
placed in the most dangerous c.		53: 9
their dangerous c. at this time.		53:15
in these c. they found that		55:23
And now, in those critical c.,		57:16
thus were our c. at this period		58: 5
we did wait in these difficult c.		58: 7
difficult c. they should be placed,	He	6:21
in whatsoever difficlut c. he may	DC	6:18
as it shall be suitable to your c.		48: 1
to his family, according to his c.,		48: 6
according to his c. and his		51: 3
whatsoever c. I, the Lord,		70:16
forth as your c. shall permit,		84:117
as your c. will admit		104:53
when c. render it impossible		107:28
to travel as their c. shall allow,		107:98
or as the c. may admit of.		127: 1
my c. in life such as to make	JS	2:22
c. of my father's family),		2:46
worldly c. were very limited,		2:55
to his own account of the c.,		2:63
the c. of my having received		2:66
the c. of having received the		2:74

CITE

I would c. your minds forward to	Al	13: 1

CITIES

Jerusalem, and also other c.	1Ne	11:13
and I beheld many c., yea, even		12: 3
saw many c. that they were sunk;		12: 4
and fair c. without inhabitant.	2Ne	15: 9
Until the c. be wasted without		16:11
and destroyed the c. thereof,		24:17
fill the face of the world with c.		24:21
and began to fortify our c.,	Jar	1: 7
building large c. and villages	Mos	27: 6
the people in their c. and villages	Al	5:hd
and their c., and their villages,		8: 7
names of the c. of the Lamanites		23:13
all their villages and all their c.		23:14

CITIES 180 CITY

named all the c. of the Lamanites	Al 23:15	beheld the great c. of Jerusalem,	1Ne 11:13
the weakest parts of their c.;	48: 5	And I beheld the c. of Nazareth;	11:13
round about their c. and the	48: 8	and in the c. of Nazareth I beheld	11:13
of earth round about all the c.,	50: 1	they call themselves of the holy c.,	20: 2
of a man, round about the c.	50: 2	O Jerusalem, the holy c.;	2Ne 8:24
to build many c. on the north,	50:15	the golden c. ceased!	24: 4
upon their towers, and in their c.,	51:20	Howl, O gate; cry, O c.;	24:31
taking possession of many c.,	51:26	or in the c. of Lehi-Nephi;	Mos 7: 1
so many c., by their numberless	51:27	come near the walls of the c.,	7:10
people should maintain those c.,	52: 4	bring their brethren into the c.,	7:16
not taken any c. save they had	52: 4	or even the c. of Lehi-Nephi,	7:21
those c. which they had taken,	52: 5	and the c. of Shilom;	7:21
those c. which had been taken out	52:10	with four of my men into the c.,	9: 5
strengthen the c. round about,	52:10	to repair the walls of the c.,	9: 8
the c. which he had taken,	52:13	the walls of the c. of Lehi-Nephi,	9: 8
the c. which they had lost—	52:15	and the c. of Shilom.	9: 8
the plains between the two c.	52:20	even into the c. of Nephi,	9:15
of a number of their c. in	53: 8	to return to the c. of Nephi,	20: 3
will retain our c. and our lands;	54:10	returned to the c. of Nephi,	21: 1
these are the c. of which the	56:13	returned again to the c. of Nephi.	21:12
are the c. which they possessed	56:15	person without the walls of the c.,	21:19
by night to maintain their c.;	56:16	been without the gates of the c.,	21:23
those c. which they had taken.	56:20	wall, on the back side of the c.	22: 6
an attack upon our other c.	56:22	and they built a c., which they	23:20
For we knew in those c.	56:23	which they called the c. of Helam.	23:20
determined to maintain those c.	56:26	yea, in the c. of Helam,	23:25
and fled to their other c.,	57: 4	together in the c. of Helam;	23:26
that we might retain our c.,	58:10	their children, towards our c.;	Al 2:25
c. which had been taken	58:31	they obtain possession of our c.,	2:25
so great a number of c.	58:32	towards their c., which was the	2:26
obtained those c. and those lands,	58:33	which was the c. of Zarahemla.	2:26
of those possessions and c.	59: 4	established in the c. of Zarahemla,	5: 2
would attack the c. round about	He 1:26	established in the c. of Zarahemla,	6: 1
taking possession of many c.	1:27	the church in the c. of Zarahemla,	6: 4
build their houses, yea, their c.,	3: 9	which was in the c. of Zarahemla,	6: 7
that they might build many c.,	3:11	there having been a c. built,	6: 7
yea, they regained many c.	4: 9	which was called the c. of Gideon,	6: 7
great c. which are round about,	7:22	c. which was called Ammonihah.	8: 6
great c. shall be taken from us,	8: 5	come to the c. of Ammonihah	8: 8
we are powerful and our c. great	8: 6	people of the c. of Ammonihah;	8: 9
wo be unto all the c. which are	13:16	the people who were in the c.;	8:10
many c. shall become desolate.	14:24	he should be cast out of their c.,	8:13
and did lay waste so many c.,	3Ne 2:11	the c. which was called Aaron.	8:13
up into this my people, your c.,	3: 6	were in the c. of Ammonihah,	8:14
c. which had been left desolate.	4: 1	return to the c. of Ammonihah,	8:16
there were many c. built anew,	6: 7	again unto the people of the c.;	8:16
there were many old c. repaired.	6: 7	he entered the c. by another way,	8:18
great and notable c. were sunk,	8:14	south of the c. of Ammonihah.	8:18
were some c. which remained;	8:15	And as he entered the c. he was	8:19
O ye people of these great c.	10: 4	who were in the c. of Ammonihah,	9: 1
I will cut off the c. of thy land,	21:15	this great c. should be destroyed	9: 4
so will I destroy thy c.	21:18	came forth into the c.	14:28
the desolate c. to be inhabited.	22: 3	to depart out of that c.,;	15: 1
that they did build b. again	4Ne 1: 7	even into the c. of Ammonihah,	16: 2
where there had been c. burned.	1: 7	and destroy the c.	16: 3
many c. which had been sunk,	1: 9	who were in the c. of Ammonihah,	16: 3
these c. could not be renewed.	1: 9	destroyed, and also their great c.,	16: 9
And there were also other c.	Mrm 5: 4	of Amulon had built a great c.,	21: 2
and villages and c. were burned	5: 5	came to the c. of Jerusalem,	21: 4
and did build many mighty c.,	Eth 9:23	went forth from c. to city,	23: 4
his father did build up many c.	10: 4	went forth from city to c.,	23: 4
he gained power over many c.;	10: 9	who were in the c. of Nephi;	23:11
that Morianton built up many c.,	10:12	Shemlon, and in the c. of Lemuel,	23:12
and he did overthrow many c.,	14:17	and in the c. of Shimnilom.	23:12
and he did burn the c.	14:17	among all the people in every c.;	35:15
and warn the people of those c.	DC 84:114	and take possession of the c.,	43:25
unto the great and notable c.	84:117	every c. throughout all the land	45:22
and build up c. unto my name,	125: 2	land of Nephi, to the c. of Nephi,	47:20
		of Nephi, which was the chief c.	47:20
CITIZEN		he entered the c. Nephi with	47:31
rebellion are unbecoming every c.	DC 134: 5	and took possession of the c.	47:31
		would spare the people of the c.;	47:33
CITIZENS		behold, the c. had been rebuilt,	49: 2
laws for the protection of all c.	DC 134: 7	army by the borders of the c.,	49: 2
a right in justice to deprive c.	134: 7	that the c. of Ammonihah had been	49: 3
rights of its members, as c., denied.	134: 9	at the c. of Ammonihah;	49:10
		at the c. of Ammonihah,	49:11
CITY		for every c. in all the land	49:13
the great c. Jerusalem must be	1Ne 1: 4	destroy the people of that c.	49:13
Jerusalem, that great c., could be	2:13	the c. of Noah. which had	49:14
I, Nephi, crept into the c. and	4: 5	strength of the c. Ammoniah.	49:14
return to the c. of Jerusalem.	4:30	at the c. Ammonihah;	49:15
even that great c. Jerusalem,	10: 3	as the c. of Noah had hitherto	49:15

CITY

captain over the men of that c.;	Al 49:16
that Lehi commanded that c.	49:17
with an oath to attack the c.;	49:17
approach near the walls of the c.	50: 5
about every c. in all the land.	50: 6
began the foundation of a c.,	50:13
the name of the c. Moroni;	50:13
a foundation for a c. between	50:14
between the c. of Moroni and	50:14
of Moroni and the c. of Aaron,	50:14
they called the name of the c.,	50:14
strong in the c. of Moroni;	51:23
took possession of the c.,	51:23
fled out of the c. of Moroni	51:24
came to the c. of Nephihah;	51:24
also the people of the c. of Lehi	51:24
go against the c. of Nephihah	51:25
men in every c. to maintain	51:25
the c. of Nephihah,	51:26
Nephihah, and the c. of Lehi,	51:26
Lehi, and the c. of Morianton,	51:26
and the c. of Omner,	51:26
of Omner, and the c. of Gid,	51:26
of Gid and the c. of Mulek,	51:26
army into the c. of Mulek,	52: 2
an attack upon the c. of Mulek,	52:16
an attack upon the c. of Mulek,	52:17
again to the c. Bountiful,	52:17
and take again the c. of Mulek.	52:19
protected the c. of Mulek,	52:20
on the west of the c. Mulek;	52:22
should march forth into the c.,	52:24
had been left to protect the c.,	52:25
possession of the c. Mulek,	52:26
came near the c. Bountiful,	52:27
left to protect the c. Bountiful.	52:27
should not obtain the c. Mulek	52:28
through to the c. of Mulek.	52:34
to the c. of Mulek with Lehi,	53: 2
and took command of the c.	53: 2
the land, or the c., Bountiful.	53: 3
encircled the c. of Bountiful	53: 4
this c. became an exceeding	53: 5
and in this c. they did guard the	53: 5
possession of the c. of Mulek,	53: 6
were guarded in the c. of Gid;	55: 7
and he sent to the c. Gid,	55:16
who were within the wall of the c.,	55:20
and took possession of the c.,	55:24
round about the c. Gid.	55:25
when he had fortified the c. Gid,	55:26
be taken to the c. Bountiful;	55:26
he also guarded that c. with	55:26
to attack the c. Morianton;	55:33
fortified the c. Morianton until	55:33
bringing new forces into that c.,	55:34
young men to the c. of Judea,	56: 9
land of Manti, or the c. of Manti,	56:14
Manti, and the c. of Zeezrom,	56:14
Zeezrom, and the c. of Cumeni,	56:14
and the c. of Antiparah.	56:14
I arrived at the c. of Judea;	56:15
with their might to fortify the c.	56:15
come against the c. of Judea,	56:18
prepared our c. and ourselves	56:20
against the c. of Zarahemla;	56:25
over to the c. of Nephihah.	56:25
little sons to a neighboring c.,	56:30
provisions to a neighboring c.	56:30
march near the c. of Antiparah,	56:31
if we were going to the c. beyond,	56:31
our provisions, to go to that c.	56:32
remainder to maintain the c.	56:33
and came near the c. antiparah.	56:33
now, in the c. Antiparah were	56:34
march back to the c. of Judea.	56:57
deliver up the c. of Antiparah	57: 1
to take the c. of Antiparah by	57: 2
up the prisoners for that c.	57: 2
to go against the c. of Antiparah.	57: 3
of Antiparah did leave the c.,	57: 4
thus the c. of Antiparah fell into	57: 4
placed to protect the c. Cumeni.	57: 7
by night, the c. Cumeni,	Al 57: 8
we did camp round about the c.	57: 9
about to enter the c. by night.	57:10
determined to maintain the c.;	57:11
they yielded up the c. unto	57:12
in obtaining the c. Cumeni.	57:12
driven back to the c. of Manti.	57:22
And we retained our c. Cumeni,	57:23
towards the c. of Cumeni;	57:31
speed towards the c. Cumeni;	57:34
our brethren in preserving the c.	57:34
was to obtain the c. of Manti;	58: 1
could lead them out of the c.	58: 1
who were in the c. of Manti;	58:13
which was near to the c.	58:13
wilderness which was near the c.,	58:14
they should not return to the c.	58:20
they ran to the c. and fell upon	58:21
who were left to guard the c.,	58:21
did take possession of the c.	58:21
concerning the c. of Manti.	58:25
before them at the c. of Manti.	58:27
possession of the c. of Manti	58:28
Lamanites did arrive near the c.,	58:29
with me in the c. of Manti;	58:39
together from the c. of Moroni	59: 5
of Moroni and the c. of Lehi	59: 5
of Lehi and the c. of Morianton,	59: 5
be men sent to the c. Nephihah,	59: 9
of the people to maintain that c.,	59: 9
easier to keep the c. from falling	59: 9
would easily maintain that c.	59: 9
that the c. of Nephihah was lost	59:11
Pahoran, in the c. of Zarahemla;	60: 1
land, or the c., of Zarahemla;	61: 8
maintain the c. of Zarahemla,	61; 8
of the c. of Zarahemla,	61:18
and went forth against the c.,	62: 7
the Lamanites in that c.	62:14
come to the c. of Nephihah,	62:18
which is near the c. of Nephihah.	62:18
to spy out in what part of the c.	62:20
down into that part of the c.,	62:22
let down into the c. by night,	62:23
all within the walls of the c.	62:23
possession of the c. of Nephihah	62:26
possession of the c. of Nephihah,	62:30
did pursue them from c. to city,	62:32
did pursue them from city to c.,	62:32
down over the walls of the c.	62:36
returned to the c. of Zarahemla;	62:42
attack that great c. Zarahemla.	He 1:18
upon the inhabitants of the c.,	1:19
watch by the entrance of the c.,	1:20
with his whole army into the c.	1:20
take possession of the whole c.	1:20
even to the walls of the c.	1:21
possession of the c. of Zarahemla,	1:22
towards the c. of Bountiful;	1:23
and had taken the capital c.	1:27
which was the c. of Zarahemla,	1:27
of the c. of Zarahemla again,	1:33
to place, and from c. to city,	4:16
to place, and from city, to c.	4:16
in the c. of Ammonihah;	5:10
beginning at the c. Bountiful;	5:14
thenceforth to the c. of Gid;	5:15
and from the c. of Gid to the	5:15
city of Gid to the c. of Mulek;	5:15
And even from one c. to another,	5:16
was in the c. of Zarahemla;	7:10
this great c., and also all those	7:22
come over and fall upon that c.,	12:17
that he should enter into the c.;	13: 4
unto this great c. of Zarahemla;	13:12
yea, wo unto this great c., for I	13:12
the more part of this great c.,	13:12
righteous who are in this great c.,	13:13
yea, wo be unto this great c.,	13:14
wo be unto the c. of Gideon,	13:15
ye, the people of this great c.,	13:21
up upon the walls of this c.,	14:11

CITY

spake upon the walls of the c.	He	16: 1
roads made, which led from c. to	3Ne	6: 8
made, which led from city to c.,		6: 8
the c. of Zarahemla did take fire.		8: 8
And the c. of Moroni did sink		8: 9
up upon the c. of Moronihah		8:10
that in the place of the c. there		8:10
in that great c. Zarahemla.		8:24
up in that great c. Moronihah.		8:25
that great c. Zarahemla have I		9: 3
that great c. Moroni have I		9: 4
that great c. Moronihah have I		9: 5
the c. of Gilgal have I caused		9: 6
tnd the c. of Onihah and the		9: 7
and the c. of Mocum and the		9: 7
and the c. of Jerusalem and the		9: 7
the c. of Gadiandi, and the city		9: 8
and the c. of Gadiomnah, and		9: 8
and the c. of Jacob, and the city		9: 8
and the c. of Gimgimno, all these		9: 8
that great c. Jacobugath, which		9: 9
the c. of Laman, and the city of		9:10
and the c. of Josh, and the city		9:10
and the c. of Gad, and the city		9:10
and the c. of Kishkumen, have		9:10
A c. that is set on a hill cannot		12:14
O Jerusalem, the holy c., for		20:36
that they may build a c., which		21:23
even that great c. Zarahemla	4Ne	1: 8
we did come to the c. of Angola,	Mrm	2: 4
we did take possession of the c.,		2: 4
did fortify the c. with our might;		2: 4
and did drive us out of the c.		2: 4
the c. of Jashon was near the		2:17
we did fortify the c. of Shem,		2:21
a c. which was in the borders,		3: 5
come down to the c. of Desolation		3: 7
possession of the c. Desolation,		4: 2
inhabitants of the c. Teancum.		4: 3
Now the c. Teancum lay in the		4: 3
was also near the c. Desolation.		4: 3
to come against the c. Teancum.		4: 6
come against the c. Teancum,		4: 7
possession of the c. Teancum		4: 7
again of the c. Desolation.		4: 8
possession of the c. Desolation,		4:13
against the c. Teancum,		4:14
down against the c. Desolation;		4:19
and they came to the c. Boaz;		4:20
we had fled to the c. of Jordan,		5: 3
did not take the c. at that time.		5: 3
and we did maintain the c.		5: 4
down from c. to city and from		8: 7
down from city to c. and from		8: 7
he returned to the c. Nehor	Eth	7: 9
they built a great c. by the		10:20
a holy c. unto the Lord;		13: 5
become a holy c. of the Lord;		13: 5
build up a holy c. unto the Lord,		13: 8
where the c. Zion shall be built,	DC	28: 9
the c. of the New Jerusalem shall		42: 9
a c. reserved until a day of		45:12
land of peace, a c. of refuge,		45:66
for an inheritance, even the c.		48: 4
lay the foundation of the c.;		48: 6
I, the Lord, will hasten the c.		52:43
and the place for the c. of Zion.		57: 2
from the mouth of the c. of the		58:13
shall be scourged from c. to city,		63:31
shall be scourged from c. to c.,		63:31
before the Lord, in the holy c.		63:49
land to land, and from c. to city,		66: 5
land to land, and from city to c.,		66: 5
to village, and from c. to city.		75:18
to village, and from city to c.		75:18
unto the c. of the living God,		76:66
have built the c. of Jerusalem		77:15
the c. of Enoch [Joseph], for a		78: 4
to place, and from c. to city,		79: 1
to place, and from city to c.,		79: 1
shall be the c. of New Jerusalem.		84: 2
Which c. shall be built,		84: 3
that the c. New Jerusalem shall		84: 4
whatsoever village or c. ye enter,		84:93
village or c. that rejecteth you,	DC	84:94
village or c. that rejecteth you,		84:95
go unto the c. of New York,		84:114
York, also to the c. of Albany,		84:114
and also to the c. of Boston,		84:114
of the c. of the stake of Zion,		94: 1
Zion is the c. of our God,		97:19
and from c. to city, to proclaim		99: 1
and from city to c., to proclaim		99: 1
There was in a c. a judge which		101:82
there was a widow in that c.,		101:83
building up of the c. of my saints,		104:36
the C. of Shinehah [Kirtland].		104:48
United Order of the C. of Zion.		104:48
c. thy servants shall enter,		109:39
and the people of that c. receive		109:39
and thy salvation be upon that c.;		109:39
gather out of that c. the righteous,		109:39
thy judgments fall upon that c.		109:40
c. thy servants shall enter,		109:41
people of that c. receive not		109:41
let it be upon that c. according		109:41
to build a holy c. to thy name,		109:58
I have much treasure in this c. for		111: 2
and many people in this c.,		111: 2
with men in this c., as you shall		111: 3
will give this c. into your hands,		111: 4
and founders of this c.;		111: 9
than one for you in this c.		111:10
Let the c., Far West, be a holy		115: 7
my will that the c. of Far West		115:17
my people in the c. of Far West,		117:10
of my saints in the c. of Far West,		118: 5
up a c. and a house unto my name,		124:51
safety and refuge out of the c.		124:109
unto you, even the c. of Nauvoo.		124:109
Let them build up a c. unto my		125: 3
land opposite the c. of Nauvoo,		125: 3
as well as in the c. of Nashville,		125: 4
or in the c. of Nauvoo,		125: 4
appointed in each ward of the c.,		128: 3
Mount Zion, and upon the holy c.,		133:56
founded a great c. and left a fame		135: 3
purposes, from Salt Lake C.,		OD
in Salt Lake C., in the Spring		OD
Salt Lake C., Utah, October 6,		OD
And he builded a c., and he	Mses	5:42
he called the name of the c.		5:42
he built a c. that was called the		7:19
the C. of Holiness, even ZION.		7:19
which I shall prepare, an Holy C.,		7:62
thou and all thy c. meet them		7:63
them to the c. of New York.	JS	2:63
"I went to the c. of New York,"		2:64

CIVIL

a c. and a delightsome people)	Mro	9:12
c. officers and magistrates	DC	134: 3
c. magistrate should restrain crime		134: 4
influence with c. government,		134: 9
appeal to the c. law for redress of		134:11

CIVILIZATION

subjecting them to peace and c.,	Al	51:22
like this, that are without c.—	Mro	9:11

CLAIM

One of Israel have c. upon them,	2Ne	9:25
mercy hath no c. on that man;	Mos	2:39
mercy could have c. on them no		3:26
deny justice when it has its c.		15:27
and c. his right to the kingdom,		29: 9
he shall have c. on mercy	Al	12:34
have no c. upon the creature?		42:21
of mercy may have c. upon them.		42:31
did c. a part of the land of Lehi;		50:26
to c. of the Father his rights of	Mro	7:27
to c. that portion which he	DC	51: 5
c. on that portion that is		51: 5
may have c. on the world,		63:27
they may c. their anointing if		68:21
ask for assistance upon		72:20
have c. on their husbands for		83: 2
children have c. upon their		83: 4
they have c. upon the church,		83: 5

CLAIM 183 CLIMATE

CLAIM
that my people should c., and DC 101:99
hold c. upon that which I have 101:99
we can fully and completely c. 123: 6
would fain c. it from Noah Abr 1:27
We c. the privilege of worshiping AoF 11

CLAIMETH
which repentance mercy c.; Al 42:22
justice c. the creature and 42:22
and mercy c. the penitent, 42:23
mercy c. all which is her own; 42:24
he c. all those who have faith Mro 7:28
on mercy and c. her own; DC 88:40
its course and c. its own; 88:40

CLAIMS
equal c. on the properties, DC 82:17

CLAPPED
they c. their hands for joy, Mos 18:11
he c. his hands upon all them Al 31:36
as he c. his hands upon them, 31:36

CLASPED
she c. her hands, being filled with Al 19:30
been c. in the arms of Jesus. Mrm 5:11

CLASS
among the poor c. of people; Al 32: 2

CLASSED
their names will be c. among DC 135: 6

CLASSES
began to be divided into c.; 4Ne 1:26
do they represent c. or orders? DC 77: 3
of the c. of beings in their 77: 3
the hands of all c. of men, JS 2:27

CLAVE
he c. the rock also and the waters 1Ne 20:21

CLAY
be esteemed as the potter's c. 2Ne 27:27
shall dwell in a tabernacle of c., Mos 3: 5
whilst in this tabernacle of c., Mro 9: 6
Anoint thine eyes with c., Mses 6:35

CLEAN
with pure hearts and c. hands, 2Ne 25:16
with a pure heart and c. hands? Al 5:19
and has made us c. thereby. 24:15
be ye c. that bear the vessels of 3Ne 20:41
and become c. before the Lord. Eth 4: 6
thy garments shall be made c. 12:37
unto you, ye are c., but not all; DC 38:10
Be ye c. that bear the vessels of 38:42
that you are c., but not all; 66: 3
that I may make you c.; 88:74
that you are c. from the blood of 88:75
are not c. from the blood of 88:85
in sin, but let your hands be c., 88:86
save he is c. from the blood 88:138
overcomes and is c. before me. 90:36
forgiven you; you are c. before 110: 5
Be ye c. that bear the vessels of 133: 5
wherefore thy garments are c. 135: 5
given every c. herb for meat; Mses 2:30

CLEANLINESS
let all things be done in c. DC 42:41

CLEANSE
to c. from all unrighteousness. Al 7:14
my blood shall not c. them if DC 29:17
c. it from all unrighteousness; 76:41
c. your feet even with water, 84:92
and c. your hands and your feet 88:74
c. your feet in the secret places 99: 4
and c. them from their blood. 109:42
C. your hearts and your garments, 112:33

CLEANSED
until they are c. from all stain, Al 5:21
garments are c. and are spotless, 5:24
your garments have been c. 5:27
inward vessel shall be c. first, 60:23
shall the outer vessel be c. also. 60:23
have first c. our inward vessel, 60:24
c. every whit from his iniquity— 3Ne 8: 1
were c. from mortality to 28:36
c. by the blood of the Lamb, Mrm 9: 6
and c. by the power of the Mro 6: 4
purified and c. from all sin. DC 50:28
purified and c. from all sin, 50:29
and c. from all their sins, 76:52
and be c. by blood, even the Mses 6:59
and be c. from the filthiness 7:48

CLEANSING
and c. your feet by the wayside. DC 24:15

CLEAR
thou wouldst c. my way before me, 2Ne 4:33
ye shall c. away the branches Jac 5:65
and ye shall not c. away the bad 5:65
ye shall c. away the bad 5:66
answer a c. conscience before God Mos 2:15
with a c. conscience before God, 2:27
and they were white and c., Eth 3: 1
c. as the moon, and fair as the DC 5:14
written to make the case c. 102:23
as the sun, and c. as the moon, 105:31
fair as the moon, c. as the sun, and 109:73
morning of a beautiful, c. day, JS 2:14

CLEARED
And thus he c. the ground, Al 2:34

CLEARLY
then shalt thou see c. to cast the 3Ne 14: 5
forth c. and understandingly DC 84:117
and that so c. and distinctly JS 2:42

CLEAVE
shall c. to the house of Jacob. 2Ne 24: 1
and c. unto God as he cleaveth Jac 6: 5
should c. unto the Lord their God, He 4:25
earth did c. together again, 3Ne 10:10
every man did c. unto that Eth 14: 2
will c. unto every good thing; Mro 7:28
Wherefore, c. unto charity, 7:46
c. unto me with all your heart, DC 11:19
and c. unto the covenants which 25:13
shalt c. unto her and none else. 42:22
mount, and it shall c. in twain, 45:48
and c. unto all good, that ye 98:11
and c. unto my servant Joseph, 132:54
and shall c. unto his wife; Mses 3:24
and shall c. unto his wife, Abr 5:18

CLEAVETH
cleave unto God as he c. unto Jac 6: 5
intelligence c. unto intelligence; DC 88:40
virtue; light c. unto light; 88:40

CLEFTS
To go unto the c. of the rocks, 2Ne 12:21

CLERGY
manifested by the respective c., JS 2: 6

CLERK
It is the duty of the Lord's c. DC 85: 1

CLERKS
as c. employed in his service; DC 57: 9
COWDERY, ORSON HYDE, C. 102:34
left my affairs with agents and c. 127: 1

CLIMATE
subject by the nature of the c.— Al 46:40

CLIMB 184 COARSENESS

CLIMB
such as should attempt to c. up — Al 49:19

CLIMBETH
that which c. upon the trees — DC 59:16
and c. up by me shall never — Mses 7:53

CLING
shall c. to thy garments, and — DC 122: 6

CLINGING
c. to the rod of iron, even until — 1Ne 8:24

CLOAK
blood upon the skirts of his c. — He 9:31
let him have thy c. also; — 3Ne 12:40

CLOSE
for the hour is c. at hand, — Al 5:29
again at the c. of their harvest; — 17:13
therefore I will c. my epistle by — 54:11
Now I c. my epistle. — 54:14
and I c. my epistle to Moroni. — 54:24
now, behold, I c. mine epistle. — 58:41
And thus I c. mine epistle. — 60:36
And now I c. mine epistle to my — 61:21
I now c. my letter for the present, — DC 127:11
but shall now c. for the present, — 128:25
near the c. of the twelfth chapter — 135: 4

CLOSED
behold, ye have c. your eyes, — 2Ne 27: 5
the waters c. upon the armies of — He 8:11
After this vision c., the — DC 110:11
After this vision had c., another — 110:13
and c. up the flesh in the stead — Mses 3:21
c. up the flesh in the stead — Abr 5:15

CLOSET
when I did turn unto my c., — Al 33: 7
thou prayest, enter into thy c., — 3Ne 13: 6

CLOSETS
pour out your souls in your c., — Al 34:26

CLOTH
linen, yea, and c. of every kind, — Mos 10: 5
all manner of good homely c. — Al 1:29
and did make all manner of c., — He 6:13
linen and c. of every kind, — 6:13
they did work all manner of c., — Eth 10:24

CLOTHE
surely c. thee with them all, — 1Ne 21:18
I c. the heavens with blackness, — 2Ne 7: 3
to do good— to c. the naked, — Jac 2:19
that we might c. our nakedness; — Mos 10: 5
nourish them, and did c. them, — Al 35: 9
kind, to c. their nakedness. — He 6:13
will c. him with costly apparel; — 13:28
God so c. the grass of the field, — 3Ne 13:30
even so will he c. you, if ye are — 13:30
that they might c. themselves — Eth 10:24
and c. you, and give you money. — DC 84:89
c. yourselves with the bond of — 88:125
and c. himself with charity; — 124:116
I c. the heavens with blackness, — 133:69

CLOTHED
righteousness, being c. with purity, — 2Ne 9:14
Ammon, and they were fed and c. — Al 21:14
and he was c. in a white robe; — 3Ne 11: 8
Wherewithal shall we be c.? — 13:31
c. after the manner of war— — Eth 15:15
c. with robes of righteousness, — DC 29:12
to be c. upon, even as I am, — 29:13
Be thou c. in robes and sit thou — 38:26
Be thou c. in rags and sit thou — 38:26
c. with power and great glory; — 45:44
c. in the brightness of his glory, — 65: 5
or wherewithal ye shall be c. — 84:81
c. with the glory of her God; — 84:101
c. with light for a covering, — 85: 7

may be c. upon with robes of — DC 109:76
thine anointed ones, be c. with — 109:80
c. in his glorious apparel, — 133:46
coats of skins, and c. them. — Mses 4:27
and I was c. upon with glory; — 7: 3
c. with power and authority; — Fac 2: 3

CLOTHES
also did take from them their c. — Al 14:22
he who feeds you, or c. you, — DC 84:90
return back to take his c.; — JS 1:15

CLOTHING
and all manner of precious c.; — 1Ne 13: 7
linen, and the precious c., and — 13: 8
Thou hast c., be thou our ruler, — 2Ne 13: 6
there is neither bread nor c.; — 13: 7
because of their fine c.; — 28:13
feeding the hungry, c. the naked, — Mos 4:26
they were dressed with thick c.— — Al 43:19
withholding their c. from the — He 4:12
who come to you in sheep's c., — 3Ne 14:15
that which is needful for c. — DC 61:11
the teams, wagons, provisions, c., — 136: 5
no other c. on but this robe, — JS 2:31

CLOUD
and upon her assemblies, a c. — 2Ne 14: 5
he descended as it were in a c.; — Mos 27:11
the c. of darkness having been — Al 19: 6
with a c. of darkness, — He 5:28
it were above the c. of darkness, — 5:29
and behold the c. of darkness, — 5:31
because of the c. of darkness — 5:34
saw through the c. of darkness — 5:36
that this c. of darkness may be — 5:40
the c. of darkness shall be — 5:41
the c. of darkness was dispersed. — 5:42
the c. of darkness was dispersed — 5:43
came a c. and overshadowed — 3Ne 18:38
and he was in a c., and the — Eth 2: 4
with them as he stood in a c., — 2: 5
stood in a c. and talked with — 2:14
that I shall come in a c. with — DC 34: 7
come forth to meet me in the c. — 45:45
and received into the c. — 76:102
he will take you up in a c., — 78:21
and a c. shall rest upon it, — 84: 5
which c. shall be even the glory of — 84: 5
caught up in the c. to meet thee, — 109:75
descended in a c. of light, — JS 2:68

CLOUDS
I will also command the c. — 2Ne 15: 6
ascend above the heights of the c.; — 24:14
in my glory in the c. of heaven, — DC 45:16
see me in the c. of heaven, — 45:44
shall come in the c. of heaven — 76:63
the Lord, in the c. of heaven, — JS 1: 1
coming in the c. of heaven, — 1:36

CLOUDY
long time, in a c. and dark day. — DC 109:61

CLOVEN
even c. tongues as of fire, — DC 109:36

CLUB
every man that lifted his c. to — Al 17:37

CLUBS
and with cimeters, and with c., — Mos 9:16
came forth with c. to slay him. — Al 17:36
fight with stones, and with c., — 57:14

COAL
having a live c. in his hand, — 2Ne 16: 6

COALS
that bloweth the c. in the fire, — 3Ne 22:16

COARSENESS
of the c. of their apparel.— — Al 32: 2

COAT

COAT
came to pass that he rent his c.;	Al 46:12
on the end thereof his rent c.,	46:13
of Joseph whose c. was rent by	46:23
the remnant of the c. of Joseph	46:24
at the law and take away thy c.,	3Ne 12:40
shall give unto any of you a c.,	DC 84:105

COATS
neither staves, neither two c.,	DC 24:18
purse or scrip, neither two c.	84:78
Lord God, make c. of skins,	Mses 4:27

COCK
the third time, the c. crowed,	JS 2:47

COCKATRICE
root shall come forth a c.,	2Ne 24:29

COCKATRICE'S
shall put his hand on the c. den.	2Ne 21: 8
shall put his hand on the c. den.	30:14

COE, Joseph
let my servant C. also take his	DC 55: 6
John Smith, C., John Johnson,	102: 3
namely 1, Oliver Cowdery; 2, C.;	102:34

COHOR
and drew away C. his brother,	Eth 7:15
the kingdom of C., the son of Noah.	7:20
And C., the son of Noah, caused	7:21
did beat them and did slay C.	7:21
C. had a son who was called	7:22
the kingdom of C. unto Shule,	7:22
fair sons and daughters of C.;	13:17

COLD
down in the c. and silent grave,	2Ne 1:14
And the love of men shall wax c.,	DC 45:27
whether, in heat or in c.,	84:92
only in times of winter, or of c.,	89:13
HE WAS MURDERED IN C. BLOOD.	135: 4
the love of many shall wax c.;	JS 1:10
the love of many shall wax c.;	1:30

COLESVILLE
unto the church which is in C.,	DC 24: 3
to confirming the church at C.,	26: 1
and more especially in C.;	37: 2
and C., Broome county, on the	128:20

COLLECTED
c. as many as were desirous to go	Mos 9: 3

COLLECTIVELY
speaking unto the church c.	DC 1:30

COLOR
of pure gold, in c. like amber.	DC 110: 2

COLORING
the least shadow or c. of justice	DC 127: 1

COLORS
will lay thy stones with fair c.,	3Ne 22:11

COLTRIN, Zebedee
and C. also take their journey.	DC 52:29

COM
And Shiblon was the son of C.	Eth 1:12
C. was the son of Coriantum.	1:13
And Heth was the son of C.	1:26
And C. was the son of Coriantum.	1:27
came to pass that he begat C.,	9:25
and C. reigned in his stead;	9:25
all his days; and he begat C.	10:31
C. drew away the half of	10:32
C. gained power over Amgid,	10:32
in the days of C. there began	10:33
C. did fight against them much;	10:34
there came also in the days of C.	11: 1

COMBINATION
they fled unto C. for protection,	Eth 11: 2
prophesied unto C. many things;	11: 3
their secret plan, and their c.)	He 2: 8
because of the secret c. of	3Ne 7: 6
Now this secret c., which	7: 9
that they formed a secret c.,	Eth 8:18
which c. is most abominable and	8:18
because of this secret c. which	8:24
because of that secret c. which	11:15
no c. of wickedness shall have	DC 109:26
of Cain, there was a secret c.,	Mses 5:51

COMBINATIONS
men unto secret c. of murder	2Ne 9: 9
And there are also secret c.,	26:22
according to the c. of the devil,	26:22
workers of darkness and secret c.	Al 37:30
workers of darkness and secret c.,	37:31
all save it were the secret c.	He 3:23
in their secret murders and c.	6:38
because of power and secret c.,	3Ne 4:29
secret, and abominable c.,	5: 6
of their secret murders and c.;	9: 9
oaths and c. of Gadianton.	4Ne 1:42
because of secret c. and	Mrm 8:27
Lord worketh not in secret c.,	Eth 8:19
the manner of their oaths and c.,	8:20
nation shall uphold such secret c.,	8:22
c. shall get above you, which	8:23
of the secret c. of Akish	9: 1
because of their wicked c.;	11: 7
by the sword of those secret c.,	13:18
his army, because of secret c.	14: 8
one of the secret c. murdered	14:10
on the earth, and of secret c.	DC 42:64

COMBINE
to c. against all righteousness.	3Ne 6:28
did c. against the people of	6:29
earth and hell c. against you,	DC 6:34
all the elements to c. to hedge	122: 7
of darkness c. against me?	JS 2:20

COMBINED
and, behold, the enemy is c.	DC 38:12

COME: *see in the APPENDIX.*

COMELINESS
he hath no form nor c.;	Mos 14: 2

COMELY
excellent and c. to them that are	2Ne 14: 2
yet they were neat and c.	Al 1:27

COMES
until the time c. that they shall	2Ne 9: 2
is good save it c. from the Lord;	Om 1:25
if the time c. that the voice of	Mos 29:27
that death c. upon mankind,	Al 12:24
which c. by the cunning plans	28:13
c. because of the traditions of	30:16
nor shall they know until he c.	DC 49: 7
hands be clean, until the Lord c.	88:86
The office of an elder c. under	107: 7
Then c. the High Priesthood,	107:64
c. the administering of ordinances	107:67
When a messenger c. saying he	129: 4

COMEST
How c. thou hither to plant	Jac 5:21
thou c. down, and the mountains	DC 133:44
art, and from whence thou c.?	Mses 6:40

COMETH
time c. that he shall manifest	1Ne 13:42
time c., saith the Lamb of God,	14: 7
when the day c. that the wrath	14:17
he c., according to the words of	19: 8
Nevertheless, when that day c.,	19:15
it meaneth that the time c. that	22: 7
the time c. speedily that Satan	22:15

COMETH

the day soon c. that all the proud	1Ne	22:15	then c. the Son of God to	He	14: 2
day c. that they must be burned.		22:15	in the night before he c. there		14: 3
For the time soon c. that the		22:16	and there c. upon them again		14:18
it c. unto men according to the		22:18	behold, by me redemption c.,	3Ne	9:17
And the time c. speedily that the		22:24	whoso c. unto me with a broken		9:20
behold, when the time c. that they	2Ne	1:10	c. unto me as a little child,		9:22
he c. to bring salvation unto men.		2: 3	the same c. of evil, and is not		11:40
redemption c. in and through the		2: 6	whatsoever c. of more than these		12:37
the Messiah c. in the fulness of		2:26	the time c., when the fulness		20:30
And the day c. that they shall be		6:10	the day c. that shall burn as		25: 1
when that day c. when they shall		6:14	the day that c. shall burn them		25: 1
and then c. the judgment,		9:15	and by and by the end c.,		27:11
And he c. into the world that		9:21	until the night c., wherein no		27:33
When the day c. that they shall		10: 7	And the day soon c. that your	Mrm	6:21
c. in the fulness of his own time.		11: 7	the time c. at that day when		8:33
of Hosts soon c. upon all naions,		12:12	the time soon c. that he		8:41
the day of the Lord c.,		23: 9	then c. the judgment of the		9:14
and when the day c. that the		25:12	then c. the time that he that is		9:14
Messiah c. in six hundred years		25:19	the fullness of his wrath c. upon	Eth	2: 9
day that c. shall burn them up,		26: 4	this c. unto you, O ye Gentiles,		2:11
day that c. shall consume them,		26: 6	until the time c. that I shall		3:21
destruction c. unto my people;		26:10	good c. of none save it be of me.		4:12
then c. speedy destruction,		26:11	For it c. to pass that whoso		8:25
And the day c. that the words		27:11	which hope c. of faith, maketh		12: 4
For the time speedily c. that		30:10	And then c. the New Jerusalem;		13:10
then c. the baptism of fire		31:13	then also c. the Jerusalem of old;		13:11
then c. a remission of your sins		31:17	which are good c. of God;	Mro	7:12
word of God which c. down	Jac	2:35	which is evil c. of the devil;		7:12
And the time speedily c.,		3: 4	which are good c. of Christ;		7:24
and the end soon c.;		5:29	the power of redemption c.		8:22
and the season speedily c.;		5:71	baptism c. by faith unto the		8:25
the season, which speedily c.;		5:76	c. the visitation of the Holy		8:26
when the time c. that evil fruit		5:77	authority which c. from God;		8:28
then c. the season and the end;		5:77	every good gift c. of Christ.		10:18
and after that the end soon c.		6: 2	despair c. because of iniquity.		10:22
which is evil c. from the devil.	Om	1:25	if the day c. that the power		10:24
the same c. out in open rebellion	Mos	2:37	the time speedily c. that ye		10:27
For behold, the time c., and is		3: 5	and the day c. that they who will	DC	1:14
behold, blood c. from every pore,		3: 7	know that the day speedily c.;		1:35
And lo, he c. unto his own, that		3: 9	it is sacred and c. from above.—		6:10
salvation c. to none such except		3:12	repenteth and c. unto me,		10:67
And behold, when that time c.,		3:21	the hour c. that I will drink of		27: 5
the means whereby salvation c.		4: 8	and the day c. that they will		31: 2
name given whereby salvation c.;		5: 8	then c. the baptism of fire and		33:11
salvation c. by the law of Moses.		13:27	And the time speedily c. that		35:10
And there c. a resurrection,		15:21	But the day soon c. that ye		38: 8
For salvation c. to none such;		15:27	be no curse when the Lord c.;		38:18
redemption c. through Christ		16:15	and then c. the baptism of fire		39: 6
whatsoever is good c. from God,	Al	5:40	For the day c. that the Lord		43:18
is evil c. from the devil.		5:40	the day c. when the thunders		43:21
that c. to take away the sins		5:48	then c. the end of the earth.		43:31
the Son of God c. in his glory,		5:50	with him that c. I will reason		45:10
my joy c. over them after		7: 5	that the end of the world c.;		45:22
liveth and c. among his people.		7: 7	that which c. of the earth,		49:19
and the Son of God c. upon the		7: 9	the Son of Man c. not in		49:22
he c. to redeem those who will		9:27	And the day c. that you shall		50:45
and salvation c. to none else.		11:40	Jesus Christ, who c. quickly,		51:20
the day c. that all shall rise from		11:41	him by whom this offense c.,		54: 5
then c. a death, even a second		12:16	the day c. that ye shall be		58: 4
for the time c., we know not		13:25	after that c. the day of my		58:11
but when the storm c. they shall		26: 6	every man that c. unto this		58:36
is no God, or that Christ c. not?		30:40	behold the Son of Man c.		58:65
heat of the sun c. and scorcheth it,		32:38	he c. in an hour you think not.		61:38
redemption c. through the Son		34: 7	behold, faith c. not by signs,		63: 9
then c. the night of darkness		34:33	at that hour c. an entire		63:54
he c. to declare glad tidings of		39:15	the day c. that all things		63:59
when this time c. no one knows;		40: 7	that which c. from above		63:64
the time c. when all shall rise,		40:10	after today c. the burning—		64:24
their resurrection c. to pass		40:19	righteous c. down from above,		67: 9
that their resurrection c. at the		40:20	Thus it c. out of the church,		72:15
awful death c. upon the wicked;		40:26	every man that c. up to Zion		72:15
reward of evil when the night c.		41: 5	that c. under the sound of		80: 1
and mercy c. because of the		42:23	man that c. into the world;		84:46
thus c. about the salvation and		42:26	voice of the Spirit c. unto God,		84:47
And when that great day c.,		45:13	whoso c. not unto me is under		84:51
the time very soon c. that		45:13	it c. quickly, saith the Lord.		87: 8
sanctification c. because of	He	3:35	after your testimony c. wrath		88:88
that he c. to redeem the world.		5: 9	For after your testimony c. the		88:89
From whence c. this blood?		9:32	also c. the testimony of the		88:90
it surely c. unto this people,		13: 6	and lo, the Bridegroom c.;		88:92
the time c., saith the Lord,		13:14	then c. the redemption of those		88:99
the time c. that he curseth		13:31	c. the battle of the great God;		88:114
five years more c., and behold,		14: 2	when he c. into the house of God,		88:130

COMETH

he that c. in and is faithful	DC 88:135
then c. the day when the arm	90:10
his sins and c. unto me,	93: 1
man that c. into the world;	93: 2
c. and taketh away light and	93:39
vengeance c. speedily upon the	97:22
more or less than this, c. of evil.	98: 7
is less than these c. of evil.	98:10
Until the day c. when there is	101:21
commandment, c. the blessing.	103:12
night c. let not the inhabitants	112: 5
vengeance c. speedily upon the	112:24
my visitation c. speedily,	124:10
more or less than this c. of evil,	124:120
the prince of this world c.,	127:11
behold and lo, the Bridegroom c.;	133:10
Who is this that c. down from	133:46
day c. that shall burn as an oven,	133:64
day that c. shall burn them up,	133:64
now c. the day of their calamity,	136:35
of transgression c. the fall,	Mses 6:59
whoso c. in at the gate and	7:53
the Son of Man c. in the flesh,	7:54
who c. in the name of the Lord,	JS 1: 1
the morning c. out of the east,	1:26
ye think not, the Son of Man c.	1:48
when he c., shall find so doing;	1:50
thus c. the end of the wicked,	1:55
the day c. that shall burn as	2:37

COMFORT

did my father, Lehi, c. my mother,	1Ne 5: 6
For the Lord shall c. Zion,	2Ne 8: 3
he will c. all her waste places;	8: 3
and by whom shall I c. thee?	8:19
and c. those that stand in need of	Mos 18: 9
those that stand in need of c.,	18: 9
up your heads and be of good c.,	24:13
Be of good c., for on the morrow	24:16
bidding them to be of good c.:	27:23
wilt thou c. my soul in Christ.	Al 31:31
O Lord, wilt thou c. my soul,	31:32
all these wilt thou c., O Lord.	31:32
wilt thou c. their souls in Christ.	31:32
be for a c. unto my servant,	DC 25: 5
Lord administered c. unto Adam,	107:55
This son shall c. us concerning	Mses 8: 9

COMFORTABLE

to get a c. maintenance.	JS 2:55

COMFORTED

joy was full, and my mother was c.	1Ne 5: 7
for the Lord hath c. his people,	21:13
lift up your heads and be c.;	Mos 7:18
the Lord hath c. his people,	12:23
the Lord hath c. his people,	15:30
and said unto them: Be c.	Al 17:10
And they were c.	17:10
behold, the Lord c. us, and said:	26:27
that mourn, for they shall be c.	3Ne 12: 4
the Lord hath c. his people,	16:19
the Father hath c. his people,	20:34
tossed with tempest, and not c.!	22:11
having heard these words, was c.,	Eth 12:29
mourned and refused to be c.	15: 3
fear not, let your hearts be c.;	DC 98: 1
Therefore, let your hearts be c.;	100:15
who have mourned shall be c.	101:14
Therefore, let your hearts be c.	101:16
I will refuse to be c.; but the	Mses 7:44

COMFORTEDST

is turned away, and thou c. me.	2Ne 22: 1

COMFORTER

which C. filleth with hope and	Mro 8:26
given him through me by the C.,	DC 21: 9
shall be given thee by the C.,	24: 5
shalt teach them by the C.,	28: 1
art led at any time by the C.	28: 4
it shall be given you by the C.	31:11
and it shall be given by the C.,	35:19

the Holy Ghost even the C.,	DC 36: 2
and the Holy Ghost, even the C.,	39: 6
lift up your voices by the C.,	42:16
the C. knoweth all things,	42:17
the C., to write these things.	47: 4
the C. which was sent forth	50:14
the word of truth by the C.,	50:17
which is taught them by the C.	52: 9
the name of the Lord for the C.,	75:10
from on high, even by the C.,	75:27
I will send upon him the C.,	79: 2
now send upon you another C.,	88: 3
which other C. is the same that	88: 3
This C. is the promise which	88: 3
by the administration of the C.,	90:11
as shall be manifested by the C.,	90:14
receive of my Spirit, even the C.,	124:97
the record of heaven; the C.;	Mses 6:61

COMFORTETH

I am he that c. you.	2Ne 8:12

COMING

the c. of a Messiah, and also the	1Ne 1:19
wait for the c. of the Messiah.	2Ne 6:13
the truth of the c. of Christ,	11: 4
for thee to meet thee at thy c.;	24: 9
many hundred years before his c.;	Jac 4: 4
years after the c. of Christ	WM 1: 2
prophecies of the c. of Christ	1: 4
unto them, concerning his c.;	Mos 3:15
unto them concerning his c.;	3:15
concerning the c. of our Lord,	4:30
yea, even the c. of Christ.	7:26
concerning the c. of the Messiah,	13:33
concerning the c. of the Lord —	15:11
of the c. of the king's army;	18:34
sent, previous to the c. of Ammon,	21:25
days before the c. of Zmmon.	21:26
And now since the c. of Ammon,	21:32
concerning the c. of Christ.	26: 2
Amlicites at the time of their c.	Al 2:13
the time of his c. in his glory.	13:24
by the mouth of angels, of his c.;	13:25
of angels, at the eime of his c.;	13:26
saw Alma and Amulek c. forth	14:29
them at the time of his c. —	16:16
the c. of the Son of God,	16:19
concerning the c. of Christ,	18:39
concerning the c. of Christ,	21: 9
that they were c. against them	24:21
look forward to the c. of Christ,	25:15
law of Moses was a type of his c.,	25:15
and c. to the Lord their God,	29:10
concerning the c. of Christ.	30: 6
concerning the c. of Christ,	34: 2
no more deny the c. of Christ;	34:37
c. into the presence of my God	36:14
the c. of one Jesus Christ,	36:17
you concerning the c. of Christ.	39:15
hear the word at the time of his c.	39:16
a soul will be at the time of his c.?	39:17
or as after the time of his c.?	39:19
until after the c. of Christ.	40: 2
Lamanites were c. upon them;	43: 4
time of the c. of the Lamanites.	43:26
saw the Nephites c. upon them	43:36
they discovered the army c.,	47: 5
they were c. to destroy them,	47: 5
against the c. of their enemies,	50: 6
c. down to battle against them,	51:13
Lamanites were c. into the	51:14
to wait for the c. of Moroni,	52:17
Lamanites c. out against him	52:23
with his army c. against them,	52:28
they saw him c. and they	55: 8
the Lamanites are c. upon us,	60:17
that Moroni was c. against them,	62:31
before the c. of Christ,	He 1:hd
down to the c. of Christ.	1:hd
down to the c. of Christ,	1:hd
concerning the c. of the Messiah.	8:13
behold, Abraham saw of his c.,	8:17

COMING

thousand years before his c.,	He	8:18
have testified of the c. of Christ,		8:22
for a sign at the time of his c.;		14: 3
know of the c. of Jesus Christ		14:12
know of the signs of his c.,		14:12
remember at the time of their c.		16: 5
or from the c. of Christ;	3Ne	2: 8
year from the c. of Christ,		3: 1
the scriptures concerning my c.		9:16
these things at the c. of Christ,		10:15
not forbid any man from c.		18:22
may abide the day of his c.,		24: 2
before the c. of the great and		25: 5
before the great and c. day		28:31
that the Lord delays his c.		29: 2
shall see these sayings c. forth		29: 4
years from the c. of Christ)	4Ne	1:21
year from the c. of Christ.		1:48
years from the c. of Christ,	Mrm	3: 4
the c. of our Lord and Savior.		8: 6
concerning the c. of Christ,	Mro	7:22
it was until the c. of Christ.		7:25
was given of the c. of Christ.		10: 1
the c. of the great and dreadful	DC	2: 1
would be utterly wasted at his c.		2: 3
and the c. forth of my church		5:14
by the brightness of my c.		5:19
years since the c. of our Lord		20: 1
right hand at the day of my c.		29:12
at the c. of the Bridegroom—		33:17
of the Lord for his second c.		34: 6
a great day at the time of my c.,		34: 8
forth for the time of my c.,		35:15
time until the time of my c.,		35:18
and shall abide the day of my c.;		35:21
my face for the time of my c.;		39:20
forth for the signs of my c.,		39:23
that which is c. on the earth,		42:64
concerning the signs of my c.,		45:16
that Christ delayeth his c. until		45:26
of the c. of the Son of Man.		45:39
kingdom of God c. in power		56:18
who are c. to this land,		58:61
for the c. of the Son of Man,		61:38
may abide the day of his c.,		61:39
may be prepared in the c. spring		63:39
of the c. of the Son of Man.		63:53
until the c. of the Son of Man,		64:23
shall not be burned at his c.		64:23
of the c. of the Son of Man;		68:11
before the time of his c.		77:12
seal, before the c. of Christ.		77:13
them for the c. of the Lord,		84:28
those who are Christ's at his c.;		88:99
which kingdom is c. forth		90: 2
lest by her continual c. she		101:84
the c. of the Lord draweth nigh,		106: 4
have obeyed my voice in c. up		108: 1
am not displeased with your c.		111: 1
in c. forth out of their graves;		128:12
c. of the great and dreadful day		128:17
who can abide the day of his c.,		128:24
bloodshed previous to the c. of the		130:12
time of the c. of the Son of Man,		130:14
decide whether this c. referred to		130:16
c. of the Son of Man will not		130:17
for the hour of his c. is nigh.—		133:17
for the c. of the Bridegroom;		133:19
things which are c. on the earth,		133:58
of the c. of the Son of Man,	Mses	7:47
forth for the time of my c.;		7:62
of the c. of the Son of Man,		7:65
and what is the sign of thy c.,	JS	1: 4
the c. of the Son of Man be.		1:26
c. in the clouds of heaven,		1:36
at the c. of the Son of Man;		1:41
the c. of the Son of Man be.		1:43
My lord delayeth his c.,		1:51
before the c. of the great and		2:38
be utterly wasted at his c.		2:39
which were c. upon the earth,		2:45
Immediately on our c. up		2:73

COMMAND

mighty man, and he can c. fifty,	1Ne	3:31
I c. you that ye touch me not,		17:48
If he should c. me that I should		17:50
save the work which I shall c. him.	2Ne	3: 8
I will also c. the clouds that		15: 6
For I c. all men, both in the		29:11
unto me, I will c. my people;	Jac	2:30
can c. in the name of Jesus		4: 6
then, why not able to c. the earth,		4: 9
in all things that he shall c. us,	Mos	5: 5
I c. you to bring Abinadi hither,		11:28
And I will go according to thy c.		22: 7
there was a strict c. throughout		27: 3
And I c. you to do these things		29:30
and I c. you to do these things,		29:30
And now I, Alma, do c. you	Al	5:61
speak by way of c. unto you		5:62
I am sent to c. thee that thou		8:16
he had authority to c. God.		11:35
I had authority to c. God		11:36
they are laid under a strict c.		12: 9
if we could c. the rocks and		12:14
I c. you that ye take the records		37: 1
also c. you that ye keep a record		37: 2
which the Lord doth c. you,		37:16
I c. you, my son Helaman, that		37:20
I c. you that ye retain all their		37:27
I c. you to take it upon you to		39:10
C. thy children to do good, lest		39:12
therefore I c. you, my son, in		39:12
took the c. of all the armies of		43:16
And Moroni took all the c., and		43:17
I c. you, in the name of that		44: 5
I c. you by all the desires which		44: 6
I will c. my men that they		44: 7
gave Amalickiah the c. of		47: 3
he had got the c. of those parts		47: 5
the king had given him c.,		47:13
he did c. that his people should		52: 4
Teancum, by the c. of Moroni—		52:15
and took c. of the city and		53: 2
to perform every word of c.		57:21
by the c. of Ammoron		59: 7
or if he should c. us so to do.		61:12
he doth not c. us that we shall		61:13
gave Lehi and Teancum c. over		62: 3
Moroni yielded up the c. of his		62:43
I c. you, that ye shall go and	He	10:11
at the c. of our great and		12: 8
brave men who are at my c.,	3Ne	3: 3
I will c. that my armies shall		3: 8
to c. them at the time that the		3:17
Zemnarihah did give c. unto		4:23
were done by c. of Gidgiddoni.		4:26
This much did the Father c. me,		15:16
I c. you that ye shall write these		16: 4
they gave me c. again of	Mrm	5: 1
at his great c. the earth shall		5:23
save it be that God shall c. you.		7: 4
at my c. the heavens are	Eth	4: 9
at my c. the inhabitants thereof		4: 9
according to the word of his c.,	Mro	7:30
And now I c. you, my servant	DC	5:21
And I the Lord c. him, my		5:26
if this be the case, I c. you,		5:29
even until I c. thee again;		5:30
and stand still until I c.,		5:34
And now I c. you, that if you		6:27
I c. you that you need not		11:15
I c. all men everywhere to repent,		18: 9
Wherefore, I c. you to repent,		19:13
Therefore I c. you to repent—		19:15
I c. you again to repent,		19:20
And I c. you that you preach		19:21
I c. thee that thou shalt not		19:25
I c. thee that thou shalt not		19:26
I c. thee that thou shalt pray		19:28
I shall c. you,		24:13
c. to be smitten in my name;		24:16
shalt not c. him who is at		28: 6
in prayer according to my c.,		29: 6

COMMAND 189 COMMANDED

until I c. you to go from hence.	DC 30:10
angels are waiting the great c.	38:12
and c. them to go hence;	51:16
Behold, I, the Lord, c.;	56: 3
I, the Lord, c. and revoke,	56: 4
that I should c. in all things;	58:26
I c. and men obey not;	58:32
given power to c. the waters,	61:27
not go until I shall c. them.	63:39
things whatsoever I shall c. you.	94:10
things whatsoever I shall c. you,	94:12
therefore I c. you to tarry,	95: 9
which I, the Lord, shall c.—	97: 8
things whatsoever I c. them.	98: 4
to do whatsoever I c. you,	98:22
as I will, when I shall c. him.	104:20
which thou didst c. us to build.	109: 4
meant by the c. in Isaiah, 52d	113: 7
c. to build a house unto me,	115: 8
not tarry, for I, the Lord, c. it.	117: 2
I c. you, all ye my saints,	124:31
I c. you again to build a house	124:55
in all things whatsoever I c. you,	124:55
c. you to send my word abroad,	126: 3
c. mine handmaid, Emma Smith,	132:54
c. the great deep, and it shall be	133:23
they shall obey thy c. as if	Mses 1:25
unto no man, until I c. you,	4:32
fled, even according to his c.;	7:13
Lord their God shall c. them;	Abr 3:25

COMMANDED

the things which I c. thee,	1Ne 2: 1
the Lord c. my father, even in a	2: 2
he did as the Lord c. him.	2: 3
they did as he c. them.	2:14
the Lord hath c. me that thou	3: 2
the Lord hath c. me that thou	3: 4
the things which the Lord hath c.,	3: 7
thing which the Lord hath c. us.	3:15
after he hath been c. to flee	3:18
I c. him in the voice of Laban,	4:20
Surely the Lord hath c. us to do	4:34
the Lord hath c. my husband to	5: 8
thing which the Lord hath c. them.	5: 8
wherewith the Lord had c. us.	5:20
records which the Lord had c. us,	5:21
the Lord c. him that I, Nephi,	7: 2
the Lord hath c. me to make	9: 5
and c. him that on the morrow	16: 9
the thing which he has c. them;	17: 3
if the Lord had not c. Moses	17:24
that Moses was c. of the Lord	17:26
the Lord c. my father that	17:44
for God had c. me that I	17:49
If God had c. me to do all	17:50
that which the Lord had c. us,	18: 6
things which had been c. us,	18: 8
the Lord c. me, wherefore I did	19: 1
that I should be c. of the Lord	19: 2
and c. my people what they should	19: 4
my molten image hath c. them.	20: 5
I have c. my sanctified ones,	2Ne 23: 3
hath he c. any that they	26:26
Hath he c. any that they	26:27
he hath c. his people that they	26:27
hath the Lord c. any that they	26:28
hath c. that men should not murder;	26:32
the words which I have c. thee,	27:22
I have been c. of him to write	33:11
for thus hath the Lord c. me,	33:15
did as the Lord had c. him,	Jac 5:70
my brother Nephi had c. me,	7:27
being c. by my father, Jarom,	Om 1: 1
according as the Lord had c. him.	1:13
and did as his father had c. him,	Mos 1:18
done as his father had c. him,	2: 1
I have not c. you to come up	2: 9
I have not c. you to come up	2:10
in all things which he hath c. you—	2:13
that ye should do as he hath c. you;	2:24
things whereof he hath c. me	2:27
hath c. me that I should declare	2:30

which was c. them of the Lord;	Mos 2:35
the Lord thy God hath c. thee,	3:22
which the Lord God hath c. me.	3:23
Thus hath the Lord c. me.	3:27
all things whatsoever he c. him.	6: 6
and were permitted, or rather c.,	7: 8
king Limhi c. his guards that	7:16
can look in them except he be c.,	8:13
whosoever is c. to look in	8:13
that is c. to do these things,	8:14
c. that I should be slain;	9: 2
he also c. that his people	9: 7
wilderness as the Lord had c. him,	10:16
and thus hath he c. me, saying,	11:20
and thus hath the Lord c. me.	11:25
thus has the Lord c. me, saying—	12: 1
he c. that the priests should	12:17
the king c. that he should be	12:18
wherewith God has c. me;	13: 4
and they were c. to repent	16:12
the king c. that the priests should	17: 1
he c. them that they should	18:19
he c. them that they should	18:20
he c. them that there should	18:21
And thus he c. them to preach.	18:22
he c. them that they should	18:23
he also c. them that the priests	18:24
Alma c. that the people of	18:27
having been c. of God;	18:29
the king c. the people that they	19: 9
the king c. them that all the	19:11
the king c. them that they should	19:20
king Limhi c. that every man	21:17
Amulon c. them that they should	24:11
being c. of God to pray	26:39
and c. him that he should keep	28:20
he c. them that they should	Al 2:10
I am c. to stand and testify	5:44
language of him who hath c. me,	5:61
the children of God were c. that	6: 6
I have been c. that I should	8:25
Alma, having been c. of God	9: 1
he has c. you to repent,	9:12
And he c. them to speak;	14:19
were c. to depart out of that city;	15: 1
they did as Ammon c. them,	17:34
the king had c. his servants,	18: 9
that Ammon did as he was c.,	19: 3
the father of Lamoni c. him that	20:14
And he also c. him that he	20:14
and c. that her servants, or the	22:19
she c. her servants that they	22:21
king c. them that they should not.	24: 6
that which the Lord hath c. me,	29: 9
that which the Lord hath c.;	29: 9
c. his men that they should stop	43:54
he c. his people that they should	44:17
c. him that he should go forth	47: 3
Amalickiah c. that his armies	47:27
found that Lehi c. the city	49:17
Moroni c. that his army should	51:17
had c. those whom he had left	52:13
Moroni c. that a part of his	52:24
And Moroni c. his men that	52:32
also c. their men that they	52:38
They were c. by Ammoron to	56:20
the Lord hath c. you that	61:20
parts which had been c. by Alma	63:12
or that which the Lord c. him	He 4:22
which Alma c. his son should	6:25
God hath c. him to prophesy	9: 2
thus hath the Lord c. me,	14: 9
he hath c. that I should prophesy	14: 9
words which the Lord hath c. me,	14:10
Gidgiddoni c. that his armies	3Ne 4:13
he c. his people that they should	7:12
c. him that he should come	11:18
Lord c. him that he should	11:20
according as I have c. you	11:28
I have c. you at this time,	12:20
I was c. to say no more of	15:18
that the Father hath c. me,	15:19

COMMANDED

thus hath the father c. me—	3Ne 16:16
am c. of the Father to speak	17: 2
he c. that their little children	17:11
c. the multitude that they should	17:13
Jesus c. his disciples that they	18: 1
he c. the multitude that they	18: 2
and c. that they should eat.	18: 3
he c. that they should give	18: 4
c. his disciples that they should	18: 8
that which I have c. you.	18:10
which the Father hath c. me	18:14
I have c. that none of you	18:25
have c. that ye should come unto	18:25
sayings which I have c. you	18:33
c. them that they should kneel	19:16
he c. his disciples that they	19:17
he c. the multitude that they	20: 1
he c. them that they should not	20: 1
c. them that they should arise	20: 2
c. them that they should break	20: 4
c. them that they should give	20: 5
which the Father hath c. me	20:10
the Father hath c. me that	20:14
even as the Father hath c. me.	20:46
I c. my servant Samuel,	23: 9
c. that it should be written;	23:13
was written according as he c.	23:13
c. them that they should teach	23:14
c. them that they should write	24: 1
which I c. unto him in Horeb	25: 4
Father c. that I should give	26: 2
things which have been c. me	26:12
things which have been c. me.	26:12
things even as Jesus had c. them.	26:20
which he hath c. me that I	30: 1
things which Ammaron c. me.	Mrm 1: 5
even as the Lord had c. me;	3:16
having been c. of the Lord that	6: 6
to that which he hath c. us,	7:10
I have been c. by my father.	8: 1
the Lord c. them that they should	Eth 2: 5
the work which thou hast c. me,	2:18
according as the Lord had c.	2:21
done even as thou hast c. me;	2:22
the Lord c. him that he should	3:28
the Lord c. the brother of Jared	4: 1
he c. that they should be made	4: 2
I am c. that I should hide	4: 3
the Lord hath c. me to write	4: 5
he c. me that I should seal them	4: 5
he also hath c. that I should	4: 5
the words which were c. me,	5: 1
he c. them that they should	6:25
I, Moroni, am c. to write	8:26
he c. that whoso should possess	9:20
therefore the Lord hath c. me,	12:22
Shiz c. his people that they	14:31
boldly; God hath c. them	Mro 8:21
I the Lord have c. them.	DC 1: 5
have c. you that you should	5: 2
persons to whom I c. you;	5: 3
c. that you should pretend to	5: 4
wherewith I have c. you;	5:22
the thing which I have c. thee.	5:34
the work which I have c. you.	6:35
this thing which I have c. you,	9:13
that part which I have c. him,	17: 6
to that which I have c. him,	18: 7
the thing which I c. him.	18: 7
in at the gate, as I have c.,	22: 4
have I not c. to repent?	29:49
by those whom I have not c.	30: 2
which I have c. them;	38:35
the things which I have c.	38:40
commandment wherewith I c.	42:12
observe to do as I have c.	42:15
work wherewith I have c. him;	43:13
the thing which I have c. you;	45:72
are c. never to cast any one	46: 3
c. not to cast any one who	46: 4
c. in all things to ask of God,	46: 7
go forth as I have c. you;	49:26
one, even as I have c. you.	51: 9
after I have c. and the	DC 56: 3
inheritance, even as I have c.;	57: 7
assist him, even as I have c.,	57:13
been c. to come to this land,	57:15
not anything until he is c.,	58:29
elders who are c. to return;	60:10
as they are c. to journey	61:24
the elders as before has been c.;	72:11
things which I have c. them.—	75: 9
the things which I have c. them;	75:13
gospel, even as I have c. them.	75:15
journey, as I have c. them,	75:18
the Lord c. us that we should	76:28
the Lord c. us to write	76:80
which we were c. to write	76:113
Which he c. us we should	76:115
the things which I have c. you	78: 7
the things which I have c. you,	78:20
according as his lord had c. him,	88:60
assembly, as I have c. you.	88:117
which I have c. to be organized;	90: 7
things which I have c. you.	90:27
I have c. you to bring up your	93:40
whatsoever I have c. her.	97:25
whatsoever I have c. her,	97:26
save I, the Lord, c. them.	98:33
was c. to offer up his only son.	101: 4
and did as their lord c. them,	101:46
have done even as I c. you,	101:53
whatsoever I have c. you;	101:60
whatsoever his lord c. him;	101:62
even as I have c. them.	103:23
which I c. to be organized	104: 1
as those whom I c. were	104: 2
this I have c. to be done	104:51
I have c. you to organize	104:58
have c. my servant Baurak Ale	105:16
to fulfil that which I have c.	105:28
which I have c. to be built	105:33
Thou who hast c. thy servants	109: 2
solemn assembly, as I have c.	109: 6
city to thy name, as thou hast c.	109:58
meet in mine eyes, and which I c.	121:16
for this cause I c. Moses	124:38
c. to build unto my holy name.	124:39
whom I c. to build up a city	124:51
who have been c. to do a work	124:53
boarding house which I have c.	124:56
doctrine which is c. you in the	128: 7
c. to be in a place underneath	128:13
God c. Abraham, and Sarah	132:34
Nay; for I, the Lord, c. it.	132:35
Abraham was c. to offer his son	132:36
than that which they were c.;	132:37
than that which they were c.,	132:37
not of that which I c. you to offer	132:51
when I c. Abraham to take Hagar	132:65
have not been c. to tarry.	133: 4
c. to be kept from the world in	133:60
and rent upon the earth, and c.,	Mses 1:19
strength, and he c., saying:	1:20
the Lord God, c. the man,	3:16
c. that they should come unto	3:19
c. that whatsoever Adam called	3:19
thou hast c. in the name of	4: 1
I c. thee that thou shouldst not	4:17
of the tree of which I c. thee,	4:23
as the Lord had c. him.	5: 1
know not, save the Lord c. me.	5: 6
and he c. them, saying:	5:13
c. them that they should repent;	5:14
And Satan c. him, saying:	5:18
forth and do as I have c. thee,	6:32
c. me that I should ask in the	7:59
c. him that he should go forth	8:19
And the Gods c. the man,	Abr 5:12
should be c. to show them;	JS 2:42
c. me to go to my father and	2:49
do as c. by the messenger.	2:50
Accordingly, as I had been c.,	2:54
he c. us to go and be baptized,	2:70
for so we were c.	2:71

COMMANDER — 191 — COMMANDMENT

COMMANDER
or their chief leader and c.;	Al 43:44
Moroni, who was the chief c. of	46:11
their leader and their chief c.	47:19
c. of the armies of the Nephites	3Ne 3:18
to be a c. and a leader of	Mrm 3:11

COMMANDEST
Why c. thou that we should slay	Al 22:20
c. that she should remain with	Mses 4:18

COMMANDETH
accomplish the thing which he c.	1Ne 3: 7
And he c. all men that	2Ne 9:23
Wherefore, he c. none that	26:24
He c. that there shall be no	26:29
his sheep; and he c. you that	Al 5:60
you that he c. you to repent;	9:12
that the Father c. all men,	3Ne 11:32
And thus c. the Father that	16:10
he c. me that I should write,	30: 1
beware lest he c. that which	Mrm 8:18
Wherefore, the Lord c. you,	Eth 8:24
of the living God c. him,	DC 61:28
c. all men everywhere to repent.	133:16

COMMANDING
even unto his c. you that	2Ne 1:27

COMMANDMENT
Written by way of c., and also	T Pg
it is a c. of the Lord.	1Ne 3: 5
I shall give c. unto my seed,	6: 6
received a c. of the Lord	9: 3
made these plates by way of c.,	19: 3
I, Nephi, received a c. of the	19: 3
thou hadst hearkened to my c.—	20:18
gave c. that all men must repent;	2Ne 2:21
unto him will I give c. that	3: 7
And I will give unto him a c. that	3: 8
Lord God hath given a c. that	26:30
Nephi gave me, Jacob, a c.	Jac 1: 1
And he gave me, Jacob, a c.	1: 2
fulfil the c. of my brother Nephi.	1: 8
because of the strict c. which I	2: 9
forgotten the c. of the Lord,	3: 5
this c. they observe to keep;	3: 6
observance, in keeping this c.,	3: 6
a c. I give unto you, which is	3: 9
the c. of my father, Enos,	Jar 1: 1
because of the c. of the queen,	Al 22:24
Giddianhi gave c. unto his	3Ne 4: 6
fulfilled the c. of Gidgiddoni.	4:13
Behold, I give unto you a c.,	12:29
hath the Father given me c. that	15:14
hath the Father given me c. that	15:15
received a c. of the Father	16: 3
I give unto you a c. that	18:12
and whosoever breaketh this c.	18:25
I give unto you another c.,	18:27
this is the c. which I give unto	18:28
now I finish the c. which	20:10
a c. I give unto you that ye	23: 1
Now this is the c.:	27:20
because of the c. which	28:16
of the c. which I have received,	Mrm 5: 9
is the c. which I have received;	5:13
according to the c. of the Lord,	5:13
and I fulfil the c. of my father.	8: 3
because of the c. of the Lord.	8:14
thou hast given us a c. that	Eth 3: 2
according to the c. of the Lord.	4: 5
according to the c. of the king,	9:29
contrary to the c. which I gave	DC 3:10
behold, I give unto you a c.,	18: 3
Whitmer, by the way of c.;	18: 9
this is a great and the last c.	19:32
by way of c. to the church	20:37
a c. I give unto you,	27: 3
by the way of c. unto the church,	28: 4
thou shalt not write by way of c.,	28: 5
but write them not by way of c.	28: 8
and I gave unto him c.,	29:35
no temporal c. gave I unto him,	DC 29:35
fruit and transgressed the c..	29:40
But now I give unto thee a c.,	35: 6
and a c. I give unto thee—	35:20
and c. give I unto you	36: 4
embracing this calling and c.,	36: 5
this c. shall be given unto	36: 7
a c. I give unto the church,	37: 3
I give unto you a c.,	38:16
I gave unto you the c.	38:32
church in these parts a c.,	38:34
unto you, I give unto you a c.,	38:40
behold I give unto you a c.,	41: 2
I give a c., that he should be	41: 9
together according to the c.	42: 3
I give unto you this first c.,	42: 4
and I give unto them a c.	42: 5
And I give unto you a c.	42:58
that ye have received a c.	43: 2
behold, I give unto you a c.,	43: 8
I give unto you a c. that you	49: 1
I give unto you a c. that ye	49:11
according to the holy c.,	49:13
this c. is given unto all	52:21
a c. that you shall forsake	53: 2
covenant and observed the c.,	54: 6
commanded and the c. is broken.	56: 3
I revoke the c. which was given	56: 5
give a new c. unto my servant	56: 5
I revoke the c. which was given	56: 6
obey the former c. which I have	56: 8
receiveth a c. with doubtful	58:29
my servant Sidney Rigdon a c.,	58:50
Wherefore, I give unto them a c.,	59: 5
wherefore, I give unto them a c.,	60:13
a c. concerning these things;	61:13
And now I give unto you a c.	61:18
this c. you shall give unto all	61:26
unto you, not by the way of c.,	63:22
either by c. or by revelation.	64:12
kept not the law, neither the c.;	64:15
I gave c. that his farm should	64:20
And a c. I give unto them—	68:33
the way of c. unto them.	70: 1
For I give unto them a c.;	70: 2
a c. I give unto them,	70: 6
this c. I give unto my servants	70:15
church, giving unto them a c.,	74: 5
a new commission and a new c.,	75: 7
Lord, give unto you this c.,	75:25
the c. which he has given—	76:51
a c. I give unto you,	78:11
I give unto you a new c.,	82: 8
Therefore, I give unto you this c.,	82:15
And I now give unto you a c.	84:43
forgive you of your sins with this c.—	84:61
But a c. I give unto them,	84:73
this revelation unto you, and c.,	84:75
I give unto you this c.,	84:77
this c. is unto all the faithful	84:86
contrary to the will and c. of God	85: 3
this c. which I give unto you,	88:62
a c. that you assemble yourselves	88:74
I give unto you a c. that	88:76
I give unto you a c. that you	88:77
not by c. or constraint, but by	89: 2
I give unto you a c. that you	90:12
that ye shall write this c.,	90:32
to the c. previously given,	92: 1
and c. concerning my servant	92: 1
now a c. I give unto you—	93:43
friends, a c. I give unto you,	94: 1
mine houses, according to the c.,	94:15
until I give unto you a c.	94:16
the great c. in all things,	95: 3
gave unto you a c.	95: 7
I gave unto you a c. that	95: 8
And I give unto you a c.,	98:11
would give unto them a c.,	98:36
But a c. I give unto you,	100: 7
hath gone forth by a former c.	101:10
a c. I give unto all the churches,	101:67
said unto you in a former c.,	101:68
the c. which I have given	101:69

COMMANDMENT 192 COMMANDMENTS

it is contrary to my c.	DC 101:96	to keep the c. of the Father?	2Ne 31:10
unto you a revelation and c.,	103: 1	that ye are willing to keep my c.,	31:14
said unto you in a former c.,	103:12	according to the c. of the Father	31:18
c. I give unto you, that ye	103:34	that they should keep his c.	Jac 2:21
I give unto you counsel, and a c.,	104: 1	this people shall keep my c.,	2:29
my servants have not kept the c.,	104: 4	these c. were given to our father,	2:34
a c. I give unto you, that ye	104:11	did obey the c. of the Lord of	5:72
a c. I give unto you concerning	104:47	according to the c. of the Lord	5:74
a c. I give unto you concerning	104:54	vineyard, and have kept my c.,	5:75
by the voice of the order, or by c.	104:64	their diligence in keeping my c.	En 1:10
for, as I said in a former c.,	105:14	Inasmuch as ye will keep my c.	Jar 1: 9
a c. I give unto you, that as	105:20	if they did not keep the c.,	1:10
agreeable to the c. which says:	107:77	to the c. of my fathers.	1:15
have done according to thy c.	109: 3	and the c. of the Lord	Om 1: 2
when I give a c. to any of the sons	124:49	according to the c. of my fathers;	1: 3
And a c. I give unto you,	124:144	as ye will not keep my c.	1: 6
by revelation and c. through	132: 7	according to the c. of our fathers.	1: 9
and I give unto you this c.—	132:12	these records and these c.,	Mos 1: 3
he received, by revelation and c.,	132:29	and so fulfilling the c. of God,	1: 4
A c. I give unto mine handmaid,	132:51	his c. always before our eyes,	1: 5
if she will not abide this c. she shall	132:54	ye should keep the c. of God,	1: 7
But if she will not abide this c.,	132:55	in keeping the c. of the Lord.	1:11
the earth, according to me c.,	132:63	them to keep the c. of God,	2: 4
spake with me, and gave me c.;	Mses 6:42	ye should keep the c. of the Lord,	2:13
for this cause, to keep the c.,	6:42	requires of you is to keep his c.;	2:22
unto you another law and c.	6:56	that if ye would keep his c.	2:22
Therefore I give unto you a c.,	6:58	if ye do keep his c. he doth	2:22
For by the water ye keep the c.;	6:60	As ye have kept my c.,	2:31
And he gave unto me a c. that	7:11	and also the c. of my father,	2:31
have I said, and also given c.,	7:33	shall keep the c. of my son,	2:31
		or the c. of God which	2:31
COMMANDMENTS		those that keep the c. of God.	2:41
in keeping the c. of the Lord!	1Ne 2:10	be diligent in keeping his c.,	4: 6
inasmuch as ye shall keep my c.,	2:20	and observe the c. of God,	4:30
inasmuch as thou shalt keep my c.,	2:22	and to be obedient to his c.	5: 5
that the Lord giveth no c. unto	3: 7	covenant with God to keep his c.	6: 1
in keeping the c. of the Lord;	3:16	hear and know the c. of God,	6: 3
because of the c. of the Lord.	3:16	did keep his c. in all things	6: 6
in keeping the c. of God.	3:21	in keeping the c. of the Lord—	10:13
in keeping the c. of the Lord;	4: 1	he did not keep the c. of God,	11: 2
hearken unto the c. of the Lord;	4:11	I know if ye keep the c. of God	12:33
as thy seed shall keep my c.,	4:14	the c. which the Lord delivered	12:33
could not keep the c. of the Lord	4:15	But I must fulfil the c.	13: 4
the records according to his c.	4:17	the remainder of the c. of God,	13:11
in keeping the c. of the Lord?	4:34	that love me and keep my c.	13:14
I and my father had kept the c.	5:20	these things for to keep these c.?	13:25
preserve the c. of the Lord	5:21	that have kept the c. of God,	15:22
to keep the c. of the Lord;	8:38	have known the c. of God,	15:26
is it that ye do not keep the c.	15:10	would not deny the c. of God,	17:20
with diligence in keeping my c.,	15:11	ye will serve him and keep his c.,	18:10
to keep his c. always in all things.	15:25	to serve him and keep his c.	21:31
to keep the c. of the Lord.	16: 4	to serve him and keep his c.	21:32
my father had fulfilled all the c.	16: 8	in his ways and keeping his c.	23:14
the c. of God must be fulfilled.	17: 3	according to the c. of God.	26:33
that the children of men keep the c.	17: 3	contrary to the c. of God,	27:10
it so be that ye shall keep my c.;	17:13	travail to keep the c. of God.	27:33
inasmuch as ye shall keep my c.	17:13	according to the c. of God,	28:11
to keep the c. of the Lord,	17:15	according to the c. of God.	29:11
and all his c., according to the law	17:22	this people according to his c.,	29:13
until further c. of the Lord.	19: 4	to teach you the c. of God,	29:14
be obedient to the c. of God.	22:30	under his feet the c. of God;	29:22
if ye shall be obedient to the c.,	22:31	repugnant to the c. of God.	29:36
serve him according to the c.	2Ne 1: 7	and he did keep his c.,	29:43
of Jerusalem shall keep his c.,	1: 9	lived to fulfil the c. of God.	29:45
that they shall keep his c.	1: 9	in keeping the c. of God,	Al 1:25
all the c. from the beginning,	1:10	who believed in the c. of God	3:11
Inasmuch as ye shall keep my c.	1:20	at defiance the c. of God?	5:43
as ye will not keep my c.	1:20	according to the c. of God.	7:15
hath kept the c. from the time	1:24	with him to keep his c.,	7:16
shall keep the c. of the Lord,	1:32	and keepeth the c. of God	7:23
according to the c. which the Lord	2:21	diligent in keeping the c. of God	8:15
according to the c. which God	2:26	faithful in keeping the c. of God	8:17
and hearken unto his great c.;	2:28	statutes and judgments, and c.	9: 8
if it so be that ye shall keep the c.	3: 2	have forgotten the c. of God,	9:13
Inasmuch as ye shall keep my c.	4: 4	as ye shall keep my c.,	9:13
inasmuch as ye will not keep my c.	4: 4	as ye will not keep my c.	9:14
statutes, and the c. of the Lord	5:10	have not kept the c. of God,	12:31
according to the c. of the Lord,	5:19	Wherefore, he gave c. unto men,	12:31
obedient to the c. of the Lord,	5:31	first transgressed the first c.	12:32
all the c. of God, like unto us,	9:27	Therefore God gave unto them c.,	12:37
keep the law because of the c.	25:25	c. which he has given unto us;	13: 1
except ye shall keep the c. of God	30: 1	these c. unto his children;	13: 6
unto him in keeping his c.	31: 7	his c. unto the children of men,	

COMMANDMENTS

he doth remember all my c.	Al	18:10
for keeping the c. of God.		21:23
and that God gave him c.,		22:12
to keep his c. and his statutes.		25:14
to keep the c. of the Lord;		30: 3
not observe to keep the c. of God,		31: 9
And we have an account of his c.,		35:16
The c. of Alma to his son,		36:hd
inasmuch as ye shall keep the c.		36: 1
I had not kept his holy c.		36:13
inasmuch as ye shall keep the c.		36:30
as ye will not keep the c.		36:30
how strict are the c. of God.		37:13
If ye will keep my c. ye shall		37:13
but if ye keep not his c. ye shall		37:13
if ye transgress the c. of God,		37:15
if ye keep the c. of God,		37:16
diligent in keeping the c. of God		37:20
learn in thy youth to keep the c.		37:35
The c. of Alma to his son,		38:hd
inasmuch as ye shall keep the c.		38: 1
as ye will not keep the c. of		38: 1
will continue in keeping his c.;		38: 2
The c. of Alma to his son,		39:hd
diligence in keeping the c. of God?		39: 1
Will ye keep my c.?		45: 6
Yea, I will keep thy c. with		45: 7
transgress the c. of God,		46:21
remember to keep the c. of God,		46:23
obey the c. of the king.		47: 2
according to the c. of the king;		47: 8
in keeping the c. of God		48:15
in keeping the c. of God,		48:16
should keep the c. of God,		48:25
if they should keep his c.		48:25
Moroni had kept the c. of God		49:27
as they shall keep my c.		50:20
as they will not keep the c.		50:20
keeping the c. of the Lord		50:22
to keep the c. of God		53:21
and his c. continually;		58:40
forgotten the c. of the Lord		60:20
and it is according to his c.		60:28
made to keep the c. of my God;		60:34
c. of the Lord his God;		63: 2
and the c. of God;	He	3:20
he did keep the c. of God,		3:37
set at naught the c. of God.		4:21
remember to keep the c. of God;		5: 6
went forth, keeping the c. of God,		5:14
trample under their feet the c.		6:31
begin to keep his statutes and c.,		6:34
laying aside the c. of God,		7: 4
firm to keep the c. of God,		7: 7
was contrary to the c. of God.		8: 3
my will, and to keep my c.		10: 4
did observe strictly to keep the c.		13: 1
they do observe to keep his c.		15: 5
was contrary to the c. of God,		16:12
of Lehi have kept his c.	3Ne	5:22
to keep the c. of the Lord.		6:14
and the c. of my Father,		12:19
ye have the c. before you,		12:19
except ye shall keep my c.,		12:20
I have given unto you the c.;		15:10
therefore keep my c.		15:10
for this is fulfilling my c.,		18:10
are ye if ye shall keep my c.		18:14
other c. which he hath given me.		18:27
I give you these c. because		18:34
c. which they had received	4Ne	1:12
according to the c. of Christ:	Mro	4: 1
keep his c. which he hath given		4: 3
fulfilling the c. unto the		8:11
faith unto the fulfilling the c.;		8:25
the fulfilling the c. bringeth		8:25
preface unto the book of my c.,	DC	1: 6
from heaven, and gave him c.;		1:17
And also gave c. to others,		1:18
these c. are of me, and were		1:24
to whom these c. were given,		1:30
does the c. of the Lord		1:32
Search these c. for they are true		1:37
but how strict were your c.;	DC	3: 5
oft you have transgressed the c.		3: 6
be firm in keeping the c.		5:22
with me that he will keep my c.,		5:28
have given unto thee these c.		5:33
art faithful in keeping my c.,		5:35
I say unto you, keep my c.,		6: 6
keep my c., and assist to		6: 9
my work, according to my c.,		6: 9
in keeping the c. of God,		6:20
be faithful, keep my c.,		6:37
these words, and keep my c.		8: 5
and give you c. concerning		10:34
not fear me, neither keep my c.		10:56
I say unto you, keep my c.,		11: 6
Keep my c., and assist to		11: 9
my work, according to my c.,		11: 9
Keep my c.; hold your peace;		11:18
this is your work, to keep my c.,		11:20
I say unto you, keep my c.,		12: 6
Keep my c. in all things.		14: 6
And, if you keep my c.		14: 7
given you according to my c.		15: 5
given unto you according to my c.		16: 5
And if you do these last c.		17: 8
be diligent in keeping my c.		18: 8
must keep my c. in all things;		18:43
if you keep not my c. you		18:46
the c. which you have received		19:13
by the will and c. of God,		20: 1
Which c. were given to		20: 2
And gave unto him c.		20: 7
And gave unto them c. that		20:19
the c. and revelations of God.		20:45
remember him and keep his c.		20:77
heed unto all his words and c.		21: 4
Keep my c. continually,		25:15
concerning the revelations and c.		28: 1
shall be appointed to receive c.		28: 2
to declare faithfully the c. and		28: 3
have loved me and kept my c.,		29:12
for my c. are spiritual;		29:35
until I give unto you further c.		30: 4
and be diligent in keeping my c.,		30: 8
Keep all the c. and covenants		35:24
inasmuch as he keepeth my c.		41: 8
on my name and keep my c.		42: 1
serve me and keep all my c.		42:29
the church, agreeable to my c.,		42:32
shall observe to keep all the c.		42:78
appointed unto you to receive c.		43: 2
appointed unto you to receive c.		43: 3
before you as revelations or c.;		43: 5
the points of my law and c.,		43: 8
Be sober. Keep all my c.		43:35
of devils, or the c. of men;		46: 7
love me and keep all my c.,		46: 9
according to the laws and c.		48: 6
c. which shall be given hereafter.		53: 4
and follow me, and keep my c.,		56: 2
together, according to the c.,		57: 1
blessed is he that keepeth my c.		58: 2
guiltless that obeys not my c.?		58:30
my glory, according to my c.		59: 1
and with c. not a few,		59: 4
things, and keep not his c.		59:21
Nevertheless, I give c.,		63:13
have turned away from my c.		63:13
observe not to keep my c.		63:22
But unto him that keepeth my c.		63:23
of the truth of these c.		67: 4
seek ye out of the Book of C.,		67: 6
to the covenants and c.,		68:13
covenants and c. of the church.		68:24
should be entrusted with the c.		69: 1
over the revelations and c.		70: 3
and prepare the way for the c.		71: 4
Wherefore, keep my c.;		71:11
the c. which have been given,		72: 7
to the revelations and c. which		75: 4
That by keeping the c. they		76:52
you may accomplish the c.		78:13
the priesthood by the c. of God,		84:16

COMMANDMENTS 194 COMMISSIONED

and the law of carnal c.,	DC 84:27	when the work shall c., that ye	Mrm 3:17
the former c. which I have	84:57	c. again to write for my servant,	DC 9: 1
to walk in all the c. of God	88:133	shalt c. from this time forth to	30: 9
walking in obedience to the c.,	98:18	shall c. a work of laying out and	94: 1
faithful in keeping all former c.	92: 2		
my voice, and keepeth my c.,	93: 1	COMMENCED	
For if you keep my c.	93:20	they who had c. in the path	1Ne 8:23
fulness unless he keepeth his c.	93:27	thus c. the reign of the judges	Mos 29:44
He that keepeth his c. receiveth	93:28	wars and contentions were c.	Al 3:25
and truth, according to the c.;	93:42	thus c. a war betwixt the	35:13
hath not kept the c. concerning	93:44	c. in your youth to look to	38: 2
You have not kept the c.,	93:47	work of death c. on both sides,	43:37
If you keep my c. you shall	95:11	that a battle c. between them,	50:35
If you keep not my c.,	95:12	c. the twenty and fifth year	51: 1
keepeth my c. from henceforth—	96: 6	and a terrible battle had c.	56:49
I shall give unto him other c.	97: 4	which first c. at our head,	60:15
inasmuch as they keep my c.	100:14	they c. a war with their brethren.	He 11:24
and keep his c., shall be saved.	100:17	And the battle c. in this the	3Ne 4:11
they hearkened not unto the c.	101:50	the Father hath already c.	21: 7
unto the precepts and c. which	103: 4	the work of the Father has c.	Eth 4:17
inasmuch as they keep not my c.,	103: 8	you did not continue as you c.,	DC 9: 5
the churches to keep the c.	103:29	it was expedient when you c.;	9:11
the laws and c. which have	103:35	It is to be c. with prayer;	88:141
obtaining the fulfilment of these c.	103:40	It c. with the Methodists,	JS 2: 5
as he is faithful in keeping my c.,	104:42	he c. quoting the prophecies of	2:36
before you, according to my c.,	104:86	He c., and again related the	2:45
those c. which I have given	105:34	I c. copying the characters off	2:62
covenants and c. of the church,	107:12	I c. to translate the Book of	2:67
agreeable to the covenants and c.	107:20		
covenants and c. of the church.	107:63	COMMENCEMENT	
concerning the revelations and c.	109:60	in the c. of the first year of the	1Ne 1: 4
and the c. which thou hast given	109:68	the c. of the reign of Zedekiah,	5:12
if my people will keep my c.,	110: 8	the c. of the reign of Zedekiah;	5:13
of my holy laws and c.	124:50	in the c. of the fifth year	Al 2: 1
here essaying to keep my c.	124:85	in the c. of the ninth year,	4:11
If ye love me, keep my c.;	124:87	in the c. of the ninth year	4:20
will do my will and keep my c.	125: 2	in the c. of the tenth year	8: 3
for this cause these c. were given;	133:60	the c. of the reign of the judges	30:32
c. which compose this book of	135: 3	in the c. of the eighteenth year	43: 4
promise to keep all the c. and	136: 2	the c. of the nineteenth year of	45:20
Be diligent in keeping all my c.,	136:42	the c. of the twentieth year of	50: 1
And he also gave me c.	Mses 1:17	in the c. of the twenty and	50:17
And he gave unto them c.,	5: 5	in the c. of the twenty and	50:25
obedient unto the c. of the Lord.	5: 5	in the c. of the twenty and	51: 1
shalt hearken unto my c.,	5:23	in the c. of the twenty and	52:19
they kept not the c. of God,	5:52	in the c. of the thirtieth year	56: 1
and have not kept the c.,	6:28	in the c. of the twenty and	56:20
to keep the c. of God,	Abr 1: 2	in the c. of the twenty and	57: 6
and from the holy c. which	1: 5	in the c. of the thirty and first	62:12
for doctrines the c. of men,	JS 2:19	in the c. of the thirty and	63: 1
and c. which I had received.	2:49	in the c. of the fortieth year of	He 1: 1
		the c. of the sixth and seventh	6:16
COMMANDS		in the c. of the eighty and first	11:30
to the strict c. of God,	Jac 2:10	in the c. of the ninety and	3Ne 1: 4
listen unto the word of his c.,	2:16	in the c. of the fourteenth year,	2:17
obedient unto the c. of God	4: 5	until the c. of my day;	5:16
he promised obedience unto the c.	7:27	the c. of the thirtieth year—	6:17
contrary to the c. of God that	Al 30: 7	and thus in the c. of this,	6:17
which was obedient unto his c.,	47: 3	in the c. of the thirty and third	7:23
contrary to the c. of the king.	47:16	many in the c. of this year	7:26
Amalickiah had fulfilled his c.,	47:21	a c. to lay the foundation of	DC 48: 6
cannot any longer enforce my c.	Mro 9:18	c. of the difficulties which will	130:12
would do according to his c.	Mses 5:30	at the c. of this record.	Abr 1:12
COMMENCE		COMMENCING	
come forth, and c. in the path	1Ne 8:22	c. with number one and so in	DC 102:12
the work of the Father shall c.,	14:17		
that day when my work shall c.	2Ne 3:13	COMMEND	
the Lord God shall c. his work	30: 8	I would c. you to seek this	Eth 12:41
thus the work of the Lord did c.	Al 19:36		
that they might c. an attack	43:24	COMMENDING	
caused that his armies should c.	50: 1	c. themselves unto the Lord	Eth 6: 4
c. in digging up heaps of earth	50: 1		
did c. his reign in the end of the	50:40	COMMISSION	
c. laboring in digging a ditch	53: 3	I revoke the c. which I gave	DC 75: 6
c. a labor in strengthening	55:25	And I give unto him a new c.	75: 1
they did c. the work of death;	He 4: 5	We believe that the c. of crime	134: 8
shall the work of the Father c.	3Ne 21:26	the Utah C., in their recent report	OD
shall the work of the Father c.	21:26		
the work shall c. among all	21:27	COMMISSIONED	
and then shall the work c.,	21:28	Having been c. of Jesus Christ,	DC 20:73
		with which I have c. you.	88:80

COMMIT

Wo unto them who c. whoredoms,	2Ne	9:36
that they should not c. whoredoms;		26:32
and all those who c. whoredoms,		28:15
for they shall not c. whoredoms,	Jac	2:33
plunder, or steal, or c. adultery;	Mos	2:13
c. any manner of wickedness,		2:13
or else thou shalt c. sin;		4:28
cause thy neighbor to c. sin also.		4:28
things whereby ye may c. sin;		4:29
he did cause his people to c. sin,		11: 2
and they did c. whoredoms		11: 2
Why do ye c. whoredoms		12:29
and cause this people to c. sin,		12:29
Thou shalt not c. adultery.		13:22
the people to c. so many sins		21:30
did cause them to c. many sins;		26: 6
also this people to c. much sin.		29: 9
that if these people c. sins		29:30
and durst not c. any wickedness	Al	1:33
to steal, nor to c. adultery,		23: 3
to c. any manner of wickedness.		23: 3
unto death rather than c. sin;		24:19
brethren lest they should c. sin;		27:23
also men, to c. whoredoms—		30:18
ye have hitherto risked to c. sin.		41: 9
began to c. secret murders,	He	6:17
c. whoredoms and all manner of		6:23
might the more easily c. adultery		7: 5
they did c. murder and plunder;		11:25
they did c. many murders,	3Ne	1:27
that thou shalt not c. adultery;		12:27
causeth her to c. adultery;		12:32
c. all manner of wickedness	Eth	8:16
to c. murder from the beginning;		8:25
whoso was found to c. iniquity,	Mro	6: 7
sent mine angels to c. unto you;	DC	27:16
Thou shalt not c. adultery;		42:24
man or woman shall c. adultery,		42:80
not steal; neither c. adultery,		59: 6
c. adultery in their hearts,		63:16
C. not adultery—		66:10
gospel to c. to every nation,		77: 8
c. no murder whereby to shed		132:19
c. no murder whereby to shed		132:19
c. any sin or transgression of the		132:26
c. no murder wherein they shed		132:26
that ye c. murder wherein ye shed		132:27
by my word, he will not c. sin,		132:59
cannot c. adultery for they are		132:61
cannot c. adultery with that		132:61
c. adultery, for they belong to him,		132:62
A disposition to c. such was	JS	2:28

COMMITTED

not be whoredoms c. among	Jac	3: 5
I have c. the unpardonable sin,		7:19
and were c. to prison.	Mos	7: 7
what great sins have thy people c.,		12:13
expedient that those who c. sin,		26: 6
to the sins which he has c.;		26:29
or to the sins which he had c.,		26:39
And whosoever has c. iniquity,		29:15
one wicked king cause to be c.,		29:17
to the crimes which he had c.	Al	1:10
many murders which we have c.		24: 9
and murders which we have c.,		24:10
many murders which we have c.,		24:11
for the murders which they had c.;		24:25
sins we have c. against them.		27: 6
sins which we have c. against		27: 8
if he c. adultery he was		30:10
and so many murders c.	3Ne	5: 6
c. adultery already in his heart.		12:28
I have c. unto you.	DC	5: 7
to whom I have c. the keys		27: 5
to whom I have c. the keys		27: 6
unto whom I have c. the keys		27: 9
Unto whom I have c. the keys		27:13
But he that has c. adultery		42:25
are c. unto man on the earth,		65: 5
which they have c. against me,		99: 5
and c. unto us the keys of the		110:11
c. the dispensation of the gospel		110:12
keys of this dispensation are c.	DC	110:16
she hath c. adultery and shall be		132:41
another man, she has c. adultery.		132:42
his vow and hath c. adultery.		132:43
if she hath not c. adultery,		132:44
c. adultery but hath been faithful;		132:44
another man, she has c. adultery,		132:63
and hath c. it unto man,		133:36
in which the offense is c.;		134: 8

COMMITTEE

to be a c. to build mine houses,	DC	94:15
c. can be appointed to find out		123: 4

COMMITTETH

her who is divorced c. adultery.	3Ne	12:32
and he that c. adultery,	DC	42:24
who c. the everlasting gospel—		88:103

COMMITTING

he will justify in c. a little sin;	2Ne	28: 8
themselves in c. whoredoms,	Jac	2:23
and the c. of whoredoms,	Mos	29:36
c. whoredoms, and murdering,	Al	1:32
murdering, c. adultery, and		16:18
lying, stealing, c. adultery,	He	4:12
they are not capable of c. sin;	Mro	8: 8
and capable of c. sin;		8:10

COMMON

it is not c. that the voice of	Mos	29:26
it is c. for the lesser part of		29:26
had all things c. among them,	3Ne	26:19
had all things c. among them;	4Ne	1: 3
and their substance no more c.		1:25
shall be done by c. consent	DC	26: 2
by c. consent in the church,		28:13
to become the c. property		82:18
and no c. or ordinary case		102:28
and c. consent of the order.		104:71
and c. consent of the order—		104:72
by c. consent or otherwise,		104:85
be a judge, even a c. judge among		107:74
before the c. council of the church,		107:82
wrath of man have been my c. lot		127: 2
was c. among all the sects—	JS	2:22
pursue my c. vocations in life		2:27

COMMOTION

the whole earth shall be in c.,	DC	45:26
And all things shall be in c.;		88:91

COMMUNE

to c. with the general assembly	DC	107:19

COMMUNICATED

things which are c. unto you.	DC	84:61

COMMUNICATION

let your c. be Yea, yea;	3Ne	12:37
treated my c. not only lightly,	JS	2:21
After this c., I saw the light in		2:43

COMMUNION

have c. with the Holy Spirit,	Jar	1: 4
enjoy the c. and presence of God	DC	107:19

COMNOR

of Shurr was near the hill C.;	Eth	14:28
together upon the hill C.,		14:28

COMPANIES

c. to go up unto the land of	DC	103:30
with them, be organized into c.,		136: 2
c. be organized with captains of		136: 3
c. are organized let them go to		136: 6

COMPANION

inasmuch as you desire a c.,	DC	80: 2
shall be thy constant c.,		121:46

COMPANIONS

having put away their c. for	DC	42:74

COMPANIONS — COMPULSION

COMPANIONS
any persons have left their c.	DC 42:75
and their c. are living,	42:75

COMPANY
there was a large c. of men,	Al 63: 4
this whole c. of mine elders	DC 61: 3
Phelps take their former c.,	61: 9
an innumerable c. of angels,	76:67
next spring, in c. with others,	114: 1
each c. provide themselves with	136: 5
each c., with their captains and	136: 7
each c. bear an equal proportion	136: 8
Let each c. prepare houses, and	136: 9
and Erastus Snow organize a c.	136:12
Wilford Woodruff organize a c.	136:13
and George A. Smith organize a c.	136:14
I happened to be in c. with	JS 2:21
associated with jovial c.,	2:28

COMPARE
we will c. the word unto a seed.	Al 32:28

COMPARED
be c. like unto an olive-tree,	1Ne 10:12
Israel was c. unto an olive-tree,	15:12

COMPASS
the c., which had been prepared	1Ne 18:12
I took the c., and it did work	18:21
and also the ball, or c.,	2Ne 5:12
c. yourselves about with	7:11
which is, being interpreted, a c.;	Al 37:38
slothful to give heed to this c.	37:43
fathers to give heed to this c.	37:44

COMPASSETH
it c. the whole land of Havilah,	Mses 3:11
c. the whole land of Ethiopia.	3:13

COMPASSION
have c. on the son of her womb?	1Ne 21:15
being filled with c. towards	Mos 15: 9
the Lamanites had c. on them,	19:14
they had c. on them	20:26
the Lamanites had c. on Amulon	23:34
they were moved with c. and	Al 27: 4
they were moved with c. and	53:13
my bowels are filled with c.	3Ne 17: 6
for I have c. upon you;	17: 7
the Lord had c. upon Jared;	Eth 1:35
the Lord had c. upon their	1:37
of Jared, and had c. upon him,	1:40
I will have c. upon you.	DC 64: 2
ye forgive not, having not c.,	64:13
mercy hath c. on mercy and	88:40
my bowels are filled with c.	101: 9
and thy bowels be moved with c.	121: 3
bowels moved with c. toward us.	121: 4
things abroad, and had not c.;	Mses 5:53
have c. upon the earth?	7:49

COMPEL
go forth and c. them to arms.	Al 47: 3
power to c. those dissenters to	51:15
did c. them to go forth and bury	53: 1
shall c. thee to go a mile,	3Ne 12:41

COMPELLED
was c. to pay that which he owed,	Al 11: 2
because ye are c. to be humble	32:13
if he is c. to be humble,	32:13
ye were c. to be humble	32:14
they who are c. to be humble	32:15
without being c. to be humble;	32:16
or even c. to know, before	32:16
been c. to humble yourselves;	32:25
the same is not c. to come;	42:27
thus the Nephites were c., alone,	43:13
c. reluctantly to contend with	48:21
c. to hoist the title of liberty	51:20
c. to march with their brethren	52:39
c. to cause the Lamanites to	53: 5
were c. to behold their brethren	53:15
c. by the orders of Ammoron	Al 56:18
c. to deliver up their weapons	56:54
c. to flee from the land of	59: 6
were c. because of their fear,	He 8:10
were c., for the safety of their	3Ne 2:12
for he that is c. in all things,	DC 58:26

COMPLAIN
my brethren did c. against me,	1Ne 17:18
murmur and c. against us.	17:22
murmur, and c. to their leaders	Mos 27: 1
and they did c. to Alma.	27: 1
we would not murmur nor c.	Al 60: 4

COMPLAINED
she also had c. against my father,	1Ne 5: 2
my mother c. against my father.	5: 3
he was c. of to the judge;	Al 11: 2
the poor have c. before me,	DC 38:16

COMPLAINING
even unto c. against the Lord	1Ne 16:22

COMPLAINT
a c. came up unto the land of	3Ne 6:25

COMPLAINTS
afflict the king sorely with their c.,	Mos 21: 6

COMPLETE
c. revolution	Mrm 2: 8
and c. the salvation of man,	DC 77:12
for a full and c. deliverance	109:32
whole and c. and perfect union,	128:18

COMPLETED
until I have c. my work,	DC 84:97

COMPLETELY
fully and c. claim that promise	DC 123: 6

COMPOSE
which c. this book of Doctrine	DC 135: 3

COMPOSED
were c. of the Lamanites and	Al 47:35
council c. of the twelve apostles,	DC 102:30
c. of the First Presidency of	120: 1

COMPOSING
several elders c. this church	DC 20:61
the several churches, c. the church	20:81
The number c. the council,	102: 5

COMPOUND
things must needs be a c. in one;	2Ne 2:11
were a c. of Laman and Lemuel,	Al 43:13

COMPREHEND
believe that man doth not c. all	Mos 4: 9
the things which the Lord can c.	4: 9
who cannot c. the marvelous works	Mrm 9:16
which c. the earth and all	DC 88:43
when you shall c. even God,	88:49

COMPREHENDED
in that he c. all things,	DC 88: 6
came unto his own was not c.	88:48
they (the Gods) c. the light,	Abr 4: 4

COMPREHENDETH
he c. all things, and he is a	Al 26:35
and the darkness c. it not.	DC 6:21
and the darkness c. it not.	10:58
and the darkness c. it not;	34: 2
and the darkness c. it not;	39: 2
and the darkness c. it not.	45: 7
He c. all things, and all things	88:41
and the darkness c. it not.	88:49
is filled with light c. all things.	88:67

COMPULSION
c. upon the souls of the children	DC 121:37

COMPULSORY   197   CONCERNING

COMPULSORY
without c. means it shall flow   DC 121:46

CONCATENATION
whole c. of diabolical rascality   DC 123: 5

CONCEALED
And he being c. for many days   Mos 17: 4
and c. them on the east, and on   Al 43:31
the remainder he c. in the west   43:32
of the army of Moroni was c.   43:34
was c. on the south of the hill,   43:35
c. their secret plans in the earth.   He 11:10

CONCEIVE
Behold, a virgin shall c.,   2Ne 17:14
shall be overshadowed and c.   Al 7:10
c. so great and marvelous things   3Ne 17:17
no one can c. of the joy which   17:17

CONCEIVED
and she c. and bare a son.   2Ne 18: 3
he was c. by the power of God;   Mos 15: 3
and whe c. and bare Cain,   Mses 5:16
c. and bare his brother Abel.   5:17
and she c. and bare Enoch,   5:42
thy children are c. in sin,   6:55

CONCEIVETH
grow up, sin c. in their hearts,   Mses 6:55

CONCEPTION
multiply thy sorrow and thy c.   Mses 4:22

CONCERN
C. not yourselves about your debts,   DC 111: 5
C. not yourselves about Zion,   111: 6
To Whom it may C.:   OD

CONCERNED
not so much c. about his people   Mos 19: 8
more diligent and c. at home,   DC 93:50
as the sectarian world was c.—   JS 2:26

CONCERNING
unto the people c. their iniquity   1Ne 1:hd
did my father read c. Jerusalem—   1:13
yea, c. the destruction of Jerusalem,   1:18
c. the things which he had both   1:18
unto me c. the elders of the Jews,   4:22
many times c. the elders of the Jews,   4:27
Jews might not know c. our flight   4:36
our fears did cease c. him.   4:37
comfort my mother, Sariah, c. us,   5: 6
and began to prophesy c. his seed—   5:17
prophesied many things c. his seed.   5:19
end of prophesying c. his seed,   7: 1
c. the destruction of Jerusalem;   7:13
c. the destruction of Jerusalem   7:13
as I have spoken c. these things,   9: 2
he spake unto them c. the Jews—   10: 2
he also spake c. the prophets,   10: 5
c. this Messiah, of whom he had   10: 5
also c. a prophet who should   10: 7
spake my father c. this thing.   10: 8
unto my brethren c. the gospel   10:11
also c. the dwindling of the   10:11
spake much c. the Gentiles,   10:12
and also c. the house of Israel,   10:12
c. the things which he saw   10:17
c. the covenants of the Lord   14: 5
write c. the end of the world.   14:22
c. the things which I saw while   14:30
c. the things which my father   15: 2
c. the natural branches of the   15: 7
and also c. the Gentiles.   15: 7
c. the grafting in of the   15:13
much unto them c. these things;   15:19
c. the restoration of the Jews   15:19
c. the restoration of the Jews,   15:20
c. the ways of the Lord;   16:29
had spoken c. the wicked.   18:11
c. the three days of darkness,   19:10
to show unto me c. them,   1Ne 19:20
all things c. them; also   19:21
he did show unto many c. us;   19:21
that we know c. them for they   19:21
c. the doings of the Lord in   19:22
have been prophesied c. them,   22: 5
and also c. all those who shall   22: 5
further as yet c. these things.   22:29
c. their rebellions upon the waters,   2Ne 1: 2
c. the land of promise,   1: 3
boldly c. your iniquities.   1:26
speak c. the prophecies of which   4: 1
c. Joseph, who was carried into   4: 1
truly prophesied c. all his seed.   4: 2
And he prophesied c. us,   4: 2
c. the prophecies of Joseph,   4: 3
which he spake c. them,   5:19
c. all things which are written,   6: 3
c. things which are, and which   6: 4
c. all the house of Israel;   6: 5
speak somewhat c. these words,   6: 8
c. the covenants of the Lord   9: 1
c. this righteous branch of which   10: 1
so great knowledge c. these things,   10:20
saw c. Judah and Jerusalem: 12: 1
c. Maher-shalal-hash-baz.   18: 1
c. the words which I have written,   25: 1
c. the manner of prophesying   25: 1
c. the manner of the Jews;   25: 2
c. the regions round about;   25: 6
c. the judgments of God,   25: 6
c. the destruction which should   25:10
delighteth to prophesy c. him,   25:13
we speak c. the law   25:27
c. the convincing of the Jews,   26:12
I prophesy unto you c. the last days;   26:14
c. the days when the Lord God   26:14
that he may whisper c. them,   26:16
c. the house of Jacob: 27:33
c. the Jews and the Gentiles.   30: 3
remnant of our seed know c. us,   30: 4
c. the doctrine of Christ;   31: 2
c. that prophet which the Lord   31: 4
c. that which ye should do   32: 1
I must speak c. this thing.   32: 8
A few words c. the history of   Jac 1:hd
commandment c. the small plates,   1: 1
c. the history of this people   1: 2
manifest unto us c. our people,   1: 5
I can tell you c. your thoughts,   2: 5
c. the wickedness of your hearts.   2: 6
much boldness of speech c. you,   2: 7
and tell you c. your wickedness   2:10
I have spoken unto you c. pride;   2:20
speaking unto you c. this pride.   2:22
unto you c. a grosser crime,   2:22
written c. David, and Solomon   2:23
small degree of knowledge c. us,   4: 2
us, or c. their fathers—   4: 2
contempt, c. their first parents.   4: 3
spake, c. the house of Israel,   6: 1
which have been spoken c. Christ,   6: 8
so many have spoken c. him;   6: 8
which I had seen c. these things;   7: 5
they have spoken c. this Christ.   7:11
father speak c. eternal life,   En 1: 3
do I write c. them.   1:23
unto you somewhat c. Mosiah,   Om 1:12
spake a few words c. his fathers.   1:22
somewhat c. a certain number who   1:27
have not since known c. them.   1:30
he may write somewhat c. them,   WM 1: 1
and somewhat c. Christ,   1: 2
I speak somewhat c. that which   1: 3
as have been prophesied c. us   1: 4
to God is c. my brethren,   1: 8
And now, c. this king Benjamin—   1:12
they might know c. the prophecies   Mos 1: 2
he also taught them c. the records   1: 3
know nothing c. these things,   1: 5
c. all the affairs of the kingdom.   1:15
gave him charge c. the records   1:16
he hath commanded me c. you.   2:27

CONCERNING

not been taught c. these things,	Mos	2:34	which he said c. the seed of the	Al	25: 9
have been taught c. the records		2:34	c. the admitting their brethren		27:21
c. that which is to come.		3: 1	c. the coming of Christ.		30: 6
knowing the will of God c. them,		3:11	And now as I said c. faith—		32:21
he unto them, c. his coming;		3:15	Now, as I said c. faith—		32:26
spake unto them c. his coming;		3:15	has said c. prayer or worship?		33: 3
c. the coming of our Lord,		4:30	c. those who were mine enemies,		33: 4
all the charges c. the kingdom,		6: 3	have spoken c. the Son of God.		33:18
desirous to know c. the people		7: 1	spoken c. the coming of Christ,		34: 2
to inquire c. their brethren.		7: 2	c. the words which had been		35: 3
to inquire c. our brethren,		7:13	c. the words which had been		35: 4
all the things c. their brethren		8: 1	the people know c. their desires;		35: 5
knew nothing c. the Lord,		10:11	c. the things pertaining unto		35:16
my people c. the Lamanites,		10:19	c. the coming of one Jesus Christ,		36:17
prophesied evil c. thy people,		12: 9	you c. those twenty-four plates,		37:21
prophesieth evil c. thy life,		12:10	unto them c. their iniquities;		37:30
this man has lied c. you,		12:14	to say c. the thing which our		37:38
what know ye c. the law of Moses?		12:31	you c. the coming of Christ.		39:15
the truth c. your iniquities.		13: 7	c. the resurrection of the dead.		40: 1
to prophesy evil c. this people.		13:26	that is c. the resurrection.		40: 3
c. the coming of the Messiah,		13:33	And now, c. this space of time,		40: 9
more or less c. these things?		13:33	c. the state of the soul between		40:11
c. the coming of the Lord—		15:11	say c. the restoration of which		41: 1
for he knew c. the iniquity		17: 2	been worried also c. this thing.		41: 1
which thou hast spoken evil c. me		17: 8	been spoken c. restoration,		41:10
spoken unto you c. this people,		17: 9	which is c. the justice of God		42: 1
Yea, c. that which was to come,		18: 2	say no more c. their preaching,		43: 2
c. the resurrection of the dead,		18: 2	c. those records which have been		45: 2
and to teach them c. the things		18:18	nothing c. his death and burial.		45:19
heard nothing c. this matter;		20:16	c. the justice of the cause		46:29
all the things c. his father,		20:23	c. the death of the king.		47:33
voice of the people c. the matter.		22: 1	c. the death of the king.		47:34
teach them anything c. the Lord		24: 5	c. their great loss.		49:25
c. the resurrection of the dead,		26: 2	c. the land of Lehi,		50:25
believe c. the coming of Christ.		26: 2	all things c. the matter,		50:31
Alma did not know c. them;		26: 9	c. their intentions to flee into		50:31
he should do c. this matter,		26:13	of Morianton c. their lands,		51: 1
of me c. the transgressor,		26:19	c. the chief judge Pahoran,		51: 2
to their leaders c. the matter;		27: 1	c. the altering of the law.		51: 3
prayed with much faith c. thee		27:14	a warm dispute c. the matter,		51: 4
to know c. those people who had		28:12	contentions c. the chief judge,		51:12
c. who should be their king.		29: 1	c. the death of his brother,		52:12
c. who should be their judges,		29:39	say c. the people of Ammon,		53:10
c. all the affairs of the church.		29:42	somewhat c. this war which		54: 5
their voices c. the matter;	Al	2: 6	somewhat c. the justice of God,		54: 6
c. the things which are to come.		5:44	c. that awful hell that awaits		54: 7
you, c. that which is to come,		5:48	to you c. these things in vain;		54:11
your faith is strong c. that		7:17	c. that God whom ye say we		54:21
c. the things which I have spoken,		7:17	c. our warfare in this part of		56: 2
against them c. their iniquities.		8:25	c. their traditions or their		56: 4
I knew c. these things;		10: 6	knowest c. all these things—		56: 4
unto you c. the things of God.		10: 8	ye also know c. the covenant		56: 6
c. the death of the mortal body,		11:45	c. these prisoners of war;		57:16
and also c. the resurrection		11:45	inquire of them c. the prisoners;		57:17
more c. the kingdom of God.		12: 8	c. the prisoners whom they		57:28
spoken c. the resurrection		12: 8	c. the affairs of our people.		58: 4
know nothing c. his mysteries;		12:11	thought c. the city of Manti.		58:25
hath spoken plainly c. death,		12:12	c. that which is to come.		58:40
man should know c. the things		12:28	c. the freedom of their country.		59:13
as I said c. the holy order of		13:10	I say much c. this matter?		60:18
which they have spoken c. him,		13:26	worried c. what we should do,		61:19
knew c. the blindness of the minds,		14: 6	regulations were made c. the law.		62:47
and also c. themselves,		15: 2	c. who should have the	He	1: 2
of the Lord c. the matter.		16: 6	c. who should fill the		2: 1
did inquire c. the place where		16:20	particular and very large, c. them.		3:13
know anything c. the Lord;		17:35	unto them c. their iniquities,		4:14
they had seen c. the matter.		18: 1	c. that which was to come.		6:14
and tell me c. these things;		18:20	c. the corruptness of their law;		8: 3
thou wilt tell me c. these things,		18:21	c. their secret works of darkness;		8: 4
all the things c. the fall of man,		18:36	unto us c. our iniquities.		8: 8
c. the rebellions of Laman and		18:38	not have testified c. those things.		8: 9
them c. the coming of Christ,		18:39	c. the judgments that shall come		8:12
c. the great power of Ammon.		19:15	c. the coming of the Messiah.		8:13
c. the things which they spake,		21: 8	he has said c. the chief judge		9: 2
them c. the coming of Christ,		21: 9	had spoken c. the chief judge.		9: 4
c. the resurrection of the dead,		21: 9	knew nothing c. the multitude		9: 8
c. things pertaining to		21:23	sent to inquire c. the chief judge		9:12
said c. the Spirit of the Lord?		22: 5	C. the five whom ye say ye have		9:12
tell me c. all these things,		22:11	to know, c. the matter,		9:13
c. the wicked traditions of their		23: 3	ye might know c. this thing;		9:23
c. the name that they should take		23:16	so much evil c. this people,		9:27
unto the people c. the matter;		24: 7	know nothing c. the matter		9:36

CONCERNING

c. their destruction if they did	He 10:12		church, c. church matters,	DC 30: 7
c. the death of the chief judge,	10:13		c. my servant Parley P. Pratt,	32: 1
spoken c. our destruction	11: 8		give I unto you c. all men—	36: 4
c. the points of doctrine	11:22		commanded c. your teaching,	42:15
c. the true points of doctrine,	11:23		my laws c. these things	42:28
said unto you c. another sign,	14:20		c. the consecration of	42:32
c. the restoration of our	15:11		hold thy peace c. them,	42:57
c. the people of the Nephites:	15:17		c. the signs of my coming,	45:16
c. the plates of brass, and all	3Ne 1: 2		which I have told you c. them	45:21
and your faith c. this thing	1: 6		I have told you c. Jerusalem;	45:24
knew the will of God c. them,	6:18		I spake c. the ten virgins.	45:56
c. the redemption which the Lord	6:20		any further c. this chapter,	45:60
c. the ministry of Christ,	7:15		this c. those who are not of	46: 5
c. their wickedness and their	9:10		c. your confirmation meetings,	46: 6
the scriptures c. my coming	9:16		c. your calling and election	53: 1
Zenock spake c. these things,	10:16		c. the place upon which he lives.	56: 8
they testified particularly c. us,	10:16		And now c. the gathering—	57:15
c. a remnant of the seed of	10:17		learn of me what I will c. you,	58: 1
had been given c. his death.	11: 2		and also c. this land	58: 1
c. the points of my doctrine,	11:28		c. those things which shall	58: 3
c. the law of Moses;	15: 2		spake c. my servant Edward	58:24
c. things which are to come.	15: 7		directions c. this land.	58:34
c. the other tribes of the house	15:15		c. my servant Martin Harris	58:38
of the Father c. this thing	15:18		c. the residue of the elders of	58:44
it was noised abroad c. Jesus;	19: 3		no more c. this matter.	59:22
commanded me c. this people,	20:10		c. your journey unto the land	60: 5
may know c. this people who	21: 2		c. Sidney Rigdon and Oliver	60:17
c. this my people who shall be	21: 2		commandment c. these things;	61:13
c. my people which are of	23: 2		your brethren c. these waters,	61:18
the people c. this matter.	27: 3		those c. whom I have spoken,	61:21
end of speaking c. these things	28:24		c. my servants, Sidney Rigdon,	61:23
c. those whom the Lord hath	28:36		And now, c. the residue,	61:33
c. their restoration to the lands	29: 1		Lord and his will c. you.	63: 1
that I should speak c. you,	30: 1		Lord your God c. his saints,	63:24
have observed c. this people;	Mrm 1: 3		and receive my will c. you,	64: 1
sacred engravings c. this people.	1: 3		unto you what I will c. you,	66: 1
have observed c. this people.	1: 4		or what is my will c. you.	66: 6
c. the destruction of my people,	6: 1		c. the items in addition to the	68:13
ye will know c. your fathers,	7: 9		c. their right of the priesthood	68:21
behold, I say no more c. them,	8: 9		and know c. my church;	69: 3
end of speaking c. this people.	8:13		c. the law of circumcision,	74: 3
c. that which must shortly	8:34		the Lord your God c. you.	75:12
speak also c. those who do not	9: 1		might know his will c. you—	75:23
have desired c. our brethren,	9:36		of my will c. all things	76: 7
speaks c. the creation of the world,	Eth 1: 3		c. those who shall hear the voice	76:16
decrees of God c. this land,	2: 9		c. all those who know my	76:31
an account c. them of old,	8: 9		C. whom I have said there is	76:34
speak somewhat c. these things;	12: 6		c. them who shall come forth	76:50
own language, c. these things;	12:39		of his economy c. this earth	77: 6
c. the destruction of the people	13: 1		may understand my will c. you;	82: 8
he spake c. a New Jerusalem	13: 4		church c. women and children,	83: 1
also c. the house of Israel,	13: 5		word of the Lord c. his church,	84: 2
been spoken c. another people	13:21		said c. the sons of Moses—	84:31
And now I speak c. baptism.	Mro 6: 1		and mine angels charge c. you.	84:42
c. the welfare of their souls.	6: 5		to beware c. yourselves,	84:43
which he spake c. faith, hope,	7: 1		words, or your testimony c. me.	84:94
c. the coming of Christ;	7:22		c. the parable of the wheat and	86: 1
would speak unto you c. hope.	7:40		c. the wars that will shortly come	87: 1
c. that which grieveth me	8: 4		to receive his will c. you:	88: 1
c. the baptism of your little	8: 5		chapter of John's testimony c. me.	88:141
of the Lord c. the matter.	8: 7		wearying me c. this matter.	90:33
c. the sufferings of this people.	9: 7		unto you c. the Apocrypha—	91: 1
he may prophesy c. all things;	10:13		c. my servant Shederlaomach	92: 1
c. the man that desires the	DC 5:23		commandments c. his children;	93:44
unto them c. these things,	5:26		a commandment c. them.	94:16
me any more c. this matter.	5:29		c. the building of mine house;	95: 3
c. the truth of these things.	6:22		how to act c. this matter;	96: 1
to your mind c. that matter?	6:23		my will c. your brethren	97: 1
c. the engravings of old records,	8: 1		c. the school in Zion,	97: 3
you shall have knowledge c. it.	8: 9		you c. the laws of the land,	98: 4
c. these things,	10:34		unto you c. your families—	98:23
unto the world c. the matter.	10:37		give unto you a word c. Zion.	100:13
c. the things which, in my	10:40		c. your brethren who have been	101: 1
c. the points of my doctrine,	10:63		hearts be comforted c. Zion;	101:16
c. the foundation of my church,	18: 4		wisdom c. the children of Zion,	101:41
even the Father c. me—	19: 2		will c. the redemption of Zion.	101:43
give unto you c. this matter;	19:32		in me c. all the churches,	101:63
c. the manner of baptism—	20:37		have given c. these things—	101:69
c. the church of Christ	20:68		c. the salvation and redemption	103: 1
I give unto you c. my will;	25: 2		c. the restoration and redemption	103:29
world began, c. the last days;	27: 6		c. all the properties which	104: 1
c. the revelations and	28: 1		c. the properties of the order—	104:19

CONCERNING 200 CONDEMNATION

I give unto you c. Zion,	DC 104:47	CONCUBINES		
unto you c. your stewardship	104:54	desiring many wives and c.,	Jac	1:15
unto you, c. your debts—	104:78	truly had many wives and c.,		2:24
my will c. the redemption of	105: 1	and c. he shall have none;		2:27
speaking c. the church and not	105: 2	and c. they should have none,		3: 5
not c. those who are appointed	105: 7	And he had many wives and c.	Mos	11: 2
speak c. my churches abroad—	105: 8	himself, and his wives and his c.;		11: 4
more perfectly c. their duty,	105:10	and their wives and their c.;		11: 4
counsel him c. this matter,	105:22	with his wives and his c.;		11:14
c. the purchasing of all the	105:28	he did have many wives and c.,	Eth	10: 5
which I have given c. Zion	105:34	their having many wives and c.—	DC	132: 1
be an end of controversy c. him.	107:83	Abraham received c., and they		132:37
soul be at rest c. your spiritual	108: 2	also received many wives and c.,		132:38
of the prophets, c. the last days.	109:23	David's wives and c. were given		132:39
terrible things c. the wicked,	109:45			
c. the revelations and	109:60	CONDEMN		
inquire diligently c. the more	111: 9	c. not the things of God	T	Pg
thy prayers c. thy brethren.	112:11	And all they who shall c. me,	2Ne	7: 9
c. the affairs of my church in	112:27	words shall c. you at the last day.		33:14
know my will c. those kings	124: 1	that he perish not, and c. him,	Mos	4:22
consolation c. all those who	124:53	For our words will c. us,	Al	12:14
c. the kindreds of the earth,	124:58	yea, all our works will c. us;		12:14
wish to know my will c. them,	124:73	and our thoughts will also c. us;		12:14
c. my servant Vinson Knight,	124:74	this people, and c. our law?		14:20
and cease to fear c. his family,	124:87	he doth c. all this people,	He	8: 5
will of the Lord c. the saints	125: 1	power to c. any one to death	3Ne	6:22
keep my commandments c. them,	125: 2	thee in judgment thou shalt c.		22:17
Lord unto you c. your dead:	127: 6	shall not c. it because of the	Mrm	8:12
revelation to you c. a recorder.	128: 2	C. me not because of mine		9:31
they have kept c. their dead.	128: 8	c. them before the elders,	Mro	6: 7
as Paul says c. the fathers—	128:15	good thing, and c. it not,		7:19
received promises c. his seed,	132:30	Behold, I do not c. you;	DC	6:35
as ye have asked c. adultery,	132:41	of that house, and c. them;		75:21
hear the word of the Lord c.	133: 1	thy neighbor, lest he c. thee.		136:25
the Camp of Israel in their	136: 1			
will of the Lord c. his people.	136: 9	CONDEMNATION		
declaration c. plural marriages	OD	no punishment there is no c.;	2Ne	9:25
and tell me c. this earth,	Mses 1:36	and where there is no c.		9:25
speak unto thee c. this earth	1:40	and ye have come unto great c.;	Jac	2:34
reveal unto you c. this heaven,	2: 1	much more just will be your c.	Mos	4:22
c. all the families of the earth,	5:10	and your c. is just		4:25
c. the children of Noah;	7:60	hath brought himself under c.		26:31
shall comfort us c. our work	8: 9	bring upon himself his own c.	Al	3:19
unto the fathers c. the seed.	Abr 1: 4	in favor of your law, to your c.		10:26
c. the land of Chaldea,	1:29	unto them by the way of c.;		60: 2
c. the right of Priesthood,	1:31	and behold it is to your c.;		60:12
said c. every plant of the field	5: 5	yourselves to come under c.,	He	14:19
show us c. the buildings of	JS 1: 2	upon themselves their own c.		14:29
c. the destruction of the temple,	1: 4	save their c. was signed by	3Ne	6:22
c. the destruction of Jerusalem,	1:12	you that ye come not under c.;		18:33
spoken unto you c. the Jews;	1:21	from them, unto their c.		26:10
the vision which I had had c. it,	2:50	or he that is under no c.,	Mro	8:22
c. the rise of this Church,	2:73	is unto them that are under c.		8:24
		we should be brought under c.;		9: 6
CONCERNS		the c. of this generation	DC	5:18
arrange their temporal c.,	DC 63:38	and c. in the day of judgment.		10:23
them and the c. thereof,	70: 5	it shall turn to their own c.—		20:15
the literary c. of my church	72:20	blessed, and art under no c.		23: 1
the c. of your stewardships,	82:17	for thou also art under no c.,		23: 3
prescribing rules on spiritual c.,	134: 6	for thou also art under no c.,		23: 4
		for thou also art under no c.,		23: 5
CONCERT		only in wrath unto their c.		63:11
act in c. also with my servant	DC 124:95	there be who are under this c.,		63:62
		and in this there is no c.,		63:64
CONCLUDE		without this there remaineth c.		63:64
wherefore, I c. this record,	Jac 7:26	of glory, otherwise, a greater c.		63:66
		ye are under c. if ye do not		67: 8
CONCLUDED		who are ordained unto this c.		76:48
c. to go down into Egypt,	Abr 2:21	light shall receive the greater c.		82: 3
Gods c. upon the seventh time,	5: 3	the whole church under c.		84:55
		And this c. resteth upon the		84:56
CONCLUDING		shall remain under this c. until		84:57
c. that if he gave wisdom to	JS 2:13	it shall turn unto your c.		88:65
		judged, and are found under c.;		88:100
CONCLUSION		are brought under c. thereby,		90: 5
any certain c. who was right	JS 2: 8	here is the c. of man;		93:31
At length I came to the c. that	2:13	receiveth not the light is under c.		93:32
		you have continued under this c.;		93:41
CONCOURSES		for they are not all under this c.;		105: 7
with numberless c. of angels	1Ne 1: 8	Was Abraham, therefore, under c.?		132:35
I saw numberless c. of people,	8:21	without c. on earth and in		132:48
with numberless c. of angels,	Al 36:22	and to the c. of the ungodly.		136:33
		offend God, and come under c.	JS	2:25

CONDEMNED 201 CONFESS

CONDEMNED
otherwise ye are c.;	Mos 4:25
that we should be c. of God	12:13
Therefore thou art c. to die,	Al 1:14
be awful, for then we shall be c.	12:13
the people, and c. unto death;	He 1: 8
saw that he was c. unto death,	1: 9
were found were c. unto death.	1:12
be c. according to the crime	8: 1
if they are c. they bring upon	14:29
c. and punished according to	3Ne 5: 5
had c. the prophets of the Lord	6:25
wherefore, he that is not c.,	Mro 8:22
with me, and behold, he is c.	DC 5:27
And neither of you have I c.	9:12
But he or she shall be c. by	42:81
standeth c. before the Lord;	64: 9
They c. for evil that thing in	64:16
in their stewardships shall be c.,	64:40
be tried or c. for any crime,	68:22
be impeached, he shall be c.;	68:23
not be c. with the unjust;	104: 7
and the wicked might be c.	136:39
felt c. for my weakness and	JS 2:29

CONDEMNETH
But he c. you, and if ye persist	Jac 2:14
more fully c. the sinner,	Al 41:15
unto him whom the Father c.	3Ne 18:33
he that c., let him be aware lest	Mrm 8:17

CONDEMNING
C. the righteous because of their	He 7: 5

CONDESCENSION
Knowest thou the c. of God?	1Ne 11:16
Look and behold the c. of God!	11:26
his c. unto the children of men	2Ne 4:26

CONDESCENSIONS
his c. unto the children of men;	2Ne 9:53
c. unto the children of men,	Jac 4: 7

CONDITION
on c. that they will give us a	Al 27:24
the c. of repentance,	He 14:18
from their wild and savage c.	DC 109:65
scattered c. among the Gentiles.	113:10
in their saved c., to all eternity;	132:17

CONDITIONS
c. whereby man can be saved	Mos 4: 8
the c. which I have told you.	4: 8
under the c. that they would	19:15
on what c. are they saved?	Al 5:10
them on the c. of repentance.	17:15
only on c. of repentance of men	42:13
for except it were for these c.,	42:13
submit to the c. which I have	44:11
on c. that ye will deliver up	54:11
tidings of the c. of repentance,	He 5:11
might know the c. of repentance;	14:11
And these were the c. also,	16:11
him, on c. of repentance.	DC 18:12
the c. of the children of men.	46:15
are certain bounds also and c.	88:38
beings who abide not in those c.	88:39
that blessing, and the c. thereof,	132: 5
the c. of this law are these:	132: 7

CONDUCT
with the c. of their fathers,	Mos 25:12
and c. him forth to the land of	Al 18: 9
for when they saw your c. they	39:11
power to c. the war in that part	61:15
c. him to the judgment-seat	He 2: 7
and c. thyself wisely before me?	DC 19:41
c. the meetings as they are led by	20:45
thus shall ye c. in all things.	42:93
to c. all meetings as they are	46: 2
their members for disorderly c.,	134:10

CONDUCTED
Alma c. his brethren back to	Al 27:20

CONDUIT
meetings were c. by the church	Mro 6: 9
which case shall there be c.,	DC 102:27
was to be c. in the last days.	JS 2:54

CONDUIT
at the end of the c. of the upper	2Ne 17: 3
a c. open right up into	JS 2:43

CONFEDERACY
Say ye not, A c.,	2Ne 18:12
whom this people shall say, A c.;	18:12

CONFEDERATE
Syria is c. with Ephraim.	2Ne 17: 2
Saying unto him: Thou art c.;	He 9:20

CONFER
he should c. the kingdom upon	Mos 1: 9
I, being old, did c. the kingdom	10:22
no one to c. the kingdom upon,	28:10
not c. the kingdom upon him;	29: 3
having no one to c. it upon,	Al 10:19
was desirous to c. upon them,	17: 6
to c. those sacred things, before	63:11
I c. the Priesthood of Aaron,	DC 13: 1
c. upon my servant Pelagoram	104:22
I c. the Priesthood of Aaron,	JS 2:69

CONFERENCE
in c. once in three months,	DC 20:61
or he may receive it from a c.	20:64
of a high council or general c.	20:67
with the church since the last c.;	20:82
to the west to hold the next c.;	26: 1
leave this place until after the c.;	28:10
appointed to preside over the c.	28:10
from this time until the next c.,	52: 2
let a c. meeting be called;	58:58
also hold a c. upon this land.	58:61
Edward Partridge direct the c.	58:62
given, and the voice of the c.	72: 7
the regions round about, until c.;	73: 1
them, by the voice of the c.,	73: 2
the regions round about until c.;	73: 4
After prayer the c. adjourned.	102:34
Let a c. be held immediately;	118: 1
instructions at my general c.,	124:88
of them at my general c.;	124:144
as a Church in General C.	OD

CONFERENCES
as said c. shall direct or	DC 20:61
said c. are to do whatever	20:62
they belong, or from the c.	20:63
teachers to attend the several c.	20:81
the elders of the church at the c.,	58:56
as shall be ruled by the c.	58:58

CONFERRED
and I c. them upon my son	Om 1: 3
c. the kingdom upon Noah,	Mos 11: 1
having the kingdom c. upon him	19:26
had been c. upon none but	25:13
had kept, and c. them upon Alma,	28:20
and c. them upon him,	28:20
having c. the office upon him,	29:42
the king c. the kingdom upon	Al 24: 3
Alma had c. them upon his son,	50:38
had been c. upon Helaman,	63:13
was c. upon you by the hands of	DC 67:14
have been c. upon you.	97:14
because it was c. upon Aaron	107:13
may be c. upon us, it is true;	121:37
the keys of this priesthood are c.)	132: 7
c. upon you the keys and power	132:45
It was c. upon me from the	Abr 1: 3
should he c. on us hereafter;	JS 2:70
and c. this Priesthood upon us,	2:72
in due time be c. upon us,	2:72

CONFESS
but I c. unto God.	Jac 7:19
and shall c. before God that	Mos 16: 1
then I will c. unto them that	26:27

CONFESS

if he c. his sins before thee   Mos 26:29
of their sins and did c. them,   26:35
those that would not c. their sins   26:36
and every tongue c. before him.   27:31
then shall they c. that he is God;   27:31
then shall they c., who live   27:31
and c. their sins before him.   Al 17: 4
came forth and did c. their sins   He 5:17
and he shall c. his fault and   9:17
and then shall he c. unto you,   9:35
according to the words he did c.   9:37
their error and did c. their faults.   3Ne 1:25
c. your sins, lest you suffer   DC 19:20
she c. thou shalt be reconciled.   42:88
And if he or she c. not   42:89
And if he or she c. not,   42:91
opportunity to c. in secret   42:92
will c. them and forsake them.   58:43
c. not his hand in all things,   59:21
unto those who c. their sins   61: 2
who c. their sins before me   64: 7
every tongue shall c. to him   76:110
and every tongue shall c.,   88:104

CONFESSED

taught them, and c. the Christ,   Jac 7:17
they c. unto him their sins and   He 16: 1
repented not, and c. not,   Mro 6: 7
And c. they were strangers and   DC 45:13

CONFESSES

and c. by the power of the   Mro 7:44

CONFESSETH

for he c. them not, and he   DC 58:60
of his sins, and c. them not,   64:12

CONFESSING

c. all their sins,   Mos 27:35
repenting and c. their sins.   He 16: 5
c. thy sins unto thy brethren,   DC 59:12
c. me before the world;   124:18

CONFESSION

In making this c., no one need   JS 2:28

CONFIDENCE

and lost the c. of your children,   Jac 2:35
upheld by the c., faith, and   DC 107:22
then shall thy c. wax strong   121:45
he may obtain the c. of men.   124:112
as to destroy all c. in settling   JS 2:12
I had full c. in obtaining   2:29

CONFINE

and c. the words unto mine own   2Ne 25: 8

CONFINED

that ye should be c. in dungeons,   Mos 2:13
and c. himself wholly to the   Al 4:20
wholly c. to the judgment-seat,   7: 1
could not be c. in dungeons;   8:31
strong cords, and c. in prison.   14:22
c. in jail by the conspiracy of   DC 135: 7

CONFIRM

unto him will I c. all my words,   Mrm 9:25
to c. those who are baptized   DC 20:41
to c. the church by the laying on   20:43
you shall c. in my church,   33:15
which I now c. upon you   84:42

CONFIRMATION

concerning your c. meetings,   DC 46: 6

CONFIRMED

c. to others by the ministering   DC 20:10
c. by the laying on of the hands   20:68
and c. you to be apostles,   27:12
c. a priesthood also upon Aaron   84:18
was c. upon Aaron and his sons,   84:30
has renewed and c. upon you,   84:48

CONFUSION

is c. upon you for your sakes,   DC 84:48
order of this priesthood was c.   107:40
all things were c. unto Adam,   Mses 5:59

CONFIRMING

c. their faith, and exhorting them   Mos 27:33
the hands and c. the churches.   DC 24: 9
to c. the church at Colesville,   26: 1
which is to come, c. our hope!   128:21

CONFLICT

Behold, we will end the c.   Al 44:10

CONFORMING

answer the will of God, by c.   DC 128: 5
earthly c. to that which is   128:13

CONFOUND

And he did c. them, that they   1Ne 2:14
I did c. him in all his words.   Jac 7: 8
did c. them in all their words.   Mos 12:19
c. the wise and the learned.   Al 32:23
many instances doth c. the wise.   37: 6
the Lord doth c. the wise and   37: 7
did c. many of those dissenters   He 5:17
insomuch that they did c. them.   9:18
that he will not c. us that we may   Eth 1:34
did not c. the language of Jared;   1:35
that he c. not their language.   1:36
and thus I will c. those who   DC 10:42
Wherefore, c. your enemies;   71: 7
We ask thee, Holy Father, to c.,   109:29
when the weak shall c. the wise,   133:58

CONFOUNDED

at the time the Lord c. the   T Pg
Israel shall no more be c.   1Ne 14: 2
they should no more be c.,   15:20
insomuch that they were c.   17:52
hereafter be scattered and be c.,   22: 5
Israel have been scattered and c.,   22: 7
those who shall not be c.   22:22
seek to destroy him shall be c.;   2Ne 3:14
He hath c. mine enemies,   4:22
therefore shall I not be c.   7: 7
the Lord c. the language of   Om 1:22
the Lord c. the language of   Mos 28:17
neither be thou c., for thou   3Ne 22: 4
the Lord c. the language of   Eth 1:33
Jared and his brother were not c.   1:35
also, that they were not c.   1:37
which ye shall write I have c.;   3:24
and they shall no more be c.,   13: 8
thou mayest no more be c.,   Mro 10:31
and no more be c. at all.   DC 35:25
midst, and you shall not be c.   49:27
against you he shall be c.   71:10
trust in me and he shall not be c.;   84:116
Be not ashamed, neither c.;   90:17
shall not be c. in this world,   93:52
shall not be c. before men;   100: 5

CONFOUNDETH

He c. them and buildeth a ship.   1Ne 1:hd
He c. a man who seeketh to   Jac 1:hd

CONFOUNDING

unto the c. of false doctrines   2Ne 3:12

CONFUSED

of the warrior is with c. noise,   2Ne 19: 5
much c., knew not whether to   Al 52:36
being c. because of the fall of   56:51

CONFUSION

they fled in much c., lest   Al 52:28
Now Moroni seeing their c.,   52:37
in haste, lest there should be c.,   DC 63:24
and to bring to shame and c.,   109:29
and filled the world with c.,   123: 7
and not a house of c.   132: 8
a scene of great c. and   JS 2: 6

CONFUSION 203 CONSEQUENCE

so great were the c. and strife	JS	2: 8
remain in darkness and c.,		2:13

CONGREGATION
also upon the mount of the c.,	2Ne	24:13
preach by the way in every c.,	DC	52:10
the c. in the house may hear		88:129
stood up in the midst of the c.;		107:56

CONGREGATIONS
my cries in the midst of thy c.	Al	33: 9
among the c. of the wicked,	DC	60: 8
among the c. of the wicked;		60:13
among the c. of the wicked,		60:14
in the c. of the wicked		61:30
for the c. of their brethren,		61:32
among the c. of the wicked.		61:32
among the c. of the wicked,		61:33
among the c. of the wicked.		62: 5
in the c. of the wicked,		68: 1
the c. in the eastern countries,		103:29

CONGRESS
as laws have been enacted by C.	DC	OD

CONNECTED
spirit and element, inseparably c.,	DC	93:33
inseparably c. with the powers		121:36
things c. with the Church,	JS	2:73

CONNECTION
Which power you hold, in c. with	DC	112:31
in c. with this quotation I will		128:17

CONNECTIONS
mercy upon all their immediate c.,	DC	109:70
and their immediate c.,		109:71
and all their immediate c.,		109:72
c., associations, or expectations,		132: 7

CONQUER
swords, and we will perish or c.	Al	44: 8
determined to c. in this place		56:17
fixed with a determination to c.		58:12
enable the Lamanites to c.		61: 8
in which we did not c.;	Mro	9: 2
c. the enemy of all righteousness,		9: 6
yea that you may c. Satan,	DC	10: 5

CONQUERED
every man c. according to	Al	30:17
be c. under the Lamanites.		61: 8
fought all that day, and c. not.	Eth	15:15
nevertheless, they c. not,		15:17

CONQUEROR
that you may come off c.;	DC	10: 5
as yet, c. of their enemies.	Jac	7:25

CONSCIENCE
answer a clear c. before God	Mos	2:15
with a clear c. before God,		2:27
their sins, and having peace of c.,		4: 3
life or death, joy or remorse of c.	Al	29: 5
brought remorse of c. unto man.		42:18
individual the free exercise of c.,	DC	134: 2
crime, but never control c.;		134: 4
sacred the freedom of c.		134: 5
c. void of offense towards God.		135: 4
to the dictates of our own c.,	AoF	11

CONSCIENCES
of worship to bind the c. of men,	DC	134: 4

CONSCIOUSNESS
tremble under a c. of his guilt,	Al	12: 1
under a c. of his own guilt;		14: 6
under a c. of your guilt?	Mrm	9: 3
souls are racked with a c. of guilt		9: 3
under a c. of your filthiness		9: 4

CONSECRATE
he shall c. thine afflictions	2Ne	2: 2

And may the Lord c. also unto	2Ne	3: 2
I, Nephi, did c. Jacob and Joseph,		5:26
I will c. this land unto thy seed,		10:19
will c. thy performance unto thee,		32: 9
the Lord God will c. my prayers		33: 4
did c. Amlici to be their king.	Al	2: 9
I will c. their gain unto the	3Ne	20:19
c. of thy properties for their	DC	42:30
I will c. of the riches of those		42:39
I c. unto them this land for a		51:16
I will c. unto my people,		52: 2
c. and dedicate this land,		58:57
of all those who c. properties,		85: 1
and c. it unto my name.		104:60
I will c. that spot that it shall		124:44

CONSECRATED
this land is c. unto him	2Ne	1: 7
the Lord hath c. this land		1:32
having been c. by my brother		6: 2
had been c. priests and teachers	Jac	1:18
and c. by my father,	Mos	2:11
had c. his son Mosiah to be		6: 3
that had been c. by his father,		11: 5
and c. new ones in their stead,		11: 5
Therefore he c. all their priests		23:17
none were c. except they were		23:17
had been c. the high priest	Al	4: 4
Alma had c. to be teachers,		4: 7
having been c. by my father,		5: 3
and c. priests and teachers		15:13
residue to be c. unto the bishop,	DC	42:33
that which he has c. unto		42:37
which is c. to the bishop,		42:71
he has c. unto the bishop		51: 5
and c. for the gathering of		57: 1
c. unto the inhabitants of Zion,		70: 8
c. to the good of the church,		72:12
have c. the land of Shinehah		82:13
the c. spot as I have appointed—		84:31
be c. for the bringing forth of		84:104
the money may be c. unto me,		90:29
lot on the south be c. unto me		94: 3
that has been c. unto me.		103:22
have c. to be the land of Zion,		103:24
my kingdom upon the c. land,		103:35
be holy and c. unto the Lord.		104:66
I have c. for the gathering		105:15
be sanctified and c. to be holy,		109:12
Far West, be a holy and c. land		115: 7

CONSECRATING
and c. priests and teachers	Al	23: 4

CONSECRATION
the c. of the properties of	DC	42:32
which he has received by c.,		42:32
their support after this first c.,		42:33
receive not their inheritance by c.,		85: 3
according to the laws of c.		105:29

CONSECRATIONS
kept by the c. of the church;	DC	83: 6
may receive the c. of mine house,		124:21

CONSENT
by common c. in the church,	DC	26: 2
by common c. in the church,		28:13
your prayer of faith with one c.		93:51
the c. of those who call themselves		101:97
united c. or voice of the order,		104:21
and common c. of the order.		104:71
and common c. of the order—		104:72
by common c. or otherwise,		104:85
without the c. of the stockholder,		124:71
the first give her c., and if he		132:61

CONSEQUENCE
in c. of that which is coming	DC	42:64
In c. of transgression,		52:37
in c. of the stiffneckedness		56: 6
In c. of evils and designs		89: 4

CONSEQUENCE 204 CONSTRAIN

CONSEQUENCE
in c. of their transgressions;	DC	101: 2
in c. of those things which I		101:98
in c. of their being driven out		104:51
in c. of the transgressions of		105: 9
rejoice in c. of the blessings which		110: 9
In c. of this alleged occurrence		OD
a boy of no c. in the world,	JS	2:22
In c. of these things, I often		2:29
(in c. of the indigent		2:46

CONSEQUENCES
that I teach you the c. of sin.	2Ne	9:48
them the awful c. of them.	Jac	3:12
a foundation for serious c.	Al	50:32
c. would lead to the overthrow		50:32

CONSEQUENTLY
c., the books spoken of must be	DC	128: 7
C., the baptismal font was		128:13

CONSIDER
I would that ye should c.	1Ne	22:30
and c. themselves fools before God,	2Ne	9:42
c. the operation of his hands.		15:12
look upon thee, and shall c. thee,		24:16
that ye should c. on the blessed	Mos	2:41
they shall c. him a man, and say		3: 9
that ye should c. the cause		29: 5
which ye are called to c.—		29: 5
let us be wise and c. these things,		29: 8
C. the lilies of the field how	3Ne	13:28
had not heard shall they c.		20:45
had not heard shall they c.		21: 8
that they may c. these things.	DC	45:73
For, c. the lilies of the field,		84:82
whom they may c. worthy		102: 7
the twelve councilors shall c.		102:13
we c. him fully authorized by		OD

CONSIDERABLE
took others to a c. number,	Om	1:29
Yea, even to a c. distance,	Al	56:37
stands a hill of c. size,	JS	2:51
top, under a stone of c. size,		2:51
I copied a c. number of them,		2:62

CONSIDERATION
we would suggest for your c.	DC	123: 1

CONSIDERED
for I c. that mine afflictions	1Ne	15: 5
which I c. to be most precious;	Jac	1: 2
that he c. that Ammoron,	Al	62:35
are c. as dead, both as to things	He	14:16
ye have not c. the great	DC	95: 3
that which they have never c.;		101:94

CONSIDEREST
c. not the beam that is in thine	3Ne	14: 3

CONSIDERING
c. himself an unworthy servant.	Mos	21:33
c. their kings to be powerful;	Al	18:13
c. that the law of Moses was a		25:15
c. the end of your salvation,	DC	46: 7

CONSIGN
c. us to an awful destruction,	Al	26:19

CONSIGNATION
their c. to happiness or misery,	Al	40:15
their c. to happiness or misery.		40:17

CONSIGNED
they are c. to an awful view of	Mos	3:25
c. to a state of endless misery	Al	9:11
are c. to a state of endless wo.		28:11
c. to partake of the fruits of		40:26
be c. to a state of misery.		42: 1
c. them forever to be cut off		42:14
have been c. to bondage,		50:22
I am c. that these are my days,	He	7: 9
c. to a state of endless misery,		12:26

CONSIST
c. of men, women, and children,	3Ne	17:25
to c. of twelve high priests,	DC	102: 1
which c. in the key of knowledge.		128:14

CONSISTED
family, which c. of my mother,	1Ne	2: 5
brethren, who c. of Nephi,	Al	3: 6
who c. of the Nephites and	Mrm	1: 8

CONSISTENT
not c. with that character	JS	2:28

CONSISTENTLY
c. with the feelings of the	DC	105:24

CONSISTING
c. of his wife, and his sons, and his	Mos	2: 5
His family c. of eleven souls,	JS	2: 4

CONSISTS
c. of the learning of the Jews	1Ne	1: 2
nature of this ordinance c. in	DC	128: 8
c. in obtaining the powers of		128:11

CONSOLATION
impart much c. to the church,	Mos	27:33
filling their souls with joy and c.,	He	3:35
c. concerning all those who have	DC	124:53
giving us c. by holding forth		128:21

CONSOLE
will c. you in your afflictions,	Jac	3: 1
may c. ourselves in this point,	Al	56:11

CONSOLING
instead of c. and healing	Jac	2: 9
in his afflictions, with c. words,	DC	25: 5

CONSPIRACY
slain by the c. of his brother,	DC	84:16
do not justify sedition nor c.		134: 7
in jail by the c. of traitors		135: 7

CONSPIRE
the billowing surge c. against thee;	DC	122: 7

CONSPIRING
will exist in the hearts of c. men	DC	89: 4

CONSTANT
shall be thy c. companion,	DC	121:46

CONSTANTLY
blessings c. from under thy hand.	DC	122: 2

CONSTELLATIONS
stars of heaven and the c. thereof	2Ne	23:10

CONSTITUTE
c. the spiritual authorities of the	DC	107:32
c. a quorum and First Presidency,		124:126

CONSTITUTED
c. what is called the Urim and	JS	2:35
what c. "sears" in ancient		2:35

CONSTITUTION
God hath ordained for the c.,	DC	89:10
to the laws and c. of the people,		101:77
established the C. of this land,		101:80
namely, the C. of our land,		109:54
And they shall form a c., whereby		124:63

CONSTITUTIONAL
that law of the land which is c.,	DC	98: 5
is the c. law of the land;		98: 6
laws have been pronounced c.		OD

CONSTRAIN
that his father should c. him,	Eth	6:25
should c. no man to be their king.		6:25

CONSTRAINED — CONTEND

CONSTRAINED
I was c. by the Spirit that I	1Ne	4:10
I, Nephi, was c. to speak unto	2Ne	4:14
and be c. to exclaim: Holy, holy		9:46
as the Spirit hath c. me;		28: 1
my soul that I should be c.,	Jac	2: 9
now behold, I, Moroni, am c.,	Al	60:34
he was c. to speak more	He	8:11
being c. by the Holy Ghost,	4Ne	1:48
may be c. to acknowledge that	DC	105:32
c. to acknowledge that thou hast		109:13

CONSTRAINETH
the Spirit of the Lord c. me	1Ne	7:15
The Spirit c. me that I must	Al	14:11

CONSTRAINT
care, and by c. of the Spirit;	DC	63:64
not by commandment or c.,		89: 2

CONSTRUCT
Thou shalt c. a ship, after the	1Ne	17: 8
may make tools to c. the ship		17: 9
that ye could not c. a ship,		17:19
I did c. it after the manner of	2Ne	5:16

CONSTRUCTION
the manner of the c. was like unto	2Ne	5:16

CONSTRUED
c. to inculcate or encourage	DC	OD

CONSULT
brethren did c. one with another.	1Ne	3:10
Limhi began to c. with the people	Mos	22: 1

CONSULTED
Mosiah c. with his priests.	Mos	27: 1
therefore the king c. with Aaron	Al	23:16
of the Zoramites had c. together		35: 3
and c. with them concerning the		35: 4
And c. for a long time,	DC	101:48

CONSUME
and it shall also c. the beard.	2Ne	17:20
shall c. the glory of his forest,		20:18
the day that cometh shall c. them,		26: 6
that ye may c. it on your lusts,	Mrm	9:28
they may c. it upon their lusts.	DC	46: 9
c. the wicked with		63:34

CONSUMED
those who must be c. as stubble;	1Ne	22:23
and the scorner is c.,	2Ne	27:31
yea, a fire which cannot be c.,	Al	5:52
of those who were c. by fire.		14: 9
been cast into the fire were c.,		14:14
ye sons of Jacob are not c.	3Ne	24: 6
the inhabitants thereof are c.	DC	5:19
and the earth shall be c.		29:23
and the scorner shall be c.;		45:50
and all flesh be c. before me.		98:17
the face of the earth, shall be c.;		101:24

CONSUMETH
and the flame c. the chaff,	2Ne	15:24
and it well nigh c. me		26: 7

CONSUMING
even unto the c. of my flesh;	1Ne	17:48
unto the c. of my flesh.	2Ne	4:21
children who were c. in the fire,	Al	14:10

CONSUMPTION
the c. decreed shall overflow with	2Ne	20:22
Lord God of Hosts shall make a c.,		20:23
until the c. decreed hath	DC	87: 6

CONTAIN
did c. the five books of Moses,	1Ne	5:11
they c. the covenants of the Lord,		13:23
which c. these prophesyings	WM	1: 6
plates, which c. these records	Mos	1: 3
of Nephi, which c. the records	Mos	1: 6
records which c. the prophecies		2:34
which c. these engravings	Al	37: 3
do c. that which is holy writ.		37: 5
things that these records do c.,		37: 9
cannot c. even a hundredth part	3Ne	5: 8
do c. all the proceedings of this		5: 9
the plates of Nephi do c. the		26: 7
which c. these records—	DC	3:19
which c. much of my gospel,		6:26
c. those parts of my scripture		8: 1
c. all those parts of my gospel		10:46

CONTAINED
c. the genealogy of my father.	1Ne	3:12
c. the plainness of the gospel		13:24
which c. the record of the Jews.	Om	1:14
c. this small account of	WM	1: 3
which c. records which had been		1:10
plates which c. the record of	Mos	8: 5
mystery is c. within these plates,		8:19
which c. the holy scriptures,	Al	14: 8
know of the mysteries c. thereon.		37: 4
cannot be c. in this work.	He	3:14
There are many things c. therein	DC	91: 1
There are many things c. therein		91: 2
the books which c. the record of		128: 7
revelation c. in the letter which		128: 7
everlasting gospel, which it c.,		135: 3
everlasting Gospel was c. in it,	JS	2:34

CONTAINETH
c. many of the prophecies	1Ne	13:23

CONTAINING
c. the fulness of my everlasting	DC	27: 5
book c. the records of our dead,		128:24

CONTAINS
c. the covenants of the Lord,	1Ne	13:23
suppose that it c. all my words;	2Ne	29:10
c. the truth and the word of God.	DC	19:26
c. a record of a fallen people,		20: 9
that it c. the revealed will,		77: 6
the first seal c. the things of		77: 7
C. writings that cannot be	Fac	2: 8

CONTEMPLATE
shall c. the word of the Lord;	DC	124:23
that he may c. the glory of Zion,		124:60

CONTEMPLATED
where you have c. building it,	DC	124:43

CONTEMPLATING
John the Revelator was c. this	DC	128: 6

CONTEMPT
not with sorrow, neither with c.,	Jac	4: 3
lightly, but with great c.,	JS	2:21

CONTEND
brethren did c. against my seed,	1Ne	12:19
and could not c. against me;		17:52
for I will c. with him that		21:25
I will c. with them that contendeth	2Ne	6:17
Who will c. with me?		7: 8
should not c. one with another;		26:32
they shall c. one with another;		28: 4
priests shall c. one with another,		28: 4
manner of Sherem c. against me.	Jac	7: 7
they did c. against their enemies,	WM	1:14
did c. against the Lamanites		1:14
they should c. with my people;	Mos	9:13
we did c. with them, face to face.		10:19
people of Limhi to c. with them,		22: 2
began to c. with him sharply,	Al	1: 7
c. warmly with their adversaries,		1:22
Amlicites did c. with the Nephites		2:17
and they did c. mightily,		2:29
sent his guards to c. with Alma.		2:32
cross and c. with the Lamanites		2:34
they began to c. with me,		9: 1
I go and c. with these men who		17:33

CONTEND — 206 — CONTINUAL

CONTEND
stood to c. with those who	Al	17:34
began to c. with him, saying:		21: 5
that ye c. no more against the		34:38
might c. with the armies of		35:13
to c. with their brethren,		43:14
to c. with the army of Lehi.		43:36
to c. more powerfully against		44:16
and the Lamanites did c. with		44:17
to c. with their brethren,		48:21
began to c. with the Nephites,		49:21
not sufficiently strong to c.		56:39
to c. with an enemy which was		58: 8
c. no more with the Lamanites		60:24
did c. for the judgment-seat,	He	1: 3
did also cause the people to c.;		1: 3
did c. for the judgment-seat,		1: 4
and did c. with them one by one,		9:18
and to c. among themselves,		16:17
c. with the tribes of the people;	3Ne	7:12
hearts of men to c. with anger,		11:29
that we did c. with an army of	Mrm	2:25
c. against the word of the Lord,	Eth	4: 8
C. against no church, save it be	DC	18:20
I the Lord, will c. with Zion,		90:36
C. thou, therefore, morning by		112: 5
c. earnestly for the redemption		117:13
thy friends do not c. against thee,		121:10
Cease to c. one with another;		136:23

CONTENDED
Therefore, I c. with my brethren		
he c. again with Amlici;	Mos	9: 2
And he also c. with the king of	Al	2:31
c. with the guards of the king of		2:32
c. with many about the word.		2:33
and they c. in their might		21:11
	Eth	15:24

CONTENDETH
with him that c. with thee,	1Ne	21:25
with them that c. with thee—	2Ne	6:17

CONTENDING
been c. with our brethren,	Mos	22: 3
in c. against those who sought to	Al	18: 2
And while they were thus c.,		19:28
c. with the Lamanites, to defend		43:47
we were c. among ourselves,		60:16
were c. for the Methodist faith,	JS	2: 5
priest c. against priest,		2: 6

CONTENT
I ought to be c. with the	Al	29: 3
then thy servant will be c.	Mses	1:36

CONTENTION
that I saw much war and c.	Om	1:10
he caused a c. among them;		1:28
after there having been much c.	WM	1:16
no more c. in all the land	Mos	1: 1
was no c. among all his people		6: 7
that there should be no c.		18:21
and there began to be a great c.		19: 3
that there should be no c.		23:15
save it be through much c.,		29:21
to be a c. among the people;	Al	2: 1
c. began to be exceeding sharp		19:28
when she saw the c. which was		19:28
seeing the c. among his people,		19:31
a great c. and a disturbance		22:22
and there began to be c. in		25: 8
a c. which took place among them		50:25
there began to be a warm c.		50:26
there began to be a c. among		51: 2
thiss matter of their c. was settled		51: 7
there began to be a serious c.	He	1: 2
because of so much c. and		1:18
there began to be a c. again		2: 1
no c. among the people of Nephi		3: 1
was no c. among the people		3: 2
neither was there much c. in		3: 2
much c. and many dissensions;		3: 3
was still great c. in the land,		3:19
was also a c. among the people,		4: 1
did cause a great c. in the land.		
he that hath the spirit of c. is		
the devil, who is the father of c.,		
no c. among all the people,		
there was no c. in the land,		
was no c. in all the land.		
there may not be so much c.;	DC	10:63
the hearts of the people to c.		10:63
a great c. among the people		74: 3
	3Ne	7: 7
		11:29
		11:29
	4Ne	1:13
		1:15
		1:18

CONTENTIONS
the wars and c. of my people;	1Ne	9: 4
the wars and c. of my people.		9: 4
of wars and c. in the land;		12: 3
c. and destructions of my people.		19: 4
and laying down of c.,	2Ne	3:12
we had already had wars and c.		5:34
wars and c. among my people.		26: 2
and their wars, and their c.,	Jac	3:13
which caused wars and c.;		7:26
and prophesying of wars, and c.,	En	1:23
after the manner of wars, and c.,	Jar	1:13
had had many wars and serious c.,	Om	1:17
of c. among his own people.	WM	1:12
beware lest there shall arise c.	Mos	2:32
but there arose c. among them,		7:25
to be wars and c. in the land.		9:13
to raise c. among my people;		11:28
no more c. in all the land		28: 2
there would rise c. among you.		29: 7
cause wars and c. among you,		29: 7
there should be no wars nor c.,		29:14
and all the wars, and c.,		29:36
wars and c. among the people.	Al	1:hd
wonderful c. one with another.		2: 5
these wars and c. were commenced		3:25
no c. nor wars in the land of		4: 1
be great c. among the people		4: 9
c. which were among his people,		4:19
having been no wars nor c. for		16: 1
c. among the Nephites,		28: 9
the c. which were among them;		35:15
they were free from wars and c.		48:20
their quarrelings and their c.,		50:21
a critical time for such c. to be		51: 9
to settle the affairs of their c.		51:12
to put an end to such c. and		51:16
breaking down the wars and c.		51:22
there had been murders, and c.,		62:40
because of so many wars and c.		62:44
Their wars and c.,	He	1:hd
their wars, and c., and dissensions,		3:14
after there had been great c.,		3:17
the wars and c. began to cease,		3:22
rising up in great c., and		4:12
and raised c. among them;		8: 7
and there began to be c.,		10:18
that the c. did increase,		11: 1
save it were a few c. concerning		11:22
go about spreading rumors and c.		16:22
And there were no c., save it	3Ne	1:24
there began to be wars and c.		2:11
their many c. and dissensions,		2:18
were no c. and disputations	4Ne	1: 2
there began to be c.	Eth	11: 7
and c. arose in the school of	DC	95:10
there were jarrings, and c.,		101: 6

CONTEST
and a c. about opinions.	JS	2: 6

CONTESTS
by the c. of these parties	JS	2:11

CONTINENT
the former inhabitants of this c.,	JS	2:34
built upon this [the American] c.;	AoF	10

CONTINENTS
means of publishing it on two c.;	DC	136: 3

CONTINUAL
people in wrath with a c. stroke,	2Ne	24: 6

CONTINUAL 207 CONTINUE

king Benjamin had c. peace	Mos 1: 1	
king Mosiah had had c. peace	7: 1	
thus we did have c. peace	10: 5	
king Limhi did have c. peace	19:29	
their c. cries did stir up	21:11	
and there was c. peace	29:43	
began to have c. peace again,	Al 1:28	
was c. peace in all that time.	4: 5	
have c. peace in all the land.	16:12	
c. peace throughout all the land.	30: 2	
of the judges, there was c. peace.	30: 5	
was c. peace among them,	49:30	
there was c. peace established in	He 3:23	
there was c. rejoicing in the land	3:31	
also there was c. peace	3:32	
and the people had c. peace.	3Ne 6: 9	
a c. scene of wickedness and	Mrm 2:18	
is one c. round of murder and	8: 8	
lest by her c. coming she	DC 101:84	

CONTINUALLY
c. running into the fountain of	1Ne 2: 9	
c. holding fast to the rod of	8:30	
thy walls are c. before me.	21:16	
and my heart pondereth c. upon	2Ne 4:16	
of hell be shut c. before me,	4:32	
and hast feared c. every day,	8:13	
pray unto him c. by day,	9:52	
For I pray c. for them by day,	33: 3	
of their arms to destroy us c.	Jac 7:24	
I cried unto him c.,	En 1:15	
were c. seeking to destroy us.	1:20	
c. reminding them of death,	1:23	
stirring them up c. to keep them	1:23	
with the word, c. stirring them up	Jar 1:12	
And they were admonished c. by	Om 1:13	
but to do good c.	Mos 5: 2	
and watch and pray c., that	Al 13:28	
watching and praying c., that	15:17	
without any respect of persons, c.	16:14	
teaching the people of Lamoni c.,	22: 1	
prayeth c. without ceasing—	26:22	
drawn out in prayer unto him c.	34:27	
ye be watchful unto prayer c.,	34:39	
righteously, and do good c.;	41:14	
were c. bringing new forces	55:34	
do put their trust in God c.	57:27	
and his commandments c.;	58:40	
keep you c. in his presence;	58:41	
pray unto the Lord their God c.,	62:51	
he did observe to do good c.,	63: 2	
was right in the sight of God c.;	He 3:20	
their deeds have been evil c.,	15: 4	
did stir them up to do iniquity c.;	16:22	
were c. marching by day and	3Ne 4:21	
the people from prospering c.,	6: 5	
weeping among all the people c.;	8:23	
persisted in their wickedness c.	Mrm 4:10	
in the shedding of blood c.	4:11	
directed c. by the hand of the	Eth 2: 6	
our natures have become evil c.;	3: 2	
and they did have light c.,	6:10	
be persuaded to do good c.,	8:26	
labor c. for their support;	10: 6	
to keep them c. watchful	Mro 6: 4	
and fighteth against him c.,	7:12	
and to do that which is evil c.	7:12	
and enticeth to do good c.;	7:13	
c. praying unto God the	8: 3	
stirreth them up c. to anger	9: 3	
I am laboring with them c.;	9: 4	
after blood and revenge c.	9: 5	
and to strengthen the church c.	DC 23: 3	
language to exhortation c.,	23: 7	
Keep my commandments c.,	25:15	
virtue and holiness before me c.	46:33	
church record and history c.;	47: 3	
your minds c. the words of life,	84:85	
and was before his face c.;	107:49	
thy holy presence may be c. in	109:12	
is that one is to travel c.,	124:140	

and are c. before the Lord.	DC 130: 7	
of his heart, being only evil c.	Mses 8:22	
multitudes were on the alert c.	JS 2:60	

CONTINUANCE
seven thousand years of its c.,	DC 77: 6	
the c. of the practice of polygamy	OD	

CONTINUATION
a c. of the seeds forever and	DC 132:19	
exaltation and c. of the lives,	132:22	
law is the c. of the works of	132:31	
a c. of a famine in the land;	Abr 2:21	

CONTINUE
and did still c. to murmur;	1Ne 4: 4	
strong drink, that c. until night,	2Ne 15:11	
and c. in the path until the end	33: 9	
c. in the way which is narrow,	Jac 6:11	
and c. in fasting and praying,	Om 1:26	
and c. in the faith	Mos 4: 6	
and c. in the faith of what ye have	4:30	
to c. in prayer and supplication	Al 31:10	
and c. in prayer unto him.	34:19	
c. in keeping his commandments;	38: 2	
that ye should c. to teach;	38:10	
therefore we did c. our march,	56:39	
and fourth year the famine did c.,	He 11: 5	
did also c. in the seventy and	11: 6	
and the people of Nephi did c.	3Ne 2:17	
c. to have those secret murders	5: 5	
such shall ye c. to minister;	18:32	
did still c., without ceasing,	19:24	
still c. to build up churches	4Ne 1:41	
and not c. in your iniquities	Eth 2:11	
and shall c. to be poured out	DC 5:19	
so I would that ye should c.	9: 1	
did not c. as you commenced,	9: 5	
c. on unto the finishing of	10: 3	
shalt c. in calling upon God	24: 5	
c. in laying on of the hands	24: 9	
shall c. in bearing my name	24:10	
C. in the spirit of meekness,	25:14	
if ye c. the gates of hell	33:13	
shall be damned if he so c.	42:60	
eternal life if they c. faithful.	46:14	
deceived, but c. in steadfastness,	49:23	
And now c. your journey.	62: 4	
C. in these things even unto	66:12	
c. in patience until ye are	67:13	
that he shall c. in writing	69: 3	
should c. preaching the gospel,	73: 1	
to c. the work of translation	73: 4	
my blessings c. with you.	82:23	
c. with the house of Aaron	84:27	
to c. faithful in all things,	84:80	
are ye if ye c. in my goodness,	86:11	
that ye shall c. in prayer	88:76	
c. in the vineyard until the	88:85	
c. in the ministry and presidency.	90:12	
c. with his family upon the	90:20	
love of the Father shall not c.	95:12	
c. to preside over the school	97: 4	
shalt c. proclaiming my gospel	99: 8	
c. your journey and let your	100:12	
c., that I may build them up	101:64	
shall c. to gather together	101:67	
c. to importune for redress,	101:76	
and c. in humility before me.	105:12	
for them, if they c. faithful.	105:18	
if he c. to be a faithful witness	106: 8	
unto you if you c. faithful.	108: 5	
Let the residue c. to preach from	118: 3	
I accept if he c., and will crown	124:17	
Wight should c. in preaching for	124:18	
and shall c. their works.	124:86	
and c. the subject another time.	128:25	
to everlasting, because they c.;	132:20	
were to c. so long as they were	132:30	
out of the world they should c.;	132:30	
out of the world should they c.	132:30	

CONTINUE 208 CONVERSING

that this right shall c. in thee,	Abr 2:11	c. to the commandments of God,	He 16:12
c. as I was until further directed.	JS 2:26	was c. to the laws of the land,	3Ne 6:24
that I should c. to do so until	2:53	c. to that which I had supposed;	Mro 1: 4
to c. the work of translation	2:75	is c. to the commandment	DC 3:10
		they read c. from that which	10:11
CONTINUED		c. to the church covenants.	28:12
and he c. his words, saying:	Mos 13: 6	c. to the will and commandment	85: 3
ye had c. in the supplicating of	Al 7: 3	it is c. to my commandment	101:96
there still c. to be peace in	4Ne 1: 4	it is c. to the order of heaven	129: 7
And the lesser priesthood c.,	DC 84:26	nor baptize them c. to the will	134:12
hath c. through the lineage of	86: 8		
but c. from grace to grace,	93:13	**CONTRITE**	
have c. under this condemnation;	93:41	a broken heart and a c. spirit;	2Ne 2: 7
you, be c. on and not cease;	127: 4	heart is broken and my spirit is c.!	4:32
is the work of my Father c.,	132:63	with faith, having a c. spirit,	He 8:15
Enoch c. his speech, saying:	Mses 6:43	a broken heart and a c. spirit.	3Ne 9:20
Enoch c. his speech, saying:	7: 1	a broken heart and a c. spirit,	9:20
Enoch c. to call upon all the	7:12	a broken heart and a c. spirit.	12:19
Enoch c. his preaching in	7:19	with broken hearts and c. spirits,	Mrm 2:14
Enoch c. his cry unto the Lord,	7:50	a broken heart and a c. spirit,	Eth 4:15
Noah c. his preaching unto	8:23	a broken heart and a c. spirit,	Mro 6: 2
therefore he c. in Haran.	Abr 2: 5	broken hearts and c. spirits,	DC 20:37
which c. to increase;	JS 2:22	of sins unto the c. heart.	21: 9
I c. to pursue my common	2:27	that prayeth, whose spirit is c.,	52:15
I c. to affirm that I had seen	2:27	that speaketh, whose spirit is c.,	52:16
which c. to increase until	2:30	truly humble before me and c.	54: 3
it c. to do so until the room was	2:43	hands, if they are c. before me,	55: 3
at which I c. to work for nearly	2:56	may go, that are c. before me,	56: 7
The excitement, however, still c.,	2:61	broken, whose spirits are not c.,	56:17
still c. the work of translation,	2:68	broken, and whose spirits are c.,	56:18
		a broken heart and a c. spirit.	59: 8
CONTINUETH		are broken, and their spirits c.	97: 8
receiveth light, and c. in God,	DC 50:24	to enlighten the humble and c.,	136:33
Which priesthood c. in the church	84:17		
which priesthood also c. and	84:18	**CONTROL**	
justice c. its course and	88:40	or to exercise c. or dominion or	DC 121:37
as he c. to abide in me	97: 4	the right and c. of property, and	134: 2
		crime, but never c. conscience;	134: 4
CONTINUING			
c. in fasting and prayer,	4Ne 1:12	**CONTROLLED**	
Owing to my c. to assert that I	JS 2:58	powers of heaven cannot be c.	DC 121:36
CONTINUOUS		**CONTROLLEST**	
by c. labor were enabled to get	JS 2:55	who c. and subjectest the devil,	DC 121: 4
CONTRACT		**CONTROVERSIES**	
according to the c. which he	DC 124:115	and a final decision upon c. in	DC 107:80
CONTRACTED		**CONTROVERSY**	
Pay the debt thou hast c.	DC 19:35	an end of c. concerning him.	DC 107:83
marriages have been c. in Utah	OD		
		CONVENED	
CONTRACTING		c. for that purpose, to act in	DC 102: 8
refrain from c. any marriage	DC OD		
		CONVENES	
CONTRACTS		Whenever this council c. to act	DC 102:13
All covenants, c., bonds,	DC 132: 7		
all c. that are not made unto	132: 7	**CONVENIENT**	
		C. to the village of Manchester,	JS 2:51
CONTRADICT			
or c. the words which he should	Al 10:16	**CONVERSATION**	
		by a godly walk and c.,	DC 20:69
CONTRADICTED		your brethren in all your c.,	108: 7
but that you have c. yourself.	DC 10:31		
		CONVERSATIONS	
CONTRARY		places wherein you receive c.,	DC 124:39
c. to his own knowledge.	Mos 2:33		
go c. to that which has been	2:36	**CONVERSE**	
c. to the will of the king of	23:39	sent angels to c. with them,	Al 12:29
c. to the commandments of God,	27:10	is it with whom these men do c.?	He 5:38
anything c. to that which is right;	29:26	do c. with the angels of God.	5:39
was c. to the word of God;	Al 1:15		
which is c. to the statutes,	8:17	**CONVERSED**	
should transgress c. to the light	9:23	having c. with angels, and	Al 9:21
is c. to the Spirit of the Lord.	11:22	therefore God c. with men,	12:30
c. to the commands of God	30: 7	angels and had c. with them;	19:34
gone c. to the nature of God;	41:11	we saw and with whom we c.	DC 76:14
c. to the nature of happiness.	41:11	with whom God, himself, c.	Mses 6:22
c. to the commands of the king.	47:16		
c. to the laws of their country	He 6:23	**CONVERSING**	
c. to the commandments of God.	8: 3	also c. about this Jesus Christ,	3Ne 11: 2
ask that which is c. to my will.	10: 5	were thus c. one with another,	11: 3
thing is c. to the nature of	13:38	c. with him on the subject of	JS 2:21
		c. with me about the plates,	2:42

CONVERSION — CORIANTON

CONVERSION
also related unto them his c.,	Al	27:25
An account of their c.	He	1:hd
of the c. of the Lamanites,		6: 3
Nephites the manner of their c.,		6: 4
in me at the time of their c.,	3Ne	9:20
expressed at the time of their c.,	JS	2: 6

CONVERT
and c. the law of Moses into	Jac	7: 7
he might c. us unto his faith,	He	9:16
and c. against convert;	JS	2: 6
and convert against c.;		2: 6

CONVERTED
and be c. and be healed.	2Ne	16:10
having been c. unto the Lord	Al	19:16
having been c. to the Lord,		19:17
and were c. unto the Lord.		19:31
household were c. unto the Lord.		22:23
king had been c. unto the Lord,		23: 3
and were c. unto the Lord,		23: 6
who were c. unto the Lord:		23: 8
which were c. unto the Lord;		23:13
And the Amalekites were not c.,		23:14
of the truth and were c.		23:15
the king and those who were c.		23:16
who had not been c. and had not		24: 1
who had been c. unto the Lord		24: 6
thus there were many of them c.		25: 6
were all c. again unto the Lord;		30:58
had been c. unto the Lord;		53:10
the Lamanites are c.	He	1:hd
c. while they were in prison.		9:39
and were c. unto the Lord.	3Ne	1:22
that they soon became c.,		1:25
had become c. unto the Lord		2:12
Lamanites who were c. unto		6:14
were but few who were c. unto		7:21
as many as were c. did truly		7:21
repent of your sins, and be c.,		9:13
be c. through their preaching.		15:22
and they were c. unto the Lord,		28:23
people were all c. unto the Lord,	4Ne	1: 2
teach them that shall be c.	DC	42:64
And many shall be c.,		44: 4
be c. from their wild and savage		109:65
be c. and redeemed with Israel,		109:70
shall be c., and I will heal them.		112:13
in order to have everybody c.,	JS	2: 6

CONVERTS
the c. to these different faiths	JS	2: 6
when the c. began to file off,		2: 6
of both the priests and the c.		2: 6

CONVEY
selected to c. the prisoners,	Al	57:22
do not sell or c. the stock away	DC	124:69
appeared to c. any such teaching,		OD

CONVEYED
and c. away out of the midst	He	10:16

CONVINCE
to c. thee of the power and	Mos	27:14
and c. them of the iniquity of		28: 2
they did c. many of their sins,	Al	21:17
to c. us of the traditions of		24: 7
ye can c. the Lamanites of		26:24
c. them of the error of their	DC	6:11
to c. all of their ungodly deeds		99: 5

CONVINCED
that the Gentiles be c. also	2Ne	26:12
c. of the truth of his words.	Mos	29:37
for he was c. more and more of	Al	12: 7
he was also c. that Alma and		12: 7
c. that they knew the thoughts		12: 7
his people might be c. concerning		23: 3
c. that they were all brethren,		23: 3
we have been c. of our sins,	Al	24: 9
may be c. that there is a God,		30:43
be c. of the truth of thy words.		30:43
Art thou c. of the power of God?		30:51
c. of the wickedness of Korihor;		30:58
and c. many of the error of		37: 8
c. so many thousands of the		37: 9
were c. of the wickedness of	He	5:19
Lamanites were c. of them,		5:50
And as were c. did		5:51
were c. of the error which they	3Ne	1:25

CONVINCING
And also to the c. of the Jew	T Pg	
unto the c. of the Gentiles	1Ne	13:39
to the c. of them unto peace		14: 7
but to the c. of my word,	2Ne	3:11
of c. them of the true Messiah,		25:18
and unto the c. of them that they		25:18
concerning the c. of the Jews,		26:12
unto the c. of many people of	Al	62:45
of the Lamanites, to the c. them,	He	5:19
because of the c. power of God	3Ne	28:29
of God unto the c. of men.	DC	11:21
the c. of many of their sins,		18:44
in power in c. the nations,		90:10

COOK
become sweet, that ye c. it not;	1Ne	17:12

COOL
the garden, in the c. of the day;	Mses	4:14

COPIED
I c. a considerable number of	JS	2:62

COPPER
of gold, and of silver, and of c.	1Ne	18:25
of iron, and of c., and of brass,	2Ne	5:15
and also in iron and c.,	Jar	1: 8
and they are of brass and of c.,	Mos	8:10
part of their ziff, and of their c.,		11: 3
and of brass, and of ziff, and of c.;		11: 8
fine wood, and of c., and of brass.		11:10
of silver, and of iron, and of c.	Eth	10:23
And with iron, with c., and	DC	124:27

COPY
to c., and to correct, and	DC	57:13
a c. of their proceedings, with		102:26

COPYING
writing, c., selecting, and	DC	69: 8
commenced c. the characters	JS	2:62

CORD
by the neck with a flaxen c.,	2Ne	26:22
And he went forth with a c.,	Al	62:36

CORDS
and they did bind me with c.,	1Ne	7:16
did take me and bind me with c.,		18:11
draw iniquity with c. of vanity,	2Ne	15:18
with his strong c. forever.		26:22
and bound them with strong c.,	Al	14: 4
they were bound with strong c.,		14:22
and Amulek were bound with c.		14:23
And they broke the c. with which		14:26
of being bound with strong c.		20:29
prison, and bound with strong c.,		20:30
taken and bound with strong c.,		26:29
in haste strong c. and ladders,		62:21
strong c. and their ladders;		62:23
lengthen thy c. and strengthen	3Ne	22: 2
is stronger than the c. of death.	DC	121:44

CORIANTON
with him were Shiblon and C.;	Al	31: 7
of Alma to his son, C.		39:hd
Helaman, and Shiblon, and C.,		49:30
C. had gone forth to the land		63:10

CORIANTON   210   CORRESPONDENCE

and he was a descendant of C.	Eth	1: 6	give battle unto the people of C.	Eth 15: 6
C. was the son of Moron.		1: 7	C. saw that he was about to fall	15: 7
of his days; and he begat C.		11:18	in which C. was wounded again,	15: 9
C. dwelt in captivity all his days.		11:19	the armies of C. did press upon	15:10
in the days of C. there also		11:20	the army of C. did pitch their	15:11
to pass that C. begat Ether,		11:23	that the people who were for C.	15:13
			together to the army of C.;	15:13
CORIANTUM			C. wrote again an epistle unto	15:18
And Com was the son of C.	Eth	1:13	fifty and two of the people of C.,	15:23
C. was the son of Amnigaddah.		1:14	seven of the people of C.	15:25
And Com was the son of C.		1:27	when the men of C. had	15:28
And C. was the son of Emer.		1:28	his wrath that he would slay C.	15:28
and daughters; and he begat C.,		9:21	save it were C. and Shiz,	15:29
anointed C. to reign in his stead.		9:21	C. had leaned upon his sword,	15:30
anointed C. to reign in his stead		9:22	that C. fell to the earth,	15:32
C. did walk in the steps of his		9:23		
C. took to wife, in his old age,		9:24	**CORIHOR**	
all his days; and he begat C.,		10:31	in his stead; and Kib begat C.	Eth 7: 3
and C. dwelt in captivity all		10:31	when C. was thirty and two years	7: 4
			wherefore C. drew away many	7: 4
CORIANTUMR			his people under C. his son,	7: 7
they gave an account of one C.,	Om	1:21	gave battle unto his brother C.,	7: 9
And C. was discovered by		1:21	C. repented of the many evils	7:13
by a man whose name was C.;	He	1:15	that C. had many sons and	7:14
that C., being a mighty man,		1:16	among the sons of C. there was	7:14
appoint C. to be their leader,		1:17	the king, and also his father C.,	7:15
C. did march forth at the head of		1:19	fair sons and daughters of C.;	13:17
C. did cut down the watch by		1:20	and they fled to the land of C.,	14:27
the chief judge, did flee before C.,		1:21	their tents in the valley of C.;	14:28
that C. did smite him against		1:21		
when C. saw that he was in		1:22	**CORINTHIANS**	
this march of C. through the		1:25	Paul hath declared, 1 C. 15:46,	DC 128:13
were slain C. was also found.		1:30	quotation of Paul, 1 C. 15:29:	128:16
thus had C. plunged the		1:32		
whom were Esrom and C.;	Eth	8: 4	**CORN**	
of Ether were in the days of C.;		12: 1	the amount of one half of our c.,	Mos 7:22
C. was king over all the land.		12: 1	with seeds of c., and of wheat,	9: 9
Ether came forth in the days of C.,		12: 2	flocks, and the c. of their fields.	9:14
and sought to destroy C.		13:15	wheat for man, and c. for the ox,	DC 89:17
And now C., having studied,		13:16		
fighting against C. that they		13:18	**CORNER**	
that the sons of C. fought much		13:19	may become the head of their c.?	Jac 4:17
should go and prophesy unto C.		13:20	the lot which is on the c. south	DC 104:39
and C. should receive a burial		13:21	from the c. stone thereof unto	115:12
be destroyed save it were C.		13:21	planted to be a c.-stone of Zion,	124: 2
C. repented not, neither his		13:22	c.-stone I have appointed for	124:23
and he also gave battle unto C.;		13:23	glory of this, the c. stone thereof;	124:60
And the sons of C., in the		13:24	for the c.-stone of Zion—	124:131
C. was exceedingly angry with		13:27		
C. beat him, and did pursue him		13:28	**CORNERS**	
and behold, he did beat C.,		13:29	from the four c. of the earth.	2Ne 21:12
And C. gave Shared battle again		13:30	and in the c. of the streets,	3Ne 13: 5
Shared wounded C. in his thigh,		13:31	world, to the four c. thereof,	DC 124: 3
and he gave battle unto C.,		14: 3	upon the four c. of the earth,	124:128
C. did beat him and did pursue		14: 3		
C. did lay siege to the wilderness;		14: 5	**CORNER-STONE:** see *CORNER* and *STONE.*	
slew a part of the army of C.,		14: 5		
himself upon the throne of C.		14: 6	**COROM**	
that C. dwelt with his army in		14: 7	And Kish was the son of C.	Eth 1:19
C. came up unto the land of		14:11	And C. was the son of Levi.	1:20
army of C. did press forward		14:12	and he also begat C., whom he	10:16
to pass that C. pursued him;		14:13	C. did that which was good in	10:17
Lib did smite the army of C.,		14:14		
And C. had taken all the people		14:15	**CORRECT**	
of Lib did come against C.		14:16	of their fathers, which are not c.	Mos 1: 5
in teh which C. fled again		14:16	you by our fathers, which are c.,	29:25
that Shiz pursued after C.,		14:17	of their fathers, which were c.,	Al 3:11
of them fled to the army of C.		14:20	their fathers, which were not c.	17: 9
Shiz did not cease to pursue C.;		14:24	their fathers, which were not c.	21:17
to avenge himself upon C.		14:24	to copy, and to c., and select,	DC 57:13
C. should not fall by the sword.		14:24	that the translation was c.,	JS 2:64
Shiz did pursue C. eastward,		14:26	had been translated was also c.	2:64
to flee before the armies of C.;		14:27		
and C. pitched his tents in		14:28	**CORRECTLY**	
C. did gather his armies together		14:28	and it is mostly translated c.;	DC 91: 1
Shiz smote upon C. that he gave		14:30	as far as it is translated c.;	AoF 8
C., having lost his blood, fainted,		14:30		
not pursue the armies of C.;		14:31	**CORRESPONDENCE**	
C. had recovered of his wounds,		15: 1	they did open a c. with them,	Al 23:18
he wrote an epistle unto C.,		15: 5	opened a c. with these brethren,	24: 8
people of C. were stirred up to		15: 6	that by opening this c. we have	24: 9
anger against the people of C.;		15: 6	into a c. with the Lamanites,	31: 4

CORRILL 211 COULD

CORRILL, John
And also my servant C., or as	DC	50:38
Lyman Wight and my servant C.		52: 7

CORRUPT
natural branches had become c.	Jac	5:39
and they had all become c.		5:39
that his vineyard was no more c.,		5:75
lucre which doth c. the soul;	Mos	29:40
in heaven, where nothing doth c.,	He	8:25
where moth and rust doth c.,	3Ne	13:19
neither moth nor rust doth c.,		13:20
a c. tree bringeth forth evil fruit.		14:17
a c. tree bring forth good fruit.		14:18
for that which moth doth c.		27:32
And their hearts are c.,	DC	10:21
all having c. minds.		33: 4
all flesh has become c. before my		112:23
The earth was c. before God,	Mses	8:28
earth, and, behold, it was c.,		8:29
those professors were all c.;	JS	2:19

CORRUPTED
perisheth not, neither can be c.,	2Ne	9:51
the way; they have become c.		28:11
their churches have become c.,		28:12
it were these had become c.	Jac	5:42
good fruit have also become c.;		5:42
the trees thereof have become c.,		5:46
is it that has c. my vineyard?		5:47
of thy vineyard have become c.?		5:48
that my vineyard is no more c.,		5:75
their language had become c.;	Om	1:17
that their laws had become c.,	He	4:22
for the laws had become c.		5: 2
c. the hearts of all the people;	Eth	9: 6
my vineyard has become c.	DC	33: 4
For all flesh is c. before me;		38:11
Also because their hearts are c.,		121:13
all flesh had c. its way upon	Mses	8:29

CORRUPTIBLE
every c. thing, both of men,	DC	101:24

CORRUPTIBLENESS
and c. to the extent thereof.	DC	19:38

CORRUPTION
death, nor c. nor incorruption,	2Ne	2:11
c. could not put on incorruption.		9: 7
this c. shall put on incorruption,	Mos	16:10
this c. raised in incorruption,	Al	5:15
that they can no more see c.		11:45
die, seeing there is no more c.		12:18
c. does not put on incorruption—		40: 2
immortality, c. to incorruption—		41: 4
which are now moldering in c.	Mrm	6:21
now the very mainspring of all c.,	DC	123: 7
save themselves from the c. of		134:12
to purify the vineyard of c.		135: 6

CORRUPTNESS
concerning the c. of their law;	He	8: 3

COST
c. the best blood of the nineteenth	DC	135: 6

COSTLINESS
of the c. of your apparel,	Jac	2:13

COSTLY
and to wear very c. apparel,	Al	1: 6
and they did not wear c. apparel,		1:27
and strife; wearing c. apparel;		1:32
began to wear very c. apparel.		4: 6
in the wearing of c. apparel		5:53
O my God, their c. apparel, and		31:28
will clothe him with c. apparel;	He	13:28
as the wearing of c. apparel,	4Ne	1:24

COULD
that great city, c. be destroyed	1Ne	2:13
I also thought that they c. not		4:15
power whereby they c. accomplish		5: 8
insomuch that we c. preserve the	1Ne	5:21
neither c. the temptations and the		15:24
that we c. obtain no food.		16:21
believe that I c. build a ship;		17:18
that ye c. not construct a ship,		17:19
that ye c. not feel his words;		17:45
to do all things I c. do them.		17:50
and c. not contend against me;		17:52
insomuch that I c. not move,		18:12
with destruction, c. soften their		18:20
which he c. not restrain,	2Ne	1:26
utterance that he c. not shut it.		1:27
righteousness c. not be brought		2:11
there c. have been no creation		2:13
man c. not act for himself save		2:16
it c. not be built like unto Solomon's		5:16
c. not put on incorruption.		9: 7
there c. have been no creation.		11: 7
What c. have been done more		15: 4
but c. not prevail against it.		17: 1
c. speak with the tongue of angels?		32: 2
And now, how c. ye speak with the		32: 2
that we c. persuade all men not	Jac	1: 8
things that they c. not understand.		4:14
What c. I have done more for		5:41
But what c. I have done more in		5:47
What c. I have done more for		5:49
he c. use much flattery,		7: 4
wherefore, I c. not be shaken.		7: 5
these words he c. say no more,		7:20
knew that God c. not lie;	En	1: 6
For what c. I write more than	Jar	1: 2
of Mosiah, c. understand them.	Om	1:17
c. have remembered all these	Mos	1: 4
he c. read these engravings,		1: 4
c. teach them to their children,		1: 4
c. not teach them all within		2: 7
they c. not all hear his words		2: 8
possible that little children c. sin		3:16
could sin they c. not be saved;		3:16
justice c. no more deny unto them		3:26
c. deny that Adam should fall		3:26
mercy c. have claim on them		3:26
that ye c. not find utterance,		4:20
we c. prophesy of all things.		5: 3
if he c. interpret languages,		8: 6
Ammon told him that he c. not.		8: 6
which otherwise c. not be known.		8:17
that they c. not overpower them		9:11
of weapons which we c. invent,		9:16
my old men that c. bear arms,		10: 9
do all they c. to destroy them;		10:17
that he c. stand upon the top		11:12
he c. even look over all the land		11:12
fifty c. stand against thousands		11:19
c. not any man be saved except		13:32
there c. have been no redemption.		16: 6
there c. have been no resurrection.		16: 7
that they c. deliver themselves		21: 5
but they c. not find it,		21:25
he c. interpret such engravings;		21:28
they c. find no way to deliver		22: 2
things, which they c. carry,		22:12
c. no longer follow their tracks;	Mos	22:16
king Noah c. not overtake them		23: 2
that ye c. always have just men		23: 8
and none c. deliver them but		23:23
c. bear up their burdens with ease,		24:15
and none c. deliver them except		24:21
all their children that c. speak		24:22
c. not all be governed by one		25:20
neither c. they all hear the word		25:20
that c. not understand the words		26: 1
they c. not understand the word		26: 3
c. shake the earth and cause it to		27:18
that he c. not open his mouth;		27:19
that he c. not move his hands;		27:19
they c. not bear that any human		28: 3
king c. not confer the kingdom		29: 3
c. have just men to be your kings,		29:13
c. have men for your kings who		29:13
if this c. always be the case		29:13
the law c. have no power on	Al	1:17

COULD

Alma c. pursue the Amlicites no	Al 2:20
that they c. not be numbered.	2:35
C. ye say, if ye were called to die	5:27
that I c. not come unto you.	7: 1
even I c. not have come now	7: 2
c. not be confined in dungeons;	8:31
that any man c. slay them;	8:31
God c. do such marvelous works,	9: 5
c. fall into sins and transgressions,	9:19
crime which they c. make appear	10:13
Amulek c. know of their designs.	10:17
glad if we c. command the rocks	12:14
there c. have been no resurrection	12:25
first parents c. have gone forth	12:26
of redemption c. have no power,	12:32
of justice c. not be destroyed,	12:32
c. not look upon sin save	13:12
Nephites c. raise a sufficient army	16: 3
they said God c. not destroy,	16: 9
that one of their men c. slay him	17:35
seeing that they c. not hit him	17:36
Ammon c. discern his thoughts;	18:18
see that Ammon c. not be slain,	19:23
what c. be the cause of this	19:24
or what all these things c. mean.	19:24
thy soul c. not be saved.	20:17
his arm that he c. not use it.	20:20
king saw that Ammon c. slay him,	20:21
that there c. be no redemption	21: 9
where they c. be admitted.	21:16
c. not merit anything of himself;	22:14
c. have no more possessions	22:34
since it has been all that we c. do,	24:11
for it was all we c. do to repent	24:11
it has been as much as we c. do	24:15
c. not overpower the Nephites	25:13
c. we have supposed when we	26: 1
Who c. have supposed that our	26:17
we c. be the means of saving some.	26:30
saw that they c. not seek revenge	27: 2
never c. be prevailed upon to	27:28
which c. be inflicted by their	27:29
c. have the wish of mine heart,	29: 1
that I c. speak unto all the ends	29: 7
law c. have no hold upon him)	30:12
there c. be no atonement made	30:17
that he c. not have utterance,	30:50
of God c. bring this upon me;	30:52
that ye c. not worship your God	33: 2
if ye c. be healed by merely casting	33:21
and none c. deliver them except	36: 2
that I c. not open my mouth,	36:10
that I c. be banished and become	36:15
I c. remember my pains no more;	36:19
there c. be nothing so exquisite	36:21
c. not have convinced so many	37: 9
believe that God c. cause that	37:40
Therefore, as the soul c. never die,	42: 9
c. not be brought about, only	42:13
mercy c. not take effect except	42:13
of justice c. not be destroyed;	42:13
of mercy c. not be brought about	42:15
repentance c. not come unto men	42:16
how c. a man repent except he	42:17
How c. he sin if there was no law?	42:17
Hos c. there be a law save there	42:17
if men sinned what c. justice do,	42:21
Alma, also, himself, c. not rest,	43: 1
c. not get Lehonti to come down	47:12
they c. not suffer to lay down	48:24
they c. not bear that their	48:25
that the Lamanites c. not cast	49: 4
neither c. they come upon them	49: 4
and they c. not come upon them.	49:11
the Lamanites c. not get into	49:18
they c. not obtain power over the	49:22
the Lamanites c. not hurt them.	50: 4
they c. cast stones from the top	50: 5
impossible that he c. overpower	52:17
the Nephites c. have slain them.	55:18
They c. not be taken in their	55:31
that we c. overpower them;	56:23
we c. not stand against them,	Al 56:40
that we c. guard them to keep	56:57
c. not come upon us by night	57: 9
they c. get into their hands,	57:14
and we c. not overtake them,	57:34
no way that we c. lead them	58: 1
we c. not decoy them away from	58: 1
c. not come to battle with them,	58: 6
that they c. easily destroy us	58:15
c. ye suppose that ye could sit	60:11
ye c. sit upon your thrones,	60:11
ye c. do nothing and he would	60:11
we c. have withstood our enemies	60:15
they c. have gained no power	60:15
it were possible that I c. get.	61: 5
gained whatsoever force he c.	62: 4
together whatsoever men he c.	62: 6
c. not obtain the judgment-seat,	He 1: 6
that no man c. overtake him.	1:10
that they all c. not be found;	1:12
c. stand against the Nephites,	1:16
the Lamanites c. not retreat	1:31
them they c. nowhere be found.	2:11
c. obtain no more possessions	4:18
c. not be governed by the law	5: 3
the Lamanites c. not flee	5:34
c. speak forth marvelous words.	5:45
that he c. not stay among them,	7: 3
Oh, that I c. have had my days	7: 7
that I c. have joyed with him in	7: 7
if my days c. have been in those	7: 8
how c. you have given away to	7:16
how c. you have forgotten your	7:20
c. not have testified concerning	8: 9
that they c. not flee from us.	9: 8
he c. not know of all things.	9:41
and they c. not take him	10:16
that they c. not be discovered,	11:25
that which ye c. not obtain;	13:38
c. not hit him with their stones	16: 2
saw this, that they c. not hit him,	16: 3
c. not hit him with their stones	16: 6
people c. not overpower them;	3Ne 1:27
and c. nowhere be found in all	2: 9
and c. not be frightened by the	3:12
the robbers c. not exist save it	4: 3
was no way that they c. subsist	4: 5
that they c. raise grain,	4: 6
they c. cause them to yield	4:16
that c. have power to condemn	6:22
that it c. not be impeded	7:13
that they c. disbelieve his words,	7:18
not any man who c. do a miracle	8: 1
c. feel the vapor of darkness;	8:20
And there c. be no light,	8:21
neither c. there be fire kindled	8:21
there c. not be any light at all;	8:21
and as many as c. come for the	17:10
that they c. not see Jesus.	18:38
there c. be nothing upon earth	19:25
I c. not show unto them so	19:35
their tongues that they c. utter.	26:14
that they c. utter the things	28:14
out of the body, they c. not tell;	28:15
they c. behold the things of God.	28:15
the prisons c. not hold them,	28:19
they c. not dig pits sufficient	28:20
that Satan c. have no power	28:39
that he c. not tempt them;	28:39
of the earth c. not hold them.	28:39
these cities c. not be renewed.	4Ne 1: 9
there c. not be a happier people	1:16
that they c. not hold them,	Mrm 1:18
no man c. keep that which was	2:10
I would that I c. persuade all	3:22
Lamanites c. have had no power	4: 4
as though I c. deliver them	5: 1
c. not get into the country	5: 4
there we c. give them battle.	6: 2
how c. ye have departed from	6:17
how c. ye have rejected that	6:17
how is it that ye c. have fallen!	6:19
in his name c. they remove	8:24

COULD

in his name c. they cause the	Mrm	8:24
fiery furnace c. not harm them,		8:24
that ye c. be happy to dwell		9: 3
we c. have written in Hebrew,		9:33
ye c. not have seen my finger.	Eth	3: 9
I c. not make a full account		3:17
he c. not be kept from beholding		3:19
he c. not be kept from within		3:20
he c. show unto him all things—		3:26
the Lord c. not withhold anything		3:26
the Lord c. show him all things.		3:26
no water that c. hurt them,		6: 7
of the sea c. break them,		6:10
neither whale that c. mar them;		6:10
she c. redeem the kingdom		8: 8
that the people c. not pass,		9:33
c. be a people more blessed		10:28
for he c. not be restrained		12: 2
c. not be kept from within the		12:19
he c. not hide it from the sight		12:20
Lord c. not withhold anything		12:21
he c. no longer be kept without		12:21
people that they c. speak much,		12:23
that we c. write but little,		12:24
it c. not be a new Jerusalem		13: 5
the morrow, he c. not find it,		14: 1
was possible that they c. receive.		15:14
strength that they c. walk,		15:28
there is no good thing come unto	Mro	7:24
if little children c. not be saved		8:13
you c. have translated;	DC	9:10
you c. not have them;		18:35
c. not be agents unto themselves;		29:39
they c. not know the sweet.		29:39
which ye c. not understand,		50:15
and c. not endure his presence;		84:24
otherwise ye c. not abound.		88:50
and then ye c. have made ready		101:54
which c. not be settled by the		102: 2
c. be distinguished from him		107:43
c. not be annulled, according		128: 9
the Holy Ghost c. not dwell in us.		130:22
seashore ye c. not number them.		132:30
not shortened at all that I c. not		133:67
Moses c. endure his presence.	Mses	1: 2
natural eyes c. not have beheld;		1:11
I c. not look upon God,		1:14
of man; and man c. behold it.		3: 9
and c. not stand in his presence.		6:47
that man c. number the particles		7:30
And the Lord c. not withhold;		7:51
he c. not have the right of	Abr	1:27
I c. not see the end thereof.		3:12
c. only bring forth the same		4:12
unless I c. get more wisdom	JS	2:12
so that I c. not speak.		2:15
c. not make it otherwise;		2:24
c. not make him think or		2:24
and I c. not deny it, neither		2:25
c. be made to appear so		2:31
I c. discover that he had no		2:31
so that I c. see into his bosom.		2:31
I c. see the place where		2:42
otherwise I c. not get them.		2:46
as we c. get opportunity.		2:55
Every stratagem that c. be		2:60
we never c. attain to previously,		2:74

COUNCIL

he might hold a c. with them	Mos	12:17
might hold a c. with Lamoni	Al	24: 5
chief captains held a c. of war—		52:19
shall be in danger of the c.	3Ne	12:22
by the direction of a high c.	DC	20:67
be appointed by the high c.		42:34
and the bishop and his c.;		42:34
sit in c. with the saints which		78: 9
benefit of the c. of high priests,		89: 1
in all your lives, to preside in c.,		90:16
be determined in c. among you.		96: 3
This day a general c. of		102: 1

COUNCILORS

proceeded to organize the high c.	DC	102: 1
The high c. was appointed		102: 2
the church or the bishop's c.		102: 2
presidents by the voice of the c.;		102: 3
were chosen to be a standing c.		102: 3
by the unanimous voice of the c.		102: 3
The number composing the c.,		102: 5
the high c. cannot have power to		102: 6
by the voice of a general c. of		102: 8
is also the president of the c.,		102: 9
that he should preside over the c.		102:10
has power to preside over the c.		102:11
a high c. of the church of Christ		102:12
Whenever this c. convenes to act		102:13
a right to one-half of the c.,		102:15
appointed to speak before the c.		102:16
in its true light before the c.;		102:16
for themselves before the c.,		102:18
the majority of the c. having		102:22
case clear to the minds of the c.,		102:23
power to call and organize a c.		102:24
the said c. of high priests shall		102:25
to preside over such c. for the		102:25
It shall be the duty of said c.		102:26
to the high c. of the seat of the		102:26
with the decision of said c.,		102:27
they may appeal to the ahigh c. of		102:27
This c. of high priests abroad		102:28
is to be sufficient to call such c.		102:28
necessary to call such a c. or not.		102:29
distinction between the high c.		102:30
and the traveling high c.		102:30
shall be agreed by this order in c.,		104:53
and the voice of the c. direct.		104:53
and it is manifest before the c.		104:74
shall be subject unto the c.		104:76
he shall be subject to the c.		104:77
a Traveling Presiding High C.,		107:33
twelve or the traveling high c.,		107:34
or to the traveling high c.		107:36
high c. in Zion form a quorum		107:37
the duty of the traveling high c.		107:38
and carried up unto the c. of the		107:78
And the Presidency of the c. of		107:79
highest c. of the church of God,		107:80
who is exempt from this c. of		107:81
the common c. of the church,		107:82
deacons, to sit in c. with them,		107:85
and to sit in c. with them,		107:86
priests, and sit in c. with them,		107:87
elders, and to sit in c. with them,		107:89
the high c. of my church in Zion,		115: 3
it shall be disposed of by a c.,		120: 1
of the bishop and his c.,		120: 1
and by my high c.;		120: 1
of the C. of the Eternal God		121:32
over the Twelve traveling c.;		124:127
I give unto you a high c.,		124:131
traveling high c., mine apostles,		124:139

COUNCILOR

bishop, high c., and high priest,	DC	20:67

COUNCILORS

bishops, high c., high priests,	DC	20:66
The above-named c. were then		102: 4
in appointing the above-named c.		102: 5
seven of the above-named c.,		102: 6
to act in the place of absent c.		102: 7
one of the above-named c.,		102: 8
shall be the duty of the twelve c.		102:12
the twelve c. shall consider		102:13
two only of the c. shall speak		102:13
the c. appointed to speak		102:16
Those c. who draw even numbers,		102:17
the c. who are appointed to speak		102:18
the c., accuser and accused		102:19
and call upon the twelve c.		102:19
But should the remaining c.,		102:20
The twelve c. then proceeded		102:34
twelve traveling c. are called		107:23

COUNCILS

COUNCILS
standing high c., at the stakes	DC 107:36
to the c. of the twelve at the	107:37
the decision of either of these c.,	107:77

COUNSEL
hearken not unto the c. of God,	2Ne 9:28
and let the c. of the Holy One	15:19
taken evil c. against thee, saying:	17: 5
Take c. together, and it shall	18:10
the spirit of c. and might,	21: 2
to hide their c. from the Lord!	27:27
and lend an ear unto my c.,	28:30
brethren, seek not to c. the Lord,	Jac 4:10
but to take c. from his hand.	4:10
said unto him: C. me not;	5:22
the Lord doth c. in wisdom,	Al 29: 8
for he doth c. in wisdom over all	37:12
C. with the Lord in all thy doings,	37:37
to c. with your elder brothers	39:10
And give heed to their c.	39:10
should not c. his fellow man	DC 1:19
the c. of thy director to be	3:15
seek not to c. your God.	22: 4
seek to c. in your own ways.	56:14
to the c. of his own will,	58:20
c. between themselves and me.	58:25
in his heart, and received not c.,	63:55
and c. wrongfully to your hurt,	64:20
receive c. and assistance from	69: 4
listen to the c. of him who has	78: 2
under the c. and direction of	78:16
as thou art faithful in c.,	81: 3
the c. which I shall give unto you.	100: 2
they esteemed lightly my c.;	101: 8
if they will hearken unto this c.	101:74
from this very hour unto the c.	103: 5
shall c. them, in obtaining the	103:40
my friends, I give unto you c.,	104: 1
according to the c. of the order,	104:21
to the c. of the order,	104:36
c. him concerning this matter,	105:22
the c. which they receive,	105:37
receive c. of him whom I	108: 1
and the virtuous, shall see, c.,	122: 2
therefore, hearken to your c.,	124:13
shall not fail if he receive c.	124:16
receive also the c. from those	124:61
he aspireth to establish his c.	124:84
instead of the c. which I have	124:84
the c. of my servant Joseph,	124:89
shall receive c. from my servant	124:95
hearken unto the c. of my	124:112
unto the c. of my servants	124:118
himself, and seeketh not my c.,	136:19
he rejected the greater c. which	Mses 5:25
and why c. ye yourselves,	6:43
Man of C. is my name;	7:35
Gods took c. among themselves	Abr 4:26

COUNSELED
having c. with his priests	Mos 17: 6
and have c. thee,	DC 24: 1
as if shall be c. by the elders	58:56
our work, which we have c.;	Abr 5: 2
all our work which we have c.	5: 2
works which they (the Gods) c.	5: 3
c. among themselves to form	5: 3
when they c. to do them,	5: 5

COUNSELETH
know that he c. in wisdom,	Jac 4:10
him that c. or sitteth upon	DC 58:20

COUNSELOR
the c., and the cunning artificer,	2Ne 13: 3
shall be called, Wonderful, C.,	19: 6
his c. over him in the church,	DC 30: 7
and a c. unto my servant	81: 1
the family of thy c. and scribe,	90:19
my c., even Sidney Rigdon,	90:21
as c. unto my servant Joseph,	124:91
be c. unto my servant Joseph,	124:103

COUNSELORS
of my church and his c.,	DC 42:31
to assist the bishop as c.	42:71
decided by the c. and bishop.	42:72
by the assistance of his c.,	58:18
he has appointed for his c.;	58:24
who is a judge, and his c.,	64:40
by the assistance of his c.,	107:72
bishop independently, without c.,	107:76
even twelve, to assist as c.;	107:79
High Priesthood and his c.	107:79
c. of the High Priesthood;	107:82
made c. for my name's sake	112:20
your c. and your leaders,	112:30
c. who are and shall be appointed	115: 1
Edward Partridge, and his c.;	115: 2
my servant Joseph and his c.,	115:16
for c. my servant Sidney Rigdon	124:126
and Noah Packard for c.,	124:136
Samuel Rolfe and his c. for	124:142
of the teachers and his c.,	124:142
of the deacons and his c.,	124:142
president of the stake and his c.	124:142
with a president and his two c.	136: 3

COUNSELS
hearken not to the voice of his c.	1Ne 19: 7
hearken unto the c. of God.	2Ne 9:29
to hide their c. from the Lord;	28: 9
and to give ear unto his c.,	He 12: 5
they do set at naught his c.,	12: 6
sets at naught the c. of God,	DC 3: 4
set at naught the c. of God,	3: 7
has set at naught the c. of God,	3:13
if thou wilt slight these c.,	19:33
and have sought their own c.	Mses 6:28

COUNT
no man c. them as small things;	DC 123:15
to c. the sand upon the seashore	132:30
canst c. the number of sands,	Abr 3:14

COUNTED
hoofs shall be c. like flint,	2Ne 15:28
be c. as naught among them—	Mrm 5: 9
not c. unto him for righteousness.	Mro 7: 7
it is c. unto him the same as	7: 8
he is c. evil before God.	7: 8
also is it c. evil unto a man,	7: 9
slothful shall not be c. worthy	DC 107:100
not approved shall not be c.	107:100

COUNTENANCE
The show of their c. doth witness	2Ne 13: 9
the c. of the king was changed;	Al 18:12
not as the hypocrites, of a sad c.,	3Ne 13:16
his c. did smile upon them,	19:25
of his c. did shine upon,	19:25
as white as the c. and also the	19:25
angel, whose c. was as lightening,	DC 20: 6
glad heart and a cheerful c.—	59:15
ye shall behold the joy of my c.	88:52
you with the joy of my c.	88:53
the light of the c. of his lord.	88:56
the light of the c. of their lord.	88:58
c. shone above the brightness of	110: 3
very wroth, and his c. fell.	Mses 5:21
wroth? Why is thy c. fallen?	5:22
his c. truly like lightning.	JS 2:32

COUNTENANCES
received his image in your c.?	Al 5:14
of God engraven upon your c.?	5:19
with cheerful hearts and c.,	DC 59:15
c. by the influence of my wife's	JS 2:75

COUNTIES
and the c. round about,	DC 101:71
the adjoining c. round about.	105:28
own place, but in the adjoining c.;	106: 2

COUNTRIES
who should be led out of other c.	2Ne 1: 5

COUNTRIES 215 COURT-HOUSE

and give ear all ye of far c.; 2Ne 18: 9
to retreat towards the north c. Mrm 2: 3
had escaped into the south c., 6:15
of all lands, nations, and c.; Eth 8:25
began to be fruit in the north c., 9:35
and in all the c. round about. 9:35
the earth, and from the north c., 13:11
Ye hear of wars in far c., DC 38:29
will soon be great wars in far c., 38:29
called to go into the eastern c., 39:14
ye forth into the western c., 45:64
him to go unto the eastern c.; 75: 6
again, Go ye into the south c. 75: 8
their journey into the eastern c., 75:13
their journey into the eastern c.; 75:14
journey unto the western c., 75:15
go again into the eastern c., 79: 1
and a knowledge also of c. 88:79
a knowledge of history, and of c., 93:53
called to go into the eastern c. 99: 1
the churches in the eastern c., 101:74
the congregations in the eastern c., 103:29
be driven back into the north c., 133:23
they who are in the north c. 133:26

COUNTRY
They come from a far c., 2Ne 23: 5
have a c. whither they might flee, Al 22:34
to defent their lands and their c., 43:26
families, and their lands, their c., 43:47
binds us to our lands and our c.; 44: 5
and the freedom of his c., 48:11
his people, his rights, and his c., 48:13
take up arms to defend their c. 51:13
dissenters to defent their c. 51:15
arms in defence of their c. 51:20
arms in the defence of their c. 53:13
weapons of war to defend their c. 53:18
have come forth to defend our c. 56: 5
died in the cause of their c. 56:11
to defend ourselves and our c. 58: 8
the freedom of their c. 59:13
ye are also traitors to your c. 60:18
ye are in the heart of our c. 60:19
support those parts of our c. 60:24
to defend the cause of my c., 60:28
in the defence of your c. and 60:29
the freedom and welfare of my c. 60:36
in the defence of their c. and 61: 6
the freedom and cause of his c. 62: 1
had rebelled against their c. 62: 2
arms in the defence of their c., 62: 9
observed for the safety of their c.; 62:10
had fought valiantly for his c., 62:37
armies to defend their north c. He 4: 7
contrary to the laws of their c. 6:23
according to the laws of their c., 6:24
yea, even unto his own c., 16: 7
your property, and your c., 3Ne 3: 2
the law and the rights of their c.; 6:30
into the c. which lay before us, Mrm 5: 4
escaped into the c. southward 8: 2
upon the face of this north c. Eth 1: 1
And the c. was divided; 7:20
agreeable to the laws of our c., DC 20: 1
this whole region of c., 58:52
journey also into the south c. 75:17
Abraham, get thee out of thy c., Abr 2: 3
all the sects in that region of c. JS 2: 5
the whole district of c. seemed 2: 5

COUNTY
can be purchased in Jackson c., DC 101:71
of all the lands in Jackson c. 105:28
by the inhabitants of Jackson c., 109:47
house unto my name, in Jackson c., 124:51
wilderness of Fayette, Seneca c., 128:20
Harmony, Susquehanna c., 128:20
and Colesville, Broome c., 128:20
Whitmer, in Fayette, Seneca c., 128:21
the town of Sharon, Windsor c., JS 2: 3
Ontario (now Wayne) c., 2: 3
in the same c. of Ontario— 2: 3

village of Manchester, Ontario c., JS 2:51
who lived in Chenango c., 2:56
Harmony, Susquehanna c., 2:56
South Bainbridge, Chenango c., 2:58
with my wife to Susquehanna c., 2:61
of Palmyra township, Wayne c., 2:61

COUPLED
will be c. with eternal glory, DC 130: 2

COURAGE
Zoram did take c. at the words 1Ne 4:35
his heart began to take c.; Al 15: 4
c. to go forth unto the Lamanites 17:12
exceeding great strength and c., 43:43
they took c. and pursued them 52:24
were exceedingly valiant for c., 53:20
that never had I seen so great c., 56:45
that the Lamanites took c., 56:52
which caused them to take c.; 57:32
And we did take c. with our 58:12
this epistle his heart did take c., 62: 1
of their exceeding great c., 62:19
his heart took c. insomuch that He 1:22
their hearts did take c. 5:24
C., brethren; and on, on to the DC 128:22

COURSE
The c. of their travels. They 1Ne 1:hd
afflictions in the c. of my days, 1: 1
c. of the Lord is one eternal round. 10:19
traveling nearly the same c. as 16:33
it lieth in a straight c. before him, 2Ne 9:41
in the c. of my days. En 1:24
knew not the c. they should travel Mos 7: 4
bent their c. towards the land of 22:11
in the c. of the land of Nephi, Al 2:24
his c. is one eternal round. 7:20
and his c. is one eternal round. 37:12
the c. which they should travel in 37:39
or did not travel a direct c., 37:42
a straight c. to eternal bliss, 37:44
a straight c. to the promised land. 37:44
our fathers, by following its c., 37:45
of Christ, if we follow their c., 37:45
which c. the Lamanites were to 43:30
to cut off the c. of Amalickiah 46:31
a straight c. from the east sea to 50: 8
being in their c. of march, 52:34
march in a straight c. after us; 56:37
we took our c. after having 58:23
they took their c. northword. 63: 6
in a straight and narrow c. He 3:29
did follow the c. of the beasts, Eth 9:34
and his c. is one eternal round. DC 3: 2
whose c. is one eternal round, 35: 1
is given the c. for the saints, 61:29
justice continueth its c. and 88:40
Missouri river in its decreed c., 121:33
rivers shall turn from their c.; Mses 6:34
were turned out of their c.; 7:13

COURSES
one place, in their several c., DC 52:33
And their c. are fixed, even the 88:43
the c. of the heavens and the 88:43

COURT
is not far from the c.-house. DC 57: 3
the length thereof, in the inner c. 94: 4
And there shall be a lower c. 94: 5
a lower court and a higher c., 94: 5
length thereof in the inner c.; 94:11
shall be a lower and a higher c. 94:11
in length, in the inner c. thereof. 95:15
the lower part of the inner c. 95:16
the higher part of the inner c. 95:17
that cannot be rejected by any c. 135: 7
pronounced constitutional by the c. OD
and also in the c. of Pharaoh; Abr 1:20
Astronomy, in the king's c. Fac 3: 6

COURT-HOUSE: *see COURT and HOUSE.*

COVENANT

upon the c. people of the Lord,	1Ne	14:14
are the c. people of the Lord;		15:14
the c. which should be fulfilled		15:18
which c. the Lord made to our		15:18
my servant for a c. of the people,		21: 8
unto the remembering of my c.	2Ne	3:21
because of this c. thou art blessed:		3:23
and the c. people of the Lord shall		6:13
God shall deliver his c. people.		6:17
the Jews, mine ancient c. people.		29: 4
the Jews, mine ancient c. people?		29: 5
as will repent are the c. people		30: 2
would be according to the c.	En	1:17
to enter into a c. with our God	Mos	5: 5
the c. which ye have made is		5: 6
ye have made is a righteous c.		5: 6
of the c. which ye have made		5: 7
have entered into the c. with God		5: 8
had entered into a c. with God		6: 1
but who had entered into the c.		6: 2
have entered into a c. with him,		18:10
have entered into a c. to serve him		18:13
had entered into a c. with God		21:31
had also entered into a c. with God,		21:32
the c. which ye have made unto me;		24:13
and I will c. with my people		24:13
and I c. with thee that thou		26:20
and enter into a c. with him	Al	7:15
yea, they had entered into a c.		43:11
and depart with a c. of peace.		44:14
and entered into a c. of peace.		44:15
as many as entered into a c.		44:15
promising that he would c. and		44:19
after they had entered into a c.		44:20
enter into a c. that they will		46:20
their garments in token, or as a c.,		46:21
this was the c. which they made,		46:22
We c. with our God, that we		46:22
entered into a c. to keep the		46:31
not enter into a c. to support		46:35
who denied the c. of freedom.		46:35
who had entered into this c.		53:15
who had not entered into a c.		53:16
they entered into a c. to fight		53:17
who entered into this c.		53:18
the c. which their fathers made,		56: 6
they were about to break the c.		56: 7
that they should break this c.		56: 8
the c. which I have made		60:34
caused them to enter into a c.		62:16
when they had entered into this c.		62:17
and they all entered into a c.,	He	1:11
who had entered into a c. that		2: 3
who had entered into the c.,		6:22
his band, who had taken this c.		6:22
enter into a c. that they would	3Ne	5: 4
who did not enter into a c.,		5: 5
shall the c. wherewith he hath		5:25
the c. that he hath covenanted		5:25
into a c. to keep the peace,		6: 3
enter into a c. one with another,		6:28
that c. which was given by		6:28
which c. was given and		6:28
enter into a c. to destroy them,		6:29
they did c. one with another		6:30
a c. to destroy the government.		7:11
time of the fulfilling of the c.		10: 7
the c. which I have made with		15: 8
then will I fulfill the c. which		16: 5
then will I remember my c.		16:11
but I will remember my c. unto		16:12
then is the fulfilling of the c.		20:12
unto the fulfilling of the c.		20:22
of the c. which the Father made		20:25
ye are the children of the c.—		20:26
then fulfilleth the Father the c.		20:27
I will remember the c. which		20:29
this c. which the father hath		20:46
c. of the Father may be fulfilled		21: 4
unto the fulfilling of the c.		21: 7
my people who are of the c.		21:11
they shall come in unto the c.		21:22
c. of my people be removed,		22:10

216

COVENANT

even the messenger of the c.,	3Ne	24: 1
the c. which the Father hath		29: 1
the Lord will remember his c.		29: 3
the Lord remembereth his c.		29: 8
unto the fulfilling of the c.		29: 9
the c. people of the Lord,	Mrm	3:21
unto the fulfilling of his c.;		5:14
c. which he made unto Abraham		5:20
among the people of the first c.;		7:10
dispersed c. people of the Lord.		8:15
against the c. people of the Lord		8:21
the Lord will not remember his c.		8:21
he will remember the c. which		8:23
the c. which he hath made		9:37
the c. which he made unto	Eth	4:15
the c. which God made with		13:11
which is in the c. of the Father	Mro	10:33
broken mine everlasting c.;	DC	1:15
mine everlasting c. might be		1:22
enter into a c. with me,		5: 3
he will break the c. which he		5:27
and c. with me that he will		5:28
a new and an everlasting c.,		22: 1
this last c. and this church		22: 3
this shall be my c. with you,		38:20
the c. which I have sent forth		39:11
Wherefore he broke my c.,		40: 3
a c. and a deed which cannot		42:30
my c. people may be gathered in		42:36
everlasting c. into the world,		45: 9
unto you mine everlasting c.,		49: 9
are heirs according to the c.		52: 2
the c. which they made unto me		54: 4
are they who have kept the c.		54: 6
receiving mine everlasting c.,		66: 2
the mediator of the new c.,		76:69
neither the everlasting c.		76:101
by a bond or everlasting c.		78:11
and c. that cannot be broken		82:11
ye bind yourselves by this c.,		82:15
soul that sins against this c.,		82:21
is according to the oath and c.		84:39
this oath and c. of my Father,		84:40
But whoso breaketh this c.		84:41
the Father teacheth him of the c.		84:48
and remember the new c.,		84:57
And c. of their fathers.		84:99
remembrance of the everlasting c.		88:131
remembrance of the everlasting c.,		88:133
in which c. I receive you to		88:133
with this same prayer and c.,		88:135
uprightly and remember the c.		90:24
unto you, with an immutable c.		98: 3
whether you will abide in my c.,		98:14
For if ye will not abide in my c.		98:15
c. with an everlasting covenant		101:39
covenant with an everlasting c.,		101:39
but have broken the c.		104: 4
shall break the c. with which		104: 5
Jesus the mediator of the new c.		107:19
God of Israel, who keepest c.		109: 1
servants the testimony of the c.,		109:38
and everlasting c. of marriage];		131: 2
you a new and an everlasting c.;		132: 4
and if ye abide not that c.,		132: 4
for no one can reject this c. and		132: 4
to the new and everlasting c.,		132: 6
he c. with her so long as he is in		132:15
their c. and marriage are not of		132:15
make a c. with her for time		132:18
if that c. is not be me or by my		132:18
by the new and everlasting c.,		132:19
if ye abide in my c., and commit		132:19
of the new and everlasting c.		132:26
my new and everlasting c.,		132:27
wife in the new and everlasting c.,		132:41
not in the new and everlasting c.,		132:42
an offering at your hand, by c.		132:51
his gospel, his everlasting c.,		133:57
with c. and promise to keep all		136: 2
And this shall be our c.—		136: 4
entered into a c. with Satan,	Mses	5:49
elect's sake, according to the c.,	JS	1:20
the elect according to the c.		1:22

COVENANTED

COVENANTED
God hath c. with thy father	1Ne 13:30
he c. with them, yea, even	17:40
which the Lord God hath c. with	2Ne 1: 5
the Lord hath c. this land unto me,	1: 5
has c. with all the house of Israel—	9: 1
have I c. with their fathers	10: 7
God, and that I c. with Abraham	29:14
he c. with me that he would	En 1:16
and he c. with me that I	Mos 9: 6
c. to maintain their rights and	Al 51: 6
they c. that they never would	53:17
his band, who had c. with him,	He 1:12
c. with all the house of Jacob,	3Ne 5:25
hath c. with the house of Jacob	5:25
of the covenant that he hath c.	5:25
who c. with my people Israel;	15: 5
with whom the Father hath c.,	20:19
I have c. with them that I	20:29
which the Father hath c. with	20:46
he hath c. with his people,	21: 4
which he has before c. with me,	DC 5:27
he c. with me that he would	40: 1
ye have c. one with another.	90:24
c. with Jehovah, and vowed to	109:68
them that had c. with Satan;	Mses 5:52
and he c. with Enoch, and	7:51
he truly c. with Enoch that	8: 2

COVENANTETH
for the Lord c. with none save it	2Ne 30: 2

COVENANTING
vouching and c. with God, that	Al 24:18
upon their c. to keep the peace	50:36

COVENANTS
may know the c. of the Lord,	T Pg
contains the c. of the Lord,	1Ne 13:23
they contain the c. of the Lord,	13:23
and also many c. of the Lord	13:26
concerning the c. of the Lord	14: 5
Rememberest thou the c. of the	14: 8
way for the fulfilling of his c.,	14:17
and he remembered the c. which he	17:40
remember the c. which he made	19:15
for thus are the c. of the Lord	22: 6
the c. of the Father of heaven	22: 9
in bringing about his c. and his	22:11
great were the c. of the Lord	2Ne 3: 4
remembered in the c. of the Lord	3: 5
of the c. which I have made	3: 7
also to the knowledge of my c.,	3:12
will fulfil his c. which he has made	6:12
concerning the c. of the Lord	9: 1
how great the c. of the Lord,	9:53
that my c. may be fulfilled	10:15
delighteth in the c. of the Lord	11: 5
remember my c. which I have	29: 1
retain all their oaths, and their c.,	Al 37:27
and their c. from this people,	37:29
and did enter into their c. and	He 6:21
it is these secret oaths and c.	6:25
those secret oaths and c. did not	6:26
and their oaths, and their c.,	6:30
work of the c. of the Father,	Mro 7:31
the c. which he hath made unto	7:32
the c. of the Eternal Father	10:31
all old c. have I caused to be	DC 22: 1
the c. which thou hast made.	25:13
contrary to the church c.	28:12
to the c. of the church,	28:14
the church articles and c.	33:14
all the commandments and c.	35:24
And they shall observe the c.	42:13
hereafter receive church c.,	42:67
all the commandments and c.	42:78
laws and c. of the church,	51: 4
the items in addition to the c.	68:13
according to the c.	68:24
to observe their c. by sacrifice—	97: 8
The c. being broken through	104:52
and the c. which ye have made	DC 104:55
agreeable to the c. and	107:12
agreeable to the c. and	107:20
appointed, according to the c. and	107:63
it is given according to the c.	107:85
of their office, as given in the c.	107:86
their office, as is given in the c.—	107:87
teach them according to the c.	107:89
in the book of Doctrine and C.	124:141
All c., contracts, bonds,	132: 7
this book of Doctrine and C.,	135: 3
this book of Doctrine and C.	135: 6
the c. of the Lord might be	Mses 8: 2

COVER
as the waters c. the sea.	2Ne 21: 9
and the worms c. thee.	24:11
and mountains shall c. them,	26: 5
as the waters c. the sea.	30:15
garments to c. their nakedness.	Al 49: 6
to c. the face of the whole earth,	He 3: 8
did c. the whole face of the land,	11:20
c. the face of the whole earth	14:27
sickness shall c. the land.	DC 45:31
calamity shall c. the mocker,	45:50
when we undertake to c. our sins,	121:37
of darkness shall c. the earth;	Mses 7:61

COVERED
and have c. thee in the shadow	2Ne 8:16
with twain he c. his face,	16: 2
and with twain he c. his feet,	16: 2
the seers hath he c. because of	27: 5
a land which was c. with bones of	Mos 8: 8
also c. with ruins of buildings	8: 8
land which was c. with dry bones;	21:26
were c. with a shallow covering.	Al 16:11
c. with large bodies of water,	50:29
Moronihah have I c. with earth,	3Ne 9: 5
had become c. with buildings,	Mrm 1: 7
the land was c. with animals of	Eth 10:19
was c. with inhabitants.	10:21
c. with the bodies of the dead.	14:21
thy hiding place no longer be c.;	DC 121: 4
never more be c. by the floods.	Mses 7:50
all around was c. with earth.	JS 2:51

COVERETH
unto you, darkness c. the earth,	DC 112:23
where is the pavillion that c. thy	121: 1
west, and c. the whole earth,	JS 1:26

COVERING
and I make sackcloth their c.	2Ne 7: 3
were covered with a shallow c.	Al 16:11
clothed with light for a c.,	DC 85: 7
the veil of the c. of my temple,	101:23
I shall unveil the face of my c.,	124: 8
and make sackcloth their c.	133:69
eternity was our c. and our rock	Abr 2:16

COVERT
a c. from storm and from rain.	2Ne 14: 6

COVET
ye c. that which ye have not	Mos 4:25
shalt not c. thy neighbor's house,	13:24
shalt not c. thy neighbor's wife,	13:24
shalt not c. thy neighbor's wife;	DC 19:25
shalt not c. thine own property,	19:26
c. that which is but the drop,	117: 8
and c. not that which is thy	136:20

COVETOUS
love one another; cease to be c.;	DC 88:123
and lustful and c. desires	101: 6
sins, and of all their c. desires,	117: 4

COVETOUSNESS
pride of their hearts, and their c.,	DC 98:20
broken the covenant through c.,	104: 4
by c. and feigned words—	104:52

COVILL 218 CREATED

COVILL, James: *see also JAMES.*
heart of my servant C. was right | DC | 40: 1

COW
both the c. and the ox, and the ass | 1Ne | 18:25
nourish a young c. and two sheep; | 2Ne | 17:21
the c. and the bear shall feed; | | 21: 7
the c. and the bear shall feed; | | 30:13

COWDERY, Oliver: *see also COWDERY'S, Oliver; and OLIVER.*
C., verily, verily, I say unto you, | DC | 8: 1
you, my servant C., have desired | | 18: 1
now, C., I speak unto you, | | 18: 9
behold, I give unto you, C., | | 18:37
C., who was also called of God, | | 20: 3
by you, C. mine apostle; | | 21:10
that I may send my servant, C., | | 25: 6
servants, Joseph Smith, Jun., and C., | | 27: 8
go with my servants, C. and | | 32: 2
my servant C. shall return unto | | 37: 3
C. I have appointed to another | | 47: 3
obtained for my servant C. also. | | 52:41
ordained to assist my servant C. | | 55: 4
let my servant C. assist him, | | 57:13
return, and also C. with them, | | 58:58
Joseph Smith, Jun., and C., | | 60: 6
Sidney Rigdon and C. | | 60:17
Joseph Smith, Jun., and C., | | 61:23
Joseph Smith, Jun., and C., | | 61:30
unto them, with my servant C. | | 63:46
let my servant C. carry these | | 68:32
should go with my servant C.; | | 69: 2
assistance from my servant C. | | 69: 4
and also unto my servant C., | | 70: 1
and Horah and Olihah [C.], | | 82:11
Carter, Jared Carter, C., | | 102: 3
was the result, namely: 1, C.; | | 102:34
C., ORSON HYDE, Clerks. | | 102:34
let my servant Olihah [C.] | | 104:28
G. Williams] and Olihah [C.] | | 104:29
named for my servant Olihah [C.] | | 104:34
him that was my servant C.; | | 124:95
C. came to my house, | JS | 2:66
days after the arrival of Mr. C. | | 2:67
that I should baptize C., and | | 2:70
and he (C.) the second. | | 2:72
no sooner had I baptized C., | | 2:73

COWDERY'S, Oliver: *see also COWDERY, Oliver.*
for my servant C. sake. | DC | 69: 1

COWDERY, Warren A.: *see also WARREN.*
C. should be appointed, and | DC 106: 1

COWS
of oxen, and c., and of sheep, | Eth | 9:18

CRACKS
be found in seams and in c., | He | 14:22
and in seams and in c., | 3Ne | 8:18

CRAFT
for it did destroy their c.; | Al | 35: 3
many words, and also in his c., | He | 2: 4
Let there be a c. made, or | DC | 60: 5

CRAFTINESS
cunning and c. of king Laman, | Mos | 7:21
and the c. of king Laman, | | 9:10
by his cunning, and lying c., | | 10:18
all the pride and c. and all the | Al | 4:19
been taken in thy lying and c., | | 12: 3
were blinded by the c. of men. | DC | 76:75
and take them in their own c.; | | 121:12
who are blinded by the subtle c. | | 123:12

CRAFTS
himself from the c. of men; | DC 106: 6

CREATE
will c. upon every dwelling-place | 2Ne 14: 5

and c. a bitter persecution; | JS | 2:22
to c. in them a spirit of the | | 2:23

CREATED
of that God who had c. them. | 1Ne | 2:12
the Lord hath c. the earth that | | 17:36
he hath c. his children that | | 17:36
They are c. now, and not from | | 20: 7
been c. for a thing of naught; | 2Ne | 2:12
and he hath c. all things, | | 2:14
he had c. our first parents, | | 2:15
all things which are c., | | 2:15
And all things which were c. | | 2:22
which they were after they were c.; | | 2:22
the Lord your God, have c. all men, | | 29: 7
unto him who c. all flesh? | Jac | 2:21
the selfsame end hath he c. them, | | 2:21
which earth was c. by the power of | | 4: 9
and to speak and man was c., | | 4: 9
to that God who has c. you, | Mos | 2:20
should serve him who has c. you | | 2:21
in the first place, he hath c. you, | | 2:23
yet ye were c. of the dust | | 2:25
if belongeth to him who c. you. | | 2:25
who c. heaven and earth, | | 4: 2
and that he c. all things, | | 4: 9
of the glory of him that c. you, | | 4:12
if God, who has c. you, on whom | | 4:21
mercy of him who c. all things, | | 5:15
the image after which man was c. | | 7:27
was c. after the image of God, | | 7:27
for it is I that hath c. them; | | 26:23
for the Lord had c. all men, | Al | 1: 4
redemption of him who c. you? | | 5:15
who is God, c. all things which | | 18:28
I believe that he c. all things | | 18:29
they all c. from the beginning. | | 18:32
was c. after the image of God, | | 18:34
and he c. all things both in | | 22:10
the Great Spirit c. all things, | | 22:11
God c. man after his own image, | | 22:12
their God, who hath c. them, | He | 12: 6
I c. the heavens and the earth, | 3Ne | 9:15
I have c. the smith that bloweth | | 22:16
I have c. the waster to destroy. | | 22:16
been c. by the hand of God. | 4Ne | 1:16
upon that Being who c. them. | Mrm | 5: 2
who c. the heavens and the earth, | | 9:11
Behold he c. Adam, and by | | 9:12
man was c. of the dust of | | 9:17
myself unto man whom I have c., | Eth | 3:15
ye are c. after mine own image? | | 3:15
Yea, even all men were c. in | | 3:15
man have I c. after the body | | 3:16
c. the heavens and the earth, | DC | 14: 9
that he c. man, male and female, | | 20:18
in his own likeness, c. he them; | | 20:18
all things whatsoever I have c. | | 29:30
power of my Spirit c. I them; | | 29:31
Adam, your father, whom I c. | | 29:34
the worlds are and were c., | | 76:24
other creature which God has c. | | 77: 2
this intent was it made and c., | | 88:20
was not c. or made, neither | | 93:29
world upon which he was c.; | Mses | 1: 8
which are, and which were c.; | | 1: 8
my power, have I c. them, | | 1:32
without number have I c.; | | 1:33
I also c. them for mine own | | 1:33
and by the Son I c. them, | | 1:33
Begotten I c. these things; | | 2: 1
the beginning I c. the heaven, | | 2: 1
And I, God, c. great whales, | | 2:21
things which I had c. were good. | | 2:21
God, c. man in mine own image, | | 2:27
mine Only Begotten c. I him; | | 2:27
male and female c. I them. | | 2:27
which I, God, had c. and made. | | 3: 3
of the earth, when they were c., | | 3: 4
the Lord God, c. all things, | | 3: 5
had c. all the children of men; | | 3: 5
for in heaven c. I them; | | 3: 5
all things were before c.; | | 3: 7

CREATED

spiritually were they c. and made	Mses 3: 7
spiritual in the day that I c. it;	3: 9
the sphere in which I, God, c. it,	3: 9
the Lord God, c. much gold;	3:11
In the day that God c. man,	6: 8
male and female, c. he them,	6: 9
in the day when they were c.	6: 9
since the day that I c. them,	6:28
the spirits that God had c.;	6:36
c. and made to bear record of me, in the day I c. them;	6:63 7:32
destroy man whom I have c.,	8:26
Noah that I have c. them,	8:26
c. no small stir and division	JS 2: 5

CREATING

every creature of his c.,	Mos 27:30

CREATION

which gave an account of the c.	1Ne 5:11
having a knowledge of the c. of	2Ne 1:10
works of the Lord from the c. of	1:10
no purpose in the end of its c.	2:12
could have been no c. of things,	2:13
written, from the c. of the world.	6: 3
for there could have been no c.	11: 7
back until the c. of Adam.	Mos 28:17
he began at the c. of the world,	Al 18:36
and also the c. of Adam,	18:36
he began from the c. of Adam,	22:12
scriptures from the c. of Adam,	22:13
concerning the c. of the world,	Eth 1: 3
from the c. of Adam even down	Mro 10: 3
might answer the end of its c.;	DC 49:16
according to his c. before the	49:17
destined order or sphere of c.,	77: 3
hath filled the measure of its c.,	88:19
it filleth the measure of its c.,	88:25
from the beginning of the c.;	112:31
from the beginning of c. until	132:38
myself to the beginning of the c.,	Abr 1:28
of the beginning of the c.,	1:31
signifying the first c.,	Fac 2: 1
next grand governing c.	2: 2

CREATIONS

let the eternal c. declare his name	DC 128:23
beginning to the number of thy c.;	Mses 7:30
own bosom, from all thy c.,	7:31
the c. which I have made;	7:36
all the c. of God mourned;	7:56
all the c. which I have made;	7:64

CREATOR

for it behooveth the great C. that	2Ne 9: 5
the merciful plan of the great C.,	9: 6
by the help of the all-powerful C.	Jac 2: 5
they, in the sight of your great C.?	3: 7
they denied the being of their C.;	Om 1:17
the C. of all things from the	Mos 3: 8
interpostion of their all-wise C.,	29:19
except ye make our C. a liar	Al 5:25
that there is a Supreme C.	30:44
the C. of all things from the	He 14:12
the c. of the first day,	DC 95: 7
When will my C. sanctify me,	Mses 7:48

CREATURE

the pains of every living c.,	2Ne 9:21
every c. of his creating,	Mos 27:30
should be declared to every c.,	28: 3
he should discover to every c.	28:15
to the management of the c.	Al 30:17
would have no claim upon the c.?	42:21
otherwise justice claimeth the c.	42:22
preach the gospel to every c.;	Mrm 9:22
preach my gospel unto every c.	DC 18:28
must be preached unto every c.,	58:64
preach the gospel to every c.,	68: 8
every other c. which God has	77: 2
preach the gospel to every c.	80: 1
into all the world unto every c.	84:62

preach my gospel unto every c.	DC 112:28
to send my word to every c.	124:128
forth abundantly the moving c.	Mses 2:20
every living c. that moveth,	2:21
the living c. after his kind,	2:24
Adam called every living c.,	3:19
every living c. that moveth,	Abr 4:21
the living c. after his kind,	4:24
Adam called every living c.,	5:20

CREATURES

houses shall be full of doleful c.;	2Ne 23:21
towards you, unworthy c.,	Mos 4:11
And thus they become new c.;	27:26
independent above all other c.	DC 78:14
made and prepared for my c.	104:13
the moving c. that have life;	Abr 4:20

CREDITORS

to which of my c. have I sold you?	2Ne 7: 1

CREEDS

riveted the c. of the fathers,	DC 123: 7
their c. were an abomination	JS 2:19

CREEP

animals that run or c. on the earth;	DC 89:14
everything which c. upon the	Mses 2:25
every creeping thing that c.	2:26
and to everything that c. upon	2:30
thing that c. upon the earth	Abr 4:25
thing that c. upon the earth.	4:26
thing that c. upon the earth,	4:30

CREEPING

of beasts, and of c. things,	DC 77: 2
his kind, cattle, and c. things,	Mses 2:24
every c. thing that creepeth	2:26
and beast, and the c. things,	8:26
his kind, cattle and c. things,	Abr 4:24
every c. thing that creepeth	4:26

CREPT

I, Nephi, c. into the city and	1Ne 4: 5
sons of Shule c. into the house	Eth 7:18

CRIED

I c. unto the Lord for them.	1Ne 2:18
the Spirit c. with a loud voice,	11: 6
and c. unto the Lord.	17: 7
had c. unto them from the dust;	2Ne 3:19
And one c. unto another, and said:	16: 3
moved at the voice of him that c.,	16: 4
I c. unto him in mighty prayer	En 1: 4
I c. unto him continually,	1:15
they all c. aloud with one voice,	Mos 4: 2
And they all c. with one voice,	5: 2
he c. unto them, saying:	17:14
and c., saying: O Lord,	18:12
the king c. out in the anguish of	19: 7
Nevertheless he c. again, saying:	27:13
they c. mightily unto him	29:20
with much faith, c., saying:	Al 2:30
Amulek, and they c. out, saying:	10:24
and c. the mightier unto them,	10:25
people c. out against him, saying:	10:28
and c. with a mighty voice,	13:21
And Alma c., saying:	14:26
And then Alma c. unto the Lord,	15:10
and c. with a loud voice, saying:	19:29
and c. mightily, saying:	22:17
up his voice to heaven, and c.,	31:26
c. unto those whom he beheld,	32: 7
I c. within my heart: O Jesus,	36:18
and they c. with one voice unto	43:49
c. unto the Lord for their freedom,	43:50
c. mightily unto Moroni,	44:19
And they c. unto us, saying:	57:31
and they c. out against him,	He 8: 1
he c. again unto the Lord, saying:	11: 9
and c. with a loud voice,	13: 4
they c. unto their captains,	16: 6

CRIED 220 CROWN

CRIED		
c. mightily to his God in behalf	3Ne	1:11
he c. mightily unto the Lord,		1:12
and c. unto them, saying:		12: 1
the slain of my people and I c.:	Mrm	6:16
long time ye have c. unto me.	Eth	1:43
brother of Jared c. unto the		2:18
And he c. again unto the Lord		2:22
and c. again unto the Lord,		3: 1
c. repentance unto the people,		11:20
you c. unto me in your heart,	DC	6:22
Satan c. with a loud voice,	Mses	1:19
that Satan c. with a loud voice,		1:22
and c. with a loud voice,		6:37
that Adam c. unto the Lord,		6:64
Mahujah, and c. unto the Lord,		7: 2
and he c. unto the Lord,		7:45
and c. unto the Lord, saying:		7:49
that Enoch c. unto the Lord,		7:54
wept and c. unto the Lord,		7:58

CRIES		
the c. of the fair daughters of	Jac	2:32
And God did hear our c. and	Mos	9:18
I will be slow to hear their c.;		11:24
their continual c. did stir up the		21:11
the Lord did hear their c.,		21:15
the Lord did hear my c.,		23:10
that they should stop their c.;		24:11
the Lord did hear their c.,	Al	2:28
quick to hear the c. of his people		9:26
and heard my c. in the midst of		33: 9
yea, thou didst hear my c.,		33:10
our prisoners did hear their c.,		57:32
known unto God were all their c.,		60:10
lift their c. to the Lord their God,	3Ne	4: 8
will not suffer their c. any longer.	Mrm	8:41
and so great were their c.,	Eth	15:16
did rend the air with their c.,		15:17
Behold, my heart c.;	Mro	9:15
ears may be opened unto your c.,	DC	101:92
the c. of their innocent ones		109:49
ear be penetrated with their c.?		121: 2
c. of the widow and the fatherless		136: 8
of thy brother's blood c. unto me	Mses	5:35

CRIETH		
unto him that c.: All is well!	2Ne	28:25
c. unto me with a mighty voice,	Al	5:51
he c. unto the four angels	DC	77: 9
c. from the ground against		136:36

CRIME		
unto you concerning a grosser c.,	Jac	2:22
c. which they could make appear	Al	10:13
whatsoever a man did was no c.		30:17
not been guilty of so great a c.		39: 7
justice according to their c.		50:39
according to the c. which he	He	8: 1
to be judged of the c. which	3Ne	6:26
tried or condemned for any c.,	DC	68:22
civil magistrate should restrain c.,		134: 4
c. should be punished according		134: 8
They were innocent of any c.,		135: 7

CRIMES		
you according to your c.,	Jac	2: 9
because of your grosser c.		2:23
punished according to their c.;	WM	1:15
punished according to their c.;		1:16
judge them according to their c.	Mos	26:11
c. which he had committed.	Al	1:10
and the c. of the people.		4:16
the trails of the c. of the people		10:14
be judged according to their c.		30:11
for the c. he had done;		30:11
I would not dwell upon your c.,		39: 7
ye cannot hide your c. from God;		39: 8

CRIMINALITY		
be punished according to their c.	DC	134: 8

CRISIS		
ye are brought to that awful c.,	Al	34:34

CRISPING		
and the wimples, and the c.-pins;	2Ne	13:22

CRISPING-PINS: see CRISPING and PINS.

CRITICAL		
this was a c. time for such	Al	51: 9
now, in those c. circumstances,		57:16

CROOKED		
that he cannot walk in c. paths;	Al	7:20
God doth not walk in c. paths,	DC	3: 2
unto a c. and perverse generation.		33: 2
unto a c. and perverse generation,		34: 6

CROPS		
Cry unto him over the c. of	Al	34:24
to destroy the c. of the earth.	DC	29:16
prepare for putting in spring c.		136: 7

CROSS		
They c. the large waters into the	1Ne	1:hd
he was lifted up upon the c.		11:33
that he can c. these great waters.		17:17
view his death, and suffer his c.	Jac	1: 8
that they might c. him,	Mos	12:19
his people might have room to c.	Al	2:34
they might make him c. his words,		10:16
Lamanites will c. the river Sidon		16: 6
c. yourself in all these things;		39: 9
and c. yourself in these things.		39: 9
and began to c. the river Sidon,		43:35
Sidon that they should not c.		43:40
durst they c. the head of Sidon,		56:25
ways that they might c. him,	He	9:19
wherein ye will take up your c.,	3Ne	12:30
might be lifted up upon the c.;		27:14
had been lifted up upon the c.,		27:14
they did c. many waters,	Eth	2: 6
c. this great water in darkness?		2:22
cannot c. this great deep save		2:25
light while we shall c. the sea.		3: 4
should be lifted up upon the c.,		4: 1
c. the great waters in darkness.		6: 3
that you must take up your c.,	DC	23: 6
take up his c. and follow me,		56: 2
gird up your loins take up your c.		112:14
Son of Man lifted up on the c.,	Mses	7:55
in attempting to c. the fence	JS	2:48

CROSSED		
after they had c. the river Jordan	1Ne	17:32
after they had c. the sea,	Mos	10:13
when they had all c. the river	Al	2:35
his sons c. over the river Sidon,		16: 7
and they c. the waters of Sidon.		43:40

CROSSES		
have endured the c. of the world,	2Ne	9:18

CROSSING		
also wronged while c. the sea;	Mos	10:12
as they were c. the river Sidon,	Al	2:27

CROSSWAYS		
two stones c. of the box,	JS	2:52

CROWED		
the cock c. and I found that	JS	2:47

CROWN		
with a scab the c. of the head	2Ne	13:17
shall receive a c. of eternal life;	DC	20:14
a c. of righteousness thou shalt		25:15
to receive a c. of righteousness,		29:13
and will c. the faithful with joy		52:43
receive a c. in the mansions of		59: 2
shall have a c. of eternal life		66:12
he shall in nowise lose his c.;		75:28
they obtain not the c. over		76:79
crowned with the c. of his glory,		76:108
unto the c. prepared for you,		78:15
will c. him again with sheaves.		79: 3

CROWN 221 CRY

shalt have a c. of immortality,	DC 81: 6
promised unto you a c. of glory	104: 7
I have prepared a c. for him in the	106: 8
will c. him with blessings and	124:17
bless you, and c. you with honor,	124:55
with a c. of eternal light upon	Fac 2: 3
a c. upon his head,	3: 1

CROWNED
ye shall be c. with much glory;	DC 58: 4
c. with blessings from above,	59: 4
and c. with honor, and glory,	75: 5
c. with the crown of his glory,	76:108
it shall be c. with glory,	88:19
be c. with the glory of his might,	88:107
lives for my name shall be c.	101:15
and be c. with celestial glory,	101:65
be c. with the same blessing,	124:95
fall down and be c. with glory,	133:32
and were c. at the right hand	Mses 7:56
c. on the right hand of God.	JS 1: 1

CROWNS
with c. upon their heads,	DC 29:12
c. of glory upon our heads,	109:76
children, and c. of eternal lives	132:55
of Man, with c. of glory;	Mses 7:56

CRUCIFIED
and to be c., according to the	1Ne 19:10
against him, that he be c.	2Ne 10: 5
he shall be led, c., and slain,	Mos 15: 7
He was c., died, and rose	DC 20:23
that Jesus was c. by sinful men	21: 9
was c. for the sins of the world,	35: 2
I am Jesus that was c.	45:52
was c. for the sins of the world.	46:13
was c. for the sins of the world,	53: 2
was c. for the sins of the world—	54: 1
having c. him unto themselves	76:35
Jesus, to be c. for the world,	76:41

CRUCIFY
because they c. the God of	1Ne 19:13
they should scourge him and c.	2Ne 6: 9
and they shall c. him—	10: 3
on earth that would c. their God.	10: 3
Behold, they will c. him;	25:13
shall scourge him, and shall c. him.	Mos 3: 9

CRUEL
| c. both with wrath and fierce | 2Ne 23: 9 |
| murder them in a most c. manner, | Mro 9:10 |

CRUELTY
| massacred by the barbarous c. | Al 48:24 |

CRUMBLE
| and to c. to its mother earth, | 2Ne 9: 7 |
| to c. and to return to their | Mrm 6:15 |

CRUSH
| shall fall upon them and c. them | 2Ne 26: 5 |

CRUSHED
| fallen upon and c. to death; | 3Ne 10:13 |

CRY
wherefore, I did c. unto the Lord;	1Ne 2:16
go forth and c. in the wilderness:	10: 8
And they shall c. from the dust;	2Ne 3:20
their c. shall go, even according	3:20
he hath heard my c. by day,	4:23
and c. unto the Lord, and say:	4:30
I will c. unto thee, my God,	4:35
Nephi, did c. much unto the Lord	5: 1
righteousness, but behold, a c.	15: 7
have knowledge to c., My father,	18: 5
C. out and shout, thou	22: 6
shall c. in their desolate houses,	23:22
Howl, O gate; c., O city;	24:31
the c. of the clood of the saints	26: 3
but I must c. unto my God:	26: 7

doth he c. unto any, saying:	2Ne 26:25
and wonder, for ye shall c. out,	27: 4
for ye shall cry out, and c.;	27: 4
the clood of the saints shall c. from	28:10
and I c. unto my God in faith,	33: 3
I know that he will hear my c.	33: 3
for he had heard my c.	Jac 7:22
the day long did I c. unto him;	En 1: 4
and I did c. unto God that he	1:16
did c. mightily to the Lord	Mos 9:17
when they shall c. unto me	11:24
and c. mightily to the Lord	11:25
did c. mightily from day to day,	21:10
and they did c. mightily to God;	21:14
did they c. unto their God that	21:14
the Lord was slow to hear their c.	21:15
and began to c. unto the Lord	23:28
they began to c. mightily to God.	24:10
to c. unto them that they must	Al 5:49
C. unto this people, saying—	7: 9
and c. mightily unto this people,	9:25
well doth he c. unto this people,	10:20
Yea, well doth he c., by the	10:21
he began to c. unto the people,	14: 7
and c. mightily against them at	14:11
there was a c. of war heard	16: 1
he began to c. unto the Lord,	18:41
they also began to c. unto God,	19:15
blood would c. from the ground	20:18
the c. of widows mourning for	28: 5
the c. of mourning was heard	28: 5
c. repentance unto every people!	29: 1
and c. with a loud voice, saying:	31:14
Behold, O God, they c. unto thee,	31:27
c. unto thee with their mouths,	31:27
yet they c. unto thee and say—	31:28
when I did c. unto thee in my field;	33: 5
I did c. unto thee in my prayer,	33: 5
children may c. unto thee,	33: 8
therefore I will c. unto thee in	33:11
Yea, c. unto him for mercy;	34:18
C. unto him when ye are in your	34:20
C. unto him in your houses, yea,	34:21
c. unto him against the power of	34:22
Yea, c. unto him against the devil,	34:23
C. unto him over the crops of	34:24
C. over the flocks of your fields,	34:25
when you do not c. unto the Lord,	34:27
did c. unto the Lord their God	37:30
c. unto God for all thy support;	37:36
until I did c. out unto the Lord	38: 8
I did c. unto him and I did find	38: 8
servants of Amalickiah raised a c.,	47:25
man did c. unto the multitude,	He 5:37
repent, and c. unto the voice,	5:41
they all did begin to c. unto the	5:42
they did c. even until the cloud	5:42
they should c. out against them.	8: 4
they did c. unto the people,	8: 5
there were some who did c. out:	8: 7
raising the c. of murder among	9: 6
and did c. out against Nephi,	9:16
Nephi did c. unto the Lord,	11: 3
c. unto the Lord our God that	11: 8
ye shall c. unto the Lord;	13:32
and in vain shall ye c., for your	13:32
C. unto this people, repent and	14: 9
people should c. unto the Lord	3Ne 3:12
and c. unto the Lord, ye will	3:15
did c. with a loud voice, saying:	4:28
and c. again with one voice,	4:30
Yea, they did c.: Hosanna to	4:32
And they did c.: Blessed be	4:32
Nephi did c. unto the people in	7:23
they were heard to c., saying:	8:24
were heard to c. and mourn,	8:25
might not c. unto me from the	9:11
did c. out with one accord,	11:16
they did c. out with one voice,	20: 9
And then shall a c. go forth:	20:41
forth into singing, and c. aloud,	22: 1
began to c. even as had been	Mrm 2:10
C. unto this people—Repent ye,	3: 2

CRY

And I did c. unto this people,	Mrm	3: 3
shall c., yea, even from the dust		8:23
from the dust will they c. unto		8:23
the blood of saints shall c. unto		8:27
to c. unto the Lord from the		8:40
c. mightily unto the Father in		9: 6
C. unto the Lord, that he will	Eth	1:34
brother of Jared did c. unto the		1:35
C. again unto the Lord, and it		1:36
brother of Jared did c. unto the		1:37
c. unto him whither we shall go.		1:38
brother of Jared did c. unto the		1:39
they did c. unto the Lord,		6: 7
c. unto him from the ground		8:22
c. from the dust for vengeance		8:24
iniquities and c. unto the Lord.		9:34
he did c. from the morning,		12: 3
yea, a c. went forth throughout		14:18
c. repentance unto this people,	DC	18:14
and c. repentance unto a crooked		34: 6
That the c. of the saints, and of		87: 7
c. they have sinned when they		121:16
those who c. transgression do		121:17
let my servant William c. aloud		124:101
and all ye valleys c. aloud;		128:23
and lo, this shall be their c.,		133: 9
let the c. go forth among all		133:10
will c. unto the Lord of Hosts		135: 4
continued his c. unto the Lord,	Mses	7:50
the c. and tumult were so great	JS	2: 9

CRYING

the voice of one c. from the dust:	2Ne	33:13
of the angel, c. unto the people.	Al	9:29
c. that these things ought not		16:18
and c. with a loud voice, saying:		46:19
c. repentance unto the people,	He	16: 4
upon all the face of this land, c.:	3Ne	9: 1
c. repentance unto them —	Eth	9:28
like as one c. from the dead,	Mro	10:27
c. repentance unto this people,	DC	18:15
with a sound of rejoicing, c. —		19:37
C. repentance, saying;		36: 6
go forth, c. with a loud voice,		39:19
heaven is at hand; c.: Hosanna!		39:19
Yea, a voice c. —		65: 3
the angels are c. unto the Lord		86: 5
of one c. in the wilderness —		88:66
heaven, c. with a loud voice,		88:92
angel c. through the midst of		133:17
some c. "Lo, here!" and others,	JS	2: 5

CRYSTAL

will be made like unto c. and will	DC	130: 9

CUBIT

can add one c. unto his stature?	3Ne	13:27
signifies one day to a c.	Fac	2: 1

CUMBER

may not c. the ground of me	Jac	5: 9
all sorts of fruit did c. the tree.		5:30
shall not c. the ground of my		5:49
they c. not the ground of my		5:66

CUMBERED

which c. this spot of ground,	Jac	5:44
Seek not to be c.	DC	66:10

CUMENI

of Zeezrom, and the city of C.,	Al	56:14
placed to protect the city C.		57: 7
surround, by night, the city C.,		57: 8
in obtaining the city C.		57:12
And we retained our city C.,		57:23
towards the city of C.;		57:31
with speed towards the city C.;		57:34

CUMOMS

elephants and cureloms and c.;	Eth	9:19
elephants and cureloms and c.		9:19

222

CURIOUS

CUMORAH

our people unto the land of C.,	Mrm	6: 2
by a hill which was called C.,		6: 2
march forth to the land of C.,		6: 4
tents around about the hill C.;		6: 4
our people unto the land of C.		6: 5
people in one to the land of C.,		6: 6
hid up in the hill C. all the		6: 6
from the top of the hill C.,		6:11
and tremendous battle at C.,		8: 2
Glad tidings from C.!	DC	128:20

CUNNING

many things by his c. arts,	1Ne	16:38
O that c. plan of the evil one!	2Ne	9:28
to the enticings of that c. one.		9:39
counselor, and the c. artificer,		13: 1
by the c. and craftiness of	Mos	7:21
the c. and the craftiness of		9:10
by his c., and lying craftiness,		10:18
began to be a c. and a wise people,		24: 7
the world, yea, a very c. people,		24: 7
Amlici, he being a very c. man,	Al	2: 1
Now this Amlici had, by his c.,		2: 2
that by their c. devices they might		10:13
the arts and c. of the people;		10:15
may, by their c. and their lyings,		20:13
c. plans which he hath devised		28:13
your c. that has preserved you		44: 9
he was a man of c. device		46:10
assistance of his c. servants,		47:35
by the c. of Amalickiah,		51:27
all the c. and the snares and	He	3:29
the c. and the mysterious arts		16:21
greater than the c. of the devil.	3Ne	21:10
because of his c. words,	Eth	8: 2
war and all the c. of the world,		13:16
has sought to lay a c. plan,	DC	10:12
thus he has laid a c. plan,		10:23
than the c. of the devil.		10:43

CUP

of the Lord the c. of his fury —	2Ne	8:17
hast drunken the dregs of the c.		8:17
of thine hand the c. of trembling,		8:22
the dregs of the c. of my fury;		8:22
out of the c. of the wrath of God,	Mos	3:26
out of the c. of the wrath of God.		5: 5
they drink the dregs of a bitter c.	Al	40:26
have drunk out of that bitter c.	3Ne	11:11
should take of the wine of the c.		18: 8
they took the c., and said:	Mro	5: 1
I might not drink the bitter c.,	DC	19:18
he shall take the c. also, and say:		20:78
the c. of mine indignation is full;		29:17
when the c. of the wrath of		43:26
all nations to drink of her c.,		86: 3
the c. of their iniquity is full.		101:11
that their c. might be full;		103: 3

CURE

they might c. them of their hatred	Mos	28: 2

CURELOMS

elephants and c. and cumoms;	Eth	9:19
elephants and c. and cumoms.		9:19

CURES

even had done all manner of c.	3Ne	26:15

CURING

and c. all manner of diseases.	Mos	3: 5

CURIOUS

a round ball of c. workmanship;	1Ne	16:10
work timbers of c. workmanship.		18: 1
manner of so c. a workmanship.	Al	37:39
he being an exceedingly c. man,		63: 5
and there were also c. workmen,	He	6:11
of exceedingly c. workmanship.	Eth	10:27

CURSE

CURSE
I will c. them even with a sore	1Ne	2:23
curse even with a sore c.,		2:23
Lord did c. the land against them,		17:35
yea, he did c. it against them unto		17:35
fret themselves, and c. their king	2Ne	18:21
I shall visit them with a sore c.,	Jac	2:33
and I c. it not save it be for	En	1:10
which was a c. upon them	Al	3: 6
bring the same c. upon his seed.		3: 9
that the c. should fall upon them.		3:18
brought upon themselves the c.;		3:19
the c. of God had fallen upon		17:15
the c. of God did no more follow		23:18
brought this great c. upon me.		30:53
the c. might be taken from him.		30:54
If this c. should be taken from		30:55
c. was not taken off of Korihor;		30:56
there is a c. upon all this land,		37:28
wroth, and he did c. God,		49:27
a c. shall come upon the land,	He	13:17
of the great c. of the land,		13:18
because of the c. of the land.		13:19
a c. should come upon the land,		13:23
because of the c. of the land.		13:35
their c. was taken from them,	3Ne	2:15
c. which was upon the land		3:24
bless them that c. you, do good		12:44
Ye are cursed with a c., for ye		24: 9
and smite the earth with a c.		25: 6
they did c. God and wish to	Mrm	2:14
bringing a c. upon the land,	Eth	7:23
to take the c. from off the land,		9:16
or there should come a c. upon		9:28
c. should come upon the land,		11: 6
be a great c. upon all the land		14: 1
great was the c. upon the land.		14: 1
the c. of Adam is taken from	Mro	8: 8
under the c. of a broken law.		8:24
may not be smitten with a c.;	DC	27: 9
no c. when the Lord cometh;		38:18
ye that hear me not will I c.,		41: 1
voices and c. God and die.		45:32
smite the whole earth with a c.,		98:17
against them, ye shall c. them;		103:24
And whomsoever ye c., I will		103:25
whomsoever ye curse, I will c.,		103:25
with a very sore and grievous c.		104: 4
earth be smitten with a c.—		110:15
come and smite the earth with a c.		128:17
earth will be smitten with a c.		128:18
whomsoever you c. I will curse,		132:47
whomsoever you curse I will c.,		132:47
down upon the world with a c.		133: 2
cursed the earth with a sore c.,	Mses	5:56
c. the land with much heat,		7: 8
out and smite them with a c.,		7:10
went forth a c. upon all people		7:15
cursed the earth with a sore c.,		8: 4
preserved the c. in the land.	Abr	1:24
and c. them that curse;		2:11
and curse them that c. thee;		2:11

CURSED
c. shall be the land for their sakes,	2Ne	1: 7
That ye may not be c. with a sore		1:22
Wherefore, if ye are c., behold, I		4: 6
c. is he that putteth his trust in		4:34
c. is he that putteth his trust in		4:34
c. shall be the seed of him that		5:23
be c. even with the same cursing.		5:23
C. is he that putteth his trust in		28:31
ye have c. them, and have hated		29: 5
or c. be the land for their sakes.	Jac	2:29
the land is c. for your sakes;		3: 3
they are c. with a sore cursing,		3: 3
and how c. are they who shall be		6: 3
them, therefore they were c.;	Al	3: 7
Behold, the Lamanites have I c.,		3:14
brethren, that they may be c. also.		3:15
even so doth every man that is c.		3:19
how much more c. is that		32:19
c. be the land forever and ever		37:31

223

C. shall be the land, yea, this	Al	45:16
and c. be they who hide not up	He	13:19
c. is he, and also the treasure,		13:19
c. be they and also their treasures,		13:20
ye are c. because of your riches,		13:21
and also are your riches c.		13:21
he hath c. the land because of		13:30
for behold the land is c., and		13:36
Ye are c. with a curse, for ye	3Ne	24: 9
the land was c. for their sake.	Mrm	1:17
the Lord had c. the land,		1:18
shall be c. by the law.	DC	24:17
Depart from me, ye c., into		29:28
I shall say: Depart, ye c.		29:41
servant John, I c. the waters.		61:14
in the beginning c. the land,		61:17
I have c. them with a very sore		104: 4
he shall be c. in his life,		104: 5
been c. and smitten because		109:65
C. are all those that shall lift		121:16
whoever he curses shall be c.;		124:93
shalt be c. above all cattle,	Mses	4:20
c. shall be the ground for thy		4:23
shalt be c. from the earth		5:36
Wherefore the Lord c. Lamech,		5:52
God c. the earth with a sore		5:56
residue of the people have I c.		7:20
the Lord c. the earth with a		8: 4
ground which the Lord hath c.		8: 9
c. him as pertaining to the	Abr	1:26

CURSES
are the c. of God upon her,	DC	113:10
whoever he c. shall be cursed;		124:93

CURSETH
and c. the land unto them for	1Ne	17:38
cometh that he c. your riches,	He	13:31

CURSING
Or, that a c. should come upon	2Ne	1:18
may not be cursed with a sore c.;		1:22
that the c. may be taken from		4: 6
caused the c. to come upon them,		5:21
yea, even a sore c.,		5:21
cursed even with the same c.		5:23
And because of their c. which		5:24
they are cursed with a sore c.,	Jac	3: 3
and the c. which hath come		3: 5
the c. and the blessing of God	Al	45:16
them a c. instead of a blessing.	DC	24: 6
them a c. instead of a blessing.		24: 6
leave a c. instead of a blessing,		24:15
they were nigh unto c.		104: 3
this is a c. which I will put	Mses	5:25

CURSINGS
with the heaviest of all c.	DC	41: 1
by your own works, bring c.,		124:48
and shall be attended with c.		124:120
visited with blessings and not c.,		132:48

CURTAIN
the c. of heaven be unfolded,	DC	88:95

CURTAINS
forth the c. of thy habitations;	3Ne	22: 2
the c. or the strength of Zion.	DC	101:21
thy c. are stretched out still;	Mses	7:30

CUSH
from C., and from Elam, and from	2Ne	21:11

CUSTOM

the c. of the people of Nephi to	Al	8: 7
their c. to bind all the Nephites		17:20
to the c. of the Lamanites.		17:25
the c. among the Lamanites,		47:17
was the c. with the Lamanites,		47:23
which c. they had taken from		47:23
the c. among all the Nephites	3Ne	3:19
the c. of the priest of Pharaoh,	Abr	1: 8

CUT 224 DAMNED

CUT
c. off from the presence of	1Ne 2:21
from thee, that I c. thee not off.	20: 9
should not have been c. off nor	20:19
fight against Zion shall be c. off.	22:19
be c. off from among the people.	22:20
that ye be c. off and destroyed	2Ne 1:17
shall be c. off from my presence.	1:20
or, by the law men are c. off.	2: 5
the temporal law they were c. off;	2: 5
shall be c. off from my presence.	4: 4
shall be c. off from the presence	5:20
were c. off from his presence.	5:20
thou not he that hath c. Rahab,	8: 9
were c. off from the presence	9: 6
the sycomores are c. down,	19:10
will the Lord c. off from Israel	19:14
and c. off nations not a few.	20: 7
he shall c. down the thickets	20:34
of Judah shall be c. off;	21:13
Art thou c. down to the ground,	24:12
and c. off from Babylon	24:22
that watch for iniquity are c. off;	27:31
c. down that which cumbered	Jac 5:44
he was c. off out of the land	Mos 14: 8
c. off from the face of the earth	Al 9:11
be c. off from the presence of	9:13
been c. off from the presence of	9:14
been c. off from his presence,	9:14
shall be c. off from his presence.	36:30
shall be c. off from his presence.	37:13
as they were c. off from the tree of	42: 6
should be c. off from the face of	42: 6
that our first parents were c. off	42: 7
were c. off from the presence of	42: 9
being c. off from the presence of	42:11
to be c. off from his presence.	42:14
he thought to c. off the people	46:30
c. off the course of Amalickiah	46:31
he c. off all the strongholds of	50:11
did seek to c. off the strength and	50:12
be c. off from the presence of	50:20
c. his way through to the city	52:34
being c. off from their support	57:11
c. them off from their support	58:15
c. off the spies of the Lamanites	58:20
when they had c. them off,	58:21
Coriantumr did c. down the watch	He 1:20
go forth and c. his way through	1:23
and c. them down to the earth.	1:24
be c. off from my presence.	12:21
being c. off from the presence of	14:16
for they are c. off again as to	14:18
c. off the people of Nephi from	3Ne 4:16
should c. them off from all their	4:16
did c. off the way of their retreat,	4:24
c. off in their places of retreat.	4:26
all thine enemies shall be c. off.	20:17
be c. off from among the people.	20:23
be c. off from among my people	21:11
all their enemies shall be c. off.	21:13
I will c. off thy horses out of the	21:14
I will c. off the cities of thy land,	21:15
I will c. off witchcrafts out of	21:16
graven images I will also c. off,	21:17
I c. off from among my people,	21:20
c. them off from the face of	Mrm 3:10
shall be c. off from the face of	3:15
strongholds did c. them off	5: 4
are fully ripe ye shall be c. off	Eth 2:15
he was c. off from the presence	10:11
be c. off while in the thought,	Mro 8:14
c. off from among the people;	DC 1:14
watches not for me shall be c. off.	45:44
be detected and shall be c. off,	50: 8
who are c. off from my church,	50: 8
if otherwise, they will be c. off.	51: 2
not faithful, they shall be c. off,	52: 6
I will c. my work short in	52:11
be c. off in mine own due time,	56: 3
shall be c. off out of my church,	56:10
otherwise they shall be c. off.	63:63
c. off out of the land of Zion,	64:35
as the stone which is c. out of	65: 2

DAMNED
be c. short in righteousness—	DC 84:97
but they shall be c. asunder,	85: 9
to have been c. off from the church,	85:11
in his time, will c. off those wicked,	101:90
Inasmuch as ye are c. off for	104: 9
that thy work may be c. short	109:59
and their hopes may be c. off;	121:14
be c. off from among the people.	133:63
And shall c. him asunder,	JS 1:54
They shall be c. off from among	1:55
be c. off from among the people,"	2:40
of mine, I should be c. off;	2:59

CUTLER, Alpheus
C., William Huntington. DC 124:132

CUTS
that it c. you to your hearts	Mos 13: 7

CUTTETH
it c. them to the very center.	1Ne 16: 2

CUTTING
c. them off by thousands and	3Ne 4:21

DAGGERS
d. placed to pierce their souls	Jac 2: 9

DAILY
calling on the name of the Lord d.,	Mos 4:11
And he did exhort them d., with	Al 21:23
and supplication to God d.,	31:10
that ye live in thanksgiving d.,	34:38
his armies, which did increase d.	50:12
thus seeing our forces increase d.,	56:29
behold, they are flocking to us d.,	61: 6
having many revelations d.,	He 11:23
receiving d. an addition to their	11:25
who do add to their numbers d.	15: 6
angels did minister unto him d.	3Ne 7:18
this shall suffice for thy d. walk,	DC 19:32
maintenance by his d. labor,	JS 2:23

DAMAGE
d. thereof was exceeding great,	3Ne 8:15

DAMAGES
d. which they have sustained,	DC 123: 2

DAMASCUS
For the head of Syria is D.,	2Ne 17: 8
and the head of D., Rezin;	17: 8
before the riches of D.	18: 4
Is not Samaria as D.?	20: 9

DAMNATION
drinketh d. to his own soul;	Mos 2:33
men drink d. to their own souls	3:18
have drunk d. to their own souls.	3:25
to the resurrection of endless d.,	16:11
hath subjected them, which is d.	16:11
shall reap the d. of their souls,	Al 9:28
evil shall have everlasting d.	He 12:26
and drinketh d. to his soul;	3Ne 18:29
evil, to the resurrection of d.;	26: 5
might bring d. upon your souls?	Mrm 8:33
Again, it is written *eternal d.*;	DC 19: 7
that believe not unto eternal d.;	29:44
vipers shall not escape the d. of	121:23

DAMNED
to the end, they must be d.;	2Ne 9:24
How shall we look when we are d.?	Al 14:21
even with the pains of a d. soul.	36:16
and is not baptized, shall be d.	3Ne 11:34
rather the sorrowing of the d.	Mrm 2:13
dwell with the d. souls in hell.	9: 4
he that believeth not shall be d.;	9:23
he that believeth not shall be d.,	Eth 4:18
that doeth them not shall be d.	DC 42:60
receiveth him not shall be d.—	49: 5
with slothfulness, the same is d.	58:29
that believeth not shall be d.	68: 9

DAMNED 225 DARKNESS

be d., and shall not come into DC 84:74
and is not baptized, shall be d. 112:29
not that covenant; then are ye d.; 132: 4
abide the law, or he shall be d., 132: 6
but shall be d., saith the Lord. 132:27
repented not, should be d.; Mses 5:15

DAMNING
the most d. hand of murder, DC 123: 7

DANCE
they began to d., and to sing, and 1 Ne 18: 9
and satyrs shall d. there. 2 Ne 23:21
together to sing, and to d., Mos 20: 1
together to sing and to d. 20: 2
gathered together to d., 20: 5
am fair, and I will d. before him, Eth 8:10

DANCED
the daughter of Jared d. before Eth 8:11

DANCING
d., and with a prayer of praise DC 136:28

DANGER
for war, according to their d.; Al 48:15
that when they saw the d., 53:13
Antipus, beholding our d., 56:38
in d. of the judgment of God; 3 Ne 12:21
shall be in d. of his judgment. 12:22
shall be in d. of the council; 12:22
shall be in d. of hell fire. 12:22
lest he shall be in d. of hell fire. Mrm 8:17
same is in d. to be hewn down 8:21
they are in d. of death, hell, and Mro 8:21

DANGEROUS
exceedingly precarious and d., Al 46: 7
Nephites in those d. circumstances 52:14
in the most d. circumstances. 53: 9
d. circumstances at this time. 53:15
unjust, and d. to the peace DC 134:12

DANGERS
are many d. upon the waters, DC 61: 4

DANIEL: see also MILES, Daniel; and STANTON, Daniel.
spoken of by D. the prophet. DC 116: 1
spoken of by D. the prophet, JS 1:12
spoken of by D. the prophet, 1:32

DARE
not d. to look up to our God; Al 12:14

DARED
not deny, it neither d. I do it; JS 2:25

DARING
d. not to give a full account of Mrm 5: 9

DARK
dream, a d. and dreary wilderness. 1 Ne 8: 4
I was in a d. and dreary waste. 8: 7
they became a d., and loathsome, 12:23
And their works are in the d.; 2 Ne 27:27
their works shall be in the d., 28: 9
the light, but must perish in the d. 32: 4
skins of the Lamanites were d., Al 3: 6
the d. veil of unbelief was being 19: 6
did slay them even until it was d. 51:32
wilderness, even until it was d. 56:40
immediately, before it was yet d., 3 Ne 19: 2
shall become a d., a filthy, and Mrm 5:15
daylight is from the d. night. Mro 7:15
long time, in a cloudy and d. day. DC 109:61
the d. and benighted dominion of 121: 4
in all their d. and hellish hue, 123: 6
Which d. and blackening deeds 123:10
and their works were in the d., Mses 5:51
their own counsels in the d.; 6:28
until the room was again left d., JS 2:43

DARKENED
is d. in the heavens thereof. 2 Ne 15:30
Lord of Hosts is the land d., 19:19
sun shall be d. in her going forth, 23:10
endless, that can never be d.; Mos 16: 9
the night shall not be d.; He 14: 4
the sun shall be d. and refuse 14:20
and your mind became d. DC 10: 2
shall come the sun shall be d., 29:14
shall come the sun shall be d., 34: 9
the sun shall be d., and the 45:42
minds in times past have been d., 84:54
be weary in mind, neither d., 84:80
day the heavens shall be d., Mses 7:61
the sun shall be d., and the JS 1:33

DARKEST
I was in the d. abyss; but now Mos 27:29
yea, even in the d. abyss, Al 26: 3

DARKNESS
for the space of many hours in d., 1 Ne 8: 8
there arose a mist of d.; 8:23
an exceeding great mist of d., 8:23
forward through the mist of d., 8:24
I saw a mist of d. on the 12: 4
I saw the vapor of d., that it passed 12: 5
the mists of d. are the temptations 12:17
concerning the three days of d. 19:10
by smoke, and vapor of d., and 19:11
to them that sit in d. 21: 9
out of obscurity and out of d.; 22:12
the bringing of them out of d. 2 Ne 3: 5
unto light—yea, out of hidden d. 3: 5
of his servant, that walketh in d. 7:10
all manner of secret works of d. 9: 9
destroy the secret works of d., 10:15
that put d. for light, and light for 15:20
and light for d., 15:20
behold, d. and sorrow, 15:30
and behold trouble, and d., 18:22
and shall be driven to d. 18:22
The people that walked in d. 19: 2
for their works were works of d., 25: 2
choose works of d. rather than light, 26:10
of murder, and works of d.; 26:22
the Lord God worketh not in d. 26:23
out of obscurity and out of d. 27:29
scales of d. shall begin to fall 30: 6
no work of d. save it shall be 30:17
of the d. of their skins; Jac 3: 9
they walked in the midst of d., Al 5: 7
the cloud of d. having been 19: 6
the Lamanites, were in d., 26: 3
encircled about with everlasting d. 26:15
then cometh the night of d. 34:33
the mysteries and the works of d., 37:21
his people began to work in d., 37:22
shall shine forth in d. unto light, 37:23
secret works, their works of d., 37:23
bring forth out of d. unto light 37:25
have been brought out of d. and 37:26
they should fall into d. also 37:27
come upon all those workers of d., 37:28
come upon these workers of d. 37:30
unto those workers of d. 37:31
shall be cast out into outer d.; 40:13
the souls of the wicked, yea, in d., 40:14
from that endless night of d., 41: 7
and fall into the works of d., 45:12
Moroni went forth in the d. 62:20
overshadowed with a cloud of d., He 5:28
as if it were above the cloud of d., 5:29
and behold the cloud of d., 5:31
the cloud of d. which did 5:34
he saw through the cloud of d. 5:36
cloud of d. may be removed 5:40
cloud of d. shall b. removed 5:41
the cloud of d. was dispersed. 5:42
the cloud of c. was dispersed 5:43
works of d. and abominations 6:28
to still carry on the work of d., 6:29

DARKNESS

doth carry on his works of d.	He	6:30
their secret works of d.;		8: 4
their secret works of d., and		10: 3
will ye choose d. rather than light?		13:29
he cometh there shall be no d.,		14: 3
that d. should cover the face of		14:27
down of the sun there was no d.;	3Ne	1:15
was no d. when the night came.		1:15
was no d. in all that night,		1:19
d. for the space of three days		8: 3
d. upon the face of the land.		8:19
thick d. upon all the face of		8:20
could feel the vapor of d.;		8:20
be no light, because of the d.,		8:21
so great were the mists of d. which		8:22
because of the d. and the great		8:23
the d. dispersed from off the face		10: 9
by the vapor of smoke and of d.		10:13
thy whole body shall be full of d.		13:23
the light that is in thee be d.,		13:23
be darkness, how great is that d.!		13:23
be brought out of d. unto light,	Mrm	8:16
and it shall shine forth out of d.,		8:16
and the works of d.		8:27
shall cross this great water in d.?	Eth	2:22
across this raging deep in d.;		3: 3
that they may shine forth in d.;		3: 4
caused stones to shine in d.,		6: 3
not cross the great waters in d.		6: 3
the people, to keep them in d.,		8:16
out of obscurity and out of d.,	DC	1:30
the light which shineth in d.,		6:21
the d. comprehendeth it not.		6:21
they love d. rather than light,		10:21
the light which shineth in d.,		10:58
the d. comprehendeth it not.		10:58
the light which shineth in d.,		11:11
light which cannot be hid in d.;		14: 9
will disperse the powers of d.		21: 6
powers of Satan and from d.!		24: 1
they love d. rather than light,		29:45
a light which shineth in d.		34: 2
the d. comprehendeth it not;		34: 2
have I kept in chains of d.		38: 5
veil of d. shall soon be rent,		38: 8
the powers of d. prevail upon		38:11
a light which shineth in d.		39: 2
the d. comprehendeth it not;		39: 2
a light that shineth in d. and		45: 7
the d. comprehendeth it not.		45: 7
forth among them that sit in d.,		45:28
edify is not of God, and is d.		50:23
may chase d. from among you;		50:25
unto those who sit in d. and		57:10
to cast down to the regions of d.		77: 8
dominions, and d. reigneth;		82: 5
in sin, and groaneth under d.		84:49
under sin and d. even now.		84:53
The light shineth in d.,		88:49
the d. comprehendeth it not;		88:49
there shall be no d. in you;		88:67
are walking in d. at noon-day.		95: 6
therefore you shall walk in d.		95:12
outer d., where there is weeping,		101:91
forth out of the wilderness of d.,		109:73
unto you, d. covereth the earth,		112:23
gross d. the minds of the people,		112:23
light all the hidden things of d.,		123:13
ye were delivered over unto d.		133:72
shall go away into outer d.,		133:73
for it is d. unto me?	Mses	1:15
and I caused d. to come up		2: 2
divided the light from the d.		2: 4
and the d., I called Night;		2: 5
to divide the light from the d.;		2:18
works of d. began to prevail		5:55
whole face of the earth with d.;		7:26
were reserved in chains of d.		7:57
d. shall cover the earth;		7:61
d. reigned upon the face of	Abr	4: 2
it to be divided, from the d.		4: 4
and the d. they called Night.		4: 5
to divide the light from the d.		4:17

DAUGHTERS

I must either remain in d.	JS	2:13
Thick d. gathered around me,		2:15
why should the powers of d.		2:20
DART		
guiver, and the d., and the javelin,	Jar	1: 8
DARTS		
the fiery d. of the adversary	1Ne	15:24
all the fiery d. of the adversary;	DC	3: 8
all the fiery d. of the wicked;		27:17
DASH		
also d. the young men to pieces,	DC	23:18
waves shall d. upon you.	Eth	2:24
DASHED		
also shall be d. to pieces	DC	23:16
for they will be d. in pieces;	Eth	2:23
DATE		
all records that are of ancient d.;	Mos	8:13
and they are of ancient d. and	3Ne	3: 9
heard with his ears, giving the d.,	DC	128: 3
DATED		
is d. September 24th, 1890,	DC	OD
DAUGHTER		
took the eldest d. of Ishmael	1Ne	16: 7
thy neck, O captive d. of Zion.	2Ne	8:25
Lift up the voice, O d. of Gallim;		20:30
the mount of the d. of Zion,		20:32
thou, nor thy son, nor thy d.,	Mos	13:18
the son and the d. mourning for		21: 9
and the d. for the brother,	Al	28: 5
thy neck, O captive d. of Zion.	3Ne	20:37
Now the d. of Jared being	Eth	8: 8
the d. of Jared was exceeding		8: 9
the d. of Jared danced before		8:11
it was the d. of Jared who put		8:17
gave unto Akish his d. to wife.		9: 4
beautiful garments, O d. of Zion;	Mro	10:31
unto you, Emma Smith my d.;	DC	25: 1
woman, who was the d. of Ham,	Abr	1:23
Ham, and the d. of Egypt,		1:23
of Egypt, the d. of Ham,		1:25
Mack, d. of Solomon Mack);	JS	2: 4
I first saw my wife (his d.),		2:57
DAUGHTERS		
take the d. of Ishmael to wife.	1Ne	1:hd
his sons should take d. to wife,		7: 1
and two of the d. of Ishmael,		7: 6
wife, and his three other d.		7: 6
one of the d. of Ishmael,		7:19
one of the d. of Ishmael to wife;		16: 7
took of the d. of Ishmael to wife;		16: 7
the d. of Ishmael did mourn		16:35
thy d. shall be carried upon their		21:22
their d. have been carried upon		22: 6
of Laman, his sons, and his d.,	2Ne	4: 3
Behold, my sons, and my d.,		4: 3
the sons and d. of my first-born,		4: 3
But behold, my sons and my d.,		4: 5
to the sons and d. of Laman,		4: 8
caused the sons and d. of Lemuel to		4: 8
behold, my sons and my d., who		4: 9
are the sons and the d. of my second		4: 9
unto the sons and d. of Laman;		4: 9
and thy d. shall be carried upon		6: 6
the d. of Zion are haughty,		13:16
of the head of the d. of Zion,		13:17
the filth of the d. of Zion,		14: 4
mourning of the d. of my people	Jac	2:31
cries of the fair d. of this people,		2:32
captive the d. of my people		2:33
his wife, and his sons, and his d.,	Mos	2: 5
and their sons, and their d.,		2: 5
of Christ, his sons, and his d.;		5: 7
have become his sons and his d.		5: 7
their fair d. should stand forth		19:13
the d. of the Lamanites did gather		20: 1

DAUGHTERS / DAY

the d. of the Lamanites	Mos	20: 4
of the d. of the Lamanites		20: 5
that their d. had been missing,		20: 6
carry away the d. of my people;		20:15
stolen the d. of the Lamanites?		20:18
the carrying away of their d.		20:23
stolen the d. of the Lamanites,		21:20
were the d. of the Lamanites,		23:33
to wife the d. of the Lamanites,		25:12
becoming his sons and d.;		27:25
should take one of his d. to wife.	Al	17:24
and his d. mourned over him,		18:43
d. became exceedingly fair,	3Ne	2:16
our mothers and our fair d.,		8:25
fair sons and d. of my people;		9: 2
O ye fair sons and d.,	Mrm	6:19
become my sons and my d.	Eth	3:14
also begat sons and d.		6:15
and they also begat sons and d.		6:16
the d. of the brother of Jared		6:20
of sons and d. of Jared		6:20
And he begat sons and d.;		7: 2
and he begat sons and d.,		7: 4
also begat many sons and d.		7:12
Corihor had many sons and d.		7:14
that Shule begat sons and d.		7:26
and Jared begat sons and d.		8: 1
that he begat sons and d.		8: 4
also to his sons and to his d.		9: 2
also his sons and his d.,		9: 3
and he begat many sons and d.;		9:21
and begat sons and d.;		9:24
he also begat other sons and d.		9:25
and he begat sons and d.		10: 2
begat sons and d. in captivity,		10:14
old age, and begat sons and d.;		10:16
and he begat many sons and d.		10:17
and begat sons and d.;		10:29
neither his fair sons nor d.;		13:17
the fair sons and d. of Cohor;		13:17
the fair sons and d. of Corihor;		13:17
none of the fair sons and d. upon		13:17
many of the d. of the Lamanites	Mro	9: 9
many widows and their d. who		9:16
are sons and d. in my kingdom.	DC	25: 1
begotten sons and d. unto God.		76:24
to the house of the d. of Zion.		124:11
bare unto him sons and d.,	Mses	5: 2
the sons and d. of Adam began		5: 3
they also begat sons and d.		5: 3
unto their sons and their d.		5:12
took one of his brothers' d. to wife,		5:28
he also begat many sons and d.		5:42
and other sons and d.		5:43
and other sons and d.		5:43
and other sons and d.		5:43
among the d. of men		5:53
he begat many sons and d.;		6:11
and begat many sons and d.		6:14
and begat many sons and d.		6:18
and begat sons and d.		6:19
and begat sons and d.		6:20
and begat sons and d.		6:21
and begat sons and d.;		8: 6
and begat sons and d.;		8:10
and d. were born unto them,		8:14
saw that those d. were fair,		8:14
The d. of thy sons have sold		8:15
unto ourselves the d. of men?		8:21
who were the d. of Onitah,	Abr	1:11
who were the d. of Haran.		2: 2

DAUNTED

have d. our freemen that they	Al	61: 4

DAVID: see also DORT, David; FULLMER, David; PATTEN, David W.; and WHITMER, David.

it was told the house of D.,	2Ne	17: 2
Hear ye now, O house of D.;		17:13
no end, upon the throne of D.,		19: 7
such as like unto D. of old	Jac	1:15
which were written concerning D.,	Jac	2:23
D. and Solomon truly had many		2:24
us forth out of the land of D.	Mrm	2: 5
thou art D., and thou art called to	DC	14:11
Behold I say unto, you D.,		30: 1
broken off from the house of D.;		109:63
as also Moses, D., and Solomon,		132: 1
D. also received many wives and		132:38

DAVID'S

D. wives and concubines	DC	132:39

DAVIES, Amos

let my servant D. pay stock into	DC	124:111

DAWN

they awoke at the d. of day	Al	47:14
before the d. of the morning,		56:39

DAY

above that of the sun at noon-d.	1Ne	1: 9
in that d. that they shall rebel		2:23
same yesterday, to-d., and forever;		10:18
merciful unto the Gentiles in that d.,		13:34
bring forth my Zion at that d.,		13:37
shall be lifted up at the last d.,		13:37
in that d. that he shall manifest		14: 1
when the d. cometh that the wrath		14:17
at that d., the work of the Father		14:17
at that d., shall the remnant of		15:14
at that d. will they not rejoice		15:15
at that d., will they not receive		15:15
for the d. should come that they		15:32
should be lifted up at the last d.;		16: 2
before them, leading them by d.		17:30
at this d. about to be destroyed;		17:43
the d. must surely come that they		17:43
the forth d., which we had been		18:14
I did praise him all the d. long;		18:16
all the house of Israel at that d.,		19:11
Nevertheless, when that d. cometh,		19:15
before the d. when thou heardest		20: 7
in a d. of salvation have I helped		21: 8
for the d. soon cometh that all the		22:15
the d. cometh that they must be		22:15
ye shall be saved at the last d.		22:31
if the d. shall come that they will	2Ne	1:10
the law at the great and last d.,		2:26
Wherefore, Joseph truly saw our d.		3: 5
in that d. when my work shall		3:13
he hath heard my cry by d.,		4:23
And by d. have I waxed bold		4:24
the d. cometh that they shall be		6:10
when that d. cometh when they		6:14
hast feared continually every d.,		8:13
at the great and judgment d.		9:22
shall smite them at the last d.		9:33
ye shall know at the last d.,		9:44
for that glorious d. when justice		9:46
even the d. of judgment,		9:46
pray unto him continually by d.,		9:52
When the d. cometh that they		10: 7
alone shall be exalted in that d.		12:11
For the d. of the Lord of Hosts		12:12
the d. of the Lord shall come		12:13
alone shall be exalted in that d.		12:17
In that d. a man shall cast		12:20
In that d. shall he swear,		13: 7
In that d. the Lord will take away		13:18
in that d., seven women shall take		14: 1
In that d. shall the branch of		14: 2
a cloud and smoke by d.		14: 5
in that d. they shall roar against		15:30
from the d. that Ephraim departed		17:17
in that d. that the Lord shall		17:18
In the same d. shall the Lord		17:20
in that d., a man shall nourish		17:21
in that d., every place shall be,		17:23
branch and rush in one d.		19:14
ye do in the d. of visitation,		20: 3
his thorns and his briers in one d.;		20:17
in that d., that the remnant of		20:20

DAY 228 DAY

in that d. that his burden shall	2Ne 20:27
shall he remain at Nob that d.;	20:32
in that d. there shall be a root	21:10
in that d. that the Lord shall	21:11
in the d. that he came up out	21:16
in that d. thou shalt say:	22: 1
in that d. shall ye say:	22: 4
the d. of the Lord is at hand;	23: 6
the d. of the Lord cometh,	23: 9
in the d. of his fierce anger.	23:13
her d. shall not be prolonged.	23:22
in that d. that the Lord shall	24: 3
in that d., that thou shalt	24: 4
in that d. shall they understand	25: 8
when the d. cometh that the Only	25:12
for I have seen his d.,	25:13
when that d. shall come that they	25:16
the d. will come that it must	25:16
shall judge them at the last d.,	25:18
great and terrible shall that d. be	26: 3
the d. that cometh shall burn them	26: 4
the d. that cometh shall consume	26: 6
when that d. shall come they	27: 2
in the d. of the wickedness	27: 8
the d. cometh that the words of	27:11
at that d. when the book shall	27:12
in that d. shall the deaf hear	27:29
in that d. that the churches which	28: 3
for this d. he is not a God	28: 6
the d. shall come that the Lord	28:16
in that d. that they are fully	28:16
at that d. shall he rage in	28:20
arm unto them from d. to day,	28:32
arm unto them from day to d.,	28:32
is lengthened out all the d. long,	28:32
at that d. when I shall proceed	29: 1
shall at that d. be revealed;	30:18
pray continually for them by d.,	33: 3
the end of the d. of probation.	33: 9
are his words, at the last d.;	33:11
at that great and last d.	33:12
until that great d. shall come.	33:13
shall condemn you at the last d.	33:14
be found spotless at the last d.	Jac 1:19
I come up into the temple this d.	2: 2
but I this d. am weighed down	2: 3
that are filthy this d. before God;	3: 3
and one d. they shall become a	3: 6
upon your heads at the last d.	3:10
mine hand almost all the d. long,	5:47
the d. that he shall set his hand	6: 2
is the d., yea, even the last time,	6: 2
hands unto them all the d. long;	6: 4
towards you in the light of the d.,	6: 5
good word of God all the d. long,	6: 7
all the d. long did I cry unto	En 1: 1
some future d. unto the Lamanites,	1:13
And I rejoice in the d. when my	1:27
the sabbath d. holy unto the Lord.	Jar 1: 5
and he wrote it in the d. that he	Om 1: 9
some d. it may profit them.	WM 1: 2
concerning us down to this d.	1: 4
as many as go beyond this d.	1: 4
judged at the great and last d.,	1:11
I shall speak unto you this d.;	Mos 2: 9
ye yourselves are witnesses this d.	2:14
conscience before God this d.	2:15
is preserving you from d. to day,	2:21
is preserving you from day to d.,	2:21
I should declare unto you this d.,	2:30
rise the third d. from the dead;	3:10
this people, at the judgment d.;	3:24
that ye remain from d. to day;	4:24
that ye remain from day to d.;	4:24
of your sins from d. to day,	4:26
of your sins from day to d.,	4:26
this d. he hath spiritually begotten	5: 7
very thankful before God this d.	7:12
And ye all are witnesses this d.,	7:21
in the d. of their transgression;	7:29
and in one d. and a night we did	9:18
they shall howl all the d. lonf.	12: 4
Remember the sabbath d., to keep	13:16
But the seventh d., the sabbath	Mos 13:18
the Lord blessed the sabbath d.,	13:19
to observe strictly from d. to day,	13:30
to observe strictly from day to d.,	13:30
have looked forward to that d.	15:11
against you at the last d.	17:10
And in that d. ye shall be hunted,	17:18
should observe the sabbath d.,	18:23
every d. they should give thanks	18:23
there was one d. in every week	18:25
the d. that they were assembling	18:32
there was one d. a small number	20: 2
did cry mightily from d. to day,	21:10
did cry mightily from day to d.,	21:10
even all the d. long did they cry	21:14
shall be lifted up at the last d.	23:22
and when they had traveled all d.	24:20
I will not receive at the last d.	26:28
Yea, even at the last d.,	27:31
should be saved at the last d.,	Al 1: 4
pursue the Amlicites all that d.,	2:19
Looking forward to that d., thus	4:14
saying unto you, in that d.:	5:16
can lie unto the Lord in that d.,	5:17
can ye look up to God at that d.	5:19
ye will know at that d. that ye	5:21
and witness it unto him this d.	7:15
and it shall be at the last d.,	7:21
should be destroyed in one d.	9: 4
for them in the d. of judgment	9:15
fourth d. of this seventh month,	10: 6
a senine of gold for a d., or a	11: 3
the d. cometh that all shall rise	11:41
the d. of salvation draweth nigh;	13:21
to God that it might be in my d.;	13:25
the d. of your repentance;	13:27
may be lifted up at the last d.	13:29
against them at the last d.	14:11
the twelfth d., in the tenth month,	14:23
the fifth d. of the second month,	16: 1
the fifth d. of the second month	16: 1
in one d. it was left desolate;	16:10
and perhaps until the d. I die.	17:23
that great d. when I made a feast	20: 9
ye shall be cast off at the last d.?	22: 6
may not be cast off at the last d.?	22:15
and be saved at the last d.	22:18
of a d. and a half's journey	22:32
testimony to our God at the last d.,	24:15
at the d. that we shall be brought	24:15
never used them, at this d.	24:16
were joined that d. by more than	24:26
behold they are hunted at this d.	25: 9
yea, all the d. long did ye labor;	26: 5
by the storm at the last d.;	26: 6
will raise them up at the last d.	26: 7
surely this was a sorrowful d.;	28: 6
Choose ye this d., whom ye will	30: 8
support his children at the last d.,	30:60
together on one d. of the week,	31:12
which d. they did call the day of	31:12
they did call the d. of the Lord;	31:12
at the last and judgment d.,	33:22
morning, mid-d., and evening.	34:21
and the d. of your salvation;	34:31
the d. of this life is the day for	34:32
the d. for men to perform their	34:32
the d. of your repentance	34:33
after this d. of life, which is given	34:33
the d. of your repentance even	34:35
become his subjects at the last d.;	34:39
firm hope that ye shall one d. rest	34:41
shall be lifted up at the last d.	36: 3
he will raise me up at the last d.,	36:28
even down to the present d.;	36:29
shall be lifted up at the last d.	37:37
by the power of God, d. by day.	37:40
by the power of God, day by d.	37:40
shall be lifted up at the last d.	38: 5
and receive you at the last d.	38:15
against you at the last d.	39: 8
all is as one d. with God,	40: 8
also, at the last d., be restored	41: 3

DAY 229 DAY

desired to do evil all the d. long	Al 41: 5
in the last d. it shall be restored	42:27
say unto you, that from that d.,	45:12
And when that great d. cometh,	45:13
in that great and dreadful d.,	45:14
they awoke at the dawn of d.	47:14
on the tenth d. of the month,	49: 1
by the labors and heat of the d.	51:33
to give them battle on that d.	52: 1
the second d. in the first month,	56: 1
had fought valiantly by d.	56:16
not pass us by night nor by d.	56:22
thus we did flee all that d.	56:40
in the morning of the third d.	56:42
great strength from d. to day,	58: 5
great strength from day to d.,	58: 5
Lord their God from d. to day;	58:40
Lord their God from day to d.;	58:40
receiving strength from d. to day,	59: 7
receiving strength from day to d.,	59: 7
did not come to battle in that d.	62:19
grow upon them from d. to day.	He 3:36
grow upon them from day to d.	3:36
the very d. that he has delivered	7:20
in his d. which is to come.	8:22
wrath against the d. of judgment.	8:25
liberated on the d. of the burial.	9:18
that it lengthen out the d. for	12:14
in the great and last d.	12:25
the d. shall come that they shall	13:20
in that d. shall they be smitten,	13:20
ye weep and howl in that d.,	13:32
Yea, in that d. ye shall say:	13:33
the d. that he gave us our riches,	13:33
in the d. we have sought them	13:34
in the d. that the word of	13:36
have procrastinated the d. of	13:38
appear unto man as if it was d.	14: 3
shall be one d. and a night and	14: 4
one day and a night and d.,	14: 4
as if it were one d. and there	14: 4
in that d. that he shall suffer	14:20
the d. that they shall give suck;	15: 2
in the d. of my wisdom they shall	15:16
did watch steadfastly for that d.	3Ne 1: 8
day and that night and that d.	1: 8
day which should be as one d.	1: 8
a d. set apart by the unbelievers,	1: 9
unto the Lord, all the d.;	1:12
as light as though it was mid-d.	1:19
it was the d. that the Lord should	1:19
from the robbers d. and night.	3:14
great and terrible was the d.	4: 7
marching out by d. and by night,	4:21
upon them by night and by d.	4:22
with all diligence d. and night.	5: 3
the commencement of my d.;	5:16
on the fourth d. of the month,	8: 5
before this great and terrible d.,	8:24
before this great and terrible d.,	8:25
Sufficient is the d. unto the evil	13:34
Many will say to me in that d.:	14:22
him will I raise up at the last d.	15: 1
in the latter d. shall the truth	16: 7
at that d. when the Gentiles	16:10
shall hang over them at that d.;	20:20
in that d. they shall know that	20:39
And when that d. whall come,	21: 8
For in that d., for my sake	21: 8
it shall come to pass in that d.,	21:14
at that d. whosoever will not	21:20
of the Father commence at that d.,	21:26
at that d. shall the work of the	21:26
at the d. that the Father should	23: 9
may abide the d. of his coming,	24: 2
in that d. when I make up my	24:17
the d. cometh that shall burn as	25: 1
the d. that cometh shall burn	25: 1
in the d. that I shall do this,	25: 3
of the great and dreadful d. of	25: 5
even unto the great and last d.,	26: 4
shall ye be called at the last d.;	27: 5
same shall be saved at the last d.	3Ne 27: 6
before my Father at that d.	27:16
spotless before me at the last d.	27:20
shall be lifted up at the last d.	27:22
in that d. will I visit them,	27:32
the d. of their transfiguration,	28:17
before the great and coming d.	28:31
by them, before that judgment d.	28:32
not receive them at the last d.;	28:34
shall take place at the last d.;	28:39
until the judgment d. of Christ;	28:40
at that d. they were to receive	28:40
at that d., if ye shall spurn at	29: 4
unto him that shall say at that d.,	29: 7
the d. of grace was passed with	Mrm 2:15
shall be lifted up at the last d.	2:19
unto my god all the d. long	3:12
the d. soon cometh that your	6:21
before him at the judgment d.	7: 7
with you in the d. of judgment.	7:10
d. when it shall be said that	8:26
it shall come in a d. when the	8:27
it shall come in a d. when the	8:28
even in a d. when leaders of	8:28
it shall come in a d. when there	8:29
it shall come in a d. when there	8:31
will uphold such at the last d.	8:31
it shall come in a d. when there	8:32
at that d. when all these things	8:33
which must shortly come at that d.	8:34
in the d. of your visitation—	9: 2
that great d. when the earth	9: 2
in that great d. when ye shall be	9: 2
at that great and last d.	9: 6
until the d. that they shall repent	Eth 4: 6
in that d. that they shall exercise	4: 7
I that speaketh, at the last d.	4:10
unto my name at the last d.,	4:19
against the world at the last d.	5: 4
stand before God at the last d.	5: 6
praise the Lord all the d. long;	6: 9
did rejoice and glory in his d.;	9:22
in the cavity of a rock by d.;	13:13
people became troubled by d.	14:23
and they fought all that d.,	15:15
great and terrible was that d.;	15:17
that they fought all that d.,	15:20
with their shields, all that d.	15:24
Lamanites, in some future d.,	Mro 1: 4
and great glory at the last d.,	7:35
has the d. of miracles ceased?	7:35
possessed of it at the last d.,	7:47
if the d. cometh that the power	10:24
the d. when the wrath of God	DC 1: 9
the d. when the Lord shall come	1:10
the d. cometh that they who	1:14
know that the d. speedily cometh;	1:35
and dreadful d. of the Lord.	2: 1
before God at the last d.	4: 2
shalt be lifted up at the last d.	5:35
and reap while the d. lasts,	6: 3
shall be lifted up at the last d.	9:14
in the d. of judgment.	10:23
and reap while the d. lasts,	11: 3
and reap while the d. lasts,	12: 3
and reap while the d. lasts,	14: 3
shall be lifted up at the last d.	17: 8
shall they be called at the last d.;	18:24
the last great d. of judgment,	19: 3
on the sixth d. of the month	20: 1
died, and rose again the third d.;	20:23
on the sixth d. of the month	21: 3
of a trump, both d. and night.	24:12
able to withstand the evil d.,	27:15
against the d. when tribulation	29: 8
is nigh and the d. soon at hand	29: 9
the d. of my coming in a pillar	29:12
before this great d. shall come	29:14
the d. cometh that they will believe	31: 2
shall be a great d. at the time of	34: 8
before that great d. shall come,	34: 9
shall abide the d. of my coming;	35:21

DAY 230 DAY

the judgment of the great d.,	DC 38: 5
But the d. soon cometh that	38: 8
purified shall not abide the d.	38: 8
d. or the hour no man	39:21
in the d. that I shall give them.	41:10
souls in the d. of judgment.	41:12
in that d. when I shall come	42:36
the great d. of the Lord is nigh	43:17
the d. cometh that the Lord	43:18
for the great d. of the Lord;	43:20
the d. cometh when the thunders	43:21
for the great d. of the Lord?	43:21
the great d. of the Lord is come?	43:22
the voice of mercy all the d. long,	43:25
Behold, the d. has come, when	43:26
in the d. that they assemble	44: 2
until a d. of righteousness	45:12
a d. which was sought for by all	45:12
the d. when I shall come in	45:16
the d. of redemption shall come,	45:17
and when that d. shall come,	45:24
in that d. shall be heard of wars	45:26
Even so it shall be in that d.	45:38
the great d. of the Lord to come,	45:39
the d. of the Lord shall come,	45:42
And at that d., when I shall	45:56
the fire, but shall abide the d.	45:57
and the d. no man knoweth,	49: 7
before the great d. of the Lord	49:24
and brighter until the perfect d.	50:24
the d. cometh that you shall	50:45
the d. is not given unto them,	51:17
will lift them up at the last d.	52:44
in the d. of visitation and of	56: 1
in the d. of visitation, and of	56:16
the d. cometh that ye shall be	58: 4
cometh the d. of my power;	58:11
prepared for the great d.	58:11
sacraments upon my holy d.;	59: 9
this is a d. appointed unto you	59:10
that on this, the Lord's d.,	59:12
on this d. thou shalt do none	59:13
in the d. when I shall make up	60: 4
them in the d. of judgment.	60:15
may abide the d. of his coming,	61:39
the d. of wrath shall come upon	63: 6
the d. of transfiguration shall	63:20
in the d. of the coming of the	63:53
in that d. will I send mine	63:54
For this is a d. of warning,	63:58
and not a d. of many words.	63:58
the d. cometh that all things	63:59
And after that d., I, the Lord,	64:22
verily it is a d. of sacrifice,	64:23
a d. for the tithing of my	64:23
the d. shall come when the	64:43
also observe the Sabbath d.	68:29
of them in the d. of judgment.	70: 4
shall be lifted up at the last d.	75:16
in the d. of judgment you shall	75:21
heathen in the d. of judgment,	75:22
and be lifted up at the last d.	75:22
on the sixteenth d. of February,	76:11
on the seventh d. he finished	77:12
until the d. of redemption.	78:12
until the d. of redemption.	82:21
upon you who are present this d.,	84:42
against the d. of vengeance and	85: 3
none inheritance in that d.,	85: 9
in that d. shall not find an	85:11
unto the Lord d. and night,	86: 5
until the d. of the Lord come;	87: 8
the sun giveth his light by d.,	88:45
the d. shall come when you	88:49
until that great and last d.,	88:102
then cometh the d. when the arm	90:10
that d., that every man shall hear	90:11
walking in darkness at noon-d.	95: 6
the creator of the first d.,	95: 7
pass over by night and by d.,	97:23
they shall be mine in that d.	101: 3
in the d. of their trouble.	101: 7
In the d. of their peace they	101: 8
but, in the d. of their trouble,	DC 101: 8
in the d. of wrath I will	101: 9
in that d. all who are found	101:12
Until the d. cometh when there is	101:21
in that d. the enmity of man,	101:26
in that d. whatsoever any man	101:27
in that d. Satan shall not have	101:28
In that d. an infant shall not die	101:30
in that d. when the Lord shall	101:32
own sins in the d. of judgment.	101:78
This d. a general council of	102: 1
Satan until the d. of redemption.	104: 9
There has been a d. of calling,	105:35
has come for a d. of choosing;	105:35
that d. shall not overtake you as	106: 5
Before his d. it was called	107: 3
be fulfilled upon you in that d.	108: 6
as thou didst in the d. of battle,	109:28
upon those on the d. of Pentecost;	109:36
not faint in the d. of trouble.	109:38
prepared against the d. of burning.	109:46
long time, in a cloudy and dark d.	109:61
be adorned as a bride for that d.	109:74
before the great and dreadful d.	110:14
dreadful d. of the Lord is near,	110:16
d. after day let thy warning	112: 5
day after d. let thy warning voice	112: 5
a d. of wrath, a day of burning,	112:24
d. of burning, a day of desolation,	112:24
a d. of desolation, of weeping,	112:24
Jesus Christ of Latter-d. Saints,	115: 3
Jesus Christ of Latter-d. Saints.	115: 4
on the fourth d. of July next;	115:10
And in one year from this d. let	115:11
the twenty-sixth d. of April next,	118: 5
the heads of the Latter-d. Saints.	121:33
visit them in the d. of visitation,	124: 8
the d. of my visitation cometh	124:10
ye are sealed up unto the d. of	124:124
d. has the god of my fathers	127: 2
of Jesus Christ of Latter-d. Saints.	127:12
great and dreadful d. of the Lord:	128:17
of Jesus Christ of Latter-d. Saints.	128:21
great d. of the Lord is at hand;	128:24
can abide the d. of his coming,	128:24
as Latter-d. Saints, offer unto	128:24
Satan unto the d. of redemption,	132:26
for the great d. of the Lord.	133:10
for ye know neither the d. nor	133:11
dwell in his presence d. and night,	133:35
upon the name of the Lord d. and	133:40
this was the d. of vengeance	133:51
sing the song of the Lamb, d. and	133:56
in the d. when the weak shall	133:58
in the d. that they were given,	133:60
the d. cometh that shall burn as	133:64
the d. that cometh shall burn	133:64
d. when I came unto mine own,	133:66
thousands of the Latter-d. Saints,	135: 3
of Jesus Christ of Latter-d. Saints,	136: 2
cometh the d. of their calamity,	136:35
of Jesus Christ of Latter-d. Saints,	OD
my advice to the Latter-d. Saints.	OD
of Jesus Christ of Latter-d. Saints.	OD
of Jesus Christ of Latter-d. Saints,	OD
in a d. when the children	Mses 1:41
And I, God, called the light D.;	2: 5
the morning were the first d.	2: 5
the morning were the second d.	2: 8
the morning were the third d.	2:13
to divide the d. from the night,	2:14
the greater light to rule the d.,	2:16
the sun to rule over the d.,	2:18
the morning were the fourth d.	2:19
the morning were the fifth d.	2:23
the morning were the sixth d.	2:31
on the seventh d. I, God, ended	3: 2
and I rested on the seventh d.	3: 2
God, blessed the seventh d.,	3: 3
in the d. that I, the Lord God,	3: 4
in the d. that I created it;	3: 9
for in the d. thou eatest thereof	3:17
in the d. ye eat thereof,	4:11

DAY 231 DAYS

garden, in the cool of the d.;	Mses 4:14	travel for the space of many d.,	1Ne 16:15
And in that d. the Holy Ghost	5: 9	traveled for the space of many d.,	16:17
in that d. Adam blessed God	5:10	traveled for the space of many d.	16:33
d. I will deliver thy brother	5:29	for the space of many d.,	17: 7
driven me out this d. from the	5:39	even for the space of many d.	17:52
In the d. that God created man,	6: 8	that thy d. may be long in the	17:55
in the d. when they were created	6: 9	for the space of many d.,	18: 9
since the d. that I created them,	6:28	for the space of three d.;	18:13
Choose ye this d., to serve	6:33	for the space of four d.,	18:15
of righteousness unto this d.	6:41	for the space of many d.	18:23
in the d. I created them;	7:32	the three d. of darkness, which	19:10
in the d. that my Chosen shall	7:39	it meaneth us in the d. to come,	22: 6
that d. they shall be in torment;	7:39	a few more d. and I go the way of	2Ne 1:14
When shall the d. of the Lord	7:45	in the d. of my tribulation	2: 1
the d. of the coming of the Son	7:47	thy d. shall be spent in the service	2: 3
the judgment of the great d.	7:57	the d. of the children of men	2:21
the d. shall come that the earth	7:61	in the last d. of my probation;	2:30
before that d. the heavens	7:61	in the d. of my greatest sorrow	3: 1
the d. of the coming of the Son	7:65	manifest unto them in the latter d.,	3: 5
that d. he saw great tribulations	7:66	of their fathers in the latter d.,	3:12
he saw the d. of the righteous,	7:67	thou shalt be blessed in all thy d.	4:11
have I kept even unto this d.,	Abr 1:31	not many d. after his death,	4:13
was a d. unto the Lord,	3: 4	for the space of many d.	5: 7
that which is to rule the d.,	3: 5	for the space of many d.	5: 7
light which is set to rule the d.,	3: 6	awake as in the ancient d.	8: 9
and, at that d., many followed	3:28	wasteth the d. of his probation,	9:27
the Gods called the light D.,	4: 5	in the last d., when the mountain	12: 2
until the evening they called d.;	4: 5	in the d. of Ahaz the son of	17: 1
which they called d. and night.	4: 5	d. that have not come from the day	17:17
evening that they called d.;	4: 8	in the d. that the prophecies of	25: 7
that they called night and d.	4: 8	worth unto them in the last d.;	25: 8
until the evening they called d.;	4:13	for the space of three d.	25:13
to divide the d. from the night;	4:14	unto you concerning the last d.;	26:14
the greater light to rule the d.,	4:16	concerning the d. when the Lord	26:14
over the d. and over the night,	4:17	in the 1st d., or in the days of	27: 1
until evening that it was d.;	4:19	or in the d. of the Gentiles—	27: 1
until evening that they called d.;	4:23	in the d. of temptation	Jac 1: 7
until evening that they called d.;	4:31	having labored in all his d.	1:10
in the d. that the Gods formed	5: 4	after many d. it bagan to put	5: 6
signifies one d. to a cubit.	Fac 2: 1	nourished for the space of many d.	7:15
One d. in Kolob is equal to	2: 1	we did mourn out our d.	7:26
neither on the Sabbath d.;	JS 1:17	in the course of my d.	En 1:24
But of that d., and hour, no one	1:40	I have declared it in all my d.,	1:26
until the d. that Noah entered	1:42	Wherefore, in my d., I would	Om 1: 2
in a d. when he looketh not	1:53	in the d. of Mosiah, there was	1:20
Jesus Christ of Latter-D. Saints,	2: 1	was born in the d. of Mosiah;	1:23
twenty-third d. of December,	2: 3	in the d. of king Benjamin,	1:24
I was one d. reading the	2:11	until the d. of king Benjamin.	WM 1:10
morning of a beautiful, clear d.,	2:14	all the remainder of his d.	Mos 1: 1
most popular sects of the d.,	2:23	to spend my d. in your service,	2:12
of the religious sects of the d.,	2:28	had spent my d. in your service,	2:16
the d. cometh that shall burn as	2:37	has spent his d. in your service,	2:19
and dreadful d. of the Lord.	2:38	all the remainder of our d.,	5: 5
the d. had not yet come when	2:40	therefore they wandered many d.	7: 4
found that d. was approaching,	2:47	even forty d. did they wander.	7: 4
the necessary labors of the d.;	2:48	they had wandered forty d.	7: 5
twenty-second d. of September,	2:59	they had been in prison two d.	7: 8
in his charge until this d.,	2:60	for the space of many d.,	8: 8
being the second d. of May,	2:60	Six d. shalt thou labor, and do	13:17
On the 5th d. of April, 1829,	2:66	For in six d. the Lord made	13:19
on a certain d. went into	2:68	that thy d. may be long upon	13:20
the fifteenth d. of May, 1829,	2:72	his seed, he shall prolong his d.,	14:10
		being concealed for many d.	17: 4
DAYLIGHT		And after three d., having	17: 6
as the d. is from the dark	Mro 7:15	after many d. there were a	18: 7
		after many d. the Lamanites	21: 2
DAY'S		not many d. before the coming of	21:26
a d. journey for a Nephite,	He 4: 7	after being many d. in the	22:13
hiring out by d. work and	JS 2:55	they had pursued them two d.,	22:16
		in the wilderness for many d.	23:30
DAYS		been in the wilderness twelve d.	24:25
afflictions in the course of my d.,	1Ne 1: 1	space of two d. and two nights,	27:23
favored of the Lord in all my d.;	1: 1	plead with their father many d.	28: 5
record of my proceedings in my d.	1: 1	your king the remainder of my d.;	29:11
dwelt at Jerusalem in all his c.);	1: 4	thus ended the d. of Alma,	29:47
of my proceedings, in my d.	1:17	not many d. after the battle	Al 3:20
when he had traveled three d.	2: 6	I have fasted and prayed many d.	5:46
in the d. of your probation,	10:21	for I had fasted many d.	8:26
in the latter d., when our seed	15:13	And Alma tarried many d.	8:27
be fulfilled in the latter d.;	15:18	your d. shall not be prolonged	9:18
of the Jews in the latter d.	15:19	And not many d. hence	9:26
in the d. of probation,	15:31	for he has fasted many d.	10: 7
in their d. of probation.	15:32	the people in the d. of Noah,	10:22
traveled for the space of four d.,	16:13		

DAYS

beginning of d. or end of years,	Al	13: 7
beginning of d. or end of years,		13: 9
people in the d. of Melchizedek,		13:14
peace in the land in his d.;		13:18
been cast into prison three d.,		14:18
they did mock them for many d.		14:22
had thus suffered for many d.,		14:23
Neverthless, after many d. their		16:11
many d. in the wilderness,		17: 9
in the service of the king three d.,		17:26
space of two d. and two nights;		18:43
after two d. and two nights		19: 1
space of two d. and two nights;		19: 5
and kept in prison for many d.,		20:30
than spend their d. in idleness		24:18
whose d. have been spent in the		26:24
also after the d. of fasting,		30: 2
of three d. and three nights		36:10
for three d. and for three nights		36:16
I was three d. and three nights		38: 8
from the d. of Adam down to the		40:18
until the end of his d.,		41: 6
and has not repented in his d.,		42:28
in the d. of Helaman,		45:hd
which he kept in his d.		45:hd
since the d. of Nephi, than in the		50:23
than in the d. of Moroni,		50:23
the cause of God all his d.,		50:39
endeth the d. of Amalickiah.		51:37
not many d. had passed away		57:12
the remainder of his d. in peace.		62:43
thus ended the d. of Pacumeni.	He	1:21
God all the remainder of his d.,		5: 4
also, all the remainder of his d.;		5: 4
been cast into prison many d.		5:22
that I could have had my d. in		7: 7
in the d. when my father Nephi		7: 7
if my d. could have been in		7: 8
days could have been in those d.,		7: 8
consigned that these are my d.,		7: 9
he will lengthen out their d.		7:24
prophets, from his d. even to		8:16
days even to the d. of Abraham.		8:16
many before the d. of Abraham		8:18
even since the d. of Abraham		8:19
that he did preach, many d.,		13: 2
If our d. had been in the days		13:25
in the d. of our fathers of old,		13:25
and in the d. of your poverty		13:31
And in the d. of your poverty		13:32
be your language in those d.		13:37
your d. of probation are past;		13:38
sought all the d. of your lives for		13:38
there shall be two d. and a night;		14: 4
for the space of three d.,		14:20
earth for the space of three d.		14:27
in the d. of their iniquities		15: 3
hath the Lord prolonged their d.		15: 4
bless them and prolong their d.,		15:10
the Lord shall prolong their d.,		15:11
unto them all the d., of our lives.		16:21
away since the d. of Mosiah,	3Ne	2: 5
it was in the d. of Lachoneus,		6:19
darkness for the space of three d.		8: 3
did last for the space of three d.		8:23
thus did the three d. pass away.		10: 9
as in the d. of old, and as in		24: 4
Even from the d. of your fathers		24: 7
for the space of three d.;		26:13
of their wickedness all my d.;	Mrm	2:19
wise in the d. of your probation;		9:28
transpired from the d. of Adam	Eth	1: 4
hundred and forty and four d.		6:11
in righteousness all his d.,		7: 1
whose d. were exceeding many.		7: 1
no more wars in the d. of Shule;		7:27
in righteousness all his d.		7:27
in the d. of the reigns of Omer		8: 4
in captivity the half of his d.		8: 4
and traveled many d., and came		9: 3
having seen exceeding many d.,		9:15
in righteousness all his d.,		9:21

unto his people in all his d.	Eth	9:23
remain in captivity all his d.;		10:14
the sight of the Lord all his d.;		10:17
and after he had seen many d.		10:17
in the d. of Lib the poisonous		10:19
all the remainder of his d.		10:30
lived in captivity all his d.		10:31
dwelt in captivity all his d.;		10:31
dwelt in captivity all his d.;		10:31
dwelt in captivity all his d.;		10:31
in the d. of Com there began		10:33
came also in the d. of Com		11: 1
in all the remainder of his d.		11: 3
to pass in the d. of Shiblom.		11: 7
did dwell in captivity all his d.		11: 9
reign over the people all his d.		11:10
manner of iniquity in his d.,		11:10
and few were his d.		11:10
that which was wicked in his d.		11:11
in the d. of Ethem there came		11:12
judgment in wickedness all his d.;		11:14
all the remainder of his d.		11:18
dwelt in captivity all his d.		11:19
in the d. of Coriantor there		11:20
dwelt in captivity all his d.		11:23
the d. of Ether were in the days		12: 1
were in the d. of Coriantumr;		12: 1
forth in the d. of Coriantumr,		12: 2
Ether saw the d. of Christ,		13: 4
for the space of three d.		13:28
for the space of three d.		14:26
I have chosen in these last d.	DC	1: 4
that thy d. may be prolonged,		5:33
that they might preach in their d.,		10:48
that you should labor all your d.		18:15
Chruch of Christ in these last d.,		20: 1
his d. of rejoicing are come unto		21: 8
up unto me, even as in d. of old.		22: 3
even unto the end of thy d.		24: 8
began, concerning the last d.;		27: 6
the prince of all, the ancient of d.;		27:11
man the d. of his probation—		29:43
the d. of thy deliverance are		39:10
have sent forth in these last d.,		39:11
as with men in d. of old,		45:10
as unto men in d. of old.		45:15
called and chosen in these last d.,		52: 1
the d. come that I will send		52:11
And the d. have come;		52:20
have raised up in these last d.		53: 1
like as it was in ancient d.,		58:17
up in righteousness on all d.		59:11
as with men in d. of old.		61:13
in the last d., by the mouth		61:14
the d. will come that no flesh		61:15
it shall be said in d. to come		61:16
in the last d. have I blessed it,		61:17
not to be mocked in the last d.		63:58
My disciples, in d. of old, sought		64: 8
for his saints in these last d.,		64:30
the land of Zion in these last d.		64:34
my church in these last d.		64:37
be prepared for the d. to come,		65: 5
to be revealed in the last d.,		66: 2
and apostles in d. of old.		66: 2
Tarry not many d. in this place;		66: 6
in the d. of the apostles		74: 2
of my kingdom from d. of old,		76: 7
God made the world in six d.,		77:12
Jewish nation in the last d.,		77:15
who is without beginning of d.		78:16
established in the last d. for		84: 2
lived in the d. of Abraham,		84:13
is without beginning of d. or		84:17
at the time he was eight d. old		84:28
in d. when I was with them,		84:77
in ancient d., built up my church		84:108
of abomination in the last d.		84:117
in the last d., even now while		86: 4
after many d., slaves shall rise		87: 4
in their hours, in their d.,		88:44
the d. will come that you shall		88:68

DAYS 233 DEAD

not many d. hence and the	DC 88:87	DAY'S		
of all saints in the last d. –	89: 2	He taketh three d. journey into	1Ne	1:hd
of conspiring men in the last d.,	89: 4	after many d. wandering in the	Mos	9: 4
and not be idle in her d. from	90:31	they fled eight d. journey into		23: 3
after many d. all things were	101:62			
have power after many d. to	105:37	DAYTIME		
the church, in ancient d., called	107: 4	for a shadow in the d.	2Ne	14: 6
was instituted in the d. of Adam,	107:41	he did hide himself in the d.	Mos	18: 5
ninety-six years and seven d. old	107:46	and traveled three d. journey	Al	8: 6
prophets, concerning the last d.	109:23			
the wicked, in the last d. –	109:45	DEACON		
the last d. and for the last time,	112:30	Every elder, priest, teacher, or d.	DC	20:60
of my people in the last d.	113: 6	Each priest, teacher, or d.,		20:64
God should call in the last d.,	113: 8	the offices of teacher and d. are		84:30
my church be called in the last d.,	115: 4	teacher, d., and member.		107:10
or the Ancient of D. shall sit,	116: 1	from d. to teacher, and from		107:63
all the appointed d., months,	121:31	president over the office of a d.		107:85
all the d. of their days, months,	121:31			
of their d., months, and years,	121:31	DEACONS		
in the d. of the dispensation of	121:31	the elders, priests, teachers, d.,	DC	20:38
Thy d. are known, and thy years	122: 9	elders, priests, teachers, and d.;		20:39
only in the d. of your poverty,	124:30	other priests, teachers, and d.		20:48
common lot all the d. of my life;	127: 2	by the d. if occasion requires.		20:57
to be revealed in the last d.,	128:17	But neither teachers nor d.		20:58
be revealed from the d. of Adam	128:18	the teachers or d. of the church.		20:84
to hold this power in the last d.,	132: 7	the d. and teachers should be		84:111
in the d. before it was divided.	133:24	priests, even down to the d. –		88:127
carried them all the d. of old.	133:53	in like manner, and also the d. –		107:62
d. previous to his assassination,	135: 4	is to preside over twelve d.,		107:85
arm is stretched out in the last d.,	136:22	· also the president of the d. and		124:142
calamity, even the d. of sorrow,	136:35			
the d. of Adam to Abraham,	136:37	DEAD		
I am without beginning of d.	Mses 1: 3	he should rise from the d., and	1Ne	10:11
even unto the end of thy d.;	1:26	saying: Our father is d.; yea, and		16:35
and for seasons, and for d.,	2:14	to pass the ressurrection of the d.,	2Ne	2: 8
dust shalt thou eat all the d.	4:20	it must needs remain as d.,		2:11
shalt thou eat of it all the d.	4:23	temporal, shall deliver up its d.;		9:11
And after many d. an angel	5: 6	death, shall deliver up its d.;		9:12
For, from the d. of Cain,	5:51	and hell must deliver up their d.,		9:12
the d. of Adam, after he had	6:11	for the living to hear from the d.?		18:19
all the d. that Adam lived	6:12	it stirreth up the d. for thee,		24: 9
and prophesied in all his d.,	6:13	he shall rise from the d.,		25:13
d. Satan had great dominion	6:15	Messiah hath risen from the d.,		25:14
All the d. of Seth were nine	6:16	the law hath become d. unto us,		25:25
the d. of Enos were nine hundred	6:18	Christ shall have risen from the d.		26: 1
d. of Cainan were nine hundred	6:19	speak as if it were from the d.		27:13
all the d. of Mahalaleel were	6:20	healing the sick, raising the d.,	Mos	3: 5
d. of Jared were nine hundred	6:24	rise the third day from the d.;		3:10
beginning of d. or end of years,	6:67	did help to bury their d.		9:19
in his d., that he built a city	7:19	to pass the resurrection of the d.,		13:35
d. of wickedness and vengeance.	7:46	and hath power over the d.;		15:20
even so will I come in the last d.,	7:60	to pass the resurrection of the d.		15:20
in the d. of wickedness and	7:60	Christ had not risen from the d.,		16: 7
Son of Man, in the last d.,	7:65	the resurrection of the d.,		18: 2
And all the d. of Zion,	7:68	until you are d. as to the mortal		18:13
d. of Enoch, were three hundred	7:68	among the number of their d.;		20:12
d. of Enoch were four hundred	8: 1	yet he was not d., having been		20:12
the d. of Methuselah were	8: 7	has fallen among their d.,		20:13
d. of Lamech were seven hundred	8:11	the resurrection of the d.,		26: 2
his d. shall be an hundred	8:17	had finished burying their d.	Al	3: 1
those d. there were giants on	8:18	of the resurrection of the d.		4:14
wisely and justly all his d.,	Abr 1:26	being d. unto all good works.		5:42
in the d. of the first patriarchal	1:26	that all shall rise from the d.		11:41
many as to its number of d.,	3: 5	the resurrection of the d.,		12: 8
that they numbered the d.;	4:13	that all shall rise from the d.,		12: 8
and for d. and for years,	4:14	that man should rise from the d.		12:20
them that give suck in those d.;	JS 1:16	after the resurrection of the d.		12:24
For then, in those d., shall be	1:18	been no resurrection of the d.;		12:25
except those d. should be	1:20	to pass the resurrection of the d.,		12:25
those d. shall be shortened.	1:20	their d. bodies were heaped up		16:11
those d. which shall come upon	1:21	also the resurrection of the d.,		16:19
in those d. there shall also	1:22	unto the earth, as if he were d.		18:42
after the tribulation of those d.,	1:33	and he lay as if he were d.		18:43
the d. will come, that heaven	1:35	the purpose of burying their d.		19: 1
after the tribulation of those d.,	1:36	and some say that he is not d.,		19: 5
But as it was in the d. of Noah,	1:41	but others say that he is d.		19: 5
as it was in the d. which were	1:42	and he knew that he was not d.		19: 7
in the last d., two shall be in	1:44	He is not d., but he sleepeth in		19: 8
few d. after I had this vision,	2:21	lay there as though they were d.;		19:18
visions or revelations in these d.;	2:21	to smite him, behold, he fell d.		19:22
to be conducted in the last d.	2:54	that the man had fallen d.,		19:24
Two d. after the arrival of	2:67	the resurrection of the d.,		21: 9

DEAD 234 DEALING

I may be raised from the d.,	Al 22:18	
he was struck as if he were d.	22:18	
she saw him lay as if he were d.,	22:19	
their d. were buried by the people	30: 1	
Now their d. were not numbered	30: 2	
were the d. of the Nephites	30: 2	
after they had buried their d.,	30: 2	
that when a man was d., that was	30:18	
down, even until he was d.	30:59	
he shall rise again from the d.,	33:22	
the resurrection of the d.	40: 1	
to pass the resurrection of the d.	40: 3	
all shall come forth from the d.	40: 4	
men shall come forth from the d.,	40: 5	
that all shall rise from the d.	40: 5	
that they shall rise from the d.;	40: 9	
resurrection of Christ from the d.	40:16	
that the d. shall come forth,	40:21	
as soon as they were d. their	42:11	
to pass the resurrection of the d.;	42:23	
the resurrection of the d. bringeth	42:23	
of their d. was not numbered	44:21	
of their d. was exceeding great,	44:21	
cast their d. into the waters of	44:22	
Now, when Lehonti was d.,	47:19	
their d. and wounded bodies.	49:22	
they found Amalickiah was d.	52: 1	
to go forth and bury their d.,	53: 1	
and also the d. of the Nephites	53: 1	
had finished burying their d.	53: 3	
also the d. of the Nephites,	53: 3	
be taken from among the d.,	57:24	
had buried our d. and also	57:28	
also the d. of the Lamanites,	57:28	
knew that Teancum was d.	62:37	
But behold, he was d.,	62:37	
that he fell d. without a groan.	He 2: 9	
chief judge be true, that he be d..	9: 2	
the chief judge whether he was d.?	9:12	
behold he was d., according to	9:15	
to pass the resurrection of the d.;	14:15	
are considered as d., both as to	14:16	
he shall rise again from the d.	14:20	
shall yield up many of their d.;	14:25	
and became as if they were d.,	3Ne 1:16	
the top thereof until he was d.	4:28	
had hanged him until he was d.	4:28	
brother did he raise from the d.,	7:19	
whom he had raised from the d.,	19: 4	
who should arise from the d.	23: 9	
and raised a man from the d.,	26:15	
heal the sick, and raise the d.,	4Ne 1: 5	
their d. were cast into the sea.	Mrm 3: 8	
survived the d. of our people,	6:11	
to pass the resurrection of the d.,	7: 6	
one should speak from the d.	8:26	
as though I spake from the d.,	9:30	
after he had risen from the d.;	Eth 12: 7	
covered with the bodies of the d.	14:21	
was none left to bury the d.,	14:22	
away as though he were d.	14:30	
and putting trust in d. works.	Mro 8:23	
like as one crying from the d.,	10:27	
Judge of both quick and d.	10:34	
he hath risen again from the d.,	DC 18:12	
neither by your d. works.	22: 2	
it is because of your d. works	22: 3	
even the d. which died in me,	29:13	
then shall all the d. awake,	29:26	
he became spiritually d.,	29:41	
are the d. that die in the Lord,	63:49	
they shall rise from the d. and	63:49	
world the resurrection of the d.	63:52	
of the resurrection of the d.,	76:16	
by the resurrection of the d.,	76:39	
of the ministry and were d.;	77: 5	
the resurrection from the d.	88:14	
the resurrection from the d. is	88:16	
And these are the rest of the d.;	88:101	
the trump shall sound for the d.,	109:75	
baptized for those who are d.—	124:29	
baptisms for your d. shall not	124:32	
as a church, with your d.,	DC 124:32
ordinance of baptizing for the d.	124:33
baptisms for your d. cannot be	124:33
your baptisms for the d.,	124:35
for your baptisms for your d.	124:36
and your baptisms for the d.,	124:39
I will that he should raise the d.,	124:100
relation to the baptism for your d.	127: 5
Lord unto you concerning your d.:	127: 6
of you are baptized for your d.,	127: 6
subject of baptism for the d.,	127:10
subject of the baptism for the d.,	128: 1
for the salvation of the d. who	128: 5
subject in ralation to the d.,	128: 6
And I saw the d., small and great,	128: 6
and the d. were judged out of	128: 6
but the d. were judged out of	128: 7
of the books shall your d. be judged,	128: 8
have kept concerning their d.	128: 8
as well for the d. as for the	128:11
answer to the likeness of the d.,	128:12
of the resurrection of the d. in	128:12
ordinance of baptism for the d.,	128:12
being in likeness of the d.	128:12
to show forth the living and the d.,	128:13
the earth in relation to your d.,	128:14
principles in relation to the d.	128:15
neither can we without our d.	128:15
relation to the baptism for the d.,	128:16
do which are baptized for the d.,	128:16
if the d. rise not at all?	128:16
are they then baptized for the d.?	128:16
namely, the baptism for the d.;	128:17
It is the baptism for the d.	128:18
glad tidings for the d.;	128:19
gladness for the living and the d.;	128:19
Let the d. speak forth anthems	128:22
containing the records of our d.,	128:24
after the resurrection from the d.;	132: 7
have an end when men are d.	132: 7
not remain after men are d.,	132:13
not of force when they are d.,	132:15
exclaiming: *I am a d. man*!	135: 1
was shot d. in the attempt,	135: 1
were both shot after they were d.,	135: 1
The testators are now d.,	135: 5
his resurrection from the d.;	Mses 7:62

DEADLY

if they drink any d. thing	Mrm 9:24
and against d. poisons;	DC 24:13
administer unto him d. poison;	124:98

DEADNESS

may know the d. of the law;	2Ne 25:27
by knowing the d. of the law,	25:27

DEAF

wo unto the d. that will not hear;	2Ne 9:31
the d. hear the words of the book,	27:29
their sight, and the d. to hear,	Mos 3: 5
that are withered, or that are d.,	3Ne 17: 7
unstopped the ears of the d.,	26:15
their sight, and the d. to hear,	4Ne 1: 5
their sight, and the d. to hear,	DC 35: 9
lame, and the blind, and the d.,	58:11
and unstop the ears of the d.;	84:69

DEAFNESS

and the d. of their ears,	Jar 1: 3

DEAL

wouldst d. very treacherously,	1Ne 20: 8
d. justly, judge righteously, and	Al 41:14
my servant shall d. prudently;	3Ne 20:43
every man did d. justly one with	4Ne 1: 2
And let every man d. honestly,	DC 51: 9
for I will d. mercifully with her.	111: 6
a right to d. with their members	134:10
excited a great d. of prejudice	JS 2:22

DEALING

man d. justly, one with another.	3Ne 26:19

DEALINGS 235 DEATH

DEALINGS
knew not the d. of that God	1Ne	2:12
not the d. of the Lord;	Mos	10:14
just are all the d. of the Lord,	Al	50:19
that such d. be for fellowship	DC	134:10

DEALT
d. with you after this manner.	DC	9: 6
d. with as the scriptures direct.		20:80
d. with according to the laws of		42:79
d. with according to the law of		42:81
d. with according to the laws of		82:21

DEAR
by all that is most d. unto us—	Al	44: 5
most d. and precious above all	Mro	9: 9
D. and well beloved brother,	DC	126: 1

DEARLY
these our d. beloved brethren,	Al	26: 9
who have so d. beloved us,		26: 9
those whom they so d. beloved,		27: 4
those who had so d. beloved them—		27: 4
My d. beloved brother, Moroni,		56: 2
Therefore, d. beloved brethren,	DC	123:17
d. beloved brethren and sisters,		128:15

DEARTH
to be a great d. upon the land,	Eth	9:30
fast because of the d.,		9:30

DEATH
after the d. of the temporal body,	1Ne	15:31
suffered all things, save it were d.;		17:20
should be a sign given of his d.		19:10
An account of the d. of Lehi.	2Ne	1:hd
having no life neither d.,		2:11
or to choose captivity and d.,		2:27
And not choose eternal d.,		2:29
not many days after his d.,		4:13
also my father, before his d.;		4:14
as d. hath passed upon all men,		9: 6
that monster, d. and hell,		9:10
which I call the d. of the body,		9:10
and also the d. of the spirit.		9:10
this d., of which I have spoken,		9:11
its dead; which d. is the grave.		9:11
this d. of which I have spoken,		9:12
which is the spiritual d.		9:12
which spiritual d. is hell;		9:12
wherefore, d. and hell must deliver		9:12
from this first d. unto life,		9:15
the devil, and d., and hell,		9:19
that awful monster, d. and hell,		9:26
to be carnally-minded is d.		9:39
choose the way of everlasting d.		10:23
may God raise you from d.		10:25
and also from everlasting d.		10:25
plan of deliverance from d.		11: 5
in the land of the shadow of d.,		19: 2
and also of his d. and resurrection;		26: 3
they are grasped with d., and hell;		28:23
and d., and hell, and the evil,		28:23
believe in Christ, and view his d.,	Jac	1: 8
of Nephi, after the d. of Nephi:		2: 1
awake from the slumber of d.;		3:11
brimstone which is the second d.		3:11
reminding them of d.,	En	1:23
and I have lived to see his d.;	Om	1:23
can suffer, except it be unto d.;	Mos	3: 7
guards should have put you to d.		7:11
said this, they did put him to d.;		7:28
and with the rich in his d.;		14: 9
hath poured out his soul into d.;		14:12
becoming subject even unto d.,		15: 7
God breaketh the bands of d.,		15: 8
having gained the victory over d.;		15: 8
having broken the bands of d.,		15: 9
the bands of d. shall be broken,		15:20
who has broken the bands of d.		15:23
or have broken the bands of d.		16: 7
and that d. should have no sting,		16: 7
the sting of d. is swallowed up		16: 8
that there can be no more d.		16: 9
cause that he should be put to d.	Mos	17: 1
and thou art worthy of d.		17: 7
this cause thou shalt be put to d.		17: 8
and I will suffer even until d.,		17:10
with faggots, yea, even unto d.		17:13
even the pains of d. by fire;		17:15
as I suffer, the pains of d. by fire.		17:18
fell, having suffered d. by fire;		17:20
having been put to d. because		17:20
the truth of his words by his d.		17:20
and sufferings, and d. of Christ,		18: 2
that ye may be in, even until d.,		18: 8
suffer, even unto d. by fire.		19:20
priests also and put them to d.,		19:21
that they should be put to d.		21:23
did mourn for the d. of Abinadi;		21:30
upon God should be put to d.		24:11
repenting nigh unto d.,		27:28
he suffered an ignominious d.	Al	1:15
murdered was punished unto d.		1:18
Christ from the bands of d.		4:14
encircled about by the bands of d.,		5: 7
were the bands of d. broken,		5: 9
loosed from the bands of d.,		5:10
for his wages he receiveth d.,		5:42
And he will take upon him d.,		7:12
he may loose the bands of d.		7:12
the loosing of the bands of d.;		11:41
Now, there is a d. which is		11:42
which is called a temporal d.;		11:42
the d. of Christ shall loose the		11:42
the bands of this temporal d.,		11:42
be raised from this temporal d.		11:42
the d. of the mortal body,		11:45
immortal body, that is from d.,		11:45
even from the first d. unto life,		11:45
spoken plainly concerning d.,		12:12
say unto you then cometh a d.,		12:16
cometh a death, even a second d.,		12:16
death, which is a spiritual d.;		12:16
in his sins, as to a temporal d.,		12:16
shall also die a spiritual d.;		12:16
there would have been no d.,		12:23
that d. comes upon mankind,		12:24
the d. which has been spoken of		12:24
Amulek, which is the temporal d.;		12:24
and after d., they must come to		12:27
thereof being a second d.,		12:32
which was an everlasting d.		12:32
the last d., as well as the first.		12:36
may not suffer the second d.		13:30
from d., and from destruction—		15:17
Son of God, his sufferings and d.,		16:19
the d. and sufferings of Christ,		21: 9
d. of Christ atone for their sins,		22:14
that he breaketh the bands of d.,		22:14
sting of d. should be swallowed		22:14
and would suffer even unto d.		24:19
that they should be put to d.		25: 7
that he should suffer d. by fire.		25: 9
the first that suffered d. by fire		25:11
many should suffer d. by fire,		25:11
should cause many to be put to d.,		25:12
everlasting gulf of d. and misery,		26:20
they never did look upon d. with		27:28
d. was swallowed up to them by		27:28
Therefore, they would suffer d.		27:29
because of d. and destruction		28:14
it be unto d. or unto life;		29: 4
desireth good or evil, life or d.,		29: 5
he was punished unto d.;		30:10
his words they stoned him to d.		33:17
your repentance even until d.,		34:35
by the everlasting chains of d.		36:18
and from bonds, and from d.;		36:27
space betwixt the time of d. and		40: 6
from this time of d. to the time		40: 7
between the time of d. and		40: 9
between d. and the resurrection—		40:11
between d. and the resurrection		40:21
an awful d. cometh upon the		40:26
reclaimed from this temporal d.,		42: 8
upon all mankind a spiritual d.		42: 9
reclaimed from this spiritual d.		42: 9

DEATH   236   DECEIT

the work of d. commenced on	Al 43:37
brought d. almost at every stroke.	43:37
work of d. among the Lamanites.	43:38
the wounds of d. in your bodies,	44: 7
the work of d. should cease again	44:20
his d. or burial we know not of.	45:18
concerning his d. and burial.	45:19
words of Jacob, before his d.,	46:24
back, and put Amalickiah to d.;	46:30
he caused to be put to d.;	46:35
concerning the d. of the king.	47:33
concerning the d. of the king.	47:34
or to put them to d.	51:15
he did cause the d. of the king	51:34
concerning the d. of his brother,	52:12
to carry on after his d.	54: 5
ye shall soon be visited with d.,	54:10
I will seek d. among them	55: 3
fought, yet they did not fear d.;	56:47
keep them, or to put them to d.	57:13
did administer d. unto all those	57:19
are spreading the work of d.	60: 7
fight against it, were put to d.	62: 9
inflicted d. upon all those who	62:11
he had delivered them from d.,	62:50
sacred things, before his d., upon	63:11
before the d. of Shiblon,	63:13
people and condemned unto d.;	He 1: 8
that he was condemned unto d.,	1: 9
found were condemned unto d.	1:12
they did commence the work of d.;	4: 5
they might accuse him to d.—	9:19
as if d. had come upon him.	9:33
the d. of the chief judge,	10:13
he doth visit them with d. and	12: 3
unto you, yea, a sign of his d.	14:14
this d. bringeth to pass the	14:16
all mankind from the first d.—	14:16
the first death-that spiritual d.;	14:16
upon them again a spiritual d.,	14:18
spiritual death, yea, a second d.,	14:18
down unto this second d.	14:19
another sign, a sign of his d.,	14:20
that day that he shall suffer d.	14:20
the time that he shall suffer d.,	14:20
that ye might choose life or d.;	14:31
should be put to d. except he	3Ne 1: 9
spread so much d. and carnage	2:11
they did testify boldly of his d.	6:20
power to condemn any one to d.	6:22
taken and put to d. secretly by	6:23
knowledge of their d. came not	6:23
of the land until after their d.	6:23
that any man should be put to d.	6:24
the prophets of the Lord unto d.,	6:25
and suffered d. by the people.	7:19
fallen upon and crushed to d.;	10:13
had been given concerning his d.	11: 2
broad the way which leads to d.,	27:33
for ye shall never taste of d.;	28: 7
never endure the pains of d.;	28: 8
who were never to taste of d.,	28:25
be that they must taste of d.;	28:37
that they might not taste of d.	28:38
and with that awful fear of d.	Mrm 6: 7
in him is the sting of d. swallowed up.	7: 5
the d. of Christ bringeth to pass	9:13
from this eternal band of d.,	9:13
which d. is a temporal death.	9:13
which death is a temporal d.	9:13
he was about to put him to d.,	Eth 7:18
no food until he had suffered d.	9: 7
brother of him that suffered d.,	9: 8
he did cause to be put to d.	10: 6
after the d. of his father,	10:15
should be put to d.;	11: 5
that they should not taste of d.;	12:17
and after the d. of Shared,	14: 3
prepared for d. on the morrow.	15:26
they put to d. every Nephite	Mro 1: 9
they are in danger of d., hell, and	8:21
that they have no fear of d.;	9: 5
their bodies even unto d.;	9:10
to weigh thee down unto d.;	Mro 9:25
and may his sufferings and d.,	9:25
give unto me power over d.,	DC 7: 2
suffered d. in the flesh;	18:11
which is the first d., even	29:41
even that same d. which is	29:41
same death which is the last d.,	29:41
not die as to the temporal d.,	29:42
by his natural d. he might be	29:43
die in me shall not taste of d.,	42:46
them, for their d. is bitter.	42:47
and is not appointed unto d.,	42:48
my voice, lest d. shall overtake you;	45: 2
and d. of him who did no sin,	45: 4
endure, whether in life or in d.,	50: 5
be cut off, either in life or in d.	50: 8
in the region and shadow of d.	57:10
whether in life or in d.;	58: 2
whether in life or in d.	61:39
brimstone, which is the second d.	63:17
who have not sinned unto d.	64: 7
second d. shall have any power;	76:37
are theirs, whether life or d.,	76:59
shall fall by the shaft of d.,	85: 8
the d. and misery of many souls;	87: 1
they shall not any more see d.	88:116
in my covenant, even unto d.,	98:14
sorrow because there is no d.	101:29
fear not even unto d.;	101:36
vacancy shall occur by the d.,	102: 8
years previous to his (Adam's) d.,	107:42
previous to the d. of Adam,	107:53
to heaven without tasting d.,	110:13
bring them into bondage and d.—	121:18
is stronger than the cords of d.	121:44
sentence of d. passed upon thee;	122: 7
assent unto my d., after ye have	132:27
in d. they were not separated!	135: 3
marveled because of his d.;	136:39
own brother, in administering d.,	Mses 6:15
brought upon themselves d.;	6:29
d. hath come upon our fathers;	6:45
and by his fall came d.;	6:48
which fall bringeth d.,	6:59
should persecute him unto d.,	JS 2:24
by the d. of my eldest brother,	2:56

DEATHS

these d. and destructions by fire,	3Ne 10:14
the way that leadeth to the d.;	DC 132:25

DEBT

Pay the d. thou hast contracted	DC 19:35
to get in d. to thine enemies;	64:27
pay the d. out of that which	72:13
answer the d. unto the bishop	72:14
enabled to discharge every d.;	90:23
of those to whom you are in d.,	104:80
of those to whom you are in d.,	104:81
in d. any more for the building	115:13

DEBTORS

our debts, as we forgive our d.	3Ne 13:11

DEBTS

forgive us our d., as we forgive	3Ne 13:11
unto you, concerning your d.—	DC 104:78
that you shall pay all your d.	104:78
yourselves about your d.,	111: 5
Kirtland be turned out for d.,	117: 5
for the d. of the Presidency of	119: 2
see that all my d. are canceled	127: 1

DECAY

and waxed old, and began to d.	Jac 5: 3
that his olive-tree began to d.;	5: 4

DECAYED

was preserved and had not d.	Al 46:24

DECEIT

neither was any d. in his mouth.	Mos 14: 9
obtaining power by fraud and d.,	Al 48: 7

DECEITS / DECLARE

DECEITS
all manner of lyings, and of d.,	3Ne 16:10

DECEIVE
that he may d. our eyes,	1Ne 16:38
a false Messiah which should d.	2Ne 25:18
d. many with their flattering	Mos 26: 6
to lie and to d. this people	Al 12: 4
cunning and their lyings, d. us,	20:13
thou that we d. this people,	30:35
not d. this people any more.	30:47
and d. the hearts of the people;	3Ne 2: 2
D. and lie in wait to catch,	DC 10:25
wo be unto him that lieth to d.	10:28
supposeth that another lieth to d.,	10:28
Satan hath sought to d. you,	50: 3
whereby they lie in wait to d.,	123:12
of heaven for a just man to d.;	129: 7
d. me not; for God said unto me:	Mses 1:16
to d. and to blind men,	4: 4
Take heed that no man d. you;	JS 1: 5
and shall d. many;	1: 6
shall arise, and shall d. many;	1: 9
they shall d. the very elect,	1:22

DECEIVED
for he cannot be d.,	2Ne 9:41
d. by the power of the devil.	Jac 7:18
being d. by the cunning and	Mos 7:21
and his fair promises, d. me, that	10:18
d. by the vain and flattering words	11: 7
behold, the devil hath d. me;	Al 30:53
He hath d. you—	DC 10:29
that you may not be d.,	43: 6
guide, and have not been d.—	45:57
Wherefore, beware lest ye are d.;	46: 8
and that ye may not be d.	46: 8
Wherefore, be not d., but continue	49:23
among you, who have d. some,	50: 7
things, that ye may not be d.;	52:14
up my word, shall not be d.,	JS 1:37

DECEIVERS
that are d. and hypocrites,	DC 50: 6

DECEIVETH
and that satan d. him;	DC 28:11

DECEIVING
his lying and d. to destroy him,	Al 12: 1
in the earth, d. the world.	DC 50: 2
he goeth forth d. the nations.—	52:14

DECEIVINGS
preach against all lyings, and d.,	Al 16:18
these lyings and d.	3Ne 1:22
lyings, and d., and envyings,	21:19
evil doings, of your lyings and d.,	30: 2
and robbing, and lying, and d.,	Mrm 8:31

DECEMBER
on the subject, D. 25th, 1832.	DC 130:13
was thirty-eight in D., 1843;	135: 6
on the twenty-third day of D.,	JS 2: 3
in the month of D., and the	2:62

DECEPTION
and no d. before God,	2Ne 31:13

DECIDE
power to d. upon testimony	DC 107:79
without being able to d. whether	130:16
d. how many can go next spring	136: 7

DECIDED
d. by the counselors and bishop.	DC 42:72
most d. against the Baptists	JS 2: 9

DECISION
shall give a d. according to	DC 102:19
in the d. of the president,	102:20
d. shall be altered accordingly.	102:21

the first d. shall stand,	DC 102:22
accompanying their d.,	102:26
with the d. of said council,	102:27
no such d. had been made.	102:27
From the d. of the former	102:31
from the d. of the latter	102:31
every d. made by either of	107:27
in case that any d. of these	107:32
can be no appeal from their d.	107:32
the d. of either of these councils,	107:77
the d. of the bishop or judges,	107:78
And after this d. it shall be	107:80
a final d. upon controversies	107:80
their d. upon his head shall	107:83

DECISIONS
the twelve apostles, in their d.	DC 102:30
quorum must be agreed to its d.,	107:27
make their d. of the same power	107:27
their d. are not entitled to the	107:29
d. of a quorum of three presidents	107:29
The d. of these quorums,	107:30
affairs of the church, in all their d.,	107:36
affairs of the church, in all their d.,	107:37
thus were their d. at the time	Abr 5: 3

DECLARATION
OFFICIAL D.	DC OD
d. concerning plural marriages	OD

DECLARE
and began to prophesy and to d.	1Ne 1:18
and will ye not d. them?	20: 6
yea, I have called him to d.,	20:15
with a voice of singing d. ye,	20:20
And now I, Nephi, d. unto you,	22:21
of thy loins shall d. it.	2Ne 3:18
I will d. unto you the remainder	9:54
d. their sin to be even as Sodom,	13: 9
d. his doings among the people,	22: 4
that I might d. unto you the word	Jac 2: 2
d. the word which I shall give	2:11
the word whichI d. unto you,	2:12
and to d. unto them that there	7: 2
I, Sherem, d. unto you that	7: 7
and the word according to	En 1:26
that I might d. unto you that	Mos 2:29
I should d. unto you this day,	2:30
to d. unto you the glad tidings	3: 3
to d. unto thee that thou mayest	3: 4
d. unto thy people, that they may	3: 4
to d. these things to every	3:13
and who shall d. his generation?	14: 8
who shall d. his generation?	15:10
they did d. unto the people that	27:37
Now I d. unto you that	29: 6
and began to d. the word of God	Al 6: 8
to d. the words of God unto them;	8:30
to d. unto them the truth of such	9: 6
with boldness to d. unto them,	9: 7
doth d. it unto all nations;	13:22
yea, doth d. it, that they may	13:22
to d. unto them the word of God.	17:12
they did all d. unto the people	19:33
many did d. unto the people	19:34
went forth again to d. the word,	21:15
he did also d. unto them that	21:21
Yea, I would d. unto every soul,	29: 2
to d. the word of God unto	30:32
save it were to d. the truth,	30:34
and having been d. to the word,	35:15
to d. unto them concerning their	37:30
unto this people and d. the word,	37:47
sent his angel to d. unto me that	38: 7
he cometh to d. glad tidings of	39:15
to d. these glad tidings unto	39:16
to d. these glad tidings unto	39:19
d. the word with truth and	42:31
to d. the word untothem.	43: 1
to d. the word unto them.	45:20
and did d. the word of God	62:45
d. unto the people these words.	He 5: 6

DECLARE   DECREED

to d. the tidings of the conditions	He 5:11
sent unto you to d. good tidings.	5:29
did d. unto the people of the	6: 4
and then he might d. it unto us,	9:16
d. unto you that he is innocent.	9:30
I d. it unto thee in the presence	10: 6
shall go and d. unto this people,	10:11
began to d. unto them the word	10:12
Nephi did d. unto them the word	10:14
should not d. wars against them;	12: 2
unto you to d. it unto you also,	13: 7
I d. unto you that except ye shall	15: 1
did d. unto them glad tidings	16:14
d. his word among his people,	3Ne 5:13
whom I did send to d. unto them	9:10
I will d. unto you my doctrine.	11:31
shall d. more or less than this,	11:40
d. the words which I have spoken,	11:41
these things which I d. unto you,	21: 2
d. unto you hereafter of myself,	21: 2
a man shall d. it unto them.	21: 9
Did I not d. my words unto you,	Mro 10:27
I d. these things unto the	10:28
will I d. it unto them.	DC 5:12
Seek not to d. my word,	11:21
also that you may d. repentance	14: 8
d. repentance unto this people,	15: 6
d. repentance unto this people,	16: 6
who are called to d. my gospel,	18:26
and teachers; to d. my gospel,	18:32
thou shalt d. glad tidings,	19:29
but thou shalt d. repentance	19:31
yea, preach, exhort, d. the truth,	19:37
d. my gospel as with the voice of	24:12
d. faithfully the commandments	28: 3
d. my gospel with the sound of	29: 4
to d. unto them repentance	29:42
And now I d. no more unto you	29:50
your mouth to d. my gospel;	30: 5
d. glad tidings of great joy	31: 3
You shall d. the things which	31: 4
for a little time, and d. my word,	31: 6
d. my gospel and learn of me,	32: 1
to d. my gospel unto a crooked	33: 2
shall d. it with a loud voice,	36: 3
d. the word in the regions	52:39
d. my word with loud voices,	60: 7
and d. the word among the	61:33
d. glad tidings unto the	62: 5
d. both by word and by flight	63:37
I, the Lord, d. unto you,	64:31
d. the things which ye have heard,	80: 4
have power to d. my word	99: 2
ye shall d. whatsoever thing	100: 7
thing ye d. in my name,	100: 7
the eternal creations d. his name	128:23
d. that these charges are false.	OD
d. my intention to submit to	OD
d. that my advice to the	OD
go forth and d. his Gospel	Mses 8:19
that ye may d. all these words.	Abr 3:15

DECLARED

d. unto this people the things	1Ne 2: 1
hast d. unto us hard things,	16: 1
I have d. the former things	20: 3
even from the beginning d. to thee;	20: 5
they were d. unto thee, lest	20: 7
hath d. these things unto them?	20:14
word which he hath d. by them;	20:14
from the time that it was d. have I	20:16
gospel of Jesus Christ shall be d.	2Ne 30: 5
I have d. it in all my days,	En 1:26
not having salvation d. unto them.	Mos 15:24
shall be d. to every nation,	15:28
should be d. to every creature,	28: 3
which were d. unto the people	Al 9:hd
these glad tidings d. unto us	13:23
hear the joyful news d. unto us	13:25
he also d. unto them that	21:22
the word of God should be d.	45:21
was d. unto them by Helaman,	49:30
d. the word, which I have given	He 10: 4
when Nephi had d. unto them the	10:15
until he had d. it unto them all,	10:17
saved, hath repentance been d.	12:22
an angel of the Lord hath d. it	13: 7
And God also d. unto prophets,	Mro 7:23
d. unto the world by them.—	DC 20:10
I d. from mine own mouth that	29:29
was d. in my former letter	128: 2
relation to the dead, when he d.,	128: 6
is heavenly, as Paul hath d.,	128:13
This a voice d. to me,	130:13
and d. these things abroad,	Mses 5:53
him whom he d. should come	5:57
being d. by holy angels	5:58

DECLARETH

d. unto you the word of the Lord,	He 13:26
Whosoever d. more mor less	DC 10:68

DECLARING

d. that I have written according	Jac 7:26
d. unto the people that every	Al 1: 3
d. unto them that they must	9:25
angels are d. it unto many	13:24
d. unto those who had believed	30:57
d. throughout all the regions	He 5:50
to multitude, d. the word of God,	10:17
by d. the word of Christ unto	Mro 7:31
d. my gospel with the sound of	DC 28:16
d. my word like unto angels of	42: 6
d. none other things than the	52:36
d. the fulfilment of the prophets—	128:20
d. the three witnesses to bear	128:20
d. themselves as possessing the	128:20
all d. their dispensation,	128:21

DECLINED

And Ammon d. doing this thing,	Mos 21:33
d., and will not take upon him	29: 6

DECOY

he might d. the Lamanites out	Al 52:21
we could not d. them away from	58: 1

DECREASE

began to d. as to their faith	3Ne 1:30

DECREE

Wo unto them that d. unrighteous	2Ne 20: 1
he sent a d. among them, that	Al 23: 2
the firm d. of a just God,	29: 4
it is the everlasting d. of God.	Eth 2:10
the d. hath gone forth from the	DC 29: 8
it hath gone forth in a firm d.,	29:12
and I revoke not the d.	61:19
by virtue of the d. concerning	68:21
the d. which God hath made.	88:61
the d. hath gone forth by	101:10
that I have decreed a d.	103: 5
mouth of God in a firm d.;	Mses 5:15
Gospel preached, and a d. sent	5:59
is a d., which I have sent forth	6:30
he sent forth an unalterable d.,	7:52

DECREED

the consumption d. shall overflow	2Ne 20:22
expressly promised and firmly d.,	Al 9:24
what I the Lord have d. in	DC 1: 7
have d. that he that receiveth	49: 5
have d. in mine anger many	61: 5
I, the Lord, have d.,	61:19
and d. wars upon the face of	63:33
I, the Lord, have d. all these	63:36
until the consumption d. hath	87: 6
it is d. that the poor and	88:17
d. that they shall be granted.	98: 2
for I have d. in my heart,	98:14
those things which I have d.	101:98
I have d. a decree	103: 5
they shall, for I have d. it,	103: 6
I have d. that your brethren	103:11

DECREED

have d. in my heart, that	DC 104: 5
d. to provide for my saints,	104:16
Missouri river in its d. course,	121:33
a law, irrevocably d. in heaven	130:20
d. it, even as it shall be sent	Mses 6:30

DECREES

that decree unrighteous d.,	2Ne 20: 1
the d. of God are unalterable;	Al 41: 8
the d. of God concerning this	Eth 2: 9
ye may know the d. of God—	2:11
to the d. of the great Jehovah.	DC 128: 9

DEDICATE

consecrate and d. this land,	DC 58:57
which we now d. to thee,	109:12

DEDICATED

d. by the hand of Joseph Smith,	DC 84: 3
it shall be d. unto the Lord	94: 6
be wholly d. unto the Lord	94: 7
be d. unto me for the building	94:10
be wholly d. unto the Lord	94:12
be d. unto me for your sacrament	95:16
be d. unto me for the school of	95:17

DEDICATION

accept the d. of this house	DC 109:78

DEED

and also in power, in very d., unto	1Ne 14: 1
much good, both in word and in d.,	2Ne 3:24
mighty in word and in d., in faith	He 10: 5
be made manifest in very d.	Eth 4:16
and a d. which cannot be broken.	DC 42:30
Zion is in very d. the kingdom	105:32
not in name but in d.,	117:11

DEEDED

that portion that is d. unto him.	DC 51: 5

DEEDS

and your words, and your d.,	Mos 4:30
to be judged according to the d.	Al 5:15
my God, to be judged of my d.	36:15
unto him according to his d.	42:27
he testifieth that your d. are evil	He 13:26
because their d. have been evil	15: 4
because their d. are evil;	DC 10:21
and the d. which he hath done.	19: 3
than light, and their d. are evil,	29:45
reward thee according to thy d.	64:11
of all their unrighteous d.,	84:87
unrighteous and ungodly d.,	84:117
convince all of their ungodly d.	99: 5
Which dark and blackening d.	123:10

DEEP

awake from a d. sleep,	2Ne 1:13
upon the waters of the great d.	4:20
the waters of the great d.;	8:10
upon you the spirit of d. sleep.	27: 5
that seek d. to hide their counsel	27:27
seek d. to hide their counsels	28: 9
pierced with d. wounds	Jac 2:35
sunk d. into my heart.	En 1: 3
the Lord caused a d. sleep to	Mos 24:19
awakened them out of a d. sleep,	Al 5: 7
will bury them d. in the earth,	24:16
did bury them up d. in the earth.	24:17
weapons of war d. in the earth,	26:32
and were in a d. sleep,	55:15
Lamanites were in a d. sleep	55:16
unto the waters of the great d.—	He 12:16
ye cannot cross this great d.	Eth 2:25
go forth across this raging d.	3: 3
when they were buried in the d.	6: 7
across the great d. into the	7:27
brought across the great d.?	8: 9
and his brother across the d.;	10: 2
he gave him many d. wounds;	14:30
if thou be cast into the d.;	DC 122: 7
d. water is what I am wont to	127: 2

DEFEAT

mighty ocean, even the great d.,	DC 133:20
He shall command the great d.,	133:23
up in the midst of the great d.	133:27
up upon the face of the d.;	Mses 2: 2
a d. sleep to fall upon Adam;	3:21
reigned upon the face of the d.,	Abr 4: 2
a d. sleep to fall upon Adam;	5:15
though my feelings were d. and	JS 2: 8
so d. were the impressions made	2:46

DEFEAT

slay Morianton and d. his army,	Al 50:35

DEFENCE: see also DEFENSE.

the glory of Zion shall be a d.	2Ne 14: 5
the sword of Laban in their d.,	Jac 1:10
in the d. of my brethren.	Om 1:10
arms in d. of their country.	Al 51:20
arms in the d. of their country.	53:13
their weapons of war in our d.	56: 7
our city and ourselves for d.	56:20
in the d. of your country	60:29
in the d. of their country	61: 6
in the d. of their freedom,	62: 5
arms in the d. of their country,	62: 9
in the d. of your liberty, and	3Ne 3: 2
in the d. of his property and	Eth 14: 2

DEFEND

in order to d. thy flocks	Al 18:16
to d. themselves against the	24: 5
taken up arms to d. themselves,	35:14
and also shields to d. their heads,	43:19
to d. themselves against the	43:23
d. their lands and their country,	43:26
he should d. them by stratagem;	43:30
Ye shall d. your families even	43:47
to d. themselves, and their	43:47
with an oath to d. his people,	48:13
were taught to d. themselves	48:14
should go to d. themselves	48:16
prepared to d. themselves	49:20
or to d. his people against	50: 1
take up arms to d. their country.	51:13
dissenters to d. their country	51:15
every city to maintain and d. it.	51:25
to d. himself against them,	52: 6
to d. themselves against their	53:16
of war to d. their country.	53:18
only sought to d. ourselves.	54:13
come forth to d. our country.	56: 5
to d. ourselves and our country	58: 8
to d. the cause of our country,	60:28
to d. their north country.	He 4; 7
to d. themselves against their	3Ne 3:22
preparations to d. ourselves	Mrm 2: 4
to d. themselves against other	DC 87: 3

DEFENDED

I d. thy servants and thy flocks,	Al 18:16
were so honorably and nobly d.,	DC 109:54

DEFENDING

while d. the flocks of the king.	Al 19:21
are justified in d. themselves,	DC 134:11

DEFENSE: see also DEFENCE.

her stakes, may be for a d.,	DC 115: 6
his d. before King Agrippa,	JS 2:24

DEFER

name's sake will I d. mine anger,	1Ne 20: 9

DEFERENCE

laws all men owe respect and d.,	DC 134: 6

DEFIANCE

set at d. the commandments of	Al 5:18
rebellion against us are set at d.,	61: 7
they did set at d. the law	3Ne 6:30

DEFILED

and churches become d. and	Mrm 8:28

DEFILED — 240 — DELIVER

DEFILED
and whatsoever temple is d., come into it, that it be not d.,	DC 93:35 97:15
But if it be d. I will not	97:17

DEFORMED
of the whole earth became d.,	3Ne 8:17

DEFY
they did d. the whole armies of	He 11:32
the truth and d. my power.—	DC 76:31
and glory d. all description,	JS 2:17

DEGREE
small d. of knowledge concerning	Jac 4: 2
listened to my words in any d.,	Mos 22: 4
upon death with any d. of terror,	Al 27:28
harrowed up to the greatest d.	36:12
with the least d. of allowance.	45:16
began to cease, in a small d.,	He 3:22
began to increase in great d.,	3Ne 1:28
in some d. they had peace in the	7:14
with the least d. of allowance;	DC 1:31
in the least d. you have tasted	19:20
in any d. of unrighteousness	121:37
but soon recovering in some d.,	JS 2:20

DEGREES
they began to prosper by d.	Mos 21:16
should administer poison by d.	Al 47:18
there are three heavens or d.	DC 131: 1

DEIGN
d. to give unto you greater riches,	DC 38:18
I d. to reveal unto my church	DC 124:41

DELAY
taken down without d.	DC OD

DELAYETH
that Christ d. his coming until	DC 45:26
My lord d. his coming,	JS 1:51

DELAYS
that the Lord d. his coming	3Ne 29: 2

DELIBERATELY
the murderer who d. killeth,	2Ne 9:35

DELICATE
and chaste and d. before God,	Jac 2: 7
souls and wound their d. minds.	2: 9

DELICIOUS
yea, it beginneth to be d. to me.	Al 32:28

DELIGHT
let your soul d. in fatness.	2Ne 9:51
and gold, nor shall they d. in it.	23:17
God, d. in the chastity of women.	Jac 2:28
and did d. in blood,	Mos 11:19
d. in the shedding of blood;	Al 26:24
that did not d. in bloodshed;	48:11
not d. in the shedding of blood;	48:23
not d. in murder or bloodshed,	55:19
the covenant, whom ye d. in;	3Ne 24: 1
d. no more in the shedding of	Mrm 7: 4
d. is in so much abomination—	Mro 9:13
they d. in everything save that	9:19
Let thy soul d. in thy husband,	DC 25:14
ye whom I d. to bless with	41: 1
d. to honor those who serve me	76: 5
we d. not in the destruction of	109:43

DELIGHTED
they d. in wars and bloodshed,	Jac 7:24
he d. in the shedding of blood;	Mos 29:40
d. in murdering the Nephites,	Al 17:14
they d. in the destruction of	17:35
he d. in the saving of his people	55:19
d. in the shedding of blood	Mrm 4:11

DELIGHTETH
my soul d. in the scriptures,	2Ne 4:15
my soul d. in the things of	2Ne 4:16
devil of all devils d. in them.	9:37
my heart d. in righteousness;	9:49
my soul d. in his words,	11: 2
my soul d. in proving unto	11: 4
my soul d. in the covenants of	11: 5
my soul d. in his grace,	11: 5
my soul d. in proving unto	11: 6
my soul d. in plainness	25: 4
my soul d. in the words of Isaiah,	25: 5
my soul d. to prophesy	25:13
my soul d. in plainness;	31: 3
my soul d. in the song of the	DC 25:12

DELIGHTFUL
let it be a d. habitation for man,	Al 124:60
d. in all manner of wickedness	Mos 24: 7

DELIGHTSOME
white, and exceeding fair and d.,	2Ne 5:21
shall be a white and d. people.	30: 6
shall also become a d. people.	30: 7
once again be a d. people.	WM 1: 8
for ye shall be a d. land,	3Ne 24:12
exceedingly fair and d. people.	4Ne 1:10
were once a d. people,	Mrm 5:17
were a civil and a d. people)	Mro 9:12

DELINEATE
d. the chronology running back	Abr 1:28

DELIVER
the Lord will d. Laban into your	1Ne 3:29
the Lord will d. Laban into our	3:31
the Lord is able to d. us, even as	4: 3
the Lord will d. my sons out of	5: 5
wilt thou d. me from the hands of	7:17
did d. you from destruction;	17:14
d. my people, O house of Israel.	2Ne 3: 9
to d. thy people out of the land	3:10
Wilt thou d. me out of the hands of	4:31
God shall d. his covenant people.	6:17
or have I no power to d.?	7: 2
shall d. up its dead;	9:11
shall d. up its dead;	9:12
and hell must d. up their dead,	9:12
must d. up its captive spirits,	9:12
must d. up its captive bodies,	9:12
must d. up the spirits of the	9:13
the grave d. up the body of	9:13
away safe, and none shall d.	15:29
shall d. the words of the book,	27: 9
shall d. these words unto another;	27: 9
which are sealed he shall not d.,	27:10
neither shall he d. the book.	27:10
to whom he shall d. the book:	27:15
and d. them to another,	27:15
God will d. again the book	27:19
I d. these plates into the hands of	Jar 1:15
did d. them out of the hands of	Om 1: 7
I did d. the plates unto	1: 8
I shall d. up these plates unto	1:25
about to d. up the record	WM 1: 1
that I d. these records into the	1: 2
that the Lord will d. them up,	Mos 1:13
will d. us out of our bondage,	7:15
to d. us out of bondage.	7:33
would d. us out of the hands of	8: 7
I will d. them into the hands of	9:17
and none shall d. them, except	11:21
d. them out of their afflictions;	11:23
we d. him into thy hands;	11:25
which the Lord sent me to d.;	12:16
that they would d. up king Noah	13: 3
and d. up their property,	19:15
d. themselves out of their hands,	19:15
d. them out of their afflictions.	21: 5
d. them out of bondage.	21:14
to d. themselves out of the hands	21:15
d. themselves out of bondage;	21:36
d. themselves out of bondage,	22: 2
to d. themselves out of bondage	22: 2

DELIVER 241 DELIVERED

d. this people out of bondage.	Mos	22: 4	I will d. thee up, and it shall be	Mses	5:23
none could d. them but the Lord		23:23	I will d. thy brother Abel into		5:29
that he did d. them,		23:24	have come down to d. thee,	Abr	1:16
their God and he would d. them.		23:27	didst send thine angel to d. me		2:13
and d. them out of bondage.		24:13	God sent his angel to d. thee		3:20
I will d. you out of bondage.		24:16	d. unto htee the works which		3:21
d. this people out of bondage.		24:17	they d. you up to be afflicted,	JS	1: 7
and none could d. them except		24:21	to d. me out of the power of		2:16
it was the Lord that did d. them.		25:16			
I d. them into thy hands		26:12	**DELIVERANCE**		
d. thy sons out of the hands of		28: 7	mighty even unto the power of d.	1Ne	1:20
behold, he did d. them because		29:20	the d. of them to the hardness of		14: 7
he did d. them out of bondage;		29:20	the way of d. of our God,	2Ne	9:11
would d. them out of the hands of	Al	2:28	eternal plan of d. from death.		11: 5
began to d. the word of God unto		5: 1	chains, from whence there is no d.		28:22
Lord did d. them out of bondage		5: 5	of the d. of our fathers,	Mos	9:17
might d. them to their judges		10:13	and d. of Jesus Christ from	Al	4:14
was about to d. up the kingdom,		10:19	according to the power of his d.;		7:13
to d. you up unto the flames?		14:19	power and d. of Jesus Christ;		9:28
why do ye not d. yourselves?		14:20	is in Christ, even unto d.		14:26
d. yourselves from these bands,		14:24	and of their power of d.		15: 2
will d. unto thee thy brethren		16: 6	exceeding sore, having no d.;		15: 3
d. his sons out of their hands;		17:35	*their sufferings and d.* –		17:hd
and I go that I may d. them.		20: 3	their d. by the hand of the Lord.		46: 7
Go and d. thy brethren,		20: 5	should hope for our d. in him.		58:11
art going to d. these Nephites,		20:13	and faith, for his and your d.;	DC	30: 6
Lord did d. them out of bondage,		29:11	the days of thy d. are come,		39:10
did d. them out of bondage.		29:11	and great glory unto their d.;		56:18
did d. them out of bondage.		29:12	I prepare a way for their d.		95: 1
and none could d. them except		36: 2	means unto you for your d.		104:80
did d. them in their afflictions.		36: 2	complete d. from under this yoke;		109:32
and he will still d. me.		36:27			
knowest that the Lord did d. thee.		38: 4	**DELIVERED**		
ye d. up your weapons of war		44: 6	d. unto them by the Spirit and	1Ne	3:20
we will d. them up unto you,		44: 8	hath d. him into thy hands.		4:11
will d. up your weapons of war		44:14	hath d. him into thy hands;		4:12
d. them up into Lehonti's hands,		47:13	had d. Laban into my hands		4:17
the Lord would d. them;		48:16	protected my sons, and d. them		5: 8
of war and d. them up,		52:37	were d. by the power of God out		13:19
who would not d. up their swords		52:39	or the lawful captives d.?		21:24
d. up a man and his wife and		54:11	prey of the terrible shall be d.;		21:25
not doubt, God would d. them.		56:47	mighty, or the lawful captive d.?	2Ne	6:16
to d. up their weapons of war		56:54	prey of the terrible shall be d.;		6:17
d. themselves up as prisoners		56:56	they are d. by the power of him.		9:25
d. up those prisoners of war		57: 1	are d. from that awful monster,		9:26
d. up the city of Antiparah		57: 1	shall not be d. in the day of		27: 8
d. up our prisoners on exchange.		57: 2	the book shall be d. unto a man,		27: 9
and d. us out of the hands of		58:10	the book shall be d. unto him		27:12
assurances that he would d. us;		58:11	him to whom the book shall be d.;		27:12
we trust God will d. us,		58:37	read the words that shall be d. him:		27:24
and d. us out of the hands of		58:37	and d. unto them many things	Jac	4:14
do nothing and he would d. you?		60:11	the day that he d. them unto me.	Om	1: 9
that the Lord will still d. us.		60:21	which had been d. into my hands,	WM	1: 3
trust in him, and he will d. us.		61:13	Amaleki had d. up these plates		1:10
fear not, for God will d. them,		61:21	d. them by the hand of the Lord.	Mos	1: 2
that ye will d. up your lands	3Ne	3:10	had d. them out of the hands of		2: 4
would d. us into their hands;		3:21	shall be d. unto you by him,		2:31
he will d. them into our hands.		3:21	words which had been d. unto him		4: 1
he would d. them in the time		3:25	*d. out of the hands of the Lamanites.*		9:hd
he would spare them and d. them		4: 8	the Lord d. him out of their hands.		11:26
to d. those who were guilty of		6:29	which the Lord d. unto Moses		12:33
temptation, but d. us from evil.		13:12	for I have not d. the message		13: 3
teareth in pieces, and none can d.		20:16	being d. up to the devil,		16:11
teareth in pieces, and none can d.		21:12	and he d. him up that he might		17:12
d. them from their afflictions.	Mrm	5: 1	been d. by the power of God		23:13
pieces, and there is none to d.		5:24	d. themselves up into their hands;		23:29
sacred records that I would d.	Mro	9:24	had d. them out of bondage;		24:21
and go forth and d. my words	DC	5: 6	had been d. out of bondage,		25: 8
shall d. you out of the hands of		8: 4	had been d. out of bondage,		25:16
d. him or her up unto the church,		42:89	d. to him by the mouth of Alma.		25:21
he shall d. up the kingdom,		76:107	and d. up unto the priests		26: 7
ye shall d. him over unto		104:10	in bondage, and he has d. them.		27:16
to d. yourself from bondage,		104:84	d. to him by the hand of Limhi;		28:11
will d. them in time of trouble,		105: 8	be d. from all manner of bondage;		29:40
to bless you and d. you forever.		108: 8	but he d. the judgment-seat unto	Al	4:18
d. thou, O Jehovah, we beseech		109:42	Alma d. up the judgment-seat to		4:20
d. thy people from the calamity		109:46	*d. to the people in their cities*		5:hd
and will d. me from henceforth;		127: 2	they were d. out of the hands of		5: 4
but he will still d. his message.		129: 7	he has d. their souls from hell?		5: 6
neither my power to d.		133:67	d. by the mouth of Abinadi?		5:11
and lo, there are none to d. you;		133:71	*he d. to the people in Gideon,*		7:hd
went to carthage to d. himself		135: 4	hast d. up the judgment-seat unto		8:12
diligent search till thou shalt d.		136:26	I am he that d. it unto you.		8:15
thou shalt d. my people from	Mses	1:26	*d. by the miraculous power of*	Al	9:hd

DELIVERED

times he d. our fathers out of	Al	9:10
and after having been d. of God		9:22
and d. them to the officers to be		14:17
they might be d. from Satan,		15:17
sho had ever d. them out of		19:27
were d. by Lamoni and Ammon.		20:30
were d. by the hand of Lamoni		21:14
and thus they were d. for the		21:15
whom thou hast d. out of prison.		22: 2
of God we have been d. again.		26:29
who d. them out of the hands of		29:12
they d. him up into the hands of		30:29
yea, God has d. me from prison,		36:27
he has d. them out of bondage		36:28
d. them out of bondage and		36:29
and ye shall be d. up unto Satan,		37:15
ye shall be d. out of your trials,		38: 5
d. from that endless night of		41: 7
and d. the message unto Moroni.		43:24
he has d. you into our hands.		44: 3
d. up his sword and his cimeter,		44: 8
that has d. us into your hands;		44: 9
d. them out of the hands of		45: 1
d. up into the hands of Moroni		46:33
he d. his men, contrary to		47:16
of the Lord were d. at all times,		50:22
d. up their weapons of war;		52:36
we are again d. out of the hands		57:35
behold, it is he that has d. ua;		57:35
the many times we have been d.		60:20
he had d. them from death,		62:50
had d. them out of the hands of		62:50
which had been d. unto Helaman		63: 1
Nephi d. up the judgment-seat	He	5: 1
which were d. unto Helaman;		6:26
the very day that he has d. you?		7:20
in nowise be d. out of the hands	3Ne	3:15
been d. from an everlasting		4:33
people having been d. up for		6:17
they that tempt God are even d.		24:15
d. out of the depths of the earth;		28:20
thrice have I d. them out of	Mrm	3:13
repented not after I had d. them,		3:15
shalt be d. up and become as	DC	3:11
because you d. up those writings		10: 1
because you have d. the		10: 8
Therefore, you have d. them up,		10: 9
been d. from all thine enemies,		24: 1
d. from the Powers of Satan		24: 1
shall be d. up and dealt with		42:79
d. up unto the law of the land.		42:84
d. up unto the law of the Inad.		42:85
d. up unto the law of the land.		42:86
d. up unto the law, even that		42:87
be d. up unto the law of God.		42:91
d. over to the buffetings of Satan		78:12
d. over to the buffetings of Satan		82:21
if you will be d. you shall set		93:43
d. thine enemy into thine hands;		98:29
shall be d. into the treasury;		104:62
that you shall be d. this once		104:83
may be d. from the hands of all		109:28
be d. from those who would		124:98
God of my fathers d. me out		127: 2
d. unto the buffetings of Satan		132:26
ye were d. over unto darkness.		133:72
Have I not d. you from your		136:40
I found myself d. from	JS	2:17
d. by the Savior to the ancient		2:34
messenger d. them up to me		2:59
for them, I d. them up to him;		2:60

DELIVEREDST
d. up that which God had	DC	3:12
d. up that which was sacred		3:12

DELIVERETH
for he d. his saints from	2Ne	9:19

DELIVERING
in d. us out of the hands of	1Ne	7:11

DENY

and his power in d. Alma	Mos	25:10
in d. the people of Limhi out of	Al	1: 8
in d. them from the hands of		49:28
d. their women and their children		53: 7
by d. up the prisoners for that		57: 2
d. them out of the hands of	He	12: 2
in d. them out of the hands of	3Ne	4:33

DELUDED
if they supposed me to be d.	JS	2:28

DEMANDED
chief captains d. their weapons	Al	55:23

DEMANDING
d. the possession of the land of	3Ne	3:11

DEMANDS
satisfieth the d. of his justice	2Ne	9:26
the d. of divine justice do awaken	Mos	2:38
and satisfied the d. of justice.		15: 9
can satisfy the d. of justice,	Al	34:16
whole law of the d. of justice;		34:16
to appease the d. of justice,		42:15
justice exerciseth all his d.,		42:24
could not be frightened by the d.	3Ne	3:12

DEMONS
Behold, we are surrounded by d.,	He	13:37

DEMONSTRATION
in the d. of my Holy Spirit.	DC	99: 2

DEN
his hand on the cockatrice's d.	2Ne	21: 8
his hand on the cockatrice's d.		30:14
cast into a d. of wild beasts:	3Ne	28:22

DENIED
for justice cannot be d.,	Jac	6:10
and d. the things which he had		7:17
lied unto God; for I d. the Christ,		7:19
d. the being of their Creator;	Om	1:17
d. that which had been spoken of	Mos	27:30
who d. the covenant of freedom.	Al	46:35
unto him their sins and d. not,	He	16: 1
church which d. the Christ;	4Ne	1:29
the power of God shall be d.,	Mrm	8:28
Having d. the Holy Spirit after	DC	76:35
having d. the Only Begotten		76:35
of its members, as citizens, d.		134: 9
gone astray, and have d. me,	Mses	6:28

DENIEST
D. thou the Christ who should	Jac	7: 9

DENIETH
he d. none that come unto him,	2Ne	26:33
and d. the power of God,		28:26
whosoever d. this is a liar and a	Al	5:39
he that d. these things	Mrm	9: 8
d. the mercies of Christ,	Mro	8:20
that is good d. the Christ,		10: 6
unto him that d. these things;	DC	11:25

DENOMINATED
the land which we d. Haran.	Abr	2: 4

DENOMINATIONS
among all sects, parties, and d.,	DC	123:12
strife among the different d.,	JS	2: 8

DENOTE
all things d. there is a God;	Al	30:44

DENS
cast them into d. of wild beasts,	4Ne	1:33

DENY
these things, and d. them not.	1Ne	10:22
believe in Christ and d. him not;	2Ne	25:28

DENY 243 DEPARTED

ye also d. the prophets	2Ne	25:28
believe in Christ, and d. him not;		25:29
and d. the Holy Ghost,		28: 4
And they d. the power of God,		28: 5
they will d. me; nevertheless,		28:32
and after this should d. me,		31:14
and d. the good word of Christ,	Jac	6: 8
be a Christ, I would not d. him;		7: 9
Yet thou wilt d. it, because thou		7:14
could no more d. unto them	Mos	3:26
than it could d. that Adam		3:26
I mean all you who d. the beggar,		4:24
for he cannot d. himself;		15:27
for he cannot d. justice		15:27
not d. the commandments of God,		17:20
and now, who can d. this?	Al	5:39
if thou wilt d. the existence of		11:22
d the true and living God,		11:25
impossible for him to d. his word.		11:34
for I cannot d. his word, and he		11:37
ye d. again that there is a God,		30:39
a God, and also d. the Christ?		30:39
they are true; and will ye d. them?		30:41
will ye d. against all these		30:45
Yea, I will d., except ye shall		30:45
therefore if thou shalt d. again,		30:47
do not d. the existence of a God,		30:48
hypocrites who do d. the faith.		34:28
no more d. the coming of Christ;		34:37
if ye d. the Holy Ghost when it		39: 6
and ye know that ye d. it,		39: 6
d. the justice of God no more.		42:30
transgression and d. our faith.		44: 4
ye not only d. my words, but	He	8:13
ye also d. all the words which		8:13
and cannot d. them except ye		8:24
behold, he shall d. unto you;		9:30
and d. no more that he has done		9:35
to the words he did d.;		9:37
d. yourselves of these things,	3Ne	12:30
shall d. the Christ and his works!		29: 5
that shall d. the revelations of		29: 6
to d.the true church of Christ.	4Ne	1:26
d. the more parts of his gospel,		1:27
will ye longer d. the Christ,	Mrm	9: 3
who d. the revelations of God,		9: 7
Who can d. his sayings?		9:26
he that shall d. these things,	Eth	4: 8
that which will not d. the Christ.	Mro	1: 2
Moroni, will not d. the Christ;		1: 3
and d. him, and serve not God,		7:17
to d. the pure mercies of God		8:19
that ye d. not the power of God;		10: 7
that ye d. not the gifts of God,		10: 8
d. yourselves of all ungodliness;		10:32
d. yourselves of all ungodliness		10:32
in nowise d. the power of God.		10:32
in Christ, and d. not his power,		10:33
But if he d. this he will break	DC	5:27
d. that which you have received,		10:62
D. not the spirit of revelation,		11:25
again begin to d. their God,		29:22
but I cannot d. my word.		39:16
lust after her shall d. the faith,		42:23
shall d. the faith and shall fear.		63:16
and to d. the truth and defy		76:31
who d. the Son after the		76:43
they who d. not the Holy Spirit.		76:83
endure chastening, but d. me,		101: 5
among you who d. my name,		114: 2
I d. that either forty or any		OD
and d. the God of heaven?	Mses	6:43
we know them, and cannot d.,		6:45
but they d. the power thereof."	JS	2:19
d. what I have actually seen?		2:25
knew it, and I could not d. it,		2:25

DENYING

for by d. him ye also deny	2Ne	25:28
or d. the Holy Ghost?	Al	39: 5
sins, by d. he justice of God;		42:30
was found d. their freedom		62:10
d. the spirit of prophecy and of	He	4:12

d. the mercies of Christ, and	Mro	8:23
and they are d. the Holy Ghost.		8:28

DEPART

The Lord warns Lehi to d. out of	1Ne	1:hd
They take their families and d. into		1:hd
take his family and d. into the		2: 2
take our tents and d. into the		16:12
that he should d. into the wilderness;		17:44
The Lord warns Nephi to d.	2Ne	1:hd
ye will not d. from it.		4: 5
I, Nephi, should d. from them		5: 5
envy of Ephraim also shall d.,		21:13
shall his yoke d. from off them,		24:25
his burden d. from off their		24:25
unto any, saying: D. from me?		26:25
should d. out of the synagogues,		26:26
should also d. out of the land	Om	1:12
people should d. out of the land,	Mos	9: 7
yet they would not d. from them;		16:12
suffer that he might d. in peace.		17: 2
might not d. into the wilderness;		19:28
and d. into the wilderness,		22: 2
Thus we will d. with our women		22: 8
did d. by night into the		22:11
they shall d. into everlasting fore		26:27
to d. out of that city;	Al	15: 1
may d. into the wilderness;		44: 8
ye shall not d. except ye depart		44:11
except ye d. with an oath that		44:11
d. with a covenant of peace.		44:14
to d. into the wilderness.		44:15
to d. into the wilderness.		44:20
should d. out of the land in peace.	He	1:33
and they would not d. from it,	3Ne	6:14
d. from me, ye that work		14:23
D. ye, depart ye, go ye out from		20:41
d. ye, go ye out from thence,		20:41
For the mountains shall d. and		22:10
kindness shall not d. from thee,		22:10
and d. from the right way,	Mrm	9:20
he should d. out of the land;	Eth	9: 3
d. from the living God;	DC	20:32
D. from me, ye cursed, into		29:28
I shall say: D., ye cursed.		29:41
d. speedily from that house,		75:20
d. to go over the great waters,		118: 1
D. hence, Satan.	Mses	1:18
saying: D. from me, Satan,		1:20
the Only Begotten, d. hence, Satan.		1:21
to the mountains— D. hence—	Abr	2: 7
servant rise up and d. in peace.		2:13

DEPARTED

he d. into the wilderness.	1Ne	2: 4
tents, and d. into the wilderness.		2: 4
angel had spoken unto us, he d.		3:30
And after the angel had d.,		3:31
and d. into the wilderness, and		4:38
day that Ephraim d. from Judah,	2Ne	17:17
And they d. out of the land	Om	1:13
because he d. into the wilderness	Mos	18:34
and d. into the wilderness		22:15
had d. out of the land by night,		23: 1
and d. into the wilderness		24:20
people d. into the wilderness;		24:24
that they d. out of the valley,		27:17
angel spake unto Alma, and he d.	Al	2:26
and d. out of the valley of		6: 7
he d. from them, yea, from the		8: 3
that Alma d. from thence and		8: 6
his work at Melek he d. thence,		8:13
he d. thence and took his journey		14:20
that they d. and went their ways,		15: 1
and they d., and came out		15: 1
who had d. out of the lnad of		17: 7
they d. out of the land of		17: 8
thus they d. into the wilderness		17:13
and d. one from another,		17:18
unto them, and he d. from them,		21:11
he d. out of their synagogue,		21:12
therefore they d. and came over		22: 1
he d. from the land of Middoni		

DEPARTED 244 DESCENDANT

herds, and d. out of the land	Al 27:14	up a land out of the d. of the sea,	Mses 7:14
d. out of the land of Jershon,	35:13	came up out of the d. of the sea.	7:14
are d. from this mortal body,	40:11		
d. out of the land of Antionum	43:22	**DEPTHS**	
they had d. into the wilderness	43:23	drowned in the d. of the fountain;	1Ne 8:32
d. out of the land Zarahemla,	45:18	and the d. thereof are the depths	12:16
and d. into the land of Nephi.	46:29	depths thereof are the d. of hell.	12:16
d. out of the land of Zarahemla,	52:12	down into the d. of sorrow.	16:25
d. out of the land of Zarahemla	63: 4	me into the d. of the sea;	17:48
d. out of the land of Zarahemla,	He 3: 3	swallowed up in the d. of the sea;	18:10
d. out of the land of Zarahemla,	3Ne 1: 2	swallowed up in the d. of the sea.	18:15
Then he d. out of the land,	1: 3	swallowed up in the d. of the sea	18:20
he d. from them, and ascended	18:39	that hath made the d. of the sea	2Ne 8:10
Jesus d. out of the midst of	19:19	come down in the d. of humility,	9:42
were to tarry, and then he d.	28:12	the d., or in the heights above.	17:11
how could ye have d. from the	Mrm 6:17	the d. of the earth shall swallow	26: 5
Omer d. out of the land with his	Eth 9: 3	the d. of the mysteries of him;	Jac 4: 8
and he d. hence, even from	Mses 1:22	even in the d. of humility,	Mos 4:11
when Satan had d. from the	1:24	even in the d. of humility;	21:14
I, Abraham, d. as the Lord	Abr 2:14	bones are in the d. of the sea,	Al 3: 3
when I d. out of Haran.	2:14	are buried in the d. of the sea.	44:22
out, and d. from the temple;	JS 1: 2	drowned in the d. of the sea.	63: 8
When the light had d., I had	2:20	of them into the d. of humility,	He 6: 5
		did sink into the d. of the sea,	3Ne 8: 9
DEPARTETH		be sunk in the d. of the sea,	9: 4
he that d. from thee shall	Al 3:17	buried up in the d. of the earth;	9: 6
		buried up in the d. of the earth,	9: 8
DEPARTURE		drowned in the d. of the sea;	10:13
and also for the d. of Alma	Mos 21:30	down into the d. of humility	12: 2
they did mourn for their d.,	21:31	out of the d. of the earth;	28:20
unto them before his d.;	Al 17:18	again out of the d. of the sea;	Eth 2:24
sacred from the d. of Lehi	3Ne 1: 2	up in the d. of the sea?	2:25
		buried in the d. of the sea,	6: 6
DEPEND		dominions, all heights and d.	DC 132:19
and on whom ye d. for safety,	2Ne 6: 2		
all d. upon the same Being,	Mos 4:19	**DERANGEMENT**	
not to d. upon the people for	18:26	this d. of your minds comes	Al 30:16
to d. upon their own strength	He 16:15		
we d. upon them to teach us	16:21	**DERISION**	
		and fools shall have thee in d.,	DC 122: 1
DEPENDED			
they d. upon their own strength.	Mos 10:11	**DESCEND**	
has d. upon his own judgment	DC 3:13	that rejoiceth, shall d. into it.	2Ne 15:14
		which shall d. upon you,	DC 78:14
DEPENDENT		who shall d. with him first,	88:98
on whom you are d. for your lives	Mos 4:21	and fall when the storms d.,	90: 5
		the winds blow, and the rains d.,	90: 5
DEPENDS		the knowledge of God d. upon	128:19
which d. upon these things.	DC 123:15	may d. upon him and not tarry	130:23
DEPOSITED		**DESCENDANT**	
there have I d. unto the Lord	Mrm 1: 3	that he was a d. of Joseph;	1Ne 5:14
Ammaron had d. the records	2:17	Laban also was a d. of Joseph,	5:16
He said there was a book d.,	JS 2:34	that we are a d. of Joseph.	6: 2
d. with the plates;	2:35	and I am a d. of Joseph	2Ne 3: 5
place where the plates were d.,	2:42	and a d. of Zarahemla;	Mos 7: 3
told me the plates were d.;	2:50	and am a d. of Zarahemla,	7:13
the plates, d. in a stone box.	2:51	he also being a d. of Nephi.	17: 2
to the place where they were d.,	2:59	who was a d. of Mulek,	25: 2
		who was a d. of Aminadi;	Al 10: 2
DEPRAVITY		Aminadi was a d. of Nephi,	10: 3
O the d. of my people!	Mro 9:18	who was a d. of Manasseh,	10: 3
		and he was a d. of Ishmael.	17:21
DEPRESSED		Ammoron, and a d. of Zoram,	54:23
Now when our hearts were d.,	Al 26:27	a man who was a d. of Laman	55: 4
d. in body as well as in spirit,	56:16	and he was a d. of Zarahemla;	He 1:15
		being a d. of Nephi who	3Ne 1:hd
DEPRIVE		Mormon, and a pure d. of Lehi.	5:20
would d. them of their rights	Al 2: 4	Mormon, being a d. of Nephi,	Mrm 1: 5
a right in justice to d. citizens	DC 134: 7	my father was a d. of Nephi.	8:13
		and he was a d. of Coriantor.	Eth 1: 6
DEPRIVED		Aaron was a d. of Heth,	1:16
d. of the privilege of assembling	Al 6: 5	was a d. of Riplakish.	1:23
		Shez, who was a d. of Heth –	10: 1
DEPRIVING		(he being a d. of Riplakish)	10: 9
after d. them of that which was	Mro 9: 9	Ethem, being a d. of Ahah,	11:11
		a d. of the brother of Jared.	11:17
DEPTH		except he be a literal d. and	DC 68:18
the d. of the ditch which had	Al 49:18	no literal d. of Aaron can	68:19
even in the d. of humility.	62:41	And a literal d. of Aaron,	68:20
been drowned in the d. of the sea.	DC 54: 5	For he is a d. of Seth [Joseph]	96: 7
the width, the height, the d., and	76:48	except he be a literal d. of Aaron.	107:16
drowned in the d. of the sea.	121:22	when no literal d. of Aaron can	107:17

DESCENDANT 245 DESIRE

DESCENDANT
he is a literal d. of Aaron;	DC	107:69
unless he is a literal d. of Aaron		107:70
who is not a literal d. of Aaron,		107:73
a literal d. of Aaron has a legal		107:76
who is partly a d. of Jesse		113: 4
a d. of Jesse, as well as of Joseph,		113: 6
a d. from the loins of Ham,	Abr	1:21

DESCENDANTS
that they are d. of the Jews.	2Ne	30: 4
those who were d. of Nephi,	Mos	25: 2
those who were d. of Nephi.		25:13
actual d. of Laman and Lemuel.	Al	24:29
and the d. of the priests of Noah.		43:13
those d. were as numerous,		43:14
that these were d. of Laman,		56: 3
were real d. of the Lamanites,	He	1:24
have fallen, who are d. of Jacob,	3Ne	10: 4
and his d. were driven out	Eth	10: 8
they be literal d. of Aaron.	DC	68:15
they be literal d. of Aaron		68:16
literal d. of the chosen seed,		107:40

DESCENDED
it d. upon the saints of the church	1Ne	14:14
the Holy Ghost d. upon him	2Ne	31: 8
he d. as it were in a cloud;	Mos	27:11
the rain d., and the floods came,	3Ne	14:25
the rain d., and the floods came,		14:27
also he d. below all things,	DC	88: 6
the Holy Ghost d. upon him		93:15
Son of Man hath d. below		122: 8
the Spirit of God d. out of	Mses	6:26
Spirit of God d. upon him,		6:65
which d. gradually until it fell	JS	2:16
messenger from heaven d.		2:68

DESCENDING
d. out of the midst of heaven,	1Ne	1: 9
behold a man d. out of heaven,		11: 7
and I saw angels d. upon the		11:30
Lamb of God d. out of heaven;		12: 6
a Man d. out of heaven;	3Ne	11: 8
saw angels d. out of heaven		17:24
d. from father to son,	DC	68:21
angels d. out of heaven;	Mses	7:25
beheld angels d. out of heaven,		7:27

DESCENDS
when the rain d., and the floods	3Ne	18:13
till he d. on the earth to	DC	49: 6

DESCENT
one of the royal d. directly	Abr	1:11
From this d. sprang all the		1:22

DESCRIBE
is impossible for the tongue to d.,	Mrm	4:11

DESCRIBING
d. heaven, the paradise of God,	DC	77: 2

DESCRIPTION
perfect d. of the horrible scene	Mrm	4:11
beyond the d. of that which		5:15
write a d. of the land of Zion,	DC	58:50
brightness and glory defy all d.,	JS	2:17
person was glorious beyond d.,		2:32

DESERET
did also carry with them d.,	Eth	2: 3

DESERT
her d. like the garden of the Lord.	2Ne	8: 3
wild beasts of the d. shall lie		23:21
Behold, he is in the d.;	JS	1:25

DESERTED
had been d. by the Nephites,	3Ne	4: 1
had been d. by the Nephites,		4: 2

DESERTING
d. away into the land of Nephi,	He	4:12

DESERTS
he led them through the d.;	1Ne	20:21
in the barren d. there shall come	DC	133:29

DESIGN
the d. of the Nephites was to	Al	43: 9
he had accomplished his d.,		48: 3
abandoned their d. in marching		52: 2
according to the d. of Moroni.		55:16
that he should accomplish his d.;	He	2: 9
they did abandon their d. to		4:19
to withdraw from their d.,	3Ne	4:22
Gidgiddoni being aware of their d.,		4:24
the Lamanites withdrew their d.,	Mrm	1:12
shall accomplish his evil d.	DC	10:14
the d. of your God concerning		58: 3
I d. to prepare mine apostles		95: 4
I d. to endow those whom		95: 8
I d. to build mine holy house.		96: 2

DESIGNATED
must be d. by this Presidency,	DC	68:20
be d. unto them by revelation—		107:39

DESIGNED
is d. for those who do not travel	DC	107:90
D. to represent the pillars	Fac	1:11
d. by the authors thereof to	JS	2: 1
I had previously d. to go,		2:15

DESIGNING
evil-disposed and d. persons,	JS	2: 1

DESIGNS
Amulek could know of their d.	Al	10:17
to the accomplishment of his d.		43: 7
his d. were to stir up the		43: 8
that he might accomplish his d.		47:16
accomplished his d. thus far,		48: 2
therefore he abandoned his d.		52:17
thus we had accomplished our d.		57:12
the d., and the purposes of God	DC	3: 1
shall not accomplish their evil d.		10:31
d. which do and will exist in		89: 4

DESIRABLE
and found that they were d.;	1Ne	5:21
a tree, whose fruit was d. to make		8:10
it was d. above all other fruit.		8:12
which was d. above all other fruit.		8:15
it is the most d. above all things.		11:22
most d. above all other fruits;		15:36
the fruit thereof would not be d.;	Al	32:39

DESIRE
I d. the room that I may write	1Ne	6: 3
I d. to behold the things which		11: 3
I d. that ye should remember to	2Ne	1:16
And when I d. to rejoice,		4:19
And if my people d. to know		5:33
d. and anxiety for the welfare of	Jac	2: 3
I d. to speak unto the people		7:16
a d. for the welfare of my	En	1: 9
this was the d. which I desired		1:13
I do not d. to boast,	Mos	2:16
I would d. that ye should		2:41
I d. to know the cause whereby		7:10
neither do they d. that she should		8:20
and yet d. to know of me what		12:25
no beauty that we should d. him.		14: 2
if this be the d. of your hearts,		18:10
This is the d. of our hearts.		18:11
I d. that thou wouldst listen to		22: 4
I d. that ye should stand fast		23:13
I d. that ye should consider		29: 5
to d. that which is not right;		29:26
I d. that this inequality should		29:32
I d. that this land be a land of		29:32
having great hopes and much d.	Al	7: 3
I do not d. that my joy over you		7: 5
I had much d. that ye were not		7:18
it was only thy d. that I should		11:25
if it were his d. to dwell in the		17:22

DESIRE

I d. to dwell among this people	Al	17:23	
I would d. him that he come		18:11	
this is the thing that I d. of thee.		18:22	
desired of him was his only d.		19: 7	
they had no more d. to do evil.		19:33	
the old king according to his d.,		20:24	
Ammon had no d. to destroy him,		20:26	
for I shall greatly d. to see thee.		20:27	
and I d. to know the cause why		22: 3	
and I d. that ye should tell me		22:11	
unto men according to their d.,		29: 4	
why should I d. more than to		29: 6	
Why should I d. that I were an		29: 7	
In whom did ye d. that Alma		30:51	
now I do not d. that ye should		32:24	
can no more than d. to believe,		32:27	
let this d. work in you, even until		32:27	
I d. that ye shall plant this		33:23	
I d. that ye should remember		34:37	
I d. that this people might not		37:28	
I d. that ye should let these		42:29	
I d. that ye should deny the		42:30	
the only d. of the Nephites to		43:30	
his army according to his d.,		43:33	
do not d. to be men of blood.		44: 1	
yet we do not d. to slay you.		44: 1	
neither do we d. to bring any one		44: 2	
this was the d. of Amalickiah;		47: 4	
he had not obtained his d. over		49:26	
this was not the d. of Moroni;		55:19	
this was the d. of Moroni.		55:24	
were disappointed in this our d.		56:23	
it was our d. to wage a battle		57: 7	
we soon accomplished our d.;		57: 8	
is so, we do not d. to murmur.		58:35	
we d. to know the cause of this		60: 6	
we d. to know the cause of your		60: 6	
not been for the d. of power and		60:16	
that has a d. for freedom,		60:27	
according to the d. of Pahoran,		62: 3	
frightened according to his d.,	He	1:27	
unto him the object of his d.,		2: 7	
I d. that ye should remember to		5: 6	
have somewhat more to d. of you,		5: 8	
which d. is, that ye may not do		5: 8	
to get gain, according to their d.		6: 8	
do not d. that the Lord		12: 6	
it became the d. of the people of	3Ne	4:22	
or shall d. to come unto me,		12:23	
ye d. that I should show unto		17: 8	
and they were filled with d.		19:24	
What is it that ye d. of me,		28: 1	
We d. that after we have lived		28: 2	
that their d. may be fulfilled,		28:29	
do not d. to harrow up the souls	Mrm	5: 8	
what they will d. of us before	Eth	6:19	
they did d. of them the things		6:21	
that he will d. me to wife;		8:10	
if he shall d. of thee that ye		8:10	
thing which I shall d. of you?		8:13	
I d. that ye should labor	Mro	8: 6	
even as you d. so it shall	DC	6: 8	
if you d. you shall be the means		6: 8	
if you d. a further witness,		6:22	
if you d. of me, to translate,		6:25	
a d. to lay up treasures for		6:27	
Peter, this was a good d.;		7: 5	
even as you d. of me so it shall		11: 8	
if you d., you shall be the means		11: 8	
if thou wilt d. of me in faith,		11:10	
all things whatsoever you d.		11:14	
then, if you d., you shall have		11:21	
d. to take upon them my name		18:27	
if they d. to take upon them		18:28	
thou shalt d. to see thy family;		19:36	
and d. to be baptized,		20:37	
of you by them who d. it,		24:14	
And if ye d. the glories of the		43:12	
that if ye d. the mysteries of the		43:13	
d. to know the truth in part,		49: 2	
if your brethren d. to escape		54: 3	
except they d. it through the		58:44	

DESIRED

if any among you d. to ride	DC	62: 7	
those who d. in their hearts,		63:57	
as you d. a companion,		80: 2	
desired, with exceedingly great d.,		127:10	
and d. to espouse another,		132:61	
thy d. shall be to thy husband,	Mses	4:22	
be unto thee according to his d.		5:23	
some d. to be united with them;	JS	2: 8	
to offer up the d. of my heart		2:15	
he d. of Laban the records	1Ne	3:12	
and d. him that he would give		3:24	
after I had d. to know the things		11: 1	
behold the things which thou hast d.		11: 6	
and it did work whither I d. it.		18:21	
brother has d. that I should speak	2Ne	6: 4	
understand, because they d. it.	Jac	4:14	
because they d. it God hath		4:14	
the desire which I d. of him—	En	1:13	
which king Benjamin d. of them;	Mos	5: 6	
Ye have spoken the words that I d.;		5: 6	
he d. that Alma should also speak		25:14	
to all who d. to hear them.		27:35	
and d. of him that he would grant		28: 1	
and d. of him to know whether	Al	16: 5	
and d. that he should come in		19: 2	
and d. to know what she would		19: 3	
Now, this was what Ammon d.,		19: 6	
what the queen d. of him was		19: 7	
as the queen had d. him;		19: 7	
Lamoni d. that Ammon should		20: 1	
this is all that thou hast d.,		20:26	
if a man d. to serve God,		30: 9	
whosoever d. to worship must		31:14	
as ye have d. to know of me		32:24	
ye have d. of my beloved brother		34: 3	
for as he has d. to do evil		41: 5	
and d. righteousness until the end		41: 6	
If he has d. to do evil,		42:28	
for he d. to speak with him.		47:10	
Amalickiah d. him to come		47:13	
very thing which Amalickiah d.		47:15	
the thing that Amalickiah d.,		47:16	
she also d. him that he should		47:33	
she also d. him that he should		47:33	
d. that a few particular points		51: 2	
d. that he should no longer be		51: 4	
d. all his forces when he		53: 5	
he d. the provisions which were		54: 2	
he also d. his own people for the		54: 2	
d. that they should be brought;	He	9:13	
and came according as ye d.,		9:15	
to the words which had been d.,		11: 9	
whithersoever he d. to carry	3Ne	6:17	
iniquity he d. they should—		6:17	
for that which they most d.;		19: 9	
they d. that the Holy Ghost		19: 9	
because ye d. this thing of me;		28: 3	
unto him the thing which they d.		28: 5	
have d. the thing which John,		28: 6	
lifted up by the Jews, d. of me.		28: 6	
thing which ye have d. of me,		28: 9	
ye have d. that ye might bring		28: 9	
d. of him that he would grant	Mrm	6: 2	
unto me the thing which I d.		6: 3	
have d. concerning our brethren.		9:36	
the people d. of them that they	Eth	6:22	
that he d. her to wife.		8:11	
the assistance which Akish d.		8:14	
to do whatsoever thing he d.		8:17	
according to that which he d.		9:10	
fighting for that which he d.		13:25	
Martin Harris has d. a witness	DC	5: 1	
he d. of me that he might bring		7: 4	
my beloved has d. that he		7: 5	
joy in that which ye have d.		7: 8	
according to that which you d.		9: 1	
my disciples, d. in their prayers		10:46	
many times you have d. of me		15: 4	
many times you have d. of me		16: 4	
have d. to know of me,		18: 1	

DESIRED 247 DESIROUS

DESIRED
d., with exceedingly great desire,	DC 127:10
a tree to be d. to make her wise,	Mses 4:12

DESIREDST
thou d. that thou mightest	DC 7: 4

DESIRES
great d. to know of the mysteries	1 Ne 2:16
d. of this great and abominable	13: 8
unto thee according to thy d.,	En 1:12
after the d. of his own heart.	Mos 11: 2
to their own carnal wills and d.;	16:12
and good d. towards God,	18:28
should do according to their d.	21: 6
to the d. of their enemies.	21:13
they relinquished their d. for a king,	29:38
that my d. have been gratified.	Al 7:18
unto them, according to their d.,	9:20
according to my faith and d.	18:35
may do according to his own d.	20:24
their God according to their d.,	21:22
might flee, according to their d.	22:34
the word according to their d.,	23: 3
to the d. of their enemies.	27: 3
ought not to harrow up in my d.,	29: 4
it is given according to his d.,	29: 5
and according to your own d.;	30:27
them according to their d.,	30:28
people bring concerning their d.;	35: 5
the d. of their hearts were good,	41: 3
according to his d. of happiness,	41: 5
good according to his d. of good;	41: 5
evil according to his d. of evil;	41: 5
God according to their d.	43: 9
the d. which ye have for life,	44: 6
that he did according to his d.,	46:32
(for he had gained his d.)	47:20
thus it was according to his d.	49:15
may do according to your d.	55:12
But he had obtained his d.;	55:20
the city Gid, according to his d.,	55:26
their great d. which they had	60: 9
who have d. to usurp power	60:27
was granted according to their d.	62:28
receive according to our d.	Eth 3: 2
of Shule according to his d.	7:22
of his own will and carnal d.,	DC 3: 4
if ye have d. to serve God	4: 3
man that d. the witness.—	5:23
the things which he d. to see.	5:24
unto thee because of thy d.;	6:20
that if you have good d.—	6:27
both have according to your d.,	7: 8
behold, according to your d.,	11:11
speak unto all who have good d.,	11:27
d. to bring forth and establish	12: 7
the d. of which I have spoken;	18:37
by their d. and their works	18:38
whose d. have come up before me.	67: 1
from all your lustful d.,	88:121
offering up of your most holy d.	95:16
and covetous d. among them;	101: 6
sins, and of all their covetous d.,	117: 4
that have d. to dwell therein,	125: 4

DESIREST
unto me: Behold, what d. thou?	1 Ne 11: 2
he said unto me: What d. thou?	11:10
What d. thou of me?	Al 18:15
whatsoever thou d. which is right,	18:17
whatsoever thou d. I will give	18:21
whatsoever thou d. of me I will	18:21
If thou d. this thing, if thou	22:16
receive the hope which thou d.	22:16
John, my beloved, what d. thou?	DC 7: 1
because thou d. this thou shalt	7: 3
a few years, if thou d. of me,	99: 7

DESIRETH
voice of the people d. anything	Mos 29:26
the king d. thee to stay.	Al 18:13
whether he d. good or evil,	29: 5
therefore he d., in the first place,	32:22

do whatsoever your heart d.—	He 13:27
d. to be baptized in my name,	3 Ne 11:23
Satan d. to have you, that he	18:18
whoso d. to reap, let him thrust	DC 6: 3
whoso d. to reap let him thrust	11: 3
whoso d. to reap let him thrust	12: 3
whoso d. to reap let him thrust	14: 3
Satan d. to sift him as chaff.	52:12
and Satan d. to have thee;	Mses 5:23

DESIRING
d. to know of them the cause of	1 Ne 15: 6
d. many wives and concubines,	Jac 1:15
d. to know of his people if	Mos 5: 1
d. to know their will concerning	29: 1
d. them to come unto him.	Al 15: 4
d. the voice of the people	27:21
d. to know whether they should	33: 1
d. them that they should cast out	35: 8
d. him that he should inquire of	43:23
d. that the leader of those who	47:10
d. him to come down.	47:11
d. that he would come down,	47:12
d. him that he would spare the	47:33
d. that he should read it,	51:15
d. him that he would be faithful	52:10
d. him that he would come out	52:20
d. that he would exchange	54: 1
d. he should cause men to	59: 3
d. that he would conduct him	He 2: 7
d. that they might be baptized	16: 1
d. that ye would yield up unto	3 Ne 3: 6
d. him that he would spare	Eth 15: 4
d. that he would not come	15:18
d. also to be one who	Abr 1: 2
and d. to receive instructions,	1: 2

DESIROUS
we were d. that he should tarry	1 Ne 4:36
d. to return unto the land of	7: 7
began to be d. that my faimily	8:12
I was d. that Laman and Lemuel	8:17
I, Nephi, was d. also that I might	10:17
they were d. to return again to	16:36
were d. that they might not labor,	17:18
were d. to throw me into the	17:48
I, Nephi, was d. that they should	2 Ne 5:18
I am d. for the welfare of your souls.	6: 3
the people were d. to retain in	Jac 1:11
who were d. to possess the land	Om 1:27
he was d. to know concerning	Mos 7: 1
For I am d. that these records	8:12
I am d. to know the cuase of	8:12
I was d. that they should not be	9: 1
as many as were d. to go up	9: 3
were d. to bring us into bondage,	9:12
as ye are d. to come into the fold	18: 8
Limhi was d. that his father	19:17
d. to go against them to battle.	21: 6
For they were d. to take them	21:21
people were d. to be baptized;	21:33
were d. to become even as Alma	21:34
They were d. to be baptized	21:35
d. that Alma should be their king,	23: 6
was d. that he might be baptized;	25:17
d. that they might be baptized	25:17
d. to take upon them the name of	25:23
they were d. that salvation should	28: 3
were d. beyond measure to know	28:12
We are d. that Aaron thy son	29: 1
for ye are d. to have a king.	29: 5
that are d. to follow the voice of	Al 5:57
d. that they might destroy Alma	14: 2
whosoever were d. to be baptized.	15:13
the Nephites were d. to obtain	16: 4
was d. to confer upon them,	17: 6
therefore he was d. to learn them.	20:27
d. that they might have a name,	23:16
was d. to be a king;	46: 4
d. that he should be their king;	46: 4
d. to maintain their liberty,	46:28
d. that the law should be altered	51: 4

DESIROUS 248 DESTROY

d. that Pahoran should be	Al	51: 5
d. that the law should be		51: 5
d. that Pahoran should remain		51: 6
Lehi was not d. to overtake them		52:30
and were d. to take up arms		53:13
more d. to drink of the wine;		55:10
d. that the Lamanites should		56:21
not d. to make an attack upon		56:21
we were d., if they should pass		56:23
d. to bring a stragagem into effect		56:30
exceedingly d. to overtake us		58:19
d. that the Lamanites should		62:19
d. to join the people of Ammon		62:27
that as many as were d.,		62:28
were d. that he should be their	He	1: 7
who were d. that he should be		1: 9
were d. to remain Lamanites,	3Ne	6: 3
people of Akish were d. for gain,	Eth	9:11
as Akish was d. for power;		9:11
d. that his children should be	DC	74: 3

DESOLATE

cause to inherit the d. heritages;	1Ne	21: 8
For thy waste and thy d. places,		21:19
have lost my children, and am d.,		21:21
and she shall be d.,	2Ne	13:26
many houses shall be d.,		15: 9
and the land be utterly d.;		16:11
all of them in the d. valleys,		17:19
fierce anger, to lay the land d.;		23: 9
shall cry in their d. houses,		23:22
behold, in one day it was left d.;	Al	16:10
and their lands remained d.		16:11
rendered d. and without timber,	He	3: 5
now no part of the land was d.,		3: 6
the land it was called d.		3: 6
and many cities shall become d.		14:24
houses shall be left unto you d.		15: 1
the cities which had been left d.	3Ne	4: 1
Nephites had left their lands d.,		4: 3
and the places were left d.		8:14
your dwellings shall become d.		10: 7
more are the children of the d.		22: 1
the d. cities to be inhabited.		22: 3
shall be left unto them d.	DC	84:115
it was formed, was empty and d.,	Abr	4: 2
down, and left unto you d.	JS	1: 2

DESOLATING

a d. scourge shall go forth	DC	5:19
for a d. sickness shall cover		45:31

DESOLATION

thy d. and destruction,	2Ne	8:19
in the d. which shall come		20: 3
And it was called D. of Nehors;	Al	16:11
the land which they called D.,		22:30
on the northward was called D.,		22:31
line Bountiful and the land D.,		22:32
which was south of the land D.,		46:17
to the borders of the land D.;		50:34
land Bountiful, by the land D.,		63: 5
your d. is already come upon you,	He	13:32
land Bountiful and the land D.	3Ne	3:23
together at the land D.	Mrm	3: 5
did come down to the city of D.		3: 7
out of the land D.		4: 1
back again to the land of D.		4: 2
take possession of the city D.,		4: 2
it was also near the city D.		4: 3
possession again of the city D.		4: 8
take possession of the city D.,		4:13
come down against the city D.;		4:19
sore battle foaght in the land D.,		4:19
near the land which is called D.	Eth	7: 6
and d. are sent forth upon	DC	29: 8
d. shall come upon this		45:19
every d. which I have told you		45:21
d. shall come upon the wicked.		63:37
the d. and utter abolishment		84:114
the d. of abomination in the		84:117
the d. of abomination which		88:85
a day of d., of weeping,		112:24

shall see the abomination of d.,	JS	1:12
shall the abomination of d.		1:32

DESOLATIONS

except d. upon Babylon,	DC	35:11
in divers places, and many d.;		45:33
d. by famine, sword, and	JS	2:45

DESPAIR

and doom us to eternal d.?	Al	26:19
hope ye must needs be in d.;	Mro	10:22
d. cometh because of iniquity.		10:22
I was ready to sink into d.	JS	2:16

DESPERATELY

and sixty fought most d.;	Al	57:19

DESPISE

they are rich they d. the poor,	2Ne	9:30
d. not the revelations of God.	Jac	4: 8
hold to the one and d. the other.	3Ne	13:24
they did d. them because of	4Ne	1:29
will d. the works of the Lord?	Mrm	9:26
will d. the children of Christ?		9:26
O then d. not, and wonder not,		9:27
of God, and d. his words.—	DC	3: 7
no man d. my servant Oliver		117:15
no man d. my servant George,		124:21

DESPISED

have d. the Holy One of Israel,	1Ne	19:14
and d. the shame of it,	2Ne	9:18
d. the word of the Holy One		15:24
they d. the words of plainness,	Jac	4:14
He is d. and rejected of men;	Mos	14: 3
was d., and we esteemed him not.		14: 3
for they are d. of all men	Al	32: 5
d. of your brethren because of		32:12
have been d. by mine enemies;		33:10
we, who are d. because we take		46:18
those who are unlearned and d.,	DC	35:13
d. by those that flattered them.		121:20
Lamech was d., and cast out,	Mses	5:54
they were d. among all people.		7: 8

DESPISERS

all ye who are d. of the works	Mrm	9:26

DESPISETH

to him whom man d., to him	1Ne	21: 7
they are they whom he d.;	2Ne	9:42

DESPISING

up with their pride, d. others,	Al	4:12

DESPITEFULLY

pray for them who d. use you	3Ne	12:44

DESTINATION

place of my d. in Pennsylvania;	JS	2:62

DESTINED

d. order or sphere of creation,	DC	77: 3
I was d. to prove a disturber	JS	2:20

DESTINIES

hold the d. of all the armies	DC	117: 6

DESTROY

and they seek to d. his life.	1Ne	1:hd
to d. Laban, even as the Egyptians.		4: 3
they should pursue us and d. us.		4:36
do they d. the saints of God,		13: 9
utterly d. the mixture of thy seed,		13:30
shall d. the seed of thy brethren.		13:31
to his word he did d. them;		17:31
not suffer that the wicked shall d.		22:16
must needs d. the wisdom of God	2Ne	2:12
and they that seek to d. him		3:14
to d. my peace and afflict my soul?		4:27
should come upon us and d. us;		5:14
and none will he d. that believe		6:14
as if he were ready to d.?		8:13
I must needs d. the secret works		10:15

DESTROY

and d. the way of thy paths.	2Ne 13:12
but in his heart it is to d.	20: 7
They shall not hurt nor d.	21: 9
the Lord shall utterly d. the	21:15
indignation, to d. the whole land.	23: 5
he shall d. the sinners thereof	23: 9
For I will d. her speedily;	23:22
the prophets, and d. them not,	26: 8
seek to d. the things of God.	26:17
and the wicked will he d.;	30:10
he must d. the wicked by fire.	30:10
They shall not hurt nor d.	30:15
seek to d. the people of Nephi,	Jac 1:14
of your hearts d. your souls!	2:16
the Lord God will not d. them,	3: 6
the power of their arms to d. us	7:24
they would d. our records	En 1:14
continually seeking to d. us.	1:20
come upon them and d. them—	Mos 9: 1
upon us again unawares and d. us;	10: 2
upon my people and d. them.	10: 7
and do all they could to d. them;	10:17
this land, that they may d. them;	10:18
the Lamanites began to d. them,	11:17
they repent I will utterly d. them	12: 8
and saith that God will d. them.	12: 9
upon those that d. his people.	17:19
he sent his army to d. them.	18:33
are upon us, and they will d. us;	19: 7
yea, they will d. my people.	19: 7
molest them nor seek to d. them.	19:29
to d. the people of Limhi.	20: 7
whom this people sought to d.?	20:18
not overtake them to d. them.	23: 2
they should not d. their husbands.	23:33
and did not d. them, because	23:34
to d. the church of God,	27:10
seeking to d. the church,	27:10
seek to d. the church no more,	27:16
and d. the souls of many people.	29: 7
we have no right to d. my son,	29: 8
we have any right to d. another	29: 8
and if he can he will d. them;	29:23
intent to d. the church of God.	Al 2: 4
came upon them to d. them.	2:27
their brethren sought to d. them,	3: 7
last, if he can, he will d. him.	5:59
repent the Lord God will d. them.	8:16
may d. the liberty of thy people,	8:17
repent, or he will utterly d. you	9:12
your iniquities, to d. his people.	9:19
Lamanites might d. all his people	9:19
those men who sought to d. them,	10:14
might d. that which was good;	11:21
thou mightest have cause to d. me.	11:25
his lying and deceiving to d.	12: 1
they might d. Alma and Amulek;	14: 2
the Lord will d. this people	14:24
slay the people and d. the city.	16: 2
which they said God could not d.,	16: 9
thou that hast sought to d. him,	20:19
Ammon had no desire to d. him,	20:26
to d. their brethren,	24: 5
if our brethren seek to d. us,	24:16
and if our brethren d. us,	24:16
threatenings to d. his church.	26:18
against them, that we d. them	26:25
lest they overrun us and d. us.	26:25
the intent to d. our brethren,	26:26
their many struggles to d. them,	27: 1
they began again to d. them.	27: 2
Behold, the Nephites will d. us,	27: 6
he may d. the children of God.	30:42
for it did d. their craft;	35: 3
seeking to d. the church of God;	36: 6
no more to d. the church of God.	36: 9
more to d. the church of God—	36:11
except they repent I will d. them	37:25
d. the great plan of happiness.	42: 8
it should d. the work of justice.	42:13
the Lamanites would d.	43:10
intention to d. their brethren,	43:29
that ye cannot d. this our faith.	44: 3
seek to d. the church of God,	Al 46:10
to d. the foundation of liberty	46:10
that they were coming to d. them,	47: 5
and had gone to d. them	48:24
would d. the people of that city.	49:13
d. all such as should attempt to	49:19
did attempt to d. the Nephites	49:23
come upon them and d. them.	50:28
behold, if ye seek to d. us more	54:13
we will seek to d. you;	54:13
d. them in their drunkenness.	55:19
they might d. them with poison	55:30
yea, and will d. our people.	57:31
resolving by stratagem to d. us;	58: 6
that they could easily d. us with	58:15
insomuch that they did d. them	58:21
to d. his righteous people.	60:31
and sought to d. the liberty of	He 1: 8
lay wait to d. Halaman also;	2: 3
sought to d. Helaman.	2: 5
the judgment-seat to d. Helaman,	2: 6
by this band to d. Helaman—	2: 6
seek no more to d. my servants	5:29
seek no more to d. my servants.	5:32
to d. them off the face of the	6:20
people who sought to d. Nephi	8:10
seeketh to d. the souls of men.	8:28
and seek to d. my life.	9:24
will in this thing week to d. me.	9:25
did no more seek to d. Nephi,	11:18
band of robbers, and to d. them.	11:28
band of robbers, and did d. many;	11:30
down out of heaven and d. it.	13:13
all manner of ways to d. him;	13:26
who hath sought to d. our souls.	13:37
with me and do seek to d. me,	14:10
I will not utterly d. them, but	15:16
my will, I will utterly d. them,	15:17
upon the Nephites and d. them.	3Ne 3: 3
and d. them in their own lands.	3:20
they did hope to d. the robbers	4: 4
enter into a covenant to d. them,	6:29
with another to d. the governor,	6:30
did d. upon the judgment seat,	7: 1
d. the government of the land.	7: 2
covenant to d. the government.	7:11
did d. the peace of my people	9: 9
to d. them from before my face,	9: 9
did send down fire and d. them,	9:11
to d. the law or the prophets.	12:17
am not come to d. but to fulfil;	12:17
I do not d. the prophets,	15: 6
I do not d. that which hath	15: 7
that he may not d. my people,	18:31
and I will d. thy chariots;	21:14
so will I d. thy cities.	21:18
I have created the waster to d.	22:16
not d. the fruits of your ground;	24:11
d. the inhabitants of our land.	Mrm 5: 4
the Lamanites would d. them)	6: 6
We will d. the work of the Lord,	8:21
again of old, to d. his father.	Eth 9:26
sought again to d. the kingdom.	10:33
the people sought to d. them.	11: 2
the Lord would utterly d. them	11:12
and sought to d. Coriantumr	13:15
unto them who sought to d. him.	13:16
lest they should d. me.	Mro 1: 1
Lamanites shall d. this people;	9: 3
d. their brethren the Nephites,	DC 3:18
the lying in wait to d. thee yea,	5:32
many that lie in wait to d. thee	5:33
they have sought to d. you;	10: 6
trusted has sought to d. you.	10: 6
has also sought to d. your gift.	10: 7
that he may d. this work;	10:12
Therefore we will d. him, and	10:19
to d. the work of God;	10:23
in wait to catch, that ye may d.;	10:25
in a lie, that they may d. him.	10:25
seeking to d. the souls of men.	10:27
that they shall c. my work;	10:43
I do not bring it to d. that	10:52

DESTROY 250 DESTROYER

not say this to d. my church	DC	10:54
to d. the crops of the earth.		29:16
enemy seeketh to d. my people.		44: 5
Satan seeketh to d. his soul;		64:17
earth, to save life and to d.;		77: 8
and they will not d. you.		82:22
lest you d. the wheat also.		86: 6
God shall d. that temple.		93:35
d. and lay waste mine enemies;		105:15
d. her if she abide not in my law.		132:54
lest an enemy come and d. him;		132:57
for Satan seeketh to d.;		132:57
for I will d. her;		132:64
sought to d. the agency of man,	Mses	4: 3
he sought to d. the world.		4: 6
the Lord said: I will d. man		8:26
behold I will d. all flesh		8:30
to d. him who hath lifted up	Abr	1:17
as to d. all confidence in	JS	2:12
all this did not d. the reality		2:24

DESTROYED

that they might not be d.—	T Pg	
great city Jerusalem must be d.	1 Ne	1: 4
Jerusalem—that it should be d.,		1:13
that great city, could be d.		2:13
knew that Jerusalem must be d.,		3:17
after this they should be d., even that		10: 3
and after thy seed shall be d., and		13:35
are at this day about to be d.;		17:43
surely come that they must be d.,		17:43
cut off nor d. from before me.		20:19
that fight against Zion shall be d.,		22:14
know that Jerusalem is d.;	2 Ne	1: 4
ye be cut off and d. forever;		1:17
seed shall not utterly be d.		3: 3
for thy seed shall not be d.,		3:23
thou shalt not utterly be d.;		4: 9
that believe not in him shall be d.,		6:15
seed shall not utterly be d.,		9:53
they who shall not be d.		10: 6
they that are led of them are d.		19:16
and the yoke shall be d.		20:27
and d. the cities thereof,		24:17
because thou hast d. thy land		24:20
one generation hath been d.		25: 9
been d. from generation to		25: 9
hath any of them been d. save		25: 9
they have been d. save it be		25:10
Jerusalem shall be d. again;		25:14
and also Babylon shall be d.;		25:15
For those who shall be d.		26:16
as those who have been d.		26:18
destroyed have been d. speedily;		26:18
they shall not be d.,		28:17
the Gentiles are utterly d.		30: 1
and by any means be d.,	En	1:13
the Lamanites should not be d.,		1:13
d. fromm off the face of the land.	Jar	1:10
being d. upon the face of the land;		1:12
part of the Nephites were d.	Om	1: 5
of the people who have been d.,	Mos	8:12
this very people who have been d.;		8:12
that they should not be d.		9: 1
army was d. in the wilderness.		9: 2
will not suffer that I shall be d.		13: 3
that his father should not be d.;		19:17
peopled and which had been d.,		21:26
those people who had been d.		28:12
account of the people who were d.,		28:17
from the time that they were d. back		28:17
obey his laws he causeth to be d.;		29:23
preserve his people from being d.	Al	2:21
of their fields of grain were d.,		3: 2
and d. by the Lamanites.		4: 2
of you, my brethren, were they d.?		5: 8
you, that ye may not be d.		5:60
great city should be d. in one day.		9: 4
preserved them from being d.,		9:10
battle, that they might not be d.,		9:22
d. from off the face of the earth?		9:24
this cause, that ye may not be d.,		9:25

works of justice could not be d.,	Al	12:32
might be burned and d. by fire.		14: 8
they had d. the people who were		16: 3
people of Ammonihah were d.;		16: 9
of the Ammonihahites was d.,		16: 9
had d. so many of their brethren,		19:27
had been peopled and been d.,		22:30
of Ammonihah, and d. them.		25: 2
our enemies, that we be not d.		27: 5
truth, that thy soul may be d.		30:46
If thou wilt of thyself be d.,		36: 9
If thou wilt be d. of thyself,		36:11
lest perhaps I should be d.,		36:11
those people who have been d.,		37:21
they should be d. from off the		37:22
therefore they have been d.,		37:26
into darkness also and be d.		37:27
that this people might not be d.		37:28
d. on account of their wickedness		37:29
work of justice could not be d.;		42:13
works of justice would be d.,		42:22
the Lamanites they would be d.		43:11
not suffer that they should be d.;		43:12
Lord suffer that we shall be d.		44: 4
they were all about to be d.,		44:19
and is not d. in that great and		45:14
shall be trodden down and d.,		46:18
that we shall be d., even as		46:22
that they might not be d.		47:15
because the Lamanites had d. it		49: 3
battle even until you are d.		54:12
perhaps d. our little army;		56:19
were not all d. by the sword;		57:23
feared lest that he should be d.;	He	2:11
they were not d. out of the land.		3:23
trodden down, and slain, and d.		4:20
d. from among the Lamanites.		6:37
utterly d. except thou shalt repent.		7:24
d. from off the face of the earth.		7:28
Jerusalem was d. according to		8:20
dispute that Jerusalem was d.?		8:21
people shall be d. by the sword;		11: 4
whom thou hast already d.		11:11
those who were about to be d.	3 Ne	1:11
with an oath, ye shall not be d.;		3: 8
of the government were d.,		7: 6
Lord, that they might not be d.	Mrm	2:17
were d. by the Lamanites,		5: 5
were swept down and d.		5: 7
Lamanites, until they were all d.		8: 2
ancient inhabitants who were d.	Eth	1: 1
tower down until they were d.		1: 5
be d. if they did not repent.		7:23
behold, they shall be d.;		8:22
where the Nephites were d.,		9: 3
or they should be d. when they		9:20
be d. if they did not repent.		9:28
the inhabitants began to be d.		9:30
the poisonous serpents were d.		10:19
lest they should be d.,		12: 3
after it should be d. it should		13: 5
Otherwise they should be d.,		13:21
and every soul should be d. save		13:21
their minds that they might be d.;		15:19
consumed away and utterly d.	DC	5:19
Joseph Smith, Jun., may not be d.,		17: 4
and this people shall be d.		45:19
and the enemy d. their works,		101:51
not by me shall be shaken and d.		132:14
they shall be d. in the flesh,		132:26
adultery and shall be d.		132:41
shall be d., saith the Lord		132:52
she shall be d., saith the Lord;		132:54
adultery, and shall be d.;		132:63
unto him, or she shall be d.,		132:64
that they shall utterly be d.;	Mses	7: 7
and utterly d. them,	Abr	1:20
if I did I should be d.	JS	2:42

DESTROYER

| the d. rideth upon the face | DC | 61:19 |

DESTROYER 251 DESTRUCTION

| from the hands of the d. | DC 101:54 |
| the d. I have sent forth to | 105:15 |

DESTROYERS
| make haste against thy d.; | 1 Ne 21:17 |

DESTROYETH
and d. the nations of the wicked.	1 Ne 17:37
and the wicked he d.,	17:38
and d. when he pleases,	DC 63: 4

DESTROYING
for the purpose of d. the king,	Al 24:20
d. the people of Anti-Nephi-Lehi	24:20
to the d. of Satan and his works	DC 19: 3
the d. angel shall pass by	89:21

DESTRUCTION
concerning the d. of Jerusalem,	1 Ne 1:18
concerning the d. of Jerusalem;	7:13
concerning the d. of Jerusalem	7:13
shall be the d. of all nations,	11:36
been digged for the d. of men	14: 3
who digged it, unto their utter d.,	14: 3
not the d. of the soul, save it be	14: 3
and also into d., both temporally	14: 7
to lead them away to d.	15:24
the Lord, did deliver you from d.;	17:14
unto the scattering them to d.	17:32
against them unto their d.,	17:35
which threatened them with d.,	18:20
and the land of thy d., shall	21:19
unto the d. of their enemies	22:17
upon you, unto the d.,	2 Ne 1:22
d. of both soul and body.	1:22
shall scourge them even unto d.	5:25
unto the d. of their enemies,	6:14
thy desolation and d.,	8:19
and mine anger in their d.	20:25
as a d. from the Almighty.	23: 6
sweep it with the besom of d.,	24:23
the d. which should come upon	25:10
a speedy d. cometh unto my	26:10
foolishness they shall reap d.;	26:10
then cometh speedy d.,	26:11
with a sore curse, even unto d.;	Jac 2:33
upon those who seek your d.	3: 1
shall scourge you even unto d.	3: 3
bring your children unto d.,	3:10
from going down speedily to d.	En 1:23
almost all the d. of my people,	WM 1: 1
witness the entire d. of my people.	1: 2
which bringeth immediate d.	Mos 7:31
to know the cause of their d.	8:12
a great d. to come upon them.	21:20
committed, yea, and what great d.!	29:17
great d. did come upon them;	29:18
he will visit you with great d.	29:27
it would prove their entire d.	Al 1:12
which would prove their d.	3: 8
bringing on the d. of the people.	4:11
everlasting d. did await them.	5: 7
which doth bind you down to d.,	7:15
ye shall be visited with utter d.;	9:18
to the utter d. of this people	10:18
they would be ripe for d.	10:19
even now be visited with utter d.;	10:22
of the d. of this people	10:27
you down to everlasting d.,	12: 6
and led by his will down to d.	12:11
down to an everlasting d.,	12:17
the everlasting d. of your souls;	12:36
it shall be to your own d.	13:20
witness the d. of those who	14: 9
fear of d. had come upon them.	14:26
and from death, and from d.—	15:17
be unbelieving, and go on to d.,	16:17
in the d. of their brethren;	17:35
with everlasting darkness and d.;	26:15
not consign us to an awful d.,	26:19
it was in vain to seek their d.,	27: 1
this work of d. among those	27: 4
save them from everlasting d.—	27: 4

saw this great work of d.,	Al 27: 4
the d. of many thousand lives;	28:10
of death and d. among men,	28:14
be unto salvation or unto d.	29: 4
bringing many souls down to d.,	30:47
in thine anger with speedy d.	33:10
rather led them away unto d.;	36:14
d. shall come upon all those	37:28
secret combinations, even unto d.,	37:31
that I must stop the work of d.	38: 7
the hearts of many people to d.;	39:12
and also their d. and misery.	42:26
of the great d. among them,	43:39
tongue, and people, unto d.,	45:16
hitherto a cause of all their d.	51:16
upon you, even to your utter d.	54: 9
the saving of his people from d.;	55:19
to our overthrow and utter d.	58: 9
plan laid to lead them on to d.;	58:24
visit you even to your utter d.	60:29
entire d. of the people of Nephi.	He 2:13
greatness of the d. of the people	3: 6
therefore they were ripening for d.,	5: 2
justice, save it were to their d.	5: 3
down the people unto d.	6:25
the people down to an entire d.,	6:28
ripening for an everlasting d.	6:40
his anger, to their utter d.	7:hd
all this people, even unto d.;	8: 5
testified of the d. of Jerusalem)	8:20
and wickedness, for everlasting d.;	8:26
mourn, because of the great d.	9:22
famine, and with pestilence, and d.,	10: 6
shall be smitten, even unto d.	10:11
concerning their d. if they	10:12
shall be smitten even unto d.	10:14
who did carry on this work of d.	11: 2
of d. did cease by the sword	11: 5
work of d. did also continue	11: 6
concerning our d. be fulfilled.	11: 8
in the d. of those wicked men	11:11
d. which has come unto them.	11:15
d. among the people of Nephi,	11:27
be a stop put to this work of d.;	11:28
were also visited with much d.	11:30
did do great d. unto them;	11:33
they were ripening again for d.	11:37
heavy d. awaiteth this people,	13: 6
enemies, to behold your utter d.;	13:10
generation shall visit your d.	13:10
you, then shall ye be ripe for d.;	13:14
you, and your d. is made sure;	13:32
and your d. is made sure!	13:38
plan of d. which they had laid	3 Ne 1:16
were threatened with utter d.	2:13
sword of d. did hang over	2:19
would visit you with utter d.	3: 4
that d. whould come upon you.	3: 6
great d. which came upon them	4:22
delivered from an everlasting d.	4:33
d. in the land southward.	8:11
d. in the land northward;	8:12
d. which had come upon them.	8:23
is the way, which leadeth to d.,	14:13
notwithstanding the great d.	Mrm 2: 8
we might save them from d.	2:21
sorrow for d. of this people;	5:11
concerning the d. of my people,	6: 1
great d. had come upon.	6:22
sad tale of the d. of my people.	8: 3
great and marvelous is the d. of	8: 7
caused the d. of this people	Eth 8:21
the d. of the people of Nephi.	8:21
the work of d. come upon you,	8:23
to your overthrow and d.	8:23
to pass the d. of all people,	8:25
who did not seek his d.	9: 2
the d. of nearly all the people	9:12
the d. of his fathers,	10: 2
the d. of that great people	11: 1
of the d. of the people	11: 5
be a great d. among them,	11: 6
that there was a great d.,	11: 7
against them to their utter d.;	11:20

DESTRUCTION 252 DEVIL

concerning the d. of the people	Eth	13: 1
a way for their everlasting d.		14:25
so terrible was the d. among		14:27
proven their d. except they	Mro	8:27
unto him, or their utter d.;		9:22
people of the d. of Jerusalem;	DC	5:20
you and bring your soul to d.		8: 4
he may lead their souls to d.		10:22
the d. of thyself and property.		19:33
to bring to pass even your d.		38:13
who are well-nigh ripened for d.		61:31
delight not in the d. of		109:43
not look back lest sudden d.		133:15
the d. of the temple,	JS	1: 4
or the d. of the wicked,		1: 4
the d. of Jerusalem,		1:12
come, or the d. of the wicked;		1:31
if I were doomed to sudden d.		2:15
and abandon myself to d.—		2:16

DESTRUCTIONS

because of the d. of my people,	1Ne	15: 5
and contentions and d. of my people.		19: 4
because of their iniquities, d.,	2Ne	10: 6
and all manner of d.,		26: 6
of wars, and contentions, and d.,	En	1:23
them their wars and their d.	Al	50:21
many great d. have I caused	3Ne	9:12
all these deaths and d. by fire,		10:14
d. which came upon the people,	Eth	13:14
great d. await the wicked.	DC	34: 9
many d. upon the waters;		61: 5

DETECT

now behold, we will d. this man,	He	9:17
you may therefore d. him.	DC	129: 8

DETECTED

But the hypocrites shall be d.	DC	50: 8

DETECTING

d. the devil when he appeared	DC	128:20

DETERMINATION

Aaron saw the d. of the queen,	Al	22:22
the land of Noah with a firm d.;		49:13
a d. to conquer our enemies		58:12
it was his d. to go forth and	He	1:23
a d. to serve him to the end.	Mro	6: 3
having a d. to serve him	DC	20:37
a d. that is fixed, immovable,		88:133
to the d. to "ask of God"	JS	2:13
this, my d. to ask of God,		2:14

DETERMINE

d. concerning these prisoners	Al	57:16
power to d. the same.	DC	102:22
to d. whether any such case,		102:33

DETERMINED

be men, and be d. in one mind	2Ne	1:21
even d. in all the land.		20:23
they were d. that he should fall;	Al	17:36
that they were d. to slay them.		46: 2
their minds with a d. resolution		47: 6
For he was d., because of the		48: 4
d. by the sword to slay them.		50:26
Lamanites were d. to maintain		52: 5
Jacob was d. to slay them		52:34
which ye are still d. to carry on		54: 5
now they were d. to conquer		56:17
were d. to maintain those cities		56:26
still d. to maintain the city;		57:11
d. to overthrow the Lamanites		62:14
be d. in council among you.	DC	96: 3
which he had d. against me,	Abr	1:30

DETESTABLE

and all their d. things,	DC	98:20

DETHRONE

ye cannot d. an iniquitous king	Mos	29:21
to d. the king of the Lamanites.	Al	47: 4

at their head and d. the king	Al	47: 8
that he did d. his father,	Eth	9:27

DETHRONED

that Pahoran should be d.	Al	51: 5

DETHRONING

his designs in d. the king.	Al	47:16

DETROIT

the same place by the way of D.	DC	52: 8

DEVIATING

servant and never d. friend,	DC	128:25

DEVICE

he was a man of cunning d.	Al	46:10

DEVICES

by their cunning d. they might	Al	10:13
was expert in the d. of the devil,		11:21
working d. that he may destroy		30:42

DEVIL

are the temptations of the d.,	1Ne	12:17
and the temptations of the d.,		12:19
and I saw the d. that he was		13: 6
founded by the d. and his children,		14: 3
to the captivity of the d.,		14: 4
to the captivity of the d.,		14: 7
whose foundation is the d.		14: 9
the other is the church of the d.;		14:10
whose foundation is the d.,		14:17
the d. is the foundation of it;		15:35
kingdom of the d., which shall		22:22
who belong to the kingdom of the d.		22:23
the will and captivity of the d.	2Ne	1:18
wherefore, he became a d.,		2:17
that old serpent, who is the d.,		2:18
the captivity and power of the d.;		2:27
the d. power to captivate,		2:29
became the d., to rise no more.		9: 8
we become devils, angels to a d.,		9: 9
they who are filthy are the d.		9:16
the d., and death, and hell,		9:19
death and hell, and the d.,		9:26
the d. of all devils delighteth		9:37
and the d. hath obtained me,		9:46
and not to the will of the d.		10:24
because they yield unto the d.		26:10
to the combinations of the d.,		26:22
the kingdom of the d. must shake,		28:19
or the d. will grasp them with		28:19
thus the d. cheateth their souls,		28:21
saith unto them: I am no d.,		28:22
and death, and hell, and the d.,		28:23
shall be of the spirit of the d.		33: 5
may not become angels to the d.,	Jac	3:11
according to the power of the d.		7: 4
because thou art of the d.		7:14
deceived by the power of the d.		7:18
which is evil cometh from the d.	Om	1:25
and say that he hath a d.,	Mos	3: 9
the d., who is the master of sin,		4:14
and the d. has power over them;		16: 3
subjecting themselves to the d.		16: 5
the d. hath all power over him.		16: 5
also is the d. an enemy to God.		16: 5
being delivered up to the d.,		16:11
prepared for the d. and his angels.		26:27
to become subjects to the d.?	Al	5:20
children of the kingdom of the d.		5:25
that the d. is your shepherd,		5:39
is a liar and a child of the d.		5:39
is evil cometh from the d.		5:40
same becometh a child of the d.,		5:41
power and captivation of the d.		9:28
laying the foundation of the d.,		10:17
that this man is a child of the d.,		10:28
was expert in the devices of the d.,		11:21
plan, as to the subtlety of the d.,		12: 4
they are taken captive by the d.,		12:11
thou also possessed with the d.?		14: 7
of Alma and Amulek to the d.;		15:15

DEVIL

got the victory over the d.,	Al	16:21
and the power of the d., which		28:13
but the d. has power over you,		30:42
behold, the d. hath deceived me;		30:53
the d. will not support his children		30:60
cry unto him against the d., who		34:23
subjected to the spirit of the d.,		34:35
the d. hath all power over you;		34:35
by the temptation of the d.,		34:39
every temptation of the d.,		37:33
suffer not the d. to lead away		39:11
the spirit of the d. did enter into		40:13
led captive by the will of the d.		40:13
inherit the kingdom of the d.,		41: 4
the d. would never have power		48:17
And if it so be that there is a d.		54:22
the snares and the wiles of the d.,	He	3:29
when the d. shall send forth his		5:12
that the d. has got so great hold		7:15
that he is a sinner, and of the d.,		13:26
bind, him for behold he hath a d.;		16: 6
the power of the d. which is in him		16: 6
men and by the power of the d.,	3Ne	2: 2
by the temptations of the d.		6:17
and administered by the d.,		6:28
the d. laugheth, and his angels		9: 2
is not of me, but is of the d.,		11:29
lest ye be tempted by the d.,		18:15
than the cunning of the d.		21:10
men, or upon the works of the d.,		27:11
kept up by the power of the d.	Eth	8:16
for it is built up by the d.,		8:25
a man being a servant of the d.	Mro	7:11
he cannot be a servant of the d.		7:11
which is evil cometh of the d.;		7:12
for the d. is an enemy unto God,		7:12
good and of God to be of the d.		7:14
knowledge it is of the d.;		7:17
this manner doth the d. work,		7:17
the d. shall have power over his	DC	1:35
the d. has sought to lay a cunning		10:12
than the cunning of the d.		10:43
build up the kingdom of the d.—		10:56
save it be the church of the d.		18:20
fire, prepared for the d. and		29:28
Adam being tempted of the d.—		29:36
behold, the d. was before Adam,		29:36
thus came the d. and his angels;		29:37
needs be that the d. should tempt		29:39
the d. tempted Adam, and he		29:40
subject to the will of the d.,		29:40
that old serpent, even the d.,		76:28
through the power of the d.		76:31
with the d. and his angels in		76:33
with the d. and his angels—		76:36
reign with the d. and his angels		76:44
not be redeemed from the d.		76:85
serpent, who is called the d.,		88:110
the d. shall gather together his		88:113
the d. and his armies shall be		88:114
controllest and subjectest the d.,		121: 4
the very d. to tremble and palsy.		123:10
detecting the d. when he appeared		128:20
be the d. as an angel of light,		129: 8
became Satan, yea, even the d.,	Mses	4: 4
saying it was all of the d.,	JS	2:21

DEVILISH

For they are carnal and d.,	Mos	16: 3
becoming carnal, sensual, d.,		16: 3
for carnal, or d. for devilish—	Al	41:13
for carnal, or devilish for d.—		41:13
become carnal, sensual, and d.,		42:10
how vain, and how evil, and d.,	He	12: 4
man became sensual and d.,	DC	20:20
to be carnal, sensual, and d.	Mses	5:13
d., and are shut out from the		6:49

DEVILS

and with d. and unclean spirits;	1Ne	11:31
and the d. and the unclean spirits		11:31
we become d., angels to a devil,	2Ne	9: 9
devil of all d. delighteth in them.		9:37
And he shall cast out d.,	Mos	3: 6

DICTATES

cast out d. and unclean spirits;	3Ne	7:19
And as many as had d. cast out		7:22
in thy name have cast out d.,		14:22
my name shall they cast out d.;	Mrm	9:24
except casting out d., healing	DC	24:13
in faith, they shall cast out d.;		35: 9
evil spirits, or doctrines of d.,		46: 7
are of men, and others of d.		46: 7
name they shall cast out d.;		84:67
heal the sick, he shall cast out d.,		124:98

DEVISE

d. a plan whereby she could	Eth	8: 8

DEVISED

many means were d. to reclaim	Jac	7:24
cunning plans which he hath d. to	Al	28:13
have they d. murder,	Mses	6:28

DEVOTE

shalt d. all thy service in Zion;	DC	24: 7
d. his moneys for the		104:26
And d. his whole time to		106: 3

DEVOTED

let your time be d. to the	DC	26: 1

DEVOTION

forms for public or private d.;	DC	134: 4

DEVOTIONS

thy d. unto the Most High;	DC	59:10

DEVOUR

shall d. Israel with open mouth.	2Ne	19:12
it shall d. the briers and thorns,		19:18
shall d. his thorns and his briers		20:17
wild beasts, shall d. their flesh.	Mos	12: 2
their land also, and d. their grain.		12: 6
wolves enter not and d. his flock?	Al	5:59
did d. the carcasses of them	Eth	9:34
d. their flesh like unto wild	Mro	9:10
fowls of the air shall d. them	DC	29:20

DEVOURED

to be d. by wild beasts.	1Ne	7:16
are d. by the beasts of the forest.	Mos	8:21
and were d. by those beasts and	Al	2:38
with them all that they had not d.,	3Ne	6: 2
until they had d. them all.	Eth	9:34

DEVOURER

rebuke the d. for your sakes,	3Ne	24:11

DEVOURETH

as the fire d. the stubble,	2Ne	15:24

DEVOURING

with the flame of d. fire.	2Ne	27: 2
shall be cast down by d. fire,	DC	29:21
with vengeance, with d. fire.		97:26

DEVOUTLY

and called on the Lord d.,	Abr	2:18

DEW

even as a d. before the sun.	Mrm	4:18

DEWS

distil upon thy soul as the d.	DC	121:45
As the d. of Carmel, so shall		128:19

DIABOLICAL

concatenation of d. rascality	DC	123: 5

DICTATE

nor d. forms for public or	DC	134: 4

DICTATED

which shall be d. by my Spirit;	DC	104:81

DICTATES

after the d. of his own will	DC	3: 4
according to the d. of our own	AoF	11

DID 254 DIED

DID: see in the APPENDIX.

DIDST

and thou d. not know them.	1Ne	20: 6
because thou d. graft in the	Jac	5:34
and thou d. turn them to me.	Al	33: 4
my prayer, and thou d. hear me.		33: 5
thou d. hear me in my prayer.		33: 6
unto thee, thou d. hear me.		33: 7
yea, thou d. hear my cries,		33:10
thou d. visit them in thine anger		33:10
And thou d. hear me because of		33:11
thou d. bear all these things with		38: 4
thou d. not give so much heed		39: 2
thou d. go on unto boasting in		39: 2
Thou d. do that which was		39: 3
for thou d. forsake the ministry,		39: 3
thou d. hearken unto my words	He	11:14
barren, thou that d. not bear;	3Ne	22: 1
that d. not travail with child;		22: 1
thus d. thou manifest thyself	Eth	12:31
thou d. show thyself unto them		12:31
Thou d. baptize by water unto	DC	35: 5
which thou d. command us to		109: 4
as thou d. in the day of battle,		109:28
that which thou d. appoint a		109:51
the lands which thou d. give to		109:64
for his offering thou d. accept	Mses	5:38
Thou d. send thine angel to	Abr	2:13

DIE

should d. in their wickedness	1Ne	15:33
shall not d., but ye shall be as God,	2Ne	2:18
and they d. because of thirst.		7: 2
therein shall d. in like manner.		8: 6
be afraid of man, who shall d.,		8:12
that he should not d. in the pit,		8:14
our flesh must waste away and d.;		9: 4
and d. for all men, that all men		9: 5
deliberately killeth, for he shall d.		9:35
all those who d. in their sins;		9:38
and be merry, for tommorrow we d.;		28: 7
these things, for tomorrow we d.;		28: 8
and he saw that he must soon d.;	Jac	1: 9
not your hearts; for why will ye d.?		6: 6
on the morrow, for I shall d.;		7:16
unto the people before I shall d.		7:16
against him and d. in their sins;	Mos	15:26
thou art condemned to d.,	Al	1:14
ye say, if ye were called to d.		5:27
life, that they can d. no more;		11:45
shall also d. a spiritual death;		12:16
shall d. as to things pertaining		12:16
they cannot d., seeing there is		12:18
that the soul can never d.?		12:20
If thou eat thou shalt surely d.		12:23
unto man that they must d.;		12:27
and perhaps until the day I d.		17:23
and d. to atone for their sins;		33:22
for all do not d. at once,		40: 8
resurrection of those who d. after		40:19
they d. as to things pertaining to		40:26
was appointed unto man to d.—		42: 6
as the soul could never d.,		42: 9
a man murdered he should d.—		42:19
would he be afraid he would d. if		42:19
to conquer in this place or d.;		56:17
ye, repent ye! Why will ye d.?	He	7:17
he surely must d. that salvation		14:15
did curse God and wish to d.	Mrm	2:14
do faint by the way and d.	Mro	9:16
shall do these things away and d.,		10:26
for they d. in their sins,		10:26
not d. as to the temporal death,	DC	29:42
but he that killeth shall d.		42:19
if they d. they shall die unto me,		42:44
if they die they shall d. unto me,		42:44
weep for the loss of them that d.,		42:45
those that d. in me shall not		42:46
they that d. not in me, wo unto		42:47
voices and curse God and d.		45:32
those that d. shall rest from all	DC	59: 2
the dead that d. in the Lord,		63:49
dead and shall not d. after,		63:49
to him to d. at the age of man.		63:50
become old; old men shall d.;		63:51
notwithstanding it shall d.,		88:26
For notwithstanding they d.,		88:27
infant shall not d. until he		101:30
is they d. let them die unto me;		124:86
if they die let them d. unto me;		124:86
who should d. without a knowledge		128: 5
whether I should d. and thus see		130:16
fish stink, and d. for thirst.		133:68
I SHALL D. INNOCENT,		135: 4
eatest thereof thou shalt surely d.	Mses	3:17
shall ye touch it, lest ye d.		4: 9
woman: Ye shall not surely d.,		4:10
if so thou shouldst surely d.?		4:17
for thou shalt surely d.—for out of it		4:25
and if thou tell it thou shalt d.;		5:29
they tell it, they shall surely d.;		5:29
sons of men, lest he should d.		5:54
them with a curse, and they d.		7:10
know that all flesh shall d.;		8:17
thereof, thou shalt surely d.	Abr	5:13

DIED

Ishmael d., and was buried in the	1Ne	16:34
better that they had d. before		17:20
he d., and was buried.	2Ne	4:12
In the year that king Uzziah d.,		16: 1
In the year that king Ahaz d.		24:28
it came to pass that Nephi d.	Jac	1:12
many hearts d., pierced with deep		2:35
branch had withered away and d.		5:40
who have d. not knowing the will	Mos	3:11
lived three years and he d.		6: 5
king Laman d., and his son began		10: 6
these are they for whom he has d.,		15:12
that have d. before Christ came,		15:24
his father d., being eighty and		29:45
Mosiah d. also, in the thiry and		29:46
that many d. in the wilderness	Al	2:38
the king d. in that selfsame year		24: 4
that there were many who d.,		46:39
were some who d. with fevers,		46:40
were many who d. with old;		46:41
who d. in the faith of Christ		46:41
degrees to Lehonti, that he d.		47:18
the second chief judge, d.,		50:37
d. in the cause of their country		56:11
awake his servant before he d.,		62:36
and Helaman d., in the thirty		62:52
to pass that Moroni d. also.		63: 3
of the judges, Shiblon d. also,		63:10
For behold, Pahoran had d., and	He	1: 2
the wall, insomuch that he d.		1:21
Helaman d., and his eldest son		3:37
d., and his son Amos kept it in	4Ne	1:19
came to pass that Amos d. also,		1:21
Amos d.; and his brother,		1:47
Jared d., and his brother also.	Eth	6:29
he d., having seen exceeding		9:15
in his day; and he d. in peace.		9:22
his wife, d. being an hundred and		9:24
And he d., and Riplakish		10: 4
eight years, and his father d.		10:13
age he begat Levi; and he d.		10:14
Coriantor begat Ether, and he d.,		11:23
of Egypt, even so he d. there;		13: 7
he smote upon him until he d.;		14:16
he had struggled for breath, he d.		15:31
how many little children have d.	Mro	8:12
He was crucified, d., and rose	DC	20:23
even the dead which d. in me,		29:13
are they who d. without law;		76:72
who have d. in the gospel also;		128:18
He lived great, and he d. great in		135: 3
they d. for glory;		135: 6
I should have withered and d.	Mses	1:11
and thirty years, and he d.		6:12
and twelve years, and he d.		6:16

DIED 255 DILIGENCE

and five years, and he d. Mses 6:18
and ten years, and he d. 6:19
and ninety-five years, and he d. 6:20
and sixty-two years, and he d. 6:24
of the inhabitants thereof d. 8: 4
and sixty-nine years, and he d. 8: 7
seventy-seven years, and he d. 8:11
smote the priest that he d.; Abr 1:20
was smitten that he d., 1:29
that Haran, my brother, d.; 2: 1
"who d. November 19th, 1824, JS 2: 4

DIES
that misery which never d.— Mrm 8:38
when he d. he shall not sleep, DC 101:31

DIETH
remaineth and d. in his sins, Mos 2:33
and d. an enemy to God, 2:38
that d. in his infancy; 3:18
that whosoever d. in his sins, Al 12:16
becometh expedient that he d., He 14:15
where their worm d. not, DC 76:44

DIFFER
and d. in glory as the moon DC 76:78

DIFFERENCE
The d. between this quorum and DC 124:140

DIFFERENCES
know the d. of administration, DC 46:15

DIFFERENT
themselves together in d. bodies, Mos 25:21
of the d. pieces of their gold, Al 11: 4
there are d. ways that these gifts Mro 10: 8
servants over d. stakes DC 124:134
a d. view of the translation, 128: 8
to the d. religious parties, JS 2: 5
the converts to these d. faiths 2: 6
among the d. denominations, 2: 8
teachers of religion of the d. sects 2:12

DIFFERENTLY
same passages of scripture so d. JS 2:12
also quoted the next verse d.: 2:39

DIFFERING
thus d. from other officers in DC 107:23
thus d. from other officers in 107:25

DIFFERS
whose glory d. from that of DC 76:71
as that of the moon d. from 76:71
as the moon d. from the sun. 76:78
the glory of the stars d. from 76:81
one star d. from another star 76:98
so d. one from another in glory 76:98

DIFFICULT
it began to be exceedingly d., 1Ne 16:21
wait in these d. circumstances Al 58: 7
whatsoever d. circumstances they He 6:21
in whatsoever d. circumstances DC 6:18
whether it is a d. one or not; 102:13
But if it is thought to be d., 102:14
and if more d., six; 102:14
be called on the most d. cases 102:28
the most d. cases of the church, 107:78
be very d. for one recorder to 128: 3

DIFFICULTIES
purpose of settling important d. DC 102: 2
to settle d., when the parties 102:24
commencement of the d. which 130:12
d. caused by the contests of JS 2:11

DIFFICULTY
many afflictions and much d., 1Ne 17: 6
because of the d. of engraving Jac 4: 1
there began to be a serious d. He 1: 1
so much d. in the government, 1:18

In case of d. respecting DC 102:23
To obviate this d., there can be 128: 3
no d. in obtaining a knowledge 128:11

DIG
d. a pit for thy neighbor; 2Ne 28: 8
I will prune it, and d. about it, Jac 5: 4
Let us prune it, and d. about it, 5:27
and d. about the trees, 5:63
d. about them, and prune them, 5:64
to d. down their banks of earth Al 49:22
they could not d. pits sufficient 3Ne 28:20
they did d. it out of the earth; Eth 10:23
into the field to d. in the field. DC 88:51
to d. for the silver mine, JS 2:56

DIGGED
pit, which hath been d. for them 1Ne 14: 3
pit which hath been d. for the 14: 3
shall be filled by those who d. it, 14: 3
the pit which they d. to ensnare 22:14
the pit from whence ye are d. 2Ne 8: 1
it shall not be pruned nor d.; 15: 6
that shall be d. with the mattock, 17:25
he pruned it, and d. about it, Jac 5: 5
that it should be d. about, 5:11
and I have d. about it, 5:47

DIGGER
of my having been a money-d. JS 2:56

DIGGETH
who d. a pit for them shall fall DC 109:25

DIGGING
in d. up heaps of earth Al 50: 1
d. a ditch round about the land, 53: 3
been d., in order, if possible, JS 2:56
to cease d. after it. 2:56

DIGNITY
according to the d. of his office DC 102:10

DILEMMA
d. that our brethren were in Al 7: 3
state of d. like your brethren, 7:18

DILIGENCE
exhorting them to all d., 1Ne 10: 2
d. in keeping my commandments, 15:11
exhort my brethren, with all d., 16: 4
according to the faith and d. and 16:28
according to the faith and d. which 16:29
brethren to faithfulness and d. 17:15
I have exhorted you with all d.; 2Ne 6: 3
and their d. unto me, in bringing 29: 4
them the word of God with all d.; Jac 1:19
thus they labored, with all d., 5:74
according to their d. in keeping En 1:10
prayed and labored with all d., 1:12
all long-suffering the people to d.; Jar 1:11
according to the heed and d. Mos 1:16
and serve him with all d. of mind, 7:33
over the church, walking in all d., 26:38
because of the exceeding d. and Al 7:26
and d. which they give unto him. 12: 9
exhort them daily, with all d.; 21:23
thus we see the great call of d. 28:14
with great d., and with patience, 32:41
And because of your d. 32:42
of your faith, and your d., 32:43
to exercise their faith and d. 37:41
of thy faithfulness and thy d., 38: 3
and his d. in keeping the 39: 1
because of their heed and d. 49:30
and preparing for war with all d.; 51: 9
with so much d. to preserve; 51:14
are striving with unwearied d. He 15: 6
and did serve God with all d. 3Ne 5: 3
willing with all d. to keep the 6:14
endureth by d. unto prayer, Mro 8:26
godliness, charity, humility, d. DC 4: 6
his d. I know, and his prayers 21: 7

DILIGENCE   256   DISADVANTAGE

their d. and for their security;	DC 70:15
through your d., faithfulness,	103:36
by your d. and humility and	104:79
which he is appointed, in all d.	107:99
work, and cease not their d.,	124:49
your d., and your perseverance,	127: 4
in this life through his d. and	130:19

DILIGENT

be d. in keeping the commandments	1 Ne 4:34
been d. in the office of my calling;	Jac 2: 3
have been d. in laboring with me	5:75
they have been a d. people	Mos 1:11
d. in keeping his commandments,	4: 6
expedient that he should be d.,	4:27
of many days, yet they were d.,	8: 8
d. in keeping the commandments	Al 7:23
d. in fulfilling all my words,	37:20
that ye be d. in keeping the	37:20
that ye would be d. and temperate	38:10
Therefore be d.; stand by my	DC 6:18
Be faithful and d. in keeping	6:20
but be d. unto the end.	10: 4
if he shall be d. in keeping my	18: 8
d. in keeping my commandments,	30: 8
are faithful and d. before me.	59: 4
every man be d. in all things.	75:29
give d. heed to the words of	84:43
more d. and concerned at home,	93:50
as you are d. and humble,	104:80
thou shalt make d. search till	136:26
be d. in preserving what thou hast,	136:27
Be d. in keeping all my	136:42

DILIGENTLY

for thou hast sought me d.,	1 Ne 2:19
all those who d. seek him,	10:17
he that d. seeketh shall find;	10:19
Hearken d. unto me,	2 Ne 9:51
For we labor d. to write,	25:23
we labored d. among our people,	Jac 1: 7
we labor d. to engraven these words	4: 3
may labor d. with our might in	5:61
have labored d. in his vineyard;	6: 3
he labored d. that he might lead	7: 3
did seek d. to restore the	En 1:20
and the teachers, did labor d.,	Jar 1:11
should remember to search them d.,	Mos 1: 1
again d. unto their labors;	Al 1:26
began to inquire of them d.,	12: 8
had searched the scriptures d.,	17: 2
which I have inquired d. of God	40: 3
have inquired d. of the Lord	40: 9
have stirred yourselves more d.	60:10
that ye search these d.;	3 Ne 23: 1
search d. in the light of Christ	Mro 7:19
I desire that ye should labor d.,	8: 6
their hardness, let us labor d.;	9: 6
sought d. to sanctify his people	DC 84:23
search d. and spare not;	84:94
seek me d. and ye shall find	88:63
Teach ye d. and my grace	88:78
Therefore, tarry ye, and labor d.,	88:84
seek ye d. and teach one	88:118
let the bishop search d. to	90:22
Search d., pray always, and	90:24
he shall seek d. to take away	96: 9
seeking d. to learn wisdom	97: 1
wise men should be sought for d.,	98:10
seek d. to turn the hearts of	98:16
seek d. that peradventure you	103:32
seek d. that peradventure ye	103:33
seeking d. the kingdom	106: 3
as all have not faith, seek ye d.	109: 7
inquire d. concerning the	111: 9
labor d. to build a house unto	115:10
labor d. until it shall be finished,	115:12
await patiently and d. for	124:88

DIMINISHING

nor d. from the prophecy of	DC 20:35

DIMMED

they be d. any more by time.	1 Ne 5:19

DIMNESS

and darkness, d. of anguish,	2 Ne 18:22
the d. shall not be such as was	19: 1

DIRECT

and he will d. thee for good;	Al 37:37
or did not travel a d. course,	37:42
I d. mine epistle to Pahoran,	60: 1
conferences shall d. or appoint;	DC 20:61
be dealt with as the scriptures d.	20:80
how to act and d. my church,	43: 8
and as wisdom shall d.	57: 6
him good or as he shall d.,	58:51
d. the conference which shall	58:62
as the Lord shall d. them,	84:103
secular business as he shall d.	84:113
[Joseph Smith, Jun.] shall d.	104:26
and the voice of the council d.	104:53

DIRECTED

thy thoughts be d. unto the Lord;	Al 37:36
d. continually by the hand of	Eth 2: 6
according as thou hast d. me.	2:18
they shall be d. by the Spirit.	DC 42:13
d. and guided by the Holy Spirit.	46: 2
moneys even as I have d.	63:46
continue as I was until further d.	JS 2:26

DIRECTION

neraly a south-southeast d.,	1 Ne 16:13
following the same d.,	16:14
by the d. of a high council	DC 20:67
and d. of the Holy One,	78:16
under the d. of the presidency,	107:10
under the d. of the Presidency	107:33
under the d. of the Twelve	107:34
the d. of the Twelve Apostles.	136: 3
under the d. of Peter, James and	JS 2:72

DIRECTIONS

did follow the d. of the ball,	1 Ne 16:16
d. which were given upon the ball.	16:30
d. whither they should travel.	Eth 2: 5
and give unto him d.;	DC 51: 1
d. how to organize this people.	51: 1
elders and members further d.	57:16
further d. concerning this land.	58:34
other d. concerning my servant	58:38
and the d. of the Spirit.	62: 8
I give unto you d. how	82: 9
gave us d. that I should	JS 2:70

DIRECTLY

d. between Jew and Gentile;	DC 57: 4
hands to heaven, yea, even d.,	88:132
d. from the loins of Ham.	Abr 1:11

DIRECTOR

and the ball or d., which led	Mos 1:16
our fathers call a ball, or d.—	Al 37:38
as surely as this d. did bring	37:45
suffered the counsel of thy d.	DC 3:15

DIRECTORS

d. which were given to Lehi	DC 17: 1

DIRECTS

moneys according as the law d.	DC 58:36
else I must do as James d.,	JS 2:13

DIRT

had cast up d. around about	Al 49: 2
they cast up d. out of the ditch	53: 4

DISABUSE

to d. the public mind, and	JS 2: 1

DISADVANTAGE

been a d. to the Nephites,	Al 53:19

DISADVANTAGES

DISADVANTAGES
all the d. they labored under, Mos 29:35

DISANNUL
and who shall d.? 2Ne 24:27

DISAPPEARED
he ascended til he entirely d., JS 2:43

DISAPPOINTED
were d. in their places of retreat Al 49:11
they were again d., 49:17
wer were d. in this our desire. 56:23
But in this thing they were d., 3Ne 4:10
That they may be d. also, DC 121:14

DISAPPOINTMENT
behold, how great was their d.; Al 49: 4
But behold he met with a d. 51:31

DISAPPROVE
or else d. of them at DC 124:144

DISBELIEVE
d. the traditions of their fathers, Al 25: 6
can ye d. on the So of God? 33:14
to d. in the spirit of prophecy He 4:23
to d. all which they had heard 3Ne 2: 1
that they could d. his words, 7:18

DISCERN
Ammon could d. his thoughts; Al 18:18
And thus we can plainly d., that 24:30
d. between the righteous and 3Ne 24:18
to d. all those gifts lest DC 46:27
enabled to d. by the Spirit 63:41
d. between the righteous and 101:95

DISCERNED
can only be d. by purer eyes; DC 131: 7
d. them by the Spirit of Mses 1:28

DISCERNER
is a d. of the thoughts and DC 33: 1

DISCERNIBLE
is light, is good, because it is d., Al 32:35

DISCERNING
to others the d. of spirits. DC 46:23
d. it by the spirit of God. Mses 1:27

DISCHARGE
be enabled to d. every debt; DC 90:23
to act in the d. of your duties 103: 1

DISCIPLE
I am a d. of Jesus Christ, 3Ne 5:13
and doeth it, the same is my d.; DC 41: 5
it not, the same is not my d., 41: 5
things, the same is not my d. 52:40
not these things is not my d.; 84:91
his life for my sake is not my d. 103:28

DISCIPLES
Behold the twelve d. of the Lamb, 1Ne 12: 8
seal the law among my d. 2Ne 18:16
a few who shall be called the d. Al 45:14
Ye are my d.; and ye are a 3Ne 15:12
Jesus commanded his d. that 18: 1
when the d. had come with bread 18: 3
and he gave unto the d. 18: 3
were filled, he said unto the d.: 18: 5
commanded his d. that they 18: 8
when the d. had done this, 18:10
spoken these words unto his d., 18:17
his eyes again upon the d. 18:26
touched with his hand the d. 18:36
but the d. bare record that he 18:37
the d. saw and did bear record 18:39
these were the names of the d. 19: 4
the d. did pray unto the Father 19: 7
were ministering unto the d., 19:15

that his d. should kneel down 3Ne 19:16
his d. that they should pray. 19:17
he came unto his d., 19:24
he came again unto his d.; 19:30
he came again to the d., 19:35
cease to pray, and also his d. 20: 1
and gave to the d. to eat. 20: 3
neither wine, brought by the d., 20: 6
his d. answered him and said: 23:10
the d. whom Jesus had chosen 26:17
the d. of Jesus were journeying 27: 1
the d. were gathered together 27: 1
sayings he said unto his d.: 27:33
spake unto his d., one by one, 28: 1
ONE OF THE D. OF JESUS 4Ne 1:hd
the d. of Jesus had formed 1: 1
wrought by the d. of Jesus, 1: 5
wrought among the d. of Jesus. 1:13
the d. of Jesus, whom he had 1:14
there were other d. ordained 1:14
authority over the d. of Jesus 1:30
were the three d. of Jesus 1:37
the d. began to sorrow for 1:44
save it were the d. of Jesus. 1:46
did take away his beloved d., Mrm 1:13
the beloved d. were taken away 1:16
whom Jesus chose to be his d. 3:18
God save it be the d. of Jesus, 8:10
unto his d. who should tarry, 9:22
yea and also to all his d., 9:22
words believeth not my d.; Eth 4:10
three d. obtained a promise that 12:17
manifest thyself unto thy d.; 12:31
which he spake unto his d., Mro 2: 1
it not, but the d. heard it; 2: 3
The manner which the d., 3: 1
people, by the mouths of my d., DC 1: 4
unto you, as I said unto my d., 6:32
prophets, yea, and also my d., 10:46
unto my d., and many there 10:59
and the Twelve shall be my d., 18:27
as I showed it unto my d. 45:16
But my d. shall stand in 45:32
spoken these words unto my d., 45:34
as my d. are enabled to 57: 5
things the d. may need to 57: 8
the d. and the children of men 58:52
let my d. in Kirtland 63:38
those of my d. who shall tarry. 63:41
unto the d. that shall tarry, 63:45
My d., in days of old, 64: 8
be made known unto my d., 64:19
by this you may know my d. 84:91
that I promised unto my d., 88: 3
Then understood his d. that he JS 1: 1
and his d. came to him, 1: 2
the d. came unto him privately, 1: 4

DISCIPLINED
be marshaled and d. for war. DC 87: 4

DISCOMFORT
all those that d. my people, DC 121:23

DISCOURSES
in public d. the leaders of DC OD

DISCOVER
did d. the genealogy of his fathers. 1Ne 5:16
that perhaps I might d. my family 8:13
Lord will d. their secret parts. 2Ne 13:17
that I might d. their preparations, Mos 10: 7
d. the abominations of this people 12: 8
preparations for war did he d.; 20: 8
he should d. to every creature 28:15
that I may d. unto my people who Al 37:23
I may d. unto them the works of 37:23
that they might d. the number 58:14
d. an error in the decision of DC 102:20
insomuch that they shall not d. 111: 4
You will d. in this quotation 128: 7
I could d. that he had no JS 2:31
if possible, to d. the mine. 2:56

DISCOVERED   258   DISPUTATIONS

DISCOVERED
they d. a people, who were called	Om	1:14
Mosiah d. that the people of		1:15
the land where Mosiah d. them;		1:16
at the time that Mosiah d. them,		1:17
And Coriantumr was d. by		1:21
d. a land which was covered with	Mos	8:8
d. a land which had been peopled		8:8
d. a movement among the people,		18:32
they were d. unto the king.		18:32
d. the daughters of the Lamanites,		20:4
Limhi had d. them from the tower,		20:8
d. Ammon and his brethren;		21:23
when they d. the land of Helam,		23:35
d. by the people of Zarahemls,	Al	22:30
for they d. the army coming,		47:5
the Lamanites had d. Teancum,		52:22
were not d. by the Lamanites.		58:19
But when Moronihah had d. this,	He	1:28
that they could not be d.,		11:25
being first d. by a woman,	Abr	1:23
When this woman d. the land		1:24
I d. a light appearing in my	JS	2:30
I suddenly d. that my room		2:44
d. something to be wrong with		2:48

DISEASES
afflicted with all manner of d.,	1Ne	11:31
and curing all manner of d.	Mos	3:5
afflicted with all manner of d.		17:16
all manner of d. of every kind;	Al	9:22
to remove the cause of d.,		46:40

DISFIGURE
for they d. their faces that they	3Ne	13:16

DISGUISE
Abinadi came among them in d.,	Mos	12:1
for he was in d. at the time that	He	1:12
and having obtained, through d.,		2:6

DISH
would hold water like unto a d.;	Eth	2:17
thereof was tight like unto a d.;		2:17
thereof were tight like unto a d.;		2:17
thereof was tight like unto a d.;		2:17
was shut, was tight like unto a d.		2:17
vessels being tight like unto a d.,		6:7

DISHONEST
some said he was d., others	JS	2:24

DISMISSED
he d. the multitude, and they	Mos	6:3
king Limhi d. the multitude,		8:4

DISOBEDIENCE
himself because of his own d.;	Al	42:12
was wroth because of their d.;		47:3
light and truth, through d., from	DC	93:39
are the children of d. themselves.		121:17

DISORDERLY
their members for d. conduct,	DC	134:10

DISOWNED
cast out, and d. by his people.	Mos	15:5

DISPATCHES
Press d. having been sent	DC	OD

DISPELLED
cloud of darkness having been d.,	Al	19:6

DISPENSATION
kingdom, and a d. of the gospel	DC	27:13
d. of the gospel of Abraham,		110:12
the keys of this d. are committed		110:16
is the d. of the fulness of times.		112:30
all those who have received a d.		112:31
keys of the d., which ye have		112:32
the d. of the fulness of times—		121:31
to the d. of the fulness of times.	DC	124:41
has given a d. of the priesthood		128:9
the d. of the fulness of times,		128:18
which d. is now beginning		128:18
the d. of the fulness of times.		128:18
the d. of the fulness of times!		128:20
all declaring their d., their rights,		128:21

DISPENSATIONS
welding together of d., and keys,	DC	128:18

DISPERSE
overshadowed them, did not d.—	He	5:31
the multitude did d., and	3Ne	19:1
will d. the powers of darkness	DC	21:6

DISPERSED
gather together the d. of Judah	2Ne	21:12
should have d. our enemies,	Al	60:16
the cloud of darkness was d.	He	5:42
the cloud of darkness was d.		5:43
whence they have been d.;	3Ne	5:26
darkness d. from off the face of		10:9
among all the d. of my people,		21:26
among all the d. of my people,		21:27
and long d. covenant people	Mrm	8:15

DISPERSION
gathered in from their long d.,	2Ne	10:8
shall gather in, from their long d.,	3Ne	21:1

DISPLAY
make a d. of thy testimony	DC	109:49

DISPLAYED
and d. the weakness of youth,	JS	2:28

DISPLEASE
yea, they feared to d. the king,	Al	47:2

DISPLEASED
were d. with the conduct of	Mos	25:12
and that ye be not d. with him,	Al	20:24
the Lord your God, am not d.	DC	111:1
and it d. God, and he	Mses	5:52

DISPLEASURE
not incur the d. of a just God	2Ne	1:22
and incurred the d. of God	Mos	1:17
And in his hot d., and in his	DC	101:90
in my hot d. will I send	Mses	7:34

DISPOSE
d. of the land, that he may	DC	63:39

DISPOSED
it shall be d. of by a council,	DC	120:1
evil-d. and designing persons,	JS	2:1

DISPOSITION
we have no more d. to do evil,	Mos	5:2
might know of the d. of the king,		9:5
more wicked and murderous d.	Al	43:6
make a d. of his merchandise,	DC	114:1
nature and d. of almost all men,		121:39
A d. to commit such was	JS	2:28

DISPROVE
own tenets and d. all others.	JS	2:9

DISPUTATIONS
know of them the cause of their d.	1Ne	15:6
doubtings and d. among the	3Ne	8:4
there shall be no d. among you.		11:22
there shall be no d. among you,		11:28
shall there be d. among you		11:28
because of the d. which have		18:34
if ye have no d. among you.		18:34
there are d. among the people	4Ne	1:2
there were no contentions and d.	Mro	8:4
should d. rise among you.		8:5
d. among you concerning the		

DISPUTE 259 DISTURBANCES

DISPUTE
he hath spoken it, and who can d.?	2Ne	10: 9
can ye d. the power of God?	Mos	27:15
much d. and wonderful contentions	Al	2: 5
and now will ye d. more?		30:51
therefore there arose a warm d.		51: 4
should ye d. among yourselves,	He	8:12
will you d. that Jerusalem was		8:21
and d. because of this thing?	3Ne	27: 4
d. not because ye see not,	Eth	12: 6

DISPUTING
they were d. one with another	1Ne	15: 2

DISPUTINGS
there began to be some d.	3Ne	6:10

DISREPUTE
may not be brought into d.	DC	90:23

DISSATISFIED
or either of them be d. with	DC	102:27
in the least to cause them to be d.		134:12

DISSENSION
much d. among the people;	Mos	27: 9
before your d. from among us.	Al	34: 2
there arose a d. among them,		45:23

DISSENSIONS
of wars, and contentions, and d.,	Jar	1:13
d. away unto the Lamanites,	WM	1:16
of the d. among the brethren	Mos	26: 5
and their wars and d.,	Al	45:hd
many little d. and disturbances		45:21
led away by Amalickiah to d.,		46: 6
Nephites, had heard of these d.,		46:11
the land where there were d.,		46:28
not long after their d. they		47:36
end to such contentions and d.		51:16
which caused d. amongst them,		53: 8
because of d. and intrigue		53: 9
yea, such as rebellions and d.,		61:14
and contentions, and d.,		62:40
and contentions, and their d.	He	1:hd
some little d. among the people,		3: 1
much contention and many d.;		3: 3
wars, and contentions, and d.,		3:14
disturbances, and wars, and d.,		3:17
were many d. in the church,		4: 1
their many contentions and d.,	3Ne	2:18
Lamanites because of their d.	DC	10:48

DISSENT
will also d. over unto them;	Mro	9:24

DISSENTED
who had d. from the Nephites,	Al	43:13
they d. even from the church;		46: 7
those who have d. from us?		46:27
and those who had d.,		46:28
and had d. from their church,		48:24
those who have d. from us,		60:32
of God but had d. from them.	He	5:35
who have d. away from you	3Ne	3:10
had d. over unto the Lamanites,	Mrm	6:15
d. over unto the Lamanites,	Mro	9:24

DISSENTER
a d. from among the Nephites;	He	1:15

DISSENTERS
were d. from the Nephites;	Al	31: 8
and all the d. of the Nephites,		47:35
Now these d., having the same		47:36
to compel those d. to defend		51:15
were four thousand of those d.		51:19
And the remainder of those d.,		51:20
go speedily against those d.,		61:17
who was the king of those d.		62: 6
some d. who had gone forth		63:14
hearken to the words of those d.	He	4: 3
there were d. who went up		4: 4

those d. of the Nephites,	He	4: 8
did confound many of those d.		5:17
and Nephites who were d.		5:27
the d. from the people of Nephi,		11:24
to anger by them, or by those d.,		11:24
there were d. that went forth		11:25
were many d. of the Nephites	3Ne	1:28
until they were joined by d.,		7:12
that there would be many d.)		7:12

DISSENTING
by d. away unto those wicked	3Ne	3:11

DISSOLVED
thou, whole Palestina, are d.;	2Ne	24:31
are d. as a united order	DC	104:53

DISTANCE
d. of a day and a half's journey	Al	22:32
Yea, even to a considerable d.,		56:37
travel to an exceeding great d.,	He	3: 4

DISTANT
time cometh, and is not far d.,	Mos	3: 5
time is at hand, or is not far d.,		7:18
behold, the time is not far d.	Al	7: 7
us, but in a land which is far d.,	He	16:20

DISTIL
priesthood shall d. upon thy soul	DC	121:45

DISTINCT
This presidency is a d. one	DC	107:90

DISTINCTION
There is a d. between the	DC	102:30

DISTINCTLY
hear his words carefully and d.,	DC	88:129
so clearly and d. that I knew	JS	2:42

DISTINCTNESS
owing to the d. of the vision	JS	2:50

DISTINGUISH
hereafter d. them by these names,	Jac	1:14
that they might d. a brother	He	6:22

DISTINGUISHED
may be d. above all the people	Mos	1:11
were d. by the name of Amlici,	Al	2:11
were d. from the Nephites,		3: 4
might be d. from the seed of		3: 8
might be d. from their brethren;		23:16
upon them, that they might be d.		23:16
were d. by that name ever after.		27:26
also d. for their zeal towards God,		27:27
people began to be d. by ranks,	3Ne	6:12
be d. from him only by his age.	DC	107:43

DISTRESS
that d. her, shall be as a dream	2Ne	27: 3

DISTRESSING
aggravating and d. manner	Al	27:29

DISTRICT
the whole d. of country	JS	2: 5

DISTURB
shall harm or d. their prosperity	2Ne	1:31
not haughtiness d. their peace;	Mos	27: 4
that it is they that I will d.,	DC	10:56

DISTURBANCE
no more d. between the Lamanites	Mos	21:22
and a d. among them;	Al	22:22
thus the people did have no d.		30: 4

DISTURBANCES
all manner of d. and wickedness,	Al	11:20
the many little dissensions and d.		45:21
had been great contentions, and d.,	He	3:17

DISTURBED   260   DOCTRINE

DISTURBED
and they were much d., for	He	16:22

DISTURBER
a d. and an annoyer of his	JS	2:20

DITCH
of the d. which had been dug	Al	49:18
in digging a d. round about		53: 3
upon the inner bank of the d.;		53: 4
they cast up dirt out of the d.		53: 4

DITCHES
instead of filling up their d. by	Al	49:22

DIVERS
for there are d. ways and means,	Mos	4:29
have been taken in d. iniquities.		26:11
began to question him in d. ways	He	9:19
and earthquakes in d. places.	Mrm	8:30
d. ways that he did manifest	Mro	7:24
and of d. kinds of tongues.		10:16
earthquakes also in d. places,	DC	45:33
d. places through all the travels		128:21
and of Raphael, and of d. angels,		128:21
and earthquakes, in d. places.	JS	1:29
led me into d. temptations,		2:28

DIVERSITIES
know the d. of operations,	DC	46:16

DIVIDE
d. the wicked from the righteous;	1Ne	15:30
shake as if it were to d. asunder.		17:45
rejoice when they d. the spoil.	2Ne	19: 3
d. him a portion with the great,	Mos	14:12
shall d. the spoil with the strong;		14:12
shall d. asunder all the cunning	He	3:29
as if it were about to d. asunder.		5:33
if it was about to d. asunder.	3Ne	8: 6
and d. unto the saints their	DC	57: 7
d. the lands of the heritage of		58:17
Let it d. the waters from the	Mses	2: 6
to d. the day from the night,		2:14
to d. the light from the darkness;		2:18
to d. two and two in the land,		5: 3
the people of Canaan shall d.		7: 7
d. the waters from the waters.	Abr	4: 6
to d. the day from the night;		4:14
to d. the light from the darkness.		4:17

DIVIDED
waters of the Red Sea and they d.	1Ne	4: 2
they d. the Gentiles from the seed		13:10
the waters of the Red Sea were d.		17:26
with their bodies, never to be d.;	Al	11:45
d. from the land of Zarahemla by		22:27
Lamanites and the Nephites d.		22:27
d. the land of Nephi from the		27:14
Therefore, he d. his army and		43:31
that they d. hither and thither	He	10: 1
they were d. against themselves		10:18
were d. one against another;	3Ne	7: 2
that they were d. into tribes,		7:14
began to be d. into classes;	4Ne	1:26
the lands of our inheritance d.	Mrm	2:28
And the country was d.;	Eth	7:20
And they were d.; and a part		14:20
Southern States shall be d.	DC	87: 3
And again, let it be d. into lots,		96: 3
in the days before it was d.		133:24
In life they were no d.,		135: 3
d. the light from the darkness.	Mses	2: 4
made the firmament and d.		2: 7
and they d. the light,	Abr	4: 4
or caused it to be d., from		4: 4
it d. the waters which were		4: 7

DIVIDEND
to the d. of their property,	DC	136: 8

DIVIDES
place where the sea d. the land.	Eth	10:20

DIVIDETH
a great and a terrible gulf d. them;	1Ne	12:18
great sea which d. the lands.	Eth	2:13

DIVIDING
and thither, to the d. asunder,	He	12: 8
to the d. asunder of both	DC	6: 2
to the d. asunder of both		11: 2
to the d. asunder of both		12: 2
to the d. asunder of both		14: 2
to the d. asunder of the joints		33: 1

DIVINE
praise him through grace d. Amen.	2Ne	10:25
demands of d. justice do awaken	Mos	2:38
honor and to thy d. acceptance;	DC	109:10
and d. laws given of heaven,		134: 6
obtaining a d. manifestation,	JS	2:29
(under D. providence),		2:75

DIVISION
a great d. among the people,	2Ne	30:10
there began to be a d. among	Mos	19: 2
thus was the d. among them,	Al	51: 6
arose a d. among the people,	He	10: 1
was a great d. among the people.	4Ne	1:35
and d. amongst the people,	JS	2: 5

DIVISIONS
cause three d. among the people.	He	1: 4
be no d. made upon the land,	DC	56: 9
there are two d. or grand heads—		107: 6

DIVORCED
whoso shall marry her who is d.	3Ne	12:32

DIVORCEMENT
the bill of your mother's d.?	2Ne	7: 1
let him give her a writing of d.	3Ne	12:31

DIVULGE
whoso should d. whatsoever	Eth	8:14

DO: *see in the APPENDIX.*

DOCTRINE
and the very points of his d.,	1Ne	15:14
that murmured shall learn d.	2Ne	27:35
of false teachers, and false d.,		28:12
concerning the d. of Christ;		31: 1
this is the d. of Christ,		31:21
the only and true d. of the Father,		31:21
this is the d. of Christ,		32: 6
be no more d. given until		32: 6
to overthrow the d. of Christ.	Jac	1:hd
might overthrow the d. of Christ.		7: 2
the gospel, or the d. of Christ.		7: 6
upon those points of d.,	Al	41: 9
concerning the points of d.	He	11:22
concerning the true points of d.,		11:23
believe that the d. of Christ was	3Ne	2: 2
concerning the points of my d.,		11:28
Behold, this is not my d.,		11:30
that such things		11:30
I will declare unto you my d.		11:31
And this is my d., and it is		11:32
the d. which the Father hath		11:32
unto you, that this is my d.,		11:35
unto you, that this is my d.,		11:39
and establish it for my d.,		11:40
of the true points of my d.,		21: 6
light the true points of my d.,	DC	10:62
the only d. which is in me.		10:62
concerning the points of my d.;		10:63
Behold, this is my d.—		10:67
may know of a surety my d.		11:16
the d. of repentance,		68:25
the d. of the kingdom.		88:77
in theory, in principle, in d.,		88:78
in theory, in principle, and in d.,		97:14
may act in d. and principle		101:78
respecting d. or principle,		102:23
the d. of the priesthood shall		121:45

DOCTRINE — DOLEFUL

DOCTRINE

the book of D. and Covenants.	DC 124:141
agreeing precisely with the d.	128: 7
seem to some to be a very bold d.	128: 9
d. of their having many wives	132: 1
this book of D. and Covenants,	135: 3
this book of D. and Covenants	135: 6

DOCTRINES

the confounding of false d.	2Ne 3:12
false and vain and foolish d.,	28: 9
and all those who preach false d.,	28:15
they went forth preaching false d.;	Al 1:16
evil spirits, or d. of devils,	DC 46: 7
they teach for d. the	JS 2:19

DOCUMENTS

other wise d. and instructions	DC 135: 3

DODDS, Asa

I say unto my servan D.,	DC 75:15

DOES

What d. this mean which Amulek	Al 12: 8
What d. the scripture mean, which	12:21
d. not put on immortality,	40: 2
d. not put on incorruption—	40: 2
d. not this testify against them?	47:34
d. not grant us more strength;	58:34
if so he d. not understand them.	Mrm 9: 8
and d. the commandments	DC 1:32
and d. not humble himself	5:24
d. contain all those parts of	10:46
and that God d. inspire men	20:11
if he d. not, he can ot obtain it.	131: 3
why d. the world think to make	JS 2:25
all that He d. now reveal,	AoF 9

DOEST

But when thou d. alms let not	3Ne 13: 3
When thou d. terrible things,	DC 133:43
thou shalt do all that thou d.	Mses 5: 8
If thou d. well, thou shalt be	5:23
And if thou d. not well, sin lieth	5:23

DOETH

He d. not anything save	2Ne 26:24
for whoso d. them shall perish.	26:32
for he d. that which is good	26:33
he d. nothing save it be plain	26:33
all ye that d. iniquity,	27: 4
that the man that d. this,	Mos 2:37
	4:18
whosoever d. this the same hath	5: 9
whosoever d. this shall be found	5:36
whosoever d. not the works of	Al 5:42
And whosoever d. this must	7:16
And whosoever d. this, and	32:19
the will of God and d. it not,	He 14:30
whosoever d. iniquity, doeth it	14:30
iniquity, d. in unto himself;	3Ne 13: 3
know what thy right hand d.;	14:21
that d. the will of my Father	14:24
sayings of mine and d. them,	14:26
sayings of mine and d. them not	15: 1
sayings of mine and d. them,	20:19
And behold, I am he who d. it.	29: 7
he that d. this shall become like	Mrm 6:22
he d. with you according to	Mro 7: 8
a gift, he d. it grudgingly;	10:25
none but god d. among you,	10:25
be one among you that d. good,	DC 33: 4
there is none which d. good save	35:12
are none that d. good except	41: 5
receiveth my law and d. it,	41: 5
he receiveth it and d. it not,	42:25
forsaketh it, and d. it no more,	42:26
But if he d. it again, he shall	42:60
he that d. according to these	42:60
he that d. them not shall be	49:14
And whoso d. this shall receive	52:40
he that d. not these things,	58:29
he that d. not anything until	59:23
who d. the works of righteousness	

DOG

like the d. to his vomit, or like	3Ne 7: 8

DOGS

vultures of the air, and the d.,	Mos 12: 2
mangled by d. and wild beasts	Al 16:10
meat for d. and wild beasts.	He 7:19
that which is holy unto the d.,	3Ne 14: 6
that are not worthy, or to d.,	DC 41: 6

DOING

d. all things for them which were	1Ne 17:30
d. no good, for they knew no sin.	2Ne 2:23
by so d. they kept them from	Jar 1:12
Ammon declined d. this thing,	Mos 21:33
d. these things, they did abound	27: 5
d. this great and marvelous work.	Al 26:15
they were d. that which they felt	43:46
by so d. God would prosper	48:15
by so d., the Lord would deliver	48:16
shedding of blood but in d. good,	48:16
lest by so d. they should lose	53:15
and begin to be up and d.,	60:24
d. no justice unto the children of	He 7: 4
d. all things for the welfare and	12: 2
for happiness in d. iniquity,	13:38
these things and not d. them	14:19
more part of them are d. this,	15: 6
went forth d. mighty miracles	4Ne 1:30
unto me, and I know your d.	Mrm 8:35
And by so d., the Lord God	Mro 7:32
be the means of d. much good	DC 6: 8
be the means of d. much good	11: 8
For by d. these things	21: 6
d. all things with prayer and	46: 7
by so d. I will bless him,	49: 4
d. these things which ye have	50:35
d. that which I have appointed	50:38
be employed in d. this business.	51:14
be not weary in well-d.,	64:33
were d. the work of translation,	76:15
by d. the things which I have	78: 7
in d. these things thou wilt do	81: 4
d. all things with an eye	82:19
when he cometh, shall find so d.;	JS 1:50
by so d. I would offend God,	2:25
and in d. good to all men;	AoF 13

DOINGS

for all thy d. thou shalt be	1Ne 10:20
the d. of the Lord in other lands,	19:22
their d. have been against the Lord,	2Ne 13: 8
shall eat the fruit of their d.	13:10
declare his d. among the people,	22: 4
and their d. were doings of	25: 2
doings were d. of abominations.	25: 2
their d. shall be as a stumbling	Mos 7:29
he did not repent of his evil d.	11:29
have repented not of their evil d.;	12: 1
let all thy d. be unto the Lord,	Al 37:36
with the Lord in all thy d.,	37:37
behold all the d. of the Father	3Ne 29: 4
spurn at the d. of the Lord,	29: 4
if ye shall spurn at his d. he	29: 5
spurneth at the d. of the Lord;	30: 2
and repent of your evil d.,	4Ne 1:18
did bless them in all their d.;	Mrm 2: 8
did not repent of their evil d.;	Eth 8: 5
because of the d. of Jared	15:13
behold all the d. of the people;	DC 76: 2
and the extent of his d.	88:121
and from all your wicked d.	88:137
give utterance in all your d.	108: 7
exhortations, and in all your d.	Mses 7:41
and told Enoch all the d. of	

DOLEFUL

houses shall be full of d. creatures;	2Ne 23:21

DOLLARS   262   DONE

DOLLARS

obtain five talents (d.) let him	DC 104:69
If it be five talents (d.),	104:73
or it it be ten talents (d.),	104:73
shall not receive less than fifty d.	124:64
to receive fifteen thousand d.	124:64
receive over fifteen thousand d.	124:65
to receive under fifty d. for	124:66
pay over fifteen thousand d. stock	124:72
that house, nor under fifty d.;	124:72
gave me fifty d. to assist us	JS 2:61

DOMINION

and she had d. over all the earth,	1 Ne 14:11
must reign in d., and might,	22:24
might, majesty, power, and d.	Al 5:50
and in his might, majesty, and d.,	12:15
have power over his own d.	DC 1:35
power, and in might, and in d.	76:91
power, and in might, and in d.	76:95
to his own works, his own d.,	76:111
glory, and in might, and in d.;	76:114
and d. forever and ever.	76:119
d., truth, justice, judgment,	109:77
dark and benighted d. of Sheol—	121: 4
or to exercise control or d.	121:37
begin to exercise unrighteous d.	121:39
thy d. shall be an everlasting	121:46
shall be an everlasting d.,	121:46
have d. over the fishes of the sea,	Mses 2:26
have d. over the fish of the sea,	2:28
to have d. over all the beasts	5: 1
Satan had great d. among men,	6:15
give them d. over the fish of	Abr 4:26
d. over the fish of the sea,	4:28

DOMINIONS

their d. upon the face of the earth	1 Ne 14:12
the adversary spreadeth his d.,	Dc 82: 5
All thrones and d., principalities	121:29
principalities, and powers, d.,	132:19

DON CARLOS: see also SMITH, Don C.

Samuel Harrison, William, D.;	JS 2: 4

DONE

what great things the Lord hath d.	T Pg
of the things which thou hast d.;	1 Ne 2: 1
this they said he had d. because	2:11
told the things which Laban had d.,	3:14
And all this he hath d. because	3:16
after I had d. this, I went forth	4:20
what great things the Lord hath d.	7:11
thing that they had d. against me.	7:20
forgive them all that they had d.,	7:21
after they had d. praying unto the	7:21
were d. as my father dwelt in a	10:16
all this have they d. that they	13:27
were d. by the temporal body	15:32
said and d. as my father dwelt in	16: 6
there was not any thing d. save it	17:31
if I should say it, it would be d.	17:50
of the thing which they had d.,	18:20
this have I d., and commanded	19: 4
say—Mine idol hath d. them,	20: 5
thou shouldst go, hath d. it.	20:17
notwithstanding he hath d. all this,	20:22
things the Lord had d. for them	2 Ne 1: 1
But behold, his will be d.;	1:19
have been d. in the wisdom of him	2:24
and it shall be d. unto thee	3:25
the Lord spake it, and it was d.	5:23
What could have been d. more	15: 4
that I have not d. in it?	15: 4
as I have d. unto Samaria	20:11
wisdom I have d. these things;	20:13
for he hath d. excellent things;	22: 5
the law ought to be d. away.	25:27
which shall be d. among them,	26:17
the Redeemer hath d. his work,	28: 5
he hath d. his work.	28: 6
ye have d. according to the	31:18
I would ask if all is d.?	31:19
for ye have d. these things which	Jac 2:34

which ye ought not to have d.	Jac 2:34
ye have d. greater iniquities than	2:35
they desired it God hath d. it,	4:14
unto myself, I have d. this thing,	5:11
What could I have d. more for	5:41
what could I have d. more in	5:47
of my vineyard, for I have d. all.	5:49
What could I have d. more for	5:49
I have d. according to my will;	5:75
Nevertheless, not my will be d.;	7:14
And thy will, O Lord, be d.,	7:14
And I said: Lord, how is it d.?	En 1: 7
it shall be d. unto them	1:18
should be d. among this people,	Jar 1: 3
the Lord as I ought to have d.	Om 1: 2
Mosiah had d. as his father had	Mos 2: 1
have not d. these things that I	2:15
should do as ye have hitherto d.	2:31
all these things are d. that a	3:10
repenteth of that which he hath d.	4:18
of the thing which thou hast d.	4:22
things are d. in wisdom and order;	4:27
all things must be d. in order.	4:27
to that which his father had d.	6: 7
that after he had d. all this,	8: 4
what great evil hast thou d.,	12:13
unto them, Have ye d. all this?	12:37
because he had d. no evil,	14: 9
even as ye have d. unto me,	17:15
that all this was d. in Mormon,	18:30
were d. in the borders of the land,	18:31
what they had d. to the king.	19:24
and whosoever has d. this thing	20:16
all this was d. that the word of	21: 4
Now this was d. because there	25:20
great things he has d. for them;	27:16
what the Lord had d. for his son,	27:21
which they had d. to the church,	27:35
of Mosiah had d. all these things,	28: 1
king Mosiah had d. these things,	28:20
Now when Mosiah had d. this he	29: 1
a man who has d. much good	Al 1:13
to that which he had d.,	1:33
And this was d. that their seed	3: 8
Now all these things were d., yea,	3:25
to the deeds which have been d.	5:15
according as he had before d.	8: 1
Now, this was d. that the Lord	8:31
and this he has d. while	10:10
that which Amulek had d.	12: 1
this was d. before the chief judge	14: 5
d. to the great astonishment of	15:11
of the things which they had d.	17:39
d. wrong in slaying his servants;	18: 5
what he had d. for his brethren;	19:14
and when whe had d. this,	19:30
d. in the presence of the queen	22:23
of the things which they had d.	24:24
what the Lord has d. for me,	29:10
be d. according to my words,	29:17
for the crimes which he had d.;	30:11
after ye have d. all these things,	34:28
that ye should do as I have d.,	36: 2
in remembrance, as I have d.,	36:29
according as I have d., upon	37: 2
they should go, behold, it was d.;	37:40
and that wrong which ye have d.	39:13
evil shall be d. unto him,	42:28
this is d. unto us because of	44: 3
And when Alma had d. this	45:18
as they had hitherto d.;	49: 6
all the things that he had d.	51:35
were d. in a profound silence.	55:17
this was d. in the night-time,	55:22
their faith it was d. unto them;	57:21
has d. this great thing for us.	57:35
that which we had hitherto d.;	58: 1
Now this was d. because the	58:22
yea, that they have d. when	60: 9
strength as we hitherto have d.;	60:16
for it would have been d.,	60:16
repent of that which ye have d.,	60:24
this was d. to fortify the land	62:13

DONE

great things the Lord had d.	Al	62:50
that all these things were d.		62:52
all this was d. in the fortieth year	He	1:13
borders as they had hitherto d.;		1:26
he had seen, and heard, and d.		2: 9
all this was d. in the fifty and		4: 8
and this I have d. that when you		5: 6
the wrongs which they had d.		5:17
strength, as he has hitherto d.,		7:22
to the crime which he has d.?		8: 1
told them all that they had d.,		9:13
we know not who has d. it;		9:15
this man that hath d. this murder?		9:20
because I have d. this, ye say		9:24
that he has d. this murder.		9:35
those things which thou hast d.;		10: 4
d. this with such unwearyingness,		10: 5
all things shall be d. unto thee		10: 5
be rent in twain, it shall be d.		10: 8
become smooth it shall be d.		10: 9
miracle which Nephi had d.		10:13
And so it was d., according to		11: 5
may be d. according to my words,		11:13
the day for many hours—it is d.;		12:14
Be thou dried up—it is d.		12:16
it be buried up—behold it is d.		12:17
accursed forever—it shall be d.		12:20
They that have d. good shall have		12:26
they that have d. evil shall have		12:26
mighty works which I have d.		15:17
many wrongs which ye have d.	3Ne	3: 4
d. by command of Gidgiddoni.		4:26
thing which he had d. for them,		4:31
was d. among so many people		5: 8
things which have been d.—		5:14
of the crime which they had d.,		6:26
Now all this was d., and there		7: 5
d. in about the space of three		8:19
offerings shall be d. away,		9:19
such things should be d. away.		11:30
Old things are d. away, and all		12:47
Thy will be d. on earth as it is		13:10
d. many wonderful works?		14:22
I have d. unto your brethren		17: 8
And when he had d. this he		17:22
observe to do, even as I have d.,		18: 6
when the disciples had d. this,		18:10
for this thing which ye have d.,		18:10
be d. even as Moses said)		21:11
and whoredoms, shall be d. away.		21:19
had d. all manner of cures		26:15
And behold, all this was d.,	Mrm	2: 9
my people, the Nephites, had d.,		3: 9
now all these things had been d.,		4: 9
not of the evil they had d.,		4:10
Behold, if ye had not d. this,		6:18
of the Lord which hath d. it.		8: 8
d. with an eye single to his glory,		8:15
shall be d. by the power of God.		8:16
said that miracles are d. away;		8:26
and say that they are d. away,		9: 7
And when thou hast d. this	Eth	1:42
of the land have hitherto d.		2:11
of the evil which he had d.,		2:15
I have d. even as thou hast		2:22
when they had d. all these things		6: 4
great things the Lord had d.		6:30
great things the Lord had d.		6:30
of the thing which Shule had d.,		7:10
many evils which he had d.;		7:13
things that the Lord had d.		7:27
that evil may be d. away,		8:26
that which his father had d.		9: 8
what the Lord had d. in		10: 2
O Lord, thy righteous will be d.,		12:29
of the evil which he hath d.;		15: 3
after ye have d. this ye shall	Mro	2: 2
or to sing, even so it was d.		6: 9
behold, it shall be d. unto you.		7:26
And because he hath d. this,		7:29
circumcision is d. away in me.		8: 8
after they had d. this thing,		9:10

263

and after they have d. this,	Mro	9:10
spiritual, never will be d. away,		10:19
gifts of God shall be d. away		10:24
repent of that which thou hast d.	DC	3:10
unto me the things that he has d.		5:28
art thou for what thou hast d.;		6:14
even as they have d. unto me,		6:30
than what he has before d.		7: 5
shall it be d. unto you.		8:11
so it shall be d. unto you;		11: 8
shall it be d. unto you.		11:17
having d. this that I might		19: 2
and the deeds which he hath d.		19: 3
necessary to be d. at the time.		20:62
all things may be d. in order.		20:68
have I caused to be d. away		22: 1
shall be d. by common consent		26: 2
having d. all, that ye may be		27:15
all things must be d. in order,		28:13
let all things be d. in cleanliness		42:41
all things may be d. according to		42:55
it shall be d. in a meeting,		42:89
be d. according to my law		44: 6
it is d. even as he asketh.		46:30
be d. in the name of Christ,		46:31
have d. unto the Son of Man		49: 6
name of Jesus and it shall be d.		50:29
be d. through the bishop or		51:12
faith it shall be d. unto them.		52:20
after you have d. journeying,		54: 9
as can be d. in righteousness,		57: 6
all these things be d. in order;		58:55
but let it be d. as it shall be		58:56
be d. away from among them;		68:32
have d. well inasmuch as they		70:17
this thing ye have d. wisely,		72: 3
law of Moses should be d. away		74: 5
the tradition might be d. away,		74: 6
They who have d. good in the		76:17
they who have d. evil in the		76:17
all things be d. unto my glory,		78: 8
be d. according to the laws of		82:15
it shall be d. unto them as		85:12
it must be d. according to the		94: 2
d. even as I commanded you,		101:53
things be d. in their time,		101:72
needs be d. in mine own way;		104:16
let all things be d. according to		104:21
I have commanded to be d.		104:51
all things may be d. in order		107:84
that thy servants have d.		109: 3
thou knowest that we have d.		109: 5
that it may be d. to thine honor		109:10
Thy will be d., O Lord,		109:44
but have d. that which was meet		121:16
seen the work which he hath d.,		124:17
love him for the work he hath d.,		124:78
is d. on the general church book,		128: 4
be d. unto them in all things		132:19
has d. more, save Jesus only,		135: 3
d. in this matter was without		OD
and it was d. as I spake;	Mses	2: 5
from the waters; and it was d.;		2: 6
Father, thy will be d., and the		4: 2
this thing which thou hast d.?		4:19
d. this thou shalt be cursed		4:20
all these things were d. in secret.		5:30
gloried in that which he had d.,		5:33
Lord said: What hast thou d.?		5:35
it was d. after the manner of	Abr	1:11
What is to be d.? Who of all	JS	2:10
I had scarcely d. so, when		2:15
which he had d. at his first		2:45
which having d., he informed me		2:45
ascended as he had d. before.		2:45
had d. what was required at		2:60

DOOM

his final d. is to endure a	Mos	2:39
and d. us to eternal despair?	Al	26:19
and wo, wo, wo, is their d.	DC	38: 6
and misery shall be their d.;	Mses	7:37

DOOMED   264   DOTH

DOOMED
d. to suffer the wrath of God,	DC 76:33
were d. to sudden destruction.	JS 2:15
who was d. to the necessity of	2:23

DOOR
and went forth to the tent d.,	1Ne 16:10
the posts of the d. moved at	2Ne 16: 4
the d. thereof towards the temple,	Mos 2: 6
obtain the outer d. of the prison;	Al 14:27
when thou hast shut thy d.,	3Ne 13: 6
the d. thereof, when it was shut,	Eth 2:17
broke down the d. of the prison	7:18
effectual d. shall be opened	DC 100: 3
to open the d. by the proclamation	107:35
to unlock the d. of the kingdom	112:17
an effectual d. shall be opened	112:19
shall have power to open the d.	112:21
an effectual d. shall be opened	118: 3
as the d. shall be open to him	124:115
sin lieth at the d., and Satan	Mses 5:23

DOORS
behold it is now even at your d.;	He 8:27
they are nigh, even at your d.,	DC 45:63
the Lord is near, even at the d.	110:16
that he is near, even at the d.;	JS 1:39

DORMANT
your faith is d.; and this because	Al 32:34

DORT, David
Grover, Newel Knight, D.,   DC 124:132

DOST
Why d. thou offer sacrifices   Mses 5: 6

DOTH
D. this thing mean the torment	1Ne 15:31
or d. it mean the final state of	15:31
or d. it speak of the things which	15:31
he d. nourish them, and strengthen	17: 3
spirit, which d. weary me even	19:20
the Lord of Hosts, d. take away	2Ne 13: 1
countenance d. witness against	13: 9
and d. declare their sin	13: 9
neither d. his heart think so;	20: 7
d. magnify his holy name.	25:13
d. he cry unto any, saying:	26:25
for after this manner d. the Lord	31: 3
d. abound most plentifully.	Jac 2:12
he never d. vary from that which	Mos 2:22
he d. bless you and prosper you.	2:22
he d. require that ye should	2:24
he d. immediately bless you;	2:24
my whole frame d. tremble	2:30
but the Lord God d. support me,	2:30
which d. cause him to shrink	2:38
and d. fill his breast with guilt,	2:38
as a child d. submit to his father.	3:19
which d. cause them to shrink	3:25
that man d. not comprehend all	4: 9
d. grant unto you whatsoever ye	4:21
d. not belong to you but to God,	4:22
according as he d. agree, or else	4:28
d. a man take an ass from	5:14
d. exact of us, or our lives.	7:22
long d. he suffer with his people;	8:20
D. salvation come by the law of	12:31
d. not come by the law alone;	13:28
Yea, even d. not Isaiah say:	14: 1
except the king d. pacify them	20:20
d. not my voice shake the earth?	27:15
the kingdom d. rightly belong	29: 6
to whom the kingdom d. belong,	29: 7
iniquity d. one wicked king	29:17
and thus d. the Lord work	29:20
whosoever d. not obey his laws	29:23
whosoever d. rebel against him	29:23
an unrighteous king d. pervert	29:23
of the people d. choose iniquity,	29:27
lucre which d. corrupt the soul;	29:40
so d. every man that is cursed	Al 3:19
d. make a mock of his brother,	Al 5:30
the good shepherd d. call you;	5:38
in his own name he d. call you,	5:38
shepherd, and he d. follow him;	5:41
unto his voice, and d. follow him.	5:41
sheep d. not watch over them,	5:59
his flock d. he not drive him out?	5:59
good shepherd d. call after you;	5:60
sin, which easily d. beset you,	7:15
d. bind you down to destruction,	7:15
neither d. he vary from that	7:20
d. not dwell in unholy temples;	7:21
my soul d. exceedingly rejoice,	7:26
well d. the Lord judge of your	10:20
well d. he cry unto this people,	10:20
well d. he cry, by the voice of	10:21
This man d. revile against our laws	10:24
d. grant unto the children of men,	12: 9
d. declare it unto all nations;	13:22
yea, d. declare it, that they may	13:22
he d. sound these glad tidings	13:22
he d. suffer that they may do	14:11
d. send such great punishments	18: 2
even he d. remember all my	18:10
for myself, to me he d. not stink.	19: 5
the thing which d. trouble me.	22: 5
in his mercy he d. visit us by	24:14
he d. work righteousness forever.	26: 8
thy joy d. carry thee away unto	26:10
Lord d. grant unto all nations,	29: 8
the Lord d. counsel in wisdom,	29: 8
what d. it profit us to labor in	30:34
and he d. carry you about,	30:42
but d. speedily drag them down	30:60
which d. bind them down to a	31:17
d. lead their hearts to wander far	31:17
d. pain my soul.	31:30
d. begin to be enlightened,	32:34
your mind d. begin to expand.	32:34
spirit which d. possess your bodies	34:34
the devil, and he d. seal you his;	34:35
of the righteous d. he dwell;	34:36
which he d. bestow upon you.	34:38
d. give me exceeding great joy in	36:25
instances d. confound the wise.	37: 6
the Lord God d. work by means to	37: 7
the Lord d. confound the wise	37: 7
for he d. counsel in wisdom	37:12
which the Lord d. command you,	37:16
of the Lord d. say unto me:	39:12
more which d. worry your mind,	42: 1
which d. hang over you except	54: 6
the government d. rightly belong,	54:18
of justice d. hang over you;	60:29
he d. not command us that we	61:13
d. not dwell in unholy temples—	He 4:24
he d. carry on his works of	6:30
and d. hand down their plots,	6:30
he d. condemn all this people,	8: 5
where nothing d. corrupt,	8:25
which at this time d. await you,	9:22
who d. prophesy so much evil	9:27
d. bless and prosper those who	12: 1
when he d. prosper his people,	12: 2
except the Lord d. chasten his	12: 3
except he d. visit them with	12: 3
voice d. the whole earth shake;	12:11
which he d. put into my heart;	13: 5
where moth and rust d. corrupt,	3Ne 13:19
moth nor rust d. corrupt,	13:20
this d. witness unto the Father	18:10
that I am he that d. speak.	20:39
what d. it profit that we have	24:14
for that which moth d. corrupt	27:32
these things d. the Spirit manifest	Mrm 3:20
unto yourselves a god who d. vary,	9:10
he that d. possess it shall serve	Eth 2:10
which d. cause you to remain in	4:15
neither d. he will that man	8:19
this manner d. the devil work,	Mro 7:17
it d. not exceed that of our	9: 9
this land d. exceed everything;	9:19
their wickedness d. exceed that	9:20

DOTH 265 DOWN

DOTH
For God d. not walk in crooked	DC	3: 2
neither d. he turn to the right		3: 2
neither d. he vary from that		3: 2
Satan d. stir up the hearts of		10:63
d. he preach it by the Spirit of		50:17
d. he receive it by the Spirit of		50:19
And that which d. not edify		50:23
in nothing d. man offend God,		59:21
For what d. it profit a man if		88:33
d. know that in the day ye eat	Mses	4:11
what hour your Lord d. come.	JS	1:46

DOUBLE
d. the number of the Nephites;	Al	43:51

DOUBLED
your reward shall be d. unto	DC	98:26

DOUBT
unto you; wherefore can ye d.?	1Ne	4: 3
we have no reason to d.	Al	24:26
if they did not d., God would		56:47
We do not d. our mothers knew		56:48
and whosoever did not d.,		57:26
sorrowful, and began to d.,		59:11
marvel not, neither should they d.	He	5:49
who did d. in the least the words	3Ne	5: 1
D. not but be believing, and	Mrm	9:27
d. not, fear not.	DC	6:36
Therefore, d. not, for it is		8: 8

DOUBTED
They d. and marveled also	Al	59:12

DOUBTFUL
he also saw that his people were d.	Al	46:29
a commandment with d. heart,	DC	58:29

DOUBTING
believeth in Christ, d. nothing,	Mrm	9:21
believe in my name, d. nothing,		9:25
for he knew, nothing d.	Eth	3:19
voices, without wrath or d.,	DC	60: 7

DOUBTINGS
there began to be great d.	3Ne	8: 4

DOUBTLESS
D. a great mystery is contained	Mos	8:19
d. prepared for the purpose of		8:19

DOVE
abide upon him in the form of a d.	1Ne	11:27
upon him in the form of a d.	2Ne	31: 8
upon him in the form of a d.,	DC	93:15
Abraham, in the form of a d.	Fac	2: 7

DOWN
they came d. and went forth upon	1Ne	1:11
he came d. by the borders near		2: 5
and bring them d. hither into the		3: 4
we will not go d. unto our father		3:15
let us go d. to the land of our		3:16
even d. unto this present time.		3:20
we went d. to the land of our		3:22
go d. in the wilderness with us.		4:33
Therefore, if thou wilt go d. into		4:34
he would go d. into the wilderness		4:35
we had come d. into the wilderness		5: 1
and bring them d. again unto us		5: 5
even d. to the commencement of		5:12
even d. to the commencement of		5:13
bring d. Ishmael and his family		7: 2
with us d. into the wilderness		7: 5
they did bow d. before me, and		7:20
we did come d. unto the tent of		7:22
had come d. unto the tent of my		7:22
fell d. and partook of the fruit		8:30
an angel came d. and stood		11:14
fall d. at his feet and worship him.		11:24
the Holy Ghost come d. out of		11:27
and he came d. and showed himself		12: 6
bindeth them d., and yoketh them		13: 5
bringeth them d. into captivity.	1Ne	13: 5
and bring them d. into captivity.		13: 9
the Spirit of God, that it came d.		13:12
no more brought d. into captivity;		14: 2
away the souls of men d. to hell—		14: 3
being brought d. into captivity,		14: 7
d. into the depths of sorrow.		16:25
they fell d. before me, and were		17:55
arise and go d. into the ship.		18: 5
we did go d. into the ship, with		18: 6
we did all go d. into the ship,		18: 6
we had all gone d. into the ship,		18: 8
they were brought d., yea, even		18:17
about to be brought d. to lie low		18:18
these plates should be handed d.		19: 4
they shall bow d. to thee with their		21:23
be brought d. into captivity;	2Ne	1: 7
d. to the eternal gulf of misery		1:13
ye must soon lay d. in the cold		1:14
hath been weighed d. with sorrow		1:17
not be brought d. with grief		1:21
not come d. into captivity;		1:21
Messiah, who layeth d. his life		2: 8
captive, to bring you d. to hell,		2:29
and laying d. of contentions,		3:12
I cannot go d. to my grave save		4: 5
angels came d. and ministered		4:24
they shall bow d. to thee with		6: 7
ye shall lie d. in sorrow.		7:11
Bow d., that we may go over—		8:23
sit d., O Jerusalem;		8:25
even from the beginning d.,		9: 2
flesh must have laid d. to rot		9: 7
for he shall be thrust d. to hell.		9:34
for they shall be thrust d. to hell.		9:36
come d. in the depths of humility,		9:42
and not hang d. our heads,		10:20
the mean man boweth not d.,		12: 9
of men shall be bowed d.,		12:11
of man shall be bowed d.,		12:17
I will break d. the wall thereof,		15: 5
and it shall be trodden d.;		15: 5
the mean man shall be brought d.,		15:15
The bricks are fallen d.,		19:10
the sycamores are cut d.,		19:10
Without me they shall bow d.		20: 4
and to tread them d. like the		20: 6
I have put d. the inhabitants		20:13
ones of stature shall be hewn d.;		20:33
he shall cut d. the thickets		20:34
leopard shall lie d. with the kid,		21: 6
young ones shall lie d. together;		21: 7
lay d. the haughtiness of		23:11
Since thou art laid d. no feller		24: 8
pomp is brought d. to the grave;		24:11
Art thou cut d. to the ground,		24:12
thou shalt be brought d. to hell,		24:15
go d. to the stones of the pit;		24:19
the needy shall lie d. in safety;		24:30
d. from generation to generation		25:16
and handed d. unto my seed,		25:21
ye must bow d. before him,		25:29
therefore they must go d. to hell.		26:10
been brought d. low in the dust,		26:15
they put d. the power and		26:20
that he layeth d. his own life		26:24
your turning of things upside d.		27:27
they shall be thrust d. to hell!		28:15
them away carefully d. to hell.		28:21
leopard shall lie d. with the kid,		30:12
young ones shall lie d. together;		30:13
your Savior d. into the water,		31:13
and hand them d. unto my seed,	Jac	1: 3
but I this day am weighed d.		2: 3
which cometh d. against you,		2:35
and send d. justice upon those who		3: 1
let us go d. into the vineyard,		5:15
servant, went d. into the vineyard		5:16
let us go d. into the vineyard,		5:29
servant went d. into the vineyard;		5:30
Let us go d. into the nethermost		5:38
they went d. into the nethermost		5:39
nothing save it be to be hewn d.		5:42

DOWN

I also cut d. that which	Jac	5:44
of no worth but to be hewn d.		5:46
I should hew d. all the trees		5:47
hew d. the trees of the vineyard		5:49
and the bad be hewn d. and cast		5:66
that ye must be hewn d. and cast		6: 7
power of God came d. upon them,		7:21
I must soon go d. to my grave;		7:27
and I kneeled d. before my Maker,	En	1: 4
their transgressions will I bring d.		1:10
going d. speedily to destruction.		1:23
I must soon go d. to my grave,		1:26
until they came d. into the land	Om	1:13
am about to lie d. in my grave;		1:30
d. to the reign of this king	WM	1: 3
d. to the reign of this king		1: 3
concerning us d. to this day		1: 4
had been handed d. by the kings,		1:10
handed d. from king Benjamin,		1:11
armies of the Lamanites came d.		1:13
even d. to this present time.	Mos	1: 4
from the eldest d. to the youngest,		2: 5
I am about to go d. to my grave,		2:28
that I might go d. in peace,		2:28
even d. to the time our father,		2:34
shall come d. from heaven among		3: 5
who shall come d. among the		4: 2
went d. into the land of Nephi.		7: 6
that God should come d. among		7:27
which brought d. the wrath of God		7:28
he put d. all the priests that		11: 5
Thou shalt not bow d. thyself		13:13
God himself should come d.		13:34
God himself shall come d. among		15: 1
God himself should come d.		17: 8
did bow himself d. before them,		20:25
he wrote them d. that he might		26:33
were handed d. from generation		28:14
handing them d. from one		28:20
had been handed d. from the time		28:20
bearing d. against the church;	Al	1: 3
trodden d. by the hosts of men.		3: 2
pull d., by the word of God,		4:19
in bearing d. in pure testimony		4:19
to sit d. in the kingdom of God,		5:24
hewn d. and cast into the fire—		5:35
hewn d. and cast into the fire,		5:52
hewn d. and cast into the fire		5:56
doth bind you d. to destruction,		7:15
brought to sit d. with Abraham,		7:25
being weighed d. with sorrow,		8:14
was thus weighed d. with sorrow,		8:14
and to bring d. the wrath of God		10:18
I will come d. among my people,		10:21
d. to everlasting destruction,		12: 6
led by his will d. to destruction.		12:11
d. to an everlasting destruction,		12:17
he sendeth d. his wrath upon you		12:36
to pull d. his wrath upon us		12:37
not bring d. his wrath upon you,		13:30
bound d. by the chains of hell,		13:30
and he has come d. at this time		18: 4
Yea, and he looketh d. upon all the		18:32
even d. to the time that their		18:36
Jerusalem d. to the present time.		18:38
and the queen also sunk d.,		19:13
d. to the land of Middoni,		20: 7
if thou wilt bow d. before God,		22:16
and will bow d. before God,		22:16
king did bow d. before the Lord,		22:17
prophecies which were handed d.		23: 5
they did lay d. the weapons of		23: 7
they that laid d. the weapons of		23:13
that they would lie d. and perish,		24:23
threw d. their weapons of war,		24:25
came d. even as their brethren,		24:25
not be beaten d. by the storm		26: 6
of these have laid d. their lives;		26:34
go d. to the land of Zarahemla		27: 5
unto us, go d. unto our brethren,		27: 7
we will go d. unto our brethren,		27: 8
therefore let us go d. and rely		27: 9
went d. into the land of Jershon,		27:26

sit d. in the kingdom of God;	Al	29:17
that are bound d. under a foolish		30:13
handed d. by holy prophets,		30:14
bind themselves d. under the		30:23
are laid d. by ancient priests,		30:23
but be brought d. according to		30:23
and ye keep them d., even as		30:27
many souls d. to destruction,		30:47
was run upon and trodden d.,		30:59
speedily drag them d. to hell.		30:60
people to bow d. to dumb idols,		31: 1
which was handed d. to them by		31:16
cast by thy wrath d. to hell;		31:17
bind them d. to a belief of Christ,		31:17
he sat d. upon the ground,		34: 1
shall sit d. in his kingdom,		34:36
even d. to the present day;		36:29
should be kept and handed d.		37: 4
when thou liest d. at night		37:37
at night lie d. unto the Lord,		37:37
his kingdom, to sit d. in peace.		38:15
d. to the resurrection of Christ		40:16
d. to the resurrection of Christ.		40:18
shall bring you d. unto repentance.		42:29
let it bring you d. to the dust		42:30
d. into the borders of the land		43:32
threw d. their weapons of war		44:15
and they began to be swept d.,		44:18
be trodden d. and destroyed,		46:18
come d. to the foot of the mount,		47:10
he durst not go d. to the foot of		47:11
desiring him to come d.		47:11
to come d. off from the mount,		47:12
desiring that he would come d.,		47:12
when Lehonti had come d. with		47:13
to come d. with his army in the		47:13
Lehonti came d. with his men		47:14
of Nephi d. to the present time.		47:35
not suffer to lay d. their lives,		48:24
if king Amalickiah had come d.		49:10
Amalickiah did not come d.		49:11
smite d. all who should attempt		49:20
to dig d. their banks of earth		49:22
pulling d. the banks of earth,		49:22
he feared not to come d. to the		51:11
Amalickiah did himself come d.,		51:12
coming d. to battle against them,		51:13
to pull d. their pride and their		51:17
and they did pull d. their pride		51:18
hewn d. and leveled to the earth.		51:18
who were hewn d. by the sword;		51:19
rather than be smitten d. to		51:20
brought d. to humble themselves		51:21
thus breaking d. the wars and		51:22
kept them d. by the seashore,		51:25
and march d. near the seashore;		52:22
to retreat d. by the seashore,		52:23
threw d. their weapons of war		52:38
d. into the land of Zarahemla,		53:10
d. into the land of Zarahemla;		53:12
the laying d. of their lives;		53:17
pull d. the wrath of that God		54: 9
if ye will lay d. your arms,		54:18
shall lay d. their weapons and		54:18
d. out of the land of Nephi—		56: 3
durst they march d. against		56:25
d. to the land of Zarahemla;		57:15
d. to the land of Zarahemla;		57:16
go d. to the land of Zarahemla.		57:16
go d. to the land of Zarahemla		57:28
to guard them d. to the land.		57:29
we did start to go d. to		57:30
not for power, but to pull it d.		60:36
Moroni and Pahoran went d.		62: 7
to be let d. from the top of		62:21
let themselves d. into that part		62:22
let d. into the city by night,		62:23
even d. upon the borders by		62:32
did let himself d. over the walls		62:36
handed d. from one generation		63:13
came d. with a numerous army		63:15
d. to the coming of Christ.	He	1:hd
d. to the coming of Christ.		1:hd

DOWN

And they came d. again that they	He	1:15	d. against the city Desolation;	Mrm	4:19
d. to the land of Zarahemla		1:17	were swept d. and destroyed.		5: 7
cut d. the watch by the entrance		1:20	been handed d. by our fathers,		6: 6
and cut them d. to the earth.		1:24	that my men were hewn d.,		6:10
And they have been handed d.		3:16	and hewn d. all my people save		6:11
sit d. with Abraham, and Isaac,		3:30	my people who were hewn d.,		6:11
did come d. against the Nephites		4: 5	must lay d. your weapons of war,		7: 4
and trodden d., and slain, and		4:20	d. from city to city and from		8: 7
d. to the gulf of misery and		5:12	hewn d. and cast into the fire;		8:21
Holy Spirit of God did come d.		5:45	handed d. and altered by us,		9:32
angels came d. out of heaven		5:48	from the tower d. until they	Eth	1: 5
lay d. their weapons of war,		5:51	d. into the valley which is		1:42
did come d. into the land of		6: 4	went d. into the valley which		2: 1
bringing d. many of them into		6: 5	d. into the valley of Nimrod		2: 4
bringing d. the people unto		6:25	the Lord came d. and talked		2: 4
d. to an entire destruction,		6:28	not bring d. the fulness of the		2:11
of man even d. to this time.		6:29	feel d. before the Lord,		3: 6
and doth hand d. their plots,		6:30	to go d. out of the mount		4: 1
come d. to believe in their works		6:38	came d. out of the mount,		6: 2
d. to everlasting misery and		7:16	they bowed themselves d. upon		6:12
fathers, even d. to this time;		8:22	must soon go d. to the grave;		6:19
cast d. because of the wickedness		10: 3	before we go d. to our graves.		6:19
Be thou cast d. and become		10: 9	they went d. to their graves.		6:21
had been laid d. by the prophets.		11:22	broke d. the door of the prison		7:18
fire should come d. out of heaven		13:13	been handed d. even from Cain,		8:15
hewn d. and cast into the fire;		14:18	until the going d. of the sun,		12: 3
hewn d. and cast into the fire;		14:18	unto the laying d. of thy life		12:33
d. unto this second death.		14:19	sitting d. in the place which I		12:37
they shall be trodden d. and slain		15: 9	should come d. out of heaven,		13: 3
cast himself d. from the wall,		16: 7	d. into the land of Egypt,		13: 7
handed d. unto us by our fathers,		16:20	did kneel d. with the church,	Mro	4: 2
will keep us d. to be servants		16:21	d. on the right hand of God,		7:27
bowed himself d. upon the earth,	3Ne	1:11	he must go d. to hell.		8:14
at the going d. of the sun		1:15	put d. all power and authority		8:28
about to be smitten d. by it,		2:19	to weigh thee d. unto death;		9:25
Go d. upon the Nephites and		3: 3	even d. unto the time that ye		10: 3
should come d. against you		3: 4	break d. the mighty and strong	DC	1:19
armies shall come d. against you,		3: 8	and shall come d. in judgment		1:36
have been handed d. unto us.		3: 9	if he will bow d. before me,		5:24
should come d. against them.		3:12	draggeth their souls d. to hell;		10:26
come d. out of the wilderness		3:17	And thus he goeth up and d.,		10:27
come d. against them to battle.		3:25	d. even till you come to the reign		10:41
to come d. and to sally forth		4: 1	you shall fall d. and worship		18:40
even d. until the present time.		5:15	to sit d. on the right hand of		20:24
send d. fire and destroy them,		9:11	shall go d. into the water with		20:73
such I have laid d. my life,		9:22	my body which was laid d.		27: 2
came d. and stood in the midst		11: 8	be cast d. by devouring fire,		29:21
did fall d. at the feet of Jesus,		11:17	And they were thrust d.,		29:37
go d. and stand in the water,		11:23	command to reap d. the earth,		38:12
d. into the depths of humility		12: 2	ye now see shall be thrown d.		45:20
hewn d., and cast into the fire.		14:19	hewn d. and cast into the fire.		45:50
tread them d., saith the Father.		16:14	hewn d. and cast into the fire,		45:57
and shall tread them d., and they		16:15	they shall come d., for that		49:10
were whole, bow d. at his feet,		17:10	able to cast the soul d. to hell.		63: 4
set them d. upon the ground		17:12	and will come d. in heaven		63:34
kneel d. upon the ground.		17:13	of one sent d. from on high,		65: 1
and they came d. and encircled		17:24	shall come d. in heaven,		65: 5
sit themselves d. upon the earth.		18: 2	cometh d. from above,		67: 9
the multitude should kneel d.		19: 6	thrust d. from the presence of		76:25
went d. unto the water's edge,		19:10	they who are thrust d. to hell.		76:84
Nephi went d. into the water		19:11	they who are cast d. to hell		76:106
and it came d. from heaven,		19:14	or to cast d. to the regions of		77: 8
and angels did come d. out of		19:14	lift up the hands which hand d.,		81: 5
kneel d. again upon the earth,		19:16	the Lord hath brought d. Zion		84:100
should kneel d. upon the earth.		19:16	forth to reap d. the fields.		86: 5
had all knelt d. upon the earth,		19:17	cast themselves d. as a fig		88:87
treadeth d. and teareth in pieces,		20:16	even d. to the deacons.—		88:127
arise, sit d., O Jerusalem;		20:37	That she may settle d. in peace		90:31
treadeth d. and teareth in pieces,		21:12	hewn d. and cast into the fire.		97: 7
throw d. all thy strongholds;		21:15	whoso layeth d. his life in my		98:13
the power of heaven come d.		21:25	are called to lay d. their lives		101:35
ye shall tread d. the wicked;		25: 3	may not be broken d. when		101:45
hewn d. and cast into the fire,		27:11	night, and broke d. the hedge;		101:51
works that they are hewn d.;		27:12	and broke d. the olive-trees.		101:51
hewn d. and cast into the fire,		27:17	from breaking d. the hedge		101:54
ye shall sit d. in the kingdom of		28:10	break d. the walls of mine		101:57
they were cast d. into the earth;		28:20	throw d. their tower, and		101:57
which had been handed d. from	4Ne	1:48	no more to be thrown d.,		101:75
saw thousands of them hewn d.	Mrm	2:15	no more to be thrown d.		103:13
come d. to the city of Desolation		3: 7	they shall be thrown d.;		103:14
did come d. again to battle.		3: 8	be afraid to lay d. his life for		103:27
did come d. against the Nephites		4:17	whoso layeth d. his life for		103:27

DOWN		
is not willing to lay d. his life	DC	103:28
be trodden d. by whom I will;		104: 5
throw d. the towers of mine		105:16
of throwing d. the towers of		105:30
to be handed d. from father to		107:40
d. by lineage in the following		107:41
he was bowed d. with age,		107:56
glory may rest d. upon thy people,		109:12
may lay d. their weapons of		109:66
cause the mountains to flow d.		109:74
have come d. from the fathers,		112:32
sent d. from heaven unto you.		112:32
pouring d. knowledge from heaven		121:33
made to bow d. with grief,		123: 7
or Adam d. to the present time,		128:21
and rills, flow d. with gladness.		128:23
thrown d., and shall not remain		132:13
the Lord who shall come d.		133: 2
shall break d. the mountains,		133:22
ice shall flow d. at their presence.		133:26
fall d. and be crowned with glory,		133:32
that thou wouldst come d.,		133:40
that the mountains might flow d.		133:40
come d. to make thy name known		133:42
Yea, when thou comest d.,		133:44
mountains flow d. at thy presence,		133:44
Who is this that cometh d.		133:46
ye shall lie d. in sorrow.		133:70
and turned d. the leaf upon it:		135: 4
even unto the sitting d. in the place		135: 5
names go d. to posterity as gems		135: 6
taken d. without delay.		OD
caused that he should be cast d.;	Mses	4: 3
was carried d. into the water,		6:64
will I send d. out of heaven;		7:62
it came d. from the fathers,	Abr	1: 3
not bow d. to worship gods of		1:11
have come d. to deliver thee,		1:16
I have come d. to visit them,		1:17
broke d. the altar of Elkehah,		1:20
concluded to go d. into Egypt,		2:21
come d. unto thee to deliver		3:21
I came d. in the beginning		3:21
We will go d., for there is space		3:24
Let us go d.		4: 1
they went d. at the beginning,		4: 1
Let us go d. and form man in		4:26
the Gods went d. to organize		4:27
the Gods came d. and formed		5: 4
They shall be thrown d., and left	JS	1: 2
that shall not be thrown d.		1: 3
I kneeled d. and began to offer		2:15

DR.		
left him and went to D. Mitchell,	JS	2:65

DRAG		
speedily d. them down to hell.	Al	30:60
to d. you down to the gulf of	He	5:12

DRAGGED		
until he d. the people down to	He	6:28
and thou be d. to prison,	DC	122: 6

DRAGGETH		
d. their souls down to hell;	DC	10:26

DRAGON		
cut Rahab, and wounded the d.?	2Ne	8: 9

DRAGONS		
and d. in their pleasant palaces;	2Ne	23:22
and like d. did they fight.	Mos	20:11
yea, they did fight like d.,	Al	43:44

DRAW		
them that d. iniquity with cords	2Ne	15:18
of the Holy One of Israel d. nigh		15:19
with joy shall ye d. water out		22: 3
that he may d. all men unto him.		26:24
as this people d. near unto me with		27:25
d. away a part of this people	Mos	29: 7
d. away a part of their forces	Al	52:13

that I might d. all men unto me,	3Ne	27:14
Father I will d. all men unto me,		27:15
D. near unto me and I will	DC	88:63
and I will d. near unto you;		88:63
councilors who d. even numbers,		102:17
"they d. near to me with	JS	2:19

DRAWETH		
For behold, the time d. near,	Jac	5:29
and the end d. nigh.		5:47
for behold the end d. nigh,		5:62
the last time, for the end d. nigh.		5:64
for the day of salvation d. nigh;	Al	13:21
your redemption d. nigh.	DC	35:26
coming of the Lord d. nigh,		106: 4

DRAWN		
d. away much people after him;	Al	2: 2
those who had not been d. away		2: 3
be full, d. out in prayer unto him		34:27
ye have d. away the forces into		58:35
yea your hearts are not d. out	He	13:22
those whom he had d. away	Eth	7: 9
if with a d. sword thine enemies	DC	122: 6
he had d. away many after him,)	Mses	4: 6
which I had d. off the plates,	JS	2:63

DREAD		
and let him be your d.	2Ne	18:13
the wicked with awful d. and fear.	Jac	6:13

DREADFUL		
d. on the part of the Lamanites,	Al	43:37
in that great and d. day,		45:14
and the d. groanings did cease,	3Ne	10: 9
great and d. day of the Lord;		25: 5
great and d. day of the Lord.	DC	2: 1
before the great and d. day		110:14
great and d. day of the Lord		110:16
great and d. day of the Lord:		128:17
the great and d. day of the Lord.	JS	2:38

DREAM		
unto my father, yea, even in a d.,	1Ne	2: 1
commanded my father, even in a d.,		2: 2
I have dreamed a d., in the which		3: 2
dreamed a d.; or, in other words,		8: 2
I saw in my d., a dark and		8: 4
all the words of his d. or vision,		8:36
of speaking the words of his d.,		10: 2
thing which our father saw in a d.?		15:21
shall be as a d. of a night vision;	2Ne	27: 3
away like as it were unto us a d.,	Jac	7:26
the Lord warned Omer in a d.	Eth	9: 3

DREAMED		
I have d. a dream, in the which	1Ne	3: 2
d. a dream; or, in other words,		8: 2

DREAMETH		
as unto a hungry man which d.,	2Ne	27: 3
like unto a thirsty man which d.,		27: 3

DREAMS		
which he saw in visions and in d.;	1Ne	1:16
by their traditions and their d.	Al	30:28

DREARY		
a dark and d. wilderness.	1Ne	8: 4
I was in a dark and d. waste.		8: 7

DREGS		
hast drunken the d. of the cup	2Ne	8:17
the d. of the cup of my fury;		8:22
they drink the d. of a bitter cup.	Al	40:26

DRESS		
manner of d. was exceeding fine;	1Ne	8:27
Eden, to d. it, and to keep it.	Mses	3:15
to d. it and to keep it.	Abr	5:11

DRESSED		
and he was d. in a white robe:	1Ne	8: 5
and he was d. in a white robe.		14:19

DRESSED / DRIVEN

were d. with thick clothing—	Al	43:19
that their wounds should be d.		57:24

DREW
beheld his sword, and I d. it forth	1Ne	4: 9
he d. his sword, and swore in	Mos	19: 4
and d. his sword and began to	Al	1: 9
d. his sword and went forth that		19:22
and he d. his sword that he might		20:16
yea, he d. out the man, and he		42: 2
Corihor d. away many people	Eth	7: 4
and d. away Cohor his brother,		7:15
by which means they d. away		9:11
Com d. away the half of the		10:32

DRIED
shall wither even as a d. reed;	1Ne	17:48
because the waters are d. up,	2Ne	7: 2
not he who hath d. the sea,		8:10
their multitude d. up with thirst.		15:13
the great deep—Be thou d.—	He	12:16

DRINK
thou shalt no more d. it again.	2Ne	8:22
that they may follow strong d.,		15:11
Wo unto the mighty to d. wine,		15:22
of strength to mingle strong d.;		15:22
shall stagger but not with strong d.		27: 4
Eat, d., and be merry, for tomorrow		28: 7
Eat, d., and be merry; nevertheless,		28: 8
and would d. the blood of beasts.	Jar	1: 6
but men d. damnation to their	Mos	3:18
we may not d. out of the cup of		5: 5
eat, and d., and rest themselves		7:16
they did d. freely of the wine		22:10
yea, ye shall eat and d. of	Al	5:34
or what they should d.,		31:37
they d. the dregs of a bitter cup.		40:26
that he would d. his blood;		49:27
sworn to d. the blood of Moroni.		51: 9
of your wine, that we may d.;		55: 9
more desirous to d. of the wine;		55:10
they did d. and were merry,		55:14
ye shall eat, or what ye shall d.;	3Ne	13:25
or, What shall we d.? or,		13:31
the wine of the cup and d. of it,		18: 8
that they might d. of it.		18: 8
and did d. of it and were filled;		18: 9
they did d., and they were filled.		18: 9
to eat and d. of my flesh and		18:29
he also gave them wine to d.,		20: 5
bread to eat, and also wine to d.		20: 7
if they d. any deadly thing	Mrm	9:24
the souls of all those who d. of it,	Mro	5: 2
might not d. the bitter cup,	DC	19:18
souls of all those who d. of it,		20:79
shall eat or what ye shall d.		27: 2
purchase wine neither strong d.		27: 3
will d. of the fruit of the vine		27: 5
all nations d. of the wine of		35:11
shall eat, or what ye shall d.,		84:81
all nations to d. of her cup,		86: 3
d. of the wine of the wrath of		88:94
d. of the wine of the wrath of		88:105
wine or strong d. among you,		89: 5
to eat and d. with the drunken,	JS	1:52

DRINKETH
behold he d. but he awaketh		
d. damnation to his own soul;	2Ne	27: 3
whoso eateth and d. my flesh	Mos	2:33
eateth and d. damnation to	3Ne	18:29
he that d. of this wine drinketh		18:29
d. of my blood to his soul;		20: 8
inasmuch as any man d. wine		20: 8
	DC	89: 5

DRINKING
d. in with the traditions of the	Al	47:36
And are we not eating and d.,	Mses	8:21
they were eating and d.,	JS	1:42

DRINKS
strong d. are not for the belly,	DC	89: 7

hot d. are not for the body	DC	89: 9
useful animals, and for mild d.,		89:17

DRIVE
king Benjamin did d. them out	Om	1:24
but will d. him away, and cast him	Mos	5:14
we did d. them again out of our		10:20
to d. the Lamanites before them;		20:11
and d. them as they would a		21: 3
to d. them out of their land.		21: 7
may d. them into the wilderness		22: 6
sent to d. them out of their land.	Al	3:21
his flock doth he not d. him out?		5:59
army to d. them out of the land,		16: 3
Lamanites d. their flocks hither,		17:26
thereby they might d. away many		18: 7
Amalickiah did d. them,		51:23
they did d. them out of the land;		62:38
d. them back out of their lands	3Ne	2:17
and did d. us out of the city.	Mrm	2: 4
they did also d. ua forth out of		2: 5
did d. the inhabitants forth		4:14
and d. them out of their lands.		4:15
whether he will d. us out of	Eth	1:38
if he will d. us out of te land,		1:38
and d. the church into the	DC	86: 3
to d. you from my goodly land,		103:24
discomfort my people, and d.,		121:23

DRIVEN
have d. him out of the land.	1Ne	7:14
exceed the whiteness of the d. snow.		11: 8
who were d. out by our fathers,		17:33
were d. forth before the wind		18: 8
And after we had been d. forth		18: 9
were d. back upon the waters		18:13
day, which we had been d. back,		18:14
And after we had been d. back		18:15
are broken off and are d. out,		21: 1
they were d. out of the garden	2Ne	2:19
after they are d. to and fro,		6:11
we have been d. out of the land		10:20
and shall be d. to darkness.		18:22
until they had d. them out of	WM	1:14
their journey, but were d. back,	Mos	1:17
and scattereth, and are d.,		8:21
we had d. them out of our land.		9:18
d. out of the land of Jerusalem		10:12
and they were d. back,		11:18
and shall be d. by men,		12: 2
be d. before like a dumb ass.		12: 5
d. forth upon the face of the land.		12:12
be d. and scattered to and fro,		17:17
is d. by wild and ferocious beasts.		17:17
but they were d. back again,		21:11
and to be d. to and fro,		21:13
who were d. into the wilderness		23: 1
and was d. out before the king,		24: 9
on every hand, and slain and d.,	Al	2:37
and d. into the wilderness;		16: 8
having been d. out of the land,		16: 9
when he had d. them afar off,		17:39
d. them from house to house,		20:30
whither the Nephites had d. them.		22:29
the which they were d. and slain.		25: 3
is d. and slain by wild beasts;		25:12
they were d. by the Lamanites,		25:12
shall they be d. with fierce winds		26: 6
Lamanites were d. and scattered,		28: 3
after the Lamanites were d. out		30: 1
were d. out of their land;		35:14
were d. by Lehi into the waters		43:40
they were d. insomuch that they		43:51
but behold, they were d. back		49:21
had d. all the Lamanites out of		50: 9
after this manner were they d.		51:32
d. back to the city of Manti.		57:22
that they had d. their whole army		58:25
have d. me out before them,		61: 5
those who had d. Pahoran from		62: 2
who had d. the freemen out of		62: 6
were beaten and d. back again		63:15

DRIVEN — DUE

DRIVEN
and hunted, and d. forth,	He 3:16
were slain and d. out of the land,	4: 2
were d. even into the land of	4: 6
and d. before the Lamanites,	4:13
d. out of the land of Jerusalem?	8:21
Lehi was d. out of Jerusalem	8:22
that same year they were d. back	11:29
they shall be d. to and fro upon	15:12
again were hunted and d.	Mrm 2:20
were d. forth until we had come	2:20
d. back again to the land of	4: 2
and d. back by the Nephites.	4: 8
that they had d. the Lamanites	4: 8
Nephites were d. and slaughtered	4:21
they were d. back that they did	5: 3
they are d. about as chaff before	5:16
as chaff is d. before the wind,	5:18
d. and scattered by the Gentiles	5:20
d. and scattered by the Gentiles,	5:20
iniquity, and hast d. us forth,	Eth 3: 3
were d. forth before the wind.	6: 8
And thus they were d. forth;	6:10
And thus they were d. forth,	6:11
his descendants were d. out of	10: 8
came forth, but were d. again;	14:29
were d. again the second time.	14:29
Being d. and smitten by	DC 103: 2
of their being d. out and	104:51
d. by the inhabitants of Jackson	109:47
mob, who have d. thy people,	109:50
d. to the ends of the earth,	109:67
great deep, and it shall be d. back	133:23
you received, me and you were d.	133:66
the nation that has d. you out.	136:34
the Lord God, had d. them out,	Mses 5: 1
thou hast d. me out this day	5:39

DRIVING
the d. out of the children of the	1Ne 17:32
were d. forth their flocks to	Al 17:27
d. the Nephites before them	51:28

DROOP
No longer d. in sin.	2Ne 4:28

DROP
covet that which is but the d.,	DC 117: 8

DROSS
esteemed by their brethren as d.;	Al 32: 3
ye are as d., which the refiners	34:29

DROVE
and d. many of their flocks out	Mos 11:17
they d. them back for a time;	11:18
and d. them back, and slew many	21: 8
until he slew and d. them back.	Al 2:33
d. the remainder of them out of	3:23
d. all the Lamanites who were	50: 7
and d. him back again to	Eth 13:29
I d. out the man, and I placed	Mses 4:31

DROWNED
d. in the waters of the Red Sea.	1Ne 4: 2
d. in the depths of the fountain;	8:32
Egyptians were d. in the Red Sea,	17:27
lest they should be d. in the sea;	18:13
we suppose that they were d. in	Al 63: 8
the inhabitants thereof were d.	3Ne 8: 9
the inhabitants thereof to be d.	9: 4
not d. in the depths of the sea;	10:13
been d. in the depth of the sea.	DC 54: 5
about their necks, and they d.	121:22

DRUNK
hast d. at the hand of the Lord	2Ne 8:17
d. damnation to their own souls.	Mos 3:25
they have d. out of the cup of	3:26
have d. out of that bitter cup	3Ne 11:11
multitude had all eaten and d.,	20: 9

DRUNKEN
for he was d. with wine.	1Ne 4: 7
shall be d. with their own blood	1Ne 21:26
shall be d. with their own blood.	22:13
shall be d. with their own blood	2Ne 6:18
thou hast d. the dregs of the cup	8:17
and d., and not with wine:	8:21
they will be d. with iniquity	27: 1
shall be d. but not with wine,	27: 4
of the Lamanites, by night are d.;	Mos 22: 6
the Lamanites, and they will be d.;	22: 7
when they are d. and asleep.	22: 7
and by and by they were all d.	Al 55:14
men saw that they were all d.,	55:15
were in a deep sleep and d.,	55:16
behold they were d. and the	55:18
of Coriantumr, as they were d.	Eth 14: 5
they were d. with anger,	15:22
as a man who is d. with wine;	15:22
to reel to and fro as a d. man,	DC 49:23
reel to and fro as a d. man;	88:87
and to eat and drink with the d.,	JS 1:52

DRUNKENNESS
and destroy them in their d.	Al 55:19
them with poison or with d.	55:30
Cease d.; and let your words	DC 136:24

DRY
out of captivity, on d. ground,	1Ne 4: 2
they passed through on d. ground.	17:26
at my rebuke I d. up the sea,	2Ne 7: 2
and make men go over d. shod.	21:15
through the Red Sea on d. ground,	Mos 7:19
even as a d. stalk of the field,	12:11
and as a root out of d. ground;	14: 2
which was covered with d. bones;	21:26
came through upon d. ground,	He 8:11
earth was smitten that it was d.,	11: 6
fine and exceedingly d. wood,	3Ne 8:21
the Red Sea on d. ground.	DC 8: 3
or to the seas, or to the d. land,	121:30
all ye seas and d. lands tell	128:23
at my rebuke I d. up the sea.	133:68
burn up the d. trees to purify the	135: 6
Let there be d. land; and it was	Mses 2: 9
I, God, called the d. land Earth;	2:10
and let the earth come up d.;	Abr 4: 9
Gods prounounced the d. land,	4:10

DUE
to come forth in d. time by	T Pg
the own d. time of the Lord,	1Ne 10: 3
the own d. time of the Lord,	14:26
until the own d. time of the Lord,	2Ne 27:10
them forth in mine own d. time;	27:21
the Lamanites in his own d. time.	En 1:16
according to that which is his d.	Mos 4:13
be fulfilled in his own d. time,	3Ne 5:25
together in mine own d. time,	20:29
come forth in mine own d. time.	Mrm 5:12
I will cause in mine own d. time	Eth 3:24
show them in mine own d. time	3:27
your words, in mine own d. time.	DC 24:16
be saved in mine own d. time;	35:25
unto you in mine own d. time	42:62
in mine own d. time will I come	43:29
be cut off in mine own d. time,	56: 3
in mine own d. time, ye shall see	67:14
in the d. time of the Lord,	68:14
in mine own d. time.	71:10
in the d. time of the Lord,	76:38
in mine own d. time for the	82:13
rewarded in mine own d. time.	90:29
over Zion in mine own d. time.	90:32
in d. time receive of his fulness.	93:19
are to be testified of in d. time.	107:57
I will gather out in d. time for	111: 2
in d. time that I will give	111: 4
in the d. time he shall be made a	117:14
mine own d. time, saith the Lord.	117:16
my debts are canceled in d. time,	127: 1
unto you all things in d. time.	132:45
be redeemed in mine own d. time.	136:18
given in the own d. time	Mses 10:12

DUE 271 DUTIES

give them meat in d. season?	JS	1:49
in d. time be conferred on us,		2:72

DUG
and pruned it, and d. about it,	Jac	5:76
the Nephites had d. up a ridge	Al	49: 4
which had been d. round about,		49:18

DULL
and their ears are d. of hearing,	Mses	6:27

DULY
d. recommended and authorized	DC	112:21

DUMB
driven before like a d. ass.	Mos	12: 5
a sheep before her shearers is d.		14: 7
a sheep before the shearer is d.,		15: 6
drive them as they would a d. ass—		21: 3
so great that he became d.,		27:19
that thou shalt become d.,	Al	30:47
sign, that thou shalt be struck d.,		30:49
of God, ye shall be struck d.,		30:49
words, Korihor was struck d.,		30:50
I know that I am d., for I		30:52
people to bow down to d. idols,		31: 1
were struck d. with amazement.	He	5:25
their blind, and with their d.,	3Ne	17: 9
to hear, and the d. to speak,	DC	35: 9
tongue of the d. shall speak;		84:70
children unto their d. idols,	Abr	1: 7

DUNBAR: see WILSON, Dunbar.

DUNG
and d. them once more,	Jac	5:64
heaped up as d. upon the face of	Mrm	2:15

DUNGED
have pruned it, and I have d. it;	Jac	5:47
and dug about it, and d. it;		5:76

DUNGEONS
that ye should be confined in d.,	Mos	2:13
they could not be confined in d.;	Al	8:31

DURATION
have remained to an endless d.	2Ne	9: 7
and the d. of eternity,	En	1:23

DURING
d. which time Com gained power	Eth	10:32
d. the seven thousand years of	DC	77: 6
d. this time your baptisms shall		124:31
last June, or d. the past year,		OD
d. that period been solemnized		OD
d. the time specified, which can		OD
D. this time of great excitement	JS	2: 8
D. the space of time which		2:28
D. the time that I was thus		2:57

DURST
that they d. not utter against him;	1Ne	2:14
neither d. they lay their hands		17:52
Now they d. not do this lest they		17:52
for I d. not speak further as yet		22:29
d. not lay their hands on him,	Mos	13: 5
d. not return to their wives		20: 3
Now they d. not slay them,		21: 3
they d. not lie, if it were known,	Al	1:17
And they d. not steal, for fear of		1:18
neither d. they rob, nor murder,		1:18
and d. not ocmmit any wickedness		1:33
he come in unto me, but I d. not.		18:11
they d. not put forth their hands		19:24
they d. hot lay their hands on		22:20
they d. not look up with boldness,		30:27
they d. not enjoy their rights		30:27
they d. not make use of that which		30:28
d. not come against the Nephites		43:22
he d. not go down to the foot of		47:11
his chief captains d. not attack		49:11

that they d. not oppose but were	Al	51: 7
They d. not pass by us with their		56:24
neither d. they with a part,		56:24
Neither d. they march down		56:25
neither d. they cross the head of		56:25
they d. not turn to the right nor		56:40
we d. not go forth and attack		58: 2
d. not come out against us		61: 7
they d. not come out against		62:19
the Lamanites d. not come into	He	1:18
the Lamanites d. not come into		1:26
d. not lay their hands upon them		5:23
d. not lay their hands upon them;		5:25
d. they come near unto them,		5:25
they d. not lay their own hands		8: 4
they d. not spread themselves	3Ne	4: 6
they d. not open their mouths,		11: 8
for they d. not speak unto him		28: 5

DUST
brought down to lie low in the d.;	1Ne	18:18
and lick up the d. of thy feet;		21:23
church, shall tumble to the d.		22:14
who must be brought low in the d.;		22:23
Awake! and arise from the d.,	2Ne	1:14
arise from the d., my sons,		1:21
and arise from the d.		1:23
cried unto them from the d.;		3:19
they shall cry from the d.;		3:20
lick up the d. of thy feet;		6: 7
lick up the d. of their feet;		6:13
Shake thyself from the d.;		8:25
and hide thee in the d.,		12:10
blossoms shall go up as d.;		15:24
brought down low in the d.,		26:15
shall be low out of the d.,		26:16
speech shall whisper out of the d.		26:16
who have slumbered in the d.,		27: 9
voice of one crying from the d.:		33:13
he can smite you to the d.:	Jac	2:15
And all flesh is of the d.;		2:21
as much as the d. of the earth;	Mos	2:25
created of the d. of the earth;		2:25
for I am also of the d.		2:26
even less than the d. of the earth.		4: 2
themselves even to the d.,		21:13
humble yourselves even to the d.,	Al	34:38
down to the d. in humility.		42:30
are less than the d. of the earth.	He	12: 7
the d. of the earth moveth hither		12: 8
Shake thyself from the d.;	3Ne	20:37
even from the d. will they cry	Mrm	8:23
created of the d. of the earth;		9:17
cry from the d. for vengeance	Eth	8:24
as one speaking out of the d.?	Mro	10:27
awake, and arise from the d.,		10:31
by casting off the d. of your feet	DC	24:15
And shake off the d. of thy feet		60:15
they shall not sleep in the d.,		63:51
shake off the d. of your feet		75:20
man out of the d. of the earth		77:12
God, formed man from the d. of	Mses	3: 7
d. shalt thou eat all the days of		4:20
for d. thou wast, and unto dust		4:25
and unto d. shalt thou return.		4:25
so became of d. a living soul,		6:59
man from the d. of the ground,	Abr	5: 7

DUTIES
and attend to all family d.	DC	20:47
and attend to all family d.		20:51
In all these d. the priest is		20:52
in all his d. in the church,		20:57
to perform the d. of his calling,		20:64
until he is called to further d.		47: 1
act in the discharge of your d.		103: 1
in the d. of their calling,		107:23
in the d. of their calling.		107:25
teaching them the d. of		107:87
teach them the d. of their office,		107:87
one of the d. of this priesthood.		107:88

DUTY

up in remembrance of their d.	Mos	1:17
of God and their d. towards him.		13:30
to a remembrance of their d.	Al	4: 3
up in remembrance of their d.,		4:19
to a sense of your d. to God,		7:22
the d. which they owed to their		43:46
of them are in the path of their d.,	He	15: 5
The d. of the elders, priests,	DC	20:38
The priest's d. is to preach,		20:46
The teacher's d. is to watch		20:53
that all the members do their d.		20:55
The d. of the members after they		20:68
the d. of the several churches,		20:81
thy d. is unto the church forever,		23: 3
this is thy d. from henceforth		23: 5
it is your d. to unite with		23: 7
the d. of the bishop shall be		72: 7
known the d. of the bishop		72: 9
that it is the d. of the church		75:24
It is the d. of the Lord's clerk,		85: 1
the d. of the twelve councilors		102:12
the d. of said council to transmit,		102:26
more perfectly concerning their d.,		105:10
d. of the traveling high council		107:38
It is the d. of the Twelve,		107:39
It is the d. of the Twelve,		107:58
This is the d. of a bishop who		107:73
d. of a president over the office		107:85
and to teach them their d.,		107:85
d. of the president over the office		107:86
the d. of the president over the		107:87
d. of the president over the office		107:89
d. of the President of the office		107:91
now let every man learn his d.,		107:99
and he that learns not his d.		107:100
d. that we owe to God,		123: 7
an imperative d. that we owe,		123: 9
imperative d. that we owe to all		123:11
not my d. to join with any	JS	2:26

DWELL

if my father should d. in the land	1Ne	3:18
no unclean thing can d. with God;		10:21
cannot d. in the kingdom of God;		15:33
to d. in the kingdom of God, or		15:35
give place to me that I may d.		21:20
for they d. in righteousness,		22:26
shall d. safely in the Holy One of		22:28
and they shall d. safely forever.	2Ne	1: 9
that they d. in prosperity long		1:31
shalt d. safely with thy brother,		2: 3
can d. in the presence of God,		2: 8
they that d. therein shall die		8: 6
have all men that d. thereon		10:19
I d. in the midst of a people of		16: 5
they that d. in the land of		19: 2
wolf also shall d. with the lamb,		21: 6
and owls shall d. there,		23:21
shall the wolf d. with the lamb;		30:12
of Mosiah who d. in the land,	Mos	1:10
that thereby they may d. with God		2:41
shall d. in a tabernacle of clay,		3: 5
evil spirits which d. in the hearts		3: 6
to d. in the land of Lehi-Nephi,		7: 1
They are raised to d. with God		15:23
began to d. in the land again		21: 1
doth not d. in unholy temples;	Al	7:21
were his desire to d. in the land		17:22
I desire to d. amont this people		17:23
have gone to d. with their God.		24:22
to d. in the land of Ishmael		25:13
to d. at the right hand of God,		28:12
shall d. here below in the flesh,		31:26
hearts of the righteous doth he d.?		34:36
last day, to d. with him in glory;		36:28
would not d. upon your crimes,		39: 7
to d. with my brother whom ye		54:22
to d. with the people of Ammon,		62:17
cement, in the which they did d.	He	3: 7
land northward did d. in tents,		3: 9
doth not d. in unholy temples—		4:24
and they did d. in one land,	3Ne	3:25

ye that d. at Jerusalem,	3Ne	10: 5
pain while ye shall d. in the flesh,		28: 9
but to d. with God eternally		28:40
d. in the hearts of the people.	4Ne	1:15
to d. in the presence of God	Mrm	7: 7
that ye shall d. with him under		9: 3
to d. with that holy Being,		9: 3
to d. with a holy and just God		9: 4
d. with the damned souls in hell.		9: 4
up to d. in the kingdom	Eth	4:19
did d. in captivity all his days.		11: 9
who d. upon the face thereof;		13: 2
blessed are they who d. therein,		13:10
all the saints shall d. with God.	Mro	8:26
I d. no longer upon this horrible		9:20
you shall d. with me in glory,	DC	6:30
salvation who d. on the earth.		7: 6
which shall d. in your heart.		8: 2
d. in righteousness with men		29:11
who d. upon this farm.		63:38
that d. upon the face thereof,		63:39
d. in the presence of God		76:62
They who d. in his presence		76:94
but where God and Christ d.		76:112
that he may d. therein even so.		96: 9
may d. upon all the earth.		101:25
be permitted to d. thereon.		101:99
say they shall not d. thereon;		101:100
kingdom they shall d. thereon.		101:100
d. in the land of Shinehah		104:21
when I shall d. with them,		104:59
d. in the regions round about		105:23
your God will not d. therein.		124:24
for the Most High to d. therein.		124:27
that have desires to d. therein,		125: 4
and the Son d. in a man's heart		130: 3
inhabitants who d. thereon,		130: 9
manifest to those who d. on it;		130: 9
the Holy Ghost could not d. in us.		130:22
d. in his presence day and night,		133:35
appear unto many that d. on		133:36
father of such as d. in tents,	Mses	5:45
for no unclean thing can d. there,		6:57
dwell there, or d. in his presence;		6:57
none other people shall d. there		7: 5
Zion shall d. in safety forever.		7:20
in the last days, to d. on the		7:65
I d. in heaven;	Abr	2: 7
I d. in the midst of them		3:21
an earth whereon these may d.;		3:24

DWELLEST

O my people that d. in Zion,	2Ne	20:24
art holy and d. in the heavens,	Eth	3: 2

DWELLETH

of Hosts, which d. in Mount Zion.	2Ne	18:18
he d. not in unholy temples.	Mos	2:37
And because he d. in flesh		15: 2
every one that d, in the land;	Al	5:49
a portion of that Spirit d. in me,		18:35
he d. not in unholy temples,		34:36
he d. eternally in the heavens.	Mro	7:28

DWELLING

will create upon every d.-place	2Ne	14: 5
d. in tents, and wandering about	En	1:20
his d. in his mortal tabernacle;	Al	7: 8

DWELLING-PLACE: see DWELLING and PLACE.

DWELLINGS

the places of your d. shall	3Ne	10: 7

DWELLS

heavens is a place where God d.	Al	18:30
voice of him who d. on high,	DC	1: 1
that d. upon all the face of		101:24
the place upon which he now d.		104:27

DWELT

Lehi, having d. at Jerusalem	1Ne	1: 4
and d. upon a rock before him;		1: 6

DWELT

Ant my father d. in a tent.	1Ne	2:15
and speak, as he d. in a tent,		9: 1
done as my father d. in a tent,		10:16
done as my father d. in a tent		16: 6
neither shall it be d. in	2Ne	23:20
of myself, have d. at Jerusalem,		25: 6
they had d. there from that time	Om	1:16
he d. with them for the space of		1:21
after we had d. in the land	Mos	9:11
this Alma hath d. at my house.	Al	10:10
the wilderness, and d. in tents;		22:28
of the land wheresoever they d.,		23:14
who d. upon the mountains,	3Ne	1:27
saints who have d. in the land.	Mrm	9:36
and they d. in tents,	Eth	2:13
d. in tents upon the seashore		2:13
and d. in the land of Nehor;		7: 4
of Moron where the king d.,		7: 5
of Moron, where the king d.,		7: 6
that Kib d. in captivity,		7: 7
came and d. in the land of Heth.		8: 2
came over and d. with Omer.		9: 9
Aaron d. in captivity all his		10:31
Amnigaddah also d. in captivity		10:31
Coriantum d. in captivity		10:31
Moron d. in captivity all the		11:18
Coriantor d. in captivity all		11:19
d. in captivity all his days.		11:23
he d. in the cavity of a rock		13:14
Ether d. in the cavity of a rock,		13:18
Coriantumr d. with his army		14: 7
and d. among the sons of men.	DC	93: 4
which came and d. in the flesh,		93:11
in the flesh, and d. among us.		93:11
was with him, for he d. in him.		93:17
or the land where Adam d.,		117: 8
brethren d. in the land of Nod,	Mses	5:41
and d. in a land of promise,		6:17
great people which d. in tents,		7: 5
of Canaan, which d. in tents.		7: 6
Lord came and d. with his people,		7:16
and they d. in righteousness.		7:16
mind, and d. in righteousness;		7:18
and he d. in the midst of Zion;		7:69
tarried in Haran and d. there,	Abr	2: 5
d. in tents as we came on		2:15

DWINDLE

should d. and perish in unbelief.	1Ne	4:13
Behold these shall d. in unbelief.		12:22
be destroyed, and d. in unbelief,		13:35
that they shall d. in unbelief,	2Ne	1:10
unto them, shall d. in unbelief.	Al	45:10
because they shall d. in unbelief		45:12
the sword, or to d. in unbelief,		50:22
the church had begun to d.;	He	4:23
did begin to d. in unbelief		6:34
if they should d. in unbelief		15:11
seed which shall d. in unbelief	3Ne	21: 5
thus they did d. in unbelief	4Ne	1:34
and they did not d. in unbelief,		1:38
from the beginning, did d.		1:38
that they d. in unbelief	Mrm	9:20

DWINDLED

after they had d. in unbelief	1Ne	12:23
seed shall have d. in unbelief,		15:13
shall have d. in unbelief,	2Ne	26:15
those who have d. in unbelief		26:15
those who have d. in unbelief		26:17
those who have d. in unbelief		26:19
would have d. in unbelief,	Mos	1: 5
them who have d. in unbelief	He	15:15
again have d. in unbelief.		15:15
who have d. in unbelief.	Mrm	9:35
they have all d. in unbelief;	Eth	4: 3
who d. in unbelief because	DC	3:18

DWINDLING

the d. of the Jews in unbelief.	1Ne	10:11

DYE

in falsehood of the blackest d.,	DC	127: 1

DYED

and they were d. in blood,	3Ne	4: 7
because of their being d. in blood.		4: 7
in heaven with d. garments;	DC	133:46

DYING

the words of thy d. father	2Ne	3:25

EACH

e. one had six wings;	2Ne	16: 2
rejoiced in e. other's safety;	Al	53: 2
they were beloved by e. other,		53: 2
fallen with their ten thousand e.	Mrm	6:14
sword with their ten thousand e.;		6:15
prepared, one in e. end thereof;	Eth	6: 2
And visit the house of e. member,	DC	20:47
And visit the house of e. member,		20:51
neither hardness with e. other,		20:54
E. priest, teacher, or deacon,		20:64
instruct and edify e. other,		43: 8
And they give light to e. other in		88:44
every member in e. quorum		107:27
appointed in e. ward of the city,		128: 3
become a Urim and Thummim to e.		130:10
a white stone is given to e. of		130:11
as will secure to e. individual		134: 2
e. company provide themselves		136: 5
e. company, with their captains		136: 7
Let e. company bear an equal		136: 8
Let e. company prepare houses,		136: 9
and e. land was called earth,	Mses	1:29
and we will kiss e. other;		7:63
I went at the end of e. year,	JS	2:54
at e. time I found the same		2:54
from him at e. of our interviews,		2:54

EAGLES

there will the e. be gathered	JS	1:27

EAGLES'

bear him up as on e. wings;	DC	124:18
of his thoughts as upon e. wings.		124:99

EAMES, Ruggles

And also my servant E.	DC	75:35

EAR

thine e. was not opened; for I	1Ne	20: 8
ye should give e. unto my words.	2Ne	4: 3
He waketh mine e. to hear		7: 4
Lord God hath opened mine e.,		7: 5
and give e. unto me, O my nation;		8: 4
brethren, give e. to my words.		9:40
and the tablets, and the e.-rings;		13:20
give e. all ye of far countries;		18: 9
and give e. unto my words;		25: 4
and lend an e. unto my counsel,		28:30
My son, give e. to my words;	Al	36: 1
My son, give e. to my words,		38: 1
and to give e. unto his counsels,	He	12: 5
seen, neither hath the e. heard,	3Ne	17:16
neither e. that shall not hear,	DC	1: 2
and give e. to the words which I		43: 1
give e. to him who laid the		45: 1
give e. to the voice of the living		50: 1
and give e. to my word,		58: 1
hearts and give e. from afar;		63: 1
heavens, and give e., O earth,		76: 1
eye has not seen, nor e. heard,		76:10
for every e. shall hear it, and		88:104
e. be penetrated with their cries.		121: 2
let thine e. be inclined;		121: 4
men heard nor perceived by the e.;		133:45

EARLY

that rise up e. in the morning,	2Ne	15:11
they who have sought me e.	DC	54:10
He that seeketh me e. shall		88:83
retire to thy bed e., that ye		88:124
arise e. that your bodies and		88:124
e. in the spring of eighteen	JS	2:14
a very e. period of my life,		2:20

EARNEST 274 EARTH

EARNEST
more e. heed unto your sayings,	DC 93:48

EARNESTLY
are e. seeking the kingdom—	DC 46: 5
e. seeking after the kingdom,	46: 6
seek ye e. the best gifts,	46: 8
also seek not e. the riches	68:31
pray e. that peradventure	103:35
contend e. for the redemption	117:13
was praying e. on the subject,	130:13
praying very e. to know the	130:14
seeking e. to imitate that	Abr 1:26
Thy servant has sought thee e.;	2:12

EARNESTNESS
began to look with great e. for	3Ne 8: 3
be attended to with great e.	DC 123:14

EAR-RINGS: see EAR and RINGS.

EARS
shall again in thine e. say;	1Ne 21:20
In mine e., said the Lord of Hosts,	2Ne 15: 9
and make their e. heavy,	16:10
and hear with their e.,	16:10
after the hearing of his e.	21: 3
thus he whispereth in their e.,	28:22
and the deafness of their e.,	Jar 1: 3
open your e. that ye may hear,	Mos 2: 9
and did open their e. to hear it;	3Ne 11: 5
unstopped the e. of the deaf,	26:15
open ye your e. and hearken	DC 33: 1
speak in your e. with a voice	38:30
to the e. of all that live,	43:21
the e. of all tingle that hear	43:22
who shall speak in your e.	78: 2
and unstop the e. of the deaf;	84:69
the e. of the Lord of Sabaoth,	87: 7
the e. of the Lord of Sabaoth,	88: 2
trump in the e. of all living,	88:108
have come up into my e.	90: 1
the e. of the Lord of Sabaoth,	95: 7
let it be read this once to her e.,	97:27
the e. of the Lord of Sabaoth,	98: 2
that their e. may be opened	101:92
shall be proclaimed in their e.;	109:29
to ascend up in thine e.,	109:49
let him hear with his e.,	127: 6
and also to hear with his e.,	128: 2
heard with his e., giving the date,	128: 3
with his eyes and heard with his e.,	128: 4
proclaiming in our e., glory,	128:23
into the e. of the Lord against	136: 8
his e. opened that he may hear;	136:32
and their e. are dull of hearing,	Mses 6:27

EARTH
forth upon the face of the e.;	1Ne 1:11
over all the inhabitants of the e.;	1:14
he is mightier than all the e.,	4: 1
had fallen to the e. before me,	4: 7
in the air, high above the e.	8:26
upon all the face of the e.	10:12
upon all the face of the e.	10:13
for he is God over all the e.,	11: 6
I saw the multitudes of the e.,	11:34
multitude of the e. was gathered	11:35
I saw the e. and the rocks,	12: 4
and I saw the plains of the e.,	12: 4
many that did tumble to the e.,	12: 4
passed from off the face of the e.;	12: 5
I saw the multitudes of the e.	12:13
upon the face of the e.,	13:39
one Shepherd over all the e.	13:41
she is the whore of all the e.	14:10
and beheld the whore of all the e.,	14:11
she had dominion over all the e.,	14:11
also upon all the face of the e.;	14:12
dominions upon the face of the e.	14:12
upon the face of all the e.,	14:13
upon all the face of the e.;	14:14
the nations and kindreds of the e.	14:15
abominable church of all the e.,	1Ne 14:17
the kindreds of the e. be blessed.	15:18
the Lord hath created the e. that	17:36
and this e. is his footstool.	17:39
which did cause the e. to shake	17:45
he can cuse the e. that it shall	17:46
say unto this water, be thou e.,	17:50
be thou earth, it should be e.;	17:50
we did begin to till the e.,	18:24
did put all our seeds into the e.,	18:24
and by the opening of the e.,	19:11
the rocks of the e. must rend;	19:12
because of the groanings of the e.,	19:12
from the four quarters of the e.	19:16
all the e. shall see the salvation	19:17
also laid the foundation of the e.,	20:13
utter to the end of the e.;	20:20
unto the ends of the e.	21: 6
to establish the e., to cause	21: 8
Sing, O heavens; and be joyful, O e.;	21:13
with their face towards the e.,	21:23
upon all the face of the e.,	22: 3
the kindreds of the e. be blessed.	22: 9
the kindreds of the e. cannot be	22:10
which is the whore of all the e.,	22:13
be upon the face of this e.;	22:18
from the four quarters of the e.;	22:25
of the creation of the e.,	2Ne 1:10
I go the way of all the e.	1:14
unto the inhabitants of the e.,	2: 8
we are not, neither the e.,	2:13
both the heavens and the e.,	2:14
the garden of Eden, to till the e.	2:19
even the family of all the e.	2:20
with their faces towards the e.,	6: 7
and look upon the e. beneath;	8: 6
the e. shall wax old like a garment;	8: 6
laid the goundations of the e.,	8:13
lay the foundations of the e.,	8:16
and to crumb.e to its mother e.,	9: 7
there is none other nation on e.	10: 3
restored in the flesh, upon the e.,	10: 7
from the four parts of the e.,	10: 8
are the whore of all the e.;	10:16
and into the caves of the e.,	12:19
ariseth to shake terribly the e.	12:19
ariseth to shake terribly the e.	12:21
the fruit of the e. excellent	14: 2
alone in the midst of the e.!	15: 8
unto them from the end of the e.;	15:26
the whole e. is full of his glory.	16: 3
they shall look unto the e.	18:22
have I gathered all the e.;	20:14
with equity for the meek of the e.;	21: 4
shall smite the e. with the rod	21: 4
for the e. shall be full of the	21: 9
from the four corners of the e.	21:12
this is known in all the e.	22: 5
the e. shall remove out of her place,	23:13
from far unto the ends of the e.;	24: 2
The whole e. is at rest,	24: 7
all the chief ones of the e.;	24: 9
that made the e. to tremble,	24:16
is purposed upon the whole e.;	24:26
the Father of heaven and of e.,	25:12
as long as the e. should stand.	25:21
as long as the e. shall stand;	25:22
depths of the e. shall swallow them	26: 5
unto me all ye ends of the e.,	26:25
upon all the lands of the e.,	27: 1
even unto the end of the e.	27:11
visit the inhabitants of the e.;	28:16
if the inhabitants of the e. shall	28:17
the whore of all the e.,	28:18
must tumble to the e.,	28:18
hiss forth unto the ends of the e.,	29: 2
and in the e. beneath;	29: 7
upon all the nations of the e.?	29: 7
speak unto all nations of the e.	29:12
of his people upon the e.	30: 8
with equity for the meek of the e.	30: 9
shall smite the e. with the rod	30: 9
for the e. shall be full of the	30:15

EARTH

which is sealed upon the e.		2Ne 30:17
Jew, and all ye ends of the e.,		33:10
Israel, and all ye ends of the e.,		33:13
For what I seal on e., shall be		33:15
Creator of heaven and e.	Jac	2: 5
man came upon the e.,		4: 9
which e. was created by the power		4: 9
why not able to command the e.,		4: 9
power, both in heaven and in e.;		7:14
insomuch that he fell to the e.		7:15
overcome that they fell to the e.		7:21
very soon go the way of all the e.;	Mos	1: 9
as much as the dust of the e.;		2:25
were created of the dust of the e.;		2:25
mortal frame to its mother e.		2:26
the Father of heaven and e.,		3: 8
behold they had fallen to the e.,		4: 1
even less than the dust of the e.		4: 2
who created heaven and e.,		4: 2
both in heaven and in e.		4: 9
both in heaven and in e.;		4: 9
all things, in heaven and in e.,		5:15
people that they should till the e.		6: 7
he also, himself, did till the e.,		6: 7
go forth upon the face of the e.—		7:27
them from off the face of the e.;		12: 8
and all the ends of the e. shall see		12:24
things which are in the e. beneath.		12:36
or which are in the e. beneath,		13:12
are in the water under the e.		13:12
the Lord made heaven and e.,		13:19
power upon the face of the e.?		13:34
Father of heaven and of e.		15: 4
and all the ends of the e. shall see		15:31
abroad upon the face of the e.,		27: 6
which caused the e. to shake		27:11
that they fell to the e.,		27:12
doth not my voice shake the e.?		27:15
were with him fell again to the e.,		27:18
as thunder, which shook the e.;		27:18
of God that could shake the e.		27:18
abroad upon the face of all the e.,		28:17
having gone the way of all the e.,	Al	1: 1
between the heavens and the e.,		1:15
have been heaped up on the e.		2:38
upon the face of the e.?		5:16
works upon the face of the e.—		5:17
Repent, all ye ends of the e.,		5:50
the glory of the King of all the e.;		5:50
cometh upon the face of the e.		7: 9
that the e. should pass away?		9: 2
that the e. should pass away.		9: 3
cut off from the face of the e.		9:11
you from off the face of the e.;		9:12
from off the face of the e.?		9:24
Father of heaven and of e.,		11:39
abroad upon the face of the e.;		13:22
their fear that they fell to the e.,		14:27
and the e. shook mightily,		14:27
twain, so that they fell to the e.;		14:27
the prison had fallen to the e.,		14:28
walls thereof had fallen to the e.,		14:29
heaped up upon the face of the e.,		16:11
are in heaven and in the e.		18:28
all things which are in the e.;		18:29
Lamoni said: Is it above the e.?		18:31
unto the e., as if he were dead.		18:42
all three had sunk to the e.		19:14
until they had all fallen to the e.,		19:16
of Lamoni had fallen to the e.,		19:17
Ammon lay prostrate upon the e.,		19:17
their servants prostrate upon the e.,		19:18
he might smite him to the e.		20:16
I will smite thee to the e.		20:24
things both in heaven and in e.		22:10
prostrate himself upon the e.,		22:17
and raised the king from the e.,		22:22
will bury them deep in the e.,		24:16
did bury them up deep in the e.		24:17
themselves before them to the e.,		24:21
weapons of war deep in the e.,		26:32
of mercy are over all the e.		26:37

275

and he fell again to the e.	Al	27:17
thousands are laid low in the e.,		28:11
in heaps upon the face of the e.;		28:11
with a voice to shake the e.,		29: 1
upon all the face of the e.		29: 2
speak unto all the ends of the e.?		29: 7
even the e., and all things that		30:44
and the whole e. did tremble		36: 7
and we all fell to the e., for the		36: 7
I fell to the e.; and it was		36:10
I fell to the e. and I did		36:11
no power of e. or hell can take		37:16
from off the face of the e.		37:22
them from off the face of the e.;		37:25
and it shook the whole e.		38: 7
cut off from the face of the e.—		42: 6
soldiers smote it even to the e.,		44:12
off his scalp and it fell to the e.		44:12
as this scalp has fallen to the e.,		44:14
so shall ye fall to the e. except		44:14
and he also blessed the e. for		45:15
and he bowed himself to the e.,		46:13
to the heart; and he fell to the e.		47:24
throwing up banks of e. round		48: 8
Nephites had dug up a ridge of e.		49: 4
to dig down their banks of e.		49:22
by pulling down the banks of e.,		49:22
in digging up heaps of e.		50: 1
upon the top of these ridges of e.		50: 2
and level them with the e.,		51:17
hewn down and leveled to the e.		51:18
than be smitten down to the e.		51:20
a strong wall of timbers and e.,		53: 4
from off the face of the e.		54:12
one soul of them fallen to the e.;		56:56
had gone the way of all the e.		62:37
and gone the way of all the e.;	He	1: 2
and cut them down to the e.		1:24
to cover the face of the whole e.,		3: 8
scattered upon the face of the e.,		3:16
the e. shook exceedingly,		5:27
were about to tumble to the e.;		5:27
behold the e. shook exceedingly,		5:31
were about to tumble to the e.;		5:31
the e. shook again and the walls		5:32
the e. shook as if it were about to		5:33
of him who had shaken the e.;		5:42
destroy them off the face of the e.		6:20
from off the face of the e.		7:28
all things which are in the e.,		8:24
chief judge had fallen to the e.,		9: 3
that they fell to the e.;		9: 4
quake, and had fallen to the e.		9: 5
five men who had fallen to the e.		9: 7
insomuch that we fell to the e.;		9:14
shall smite the e. with famine,		10: 6
whatsoever ye shall seal on e.		10: 7
whatsoever ye shall loose on e.		10: 7
e. was smitten that it was dry,		11: 6
and the whole e. was smitten,		11: 6
their secret plans in the e.		11:10
rain upon the face of the e.,		11:13
that rain should fall upon the e.,		11:17
are less than the dust of the e.		12: 7
the dust of the e. moveth hither		12: 8
voice doth the shole e. shake;		12:11
and if he say unto the e.—Move—		12:13
if he say unto the e.—Thou		12:14
to his word the e. goeth back,		12:15
surely it is the e. that moveth		12:15
man hide up a treasure in the e.,		12:18
shall hide up treasures in the e.		13:18
that ye shall fall to the e.		14: 7
the Father of heaven and of e.,		14:12
the e. shall shake and tremble;		14:21
are upon the face of this e.,		14:21
both above the e. and beneath,		14:21
upon the face of the whole e.,		14:22
both above the e. and beneath.		14:22
cover the face of the whole e.		14:27
and fro upon the face of the e.,		15:12
the Father of heaven and of e.,		16:18

EARTH

bowed himself down upon the e.,	3Ne	1:11
fell to the e. and became as if		1:16
upon the face of the whole e.		1:17
that they fell to the e.		1:17
had all fallen to the e., and did		4: 8
they did fell the tree to the e.,		4:28
may cause to be felled to the e.		4:29
man hath been felled to the e.		4:29
from the four quarters of the e.		5:24
abroad upon all the face of the e.		5:24
from the four quarters of the e.		5:26
that it did shake the whole e.		8: 6
the e. was carried up upon the		8:10
great quaking of the whole e.;		8:12
thereof had fallen to the e.,		8:14
the whole e. became deformed,		8:17
and the quaking of the e.		8:17
upon the face of the whole e.,		8:18
quakings of the e. did cease—		8:19
all the inhabitants of the e.,		9: 1
the inhabitants of the whole e.		9: 2
Moronihah have I covered with e.,		9: 5
buried up in the depths of the e.;		9: 6
buried up in the depths of the e.,		9: 8
all the wickedness of the whole e.,		9: 9
created the heavens and the e.,		9:15
come unto me ye ends of the e.,		9:22
the e. did cease to tremble,		10: 9
the e. did cleave together		10:10
not sunk and buried up in the e.;		10:13
and by the opening of the e.		10:14
the whole multitude fell to the e.;		11:10
and the God of the whole e.,		11:14
spoken, unto the ends of the e.		11:41
for they shall inherit the e.		12: 5
unto you to be the salt of the e.;		12:13
wherewith shall the e. be salted?		12:13
Nor by the e., for it is his		12:35
Thy will be done on e. as it is in		13:10
for yourselves treasures upon e.,		13:19
forth upon the face of the e.		16: 4
from the four quarters of the e.;		16: 5
all the people of the whole e.,		16:10
all the ends of the e. shall see		16:20
himself also knelt upon the e.;		17:15
And they arose from the e.,		17:20
sit themselves down upon the e.		18: 2
down upon the face of the e.,		19: 6
kneel down again upon the e.,		19:16
should kneel down upon the e.		19:16
had all knelt down upon the e.,		19:17
them and bowed himself to the e.,		19:19
nothing upon e. so white as the		19:25
off and bowed himself to the e.,		19:27
abroad upon the face of the e.,		20:13
unto the Lord of the whole e.		20:19
the kindreds of the e. be blessed.		20:25
kindreds of the e. be blessed—		20:27
all the ends of the e. shall see		20:35
the God of the whole e. shall he		22: 5
should no more go over the e.,		22: 9
and smite the e. with a curse.		25: 6
come upon the face of the e.,		26: 3
e. should be wrapt together as		26: 3
and the e. should pass away;		26: 3
Repent, all ye ends of the e.,		27:20
minister upon the face of the e.;		28:16
they were cast down into the e.;		28:20
did smite the e. with the word		28:20
out of the depths of the e.;		28:20
powers of the e. could not hold		28:39
hide up their treasures in the e.;	Mrm	1:18
cut off from the face of the e.		3:15
write unto all the ends of the e.,		3:18
persuade all ye ends of the e.		3:22
the e. shall be rolled together		5:23
blood lay upon the face of the e.,		6:15
and to return to their mother e.		6:15
and hide up the records in the e.;		8: 4
it shall be brought out of the e.,		8:16
could they cause the e. to shake;		8:24
prisons to tumble to the e.;		8:24
out of the e. shall they come,		8:26
upon the face of the e.;	Mrm	8:31
the e. shall be rolled together		9: 2
who created the heavens and the e.,		9:11
the heaven and the e. should be;		9:17
was created of the dust of the e.;		9:17
all, even unto the ends of the e.		9:21
even unto the ends of the e.		9:25
upon all the face of the e.;	Eth	1:33
is choice above all the e.?		1:38
the seed of the e. of every kind;		1:41
above all the lands of the e.		1:42
seed, upon all the face of the e.		1:43
of Jared had fallen to the e.;		3: 7
all the inhabitants of the e.		3:25
even unto the ends of the e.		3:25
hide them up again in the e.		4: 3
of the heavens and of the e.,		4: 7
at my word the e. shall shake;		4: 9
repent all ye ends of the e.,		4:18
and began to till the e.		6:13
to multiply and to till the e.;		6:18
the heavens, and also by the e.,		8:14
no rain upon the face of the e.		9:30
rain upon the face of the e.;		9:35
like unto the rest of the e.;		10:17
they did dig it out of the e.;		10:23
did cast up mighty heaps of e.		10:23
all manner of tools to till the e.,		10:25
been upon the face of the e.,		11: 6
as heaps of e. upon the face of		11: 6
known upon the face of the e.;		11: 7
from off the face of the e.		11:12
the prison to tumble to the e.		12:13
when the e. shall pass away.		13: 8
a new heaven and a new e.;		13: 9
the four quarters of the e.,		13:11
upon the face of the whole e.		13:17
he sweepeth the e. before him!		14:18
Coriantumr fell to the e.,		15:32
Repent all ye ends of the e.,	Mro	7:34
shall last, or the e. shall stand,		7:36
unto all the ends of the e.—		10:24
O inhabitants of the e.	DC	1: 6
unto the inhabitants of the e.,		1: 8
seal both on e. and in heaven,		1: 8
is unto the ends of the e.,		1:11
upon the inhabitants of the e.,		1:13
upon the inhabitants of the e.,		1:17
also might increase in the e.;		1:21
upon the face of the whole e.,		1:30
O inhabitants of the e.:		1:34
peace shall be taken from the e.,		1:35
the heavens and the e. pass away,		1:38
whole e. would be utterly wasted		2: 3
unto the inhabitants of the e.,		5: 5
among the inhabitants of the e.,		5:19
until the e. is empty,		5:19
from off the face of the e.;		5:33
let e. and hell combine against		6:34
salvation who dwell on the e.		7: 6
and down, to and fro in the e.,		10:27
never be taken again from the e.,		13: 1
created the heavens and the e.,		14: 9
for mine arm is over all the e.		15: 2
for mine arm is over all the e.		16: 2
should obtain treasures of e.		19:38
the framer of heaven and e.,		20:17
which shall be built up on the e.		27: 4
of the vine with you on the e.,		27: 5
whole e. may not be smitten		27: 9
in heaven, and which are on e.;		27:13
at hand when the e. is ripe;		29: 9
shall not be upon the e.		29: 9
righteousness with men on e.		29:11
and all the e. shall quake		29:13
above and in the e. beneath;		29:14
to destroy the crops of the e.		29:16
flies upon the face of the e.,		29:18
which is the whore of all the e.,		29:21
then will I spare the e. but for		29:22
and the e. shall be consumed		29:23
a new heaven and a new e.		29:23
even the heaven and the e.,		29:24

EARTH

before the e. shall pass away,	DC 29:26
has been on the things of the e.	30: 2
from the four quarters of the e.,	33: 6
shall come at the end of the e.;	38: 5
of darkness prevail upon the e.,	38:11
command to reap down the e.,	38:12
And I have made the e. rich,	38:17
forever, while the e. shall stand,	38:20
that which shall shake the e.;	38:30
the riches of the e. are mine	38:39
which is coming on the e.,	42:64
and the e. shall tremble,	43:18
voices from the ends of the e.,	43:21
Hearken, O ye hations of the e.,	43:23
O, ye nations of the e.,	43:24
upon the inhabitants of the e.	43:28
come upon the e. in judgment,	43:29
and shall reign with me on e.	43:29
then cometh the end of the e.	43:31
e. shall pass away so as by fire.	43:32
their end no man knoweth on e.,	43:33
laid the foundation of the e.,	45: 1
Who were separated from the e.,	45:12
strangers and pilgrims on the e.;	45:13
and the e. shall pass away;	45:22
whole e. shall be in commotion,	45:26
coming until the end of the e.	45:26
above, and in the e. beneath.	45:40
from the four quarters of the e.	45:46
and the e. shall tremble,	45:48
the ends of the e. shall hear it;	45:49
nations of the e. shall mourn,	45:49
the e. shall be given unto them	45:58
till he descends on the e.	49: 6
the nations of the e. shall bow	49:10
Lord Jesus, who was on the e.,	49:12
the e. might answer the end	49:16
that which cometh of the e.,	49:19
of a man traveling on the e.	49:22
the e. to tremble and to reel	49:23
have gone abroad in the e.	50: 1
which have gone forth in the e.	50: 2
both in heaven and on the e.,	50:27
even the Lord of the whole e.,	55: 1
heaven and the e. pass away,	56:11
fatness of the e. shall be theirs.	56:18
generations shall inherit the e.	56:20
that the e. may know that the	58: 8
together from the ends of the e.	58:45
inhabitants of the e. will repent.	58:48
uttermost parts of the e.—	58:64
that live shall inherit the e.,	59: 2
reward the good things of the e.,	59: 3
the fulness of the e. is yours,	59:16
trees and walketh upon the e.;	59:16
things which come of the e.,	59:17
all things which come of the e.,	59:18
among the armies of the e.;	60: 4
unto the inhabitants of the e.,	62: 5
an inheritance upon the e.	63:20
the e. shall be transfigured,	63:21
from the inhabitants of the e.	63:32
wars upon the face of the e.,	63:33
things upon the face of the e.,	63:36
unto the inhabitants of the e.;	63:37
nations of the e. shall tremble	64:43
is unto the ends of the e.,	65: 1
committed unto man on the e.,	65: 2
forth unto the ends of the e.,	65: 2
until it has filled the whole e.	65: 2
may go forth upon the e.,	65: 5
which is set up on the e.	65: 5
glorified in heaven so on e.,	65: 6
and the e. are in mine hands,	67: 2
who are abroad in the e.	69: 5
upon the inhabitants of the e.,	71: 4
forth unto the ends of the e.;	72:21
ye heavens, and give ear, O e.,	76: 1
reign on the e. over his people.	76:63
are honorable men of the e.,	76:75
suffer the wrath of God on e.	76:104
It is the e., in its sanctified,	77: 1
his economy concerning this e.	77: 6
over the four parts of the e.,	DC 77: 8
Hurt not the e., neither the sea,	77: 9
over the nations of the e.,	77:11
man out of the dust of the e.,	77:12
the Lord God sanctify the e.,	77:12
things of this e. shall be added	78:19
against the inhabitants of the e.;	82: 6
shall not be taken from the e.	84:97
The e. hath travailed and	84:101
I will not only shake the e.,	84:118
the inhabitants of the e. shall	87: 6
the inhabitants of the e. be	87: 6
Lord of Sabaoth, from the e.,	87: 7
And the e. also, and the	88:10
the e. upon which you stand.	88:10
the meek of the e. shall inherit	88:17
the e. abideth the law of	88:25
of the heavens and the e.,	88:43
which comprehend the e.; and	88:43
The e. rolls upon her wings,	88:45
both in heaven and in the e.,	88:79
in the earth, and under the e.;	88:79
the e. shall tremble and reel	88:87
O inhabitants of the e.;	88:92
she is the tares of the e.;	88:94
the saints that are upon the e.,	88:96
and they who are on the e.	88:98
again, until the end of the e.	88:101
people, both in heaven and in e.,	88:104
and that are under the e.—	88:104
that run or creep on the e.;	89:14
forth unto the ends of the e.,	90: 9
both in heaven and on e.,	93:17
kingdom of God on the e.,	97:14
nations of the e. shall honor	97:19
smite the whole e. with a curse,	98:17
things of my kingdom on the e.	100:11
tabernacle, which hideth the e.,	101:23
upon all the face of the e.,	101:24
may dwell upon all the e.	101:25
sleep, that is to say in the e.,	101:31
things of the e., by which it	101:33
things that are in the e.,	101:34
in the earth, and upon the e.,	101:34
accounted as the salt of the e.	101:39
if that salt of the e. lose its	101:40
the e. is given unto the saints,	103: 7
the heavens, and built the e.,	104:14
For the e. is full, and there is	104:17
church and kingdom on the e.,	104:59
peace unto the ends of the e.;	105:39
preserved unto the end of the e.;	107:42
in truth, unto the ends of the e.,	109:23
upon the inhabitants of the e.,	109:38
upon all the nations of the e.;	109:54
and the great ones of the e.,	109:55
and afflicted ones of the e.;	109:55
all the ends of the e. may know	109:57
driven to the ends of the e.,	109:67
all the poor and meek of the e.;	109:72
great mountain and fill the whole e.;	109:72
that thy glory may fill the e.;	109:74
from the four parts of the e.,	110:11
lest the whole e. be smitten	110:15
my word unto the ends of the e.	112: 4
let not the inhabitants of the e.	112: 5
darkness covereth the e., and	112:23
upon the inhabitants of the e.,	112:24
come upon all the face of the e.,	112:24
upon the whole e.	115: 6
send again the snows upon the e.	117: 6
Have I not made the e.?	117: 6
armies of the nations of the e.?	117: 6
Almighty, maker of heaven, e.,	121: 4
The ends of the e. shall inquire	122: 1
whole e. groans under the weight	123: 7
yet on the e. among all sects,	123:12
through the weak things of the e.	124: 1
nations of the e. scattered abroad.	124: 3
Awake, O kings of the e.!	124:11
to the kings and people of the e.,	124:16
all the precious trees of the e.;	124:26
all your precious things of the e.;	124:27

EARTH

not a place found on e. that	DC 124:28
font there is not upon the e.,	124:29
concerning the kindreds of the e.,	124:58
seed shall the kindred of the e.	124:58
unto the inhabitants of the e.	124:89
whatsoever he shall bind on e.	124:93
whatsoever he shall loose on e.	124:93
warn the inhabitants of the e.	124:106
unto the kings of the e.,	124:107
upon the e.,	124:128
whatsoever you bind on e.,	127: 7
whatsoever you loose on e.,	127: 7
to restore many things to the e.,	127: 8
records which are kept on the e.	128: 7
whatsoever you bind on e.	128: 8
whatsoever you loose on e.	128: 8
whatsoever you record on e.	128: 8
you do not record on e. shall not	128: 8
which records or binds on e.	128: 9
a law on e. and in heaven,	128: 9
whatsoever thou shalt bind on e.	128:10
whatsoever thou shalt loose on e.	128:10
The first man is of the e., earthy;	128:14
records on the e. in relation to	128:14
lest I come and smite the e. with	128:17
e. will be smitten with a curse	128:18
and a voice of truth out of the e.;	128:19
the e. break forth into singing.	128:22
angels who minister to this e.	130: 5
not reside on a planet like this e.	130: 6
e., in its sanctified and immortal	130: 9
and this e. will be Christ's.	130: 9
have appointed on the e. to hold	132: 7
but one on the e. at a time	132: 7
whatsoever you seal on e. shall	132:46
whatsoever you bind on e.	132:46
whosoever sins you remit on e.	132:46
whosoever sins you retain on e.	132:46
that whatsoever you give on e.,	132:48
give any one on e., by my word	132:48
be without condemnation on e. and	132:48
to multiply and replenish the e.,	132:63
all the ends of the e. shall see	133: 3
hear, O ye inhabitants of the e.	133:16
the e. shall be like as it was	133:24
O inhabitants of the e.,	133:36
unto many that dwell on the e.	133:36
him that made heaven, and e.,	133:39
things which are coming on the e.,	133:58
And by the weak things of the e.	133:59
gospel to the nations of the e.,	134:12
to the four quarters of the e.;	135: 3
be rejected by any court on e.,	135: 7
he avenges that blood on the e.	135: 7
e. at the present time who holds	OD
remain in the flesh on the e.	Mses 1: 5
unto himself, he fell unto the e.	1: 9
loud voice, and rent upon the e.,	1:19
to tremble, and the e. shook;	1:21
his eyes and beheld the e.,	1:27
and each land was called e.,	1:29
But only an account of this e.,	1:35
and tell me concerning this e.,	1:36
And as one e. shall pass away,	1:38
speak unto thee concerning this e.	1:40
this heaven, and this e.;	2: 1
I created the heaven, and the e.	2: 1
And the e. was without form,	2: 2
I, God, called the dry land E.;	2:10
Let the e. bring forth grass,	2:11
seed should be in itself upon the e.,	2:11
And the e. brought forth grass,	2:12
heaven to give light upon the e.;	2:15
geaven to give light upon the e.,	2:17
which may fly above the e.	2:20
and let fowl multiply in the e.;	2:22
Let the e. bring forth the living	2:24
beasts of the e. after their kind,	2:24
beasts of the e. after their kind,	2:25
upon the e. after his kind	2:25
the cattle, and over all the e.,	2:26
thing that creepeth upon the e.	2:26
multiply, and replenish the e.,	2:28

thing that moveth upon the e.	Mses 2:28
is upon the face of all the e.,	2:29
And to every beast of the e.,	2:30
that creepeth upon the e.,	2:30
heaven and the e. were finished,	3: 1
of the heaven and of the e.,	3: 4
God, made the heaven and the e.;	3: 4
the field before it was in the e.,	3: 5
upon the face of the e.	3: 5
to rain upon the face of the e.	3: 5
was not yet flesh upon the e.,	3: 5
went up a mist from the e.,	3: 6
the first flesh upon the e.,	3: 7
that Adam began to till the e.,	5: 1
and to replenish the e.	5: 2
all the families of the e.,	5:10
shalt be cursed from the e.	5:36
vagabond shalt thou be in the e.	5:37
and a vagabond in the e.;	5:39
cursed the e. with a sore curse,	5:56
he bowed himself to the e.,	6:31
the e. is his footstool;	6:44
and things which are on the e.,	6:63
things which are in the e.,	6:63
and things which are under the e.,	6:63
Lord, and the e. trembled,	7:13
all the inhabitants of the e.;	7:21
nations of the e. were before him;	7:23
was upon all the face of the e.	7:24
unto the inhabitants of the e.	7:25
veiled the whole face of the e.	7:26
number the particles of the e.,	7:30
beheld all the families of the e.;	7:45
that Enoch looked upon the e.;	7:48
when Enoch heard the e. mourn,	7:49
have compassion upon the e.?	7:49
e. might never more be covered	7:50
nations, while the e. should stand;	7:52
in the flesh, shall the e. rest?	7:54
mourned; and e. groaned;	7:56
saying: When shall the e. rest?	7:58
thou not come agin upon the e.?	7:59
wilt not come again on the e.	7:59
shall come that the e. shall rest	7:61
darkness shall cover the e.;	7:61
shall shake, and also the e.;	7:61
will I send forth out of the e.,	7:62
will I cause to sweep the e. as	7:62
the four quarters of the e.,	7:62
thousand years the e. shall rest.	7:64
dwell on the e. in righteousness	7:65
all the kingdoms of the e.	8: 3
the Lord cursed the e. with a	8: 4
multiply on the face of the e.,	8:14
there were giants on the e.,	8:18
men had become great in the e.;	8:22
Lord had made man on the e.,	8:25
created, from the face of the e.,	8:26
The e. was corrupt before God,	8:28
And God looked upon the e.,	8:29
corrupted its way upon the e.	8:29
for the e. is filled with violence,	8:30
all flesh from off the e.	8:30
before the foundations of the e.	Abr 1: 3
be known in the e. forever,	1:19
with the blessings of the e.,	1:26
the e. is my footstool;	2: 7
families of the e. be blessed,	2:11
e. upon which thou standest,	3: 5
e. upon which thou standest,	3: 6
e. upon which thou standest.	3: 7
and the moon be above the e.,	3:17
and in the e. beneath,	3:21
and we will make an e.	3:24
formed the heavens and the e.	4: 1
And the e., after it was formed,	4: 2
formed anything but the e.;	4: 2
and let the e. come up dry;	4: 9
prounounced the dry land, e.;	4:10
Let us prepare the e. to bring	4:11
its own likeness upon the e.,	4:11
the Gods organized the e. to	4:12
the e. to bring forth the tree	4:12

EARTH / EAST

to give light upon the e.;	Abr	4:15
to give light upon the e.,		4:17
that they may fly above the e.		4:20
fowl to multiply in the e.		4:22
the Gods prepared the e. to		4:24
beasts of the e. after their kind;		4:24
the Gods organized the e. to		4:25
thing that creepeth upon the e.		4:25
the cattle, and over all the e.,		4:26
that creepeth upon the e.		4:26
multiply, and replenish the e.,		4:28
thing that moveth upon the e.		4:28
upon the e.,		4:29
And to every beast of the e.,		4:30
that creepeth upon the e.,		4:30
finish the heavens and the e.		5: 1
form the heavens and the e.		5: 3
of the heavens and of the e.,		5: 4
formed the e. and the heavens,		5: 4
the field before it was in the e.,		5: 5
caused it to rain upon the e.		5: 5
went up a mist from the e.,		5: 6
measurement of this e.,	Fac	2: 1
the E. and the Sun in		2: 5
e. in its four quarters.		2: 6
he should come again on the e.,	JS	1: 1
and covereth the whole e.,		1:26
from the four quarters of the e.		1:27
heaven and e. shall pass away;		1:35
the tribes of the e. mourn;		1:36
but the end of the e. is not yet,		1:55
whole e. would be utterly wasted		2:39
which were coming upon the e.,		2:45
judgments would come on the e.		2:45
all around was covered with e.		2:51
Having removed the e.,		2:52
never be taken again from the e.		2:69
reign personally upon the e.;	AoF	10
that the e. will be renewed and		10

EARTHLY

things, yea, and e. things also,	DC	78: 5
ye are not equal in e. things		78: 6
as a steward over e. blessings,		104:13
that which is e. conforming		128:13
beyond anything e. I had ever	JS	2:31
that any e. thing could be made		2:31

EARTHQUAKE

with thunder and with e.,	2Ne	27: 2
with famine, and plague, and e.,	DC	87: 6

EARTHQUAKES

and I heard thunderings, and e.,	1Ne	12: 4
by tempest, and by e.,	2Ne	6:15
thunderings, and lightnings, and e.,		26: 6
and e. in divers places.	Mrm	8:30
and by the voice of e., and	DC	43:25
be e. also in divers places,		45:33
cometh the testimony of e.,		88:89
famines, and pestilences, and e.,	JS	1:29

EARTHS

yea, millions of e. like this,	Mses	7:30

EARTHY

The first man is of the earth, e.;	DC	128:14
As is the e., such are they also		128:14
such are they also that are e.;		128:14

EASE

unto him that is at e. in Zion!	2Ne	28:24
they began to e. their burdens;	Mos	21:15
And I will also e. the burdens		24:14
bear up their burdens with e.,		24:15
I will e. your mind somewhat on	Al	39:17
he might with e. maintain that		59: 3
and this because of their e.,	He	12: 2
did e. the burden of the people,	Eth	10:10

EASED

and e. their burdens,	Mos	24:21

EASIER

e. to keep the city from falling	Al	59: 9

EASILY

sins which do so e. beset me.	2Ne	4:18
sin, which e. doth beset you,	Al	7:15
that they should e. overpower		49: 7
that they could e. destroy us		58:15
they would e. maintain that city.		59: 9
the more e. commit adultery,	He	7: 5
not her own, is not e. provoked,	Mro	7:45
more e. obtain knowledge.—	DC	69: 7

EASINESS

simpleness of the way, or the e. of	1Ne	17:41
because of the e. of the way;	Al	37:46
e. and willingness to believe	He	6:36

EAST

the feet of those who are in the e.	1Ne	21:13
they be replenished from the e.,	2Ne	12: 6
shall spoil them of the e. together;		21:14
both in the e. and in the west,		29:11
they shall reap the e. wind,	Mos	7:31
also be smitten with the e. wind;		12: 6
on the e. and on the west,		27: 6
which was e. of the river Sidon,	Al	2:15
upon the hill e. of Sidon.		2:17
upon the e. of the river Sidon,		6: 7
on the e. of the garden of Eden,		12:21
on the e. of the river Sidon,		16: 6
the e. side of the river Sidon.		16: 7
the sea, on the e. and on the west,		22:27
the sea e. even to the sea west,		22:27
from the e. towards the west—		22:27
on the e. by the seashore,		22:29
Sidon, from the e. to the west,		22:29
from the e. to the west sea;		22:32
from the e. unto the west sea,		22:33
having fled into the e. wilderness,		25: 5
they fled into the e. wilderness.		25: 8
which is on the e. by the sea,		27:22
e. of the land of Zarahemla,		31: 3
the e. end of the garden of Eden,		42: 2
and concealed them on the e.,		43:31
the Lamanites about on the e.		43:35
on the e. were the men of Lehi.		43:52
Lehi on the e. of the river Sidon,		43:53
on the e. of the river Sidon.		49:16
go forth into the e. wilderness;		50: 7
who were in the e. wilderness		50: 7
from the e. sea to the west.		50: 8
out of the e. wilderness,		50: 9
go forth into the e. wilderness,		50: 9
Lamanites in the e. wilderness,		50:11
and it was by the e. sea;		50:13
on the west and on the e.		50:34
on the e. borders by the seashore.		51:26
on the borders by the e. sea,		52:13
to pass that they were on the e.,		62:21
by the wilderness on the e.		62:34
nor on the south, nor on the e.,	He	1:31
from the west sea to the sea e.		3: 8
the west sea, even unto the e.;		4: 7
from the west sea to the sea e.		11:20
earth from the west to the e.,	3Ne	1:17
in from the e. and from the west,		20:13
forth from the e. and to the west,	DC	42:63
let him that goeth to the e.		42:64
forth from the e. unto the west,		43:22
from the e. and from the west,		44: 1
your brethren come from the e.		48: 5
whether to the e. or to the west,		75:26
the angel ascending from the e.,		77: 9
the angel ascending from the e.		77: 9
to the e. or to the west,		80: 3
who have families in the e.,		105:21
let all those who come from the e.		125: 4
goeth toward the e. of Assyria.	Mses	3:14
at the e. of the Garden of Eden,		4:31
of Nod, on the e. of Eden.		5:41
of Cainan, by the sea e.,		6:42

EAST — EDGED

mountain on the e. of Behel, Abr 2:20
on the west, and Hai on the e.; 2:20
morning cometh out of the e., JS 1:26

EASTERN
called to go into the e. countries, DC 39:14
gather ye out from the e. lands, 45:64
impart to the e. brethren; 48: 2
their journey into the e. lands; 52:35
Go unto the e. lands, bear 66: 7
him to go unto the e. countries; 75: 6
journey into the e. countries, 75:13
journey into the e. countries; 75:14
go again into the e. countries, 79: 1
to go into the e. countries 99: 1
round about in this e. land. 100: 3
the churches in the e. countries, 101:74
congregations in the e. countries, 103:29
not take his family unto the e. 124:83
not remove his family unto the e. 124:108

EASTWARD
and we did travel nearly e. 1 Ne 17: 1
destroyed, and from thence e., Eth 9: 3
Shiz did pursue Coriantumr e., 14:26
planted a garden e. in Eden, Mses 3: 8
planted a garden, e. in Eden, Abr 5: 8

EASY
e. to the understanding of all men. 1 Ne 14:23
and gentle; e. to be entreated; Al 7:23
it is as e. to give heed to the 37:44
it is not e. for him to obtain 39: 6
it is not e. for him to obtain 39: 6
Is it not as e. at this time for 39:19
become an e. prey for them. 49: 3
because it was e. to guard them 53: 5
his people e. to be entreated, He 7: 7
e. it will burn up the dry trees DC 135: 6

EAT
and the moth shall e. them up. 2Ne 7: 9
For the moth shall e. them up 8: 8
the worm shall e. them like wool. 8: 8
hath no money, come buy and e.; 9:50
shall e. the fruit of their doings. 13:10
We will e. our own bread, 14: 1
of the fat ones shall strangers e. 15:17
Butter and honey shall he e., 17:15
he shall e. butter; for butter 17:22
butter and honey shall every one e. 17:22
and he shall e. on the left hand 19:20
they shall e. every man the flesh 19:20
the lion shall e. straw like the ox. 21: 7
E., drink, and be merry, for 28: 7
E., drink, and be merry; 28: 8
the lion shall e. straw like the ox. 30:13
did e. nothing save it was raw meat; En 1:20
thereby they might e., and drink, Mos 7:16
yea, ye shall e. and drink of the Al 5:34
servant of God something to e.? 8:19
If thou e. thou shalt surely die. 12:23
themselves what they should e., 31:37
of life, and e. and live forever, 42: 3
for your life, what ye shall e., 3Ne 13:25
saying, What shall we e.? or, 13:31
commanded that they should e. 18: 3
is unworthy to e. and drink of 18:29
and gave to the disciples to e. 20: 3
gave unto them bread to e., 20: 7
they may e. in remembrance of Mro 4: 3
may e. in remembrance of DC 20:77
mattereth not what ye shall e. 27: 2
and shall e. their flesh and shall 29:18
that is idle shall not e. the bread 42:42
that man should not e. the same, 49:18
e. the good of the land of Zion 64:34
for what ye shall e., or what 84:81
they shall e. the fruit thereof. 101:101
the garden thou mayest freely e., Mses 3:16
evil, thou shalt not e. of 3:17
Ye shall not e. of every tree of 4: 7
We may e. of the fruit of the trees 4: 8

Ye shall not e. of it, neither Mses 4: 9
ye e. thereof, then your eyes shall 4:11
of the fruit thereof, and did e., 4:12
husband with her, and he did e. 4:12
thee that hou shouldst not e., 4:17
the fruit of the tree and I did e. 4:18
serpent beguiled me, and I did e. 4:19
dust shalt thou e. all the days of 4:20
Thou shalt not e. of it, 4:23
in sorrow shalt thou e. of it all 4:23
shalt e. the herb of the field. 4:24
of thy face shalt thou e. bread, 4:25
tree of life, and e. and live forever, 4:28
to e. his bread by the sweat of 5: 1
the garden thou mayest freely e., Abr 5:12
and evil, thou shalt not e. of it; 5:13
to e. and drink with the drunken, JS 1:52

EATEN
for ye have e. up the vineyard 2Ne 13:14
and it shall be e. up; 15: 5
and shall be e., as a teil-tree, 16:13
after he had e. and was filled Al 8:23
not e. up all their provisions; 3Ne 18: 4
they had e. and were filled, 18: 4
multitude had e. and were filled, 18: 5
when they had e. he commanded 20: 4
multitude had all e. and drunk, 20: 9
book which was e. by John, DC 77:14
Hast thou e. of the tree whereof Mses 4:17
voice of thy wife, and hast e. 4:23

EATEST
e. thereof thou shalt surely die. Mses 3:17
in the time that thou e. thereof, Abr 5:13

EATETH
behold he e. but he awaketh 2Ne 27: 3
e. and drinketh my flesh and 3Ne 18:29
e. and drinketh damnation 18:29
He that e. this bread eateth of 20: 8
bread e. of my body to his soul; 20: 8

EATING
and are we not e. and drinking, Mses 8:21
they were e. and drinking, JS 1:42

ECONOMY
the hidden things of his e. DC 77: 6

EDEN: see also SMITH, Eden.
driven out of the garden of E., 2Ne 2:19
have remained in the garden of E. 2:22
he will make her wilderness like E., 8: 3
on the east of the garden of E., Al 12:21
forth from the garden of E., 42: 2
the east end of the garden of E., 42: 2
cast out from the Garden of E., DC 29:41
a garden eastward in E., Mses 3: 8
caused a river to go out of E. 3:10
put him into the Garden of E., 3:15
forth from the Garden of E., 4:29
at the east of the Garden of E., 4:31
toward the Garden of E., 5: 4
land of Nod, on the east of E. 5:41
in the Garden of E. 6:53
in the Garden of E., gave I 7:32
a garden, eastward in E., Abr 5: 8
was a river running out of E., 5:10
put him in the Garden of E., 5:11
to Adam in the Garden of E., Fac 2: 3

EDGE
arms with the e. of his sword, Al 17:37
went down unto the water:s e., 3Ne 19:10
sharper than a two-e. sword, DC 6: 2
sharper than a two-e. sword, 11: 2
sharper than a two-e. sword, 12: 2
the e. all around was covered JS 2:51
fixed under the e. of the stone, 2:52

EDGED
sharper than a two-e. sword, DC 14: 2
sharper than a two e. sword, 33: 1

EDGES

EDGES
thinner towards the e.,   JS   2:51

EDIFICATION
of the Holy Spirit to your e.   DC 88:137
to the e. of the school,   97: 5

EDIFIED
both are e. and rejoice together.   DC 50:22
he may be e. in all meekness,   84:106
that all may be e. together,   84:110
that all may be e. of all,   88:122

EDIFIETH
whose language is meek and e.,   DC 52:16

EDIFY
shall instruct and e. each other,   DC 43: 8
which doth not e. is not of God,   50:23

EDIFYING
e. one another, as it is given   DC 107:85
words tend to e. one another.   136:24

EDOM
they shall lay their hand upon E.   2Ne 21:14

EDSON: see FULLER, Edson.

EDWARD: see also PARTRIDGE, Edward.
I say unto you, my servant E.,   DC 36: 1

EFFECT
and the e. thereof is poison.   Mos   7:30
have been void, taking none e.   Al   12:26
is the e. of a frenzied mind;   30:16
powerful e. upon the minds of   31: 5
mercy could not take e. except it   42:13
at them that they might take e.;   49: 4
have carried this plan into e.,   50:30
to bring a stratagem into e.   56:30
have any e. upon the Nephites,   3Ne   4:18
has become void and of none e.   DC 54: 4
to the e. that the Utah Commission,   OD

EFFECTUAL
an e. struggle to be made.   Mos   7:18
an e. door shall be opened in   DC 100: 3
an e. door shall be opened   112:19
an e. door shall be opened   118: 3

EFFICACY
are of no e., virtue, or force   DC 132: 7

EFFORT
the last e. which is enjoined   DC 123: 6

EGGS
as one gathereth e. that are left   2Ne 20:14

EGYPT
who was sold into E., and who   1Ne   5:14
and out of the land of E.,   5:15
bring them out of the land of E.   17:40
were led out of E., out of bondage,   19:10
who was carried captive into E.   2Ne   3: 4
thy people out of the land of E.   3:10
Joseph, who was carried into E.   4: 1
is in the uttermost part of E.,   17:18
thee, after the manner of E.   20:24
lift it up after the manner of E.   20:26
left, from Assyria, and from E.,   21:11
came up out of the land of E.   21:16
Israel up out of the land of E.,   25:20
of Israel out of the land of E.,   Mos   7:19
brought thee out of the land of E.,   12:34
of Joseph who was sold into E.   Al   10: 3
has brought our fathers out of E.,   36:28
father down into the land of E.   Eth 13: 7
Israel out of the land of E.;   DC 136:22
god of Pharaoh, king of E.;   Abr   1: 6
of Pharaoh, the king of E.,   1: 8

281   EIGHTEENTH

that of Pharaoh, king of E.,   Abr   1:13
god of Pharaoh, king of E.;   1:17
this king of E. was a descendant   1:21
The land of E. being first   1:23
in the Chaldean signifies E.,   1:23
the first government of E. was   1:25
concluded to go down into E.,   2:21
was come near to enter into E.,   2:22
unto thee before ye go into E.,   3:15
Abraham in E.   Fac   1:10
Signifies Abraham in E.—   3: 3
of Pharaoh, King of E.,   3: 4

EGYPTIAN
destroy the tongue of the E. sea;   2Ne 21:15
among us the reformed E.,   Mrm   9:32
in E. signifying one thousand;   Fac   2: 4
called in E. Enish-go-on-dosh;   2: 5
seen translated from the E.   JS   2:64
and he said that they were E.,   2:64

EGYPTIANS
and the language of the E.   1Ne   1: 2
to destroy Laban, even as the E.   4: 3
out of the hands of the E.   17:23
E. were drowned in the Red Sea,   17:27
taught in the language of the E.   Mos   1: 4
them out of the hands of the E.   Al   29:12
he has swallowed up the E. in   36:28
closed upon the armies of the E.   He   8:11
after the manner of the E.   Abr   1: 9
after the manner of the E.   1:11
this descent sprang all the E.,   1:22
when the E. shall see her,   2:23
Let her say unto the E.,   2:24
as understood by the E.   Fac   1:11
the E. meant it to signify   1:12
called by the E. Jah-oh-eh.   2: 1
called by the E. Oliblish,   2: 2
by the E. to be the Sun,   2: 5

EGYPTUS
Ham, and the daughter of E.,   Abr   1:23
Pharaoh, the eldest son of E.,   1:25

EIGHT
even e. years in the wilderness.   1Ne 17: 4
two hundred and thirty and e.   Jar   1:13
And they fled e. days' journey   Mos 23: 3
e. thousand of the Lamanites   He   5:19
had been prepared was e.)   Eth   3: 1
and he did reign e. years,   10:13
one thousand e. hundred and   DC 20: 1
of the hands, when e. years,   68:25
of their sins even e. years old,   68:27
one thousand e. hundred and   76:11
at the time he was e. days old   84:28
is to preside over forty-e. priests,   107:87
and Joseph Smith was thirty-e.   135: 6
e. hundred years, and he begat   Mses 6:11
Enos, e. hundred and seven   6:14
Cainan, e. hundred and fifteen   6:18
Mahalaleel e. hundred and   6:19
begat Jared, e. hundred and   6:20
Mahalaleel were e. hundred   6:20
he begat Enoch, e. hundred   6:21
thousand e. hundred and five,   JS   2: 3
one thousand e. hundred and   2:27
one thousand e. hundred and   2:59
one thousand e. hundred and   2:60
eight hundred and thirty-e.   2:60

EIGHTEEN
e. hundred and thirty,   DC 21: 3
of e. hundred and twenty.   JS   2:14
e. hundred and twenty-three—   2:28

EIGHTEENTH
in the e. year of the reign of   Al   35:13
in the e. year of the reign of   43: 3
commencement of the e. year   43: 4
thus ended the e. year of   44:24

EIGHTEENTH

in the latter end of the e. year	3Ne	4: 1
thus the e. year did pass away.		4: 4

EIGHTH

in the e. year of the reign of	Al	4: 6
in this e. year of the reign of		4: 9
ended the e. year of the reign of		4:10
of the twenty and e. year,		52:19
ended the twenty and e. year of		53:23
ended the twenty and e. year of		57: 5
And in the thirty and e. year,		63: 7
ended the thirty and e. year.		63: 9
and also in the forty and e. year.	He	3:19
end of the forty and e. year		3:22
that in the fifty and e. year of		4: 5
the fifty and e. and ninth years		4: 8
in the sixty and e. year also,		6:33
thus ended the sixty and e. year		6:41
peace in the seventy and e. year,		11:22
in the eighty and e. year of		16:11
and also the ninety and e. year;	3Ne	2: 4
away the twenty and e. year,		6: 9
thirty and e. year pass away,	4Ne	1: 6
being now the e. year since	JS	2: 2
from the twenty-e. verse to		2:41

EIGHTIETH

in the e. year of the reign	He	11:24
thus ended the e. year of the		11:29
in the three hundred and e. year	Mrm	5: 6

EIGHTY

two hundred and e. and two	Om	1: 3
died, being e. and two years old,	Mos	29:45
of the e. and first year they did	He	11:30
thus ended the e. and first year		11:35
And in the e. and second year		11:36
And in the e. and third year		11:36
And in the e. and fourth year		11:36
in the e. and fifth year		11:37
thus ended the e. and fifth year.		11:38
in the e. and sixth year,		13: 1
thus ended the e. and sixth year		16: 9
also the e. and seventh year		16:10
also, in the e. and eighth year		16:11
in the e. and ninth year of		16:12
he kept it e. and four years,	4Ne	1:20
hundred and e. and four years	Mrm	6: 5
He was e.-seven years old when	DC	107:45
thou livest until thou art e.-five		130:15
lived one hundred and e.-seven	Mses	8: 5
seven hundred and e.-two years,		8: 6
one hundred and e.-two years,		8: 8

EIGHTY-FOUR: see EIGHTY and FOUR.

EIGHTY-FIVE: see EIGHTY and FIVE.

EIGHTY-SEVEN: see EIGHTY and SEVEN.

EIGHTY-TWO: see EIGHTY and TWO.

EITHER

e. on the one hand or on the other—	1Ne	14: 7
e. to the convincing of them unto		14: 7
ask it e. in the depths, or	2Ne	17:11
and e. for a measure of barley,	Al	11: 7
nor e. of their brethren who		23: 1
what could justice do, or mercy e.,		42:21
e. to the subjecting the Nephites		54:20
could not retreat e. way,	He	1:31
for e. he will hate the one and	3Ne	13:24
e. a stewardship or otherwise,	DC	42:72
cut off, e. in life or in death,		50: 8
the inhabitants on e. side		61: 3
e. by commandment or by		64:12
e. a greater or a lesser kingdom.		88:37
his stead, both or e. of them.		102:11
or e. of them shall request it.		102:24
or e. of them be dissatisfied		102:27
every decision made by e. of		107:27
of these quorums, or e. of them,		107:30
decision of e. of these councils,		107:77

282

if one or e. of the ten virgins,	DC	132:63
in jeopardy of e. life or limb,		134:10
I deny that e. forty or any		OD
I must e. remain in darkness	JS	2:13

ELAM

and from Dush, and from E., and	2Ne	21:11

ELDER

my e. brothers, who were Laman,	1Ne	2: 5
to my e. brethren, who were		4:24
Behold ye are mine e. brethren,		7: 8
teacher, who are his e. brethren.		16:37
the e. was called Jacob		18: 7
us, who are the e. brethren,	2Ne	5: 3
and Sam, mine e. brother and his		5: 6
to counsel with your e. brothers	Al	39:10
e. or priest did minister it—	Mro	4: 1
to be the first e. of this church:	DC	20: 2
be the second e. of this church,		20: 3
manifested unto this first e.		20: 5
An apostle is an e., and it is		20:38
when there is no e. present;		20:49
But when there is an e. present,		20:50
assist the e. if occasion requires.		20:52
the absence of the e. or priest.—		20:56
Every e., priest, teacher, or		20:60
when presented to an e., shall		20:64
high priesthood (or presiding e.),		20:67
the e. or priest shall administer		20:76
be signed by any e. or priest		20:84
acquainted with the e. or priest,		20:84
an e. of the church through		21: 1
you are an e. under his hand,		21:11
an e. unto this church of Christ,		21:11
every man, both e., priest,		38:40
ordination, even that of an e.,		53: 3
to be an e. unto this church,		55: 2
every e. in this part of the		72:16
let every e. who shall give an		72:19
the offices of e. and bishop are		84:29
or presiding e. of the church.		88:140
office of an e. comes under the		107: 7
and also in the office of an e.,		107:10
An e. has a right to officiate		107:11
The high priest and e. are to		107:12
who are of the office of an e.;		107:60
to priest, and from priest to e.,		107:63
thine offspring, and thine e. son,		122: 6
Joseph to be a presiding e.		124:125
when any E. of the Church		OD
the first E. of the Church,	JS	2:72

ELDERS

concerning the e. of the Jews,	1Ne	4:22
concerning the e. of the Jews,		4:27
priests, and e. over the church;	Al	4: 7
was among the e. of the church,		4:16
he ordained priests and e.,		6: 1
were called the e. of the church,	Mro	3: 1
The manner of their e. and		4: 1
e., priests, and teachers were		6: 1
condemn them before the e.,		6: 7
and we, the e. of the church,	DC	20:16
The duty of the e., priests,		20:38
And to ordain other e.,		20:39
e. are to conduct the meetings		20:45
The several e. composing this		20:61
The e. are to receive their		20:63
their licenses from other e.,		20:63
But the presiding e., traveling		20:66
councilors, high priests, and e.,		20:66
The e. or priests are to have		20:68
laying on of the hands of the e.,		20:68
church, and also before the e.,		20:69
unto the e. before the church,		20:70
held by the e. of the church,		20:81
in a book by one of the e.,		20:82
the other e. shall appoint from		20:82
given unto the e. of my church,		36: 5
Hearken, O ye e. of my church		41: 2
Hearken, O ye e. of my church,		42: 1
the e., priests, and teachers		42:12

ELDERS

his counselors, two of the e.,	DC 42:31
And the e. of the church,	42:44
And the e. or high priests	42:71
before two e. of the church,	42:80
the e. shall lay the case before	42:81
to the members, but to the e.	42:89
O hearken, ye e. of my church,	43: 1
hearken ye e. of my church,	43:15
the e. of my church should be	44: 1
and ye e. listen together,	45: 6
together ye e. of my church;	45:64
given to the e. of my church	46: 2
to be e. unto the church,	46:27
hands of the e. of the church.	49:14
O ye e. of my church,	50: 1
unto the e. of his church,	50:10
the e. whom he hath called	52: 1
all the e. whom I have chosen.	52:21
residue of the e. watch over	52:39
O ye e. of my church,	57: 1
of both e. and members	57:16
O ye e. of my church,	58: 1
residue of the e. of my church,	58:44
by the e. of the church at	58:56
of the e. of this church,	58:61
unto the e. of his church,	60: 1
mine e. who are commanded	60:10
O ye e. of my church,	61: 2
this whole company of mine e.	61: 3
O ye e. of my church,	62: 1
O ye e. of my church,	64: 1
O ye e. of my church,	67: 1
the faithful e. of my church.—	68: 7
the e. of the church in this	72: 5
To take an account of the e.	72:11
from three e. of the church,	72:25
this be a pattern unto the e.	73: 5
O ye e. of my church,	75:23
by the four and twenty e.,	77: 5
these e. whom John saw,	77: 5
e. who had been faithful in	77: 5
Joseph Smith, Jun., and six e.,	84: 1
should travel, and also the e.,	84:111
and will raise up e. and send	88:72
those who are not the first e.	88:85
nine high priests, seventeen e.,	102: 5
are the first e. of my church,	105: 7
that mine e. should wait for	105: 9
until mine e. are endowed	105:11
that mine e. should wait for	105:13
and Baneemy [mine e.],	105:27
that the first e. of my church	105:33
there must needs be presiding e.	107:60
or will choose among the e.	107:72
the president over the office of e.	107:89
is to preside over ninety-six e.,	107:89
with the first of mine e.,	108: 4
with the rest of mine e. whom	108: 4
and unto all the e. and people	115: 3
preside over the quorum of e.,	124:137
is instituted for traveling e.	124:139
and the quorum of e.	124:140
Send forth the e. of my church	133: 8
Listen, ye e. of my church	133:16
and ye e. listen together;	136:41

ELDEST

(beginning at the e.) Laman,	1Ne 1:hd
Laman and Lemuel, being the e.,	2:12
Zoram took the e. daughter of	16: 7
from the e. down to the youngest,	Mos 2: 5
the e. of his sons he took not with	Al 31: 7
was the e. son of our father Lehi;	56: 3
unto the e. the name of Nephi,	He 3:21
his e. son Nephi began to reign	3:37
son Nephi, who was his e. son,	3Ne 1: 2
his e. son, whose name was	Eth 10: 3
Pharoah, the e. son of Egypt,	Abr 1:25
by the death of my e. brother,	JS 2:56

ELECT

and thou art an e. lady, whom	DC 25: 3
to pass the gathering of mine e.;	29: 7
for mine e. hear my voice	DC 29: 7
even so will I gather mine e.	33: 6
the salvation of mine own e.;	35:20
kingdom, and the e. of God.	84:34
to the honorable president-e.,	124: 3
to gather out mine e. from the	Mses 7:62
they shall deceive the very e.,	JS 1:22
the e. according to the covenant.	1:22
shall mine e. be gathered	1:27
the remainder of his e. from	1:37
mine e., when they shall see	1:39

ELECTED

hast e. us to be thy holy children;	Al 31:16
e. us that we shall be saved,	31:17
e. to be cast by thy wrath down	31:17
thank thee that thou hast e. us,	31:17

ELECTION

calling and e. in the church,	DC 53: 1
according to the e. of grace,	84:99

ELECT'S

for the e. sake, according to	JS 1:20
unto you for the e. sake;	1:23
I speak for mine e. sake;	1:29

ELEGANT

many e. and spacious buildings;	Mos 11: 8

ELEMENT

and spirit and e., inseparably	DC 93:33
And also that of e. shall melt	101:25

ELEMENTS

even until the e. should melt	3Ne 26: 3
e. shall melt with fervent heat,	Mrm 9: 2
The e. are eternal, and spirit	DC 93:33
The e. are the tabernacle of	93:35
e. combine to hedge up the way;	122: 7

ELEPHANTS

there were e. and cureloms	Eth 9:19
more especially the e. and	9:19

ELEVATED

and the most e. of nay in	JS 2:51

ELEVEN

that I, being e. years ole,	Mrm 1: 6
family consisting of e. souls,	JS 2: 4

ELEVENTH

in the e. year of the reign of the	Al 16: 1
second month in the e. year,	16: 1
ended the e. year of the judges,	16: 9
in the e. month of the	49: 1
the e. year also passed away	3Ne 2:10
and it is the e. hour,	DC 33: 3
the e. chapter of Revelation?	77:15
quoted the e. chapter of Isaiah,	JS 2:40

ELIAS: see also HIGBEE, Elias.

And also with E., to whom	DC 27: 6
which Zacharias he (E.) visited	27: 7
be filled with the spirit of E.;	27: 7
some of Moses, and some of E.,	76:100
this is E. which was to come	77: 9
this is E., who, as it is written,	77:14
After this, E. appeared,	110:12

ELIHU

under the hand of E.;	DC 84: 8
E. under the hand of Jeremy;	84: 9

ELIJAH

I will send you E. the prophet	3Ne 25: 5
by the hand of E. the prophet,	DC 2: 1
And also E., unto whom I have	27: 9
before E. which should come,	35: 4
for E. the prophet, who was taken	110:13
that he [E.] should be sent,	110:14

ELIJAH

I will send you E. the prophet DC 128:17
And from Moses to E., 133:55
and from E. to John, 133:55
by the hand of E. the prophet, JS 2:38

ELKENAH
wholly turned to the god of E., Abr 1: 6
by the hand of the priest of E. 1: 7
priest of E. was also the priest of 1: 7
and it stood before the gods of E., 1:13
to worship the god of E., 1:17
the Lord broke down the altar of D., 1:20
after the priest of E. was smitten 1:29
to deliver me from the gods of E. 2:13
from the hands of the priest of E. 3:20
idolatrous priest of E. Fac 1: 3
standing before the gods of E., 1: 4
idolatrous god of E. 1: 5

ELOQUENT
artificer, and the e. orator. 2Ne 13: 3

ELSE
unto none e. can the ends of 2Ne 2: 7
or e. thou shalt commit sin; Mos 4:28
or e. I should have caused that 7:11
and salvation cometh to none e. Al 11:40
than the sword, or anything e., 31: 5
or e. all mankind must 34: 9
or e. he will hold to the one and 3Ne 13:24
or e. it needs be that they must 28:37
to none e. will I grant this DC 5:14
is none e. save God that 6:16
commandments, and none e. 29:12
there is none e. with whom I am 38:10
shalt cleave unto her and none e. 42:22
none e. shall be appointed unto 43: 4
e. were your children unclean, 74: 1
mine, or e. your faith is vain, 104:55
of that stock anywhere e., 124:71
they appropriate anywhere e., 124:71
or e. disapprove of them at 124:144
E. what shall they do which are 128:16
Joseph, and to none e. 132:54
unto him and to no one e. 132:61
or e. where is thy glory, Mses 1:15
or e. I must do as James JS 2:13
e. why should the powers of 2:20

ELSEWHERE
bishops or judges in Zion or e. DC 107:74
the necessity of taking her e.; JS 2:58

EMBARK
that e. in the service of God, DC 4: 2

EMBARRASSMENTS
now the cause of these our e., Al 58: 9

EMBASSIES
they sent e. to the army of Al 52:20

EMBASSY
secret e. into the mount Antipas, Al 47:10
had sent an e. to the queen 47:32
did send an e. to the governor 58: 4

EMBLEMATICAL
e. of the grand Presidency in Fac 3: 1

EMBLEMS
the e. of the flesh and blood DC 20:40

EMBRACE
to e. the secret plans again Eth 9:26
e. it with singleness of heart DC 36: 7
of those who e. my gospel 42:39

EMBRACETH
truth e. truth; virtue loveth DC 88:40

ENCAMP

EMBRACING
e. this calling and DC 36: 5

EMER: *see also HARRIS, Emer.*
Coriantum was the son of E. Eth 1:28
And E. was the son of Omer. 1:29
in his old age he begat E.; 9:14
he anointed E. to be king to 9:14
after that he had anointed E. 9:15
that E. did reign in his stead, 9:15
and the house of E. did prosper 9:16
exceedingly under the reign of E.; 9:16
E. did execute judgment in 9:21

EMMA: *see SMITH, Emma.*

EMPLOY
got gain according to their e. Al 10:32
their wages according to their e., 11:20
that they might have more e., 11:20
did e. him men in preparing 53: 7
were obliged to e. all our force 57:13
that we should e. our men to 58: 3
Moronihah did e. all his armies He 4:19
He should also e. an agent to DC 84:113

EMPLOYED
behold, I had e. my people, Mrm 3: 1
be e. in doing this business. DC 51:14
will as clerks e. in his service; 57: 9
the time that I was thus e., JS 2:57
e. in the service of Mr. Stoal. 2:57
e. in circulating falsehoods 2:61
While we were thus e., praying 2:68

EMPLOYETH
and he e. no servant there; 2Ne 9:41

EMPTIED
and it e. into the Red Sea; 1Ne 2: 8
the waters of the river e. into 2: 9

EMPTY
he awaketh and his soul is e.; 2Ne 27: 3
until the earth is e., and the DC 5:19
was formed, was e. and desolate, Abr 4: 2

EMRON
sword, and also Luram and E.; Mro 9: 2

ENABLE
e. them that they might be skillful Al 10:15
e. the Lamanites to conquer 61: 8
they did e. the people in the land He 3:11
provided to e. you to translate; DC 10: 4
e. thy servants to seal up the law, 109:46
would en us to redeem them out 128:22

ENABLED
may be e. to keep my laws; DC 44: 5
may be e. to purchase land 48: 4
disciples are e. to buy lands. 57: 5
e. to discern by the Spirit 63:41
he may be e. to discharge every 90:23
were e. to get a comfortable JS 2:55
was I e. to reach the place of 2:62

ENACT
he might have power to e. laws Al 4:16
governments have a right to e. DC 134: 5
to e. laws for the protection of 134: 7

ENACTED
as laws have been e. by Congress DC OD

ENACTETH
he e. laws, and sendeth them forth Mos 29:23

ENCAMP
did e. with their armies Al 62:34
thus they did e. for the night. 62:35

ENCIRCLE

ENCIRCLE
O Lord, wilt thou e. me around	2Ne 4:33
e. you about with his chains,	Al 12: 6
E. the flocks round about that	17:33
walls of stone to e. them about,	48: 8
attempt to e. them about	55:29
I will e. thee in the arms of	DC 6:20

ENCIRCLED
and I am e. about eternally	2Ne 1:15
e. about by the bands of death,	Al 5: 7
of hell which e. them about,	5: 9
be e. about by the pains of hell.	14: 6
e. about with everlasting darkness	26:15
are e. about with the matchless	26:15
am e. about by the everlasting	36:18
and e. the Lamanites about	43:35
armies of Moroni e. them about,	43:52
were e. about by the Nephites,	43:53
had e. the city of Bountiful	53: 4
the Lamanites were e. about	62:34
Nephi and Lehi were e. about	He 5:23
were e. about with a pillar of fire,	5:24
they saw that they were e. about,	5:43
yea, they were e. about;	5:44
we are e. about by the angels of	13:37
and e. those little ones about,	3Ne 17:24
they were e. about with fire;	17:24
e. about as if it were by fire;	19:14

ENCIRCLES
e. them in the arms of safety,	Al 34:16

ENCLOSE
round about to e. his armies,	Al 48: 8

ENCOMPASSED
I am e. about, because	2Ne 4:18
must be e. about by the floods.	Eth 3: 2
were e. about by many waters	6: 7

ENCOMPASSETH
and e. them round about.	DC 76:29

ENCOURAGE
to inculcate or e. polygamy;	DC OD

ENCOURAGED
e. and urged the continuance	DC OD

ENCROACHMENTS
from the unlawful assults and e.	DC 134:11

ENCYCLOPEDIAS
in the magazines, and in the e.,	DC 123: 5

END
father, Lehi, had made an e. of	1Ne 7: 1
hold of the e. of the rod of iron;	8:24
hold of the e. of the rod of iron;	8:30
father had made an e. of speaking	10: 2
and if they endure unto the e.	13:37
into that hell which hath no e.	14: 3
concerning the e. of the world.	14:22
now I make an e. of speaking	14:30
forever and ever, and hath no e.	15:30
I, Nephi, had made an e. of	16: 1
utter to the e. of the earth;	20:20
And now I, Nephi, make an e.;	22:29
and endure to the e.,	22:31
an e. of teaching my brethren,	2Ne 1: 1
no purpose in the e. of its creation.	2:12
purposes in the e. of man,	2:15
remained forever, and had no e.	2:22
had made an e. of speaking	4: 3
had made an e. of speaking	4: 8
in the e. thy seed shall be blessed.	4: 9
had made an e. of speaking	4:10
had made an e. of speaking	4:11
forever and ever and has no e.	9:16
in his name, and endure to the e.,	9:24
for, for this e. hath the law of	11: 4
is there any e. of their treasures;	12: 7
is there any e. of their chariots.	2Ne 12: 7
them from the e. of the earth;	15:26
thy son, at the e. of the conduit	17: 3
and peace there is no e.,	19: 7
from the e. of heaven,	23: 5
For, for this e. was the law	25:25
for what e. the law was given.	25:27
of the world unto the e. thereof.	27:10
be even unto the e. of the earth.	27:11
until the e. of man, neither from	29: 9
I must make an e. of my sayings.	30:18
make an e. of my prophesying	31: 1
He that endureth to the e.,	31:15
a man shall endure to the e.,	31:16
of Christ, and endure to the e.,	31:20
which is one God, without e. Amen.	31:21
in him, and to endure to the e.,	33: 4
the e. of the day of probation.	33: 9
and for the selfsame e. hath he	Jac 2:21
And now I make an e. of speaking	2:22
And I make an e. of speaking	3:14
and the e. soon cometh;	5:29
and the e. draweth nigh.	5:47
for behold the e. draweth nigh,	5:62
last time, for the e. draweth nigh.	5:64
for the e. is nigh at hand,	5:71
cometh the season and the e.;	5:77
after that the e. soon cometh.	6: 2
And I make an e. of my writing	7:27
And I make an e.	Om 1: 3
And I make an e.	1: 9
And I make an e.	1:11
praying, and endure to the e.;	1:26
I make an e. of my speaking.	1:30
made an e. of teaching his sons,	Mos 1: 9
had made an e. of these sayings	1:15
if they hold out faithful to the e.	2:41
had made an e. of speaking the	4: 1
even unto the e. of his life,	4: 6
even unto the e. of the world.	4: 7
even unto the e. of your lives,	4:30
obedient unto the e. of your lives.	5: 8
made an e. of all these things,	6: 3
an e. of speaking to his people,	8: 1
an e. of speaking these words	8:19
had made an e. of these sayings	13:25
an e. of reading the records,	25: 7
an e. of speaking and reading to	25:14
made an e. of speaking to them,	25:17
him that believeth unto the e.	26:23
and, in the e., all men should	Al 1: 4
e. to the spreading of priestcraft	1:16
they were faithful until the e.;	5:13
Alma had made an e. of speaking	6: 1
he is the beginning and the e.,	11:39
an e. of speaking these words,	12:19
we have spoken, which is the e.	12:27
beginning of days or e. of years,	13: 7
is without beginning or e.—	13: 8
beginning of days or e. of years,	13: 9
he had made an e. of speaking	14: 1
had made an e. of these sayings,	24:17
faith of Christ, even unto the e.	27:27
latter e. of the seventeenth year,	30: 6
was dead, that was the e. thereof.	30:18
and this put an e. to the iniquity	30:58
thus we see the e. of him who	30:60
that after the e. of Korihor,	31: 1
and endureth to the e. the same	32:13
his sins, and endureth to the e.,	32:15
of your repentance until the e.;	34:33
had made an e. of these words,	35: 1
is he that endureth to the e.	38: 2
until the e. of his days,	41: 6
the east e. of the garden of Eden,	42: 2
an e. of speaking these words,	44:10
Behold, we will e. the conflict.	44:10
fastened it upon the e. of a pole.	46:12
on the e. thereof his rent coat,	46:13
the e. of the nineteenth year of	46:37
that in the latter e. of the	48: 2
in the latter e. of the	48:21
in the e. of the twenty and	50:40

END 286 ENDEAVOR

put an e. to such contentions	Al 51:16
put an e. to those king-men,	51:21
put an e. to the stubbornness	51:21
in the latter e. of the twenty	52:18
to put an e. to our receiving	56:29
should put an e. to their lives,	57:15
and ninth year, in the latter e.,	58:38
put an e. to this great iniquity.	61:18
of the judges; and it had an e.	He 1:13
in the e. of this book ye shall	2:13
the e. of the book of Helaman,	2:14
the e. of the book of Nephi,	2:14
in the latter e. of the forty and	3:22
and sixth year did e. in peace.	11:21
did put an e. to their strife	11:23
in the latter e. of the year,	3Ne 3:22
the latter e. of the eighteenth	4: 1
the e. of Giddianhi the robber.	4:14
put an e. to all those wicked,	5: 6
now I make an e. of my saying,	5:19
Omega, the beginning and the e.	9:18
for this time I make an e. of my	10:19
the law; therefore it hath an e.	15: 5
unto Moses hath an e. in me.	15: 8
unto me, and endure to the e.,	15: 9
unto him that endureth to the e.	15: 9
Jesus had made an e. of praying	17:18
had made an e. of these sayings,	18:36
Jesus had made an e. of praying	19:35
I, Mormon, make an e. of my	26:12
name, and endureth to the e.,	27: 6
and by and by the e. cometh,	27:11
and if he endureth to the e.,	27:16
he that endureth not unto the e.,	27:17
their faithfulness unto the e.	27:19
hast called us, may have an e.,	28: 2
now I, Mormon, make an e. of	28:24
thus is the e. of the record of	4Ne 1:49
they did not put an e. to my life.	Mrm 6:10
of happiness which hath no e.	7: 7
one knoweth the e. of the war.	8: 8
I make an e. of speaking	8:13
Has the e. come yet?	9:15
ye do this, and endure to the e.,	9:29
at the e. of four years that	Eth 2:14
prepared, one in each e. thereof;	6: 2
until the e. come when the earth	13: 8
made an e. of abridging the	Mro 1: 1
of faith on his name to the e.	3: 3
to serve him to the e.	6: 3
of faith on his name to the e.	8: 3
prayer, until the e. shall come.	8:26
and hold out faithful to the e.,	DC 6:13
but be diligent unto the e.	10: 4
may not be ashamed in the e.,	10:19
endureth of my church to the e.,	10:69
and endure to the e. you shall	14: 7
and endure to the e., the same	18:22
the beginning and the e.,	19: 1
his works at the e. of the world,	19: 3
shall be no e. to this torment,	19: 6
even unto the e. of thy life.	19:32
and endure in faith to the e.,	20:25
infinite and eternal, without e.	20:28
in faith on his name to the e.,	20:29
to serve him to the e.,	20:37
even unto the e. of thy days.	24: 8
and lo, I am with him to the e.	24:10
And the e. shall come, and the	29:23
unto myself my works have no e.,	29:33
Be faithful unto the e., and lo,	31:13
Omega, the beginning and the e.,	35: 1
Omega, the beginning and the e.,	38: 1
shall come at the e. of the earth;	38: 5
then cometh the e. of the earth.	43:31
and their e. no man knoweth	43:33
the beginning and the e.,	45: 7
that the e. of the world cometh;	45:22
until the e. of the earth.	45:26
the e. of your salvation,	46: 7
the beginning and the e.;	49:12
answer the e. of its creation;	49:16
saved who endureth unto the e.	DC 53: 7
the beginning and the e.,	54: 1
I make an e. of speaking unto	56:20
unto this e. were they made to	59:20
the beginning and the e.	61: 1
these things even unto the e.,	66:12
I make an e. of my sayings.	72:23
be with them even unto the e.	75:11
be with them even unto the e.	75:13
with them also, even unto the e.	75:14
and in truth unto the e.	76: 5
And the e. thereof, neither	76:45
the e., the width, the height,	76:48
this is the e. of the vision of	76:49
this is the e. of the vision which	76:80
cannot come, worlds without e.	76:112
This is the e. of the vision	76:113
unto the e. of all things;	77:12
beginning of days or e. of life.	78:16
if thou art faithful unto the e.	81: 6
of days or e. of years.	84:17
the beginning and the e.	84:120
made a full e. of all nations;	87: 6
truth abideth and hath no e.;	88:66
again, until the e. of the earth.	88:101
great and last day, even the e.,	88:102
unto this e. was the ordinance of	88:139
the beginning and the e.	95: 7
I am with you even unto the e.	100:12
purpose and the e. thereof—	101:33
am with you even unto the e.	105:41
preserved unto the e. of the earth;	107:42
shall be an e. of controversy	107:83
that there may be an e. to lyings	109:30
the finishing and the e. thereof,	121:32
unto this e. have I raised you up,	124: 1
at the e. of this appointment	124:32
at the e. of the appointment	124:32
for some good e., or bad,	127: 2
that is the e. of his kingdom;	131: 4
that are not made unto this e.	132: 7
have an e. when men are dead.	132: 7
be gods, because they have no e.;	132:20
even unto the e. of the world,	132:49
from one e. of heaven to the other.	133: 7
without beginning of days or e.	Mses 1: 1
for my works are without e.,	1: 4
even unto the e. of thy days;	1:26
there is no e. to my works,	1:38
I am the Beginning and the E.,	2: 1
in the world, until the e. thereof;	5:59
be in the e. of the world also.	6: 7
beginning of days or e. of years,	6:67
before thy face and have no e.;	7:31
even unto the e. of the world;	7:67
e. of all flesh is come before me,	8:30
I know the e. from the beginning;	Abr 2: 8
could not see the e. thereof.	3:12
they shall have no e.,	3:18
seventh time we will e. our work,	5: 2
and of the e. of the world,	JS 1: 4
which is the e. of the world?	1: 4
but the e. is not yet.	1:23
and then shall the e. come,	1:31
from one e. of heaven to the	1:37
cometh the e. of the wicked,	1:55
but the e. of the earth is not yet,	1:55
I went at the e. of each year,	2:54
at the e. of another year	2:59
ENDANGERED	
and thy life is e. by him,	DC 98:31
ENDEAVOR	
I will e. to speak with boldness;	Mos 7:12
e. to establish Amlici to be king	Al 2: 2
Do not e. to excuse yourself	42:30
did e. to stir up the Lamanites	He 4: 3
to e. to repair unto them the	5:17
I did e. to preach unto this	Mrm 1:16
But I shall e., hereafter,	Abr 1:28
I shall e. to write some of	1:31

ENDEAVORED 287 ENDS

ENDEAVORED
e. to enforce it by the sword;	Al	1:12
Ye e. to believe that ye should	DC	67: 3
but e. to take away my life	Abr	1: 7
to have e. in a proper and	JS	2:28

ENDEAVORING
was e. to harass the Nephites,	Al	52:13
e. to prove by the scriptures that	3Ne	1:24
in e. to establish their own	JS	2: 9

ENDEAVORS
all my e. to preserve them,	JS	2:59

ENDED
after they had e. the ceremony,	Mos	19:24
thus e. the reign of the kings		29:47
and thus e. the days of Alma,		29:47
and e. in the fifth year of	Al	3:25
thus e. the eighth year of the reign		4:10
thus e. the ninth year of the reign		8: 2
thus e. the words of Amulek,		11:46
thus e. the tenth year of the reign		15:19
And thus e. the eleventh year of		16: 9
thus e. the fourteenth year of the		16:21
of the reign of the judges is e.		28: 9
e. the seventeenth year of the reign		35:12
thus e. the eighteenth year of		44:24
thus e. the record of Alma,		44:24
thus e. the nineteenth year of		49:29
thus e. the twentieth year.		50:16
of the judges also e. in peace;		50:24
thus e. the twenty and fourth		50:35
thus e. the twenty and eighth		53:23
thus e. the twenty and ninth		55:35
thus e. the twenty and sixth		56:20
thus e. the twenty and eighth		57: 5
thus e. the thirtieth year of		62:11
thus e. the thirty and first		62:39
thus e. the thirty and sixth year		63: 3
thus e. the thirty and seventh		63: 6
thus e. the thirty and eighth		63: 9
thus e. the thirty and ninth year		63:16
thus e. the account of Alma,		63:17
thus e. the days of Pacumeni.	He	1:21
thus e. the forty and first year of		1:34
thus e. the forty and second year		2:12
year of the reign of the judges e.;		3:18
and the second year e. in peace also,		3:36
thus e. the sixty and first year of		4:17
the reign of the judges had e.,		6: 1
thus e. the sixty and third year.		6: 6
thus e. the sixty and sixth year.		6:15
thus e. the sixty and eighth year of		6:41
thus e. the seventy and first year of		10:19
thus e. the seventy and seventh		11:21
thus e. the eightieth year of		11:29
to pass that thus e. this year.		11:32
thus e. the eighty and first year		11:35
thus e. the eighty and fifth year.		11:38
thus e. the eighty and sixth year		16: 9
thus e. also the eighty and		16:10
thus e. the ninetieth year		16:24
thus e. the book of Helaman,		16:25
And thus e. the thirteenth year.	3Ne	2:16
And thus e. the fourteenth year.		2:18
And thus e. the fifteenth year,		2:19
And thus e. the thirtieth year;		7:13
when Jesus had e. these sayings		15: 1
when Jesus had e. these sayings		27:33
when the thousand years are e.,	DC	29:22
be past, and the harvest e.,		45: 2
harvest is past, the summer is e.,		56:16
until the thousand years are e.,		88:101
day I, God, e. my work,	Mses	3: 2

ENDETH
thus e. the fifth year of the reign	Al	3:27
And thus e. the seventh year of		4: 5
thus e. the fifteenth year of		28: 7
thus e. the twenty and fifth		51:37
thus e. the days of Amalickiah.		51:37

ENDING
of the world to the e. thereof.	2Ne	27: 7
is to endure a never-e. torment.	Mos	2:39
in a state of never-e. happiness.		2:41
ourselves a never-e. torment,		5: 5
a state of never-e. happiness.	Al	28:12
in the e. of the twenty and		52:14
the e. of the forty and third year.	He	3: 1
in the e. of the thirty and	3Ne	10:18

ENDLESS
have remained to an e. duration.	2Ne	9: 7
and brimstone, which is e. torment.		9:19
and brimstone, which is e. torment;		9:26
and brimstone, which is e. torment.		28:23
fire and brimstone is e. torment.	Jac	6:10
state of misery and e. torment,	Mos	3:25
yea, a light that is e., that can		16: 9
yea, a light that is also a life which is e.,		16: 9
of e. life and happiness;		16:11
resurrection of e. damnation,		16:11
soul should endure e. torment		28: 3
to a state of e. misery and woe.	Al	9:11
time to prepare for that e. state		12:24
consigned to a state of e. wo.		28:11
raised to e. happiness to inherit		41: 4
or to e. misery to inherit the		41: 4
from that e. night of darkness;		41: 7
to the gulf of misery and e. wo,	He	5:12
to everlasting misery and e. wo?		7:16
to a state of e. misery,		12:26
is the value of an e. happiness	Mrm	8:38
a redemption from an e. sleep,		9:13
must have gone to an e. hell.	Mro	8:13
death, hell, and an e. torment.		8:21
of suffer, for I, God, am e.	DC	19: 4
but it is written *e. torment.*		19: 6
For, behold, I am e., and the		19:10
from my hand is e. punishment,		19:10
for E. is my name wherefore.		19:10
E. punishment is God's		19:12
which is e. punishment, which		76:44
and E. is my name;	Mses	1: 3
end of years; and is not this e.?		1: 3
E. and Eternal is my name,		7:35

ENDLESSLY
they would have been e. lost	Mos	16: 4

ENDOW
e. those whom I have chosen	DC	95: 8

ENDOWED
be e. with power from on high;	DC	38:32
when men are e. with power		38:38
and ye shall be e. with power,		43:16
e. with power from on high.		105:11
which my servants have been e.		110: 9
I have e. him with the keys		132:59

ENDOWMENT
I have prepared a great e.	DC	105:12
blessing and e. for them,		105:18
receive their e. from on high		105:33
and the e. with which		110: 9
for the glory, honor, and e.		124:39
was performed in the E. House,		OD
E. House was, by my instructions,		OD

ENDS
unto the e. of the earth.	1Ne	21: 6
to answer the e. of the law,	2Ne	2: 7
can the e. of the law be answered.		2: 7
the e. of the law which the Holy		2:10
answer the e. of the atonement—		2:10
from far unto the e. of the earth;		24: 2
unto me all ye e. of the earth,		26:25
hiss forth unto the e. of the earth,		29: 2
Jew, and all ye e. of the earth,		33:10
Israel, and all ye e. of the earth,		33:13
and all the e. of the earth shall	Mos	12:24
and all the e. of the earth shall		15:31

ENDS

Repent, all ye e. of the earth,	Al	5:50
unto all the e. of the earth?		29: 7
come unto me ye e. of the earth,	3Ne	9:22
spoken, unto the e. of the earth.		11:41
all the e. of the earth shall see		16:20
all the e. of the earth shall see		20:35
Repent, all ye e. of the earth,		27:20
unto all the e. of the earth;	Mrm	3:18
persuade all ye e. of the earth		3:22
even unto the e. of the earth.		9:21
even unto the e. of the earth.		9:25
and the e. thereof were peaked;	Eth	2:17
even unto the e. of the earth,		3:25
repent all ye e. of the earth,		4:18
hath answered the e. of the law,	Mro	7:28
Repent all ye e. of the earth,		7:34
unto all the e. of the earth—		10:24
is unto the e. of the earth,	DC	1:11
unto the e. of the world,		1:23
voices from the e. of the earth,		43:21
the e. of the earth shall hear it;		45:49
from the e. of the earth.		58:45
is unto the e. of the earth,		65: 1
forth unto the e. of the earth,		65: 2
forth unto the e. of the earth;		72:21
forth unto the e. of the earth,		90: 9
peace unto the e. of the earth;		105:39
truth, unto the e. of the earth,		109:23
the e. of the earth may know		109:57
driven to the e. of the earth,		109:67
my word unto the e. of the earth.		112: 4
The e. of the earth shall inquire		122: 1
all the e. of the earth shall see		133: 3
the world and the e. thereof,	Mses	1: 8
the world, unto the e. thereof.		6:30

ENDURANCE

the e. of faith on his name	Mro	3: 3
the e. of faith on his name		8: 3

ENDURE

and if they e. unto the end	1Ne	13:37
and e. to the end, ye shall		22:31
in his name, and e. to the end,	2Ne	9:24
unless a man shall e. to the end,		31:16
word of Christ, and e. to the end,		31:20
in him, and to e. to the end,		33: 4
and praying, and e. to the end;	Om	1:26
to e. a never-ending torment.	Mos	2:39
soul should e. endless torment		28: 3
unto me, and e. to the end,	3Ne	15: 9
never e. the pains of death;		28: 8
do this, and e. to the end,	Mrm	9:29
and e. to the end you shall	DC	14: 7
and e. to the end, the same		18:22
and e. in faith to the end,		20:25
and e. in faith on his name		20:29
e. them, for, lo, I am with thee,		24: 8
are faithful and e.,		50: 5
and could not e. his presence;		84:24
those who will not e. chastening,		101: 5
for my name, and e. in faith,		101:35
And then, if thou e. it well,		121: 8
Moses could e. his presence.	Mses	1: 2
hope to be able to e. all things.	AoF	13

ENDURED

they who have e. the crosses of	2Ne	9:18
upon all who have e. valiantly	DC	121:29
things, we have e. many things,	AoF	13

ENDURETH

He that e. to the end,	2Ne	31:15
findeth mercy and e. to the end	Al	32:13
of his sins, and e. to the end,		32:15
blessed is he that e. to the end.		38: 2
unto him that e. to the end	3Ne	15: 9
my name, and e. to the end,		27: 6
and if he e. to the end, behold,		27:16
he that e. not unto the end,		27:17
hopeth all things, e. all things.	Mro	7:45
of Christ, and it e. forever;		7:47
love e. by diligence unto prayer,		8:26
and e. of my church to the end,	DC	10:69

ENEMIES

saved who e. unto the end.	DC	53: 7
he that e. in faith and doeth		63:20
He that is faithful and e. shall		63:47

ENEMIES

unto the destruction of their e.	1Ne	22:17
He hath confounded mine e.,	2Ne	4:22
again because of mine e.		4:29
me out of the hands of mine e.?		4:31
mine escape before mine e.!		4:33
unto the destruction of their e.,		6:14
and join his e. together;		19:11
as yet conquerors of their e.	Jac	7:25
falling into the hands of their e.,	Om	1: 2
falling into the hands of their e.,		1: 6
out of the hands of their e.		1: 7
they did contend against their e.,	WM	1:14
out of the hands of their e.,	Mos	2: 4
into the hands of your e.,		2:31
your e. shall have no power over		2:31
be in subjection to our e.,		7:18
us out of the hands of our e.,		9:17
into the hands of our e.		10: 2
them into the hands of their e.;		11:21
afflicted by the hand of their e.		11:21
that they be smitten by their e.		11:24
or be taken captive by our e.;		12:15
be taken by the hand of your e.,		17:18
to the desires of their e.		21:13
them out of the hands of their e.,	Al	2:28
no more for a time with their e.		3:24
out of the hands of their e.,		9:10
be slain by the e. of the king;		18: 3
to the desires of their e.		27: 3
flee out of the hands of our e.,		27: 5
will guard them from their e.		27:24
those who were mine e.,		33: 4
have been despised by mine e.,		33:10
and wast angry with mine e.,		33:10
him against the power of your e.		34:22
them from the hands of their e.;		43: 9
be slain by the hands of your e.		43:46
out of the hands of their e.;		45: 1
may cast us at the feet of our e.,		46:22
which was called by their e.		48:10
themselves against their e.,		48:14
themselves against their e.,		48:16
had all power over their e.;		49:23
them from the hands of their e.		49:28
against the coming of their e.,		50: 6
people from the hands of their e.		50:10
themselves against their e.;		53:16
out of the hands of our e.		57:35
falling into the hands of our e.,		58: 8
us out of the hands of our e.,		58:10
determination to conquer our e.,		58:12
us out of the hands of our e.		58:37
while your e. are spreading the		60: 7
we could have withstood our e.		60:15
and gone forth against our e.,		60:16
should have dispersed our e.,		60:16
out of the hands of our e.?		60:20
subject ourselves to our e.,		61:13
out of the hands of their e.		62:50
to withstand against your e.	He	7:22
our e. can have no power over us.		8: 6
out of the hands of their e.;		12: 2
softening the hearts of their e.		12: 2
who shall live, of your e.,		13:10
they shall flee before their e.;		13:20
and slain by their e.,		15: 9
themselves against their e.	3Ne	3:22
themselves against their e.;		3:25
e. should come down against		3:25
them out of the hands of their e.		4: 8
falling into the hands of their e.		4:31
them out of the hands of their e.;		4:33
nevertheless they were e.;		7:11
their e. were more numerous		7:12
love your e., bless them that		12:44
all thine e. shall be cut off.		20:17
and all their e. shall be cut off.		21:13
who had been slain by their e.	Mrm	3: 9
go up to battle against their e.,		3:10

ENEMIES / ENGRAVEN

out of the hands of their e.,	Mrm 3:13		the e. in the secret chambers	DC 38:28
go up unto their e. to battle,	3:14		might escape the power of the e.,	38:31
refused to go up against mine e.;	3:16		and that not by the hand of an e.	42:43
out of the hands of your e.,	DC 8: 4		the church, and not of the e.;	42:80
been delivered from all thine e.,	24: 1		the e. seeketh to destroy my	44: 5
neither strong drink of your e.;	27: 3		the e., even Satan, sitteth to	86: 3
their e. shall be under their	35:14		if your e. shall smite you the	98:25
your e. may not have power	44: 5		you revile not against your e.,	98:25
your e. say that this house	45:18		shall stand against your e.	98:27
and in the eyes of your e.,	45:72		if that e. shall excape my	98:28
to put all e. under his feet,	49: 6		I have delivered thine e. into	98:29
is now the land of your e.	52:42		thine e. is in thine hands;	98:31
brethren desire to escape their e.,	54: 3		thine e. is in thine hands	98:31
lest your e. come upon you;	54: 7		if after thine e. has come	98:39
subdues all e. under his feet.	58:22		a testimony against thine e.—	98:39
lo, your e. are upon you,	63:31		as oft as thine e. repenteth	98:40
to get in debt to thine e.;	64:27		will avenge thee of thine e.	98:45
that thine e. may be subdued;	65: 6		when the e. shall come to spoil	101:45
Wherefore, confound your e.;	71: 7		And the e. came by night,	101:51
subdue all e. under his feet.	76:61		the e. destroyed their works,	101:51
subdued all e. under his feet,	76:106		lest the e. should come	101:53
to be avenged of their e.	87: 7		would have seen the e. while	101:54
be not afraid of your e.,	98:14		kept the e. from breaking down	101:54
avenged themselves on all their e.,	98:37		lest he esteem thee to be his e.;	121:43
break down the walls of mine e.;	101:57		if fierce winds become thine e.;	122: 7
avenge me of mine e.,	101:58		for the e. is on the alert,	127:11
have been scattered by their e.,	101:76		lest an e. come and destroy	132:57
into the hands of mine e.	101:96		of the power of this e.	JS 2:16
be polluted by mine e.,	101:97		the e. which held me bound.	2:17
smitten by the hands of mine e.,	103: 2			
to prevail against mine e.	103: 6		ENERGIES	
as mine e. come against you	103:24		with all the e. of my soul	1Ne 15:25
ye shall avange me of mine e.	103:25			
even in avenging me of mine e.,	103:26		ENERGY	
destroy and lay waste mine e.;	105:15		in the e. of my soul.	1Ne 16:24
down the towers of mine e.,	105:16		for I speak in the e. of my soul;	Al 5:43
down the towers of mine e.	105:30		and did urge them with great e.,	Mrm 2:23
and avenging me of mine e.	105:30		Father with all the e. of heart,	Mro 7:48
from the hands of all their e.	109:28			
anger be kindled against our e.;	121: 5		ENFORCE	
terrible in the midst of thine e.	122: 4		to e. it by the sword;	Al 1:12
if thine e. fall upon thee;	122: 6		any longer e. my commands.	Mro 9:18
with a drawn sword thine e. tear	122: 6		and magistrates to e. the laws	DC 134: 3
e. prow l around thee like wolves	122: 6			
e. come upon them and hinder	124:49		ENFORCED	
and were hindered by their e.,	124:51		were priestcraft to be e. among	Al 1:12
hindered by the hands of their e.,	124:53			
revealed unto me that me e.,	127: 1		ENGAGED	
shall triumph over all my e.,	127: 2		anxiously e. in a good cause,	DC 58:27
I have been pursued by my e.	128: 1			
e. shall become a prey unto	133:28		ENGRAVE	
and fear not thine e.;	136:17		shall e. on the plates of Nephi	Mrm 1: 4
Fear not thine e.,	136:30			
delivered you from your e.,	136:40		ENGRAVED	
and your e. triumph over you.	136:42		I e. that which is pleasing unto	2Ne 5:32
e. came to battle against them;	Mses 7:13			
fear of the e. of the people of	7:14		ENGRAVEN	
			are e. upon plates of brass.	1Ne 3: 3
ENEMY			e. upon the plates of brass,	3:12
angry because of mine e.?	2Ne 4:27		e. upon the plates of brass,	3:24
no more for the e. of my soul.	4:28		e. upon the plates of brass.	4:16
my way, but the ways of mine e.	4:33		e. upon the plates of brass,	5:10
an e. to all righteousness;	Mos 2:37		there should be an account e.	9: 3
and shall be an e. to God,	2:38		should be e. an account of the	9: 4
the natural man is an e. to God,	3:19		that I might e. upon them the	19: 1
an e. to all righteousness.	4:14		I did e. the record of my father,	19: 1
being an e. to God;	16: 5		prophecies have I e. upon them.	19: 1
also is the devil an e. to God.	16: 5		e. upon those plates of which I	19: 2
and an e. to the king,	19: 4		e. upon the plates of brass,	19:22
a chance for the e. of God to	27: 9		e. upon the plates of brass,	22: 1
Lamanites were an e. to them,	Al 22:34		are e. upon the plates of brass.	2Ne 4:15
the e. listeth to carry them.	26: 6		were e. upon the plates of brass;	5:12
even to take the life of their e.;	26:32		shalt e. many things upon them	5:30
who is an e. to all righteousness.	34:23		upon which I have e. these things.	5:31
except it were against an e.,	48:14		upon which these things are e.	Jac 1: 1
an e. which was innumerable.	58: 8		be e. upon his other plates,	1: 3
sorrowful because of their e.	3Ne 3:26		I should e. the heads of them	1: 4
thy neighbor and hate thine e.;	12:43		labor diligently to e. these words	4: 3
the devil is an e. unto God,	Mro 7:12		the records of our wars are e.	Jar 1:14
the e. of all righteousness,	9: 6		the record of this people is e.	Om 1:11
and this because of the e.	DC 37: 1		were e. on the plates of brass,	Mos 1: 3
and the e. shall not overcome.	38: 9		were e. on the plates of brass;	1:16
behold, the e. is combined.	38:12		were e. on the plates of brass,	10:16

ENGRAVEN 290 ENOCH

ENGRAVEN
and it was e. on plates of ore.	Mos 21:27
were e. on the plates of brass,	28:11
e. upon your countenances?	Al 5:19
e. on the plates which were called	3Ne 5:10
e. upon the plates of Nephi,	26:11
e. upon the plates of Nephi;	DC 10:38
e. upon the plates of Nephi	10:40
e. upon the plates of Nephi	10:45

ENGRAVING
because of the difficulty of e.	Jac 4: 1

ENGRAVINGS
e., which were upon the plates of	1Ne 4:24
e. which are upon the plates of	13:23
they will be pleased with mine e.	2Ne 5:32
brought unto him with e. on it;	Om 1:20
and he did interpret the e. by	1:20
therefore he could read these e.,	Mos 1: 4
plates which are filled with e.,	8: 9
e. that are on the plates.	8:11
whereby he could interpret such e.;	21:28
of brass, which contain these e.,	Al 37: 3
all those e. which were in the	63:12
sacred e. concerning this people.	Mrm 1: 3
concerning the e. of old	DC 8: 1
you shall translate the e. which	10:41
first part of the e. of Nephi,	10:45

ENGULF
is prepared to e. the wicked—	He 3:29

ENISH-GO-ON-DOSH
Is called in Egyptian E.;	Fac 2: 5

ENJOINED
last effort which is e. on us	DC 123: 6

ENJOY
and every man may e. his rights	Mos 29:32
not e. their rights and privileges.	Al 30:27
to e. that which they are	DC 88:32
to e. that which they might	88:32
and to e. the communion and	107:19
which glory we do not now e.	130: 2
e. the words of eternal life	Mses 6:59

ENJOYED
might have e. our possessions	1Ne 17:21
had e. peace but a few years.	3Ne 6:16

ENJOYMENT
a perfect knowledge of their e.,	2Ne 9:14
the e. of their eternal felicity.	DC 77: 3

ENLARGE
to e. the wounds of those who	Jac 2: 9
for it beginneth to e. my soul;	Al 32:28
E. the place of thy tent, and	3Ne 22: 2
and e. thy borders forever,	Mro 10:31
which shall greatly e. the soul	DC 121:42

ENLARGED
Therefore, hell hath e. herself,	2Ne 15:14
have e. the memory of this people,	Al 37: 8
her borders must be e.,	DC 82:14
until the borders of Zion are e.	107:74
therefore, they cannot be e.,	132:17
borders of my people may be e.,	133: 9

ENLIGHTEN
to e. my understanding,	Al 32:28
of me and I did e. thy mine;	DC 6:15
which shall e. your mind,	11:13
For by my Spirit will I e. them,	76:10
sent forth into the world to e.	136:33

ENLIGHTENED
once e. by the Spirit of God,	Al 24:30
understanding doth begin to be e.,	32:34
firmness when they are once e.,	He 15:10
been e. by the Spirit of truth;	DC 6:15
out understandings were e.,	76:12

And whoso is e. by the Spirit	DC 91: 5
Our minds being now e.,	JS 2:74

ENLIGHTENETH
the Spirit e. every man through	DC 84:46
him who e. your eyes,	88:11

ENLIVEN
the body and to e. the soul.	DC 59:19

ENMITY
in that day the e. of man,	DC 101:26
of man, and the e. of beasts,	101:26
yea, the e. of all flesh, shall	101:26
e. between thee and the woman,	Mses 4:21

ENOCH
taken the Zion of E. into mine	DC 38: 4
whom ye say is the God of E.,	45:11
which was after the order of E.,	76:57
assembly and church of E.,	76:67
some of Isaiah, and some of E.;	76:100
The Lord spake unto E.	78: 1
the city of E. [Joseph], for a	78: 4
and my servant Gazelam, or E.	78: 9
And from Noah till E., through	84:15
And from E. to Abel,	84:16
E. was twenty-five years old	107:48
Jared, E., and Methuselah,	107:53
all written in the book of E.,	107:57
E. also, and they who were with	133:54
and she conceived and bare E.,	Mses 5:42
after the name of his son, E.	5:42
And unto E. was born Irad,	5:43
and Irad, the son of E.,	5:49
and begat E.; and Jared lived,	6:21
Jared lived, after he begat E.,	6:21
taught E. in all the ways of	6:21
And E. lived sixty-five years,	6:25
that E. journeyed in the land,	6:26
E., my son, prophesy unto this	6:27
when E. had heard these words,	6:31
And the Lord said unto E.:	6:32
And the Lord spake unto E.,	6:35
that E. went forth in the land,	6:37
And E. continued his speech, saying:	6:43
E. spake forth the words of God,	6:47
that E. continued his speech,	7: 1
time forth E. began to prophesy,	7: 2
land of Sharon, and the land of E.,	7: 9
E. continued to call upon all the	7:12
And so great was the faith of E.,	7:13
so powerful was the word of E.,	7:13
And E. continued his preaching	7:19
that E. talked with the Lord;	7:20
But the Lord said unto E.:	7:20
that the Lord showed unto E.	7:21
And the Lord said unto E.:	7:21
E. also beheld the residue of	7:22
E. beheld, and lo, all the	7:23
and E. was high and lifted up,	7:24
E. beheld angels descending out	7:27
and E. bore record of it, saying:	7:28
And E. said unto the Lord:	7:29
The Lord said unto E.: Behold	7:32
that the Lord spake unto E.,	7:41
told E. all the doings of the	7:41
wherefore E. knew, and looked upon	7:41
E. also saw Noah, and his family;	7:42
E. saw that Noah built an ark;	7:43
E. saw this, he had bitterness	7:44
but the Lord said unto E.:	7:44
came to pass that E. looked;	7:45
E. saw the day of the coming of	7:47
that E. looked upon the earth;	7:48
when E. heard the earth mourn,	7:49
E. continued his cry unto the	7:50
and he covenanted with E.,	7:51
that E. cried unto the Lord,	7:54
the Lord said unto E.;	7:55
again E. wept and cried unto	7:58
And E. beheld the Son of Man	7:59
And the Lord said unto E.:	7:60

ENOCH

And the Lord said unto E.:	Mses 7:63
E. saw the day of the coming of	7:65
the Lord showed E. all things,	7:67
days of Zion, in the days of E.,	7:68
E. and all his people walked	7:69
days of E. were four hundred	8: 1
that Methuselah, the son of E.,	8: 2
fulfilled, which he made to E.;	8: 2
covenanted with E. that Noah	8: 2
even as it was given unto E.	8:19

ENORMITY
seeing the e. of their number,	Al 52: 5
the e. of our numbers,	57:13

ENOS
wherefore, I said unto my son E.:	Jac 7:27
THE BOOK OF E.	En 1:hd
I, E., knowing my father that he	1: 1
E., thy sins are forgiven thee,	1: 5
I, E., knew that God could not	1: 6
after I, E., had heard these words,	1:11
I, E., knew it would be according	1:17
I, E., went about among the people	1:19
commandment of my father, E.,	Jar 1: 1
E. was ordained at the age of	DC 107:44
he called Seth, E., Cainan,	107:53
a son, and he called his name E.	Mses 6: 3
and begat E., and prophesied	6:13
taught his son E. in the ways	6:13
wherefore E. prophesied also.	6:13
Seth lived, after he begat E.,	6:14
E. lived ninety years, and	6:17
E. and the residue of the people	6:17
E. lived, after he begat Cainan,	6:18
days of E. were nine hundred	6:18

ENOUGH
the word of God, for we have e.!	2Ne 28:29
them that shall say, We have e.,	28:30
Thou hast had signs e.; will ye	Al 30:44
not be room e. to receive it.	3Ne 24:10
that he can say e. in my cause;	DC 24:10
and there is e. and to spare;	104:17
loan e. to deliver yourself from	104:84
Is there not room e. on the	117: 8
blackening deeds are e. to	123:10
I am well e. off."	JS 2:20

ENROLLED
names e. with the people of God.	DC 85: 3
e. in the book of the law of God;	85: 7

ENSAMPLE
this is an e. unto all those	DC 68: 2
And this is the e. unto them,	68: 3
this shall be an e. for all the	72:23
this is also an e.	72:26
the e. which I give unto you,	78:13
this is an e. unto you for	88:136
this is an e. unto all people,	98:38
be an e. unto all the stakes	119: 7

ENSIGN
lift up an e. to the nations	2Ne 15:26
stand for an e. of the people;	21:10
shall set up an e. for the nations,	21:12
be an e. unto the people,	DC 64:42
And lift up an e. of peace,	105:39
for an e., and for the gathering	113: 6

ENSNARE
to e. the people of the Lord.	1Ne 22:14
devised to e. the hearts of men.	Al 28:13

ENSUED
confusion and bad feeling e.—	JS 2: 6

ENSUING
in the e. month "May, 1829",	JS 2:68

ENTANGLE
e. not yourselves in sin, but let	DC 88:86

ENTANGLED
was e. again in the vanities of	DC 20: 5

ENTER
did e. into that strange building.	1Ne 8:33
after they did e. into that building	8:33
e. into the kingdom of God;	15:34
ye wicked ones, e. into the rock,	2Ne 12:10
The Lord will e. into judgment	13:14
the gate, by which they should e.,	31: 9
the gate by which ye should e.	31:17
the gate by which ye should e.	31:17
if ye will e. in by the way,	32: 5
and e. into the narrow gate	33: 9
that they might e. into his rest,	Jac 1: 7
in his wrath they should not e. in,	1: 7
and e. in at the strait gate,	6:11
are willing to e. into a covenant	Mos 5: 5
wolves e. not and devour his flock?	Al 5:59
if a wolf e. his flock doth he not	5:59
no ravenous wolf to e. among you,	5:60
and e. into a covenant with him	7:15
e. and partake of the fruit of	12:21
and these shall e. into my rest.	12:34
that he shall not e. into my rest.	12:35
not e. into the rest of the Lord;	12:36
let us e. into the rest of God,	12:37
they also might e. into his rest—	13: 6
that ye may also e. into that rest.	13:13
might e. into the rest of the Lord.	13:16
the last day and e. into his rest.	13:29
might e. into the rest of the Lord	16:17
would e. into a correspondence	31: 4
they might not e. into temptation.	31:10
to e. into their synagogues to	32: 3
of the devil did e. into them,	40:13
e. into a covenant that they will	46:20
that would not e. into a covenant	46:35
to e. the fort by any other way,	49:19
about to e. the city by night.	57:10
do e. into the rest of the Lord	60:13
in whatsoever place he did e.,	62: 4
to e. into a covenant that they	62:16
the Nephites who did e. therein	63: 6
many more people did e. into it;	63: 7
began to e. into the church—	He 3:33
and did e. into their hearts,	5:45
did e. into their covenants and	6:21
ye have suffered to e. your hearts,	7:26
that he should e. into the city;	13: 4
and e. into a covenant that they	3Ne 5: 4
who did not e. into a covenant,	5: 5
they did e. into a covenant	6:28
e. into a covenant to destroy	6:29
e. into the kingdom of heaven.	12:20
these things to e. into your heart;	12:29
e. into thy closet, and when	13: 6
E. ye in at the strait gate;	14:13
e. into the kingdom of heaven;	14:21
lest ye e. into temptation;	18:18
no unclean thing can e. into his	27:19
E. ye in at the strait gate;	27:33
e. into the rest of the Lord,	Mro 7: 3
e. into a covenant with me,	DC 5: 3
that you may e. into my rest.	19: 9
cannot e. in at the strait gate	22: 2
e. ye in at the gate, as I have	22: 4
shouldst e. into temptation.	23: 1
in whatsoever place ye shall e.,	24:15
lest you e. into temptation	31:12
e. into the joy of his Lord,	51:19
you e. not into temptation,	61:39
e. into the joy of these things.	70:18
And in whatsoever house ye e.,	75:19
And in whatsoever house ye e.,	75:20
should not e. into his rest	84:24
whatsoever village or city ye e.,	84:93
who shall e. upon the threshold	109:13
city thy servants shall e.,	109:39
city thy servants shall e.,	109:41
when every man shall e. into his	121:32
general church recorder can e.	128: 4
a man must e. into this order	131: 2

ENTER / EPHAH

ENTER
He may e. into the other,	DC 131: 4
permitted to e. into my glory.	132: 4
and e. into their exaltation;	132:26
can in nowise e. into my glory,	132:27
e. ye into my law and ye shall be	132:32
if ye e. not into my law ye cannot	132:33
not permitting any person to e. into	OD
was come near to e. into Egypt,	Abr 2:22
It seemed to e. with great force	JS 2:12

ENTERED
ye have e. in by the gate;	2Ne 31:18
if ye e. in by the way ye shoul	31:18
after ye have e. in by the way.	32: 1
you that have e. into the covenant	Mos 5: 8
had e. into a covenant with God	6: 1
but who had e. into the covenant	6: 2
who having e. into a treaty with	7:21
have e. into a covenant with him,	18:10
have e. into a covenant to serve	18:13
had e. into a covenant with God	21:31
also e. into a covenant with God,	21:32
he e. the city by another way,	Al 8:18
And as he e. the city he was	8:19
and e. into the rest of the Lord	13:12
as Ammon e. the land of Ishmael,	17:20
e. into one of their synagogues,	21: 5
And we have e. into their houses	26:29
have also e. into their temples	26:29
they had e. into a covenant	43:11
and e. into a covenant of peace.	44:15
as many as e. into a covenant	44:15
e. into a covenant with him	44:20
e. into a covenant to keep the	46:31
he e. the city Nephi with his	47:31
who had e. into this covenant	53:15
who had not e. into a covenant	53:16
they e. into a covenant to fight	53:17
who e. into this covenant and	53:18
e. into the rest of their God.	57:36
they had e. into this covenant	62:17
and they all e. into a covenant,	He 1:11
band, who had e. into a covenant	2: 3
who had e. into the covenant,	6:22
who had e. into a covenant to	3Ne 6: 3
those who had e. into a covenant	7:11
yet e. into the heart of man.	DC 76:10
e. into the ears of the Lord	98: 2
and e. into and sealed by the	132: 7
and hath e. into his exaltation	132:29
have e. into his exaltation,	132:37
e. into a covenant with Satan,	Mses 5:49
day that Noah e. into the ark	JS 1:42

ENTERETH
nothing e. into his rest save	3Ne 27:19

ENTERING
e. into their synagogues,	Al 32: 1

ENTHRONED
where thou sittest e., with glory,	DC 109:77

ENTICE
e. our first parents to partake	He 6:26

ENTICED
was e. by the one or the other.	2Ne 2:16

ENTICETH
and inviteth and e. to sin,	Mro 7:12
inviteth and e. to do good	7:13
inviteth and e. to do good,	7:13

ENTICING
might not be e. unto my people	2Ne 5:21
given away to the e. of him	He 7:16

ENTICINGS
to the e. of that cunning one.	2Ne 9:39
to the e. of the Holy Spirit,	Mos 3:19

ENTIRE
the e. destruction of my people.	WM 1: 2
would prove their e. destruction.	Al 1:12
not long maintain an e. peace	51: 2
slmost the e. destruction of the	He 2:13
people down to an e. destruction,	6:28
an e. separation of the righteous	DC 63:54

ENTIRELY
e. forgetting the Lord their God.	Al 47:36
e. lost in a strife of words and	JS 2: 6
power which e. overcame me,	2:15
ascended till he e. disappeared,	2:43
as to render me e. unable.	2:48
my strength e. failed me,	2:48

ENTITLE
shall e. him to a license,	DC 20:64

ENTITLED
is justly e. to a re-hearing,	DC 102:33
their decisions are not e. to the	107:29

ENTRANCE
save it was by their place of e.	Al 49: 4
any other way save by the e.,	49:18
about, save it were by the e.	49:18
of security by the place of e.;	49:20
armies before the place of e.,	49:21
they were on the east, by the e.;	62:21
the watch by the e. of the city,	He 1:20

ENTREATED
and gentle; easy to be e.;	Al 7:23
were his people easy to be e.,	He 7: 7

ENTRUSTED
which have been e. with me;	Al 37: 1
God has e. you with these things,	37:14
ministry wherewith thou wast e.	39: 4
whatsoever thing they were e.	53:20
been e. to me by the hand of	Mrm 6: 6
been e. with these things,	DC 3: 5
things which I have e. unto you,	5: 9
which I have e. with thee.	5:31
which I have e. unto him.	9: 1
wherewith you have been e.;	10: 7
whatsoever shall be e. to his	12: 8
e. with the commandments	69: 1
that shall be e. unto his care,	124:113

ENUMERATED
iniquities which cannot be e.—	Mos 29:36

ENVIETH
long, and is kind, and e. not,	Mro 7:45

ENVY
The e. of Ephraim also shall	2Ne 21:13
Ephraim shall not e. Judah,	21:13
that they should not e.;	26:32
you who is not stripped of e.?	Al 5:29
as the e. and wrath of man have	DC 127: 2

ENVYING
to the e. of them who belong	Mrm 8:28
unto e., and strifes, and malice,	8:36

ENVYINGS
churches built up which cause e.,	2Ne 26:21
babblings, and in e. and strife;	Al 1:32
yea, there were e., and strife,	4: 9
lyings, and deceivings, and e.,	16:18
e., strifes, malice, persecutions	He 13:22
lyings, and deceivings, and e.,	3Ne 21:19
your priestcrafts, and your e.,	30: 2
And there were no e., nor	4Ne 1:16
contentions, and e., and strifes,	DC 101: 6

EPHAH
seed of a homer shall yield an e.	2Ne 15:10

EPHRAIM

EPHRAIM
Syria is confederate with E.	2Ne	17: 2
Syria, E., and the son of Remaliah,		17: 5
shall E. be broken that it be not		17: 8
the head of E. is Samaria,		17: 9
from the day that E. departed		17:17
all the people shall know, even E.		19: 9
Manasseh, E.; and Ephraim, Manasseh;		19:21
Manasseh, Ephraim; and E., Manasseh;		19:21
The envy of E. also shall depart,		21:13
E. shall not envy Judah,		21:13
and Judah shall not vex E.		21:13
he came to the hill E.,	Eth	7: 9
of the record of the stick of E.	DC	27: 5
are not of the blood of E.,		64:36
of Jesse as well as of E.,		113: 4
treasures unto the children of E.,		133:30
even the children of E.		133:32
blessing upon the head of E.		133:34

EPISTLE
Therefore he wrote an e.,	Al	54: 4
had brought an e. to Moroni.		54: 4
therefore I will close my e. by		54:11
Now I close my e.		54:14
when he had received this e.,		54:15
wrote another e. unto Moroni,		54:15
and I close my e. to Moroni.		54:24
when Moroni had received this e.		55: 1
as I have stated in my e.;		55: 2
would not grant unto me mine e.,		55: 3
received an e. from Helaman,		56: 1
an e. from Ammoron, the king,		57: 1
But I sent an e. unto the king,		57: 2
And Ammoron refused mine e.,		57: 3
And now, behold, close mine e.		58:41
and had read Helaman's e.,		59: 1
sent an e. to Pahoran,		59: 3
when Moroni had sent this e.		59: 4
I direct mine e. to Pahoran,		60: 1
And except ye grant mine e.,		60:25
And thus I close mine e.		60:36
after Moroni had sent his e.		61: 1
received an e. from Pahoran,		61: 1
in your e. you have censured		61: 9
I do joy in receiving your e.,		61:19
And now I close mine e. to my		61:21
when Moroni had received this e.		62: 1
received an e. from the leader	3Ne	3: 1
I write this e. unto you,		3: 2
Therefore I have written this e.,		3: 5
I write this e. unto you,		3:10
when Lachoneus received this e.		3:11
hearken to the e. of Giddianhi,		3:12
king of the Lamanites sent an e.	Mrm	3: 4
I, Mormon, wrote an e. unto		6: 2
that he wrote an e. unto Shiz,	Eth	15: 4
when Shiz had received this e.		15: 5
wrote an e. unto Coriantumr,		15: 5
wrote again an e. unto Shiz,		15:18
An e. of my father Mormon,	Mro	8: 1
intent I have written this e.		8: 6
The second e. of Mormon to		9:hd
And an e. and subscription,	DC	58:51
reading the E. of James,	JS	2:11

EQUAL
the root and the top may be e. in	Jac	5:66
the root and the top thereof e.,		5:73
and the fruits were e.;		5:74
man should have an e. chance	Mos	29:38
and thus they were all e.,	Al	1:26
which is e. to a senine of gold;		11: 5
silver was e. to a senine of gold,		11: 7
of gold is e. to three shiblons.		11:19
all men were on e. grounds.		30:11
have an e. chance to fight;		49:22
this change was not e. to that	3Ne	28:39
every man e. according to his	DC	51: 3
temporal things you shall be e.,		70:14
he makes them e. in power,		76:95
may be e. in the bonds of		78: 5
are not e. in earthly things		78: 6

ERROR
e. in obtaining heavenly things;	DC	78: 6
And you are to be e.,		82:17
e. claims on the properties,		82:17
and be made e. with him.		88:107
man may have an e. privilege.		88:122
are accounted as e. with thee		90: 6
e. in authority and power		107:24
e. in authority to that of		107:26
e. in authority in the affairs of		107:36
e. in authority in the affairs of the		107:37
office of a bishop is not e. unto		107:68
company bear an e. proportion,		136: 8
one day in Kolob is e. to	Fac	2: 1
which is e. with Kolob in		2: 4

EQUALITY
should be an e. among all men;	Mos	27: 3

EQUALLY
e. zealous in endeavoring to	JS	2: 9

EQUITY
and reprove with e. for the meek	2Ne	21: 4
and reprove with e. for the meek		30: 9
full of grace, e., and truth,	Al	9:26
with e. and justice in my hands.		10:21
who is full of grace, e., and truty.		13: 9
judgment-seat with justice and e.;	He	3:20
judgment-seat with justice and e.;		3:37
according to e. and justice.	3Ne	6: 4
according to e. and justice.	DC	102:16
as will administer the law in e.		134: 3

ERASTUS: see SNOW, Erastus.

ERE
e. he is aware, he is left	DC	121:38

ERECT
caused them to e. fortifications	Al	50:10
he did e. him an exceedingly	Eth	10: 6

ERECTED
he caused a tower to be e.,	Mos	2: 7
And he caused towers to be e.	Al	50: 4

ERECTING
e. small forts, or places of	Al	48: 8

ERR
And now, if I do e., even did they	1Ne	19: 6
even did they e. of old; not that I		19: 6
who lead thee cause thee to e.	2Ne	13:12
of this people cause them to e.;		19:16
I know that no man can e.;		25: 7
plainly that ye cannot e.		25:20
in many instances they do e.,		28:14
you plainly that ye cannot e.,	Al	5:43
understand, that we cannot e.;		13:23
ye do greatly e., and ye ought to		33: 2
Now in this thing they did e.,	3Ne	1:24
and in these things they do e.,	DC	10:63
and they e. in many instances		33: 4

ERRAND
obtained mine e. from the Lord.	Jac	1:17
haste upon their e. and mission.	DC	61: 7
agents, ye are on the Lord's e.;		64:29
the Lord's e. in the day when		133:58

ERRED
They also that e. in spirit	2Ne	27:35
And inasmuch as they e.	DC	1:25

ERROR
many of the e. of their ways,	Al	37: 8
of the e. which they were in,	3Ne	1:25
to a knowledge of their e.		1:25
this gross e. should be removed	Mro	8: 6
them of the e. of their ways.	DC	6:11
discover an e. in the decision		102:20
people think they were in e.	JS	2: 9

ERRORS

ERRORS
they had fallen into great e.,	Al	31: 9
and sophistry to prove their e.,	JS	2: 9
fell into many foolish e.,		2:28

ESAIAS
some of Elias, and some of E.,	DC	76:100
And God under the hand of E.;		84:11
And E. received it under the		84:12
E. also lived in the days of		84:13

ESCAPE
wilt thou make a way for mine e.	2Ne	4:33
who prepareth a way for our e.		9:10
and they had made their e.—	Al	47:32
and they would make their e.;		56:40
none did e. who were not slain,	3Ne	5: 4
swifter than the Lamanites' did e.,	Mrm	5: 7
and there is none to e.;	DC	1: 2
that you may e. the hands of		10: 5
might e. the power of the enemy,		38:31
desire to e. their enemies,		54: 3
the saints also shall hardly e.;		63:34
their souls may e. the wrath		88:85
and who shall e. it?		97:22
Zion shall e. if she observe		97:25
enemy shall e. my vengeance,		98:28
guilty among you may not e.;		104: 7
you cannot e. my wrath in		104: 8
ye cannot e. the buffetings		104: 9
generation of vipers shall not e.		121:23
I make a way for your e.,		132:50

ESCAPED
to them that are e. of Israel.	2Ne	14: 2
as are e. of the house of Jacob,		20:20
we have e. from the Nephites,	Al	55: 8
had e. into the south countries,	Mrm	6:15
e. into the country southward		8: 2
through the providence of God, e.,	DC	135: 2

ESCUTCHEON
on the e. of the State of Illinois,	DC	135: 7

ESPECIAL
and e. witnesses of my name,	DC	27:12
to be e. witnesses unto the		107:25
take e. care of your family		126: 3
and in an e. manner		128:17

ESPECIALLY
more e. given unto those who are	1Ne	19:10
and e. unto our seed,	2Ne	28: 2
and e. unto my people.		33: 3
e. among this my people;	Mos	29:32
yea, and more e. by our priests;	Al	32: 5
and more e. their women and	He	11:33
e. among the people of Nephi.	Mrm	2:11
and more e. the elephants	Eth	9:19
and more e. in Colesville;	DC	37: 2
more e. for those that have not		42:45
waters, and more e. hereafter;		61: 4
yea, and more e. upon these waters.		61: 5
e. mine aged servant Joseph		90:25

ESPOUSE
if any man e. a virgin,	DC	132:61
and desire to e. another,		132:61
and if he e. the second,		132:61

ESPOUSED
the cause, which ye have e.,	DC	78: 4
of the ten virgins, after she is e.,		132:63

ESROM
among whom were E. and	Eth	8: 4

ESSAYING
e. to keep my commandments.	DC	124:85
and are e. to be my saints,		125: 2

ESSENTIAL
and e. to our salvation,	DC	128:15

ESTABLISHED

ESTABLISH
shall e. the truth of the first,	1Ne	13:40
to e. the earth, to cause to		21: 8
hath said, I will e. my word.	2Ne	11: 3
and to e. it with judgment		19: 7
him good will he e. his word;		27:14
once more e. peace in the land.	WM	1:18
again began to e. the kingdom	Mos	10: 1
Limhi began to e. the kingdom		19:27
to e. peace among his people.		19:27
that he might e. churches		25:19
This is my church, and I will e. it;		27:13
who would e. the laws of God,		29:13
to e. peace throughout the land,		29:14
even began to e. a church	Al	1: 6
did e. the affairs of the church;		1:28
endeavor to e. Amlici to be king		2: 2
began to e. peace in the land,		3:24
began to e. the church more fully;		4: 4
began to e. a church in the land		5: 3
began to e. the church of God		5: 5
to e. the order of the church		6: 4
and to e. the words of Amulek,		12: 1
e. peace in the land in his days;		13:18
thy brethren, and e. my word;		17:11
did e. a church among them.		19:35
and by this did e. his church;		29:11
did e. his church among them;		29:13
that they might e. a kingdom		43:29
went forth to e. the church		45:22
and e. him to be their king		46: 5
to e. and to exercise authority		46:34
and to e. a king over the land.		51: 5
did e. again the church of God,		62:46
in which Alma did e. the church	3Ne	5:12
did e. peace in all the land.		6: 3
and to e. a king over the land,		6:30
not e. a king over the land;		7: 1
their leaders did e. their laws,		7:11
But they did e. very strict laws		7:14
and e. it for my doctrine,		11:40
that I will e. my people,		20:21
this people will I e. in this land,		20:22
e. again among them my Zion;		21: 1
will e. my church among them,		21:22
and did e. himself king over	Eth	10: 9
to e. his righteousness,	DC	1:16
and e. the cause of Zion;		6: 6
I will e. my church among		10:53
I do that I may e. my gospel,		10:63
him will I e. upon my rock,		10:69
and e. the cause of Zion.		11: 6
and e. the cause of Zion.		12: 6
bring forth and e. this work;		12: 7
bring forth and e. my Zion.		14: 6
I will e. a church by your hand;		31: 7
shall be sufficient to e. you,		42:67
in this place, and e. a store,		57: 8
and e. a house, even a house		88:119
in this way they may e. Zion.		101:74
Zion, and e. her waste places,		101:75
e. the children of Zion upon		103:35
e. a house, even a house of prayer,		109: 8
We ask thee, Holy Father, to e.		109:24
he aspireth to e. his counsel		124:84
to e. their own tenets and	JS	2: 9

ESTABLISHED
be e. by the mouth of the Lamb;	1Ne	13:41
they both shall be e. in one;		13:41
who are in the east shall be e.;		21:13
which kingdom is e. among them		22:22
shall be e. in all their lands	2Ne	9: 2
of the Lord's house shall be e.		12: 2
surely ye shall not be e.		17: 9
e. peace in the land of Zarahemla,	Mos	2: 4
because thou hast e. a church		26:17
and they shall be e.,		26:17
but he had e. peace in the land,		29:40
nevertheless he had e. laws,	Al	1: 1
e. by the voice of the people		2: 3
in the church which was e.		5: 2
of the church, which was e. in		6: 1

ESTABLISHED 295 ETERNAL

unto the church which was e.	Al	6: 8
they are e. again in the way of		7: 4
e. the order of the church,		8: 1
the church which thou hast e.		8:11
having been e. by king Mosiah.		11: 4
And Alma e. a church in the		15:13
having e. the church at Sidom,		15:17
after the church had been e.		16:21
when they had e. a church in		20: 1
which was e. by my father,		27: 9
were e. in the land of Jershon,		28: 1
and a church also e. in the land		28: 1
were e. in the land of Jershon,		30: 1
they having e. peace between		51: 1
who had e. armies to protect		52:15
there was once more peace e.		62:42
had e. again peace between	He	2: 1
continual peace e. in the land,		3:23
Gadianton the robber had e.		3:23
were e. by the voice of the people,		5: 2
which had been e. among them.		6: 3
which was e. by Gadianton!		7:25
the first church which was e.	3Ne	5:12
e. this great peace in the land.		6: 6
e. according to the minds of		7:14
should be e. in this land,		21: 4
In righteousness shalt thou be e.;		22:14
witnesses shall these things be e.;	Eth	5: 4
that he had e. himself king		10:10
everlasting covenant might be e.;	DC	1:22
witnesses shall every word be e.		6:28
shall be e. by the testimony		6:31
being regularly organized and e.		20: 1
church was organized and e.		21: 3
church to be e. among them;		28: 8
that this church have I e.		33: 5
every word shall be e. against		42:80
be e. as a printer unto the		57:11
whatsoever land they shall be e.		72:23
hath e. the foundations of		78:15
and e. his feet, and set him		78:16
his church, e. in the last days		84: 2
And truth is e. in her bowels;		84:101
e. for their instruction in all		88:127
which I have suffered to be e.,		101:77
have I e. the Constitution of		101:80
to the land of Zion, to be e.,		103:13
to be organized and e.,		104: 1
which I have e. for my stake		104:40
by our fathers, be e. forever.		109:54
every word may be e.		128: 3
of Egypt was e. by Pharaoh,	Abr	1:25
e. his kingdom and judged his		1:26
that order e. by the fathers		1:26

ESTABLISHING

e. peace among the fruit of thy	2Ne	3:12
e. churches, and consecrating	Al	23: 4
e. the affairs of the storehouse	DC	78: 3
printing thereof, and for e. Zion.		84:104

ESTABLISHMENT

e. of the church became general	Al	16:15
permanent and everlasting e.	DC	78: 4
Ozondah [mercantile e.] stands,		104:39
of the Ozondah [mercantile e.],		104:39
of the Ozondah [mercantile e.]		104:40
whole Ozondah [mercantile e.],		104:41

ESTATE

they who keep their first e.	Abr	3:26
they who keep not their first e.		3:26
those who keep their first e.;		3:26
they who keep their second e.		3:26
and kept not his first e.;		3:28

ESTEEM

things which some men e. to be	1Ne	19: 7
and e. them as things of naught.	2Ne	33: 2
and I e. it as of great worth,		33: 3
yet we did e. him stricken,	Mos	14: 4
not e. one flesh above another,		23: 7
should e. his neighbor as himself,		27: 4

my brethren, for I e. you as such,	Mos	29: 5
e. him more than any other man;		29:40
they did e. him, yea, exceedingly,		29:40
did e. him as a great prophet,	He	11:18
let every man e. his brother as	DC	38:24
let every man e. his brother as		28:25
lest he e. thee to be his enemy;		121:43
shall e. my words as naught	Mses	1:41

ESTEEMED

and he shall be e. highly among	2Ne	3: 7
shall be e. as the potter's clay.		27:27
field shall be e. as a forest.		27:28
was despised, and we e. him not.	Mos	14: 3
being e. as filthiness;	Al	32: 3
e. by their brethren as dross;		32: 3
e. by Alma and his fathers to be		50:38
but they e. him as naught,	Eth	13:13
they e. lightly my counsel;	DC	101: 8

ESTEEMETH

the Lord e. all flesh in one;	1Ne	17:35

ESTEEMING

not e. himself above his hearers,	Al	1:26

ETC

into the promised land e.	1Ne	1:hd
journeyings in the wilderness e.	2Ne	1:hd
is called the Book of Helaman e.	He	1:hd
of power, to move, to act, e.	DC	77: 4
with jovial company, e.,	JS	2:28
pastors, teachers, evangelists, e.	AoF	6
interpretation of tongues, e.		7

ETERNAL

JESUS is the CHRIST, the E. GOD,	T Pg	
course of the Lord is one e. round.	1Ne	10:19
even the Son of the E. Father!		11:21
of the justice of the E. God,		12:18
is the Son of the E. Father,		13:40
unto peace and life e., or		14: 7
the e. gulf of misery and woe.	2Ne	1:13
the e. destruction of both soul		1:22
and your own e. welfare.		1:25
of God and his e. purposes,		2:12
to bring about his e. purposes		2:15
to choose liberty and e. life,		2:27
his words, and choose e. life,		2:28
And not choose e. death,		2:29
the presence of the E. God,		9: 8
and it is his e. word,		9:16
spiritually-minded is life e.		9:39
death or the way of e. life.		10:23
into the e. kingdom of God,		10:25
e. plan of deliverance from death.		11: 5
Jesus is the Christ, the E. God;		26:12
path which leads to e. life;		31:18
Ye shall have e. life.		31:20
endure to the end, which is life e.		33: 4
until ye shall obtain e. life.	Jac	6:11
of eternity, and of e. punishment.		7:18
they had an e. hatred against us,		7:24
speak concerning e. life,	En	1: 3
everlasting salvation and e. life,	Mos	5:15
they have an e. hatred towards		10:17
the very E. Father of heaven and		15: 4
they have e. life through Christ,		15:23
or have e. life, being redeemed by		15:24
little children also have e. life.		15:25
who is the very E. Father.		16:15
that ye may have e. life—		18: 9
may he grant unto you e. life,		18:13
that thou shalt have e. life;		26:20
soul was racked with e. torment;		27:29
and they shall have e. life.		28: 7
all men should have e. life.	Al	1: 4
of souls sent to the e. world,		3:26
to reap e. happiness or eternal		3:26
or e. misery, according to the		3:26
and such an one hath not e. life.		5:28
unto him, he shall have e. life,		7:16
his course is one e. round.		7:20

ETERNAL   ETERNITY

Son of God the very E. Father?	Al	11:38
Yea, he is the very E. Father		11:39
are they that shall have e. life,		11:40
Holy Spirit, which is one E. God,		11:44
hope that ye shall receive e. life;		13:29
I do that I may have this e. life		22:15
through faith, unto e. salvation,		25:16
and doom us to e. despair?		26:19
to the great plan of the E. God		34: 9
be an infinite and e. sacrifice.		34:10
Son of God, yea, infinite and e.		34:14
great and e. plan of redemption.		34:16
your body in that e. world.		34:34
I was racked with e. torment,		36:12
about his great and e. purposes;		37: 7
and his course is one e. round.		37:12
a straight course to e. bliss,		37:44
punishment, which also was e.		42:16
as e. also as the life of the woul.		42:16
about his great and e. purposes,		42:26
of this world into an e. world,		48:23
will wage a war which shall be e.,		54:20
or to their e. extinction.		54:20
which is e., and which fadeth not	He	5: 8
that precious gift of e. life,		5: 8
even unto that life which is e.		8:15
which is in our great and E. Head.		13:38
unto me ye shall have e. life.	3Ne	9:14
to the end will I give e. life.		15: 9
his great and e. purpose, in	Mrm	5:14
yea, the E. Father of heaven,		6:22
For the e. purposes of the Lord		8:22
from this e. band of death,		9:13
sword of the justice of the E. God	Eth	8:23
O God, the E. Father,	Mro	4: 3
O God, the E. Father,		4: 3
O God, the E. Father,		5: 2
O God, the E. Father,		5: 2
to be raised unto life e.,		7:41
hope of his glory and of e. life,		9:25
ask God, the E. Father,		10: 4
the covenants of the E. Father		10:31
the E. Judge of both quick and		10:34
and his course is one e. round.	DC	3: 2
behold I grant unto you e. life,		5:22
he that hath e. life is rich.		6: 7
in this land might have e. life;		10:50
he that hath e. life is rich.		11: 7
the end you shall have e. life,		14: 7
shall be blessed unto e. life;		18: 8
Again, it is written *e. damnation*;		19: 7
E. punishment is God's		19:11
shall receive a crown of e. life;		20:14
in heaven, who is infinite and e.,		20:17
in all things, whould have e. life,		20:26
are one God, infinite and e.,		20:28
O God, the E. Father, we ask		20:77
thee, O God, the E. Father,		20:77
O God, the E. Father, we ask		20:79
thee, O God, the E. Father,		20:79
on my right hand unto e. life;		29:27
raised in immortality unto e. life,		29:43
believe not unto e. damnation;		29:44
you shall be blessed unto e. life.		30: 8
whose course is one e. round,		35: 1
that which bringeth life e.		42:61
honor and the riches of e. life,		43:25
gave I power to obtain e. life.		45: 8
they also might have e. life if		46:14
for they shall inherit e. life.		50: 5
and shall inherit e. life.		51:19
and e. life in the world to come.		59:23
and e. weight of glory,		63:66
shall have a crown of e. life		66:12
to seal them up unto e. life.		68:12
and immortality, and e. life.		75: 5
and e. shall be their glory.		76: 6
which is e. punishment,		76:44
of his fulness in the e. world,		76:86
the vengeance of e. fire.		76:105
immortal, and e. state.		77: 1
enjoyment of their e. felicity.		77: 3
e. life in the mansions which		81: 6
heed to the words of e. life.		84:43
shall utter words, e. words;	DC	85: 7
I give unto you of e. life,		88: 4
The elements are e., and spirit		93:33
whom I give a promise of e. life		96: 6
shall find it again, even life e.		98:13
the words of wisdom and e. life		98:20
and ye shall have e. life.		101:38
in the garners to possess e. life,		101:65
reap e. joy for all our sufferings.		109:76
behold from the e. heavens		121: 2
midst of the Council of the E. God		121:32
shall enter into his e. presence		121:32
honor, immortality, and e. life.		124:55
and immortality and e. life—		128:12
speak forth anthems of e. praise		128:22
the wonders of your E. King!		128:23
And let the e. creations declare		128:23
and immortality and e. life;		128:23
will be coupled with e. glory,		130: 2
that he is sealed up unto e. life,		131: 5
and an e. weight of glory.		132:16
This is e. lives—to know the		132:24
and crowns of e. lives in the		132:55
of eternal lives in the e. worlds.		132:55
their exaltation in the e. worlds,		132:63
shall be given e. life.		133:62
and glory is their e. reward.		135: 6
immortality and e. life of man.	Mses	1:39
e. life which God giveth unto		5:11
enjoy the words of e. life in		6:59
and e. life in the world to come,		6:59
Endless and E. is my name,		7:35
be sanctified and have e. life?		7:45
of salvation, even of life e.	Abr	2:11
for they are gnolaum, or e.	Fac	2: 3
of e. light upon his head;		3:18
believe in God, the E. Father,	AoF	1

ETERNALLY

e. in the arms of his love.	2Ne	1:15
knoweth that ye are e. indebted	Mos	2:34
have a place e. at my right hand.		26:24
dwell with God e. in the heavens.	3Ne	28:40
mankind have light, and that e.,	Eth	3:14
he dwelleth e. in the heavens,	Mro	7:28
be e. bound in the heavens;		DC 132:46
remit on earth shall be remitted e.		132:46

ETERNITY

And he spake of hell, and of e.,	Jac	7:18
and the duration of e.,	En	1:23
who was, and is from all e. to	Mos	3: 5
and is from all eternity to all e.,		3: 5
prepared from e. to all eternity,	Al	13: 7
prepared from eternity to all e.,		13: 7
is given us to prepare for e.,		34:33
is unchangeable from all e.	Mro	8:18
from all eternity to all e.		8:18
upon the wide expanse of e.,	DC	38: 1
to reign, and all e. is pained,		38:12
Ye shall possess it again in e.,		38:20
ye shall have the riches of e.;		38:39
who is from all e. to all eternity,		39: 1
who is from all eternity to all e.,		39: 1
unto me in time and in e.		39:22
let the solemnities of e. rest		43:34
riches of e. are mine to give.		67: 2
not earnestly the riches of e.,		68:31
both in time and in e.		72: 3
From e. to eternity he is the		76: 4
eternity to e. he is the same,		76: 4
wonders of e. shall they know,		76: 8
the devil and his angels in e.;		76:33
the devil and his angels in e.,		76:44
the riches of e. are yours.		78:18
who is in the bosom of e.,		88:13
to all generations and for e.		109:24
as well for time and for all e.,		132: 7
their saved condition, to all e.;		132:17
with her for time and for all e.,		132:18
in time, and through all e.;		132:19
of the world, and through all e.;		132:49
from all e. to all eternity.	Mses	6:67
from all eternity to all e.		6:67

ETERNITY 297 EVER

from all e. to all eternity?	Mses	7:29
from all eternity to all e.		7:29
from all e. to all eternity;		7:31
from all eternity to all e.;		7:31
his heart swelled wide as e.;		7:41
yearned; and all e. shook.		7:41
which is broad as e.;		7:53
e. was our covering and	Abr	2:16

ETHEM

And Moron was the son of E.	Eth	1: 8
And E. was the son of Ahah.		1: 9
And E., being a descendant		11:11
in the days of E. there came		11:12
E. did execute judgment in		11:14

ETHER

taken from the Book of E.	T Pg	
THE BOOK OF E.	Eth	1:hd
which is called the book of E.		1: 2
that wrote this record was E.,		1: 6
that Coriantor begat E.,		11:23
the days of E. were in the days		12: 1
E. was a prophet of the Lord;		12: 2
E. came forth in the days of		12: 2
E. did prophesy great and		12: 5
rejected all the words of E.;		13: 2
E. saw the days of Christ,		13: 4
were the prophecies of E.;		13:13
E. dwelt in the cavity of a rock,		13:18
the word of the Lord came to E.,		13:20
and they sought to kill E.,		13:22
of the Lord which came to E.		14:24
words which E. had spoken		15: 1
not been slain, save it was E.		15:12
E. did behold all the doings		15:13
And the Lord spake unto E.,		15:33
words which are written by E.		15:34
close of the twelfth chapter of E.,	DC	135: 4

ETHIOPIA

compasseth the whole land of E.	Mses	3:13

EUPHRATES

the fourth river was the E.	Mses	3:14

EVANGELICAL

to ordain e. ministers,	DC	107:39

EVANGELISTS

prophets, pastors, teachers, e.,	AoF	6

EVE

and E., who were our first parents;	1Ne	5:11
Wherefore, he said unto E.,	2Ne	2:18
after Adam and E. had partaken		2:19
he sought also to beguile E.,	Mses	4: 6
Adam called his wife's name E.,		4:26
E., also, his wife, did labor		5: 1
Adam and E., his wife, called		5: 4
E., his wife, heard all these		5:11
and E. blessed the name of God,		5:12
And Adam and E., his wife,		5:16
And Adam knew E. his wife, and		5:16

EVEN: see in the *APPENDIX*.

EVENING

both morning, mid-day, and e.	Al	34:21
when it was e. Laman went to		55: 8
e. and the morning were the first	Mses	2: 5
the e. and the morning were		2: 8
the e. and the morning were		2:13
the e. and the morning were		2:19
the e. and the morning were		2:23
the e. and the morning were		2:31
from the e. until morning	Abr	4: 5
from the morning until the e.		4: 5
it was from e. until morning		4: 8
it was from morning until e.		4: 8
from the e. until the morning		4:13
from the morning until the e.		4:13
it was from e. until morning		4:19

it was from morning until e.	Abr	4:19
it was from e. until morning		4:23
it was from morning until e.		4:23
it was from e. until morning		4:31
it was from morning until e.		4:31
the e. of the above-mentioned	JS	2:29

EVENTS

various e. in relation to this	JS	2: 2

EVENTUALLY

e. terminate in the death and	DC	87: 1

EVER

above all that I e. before tasted.	1Ne	8:11
the whiteness that I had e. seen.		8:11
in a fallen state, and e. would be		10: 6
forever and e., and hath no end.		15:30
know that it e. has been.	2Ne	6: 3
forever and e. and has no end.		9:16
which e. have been among the		27:11
and which e. will be even unto		27:11
foundation, can e. build upon it,	Jac	4:17
ascendeth up forever and e.,		6:10
neither has been, nor e. will be.		7: 9
are, and will be, forever and e.;	Mos	2:24
ascendeth up forever and e.		2:38
and will be, forever and e.,		3:19
ascendeth up forever and e.		3:27
which e. were since the fall of		4: 7
or who are, or who e. shall be,		4: 7
e. since the world began—		13:33
e. since the world began?		15:13
e. since the world began,		15:26
and remained so e. after,		26: 6
have been e. since the world began,	Al	7:25
ascendeth up forever and e.;		12:17
who had e. delivered them out of		19:27
by that name e. after.		27:26
who never was nor e. will be.		30:28
cursed be the land forever and e.		37:31
and were, and e. would be,		48:17
exceeding stronghold e. after;		53: 5
and had e. since been protected by		53:10
they e. had been protected by		53:12
as I had e. called them my sons		56:46
shall e. after be found in seams	He	14:22
e. since I have been sufficient	Mrm	2:18
which e. hath been amongst us,		5:15
that ye have e. abused his laws?		9: 3
the truth abideth forever and e.	DC	1:39
to whom be glory forever and e.		20:16
his holy name, both now and e.		20:36
e. lifting up your heart unto		30: 6
you shall e. open your mouth		30:11
on earth, nor e. shall know,		43:33
the beginning, and e. shall be,		46: 2
to generation forever and e.,		56:20
power and glory, forever and e.		65: 8
to generation, forever and e.		69: 8
worship him forever and e.		76:21
and his Christ forever and e.		76:62
upon his throne forever and e.;		76:92
give him glory forever and e.		76:93
power to reign forever and e.		76:108
upon the throne forever and e.;		76:110
and dominion forever and e.		76:119
Forever and e., Amen.		84:102
may possess it forever and e.;		88:20
even God, forever and e.		88:41
upon the throne, forever and e.		88:104
thanksgiving, forever and e.		88:133
generations forever and e.,		97:28
to possess it forever and e.		103: 7
that we may e. be with the Lord;		109:75
to generation, forever and e.		117:12
people be on him forever and e.		117:15
flow unto thee forever and e.		121:46
stand by thee forever and e.		122: 4
be with you forever and e.		122: 9
to generation, forever and e.,		124:59
to generation, forever and e.		124:96
upon the throne forever and e.,		124:101

be well with him forever and e.	DC	124:118
declare his name forever and e.!		128:23
I am, as e., your humble servant		128:25
angels of God forever and e.		132:17
of the seeds forever and e.		132:19
day and night, forever and e.		133:35
loving kindness, forever and e.		133:52
day and night forever and e.		133:56
than any other man that e. lived		135: 3
e. since the day that I created	Mses	6:28
added upon their heads for e.	Abr	3:26
upon their heads for ever and e.		3:26
no, nor e. shall be sent again	JS	1:18
for another, if they e. had any,		2: 6
anything earthly I had e. seen;		2:31
that we would e. be otherwise—		2:61
nor e. before had thought of.		2:74

EVERLASTING

yea, the Son of the e. God was	1Ne	11:32
the e. kingdom of the Lamb;		13:37
a work which shall be e.,		14: 7
give praise unto their e. God,		15:15
the e. welfare of your souls.	2Ne	2:30
my rock and mine e. God.		4:35
e. joy and holiness shall be upon		8:11
they shall go away into e. fire;		9:16
to choose the way of e. death		10:23
and also from e. death		10:25
E. Father, The Prince of Peace.		19: 6
will grasp them with his e. chains,		28:19
I bid you an e. farewell,		33:14
for his wages an e. punishment,	Mos	2:33
have e. salvation and eternal life,		5:15
and they shall depart into e. fire		26:27
to snatch me out of an e. burning,		27:28
judgment of an e. punishment		27:31
by the light of the e. word;	Al	5: 7
an e. destruction did await them.		5: 7
of your sins, with an e. faith,		7: 6
you down to e. destruction,		12: 6
acknowledge to our e. shame that		12:15
down to an e. destruction,		12:17
which was an e. death as to		12:32
the e. destruction of your souls;		12:36
that the light of e. life was		19: 6
encircled about with e. darkness		26:15
brought them into his e. light,		26:15
light, yea, into e. salvation;		26:15
over that e. gulf of death and		26:20
and my redemption from e. wo.		26:36
save them from e. destruction—		27: 4
a tree springing up unto e. life.		32:41
springing up in you unto e. life.		33:23
about by the e. chains of death.		36:18
by his e. power, delivered them		36:29
e. hatred against sin and iniquity.		37:32
swearing by their e. Maker,	He	1:11
across that e. gulf of misery		3:29
destruction, and to an e. hell.		6:28
ripening for an e. destruction.		6:40
to e. misery and endless wo?		7:16
wickedness, for e. destruction;		8:26
of our great and e. God.		12: 8
have done good shall have e. life;		12:26
done evil shall have e. damnation.		12:26
the same shall have e. life.		14: 8
their e. hatred towards you	3Ne	3: 4
delivered from an e. destruction.		4:33
that they might have e. life.		5:13
but with e. kindness will I have		22: 8
to the resurrection of e. life;		26: 5
it is the e. decree of God.	Eth	2:10
a way for their e. destruction.		14:25
being from e. to everlasting,	Mro	7:22
being from everlasting to e.,		7:22
with charity, which is e. love;		8:17
out of the mouth of the e. God;		10:28
broken mine e. covenant;	DC	1:15
That mine e. covenant might		1:22
e. salvation in the kingdom		6: 3
e. salvation in the kingdom		11: 3
e. salvation in the kingdom		12: 3
e. salvation in the kingdom	DC	14: 3
from e. to everlasting the same		20:17
from everlasting to e. the same		20:17
a new and an e. covenant,		22: 1
the fulness of my e. gospel,		27: 5
from me, ye cursed, into e. fire,		29:28
preach the e. gospel among		36: 5
saved you with an e. salvation,		43:25
unto me and have e. life.		45: 5
I have sent mine e. covenent		45: 9
singing with songs of e. joy.		45:71
sent unto you mine e. covenant,		49: 9
obtain it for an e. inheritance.		57: 5
who is from e. to everlasting,		61: 1
who is from everlasting to e.,		61: 1
water, sptinging up unto e. life.		63:23
receiving mine e. covenant,		66: 2
to Zion with songs of e. joy		66:11
to proclaim the e. gospel,		68: 1
go away into e. punishment,		76:44
neither the e. covenant.		76:101
they who have the e. gospel		77: 8
angels having the e. gospel,		77: 9
to administer the e. gospel;		77:11
e. establishment and order		78: 4
by a bond or e. covenant		78:11
great joy, even the e. gospel.		79: 1
to be an e. order unto you,		82:20
to proclaim mine e. gospel,		84:103
committeth the e. gospel—		88:103
remembrance of the e. covanant.		88:131
remembrance of the e. covanant,		88:133
to proclaim mine e. gospel unto		99: 1
children, with songs of e. joy,		101:18
according to mine e. gospel,		101:22
are called unto mine e. gospel,		101:39
covenant with an e. covenant,		101:39
an e. order for the benefit of		104: 1
should preach my e. gospel,		106: 2
e. gospel shall be proclaimed		109:29
with songs of e. joy;		109:39
the fulness of the e. gospel;		109:65
and had in e. remembrance		109:71
of fulness, from e. to everlasting.		109:77
of fulness, from everlasting to e.		109:77
shall be an e. dominion,		121:46
and proclaim my e. gospel		124:88
belonging to the e. gospel,		128:17
new and e. covenant of marriage];		131: 2
a new and an e. covenant,		132: 4
to the new and e. covenant,		132: 6
by the new and e. covenant,		132:19
therefore shall they be from e.		132:20
be from everlasting to e.,		132:20
of the new and e. covenant		132:26
received my new and e. covenant,		132:27
wife in the new and e. covenant,		132:41
in the new and e. covenant,		132:42
the boundaries of the e. hills		133:31
be filled with songs of e. joy.		133:33
is the blessing of the e. God		133:34
having the e. gospel,		133:36
his gospel, his e. covenant,		133:57
the fulness of the e. gospel,		135: 3
to the truth of the e. gospel		135: 7
forth with songs of e. joy.	Mses	7:53
after thee for an e. possession,	Abr	2: 6
the fulness of the e. Gospel	JS	2:34

EVERLASTINGLY

salvation until it is e. too late,	He	13:38

EVERMORE

be comforted; yea, rejoice e.,	DC	98: 1

EVERY

yea, even e. whit; and I did gird	1Ne	4:19
all manner of seeds of e. kind,		8: 1
both of grain of e. kind, and also		8: 1
of the seeds of fruit of e. kind.		8: 1
we did take seed of e. kind		16:11
had rejected e. word of God,		17:35
e. one according to his age;		18: 6

EVERY

beasts in the forests of e. kind,	1Ne 18:25
e. nation, kindred, tongue and	19:17
And e. nation which shall war	22:14
herds, and animals of e. kind.	2Ne 5:11
hast feared continually e. day,	8:13
the pains of e. living creature,	9:21
e. one that thirsteth, come ye	9:50
astray, e. one to his wicked ways.	12: 5
upon all nations, yea, upon e. one;	12:12
upon e. one who is lifted up,	12:12
are lifted up, and upon e. people;	12:14
And upon e. high tower,	12:15
and upon e. fenced wall;	12:15
oppressed, e. one by another,	13: 5
and e. one by his neighbor;	13: 5
e. one that is written among the	14: 3
upon e. dwelling-place of mount	14: 5
butter and honey shall e. one eat	17:22
e. place shall be, where there were	17:23
For e. battle of the warrior is	19: 5
for e. one of them is a hypocrite	19:17
and e. mouth speaketh folly.	19:17
e. man the flesh of his own arm—	19:20
e. man's heart shall melt;	23: 7
e. man turn to his own people,	23:14
flee e. one into his own land.	23:14
E. one that is proud shall	23:15
e. one that is joined to the wicked	23:15
e. one of them in his own house.	24:18
unto e. nation, kindred, tongue,	26:13
and thus shall e. one say	28: 3
e. man according to their works,	29:11
and e. kind of sin,	Jac 3:12
e. sort according to its number.	5:31
all manner of cattle of e. kind,	En 1:21
all manner of tools of e. kind	Jar 1: 8
e. one according to the heed	Mos 1:16
e. man according to his family,	2: 5
e. family being separate from	2: 5
e. man having his tent with the	2: 6
blood cometh from e. pore,	3: 7
to e. kindred, nation, and tongue,	3:13
e. nation, kindred, tongue, and	3:20
e. man according to his works,	3:24
to render to e. man according to	4:13
riches which we have of e. kind?	4:19
e. man according to that which	4:26
e. one, according to their families,	6: 3
and even all our grain of e. kind,	7:22
e. one unto his own house.	8: 4
with ruins of buildings of e. kind,	8: 8
weapons of war made of e. kind,	10: 1
all manner of fruit of e. kind.	10: 4
linen, yea, and cloth of e. kind,	10: 5
e. man according to his age.	10: 9
turned e. one to his own way;	14: 6
e. one that has opened his mouth	15:13
e. nation, kindred, tongue, and	15:28
e. nation, kindred, tongue, and	16: 1
ye shall be smitten on e. hand,	17:17
baptize e. one that went forth	18:16
to e. fifty of their number	18:18
e. day they should give thanks	18:23
there was one day in e. week	18:25
e. one according to that which	18:27
yea, and to e. needy, naked soul.	18:28
had surrounded them on e. side.	21: 5
commanded that e. man should	21:17
e. man should love his neighbor	23:15
in e. land which was possessed by	24: 4
priests and teachers over e. church.	25:19
e. church having their priests and	25:21
and e. priest preaching the word	25:21
e. one by the word of God,	26:39
e. man should esteem his neighbor	27: 4
he remembereth e. creature	27:30
Yea, e. knee shall bow,	27:31
and e. tongue confess before him.	27:31
be declared to e. creature,	28: 3
he should discover to e. creature	28:15
and e. man may enjoy his rights	29:32
that e. man might bear his part.	29:34
that e. man should have an equal	29:38
e. man expressed a willingness to	Mos 29:88
that e. priest and teacher ought	Al 1: 3
e. man according to his strength.	1:26
e. man according to that which	1:27
herds, and fatlings of e. kind,	1:29
e. man suffering according to	1:33
e. man according to his mind,	2: 5
of weapons of war, of e. kind.	2:12
of weapons of war of e. kind;	2:14
Yea, they were met on e. hand,	2:37
even so doth e. man that is cursed	3:19
e. man receiveth wages of him	3:27
that e. soul had cause to mourn;	4: 3
yea, the sins of e. man who	5:48
e. one that dwelleth in the land;	5:49
e. tree that bringeth not forth	5:52
and temptations of e. kind;	7:11
fear not, and lay aside e. sin,	7:15
been favored above e. other nation,	9:20
all manner of diseases of e. kind;	9:22
e. man who was a judge of the law,	11: 1
of the people, in e. generation,	11: 4
a measure of e. kind of grain.	11: 7
but e. thing shall be restored to	11:44
to save e. man that believeth	12:15
e. soul within the walls thereof,	14:28
yea, e. living soul of the	16: 9
forth among them, e. man alone,	17:17
e. man that lifted his club up	17:37
in e. synagogue of the Amalekites,	21:16
in e. assembly of the Lamanites	21:16
of wild animals of e. kind,	22:31
suffer their afflictions on e. hand,	22:34
word unto them in e. particular.	25:17
we have suffered e. privation;	26:28
that God is mindful of e. people,	26:37
cry repentance unto e. people!	29: 1
I would declare unto e. soul,	29: 2
but e. man fared in this life	30:17
e. man prospered according to	30:17
e. man conquered according to	30:17
e. man did go forth and offer up	31:20
offer up, e. man, the selfsame	31:22
shall be unto e. man according	32:20
for e. seed bringeth forth unto its	32:31
be all fulfilled, e. jot and tittle,	34:13
e. whit pointing to that great and	34:14
among all the people in e. city;	35:15
give unto them e. one his charge,	35:16
trials and troubles of e. kind,	36:27
unto e. nation, kindred, tongue,	37: 4
unto e. nation that shall hereafter	37:25
to withstand e. temptation of	37:33
e. limb and joint shall be restored	40:23
that e. part of the body should	41: 2
e. thing to its natural frame—	41: 4
sword which turned e. way,	42: 2
brought death almost at e. stroke.	43:37
unto e. nation, kindred, tongue,	45:16
in e. city throughout all the	45:22
to be hoisted upon e. tower	46:36
for e. city in all the land round	49:13
about e. city in all the land.	50: 6
men in e. city to maintain and	51:25
for e. man of Teancum did	51:31
power to harass them on e. side.	52: 9
seek e. opportunity to scourge	52:10
great afflictions of e. kind.	56:16
perform e. word of command	57:21
of weapons of war of e. kind,	60: 2
manner of afflictions of e. kind.	60: 3
and flocks and herds of e. kind;	62:29
all manner of shields of e. kind.	He 1:14
slay e. one who did oppose them,	1:20
were surrounded on e. hand	1:31
and many records of e. kind,	3:15
encircled about, yea, e. soul, by	5:43
of precious ore of e. kind;	6:11
linen and cloth of e. kind,	6:13
did use e. means in their power	6:20
of precious things of e. kind	12: 2
all things, e. whit, according to	3Ne 1:20
it must be fulfilled in e. whit;	1:25

EVERY

EVERY   300   EVERY

weapons of war of e. kind,	3Ne 3:26	
and cattle, and flocks of e. kind,	4: 4	
should hem them in on e. side,	4:16	
e. man, with his family, his	6: 1	
of all their grain of e. kind,	6: 2	
e. man according to his family	7: 2	
e. tribe did appoint a chief or	7: 3	
e. one according to his tribe;	7:11	
e. man according to his family,	7:14	
save he were cleansed e. whit	8: 1	
e. one that asketh, receiveth;	14: 8	
e. good tree bringeth forth	14:17	
E. tree that bringeth not forth	14:19	
Not e. one that saith unto me,	14:21	
e. one that heareth these sayings	14:26	
and he did heal them e. one	17: 9	
see and hear, e. man for himself;	17:25	
e. man did take his wife and	19: 1	
e. soul who will not hear that	20:23	
turning away e. one of you from	20:26	
and e. tongue that shall rise	22:17	
e. man dealing justly, one with	26:19	
he touched e. one of them with	28:12	
e. man did deal justly one with	4Ne 1: 2	
e. soul who belongs to the whole	Mrm 3:20	
and e. heart was hardened,	4:11	
e. soul was filled with terror	6: 8	
your churches, yea, even e. one,	8:36	
preach the gospel to e. creature;	9:22	
both male and female, of e. kind;	Eth 1:41	
the seed of the earth of e. kind;	1:41	
male and female, of e. kind.	2: 1	
of the land, seeds of e. kind.	2: 3	
e. soul should be destroyed	13:21	
e. man with his band fighting	13:25	
e. man did cleave unto that	14: 2	
e. man kept the hilt of his sword	14: 2	
were fulfilled thus far, e. whit;	15: 3	
e. one to the army which he	15:15	
they put to death e. Nephite	Mro 1: 2	
e. thing which inviteth and	7:13	
of Christ is given to e. man,	7:16	
e. thing which inviteth to do	7:16	
lay hold upon e. good thing,	7:19	
lay hold upon e. good thing?	7:20	
may lay hold on e. good thing.	7:21	
there should come e. good thing.	7:22	
e. word which proceeded forth	7:25	
lay hold upon e. good thing;	7:25	
will cleave unto e. good thing;	7:28	
mind in e. form of godliness.	7:30	
they come unto e. man severally,	10:17	
e. good gift cometh of Christ.	10:18	
lay hold upon e. good gift,	10:30	
to recompense unto e. man	DC 1:10	
measure to e. man according to	1:10	
e. man walketh in his own way,	1:16	
that e. man might speak in the	1:20	
with you in e. time of trouble.	3: 8	
shall e. word be established.	6:28	
Look unto me in e. thought;	6:36	
my gospel unto e. creature.	18:28	
e. according to his works	19: 3	
e. man must repent or suffer,	19: 4	
and to bleed at e. pore.	19:18	
and upon e. high place,	19:29	
among e. people that thou shalt	19:29	
E. elder, priest, teacher, or	20:60	
E. president of the high	20:67	
E. member of the church of	20:70	
become corrupted e. whit;	33: 6	
be baptized, e. one of you,	33:11	
e. man which will embrace it	36: 7	
let e. man choose for himself	37: 4	
e. man esteem his brother as	38:24	
e. man esteem his brother as	38:25	
that e. man, both elder, priest,	38:40	
e. man to his neighbor,	38:41	
in my name, e. one of you,	42: 4	
up my church in e. region—	42: 8	
e. man shall be made accountable	42:32	
e. man who has need may be	42:33	

e. person who belongeth to this	DC	42:78
e. word shall be established		42:80
famines and pestilences of e. kind,		43:25
that e. bond may be broken		44: 5
until e. desolation which I		45:21
e. man that will not take his		45:68
of e. nation under heaven,		45:69
all have not e. gift given unto		46:11
to e. man is given a gift by		46:11
given to e. man to profit withal.		46:16
that e. member may be profited		46:29
e. man according to his family,		48: 6
let e. man beware lest he do		50: 9
e. man equal according to his		51: 3
let e. man deal honestly,		51: 9
by the way in e. congregation,		52:10
and he shall reward e. man,		56:19
also e. tract lying westward,		57: 4
also e. trace bordering by		57: 5
this is a law unto e. man		58:36
be preached unto e. creature,		58:64
fear shall come upon e. man;		63:33
And that e. man should take		63:37
out of e. nation under heaven.		64:42
bear testimony in e. place,		66: 7
unto e. people and in their		66: 7
be made strong in e. place;		66: 8
the gospel to e. creature,		68: 8
of e. man in his stewardship,		70: 9
at the hand of e. steward,		72: 3
e. man that cometh up to Zion		72:15
e. elder in this part of the		72:16
rendereth e. man acceptable,		72:17
let e. elder who shall give an		72:19
e. man who is obliged to		75:28
Let e. man be diligent in all		75:29
and e. tongue shall confess to		76:110
e. man shall receive according		76:111
e. other creature which God		77: 2
gospel to commit to e. nation,		77: 8
twelve thousand out of e. tribe?		77:11
are ordained out of e. nation,		77:11
appoint e. man his portion.		78:21
preach the gospel to e. creature		80: 1
e. man according to his wants		82:17
e. man may improve upon		82:18
e. man may gain other talents,		82:18
E. man seeking the interest of		82:19
e. word that proceedeth forth		84:44
Spirit giveth light to e. man		84:46
the Spirit enlighteneth e. man		84:46
And e. one that hearkeneth to		84:47
all the world unto e. creature.		84:62
e. soul who believeth on		84:64
shall be meted unto e. man.		84:85
that e. man who goes forth		84:103
let e. man stand in his own		84:109
body hath need of e. member,		84:110
And unto e. kingdom is given		88:38
unto e. law there are certain		88:38
e. man in his hour, and in his		88:58
E. man in his own order,		88:60
e. kingdom in its hour, and in		88:61
it becometh e. man who hath		88:81
for e. ear shall hear it,		88:104
and e. knee shall bow,		88:104
and e. tongue shall confess,		88:104
prepare e. needful thing;		88:119
that e. man may have an equal		88:122
E. herb in the season thereof,		89:11
e. fruit in the season thereof,		89:11
e. man shall hear the fulness of		90:11
enabled to discharge e. debt;		90:23
e. soul who forsaketh his sins		93: 1
true light that lighteth e. man		93: 2
e. man whose spirit receiveth		93:32
E. spirit of man was innocent		93:38
e. tree that bringeth not forth		97: 7
e. sacrifice which I, the Lord,		97: 8
e. word which proceedeth forth		98:11
And e. corruptible thing,		101:24
to reward e. man according		101:65

EVERY 301 EVIL

That e. man may act in doctrine	DC 101:78
that e. man may be accountable	101:78
e. man is to speak according	102:16
appoint e. man his stewardship;	104:11
e. man may give an account	104:12
make e. man accountable,	104:13
e. decision made by either of these	107:27
e. member in each quorum must	107:27
now let e. man learn his duty,	107:99
prepare e. needful thing,	109: 8
be prepared to obtain e. needful	109:15
preach my gospel unto e. creature	112:28
to recompense e. man according	112:34
a time appointed for e. man,	121:25
when e. man shall enter into	121:32
And let e. man who pays stock	124:122
send my word to e. creature.	124:128
e. word may be established.	128: 3
let e. man call upon the name	133: 6
shall be preached unto e. nation,	133:37
e. citizen thus protected,	134: 5
e. man should be honored in his	134: 6
to the peace of e. government	134:12
the reader in e. nation will be	135: 6
Let e. man use all his influence	136:10
e. herb yielding seed after his	Mses 2:12
e. living creature that moveth,	2:21
e. winged fowl after his kind;	2:21
and over e. creeping thing that	2:26
e. living thing that moveth	2:28
I have given you e. herb bearing	2:29
e. tree in the which shall be	2:29
And to e. beast of the earth,	2:30
and to e. fowl of the air,	2:30
be given e. clean herb for meat;	2:30
e. plant of the field before it was	3: 5
e. herb of the field before it	3: 5
the Lord God, to grow e. tree,	3: 9
of e. tree of the garden thou	3:16
formed e. beast of the field,	3:19
and e. fowl of the air;	3:19
Adam called e. living creature,	3:19
and to e. beast of the field,	3:20
not eat of e. tree of the garden?	4: 7
and above e. beast of the field;	4:20
sword, which turned e. way to	4:31
of e. artificer in brass and iron.	5:46
and they knew e. man his brother.	5:51
and e. man was lifted up in the	8:22
e. living creature that moveth,	Abr 4:21
e. winged fowl after their kind.	4:21
and e. thing that creepeth	4:25
and over e. creeping thing	4:26
and over e. living thing	4:28
give them e. herb bearing seed	4:29
e. tree which shall have fruit	4:29
And to e. beast of the earth,	4:30
and to e. fowl of the air,	4:30
and to e. thing that creepeth	4:30
e. green herb for meat,	4:30
concerning e. plant of the field	5: 5
and e. herb of the field	5: 5
e. tree that is pleasant	5: 9
of e. tree of the garden thou	5:12
formed e. beast of the field,	5:20
e. fowl of the air,	5:20
Adam called e. living creature,	5:20
to e. beast of the field;	5:21
into e. feeling of my heart.	JS 2:12
E. stratagem that could be	2:60

EVERYBODY
in order to have e. converted,	JS 2: 6

EVERYTHING
in e. save that which is good;	Mro 9:19
of this land doth exceed e.;	9:19
and in e. give thanks;	DC 98: 1
And e. that is in the world,	132:13
e. which creepeth upon the	Mses 2:30
to e. that creepeth upon the	2:30
God saw e. that I had made,	2:31
We will do e. that we have said,	Abr 4:31

EVERYWHERE
all men, e., to repent and	3Ne 11:32
command all men e. to repent,	DC 18: 9
commandeth all men e. to repent.	133:16
men by the Holy Ghost e.	Mses 5:14
upon all men, e., to repent	6:23
that all men, e., must repent,	6:57

EVIDENCE
what e. have ye that there is no	Al 30:40
after the e. is examined,	DC 102:16

EVIDENCES
e. which were brought against	Al 11: 2
the e. which they had received.	He 5:50
many e. which ye have received;	8:24
after the e. are heard and	DC 102:18
After the e. are heard,	102:19
after hearing the e. and	102:20
and the e. and statements	102:33

EVIL
that they know good from e.	2Ne 2: 5
that which was e. before God.	2:17
be as God, knowing good and e.	2:18
free forever, knowing good from e.;	2:26
and the e. which is therein,	2:29
the e. one have place in my heart	4:27
that cunning plan of the e. one!	9:28
have rewarded e. unto themselves!	13: 9
Wo unto them that call e. good,	15:20
that call evil good, and good e.,	15:20
have taken e. counsel against thee,	17: 5
that he may know to refuse the e.	17:15
child shall know to refuse the e.	17:16
I will punish the world for e.,	23:11
for the e. spirit teacheth not a man	32: 8
long as it shall bring forth e. fruit.	Jac 5:35
hath brought forth much e. fruit;	5:37
brought forth so much e. fruit	5:37
have also brought forth e. fruit.	5:38
the good may overcome the e.	5:59
that e. fruit shall again come into	5:77
will ye bring forth e. fruit, that ye	6: 7
they were led by their e. nature	En 1:20
and that which is e. cometh from	Om 1:25
and ye list to obey the e. spirit,	Mos 2:32
he listeth to obey the e. spirit,	2:37
cast out devils, or the e. spirits	3: 6
be good, or whether they be e.	3:24
if they be e. they are consigned to	3:25
or who is the e. spirit which hath	4:14
no more disposition to do e.,	5: 2
great e. should come upon them.	7:25
he did not repent of his e. doings.	11:29
repented not of their e. doings;	12: 1
who has prophesied e. concerning	12: 9
prophesieth e. concerning thy life,	12:10
what great e. hast thou done,	12:13
a great e. against this people?	12:29
to prophesy e. concerning this	13:26
because he had done no e.,	14: 9
knowing e. from good,	16: 3
be good or whether they be e.—	16:10
and if they be e., to the	16:29
thou hast spoken e. concerning me	17: 8
is e. cometh from the devil.	Al 5:40
bringeth forth e. works,	5:41
and if they have been e. they	9:28
for this great e. thou shalt have	11:25
they be good or whether they be e.	11:44
as Gods, knowing good from e.,	12:31
whether to do e. or to do good—	12:31
that they should not do e.,	12:32
being left to choose good or e.;	13: 3
it was a great e. that had come	19:19
brought this e. upon them,	19:20
they had no more desire to do e.	19:33
should some e. come upon her.	22:21
good and e. have come before	29: 5
that knoweth not good from e.	29: 5
but he that knoweth good and e.,	29: 5
whether he desireth good or e.,	29: 5

EVIL — 302 — EXALTED

men, whether they be good or e.,	Al	40:11
the wicked, yea, who are e.—		40:13
chose e. works rather than good;		40:13
their works, which have been e.;		40:26
if their works are e. they shall be		41: 4
shall be restored unto them for e.		41: 4
and the other to e. according to		41: 5
according to his desires of e.;		41: 5
desired to do e. all the day long		41: 5
so shall he have his reward of e.		41: 5
whether to do good or do e.		41: 7
is to bring back again e. for evil,		41:13
is to bring back again evil for e.,		41:13
as God, knowing good and e.;		42: 3
If he has desired to do e.,		42:28
behold, e. shall be done unto him,		42:38
to be led away by the e. one.		46: 8
being a very subtle man to do e.		47: 4
brother, Moroni, let us resist e.,		61:14
whatsoever e. we cannot resist		61:14
Now this was a great e., which	He	3:34
and they who chose e. were more		5: 2
the e. one who seeketh to destroy		8:28
so much e. concerning this people,		9:27
Now this great e., which came		11:34
foolish, and how vain, and how e.,		12: 4
unto the words of the e. one,		12: 4
they that have done e. shall		12:26
testifieth that your deeds are e.		13:26
that ye might know good from e.,		14:31
or ye can do e., and have that		14:31
which is e. restored unto you.		14:31
deeds have been e. continually,		15: 4
the mysterious arts of the e. one,		16:21
doctrine, the same cometh of e.,	3Ne	11:40
shall say all manner of e. against		12:11
cometh of more than these is e.		12:37
that ye shall not resist e.,		12:39
rise on the e. and the good.		12:45
but deliver us from e.		13:12
But if thine eye be e., thy whole		13:23
is the day unto the e. thereof.		13:34
If ye then, being e., know how		14:11
a corrupt tree bringeth forth e.		14:17
tree cannot bring forth e. fruit,		14:18
be good or whether they be e.—		26: 4
if they be e., to the resurrection		26: 5
be good or whether they be e.—		27:14
and repent of your e. doings,		30: 2
power of the e. one was wrought	Mrm	1:19
not repent of their e. doings;		2: 8
whether they be good or e.;		3:20
not of the e. they had done,		4:10
and turn from your e. ways?		5:22
of the e. which he had done,	Eth	2:15
have become e. continually;		3: 2
that e. may be done away,		8:26
of the e. which he had done;		15: 3
a man being e. cannot do that	Mro	7: 6
if a man being e. giveth a gift,		7: 8
he is counted e. before God.		7: 8
is it counted e. unto a man,		7: 9
a man being e. cannot do that		7:10
which is e. cometh of the devil;		7:12
do that which is e. continually.		7:12
that which is e. to be of God,		7:14
ye may know good from e.;		7:15
that he may know good from e.;		7:16
thing that persuadeth men to do e.,		7:17
that ye may know good from e.;		7:19
easily provoked, thinketh no e.,		7:45
and touch not the e. gift,		10:30
shall accomplish his e. design	DC	10:14
because their deeds are e.		10:21
not accomplish their e. designs		10:31
backbiting nor e. speaking;		20:54
able to withstand the e. day,		27:15
and their deeds are e.,		29:45
not speak e. of thy neighbor,		42:27
not be seduced by e. spirits,		46: 7
for this e. they were afflicted		64: 6
They sought e. in their hearts,		64:16
They condemned for e. that		64:16

thing in which there was no e.;	DC	64:16
and they repent of the e.,		64:17
they who have done e. in the		76:17
repent of their former e. works;		84:76
for their e. hearts of unbelief,		84:76
and truth forsake that e. one.		93:37
or less than this, cometh of e.		98: 7
is less than these cometh of e.		98:10
that ye shall forsake all e. and		98:11
is the cause of this great e.?		101:52
and repentent not of the e.,		104:10
power to bring e. upon you.		104:10
but are full of all manner of e.,		105: 3
and cease to do e., and lay aside all		124:116
more or less than this cometh of e.,		124:120
their tendency to e. among men,		134: 8
Keep yourselves from e.		136:21
cease to speak e. one of another.		136:23
tree of knowledge of good and e.	Mses	3: 9
tree of the knowledge of good and e.,		3:17
as gods, knowing good and e.		4:11
one of us to know good and e.;		4:28
should have known good and e.,		5:11
unto them to know good from e.;		6:56
of his heart, being only e.		8:22
their hearts were set to do e.,	Abr	1: 6
the e. which he had determined		1:30
of knowledge of good and e.		5: 9
of knowledge of good and e.,		5:13
if that e. servant shall say in	JS	1:51
in circulation by e.-disposed		2: 1
all manner of e. against me		2:25
should be had for good and e.		2:33
both good and e. spoken of		2:33

EVIL-DISPOSED: see EVIL and DISPOSED.

EVILDOER

a hypocrite and an e.,		2Ne 19:17

EVILDOERS

the seed of e. shall never be		2Ne 24:20

EVILS

the many e. which he had done;	Eth	7:13
In consequence of e. and	DC	89: 4

EXACT

doth e. of us, or our lives.		Mos 7:22

EXACTED

he had not e. riches of them,		Mos 29:40

EXACTLY

pillar of light e. over my head,	JS	2:16

EXACTNESS

every word of command with e.;	Al	57:21

EXALT

e. the voice unto them,		2Ne 23: 2
I will e. my throne above the stars		24:13
that thy right hand may e. them,		DC 109:71
E. not yourselves;		112:15
God shall e. thee on high;		121: 8

EXALTATION

and the Gentiles to the e. or	DC	124: 9
separately and singly, without e.,		132:17
to their e. and glory in all things,		132:19
the way that leadeth unto the e.		132:22
and shall receive your e.		132:23
and enter into their e.;		132:26
and hath entered into his e.		132:29
they have entered into their e.,		132:37
he hath fallen from his e.,		132:39
verily I seal upon you your e.,		132:49
even unto his e. and glory.		132:57
for their e. in the eternal worlds,		132:63

EXALTED

and my highways shall be e.		1Ne 21:11
and shall be e. above the hills,		2Ne 12: 2

EXALTED 303 EXCEEDING

alone shall be e. in that day.	2Ne	12:11	the fall thereof was e. great.	1Ne 11:36
alone shall be e. in that day.		12:17	they were white, and e. fair	13:15
of Hosts shall be e. in judgment,		15:16	an e. great many do stumble,	13:29
mention that his name is e.		22: 4	and they were all e. sorrowful,	16:20
he shall be e. and extolled and	3Ne	20:43	I, Nephi, was e. sorrowful	17:19
that which is now e. of itself	DC	49:10	workmanship thereof was e. fine;	18: 4
and for the valleys to be e.,		49:23	lifted up unto e. rudeness.	18: 9
he e. himself in his heart,		63:55	the tempest began to be e. sore.	18:14
that abaseth himself shall be e.		101:42	in the hands of God, with e. faith,	2Ne 3:24
that the poor shall be e.,		104:16	away upon e. high mountains.	4:25
they may be e. in thy presence,		109:69	workmanship thereof was e. fine.	5:16
and the valleys to be e.,		109:74	were white, and e. fair	5:21
abased thyself thou shalt be e.;		112: 3	spoken unto you e. many things.	6: 2
many low ones shall be e.		112: 8	and pray unto him with e. faith,	Jac 3: 1
abase himself that he may be e.		124:114	were e. many prophets among us.	En 1:22
			nothing save it was e. harshness,	1:23
EXALTETH			e. great plainness of speech,	1:23
He that e. himself shall be	DC	101:42	God is e. merciful unto them,	Jar 1: 3
			they were e. more numerous than	1: 6
EXALTS			and became e. rich in gold,	1: 8
he e. himself and does not	DC	5:24	they had become e. numerous.	Om 1:17
			and rejoice with e. great joy,	Mos 3:13
EXAMINE			because of the e. faith which	4: 3
But behold, ye shall e. him, and	He	9:31	which causeth such e. great joy	4:11
			so e. great was your joy.	4:20
EXAMINED			rejoice with such e. great joy.	5: 4
case, after the evidence is e.,	DC	102:16	he was e. glad, and said:	7:14
			and his face shone with e. luster,	13: 5
EXAMINING			that the battle became e. sore,	20:10
after e. the appeal and the	DC	102:33	he was filled with e. great joy.	21:24
			they were filled with e. great joy.	25: 8
EXAMPLE			because of thy e. faith in the words	26:15
yea, and set an e. for you?	1Ne	7: 8	their e. faith in the words alone	26:16
having set the e. before them.	2Ne	31: 9	they began to be e. rich,	Al 1:29
the e. of the Son of the living God,		31:16	because of their e. riches,	4: 6
because of the e. that ye have	Jac	3:10	the e. great joy of knowing that	7: 4
also that the e. of the church	Al	4:11	because of the e. diligence	7:26
he not set a good e. for thee?		39: 1	on account of their e. faith	13: 3
I have set an e. for you.	3Ne	18:16	exercising e. great faith,	13: 3
following the e. of our Savior,	Mrm	7:10	on account of their e. faith	13:10
be an e. unto my servant	DC	51:18	there were many, e. great many,	13:12
be an e. unto the church,		58:35	mind until it did become e. sore,	15: 3
that he may be an e.—		88:130	and his mind also was e. sore	15: 5
this I make an e. unto you,		124:53	art thou because of thy e. faith;	19:10
			being e. angry with Ammon,	19:22
EXAMPLES			contention began to be e. sharp	19:28
because of your bad e. before	Jac	2:35	e. sorrowful, even unto tears.	19:28
that ye may show forth good e.	Al	17:11	meet them he was e. sorrowful,	20:29
			their hatred became e. sore	24: 2
EXCEED			of their loss, were e. angry.	27: 2
brightness did e. that of the stars	1Ne	1:10	Now was not this e. joy?	27:18
white, to e. all the whiteness		8:11	his heart was e. sorrowful	31: 2
e. the whiteness of the driven		11: 8	Lord, my heart is e. sorrowful;	31:31
to e. the pride of those who	Al	4: 9	us out because of our e. poverty;	32: 5
was not that to e. their strength.		27:19	because of your e. poverty,	32:12
to e. the strength of the city		49:14	because of their e. poverty.	32:15
did e. the Lamanites in their		51:31	out because of your e. poverty,	34:40
did e. that of the Nephites	He	6: 1	his heart was e. sorrowful.	35:15
did e. all the whiteness, yea, even	3Ne	19:25	with joy as e. as was my pain!	36:20
even to e. the number of	Mrm	1:11	bring them to taste of the e. joy	36:24
e. the number of the Nephites.		4:13	Lord doth give me e. great joy	36:25
flight did not e. the Lamanites'		5: 7	fight with such e. great strength	43:43
is large, or to e. all;	Eth	15: 8	that Zerahemnah was e. wroth,	44:16
it doth not e. that of our	Mro	9: 9	of their dead was e. great,	44:21
this land doth e. everything;		9:19	worship God with e. great joy.	45: 1
doth e. that of the Lamanites.		9:20	because of their e. great riches;	45:24
			now behold, they were e. wroth,	46: 2
EXCEEDED			e. great care over the church,	46: 6
e. more than the number of those	Al	52:40	e. great prosperity in the church	49:30
			he was e. wroth because of	51:14
EXCEEDING			yea, he was e. wroth;	51:14
I, Nephi, being e. young,	1Ne	2:16	forth to battle with e. fury	52:33
he was e. glad, for he knew		3: 8	on both hands with e. fury;	52:35
we began to be e. sorrowful,		3:14	and earth to an e. height.	53: 4
property, and that it was e. great,		3:25	this city became an e. stronghold	53: 5
workmanship thereof was e. fine,		4: 9	the pity and the e. love which	53:11
my mother, Sariah, was e. glad,		5: 1	that city with an e. strong force.	55:26
for behold, they were e. wroth,		7:16	had become an e. stronghold.	55:33
filled my soul with e. great joy;		8:12	because of their e. faith in	57:26
an e. great mist of darkness,		8:23	I was filled with e. joy because	57:36
their manner of dress was e. fine;		8:27	the e. success which Helaman	59: 1
into an e. high mountain,		11: 1	And thus being e. numerous,	59: 7
far beyond, yea, e. of all beauty;		11: 8		

EXCEEDING — 304 — EXCEEDINGLY

them with an e. great slaughter.	Al 59: 7
was lost he was e. sorrowful,	59:11
have suffered e. great sufferings;	60: 3
cause of this e. great neglect;	60: 6
e. great neglect towards them.	60: 9
of the e. goodness of God	60:11
because of their e. slothfulness,	60:14
their e. great neglect towards	60:14
this because of their e. faith,	60:26
have risen up are e. numerous.	61: 3
was filled with e. great joy	62: 1
they became e. strong,	62: 6
knowing of their e. great courage,	62:19
dead they were e. sorrowful;	62:37
because of the e. great length	62:41
because of the e. great length	62:41
wax e. strong again in the land.	62:48
And they began to grow e. rich.	62:48
be their governor, was e. wroth	He 1: 7
who was e. expert in many words,	2: 4
there were an e. great many who	3: 3
did travel to an e. great distance,	3: 4
e. expert in the working of cement;	3: 7
timber was e. scarce in the land	3:10
there was e. great prosperity in	3:24
there was peace and e. great joy	3:32
save it were the e. great pride	3:36
because of their e. great riches	3:36
hearts, because of their e. riches,	4:12
that they became e. rich, both	6: 9
they did have an e. plenty of gold,	6: 9
them they were e. sorrowful;	6:20
of the e. sorrow of my heart,	7:14
because of your e. great riches!	7:26
have e. great peace in the land;	11:21
an e. great band of robbers;	11:26
the e. greatness of the numbers	11:31
give unto you e. great praise	3Ne 3: 2
thereof should be e. great.	3:14
because of their e. great riches,	6:10
who were e. angry because of	6:21
their tribes became e. great.	7: 4
there were e. sharp lightnings,	8: 7
e. great quaking of the whole	8:12
the damage thereof was e. great,	8:15
have great joy and be e. glad,	12:12
many, yea, an e. great number,	19: 3
they had become e. rich,	4Ne 1:23
because of their e. riches,	1:43
become e. wicked more like	1:45
upon us with e. great power,	Mrm 2: 3
Lamanites with e. great anger,	4:15
the Lamanites with e. boldness,	4:20
that they were e. tight,	Eth 2:17
Shelem, because of its e. height,	3: 1
such e. faith as thou hast;	3: 9
whose days were e. many.	7: 1
and they became e. fair;	7: 4
until he became e. old;	7: 7
had become e. numerous.	7:11
Jared became e. sorrowful	8: 7
daughter of Jared being e. expert,	8: 8
daughter of Jared was e. fair.	8: 9
having seen e. many days,	9:15
they had become e. rich—	9:16
that they became e. rich—	9:16
even until he was e. old.	9:23
an e. great wickedness upon	9:26
began to be destroyed e. fast	9:30
because of his e. riches,	10: 3
did live to an e. old age;	10: 4
the war became e. sore,	10: 9
and the people became e. rich	10:12
did live to an e. great age,	10:13
began to be an e. great war	11: 4
whose faith was so e. strong,	12:19
and the battle became e. sore.	13:27
and the battle became e. sore,	14: 4
and the battle became e. sore,	14:16
and the battle became e. sore.	14:29
And to another, e. great faith;	Mro 10:11
a more e. and eternal weight	DC 63:66
blessed with e. great blessings.	DC 108: 8
e., and an eternal weight of glory.	132:16

EXCEEDINGLY

he did quake and tremble e.	1Ne 1: 6
he was e. frightened,	4:28
they did rejoice e., and did offer	5: 9
I fear e. because of you;	8: 4
he e. feared for Laman and Lemuel;	8:36
she was e. fair and white.	11:13
after the Gentiles do stumble e.,	13:34
had been blessed of the Lord e.	16: 8
did begin to murmur e.,	16:20
it began to be e. difficult,	16:21
he did fear and tremble e.,	16:27
daughters of Ishmael did mourn e.,	16:35
and did chasten them e.;	16:39
we were e. rejoiced when we	17: 6
And I, Nephi, began to fear e.	18:10
they began to be frightened e.	18:13
and behold they had swollen e.;	18:15
they did grow e.; wherefore,	18:24
I e. fear and tremble	2Ne 1:25
and we did prosper e.;	5:11
we began to prosper e.,	5:13
The people having loved Nephi e.,	Jac 1:10
whose feelings are e. tender	2: 7
my heart would rejoice e. because	2:22
and, perhaps, that I may rejoice e.	5:60
began to grow and thrive e.;	5:73
they were astonished e.;	7:21
laws of the land were e. strict.	Jar 1: 5
And we multiplied e.,	1: 8
also Zarahemla did rejoice e.,	Om 1:14
for they had multiplied e.	Mos 2: 2
my whole frame doth tremble e.	2:30
the king rejoiced e., and gave	8:19
labor e. to support iniquity.	11: 6
industrious, and did labor e.	23: 5
to prosper e. in the land;	23:19
they did multiply and prosper e.	23:20
to prosper e. in the affairs of	26:37
the people of Mosiah to mourn e.,	28:18
and became e. anxious that	29:38
and they were e. rejoiced	29:39
yea, e. beyond measure,	29:40
and my soul doth e. rejoice,	Al 7:26
began to tremble more e.,	12: 7
therefore Alma did rejoice e.	17: 2
And they began to weep e.,	17:28
he was astonished e., and said:	18: 2
Lamoni began to fear e., with	18: 5
he was astonished e., and said:	20:26
and their skins were worn e.	20:29
she also began to fear e., lest	22:21
their brethren did rejoice e.,	25:17
Behold, they have labored e.,	29:15
therefore, they were e. afraid	43:21
the Lamanites did fight e.;	43:43
did fall e. fast before the	44:18
of Nephi were e. rejoiced,	45: 1
e. precarious and dangerous,	46: 7
them they were e. afraid;	47: 2
labor e. for the welfare and	48:12
Lamanites were astonished e.,	49: 5
e. astonished at their manner of	49: 9
for they feared Lehi e.;	49:17
was e. angry with his people,	49:26
Yea, he was e. wroth, and he	49:27
And they did prosper e.,	50:18
and they became e. rich;	50:18
they were e. fearful lest the	50:28
were e. valiant for courage,	53:20
Moroni felt to rejoice e. at this	54: 2
Antipus did rejoice e.,	56:10
and began to slay them e.,	56:52
were e. desirous to overtake	58:19
they were e. afraid, lest	58:24
astonished e. and struck with	58:29
he was e. rejoiced because	59: 1
I fear e. that the judgments of	60:14
But he did also mourn e.	62: 2
they were affrighted e.,	62:24

EXCEEDINGLY 305 EXCEPT

and did begin to labor e.,	Al	62:29
the armies of the Lamanites e.,		62:30
the army of Moroni e.;		62:30
was e. angry with Ammoron,		62:35
very many e. sore afflictions		62:37
they did humble themselves e.		62:49
he being an e. curious man,		63: 5
built him an e. large ship,		63: 5
was with such e. great speed	He	1:19
became an e. bloody battle;		1:30
this did please Kishkumen e.,		2: 9
the Lamanites were e. afraid,		4: 3
were e. more numerous than they,		4:25
these words, the earth shook e.,		5:27
behold the earth shook e., and		5:31
and behold, they did shine e.,		5:36
with e. great power and authority,		6: 5
and they did flourish e., both in		6:12
did multiply and wax e. strong		6:12
began to grow e. wicked again.		6:16
they had become e. wicked;		6:31
grow e. in the knowledge of		6:34
saw this they were astonished e.,		9: 4
and their e. great prosperity.		12: 2
his heart was e. sorrowful.	3Ne	1:10
so e. astonished that they fell		1:17
war, which had become e. sore.		2:13
daughters became e. fair,		2:16
and did become e. sore;		2:17
he was e. astonished,		3:11
And they were e. sorrowful		3:26
and others were e. humble;		6:13
their fine and e. dry wood,		8:21
did labor e. all that night,		19: 3
the Lord did prosper them e.	4Ne	1: 7
and did multiply e. fast,		1:10
and became an e. fair and		1:10
this church did multiply e.		1:28
became e. more numerous		1:40
was an e. sore battle fought	Mrm	4:19
with an e. great slaughter;		4:21
and they became e. rich.	Eth	6:28
did prosper e. and wax great.		7:19
they were e. angry because of		8: 5
the house of Emer did prosper e.		9:16
an e. beautiful throne;		10: 6
And they were e. industrious,		10:22
of e. curious workmanship.		10:27
Coriantumr was e. angry		13:27
they fought an e. sore battle,		15: 9
that they did rend the air e.		15:16
their wars are e. fierce among	Mro	1: 2
I rejoice e. that your Lord		8: 2
that which grieveth me e.;		8: 4
For so e. do they anger that		9: 5
e. blessed even above measure,	DC	58:61
among you who have sinned e.;		82: 2
and shall become e. angry,		87: 5
stars shall become e. angry,		88:87
e. great and glorious tidings,		109:23
and be e. glad;		127: 3
I desired, with e. great desire,		127:10
your hearts rejoice, and be e. glad.		128:22
up into an e. high mountain,	Mses	1: 1
pass that Moses began to fear e.;		1:20
so e. white and brilliant.	JS	2:31
Not only was his robe e. white,		2:32
The room was e. light, but not		2:32

EXCEL

images did e. them of Jerusalem	2Ne	20:10
with him, for he seeketh to e.,	DC	58:41

EXCELLENCY

the beauty of the Chaldees' e.,	2Ne	23:19

EXCELLENT

fruit of the earth e. and comely	2Ne	14: 2
for he hath done e. things;		22: 1
because of the e. qualities of	Al	46:40
God prepared a more e. way;	Eth	12:11
might have a more e. hope;		12:32

EXCELLETH

my wisdom e. them all,	Abr	3:21

EXCELS

e. in all things the glory of	DC	76:91
which e. in all things—		76:92

EXCEPT

e. they shall rebel against me also.	1Ne	2:23
And e. they should have charity	2Ne	26:30
e. ye shall keep the commandments		30: 1
e. they shall be reconciled unto		33: 9
for e. ye repent the land is cursed	Jac	3: 3
e. ye repent they shall possess		3: 4
e. we should do something for it		5:37
e. it were for the help of these	Mos	1: 4
e. it be through transgression.		1:12
e. it be your little children		2:34
e. it be unto death;		3: 7
e. it be through repentance and		3:12
e. it were through the atonement		3:15
e. they humble themselves and		3:18
e. it be little children,		3:21
e. the conditions which I have		4: 8
e. he repenteth of that which he		4:18
e. it be through transgression;		5:11
e. it were little children,		6: 2
e. he be commanded, lest he		8:13
e. he should possess the power of		8:16
e. they repent I will visit		11:20
e. they repent and turn to the		11:21
e. this people repent and turn		11:23
e. it be the Lord the Almighty		11:23
e. they repent in sackcloth and		11:25
e. they repent I will utterly		12: 8
come upon thee e. thou repent,		12:12
e. it were through the redemption		13:32
e. the king doth pacify them		20:20
e. it were to take their women		22: 2
e. he be a man of God, walking		23:14
e. it were by him from God.		23:17
e. they were just men.		23:17
e. it were among their own		24: 7
e. it were the Lord their God.		24:21
e. it were repentance and faith		25:22
and e. we make haste they	Al	2:25
e. they repent of their wickedness		3:14
e. his garments are washed white;		5:21
e. ye make our Creator a liar		5:25
for e. ye repent ye can in nowise		5:51
the fire e. they speedily repent.		5:56
e. they repent the Lord God will		8:16
e. ye repent I will visit this		8:29
e. ye repent, ye can in nowise		9:12
than for you, e. ye repent.		9:15
time is soon at hand e. ye repent.		10:23
e. ye inherit the kingdom of		11:37
e. it be the loosing of the bands		11:41
I will smite thee e. thou wilt grant		20:22
e. we repent we shall perish.		21: 6
deny, e. ye shall show me a sign.		30:45
and e. ye show me a sign,		30:48
e. it be through the atonement		34: 9
e. it was the God of Abraham,		36: 2
e. they repent I will destroy		37:25
e. they repent before they are		37:31
e. ye repent they will stand as a		39: 8
e. ye do this ye can in nowise		39: 9
e. it were for these conditions,		42:13
e. it should destroy the work of		42:13
e. an atonement should be made;		42:15
e. there were a punishment,		42:16
a man repent e. he should sin?		42:17
e. that they preached the word,		43: 2
destroyed e. we should fall into		44: 4
e. ye depart with an oath that		44:11
e. ye will deliver up your		44:14
e. it were against an enemy,		48:14
e. it were to preserve their		48:14
e. ye repent and withdraw		54: 6
e. ye repent and withdraw		54: 7
e. you withdraw your purposes,		54: 9

EXCEPT			306		EXCUSABLE	
come upon you e. ye withdraw,	Al	54:10	he saves all e. them—		DC	76:44
e. they should come out to		58:15	e. to them who are made			76:46
e. ye do repent of that which		60:24	e. those who are ordained			76:48
And e. ye grant mine epistle,		60:25	e. him to whom God has			76:90
e. ye do bestir yourselves in		60:29	e. that which he hath not put			77:12
e. ye do administer unto our		60:30	e. judgment shall immediately			82:11
e. they repent the Lord hath		61:20	e. he be a literal descendant of			107:16
and e. they should cleave unto	He	4:25	without counselors, e. in a case			107:76
destruction e. they repent		7:hd	e. ye perform them in a house			124:37
e. ye will repent, behold, he		7:19	e. the same shall pay his stock			124:67
come unto you e. ye shall repent.		7:22	e. it be by law, even as I and			132:11
than for you e. ye shall repent.		7:23	e. ye abide my law ye cannot			132:21
destroyed e. thou shalt repent.		7:24	e. such laws are framed and			134: 2
And e. ye repent ye shall perish;		7:28	e. he behold all my glory;		Mses	1: 5
come to pass e. we repent;		8: 7	e. his glory should come upon			1:14
come upon you e. ye repent?		8:12	Show them not unto any e.			1:42
not slain, all e. it were Mulek?		8:21	e. to them that believe.			4:32
cannot deny them e. ye shall lie,		8:24	e. thou shalt hearken unto			5:23
e. ye repent it will come unto		8:26	upon thee, e. thou repent.			5:25
await you, e. ye shall repent.		9:22	And e. those days should be		JS	1:20
for e. he was a god he could not		9:41	left dark, e. just around him;			2:43
e. ye repent ye shall be smitten,		10:11				
E. ye repent, thus saith the Lord,		10:14	EXCEPTING			
e. the Lord doth chasten his		12: 3	e. my servant Joseph Smith,		DC	28: 2
e. he doth visit them with death		12: 3	e. my servants Joseph Smith,			42: 4
e. they repent I will take away		13: 8	e. those whom I shall reserve			63:39
shall surely come e. ye repent,		13:10				
e. ye shall repent your houses		15: 1	EXCESS			
e. ye repent, your women shall		15: 2	with judgment, not to e.,		DC	59:20
of Nephi e. they shall repent,		15: 3	your e. of laughter far from you.			88:69
them than for you e. ye repent.		15:14	of famine and e. of hunger.			89:15
e. the sign should come to pass,	3Ne	1: 9				
and e. ye do this, I will avenge		3:10	EXCHANGE			
e. ye repent of all your		3:15	that he would e. prisoners.		Al	54: 1
e. they should fall into		6: 5	that I will not e. prisoners,			54:11
e. they had power from the		6:24	case that ye will do it, will e.			54:11
whole earth e. they shall repent;		9: 2	to e. prisoners according to your			54:20
that e. ye shall keep my		12:20	not e. prisoners with Ammoron			55: 2
e. they repent it shall fall upon		20:20	deliver up our prisoners on e.			57: 2
the Gentiles e. they repent;		21:14	for he would not e. prisoners;			57: 3
e. ye shall repent and turn from	Mrm	5:22	in e. for his former inheritance,		DC	104:24
e. by and by it shall be	Eth	5: 1				
people e. they should repent,		11: 1	EXCHANGERS			
e. they should repent of their		11: 6	this money be given to the e.?		DC	101:49
e. they repented of their		11:12				
and e. they should repent		11:20	EXCITE			
e. men shall have charity		12:34	to e. the public mind against		JS	2:22
e. he shall do it with real	Mro	7: 6				
they shall perish e. they repent.		8:16	EXCITED			
e. they should repent.		8:27	My mind at times was greatly e.,		JS	2: 9
they must perish e. they repent		9:22	had e. a great deal of prejudice			2:22
e. ye have charity ye can in		10:21				
E. thou do this, thou shalt be	DC	3:11	EXCITEMENT			
e. to those persons to whom		5: 3	e. on the subject of religion.		JS	2: 5
e. I grant it unto you.		5: 3	During this time of great e.			2: 8
these things, e. he shall say:		5:26	before mentioned religious e.;			2:21
e. he humble himself and		5:28	The e., however, still continued,			2:61
And e. thou do this, behold,		5:31				
e. he shall be humble and full		12: 8	EXCLAIM			
e. when thou shalt desire to see		19:36	did e. many things unto the Lord;		1Ne	1:14
e. I shall command you,		24:13	to e.; The God of nature suffers.			19:12
e. casting out devils, healing		24:13	and be constrained to e.: Holy,		2Ne	9:46
e. it be required of you by them		24:14	did e. in the agony of his soul:		He	7: 6
And e. thou do this, where I am		25:15				
e. it is made new among you;		27: 4	EXCLAIMED			
e. it is his brother, Joseph Smith,		30: 7	their hands for joy, and e.:		Mos	18:11
e. desolations upon Babylon,		35:11				
e. those who are ready to		35:12	EXCLAIMETH			
e. he be ordained by some one		42:11	my heart e.: O wretched man		2Ne	4:17
this gift e. it be through him;		43: 4				
power e. to appoint another		43: 4	EXCLAIMING			
e. those which I have reserved		49: 8	e.: I am a dead man!		DC	135: 1
e. he be purified and cleansed		50:28	e.: O Lord my God!			135: 1
e. they desire it through the		58:44				
e. he bear record by the way,		58:59	EXCLUSIVE			
e. quickened by the Spirit of		67:11	e. of the sacred things,		DC	104:63
e. they be literal descendants of		68:15				
e. he be a literal descendant		68:18	EXCOMMUNICATE			
e. one go with him who will		69: 1	They can only e. them from		DC	134:10
e. the law of Moses should be		74: 5				
e. he repent and mend his		75:29	EXCUSABLE			
e. those sons of perdition who		76:43	are not e. in thy transgressions;		DC	24: 2

EXCUSE 307 EXHORTED

EXCUSE
not that I would e. myself because	1 Ne	19: 6
to the flesh I would e. myself.		19: 6
for they seek to e. themselves in	Jac	2:23
this was no e. for thee, my son.	Al	39: 4
Do not endeavor to e. yourself		42:30
spoken, and I e. not myself;	DC	1:38
they are left without e.,		88:82
all men may be left without e.;		101:93
nation may be left without e.		123: 6
they may be left also without e.—		124: 7

EXECUTE
shall e. judgment in righteousness.	1 Ne	22:21
my commandments to e. them.	Al	18:10
I will e. vengeance and fury	3 Ne	21:21
he may not e. judgment unto		29: 9
Orihah did e. judgment upon	Eth	7: 1
e. judgment in righteousness;		7:11
Shule did e. judgment against		7:24
he did e. a law throughout all		7:25
did e. judgment in righteousness		7:27
did e. judgment in righteousness		9:21
did e. judgment in wickedness		11:14
e. judgment against them		11:20
E. judgment and justice for us	DC	105:25

EXECUTED
who was e. according to the law—	Al	2: 1
and the judge e. authority,		11: 2
were e. according to the law;		62: 9
speedily e. according to the law.		62:10
be e. according to the law.	He	2:10
her law be e. and fulfilled,	DC	105:34

EXECUTETH
For he e. all his words,	2 Ne	9:17
Thus God e. vengeance upon	Mos	17:19
the creature and e. the law,	Al	42:22
governeth and e. all things.	DC	88:40

EXEMPT
not e. from the justice of God.	DC	10:28
none are e. from this law		70:10
who is e. from this council of		107:81
he is e. from the law of Sarah,		132:65

EXEMPTED
none shall be e. from the	DC	107:84

EXERCISE
that they e. faith in him?	1 Ne	7:12
and to e. their hatred upon them.	Mos	11:17
and e. authority over them;		21: 3
to e. authority over Alma and		24: 8
to e. his power over them.		27: 9
Do ye e. faith in the redemption	Al	5:15
they did not e. their power until		8:31
and e. the power of God which is		14:10
which he shall e. upon them		14:11
did not e. his justice upon us,		26:20
and e. a particle of faith,		32:27
should begin to e. their faith.		33: 1
ye may begin to e. your faith		34:17
and forgot to e. their faith and		37:41
and to e. authority over them.		46:34
they did e. power and authority	4 Ne	1:30
that ahey shall e. faith in me,	Eth	4: 7
began to e. faith in Christ;	Mro	7:25
and e. faith in me, behold,	DC	5:28
therefore thou shalt e. thy gift,		6:11
faithful, and e. faith in me,		44: 2
and e. the prayer of faith,		104:80
to e. control or dominion or		121:37
begin to e. unrighteous dominion.		121:39
the free e. of conscience,		134: 2
and to him only, for the e. of it,		134: 4
free e. of their religious belief;		134: 7

EXERCISED
yet he e. authority over them,	Mos	24: 9
being e. with much faith, cried,	Al	2:30
and he hath e. his power in thee.		12: 5

having e. mighty faith,	Al	13:18
for ye have only e. your faith		32:36

EXERCISES
while he that e. no faith	Al	34:16

EXERCISETH
he that repenteth and e. faith,	Al	26:22
justice e. all his demands,		42:24

EXERCISING
by thus e. the law upon them,	Al	1:33
and e. exceeding great faith,		13: 3

EXERT
e. themselves in their might	3 Ne	3:16
to e. the powers of heaven;	DC	84:119

EXERTED
therefore they e. themselves	Mos	20:11

EXERTING
But e. all my powers to call upon	JS	2:16

EXERTION
with a little e. raised it up.	JS	2:52

EXERTIONS
most strenuous e. were used	JS	2:60

EXHAUSTED
I found my strength so e. as	JS	2:48

EXHAUSTING
even to the e. of his strength;	Al	27:17

EXHORT
I did e. them that they would	1 Ne	7:21
he did e. them then with all the		8:37
I, Nephi, did e. them to give heed		15:25
I did e. them with all the		15:25
I, Nephi, did e. my brethren,		16: 4
did e. my brethren to faithfulness		17:15
he did e. the people of Limhi	Mos	25:16
And he did e. them daily, with	Al	21:23
and I also e. you, my brethren,		34:39
I would e. you to have patience,		34:40
and did e. them to faith and	He	6: 4
whether to preach, or to e., or	Mro	6: 9
I would e. you that when ye		10: 3
I would e. you that ye would		10: 4
I would e. you that ye deny		10: 7
I e. you, my brethren, that ye		10: 8
I would e. you, my beloved		10:18
to e. authority over Alma and		10:19
I e. you to remember these		10:27
I would e. you that ye would		10:30
preach, e., declare the truth,	DC	19:37
to teach, expound, e., baptize,		20:42
teach, expound, e., and baptize,		20:46
e. them to pray vocally and in		20:47
preach, teach, expound, e.,		20:50
to warn, expound, e., and teach,		20:59
and to e. the church, according		25: 7

EXHORTATION
few words by way of e. unto	Mro	10: 2
and thy calling is to e., and to	DC	23: 3
and thy calling is to e., and to		23: 4
and thy calling also is to e.,		23: 5
language to e. continually,		23: 7
them by the word of e.;		50:37
in e. to the churches in the		73: 1

EXHORTATIONS
in all your prayers, in all your e.,	DC	108: 7

EXHORTED
I have e. you with all diligence;	2 Ne	6: 3
stood among them, and e. them	Mos	23:27
and he hath e. you unto faith	Al	34: 3
are e. to return to the Lord	DC	113:10

EXHORTING 308 EXPEDIENT

EXHORTING
of e. them to all diligence,	1Ne 10: 2
e. with all long-suffering	Jar 1:11
e. all men to come unto God,	Om 1:25
e. them with long-suffering and	Mos 27:33
e. the people to believe in God	Eth 12: 3
e. them to pray vocally and in	DC 20:51

EXIGENCY
of all persons in times of e.,	DC 134:11

EXILE
The captive e. hasteneth,	2Ne 8:14

EXIST
the robbers could not e. save it	3Ne 4: 3
robbers that do e. upon the	Mrm 8: 9
designs which do and will e. in	DC 89: 4
will e. among us there,	130: 2
no government can e. in peace,	134: 2
where such laws e. as will protect	134:11
Abraham, these two facts e.,	Abr 3: 6
And where these two facts e.,	3: 8
If two things e.,	3:16
or a star may e. above;	3:17
no end, they shall e. after,	3:18
These two facts do e., that there	3:19
or as they at present e.,	JS 2: 2

EXISTED
they e. before, they shall have	Abr 3:18
that e. in the Primitive Church,	AoF 6

EXISTENCE
and prolong their e. in the land.	Al 9:16
deny the e. of a Supreme Being.	11:22
I do not deny the e. of a God,	30:48
continuance, or its temporal e.	DC 77: 6
otherwise there is no e.	93:30

EXISTS
that same sociality which e.	DC 130: 2

EXPAND
and their souls did e.,	Al 5: 9
and your mind doth begin to e.	32:34

EXPANSE
upon the wide e. of eternity,	DC 38: 1
an e. in the midst of the waters,	Abr 4: 6
And the Gods ordered the e.,	4: 7
waters which were under the e.	4: 7
waters which were above the e.;	4: 7
the Gods called the e., Heaven.	4: 8
lights in the e. of the heaven,	4:14
lights in the e. of the heaven	4:15
them in the e. of the heavens,	4:17
earth in the open e. of heaven.	4:20
Raukeeyang, signifying e.,	Fac 1:12
Raukeeyang, signifying e.,	2: 4

EXPECT
so I may e. you will do it again.	Al 54: 8
How can we e. that God will	Mro 9:14
fulfil the promises which ye e.	DC 124:47

EXPECTATION
have awaited with anxious e.	DC 121:27

EXPECTATIONS
connections, associations, or e.,	DC 132: 7

EXPEDIENT
as many of them as were e.	1Ne 10:15
which were e. for man to receive,	17:30
which are e. unto man.	2Ne 2:27
words which are e. in my wisdom	3:19
for it is e. that it should be	9: 5
is it e. that I should awake you	9:47
it must needs be e. that I teach	9:48
it must needs be e. that Christ—	10: 3
it must needs be e. that they	25:16
inasmuch as it shall be e.,	25:30
it is e. that much should be	Jar 1: 3
he thought it e. that he should	Mos 1: 9
it is e, that he should be diligent,	4:27
were it e., we could prophesy of	5: 3
king Benjamin thought it was e.,	6: 1
it is e. that ye should keep the	13:27
e. to keep the law of Moses.	13:27
e. that there should be a law given	13:29
not e. that we should have a king;	23: 7
not e. that ye should have a king.	23: 7
e. that those who committed sin,	26: 6
it is e. that all people should know	28:19
it would be e. that ye should	29:13
not e. that ye should have a king	29:16
it is not e. that such abominations	29:24
e. that the curse should fall	Al 3:18
e. that man should know	12:28
e. that thou shouldst forbear;	20:18
for it was e. that they should	25:15
Alma thought it was e. that	31: 5
it is e. that an atonement should	34: 9
which it is e. should be made.	34: 9
For it is e. that there should	34:10
it is e. that there should be a	34:13
or it is e. there should be, a stop	34:13
it was not e. that man should	42: 8
it was e. that mankind should	42: 9
it became e. that the word of	45:21
Moroni thought it was not e.	46:30
Moroni thought it was e. that	46:31
not e. that he should attempt	52: 5
not e. that they should fight	55:23
was e. for Moroni to make	55:33
it became e. that we should	57:11
Therefore it became e. for us,	57:15
it became e. that we should	58: 3
it became e. that we should	58: 3
it will be e. that we contend	60:24
it became e. that this law	62:10
become e. that a regulation	62:44
it became e. for Shiblon to	63:11
it was e. that there should be	He 11:28
and cometh e. that he dieth,	14:15
no more e. to observe the law	3Ne 1:24
became e. that all the people,	2:11
e. that he should go up to battle	4: 5
be e. that Christ had come,	5: 2
it hath become e. that I,	5:14
it is e. that I should go unto	18:35
e. that they should have first,	26: 9
whatsoever thing is e. in me.	Mro 7:33
things which are e. unto me.	10:23
it is not e. that you should	DC 9: 3
not e. that you should translate	9:10
was e. when you commenced;	9:11
is past, and it is not e. now;	9:11
all things which are e. unto	18:18
It is e. that the church meet	20:75
it is e. in me that you shall	30: 5
not e. in me that ye should	37: 1
it is e. in me that they should	37: 3
it is e. that thou shouldst hold	42:57
it is e. in me that the elders	44: 1
the world until it is e. in me,	45:72
it is e. in me that my servant	47: 1
meetings, whenever it shall be e.	47: 2
it is e. that my servant Sidney	61: 7
it is e. in me that my servant	64:18
it is necessary and e. in me	71: 1
it is e. in me for a bishop to	72: 2
it is e. in me that they should	73: 1
it is e. to translate again;	73: 3
it is e. to continue the work of	73: 4
all things that are e. for them.—	75:10
it is e. that all things be done	78: 8
it is e. for my servants Alam	82:11
it is e. that I give unto you	84:77
it is e. that every man who	84:103
unto you, that is e. for you;	88:64
that is not e. for you,	88:65
are e. for you to understand;	88:78
all things that are e. for them,	88:127
it is e. in me that this stake	96: 1
this is the most e. in me,	96: 5

EXPEDIENT — 309 — EXTINCT

EXPEDIENT
it is wisdom and e. in me,	DC 96: 6
it is e. in me that he should	96: 8
it is not e. that you should	99: 6
thus it was e. in me for the	100: 4
And it is e. in me that you,	100: 9
it is e. that I, the Lord, should	104:13
it is e. in me that mine elders	105: 9
it is e. in me that mine elders	105:13
it is e. in me that they should	105:19
it is e. in me that the first	105:33
it is e. that you should form	111: 3
I have thought it e. and wisdom	127: 1

EXPELLED
have been e. from the church,	DC 20:83

EXPENSES
receive money to bear her e.,	DC 90:28

EXPERIENCE
more perfectly, and have e.,	DC 105:10
We have learned by sad e.	121:39
these things shall give thee e.,	122: 7

EXPERIENCED
Have ye e. this mighty change in	Al 5:14
if ye have e. a change of heart,	5:26
of what I had just e.;	JS 2:47
we e. great and glorious	2:73

EXPERIMENT
even to an e. upon my words,	Al 32:27
because ye have tried the e.,	32:33
that ye might try the e.	32:36
ye may try the e. of its goodness.	34: 4

EXPERT
one of the most e. among them,	Al 10:31
e. in the devices of the devil,	11:21
was exceeding e. in many words,	He 2: 4
e. in the working of cement;	3: 7
of Jared being exceeding e.,	Eth 8: 8
number of able-bodied and e. men,	DC 136: 7

EXPERTNESS
because of his e. and great	Al 18: 3

EXPLAIN
and to e. things beyond, or to	Al 12: 1
thing which I was about to e.	12:22
behold, I will e. it unto thee.	41: 1
I will e. this thing unto thee,	42: 2
I will e. unto you this mystery,	DC 19: 8

EXPLAINED
and e. them to the people of	Mos 8: 3
and he e. it all unto them.	29:33

EXPLAINING
and e. the prophecies and	Mos 27:35

EXPLANATIONS
offered many e. which cannot	JS 2:41

EXPOSED
is e. to the whole law of the	Al 34:16
e. to the heavy blows of the	43:37
were e. to the sharp swords of	44:18
who had been e. to the arrows	49:24
were most e. to the Lamanites,	62:42

EXPOUND
Alma began to e. these things	Al 12: 9
as he began to e. these things	21:10
did e. unto him the scriptures	22:13
Aaron did e. all these things	22:14
judges did e. the matter	He 9:16
did e. all things unto them,	3Ne 26: 1
And he did e. all things,	26: 3
to teach, e., exhort, baptize,	DC 20:42
to preach, teach, e., exhort,	20:46
to preach, teach, e., exhort,	20:50
to warn, e., exhort, and teach,	20:59
sufficient time to e. all things	20:68
and to e. all scriptures,	24: 9
his hand to e. scriptures,	25: 7

EXPOUNDED
he e. unto them all the records	Al 18:38
he e. unto them the plan of	18:39
and e. them to the king,	18:40
after Aaron had e. these things	22:15
e. all the scriptures unto them	3Ne 23: 6
had e. all the scriptures in one,	23:14
which he had e. unto them.	23:14
they were written he e. them.	24: 1
he e. them unto the multitude;	26: 1

EXPOUNDING
and e. all scriptures unto	DC 24: 5
e. these things unto them,	63:46
and e. all scriptures unto them.	68: 1
Preaching and e., writing,	69: 8
e. the mysteries thereof out of	71: 1
in e. all scriptures and	97: 5
mighty in e. all scriptures,	100:11

EXPRESS
more e. than other scriptures,	DC 19: 7
might e. beyond his language;	67: 5
his likeness was the e. likeness	107:43
being instituted for the e. purpose	134: 6

EXPRESSED
every man e. a willingness to	Mos 29:38
e. at the time of their conversion,	JS 2: 6

EXPRESSIONS
They are figurative e., used	DC 77: 2

EXPRESSLY
that they were e. repugnant to	Mos 29:36
has not the Lord e. promised	Al 9:24

EXQUISITE
be nothing so e. and so bitter	Al 36:21
can be nothing so e. and sweet as	36:21
how e. you know not, yea,	DC 19:15
loose robe of most e. whiteness.	JS 2:31

EXTENDED
it e. along the bank of the river,	1Ne 8:19
And while his arm of mercy is e.	Jac 6: 5
if he had not e. his arm in	Mos 1:14
while the arms of mercy were e.	16:12
for the arms of mercy were e.	16:12
for the arms of mercy were e.	Al 5:33
many promises which are e.	9:16
the promises of the Lord are e.	9:24
the promises of the Lord were e.	17:15
his arm is e. to all people who	19:36
arm which he e. towards me,	29:10
have been e. to our brethren,	He 15:12
arm of mercy is e. towards you,	3Ne 9:14
he whould have e. his arm and	DC 3: 8

EXTENDING
e. the arm of mercy towards	Mos 29:20

EXTENSIVE
the e. branches of my church,	DC 72:23

EXTENT
corruptibleness to the e. thereof.	DC 19:38
the e. of his doings none can	76: 2

EXTINCT
become e. both soul and body,	Al 36:15
that ye may become e.;	44: 7
of Nephi shall become e.—	45:11
even until they shall become e.	45:14
and authority shall become e.	60:27
that they have become e.,	He 11:10
even until ye shall become e.	3Ne 3: 8

EXTINCTION 310 EYES

EXTINCTION
authority or to their eternal e.   Al   54:20

EXTOLLED
he shall be exalted and e.   3Ne   20:43

EXTORTION
not to excess, neither by e.   DC   59:20

EXTRAORDINARY
this e. scene of religious feeling,   JS   2: 6
told to me by this e. messenger;   2:44

EXTREME
the e. hatred of the Lamanites   Al   43:11
laboring under the e. difficulties   JS   2:11

EXULT
yet they rejoice and e. in the hope,   Al   28:12

EYE
view me with his all-searching e.;   2Ne   9:44
piercing e. of the Almighty God.   Jac   2:10
with one glance of his e. he can   2:15
for they shall see e. to eye   Mos   12:22
to e. when the Lord shall bring   12:22
for they shall see e. to eye,   15:29
to e., when the Lord shall bring   15:29
and people shall see e. to eye   16: 1
and people shall see eye to e.   16: 1
should look forward with one e.,   18:21
the glance of his all-searching e.   27:31
look forward with an e. of faith,   Al   5:15
forward with an e. of faith   32:40
have seen e. to eye as I have   36:26
have seen eye to e. as I have   36:26
angels, and being e.-witness,   3Ne   7:15
being e.-witness to their quick   7:15
it is written, an e. for an eye,   12:38
it is written, an eye for an e.,   12:38
The light of the body is the e.;   13:22
if, therefore, thine e. be single,   13:22
But if thine e. be evil,   13:23
mote that is in thy brother's e.,   14: 3
the beam that is in thine own e.?   14: 3
pull the mote out of thine e.—   14: 4
behold, a beam is in thine own e.?   14: 4
the beam out of thine own e.;   14: 5
the mote out of thy brother's e.   14: 5
for they shall see e. to eye   16:18
they shall see eye to e. when   16:18
in the e. of all the nations;   16:20
The e. hath never seen, neither   17:16
for they shall see. to eye.   20:32
for they shall see eye to e.   20:32
changed in the twinkling of an e.   28: 8
with an e. single to his glory,   Mrm   8:15
had beheld with an e. of faith,   Eth   12:19
there is no e. that shall not see,   DC   1: 2
an e. single to the glory of God,   4: 5
with an e. single to my glory—   27: 2
changed in the twinkling of an e.,   43:32
with an e. single to my glory,   55: 1
with an e. single to my glory,   59: 1
both to please the e. and to   59:18
in the twinkling of an e.   63:51
things which e. has not seen,   76:10
an e. single to the glory of God.   82:19
and shall see e. to eye,   84:98
and shall see eye to e.,   84:98
if your e. be single to my glory,   88:67
in the twinkling of an e.,   101:31
and thine e., yea thy pure eye,   121: 2
and thine eye, yea thy pure e.,   121: 2
let thine e. pierce;   121: 4
be e.-witness of your baptisms;   127: 6
who should be e.-witness,   128: 2
had his e. fixed on the restoration   128:17
neither hath any e. seen,   133:45
were not visible to the natural e.;   Mses   6:36
mine e. can pierce them also,   7:36

EYES
as I cast my e. round about,   1Ne   8:13
I cast mine e. towards the head of   8:17
they did cast their e. about as if   8:25
I also cast my e. round about,   8:26
blindeth the e., and hardeneth   12:17
that they might blind the e. and   13:27
that he may deceive our e.,   16:38
glorious in the e. of the Lord,   21: 5
Lift up thine e. round about   21:18
his arm in the e. of the nations.   22:10
arm in the e. of all the nations,   22:11
popular in the e. of the world,   22:23
I will make him great in mine e.;   2Ne   3: 8
mine e. have beheld great things,   4:25
Lift up your e. to the heavens,   8: 6
shall be great in the e. of me,   10: 8
to provoke the e. of his glory.   13: 8
necks and wanton e.,   13:16
the e. of the lofty shall be humbled.   15:15
Wo unto the wise in their own e.   15:21
for mine e. have seen the King,   16: 5
their ears heavy and shut their e.—   16:10
lest they see with their e.,   16:10
not judge after the sight of his e.,   21: 3
dashed to pieces before their e.;   23:16
their e. shall not spare children.   23:18
mine e. hath beheld the things of   25: 5
cast their e. unto the serpent   25:20
lifted up in the pride of their e.,   26:20
behold, ye have closed your e.,   27: 5
be his from the e. of the world,   27:12
the e. of none shall behold it   27:12
the e. of the blind shall see out   27:29
shall begin to fall from their e.;   30: 6
mine e. water my pillow by night,   33: 3
always before our e.,   Mos   1: 5
we have them before our e.   1: 6
he cast his e. round about on   4: 1
the e. of the people were blinded;   11:29
in the e. of all the nations,   12:24
in the e. of all the nations;   15:31
to the e. of them who there came   18:30
the king cast his e. round about   19: 6
gain favor in the e. of the king   24: 1
with their own e. they had   27:18
e. of the people might be opened   27:22
were not proud in their own e.,   Al   1:20
up in the pride of their own e.;   1:32
lifted up in the pride of their e.,   4: 6
lifted up in the pride of their e.,   4: 8
power over you, to blind your e.,   10:25
found favor in the e. of the king   20:28
by merely casting about your e.   33:21
ye would not cast about your e.,   33:21
if not so, then cast about your e.   33:22
no more after the lusts of your e.,   39: 9
they grew rich in their own e.,   45:24
up in the pride of their e.;   62:49
they did lift their e. to heaven;   He   5:36
when they cast their e. about,   5:43
they cast up their e. as if to   5:48
gained favor in the e. of some,   8:10
walked after the pride of your e.,   13:27
cannot witness with our own e.   16:20
that he did blind their e. and   3Ne   2: 2
in the e. of some, would be   5: 8
I have seen with mine own e.   5:17
they cast their e. round about,   11: 3
e. were towards the sound   11: 5
cast their e. up again towards   11: 8
the e. of the whole multitude   11: 8
and did see with their e. and   11:15
he cast his e. round about on   15: 1
he cast his e. round about again   17: 5
cast their e. towards heaven,   17:24
he turned his e. again upon the   18:26
in the e. of all the nations;   20:35
cast his e. upon them and said: 23: 8
opened the e. of their blind   26:15
has been before mine e. ever   Mrm   2:18
as was laid before mine e.;   5: 8

EYES 311 FACE

wrought marvelous in our e.?	Mrm	9:16
the e. of the brother of Jared,	Eth	3: 6
magnify to the e. of men		3:24
in the e. of all the people.		4:16
gain favor in the e. of Shule;		7:22
favor in the e. of the people,		10:10
but truly saw with their e.		12:19
and whose e. are upon all men;	DC	1: 1
and have seen them with your e.		17: 3
and their e. from their sockets;		29:19
manifest in the e. of all people.		35: 7
things are present before mine e.;		38: 2
that mine e. are upon you.		38: 7
and ye see them with your e.,		45:37
this work in the e. of the people,		45:72
and in the e. of your enemies,		45:72
whose e. are full of greediness,		56:17
behold with your natural e.,		58: 3
mine e. are upon those who		62: 2
in the e. of the people.		63:15
justified in the e. of the law,		64:13
and lo, mine e. are upon you,		67: 2
Your e. have been upon my		67: 5
their e. are full of greediness.		68:31
the Spirit our e. were opened		76:12
the e. of our understandings		76:19
by the e. and wings, which		77: 4
Their e. are a representation		77: 4
shall open the e. of the blind,		84:69
him who enlighteneth your e.,		88:11
before the e. of the people.		90:23
it is meet in mine e. that she		90:30
lift up his e. in hell, being in		104:18
favor and grace in their e.,		105:25
favor in the e. of the people,		105:26
and the e. of our understanding		110: 1
His e. were as a flame of fire;		110: 3
that which was meet in mine e.,		121:16
e. see and know all their works,		121:24
that ye may find grace in their e.,		124: 9
and he shall be great in mine e.;		124:13
record that he saw with his e.,		128: 3
same as if he had seen with his e.		128: 4
can only be discerned by purer e.;		131: 7
in the e. of all the nations,		133: 3
he died great in the e. of God		135: 3
that his e. may be opened		136:32
mine own e. have beheld God;	Mses	1:11
my natural, but my spiritual e.,		1:11
natural e. could not have beheld;		1:11
lifted up his e. unto heaven,		1:24
Moses cast his e. and beheld		1:27
then your e. shall be opened,		4:11
became pleasant to the e.,		4:12
e. of them both were opened,		4:13
transgression my e. are opened,		5:10
and their e. cannot see afar off;		6:27
Anoint thine e. with clay,		6:35
behold, these which thine e. are		7:38
grace in the e. of the Lord;		8:27
behold thine e. see it;	Abr	3: 6
he put his hand upon mine e.,		3:12
they multiplied before mine e.,		3:12
intelligences thine e. have seen		3:21
that sleep had fled from my e.,	JS	2:46

EYE-WITNESS: see EYE and WITNESS.

EZEKIEL
by the mouth of E. the prophet, DC 29:21

EZIAS
behold, also Zenock, and also E., He 8:20

EZRA: see also BENSON, Ezra T.; BOOTH, Ezra; PULSIPHER, Ezra; and THAYRE, Ezra.
my servants E. and Northrop,	DC	33: 1
and second verses of E.		85:12

EZROM
an e. of silver, and an onti of	Al	11: 6
And an e. of silver was as great		11:12

FACE
went forth upon the f. of the earth	1Ne	1:11
upon all the f. of the earth,		10:12
upon all the f. of the earth.		10:13
in the Spirit from before my f.,		11:29
darkness on the f. of the land		12: 4
from off the f. of the earth;		12: 5
multitudes upon the f. of the land.		12:20
nations, upon the f. of the land		13:30
upon all the f. of the earth,		13:39
upon all the f. of the earth;		14:12
upon the f. of the earth		14:12
upon the f. of all the earth,		14:13
upon all the f. of the earth;		14:14
with their f. towards the earth,		21:23
upon all the f. of the earth.		22: 3
even upon the f. of this land;		22: 7
be upon the f. of this earth;		22:18
prosper upon the f. of this land;	2Ne	1: 9
blessed upon the f. of this land,		1: 9
long upon the f. of this land;		1:31
prosperity upon the f. of this land		1:31
I hid not my f. from shame		7: 6
have I set my f. like a flint,		7: 7
return to God, and behold his f.,		9:38
with twain he covered his f.,		16: 2
the Lord, that hideth his f.		18:17
fill the f. of the world with cities.		24:21
and grind upon the f. of the poor.		26:20
neither shall his f. now wax pale.		27:33
gather in upon the f. of this land;		30: 7
you and I shall stand f. to face		33:11
face to f. before his bar;		33:11
came upon the f. of the earth,	Jac	4: 9
of his hands upon the f. of it,		4: 9
shall I see his f. with pleasure,	En	1:27
off from the f. of the land.	Jar	1: 3
upon much of the f. of the land,		1: 6
spread upon the f. of the land,		1: 8
from off the f. of the land.		1:10
destroyed upon the f. of the land;		1:12
go forth upon the f. of the earth—	Mos	7:27
did contend with them, f. to face.		10:19
did contend with them, face to f.		10:19
them from off the f. of the earth;		12: 8
forth upon the f. of the land.		12:12
his f. shone with exceeding luster,		13: 5
power upon the f. of the earth?		13:34
we hid as it were our f. from him;		14: 3
abroad upon the f. of the earth,		27: 6
upon the f. of all the earth,		28:17
remains upon the f. of the land.		29:32
Amlici with the sword, f. to face;	Al	2:29
Amlici with the sword, face to f.;		2:29
upon the f. of the earth?		5:16
works upon the f. of the earth—		5:17
upon the f. of the earth.		7: 9
cut off from the f. of the earth		9:11
from off the f. of the earth;		9:12
from off the f. of the earth?		9:24
abroad upon the f. of the earth;		13:22
up upon the f. of the earth,		16:11
his Spirit on all the f. of the land		16:16
in heaps upon the f. of the earth;		28:11
upon all the f. of the earth.		29: 2
things that are upon the f. of it,		30:44
his f. immediately towards him,		32: 6
from off the f. of the earth.		37:22
from off the f. of the earth;		37:25
I have seen an angel f. to face,		38: 7
I have seen an angel face to f.,		38: 7
off from the f. of the earth—		42: 6
had sent upon the f. of the land		46:10
from off the f. of the earth.		54:12
timber upon the f. of the land,	He	3: 7
cover the f. of the whole earth,		3: 8
up upon the f. of the land		3: 9
upon the f. of the earth,		3:16
of God did stare them in the f.		4:23
them off the f. of the earth.		6:20
over all the f. of the land,		6:28
from off the f. of the earth.		7:28
which has come upon your f.,		9:34

FACE 312 FACE

about upon the f. of the land,	He	10:12
rain upon the f. of the earth		11:13
the whole f. of the land was filled		11:18
cover the whole f. of the land,		11:20
throughout the f. of all the land;		11:21
people upon all the f. of the land.		11:32
no light upon the f. of this land,		14:20
are upon the f. of this earth		14:21
upon the f. of the whole earth,		14:22
cover the whole f. of the earth		14:27
pass upon all the f. of this land,		14:28
and fro upon the f. of the earth,		15:12
upon all the f. of the land,		16:22
upon all the f. of the land.		16:23
upon the f. of the whole earth	3Ne	1:17
all the f. of the land,		3:22
from off the f. of the land;		4: 4
upon the f. of the land		4: 6
upon all the f. of the earth.		5:24
three days over the f. of the land.		8: 3
whole f. of the land was changed,		8:12
thus the f. of the whole earth		8:17
upon the f. of the whole earth,		8:18
upon all the f. of the land.		8:18
darkness upon the f. of the land.		8:19
upon all the f. of the land,		8:20
were upon the f. of the land.		8:22
upon all the f. of this land,		9: 1
abominations from before my f.,		9: 5
abominations from before my f.,		9: 7
abominations from before my f.,		9: 8
destroy them from before my f.,		9: 9
might be hid from before my f.,		9:11
from off the f. of the land,		10: 9
thy head, and wash thy f.;		13:17
forth upon the f. of the earth		16: 4
forth upon the f. of this land,		16: 8
down upon the f. of the earth,		19: 6
upon the f. of the earth,		20:13
upon all the f. of the earth,		21:24
I hid my f. from thee for a		22: 8
come upon the f. of the earth,		26: 3
upon the f. of the earth;		28:16
forth upon the f. of the land,		28:18
people upon the f. of the land;		28:23
upon all the f. of the land,	4Ne	1: 2
upon all the f. of the land,		1:23
over all the f. of the land;		1:46
The whole f. of the land had	Mrm	1: 7
upon all the f. of the whole land,		1:13
upon all the f. of the land,		1:19
throughout all the f. of the land,		2: 8
throughout all the f. of the land.		2: 8
as dung upon the f. of the land.		2:15
them off from the f. of the land.		3:10
cut off from the f. of the earth.		3:15
lay upon the f. of the land,		6:15
the whole f. of this land is one		8: 8
do exist upon the f. of the land.		8: 9
they be upon the f. of the land		8:10
upon the f. of the earth;		8:31
the f. of this north country.	Eth	1: 1
upon all the f. of the earth;		1:33
upon all the f. of the earth.		1:43
was upon the f. of the land,		2: 3
upon all the f. of the land.		4:17
blow upon the f. of the waters,		6: 5
down upon the f. of the land,		6:12
forth upon the f. of the land,		6:13
spread upon the f. of the land,		6:18
upon all the f. of the land,		7:11
over all the f. of the land,		9:26
upon the f. of the land,		9:26
curse upon the f. of the land;		9:28
no rain upon the f. of the earth.		9:30
also upon the f. of the land,		9:31
rain upon the f. of the earth;		9:35
cities upon the f. of the land,		10: 4
spread over all the f. of the land.		10: 4
whole f. of the land northward		10:21
been upon the f. of the earth,		11: 6
earth upon the f. of the land		11: 6
upon the f. of the earth;		11: 7
from off the f. of the earth		11:12

hath talked with me f. to face,	Eth	12:39
hath talked with me face to f.,		12:39
from off the f. of this land		13: 2
who dwell upon the f. thereof;		13: 2
upon the f. of the whole earth		13:17
a war upon all the f. of the land,		13:25
upon all the f. of the land.		13:26
people upon the f. of the land		13:31
throughout all the f. of the land.		14:19
whole f. of the land was covered		14:21
strewed upon the f. of the land,		14:22
forth upon the f. of the land,		14:23
upon all the f. of the land;		14:23
upon all the f. of the land,		15:12
were upon the f. of the land,		15:14
be one man upon the f. thereof	Mro	7:36
abominations from before thy f.!		9:15
upon all the f. of this land		9:19
upon the f. of the whole earth,	DC	1:30
from off the f. of the earth;		5:33
talked with the Lord f. to face,		17: 1
talked with the Lord face to f.,		17: 1
place upon the f. of this land,		29: 8
flies upon the f. of the earth,		29:18
with thee and go before thy f.		39:12
preparing the way before my f.		39:20
be a messenger before my f.		45: 9
one with another f. to face.		50:11
one with another face to f.		50:11
rideth upon the f. thereof,		61:19
wars upon the f. of the earth,		63:33
things upon the f. of the earth,		63:36
that dwell upon the f. thereof,		63:39
man can see the f. of God,		84:22
might behold the f. of God;		84:23
before the f. of his people,		84:28
also, for I will go before your f.		84:88
the f. of him who sitteth upon		88:40
he will unveil his f. unto you,		88:68
and the sun shall hide his f.,		88:87
and the f. of the Lord shall be		88:95
shall see my f. and know that		93: 1
stand rebuked before my f.;		95: 2
upon all the f. of the earth,		101:24
shall cease from before my f.		101:26
seek the f. of the Lord always,		101:38
was before his f. continually;		107:49
upon the f. of thine Anointed.		109:53
be of good cheer before my f.;		112: 4
become corrupt before my f.		112:23
come up all the f. of the earth,		112:24
unveil the f. of my covering,		124: 8
be a spokesman before my f.		124:104
to prepare a way before my f.		124:139
see that f. of the Son of Man;		130:15
should die and thus see his f.		130:16
sun shall hide his f. in shame,		133:49
And he saw God f. to face,	Mses	1: 2
And he saw God face to f.,		1: 2
was upon me; and I beheld his f.,		1:11
inhabitants on the f. thereof.		1:29
and talked with him f. to face.		1:31
and talked with him face to f.		1:31
come up upon the f. of the deep;		2: 2
moved upon the f. of the water;		2: 2
is upon the f. of all the earth,		2:29
upon the f. of the earth.		3: 5
to rain upon the f. of the earth.		3: 5
the whole f. of the ground.		3: 6
By the sweat of thy f. shalt		4:25
this day from the f. of the Lord,		5:39
and from thy f. shall I be hid;		5:39
upon all the f. of the land.		6:15
he brought in upon the f. thereof.		6:44
and he stood before my f.,		7: 4
one with another, f. to face;		7: 4
one with another, face to f.;		7: 4
was upon all the f. of the earth.		7:24
veiled the whole f. of the earth		7:26
mercy shall go before thy f.		7:31
hath plead before my f.		7:39
for a season abide upon my f.?		7:48
multiply on the f. of the earth,		8:14
from the f. of the earth,		8:26

FACE 313 FAITH

FACE
and withdrawn his f. from me,	Abr	2:12
talked with the Lord, f. to face,		3:11
face to f., as one man talketh		3:11
reigned upon the f. of the deep,		4: 2
upon the f. of the waters.		4: 2
upon the f. of all the earth,		4:29
the whole f. of the ground.		5: 6

FACES
with their f. towards the earth,	2Ne	6: 7
and grind the f. of the poor,		13:15
their f. shall be as flames.		23: 8
the f. of Nephi and Lehi;	He	5:36
even as the f. of angels.		5:36
the f. of Nephi and Lehi.		5:37
they disfigure their f. that they	3Ne	13:16

FACSIMILE
the first f. of this book.)	Fac	3: 3

FACT
shall be another f. above them,	Abr	3: 8
it was nevertheless a f. that	JS	2:24

FACTION
some f. in the government,	Al	58:36

FACTS
a knowledge of all the f.,	DC	123: 1
in obtaining a knowledge of f.		128:11
Abraham, these two f. exist,	Abr	3: 6
And where these two f. exist,		3: 8
These two f. do exist, that there		3:19
in possession of the f.,	JS	2: 1
have such f. in my possession.		2: 1

FACULTIES
arouse the f. of your soul;	Jac	3:11
and f. which I have possessed,	Mos	29:14
ye will awake and arouse your f.,	Al	32:27

FACULTY
with all the f. which I possessed,	1Ne	15:25
and the f. of his whole soul,	WM	1:18

FADETH
eternal, and which f. not away;	He	5: 8

FAGGOTS
and scourged his skin with f.,	Mos	17:13

FAIL
nor that his bread should f.	2Ne	8:14
church began to f. in its progress.	Al	4:10
Spirit of the Lord did not f. him.		4:15
of all, for all things must f.—	Mro	7:46
over him that his faith f. not,	DC	35:19
and men's hearts shall f. them,		45:26
of the prophets shall not f.;		58: 8
lest their faith f. and they are		61:18
words are sure and shall not f.,		64:31
not f. to go into the world,		75:26
His purposes f. not, neither are		76: 3
the same, and his years never f.		76: 4
f. not to continue faithful		84:80
men's hearts shall f. them,		88:91
cause of thy people may not f.		109:52
and his reward shall not f.		124:16
let him not f., neither let		124:75
upon you, and your faith f. you,		136:42

FAILED
my strength entirely f. me,	JS	2:48

FAILETH
are nothing, for charity never f.	Mro	7:46

FAILING
and men's hearts f. them,	Mses	7:66

FAIN
we would f. be glad if we could	Al	12:14
would f. claim it from Noah,	Abr	1:27

FAINT
fear not, neither be f.-hearted	2Ne	17: 4
Therefore shall all hands be f.,		23: 7
he awaketh and behold he is f.,		27: 3
ye must pray always, and not f.;		32: 9
women do f. by the way and die.	Mro	9:16
Praying always that they f. not;	DC	75:11
Pray always, that ye may not f.,		88:126
and shall walk and not f.		89:20
always to pray and not to f.,		101:81
let not your hearts f.,		103:19
that thy people may not f.		109:38
not fail, neither let his heart f.;		124:75

FAINTED
Thy sons have f., save these two;	2Ne	8:20
f. because of the loss of blood;	Al	57:25
having lost his blood, f.,	Eth	14:30
and he f. with the loss of blood.		15: 9
they f. with the loss of blood.		15:27
had f. with the loss of blood.		15:29

FAINTETH
as when a standard-bearer f.	2Ne	20:18

FAINT-HEARTED: see FAINT and HEARTED.

FAIR
she was exceedingly f. and white.	1Ne	11:13
and f. above all other virgins.		11:15
they were white, and exceeding f.		13:15
and exceeding f. and delightsome,	2Ne	5:21
and f. cities without inhabitant.		15: 9
of the f. daughters of this people,	Jac	2:32
his f. promises, deceived me, that	Mos	10:18
their f. daughters should stand		19:13
meeting them upon f. grounds,	Al	52:21
became exceedingly f., and	3Ne	2:16
mothers and our f. daughters,		8:25
of the f. sons and daughters of		9: 2
lay thy stones with f. colors,		22:11
f. and delightsome people.	4Ne	1:10
O ye f. ones, how could ye have	Mrm	6:17
O ye f. ones, how could ye have		6:17
O ye f. sons and daughters,		6:19
ye f. ones, how is it that ye could		6:19
may be found spotless, pure, f.,		9: 6
and they became exceeding f.;	Eth	7: 4
of Jared was exceeding f.		8: 9
I am f., and I will dance before		8:10
them away by f. promises		8:17
neither his f. sons nor		13:17
the f. sons and daughters of		13:17
the f. sons and daughters of		13:17
of the f. sons and daughters		13:17
as the moon, and f. as the sun,	DC	5:14
may become f. as the sun,		105:31
and shine forth f. as the moon,		109:73
saw that those daughters were f.,	Mses	8:14
a very f. woman to look upon;	Abr	2:22

FAITH
hath chosen, because of their f.,	1Ne	1:20
art thou, Nephi, because of thy f.,		2:19
be that they exercise f. in him?		7:12
to my f. which is in thee,		7:17
received by f. on the Son of God—		10:17
because of their f. in the Lamb		12:10
because of their f. in him.		12:11
and ask me in f., believing that		15:11
they did work according to the f.		16:28
according to the f. and diligence		16:29
given them to do all things by f.;	2Ne	1:10
from the dust; for I know their f.		3:19
Because of their f. their words shall		3:21
will I make strong in their f.,		3:21
f., to work mighty wonders,		3:24
having perfect f. in the Holy One		9:23
alive in Christ because of our f.;		25:25
of men according to their f.		26:13
save it be according to their f.		27:23
Christ with unshaken f. in him,		31:19

FAITH

I cry unto my God in f.,	2Ne	33: 3
and great f. in Christ		33: 7
because of f. and great anxiety,	Jac	1: 5
pray unto him with exceeding f.,		3: 1
and our f. becometh unshaken,		4: 6
of Christ unto God, having f.,		4:11
that I, Jacob, had f. in Christ		7: 3
had hope to shake me from the f.,		7: 5
Because of thy f. in Christ,	En	1: 8
thy f. hath made thee whole.		1: 8
my f. began to be unshaken		1:11
to thy desires, because of thy f.		1:12
in restoring them to the true f.		1:14
thing ye shall ask in f.,		1:15
I had f., and I did cry unto God		1:16
unto them according to their f.;		1:18
for their f. was like unto thine.		1:18
unto the true f. in God.		1:20
not stiffnecked and have f.,	Jar	1: 4
of men, according to their f.		1: 4
mighty men in the f. of the Lord;		1: 7
even through f. on his name;	Mos	3: 9
and f. on the Lord Jesus Christ.		3:12
and f. on the name of the Lord God		3:21
because of the exceeding f. which		4: 3
in the f. even unto the end of		4: 6
and standing steadfastly in the f.		4:11
in f., believing that ye shall		4:21
in the f. of what ye have heard		4:30
And it is the f. which we have had		5: 4
changed through f. on his name;		5: 7
that man, through f., might work		8:18
redemption, and f. on the Lord.		18: 7
repentance and f. on the Lord,		18:20
having one f. and one baptism,		18:21
and f. on the words which had		21:30
trieth their patience and their f.		23:21
so great was their f. and their		24:16
repentance and f. on the Lord.		25:15
were repentance and f. in God.		25:22
a separate people as to their f.,		26: 4
because of thy exceeding f. in the		26:15
because of their exceeding f. in		26:16
for he has prayed with much f.		27:14
answered according to their f.		27:14
confirming their f., and		27:33
that did stand fast in the f.;	Al	1:25
being exercised with much f.,		2:30
according to his f. there was		5:12
exercise f. in the redemption		5:15
look forward with an eye of f.,		5:15
your sins, with an everlasting f.,		7: 6
may have f. on the Lamb of God,		7:14
now because your f. is strong		7:17
And see that ye have f., hope, and		7:24
according to your f. and good		7:27
desires, and their f., and prayers,		9:20
through f. on his name.		9:27
unto them according to their f.		12:30
on account of their exceeding f.		13: 3
exercising exceeding great f.,		13: 3
calling on account of their f.,		13: 4
on account of their exceeding f.		13:10
having exercised mighty f.,		13:18
Having f. on the Lord;		13:29
them because they were of thy f.		14:15
after the order and f. of Nehor,		14:16
to our f. which is in Christ,		14:26
to their f. which was in Christ.		14:28
to his f. which is in Christ.		15:10
according to my f. and desires		18:35
because of thy exceeding f.;		19:10
has not been such great f. among		19:10
unto him according to thy f.—		19:23
through f. and repentance,		22:14
and call on his name in f.,		22:16
to strengthen their f. in Christ;		25:16
they did retain a hope through f.,		25:16
that repenteth and exerciseth f.,		26:22
they were firm in the f. of Christ,		27:27
and this because he prayed in f.		31:38
Now I ask, is this f.?		32:18
now as I said concerning f.—	Al	32:21
f. is not to have a perfect		32:21
if ye have f. ye hope for things		32:21
Now as I said concerning f.—		32:26
any more than f. is a perfect		32:26
and exercise a particle of f.,		32:27
would not this increase your f.?		32:29
and your f. is dormant;		32:34
neither must ye lay aside your f.,		32:36
exercised your f. to plant the seed		32:36
forward with an eye of f. to		32:40
by your f. with great diligence,		32:41
of your diligence and your f.		32:42
reap the rewards of your f.,		32:43
should begin to exercise their f.		33: 1
even so nourish it by your f.		33:23
he hath exhorted you unto f.		34: 3
ye would have so much f. as		34: 4
they may have f. unto repentance.		34:15
while he that exercises no f. unto		34:16
only unto him that has f. unto		34:16
ye may begin to exercise your f.		34:17
hypocrites who do deny the f.		34:28
and f. on the Lord Jesus Christ;		37:33
their f. on the Lord Jesus Christ.		37:33
according to their f. in God;		37:40
if they had f. to believe that		37:40
and forgot to exercise their f.		37:41
religion and our f. in Christ.		44: 3
ye cannot destroy this our f.		44: 3
that this is the true f. of God;		44: 4
unto our f., and our religion;		44: 4
transgression and deny our f.		44: 4
by our f., by our religion, and		44: 5
Behold, we are not of your f.;		44: 9
who should stand fast in the f.		45:17
stand fast in the f. of Christ.		46:27
who died in the f. of Christ		46:41
was firm in the f. of Christ,		48:13
And this was their f., that by		48:15
and this was the f. of Moroni,		48:16
according to their f. it was done		57:21
because of their exceeding f. in		57:26
this was the f. of these of whom		57:27
did grant unto us great f.,		58:11
f. is strong in the prophecies		58:40
because of their exceeding f.,		60:26
according to the f. which is in us.		61:17
and firmer in the f. of Christ,	He	3:35
until ye shall have f. in Christ,		5:41
of your f. in my Well Beloved,		5:47
and their steadiness in the f.		6: 1
and did exhort them to f.		6: 4
upon the Son of God with f.,		8:15
he might convert us unto his f.,		9:16
and in deed, in f. and in works;		10: 5
rapentance and f. on the Lord		13: 6
leadeth them to f. on the Lord,		15: 7
which f. and repentance bringeth		15: 7
are firm and steadfast in the f.,		15: 8
this because of their f. in Christ.		15: 9
and your f. concerning this thing	3Ne	1: 6
that their f. had not been vain.		1: 8
destroyed because of their f.		1:11
as to their f. and righteousness,		1:30
be fulfilled according to their f.,		5:14
converted unto the true f.;		6:14
remission of sins through f. on		7:16
great was his f. on the Lord		7:18
because of their f. in me at		9:20
if ye are not of little f.		13:30
your f. is sufficient that I should		17: 8
are ye because of your f.		17:20
have chosen, because of their f.,		19:28
through f. on their words,		19:28
of the world, because of their f.,		19:29
So great f. have I never seen		19:35
should have first, to try their f.,		26: 9
I will try the f. of my people.		26:11
in my blood, because of their f.,		27:19
nevertheless, it was without f.,	Mrm	3:12
and he knoweth their f., for		8:24

FAITH

answered according to their f.;	Mrm 9:37
f. on the name of Jesus Christ.	9:37
because of thy f. thou hast	Eth 3: 9
before me with such exceeding f.	3: 9
and he had f. no longer,	3:19
they shall exercise f. in me,	4: 7
by f. all things are fulfilled—	12: 3
which hope cometh of f.,	12: 4
f. is things which are hoped for	12: 6
until after the trial of your f.	12: 6
by f. that Christ showed himself	12: 7
until after they had f. in him;	12: 7
that some had f. in him,	12: 7
But because of the f. of men	12: 8
if ye will but have f.	12: 9
it was by f. that they of old	12:10
by f. was the law of Moses	12:11
by f. that it hath been fulfilled.	12:11
if there be no f. among the	12:12
himself until after their f.	12:12
it was the f. of Alma and	12:13
it was the f. of Nephi and	12:14
it was the f. of Ammon and	12:15
miracles wrought them by f.,	12:16
it was by f. that the three	12:17
the promise until after their f.	12:17
miracles until after their f.;	12:18
f. was so exceeding strong,	12:19
had beheld with an eye of f.,	12:19
for so great was his f. in God,	12:20
word he had obtained by f.	12:20
of Jared had obtained by f.,	12:21
it is by f. that my fathers have	12:22
made us mighty in word by f.,	12:23
before me, and have f. in me,	12:27
f., hope and charity bringeth	12:28
of men according to their f.;	12:29
if he had not had f. it would	12:30
thou workest after men have f.	12:30
after they had f., and did	12:31
endurance of f. on his name	Mro 3: 3
and the finisher of their f.	6: 4
concerning f., hope, and charity;	7: 1
And now I come to that f.,	7:21
began to exercise f. in Christ;	7:25
thus by f., they did lay hold	7:25
were saved by f. in his name;	7:26
by f., they become the sons of	7:26
in f. believing that ye shall	7:26
all those who have f. in him;	7:28
they who have f. in him will	7:28
of strong f. and a firm mind	7:30
of men may have f. in Christ,	7:32
If ye will have f. in me	7:33
my name, and have f. in me,	7:34
it is by f. that miracles are	7:37
it is by f. that angels appear	7:37
save they shall have f. in his	7:38
then has f. ceased also;	7:38
judge that ye have f. in Christ	7:39
for if ye have not f. in him	7:39
that ye can attain unto f.,	7:40
this because of your f. in him	7:41
if a man have f. he must needs	7:42
without f. there cannot be any	7:42
he cannot have f. and hope,	7:43
If so, his f. and hope is vain,	7:44
through the endurance of f.	8: 3
neither f., hope, nor charity;	8:14
baptism cometh by f. unto the	8:25
real intent, having f. in Christ,	10: 4
the f. of the children of men,	10: 7
to another, exceeding great f.;	10:11
Wherefore, there must be f.;	10:20
if there must be f. there must	10:20
of God if ye have not f.;	10:20
If ye have f. ye can do all	10:23
That f. also might increase in	DC 1:21
glorified through f. in his name,	3:20
And f., hope, charity and love,	4: 5
Remember f., virtue, knowledge,	4: 6
himself in mighty prayer and f.,	5:24
and exercise f. in me,	5:28
it be those who are of thy f.	DC 6:12
patience, f., hope and charity.	6:19
things you shall ask in f.,	8: 1
without f. you can do nothing;	8:10
therefore ask in f.	8:10
according to your f. shall it	8:11
according to their f. in their	10:47
Yea, and this was their f.—	10:48
their f. in their prayers was	10:49
according to their f. in their	10:52
if thou wilt desire of me in f.,	11:10
in f. believing in me that you	11:14
according to your f. shall it	11:17
having f., hope, and charity,	12: 8
in my name, in f. believing,	14: 8
it is by your f. that you shall	17: 2
by that f. which was had by the	17: 2
after that you have obtained f.,	17: 3
and it is because he had f.	17: 5
the same power, and the same f.,	17: 7
in f. believing that you shall	18:18
And if you have not f., hope,	18:19
declare repentance and f. on	19:31
himself sincerely, through f.,	20: 6
And those who receive it in f.,	20:14
and endure in f. to the end,	20:25
in f. on his name to the end,	20:29
works and f. agreeable to the	20:69
build it up unto the most holy f.	21: 2
in all patience and f.	21: 5
I will, according to their f.	25: 9
by much prayer and f.,	26: 2
things you shall receive by f.	26: 2
Taking the shield of f. wherewith	27:17
by the prayer of f.	28:13
Whatsoever ye shall ask in f.,	29: 6
through f. on the name of mine	29:42
heart unto me in prayer and f.,	30: 6
because of your f. in my work.	31: 1
that they shall have f. in me	33:12
And whoso having f. you shall	33:15
shall ask it in my name in f.,	35: 9
without f. shall not anything be	35:11
over him that his f. fail not,	35:19
they pray unto me in much f.	37: 2
thou shalt have great f.,	39:12
Ohio call upon me in much f.,	39:16
by the prayer of your f. ye shall	41: 3
unto you by the prayer of f.;	42:14
lust after her shall deny the f.,	42:23
and have not f. to be healed,	42:43
that hath f. in me to be healed,	42:48
He which hath f. to see shall see.	42:49
He who hath f. to hear shall hear.	42:50
who hath f. to leap shall leap.	42:51
have not f. to do these things,	42:52
before me by the prayer of f.	43:12
faithful, and exercise f. in me,	44: 2
given to have f. to be healed;	46:19
it is given to have f. to heal.	46:20
through the prayer of f.	52: 9
according to men's f. it shall	52:20
to preach f. and repentance and	53: 3
through the prayer of f.,	58:44
through f. they shall overcome;	61: 9
lest their f. fail and they are	61:18
behold, f. cometh not by signs,	63: 9
signs come by f., not by the	63:10
signs come by f., unto mighty	63:11
without f. no man pleaseth God;	63:11
after signs and wonders for f.,	63:12
deny the f. and shall fear.	63:16
he that endureth in f. and	63:20
come, and hath kept the f.,	63:50
f. in Christ the Son of the	68:25
And who overcome by f.,	76:53
brought to pass by the f.	84:99
their manner of life, their f.,	85: 2
(for verily your f. is weak),	86: 6
And as all have not f., seek ye	88:118
even by study and also by f.	88:118
house of fasting, a house of f.,	88:119
man of God, and of strong f.—	90:22

FAITH / FAITHFULLY

prayer of f. with one consent	DC 93:51
according to the prayer of f.;	93:52
and endure in f., though they	101:35
faithfulness, and prayers of f.	103:36
are mine, or else your f. is vain,	104:55
humility and the prayer of f.	104:79
exercise the prayer of f.,	104:80
thus far for a trial of their f.	105:19
neither boast of f. nor of	105:24
upheld by the confidence, f.,	107:22
in f., and virtue, and knowledge,	107:30
And as all have not f.,	109: 7
even by study and also by f.;	109: 7
a house of fasting, a house of f.,	109: 8
even by study, and also by f.,	109:14
a house of fasting, a house of f.,	109:16
and to the house hold of f.,	121:45
rules on spiritual concerns, for f.	134: 6
with the broken f. of the State	135: 7
upon you, and your f. fail you,	136:42
f. was taught unto the children	Mses 6:23
so great was the f. of Enoch	7:13
through f. I am in the bosom of	7:47
contending for the Methodist f.,	JS 2: 5
to the Presbyterian f.,	2: 7
F. in the Lord Jesus Christ;	AoF 4

FAITHFUL

because thou hast been f.	1Ne 2: 1
let us be f. in keeping the	3:16
that they might be f. in keeping	3:21
let us be f. in keeping the	4: 1
Wherefore, let us be f. to him.	7:12
if it so be that we are f. to him,	7:13
because of the Lord that is f.	21: 7
because thou hast been f.	2Ne 1:31
and be f. unto his words,	2:28
because of the prayers of the f.;	6:11
I took unto me f. witnesses	18: 2
prayers of the f. shall be heard,	26:15
the words of the f. should speak	27:13
words of my Beloved are true and f.	31:15
if they hold out f. to the end	Mos 2:41
f. in keeping the commandments	10:13
they were f. until the end;	Al 5:13
f. in keeping the commandments	8:15
that has been so f. as this man;	18:10
so long as we are f. unto him,	44: 4
did belong to the church were f.;	46:15
be f. unto the Lord their God.	48: 7
if they were f. in keeping	48:15
those who were f. in keeping	50:22
f. in maintaining that quarter	52:10
let us be f. unto the Lord,	Eth 1:38
that is found f. unto my name	4:19
that ye will be f. unto me in	8:13
not unto thee, thou hast been f.;	12:37
My son, be f. in Christ;	Mro 9:25
for they are true and f.,	DC 1:37
Yet you should have been f.;	3: 8
And if thou art f. in keeping	5:35
and hold out f. to the end,	6:13
Be f. and diligent in keeping	6:20
be f., keep my commandments,	6:37
Be f., and yield to no temptation.	9:13
therefore see that you are f.	10: 3
which thing if ye do, and are f.,	14:11
and if thou art f. and walk in	25: 2
and be f. until I come,	27:18
Be f. unto the end, and lo,	31:13
be f., praying always, having	33:17
And if you are f., behold,	34:11
f. laborers into my vineyard,	39:17
which ye have received and be f.	42:66
that inasmuch as they are f.,	44: 2
eternal life it they continue f.	46:14
given him, inasmuch as he is f.,	47: 4
blessed are they who are f.	50: 5
And whoso is found a f.,	51:19
as they are f. unto me,	52: 4
inasmuch as they are f.,	52: 5
inasmuch as they are not f.,	52: 6
he that is f. shall be made	52:13

He that is f., the same shall	DC 52:34
if ye are f. ye shall assemble	52:42
and will crown the f. with joy	52:43
he that is f. in tribulation,	58: 2
they that are f. and diligent	59: 4
if they are not more f.	60: 3
and he that is f. among you	61: 6
And inasmuch as they are f.	61:10
be f., and declare glad tidings	62: 5
the f. among you should be	62: 6
I, the Lord, promise the f.	62: 6
lo, I am with the f. always.	62: 9
He that is f. and endureth	63:47
not f. in their stewardships	64:40
he that is f. shall be made	66: 8
for they are true and f.;	66:11
the f. elders of my church—	68: 7
These sayings are true and f.;	68:34
him who will be true and f.	69: 1
been f. over many things,	70:17
and inasmuch as ye are f.	71: 7
they are true and f.	71:11
he who is f. and wise in time	72: 4
And the labors of the f. who	72:14
steward and as a f. laborer;	72:17
if ye are f. ye shall be laden	75: 5
and inasmuch as they are f.,	75:13
he who is f. shall overcome	75:16
gird up your loins and be f.,	75:22
elders who had been f. in	77: 5
he that is f. and wise	78:22
And inasmuch as he is f.,	79: 3
as thou art f. in counsel,	81: 3
Wherefore, be f.; stand in	81: 5
if thou art f. unto the end	81: 6
And if they are not f.	83: 3
whoso is f. unto the obtaining	84:33
to continue f. in all things,	84:80
the f. who are called of God	84:86
cometh in and is f. before me,	88:135
in peace inasmuch as she is f.,	90:31
inasmuch as you are f. in	92: 2
if you are f. you shall receive	93:18
give unto the f. line upon line,	98:12
a f. and wise steward in the	101:61
whom I commanded been f.	104: 2
inasmuch as they were not f.	104: 3
And inasmuch as he is f.,	104:25
inasmuch as they are f.,	104:31
And, inasmuch as they are f.,	104:33
And inasmuch as he is f.,	104:35
And inasmuch as he is f.,	104:38
And inasmuch as he is f. in	104:42
inasmuch as he is f.,	104:46
f. and wise in his stewardship,	104:75
as ye are humble and f. and	104:82
inasmuch as they are f. and	105:12
for them, if they continue f.	105:18
be very f., and prayerful,	105:23
Therefore, be f.; and behold,	105:41
continue to be a f. witness	106: 8
if you continue f.	108: 5
and be ye f. before me	112:12
Be f. until I come,	112:34
also unto my f. servants	115: 3
be f. over a few things,	117:10
be f. and true in all things	124:13
that ye are f. in all things	124:55
when he shall prove himself f.	124:113
kept a proper and f. record	128: 9
This is a f. saying.	128: 9
but hath been f.;	132:44
hath been f. over a few things,	132:53
thou hast been f.;	135: 5
f. in keeping all my words	136:37
foundation he did lay, and was f.;	136:38
then, is a f. and wise servant,	JS 1:49

FAITHFULLY

stand by my servant Joseph, f.,	DC 6:18
declare f. the commandments	28: 3
and did it truly and f.,	128: 9

FAITHFULNESS — FALL

FAITHFULNESS
I did exhort my brethren to f.	1 Ne 17:15
and f. the girdle of his reins.	2 Ne 21: 5
and f. the girdle of his reins.	30:11
had learned of the f. of Ammon	Al 18: 2
because of the f. of Ammon,	18:10
steadiness and your f. unto God;	38: 2
because of thy f. and thy diligence,	38: 3
steadiness of thy brother, his f.,	39: 1
because of the f. of Pahoran,	62: 1
and their f. unto the end.	3 Ne 27:19
and f. upon his loins,	DC 63:37
are appointed to labor, in all f.;	68:30
diligence, f., and prayers of faith.	103:36
may know that thy f. is stronger	121:44
do this with a pure heart, in all f.,	136:11

FAITHS
converts to these different f.	JS 2: 6

FALL
f. down at his feet and worship him.	1 Ne 11:24
the f. thereof was exceeding great.	11:36
people, for I had beheld their f.	15: 5
shall f. upon their own heads,	22:13
they shall f. into the pit which	22:14
and great shall be the f. of it.	22:14
way is prepared from the f. of men,	2 Ne 2: 4
the children of men from the f.	2:26
they are redeemed from the f.	2:26
unto man by reason of the e.;	9: 6
and the f. came by reason of	9: 6
Thy men shall f. by the sword	13:25
shall stumble and f., and be broken,	18:15
they shall f. under the slain.	20: 4
Lebanon shall f. by a mighty one.	20:34
to the wicked shall f. by the sword.	23:15
and buildings shall f. upon them	26: 5
and great must be the f. thereof.	28:18
trembleth lest he shall f.	28:28
scales of darkness shall begin to f.	30: 6
they must needs f.;	Jac 4:14
should f. into transgression,	En 1:13
but should f. into transgression,	Jar 1:10
should f. into transgression,	Mos 1:13
as in Adam, or by nature, they f.,	3:16
has been from the f. of Adam,	3:19
could deny that Adam should f.	3:26
ever were since the f. of Adam,	4: 7
which was the cause of their f.;	16: 3
of Limhi began to f. upon them	20: 9
f. into the hands of the Lamanites.	21:19
did f. before the Amlicites.	Al 2:17
the Amlicites did f. before them.	2:28
the curse should f. upon them.	3:18
f. into sins and transgressions,	9:19
they should f. into transgression,	9:23
should f. into transgression,	10:19
the mountains to f. upon us	12:14
Adam did f. by the partaking	12:22
by his f., all mankind became	12:22
were slain by the f. thereof.	14:27
determined that he should f.,	17:36
things concerning the f. of man,	18:36
he might let it f. upon Ammon,	19:22
better had he should than thee,	20:17
if thou shouldst f. at this time,	20:17
laying the f. of man before him,	22:13
had been the cause of his f.,	22:19
had seen the cause of the king's f.,	22:20
Therefore we shall f. before them.	22:20
unto the Lord, never did f. away.	23: 6
Lamanites began to f. upon them,	24:21
the sword of his justice f. upon us,	26:19
they should f. into darkness also	37:27
and thus they stand or f.;	41: 9
and the f. had brought upon all	42: 9
if they should f. into the hands	43:10
if they should f. into the hands	43:11
f. upon them and to slay them.	43:41
we should f. into transgression	44: 4
that they shall f. upon you,	Al 44: 7
so shall ye f. to the earth	44:14
f. upon them and slay them.	44:17
did f. exceedingly fast before	44:18
f. into the works of darkness,	45:12
or f. into transgression,	46:21
if we shall f. into transgression;	46:22
if we shall f. into transgression.	46:22
to f. in with their brethren,	47:15
that they should f. upon them	52:32
not f. upon the Lamanites	55:19
to f. upon them in their rear,	56:23
strong and they should f.	56:24
sons should f. into their hands;	56:39
not suffer that we should f.;	56:46
about to f. into the hands of	56:50
because of the f. of their leaders,	56:51
did they f. upon the Lamanites,	56:56
behold, they will f. upon them,	57:31
and were about to f. upon us	58:18
not f. into the hands of	59:11
yea, and it shall f. upon you	60:29
they did f. upon them and cut	He 1:24
if men build they cannot f.	5:12
earth; but behold they did not f.	5:27
rain should f. upon the earth,	11:17
come over and f. upon that city,	12:17
that ye shall f. to the earth.	14: 7
by the f. of Adam being cut off	14:16
shall let f. the sword upon you	3 Ne 3: 8
we may f. upon the robbers	3:20
did f. back from before them.	4:12
f. into their hands by the way;	4:13
they should f. into transgression.	6: 5
did f. down at the feet of Jesus,	11:17
and great was the f. of it.	14:27
beat upon them, they shall f.,	18:13
Holy Ghost did f. upon them,	19:13
repent it shall f. upon them,	20:20
together against thee shall f.	22:15
to f. into the hands of the	Mrm 6: 6
they did f. upon my people	6: 9
more who did f. by the sword,	6:15
and great has been their f.;	8: 7
by Adam came the f. of man.	9:12
because of the f. of man came	9:12
because of the f. our natures	Eth 3: 2
ye are redeemed from the f.;	3:13
Eternal God shall f. upon you,	8:23
f. by the poisonous serpents.	9:33
should not f. by the sword.	14:24
saw that he was about to f.	15: 7
it shall f. upon the inhabitants	DC 1:13
Babylon the great, which shall f.	1:16
he must f. and incur the	3: 4
if thou art not aware thou wilt f.	3: 9
he will f. into transgression;	5:32
you shall f. down and worship	18:40
that man f. from grace	20:32
lest they f. into temptation;	20:33
the stars shall f. from heaven,	29:14
flesh shall f. from off their bones,	29:19
redeemed from their spiritual f.,	29:44
their shining, and some shall f.,	34: 9
let f. the sword in their behalf,	35:14
that this house shall never f.	45:18
and the stars f. from heaven.	45:42
the arm of the Lord shall f.,	45:45
shall the arm of the Lord f.	45:47
upon this rock shall never f.	50:44
let him take heed lest he f.	58:15
judgments f. upon your heads.	82: 2
f. not from your steadfastness.	82:24
a hair of his head shall not f. to	84:80
a hair of his head shall not f.	84:116
shall f. by the shaft of death,	85: 8
men shall f. upon the ground	88:89
and f. when the storms descend,	90: 5
redeemed man from the f.,	93:38
and surely Zion cannot f.,	97:19
would let f. the sword of mine	101:10

FALL   318   FALSE

diggeth a pit for them shall f.	DC 109:25
thy judgments f. upon that city.	109:40
thine indignation f. upon them,	109:52
if thine enemies f. upon thee;	122: 6
that ye may not f.	124:124
shall they f. down and be crowned	133:32
a deep sleep to f. upon Adam;	Mses 3:21
and by his f. came death;	6:48
of transgression cometh the f.,	6:59
which f. bringeth death,	6:59
climbeth up by me shall never f.;	7:53
and we will f. upon their necks,	7:63
they shall f. upon our necks,	7:63
a deep sleep to f. upon Adam;	Abr 5:15
the stars shall f. from heaven,	JS 1:33

FALLEN

he had f. to the earth before me,	1Ne 4: 7
many as heeded them, had f. away.	8:34
in a lost and in a f. state,	10: 6
I saw multitudes who had f.	12: 5
is written, had f. from heaven;	2Ne 2:17
because he had f. from heaven,	2:18
he would not have f., but he	2:22
and because man became f. they	9: 6
is ruined, and Judah is f.,	13: 8
The bricks are f. down,	19:10
How art thou f. from heaven,	24:12
from their lost and f. state.	25:17
and had f. by the sword from	Om 1:17
until they have f. into my hands.	WM 1:11
f. into the hands of the Lamanites,	Mos 1:14
that have f. into transgression.	2:40
for the sins of those who have f.	3:11
behold they had f. to the earth,	4: 1
and your worthless and f. state—	4: 5
if this people had not f. into	7:25
that has not f. into transgression,	15:13
people from their lost and f. state.	16: 4
remaineth in his f. state and	16: 5
that I have f. into your hands.	17: 9
having received a wound has f.	20:13
from their carnal and f. state,	27:25
that ye are a lost and a f. people.	Al 9:30
they were a lost and a f. people	9:32
became a lost and f. people.	12:22
the prison had f. to the earth,	14:28
walls thereof had f. to the earth,	14:29
curse of God had f. upon them	17:15
six of them had f. by the sling,	17:38
had seen that they had f.,	19:15
until they had all f. to the earth,	19:16
of Lamoni had f. to the earth,	19:17
beheld that the man had f. dead,	19:24
him or any of those who had f.;	19:24
lot to have f. into the hands of	20:30
of transgression, man had f.	22:12
since man had f. he could not	22:14
who had f. under the sword,	24:24
then have f. away into sin	24:30
is a guilty and a f. people,	30:25
they had f. into great errors,	31: 9
yea, all are f. and are lost,	34: 9
yea, they became f. man.	42: 6
to reclaim men from this f. state,	42:12
we see that all mankind were f.,	42:14
this scalp has f. to the earth,	44:14
and he has f. and they have fled;	47:26
had not f. into the hands of	52:10
to have f. into the hands of	53:11
For Antipus had f. by the sword,	56:51
one soul of them f. to the earth;	56:56
thousands have f. by the sword,	60: 5
many who have f. by the sword;	60:12
they have f. into transgression	He 3:16
cities which had f. into the hands	4: 9
had f. into a state of unbelief	4:25
f. into this great transgression;	4:26
chief judge had f. to the earth,	9: 3
quake, and had f. to the earth.	9: 5
five men who had f. to the earth.	9: 7
had all f. to the earth, and did	3Ne 4: 8
the Nephites had f. with fear	4: 9

thereof had f. to the earth,	3Ne 8:14
thereof who had not f.	8:20
and abominations that they are f.!	9: 2
great cities which have f.,	10: 4
the house of Israel, who have f.;	10: 5
Jerusalem, as ye that have f.;	10: 5
neither were they f. upon and	10:13
of Gidgiddonah had f.,	Mrm 6:13
And Lamah had f. with his ten	6:14
and Gigal had f. with his ten	6:14
and Limhah had f. with his ten	6:14
and Joneam had f. with his ten	6:14
f. with their ten thousand each.	6:14
over unto the Lamanites, had f.;	6:15
done this, ye would not have f.	6:18
behold, ye are f., and I mourn	6:18
how is it that ye could have f.!	6:19
that the brother of Jared had f.	Eth 3: 7
Arise, why hast thou f.?	3: 7
they had all f. by the sword	15:23
they had all f. by the sword,	15:29
otherwise men were f., and there	Mro 7:24
Archeantus has f. by the	9: 2
have f. victims to their awful	9:17
contains a record of a f. people,	DC 20: 9
devilish, and became f. man.	20:20
And we beheld, and lo, he is f.!	76:27
is f., even a son of the morning!	76:27
And after they have f. asleep	86: 3
She is f. who made all nations	88:105
she is f., is fallen!	88:105
she is fallen, is f.!	88:105
and not have f. asleep, lest the	101:53
from whence they have f.;	113:10
the place of those who are f.	118: 1
the places of those who have f.,	118: 6
he hath f. from his exaltation,	132:39
as thou hast f. thou mayest be	Mses 5: 9
Why is thy countenance f.?	5:22

FALLETH

believe, and f. into transgression?	Al 32:19
of justice f. upon this people.	He 13: 5
a fig that f. from off a fig-tree.	DC 88:87
the flower thereof which soon f.,	124: 7
of my brother f. into my hands.	Mses 5:33

FALLING

from f. into the hands of	Om 1: 2
from f. into the hands of	1: 6
f. into the hands of your enemies,	Mos 2:31
f. into the hands of our enemies.	10: 2
from f. into their hands.	Al 57:17
country from f. into the hands	58: 8
them from f. by the sword,	58:39
city from f. into the hands of	59: 9
of them from f. by the sword.	60: 8
who are f. by the sword,	60:22
and f. upon their armies,	3Ne 4:21
preserving them from f. into	4:31

FALLS

when he f. he shall rise again,	DC 117:13

FALSE

confounding of f. doctrines,	2Ne 3:12
save it should be a f. Messiah	25:18
f. and vain and foolish doctrines,	28: 9
because of f. teachers,	28:12
false teachers, and f. doctrine,	28:12
those who preach f. doctrines,	28:15
after there had been f. Christs,	WM 1:15
after there had been f. prophets,	1:16
false prophets, and f. preachers	1:16
Thou shalt not bear f. witness	Mos 13:23
went forth preaching f. doctrines;	Al 1:16
and bear f. witness against your	He 7:21
And thus we can behold how f.,	12: 1
will say that he is a f. prophet,	13:26
Beware of f. prophets, who come	3Ne 14:15
adulterers, and against f. swearers,	24: 5
many priests and f. prophets	4Ne 1:34
many spirits which are f. spirits,	DC 50: 2

FALSE 319 FAMINE

in perils among f. brethren; DC 122: 5
with all manner of f. accusations; 122: 6
an old sectarian notion, and is f. 130: 3
declare that these charges are f. OD
many f. prophets shall arise, JS 1: 9
there shall also arise f. Christs, 1:22
false Christs, and f. prophets, 1:22

FALSEHOOD
founded in f. of the blackest dye, DC 127: 1

FALSEHOODS
circulating f. about my father's JS 2:61

FALSELY
manner of evil against you f., 3Ne 12:11
swear f. against my servants, DC 121:18
of evil against me f. for JS 2:25

FAME
having heard of the f. of Ammon, Al 19: 2
the f. of this house shall spread DC 110:10
f. and name that cannot be slain. 135: 3

FAMILIAR
unto them that have f. spirits, 2Ne 18:19
as one that hath a f. spirit; 26:16
and be f. with all and free with Jac 2:17

FAMILIES
They take their f. and depart 1Ne 1:hd
sons of Ishmael and their f., did rebel 7: 6
to slay food for our f.; 16:14
after we had slain food for our f. 16:14
we did return again to our f. 16:14
and obtain food for our f. 16:17
did return without food to our f., 16:19
that I did obtain food for our f. 16:31
every one, according to their f., Mos 6: 3
took their tents and their f. 18:34
Ye shall defend your f. even Al 43:47
defend themselves, and their f., 43:47
Pray in your f. unto the Father, 3Ne 18:21
with his brother and their f., Eth 1:33
with some others and their f., 1:33
their friends and their f. also, 1:37
of every kind; and thy f.; 1:41
also thy friends and their f., 1:41
friends of Jared and their f., 1:41
and his brother, and their f., 2: 1
and his brother and their f., 2: 1
have their f. supported out of DC 42:71
to be gathered with your f., 48: 6
Let them labor with their f., 52:36
speedily as can be, with their f., 57:14
make preparations for those f. 57:15
bring their f. to this land, 58:25
supporting the f. of those, 75:24
the f. of those who are called 75:24
ye obtain places for your f., 75:25
can obtain places for their f., 75:26
that inasmuch as they have f., 84:103
let all those who have not f., 84:104
Let your f. be small, especially 90:25
who do not belong to your f.; 90:25
unto you concerning your f.— 98:23
smite you, or your f., once, 98:23
and Joseph, your f. are well; 100: 1
who have f. in the east, 105:21
may exalt them, with all their f., 109:71
with all their f., 109:72
I will provide for their f.; 118: 3
the f. of those who have gone 136: 8
in your houses, and in your f. 136:11
concerning all the f. of the earth, Mses 5:10
beheld all the f. of the earth; 7:45
the f. of the earth be blessed, Abr 2:11

FAMILY
into the wilderness with his f. 1Ne 1:hd
he should take his f. and depart 2: 2
with him, save it were his f., and 2: 4
travel in the wilderness with his f., 2: 5
take his f. into the wilderness 7: 1

bring down Ishmael ane his f. 1Ne 7: 2
my f. should partake of it also; 8:12
perhaps I might discover my f. also, 8:13
the f. of all the earth. 2Ne 2:20
I, Nephi, did take my f., 5: 6
and also Zoram and his f., 5: 6
mine elder brother and his f., 5: 6
who belong to the f. of Adam. 9:21
every man according to his f., Mos 2: 5
every f. being separate one from 2: 5
every man, with his f., his 3Ne 6: 1
every man according to his f. 7: 2
save he had much f. and 7: 4
every man according to his f., 7:14
whole human f. of Adam; Mrm 3:20
Jared thy brother and his f.; Eth 1:41
out of the land with his f., 9: 3
save it were Jared and his f. 9: 3
all save the support of thy f. DC 19:34
thou shalt desire to see thy f.; 19:36
and attend to all f. duties. 20:47
and attend to all f. duties. 20:51
and this because of thy f. 23: 3
well as in secret, and in your f., 23: 6
afflictions because of your f.; 31: 2
I will bless you and your f., 31: 2
Wherefore your f. shall live. 31: 5
is sufficient for himself and f. 42:32
every man according to his f., 48: 6
equal according to his f., 51: 3
and for the wants of his f., 51:14
to provide for his own f., 75:28
for the f. of thy counselor 90:19
continue with his f. upon the 90:20
Your f. must needs repent and 93:48
and set in order his f., 93:50
upon you, neither upon your f., 98:28
Let his f. rejoice 124:76
let him not take his f. unto 124:83
cease to fear concerning his f., 124:87
Let him come and locate his f. 124:105
let him not remove his f. unto 124:108
at your hand to leave your f. 126: 1
take especial care of your f. 126: 3
also saw Noah, and his f.; Mses 7:42
he moved with his f. into JS 2: 3
His f. consisting of eleven 2: 4
My father's f. was proselyted 2: 7
circumstances of my father's f.), 2:46
my father's f. met with a 2:56
my wife's father's f. were very 2:58
falsehoods about my father's f., 2:61
the f. related to him the 2:66
influence of my wife's father's f. 2:75

FAMINE
household from perishing with f. 1Ne 5:14
are visited by sword, and by f., 2Ne 1:18
and by pestilence, and by f. 6:15
and the f. and the sword— 8:19
I will kill thy root with f., 24:30
smitten with f. and sore afflictions, Mos 1:17
smitten with f. and sore afflictions; 9: 3
yea, with f. and with pestilence; 12: 4
having been saved from f., Al 9:22
but it would be by f., and by 10:22
then ye shall be smitten by f., 10:23
children from f. and affliction, 53: 7
bloodshed, yea, and so much f. 62:35
had wars, and bloodsheds, and f., 62:39
shall smite the earth with f., He 10: 6
let there be a f. in the land, 11: 4
was a great f. upon the land, 11: 5
fourth year the f. did continue, 11: 5
the sword but became sore by f. 11: 5
they were about to perish by f., 11: 7
he turn away from us this f., 11: 8
and cause that this f. may cease 11:12
when I said, let there be a f., 11:14
have repented, because of the f. 11:15
and with f. and with all manner 12: 3
with the sword and with f. 13: 9
even there should be a great f., Eth 9:28
in preserving them from f. 9:35
Heth had perished by the f., 10: 1

FAMINE 320 FASTER

FAMINE
and with f., and plague, and	DC	87: 6
of winter, or of cold, or f.		89:13
only in times of f. and excess		89:15
a great f. into the land,	Mses	8: 4
there should be a f. in the land.	Abr	1:29
Accordingly a f. prevailed		1:30
tormented because of the f.,		1:30
caused the f. to wax sore in		2: 1
And the f. abated;		2: 5
the f. might be turned away		2:17
was a continuation of a f.		2:21
for the f. became very grievous.		2:21
with great desolations by f.,	JS	2:45

FAMINES
f., pestilences, and bloodshed	2Ne	10: 6
yea, f. and bloodshed,	Al	45:11
also many f. and pestilences,	Eth	11: 7
the voice of f. and pestilences	DC	43:25
shall be f., and pestilences,	JS	1:29

FAMISHED
their honorable men are f.,	2Ne	15:13

FAR
thus f. I and my father had kept	1Ne	5:20
the beauty thereof was f. beyond,		11: 8
and hearken ye people from f.;		21: 1
behold, these shall come from f.;		21:12
swallowed thee up shall be f. away.		21:19
I had made, of my people thus f.	2Ne	5:29
ensign to the nations from f.,		15:26
Lord have removed men f. away,		16:12
give ear all ye of f. countries;		18: 9
which shall come from f.?		20: 3
They come from a f. country,		23: 5
from f. unto the ends of the earth;		24: 2
removed their hearts f. from me,		27:25
have not come thus f. save it were		31:19
cometh, and is not f. distant,	Mos	3: 5
and it f. from the thoughts and		5:13
is at hand, or is not f. distant,		7:18
and become f. more wealthy than	Al	1:31
behold, the time is not f. distant		7: 7
it would be f. more tolerable		9:23
it being so f. northward that		22:30
to wander f. from thee, our God.		31:17
thus f. the word of God has been		37:26
into a f. better land of promise.		37:45
have gone f. astray because of		41: 1
accomplished his designs thus f.,		48: 2
Lamanites had retreated f.		52:31
they did not pursue us f. before		56:42
but in a land which is f. distant,	He	16:20
as f. as the borders of the	3Ne	4:13
And thus f. were the scriptures		10:11
thou shalt be f. from oppression		22:14
that they were fulfilled thus f.,	Eth	15: 3
hear of wars in f. countries,	DC	38:29
be great wars in f. countries,		38:29
is not f. from the court-house.		57: 3
excess of laughter f. from you.		88:69
and uncleanness f. from you.		90:18
I have suffered them thus f.,		103: 3
they should be brought thus f.		105:19
Let the city, F. West, be a holy		115: 7
F. West should be built up speedily		115:17
my people in the city of F. West,		117:10
my saints in the city of F. West,		118: 5
as f. as they can get hold of		123: 3
who are worthy of f. more,		132:16
as f. as we have any right	Fac	2:12
so f. as I have such facts in my	JS	2: 1
but their hearts are f. from me,		2:19
so f. as the sectarian world was		2:26
this hill, not f. from the top,		2:51
as f. as in them lay.		2:75
as f. as it is translated correctly;	AoF	8

FARED
man f. in this life according to	Al	30:17

FAREWELL
F. until that great day shall	2Ne	33:13
I bid you an everlasting f.,		33:14
Finally, I bid you f., until I shall	Jac	6:13
and to the reader I bid f.,		7:27
and be sober. My son, f.	Al	37:47
Be sober. My son, f.		38:15
bid f. unto the Gentiles,	Eth	12:38
F., my son, until I shall write	Mro	8:30
And now I bid unto all, f.		10:34
bid f. unto the Gentiles;	DC	135: 5

FARM
concerns, who dwell upon this f.	DC	63:38
that his f. should be sold.		64:20
Williams should sell his f.,		64:21

FARMED
and f. with him that season.	JS	2:58

FARMER
and a f. of respectability.	JS	2:61

FARMING
take teams, seeds, and f. utensils,	DC	136: 7

FARMS
have f. that cannot be sold,	DC	38:37

FARTHER
from them f. into the wilderness.	Mos	19:23

FASHION
I have given you the f. of them	Abr	1:14

FAST
holding f. to the rod of iron,	1Ne	8:30
and would hold f. unto it,		15:24
of him that would bind you f.;	2Ne	9:45
should stand f. in this liberty	Mos	23:13
and they began to f., and to pray		27:22
that did stand f. in the faith;	Al	1:25
did fall exceedingly f. before		44:18
did f. much and pray much,		45: 1
who should stand f. in the faith		45:17
stand f. in the faith of Christ.		46:27
stand f. in that liberty		58:40
soul standeth f. in that liberty		61: 9
who stand f. in that liberty		61:21
they did f. and pray oft,	He	3:35
together to mourn and to f.,		9:10
Moreover, when ye f. be not	3Ne	13:16
may appear unto men to f.		13:16
thou appear not unto men to f.,		13:18
and did multiply exceedingly f.,	4Ne	1:10
people as f. as it were possible,	Mrm	2: 7
to be destroyed exceeding f.	Eth	9:30
together oft, to f. and to pray,	Mro	6: 5
Stand f. in the work wherewith	DC	9:14
stand f. in the office whereunto		54: 2
as f. as you receive moneys,		104:68
as f. as ye are able to receive		111:11

FASTED
after they had f. and prayed	Mos	27:23
I have f. and prayed many days	Al	5:46
for I had f. many days.		8:26
for he has f. many days because		10: 7
they f. much and prayed much		17: 9

FASTENED
f. into the two rims of a bow.	Mos	28:13
he f. it upon the end of a pole.	Al	46:12
he f. on his head-plate.		46:13
Abraham f. upon an altar.	Fac	1: 2
these stones, f. to a breastplate,	JS	2:35

FASTER
they grew f. than the strength of	Jac	5:48
should run f. than he has strength.	Mos	4:27
Do not run f. or labor more	DC	10: 4

FASTEST 321 FATHER

FASTEST
when thou f., anoint thy head,	3Ne	13:17

FASTING
and continue in f. and praying,	Om	1:26
and join in f. and mighty prayer	Al	6: 6
to much prayer, and f.;		17: 3
a time of much f. and prayer.		28: 6
and also after the days of f.,		30: 2
united in mighty prayer and f.	3Ne	27: 1
continuing in f. and prayer,	4Ne	1:12
that thy f. may be perfect,	DC	59:13
Verily, this is f. and prayer,		59:14
continue in prayer and f.		88:76
a house of prayer, a house of f.,		88:119
for your preaching, and your f.,		95:16
house of prayer, a house of f.,		109: 8
a house of prayer, a house of f.,		109:16

FASTINGS
that your f. and your mourning	DC	95: 7

FAT
the waste places of the f. ones	2Ne	15:17
Make the heart of this people f.,		16:10
send among his f. ones, leanness;		20:16
that a feast of f. things might be	DC	58: 8
a feast of f. things, of wine on		58: 8
of his flock, and of the f. thereof,	Mses	5:20

FATHER
in all the learning of my f.;	1Ne	1: 1
a record in the language of my f.,		1: 2
(my f., Lehi, having dwelt at		1: 4
my f., Lehi, as he went forth		1: 5
first came and stood before my f.,		1:11
and many things did my f. read		1:13
when my f. had read and seen		1:14
language of my f. in the praising		1:15
things which my f. hath written,		1:16
abridgment of the record of my f.,		1:17
have abridged the record of my f.		1:17
marvelous things unto my f., Lehi,		1:18
the Lord spake unto my f.,		2: 1
the Lord commanded my f., even		2: 2
when my f. saw that the waters		2: 9
in many things against their f.,		2:11
did murmur against their f.		2:12
to take away the life of my f.		2:13
my f. did speak unto them in the		2:14
And my f. dwelt in a tent.		2:15
which had been spoken by my f.;		2:16
to the tent of my f.		3: 1
I, Nephi, said unto my f.: I will		3: 7
when my f. had heard these words		3: 8
contained the genealogy of my f.		3:12
unto my f. in the wilderness.		3:14
unto our f. in the wilderness		3:15
if he should dwell in the land		3:18
with me, and also with my f.;		3:28
down into the wilderness to my f.		4:34
into the wilderness unto my f.		4:35
journeyed unto the tent of our f.		4:38
into the wilderness unto our f.,		5: 1
had complained against my f.,		5: 2
my mother complained against my f.		5: 3
my f. spake unto her, saying:		5: 4
did my f., Lehi, comfort my mother,		5: 6
had returned to the tent of my f.,		5: 7
my f., Lehi, took the records		5:10
my f., Lehi, also found upon the		5:14
that he might preserve his f., Jacob,		5:14
thus my f., Lehi, did discover		5:16
when my f. saw all these things,		5:17
my f. had kept the commandments		5:20
which has been kept by my f.;		6: 1
account of all the things of my f.,		6: 3
after my f., Lehi, had made an		7: 1
wilderness to the tent of our f.		7: 5
me, Nephi, and Sam, and their f..		7: 6
take away the life of my f.,		7:14
journey towards the tent of our f.		7:21
come down unto the tent of our f.		7:22
come down unto the tent of my f.,		7:22
my f. tarried in the wilderness	1Ne	8: 2
not speak all the words of my f.		8:29
These are the words of my f.:		8:34
not of the fruit, said my f.		8:35
after my f. had spoken all the		8:36
my f. did preach unto them.		8:37
things did my f. see, and hear, and		9: 1
somewhat of the things of my f.,		10: 1
after my f. had made an end of		10: 2
from the time that my f. left		10: 4
spake my f. concerning this thing.		10: 8
my f. said he should baptize in		10: 9
after my f. had spoken these		10:11
my f. spake much concerning the		10:12
did my f. prophesy and speak unto		10:15
done as my f. dwelt in a tent,		10:16
heard all the words of my f.,		10:17
the things that my f. had seen,		11: 1
behold the things which my f. saw.		11: 3
Believest thou that thy f. saw		11: 4
I believe all the words of my f.		11: 5
the fruit which thy f. tasted,		11: 7
the tree which my f. had seen;		11: 8
even the Son of the Eternal F.!		11:21
of the tree which thy f. saw?		11:21
of iron, which my f. had seen,		11:25
of whom my f. had spoken;		11:27
the building which my f. saw.		11:35
of filthy water which thy f. saw;		12:16
spacious building, which thy f. saw,		12:18
God hath covenanted with thy f.		13:30
is the seed of thy f.—		13:34
is the Son of the Eternal F.,		13:40
numbered among the seed of thy f.;		14: 2
of the F. unto the house of Israel?		14: 8
the work of the F. shall commence,		14:17
I saw the things which my f. saw,		14:29
I returned to the tent of my f.		15: 1
things which my f. had spoken		15: 2
words which our f. hath spoken		15: 7
the thing which our f. meaneth		15:13
And this is what our f. meaneth;		15:17
our f. hath not spoken of our		15:18
Lord made to our f. Abraham,		15:18
this thing which our f. saw in a		15:21
the rod of iron which our f. saw,		15:23
river of water which our f. saw?		15:26
the water which my f. saw was		15:27
our f. also saw that the		15:30
done as my f. dwelt in a tent		16: 6
my f. had fulfilled all the		16: 8
the Lord spake unto my f. by		16: 9
as my f. arose in the morning,		16:10
my f. began to murmur against		16:20
I said unto my f.: Whither		16:23
voice of the Lord came unto my f.;		16:25
when my f. beheld the things		16:27
because of the loss of their f.,		16:35
they did murmur against my f.,		16:35
saying: Our f. is dead;		16:35
they did murmur against my f.,		16:36
Behold, let us slay our f.,		16:37
thou art like unto our f.,		17:20
and our f. hath judged them,		17:22
the Lord commanded my f. that		17:44
murmur no more against their f.;		17:49
honor thy f. and thy mother, that		17:55
voice of the Lord came unto my f.,		18: 5
my f. had begat two sons in the		18: 7
my f., Lehi, had said many things		18:17
did engraven the record of my f.,		19: 1
and the prophecies of my f.; and		19: 1
wherefore, the record of my f.,		19: 2
years from the time my f. left		19: 8
covenants of the F. of heaven unto		22: 9
need not suppose that I and my f.		22:31
our f., Lehi, also spake many	2Ne	1: 1
devil, who is the f. of all lies,		2:18
shall be after the name of his f.		3:15
did my f. of old prophesy.		3:22
the words of thy dying f. Amen.		3:25
of which my f. hath spoken,		4: 1
after my f. had made an end of		4: 3

FATHER 322 FATHER

after my f. had made an end of	2Ne 4: 8
when my f. had made an end of	4:10
after my f., Lehi, had spoken	4:12
and also my f., before his death;	4:14
which was prepared for my f.	5:12
taught you the words of my f.;	6: 3
Look unto Abraham, your f.,	8: 2
to remain with the f. of lies,	9: 9
be like unto a f. to them;	10:18
brother of the house of his f.,	13: 6
not have knowledge to cry, My f.,	18: 4
Mighty God, The Everlasting F.,	19: 6
from Jerusalem with my f.;	25: 4
after my f. left Jerusalem;	25:10
the Only Begotten of the F.,	25:12
the F. of heaven and of earth,	25:12
and worship the F. in his name,	25:16
time that my f. left Jerusalem;	25:19
thee, Nephi, and also unto thy f.,	29: 2
he humbleth himself before the F.,	31: 7
and witnesseth unto the F. that	31: 7
the commandments of the F.?	31:10
And the F. said: Repent ye,	31:11
will the F. give the Holy Ghost,	31:12
witnessing unto the F. that ye	31:13
and witnessed unto the F. that ye	31:14
I heard a voice from the F.,	31:15
the commandments of the F.	31:18
Ghost, which witnesses of the F.	31:18
Behold, thus saith the F.:	31:20
and true doctrine of the F.,	31:21
pray unto the F. in the name of	32: 9
I pray the F. in the name of	33:12
were given to our f., Lehi;	Jac 2:34
and worshiped the F. in his name,	4: 5
also we worship the F. in his name.	4: 5
of my F. who was in heaven;	7:22
knowing my f. that he was a just	En 1: 1
I had often heard my f. speak	1: 3
that our f. Lehi left Jerusalem.	1:25
you in the mansions of my F.	1:27
commandment of my f., Enos,	Jar 1: 1
commanded by my f., Jarom,	Om 1: 1
are few, in the book of my f.	1: 4
not possible that our f., Lehi,	Mos 1: 1
as his f. had commanded him,	1:18
the words which his f. should speak	1:18
as his f. had commanded him,	2: 1
and consecrated by my f.,	2:11
also the commandments of my f.,	2:31
was spoken of by my f. Mosiah,	2:32
indebted to your heavenly F.,	2:34
time our f., Lehi, left Jerusalem;	2:34
of God, the F. of heaven and earth,	3: 8
as a child doth submit to his f.	3:19
to that which his f. had done	6: 7
was the God, the F. of all things,	7:27
for f. fought against father,	9: 2
for father fought against f.,	9: 2
did not walk in the ways of his f.	11: 1
had been consecrated by his f.,	11: 5
Honor thy f. and thy mother,	13:20
the flesh to the will of the F.,	15: 2
being the F. and the Son—	15: 2
The F., because he was conceived	15: 3
thus becoming the F. and son—	15: 3
Eternal F. of heaven and of earth.	15: 4
the Son to the F., being one God,	15: 5
swallowed up in the will of the F.	15: 7
who is the very Eternal F.	16:15
his f. should not be destroyed;	19:17
of the iniquities of his f.,	19:17
remember the priests of thy f.,	20:18
all the things concerning his f.,	20:23
daughter mourning for their f.,	21: 9
called after the name of his f.;	24: 3
being called Alma, after his f.;	27: 8
his servant, Alma, who is thy f.;	27:14
even until he was laid before his f.	27:19
they rehearsed unto his f. all that	27:20
and his f. rejoiced, for he knew	27:20
and returned to their f.,	28: 1
that they did plead with their f.	28: 5
do even as my f. Benjamin did	Mos 29:13
his f. having conferred the	29:42
his f. died, being eighty and two	29:45
by the hand of his f. Alma.	Al 4: 4
been consecrated by my f., Alma,	5: 3
did not my f. Alma believe in	5:11
and my f. Alma believe them?	5:11
the Only Begotten of the F.,	5:48
not remember that our f., Lehi,	9: 9
of the Only Begotten of the F.,	9:26
and my f. and my kinsfolk;	10:11
Son of God the very Eternal F.?	11:38
he is the very Eternal F. of	11:39
Christ the Son, and God the F.,	11:44
the Only Begotten of the F.,	13: 9
even our f. Abraham paid tithes	13:15
and he did reign under his f.	13:18
also by his f. and his kindred;	15:16
taken leave of their f., Mosiah,	17: 6
the kingdom which their f. was	17: 6
which he had received from his f.,	18: 5
by the f. of Lamoni, who was	18: 9
to the time that their f., Lehi,	18:36
a remarkable vision of her f.—	19:16
had said unto Mosiah, his f.:	19:23
he might show him unto his f.	20: 1
they met the f. of Lamoni,	20: 8
the f. of Lamoni said unto him:	20: 9
that he did not go unto his f.	20:12
his f. was angry with him, and	20:13
the f. of Lamoni commanded him	20:14
when his f. had heard these words,	20:16
oppressions of the king, his f.;	21:21
his f. had granted unto him that	21:21
and he was the f. of Lamoni.	22: 1
which was established by my f.,	27: 9
yea, the brother for the f.;	28: 5
also to have heard my f. prophesy	36:17
I saw, even as our f. Lehi saw,	36:22
in the stead of his f.;	50:39
did fill the seat of his f.,	50:40
the eldest son of our f. Lehi;	56: 3
F., behold our God is with,	56:46
called after the name of his f.	63:11
did walk after the ways of his f.,	He 3:20
did walk in the ways of his f.	3:37
which their f. Helaman spake	5: 5
power given unto him from the F.	5:11
when my f. Nephi first came out	7: 7
Our f. Lehi was driven out of	8:22
the F. of heaven and of earth,	14:12
the F. of heaven and of earth,	16:18
both of the F. and of the Son—	3Ne 1:14
of the F. because of me, and of	1:14
Nephi, who was the f. of Nephi,	2: 9
did fill the seat of his f. and did	6:19
with the F. from the beginning.	9:15
I am in the F., and the Father	9:15
the Father, and the F. in me;	9:15
in me hath the F. glorified his	9:15
Behold, our f. Jacob also testified	10:17
which our f. Lehi brought out of	10:17
cup which the F. hath given me,	11:11
have glorified the F. in taking	11:11
I have suffered the will of the F.	11:11
in the name of the F., and of	11:25
that the F., and the Son, and	11:27
and I am in the F., and the	11:27
in the Father, and the F. in me,	11:27
and the F. and I are one.	11:27
devil, who is the f. of contention.	11:29
doctrine which the F. hath given	11:32
and I bear record of the F.,	11:32
and the F. beareth record of me,	11:32
beareth record of the F. and me;	11:32
the F. commandeth all men,	11:32
I bear record of it from the F.;	11:35
in me believeth in the F. also;	11:35
will the F. bear record of me,	11:35
will the F. bear record of me,	11:36
bear record unto him of the F.	11:36
the F., and I, and the Holy Ghost	11:36
glorify your F. who is in heaven.	12:16

FATHER

the commandments of my F.,	3Ne 12:19
be the children of your F.	12:45
as I, or your F. who is in heaven	12:48
of your F. who is in heaven.	13: 1
and thy F. who seeth in secret,	13: 4
pray to thy F. who is in secret;	13: 6
and thy F., who seeth in secret,	13: 6
your F. knoweth what things	13: 8
Our F. who art in heaven,	13: 9
heavenly F. will also forgive you;	13:14
your F. forgive your trespasses.	13:15
unto men to fast, but unto thy F.,	13:18
and thy F., who seeth in secret,	13:18
your heavenly F. feedeth them.	13:26
your heavenly F. knoweth that	13:32
shall your F. who is in heaven	14:11
will of my F. who is in heaven.	14:21
before I ascended to my F.;	15: 1
the F. hath given it unto you.	15:13
the F. given me commandment	15:14
the F. given me commandment	15:15
whom the F. hath led away out	15:15
This much did the F. command	15:16
to say no more of the F.	15:18
that the F. hath commanded me,	15:19
hath the F. separated from them;	15:20
whom the F. hath given me.	15:24
a commandment of the F.	16: 3
do not ask the F. in my name,	16: 4
which the F. hath made unto	16: 5
unto them of me and of the F.	16: 6
their belief in me, saith the F.,	16: 7
But wo, saith the F., unto the	16: 8
because of the mercies of the F.	16: 9
also the judgments of the F.	16: 9
thus commandeth the F. that I	16:10
behold, saith the F., I will bring	16:10
and return unto me, saith the F.,	16:13
tread them down, saith the F.	16:14
hath the F. commanded me—	16:16
commanded of the F. to speak	17: 2
and ask of the F., in my name,	17: 3
But now I go unto the F.,	17: 4
they are not lost unto the F.,	17: 4
F., I am troubled because of	17:14
behold he prayed unto the F.	17:15
heard Jesus speak unto the F.;	17:16
him pray for us unto the F.	17:17
an end of praying unto the F.,	17:18
and prayed unto the F. for them.	17:21
it shall be a testimony unto the F.	18: 7
doth witness unto the F. that	18:10
may witness unto the F. that ye	18:11
the F. hath commanded me	18:14
pray unto the F. in my name;	18:19
shall ask the F. in my name,	18:20
Pray in your families unto the F.,	18:21
shall pray for them unto the F.,	18:23
that I have prayed unto the F.,	18:24
and then I must go unto my F.	18:27
shall pray for him unto the F.	18:30
him whom the F. condemneth.	18:33
And now I go unto the F.,	18:35
go unto the F. for your sakes.	18:35
and should pray unto the F.	19: 6
disciples did pray unto the F.	19: 7
knelt again and prayed to the F.	19: 8
F., I thank thee that thou hast	19:20
F., I pray thee that thou wilt	19:21
F., thou hast given them the	19:22
F., I pray unto thee for them,	19:23
in them as thou, F., art in me,	19:23
had thus prayed unto the F.,	19:24
and he prayed again unto the F.,	19:27
F., I thank thee that thou hast	19:28
F., I pray not for the world,	19:29
in them as thou, F., art in me,	19:29
way off and prayed unto the F.;	19:31
which the F. hath commanded	20:10
covenant which the F. hath	20:12
the F. hath commanded	20:14
whom the F. hath covenanted,	20:19
shall come to pass, saith the F.,	3Ne 20:20
fall upon them, saith the F.,	20:20
which I made with your f. Jacob;	20:22
the F. made with your fathers,	20:25
The F. having raised me up unto	20:26
fulfilleth the F. the covenant	20:27
their own heads, saith the F.	20:28
unto them forever, saith the F.	20:29
pray unto the F. in my name.	20:31
Then will the F. gather them	20:33
the F. hath comforted his	20:34
The F. hath made bare his holy	20:35
see the salvation of the F.;	20:35
and the F. and I are one.	20:35
as the F. hath commanded me.	20:46
which the F. hath covenanted	20:46
be given unto you of the F.,	21: 3
made known unto them of the F.,	21: 3
and shall come forth of the F.	21: 3
it is wisdom in the F. that they	21: 4
people by the power of the F.,	21: 4
that the covenant of the F. may	21: 4
thus it behooveth the F. that it	21: 6
work of the F. hath already	21: 7
shall the F. work a work,	21: 9
which the F. shall cause him	21:11
to pass in that day, saith the F.,	21:14
shall come to pass, saith the F.,	21:20
shall the work of the F. commence	21:26
shall the work of the F. commence	21:26
which the F. hath led away out	21:26
with the F., to prepare the way	21:27
may call on the F. in my name.	21:27
the work commence, with the F.,	21:28
will go before them, saith the F.,	21:29
the time and the will of the F.	23: 4
the F. should glorify his name	23: 9
the F. had given unto Malachi,	24: 1
said the F. unto Malachi—	24: 1
the F. commanded that I should	26: 2
and had gone unto the F.,	26:15
and had ascended unto the F.—	26:15
praying unto the F. in his name;	27: 2
shall call upon the F. in my name	27: 7
therefore if ye call upon the F.,	27: 9
my name the F. will hear you;	27: 9
then will the F. show forth his	27:10
world to do the will of my F.,	27:13
because my F. sent me.	27:13
my F. sent me that I might be	27:14
men be lifted up by the F.,	27:14
according to the power of the F.	27:15
I hold guiltless before my F.	27:16
because of the justice of the F.	27:17
all things are written by the F.;	27:26
And now I go unto the F.	27:28
ye shall ask the F. in my name	27:28
and even the F. rejoiceth,	27:30
after that I am gone to the F.?	28: 1
when I am gone unto the F.?	28: 4
to behold all the doings of the F.	28: 7
according to the will of the F.,	28: 7
blessed in the kingdom of my F.	28: 8
sit down in the kingdom of my F.;	28:10
the F. hath given me fulness of	28:10
and I am even as the F.;	28:10
and the F. and I are one;	28:10
beareth record of the F. and me;	28:11
the F. giveth the Holy Ghost	28:11
if they shall pray unto the F.	28:30
into the kingdom of the f.	28:40
which the F. hath made with	29: 1
carried by my f. into the land	Mrm 1: 6
that the F. may bring about,	5:14
were led even by God the F.	5:17
and the F., yea, the Eternal	6:22
yea, the Eternal F. of heaven,	6:22
by the power of the F. he hath	7: 5
unto the F., and unto the Son,	7: 7
do finish the record of my f.,	8: 1
been commanded by my f.	8: 1
my f. also was killed by them,	8: 3

FATHER 324 FATHER

fulfil the commandment of my f.	Mrm 8: 3
my f. hath made this record,	8: 5
My f. hath been slain in battle,	8: 5
my f. and I have seen them,	8:11
my f. was a descendant of Nephi.	8:13
cry mightily unto the F. in the	9: 6
even the F. and the Son;	9:12
whatsoever he shall ask the F.	9:21
ask the F. in the name of Jesus	9:27
mine imperfection, neither my f.,	9:31
may God the F. remember the	9:37
I am the F. and the Son.	Eth 3:14
the F. of the heavens and of	4: 7
not believe the F. who sent me.	4:12
For behold, I am the F.,	4:12
the F. hath laid up for you,	4:14
call upon the F. in my name,	4:15
the F. hath remembered the	4:15
work of the F. has commenced	4:17
of which the F., and the Son,	5: 4
unto the F. in the name of Jesus,	5: 5
that his f. should constrain him,	6:25
but his f. would not;	6:25
the Lord had done for his f.,	6:30
he rebelled against his f.,	7: 4
and restored it unto his f. Kib.	7: 9
his f. bestowed upon him the	7:10
to reign in the stead of his f.	7:10
the king, and also his f. Corihor,	7:15
prison and brought out their f.,	7:18
Jared rebelled against his f.,	8: 2
he gave battle unto his f.,	8: 3
carry away his f. into captivity,	8: 3
give up the kingdom unto his f.	8: 6
seeing the sorrows of her f.,	8: 8
the kingdom unto her f.	8: 8
that she did talk with her f.,	8: 9
hath my f. so much sorrow?	8: 9
let my f. send for Akish,	8:10
the head of my f., the king.	8:10
the head of my f., the king.	8:12
devil, who is the f. of all lies;	8:25
sought the life of his f.-in-law;	9: 5
the head of his f.-in-law,	9: 5
angry with his f. because of	9: 8
that which his f. had done	9: 8
and did fill the steps of his f.	9:15
did walk in the steps of his f.,	9:23
again of old, to destroy his f.	9:26
that he did dethrone his f.,	9:27
brought peace again unto his f.	10: 3
his f. did build up many cities	10: 4
did reign in the stead of his f.;	10:13
eight years, and his f. died.	10:13
after the death of his f.,	10:15
reigned in the stead of his f.	10:30
and glorified the name of the F.,	12: 8
among the mansions of thy F.,	12:32
in the mansions of thy F.	12:34
in the mansions of my F.	12:37
that the grace of God the F.,	12:41
as Joseph brought his f. down	13: 7
merciful unto the f. of Joseph	13: 7
made with their f., Abraham.	13:11
kingdom again unto their f.	13:24
where my f. Mormon did hide	15:11
call on the F. in my name,	Mro 2: 2
prayed unto the F. in the name	3: 2
pray to the F. in the name of	4: 2
O God, the Eternal F.,	4: 3
O God, the Eternal F.,	4: 3
O God, the Eternal F.,	5: 2
O God, the Eternal F.,	5: 2
the words of my f. Mormon,	7: 1
it is by the grace of God the F.,	7: 2
ye shall ask the F. in my name,	7:26
to claim of the F. his rights of	7:27
work of the covenants of the F.,	7:31
manner bringeth to pass the F.,	7:32
pray unto the F. with all the	7:48
An epistle of my f. Mormon,	8: 1
praying unto God the F. in	8: 3
may the grace of God the F.,	9:26
would ask God, the Eternal F.,	Mro 10: 4
the covenants of the Eternal F.	10:31
is in the covenant of the F.	10:33
shall ask the F. in my name,	DC 14: 8
in the kingdom of my F.	15: 6
in the kingdom of my F.	16: 6
in the kingdom of my F.!	18:15
into the kingdom of my F.,	18:16
Ask the F. in my name,	18:18
name which is given of the F.,	18:23
name which is given of the F.,	18:24
place in the kingdom of my F.	18:25
and worship the F. in my name.	18:40
come unto the kingdom of my F.	18:44
saved in the kingdom of my F.	18:46
of him whose I am, even the F.,	19: 2
Nevertheless, glory be to the F.,	19:19
I came by the will of the F.,	19:24
down on the right hand of the F.,	20:24
according to the will of the F.;	20:24
which beareth record of the F.	20:27
F., Son, and Holy Ghost are	20:28
worship the f. in his name,	20:29
baptize you in the name of the F.,	20:73
call upon the F. in solemn prayer,	20:76
O God, the Eternal F.,	20:77
O God, the Eternal F.,	20:77
O God, the Eternal F.,	20:79
O God, the Eternal F.,	20:79
through the will of God the F.,	21: 1
remembering unto the F. my	27: 2
Michael, or Adam, the F. of all,	27:11
those whom my F. hath given me	27:14
am your advocate with the F.;	29: 5
hath gone forth from the F.	29: 8
decree, by the will of the F.,	29:12
ashamed to own before the F.;	29:27
Adam, your F., whom I created.	29:34
Redeemer, by the will of the F.	31:13
I am their advocate with the F.,	32: 3
one in me as I am one in the F.,	35: 2
as the F. is one in me,	35: 2
pleaded before the F. for them.	38: 4
will of the F. to give unto you,	38:39
asked the F. in my name,	42: 3
and beareth record of the F.	42:17
is the advocate with the F.,	45: 3
F., behold the sufferings and	45: 4
F., spare these my brethren	45: 5
sent forth by the will of the F.	50:27
ask of the F. in the name of	50:31
kingdom is given you of the F.,	50:35
them that my F. hath given me;	50:41
them that my F. hath given me	50:42
And the F. and I are one.	50:43
I am in the F. and the Father	50:43
in the Father and the F. in me;	50:43
crown in the mansions of my F.,	59: 2
from the presence of my F.	63:34
at the right hand of my F.,	66:12
above, from the F. of lights.	67: 9
in the name of the F., and of	68: 8
of as many as the F. shall	68:12
descending from f. to son,	68:21
prepared for him of my F.	72: 4
which were ordained of the f.,	76:13
who was in the bosom of the F.,	76:13
Son, on the right hand of the F.,	76:20
the Only Begotten of the F.—	76:23
Son whom the F. loved	76:25
who was in the bosom of the F.,	76:25
Only Begotten Son of the F.,	76:35
who was in the bosom of the F.	76:39
the F. had put into his power	76:42
Who glorifies the F., and saves	76:43
after the F. has revealed him.	76:43
which the F. sheds forth upon	76:53
the F. has given all things.—	76:55
received the fulness of the F.,	76:71
but not of the fulness of the F.	76:77
where God, even the F., reigns	76:92
and present it unto the F.,	76:107
of your F. who is in heaven;	78: 4

FATHER

how great blessings the F. hath	DC 78:17
prepared in the house of my F.	81: 6
under the hand of his f.-in-law,	84: 6
by the hand of his f. Adam,	84:16
the face of God, even the F.,	84:22
receiveth me receiveth my F.;	84:37
that receiveth my F. receiveth	84:38
all that my F. hath shall be	84:38
this oath and covenant of my F.,	84:40
cometh unto God, even the F.	84:47
And the F. teacheth him of	84:48
they whom my F. hath given me;	84:63
kingdom where my F. and I am.	84:74
For your F., who is in heaven,	84:83
your F. which is in heaven,	84:92
the presence of God the F.;	88:19
Whatsoever ye ask the F. in	88:64
I may testify unto your F.,	88:75
meet in the sight of your F.,	89: 5
And that I am in the F.,	93: 3
the Father, and the F. in me,	93: 3
and the F. and I are one—	93: 3
The F. because he gave me of	93: 4
world and received of my F.,	93: 5
of the Only Begotten of the F.,	93:11
fulness of the glory of the F.;	93:16
and the glory of the F. was	93:17
come unto the F. in my name,	93:19
glorified in me as I am in the F.;	93:20
in the beginning with the F.,	93:21
in the beginning with the F.;	93:23
promise of the F. unto you;	95: 9
the love of the F. shall not	95:12
and where my F. and I am,	98:18
shall be rejected of my F.	99: 4
come in the kingdom of my F.	101:65
lot upon which his f. resides.	104:28
upon which his f. now resides;	104:43
upon him, and upon his f.	104:44
an inheritance for his f.,	104:45
for him in the mansions of my F.	106: 8
and presence of God the F.,	107:19
handed down from f. to son,	107:40
the promise of God by his f.,	107:42
the express likeness of his f.,	107:43
be like unto his f. in all things,	107:43
the promise of the F. unto you	108: 5
now we ask thee, Holy F.,	109: 4
Holy F., we ask thee to assist us,	109:10
grant, Holy F., that all those	109:14
we ask thee, Holy F.,	109:22
We ask thee, Holy F., to establish	109:24
We ask thee, Holy F., to confound	109:29
ask thee, Holy F., to remember	109:47
didst give to Abraham, their f.	109:64
I am your advocate with the F.	110: 4
from the society of thy f. and	122: 6
and shall say, My f., my father,	122: 6
my f., why can't you stay	122: 6
f., what are the men going to	122: 6
on us by our Heavenly F.,	123: 6
appointed unto him by his f.,	124:91
the chamber of old F. Whitmer,	128:21
The appearing of the F. and	130: 3
idea that the F. and the Son	130: 3
The f. has a body of flesh and	130:22
even as I and my F. ordained	132:11
no man shall come unto the F.	132:12
was ordained by me and my F.	132:28
of the works of my F.,	132:31
receive the promise of my F.,	132:33
for you in the kingdom of my F.,	132:49
with Abraham your f.	132:49
as I was with Abraham, thy f.,	132:57
if a man be called of my F.,	132:59
which was given by my F.	132:63
is the work of my F. continued,	132:63
prepared in the mansions of my F.	135: 5
which beareth record of the F.	Mses 1:24
shall a man leave his f. and his	3:24
F., thy will be done, and the	4: 2
the devil, the f. of all lies,	4: 4
the Only Begotten of the F.,	5: 7

beareth record of the F. and the	Mses 5: 9
am the Only Begotten of the F.	5: 9
shalt be the f. of his lies;	5:24
that thy f. may not know it;	5:29
the f. of such as dwell in tents,	5:45
the f. of all such as handle the	5:45
gave unto their f., Adam.	6:28
my f. taught me in all the ways	6:41
he called upon our f. Adam	6:51
our f. Adam spake unto the	6:53
had spoken with Adam, our f.,	6:64
the record of the F., and the Son,	6:66
our f. Adam taught these	7: 1
name of the F., and of the Son,	7:11
record of the F. and the Son.	7:11
even in the bosom of the F.,	7:24
testimony of the F. and Son;	7:27
they should choose me, their F.;	7:33
Satan shall be their f.,	7:37
I am in the bosom of the F.,	7:47
of Man ascend up unto the F.;	7:59
at the residence of my f.,	Abr 1: 1
to be a f. of many nations,	1: 2
who is Adam, our first f.,	1: 3
even the priesthood of thy f.,	1:18
Adam, and also of Noah, his f.,	1:26
my f. was led away by their	1:27
my f. was sorely tormented	1:30
Terah, my f., yet lived in the	2: 1
also my f. followed after me,	2: 4
my f. tarried in Haran and dwelt	2: 5
my f. turned again unto his	2: 5
up and bless thee as their f.;	2:10
man leave his f. and his mother,	5:18
God in heaven, but my F. only.	JS 1:40
My f., Joseph Smith, Sen.,	2: 3
my f., Joseph Smith;	2: 4
My f., who was laboring along	2:48
commanded me to go to my f.	2:49
I returned to my f. in the field,	2:50
at the house of my wife's f.,	2:62
where my f. resided,	2:66
my f. being one of those who	2:66
blessings from our Heavenly F.	2:73
believe in God, the Eternal F.,	AoF 1

FATHER-IN-LAW: see *FATHER, IN,* and *LAW*.

FATHERLESS

shall have mercy on their f.	2Ne 19:17
and that they may rob the f.!	20: 2
the widow and the f., and that	3Ne 24: 5
but to the widows and f.,	DC 123: 9
the poor, the widows, the f.,	136: 8
the cries of the widow and the f.	136: 8

FATHERS

the Lord hath done for their f.;	T Pg
the language of our f.;	1Ne 3:19
f. came through, out of captivity,	4: 2
to deliver us, even as our f.,	4: 3
a genealogy of his f.;	5:14
discover the genealogy of his f.	5:16
and his f. had kept the records.	5:16
not give the genealogy of my f.	6: 1
of the Lord which was in our f.;	15:12
was ministered unto their f.	15:14
Do ye believe that our f.,	17:23
who were driven out by our f.,	17:33
Do ye suppose that our f.	17:34
and bless it unto our f.	17:35
he did bless it unto our f.	17:35
Behold, he loved our f., and he	17:40
and the genealogy of his f..	19: 2
God of our f., who were led	19:10
which he made to their f.	19:15
kings shall be thy nursing f.,	21:23
covenants of the Lord with our f.;	22: 6
which I have made with thy f.	2Ne 3: 7
to the knowledge of their f.	3:12
which I made unto thy f.	3:21
kings shall be thy nursing f.,	6: 7
have I covenanted with their f.	10: 7

FATHERS

shall be nursing f. unto them,	2Ne	10: 9
which he hath made to our f.;		11: 5
for the iniquities of their f.,		24:21
unto the knowledge of their f..		30: 5
which was had among their f.		30: 5
known unto them of their f.;		33: 4
which was given unto our f.—	Jac	3: 5
of the iniquity of their f.;		3: 7
filthiness came because of their f.		3: 9
or concerning their f.—		4: 2
also all the traditions of our f.	En	1:14
Thy f. have also required		1:18
more than my f. have written?	Jar	1: 2
which he spake unto our f.,		1: 9
to the commandments of my f.		1:15
to the commandments of my f.;	Om	1: 3
which he spake unto our f.,		1: 6
to the commandments of our f.		1: 9
gave a genealogy of his f.,		1:18
a few words concerning his f.		1:22
my f. knowing that many of them	WM	1: 4
in all the language of his f.,	Mos	1: 2
spoken by the mouths of their f.,		1: 2
even our f. would have dwindled		1: 5
of the traditions of their f.,		1: 5
and the sayings of our f.		1: 6
which the Lord made unto our f.		1: 7
he has hitherto preserved our f.		1:13
in the preservation of our f.		1:14
our f. through the wilderness,		1:16
all that has been spoken by our f.		2:35
hath been spoken of by our f.,		4:14
which was the land of their f.,		7: 9
brought our f. out of the land of		7:20
to inherit the land of his f.,		7:21
to inherit the land of our f.,		9: 3
was near to the land of our f.		9: 4
of the deliverance of our f.		9:17
we did inherit the land of our f.		10: 3
in the tradition of their f.,		10:12
of the iniquities of their f.,		10:12
which have been taught by our f.,		12:20
the iniquities of the f. upon the		13:13
with the conduct of their f.,		25:12
be called by the names of their f.,		25:12
believe the tradition of their f.		26: 1
remember the captivity of thy f.		27:16
had been spoken of by our f.;		27:30
them of the iniquity of their f.;		28: 2
has been given to us by our f.		29:15
have been given you by our f.,		29:25
and our f., and our wives, and	Al	2:25
which was set upon their f.,		3: 6
also in the tradition of their f.,		3:11
the captivity of your f.?		5: 6
preached the word unto your f.,		5:13
it has been spoken by our f.,		5:21
which have been spoken by our f.		5:44
which have been spoken by our f.		5:47
which had been spoken by his f.,		6: 8
the tradition of your f.;		9: 8
many times he delivered our f.		9:10
of the traditions of their f.		9:16
of the traditions of their f.		9:17
words of our f. may be fulfilled,		13:26
of the traditions of their f.,		17: 9
of the traditions of their f.;		17:15
of whom our f. have spoken.		18: 4
all the journeyings of their f.		18:37
Behold, he robbed our f.;		20:13
that thy f. and also that our		21: 8
that our f. did know concerning		21: 8
and of the traditions of their f.,		21:17
brought our f. out of the land		22: 9
the wicked traditions of their f.,		23: 3
the traditions of our wicked f.		24: 7
the traditions of their f.,		25: 6
of the traditions of their f.,		26:24
also of f. mourning for their sons,		28: 5
remember the captivity of my f.;		29:11
the captivity of my f.;		29:12
are foolish traditions of your f.		30:14
of the traditions of your f.,		30:16
the foolish traditions of your f.,		30:23
the foolish tradition of your f.,	Al	30:27
the silly traditions of their f.,		30:31
by the childishness of their f.;		31:16
the captivity of our f.;		36: 2
has brought our f. out of Egypt,		36:28
f. out of the land of Jerusalem;		36:29
has been prophesied by our f.,		37: 4
incorrect tradition of their f.;		37: 9
which he has made unto our f.		37:17
thing which our f. call a ball,		37:38
or our f. called it Liahona,		37:38
to show unto our f. the course		37:39
our f. were slothful to give heed		37:43
f. to give heed to this compass,		37:44
this director did bring our f.,		37:45
for so was it with our f.;		37:46
unto them, and also unto their f.,		43:46
esteemed by Alma and his f.		50:38
your f. did wrong their		54:17
Zoram, whom your f. pressed		54:23
covenant which their f. made,		56: 6
from the f. of those my two		56:27
upon the liberty of their f.		56:47
our f. and our women and		58:31
forgotten the captivity of our f.?		60:20
it is the tradition of their f.		60:32
and with all our holy f.	He	3:30
hath been given to our f.		5: 8
of the traditions of their f.		5:19
and the tradition of their f.		5:51
the Israelites, who were our f.,		8:11
have been spoken by our f.,		8:13
and also almost all of our f.,		8:22
in the days of our f. of old,		13:25
of the tradition of their f.		15: 4
abominable traditions of their f.,		15: 7
hath been spoken of by our f.,		15:11
of the traditions of their f.,		15:15
handed down unto us by our f.,		16:20
faith in the tradition of their f.	3Ne	1:11
f. out of the land of Jerusalem,		5:20
of the covenant to your f.		10: 7
the Father made with your f.,		20:25
them again the land of their f.		20:29
Even from the days of your f.		24: 7
heart of the f. to the children,		25: 6
heart of the children to their f.,		25: 6
they did speak unto their f.		26:14
as their f., from the beginning,	4Ne	1:38
and abomination of their f.,		1:39
ceased to strive with their f.;	Mrm	5:16
been handed down by our f.,		6: 6
ye f. and mothers, ye husbands		6:19
then are ye blessed with your f.		6:21
know of the things of their f.:		7: 1
come to the knowledge of your f.,		7: 5
will know concerning your f.,		7: 9
the blood of their f. and their		8:40
which he made unto your f.	Eth	4:15
the Lord had done for their f.		6:30
that the Lord had done for his f.		7:27
the record which our f. brought		8: 9
the destruction of his f.,		10: 2
by which he brought their f.		11:21
showed himself unto our f.,		12: 7
that my f. have obtained		12:22
spake these words unto our f.,	Mro	7:26
the husbands and f. of those		9: 8
upon the flesh of their f.;		9: 8
showing his body unto our f.,		9:25
Christ truly said unto our f.:		10:23
the promises made to the f.,	DC	2: 2
children shall turn to their f.		2: 2
the testimony of their f.—		3:17
of the iniquity of their f.,		3:18
to the knowledge of their f.,		3:20
hearts of the f. to the children,		27: 9
hearts of the children to the f.,		27: 9
Isaac, and Abraham, your f.,		27:10
required at the hand of their f.		29:48
that I have made unto your f.,		45:16
to the traditions of their f.		74: 4
in the land of their f.		77:15
have lost their husbands or f.;		83: 1

FATHERS

through the lineage of his f.,	DC 84:14
through the lineage of their f.;	84:15
And covenant of their f.	84:99
neither the names of the f.,	85: 5
and the names of their f.,	85: 7
the lineage of your f.—	86: 8
of the tradition of their f.	93:39
promise made unto his f.—	96: 7
hearts of the children to their f.,	98:16
hearts of the f. to the children;	98:16
and thy f., Joseph, and Jacob,	98:32
their f. have trespassed,	98:47
trespassed, or their father's f.,	98:47
your f. were led at the first,	103:18
you as I said unto your f.:	103:19
by our f., be established forever.	109:54
hearts of the f. to the children,	110:15
and the children to the f.,	110:15
have come down from the f.,	112:32
riveted the creeds of the f.,	123: 7
and f. have been murdered	123: 9
God of my f. delivered me out	127: 2
as Paul says concerning the f.—	128:15
he shall turn the heart of the f.	128:17
heart of the children to their f.,	128:17
between the f. and the	128:18
of f. and mothers, brothers and	132:55
even the God of your f.,	136:21
mouths of my servants, thy f.,	Mses 6:30
of Cainan, the land of my f.,	6:41
death hath come upon our f.;	6:45
hath made known unto our f.	6:50
upon the heads of their f.;	7:37
the Son of God, even as our f.,	8:24
for the blessings of the f.,	Abr 1: 2
the right belonging to the f.	1: 2
conferred upon me from the f.;	1: 3
it came down from the f. from	1: 3
through the f. unto me.	1: 3
appointment of God unto the f.	1: 4
My f. having turned from their	1: 5
order established by them,	1:26
But the records of the f.,	1:31
were made known unto the f.,	1:31
the promises made to the f.,	JS 2:39
children shall turn to their f.	2:39

FATHER'S

the land of our f. inheritance,	1Ne 3:16
and upon thy f. house,	2Ne 17:17
began to reign in his f. stead.	Mos 6: 4
my f. name was Mormon)	Mrm 1: 5
home shall be at your f. house,	DC 30: 4
my f. kingdom which shall be	27: 4
receiveth my F. kingdom;	84:38
meet for their F. kingdom;	84:58
not come into my F. kingdom	84:74
for in my F. house are many	98:18
trespassed, or their f. fathers,	98:47
his F. name written on their	133:18
away from thy f. house,	Abr 1:16
kindred, and from thy f. house,	2: 3
turned away from my f. house,	2:17
my f. arrival in Palmyra,	JS 2: 3
My f. family was proselyted	2: 7
circumstances of my f. family),	2:46
my f. worldly circumstances	2:55
my f. family met with a	2:56
my wife's f. family were very	2:58
Mr. Stoal's, and went to my f.,	2:58
falsehoods about my f. family,	2:61
influence of my wife's f. family	2:75

FATHERS'

land of our f. first inheritance,	Mos 9: 1
the land of their f. nativity;	Al 21: 1
place of their f. first inheritance,	22:28

FATIGUE

affliction, hunger, thirst, and f.;	1Ne 16:35
of body, hunger, thirst, and f.,	Mos 3: 7
suffered hunger, thirst, and f.	7:16
such as hunger, thirst and f.,	Al 17: 5
them because of their much f.,	51:33
even hunger, thirst, and f.,	60: 3

FATIGUED

f., because of their journeying	1Ne 16:19

FATLING

the young lion and f. together;	2Ne 21: 6
the young lion, and f., together;	30:12

FATLINGS

and a fifth part of their f.;	Mos 11: 3
and herds, and f. of every kind,	Al 1:29
flocks and herds, yea, many f.	He 6:12

FATNESS

and let your soul delight in f.	2Ne 9:51
the f. of the earth shall be	DC 56:18
may partake the f. thereof.	61:17

FAULT

and he shall confess his f. and	He 9:17
tell us, and acknowledge thy f.;	9:20
then ye will not find f. with him.	13:28
But behold, we know no f.;	Mrm 8:17
or being overtaken in a f.,	DC 20:80
cease to find f. one with another;	88:124

FAULTS

if there are f. they are the	T Pg
and acknowledge your f. and	Al 39:13
error and did confess their f.	3Ne 1:25
And if there be f. they be the	Mrm 8:17
faults they be the f. of man.	8:17
Admonish him in his f.,	DC 6:19

FAVOR

gain f. in the sight of Ishmael,	1Ne 7: 4
gain f. in the eyes of the king	Mos 24: 1
stir up those who were in his f.	Al 2: 8
those who were not in his f.	2: 8
I have spoken in f. of your law,	10:26
found f. in the eyes of the king	20:28
those who were in f. of the words	35: 6
who were in f. of the king;	47: 5
he sought to gain f. of those who	47: 5
to gain f. with the armies of the	47: 8
sought the f. of the queen,	47:35
came in f. of the freemen,	51: 7
those who were in f. of kings	51: 8
yea, and may he f. this people,	58:41
gained f. in the eyes of some,	He 8:10
did gain f. in the eyes of Shule;	Eth 7:22
gain f. in the eyes of the people,	10:10
I will give unto you f. and	DC 105:25
find f. in the eyes of the people,	105:26
and find f. in thy sight,	109:21
may obtain f. in the sight of all;	109:56
the set time has come to f. her.	124: 6
I have found f. in thy sight,	Mses 6:31

FAVORED

having been highly f. of the Lord	1Ne 1: 1
thou shalt be f. of the Lord,	3: 6
he that is righteous is f. of God.	17:35
and a f. people of the Lord.	2Ne 1:19
highly f. people of the Lord	Mos 1:13
therefore he was f. of the Lord,	10:13
a highly f. people of the Lord;	Al 9:20
been f. above every other nation,	9:20
therefore, we are thus highly f.,	13:23
a highly f. people of the Lord.	27:30
of the land might be f.	46:16
they were highly f. of the Lord,	48:20
And thus were we f. of the Lord;	56:19
a man highly f. of the Lord,	Eth 1:34
he was not f. of the Lord.	10:13

FAVORS   328   FEAR

FAVORS
great f. shown unto them,	3Ne	10:18
did bestow great f. upon him,	Eth	7:22

FAYETTE
Colesville, F., and Manchester,	DC	24: 3
wilderness of F., Seneca county		128:20
old Father Whitmer, in F.,		128:21

FEAR
with an oath, that he need not f.;	1Ne	4:33
I f. exceedingly because of you;		8: 4
did f. and tremble exceedingly,		16:27
I f. lest ye shall be cast off forever.		17:47
I, Nephi, began to f. exceedingly		18:10
for f. lest thou shouldst say—		20: 5
Wherefore, the righteous need not f.;		22:17
And the righteous need not f.,		22:22
they who need f., and tremble,		22:23
I exceedingly f. and tremble	2Ne	1:25
f. ye not the reproach of men,		8: 7
but the righteous f. them not,		9:40
ye may not shrink with awful f.;		9:46
for the f. of the Lord		12:10
for the f. of the Lord shall come		12:19
for the f. of the Lord shall come		12:21
f. not, neither be faint-hearted		17: 4
thither the f. of briers and thorns;		17:25
neither f. ye their fear,		18:12
fear ye their f., nor be afraid.		18:12
and let him be your f.,		18:13
and of the f. of the Lord;		21: 2
understanding in the f. of the Lord;		21: 3
from thy sorrow, and from thy f.,		24: 3
their f. towards me is taught by		27:25
and shall f. the God of Israel.		27:34
f. God—he will justify us		28: 8
I f. that unless ye shall repent	Jac	3: 8
wicked with awful dread and f.		6:13
I f. lest I have committed the		7:19
I greatly f. lest my case shall be		7:19
keep him in the f. of the Lord.	En	1:23
up hither that ye should f. me,	Mos	2:10
for the f. of the Lord had come		4: 1
and f., and tremble before God,		15:26
a great f. of the Lamanites had		21:10
I f. there would rise contentions		29: 7
things in the f. of the Lord;		29:30
they need not f. nor tremble,	Al	1: 4
if it were known, for f. of the law,		1:17
durst not steal, for f. of the law,		1:18
and struck with much f., saying:		2:23
I say unto you come and f. not,		7:15
the f. of destruction had come		14:26
so great was their f. that they fell		14:27
they were struck with great f.,		14:29
because of the f. of being slain.		17:29
Therefore they did not f. Ammon,		17:35
Lamoni began to f. exceedingly,		18: 5
with f. lest he had done wrong		18: 5
the f. of the Lord had come		19:15
f. came upon them all, and they		19:24
queen saw the f. of the servants		22:21
she also began to f. exceedingly,		22:21
greatly marveled, and began to f.		22:23
Ammon, I f. that thy joy doth		26:10
of their f. to take up arms		27:23
this their great f. came because of		27:23
because they have reason to f.,		28:11
salvation with f. before God,		34:37
of Ammon did not f. their words;		35: 9
the f. of the Lord came upon us.		36: 7
I was struck with such great f.		36:11
my son, in the f. of God, that		39:12
that were struck with f.;		44:15
for I f. not your threatenings.		54:16
we f. not your threatenings.		54:19
F. not; behold, I am a		55: 8
yet they did not f. death;		56:47
grieved and also filled with f.,		58: 9
and struck with great f.,	Al	58:29
we f. that there is some		58:36
I f. exceedingly that the		60:14
I do not f. your power nor		60:28
but it is my God whom I f.;		60:28
insomuch that they do f. us		61: 7
tell them to f. not, for God will		61:21
the Nephites were in great f.,	He	4:20
for f. lest they should be		5:23
F. not, for behold, it is God that		5:26
awful solemn f. came upon them.		5:28
the f. which did come upon them.		5:34
compelled because of their f.,		8:10
the remainder of them did f.		8:10
and f. came upon them lest all		9: 5
And he shall stand with f., and		9:30
Because of this f. and this		9:34
shall greater f. come upon him;		9:35
they did cause great f. to come		11:32
and they f. to take them up lest		15: 9
can see that they f. to sin—		15: 9
and they began to f. because of	3Ne	1:18
they did cause f. to come upon		3:16
did f. the words which had been		3:25
the Nephites had fallen with f.		4: 9
the Nephites did not f. them;		4:10
but they did f. their God and		4:10
F. not, for thou shalt not be		22: 4
oppression for thou shalt not f.,		22:14
and f. not me, saith the Lord		24: 5
But unto you that f. my name,		25: 2
that awful f. of death which fills	Mrm	6: 7
with f. and trembling before him.		9:27
for he was struck with f.	Eth	3: 6
when he saw, he fell with f.;		3:19
I f. lest the Gentiles shall		12:25
And there went a f. of Shiz		14:18
I f. not what man can do;	Mro	8:16
perfect love casteth out all f.		8:16
I f. lest the Spirit hath ceased		8:28
I f. lest the Lamanites shall		9: 3
I f. lest the Spirit of the Lord		9: 4
that they have no f. of death;		9: 5
Wherefore, f. and tremble,	DC	1: 7
F. not to do good, my sons,		6:33
Therefore, f. not, little flock;		6:34
doubt not, f. not.		6:36
to my church need not f.,		10:55
But it is they who do not f.,		10:56
And thou needest not f., for thy		25: 9
therefore, f. not, but give heed		30: 5
F. not, little flock, the kingdom		35:27
f. not, for the kingdom is yours.		38:15
ye are prepared ye shall not f.		38:30
and the f. of persecution and		40: 2
that f. may seize upon them,		45:74
F. not, little children, for you		50:41
because of the f. of man.		60: 2
the rebellious f. and tremble;		63: 6
shall deny the faith and shall f.		63:16
f. shall come upon every man;		63:33
f. because of their terrible ones.		64:43
be of good cheer, and do not f.,		68: 6
gracious unto those who f. me,		76: 5
and f. not, saith your Lord,		79: 4
f. shall come upon all people.		88:91
F. God, and give glory to him		88:104
f. not, let your hearts be		98: 1
f. not even unto death;		101:36
Though I f. not God, nor		101:84
f. not what man can do,		122: 9
cease to f. concerning his family,		124:87
F. God, and give glory to him,		133:38
and f. not thine enemies;		136:17
F. not thine enemies,		136:30
Moses began to f. exceedingly;	Mses	1:20
as he began to f., he saw the		1:20
f. came on all them that heard		6:39
looking forth with f., in torment,		7: 1
the f. of the enemies of the people		7:14
The f. of the Lord was upon all		7:17

FEAR 329 FEELINGS

FEAR
looking forth with f. for the	Mses	7:66
but the f. soon left me.	JS	2:32

FEARED
he exceedingly f. for Laman and	1 Ne	8:36
he f. lest they should be cast off		8:36
for I have f., lest for the	2 Ne	1:17
hast f. continually every day,		8:13
release him, for he f. his word;	Mos	17:11
he f. that the judgments of God		17:11
he f. that he should do wrong		26:13
for he f. to offend him.	Al	20:11
f. lest that a multitude should		22:22
the Nephites greatly f. that the		31: 4
they f. to displease the king,		47: 2
f. to go to battle against the		47: 2
for they f. Lehi exceedingly;		49:17
f. that they would hearken to		50:32
that he f. not to come down to		51:11
all they f. was Lehi and his men.		52:29
Helaman f. lest by so doing		53:15
he f. lest that he should be	He	2:11
for they f. the people lest they		8: 4
And thou hast not f. them,		10: 4
Then they that f. the Lord spake	3 Ne	24:16
him for them that f. the Lord,		24:16
I f. lest he should smite me;	Eth	3: 8
have f. man more than God.	DC	3: 7
you f., and the time is past,		9:11
you have f. man and have		30: 1
city a judge which f. not God,		101:82
and all nations f. greatly,	Mses	7:13

FEARETH
is among you that f. the Lord,	2 Ne	7:10
he that f. me shall be looking	DC	45:39

FEARFUL
and a state of awful, f. looking	Al	40:14
f. lest the army of Moroni		50:28
they began to be f., and began		56:29
the f., and the unbelieving,	DC	63:17

FEARING
and also f. that the people would	Mos	20: 3
f. that he might by some means		21:19
f. that they should be cast off		28: 4
f. he should lose his life, said:	Al	20:23
f. that he should not gain the		46:29
f. lest there were many of them		56:55
f. that we should cut them off		58:15
not f. what man can do	DC	30:11
f. them not, for they are as grass,		124: 7

FEARS
our f. did cease concerning him.	1 Ne	4:37
Therefore they hushed their f.,	Mos	23:28
there were f. in your hearts,	DC	67: 3
yourselves from jealousies and f.,		67:10

FEAST
f. upon that which perisheth not,	2 Ne	9:51
f. upon the words of Christ;		32: 3
and f. upon his love;	Jac	3: 2
f. themselves upon the flocks of	Mos	9:12
had been a great f. appointed	Al	18: 9
Why did ye not come to the f.		20: 9
when I made a f. unto my sons,		20: 9
to the f. which he had prepared.		20:12
and ye shall f. upon this fruit		32:42
a f. of fat things might be	DC	58: 8
a f. of fat things, of wine on		58: 8

FEASTING
f. upon the word of Christ,	2 Ne	31:20
instead of f. upon the pleasing	Jac	2: 9

FEASTS
pipe, and wine are in their f.;	2 Ne	15:12

FEBRUARY
on the sixteenth day of F.,	DC	76:11
was forty-four years old in F., 1844		135: 6
December, and the F. following,	JS	2:62
Sometime in this month of F.,		2:63

FED
they were f. with manna in the	1 Ne	17:28
and f. them with manna that		7:19
Amulek, because thou hast f. me	Al	8:26
and they were f. and clothed.		21:14

FEEBLE
and strengthen the f. knees.	DC	81: 5

FEED
They shall f. in the ways, and	1 Ne	21: 9
I will f. them that oppress thee		21:26
and he shall f. his sheep,		22:25
I will f. them that oppress thee,	2 Ne	6:18
Then shall the lambs f. after		15:17
the cow and the bear shall f.;		21: 7
first-born of the poor shall f.,		24:30
the cow and the bear shall f.;		30:13
and to f. the hungry,	Jac	2:19
he shall f. among his flocks,	Mos	5:14
shalt f. a prophet of the Lord;	Al	10: 7
him into thy house and f. him,		10: 7
they f. the women upon the flesh	Mro	9: 8
and the same will f. you,	DC	84:89
follow me, and f. my sheep.		112:14

FEEDETH
heavenly Father f. them.	3 Ne	13:26

FEEDING
f. upon beasts of prey;	En	1:20
such as f. the hungry,	Mos	4:26
were watering and f. their flocks,		9:14
f. the hungry, and suffering all	Al	4:13
Behold, he is f. thy horses.		18: 9

FEEDS
he who f. you, or clothes you,	DC	84:90

FEEL
that ye could not f. his words;	1 Ne	17:45
I began to f. a desire for	En	1: 9
cannot f. them upon your backs,	Mos	24:14
brethren, how will any of you f.,	Al	5:22
I would ask, can ye f. so now?		5:26
say the smallest part which I f.		26:16
when you f. these swelling motions,		32:28
could f. the vapor of darkness;	3 Ne	8:20
ye may f. the prints of the nails		11:14
did f. the prints of the nails in		11:15
and did f. with their hands,		11:15
that ye might f. and see;		18:25
you shall f. that it is right.	DC	9: 8
earth be made to f. the wrath,		87: 6
of necessity they f. after me.		101: 8
may f. thy power, and feel		109:13
and f. constrained to acknowledge		109:13
I, the Lord, will f. after them,		112:13
I f., like Paul, to glory in		127: 2
do so, and you will f. his hand.		129: 5
and you will not f. anything;		129: 8

FEELING
other multitudes f. their way	1 Ne	8:31
all the f. of a tender parent,		8:37
but ye were past f., that ye		17:45
f. for your welfare, because of	3 Ne	3: 5
without principle, and past f.;	Mro	9:20
scene of religious f.,	JS	2: 6
confusion and bad f. ensued—		2: 6
force into every f. of my heart.		2:12

FEELINGS
according to the f. of his heart	2 Ne	4:12
whose f. are exceedingly tender	Jac	2: 7
you shall have no such f.,	DC	9: 9
with the f. of the people;		105:24
and press itself upon my f.		128: 1
seemingly good f. of both the	JS	2: 6
their good f. one for another,		2: 6
though my f. were deep and	JS	2: 8

FEET

FEET		
loosed from off my hands and f.,	1 Ne	7:18
I saw many fall down at his f.		11:24
and trample under their f.		19: 7
do men trample under their f.;		19: 7
I say, trample under their f.		19: 7
for the f. of those who are in		21:13
and lick up the dust of thy f.;		21:23
and lick up the dust of thy f.;	2 Ne	6: 7
shall lick up the dust of their f.;		6:13
making a tinkling with their f.—		13:16
and with twain he covered his f.,		16: 2
the head, and the hair of the f.;		17:20
as a carcass trodden under f.		24:19
are the f. of him that bringeth	Mos	12:21
upon the mountains were their f.!		15:15
are the f. of those that are still		15:16
are the f. of those who shall		15:17
are the f. of him that bringeth		15:18
he trampleth under his f. the		29:22
the Holy One under your f.;	Al	5:53
they rose and stood upon their f.		14:25
Zeezrom leaped upon his f.,		15:11
she arose and stood upon her f.,		19:29
he arose and stood upon his f.		19:30
And he stood upon his f.,		22:22
did tramble beneath our f.;		36: 7
again, and I stood upon my f.,		36:23
of war at the f. of Moroni,		44:15
garments at the f. of Moroni,		46:22
cast us at the f. of our enemies,		46:22
cast our garments at thy f.		46:22
of war at the f. of Moroni,		52:38
them at the foot of the Nephites,		55:23
trample them under your f.		60:33
trampled under their f. the laws	He	4:22
and did trample under their f.		6:31
they did trample under their f.		6:39
and do trample under their f.		12: 2
nails in my hands and in my f.,	3 Ne	11:14
nails in his hands and in his f.;		11:15
did fall down at the f. of Jesus,		11:17
the Lord and did kiss his f.		11:19
they trample them under their f.,		14: 6
been trodden under f. by them;		16: 8
were whole, bow down at his f.,		17:10
for the multitude did kiss his f.,		17:10
did bathe his f. with their tears.		17:10
arise and stand up upon their f.		20: 2
arose up and stood upon their f.		20: 2
are the f. of him that bringeth		20:40
ashes under the soles of your f.		25: 3
been trampled under f. of men,		28:35
of the Nephites under their f.	Mrm	5: 6
set their f. upon the shores of	Eth	6:12
the nails in my hands and f.;	DC	6:37
casting off the dust of your f.		24:15
cleansing your f. by the wayside.		24:15
your f. shod with the preparation		27:16
enemies shall be under their f.;		35:14
in thine hands and in thy f.?		45:51
put all enemies under his f.,		49: 6
all enemies under his f.		58:22
whose f. stand upon the land		59: 3
shake off the dust of thy f.		60:15
wash thy f., as a testimony		60:15
shake off the dust of your f.		75:20
subdue all enemies under his f.		76:61
all enemies under his f.,		76:106
and established his f.,		78:16
cleanse your f. even with water,		84:92
not the head say unto the f.		84:109
it hath no need of the f.;		84:109
without the f. how shall the		84:109
hands and your f. before me,		88:74
ordinance of the washing of f.,		88:139
ordinance of the washing of f.		88:139
the ordinance of washing f. is to		88:140
built fifty-five by sixty-five f.		94: 4
by fifty-five by sixty-five f.		94:11
be fifty and five f. in width,		95:15

FELL

let it be sixty-five f. in length,	DC	95:15
cleanse your f. in the secret		99: 4
trodden under the f. of men.		101:40
importune at the f. of the judge;		101:86
at the f. of the governor;		101:87
at the f. of the president;		101:88
world are subdued under my f.,		103: 7
under his f. was a paved work of		110: 2
Let thy f. be shod also, for thou		112: 7
f. of those that bring glad tidings		128:19
for his f. did not touch the floor.	JS	2:30
so, also, were his f. naked, as		2:31

FEIGNED

covetousness, and with f. words,	DC	104: 4
covetousness and f. words—		104:52

FELICITY

enjoyment of their eternal f.	DC	77: 3

FELL

the lot f. upon Laman;	1 Ne	3:11
it f. into the hands of Laban.		3:26
they f. away into forbidden paths		8:28
came forth and f. down and partook		8:30
the pride of the world; and it f.,		11:36
Holy Ghost f. upon twelve others;		12: 7
they f. down before me, and were		17:55
Adam f. that men might be;	2 Ne	2:25
that angel who f. from before the		9: 8
insomuch that he f. to the earth.	Jac	7:15
overcome that they f. to the earth.		7:21
the severity of the Lord f. upon	Om	1:22
he f., having suffered death by	Mos	17:20
that they f. to the earth,		27:12
with him f. again to the earth,		27:18
their fear that they f. to the earth,	Al	14:27
twain, so that they f. to the earth;		14:27
who f. into their hands,		17:20
said this, he f. unto the earth,		18:42
he f. upon his knees, and began		19:14
to smite him, behold, he f. dead.		19:22
and f. upon the people who were		25: 2
and he f. again to the earth.		27:17
and we all f. to the earth,		36: 7
I f. to the earth; and it was		36:10
that I f. to the earth and I did		36:11
a man f. among the Nephites,		43:38
his scalp and it f. to the earth.		44:12
and he f. to the earth.		47:17
and he f. upon her and beat her		50:30
prisoners who f. into his hands;		52: 8
of Antiparah f. into our hands.		57: 4
f. upon the guards who were left		58:21
that he f. dead without a groan.	He	2: 9
that they f. to the earth;		9: 4
that we f. to the earth;		9:14
f. to the earth and became as	3 Ne	1:16
that they f. to the earth.		1:17
did f. the tree to the earth,		4:28
whole multitude f. to the earth;		11:12
and it f. not, for it was founded		14:25
it f., and great was the fall of it.		14:27
I f. wounded in the midst;	Mrm	6:10
f. down before the Lord,	Eth	3: 6
when he saw, he f. with fear;		3:19
of them which f. by the way,		9:34
many thousands f. by the sword.		14: 4
raised upon his hands and f.;		15:31
Coriantumr f. to the earth,		15:32
their hands, f. the Holy Ghost.	Mro	2: 3
and f. calmly, exclaiming:	DC	135: 1
unto himself, he f. unto the earth.	Mses	1: 9
the Holy Ghost f. upon Adam,		5: 9
wroth, and his countenance f.		5:21
Because that Adam f.,		6:48
the Holy Ghost f. on many,		7:27
gradually until it f. upon me.	JS	2:16
f. into many foolish errors,		2:28
and I f. helpless on the ground,		2:48
the Holy Ghost f. upon him,		2:73

FELLED 331 FEW

FELLED
may cause to be f. to the earth	3Ne 4:29
man hath been f. to the earth.	4:29

FELLER
no f. is come up against us.	2Ne 24: 8

FELLOW
in the service of your f. beings	Mos 2:17
a great benefit to his f. beings.	8:18
Away with this f., and slay him;	13: 1
did Alma and his f. laborers do	26:38
power unto these my f.-servants,	Al 17:29
hearts of these my f.-servants,	17:29
my f. laborers who are with me—	31:32
Take this f. and bind him, for	He 16: 6
he has measured to his f. man.	DC 1:10
should not counsel his f.,	1:19
Upon you my f. servants,	13: 1
good unto thy f. beings,	81: 4
destruction of our f. men,	109:43
begin to smite his f.-servants.	JS 1:52
Upon you my f. servants	2:69

FELLOWS
the head of Ephraim and his f.	DC 133:34

FELLOW-SERVANTS: see FELLOW and SERVANTS.

FELLOWSHIP
they did f. one with another	He 6: 3
shall have f. in the church.	DC 83: 2
not have f. in the church;	83: 3
covenant I receive you to f.,	88:133
But so long as he is in full f.,	104:75
that such dealings be for f.	134:10
withdraw from them their f.	134:10

FELT
if ye have f. to sing the song of	Al 5:26
that which they f. was the duty	43:46
Moroni f. to rejoice	54: 2
I f. some desire to be united	JS 2: 8
never before f. in any being—	2:16
that I f. much like Paul, when	2:24
I often f. condemned for my	2:29

FEMALE
old and young, both male and f.;	1Ne 8:27
both male and f., shall perish;	2Ne 10:16
bond and free, male and f.;	26:33
bond and free, both male and f.,	Al 1:30
bond and free, both male and f.,	11:44
thy flocks, both male and f.,	Eth 1:41
gathered together, male and f.,	2: 1
he created man, male and f.,	DC 20:18
male and f. created I them.	Mses 2:27
male and f., created he them,	6: 9
male and f. to form they them.	Abr 4:27

FENCE
in attempting to cross the f.	JS 2:48

FENCED
tower, and upon every f. wall;	2Ne 12:15
he f. it, and gathered out the	15: 2

FEROCIOUS
they became wild, and f.,	En 1:20
and f., and a blood-thirsty people,	Mos 10:12
is driven by wild and f. beasts.	17:17
and a hardened and a f. people;	Al 17:14
and more wild, wicked and f.	47:36
becoming wicked, and wild, and f.,	He 3:16

FERTILE
most f. parts of the wilderness,	1Ne 16:14
more f. parts of the wilderness.	16:16

FERVENT
elements should melt with f. heat,	3Ne 26: 3
elements shall melt with f. heat,	Mrm 9: 2
shall melt with f. heat;	DC 101:25

FETTERS
and shackles, and f. of hell.	DC 123: 8

FEVER
sick at Sidom, with a burning f.,	Al 15: 3
being very low with a burning f.;	15: 5

FEVERS
there were some who died with f.,	Al 46:40
but not so much so with f.,	46:40

FEW
and its numbers were f., because	1Ne 14:12
must be destroyed, save a f. only,	17:43
a f. more days and I go the way	2Ne 1:14
I have spoken these f. words	2:30
and cut off nations not a f.	20: 7
the trees of his forest shall be f.,	20:19
which shall view it, save it be a f.	27:13
God will beat us with a f. stripes,	28: 8
all gone astray save it be a f.,	28:14
I cannot write but a f. things,	31: 1
can I write but a f. of the words	31: 1
save it be a f. words which I	31: 2
A f. words concerning the history	Jac 1:hd
a f. of the things which I	1: 2
can write a f. words upon plates,	4: 2
other servants; and they were f.	5:70
I, Jarom, write a f. words	Jar 1: 1
whatsoever I write, which are f.,	Om 1: 4
I, Chemish, write what f. things	1: 9
a f. words concerning his fathers.	1:22
only a f. of them have I written	Mos 8: 1
were but f. of them gathered	20: 5
behold also there are but f. of us.	20:19
Will ye answer me a f. questions	Al 11:21
they were in number not a f.	17:34
they were not f. in number;	17:37
him, and they were not a f.	17:38
and f. believed on the words	21:12
might save some f. of their souls.	26:26
of our labors; and are the f.?	26:31
f. understood the meaning of	33:20
save it be a f. who shall be	45:14
there were but f. who denied	46:35
a f. particular points of the law	51: 2
army, save a f. guards only,	58:22
speedily with a f. of your men,	61:15
sent a f. provisions unto them,	61:16
save it were a f. contentions	He 11:22
were a f. that began to preach,	3Ne 1:24
among a f. of the Lamanites	6:14
enjoyed peace but a f. years.	6:16
there were but f. righteous men	7: 7
were but f. who were converted	7:21
and f. there be that find it.	14:14
and f. there be that find it;	27:33
passed away save it were a f.	4Ne 1:22
save it were these f. plates	Mrm 6: 6
a f. who had escaped into the	6:15
a f. who had dissented over unto	6:15
I have but f. things to write,	8: 1
none save a f. only who do not	8:36
and f. who his days.	Eth 11:10
And only a f. have I written,	12:40
I write a f. more things,	Mro 1: 4
but I write a f. more things,	1: 4
a f. of the words of my father	7: 1
only a f. years have passed	9:12
write somewhat a f. things,	9:24
spoken a f. words by way of	10: 2
hast translated a f. more pages	DC 5:30
unto you, Oliver, a f. words.	23: 1
unto you, Hyrum, a f. words;	23: 3
I speak a f. words unto you,	23: 4
I speak a f. words unto you,	23: 5
doeth good save it be a f.;	33: 4
with commandments not a f.,	59: 4
f. shall stand to receive an	63:31
after a f. weeks, shall return	64:18
A f. words in addition to the	72:24
called but f. of them are chosen.	95: 5
And after a f. years, if thou	DC 99: 7
there have been some f. things in	112: 2

FEW 332 FIFTH

be faithful over a f. things,	DC 117:10	fruit before the time in the f.,	3Ne	24:11
many called, but f. are chosen.	121:34	after thou hast sowed thy f.	DC	24: 3
many are called, but f. are chosen.	121:40	sent forth to reap down the f.;		86: 5
his care, yea, even a f. things,	124:113	and f. for raising grain,		136: 9
I wrote a f. words of revelation	128: 2	in your f., and in your houses,		136:11
have had a f. additional views	128: 2			
and f. there be that find it,	132:22	**FIERCE**		
been faithful over a f. things,	132:53	for the f. anger of Rezin	2Ne	17: 4
Some f. days after I had this	JS 2:21	both with wrath and f. anger,		23: 9
were but f. who believed him;	2:24	and in the day of his f. anger.		23:13
		in my f. anger will I visit them	Mos	12: 1
FIELD		will not turn my f. anger away.	Al	8:29
I beheld a large and spacious f.	1Ne 8: 9	and in his f. anger he will not		9:12
unto a large and spacious f.,	8:20	to the f. anger of the Lord.		9:18
and the beasts of the f.	2Ne 2:15	but in his f. anger he will come		10:23
in the highway of the fuller's f.;	17: 3	shall they be driven with f. winds		26: 6
and of his fruitful f.,	20:18	did smite in their f. anger.		43:44
shall be turned into a fruitful f.;	27:28	thine anger, yea, thy f. anger,	He	11:12
the fruitful f. shall be esteemed as	27:28	I will visit them in my f. anger,		13:10
even as a dry stalk of the f.,	Mos 12:11	their wars are exceedingly f.	Mro	1: 2
Behold, the f. was ripe,	Al 26: 5	the f. and vivid lightning also,	DC	87: 6
when I did cry unto thee in my f.;	33: 5	displeasure, and in his f. anger,		101:90
proved them in the f. of battle,	3Ne 3: 4	than the f. lion, because of thy		122: 4
noble spirit in the f. of battle.	3: 5	if f. winds become thine enemy;		122: 7
Consider the lilies of the f. how	13:28	and my f. anger is kindled	Mses	6:27
God so clothe the grass of the f.,	13:30	for my f. anger is kindled		7:34
For behold the f. is white	DC 4: 4			
Behold, the f. is white already	6: 3	**FIERCENESS**		
Behold, the f. is white already	11: 3	saw the f. and the anger of	Al	43:48
Behold, the f. is white already	12: 3	caused by the f. of the wind.	Eth	6: 6
Behold, the f. is white already	14: 3	of the f. of the wrath of	DC	76:107
feap in the f. which is white	31: 4	the f. of the wrath of Almighty		88:106
For behold, the f. is white	33: 3			
the f. is white already to	33: 7	**FIERY**		
the beasts of the f. and the	49:19	the f. darts of the adversary	1Ne	15:24
the beasts of the f. and the	59:16	He sent f. flying serpents among		17:41
For consider the lilies of the f.,	84:82	shall be a f. flying serpent.	2Ne	24:29
I say, the f. was the world,	86: 2	the f. indignation of the wrath	Al	40:14
the f. remaineth to be burned.	86: 7	the f. furnace could not harm	Mrm	8:24
unto a man having a f.,	88:51	the f. darts of the adversary;	DC	3: 8
forth his servants into the f.	88:51	all the f. darts of the wicked;		27:17
into the field to dig in the f.	88:51	the f. indignation of the wrath	Mses	7: 1
Go ye and labor in the f.,	88:52			
Go ye also into the f., and in	88:53	**FIFTEEN**		
And the lord of the f. went	88:56	And I, being f. years of age and	Mrm	1:15
but for the beasts of the f.,	89:14	to receive f. thousand dollars	DC	124:64
and for all beasts of the f.,	89:17	receive over f. thousand dollars		124:65
man, or of the beasts of the f.,	101:24	pay over f. thousand dollars stock		124:72
the woods and all the trees of the f.	128:23	eight hundred and f. years,	Mses	6:18
every plant of the f. before it was	Mses 3: 5	governs f. other fixed planets	Fac	2: 5
herb of the f. before it grew.	3: 5	between fourteen and f. years	JS	2:22
formed every beast of the f.,	3:19			
and to every beast of the f.;	3:20	**FIFTEENTH**		
than any beast of the f.	4: 5	thus endeth the f. year of	Al	28: 8
and above every beast of the f.;	4:20	the f. year of the reign of		28: 9
shalt eat the herb of the f.	4:24	from the first year to the f. has		28:10
over all the beasts of the f.,	5: 1	And in the f. year they did	3Ne	2:18
And Cain went into the f.,	5:32	And thus ended the f. year,		2:19
that while they were in the f.,	5:32	was at this time in my f. year.	JS	2: 7
concerning every plant of the f.	Abr 5: 5	It was on the f. day of May,		2:72
and every herb of the f. before	5: 5			
formed every beast of the f.,	5:20	**FIFTH**		
to every beast of the f.;	5:21	one f. part of all they possessed,	Mos	11: 3
Neither let him who is in the f.	JS 1:15	a f. part of their gold and of		11: 3
two shall be in the f.,	1:44	and a f. part of their ziff,		11: 3
to cross the fence out of the f.	2:48	and a f. part of their fatlings,		11: 3
returned to my father in the f.,	2:50	also a f. part of all their grain.		11: 3
I left the f., and went to the	2:50	until the f. year of the reign of	Al	1:33
		commencement of the f. year of		2: 1
FIELDS		and ended in the f. year of		3:25
upon the flocks of our f.	Mos 9:12	endeth the f. year of the reign of		3:27
and the corn of their f.	9:14	the f. day of the second month,		16: 1
and to slay them in their f.,	11:16	the f. day of the second month		16: 1
and laid wait for them in the f.	20: 8	of the twenty and f. year of		51: 1
of Alma fled from their f.,	23:26	the twenty and f. year in peace;		51: 1
their f. of grain were destroyed,	Al 3: 2	in the twenty and f. year of		51:12
for the loss of their f. of grain,	4: 2	the twenty and f. year of		51:37
unto him when ye are in your f.,	34:20	in the thirty and f. year of		62:52
him over the crops of your f.,	34:24	contention in the forth and f. year.	He	3: 2
Cry over the flocks of your f.,	34:25	And in the sixty and f. year they		6:14
yea, in the increase of their f.,	He 12: 2	passed away the sixty and f. year.		6:14

FIFTH 333 FILL

in the seventy and f. year.	He 11: 6	wo unto them that f. against God	2Ne 25:14
in the eighty and f. year they	11:37	all the nations that f. against Zion,	27: 3
thus ended the eighty and f. year.	11:38	be that f. against Mount Zion.	27: 3
away the ninety and f. year also,	3Ne 2: 1	unto them that f. against my word	29:14
fourth, and the twenty and f.;	5: 7	he did f. with the strength of his	WM 1:13
and also the thirty and f.,	4Ne 1: 1	f. and quarrel one with another,	Mos 4:14
hundred and forty and f. year	Mrm 2:16	and like dragons did they f.	20:11
hundred and seventy and f. year.	4:16	did not f. against God any more,	Al 23: 7
verse of the f. chapter of John,	DC 76:15	Lamanites did f. exceedingly;	43:43
shall sound, which is the f. trump,	88:103	to f. with such exceeding great	43:43
is the f. angel who committeth	88:103	yea, they did f. like dragons,	43:44
and the morning were the f. day.	Mses 2:23	might have an equal chance to f.;	49:22
day; and it was the f. time.	Abr 4:23	to f. against the men of Moroni	51:18
first chapter and f. verse,	JS 2:11	to f. valiantly for their freedom	51:21
he quoted the f. verse thus;	2:38	a covenant to f. for the liberty	53:17
		f. in all cases to protect the	53:17
FIFTIES		they should f. with the Nephites;	55:23
tens, or by twenties, or by f.,	DC 103:30	and would f. with stones,	57:14
by hundreds, or by f., or by	104:68	but would f. against it,	62: 9
of hundreds, captains of f.,	136: 3	therefore they would not f.,	Mrm 2: 3
captains of hundreds, and of f.,	136:15	and f. for their wives, and their	2:23
		Com did f. against them much;	Eth 10:34
FIFTIETH		they shall f. manfully for me;	DC 35:14
f. year of the reign of the judges.	He 3:32	Michael shall f. their battles,	88:115
the three hundred and f. year	Mrm 2:28	the Lord, would f. their battles,	98:37
		to f. the battles of Zion;	105:14
FIFTY		I will f. your battles.	105:14
and he can command f., yea, even	1Ne 3:31	thou wilt f. for thy people as	109:28
he can slay f.; then why not us?	3:31	and to f. against God.	121:38
mightier than Laban and his f.,	4: 1		
The captain of f.,	2Ne 13: 3	FIGHTETH	
f. and five years had passed	Jac 1: 1	he that f. against Zion shall	2Ne 10:13
and they were all slain, save f.,	Om 1:28	ht that f. against Zion,	10:16
that their f. could stand against	Mos 11:19	upon him that f. against thee	Al 3:16
one priest to every f. of their	18:18	and f. against him continually,	Mro 7:12
about four hundred and f. souls.	18:35		
were about f. who were wounded,	Al 49:24	FIGHTING	
And in the f. and first year of	He 3:33	they were not f. for monarchy	Al 43:45
f. and second year ended in	3:36	they were f. for their homes	43:45
in the f. and third year of the	3:37	weary because of his much f.	3Ne 4:14
in the f. and fourth year there	4: 1	f. against Coriantumr that they	Eth 13:18
in the f. and sixth year of the	4: 4	f. for that which he desired.	13:25
And in the f. and seventh year	4: 5		
in the f. and eighth year of	4: 5	FIGS	
the f. and eighth and ninth years	4: 8	of thorns, or f. of thistles?	3Ne 14:16
and also the f. and first,	4Ne 1: 6		
and the f. and second;	1: 6	FIG-TREE: see FIG and TREE.	
until the f. and nine years had	1: 6		
two hundred and f. years pass	1:41	FIG-TREES: see FIG and TREES.	
against an army of f. thousand.	Mrm 2:25		
f. and two of the people of	Eth 15:23	FIGURATIVE	
it shall be built f.-five by	DC 94: 4	They are f. expressions,	DC 77: 2
it shall be f.-five by sixty-five	94:11		
be f. and five feet in width,	95:15	FIGURE	
or twenty, or f., or an hundred,	104:69	also a numerical f.,	Fac 2: 4
or twenty, or f., or a hundred,	104:73		
not receive less than f. dollars	124:64	FIGURES	
to receive under f. dollars	124:66	in the f. at the beginning,	Abr 1:14
nor under f. dollars;	124:72	which manner of the f. is called	1:14
four hundred and f. years old,	Mses 8:12		
gave me f. dollars to assist us	JS 2:61	FILE	
		when the converts began to f. off,	JS 2: 6
FIFTY-FIVE: see FIFTY and FIVE.			
		FILL	
FIG		shall f. the breadth of thy land,	2Ne 18: 8
learn the parable of the f.-tree,	DC 35:16	nor f. the face of the world with	24:21
Ye look and behold the f.-trees,	45:37	and doth f. his breast with guilt,	Mos 2:38
cast themselves down as a f.	88:87	and my words f. you with wonder	13: 8
fig that falleth from off a f.-tree.	88:87	to f. the judgment-seat,	Al 50:39
they sewed f.-leaves together	Mses 4:13	Pahoran did f. the seat of his	50:40
learn a parable of the f.-tree—	JS 1:38	no one to f. the judgment-seat.	He 2: 1
		who should f. the judgment-seat.	2: 1
FIG-LEAVES: see FIG and LEAVES		appointed to f. the judgment-seat,	2: 2
		f. the judgment-seat with justice	3:20
FIGHT		f. the judgment-seat with justice	3:37
to f. against the apostles of the	1Ne 11:34	did f. the seat of his father and	3Ne 6:19
to f. against the twelve apostles	11:35	did f. the steps of his father.	Eth 9:15
shall f. against the twelve apostles	11:36	which shall f. your soul with joy;	DC 11:13
to f. against the Lamb of God.	14:13	that they may f. their mission,	61: 9
And all that f. against Zion	22:14	so be that they f. their mission,	61:22
all they who f. against Zion shall	22:19	Lord, which shall f. the house.	84: 5
repent and f. not against Zion,	2Ne 6:12	and to f. appointments that you	84:107
they that f. against Zion and	6:13	you yourselves are not able to f.	84:107

FILL 334 FILTHY

to f. the immensity of space.—	DC 88:12	were f. with the Holy Ghost,		3Ne 26:17
would f. their offices according to	102: 4	in my name shall be f.;		27:16
they might f. up the measure of	103: 3	be f. with the Holy Ghost,		30: 2
f. the several calls for preaching	107:38	the land was f. with robbers	Mrm	2: 8
mountain and f. the whole earth;	109:72	heart has been f. with sorrow		2:19
that thy glory may f. the earth;	109:74	every soul was f. with terror		6: 8
be appointed to f. the places of	118: 6	ye may be f. with this love,	Mro	7:48
that you should f. all these offices	124:144	And I am f. with charity,		8:17
and multiply, and f. the waters	Mses 2:22	be f. with the spirit of Elias;	DC	27: 7
and f. the waters in the seas or	Abr 4:22	mouths and they shall be f.,		33: 8
it would f. up volumes.	JS 2:61	mouths and they shall be f.,		33:10
		be f. with the measure of man,		49:17
FILLED		until it has f. the whole earth.		65: 2
f. with the Spirit of the Lord.	1Ne 1:12	shall be f. with joy and gladness;		75:21
his whole heart was f., because	1:15	being f. with the Holy Ghost		84:27
power, being f. with the Spirit,	2:14	be f. with the glory of the Lord,		84:32
behold, he was f. with joy,	5: 1	be f. with the knowledge of the		84:98
he was f. with the Spirit, and	5:17	f. the measure of its creation,		88:19
it f. my soul with exceeding great	8:12	bodies shall be f. with light,		88:67
it was f. with people,	8:27	that body which is f. with light		88:67
shall be f. by those who digged it,	14: 3	saints shall be f. with his glory,		88:107
I am f. with the power of God,	17:48	bowels are f. with compassion		101: 9
He hath f. me with his love,	2Ne 4:21	be f. by the nomination of		102: 8
and his train f. the temple.	16: 1	And let thy house be f.,		109:37
and the house was f. with smoke.	16: 4	f. the world with confusion,		123: 7
are f. with the spirit of prophecy.	25: 4	f. with songs of everlasting joy.		133:33
and be f. with love towards God	Mos 2: 4	being f. with the Holy Ghost,	Mses	1:24
they may also be f. with joy.	3: 4	Adam blessed God and was f.,		5:10
and they were f. with joy,	4: 3	thy mouth, and it shall be f..		6:32
and be f. with the love of God,	4:12	and it was f. with violence.		8:28
your hearts should be f. with joy,	4:20	the earth is f. with violence,		8:30
which are f. with engravings,	8: 9	he f. me with the vision of	Abr	1:15
being f. with compassion	15: 9	were f. with the Holy Ghost,	JS	2:73
rejoicing, being f. with the Spirit.	18:14			
were f. with the grace of God.	18:16	**FILLETH**		
was f. with exceeding great joy.	21:24	which Comforter f. with hope	Mro	8:26
now Limhi was again f. with joy	21:28	it f. the measure of its creation,	DC	88:25
brethren were f. with sorrow	21:29			
were f. with exceeding great joy.	25: 8	**FILLING**		
they were f. with sorrow,	25: 9	instead of f. up their ditches by	Al	49:22
were f. with pain and anguish	25:11	unto the f. their souls with joy	He	3:35
yea, they were f. with sorrow;	28:18	robbers f. the judgment-seats—		7: 4
being f. with great joy because of	Al 4:14			
souls f. with guilt and remorse,	5:18	**FILLS**		
his bowels may be f. with mercy,	7:12	f. the breasts of all the wicked,	Mrm	6: 7
that Alma ate bread and was f.;	8:22			
after he had eaten and was f.	8:23	**FILTH**		
they were f. with the Holy Ghost.	8:30	the f. of the daughters of Zion,	2Ne	14: 4
being f. with the Spirit of God,	18:16			
her hands, being f. with joy,	19:30	**FILTHINESS**		
that I may be f. with joy,	22:15	water which my father saw was f.;	1Ne	15:27
f. with all manner of wild	22:31	beheld not the f. of the water.		15:27
then is my soul f. with joy;	29:10	if their works have been f. they		15:33
they were f. with the Holy Spirit.	31:36	there must needs be a place of f.		15:34
this fruit even until ye are f.,	32:42	whom ye hate because of their f.	Jac	3: 5
my soul was f. with joy	36:20	against them because of their f.;		3: 9
and be f. with the Holy Ghost.	36:24	ye shall remember your own f.,		3: 9
that ye may be f. with love;	38:12	their f. came because of their		3: 9
they were f. up in a measure	49:22	that ye may, because of your f.,		3:10
having f. the judgment-seat	50:37	full of idolatry and f.;	En	1:20
his soul was f. with anger	51:14	If my people shall sow f.	Mos	7:30
I was f. with exceeding joy	57:36	If my people shall sow f.		7:31
grieved and also f. with fear,	58: 9	with blood and all manner of f.?	Al	5:22
was f. with exceeding great joy	62: 1	f. of anything which is unclean		7:21
they were f. with that joy which	He 5:44	is filthy shall remain in his f.		7:21
and they were f. as if with fire,	5:45	being esteemed as f.;		32: 3
my soul shall be f. with sorrow	7: 9	under a consciousness of your f.	Mrm	9: 4
and was f. with gladness and did	8:17	and be cleansed from the f.	Mses	7:48
the land was f. with rejoicing;	11:18			
shall be f. with the Holy Ghost.	3Ne 12: 6	**FILTHY**		
be f. with all manner of lyings,	16:10	Behold the fountain of f. water	1Ne	12:16
bowels are f. with compassion	17: 6	and loathsome, and a f. people,		12:23
my bowels are f. with mercy.	17: 7	they must needs be f.; and if they		15:33
the joy which f. our souls at the	17:17	if they be f. it must needs be		15:33
when they had eaten and were f.,	18: 4	kingdom of God must be f. also.		15:33
multitude had eaten and were f.,	18: 5	the kingdom of God is not f.,		15:34
and did drink of it and were f.;	18: 9	prepared for that which is f.		15:34
they did drink, and they were f.	18: 9	they who are f. shall be filthy	2Ne	9:16
were f. with the Holy Ghost and	19:13	shall be f. still; wherefore,		9:16
they were f. with desire.	19:24	they who are f. are the devil and		9:16
hunger nor thirst, but shall be f.	20: 8	that are f. this day before God;	Jac	3: 3
they were f. with the Spirit;	20: 9	which are not f. like unto you,		3: 3

FILTHY   335   FINGER

that he who is f. shall remain in	Al 7:21
a f., and a loathsome people,	Mrm 5:15
he that is f. shall be filthy still;	9:14
he that is filthy shall be f. still;	9:14
they must remain f. still.	DC 88:35
end, who shall remain f. still.	88:102

FINAL

the f. state of the soul after the	1Ne 15:31
the f. state of the souls of men	15:35
his f. doom is to endure a	Mos 2:39
this is the f. state of the wicked.	Al 34:35
a f. decision upon controversies	DC 107:80

FINALLY

F., I bid you farewell, until I shall	Jac 6:13
And f., I cannot tell you all	Mos 4:29
And f., all ye that will persist	Al 5:56
f. I prevailed with the	JS 2:56

FIND

that diligently seeketh shall f.;	1Ne 10:19
whither shall I go that I may f. ore	17: 9
whither I should go to f. ore,	17:10
did f. upon the land of promise,	18:25
And we did f. all manner of ore,	18:25
and in him they shall f. pasture.	22:25
man should f. out all his ways.	Jac 4: 8
that ye could not f. utterance,	Mos 4:20
might f. the land of Zarahemla,	8: 7
but they could not f. it,	21:25
they did f. a land which had been	21:26
they could f. no way to deliver	22: 2
f. that ye had humbled yourselves	Al 7: 3
f. that ye were blameless before	7: 3
f. that ye were not in the awful	7: 3
might f. witness against them,	10:13
repenteth shall f. mercy;	32:13
for such shall f. rest to their souls.	37:34
and I did f. peace to my soul.	38: 8
perhaps he might f. a man who	55: 4
that he did f. the king;	62:36
ye shall f. blood upon the skirts	He 9:31
accursed, that no man shall f. thee	12:19
shall f. them again no more,	13:18
then ye will not f. fault with him.	13:28
seek, and ye shall f.;	3Ne 14: 7
and few there be that f. it.	14:14
and few there be that f.;	27:33
and with me ye shall f. rest.	28: 3
the morrow, he could not f. it,	Eth 14: 1
the people of Limhi did f. them.	15:33
thou mayest f. out mysteries,	DC 6:11
inasmuch as ye shall f. them	42: 8
if ye shall f. that any persons	42:75
a promise that they should f. it	45:14
shall f. rest to their souls.	54:10
of his doings none can f. out.	76: 2
shall f. none inheritance in	85: 9
not f. an inheritance among	85:11
diligently and ye shall f. me;	88:63
seeketh me early shall f. me,	88:83
cease to f. fault one with	88:124
And shall f. wisdom and great	89:19
learn wisdom and to f. truth.	97: 1
shall f. it again, even life	98:13
for my sake shall f. it again.	103:27
in this way you may f. favor in	105:26
and f. favor in thy sight,	109:21
hold of them and f. them out.	123: 3
appointed to f. out these things,	123: 4
they know not where to f. it—	123:12
that ye may f. grace in their eyes,	124: 9
traveler may f. health and safety	124:23
seek to f. safety and refuge	124:109
f. recorded in Revelation 20:12—	128: 6
and few there be that f. it,	132:22
f. that which thy neighbor has	136:26
If the world can f. out	Fac 2:11
when he cometh, shall f. so doing;	JS 1:50

FINDETH

he f. himself on the left hand of	Mos 5:10

he that f. mercy and endureth	Al 32:13
and he that seeketh, f.;	3Ne 14: 8
whoso f. them, the same will	Eth 1: 4
he that f. me will slay me,	Mses 5:39

FINDING

lest any f. him should kill him.	Mses 5:40
f. there was greater happiness	Abr 1: 2
f. myself alone, I kneeled down	JS 2:15

FINE

thereof was exceeding f.,	1Ne 4: 9
manner of dress was exceeding f.;	8:27
or, in f., after the Gentiles had	10:14
and scarlets, and f.-twined linen,	13: 7
scarlets, and the f.-twined linen,	13: 8
and it was of f. brass.	16:10
bow, which was made of f. steel;	16:18
thereof was exceeding f.;	18: 4
yea, in f., all those who belong to	22:23
in f., all things which are created,	2Ne 2:15
thereof was exceeding f.	5:16
in f., wo unto all those who	9:38
and the f. linen, and hoods,	13:23
more precious than f. gold;	23:12
because of their f. sanctuaries;	28:13
because of their f. clothing;	28:13
in f., wo unto all those who	28:28
and in f. workmanship of wood,	Jar 1: 8
Yea, and in f., two hundred and	Om 1: 3
and work all manner of f. linen,	Mos 10: 5
them with f. work of wood,	11: 8
all of which was of f. wood and	11: 9
should work all manner of f. work	11:10
of f. wood, and of copper, and of	11:10
of silk and f.-twined linen,	Al 1:29
exceeding riches, and their f. silks,	4: 6
silks, and their f.-twined linen,	4: 6
Or in f., in the first place they	13: 5
and in f., in all the land round	24: 1
Yea, in f., they did pervert	31:11
and upon all manner of f. goods.	31:24
yea, and in f. so great had been	36:14
yea, and in f., all the land,	46:17
Yea and in f., their wars never	48:22
in f. because of those who had	62: 2
of f.-twined linen and cloth of	He 6:13
and in f. doing all things for the	12: 2
yea, in f., all the people upon	3Ne 1:17
f. and exceedingly dry wood,	8:21
yea, and in f., till the seventy	4Ne 1:14
and all manner of f. pearls,	1:24
of the f. things of the world.	1:24
the wearing of very f. apparel,	Mrm 8:36
substance, and your f. apparel,	8:37
and of silks, and of f. linen,	Eth 9:17
he did obtain all his f. work,	10: 7
his f. gold he did cause to be	10: 7
all manner of f. workmanship	10: 7
did work all manner of f. work.	10:23
have silks, and f.-twined linen;	10:24
and in f., there were none of	13:17
and in f., all manner of	13:26
is matter, but it is more f.	DC 131: 7

FINE-TWINED: see FINE and TWINED.

FINGER

did point the f. of scorn at me	1Ne 8:33
by the f. of mine own hand;	2Ne 3:17
was written by the f. of God.	Al 10: 2
every one of them with his f.	3Ne 28:12
stones, O Lord, with thy f.,	Eth 3: 4
stones one by one with his f.	3: 6
and he saw the f. of the Lord;	3: 6
and it was as the f. of a man,	3: 6
I saw the f. of the Lord,	3: 8
ye could not have seen my f.	3: 9
and he saw the f. of Jesus,	3:19
that it was the f. of the Lord;	3:19
that when God put forth his f.	12:20
had beheld the f. of the Lord,	12:21
appointed by the f. of the Lord,	DC 84: 3
pattern given by the f. of God;	Mses 6:46

FINGERS 336 FIRE

FINGERS
pointing their f. towards those	1Ne 8:27
nor touch me with their f.,	17:52
which their own f. have made.	2Ne 12: 8

FINISH
to f. my record upon them,	WM 1: 5
proceed to f. out my record,	1: 9
therefore I f. my message.	Mos 13: 7
But I f. my message;	13: 9
now I f. the commandment	3Ne 20:10
now I f. my record concerning	Mrm 6: 1
do f. the record of my father,	8: 1
proceed to f. my record	Eth 13: 1
That when he shall f. his work	DC 124:19
f. the heavens and the earth,	Abr 5: 1

FINISHED
after I had f. the ship,	1Ne 18: 4
for my work is not yet f.;	2Ne 29: 9
after having f. speaking to the	Mos 6: 1
Abinadi had f. these sayings,	17: 1
had f. translating these records,	28:17
After they had f. burying their	Al 3: 1
when he had f. his work at Melek	8: 6
when Amulek had f. these words	11:46
But, behold, our work is not f.;	14:13
had f. burying their dead	53: 3
and he f. his record;	Eth 15:33
no other gift until it is f.	DC 5: 4
until you have f. this record,	9: 1
and f. the will of him whose	19: 2
partook and f. my preparations	19:19
work of translation until it be f.	73: 4
Lamb, shall have f. his work.	76:85
on the seventh day he f. his work,	77:12
order, until his hour was f.,	88:60
It is f.; it is finished!	88:106
It is finished; it is f.!	88:106
And when you have f. the	90:13
have f. their remarks.	102:18
labor diligently until it shall be f.,	115:12
anything remain that is not f.	115:12
holy temple, when it is f.,	128:24
heaven and the earth were f.,	Mses 3: 1
things which I had made were f.,	3: 2

FINISHER
author and the f. of their faith.	Mro 6: 4

FINISHING
unto the f. of the remainder of	DC 10: 3
preparing and f. of his work,	77:12
unto the f. and the end thereof,	121:32

FIR
the f.-trees rejoice at thee,	2Ne 24: 8
bring the box-tree, and the f.-tree,	DC 124:26

FIRE
there came a pillar of f. and dwelt	1Ne 1: 6
that they were burned with f.;	12: 4
the brightness of a flaming f.,	15:30
bellows wherewith to blow the f.,	17:11
have wherewith to blow the f.,	17:11
together that I might make f.	17:11
that we should make much f.,	17:12
by tempest, by f., and by smoke,	19:11
destruction of their enemies by f.	22:17
saved, even if it so be as by f.	22:17
blood, and f., and vapor of smoke	22:18
both by f., and by tempest,	2Ne 6:15
Behold all ye that kindle f.,	7:11
walk in the light of your f.	7:11
shall go away into everlasting f.;	9:16
as a lake of f. and brimstone,	9:16
and that lake of f. and brimstone,	9:19
and the lake of f. and brimstone,	9:26
and the shining of a flaming f.	14: 5
as the f. devoureth the stubble,	15:24
tails of these smoking f. brands,	17: 4
be with burning and fuel of f.	19: 5

For wickedness burneth as the f.;	2Ne 19:18
shall be as the fuel of the f.;	19:19
a burning like the burning of a f.	20:16
light of Israel shall be for a f.,	20:17
the f. of the anger of the Lord	26: 6
with the flame of devouring f.	27: 2
even a lake of f. and brimstone,	28:23
he must destroy the wicked by f.	30:10
then cometh the baptism of f.	31:13
have received the baptism of f.	31:14
a remission of your sins by f.	31:17
into that lake of f. and brimstone	Jac 3:11
and we will cast them into the f.	5: 7
I will cast into the f. and burn	5: 9
and cast them into the f.	5:26
that it may be cast into the f.,	5:37
hewn down and cast into the f.	5:42
and cast them into the f.,	5:45
hewn down and cast into the f.;	5:46
and cast them into the f.	5:47
and cast them into the f.,	5:49
and cast them into the f.	5:58
hewn down and cast into the f.,	5:66
will I cause to be burned with f.	5:77
the world shall be burned with f.	6: 3
hewn down and cast into the f.?	6: 7
into that lake of f. and brimstone	6:10
which lake of f. and brimstone is	6:10
which is like an unquenchable f.,	Mos 2:38
is as a lake of f. and brimstone,	3:27
as a garment in a furnace of f.	12:10
even the pains of death by f.;	17:15
I suffer, the pains of death by f.	17:18
having suffered death by f.;	17:20
suffer, even unto death by f.	19:20
shall depart into everlasting f.	26:27
hewn down and cast into the f.—	Al 5:35
hewn down and cast into the f.,	5:52
a f. which cannot be consumed,	5:52
even an unquenchable f.	5:52
hewn down and cast into the f.	5:56
be as a lake of f. and brimstone,	12:17
they should be cast into the f.,	14: 8
and cast them into the f. also,	14: 8
be burned and destroyed by f.	14: 8
those who were consumed by f.	14: 9
who were consuming in the f.,	14:10
who had been cast into the f.	14:14
into a lake of f. and brimstone?	14:14
who had been cast into the f.;	14:15
Lamanites should perish by f.	25: 5
that he should suffer death by f.	25: 9
the first that suffered death by f.	25:11
many should suffer death by f.,	25:11
were encircled about as if by f.,	He 5:23
as standing in the midst of f.	5:23
encircled about with a pillar of f.,	5:24
yea every soul, by a pillar of f.	5:43
if in the midst of a flaming f.,	5:44
and they were filled as if with f.,	5:45
cause that f. should come down	13:13
hewn down and cast into the f.;	14:18
hewn down and cast into the f.;	14:18
the city of Zarahemla did take f.	3Ne 8: 8
neither could there be f. kindled	8:21
was not any light seen, neither f.,	8:22
Zarahemla have I burned with f.,	9: 3
I caused to be burned with f.	9: 9
I caused to be burned with f.,	9:10
I did send down f. and destroy	9:11
him will I baptize with f. and	9:20
were baptized with f. and with	9:20
they were not burned by f.,	10:13
deaths and destructions by f.,	10:14
for he will visit them with f. and	11:35
I will baptize you with f. and	12: 1
they shall be visited with f.	12: 2
fool, shall be in danger of hell f.	12:22
hewn down, and cast into the f.	14:19
as it were in the midst of f.;	17:24
they were encircled about with f.;	17:24
with the Holy Ghost and with f.	19:13

FIRE 337 FIRST

encircled about as if it were by f.;	3Ne	19:14
that bloweth the coals in the f.,		22:16
For he is like a refiner's f.,		24: 2
hewn down and cast into the f.,		27:11
hewn down and cast into the f.,		27:17
cast them into furnaces of f.,	4Ne	1:32
and cities were burned with f.;	Mrm	5: 5
first with water, then with f.		7:10
he shall be in danger of hell f.		8:17
hewn down and cast into the f.;		8:21
a flame of unquenchable f.		9: 5
shall ye take f. with you,	Eth	2:23
shall not go by the light of f.		2:23
pass away, even so as by f.		4: 9
that they were baptized with f.		12:14
I will make him as flaming f.	DC	7: 6
of sins by baptism, and by f.,		19:31
of hands for the baptism of f.		20:41
of my coming in a pillar of f.,		29:12
be cast down by devouring f.,		29:21
ye cursed, into everlasting f.,		29:28
then cometh the baptism of f.		33:11
by the f. of mine indignation		35:14
and come forth out of the f.,		36: 6
then cometh the baptism of f.		39: 6
shall pass away so as by f.		43:32
go away into unquenchable f.,		43:33
they shall behold blood, and f.,		45:41
be hewn down and cast into the f.		45:50
be hewn down and cast into the f.,		45:57
burneth with f. and brimstone,		63:17
wicked with unquenchable f.		63:34
cast them into unquenchable f.		63:54
into the lake of f. and brimstone,		76:36
and the f. is not quenched,		76:44
the vengeance of eternal f.		76:105
hewn down and cast into the f.		97: 7
vengeance, with devouring f.		97:26
be burned with unquenchable f.		101:66
even cloven tongues as of f.,		109:36
His eyes were as a flame of f.;		110: 3
For he is like a refiner's f.,		128:24
on a globe like a sea of glass and f.,		130: 7
be as the melting f. that burneth,		133:41
f. which causeth the waters to		133:41
if the f. can scathe a green tree		135: 6
Thou art baptized with f.,	Mses	6:66
the f. of mine indignation is		7:34
and the f. to be my chariot;	Abr	2: 7

FIRE-BRANDS: see FIRE and BRANDS.

FIREPLACE
And as I leaned up to the f.,	JS	2:20

FIRES
when there shall be heard of f.,	Mrm	8:29

FIRM
f. and steadfast, and immovable	1Ne	2:10
for ye may, if your minds are f.,	Jac	3: 2
they were f., and would suffer	Al	24:19
they were f. in the faith of Christ,		27:27
the f. decree of a just God,		29: 4
f. hope that ye shall one day rest		34:41
a man who was f. in the faith		48:13
of Noah with a f. determination;		49:13
were f. before the Lamanites,		57:19
and sixty were f. and undaunted.		57:20
young, and their minds are f.,		57:27
f. to keep the commandments of	He	7: 7
are f. and steadfast in the faith,		15: 8
they were f., and steadfast,	3Ne	6:14
of strong faith and a f. mind	Mro	7:30
f. in keeping the commandments	DC	5:22
hath gone forth in a f. decree,		29:12
mouth of God in a f. decree;	Mses	5:15

FIRMAMENT
exceed that of the stars in the f.	1Ne	1:10
the sun of the f. is written of	DC	76:70
differs from the sun in the f.	DC	76:71
the glory of the moon in the f.		76:81
as the stars in the f. of heaven,		76:109
a f. in the midst of the water,	Mses	2: 6
I, God, made the f.		2: 7
the great waters under the f.		2: 7
waters which were above the f.,		2: 7
called the f. Heaven;		2: 8
Let there be lights in the f.		2:14
let them be for lights in the f.		2:15
set them in the f. of the		2:17
in the open f. of heaven.		2:20
were in the f. of heaven.	Abr	3:13
the f. over our heads;	Fac	1:12
or the f. of the heavens;		2: 4

FIRMER
and f. and firmer in the faith	He	3:35
and f. in the faith of Christ,		3:35

FIRMLY
expressly promised and f. decreed,	Al	9:24
f. believing that their souls were		46:39

FIRMNESS
Look unto God with f. of mind,	Jac	3: 1
shaken from my f. in the Spirit,		4:18
because of their f. and their	He	6: 1
because of their f. when they		15:10
great praise because of your f.,	3Ne	3: 2
and also the f. of your people,		3: 2
because of your f. in that which		3: 5
stand before them with such f.	Mrm	2:25
but ask with a f. unshaken,		9:28

FIRST
THE F. BOOK OF NEPHI	1Ne	1:hd
the f. year of the reign of Zedekiah,		1: 4
the f. came and stood before my		1:11
Eve who were our f. parents;		5:11
shall establish the truth of the f.,		13:40
the last shall be f., and the first		13:42
first, and the f. shall be last.		13:42
made mention upon the f. plates.		19: 2
for I am he; I am the f.,		20:12
after thou hast lost the f.,		21:20
yea, even my f. blessing.	2Ne	1:28
I take away my f. blessing,		1:29
thou art my f.-born in the days		2: 1
being the f. that should rise.		2: 8
he is the f.-fruits unto God,		2: 9
my f.-born in the wilderness,		2:11
after he had created our f. parents,		2:15
sons and daughters of my f.-born,		4: 3
the f. judgment which came upon		9: 7
being who beguiled our f. parents,		9: 9
passed from this f. death unto life,		9:15
when at f. he lightly afflicted		19: 1
the f.-born of the poor shall feed,		24:30
save in the f. place ye shall pray		32: 9
having f. obtained mine errand	Jac	1:17
concerning their f. parents.		4: 3
the f.-fruits of Christ unto God,		4:11
he beheld the f. that it had		5:20
of ground was poorer than the f.		5:23
yea, the f. and the second		5:39
and the branches of the f. fruit—		5:60
at the last that they may be f.,		5:63
and that the f. may be last,		5:63
old and young, the f. and the last;		5:63
and the last and the f.,		5:63
And his f. parents came out from	Om	1:22
in the f. place, he hath created you,	Mos	2:23
of our fathers' f. inheritance		9: 1
in the land of their f. inheritance,		10:13
even a f. resurrection;		15:21
come forth in the f. resurrection;		15:22
they are the f. resurrection.		15:22
have part in the f. resurrection.		15:24
have a part in the f. resurrection,		15:24
no part in the f. resurrection.		15:26

FIRST 338 FIRST

that did beguile our f. parents,	Mos	16: 3
with those of the f. resurrection,		18: 9
Helam, he being one of the f.,		18:12
baptized him according to the f.,		18:15
to be the f. chief judge,		29:42
Alma was the f. and chief judge.		29:44
was the son of Alma the f.,	Al	1:hd
of Alma, the f. and chief Judge.		1:hd
in the f. year of the reign of the		1: 1
in the f. year of the reign of Alma		1: 2
this is the f. time that priestcraft		1:12
the f. army met the Amlicites.		3:20
f. in the land of Zarahemla,		5: 1
it is the f. time that I have		7: 1
of him who f. possessed them;		8: 7
thy f. message from him.		8:15
and the end, the f. and the last;		11:39
even from the f. death unto life,		11:45
lest our f. parents should enter		12:21
that our f. parents could have		12:26
they having f. transgressed the		12:31
as in the f. provocation,		12:36
last provocation as well as the f.,		12:36
the last death, as well as the f.		12:36
in the f. place being left to		13: 3
in the f. place they were on the		13: 5
at the time the angel f. appeared		17: 2
in the f. year of the judges;		17: 6
and f. began to preach to the		21: 4
delivered for the f. time out of		21:15
of their fathers' f. inheritance,		22:28
being the place of their f. landing.		22:30
Abinadi was the f. that suffered		25:11
from the f. year to the fifteenth		28:10
he desireth, in the f. place, that		32:22
cannot know of their surety at f.,		32:26
was a f. resurrection.		40:15
that there is a f. resurrection,		40:16
suppose that this f. ressurrection,		40:17
Lord God sent our f. parents forth		42: 2
that our f. parents were cut off		42: 7
ye are not guilty of the f. offense,		43:46
had raised the f. from the ground,		47:24
of the twenty and f. year		50:17
in the twenty and f. year of		50:23
it was his f. care to put an end		51:16
the f. morning of the first month,		52: 1
first morning of the f. month,		52: 1
the land of our f. inheritance;		54:12
the land of our f. inheritance.		54:13
save they had f. given to some of		55:31
the second day in the f. month,		56: 1
where we had f. pitched our tents		58:17
f. commenced at our head,		60:10
inward vessel shall be cleansed f.,		60:23
have f. cleansed our inward vessel,		60:24
of the thirty and f. year of		62:12
the thirty and f. year of the		62:39
And the f. ship did also return,		63: 7
in the forty and f. year of the	He	1:14
thus ended the forty and f. year		1:34
in the fifty and f. year of the		3:33
in the sixty and f. year of		4:10
thus ended the sixty and f. year		4:17
the names of our f. parents who		5: 6
who did entice our f. parents to		6:26
Nephi f. came out of the land of		7: 7
thus ended the seventy and f. year		10:19
of the eighty and f. year		11:30
thus ended the eighty and f. year		11:35
all mankind from the f. death—		14:16
in the f. year of the reign	3Ne	1:hd
that the ninety and f. year had		1: 1
in the twenty and f. year they		4:16
f. church which was established		5:12
in the thirty and f. year that		7:14
the thirty and f. year did pass		7:21
fourth year, in the f. month,		8: 5
f. be reconciled to thy brother,		12:24
seek ye f. the kingdom of God		13:33
f. cast the beam out of thine		14: 5
having raised me up unto you f.,		20:26
that they should have f.,		26: 9
and ninth, and forty and f.,	4Ne	1: 6
and also the fifty and f.,		1: 6
the seventy and f. year passed		1:14
the f. generation from Christ		1:18
this two hundred and f. year		1:24
hundred and thirty and f. year,		1:35
hundred and sixty and f. year	Mrm	3: 7
the people of the f. covenant;		7:10
are baptized, f. with water,		7:10
that the f. part of this record,	Eth	1: 3
land of their f. inheritance;		7:16
who beguiled our f. parents,		8:25
f. believed in the Son of God.		12:18
there are they were f.,		13:12
who were last, who shall be f.		13:12
the f. year that Ether dwelt in		13:18
that in the f. year of Lib,		14:11
at the time of his f. appearing;	Mro	2: 3
the f. fruits of repentance is		8:25
this is the f. gift that I bestowed	DC	5: 4
this f. part of the engravings		10:45
but f. seek to obtain my word,		11:21
to be the f. elder of this church;		20: 2
manifested unto this f. elder		20: 5
he being the f. unto you,		21:11
the f. preacher of this church		21:12
unto the f. priesthood which		27: 8
that the f. shall be last,		29:30
the last shall be f. in all things		29:30
F. spiritual, secondly temporal,		29:32
f. temporal, and secondly		29:32
which is the f. death,		29:41
unto you this f. commandment,		42: 4
after this f. consecration,		42:33
have part in the f. resurrection;		45:54
these are the f. ordinances		53: 6
F., the rich and the learned,		58:10
have part in the f. resurrection.		63:18
minister even according to the f.;		68:14
appointed by the F. Presidency		68:15
the hands of the F. Presidency		68:19
the F. Presidency of the church;		68:22
part in the f. resurrection.		76:64
the f. seal contains the things of		77: 7
the things of the f. thousand years,		77: 7
Adam, who was the f. man.—		84:16
and sixty-f. and second verses of		85:12
shall f. gather out the wheat		86: 7
And he said unto the f.:		88:52
in the f. hour I will come unto		88:52
went unto the f. in the first		88:56
unto the first in the f. hour,		88:56
then he withdrew from the f.		88:57
Beginning at the f., and so on		88:59
and from the last unto the f.,		88:59
and from the f. unto the last;		88:59
those who are the f. laborers in		88:70
who are the f. laborers in		88:74
those who are not the f. elders		88:85
They are Christ's, the f. fruits,		88:98
who shall descend with him f.,		88:98
are f. caught up to meet him;		88:98
then shall the f. angel again		88:108
of God in the f. thousand years.		88:108
he shall be f. in the house of God,		88:129
should be f. in the house—		88:130
unto the Gentiles f., and then,		90: 9
not of the fulness at the f.,		93:12
not of the fulness at f.,		93:13
not of the fulness at the f.		93:14
f. set in order thy house.		93:44
let the f. lot on the south be		94: 3
on the f. and second lots on		94:14
the creator of the f. day,		95: 7
they should f. lift a standard of		98:34
come upon thee the f. time,		98:39
and repent not the f. time,		98:41
of the twelve shall speak f.,		102:12
the f. decision shall stand,		102:22
of the seat of the F. Presidency		102:26
of the seat of the F. Presidency		102:27
of the seat of the F. Presidency		102:33
ascertain who should speak f.,		102:34

FIRST

your fathers were led at the f.,	DC 103:18
are the f. elders of my church,	105: 7
But f. let my army become	105:31
that the f. elders of my church	105:33
the f. is called the Melchizedek	107: 2
f. unto the Gentiles	107:33
f. unto the Gentiles and then	107:34
f. unto the Gentiles and then	107:35
other seventy besides the f.	107:95
Gentiles f. and also unto the Jews.	107:97
with the f. of mine elders,	108: 4
I am the f. and the last;	110: 4
receiveth those, the F. Presidency,	112:20
F. among those among you,	112:26
and those, the F. Presidency,	112:30
rod spoken of in the f. verse of	113: 3
redemption of the F. Presidency	117:13
composed of the F. Presidency	120: 1
F., I give unto you Hyrum	124:124
a quorum and F. Presidency,	124:126
that was not f. which is spiritual	128:14
The f. man is of the earth, earthy;	128:14
come forth in the f. resurrection,	132:19
if it be after the f. resurrection,	132:19
come forth in the f. resurrection,	132:26
and the f. give her consent,	132:61
all nations, f. upon the Gentiles,	133: 8
Hyrum was shot f. and fell	135: 1
the f. man of all men	Mses 1:34
and the morning were the f. day.	2: 5
the f. flesh upon the earth,	3: 7
the earth, the f. man also;	3: 7
called the name of the f. Pison,	3:11
called the f. of all women,	4:26
and even the f. of all we know,	6:45
on the f. man, who is Adam,	Abr 1: 3
who is Adam, our f. father,	1: 3
f. discovered by a woman,	1:23
the f. government of Egypt was,	1:25
fathers in the f. generations,	1:26
days of the f. patriarchal reign,	1:26
they who keep their f. estate	3:26
who keep not their f. estate	3:26
those who keep their f. estate;	3:26
I will send the f.	3:27
and kept not his f. estate;	3:28
this was the f., or the beginning,	4: 5
signifying the f. creation,	Fac 2: 1
F. in government,	2: 1
the f. facsimile of this book.)	3: 3
f. chapter and fifth verse,	JS 2:11
It was the f. time in my life	2:14
the twenty-f. of September,	2:27
twenty-f. of September, after	2:29
When I f. looked upon him,	2:32
He f. quoted part of the third	2:36
Instead of quoting the f. verse	2:36
he had done at his f. visit,	2:45
The f. thing that I can recollect	2:49
was there I f. saw my wife	2:57
I baptized him f., and	2:71
the f. Elder of the Church,	2:72
the f. principles and ordinances of	AoF 4
f., Faith in the Lord Jesus	4

FIRSTBORN

my f. in the wilderness,	2Ne 2: 2
the f. of the brother of Jared;	Eth 6:25
f. among the sons of Aaron;	DC 68:16
the f. holds the right of the	68:17
and the f. of Aaron.	68:18
who are the church of the F.	76:54
church of Enoch, and of the F.	76:67
that of the church of the F.	76:71
are the church of the F.;	76:94
up unto the church of the F.,	76:102
come to the church of the F.	77:11
ye are the church of the F.,	78:21
that of the church of the F.,	88: 5
the Father, and am the F.;	93:21
and are the church of the F.	93:22
assembly and church of the F.,	107:19
time, even the right of the f.,	Abr 1: 3

FIRST-BORN: *see FIRST and BORN.*

FIRST-FRUITS: *see FIRST and FRUITS.*

FIRSTLINGS

took of the f. of their flocks,	Mos 2: 3
offer the f. of their flocks,	Mses 5: 5
brought of the f. of his flock,	5:20

FIR-TREES: *see FIR and TREES.*

FISH

and their f. to stink because	2Ne 7: 2
Or if he ask a f., will he give	3Ne 14:10
with them the f. of the waters.	Eth 2: 2
heavens, or of the f. of the sea,	DC 101:24
and also the f. of the sea,	117: 6
their f. stink, and die for thirst.	133:68
dominion over the f. of the sea,	Mses 2:28
dominion over the f. of the sea,	Abr 4:26
dominion over the f. of the sea,	4:28

FISHES

and the f. of the sea;	DC 29:24
dominion over the f. of the sea,	Mses 2:26

FISTS

smite one another with their f.	Al 1:22

FIT

see f. in mine own wisdom	2Ne 27:22
Lord seeth f. to inflict upon him,	Mos 3:19
did not see f. to deliver them	21:15
Lord seeth f. to chasten his people;	23:21
hath seen f. to snatch me out of	27:28
Lord saw f. in his infinite mercy	28: 4
as the Lord sees f. that we may live	29:32
f. discovered by a woman,	1:23
he seeth f. that they should have;	Al 29: 8
when the Lord seeth f. in his	3Ne 28:29
that when the Lord shall see f.,	29: 1
he shall see f., in his wisdom.	Mrm 5:13
are not f. to be numbered among	Mro 7:39
until I shall see f. to make all	DC 10:37

FIVE

did contain the f. books of Moses,	1Ne 5:11
within three score and f. years	2Ne 17: 8
fifty and f. years had passed	Jac 1: 1
f. hundred and nine years from	Mos 29:46
twelve thousand f. hundred	Al 2:19
six thousand f. hundred sixty	2:19
three thousand f. hundred souls	4: 5
slay a thousand and f. of them;	24:22
was only twenty and f. years old	43:17
to the amount of f. thousand	63: 4
even there were f. who went,	He 9: 1
those f. men who had fallen to	9: 7
Where are the f. who were sent to	9:12
Concerning the f. whom ye say ye	9:12
are f. who are the murderers,	9:12
they were the f. who were sent;	9:13
the f. were liberated on the	9:18
that the f. were set at liberty,	9:38
because of the testimony of the f.,	9:39
for f. years more cometh, and	14: 2
twenty and f. years passed away.	3Ne 5: 7
space of twenty and f. years;	5: 8
thousand and f. hundred souls;	17:25
three hundred and f. years	4Ne 1:47
for the space of f. years,	DC 64:21
built fifty-f. by sixty-five	94: 4
sixty-f. feet in the width	94: 4
shall be fifty-f. by sixty-five feet	94:11
by sixty-f. feet in the width	94:11
be fifty and f. feet in width,	95:15
let it be sixty-f. feet in length,	95:15
to the number of f. hundred of	103:30
if you cannot obtain f. hundred,	103:32
among you obtain f. talents	104:69
If it be f. talents [dollars],	104:73
Enoch was twenty-f. years old	107:48
sixty-f. and Adam blessed him.	107:48
three hundred and sixty-f. years,	107:49

FIVE   340   FLED

until thou art eighty-f. years old,	DC 130:15	his wickedness and his f. words)	Al	50:35
June, 1844, about f. o'clock p.m.,	135: 1	he speaketh f. words unto you,	He	13:28
lived one hundred and f. years,	Mses 6:13	their lyings and their f. words,	3Ne	1:29
were nine hundred and f. years,	6:18			
Mahalaleel lived sixty-f. years,	6:20	**FLATTERY**		
eight hundred and ninety-f.	6:20	wherefore, he could use much f.,	Jac	7: 4
Enoch lived sixty-f. years,	6:25	did speak much f. to the people;	Mos	27: 8
three hundred and sixty-f. years.	7:68	for they have used great f.,	Al	61: 4
f. hundred and ninety-five years,	8:10			
five hundred and ninety-f. years,	8:10	**FLAXEN**		
he was f. hundred years old	8:12	by the neck with a f. cord,	2Ne	26:22
thousand eight hundred and f.,	JS 2: 3			
		FLED		
FIVES		But Laman f. out of his presence,	1Ne	3:14
twenties, or by tens, or by f.	DC 104:68	we f. into the wilderness,		3:27
		they f. from before my presence;		4:28
FIXED		Gibeah of Saul is f.	2Ne	20:29
their hatred was f.,	En 1:20	they f., all that were not	Mos	9:15
being f. in their minds with a	Al 47: 6	the time they f. out of the land;		11:13
were f. with a determination	58:12	But he f. from before them		17: 4
And their courses are f., even the	DC 88:43	who had f. from the servants of		18: 1
in a determination that is f.,	88:133	he f. and ran and got upon		19: 5
eye f. on the restoration of the	128:17	wives and their children and f.		19:12
governs fifteen other f. planets	Fac 2: 5	and they f. before them.		19:21
f. under the edge of the stone,	JS 2:52	and his priests had f. from them		19:23
		and the priests that had f. into		20:23
FLAME		priests that f. into the wilderness,		21:20
whose f. ascendeth up forever	2Ne 9:16	knew not whither they had f.		21:31
and the f. consumeth the chaff,	15:24	who had f. into the wilderness.		21:34
and his Holy One for a f.,	20:17	they f. eight days' journey into		23: 3
with the f. of devouring fire.	27: 2	the brethren of Alma f. from		23:26
whose f. ascendeth up forever	Mos 2:38	the king of the Lamanites f. back	Al	2:32
whose f. ascendeth up forever	Al 12:17	they f. before the Nephites		2:36
kindle a f. of unquenchable fire	Mrm 9: 5	f. from the presence of Alma and		14:29
His eyes were as a f. of fire;	DC 110: 3	insomuch that they f. many ways.		17:27
		f. out of the land of Middoni		21:13
FLAMES		having f. into the east wilderness.		25: 5
their faces shall be as f.	2Ne 23: 8	they f. into the east wilderness.		25: 8
whose f. are unquenchable,	Jac 6:10	f. even to the waters of Sidon.		43:50
whose f. are unquenchable,	Mos 3:27	came to pass that Amalickiah f.		46:33
when the f. began to scorch him,	17:14	and those who had f. with him		47: 1
and save them from the f.	Al 14:10	thither had all the Lamanites f.;		47: 5
to deliver you up unto the f.?	14:19	therefore they f. to Onidah,		47: 5
		Now the servants of the king f.;		47:25
FLAMING		he has fallen and they have f.;		47:26
unto the brightness of a f. fire,	1Ne 15:30	and f. into the wilderness,		47:29
the shining of a f. fire	2Ne 14: 5	They have f.; does not this		47:34
cherubim and a f. sword on	Al 12:21	they f. into the wilderness.		49:25
cherubim, and a f. sword which	42: 2	f. to the camp of Moroni,		50:27
placed cherubim and the f. sword,	42: 3	had f. to the camp of Moroni,		50:28
as if in the midst of a f. fire,	He 5:44	she f., and came over to the		50:31
I will make him as f. fire	DC 7: 6	who f. out of the city of Moroni		51:26
cherubim and a f. sword,	Mses 4:31	they f. in much confusion,		52:28
		and f. to their other cities,		57: 4
FLATTER		that after the Lamanites had f.,		57:24
I may f. the king of the land,	Al 20: 4	broke through and f. from us.		57:33
f. them out of their strongholds,	52:19	when they had f. and we could		57:34
about to f. away those people	He 1: 7	Lamanites have f. to the land		58:38
did f. them, and also Kishkumen,	2: 5	have f. to the land of Gideon,		61: 5
that he did f. many people,	Eth 8: 2	f. into the land of Moroni,		62:25
		f. before the army of Moroni.		62:31
FLATTERED		Lamanites f. from Lehi and		62:32
that he f. them by his words,	Al 17:31	the Nephites had f. before them,	He	1:22
he f. them that there would	3Ne 7:12	by a garb of secrecy, and he f.,		9: 6
despised by those that f. them.	DC 121:20	boldness, was pursued as he f.;	3Ne	4:14
		that he f. before me.	Mrm	2: 9
FLATTERETH		when they had f. we did pursue		2:26
And behold, others he f. away,	2Ne 28:22	they f. again from before them,		4:20
And thus he f. them,	DC 10:25	we had f. to the city of Jordan;		5: 3
And thus he f. them,	10:26	and f. out of the land,	Eth	9: 9
thus he f. them away to	10:29	who f. with the house of Omer.		9:12
		which f. into the land southward.		9:32
FLATTERIES		they f. unto Com for protection,		11: 2
led by the f. of Amalickiah,	Al 46: 5	but he f. from before them		13:22
		he f. to the borders upon		14:12
FLATTERING		they f. again to the wilderness		14:14
which were f. unto the people;	Jac 7: 2	with him as he f. before Lib		14:15
the vain and f. words of the king	Mos 11: 7	of the land whither he f.		14:15
did speak f. things unto them.	11: 7	Coriantumr f. again before		14:16
deceive many with their f. words,	26: 6	f. to the army of Shiz,		14:20
by thy lying and thy f. words;	Al 30:47	f. to the army of Coriantumr,		14:20
in the f. words of Amalickiah,	46: 7	they f. to the land of Corihor,		14:27
and a man of many f. words,	46:10	he f. again before the people of		15: 7

FLED 341 FLESH

have f. to the army of Aaron	Mro	9:17
and were affrighted, and f.;	DC	101:51
trembled, and the mountains f.,	Mses	7:13
that they f. and stood afar off		7:14
forth the saying, ZION is F.		7:69
sleep had f. from my eyes,	JS	2:46

FLEE

commanded to f. out of the land,	1Ne	3:18
needs be that he f. out of the land.		3:18
did f. before the servants of Laban,		3:26
did cease to f. from my presence.		4:29
was about to f. from before me		4:30
held him, that he should not f.		4:31
hath commanded my husband to f.		5: 8
f. ye from the Chaldeans,		20:20
in warning us that we should f.	2Ne	1: 3
and f. into the wilderness,		5: 5
sorrow and mourning shall f. away.		8:11
to whom will ye f. for help?		20: 3
of Gebim gather themselves to f.		20:31
and f. every one into his own land.		23:14
that he should f. out of the land	Om	1:12
should f. before the Lamanites,	Mos	19: 9
they did f. into the wilderness,		19: 9
and f. before the Lamanites.		19:11
that they began to f. before them.	Al	2:18
the Amlicites began to f. before		2:35
people saw this, they began to f.,		14:26
did f. from the presence of Alma		14:29
round about that they f. not;		17:33
and began to f. before him;		17:37
and he caused them to f. by		17:37
a country whither they might f.,		22:34
would not f. from the sword,		24:23
and f. out of the hands of our		27: 5
to f. towards the river Sidon.		43:39
And the Lamanites did f. again		43:42
about to shrink and f. from them.		43:48
the Lamanites began to f. before		43:50
warn them to f., or to prepare		48:15
should f. to the land which was		50:29
to f. into the land northward.		50:31
saw that he began to f.,		52:24
that we did f. before them,		56:36
thus we did f. all that day into		56:40
and we did f. before them.		56:41
they did f. into the wilderness.		58:29
did f. out of all this quarter of		58:30
who had been compelled to f.		59: 6
were obliged to f. before them;		59: 8
that they did f. out by the pass.		62:24
and they did f. even that they		62:38
did f. before Coriantumr, even to	He	1:21
that the Lamanites could not f.		5:34
that they could not f. from us.		9: 8
they shall f. before their enemies;		13:20
for ye shall attempt to f. and		15: 2
shall be heavy and cannot f.;		15: 2
and did f. out of their lands,		16: 7
Nephites who did f. unto them,	3Ne	1:28
to f. before the Lamanites;	Mrm	2:16
f. from before the Lamanites,		2:24
that they did f. from before us.		2:25
the remainder did f. and join		4: 3
did again f. from before them,		4:22
began to f. before the poisonous	Eth	9:31
began to f. before the armies		14:27
caused them to f. before them;		15:10
and they did f. southward,		15:10
were about to f. for their lives;		15:28
be converted to f. to the west,	DC	42:64
must needs f. unto Zion		45:68
go to now and f. the land,		54: 7
the inhabitants of the earth to f.		124:106
among the Gentiles f. unto Zion.		133:12
be of Judah f. unto Jerusalem,		133:13
the Nephites shall f. before you,	Mses	6:34
in Judea f. into the mountains;	JS	1:13
him who is on the housetop f.,		1:14

FLEEING

and they are f. before them	Al	2:25
saw that they were f. before him,		62:25

FLEETH

which f. from the shepherd,	Mos	8:21
as a goat f. with her young	Al	14:29
as it were, f. at the thought.		26:20

FLESH

after the manner of the f.	1Ne	11:18
the Lord esteemeth all f. in one;		17:35
even unto the consuming of my f.;		17:48
which is in me, according to the f.,		19: 6
shall wander in the f., and perish,		19:14
with their own f.;		21:26
all f. shall know that I, the Lord,		21:26
according to the spirit and not the f.?		22: 1
children of men according to the f.		22: 2
cometh unto men according to the f.		22:18
among them which are in the f.—		22:22
built up to get power over the f.,		22:23
those who seek the lusts of the f.		22:23
must come according to the f.		22:27
whom he shall minister in the f.	2Ne	2: 4
by the law no f. is justified;		2: 5
there is no f. that can dwell in		2: 8
down his life according to the f.,		2: 8
they might repent while in the f.;		2:21
men are free according to the f.;		2:27
according to the will of the f.		2:29
heart sorroweth because of my f.,		4:17
even unto the consuming of my f.		4:21
and my f. waste away,		4:26
I yield to sin, because of my f.?		4:27
not put my trust in the arm of f.;		4:34
putteth his trust in the arm of f.		4:34
trust in man or maketh f. his arm.		4:34
himself unto them in the f.;		6: 9
many shall be afflicted in the f.,		6:11
oppress thee, with their own f.;		6:18
all f. shall know that I the Lord		6:18
our f. must waste away and die;		9: 4
become subject unto man in the f.,		9: 5
this f. must have laid down to rot		9: 7
if the f. should rise no more		9: 8
like unto us in the f., save it be		9:13
be destroyed, according to the f.,		9:53
unto us according to the f.;		10: 2
our children shall perish in the f.		10: 2
they shall be restored in the f.,		10: 7
unto them while they are in the f.,		10:15
unto them while they are in the f.—		10:17
the will of the devil and the f.;		10:24
every man the f. of his own arm—		19:20
himself unto them in the f.,		25:12
in man, or maketh f. his arm,		28:31
according to the f. he humbleth		31: 7
himself unto you in the f.		32: 6
himself unto in the f.,		32: 6
unto him who created all f.?	Jac	2:21
And all f. is of the dust;		2:21
he manifesteth himself in the f.		4:11
shall manifest himself in the f.;	En	1: 8
take upon him f. and blood,	Mos	7:27
wild beasts, shall devour their f.		12: 2
subjected the f. to the will of		15: 2
and the Son, because of the f.;		15: 3
f. becoming subject to the Spirit,		15: 5
the f. becoming subject even		15: 7
not esteem one f. above another,		23: 7
with mercy, according to the f.,	Al	7:12
he may know according to the f.		7:12
suffereth according to the f.		7:13
shall dwell here below in the f.,		31:26
of the Son because of my f.	3Ne	1:14
my f. and blood unworthily,		18:28
my f. and blood unworthily		18:29
to eat and drink of my f.		18:29
unto him of my f. and blood.		18:30
pain while ye shall dwell in the f.,		28: 9
changed from this body of f.		28:15
they were sanctified in the f.,		28:39
their f., and bones, and blood lay	Mrm	6:15
a man, like unto f. and blood;	Eth	3: 6
that the Lord had f. and blood.		3: 8
shall take upon me f. and blood;		3: 9

FLESH 342 FLOCKS

unto my people in the f.	Eth 3:16	had headed his people in his f.	Al	51:29
shall glorify my name in the f.;	3:21	speedy was the f. of Kishkumen	He	1:10
a prey to the worms of the f.	14:22	they took their f. out of the land,		2:11
the will of the Lord in the f.,	15:34	should take their f. into the	3Ne	7:12
the f. and blood of Christ unto	Mro 4: 1	go out with haste nor go by f.;		20:42
upon the f. of their husbands,	9: 8	not go out in haste, nor go by f.,		21:29
upon the f. of their fathers;	9: 8	that we did again take to f.,	Mrm	5: 7
they devour their f. like unto	9:10	those whose f. was swifter than		5: 7
neither trust in the arm of f.—	DC 1:19	those whose f. did not exceed		5: 7
these things known unto all f.;	1:34	be not in haste, nor by f.,	DC	58:56
Redeemer suffered death in the f.;	18:11	both by word and by f.		63:37
Savior Jesus Christ in the f.,	20: 1	be in haste, nor by f.;		101:68
the meridian of time, in the f.,	20:26	let not your f. be in haste,		133:15
of the f. and blood of Christ—	20:40	put their tens of thousands to f.		133:58
and shall eat their f., and shall	29:18	your f. be not in the winter	JS	1:17
and their f. shall fall from off	29:19			
garments spotted with the f.	36: 6	FLINT		
all f. is corrupted before me;	38:11	they had become like unto a f;	2Ne	5:21
and all f. is mine, and I am	38:16	have I set my face like a f.,		7: 7
find it and see it in their f.	45:14	hoofs shall be counted like f.,		15:28
I stood before them in the f.,	45:16			
and they twain shall be one f.,	49:16	FLOCK		
that wasteth f. and hath no need.	49:21	Yea, they are as a wild f.	Mos	8:21
all f. is in mine hand,	61: 6	even as a wild f. is driven by		17:17
no f. shall be safe upon the	61:15	enter not and devour his f.?	Al	5:59
all f. shall know that I am God.	63: 6	if a wolf enter his f. doth he not		5:59
seen God at any time in the f.,	67:11	many; for they did f. in from		15:14
according to men in the f.;	76:73	did f. unto his standard,		62: 5
testimony of Jesus in the f.,	76:74	began to f. together in armies,	Eth	14:19
of the Spirit, while in the f.,	76:118	Therefore, fear not, little f.;	DC	6:34
not manifest unto men in the f.;	84:21	Fear not, little f., the kingdom		35:27
heirs, according to the f.,	86: 9	brought of the firstlings of his f.,	Mses	5:20
according to men in the f.	88:99			
f. also of beasts and of the	89:12	FLOCKING		
and made f. my tabernacle,	93: 4	behold, they are f. to us daily,	Al	61: 6
which came and dwelt in the f.,	93:11			
out my Spirit upon all f.—	95: 4	FLOCKS		
all f. be consumed before me.	98:17	we began to raise f., and herds,	2Ne	5:11
for all f. is in mine hands,	101:16	and f. of herds,	En	1:21
all f. shall see me together.	101:23	and f. of all manner of cattle		1:21
beasts, yea, the enmity of all f.,	101:26	took of the firstlings of their f.,	Mos	2: 3
rights and protection of all f.,	101:77	that he shall feed among his f.,		5:14
and all f. has become corrupt	112:23	one half of the increase of our f.		7:22
having bodies of f. and bones.—	129: 1	upon the f. of our fields.		9:12
for a spirit hath not f. and bones,	129: 2	were watering and feeding their f.,		9:14
The Father has a body of f. and	130:22	and to take off their f.,		9:14
has not a body of f. and bones,	130:22	I did guard my people and my f.,		10: 2
they shall be destroyed in the f.,	132:26	again began to tend their f.,		10:21
and shall reign over all f.	133:25	while they were tending their f.		11:16
now are to go forth unto all f.—	133:60	drove many of their f. out of		11:17
the Lord, who ruleth over all f.	133:61	and f., and herds, that they did		21:16
remain in the f. on the earth.	Mses 1: 5	secured their grain and their f.;		21:18
was not yet f. upon the earth,	3: 5	and their f., and their herds,		22: 2
the first f. upon the earth,	3: 7	gather together their f. and herds,		22: 6
of his ribs and closed up the f.	3:21	our f., and our herds into the		22: 8
of my bones, and f. of my flesh;	3:23	should gather their f. together;		22:10
of my bones, and flesh of my f.;	3:23	with their f. and their herds,		22:11
and they shall be one f.	3:24	they gathered together their f.,		23: 1
again in the f. I shall see God.	5:10	gathered their f. together,		24:18
for all f. is in my hands,	6:32	gethering their f. together		24:18
men before they were in the f.	6:51	and abundance of f. and herds,	Al	1:29
the Son of Man, even in the f.;	7:47	fleeing before them with their f.,		2:25
the Son of Man cometh in the f.,	7:54	many of their f. and their herds;		3: 2
know that all f. shall die;	8:17	and also for the loss of their f.		4: 2
for all f. had corrupted its way	8:29	because of their many f. and herds,		4: 6
The end of all f. is come before me,	8:30	and upon your f. and herds,		7:27
I will destroy all f. from off	8:30	to watch the f. of Lamoni,		17:25
closed up the f. in the stead	Abr 5:15	going forth with their f.		17:26
of my bones, and f. of my flesh,	5:17	Lamanites drive their f. hither,		17:26
of my bones, and flesh of my f.,	5:17	were driving forth their f. to this		17:27
his wife, and they shall be one f.	5:18	had been with their f. to water,		17:27
should none of their f. be saved;	JS 1:20	scattered the f. of Ammon and		17:27
		because their f. were scattered by		17:28
FLEW		our f. are scattered already.		17:28
Then f. one of the seraphim	2Ne 16: 6	restoring these f. unto the king,		17:29
		let us go in search of the f.,		17:31
FLIES		will preserve the f. unto the king		17:31
f. upon the face of the earth,	DC 29:18	that they went in search of the f.,		17:32
		and did head the f. of the king,		17:32
FLIGHT		again stood to scatter their f.;		17:33
concerning our f. into the	1Ne 4:36	Encircle the f. round about		17:33
so speedy was the f. of his people.	Mos 20:12	these men who do scatter our f.		17:33
to stop their f. into the land	Al 50:33			

FLOCKS 343 FOLLOW

stood to scatter the f. of the king.	Al 17:35	all nations shall f. unto it.	2Ne 12: 2
and they watered their f.	17:39	our hearts f. out with sorrow	DC 109:48
of Ammon in preserving his f.,	18: 2	cause the mountains to f. down	109:74
can they scatter the king's f.	18: 3	my Spirit, that shall f. unto you.	111: 8
brethren had scattered their f. at	18: 6	it shall f. unto thee forever	121:46
they had had their f. scattered	18: 6	and rills, f. down with gladness.	128:23
to scatter the f. of the people,	18: 7	ice shall f. down at their presence.	133:26
time of the watering of their f.,	18: 9	the mountains might f. down	133:40
defended thy servants and thy f.,	18:16	the mountains f. down at thy	133:44
in order to defend thy f. and	18:16		
brethren that scattered my f.—	18:20	**FLOWER**	
who had had their f. scattered	19:20	the f. thereof which soon falleth,	DC 124: 7
f. which belonged to the king,	19:21		
while defending the f. of the king.	19:21	**FLOWING**	
did gather together all their f.	27:14	land f. with milk and honey,	DC 38:18
your fields, yea, over all your f.	34:20		
Cry over the f. of your fields,	34:25	**FLY**	
and f. and herds of every kind;	62:29	and with twain he did f.	2Ne 16: 2
they did raise many f. and herds,	He 6:12	for the f. that is in the uttermost	17:18
fields, their f. and their herds,	12: 2	they shall f. upon the shoulders of	21:14
their f. and their herds, and all	3Ne 3:13	f. through the midst of heaven,	DC 88:92
and all their f., and their herds,	3:22	and fowl which may f. above	Mses 2:20
gathered their f. and their herds	4: 3	that they may f. above the earth	Abr 4:20
cattle, and f. of every kind,	4: 4		
his family, his f. and his herds,	6: 1	**FLYING**	
lion among the f. of sheep,	20:16	sent fiery f. serpents among them;	1Ne 17:41
lion among the f. of sheep,	21:12	fruit shall be a fiery f. serpent.	2Ne 24:29
and gather together thy f.,	Eth 1:41	f. through the midst of heaven,	DC 88:103
with their f. which they had	2: 1	have sent forth mine angel f.	133:36
food for their f. and herds,	6: 4		
their f. began to flee before	9:31	**FOES**	
grain, and in f., and herds,	10:12	also the f. of our whole army,	Al 57:25
lo, I will take care of your f.,	DC 88:72	thou shalt triumph over all thy f.	DC 121: 8
you shall be blessed in your f.,	136:11		
to till the land, and to tend f.,	Mses 5: 3	**FOIBLES**	
offer the firstlings of their f.,	5: 5	and the f. of human nature;	JS 2:28
f. of my brother falleth into	5:33		
because of my brother's f.	5:38	**FOLD**	
there were many f. in Haran;	Abr 2: 5	not come unto the true f. of God?	1Ne 15:15
		shall be one f. and one shepherd;	22:25
FLOEESE		to the true church and f. of God;	2Ne 9: 2
as also F. or the Moon,	Fac 2: 5	shepherds make their f. there.	23:20
		to come into the f. of God,	Mos 18: 8
FLOOD		good shepherd, of what f. are ye?	Al 5:39
yet it would not be by f., as	Al 10:22	shepherd, and ye are of his f.;	5:39
that ye may not perish in the f.	Eth 2:20	he will bring you into his f.,	5:60
and swept away as with a f.;	DC 109:70	been brought into the f. of God.	26: 4
to sweep the earth as with a f.,	Mses 7:62	I have which are not of this f.;	3Ne 15:17
days which were before the f.;	JS 1:42	and there shall be one f., and	15:17
knew not until the f. came,	1:43	I have which are not of this f.;	15:21
		and there shall be one f., and	15:21
FLOODS		may be one f. and one shepherd;	16: 3
when the f. come and the winds	3Ne 11:40	which are not of this f.—	DC 10:59
rain descended, and the f. came,	14:25	unto him, even an hundred f.,	78:19
rain descended, and the f. came,	14:27	yea, even an hundred f.,	82:18
rain descends, and the f. come,	18:13	your reward shall be an hundred-f.	98:25
and the f. have I sent forth.	Eth 2:24	be doubled unto you four-f.	98:26
and the f. which shall come,	2:25	and reward thee four-f. in all	98:44
encompassed about by the f.	3: 2	of thine enemy an hundred-f.;	98:45
will I send in the f.	Mses 7:34	restore four-f. for all their	98:47
shall perish in the f.;	7:38	shall be seventy and seven f.;	Mses 5:48
the f. came and swallowed them up.	7:43		
more be covered by the f.	7:50	**FOLK**	
that he would stay the f.;	7:51	house, and from all thy kins-f.,	Abr 1:16
I will send in the f. upon them.	8:17		
the f. will come in upon you;	8:24	**FOLLIES**	
		notwithstanding your f.	DC 111: 1
FLOOR		upon your own heads, by your f.,	124:48
gathereth his sheaves into the f.	3Ne 20:18	of all my sins and f.,	JS 2:29
their *innocent blood* on the f. of	DC 135: 7		
his feet did not touch the f.	JS 2:30	**FOLLOW**	
		and the armies of Pharaoh did f.	1Ne 4: 2
FLOURISH		they did f. me up until we came	4: 4
and they did f. exceedingly,	He 6:12	bade him that he should f. me.	4:25
rejoice upon the hills and f.;	DC 35:24	wherefore he did f. me.	4:26
rejoice upon the hills and f.	39:13	unto me, and bade me f. him.	8: 6
Jacob shall f. in the wilderness,	49:24	did f. the directions of the ball,	16:16
Zion shall f. upon the hills	49:25	ye that f. after righteousness,	2Ne 8: 1
say unto you that Zion shall f.,	64:41	that they may f. strong drink,	15:11
upon the high places, and did f.	Mses 7:17	children of men: F. thou me,	31:10
		brethren, can we f. Jesus save	31:10
FLOW		f. me, and do the things which	31:12
the waters to f. out of the rock	1Ne 20:21	if ye shall f. the Son,	31:13

FOLLOW 344 FOOLISH

could no longer f. their tracks; Mos 22:16
Alma sent spies to f. their tracks; Al 2:21
shepherd, and he doth f. him; 5:41
unto his voice, and doth f. him. 5:41
are desirous to f. the voice of 5:57
and they did f. Ammon, and they 17:32
curse of God did no more f. them. 23:18
of Christ, if we f. their course, 37:45
to f. after their own will. 42: 7
and I will f. you even into your 54:12
the Lamanites did f. after us 58:19
did f. us into the wilderness; 58:19
that his band should f. him. He 2:11
Samuel and those that f. after, 3Ne 20:24
For their works do f. them, 27:12
these signs shall f. them that Mrm 9:24
signs shall f. them that believe Eth 4:18
did f. the course of the beasts, 9:34
of the devil cannot f. Christ; Mro 7:11
if he f. Christ he cannot be a 7:11
hear my voice and f. me, DC 38:22
not take up his cross and f. me, 56: 2
shall f. after much tribulation. 58: 3
receive that which is to f. 58: 5
and their works shall f. them; 59: 2
but signs f. those that believe. 63: 9
their works shall f. them in 63:15
and his works shall f. him, 63:48
judgment shall immediately f., 82:11
shall f. them that believe.— 84:65
Therefore, f. me, and listen to 100: 2
as they f. the counsel which 105:37
take up your cross, f. me, 112:14
And these signs shall f. him— 124:98
we f. the admonition of Paul— AoF 13

FOLLOWED
as I f. him I beheld myself 1Ne 8: 7
they f. the king, and went forth Mos 20:25
f. after the people of king Limhi, 23:30
we f. the camp of the Amlicites, Al 2:24
Lamanites had f. their brethren 28: 1
and the multitude f. them. 3Ne 19:10
also my father f. after me, Abr 2: 4
that day, many f. after him. 3:28
vision, persecution still f. me, JS 2:58

FOLLOWER
myself a f. of righteousness, Abr 1: 2
a greater f. of righteousness, 1: 2

FOLLOWERS
who are the humble f. of Christ; 2Ne 28:14
of the humble f. of God, Al 4:15
humble f. of God and the Lamb. He 6: 5
did plot with Cain and his f. 6:27
and the humble f. of God. 6:39
are the peaceable f. of Christ, Mro 7: 3
true f. of his Son, Jesus Christ; 7:48

FOLLOWING
he also saw twelve others f. him, 1Ne 1:10
I also beheld twelve others f. him, 11:29
the wilderness, f. the same direction, 16:14
by f. your Lord and your Savior 2Ne 31:13
in f. the example of the Son 31:16
our fathers, by f. its course, Al 37:45
f. the example of our Savior, Mrm 7:10
administered in the f. manner DC 20:72
signs f. them that believe. 58:64
shall be blest with signs f., 68:10
first, and the f. was the result, 102:34
by lineage in the f. manner: 107:41
preparatory work, this f. summer; 115: 9
on the f. Sabbath. 127:10
I heard a voice repeat the f.: 130:14
he read the f. paragraph, 135: 4
Lorenzo Snow offered the f.; OD
December, and the February f. JS 2:62

FOLLOWS
f. after the dictates of his own DC 3: 4
which was given unto us as f.: 76:15

councilors were forty-three, as f.: DC 102: 5
his return, which was as f.: JS 2:63

FOLLY
and every mouth speaketh f. 2Ne 19:17
their f. and their abominations DC 35: 7
have laughed shall see their f. 45:49
their f. shall be made manifest, 63:15
And let him repent of all his f., 124:116
his f. shall be made manifest. 136:19

FONT
For a baptismal f. there is not DC 124:29
baptismal f. was instituted as 128:13

FOOD
to slay f. for our families; 1Ne 16:14
we had slain f. for our families 16:14
slaying f. by the way, with our 16:15
and obtain f. for our families. 16:17
as I, Nephi, went forth to slay f., 16:18
my bow, for we did obtain no f. 16:18
return without f. to our families, 16:19
did suffer much for the want of f. 16:19
insomuch that we could obtain no f. 16:21
Whither shall I go to obtain f.? 16:23
I did obtain f. for our families. 16:31
they beheld that I had obtained f., 16:32
the Lord did bless us again with f., 16:39
I will make thy f. become sweet, 17:12
will not give unto him of my f., Mos 4:17
we have, for both f. and raiment, 4:19
I will impart unto thee of my f.; Al 8:20
they did withhold f. from them 14:22
might provide f. for themselves 17: 7
from the land northward for f. 22:31
house to house begging for his f. 30:56
begging f. for his support. 30:58
and providing f. for their armies. 53: 7
that I may preserve my f. for 54:20
to perish for the want of f. 58: 7
to pass that we did receive f., 58: 8
do not cause f. to be sent unto us, 60:19
send forth f. and men unto us, 60:24
unto them f. for their support, 60:25
he will give unto us of your f., 60:35
that we may obtain more f. 61:18
with a sufficient quantity of f., 62:13
their f. from the hungry, He 4:12
prison many days without f., 5:22
wilderness, for the want of f.; 3Ne 4: 3
to plunder and to obtain f., 4: 4
because of the want of f., 4:24
had prepared all manner of f., Eth 6: 4
f. for their flocks and herds, 6: 4
kept him upon little or no f. 9: 7
were useful for the f. of man. 9:18
to hunt f. for the people of 10:19
whithersoever they can for f.; Mro 9:16
what thou needest for f. and DC 24:18
with herbs and mild f., 42:43
provide for him f. and raiment, 43:13
of man for f. and for raiment, 49:19
to provide f. and raiment, 51: 8
let they f. be prepared with 59:13
whether for f. or for raiment, 59:17
Yea, for f. and for raiment, 59:19
For f. and for raiment, 70:16
is good for the f. of man; 89:16
man saw that it was good for f. Mses 3: 9
saw that the tree was good for f., 4:12
to the sight and good for f.; Abr 5: 9

FOOL
saying: Our brother is a f. 1Ne 17:17
Thou f., that shall say: 2Ne 29: 6
whosoever shall say, Thou f., 3Ne 12:22

FOOLISH
the f. imaginations of his heart. 1Ne 2:11
the f. imaginations of his heart; 17:20
false and f. doctrines, 2Ne 28: 9
not believe in such f. traditions. Al 8:11

FOOLISH 345 FOREGOING

FOOLISH
not believe in these f. traditions,	Al 21: 8
down under a f. and a vain hope,	30:13
yourselves with such f. things?	30:13
are f. traditions of your fathers,	30:14
the f. traditions of your fathers,	30:23
down under the f. ordinances	30:23
the f. traditions of your fathers,	30:27
the f. traditions of our brethren,	31:17
led away by any vain or f. thing;	39:11
O how f., and how vain, and	He 12: 4
be led by f. and blind guides?	13:29
hearts, which were f. and vain;	16:22
was a f. and a vain thing.	3Ne 2: 2
that ye should be so f. and vain	3: 3
shall be likened unto a f. man,	14:26
be f. virgins among the wise;	DC 63:54
fell into many f. errors,	JS 2:28

FOOLISHNESS
the frailties, and the f. of men!	2Ne 9:28
wherefore, their wisdom is f.	9:28
reward of their pride and their f.	26:10
suppose that this is f. in me;	Al 37: 6

FOOLS
consider themselves f. before God,	2Ne 9:42
O f., they shall have a Bible;	29: 4
O ye f., ye uncircumcised of	He 9:21
F. mock, but they shall mourn;	Eth 12:26
f. shall have thee in derision,	DC 122: 1

FOOT
which I never had before set my f.	1Ne 11: 1
mountains tread him under f.;	2Ne 24:25
the beasts and trodden under f.	Mos 12:11
which were trodden under f.	Al 4: 2
and is trodden under f. of men.	34:29
thy feet to be trodden under f.,	46:22
come down to the f. of the mount,	47:10
go down to the f. of the mount.	47:11
to be trodden under f. of men.	3Ne 12:13
trodden under f. of my people,	16:15
Lord set his f. upon this mount,	DC 45:48
and trodden under f. of men.	103:10

FOOTSTOOL
his throne, and this earth is his f.	1Ne 17:39
Nor by the earth, for it is his f.;	3Ne 12:35
and behold it is my f.,	DC 38:17
in the land upon the f. of God.	Mses 6: 9
the earth is his f.;	6:44
in heaven; the earth is my f.;	Abr 2: 7

FOR: *see in the APPENDIX.*

FORASMUCH
F. as this people refuseth	2Ne 18: 6
F. as this people draw near	27:25
F. as the Lord has revealed	DC 127: 1
F. as thou art God, and I know	Mses 7:59

FORBADE
but the Lord f. it, saying:	3Ne 26:11
taste of death, but the Lord f.;	28:25
He again f. me to join with	JS 2:20
This f. me, saying that	2:46

FORBEAR
I pray thee f., and do not	Mos 20:17
expedient that thou shouldst f.;	Al 20:18
they did f. from slaying them;	24:24
unto me; therefore I shall f.	37:11
we will f. shedding your blood.	52:37
I did f. to make a full account	Mrm 2:18

FORBID
The Lord f.; for if we should	3Ne 3:21
ye shall not f. any man from	18:22
come unto you and f. them not;	18:22
flesh and blood ye shall f. him.	18:29
but, remember that I f. it,	Mses 3:17

FORBIDDEN
they fell away into f. paths	1Ne 8:28

Nephi, am f. that I should write	1Ne 14:28
the f. fruit in opposition to the	2Ne 2:15
Partake of the f. fruit,	2:18
had partaken of the f. fruit	2:19
unto the other, and none are f.	26:28
the Lord hath f. this thing;	26:30
his partaking of the f. fruit;	Mos 3:26
by the partaking of the f. fruit,	Al 12:22
to partake of the f. fruit—	He 6:26
f. that there should not any	3Ne 26:16
save it be those which are f.	27:23
And it was f. them that	28:14
him to whom it had been f.	4Ne 1:27
f. that I should preach unto	Mrm 1:16
was f. to preach unto them,	1:17
by all that had been f. them	3:14
that which is f. of the Lord.	8:18
they were f. to come unto	Eth 4: 1
that thing is f. you, except	5: 1
but in all things hath f. it,	8:19
to write more, but I am f.;	13:13
and he partook of the f. fruit	DC 29:40
as you are f. to shed blood,	63:31
or f., to get in debt to thine	64:47
from contracting any marriage f. by	OD
which signifies that which is f.	Abr 1:23
having been f. to join any of	JS 2:28
but was f. by the messenger,	2:53
I was f. to bring them.	2:65

FORBIDDETH
whoso f. to marry is not	DC 49:15
whoso f. to abstain from meats,	49:18

FORBIDDING
by Congress f. plural marriages,	DC OD

FORCE
the law was put in f. upon all	Al 1:32
put them in f. according to the	4:16
city with an exceeding strong f.	55:26
little f. which I brought with me,	56:17
the city of Antiparah by our f.;	57: 7
yea, with our strong f., or with	57: 8
or with a part of our strong f.,	57: 8
to employ all our f. to keep them,	57:13
small f. which we had received,	58:12
Therefore he retained all his f.	59:10
whatsoever f. ye can upon	61:17
gained whatsoever f. he could	62: 4
against them with all our f.	Mrm 3: 6
is in f. from this very hour	DC 84:75
are of no efficacy, virtue, or f.	132: 7
not of f. when they are dead,	132:15
then it is not valid neither of f.	132:18
shall be of full f. when they are	132:19
and their testament is in f.	135: 5
seemed to enter with great f.	JS 2:12

FORCED
we were f. to keep secret	JS 2:74

FORCES
that I might spy out their f.,	Mos 9: 1
the f. of the king were small,	19: 2
draw away a part of their f.	Al 52:13
he desired all his f. when he	53: 5
continually bringing new f. into	55:34
their f. had slain a vast number	56:10
And thus, with their f., they were	56:26
seeing our f. increase daily,	56:29
our f. were sufficient to take the	57: 2
drawn away the f. into that	58:35
uniting his f. with those of	62: 6

FOREFATHERS
and also a genealogy of thy f.,	1Ne 3: 3
come to the knowledge of their f.,	15:14
which is the land of our f.,	Al 7:10
have the genealogy of our f.,	37: 3
Which our f. have awaited	DC 121:27

FOREGOING
according to the f. pattern,	DC 102:12

FOREGOING

after the manner of the f.,	DC 102:24
vote to sustain the f. motion	OD

FOREHEADS

themselves with red in their f.	Al	3: 4
a mark of red upon their f.		3:13
to mark themselves in their f.;		3:18
servants of our God in their f.	DC	77: 9
Father's name written on their f.		133:18

FOREIGN

and vapors of smoke in f. lands;	Mrm	8:29
Ye hear of wars in f. lands;	DC	45:63
shall spread to f. lands;		110:10
send forth unto f. lands;		133: 8

FOREKNOWLEDGE

according to the f. of God,	Al	13: 3
according to his f. of all things—		13: 7

FOREMOST

the f. to accuse Amulek and	Al	10:31
f. among them said unto him:		32: 5

FORESEE

that they may f. that he will come,	Mos	27:30
because I f. the lying in wait	DC	5:32
I f. that if my servant Martin		5:32

FOREST

shall consume the glory of his f.,	2Ne	20:18
the rest of the trees of his f.		20:19
field shall be esteemed as a f.		27:28
devoured by the beasts of the f.	Mos	8:21
in the f. that was near the		18:30
the f. of Mormon, how beautiful		18:30
lion among the beasts of the f.,	3Ne	20:16
lion among the beasts of the f.		21:12
covered with animals of the f.	Eth	10:19
that the beasts of the f. and	DC	29:20

FORESTS

were beasts in the f. of every kind,	1Ne	18:25
in the thickets of the f.,	2Ne	19:18
cut down the thickets of the f.		20:34
I went to hunt beasts in the f.;	En	1: 3
in the fields and in the f.	Mos	20: 8

FORESWORN

they have f. themselves,	Mses	6:29

FORETOLD

it were f. them by the prophets	2Ne	25: 9

FOREVER

that they are not cast off f.—	T Pg	
the same yesterday, to-day, and f.;	1Ne	10:18
wherefore, we must be cast off f.		10:21
behold, they are righteous f.;		12:10
from this time henceforth and f.		12:18
f. remain in that awful state		13:32
people upon the promised land f.;		14: 2
which ascendeth up unto God f.		15:30
fear lest ye shall be cast off f.		17:47
unto me, and to my children f.,	2Ne	1: 5
righteous it shall be blessed f.		1: 7
and they shall dwell safely f.		1: 9
ye be cut off and destroyed f.;		1:17
for his ways are righteousness f.		1:19
true friend unto my son, Nephi, f.		1:30
upon the face of this land f.		1:31
the same, yesterday, today, and f.		2: 4
and become miserable f.		2: 5
and had become miserable f.,		2:18
they must have remained f.,		2:22
they have become free f.,		2:26
brethren, for thy security f.,		3: 2
may the Lord bless thee f.,		3: 3
I will preserve thy seed f.		3:16
you and unto your seed f.		4: 7
O Lord, I will praise thee f.;		4:30
and I will trust in thee f.		4:34
my voice shall ascend up unto		4:35

FOREVER

or have I cast thee off f.?	2Ne	7: 1
But my salvation shall be f.,		8: 6
my righteousness shall be f.,		8: 8
and lift up your heads f.,		9: 3
whose flame ascendeth up f.		9:16
and their joy shall be full f.		9:18
shall be hid from them f.—		9:43
I will be a light unto them f.,		10:14
be numbered among thy seed, f.,		10:19
from henceforth, even f.		19: 7
them with his strong cords f.		26:22
the same yesterday, today, and f.;		27:23
the same yesterday, today, and f.;		29: 9
from that time henceforth and f.		29: 9
that I would remember his seed f.		29:14
and glorify him f.	Jac	2:21
ye may, if your minds are firm, f.		3: 2
and whose smoke ascendeth up f.		6:10
and will be, f. and ever;	Mos	2:24
ascendeth up f. and ever.		2:38
and will be f. and ever,		3:19
have claim on them no more f.		3:26
ascendeth up f. and ever.		3:27
he hath done he perisheth f.,		4:18
from this time henceforth and f.!		15:17
they shall sing to his praise f.		18:30
that they should be cast off f.		28: 4
from this time henceforth and f.,	Al	3:14
thy seed, henceforth and f.;		3:17
works, from this time forth and f.		7:27
set my back towards this land f.		8:24
flame ascendeth up f. and ever;		12:17
fruit of the tree of life, and live f.?		12:21
chance that they should live f.		12:21
would have been f. miserable,		12:26
Thus they become high priests f.,		13: 9
upon him the high priesthood f.		13:14
kingdom from this time and f.;		20:26
he doth work righteousness f.		26: 8
we will praise his name f.		26:12
we have reason to praise him f.,		26:14
yea, we will praise our God f.		26:16
will give thanks unto my God f.		26:37
of all men, bless their souls f.		28: 8
but that they may praise him f.,		29:17
thou wilt be a spirit		31:15
the same yesterday, today, and f.;		31:17
and I will praise him f.;		36:28
cursed be the land f. and ever		37:31
heart be placed upon the Lord f.		37:36
and if we will look we may live f.		37:46
tree of life, and eat and live f.,		42: 3
of live, he would have lived f.,		42: 5
and man became lost f.,		42: 6
f. to be cut off from his presence.		42:14
could have been shaken f.;		48:17
behold, I will bless thee f.;	He	10: 5
this time henceforth and f.		12:19
man getteth it henceforth and f.		12:19
thou shalt be accursed f.—		12:20
the power, and the glory, f.	3Ne	13:13
the promised land unto them f.,		20:39
same yesterday, today, and f.,	Mrm	9: 9
may he bless them f., through		9:37
from that time henceforth and f.,	Eth	2: 8
may be and abide in you f.		12:41
of Christ, and it endureth f.;	Mro	7:47
eternal life, rest in your mind f.		9:25
be, and abide with you f.		9:26
today and tomorrow, and f.		10: 7
same yesterday, today, and f.,		10:19
and enlarge thy borders f.,		10:31
the truth abideth f. and ever.	DC	1:39
be all glory, both now and f.		20: 4
God yesterday, today, and f.		20:12
to whom be glory f. and ever.		20:16
truth from henceforth and f.		23: 2
thy duty is unto the church f.,		23: 3
duty from henceforth and f.		23: 5
today as yesterday, and f.		35: 1
inheritance of your children f.,		38:07
to generation, f. and ever.		56:20
power and glory, f. and ever.		65: 6
to generation, f. and ever.		69: 8

FOREVER — FORGIVENESS

who worship him f. and ever.	DC 76:21
and his Christ f. and ever.	76:62
upon his throne f. and ever;	76:92
give him glory f. and ever.	76:93
his power to reign f. and ever.	76:108
upon the throne f. and ever;	76:110
and dominion f. and ever.	76:119
kingdom is yours, and shall be f.,	82:24
also continueth and abideth f.	84:18
and peace, F. and ever,	84:102
may possess it f. and ever;	88:20
of him, even God, f. and ever.	88:41
upon the throne, f. and ever;	88:104
in thanksgiving, f. and ever.	88:133
you shall be blessed f.	92: 2
her generations f. and ever,	97:28
to possess it f. and ever.	103: 7
thou art a prince over them f.	107:55
bless you and deliver you f.	108: 8
and let them be blotted out f.	109:34
by our fathers, be established f.	109:54
f. and ever, saith the Lord.	117:12
of my people be on him f.	117:15
be a standing law unto them f.,	119: 4
will rejoice in thy name f.	121: 6
shall flow unto thee f. and ever.	121:46
God shall stand by thee f.	122: 4
for God shall be with you f.	122: 9
f. and ever, saith the Lord.	124:59
from generation to generation, f.	124:96
sitteth upon the throne f.	124:101
and it shall be well with him f.	124:118
this time, henceforth and f.	126: 3
creations declare his name f.	128:23
but are angels of God f.	132:17
a continuation of the seeds f.	132:19
in his presence day and night, f.	133:35
to his loving kindness, f.	133:52
of the Lamb, day and night f.	133:56
and the glory be thine f.	Mses 4: 2
tree of life, and eat and live f.,	4:28
beginning, henceforth and f.,	5: 9
the Son, from henceforth and f.;	6:66
thereof shall go forth f.;	7: 8
Zion shall dwell in safety f.	7:20
Enoch: Behold mine abode f.	7:21
thou art merciful and kind f.;	7:30
shall be known in the earth f.,	Abr 1:19

FOREVERMORE

in the name of the Son f.	Mses 5: 8

FOREWARN

f. your brethren concerning	DC 61:18
I have warned you, and f. you,	89: 4

FORGAVE

and f. not one another in	DC 64: 8

FORGET

they did f. by what power they	1 Ne 18: 9
can a woman f. her sucking child,	21:15
they may f., yet will I not	21:15
yet will I not f. thee, O house	21:15
do f. the Lord their God,	Al 46: 8
again to f. the Lord their God.	He 11:36
and do f. the Lord their God,	12: 2
people began to f. those signs	3 Ne 2: 1
shalt f. the shame of thy youth,	22: 4
to f. the thing which is wrong;	DC 9: 9
upon all the nations that f. God,	133: 2

FORGETTEST

And f. the Lord thy maker,	2 Ne 8:13

FORGETTING

entirely f. the Lord their God.	Al 47:36

FORGIVE

plead with me that I would f.	1 Ne 7:20
I did frankly f. them all	7:21
himself not, therefore, f. him not.	2 Ne 12: 9
of heart that he would f. you;	Mos 4:10
and him will I freely f.	26:22
him shall ye f., and I will	26:29
and I will f. him also.	26:29
will I f. them their trespasses	26:30
ye shall also f. one another	26:31
O Lord, f. my unworthiness,	Al 38:14
And f. us our debts, as we	3 Ne 13:11
our debts, as we f. our debtors.	13:11
if ye f. men their trespasses	13:14
heavenly Father will also f. you;	13:14
if ye f. not men their trespasses	13:15
your Father f. your trespasses.	13:15
I will f. thee and thy brethren	Eth 2:15
doeth it no more, thou shalt f.;	DC 42:25
for I, the Lord, f. sins,	61: 2
I, the Lord, f. sins unto those	64: 7
ye ought to f. one another;	64: 9
I, the Lord, will f. whom I	64:10
will forgive whom I will f.,	64:10
it is required to f. all men.	64:10
not because ye f. not,	64:13
I f. him and say unto him	75: 8
even so I, the Lord, f. you.	82: 1
For I will f. you of your sins	84:61
thou shalt f. him, and shalt	98:39
against thee, thou shalt f. him,	98:40
nevertheless thou shalt f. him.	98:41
nevertheless thou shalt f. him.	98:42
not, thou shalt also f. him.	98:43
thou shalt not f. him, but shalt	98:44
f. him with all thine heart;	98:45
f. the transgressions of thy people,	109:34
for I will f. all his sins,	124:76
and will f. all his sins;	124:78
and will f. all your sins;	132:50
handmaid f. my servant Joseph	132:56

FORGIVEN

Enos, thy sins are f. thee,	En 1: 5
also that he hath f. us of those	Al 24:10
you shall be f. of your sins.	Mrm 8:32
with real intent, they were f.	Mro 6: 8
of the Lord shall be f.;	DC 1:32
Behold, thy sins are f. thee,	25: 3
time your sins are f. you,	29: 3
and your sins are f. you,	31: 5
and your sins are f. you,	36: 1
he shall not be f., but shall	42:26
for your sins are f. you.	50:36
repent and he shall be f.	50:39
of his sins, the same is f.,	58:42
and your sins are f. you.	60: 7
whose sins are now f. you,	61: 2
and your sins are f. you.	62: 3
I have f. you your sins.	64: 3
f. my servant Isaac Morley.	64:16
of the evil, then shall be f.	64:17
And if he repent he shall be f.,	68:24
f. one another your trespasses,	82: 1
my son, thy sins are f. thee,	90: 1
their sins are f. them also,	90: 6
that their sins may be f.,	95: 1
Your sins are f. you,	108: 1
your sins are f. you,	110: 5
therefore, all thy sins are f. thee.	112: 3
not be f. in the world nor out	132:27
shall she be f. her trespasses,	132:56
I have f. thee thy transgression	Mses 6:53

FORGIVENESS

unto the Lord their God for f.	1 Ne 7:21
we may receive f. of our sins,	Mos 4: 2
is not easy for him to obtain f.;	Al 39: 6
is not easy for him to obtain a f.	39: 6
as they repented and sought f.,	Mro 6: 8
he that kills shall not have f.	DC 42:18
remember that he hath no f.;	42:79
their sins before me and ask f.,	64: 7
no f. in this world nor in the	76:34
shall not have f. of sins in	84:41
come unto thee praying thy f.,	98:39
for f. of all my sins and follies,	JS 2:29

FORGIVETH 348 FORT

FORGIVETH
f. not his neighbor's trespasses	Mos 26:31
he that f. not his brother his	DC 64: 9

FORGOT
and f. to exercise their faith and	Al 37:41

FORGOTTEN
How is it that ye have f.	1Ne 7:10
how is it that ye have f.	7:11
how is it that ye have f.	7:12
and my Lord hath f. me—	21:14
in unbelief shall not be f.	2Ne 26:15
I the Lord have not f. my people.	29: 5
not f. the commandment of	Jac 3: 5
f. the tradition of your fathers;	Al 9: 8
f. the commandments of God.	9: 8
f. so soon how many times he	9:10
Have ye f. the commandments	60:20
have ye f. the captivity of	60:20
Have ye f. the many times	60:20
how could you have f. your God	He 7:20

FORM
that he was in the f. of a man;	1Ne 11:11
abide upon him in the f. of dove.	11:27
upon him in the f. of a dove.	2Ne 31: 8
and take upon him the f. of man,	Mos 13:34
he hath no f. nor comeliness;	14: 2
f. themselves into a church,	21:34
reunited again in its perfect f.;	Al 11:43
which move in their regular f.	30:44
unto me in the f. of an angel,	30:53
and his f. more than the sons of	3Ne 20:44
mind in every f. of godliness.	Mro 7:30
not in the f. of woman,	DC 49:22
upon him in the f. of a dove,	93:15
to the f. above written.	102:13
f. a quorum of the Presidency	107:22
f. a quorum, equal in authority	107:24
f. a quorum, equal in authority	107:26
A majority may f. a quorum	107:28
f. a quorum equal in authority	107:36
f. a quorum equal in authority	107:37
f. acquaintance with men in	111: 3
And they shall f. a constitution,	124:63
was instituted to f. a relationship	128:12
earth was without f., and void;	Mses 2: 2
made after the f. of a bedstead,	Abr 1:13
and f. man in our image,	4:26
image of the Gods to f. they him,	4:27
and female to f. they them.	4:27
among themselves to f.;	5: 3
f. the heavens and the earth.	5: 3
will f. an help meet for him.	5:14
Abraham, in the f. of a dove.	Fac 2: 7
having a f. of godliness, but	JS 2:19

FORMATION
church whose f. thou hast seen.	1Ne 13:32

FORMED
Lord— that f. me from the womb	1Ne 21: 5
who had f. a church of God	Mos 21:30
a band who had been f. by	He 6:18
had f. their laws according to	3Ne 6: 4
No weapon that is f. against thee	22:17
had f. a church of Christ	4Ne 1: 1
they f. a secret combination,	Eth 8:18
weapon that is f. against you	DC 71: 9
f. man out of the dust of	77:12
That no weapon f. against	109:25
I, the Lord God, f. man	Mses 3: 7
I put the man whom I had f.	3: 8
God, f. every beast of the field,	3:19
f. the heavens and the earth.	Abr 4: 1
And the earth, after it was f.,	4: 2
not f. anything but the earth;	4: 2
f. these the generations of	5: 4
when they were f. in the day	5: 4
f. the earth and the heavens,	5: 4
not f. a man to till the ground.	5: 5

Gods f. man from the dust of	Abr 5: 7
into the body which they had f.	5: 8
from man, f. they a woman,	5:16
the ground the gods f. every beast of	5:20
f. by laying stones together	JS 2:52

FORMER
I have declared the f. things	1Ne 20: 3
the f. three he took with him,	Al 31: 6
days of old, and as in f. years.	3Ne 24: 4
and obey the f. commandment	DC 56: 8
take their f. company,	61: 9
shall the f. sins return,	82: 7
the f. commandments which	84:57
repent of their f. evil works;	84:76
keeping all f. commandments	92: 2
forth by a f. commandment	101:10
you in a f. commandment,	101:68
to the f. pattern written,	102:27
From the decision of the f.	102:31
unto you in a f. commandment,	103:12
exchange for his f. inheritance,	104:24
I said in a f. commandment,	105:14
was declared in my f. letter	128: 2
the f. was wounded in a savage	135: 2
an account of the f. inhabitants	JS 2:34
"seers" in ancient or f. times;	2:35

FORMS
f. for public or private devotion;	DC 134: 4

FORNICATION
warning them against f. and	Jac 3:12
of your murders and your f.	He 8:26
saving for the cause of f.,	3Ne 12:32
the wine of the wrath of her f.	DC 35:11
companions for the cause of f.,	42:74
wine of the wrath of her f.,	88:94
wine of the wrath of her f.;	88:105

FORSAKE
repent of your sins and f. them,	Mos 4:10
yea, I will f. my kingdom,	Al 22:15
for thou didst f. the ministry,	39: 3
ye should repent and f. your sins,	39: 9
not f. the Lord their God;	46:21
they did f. all their sins,	3Ne 5: 3
and f. their murders and	Eth 11: 1
f. him not, and surely these	DC 35:22
that you shall f. the world.	53: 2
will confess them and f. them.	58:43
go with you, and f. him not,	66: 8
F. all unrighteousness.	66:10
and forth f. that evil one.	93:37
needs repent and f. some things,	93:48
that ye shall f. all evil and	98:11
For they do not f. their sins,	98:20

FORSAKEN
hath said: The Lord hath f. me,	1Ne 21:14
O Lord, thou hast f. thy people,	2Ne 12: 6
shall be f. of both her kings.	17:16
Amulek having f. all his gold,	Al 15:16
Why has he f. you?	He 7:17
woman f. and grieved in spirit,	3Ne 22: 6
a small moment have I f. thee,	22: 7
midst, and I have not f. you;	DC 61:36
find me, and shall not be f.	88:83
that he shall not be f.,	124:90

FORSAKETH
and f. it, and doeth it no more,	DC 42:25
every soul who f. his sins	93: 1

FORSAKING
for there shall be a great f.	2Ne 16:12

FORSWEAR
thou shalt not f. thyself, but	3Ne 12:33

FORT
to enter the f. by any other way,	Al 49:19

FORTH

To come f. by the gift and power	T Pg
to come f. in due time by	T Pg
Lehi, as he went f. prayed unto	1Ne 1: 5
went f. upon the face of the earth:	1:11
he went f. among the people,	1:18
went f. towards the house of	4: 5
I went f., and as I came near	4: 7
I drew it f. from the sheath	4: 9
to bring f. his righteous purposes.	4:13
I went f. unto the treasury and	4:20
as I went f. towards the treasury	4:20
as I went f. unto my brethren,	4:27
tarry with us from that time f.	4:35
thou hast led us f. from the land	5: 2
these plates of brass should go f.	5:18
did again, with my brethren, go f.	7: 3
did go f. and partake of the fruit	8:11
come f., and commence in the path	8:22
came f. and caught hold of the end	8:24
come f. and partake of the fruit	8:24
came f. and fell down and partook	8:30
go f. and cry in the wilderness:	10: 8
beheld the Son of God going f.	11:24
of God went f. and was baptized	11:27
he went f. ministering unto the	11:28
beheld the Lamb of God going f.	11:31
they went f. in multitudes	12:20
he went f. upon the many waters,	13:12
they went f. out of captivity,	13:13
who had gone f. out of captivity	13:16
it was carried f. among them.	13:20
beheld that the book proceeded f.	13:24
when it proceeded f. from the	13:24
these things go f. from the Jews	13:25
go f. by the hand of the twelve	13:26
book hath gone f. through the	13:28
it goeth f. unto all the nations	13:29
it goeth f. unto all the nations	13:29
have gone f. out of captivity,	13:29
have gone f. out of captivity,	13:30
I will bring f. unto them, in mine	13:34
to come f. unto the Gentiles,	13:35
who shall seek to bring f. my Zion	13:37
which had preceeded f. from the	13:38
it came f. from the Gentiles unto	13:38
after it had come f. unto them	13:39
other books, which came f. by	13:39
to come f. in their purity,	14:26
and went f. to the tent door,	16:10
and go f. into the wilderness	16:14
did go f. again in the wilderness,	16:14
as I, Nephi, went f. to slay food,	16:18
I, Nephi, did go f. up into the	16:30
nearly eastward from that time f.	17: 1
the rock, and there came f. water,	17:29
led f. by his matchless power	17:42
came f. to lay their hands upon me	17:48
Stretch f. thine hand again unto	17:53
I stretched f. my hand unto my	17:54
and did go f. with me;	18: 1
we did put f. into the sea	18: 8
and were driven f. before the wind	18: 8
had been driven f. before the wind	18: 9
that he might show f. his power,	18:11
we went f. upon the land,	18:23
are come f. out of the waters	20: 1
they went f. out of my mouth,	20: 3
Go ye f. of Babylon, flee ye	20:20
mayest say to the prisoners: Go f.;	21: 9
break f. into singing, O mountains;	21:13
made thee waste shall go f. of thee.	21:17
and come f. out of obscurity,	2Ne 1:23
bringing us f. into the land	1:24
they have brought f. children;	2:20
I give power to bring f. my word	3:11
to the bringing f. my word only,	3:11
already gone f. among them.	3:11
Lord shall bring f. by his hand,	3:15
go f. unto the fruit of thy loins.	3:19
shall proceed f. out of my mouth	3:21
my salvation is gone f.,	8: 5
hath stretched f. the heavens,	8:13
all the sons she hath brought f.;	2Ne 8:18
have gone f. out of his mouth,	9:17
in carrying them f. to the lands	10: 8
send them f. unto all my children,	11: 2
their words f. unto my children	11: 3
out of Zion shall go f. the law,	12: 3
and walk with stretched-f. necks	13:16
that it should bring f. grapes,	15: 2
and it brought f. wild grapes.	15: 2
that it should bring f. grapes	15: 4
grapes it brought f. wild grapes.	15: 4
stretched f. his hand against them,	15:25
Go f. now to meet Ahaz,	17: 3
be for the sending f. of oxen,	17:25
there shall come f. a rod out of	21: 1
shall be darkened in her going f.,	23:10
they break f. into singing.	24: 7
shall come f. a cockatrice,	24:29
he shall bring f. his words unto	25:18
and the water should come f.;	25:20
shall bring these things f. unto	26:14
shall bring f. unto you the words	27: 6
the Lord, that they may come f.;	27:10
proceed to bring f. the words	27:14
I will bring them f. in mine own	27:21
should proceed f. out of my mouth	29: 2
my words shall hiss f. unto the	29: 2
because my words shall hiss f.—	29: 3
it shall proceed f. from the Jews,	29: 4
unto me, in bringing f. salvation	29: 4
and I bring f. my word unto the	29: 7
and that I speak f. my words	29: 9
which I have spoken shall come f.,	30: 3
they shall carry them f. unto the	30: 3
words which shall proceed f. out	33:14
Nephi, third Nephi, and so f.,	Jac 1:11
I have led this people f. out of	2:25
master of the vineyard went f.,	5: 4
that perhaps it may shoot f.	5: 4
began to put f. somewhat a little,	5: 6
and it had sprung f.	5:17
hath brought f. much strength;	5:18
have brought f. tame fruit.	5:18
the tree thereof hath brought f.;	5:18
not brought f. much fruit also,	5:19
went f. whither the master had	5:20
that it had brought f. much fruit;	5:20
and it hath brought f. much fruit.	5:20
that it hath brought f. much fruit.	5:22
and it hath brought f. much fruit;	5:23
and it hath brought f. fruit.	5:24
tree hath brought f. tame fruit.	5:25
tree hath brought f. wild fruit;	5:25
have not brought f. good fruit,	5:26
may bring f. good fruit unto thee,	5:27
it hath brought f. much fruit,	5:32
long as it shall bring f. evil fruit.	5:35
they have hitherto brought f.,	5:36
hath brought f. much evil fruit;	5:37
hath brought f. so much evil fruit	5:37
have also brought f. evil fruit.	5:38
tree which brought f. good fruit,	5:40
have once brought f. good fruit	5:42
part thereof brought f. good fruit,	5:45
part thereof brought f. wild fruit;	5:45
that they bring f. no good fruit;	5:46
I have stretched f. mine hand	5:47
may bring f. good fruit unto me,	5:54
may bring f. again good fruit;	5:60
bring f. again the natural fruit,	5:61
and bring f. the natural fruit,	5:64
which bring f. bitter fruit,	5:65
shall bring f. the natural fruit,	5:68
go f. in his power, to nourish	6: 2
and he stretches f. his hands	6: 4
will ye bring f. evil fruit,	6: 7
that it might be brought f.	En 1:13
that he would bring them f.	1:16
had dwelt there from that time f.	Om 1:16
should be written and sent f.	Mos 2: 8
and shall go f. amongst men,	3: 5
he went f. and bowed himself	7:12
go f. upon the face of the earth—	7:27

FORTH

did go f. against the Lamanites	Mos	9:16
f. to battle against the Lamanites;		9:17
and we did go f. in his might;		9:18
did go f. against the Lamanites,		9:18
and he went f. among them,		11:20
Go f., and say unto this people,		11:20
Stretch f. thy hand and		12: 2
I will send f. hail among them,		12: 6
f. upon the face of the land.		12:12
Break f. into joy; sing together		12:23
And they stood f. and attempted		13: 2
to come f. and to prophesy evil		13:26
and go f. in mighty power upon		13:34
come f. in the first resurrection;		15:22
Break f. into joy, sing together,		15:30
he stretched f. his hand and said:		16: 1
did go f. to a place which was		18: 4
went and stood f. in the water,		18:12
and came f. out of the water		18:14
and went f. a second time into		18:15
went f. to the place of Mormon;		18:16
fair daughters should stand f.		19:13
came f. out of their secret places		20: 5
they sent their armies f.;		20: 7
he went f. and said unto the king:		20:17
Let us go f. to meet my people,		20:24
and went f. without arms to		20:25
went f. against the Lamanites		21: 7
Gideon went f. and stood before		22: 3
did show f. his mighty power		23:24
went f. and stood among them,		23:27
went f. and delivered themselves		23:29
and he also sent f. their wives,		23:33
Alma did go f. into the water		25:18
serve me and go f. in my name,		26:20
they know me thay shall come f.,		26:24
they that never knew me come f.		26:25
Alma, arise and stand f., for why		27:13
sendeth them f. among his people,		29:23
these things f. among the people		29:37
went f. preaching false doctrines;	Al	1:16
stones, and their slings, and so f.		3: 5
of Nephi, from that time f.—		3:11
might go f. among his people,		4:19
bring f. works of righteousness,		5:35
bringeth f. not good fruit,		5:36
a man bringeth f. good works		5:41
whosoever bringeth f. evil works,		5:41
shine f. among all the children of		5:50
Go f. and say unto this people—		5:51
that bringeth not f. good fruit		5:52
and they do bring f. works which		5:54
and bring f. a son, yea, even		7:10
he shall go f., suffering pains		7:11
yea, come and go f., and show		7:15
from this time f. and forever.		7:27
and he brought f. bread and meat		8:21
go f. and prophesy unto this		8:29
Alma went f., and also Amulek,		8:30
Lord might show f. his power		8:31
went f. and began to preach		8:32
and go f. and preach again unto		9: 1
stood f. to lay their hands on me;		9: 7
must go f. and cry mightily unto		9:25
ye ought to bring f. works which		9:30
that Amulek went and stood f.,		9:34
But Amulek stretched f. his hand,		10:25
and sent f. officers that the man		11: 2
come f. and stand before him		12:15
and bringeth f. fruit meet for		12:15
came f. and said unto him:		12:20
gone f. and partaken of the		12:26
from that time f. to call on his		12:30
bring f. fruit meet for repentance		13:13
stretched f. his hand unto them		13:21
went f. and witnessed against		14: 5
plead for them from that time f.;		14: 7
they also brought f. their records		14: 8
them f. to the place of martyrdom,		14: 9
let us stretch f. our hands, and		14:10
must not stretch f. mine hand;		14:11
And many came f. also, and smote		14:20
they all went f. and smote them,	Al	14:25
Amulek came f. out of the prison,		14:28
came f. out of the prison;		14:28
straightway came f. into the city.		14:28
coming f. out of the prison,		14:29
he stretched f. his hand, and		15: 5
went f. throughout all the land		15:11
began from that time f. to preach		15:12
went f. preaching repentance to		16:13
thus did Alma and Amulek go f.,		16:15
who did go f. among the people		16:18
Holding f. things which must		16:19
holding f. the coming of the Son		16:19
Go f. among the Lamanites,		17:11
ye may show f. good examples		17:11
to go f. unto the Lamanites to		17:12
and went f. among them,		17:17
going f. with their flocks to the		17:26
driving f. their flocks to this place		17:27
I will show f. my power unto		17:29
rushed f. with much swiftness		17:32
he went f. and stood to contend		17:34
stood f. and began to cast stones		17:36
came f. with clubs to slay him.		17:36
should stand f. and testify to		18: 1
conduct him f. to the land of		18: 9
thirst, and their travail, and so f.		18:37
he stretched f. his hand unto		19:12
he shall come f., and be born of		19:13
she ran f. from house to house,		19:17
went f. that he might let it fall		19:22
they durst not put f. their hands		19:24
went f. and began to rebuke them,		19:31
But Ammon stood f. and said		20:17
he stretched f. his hand to slay		20:20
were brought f. out of prison.		20:28
went f. again to declare the word,		21:15
went f. whithersoever they were		21:16
faith and repentance, and so f.;		22:14
therefore he put f. his hand and		22:22
And the king stood f., and began		22:23
the king stood f. among them		22:25
should stand f. in the midst of		22:26
their brethren who should go f.		23: 1
thus they might go f. and preach		23: 3
go f. throughout all the land,		23: 3
had sent f. this proclamation,		23: 4
went f. from city to city,		23: 4
came f. to the land of Midian,		24: 5
Behold, we went f. even in wrath,		26:18
and bringeth f. good works,		26:22
come, and been f. amongst them;		26:28
we can look f. and see the fruits		26:31
I and my brethren will go f. into		27:15
as Ammon was going f. into the		27:16
that I might go f. and speak with		29: 1
and have brought f. much fruit;		29:15
he put f. his hand and wrote		30:51
Alma should show f. his sign?		30:51
Korihor put f. his hand and wrote,		30:52
the proclamation was sent f. by		30:57
as he went f. among the people,		30:59
and as he went f. amongst them,		30:59
must go f. and stand upon the		31:14
and stretch f. his hands towards		31:14
every man did go f. and offer up		31:20
they did go f., and began to		32: 1
but he stretched f. his hand,		32: 7
every seed bringeth f. unto its own		32:31
may grow up, and bring f. fruit		32:37
and grow up and bring f. fruit.		32:37
waiting for the tree to bring f. fruit		32:43
they sent f. unto him desiring to		33: 1
come f. and bring fruit unto		34:30
come f. and harden not your hearts		34:31
should go f. unto every nation,		37: 7
that he may show f. his power		37:14
that he might show f. his power		37:18
and he hath shown f. his power		37:19
will also still show f. his power		37:19
a stone, which shall shine f.		37:23
I will bring f. out of darkness		37:25

FORTH 351 FORTH

all shall come f. from the dead.	Al	40: 4	gone f. to the land northward	Al 63:10
men shall come f. from the dead,		40: 5	to carry f. provisions unto the	63:10
that I say that they all come f.;		40:19	who had gone f. into that land.	63:10
that the dead shall come f.,		40:21	written and sent f. among the	63:12
then shall the righteous shine f.		40:25	by Alma should not go f.	63:12
God sent our first parents f. from		42: 2	had gone f. unto the Lamanites;	63:14
lest he should put f. his hand,		42: 3	they sent f. one Kishkumen,	He 1: 9
if Adam had put f. his hand		42: 5	by sending him f. he should gain	1:16
the sons of Alma did go f.		43: 1	that Coriantumr did march f.	1:19
could not rest, and he also went f.		43: 1	did march f. with his whole army	1:20
he led his army f. and encircled		43:35	to go f. against all the land.	1:22
sent f. and inspired their hearts		43:48	did march f. with a large army,	1:23
he came f. and delivered up his		44: 8	to go f. and cut his way through	1:23
and stretched it f. unto them,		44:13	therefore he did march f.,	1:24
many came f. and threw down		44:15	he immediately sent f. Lehi with	1:28
they have gone f. and are buried		44:22	went f. towards the judgment-seat	2: 6
Helaman went f. among the		45:20	go f. unto the judgment-seat.	2: 8
went f. to establish the church		45:22	going f. unto the judgment-seat,	2: 9
he went f. among the people,		46:19	that Helaman did send f. to take	2:10
come f. in the strength of		46:20	Helaman sent f. to take them	2:11
had said these words he went f.,		46:28	went f. unto the land northward	3: 3
sent f. in all the parts of the		46:28	they did spread f. into all parts	3: 5
marched f. into the wilderness,		46:32	the people who went f. became	3: 7
the proclamation had gone f.		47: 2	go f. from the land southward	3: 8
go f. and compel them to arms.		47: 3	did send f. much by the way of	3:10
should go f. to meet the king.		47:22	did also go f. into this land.	3:12
king put f. his hand to raise		47:23	and hunted, and driven f.,	3:16
that his armies should march f.		47:27	lead them f. from place to place,	4:16
go f., and pursue his servants		47:27	shall send f. his mighty winds,	5:12
came f. and pursued after the		47:28	and therefore they went f.,	5:14
moved f. toward the land of		48: 6	gone f. among all the people of	5:16
And thus they went f.,		48:20	came f. and did confess their sins	5:17
and sent f. to preach among		49:30	they went f. into the prison to	5:22
that his armies should go f.		50: 7	Nephi and Lehi did stand f. and	5:26
and they went f. and drove all		50: 7	could speak f. marvelous words.	5:45
go f. into the east wilderness,		50: 9	bidden to go f. and marvel not,	5:49
works did bring f. unto them,		50:12	they did go f., and did minister	5:50
armies did march f. against		51:18	should not go f. unto the world,	6:25
marching f. with his numerous		51:30	come f. unto Gadianton from	6:26
stole f. and went out by night,		51:33	his followers from that time f.	6:27
marched f. against the Nephites		52:12	f. from the beginning of man	6:29
march f. with his army against		52:17	had been f. among the people	7: 2
did march f. against Teancum,		52:23	he shall scatter you f. that ye	7:19
should march f. into the city,		52:24	upon this man and forbid him f.,	8: 1
led the Lamanites f. to battle		52:33	he did go f. in the Spirit,	10:17
bring f. your weapons of war		52:37	sent it f. among all the people.	10:17
came f. and threw down their		52:38	and did not yield f. grain in the	11: 6
f. into the land Bountiful.		52:39	send f. rain upon the face of	11:13
to go f. and bury their dead,		53: 1	that she may bring f. her fruit,	11:13
go f. unto the guards who were		55: 6	bring f. her fruit in the season	11:17
they brought them f. and cast		55:23	bring f. her grain in the season	11:17
come f. to defend our country.		56: 5	dissenters that went f. unto them.	11:25
fearful, and began to sally f.,		56:29	did go f. again against this band	11:30
march f. with my little sons		56:30	stretched f. his hand and cried	13: 4
we did march f., as if with		56:32	went f. and sought for Nephi;	16: 1
Antipus did march f. with a part		56:33	when they had come f. and	16: 1
he did not march f. until I		56:33	went f. unto him to be baptized,	16: 5
had gone f. with my little army,		56:33	went f. to lay their hands on him,	16: 7
they came f. with their army		56:35	from this time f. there began	3Ne 1:22
then let us go f.; we should not		56:46	began to be lyings sent f. among	1:22
we durst not go f. and attack		58: 2	Nephi went f. among the people,	1:23
the Lamanites were sallying f.		58: 6	did come f. against the people of	2:18
we did go f. with all our might		58:13	gone f. throughout all the face	3:22
came f. against the people of		59: 7	and did march f. by thousands	3:22
send f. against the Lamanites,		60: 2	all gone f. to the place which	3:22
gone f. against our enemies,		60:16	and to sally f. from the hills,	4: 1
if we had gone f. against them		60:16	they did break f., all as one,	4:31
send f. food and men unto us,		60:24	inspired from heaven and sent f.,	6:20
food to send f. unto Lehi and		61:18	had gone f. out of the reach of	7:13
we will go f. against them in		61:18	went f. among them in that	7:16
and went f. against the city,		62: 7	they did show f. signs also	7:22
Moroni went f. in the darkness		62:20	that he stretched f. his hand	11: 9
that his men should march f.		62:22	Arise and come f. unto me,	11:14
his men should march f.		62:25	that the multitude went f.,	11:15
Moroni went f. from the land,		62:30	going f. one by one until they	11:15
Teancum in his anger did go f.		62:36	until they had all gone f.,	11:15
And he went f. with a cord,		62:36	when they had all gone f.	11:16
Moroni marched f. on the		62:38	him that he should come f.	11:18
and his brethren went f.,		62:45	And Nephi arose and went f.,	11:19
therefore he went f. and built		63: 5	come f. again out of the water.	11:26
launched it f. into the west sea,		63: 5	go f. unto this people, and	11:41
did enter therein and did sail f.		63: 6	he stretched f. his hand unto	12: 1
one other ship also did sail f.;		63: 8	good tree bringeth f. good fruit;	14:17
went f. into the land northward.		63: 9	corrupt tree bringeth f. evil fruit.	14:17

FORTH   352   FORTH

tree cannot bring f. evil fruit,	3Ne	14:18
corrupt tree bring f. good fruit.		14:18
that bringeth not f. good fruit		14:19
acattered f. upon the face of		16: 4
come f. upon the face of this		16: 8
Break f. into joy, sing together,		16:19
did go f. with their sick and		17: 9
they were brought f. unto him.		17: 9
bring f. some bread and wine		18: 1
did they send f. unto the people		19: 3
went f. and stood in the midst		19: 4
of Jacob, go f. among them;		20:16
shall they break f. into joy—		20:34
And then shall a cry go f.:		20:41
and shall come f. of the Father,		21: 3
might come f. from them unto		21: 4
come f. from the Gentiles,		21: 5
come f. from the Gentiles,		21: 6
that he may show f. his power		21: 6
to bring f. unto the Gentiles,		21:11
bring them f. unto the Gentiles,		21:11
break f. into singing, and cry		22: 1
let them stretch f. the curtains		22: 2
break f. on the right hand and		22: 3
that bringeth f. an instrument		22:16
shall go f. unto the Gentiles.		23: 4
Bring f. the record which ye		23: 7
Nephi had brought f. the records,		23: 8
ye shall go f. and grow up as		25: 2
shown f. his power unto them,		26:15
began from that time f. to		26:17
Father show f. his own works		27:10
go f. upon the face of the land,		28:18
thus they did go f. among all		28:23
sayings coming f. among you,		29: 4
from that time f. they did have	4Ne	1:25
they went f. doing mighty		1:30
they came f. receiving no harm.		1:32
did come f. from among them,		1:33
did go f. at the head of an army	Mrm	2: 2
f. out of the land of David.		2: 5
And we marched f. and came		2: 6
were driven f. until we had come		2:20
did go f. against the Lamanites		2:27
utterly refuse from this time f.		3:11
went f. in their own might,		4: 8
the inhabitants f. out of her,		4:14
this time f. did the Nephites		4:18
I did go f. among the Nephites,		5: 1
not bring them f. unto them;		5:12
may come f. in his own due time.		5:12
shall come f. according to		5:13
shall go f. unto them from the		5:15
shall go f. among you as a lion,		5:24
march f. before the Lamanites.		6: 1
march f. to the land of Cumorah,		6: 4
it shall shine f. out of darkness,		8:16
suffer to bring these things f.		8:25
things shall come f. among you.		8:34
come f., both small and great,		9:13
Jared came f. with his brother	Eth	1:33
carry us f. into a land which		1:38
should go f. into the wilderness,		2: 5
would that they should come f.		2: 7
bring Jared and his brethren f.		2:13
have gone f. out of my mouth,		2:24
and the floods have I sent f.		2:24
the winds which have gone f.,		2:25
went f. unto the mount,		3: 1
and hast driven us f.,		3: 3
go f. across this raging deep		3: 3
may shine f. in darkness;		3: 4
shine f. unto us in the vessels		3: 4
able to show f. great power,		3: 5
the Lord stretched f. his hand		3: 6
to go f. unto the world,		3:21
They shall not go f. unto the		4: 6
assist to bring f. this work;		5: 2
be shown f. the power of God		5: 4
he did put f. the stones into		6: 2
and set f. into the sea,		6: 4
and he did bring them f. again		6: 7
were driven f. before the wind.		6: 8

And thus they were driven f.;	Eth	6:10
And thus they were driven f.,		6:11
they went f. upon the face of		6:13
came f. poisonous serpents		9:31
the Lord did show f. his power		9:35
and went f. and gave bettle		10: 9
or bring f. another people to		11:21
Ether came f. in the days of		12: 2
when God put f. his finger		12:20
and by night he went f.		13:13
brother of Shared did march f.		14: 5
came f. to the land of Moron,		14: 6
a cry went f. throughout the		14:18
they did march f. from the		14:22
the scent thereof went f. upon		14:23
to invite them f. to battle.		14:28
they came f., but were driven		14:29
march f. one against another		15:15
and said unto him: Go f.		15:33
And he went f., and beheld		15:33
they brought f. fruit meet that	Mro	6: 1
came f. with a broken heart and		6: 2
cannot bring f. good water;		7:11
fountain bring f. bitter water;		7:11
sent f. by the power and gift of		7:16
proceeded f. out of the mouth		7:25
proceed f. out of the mouth of		10:28
hiss f. from generation to		10:28
brought f. triumphant through		10:34
And they shall go f. and none	DC	1: 5
unto you, that they who go f.,		1: 8
things of the world shall come f.		1:19
to bring it f. out of obscurity		1:30
my work shall go f.,		3:16
work is about to come f.		4: 1
go f. and deliver my words		5: 6
they shall go f. with my words		5:11
the coming f. of my church		5:14
three witnesses will I send f.		5:15
their testimony shall also go f.		5:18
a desolating scourge shall go f.		5:19
work is about to come f.		6: 1
seek to bring f. and establish		6: 6
and assist to bring f. my work,		6: 9
he bringeth f. the same words,		10:17
have gone f. out of your hands;		10:30
should bring f. the same words		10:31
the work may not come f.		10:33
and send f. in this work.		10:45
should come f. unto this people.		10:46
work is about to come f.		11: 1
seek to bring f. and establish		11: 6
assist to bring f. my work,		11: 9
my word which hath gone f.		11:22
my word which shall come f.		11:22
wisdom that you shall go f.		11:26
work is about to come f.		12: 1
seek to bring f. and establish		12: 6
who have desires to bring f.		12: 7
work is about to come f.		14: 1
Seek to bring f. and establish		14: 6
bring f. the fulness of my		14:10
but woes shall go f., weeping,		19: 5
come f. with broken hearts		20:37
come f. again out of the water.		20:74
the decree hath gone f. from		29: 8
and desolation are sent f. upon		29: 8
hath gone f. in a firm decree,		29:12
and they shall come f.—		29:13
be a great hailstorm sent f.		29:16
send f. flies upon the face of		29:18
opened and they shall come f.—		29:26
and as the words have gone f.		29:30
send f. angels to declare unto		29:42
shalt commence from this time f.		30: 9
to preach from this time f.,		31: 1
called f. out of the wilderness.		33: 5
thou wast sent f., even as John,		35: 4
great things are to be shown f.		35:10
shall not anything be shown f.		35:11
sent f. unto this generation.		35:12
they shall be looking f. for		35:15
I have sent f. the fulness of		35:17

FORTH

ordained and sent f. to preach	DC 36: 5
and come f. out of the fire,	36: 6
may be ordained and sent f.,	36: 7
I hold f. and deign to give unto	38:18
shall go f. among all nations,	38:33
send them f. to the place	38:35
power from on high and sent f.,	38:38
have sent f. in these last days,	39:11
covenant which I have sent f.	39:11
and to bring f. Zion,	39:13
be poured f. upon their heads.	39:15
shall go f. into all nations.	39:15
Wherefore, go f., crying with	39:19
Go f. baptizing with water,	39:20
looking f. for the signs of my	39:23
that ye shall go f. in my name,	42: 4
shall go f. for a little season,	42: 5
go f. in the power of my Spirit,	42: 6
go f. baptizing with water,	42: 7
ye shall go f. into the regions	42: 8
to go f. to preach my gospel,	42:11
shall be sent f. to the east and	42:63
Ye are not sent f. to be taught,	43:15
shall streak f. from the east	43:22
shall utter f. their voices unto	43:22
shall go f. into the regions	44: 3
light shall break f. among them	45:28
the light shall begin to break f.,	45:36
say when they begin to shoot f.,	45:37
be looking f. for the great day	45:39
shown f. in the heavens above,	45:40
shall come f. to meet me in	45:45
the saints shall come f. from	45:46
go ye f. into the western	45:64
looking f. for the heavens to	49:23
go f. as I have commanded	49:26
which have gone f. in the earth,	50: 2
was sent f. to teach the truth.	50:14
sent f. to preach the word of	50:17
ordained of God and sent f.,	50:26
sent f. by the will of the	50:27
go f. among the churches and	50:37
send f. judgment unto victory.	52:11
and he goeth f. deceiving	52:14
shall bring f. fruits of praise	52:17
and bringeth not f. fruits,	52:18
might go f. from Zion,	58:13
light ye shall hold them f.	58:23
workmen sent f. of all kinds	58:54
the sound must go f. from this	58:64
it shall bring f. in its strength.	59: 3
looking f. for the coming of	61:38
whose going f. is unto the ends	65: 1
thence shall the gospel roll f.	65: 2
without hands shall roll f.,	65: 2
that his kingdom may go f.	65: 5
kingdom of God go f.,	65: 6
sent f. unto the children of	66: 2
appointed unto them to go f.—	68: 2
should send f. the accounts of	69: 5
bring f. their strong reasons	71: 8
go f. unto the ends of the earth;	72:21
go f. to proclaim my gospel,	75: 2
you should go f. and tarry,	75: 3
Son of Man, and shall come f.—	76:16
all the rest shall be brought f.	76:39
come f. in the resurrection of	76:50
which the Father sheds f. upon	76:53
come f. in the resurrection of	76:65
four angels sent f. from God,	77: 8
sent f. to build up my church.	84:32
proceedeth f. from the mouth	84:44
That they may bring f. fruit meet	84:58
goeth f. to proclaim this gospel	84:86
And plagues shall go f.,	84:97
and brought f. her strength;	84:101
who goes f. to proclaim mine	84:103
bringing f. of the revelations	84:104
go ye f. as your circumstances	84:117
setting f. clearly and	84:117
the Lord, have put f. my hand	84:119
putteth f. his hand to steady	85: 8
beginning to bring f. the word,	86: 4
sent f. to reap down the fields;	DC 86: 5
Which light proceedeth f. from	88:12
he sent f. his servants into	88:51
and fasting from this time f.	88:76
to go f. among the Gentiles	88:84
in their graves shall come f.,	88:97
he shall stand f. upon the land	88:110
showing f. the order and will	89: 2
is coming f. for the last time.	90: 2
the word may go f. unto the	90: 9
shed f. upon them for the	90:11
I sent them f. to be chastened.	95:10
of bringing f. my word to the	96: 4
my word should go f. unto the	96: 5
assist in bringing f. my word	96: 8
bringeth not f. good fruit	97: 7
cause them to bring f. as a	97: 9
every word which proceedeth f.	98:11
the Holy Ghost shall be shed f.	100: 8
the decree hath gone f. by	101:10
will the Lord arise and come f.	101:89
inasmuch as they bring f. fruit	101:100
the destroyer I have sent f.	105:15
servants may go f. from this	109:22
that thou hast put f. thy hand,	109:23
that they may come f. to Zion,	109:39
That thy church may come f.	109:73
and shine f. fair as the moon,	109:73
shalt send f. my word unto	112: 4
let thy warning voice go f.;	112: 5
and from my house shall it go f.,	112:25
Arise and shine f.,	115: 5
from that time f. let my people	115:10
from that time f. labor diligently	115:12
awake, and arise, and come f.,	117: 1
and to bring f. in abundance?	117: 7
stretch f. thy hand; let thine eye	121: 4
shall be revealed and set f.	121:29
stretch f. his puny arm	121:33
showing f. afterwards an increase of	121:43
promise which shall call him f.	123: 6
before he can send f. the power	123: 6
that I might show f. my wisdom	124: 1
from this time f. I appoint	124:94
the date, and names, and so f.,	128: 3
in the water and come f. out	128:12
in coming f. out of their graves;	128:12
to show f. the living and the dead,	128:13
holding f. that which is to come,	128:21
the earth break f. into singing.	128:22
the dead speak f. anthems of	128:22
come f. in the first resurrection;	132:19
come f. in the first resurrection,	132:26
Send f. the elders of my church	133: 8
send f. unto foreign lands;	133: 8
Go ye f. unto the land of Zion,	133: 9
Zion may go f. unto the regions	133: 9
the cry go f. among all people:	133:10
Awake and arise and go f.	133:10
God hath sent f. the angel	133:17
come f. pools of living water;	133:29
shall bring f. their rich treasures	133:30
I have sent f. mine angel	133:36
the servants of God shall go f.,	133:38
they shall come f. and stand	133:56
sent f. the fulness of his gospel,	133:57
now are to go f. unto all flesh.—	133:60
brought f. the Book of Mormon,	135: 3
has brought f. the revelations	135: 3
to bring them f. for the salvation	135: 6
Spirit is sent f. into the world	136:33
to bring f. my work;	136:37
Let the earth bring f. grass,	Mses 2:11
And the earth brought f. grass,	2:12
Let the waters bring f.	2:20
which the waters brought f.	2:21
Let the earth bring f. the living	2:24
sorrow thou shalt bring f. children,	4:22
thistles shall it bring f. to thee,	4:24
now lest he put f. his hand and	4:28
will send him f. from the Garden	4:29
as they go f. out of my mouth	4:30
from that time f., the sons and	5: 3

FORTH 354 FORWARD

from that time f. to be carnal,	Mses 5:13	had possession of, to f. them;	Al	57: 4
went f. out of the mouth of God	5:15	strengthen and f. our armies,		60:25
from this time f. thou shalt be	5:24	this was done to f. the land		62:13
sent f. from the presence of God,	5:58	did f. against the Lamanites,	He	4: 7
a decree sent f., that it should	5:59	they did f. themselves against	3Ne	3:25
I have sent f. in the beginning	6:30	did f. the city with our might;	Mrm	2: 4
as it shall be sent f. in the world,	6:30	that we did f. the city of Shem,		2:21
Go f. and do as I have commanded	6:32	we did f. against them with		3: 6
that Enoch went f. in the land	6:37			
And they came f. to hear him,	6:38	FORTIFYING		
I speak f. these words.	6:42	f. the line between the Nephites	Al	50:11
spake f. the words of God,	6:47			
was brought f. out of the water.	6:64	FORTS		
and are looking f. with fear,	7: 1	and raised f. against them;	2Ne	26:15
from that time f. Enoch began	7: 2	erecting small f., or places of	Al	48: 8
shall go f. in battle array	7: 7	or had built f. of security,		49:13
barrenness thereof shall go f.	7: 8	not get into their f. of security		49:18
went f. a curse upon all people	7:15	to attack them in their f.		52: 5
that time f. there were wars	7:16			
shed f. their tears as the rain	7:28	FORTY		
I can stretch f. mine hands and	7:36	f. years had passed away,	2Ne	5:34
and wept and stretched f. his arms,	7:41	even f. days did they wander.	Mos	7: 4
the filthiness which is gone f. out	7:48	when they had wandered f. days		7: 5
he sent f. an unalterable decree	7:52	that f. and three of my people		8: 7
they shall come f. with songs	7:53	slay three thousand and f.-three;		9:18
as were in prison came f.,	7:57	in the f. and first year of the	He	1:14
truth will I send f. out of the	7:62	thus ended the f. and first year		1:34
be looking f. for the time of	7:62	in the f. and second year of		2: 1
which shall come f. out of all the	7:64	thus ended the f. and second		2:12
looking f. with fear for the	7:66	in the f. and third year of		3: 1
from thence went f. the saying,	7:69	ending of the f. and third year.		3: 1
there came f. a great famine	8: 4	in the f. and fourth year;		3: 2
go f. and declare his Gospel	8:19	in the f. and fifth year.		3: 2
came f. in the way to the land	Abr 2:15	in the f. and sixth, yea, there		3: 3
the earth to bring f. grass;	4:11	The f. and sixth year of the		3:18
the earth to bring f. grass from	4:12	even in the f. and seventh year,		3:19
the herb to bring f. herb from	4:12	also in the f. and eighty year.		3:19
the earth to bring f. the tree	4:12	end of the f. and eighty year		3:22
could only bring f. the same	4:12	in the f. and ninth year of the		3:23
waters to bring f. abundantly	4:20	of the f. and ninth year;		3:32
might bring f. great whales,	4:21	and ninth, and f. and first,	4Ne	1: 6
waters were to bring f. abundantly	4:21	and the f. and second,		1: 6
to bring f. the living creature	4:24	until f. and nine years had		1: 6
to bring f. the beasts after	4:25	two hundred and f. and four		1:40
is in the desert; go not f.:	JS 1:25	an army of f. and four thousand.	Mrm	2: 9
these things shall be shown f.,	1:34	him with f. and two thousand.		2: 9
and it begins to put f. leaves,	1:38	hundred and f. and four years		2:15
the time for bringing them f.	2:53	hundred and f. and fifth year		2:16
		hundred and f. and sixth year		2:22
FORTIETH		hundred and f. and ninth year		2:28
commencement of the f. year	He 1: 1	hundred and f. and four days	Eth	6:11
all this was done in the f. year	1:13	hundred and f. and two years		9:24
in the f. year of his age;	DC 107:45	he reigned f. and nine years,		9:25
		the space of f. and two years		10: 8
FORTIFICATIONS		the space of f. and two years.		10:15
in their weakest f. he did	Al 48: 9	the kingdom f. and two years;		10:32
and caused them to erect f.	50:10	hundred and f.-four thousand,	DC	77:11
yea, possession of all their f.	51:23	were f.-three, as follows:		102: 5
manner of the f. of Moroni;	51:27	which is f. rods long and twelve		104:43
sought protection in their f.	52: 2	to preside over f.-eight priests,		107:87
while they were in their f.;	52:17	hundred and f.-four thousand,		133:18
in making f. to guard against	53: 7	Hyrum Smith was f.-four years		135: 6
strengthening the f. round	55:25	f. or more such marriages have		OD
that f. should be built round	3Ne 3:14	deny that either f. or any		OD
but notwithstanding all our f.	Mrm 2: 4	eight hundred and f. years,	Mses	6:19
		f.-two years afterward he begat		8:12
FORTIFIED				
Moroni had f., or had built	Al 49:13	FORTY-EIGHT: see FORTY and EIGHT.		
all of which were strongly f.	51:27			
when he had f. the city Gid,	55:26	FORTY-FOUR: see FORTY and FOUR.		
f. the city Morianton until it	55:33			
after Moroni had f. those parts	62:42	FORTY-THREE: see FORTY and THREE.		
on the line which they had f.	He 4: 7			
		FORTY-TWO: see FORTY and TWO.		
FORTIFY				
I will f. this land against all	2Ne 10:12	FORWARD		
people of Nephi did f. against	Jac 7:25	many of whom were pressing f.,	1Ne	8:21
and began to f. our cities,	Jar 1: 7	I beheld others pressing f.,		8:24
did f. and strengthen the land	Al 48: 9	did press f. through the mist		8:24
should f. the land Bountiful,	52: 9	he saw other multitudes pressing f.;		8:30
f. and strengthen the cities	52:10	and they did press their way f.,		8:30
with their might to f. the city.	56:15	and look not f. any more for	2Ne	25:16

FORWARD 355 FOUND

need not look f. any more for	2Ne 25:18
look f. with steadfastness unto	25:24
may look f. unto that life which	25:27
but look f. unto Christ with	26: 8
Wherefore, ye must press f. with	31:20
Wherefore, if ye shall press f.,	31:20
to look f. unto the Messiah,	Jar 1:11
from that time f. to take him.	Mos 11:29
and have looked f. to that day	15:11
of Christ, from that time f.	18:17
but that they should look f.	18:21
shall be observed from this time f.	26:32
Alma began from this time f. to	27:32
wise and look f. to these things,	29:10
of Nephi, from this time f.,	Al 1: 1
Looking f. to that day, thus	4:14
you look f. with an eye of faith,	5:15
f. for the remission of your sins,	7: 6
cite your minds f. to the time	13: 1
look f. to his Son for redemption.	13: 2
might look f. on the Son of God,	13:16
look f. to him for a remission of	13:16
look f. to the coming of Christ,	25:15
Ye look f. and say that ye see	30:16
looking f. with an eye of faith	32:40
looking f. to the fruit thereof,	32:41
he rushed f. that he might slay	44:12
he sent f. to the place which	47: 5
marched f. to the land of Noah	49:13
their chief captians came f. and	49:13
march f. by another way	58:26
of Christ, and have looked f.,	He 8:22
f. against the city Teancum,	Mrm 4:14
army of Coriantumr did press f.	Eth 14:12
Go f. and not backward.	DC 128:22
all men should step f.	134: 8

FOSTER, James
F., to preside over the   DC 124:138

FOSTER, Robert D.
will obey my voice,   DC 124:115

FOSTERED
one religious society is f.   DC 134: 9

FOSTERING
and preserved by thy f. hand.   DC 109:69

FOUGHT	
that I f. much with the sword	Om 1: 2
for father f. against father,	Mos 9: 2
that he f. with the king;	19: 5
for they f. like lions	20:10
But they f. for their lives,	20:11
Alma f. with Amlici with the	Al 2:29
was f. in the land of Zarahemla,	3:20
f. with stones and with arrows.	49: 2
Lehi who f. with the Lamanites	49:16
they f. on both hands with	52:35
have f. against the people of	54: 8
they had f. vailiantly by day	56:16
Now they never had f., yet they	56:47
young men who had f. with me,	56:55
had f. as if with the strength	56:56
to have f. with such miraculous	56:56
and sixty f. most desperately;	57:19
many have f. and bled out their	60: 9
had f. valiantly for his country,	62:37
had stood and f. with boldness,	3Ne 4:14
sore battle f. in the land	Mrm 4:19
they f. for the space of many	Eth 10:32
the sons of Coriantumr f. much	13:19
that Shared f. against him for	13:28
he f. with Lib, in which Lib did	14:12
they f. an exceedingly sore	15: 9
and they f. all that day,	15:15
that they f. all that day,	15:20
they f. even until the night	15:21
on the morrow they f. again;	15:23
on the morrow they f. again,	15:24
they f. for the space of three	15:27
they f. again with the sword.	15:29
a curse upon all people that f.	Mses 7:15

FOUND	
that ye may be f. spotless at the	T Pg
I f. that it was Laban	1Ne 4: 8
also f. upon the plates of brass	5:14
and f. that they were desirable;	5:21
then ye are f. unclean before the	10:21
not to be f. upon the land,	2Ne 5:16
and gladness shall be f. therein,	8: 3
my hand hath f. as a nest	20:14
and we would not be f. spotless	Jac 1:19
and I f. these plates,	WM 1: 3
that I might be f. blameless,	Mos 2:27
shall be f. blameless before God,	3:21
then are they f. no more blameless	3:22
be f. at the right hand of God,	5: 9
not f. on the left hand of God,	5:12
and f. not the land of Zarahemla	8: 8
hid himself that they f. him not.	17: 4
f. an accusation against thee,	17: 7
when the Lamanites f. that their	20: 6
f. the king of the Lamanites	20:12
when he f. that they were not,	21:24
people whose bones they had f.;	21:27
if thou hast not f. me to be an	22: 4
been f. by the people of Limhi.	22:14
when the Lamanites had f. that	22:15
had f. those priests of king Noah,	23:31
should be f. calling upon God	24:11
been f. by the people of Limhi,	28:11
and their bones have been f.,	Al 2:38
for such an one is not f. guiltless.	5:29
have f. that my desires have been	7:18
I f. the man whom the angel said	10: 8
that it has not been f. in us,	12:13
we shall not be f. spotless;	12:14
there they f. all the people who	15: 1
they f. him upon his bed, sick,	15: 5
Lamoni f. favor in the eyes of	20:28
there he f. Muloki preaching the	21:11
had f., after their many struggles	27: 1
they f. that the Zoramites had	31:12
they f. out privily the minds of	35: 5
after they had f. out the minds	35: 6
he f. by his spies which course	43:30
when Amalickiah f. that he could	47:12
and f. the king lying in his gore,	47:27
the Lamanites had f. that Lehi	49:17
when they f. that they could not	49:22
f. that the people of Lehi had	50:28
they f. Amalickiah was dead	52: 1
f. one, whose name was Laman;	55: 5
they f. that it was not expedient	55:23
f. Antipus and his men toiling	56:15
whosoever was f. denying their	62:10
that they all could not be f.;	He 1:12
but as many as were f.	1:12
slain Coriantumr was also f.	1:30
when Gadianton had f. that	2:11
them they could nowhere be f.	2:11
and behold, they were not f.	6:19
when the Lamanites f. that there	6:20
be f. in seams and in cracks,	14:22
they had come forth and f. him	16: 1
nowhere to be f. in all the land.	3Ne 2: 9
Giddianhi f. that it was expedient	4: 5
f. breathing out threatenings	5: 5
were f. in broken fragments,	8:18
he that is f. guiltless before	Mrm 7: 7
perhaps ye may be f. spotless,	9: 6
were f. by the people of Limhi,	Eth 1: 2
blessed is he that is f. faithful	4:19
was f. to commit iniquity,	Mro 6: 7
whoso is f. possessed of it	7:47
And when you have f. them	DC 18:39
who are f. on my left hand.	19: 5
church whithersoever it is f.,	37: 2
lest ye be f. among the wicked.	43:19
and they f. it not because of	45:12
And whoso is f. a faithful,	51:19
descendant of Aaron can be f.,	68:19
and f. worthy, and anointed,	68:20
f. guilty before this Presidency,	68:23
they are not f. transgressors	83: 2

FOUND 356 FOUNTAIN

be f. on any of the records or	DC 85: 4	a f. for serious consequences	Al 50:32
Their names shall not be f.,	85: 5	that ye must build your f.;	He 5:12
the saints whose names are f.,	85: 7	ye are built, which is a sure f.,	5:12
they who are not f. written in	85: 9	a f. whereon if men build they	5:12
whose names are not f. written	85:11	was from the f. of the world.	5:47
that are f. to have apostatized,	85:11	men from the f. of the world,	3Ne 1:14
as will be f. recorded in the	85:12	he buildeth upon a sandy f.,	11:40
are f. under condemnation;	88:100	but are built upon a sandy f.;	18:13
There are f. among those who	88:102	from the f. of the world	Eth 3:14
shall be f. standing in his place,	88:128	from the f. of the world;	4:14
And he that is f. unworthy of	88:134	from the f. of the world	4:15
that you may be f. worthy.	98:14	from the f. of the world.	4:19
who are f. upon the watch-tower,	101:12	from the f. of the world;	Mro 8:12
is f. no more room for them;	101:21	to lay the f. of this church,	DC 1:30
they were f. transgressors,	101:41	the f. of my church,	18: 4
shall be f. a transgressor,	104: 5	upon the f. of my gospel	18: 5
as you are f. transgressors,	104: 8	to lay the f. thereof,	21: 2
is f. a transgressor and	104:10	from the f. of the world	29:46
and ye are f. hypocrites,	104:55	were from the f. of the world,	35:18
Until he be f. a transgressor,	104:74	who laid the f. of the earth,	45: 1
is f. an unfaithful and an unwise	104:77	to lay the f. of the city;	48: 6
descendant of Aaron can be f.,	107:17	shall not build upon another's f.,	52:33
that we may be f. worthy,	109:11	be honored in laying the f.,	58: 7
if repentance is to be f.;	109:50	laying the f. of a great work.	64:33
or they shall not be f. worthy	119: 5	and the f., and the ensample,	78:13
not a place f. on earth that	124:28	beginning and f. of the city of	94: 1
nor his seed be f. begging bread.	124:90	the Lord from the f. thereof,	94: 6
and the valleys shall not be f.	133:22	the Lord from the f. thereof,	94:12
was not f. an help meet for him.	Mses 3:20	were yet laying the f. thereof,	101:47
that I have f. favor in thy sight,	6:31	a f., and a preparatory work,	115: 9
of his seed should always be f.	7:52	laying the f. of my house.	115:11
thus Noah f. grace in the eyes of	8:27	for the laying of the f. of Zion	119: 2
earnestly; now I have f. thee;	Abr 2:12	before the f. of the world,	124:33
was f. an help meet for him.	5:21	the revelations and f. of Zion,	124:39
I f. myself delivered from the	JS 2:17	before the f. of the world,	124:41
I f. myself lying on my back,	2:20	called to lay the f. of Zion;	124:118
I soon f.. however, that my	2:22	before the f. of the world	127: 2
I had f. the testimony of James	2:26	before the f. of the world,	128: 5
I f. that day was approaching,	2:47	before the f. of the world,	128: 8
I f. my strength so exhausted	2:48	from the f. of the world,	128:18
I f. the same messenger there,	2:54	before the f. of the world,	132: 5
I soon f. out the reason why	2:60	before the f. of the world,	132:63
we f. a friend in a gentleman	2:61	Which f. he did lay,	136:38
how the young man f. out that	2:64	from before the f. of the world.	Mses 5:57
the place where he f. them.	2:64	from my own mouth, from the f.	6:30
that we f. mentioned in the	2:68	footstool; and the f. thereof is his.	6:44
		are whole from the f. of the world.	6:54
FOUNDATION		slain from the f. of the world;	7:47
all men from the f. of the world,	1Ne 10:18		
the f. of a great church.	13: 4	FOUNDATIONS	
the f. of a church which is most	13: 5	and laid the f. of the earth,	2Ne 8:13
devil that he was the f. of it.	13: 6	and lay the f. of the earth,	8:16
the f. of a great and abominable	13:26	of his voice, do the f. rock,	He 12:12
whose f. is the devil,	14: 9	and lay thy f. with sapphires.	3Ne 22:11
whose f. is the devil,	14:17	who hath established the f. of	DC 78:15
the devil is the f. of it;	15:35	before the f. of this world,	130:20
hath also laid the f. of the earth,	20:13	or before the f. of the earth	Abr 1: 3
them from the f. of the world,	2Ne 9:18		
he is the f. of all these things;	26:22	FOUNDED	
yea, the f. of murder,	26:22	church, which was f. by the devil	1Ne 14: 3
things from the f. of the world	27:10	As my hand hath f. the kingdoms	2Ne 20:10
he that is built upon a sandy f.	28:28	That the Lord hath f. Zion,	24:32
might build and have safe f.	Jac 4:15	for it was f. upon a rock.	3Ne 14:25
the last, and the only sure f.,	4:16	pretensions are all f. in falsehood	DC 127: 1
after having rejected the sure f.,	4:17	f. a great city, and left a fame	135: 3
from the f. of the world,	Mos 4: 6		
from the f. of the world	4: 7	FOUNDER	
from the f. of the world,	15:19	that is the f. of peace,	Mos 15:18
from the f. of the world,	18:13	he being the f. of their church.	23:16
are laying the f. of the devil;	Al 10:17	who was the f. of their church.	29:47
the f. of the destruction of this	10:27		
laid from the f. of the world,	12:25	FOUNDERS	
from the f. of the world;	12:30	inhabitants and f. of this city;	DC 111: 9
from the f. of the world	13: 3		
from the f. of the world	13: 5	FOUNTAIN	
was from the f. of the world;	13: 7	emptied into the f. of the Red Sea,	1Ne 2: 9
from the f. of the world;	18:39	into the f. of all righteousness!	2: 9
from the f. of the world,	22:13	it also led by the head of the f.,	8:20
prepared from the f. of the world.	42:26	drowned in the depths of the f.;	8:32
to destroy the f. of liberty	46:10	led to the f. of living waters,	11:25
began the f. of a city,	50:13	Behold the f. of filthy water	12:16
also began a f. for a city	50:14	a f. of pure water,	Mos 18: 5

FOUNTAIN

the f. of all righteousness	Eth 8:26
the f. of all righteousness.	12:28
a bitter f. cannot bring forth	Mro 7:11
can a good f. bring forth	7:11
bowels shall be a f. of truth,	DC 85: 7

FOUNTAINS

of many waters, rivers, and f.;	Mrm 6: 4
the sea, and the f. of waters.—	DC 133:39

FOUR

his wife Sariah, and his f. sons,	1Ne 1:hd
traveled for the space of f. days,	16:13
the waters for the space of f. days,	18:15
from the f. quarters of the earth.	19:16
from the f. quarters of the earth;	22:25
and from the f. parts of the earth;	2Ne 10: 8
from the f. corners of the earth.	21:12
f. hundred and seventy-six years	Mos 6: 4
they have brought twenty-f. plates	8: 9
I went again with f. of my men	9: 5
about two hundred and f. souls;	18:16
about f. hundred and fifty souls.	18:35
twenty and f. of the daughters of	20: 5
f. of them were the sons of	27:34
was as great as f. senums.	Al 11:12
concerning those twenty-f. plates,	37:21
in f. hundred years from the	45:10
even for the space of f. years	46:38
even for the space of f. years.	48:20
f. thousand of those dissenters	51:19
f. thousand who had not been	62:17
thousand and f. hundred men,	63: 4
f. hundred years pass not away	He 13: 5
f. hundred years shall not pass	13: 9
from the f. quarters of the earth	3Ne 5:24
from the f. quarters of the earth	5:26
from the f. quarters of the earth;	16: 5
he kept it eighty and f. years,	4Ne 1:20
hundred and ninety and f. years	1:21
hundred and forty and f. years	1:40
are about twenty and f. years old	Mrm 1: 3
for the space of about f. years,	1:12
army of forty and f. thousand.	2: 9
hundred and forty and f. years	2:15
hundred and eighty and f. years	6: 5
it were twenty and f. of us,	6:11
save it were those twenty and f.	6:15
f. hundred years have passed	8: 6
from the twenty and f. plates	Eth 1: 2
for the space of f. years.	2:13
at the end of f. years that the	2:14
hundred and forty and f. days	6:11
And Jared had f. sons;	6:14
were twelve, he having f. sons.	6:20
he lived f. years, and he saw	9:22
had reigned twenty and f. years,	10:30
the f. quarters of the earth,	13:11
were for the space of f. years	15:14
f. hundred and twenty years	Mro 10: 1
the f. quarters of the earth.	DC 33: 6
the f. quarters of the earth.	45:46
to understand by the f. beasts,	77: 2
Are the f. beasts limited to	77: 3
limited to f. individual beasts,	77: 3
by the f. and twenty elders,	77: 5
understand by the f. angels,	77: 8
f. angels sent forth from God,	77: 8
over the f. parts of the earth,	77: 8
he crieth unto the f. angels	77: 9
hundred and forty-f. thousand,	77:11
be doubled unto you f.-fold;	98:26
and reward thee f.-fold in	98:44
and restore f.-fold for all their	98:47
council of twenty-f. high priests	102: 1
seventeen elders, f. priests, and	102: 5
difficult, f. shall be appointed;	102:14
one hundred and thirty-f. years	107:44
thirty-four years and f. months,	107:44
Mahalaleel was f. hundred and	107:46
f. hundred and thirty years old	107:49
over twenty-f. of the teachers,	107:86
from the f. parts of the earth,	DC 110:11
world, to the f. corners thereof,	124: 3
upon the f. corners of the earth,	124:128
f. winds, from one end of heaven	133: 7
hundred and forty-f. thousand,	133:18
and both received f. balls.	135: 1
in a savage manner with f. balls,	135: 2
to the f. quarters of the earth;	135: 3
Hyrum Smith was forty-f. years	135: 6
parted, and became into f. heads.	Mses 3:10
the f. quarters of the earth,	7:62
f. hundred and thirty years.	8: 1
f. hundred and fifty years old,	8:12
parted and became into f. heads.	Abr 5:10
earth in its f. quarters.	Fac 2: 6
the f. quarters of the earth.	JS 1:27
of his elect from the f. winds,	1:37
In about f. years after my	2: 3
f. of them joined that church,	2: 7
until f. years from that time;	2:53

FOURFOLD

not repay f. for the stock	DC 124:71

FOUR-FOLD: see FOUR and FOLD.

FOURTEEN

for the space of f. years among	Al 17: 4
between f. and fifteen years	JS 2:22
a little over f. years of age,	2:23

FOURTEENTH

until the f. year of the reign of	Al 16:12
thus ended the f. year of the reign	16:21
the commencement of the f. year,	3Ne 2:17
And thus ended the f. year.	2:18

FOURTH

saw many of the f. generation	1Ne 12:12
f. day, which we had been driven	18:14
and many of the f. generation	2Ne 26: 9
unto the third and f. generations	Mos 13:13
the f. day of this seventh month,	Al 10: 6
even the f. generation shall not	45:12
sent again the f. time his message	47:12
of the twenty and f. year of	50:25
ended the twenty and f. year of	50:35
end of the the twenty and f. year,	50:40
in the forty and f. year;	He 3: 2
in the fifty and f. year there	4: 1
thus the sixty and f. year did	6:13
thus in the seventy and f. year	11: 5
in the eighty and f. year they	11:36
be those of the f. generation	13:10
those of the f. generation shall	13:10
that in the ninety and f. year,	3Ne 1:28
also, and the twenty and f.,	5: 7
in the thirty and f. year,	8: 5
on the f. day of the month,	8: 5
of the thirty and f. year,	10:18
because of the f. generation	27:32
thirty and f. year passed away,	4Ne 1: 1
hundred and sixty and f. year	Mrm 4: 7
in the f. year, did beat Shared,	Eth 13:24
in the f. month, and on the	DC 20: 1
in the f. month, and on the	21: 3
And unto the f., and so on	88:55
also, and the third, and the f.,	88:57
shall sound, which is the f. trump,	88:102
the third and f. generation.	98:28
the third and f. generation,	98:29
the third and f. generation.	98:30
to the third and f. generation.	98:37
against thee the f. time	98:44
the third and f. generation.	98:46
the third and f. generation of	103:26
the third and f. generation of	105:30
made on the f. day of July next;	115:10
unto the third and f. generation,	124:50
unto the third and f. generation,	124:52
and the morning were the f. day.	Mses 2:19
the f. river was the Euphrates.	3:14

FOURTH 358 FREEDOM

day; and it was the f. time.	Abr	4:19
also the f. or last chapter	JS	2:36
f., Laying on of hands for the	AoF	4

FOWL

neither of any manner of f.;	Al	34:10
like unto the lightness of a f.	Eth	2:16
beast or animal or f.		6: 4
and f. which may fly above	Mses	2:20
every winged f. after his kind;		2:21
and let f. multiply in the earth;		2:22
and over the f. of the air,		2:26
and over the f. of the air,		2:28
and to every f. of the air,		2:30
the field, and every f. of the air;		3:19
cattle, and to the f. of the air,		3:20
and the f., that they may fly	Abr	4:20
every winged f. after their kind.		4:21
and cause the f. to multiply		4:22
and over the f. of the air,		4:26
and over the f. of the air,		4:28
and to every f. of the air,		4:30
and every f. of the air,		5:20
all cattle, to the f. of the air,		5:21
and the f. of the air,	2Ne	2:15
Behold the f. of the air,	3Ne	13:26
snares and catch f. of the air;	Eth	2: 2
and the f. of the air shall	DC	29:20
and beasts, and f. of the air,		29:24
the field and the f. of the air,		49:19
the field and the f. of the air,		59:16
and of the f. of the air;		77: 2
beasts and of the f. of the air,		89:12
the field, and the f. of heaven,		89:14
rye for the f. and for swine,		89:17
or of the f. of the heavens,		101:24
For have I not the f. of heaven,		117: 6
and the f. of the air;	Mses	8:26

FRAGMENTS

and in broken f. upon the face	He	14:22
they were found in broken f.,	3Ne	8:18

FRAILTIES

O the vainness, and the f.,	2Ne	9:28

FRAME

that my f. has no strength.	1Ne	17:47
about to yield up this mortal f.	Mos	2:26
my whole f. doth tremble		2:30
shall be restored to its proper f.,	Al	11:43
shall be restored to its perfect f.,		11:44
this had overcome his natural f.,		19: 6
to their proper and perfect f.		40:23
every thing to its natural f.—		41: 4
should be a f. of pickets built		50: 3
no part of their f. that it did	3Ne	11: 3

FRAMED

shall the thing f. say of him that	2Ne	27:27
say of him that f. it, he had no		27:27
except such laws are f. and	DC	134: 2

FRAMER

the f. of heaven and earth,	DC	20:17

FRAMES

their f. did shake before him.	1Ne	2:14

FRANKLY

I did f. forgive them	1Ne	7:21

FRAUD

thus Amalickiah, by his f.,	Al	47:30
by his f.. and by the assistance		47:35
thus become obtaining power by f.		48: 7
had a perfect knowledge of his f.;		55: 1
he may sell goods without f.,	DC	57: 8

FREDERICK: see WILLIAMS, Frederick G.

FREE

should be a f. man like unto us	1Ne	4:33
and salvation is f.	2Ne	2: 4
they have become f. forever,		2:26
men are f. according to the flesh;		2:27
they are f. to choose liberty and		2:27
Jew and Gentile, both bond and f.,		10:16
ye are f. to act for yourselves—		10:23
he hath given it f. for all men;		26:27
black and white, bond and f.,		26:33
and f. with your substance,	Jac	2:17
under this head ye are made f.,	Mos	5: 8
head whereby ye can be made f.		5: 8
of their own f. will		18:28
wherewith ye have been made f.,		23:13
old and young, both bond and f.,	Al	1:30
old and young, both bond and f.;		5:49
old and young, both bond and f.,		11:44
and that they were a f. people,		21:21
were f. from the oppressions of		21:21
have f. access to their houses,		23: 2
that this people is a f. people.		30:24
might maintain a f. government,		46:35
f. from wars and contentions		48:20
overthrow the f. government		51: 5
religion by a f. government.		51: 6
God has made them f.;		58:40
redeemed us and made us f.,		58:41
the which God hath made us f.		61: 9
God hath made them f.		61:21
Ammon and become a f. people.		62:27
f. intercourse one with another,	He	6: 8
for behold, ye are f.; ye are		14:30
and he hath made you f.		14:30
they have been made f.		15: 8
and be set up as a f. people by	3Ne	21: 4
not rich and poor, bond and f.,	4Ne	1: 3
they were all made f.,		1: 3
shall be f. from bondage,	Eth	2:12
that it might be f. unto all of	DC	10:51
strength, whether in bonds or f.;		24:11
and you shall be a f. people,		38:22
and young, both bond and f.,		43:20
things of their own f. will,		58:27
wherewith ye are made f.;		88:86
I, the Lord God, make you f.,		98: 8
therefore ye are f. indeed;		98: 8
and the law also maketh you f.		98: 8
by their own f. will and act,		124:69
for the prisoners shall go f.		128:22
the f. exercise of conscience,		134: 2
the f. exercise of their religious		134: 7
the f. gift of the Lord thy God,		136:27
saying: I am f.; surely the flocks	Mses	5:33

FREED

if ye were f. from sin?	2Ne	9:47

FREEDOM

and out of captivity unto f.	2Ne	3: 5
yea, their f. from bondage.	Al	43:48
liberty and their f. from bondage.		43:49
cried unto the Lord for their f.,		43:50
of our God, our religion, and f.,		46:12
the f. of the land might be		46:16
to support the cause of f.,		46:35
who denied the covenant of f.		46:35
and the f. of his country,		48:11
and the f. of the people,		50:39
to maintain the cause of f.		51: 7
to fight valiantly for their f.		51:21
the f. of their country.		59:13
and the f. of this people;		60:10
been true to the cause of our f.,		60:16
show unto me a true spirit of f.,		60:25
you that has a desire for f.,		60:27
even a spark of f. remaining,		60:27
this people in the cause of our f.		60:30
f. and welfare of my country.		60:36
of their country and their f.,		61: 6
that we may retain our f.,		61:14
Spirit of f. which is in them.		61:15
not also a traitor to the f.		62: 1
swords in the defence of their f.,		62: 5
was found denying their f.		62:10

FREEDOM

not true to the cause of f.	Al	62:11
and their f. and their liberty.	3Ne	2:12
overthrow the f. of all lands,	Eth	8:25
supporting that principle of f.	DC	98: 5
over my church, in the land of F.		106: 1
never suppress the f. of the soul.		134: 4
sacred the f. of conscience.		134: 5

FREELY

they did drink f. of the wine	Mos	22:10
and him will I f. forgive.		26:22
the bread and the waters of life f.;	Al	5:34
partake of the waters of life f.;		42:27
they did take of the wine f.;		55:13
they took of it more f.;		55:13
partake of the waters of life f.	DC	10:66
impart it f. to the printing of		19:26
And speak f. to all; yea, preach,		19:37
of the garden thou mayest f. eat,	Mses	3:16
these things f. unto your children,		6:58
of the garden thou mayest f. eat,	Abr	5:12

FREEMEN

took upon them the name of f.;	Al	51: 6
the f. had sworn or covenanted		51: 6
the people came in favor of the f.,		51: 7
I will leave a part of my f. to		60:25
those of my people who are f.,		61: 3
and have daunted our f. that		61: 4
driven the f. out of the land		62: 6

FRENZIED

it is the effect of a f. mind;	Al	30:16

FREQUENT

were very f. in the land—	Al	46:40
avoid the too f. repetition of his	DC	107: 4

FREQUENTLY

I f. fell into many foolish	JS	2:28

FRESH

and the men of Lehi were f.	Al	52:28
were f. and full of strength;		52:31
a f. army of the Lamanites did	Mrm	4: 2

FRET

hungry, they shall f. themselves,	2Ne	18:21

FRIEND

art a true f. unto my son, Nephi,	2Ne	1:30
know that he is a f. to the king.	Al	18: 3
Antiomno, is a f. unto me;		20: 4
yea, a true f. to liberty;		62:37
now Omer was a f. to Akish;	Eth	8:11
to be your f. and brother	DC	88:133
never deviating f., JOSEPH SMITH.		128:25
we found a f. in a gentleman	JS	2:61

FRIENDLY

and those who are f. to Nephi	Jac	1:14
people f. one with another;	Mos	24: 5
might become f. to one another,		28: 2
they were f. with the Nephites;	Al	23:18
warm hearts and f. hands.	DC	121: 9
had become very f. to me,	JS	2:75

FRIENDS

saying: My f. and my brethren,	Mos	4: 4
he has his f. in iniquity,		29:22
I have many kindreds and f.,	Al	10: 4
by those who were once his f.		15:16
that those judges had many f.	3Ne	6:27
family and his kindred and f.;		7: 2
and many kindreds and f.;		7: 4
the f. and kindreds of those who		7: 6
his family, kindred and f.;		7:14
loss of their kindred and f.		10: 8
have not f. nor whither to go;	Mrm	8: 5
from them who are our f.,	Eth	1:36
had compassion upon their f.		1:37
also thy f. and their families,		1:41
and the f. of Jared and		1:41
and also the f. of Jared and		2: 1
the f. of Jared and his brother		6:16
unto his kindred and f.,		8:17
of Akish and his f.,		9: 1
among your f., and in all places.	DC	23: 6
in the house of my f.		45:52
make unto yourselves f. with		82:22
hath given me; ye are my f.;		84:63
again I say unto you, my f.,		84:77
henceforth I shall call you f.,		84:77
become even as my f. in days		84:77
even upon you my f.,		88: 3
verily I say unto you, my f.,		88:62
verily I say unto you, my f.,		88:117
other words, I will call you f.,		93:45
friends, for you are my f.,		93:45
Now, I say unto you, my f.,		93:51
verily I say unto you, my f.,		94: 1
Verily I say unto you my f.,		97: 1
Verily I say unto you my f.,		98: 1
my f. Sidney and Joseph,		100: 1
Verily I say unto you, my f.,		103: 1
Verily I say unto you, my f.,		104: 1
behold, I say unto you, my f.,		105:26
calling us thy f., saying—		109: 6
Thy f. do stand by thee,		121: 9
thy f. do not contend against thee,		121:10
in defending themselves, their f.,		134:11
ought to have been my f.	JS	2:28

FRIGHTEN

Lamanites, that they did f. them;	Al	56:56
that they did f. my armies;	Mrm	2: 3

FRIGHTENED

saw me he was exceedingly f.,	1Ne	4:28
they began to be f. exceedingly		18:13
and they were much f. because	Mos	23:26
that they should not be f.,		23:27
that the Lamanites became f.,	Al	43:39
after them, they were f. again,		47:29
f. at the city Ammonihah;		49:15
they were again f. and fled		62:31
the Lamanites were not f.	He	1:27
could not be f. by the demands	3Ne	3:12
that the people began to be f.,	Eth	14:27

FRO

captive, and removing to and f.?	1Ne	21:21
they are scattered to and f. upon		22: 4
after they are driven to and f.,	2Ne	6:11
driven and scattered to and f.,	Mos	17:17
and to be driven to and f.,		21:13
they shall be driven to and f.	He	15:12
to and f. in the earth, seeking	DC	10:27
tremble, and reel to and f.,		45:48
to and f. as a drunken man,		49:23
to and f. as a drunken man;		88:87

FROM: *see in the APPENDIX.*

FRONT

time they were met in the f.	Al	56:23
both in their f. and in their rear.	3Ne	4:25
being led in the f. by me.	Mrm	6:11

FROST

melt away as the hoar f. melteth	DC	121:11

FRUIT

of the seeds of f. of every kind.	1Ne	8: 1
a tree, whose f. was desirable		8:10
and partake of the f. thereof;		8:11
that the f. thereof was white,		8:11
as I partook of the f. thereof		8:12
it was desirable above all other f.		8:12
tree of which I was partaking the f.		8:13
come unto me, and partake of the f.,		8:15
was desirable above all other f.		8:15
come unto me and partake of the f.		8:16
should come and partake of the f.		8:17

FRUIT

come unto me and partake of the f.	1Ne	8:18
come forth and partake of the f.		8:24
after they had partaken of the f.		8:25
and were partaking of the f.		8:27
after they had tasted of the f.		8:28
and fell down and partook of the f.		8:30
those that were partaking of the f.		8:33
and Lemuel partook not of the f.,		8:35
beheld the tree which bore the f.		11: 7
of life, whose f. is most precious		15:36
Bountiful, because of its much f.		17: 5
Bountiful, because of its much f.		17: 6
the forbidden f. in opposition to	2Ne	2:15
Partake of the forbidden f.		2:18
had partaken of the forbidden f.		2:19
thou art the f. of my loins;		3: 4
out of the f. of his loins		3: 5
choice Seer unto the f. of my loins.		3: 6
out of the f. of thy loins;		3: 7
among the f. of thy loins.		3: 7
a work for the f. of thy loins,		3: 7
out of the f. of thy loins;		3:11
the f. of thy loins shall write;		3:12
the f. of the loins of Judah		3:12
written by the f. of thy loins,		3:12
by the f. of the loins of Judah,		3:12
peace among the f. of thy loins,		3:12
of the Lord, of the f. of my loins,		3:14
unto the f. of thy loins		3:18
writing of the f. of thy loins,		3:18
unto the f. of thy loins		3:18
unto the f. of thy loins.		3:19
as if the f. of thy loins had cried		3:19
who are the f. of thy loins;		3:21
shall eat the f. of their doings.		13:10
the f. of the earth excellent		14: 2
I will punish the f. of the stout		20:12
no pity on the f. of the womb;		23:18
his f. shall be a fiery flying		24:29
from the f. of the loins of Joseph.	Jac	2:25
I may preserve the f. thereof		5: 8
that I may lay up f. thereof		5:13
lose this tree and the f. thereof.		5:13
sprung forth and begun to bear f.		5:17
the f. thereof was like unto		5:17
was like unto the natural f.		5:17
have brought forth tame f.		5:18
behold, I shall lay up much f.,		5:18
the f. thereof I shall lay up		5:18
have not brought forth much f.		5:19
I may lay up of the f. thereof		5:19
that it had brought forth much f.;		5:20
Take of the f. thereof, and lay it		5:20
and it hath brought forth much f.		5:20
that it hath brought forth much f.		5:22
and it hath brought forth much f.;		5:23
and it hath brought forth f.		5:24
tree hath brought forth tame f.,		5:25
tree hath brought forth wild f.;		5:25
have not brought forth good f.,		5:26
may bring forth good f. unto thee,		5:27
nourish all the f. of the vineyard.		5:28
must lay up f. against the season,		5:29
all sorts of f. did cumber the tree.		5:30
of the vineyard did taste of the f.,		5:31
myself against the season much f.		5:31
it hath brought forth much f.,		5:32
there are all kinds of good f.;		5:32
preserve again good f. thereof		5:33
long as it shall bring forth evil f.		5:35
from the wild branches, good f.		5:36
hath brought forth much evil f.;		5:37
brought forth so much evil f.		5:37
have also brought forth evil f.		5:38
the f. of the natural branches		5:39
And the wild f. of the last had		5:40
tree which brought forth good f.,		5:40
that all the f. of the vineyard,		5:42
have once brought forth good f.		5:42
part thereof brought forth good f.,		5:45
part thereof brought forth wild f.;		5:45
that they bring forth no good f.;		5:46
to have laid up f. thereof against		5:46
branches whose f. is most bitter,	Jac	5:52
may bring forth good f. unto me,		5:54
glory in the f. of my vineyard.		5:54
may bring forth again good f.;		5:60
again in the f. of my vineyard,		5:60
and the branches of the first f.−		5:60
bring forth again the natural f.,		5:61
which natural f. is good		5:61
most precious above all other f.		5:61
and bring forth the natural f.,		5:64
which bring forth bitter f.,		5:65
shall bring forth the natural f.,		5:68
ye shall have joy in the f. which		5:71
began to be the natural f. again in		5:73
had become again the natural f.;		5:74
unto himself the natural f.,		5:74
saw that his f. was good,		5:75
I have preserved the natural f.,		5:75
unto me again the natural f.,		5:75
because of the f. of my vineyard.		5:75
lay up of the f. of my vineyard		5:76
up unto mine own self of the f.,		5:76
evil f. shall again come into my		5:77
will ye bring forth evil f.,		6: 7
and of f., and flocks of herds,	En	1:21
his partaking of the forbidden f.;	Mos	3:26
all manner of f. of every kind.		10: 4
of the f. of the tree of life;	Al	5:34
bringeth forth not good f.,		5:36
that bringeth not forth good f.		5:52
of the f. of the tree of life.		5:62
forth f. meet for repentance.		12:15
of the f. of the tree of life,		12:21
the partaking of the forbidden f.,		12:22
of the f. of the tree of life		12:23
bring forth f. meet for repentance,		13:13
and have brought forth much f.;		29:15
who are the f. of their labors		29:17
and bring forth f. unto us.		32:37
and grow up, and bring forth f.		32:37
neither is it because the f. thereof		32:39
ye cannot have the f. thereof.		32:39
with an eye of faith to the f.		32:40
pluck of the f. of the tree of life.		32:40
looking forward to the f. thereof,		32:41
ye shall pluck the f. thereof,		32:42
and ye shall feast upon this f.		32:42
the tree to bring forth f. unto you.		32:43
that they might obtain this f.		33: 1
and bring f. unto repentance.		34:30
great joy in the f. of my labors;		36:25
he should not partake of the f.−		42: 3
partake of the forbidden f.	He	6:26
that she may bring forth her f.,		11:13
that it did bring forth her f.		11:17
fruit in the season thereof.		11:17
good tree bringeth forth good f.;	3Ne	14:17
corrupt tree bringeth forth evil f.		14:17
tree cannot bring forth evil f.		14:18
corrupt tree bring forth good f.		14:18
that bringeth not forth good f.		14:19
shall your vine cast her f.		24:11
Having all manner of f.,	Eth	9:17
to be f. in the north countries,		9:35
save they brought forth f. meet	Mro	6: 1
joy in the f. of your labors.	DC	6:31
drink of the f. of the vine		27: 5
he partook of the forbidden f.		29:40
kept and blessed with much f.		52:34
That they may bring forth f.		84:58
every f. in the season thereof;		89:11
as also the f. of the vine;		89:16
that which yieldeth f., whether		89:16
that bringeth not forth good f.		97: 7
that yieldeth much precious f.		97: 9
the f. of my vineyard.		101:45
bring forth f. and works		101:100
they shall eat the f. thereof.		101:101
his seed, and of the f. of his loins−		132:30
the f. tree yielding fruit,	Mses	2:11
the fruit tree yielding f.,		2:11
and the tree yielding f.,		2:11
and the tree yielding f.,		2:12

FRUIT — FULFILLED

FRUIT
the f. of a tree yielding seed;	Mses	2:29
may eat of the f. of the trees		4: 8
of the f. of the tree which thou		4: 9
she took of the f. thereof, and did		4:12
she gave me of the f. of the tree		4:18
hast eaten of the f. of the tree		4:23
Cain brought of the f. of the		5:19
should be of the f. of his loins.		8: 2
the f. tree yielding fruit, after	Abr	4:11
yielding f., after his kind,		4:11
tree from its own seed, yielding f.,		4:12
which shall have f. upon it;		4:29
the f. of the tree yielding seed		4:29

FRUITFUL
a vineyard in a very f. hill.	2Ne	15: 1
and of his f. field,		20:18
shall be turned into a f. field;		27:28
the f. field shall be esteemed as		27:28
bring forth as a very f. tree	DC	97: 9
Be f., and multiply, and fill	Mses	2:22
Be f., and multiply, and		2:28
cause them to be f. and multiply,	Abr	4:22
them to be f. and multiply,		4:28

FRUITS
desirable above all other f.;	1Ne	15:36
f. and meat from the wilderness,		18: 6
he is the first-f. unto God,	2Ne	2: 9
the first-f. of Christ unto God,	Jac	4:11
and the f. were equal;		5:74
with seeds of all manner of f.;	Mos	9: 9
and see the f. of our labors;	Al	26:31
to partake of the f. of their labors		40:26
shall know them by their f.	3Ne	14:16
by their f. ye shall know them.		14:20
destroy the f. of your ground;		24:11
the first f. of repentance is	Mro	8:25
f. of praise and wisdom,	DC	52:17
and bringeth not forth f.,		52:18
They are Christ's, the first f.,		88:98

FRUSTRATED
redemption would have been f.,	Al	12:26
of salvation would have been f.		42: 5
of the prophets had been f.;	3Ne	1:16
purposes of God cannot be f.,	DC	3: 1
not the work of God that is f.,		3: 3

FUEL
with burning and f. of fire.	2Ne	19: 5
shall be as the f. of the fire;		19:19

FUGITIVE
A f. and a vagabond shalt thou	Mses	5:37
I shall be a f. and a vagabond		5:39

FULFIL: see also FULFILL.
God will f. his covenants which	2Ne	6:12
to f. the merciful plan of the		9: 6
For I will f. my promises		10:17
by water, to f. all righteousness,		31: 5
of God did f. all righteousness		31: 6
to f. the commandment of my	Jac	1: 8
I must f. the commandments	Mos	13: 4
and we f. the oath which we have		20:22
to f. the commandments of God.		29:45
For he will f. all his promises	Al	37:17
see that ye f. the word of God.		60:35
not come to destroy but to f.;	3Ne	12:17
I have come to f. the law;		15: 5
I may f. other commandments		18:27
I f. the commandment of my	Mrm	8: 3
to f. the promises that I have	DC	45:16
Lord speaketh, he will also f.		85:10
that I may f. this promise,		88:75
even so will I f.—		105:14
f. that which I have commanded		105:28
f. that which thou hast spoken		109:23
f. the promises which ye expect		124:47
f. the promise which was given		132:63
f. the oath which I have made	Mses	7:60

FULFILL: see also FULFIL.
he will f. his word which he hath	1Ne	20:14
I will f. all that which I have	3Ne	1:13
to f. all things which I have		1:14
then will I f. the covenant		16: 5
to f. and to do the work of	Mro	7:31

FULFILLED
the word of the Lord shall be f.	1Ne	7:13
destruction of Jerusalem must be f.		7:13
the covenant which should be f.		15:18
had f. all the commandments		16: 8
commandments of God must be f.		17: 3
fruit of my loins, shall be f.	2Ne	3:14
words of the Lord had been f.		5:19
the word of the Lord was f.		5:20
and his law must be f.		9:17
that my covenants may be f.		10:15
prophecies of Isaiah shall be f.		25: 7
promise may be f. unto Joseph,		25:21
until the law shall be f.		25:24
after the law is f. in Christ,		25:27
until the law shall be f.		25:30
that many of them have been f.;	WM	1: 4
down to this day have been f.,		1: 4
the promise of the Lord is f.,	Mos	7:32
are not the words of Abinadi f.,		20:21
the word of the Lord might be f.		21: 4
Thus the word of God is f.,	Al	3:14
that the word of God may be f.,		5:57
for the word of God must be f.		5:58
this that the word might be f.		7:11
words of our fathers may be f.,		13:26
as yet, for it was not all f.		25:15
of Moses until it should be f.		30: 3
shall the law of Moses be f.;		34:13
yea, it shall be all f., every jot		34:13
for he has f. his promises which		37:17
behold, one purpose hath he f.,		37:17
the word of God might be f.,		37:24
the word of God has been f.;		37:26
even until the prophecy is f.;		45: 9
this prophecy shall be f.		45:14
Amalickiah had f. his commands,		47:21
our destruction be f.	He	11: 8
of the prophets began to be f.		16:13
the scriptures began to be f.		16:14
of the prophets began to be f.	3Ne	1: 4
was past for the words to be f.,		1: 5
words of Samuel are not f.;		1: 6
which came unto Nephi were f.,		1:15
that the law was not yet f.,		1:25
it must be f. in every whit;		1:25
unto them that it must be f.,		1:25
pass away till it should all be f.;		1:25
they had f. the commandment		4:13
needs be that they must be f.		5: 1
be f. according to their faith,		5:14
be f. in his own due time,		5:25
concerning my coming are f.		9:16
in me is the law of Moses f.		9:17
thus far were the scriptures f.		10:11
but in me it hath all been f.		12:18
before you, and the law is f.		12:19
under the law, in me are all f.		12:46
say unto you that the law is f.		15: 4
therefore, the law in me is f.,		15: 5
many as have not been f. in me,		15: 6
I say unto you, shall all be f.		15: 6
with my people is not all f.;		15: 8
of the prophet Isaiah shall be f.,		16:17
words of Isaiah should be f.—		20:11
that when they shall be f. then		20:12
covenanted with his people be f.;		20:46
covenant of the Father may be f.		21: 4
thy words, and they were all f.		23:10
even until all things shall be f.		28: 7
that their desire may be f.,		28:29
is already beginning to be f.		29: 1
holy prophets, shall all be f.;		29: 2
until all his promises shall be f.	Mrm	8:22
when all these things must be f.		8:33

FULFILLED 362 FULL

that by faith all things are f.—	Eth 12: 3	unto the f. the commandments;	Mro	8:25
is by faith that it hath been f.	12:11	the f. the commandments		8:25
that they were f. thus far,	15: 3	unto the f. of the prophecies		8:29
of the Lord had all been f.;	15:33	unto the f. of the prophecies.		10:28
O house of Israel, may be f.	Mro 10:31	f., among other things, the	DC 132:34
decreed in them shall be f.	DC 1: 7			
and all this that it might be f.,	1:18	**FULFILMENT**		
which are in them shall all be f.	1:37	f. of these commandments	DC 103:40
not pass away, but shall all be f.,	1:38	secure a f. of the promises		109:11
promises of the Lord might be f.,	3:19	declaring the f. of the prophets—	128:20
until my purpose is f. in this;	5: 4	a f. of those things which were	Abr 1:29
he hath f. the thing which	18: 7			
that the scriptures might be f.;	24:14	**FULL**		
by mine apostles must be f.;	29:10	I, Nephi, do not make a f. account	1Ne 1:16
even so shall they be f.,	29:30	I shall not make a f. account.		1:16
surely these things shall be f.	35:22	their joy was f., and my mother was	5: 7
of my prophets shall be f.;	42:39	a f. account of all the things of	6: 3
pass away until all shall be f.	45:23	upon which I make a f. account	9: 2
the times of the Gentiles be f.	45:25	upon which I make a f. account	9: 2
the times of the Gentiles be f.	45:30	f. of idleness and all manner of	12:23
been made un to you shall be f.	45:35	I am f. of the Spirit of God,	17:47
the parable be f. which I spake	45:56	for he is f. of grace and truth.	2Ne 2: 6
I have promised I have so f.,	49:10	an idle people, f. of mischief	5:24
that the prophecies may be f.	52:36	they are f. of the fury of the Lord,	8:20
not pass away, but shall be f.	56:11	and their joy shall be f. forever.	9:18
have promised and have not f.?	58:31	Their land also is f. of silver	12: 7
for his promises are not f.	58:33	their land is also f. of horses,	12: 7
that the promise might be f.,	62: 6	Their land is also f. of idols;	12: 8
law of Moses, which law was f.	74: 3	the whole earth is f. of his glory.	16: 3
covenant that they shall be f.;	98: 3	earth shall be f. of the knowledge	21: 9
that the prophets might be f.	101:19	shall be f. of doleful creatures;	23:21
many days all things were f.	101:62	earth shall be f. of the knowledge	30:15
and my word must needs be f.	101:64	the Son, with f. purpose of heart,	31:13
appoint unto them shall be f.	105:22	come with f. purpose of heart,	Jac 6: 5
her law be executed and f.,	105:34	f. of idolatry and filthiness;	En 1:20
it shall be f. upon you	108: 6	and these plates are f.	Om 1:30
Let it be f. upon them,	109:36	meek, humble, patient, f. of love,	Mos 3:19
But thy word must be f.	109:44	with f. purpose of heart,	7:33
f. that which was written	133:63	f. of grace, and mercy, and	Al 5:48
of my mouth they must be f.	Mses 4:30	f. of patience and long-suffering,	7:23
wherefore they must be f.	5:15	f. of grace, equity, and truth,	9:26
of the Lord might be f.,	8: 2	f. of patience, mercy, and	9:26
by Daniel the prophet, be f.	JS 1:32	of God until he know them in f.	12:10
all I have told you shall be f.	1:34	is f. of grace, equity, and truth.	13: 9
not pass away but all shall be f.	1:35	f. of all manner of wickedness;	13:17
Then shall be f. that which	1:44	f. of love and all long-suffering;	13:28
that it was about to be f.	2:40	but behold, my joy is f.,	26:11
said that this was not yet f.,	2:41	we will rejoice, for our joy is f.;	26:16
be obtained was not yet f.—	2:42	our joy would be f. if perhaps we	26:30
		was so great even that he was f.;	27:17
FULFILLETH		success, in the which my joy is f.	29:13
then f. the Father the covenant	3Ne 20:27	my joy is more f. because of the	29:14
for this cause he f. the words	27:18	was f. of the Lamanites.	31: 3
he lieth not, but f. all his words.	27:18	let your hearts be f., drawn out in	34:27
		let thy heart be f. of thanks unto	37:37
FULFILLING		his long-suffering have f. sway	42:30
unto the f. of all his words.	1Ne 9: 6	were fresh and f. of strength;	52:31
unto the f. of the word of the Lord,	10:13	is unspeakable and f. of glory.	He 5:44
way for the f. of his covenants,	14:17	unto me with f. purpose of heart.	3Ne 10: 6
power, unto the f. of his word	18:11	unto me with f. purpose of heart,	12:24
unto the f. of the words of Moses,	22:20	whole body shall be f. of light.	13:22
I am sure of the f. of this promise;	2Ne 3:14	body shall be f. of darkness.	13:23
unto the f. of the promise which	31:18	And now behold, my joy is f.	17:20
so f. the commandments of God,	Mos 1: 1	unto me with f. purpose of heart,	18:32
they were f. the words of God	Al 3:18	yea, your joy shall be f., even	28:10
to the f. of all his words.	37:16	I did make a f. account of all	Mrm 2:18
diligent in f. all my words,	37:20	forbear to make a f. account of	2:18
to the f. of all his words unto	50:19	daring not to give a f. account	5: 9
because of the f. the oath which	56: 8	he may get the f. account.	Eth 1: 4
according to the f. of his word.	60:16	I give not the f. account,	1: 5
misery, f. the words which say:	He 12:26	could not make a f. account	3:17
time of the f. of the covenant	3Ne 10: 7	days, which were f. of sorrow.	9:15
unto the f. of the prophecies of	10:14	Satan had f. power over the	15:19
this is f. my commandments,	18:10	and f. of wickedness and	DC 10:21
then is the f. of the covenant	20:12	shall be humble and f. of love,	12: 8
unto the f. of the covenant	20:22	do with f. purpose of heart,	17: 1
unto the f. of the covenant	21: 7	name with f. purpose of heart.	18:27
unto the f. of the covenant	29: 9	name with f. purpose of heart,	18:28
unto the f. of all the words	Mrm 1:19	cup of mine indignation is f.;	29:17
unto the f. of his covenant;	5:14	ye have received them in f.	42:57
the f. of the covenant which	Eth 13:11	wrath of mine indignation is f.	43:26
see the f. of the prophecies	13:21	whose eyes are f. of greediness,	56:17
to the f. the commandments	Mro 8:11	that thy joy may be f.	59:13

FULL 363 FURNACE

your mission is not yet f.	DC 62: 2
who is f. of grace and truth.	66:12
their eyes are f. of greediness.	68:31
they are f. of knowledge;	77: 4
our God; for he is f. of mercy,	84:102
made a f. end of all nations;	87: 6
f. of grace and truth,	93:11
the cup of their iniquity is f.	101:11
in this world your joy is not f.,	101:36
but in me your joy is f.	101:36
a f. statement of the testimony	102:26
that their cup might be f.;	103: 3
For the earth is f., and there is	104:17
so long as he is in f. fellowship,	104:75
but are f. of all manner of evil,	105: 3
being f. of the Holy Ghost,	107:56
a f. and complete deliverance	109:32
Their basket shall not be f.,	121:20
Let thy bowels also be f. of charity	121:45
shall be of f. force when they are	132:19
for he is f. of grace and truth;	Mses 1: 6
who is f. of grace and truth.	1:32
which is f. of grace and truth.	5: 7
who is f. of grace and truth,	6:52
which is f. of grace and truth,	7:11
had f. confidence in obtaining	JS 2:29

FULLER, Edson
Let my servants F. and	DC 52:28

FULLER'S
in the highway of the f. field;	2Ne 17: 3
a refiner's fire, and like f. soap.	3Ne 24: 2
refiner's fire, and like f. soap;	DC 128:24

FULLMER, David
unto this calling in his stead—F.,	DC 124:132

FULLY
I might more f. persuade them	1Ne 19:23
they are f. ripe in iniquity	2Ne 28:16
which, when it is f. ripe,	Mos 12:12
to establish the church more f.;	Al 4: 4
not yet f. made known unto me;	37:11
of God, when they are f. ripe;	37:28
repent before they are f. ripe.	37:31
more f. condemneth the sinner,	41:15
wickedly, when they are f. ripe;	45:16
began to be fulfilled more f.;	3Ne 1: 4
may more f. believe his gospel,	Mrm 5:15
sin until ye are f. ripe ye shall	Eth 2:15
more f. keep thyself unspotted	DC 59: 9
until the harvest is f. ripe;	86: 7
Behold, the time has f. come,	110:14
can f. and completely claim that	123: 6
that the storm is f. blown over,	127: 1
we consider him f. authorized	OD

FULNESS
the f. of mine intent is that	1Ne 6: 4
had received the f. of the Gospel,	10:14
through the f. of the Gentiles,	15:13
then shall the f. of the gospel of	15:13
the f. of the wrath of God was	17:35
the f. of the wrath of God shall	22:16
the f. of his wrath must come,	22:17
come out in the f. of his wrath	2Ne 1:17
in the f. of time he cometh	2: 3
cometh in the f. of time,	2:26
in the f. of his own time.	11: 7
may God grant, in his great f.,	He 12:24
through the f. of the Gentiles,	3Ne 16: 4
the f. of these things shall be	16: 7
shall reject the f. of my gospel,	16:10
I will bring the f. of my gospel	16:10
knowledge of the f. of my gospel.	16:12
received the f. of my gospel,	20:28
when the f. of my gospel shall	20:30
my joy is great, even unto f.,	27:30
and in them I have f. of joy.	27:31
cause ye shall have f. of joy;	28:10
Father hath given me f. of joy;	28:10
the f. of his wrath should come	Eth 2: 8

the f. of his wrath shall come	Eth 2: 9
the f. of his wrath cometh	2: 9
is not until the f. of iniquity	2:10
your iniquities until the f. come,	2:11
the f. of the wrath of God	2:11
pour out the f. of my wrath.	9:20
in the f. of his wrath,	14:25
that the f. of my gospel	DC 1:23
bring forth the f. of my gospel	14:10
the f. of the gospel of Jesus	20: 9
containing the f. of my	27: 5
and for the f. of times,	27:13
earth, and all the f. thereof,	29:24
to receive the f. of my gospel,	35:12
sent forth the f. of my gospel	35:17
preach the f. of my gospel,	39:11
and receive the t. of my gospel,	39:18
which is the f. of the gospel.	42:12
the f. of my scriptures is	42:15
shall be the f. of my gospel;	45:28
the f. of the earth is yours,	59:16
the f. ye have not yet received.	63:21
even the f. of my gospel,	66: 2
the f. of the gospel of Jesus	76:14
Father, and received of his f.;	76:20
who have received of his f.,	76:56
received the f. of the Father,	76:71
his glory, but not of his f.	76:76
but not of the f. of the Father.	76:77
who receive not of his f. in	76:86
of his f. and of his grace;	76:94
until the f. of times, when	76:106
which rest is the f. of his glory.	84:24
receive of the same, even a f.	88:29
receive of the same, even a f.	88:30
receive of the same, even a f.	88:31
shall hear the f. of the gospel	90:11
because he gave me of his f.,	93: 4
record of the f. of my glory,	93: 6
and the f. of John's record is	93: 6
not of the f. at the first,	93:12
received not of the f. at first,	93:13
grace, until he received a f.;	93:13
not of the f. at the first.	93:14
a f. of the glory of the Father;	93:16
the f. of the record of John.	93:18
in due time receive of his f.	93:19
you shall receive of his f.,	93:20
he received a f. of truth,	93:26
no man receiveth a f. unless	93:27
connected, receive a f. of joy;	93:33
man cannot receive a f. of joy.	93:34
words, the f. of my scriptures,	104:58
receive a f. of the Holy Ghost,	109:15
f. of the everlasting gospel;	109:65
mercy, and an infinity of f.,	109:77
dispensation of the f. of times.	112:30
my gospel, the f. thereof,	118: 4
reserve for the f. of their glory;	121:27
dispensation of the f. of times—	121:31
even the f. of the priesthood.	124:28
dispensation of the f. of times,	124:41
dispensation of the f. of times,	128:18
dispensation of the f. of times.	128:18
dispensation of the f. of times!	128:20
for the f. of my glory;	132: 6
he that receiveth a f. thereof	132: 6
which glory shall be a f. and	132:19
sent forth the f. of his gospel,	133:57
the f. of the everlasting gospel,	135: 3
and received a f. of joy;	Mses 7:67
the f. of the everlasting	JS 2:34
the f. of the Gentiles was soon	2:41

FUNDS
to receive the f. of the church	DC 72:10
that they also may obtain f.	72:21

FURIOUS
there should be a f. wind blow	Eth 6: 5

FURNACE
chosen thee in the f. of affliction.	1Ne 20:10
even as a garment in a hot f.;	Mos 12: 3

FURNACE 364 GAINED

be as a garment in a f. of fire.	Mos 12:10	to the secret band of G.,	He	8: 1
thrice they were cast into a f.	3Ne 28:21	secret band, whose author is G.		8:28
fiery f. could not harm them,	Mrm 8:24	swept away the band of G.		11:10
		out all the secret plans of G.;		11:26
FURNACES		thus they became robbers of G.		11:26
did cast them into f. of fire,	4Ne 1:32	it were for the G. robbers,	3Ne	1:27
		to join those G. robbers.		1:29
FURTHER		the G. robbers had become so		2:11
until f. commandments of the	1Ne 19: 4	arms against those G. robbers,		2:12
I durst not speak f. as yet	22:29	the G. robbers did gain many		2:18
no f. in pursuit of this people.	Mos 24:23	of this the secret society of G.;		3: 9
if you desire a f. witness,	DC 6:22	the hands of those G. robbers.		3:15
unto you f. commandments.	30: 4	oaths and combinations of G.	4Ne	1:42
to know any f. concerning this	45:60	the robbers of G. did spread		1:46
until he is called to f. duties.	47: 1	And these G. robbers, who	Mrm	1:18
f. directions shall be given	57:16	and the robbers of G.,		2:27
I give unto you f. directions	58:34	and the robbers of G.,		2:28
the elders until f. knowledge,	73: 5			
for f. instructions at my	124:88	**GADIANTON'S**		
f., I want you to remember	128: 6	among the Nephites, of G. band.	He	6:18
as I was until f. directed.	JS 2:26	they were called G. robbers		6:18
he f. stated that the fulness of	2:41			
		GADIOMNAH		
FURTHERMOST		and the city of G.,	3Ne	9: 8
march into the f. parts of	3Ne 4:23			
		GAIN		
FURY		did g. favor in the sight of Ishmael,	1Ne	7: 4
because of the f. of the oppressor,	2Ne 8:13	which are built up to get g.,		22:23
where is the f. of the oppressor?	8:13	thine afflictions for thy g.	2Ne	2: 2
of the Lord the cup of his f.—	8:17	own learning, that they may get g.		26:20
are full of the f. of the Lord,	8:20	that they may get g. and praise		26:29
the dregs of the cup of my f.;	8:22	and to get g. will they say this,		27:16
exceeding f. against Moroni.	Al 52:33	my prayers for the g. of my people.		33: 4
on both hands with exceeding f.;	52:35	g. favor in the eyes of the king	Mos	24: 1
with such f. with his strong men,	52:36	a tyrant who was seeking for g.,		29:40
vengeance and f. upon them,	3Ne 21:21	should g. the voice of the people,	Al	2: 4
and in his f. vex the nation;	DC 101:89	of these lawyers was to get g.;		10:32
and, in the f. of thine heart,	121: 5	got g. according to their employ.		10:32
I have trampled them in my f.,	133:51	was for the sole purpose to get g.,		11:20
		preach unto this people to get g.,		30:35
FUTURE		knowest that we receive no g.?		30:35
ye shall know at some f. period	1Ne 7:13	might g. power over the Nephites		43: 9
us, and our f. generations;	2Ne 4: 2	that he should not g. the point,		46:29
in f. generations they shall	9:53	he sought to g. favor of those		47: 5
be brought forth at some f. day	En 1:13	it was his intention to g. favor		47: 8
as well as unto f. generations.	Al 24:14	that they did g. advantage		51:31
his power unto f. generations.	37:14	might g. advantage over them		52:19
his power unto f. generations.	37:18	power to g. possession of those		55:20
in them unto f. generations;	37:19	g. power over the Nephites—	He	1:16
be given unto f. generations.	3Ne 26: 2	and to rob, and to g. power,		2: 8
the Lamanites, in some f. day,	Mro 1: 4	to buy and to sell, and to get g.,		6: 8
made known unto f. generations;	DC 5: 9	they began to seek to get g.		6:17
are manifest, past, present, and f.,	130: 7	plunder, that they might get g.		6:17
		get g. and glory of the world,		7: 5
FUTURITY		But behold, it is to get g.,		7:21
and principle pertaining to f.,	DC 101:78	g. some advantage of the robbers,	3Ne	2:17
there is much which lieth in f.,	123:15	g. many advantages over them.		2:18
		I will consecrate their g. unto		20:19
GABRIEL		shall say at that day, to get g.,		29: 7
the voice of G., and of Raphael,	DC 128:21	unto themselves to get g.,	4Ne	1:26
		the Nephites g. no power over	Mrm	4:18
GAD		to g. advantage over the		6: 4
city of Josh, and the city of G.,	3Ne 9:10	one shall have them to get g.;		8:14
Jeremy under the hand of G.;	DC 84:10	unto yourselves to get g.?		8:33
G. under the hand of Esaias;	84:11	secret abominations to get g.,		8:40
		g. power any more over Shule	Eth	7:19
GADIANDI		he did g. favor in the eyes of		7:22
And behold, the city of G.,	3Ne 9: 8	to g. power, and to murder, and		8:16
		to get power and g., until they		8:22
GADIANTON		built up to get power and g.—		8:23
For there was one G., who was	He 2: 4	of Akish were desirous for g.,		9:11
when G. had found that	2:11	did g. power over all the land,		10: 9
more of this G. shall be	2:12	he did g. favor in the eyes of		10:10
G. did prove the overthrow,	2:13	that they might get g.		10:22
which G. the robber had established	3:23	built up to get power and g.;		11:15
formed by Kishkumen and G.	6:18	unto themselves to get g.,	DC	10:56
given by G. and Kishkumen.	6:24	every man may g. other talents,		82:18
did not come forth unto G. from	6:26	that I may murder and get g.	Mses	5:31
put into the heart of G. by	6:26	Abel, for the sake of getting g.,		5:50
who put it into the heart of G.	6:29			
hunt the band of robbers of G.;	6:37	**GAINED**		
and those G. robbers filling the	7: 4	having g. the victory over death;	Mos	15: 8
which was established by G.!	7:25	that we have g. power over you,	Al	44: 5

GAINED 365 GATE

(for he had g. his desires)	Al	47:20
g. the hearts of the people.		47:30
Moroni had thus g. a victory over		53: 6
had g. some ground over the		53: 8
could have g. no power over us.		60:15
and g. whatsoever force he could		62: 4
had g. favor in the eyes of some,	He	8:10
g. the victory over the grave;	Mrm	7: 5
had g. the half of the kingdom.	Eth	8: 2
had g. the half of the kingdom		8: 3
he g. power over many cities;		10: 9
Com g. power over Amgid,		10:32

GAINS
if a person g. more knowledge and DC 130:19

GAINSAYING
a stiffnecked and a g. people; Jac 6: 4

GALILEE
beyond Jordan in G. of the nations. 2Ne 19: 1

GALL
from the g. of bitterness	Mos	27:29
who am in the g. of bitterness,	Al	36:18
are in the g. of bitterness and		41:11
they are in the g. of bitterness	Mrm	8:31
is in the g. of bitterness and	Mro	8:14

GALLAND, Isaac
Let my servant G. put stock into	DC 124:78
Let my servant G. be appointed	124:79

GALLIM
the voice, O daughter of G.; 2Ne 20:30

GAME
were no wild beasts nor g. in	3Ne	4: 2
was no g. for the robbers save		4: 2
the wild g. became scarce in		4:20
nor make g. of the Jews,		29: 8
for a wilderness, to get g.	Eth	10:21

GAPE
the very jaws of hell shall g. open DC 122: 7

GARB
by his brother by a g. of secrecy, He 9: 6

GARDEN
driven out of the g. of Eden,	2Ne	2:19
he would have remained in the g.		2:22
her desert like the g. of the Lord.		8: 3
on the east of the g. of Eden,	Al	12:21
forth from the g. of Eden,		42: 2
the east end of the g. of Eden,		42: 2
which was in the g. of Nephi,	He	7:10
the tower which was in his g.,		7:10
was also near unto the g. gate		7:10
together at the g. of Nephi;		9: 8
judges who were at the g. of Nephi,		9:11
cast out from the G. of Eden,	DC	29:41
a g. eastward in Eden,	Mses	3: 8
also in the midst of the g.,		3: 9
out of Eden to water the g.;		3:10
put him into the G. of Eden,		3:15
Of every tree of the g.		3:16
not eat of every tree of the g.?		4: 7
the fruit of the trees of the g.;		4: 8
beholdest in the midst of the g.,		4: 9
as they were walking in the g.,		4:14
amongst the trees of the g.		4:14
I heard thy voice in the g.,		4:16
forth from the G. of Eden,		4:29
at the east of the G. of Eden,		4:31
way toward the G. of Eden,		5: 4
in the G. of Eden.		6:53
and in the G. of Eden,		7:32
And the Gods planted a g.,	Abr	5: 8
also, in the midst of the g.,		5: 9
out of Eden, to water the g.,		5:10
and put him in the G. of Eden,		5:11

Of every tree of the g. thou	Abr	5:12
to Adam in the G. of Eden,	Fac	2: 3

GARDENS
or for g. or for vineyards; DC 59:17

GARMENT
all they shall wax old as a g.,	2Ne	7: 9
the earth shall wax old like a g.;		8: 6
moth shall eat them up like a g.,		8: 8
even as a g. in a hot furnace;	Mos	12: 3
be as a g. in a furnace of fire.		12:10
waving the rent part of his g.	Al	46:19
remnant of g. of my son hath		46:24
even as the remnant of his g.		46:24
which shall perish as his g.,		46:27
shalt not take thy brother's g.;	DC	42:54

GARMENTS
I took the g. of Laban and put	1Ne	4:19
for he beheld the g. and also the		4:21
g. are made white in his blood.		12:10
their g. were white even like		12:11
on thy beautiful g., O Jerusalem,	2Ne	8:24
I take off my g., and I shake them		9:44
and g. rolled in blood;		19: 5
might not come upon our g.;	Jac	1:19
blood would come upon our g.,		1:19
might rid my g. of your sins,		2: 2
might rid my g. of your blood,	Mos	2:28
except his g. are washed white;	Al	5:21
his g. must be purified until		5:21
your g. stained with blood		5:22
prophets, whose g. are cleansed		5:24
your g. have been cleansed		5:27
and keep your g. spotless,		7:25
having your g. spotless even		7:25
even as their g. are spotless,		7:25
and their g. were washed white		13:11
having their g. made white,		13:12
their g. should be made white		34:36
rending their g. in token,		46:21
even as they had rent their g.		46:21
they cast their g. at the feet of		46:22
have cast our g. at thy feet		46:22
g. shall be rent by our brethren,		46:23
themselves with g. of skins,		49: 6
thick g. to cover their nakedness.		49: 6
and also the g. of Jesus;	3Ne	19:25
put on they beautiful g., O		20:36
washed their g. in my blood,		27:19
rid our g. of the blood of	Mrm	9:35
thy g. shall be made clean.	Eth	12:37
my g. are not spotted with		12:38
whose g. are white through		13:10
and put on thy beautiful g.,	Mro	10:31
whose g. were pure and white	DC	20: 6
the g. spotted with the flesh.		36: 6
let all thy g. be plain,		42:40
nor wear the g. of the laborer.		42:42
they shall rid their g.,		61:34
and put on her beautiful g.		82:14
their g. are not clean from		88:85
That our g. may be pure,		109:76
Cleanse your hearts and your g.,		112:33
shall cling to thy g.,		122: 6
from God in heaven with dyed g.;		133:46
his g. like him that treadeth		133:48
have I sprinkled upon my g.,		133:51
wherefore thy g. are clean.		135: 5
g. are not spotted with your blood.		135: 5

GARNERS
shall be gathered into the g.,	Al	26: 5
wheat may be secured in the g.	DC 101:65

GARNISH
let virtue g. thy thoughts DC 121:45

GATE
the keeper of the g. is the Holy	2Ne	9:41
other way save it be by the g.;		9:41

GATE — 366 — GATHERED

GATE
Howl, O g.; cry, O city;	2Ne	24:31
for him that reproveth in the g.,		27:32
and the narrowness of the g.,		31: 9
the g. by which ye should enter.		31:17
the g. by which ye should enter is		31:17
yea, ye have entered in by the g.;		31:18
and enter into the narrow g.,		33: 9
and enter in at the strait g.,	Jac	6:11
was with my guards without the g.?	Mos	7:10
the g. of heaven is open unto all,	He	3:28
was also near unto the garden g.		7:10
Enter ye in at the strait g.;	3Ne	14:13
for wide is the g., and broad is		14:13
Because strait is the g., and		14:14
Enter ye in at the strait g.;		27:33
for strait is the g., and narrow is		27:33
wide is the g., and broad the way		27:33
enter in at the strait g. by	DC	22: 2
Wherefore, enter ye in at the g.,		22: 4
shall come in at the g. and be		43: 7
strait is the g., and narrow the		132:22
Broad is the g., and wide		132:25
whoso cometh in at the g. and	Mses	7:53

GATES
May the g. of hell be shut	2Ne	4:32
shut the g. of thy righteousness		4:32
her g. shall lament and mourn;		13:26
may go into the g. of the nobles.		23: 2
thy stranger that is within thy g.;	Mos	13:18
been without the g. of the city		21:23
the g. of hell shall not prevail	3Ne	11:39
the g. of hell stand open to		11:40
the g. of hell are ready open		18:13
and thy g. of carbuncles,		22:12
the g. of hell shall not prevail	DC	10:69
the g. of hell shall not prevail		17: 8
the g. of hell shall not prevail		18: 5
the g. of hell shall not prevail		21: 6
the g. of hell shall not prevail		33:13
the g. of hell shall not prevail		98:22
the g. of hell shall not prevail		128:10

GATHER
we did g. together our gold,	1Ne	3:22
did g. together multitudes upon		14:13
did g. together whatsoever things		16:11
the house of Israel, will I g. in,		19:16
all these g. themselves together,		21:18
of Gebim g. themselves to flee.	2Ne	20:31
g. together the dispersed of Judah		21:12
g. in upon the face of the land;		30: 7
g. it, and lay it up against the	Jac	5:23
G. together on the morrow,		7:16
might g. themselves together	Mos	1:18
might g. themselves together		7:17
should g. themselves together		10: 9
should g. themselves together		12:17
should g. themselves together		18:25
did g. themselves together		20: 1
should g. themselves together;		22: 1
that they g. together their flocks		22: 6
people should g. their flocks together;		22:10
and shalt g. together my sheep.		26:20
g. themselves together oft,	Al	6: 6
and we will g. them together		17:31
and did g. them together again		17:32
Let us g. together this people		27: 5
did g. together all their flocks		27:14
they did g. themselves together on		31:12
should g. themselves together to		43:26
should g. themselves together		47: 1
appointed to g. together men,		60: 2
G. together whatsoever force		61:17
and he did g. together his armies,	He	1:17
Nephites to g. together their armies.		1:19
people did g. themselves together		9: 7
should g. together their women,	3Ne	3:13
will g. all our armies together,		3:21
should g. themselves together,		3:22
who did g. themselves together		3:24
should g. themselves together in		3:24
g. in from the four quarters of		5:24
did g. themselves together,	3Ne	6:27
did g. themselves together,		7: 9
how oft will I g. you as a hen		10: 6
do they reap nor g. into barns;		13:26
Do men g. grapes of thorns,		14:16
And then will I g. them in		16: 5
I will g. my people together as		20:18
that I would g. them together		20:29
Then will the Father g. them		20:33
that I shall g. in, from their long		21: 1
with great mercies will I g. thee.		22: 7
surely g. together against thee,		22:15
shall g. together against thee		22:15
we did g. in our people as fast	Mrm	2: 7
did g. in our people as much as		2:21
should g. themselves together		3: 5
might g. together our people		6: 2
Go to and g. together thy flocks,	Eth	1:41
Let us g. together our people		6:19
did g. his armies together upon		14:28
did g. together all the people		15:12
I will g. them as a hen	DC	10:65
g. together in one all things,		27:13
Who will g. his people even as		29: 2
even so will I g. mine elect		33: 6
to g. the tares that they may		38:12
g. ye out from the eastern		45:64
g. up your riches that ye may		45:65
g. together the tribes of Israel		77: 9
him to g. the tribes of Israel;		77:14
ye shall first g. out the wheat		86: 7
he may g. together his armies.		88:111
shall g. together his armies,		88:112
shall g. together his armies,		88:113
should g. together, and stand		101:22
Go and g. together the residue		101:55
inasmuch as they g. together		101:58
I must g. together my people,		101:65
to g. together unto the places		101:67
g. together all their moneys;		101:72
lands and g. together upon them;		101:74
G. yourselves together unto		103:22
to g. together for the redemption		105:16
but carefully g. together,		105:24
g. up the strength of my house,		105:27
may g. out of that city the		109:39
g. out the righteous to build		109:58
whom I will g. out in due time		111: 2
who g. unto the land of Zion		119: 5
if the heavens g. blackness,		122: 7
g. up the libelous publications		123: 4
g. themselves together unto the		125: 2
g. ye together, O ye people of my		133: 4
g. ye out from among the		133: 7
to g. out mine elect from the	Mses	7:62
g. together the remainder of	JS	1:37
the light in the room begin to g.		2:43

GATHERED
after we had g. these things	1Ne	3:23
we had g. together all manner		8: 1
they should be g. together again;		10:14
the multitudes were g. together		11:28
they were g. together to fight		11:34
multitude of the earth was g.		11:35
Israel hath g. together to fight		11:35
multitudes g. together to battle,		12: 2
multitudes of the earth g. together.		12:13
the people of my seed g. together		12:15
they were g. together to battle.		12:15
saw them g. together in multitudes;		12:21
mother Gentiles were g. together		13:17
upon all those that were g. together		13:18
though Israel be not g.,		21: 5
they shall be g. together to the		22:12
they shall be g. together again	2Ne	6:11
they shall be g. home to the lands		9: 2
g. in from their long dispersion,		10: 8
fenced it, and g. out the stones		15: 2
have I g. all the earth;		20:14
kingdoms of nations g. together,		23: 4
shall be g. home unto the lands of		29:11
my word also shall be g. in one.		29:14

GATHERED 367 GAVE

the good and the bad to be g.;	Jac	5:77	g. unto the bosom of the church.	DC	38:38
the multitude were g. together;		7:17	shall be g. unto me in time		39:22
king Benjamin g. together his	WM	1:13	that ye may be g. in one,		42: 9
thereby they may be g. together;	Mos	1:10	covenant people may be g. in one		42:36
people g. themselves together		2: 1	how often would I have g. you		43:24
when they had g. themselves		7:18	But they shall be g. again;		45:25
a goodly number g. together		18: 7	shall be g. unto this place;		45:43
Yea, all were g. together that		18: 7	there shall be g. unto it out of		45:69
a small number of them g.		20: 2	g. out from among all nations,		45:71
were but few of them g. together		20: 5	to be g. with your families,		48: 6
he g. his people together,		20: 8	will not be g. with the saints,		76:102
they g. themselves together again,		21: 7	to the Jews after they are g.		77:15
they g. together their flocks,		23: 1	The Lord hath g. all things		84:100
and g. themselves together		23:26	have been scattered shall be g.		101:13
g. their flocks together,		24:18	g. many thousands of the		135: 3
the people should be g. together.		25: 1	be g. together unto one place,	Mses	2: 9
and they were g. together		25: 4	our substance that we had g.,	Abr	2:15
multitude should be g. together		27:21	be g. together unto one place,		4: 9
lower judges should be g. together,		29:29	will the eagles be g. together;	JS	1:27
they g. themselves together,	Al	2: 9	g. from the four quarters of		1:27
multitude to be g. together		19:28	Thick darkness g. around me,		2:15
was a multitude g. together		22:24			
they shall be g. into the garners,		26: 5	**GATHERETH**		
shall be g. together in their place,		26: 6	he g. his children from the four	1Ne	22:25
they g. together all their people,		27:14	and as one g. eggs that are left	2Ne	20:14
the Zoramites had g. themselves		31: 3	as a hen g. her chickens under	3Ne	10: 4
And they sent and g. together		35: 4	as a hen g. her chickens under		10: 5
his sons should be g. together,		35:16	as a hen g. her chickens,		10: 5
they g. together their armies in		43: 4	as a hen g. her chickens under		10: 6
armies of the Lamanites had g.		43:15	as a man g. his sheaves into		20:18
they were g. together in one body		43:51	as a hen g. her chickens	DC	10:65
g. together against their brethren.		46: 1	as a hen g. her chickens		29: 2
g. together all the people who		46:28	as a hen g. her chickens		43:24
had g. themselves together,		46:31			
they had g. themselves together		47: 7	**GATHERING**		
g. together so great an army		47:21	g. their flocks together.	Mos	24:18
g. together a numerous host		48: 3	and he was g. together soldiers	Al	51: 9
had g. together a wonderfully		51:11	And behold, instead of g. you,	He	7:19
of Lehi g. themselves together,		51:24	space of four years g. together	Eth	15:14
g. together a large number of		52:12	to pass the g. of mine elect;	DC	29: 7
they g. together their men and		56:53	for the g. of the saints.		57: 1
cause men to be g. together		59: 3	And now concerning the g.—		57:15
were g. together from the city		59: 5	work of the g. be not in haste,		58:56
g. together whatsoever men		62: 6	and for the g. of his saints to		84: 2
Lamanites were all g. together,		62:33	be built by the g. of the saints,		84: 4
g. together an innumerable army	He	1:14	and after the g. of the wheat,		86: 7
of people who had g. together.		7:12	work of the g. of my saints—		101:20
have ye g. yourselves together?		7:13	the g. together of my saints		101:64
ye have g. yourselves together,		7:15	let not your g. be in haste,		101:68
multitude who had g. together		9: 8	of the g. of my saints;		101:70
were also g. together at the burial.		9:11	the g. together of my saints.		105:15
g. their flocks and their herds	3Ne	4: 3	the g. of thy people may roll on		109:59
g. in from the four quarters of		5:26	the keys of the g. of Israel		110:11
how oft have I g. you as a hen		10: 5	g. of my people in the last days.		113: 6
how oft would I have g. you as		10: 5	g. together upon the land of Zion,		115: 6
how oft would I have g. you as		10: 5	for the g. together of my saints,		115: 8
g. together in the land Bountiful,		11:hd	by the g. of my saints;		115:17
a great multitude g. together,		11: 1	g. up a knowledge of all the facts,		123: 1
the multitude was g. together,		19: 4	the g. together of the waters,	Mses	2:10
g. in from the east and from		20:13	the g. together of the waters,	Abr	4:10
my people that they may be g. in,		21:24	in the literal g. of Israel and	AoF	10
his people may be g. home to		21:28			
multitude g. themselves together,		26:16	**GAVE**		
the disciples were g. together		27: 1	and g. unto him a book,	1Ne	1:11
Nephites had g. together a	Mrm	1:11	g. thanks unto the Lord our God.		2: 7
inhabitants thereof were not g. in,		5: 5	g. thanks unto the God of Israel.		5: 9
g. in all the remainder of our		6: 5	which g. an account of the creation		5:11
had g. in all our people in one		6: 6	and diligence which we g. unto it.		16:29
flocks which they had g. together,	Eth	2: 1	God g. unto man that he should	2Ne	2:16
the people were g. together.		6:20	God g. unto the children of men.		2:21
he had g. together an army		7: 5	he g. commandment that all men		2:21
Akish g. in unto the house of		8:13	I g. my back to the smiter,		7: 6
Numrah g. together a small		9: 9	to that God who g. them breath,		9:26
g. together an army of outcasts,		10: 9	and g. unto Moses power that		25:20
g. in from the four quarters of		13:11	also g. him power that he should		25:20
g. together to the army of		15:13	Nephi g. me, Jacob, a	Jac	1: 1
g. together to the army of Shiz.		15:13	And he g. me, Jacob, a		1: 2
when they were all g. together,		15:15	Jacob, g. unto them these words		1:17
are g. together in my name,	DC	6:32	and he g. up the ghost.		7:20
shall be g. unto one place		29: 8	g. a genealogy of his fathers,	Om	1:18
shall be g. on my right hand		29:27	g. an account of one Coriantumr,		1:21
the time when they shall be g.		31: 8	that g. him charge concerning	Mos	1;15
g. unto me a righteous people,		38:31	he also g. him charge concerning		1:16

GAVE — GENERAL

diligence which they g. unto him.	Mos	1:16	I g. unto him commandment,	DC	29:35
and g. thanks to God, saying:		8:19	no temporal commandment g. I		29:35
And they g. thanks to God,		24:22	g. unto Adam and unto his		29:42
g. him power to ordain priests		25:19	world that he g. his own life,		34: 3
it g. an account of the people		28:17	g. unto you the commandment		38:32
it g. them much knowledge,		28:18	g. I power to become my sons;		39: 4
and g. him power according to	Al	4:16	g. I power to do many		45: 8
and he g. thanks unto God.		8:22	g. I power to obtain eternal life.		45: 8
he g. commandments unto men,		12:31	I g. unto you a commandment		61:13
God g. unto them commandments,		12:32	I g. commandment that his		64:20
God g. these commandments unto		13: 1	g. heed to the traditions of		74: 4
and they g. heed unto his word,		21:23	commission which I g. unto him		75: 6
that God g. him commandments,		22:12	because he g. me of his fulness,		93: 4
g. great power unto the Nephites;		25: 6	I g. unto you a commandment		95: 7
and he also g. them strength,		31:38	I g. unto you a commandment		95: 8
g. place in the land of Jershon for		35:13	the law I g. unto my servant		98:32
which he g. unto them according		35:16	that I g. unto mine ancients,		98:33
to that God who g. them life.		40:11	and commandments which I g.		103: 4
therefore they g. them lands		43:12	Sarah g. Hagar to Abraham		132:34
they g. thanks unto the Lord		45: 1	for I g. them unto another,		132:39
he g. Amalickiah the command		47: 3	I g. unto thee, my servant Joseph,		132:40
heed and diligence which they g.		49:30	he also g. me commandments	Mses	1:17
of the city and g. it unto Lehi.		53: 2	And Adam g. names to all cattle,		3:20
g. them great hopes and much		56:17	and also g. unto her husband		4:12
and g. them charge over our		57:16	she g. me of the fruit of the tree		4:18
g. orders that my men who had		57:24	he g. unto them commandments,		5: 5
g. Lehi and Teancum command		62: 3	which I g. unto their father, Adam.		6:28
g. Moronihah great advantage	He	1:25	the Lord spake with me, and g.		6:42
and g. unto them battle,		1:29	he g. unto me a commandment		7:11
and he g. unto him a sign;		2: 7	I g. unto them their knowledge,		7:32
He g. unto the eldest the name		3:21	Eden, g. I unto man his agency;		7:32
God g. power unto one man,		8:11	unto the Lord, and g. heed,		8:13
God g. unto this man such power,		8:12	Adam g. names to all cattle,	Abr	5:21
and they g. unto him glory,		8:23	if he g. wisdom to them that	JS	2:13
of him and g. them unto you.		13:21	and g. me fifty dollars to assist		2:61
the day that he g. us our riches,		13:33	He g. me a certificate, certifying		2:64
Giddianhi g. commandment	3Ne	4: 6	of my pocket and g. it to him,		2:65
he g. unto them power to		11:22	g. us directions that I should		2:70
I am he that g. the law,		15: 5			
and the multitude g. way till		17:12	**GAVEST**		
he g. unto the disciples and		18: 3	the blood of him whom thou g.	DC	45: 4
they g. unto the multitude,		18: 9	said: The woman thou g. me,	Mses	4:18
he g. them power to give		18:37			
and g. to the disciples to eat.		20: 3	**GAZELAM**		
he also g. them wine to drink,		20: 5	G., or Enoch [Joseph Smith, Jun.]	DC	78: 9
truly g. unto them bread to eat,		20: 7	my servant G. [Joseph Smith],		82:11
one voice, and g. glory to Jesus,		20: 9	servant G. [Joseph Smith, Jun.]		104:26
g. unto me to know that they	Mrm	3: 4	servant G. [Joseph Smith, Jun.]		104:43
they g. me command again of		5: 1	servant G. [Joseph Smith, Jun.].		104:45
which I g. unto my son Moroni.		6: 6	servant G. [Joseph Smith, Jun.],		104:46
g. directions whither they should	Eth	2: 5			
and g. battle unto his brother		7: 9	**GAZELEM**		
Shule g. him power in his		7:13	will prepare unto my servant G.,	Al	37:23
And he g. battle unto Shule		7:16			
he g. battle again unto Shule,		7:17	**GEBA**		
Nimrod g. up the kingdom of		7:22	have taken up their lodging at G.;	2Ne	20:29
which g. power unto the prophets		7:25			
he g. battle unto his father,		8: 3	**GEBIM**		
army and g. battle unto Jared.		8: 5	the inhabitants of G. gather	2Ne	20:31
he g. unto Akish his daughter		9: 4			
and g. battle unto the people;		10: 9	**GEMS**		
and g. battle unto Moron,		11:15	names go down to posterity as g.	DC	135: 6
he g. battle unto them who		13:16			
also g. battle unto Coriantumr		13:23	**GENEALOGY**		
Shared g. him battle again		13:29	also a g. of thy forefathers,	1Ne	3: 3
Coriantumr g. Shared battle		13:30	contained the g. of my father.		3:12
he g. battle unto Coriantumr,		14: 3	found upon the plates of brass a g.		5:14
and g. battle unto Lib.		14:11	did discover the g. of his fathers.		5:16
Lib g. battle unto him upon		14:13	do not give the g. of my fathers		6: 1
he g. battle unto Lib,		14:16	record of my father, and the g. of		19: 2
there he g. battle unto Shiz		14:26	Enos, that our g. may be kept.	Jar	1: 1
he g. him many deep wounds;		14:30	these plates, to preserve our g.—	Om	1: 1
and g. him commandments;	DC	1:17	gave a g. of his fathers,		1:18
g. commandments to others,		1:18	have the g. of our forefathers,	Al	37: 3
commandment which I g. you,		3:10	Neither is their g. to be kept,	DC	85: 4
gospel, which I g. unto them		10:48	a g. was kept of the children of	Mses	6: 8
g. unto him commandments		20: 7	the g. of the sons of Adam,		6:22
And g. him power from on high,		20: 8			
g. unto them commandments		20:19	**GENERAL**		
God g. his Only Begotten Son,		20:21	became g. throughout the land,	Al	16:15
but g. no heed unto them.		20:22	high council or g. conference.	DC	20:67
g. promise that he should have		27: 7	the g. church record of names.		20:83
I g. unto him that he should		29:35	the g. assembly and church of		76:67

GENERAL

a g. church record of all things	DC	85: 1
a g. council of twenty-four		102: 1
of a g. council of high priests,		102: 8
the g. authorities of the church		102:32
commune with the g. assembly		107:19
brought before a g. assembly		107:32
instructions at my g. conference,		124:88
at my g. conference;		124:144
let there be a g. recorder,		128: 4
the g. church recorder can enter		128: 4
on the g. church book,		128: 4
knowledge of the g. character		128: 4
is done on the g. church book,		128: 4
same on the g. church book.		128: 4
and the breach of the g. peace,		134: 8
as a Church in G. Conference		OD
became g. among all the sects	JS	2: 5

GENERATION

also saw many of the fourth g.	1 Ne	12:12
down from one g. to another,		19: 4
as one g. passeth to another	2 Ne	1:12
salvation from g. to generation.		8: 8
salvation from generation to g.		8: 8
down, from g. to generation,		9: 2
down, from generation to g.,		9: 2
shall it be dwelt in from g.		23:20
dwelt in from generation to g.:		23:20
as one g. hath been destroyed		25: 9
have they been destroyed from g.		25: 9
destroyed from generation to g.		25: 9
even down from g. to generation		25:16
even down from generation to g.		25:16
my seed, from g. to generation,		25:21
my seed, from generation to g.,		25:21
shall go from g. to generation		25:22
shall go from generation to g.		25:22
many of the fourth g. shall have		26: 9
my seed, from g. to generation.	Jac	1: 3
my seed, from generation to g.		1: 3
from g. to generation	WM	1:10
to g. until the days of king		1:10
from g. to generation until		1:11
to g. until they have fallen		1:11
Yea, wo be unto this g.!	Mos	12: 2
this g., because of their iniquities,		12: 2
and who shall declare his g.?		14: 8
unto you, who shall declare his g.?		15:10
many of the rising g. that could		26: 1
and were handed down from g. to		28:14
down from generation to g.,		28:14
down from one g. to another,		28:20
middle aged, and the rising g.;	Al	5:49
O ye wicked and perverse g.,		9: 8
O ye wicked and perverse g.,		10:17
O ye wicked and perverse g.,		10:25
of the people, in every g., until		11: 4
blessed are this people in this g.,		27:12
down from one g. to another,		37: 4
even the fourth g. shall not		45:12
down from one g. to another;		63:13
down from one g. to another	He	3:16
awful wickedness, from g. to		6:30
from generation to g.		6:30
of the fourth g. who shall live,		13:10
those of the fourth g. shall visit		13:10
ye wicked and ye perverse g.;		13:29
the wickedness of the rising g.	3 Ne	1:30
because of you, and also this g.;		27:30
because of you and this g.;		27:30
them who are now alive of this g.;		27:31
because of the fourth g. from		27:32
fourth generation from this g.,		27:32
people of that g. were blessed,		28:23
many of that g. had passes	4 Ne	1:14
the first g. from Christ had		1:18
the second g. had all passed		1:22
down from g. to generation,		1:48
down from generation to g.,		1:48
word shall hiss forth from g. to	Mro	10:28
hiss forth from generation to g.		10:28
unbelieving and stiffnecked g.—	DC	5: 8
this g. shall have my word		5:10
same testimony among this g.,	DC	5:14
the condemnation of this g.		5:18
unto the people of this g.:		5:25
doing much good in this g.		6: 8
but repentance unto this g.;		6: 9
your testimony in this g.,		10:33
may not come forth in this g.		10:33
this g. harden not their hearts,		10:53
doing much good in this g.		11: 8
but repentance unto this g.		11: 9
the children of men in this g.,		11:22
declare repentance unto this g.		14: 8
holy work in this age and g.,		20:11
of great joy unto this g.		31: 3
a crooked and perverse g.		33: 2
a crooked and perverse g.,		34: 6
I have sent forth unto this g.		35:12
from this untoward g.,		36: 6
shall come upon this g. as		45:19
this g. of Jews shall not pass		45:21
in that g. shall the times of		45:30
be men standing in that g.,		45:31
inherit the earth from g. to		56:20
earth from generation to g.,		56:20
to possess it from g. to		69: 8
from generation to g.,		69: 8
temple shall be reared in this g.		84: 4
this g. shall not all pass away		84: 5
built unto the Lord in this g.,		84:31
from the blood of this wicked g.;		88:75
clean from the blood of this g.		88:85
clean from the blood of this g.;		88:138
unto the third and fourth g.		98:28
unto the third and fourth g.,		98:29
unto the third and fourth g.		98:30
to the third and fourth g.		98:37
unto the third and fourth g.		98:46
unto the third and fourth g.		103:26
unto the third and fourth g.		105:30
posterity unto the latest g.		107:56
rise up in the midst of this g.		109:33
from this untoward g.,		109:41
everlasting remembrance from g.		109:71
from generation to g.		109:71
blood of this g. be required		112:33
in sacred remembrance from g.		117:12
from generation to g., forever		117:12
posterity after them from g.		121:21
from generation to g.		121:21
a g. of vipers shall not escape		121:23
that we owe to all the rising g.,		123:11
unto the third and fourth g.,		124:50
unto the third and fourth g.,		124:52
have place therein, from g. to		124:56
from generation to g.		124:56
place in that house, from g.		124:59
from generation to g., forever		124:59
and for his g. after him,		124:69
from g. to generation, so long as		124:69
g., so long as he and his heirs shall		124:69
himself, and for his g. after him,		124:74
after him, from g. to generation.		124:74
after him, from generation to g.		124:77
for himself, and his g. after him,		124:77
after him, from g. to generation.		124:77
after him, from generation to g.		124:78
interest in that house from g.		124:78
from generation to g.		124:78
good, for himself, and his g.,		124:80
himself, and his generation, from g.		124:80
from generation to g.		124:80
and his seed after him, from g.		124:81
after him, from generation to g.		124:81
and his seed after him, from g.		124:82
after him, from generation to g.		124:82
in honorable remembrance from g.		124:96
from generation to g., forever		124:96
himself and for his g. after him,		124:117
after him, from g. to generation;		124:117
after him, from generation to g.;		124:117
be held in remembrance from g.		127: 9
from generation to g.,		127: 9
there came g. upon generation;	Mses	7:24

GENERATION GENTILES

there came generation upon g.;	Mses 7:24	G. who have gone forth out of	1Ne 13:30
and perfect in his g.;	8:27	that the G. will utterly destroy the	13:30
this g., in which these things	JS 1:34	that the G. shall destroy the seed	13:31
come on the earth in this g.	2:45	that the G. shall forever remain	13:32
this g. of the children of men.	2:73	I will be merciful unto the G.,	13:33
		them by the hand of the G.,	13:34
GENERATIONS		and after the G. do stumble	13:34
I beheld many g. pass away,	1Ne 12: 3	I will be merciful unto the G.	13:34
beheld three g. pass away	12:11	hid up, to come forth unto the G.,	13:35
I saw many g. pass away.	12:21	from the G. unto the remnant	13:38
many g. after the Messiah shall	15:13	from the G. unto them,	13:39
you for the space of many g.;	2Ne 1:18	unto the convincing of the G.	13:39
even after many g. have gone	3:20	which thou hast seen among the G..	13:40
us, and our future g.;	4: 2	unto the Jews and also unto the G.?	13:42
in future g. they shall become	9:53	unto the Jews and also unto the G.,	13:42
nations for the space of many g.,	25:16	unto the G. and also unto the Jews,	13:42
that many g. shall pass away,	26: 2	if the G. shall hearken unto the	14: 1
until three g. shall have passed	26: 9	if the G. repent it shall be well	14: 5
many g. shall not pass away	30: 6	wo be unto the G. if it so be	14: 6
the kings, according to the g.;	Om 1:11	among all the nations of the G.,	14:13
unto the third and fourth g.	Mos 13:13	and also concerning the G.	15: 7
unto us as well as unto future g.	Al 24:14	through the fulness of the G.,	15:13
forth his power unto future g.	37:14	of the Messiah come unto the G.,	15:13
forth his power unto future g.	37:18	from the G. unto the remnant of	15:13
power in them unto future g.;	37:19	after they are scattered by the G.;	15:17
should be given unto future g.	3Ne 26: 2	it shall come by way of the G.,	15:17
be made known unto future g.;	DC 5: 9	may show his power unto the G.,	15:17
as well as in g. of old;	20:11	give thee for a light to the G.,	21: 6
their g. shall inherit the earth	56:20	I will lift up mine hand to the G.,	21:22
the church, and for the rising g.	69: 8	they shall be nursed by the G.,	22: 6
of Zion, and unto their g.,	70: 8	lifted up his hand upon the G.	22: 6
even the things of many g.	76: 8	up a mighty nation among the G.,	22: 7
in the church of God in all g.,	84:17	a marvelous work among the G.,	22: 8
throughout all their g.,	84:18	their being nourished by the G.	22: 8
her g. forever and ever,	97:28	also be of worth unto the G.;	22: 9
his seed, throughout all their g.	107:13	and not only unto the G. but	22: 9
to all g. and for eternity;	109:24	will lift up mine hand to the G.,	2Ne 6: 6
all g. after us should be blessed.	110:12	And blessed are the G.,	6:12
g. of the heaven and of the earth,	Mses 3: 4	nations of the G. shall be great	10: 8
the book of the g. of Adam,	6: 8	kings of the G. shall be nursing	10: 9
And for these many g.,	6:28	of the Lord are great unto the G.,	10: 9
world for the space of many g.	7: 4	and the G. shall be blessed upon	10:10
by the fathers in the first g.,	Abr 1:26	be a land of liberty unto the G.,	10:11
these the g. of the heavens	5: 4	who shall raise up unto the G.	10:11
		thy seed by the hand of the G.;	10:18
GENEROSITY		I will soften the hearts of the G.,	10:18
the g. and the greatness of the	Al 22: 3	wherefore, the G. shall be blessed	10:18
		to it shall the G. seek;	21:10
GENIUS		that the G. be convinced also	26:12
prospered according to his g.,	Al 30:17	shall have been smitten by the G.;	26:15
		be smitten by the hand of the G.	26:19
GENTILE		the G. are lifted up in the pride of	26:20
and also to Jew and G.—	T Pg	days, or in the days of the G.—	27: 1
in due time by way of the G.—	T Pg	behold all the nations of the G.	27: 1
convincing of the Jew and G.	T Pg	Wo be unto the G.,	28:32
both Jew and G., both bond and	2Ne 10:16	many of the G. shall say:	29: 3
alike unto God, both Jew and G.	26:33	Yea, what do the G. mean?	29: 4
both unto G. and unto Jew;	DC 18:26	forth salvation unto the G.?	29: 4
Which is my word to the G.,	19:27	O ye G., have ye remembered	29: 5
directly between Jew and G.;	57: 4	more righteous than the G. shall be.	30: 1
		that the G. are utterly destroyed.	30: 1
GENTILES		as many of the G. as will repent	30: 2
by the Holy Ghost, unto the G.	1Ne 10:11	concerning the Jews and the G.	30: 3
spake much concerning the G.,	10:12	and be written unto the G.,	30: 3
after the G. had received the	10:14	I also have charity for the G.	33: 9
the nations and kingdoms of the G.	13: 3	supposed it had been the G.;	3Ne 15:22
saw among the nations of the G.	13: 4	G. should be converted through	15:22
divided the G. from the seed	13:10	the G. should not at any time	15:23
beheld a man among the G.,	13:12	shall be manifested unto the G.,	16: 4
that it wrought upon other G.;	13:13	through the fulness of the G.,	16: 4
beheld many multitudes of the G.	13:14	And blessed are the G.,	16: 6
they were scattered before the G.	13:14	shall the truth come unto the G.,	16: 7
it was upon the G., and they did	13:15	the unbelieving of the G.—	16: 8
the G. who had gone forth out	13:16	of the Father unto the G.,	16: 9
mother G. were gathered together	13:17	At that day when the G. shall	16:10
G. that had gone out of captivity	13:19	the G. shall not have power	16:12
they are of great worth unto the G.	13:23	if the G. will repent and	16:13
from the Jews in purity unto the G.,	13:25	if the G. do not repent after	20:15
from the Jews unto the G.,	13:26	upon all the nations of the G.	20:20
unto all the nations of the G.;	13:29	through me upon the G.,	20:27
unto all the nations of the G.,	13:29	blessing upon the G. shall	20:27
which thou hast seen with the G.	13:29	be made known unto the G.	21: 2
		shall come forth from the G.,	21: 5

GENTILES

should come forth from the G.,	3Ne	21: 6
forth his power unto the G.,		21: 6
the G., if they will not harden		21: 6
him to bring forth unto the G.,		21:11
bring them forth unto the G.,		21:11
of Jacob shall be among the G.,		21:12
wo be unto the G. except they		21:14
thy seed shall inherit the G.		22: 3
he must speak also to the G.		23: 2
they shall go forth unto the G.		23: 4
unto this people, from the G.,		26: 8
they will be among the G.,		28:27
and the G. shall know them not.		28:27
among the G. shall there be		28:32
shall come unto the G.		29: 1
Hearken, O ye G., and hear		30: 1
Turn, all ye G., from your wicked		30: 2
Therefore I write unto you, G.,	Mrm	3:17
these people, and also unto the G.,		5: 9
to the G. who have care for		5:10
go forth unto them from the G.;		5:15
G. who shall possess the land.		5:19
driven and scattered by the G.;		5:20
driven and scattered by the G.,		5:20
O ye G., how can ye stand		5:22
come unto the G. from the Jews,		7: 8
come from the G. unto you.		7: 8
this cometh unto you, O ye G.,	Eth	2:11
shall not go forth unto the G.		4: 6
Come unto me, O ye G.,		4:13
Wherefore, O ye G., it is		8:23
their brethren through the G.;		12:22
the G. will mock at these things,		12:23
I fear lest the G. shall mock		12:25
show unto the G. their weakness		12:28
that if the G. have not charity,		12:35
would give unto the G. grace,		12:36
Moroni, bid farewell unto the G.,		12:38
fulness of my gospel from the G.	DC	14:10
both the G. and also the house of		18: 6
to the G. and to the Jews also;		20: 9
the world, yea, before the G.;		21:12
in the land, even among the G.,		35: 7
my gospel among the G.		42:39
and for the G. to seek to it,		45: 9
times of the G. be fulfilled.		45:25
the times of the G. is come in,		45:28
times of the G. be fulfilled.		45:30
a light unto the G.,		86:11
vex the g. with a sore vexation.		87: 5
to go forth among the G. for		88:84
nations of Israel, and of the G.,		90: 8
unto the G. first, and then,		90: 9
be especial witnesses unto the G.		107:25
first unto the G. and secondly		107:33
first unto the G. and then to		107:34
first unto the G. and then unto		107:35
unto the G. first and also unto		107:97
who are identified with the G.		109:60
my name, not only unto the G.,		112: 4
condition among the G.		113:10
G. to the exaltation or lifting		124: 9
all nations, first upon the G.,		133: 8
among the G. flee unto Zion.		133:12
he would give unto the G. grace,		135: 5
I . . . . bid farewell unto the G.;		135: 5
the fulness of the G. was soon	JS	2:41

GENTLE

and be submissive and g.;	Al	7:23

GENTLEMAN

I hired with an old g. by	JS	2:56
I prevailed with the old g. to		2:56
in a g. by the name of Martin		2:61
a g. celebrated for his literary		2:64

GENTLENESS

by g. and meekness, and by love	DC	121:41

GEORGE: *see also HARRIS, George; JAMES, George; MILLER, George; and SMITH, George A.*

GET

no man despise my servant G.,	DC	124:21
Let my servant G., and my		124:22

GET

building a tower to g. to heaven—	T Pg	
and g. thee into the mountain.	1Ne	17: 7
which are built up to g. gain,		22:23
who are built up to g. power		22:23
learning, that they may g. gain	2Ne	26:20
that they may g. gain and priase		26:29
and to g. gain will they say this,		27:16
Jacob g. thou up into the temple	Jac	2:11
g. shaken from my firmness in the		4:18
was about to g. upon the tower	Mos	19: 6
g. thou and this people out of		24:23
g. thee out of this land,		24:23
of these lawyers was to g. gain;	Al	10:32
for the love of money, to g. gain,		11:20
they might g. money according to		11:20
to g. God to take them away		24:11
to g. our stains taken away		24:15
G. this people out of this land,		27:12
therefore g. thee out of this land;		27:12
unto this people to g. gain,		30:35
with great care, that it may g. root,		32:37
it will g. root, and grow up,		32:37
behold it will not g. any root;		32:38
not g. Lehonti to come down		47:12
not g. into their forts of security		49:18
to g. into their place of security;		49:21
whatsoever thing they could g.		57:14
it were possible that I could g.		61: 5
buy and to sell, and to g. gain,	He	6: 8
they began to seek to g. gain		6:17
plunder, that they might g. gain.		6:17
that they might g. to heaven.		6:28
as he can g. hold upon the		6:30
g. gain and glory of the world,		7: 5
But behold, it is to g. gain,		7:21
that ye might g. gold and silver,		7:21
g. great hold upon the hearts of		16:23
thus did Satan g. possession of	3Ne	2: 2
at any time he shall g. thee,		12:25
can g. rid of the justice of an		28:35
shall say at that day, to g. gain,		29: 7
unto themselves to g. gain,	4Ne	1:26
did g. hold upon their hearts.		1:28
g. them together in one body.	Mrm	2: 7
which we did g. the lands of		2:28
g. possession of any of our lands;		3: 6
could not g. into the country		5: 4
one shall have them to g. gain;		8:14
unto yourselves to g. gain?		8:33
secret abominations to g. gain,		8:40
he may g. the full account.	Eth	1: 4
to g. power and gain, until		8:22
combinations shall g. above you,		8:23
built up to g. power and gain—		8:23
for a wilderness, to g. game.		10:21
that they might g. gain.		10:22
to g. ore, of gold, and of silver,		10:23
built up to g. power and gain;		11:15
they might g. all who were upon		15:14
to g. to tempt the Lord	DC	10:15
we may g. glory of the world.		10:19
to g. thee to tempt the Lord		10:29
unto themselves to g. gain,		10:56
to g. in debt to thine enemies;		64:27
g. ye straightway unto my land;		101:57
g. in debt any more for the		115:13
soon as they g. a little authority,		121:39
far as they can g. hold of them		123: 3
G. thee hence Satan;	Mses	1:16
that I may murder and g. gain.		
g. ye upon the mount Simeon.		7: 2
g. thee out of thy country,	Abr	2: 3
unless I could g. more wisdom	JS	2:12
did I g. possession of myself,		2:18
again beginning to g. lighted,		2:44
to g. the plates for the purpose		2:46
otherwise I could not g. them.		2:46
as we could g. opportunity.		2:55
g. a comfortable maintenance.		2:55

GET 372 GHOST

were used to g. them from me.	JS 2:60	or by the power of the Holy G.!	3Ne 29: 6
to g. them from me if possible.	2:60	be filled with the Holy G.,	30: 2
		did also receive the Holy G.	4Ne 1: 1
GETTETH		being constrained by the Holy G.,	1:48
no man g. it henceforth and	He 12:19	Holy G. did not come upon any,	Mrm 1:14
		the Son, and unto the Holy G.,	7: 7
GETTING		with fire and with the Holy G.,	7:10
g. up of their prosecutions	DC 127: 1	and the Holy G. bear record—	Eth 5: 4
Abel, for the sake of g. gain,	Mses 5:50	with fire and with the Holy G.	12:14
in g. up and promoting this	JS 2: 6	because of the Holy G. which	12:23
for the purpose of g. rich.	2:46	Jesus Christ, and the Holy G.,	12:41
object in view in g. the plates	2:46	ye shall give the Holy G.;	Mro 2: 2
		their hands, fell the Holy G.	2: 3
GHOST		by the power of the Holy G.,	3: 4
himself manifest, by the Holy G.,	1Ne 10:11	by the power of the Holy G.,	6: 4
by the power of the Holy G.,	10:17	by the power of the Holy G.;	6: 9
by the power of the Holy G.,	10:17	power of the Holy G. led them	6: 9
by the power of the Holy G.,	10:19	the Holy G. may have place	7:32
the Holy G. giveth authority	10:22	the power of the holy G.	7:36
the Holy G. come down out of	11:27	by the power of the Holy G.	7:44
Holy G. fell upon twelve others;	12: 7	by the power of the Holy G.,	8: 7
of whom the Holy G. beareth	12:18	did the Holy G. manifest the	8: 9
the power of the Holy G.;	13:37	the visitation of the Holy G.,	8:26
by the power of the Holy G.;	2Ne 26:13	they are denying the Holy G.	8:28
learning, and deny the Holy G.,	28: 4	by the power of the Holy G.	10: 4
and the gift of the Holy G.!	28:26	by the power of the Holy G.	10: 5
by the power of the Holy G.	28:31	by the power of the Holy G.;	10: 7
the Holy G. descended upon him	31: 8	in your heart, by the Holy G.,	DC 8: 2
will the Father give the Holy G.,	31:12	you shall receive the Holy G.,	14: 8
then shall ye receive the Holy G.;	31:13	you shall have the Holy G.,	18:18
of fire and of the Holy G.;	31:13	to the power of the Holy G.	18:32
of fire and of the Holy G.,	31:14	by fire, yea, even the Holy G.	19:31
by fire and by the Holy G.	31:17	by the gift of the Holy G.,	20:26
and ye have received the Holy G.,	31:18	callings of God by the Holy G.,	20:27
of the Son, and of the Holy G.,	31:21	Father, Son, and Holy G. are	20:28
after ye had received the Holy G.	32: 2	gift and power of the Holy G.,	20:35
save it were by the Holy G.?	32: 2	baptism of fire and the Holy G.,	20:41
by the power of the Holy G.;	32: 3	and the giving of the Holy G.;	20:43
the way, and receive the Holy G.,	32: 5	they are led by the Holy G.,	20:45
by the power of the Holy G.	33: 1	by the power of the Holy G.,	20:60
the power of the Holy G. carrieth	33: 1	of the Son, and of the Holy G.	20:73
and the gift of the Holy G.,	Jac 6: 8	Being inspired of the Holy G.,	21: 2
by the power of the Holy G.;	7:12	thou shalt receive the Holy G.,	25: 8
by this power of the Holy G.,	7:13	of fire and of the Holy G.	33:11
and the power of the Holy G.,	7:17	bestow the gift of the Holy G.	33:15
and he gave up the g.	7:20	by the power of the Holy G.	34:10
as he was about to give up the g.,	7:21	they received not the Holy G.;	35: 5
by the power of the Holy G.,	Al 7:10	they shall receive the Holy G.	35: 6
they were filled with the Holy G.	8:30	by the Comforter, the Holy G.,	35:19
and the gift of the Holy G.,	9:21	receive my Spirit, the Holy G.,	36: 2
being sanctified by the Holy G.,	13:12	baptism of fire and the Holy G.,	39: 6
no more against the Holy G.,	34:38	receive the gift of the Holy G.,	39:23
and be filled with the Holy G.	36:24	some it is given by the Holy G.	46:13
blood or denying the Holy G.?	39: 5	some it is given by the Holy G.	46:15
if ye deny the Holy G. when it	39: 6	given by the Holy G. to some	46:16
that he shall yield up the g.	He 14:21	receive the gift of the Holy G.,	49:14
with fire and with the Holy G.,	3Ne 9:20	moved upon by the Holy G.	68: 3
with fire and with the Holy G.,	9:20	moved upon by the Holy G.	68: 4
of the Son, and of the Holy G.,	11:25	of the Son, and of the Holy G.	68: 8
Son, and the Holy G. are one;	11:27	and the gift of the Holy G.	68:25
the Holy G. beareth record of the	11:32	being filled with the Holy G.	84:27
with fire and with the Holy G.	11:35	shall receive the Holy G.	84:64
the Holy G. will bear record unto	11:36	they may receive the Holy G.,	84:74
and I, and the Holy G. are one.	11:36	the Holy G. descended upon	93:15
with fire and with the Holy G.;	12: 1	the Holy G. shall be shed forth	100: 8
with fire and with the Holy G.,	12: 2	being full of the Holy G.,	107:56
shall be filled with the Holy G.	12: 6	receive a fulness of the Holy G.,	109:15
save it were by the Holy G.	15:23	unspeakable gift of the Holy G.,	121:26
knowledge of you by the Holy G.,	16: 4	when moved upon by the Holy G.,	121:43
in me, in and of the Holy G.,	16: 6	The Holy G. shall be thy	121:46
power to give the Holy G.	18:37	and by the power of the Holy G.,	124: 4
the Holy G. should be given	19: 9	shall be given you by the Holy G.	124: 5
the Holy G. did fall upon them,	19:13	the Holy G. has not a body of	130:22
were filled with the Holy G.	19:13	the Holy G. could not dwell in us.	130:22
that thou hast given the Holy G.	19:20	man may receive the Holy G.,	130:23
that thou wilt give the Holy G.	19:21	blasphemy against the Holy G.,	132:27
hast given them the Holy G.	19:22	being filled with the Holy G.,	Mses 1:24
the pouring out of the Holy G.	20:27	day the Holy G. fell upon Adam,	5: 9
by the power of the Holy G.	21: 2	called upon men by the Holy G.	5:14
were filled with the Holy G.	26:17	and by the gift of the Holy G.	5:58
the reception of the Holy G.,	27:20	was moved upon by the Holy G.,	6: 8
the Holy G. beareth record of the	28:11	receive the gift of the Holy G.,	6:52
the Father giveth the Holy G.	28:11	with fire, and with the Holy G.	6:66
baptized did receive the Holy G.	28:18		

GHOST   373   GIFT

and truth, and of the Holy G.,	Mses	7:11
and the Holy G. fell on many,		7:27
ye shall receive the Holy G.,		8:24
the sign of the Holy G. unto	Fac	2: 7
hands for the gift of the Holy G.,	JS	2:70
than the Holy G. fell upon him,		2:73
We were filled with the Holy G.,		2:73
Jesus Christ, and in the Holy G.	AoF	1
hands for the gift of the Holy G.		4

GIANTS

g. of the land, also, stood afar	Mses	7:15
days there were g. on the earth,		8:18

GIBEAH

G. of Saul is fled.	2Ne	20:29

GID

of Omner, and the city of G.,	Al	51:26
were guarded in the city of G.;		55: 7
and he sent to the city G.,		55:16
round about the city G.		55:25
when he had fortified the city G.,		55:26
we did inquire of G. concerning		57:28
G. was the chief captain over		57:29
words which G. said unto me:		57:30
had heard these words of G.,		57:36
I caused that G., with a small		58:16
G. and his men were on the right		58:17
in the midst of G. and Teomner,		58:19
G. and Teomner did rise up		58:20
G. and Teomner by this means		58:23
thenceforth to the city of G.;	He	5:15
and from the city of G. to the		5:15

GIDDIANHI

And behold, I am G.;	3Ne	3: 9
avenge their wrongs. I am G.		3:10
because of the boldness of G.		3:11
not hearken to the epistle of G.,		3:12
G. found that it was expedient		4: 5
G. gave commandment unto his		4: 6
appearance of the armies of G.,		4: 7
appearance of the army of G.,		4: 8
when the armies of G. saw this		4: 9
when the armies of G. did rush		4:10
the oaths which G. had made,		4:12
G., who had stood and fought		4:14
was the end of G. the robber.		4:14

GIDDONAH

I am Amulek. I am the son of G.,	Al	10: 2
Now the high priest's name was G.		30:23

GIDEON: *see also CARTER, Gideon.*

among them whose name was G.,	Mos	19: 4
And G. pursued after him and		19: 6
saying: G., spare me,		19: 7
nevertheless, G. did spare his life.		19: 8
the name of the man was G.;	Al	1: 8
because G. withstood him with		1: 9
he was wroth with G., and drew		1: 9
G. being stricken with many years,		1: 9
man that slew G. by the sword,		2: 1
their tents in the valley of G.,		2:20
called after that G. who was slain		2:20
departed out of the valley of G.		2:26
river Sidon, into the valley of G.,		6: 7
which was called the city of G.,		6: 7
in the valley that was called G.,		6: 7
established in the valley of G.,		6: 8
he delivered to the people in G.,		7:hd
returned from the land of G.,		8: 1
taught the people of G. many things		8: 1
and faith of Nehor, who slew G.		14:16
journeying from the land of G.		17: 1
G. sent men into the wilderness		19:18
and they met the men of G.		19:22
And the men of G. told them of		19:22
the people told the men of G. that		19:23
they told G. what they had done		19:24
when G. had heard these things,		20:17
G. went forth and stood before		22: 3

And G. said unto him:	Al	22; 5
hearkened unto the words of G.		22: 9
came over into the land of G.,		30:21
as he did in the land of G.;		30:30
I have fled to the land of G.,		61: 5
march towards the land of G.		62: 3
march towards the land of G.		62: 4
he came to the land of G.;		62: 6
and wo be unto the city of G.,	He	13:15

GIDGIDDONAH

ten thousand of G. had fallen,	Mrm	6:13

GIDGIDDONI

appointed, and his name was G.	3Ne	3:18
G. was a great prophet among		3:19
Now the people said unto G.		3:20
But G. saith unto them:		3:21
G. did cause that they should		3:26
G. commanded that his armies		4:13
the commandment of G.		4:13
G. being aware of their design,		4:24
were done by command of G.		4:26
G., and the judge, Lachoneus,		6: 6

GIFT

by the g. and power of God	T Pg	
thereof by the g. of God.	T Pg	
Holy Ghost, which is the g. of God	1Ne	10:17
by the g. and power of the Lamb.		13:35
the g. and power of the		13:37
and the g. of the Holy Ghost!	2Ne	28:26
and the g. of the Holy Ghost,	Jac	6: 8
by the g. and power of God.	Om	1:20
the g. of speaking with tongues,		1:25
in the g. of interpreting languages,		1:25
and it is a g. from God.	Mos	8:13
who has this high g. from God.		8:14
a g. which is greater can no man		8:16
king Mosiah had a g. from God.		21:28
the g. of speaking with tongues,	Al	9:21
and the g. of preaching,		9:21
and the g. of the Holy Ghost,		9:21
and the g. of translation;		9:21
that precious g. of eternal life,	He	5: 8
partakers of the heavenly g.	4Ne	1: 3
partakers of the heavenly g.	Eth	12: 9
hope, and be partakers of the g.,		12:11
in the g. of his Son hath God		12:11
of the g. of his calling unto me,	Mro	7: 2
if he offereth a g., or prayeth		7: 6
if a man being evil giveth a g.,		7: 8
as if he had retained the g.;		7:10
neither will he give a good g.		7:10
by the power and g. of Christ;		7:16
every good g. cometh of Christ.		10:18
and lay hold upon every good g.,		10:30
and touch not the evil g., nor		10:30
a g. to translate the plates;	DC	3:11
this is the first g. that I bestowed		5: 4
should pretend to no other g.		5: 4
will grant unto you no other g.		5: 4
thou shalt have no more g.,		5:31
Behold thou hast a g.,		6:10
art thou because of thy g.		6:10
thou shalt exercise thy g.,		6:11
Make not thy g. known unto any		6:12
there is no g. greater than the		6:13
greater than the g. of salvation.		6:13
behold, I grant unto you a g.,		6:25
bringing to light, with your g.,		6:27
Joseph, the keys of this g.,		6:28
Therefore this is thy g.;		8: 8
Remember, this is your g.		8: 5
Now this is not all thy g.;		8: 6
you have another g., which is		8: 6
which is the g. of Aaron;		8: 6
this g. of Aaron to be with you.		8: 7
doubt not, for it is the g. of God;		8: 8
lost your g. at the same time,		10: 2
also sought to destroy your g.		10: 7
and that he has no g.,		10:18

GIFT

thou hast a g., or thou shalt	DC 11:10
thou shalt have a g. if thou wilt	11:10
which g. is the greatest of all	14: 7
and the same g. like unto him;	17: 7
by the g. of the Holy Ghost,	20:26
g. and power of the Holy Ghost,	20:35
bestow the g. of the Holy Ghost	33:15
the g. of the Holy Ghost,	39:23
shall be appointed unto this g.	43: 4
For all have not every g. given	46:11
to every man is given a g. by	46:11
the g. of the Holy Ghost,	49:14
he shall not retain the g.,	51: 5
and the g. of the Holy Ghost	68:25
and receive money by g.,	84:103
if a g. is bestowed upon him,	88:33
and he receive not the g.?	88:33
him who is the giver of the g.	88:33
the g. of tongues be poured out	109:36
unspeakable g. of the Holy Ghost,	121:26
translated by the g. and power	135: 3
the free g. of the Lord thy God,	136:27
by the g. of the Holy Ghost.	Mses 5:58
receive the g. of the Holy Ghost,	6:52
for the g. of the Holy Ghost,	JS 2:70
for the g. of the Holy Ghost.	AoF 4
We believe in the g. of tongues,	7

GIFTS

the greatest of all the g. of God.	1Ne 15:36
of revelation, and also many g.,	Al 9:21
give good g. unto your children,	3Ne 14:11
or by prophecy, or by g.,	29: 6
there were no g. from the Lord,	Mrm 1:14
revelations, nor prophecies, nor g.,	9: 7
to the g. and callings of God	Mro 3: 4
ye deny not the g. of God,	10: 8
that these g. are administered;	10: 8
the g. of healing by the same	10:11
all these g. come by the Spirit	10:17
g. of which I have spoken,	10:19
g. of God shall be done away	10:24
by the power and g. of God.	10:25
greatest of all the g. of God;	DC 6:13
greatest of all the g. of God.	14: 7
to the callings and g. of God	18:32
in the g. and callings of God	20:27
to the g. and callings of God	20:60
seek ye earnestly the best g.,	46: 8
your minds what those g. are,	46:10
for there are many g., and to	46:11
all these g. come from God,	46:26
to discern all those g. lest	46:27
given to have all those g.,	46:29
having all the g. of God which	107:92
and g. of the priesthood,	124:95

GIHON

the second river was called G.;	Mses 3:13

GILBERT, Sidney

I say unto you, my servant G.,	DC 53: 1
let my servant G. stand in the	57: 6
let my servant G. plant himself	57: 8
servant G. obtain a license—	57: 9
expedient that my servant G. and	61: 7
let my servants G. and	61: 9
Let my servant G. take that	61:12
G., after a few weeks, shall return	64:18
Newel K. Whitney and G.,	64:26
neither with my servant G.;	90:35
G. should sell my storehouse,	101:96

GILEAD

of Shared, whose name was G.,	Eth 14: 8

GILGAH

they were called Jacom, and G.,	Eth 6:14

GILGAL

the city of G. have I caused to	3Ne 9: 6
G. had fallen with his ten	Mrm 6:14

374

GIVE

did meet in the valley of G.;	Eth 13:27
back again to the valley of G.	13:29
battle again in the valley of G.,	13:30

GIMGIMNO

of Jacob, and the city of G.,	3Ne 9: 8

GIN

for a g. and a snare to the	2Ne 18:14

GIRD

I did g. on his armor about	1Ne 4:19
g. yourselves, and ye shall be	2Ne 18: 9
g. yourselves, and ye shall be	18: 9
rejoice, and g. up your loins,	DC 27:15
and I will g. up their loins,	35:14
g. up your loins and I will	36: 8
Wherefore, g. up your loins	38: 9
g. up your loins lest ye be	43:19
G. up your loins and be watchful	61:38
G. up your loins and be sober.	73: 6
g. up your loins and be faithful,	75:22
he is to g. himself according to	88:141
Therefore, g. up your loins,	106: 5
g. up thy loins for the work.	112: 7
Arise and g. up your loins,	112:14
my people may g. up their loins,	Mses 7:62

GIRDED

the sword g. about my loins.	1Ne 4:21
were g. with a leathern girdle	Mos 10: 8
which was g. about their loins,	Al 3: 5
armor, which was g. about them,	3: 5
which was g. about their loins;	43:20
g. on his armor about his loins;	46:13
their armor g. about their loins,	46:21
were g. about after the manner	3Ne 4: 7

GIRDING

a g. of sackcloth;	2Ne 13:24

GIRDLE

instead of a g., a rent;	2Ne 13:24
the g. of their loins be loosed,	15:27
shall be the g. of his loins,	21: 5
faithfulness the g. of his reins.	21: 5
shall be the g. of his loins,	30:11
faithfulness the g. of his reins.	30:11
a short skin g. about their loins	En 1:20
a leathern g. about their loins.	Mos 10: 8

GIRT

your loins g. about with truth,	DC 27:16

GIVE

he would g. unto us the records	1Ne 3:24
we would g. unto him our gold,	3:24
do not g. the genealogy of my	6: 1
neither at any time shall I g. it	6: 1
to g. a full account of all the	6: 3
I shall g. commandment unto my	6: 6
g. me strength that I may	7:17
they did g. thanks unto the Lord	7:22
Nephi, proceed to g. an account	10: 1
will they not rejoice and g. praise	15:15
Nephi, did exhort them to g. heed	15:25
would g. heed to the word of God	15:25
to the truth, and g. heed unto it,	16: 3
heed which we did g. unto them.	16:28
which did g. us understanding	16:29
and did g. thanks unto him.	16:32
our women did g. plenty of suck	17: 2
the Lord thy God shall g. thee.	17:55
will not g. my glory unto another.	20:11
I will also g. thee for a light to	21: 6
g. thee my servant for a covenant	21: 8
g. place to me that I may dwell.	21:20
and he will g. unto them power,	2Ne 1:11
unto him will I g. commandment	3: 7
will g. unto him a commandment	3: 8
and unto him will I g. power to	3:11
and I will g. power unto him in	3:17

GIVE

and I will g. judgment unto him	2Ne 3:17
I will g. unto him that he shall	3:18
ye should g. ear unto my words.	4: 3
should I g. way to temptations,	4:27
g. place no more for the enemy	4:28
God will g. liberally to him that	4:35
God will g. me, if I ask not amiss;	4:35
g. ear unto me, O my nation;	8: 4
brethren, g. ear to my words.	9:40
and g. thanks unto his holy name	9:52
will g. them the true knowledge of	10: 2
I will g. children unto them	13: 4
Lord himself shall g. you a sign—	17:14
abundance of milk they shall g.	17:22
g. ear all ye of far countries;	18: 9
will I g. him a charge to take	20: 6
thereof shall not g. their light;	23:10
the Lord shall g. thee rest,	24: 3
and g. ear unto my words;	25: 4
But I g. unto you a prophecy,	25: 4
God will g. unto him power,	26:16
words which I shall g. unto thee.	27:20
I will g. unto the children of men	28:30
him that receiveth I will g. more;	28:30
will the Father g. the Holy Ghost,	31:12
the word which I shall g. thee	Jac 2:11
a commandment I g. unto you,	3: 9
which will g. our children,	4: 2
as he was about to g. up the ghost,	7:21
I shall g. this people a name,	Mos 1:11
And I g. unto them a name that	1:12
g. thanks to the Lord their God,	2: 4
will not g. unto him of my food,	4:17
I g. not because I have not,	4:24
but if I had I would g.	4:24
that I said I should g. unto you	5:11
g. us a knowledge of a remnant	8:12
g. us a knowledge of this very	8:12
g. thanks to the Lord their God.	18:23
their voices and g. thanks to God.	25:10
and to g. thanks in all things.	26:39
and I shall g. an account of	28: 9
support him and g. him money.	Al 1: 5
Will ye g. to an humble servant	8:19
all these will I g. thee if thou	11:22
great worth, I will g. unto thee—	11:25
diligence which they g. unto him.	12: 9
O Lord, g. us strength according	14:26
thou desirest I will g. unto thee;	18:21
I will g. up all that I possess,	22:15
will g. away all my sins to know	22:18
they would g. up their own lives;	24:18
they would g. unto him;	24:18
g. thanks to his holy name,	26: 8
and I will g. unto you success.	26:27
I will g. thanks unto my God	26:37
we will g. up the land of Jershon,	27:22
land which we will g. unto our	27:22
that they will g. us a portion of	27:24
This will I g. unto thee for a sign,	30:49
Lord, wilt thou g. me strength,	31:30
and g. unto me success, and also	31:32
g. unto us, O Lord, power and	31:35
ye can g. place for a portion of	32:27
Now, if ye g. place, that a seed	32:28
and did g. unto them lands	35: 9
that he might g. unto them	35:16
My son, g. ear to my words;	36: 1
doth g. me exceeding great joy	36:25
to g. heed to this compass	37:43
g. heed to the word of Christ,	37:44
to g. heed to this compass,	37:44
My son, g. ear to my words,	38: 1
g. so much heed unto my words	39: 2
And g. heed to their counsel.	39:10
behold, I g. it as my opinion,	40:20
did g. unto the Nephites a large	43:13
not g. heed to the words of	45:23
would not g. heed to their words,	45:24
to g. them battle according to	47: 8
taught never to g. an offense,	48:14
and g. him (Moroni) power to	51:15
was ready to g. them battle	52: 1
not g. way before the Lamanites.	Al 52:34
never would g. up their liberty,	53:17
I will g. you battle even until	54:12
I will g. unto him according to	55: 3
G. us of your wine, that we may	55: 9
to g. way before the Lamanites.	56:51
to g. way before the Lamanites,	57:20
and also g. us strength that we	58:10
he will g. unto us of your food,	60:35
g. unto them power to conduct	61:15
and did g. unto them battle,	He 1:30
to g. unto the people;	4:22
Behold, I g. unto you power,	10: 7
and to g. ear unto his counsels,	12: 5
g. unto him of your substance;	13:28
ye will g. unto him of your gold,	13:28
Behold, I g. unto you a sign;	14: 2
this will I g. unto you for a sign	14: 3
another sign I g. unto you,	14:14
refuse to g. his light unto you;	14:20
the day that they shall g. suck;	15: 2
do g. unto you exceeding great	3Ne 3: 2
Zemnarihah did g. command	4:23
to g. my account of the things	5:19
I g. unto you power that ye	11:21
Blessed are ye if ye shall g. heed	12: 1
I g. unto you to be the salt of	12:13
I g. unto you to be the light of	12:14
I g. unto you a commandment,	12:29
g. her a writing of divorcement.	12:31
G. to him that asketh thee,	12:42
G. not that which is holy unto the	14: 6
ask bread, will g. him a stone?	14: 9
a fish, will he g. him a serpent?	14:10
know how to g. good gifts unto	14:11
g. good things to them that ask	14:11
to the end will I g. eternal life.	15: 9
g. unto this people this land	16:16
should g. unto the multitude.	18: 4
to him will I g. power that he	18: 5
and g. it unto the people of	18: 5
also g. unto the multitude	18: 8
I g. unto you a commandment	18:12
me that I should g. unto you.	18:14
I g. unto you another	18:27
which I g. unto you,	18:28
I g. you these commandments	18:34
power to g. the Holy Ghost.	18:37
that thou wilt g. the Holy Ghost	19:21
and g. unto the multitude.	20: 4
should g. unto the multitude.	20: 5
I should g. unto you this land,	20:14
g. unto them again the land of	20:29
and g. unto them Jerusalem	20:33
I g. unto you a sign, that ye	21: 1
I will g. unto you for a sign—	21: 2
shall g. unto him power that he	21:11
a commandment I g. unto you	23: 1
Therefore g. heed to my words;	23: 4
that I should g. unto you;	26: 2
bless it, and g. it unto them.	26:13
What will ye that I shall g. unto	27: 2
which I shall g. unto you,	27:27
scriptures which g. an account	28:33
the Lamanites did g. unto us	Mrm 2:29
we did g. unto the Lamanites	2:29
daring not to g. a full account	5: 9
there we could g. them battle.	6: 2
may g. unto them my words,	7: 1
rather g. thanks unto God that	9:31
proceed to g. an account of	Eth 1: 1
I g. not the full account,	1: 5
a part of the account I g.,	1: 5
this wise do I g. the account.	1: 6
the land which I shall g. you	2:15
two stones will I g. unto thee,	3:23
proceed to g. the record of Jared	6: 1
did g. light unto the vessels.	6: 2
to g. light unto men, women,	6: 3
should g. battle unto Shule,	7:21
did g. battle unto him by night.	8: 5
he would g. up the kingdom	8: 6
shall g. unto him me to wife,	8:10

GIVE

I will g. her if ye will bring	Eth 8:10
G. her unto me to wife.	8:11
I will g. her unto you, if ye will	8:12
I g. unto men weakness that	12:27
g. unto them who shall have	12:35
would g. unto the Gentiles grace,	12:36
would g. unto him his kingdom	13:20
did g. battle unto him in	14: 4
he would g. up the kingdom	15: 4
if he would g. himself up,	15: 5
did g. battle unto the people of	15: 6
ye shall g. the Holy Ghost;	Mro 2: 2
and in my name shall ye g. it,	2: 2
neither will he g. a good gift.	7:10
Listen unto them and g. heed,	8:21
a little, do they g. unto them.	9: 8
neither g. heed to the words of	DC 1:14
I will g. them power that	5:13
g. heed unto my words, which is	6: 2
g. heed unto my words.	6: 2
I g. unto you, and also unto	6:28
g. unto me power over death,	7: 2
I will g. this power and the	7: 7
that I will g. unto you power	9: 2
that I would g. it unto you,	9: 7
he will also g. him power again;	10:16
and g. you commandments	10:34
g. heed to my word, which is	11: 2
g. heed unto my word.	11: 2
I g. these words unto thee.	11:11
to them will I g. power to	11:30
g. heed to my word, which is	12: 2
g. heed unto my word.	12: 2
g. heed with your might,	12: 9
g. heed to my word, which is	14: 2
g. heed unto my word.	14: 2
I g. unto you these words:	18: 1
I g. unto you a commandment,	18: 3
I g. unto you, Oliver Cowdery,	18:37
blessings which I g. unto you	18:45
which I shall g. unto you	19:32
shalt g. heed unto all his words	21: 4
which he shall g. unto you	21: 4
g. your language to exhortation	23: 7
And I will g. unto him strength	24:12
the church shall g. unto thee in	24:18
A revelation I g. unto you	25: 2
commandment I g. unto you,	27: 3
which I shall g. unto him,	28: 3
will to g. you the kingdom.	29: 5
saying, G. me thine honor,	29:36
until I g. unto you further	30: 4
but g. heed unto the words	30: 5
brother, which he shall g. you.	30:15
g. heed unto these things and	30: 8
they shall g. heed to that which	32: 4
shall g. heed unto these words	32: 5
I g. unto thee a commandment,	35: 6
commandment I g. unto thee—	35:20
commandment g. I unto you	36: 6
a commandment g. I unto	37: 3
I g. unto you a commandment,	38:16
to g. unto you greater riches,	38:18
I will g. it unto you for the land	38:19
I will g. unto you my law;	38:32
I g. unto the church in these	38:34
of the Father to g. unto you,	38:39
of the earth are mine to g.;	38:39
I g. unto you a commandment,	38:40
so will I g. unto as many as	39: 4
I g. unto you a commandment,	41: 2
and I g. a commandment,	41: 9
the day that I shall g. them.	41:10
law which I shall g. unto you.	42: 2
I g. unto you this first	42: 4
g. unto them a commandment	42: 5
shalt g. it into my storehouse,	42:55
I g. unto you a commandment	42:58
and I will g. him liberally	42:68
and g. ear to the words which	43: 1
this I g. unto you that you	43: 6
I g. unto you a commandment,	43: 8
may g. even as I have spoken.	43:16
g. ear to him who laid the	DC 45: 1
I g. unto you that ye may now	45:61
ye must g. thanks unto God	46:32
I g. unto you a commandment	49: 1
I g. unto you a commandment	49:11
g. ear to the voice of the living	50: 1
if he g. not unto you that	50:31
and g. unto him directions;	51: 1
g. unto him a writing that	51: 4
I will g. unto you a pattern	52:14
g. unto you a commandment	53: 2
power to g. the Holy Spirit.	55: 3
a new commandment unto	56: 5
will not g. your substance to	56:16
and g. ear to my word,	58: 1
I g. unto you further directions	58:34
I g. unto my servant Sidney	58:50
I g. unto them a commandment,	59: 5
I g. unto them a commandment,	60:13
I g. unto you a commandment	61:18
shall g. unto all your brethren.	61:26
hearts and g. ear from afar;	63: 1
I g. commandments, and	63:13
I will g. the mysteries of	63:23
g. unto my servant Joseph	63:41
and g. him thine instructions;	66: 8
of eternity are mine to g.	67: 2
g. unto you a testimony of	67: 4
a promise I g. unto you	67:10
commandment I g. unto them—	68:33
I g. unto my servant Joseph	70: 1
I g. unto them a commandment;	70: 2
I shall hereafter g. unto them;	70: 3
a commandment I g. unto them,	70: 6
shall not g. these things unto	70: 6
this commandment I g. unto	70:15
a season, which I g. unto you.	71: 3
g. an account of his stewardship	72:16
g. an account unto the bishop	72:19
I g. no more unto you at this	73: 6
I g. unto him a new commission	75: 7
g. unto you this commandment,	75:25
heavens, and g. ear, O earth,	76: 1
last of all, which we g. of him:	76:22
g. him glory forever and ever.	76:93
g. unto you a place in the	78: 7
commandment I g. unto you,	78:11
ensample which I g. unto you	78:13
I will g. unto you my servant	80: 2
and I g. them unto you,	82: 4
sayings, which I g. unto you,	82: 4
I g. unto you a new	82: 8
I g. unto you directions how	82: 9
g. unto you this commandment,	82:15
to g. them inheritances.	83: 5
g. unto you a commandment	84:43
to g. diligent heed to the words	84:43
commandment I g. unto them,	84:73
g. unto you this commandment,	84:77
clothe you, and g. you money,	84:89
shall g. unto any of you a coat,	84:105
promise which I g. unto you	88: 4
And they g. light to each other	88:44
and the stars also g. their light,	88:45
which I g. unto you,	88:62
And I g. unto you, who are the	88:74
I g. unto you a commandment	88:76
I g. unto you a commandment	88:77
and shall refuse to g. light;	88:87
Fear God, and g. glory to him	88:104
as the Spirit shall g. utterance	88:137
Lord, g. unto them a promise,	89:21
I g. unto you a commandment	90:12
I g. unto the united order,	92: 1
I g. unto you these sayings	93:19
commandment I g. unto you—	93:43
g. more earnest heed unto your	93:48
as I shall g. him utterance;	93:51
commandment I g. unto you,	94: 1
I g. unto you a commandment	94:16
I g. unto you no more at this	94:17
I g. not unto you that ye shall	95:13
I g. a promise of eternal life	96: 6

GIVE

until I shall g. unto him other	DC 97: 4
and in everything g. thanks;	98: 1
I g. unto you a commandment,	98:11
For he will g. unto the faithful	98:12
g. unto them a commandment,	98:36
to the counsel which I shall g.	100: 2
a commandment I g. unto you,	100: 7
I g. unto you this promise,	100: 8
I will g. unto him power to be	100:10
I will g. unto thee power to be	100:11
I g. unto you a word concerning	100:13
I g. unto all the churches,	101:67
president shall g. a decision	102:19
I will g. unto you a revelation	103: 1
their God, shall g. unto them.	103: 5
a commandment I g. unto you,	103:34
I g. unto you counsel,	104: 1
I now g. unto you power	104:10
commandment I g. unto you,	104:11
every man may g. an account	104:12
a commandment I g. unto you,	104:47
a commandment I g. unto you	104:54
from time to time g. unto you—	104:58
And I g. it unto you from this	104:63
shall g. unto him the sum	104:73
I will g. you the victory.	104:82
I g. unto you a promise, that	104:83
I g. unto you this privilege,	104:86
commandment I g. unto you,	105:20
I will g. unto you favor and	105:25
calling, which I now g. unto him,	106: 3
I will g. him grace and assurance	106: 8
that their prejudices may g. way	109:56
which thou didst g. to Abraham,	109:64
will g. this city into your hands,	111: 4
I will g. you power to pay them.	111: 5
g. thee answer to thy prayers.	112:10
or g. them revelation.	113:10
g. unto them a promise that I will	118: 3
God shall g. unto you knowledge	121:26
things shall g. thee experience,	122: 7
to g. heed to the light and glory	124: 6
holy words which I g. unto them.	124:46
when I g. a commandment to any	124:49
shall g. him, in the very hour,	124:97
I now g. unto you the officers	124:123
I g. unto you Hyrum Smith,	124:124
I g. unto you my servant Joseph	124:125
I g. unto him for counselors	124:126
g. unto you my servant Brigham	124:127
I g. unto you a high council,	124:131
I g. unto you Don C. Smith	124:133
I g. unto him Amasa Lyman	124:136
I g. unto you John A. Hicks,	124:137
I g. unto you Joseph Young,	124:138
I g. unto you Vinson Knight,	124:141
a commandment I g. unto you,	124:144
I g. unto you a word in relation	127: 5
g. you information in relation to	128: 1
And I will g. unto thee the keys	128:10
I will g. you another quotation	128:16
I will g. you a quotation from	128:17
which I am about to g. you;	132: 3
g. unto you this commandment—	132:12
will g. unto thee the law of	132:28
take her and g. her unto him	132:44
that whatsoever you g. on earth,	132:48
to whomsoever you g. any one	132:48
A commandment I g. unto mine	132:51
I g. unto my servant Joseph	132:53
multiply him and g. unto him an	132:55
and the first g. her consent,	132:61
g. unto him, because she did not	132:65
Fear God and g. glory to him,	133:38
he would g. unto the Gentiles grace,	135: 5
inhabitants thereof, g. I unto	Mses 1:35
heaven to g. light upon the earth;	2:15
heaven to g. light upon the earth,	2:17
wherefore g. me thine honor.	4: 1
g. unto him mine own power;	4: 3
and I will g. thee utterance,	6:32
I g. unto you a commandment	6:58
amd g. heed unto my words;	8:23

GIVEN

will g. unto thy seed after thee	Abr. 2: 6
I g. unto thee a promise that	2:11
Unto thy seed will I g. this land.	2:19
stars that are set to g. light,	3:10
to g. light upon the earth;	4:15
to g. light upon the earth,	4:17
we will g. them dominion over	4:26
will g. them every herb bearing	4:29
to them we will g. it;	4:29
behold, we will g. them life,	4:30
we will g. to them every green	4:30
as we have any right to g.	Fac 2:12
and unto them that g. suck	JS 1:16
the moon shall not g. her light,	1:33
to g. them meat in due season?	1:49
wisdom, and would g. liberally,	2:13
g. him an account of the vision	2:21

GIVEN

g. them power whereby they could	1Ne 5: 8
g. thanks unto the God of Israel	5:10
for it is g. in the record which	6: 1
I have g. the name of Nephi;	9: 2
shall be g. unto thee for a sign,	11: 7
which had been g. unto him.	16: 8
which the Lord had g. unto us;	16:11
which were g. upon the ball.	16:30
shall be g. hereafter;	19: 5
should be a sign g. of his death	19:10
more especially g. unto those who	19:10
commandments which he hath g.,	2Ne 1: 7
having power g. them to do all	1:10
And the law is g. unto men.	2: 5
law which the Holy One hath g.,	2:10
commandments which God hath g.	2:26
and all things are g. them	2:27
and he hath g. me knowledge	4:23
God hath g. me the tongue of the	7: 8
Wherefore, he has g. a law;	9:25
where there is no law g. there is	9:25
who have not the law g. to them,	9:26
unto him that has the law g.,	9:27
God has g. us so great knowledge	10:20
hath the law of Moses been g.;	11: 4
things which have been g. of God	11: 4
children whom the Lord hath g.	18:18
unto us a son is g.;	19: 6
for they shall be g. them	25:18
none other name g. under heaven	25:20
For, for this end was the law g.;	25:25
for what end the law was g.	25:27
fulfilled which was g. unto Moses.	25:30
shall be signs g. unto my people	26: 3
for the signs which are g.,	26: 8
but he hath g. it free for all	26:27
God hath g. a commandment	26:30
he hath g. his power unto men;	28: 5
precepts shall be g. by the power	28:31
way nor name g. under heaven	31:21
will be no more doctrine g.	32: 6
it is g. unto them in plainness,	32: 7
and he hath g. them unto me;	33:10
which I have g. unto you.	Jac 2: 4
things which God hath g. you,	2:20
were g. to our father, Lehi;	2:34
which was g. unto our fathers—	3: 5
I have g. unto them this land,	En 1:10
the intent for which it was g.	Jar 1:11
which God has g. me.	WM 1: 9
the Lord our God hath g. us.	Mos 1:10
there shall be no other name g.	3:17
There is no other name g.	5: 8
g. him all the charges concerning	6: 3
have great power g. him from God.	8:16
that there should be a law g.	13:29
Therefore there was a law g. them,	13:30
to him that had not should be g.	18:27
shall be g. hereafter.	21:35
had g. Alma the authority over	26: 8
the Lord their God had g. them.	28: 2
to the law which has been g. to us	29:15
the laws which have been g. you	29:25
g. them by the hand of the Lord.	29:25

GIVEN

to the law which has been g.,	Mos 29:28
the law which had been g. them;	29:39
g. him the charge concerning all	29:42
which has been g. us by Mosiah,	Al 1:14
to the laws which had been g.,	4:16
hath been g. to another,	7: 2
that he hath g. me to know,	7: 4
hath g. unto me the exceeding	7: 4
which ye have g. unto my word.	7:26
which he has g. unto his people.	8:17
they had power g. unto them,	8:31
which the Lord had g. them.	8:32
so much knowledge g. unto them	11: 3
according to the law which was g.	11: 4
names are g. by the Nephites,	11: 4
for power was g. unto them that	12: 7
It is g. unto many to know the	12: 9
to him is g. the greater portion	12:10
until it is g. unto him to know	·12:10
to them is g. the lesser portion	12:11
which he has g. unto us;	12:37
were g. after this manner,	13:16
g. themselves to much prayer,	17: 3
of God which was g. unto him.	17:17
has g. us a portion of his Spirit	24: 8
unto such it is g. to know, the	26:22
unto such it shall be g. to reveal	26:22
it shall be g. unto such to bring	26:22
even as it has been g. unto us to	26:22
to him it is g. according to his	29: 5
and hath g. me much success,	29:13
do have words g. unto them	32:23
g. us to prepare for eternity,	34:33
account shall be g. of their wars	35:13
affixed, and a just law g.,	42:18
Now, if there was no law g.—	42:19
if there was no law g. against sin	42:20
And if there was no law g.,	42:21
But there is a law g., and a	42:22
the king had g. him command,	47:13
had g. up their weapons of war.	52:32
g. them power to gain possession	55:20
first g. to some of the Lamanite	55:31
God who has g. us victory over	58:33
I have g. unto you the names of	He 5: 6
hath been g. to our fathers.	5: 8
he hath power g. unto him from	5:11
and authority, g. unto them that	5:18
they should speak g. unto them—	5:18
power g. unto them that they did	5:37
which had been g. by Gadianton	6:24
marvel because ye are g. away	7:15
how could you have g. away to	7:16
that he hath g. me no power	8:12
had such great power g. unto him,	8:13
g. unto me by the power of God.	9:36
word, which I have g. unto thee,	10: 4
authority g. unto him from God.	11:18
God hath g. unto you a knowledge	14:30
He hath g. unto you that ye	14:31
he hath g. unto you that ye	14:31
great signs g. unto the people,	16:13
been g. by Samuel the prophet.	3Ne 1: 9
on this night shall the sign be g.,	1:13
this night shall the sign be g.	1:14
for the signal which had been g.	1:16
that the sign which had been g.	1:18
of the sign which had been g.	1:19
any more signs or wonders g.;	2: 3
the time when the sign was g.,	2: 7
period when the sign was g.,	2: 8
many signs which had been g.,	5: 2
true account was g. by Nephi.	5: 9
g. by those who were before me,	5:16
hath g. me and my people so	5:20
to the law which had been g.	6:26
which he has g. by them of old,	6:28
g. and administered by the	6:28
who had g. his voice against	7:10
having had power g. unto him	7:15
been g. by the prophet Samuel,	8: 3
so many signs had been g.	8: 4
have I g. to become the sons	9:17
ministry shall be g. hereafter.	3Ne 10:19
of whom the sign had been g.	11: 2
cup which the Father hath g. me,	11:11
authority g. me of Jesus Christ,	11:25
the Father hath g. unto me;	11:32
unto them I have g. power that	12: 1
I have g. you the law and the	12:19
Ask, and it shall be g. unto you;	14: 7
fulfilled that was g. unto Moses.	15: 4
law which was g. unto Moses	15: 8
I have g. unto you the	15:10
the Father hath g. it unto you.	15:13
g. me commandment that I	15:14
g. me commandment that I	15:15
whom the Father g. me.	15:24
blessed it and g. it unto you.	18: 6
behold it shall be g. unto you.	18:20
which he hath g. me.	18:27
Ghost should be g. unto them.	19: 9
thou hast g. the Holy Ghost	19:20
hast g. them the Holy Ghost	19:22
it was g. unto them what they	19:24
for those whom thou hast g. me	19:29
they had g. unto the multitude	20: 5
had all g. glory unto Jesus,	20:10
be g. unto you of the Father,	21: 2
I have g. this land for their	21:22
Father had g. unto Malachi,	24: 1
be g. unto future generations.	26: 2
I have g. unto you my gospel,	27:13
which I have g. unto you—	27:13
the word which he hath g. unto	27:18
the words which he hath g.,	27:18
my name shall be g. unto you.	27:28
hath g. me fulness of joy;	28:10
neither was it g. unto them	28:14
which was g. them in heaven.	28:16
the record which hath been g.—	28:18
were married, and g. in marriage,	4Ne 1:11
Lord their God hath g. them,	Mrm 5:14
g. unto him to dwell in the	7: 7
save it be g. him of God;	8:15
hast g. us a commandment	Eth 3: 2
which were g. by them of old	8:15
faith was the law of Moses g.	12:11
which thou hast g. them;	12:23
g. up unto the hardness of	15:19
which he hath g. them,	Mro 4: 3
it is g. unto you to judge,	7:15
of Christ is g. to every man,	7:16
the sign was g. of the coming of	10: 1
are g. by the manifestateons of	10: 8
one is g. by the Spirit of God,	10: 9
I have g. them to publish	DC 1: 6
to them is power g. to seal	1: 8
were g. unto my servants in	1:24
these commandments were g.,	1:30
g. thee sight and power to	3:12
have g. these things unto you,	5: 2
words that are g. through you.	5:11
I have g. unto thee these	5:33
testimony which shall be g.,	6:31
save it be g. you from me.	9: 9
g. unto my servant Joseph	9:12
power g. unto you to translate	10: 1
if God has g. him power to	10:16
more particular account was g.	10:39
my words which I have g. you	15: 5
my words which I have g.	16: 5
g. to the brother of Jared	17: 1
which were g. to Lehi while	17: 1
which I have g. you,	17: 8
which is g. of the Father,	18:23
none other name g. whereby	18:23
which is g. of the Father,	18:24
for they are g. by my Spirit	18:35
the punishment which is g. from	19:10
were g. to Joseph Smith, Jun.,	20: 2
Which was g. by inspiration,	20:10
which have been g. of him.	20:21
which he has g. them;	20:77
which are g. him through me	21: 9
be g. thee by the Comforter,	24: 5

GIVEN 379 GIVEN

be g. thee in the very moment	DC 24: 6	this commandment is g. unto all	DC 52:21
shall be g. thee by my Spirit.	25: 7	which shall be g. hereafter.	53: 4
thy time shall be g. to writing,	25: 8	which was g. unto my servants	56: 5
And it shall be g. thee, also,	25:11	which was g. unto my servants	56: 6
hymns, as it shall be g. thee,	25:11	which I have g. him	56: 8
whom my father hath g. me	27:14	further directions shall be g.	57:16
it shall be g. unto thee that	28: 1	his mission is g. unto him,	58:16
commandments which I have g.	28: 1	and it shall not be g. again.	58:16
I have g. him the keys of	28: 7	are g. by the prophets of God.	58:18
but it shall be g. hereafter.	28: 9	shall be g. him of the Spirit,	58:38
And it shall be g. thee from	28:15	g. all these things unto man;	59:20
judgments are not g. unto men;	29:30	which I have g. unto them,	60: 2
it is g. unto you that ye may	29:33	money which I have g. him,	60:10
have I g. unto you a law which	29:34	unto whom is g. power to	61:27
power is not g. unto Satan	29:47	unto him it is g. by the Spirit	61:27
is g. unto them even as I will,	29:48	is g. the course for the saints,	61:29
not g. heed unto my Spirit,	30: 2	inasmuch as it is g.;	61:33
I have g. unto him power	30: 6	g. unto you the kingdom.	64: 4
be g. you by the Comforter	31:11	authority which I have g. you,	68: 8
the holy scriptures are g. of me	33:16	be g. to know the signs of	68:11
it shall be g. by the power of	34:10	be g. power to seal them up	68:12
I have g. unto him the keys	35:18	which I have g. unto them,	70: 3
shall be g. by the Comforter,	35:19	shall be g. into my storehouse;	70: 7
and the scriptures shall be g.,	35:20	which shall be g. unto you,	71: 1
be g. unto him to prophesy;	35:23	shall be g. more abundantly,	71: 6
as they shall be g. him.	35:23	and power have been g.	72: 1
by the keys which I have g.	35:25	which have been g.,	72: 7
this commandment shall be g.	36: 7	to the law which has been g.,	72: 9
have g. unto you as a parable,	38:27	have g. your names to go forth	75: 2
be g. to them that are not	41: 6	which I have g. you.	75: 4
These words are g. unto you,	41:12	have g. your names that you	75:23
g. by the power of the Spirit	42: 5	was g. unto us as follows:	76:15
not be g. to any one to go	42:11	it was g. unto us of the Spirit.	76:18
the Spirit shall be g. unto you	42:14	which have been g. of him,	76:22
fulness of my scriptures is g.	42:15	commandment which he has g.—	76:51
are g. in my scriptures;	42:28	the Father has g. all things.—	76:55
and my scriptures shall be g.	42:56	to whom is g. power over the	77: 8
which have been g. unto thee	42:59	to whom is g. the seal of the	77: 9
is g. to know the mysteries of	42:65	g. power over the nations of	77:11
world it is not g. to know them.	42:65	commandments which are g. you;	78:13
keys of the church have been g.	42:69	and g. unto him the keys of	78:16
commandments, which I have g.	43: 8	whom I have g. the keys of	81: 2
whom the kingdom has been g.;	45: 1	him unto whom much is g.	82: 3
earth shall be g. unto them	45:58	in whose hand is g. all power.	84:28
shall not be g. unto you to know	45:60	shall be g. unto him.	84:38
g. to the elders of my church	46: 2	I have g. the heavenly hosts	84:42
for what they are g.;	46: 8	which I have g. them,	84:57
they are g. for the benefit of	46: 9	whom my Father hath g. me;	84:63
that are g. unto the church.	46:10	these things are g. unto you	84:73
not every gift g. unto them;	46:11	the kingdom has been g.—	84:76
to every man is g. a gift by	46:11	be g. you in the very hour	84:85
To some is g. one, and to some	46:12	to his law, which he has g.,	85: 3
and to some is g. another,	46:12	law which I have g. unto you;	88:21
To some it is g. by the Holy	46:13	in that which is g. unto him,	88:33
To others it is g. to believe	46:14	All kingdoms have a law g.;	88:36
to some it is g. by the Holy	46:15	every kingdom is g. a law;	88:38
it is g. by the Holy Ghost to	46:16	hath g. a law unto all things,	88:42
be g. to every man to profit	46:16	it shall be g. unto you,	88:64
to some is g., by the Spirit of	46:17	g. in the thirteenth chapter of	88:141
To another is g. the word of	46:18	G. for a principle with promise,	89: 3
to some it is g. to have faith	46:19	of the kingdom g. unto you;	90: 2
to others it is g. to have faith	46:20	the oracles be g. to another,	90: 4
to some is g. the working of	46:21	and g. to those that are not	90:26
to others it is g. to prophesy;	46:22	commandment previously g.,	92: 1
it is g. to some to speak with	46:24	be g. them even according to	93:52
is g. the interpretation of	46:25	which I have g. unto you.	94: 2
are to have it g. unto them	46:27	shall be g. unto you hereafter.	94: 5
unto some it may be g. to have	46:29	shall be g. unto you hereafter.	94: 6
all things which shall be g. you,	47: 1	as it shall be g. unto you.	94:12
Wherefore, it shall be g. him,	47: 4	Lord God, have g. unto you.	94:15
shall be g. to know the place,	48: 5	I have g. unto you concerning	95: 3
not g. that one man should	49:20	pattern which I have g. you.	97:10
which shall be g. unto you,	50: 1	which I have g. unto them.	98:20
has g. the adversary power;	50: 7	be g. you in the very hour,	100: 6
be g. you what you shall ask;	50:30	which I have g. unto you,	101:10
And it shall be g. unto you,	50:32	they who have g. their lives	101:15
and the kingdom is g. you of	50:35	shall ask, it shall be g. unto him.	101:27
that my Father hath g. me;	50:41	be g. to the exchangers?	101:49
that my Father hath g. me	50:42	g. concerning these things—	101:69
g. unto that of another church.	51:10	moral agency which I have g.	101:78
the day is not g. unto them,	51:17	in case no additional light is g.,	102:22
truths which I have g. you.	52:17	the earth is g. unto the saints,	103: 7

GIVEN 380 GLAD

which I have g. unto you.	DC 103:21	Holy Ghost g. authority that	1Ne 10:22
which I have g. unto them	103:29	which g. the spirit of the devil	2Ne 2:29
and which shall be g. unto you.	103:35	Holy Ghost, which g. utterance.	28: 4
which I have g. unto you,	103:40	the Lord God g. light unto the	31: 3
g. unto the children of men	104:17	which the Lord thy God g. thee.	Mos 13:20
which I have g. unto him,	104:42	which g. me knowledge, and also	Al 18:35
which I have g. unto you,	104:58	behold, this g. my soul sorrow;	46:25
consecration which I have g.	105:29	it g. light to all that are in	3Ne 12:15
I have g. concerning Zion	105:34	the Father g. the Holy Ghost	28:11
g. according to the covenants.	107:85	if a man being evil g. a gift,	Mro 7: 8
their office, as g. in the covenants.	107:86	if God g. him power again,	DC 10:17
office, as is g. in the covenants—	107:87	Holy Ghost, which g. utterance,	14: 8
have g. of our substance to build	109: 5	ask of God, who g. liberally;	46: 7
said in a revelation, g. to us,	109: 6	the Spirit g. light to every	84:46
in the revelations g. unto us;	109:11	shineth, which g. you light,	88:11
which thou hast g. unto us,	109:60	which g. life to all things,	88:13
which thou hast g. unto him,	109:68	the sun g. his light by day,	88:45
and as it shall be g. you.	111: 3	the moon g. her light by night,	88:45
keys which I have g. unto him,	112:15	he g. this promise unto you,	98: 3
the power of this priesthood g.,	112:30	God g. unto all the obedient.	Mses 5:11
unto him have I g. the keys	115:19	that g. to all men liberally,	JS 2:11
be g. you by the Holy Ghost	124: 5		
revelations I have g. unto you,	124:119	GIVING	
knowledge of said bishopric is g.	124:141	and g. light unto them by night,	1Ne 17:30
above offices I have g. unto you,	124:143	g. the Son power to make	Mos 15: 8
g. a dispensation of the priesthood	128: 9	g. a chance for the enemy of	27: 9
this power has always been g.	128: 9	g. way to indolence, and all	Al 47:36
For him to whom these keys are g.	128:11	g. them no time to assemble	He 1:24
a white stone is g. to each of	130:11	g. charge unto his son Nephi,	3Ne 1: 2
marry nor are g. in marriage;	132:16	g. audience to his people.	Eth 9: 5
because they were g. unto him,	132:37	and the g. of the Holy Ghost;	DC 20:43
wives and concubines were g.	132:39	by g. heed and doing these	50:35
it shall be g. unto you according	132:40	g. unto them a commandment,	74: 5
your wife, whom I have g.	132:51	by g. unto you this word of	89: 4
been g. unto my servant Joseph,	132:52	by g. your names by common	104:85
for they are g. unto him;	132:61	g. the date, and names,	128: 3
virgins g. unto him by this law,	132:62	g. line upon line, precept upon	128:21
belong to him, and they are g.	132:62	g. us consolation by holding	128:21
they are g. unto him to multiply	132:63	marrying and g. in marriage?	Mses 8:21
fulfil the promise which was g.	132:63	marrying and g. in marriage;	JS 1:42
these commandments were g.;	133:60	g. an account of the former	2:34
in the day that they were g.,	133:60		
shall be g. eternal life.	133:62	GLAD	
and divine laws g. of heaven,	134: 6	he was exceeding g., for he knew	1Ne 3: 8
my words that I have g. you,	136:37	mother, Sariah, was exceeding g.,	5: 1
g. you every herb bearing seed,	Mses 2:29	they were g. in their hearts,	17:19
be g. every clean herb for meat;	2:30	you the g. tidings of great joy.	Mos 3: 3
for thyself, for it is g. unto thee;	3:17	he was exceeding g., and said:	7:14
the Lord God, had g. him,	4: 3	we would fain be g. if we could	Al 12:14
g. unto as many as called	6: 5	may have g. tidings of great joy;	13:22
according to the pattern g. by	6:46	g. tidings among all his people,	13:22
and it is g. in our own language.	6:46	these g. tidings declared unto us	13:23
which shall be g. under heaven,	6:52	to declare g. tidings of salvation	39:15
ye shall ask it, shall be g. you.	6:52	to declare these g. tidings unto	39:16
g. unto them to know good from	6:56	declare these g. tidings unto us	39:19
have g. unto you another law	6:56	they were g. in their hearts;	51:13
it is g. to abide in you;	6:61	we are g. that ye have thus	55: 9
language which God had g. him.	7:13	did bring g. tidings to my soul.	He 13: 7
said, and also g. commandment,	7:33	that ye might have g. tidings;	13: 7
g. unto me a right to thy throne,	7:59	unto them g. tidings of great joy;	16:14
even as it was g. unto Enoch.	8:19	g. tidings unto the people	3Ne 1:26
their God had g. unto them,	Abr 1: 5	great joy and be exceeding g.,	12:12
I have g. you the fashion of	1:14	eye of faith, and they were g.	Eth 15: 7
Lord my God had g. unto me,	3: 1	thou shalt declare g. tidings,	DC 19:29
it is g. unto thee to know the	3: 6	Lift up your hearts and be g.,	29: 5
it is g. unto thee to know the	3:10	you shall declare g. tidings	31: 3
g. in the own due time	Fac 2:12	Lift up your hearts and be g.,	35:26
The above translation is g.	2:12	but with a g. heart and a	59:15
g. in the characters above	3: 2	declare g. tidings unto the	62: 5
g. in the ninth number	3: 3	is the gospel, the g. tidings,	76:40
g. in the first facsimile	3: 3	g. tidings of great joy,	79: 1
and it shall be g. him.	JS 2:11	Wherefore, let your heart be g.,	79: 4
		he was made g. with the light	88:56
GIVER		bear g. tidings unto all the world.	114: 1
in him who is the g. of the gift.	DC 88:33	and be exceedingly g.;	127: 3
		g. tidings for the dead;	128:19
GIVES		g. tidings of great joy.	128:19
which g. an account, or which	1Ne 19: 4	bring g. tidings of good things,	128:19
or which g. a greater account	19: 4	G. tidings from Cumorah!	128:20
or clothes you, or g. you money,	DC 84:90	rejoice, and be exceedingly g.	128:22
		all these things and was g.,	Mses 5:11
GIVETH		Lift up your heart, and be g.;	7:44
for I know that the Lord g.	1Ne 3: 7		

GLADDEN 381 GLORY

GLADDEN
the eye and to g. the heart; DC 59:18

GLADLY
would have g. joined with them, Mos 21:31
upon them, g., the name of Christ, Al 46:15
according to your request, g., 54:20

GLADNESS
might leave this world with g. 2Ne 1:21
and g. shall be found therein, 8: 3
and they shall obtain g. 8:11
receiveth it with g.; 28:28
did hear with great joy and g. Al 16:20
filled with g. and did rejoice. He 8:17
and lifting up thy heart for g.? DC 19:39
he received the word with g., 40: 2
be filled with joy and g.; 75:21
A voice of g.! 128:19
a voice of g. for the living 128:19
and rills, flow down with g. 128:23

GLANCE
under the g. of the piercing eye Jac 2:10
with one g. of his eye he can 2:15
the g. of his all-searching eye. Mos 27:31

GLASS
and clear, even as transparent g.; Eth 3: 1
What is the sea of g. spoken of DC 77: 1
on a globe like a sea of g. and fire, 130: 7

GLASSES
The g., and the fine linen, 2Ne 13:23

GLIMMER
fire, nor g., neither the sun, 3Ne 8:22

GLOBE
on a g. like a sea of glass and fire, DC 130: 7

GLORIED
and he g. in his wickedness. Mses 5:31
Cain g. in that which he had 5:33

GLORIES
desire the g. of the kingdom, DC 43:12
the g. which are to be revealed 66: 2
all their g., laws, and set times, 121:31
g. to be revealed in the last days, 128:17
powers, and g. should take place, 128:18
g. which were to be revealed, 133:57

GLORIFIED
in whom I will be g. 1Ne 21: 3
hath the Father g. his name. 3Ne 9:15
in whom I have g. my name— 11: 7
have g. the Father in taking 11:11
that I may be g. in them. 19:29
and g. the name of the Father, Eth 12: 8
be g. through faith in his name, DC 3:20
gavest that thyself might be g.; 45: 4
shall do that God may be g. 64:13
mayest be g. in heaven so 65: 6
his lord might be g. in him, 88:60
that they all might be g. 88:60
and be g. in me as I am in 93:20
until he is g. in truth and 93:28
continued, that he may be g. 132:63
And Adam g. the name of God; Mses 6: 2
he was g. and crowned on the right JS 1: 1

GLORIFIES
Who g. the Father, and saves DC 76:43

GLORIFIETH
my Father, wherein he g. himself. DC 132:31

GLORIFY
and g. the name of your God. 2Ne 6: 4
and g. him forever. Jac 2:21
the people did rejoice and g. God, He 11:18
g. your Father who is in heaven. 3Ne 12:16

Father should g. his name in me 3Ne 23: 9
I shall g. my name in the flesh; Eth 3:21
good works, being led to g. God. 12: 4
the plates but to g. God, JS 2:46

GLORIOUS
be g. in the eyes of the Lord, 1Ne 21: 5
brother, whose views have been g., 2Ne 1:24
that g. day when justice shall 9:46
of the Lord be beautiful and g.; 14: 2
and his rest shall be g. 21:10
of the g. Majesty on high, DC 20:16
not hope of a g. resurrection. 42:45
thankfulness shall be made g.; 78:19
become very g., very great, 97:18
and his rest shall be g. 101:31
exceedingly great and g. tidings, 109:23
and g. vision burst upon us; 110:13
this most g. of all subjects 128:17
how g. is the voice we hear 128:23
clothed in his g. apparel, 133:46
was g. beyond description, JS 2:32
great and g. blessings from 2:73

GLORY
in power and great g.; 1Ne 11:28
the power of God in great g. 14:14
and g. of the God of Israel. 19:13
will not give my g. unto another. 20:11
might, and power, and great g. 22:24
I have beheld his g., 2Ne 1:15
he hath sought the g. of God, 1:25
hast beheld in thy youth his g.; 2: 4
unto them in power and great g., 6:14
the g. of his majesty shall smite 12:10
the g. of his majesty shall smite 12:19
the majesty of his g. shall smite 12:21
to provoke the eyes of his g. 13: 8
upon all the g. of Zion shall be 14: 5
and their g., and their multitude, 15:14
the whole earth is full of his g. 16: 3
king of Assyria and all his g.; 18: 7
and where will ye leave your g.? 20: 3
and the g. of his high looks. 20:12
and under his g. he shall kindle 20:16
shall consume the g. of his forest, 20:18
Babylon, the g. of kingdoms, 23:19
yea, all of them, lie in g., 24:18
because of the g. of the world 27:16
and not for the g. of God. 27:16
I g. in plainness; 33: 6
I g. in truth; 33: 6
I g. in my Jesus, for he hath 33: 6
unto you, with power and great g.; 33:11
and we had a hope of his g. Jac 4: 4
ourselves had a hope of his g., 4: 4
a good hope of g. in him 4:11
I may yet have g. in the fruit of 5:54
the knowledge of the g. of God Mos 4:11
the knowledge of the g. of him 4:12
Nevertheless, in this I do not g., 23:11
I am unworthy to g. of myself. 23:11
of the goodness and g. of God. 27:22
the Son of God cometh in his g., Al 5:50
the g. of the King of all the earth; 5:50
Son of God shall come in his g.; 9:26
and his g. shall be the glory of 9:26
the g. of the Only Begotten of the 9:26
and stand before him in his g., 12:15
who caused men to behold of his g. 12:29
the time of his coming in his g. 13:24
them up unto himself, in g.; 14:11
was the light of the g. of God, 19: 6
swallowed up in the hopes of g.; 22:14
Therefore, let us g., yea, we 26:16
yea, we will g. in the Lord; 26:16
can g. too much in the Lord? 26:16
commanded me, and I g. in it. 29: 9
I do not g. of myself, but I 29: 9
I g. in that which the Lord hath 29: 9
yea, and this is my g., that 29: 9
last day, to dwell with him in g.; 36:28
and his heart did g. in it; 48:16

GLORY

for the cause of your love of g.	Al 60:32	the g. of the telestial is one,	DC 76:98
but for the g. of my God,	60:36	as the g. of the stars is one;	76:98
is unspeakable and full of g.	He 5:44	differs from another star in g.,	76:98
get gain and g. of the world,	7: 5	so differs one from another in g.	76:98
and they gave unto him g.,	8:23	crowned with the crown of his g.,	76:108
that they may have g. of men.	3Ne 13: 2	we saw the g. and the	76:109
and the power, and the g.,	13:13	surpass all understanding in g.,	76:114
even Solomin, in all his g.,	13:29	his presence in the world of g.	76:118
and gave g. to Jesus, whom	20: 9	And to God and the Lamb be g.,	76:119
had all given g. unto Jesus,	20:10	represent the g. of the classes	77: 3
that he should come in his g.—	26: 3	to the g. of your Father who	78: 4
when I shall come in my g.	28: 7	all things be done unto my g.,	78: 8
when I shall come in my g.	28: 8	the g. of him who is your Lord.	81: 4
done with an eye single to his g.,	Mrm 8:15	an eye single to the g. of God.	82:19
and also the g. of God, and the	9: 5	be even the g. of the Lord,	84: 5
and upon the g. of the world.	Eth 8: 7	which rest is the fulness of his g.	84:24
obtain kingdoms and great g.?	8: 9	filled with the g. of the Lord,	84:32
did rejoice and g. in his day;	9:22	of the world, in all their g.,	84:82
and great g. at the last day,	Mro 7:35	clothed with the g. of her God;	84:101
hope of his g. and of eternal life,	9:25	G., and honor, and power,	84:102
an eye single to the g. of God,	DC 4: 5	the g. of the celestial kingdom;	88: 4
you shall dwell with me in g.	6:30	Which g. is that of the church	88: 5
tarry until I come in my g.,	7: 3	prepared for the celestial g.;	88:18
we may get g. of the world.	10:19	it shall be crowned with g.,	88:19
altogether for my name's g.	19: 7	cannot abide a celestial g.	88:22
g. be to the Father and I	19:19	cannot abide a terrestrial g.	88:23
Jesus Christ, to whom be all g.,	20: 4	cannot abide a telestial g.;	88:24
to whom be g. forever and ever.	20:16	not meet for a kingdom of g.	88:24
power and g. be rendered to	20:36	which is not a kingdom of g.	88:24
your good, and his name's g.	21: 6	and your g. shall be that	88:28
In me hs shall have g.,	24:11	that g. by which your bodies are	88:28
the g. which shall come upon	25:14	by a portion of the celestial g.	88:29
with an eye single to my g.—	27: 2	a portion of the terrestrial g.	88:30
with power and great g.,	29:11	by a portion of the telestial g.	88:31
in g. even as I am, to judge	29:12	upon their wings in their g.,	88:45
cloud with power and great g.	34: 7	if your eye be single to my g.,	88:67
g. shall be added to the kingdom	43:10	give g. to him who sitteth upon	88:104
by the voice of g. and honor	43:25	with the g. of his might,	88:107
when I shall come in my g.	45:16	shall be filled with his g.,	88:107
clothed with power and great g.;	45:44	This is the g. of God,	88:116
when I shall come in my g.,	45:56	a house of g., a house of order,	88:119
his g. shall be upon them,	45:59	record of the fulness of my g.,	93: 6
the g. of the Lord shall be	45:67	I saw his g., that he was in	93: 7
on the right hand of his g.,	49: 6	record that I beheld his g.,	93:11
with an eye single to my g.,	55: 1	as the g. of the Only Begotten	93:11
coming in power and great g.	56:18	he received a fulness of the g. of	93:16
the g. which shall follow after	58: 3	the g. of the Father was with	93:17
be crowned with much g.;	58: 4	partakers of the g. of the same,	93:22
with an eye single to my g.,	59: 1	The g. of God is intelligence,	93:36
the good of men unto my g.	63:12	and my g. shall be there,	94: 8
and eternal weight of g.,	63:66	my g. shall not be there;	94: 9
for this once, for mine own g.,	64: 3	my g. shall rest upon it;	97:15
the g. of the Lord shall be	64:41	and my g. shall not be there;	97:17
in the brightness of his g.,	65: 5	your good, and to my name's g.,	98: 3
thine is the honor, power and g.,	65: 6	my knowledge and g. may	101:25
crowned with honor, and g.,	75: 5	shall they partake of all this g.	101:35
and eternal shall be their g.	76: 6	be crowned with celestial g.,	101:65
the g. of the Lord shone round	76:19	All victory and g. is brought	103:36
we beheld the g. of the Son,	76:20	unto you a crown of g. at	104: 7
and the g. of the Lamb,	76:39	a house of g., a house of order,	109: 8
of his fulness, and of his g.;	76:56	That thy g. may rest down	109:12
let no man g. in man,	76:61	a house of g. and of God,	109:16
but rather let him g. in God,	76:61	and thy g. be round about them,	109:22
whose g. is that of the sun,	76:70	rushing mighty wind, with thy g.	109:37
even the g. of God, the highest	76:70	that thy g. may fill the earth;	109:74
whose g. the sun of the	76:70	crowns of g. upon our heads,	109:76
whose g. differs from that of	76:71	thou sittest enthroned, with g.,	109:77
are they who receive of his g.,	76:76	reserve for the fulness of their g.;	121:27
differ in g. as the moon differs	76:78	heed to the light and g. of Zion,	124: 6
we saw the g. of the telestial,	76:81	g. as the flower thereof which	124: 7
which g. is that of the lesser,	76:81	him with blessings and great g.	124:17
as the g. of the stars differs	76:81	beget g. and honor to himself	124:18
that of the g. of the moon	76:81	you may receive honor and g.	124:34
the g. of the telestial, which	76:89	for the g., honor, and endowment	124:39
saw the g. of the terrestrial,	76:91	contemplate the g. of Zion,	124:60
the g. of the telestial,	76:91	the g. of this, the corner-stone	124:60
even in g., and in power, and	76:91	land shall redound to your g.	124:87
we saw the g. of the celestial,	76:92	with the same blessing, and g.,	124:95
give him g. forever and ever.	76:93	like Paul, to g. in tribulation;	127: 2
the g. of the celestial is one,	76:96	Herein is g. and honor,	128:12
as the g. of the sun is one.	76:96	honors, their majesty and g.,	128:21
the g. of the terrestrial is one,	76:97	proclaiming in our ears, g.,	128:23
as the g. of the moon is one.	76:97	but inherit the same g.	129: 3

GLORY

he will come in his g.;	DC	129: 6
will be coupled with eternal g.,		130: 2
which g. we do not now enjoy.		130: 2
for their g. are manifest,		130: 7
the celestial g. there are three		131: 1
permitted to enter into my g.		132: 4
instituted for the fulness of my g.;		132: 6
and an eternal weight of g.		132:16
cannot, therefore, inherit my g.;		132:18
exaltation and g. in all things,		132:19
which g. shall be a fulness and		132:19
ye cannot attain to this g.		132:21
can in nowise enter into my g.,		132:27
even unto his exaltation and g.		132:57
fall down and be crowned with g.,		133:32
Fear God and give g. to him,		133:38
And so great shall be the g. of		133:49
scathe a green tree for the g. of		135: 6
they lived for g.;		135: 6
they died for g.;		135: 6
g. is their eternal reward.		135: 6
be prepared to receive the g.		136:31
even the g. of Zion;		136:31
ye can not yet bear my g.;		136:37
the g. of God was upon Moses;	Mses	1: 2
except he behold all my g.;		1: 5
no man can behold all my g.,		1: 5
that his g. was not upon Moses;		1: 9
but his g. was upon me;		1:11
and where is thy g., that I		1:13
except his g. should come upon		1:14
g., for it is darkness unto me?		1:15
for his g. has been upon me,		1:18
worship, which is the God of f.		1:20
of God, he beheld his g. again,		1:25
g. of the Lord was upon Moses,		1:31
this is my work and my g.—		1:39
and the g. be thine forever.		4: 2
world to come, even immortal g.;		6:59
peaceable things of immortal g.;		6:61
and I was clothed upon with g.;		7: 3
great was the g. of the Lord,		7:17
Son of Man, with crowns of g.;		7:56
and he took g. unto himself.		8: 3
have g. in the same kingdom	Abr	3:26
have g. added upon their heads		3:26
with power and great g.;	JS	1:36
and g. defy all description,		2:17
and receive its paradisiacal g.	AoF	10

GLUT

g. themselves with the labors of	Mos	9:12
g. yourselves with the labors of	Al	30:27
not g. ourselves upon the labors of		30:32

GLUTTING

of g. on the labors of the people.	Al	30:31

GNASH

weep, and wail, and g. their teeth;	Mos	16: 2

GNASHING

g. their teeth upon them,	Al	14:21
and wailing, and g. of teeth,		40:13
wailing and g. of teeth,	DC	19: 5
are wailing and g. of teeth.		85: 9
and wailing, and g. of teeth,		101:91
where there is g. of teeth,		124: 8
g. of teeth upon their heads,		124:52
and wailing, and g. of teeth,		133:73
and wailing, and g. of teeth;	Mses	1:22
shall be weeping and g. of teeth.	JS	1:54

GNOLAUM

for they are g., or eternal.	Abr	3:18

GO

should g. unto the house of Laban,	1Ne	3: 4
g., my son, and thou shalt be		3: 6
I will g. and do the things which		3: 7
to g. up to the land of Jerusalem.		3: 9
g. in unto the house of Laban.		3:11
will not g. down unto our father	1Ne	3:15
let us g. down to the land of our		3:16
ye shall g. up to Jerusalem again,		3:29
us g. up again unto Jerusalem,		4: 1
let us g. up; let us be strong		4: 2
Let us g. up; the Lord is able to		4: 3
should g. with me into the treasury.		4:20
g. down in the wilderness with us.		4:33
if thou wilt g. down into the		4:34
he promised that he would g.		4:35
should g. forth unto all nations,		5:18
again, with my brethren, g. forth		7: 3
wilderness to g. up to Jerusalem.		7: 3
g. up to the land, and remember		7:15
if ye g. ye will also perish;		7:15
I did g. forth and partake of the		8:11
knew not whither they should g.		8:14
he should g. forth and cry in the		10: 8
these things g. forth from the Jews		13:25
after they g. forth by the hand		13:26
the way whither we should g.		16:10
g. forth into the wilderness to		16:14
g. forth again in the wilderness,		16:14
Whither shall I g. to obtain		16:23
I, Nephi, did g. forth up into		16:30
whither shall I g. that I may find		17: 9
whither I should g. to find ore,		17:10
and did g. forth with me; and we		18: 1
I, Nephi, did g. into the mount		18: 3
arise and g. down into the ship.		18: 5
we did g. down into the ship,		18: 6
we did all g. down into the ship,		18: 6
by the way thou shouldst g.,		20:17
G. ye forth of Babylon,		20:20
say to the prisoners: G. forth;		21: 9
shall g. forth of thee.		21:17
I g. the way of all the earth.	2Ne	1:14
in my wisdom should g. forth		3:19
their cry shall g. even according		3:20
I cannot g. down to my grave		4: 5
up in the way ye should g.		4: 5
all those who would g. with me.		5: 5
all those who would g. with me.		5: 6
all those who would g. with me		5: 6
Bow down, that we may g. over—		8:23
and they shall g. away into		9:16
many people shall g. and say,		12: 3
let us g. up to the mountain of		12: 3
out of Zion shall g. forth the law,		12: 3
they shall g. into the holes of the		12:19
To g. into the clefts of the rocks,		12:21
walking and mincing as they g.,		13:16
now g. to; I will tell you what I		15: 5
blossoms shall g. up as dust;		15:24
and who will g. for us?		16: 8
G. and tell this people—		16: 9
G. forth now to meet Ahaz,		17: 3
Let us g. up against Judah		17: 6
waters of Shiloah that g. softly,		18: 6
channels, and g. over all his banks.		18: 7
he shall overflow and g. over,		18: 8
and make men g. over dry shod.		21:15
that they may g. into the gates of		23: 2
that g. down to the stones of the		24:19
g. from generation to generation		25:22
and they shall g. according to the		25:22
therefore they must g. down to hell.		26:10
must g. into the place prepared		28:23
g. and pluck the branches from a	Jac	5: 7
g. thy way; watch the tree,		5:12
let us g. down into the vineyard,		5:15
let us g. to the nethermost part of		5:19
let us g. down into the vineyard,		5:29
us g. down into the nethermost		5:38
Let us g. down and hew down		5:49
g. to, and call servants,		5:61
let us g. to and labor with our		5:62
G. to, and labor in the vineyard,		5:71
the servants did g. and labor with		5:72
shall g. forth in his power,		6: 2
ye must g. away into that lake of		6:10
I must soon g. down to my grave;		7:27

g. to, thy faith hath made thee	En	1: 8
I must soon g. down to my grave,		1:26
I soon g. to the place of my rest,		1:27
ye can g. to the other plates of	Jar	1:14
as many as g. beyond this day	WM	1: 4
soon g. the way of all the earth;	Mos	1: 9
to g. up to the temple to hear the		1:18
might g. up to the temple to hear		2: 1
about to g. down to my grave,		2:28
that I might g. down in peace,		2:28
and g. contrary to that which has		2:36
and shall g. forth amongst men,		3: 5
your children that they g. hungry,		4:14
g. up to the land of Lehi-Nephi		7: 2
the morrow they started to g. up,		7: 3
g. up to the land of Lehi-Nephi;		7: 4
that they should g. to the hill		7:16
and g. forth upon the face of the		7:27
to g. up to possess the land,		9: 3
wilderness to g. up to the land;		9: 3
if I might g. in with my people		9: 5
did g. forth against the Lamanites		9:16
did we g. forth to battle against		9:17
and we did g. forth in his might;		9:18
g. forth against the Lamanites,		9:18
g. to battle against the Lamanites;		10: 9
we did g. up to battle against		10:10
did g. up to battle against the		10:10
g. up in the strength of the Lord		10:10
to g. to battle with their might,		10:19
G. forth, and say unto this people,		11:20
Abinadi, g. and prophesy unto		12: 1
then it matters not whither I g.,		13: 9
and g. forth in mighty power upon		13:34
did g. forth to a place which was		18: 4
he himself did g. before them,		19: 9
us g. forth to meet my people,		20:24
to g. against them to battle.		21: 6
will g. according to thy command		22: 7
Thou shalt g. before this people,		24:17
I will g. with thee and deliver		24:17
Alma did g. forth into the water		25:18
and g. forth in my name,		26:20
Therefore I say unto you, G.;		26:29
Now I say unto you, G.;		26:32
for he did g. about secretly with		27:10
Now I say unto thee: G., and		27:16
say unto thee, Alma, g. thy way,		27:16
g. up to the land of Nephi that		28: 1
might g. up to the land of Nephi.		28: 5
sons g. up among the Lamanites		28: 6
Let them g. up, for many shall		28: 7
Mosiah granted that they might g.		28: 8
to g. up to preach the word		28: 9
not g. up to battle at this time	Al	3:22
might g. forth among his people,		4:19
G. forth and say unto this		5:51
And he shall g. forth, suffering		7:11
yea, come and g. forth, and show		7:15
of heaven to g. no more out.		7:25
g. with me into my house and I		8:20
G.; and also say unto my servant		8:29
g. forth and prophesy unto this		8:29
g. forth and preach again unto		9: 1
g. forth and cry mightily unto this		9:25
g. into the wilderness in search of		16: 5
did not g. in to possess the land		16:11
did Alma and Amulek g. forth,		16:15
and g. on to destruction, but		16:17
those priests who did g. forth		16:18
to g. up to the land of Nephi,		17: 8
of his Spirit to g. with them,		17: 9
G. forth among the Lamanites,		17:11
to g. forth unto the Lamanites		17:12
let us g. in search of the flocks,		17:31
I g. and contend with these men		17:33
should g. in and see my husband,		19: 5
g. with him to the land of Nephi,		20: 1
not g. up to the land of Nephi,		20: 2
shalt g. to the land of Middoni;		20: 2
and I g. that I may deliver them.		20: 3
I will g. with thee to the land of		20: 4
I g. to the land of Middoni,		20: 4
G. and deliver thy brethren,	Al	20: 5
Come, I will g. with thee down to		20: 7
that he did not g. unto his father		20:12
not g. to the land of Middoni,		20:14
I g. to the land of Middoni		20:15
should g. and call the people,		22:21
who should g. forth preaching the		23: 1
they might g. forth and preach		23: 3
but that ig might g. forth		23: 3
we shall g. to our God and shall be		24:16
we g. up to the land of Nephi,		26:23
g. amongst thy brethren, the		26:27
let us g. down to the land of		27: 5
I will g. and inquire of the Lord,		27: 7
g. down unto our brethren,		27: 7
unto our brethren, will ye g.?		27: 7
Yea, if the Lord saith unto us g.,		27: 8
will g. down unto our brethren,		27: 8
therefore let us g. down and rely		27: 9
and if he saith unto us g., we will		27:10
if he saith unto us go, we will g.;		27:10
I and my brethren will g. forth		27:15
that I might g. forth and speak		29: 1
that they may g. no more out,		29:17
Why do ye g. about perverting		30:22
he did g. on in the same manner		30:30
And yet do ye g. about, leading		30:45
g. and reclaim this people,		30:53
And Korihor did g. about from		30:58
must g. forth and stand upon the		31:14
every man did g. forth and offer		31:20
they did g. forth, and began to		32: 1
the time that ye g. out of this life,		34:34
his kingdom, to g. no more out;		34:36
should g. forth unto every nation,		37: 4
point the way they should g.,		37:40
G. unto this people and declare		37:47
Now, g., my son, and teach the		38:15
thou didst g. on unto boasting in		39: 2
g. over into the land of Siron,		39: 3
and g. no more after the lusts of		39: 9
And now, my son, g. thy way,		42:31
did g. forth among the people,		43: 1
should g. to defend themselves		43:23
if ye will g. your way and come		44: 6
as if to g. into the land of Melek.		45:18
to g. to battle against the		47: 1
also feared to g. to battle		47: 2
g. forth and compel them to		47: 3
to g. against the Nephites.		47: 6
he durst not g. down to the foot		47:11
army to g. against the Nephites		47:21
should g. forth to meet the king.		47:22
loved the king, let him g. forth,		47:27
a numerous host to g. to battle		48: 3
should g. to defend themselves		48:16
that his armies should g. forth		50: 7
g. forth into the east wilderness,		50: 9
g. against those king-men,		51:17
g. against the city of Nephihah		51:25
and behold, I g. against them,		52:11
knew not whether to g. or to		52:36
and did compel them to g. forth		53: 1
should g. forth unto the guards		55: 6
of men should g. with him.		55: 7
till we g. against the Nephites		55:10
will strengthen us to g. against		55:11
our provisions, to g. to that city.		56:32
will ye g. against them to battle?		56:44
then let us g. forth;		56:46
let us g. lest they should		56:46
g. against the city of Antiparah.		57: 3
to g. down to the land of		57:16
started to g. down to the land of		57:28
we did start to g. down to the		57:30
we durst not g. forth and attack		58: 2
did g. forth with all our might		58:13
to g. against the Lamanites to		59: 5
shall g. up to battle against them.		60:33
will g. speedily against those		61:17
we will g. forth against them		61:18
in us to g. against our brethren.		61:19
that ye should g. against them.		61:20

GO 385 GO

	Al				
Teancum in his anger did g. forth		62:36	shall g. forth unto them from	Mrm	5:15
whither she did g. we know not.		63: 8	g. forth among you as a lion,		5:24
by Alma should not g. forth		63:12	whither I g. it mattereth not.		8: 4
that he was about to g. forth	He	1:22	not friends nor whither to g.;		8: 5
was his determination to g. forth		1:23	G. ye into all the world, and		9:22
g. forth unto the judgment-seat		2: 8	G. and inquire of the Lord	Eth	1:38
and did g. forth from the land		3: 8	unto him whither we shall g.		1:38
did also g. forth into this land.		3:12	G. to and gather together thy		1:41
holy fathers, to g. no more out.		3:30	thou shalt g. at the head of them		1:42
they did g. unto the king of the		4: 2	and I will g. before thee into		1:42
to g. to the land of Nephi.		5:20	and they who shall g. with thee,		1:43
and they were bidden to g. forth		5:49	g. forth into the wilderness,		2: 5
did g. forth, and did minister		5:50	the Lord did g. before them,		2: 5
did g. into the land northward;		6: 6	G. to work and build, after the		2:16
did g. into whatsoever part of		6: 7	brother of Jared did g. to work,		2:16
g. whithersoever they would,		6: 8	ye shall not g. by the light of fire.		2:23
not g. forth unto the world,		6:25	g. forth across this raging deep		3: 3
and the wicked g. unpunished		7: 5	to g. forth unto the world,		3:21
g. ye in unto the judgment-seat,		8:27	to g. down out of the mount		4: 1
g. on in this your way of sin?		9:21	They shall not g. forth unto the		4: 6
g. to the house of Seantum,		9:26	must soon g. down to the grave;		6:19
that ye shall g. and declare unto		10:11	before we g. down to our graves.		6:19
did not g. unto his own house,		10:12	g. whithersoever they would;		7:25
he did g. forth in the Spirit,		10:17	did g. into the land southward,		10:19
g. forth again against this band		11:30	that he should g. and prophesy		13:20
Thou shalt g. back, that it		12:14	did not g. to battle again for		13:31
he did g. about spreading rumors		16:22	they did g. again to battle,		15:17
and satan did g. about, leading	3Ne	2: 3	and said unto him: G. forth.		15:33
G. down unto the Nephites and		3: 3	he must g. down to hell.	Mro	8:14
and let us g. up upon the		3:20	if I g. not out soon against the		8:27
if we should g. up against them		3:21	I soon g. to rest in the paradise		10:34
we will not g. against them,		3:21	And they shall g. forth and	DC	1: 8
should g. up to battle against		4: 5	my work shall g. forth,		3:16
should g. up to battle against the		4: 6	shall be ordained and g. forth		5: 6
not g. to war one with another;		7:14	they shall g. forth with my words		5:11
g. down and stand in the water,		11:23	testimony shall also g. forth		5:18
g. forth unto this people, and		11:41	desolating scourge shall g. forth		5:19
G. thy way unto thy brother,		12:24	g. your ways and sin no more;		6:35
compel thee to g. a mile,		12:41	wisdom that you shall g. forth.		11:26
to go a mile, g. with him twain.		12:41	called to g. into all the world		18:28
many there be who g. in thereat;		14:13	woes shall g. forth, weeping,		19: 5
that I shall g. unto them,		16: 3	that soon it may g. to the Jew,		19:27
I g. to show myself unto them.		16: 3	shall g. down into the water with		20:73
to g. through among them,		16:14	g. thy way and sin no more.		24: 2
shall g. through among them,		16:15	g. speedily unto the church		24: 3
Therefore, g. ye unto your homes,		17: 3	And whosoever shall g. to law		24:17
But now I g. unto the Father,		17: 4	And thou shalt g. with him at		25: 6
did g. forth with their sick and		17: 9	after you shall g. to the west		26: 1
none of you should g. away,		18:25	you shall g. unto the Lamanites		28: 8
then I must g. unto my Father		18:27	from the time thou shalt g.,		28:15
And now I g. unto the Father,		18:35	command you to g. from hence.		30:10
that I should g. unto the Father		18:35	g. from them only for a little		31: 6
of Jacob, g. forth among them;		20:16	G. your way whithersoever		31:11
And then shall a cry g. forth:		20:41	shall do and whither you shall g.		31:11
depart ye, g. ye out from thence,		20:41	he shall g. with my servants,		32: 2
g. ye out of the midst of her;		20:41	also shall g. with them;		32: 3
ye shall not g. out with haste		20:42	and I myself will g. with them		32: 3
out with haste nor g. by flight;		20:42	until ye shall g. to the Ohio,		37: 1
for the Lord will g. before you,		20:42	ye shall not g. until ye have		37: 2
if he g. through both treadeth		21:12	that ye should g. to the Ohio;		38:32
they shall g. out from all nations;		21:29	shall g. forth among all nations,		38:33
they shall not g. out in haste,		21:29	g. to with his might, with the		38:40
go out in haste, nor g. by flight,		21:29	And g. ye out from among the		38:42
for I will g. before them,		21:29	with thee and g. before thy face.		39:12
should no more g. over the earth,		22: 9	to g. into the eastern countries,		39:14
shall g. forth unto the Gentiles.		23: 4	art called to g. to the Ohio.		39:14
ye shall g. forth and grow up as		25: 2	shall g. forth into all nations.		39:15
And now I g. unto the Father.		27:28	Wherefore, g. forth, crying with		39:19
did g. forth upon the face of		28:18	G. forth baptizing with water,		39:20
thus they did g. forth among all		28:23	ye shall g. forth in my name,		42: 4
of the Father to g. no more out,		28:40	g. forth for a little season,		42: 5
that age g. to the land Antum,	Mrm	1: 1	ye shall g. forth in the power of		42: 6
I did g. forth at the head of an		2: 2	ye shall g. forth baptizing with		42: 7
g. forth against the Lamanites		2:27	shall g. forth into the regions		42: 8
would g. up to battle against		3:10	to g. forth to preach my gospel,		42:11
would g. up into their enemies		3:14	the wicked shall g. away into		43:33
I utterly refused to g. up against		3:16	shall g. forth into the regions		44: 3
did g. up with their armies to		4: 1	g. forth into the western		45:64
did g. against the Lamanites		4:15	Let us not g. up to battle against		45:70
I did G. to the hill Shim,		4:23	shall g. and preach my gospel		49: 1
did g. forth among the Nephites,		5: 1	that ye g. among this people,		49:11
shall g. unto the unbelieving of		5:14	g. forth as I have commanded		49:26
for this intent shall they g. –		5:14	I will g. before you and be your		49:27

GO — 386 — GOD

g. forth among the churches	DC 50:37
command them to g. hence;	51:16
Let them g. two by two,	52:10
g. to now and flee the land,	54: 7
Griffin shall also g. with him.	56: 5
and as many as will g. may go,	56: 7
and as many as will go may g.,	56: 7
to g. to the land of Missouri;	56: 9
might g. forth from Zion,	58:13
must g. forth from this place	58:64
shalt g. to the house of prayer	59: 9
able to g. up to the land of Zion	61:16
they g. by water or by land;	61:22
and g. up unto the land of Zion;	61:24
not g. until I shall command	63:39
shall g. up unto the land of Zion,	63:41
shall g. with an open heart up	64:22
shall g. up unto the land of Zion.	64:26
that his kingdom may g. forth	65: 5
the kingdom of God g. forth,	65: 6
g. not up unto the land of Zion	66: 6
G. unto the eastern lands, bear	66: 7
Samuel H. Smith g. with you,	66: 8
I, the Lord, will g. with you.	66: 8
unto them to g. forth.—	68: 2
G. ye into all the world,	68: 8
except one g. with him who will	69: 1
should g. with my servant Oliver	69: 2
and g. forth unto the ends of	72:21
to g. up unto Zion,	72:24
privileged to g. up unto Zion.—	72:24
shall g. up unto the land of Zion	72:26
have given your names to g. forth	75: 2
should g. forth and not tarry,	75: 3
to g. unto the eastern countries;	75: 6
G. ye into the south countries.	75: 8
Luke Johnson g. with him,	75: 9
not fail to g. into the world,	75:26
comforter, whither they shall g.	75:27
g. away into the lake of fire and	76:36
shall g. away into everlasting	76:44
should g. again into the eastern	79: 1
and the way whither he shall g.;	79: 2
G. ye, go ye into the world	80: 1
g. ye into the world and preach	80: 1
g. ye and preach my gospel,	80: 3
for ye cannot g. amiss.	80: 3
g. your ways and sin no more;	82: 7
g. ye into all the world;	84:62
whatsoever place ye cannot g.	84:62
the testimony may g. from you	84:62
shall g. and preach this gospel of	84:80
And they shall not g. hungry,	84:80
for I will g. before your face.	84:88
g. away from him alone by	84:92
And plagues shall g. forth,	84:97
and g. on your way rejoicing.	84:105
let the bishop g. unto the city	84:114
g. ye forth as your circumstances	84:117
G. ye and labor in the field,	88:52
G. ye also into the field, and in	88:53
to g. forth among the Gentiles	88:84
g. ye out to meet him.	88:92
the word may g. forth unto the	90: 9
and g. up unto the land of Zion;	90:28
g. up unto the land of Zion,	90:30
Sidney Rigdon g. on his journey,	93:51
g. forth unto the children of	96: 5
should not g. out unto battle	98:33
thou art called to g. into the	99: 1
not expedient that you should g.	99: 6
thou mayest g. up also unto the	99: 7
G. ye unto my vineyard, even	101:44
G. and gather together the	101:55
g. ye straightway unto the land	101:56
g. ye straightway, and do all	101:60
Mine angel shall g. up before	103:19
Mine angels shall g. up before	103:20
to g. up unto the land of Zion,	103:30
not g. up unto the land of Zion	103:34
to g. up with you unto the land	103:34
may g. with you, and preside	103:35
ye g. to and make use of the	104:63

we will not g. up unto Zion,	DC 105: 8
that thy servants may g. forth	109:22
when they g. out and proclaim	109:38
when thy servants shall g. out	109:56
let thy warning voice g. forth;	112: 5
g. ye, and I will be with you;	112:19
and from my house shall it g. forth,	112:25
and then g. ye into all the world,	112:28
Let them g., saith the Lord,	117: 5
to g. over the great waters,	118: 4
men g. with all their might and	124:49
to g. with my servant Hyrum	124:79
Let no man g. from this place	124:85
Let my servant William g. and	124:88
g. on in so great a cause?	128:22
G. forward and not backward.	128:22
for the prisoners shall g. free.	128:22
many there are that g. in thereat,	132:25
G. ye, therefore, and do	132:32
G., therefore, and I make a way	132:50
G. ye out from Babylon.	133: 5
G. ye out of Babylon;	133: 7
G. ye forth unto the land of	133: 9
that Zion may g. forth unto the	133: 9
let the cry g. forth among all	133:10
Awake and arise and g. forth to	133:10
g. ye out to meet him,	133:10
G. ye out from among the nations,	133:14
g. ye, go ye out to meet him.	133:19
go ye, g. ye out to meet him.	133:19
the servants of God shall g. forth,	133:38
but now are to g. forth unto all	133:60
g. away into outer darkness,	133:73
had made ready to g.—	135: 4
to age shall their names g. down	135: 6
let them g. to with their might,	136: 6
how many can g. next spring;	136: 7
to g. as pioneers to prepare	136: 7
g. and teach this, my will, to	136:16
be ready to g. to a land of peace.	136:16
G. thy way and do as I have	136:17
then g. straightway and tell	136:25
caused a river to g. out of Eden	Mses 3:10
upon thy belly shalt thou g.,	4:20
they g. forth out of my mouth	4:30
Enoch: G. forth and do as I have	6:32
while we g. yonder to behold	6:38
g. forth in battle array against	7: 7
the barrenness thereof shall g. forth	7: 8
G. to this people, and say unto	7:10
mercy shall g. before thy face	7:31
g. forth and declare his Gospel	8:19
to g. into the land of Canaan;	Abr 2: 4
concluded to g. down into Egypt,	2:21
thee before ye g. into Egypt,	3:15
We will g. down, for there is	3:24
the Lord said: Let us g. down.	4: 1
Let us g. down and form man	4:26
is in the desert; g. not forth:	JS 1:25
had previously designed to g.,	2:15
and told me to g. home.	2:48
to g. to my father and tell him	2:49
to g. and do as commanded	2:50
I should let them g. carelessly,	2:59
us to g. and be baptized,	2:70

GOAT

ass and the horse, and the g. and	1 Ne 18:25
and the goat, and the wild g., and	18:25
as a g. fleeth with her young	Al 14:29

GOATS

and g., and wild goats,	En 1:21
wild g., and also many horses.	1:21
sheep, and of swine, and of g.,	Eth 9:18

GOD

by the bift and power of G.	T Pg
htereof by the gift of G.	T Pg
the CHRIST, the ETERNAL G.,	T Pg
condemn not the things of G.,	T Pg
goodness and the mysteries of G.,	1 Ne 1: 1
he saw G. sitiing upon his throne,	1: 8

of singing and praising their G.	1Ne 1: 8		the church of the Lamb of G.,	1Ne 14:12
thy works, O Lord G. Almighty!	1:14		who were the saints of G.,	14:12
in the praising of his G.;	1:15		to fight against the Lamb of G.	14:13
thanks unto the Lord our G.	2: 7		the power of the Lamb of G.,	14:14
knew not the dealings of that G.	2:12		and with the power of G.	14:14
to know of the mysteries of G.,	2:16		wrath of G. was poured out	14:15
is wisdom in G. that we should	3:19		Behold, the wrath of G. is upon	14:16
by the Spirit and power of G.,	3:20		the wrath of G. is poured out upon	14:17
keeping the commandments of G.	3:21		G. hath ordained the apostle of	14:25
seen the things of G. in a vision	5: 4		the apostle of the Lamb of G.	14:25
known the goodness of G.,	5: 4		praise unto their everlasting G.,	15:15
thanks unto the G. of Israel.	5: 9		come unto the true fold of G.?	15:15
thanks unto the G. of Israel,	5:10		that it was the word of G.;	15:24
same G. who had preserved them.	5:15		hearken unto the word of G.,	15:24
I may write of the things of G.	6: 3		give heed to the word of G.	15:25
come unto the G. of Abraham,	6: 4		and also from the saints of G.	15:28
Abraham, and the G. of Isaac,	6: 4		saw that the justice of G.	15:30
and the G. of Jacob, and be	6: 4		fire, which ascendeth up unto G.	15:30
things which are pleasing unto G.	6: 5		be brought to stand before G.,	15:33
would pray unto the Lord their G.	7:21		cannot dwell in the kingdom of G.;	15:33
thanks unto the Lord their G.;	7:22		if so, the kingdom of G. must be	15:33
prophet would the Lord G. raise	10: 4		the kingdom of G. is not filthy,	15:34
he had baptized the Lamb of G.,	10:10		enter into the kingdom of G.;	15:34
by faith on the Son of G.—	10:17		to dwell in the kingdom of G.,	15:35
the Son of G. was the Messiah	10:17		greatest of all the gifts of G.	15:36
Holy Ghost, which is the gift of G.	10:17		might walk uprightly before G.,	16: 3
and the mysteries of G. shall be	10:19		murmur against the Lord his G.;	16:20
before the judgment-seat of G.;	10:21		against the Lord their G.	16:22
unclean thing can dwell with G.;	10:21		commandments of G. must be	17: 3
to the Lord, the most high G.;	11: 6		keep the commandments of G.	17: 3
for hs is G. over all the earth,	11: 6		know that I, the Lord, am G.;	17:14
in the Son of the most high G.;	11: 6		according to the power of G.	17:29
record that it is the Son of G.	11: 7		Lord their G., their Redeemer,	17:30
thou the condescension of G.?	11:16		against the true and living G.	17:30
is the mother of the Son of G.,	11:18		that is righteous is favored of G.	17:35
Behold the Lamb of G.,	11:21		had rejected every word of G.,	17:35
it is the love of G.,	11:22		the fulness of the wrath of G.	17:35
and I beheld the Son of G.	11:24		who will have him to be their G.	17:40
was the word of G., which led	11:25		against Moses, and also against G.;	17:42
representation of the love of G.;	11:25		slow to remember the Lord your G.	17:45
representation of the love of G.	11:25		I am full of the Spirit of G.,	17:47
behold the condescension of G.!	11:26		In the name of the Almighty G.,	17:48
the Lamb of G. went forth	11:27		I am filled with the power of G.,	17:48
and beheld the Lamb of G.	11:31		as naught before the power of G.,	17:48
by the power of the Lamb of G.;	11:31		for G. shall smite him.	17:48
and beheld the Lamb of G.,	11:32		for G. had commanded me that	17:49
the Son of the everlasting G.	11:32		If G. had commanded me to	17:50
the Lamb of G. descending out	12: 6		so powerful was the Spirit of G.;	17:52
were ordained of G., and chosen.	12: 7		that I am the Lord their G.	17:53
their faith in the Lamb of G.	12:10		wherefore, worship the Lord thy G.,	17:55
even like unto the Lamb of G.	12:11		land which the Lord thy G. shall	17:55
the justice of the Eternal G.,	12:18		judgments of G. were upon them,	18:15
Messiah who is the Lamb of G.,	12:18		I did look unto my G., and I did	18:16
which slayeth the saints of G.,	13: 5		out of this time to meet their G.;	18:18
do they destroy the saints of G.,	13: 9		save it were the power of G.,	18:20
wrath of G. is upon the seed	13:11		G. of Israel do men trample	19: 7
I beheld the Spirit of G.,	13:12		the G. of our fathers, who were	19:10
I beheld the Spirit of G.,	13:13		the G. of Abraham, and of Isaac,	19:10
I beheld the wrath of G.	13:14		of Isaac, and the G. of Jacob,	19:10
the power of G. was with them,	13:18		The Lord G. surely shall visit	19:11
the wrath of G. was upon all	13:18		wrought upon by the Spirit of G.,	19:12
delivered by the power of G.	13:19		exclaim: The G. of nature suffers.	19:12
truth which is in the Lamb of G.	13:24		they crucify the G. of Israel,	19:13
to the truth which is in G.	13:25		and glory of the G. of Israel.	19:13
is the book of the Lamb of G.	13:28		mention of the G. of Israel,	20: 1
which is of G.—	13:29		themselves upon the G. of Israel,	20: 2
lifted up by the power of G.	13:30		the Lord G., and his Spirit, hath	20:16
the land that the Lord G. hath	13:30		the Lord thy G. who teacheth	20:17
the Lord G. will not suffer that	13:30		and my work with my G.	21: 4
Neither will the Lord G. suffer	13:32		my G. shall be my strength.	21: 5
Wherefore saith the Lamb of G.:	13:33		Thus saith the Lord G.:	21:22
Behold, saith the Lamb of G.,	13:34		G. will raise up a mighty nation	22: 7
also the book of the Lamb of G.,	13:38		G. will proceed to do a marvelous	22: 8
the Lamb of G. is the Son of	13:40		G. will proceed to make bare his	22:11
is one G. and one Shepherd	13:41		the fulness of the wrath of G.	22:16
hearken unto the Lamb of G.	14: 1		prophet shall the Lord your G.	22:20
hearts against the Lamb of G.,	14: 2		to the commandments of G.	22:30
destruction, saith the Lamb of G.;	14: 3		mercies of G. in sparing their lives,	2Ne 1: 2
according to the justice of G.,	14: 4		a land which the Lord G. hath	1: 5
hearts against the Lamb of G.	14: 6		whom the Lord G. shall bring out	1: 9
cometh, saith the Lamb of G.,	14: 7		their Redeemer and their G.,	1:10
the church of the Lamb of G.	14:10		the Lord your G. should come out	1:17
the church of the Lamb of G.	14:10		displeasure of a just G. upon you,	1:22

GOD

an instrument in the hands of G.,	2 Ne 1:24
he hath sought the glory of G.,	1:25
of the power of the word of G.,	1:26
according to that which is in G.,	1:26
the power of G. must be with him,	1:27
thou knowest the greatness of G.;	2: 2
be spent in the service of thy G.	2: 3
can dwell in the presence of G.,	2: 8
he is the first-fruits unto G.,	2: 9
all men come unto G.;	2:10
needs destroy the wisdom of G.	2:12
the mercy, and the justice of G.	2:12
these things are not there is no G.	2:13
if there is no G. we are not,	2:13
for there is a G., and he hath	2:14
G. gave unto man that he should	2:16
suppose that an angel of G.,	2:17
that which was evil before G.	2:17
but ye shall be as G., knowing	2:18
according to the will of G.,	2:21
which the Lord G. gave unto the	2:21
the commandments which G. hath	2:26
Lord G. would rise up a righteous	3: 5
seer shall the Lord my G. raise	3: 6
instrument in the hands of G.,	3:24
which is great in the sight of G.,	3:24
For the Lord G. hath said	4: 4
the Lord G. will not suffer that	4: 7
My G. hath been my support;	4:20
will rejoice in thee, my G.,	4:30
that G. will give liberally to him	4:35
my G. will give me, if I ask	4:35
yea, I will cry unto thee, my G.,	4:35
and mine everlasting G. Amen.	4:35
cry much unto the Lord my G.,	5: 1
and the revelations of G.;	5: 6
the Lord G. did cause a skin of	5:21
And thus saith the Lord G.:	5:22
And the Lord G. said unto me:	5:25
the Lord G. said unto me:	5:30
that which is pleasing unto G.	5:32
pleased with the things of G.	5:32
Jacob, having been called of G.,	6: 2
and glorify the name of your G.	6: 4
Thus saith the Lord G.:	6: 6
the Lord G., the Holy One of Israel,	6: 9
Lord G. will fulfil his covenants	6:12
shall know that the Lord is G.,	6:15
for the Mighty G. shall deliver his	6:17
The Lord G. hath given me the	7: 4
The Lord G. hath opened mine	7: 5
For the Lord G. will help me,	7: 7
For the Lord G. will help me.	7: 9
But I am the Lord thy G.,	8:15
of the Lord, the rebuke of thy G.	8:20
thy G. pleadeth the cause of his	8:22
to the true church and fold of G.;	9: 2
which the Lord G. shall bestow	9: 3
in our bodies we shall see G.	9: 4
O the wisdom of G., his mercy	9: 8
the presence of the Eternal G.,	9: 8
out from the presence of our G.,	9: 9
how great the goodness of our G.,	9:10
the way of deliverance of our G.,	9:11
O how great the plan of our G.!	9:13
the paradise of G. must deliver up	9:13
to the holy judgment of G.	9:15
for the Lord G. hath spoken it,	9:16
greatness and the justice of our G.!	9:17
shall inherit the kingdom of G.,	9:18
greatness of the mercy of our G.,	9:19
O how great the holiness of our G.!	9:20
be saved in the kingdom of G.	9:23
for the Lord G., the Holy One	9:24
to that G. who gave them breath,	9:26
has all the commandments of G.,	9:27
not unto the counsel of G.,	9:28
hearken unto the counsels of G.	9:29
wherefore, their treasure is their G.	9:30
for they shall return to G.,	9:38
against that Holy G.,	9:39
for the Lord G. is his name.	9:41
consider themselves fools before G.,	9:42
I pray the G. of my salvation	2 Ne 9:44
the G. of Israel did witness that	9:44
come unto that G. who is the	9:45
judgments, O Lord G. Almighty—	9:46
will praise the holy name of my G.	9:49
remember the words of your G.;	9:52
G. will be merciful unto many;	10: 2
for thus it behooveth our G.,	10: 3
earth that would crucify their G.	10: 3
and know that he be their G.	10: 4
behold, thus saith the Lord G.:	10: 7
great in the eyes of their G.,	10: 8
behold, this land, said G., shall be	10:10
against Zion shall perish, saith G.	10:13
for me are against me, saith our G.	10:16
brethren, thus saith our G.:	10:18
for it is a choice land, saith G.	10:19
they shall worship me, saith G.	10:19
that our merciful G. has given us	10:20
behold, the Lord G. has led away	10:22
yourselves to the will of G.,	10:24
after ye are reconciled unto G.,	10:24
only in and through the grace of G.	10:24
may G. raise you from death	10:25
into the eternal kingdom of G.,	10:25
G. hath said, I will establish	11: 3
G. sendeth more witnesses,	11: 3
which have been given of G.	11: 4
there be no Christ there be no G.;	11: 7
and if there be no G. we are not,	11: 7
there is a G., and he is Christ,	11: 7
the house of the G. of Jacob;	12: 3
saith the Lord G. of Hosts.	13:15
and G. that is holy shall be	15:16
Thus saith the Lord G.:	17: 7
thee a sign of the Lord thy G.;	17:11
but will ye weary my G. also?	17:13
shall not stand; for G. is with us.	18:10
seek unto their G. for the living	18:19
and curse their king and their G.,	18:21
Counselor, The Mighty G.,	19: 6
of Jacob, unto the mighty G.	20:21
For the Lord G. of Hosts shall	20:23
thus saith the Lord G. of Hosts;	20:24
Behold, G. is my salvation;	22: 2
be as when G. overthrew Sodom	23:19
my throne above the stars of G.;	24:13
may know the judgments of G.,	25: 3
concerning the judgments of G.,	25: 6
be saved in the kingdom of G.	25:13
unto them that fight against G.	25:14
the Lord G. hath scourged them	25:16
believe in Christ, the son of G.,	25:16
also the word of the angel of G.,	25:19
be Jesus Christ, the Son of G.	25:19
And as the Lord G. liveth that	25:20
and as the Lord G. liveth,	25:20
the Lord G. promised unto me	25:21
to the will and pleasure of G.;	25:22
and to be reconciled to G.;	25:23
performances and ordinances of G.	25:30
to G. from the ground against them.	26: 3
but I must cry unto my G.:	26: 7
Jesus is the Christ, the Eternal G.;	26:12
when the Lord G. shall bring these	26:14
after the Lord G. shall have	26:15
Lord G. will give unto him power,	26:16
For thus saith the Lord G.:	26:17
seek to destroy the things of G.	26:17
yea, thus saith the Lord G.:	26:18
the power and miracles of G.,	26:20
Lord G. worketh not in darkness.	26:23
the Lord G. hath given a	26:30
the Lord G. hath commanded	26:32
name of the Lord their G. in vain;	26:32
and all are alike unto G.,	26:33
the Lord G. shall bring forth	27: 6
shall be a revelation from G.,	27: 7
be sealed by the power of G.,	27:10
behold it, by the power of G.,	27:12
according to the will of G.,	27:13
for the Lord G. hath said that	27:13
the Lord G. will proceed to bring	27:14

GOD 389 GOD

that rejecteth the word of G.!	2 Ne 27:14
the Lord G. shall say unto him	27:15
and not for the glory of G.	27:16
the Lord G. will deliver again the	27:19
Then shall the Lord G. say	27:20
For behold, I am G.; and I am a	27:23
and I am a G. of miracles;	27:23
and shall fear the G. of Israel.	27:34
And they deny the power of G.,	28: 5
behold there is no G. today,	28: 5
he is not a G. of miracles;	28: 6
be merry; nevertheless, fear G.—	28: 8
G. will beat us with a few stripes,	28: 8
be saved in the kingdom of G.	28: 8
saith the Lord G. Almighty,	28:15
the Lord G. will speedily visit	28:16
stand before the throne of G.,	28:23
and denieth the power of G.,	28:26
angry because of the truth of G.!	28:28
We have received the word of G.,	28:29
need no more of the word of G.,	28:29
behold, thus saith the Lord G.:	28:30
saith the Lord G. of Hosts!	28:32
unto them, saith the Lord G.	28:32
saith the Lord G. of Hosts.	28:32
thus saith the Lord G.: O fools,	29: 4
I, the Lord your G., have created	29: 7
a witness unto you that I am G.,	29: 8
the house of Israel, that I am G.,	29:14
keep the commandments of G.	30: 1
unto them from the hand of G.;	30: 6
the Lord G. shall commence his	30: 8
shall the Lord G. judge the poor,	30: 9
the Lord G. shall cause a great	30:10
doth the Lord G. work among	31: 3
For the Lord G. giveth light unto	31: 3
should baptize the Lamb of G.	31: 4
if the Lamb of G., he being holy,	31: 5
the Lamb of G. did fulfil all	31: 6
and no deception before G.,	31:13
of the Son of the living G.,	31:16
a love of G. and of all men.	31:20
be saved in the kingdom of G.	31:21
which is one G., without end.	31:21
and I cry unto my G. in faith,	33: 3
that the Lord G. will consecrate	33: 4
not partake of the goodness of G.,	33:14
of the mouth of the Lamb of G.,	33:14
and partake of the goodness of G.,	Jac 1: 7
Wherefore, we would to G. that we	1: 8
all men not to rebel against G.,	1: 8
teach them the word of G. with	1:19
which I am under to G.,	2: 2
declare unto you the word of G.	2: 2
yea, and abominable unto G.	2: 5
and chaste and delicate before G.,	2: 7
which thing is pleasing unto G.;	2: 7
to hear the pleasing word of G.,	2: 8
which I have received from G.,	2: 9
upon the pleasing word of G.	2: 9
to the strict commands of G.,	2:10
piercing eye of the Almighty G.	2:10
the plainness of the word of G.	2:11
G. justifieth you in this thing?	2:14
seek ye for the kingdom of G.	2:18
things which G. hath given you,	2:20
the word of G. burthens me	2:23
I the Lord G. will not suffer that	2:26
For I, the Lord G., delight in	2:28
ascend up to G. against you.	2:35
the strictness of the word of G.,	2:35
Look unto G. with firmness of	3: 1
receive the pleasing word of G.,	3: 2
are filthy this day before G.;	3: 3
the Lord G. will lead away the	3: 4
the Lord G. will not destroy	3: 6
with them before the throne of G.	3: 8
which is the word of G.,	3: 9
obedient unto the commands of G.	4: 5
which is a similitude of G. and his	4: 5
Nevertheless, the Lord G. showeth	4: 7
despise not the revelations of G.	4: 8

Wherefore, if G. being able to	Jac 4: 9
the first-fruits of Christ unto G.,	4:11
for G. also spake them unto	4:13
for G. hath taken away his	4:14
they desired it g. hath done it,	4:14
how merciful is our G. unto us,	6: 4
be saved in the kingdom of G.	6: 4
and cleave unto G. as he	6: 5
by the good word of G.	6: 7
and the power of G.,	6: 8
awful guilt before the bar of G.?	6: 9
before the pleasing bar of G.,	6:13
they pervert the right way of G.,	7: 7
the Lord G. poured in his	7: 8
What am I that I should tempt G.	7:14
but if G. shall smite thee, let that	7:14
for I have lied unto G.;	7:19
I have thus lied unto G.	7:19
but I confess unto G.	7:19
the power of G. came down upon	7:21
and the love of G. was restored	7:23
trusting in the G. and rock of	7:25
blessed be the name of my G.	En 1: 1
the wrestle which I had before G.,	1: 2
knew that G. could not lie;	1: 6
my whole soul unto G. for them.	1: 9
the Lord G. would preserve a	1:13
the Lord G. was able to preserve	1:15
I did cry unto G. that he would	1:16
unto the true faith in G.	1:20
the judgments and the power of G.,	1:23
wrought upon by the power of G.	1:26
G. is exceeding merciful unto them,	Jar 1: 3
according to the word of G.,	1:10
continually by the word of G.;	Om 1:13
by the gift and power of G.	1:20
may G. grant that he may survive	WM 1:25
And my prayer to g. is	1: 2
come to the knowledge of G.,	1: 8
which G. has given me.	1: 8
And I, Mormon, pray to G. that	1: 9
according to the word of G.	1:11
they did speak the word of G.	1:11
not knowing the mysteries of G.	1:17
the commandments of G., even	Mos 1: 3
and preserved by the hand of G.,	1: 4
keep the commandments of G.,	1: 5
whom the Lord our G. hath given	1: 7
which the Lord G. hath brought	1:10
the displeasure of G. upon them;	1:11
give thanks to the Lord their G.,	1:17
keep the commandments of G.,	2: 4
with love towards G. and all men.	2: 4
mysteries of G. may be unfolded	2: 9
a clear conscience before G.	2:15
only been in the service of G.	2:16
are only in the service of your G.	2:17
yet has been in the service of G.	2:19
to that G. who has created you,	2:20
with a clear conscience before G.	2:27
I shall stand to be judged of G.	2:27
singing the praises of a just G.	2:28
but the Lord G. doth support me,	2:30
or the commandments of G.	2:31
transgressed the law of G.	2:33
in open rebellion against G.;	2:37
and dieth an enemy to G.,	2:38
keep the commandments of G.	2:41
thereby they may dwell with G. in	2:41
unto me by an angel from G.	3: 2
called Jesus Christ, the Son of G.,	3: 8
the will of G. concerning them,	3:11
that he rebelleth against G.!	3:12
And the Lord G. hath sent his	3:13
the Lord G. saw that his people	3:14
natural man is an enemy to G.,	3:19
shall be found blameless before G.,	3:21
name of the Lord G. Omnipotent.	3:21
which the Lord thy G. hath	3:22
blameless in the sight of G.,	3:22
the Lord G. hath commanded	3:23

GOD 390 GOD

out of the cup of the wrath of G.	Mos 3:26	Son to the Father, being one G.,	Mos 15: 5
in Jesus Christ, the Son of G.,	4: 2	G. breaketh the bands of death,	15: 8
knowledge of the goodness of G.	4: 5	the heirs of the kingdom of G.	15:11
knowledge of the goodness of G.,	4: 6	unto Zion: Thy G. reigneth!	15:14
Believe in g.; believe that he is,	4: 9	kept the commandments of G.,	15:22
humble yourselves before G.;	4:10	They are raised to dwell with G.	15:23
the knowledge of the glory of G.,	4:11	and fear, and tremble before G.,	15:26
the greatness of G., and your own	4:11	have wilfully rebelled against G.,	15:26
be filled with the love of G.,	4:12	known the commandments of G.,	15:26
they transgress the laws of G.,	4:14	shall see the salvation of our G.	15:31
no interest in the kingdom of G.	4:18	and shall confess before G. that	16: 1
upon the same Being, even G.,	4:19	G. redeemed his people from	16: 4
now, if G., who has created you,	4:21	of sin and rebellion against G.,	16: 5
doth not belong to you but to G.,	4:22	being an enemy to G.;	16: 5
ye may walk builtless before G.—	4:26	also is the devil an enemy to G.	16: 5
observe the commandments of G.,	4:30	to stand before the bar of G.,	16:10
through the infinite goodness of G.,	5: 3	G. himself should come down	17: 8
enter into a covenant with our G.	5: 5	the judgments of G. would come	17:11
out of the cup of the wrath of G.	5: 5	salvation of the Lord their G.	17:15
entered into the covenant with G.	5: 8	Thus G. executeth vengeance	17:19
be found at the right hand of G.,	5: 9	O G., receive my soul.	17:19
himself on the left hand of G.	5:10	deny the commandments of G.,	17:20
not found on the left hand of G.,	5:12	to come into the fold of G.,	18: 8
Christ, the Lord G. Omnipotent,	5:15	and to stand as witnesses of G.	18: 9
who is G. above all.	5:15	that ye may be redeemed of G.	18: 9
entered into a covenant with G.	6: 1	authority from the Almighty G.,	18:13
know the commandments of G.,	6: 3	were filled with the grace of G.	18:16
I am very thankful before G.	7:12	they were called the church of G.,	18:17
rejoice, and put your trust in G.,	7:19	the power and authority of G.	18:17
in that G. who was the God of	7:19	Alma, having authority from G.,	18:18
who was the G. of Abraham,	7:19	pertaining to the kingdom of G.	18:18
also, that G. who brought the	7:19	they became the children of G.	18:22
again, that same G. has brought	7:20	give thanks to the Lord their G.	18:23
yea, a chosen man of G., who	7:26	to worship the Lord their G.,	18:25
them that Christ was the G.,	7:27	were to receive the grace of G.,	18:26
was created after the image of G.,	7:27	having the knowledge of G., that	18:26
that G. should come down among	7:27	power and authority from G.	18:26
down the wrath of G. upon them.	7:28	and good desires towards G.,	18:28
and it is a gift from G.	8:13	having been commanded of G.;	18:29
who has this high gift from G.	8:14	did walk uprightly before G.,	18:29
should possess the power of G.,	8:16	and they did cry mightily to G.;	21:14
great power given him from G.	8:16	did they cry unto their G. that	21:14
Thus G. has provided a means	8:18	king Mosiah had a gift from G.,	21:28
and gave thanks to G., saying:	8:19	sins and iniquities against G.;	21:30
slow to remember the Lord our G.	9: 3	who had formed a church of G.	21:30
And G. did hear our cries and	9:18	the strength and power of G.,	21:30
keep the commandments of G.,	11: 2	entered into a covenant with G.	21:31
and turn to the Lord their G.,	11:21	also entered into a covenant with G.,	21:32
that I am the Lord their G.,	11:22	that had authority from G.	21:33
their God, and am a jealous G.,	11:22	to serve G. with all their hearts;	21:35
and turn unto the Lord their G.,	11:23	been delivered by the power of G.	23:13
it be the Lord the Almighty G.	11:23	except he be a man of G.	23:14
cry mightily to the Lord their G.,	11:25	except it were by him from G.	23:17
saith that G. will destroy them.	12: 9	the Lord their G., yea, even the	23:23
we should be condemned of G.	12:13	even the G. of Abraham and	23:23
saith unto Zion, Thy G. reigneth;	12:21	remember the Lord their G.	23:27
shall see the salvation of our G.?	12:24	nevertheless they knew not G.;	24: 5
you ought to tremble before G.	12:30	concerning the Lord their G.,	24: 5
keep the commandments of G.	12:33	they began to cry mightily to G.	24:10
I am the Lord thy G., who	12:34	should be found calling upon G.	24:11
shalt have no other G. before me.	12:35	their voices to the Lord their G.,	24:12
for G. shall smite you if	13: 3	of a surety that I the Lord G.,	24:14
therefore, G. will not suffer that	13: 3	poured out their thanks to G.	24:21
G. has commanded me;	13: 4	except it were the Lord their G.	24:21
I have spoken the word of G.	13: 4	And they gave thanks to G.,	24:22
power and authority from G.;	13: 6	voices in the praises of their G.	24:22
of the commandments of G.,	13:11	the immediate goodness of G.,	25:10
for I the Lord thy G. am a	13:13	their voices and give thanks to G.	25:18
Lord thy God am a jealous G.,	13:13	did belong to the church of G.;	25:18
name of the Lord thy G. in vain;	13:15	could they all hear the word of G.	25:20
the sabbath of the Lord thy G.,	13:18	yea, even the church of G.;	25:22
the Lord thy G. giveth thee.	13:20	were repentance and faith in G.	25:22
which G. himself shall make for	13:28	the name of Christ, or of G.,	25:23
to remember the Lord their G.;	13:29	they did join the churches of G.;	25:23
keep them in remembrance of G.	13:30	they were called the people of G.	25:24
through the redemption of G.	13:32	not understand the word of G.;	26: 3
G. should redeem his people?	13:33	not call upon the lord their G.	26: 4
G. himself should come down	13:34	so numerous as the people of G.;	26: 5
smitten of G., and afflicted.	14: 4	should do wrong in the sight of G.	26:13
G. himself shall come down among	15: 1	poured out his whole soul to G.,	26:14
he shall be called the Son of G.,	15: 2	that I am the Lord their G.,	26:26
was conceived by the power of G.;	15: 3	to the commandments of G.	26:33
And they are one G., yea, the	15: 4	walking circumspectly before G.,	26:37

GOD

teaching the word of G. in all	Mos	26:38
not belong to the church of G.		26:38
every one by the word of G.,		26:39
being commanded of God to pray		26:39
who belonged to the church of G.		27: 2
they did abound in the grace of G.		27: 5
prosperity of the church of G.;		27: 9
a chance for the enemy of G.		27: 9
about to destroy the church of G.,		27:10
to the commandments of G.,		27:10
going about rebelling against G.,		27:11
persecutest thou the church of G.?		27:13
of the power and authority of G.,		27:14
can ye dispute the power of G.?		27:15
And I am sent from G.		27:15
nothing save the power of G. that		27:18
knew that it was the power of G.		27:20
and to pray to the Lord their G.		27:22
of the goodness and glory of G.		27:22
be born again; yea, born of G.,		27:25
being redeemed of G., becoming		27:25
nowise inherit the kingdom of G.		27:26
burning, and I am born of G.		27:28
behold the marvelous light of G.		27:29
shall they confess that he is G.;		27:31
who live without G. in the world,		27:31
and preaching the word of G.		27:32
keep the commandments of G.		27:33
instruments in the hands of G.		27:36
might impart the word of G. to		28: 1
knowledge of the Lord their G.,		28: 2
to rejoice in the Lord their G.,		28: 2
the Lord their G. had given them.		28: 2
to the commandments of G.,		28:11
to the commandments of G.		29:11
that a man should be judged of G.		29:12
judgments of G. are always just,		29:12
would establish the laws of G.,		29:13
you the commandments of G.,		29:14
his feet the commandments of G.;		29:22
the judgments of G. will come		29:27
to the commandments of G.		29:36
to fulfil the commandments of G.		29:45
walking uprightly before G.,	Al	1: 1
he termed to be the word of G.,		1: 3
belonged to the church of G.,		1: 7
him with the words of G.		1: 7
an instrument in the hands of G.		1: 8
him with the words of G.		1: 9
was contrary to the word of G.;		1:15
not belong to the church of G.		1:19
did belong to the church of G.,		1:19
they did impart the word of G.,		1:20
no more among the people of G.		1:24
keeping the commandments of G.,		1:25
the word of G. unto the people,		1:26
labors to hear the word of G.		1:26
unto them the word of G.		1:26
intent to destroy the church of G.		2: 4
Nephites, or the people of G.		2:11
Alma, being a man of G., being		2:30
the Lord G. set a mark upon		3: 7
the Lord G. might preserve his		3: 8
in the commandments of G. and		3:11
Thus the word of G. is fulfilled,		3:14
were fulfilling the words of G.		3:18
out in open rebellion against G.;		3:18
judgments of G. sent upon them		4: 3
were joined to the church of G.;		4: 4
themselves to the church of G.		4: 5
not belong to the church of G.		4: 9
of the humble followers of G.,		4:15
he might preach the word of G.		4:19
pull down, by the word of G.		4:19
priesthood of the holy order of G.,		4:20
according to the holy order of G.,		5:hd
the word of G. unto the people,		5: 1
a high priest over the church of G.,		5: 3
power and authority from G.		5: 3
by the mercy and power of G.		5: 4
to establish the church of G.		5: 5
sleep, and they awoke unto G.		5: 7
he not speak the words of G.,		5:11
trust in the true and living G.		5:13
ye spiritually been born of G.?	Al	5:14
to stand before G. to be judged		5:15
brought before the tribunal of G.		5:18
the commandments of G.?		5:18
can ye look up to G. at that day		5:19
the image of G. engraven upon		5:19
shall stand before the bar of G.,		5:22
to sit down in the kingdom of G.,		5:24
yourselves blameless before G.?		5:27
ye are not prepared to meet G.		5:28
for the Lord G. hath spoken it!		5:32
is good cometh from G., and		5:40
to the commandments of G.		5:43
according to the holy order of G.,		5:44
unto me by the Holy Spirit of G.		5:46
the Lord G. hath made them		5:46
the manifestation of the Spirit of G.		5:47
the Son of G. cometh in his glory,		5:50
walk after the holy order of G.,		5:54
the word of G. may be fulfilled,		5:57
the word of G. must be fulfilled.		5:58
according to the order of G.,		6: 1
and humble themselves before G.—		6: 3
word of G. was liberal unto all,		6: 5
together to hear the word of G.		6: 5
children of G. were commanded		6: 6
souls of those who knew not G.		6: 6
began to declare the word of G.		6: 8
of Jesus Christ, the Son of G.,		6: 8
had humbled yourselves before G.,		7: 3
And blessed be the name of G.,		7: 4
according to the Spirit of G.,		7: 5
worship the true and living G.,		7: 6
the Lord G. hath power to do all		7: 8
and the Son of G. cometh upon		7: 9
a son, yea, even the Son of G.		7:10
the Son of G. suffereth		7:13
have faith on the Lamb of G.,		7:14
show unto your G. that ye are		7:15
keepeth the commandments of G.		7:16
which leads to the kingdom of G.;		7:19
received into the kingdom of G.;		7:21
to a sense of your duty to G.,		7:22
walk after the holy order of G.,		7:22
keeping the commandments of G.		7:23
always returning thanks unto G.		7:23
the peace of G. rest upon you.		7:27
according to the holy order of G.,		8: 4
he began to preach the word of G.		8: 8
with G. in mighty prayer		8:10
keeping the commandments of G.		8:15
the Lord G. will destroy them.		8:16
servant of G. something to eat?		8:19
thou art a holy prophet of G.,		8:20
and he gave thanks unto G.		8:22
high priest over the church of G.		8:23
called to preach the word of G.		8:24
declare the words of G. unto them;		8:30
by the miraculous power of G.		9:hd
having been commanded of G.		9: 1
they knew not that G. could do		9: 5
Who is G., that sendeth no		9: 6
the commandments of G.		9: 8
of Jerusalem by the hand of G.?		9: 9
inherit the kingdom of G.		9:12
kept the commandments of G.;		9:14
unto them of the Lord their G.;		9:19
been visited by the Spirit of G.;		9:21
after having been delivered of G.		9:22
the Son of G. shall come in his		9:26
hardened against the word of G.,		9:30
was written by the finger of G.		10: 2
I went on rebelling against G.,		10: 6
man, who is a chosen man of G.;		10: 7
you concerning the things of G.		10: 8
it was said by an angel of G.		10: 9
snares to catch the holy ones of G.		10:17
the wrath of G. upon your heads,		10:18
Believest thou that there is no G.?		11:24
thou knowest that there is a G.,		11:24
hast lied before G. unto me.		11:25
should deny the true and living G.,		11:25
sayest there is a true and living G.?		11:26

GOD

Yea, there is a true and living G.	Al	11:27
Is there more than one G.?		11:28
Is it the Son of G.?		11:32
for he said there is but one G.;		11:35
that the Son of G. shall come,		11:35
had authority to command G.		11:35
I had authority to command G.		11:36
Is the Son of G. the very		11:38
the dead and stand before G.,		11:41
be brought to stand before G.,		11:43
the Son, and G. the Father,		11:44
Spirit, which is one Eternal G.,		11:44
but thou hast lied unto G.;		12: 3
and more of the power of G.;		12: 7
concerning the kingdom of G.		12: 8
are brought to stand before G.		12: 8
to know the mysteries of G.;		12: 9
to know the mysteries of G. until		12:10
brought before the bar of G.,		12:12
not dare to look up to our G.;		12:14
saith that G. placed cherubim		12:21
according to the word of G.,		12:22
been void, making G. a liar,		12:23
a time to prepare to meet G.;		12:24
word of G. would have been void,		12:26
And after G. had appointed		12:28
therefore G. conversed with men,		12:30
Therefore G. gave unto them		12:32
to the supreme goodness of G.		12:32
But G. did call on men,		12:33
we provoke not the Lord our G.		12:37
let us enter into the rest of G.,		12:37
time when the Lord G. gave		13: 1
the Lord G. ordained priests,		13: 1
to the foreknowledge of G.,		13: 3
would reject the Spirit of G.		13: 4
of the holy order of G.,		13: 6
and became high priests of G.;		13:10
their righteousness before G.,		13:10
pure and spotless before G.,		13:12
into the rest of the Lord their G.		13:12
humble yourselves before G.,		13:13
look forward on the Son of G.,		13:16
according to the holy order of G.,		13:18
Would to G. that it might be in		13:25
love of G. always in your hearts,		13:29
testified that there was but one G.,		14: 5
these men are spotless before G.		14: 7
to believe in the word of G.		14: 8
the power of G. which is in us,		14:10
neither has G. saved them		14:15
If ye have the power of G.		14:24
the power of G. was upon Alma		14:25
O Lord our G., have mercy on		15:10
Ammonihah, for the word of G.,		15:16
to humble themselves before G.,		15:17
to worship G. before the altar,		15:17
they said G. could not destroy,		16: 9
they did impart the word of G.,		16:14
into the rest of the Lord their G.		16:17
forth the coming of the Son of G.,		16:19
the Son of G. should come;		16:20
the word of G. being preached		16:21
the kingdom for the word of G.,		17:hd
they might know the word of G.		17: 2
with power and authority of G.		17: 3
had been teaching the word of G.		17: 4
brought before the altar of G.,		17: 4
to preach the word of G. unto		17: 8
an instrument in the hands of G.		17: 9
declare unto them the word of G.		17:12
preach the word of G. to a wild		17:14
curse of G. had fallen upon them		17:15
to the word and power of G.		17:17
having imparted the word of G.		17:18
being filled with the Spirit of G.,		18:16
Believest thou that there is a G.?		18:24
And Ammon said: This is G.		18:28
this Great Spirit, who is G.;		18:28
heavens is a place where G. dwells		18:30
Art thou sent from G.?		18:33
was created after the image of G.,		18:34
faith and desires which are in G.	Al	18:35
thou art a prophet of a holy G.,		19: 4
was under the power of G.;		19: 6
was the light of the glory of G.,		19: 6
and he was carried away in G.—		19: 6
not dead, but he sleepeth in G.,		19: 8
Blessed be the name of G.,		19:12
or among all the people of G.		19:14
in prayer and thanksgiving to G.		19:14
they also began to cry unto G.,		19:15
that it was the power of G.;		19:17
to believe in the power of G.,		19:17
O blessed G., have mercy on this		19:29
they had told them things of G.,		19:34
one hath told me, save it be G.;		20: 5
and holy prophets of the true G.		20:15
from the ground to the Lord his G.,		20:18
together to worship G.		21: 6
that G. will save all men.		21: 6
that the Son of G. shall come		21: 7
preaching the word of G. in every		21:16
of worshiping the Lord their G.		21:22
keeping the commandments of G.		21:23
Believest thou that there is a G.?		22: 7
Amalekites say that there is a G.,		22: 7
if now thou sayest there is a G.,		22: 7
as thou livest, O king, there is a G.		22: 8
Is G. that Great Spirit that		22: 9
how G. created man after his		22:12
that G. gave him commandments,		22:12
I do that I may be born of G.,		22:15
if thou wilt bow down before G.,		22:16
and will bow down before G.,		22:16
O G., Aaron hath told me that		22:18
hath told me that there is a G.;		22:18
and if there is a G., and if thou		22:18
and if thou art G., wilt thou		22:18
forth preaching the word of G.,		23: 1
that the word of G. might have no		23: 3
and to teach the word of G.		23: 4
power of G. working miracles		23: 6
not fight against G. any more,		23: 7
the curse of G. did no more follow		23:18
for war against the people of G.		24: 4
I thank my G., my beloved people,		24: 7
our great G. has in goodness sent		24: 7
I thank my great G. that he has		24: 8
And behold, I also thank my G.,		24: 9
And I also thank my G., yea my		24:10
my great G., that he hath granted		24:10
to get G. to take them away		24:11
to repent sufficiently before G.		24:11
G. hath taken away our stains,		24:12
blood of the Son of our great G.,		24:13
great G. has had mercy on us,		24:14
Oh, how merciful is our G.!		24:15
as a testimony to our G. at the		24:15
go to our G. and shall be saved.		24:16
in their view a testimony to G.,		24:18
vouching and covenanting with G.,		24:18
have gone to dwell with their G.		24:22
praised G. even in the very act of		24:23
the people of G. were joined		24:26
enlightened by the Spirit of G.,		24:30
by fire because of his belief in G.;		25:11
themselves to the people of G.,		25:13
G. would have granted unto us		26: 1
behold the marvelous light of G.!		26: 3
instruments in the hands of G.		26: 3
been brought into the fold of G.		26: 4
Blessed be the name of our G.;		26: 8
also have been strangers to G.		26: 9
joy, and I will rejoice in my G.		26:11
but I will boast of my G., for in		26:12
for he is the Most High G.,		26:14
yea, we will praise our G. forever.		26:16
G. would have been so merciful as		26:17
to know the mysteries of G.;		26:22
alone but upon the mercies of G.		26:28
the power and wisdom of G.		26:29
that they have gone to their G.,		26:34
even unto boasting in my G.;		26:35

GOD

blessed is the name of my G.,	Al	26:36
blessed be the name of my G.,		26:36
G. is mindful of every people,		26:37
give thanks unto my G. forever.		26:37
they were angels sent from G.		27: 4
swallowed up in the joy of his G.,		27:17
who were of the church of G.		27:27
for their zeal towards G.,		27:27
dwell at the right hand of G.,		28:12
speak with the trump of G.,		29: 1
repent and come unto our G.,		29: 2
the firm decree of a just G.,		29: 4
instrument in the hands of G.		29: 9
coming to the Lord their G.,		29:10
yea, the Lord G., the God of		29:11
the G. of Abraham, the God of		29:11
the G. of Isaac, and the God of		29:11
the G. of Jacob, did deliver		29:11
that same G. who delivered		29:12
that same G. did establish his		29:13
that same G. hath called me by		29:13
now may G. grant unto these,		29:17
sit down in the kingdom of G.;		29:17
may G. grant that it may be		29:17
observing the ordinances of G.,		30: 3
contrary to the commands of G.		30: 7
if a man desired to serve G.,		30: 9
if he believed in G. it was his		30: 9
being, who they say is G.—		30:28
he would revile even against G.,		30:29
to declare the word of G. unto		30:32
believest thou that there is a G.?		30:37
ye deny again that there is a G.,		30:39
I know there is a G.,		30:39
have ye that there is no G.,		30:40
ye have put off the Spirit of G.		30:42
may destroy the children of G.		30:42
be convinced that there is a G.,		30:43
enough; will ye tempt your G.?		30:44
all things denote there is a G.;		30:44
testifying unto them there is no G.?		30:45
again, behold G. shall smite thee,		30:47
do not deny the existence of a G.,		30:48
do not believe that there is a G.;		30:48
do not know that there is a G.;		30:48
in the name of G., ye shall be		30:49
thou convinced of the power of G.?		30:51
save it were the power of G.		30:52
I also knew that there was a G.		30:52
gone astray after an unknown G.		30:53
said unto me: There is no G.;		30:53
that Alma should pray unto G.,		30:54
try the virtue of the word of G.		31: 5
had had the word of G. preached		31: 8
keep the commandments of G.,		31: 9
and supplication to G. daily,		31:10
Holy, holy G.; we believe		31:15
we believe that thou art G.,		31:15
Holy G., we believe that thou		31:16
holiness, O G., we thank thee;		31:17
to wander far from thee, our G.		31:17
And again we thank thee, O G.,		31:18
the selfsame prayer unto G..		31:22
thanking their G. that they were		31:22
never speaking of their G. again		31:23
Behold, O G., they cry unto thee,		31:27
Behold, O G., they cry unto thee		31:27
Behold, O my G., their costly		31:28
We thank thee, O G., for we are		31:28
O Lord G., how long wilt thou		31:30
began to preach the word of G.		32: 1
their synagogues to worship G.,		32: 3
have no place to worship our G.;		32: 5
that we cannot worship our G.		32: 9
that ye cannot worship G.		32:10
worship G. only once in a week?		32:11
that believeth in the word of G.,		32:16
he that knoweth the will of G.		32:19
that G. is merciful unto all who		32:22
they should believe in one G.,		33: 1
that ye could not worship your G.		33: 2
suppose that ye cannot worship G.,		33: 2
Thou are merciful, O G., for		33: 4

Yea, O G., and thou wast merciful	Al	33: 5
And again, O G., when I did		33: 6
Yea, O G., thou hast been merciful		33: 9
ye disbelieve on the Son of G.?		33:14
has testified of the Son of G.,		33:17
spoken concerning the Son of G.		33:18
begin to believe in the Son of G.,		33:22
may G. grant unto you that		33:23
taught by us to be the Son of G.;		34: 2
the word be in the Son of G.,		34: 5
cometh through the Son of G.,		34: 7
for the Lord G. hath spoken it.		34: 8
the great plan of the Eternal G.		34: 9
sacrifice will be the Son of G.,		34:14
Therefore may G. grant unto you,		34:17
for men to prepare to meet G.;		34:32
that I will return to my G.		34:34
salvation with fear before G.,		34:37
even to the dust, and worship G.,		34:38
instruments in the hands of G.		35:14
keep the commandments of G.		36: 1
except it was the G. of Abraham		36: 2
and the G. of Isaac and the		36: 2
and the G. of Jacob;		36: 2
put their trust in G. shall be		36: 3
not of the carnal mind but of G.		36: 4
if I had not been born of G.		36: 5
but G. has, by the mouth of his		36: 5
to destroy the church of G.,		36: 6
G. sent his holy angel to stop us		36: 6
more to destroy the church of G.		36: 9
to destroy the church of G.—		36:11
I had rebelled against my G.,		36:13
into the presence of my G.		36:14
stand in the presence of my G.,		36:15
one Jesus Christ, a Son of G.		36:17
O Jesus, thou Son of G., have		36:18
G. sitting upon his throne,		36:22
of singing and praising their G.;		36:22
that I had been born of G.		36:23
they might also be born of G.,		36:24
many have been born of G.,		36:26
knowledge which I have is of G.		36:26
G. has delivered me from prison,		36:27
keep the commandments of G.		36:30
keep the commandments of G.		36:30
the Lord G. doth work by means		37: 7
has hitherto been wisdom in G.		37: 8
them to the knowledge of their G.		37: 8
knowledge of the lord their G.,		37: 9
which purpose is known unto G.;		37:12
are the commandments of G.		37:13
G. has entrusted you with these		37:14
the commandments of G.,		37:15
from you by the power of G.,		37:15
keep the commandments of G.,		37:16
G. is powerful to the fulfilling		37:16
the commandments of G. as		37:20
word of G. might be fulfilled,		37:24
the word of G. has been fulfilled;		37:26
according to the power of G.,		37:28
did cry unto the Lord their G.		37:30
the judgments of G. did come		37:30
keep the commandments of G.		37:35
cry unto G. for all thy support;		37:36
heart be full of thanks unto G.;		37:37
according to their faith in G.;		37:40
to believe that G. could cause		37:40
wrought by the power of G.,		37:40
see that ye look to G. and live.		37:47
keep the commandments of G.		38: 1
keep the commandments of G.		38: 1
and your faithfulness unto G.;		38: 2
to look to the Lord your G.,		38: 2
as ye shall put your trust in G.		38: 5
the Spirit of G. which is in me		38: 6
if I had not been born of G.		38: 6
O G., I thank thee that we are		38:14
your unworthiness before G.		38:14
keeping the commandments of G.?		39: 1
the light and knowledge of G.,		39: 6
I would to G. that ye had not been		39: 7
cannot hide your crimes from G.;		39: 8

GOD 394 GOD

inherit the kingdom of G.	Al	39: 9
in the fear of G., that ye refrain		39:12
at this time as precious unto G.		39:17
knoweth them save G. himself.		40: 3
I have inquired diligently of G.		40: 3
but G. knoweth the time which		40: 4
for G. knoweth all these things;		40: 5
all is as one day with G.,		40: 8
G. knoweth all the times which		40:10
to that G. who gave them life.		40:11
of the wrath of G. upon them;		40:14
time which is appointed of G.		40:21
be brought to stand before G.,		40:21
shine forth in the kingdom of G.		40:25
can inherit the kingdom of G.;		40:26
requisite with the justice of G.;		41: 2
requisite with the justice of G.		41: 3
to inherit the kingdom of G.,		41: 4
the decrees of G. are unalterable;		41: 8
one more offense against your G.		41: 9
are without G. in the world,		41:11
contrary to the nature of G.		41:11
is concerning the justice of G.		42: 1
after the Lord G. sent our first		42: 2
that the man had become as G.		42: 3
the Lord G. placed cherubim and		42: 3
a time to repent and serve G.		42: 4
according to the word of G.,		42: 5
word of G. would have been void,		42: 5
if so, G. would cease to be God.		42:13
if so, God would cease to be G.		42:13
yea, the justice of G., which		42:14
G. himself atoneth for the sins		42:15
that G. might be a perfect, just		42:15
God might be a perfect, just G.,		42:15
just God, and a merciful G. also.		42:15
and G. would cease to be God.		42:22
and God would cease to be G.		42:22
But G. ceaseth not to be God,		42:23
But God ceaseth not to be G.,		42:23
men into the presence of G.;		42:23
If so, G. would cease to be God.		42:25
If so, God would cease to be G.		42:25
thus G. bringeth about his great		42:26
to the restoration of G.		42:28
deny the justice of G. no more.		42:30
by denying the justice of G.;		42:30
do you let the justice of G.,		42:30
ye are called of G. to preach the		42:31
And may G. grant unto you even		42:31
after the holy order of G.		43: 2
might worship G. according to		43: 9
that whosoever should worship G.		43:10
truth, the true and the living G.,		43:10
which they owed to their G.;		43:46
one voice unto the Lord their G.,		43:49
that this is the true faith of G.;		44: 4
yea, ye see that G. will support,		44: 4
name of that all-powerful G.,		44: 5
of the sacred word of G.,		44: 5
it is G. that has delivered us		44: 9
thanks unto the Lord their G.;		45: 1
and they did worship G. with		45: 1
Thus saith the Lord G.—		45:16
the blessing of G. upon the land,		45:16
word of G. should be declared		45:21
to walk uprightly before G.		45:24
men do forget the Lord their G.,		46: 8
seek to destroy the church of G.,		46:10
of liberty which G. had granted		46:10
which blessing G. had sent upon		46:10
In memory of our G.,		46:12
he prayed mightily unto his G.		46:13
who belonged to the church of G.,		46:14
had poured out his soul to G.,		46:17
Surely G. shall not suffer that		46:18
the Lord G. may bless them.		46:20
not forsake the Lord their G.;		46:21
the commandments of G.,		46:21
We covenant with our G., that		46:22
keep the commandments of G.,		46:23
be preserved by the hand of G.,		46:24
which shall be taken unto G.		46:25
and roots which G. had prepared	Al	46:40
forgetting the Lord their G.		47:36
faithful unto the Lord their G.		48: 7
live unto the Lord their G.,		48:10
swell with thanksgiving to his G.,		48:12
G. would prosper them in the		48:15
the commandments of G.		48:15
that G. would make it known		48:16
the commandments of G.,		48:16
for they were all men of G.		48:18
they did preach the word of G.,		48:19
unprepared to meet their G.		48:23
keep the commandments of G.,		48:25
he did curse G., and also Moroni,		49:27
kept the commandments of G.		49:27
did thank the Lord their G.,		49:28
they gave unto the word of G.		49:30
by the holy order of G.,		49:30
perfect uprightness before G.		50:37
to worship the Lord their G.,		50:39
and maintain the cause of G.		50:39
by the power and word of G.,		53:10
keep the commandments of G.		53:21
concerning the justice of G.,		54: 6
that G. whom you have rejected		54: 9
religion and the cause of our G.		54:10
concerning that G. whom ye say		54:21
to remember the Lord their G.		55:31
that G. would strengthen us,		56: 8
of their country and of their G.,		56:11
Father, behold our G. is with us,		56:46
not doubt, G. would deliver them,		56:47
as if with the strength of G.;		56:56
according to the goodness of G.,		57:25
to the miraculous power of G.,		57:26
that there was a just G.,		57:26
they do put their trust in G.		57:27
blessed be the name of our G.;		57:35
because of the goodness of G.		57:36
entered into the rest of their G..		57:36
judgments of G. should come		58: 9
out our souls in prayer to G.,		58:10
the Lord our G. did visit us		58:11
we trust in our G. who has		58:33
we trust G. will deliver us,		58:37
G. has made them free;		58:40
to remember the Lord their G.		58:40
may the Lord our G., who has		58:41
known unto G. were all their		60:10
the exceeding goodness of G.		60:11
the rest of the Lord their G.		60:13
judgments of G. will come upon		60:14
of the Lord your G.?		60:20
Do we suppose that G. will look		60:23
G. has said that the inward		60:23
the blessings of G. upon them,		60:25
but it is my G. whom I fear;		60:28
ye do transgress the laws of G.,		60:33
the commandments of my G.;		60:34
should adhere to the word of G.,		60:34
G. will not suffer that we should		60:35
see that ye fulfil the word of G.		60:35
but for the glory of my G.,		60:36
the which G. hath made us free.		61: 9
requisite with the justice of G.,		61:12
of our Redeemer and our G.		61:14
according to the Spirit of G.,		61:15
in the strength of our G.		61:17
fear not, for G. will deliver them,		61:21
G. hath made them free.		61:21
their country and also their G.		62: 2
humble themselves before G.,		62:41
unto the people the word of G.;		62:44
and did declare the word of G.		62:45
baptized unto the Lord their G.		62:45
establish again the church of G.,		62:46
to remember the Lord their G.;		62:49
pray unto the Lord their G.		62:51
he did walk uprightly before G.,		63: 2
of the Lord his G.;		63: 2
and the commandments of G.;	He	3:20
which was right in the sight of G.		3:20
and uniting to the church of G.		3:26

GOD 395 GOD

Jesus Christ, who is the Son of G.	He 3:28	shall believe on the Son of G.,	He	14: 8
may lay hold upon the word of G.,	3:29	know of the judgments of G.		14:11
souls, at the right hand of G.	3:30	of Jesus Christ, the Son of G.,		14:12
not into the church of G., but	3:33	G. hath given unto you a		14:30
to belong to the church of G.	3:33	walk circumspectly before G.,		15: 5
their yielding their hearts unto G.	3:35	more circumspectly before G.		16:10
keep the commandments of G.,	3:37	to the commandments of G.,		16:12
to belong to the church of G.	4:11	if so, and he be the Son of G.,		16:18
the commandments of G.	4:21	and cried mightily to his G.	3Ne	1:11
the judgments of G. did stare	4:23	Son of G. must shortly appear;		1:17
cleave unto the Lord their G.,	4:25	supported by the hand of a G.,		3: 2
him to preach the word of G.	5: 4	prayers unto the Lord their G.,		3:25
keep the commandments of G.;	5: 6	their cries to the Lord their G.,		4: 8
who is Christ, the Son of G.,	5:12	but they did fear their G.		4:10
the commandments of G.,	5:14	May the G. of Abraham, and		4:30
to teach the word of G. among	5:14	of Abraham, and the G. of Isaac,		4:30
it is G. that has shown unto you	5:26	of Isaac, and the G. of Jacob,		4:30
belonged to the church of G.	5:35	shall call on the name of their G.		4:30
do converse with the angels of G.	5:39	in singing, and praising their G.		4:31
the Holy Spirit of G. did come	5:45	Hosanna to the Most High G.		4:32
they did reject the word of G.	6: 2	of the Lord G. Almighty,		4:32
because of the church of G.	6: 3	Almighty, the Most High G.		4:32
be the humble followers of G.	6: 5	of the great goodness of G. in		4:33
and also the laws of their G.	6:23	did serve G. with all diligence		5: 3
feet the commandments of G.,	6:31	the word of G. to be preached		5: 4
in the knowledge of their G.;	6:34	of Jesus Christ, the Son of G.		5:13
they did preach the word of G.	6:37	I, according to the will of G.,		5:14
and the humble followers of G.	6:39	I have reason to bless my G.		5:20
G. threatens the people of Nephi	7:hd	knowledge of the Lord their G.		5:23
G. smiteth the people of Nephi	7:hd	is Jesus Christ, the Son of G.;		5:26
and did preach the word of G.	7: 2	humble and penitent before G.		6:13
aside the commandments of G.,	7: 4	the will of G. concerning them,		6:18
keep the commandments of G.,	7: 7	did wilfully rebel against G.		6:18
was pouring out his soul unto G.	7:11	turned from the Lord their G.,		7:14
pour out my soul unto my G.,	7:14	by the power and Spirit of G.,		7:21
turn ye unto the Lord your G.	7:17	upon by the Spirit of G.,		7:22
you have forgotten your G.	7:20	and a testimony before G.,		7:25
the Lord G. has made them known	7:29	I am Jesus Christ the Son of G.		9:15
to the commandments of G.	8: 3	given to become the sons of G.		9:17
G. gave power unto one man,	8:11	for of such is the kingdom of G.		9:22
if G. gave unto this man such	8:12	know that I am the G. of Israel,		11:14
that the Son of G. should come?	8:14	the G. of the whold earth,		11:14
upon the Son of G. with faith,	8:15	the name of the Most High G.!		11:17
were called by the order of G.;	8:18	shall inherit the kingdom of G.		11:33
why not the Son of G. come,	8:20	nowise inherit the kingdom of G.		11:38
And behold, he is G., and he is	8:23	in heart, for they shall see G.		12: 8
rebelled against your holy G.;	8:25	shall be called the children of G.		12: 9
and G. hath commanded him	9: 2	danger of the judgment of G.;		12:21
and G. has smitted them that	9: 8	cannot serve G. and Mammon.		13:24
to be a great man, chosen of G.,	9:16	if G. so clothe the grass of the		13:30
the Lord your G. will suffer you	9:21	seek ye first the kingdom of G.		13:33
given unto me by the power of G.	9:36	earth shall see the salvation of G.		16:20
that I am sent unto you from G.	9:36	him their Lord and their G.		19:18
Behold, he is a G., for except he	9:41	knowledge of the Lord their G.,		20:13
except he was a G. he could not	9:41	shall the Lord your G. raise up		20:23
thou art Nephi, and I am G.	10: 6	I am Jesus Christ, the Son of G.,		20:31
if ye shall say that G. shall smite	10:10	unto Zion: Thy G. reigneth!		20:40
that thus saith the Lord G.,	10:11	the G. of Israel shall be your		20:42
the power of G. was with him,	10:16	the G. of the whole earth shall		22: 5
declaring the word of G.,	10:17	thou wast refused, saith thy G.		22: 6
of the Lord their G.,	11: 4	Will a man rob G.?		24: 8
to remember the Lord their G.;	11: 7	It is vain to serve G., and what		24:14
we know that thou art a man of G.,	11: 8	they that tempt G. are even		24:15
cry unto the Lord our G. that	11: 8	him that serveth G. and him		24:18
people did rejoice and glorify G.,	11:18	and tongues shall stand before G.,		26: 4
a great prophet, and a man of G.,	11:18	could behold the things of G.		28:15
authority given unto him from G.	11:18	the earth with the word of G.,		28:20
of the Lord their G.	11:34	power of G. which is in them.		28:29
to forget the Lord their G.	11:36	And they are as the angels of G.,		28:30
and do forget the Lord their G.,	12: 2	the justice of an offended G.,		28:35
to remember the Lord their G.,	12: 5	but to dwell with G. eternally		28:40
desire that the Lord their G.,	12: 6	Christ, the Son of the living G.,		30: 1
of our great and everlasting G.	12: 8	from their Lord and their G.,	4Ne	1:12
the voice of the Lord their G.;	12:23	all gone to the paradise of G.,		1:14
G. grant, in his great fulness,	12:24	because of the love of G. which		1:15
keep the commandments of G.	13: 1	been created by the hand of G.		1:16
and return unto the Lord your G.	13:11	and heirs to the kingdom of G.		1:17
yea, our great and true G.,	13:18	by the power of the word of G.,		1:30
not remember the Lord your G.	13:22	taught to hate the children of G.,		1:39
not to thank the Lord your G.	13:22	than were the people of G.		1:40
hath the Lord G. caused that a	13:23	wilfully rebelled against their G.;	Mrm	1:16
had remembered the Lord our G.	13:33	because of the goodness of G.;		2:13
then cometh the Son of G. to	14: 2	did curse G., and wish to die.		2:14

GOD

open rebellion against their G.,	Mrm	2:15
hearts against the Lord their G.		3: 3
and also by the throne of G.,		3:10
the love of G. which was in me,		3:12
poured out in prayer unto my G.		3:12
the very Christ and the very G.		3:21
judgments of G. will overtake		4: 5
because it is known of G. that		5:12
Christ, the Son of the living G.;		5:14
Lord their G. hath given them,		5:14
they are without Christ and G.		5:16
were led even by G. the Father.		5:17
stand before the power of G.,		5:22
that ye are in the hands of G.?		5:23
if it so be that G. may give unto		7: 1
be that G. shall command you.		7: 4
Christ, that he is the Son of G.,		7: 5
to dwell in the presence of G. in		7: 7
Holy Ghost, which are one G.,		7: 7
wrought by the power of G.		7: 9
none that do know the true G.		8:10
save it be given him of G.;		8:15
G. wills that it shall be done with		8:15
according to the word of G.;		8:16
shall be done by the power of G.		8:16
G. knoweth all things;		8:17
the power of G. shall be denied,		8:28
transfigured the holy word of G.,		8:33
unto the revelations of G.		8:33
polluted the holy church of G.?		8:38
stand before the Lamb of G.—		9: 2
will ye say that there is no G.?		9: 2
can ye behold the Lamb of G.?		9: 3
to dwell with a holy and just G.,		9: 4
see your nakedness before G.,		9: 5
and also the glory of G.,		9: 5
who deny the revelations of G.,		9: 7
that G. is the same yesterday,		9: 9
yourselves a g. who doth very,		9:10
a g. who is not a God of		9:10
god who is not a G. of miracles.		9:10
show unto you a G. of miracles,		9:11
even the G. of Abraham, and the		9:11
of Abraham, and the G. of Isaac,		9:11
of Isaac, and the G. of Jacob;		9:11
that same G. who created the		9:11
be awakened by the power of G.		9:13
a g. who can do no miracles,		9:15
G. has not ceased to be a God		9:15
ceased to be a G. of miracles.		9:15
the things that G. hath wrought		9:16
the marvelous works of G.?		9:16
why has G. ceased to be a God of		9:19
ceased to be a G. of miracles		9:19
if so he would cease to be G.;		9:19
and he ceaseth not to be G.,		9:19
and is a G. of miracles.		9:19
the G. in whom they should trust.		9:20
said Jesus Christ, the Son of G.,		9:22
will serve the true and living G.		9:28
Christ, the Son of the living G.;		9:29
give thanks unto G. that he hath		9:31
may G. the Father remember		9:37
which the Lord G. had preserved	Eth	2: 7
serve him, the true and only G.,		2: 8
we can behold the decrees of G.		2: 9
shall possess it shall serve G.,		2: 9
serve G. or shall be swept off;		2:10
is the everlasting decree of G.		2:10
ye may know the decrees of G.—		2:11
the fulness of the wrath of G.		2:11
but serve the G. of the land,		2:12
for thou art a G. of truth,		3:12
might know that he was G.,		3:18
this perfect knowledge of G.,		3:20
saith Jesus Christ, the Son of G.,		4: 7
it shall be wisdom in G.		5: 1
be shown by the power of G.;		5: 3
be shown forth the power of G.		5: 4
received into the kingdom of G.		5: 5
stand before G. at the last day.		5: 6
themselves unto the Lord their G.		6: 4

the Lord G. caused that there	Eth	6: 5
unto him, by the G. of heaven,		8:14
above all, in the sight of G.;		8:18
wisdom in G. that these things		8:23
of the justice of the Eternal G.		8:23
the Lord G. would execute		11:20
the Lord G. would send or bring		11:21
believe in G. unto repentance		12: 3
whoso believeth in G. might with		12: 4
a place at the right hand of G.,		12: 4
works, being led to glorify G.		12: 4
called after the holy order of G.		12:10
G. prepared a more excellent		12:11
G. can do no miracle among		12:12
first believed in the Son of G.		12:18
for so great was his faith in G.,		12:20
when G. put forth his finger		12:20
that the grace of G. the Father,		12:41
of the covenant which G. made		13:11
am saved in the kingdom of G.		15:34
and callings of G. unto men;	Mro	3: 4
O G., the Eternal Father,		4: 3
O G., the Eternal Father,		4: 3
O G., the Eternal Father,		5: 2
O G., the Eternal Father,		5: 2
nourished by the good word of G.,		6: 4
is by the grace of G. the Father,		7: 2
For I remember the word of G.,		7: 5
G. hath said a man being evil		7: 6
a gift, or prayeth unto G.,		7: 6
he is counted evil before G.		7: 8
for G. receiveth none such.		7: 9
which are good cometh of G.;		7:12
for the devil is an enemy unto G.,		7:12
that which is of G. inviteth and		7:13
to do good, and to love G.,		7:13
to serve him, is inspired of G.		7:13
that which is evil to be of G.,		7:14
good and of G. to be of the devil.		7:14
a perfect knowledge it is of G.		7:16
and deny him, and serve not G.,		7:17
G. knowing all things, being		7:22
G. also declared unto prophets,		7:23
forth out of the mouth of G.,		7:25
they become the sons of G.		7:26
down on the right hand of G.,		7:27
the Lord G. prepareth the way		7:32
and G. will show unto you,		7:35
none is acceptable before G.,		7:44
may become the sons of G.;		7:48
praying unto G. the Father		8: 3
your Lord and your G.		8: 8
the word of G. unto me;		8: 9
it is solemn mockery before G.,		8: 9
if not so, G. is a partial God,		8:12
if not so, God is a partial G.,		8:12
and also a changeable G., and		8:12
suppose that G. saveth one child		8:15
having authority from G.;		8:16
For I know that G. is not a		8:18
that God is not a partial G.,		8:18
pure mercies of G. unto them,		8:19
G. hath commanded me.		8:21
But it is mockery before G.,		8:23
all the saints shall dwell with G.		8:26
authority which cometh from G.;		8:28
when I speak the word of G.		9: 4
our souls in the kingdom of G.		9: 6
that G. will stay his hand in		9:14
Come out in judgment, O G.,		9:15
cannot recommend them unto G.		9:21
I recommend thee unto G.,		9:22
I pray unto G. that he will		9:22
may the grace of G. the Father,		9:26
if it be wisdom in G. that ye		10: 3
ask G., the Eternal Father, in		10: 4
ye deny not the power of G.;		10: 7
that ye deny not the gifts of G.,		10: 8
and they come from the same G.		10: 8
is the same G. who worketh all		10: 8
of the Spirit of G. unto men,		10: 8
to one is given by the Spirit of G.,		10: 9

GOD 397 GOD

be saved in the kingdom of G.;	Mro 10:21		souls is great in the sight of G.;	DC 18:10
be saved in the kingdom of G.	10:21		to the callings and gifts of G.	18:32
that the power and gifts of G.	10:24		Christ, your Lord and your G.,	18:33
work by the power and gifts of G.	10:25		Christ, your Lord and your G.,	18:47
be saved in the kingdom of G.;	10:26		or suffer, for I, G., am endless.	19: 4
shall see me at the bar of G.;	10:27		I, G., have suffered these things	19:16
the Lord G. will say unto you	10:27		suffering caused myself, even G.,	19:18
mouth of the everlasting G.;	10:28		the truth and the word of G.—	19:26
And G. shall show unto you,	10:29		be the name of the Lord G.!	19:37
and love G. with all your might,	10:32		will and commandments of G.,	20: 1
if by the grace of G. ye are	10:32		was called of G., and ordained	20: 2
in nowise deny the power of G.	10:32		who was also called of G.,	20: 3
if ye by the grace of G. are	10:33		G. ministered unto him by an	20: 6
in Christ by the grace of G.,	10:33		that G. does inspire men and	20:11
go to rest in the paradise of G.,	10:34		showing that he is the same G.	20:12
the wrath of G. shall be poured	DC 1: 9		For the Lord G. has spoken it;	20:16
after the image of his own G.,	1:16		that there is a G. in heaven,	20:17
in the name of G. the Lord,	1:20		the same unchangeable G.,	20:17
I am G. and have spoken it;	1:24		the only living and true G.,	20:19
translate through the mercy of G.,	1:29		the Almighty G. gave his Only	20:21
by the power of G.,	1:29		in the gifts and callings of G.	20:27
behold, and lo, the Lord is G.,	1:39		and Holy Ghost are one G.,	20:28
designs, and the purposes of G.	3: 1		be saved in the kingdom of G.	20:29
G. doth not walk in crooked	3: 2		all those who love and serve G.	20:31
the work of G. that is frustrated,	3: 3		and depart from the living G.;	20:32
at naught the counsels of G.,	3: 4		or the revelations of G. which	20:35
incur the vengeance of a just G.	3: 4		the Holy Ghost, the voice of G.,	20:35
and the laws of G., and have	3: 6		And the Lord G. has spoken it;	20:36
have feared man more than G.,	3: 7		humble themselves before G.,	20:37
at naught the counsels of G.,	3: 7		and revelations of G.	20:45
But remember, G. is merciful;	3:10		to the gifts and callings of G.	20:60
that which G. had given thee	3:12		years of accountability before G.,	20:71
at naught the counsels of G.,	3:13		The person who is called of G.	20:73
which were made before G.,	3:13		O G., the Eternal Father,	20:77
embark in the service of G.,	4: 2		O G., the Eternal Father,	20:77
may stand blameless before G.	4: 2		O G., the Eternal Father, we ask	20:79
if ye have desires to serve G.	4: 3		O G., the Eternal Father,	20:79
an eye single to the glory of G.,	4: 5		the will of G. the Father,	21: 1
I, the Lord, am G., and have	5: 2		and the Lord G. will disperse the	21: 6
unto me by the power of G.	5:25		For thus saith the Lord G.:	21: 7
unto me by the power of G.;	5:26		thus saith the Lord G., lo, lo!	21:12
Behold, I am G.; give heed	6: 2		seek not to counsel your G.	22: 4
salvation in the kingdom of G.	6: 3		in calling upon G. in my name,	24: 5
reap, the same is called of G.	6: 4		the voice of the Lord your G.,	25: 1
the mysteries of G. shall be	6: 7		Jesus Christ, your Lord, your G.,	27: 1
saved in the kingdom of G.,	6:13		I the Lord G. will send forth	29:18
greatest of all the gifts of G.;	6:13		again begin to deny their G.,	29:22
none else save G. that knowest	6:16		I, the Lord G., caused that he	29:41
keeping the commandments of G.,	6:20		I, the Lord G., gave unto Adam	29:42
I am Jesus Christ, the Son of G.	6:21		until I, the Lord G., should	29:42
can you have than from G.?	6:23		thus did I, the Lord G., appoint	29:43
is your G. and your Redeemer,	8: 1		to the voice of the Lord your G.,	33: 1
power, save the power of G.,	8: 7		what I, the Lord G., shall say	34: 1
doubt not, for it is the gift of G.;	8: 8		might become the sons of G.	34: 3
hands, for it is the work of G.	8: 8		for the Lord G. hath spoken;	34:10
may know the mysteries of G.,	8:11		the voice of the Lord your G.,	35: 1
thee to tempt the Lord thy G.,	10:15		am Jesus Christ, the Son of G.,	35: 2
We will see if G. has given him	10:16		they may become the sons of G.,	35: 2
if G. giveth him power again,	10:17		For I am G., and mine arm is	35: 8
to destroy the work of G.;	10:23		Thus saith the Lord G.,	36: 1
exempt from the justice of G.	10:28		the name of the most high G.	36: 3
thee to tempt the Lord thy G.	10:29		I am Jesus Christ, the Son of G.;	36: 8
I am Jesus Christ, the Son of G.	10:57		Thus saith the Lord your G.,	38: 1
your Lord and your G.	10:70		of the Most High G.	39:19
Behold, I am G.; give heed	11: 2		saith the Lord and your G.,	41: 1
salvation in the kingdom of G.	11: 3		Christ the Son of the living G.,	42: 1
reap, the same is called of G.	11: 4		my word like unto angels of G.	42: 6
the mysteries of G. shall be	11: 7		people and I will be your G.	42: 9
yea, the power of G. unto the	11:21		according to the law of G.	42:82
seek the kingdom of G., and all	11:23		unto the law, even that of G.	42:87
I am Jesus Christ, the Son of G.	11:28		delivered up unto the law of G.	42:91
power to become the sons of G.,	11:30		has offended, and to G.,	42:92
Behold, I am G.; give heed	12: 2		and the trump of G. shall sound	43:18
salvation in the kingdom of G.	12: 3		hear the words of that G.	43:23
reap, the same is called of G.	12: 4		the words of the Lord your G.	43:27
Behold, I am G.; give heed	14: 2		and to become the sons of G.;	45: 8
salvation in the kingdom of G.	14: 3		whom ye say is the G. of Enoch,	45:11
reap, the same is called of G.	14: 4		which ye call the house of G.,	45:18
greatest of all the gifts of G.	14: 7		voices and curse G. and die.	45:32
Christ, the Son of the living G.;	14: 9		I am the Son of G.	45:52
of them, by the power of G.;	17: 3		saints of the Most High G.;	45:66
as your Lord and your G. liveth	17: 6		in all things to ask of G.,	46: 7
Christ, your Lord and your G.,	17: 9		given a gift by the Spirit of G.	46:11

GOD

Jesus Christ is the Son of G.,	DC 46:13	
whether they be of G., that the	46:16	
is given, by the Spirit of G.,	46:17	
all these gifts come from G.,	46:26	
the benefit of the children of G.	46:26	
unto such as G. shall appoint	46:27	
professing and yet be not of G.	46:27	
according to the will of G.;	46:30	
give thanks unto G. in the Spirit	46:32	
for I am G., and have sent	49: 5	
I, the Lord G., have spoken	49: 7	
to marry is not ordained of G.,	49:15	
for marriage is ordained of G.	49:15	
the same, is not ordained of G.;	49:18	
ear to the voice of the living G.;	50: 1	
and received them to be of G.;	50:15	
some other way it is not of G.	50:18	
some other way it is not of G.	50:20	
doth not edify is not of G.	50:23	
That which is of G. is light;	50:24	
light, and continueth in G.,	50:24	
He that is ordained of G. and	50:26	
may know that it is not of G.	50:31	
loud voice that it is not of G.	50:32	
He that receiveth of G., let him	50:34	
let him account it of G.;	50:34	
is accounted of G. worthy to	50:34	
unto me, saith the Lord your G.,	51: 1	
the same is of G. if he obey	52:16	
I am Jesus Christ, the Son of G.,	52:44	
unto you, of the Lord your G.,	53: 1	
Christ, the Son of the living G.	55: 2	
name, saith the Lord your G.;	56: 1	
saith the Lord G. of hosts;	56:10	
they shall see the kingdom of G.	56:18	
church, saith the Lord your G.,	57: 1	
thus saith the Lord your G.,	57: 3	
design of your G. concerning	58: 3	
the Zion of G. shall stand;	58: 7	
the city of the heritage of G.—	58:13	
heritage of G. unto his children;	58:17	
are given by the prophets of G.	58:18	
let G. rule him that judgeth,	58:20	
he that keepeth the laws of G.	58:21	
a statement of the will of G.,	58:50	
for the children of G.	58:51	
to labor for the saints of G.	58:54	
Thou shalt love the lord thy G.	59: 5	
Thou shalt thank the Lord thy G.	59: 7	
a sacrifice unto the Lord thy G.	59: 8	
it pleaseth G. that he hath	59:20	
in nothing doth man offend G.,	59:21	
that bespeaketh the power of G.	60: 4	
as the Spirit of the living G.	61:28	
lift up their voices unto G.	61:31	
church, saith the Lord your G.,	62: 1	
flesh shall know that I am G.	63: 6	
they please, but by the will of G.	63:10	
without faith no man pleaseth G.;	63:11	
with whom G. is angry he is	63:11	
is the will of the Lord your G.	63:24	
thus saith the Lord your G.	64: 1	
let G. judge between me and	64:11	
do that G. may be glorified—	64:13	
The keys of the kingdom of G.	65: 2	
to meet the kingdom of G.	65: 5	
the kingdom of G. go forth,	65: 6	
thou, O G., mayest be glorified	65: 6	
thus saith the Lord your G.,	66:13	
no man has seen G. at any time	67:11	
quickened by the Spirit of G.	67:11	
man abide the presence of G.,	67:12	
to abide the presence of G. now,	67:13	
by the Spirit of the living G.,	68: 1	
the power of G. unto salvation.	68: 4	
I am the Son of the living G.,	68: 6	
Christ the Son of the living G.,	68:25	
unto me, saith the Lord your G.,	69: 1	
business in the church of G.,	70: 5	
to the church of the living G.;	70:10	
the will of the Lord your G.,	72: 8	
Omega, your Lord and your G.—	75: 1	
is the will of the Lord your G.	75:12	
for the Lord is G., and beside	DC 76: 1
understand the things of G.—	76:12
worshiping G., and the Lamb,	76:21
even on the right hand of G.;	76:23
sons and daughters unto G.	76:24
that an angel of G. who was	76:25
authority in the presence of G.,	76:25
down from the presence of G.	76:25
devil, who rebelled against G.,	76:28
to take the kingdom of our G.	76:28
war with the saints of G.,	76:29
to suffer the wrath of G.,	76:33
are gods, even the sons of G.—	76:58
but rather let him glory in G.,	76:61
dwell in the presence of G.	76:62
unto the city of the living G.,	76:66
G. and Christ are the judge of	76:68
of the sun, even the glory of G.,	76:70
over the kingdom of our G.	76:79
to whom G. has revealed it.	76:90
G., even the Father, reighs	76:92
suffer the wrath of G. on earth.	76:104
suffer the wrath of Almighty G.,	76:106
of the wrath of Almighty G.	76:107
but where G. and Christ dwell	76:112
G. bestows on those who love	76:116
And to G. and the Lamb be glory,	76:119
heaven, the paradise of G.,	77: 2
creature which G. has created.	77: 2
were then in the paradise of G.	77: 5
mysteries, and the works of G.;	77: 6
four angels sent forth from G.,	77: 8
given the seal of the living G.	77: 9
sealed the servants of our G.	77: 9
unto the holy order of G.,	77:11
G. made the world in six days,	77:12
the Lord G. sanctify the earth,	77:12
unto me, saith the Lord your G.,	78: 1
before me, saith the Lord G.	78: 2
kingdoms, saith the Lord G.,	78:15
to the word of the Lord your G.,	81: 1
And the anger of G. kindleth	82: 6
return, saith the Lord your G.	82: 7
of the church of the living G.,	82:18
an eye single to the glory of G.	82:19
received it under the hand of G.	84:12
by the commandments of G.,	84:16
continueth in the church of G.	84:17
is after the holiest order of G.	84:18
the key of the knowledge of G.	84:19
no man can see the face of G.,	84:22
might behold the face of G.;	84:23
John, whom G. raised up,	84:27
was ordained by the angel of G.	84:28
kingdom, and the elect of G.	84:34
forth from the mouth of G.	84:44
of the Spirit cometh unto G.,	84:47
the faithful who are called of G.	84:86
with the glory of her G.;	84:101
might, Be ascribed to our G.;	84:102
will and commandment of G.	85: 3
enrolled with the people of G.	85: 3
in the book of the law of G.,	85: 5
I, the Lord G., will send one	85: 7
set in order the house of G.,	85: 7
in the book of the law of G.;	85: 7
was called of G. and appointed,	85: 8
hand to steady the ark of G.,	85: 8
the world with Christ in G.—	86: 9
hand of an Almighty G.,	87: 6
even of G., the holiest of all,	88: 5
forth from the presence of G.	88:12
the power of G. who sitteth	88:13
presence of G. the Father;	88:19
by him, and of him, even G.,	88:41
all these are one year with G.,	88:44
in the midst of the power of G.	88:45
seen G. moving in his majesty	88:47
you shall comprehend even G.,	88:49
the decree which G. hath made.	88:61
your minds become single to G.,	88:68
unto your Father, and your G.,	88:75
and your God, and my G.,	88:75

pertain unto the kingdom of G.,	DC 88:78	G. hath set his hand and seal	DC 121:12
may escape the wrath of G.,	88:85	saith G., that not one of them	121:15
sounding the trump of G.,	88:92	G. shall give unto you	121:26
the judgment of our G. is come.	88:92	there be one G. or many gods,	121:28
persecuteth the saints of G.,	88:94	of the Council of the Eternal G.	121:32
of the trump of the angel of G.	88:98	and to fight against G.	121:38
Fear G., and give glory to him	88:104	in the presence of G.;	121:45
The Lamb of G. hath overcome	88:106	thy G. shall stand by thee	122: 4
of the wrath of Almighty G.	88:106	G. shall be with you forever	122: 9
and the mighty works of G.	88:108	duty that we owe to G.,	123: 7
and the mighty works of G.	88:109	to see the salvation of G.,	123:17
the battle of the great G.;	88:114	your G. will not dwell therein.	124:24
This is the glory of G.,	88:116	saith the Lord your G.	124:32
a house of order, a house of G.;	88:119	and hate me, saith the Lord G.	124:50
shall be first in the house of G.,	88:129	saith the Lord your G.	124:51
he cometh into the house of G.,	88:130	hate me, saith the Lord your G.	124:52
prayer upon his knees before G.,	88:131	saith the Lord your G.	124:53
through the grace of G. in	88:133	For I am the Lord your G.,	124:54
all the commandments of G.	88:133	my will, saith the Lord your G.	124:69
one another in the house of G.,	88:136	their place, saith the Lord G.;	124:71
forth the order and will of G.	89: 2	for I, the Lord, am G.,	124:71
herbs G. hath ordained for the	89:10	ever, saith the Lord your G.	124:101
hath G. made for the use of	89:15	behold, I, the Lord your G.,	124:104
who receive the oracles of G.,	90: 5	saith the Lord your G.;	124:119
man of G., and of strong faith—	90:22	saith the Lord your G.	124:120
was called the Son of G.,	93:14	saith the Lord your G.	124:135
The Spirit of truth is of G.	93:26	saith the Lord your G.	124:140
also in the beginning with G.	93:29	saith the Lord your G.	124:145
in which G. has placed it,	93:30	G. knoweth all these things,	127: 2
are the tabernacle of G.;	93:35	for to this day has the G. of	127: 2
man is the tabernacle of G.,	93:35	for the Lord G. hath spoken it.	127: 2
G. shall destroy that temple.	93:35	for Israel's G. is their God,	127: 3
The glory of G. is intelligence,	93:36	for Israel's God is their G.,	127: 3
G. having redeemed man from	93:38	my prayer to G. is that you	127:12
infant state, innocent before G.	93:38	is only to answer the will of G.,	128: 5
of laws of G. and man,	93:53	*small and great, stand before G.;*	128: 6
which I the Lord G., have given	94:15	ordinance which G. has prepared	128: 8
the kingdom of G. on the earth,	97:14	Behold, thy G. reigneth!	128:19
shall come into it shall see G.	97:16	knowledge of G. descend upon	128:19
Zion is the city of our G.,	97:19	the voice of G. in the chamber	128:21
for G. is there, and the hand	97:19	the sons of G. shout for joy!	128:23
ever, saith the Lord your G.	97:28	he has a message from G.,	129: 4
I, the Lord G., make you free,	98: 8	administration is from G.	129: 9
forth out of the mouth of G.	98:11	they reside in the presence of G.,	130: 7
people, saith the Lord your G.,	98:38	The place where G. resides	130: 8
and turn to the Lord their G.,	98:47	in the name of the Lord G.,	130:12
upon them, saith the Lord thy G.,	98:48	we obtain any blessing from G.,	130:21
the voice of the Lord their G.;	101: 7	I am the Lord thy G.,	132: 2
the Lord their G. is slow to	101: 7	be damned, saith the Lord G.	132: 6
be still and know that I am G.	101:16	house of order, saith the Lord G.,	132: 8
a judge which feared not G.,	101:82	I am the Lord thy G.;	132:12
Though I fear not G., nor	101:84	saith the Lord your G.	132:13
and the wicked, saith your G.	101:95	but are angels of G. forever	132:17
according to the grace of G.	102: 4	house of order, saith the Lord G.	132:18
I, the Lord their G., shall give	103: 5	to know the only wise and true G.,	132:24
I, the Lord their G., shall speak	103: 7	redemption saith the Lord G.	132:26
Where is their G.?	105: 8	covenant, saith the Lord G.;	132:27
kingdom of our G. and his Christ;	105:32	I am the Lord thy G.,	132:28
after the Order of the Son of G.	107: 3	G. commanded Abraham,	132:34
and presence of G. the Father,	107:19	I am the Lord thy G.,	132:40
and received the promise of G.	107:42	for I, the Lord, am thy G.	132:47
G. called upon Cainan in the	107:45	For I am the Lord thy G.,	132:49
he walked with G. three hundred	107:49	be destroyed, saith the Lord G.	132:52
highest council of the church of G.,	107:80	For I am the Lord thy G.,	132:53
the justice and the laws of G.,	107:84	for I am the Lord thy G.,	132:54
having all the gifts of G. which	107:92	I, the Lord thy G., will bless her,	132:56
thy name, O Lord G. of Israel,	109: 1	for I am the Lord thy G.,	132:57
a house of order, a house of G.;	109: 8	saith the Lord your G.	132:60
a house of glory and of G.,	109:16	saith the Lord your G.;	132:64
O Mighty G. of Jacob—	109:68	whatsoever I, the Lord his G.,	132:65
and know that thou art G.	109:70	church, saith the Lord your G.,	133: 1
O Lord G. Almighty, hear us	109:77	all the nations that forget G.,	133: 2
praise, singing Hosanna to G.	109:79	see the salvation of their G.	133: 3
I, the Lord your G., am not	111: 1	G. hath sent forth the angel	133:17
the Lord thy G. shall lead thee	112:10	the blessing of the everlasting G.	133:38
those whom G. should call in the	113: 8	the servants of G. shall go forth,	133:38
are the curses of G. upon her,	113:10	Fear G. and give glory to him,	133:38
remember the Lord their G.	117:16	neither hath any eye seen, O G.,	133:45
O G., where art thou?	121: 1	cometh down from G. in heaven	133:46
O Lord G. Almighty, maker of	121: 4	the Lord your G. hath spoken it.	133:74
thy suffering saints, O our G.;	121: 6	governments were instituted of G.	134: 1
G. shall exalt thee on high;	121: 8	that religion is instituted of G.;	134: 4

GOD

exclaiming: *O Lord my G.!*	DC 135: 1
through the providence of G.,	135: 2
by the gift and power of G.,	135: 3
he died great in the eyes of G.	135: 3
void of offense towards G.,	135: 4
for the glory of G.,	135: 6
and statutes of the Lord our G.	136: 2
for I am the Lord your G.,	136:21
even the G. of your fathers,	136:21
the g. of Abraham and of Isaac	136:21
the free gift of the Lord thy G.,	136:27
call on the Lord thy G. with	136:29
calling upon the lord his G..	136:32
The words of G., which he spake	Mses 1: 1
And he saw G. face to face,	1: 2
the glory of G. was upon Moses,	1: 2
And G. spake unto Moses, saying:	1: 3
I am the Lord G. Almighty,	1: 3
but there is no G. beside me,	1: 6
the presence of G. withdrew	1: 9
mine own eyes have beheld G.;	1:11
for behold, I am a son of G.,	1:13
could not look upon G., except	1:14
Blessed be the name of my G.,	1:15
can judge between thee and G.;	1:15
for G. said unto me: Worship	1:15
Worship G., for him only shalt	1:15
deceive me not; for G. said unto	1:16
Call upon G. in the name of	1:17
I will not cease to call upon G.,	1:18
calling upon G., he received	1:20
this one G. only will I worship,	1:20
worship, which is the G. of glory.	1:20
strength, and called upon G.,	1:21
And calling upon the name of G.,	1:25
thy command as if thou wert G.	1:25
discerning it by the spirit of G.	1:27
them by the Spirit of G.;	1:28
pass that Moses called upon G.,	1:30
stood in the presence of G.,	1:31
the Lord G. said unto Moses:	1:31
merciful unto thy servant, O G.,	1:36
the Lord G. spake unto Moses,	1:37
and the End, the Almighty G.,	2: 1
face of the water; for I am G.	2: 2
I, G., said: Let there be light;	2: 3
And I, G., saw the light;	2: 4
the light and that light	2: 4
And I, G., called the light Day;	2: 5
I, G., said: Let there be a	2: 6
I, G., made the firmament	2: 7
I, G., called the firmament	2: 8
G., said: Let the waters under the	2: 9
G., said: Let there be dry land;	2: 9
I, G., called the dry land Earth;	2:10
G., saw that all things which	2:10
I, G., said: Let the earth bring	2:11
I, G., saw that all things which	2:12
I, G., said: Let there be lights	2:14
I, G., made two great lights;	2:16
I, G., set them in the firmament	2:17
I, G., saw that all things which	2:18
G., said: Let the waters bring	2:20
And I, G., created great whales,	2:21
I, G., saw that all things which	2:21
And I, G., blessed them, saying:	2:22
G., said: Let the earth bring	2:24
And I, G., made the beasts	2:25
I, G., saw that all these things	2:25
G., said unto mine Only Begotten,	2:26
And I, G., said: Let them have	2:26
I, G., created man in mine own	2:27
And I, G., blessed them, and said	2:28
And I, G., said unto man: Behold,	2:29
I, G., saw everything that I had	2:31
on the seventh day I, G., ended	3: 2
I, G., saw that they were good;	3: 2
I, G., blessed the seventh day,	3: 3
G., had created and made.	3: 3
G., made the heaven and the	3: 4
the Lord G., created all things,	3: 5
G., had not caused it to rain	3: 5
G., had created all the children	3: 5

G., spake, and there went up a	Mses 3: 6
G., formed man from the dust of	3: 7
G., planted a garden eastward	3: 8
the Lord G., to grow every tree,	3: 9
sphere in which I, G., created it,	3: 9
G., planted the tree of life also in	3: 9
G., caused a river to go out of	3:10
G., called the name of the first	3:11
Lord G., created much gold;	3:11
G., took the man, and put him	3:15
G., commanded the man, saying:	3:16
G., said unto mine Only Begotten,	3:18
Lord G., formed every beast of	3:19
G., breathed into them the breath	3:19
B., caused a deep sleep to fall	3:21
rib which I, the Lord G., had	3:22
G., spake unto Moses, saying:	4: 1
I, the Lord G., had given him,	4: 3
which I, the Lord G., had made.	4: 5
for he knew not the mind of G.,	4: 6
G. said—Ye shall not eat of	4: 7
G. hath said—Ye shall not eat	4: 9
G. doth that in the day ye	4:11
heard the voice of the Lord G.,	4:14
the presence of the Lord G.	4:14
I, the Lord G., called unto Adam,	4:15
I, the Lord G., said unto Adam:	4:17
Lord G., said unto the woman:	4:19
the Lord G., said unto the serpent:	4:20
woman, I, the Lord G., said:	4:22
Adam, I, the Lord G., said:	4:23
G., called the first of all women,	4:26
the Lord G., make coats of skins,	4:27
G., said unto mine Only Begotten:	4:28
G., will send him forth from the	4:29
For as I, the Lord G., liveth,	4:30
the Lord G., had driven them out,	5: 1
should worship the Lord their G.	5: 5
call upon G. in the name of the	5: 8
in that day Adam blessed G.	5:10
Blessed be the name of G., for	5:10
again in the flesh I shall see G.	5:10
the eternal life which G. giveth	5:11
and Eve blessed the name of G.,	5:12
saying: I am also a son of G.	5:13
they loved Satan more than G.	5:13
Lord G. called upon men by	5:14
forth out of the mouth of G.	5:15
ceased not to call upon G.	5:16
Cain loved Satan more than G.	5:18
counsel which was had from G.;	5:25
they loved Satan more than G.	5:28
their heads, and by the living G.,	5:29
not the commandments of G.,	5:52
and it displeased G., and he	5:52
And G. cursed the earth with a	5:56
sent forth from the presence of G.,	5:58
hearkened unto the voice of G.,	6: 1
Adam glorified the name of G.;	6: 2
G. hath appointed me another	6: 2
G. revealed himself unto Seth,	6: 3
unto as many as called upon G.	6: 5
was kept of the children of G.	6: 8
In the day that G. created man,	6: 8
in the likeness of G. made he him;	6: 8
the land upon the footstool of G.	6: 9
his son Enos in the ways of G.;	6:13
the residue of the people of G.	6:17
Enochiin all the ways of G.	6:21
Adam, who was the son of G.,	6:22
with whom G., himself, conversed.	6:22
the Spirit of G. descended	6:26
serve the Lord G. who made you.	6:33
the spirits that G. had created;	6:36
for he walked with G.	6:39
taught me in all the ways of G.	6:41
the same is the G. of heaven,	6:43
and he is my G., and your God,	6:43
your G., and ye are my brethren,	6:43
and deny the G. of heaven?	6:43
given by the finger of G.;	6:46
spake forth the words of G.,	6:47
out from the presence of G.	6:49

GOD

But G. hath made known unto	Mses	6:50
I am G.; I made the world,		6:51
that the Son of G. hath atoned		6:54
nowise inherit the kingdom of G.,		6:57
Spirit of G. descended upon him,		6:65
thou art one in me, a son of G.;		6:68
and become the sons of G.,		7: 1
wrath of G. to be poured out upon		7: 1
that he led the people of G.,		7:13
language which G. had given		7:13
enemies of the people of G.,		7:14
people that fought against G.;		7:15
unto the people of G.		7:19
tne g. of heaven looked upon		7:28
I am G.; Man of Holiness		7:35
all the creations of G. mourned;		7:56
stood on the right hand of G.;		7:57
Forasmuch as thou art G.,		7:59
judgments of the Almighty G.,		7:66
all his people walked with G.,		7:69
for G. received it up into his own		7:69
they were called the sons of G.		8:13
and taught the things of G.,		8:16
Behold, we are the sons of G.;		8:21
G. saw that the wickedness of		8:22
of Jesus Christ, the Son of G.,		8:24
and he walked with G., as did		8:27
earth was corrupt before G.,		8:28
And G. looked upon the earth,		8:29
And G. said unto Noah:		8:30
keep the commandments of G.,	Abr	1: 2
to the appointment of G. unto		1: 4
which the Lord their G. had given		1: 5
turned to the g. of Elkenah,		1: 6
Elkenah, and the g. of Libnah,		1: 6
and the g. of Mahmackrah,		1: 6
and the g. of Korash, and the		1: 6
Korash, and the g. of Pharaoh,		1: 6
offering unto the g. of Pharaoh,		1: 9
also unto the g. of Shagreel,		1: 9
the g. of Shagreel was the sun.		1: 9
a g. like unto that of Pharaoh,		1:13
my voice unto the Lord my G.,		1:15
to worship the g. of Elkenah,		1:17
Elkenah, and the g. of Libnah,		1:17
and the g. of Mahmackrah,		1:17
and the g. of Korash, and the		1:17
Korash, and the g. of Pharaoh,		1:17
earth forever, for I am thy G.		1:19
the Lord my G. preserved to		1:31
the Lord G. caused the famine		2: 1
For I am the Lord thy G.;		2: 7
the Lord my G. had given		3: 1
nearest unto the throne of G.;		3: 2
for I am the Lord thy G.:		3: 3
set nigh unto the throne of G.,		3: 9
near unto the throne of G.		3:10
that the Lord thy G. shall take		3:17
I am the Lord thy G.,		3:19
The Lord thy G. sent his angel to		3:20
And G. saw these souls that they		3:23
them that was like unto G.,		3:24
the Lord their G. shall command		3:25
The idolatrous g. of Elkenah.	Fac	1: 5
The idolatrous g. of Libnah.		1: 6
g. of Mahmackrah		1: 7
The idolatrous g. of Korash.		1: 8
The idolatrous g. of Pharaoh.		1: 9
or the residence of G.		2: 1
or the place where G. resides;		2: 2
revealed from G. to Abraham,		2: 2
Is made to represent G.,		2: 3
Represents G. sitting upon his		2: 7
in the Holy Temple of G.		2: 8
crowned on the right hand of G.	JS	1: 1
before sent upon Israel, of G.,		1:18
not the angels of G. in heaven,		1:40
let him ask of G., that giveth		2:11
person needed wisdom from G.,		2:12
directs, that is, ask of G.		2:13
determination to "ask of G.,"		2:13
my determination to ask of G.,		2:14
the desire of my heart to G.		2:15

all my powers to call upon G.	JS	2:16
am I that I can withstand G.,		2:25
and I knew that G. knew it,		2:25
by so doing I would offend G.,		2:25
lacked wisdom might ask of G.,		2:26
offensive in the sight of G.		2:28
was called of G. as I had been.		2:28
supplication to Almighty G.		2:29
in the act of calling upon G.,		2:30
sent from the presence of G.,		2:33
G. had a work for me to do;		2:33
that G. had prepared them for		2:35
the plates but to glorify G.,		2:46
to me that it was of G.,		2:50
But by the wisdom of G.,		2:60
an angel of G. had revealed it		2:64
in the G. of our salvation.		2:73
We believe in G., the Eternal	AoF	1
that a man must be called of G.,		5
the Bible to be the word of G.		8
of Mormon to be the word of G.		8
believe all that G. has revealed,		9
pertaining to the Kingdom of G.		9
of worshiping Almighty G.		11

GODLINESS

a firm mind in every form of g.	Mro	7:30
patience, brotherly kindness, g.,	DC	4: 6
mystery of g., how great is it!		19:10
the power of g. is manifest.		84:20
power of g. is not manifest		84:21
patience, g., brotherly kindness		107:30
having a form of g., but they	JS	2:19

GODLY

by a g. walk and conversion,	DC	20:69

GOD'S

according to G. justice;	Al	12:18
by heaven, for it is G. throne;	3Ne	12:34
punishment is G. punishment.	DC	19:11
punishment is G. punishment.		19:12
are Christ's, and Christ is G.		76:59
apostles, even G. high priests;		84:63
reckoning of G. time, angel's time,		130: 4

GODS

and becoming as G., knowing	Al	12:31
as sacrifices unto their idol g.	Mrm	4:14
as it is written, they are g.,	DC	76:58
there be one God or many g.,		121:28
of the Eternal God of all other g.		121:32
and from henceforth are not g.,		132:17
and the g. are appointed there,		132:18
pass by the angels, and the g.,		132:19
Then shall they be g.,		132:20
Then shall they be g.,		132:20
are not angels but are g.		132:37
and ye shall be as g., knowing	Mses	4:11
of the heathen,	Abr	1: 5
offering unto these strange g.,		1: 8
worship g. of wood or of stone,		1:11
stood before the g. of Elkenah,		1:13
an understanding of these g.,		1:14
and of the g. of the land,		1:20
from the g. of Elkenah,		2:13
they, that is the G., organized		4: 1
the Spirit of the G. was brooding		4: 2
And they (the G.) said:		4: 3
they (the G.) comprehended		4: 4
the G. called the light Day,		4: 5
And the G. also said:		4: 6
And the G. ordered the expanse.		4: 7
And the G. called the expanse,		4: 8
And the G. ordered, saying:		4: 9
the G. prnounced the dry land,		4:10
the G. saw that they were		4:10
And the G. said:		4:11
And the G. organized the earth		4:12
the G. saw that they were		4:12
the G. organized the lights in		4:14
And the G. organized the two		4:16
And the G. set them in the		4:17

GODS — 402 — GOLDEN

the G. watched those things	Abr	4:18
And the G. said:		4:20
And the G. prepared the waters		4:21
And the G. saw that they		4:21
And the G. said:		4:22
And the G. prepared the earth		4:24
And the G. organized the earth		4:25
the G. saw they would obey.		4:25
And the G. took counsel among		4:26
the G. went down to organize		4:27
in the image of the G. to form		4:27
And the G. said:		4:28
And the G. said:		4:28
And the G. said:		4:29
And the G. said:		4:31
the G. said among themselves:		5: 2
And the G. concluded upon		5: 3
which they (the G.) counseled		5: 3
the G. came down and formed		5: 4
that the G. formed the earth		5: 4
the G. had not caused it to rain		5: 5
And the G. formed man from		5: 7
And the G. planted a garden,		5: 8
made the G. to grow every tree		5: 9
And the G. took the man		5:11
the G. commanded the man,		5:12
yet the G. had not appointed		5:13
And the G. said:		5:14
And the G. caused a deep		5:15
the rib which the G. had taken		5:16
the G. formed every beast of		5:20
before the g. of Elkenah,	Fac	1: 4

GOES
and g. on in the ways of sin and	Mos	16: 5
every man who g. forth to	DC	84:103

GOEST
know that thou g. about much,	Jac	7: 6
whithersoever thou g. let it be in	Al	37:36
said unto him: Where g. thou?	Mses	4:15

GOETH
it g. forth unto all the nations	1Ne	13:29
it g. forth unto all the nations		13:29
to his word the earth g. back,	He	12:15
if he g. through both treadeth	3Ne	20:16
And thus he g. up and down,	DC	10:27
let him that g. to the east		42:64
g. forth deceiving the nations		52:14
that g. forth to proclaim this		84:86
judgment g. before the face of		88:40
he that g., let him not look		133:15
g. toward the east of Assyria.	Mses	3:14

GOING
the Son of God g. forth among	1Ne	11:24
the Lamb of God g. forth among		11:31
their Redeemer, g. before,		17:30
shall be darkened in her g. forth,	2Ne	23:10
would keep them from g. down	En	1:23
while he was g. about to destroy	Mos	27:10
g. about rebelling against God,		27:11
as he was g., to preach to many	Al	1: 7
by g. into the waters of baptism.		7:15
as I was g. thither I found		10: 8
g. forth with their flocks to		17:26
art thou g. with this Nephite,		20:10
unto him whither he was g.,		20:11
art g. to deliver these Nephites,		20:13
as Ammon was g. forth into the		27:16
as if we were g. to the city		56:31
g. forth unto the judgment-seat,	He	2: 9
at the g. down of the sun	3Ne	1:15
g. forth one by one until they		11:15
until the g. down of the sun,	Eth	12: 3
if g. to a church where they	DC	20:84
with him at the time of his g.,		25: 6
from g. abroad unto the world		45:72
whose g. forth is unto the ends		65: 1
g. from house to house, and		76:18
in g. out to battle against		98:36
the men g. to do with you?		122: 6

g. like a lamb to the slaughter;	DC	135: 4
g. on still towards the south;	Abr	2:21
in g. to inquire of the Lord	JS	2:18
intention of g. to the house;		2:48
what the Lord was g. to do,		2:54
g. with my wife to Susquehanna		2:61

GOLD
his g., and his silver, and his	1Ne	2: 4
their g., and their silver, and their		2:11
he left g. and silver, and all		3:16
we did gather together our g.,		3:22
we would give unto him our g.,		3:24
the hilt thereof was of pure g.,		4: 9
I also saw g., and silver, and silks,		13: 7
Behold the g., and the silver,		13: 8
of ore, both of g., and of silver,		18:25
of steel, and of g., and of silver,	2Ne	5:15
also is full of silver and g.,		12: 7
of silver, and his idols of g.,		12:20
a man more precious than fine g.;		23:12
shall not regard silver and g.,		23:17
to search much g. and silver,	Jac	1:16
you have begun to search for g.,		2:12
became exceeding rich in g.,	Jar	1: 8
and have not sought g. nor silver	Mos	2:12
and for g., and for silver,		4:19
engravings, and they are of pure g.		8: 9
a fifth part of their g. and of		11: 3
manner of precious things, of g.,		11: 8
ornamented with g. and silver		11: 9
he did ornament with pure g.;		11:11
half of their g., and their silver,		19:15
had taken all their g., and silver,		22:12
which were on the plates of g.		28:11
of grain, and of g., and of silver,	Al	1:29
herds, and their g. and their silver,		4: 6
a senine of g. for a day,		11: 3
which is equal to a senine of g.;		11: 3
of the different pieces of their g.,		11: 5
a senine of g., a seon of gold,		11: 5
a seon of g., a shum of gold,		11: 5
a shum of g., and a limnah of gold.		11: 5
a shum of gold, and a limnah of g.		11: 5
silver was equal to a senine of g.,		11: 7
a seon of g. was twice the value		11: 8
a shum of g. was twice the value		11: 9
a limnah of g. was the value of		11:10
an antion of g. is equal to three		11:19
having forsaken all his g.,		15:16
upon riches, or upon g. and silver,		17:14
that their hearts were set upon g.,		31:24
and their ornaments of g.,		31:28
have an exceeding plenty of g.,	He	6: 9
there was all manner of g. in		6:11
idols of their g. and their silver.		6:31
that ye might get g. and silver.		7:21
and in g., and in silver, and in		12: 2
ye will give unto him of your g.,		13:28
and their g., and their silver,	3Ne	6: 2
purge them as g. and silver,		24: 3
sell me for silver and for g.,		27:32
g. and silver did they lay up	4Ne	1:46
and of fine linen, and of g.,	Eth	9:17
find g. he did cause to be refined		10: 7
in buildings, and in g. and silver,		10:12
they did make g., and silver,		10:23
to get ore, of g., and of silver,		10:23
was a paved work of pure g.,	DC	110: 2
wealth pertaining to g. and silver		111: 4
come ye, with your g. and		124:11
Come ye, with all your g., and		124:26
and purge them as g. and silver,		128:24
Lord God, created much g.,	Mses	3:11
the g. of that land was good,		3:12
written upon g. plates, giving	JS	2:34
that there were g. plates in the		2:64

GOLDEN
man than the g. wedge of Ophir.	2Ne	23:12
ceased, the g. city ceased!		24: 4
a g. calf for the worship of	DC	124:84

GOMORRAH

GOMORRAH
God overthrew Sodom and G. — 2 Ne 23:19

GONE
had g. from before my presence. — 1 Ne 11:12
the Gentiles who had g. forth — 13:16
the Gentiles that had g. out of — 13:19
after the book hath g. forth — 13:28
the Gentiles which have g. forth — 13:29
the Gentiles who have g. forth — 13:30
we had all g. down into the ship, — 18: 8
what they should do after I was g.; — 19: 4
have already g. forth among them. — 2 Ne 3:11
generations have g. by them. — 3:20
my salvation is g. forth, — 8: 5
have g. forth out of his mouth, — 9:17
for ye have all g. astray, — 12: 5
my people are g. into captivity, — 15:13
They are g. over the passage; — 20:29
they have all g. out of the way; — 28:11
they have all g. astray save — 28:14
All we, like sheep, have g. astray; — Mos 14: 6
Having g. according to their own — 16:12
had g. up to the land of Nephi, — 29: 3
having g. the way of all the earth, — Al 1: 1
had g. about among the people, — 1: 3
nevertheless have g. astray, — 5:37
first parents could have g. forth — 12:26
yea, they had all g. astray; — 13:17
he has g. to the land of Ishmael, — 22: 4
have g. to dwell with their God. — 24:22
that they have g. to their God, — 26:34
had g. to war against the Nephites — 27: 1
g. astray after an unknown God. — 30:53
and have g. far astray because — 41: 1
g. contrary to the nature of God; — 41:11
would know whither they had g. — 43:22
have g. forth and are buried — 44:22
the proclamation had g. forth — 47: 2
and had g. to destroy them — 48:24
that he hath g. to such a place? — 54:22
until I had g. forth with my — 56:33
g. forth against our enemies, — 60:16
if we had g. forth against them — 60:16
had g. the way of all the earth. — 62:37
Corianton had g. forth to the — 63:10
who had g. forth into that land. — 63:10
g. forth unto the Lamanites; — 63:14
and g. the way of all the earth; — He 1: 2
until they had g. forth among — 5:16
had g. over from the Nephites, — 5:17
g. over unto the Lamanites, — 11:24
our riches are g. from us.; — 13:33
and on the morrow it is g.; — 13:34
of Lachoneus had g. forth — 3 Ne 3:22
until they had all g. forth to — 3:22
of those who have g. hence, — 5:14
g. forth out of the reach of — 7:13
until they had all g. forth, — 11:15
when they had all g. forth — 11:16
write these sayings after I am g., — 16: 4
while they were g. for bread — 18: 2
ye are g. away from mine — 24: 7
and had g. unto the Father, — 26:15
that I am g. to the Father? — 28: 1
when I am g. unto the Father? — 28: 4
all g. to the paradise of God, — 4 Ne 1:14
I had g. according to the word — Mrm 2:17
when they had g. through and — 6:11
ye are g., and my sorrows — 6:20
fathers who have g. before you. — 6:21
ye are g., and the Father, yea, — 6:22
they are g., and I fulfil the — 8: 3
saints who have g. before me, — 8:23
the winds have g. forth out of — Eth 2:24
the winds which have g. forth, — 2:25
must have g. to an endless hell. — Mro 8:13
g. on in the persuasions of men. — DC 8:13
which have g. out of your hands. — 10:10
have g. forth out of your hands; — 10:30
which have g. out of your hands, — 10:38
my word which hath g. forth — 11:22
the decree hath g. forth from — DC 29: 8
hath g. forth in a firm decree, — 29:12
as the words have g. forth out — 29:30
have g. abroad in the earth. — 50: 1
which have g. forth inthe earth, — 50: 2
g. up unto the land of Zion; — 62: 2
all have g. out of the way. — 82: 6
and the decree hath g. forth — 101:10
who have g. into the army, — 136: 8
g. astray, and have denied me, — Mses 6:28
filthiness which is g. forth out of — 7:48
having g. as usual at the end — JS 2:59

GOOD

it must needs be a g. thing for — 1 Ne 17:25
brethren beheld that it was g., — 18: 4
that they know g. from evil. — 2 Ne 2: 5
they perish from that which is g., — 2: 5
nor misery, neither g. nor bad. — 2:11
be as God, knowing g. and evil. — 2:18
doing no g., for they knew no sin. — 2:23
free forever, knowing g. from evil; — 2:26
and I have chosen the g. part, — 2:30
among them, who shall do much g., — 3:24
upon them which are g. in my sight, — 5:30
to be learned is g. if they hearken — 9:29
Wo unto them that call evil g., — 15:20
that call evil good, and g. evil, — 15:20
the evil and to choose the g. — 17:15
refuse the evil and choose the g., — 17:16
for their g. have I written them. — 25: 8
for he doeth that which is g. — 26:33
witnesses as seemeth him g. — 27:14
revile against that which is g., — 28:16
anger against that which is g. — 28:20
for it persuadeth them to do g.; — 33: 4
all men that they should do g. — 33:10
seek them for the intent to do g. — Jac 2:19
and obtained a g. hope of glory — 4:11
And he beheld that it was g.; — 5:17
and he beheld also that it was g. — 5:20
I planted in a g. spot of ground; — 5:25
have not brought forth g. fruit, — 5:26
may bring forth g. fruit unto thee, — 5:27
there is none of it which is g. — 5:32
I may preserve again g. fruit — 5:33
beholdest that they are yet g. — 5:34
I know that the roots are g., — 5:36
from the wild branches, g. fruit. — 5:36
which brought forth g. fruit, — 5:40
have once brought forth g. fruit — 5:42
are g. for nothing save it be to — 5:42
plant in a g. spot of ground; — 5:43
part thereof brought forth g. fruit, — 5:45
have overcome the g. branch — 5:45
that they bring forth no g. fruit; — 5:46
overcome the roots which are g.? — 5:48
may bring forth g. fruit unto me, — 5:54
that the g. may overcome the evil. — 5:59
may bring forth again g. fruit; — 5:60
which natural fruit is g. and — 5:61
according to the strength of the g. — 5:65
according as the g. shall grow, — 5:66
the g. shall overcome the bad, — 5:66
saw that his fruit was g., — 5:75
the natural fruit, that it is g., — 5:75
the g. and the bad to be gathered; — 5:77
the g. will I preserve unto myself, — 5:77
by the g. word of God — 6: 7
and deny the g. word of Christ, — 6: 8
and in all things which are g.; — Om 1:25
there is nothing which is g. save — 1:25
whether they be g., or whether — Mos 3:24
do evil, but to do g. continually. — 5: 2
always abounding in g. works, — 5:15
that which was g. among them — 9: 1
do with him as seemeth thee g. — 12:16
of him that bringeth, g. tidings, — 12:21
that bringeth g. tidings of good; — 12:21
that bringeth good tidings of g.; — 12:21
have brought g. tidings of good, — 15:14
have brought good tidings of g., — 15:14

GOOD

of him that bringeth g. tidings,	Mos 15:18
devilish, knowing evil from g.,	16: 3
whether they be g. or whether	16:10
If they be g., to the	16:11
and g. desires towards God,	18:28
and be of g. comfort, for	24:13
again, saying: Be of g. comfort,	24:16
bidding them to be of g. comfort:	27:23
did publish g. tidings of good;	27:37
did publish good tidings of g.;	27:37
having warred a g. warfare,	Al 1: 1
done much g. among this people;	1:13
all manner of g. homely cloth.	1:29
whether they were g. or whether	3:26
it be a g. spirit or a bad one.	3:26
bringeth forth not g. fruit,	5:36
the g. shepherd doth call you;	5:38
the voice of the g. shepherd,	5:38
not the sheep of the g. shepherd.	5:38
not the sheep of the g. shepherd,	5:39
whatsoever is g. cometh from God,	5:40
a man bringeth forth g. works	5:41
the voice of the g. shepherd,	5:41
being dead unto all g. works.	5:42
bringeth not forth g. fruit	5:52
the voice of the g. shepherd,	5:57
g. shepherd doth call after you;	5:60
will always abound in g. works.	7:24
to your faith and g. works,	7:27
destroy that which was g.;	11:21
they be g. or whether they be evil.	11:44
as Gods, knowing g. from evil,	12:31
whether to do evil or to do g.–	12:31
their exceeding faith and g. words;	13: 3
being left to choose g. or evil;	13: 3
therefore they having chosen g.,	13: 3
ye may show forth g. examples	17:11
My brethren, be of g. cheer and	17:31
this people as g. as thy people?	21: 5
and bringeth forth g. works,	26:22
I know that g. and evil have	29: 5
he that knoweth not g. from evil	29: 5
but he that knoweth g. and evil,	29: 5
whether he desireth g. or evil,	29: 5
if it be a true seed, or a g. seed,	32:28
needs be that this is a g. seed,	32:28
good seed, or that the word is g.,	32:28
needs say the seed is g.;	32:30
are ye sure that this is a g. seed?	32:31
if a seed groweth it is g.,	32:32
it groweth not, behold it is not g.,	32:32
needs know that the seed is g.	32:33
and whatsoever is light, is g.,	32:35
ye must know that it is g.;	32:35
to know if the seed was g.	32:36
not because the seed was not g.,	32:39
he rewardeth you no g. thing.	34:39
to never be weary of g. works,	37:34
and he will direct thee for g.;	37:37
has he not set a g. example for	39: 1
soul, if it were not for your g.	39: 7
Command thy children to do g.,	39:12
whether they be g. or evil,	40:11
chose evil works rather than g.;	40:13
if their works were g. in this life,	41: 3
the desires of their hearts were g.,	41: 3
be restored unto that which is g.,	41: 3
or according to his desires of	41: 5
good according to his desires of g.;	41: 5
whether to do g. or do evil.	41: 7
g. for that which is good;	41:13
good for that which is g.;	41:13
and do g. continually;	41:14
have g. rewarded unto you again.	41:14
as God, knowing g. and evil;	42: 3
but in doing g., in preserving	48:16
observe to do g. continually,	63: 2
than they who chose g.,	He 5: 2
also written, that they were g.	5: 6
ye should do that which is g.,	5: 7
unto you to declare g. tidings.	5:29
the voice of the g. shepherd;	7:18
up beyond that which is g.	7:26
alone, for he is a g. man,	He 8: 7
do iniquity, and how slow to do g.,	12: 4
unto repentance and g. works,	12:24
They that have done g. shall have	12:26
that ye might know g. from evil,	14:31
ye can do g. and be restored	14:31
restored unto that which is g.,	14:31
have that which is g. restored	14:31
people against that which was g.	16:22
your head and be of g. cheer;	3Ne 1:13
works thereof I know to be g.;	3: 9
be thenceforth g. for nothing,	12:13
that they may see your g. works	12:16
do g. to them that hate you,	12:44
rise on the evil and on the g.	12:45
give g. gifts unto your children,	14:11
g. things to them that ask him?	14:11
every g. tree bringeth forth good	14:17
good tree bringeth forth g. fruit;	14:17
A g. tree cannot bring forth evil	14:18
corrupt tree bring forth g. fruit.	14:18
that bringeth not forth g. fruit	14:19
g. for nothing but to be cast out,	16:15
bringeth g. tidings unto them,	20:40
bringeth g. tidings unto them	20:40
good tidings unto them of g.,	20:40
whether they be g. or whether	26: 4
If they be g., to the	26: 5
whether they be g. or whether	27:14
man it seemeth them g.	28:30
whether they be g. or evil;	Mrm 3:20
for it persuadeth men to do g.	Eth 4:11
persuadeth men to do g.	4:12
g. cometh of none save it be	4:12
same that leadeth men to all g.;	4:12
persuaded to do g. continually,	8:26
did administer that which was g.	9:23
he did live to a g. old age,	10:16
Corom did that which was g. in	10:17
Lib also did that which was g.	10:19
And he lived to a g. old age,	11: 4
always abounding in g. works,	12: 4
by the g. word of God,	Mro 6: 4
for if their works be g., then	7: 5
be good, then they are g. also.	7: 5
evil cannot do that which is g.;	7: 6
evil cannot do that which is g.;	7:10
neither will he give a g. gift.	7:10
cannot bring forth g. water;	7:11
neither can a g. fountain bring	7:11
which are g. cometh of God;	7:12
enticeth to do g. continually;	7:13
inviteth and enticeth to do g.,	7:13
or that which is g. and of God	7:14
that ye may know g. from evil;	7:15
that he may know g. from evil;	7:16
thing which inviteth to do g.,	7:16
he persuadeth no man to do g.,	7:17
that ye may know g. from evil;	7:19
lay hold upon every g. thing,	7:19
lay hold upon every g. thing?	7:20
may lay hold on every g. thing.	7:21
there should come every g. thing.	7:22
children of men, which were g.;	7:24
which are g. cometh of Christ;	7:24
no g. thing come unto them.	7:24
lay hold upon every g. thing;	7:25
Father in my name, which is g.,	7:26
cleave unto every g. thing;	7:28
everything save that which is g.;	9:19
somewhat as seemeth me g.;	10: 1
thing is g. is just and true;	10: 6
that is g. denieth the Christ,	10: 6
every g. gift cometh of Christ.	10:18
none that doeth g. among you,	10:25
one among you that doeth g.,	10:25
lay hold upon every g. gift,	10:30
be the means of doing much g.	DC 6: 8
If thou wilt do g., yea, and	6:13
that if you have g. desires–	6:27
Fear not to do g., my sons,	6:33
if ye sow g. ye shall also reap	6:33
also reap g. for your reward.	6:33

GOOD

fear not, little flock; do g.,	DC 6:34
Peter, this was a g. desire;	7: 5
iniquity against that which is g.,	10:20
the means of doing much g.	11: 8
Spirit which leadeth to do g.—	11:12
unto all who have g. desires,	11:27
members and in g. standing,	20:84
heavens to shake for your g.,	21: 6
Zion in mighty power for g.,	21: 7
it is his g. will to give you	29: 5
there is none which doeth g.	33: 4
there are none that doeth g.	35:12
heavens to shake for your g.,	35:24
or rented as seemeth them g.	38:37
do with him as seemeth me g.	40: 3
should live as seemeth him g.,	41: 8
and prophesy as seemeth me g.,	42:16
for the g. of the poor,	42:71
about, as seemeth them g.,	48: 3
and I am the g. shepherd,	50:44
turn unto them for their g.	51:17
as I will, as seemeth me g.	52: 6
and revoke, as it seemeth me g.;	56: 4
lands for the g. of the saints,	57: 8
for the g. of the saints.	57:12
anxiously engaged in a g. cause,	58:27
And inasmuch as men do g.	58:28
inheritance as seemeth him g.;	58:38
the agent, as seemeth him g.	58:51
the g. things of the earth,	59: 3
the g. things which come of	59:17
or bought, as seemeth you g.,	60: 5
this for the g. for the churches;	60: 9
for your g. I gave unto you	61:13
two by two, as seemeth them g.,	61:35
be of g. cheer, little children;	61:36
two by two, as seemeth you g.,	62: 5
and not for the g. of men	63:12
and pay as seemeth him g.	64:28
eat the g. of the land of Zion	64:34
be of g. cheer, and do not fear,	68: 6
be for the g. of the church,	69: 8
to the g. of the church,	72:12
the g. pleasure of my will	76: 7
They who have done g. in	76:17
nevertheless, be of g. cheer,	78:18
wilt do the greatest g. unto	81: 4
and none doeth g., for all have	82: 6
wisdom also in me for your g.	82:16
for thus it seemeth me g.	84:103
behold it is not g., neither meet	89: 5
and is not g. for man, but is	89: 8
grain is g. for the food of man;	89:16
acquainted with all g. books,	90:15
work together for your g.,	90:24
children of men for your g.	96: 5
that bringeth not forth g. fruit	97: 7
work together for your g.,	98: 3
g. men and wise men ye should	98:10
all evil and cleave unto all g.,	98:11
do with them as seemeth me g.;	100: 1
shall work together for g.	100:15
thenceforth g. for nothing only	101:40
thenceforth g. for nothing but	103:10
as it shall seem g. unto you.	104:85
work together for your g.	105:40
will order all things for your g.,	111:11
Let thy heart be of g. cheer	112: 4
experience, and shall be for thy g.	122: 7
many of them for your g.,	124: 9
therefore let it be a g. house,	124:23
of that house, as seemeth him g.;	124:72
that house as seemeth him g.,	124:77
that house, as seemeth him g.	124:80
that house, as seemeth him g.,	124:81
world for some g. end, or bad,	127: 2
whether it be g. or bad.	127: 2
bring glad tidings of g. things,	128:19
for the g. and safety of society.	134: 1
bringing offenders against g. laws	134: 8
be for fellowship and g. standing;	134:10
the light; and that light was g.	Mses 2: 4
which I had made were g.	2:10

things which I had made were g.;	Mses 2:12
which I had made were g.;	2:18
which I had created were g.	2:21
that all these things were g.	2:25
which I had made were very g.;	2:31
I, God, saw that they were g.;	3: 2
man saw that it was g. for food.	3: 9
tree of knowledge of g. and evil.	3: 9
the gold of that land was g.,	3:12
tree of the knowledge of g. and evil,	3:17
not g. that the man should be	3:18
as gods, knowing g. and evil.	4:11
saw that the tree was g. for food,	4:12
one of us to know g. and evil;	4:28
never should have known g. and	5:11
I will do as seemeth me g.	6:32
may know to prize the g.	6:55
unto them to know g. from evil;	6:56
these souls that they were g.,	Abr 3:23
and he saw that they were g.;	3:23
and that their plan was g.	4:21
tothe sight and g. for food;	5: 9
of knowledge of g. and evil.	5: 9
of knowledge of g. and evil,	5:13
is not g. that the man should	5:14
if the g. man of the house had	JS 1:47
the seemingly g. feelings of	2: 6
g. feelings one for another,	2: 6
should be had for g. and evil	2:33
both g. and evil spoken of	2:33
and in doing g. to all men;	AoF 13
of g. report or praiseworthy,	13

GOODLY

having been born of g. parents,	1Ne 1: 1
were a g. number gathered	Mos 18: 7
which is planted in a g. land,	DC 97: 9
go up also unto the g. land,	99: 7
ye shall possess the g. land.	103:20
to drive you from my g. land,	103:24

GOODNESS

the g. and the mysteries of God,	1Ne 1: 1
thy power, and g., and mercy are	1:14
not have known the g. of God,	5: 4
been brought by his infinite g.	2Ne 1:10
the great g. of the Lord,	4:17
how great the g. of our God,	9:10
they should not partake of his g.?	26:28
unto him and partake of his g.;	26:33
not partake of the g. of God,	33:14
and partake of the g. of God,	Jac 1: 7
take strangth because of their g.;	5:59
the wickedness of the g. of God	Mos 4: 5
a knowledge of the g. of God,	4: 6
or if ye have known of his g.	4:11
his g. and long-suffering towards	4:11
through the infinite g. of God,	5: 3
of the immediate g. of God,	25:10
know of the g. and glory of God.	27:22
to the supreme g. of God.	Al 19: 6
a marvelous light of his g.—	24: 7
our great God has in g. sent	34: 4
may try the experiment of its g.	57:25
according to the g. of God,	57:36
joy because of the g. of God	60:11
of the exceeding g. of God	He 12: 1
the Lord in his great infinite g.	12: 6
notwithstanding his great g.	3Ne 4:33
because of the great g. of God	Mrm 1:15
and knew of the g. of Jesus.	2:13
because of the g. of God;	Mro 8: 3
his infinite g. and grace,	DC 86:11
are ye if ye continue in my g.,	133:52
upon them according to his g.,	

GOODS

and upon all manner of fine g.	Al 31:24
their g. and their substance	4Ne 1:25
hold upon other men's g.,	DC 56:17
he may sell g. without fraud,	57: 8
send g. also unto the people,	57: 9
take from them this world's g.,	134:10
make him ruler over all his g.	JS 1:50

GORE

GORE
found the king lying in his g., Al 47:27

GOSPEL
the g. which should be preached	1Ne	10:11
had received the fulness of the G.,		10:14
contained the plainness of the g.		13:24
they have taken away from the g.		13:26
which are taken away out of the g.		13:29
and most precious parts of the g.		13:32
plain and precious parts of the g.		13:34
much of my g., which shall be plain		13:34
in them shall be written my g.,		13:36
then shall the fulness of the g.		15:13
also to the knowledge of the g.		15:14
about his covenants and his g.		22:11
the g. of Jesus Christ shall be	2Ne	30: 5
that which ye call the g.,	Jac	7: 6
Gentiles shall sin against my g.,	3Ne	16:10
reject the fulness of my g.,		16:10
fulness of my g. from among them		16:10
I will bring my g. unto them.		16:11
knowledge of the fulness of my g.		16:12
received the fulness of my g.,		20:28
the fulness of my g. shall be		20:30
when this g. shall be preached		21:26
that they are built upon my g.		27: 8
that ye are built upon my g.;		27: 9
the church is built upon my g.		27:10
if it be not built upon my g.,		27:11
I have given unto you my g.,		27:13
this is the g. which I have given		27:13
I say unto you, this is my g.;		27:21
and did preach the g. of Christ		28:23
deny the more parts of his g.,	4Ne	1:27
they who rejected the g. were		1:38
rebel against the g. of Christ;		1:38
believe the g. of Jesus Christ,	Mrm	3:21
may more fully believe his g.,		5:15
hold upon the g. of Christ;		7: 8
knoweth not the g. of Christ;		9: 8
preach the g. to every creature;		9:22
have rejected the g. of Christ;	Eth	4: 3
unto me, and believe in my g.,		4:18
the fulness of my g. might be	DC	1:23
that they may believe the g.		3:20
which contain much of my g.,		6:26
part of my g. and ministry,		6:29
greater views upon my g.;		10:45
contain all those parts of my g.		10:46
that my g., which I gave		10:48
this g. should be made known		10:49
believe in this g. in this land		10:50
bring this part of my g. to		10:52
will also bring to light my g.		10:62
that I may establish my g.,		10:63
rock, my church, and my g.,		11:16
upon my rock, which is my g.;		11:24
and of the g. of repentance,		13: 0
the fulness of my g. from		14:10
church, my g., and my rock.		18: 4
upon the foundation of my g.		18: 5
you have my g. before you,		18:17
who are called to declare my g,		18:26
all the world to preach my g.		18:28
to declare my g., according to		18:32
that they may believe the g.,		19:27
fulness of the g. of Jesus Christ,		20: 9
declare my g. as with the voice		24:12
all those who receive my g.		25: 1
fulness of my everlasting g.,		27: 5
a dispensation of the g.		27:13
preparation of the g. of peace,		27:16
and preach my g. unto them;		28: 8
declaring my g. with the sound		28:16
declare my g. with the sound		29: 4
your mouth to declare my g.;		30: 5
time forth to proclaim my g.,		30: 9
will that he shall declare my g.		32: 1
declare my g. unto a crooked		33: 2
I say unto you, this is my g.;		33:12
called of me to preach my g.		34: 5

GOSPEL

receive the fulness of my g.,	DC	35:12
shall have the g. preached unto		35:15
sent forth the fulness of my g.		35:17
and thou shalt preach my g.		35:23
you are called to preach my g.		36: 1
to preach the everlasting g.		36: 5
until ye have preached my g.		37: 2
receiveth my g. receiveth me;		39: 5
he that receiveth not my g.		39: 5
And this is my g.—		39: 6
preach the fulness of my g.,		39:11
receive the fulness of my g.,		39:18
preaching my g., two by two,		42: 6
to go forth to preach my g.,		42:11
teach the principles of my g.,		42:12
which is the fulness of the g.		42:12
of those who embrace my g.		42:39
shall be the fulness of my g.;		45:28
shall go and preach my g.		49: 1
to preach the g. unto them.		49: 3
To preach my g. by the Spirit,		50:14
that my g. may be preached		57:10
let them preach the g. in the		58:46
preaching the g. by the way,		58:63
the g. must be preached unto		58:64
who have obeyed my g.;		59: 3
been sent to preach my g.		60:13
thence shall the g. roll forth		65: 2
even the fulness of my g.,		66: 2
that you should proclaim my g.		66: 5
to proclaim the everlasting g.,		68: 1
preach the g. to every creature,		68: 8
mouths in proclaiming my g.;		71: 1
in administering the g. and the		72:14
continue preaching the g.,		73: 1
not the g. of Jesus Christ.		74: 2
believed not the g. of Christ,		74: 4
to go forth to proclaim the g.,		75: 2
and proclaim the g., even as		75:15
proclaim the g. unto the world.		75:24
of the g. of Jesus Christ,		76:14
this is the g., the glad tidings,		76:40
testimony of the g. of Christ		76:50
and preached the g. unto them,		76:73
received not the g. of Christ,		76:82
But received not the g., neither		76:101
who have the everlasting g.		77: 8
having the everlasting g.,		77: 9
administer the everlasting g.;		77:11
joy, even the everlasting g.		79: 1
preach the g. to every creature		80: 1
go ye and preach my g.,		80: 3
proclaiming the g. in the land		81: 3
priesthood administereth the g.		84:19
angels and the preparatory g.		84:26
Which g. is the gospel of		84:27
is the g. of repentance and		84:27
the g. is unto all who have not		84:75
to preach the g. in my power;		84:77
preach this g. of the kingdom,		84:80
goeth forth to proclaim this g.		84:86
proclaim mine everlasting g.,		84:103
with the sound of the g.,		84:114
doctrine, in the law of the g.,		88:78
that they might receive the g.,		88:99
committeth the everlasting g.—		88:103
to another as the g. requires.		88:123
of the g. of their salvation.		90:10
shall hear the fulness of the g.		90:11
and the g. of salvation,		93:51
proclaim mine everlasting g.		99: 1
continue proclaiming my g.		99: 8
to mine everlasting g.,		101:22
called unto mine everlasting g.,		101:39
according to the law of my g.,		104:18
should preach my everlasting g.,		106: 2
the letter of the g.,		107:20
are also called to preach the g.,		107:25
of the g. of Jesus Christ,		107:35
and administering the g.,		107:38
have right to preach my g.		108: 6
when the everlasting g. shall		109:29

GOSPEL 407 GOVERNOR

the fulness of the everlasting g.;	DC 109:65
the dispensation of the g. of	110:12
preach my g. unto every creature	112:28
and there promulgate my g.,	118: 4
have endured valiantly for the g.	121:29
solemn proclaimation of my g.,	124: 2
proclaim my everlasting g.	124:88
die without a knowledge of the g.	128: 5
belonging to the everlasting g.,	128:17
who have died in the g. also;	128:18
what do we hear in the g.	128:19
having the everlasting g.,	133:36
g. shall be preached unto every	133:37
sent forth the fulness of his g.,	133:57
g. to the nations of the earth,	134:12
neither preach the g. to,	134:12
the fulness of the everlasting g.,	135: 3
to the truth of the everlasting g.	135: 7
the G. began to be preached,	Mses 5:58
ordinance, and the G. preached,	5:59
go forth and declare his G. unto	8:19
for as many as receive this G.	Abr 2:10
with the blessings of the G.,	2:11
this G. of the Kingdom shall be	JS 1:31
everlasting G. was contained	2:34
and of the g. of repentance,	2:69
the laws and ordinances of the G.	AoF 3
and ordinances of the G. are:	4
in authority to preach the G.	5

GOT
A Bible! We have g. a Bible,	2Ne 29: 3
A Bible, we have g. a Bible,	29: 6
ran and g. upon the tower which	Mos 19: 5
why hath satan g. such great hold	Al 10:25
they g. gain according to their	10:32
g. the victory over the devil,	16:21
he had g. the command of those	47: 5
power than what he hath g.	55: 2
have g. possession of the land,	61: 8
g. great hold upon the hearts of	He 6:31
I have g. upon my tower that	7:14
devil has g. so great hold upon	7:15
and g. upon the wall thereof,	13: 4
and g. on their march beyond	3Ne 4:25
they g. aboard of their vessels	Eth 6: 4
have g. the plates of which you	DC 5: 1
they have only g. a part,	10:44
who has g. riches in store—	90:22
had now g. my mind satisfied	JS 2:26
when I g. those plates of which	2:42
which I g. fixed under the edge	2:52
g. the characters which I had	2:63

GOTTEN
after ye have g. into this straight	2Ne 31:19
Satan had g. great hold upon	Al 8: 9
which had g. into the hearts of	He 3:36
I have g. a man from the Lord;	Mses 5:16

GOULD, John
my servants Orson Hyde and G.,	DC 100:14

GOVERN
to judge and to g. the people.	Al 4:17
and I will g. him no more—	20:26
to g. and manage the affairs	60: 1
and did g. the people that year.	3Ne 6:19
g. your house in meekness,	DC 31: 9
to g. the affairs of the property	38:36
may know how to g. my church	41: 3
be my law to g. my church;	42:59
to g. all those which belong to	Abr 3: 3
to g. all those planets which	3: 9

GOVERNED
not all be g. by one teacher;	Mos 25:20
should be g. by their own voices—	Al 10:19
to be g. by those to whom the	54:18
not be g. by the law nor justice,	He 5: 3
by which all things are g.,	DC 88:13
that which is g. by law is	88:34

GOVERNETH
g. and executeth all things.	DC 88:40

GOVERNING
These are the g. ones;	Abr 3: 3
next grand g. creation near	Fac 2: 2
one of the g. planets also,	2: 5
the g. power, which governs	2: 5

GOVERNMENT
the g. shall be upon his shoulder;	2Ne 19: 6
the increase of g. and peace	19: 7
and the g. of their wars.	Al 43:17
they might maintain a free g.,	46:35
to overthrow the free g. and	51: 5
of their religion by a free g.	51: 6
rob them of their right to the g.	54:17
the g. doth rightly belong,	54:18
to obtain their rights to the g.;	54:24
the g. does not grant us more	58:34
is some faction in the g.,	58:36
Moroni was angry with the g.,	59:13
even the slothfulness of our g.,	60:14
even the great head of our g.	60:24
so much difficulty in the g.,	He 1:18
those who were at the head of g.;	3:23
the sole management of the g.,	6:39
held in office at the head of g.,	7: 5
may recover their rights and g.,	3Ne 3:10
from them their rights of g.,	3:10
did destroy the g. of the land.	7: 2
the regulations of the g. were	7: 6
into a covenant to destroy the g.	7:11
laws, and their manner of g.,	7:14
people and the g. of the land;	9: 9
the bonds of this church g.,	DC 102: 8
present them to the heads of g.	123: 6
no g. can exist in peace, except	134: 2
laws of that g. in which the	134: 8
religious influence with civil g.,	134: 9
g., from the unlawful assaults	134:11
the peace of every g. allowing	134:12
Now the first g. of Egypt was	Abr 1:25
manner of the g. of Ham,	1:25
First in g., the last	Fac 2: 1

GOVERNMENTS
and their g. were established by	He 5: 2
keys thereof, for helps and for g.,	DC 124:143
g. were instituted of G.	134: 1
We believe that all g. necessarily	134: 3
and uphold the respective g.	134: 5
rights by the laws of such g.;	134: 5
all g. have a right to enact	134: 5
states, and g. have a right,	134: 7

GOVERNOR
the g. of the people of Nephi,	Al 2:16
who was g. over all the land.	30:29
judge and g. over the people,	50:39
unto the g. of the land,	51:15
embassy to the g. of our land,	58: 4
he wrote again to the g. of the	60: 1
judge and the g. over the land,	60: 1
sent his epistle unto the chief g.,	61: 1
from Pahoran, the chief g.	61: 1
am the chief g. of this land,	61: 2
a g. over the people of Nephi.	He 1: 5
that he should be their g.,	1: 7
that he should be their g.	1: 9
to be a chief judge and a g. over	1:13
judge and the g. over the land.	3Ne 1: 1
Lachoneus, the g. of the land,	3: 1
the g. of this band of robbers;	3: 1
noble and chief g. of the land,	3: 2
I am the g. of this the secret	3: 9
Lachoneus, the g., was a just	3:12
Giddianhi, the g. of the robbers,	3:12
signed by the g. of the land.	6:22
came not unto the g. of the land	6:23
power from the g. of the land—	6:24
to the g. of the land, against	6:25

GOVERNOR 408 GRAND

GOVERNOR
with another to destroy the g.,	3Ne	6:30
importune at the feet of the g.;	DC	101:87
And if the g. heed them not,		101:88
g. which shall be appointed		124:24
the State as pledged by the g.,		135: 7

GOVERNORS
whom ye have appointed your g.	Al	60:33
high-minded g. of the nation	DC	124: 3

GOVERNS
which g. fifteen other fixed	Fac	2: 5

GRACE
for he is full of g. and truth.		
mercy, and g. of the Holy Messiah,	2Ne	2: 6
wisdom of God, his mercy and g.!		2: 8
greatness, and his g. and mercy,		9: 8
in and through the g. of God		9:53
may praise him through g. divine.		10:24
my soul delighteth in his g.,		10:25
it is by g. that we are saved,		11: 5
that it is by his g., and his		25:23
were filled with the g. of God.	Jac	4: 7
they were to receive the g. of God,	Mos	18:16
they did abound in the g. of God.		18:26
full of g., and mercy, and truth.		27: 5
in the supplicating of his g.,	Al	5:48
full of g., equity, and truth,		7: 3
who is full of g., equity, and truth.		9:26
they might be restored unto g.		13: 9
be restored unto grace for g.,	He	12:24
day of g. was passed with them,		12:24
my g. is sufficient for the meek,	Mrm	2:15
my g. is sufficient for all men	Eth	12:26
would give unto the Gentiles g.,		12:27
that the g. of God the Father,		12:36
by the g. of God the Father,		12:41
his infinite goodness and g.,	Mro	7: 2
may the g. of God the Father,		8: 3
then is his g. sufficient for you,		9:26
by his g. ye may be perfect in		10:32
if by the g. of God ye are		10:32
by the g. of God are perfect in		10:33
in Christ by the g. of God,		10:33
for my g. is sufficient for you,	DC	17: 8
my g. is sufficient for you;		18:31
according to the g. of our Lord		20: 4
through the g. of our Lord and		20:30
through the g. of our Lord and		20:31
that man may fall from g.		20:32
and the g. of your Lord Jesus		21: 1
ye must grow in g. and in		50:40
who is full of g. and truth.		66:12
of his fulness and of his g.;		76:94
According to the election of g.,		84:99
Justice, g. and truth, and peace,		84:102
and my g. shall attend you,		88:78
through the g. of God in the		88:133
Father, full of g. and truth,		93:11
but received g. for grace;		93:12
but received grace for g.;		93:12
but continued from g. to grace,		93:13
but continued from grace to g.,		93:13
you shall receive grace for g.		93:20
you shall receive grace for g.		93:20
according to the g. of God		102: 4
favor and g. in their eyes,		105:25
I will give him g. and assurance		106: 8
assist us, thy people, with thy g.,		109:10
with thy g. assisting them:		109:44
that ye may find g. in their eyes,		124: 9
he would give unto the Gentiles g.,		135: 5
for he is full of g. and truth,	Mses	1: 6
who is full of g. and truth.		1:32
which is full of g. and truth.		5: 7
Son, who is full of g. and truth,		6:52
which is full of g. and truth,		7:11
but through thine own g.;		7:59
Noah found g. in the eyes of the		8:27

GRACIOUS
g. unto those who fear me,	DC	76: 5
thou art g. and merciful,		109:53

GRADUALLY
which descended g. until it	JS	2:16

GRAFT
I will g. them whithersoever	Jac	5: 8
I will g. them whithersoever		5: 8
and g. them in, in the stead		5: 9
thou didst g. in the branches of		5:34
let us g. them into the tree		5:52
and g. in the natural branches of		5:52
I will g. them in unto them.		5:54
I will g. in unto them the branches		5:54
in them ye shall g. according		5:57
G. in the branches; begin at the		5:63
should be too strong for the g.,		5:65
and the g. thereof shall perish,		5:65
will I g. in again into the natural		5:67
will I g. into the natural branches		5:68

GRAFTED
g. in, or come to the knowledge	1Ne	10:14
shall be g. in, being a natural		15:16
and g. in the branches of	Jac	5:10
wild olive branches had been g.;		5:17
if we had not g. in these		5:18
the wild branches had been g. in;		5:30
and g. in unto the natural trees,		5:55
and g. into their mother tree.		5:56
I have g. in the natural branches		5:60
branch be g. into the true vine,	Al	16:17

GRAFTING
concerning the g. in of the natural	1Ne	15:13

GRAFTS
be so that these last g. shall grow,	Jac	5:64

GRAIN
seeds of every kind, both of g.	1Ne	8: 1
and raise all manner of g.,	En	1:21
even all our g. of every kind,	Mos	7:22
and raise all manner of g.		10: 4
also a fifth part of all their g.		11: 3
land also, and devour their g.		12: 6
to raise g. more abundantly,		21:16
secured their g. and their flocks;		21:18
and carried off their g. and		21:21
and took of their g., and		23: 1
together, and also of their g.;		24:18
abundance of g., and of gold,	Al	1:29
of their fields of g. were destroyed,		3: 2
for the loss of their fields of g.,		4: 2
for a measure of every kind of g.		11: 7
raising all manner of g.,		62:29
They did raise g. in abundance,	He	6:12
and did not yield forth g.		11: 6
forth grain in the season of g.;		11: 6
forth her fruit, and her g. in		11:13
and her grain in the season of g.		11:13
that it did bring forth her g.		11:17
her grain in the season of her g.		11:17
and their herds, and their g.,	3Ne	3:22
that they could raise g.,		4: 6
of all their g. of every kind,		6: 2
all manner of fruit, and of g.,	Eth	9:17
and in raising g., and in flocks,		10:12
All g. is ordained for the use	DC	89:14
All g. is good for the food		89:16
mild drinks, also as other g.		89:17
and fields for raising g.,		136: 9

GRAND
there are two divisions or g. heads—	DC	107: 6
and g. secret of the whole matter,		128:11
These are three g. keys whereby		129: 9
the next g. governing creation	Fac	2: 2
also the g. Key-words of the		2: 3

GRAND

which is the g. Key, or,	Fac	2: 5
the g. Key words of the		2: 7
the g. Presidency in Heaven;		3: 1

GRANGER, Oliver
I remember by servant G.;	DC	117:12
no man despise my servant G.,		117:15

GRANT
I will g. unto thee according to	En	1:12
may God g. that he may survive	WM	1: 2
doth g. unto you whatsoever ye	Mos	4:21
may he g. unto you eternal life,		18:13
would g. unto them their lives		23:36
that he would g. unto them that		28: 1
did not g. unto him the office of	Al	4:18
will I g. an inheritance at		5:58
g. that he might baptize them		8:10
doth g. unto the children of men,		12: 9
the Lord g. unto you repentance,		13:30
g. unto them a portion of his Spirit		17: 9
desirest of me I will g. it unto thee.		18:21
except thou wilt g. unto me that		20:22
I will g. unto thee whatsoever		20:23
thou wilt g. that my brethren		20:24
but g. that he may do according		20:24
I will g. unto you that my son		20:26
I will also g. unto thee that thy		20:27
for I will g. unto you your lives,		22: 3
the Lord doth g. unto all nations,		29: 8
And now may God g. unto these,		29:17
And may God g. that it may be		29:17
O Lord, wilt thou g. unto me that		31:31
Wilt thou g. unto them that they		31:33
O Lord, wilt thou g. unto us		31:34
And then may God g. unto you		33:23
Therefore may God g. unto you		34:17
And may God g. unto you even		42:31
to g. unto them their sacred		50:39
I will g. to exchange prisoners		54:20
I will not g. unto him that he		55: 2
not g. unto me mine epistle,		55: 3
did g. unto us great faith,		58:11
does not g. us more strength;		58:34
And except ye g. mine epistle,		60:25
and g. unto them food for		60:25
he would g. unto those who	He	2: 5
will not g. unto you strength,		7:22
we will g. unto thee thy life if		9:20
may God g., in his great fulness,		12:24
g. unto us that we might gather	Mrm	6: 2
g. unto me the thing which I		6: 3
g. that their prayers may be		9:37
they did g. unto him his life.	Eth	8: 6
except I g. it unto you.	DC	5: 3
I will g. unto you no other gift		5: 4
none else will I g. this power,		5:14
I g. unto you eternal life,		5:22
then will I g. unto him a view		5:24
I will g. unto him no views of		5:28
behold, I g. unto you a gift,		6:25
that will I g. unto you,		8: 9
g. unto the children of men		11:22
I g. unto this people a privilege		51:15
do thou g., Holy Father, that		109:14
I g. unto you a sufficient time		124:31
the earth, wherein I g. life,	Mses	2:30

GRANTED
which the Lord hath g. unto me.	Mos	2:11
g. that ye should live in peace		2:20
and g. unto you your lives,		2:23
king Mosiah g. that sixteen of		7: 2
g. salvation unto his people;		15:18
and g. unto them that they		19:15
Lamanites had g. unto them		19:22
he g. unto them that they should		21: 6
g. unto him that he might speak.		22: 5
had g. unto Amulon that he		23:39
G. unto him and his brethren that		24: 1
king Mosiah g. unto Alma that		25:19
Mosiah g. that they might go and		28: 8
which had been g. unto them.		29:39
he had g. unto his people that		29:40

409

g. that I should come unto you.	Al	7: 2
a space g. unto man in which he		12:24
Lord had g. unto them power,		14:28
his father had g. unto him that		21:21
and I have g. unto them that		22: 7
that he hath g. unto us that we		24:10
the lord had g. unto them		25:17
that God would have g. unto us		26: 1
a time g. unto man to repent,		42: 4
affixed and a repentance g.;		42:22
which God had g. unto them,		46:10
it was g. according to the voice		51:16
was g. according to their desires.		62:28
they g. unto those robbers who	3Ne	6: 3
g. unto them a chance for	Mrm	3: 3
of Christ it shall be g. him;		9:21
you will, it shall be g. unto you.	DC	7: 1
that it should be g. unto them		10:47
decreed that they shall be g.		98: 2
is g. that whatsoever you bind		128: 8

GRANTETH
that g. unto him that believeth	Mos	26:23
he g. unto men according to their	Al	29: 4

GRANTS
To whom he g. this privilege	DC	76:117

GRAPE
pure wine of the g. of the vine,	* DC	89: 6

GRAPES
that it should bring forth g.,	2Ne	15: 2
and it brought forth wild g.		15: 2
that it should bring forth g.		15: 4
it brought forth wild g.		15: 4
Do men gather g. of thorns,	3Ne	14:16

GRASP
the g. of this awful monster;	2Ne	9:10
or the devil will g. them with his		28:19
and they were in the g. of justice;	Al	42:14
murder from the g. of justice,	3Ne	6:29

GRASPED
they are g. with death, and hell;	2Ne	28:23

GRASPS
until he g. them with his awful	2Ne	28:22

GRASS
who shall be made like unto g.?	2Ne	8:12
so clothe the g. of the field,	3Ne	13:30
them not, for they are as g.,	DC	124: 7
Let the earth bring forth g.,	Mses	2:11
And the earth brought forth g.,		2:12
the earth to bring forth g.;	Abr	4:11
bring forth g. from its own seed,		4:12

GRATIFIED
that my desires have been g.	Al	7:18

GRATIFY
cover our sins, or to g. our pride,	DC	121:37

GRAVE
cast with sorrow into a watery g.	1Ne	18:18
lay down in the cold and silent g.,	2Ne	1:14
with grief and sorrow to the g.,		1:21
I cannot go down to my g. save		4: 5
its dead; which death is the g.		9:11
g. must deliver up its captive		9:12
the g. deliver up the body of		9:13
pomp is brought down to the g.;		24:11
thou art cast out of thy g.		24:19
I must soon go down to my g.;	Jac	7:27
I must soon go down to my g.,	En	1:26
am about to lie down in my g.,	Om	1:30
am about to go down to my g.,	Mos	2:28
he made his g. with the wicked,		14: 9
that the g. should have no victory,		16: 7
therefore the g. hath no victory,		16: 8
the g. shall have no victory,	Al	22:14
gained the victory over the g.;	Mrm	7: 5

GRAVE 410 GREAT

he must soon go down to the g.;	Eth 6:19	if the Lord has such g. power,	1Ne 17:51
as a similitude of the g.,	DC 128:13	the Lord showed unto me g. things.	18: 3
		that there arose a g. storm,	18:13
GRAVEL		yea, a g. and terrible tempest,	18:13
offspring of thy bowels like the g.	1Ne 20:19	and g. was the soreness thereof.	18:15
		and there was a g. calm.	18:21
GRAVEN		men esteem to be of g. worth,	19: 7
my g. image, and my molten image	1Ne 20: 5	unto their g. joy and salvation,	19:11
I have g. thee upon the palms	21:16	be of g. worth unto our seed;	22: 8
whose g. images did excel them	2Ne 20:10	that g. and abominable church,	22:13
not make unto thee any g. image,	Mos 12:36	that g. whore, who hath perverted	22:14
not make unto thee any g. image,	13:12	that g. and abominable church,	22:14
Thy g. images I will also cut off,	3Ne 21:17	and g. shall be the fall of it.	22:14
		might, and power, and g. glory.	22:24
GRAVES		how g. things the Lord had done	2Ne 1: 1
And many g. shall be opened,	He 14:25	received so g. blessings from	1:10
before we go down to our g.	Eth 6:19	the g. and marvelous works of	1:10
they went down to their g.	6:21	bloodsheds, and g. visitations	1:12
for their g. shall be opened,	DC 29:26	how g. the importance to	2: 8
they who have slept in their g.	88:97	of the law at the g. and last day,	2:26
for their g. shall be opened;	88:97	the g. mediation of all men,	2:27
on the earth and in their g.,	88:98	should look to the g. Mediator,	2:28
in coming forth out of their g.;	128:12	unto his g. commandments;	2:28
g. of the saints shall be opened;	133:56	g. were the covenants of the Lord	3: 4
		shall be of g. worth unto them,	3: 7
GREAT		I will make him g. in mine eyes;	3: 8
what g. things the Lord hath	T Pg	he shall be g. like unto Moses,	3: 9
having had a g. knowledge of the	1Ne 1: 1	which is g. in the sight of God,	3:24
or the g. city Jerusalem must be	1: 4	the g. goodness of the Lord,	4:17
many g. and marvelous things,	1:14	his g. and marvelous works,	4:17
G. and marvelous are thy works,	1:14	upon the waters of the g. deep.	4:20
that g. city, could be destroyed	2:13	mine eyes have beheld g. things,	4:25
having g. desires to know of the	2:16	yea, even too g. for man;	4:25
and that it was exceeding g.,	3:25	O then, if I have seen so g. things,	4:26
desirable; yea, even of g. worth	5:21	ores, which were in g. abundance.	5:15
what g. things the Lord hath done	7:11	Yea, mine anxiety is g. for you;	6: 3
my soul with exceeding g. joy;	8:12	that g. and abominable church,	6:12
an exceeding g. mist of darkness,	8:23	them in power and g. glory,	6:14
a g. and spacious building;	8:26	the waters of the g. deep;	8:10
that g. and spacious building.	8:31	it behooveth the g. Creator	9: 5
g. was the multitude that did	8:33	merciful plan of the g. Creator,	9: 6
and also a g. many more things,	9: 1	O how g. the goodness of	9:10
even that g. city Jerusalem,	10: 3	O how g. the plan of our God!	9:13
how g. a number had testified	10: 5	O how g. the holiness of	9:20
beheld the g. city of Jerusalem,	11:13	at the g. and judgment day.	9:22
people, in power and g. glory;	11:28	how g. the covenants of the Lord,	9:53
that the g. and spacious building	11:36	how g. his condescensions unto	9:53
the fall thereof was exceeding g.	11:36	shall be g. in the eyes of me,	10: 8
rumors of wars, and g. slaughters	12: 2	promises of the Lord are g. unto	10: 9
the g. and terrible judgments	12: 5	God has given us so g. knowledge	10:20
a g. and a terrible gulf divideth	12:18	g. are the promises of the Lord	10:21
the foundation of a g. church.	13: 4	in the g. and eternal plan of	11: 5
this g. and abominable church;	13: 6	the g. man humbleth himself not,	12: 9
this g. and abominable church.	13: 8	and g. and fair cities without	15: 9
of g. worth unto the Gentiles.	13:23	there shall be a g. forsaking in	16:12
of a g. and abominable church,	13:26	Take thee a g. roll, and write in it	18: 1
of the g. and abominable church,	13:28	in darkness have seen a g. light;	19: 2
an exceeding g. many do stumble,	13:29	for g. is the Holy One of Israel	22: 6
Satan hath g. power over them.	13:29	mountains like as of a g. people,	23: 4
house of Israel in g. judgment.	13:33	shall be of g. worth unto them	25: 8
peace, yea, tidings of g. joy,	13:37	there shall be g. wars and	26: 2
g. pit, which hath been digged	14: 3	g. and terrible shall that day be	26: 3
that g. and abominable church,	14: 3	with g. noise, and with storm,	27: 2
g. pit which hath been digged	14: 3	the book shall be of g. worth unto	28: 2
a g. and a marvelous work	14: 7	that g. and abominable church,	28:18
that g. and abominable church,	14: 9	g. must be the fall thereof.	28:18
belongeth to that g. church,	14:10	shall cause a g. division among	30:10
the wickedness of the g. whore	14:12	nor understand g. knowledge,	32: 7
the g. mother of abominations	14:13	I esteem it as of g. worth,	33: 3
the power of God in g. glory.	14:14	and g. faith in Christ that I shall	33: 7
the g. and abominable church,	14:15	unto you, with power and g. glory,	33:11
the g. and abominable church	14:17	kingdom at that g. and last day.	33:12
spake many g. things unto them,	15: 3	until that g. day shall come.	33:13
because of the g. wickedness of	15: 4	or revelation which was g.,	Jac 1: 4
mine afflictions were g. above all,	15: 5	because of faith and g. anxiety,	1: 5
I had joy and g. hopes of them,	16: 5	he having been a g. protector for	1:10
to his g. astonishment he beheld	16:10	have come unto g. condemnation;	2:34
Lord can bring about g. things.	16:29	in the sight of your g. Creator?	3: 7
how g. was their joy!	16:32	grace, and his g. condescensions	4: 7
so g. were the blessings of the	17: 2	g. and marvelous are the works of	4: 8
that he can cross these g. waters.	17:17	and in justice, and in g. mercy,	4:10
canst not accomplish so g. a work.	17:19	shall become the g., and the last,	4:16
of the Lord to do that g. work;	17:26	of the g. plan of redemption,	6: 8

GREAT 411 GREAT

exceeding g. plainness of speech,	En	1:23
Lord did visit them in g. judgment;	Om	1: 7
was g. rejoicing among the people		1:14
of the lord across the g. waters,		1:16
are g. things written upon them,	WM	1:11
be judged at the g. and last day,		1:11
And there were a g. number,	Mos	2: 2
and waxed g. in the land.		2: 2
For the multitude being so g. that		2: 7
the glad tidings of g. joy.		3: 3
so g. shall be his anguish		3: 7
rejoice with exceeding g. joy,		3:13
causeth such exceeding g. joy		4:11
the same hath g. cause to repent;		4:18
so exceeding g. was your joy.		4:20
g. views of that which is to come;		5: 3
brought us to this g. knowledge,		5: 4
rejoice with such exceeding g. joy.		5: 4
And is not this, our affliction, g.?		7:23
how g. reason we have to mourn.		7:23
g. are the reasons which we have		7:24
that this g. evil should come		7:25
g. power given him from God.		8:16
a g. benefit to his fellow beings.		8:18
a g. mystery is contained within		8:19
to our g. sorrow and lamentation,		9:19
we slew them with a g. slaughter,		10:20
he caused a g. tower to be built		11:13
now, because of this g. victory		11:19
upon my people such g. affliction?		11:27
be smitten with a g. pestilence—		12: 7
what g. evil hast thou done,		12:13
g. sins have thy people committed,		12:13
a g. evil against this people?		12:29
divide him a portion with the g.,		14:12
be a g. contention among them.		19: 3
afflictions of the Nephites were g.,		21: 5
now there was a g. mourning		21: 9
a g. many widows in the land,		21:10
a g. fear of the Lamanites		21:10
was a g. number of women,		21:17
had caused such a g. destruction		21:20
was filled with exceeding g. joy.		21:24
and g. were their rejoicings.		23:24
one with another and wax g.,		24: 7
so g. were their afflictions that		24:10
so g. was their faith and their		24:16
were filled with exceeding g. joy.		25: 8
by the unbelievers became so g.		27: 1
he became a g. hinderment to		27: 9
so g. was their astonishment,		27:12
how g. things he has done for		27:16
for g. was their astonishment;		27:18
was so g. that he became dumb,		27:19
of the g. anxiety of his people;		28:12
the building of the g. tower,		28:17
yea, and what g. destruction!		29:17
Behold what g. destruction did		29:18
will visit you with g. destruction		29:27
Now this was a g. trial to those	Al	1:25
with the Nephites with g. strength,		2:17
the Amlicites with g. slaughter,		2:18
camp of the Nephites in g. haste,		2:23
and to our g. astonishment,		2:24
And so g. were their afflictions		4: 3
saw and beheld with g. sorrow		4: 8
there began to be g. contentions		4: 9
was a g. stumbling-block to those		4:10
g. inequality among the people,		4:12
was a g. cause for lamentations		4:13
being filled with g. joy because		4:14
having g. hopes and much desire		7: 3
the exceeding g. joy of knowing		7: 3
which I have spoken, g. is my joy.		7:17
g. hold upon the hearts of		8: 9
for thou hast g. cause to rejoice;		8:15
this g. city should be destroyed		9: 4
of such g. and marvelous things;		9: 4
such g. hold upon your hearts;		10:25
was as g. as two senums.		11:11
was as g. as four senums.		11:12
an onti was as g. as them all.		11:13
six onties, which are of g. worth,		11:25
for this g. evil thou shalt have	Al	11:25
for the multitude was g., and he		12: 2
exercising exceeding g. faith,		13: 3
as g. privilege as their brethren.		13: 4
were many, exceeding g. many,		13:12
may have glad tidings of g. joy;		13:22
g. anxiety even unto pain,		13:27
If ye have such g. power why do		14:20
suffer these g. afflictions, O Lord?		14:26
so g. was their fear that they fell		14:27
people having heard a g. noise		14:29
they were struck with g. fear,		14:29
the g. tribulations of his mind		15: 3
And this g. sin, and his many		15: 3
to the g. astonishment of all		15:11
seeing a g. check, yea,		15:17
and also their g. city, which they		16: 9
so g. was the scent thereof		16:11
did hear with g. joy and gladness.		16:20
g. was the work which they had		17:13
And assuredly it was g., for they		17:14
also of his g. power in contending		18: 2
is not this the G. Spirit who		18: 2
doth send such g. punishments		18: 2
he be the G. Spirit or a man,		18: 3
of his expertness and g. strength;		18: 3
that a man has such g. power,		18: 3
I know that it is the G. Spirit;		18: 4
Now this if the g. Spirit of whom		18: 4
that there was a G. Spirit.		18: 5
they believed in a G. Spirit		18: 5
this man that has such g. power?		18: 8
had been a g. feast appointed at		18: 9
know that this is the G. Spirit,		18:11
interpreted, powerful or g. king,		18:13
that thy marvelings are so g.?		18:17
Art thou that G. Spirit, who		18:18
thou that there is a G. Spirit?		18:26
Believest thou that this G. Spirit,		18:28
not been such g. faith among all		19:10
the g. power of Ammon.		19:15
it was a g. evil that had come		19:19
be the cause of this g. power,		19:24
that Ammon was the G. Spirit,		19:25
said he was sent by the G. Spirit;		19:25
sent by the G. Spirit to afflict		19:27
and that it was the G. Spirit that		19:27
that it was this G. Spirit who had		19:27
that g. day when I made a feast		20: 9
the g. love he had for his son		20:26
of Amulon had built a g. city,		21: 2
Is God that G. Spirit that		22: 9
Yea, he is that G. Spirit, and he		22:10
the G. Spirit created all things,		22:11
that I may receive this g. joy.		22:15
there should be a g. contention		22:22
there began to be g. murmurings		22:24
they began to have g. success.		23: 3
that our g. God has in goodness		24: 7
I thank my g. God that he has		24: 8
thank my God, yea, my g. God,		24:10
blood of the Son of our g. God,		24:13
the g. God has had mercy on us,		24:14
have had g. knowledge of things		24:30
gave g. power unto the Nephites;		25: 6
how g. reason have we to rejoice;		26: 1
granted unto us such g. blessings?		26: 1
what g. blessings has he bestowed		26: 2
to bring about this g. work.		26: 3
have we not g. reason to rejoice?		26:13
doing this g. and marvelous work.		26:15
can say too much of his g. power,		26:16
in his g. mercy hath brought us		26:20
has there been so g. love in all		26:33
that has no g. reason to rejoice		26:35
my joy, and my g. thanksgiving;		26:37
saw this g. work of destruction,		27: 4
Satan has g. hold on the hearts		27:12
now the joy of Ammon was so g.		27:17
meeting his brethren was truly g.,		27:19
this their g. fear came because of		27:23
it did cause g. joy among them.		27:26
a g. mourning and lamentation		28: 4

GREAT

how g. the inequality of man is	Al 28:13	
thus we see the g. call of diligence	28:14	
we see the g. reason of sorrow,	28:14	
and how g. shall be their reward!	29:15	
as it were, so g. is my joy.	29:16	
did rise up in g. swelling words	30:31	
brought this g. curse upon me.	30:53	
the cause of g. sorrow to Alma	31: 2	
it would be the means of g. loss	31: 4	
a g. tendency to lead the people	31: 5	
they had fallen into g. errors	31: 9	
were lifted up unto g. boasting,	31:25	
came a g. multitude unto him,	32: 4	
and he beheld with g. joy;	32: 6	
Let us nourish it with g. care,	32:37	
by your faith with g. diligence,	32:41	
that the g. question which is in	34: 5	
the g. plan of the Eternal God	34: 9	
should be a g. and last sacrifice;	34:10	
should be a g. and last sacrifice;	34:13	
to that g. and last sacrifice;	34:14	
that g. and last sacrifice will be	34:14	
about the g. and eternal plan of	34:16	
shall the g. plan of redemption be	34:31	
with such g. fear and amazement	36:11	
so g. had been my iniquities,	36:14	
exceeding g. joy in the fruit of	36:25	
are g. things brought to pass;	37: 6	
his g. and eternal purposes;	37: 7	
that I shall have g. joy in you,	38: 2	
have had g. joy in thee already,	38: 3	
the Lord in his g. mercy sent his	38: 7	
not been guilty of so g. a crime.	39: 7	
how g. iniquity ye brought upon	39:11	
and the g. plan of salvation	42: 5	
destroy the g. plan of happiness.	42: 8	
his g. and eternal purposes,	42:26	
that the g. plan of mercy may	42:31	
might usurp g. power over them,	43: 8	
because of the g. destruction	43:39	
with such exceeding g. strength	43:43	
of their dead was exceeding g.,	44:21	
God with exceeding g. joy.	45: 1	
shall sin against so g. light	45:12	
before this g. iniquity shall come.	45:12	
And when that g. day cometh,	45:13	
in that g. and dreadful day,	45:14	
of their exceeding g. riches;	45:24	
g. care over the church,	46: 6	
g. victory which they had had	46: 7	
g. rejoicings which they had had	46: 7	
we also see the g. wickedness	46: 9	
gathered together so g. an army	47:21	
how g. was their disappointment;	49: 4	
concerning their g. loss.	49:25	
and exceeding g. prosperity in	49:30	
his armies were not so g. as they	51:11	
notwithstanding their g. loss,	51:11	
together a wonderfully g. army,	51:11	
men, for they were g. warriors;	51:31	
period of time also a g. support;	53:19	
were a g. strength to his army.	55:24	
in which we may have g. joy.	56: 9	
they had suffered g. afflictions	56:16	
gave these g. hopes and much	56:17	
never had I seen so g. courage,	56:45	
pursuing them with g. vigor	56:52	
But behold, to my g. joy,	56:56	
would break out in g. numbers,	57:14	
to whom we owe this g. victory;	57:22	
we had suffered g. loss.	57:23	
and to our g. astonishment,	57:25	
has done this g. thing for us.	57:35	
were also receiving g. strength	58: 5	
did grant unto us g. faith,	58:11	
follow after us with g. speed,	58:19	
and struck with g. fear,	58:29	
to maintain so g. a number of	58:32	
of cities and so g. possessions.	58:32	
with an exceeding g. slaughter.	59: 9	
suffered exceeding g. sufferings;	60: 3	
g. has been the slaughter among	60: 5	
g. has been your neglect towards	60: 5	

412

GREAT

of this exceeding g. neglect;	Al 60: 6	
because of their g. desires	60: 9	
of your exceeding g. neglect	60: 9	
and their exceeding g. neglect	60:14	
this because of the g. wickedness	60:17	
the g. head of our government.	60:24	
do not joy in your g. afflictions,	61: 2	
the cause of this g. iniquity;	61: 4	
for they have used g. flattery,	61: 4	
in the g. privilege of our church,	61:14	
put an end to this g. iniquity.	61:18	
was filled with exceeding g. joy	62: 1	
of their exceeding g. courage,	62:19	
relieved from a g. burthen;	62:29	
cause of this g. and lasting war	62:35	
slay them with a g. slaughter;	62:38	
exceeding g. length of the war	62:41	
exceeding g. length of the war;	62:41	
how g. things the Lord had done	62:50	
own lands, suffering g. loss.	63:15	
and also with his g. wisdom,	He 1:16	
attack that g. city Zarahemla.	1:18	
was with such exceedingly g. speed	1:19	
gave Moronihah g. advantage	1:25	
the people with a g. slaughter,	1:27	
g. many who departed out of	3: 3	
travel to an exceeding g. distance,	3: 4	
there had been g. contentions,	3:17	
still g. contention in the land,	3:19	
was exceeding g. prosperity	3:24	
so g. was the prosperity of	3:25	
was peace and exceeding g. joy	3:32	
was continual peace and g. joy	3:32	
Now this was a g. evil, which did	3:34	
people to suffer g. persecutions,	3:34	
the exceeding g. pride which	3:36	
their exceeding g. riches and	3:36	
Now this g. loss of the Nephites,	4:11	
g. slaughter which was among	4:11	
rising up in g. contentions,	4:12	
of this their g. wickedness,	4:13	
the Nephites were in g. fear,	4:20	
was as g. as their strength,	4:26	
fallen into this g. transgression;	4:26	
they did preach with g. power,	5:17	
such g. power and authority,	5:18	
speak unto the g. astonishment of	5:19	
a voice of a g. tumultuous noise,	5:30	
of the church did have g. joy	6: 3	
with another, and did have g. joy.	6: 3	
preach with exceedingly g. power	6: 5	
did also have g. joy and peace,	6:14	
had got g. hold upon the hearts of	6:31	
the g. sorrow and lamentation of	6:33	
this g. iniquity had come upon	7: 6	
the cause of so g. mourning	7:11	
and ye have g. need to marvel;	7:15	
got so g. hold upon your hearts.	7:15	
behold, this g. city, and also all	7:22	
all those g. cities which are	7:22	
sinned against that g. knowledge	7:24	
because of that g. abomination	7:25	
of your exceeding g. riches!	7:26	
these our g. cities shall be taken	8: 5	
we are powerful, and our cities g.,	8: 6	
had such g. power given unto him,	8:13	
a g. many thousand years before	8:18	
at the burial of the g. chief judge	9:10	
raise himself to be a g. man,	9:16	
because of the g. destruction	9:22	
notwithstanding that g. miracle	10:13	
was a g. famine upon the land,	11: 5	
did esteem him as a g. prophet,	11:18	
having g. power and authority	11:18	
exceeding g. peace in the land,	11:21	
an exceeding g. bend of robbers;	11:26	
these robbers did make g. havoc,	11:27	
g. destruction among the people	11:27	
they did cause g. fear to come	11:32	
did do g. destruction unto them;	11:33	
this g. evil, which came unto the	11:34	
Lord in his g. infinite goodness	12: 1	
their exceedingly g. prosperity.	12: 2	

GREAT 413 GREAT

his g. goodness and his mercy	He	12: 6
O how g. is the nothingness of		12: 7
of our g. and everlasting God.		12: 8
unto the waters of the g. deep—		12:16
may God grant, in his g. fulness,		12:24
in the g. and last day there are		12:25
yea, in g. wickedness, while		13: 1
unto this g. city of Zarahemla;		13:12
yea, wo be unto this g. city, for I		13:12
even the more part of this g. city,		13:12
righteous who are in this g. city,		13:13
yea, wo be unto this g. city,		13:14
yea, our g. and true God,		13:18
of the g. curse of the land,		13:18
ye, the people of this g. city,		13:21
but they do swell with g. pride,		13:22
unto g. swelling, envyings, strifes,		13:22
Behold, our iniquities are g.		13:37
is in our g. and Eternal Head.		13:38
prophesy a g. many more things		14: 1
shall be g. lights in heaven,		14: 3
there shall be g. tempests,		14:23
mountains, whose height is g.		14:23
shall have g. cause to mourn		15: 2
and their g. and true shepherd,		15:13
g. signs given unto the people,		16:13
unto them glad tidings of g. joy;		16:14
all these g. and marvelous works		16:16
in some g. and marvelous thing		16:20
some g. mystery which we cannot		16:21
get g. hold upon the hearts of		16:23
a g. uproar throughout the land;	3Ne	1: 7
the g. plan of destruction which		1:16
was a g. remission of sins.		1:23
began to increase in g. degree,		1:28
do g. wickedness in the land.		2: 3
unto you exceeding g. priase		3: 2
with g. anxiety for the word—		3: 3
thereof should be exceeding g.		3:14
so g. and marvelous were		3:16
the g. commander of the armies		3:18
was a g. prophet among them,		3:19
were a g. many thousand people		3:24
because of the g. curse which was		3:24
and having so g. a number,		4: 4
g. and terrible was the day that		4: 7
and g. terrible was the		4: 7
g. and terrible was the battle		4:11
g. and terrible was the slaughter		4:11
was known so g. a slaughter		4:11
because of the g. destruction		4:22
the g. slaughter which had been		4:24
the g. thing which he had done		4:31
of the g. goodness of God in		4:33
would be g. and marvelous;		5: 8
again to prosper and to wax g.;		6: 4
there was g. order in the land;		6: 4
had established this g. peace		6: 6
of their exceeding g. riches,		6:10
even unto g. persecutions;		6:10
others did receive g. learning		6:12
a g. inequality in all the land,		6:14
Satan had g. power, unto the		6:15
their tribes became exceeding g.		7: 4
cause a g. contention in the land,		7: 7
had brought so g. iniquity upon		7: 9
power and with g. authority.		7:17
so g. was his faith on the Lord		7:18
began to look with g. earnestness		8: 3
began to be g. doubtings		8: 4
there arose a g. storm,		8: 5
also a g. and terrible tempest;		8: 6
there became a g. mountain.		8:10
was a g. and terrible destruction		8:11
more g. and terrible destruction		8:12
g. quaking of the whole earth;		8:12
many g. and notable cities were		8:14
damage thereof was exceeding g.,		8:15
all these g. and terrible things		8:19
so g. were the mists of darkness		8:22
was g. mourning and howling		8:23
g. were the groanings of the		8:23
darkness and the g. destruction		8:23
before this g. and terrible day,	3Ne	8:24
burned in that g. city Zarahemla.		8:24
before this g. and terrible day,		8:25
up in that g. city Moronihah.		8:25
of the people g. and terrible.		8:25
that g. city Zarahemla have I		9: 3
that g. city Moroni have I		9: 4
that g. city Moronihah have I		9: 5
that g. city Jacobugath, which		9: 9
many g. destructions have I		9:12
so g. was the astonishment of		10: 2
O ye people of these g. cities		10: 4
have g. favors shown unto them,		10:18
g. blessings poured out upon		10:18
were a g. multitude gathered		11: 1
the g. and marvelous change		11: 1
For ye shall have g. joy and		12:12
for g. shall be your reward in		12:12
how g. is that darkness!		13:23
it fell, and g. was the fall of it.		14:27
so g. and marvelous things as		17:16
so g. and marvelous things as		17:17
g. was the joy of the multitude		17:18
yea, an exceeding g. number,		19: 3
the multitude was so g. that		19: 5
so g. and marvelous were the		19:34
So g. faith have I never seen		19:35
show unto them so g. miracles,		19:35
so g. things as ye have seen;		19:36
so g. things as ye have heard.		19:36
be a g. and a marvelous work		21: 9
with g. mercies will I gather thee.		22: 7
g. shall be the peace of thy		22:13
for g. are the words of Isaiah.		23: 1
of the g. and dreadful day of		25: 5
unto them, both g. and small.		26: 1
even unto the g. and last day,		26: 4
g. and marvelous things,		26:14
And now, behold, my joy is g.,		27:30
g. and marvelous works shall		28:31
before the g. and coming day		28:31
be a g. and marvelous work		28:32
g. and marvelous works wrought	4Ne	1: 5
that g. city Zarahemla did they		1: 8
a g. division among the people.		1:35
together g. a number of men,	Mrm	1:11
upon us with exceeding g. power,		2: 3
the g. destruction which hung		2: 8
did urge them with g. energy,		2:23
the g. calamity of my people,		2:27
did slay a g. number of them,		3: 8
because of this g. thing which		3: 9
never had been so g. wickedness		4:12
with exceeding g. anger,		4:15
with an exceedingly g. slaughter;		4:21
so g. were their numbers that		5: 6
might not have too g. sorrow		5: 9
his g. and eternal purpose,		5:14
at his g. command the earth		5:23
before this g. destruction had		6:22
the g. and tremendous battle		8: 2
and g. has been their fall;		8: 7
yea, so g. and marvelous is the		8: 7
so g. that the Lord would not		8:10
record thereof is of g. worth;		8:14
be g. pollutions upon the face		8:31
g. and marvelous things		8:34
that g. day when the earth		9: 2
in that g. day when ye shall be		9: 2
Lamb, at that g. and last day.		9: 6
come forth, both small and g.,		9:13
that time even to the g. tower,	Eth	1: 3
their familes, from the g. tower,		1:33
shall go with thee, a g. nation.		1:43
to that g. sea which divideth		2:13
cross this g. water in darkness?		2:22
cannot cross this g. deep save		2:25
able to show forth g. power,		3: 5
many g. works which the Lord		3:18
how g. things the Father hath		4:14
the g. and marvelous things		4:15
cross the g. waters in darkness.		6: 3
the g. and terrible tempests		6: 6

GREAT

how g. things the Lord had done	Eth	6:30
how g. things the Lord had done		6:30
prosper exceedingly and wax g.		7:19
Shule did bestow g. favors upon		7:22
the g. things that the Lord had		7:27
bringing them across the g. deep		7:27
brought across the g. deep?		8: 9
obtain kingdoms and g. glory?		8: 9
so g. had been the spreading of		9: 6
exceeding g. wickedness upon		9:26
there should be a g. famine,		9:28
be a g. dearth upon the land,		9:30
did live to an exceeding g. age,		10:13
himself became a g. hunter.		10:19
And they built a g. city by		10:20
destruction of that g. people		11: 1
exceeding g. war in all the land.		11: 4
g. calamity in all the land,		11: 6
a g. curse should come upon		11: 6
a g. destruction among them,		11: 6
there was a g. destruction,		11: 7
of g. and marvelous things,		11:20
g. and marvelous things unto		12: 5
wrought so g. a miracle among		12:15
so g. was his faith in God,		12:20
our words powerful and g.,		12:25
thyself unto them in g. power.		12:31
but g. and marvelous were the		13:13
there began to be a g. war		13:15
and they did meet in g. anger,		13:27
a g. curse upon all the land		14: 1
so g. was the curse upon the land.		14: 1
receive g. strength to his army.		14: 7
received g. strength in his army,		14: 8
Lib was a man of g. stature,		14:10
so g. and lasting had been the		14:21
children on both sides was so g.		14:31
and so g. were their cries,		15:16
g. and terrible was that day;		15:17
and g. glory at the last day,	Mro	7:35
rejecting so g. a knowledge,		8:29
a g. number of our choice men.		9: 2
this g. abomination of the		9: 9
to another, exceeding g. faith;		10:11
pleasing bar of the g. Jehovah,		10:34
Babylon, even Babylon the g.,	DC	1:16
of the g. and dreadful day of		2: 1
A g. and marvelous work		6: 1
which are g. and marvelous;		6:11
that Satan has g. hold upon		10:20
unto them this g. mystery;		10:64
A g. and marvelous work is		11: 1
A g. and marvelous work is		12: 1
A g. and marvelous work is		14: 1
and g. shall be your reward,		14:11
the worth of souls is g. in		18:10
how g. is his joy in the soul		18:13
g. shall be your joy with him		18:15
if your joy will be g. with one		18:16
how g. will be your joy if		18:16
the last g. day of judgment,		19: 3
of godliness, how g. is it!		19:10
a g. and the last commandment		19:32
and g. shall be your blessing—		19:38
Therefore, having so g. witnesses,		20:13
your Redeemer, the G., I AM,		29: 1
with power and g. glory,		29:11
before his g. day shall come		29:14
be a g. hailstorm sent forth		29:16
the g. and abominable church,		29:21
g. things may be required at		29:48
declare glad tidings of g. joy		31: 3
with power and g. glory.		34: 7
it shall be a g. day at the time		34: 8
before that g. day shall come,		34: 9
g. destructions await the wicked		34: 9
for thou shalt do g. things.		35: 4
shall be a g. work in the land,		35: 7
g. things are to be shown forth		35:10
Jesus Christ, the G. I AM,		38: 1
the judgment of the g. day,		38: 5
the g. command to reap down		38:12
be g. wars in far countries,		38:29

GREAT

a g. work laid up in store,	DC	38:33
the G. I AM, even Jesus Christ—		39: 1
I have bestowed g. blessings		39: 8
thou hast seen g. sorrow,		39: 9
a blessing so g. as you never		39:10
thou shalt have g. faith,		39:12
and g. shall be thy reward;		42:65
the g. day of the Lord is nigh		43:17
for the g. day of the lord;		43:20
for the g. day of the lord?		43:21
the g. day of the lord is come?		43:22
earthquakes, and g. hailstorms,		43:25
by the g. sound of a trump,		43:25
the g. Millennium, of which I		43:30
forth for the g. day of the Lord		45:39
clothed with power and g. glory;		45:44
that g. things await you;		45:62
before the g. day of the Lord		49:24
coming in power and g. glory		56:18
for the g. day to come.		58:11
the foundation of a g. work.		64:33
proceedeth that which is g.		64:33
a g. contention among the people		74: 3
G. is his wisdom, marvelous are		76: 2
G. shall be their reward and		76: 6
And their wisdom shall be g.,		76: 9
But g. and marvelous are the		76:114
how g. blessings the Father hath		78:17
glad tidings of g. joy,		79: 1
unto the g. and notable cities		84:117
the g. persecutor of the church,		86: 3
even the nation of G. Britain,		87: 3
the g. and last promise which		88:69
this g. and last promise, which		88:75
appear a g. sign in heaven,		88:93
that g. church, the mother of		88:94
until that g. and last day,		88:102
the battle of the g. God;		88:114
g. treasures of knowledge,		89:19
the g. commandment in all		95: 3
become very glorious, very g.,		97:18
is the cause of this g. evil?		101:52
have prepared a g. endowment		105:12
of Israel becomes very g.		105:26
my army become very g.,		105:31
was such a g. high priest.		107: 2
with exceeding g. blessings.		108: 3
this work through g. tribulation;		109: 5
g. and glorious tidings, in truth,		109:23
and the g. ones of the earth,		109:55
roll on in g. power and a majesty,		109:59
g. love for the children of Jacob,		109:61
may become a g. mountain and fill		109:72
sound of the rushing of g. waters,		110: 3
another g. and glorious vision		110:13
before the g. and dreadful day		110:14
that the g. and dreadful day		110:16
have a g. work for them to do,		112: 6
behold how g. is your calling.		112:33
depart to go over the g. waters,		118: 4
attended to with g. earnestness.		123:14
he shall be g. in mine eyes;		124:13
And for his love he shall be g.,		124:17
with blessings and g. glory.		124:17
a loud voice, and with g. joy,		124:88
with exceedingly g. desire,		127:10
I saw the dead, small and g.,		128: 6
to the decrees of the g. Jehovah.		128: 9
Now the g. and grand secret of		128:11
coming of the g. and dreadful day		128:17
glad tidings of g. joy.		128:19
not go on in so g. a cause?		128:22
the g. day of the Lord is at hand;		128:24
is a g. Urim and Thummim.		130: 8
for the g. day of the Lord.		133:10
mighty ocean, even the g. deep,		133:20
as the voice of a g. thunder,		133:22
He shall command the g. deep,		133:23
up in the midst of the g. deep.		133:27
how g. things thou hast prepared		133:45
so g. shall be the glory of his		133:49
founded a g. city,		135: 3
He lived g., and he died great		135: 3

GREAT

and he died g. in the eyes of God	DC 135: 3
their sorrow shall be g. unless	136:35
and their numbers were g.,	Mses 1:28
g. waters under the firmament	2: 7
I, God, made two g. lights;	2:16
And I, God, created g. whales;	2:21
the master of this g. secret,	5:31
master of that g. secret which was	5:49
Satan had g. dominion among	6:15
a g. people which dwelt in tents,	7: 5
And so g. was the faith of Enoch,	7:13
so g. was the power of the	7:13
g. was the fear of the enemies	7:14
g. was the glory of the Lord,	7:17
he had a g. chain in his hand,	7:26
has not been so g. wickedness as	7:36
until the judgment of the g. day.	7:57
g. tribulations shall be among	7:61
that day he saw g. tribulations	7:66
forth a g. famine into the land,	8: 4
men of old, men of g. renown.	8:21
had become g. in the earth;	8:22
who possessed g. knowledge,	Abr 1: 2
was g. mourning in Chaldea,	1:20
will make of thee a g. nation,	2: 9
make thy name g. among all	2: 9
the stars, that they were very g.,	3: 2
and there were many g. ones	3: 2
the name of the g. one is Kolob,	3: 3
stars, or all the g. lights,	3:13
many of the noble and g. ones;	3:22
pronounced they g. waters;	4:10
organized the two g. lights,	4:16
might bring forth g. whales,	4:21
waters in the seas or g. waters;	4:22
be g. tribulation on the Jews,	JS 1:18
shall show g. signs and wonders,	1:22
with power and g. glory;	1:36
with the g. sound of a trumpet,	1:37
g. multitudes united themselves	2: 5
the g. love which the converts	2: 6
the g. zeal manifested by the	2: 6
a scene of g. confusion and	2: 6
this time of g. excitement	2: 8
reflection and g. uneasiness;	2: 8
so g. were the confusion and	2: 8
tumult were so g. and incessant.	2: 9
seemed to enter with g. force	2:12
at this moment of g. alarm,	2:16
lightly, but with g. contempt,	2:21
excited a g. deal of prejudice	2:22
the cause of g. persecution,	2:22
the attention of the g. ones	2:23
cause of g. sorrow to myself.	2:23
of any g. or malignant sins.	2:28
of the g. and dreadful day of	2:38
g. judgments which were coming	2:45
with g. desolations by famine,	2:45
met with a g. affliction by	2:56
g. and glorious blessings	2:73
many g. and important things	AoF 9

GREATER

gives a g. account of the wars	1Ne 19: 4
hath done all this, and g. also,	20:22
he wrote, there are not many g.	2Ne 4: 2
ye have done g. iniquities than	Jac 2:35
a seer is g. than a prophet.	Mos 8:15
gift which is g. can no man have,	8:16
the g. number of our army was	9: 2
the g. portion of the word,	Al 12:10
afterwards, but none were g.;	13:19
so much g. than the Nephites.	43:21
they were the g. part of them	46: 4
did place the g. number of men;	48: 9
a g. strength to his army,	56:18
g. number of them were slain;	57:33
we have not received g. strength.	58:34
then shall g. fear come upon him;	He 9:35
shall see g. things than these,	14:28
for there began to be g. signs	3Ne 1: 4
greater signs and g. miracles	1: 4

415

GREATLY

he had g. power than they,	3Ne 7:18
by some that the time was g.;	8:19
that my wisdom is g. than the	21:10
then shall the g. things be	26: 9
shall the g. things be withheld	26:10
even g. than he had revealed	26:14
they were to receive a g. change,	28:40
know of g. things than these.	Mrm 8:12
g. is the value of an endless	8:38
And there shall be none g.	Eth 1:43
and there never were g. things	4: 4
them will I show no g. things,	4: 8
show unto you the g. things,	4:13
there is no gift g. than the	DC 6:13
What g. witness can you have	6:23
a g. work yet among men than	7: 5
he has undertaken a g. work;	7: 6
wisdom is g. than the cunning	10:43
g. views upon my gospel;	10:45
shall be g. signs in heaven above	29:14
and prepared thee for a g. work.	35: 3
deign to give unto you g. riches,	38:18
have prepared thee for a g. work.	39:11
g. in the kingdom of heaven.	58: 2
otherwise, a g. condemnation.	63:66
remaineth in him the g. sin.	64: 9
who sins against the g. light	82: 3
receive the g. condemnation.	82: 3
and this g. priesthood	84:19
a g. or a lesser kingdom.	88:37
it is no appendage to the g.,	107:14
Art thou g. than he?	122: 8
the g. light to rule the day,	Mses 2:16
and the g. light was the sun,	2:16
rejected the g. counsel which was	5:25
punishment is g. than I can bear.	5:38
g. happiness and peace and rest	Abr 1: 2
a g. follower of righteousness,	1: 2
and to possess a g. knowledge,	1: 2
g. than that upon which thou	3: 5
the set time of the g. light	3: 6
be g. things above them;	3:16
that he made the g. star;	3:18
the g. light to rule the day,	4:16

GREATEST

is the g. of all the gifts of God.	1Ne 15:36
in the days of my g. sorrow	2Ne 3: 1
Now the g. number of those of	Al 24:28
the g. number of whom were after	24:28
with the g. abhorrence;	27:28
harrowed up to the g. degree	36:12
one of the g. of the armies of	53: 6
that their g. strength was	He 1:24
charity, which is the g. of all,	Mro 7:46
the g. of all the gifts of God;	DC 6:13
the g. of all the gifts of God.	14: 7
myself, even God, the g. of all,	19:18
bless with the g. of all blessings,	41: 1
is appointed to be the g.,	50:26
thou wilt do the g. good unto	81: 4
from the least unto the g.,	84:98
which is the g. of all.	107:64
the g. of all the Kokaubeam	Abr 3:16

GREATLY

I g. fear lest my case shall be	Jac 7:19
being g. persecuted by those who	Mos 27:32
being g. astonished, and struck	Al 2:23
g. afflicted for the loss of their	4: 2
g. lamenting his loss.	18:43
for I shall g. desire to see thee.	20:27
For the king was g. astonished at	20:27
they saw it they g. marveled,	22:23
the Nephites g. feared that the	31: 4
cannot worship God, ye do g. err,	33: 2
they have been g. oppressed	DC 109:48
shall g. rejoice in consequence	110: 9
which shall g. enlarge the soul	121:42
and they shall be g. blessed.	124:79
he g. marveled and wondered.	Mses 1: 8
I will g. multiply thy sorrow	4:22

GREATLY 416 GROANETH

and all nations feared g., Mses 7:13
mind at times was g. excited, JS 2: 9
I was g. surprised at his 2:21
marveling g. at what had 2:44

GREATNESS
thou knowest the g. of God; 2Ne 2: 2
O the g. and the justice of 9:17
O the g. of the mercy of 9:19
the g. of the Holy One of Israel. 9:40
because of his g., and his grace 9:53
of the g. of their stumbling 26:20
the g. of the task, Jac 2:10
because of the g. of the multitude; Mos 2: 8
in remembrance, the g. of God, 4:11
because of the g. of their number 21:17
of the g. of their number— Al 3: 1
not destroy, because of its g. 16: 9
the g. of the words of thy 22: 3
of the g. of their numbers; 30: 2
they are puffed up, even to g., 31:27
because of the g. of the number; 44:21
reverence him because of his g. 47:22
because of the g. of the number 48: 4
of the g. of their numbers, 49: 6
rejoice in the g. of your heart. 61: 9
the g. of their numbers, 62:19
because of the g. of the march; 62:35
the g. of the number of the He 1:25
of the g. of the destruction of 3: 6
because of the g. of the number 4:20
because of the g. of the evidences 5:50
the exceeding g. of the numbers 11:31
of the g. of their number. Mrm 4:17
of the g. of their numbers. 6: 8
in the g. of his strength. DC 133:46

GREEDINESS
whose eyes are full of g., DC 56:17
but their eyes are full of g. 68:31

GREEN
if the fire can scathe a g. tree DC 135: 6
every g. herb for meat, Abr 4:30

GREETING
To be sent g.; not by DC 89: 2
brethren in Zion, in love g., 90:32

GREW
and it g., and waxed old, Jac 5: 3
they g. faster than the strength of 5:48
But they g. proud, being lifted Al 45:24
they g. rich in their own eyes, 45:24
herb of the field before it g. Mses 3: 5
herb of the field before it g.; Abr 5: 5

GREY
their g. hairs were about to be 1Ne 18:18

GRIEF
having suffered much g. because 1Ne 18:17
Because of their g. and much 18:18
with g. and sorrow to the grave, 2Ne 1:21
sorrows, and acquainted with g.; Mos 14: 3
he hath put him to g.; 14:10
made to bow down with g., DC 123: 7

GRIEFS
Surely he has borne our g., Mos 14: 4

GRIEVANCES
redress of all wrongs and g., DC 134:11

GRIEVE
which I have written g. thee, Mro 9:25

GRIEVED
g. because of the hardness 1Ne 2:18
being g. for the hardness 7: 8
was g. because of the hardness 15: 4
g. because of the afflictions 18:19
how that ye have g. their hearts Jac 3:10

Being g. for the afflictions of Mos 8: 7
many of them were sorely g. for Al 4: 7
Behold, I am g. because of the 30:46
Alma saw this his heart was g.; 31:24
Alma, being g. for the iniquity of 35:15
were g. and also filled with fear 58: 9
being g. for the hardness of 3Ne 7:16
forsaken and g. in spirit, 22: 6
not counsel, but g. the Spirit; DC 63:55
the Spirit of the Lord is g.; 121:37
and it g. him at the heart. Mses 8:25

GRIEVES
yea, it g. my soul. Al 61: 2

GRIEVETH
my soul g. because of mine 2Ne 4:17
and this g. my soul. 26:11
it g. me that I must speak 32: 8
Yea, it g. my soul Jac 2: 6
And also it g. me that I must 2: 7
It g. me that I should lose 5: 7
It g. me that I should lose 5:11
for it g. me that I should lose 5:13
it g. me that I should lose 5:32
it g. me that I should lose them. 5:46
it g. me that I should hew down 5:47
it g. me that I should lose the 5:51
it g. me that I should lose the 5:66
that which g. me exceedingly; Mro 8: 4
it g. me that there should 8: 4

GRIEVOUS
tasks, which were g. to be borne; 1Ne 17:25
which was g. to be borne— Mos 2:14
a tax which is g. to be borne. 7:15
now, is not this g. to be borne? 7:23
do that which was g. unto me; Al 39: 3
behold, this was g. unto them. Eth 6:23
which was g. to be borne; 10: 5
somewhat of that which is g. Mro 9: 1
sinned against me a very g. sin, DC 95: 3
have sinned a very g. sin, 95: 6
servants sinned a very g. sin; 95:10
which was very g. unto me, 95:10
sore and g. sin against me, 101:98
a sore and g. chastisement, 103: 4
with a very sore and g. curse. 104: 4
because of their g. burdens. 109:48
for the famine became very g. Abr 2:21
these g. judgments would come JS 2:45

GRIEVOUSLY
did more g. afflict by the way of 2Ne 19: 1

GRIEVOUSNESS
and that write g. which they 2Ne 20: 1

GRIFFIN, Selah J.
servants Newel Knight and G. DC 52:32
G. shall also go with him. 56: 5
given unto my servants G. and 56: 6

GRIND
and g. the faces of the poor, 2Ne 13:15
to pieces and g. them to powder. 26: 5
and g. upon the face of the poor. 26:20

GRINDING
Two shall be g. at the mill, JS 1:45

GROAN
that he fell dead without a g. He 2: 9

GROANED
Jesus g. within himself, 3Ne 17:14
mourned; and the earth g.; Mses 7:56

GROANETH
my heart g. because of my sins; 2Ne 4:19
and g. under darkness and DC 84:49
the whold world g. under sin 84:53

GROANINGS

GROANINGS
because of the g. of the earth,	1Ne	19:12
great were the g. of the people,	3Ne	8:23
and the dreadful g. did cease,		10: 9
cause g. in the midst of her,	DC	88:89

GROANS
the whole earth g. under	DC	123: 7

GROSS
did wax more g. in their iniquities.	Al	8:28
to behold such g. wickedness		31:26
this g. error should be removed	Mro	8: 6
g. darkness the minds of the	DC	112:23

GROSSER
unto you concerning a g. crime,	Jac	2:22
because of your g. crimes.		2:23

GROSSEST
been spent in the g. iniquity;	Al	26:24

GROSSLY
hearts have been g. hardened	Al	9:30
and impenitent and g. wicked,		6: 2

GROUND
our of captivity, on dry g.,	1Ne	4: 2
upon the g. a round ball		16:10
they passed through on dry g.		17:26
hast laid thy body as the g.	2Ne	8:23
and shall sit upon the g.		13:26
Art thou cut down to the g.,		24:12
ascend up to God from the g.		26: 3
speak unto them out of the g.,		26:16
even as it were out of the g.;		26:16
shall cry from the g. against them.		28:10
cumber the g. of my vineyard.	Jac	5: 9
I knew that it was a poor spot of g.;		5:22
this spot of g. was poorer than		5:23
I planted in a good spot of g.;		5:25
did plant in a good spot of g.;		5:43
which cumbered this spot of g.,		5:44
not cumber the g. of my vineyard,		5:49
cumber not the g. of my vineyard;		5:66
tools of every kind to till the g.,	Jar	1: 8
through the Red Sea on dry g.,	Mos	7:19
And we began to till the g.,		9: 9
that the men should till the g.,		10: 4
their flocks, and to till their g.		10:21
and as a root out of dry g.;		14: 2
wounded and left upon the g.,		20:12
and began to till the g.,		23: 5
and had begun to till the g.		23:31
And thus he cleared the g.,	Al	2:34
she might raise her from the g.;		19:29
his blood would cry from the g.		20:18
it is because your g. is barren,		32:39
he sat down upon the g.,		34: 1
the garden of Eden, to till the g.,		42: 2
spill your blood upon the g.,		44:11
scalp from off the g. by the hair,		44:13
had raised the first from the g.,		47:24
gained some g. over the Nephites,		53: 8
and also maintain all the g. and		55:27
labor exceedingly, tilling the g.,		62:29
came through upon dry g.,	He	8:11
not cry unto me from the g.	3Ne	9:11
and set them down upon the g.		17:12
should kneel down upon the g.		17:13
when they had knelt upon the g.,		17:14
destroy the fruits of your g.;		24:11
cry unto the Lord from the g.,	Mrm	8:40
cry unto him from the g.,	Eth	8:22
through the Red Sea on dry g.	DC	8: 3
not fall to the g. unnoticed.		84:80
not fall to the g. unnoticed.		84:116
men shall fall upon the g.		88:89
whether in the g. or above		89:16
the ground or above the g.—		89:16
the g. which has been reserved		104:34
g. upon which thou standest is holy.		115: 7
the parched g. shall no longer		133:29

GROWETH

crieth from the g. against them.	DC	136:36
not yet a man to till the g.;	Mses	3: 5
watered the whole face of the f.		3: 6
man from the dust of the g.;		3: 7
out of the g. made I, the Lord		3: 9
out of the g. I, the Lord God,		3:19
cursed shall be the g. for thy		4:23
thou shalt return unto the g.—		4:25
g. from whence he was taken;		4:29
but Cain was a tiller of the g.		5:17
brought of the fruit of the g. an		5:19
blood cries unto me from the g.		5:35
When thou tillest the g. it		5:37
g. which the Lord hath cursed.		8: 9
not formed a man to till the g.	Abr	5: 5
watered the whole face of the g.		5: 6
man from the dust of the g.,		5: 7
out of the g. made the Gods		5: 9
out of the g. the Gods formed		5:20
and I fell helpless on the g.,	JS	2:48
was visible above the g.,		2:51

GROUNDS
what g. had they to hope for	Al	5:10
should bring men on to unequal g.		30: 7
all men were on equal g.		30:11
meeting them upon fair g.,		52:21
they pollute mine holy g.,	DC	124:46

GROVER, Thomas
G., Newel Knight, David Dort,	DC	124:132

GROVES
I will pluck up thy g. out of	3Ne	21:18

GROW
that they did g. exceedingly;	1Ne	18:24
shall g. together, unto the	2Ne	3:12
a branches shall g. out of his roots.		21: 1
began to g. hard in their hearts,	Jac	1:15
so that these last grafts shall g.,		5:64
way for them, that they may g.		5:64
And as they begin to g. ye shall		5:65
bad according as the good shall g.,		5:66
the natural branches began to g.		5:73
ye shall g. in the knowledge of	Mos	4:12
king Laman began to g. uneasy,		9:11
he shall g. up before him as a		14: 2
sprouteth, and beginneth to g.,	Al	32:30
sprouteth, and beginneth to g.		32:30
sprouteth, and beginneth to g.,		32:33
as the tree beginneth to g.,		32:37
may get root, that it may g. up,		32:37
it will get root, and g. up,		32:37
the tree as it beginneth to g.,		32:41
Lamanites began to g. uneasy		56:30
they began to g. exceeding rich.		62:48
of the land that it should g. up,	He	3: 9
began to g. up unto the Lord.		3:21
g. upon them from day to day.		3:36
began to g. exceedingly wicked		6:16
they did g. in their iniquities		6:33
and g. in wickedness and		6:34
began to g. exceedingly in the		6:34
many children who did g. up	3Ne	1:29
the lilies of the field how they g.;		13:28
and g. up as calves in the stall.		25: 2
shall g. up without sin unto	DC	45:58
ye must g. in grace and in		50:40
children shall g. up until they		63:51
g. up on the land of Zion,		69: 8
lilies of the field, how they g.,		84:82
wheat and the tares g. together		86: 7
that they may g. up in thee,		109:15
God, to g. every tree, naturally,	Mses	3: 9
even so when they begin to g. up,		6:55
to g. every tree that is pleasant	Abr	5: 9

GROWETH
if a seed g. it is good,	Al	32:32
but if it g. not, behold it is not		32:32
and that light g. brighter and	DC	50:24

GROWING 418 HABITATION

GROWING
also g. up in wickedness;	DC	68:31
presiding officers g. out of,		107:21
has been g. stronger and		123: 7

GROWN
the wild branches have g.	Jac	5:37
not g. up to a perfect knowledge.	Al	32:29

GRUDGINGLY
evil giveth a gift, he doeth it g.;	Mro	7: 8
shall be equal, and this not g.,	DC	70:14

GUARD
were surrounded by the king's g.	Mos	7: 7
and thus I did g. my people		10: 2
that I might g. against them,		10: 7
the gates of the city with his g.,		21:23
might g. himself against them,	Al	2:21
would g. thee with my armies;		18:21
will g. them from their enemies		27:24
men over them to g. them		53: 1
g. the prisoners of the Lamanites;		53: 5
to g. them while at their labor;		53: 5
to g. against the Lamanites,		53: 7
the Lamanites do g. my people		55: 3
g. them to keep them from the		56:57
or g. them, sword in hand,		57:15
to g. them down to the land.		57:29
who were left to g. the city,		58:21
to g. them from the robbers	3Ne	3:14

GUARDED
Nephites were g. in the city	Al	55: 7
he also g. that city with an		55:26
food, which was g. to us by an		58: 8

GUARDS
with my g. without the gate?	Mos	7:10
g. should have put you to death.		7:11
Limhi commanded his g. that		7:16
I set g. round about the land,		10: 2
sent g. round about the land		11:17
his g. should surround Abinadi		17: 5
set g. round about the land,		19:28
support his g. out of the tribute		19:28
unless he took his g. with him,		21:19
or the g. of the Lamanites,		22: 6
they set g. round about the Land		23:37
wives and the children of the g.		23:38
and he put g. over them		24:11
he keepeth his g. about him;		29:22
sent his g. to contend with Alma.	Al	2:32
But Alma, with his g., contended		2:33
contended with the g. of the king		2:33
with their g. and their armies,		22:33
he would bring his g. with him.		47:12
down with his g. to Amalickiah,		47:13
came out to meet him with his g.,		47:21
when the g. of the Lamanites had		52:22
did set g. over the prisoners		53: 1
g. who were over the Nephites.		55: 6
Laman went to the g. who were		55: 8
upon our swords, and keep g.,		57: 9
fell upon the g. who were left to		58:21
whole army, save a few g. only,		58:22
not kept sufficient g. in the land	He	1:18
be placed as g. round about	3Ne	3:14

GUESSED
things they may have g. right,	He	16:16

GUIDE
I, Nephi, did g. the ship,	1Ne	18:22
springs of water shall he g. them.		21:10
And none to g. her among	2Ne	8:18
to g. you in wisdom's paths	Mos	2:36
not that he should be their g.	He	12: 5
run could no longer as a blind g.?	DC	19:40
the Holy Spirit for their g.,		45:57

GUIDED
and g. by the Holy Spirit.	DC	46: 2
g. in a right and proper way		101:63

GUIDES
be led by foolish and blind g.?	He	13:29

GUILE
And thus he was caught with g.	Al	18:23
of old, in whom there is no g.	DC	41:11
hypocrisy, and without g.—		121:42
George Miller is without g.;		124:20
be without g., and he shall receive		124:97

GUILT
perfect knowledge of all our g.,	2Ne	9:14
may not remember your awful g.		9:46
but I know my g.;		9:46
stand with shame and awful g.	Jac	6: 9
wherefore, my g. was swept away.	En	1: 6
to a lively sense of his own g.,	Mos	2:38
and doth fill his breast with g.,		2:38
to an awful view of their own g.		3:25
filled with g. and remorse,	Al	5:18
a remembrance of all your g.,		5:18
bright recollection of all our g.		11:43
under a consciousness of his g.,		12: 1
a consciousness of his own g.;		14: 6
and taken away the g. from our		24:10
a consciousness of your g.?	Mrm	9: 3
racked with a consciousness of g.		9: 3
punish g., but never suppress the	DC	134: 4
God hath atoned for original g.,	Mses	6:54

GUILTLESS
in your hearts ye remain g.,	Mos	4:25
ye may walk g. before God—		4:26
now, O king, behold, we are g.,		12:14
the Lord will not hold him g. that		13:15
such an one is not found g.	Al	5:29
God will look upon you as g.		60:23
him will I hold g. before my	3Ne	27:16
that is found g. before him	Mrm	7: 7
hold him g. that obeys not	DC	58:30
will hold the armies of Israel g.		105:30

GUILTY
the g. taketh the truth to be hard,	1Ne	16: 2
if it so be that we are g.,	2Ne	28: 8
thou are not only g. of priestcraft,	Al	1:12
g. of all manner of wickedness?		5:23
Behold, I am g., and these men		14: 7
is a g. and a fallen people,		30:25
a child is not g. because of its		30:25
not been g. of so great a crime.		39: 7
ye are not g. of the first offense,		43:46
letting the g. and the wicked go	He	7: 5
behold, we know that thou art g.		9:34
those who were g. of murder	3Ne	6:29
some of you are g. before me,	DC	38:14
not hold any g. that shall go		64:22
found g. before this Presidency,		68:23
that the g. among you may not		104: 7
and the punishment of the g.;		134: 6
g. of any great or malignant	JS	2:28
But I was g. of levity, and		2:28

GULF
a great and a terrible g. divideth	1Ne	12:18
was an awful g., which separated		15:28
the eternal g. of misery and woe.	2Ne	1:13
everlasting g. of death a misery,	Al	26:20
that everlasting g. of misery	He	3:29
the g. of misery and endless wo,		5:12

GUSHED
rock also and the waters g. out.	1Ne	20:21

GUSHING
unto the g. out of many tears,	3Ne	4:33

HABITATION
from heaven, thy holy h.,	DC	109:77
Let thy h. be known in Zion,		112: 6
house shall be a healthful h.		124:24
let it be a delightful h. for man,	DC	124:60
but let him change their h.,		124:108
truth is the h. of thy throne;	Mses	7:31

HABITATIONS 419 HAND

HABITATIONS
forth the curtains of thy h.; 3Ne 22: 2

HAD: see in the APPENDIX.

HADST
O that thou h. hearkened 1Ne 20:18
when thou h. it in thy heart to Al 11:25

HAGAR
Sarah gave H. to Abraham DC 132:34
from H. sprang many people. 132:34
commanded Abraham to take H. 132:65

HAGOTH
H. he being an exceedingly Al 63: 5

HAH-KO-KAU-BEAM
medium of Kli-flos-is-es, or H., Fac 2: 5

HAI
on the west, and H. on the east; Abr 2:20

HAIL
I will send forth h. among them, Mos 12: 6
all his h. and his mighty storm He 5:12
and be swept away by the h., DC 109:30
h. thee again with warm hearts 121: 9

HAILED
saw him coming and they h. him; Al 55: 8

HAILSTORM
shall be a great h. sent forth DC 29:16

HAILSTORMS
of earthquakes, and great h., DC 43:25

HAIR
Laban by the h. of the head, 1Ne 4:18
to them that plucked off the h. 2Ne 7: 6
instead of well set h., baldness; 13:24
and the h. of the feet; 17:20
as a h. of their heads be lost; Al 11:44
a h. of the head shall not be lost; 40:23
from off the ground by the h., 44:13
not make one h. black or white; 3Ne 12:36
a h. of your head shall not be DC 9:14
And not one h., neither mote, 29:25
a h. of his head shall not fall 84:80
a h. of his head shall not fall 84:116
the h. of his head was white 110: 3

HAIRS
their grey h. were about to be 1Ne 18:18

HALE, Emma
saw my wife (his daughter), H. JS 2:57

HALE, Isaac
was put to board with a Mr. H., JS 2:57

HALF
one h. of our corn, and our barley, Mos 7:22
one h. of the increase of our flocks 7:22
one h. of all we have or possess 7:22
one h. of all they possessed, 19:15
one h. of their gold, and their 19:15
of one h. of all they possessed. 19:22
one h. of all they possessed. 19:26
they were not h. so numerous as 20:11
yea, they were not h. so numerous. 25: 3
they were not h. so numerous as 26: 5
A shiblon is h. of a senum; 11:15
shiblon for h. a measure of barley. 11:15
a shiblum is a h. of a shiblon. 11:16
a leah is the h. of a shiblum. 11:17
wilt ask, even to h. of the kingdom. 20:23
the h. of all their possessions. He 4:10
the one h. of their property 4:16
and the one h. of all their lands. 4:16

had gained the h. of the kingdom. Eth 8: 2
had gained the h. of the kingdom 8: 3
in captivity the h. of his days. 8: 4
drew away the h. of the kingdom. 10:32
over the h. of the kingdom 10:32
overthrow the h. of the kingdom; 11:15
maintain the h. of the kingdom 11:15
for the space of h. an hour; DC 88:95
to one-h. of the council, 102:15

HALF'S
of a day and a h. journey Al 22:32

HALLOWED
blessed the sabbath day, and h. it. Mos 13:19
art in heaven, h. be thy name. 3Ne 13: 9

HALT
or blind, or h., or maimed, 3Ne 17: 7

HALTED
not pursue us far before they h.; Al 56:42
but they have h. for the purpose 56:43
whole army of the Lamanites h. 56:52

HAM
hundred years old he begat H. Mses 8:12
three sons, Shem, H., and Japheth. 8:27
directly from the loins of H. Abr 1:11
descendant from the loins of H., 1:21
who was the daughter of H., 1:23
from H., sprang that race which 1:24
of Egypt the daughter of H., 1:25
of the government of H., 1:25
claim it from Noah, through H., 1:27

HAMATH
Is not H. as Arpad? 2Ne 20: 9
and from Shinar, and from H., 21:11

HANANNIHAH
the land of H., and all the Mses 7: 9

HANCOCK, Levi W.
Let my servants H. and DC 52:29
H., James Foster, to preside 124:138

HANCOCK, Solomon
And let my servants H. and DC 52:27

HAND
Written by THE H. OF MORMON T Pg
Sealed by the h. of Moroni, T Pg
I make it with mine own h.; 1Ne 1: 3
preserved by the h. of the Lord, 5:14
go forth by the h. of the twelve 13:26
them by the h. of the Gentiles, 13:34
on the one h. or on the other— 14: 7
Stretch forth thine h. again unto 17:53
I stretched forth my h. unto my 17:54
Mine h. hath also laid the 20:13
right h. hath spanned the heavens. 20:13
in the shadow of his h. hath he 21: 2
lift up mine h. to the Gentiles, 21:22
lifted up his h. upon the Gentiles 22: 6
countries by the h. of the Lord. 2Ne 1: 5
be brought by the h. of the Lord. 1: 6
blessings from the h. of the Lord— 1:10
Lord shall bring forth by his h.,— 3:15
by the finger of mine own h.; 3:17
my father is by the h. of the Lord, 5:12
will lift up mine h. to the Gentiles, 6: 6
is my h. shortened at all that 7: 2
This shall ye have of mine h.— 7:11
thee in the shadow of mine h., 8:16
hast drunk at the h. of the Lord 8:17
that taketh her by the h., 8:18
have taken out of thine h. the cup 8:22
put it into the h. of them that 8:23
For on the other h., 9:13
seed by the h. of the Gentiles; 2Ne 10:18

HAND

not this ruin comes under thy h.—	2Ne 13: 6	and the time is soon at h. except	Al 10:23
stretched forth his h. against them,	15:25	But Amulek stretched forth his h.	10:25
but his h. is stretched out still	15:25	he stretched forth his h. unto	13:21
having a live coal in his h.,	16: 6	I must not stretch forth mine h.;	14:11
spake thus to me with a strong h.,	18:11	and he smote them with his h.	14:14
but his h. is stretched out still.	19:12	he stretched forth his h., and	15: 5
but his h. is stretched out still.	19:17	unto him, taking him by the h.:	15: 6
he shall snatch on the right h.	19:20	by his h. were they all created	18:32
he shall eat on the left h.	19:20	he stretched forth his h. unto	19:12
but his h. is stretched out still.	19:21	and took the queen by the h.,	19:29
but his h. is stretched out still.	20: 4	and as soon as she touched her h.	19:29
in their h. is their indignation.	20: 5	took the king, Lamoni, by the h.,	19:30
As my h. hath founded the	20:10	he stretched forth his h. to slay	20:20
By the strength of my h. and	20:13	delivered by the h. of Lamoni	21:14
And my h. hath found as a nest	20:14	he put forth his h. and raised the	22:22
shake his h. against the mount	20:32	suffer their afflictions on every h.,	22:34
put his h. on the cockatrice's den.	21: 8	aside to the right h. or to the left,	24:23
set his h. again the second time	21:11	to dwell at the right h. of God,	28:12
they shall lay their h. upon Edom	21:14	he put forth his h. and wrote unto	30:51
shall shake his h. over the river,	21:15	Korihor put forth his h. and wrote,	30:52
shake the h., that they may go into	23: 2	but he stretched forth his h.,	32: 7
for the day of the Lord is at h.;	23: 6	it is on the one h. even as it is on	32:20
the h. that is stretched out upon	24:26	that on the other h., there can be	36:21
And his h. is stretched out,	24:27	and preserved by the h. of the Lord	37: 4
set his h. again the second time	25:17	the one on one h., the other on	41: 4
smitten by the h. of the Gentiles.	26:19	And so it is on the other h.	41: 6
wrought by the h. of the Lord,	28: 6	lest he should put forth his h.,	42: 3
set my h. again the second time	29: 1	if Adam had put forth his h.	42: 5
unto them from the h. of Nephi.	30: 6	While on the other h., there was	43:38
put his h. on the cockatrice's den.	30:14	or buried by the h. of the Lord,	45:19
and h. them down unto my seed,	Jac 1: 3	by the h. of the Lord.	46: 7
this people, by the h. of Nephi.	1:18	be preserved by the h. of God,	46:24
the h. of providence hath smiled	2:13	put forth his h. to raise them,	47:23
were made by the h. of Nephi.	3:14	Moroni, on the other h., had been	48: 7
but to take counsel from his h.	4:10	on the other h., there was not a	49:23
have I slackened mine h., that I	5:47	on the other h., the people of	49:28
and I have stretched forth mine h.	5:47	slain by the h. of the Nephites;	51:11
for the end is nigh at h.,	5:71	the men of Moroni on one h.,	52:31
set his h. again the second time	6: 2	or guard them, sword in h.,	57:15
that he wrote it with his own h.;	Om 1: 9	yea, the time is now at h.,	60:29
brought by the h. of the Lord	1:16	were surrounded on every h.	He 1:31
by the h. of the Lord.	Mos 1: 2	souls, at the right h. of God	3:30
and preserved by the h. of God,	1: 5	the kingdom of heaven is at h.;	5:32
prepared by the h. of the Lord	1:16	was murdered by an unknown h.	6:15
suffered by the h. of the Lord	2:11	and doth h. down their plots,	6:30
therefore I will stay my h.,	4:17	on the other h., that the Nephites	6:38
be found at the right h. of God,	5: 9	stretched forth his h. and cried	13: 4
himself on the left h. of God.	5:10	for behold, the time is at h.,	3Ne 1:13
not found on the left h. of God,	5:12	And behold, the time is at h.,	1:14
for behold, the time is at h.,	7:18	had been given was already at h.	1:16
by the h. of their enemies.	11:21	had been given was already at h.;	1:18
Stretch forth thy h. and	12: 2	supported by the h. of a god,	3: 2
of the Lord shall prosper in his h.	14:10	sealing it with mine own h.,	3: 5
he stretched forth his h. and said:	16: 1	and they shall not stay their h.	3: 8
ye shall be smitten on every h.,	17:17	that he stretched forth his h.	11: 9
be taken by the h. of your enemies,	17:18	he stretched forth his h. unto	12: 1
a place at my right h.	26:23	let not thy left h. know what thy	13: 3
a place eternally at my right h.	26:24	know what thy right h. doeth;	13: 3
to him by the h. of Limhi;	28:11	Behold, my time is at h.	17: 1
preserved by the h. of the Lord,	28:15	touched with his h. the disciples	18:36
given them by the h. of the Lord.	29:25	Thy h. shall be lifted up upon	20:17
the h. of the Nephites,	Al 2:18	my servant shall be in my h.;	21:10
who was slain by the h. of Henor	2:20	Their h. shall be lifted up upon	21:13
by the h. of the Lord,	2:28	shalt break forth on the right h.	22: 3
they were met on every h.,	2:37	the one on the one h. and	26: 5
were baptized by the h. of Alma,	4: 4	and the other on the other h.,	26: 5
by the h. of his father Alma.	4: 4	of his justice is in his right h.;	29: 4
kingdom of heaven is soon at h.,	5:28	turn the right h. of the Lord	29: 9
quickly, for the hour is close at h.,	5:29	been created by the h. of God.	4Ne 1:16
time is at h. that he must repent	5:31	to me by the h. of the Lord,	Mrm 6: 6
For behold, the time is at h. that	5:36	it is the h. of the Lord which	8: 8
kingdom of heaven is soon at h.;	5:50	they come, by the h. of the Lord,	8:26
an inheritance at my right h.	5:58	destroyed by the h. of the Lord	Eth 1: 1
who was slain by the h. of Nehor	6: 7	continually by the h. of the Lord.	2: 6
the kingdom of heaven is at h.,	7: 9	the Lord stretched forth his h.	3: 6
out of Jerusalem by the h. of God?	9: 9	know what the time is at h.	4:16
of Jerusalem, by the h. of the Lord;	9:22	by the h. of wickedness;	9: 4
from the h. of the Lord,	9:23	smitten by the h. of a robber,	10: 3
kingdom of heaven is nigh at h.;	9:25	prospered by the h. of the Lord.	10:28
for the time is at h. that all men	9:28	a place at the right h. of God,	12: 4
riches by the h. of my industry.	10: 4	hilt of his sword in his right h.,	14: 2
for the kingdom of heaven is at h.	10:20	down on the right h. of God,	Mro 7:27
will not the Lord stay his h.;	10:23	expect that God will stay his h.	9:14

HAND 421 HANDLE

on the right h. of his power,	Mro	9:26
is not yet, but is high at h.,	DC	1:35
by the h. of Elijah the prophet,		2: 1
doth he turn to the right h.		3: 2
has desired a witness at my h.,		5: 1
receive a witness from my h.,		5:32
who are found on my left h.		19: 5
which is given from my h.		19:10
by the h. of my servant Joseph		19:13
and ordained under his h.;		20: 3
on the right h. of the Father,		20:24
send by the h. of some priest;		20:82
you are an elder under his g.,		21:11
shalt be ordained under his h.		25: 7
is nigh and the day soon at h.		29: 9
shall stand at my right h. at		29:12
is the workmanship of mine h.		29:25
be gathered on my right h.		29:27
the wicked on my left h. will		29:27
at the h. of their fathers.		29:48
to inquire for yourself at my h.,		30: 3
establish a church by your h.;		31: 7
the kingdom of heaven is at h.;		33:10
the time is soon at h. that I		34: 7
coming, for it is nigh at h.—		35:15
by the h. of my servant Joseph;		35:17
I will lay my h. upon you		36: 2
by the h. of my servant Sidney		36: 2
and what can stay my h.?		38:22
and no power shall stay my h.		38:33
I will stay my h. in judgment		39:16
will stay mine h. in judgment.		39:18
The kingdom of heaven is at h.;		39:19
For the time is at h.;		39:21
the kingdom of heaven is at h.		42: 7
that not by the h. of an enemy.		42:43
and revelations from my h.		43: 2
day of the Lord is nigh at h.		43:17
that summer is now nigh at h.;		45:37
on the right h. of his glory,		49: 6
which time is nigh at h.—		49: 6
by the h. of my servant		55: 2
is not yet, but is nigh at h.		58: 4
ye have received from my h.		58:23
confess not his h. in all things,		59:21
all flesh is in mine h.,		61: 6
from the h. of the Lord,		62: 7
they are now nigh at h.,		63:53
at the right h. of my Father,		66:12
at the h. of every steward,		72: 3
there any who can stay his h.		76: 3
on the right h. of the Father,		76:20
even on the right h. of God;		76:23
has come, and is now at h.;		78: 3
by the h. of Joseph Smith, Jun.,		84: 3
under the h. of his father-in-law,		84: 6
under the h. of Caleb;		84: 7
it under the h. of Elihu.		84: 8
Elihu under the h. of Jeremy;		84: 9
Jeremy under the h. of Gad;		84:10
Gad under the h. of Esaias;		84:11
under the h. of God.		84:12
by the h. of his father Adam,		84:16
whose h. is given all power.		84:28
I will be on your right h.		84:88
Lord, have put forth my h.		84:119
the scepter of power in his h.,		85: 7
putteth forth his h. to steady		85: 8
chastening h. of an Almighty		87: 6
from the h. of the bishop;		90:30
the h. of the Lord is there;		97:19
leave the residue in mine h.		101:71
crown of glory at my right h.		104: 7
with them, which is nigh at h.		104:59
by the h. of Adam.		107:44
ordained be the h. of Adam,		107:46
ordained under the h. of Adam,		107:47
ordained under the h. of Adam;		107:48
ordained under the h. of Adam.		107:50
ordained under the h. of Seth.		107:51
under the h. of Methuselah.		107:52
that thou hast put forth thy h.,		109:23
and preserved by thy fostering h.		109:69
that thy right h. may exalt them,	DC	109:71
God shall lead thee by the h.,		112:10
and my h. shall be over him;		112:15
How long shall thy h. be stayed,		121: 2
stretch forth thy h.;		121: 4
God hath set his h. and seal to		121:12
constantly from under thy h.		122: 2
have had a h. in their oppressions,		123: 3
the most damning h. of murder,		123: 7
murdered under its iron h.;		123: 9
with Abraham at his right h.,		124:19
required at your h. to leave		126: 1
great day of the Lord is at h.;		128:24
offer him your h. and request		129: 4
do so, and you will feel his h.		129: 5
he will offer you his h.,		129: 8
as you have inquired of my h.		132: 1
of me, by the h. of Nathan,		132:39
require an offering at your h.,		132:51
stand on the right h. of the Lamb,		133:56
this shall ye have of my h.—		133:70
lest he put forth his h. and	Mses	4:28
thy brother's blood from thy h.		5:36
h. was against his own brother,		6:15
he had a great chain in his h.,		7:26
it, and held it in his own h.;		7:43
at the right h. of the Son of Man,		7:56
stood on the right h. of God;		7:57
by the h. of the priest of	Abr	1: 7
lifted up his h. against thee,		1:17
I will lead thee by my h.,		1:18
I stretch my h. over the sea,		2: 7
my h. shall be over thee.		2: 8
(and his h. was stretched out),		3:12
he put his h. upon mine eyes,		3:12
and judgment in his h.	Fac	3: 1
as written above the h.		3: 4
the characters above his h.		3: 5
on the right h. of God.	JS	1: 1
know that summer is nigh at h.;		1:38
On the other h., the Baptists		2: 9
by the h. of Elijah the prophet,		2:38
what was required at my h.,		2:60
what was required at my h.		2:60
under the h. of this messenger,		2:72

HANDCUFFS
they are the very h., and chains	DC	123: 8

HANDED
these plates should be h. down	1Ne	19: 4
kept and preserved, and h. down	2Ne	25:21
had been h. down by the kings,	WM	1:10
were h. down from king Benjamin,		1:11
were h. down from generation	Mos	28:14
even as they had been h. down		28:20
prophecies which were h. down	Al	23: 5
are h. down by holy prophets,		30:14
which was h. down to them by		31:16
should be kept and h. down		37: 4
h. down from one generation		63:13
And they have been h. down	He	3:16
h. down unto us by our fathers,		16:20
they have been h. down unto us.	3Ne	3: 9
been h. down from generation	4Ne	1:48
been h. down by our fathers,	Mrm	6: 6
h. down and altered by us,		9:32
been h. down even from Cain,	Eth	8:15
to be h. over unto the bishop	DC	72: 6
and h. over to the bishop of		72:13
h. down from father to son,		107:40
h. over and carried up unto the		107:78
these other records can be		128: 4

HANDING
h. them down from one	Mos	28:20

HANDIWORK
built the earth, my very h.;		DC 104:14

HANDLE
Jesus said: H. me and see,	DC	129: 2
such as h. the harp and organ.	Mses	5:45

HANDLED 422 HANDS

HANDLED
cannot be controlled nor h.	DC	121:36

HANDMAID
that my h. Vienna Jaques should	DC	90:28
I give unto mine h., Emma		132:51
let mine h., Emma Smith, receive		132:52
I command mine h., Emma		132:54
let mine h. forgive my servant		132:56

HANDMAIDS
shall be for servants and h.;	2Ne	24: 2

HANDS
I have made with mine own h.;	1Ne	1:17
it fell into the h. of Laban.		3:26
will deliver Laban into your h.		3:29
will deliver Laban into our h.?		3:31
hath delivered him into thy h.		4:11
hath delivered him into thy h.;		4:12
had delivered Laban into my h.		4:17
my sons out of the h. of Laban,		5: 5
them out of the h. of Laban,		5: 8
us out of the h. of Laban,		7:11
they did lay their h. upon me,		7:16
me from the h. of my brethren;		7:17
loosed from off my h. and feet,		7:18
and sought to lay h. upon me;		7:19
out of the h. of all other nations.		13:19
h. of the great and abominable		13:28
out of the h. of the Egyptians		17:23
forth to lay their h. upon me		17:48
whoso shall lay his h. upon me		17:48
durst they lay their h. upon me		17:52
a man, into the h. of wicked men,		19:10
thee upon the palms of my h.;		21:16
sword of their own h. shall fall		22:13
instrument in the h. of God,	2Ne	1:24
instrument in the h. of God,		3:24
out of the h. of mine enemies?		4:31
and to labor with their h.		5:17
worship and work of their own h.,		12: 8
for the reward of their h. shall be		13:11
consider the operation of his h.		15:12
Therefore shall all h. be faint,		23: 7
with pure hearts and clean h.,		25:16
his children, the work of my h.,		27:34
or the workmanship of his h.	Jac	4: 9
he stretches forth his h. unto them		6: 4
into the h. of my son Omni,	Jar	1:15
into the h. of their enemies	Om	1: 2
into the h. of their enemies		1: 6
out of the h. of their enemies.		1: 7
into the h. of my son Moroni,	WM	1: 1
records into the h. of my son;		1: 2
had been delivered into my h.,		1: 3
into the h. of King Benjamin,		1:10
until they have fallen into my h.		1:11
into the h. of the Lamanites,	Mos	1:14
out of the h. of their enemies,		2: 4
have labored with mine own h.		2:14
into the h. of your enemies,		2:31
or out of the h. of the Lamanites,		7:15
into his h. the possessions of		7:21
out of the h. of the Lamanites.		9:hd
with the labors of our h.;		9:12
us out of the h. of our enemies,		9:17
I, myself, with mine own h., did		9:19
into the h. of our enemies.		10: 2
of the people out of their h.;		10:15
into the h. of their enemies;		11:21
delivered him out of their h.		11:26
we deliver him into thy h.;		12:16
attempted to lay their h. on him;		13: 2
if ye lay your h. upon me,		13: 3
durst not lay their h. on him,		13: 5
that I have fallen into your h.		17: 9
they clapped their h. for joy,		18:11
should labor with their own h.		18:24
into the h. of the Lamanites,		19:15
deliver themselves out of their h.,		21: 5
into the h. of the Lamanites.		21:19
out of the h. of the Lamanites		21:36
made me an instrument in his h.	Mos	23:10
even out of the h. of King Noah		23:13
themselves up into their h.;		23:29
out of the h. of the Lamanites		25:10
I deliver them into thy h.		26:12
laboring with their own h. for		27: 4
should labor with their own h.		27: 5
that he could not move his h.;		27:19
instruments in the h. of God		27:36
out of the h. of the Lamanites.		28: 7
ought not to labor with their h.,	Al	1: 3
an instrument in the h. of God		1: 8
out of the h. of their enemies,		2:28
may be an instrument in thy h.		2:30
out of the h. of the people of		5: 4
by the h. of the Lamanites		5: 5
with a pure heart and clean h.?		5:19
and elders, by laying on his h.		6: 1
stood forth to lay their h. on me;		9: 7
out of the h. of their enemies,		9:10
the h. of their own brethren?		9:10
sought to lay their h. upon me,		9:32
Egypt by the h. of his brethren.		10: 3
equity and justice in my h.		10:21
let us stretch forth our h.,		14:10
an instrument in the h. of God		17: 9
an instrument of thee in my h.		17:11
for them with their own h.		17:14
Nephites who fell into their h.,		17:20
deliver his sons out of their h.;		17:35
they durst not put forth their h.		19:24
ever delivered them out of their h.;		19:27
clasped her h., being filled with		19:30
the h. of a more hardened and a		20:30
durst not lay their h. on Aaron		22:20
not lay their h. on Ammon,		23: 1
should not lay their h. on them		23: 2
labor abundantly with their h.		24:18
slain by the h. of the Nephites;		25: 4
instruments in the h. of God		26: 3
they are in the h. of the Lord		26: 7
we have been instruments in his h.		26:15
flee out of the h. of our enemies,		27: 5
an instrument in the h. of God		29: 9
out of the h. of the Egyptians		29:12
with the labors of their h.,		30:27
up into the h. of the officers,		30:29
with mine own h. for my support,		30:32
stretch forth his h. towards		31:14
he clapped his h. upon all them		31:36
as he clapped his h. upon them,		31:36
to build with our own h.;		32: 5
instruments in the h. of God		35:14
from the h. of their enemies;		43: 9
into the h. of the Lamanites,		43:10
fall into the h. of the Lamanites		43:11
Nephites were slain by their h.,		43:44
slain by the h. of your enemies.		43:46
Ye know that ye are in our h.,		44: 1
has delivered you into our h.		44: 3
behold, ye are in our h., and I		44: 7
his bow into the h. of Moroni,		44: 8
has delivered us into your h.;		44: 9
as ye are in our h. we will spill		44:11
out of the h. of their enemies;		45: 1
up into the h. of Moroni and		46:33
deliver them up into Lehonti's h.,		47:13
from the h. of their enemies.		49:28
from the h. of their enemies.		50:10
the prisoners who fell into his h.;		52: 8
had been taken out of their h.;		52:10
into the h. of the Lamanites.		52:10
on both h. with exceeding fury;		52:35
to build with their own h.		53: 5
into the h. of their brethren,		53:11
sons should fall into their h.,		56:39
into the h. of the Lamanites;		56:50
city of Antiparah fell into our h.		57: 4
yielded up the city unto our h.;		57:12
they could get into their h.,		57:14
from falling into their h.		57:17
out of the h. of our enemies.		57:35
into the h. of our enemies,		58: 8
out of the h. of our enemies,		58:10

HANDS

out of the h. of our enemies,	Al 58:37
into the h. of the Lamanites	59: 9
into the h. of their brethren.	59:11
out of the h. of our enemies?	60:20
armies into the h. of his son,	62:43
out of the h. of their enemies.	62:50
into the h. of the Nephites.	He 1:32
into the h. of the Lamanites	4: 9
durst not lay their h. upon them	5:23
durst not lay their h. upon them;	5:25
that ye cannot lay your h. on us	5:26
not lay their own h. upon him,	8: 4
did not lay their h. on him;	8:10
did seek to lay their h. upon him	10:15
out of the h. of their enemies;	12: 2
went forth to lay their h. on him,	16: 7
of the h. of those Gadianton	3Ne 3:15
would deliver us into their h.;	3:21
will deliver them into our h.	3:21
out of the h. of their enemies.	4: 8
fall into their h. by the way;	4:13
into the h. of their enemies.	4:31
out of the h. of their enemies;	4:33
I have made with mine own h.	5:11
thrust your h. into my side,	11:14
nails in my h. and in my feet,	11:14
thrust their h. into his side,	11:15
nails in his h. and in his feet;	11:15
eyes and did feel with their h.,	11:15
worship the works fo thy h.;	21:17
out of the h. of their enemies,	Mrm 3:13
that ye are in the h. of God?	5:23
into the h. of the Lamanites,	6: 6
left by the h. of those who slew	6:15
by the h. of the apostles.	9:18
they shall lay h. on the sick	9:24
he did carry them in his h. upon	Eth 3: 1
of the awkwardness of our h.	12:24
which he was his own, with his h.,	14: 2
Shiz raised upon his h. and fell;	15:31
as he laid his h. upon them—	Mro 2: 1
upon whom ye shall lay your h.,	2: 2
as many as they laid their h.,	2: 3
they laid their h. upon them,	3: 2
into the h. of a wicked man,	DC 3:12
the prints of the nails in my h.	6:37
out of the h. of your enemies,	8: 4
you shall hold it in your h.,	8: 8
to take it away out of your h.,	8: 8
into the h. of a wicked man,	10: 1
the h. of the servants of Satan	10: 5
the writings into his h.,	10: 8
have gone out of your h.	10:10
I will require this at their h.,	10:23
have gone forth out of your h.;	10:30
which have gone out of your h.,	10:38
by the h. of my servant Joseph	18: 7
by your h. I will work a	18:44
by the laying on of h. for the	20:41
by the laying on of the h.,	20:43
the sacrament, or lay on h.;	20:58
by the laying on of the h. of	20:68
are to lay their h. upon them	20:70
continue in laying on of the h.	24: 9
shall lay their h. upon you	24:16
he shall lay his h. upon thee,	25: 8
by the laying on of the h.,	33:15
by the laying on of the h.,	35: 6
with the labor of his h.,	38:40
water, ye shall lay your h.,	39:23
in the h. of the church,	42:33
of the work of thine own h.;	42:40
and lay their h. upon them in	42:44
lift up their h. against him or	42:81
which I have put into your h.	43:15
in thine h. and in thy feet?	45:51
by the laying on of the h. of	49:14
kept in the h. of the bishop.	51:13
and the laying on of the h.	52:10
labor with their own h. that	52:39
by the laying on of h.;	53: 3
by the laying on of h.;	55: 1
you shall lay your h.,	55: 3
whose h. are not stayed from	56:17
not labor with your own h.!	DC 56:17
put into the h. of the bishop,	58:51
and labor with his own h.,	58:60
lifting up holy h. upon them.	60: 7
hold it in mine own h.;	63:25
take righteousness in his h.	63:37
these things are in his own h.,	63:44
out of the mountain without h.	65: 2
Lay your h. upon the sick,	66: 9
and the earth are in mine h.,	67: 2
the h. of my servant Joseph	67:14
under the h. of the First	68:19
under the h. of this Presidency,	68:20
under the h. of the above	68:21
by the laying on of the h.,	68:25
receive the laying on of the h.	68:27
the Lord shall put into his h.	72:13
saves all the works of his h.,	76:43
by the laying on of the h. of	76:52
into whose h. the Father has	76:55
the Father hath in his own h.	78:17
lift up the h. which hang	81: 5
laid my h. upon the nations,	84:96
cleanse your h. and your feet	88:74
but let your h. be clean,	88:86
uplifted h. unto the Most High.	88:120
with uplifted h. to heaven,	88:132
with uplifted h. to heaven,	88:135
by the h. of men.	91: 2
the Lord, require at their h.,	97:12
thine enemy into thine h.,	98:29
thine enemy is in thine h.;	98:31
thine enemy is in thine h.	98:31
they are in mine h.,	100: 1
and John Gould, are in my h.;	100:14
for all flesh is in mine h.;	101:16
from the h. of the destroyer.	101:54
the h. of those who are placed	101:76
by the h. of wise men whom	101:80
into the h. of mine enemies.	101:96
by the h. of mine enemies,	103: 2
and leave the residue in my h.	103:40
which I have put into your h.,	104:85
which I required at their h.,	105: 3
which I require at their h.	105:10
I do not require at their h.	105:14
by the h. of the Presidency of	107:17
by the laying on of the h.	107:67
workmanship of the h. of us,	109: 4
uplifted h. unto the Most High—	109: 9
holy h., uplifted to the Most High;	109:19
from the h. of all their enemies.	109:28
thy servants from their h.,	109:42
which thou hast set up without h.,	109:72
palms in our h., and crowns	109:76
unto thee, the work of our h.,	109:78
are committed into your h.;	110:16
will give this city into your h.,	111: 4
be required at your h.	112:33
a servant in the h. of Christ,	113: 4
will not accept it at their h.	115:15
accept it at the h. of my people	115:16
let it remain in your h.,	117: 5
be put into the h. of the bishop	119: 1
warm hearts and friendly h.	121: 9
or into the h. of murderers,	122: 7
h. of the very devil to tremble	123:10
stewardship will I require at his h.	124:14
which ye expect at my h.,	124:47
at the h. of those sons of men,	124:49
by the h. of their enemies,	124:53
shall pay his stock into their h.	124:67
of stock he pays into their h.	124:68
if he pays nothing into their h.	124:68
if any pay stock into their h.	124:69
the stock away out of their h.	124:69
receive any stock into their h.,	124:70
Joseph pay stock into their h.	124:72
for they have asked it at my h.	124:73
pay stock into the h. of those	124:111
and labor with his own h.	124:112
pay stock also into the h. of	124:117
request him to shake h.	129: 4
Ask him to shake h. with you,	129: 7

HANDS

when you ask him to shake h.	DC	129: 8
a blessing at my h. shall abide		132: 5
receive at your h. that which I		132:10
put his property out of his h.,		132:57
sacrifice which I require at his h.		132:60
h. of the servants of the Lord,		133:32
enemies, for they are in mine h.,		136:30
the workmanship of mine h.;	Mses	1: 4
thy brother Abel into thine h.		5:29
of my brother falleth into my h.		5:33
for all flesh is in my h.,		6:32
no man laid h. on him;		6:39
the workmanship of mine own h.,		7:32
I can stretch forth mine h. and		7:36
the workmanship of mine h.		7:36
the workmanship of mine h.;		7:37
all the workmanship of mine h.		7:40
our work and toil of our h.,		8: 9
lifted up their h. upon me,	Abr	1:15
records have come into my h.,		1:28
preserved in mine own h.		1:31
in their h. they shall bear this		2: 9
works which his h. had made;		3:11
things which his h. had made,		3:12
the h. of the priest of Elkenah.		3:20
works which my h. have made,		3:21
at the h. of all classes of men,	JS	2:27
His h. were naked, and his arms		2:31
of laboring with our h.,		2:55
took me, with the rest of his h.,		2:56
they remained safe in my h.,		2:60
having laid his h. upon us,		2:68
the power of laying on h. for		2:70
I laid my h. upon his head		2:71
he laid his h. on me and		2:71
Laying on of h. for the gift of	AoF	4
and by the laying on of h.,		5

HANER
of Shem, and the land of H.,	Mses	7: 9

HANG
and not h. down our heads,	2Ne	10:20
wrath, which doth h. over you	Al	54: 6
of justice doth h. over you;		60:29
destruction did h. over them,	3Ne	2:19
of my justice shall h. over them		20:20
up the hands which h. down,	DC	81: 5

HANGED
was taken and h. upon a tree,	3Ne	4:28
had h. him until he was dead		4:28
a millstone had been h. about	DC	121:22

HANGETH
of justice h. over this people;	He	13: 5
sword of vengeance h. over you;	Mrm	8:41

HAPPEN
what things should h. unto them.	Jac	1: 5

HAPPENED
that had h. unto their brethren	Mos	8: 2
that had h. to their wives and		19:22
had not any such thing h. before		26:10
all that had h. unto them;		27:20
all that had h. unto their wives	Al	15: 2
people what had h. among them,		19:17
And, as it h., it was their lot to		20:30
all that had h. unto the king.		22:19
the things that had h. unto them		27:20
of what had h. unto Korihor		30:57
or anything else, which had h.		31: 5
see what had h. to the king;		47:27
him all the things that had h.		55:15
not have h. had it not been	He	4:11
all these things had h. and		6: 1
I h. to be in company with	JS	2:21

HAPPIER
there never was a h. time	Al	50:23
there could not be a h. people	4Ne	1:16

HARD

HAPPINESS
in opposition to that of the h.	2Ne	2:10
h. nor misery, neither sense nor		2:11
no righteousness there be no h.,		2:13
there be no righteousness nor h.		2:13
lived after the manner of h.		5:27
that h. which is prepared for the		9:43
in a state of never-ending h.	Mos	2:41
resurrection of endless life and h.;		16:11
eternal h. or eternal misery,	Al	3:26
penitent and humble seeker of h.		27:18
in a state of never-ending h.		28:12
are received into a state of h.,		40:12
understood that this state of h.		40:15
their consignation to h. or misery,		40:15
their consignation to h. or misery.		40:17
and a state of the soul in h. or		40:21
raised to endless h. to inherit		41: 4
The one raised to h. according		41: 5
according to his desires of h.,		41: 5
shall be restored from sin to h.		41:10
wickedness never was h.		41:10
contrary to the nature of h.		41:11
would destroy the great plan of h.		42: 8
affixed opposite to the plan of h.,		42:16
to which we owe all our h.;		44: 5
the welfare and h. of his people;	He	12: 2
sought for h. in doing iniquity,		13:38
suffer them to take h. in sin.	Mrm	2:13
state of h. which hath no end.		7: 7
is the value of an endless h.		8:38
the h. of man, and of beasts,	DC	77: 2
there was greater h. and peace	Abr	1: 2

HAPPY
fruit was desirable to make one h.	1Ne	8:10
yea, and we might have been h.		17:21
and h. state of those that keep	Mos	2:41
faith of Christ are h. in him,	Al	46:41
their God, yea, and they are h.		56:11
And now we call the proud h.;	3Ne	24:15
h. to dwell with that holy Being,	Mrm	9: 3
he that is h. shall be happy		9:14
that is happy shall be h. still;		9:14

HARAN
that H., my brother, died;	Abr	2: 1
who were the daughters of H.		2: 2
which we denominated H.		2: 4
and my father tarried in H.		2: 5
there were many flocks in H.;		2: 5
therefore he continued in H.		2: 5
to take thee away out of H.,		2: 6
when I departed out of H.		2:14
the souls that we had won in H.,		2:15
from H. by the way of Jershon,		2:16

HARASS
they did h. them, insomuch	Al	51:32
power to h. them on every side.		52: 9
endeavoring to h. the Nephites,		52:13
should also h. the Nephites		52:13

HARD
it is a h. thing which I have	1Ne	3: 5
did speak many h. words unto us,		3:28
that ye are so h. in your hearts,		7: 8
which were h. to be understood,		15: 3
and they being h. in their hearts,		15: 3
hast declared unto us h. things,		16: 1
knew that I had spoken h. things		16: 2
guilty taketh the truth to be h.,		16: 2
speakest h. things against us.		16: 3
ye can be so h. in your hearts?		17:46
say that I have spoken h. things	2Ne	9:40
the words of truth are h. against all		9:40
from the h. bondage wherein thou		24: 3
many things which were h. for		25: 1
began to grow h. in their hearts,	Jac	1:15
people, h. to understand.	En	1:22
a h. hearted and a stiffnecked	Al	9: 5
a h. hearted and a stiffnecked		9:31

HARD

a h.-hearted and a stiffnecked   Al   15:15
of the people began to wax h.,   35:15
because it was h. against you,   He   14:10
began to be h. in their hearts,   3Ne   2: 1
how h. to bear you know not.   DC   19:15
lay aside all his h. speeches;   124:116
for their hearts have waxed h.,   Mses   6:27

HARDEN

blind the eyes and h. the hearts   1Ne 13:27
h. not their hearts against   14: 2
it so be that they h. their hearts   14: 6
If ye will not h. your hearts,   15:11
And they did h. their hearts   17:42
him will they h. their hearts;   22: 5
be that they will h. their hearts   22:18
that they need not h. their hearts 2Ne 25:27
there are many that h. their hearts   33: 2
many as will not h. their hearts   Jac   6: 4
of the day, h. not your hearts.   6: 5
hear his voice, h. not your hearts;   6: 6
I did h. my heart, for I was   Al   10: 6
he that will h. his heart,   12:10
he that will not h. his heart,   12:10
they that will h. their hearts,   12:11
repent, and h. not your hearts,   12:33
h. his heart and will do iniquity,   12:35
that if ye will h. your hearts   12:36
repent, and h. not our hearts,   12:37
such as would not h. their hearts,   13: 5
that they should h. their hearts,   21: 3
the people would h. their hearts,   21:12
but they did h. their hearts,   23:14
rather h. your hearts in unbelief,   33:21
h. not your hearts any longer;   34:31
repent and h. not your hearts,   34:31
they did h. their hearts and did   He 10:13
they did still h. their hearts   10:15
that they do h. their hearts,   12: 2
will h. their hearts against me,   13:12
people began to h. their hearts,   16:15
might h. the hearts of the people   16:22
by Satan, to h. their hearts,   3Ne   1:22
shall h. their hearts against me   20:28
if they will not h. their hearts,   21: 6
and h. not their hearts,   21:22
the people did h. their hearts,   4Ne   1:31
the people did h. their hearts,   1:34
they did h. their hearts against   Mrm   3: 3
they h. their hearts against it;   Mro   9: 4
if they h. their hearts against   DC   5:18
Satan will h. the hearts of   10:32
generation h. not their hearts,   10:53
if they will not h. their hearts,   10:65
who h. their hearts in unbelief,   20:15
and h. not their hearts;   29: 7
my voice but h. their hearts,   38: 6
and h. not your hearts;   45: 6
yet men will h. their hearts   45:33
if they h. not their hearts,   112:13

HARDENED

they had h. their hearts again,   1Ne 16:22
they h. their hearts and blinded   17:30
for they h. their hearts,   17:41
they had h. their hearts against   2Ne   5:21
after they have h. their hearts   6:10
nevertheless, they h. their hearts;   25:10
and yet they h. their hearts,   Mos   3:15
because they h. their hearts   10:14
therefore they h. their hearts   11:29
And king Noah h. his heart   11:29
for they have h. their hearts   12: 1
and their hearts were h.   26: 3
For the hearts of many were h.,   Al   1:24
Nevertheless, they h. their hearts,   8:11
your hearts have been grossly h.   9:30
Then if our hearts have been h.,   12:13
if we have h. our hearts against   12:13
might not be h. against the word,   16:17
and a h. and a ferocious people;   17:14
a more h. and a more stiffnecked   20:30

HARM

of themselves were sufficiently h., Al 21: 3
they become more h., and thus   24:30
so h. that they would not look,   33:20
yea, all are h.; yea, all are fallen   34: 9
became more h. and impenitent,   47:36
h. the hearts of the Lamanites   48: 3
many had become h., because   62:41
had become h. and impenitent   He   6: 2
because you have h. your hearts;   7:18
ye h. and ye stiffnecked people,   13:29
began to be more h. in iniquity,   16:12
and every heart was h., so that   Mrm   4:11
who hath h. the hearts of men   Eth   8:25
that the people h. their hearts,   11:13
But they h. their hearts and   DC   84:24

HARDENETH

h. the hearts of the children of   1Ne 12:17
repenteth, and h. not his heart,   Al   12:34
h. his heart against it,   DC   82:21

HARDENING

are now h. their hearts in sin   Al   37:10

HARDER

and the Amulonites were still h.; Al   21: 3

HARD-HEARTED: see HARD and
HEARTED.

HARDLY

shall pass through it h. bestead   2Ne 18:21
the saints also shall h. escape;   DC   63:34

HARDNESS

because of the h. of their hearts   1Ne 2:18
grieved for the h. of their hearts,   7: 8
h. of their hearts and the blindness   14: 7
because of the h. of their hearts,   15: 4
because of the h. of your hearts?   15:10
because of the h. of their hearts;   17:19
lest for the h. of your hearts   2Ne   1:17
and the h. of their hearts,   25:12
because of the h. of their hearts, Jar   1: 3
because of the h. of their hearts; Mos 13:32
on account of the h. of their hearts Al 13: 4
to the h. of their hearts,   14:11
the h. of the hearts of the people,   22:22
judge saw the h. of his heart,   30:29
because of the h. of your heart,   30:46
because of the h. of their hearts.   33:20
and the h. of their hearts.   He   6:35
Because of the h. of the hearts of   13: 8
grieved for the h. of their hearts 3Ne   7:16
because of the h. of their hearts; Mrm   1:17
because of the h. of their hearts   1:17
because of the h. of their hearts.   3:12
of wickedness, and h. of heart,   Eth   4:15
up unto the h. of their hearts,   15:19
notwithstanding their h.,   Mro   9: 6
of the h. of their hearts;   9:10
neither h. with each other,   DC   20:54

HARLOT

Lamanites after the h. Isabel.   Al   39: 3

HARLOTS

and I saw many h.   1Ne 13: 7
the precious clothing, and the h.,   13: 8
which is the mother of h.,   13:34
is the mother of h.;   14:16
out upon the mother of h..   14:17
priests spend their time with h.   Mos 11:14
and spend your strength with h.,   12:29
heart again after those wicked g., Al   39:11

HARM

h. or disturb their prosperity   2Ne   1:31
there is no h. in this;   28: 8
yet it did h. them not, neither   He   5:44
into a furnace and received no h. 3Ne 28:21
suckling lamb, and received no h.   28:22

HARM 426 HAST

HARM
they came forth receiving no h.	4Ne 1:32
among them, receiving no h.	1:33
fiery furnace could not h. them,	Mrm 8:24
destroy; behold this is no h.	DC 10:25
neighbor, nor do him any h.	42:27
not have power to h. them.	84:72

HARMLESS
Now Ammon being wise, yet h.,	Al 18:22

HARMONY
in the wilderness between H.,	DC 128:20
h. would be supplanted by	134: 6
opened by the Spaniards in H.,	JS 2:56

HARP
And the h., and the viol,	2Ne 15:12
such as handle the h. and organ.	Mses 5:45

HARRIS, Emer
my servant H. be united in	DC 75:30

HARRIS, George W.
H., Charles C. Rich,	124:132

HARRIS, Martin
my servant H. has desired	DC 5: 1
command him, my servant H.,	5:26
servant H. humbleth no himself	5:32
Edward Partridge and H.	52:24
servant H. should be an example	58:35
concerning my servant H. shall	58:38
and also unto my servant H.,	70: 1
and Mahemson [H.], to be bound	82:11
Joseph Coe, John Johnson, H.,	102: 3
11, John Smith; 12, H.	102:34
let my servant Mahemson [H.]	104:24
let my servant Mahemson [H.]	104:26
a gentleman by the name of H.,	JS 2:61

HARRIS
Mr. H. was a resident of	JS 2:61
the aforementioned Mr. H. came	2:63

HARRISON: see SAMUEL HARRISON.

HARROW
Would I h. up your souls if your	2Ne 9:47
sins, did h. up his mind until it	Al 15: 3
I ought not to h. up in my	29: 4
crimes, to h. up your soul,	39: 7
desire to h. up the souls of men	Mrm 5: 8

HARROWED
and his soul began to be h. up	Al 14: 6
neither shall they be h. up by	26: 6
my soul was h. up to the greatest	36:12
while I was h. up by the memory	36:17
I was h. up by the memory of	36:19

HARSH
and it was not a h. voice,	3Ne 11: 3

HARSHLY
And it speaketh h. against sin,	2Ne 33: 5

HARSHNESS
they did treat me with much h.;	1Ne 18:11
nothing save it was exceeding h.,	En 1:23

HARVEST
according to the joy in h.,	2Ne 19: 3
meet again at the close of their h.;	Al 17:13
the hands of the Lord of the h.,	26: 7
the field is white already to h.;	DC 4: 4
the field is white already to h.;	6: 3
the field is white already to h.;	11: 3
the field is white already to h.;	12: 3
the field is white already to h.;	14: 3
the field is white already to h.;	33: 3
the field is white already to h.;	33: 3
shall be past, and the h. ended,	45: 2
The h. is past, the summer is	56:16
until the h. is fully ripe;	DC 86: 7
for the time of h. is come,	101:64

HARVEY: see WHITLOCK, Harvey.

HAS: see in the APPENDIX.

HAST
of the things which thou h. done;	1Ne	2: 1
because thou h. been faithful		2: 1
for thou h. sought me diligently,		2:19
because thou h. not murmured.		3: 6
Behold thou h. led us forth		5: 2
the things which thou h. desired.		11: 6
after thou h. beheld the tree		11: 7
thou h. shown unto me the tree		11: 9
h. beheld that the book proceeded		13:24
many waters which thou h. seen		13:29
whose formation thou h. seen.		13:32
last records, which thou h. seen		13:40
Thou h. beheld that if the		14: 5
thou also h. heard that whoso		14: 5
many things which thou h. seen;		14:24
h. declared unto us hard things,		16: 1
which thou h. shown unto me?		17: 9
Thou h. seen and heard all this;		20: 6
after thou h. lost the first,		21:20
thou h. been brought out of the	2Ne	1:30
because thou h. been faithful		1:31
thou h. suffered afflictions		2: 1
thou h. beheld that in the fulness		2: 3
thou h. beheld in thy youth		2: 4
h. feared continually every day,		8:13
h. drunk at the hand of the Lord		8:17
h. drunken the dregs of the cup		8:17
h. laid thy body as the ground		8:23
thou h. forsaken thy people,		12: 6
and shall say: Thou h. clothing,		13: 6
Thou h. multiplied the nation,		19: 3
thou h. broken the yoke of his		19: 4
For thou h. said in thy heart:		24:13
because thou h. destroyed thy land		24:20
when thou h. read the words		27:22
the words which thou h. not read,		27:22
whom thou h. never before heard	En	1: 8
of the thing which thou h. done.	Mos	4:22
which thou h. spoken unto us;		5: 2
what great evil h. thou done,		12:13
and thou, O king, h. not sinned;		12:14
thou h. prospered in the land,		12:15
For thou h. said that God himself		17: 8
words which thou h. spoken evil		17: 8
thou h. hitherto hearkened unto		22: 3
if thou h. not found me to be an		22: 4
or if thou h. hitherto listened		22: 4
which thou h. spoken unto them.		26:16
thou h. established a church		26:17
because thou h. inquired of me		26:19
but h. enceavored to enforce it	Al	1:12
and thou h. shed the blood of		1:13
which thou h. established in		8:11
that thou h. no power over us;		8:12
and thou h. delivered up the		8:12
for thou h. great cause to rejoice;		8:15
for thou h. been faithful in		8:15
thou h. fed me and taken me in,		8:26
And now thou h. lied before God		11:25
Behold thou h. lied, for thou		11:36
thou h. been taken in thy lying		12: 3
thou h. not lied unto men only		12: 3
but thou h. lied unto God;		12: 3
What is this that thou h. said,		12:20
all the words that thou h. taught.		15: 7
thou h. heard that I defended		18:16
things which thou h. spoken.		18:33
mercy which thou h. had upon		18:41
thou h. power to do many mighty		19: 4
be according as thou h. said.		19: 9
that h. sought to destroy him.		20:19
this is all that thou h. desired,		20:26
What is this that thou h. testified?		21: 5
H. thou seen an angel?		21: 5
thou h. delivered out of prison.		22: 2

HAST 427 HASTENETH

life of which thou h. spoken?	Al 22:15	those whom thou h. ordained,	DC 24:19
Thou h. had signs enough; will ye	30:44	things which thou h. not seen,	25: 4
we believe that thou h. separated	31:16	covenants which thou h. made.	25:13
we believe that thou h. elected us	31:16	thou h. seen great sorrow,	39: 9
also thou h. made it known unto	31:16	thou h. rejected me many times	39: 9
thou h. elected us that we shall	31:17	that which thou h. to impart	42:30
thou h. elected us, that we may	31:17	things which thou h. received,	42:59
say that thou h. made it known	31:29	after thou h. been baptized	55: 1
for thou h. heard my prayer,	33: 4	after thou h. come up unto	60:14
thou h. been merciful unto me,	33: 9	and h. proclaimed my word,	60:14
Yea, and thou h. also heard	33:10	which thou h. been troubled.	66:10
thou h. been thus merciful unto me,	33:11	Thou who h. commanded thy	109: 2
thou h. turned thy judgments	33:11	as thou h. said in a revelation,	109: 6
h. turned away thy judgments	33:13	promises which thou h. made	109:11
mercies which thou h. bestowed	33:16	that thou h. sanctified it,	109:13
the words which thou h. spoken.	45: 5	also by faith, as thou h. said;	109:14
which thou h. made with him.	He 9:20	blessings which thou h. ordained	109:21
things which thou h. done;	10: 4	that thou h. put forth thy hand,	109:23
how thou h. with unwearyingness	10: 4	fulfil that which thou h. spoken	109:23
And thou h. not feared them,	10: 4	to that which thou h. spoken	109:41
h. not sought thine own life,	10: 4	We know that thou h. spoken	109:45
own life, but h. sought my will,	10: 4	and that thou h. sent us;	109:57
because thou h. done this	10: 5	as thou h. commanded them.	109:58
all the words which thou h. spoken	11: 8	one which thou h. appointed,	109:59
thou h. already destroyed.	11:11	which thou h. given unto us,	109:60
to thy words which thou h. said.	11:16	h. a great love for the children of	109:61
until thou h. paid the uttermost	3Ne 12:26	the commandments which thou h.	109:68
when thou h. shut thy door,	13: 6	kingdom, which thou h. set up	109:72
thou h. given the Holy Ghost	19:20	as thou h. abased thyself	112: 3
thou h. given them the Holy	19:22	him whom thou h. reproved,	121:43
that thou h. purified those whom	19:28	great things thou h. prepared for	133:45
whom thou h. given me out of	19:29	*thou h. been faithful;*	135: 5
wherein thou h. called us,	28: 2	*because thou h. seen thy weakness,*	135: 5
And when thou h. done this	Eth 1:42	that which thou h. borrowed;	136:25
which thou h. commanded me,	2:18	in preserving what thou h.,	136:27
according as thou h. directed me.	2:18	That Satan, whom thou h.	Mses 4: 1
as thou h. commanded me;	2:22	H. thou eaten of the tree whereof	4:17
O Lord, thou h. said that we	3: 2	this thing which thou h. done?	4:19
h. given us a commandment	3: 2	Because thou h. done this thou	4:20
O Lord, thou h. smitten us	3: 3	Because thou h. hearkened unto	4:23
and h. driven us forth, and for	3: 3	h. eaten of the fruit of the tree	4:23
thou h. been merciful unto us.	3: 3	as thou h. fallen thou mayest be	5: 9
O Lord, that thou h. all power,	3: 4	Lord said: What h. thou done?	5:35
Arise, why h. thou fallen?	3: 7	thou h. drivin me out this day	5:39
thou h. seen that I shall take	3: 9	h. taken Zion to thine own bosom,	7:31
such exceeding faith as thou h.;	3: 9	and thou h. sworn unto me,	7:59
man believed in me as thou h.	3:15	thou h. made me, and given unto	7:59
Lord thou h. made us mighty	12:23	Kokaubeam that thou h. seen,	Abr 3:16
thou h. not made us mighty in	12:23	the intelligences thou h. seen.	3:21
thou h. made all this people	12:23	of the temple, as thou h. said—	JS 1: 2
which thou h. given them;	12:23	which thou h. said concerning	1: 4
thou h. made us that we could	12:24		
thou h. not made us mighty in	12:24	HASTE	
Thou h. also made our words	12:25	Thy children shall make h.	1Ne 21:17
thou h. said that thou hast	12:32	H. thee and get thou and this	Mos 24:23
thou h. prepared a house for	12:32	camp of the Nephites in great h.,	Al 2:23
place which thou h. prepared.	12:32	except we make h. they obtain	2:25
thou h. said that thou hast	12:33	prepare in h. strong cords and	62:21
that thou h. loved the world,	12:33	For ye shall not go out with h.	3Ne 20:42
this love which thou h. had for	12:34	and they shall not go out in h.,	21:29
place which thou h. prepared	12:34	of the gathering be not in h.,	DC 58:56
this thing which thou h. said,	12:35	and preach the word, not in h.,	60: 8
unto thee, thou h. been faithful;	12:37	of the wicked, not in h.,	60:14
thou h. seen thy weakness	12:37	be in h. upon their errand	61: 7
of that which thou h. done	DC 3:10	take their journey in h. that	61: 9
that thou h. lost thy privileges	3:14	take their journey in h.—	61:21
thou h. suffered the counsel of	3:15	them take their journey in h.	61:21
h. translated a few more pages	5:30	unto the land of Zion, not in h.,	63:24
Behold thou h. a gift,	6:10	on his journey, and make h.,	93:51
art thou for what thou h.;	6:14	Williams make h. also,	93:52
for thou h. inquired of me,	6:14	let your gathering be in h.,	101:68
as often as thou h. inquired	6:14	in their time, but not in h.,	101:72
thou h. received instruction of	6:14	let not your flight be in h.,	133:15
that thou h. inquired of me	6:15		
thou h. been enlightened by	6:15	HASTEN	
work which thou h. been writing	6:17	Let him make speed, h. his work,	2Ne 15:19
Behold, thou h. a gift,	11:10	will h. the city in its time,	DC 52:43
as thou h. been baptized by	18: 7	I will h. my work in its time.	88:73
Pay the debt thou h. contracted	19:35	that you should h. to translate	93:53
thou h. been delivered from all	24: 1		
thou h. been delivered from	24: 1	HASTENETH	
after thou h. sowed thy fields	24: 3	The captive exile h.,	2Ne 8:14

HATE 428 HAVING

HATE
your brethren, whom ye h.	Jac	3: 5
that they should h. them,	Mos	10:17
generations of them that h. me;		13:13
thy neighbor and h. thine enemy;	3Ne	12:43
do good to them that h. you,		12:44
either he will h. the one and		13:24
to h. the children of God,	4Ne	1:39
to h. the children of Nephi		1:39
and ye h. me, what will ye say	DC	43:21
children of all them that h. me,		98:46
generation of them that h. me.		103:26
generation of them that h. me.		105:30
they repent not, and h. me,		124:50
they repent not, and h. me,		124:52
a lad, and all the people h. me;	Mses	6:31
and they h. their own blood;		7:33

HATED
and be h. among all nations.	1Ne	19:14
and shall be h. of all men.		22: 5
and are h., and are led	2Ne	1:18
be scattered, and smitten, and h.;		6:11
cursed them, and have h. them,		29: 5
and h. of our brethren,	Jac	7:26
the Lamanites hath he h. because	He	15: 4
and to become h. by them,	3Ne	16: 9
ye shall be h. of all nations,	JS	1: 7
I was h. and persecuted for		2:25

HATH: *see in the APPENDIX.*

HATING
h. even the garments spotted	DC	36: 6

HATRED
for I knew their h. towards me	2Ne	5:14
and their h. towards you	Jac	3: 7
they had an eternal h. against us,		7:24
their h. was fixed,	En	1:20
and become victims to their h.	Mos	1:14
they have an eternal h. towards		10:17
and to exercise their h. upon them.		11:17
cure them of their h. towards		28: 2
their h. became exceeding sore	Al	24: 2
been racked with h. against us,		26: 9
of their love and of their h. to sin.		26:34
h. against sin and iniquity.		37:32
their h. towards the Nephites,		43: 7
extreme h. of the Lamanites		43:11
fathers that has caused their h.,		60:32
weapons of war, and also their h.	He	5:51
their everlasting h. towards you	3Ne	3: 4
united in the h. of those who		7:11
because of their h. they put	Mro	1: 2

HAUGHTINESS
the h. of men shall be bowed	2Ne	12:11
h. of men shall be made low;		12:17
h. of the terrible.		23:11
pride nor h. disturb their peace;	Mos	27: 4

HAUGHTY
the daughters of Zion are h.,	2Ne	13:16
and the h. shall be humbled.		20:33

HAVE: *see in the APPENDIX.*

HAVILAH
compasseth the whole land of H.,	Mses	3:11

HAVING
h. been born of goodly parents,	1Ne	1: 1
and h. seen many afflictions		1: 1
nevertheless, h. been highly favored		1: 1
h. had a great knowledge of the		1: 1
Lehi, h. dwelt at Jerusalem		1: 4
h. great desires to know of the		2:16
also h. received much strength		4:31
h. heard all the words of my		10:17
h. been afflicted with my brethren		16:21
their bows h. lost their springs,		16:21
and h. suffered much grief		18:17

h. need of much nourishment,	1Ne	18:19
h. a knowledge of the creation	2Ne	1:10
h. power given them to do all		1:10
h. all the commandments from		1:10
h. been brought by his infinite		1:10
h. no life neither death,		2:11
h. sought that which was evil		2:17
h. no joy, for they knew no		2:23
I, Jacob, h. been called of God,		6: 2
and h. been consecrated by my		6: 2
h. a perfect knowledge like unto		9:13
h. perfect faith in the Holy One		9:23
h. a live coal in his hand,		16: 6
h. set the example before them.		31: 9
h. a perfect brightness of hope,		31:20
The people h. loved Nephi	Jac	1:10
he h. been a great protector		1:10
h. wielded the sword of Laban in		1:10
h. labored in all his days for		1:10
h. first obtained mine errand		1:17
h. ministered much unto		4: 1
and h. all these witnesses		4: 6
of Christ unto God, h. faith,		4:11
h. rejected the sure foundation,		4:17
h. been wrought upon by the	En	1:26
began to be old; and, h. no seed,	Om	1:25
all these h. been punished	WM	1:16
there h. been much contention		1:16
h. been taught in the language	Mos	1: 4
h. his tent with the door thereof		2: 6
h. transgressed the law of God		2:33
h. received a remission of		4: 3
and h. peace of conscience,		4: 3
after h. finished speaking to		6: 1
h. with them one Ammon,		7: 3
who h. entered into a treaty with		7:21
and h. yielded up into his hands		7:21
h. traveled in a land among		8: 8
h. discovered a land which was		8: 8
h. discovered a land which had		8: 8
h. been taught in all the		9: 1
and h. had a knowledge of		9: 1
and h. been sent as a spy among		9: 1
after h. told all these things		10:19
and h. subjected the flesh to		15: 2
h. gained the victory over death;		15: 9
H. ascended into heaven,		15: 9
h. the bowels of mercy;		15: 9
h. broken the bands of death,		15: 9
h. redeemed them, and satisfied		15: 9
h. salvation declared unto them.		15:24
H. gone according to their own		16:12
h. never called upon the Lord		16:12
h. counseled with his priests,		17: 6
h. suffered death by fire;		17:20
h. been put to death because he		17:20
h. sealed the truth of his words by		17:20
h. received its name from the king,		18: 4
h. been infested, by times or at		18: 4
h. authority from the Almighty		18:13
Alma, h. authority from God,		18:18
h. one faith and one baptism,		18:21
h. their hearts knit together in		18:21
h. the knowledge of God,		18:26
h. been commanded of God;		18:29
h. discovered a movement among		18:32
returned, h. searched in vain		19: 1
were small, h. been reduced,		19: 2
h. the kingdom conferred upon		19:26
h. tarried in the wilderness,		20: 4
h. decreed the daughters of the		20: 4
h. been wounded and left upon		20:12
he h. received a wound		20:13
the king h. been without the gates		21:23
h. supposed it to be the land of		21:26
h. arrived in the borders of		21:26
h. been warned of the Lord that		23: 1
h. made it known to his people,		23: 1
every church h. their priests and		25:21
after h. translated and caused to		28:11
by h. an unrighteous king to		29:35
h. conferred the office upon him,		29:42

HAVING

and h. given him the charge	Mos 29:42
h. lived to fulfil the	29:45
h. gone the way of all the earth,	Al 1: 1
h. warred a good warfare,	1: 1
h. abundance of all things	1:29
h. no respect to persons as to	1:30
h. much dispute and wonderful	2: 5
h. prayed mightily to him that	2:28
after h. buried those who had	3: 1
h. seen the afflictions of the	4:15
h. been consecrated by my father,	5: 3
he h. power and authority from	5: 3
h. a remembrance of all your	5:18
h. the image of God engraven	5:19
h. your garments stained with	5:22
astray, as sheep h. no shepherd,	5:37
h. been sanctified by the Holy	5:54
h. many sheep doth not watch	5:59
there h. been a city built,	6: 7
I h. been wholly confined to	7: 1
h. had much business that I	7: 1
h. great hopes and much desire	7: 3
h. your garments spotless even as	7:25
after h. taught the people of	8: 1
h. established the order of the	8: 1
h. been commanded of God that	9: 1
after h. had so much light	9:19
h. been such a highly favored	9:20
after h. been favored above every	9:20
after h. had all things made known	9:20
H. been visited by the Spirit of	9:21
h. conversed with angels, and	9:21
h. been spoken unto by the voice	9:21
and h. the spirit of prophecy,	9:21
after h. been delivered of God	9:22
h. been saved from famine,	9:22
they h. waxed strong in battle,	9:22
h. been brought out of bondage	9:22
h. been kept and preserved until	9:22
h. no one to confer it upon,	10:19
h. much business to do among	10:31
they h. been established by king	11: 4
he h. subjected them according to	12:17
miserable, h. no preparatory state;	12:26
they h. first transgressed the	12:31
after h. made known unto them	12:32
therefore they h. chosen good,	13: 3
h. their garments made white,	13:12
h. exercised mighty faith,	13:18
H. faith on the Lord;	13:29
h. a hope that ye shall receive	13:29
h. the love of God always in your	13:29
the people h. heard a great noise	14:29
exceeding sore, h. no deliverance;	15: 3
h. forsaken all his gold,	15:16
Alma h. established the church	15:17
Alma h. seen all these things,	15:18
h. been much peace in the land	16: 1
h. been no wars nor contentions	16: 1
h. heard that he had the spirit of	16: 5
the Lamanites h. been driven out	16: 9
h. got the victory over the devil,	16:21
h. had much success in bringing	17: 4
H. taken leave of their father,	17: 6
h. refused the kingdom which	17: 6
h. blessed them according to	17:18
h. imparted the word of God	17:18
h. heard of the fame of Ammon,	19: 2
of darkness h. been dispelled,	19: 6
she h. been converted unto	19:16
h. been converted to the Lord,	19:17
and never h. made it known,	19:17
h. this wicked spirit rooted out of	22:15
And now I, after h. said,	22:35
h. fled into the east wilderness,	25: 5
and h. usurped the power and	25: 5
after h. suffered much loss and	25: 6
even as a sheep h. no shepherd is	25:12
Alma h. received tidings that the	31: 1
after h. been instruments in the	35:14
and h. been to declare the word,	35:15
h. no space for repentance;	42: 5
h. placed his army according to	Al 43:33
h. pursued after them in vain;	47:30
h. the same instruction and the	47:36
h. been instructed in the same	47:36
he h. accomplished his designs	48: 2
h. been made king over the	48: 2
h. filled the judgment-seat with	50:37
h. established peace between	51: 1
h. commenced the twenty and	51: 1
h. no hopes of meeting them	52:21
and h. an unconquerable spirit,	52:33
h. been prepared in its strength.	55:13
after h. traveled much in the	58:23
h. restored peace to the land	62:11
h. inflicted death upon all those	62:11
h. taken many prisoners,	62:30
h. regained many of the Nephites	62:30
h. been out by night, and	He 2: 6
h. obtained, through disguise,	2: 6
h. usurped the power and	7: 4
with faith, h. a contrite spirit,	8:15
h. great power and authority	11:18
h. many revelations daily,	11:23
h. no place for refuge,	15:12
h. not understood the scriptures.	3Ne 1:24
h. proved them in the field of	3: 4
and h. so great a number,	4: 4
h. reserved for themselves	4: 4
people h. been delivered up	6:17
h. been visited by angels and	7:15
therefore h. seen angels, and	7:15
h. had power given unto him	7:15
H. authority given me of Jesus	11:25
The Father h. raised me up	20:26
after h. healed all their sick,	26:15
h. been commanded of the Lord	Mrm 6: 6
we h. survived the dead of	6:11
h. been cleansed by the blood	9: 6
h. this perfect knowledge of	Eth 3:20
were twelve, he h. four sons.	6:20
h. seen exceeding many days,	9:15
H. all manner of fruit, and of	9:17
h. dwelt in captivity all his days.	11:23
I, Moroni, h. heard these words,	12:29
h. studied, himself, in all the arts	13:16
Coriantumr, h. lost his blood,	14:30
h. shields, and breastplates, and	15:15
h. made an end of abridging	Mro 1: 1
h. a determination to serve him	6: 3
h. authority from God;	8:16
real intent, h. faith in Christ,	10: 4
after h. received the record of	DC 1:29
h. faith, hope, and charity,	12: 8
I h. accomplished and finished	19: 2
h. done this that I might	19: 2
Therefore, h. so great witnesses,	20:13
h. a determination to serve	20:37
church of Christ h. children	20:70
H. been commissioned of Jesus	20:73
h. done all, that ye may be	27:15
h. your loins girt about with	27:16
h. on the breastplate of	27:16
that whoso h. knowledge,	29:49
all h. corrupt minds.	33: 4
whoso h. faith you shall confirm	33:15
h. your lamps trimmed and	33:17
among you h. twelve sons,	38:26
h. put away their companions	42:74
use it in vain, h. not authority.	63:62
forgive not, h. not compassion,	64:13
H. denied the Holy Spirit after	76:35
Holy Spirit after h. received it,	76:35
h. denied the Only Begotten	76:35
h. crucified him unto	76:35
h. received of his fulness	76:94
h. power to shut up the heavens,	77: 8
angels h. the everlasting gospel,	77: 9
unto a man h. a field,	88:51
God h. redeemed man from the	93:38
h. power to determine the	102:22
h. a knowledge of them by the	107:71
h. all the gifts of God which he	107:92

HAVING

h. bodies of flesh and bones.—	DC	129: 1
h. many wives and concubines.—		132: 1
h. his Father's name written		133:18
h. the everlasting gospel,		133:36
Press dispatches h. been sent		OD
h. entered into a covenant with	Mses	5:49
Enoch, h. known their secret,		5:49
h. a language which was pure		6: 6
h. been myself a follower of	Abr	1: 2
My fathers h. turned from		1: 5
to go, h. looked around me,	JS	2:15
h. a form of godliness, but		2:19
h. been forbidden to join any		2:28
which h. done, he informed me		2:45
H. related these things,		2:45
H. removed the earth, I obtained		2:52
a silver mine h. been opened		2:56
my h. been a money-digger.		2:56
h. gone as usual at the end of		2:59
h. been teaching school in		2:66
of my h. received the plated,		2:66
and h. laid his hands upon us,		2:68
of h. received the Priesthood		2:74
and our h. been baptized,		2:74

HAVOC
these robbers did make great h.,	He	11:27

HAWS, Peter
servant H., organize themselves,	DC	124:62
servant H., receive any stock		124:70

HE: see in the APPENDIX.

HEAD

Laban by the hair of the h.,	1Ne	4:18
I smote off his h. with his own		4:18
after I had smitten off his h.		4:19
saw the h. thereof a little way off;		8:14
and at the h. thereof I beheld		8:14
eyes towards the h. of the river,		8:17
also led by the h. of the fountain,		8:20
lie at the h. of all the streets;	2Ne	8:20
crown of the h. of the daughters		13:17
and the h.-bands, and the tablets,		13:20
the h. of Syria is Damascus,		17: 8
and the h. of Damascus, Rezin;		17: 8
the h. of Ephraim is Samaria,		17: 9
the h. of Samaria is Remaliah's son.		17: 9
the h., and the hair of the feet;		17:20
h. and tail, branch and rush		19:14
The ancient, he is the h.;		19:15
may become the h. of their corner?	Jac	4:17
under this h. ye are made free,	Mos	5: 8
and there is no other h. whereby		5: 8
yea, at the h. of his armies,	Al	2:16
was called under that h., and		3:10
lift up thy h. and rejoice,		8:15
and did h. the flocks of the king,		17:32
by the h. of the river Sidon,		22:27
at the h. of the river Sidon,		22:29
which was high above the h.,		31:13
a hair of the h. shall not be lost;		40:23
by the h. of the river Sidon,		43:22
arm-shields,a nd their h.-plates;		43:38
in two many of their h.-plates,		43:44
he fastened on his h.-plate,		46:13
might place himself at their h.		47: 8
at the h. of his army, perhaps he		49:10
breastplates, and their h.-plates,		49:24
by the h. of the river Sidon—		50:11
to h. the people of Moriantom,		50:33
they did not h. them until they		50:34
and there they did h. them,		50:34
down, at the h. of the Lamanites.		51:12
Helaman did march at the h. of		53:22
did march at the h. of these		56: 9
durst they cross the h. of Sidon,		56:25
first commenced at our h.,		60:15
the great h. of our government.		60:24
with arrows, and with h.-plates,	He	1:14
at the h. of his numerous host,		1:19
an army round about to h. them		1:28

430 HEADS

and he did h. them before they	He	1:29
did h. them in their retreat,		1:30
were at the h. of government;		3:23
office at the h. of government,		7: 5
is in our great and Eternal H.		13:38
Lift up your h. and be of good	3Ne	1:13
they had h.-plates upon them;		4: 7
did place at their h. a man		7: 9
shalt thou swear by the h.,		12:36
when thou fastest, anoint thy h.,		13:17
forth at the h. of an army of	Mrm	2: 2
thou shalt go at the h. of them	Eth	1:42
unto me the h. of my father,		8:10
unto me the h. of my father,		8:12
Akish desired should lose his h.;		8:14
the h. of his father-in-law,		9: 5
and breastplates, and h.-plates,		15:15
he smote off the h. of Shiz.		15:30
had smitten off the h. of Shiz,		15:31
a hair of your h. shall not be	DC	9:14
him who is at thy h.,		28: 6
and at the h. of the church;		28: 6
great blessings upon thy h.;		39: 8
that there may be a h.,		46:29
as ye are appointed to the h.,		50:30
upon the h. of Simonds Ryder.		52:37
a hair of his h. shall not fall to		84:80
let not the h. say unto the		84:109
a hair of his h. shall not fall to		84:116
I have set thee to be at the h.;		107:55
their decision upon his h. shall		107:83
upon the h. of the church.		107:92
the hair of his h. was white		110: 3
I seal upon his h. the office of		124:57
anointing have I put upon his h.,		124:57
put upon the h. of his posterity		124:57
blessing upon the h. of Ephraim		133:34
his two counselors at their h.,		136: 3
and he shall bruise thy h.,	Mses	4:21
at the h. of the plain of Olishem.	Abr	1:10
of eternal light upon his h.;	Fac	2: 3
with a crown upon his h.,		3: 1
the characters above his h.		3: 2
of light exactly over my h.,	JS	2:16
His h. and neck were also bare.		2:31
messenger standing over my h.,		2:49
I laid my hands upon his h.		2:71

HEAD-BANDS: see HEAD and BANDS.

HEADED

and h. the armies of Amalickiah.	Al	46:32
had h. his people in his flight.		51:29
that he h. Amalickiah also,		51:30

HEAD-PLATE: see HEAD and PLATE.

HEAD-PLATES: see HEAD and PLATES.

HEADS

shall turn upon their own h.;	1Ne	22:13
shall fall upon their own h.,		22:13
upon the h. of your parents.	2Ne	4: 6
holiness shall be upon their h.;		8:11
and lift up your h. forever,		9: 3
and not hang down our h.,		10:20
They wear stiff necks and high h.;		28:14
these things upon your own h.;		29: 5
I should engraven the h. of them	Jac	1: 4
sins of the people upon our own h.		1:19
and wear stiff necks and high h.		2:13
lift up your h. and receive the		3: 2
their sins be heaped upon your g.		3:10
with sorrow upon their own h.	En	1:10
and their h. shaven;		1:20
lift up your h. be comforted;	Mos	7:18
lift up your h., and rejoice,		7:19
and they had their h. shaved		10: 8
Lift up your h. and be of good		24:13
be answered upon their own h.		29:30
upon the h. of their kings.		29:31
might lift up their h. and rejoice;	Al	1: 4
had not shorn their h. like unto		3: 4

HEADS 431 HEAR

h. of the Lamanites were shorn; Al 3: 5
the wrath of God upon their h., 10:18
as a hair of their h. be lost; 11:44
causing them to lift up their h. 30:18
that they may not lift up their h., 30:23
also shields to defend their h., 43:19
their bare h. were exposed to 44:18
upon your h. for vengeance; 60:10
and their h. were shorn, 3Ne 4: 7
poured out upon their h., 10:18
their iniquities upon their own h., 20:28
their works upon their own h. 27:32
for vengeance upon your h.? Mrm 8:40
by the earth, and by their h., Eth 8:14
with a blessing upon their h. DC 25:12
with crowns upon their h., 29:12
be poured forth upon their h. 39:15
by the h. of the church. 42:11
upon the h. of the rebellious, 56: 4
everlasting joy upon their h. 66:11
be upon the h. of the parents. 68:25
of my blessings upon their h., 70:15
judgments fall upon your h. 82: 2
sins are upon their own h. 88:82
are two divisions or grand h.— 107: 6
crowns of glory upon our h., 109:76
lift up your h. and rejoice. 110: 5
upon the h. of my people. 110:10
the h. of the Latter-day Saints. 121:33
to the h. of government in all 123: 6
blessings upon the h. of the poor 124:21
and judgments upon your own h., 124:48
h. of those who hindered my work, 124:50
gnashing of teeth upon their h., 124:52
upon the h. of all my people, 124:92
the h. of all their oppressors. 127: 3
hath been sealed upon their h., 132:19
shall be answered upon their h.; 133:41
parted, and became into four h. Mses 3:10
swear thy brethren by their h., 5:29
upon the h. of the children, 6:54
be upon the h. of their fathers; 7:37
have glory added upon their h. Abr 3:26
parted and became into four h. 5:10
the firmament over our h.; Fac 1:12

HEAL
that he should h. the nations 2Ne 25:20
and he shall h. them, 26: 9
them that they would h. him. Al 15: 5
h. him according to his faith 15:10
not believe that it would h. them. 33:20
converted, that I may h. him. 3Ne 9:13
them hither and I will h. them, 17: 7
sufficient that I should h. you. 17: 8
and he did h. them every one 17: 9
of heart, and I shall h. them; 18:32
Yet I will h. him, for I will show 21:10
that they did h. the sick, 4Ne 1: 5
they shall h. the sick; DC 35: 9
it is given to have faith to h. 46:20
name they shall h. the sick; 84:68
be converted, and I will h. them. 112:13
h. the sick, he shall cast out devils, 124:98
will h. him that he shall be healed; 124:104

HEALED
h. by the power of the Lamb 1Ne 11:31
a way that they might be h.; 17:41
and be converted and be h. 2Ne 16:10
and with his stripes we are h. Mos 14: 5
of Christ thou canst be h. Al 15: 8
if ye could be h. by merely casting 33:21
your eyes that ye might be h., 33:21
and were h. of their sicknesses 3Ne 7:22
Spirit of God, and had been h.; 7:22
they who had been h. and they 17:10
after having h. all their sick, 26:15
and have not faith to be h., DC 42:43
hath faith in me to be h., 42:48
unto death shall be h. 42:48
is given to have faith to be h.; 46:19
will heal him that he shall be h.; 124:104

HEALER
saying: I will not be a h.; 2Ne 13: 7

HEALETH
word which h. the wounded soul. Jac 2: 8

HEALING
with h. in his wings; 2Ne 25:13
consloing and h. their wounds; Jac 2: 9
miracles, such as h. the sick, Mos 3: 5
arise with h. in his wings; 3Ne 25: 2
of miracles and of h. did cease Mrm 1:13
nor prophecies, nor gifts, nor h., 9: 7
gifts of h. by the same Spirit; Mro 10:11
casting out devils, h. the sick, DC 24:13
prophecy, revelation, visions, h., AoF 7

HEALINGS
by gifts, or by tongues, or by h., 3Ne 29: 6

HEALTH
shall receive h. in their navel DC 89:18
the weary traveler may find h. 124:23

HEALTHFUL
house shall be a h. habitation DC 124:24

HEAPED
their sins be h. upon your heads Jac 3:10
which was h. upon them. Al 1:25
and have been h. up on the earth. 2:38
which were h. upon them by 4:15
h. up upon the face of the earth, 16:11
h. up as dung upon the face of Mrm 2:15

HEAPETH
that h. upon him persecutions? Al 5:30

HEAPING
ye are h. up for yourselves wrath He 8:25

HEAPS
thousands are moldering in h., Al 28:11
h. of earth round about all the 50: 1
cast up mighty h. of earth Eth 10:23
should become as h. of earth 11: 6

HEAR
after them, and they did h. me; 1Ne 4:29
things did my father see, and h., 9: 1
I might see, and h., and know 10:17
were gathered together to h. him; 11:28
H. ye the words of the prophet, 19:24
h. ye the words of the prophet, 19:24
h. this, O house of Jacob, 20: 1
assemble yourselves, and h.; 20:14
him shall ye h. in all things 22:20
who will not h. that prophet 22:20
h. the words of a trembling parent, 2Ne 1:14
mine ear to h. as the learned. 7: 4
h. now this, thou afflicted, 8:21
wo unto the deaf that will not h.; 9:31
them forever, that h. my words. 10:14
and tell this people—H. ye indeed, 16: 9
h. with their ears, and understand 16:10
H. ye now, O house of David; 17:13
for the living to h. from the dead? 18:19
the deaf h. the words of the book, 27:29
unto us, and h. ye our precept; 28: 5
I know that he will h. my cry. 33: 3
to h. the pleasing word of God, Jac 2: 8
Wherefore, my brethren, h. me, 2:27
h. the words of me, a prophet of 5: 2
Yea, today, if ye will h. his voice, 6: 6
to the temple to h. the words Mos 1:18
to the temple to h. the words 2: 1
in their tents and h. the words 2: 6
his people might h. the words 2: 7
they could not all h. his words 2: 8
you that can h. my words 2: 9
open your ears that ye may h., 2: 9
and h. the words which I shall 3: 3
and the deaf to h., 3: 5

HEAR

call your attention, that ye may h.	Mos	4: 4
but that ye h. and know the		5:12
that thereby they might h. and		6: 3
to the temple to h. the words		7:17
And God did h. our cries and did		9:18
I will be slow to h. their cries;		11:24
I will not h. their prayers, neither		11:25
as many as would h. his word		18: 3
went thither to h. his words.		18: 6
to h. the words of Alma.		18: 7
believed on his word, to h. him.		18: 7
to h. the word of the Lord		18:32
Lord was slow to h. their cry		21:15
the Lord did h. their cries,		21:15
the Lord did h. my cries,		23:10
could they all h. the word of God		25:20
he that will h. my voice shall		26:21
that he that will not h. my voice,		26:28
to all who desired to h. them.		27:35
to h. the word of God.	Al	1:26
the Lord did h. their cries,		2:28
that ye h. the voice of the Lord,		5:16
I would that ye should h. me,		5:43
together to h. the word of God.		6: 5
quick to h. the cries of his people		9:26
many times and I would not h.;		10: 6
only wait to h. the joyful news		13:25
as many as would h. their words,		16:14
did h. with great joy and gladness.		16:20
who would not h. his words;		19:32
not h. the words which he spake.		21:10
that they would not h. his words,		21:11
a preparation to h. the word.		32: 6
my prayer, and thou didst h. me.		33: 5
thou didst h. me in my prayer.		33: 6
unto thee thou didst h. me.		33: 7
of men, and thou wilt h. them.		33: 8
yea, thou didst h. my cries,		33:10
thou didst h. me because of		33:11
that thou wilt h. my words and		36: 3
but I did not h. them		36:11
the earth and I did h. no more.		36:11
of their children to h. the word		39:16
our prisoners did h. their cries,		57:32
that ye would h. my words!	He	13:39
And ye shall h. my words, for, for		14:11
that ye might h. and know of		14:11
of the land did h. these sayings,	3Ne	10: 3
and all the people did h.,		11: 3
it did pierce them that did h.		11: 5
third time they did h. the voice,		11: 5
did open their ears to h. it;		11: 5
glorified my name—h. ye him.		15:17
and they shall h. my voice;		15:21
and they shall h. my voice;		15:23
I said they shall h. my voice;		15:23
not at any time h. my voice—		16: 3
and that they shall h. my voice,		17:25
see and h. and bear record;		17:25
they all of them did see and h.,		19:33
And the multitude did h. and		20:23
him shall ye h. in all things		20:23
who will not h. that prophet		27: 9
my name the Father will h. you;		30: 1
h. the words of Jesus Christ,	4Ne	1: 5
their sight, and the deaf to h.;		1:12
and to h. the word of the Lord.	Mrm	9:30
know that ye shall h. my words.	Eth	1:40
Lor did h. the brother of Jared,	DC	1: 2
neither ear that shall not h.,		1:11
that all that will h. may hear:		1:11
that all that will h. may h.:		1:14
will not h. the voice of the Lord,		14: 8
you shall both h. and see,		24: 6
and write, and they shall h. it,		29: 7
for mine elect h. my voice		29:17
cleanse them if they h. me not.		34: 1
hearken and h. and behold		35: 9
and the deaf to h.,		35:21
For they will h. my voice,		38: 6
that will not h. my voice but		38:22
h. my voice and follow me,		38:29
h. of wars in far countries,		

432

Hearken and h., O ye my	DC	41: 1
all blessings, ye that h. me;		41: 1
ye that h. me not will I curse,		41: 1
hearken and h. and obey the		42: 2
He who hath faith to h. shall		42:50
who hath faith to hear shall h.		42:50
the ears of all tingle that h.,		43:22
h. the words of that God who		43:23
h. my voice while it is		45: 6
the ends of the earth shall h. it;		45:49
Ye h. of wars in foreign lands;		45:63
h. of wars in your own lands.		45:63
shall h. my voice and see me,		50:45
and h. the word of the Lord		63: 1
h. the word of him whose anger		63: 2
my church, hearken ye and h.,		64: 1
and h. the word of the Lord		70: 1
wherefore hearken and h.,		70: 2
H., O ye heavens, and give ear,		76: 1
h. the voice of the Son of Man,		76:16
you who now h. my words,		84:60
that which you h. is as the		88:66
and all nations shall h. it.		88:94
for every ear shall h. it,		88:104
they h. the sound of the trump,		88:104
may h. his words carefully		88:129
every man shall h. the fulness of		90:11
wise men and rulers may h.		101:94
h. us in these our petitions,		109:77
O h., O hear, O hear us, O Lord!		109:78
O hear, O h., O hear us, O Lord!		109:78
O hear, O hear, O h. us, O Lord!		109:78
let him h. with his ears,		127: 6
and also to h. with his ears,		128: 2
Who can h. it?		128: 9
what do we h. in the gospel		128:19
And again, what do we h.?		128:20
how glorious is the voice we h.		128:23
h. the word of the Lord		133: 1
Hearken and h., O ye inhabitants		133:16
and h. the voice of the Lord;		133:16
their prophets shall h. his voice,		133:26
his ears opened that he may h.;		136:32
H. my voice, ye wives of Lamech,	Mses	5:47
And they came forth to h. him,		6:38
to him, for to h. him, saying:	JS	1: 1
and you also shall h. of wars,		1:23
And they shall h. of wars,		1:28
is My Beloved Son. H. Him!		2:17
who would not h. his voice		2:40

HEARD

and he saw and h. much;	1Ne	1: 6
the things which he saw and h.		1: 6
which he had both seen and h.		1:18
the things which he saw and h.,		1:19
when the Jews h. these things		1:20
when my father had h. these words		3: 8
when I, Nephi, had h. these words,		4:14
h. all the words of my father,		10:17
I h. thunderings, and earthquakes,		12: 4
thou also hast h. that whoso		14: 5
I, Nephi, h. and bear record,		14:27
of the things which I saw and h.;		14:28
ye have h. his voice from time		17:45
Thou hast seen and h. all this;		20: 6
acceptable time have I h. thee,		21: 8
things which I have seen and h.	2Ne	4:16
he hath h. my cry by day,		4:23
I h. the voice of the Lord, saying:		16: 8
cause it to be h. unto Laish,		20:30
the noise of thy viols is not h.;		24:11
prayers of the faithful shall be h.,		26:15
I h. a voice from the Father,		31:15
h. the mourning of the daughters	Jac	2:31
I had h. the voice of the Lord		7: 5
for I have h. and also know that		7: 6
for I have h. and seen;		7:12
for he had h. my cry and		7:22
I had often h. my father speak	En	1: 3
hast never before h. nor seen.		1: 8
when I had h. these words		1: 9
I, Enos, had h. these words,		1:11

HEARD 433 HEARD

things which I had h. and seen.	En	1:19
the Lord hath h. thy prayers,	Mos	3: 4
in the faith of what ye have h.		4:30
people had h. nothing from them		7: 1
after Limhi had h. the words of		7:14
for the Lord h. his prayers and		10:13
when king Noah had h. of the		11:27
when the king had h. these words,		13: 1
has h. the words of the prophets,		15:11
when the people had h. these		18:11
Limhi had h. nothing concerning		20:16
when Gideon had h. these things		20:17
when Alma had h. these words		26:33
the Lord hath h. the prayers of		27:14
which they had h. and seen,		27:32
the things which they had h.,		28: 1
h. by the people round about;	Al	12: 2
people having h. a great noise		14:29
when he h. that Alma and		15: 4
there was a cry of war h.		16: 1
having h. that he had the spirit of		16: 5
when the king h. these words,		18: 4
h. that Ammon was preparing		18:10
thou hast h. that I defended		18:16
when the king had h. these words,		18:18
having h. of the fame of Ammon,		19: 2
h. from the mouth of Ammon;		19:31
as many as h. his words believed,		19:31
that when Ammon had h. this,		20: 3
when Lamoni had h. this he caused		20: 6
when his father had h. these words,		20:16
And now when Aaron h. this,		22: 8
that when Ammon had h. this,		27:25
mourning and lamentation h.		28: 4
thus the cry of mourning was h.		28: 5
even that he hath h. my prayer;		29:10
and his sons had h. these prayers,		31:19
And now when Alma h. this,		32: 6
for thou hast h. my prayer,		33: 4
to be h. of thee and not of men,		33: 8
and h. my cries in the midst of		33: 9
thou hast also h. me when I have		33:10
which were h. by my brethren,		36:11
for when I h. the words—If thou		36:11
h. my father prophesy unto		36:17
that they pray to be h. of men,		38:13
that when Zerahemnah had h.		44: 8
many, when they h. these words		44:15
that he was never h. of more;		45:18
had h. of these dissensions,		46:11
when they h. these words,		47:28
had h. that the king was slain—		47:32
h. that the Lamanites were		51:13
Lamanites had h. these words,		52:38
the Lamanites h. these words		55: 9
had h. these words of Gid,		57:36
that they were never h. of more.		63: 8
things which he had seen, and h.,	He	2: 9
when they h. this voice, and beheld		5:30
when they h. this they cast up		5:48
who saw and h. these things;		5:49
which they had h. and seen,		5:50
garden of Nephi, and h. his words,		9:11
who h. the words of Samuel,		16: 1
he was never h. of more among		16: 8
and wonders which they had h.,	3Ne	2: 1
all which they had h. and seen—		2: 1
one place they were h. to cry,		8:24
they were h. to cry and mourn,		8:25
there was a voice h. among all		9: 1
the people had h. these words,		10: 8
they h. a voice as if it came out		11: 3
not the voice which they h.;		11: 3
that again they h. the voice,		11: 4
the voice which they h.;		11: 6
Ye have h. that it hath been said		12:21
be h. for their much speaking.		13: 7
ye have h. the things which I		15: 1
both h. my voice, and seen me;		15:24
have not as yet h. my voice;		16: 2
did bear record who h. him.		17:15
seen, neither hath the ear h.,		17:16

as we saw and h. Jesus speak	3Ne	17:16
we both saw and h. Jesus speak;		17:17
the time we h. him pray for us		17:17
the multitude h. not the words		18:37
have they h. so great things as		19:36
so great things as ye have h.		19:36
Jesus, whom they both saw and h.		20: 9
and that which they had not h.		20:45
and that which they had not h.		21: 8
heathen, such as they have not h.		21:21
and the Lord hearkened and h.;		24:16
both saw and h. these children;		26:16
saw and h. unspeakable things,		26:18
which they had both h. and seen,		27: 1
things which ye have ssen and h.,		27:23
saw and h. unspeakable things.		28:13
things which they saw and h.;		28:14
things which they had h. and seen,		28:16
which I have both seen and h.,	Mrm	1: 1
the things which I saw and h.,		3:16
him whom they saw and h.,		3:21
shall be h. of fires, and tempests,		8:29
there shall also be h. of wars,		8:30
things which ye have seen and h.	Eth	3:21
things which ye have seen and h.,		3:21
Moroni, having h. these words,		12:29
and the multitude h. it not,	Mro	2: 3
but the disciples h. it;		2: 3
that you have h. my voice,	DC	18:36
have h. and bear witness to		20:16
and his prayers I have h.		21: 7
thou shalt be h. by the church		28: 1
yea, wherever you can be h.,		30:10
I have h. thy prayers,		35: 3
for I have h. your prayers,		38:16
h. of wars and rumors of wars,		45:26
which they have seen and h.		52:36
that I have h. your prayers;		53: 1
that which he hath seen and h.		64:19
whose prayers I have h.,		67: 1
eye hath not seen, nor ear h.,		76:10
we h. the voice bearing record		76:23
And we h. the voice, saying:		76:49
for we saw and h.,		76:50
And h. the voice of the Lord		76:110
the things which ye have h.,		80: 1
whose prayers I have h.,		96: 6
after the evidences are h.		102:18
After the evidences are h.,		102:19
I have h. their prayers,		105:19
thy servants, have h. thy voice,		109:57
I have h. thy prayers;		112: 1
have h. thy prayers concerning		112:11
h. with his ears, giving the date,		128: 3
with his eyes and h. with his ears,		128: 4
h. a voice repeat the following:		130:14
shall be h. among all people;		133:21
have not men h. nor perceived		133:45
And his voice shall be h.:		133:50
and he h. a voice, saying:	Mses	1:25
they h. the voice of the Lord God,		4:14
I h. thy voice in the garden,		4:16
they h. the voice of the Lord		5: 4
his wife, h. all these things and		5:11
And he h. a voice from heaven,		6:27
when Enoch had h. these words,		6:31
came to pass when they h. him,		6:39
fear came on all them that h. him;		6:39
And he h. a voice out of heaven,		6:66
the roar of the lions was h. out		7:13
and he h. a loud voice saying:		7:25
he h. a voice from the bowels		7:48
when Enoch h. the earth mourn,		7:49
And he h. a loud voice;		7:56
also, after that they had h. him,		8:21
the Lord hearkened and h.,	Abr	1:15
Jehovah, and I have h. thee,		1:16
saw a light, and h. a voice;	JS	2:24
h. a voice speaking unto him,		2:24
what I had both seen and h.		2:46
and h. him rehearse or repeat		2:46
He had h. something of a		2:56

HEARDEST 434 HEARKEN

HEARDEST
the day when thou h. them not   1Ne 20: 7
Yea, and thou h. not;   20: 8

HEARER
was no better then the h.,   Al 1:26

HEARERS
esteeming himself above his h.,   Al 1:26

HEAREST
h. him revile against this people   He 8: 2
in me because thou h. them,   3Ne 19:22

HEARETH
whoso h. these sayings of mine   3Ne 14:24
one that h. these sayings of mine   14:26

HEARING
reprove after the h. of his ears.   2Ne 21: 3
in the h. of the multitude: Mrm 9:22
are now h. these words of mine   DC 50:36
after h. the evidences and   102:20
has been read in our h.,   OD
and their ears are dull of h.,   Mses 6:27

HEARKEN
would not h. unto my words;   1Ne 2:18
not h. unto the commandments   4:11
if he would h. unto my words,   4:32
if he would h. unto our words,   4:32
that they would h. to his words,   8:37
shall h. unto the Lamb of God   14: 1
would h. unto the word of God,   15:24
were willing to h. to the truth,   16: 3
we would h. unto his words;   17:22
h. not to the voice of his counsels.   19: 7
H. and hear this, O house   20: 1
H. unto me, O Jacob,   20:12
H., O ye house of Israel,   21: 1
and h. ye people from far;   21: 1
that ye would h. unto my words.   2Ne 1:12
will h. unto the voice of Nephi   1:28
And if ye will h. unto him   1:28
if ye will not h. unto him   1:29
h. unto his great commandments;   2:28
h. unto the words of the book.   3:23
h. unto the words of thy brother,   3:25
they did h. unto my words.   5: 6
they will not h. unto thy words   5:20
and h. unto my words,   5:25
H. unto me, ye that follow   8: 1
H. unto me, my people;   8: 4
H. unto me, ye that know   8: 7
if they will h. unto his voice;   9:21
they h. not unto the counsel of   9:28
they h. unto the counsels of God.   9:29
H. diligently unto me,   9:51
and h. unto soothsayers   12: 6
Wherefore, h., O my people,   25: 4
righteous that h. unto the words   26: 8
unto the people: H. unto us,   28: 5
h. unto my precept;   28: 6
those who h. unto my precepts,   28:30
h. unto the precepts of men,   28:31
if ye would h. unto the Spirit   32: 8
h. unto these words and believe   33:10
But behold, h. ye unto me,   Jac 2: 5
and h. to the word of the Lord: 2:27
they shall h. unto these things.   2:30
my brethren, h. unto my word;   3:11
H., O ye house of Israel,   5: 2
h. unto the voice of the Lord   Om 1:12
h. unto the voice of the Lord;   1:13
that you should h. unto me,   Mcs 2: 9
would not h. unto his words;   7:25
h. unto the voice of the Lord;   16: 2
h. unto the words of the Lord,   20:21
ye will not h. unto his voice!   Al 5:37
if ye will not h. unto the voice of   5:38
and if you will h. unto his voice   5:60
not h. unto the words of Alma.   8: 9
that ye would h. unto my words,   Al 13:27
Wilt thou h. unto my words,   18:22
would not h. unto their words,   20:30
would not h. unto the words.   35: 3
not h. to the words of Helaman   46: 1
would h. unto their words.   48:19
h. to the words of Morianton   50:32
he did not h. to those who had   51: 3
they would not h. to the words   He 4: 3
h. unto the words of the Lord—   7: 7
ye will not h. unto the voice of   7:18
their sins, and h. unto my words.   7:23
h. unto the words of the Lord.   10:13
would not h. unto his words;   10:15
they would not h. unto his words;   10:18
O Lord, wilt thou h. unto me,   11:13
thou didst h. unto my words   11:14
at this time, h. unto my words,   11:14
h. unto the words of the evil one,   12: 4
and h. unto the voice of the Lord   12:23
great city, and h. unto my words;   13:21
h. unto the words which the Lord   13:21
not h. to the epistle of Giddianhi,   3Ne 3:12
unto me, and h. unto my voice,   16:15
repent and h. unto my words,   21:22
whosoever will h. unto my words   23: 5
not h. unto the words of Jesus,   28:34
H., O ye Gentiles, and hear the   30: 1
h. unto the words of the Lord.   Mrm 9:27
would not h. unto their words;   Eth 11:13
H., O ye people of my church,   DC 1: 1
H. ye people from afar;   1: 1
will not h. unto my words;   5: 5
H., my servant John, and listen   15: 1
H., my servant Peter, and listen   16: 1
H. unto the voice of the Lord   25: 1
as many as will h. to my voice   29: 2
h. to the voice of the Lord   33: 1
and h. unto my voice.   33: 6
My son Orson, h. and hear   34: 1
H. and listen to the voice of   39: 1
if thou wilt h. to my voice,   39:10
H. and hear, O ye my people,   41: 1
H., O ye elders of my church   41: 2
H., O ye elders of my church,   42: 1
h. and hear and obey the law   42: 2
O h., ye elders of my church,   43: 1
h. ye elders of my church,   43:15
H. ye, for, behold, the great   43:17
H., O ye nations of the earth,   43:23
H. ye to these words.   43:34
H., O ye people of my church,   45: 1
h. ye and give ear to him who   45: 1
again I say, h. unto my voice,   45: 2
H., O ye people of my church,   45: 6
h. ye together and let me show   45:11
h. and I will reason with you,   45:15
H., O ye people of my church;   46: 1
H. unto my word, my servants   49: 1
H., O ye elders of my church,   50: 1
H. unto me, saith the Lord your   51: 1
H., O ye people who profess   56: 1
H., O ye elders of my church,   57: 1
H., O ye elders of my church,   58: 1
h. unto the voice of him who   61: 1
h., O ye elders of my church,   62: 1
H., O ye people, and open your   63: 1
h. ye and hear, and receive my   64: 1
H., and lo, a voice as of one   65: 1
h., O ye elders of my church,   67: 1
H. unto me, saith the Lord your   69: 1
h., O ye inhabitants of Zion,   70: 1
wherefore h. and hear, for thus   70: 2
H., and listen to the voice of   72: 1
H., O ye who have given your   75: 2
H. unto me, saith the Lord your   78: 1
h. to the calling wherewith   81: 1
They were slow to h. unto   101: 7
slow to h. unto their prayers,   101: 7
they will h. unto this counsel   101:74
willing to h. to my voice.   101:75
they did not h. altogether   103: 4

HEARKEN 435 HEART

inasmuch as they h. from this	DC 103: 5
h. not to observe all my words,	103: 8
and h. to the voice of my Spirit.	112:22
therefore, h. to your counsel,	124:13
And if my people will h.	124:45
But if they will not h. to	124:46
h. to the counsel of my servant	124:89
if he will h. unto my voice,	124:110
let him h. unto the counsel	124:112
h. unto the counsel of my	124:118
H., O ye people of my church,	133: 1
H. and hear, O ye inhabitants	133:16
them that h. not to the voice	133:63
h., O ye people of my church;	136:41
even as many as would not h.	Mses 4: 4
except thou shalt h. unto	5:23
of Lamech, h. unto my speech;	5:47
would not h. unto his voice,	5:57
turn unto me, and h. unto my	6:52
for they will not h. to my voice.	8:15
H., and give heed unto my	8:23
refused to h. to my voice;	Abr 1: 5
when they h. to my voice.	2: 6
do well to h. unto thy voice,	2:13

HEARKENED
he h. unto the words of Laman.	1Ne 3:28
not h. unto the word of the Lord?	7: 9
not h. unto the words of the Lord?	17:23
O that thou hadst h. to my	20:18
and h. no more to the words of	Jac 7:23
who have h. unto their words,	Mos 15:11
hast hitherto h. unto my words	22: 3
king h. unto the words of Gideon.	22: 9
not h. unto the words of him who	He 13:21
and the Lord h. and heard;	3Ne 24:16
they h. not unto the voice of	Eth 11: 7
and they h. not unto the	DC 101:50
have not h. unto my words.	105:17
who have h. unto my words,	105:18
h. unto the voice of thy wife,	Mses 4:23
But behold, Cain h. not,	5:16
h. unto the voice of the Lord.	5:17
Adam h. unto the voice of God,	6: 1
and his sons h. unto the Lord,	8:13
they h. not unto his words;	8:20
h. not unto the words of Noah.	8:21
upon you; nevertheless they h. not.	8:24
and h. not unto my voice,	Abr 1: 7
and the Lord h. and heard,	1:15

HEARKENETH
wo be unto him that h. unto	2Ne 28:26
he h. unto the voice of	Al 5:41
the devil, for he h. unto his voice,	5:41
h. to the voice of the Spirit.	DC 84:46
that h. to the voice of the Spirit	84:47

HEARKENING
were capable of h. unto them;	Al 54: 7
by h. to observe all the words	DC 103: 7

HEART
with all his h., in behalf of his	1Ne 1: 1
and his whole h. was filled,	1:15
foolish imaginations of his h.	2:11
soften my h. that I did believe	2:16
diligently, with lowliness of h.	2:19
kill Laban; but I said in my h.:	4:10
did soften the h. of Ishmael,	7: 5
as I sat pondering in mine h.	11: 1
foolish imaginations of his h.;	17:20
because of you, and my h. is pained;	17:47
Then shalt thou say in thine h.:	21:21
My h. hath been weighed down	2Ne 1:17
that my h. might leave this world	1:21
in one mind and in one h.,	1:21
broken h. and a contrite spirit;	2: 7
according to the feelings of his h.	4:12
and my h. pondereth them,	4:15
and my h. pondereth continually	4:16
my h. exclaimeth:	4:17
my h. sorroweth because of	4:17

my h. groaneth because of	2Ne 4:19
why should my h. weep	4:26
have place in my h. to destroy	4:27
Rejoice, O my h., and give place	4:28
Rejoice, O my h., and cry unto	4:30
my h. is broken and my spirit is	4:32
in whose h. I have written my law,	8: 7
unto the uncircumcised of h.,	9:33
my h. delighteth in righteousness;	9:49
Make the h. of this people fat,	16:10
and understand with their h.,	16:10
And his h. was moved,	17: 2
the h. of his people, as the trees	17: 2
in the pride and stoutness of h.:	19: 9
neither doth his h. think so;	20: 7
but in his h. it is to destroy	20: 7
the stout h. of the king of Assyria,	20:12
every man's h. shall melt;	23: 7
For thou hast said in thy h.:	24:13
my h. doth magnify his holy name.	25:13
the meek and the poor in h.,	28:13
the Son, with full purpose of h.,	31:13
in the presence of the pure in h.,	Jac 2:10
in heart, and the broken h.,	2:10
my h. would rejoice exceedingly	2:22
unto you that are pure in h.	3: 1
O all ye that are pure in h.,	3: 2
unto you that are not pure in h.,	3: 3
come with full purpose of h.,	6: 5
sunk deep into my h.	En 1: 3
and ask in sincerity of h. that	Mos 4:10
the thoughts and intents of his h.?	5:13
the Lord with full purpose of h.,	7:33
after the desires of his own h.	11: 2
he placed his h. upon his riches,	11:14
And king Noah hardened his h.	11:29
do this work with holiness of h.	18:12
repenteth in the sincerity of his h.,	26:29
lifted up in the pride of his h.,	Al 1: 6
mighty change wrought in his h.	5:12
with a pure h. and clean hands?	5:19
experienced a change of h.,	5:26
Nevertheless, I did harden my h.,	10: 6
in the wickedness of my h.,	10: 6
thou hadst in thy h. to retain	11:25
thoughts and intents of his h.;	12: 7
he that will harden his h.,	12:10
he that will not harden his h.,	12:10
and hardeneth not his h.,	12:34
whosoever will harden his h.	12:35
from the inmost part of my h.,	13:27
his h. began to take courage;	15: 4
his h. was swollen within him	17:29
thou the thoughts of my h.?	18:20
the thoughts and intents of the h.;	18:32
his h. was swollen within him,	19:13
his h. began to rejoice, and he	22: 8
full, yea, my h. is brim with joy,	26:11
could have the wish of mine h.	29: 1
judge saw the hardness of his h.,	30:29
because of the hardness of your h.,	30:46
his h. again began to sicken	31: 1
his h. was exceeding sorrowful	31: 2
Alma saw this his h. was grieved;	31:24
my h. is exceeding sorrowful;	31:31
and also they were poor in h.	32: 3
of whom were poor in h.,	32: 4
I behold that ye are lowly in h.;	32: 8
are brought to a lowliness of h.;	32:12
without stubbornness of h.,	32:16
seed may be planted in your h.,	32:28
his h. was exceeding sorrowful.	35:15
I cried within my h.: O Jesus,	36:18
and to be meek and lowly in h.,	37:33
but to be meek and lowly in h.;	37:34
the affections of thy h. be placed	37:36
let thy h. be full of thanks unto	37:37
to lead away your h. again	39:11
have full sway in your h.,	42:30
commandments with all my h.	45: 7
he laid the plan in his h. to	47: 4
he stabbed the king to the h.;	47:24
have stabbed him to the h.,	47:26

HEART

a man whose h. did swell with	Al	48:12
and his h. did glory in it;		48:16
and put a javelin to his h.;		51:34
ye are in the h. of our country		60:19
rejoice in the greatness of your h.		61: 9
his h. did take courage,		62: 1
which did pierce him near the h.		62:36
not come into the h. of their lands	He	1:18
his h. took courage insomuch		1:22
known all the h. of Kishkumen,		2: 8
stab Kishkumen even to the h.,		2: 9
put into the h. of Gadianton		6:26
it into the h. of Gadianton		6:29
his h. was swollen with sorrow		7: 6
the exceeding sorrow of my h.,		7:14
ye fools, ye uncircumcised of h.,		9:21
was thus pondering in his h.,		10: 3
things should come into his h.		13: 3
things the Lord put into his h.		13: 4
which he doth put into my h.;		13: 5
he hath put it into my h. to say		13: 5
whatsoever your h. desireth—		13:27
a change of h. unto them—		15: 7
his h. was exceedingly sorrowful.	3Ne	1:10
and in holiness of h., that they		4:29
a broken h. and a contrite spirit.		9:20
a broken h. and a contrite spirit,		9:20
unto me with full purpose of h.		10: 6
blessed are all the pure in h.,		12: 8
a broken h. and a contrite spirit.		12:19
unto me with full purpose of h.,		12:24
adultery already in his h.		12:28
these things to enter into your h.;		12:29
there will your h. be also.		13:21
unto me with full purpose of h.,		18:32
turn the h. of the fathers to		25: 6
and the h. of the children to		25: 6
my h. did begin to rejoice	Mrm	2:12
my h. had been filled with sorrow		2:19
my h. did sorrow because of		2:27
which was in me, with all my h.;		3:12
and every h. was hardened, so		4:11
unto the Lord with all your h.,		9:27
of wickedness, and hardness of h.,	Eth	4:15
broken h. and a contrite spirit,		4:15
had set his h. upon the kingdom		8: 7
put it into his h. to search up		8:17
Jared put it into the h. of Akish;		8:17
he began to sorrow in his h.;		15: 2
a broken h. and a contrite spirit,	Mro	6: 2
and not with real intent of h.;		7: 9
shall be meek, and lowly of h.		7:43
save the meek and lowly in h.;		7:44
a man be meek and lowly in h.,		7:44
Father with all the energy of h.,		7:48
meekness, and lowliness of h.;		8:26
meekness and lowliness of h.		8:26
Behold, my h. cries:		9:15
ye shall ask with a sincere h.,		10: 4
h. that shall not be penetrated.	DC	1: 2
serve him with all your h.,		4: 2
faith, in the sincerity of his h.,		5:24
and the intents of thy h.		6:16
treasure up these words in thy h.		6:20
you cried unto me in your h.,		6:22
ask in faith, with an honest h.,		8: 1
in your mind and in your h.,		8: 2
which shall dwell in your h.		8: 2
in faith, with an honest h.,		11:10
cleave unto me with all your h.,		11:19
treasure up in your h. until		11:26
do with full purpose of h.,		17: 1
name with full purpose of h.		18:27
name with full purpose of h.,		18:28
vocally as well as in thy h.;		19:28
lifting up thy h. for gladness?		19:39
of sins unto the contrite h.		21: 9
thy h. shall be opened to preach		23: 2
and thy h. is opened, and thy		23: 3
delighteth in the song of the h.;		25:12
lift up thy h. and rejoice,		25:13
ever lifting up your h. unto me		30: 6
Lift up your h. and rejoice,	DC	31: 3
and be meek and lowly of h.		32: 1
thoughts and intents of the h.		33: 1
embrace it with singleness of h.		36: 7
thine h. is now right before me		39: 8
the h. of my servant James		40: 1
his h. is pure before me,		41:11
love thy wife with all thy h.,		42:22
and repents with all his h.,		42:25
shalt not be proud in thy h.;		42:40
before you in all lowliness of h.		42:74
with one h. and with one mind,		45:65
should do in all holiness of h.,		46: 7
the poor who are pure in h.,		56:18
that you may lay it to h.,		58: 5
unbelief and blindness of h.,		58:15
commandment with doubtful h.,		58:29
Lord thy God with all thy h.,		59: 5
even that of a broken h. and		59: 8
prepared with singleness of h.		59:13
but with a glad h. and a		59:15
the eye and to gladden the h.;		59:18
but he that is upright in h.		61:16
a thankful h. in all things.		62: 7
he exalted himself in his h.,		63:55
that shall go with an open h.		64:22
the Lord requireth the h. and a		64:34
for the murmurings of his h.;		75: 7
entered into the h. of man.		76:10
Wherefore, let your h. be glad,		79: 4
always, vocally and in thy h.,		81: 3
hardeneth his h. against it,		82:21
all the pure in h. that		97:16
THE PURE IN H.;		97:21
I have decreed in my h.,		98:14
forgive him with all thine h.;		98:45
in my name, in solemnity of h.,		100: 7
that remain, and are pure in h.,		101:18
Lord, have decreed in my h.,		104: 5
as I did the h. of Pharaoh,		105:27
the vanity of his h.,		106: 7
holiness, and lowliness of h.,		107:30
been sore few things in thine h.		112: 2
Let thy h. be of good cheer		112: 4
I know thy h., and have heard		112:11
will do this in all lowliness of h.,		118: 3
thing h. shall be softened		121: 3
let thine h. be softened,		121: 4
in the fury of thine h.,		121: 5
While the pure in h., and the wise,		122: 2
and to all the pure in h.—		123:11
because of the integrity of his h.,		124:15
because of the integrity of his h.,		124:20
who have been pure in h.,		124:54
neither let his h. faint;		124:75
he shall turn the h. of the fathers		128:17
h. of the children to their fathers,		128:17
and the Son dwell in a man's h.		130: 3
prepare thy h. to receive and		132: 3
and make her h. to rejoice.		132:56
vengeance which was in my h.		133:51
if ye do this with a pure h.,		136:11
Satan put it into the h. of the	Mses	4: 6
were of one h. and one mind,		7:18
his h. swelled wide as eternity;		7:41
Lift up your h., and be glad;		7:44
of the thoughts of his h.,		8:22
Noah, and his h. was pained		8:25
and it grieved him at the h.		8:25
I said in my h.:	Abr	2:12
God shall take in his h. to do		3:17
evil servant shall say in his h.:	JS	1:51
more power to the h. of man		2:12
into every feeling of my h.		2:12
offer up the desire of my h.		2:15
I was led to say in my h.:		2:25

HEARTED

fear not, neither be faint-h.	2Ne	17: 4
hard-h. and a stiffnecked people.	Al	9: 5
hard-h. and a stiffnecked people.		9:31
hard h. and a stiffnecked people;		15:15

HEARTHOM

HEARTHOM
Heth, who was the son of H.	Eth	1:16
And H. was the son of Lib.		1:17
and he also begat H.		10:29
H. reigned in the stead of his		10:30
when H. had reigned twenty		10:30

HEARTS
because of the hardness of their h.	1 Ne	2:18
grieved for the hardness of their h.,		7: 8
it that ye are so hard in your h.,		7: 8
that they did soften their h.;		7:19
in the h. of the children of men;		11:22
hardeneth the h. of the children		12:17
blind the eyes and harden the h.		13:27
harden not their h. against him		14: 2
be that they harden their h. against		14: 6
them to the hardness of their h.		14: 7
they being hard in their h.,		15: 3
because of the hardness of their h.,		15: 4
because of the hardness of your h.?		15:10
If ye will not harden your h.,		15:11
because they had hardened their h.		16:22
Laman stir up their h. to anger.		16:38
because of the hardness of their h.;		17:19
they were glad in their h.,		17:19
they hardened their h. and blinded		17:30
for they hardened their h.,		17:41
And they did harden their h.		17:42
ye are murderers in your h.		17:44
that ye can be so hard in your h.?		17:46
not soften the h. of my brethren		18:19
destruction, could soften their h.;		18:20
turn their h. aside, rejecting signs		19:13
because they turn their h. aside,		19:14
no more turn aside their h.		19:15
him will they harden their h.;		22: 5
have no more power over the h.		22:15
that they will harden their h.		22:18
for he hath no power over the h.		22:26
lest for the hardness of your h.	2 Ne	1:17
they had hardened their h.		5:21
they have hardened their h.		6:10
their h. are upon their treasures;		9:30
Let your h. rejoice.		9:52
soften the h. of the Gentiles,		10:18
cheer up your h., and remember		10:23
these words may lift up their h.		11: 8
nevertheless, they hardened their h.;		25:10
and the hardness of their h.,		25:12
with pure h. and clean hands,		25:16
that they need not harden their h.		25:27
removed their h. far from me,		27:25
shall be puffed up in their h.,		28: 9
puffed up in the pride of their h.,		28:15
shall he rage in the h. of the		28:20
shall have power over the h. of		30:18
ye ponder somewhat in your h.		32: 1
ye ponder these things in your h.?		32: 1
that ye ponder still in your h.;		32: 8
carrieth it untothe h. of the		33: 1
are many that harden their h.		33: 1
began to grow hard in their h.,	Jac	1:15
the wickedness of your h.		2: 6
lifted up in the pride of your h.,		2:13
not this pride of your h. destroy		2:16
because ye were proud in your h.,		2:20
broken the h. of your tender wives,		2:35
sobbings of their h. ascend up		2:35
many h. died, pierced with deep		2:35
how that ye have grieved their h.		3:10
receive them with thankful h.,		4: 3
many as will not harden their h.		6: 4
of the day, harden not your h.		6: 5
hear his voice, harden not your h.;		6: 6
lead away the h. of the people,		7: 3
that he did lead away many h.;		7: 3
because of the hardness of their h.,	Jar	1: 3
did prick their h. with the word,		1:12
your h. that ye may understand,	Mos	2: 9
in the h. of the children of men.		3: 6
and yet they hardened their h.,		3:15
and our h. may be purified;		4: 2
your h. should be filled with joy,	Mos	4:20
I would that ye say in your h.		4:24
And now, if ye say this in your h.		4:25
a mighty change in us, or in our h.,		5: 2
ye say that your h. are changed		5: 7
name be not blotted out of your h.		5:11
name written always in your h.,		5:12
because they hardened their h.		10:14
lifted up in the pride of their h.		11: 5
lifted up in the pride of their h.;		11:19
therefore they hardened their h.		11:29
for they have hardened their h.		12: 1
applied your h. to understanding;		12:27
do ye set your h. upon riches?		12:29
it cuts you to your h. because I		13: 7
they are not written in your h.;		13:11
because of the hardness of their h.;		13:32
if this be the desire of your h.,		18:10
This is the desire of our h.		18:11
having their h. knit together		18:21
they had sworn in their h. that		19:19
to soften the h. of the Lamanites		21:15
to serve God with all their h.;		21:35
soften the h. of the Lamanites,		23:28
did soften the h. of the Lamanites.		23:29
did pour out their h. to him;		24:12
did know the thoughts of their h.		24:12
and their h. were hardened.		26: 3
stealing away the h. of the people;		27: 9
the h. of many were hardened,	Al	1:24
not set their h. upon riches;		1:30
much joy in the h. of those who		2: 8
and to set their h. upon riches		4: 8
Behold, he changed their h.;		5: 7
change was also wrought in their h.,		5:13
this mighty change in your h.?		5:14
puffed up in the pride of your h.;		5:53
your h. upon the vain things of		5:53
lifted up in the pride of their h.–		6: 3
lifted up in the pride of your h.;		7: 6
have not set your h. upon riches		7: 6
hold upon the h. of the people		8: 9
they hardened their h.,		8:11
seeing that your h. have been		9:30
got such great hold upon your h.?		10:25
the lawyers put it into their h. that		10:30
And they that will harden their h.,		12:11
if our h. have been hardened,		12:13
hardened our h. against the word,		12:13
repent, and harden not your h.,		12:33
that if ye will harden your h.		12:36
repent, and harden not our h.,		12:37
account of the hardness of their h.		13: 4
such as would not harden their h.,		13: 5
the h. of the children of men		13:24
the love of God always in your h.,		13:29
to the hardness of their h.,		14:11
checked as to the pride of their h.,		15:17
to prepare their h. to receive		16:16
the h. of the sons of Mosiah,		17:12
their h. were set upon riches,		17:14
that I may win the h. of these		17:29
that their h. had been changed;		19:33
that they should harden their h.,		21: 3
the thought and intent of our h.?		21: 6
the people would harden their h.,		21:12
hardness of the h. of the people,		22:22
but they did harden their h.,		23:14
and also the h. of the Lamanites		23:14
of his spirit to soften our h.,		24: 8
taken away the guilt from our h.,		24:10
to take them away from our h.,		24:11
whose h. had swollen in them		24:24
whose h. delight in the shedding		26:24
Now when our h. were depressed,		26:27
hold on the h. of the Amalekites,		27:12
will try the h. of our brethren,		27:15
to ensnare the h. of men.		28:13
leading away the h. of many,		30:18
that causes such joy in their h.?		30:35
away the h. of this people,		30:45
lead away the h. of this people;		30:55
leading the h. of the people to		31: 1

HEARTS

doth lead their h. to wander far	Al	31:17
their h. were not stolen away		31:22
that their h. were set upon gold,		31:24
that their h. were lifted up unto		31:25
yet their h. are swallowed up in		31:27
their h. are set upon them,		31:28
said must be planted in their h.;		33: 1
ot the hardness of their h.,		33:20
rather harden your h. in unbelief,		33:21
shall plant this word in your h.,		33:23
to plant the word in your h.,		34: 4
unto the Lord, let your h. be full,		34:27
harden not your h. any longer;		34:31
repent and harden not your h.,		34:31
but in the h. of the righteous		34:36
seeing that the h. of the people		35:15
who are now hardening their h.		37:10
did steal away the h. of many;		39: 4
lead away the h. of many people		39:12
ye lead away the h. of no more		39:13
the desires of their h. were good,		41: 3
and inspired their h. with these		43:48
proud, being lifted up in their h.,		45:24
he led away the h. of many		46:10
gained the h. of the people.		47:30
inspire the h. of the Lamanites		48: 1
inspire their h. against them		48: 2
had hardened the h. of the		48: 3
the h. of the children of men.		48:17
Morianton put it into their h.		50:29
stirred up the h. of the people of		51: 9
they were glad in their h.;		51:13
led away the h. of many people,		61: 4
in the sincerity of their h.,	He	3:27
into the h. of the people who		3:33
the sanctification of their h.,		3:35
their yielding their h. unto God.		3:35
into the h. of the people;		3:36
because of the pride of their h.,		4:12
their h. did take courage.		5:24
and did enter into their h.,		5:45
set their h. upon their riches;		6:17
Satan did stir up the h. of the		6:21
put it into the h. of the people		6:28
the h. of the children of men.		6:30
upon the h. of the Nephites;		6:31
and the hardness of their h.		6:35
got so great hold upon your h.		7:15
you have hardened your h.;		7:18
set your h. upon the riches		7:21
ye have suffered to enter your h.,		7:26
told us the thoughts of our h.,		9:41
they did harden their h. and		10:13
they did still harden their h.		10:15
the h. of the children of men;		12: 1
softening the h. of their enemies		12: 2
that they do harden their h.,		12: 2
set their h. upon the vain things		12: 4
hardness of the h. of the people		13: 8
turn the h. of their brethren		13: 8
will harden their h. against me,		13:12
have set their h. upon riches;		13:20
set their h. upon their riches,		13:20
ye have set your h. upon them,		13:21
h. are not drawn out unto the Lord,		13:22
after the pride of your own h.;		13:27
people began to harden their h.,		16:15
people imagine up in their h.,		16:22
harden the h. of the people		16:22
hold upon the h. of the people		16:23
by Satan, to harden them h.,	3Ne	1:22
they began to be hard in their h.,		2: 1
up some vain thing in their h.,		2: 2
deceive the h. of the people;		2: 2
of the h. of the people again,		2: 2
leading away the h. of the people,		2: 3
their h. were swollen with joy,		4:33
those secret murders in their h.,		5: 5
lead away the h. of the people		6:16
h. were turned from the Lord		7:14
for the hardness of their h.		7:16
and did cause their h. to burn.		11: 3
he stirreth up the h. of men		11:29

stir up the h. of men with anger,	3Ne	11:30
up in the pride of their h.		16:10
can the h. of men conceive so		17:17
and their h. were open and they		19:33
they did understand in their h.		19:33
not cease to pray in their h.		20: 1
shall harden their h. against me		20:28
if they will not harden their h.,		21: 6
words, and harden not their h.,		21:22
And they sorrowed in their h.,		28: 5
ye need not imagine in your h.		29: 3
dwell in the h. of the people.	4Ne	1:15
who did get hold upon their h.		1:28
the people did harden their h.,		1:31
the people did harden their h.,		1:34
began to be proud in their h.,		1:43
of the hardness of their h.;	Mrm	1:17
of the hardness of their h.		1:17
broken h. and contrite spirits,		2:14
harden their h. against the Lord		3: 3
of the hardness of their h.		3:12
stir up the h. of the children of		4: 5
up in the pride of their h.;		8:28
shall rise in the pride of their h.,		8:28
do walk in the pride of your h.;		8:36
up in the pride of their h.,		8:36
because of the pride of your h.		8:36
hath hardened the h. of men	Eth	8:25
the h. of the children of men,		8:26
had corrupted the h. of all the		9: 6
they won the h. of the people,		9:10
the people hardened their h.,		11:13
power over the h. of the people;		15:19
up unto the hardness of their h.,		15:19
may have place in their h.,	Mro	7:32
they harden their h. against it;		9: 4
of the hardness of their h.;		9:10
of the wilfulness of their h.,		9:23
and ponder it in your h.		10: 3
plant in the h. of the children	DC	2: 2
the h. of the children shall		2: 2
harden their h. against them;		5:18
Satan hath put it into their h.		10:10
put into their h. to do this,		10:13
put it into their h. to get thee		10:15
say and think in their h.–		10:16
has great hold upon their h.;		10:20
And their h. are corrupt,		10:21
stirreth up their h. to anger		10:24
harden the h. of the people		10:32
generation harden not their h.,		10:53
stir up the h. of the people		10:63
they will not harden their h.;		10:65
the h. of the children of men,		19: 7
harden their h. in unbelief,		20:15
come forth with broken h.		20:37
turning the h. of the fathers		27: 9
the h. of the children to the fathers,		27: 9
lift up your h. and rejoice,		27:15
Lift up your h. and be glad,		29: 5
and harden not their h.;		29: 7
to prepare their h. and be		29: 8
will open the h. of the people,		31: 7
Lift up your h. and be glad,		35:26
my voice but harden their h.,		38: 6
neither your h. of unbelief,		38:14
if you seek it with all your h.		38:19
ye know not the h. of men in		38:29
Lift up your h. and rejoice,		42:69
these things up in your h.,		43:34
and harden not your h.;		45: 6
and men's h. shall fail them,		45:26
they turn their h. from me		45:29
harden their h. against me,		45:33
the h. of the children of men.		45:55
And your h. are not satisfied.		56:15
whose h. are not broken,		56:17
whose h. are broken, and whose		56:18
that your h. might be prepared		58: 6
Then they say in their h.:		58:33
of men should open their h.		58:52
cheerful h. and countenances,		59:15
their sins with humble h.,		61: 2

HEARTS

open your h. and give ear from	DC 63: 1
commit adultery in their h.,	63:16
Satan putteth it into their h.	63:28
those who desire in their h.,	63:57
not one another in their h.;	64: 8
ye ought to say in your h.—	64:11
They sought evil in their h.,	64:16
the h. of the children of men.	64:22
heard, and whose h. I know,	67: 1
there were fears in your h.,	67: 3
sought in your h. knowledge	67: 5
are willing to open their h.	75:25
seeketh to turn their h. away	78:10
as they united their h. and	84: 1
But they hardened their h.	84:24
for their evil h. of unbelief,	84:76
my Spirit shall be in your h.,	84:88
in whose h. the enemy,	86: 3
that it may abide in your h.,	88: 3
with you to ponder in your h.,	88:62
ponder the warning in their h.	88:71
yea, purify your h., and	88:74
men's h. shall fail them;	88:91
thoughts and intents of their h.,	88:109
in the h. of conspiring men	89: 4
the h. of the children of men	96: 5
who know their h. are honest,	97: 8
let your h. be comforted;	98: 1
turn the h. of the children to	98:16
and the h. of the fathers to	98:16
the h. of the Jews unto the	98:17
Let not your h. be troubled;	98:18
ways, the pride of their h.,	98:20
with all their h. and with all	98:47
that I shall put into your h.,	100: 5
and let your h. rejoice;	100:12
let your h. be comforted;	100:15
let your h. be comforted	101:16
let not your h. faint,	103:19
I will soften the h. of those	104:80
I will soften the h. of those	104:81
will soften the h. of the people,	105:27
before thee, with all their h.—	109: 1
prepare the h. of thy saints	109:38
our h. flow out with sorrow	109:48
That their h. may be softened	109:56
Let the h. of your brethren rejoice,	110: 6
let the h. of all my people rejoice,	110: 6
Yea the h. of thousands and tens	110: 9
h. of the fathers to the children,	110:15
if they harden not their h.,	112:13
purify your h. before me;	112:28
Cleanse your h. and your	112:33
warm h. and friendly hands.	121: 9
because their h. are corrupted,	121:13
Because their h. are set so much	121:35
upon the h. of the children,	123: 7
will visit and soften their h.,	124: 9
away their h. from affliction;	124:76
Let your h. rejoice,	128:22
will touch the h. of honest men	135: 7
men, and raged in their h.;	Mses 6:15
for their h. have waxed hard,	6:27
grow up, sin conceiveth in their h.,	6:55
and men's h. failing them,	7:66
For their h. were set to do evil,	Abr 1: 6
Therefore they turned their h. to	1: 7
turned their h. away from me,	1:17
but their h. are far from me,	JS 2:19
plant in the h. of the children	2:39
the h. of the children shall turn	2:39

HEAT

shall the h. nor the sun smite;	1Ne 21:10
in the daytime from the h.,	2Ne 14: 6
be scorched with a burning h.	Al 15: 3
when the h. of the sun cometh	32:38
by the labors and h. of the day.	51:33
should melt with fervent h.,	3Ne 26: 3
shall melt with fervent h.	Mrm 9: 2
water, whether in h. or in cold,	DC 84:92
shall melt with fervent h.;	101:25
curse the land with much h.,	Mses 7: 8

HEATHEN

and he remembereth the h.;	2Ne 26:33
not vain repetitions, as the h.,	3Ne 13: 7
upon them, even as upon the h.,	21:21
the h. nations be redeemed,	DC 45:54
more tolerable for the h.	75:22
the nations, the h. nations,	90:10
of the gods of the h.,	Abr 1: 5
hearts to the sacrifice of the h.	1: 7

HEAVEN

building a tower to get to h.—	T Pg
descending out of the midst of h.,	1Ne 1: 9
a man descending out of h.,	11: 7
Holy Ghost come down out of h.	11:27
of God descending out of h.,	12: 6
the covenants of the Father of h.	22: 9
is written, had fallen from h.;	2Ne 2:17
because he had fallen from h.,	2:18
I, the Lord, the king of h.,	10:14
a far country, from the end of h.,	23: 5
For the stars of h. and the	23:10
How art thou fallen from h.,	24:12
I will ascend into h.,	24:13
the Father of h. and of earth,	25:12
none other name given under h.	25:20
way nor name given under h.	31:21
Creator of h. and earth	Jac 2: 5
power, both in h. and in earth;	7:14
of my Father who was in h.;	7:22
they are received into h.,	Mos 2:41
shall come down from h. among	3: 5
the Father of h. and earth,	3: 8
who created h. and earth,	4: 2
both in h. and in earth;	4: 9
power, both in h. and in earth;	4: 9
that you may be brought to h.,	5:15
all things, in h. and in earth,	5:15
likeness of any thing in h. above,	12:36
of things which are in h. above,	13:12
the Lord made h. and earth,	13:19
Father of h. and of earth.	15: 4
Having ascended into h.,	15: 9
and ascension into h.	18: 2
have place in the kingdom of h.;	Al 5:25
the kingdom of h. is soon at hand,	5:28
the kingdom of h. is soon at hand;	5:50
King of h. shall very soon shine	5:50
inherit the kingdom of h.	5:51
the kingdom of h. is at hand,	7: 9
inherit the kingdom of h.;	7:14
in the kingdom of h.	7:25
the kingdom of h. is nigh at hand;	9:25
for the kingdom of h. is at hand.	10:20
can inherit the kingdom of h.;	11:37
ye inherit the kingdom of h.?	11:37
Father of h. and of earth,	11:39
created all things which are in h.	18:28
all things both in h. and in	22:10
forth his hands towards h.,	31:14
And he lifted up his voice to h.,	31:26
wilt show unto us a sign from h.,	32:17
Christ, and his ascension into h.	40:20
the gate of h. is open unto all,	He 3:28
of God in the kingdom of h.,	3:30
up for yourselves a treasure in h.,	5: 8
for the kingdom of h. is at hand;	5:32
that they did lift their eyes to h.;	5:36
of God did come down from h.,	5:45
angels came down out of h.	5:48
high that they might get to h.	6:28
all things, both things in h.,	8:24
up for yourselves treasures in h.,	8:25
seal on earth shall be sealed in h.;	10: 7
on earth shall be loosed in h.;	10: 7
fire should come down out of h.	13:13
there shall be great lights in h.,	14: 3
many signs and wonders in h.	14: 6
the Father of h. and of earth,	14:12
the Father of h. and of earth,	16:18
at a sign or a wonder from h.,	3Ne 2: 1
began to be men inspired from h.	6:20

HEAVEN

the ascension of Christ into h.	3Ne 10:18	glorified in h. so on earth,	DC 65: 6
a voice as if it came out of h.;	11: 3	their understanding reach to h.;	76: 9
did look steadfastly towards h.,	11: 5	he shall come in the clouds of h.	76:63
their eyes up again towards h.;	11: 8	whose names are written in h.,	76:68
a Man descending out of h.;	11: 8	the stars in the firmament of h.,	76:109
them after his ascension into h.	11:12	Revelator, John, in describing h.,	77: 2
when I am again ascended into h.	11:21	of your Father who is in h.;	78: 4
for theirs is the kingdom of h.	12: 3	For your Father, who is in h.,	84:83
for theirs is the kingdom of h.	12:10	your Father which is in h.,	84:92
great shall be your reward in h.;	12:12	to exert the powers of h.;	84:119
glorify your Father who is in h.	12:16	and the thunder of h.,	87: 6
enter into the kingdom of h.	12:20	both in h. and in the earth,	88:79
by h., for it is God's throne;	12:34	fly through the midst of h.,	88:92
of your Father who is in h.;	12:45	appear a great sign in h.,	88:93
Father who is in h. is perfect.	12:48	there shall be silence in h. for	88:95
of your father who is in h.	13: 1	the curtain of h. be unfolded,	88:95
Our Father who art in h., hallowed	13: 9	the midst of the pillar of h.—	88:97
be done on earth as it is in h.	13:10	flying through the midst of h.,	88:103
for yourselves treasures in h.,	13:20	both in h. and in earth,	88:104
shall your Father who is in h.	14:11	armies, even the hosts of h.	88:112
enter into the kingdom of h.	14:21	and, with uplifted hands to h.,	88:132
will of my Father who is in h.	14:21	with uplifted hands to h.,	88:135
they cast their eyes towards h.,	17:24	the field, and the fowls of h.,	89:14
saw angels descending out of h.	17:24	a voice out of h. saying:	93:15
from them, and ascended into h.	18:39	power, both in h. and on earth,	93:17
that he ascended again into h.	18:39	and upon the earth, and in h.	101:34
when Jesus had ascended into h.,	19: 1	according to the law of h.,	102: 4
and it came down from h.,	19:14	diligently the kingdom of h.	106: 3
angels did come down out of h.	19:14	there was joy in h. when	106: 6
powers of h. shall be in the	20:22	mysteries of the kingdom of h.,	107:19
the power of h. come down	21:25	agreeable to the institution of h.;	107:33
not open you the windows of h.,	24:10	root and branch, from under h.;	109:52
after he had ascended into h.—	26:15	and answer us from h.,	109:77
my glory with the powers of h.	28: 7	to h. without tasting death,	110:13
they were caught up into h.,	28:13	sent down from h. unto you.	112:32
which has given them in h.	28:16	For have I not the fowls of h.,	117: 6
yea, the Eternal Father of h.,	Mrm 6:22	Lord God Almighty, maker of h.,	121: 4
the h. and the earth should be;	9:17	shall be swept from under h.,	121:15
from all other nations under h.,	Eth 2:12	pouring down knowledge from h.	121:33
unto him, by the God of h.,	8:14	connected with the powers of h.,	121:36
should come down out of h.,	13: 3	the powers of h. cannot be	121:36
be a new h. and a new earth;	13: 9	as the dews from h.	121:45
until ye shall rest with him in h.	Mro 7: 3	they are truly manifest from h.—	123:13
Christ hath ascended into h.,	7:27	on earth shall be bound in h.;	124:93
seal both on earth and in h.,	DC 1: 8	on earth shall be loosed in h.	124:93
his sword is bathed in h.,	1:13	For all this there is a reward in h.	127: 4
spake unto him from h.,	1:17	it may be recorded in h.;	127: 7
for from h. will I declare it	5:12	on earth, may be bound in h.;	127: 7
treasures for yourself in h.—	6:27	on earth, may be loosed in h.;	127: 7
inherit the kingdom of h.	6:37	is the record which is kept in h.;	128: 7
inherit the kingdom of h.	10:55	it may be recorded in h.	128: 7
that there is a God in h.,	20:17	on earth shall be bound in h.,	128: 8
the framer of h. and earth,	20:17	on earth shall be loosed in h.	128: 8
And ascended into h., to sit	20:24	on earth shall be recorded in h.,	128: 8
both which are in h., and	27:13	shall not be recorded in h.;	128: 8
I will reveal myself from h.	29:11	binds on earth and binds in h.	128: 9
the stars shall fall from h.,	29:14	a law on earth and in h.,	128: 9
be greater signs in h. above	29:14	*the keys of the kingdom of h.:*	128:10
the h. and the earth shall be	29:23	*on earth shall be bound in h.;*	128:10
a new h. and a new earth.	29:23	*on earth shall be loosed in h.*	128:10
even the h. and the earth,	29:24	*the second man is the Lord from h.*	128:14
a third part of the hosts of h.	29:36	so also are the records in h.	128:14
the kingdom of h.;	33:10	A voice of mercy from h.,	128:19
all the seraphic hosts of h.,	38: 1	Moroni, an angel from h.,	128:20
presence of all the hosts of h.—	38:11	the voice we hear from h.,	128:23
The kingdom of h. is at hand.—	39:19	are two kinds of beings in h.	129: 1
the kingdom of h. is at hand.	42: 7	it is contrary to the order of h.	129: 7
shall utter his voice out of h.,	43:18	a law, irrevocably decreed in h.	130:20
shall utter his voice out of h.,	43:23	but are appointed angels in h.;	132:16
in my glory in the clouds of h.,	45:16	on earth shall be sealed in h.,	132:46
and the stars fall from h.	45:42	on earth shall be retained in h.	132:46
see me in the clouds of h.,	45:44	condemnation on earth and in h.	132:48
out of every nation under h.;	45:69	from one end of h. to the other.	133: 7
neither the angels in h.,	49: 7	crying through the midst of h.,	133:17
both in h. and on the earth,	50:27	flying through the midst of h.,	133:36
the h. and the earth pass away,	56:11	And worship him that made h.,	133:39
greater in the kingdom of h.	58: 2	cometh down from God in h.	133:46
recorded in h. for the angels	62: 3	and divine laws given of h.,	134: 6
and will come down in h.	63:34	lifted up his eyes unto h.,	Mses 1:24
out of every nation under h.	64:42	unto you concerning this h.,	2: 1
shall come down in h.,	65: 5	the beginning I created the h.,	2: 1
the kingdom of h. may come,	65: 6	God, called the firmament h.;	2: 8

HEAVEN 441 HEAVENS

Let the waters under the h. be	Mses 2: 9		right hand hath spanned the h.	1Ne 20:13
lights in the firmament of the h.,	2:14		Sing, O h.; and be joyful,	21:13
lights in the firmament of the h.	2:15		both the h. and the earth,	2Ne 2:14
the firmament of the h. to give	2:17		I clothe the h. with blackness,	7: 3
in the open firmament of h.	2:20		Lift up your eyes to the h.,	8: 6
h. and the earth were finished,	3: 1		for the h. shall vanish away	8: 6
are the generations of the h.	3: 4		that hath stretched forth the h.,	8:13
God, made the h. and the earth;	3: 4		that I may plant the h.	8:16
for in h. created I them;	3: 5		is darkened in the h. thereof.	15:30
God descended out of h.,	6:26		Therefore, I will shake the h.,	23:13
he heard a voice from h.,	6:27		that I rule in the h. above	29: 7
the same is the God of h.,	6:43		voice high that it reached the h.	En 1: 4
and deny the God of h.?	6:43		between the h. and the earth,	Al 1:15
which shall be given under h.,	6:52		but I do not know the h.	18:29
again into the kingdom of h.,	6:59		The h. is a place where God dwells	18:30
the record of h.; the Comforter;	6:61		behold, they saw the h. open;	He 5:48
And he heard a voice out of h.,	6:66		I created the h. and the earth,	3Ne 9:15
there came a voice out of h.,	7: 2		and they saw the h. open,	17:24
time, was taken up into h.	7:21		the h. and the earth should pass	26: 3
that Zion was taken up into h.,	7:23		behold, the h. were opened,	28:13
angels descending out of h.;	7:25		who were caught up into the h.,	28:36
angels descending out of h.,	7:27		with God eternally in the h.	28:40
by the powers of h. into Zion.	7:27		began to swear before the h.	Mrm 3: 9
God of h. looked upon the	7:28		And they did swear by the h.,	3:10
King of Zion, the Rock of H.,	7:53		created the h. and the earth,	9:11
will I send down out of h.;	7:62		art holy and dwellest in the h.,	Eth 3: 2
I dwell in h.; the earth is	Abr 2: 7		the Father of the h. and of	4: 7
were in the firmament of h.	3:13		my command the h. are opened	4: 9
the Gods called the expanse, H.	4: 8		of heaven, and also by the h.,	8:14
Let the waters under the h. be	4: 9		he dwelleth eternally in the h.	Mro 7:28
lights in the expanse of the h.,	4:14		whose throne is high in the h.,	9:26
lights in the expanse of the h.	4:15		the h. and the earth pass	DC 1:38
earth in the open expanse of h.	4:20		created the h. and the earth,	14: 9
represent the pillars of h.,	Fac 1:11		and cause the h. to shake	21: 6
the grand Presidency in H.;	3: 1		I will cause the h. to shake	35:24
in the clouds of h., and all	JS 1: 1		the h. shall shake and the	43:18
and the stars shall fall from h.,	1:33		who made the h. and all the	45: 1
powers of h. shall be shaken.	1:33		the h. and the earth shall pass	45:22
h. and earth shall pass away;	1:35		shown forth in the h. above,	45:40
sign of the Son of Man in h.,	1:36		and the h. also shall shake.	45:48
coming in the clouds of h., with	1:36		and now reigneth in the h.,	49: 6
from one end of h. to the other.	1:37		forth for the h. to be shaken,	49:23
not the angels of God in h.,	1:40		all cases under the whole h.	52:19
my back, looking up into h.	2:20		the Lord, rule in the h. above,	60: 4
all the persecution under h.	2:24		the h. and the earth are in mine	67: 2
conduit open right up into h.,	2:43		Hear, O ye h., and give ear,	76: 1
ascended into h. as before,	2:47		for the h. wept over him—	76:26
messenger from h. descended	2:68		voice out of the h. bore record	76:40
			having power to shut up the h.,	77: 8
HEAVENLY			mine own voice out of the h.;	84:42
you ought to thank your h. King!	Mos 2:19		and the h. have smiled upon	84:101
indebted to your h. Father,	2:34		the starry h. shall tremble.	84:118
your h. Father will also forgive	3Ne 13:14		even the courses of the h. and	88:43
your h. Father feedeth them.	13:26		and lo, the h. were opened,	93:15
your h. Father knoweth that ye	13:32		field, or of the fowls of the h.,	101:24
and partakers of the h. gift.	4Ne 1: 3		the Lord, stretched out the h.	104:14
be partakers of the h. gift.	Eth 12: 8		to have the h. opened unto	107:19
we conversed in the h. vision.	DC 76:14		when thou shalt unveil the h.,	109:74
the h. place, the holiest of all.	76:66		h. were again opened unto us;	110:11
thus we saw, in the h. vision,	76:89		behold from the eternal h.	121: 2
equal in the bonds of h. things,	78: 5		if there be bounds set to the h.	121:30
for the obtaining of h. things.	78: 5		What power shall stay the h.?	121:33
equal in obtaining h. things;	78: 6		behold, the h. withdraw themselves;	121:37
I have given the h. hosts	84:42		if the h. gather blackness,	122: 7
on us by our H. Father,	123: 6		there are three h. or degrees;	131: 1
conforming to that which is h.,	128:14		be eternally bound in the h.;	132:46
and as is the h., such are	128:14		remitted eternally in the h.;	132:46
such are they also that are h.	128:14		that thou wouldst rend the h.,	133:40
before this h. light had	JS 2:43		I clothe the h. with blackness,	133:69
the same h. messenger was	2:44		when I called to you out of the h.;	133:71
after the h. messenger had	2:47		by mine own voice out of the h.,	136:37
same h. messenger delivered	2:59		thereof, and also the h.,	Mses 1:36
blessings from our H. Father.	2:73		The h., they are many, and	1:37
			earth shall pass away, and the h.	1:38
HEAVENS			and lo, and the	6:42
that he saw the h. open,	1Ne 1: 8		he made; the earth is	6:44
Thy throne is high in the h.,	1:14		things which are in the h. above,	6:63
that I saw the h. open;	1:14		I beheld the h. open, and I was	7: 3
I beheld the h. open,	11:27		How is it that the h. weep,	7:28
I beheld the h. open again,	11:30		the whole h. shall weep over them,	7:37
I saw the h. open,	12: 6		should not the h. weep,	7:37
He ruleth high in the h.,	17:39		for this shall the h. weep, yea,	7:40

HEAVENS / HELAMAN

his brethren, and said unto the h.:	Mses	7:44
and the h. were veiled;		7:56
day the h. shall be darkened,		7:61
h. shall shake, and also the earth;		7:61
for I rule in the h. above,	Abr	3:21
and formed the h. and the earth.		4: 1
them in the expanse of the h.,		4:17
will finish the h. and the earth,		5: 1
to form the h. and the earth.		5: 3
of the h. and of the earth,		5: 4
formed the earth and the h.,		5: 4
to be high, or the h.,	Fac	1:12
or the firmament of the h.;		2: 4
revealing through the h. the		2: 7
of the h. shall be shaken,	JS	9:36

HEAVIEST
with the h. of all cursings.	DC	41: 1

HEAVING
waves of the sea h. themselves	DC	88:90

HEAVY
and make their ears h.,	2Ne	16:10
put h. burdens upon their backs,	Mos	21: 3
the h. blows of the Nephites	Al	43:37
h. destruction awaiteth this people,	He	13: 6
they shall be h. and cannot flee;		15: 2
he did tax them with h. taxes;	Eth	10: 5
the persecution so h. upon us	JS	2:61

HEBER: see KIMBALL, Heber C.

HEBREW
we should have written in H.;	Mrm	9:33
the H. hath been altered by us		9:33
if we could have written in H.,		9:33
answering to the H. word,	Fac	1:12
Answers to the H. word		2: 4

HEDGE
and h. not up my way,	2Ne	4:33
I will take away the h. thereof,		15: 5
but I will h. up their ways	Mos	7:29
they should h. up the way	Eth	9:33
and built a h. round about,	DC	101:46
by night, and broke down the h.;		101:51
and built the h. round about,		101:53
breaking down the h. thereof,		101:54
combine to h. up the way;		122: 7

HEED
give h. unto the word of the Lord;	1Ne	15:25
would give h. to the word of God		15:25
the truth, and give h. unto it,		16: 3
to the faith and diligence and h.		16:28
And say unto him: Take h.,	2Ne	17: 4
the h. and diligence which they	Mos	1:16
take h. that ye do not transgress,		5:11
the exceeding diligence and h.	Al	7:26
the h. and diligence which they		12: 9
and they gave h. unto his word,		21:23
slothful to give h. to this compass		37:43
as easy to give h. to the word of		37:44
to give h. to this compass,		37:44
give so much h. unto my words		39: 2
And give h. to their counsel.		39:10
give h. to the words of Helaman		45:23
would not give h. to their words,		45:24
because of their h. and diligence		49:30
give h. unto the words of these	3Ne	12: 1
take h. that ye do not your alms		13: 1
Therefore give h. to my words;		23: 4
take h., my beloved brethren,	Mro	7:14
Listen unto them and give h.,		8:21
neither give h. to the words of	DC	1:14
give h. unto my word, which is		6: 2
give h. unto my words.		6: 2
give h. to my word, which is		11: 2
give h. unto my word.		11: 2
give h. to my word, which is		12: 2
give h. unto my word.		12: 2
give h. with your might,		12: 9
give h. to my word, which is	DC	14: 2
give h. unto my word.		14: 2
but gave no h. unto them.		20:22
church take h. and pray always,		20:33
who are sanctified take h. also.		20:34
give h. unto all his words		21: 4
not given h. unto my Spirit,		30: 2
give h. unto the words and		30: 5
give h. unto these things and		30: 8
give h. to that which is written,		32: 4
shall give h. unto these words		32: 5
by giving h. and doing these		50:35
let him take h. lest he fall.		58:15
I say, let the wicked take h.,		63: 6
gave h. to the traditions of		74: 4
to give diligent h. to the		84:43
earnest h. unto your sayings,		93:48
take h. that ye see to this		96: 4
And if he h. them not,		101:87
if the governor h. them not,		101:88
if the president h. them not,		101:89
to give h. to the light and glory		124: 6
unto the Lord, and gave h.,	Mses	8:13
and give h. unto my words;		8:23
Take h. that no man deceive	JS	1: 5

HEEDED
but we h. them not.	1Ne	8:33
For as many as h. them, had		8:34

HEEL
those that shall lift up the h.	DC	121:16
cannot lay hold upon his h.,		124:99
and thou shalt bruise his h.	Mses	4:21

HEIGHT
built up to the h. of a man,	Al	50: 2
and earth, to an exceeding h.		53: 4
mountains, whose h. is great.	He	14:23
because of its exceeding h.,	Eth	3: 1
the width, the h., the depth,	DC	76:48

HEIGHTS
depths, or in the h. above.	2Ne	17:11
I will ascend above the h. of		24:14
dominions, all h. and depths—	DC	132:19

HEIR
I became a rightful h.,	Abr	1: 2

HEIRS
are the h. of the kingdom of God.	Mos	15:11
and h. to the kingdom of God.	4Ne	1:17
who shall be h. of salvation	DC	7: 6
h. according to the covenant.		52: 2
h. according to the laws of		70: 8
they shall be h. of salvation.		76:88
For ye are lawful h., according		86: 9
he and his h. shall hold that stock,		124:69

HELAM
Alma took H., he being one of	Mos	18:12
H., I baptize thee, having		18:13
both Alma and H. were buried in		18:14
and they called the land H.		23:19
exceedingly in the land of H.;		23:20
which they called the city of H.		23:20
while they were in the land of H.,		23:25
Helam, yea, in the city of H.,		23:25
together in the city of H.;		23:26
took possession of the land of H.		23:29
they discovered the land of H.,		23:35
round about the land of H.,		23:37
of them returned to the land of H.,		23:38
who were in the land of H.,		23:39
of thy fathers in the land of H.,		27:16
and also in the land of H.,	Al	24: 1

HELAMAN
Mosiah, and Helorum, and H.	Mos	1: 2
with him, and his name was H.;	Al	31: 7
of Alma to his son H.,		36:hd
And now, O my son H., behold,		36: 3

HELAMAN 443 HELL

And now, my son H.,	Al	37: 1
O remember, remember my son H.,		37:13
I command you, my son H.,		37:20
unto you, even as I said unto H.,		38: 1
dissensions, in the days of H.,		45:hd
according to the record of H.,		45:hd
that Alma came unto his son H.		45: 2
And H. said unto him:		45: 3
Alma had said these things to H.,		45:15
h. went forth among the people		45:20
H. and his brethren went forth		45:22
after H. and his brethren had		45:23
words of H. and his brethren;		45:23
not hearken to the words of h.		46: 1
preaching of H. and his brethren,		46: 6
H. and the high priests did also		46:38
H. and his brethren were no less		48:19
was declared unto them by H.,		49:30
conferred them upon his son, H.		50:38
by the persuasions of H. and		53:14
H. feared lest by so doing they		53:15
that H. should be their leader.		53:19
H. did march at the head of		53:22
received an epistle from H.,		56: 1
I, H., did march at the head of		56: 9
when H. came upon their rear		56:52
halted and turned upon H.		56:52
I, H., had heard these words of		57:36
I am H., the son of Alma.		58:41
success which H. had had,		59: 1
together to strengthen H.,		59: 3
Helaman, or the armies of H.,		59: 3
and also H. and his men,		60: 3
men unto us, and also unto H..		60:24
and of your men, and also to H.		60:34
men should be sent unto H.,		62:12
also H. returned to the place of		62:42
H. did take upon him again to		62:44
H. and his brethren went forth,		62:45
And H. died, in the thirty and		62:52
been delivered unto H. by Alma.		63: 1
his death, upon the son of H.,		63:11
of Helaman, who was called H.,		63:11
were in the possession of H.		63:12
had been conferred upon H.,		63:13
of Alma, and H. his son,		63:17
THE BOOK OF H.	He	1:hd
according to the records of H.,		1:hd
who was the son of H.,		1:hd
according to the record of H.		1:hd
which is called the book of H.,		1:hd
H., who was the son of Helaman,		2: 2
Helaman, who was the son of H.,		2: 2
did lay wait to destroy H. also;		2: 3
Kishkumen sought to destroy H.		2: 5
the judgment-seat to destroy H.,		2: 6
behold one of the servants of H.,		2: 6
by this band to destroy H.—		2: 6
that he might murder H.		2: 7
servant of H. had known		2: 8
the servant of H. said unto		2: 8
but behold, the servant of H.,		2: 9
he ran and told H. all the things		2: 9
H. did send forth to take this		2:10
when H. sent forth to take them		2:11
mean the end of the book of H.,		2:14
H. did fill the judgment-seat		3:20
H. died, and his eldest son Nephi		3:37
who were the sons of H.,		4:14
their father H. spake unto them.		5: 5
the words which H. taught to		5:13
which were delivered unto H.;		6:26
OF NEPHI, THE SON OF H.—		7:hd
Nephi, the son of H., returned		7: 1
And thus ended the book of H.,		16:25
according to the record of H.		16:25
WAS THE SON OF H.	3Ne	1:hd
And H. was the son of		1:hd
was the son of H.,		1:hd
And Nephi, the son of H., had		1: 2
HELAMAN'S		
and had read H. epistle,	Al	59: 1

HELD		
h. him, that he should not flee.	1Ne	4:31
captains h. a council of war—	Al	52:19
to be h. in office at the head of	He	7: 5
h. by the elders of the church,	DC	20:81
which are h. before the world.		46: 3
which shall be h. in Missouri,		52: 2
which shall be h. by them.		58:62
conference be h. immediately;		118: 1
h. in reserve for the fulness of		121:27
to be h. in remembrance from		127: 9
laws are framed and h. inviolate		134: 2
beings to be h. in servitude.		134:12
and h. it in his own hand;	Mses	7:43
the enemy which h. me bound.	JS	2:17
h. the keys of the Priesthood of		2:72
HELEM		
were Amaleki, H., and Hem,	Mos	7: 6
HELL		
depths thereof are the depths of h.	1Ne	12:16
away the souls of men down to h.—		14: 3
the casting of it into that h.		14: 3
representation of that awful h.,		15:29
awful h. of which I have spoken,		15:35
yea, even from the sleep of h.,	2Ne	1:13
hath redeemed my soul from h.;		1:15
captivate, to bring you down to h.,		2:29
May the gates of h. be shut		4:32
yea, that monster, death and h.,		9:10
which spiritual death is h.;		9:12
death and h. must deliver up		9:12
and h. must deliver up its captive		9:12
the devil, and death, and h.,		9:19
death and h., and the devil,		9:26
he shall be thrust down to h.		9:34
they shall be thrust down to h.		9:36
h. hath enlarged herself,		15:14
H. from beneath is moved		24: 9
shalt be brought down to h.,		24:15
therefore they must go down to h.		26:10
they shall be thrust down to h.!		28:15
them away carefully down to h.		28:21
and telleth them there is no h.;		28:22
are grasped with death, and h.;		28:23
and death, and h., and the devil,		28:23
hath redeemed my soul from h.		33: 6
yourselves from the pains of h.	Jac	3:11
he spake of h., and of eternity,		7:18
has delivered their souls from h.?	Al	5: 6
of death, and the chains of h.,		5: 7
the chains of h. which encircled		5: 9
yea, and also the chains of h.?		5:10
O thou child of h., why tempt ye		11:23
what is meant by the chains of h.		12:11
down by the chains of h.,		13:30
encircled about by the pains of h.		14: 6
has saved me from an awful h.!		19:29
he loosed from the pains of h.;		26:13
brethren from the chains of h.		26:14
speedily drag them down to h.		30:60
cast by thy wrath down to h.;		31:17
tormented with the pains of h.;		36:13
no power of earth or h. can take		37:16
the very powers of h. would have		48:17
that awful h. that awaits to		54: 7
that thou art a child of h.;		54:11
be that there is a devil and a h.,		54:22
and to an everlasting h.	He	6:28
the gates of h. shall not prevail	3Ne	11:39
and the gates of h. stand open		11:40
shall be in danger of h. fire.		12:22
that ye should be cast into h.		12:30
the gates of h. are ready open		18:13
he shall be in danger of h. fire.	Mrm	8:17
with the damned souls in h.		9: 4
must have gone to an endless h.	Mro	8:13
thought, he must go down to h.		8:14
they are in danger of death, h.,		8:21
let earth and h. combine against	DC	6:34
their souls down to h.;		10:26
the gates of h. shall not prevail		10:69

HELL 444 HER

the gates of h. shall not prevail	DC 17: 8	as a h. gathereth her chickens	DC 29: 2
the gates of h. shall not prevail	18: 5	as a h. gathereth her chickens	43:24
the gates of h. shall not prevail	21: 6		
beginning, which place is h.	29:38	**HENCE**	
the gates of h. shall not prevail	33:13	come many hundred years h.	Jac 7: 7
able to cast the soul down to h.	63: 4	And not many days h. the Son	Al 9:26
who are thrust down to h.	76:84	of those who have gone h.,	3Ne 5:14
they who are cast down to h.	76:106	I command you to go from h.	DC 30:10
armies; even the hosts of h.,	88:113	not many years h. ye shall	45:63
the gates of h. shall not prevail	98:22	and command them to go h.;	51:16
lift up his eyes in h., being in	104:18	For not many days h. and	88:87
not escape the damnation of h.	121:23	not many years h. they shall	105:15
and h. shall rage against thee;	122: 1	And not many years h.,	121:15
if the very jaws of h. shall gape	122: 7	H. many are called, but few are	121:40
and shackles, and fetters of h.	123: 8	H., whatsoever those men did	128: 9
enough to make h. itself shudder,	123:10	h., this ordinance was instituted	128:12
the gates of h. shall not prevail	128:10	thee h. Satan; deceive me not;	Mses 1:16
fear, he saw the bitterness of h.	Mses 1:20	Depart h., Satan.	1:18
a h. I have prepared for them,	6:29	depart h., Satan.	1:21
		and he departed h., even from	1:22
HELLISH		H. came the saying abroad	6:54
in all their dark and h. hue,	DC 123: 6	to the mountains—Depart h.—	Abr 2: 7
		H. arose the very prevalent story	JS 2:56
HELM			
by a very small h.	DC 123:16	**HENCEFORTH**	
		from this time h. and forever.	1Ne 12:18
HELMET		h. there shall no more come into	2Ne 8:24
And take the h. of salvation,	DC 27:18	justice from h., even forever.	19: 7
		neither from that time h. and	29: 9
HELORUM		be preserved from this time h.	WM 1:11
Mosiah, and H., and Helaman.	Mos 1: 2	from this time h. and forever;	Mos 15:17
		from this time h. and forever,	Al 3:14
HELP		thy seed, h. and forever;	3:17
For the Lord God will h. me,	2Ne 7: 7	in the faith from that time h.	45:17
For the Lord God will h. me.	7: 9	from this time h. and forever—	He 12:19
to whom will ye flee for h.?	20: 3	no man getteth it h. and forever.	12:19
the h. of the all-powerful Creator	Jac 2: 5	h. there shall no more come into	3Ne 20:36
		from that time h. and forever,	Eth 2: 8
HELP		of the Lord, from this time h.	Mro 7: 3
Wherefore, with the h. of these,	WM 1:18	truth from h. and forever.	DC 23: 2
were for the h. of these plates;	Mos 1: 4	thy duty from h. and forever.	23: 5
did h. to bury their dead.	9:19	with all your soul, from h.;	30:11
with the h. of a numerous army	He 4: 8	be ye strong from h.;	38:15
to h. such as sought power	Eth 8:16	from h., when the Lord shall	63:49
to h. me in my stewardship—	DC 104:72	beware from h., and refrain	82: 2
to h. him in his stewardship—	104:73	from h. I shall call you friends,	84:77
H. thy servants to say, with thy	109:44	thou art blessed from h. that	90: 2
h. us by the power of thy Spirit,	109:79	my commandments from h.—	96: 6
to the h. of my people,	124:11	arise up and be more careful h.	108: 3
h. you to write this proclamation,	124:12	send you, from h. from that	108: 6
h. you in your labor in sending	124:16	shall be opened for them, from h.	118: 3
I will make an h. meet for him.	Mses 3:18	and true in all things from h.,	124:13
was not found an h. meet for him.	3:20	let him from h. hearken	124:89
Let us make an h. meet for	Abr 5:14	h. he shall hold the keys of	124:92
will form an h. meet for him.	5:14	from this time, h. and forever.	126: 3
was found an h. meet for him.	5:21	and will deliver me from h.;	127: 2
		from h. are not gods, but	132:17
HELPED		from h. I will strengthen him.	132:53
I h. thee; and I will preserve thee,	1Ne 21: 8	beginning, h. and forever,	Mses 5: 9
		it shall not h. yield unto	5:37
HELPLESS		the Son, from h. and forever;	6:66
carried h., even until he was laid	Mos 27:19	ye shall not see me h. and	JS 1: 1
and I fell h. on the ground,	JS 2:48		
		HENCEFORWARD	
HELPS		h. their names will be classed	DC 135: 6
for h. and for governments,	DC 124:143		
		HENI	
HEM		of Omner, and the land of H.,	Mses 7: 9
were Amaleki, Helem, and H.,	Mos 7: 6		
should h. them in on every side,	3Ne 4:16	**HENRY**: *see HERRIMAN, Henry and SHERWOOD, Henry G.*	
HEMAN: *see BASSET, Heman.*			
		HER	
HEMMED		my father spake unto h., saying:	1Ne 5: 4
h. in the Lamanites on the south,	Al 22:33	also h. mother, and one of the sons	7:19
		again, bearing a child in h. arms.	11:20
HEN		also my wife with h. tears	18:19
as a h. gathereth her chickens	3Ne 10: 4	can a woman forget h. sucking child,	21:15
as a h. gathereth her chickens	10: 5	compassion on the son of h. womb?	21:15
as a h. gathereth her chickens,	10: 5	he will comfort all h. waste places;	2Ne 8: 3
as a h. gathereth her chickens	10: 6	will make h. wilderness like Eden,	8: 3
as a h. gathereth her chickens	DC 10:65	and h. desert like the garden of the	8: 3

HER 445 HER

And none to guide h. among all	2Ne 8:18	shalt take him or h. between	DC 42:88
that taketh h. by the hand,	8:18	him or h. and thee alone;	42:88
And h. gates shall lament	13:26	shalt deliver him or h. up unto	42:89
and upon h. assemblies, a cloud	14: 5	confess in secret to him or h.	42:92
opened h. mouth without measure;	15:14	speak reproachfully of him or h.	42:92
shall be forsaken of both h. kings.	17:16	as a hen gathereth h. chickens	43:24
not be such as was in h. vexation,	19: 1	her chickens under h. wings,	43:24
done unto Samaria and h. idols,	20:11	on a woman to lust after h.,	63:16
so do to Jerusalem and to h. idols?	20:11	of the Lord shall be upon h.;	64:41
be darkened in h. going forth,	23:10	come unto h. out of every nation	64:42
shall not cause h. light to shine.	23:10	shall tremble because of h.,	64:43
earth shall remove out of h. place,	23:13	fear because of h. terrible ones.	64:43
and h. time is near to come,	23:22	Zion, or in any of h. stakes	68:25
and h. day shall not be prolonged.	23:22	Zion, or in any of h. stakes	68:26
For I will destroy h. speedily;	23:22	h. borders must be enlarged;	82:14
against Zion, and that distress h.,	27: 3	h. stakes must be strengthened;	82:14
as a sheep before h. shearers is	Mos 14: 7	put on h. beautiful garments.	82:14
widow mourning for h. husband,	21: 9	and brought forth h. strength;	84:101
as a goat fleeth with h. young	Al 14:29	is established in h. bowels;	84:101
that he should come in unto h.	19: 2	heavens have smiled upon h.;	84:101
And Ammon said unto h.:	19: 9	with the glory of h. God;	84:101
And Ammon said unto h.:	19:10	all nations to drink of h. cup,	86: 3
over the bed of h. husband,	19:11	mercy and claimeth h. own;	88:40
a remarkable vision of h. father—	19:16	The earth rolls upon h. wings,	88:45
and also h. mistress, the queen,	19:17	moon giveth h. light by night,	88:45
might raise h. from the ground;	19:29	groanings in the midst of h.,	88:89
as soon as she touched h. hand	19:29	of the wrath of h. fornication,	88:94
arose and stood upon h. feet,	19:29	h. bands are made strong,	88:94
clasped h. hands, being filled with	19:30	of the wrath of h. fornication;	88:105
commanded that h. servants,	22:19	money to bear h. expenses,	90:28
should some evil come upon h.	22:21	idle in h. days from thenceforth.	90:31
she commanded h. servants that	22:21	and plead with h. strong ones,	90:36
claimeth all which is h. own;	42:24	chasten h. until she overcomes	90:36
informing h. that the king had	47:32	be removed out of h. place.	90:37
that he should come in unto h.;	47:33	of the earth shall honor h.,	97:19
they all testified unto h. that the	47:34	be moved out of h. place,	97:19
and took h. unto him to wife	47:35	to be h. salvation and her	97:20
and he fell upon h. and beat	50:30	salvation and h. high tower.	97:20
fell upon her and beat h. much.	50:30	I have commanded h.	97:25
that she may bring forth h. fruit,	He 11:13	I have commanded h.,	97:26
and h. grain in the season of grain.	11:13	I will visit h. according to all	97:26
that it did bring forth h. fruit	11:17	according to all h. works,	97:26
fruit in the season of h. fruit.	11:17	be read this once to h. ears,	97:27
that it did bring forth h. grain	11:17	have accepted of h. offering;	97:27
her grain in the season of h. grain.	11:17	these things shall come upon h.;	97:27
and abominations which are in h.	13:14	I will bless h. with blessings,	97:28
and abominations which are in h.	13:15	of blessings upon h.,	97:28
sow to h. wallowing in the mire.	3Ne 7: 8	and upon h. generations forever	97:28
as a hen gathereth h. chickens	10: 4	not be moved out of h. place,	101:17
her chickens under h. wings,	10: 4	h. children are scattered.	101:17
as a hen gathereth h. chickens	10: 5	and establish h. waste places,	101:75
her chickens under h. wings,	10: 5	troubleth me I will avenge h.,	101:84
as a hen gathereth h. chickens,	10: 5	lest by h. continual coming	101:84
as a hen gathereth h. chickens	10: 6	I cannot receive it unto myself.	105: 5
her chickens under h. wings,	10: 6	that h. banners may be terrible	105:31
on a woman, to lust after h.,	12:28	become subject unto h. laws.	105:32
give h. a writing of divorcement.	12:31	concerning Zion and h. law	105:34
causeth h. to commit adultery;	12:32	fulfilled, after h. redemption,	105:34
shall marry h. who is divorced	12:32	forth to Zion, or to h. stakes,	109:39
go ye out of the midst of h.;	20:41	for I will deal mercifully with h.	111: 6
cast h. fruit before the time	24:11	to put on h. strength is to	113: 8
the inhabitants forth out of h.,	Mrm 4:14	from the bands of h. neck;	113: 9
anything wherewith to steer h.;	5:18	The bands of h. neck are the	113:10
seeing the sorrows of h. father,	Eth 8: 8	are the curses of God upon h.,	113:10
the kingdom unto h. father.	8: 8	land of Zion, and upon h. stakes,	115: 6
that she did talk with h. father,	8: 9	set time has come to favor h.	124: 6
I will give h. if ye will bring	8:10	that in Zion, and in h. stakes,	124:36
that he desired h. to wife.	8:11	endowment of all h. municipals,	124:39
Give h. unto me to wife.	8:11	and as watchmen upon h. walls.	124:61
I will give h. unto you, if ye will	8:12	and he marry h. not by me nor	132:15
seeketh not h. own, is not easily	Mro 7:45	he covenant with h. so long as	132:15
as a hen gathereth h. chickens	DC 10:65	a covenant with h. for time and	132:18
her chickens under h. wings,	10:65	I have not appointed unto h.	132:41
calling him or h. by name:	20:73	if h. husband be with another	132:43
immerse him or h. in the water,	20:74	innocent and hath not broken h. vow,	132:44
he shall mourn for h. no longer;	21: 8	to take h. and give her unto	132:44
as a hen gathereth h. chickens	29: 2	give h. unto him that hath not	132:44
her chickens under h. wings,	29: 2	commanded you to offer unto h.;	132:51
of the wrath of h. fornication.	35:11	destroy h. if she abide not in my	132:54
cleave unto h. and none else.	42:22	servant Joseph do all things for h.,	132:55
upon a woman to lust after h.	42:23	she be forgiven h. trespasses,	132:56
established against him or h.	42:80	will bless h., and multiply her,	132:56
their hands against him or h.,	42:81	will bless her, and multiply h.,	132:56

HER 446 HEREAFTER

and make h. heart to rejoice. DC 132:56
and the first give h. consent, 132:61
and he teaches unto h. the law 132:64
for I will destroy h.; 132:64
h. stakes may be strengthened, 133: 9
and brought h. unto the man. Mses 3:22
tree to be desired to make h. wise, 4:12
and also gave unto h. husband 4:12
gave unto her husband with h., 4:12
between thy seed and h. seed; 4:21
which hath opened h. mouth 5:36
yield unto thee h. strength. 5:37
begat Shem of h. who was the 8:12
afterward settled h. sons in it; Abr 1:24
when the Egyptians shall see h., 2:23
kill you, but they will save h. 2:23
Let h. say unto the Egyptians, 2:24
and brought h. unto the man. 5:16
the moon shall not give h. light, JS 1:33
name, previous to h. marriage, 2: 4
necessity of taking h. elsewhere; 2:58
rumor with h. thousand tongues 2:61

HERB
and the h., and the good things DC 59:17
but is an h. for bruises and 89: 8
Every h. in the season thereof, 89:11
forth grass, the h. yielding seed, Mses 2:11
h. yielding seed after his kind, 2:12
given you every h. bearing seed, 2:29
given every clean h. for meat; 2:30
h. of the field before it grew. 3: 5
shalt eat the h. of the field. 4:24
the h. yielding seed; the fruit Abr 4:11
the h. to bring forth herb from 4:12
bring forth h. from its own seed, 4:12
give them every h. bearing seed 4:29
to them every green h. for meat, 4:30
h. of the field before it grew; 5: 5

HERBS
with h. and mild food, DC 42:43
all wholesome h. God hath 89:10

HERDS
we began to raise flocks, and h., 2Ne 5:11
and of fruit, and flocks of h., En 1:21
increase of our flocks and our h.; Mos 7:22
abundantly, and flocks, and h., 21:16
and their flocks, and their h., 22: 2
gather together their flocks and h., 22: 6
our children, our flocks, and our h. 22: 8
with their flocks and their h., 22:11
and abundance of flocks and h., Al 1:29
many of their flocks and their h.; 3: 2
for the loss of their flocks and h., 4: 2
of their many flocks and h., 4: 6
and upon your flocks and h., 7:27
together all their flocks and h., 27:14
flocks and h. of every kind; 62:29
they did raise many flocks and h., He 6:12
fields, their flocks and their h., 12: 2
their flocks and their h., and all 3Ne 3:13
and all their flocks, and their h., 3:22
their h. and all their substance, 4: 3
his family, his flocks and his h., 6: 1
food for their flocks and h., Eth 6: 4
grain, and in flocks, and h., 10:12
your flocks, and in your h., DC 136:11

HERE
Then I said: H. am I; send me. 2Ne 16: 8
h. a little and there a little; 28:30
look h.; behold the tree. Jac 5:16
Behold, h. is the man, Mos 12:16
h. are the waters of Mormon 18: 8
h. is the king of the Lamanites; 20:13
h. are many whom we have 26:11
and h. we began to establish the Al 5: 5
h. are six onties of silver, 11:22
shall remain h. until we return; 27:15
h. he did not have much success, 30:21

shall dwell h. below in the flesh, Al 31:26
h. is somewhat more I would 40: 1
h. are our weapons of war; 44: 8
h. is one thing in which we 56: 9
Behold h. is money; and also He 9:20
we lay a tool h. and on the 13:34
and h. we had hope to gain Mrm 6: 4
But behold, h. is wisdom, DC 10:34
H. is wisdom, show it not unto 10:35
Behold, h. is wisdom, and let 37: 4
clothed in robes and sit thou h.; 38:26
h. and in the New Jerusalem. 42:67
receive wisdom h. is wisdom. 57: 3
behold h. is wisdom, 57: 9
behold h. is wisdom— 57:12
Behold, h. is wisdom. 58:23
Behold, h. is wisdom. 58:53
store and their possessions h.; 64:26
h. is wisdom also in me for 82:16
h. is the agency of men, 93:31
h. is the condemnation of man; 93:31
h. in the land of Kirtland, 94: 1
Now h. is wisdom, and the 95:13
say unto you, h. is wisdom, 96: 1
h. is wisdom concerning the 101:41
Behold, h. is wisdom; 107:92
and my name shall be h.; 110: 7
has come h. essaying to keep 124:85
If they live h. let them live unto 124:86
rest from all their labors h., 124:86
h. a little, and there a little; 128:21
sociality which exists among us h. 130: 2
H. is wisdom and it remaineth Mses 1:31
h. am I, send me, I will be thy 4: 1
Tarry ye h. and keep the tents, 6:38
Son of Man: H. am I, send me. Abr 3:27
and said: H. am I, send me. 3:27
there shall not be left h., JS 1: 3
Lo, h. is Christ, or there, 1:21
some crying, "Lo, h.!" and 2: 5
which cannot be mentioned h. 2:41

HEREAFTER
the things which thou shalt see h. 1Ne 14:25
shall be given h.; and then, 19: 5
those who shall h. be scattered 22: 5
that shall receive h. these things 2Ne 25: 3
shall not h. distinguish them Jac 1:14
those who shall h. publish peace, Mos 15:17
their baptism shall be given h. 21:35
stand as witnesses for me h., 24:14
account of their proceedings h. 28: 9
this account shall be written h.; 28:19
shall be given of their wars h. Al 35:13
that shall h. possess the land. 37:25
Gadianton shall be spoken h. He 2:12
of his ministry shall be given h. 3Ne 10:19
I will show unto you h. that 18:37
declare unto you h. of myself, 21: 2
shall be wrought among you h. 21: 5
For h. you shall be ordained DC 5: 6
as many as shall h. come to 20:13
shall come h. by the gift and 20:35
be built, but it shall be given h. 28: 9
which is h. to be revealed— 42:35
ye shall h. receive church 42:67
shall h. be appointed unto you. 45:65
and which ye shall h. receive. 48: 6
h. shall be made strong. 50:16
and which ye shall h. receive— 50:35
which shall be given h. 53: 4
residue shall be made known h., 55: 6
directions shall be given h. 57:16
things which shall come h., 58: 3
The residue h. 60:17
waters, and more especially h.; 61: 4
to their judgments h. 61:22
remaineth with me to do h. 61:28
that h. shall be revealed. 63:14
There remain h., in the due 68:14
I shall h. give unto them; 70: 3
shall h. appoint unto any man. 70: 9

HEREAFTER 447 HIDE

record is h. to be revealed.	DC 93: 6	h. down and cast into the fire;	He	14:18
shall be given unto you h.	94: 5	h. down, and cast into the fire.	3Ne	14:19
shall be given unto you h.	94: 6	h. down and cast into the fire,		27:11
h., from time to time give unto	104:58	works that they are h. down;		27:12
are and shall be appointed h.;	115: 1	h. down and cast into the fire,		27:17
I will show unto you h.	124:102	h. down in open rebellion against	Mrm	2:15
I will reveal more unto you, h.;	132:66	that my men were h. down,		6:10
endeavor, h., to delineate the	Abr 1:28	and h. down all my people save		6:11
should be conferred on us h.;	JS 2:70	my people who were h. down,		6:11
		same is in danger to be h. down		8:21
HEREBY		h. down and cast into the fire.	DC	45:50
do h., in the most solemn	DC OD	h. down and cast into the fire.		45:57
I h. declare my intention to	OD	h. down and cast into the fire.		97: 7
HEREIN		**HICKS, John A.**		
H. is glory and honor,	DC 128:12	I give unto you H.,	DC 124:137	
h. is the work of my Father	132:63	**HID**		
HEREWITH		and h. up unto the Lord,	T Pg	
and prove me now h., saith the	3Ne 24:10	and h. up unto the Lord,	T Pg	
I will try you and prove you h.	DC 98:12	we h. ourselves in the cavity	1Ne	3:27
And we will prove them h.,	Abr 3:25	after they had h. themselves,		4: 5
		shall be h. up, to come forth		13:35
HERITAGE		of his hand hath he h. me,		21: 2
This is the h. of the servants of	3Ne 22:17	in his quiver hath he h. me;		21: 2
of the city of the h. of God—	DC 58:13	I h. not my face from shame	2Ne	7: 6
divide the lands of the h. of God	58:17	shall be h. from them forever—		9:43
not be left to pollute mine h.,	105:15	book shall be h. from the eyes of		27:12
		of their prudent shall be h.		27:26
HERITAGES		and h. the natural branches of	Jac	5:14
to cause to inherit the desolate h.;	1Ne 21: 8	had h. the natural branches of		5:20
		should be h. in the wilderness;	Mos 10: 9	
HERMOUNTS		we h. as it were our face from him;		14: 3
wilderness, which was called H.;	Al 2:37	and h. himself that they found		17: 4
		of him who hath h. it up—	He	12:18
HERRIMAN, Henry		Yea, we have h. up our treasures		13:35
H., Zera Pulsipher, Levi Hancock,	DC 124:138	be h. from before my face,	3Ne	9:11
		that is set on a hill cannot be h.		12:14
HERSELF		In a little wrath I h. my face		22: 8
Therefore, hell hath enlarged h.,	2Ne 15:14	for they are h. from the world.		28:25
who has presented himself or h.	DC 20:73	Ammaron h. up the records	Mrm	1: 2
she shall prosper, and spread h.,	97:18	records which Ammaron had h.		4:23
Zion loosing h. from the bands	113: 9	all things which are h. must be		5: 8
stay h. and partake not of that	132:51	are to be h. up unto the Lord		5:12
		and h. up in the hill Cumorah		6: 6
HESHLON		knowledge which is h. up	Eth	4:13
until he came to the plains of H.	Eth 13:28	things which have been h. up		4:15
		he h. himself in the cavity of		13:13
HETH		and h. again in the cavity of		13:22
Aaron was a descendant of H.,	Eth 1:16	he h. them in a manner that		15:33
And Shez was the son of H.	1:25	records which have been h. up,	DC	8:11
And H. was the son of Com.	1:26	which cannot be h. in darkness;		14: 9
came and dwelt in the land of H.	8: 2	have been h. from the world		86: 9
and nine years, and he begat H.;	9:25	h. from before the world was.		124:38
H. began to embrace the secret	9:26	h. from before the foundation of		124:41
the commandment of the king, H.	9:29	h. from the wise and prudent,		128:18
who was a descendant of H.—	10: 1	I was naked, and I h. myself.	Mses 4:16	
H. had perished by the famine,	10: 1	and from my face shall I be h.;		5:39
And he begat H., and Heth	10:31	things are not h. from the Lord.		5:39
H. lived in captivity all his days.	10:31			
And H. begat Aaron, and Aaron	10:31	**HIDDEKEL**		
		name of the third river was H.;	Mses 3:14	
HEW				
that I should h. down all the trees	Jac 5:47	**HIDDEN**		
and h. down the trees of the	5:49	from this time, even h. things,	1Ne 20: 6	
		yea, out of h. darkness	2Ne	3: 5
HEWETH		h. things shall come to light,	Mos	8:17
against him that h. therewith?	2Ne 20:15	been h. because of iniquity.	DC	6:27
		the h. mysteries of my kingdom		76: 7
HEWN		the h. things of his economy		77: 6
the rock from whence ye are h.,	2Ne 8: 1	knowledge, even h. treasures;		89:19
but we will build with h. stones;	19:10	h. things which no man knew,		101:33
ones of stature shall be h. down;	20:33	bringing to light all the h. things		123:13
nothing save it be to be h. down	Jac 5:42			
of no wroth but to be h. down	5:46	**HIDE**		
and the bad be h. down	5:66	and I caused that they should h.	1Ne	4: 5
that ye must be h. down	6: 7	and h. thee in the dust,	2Ne 12:10	
h. down and cast into the fire—	Al 5:35	as Sodom, and they cannot h. it.		13: 9
h. down and cast into the fire,	5:52	book again, and h. it up unto me,		27:22
h. down and cast into the fire	5:56	to h. their counsel from the Lord!		27:27
they were h. down and leveled	51:18	to h. their counsels from the Lord;		28: 9
who were h. down by the sword;	51:19	he did h. himself in the daytime	Mos 18: 5	
h. down and cast into the fire;	He 14:18	upon us to h. us from his presence.	Al	12:14

HIDE 448 HIGH

let us h. them away that they	Al	24:15	thou art h. priest over the church	Al 8:11
we will h. away our swords, yea,		24:16	am the h. priest over the church	8:23
cannot h. your crimes from God;		39: 8	ordained unto the h. priesthood	13: 6
if a man h. up a treasure in the	He	12:18	This h. priesthood being after the	13: 7
whoso shall h. up treasures in		13:18	upon them the h. priesthood of	13: 8
and shall h. it up unto the Lord.		13:18	and ordinance, and h. priesthood,	13: 8
h. up their treasures unto me;		13:19	they become h. priests forever,	13: 9
h. not up their treasures unto		13:19	holy order of this h. priesthood,	13:10
they shall h. up their treasures,		13:20	and became h. priests of God;	13:10
I will h. up their treasures when		13:20	a h. priest after this same order	13:14
they will not h. them up unto me,		13:20	took upon him the h. priesthood	13:14
to h. their iniquities and their	3Ne	9: 5	the office of the h. priesthood	13:18
to h. their wickedness and		9: 7	was h. priest over the church,	16: 5
to h. their wickedness and		9: 8	for he is the Most H. God, and	26:14
h. up the records which were	4Ne	1:48	Ammon, who was a h. priest	30:20
did h. them up unto the Lord		1:49	and carried before the h. priest,	30:21
began to h. up their treasures in	Mrm	1:18	the h. priest said unto him:	30:22
h. up the records in the earth;		8: 4	the h. priest's name was Giddonah.	30:23
that I should h. them up again	Eth	4: 3	Now when the h. priest and the	30:29
could not h. it from the sight of		12:20	which was h. above the head,	31:13
Mormon did h. up the records		15:11	were h. priests over the church.	46: 6
h. their sins, and wickedness,	Mro	9:15	Helaman and the h. priests did	46:38
and he thinketh to h. them.	DC	58:60	so h. that the Lamanites could	49: 4
but they h. the talent which I		60: 2	and they were strong and h.	50: 3
and the sun shall h. his face,		88:87	of kings were those of h. birth,	51: 8
the sun shall h. his face in shame,		133:49	the h. priests and the teachers	He 3:25
Adam and his wife went to h.	Mses	4:14	build a tower sufficiently h. that	6:28
			Hosanna to the Most H. God.	3Ne 4:32
HIDETH			Almighty, the Most H. God.	4:32
the Lord, that h. his face from	2Ne	18:17	they who had been h. priests	6:21
none h. up their treasures unto me	He	13:19	lawyer nor judge nor h. priest	6:22
h. not up his treasures unto me,		13:19	the lawyers and the h. priests,	6:27
h. up this record unto the Lord;	Mrm	8:14	the name of the Most H. God!	11:17
tabernacle, which h. the earth,	DC	101:23	and extolled and be very h.	20:43
			they were also taught from on h.	Eth 6:17
HIDING			his h. priest murdered him as	14: 9
h. themselves that they could not	He	11:25	throne is h. in the heavens,	Mro 9:26
forth out of his h. place,	DC	101:89	voice of him who dwells on h.,	DC 1: 1
that covereth thy h. place?		121: 1	strong, and blessed from on h.,	1:28
thy h. place no longer be covered;		121: 4	and upon every h. place,	19:29
call him forth from his h. place;		123: 6	And gave him power from on h.,	20: 8
			of the glorious Majesty on h.,	20:16
HIEROGLYPHICS			h. councilors, high priests,	20:66
Rahleenos, which signifies h.	Abr	1:14	h. priests, and elders, may	20:66
			president of the h. priesthood	20:67
HIGBEE, Elias			bishop, h. councilor, and	20:67
Questions by H.:	DC	113: 7	high councilor, and h. priest,	20:67
			the direction of a h. council	20:67
HIGH			the name of the most h. God.	36: 3
thy throne is h. in the heavens,	1Ne	1:14	with power from on h.;	38:32
in the air, h. above the earth.		8:26	with power from on h. and	38:38
into an exceeding h. mountain,		11: 1	the name of the Most H. God.	39:19
to the Lord, the most h. God.		11: 6	revealed unto you from on h.,	42: 9
in the Son of the most h. God;		11: 6	two of the elders, or h. priests,	42:31
He ruleth h. in the heavens,		17:39	appointed by the h. council of	42:34
pastures shall be in all h. places.		21: 9	the elders or h. priests who	42:71
my voice have I sent up on h.;	2Ne	4:24	are to be taught from on h.	43:16
away upon exceeding h. mountains.		4:25	the saints of the Most H. God;	45:66
for they are h. and lifted up;		12:13	the rich, the h. and the low,	58:47
And upon all the h. mountains,		12:14	devotions unto the Most H.;	59:10
And upon every h. tower,		12:15	sacraments unto the Most H.,	59:12
upon a throne, h. and lifted up,		16: 1	a sacrament unto the Most H.	62: 4
and the glory of his h. looks.		20:12	on a hill, or in a h. place,	64:37
the h. ones of stature shall be hewn		20:33	of one sent down from on h.,	65: 1
a banner upon the h. mountain,		23: 2	be h. priests who are worthy,	68:15
I will be like the Most H.		24:14	as a h. priest of the Melchizedek	68:19
They wear stiff necks and h. heads;		28:14	no bishop or h. priest who shall	68:22
and wear stiff necks and h. heads	Jac	2:13	the h. priests of my church,	72: 1
raise my voice h. that it reached	En	1: 4	be made known from on h.,	75:27
who has this h. gift from God.	Mos	8:14	are priests of the Most H.,	76:57
were set apart for the h. priests,		11:11	be servants of the Most H.;	76:112
yea, a very h. tower, even so		11:12	who are sealed are h. priests,	77:11
even so h. that he could stand		11:12	ordained unto the h. priesthood	78: 1
now, Alma was their h. priest,		23:16	has ordained you from on h.,	78: 2
Alma, who was the h. priest.		26: 7	his feet, and set him upon h.,	78:16
he being also the h. priest,		29:42	be a h. priest in my church,	81: 1
the H. Priest over the Church.	Al	1:hd	Presidency of the H. Priesthood:	81: 2
the h. priest over the people of		4: 4	of the saints of the Most H.,	82:13
the office of being h. priest over		4:18	and lifted their voices on h.	84: 1
retained the office of h. priest		4:18	unto the h. priesthood.	84:29
wholly to the h. priesthood of		4:20	apostles, even God's h. priests;	84:63
Alma, the H. Priest according to		5:hd	the h. priests should travel,	84:111
to be a h. priest over the church		5: 3	who are of the H. Priesthood,	85:11

HIGH 449 HILL

among the saints of the Most H.;	DC 85:11
He that ascended up on h.,	88: 6
uplifted hands unto the Most H.	88:120
beginning at the h. priests,	88:127
of the council of h. priests,	89: 1
your h.-mindedness and pride,	90:17
chosen with power from on h.;	95: 8
salvation and her h. tower.	97:20
of twenty-four h. priests	102: 1
to organize the h. council of	102: 1
to consist of twelve h. priests,	102: 1
The h. council was appointed	102: 2
h. priests, were chosen to be	102: 3
nine h. priests, seventeen elders,	102: 5
that the h. council cannot	102: 6
to appoint other h. priests,	102: 7
a general council of h. priests,	102: 8
Whenever a h. council of the	102:12
The h. priests when abroad,	102:24
the said council of h. priests	102:25
to the h. council of the seat of	102:26
may appeal to the h. council	102:27
This council of h. priests abroad	102:28
or located h. priests abroad	102:29
between the h. council or	102:30
traveling h. priests abroad,	102:30
traveling h. council composed of	102:30
with power from on h.	105:11
their endowment from on h.	105:33
ordained a presiding h. priest	106: 1
time to this h. and holy calling,	106: 3
was such a great h. priest.	107: 2
Presidency of the H. Priesthood	107: 9
H. priests after the order of	107:10
when the h. priest is not present.	107:11
The h. priest and elder are to	107:12
as a h. priest of the Melchizedek	107:17
three Presiding H. Priests,	107:22
Traveling Presiding H. Council,	107:33
or the traveling h. council,	107:34
The standing h. councils,	107:36
or to the traveling h. council.	107:36
h. council in Zion form a quorum	107:37
duty of the traveling h. council	107:38
who were all h. priests,	107:53
Then comes the H. Priesthood,	107:64
be appointed of the H. Priesthood	107:65
President of the H. Priesthood of	107:65
Presiding H. Priest over the	107:66
the H. Priesthood of the Church.	107:66
be chosen from the H. Priesthood,	107:69
a h. priest, that is, after the order	107:71
ordained to the H. Priesthood	107:73
President of the H. Priesthood,	107:76
Presidency of the H. Priesthood.	107:78
the council of the H. Priesthood	107:79
power to call other h. priests,	107:79
Presidency of the H. Priesthood	107:79
President of the H. Priesthood	107:82
counselors of the H. Priesthood;	107:82
the office of the H. Priesthood	107:91
hold as h. and responsible offices	107:98
uplifted hands unto the Most H.–	109: 9
hands, uplifted to the Most H.,	109:19
upon them with power from on h.	109:35
h. ones shall be brought low,	112: 8
of the h. council of my church	115: 3
and by my h. council;	120: 0
God shall exalt thee on h.;	121: 8
h.-minded governors of the nation	124: 3
for the Most H. to dwell therein.	124:27
I give unto you a h. council,	124:131
over a quorum of h. priests;	124:133
over the quorum of h. priests	124:136
wherever the traveling h. council,	124:139
into an exceedingly h. mountain,	Mses 1: 1
upon the hills and the h. places,	6:37
forth to hear him, upon the h. places,	6:38
the h. places, and did flourish.	7:17
and Enoch was h. and lifted up,	7:24
a rightful heir, a H. Priest,	Abr 1: 2
to be h., or the heavens,	Fac 1:12
yet men of h. standing would	JS 2:22

HIGHER	
they may be judged of a h. judge.	Mos 29:28
If your h. judges do not	29:29
they shall judge your h. judges,	29:29
appointed captains, and h. captains,	Al 2:13
a lower court and a h. court,	DC 94: 5
shall be a lower and a h. court.	94:11
the h. part of the inner court	95:17
are no h. authorities present.	107:12
power and authority of the h.,	107:18
to a h. order of kingdoms	130:10

HIGHEST	
the glory of God, the h. of all,	DC 76:70
h. council of the church of God,	107:80
And in order to obtain the h.,	131: 2

HIGHLY	
having been h. favored of the Lord	1Ne 1: 1
he shall be esteemed h. among	2Ne 3: 7
h. favored people of the Lord	Mos 1:13
a h. favored people of the Lord;	Al 9:20
we are thus h. favored, for we	13:23
a h. favored people of the Lord.	27:30
were h. favored of the Lord,	48:20
of whom I have so h. spoken,	58:39
a man h. favored of the Lord,	Eth 1:34

HIGH-MINDEDNESS: see *HIGH* and
MINDEDNESS.

HIGHNESS	
upon them that rejoice in my h.	2Ne 23: 3
because of the h. of the bank	Al 49:18

HIGHWAY	
in the h. of the fuller's field;	2Ne 17: 3
there shall be a h. for the remnant	21:16
which was by the h. which led	He 7:10
garden gate by which led the h.	7:10
h. shall be cast up in the midst	DC 133:27

HIGHWAYS	
and my h. shall be exalted.	1Ne 21:11
many h. shall be broken up,	He 14:24
there were many h. cast up,	3Ne 6: 8
And the h. were broken up,	8:13

HILL	
a vineyard in a very fruitful h.	2Ne 15: 1
of Zion, the h. of Jerusalem.	20:32
they came to a h., which is north	Mos 7: 5
the h. which was north of Shilom,	7:16
the h. north of the land Shilom,	11:13
upon the top of the h. Manti,	Al 1:15
came upon the h. Amnihu,	2:15
upon the h. east of Sidon.	2:17
the people upon the h. Onidah,	32: 4
on the south of the h. Riplah;	43:31
came up on the north of the h.,	43:34
had passed the h. Riplah,	43:35
concealed on the south of the h.,	43:35
A city that is set on a h. cannot	3Ne 12:14
a h. which shall be called Shim;	Mrm 1: 3
I did go to the h. Shim,	4:23
a h. which was called Cumorah,	6: 2
around about the h. Cumorah;	6: 4
his up in the h. Cumorah all	6: 6
from the top of the h. Cumorah,	6:11
he came to the h. Ephraim,	Eth 7: 9
and he did molten out of the h.,	7: 9
and passed by the h. of Shim,	9: 3
Shurr was near the h. Comnor;	14:28
together upon the h. Comnor,	14:28
their tents by the h. Ramah;	15:11
that same h. where my fahter	15:11
unto a judge sitting on a h.,	DC 64:37
the altar which stood by the h.	Abr 1:10
by the hill called Potiphar's H.,	1:10
Potiphar's H. was in the land of	1:20
stands a h. of considerable size,	JS 2:51
On the west side of this h.,	2:51

HILLS — 450 — HIMSELF

HILLS
shall be exalted above the h.,	2Ne	12: 2
and upon all the h.,		12:14
and the h. did tremble,		15:25
And all h. that shall be digged		17:25
have taught them upon their h.;	Al	26:29
h. and the mountains tremble	He	12: 9
and to sally forth from the h.,	3Ne	4: 1
made h. and valleys in the places		9: 8
depart and the h. be removed,		22:10
Zion shall rejoice upon the h.	DC	35:24
it may rejoice upon the h.		39:13
Zion shall flourish upon the h.		49:25
boundaries of the everlasting h.		133:31
upon the h. and the high places,	Mses	6:37

HILT
the h. thereof was of pure gold,	1Ne	4: 9
the earth, and it broke by the h.;	Al	44:12
kept the h. of his sword in his	Eth	14: 2

HILTS
the h. thereof have perished,	Mos	8:11

HIM: see in the APPENDIX.

HIMNI
and Aaron, and Omner, and H.;	Mos	27:34
and Aaron, Omner and H.,	Al	22:35
or Aaron, or Omner, or H.,		23: 1
and Aaron, and Omner, and H.,		25:17
of Aaron, of Omner, and H.;		27:19
H. he did leave in the church in		31: 6

HIMSELF
manifesting h. unto all nations	T Pg	
and he cast h. upon his bed,	1Ne	1: 7
and should make h. manifest,		10:11
that he should manifest h. unto		10:17
down and showed h. unto them.		12: 6
shall manifest h. unto all nations,		13:42
he has manifested h. unto the Jews		13:42
shall manifest h. unto the Gentiles		13:42
shall manifest h. unto them in word,		14: 1
he has thought to make h. a king		16:38
the God of Jacob, yieldeth h.,		19:10
he offereth h. a sacrifice	2Ne	2: 7
that he should act for h.		2:16
man could not act for h. save		2:16
might be miserable like unto h.		2:27
should manifest h. unto them		6: 9
after he should manifest h. they		6: 9
will set h. again the second time		6:14
will manifest h. unto them in power		6:14
show h. unto those at Jerusalem,		9: 5
he suffereth h. to become subject		9: 5
in misery, like unto h.;		9: 9
transformeth h. nigh unto an angel		9: 9
the great man humbleth h. not,		12: 9
he hath made for h. to worship,		12:20
the child shall behave h. proudly		13: 5
Lord h. shall give you a sign—		17:14
Sanctify the Lord of Hosts h.,		18:13
shall manifest h. unto his people,		25:12
manifested h. unto his people,		25:14
show h. unto you, my children,		26: 1
manifesteth h. unto all those who		26:13
he humbleth h. before the Father,		31: 7
he shall manifest h. unto you		32: 6
he shall manifest h. unto you		32: 6
he manifesteth h. in the flesh.	Jac	4:11
the Lord had preserved unto h.		5:74
preserved unto h. the natural fruit,		5:74
shall manifest h. in the flesh,	En	1: 8
has brought upon h. his misery;	Mos	4:17
he findeth h. on the left hand		5:10
he also, h., did till the earth,		6: 7
and bowed h. before the king;		7:12
he h. came up out of the land.		8: 2
all this did he take to support h.,		11: 4
which God h. shall make for		13:28
God h. should come down among		13:34
that he, h., should be oppressed	Mos	13:35
God h. shall come down among		15: 1
but suffereth h. to be mocked,		15: 5
taken upon h. their iniquity and		15: 9
for he cannot deny h.;		15:27
hid h. that they found him not.		17: 4
God h. should come down among		17: 8
small trees, where he did hide h.		18: 5
not bury h. again in the water.		18:15
and he h. did go before them,		19: 9
he h. being a just man.		19:17
the king h. went before his people;		20: 7
did bow h. down before them,		20:25
And the king h. did not trust		21:19
considering h. an unworthy servant.		21:33
shall not think h. above another;		23: 7
should love his neighbor as h.,		23:15
brought h. under condemnation.		26:31
should esteem his neighbor as h.,		27: 4
will make h. manifest unto all.		27:30
pleaded for h. with much boldness.	Al	1:11
esteeming h. above his hearers,		1:26
might guard h. against them,		2:21
suffered h. to be led away by		3:10
upon h. his own condemnation.		3:19
h. being afflicted with a wound		3:22
the office of high priest unto h.;		4:18
that he h. might go forth		4:19
and confined h. wholly to the		4:20
to rest h. from the labors which		8: 1
Lord receiveth them up unto h.,		14:11
Ammon turned h. unto the king,		18:14
and bowed h. before the king,		22: 2
could not merit anything of h.;		22:14
did prostrate h. upon the earth,		22:17
Yea, he that truly humbleth h.,		32:15
knoweth them save God h.		40: 3
which man had brought upon h.		42:12
God h. atoneth for the sins of		42:15
Alma, also, h., could not rest,		43: 1
Jesus Christ shall manifest h.		45:10
the Lord took Moses unto h.;		45:19
Alma in the spirit, unto h.;		45:19
and he bowed h. to the earth,		46:13
of God, and be taken unto h.,		46:24
he might place h. at their head		47: 8
did not come down h. to battle.		49:11
he did prepare h. and his armies		51:10
Amalickiah did h. come down,		51:12
to defend h. against them,		52: 6
secrete h. in the wilderness,		58:16
did let h. down over the walls of		62:36
Nephites, and he h. was slain,	He	1:32
had bowed h. upon the tower		7:10
he did manifest h. unto them,		8:23
might raise h. to be a great man,		9:16
he h. was the very murderer,		9:38
perisheth, perisheth unto h.;		14:30
doeth iniquity, doeth it unto h.,		14:30
did cast h. down from the wall,		16: 7
will he not show h. unto us		16:18
will he not show h. in this land		16:19
bowed h. down upon the earth,	3Ne	1:11
no one knew it save it were h.		5:20
truly manifest h. unto them—		10:18
Jesus Christ did show h. unto		11:hd
did he show h. unto them.		11:hd
Christ should show h. unto them		11:12
and bowed h. before the Lord		11:19
h. shall reward thee openly.		13: 4
Jesus groaned within h.,		17:14
he h. also knelt upon the earth;		17:15
see and hear, every man for h.;		17:25
suffereth h. to be led into		18:25
also show h. on the morrow		19: 2
should show h. unto the multitude.		19: 3
and bowed h. to the earth,		19:19
and bowed h. to the earth;		19:27
he did show h. unto them oft,		26:13
that he showed h. unto them,		26:15
And Jesus again showed h.		27: 2
he turned h. unto the three,		28: 4

HIMSELF

the Lord showed h. unto him,	Eth	3:13
Jesus showed h. unto this man		3:17
showed h. unto the Nephites.		3:17
after Christ should show h.		4: 1
after Christ truly had showed h.		4: 2
and did establish h. king over		10: 9
that he had established h. king		10:10
but not unto h. because of his		10:11
obtain unto h. the kingdom.		10:15
obtained unto h. the kingdom		10:16
Lib also h. became a great		10:19
by faith that Christ showed h.		12: 7
he showed not h. unto them		12: 7
showed h. not unto the world.		12: 7
he has shown h. unto the world,		12: 8
he showed not h. until after		12:12
hid h. in the cavity of a rock		13:13
Coriantumr, having studied, h.,		13:16
his household save it were h.		13:21
and placed h. upon the throne		14: 6
obtained unto h. the kingdom;		14:10
to avenge h. upon Coriantumr		14:24
that if he would give h. up,		15: 5
as the words of our Savior h.	Mro	8:29
he exalts h. and does not	DC	5:24
not humble h. sufficiently		5:24
humble h. in mighty prayer		5:24
And now, except he humble h.		5:28
Martin Harris humbleth not h.		5:32
and humbling h. sincerely,		20: 6
person who has presented h.		20:73
have glory, and not of h.,		24:11
he should be an agent unto h.;		29:35
let every man choose for h.		37: 4
esteem his brother as h.,		38:24
esteem his brother as h.		38:25
sufficient for h. and family.		42:32
let him also reserve unto h.		51:14
plant h. in this place,		57: 8
the bishop, of h. or the agent,		58:51
he exalted h. in his heart,		63:55
render h. and his accounts		72:19
not of the Lord, but of h.,		74: 5
Let him offer h. in prayer upon		88:131
he is to gird h. according to		88:141
He that exalteth h. shall be		101:42
he that abaseth h. shall be		101:42
but afterward he said within h.;		101:84
that he h. was appointed.		102:10
in case he h. is absent,		102:11
separated h. from the crafts of		106: 6
inasmuch as he will humble h.		106: 7
shows h. not approved		107:100
to manifest h. to his people.		109: 5
shall fall into the same h.;		109:25
twelve including h., to testify		114: 1
ere he is aware, he is left unto h.,		121:38
honor to h. and unto my name.		124:18
for stock in that house, for h.		124:69
stock into that house for h.,		124:74
house as seemeth him good, for h.		124:77
house, as seemeth him good, for h.		124:80
house, as seemeth him good, for h.		124:81
pay stock into that house, for h.		124:82
and humble h. before me.		124:103
when he shall prove h. faithful		124:113
Let him therefore abase h.		124:114
and clothe h. with charity;		124:116
for h. and for his generation after		124:117
wherein he glorifieth h.		132:31
repenteth and sanctifieth h.		133:62
to deliver h. up to the pretended		135: 4
man shall seek to build up h.,		136:19
learn wisdom by humbling h.		136:32
and Moses was left unto h.	Mses	1: 9
And as he was left unto h.,		1: 9
and he said unto h.: Now,		1:10
took unto h. two wives;		5:44
And God revealed h. unto Seth,		6: 3
with whom God, h., conversed.		6:22
he bowed h. to the earth,		6:31
and he took glory unto h.		8: 3

451

HINDER

to h. the people from prospering	3Ne	6: 5
let no man h. them doing that	DC	50:38
as to h. the Almighty from		121:33
h. them from performing that		124:49

HINDERED

be h. in accomplishing	DC	90:27
upon the heads of those who h. my		124:50
and were h. by their enemies,		124:51
h. by the hands of their enemies,		124:53

HINDERETH

is persecuted, and none h.	2Ne	24: 6

HINDERMENT

And he became a great h. to	Mos	27: 9

HINTED

ye have h. that he hath gone to	Al	54:22

HIRAM: see PAGE, Hiram.

HIRE

the laborer is worthy of his h.	DC	31: 5
the same is worthy of his h.,		70:12
the laborer is worthy of his h.		84:79
the laborer is worthy of his h.		106: 3
This place you may obtain by h.		111: 9

HIRED

shave with a razor that is h.,	2Ne	17:20
who were h. or appointed	Al	10:14
I h. with an old gentleman by	JS	2:56

HIRELING

oppress the h. in his wages,	3Ne	24: 5

HIRING

h. out by day's work and	JS	2:55
previous to my h. to him,		2:56

HIS: see in the APPENDIX.

HISS

and become a h. and a by-word,	1Ne	19:14
will h. unto them from the end	2Ne	15:26
in that day that the Lord shall h.		17:18
and my words shall h. forth unto		29: 2
because my words shall h. forth—		29: 3
to become a h. and a by-word	3Ne	16: 9
and ye need not any longer h.,		29: 8
and his word shall h. forth	Mro	10:28

HISTORIES

libelous h. that are published,	DC	123: 5

HISTORY

account of the h. of my people;	1Ne	9: 2
a more h. part are written upon	2Ne	4:14
part of the h. of my people		5:33
the h. of the people of Nephi.	Jac	1:hd
concerning the h. of this people		1: 2
the h. of his people should be		1: 3
write and keep a regular h.,	DC	47: 1
record and h. continually;		47: 3
in writing and making a h.		69: 3
has appointed, to keep a h.,		85: 1
the records or h. of the church.		85: 4
to obtain a knowledge of h.,		93:53
the h. of the whole transaction;		128: 3
been induced to write this h.,	JS	2: 1
In this h. I shall present the		2: 2

HIT

not h. him with their stones,	Al	17:36
could not h. him with their stones	He	16: 2
that they could not h. him,		16: 3
could not h. him with their stones		16: 6
we cannot h. him with our stones		16: 6

HITHER

them down h. into the wilderness.	1Ne	3: 4

HITHER 452 HOLDING

they divided h. and thither,	1 Ne 4: 2
Sea were divided h. and thither,	17:26
Bring h. the book, and I will read	2 Ne 27:15
that they have come up h. to	Jac 2: 8
and bring them h. unto me;	5: 7
How comest thou h. to plant this	5:21
Look h.; behold I have planted	5:23
Look h., and behold another branch	5:24
Look h. and behold the last.	5:25
to come up h. to trifle with the	Mos 2: 9
to come up h. that ye should	2:10
bring Abinadi h., that I may slay	11:28
bring him h. that we may question	12:18
bring him h. that I may see him.	20:14
Lamanites drive their flocks h.,	Al 17:26
ye can upon your march h.,	61:17
and they parted h. and thither,	He 8:11
that they divided h. and thither	10: 1
of the earth moveth h. and thither,	12: 8
sick among you? Bring them h.	3Ne 17: 7
Bring them h. and I will heal	17: 7
this cause I have sent you h.,	DC 58:14
that you have come up h.;	60: 1
as many as have come up h.,	105:20
obeyed my voice in coming up h.	108: 1
come up h. unto the land of my	117: 9
let him come up h. speedily,	117:14

HITHERTO
had not h. suffered that we	1 Ne 17:12
I have h. been diligent in the	Jac 2: 3
your souls than I have h. been.	2: 3
strength they have h. brought	5:36
he has h. preserved our fathers.	Mos 1:13
ye should do as ye have h. done.	2:31
hast h. hearkened unto my words	22: 3
hast h. listened to my words	22: 4
as he has h. visited this land.	29:27
it has h. been wisdom in God	Al 37: 8
ye have h. risked to commit sin.	41: 9
upon them as they had h. done;	49: 6
which had h. been a weak place,	49:14
had h. been the weakest part of	49:15
not so great as they had h. been,	51:11
this had been h. a cause of	51:16
had h. been a disadvantage	53:19
that which we had h. done;	58: 1
our strength as we h. have done;	60:16
the borders as they had h. done;	He 1:26
strength, as he has h. done,	7:22
as there have h. been;	3Ne 11:28
doctrine, as there have h. been.	11:28
of the land have h. done.	Eth 2:11
barges which ye have h. built.	2:16
as it hath h. been verified.	DC 5:20

HOAR
| melt away as the h. frost melteth | DC 121:11 |

HOE
| and to sow, to reap and to h., | Eth 10:25 |

HOIST
| to h. the title of liberty upon | Al 51:20 |

HOISTED
| the title of liberty to be h. | Al 46:36 |

HOLD
caught h. of the end of the rod	1 Ne 8:24
caught h. of the end of the rod	8:30
and would h. fast unto it,	15:24
a man shall take h. of his brother	2 Ne 13: 6
seven women shall take h. of one	14: 1
roar, and lay h. of the prey,	15:29
sorrows shall take h. of them;	23: 8
have taken h. of the moisture of	Jac 5:18
if they h. out faithful to the end	Mos 2:41
he might h. a council with them	12:17
the Lord will not h. him guiltless	13:15
Satan had gotten great h. upon	Al 8: 9
such great h. upon your hearts?	10:25
h. a council with Lamoni	24: 5
Satan has great h. on the hearts	27:12

law could have no h. upon him)	Al 30:12
mind caught h. upon this thought,	36:18
the strongest h. in all the land,	He 1:22
lay h. upon the word of God,	3:29
h. upon the walls of the prison;	5:44
get h. upon the hearts of the	6:30
got great h. upon the hearts of the	6:31
got so great h. upon your hearts.	7:15
that they laid h. on them,	9: 9
slippery, that ye cannot h. them;	13:31
slippery, and we cannot h. them.	13:36
get great h. upon the hearts of	16:23
he will h. to the one and despise	3Ne 13:24
h. up your light that it may	18:24
the light which ye shall h. up—	18:24
him will I h. guiltless before	27:16
the prisons could not h. them,	28:19
dig pits sufficient to h. them.	28:20
of the earth could not h. them.	28:39
who did get h. upon their hearts.	4Ne 1:28
that they could not h. them,	Mrm 1:18
lay h. upon the gospel of Christ,	7: 8
would h. water like unto a dish;	Eth 2:17
lay h. upon every good thing,	Mro 7:19
lay h. upon every good thing?	7:20
may lay h. on every good thing.	7:21
lay h. upon every good thing;	7:25
lay h. upon every good gift,	10:30
and h. out faithful to the end,	DC 6:13
you shall h. it in your hands,	8: 8
Satan has great h. upon their	10:20
h. your peace until I shall see	10:37
h. your peace; appeal unto my	11:18
But now h. your peace;	11:22
to h. the next conference;	26: 1
take h. of the inhabitants	29:18
I h. forth and deign to give	38:18
beware how you h. them,	41:12
h. thy peace concerning them,	42:57
his portion, that he shall h. it,	51: 4
h. upon other men's goods,	56:17
light ye shall h. them forth.	58:23
that will h. him guiltless that	58:30
h. a conference upon this land.	58:61
and h. a meeting and rejoice	62: 4
let the unbelieving h. their lips,	63: 6
h. it in your own hands;	63:25
retain a strong h. in the land	64:21
not h. any guilty that shall go	64:22
h. the keys of this priesthood,	68:18
beware how they h. them	90: 5
h. no more as a testimony	98:39
and h. claim upon that which	101:99
h. the armies of Israel guiltless	105:30
to h. the keys of this priesthood,	107:16
to h. the keys of all the spiritual	107:18
h. the keys of the ministering of	107:20
he cannot h. the keys of that	107:70
h. as high and responsible offices	107:98
and honorably h. a name and	109:24
I have chosen to h. the keys of	112:16
Which power you h., in connection	112:31
h. the power of priesthood to bring	113: 8
Do I not h. the destinies of all	117: 6
Therefore, h. on thy way,	122: 9
get h. of them and find them out.	123: 3
he and his heirs shall h. that stock,	124:69
h. the keys of the patriarchal	124:92
poisonous serpent cannot lay h.	124:99
that ye may h. the keys thereof,	124:123
to h. the sealing blessings of my	124:124
Which Twelve h. the keys to	124:128
on the earth to h. this power	132: 7
Joseph to h. this power in the	132: 7
hands and h. all the creations	Mses 7:36
which I h. unto this present time.	Abr 1:28

HOLDETH
| h. the key of the mysteries | DC 84:19 |
| h. the key of the ministering | 84:26 |

HOLDING
| continually h. fast to the rod | 1 Ne 8:30 |
| H. forth things which must shortly | Al 16:19 |

HOLDING

h. forth the coming of the Son of	Al	16:19
I am h. my Spirit from the	DC	63:32
h. the scepter of power in his		85: 7
in h. the keys of this last		90: 6
Twelve being sent out, h. the keys,		107:35
h. forth that which is to come,		128:21
h. sacred the freedom of		134: 5
h. the right belonging to the	Abr	1: 2
h. the key of power also,	Fac	2: 2

HOLDS

the strongest h. of the Lamanites	Al	53: 6
so strong were their h. and	3Ne	1:27
which h. the keys of the	DC	13: 0
the firstborn h. the right of		68:17
h. the right of presidency,		107: 8
h. the keys or authority of		107:15
who h. the keys of this power,		132:64
h. men accountable for their acts		134: 1
h. the keys of the sealing ordinances,		OD
h. the keys of the ministering	JS	2:69

HOLE

to the h. of the pit from whence	2Ne	8: 1
shall play on the h. of the asp,		21: 8
shall play on the h. of the asp,		30:14
thou shalt make a h. in the top,	Eth	2:20
unstop the h. and receive air.		2:20
ye shall stop the h., that ye		2:20
without even a h. in his robe.	DC	135: 2

HOLES

go into the h. of the rocks,	2Ne	12:19
and in the h. of the rocks,		17:19

HOLIEST

heavenly place, the h. of all.	DC	76:66
is after the h. order of God.		84:18
even of God, the h. of all,		88: 5

HOLINESS

the truth and h. which is in him.	2Ne	2:10
neither h. nor misery,		2:11
and h. shall be upon their heads;		8:11
O how great the h. of our God!		9:20
I would speak unto you of h.;		9:48
do this work with h. of heart.	Mos	18:12
for the which h., O God, we	Al	31:17
righteousness and in h. of heart,	3Ne	4:29
and the h. which is in Christ,		26: 5
and the h. of Jesus Christ,	Mrm	9: 5
walking in h. before the Lord.	DC	20:69
walking in all h. before me;		21: 4
virtue and h. before me.		38:24
to act in all h. before me—		43: 9
should do in all h. of heart,		46: 7
virtue and h. before me		46:33
increase in beauty, and in h.;		82:14
made in all righteousness, in h.,		107:30
it is thy house, a place of thy h.		109:13
pain shall be sanctified in h.		133:35
who walked in h. before the Lord.	Mses	5:26
Man of H. is his name,		6:57
called the City of H., even ZION.		7:19
am God; Man of H. is my name;		7:35

HOLY

unto me by his H. Spirit.	1Ne	2:17
the mouth of all the h. prophets,		3:20
the prophecies of the h. prophets,		5:13
manifest, by the H. Ghost,		10:11
by the power of the H. Ghost,		10:17
by the power of the H. Ghost,		10:17
by the power of the H. Ghost,		10:19
the H. Ghost giveth authority		10:22
the H. Ghost come down out of		11:27
the H. Ghost fell upon twelve		12: 7
whom the H. Ghost beareth record,		12:18
the prophecies of the h. prophets;		13:23
and the power of the H. Ghost;		13:37
despised the H. One of Israel,		19:14
against the H. One of Israel,		19:15
call themselves of the h. city,		20: 2
Redeemer, the H. One of Israel;	1Ne	20:17
Redeemer of Israel, his H. One,		21: 7
because of the H. One of Israel;		22: 5
against the H. One of Israel.		22:18
was the H. One of Israel,		22:21
and the H. One of Israel		22:24
the H. One of Israel reigneth.		22:26
in the H. One of Israel		22:28
will reject the H. One of Israel,	2Ne	1:10
in and through the H. Messiah;		2: 6
and grace of the H. Messiah,		2: 8
law which the H. One hath given,		2:10
to the will of his H. Spirit;		2:28
commandments of the H. One		3: 2
after the manner of his h. order,		6: 2
Lord God, the H. One of Israel,		6: 9
necks against the H. One of Israel,		6:10
judgments of the H. One of Israel		6:10
is God, the H. One of Israel.		6:15
O Jerusalem, the h. city;		8:24
by the mouth of his h. prophets,		9: 2
our God, the H. One of Israel,		9:11
resurrection of the H. One of Israel.		9:12
seat of the H. One of Israel;		9:15
to the h. judgment of God.		9:15
saints of the H. One of Israel,		9:18
believed in the H. One of Israel,		9:18
our God, the H. One of Israel!		9:19
faith in the H. One of Israel,		9:23
Lord God, the H. One of Israel,		9:24
mercies of the H. One of Israel		9:25
which is the H. One of Israel.		9:26
against that H. God,		9:39
greatness of the H. One of Israel.		9:40
come unto the Lord, the H. One.		9:41
is the H. One of Israel;		9:41
constrained to exclaim: H., holy		9:46
Holy, h. are thy judgments,		9:46
if ye were h. I would speak		9:48
but as ye are not h.,		9:48
praise the h. name of my God.		9:49
come unto the H. One of Israel,		9:51
and give thanks unto his h. name		9:52
in Jerusalem shall be called h.,		14: 3
and God that is h. shall be		15:16
counsel of the H. One of Israel		15:19
word of the H. One of Israel.		15:24
H., holy, holy, is the Lord of Hosts;		16: 3
Holy, h., holy, is the Lord of Hosts;		16: 3
Holy, holy, h., is the Lord of Hosts;		16: 3
so the h. seed shall be the		16:13
and his H. One for a flame,		20:17
the Lord, the H. One of Israel,		20:20
in all my h. mountain,		21: 9
great is the H. One of Israel		22: 6
heart doth magnify his h. name.		25:13
Christ is the H. One of Israel.		25:29
by the power of the H. Ghost;		26:13
rejoice in the H. One of Israel.		27:30
sanctify the H. One of Jacob,		27:34
and deny the H. Ghost, which		28: 4
of God, the H. One of Israel;		28: 5
and the gift of the H. Ghost!		28:26
by the power of the H. Ghost.		28:31
who is the H. One of Israel.		30: 2
in all my h. mountain;		30:15
Lamb of God, he being h.,		31: 5
Know ye not that he was h.?		31: 7
notwithstanding he being h.,		31: 7
the H. Ghost descended upon him		31: 8
will the Father give the H. Ghost,		31:12
then shall ye receive the H. Ghost;		31:13
of fire and of the H. Ghost;		31:13
praises unto the H. One of Israel.		31:13
of fire and of the H. Ghost,		31:14
by fire and by the H. Ghost.		31:17
ye have received the H. Ghost,		31:18
the Son, and of the H. Ghost,		31:21
ye had received the H. Ghost		32: 2
save it were by the H. Ghost?		32: 2
by the power of the H. Ghost;		32: 3
and receive the H. Ghost,		32:15
by the power of the H. Ghost		33: 1

HOLY 454 HOLY

power of the H. Ghost carrieth it	2Ne	33: 1
their hearts against the H. Spirit,		33: 2
but also all the h. prophets	Jac	4: 4
and the gift of the H. Ghost,		6: 8
and quench the H. Spirit,		6: 8
me by the power of the H. Ghost;		7:12
sign by this power of the H. Ghost,		7:13
and the power of the H. Ghost,		7:17
this land, and it is a h. land;	En	1:10
be by the power of his h. arm,		1:13
communion with the H. Spirit.	Jar	1: 4
sabbath day h. unto the Lord.		1: 5
unto God, the H. One of Israel,	Om	1:25
Christ, who is the H. One of Israel,		1:26
assistance of the h. prophets	WM	1:16
king Benjamin was a h. man,		1:17
and there were many h. men in		1:17
been spoken by the h. prophets,	Mos	2:34
God hath sent his h. prophets		3:13
h. prophets spake many h. words		3:15
to the enticings of the H. Spirit,		3:19
hath made bare his h. arm		12:24
the sabbath day, to keep it h.		13:16
h. prophets who have prophesied		15:11
I mean all the h. prophets		15:13
hath made bare his h. arm		15:31
by the mouth of the h. prophets.		18:19
the sabbath day, and keep it h.,		18:23
who were just and h. men.	Al	3: 6
priesthood of the h. order of God,		4:20
according to the h. order of God,		5:hd
And was he not a h. prophet?		5:11
and also all the h. prophets,		5:24
according to the h. order of God,		5:44
unto me by the H. Spirit of God.		5:46
unto me by his H. Spirit;		5:46
the H. One hath spoken it.		5:52
and trample the H. One under		5:53
walk after the h. order of God,		5:54
been sanctified by the H. Spirit,		5:54
the h. order by which he was		6: 8
by the power of the H. Ghost,		7:10
the testimony of the H. Spirit,		7:16
walk after the h. order of God,		7:22
the h. prophets who have been		7:25
according to the h. order of God,		8: 4
thou art a h. prophet of God,		8:20
they were filled with the H. Ghost.		8:30
and the gift of the H. Ghost,		9:21
yea, a h. man, who is a chosen man		10: 7
said unto me he is a h. man;		10: 9
wherefore I know he is a h. man		10: 9
to catch the h. ones of God.		10:17
the Father, and the H. Spirit,		11:44
repentance and their h. works.		12:30
priests, after his h. order,		13: 1
are called with a h. calling,		13: 3
with that h. calling which was		13: 3
been called to this h. calling		13: 4
thus this h. calling being prepared		13: 5
being called by this h. calling,		13: 6
priesthood of the h. order of God,		13: 6
being called with a h. calling,		13: 8
and ordained with a h. ordinance,		13: 8
the high priesthood of the h. order,		13: 8
h. order of this high priesthood,		13:10
were called after this h. order,		13:11
being sanctified by the H. Ghost,		13:12
according to the h. order of God,		13:18
known unto just and h. men,		13:26
and call on his h. name,		13:28
and thus be led by the H. Spirit,		13:28
contained the h. scriptures,		14: 8
God dwells and all his h. angels.		18:30
called by his H. Spirit to teach		18:34
the records and the h. scriptures		18:36
thou art a prophet of a h. God,		19: 4
and h. prophets of the true God.		20:15
let us give thanks to his h. name,		26: 8
hath called me by a h. calling,		29:13
are handed down by h. prophets,		30:14
prophecies of the h. prophets?		30:22

and also all the h. prophets?	Al	30:44
H., holy God; we believe		31:15
h. God; we believe that thou		31:15
we believe that thou art h.,		31:15
H. God, we believe that thou		31:16
elected us to be thy h. children;		31:16
we are a chosen and a h. people.		31:18
being interpreted, is the h. stand.		31:21
together again to the h. stand,		31:23
they were filled with the H. Spirit.		31:36
ye begin to call upon his h. name,		34:17
the h. scriptures testify of these		34:30
no more against the H. Ghost,		34:38
by the mouth of his h. angel,		36: 5
God sent his h. angel to stop us		36: 6
not kept his h. commandments.		36:13
and be filled with the H. Ghost.		36:24
the records of the h. scriptures		37: 3
do contain that which is h. writ.		37: 5
or denying the H. Ghost?		39: 5
if ye deny the H. Ghost when it		39: 6
after the h. order of God		43: 2
ordained by the h. order of God,		49:30
prophecies of many h. prophets,	He	1:hd
hearts, call upon his h. name.		3:27
and with all our h. fathers,		3:30
the H. Spirit of God did come		5:45
but also all the h. prophets,		8:16
rebelled against your h. God;		8:25
under their feet the H. One—		12: 2
led to believe the h. scriptures,		15: 7
prophecies of the h. prophets,		15: 7
by the mouth of my h. prophets.	3Ne	1:13
prophecy of all the h. prophets.		1:26
the h. prophets who had spoken;		5: 1
gone hence, who were the h. ones,		5:14
with fire and with the H. Ghost,		9:20
with fire and with the H. Ghost,		9:20
of many of the h. prophets.		10:14
of the Son, and of the H. Ghost.		11:25
Son, and the H. Ghost are one;		11:27
the H. Ghost beareth record of		11:32
with fire and with the H. Ghost.		11:35
the H. Ghost will bear record		11:36
and I, and the H. Ghost are one.		11:36
with fire and with the H. Ghost;		12: 1
with fire and with the H. Ghost,		12: 2
be filled with the H. Ghost.		12: 6
that which is h. unto the dogs,		14: 6
save it were by the H. Ghost.		15:23
of you by the H. Ghost,		16: 4
in me, in and of the H. Ghost,		16: 6
Lord hath made bare his h. arm		16:20
power to give the H. Ghost.		18:37
the H. Ghost should be given		19: 9
the H. Ghost did fall upon them,		19:13
with the H. Ghost and with fire.		19:13
given the H. Ghost unto these		19:20
wilt give the H. Ghost unto all		19:21
hast given them the H. Ghost		19:22
pouring out of the H. Ghost		20:27
Father hath made bare his h. arm		20:35
O Jerusalem, the h. city, for		20:36
by the power of the H. Ghost		21: 2
Redeemer, the H. One of Israel—		22: 5
were filled with the H. Ghost.		26:17
the reception of the H. Ghost,		27:20
and also all the h. angels,		27:30
the H. Ghost beareth record of		28:11
the Father giveth the H. Ghost		28:11
did receive the H. Ghost.		28:18
in the flesh, that they were h.,		28:39
spoken by the h. prophets,		29: 2
or by the power of the H. Ghost!		29: 6
be filled with the H. Ghost,		30: 2
did also receive the H. Ghost.	4Ne	1:1 1
constrained by the H. Ghost,		1:48
the H. Ghost did not come upon	Mrm	1:14
the Son, and unto the H. Ghost,		7: 7
fire and withthe H. Ghost,		7:10
transfigured the h. word of God,		8:33
polluted the h. church of God?		8:38

HOLY

Reference	Citation	Location
to dwell with that h. Being,		Mrm 9: 3
to dwell with a h. and just God,		9: 4
the judgment of the H. One		9:14
for we know that thou art h.		Eth 3: 2
and the H. Ghost bear record—		5: 4
called after the h. order of God.		12:10
with fire and with the H. Ghost.		12:14
because of the H. Ghost which		12:23
Jesus Christ, and the H. Ghost,		12:41
the h. sanctuary of the Lord.		13: 3
a h. city unto the Lord;		13: 5
become a h. city of the Lord;		13: 5
up a h. city unto the Lord,		13: 8
ye shall give the H. Ghost;		Mro 2: 2
their hands, fell the H. Ghost.		2: 3
by the power of the H. Ghost,		3: 4
by the power of the H. Ghost,		6: 4
by the power of the H. Ghost;		6: 9
power of the H. Ghost led them		6: 9
Jesus Christ, and his h. will,		7: 2
the H. Ghost may have place		7:32
the power of the H. Ghost		7:36
by the power of the H. Ghost		7:44
ministry, and to his h. work.		8: 2
the name of his H. Child, Jesus,		8: 3
by the power of the H. Ghost,		8: 7
did the H. Ghost manifest the		8: 9
and the power of his H. Spirit,		8:23
the visitation of the H. Ghost,		8:26
they are denying the H. Ghost.		8:28
by the power of the H. Ghost.		10: 4
by the power of the H. Ghost		10: 5
by the power of the H. Ghost;		10: 7
that ye become h., without spot.		10:33
in your heart, by the H. Ghost,		DC 8: 2
gospel which my h. prophets,		10:46
you shall receive the H. Ghost,		14: 8
you shall have the H. Ghost,		18:18
to the power of the H. Ghost		18:32
by fire, yea, even the H. Ghost.		19:31
unto him by an h. angel,		20: 6
that the h. scriptures,		20:11
and call them to his h. work		20:11
transgression of these h. laws		20:20
be baptized in his h. name,		20:25
in the words of the h. prophets,		20:26
by the gift of the H. Ghost,		20:26
of God by the H. Ghost,		20:27
and H. Ghost are one God,		20:28
of his book, the h. scriptures,		20:35
gift and power of the H. Ghost,		20:35
be rendered to his h. name,		20:36
of fire and the H. Ghost,		20:41
and the giving of the H. Ghost;		20:43
they are led by the H. Ghost.		20:45
by the power of the H. Ghost,		20:60
agreeable to the h. scriptures—		20:69
of the Son, and of the H. Ghost.		20:73
Being inspired of the H. Ghost		21: 2
up unto the most h. faith.		21: 2
thou shalt receive the H. Ghost,		25: 8
mouth of all the h. prophets		27: 6
of fire and of the H. Ghost.		33:11
bestow the gift of the H. Ghost		33:15
and the h. scriptures are given		33:16
by the power of the H. Ghost.		34:10
they received not the H. Ghost;		35: 5
they shall receive the H. Ghost		35: 6
by the Comforter, the H. Ghost,		35:19
call on the h. prophets to		35:23
receive my Spirit, the H. Ghost,		36: 2
of fire and the H. Ghost,		39: 6
the gift of the H. Ghost,		39:23
was sought for by all h. men,		45:12
shall stand in h. places,		45:32
with all the h. angels;		45:44
have taken the H. Spirit for		45:57
and guided by the H. Spirit.		46: 2
it is given by the H. Ghost to		46:13
it is given by the H. Ghost to		46:15
it is given by the H. Ghost to		46:16
h. men that ye know not of.		49: 8
to the h. commandment,		49:13
the gift of the H. Ghost,		DC 49:14
the reception of the H. Spirit		53: 3
a reception of the H. Spirit		55: 1
power to give the H. Spirit.		55: 3
sacraments upon my h. day;		59: 9
lifting up h. hands upon them.		60: 7
I am able to make you h.,		60: 7
before the Lord, in the h. city.		63:49
call upon his h. name,		65: 4
moved upon by the H. Ghost.		68: 3
moved upon by the H. Ghost		68: 4
the Son, and of the H. Ghost.		68: 8
and the gift of the H. Ghost by		68:25
the Sabbath day to keep it h.		68:29
are appointed by the H. Spirit		72:24
unclean, but now are they h.		74: 1
But little children are h.,		74: 7
saw the h. angels, and them		76:21
Having denied the H. Spirit		76:35
and receive the H. Spirit by		76:52
by the H. Spirit of promise,		76:53
they who deny not the H. Spirit.		76:83
but of the H. Spirit through		76:86
by the power of the H. Spirit,		76:116
unto the h. order of God,		77:11
Lord God, the H. One of Zion,		78:15
and direction of the H. One,		78:16
according to the H. Priesthood		84: 6
and the H. Priesthood also;		84:25
being filled with the H. Ghost		84:27
kingdom pollute my h. land?		84:59
shall receive the H. Ghost.		84:64
may receive the H. Ghost,		84:74
mouths of all the h. prophets		86:10
stand ye in h. places,		87: 8
even the H. Spirit of promise;		88: 3
a tabernacle of the H. Spirit		88:137
the H. Ghost descended upon		93:15
to be h., undefiled, according to		94:12
your most h. desires unto me,		95:16
to build mine h. house.		96: 2
demonstration of my H. Spirit.		99: 2
the H. Ghost shall be shed forth		100: 8
and stand in h. places;		101:22
unto my name upon h. places;		101:64
to just and h. principles;		101:77
for sacred and h. purposes.		104:65
it may be h. and consecrated		104:66
be the h. and sacred writings,		104:68
for h. and sacred purposes,		104:68
to this high and h. calling,		106: 3
H. Priesthood, after the Order of		107: 3
and were righteous and h. men.		107:29
being full of the H. Ghost,		107:56
now we ask thee, H. Father,		109: 4
now, H. Father, we ask thee to		109:10
and consecrated to be h.,		109:12
h. presence may be continually in		109:12
And do thou grant, H. Father,		109:14
receive a fulness of the H. Ghost,		109:15
with h. hands, uplifted to the		109:19
And we ask thee, H. Father,		109:22
We ask thee, H. Father,		109:24
ask thee, H. Father, to confound		109:29
ask thee, H. Father, to remember		109:47
to build a h. city to thy name,		109:58
from heaven, thy h. habitation,		109:77
and do not pollute this h. house.		110: 8
Let the city, Far West, be a h.		115: 7
and it shall be called most h.,		115: 7
upon which thou standest is h.		115: 7
to keep and preserve it h.,		117:16
for my h. priesthood,		119: 4
this law, to become h.,		119: 6
that it may be most h.,		119: 6
you knowledge by his H. Spirit,		121:26
unspeakable gift of the H. Ghost,		121:26
when moved upon by the H. Ghost,		121:43
H. Ghost shall be thy constant		121:46
by the power of the H. Ghost,		124: 4
given you by the H. Ghost.		124: 5
blessed and h. is he, for he is mine.		124:19
It shall be h., or the Lord		124:24
The keys of the h. priesthood		124:34

HOLY 456 HOODS

your oracles in your most h. places	DC 124:39
the ordinance of my h. house,	124:39
to build unto my h. name.	124:39
that spot that it shall be made h.	124:44
they pollute mine h. grounds,	124:46
and mine h. ordinances,	124:46
my h. words which I give unto	124:46
transgression of my h. laws	124:50
new translation of my h. word	124:89
even the H. Spirit of promise,	124:124
put in the archives of my h. temple,	127: 9
the record shall be just as h.,	128: 4
the powers of the H. Priesthood.	128:11
let us present in his h. temple,	128:24
the H. Ghost has not a body of	130:22
the H. Ghost could not dwell in us.	130:22
man may receive the H. Ghost,	130:23
the power of the H. Priesthood.	131: 5
sealed by the H. Spirit of promise,	132: 7
and that too most h.,	132: 7
is not sealed by the H. Spirit of	132:18
them by the H. Spirit of promise,	132:19
sealed by the H. Spirit of promise,	132:26
blasphemy against the H. Ghost,	132:27
the law of my H. Priesthood,	132:28
unto her by the h. anointing,	132:41
by the power of my H. Priesthood,	132:44
he shall make bare his h. arm	133: 3
and the h. apostles, with Abraham,	133:55
Mount Zion, and upon the h. city,	133:56
being filled with the H. Ghost,	Mses 1:24
day the H. Ghost fell upon Adam,	5: 9
called upon men by the H. Ghost	5:14
being declared by h. angels	5:58
and by the gift of the H. Ghost.	5:58
unto Adam, by an h. ordinance,	5:59
was moved upon by the H. Ghost,	6: 8
the gift of the H. Ghost,	6:52
with fire, and with the H. Ghost.	6:66
and truth, and of the H. Ghost,	7:11
and the H. Ghost fell on many,	7:27
canst weep, seeing thou art h.,	7:29
I shall prepare, an H. City,	7:62
ye shall receive the H. Ghost,	8:24
and from the h. commandments	Abr 1: 5
of the H. Priesthood,	Fac 2: 3
the sign of the H. Ghost unto	2: 7
in the H. Temple of God.	2: 8
and all the h. angels with him.	JS 1: 1
shall stand in the h. place;	1:12
hands for the gift of the H. Ghost,	2:70
the H. Ghost fell upon him,	2:73
filled with the H. Ghost,	2:73
Christ, and in the H. Ghost.	AoF 1
for the gift of the H. Ghost.	4

HOME
when they shall be gathered h.	2Ne 9: 2
house of Israel, shall be gathered h.	29:14
h. to that God who gave them	Al 40:11
and did return to his own h.	3Ne 19: 1
his people may be gathered h.	21:28
Leave thy house and h., except	DC 19:36
And your h. shall be at your	30: 4
Sidney Rigdon, seek them a h.,	63:65
things which are at h., things	88:79
diligent and concerned at h.,	93:50
let my servant Joseph tarry at h.,	124:102
in some degree, I went h.	JS 2:20
and told me to go h.	2:48
Sometimes we were at h.,	2:55

HOMELY
and all manner of good h. cloth.	Al 1:29

HOMER
seed of a h. shall yield an ephah.	2Ne 15:10

HOMES
they returned to their h.,	Al 31:23
they were fighting for their h.	43:45
children are returning to their h.,	58:31
Therefore, go ye unto your h.,	3Ne 17: 3

and their houses, and their h.	Mrm 2:23
be made to leave their h.,	DC 52: 3
let them return to their h.	58:46
while journeying unto their h.;	61:23
until they return to their h.,	61:35

HONEST
were perfectly h. and upright	Al 27:27
shall ye know that I am an h. man,	He 9:36
ask in faith, with an h. heart,	DC 8: 1
in faith, with an h. heart,	11:10
who know their hearts are h.,	97: 8
h. men and wise men should	98:10
that will touch the hearts of h. men	135: 7
We believe in being h., true,	AoF 13

HONESTLY
And let every man deal h.,	DC 51: 9

HONEY
its much fruit and also wild h.,	1Ne 17: 5
and h. in abundance, and provisions	18: 6
Butter and h. shall he eat,	2Ne 17:15
butter and h. shall every one eat	17:22
buy milk and h., without money	26:25
by interpretation, is a h. bee;	Eth 2: 3
land flowing with milk and h.,	DC 38:18

HONOR
h. thy father and thy mother,	1Ne 17:55
and with their lips do h. me,	2Ne 27:25
H. thy father and thy mother,	Mos 13:20
did for the sake of riches and h.	Al 1:16
I seek not for h. of the world,	60:36
and h., power and glory be	DC 20:36
Give me thine h., which is my	29:36
by the voice of glory and h.	43:25
thine is the h., power and glory,	65: 6
crowned with h., and glory,	75: 5
delight to h. those who serve	76: 5
and h., and dominion forever	76:119
Glory, and h., and power, and	84:102
nations of the earth shall h. her,	97:19
that it may be done to thine h.	109:10
sittest enthroned, with glory, h.,	109:77
thou shalt be had in h.;	122: 4
beget glory and h. to himself	124:18
for he shall h. me.	124:21
you may receive h. and glory.	124:34
for the glory, h., and endowment	124:39
crown you with h., immortality,	124:55
blessing, and glory, and h.,	124:95
Herein is glory and h.,	128:12
glory, and salvation, and h.,	128:23
do it; wherefore give me thing h.	Mses 4: 1

HONORABLE
captain of fifty, and the h. man,	2Ne 13: 3
and the base against the h.	13: 5
their h. men are famished,	15:13
who are h. men of the earth,	DC 76:75
And let h. men be appointed,	101:73
to the h. president-elect,	124: 3
name may be had in h. remembrance	124:96

HONORABLY
h. hold a name and standing	DC 109:24
so h. and nobly defended,	109:54

HONORED
h. in laying the foundation,	DC 58: 7
he shall be h. in the midst	124:76
man should be h. in his station,	134: 6
that he might be h. and the	136:39

HONORING
h., and sustaining the law.	AoF 12

HONORS
and aspire to the h. of men,	DC 121:35
their rights, their keys, their h.,	128:21

HOODS
glasses, and the fine linen, and h.,	2Ne 13:23

HOOFS 457 HOSTS

HOOFS
horses' h. shall be counted like	2Ne 15:28
and I will make thy h. brass.	3Ne 20:19

HOOKS
and their spears into pruning-h.—	2Ne 12: 4

HOPE
that ye may have h. as well as	1Ne 19:24
having a perfect brightness of h.,	2Ne 31:20
for none of these can I h. except	33: 9
ye have obtained a h. in Christ	Jac 2:19
and we had a h. of his glory	4: 4
ourselves had a h. of his glory,	4: 4
we obtain a h., and our faith	4: 6
obtained a good h. of glory	4:11
he had h. to shake me from the	7: 5
they to h. for salvation?	Al 5:10
ye have faith, h., and charity,	7:24
having a h. that ye shall	13:29
receive the h. which thou desirest.	22:16
they did retain a h. through faith,	25:16
for their h. and views of Christ	27:28
they rejoice and exult in the h.,	28:12
under a foolish and a vain h.,	30:13
if ye have faith ye h. for things	32:21
with a firm h. that ye shall one day	34:41
even so I h. that you will	38: 2
we should h. for our deliverance	58:11
I h. that ye will deliver up	3Ne 3:10
did h. to destroy the robbers	4: 4
But behold, I was without h.,	Mrm 5: 2
we had h. to gain advantage	6: 4
with surety h. for a better world,	Eth 12: 4
which h. cometh of faith,	12: 4
they might h. for those things	12: 8
Wherefore, ye may also have h.,	12: 9
faith, h. and charity bringeth	12:28
might have a more excellent h.;	12:32
wherefore man must h., or he	12:32
concerning faith, h., and charity;	Mro 7: 1
have obtained a sufficient h.	7: 3
speak unto you concerning h.	7:40
unto his faith, save ye shall have h.?	7:40
what is it that ye shall h. for?	7:41
h. through the atonement of	7:41
faith he must needs have h.;	7:42
faith there cannot be any h.	7:42
he cannot have faith and h.,	7:43
If so, his faith and h. is vain,	7:44
that we may have this h.;	7:48
neither faith, h., nor charity;	8:14
which Comforter filleth with h.	8:26
the h. of his glory and of eternal	9:25
be faith there must also be h.;	10:20
if there must be h. there must	10:20
neither can ye if ye have no h.	10:21
if ye have no h. ve must needs	10:22
And faith, h., charity and love,	DC 4: 5
patience, faith, h. and charity.	6:19
having faith, h., and charity,	12: 8
And if you have not faith, h.,	18:19
h. of a glorious resurrection.	42:45
their h. shall be blasted,	121:11
is to come, confirming our h.	128:21
we h. all things, we have endured	AoF 13
and h. to be able to endure all	13

HOPED
and these I had h. to preserve,	Jac 5:46
faith is things which are h. for	Eth 12: 6

HOPES
I had joy and great h. of them,	1Ne 16: 5
having great h. and much desire	Al 7: 3
swallowed up in the h. of glory;	22:14
having no h. of meeting them	52:21
gave them great h. and much	56:17
began to lose all h. of succor;	57:12
and their h. may be cut off;	DC 121:14

HOPETH
h. all things, endureth all things.	Mro 7:45

HOPING
h. that our beloved brethren and	Jac 4: 3
h. that many of my brethren may	7:27

HORAH
H. and Olihah [Oliver Cowdery],	DC 82:11

HOREB
I commanded unto him in H.	3Ne 25: 4

HORN
yea, I will make thy h. iron,	3Ne 20:19

HORRIBLE
of the h. scene of the blood and	Mrm 4:11
dwell no longer upon this h. scene.	9:20

HORROR
rack my soul with inexpressible h.	Al 36:14

HORSE
the ox, and the ass and the h.,	1Ne 18:25
for the ox, and oats for the h.,	DC 89:17

HORSES
their land is also full of h.,	2Ne 12: 7
wild goats, and also many h.	En 1:21
Behold, he is feeding thy h.	Al 18: 9
should prepare his h. and chariots,	18: 9
Ammon was preparing his h.	18:10
Ammon had made ready the h.	18:12
ready his h. and his chariots.	20: 6
and they had taken their h.,	3Ne 3:22
provisions, and h. and cattle,	4: 4
herds, his h. and his cattle,	6: 1
I will cut off thy h. out of the	21:14
And they also had h., and asses,	Eth 9:19
to ride upon h., or upon mules,	DC 62: 7

HORSES'
h. hoofs shall be counted like	2Ne 15:28

HOSANNA
H. to the Lord, the most high God;	1Ne 11: 6
H. to the Most High God.	3Ne 4:32
H.! Blessed be the name of	11:17
H., hosanna, blessed be the	DC 19:37
h., blessed be the name of the	19:37
H., blessed be the name of	36: 3
H.! blessed be the name of	39:19
singing H. to God and the Lamb!	109:79

HOSANNAS
with h. to him that sitteth upon	DC 124:101

HOST
a numerous h. of Lamanites	Mos 9:14
numerous h. of the Lamanites;	Al 2:24
a numerous h. to go to battle	48: 3
at the head of his numerous h.,	He 1:19
finished, and all the h. of them.	Mses 3: 1
an h. of men hath he brought in	6:44

HOSTS
who is the Lord of H.; yea, the	1Ne 20: 2
yea, the Lord of H. is his name.	20: 2
the Lord of H. is my name.	2Ne 8:15
the day of the Lord of H.	12:12
behold, the Lord, the Lord of H.,	13: 1
saith the Lord God of H.	13:15
the vineyard of the Lord of H.	15: 7
In mine ears, said the Lord of H.,	15: 9
the Lord of H. shall be exalted	15:16
the law of the Lord of H.	15:24
Holy, holy, holy, is the Lord of H.;	16: 3
have seen the King, the Lord of H.	16: 5
Sanctify the Lord of H. himself,	18:13
in Israel from the Lord of H.,	18:18
The zeal of the Lord of H.	19: 7
do they seek the Lord of H.	2Ne 19:13
the wrath of the Lord of H.,	19:19
shall the Lord, the Lord of H.,	20:16

HOSTS — HOUSE

For the Lord God of H. shall	2Ne 20:23
thus saith the Lord God of H.;	20:24
the Lord of H. shall stir up a	20:26
the Lord, the Lord of H. shall	20:33
the Lord of H. mustereth	23: 4
mustereth the h. of the battle.	23: 4
in the wrath of the Lord of H.,	23:13
saith the Lord of H.,	24:22
saith the Lord of H.	24:23
The Lord of H. hath sworn,	24:24
the Lord of H. hath purposed,	24:27
saith the Lord of H.,	26: 4
saith the Lord of H.;	26: 5
saith the Lord of H.	26: 6
be visited of the Lord of H.,	27: 2
saith the Lord of H.,	27:27
saith the Lord of H.:	27:28
saith the Lord of H.	28:17
saith the Lord God of H.!	28:32
saith the Lord God of H.	28:32
thus saith the Lord of H.	Jac 2:28
saith the Lord of H.,	2:29
if I will, saith the Lord of H.,	2:30
not suffer, saith the Lord of H.,	2:32
my people, saith the Lord of H.	2:32
them of old, saith the Lord of H.	2:33
as numerous as the h. of Israel.	Mos 8: 8
with their numerous h.,	10: 8
come with their numerous h.;	20:20
trodden down by the h. of men.	Al 3: 2
cities, by their numberless h.,	51:27
us with their numerous h.,	58:15
the land, saith the Lord of H.,	He 13:17
saith the Lord of H., yea, our	13:18
that day, saith the Lord of H.	13:32
the Lord of H. is his name;	3Ne 22: 5
shall come, saith the Lord of H.	24: 1
not me, saith the Lord of H.	24: 5
unto you, saith the Lord of H.	24: 7
herewith, saith the Lord of H.,	24:10
the fields, saith the Lord of H.	24:11
land, saith the Lord of H.	24:12
mournfully before the Lord of H.?	24:14
be mine, saith the Lord of H.,	24:17
them up, saith the Lord of H.,	25: 1
do this, saith the Lord of H.	25: 3
with man, saith the Lord of H.	DC 1:33
them up, saith the Lord of H.,	29: 9
glory, with all the h. thereof,	29:11
wailing among the h. of men;	29:15
third part of the h. of heaven	29:36
all the seraphic h. of heaven,	38: 1
of all the h. of heaven—	38:11
heavens and all the h. thereof,	45: 1
saith the Lord God of h.;	56:10
for I am the Lord of H.;	64:24
I have given the heavenly h.	84:42
of God, saith the Lord of H.	85: 5
armies, even the h. of heaven.	88:112
armies; even the h. of hell,	88:113
unto you, saith the Lord of H.,	107:60
against them, saith the Lord of H.;	121:23
your reward, saith the Lord of H.	127: 4
priesthood, saith the Lord of H.	127: 8
generation, saith the Lord of H.	127: 9
burn them up, saith the Lord of h.,	133:64
cry unto the Lord of H. till he	135: 7
earth, and all the h. of them.	Abr 5: 1
burn them, saith the Lord of H.,	JS 2:37

HOT

as a garment in a h. furnace;	Mos 12: 3
h. drinks are not for the body	DC 89: 9
And in his h. displeasure,	101:90
in my h. displeasure will I send	Mses 7:34

HOUR

for the h. is close at hand,	Al 5:29
him not for the space of an h.,	18:14
in that selfsame h. that they cried	43:50
the h. is not yet, but is nigh	DC 1:35
the very h. what thou needest	24:18
the h. cometh that I will	DC 27: 5
the h. is nigh and the day	29: 9
For the h. is nigh, and that	29:10
for the h. of your mission is	31: 3
and it is the eleventh h.,	33: 3
or the h. no man knoweth;	39:21
in an h. when ye think not	45: 2
they know that hte h. is nigh.	45:38
but the h. and the day no man	49: 7
the h. and the day is not	51:17
quickly, in an h. you think not.	51:20
the h. is not yet, but is nigh	58: 4
cometh in an h. you think not.	61:38
And until that h. there will be	63:54
at that h. cometh an entire	63:54
is in force from this very h.	84:75
shall be given you in the very h.	84:85
this h. take purse or scrip,	84:86
the h. of their judgment is	84:115
in the first h. I will come unto	88:52
in the second h. I will visit	88:53
unto the first in the first h.,	88:56
tarried with him all that h.,	88:56
their lord, every man in his h.,	88:58
until his h. was finished,	88:60
every kingdom in its h.,	88:61
for the h. of judgment which is	88:84
for the space of half an h.;	88:95
for the h. of his judgment is	88:104
be given you in the very h.,	100: 6
hearken from this very h. unto	103: 5
mine enemies from this very h.	103: 6
power from this very h.,	104:10
only up to this h. unto them,	104:53
unto you from this very h.;	104:63
that Jerusalem from this h., may	109:62
continue to preach from that h.,	118: 3
in an h. when ye think not of;	124:10
in the h. of affliction;	124:16
and shall give him, in the very h.,	124:97
h. of temptation that may come	124:124
neither the day nor the h.	133:11
for the h. of his coming is nigh.—	133:17
the h. of his judgment is come;	133:38
the h. of their redemption;	Mses 7:67
But of that day, and h., no one	JS 1:40
at what h. your Lord doth come.	1:46
in such an h. as ye think not,	1:48
in an h. that he is not aware of,	1:53

HOURS

traveled for the space of many h.	1Ne 8: 8
lengthen out the day for many h.—	He 12:14
for the space of many h.	14:21
for the space of many h.	14:26
for about the space of three h.;	3Ne 8:19
in about the space of three h.—	8:19
land for the space of many h.;	10: 1
land for the space of many h.	10: 2
And for the space of three h.	Eth 2:14
fought for the space of three h.,	15:27
in their minutes, in their h.,	DC 88:44
it was for the space of many h.	Mses 1:10

HOUSE

a remnant of the h. of Israel;	T Pg
the remnant of the H. of Israel	T Pg
he returned to his own h.	1Ne 1: 7
And he left his h., and the land	2: 4
should go unto the h. of Laban.	3: 4
go in unto the h. of Laban.	3:11
went in unto the h. of Laban,	3:11
talked with him as he sat in his h.	3:11
again unto the h. of Laban.	3:23
forth towards the h. of Laban.	4: 5
came near unto the h. of Laban	4: 7
went up unto the h. of Ishmael,	7: 4
all the h. of Ishmael had come	7:22
also concerning the h. of Israel,	10:12
after the h. of Israel should be	10:14
the remnants of the h. of Israel,	10:14

HOUSE

the h. of Israel hath gathered	1 Ne 11:35
ye are of the h. of Israel.	12: 9
hath made unto the h. of Israel;	13:23
hath made unto the h. of Israel;	13:23
the remnant of the h. of Israel	13:33
the remnant of the h. of Israel—	13:34
numbered among the h. of Israel;	14: 2
the h. of Israel shall no more be	14: 2
the Lord unto the h. of Israel;	14: 5
the Father unto the h. of Israel?	14: 8
people who are of the h. of Israel.	14:17
the Lord, unto the h. of Israel.	14:26
the h. of Israel was compared unto	15:12
broken off from the h. of Israel,	15:12
not a branch of the h. of Israel?	15:12
they are of the h. of Israel,	15:14
again among the h. of Israel;	15:16
the Jews, or of the h. of Israel.	15:17
also of all the h. of Israel,	15:18
the Jews, or of the h. of Israel;	15:20
those who are of the h. of Israel.	19:10
shall visit all the h. of Israel	19:11
people who are of the h. of Israel,	19:16
speak unto all the h. of Israel,	19:19
a remnant of the h. of Israel,	19:24
written unto all the h. of Israel,	19:24
hear this, O h. of Jacob,	20: 1
Hearken, O ye h. of Israel,	21: 1
are of my people, O h. of Israel.	21: 1
then, O h. of Israel, behold,	21:12
not forget thee, O h. of Israel.	21:15
it appears that the h. of Israel,	22: 3
who are of the h. of Israel.	22: 6
after all the h. of Israel have	22: 7
but unto all the h. of Israel,	22: 9
those who are of the h. of Israel.	22:11
war against thee, O h. of Israel,	22:14
unto the h. of Israel;	2 Ne 3: 5
my people, O h. of Israel.	3: 9
restoring thee, O h. of Israel,	3:13
restoration unto the h. of Israel,	3:24
concerning all the h. of Israel;	6: 5
ye are of the h. of Israel.	6: 5
ye are of the h. of Israel.	6: 5
O h. of Israel, is my hand	7: 2
unto thee, O h. of Israel.	7: 4
with all the h. of Israel—	9: 1
unto the h. of Israel.	9:53
numbered among the h. of Israel.	10:18
from the h. of Israel,	10:22
the mountain of the Lord's h.	12: 2
to the h. of the God of Jacob;	12: 3
O h. of Jacob, come ye	12: 5
thy people, the h. of Jacob,	12: 6
his brother of the h. of his father,	13: 6
in my h. there is neither bread	13: 7
of Hosts is the h. of Israel,	15: 7
unto them that join h. to house,	15: 8
unto them that join house to h.,	15: 8
and the h. was filled with smoke.	16: 4
it was told the h. of David,	17: 2
Hear ye now, O h. of David;	17:13
people, and upon thy father's h.,	17:17
face from the h. of Jacob,	18:17
escaped of the h. of Jacob,	20:20
shall cleave to the h. of Jacob.	24: 1
the h. of Israel shall possess them,	24: 2
opened not the h. of his prisoners?	24:17
every one of them in his own h.	24:18
which are of the h. of Israel,	25: 4
shall be read upon the h. tops;	27:11
concerning the h. of Jacob:	27:33
a remnant of the h. of Israel.	28: 2
which are of the h. of Israel;	29: 1
which are of the h. of Israel;	29: 2
other tribes of the h. of Israel,	29:12
which are of the h. of Israel,	29:14
who are of the h. of Israel,	29:14
who are of the h. of Israel.	33:13
he spake unto the h. of Israel,	Jac 5: 1
Hearken, O ye h. of Israel,	5: 2
I will liken thee, O h. of Israel,	5: 3
concerning the h. of Israel,	6: 1
he remembereth the h. of Israel,	Jac 6: 4
every one unto his own h.	Mos 8: 4
out of the h. of bondage.	12:34
shalt not covet thy neighbor's h.,	13:24
to his own h. at Zarahemla	Al 8: 1
Therefore, go with me into my h.	8:20
a blessing unto me and my h.	8:20
the man received him into his h.;	8:21
he blessed Amulek and his h.,	8:22
Amulek, return to thine own h.,	10: 7
thou shalt receive him into thy h.	10: 7
he shall bless thee and thy h.;	10: 7
shall rest upon thee and thy h.	10: 7
and returned towards my h.	10: 8
Thou shalt receive into thy h.—	10: 8
this Alma hath dwelt at my h.	10:10
behold, he hath blessed mine h.,	10:11
went in unto the h. unto Zeezrom;	15: 5
and took him to his own h.,	15:18
she ran forth from h. to house,	19:17
she ran forth from house to h..	19:17
together unto the h. of the king.	19:18
or upon the king and his h.,	19:19
hath brought this evil upon his h.,	19:20
had driven them from h. to house,	20:30
had driven them from house to h.,	20:30
even to the h. of the king	22: 1
from one h. of worship to another,	23: 4
we have traveled from h. to house,	26:28
we have traveled from house to h.,	26:28
Zarahemla; even to his own h.	27:20
and went about from h. to house	30:56
from house to h. begging for	30:56
did go about from h. to house,	30:58
house to h., begging food for	30:58
when I did turn to my h. thou	33: 6
and take possession of their h.—	40:13
and he retired to his own h.	62:43
Go to the h. of Seantum, who	He 9:26
went his way towards his own h.,	10: 2
and did not go unto his own h..	10:12
he hath blessed the h. of Jacob,	3 Ne 5:21
covenanted with all the h. of Jacob,	5:25
covenanted with the h. of Jacob	5:25
restoring all the h. of Jacob	5:25
yea, who are of the h. of Israel,	10: 4
O ye people of the h. of Israel,	10: 5
O ye people of the h. of Israel,	10: 5
O ye h. of Israel whom I have	10: 6
But if not, O h. of Israel,	10: 7
light to all that are in the h.;	12:15
who built his h. upon a rock—	14:24
blew, and beat upon that h.;	14:25
who built his h. upon the sand—	14:26
blew, and beat upon that h.;	14:27
a remnant of the h. of Joseph.	15:12
other tribes of the h. of Israel,	15:15
all the people of the h. of Israel.	16: 5
unbelief of you, O h. of Israel,	16: 7
people who are of the h. of Israel;	16: 8
people who are of the h. of Israel,	16: 8
people who are of the h. of Israel,	16: 9
people who are of the h. of Israel	16: 9
unto my people, O h. of Israel,	16:11
show unto thee, O h. of Israel,	16:12
unto you, O h. of Israel,	16:12
among my people, O h. of Israel.	16:13
people, who are of the h. of Israel,	16:14
suffer my people, O h. of Israel,	16:15
of my people, O h. of Israel,	16:15
of the people of the h. of Israel.	17:14
a remnant of the h. of Israel.	20:10
unto his people, O h. of Israel.	20:12
a remnant of the h. of Jacob,	20:16
my people, O h. of Israel.	20:21
and ye are of the h. of Israel;	20:25
of my people, O h. of Israel.	20:27
my people, O h. of Israel.	21: 1
a remnant of the h. of Jacob,	21: 2
with his people, O h. of Israel;	21: 4
among my people, O h. of Israel;	21: 6
who are of the h. of Israel.	21: 7
among my people, O h. of Israel;	21:20
of the h. of Israel as shall come,	21:23

HOUSE

which are of the h. of Israel;	3Ne 23: 2	the congregation in the h. may	DC 88:129
that there may be meat in my h.;	24:10	he cometh into the h. of God,	88:130
his people of the h. of Israel.	29: 3	should be first in the h.—	88:130
the remnant of the h. of Israel;	29: 8	that mine h. shall be polluted	88:134
hath made unto the h. of Israel.	29: 9	one another in the h. of God,	88:136
who are of the h. of Israel.	30: 2	doings in the h. of the Lord,	88:137
remnant of the h. of Jacob	4Ne 1:49	descend, and beat upon their h.	90: 5
and also unto you, h. of Israel,	Mrm 3:17	the h. of Joseph, of the	90:10
even among all the h. of Israel,	4:12	set in order your own h., ,	93:43
be revealed upon the h.-tops—	5: 8	that are not right in your h.	93:43
have care for the h. of Israel,	5:10	first set in order thy h.	93:44
the calamity of the h. of Israel;	5:11	Kirtland, beginning at my h.	94: 1
remnant of the h. of Jacob;	5:12	of a h. for the presidency,	94: 3
the Jews, or all the h. of Israel,	5:14	the building of a h. unto me,	94:10
and unto all the h. of Israel.	5:20	this h. shall be wholly dedicated	94:12
ye remnant of the h. of Israel;	7: 1	the building of mine h.;	95: 3
ye that ye are of the h. of Israel.	7: 2	that you should build a h.,	95: 8
Lord who are the h. of Israel,	8:21	in the which h. I design to	95: 8
made unto the h. of Israel—	8:21	that you should build a h.	95:11
hath made with the h. of Israel;	9:37	let the h. be built, not after	95:13
Come unto me, O ye h. of Israel,	Eth 4:14	design to build mine holy h.	96: 2
unto your fathers, O h. of Israel.	4:15	upon the h. named among you	96: 9
into the h. of Noah by night	7:18	a h. should be built unto me	97:10
gathered in unto the h. of Jared	8:13	may be a h. built unto me	97:12
who fled with the h. of Omer.	9:12	my people build a h. unto me	97:15
and the h. of Emer did prosper	9:16	in my Father's h. are many	98:18
hast prepared a h. for man,	12:32	countries from h. to house,	99: 1
concerning the h. of Israel,	13: 5	from house to h., from village	99: 1
be built unto the h. of Israel.	13: 5	of my Father and his h.;	99: 4
the remnant of the h. of Joseph	13: 8	take all the strength of mine h.,	101:55
who were of the h. of Israel.	13:10	are the strength of mine h.,	101:55
made unto thee, O h. of Israel,	Mro 10:31	with the residue of mine h.	101:58
a branch of the h. of Jacob;	DC 10:60	steward in the midst of mine h.,	101:61
Gentiles unto the h. of Israel.	14:10	at the h. of Joseph Smith, Jun.,	102: 1
and also the h. of Israel.	18: 6	unto the strength of my h.,	103:22
Leave thy h. and home, except	19:36	of the strength of my h.	103:30
visit the h. of each member,	20:47	of the strength of my h.,	103:34
visit the h. of each member,	20:51	which is set off joining the h.,	104:28
judge the whole h. of Israel,	29:12	is to be for the Laneshine h.	104:28
shall be at your father's h.,	30: 4	the Laneshine h. [printing office]	104:29
Govern your h. in meekness,	31: 9	have the h. in which he lives,	104:34
which are of the h. of Israel.	39:11	off for the building of my h.,	104:43
should have a h. built,	41: 7	the h. of my servant Gazelam	104:45
who are of the h. of Israel.	42:39	the h. of my servant Gazelam	104:46
which ye call the h. of God,	45:18	to be stewards over mine h.,	104:57
say that this h. shall never fall.	45:18	suffer his h. to be broken up.	104:86
in the h. of my friends.	45:52	unto the strength of my h.,	105:16
is not far from the court-h.	57: 3	the strength of mine h. have	105:17
a supper of the h. of the Lord,	58: 9	gather up the strength of my h.,	105:27
also for the h. of the printing.	58:37	from on high in my h.,	105:33
shalt go to the h. of prayer	59: 9	to build a h. to thy name in	109: 2
going from h. to house,	75:18	O Lord, to accept of this h.,	109: 4
from house to h., and from	75:18	to build a h. to thy name,	109: 5
And in whatsoever h. ye enter,	75:19	needful thing, and establish a h.,	109: 8
your blessing upon that h.	75:19	even a h. of prayer,	109: 8
And in whatsoever h. ye enter,	75:20	a h. of fasting,	109: 8
depart speedily from that h.,	75:20	a h. of faith,	109: 8
shall be judges of that h.,	75:21	a h. of learning,	109: 8
of judgment, than for that h.;	75:22	a h. of glory,	109: 8
in the h. of my Father.	81: 6	a h. of order,	109: 8
until an h. shall be built unto	84: 5	a h. of God;	109: 8
the Lord, which shall fill the h.	84: 5	thy people, and upon this thy h.,	109:12
continue with the h. of Aaron	84:27	may be continually in this h.;	109:12
sacrifice in the h. of the Lord,	84:31	the threshold of the Lord's h.	109:13
which h. shall be built unto	84:31	thy h., a place of thy holiness.	109:13
Mount Zion in the Lord's h.,	84:32	who shall worship in this h.	109:14
and wo unto that h.,	84:94	And that this h. may be	109:16
Wo, I say again, unto that h.,	84:95	a h. of prayer,	109:16
their h. shall be left unto	84:115	a h. of fasting,	109:16
set in order the h. of God,	85: 7	a h. of faith,	109:16
and establish a h., even a	88:119	a h. of glory and of God,	109:16
even a h. of prayer, a house	88:119	glory and of God, even thy h.;	109:16
a h. of fasting, a house of	88:119	of thy people, into this h.,	109:17
a h. of faith, a house of	88:119	all their outgoings from this h.	109:18
a h. of learning, a house of	88:119	come into thy h. to pollute it;	109:20
a h. of glory, a house of	88:119	who shall reverence thee in thy h.	109:21
a h. of order, a house of	88:119	servants may go forth from this h.	109:22
house of order, a h. of God;	88:119	name and standing in this thy h.,	109:24
the order of the h. prepared	88:127	thy name shall be put in this h.;	109:26
shall be the order of the h.	88:128	And let thy h. be filled, with	109:37
the h. which shall be prepared	88:128	servants shall go out from thy h.,	109:56
shall be first in the h. of God,	88:129	broken off from the h. of David;	109:63

HOUSE

dedication of this h. unto thee,	DC 109:78	the mountains of the Lord's h.	DC 133:13
built this h. to my name.	110: 6	performed in the Endowment H.,	OD
behold, I have accepted this h.,	110: 7	occurrence the Endowment H. was,	OD
to my people in mercy in this h.	110: 7	Lord cursed Lamech, and his h.,	Mses 5:52
and do not pollute this holy h.	110: 8	thee away from thy father's h.,	Abr 1:16
have been endowed in this h.	110: 9	and from thy father's h., unto	2: 3
the fame of this h. shall spread	110:10	turned away from my father's h.,	2:17
in Zion, and remove not thy h.;	112: 6	to take anything out of his h.;	JS 1:14
And upon my h. shall it begin,	112:25	if the good man of the h. had	1:47
and from my h. shall it go forth,	112:25	suffered his h. to have been	1:47
against me in the midst of my h.,	112:26	intention of going to the h.;	2:48
Ephraim, or of the h. of Joseph,	113: 4	at the h. of Squire Tarbill,	2:58
you to build a h. unto me,	115: 8	at the h. of my wife's father,	2:62
to build a h. unto my name;	115:10	and was just leaving the h.,	2:64
laying the foundation of my h.	115:11	Oliver Cowdery came to my h.,	2:66
building of a h. unto my name;	115:13	to board for a season at my h.,	2:66
let a h. be built unto my name	115:14		
their God, and mine h. also,	117:16	HOUSEHOLD	
on the building-spot of my h.,	118: 5	all his h. from perishing	1Ne 5:14
For the building of mine h.,	119: 2	of Ishmael, and also his h.,	7: 5
from the ordinances of mine h.	121:19	yea, and even all his h.	2Ne 4:10
to the h. of the daughters of Zion.	124:11	had spoken unto all his h.,	4:12
the consecrations of mine h.,	124:21	his whole h. were converted	Al 22:23
build a h. unto my name,	124:22	unto the Lord, and all his h.;	23: 3
it shall be for a h. for boarding,	124:23	in your houses, yea, over all your h.,	34:21
a h. that strangers may come	124:23	his daughters, and all his h.,	Eth 9: 3
therefore let it be a good h.,	124:23	all his h. save it were Shez—	10: 1
h. shall be a healthful habitation	124:24	if he would repent, and all his h.,	13:20
and build a h. to my name,	124:27	all his h. save it were himself.	13:21
ordinance belongeth to my h.,	124:30	neither his h., neither the people;	13:22
not able to build a h. unto me.	124:30	men, and to the h. of faith,	DC 121:45
saints, to build a h. unto me;	124:31	hath made ruler over his h.,	JS 1:49
time to build a h. unto me;	124:31		
time to build a h. to me,	124:33	HOUSES	
except ye perform them in a h.	124:37	the spoil of the poor in your h.	2Ne 13:14
build a h. in the land of promise,	124:38	many h. shall be desolate,	15: 9
by the ordinance of my holy h.,	124:39	and the h. without man,	16:11
this h. be built unto my name,	124:40	offense to both the h. of Israel,	18:14
all things pertaining to this h.,	124:42	their h. shall be spoiled	23:16
you build a h. unto my name,	124:47	their h. shall be full of doleful	23:21
a city and a h. unto my name,	124:51	shall cry in their desolate h.,	23:22
again to build a h. to my name,	124:55	or out of the h. of worship?	26:26
pertaining to my boarding h.	124:56	their families, to their own h.	Mos 6: 3
my servant Joseph and his h.	124:56	to their lands, and to their h.,	Al 3: 1
after him have place in that h.,	124:59	and upon your h. and lands,	7:27
And let the name of that h. be	124:60	have free access to their h.,	23: 2
that house be called Nauvoo H.;	124:60	we have entered into their h. and	26:29
the purpose of building that h.	124:62	synagogues, and into their h.;	32: 1
stock for the building of that h.	124:63	Cry unto him in your h., yea,	34:21
for a share of stock in that h.,	124:64	support their lands, and their h.,	43: 9
any one man for stock in that h.	124:64	came to their h. and their lands.	44:23
from any one man in that h.	124:66	they did build h. of cement,	He 3: 7
as a stockholder in this h.,	124:67	in tents, and in h. of cement,	3: 9
he shall receive stock in that h.;	124:68	have timber to build their h.,	3: 9
not receive any stock in that h.	124:68	your h. shall be left unto you	15: 1
it shall be for stock in that h.,	124:69	and their children, and their h.,	Mrm 2:23
other purpose, only in that h.	124:70	and building h. of worship,	DC 42:35
anywhere else, only in that h.,	124:71	food or for raiment, or for h.,	59:17
anywhere else, only in that h.,	124:71	for h. and for lands,	70:16
hands for the building of that h.,	124:72	Set in order your h.;	90:18
thousand dollars stock in that h.,	124:72	a committee to build mine h.,	94:15
stock into that h. for himself,	124:74	two h. are not to be built	94:16
honored in the midst of his h.,	124:76	for the building of my h.,	104:34
Hyrum put stock into that h.	124:77	appointed unto him the h.	104:39
Galland put stock into that h.;	124:78	have appointed unto you, in h.,	104:68
for an interest in that h.	124:78	h. and their barns shall perish,	121:20
Marks pay stock into that h.,	124:80	h. and lands, wives and children,	132:55
Sherwood pay stock into that h.,	124:81	Let each company prepare h.,	136: 9
Law pay stock into that h.,	124:82	in your fields, and in your h.,	136:11
to build a h. for boarding,	124:111		
for boarding, even the Nauvoo H.	124:111	HOUSETOP	
build a h. for my servant Joseph,	124:115	him who is on the h. flee,	JS 1:14
of the quorum of the Nauvoo H.,	124:117		
to the quorum of the Nauvoo H.	124:119	HOUSE-TOPS: see HOUSE and TOPS.	
quorum of the Nauvoo H. have	124:121	HOUSETOPS	
do in building the Nauvoo H.;	124:121	shall be spoken upon the h.,	DC 1: 3
unto them for stock in that h.	124:122		
rooms for all these offices in my h.	124:145	HOW	
mine h. is a house of order,	132: 8	H. is it possible that the Lord will	1Ne 3:31
mine house is a h. of order,	132: 8	h. is it that ye are so hard in	7: 8
and not a h. of confusion.	132: 8	H. is it that ye have not hearkened	7: 9
for my h. is a house of order,	132:18	H. is it that ye have forgotten	7:10
for my house is a h. of order,	132:18		

h. is it that ye have forgotten	1 Ne	7:11
h. is it, that ye have forgotten		7:12
h. great a number had testified		10: 5
h. beautiful upon the mountains		13:37
H. is that ye do not keep the		15:10
H. is it that ye will perish,		15:10
h. come unto him and be saved.		15:14
food, h. great was their joy!		16:32
h. is it that he cannot instruct		17:51
h. great things the Lord had done	2 Ne	1: 1
h. merciful the Lord had been		1: 3
h. great the importance to make		2: 8
that I should know h. to speak		7: 4
O h. great the goodness of		9:10
O h. great the plan of our		9:13
O h. great the holiness of		9:20
h. great the covenants of the Lord,		9:53
h. great his condescensions unto		9:53
Then said I: Lord, h. long?		16:11
H. hath the oppressor ceased,		24: 4
H. art thou fallen from heaven,		24:12
h. that we came out from		30: 4
h. much more need have we,		31: 5
And now, h. could ye speak with		32: 2
h. that ye are beginning to labor	Jac	2: 5
h. much better are you than they,		3: 7
h. that ye have grieved their hearts		3:10
H. unsearchable are the depths of		4: 8
h. is it possible that these,		4:17
H. comest thou hither to plant		5:21
And h. blessed are they who have		6: 3
and h. cursed are they who shall		6: 3
And h. merciful is our God unto us,		6: 4
And I said: Lord, h. is it done?	En	1: 7
O h. you ought to thank your	Mos	2:19
O then, h. ye ought to impart of		4:21
h. much more just will be your		4:22
For h. knoweth a man the master		5:13
h. great reason we have to mourn.		7:23
h. many of our brethren have		7:24
O h. marvelous are the works		8:20
and h. long doth he suffer with		8:20
h. blind and impenetrable are		8:20
H. beautiful upon the mountains		12:21
O h. beautiful upon the mountains		15:15
h. beautiful upon the mountains		15:16
h. beautiful upon the mountains		15:17
O h. beautiful upon the mountains		15:18
h. beautiful are they to the eyes		18:30
yea, and h. blessed are they,		18:30
h. they should deliver		22: 1
h. great things he has done for		27:16
And h. blessed are they!		27:37
h. much iniquity doth one		29:17
h. will any of you feel, if ye shall	Al	5:22
h. do ye suppose that I know		5:45
h. to succor his people according		7:12
h. have ye forgotten the		9: 8
yea, h. soon ye have forgotten		9: 8
h. many times he delivered		9:10
H. knowest thou these things?		11:30
therefore, h. can ye be saved,		11:37
cometh, we know not h. soon.		13:25
H. can we witness this awful scene?		14:10
H. shall we look when we are		14:21
H. long shall we suffer these		14:26
H. knowest thou the thoughts of		18:20
H. knowest thou the thought and		21: 6
H. knowest thou that we have		21: 6
H. knowest thou that we are not		21: 6
h. God created man after his		22:12
Oh, h. merciful is our God!		24:15
h. great reason have we to rejoice;		26: 1
h. many of them are brought to		26: 3
h. many thousands of our		26:13
h. many of these have laid		26:34
h. great the inequality of man is		28:13
h. great shall be their reward!		29:15
H. do ye know of their surety?		30:15
O, h. long, O Lord, wilt thou		31:26
O Lord God, h. long wilt thou		31:30
h. much more cursed is he that		32:19
or h. they should plant the seed,		33: 1
h. can ye disbelieve on the Son	Al	33:14
h. strict are the commandments		37:13
h. great iniquity ye brought upon		39:11
h. could a man repent except he		42:17
H. could he sin if there was no		42:17
H. could there be a law save		42:17
h. quick the children of men do		46: 8
yea, h. quick to do iniquity,		46: 8
h. great was their disappointment;		49: 4
we see h. merciful and just are		50:19
did remember h. great things		62:50
and h. that it was his object to	He	2: 8
ye may know h. that it is said,		5: 6
h. could you have given away to		7:16
h. could you have forgotten your		7:20
h. long the Lord your God will		9:21
h. thou hast with unwearyingness		10: 4
And thus we can behold h. false,		12: 1
O h. foolish, and how vain,		12: 4
and h. vain, and how evil,		12: 4
vain, and h. evil, and devilish,		12: 4
and h. quick to do iniquity,		12: 4
and h. slow to do good, are the		12: 4
h. quick to hearken unto the		12: 4
h. quick to be lifted up in pride;		12: 5
yea, h. quick to boast,		12: 5
h. slow are they to remember		12: 5
h. slow to walk in wisdom's		12: 5
O h. great is the nothingness		12: 7
h. long will ye suppose that the		13:29
h. long will ye suffer yourselves		13:29
h. long will ye choose darkness		13:29
h. oft have I gathered you as a	3 Ne	10: 4
h. oft would I have gathered you		10: 5
h. oft would I have gathered you		10: 5
h. oft will I gather you as a		10: 6
h. great is that darkness!		13:23
lilies of the field h. they grow;		13:28
h. wilt thou say to thy brother:		14: 4
know h. to give good gifts unto		14:11
h. much more shall your Father		14:11
H. beautiful upon the mountains		20:40
H. be it that ye have not written		23:11
h. be it my church save it be		27: 5
And h. blessed were they!	4 Ne	1:18
h. can ye stand before the	Mrm	5:22
h. could ye have departed from		6:17
h. could ye have rejected that		6:17
h. is it that ye could have fallen!		6:19
h. long the Lord will suffer that		8: 5
h. great things the Father hath	Eth	4:14
h. great things the Lord had done		6:30
h. great things the Lord had done		6:30
h. is it possible that ye can	Mro	7:20
H. is it that ye can attain unto		7:40
h. many little children have died		8:12
h. can a people like this, that		9:11
h. can a people like this, whose		9:13
H. can we expect that God will		9:14
h. merciful the Lord hath been		10: 3
but h. strict were your	DC	3: 5
h. oft you have transgressed		3: 6
h. great is his joy in the soul		18:13
h. great shall be your joy with		18:15
h. great will be your joy if		18:16
of godliness, h. great is it!		19:10
h. oft you know not,		19:15
h. exquisite you know not,		19:15
h. hard to bear you know not.		19:15
know h. to govern my church		41: 3
beware h. you hold them		41:12
h. to act and direct my church,		43: 8
h. to act upon the points of		43: 8
h. often would I have gathered		43:24
H. oft have I called upon you		43:25
h. the day of redemption shall		45:17
h. to organize this people.		51: 1
h. to succor them who are		62: 1
beware h. they take my name		63:61
h. great blessings the Father		78:17
h. you may act before me,		82: 9
of the field, h. they grow,		84:82
h. shall the body be able to		84:109

HOW 463 HUMBLED

beware h. they hold them DC 90: 5
and know h. to worship, 93:19
know h. to act concerning this 96: 1
know h. to act in the discharge 103: 1
h. long wilt thou suffer this 109:49
h. he has covenanted with 109:68
behold h. great is your calling. 112:33
H. long shall thy hand be stayed, 121: 2
h. long shall they suffer these 121: 3
H. long can rolling waters remain 121:33
h. shall your washings be 124:37
H. beautiful upon the mountains 128:19
h. glorious is the voice we hear 128:23
h. great things thou hast prepared 133:45
h. easy it will burn up the dry 135: 6
h. many can go next spring; 136: 7
H. is it that the heavens weep, Mses 7:28
H. is it that thou canst weep, 7:29
h. is it thou canst weep? 7:31
is it, and h. shall I know it? JS 2:10
h. to act I did not know, 2:12
h. very strange it was that an 2:23
h. and in what manner his 2:54
h. the young man found out that 2:64
let them worship h., where, or AoF 11

HOWBEIT
H. he meaneth not so, 2Ne 20: 7
H. that was not first which is DC 128:14
H. that he made the greater star; Abr 3:18

HOWEVER
They are, h., to warn, DC 20:59
Abraham, h., did not refuse, 132:36
h., holding sacred the freedom 134: 5
I soon found, h., that my telling JS 2:22
H., it was nevertheless a fact 2:24
excitement, h., still continued, 2:61
The persecution, h., became so 2:61

HOWL
H. ye, for the day of the Lord is 2Ne 23: 6
H., O gate; cry, O city; 24:31
they shall h. all the day long. Mos 12: 4
and they shall have cause to h., 16: 2
ought to begin to h. and mourn, He 9:22
and then shall ye weep and h. 13:32
they began to weep and h. again 3Ne 10: 8

HOWLING
there was great mourning and h. 3Ne 8:23
they did cease lamenting and h. 10: 2
took up a h. and a lamentation Eth 15:16

HOWLINGS
thus were the h. of the people 3Ne 8:25
their h. and lamentations, Eth 15:16
their h., and their mournings, 15:17

HUE
in all their dark and hellish h., DC 123: 6

HUMAN
that any h. soul should perish; Mos 28: 3
for it shall not be a h. sacrifice; Al 34:10
the whole h. family of Adam; Mrm 3:20
we do not believe that the law DC 134: 4
h. laws being instituted for 134: 6
h. beings to be held in servitude. 134:12
and the foibles of h. nature; JS 2:28

HUMBLE
did h. themselves before the Lord; 1Ne 13:16
did h. themselves before the Lord. 15:20
did h. themselves before the Lord; 16: 5
did h. themselves before the Lord, 16:32
h. themselves again before the Lord. 18: 4
are the h. followers of Christ; 2Ne 28:14
except they h. themselves Mos 3:18
submissive, meek, h., patient, 3:19
and h. yourselves before God; 4:10
and h. yourselves even in the 4:11
And they did h. themselves 21:13

And they did h. themselves Mos 21:14
because they did h. themselves 29:20
of the h. followers of God, Al 4:15
ye have been sufficiently h.? 5:27
who h. themselves and do walk 5:54
and h. themselves before God— 6: 3
I would that ye should be h., 7:23
ye give to an h. servant of God 8:19
should h. yourselves before God, 13:13
h. yourselves even as the people in 13:14
h. yourselves before the Lord, 13:28
becoming h., meek, submissive, 13:28
to h. themselves before God, 15:17
and h. seeker of happiness. 27:18
synagogues, that ye may be h., 32:12
are necessarily brought to be h. 32:12
ye are compelled to be h. 32:13
if he is compelled to be h., 32:13
ye were compelled to be h. 32:14
blessed who truly h. themselves 32:14
they who are compelled to be h. 32:15
blessed are they who h. themselves 32:16
without being compelled to be h.; 32:16
been compelled to h. yourselves; 32:25
who would h. themselves, 32:25
Yea, h. yourselves, and continue in 34:19
h. yourselves even to the dust, 34:38
teach them to h. themselves and 37:33
the people did h. themselves 48:20
brought down to h. themselves 51:21
did h. themselves before God, 62:41
did h. themselves exceedingly 62:49
the more h. part of the people He 3:34
and smiting their h. brethren 4:12
to be the h. followers of God 6: 5
and the h. followers of God. 6:39
did h. themselves in sackcloth, 11: 9
and others were exceedingly h.; 3Ne 6:13
were h. and penitent before God. 6:13
and h. yourselves before him, Mrm 5:24
h. themselves before the Lord, Eth 6:12
weakness that they may be h.; 12:27
that h. themselves before me; 12:27
for if they h. themselves 12:27
h. themselves as their little Mro 8:10
inasmuch as they were h. DC 1:28
not h. himself sufficiently 5:24
h. himself in mighty prayer 5:24
now, except he h. himself 5:28
shall be h. and full of love, 12: 8
lest I h. you with my 19:20
canst thou be h. and meek, 19:41
All those who h. themselves 20:37
h. themselves before me, 29: 2
truly h. before me and contrite 54: 3
their sins with h. hearts; 61: 2
h. yourselves before me, 67:10
for ye are not sufficiently h., 67:10
all things bow in h. reverence, 76:93
many of whom are truly h. 97: 1
as he will be h. before me. 104:23
shall h. yourselves before me, 104:79
as you are diligent and h., 104:80
as ye are h. and faithful 104:82
prayerful, and h. before me, 105:23
as he will h. himself before me. 106: 7
Be thou h.; and the Lord 112:10
shall h. themselves before me, 112:22
let him be h. before me, 124:97
and h. himself before me. 124:103
I am, as ever, your h. servant, 128:25
enlighten the h. and contrite, 136:33

HUMBLED
for they had h. themselves 1Ne 16:24
lofty looks of man shall be h., 2Ne 12:11
the mighty man shall be h., 15:15
the eyes of the lofty shall be h. 15:15
and the haughty shall be h. 20:33
and they h. themselves Al 5:13
ye had h. yourselves before God, 7: 3
afflictions had truly h. them 32: 6
had h. themselves sufficiently Eth 9:35
have h. yourselves before me, DC 61:37

HUMBLETH

the great man h. himself not,	2Ne	12: 9
he h. himself before the Father,		31: 7
Yea, he that truly h. himself,	Al	32:15
Martin Harris h. not himself	DC	5:32

HUMBLING

and h. himself sincerely,	DC	20: 6
by h. the rich and the proud.		84:112
learn wisdom by h. himself		136:32

HUMBLY

to walk h. before the Lord;	Eth	6:17
did walk h. before the Lord,		6:30
yea, to do justly, to walk h.,	DC	11:12

HUMILITY

come down in the depths of h.,	2Ne	9:42
even in the depths of h.,	Mos	4:11
even in the depths of h.;		21:14
and this because of their h.;	Al	1:20
bring you down to the dust in h.		42:30
God, even in the depth of h.		62:41
stronger and stronger in their h.,	He	3:35
of them into the depths of h.,		6: 5
because of this their h.		11:11
of their repentance and their h.	3Ne	4:33
come down into the depths of h.		12: 2
because of their h. and their	4Ne	1:29
and that he told me in plain h.,	Eth	12:39
godliness, charity, h., diligence.	DC	4: 6
thou shalt do it with all h.,		19:30
by your diligence and h. and		104:79
and continue in h. before me.		105:12
in meekness and h.,		113: 3

HUMPHREY, Solomon

Joseph Wakefield and H.	DC	52:35

HUNDRED

six h. years from the time that	1Ne	10: 4
in six h. years from the time		19: 8
Messiah cometh in six h. years	2Ne	25:19
many h. years before his coming;	Jac	4: 4
shall come many h. years hence.		7: 7
an h. and seventy and nine years	En	1:25
two h. years had passed away,	Jar	1: 5
two h. and thirty and eight		1:13
two h. and seventy and six years	Om	1: 3
two h. and eighty and two years		1: 3
three h. and twenty years had		1: 5
And it is many h. years after	WM	1: 2
four h. and seventy-six years	Mos	6: 4
two h. and seventy-nine of our		9:19
about two h. and four souls		18:16
about four h. and fifty souls.		18:35
five h. and nine years from		29:46
twelve thousand five h. thirty	Al	2:19
six thousand five h. sixty and		2:19
about three thousand five h. souls		4: 5
four h. years from the time that		45:10
there were two h., out of my		57:25
of five thousand and four h.		63: 4
about three h. souls who saw	He	5:49
four h. years pass not away save		13: 5
four h. years shall not pass away		13: 9
it was six h. years from the	3Ne	1: 1
an h. years had passed away		2: 5
six h. and nine years had		2: 6
two thousand and five h. souls;		17:25
an h. years had passed away,	4Ne	1:14
an h. and ten years had passed		1:18
an h. and ninety and four		1:21
two h. years had passed		1:22
in this two h. and first year		1:24
two h. and ten years had		1:27
two h. and thirty years had		1:34
two h. and thirty and first		1:35
two h. and forty and four		1:40
two h. and fifty years pass		1:41
also two h. and sixty years.		1:41
three h. years had passed		1:45

three h. and five years had	4Ne	1:47
three h. and twenty years had		1:48
three h. and twentieth year		1:48
three h. and twenty and	Mrm	2: 2
the three h. and twenty and		2: 3
and three h. and thirty years		2: 9
three h. and forty and four		2:15
the three h. and forty and		2:16
the three h. and forty and		2:22
the three h. and forty and		2:28
the three h. and fiftieth year		2:28
three h. and sixty years from		3: 4
the three h. and sixty and		3: 7
in the three h. and sixty and		3: 8
in the three h. and sixty and		4: 1
in the three h. and sixty and		4: 7
the three h. and sixty and		4:10
in the three h. and sixty and		4:15
the three h. and seventy and		4:16
three h. and seventy and nine		5: 5
the three h. and eightieth year		5: 6
when three h. and eighty and		6: 5
four h. years have passed away		8: 6
three h. and forty and four	Eth	6:11
being an h. and two years old.		9:24
an h. and forty and two years		9:24
four h. and twenty years have	Mro	10: 1
one thousand eight h. and	DC	20: 1
Lord eighteen h. and thirty,		21: 3
should be baptized an h. times		22: 2
eight h. and thirty-two.—		76:11
one h. and forty-four thousand,		77:11
unto him, even an h. fold,		78:19
talents, yea, even an h. fold,		82:18
your reward shall be an h.-fold.		98:25
of thine enemy an h.-fold;		98:45
or by fifties, or by an h.,		103:30
to the number of five h. of		103:30
if you cannot obtain five h.,		103:32
you may obtain three h.		103:32
if ye cannot obtain three h.,		103:33
ye may obtain one h.		103:33
until you have obtained a h. of		103:34
or twenty, or fifty, or an h.,		104:69
or twenty, or fifty, or a h.,		104:73
one h. and thirty-four years		107:44
four h. and ninety-six years		107:46
Jared was two h. years old		107:47
three h. and sixty-five years,		107:49
four h. and thirty years old		107:49
Methuselah was one h. years		107:50
h. and forty four thousand,		133:18
lived one h. and thirty years,	Mses	6:10
were eight h. years, and he		6:11
were nine h. and thirty years,		6:12
lived one h. and five years,		6:13
eight h. and seven years, and		6:14
were nine h. and twelve years,		6:16
eight h. and fifteen years, and		6:18
Enos were nine h. and five years,		6:18
eight h. and forty years,		6:19
were nine h. and ten years,		6:19
eight h. and thirty years,		6:20
eight h. and ninety-five years,		6:20
one h. and sixty-two years,		6:21
eight h. years, and begat		6:21
were nine h. and sixty-two years,		6:24
three h. and sixty-five years.		7:68
were four h. and thirty years.		8: 1
one h. and eighty-seven years,		8: 5
seven h. and eighty-two years,		8: 6
nine h. and sixty-nine years,		8: 7
one h. and eighty-two years,		8: 8
five h. and ninety-five years,		8:10
seven h. and seventy-seven years,		8:11
was four h. and fifty years old,		8:12
five h. years old he begat Ham.		8:12
shall be an h. and twenty years;		8:17
thousand eight h. and five,	JS	2: 3
of eighteen h. and twenty.		2:14
eight h. and twenty-three,		2:27
eighteen h. and twenty-three—		2:28

HUNDRED   465   HYMNS

eight h. and twenty-seven,	JS	2:59
eight h. and thirty-eight,		2:60

HUNDREDFOLD
unto him an h. in this world,	DC	132:55

HUNDRED-FOLD: see HUNDRED and FOLD.

HUNDREDS
by h., or by fifties, or by	DC	104:68
a chance to loan money by h.,		104:84
organized with captains of h.,		136: 3
presidents, and captains of h.,		136:15

HUNDREDTH
a h. part of the proceedings of	Jac	3:13
I cannot write the h. part of	WM	1: 5
a h. part of the proceedings of	He	3:14
cannot contain even a h. part	3Ne	5: 8
even a h. part of the things		26: 6
the h. part I have not written)	Eth	15:33

HUNG
great destruction which h. over	Mrm	2: 8

HUNGER
suffered much affliction, h., thirst,	1Ne	16:35
perish in the wilderness with h.		16:35
They shall not h. nor thirst,		21:10
we must have perished with h.	2Ne	1:24
h., thirst, and fatigue,	Mos	3: 7
suffered h., thirst, and fatigue.		7:16
that they did not suffer with h.		21:16
they might not perish with h.;		21:17
from them that they might h.,	Al	14:22
such as h., thirst and fatigue,		17: 5
their sufferings with h. and thirst,		18:37
they also had suffered h., thirst,		20:29
them that they should h. not,		31:38
until ye are filled, that ye h. not,		32:42
were afflicted with h. and thirst,		37:42
even h., thirst, and fatigue,		60: 3
they were about to perish with h.,		60: 9
that we should perish with h.;		60:35
were about to perish with h.	3Ne	4:20
h. and thirst after righteousness,		12: 6
soul shall never h. nor thirst,		20: 8
of famine and excess of h.	DC	89:15

HUNGERED
And my soul h.;	En	1: 4
he entered the city he was an h.,	Al	8:19
I was an h., for I had fasted		8:26
and he is an h., and thou shalt		10: 7

HUNGRY
through it hardly bestead and h.;	2Ne	18:21
when they shall be h., they shall		18:21
on the right hand and be h.;		19:20
as unto a h. man which dreameth,		27: 3
and to feed the h.,	Jac	2:19
your children that they go h.,	Mos	4:14
such as feeding the h.,		4:26
who were naked, or that were h.,	Al	1:30
the naked and those who were h.,		4:12
and the needy, feeding the h.,		4:13
their food from the h.,	He	4:12
suffer the h., and the needy,	Mrm	8:39
And they shall not go h.,	DC	84:80

HUNT
I went to h. beasts in the forests;	En	1: 3
began to h. the seed of Amulon	Al	25: 8
did h. the band of robbers of	He	6:37
to h. food for the people of	Eth	10:19

HUNTED
And in that day ye shall be h.,	Mos	17:18
h. at this day by the Lamanites.	Al	25: 9
and they were h., and they were		25:12
plundered, and h., and driven	He	3:16

and be h., and shall be smitten	He	15:12
people of Nephi again were h.	Mrm	2:20
were h. by the Lamanites,		8: 2
Lamanites have h. my people,		8: 7

HUNTER
being called after the mighty h.)	Eth	2: 1
also himself became a great h.		10:19

HUNTINGTON, William
Alpheus Cutler, H.   DC 124:132

HURL
to h. away your souls down to	He	7:16

HURLED
stars shall be h. from their places.	DC	133:49

HURT
They shall not h. nor destroy	2Ne	21: 9
They shall not h. nor destroy		30:15
the prison, and they were not h.;	Al	14:28
the Lamanites could not h. them.		50: 4
therefore they shall not h. him,	3Ne	21:10
thing it shall not h. them;	Mrm	9:24
no water that could h. them,	Eth	6: 7
counsel wrongfully to your h.,	DC	64:20
H. not the earth, neither the		77: 9
it shall not h. them;		84:71
and a young man to my h.	Mses	5:47

HUSBAND
the Lord hath commanded my h.	1Ne	5: 8
the widow mourning for her h.,	Mos	21: 9
The servants of my h. have made	Al	19: 4
that ye should go in and see my h.,		19: 5
she watched over the bed of her h.,		19:11
For thy maker, thy h., the	3Ne	22: 5
Joseph Smith, Jun., thy h.,	DC	25: 5
thy h. shall support thee in		25: 9
Let thy soul delight in thy h.,		25:14
For the unbelieving h. is		74: 1
wife is sanctified by the h.;		74: 1
for the unbelieving h. was		74: 3
if her h. be with another woman,		132:43
also gave unto her h. with her,	Mses	4:12
thy desire shall be to thy h.,		4:22

HUSBANDS
and abominations of their h.	Jac	2:31
their h. love their wives,		3: 7
and their wives love their h.;		3: 7
their h. and their wives love		3: 7
they should not destroy their h.	Mos	23:33
widows mourning for their h.,	Al	28: 5
and mothers, ye h. and wives,	Mrm	6:19
their h. to cry unto the Lord		8:40
the h. and fathers of those	Mro	9: 8
women upon the flesh of their h.,		9: 8
lost their h. or fathers:	DC	83: 1
Women have claim on their h.,		83: 2
until their h. are taken;		83: 2
h. and fathers have been murdered,		123: 9

HUSHED
Therefore they h. their fears,	Mos	23:28

HYDE, Orson
My servant, H., was called by	DC	68: 1
the Lord unto you, my servant H.,		68: 7
let my servant H. and my		75:13
servants H. and John Gould,		100:14
Cowdery, Samuel H. Smith, H.,		102: 3
7, John Johnson; 8, H.;		102:34
OLIVER COWDERY, H., clerks.		102:34
Let my servant H. journey		103:40
Orson Pratt, H., William Smith,		124:129

HYMNS
make a selection of sacred h.,	DC	25:11

HYPOCRISY 466 ILLUMINATED

HYPOCRISY
acting no h. and no deception	2Ne 31:13
mischiefs, and all manner of h.,	3Ne 16:10
without h., and without guile—	DC 121:42

HYPOCRITE
for every one of them is a h.	2Ne 19:17
Thou h., first cast the beam	3Ne 14: 5

HYPOCRITES
ye lawyers and h., for ye are	Al 10:17
as h. who do deny the faith.	34:28
will h. do in the synagogues	3Ne 13: 2
thou shalt not do as the h.,	13: 5
when ye fast be not as the h.,	13:16
pollutions, ye h., ye teachers,	Mrm 8:38
them that are deceivers and h.,	DC 50: 6
there are h. among you,	50: 7
But the h. shall be detected	50: 8
h. shall be proved by them,	64:39
them their portion among h.,	101:90
and ye are found h.,	104:55
portion of the oppressor among h.,	124: 8
him his portion with the h.;	JS 1:54

HYPOCRITICAL
send him against a h. nation,	2Ne 20: 6

HYRUM: see also SMITH, Hyrum.
Behold thou art H., my son;	DC 11:23
Behold, I speak unto you, H.,	23: 3
Sidney, and my servant H.,	112:17
Sidney, neither my servant H.,	115:13
H. put stock into that house	124:77
to go with my servant H. to	124:79
in the room of my servant H.,	124:91
that my servant H. may take	124:91
H. may bear record of the	124:96
servant H., and for them alone;	124:102
of my servants Joseph, and H.,	124:118
H. was shot first and fell	135: 1
and so has his brother H.	135: 3
H. had made ready to go—	135: 4
H., myself, Samuel Harrison,	JS 2: 4
H. and Samuel Harrison;	2: 7

I: *see in the APPENDIX.*

ICE
and the i. shall flow down at	DC 133:26

IDEA
i. that the Father and the Son	DC 130: 3

IDENTIFIED
who are i. with the Gentiles.	DC 109:60

IDLE
they did become an i. people,	2Ne 5:24
the more i. part of the Lamanites	Al 22:28
and I did stand as an i. witness	Mrm 3:16
Thou shalt not be i.;	DC 42:42
he that is i. shall not eat the	42:42
shalt not i. away thy time.	60:13
and not tarry, neither be i.	75: 3
cast away your i. thoughts and	88:69
Cease to be i.; cease to be	88:124
and not be i. in her days	90:31

IDLENESS
a filthy people, full of i.	1Ne 12:23
sorceries, and in idolatry or i.,	Al 1:32
than spend their days in i.	24:18
see that ye refrain from i.	38:12
will ye sit in i. while ye are	60:22
thousands, who do also sit in i.,	60:22

IDLER
for the i. shall be had in	DC 68:30
And the i. shall not have place	75:29

IDLERS
for there are i. among them;	DC 68:31

IDOL
say—Mine i. hath done them,	1Ne 20: 5
as sacrifices unto their i. gods.	Mrm 4:14
whose substance is that of an i.,	DC 1:16

IDOLATRIES
abominations, and your i.,	3Ne 30: 2
repent of their iniquities and i.	Eth 7:26

IDOLATROUS
a lazy and an i. people;	Mos 9:12
Yea, and they also became i.,	11: 7
a very wicked and an i. man.	27: 8
into the land of this i. nation.	Abr 2:18
The i. priest of Elkenah	Fac 1: 3
for sacrifice by the i. priests,	1: 4
The i. god of Elkenah.	1: 5
The i. god of Libnah.	1: 6
The i. god of Mahmackrah.	1: 7
The i. god of Korash.	1: 8
The i. god of Pharaoh.	1: 9

IDOLATRY
full of i. and filthiness;	En 1:20
in their laziness, and in their i.,	Mos 11: 6
sorceries, and in i. or idleness,	Al 1:32
their i., their whoredoms,	50:21
of their unbelief and i.	Mrm 5:15
wickedness and i. of the people	Eth 7:23
no i. nor wickedness practised.	DC 52:39
was led away by their i.;	Abr 1:27
father turned again unto his i.,	2: 5

IDOLS
wo unto those that worship i.,	2Ne 9:37
Their land is also full of i.;	12: 8
the i. he shall utterly abolish.	12:18
a man shall cast his i. of silver,	12:20
and his i. of gold,	12:20
founded the kingdoms of the i.,	20:10
have done unto Samaria and her i.,	20:11
so do to Jerusalem and to her i.?	20:11
that you do not worship i.,	Al 7: 6
many of whom did worship i.,	17:15
people to bow down to dumb i.,	31: 1
i. of their gold and their silver.	He 6:31
were again sacrificed unto i.	Mrm 4:21
children unto their dumb i.,	Abr 1: 7

IDUMEA
down in judgment upon I.,	DC 1:36

IF: *see in the APPENDIX.*

IGNOMINIOUS
there he suffered an i. death.	Al 1:15

IGNORANCE
the wickedness, and the i.,	2Ne 32: 7
we must have suffered in i.,	Mos 1: 3
before Christ came, in their i.,	15:24
to remain in their state of i.;	Al 9:16
over them, to keep them in i.,	30:23
they can keep us in i.,	He 16:20
and thus will they keep us in i.	16:21
for a man to be saved in i.	DC 131: 6

IGNORANT
was not i. of the iniquities of	Mos 19:17
that ye should be i. of the	Al 34: 2
were i. because of their poverty,	3Ne 6:12
him that is i. learn wisdom	DC 136:32

IGNORANTLY
or who have i. sinned.	Mos 3:11
Now they did not sin i.,	3Ne 6:18

ILLINOIS
the escutcheon of the State of I.,	DC 135: 7

ILLUMINATED
i. by the light of the everlasting	Al 5: 7

IMAGE

IMAGE
my graven i., and my molten	1Ne 20: 5
molten i. hath commanded them.	20: 5
take upon him the i. of man,	Mos 7:27
i. after which man was created	7:27
was created after the i. of God,	7:27
make unto thee any graven i.,	12:36
make unto thee any graven i.,	13:12
his i. in your countenances?	Al 5:14
the i. of God engraven upon	5:19
was created after the i. of God,	18:34
created man after his own i.,	22:12
are created after mine own i.?	Eth 3:15
beginning after mine own i.	3:15
after the i. of his own God,	DC 1:16
whose i. is in the likeness of	1:16
after his own i. and in his	20:18
Let us make man in our i.,	Mses 2:26
created man in mine own i.,	2:27
in the i. of mine Only Begotten	2:27
In the i. of his own body,	6: 9
own likeness, after his own i.,	6:10
go down and form man in our i.,	Abr 4:26
to organize man in their own i.,	4:27
i. of the Gods to form they him,	4:27

IMAGES
whose graven i. did excel them of	2Ne 20:10
graven i. I will also cut off,	3Ne 21:17
standing i. out of the midst of	21:17

IMAGINARY
not to an i. ruin, but to the	JS 2:16

IMAGINATION
up in the i. of his thoughts	DC 124:99
the i. of the thoughts of his heart,	Mses 8:22

IMAGINATIONS
the foolish i. of his heart.	1Ne 2:11
vain i. and the pride of the	12:18
the foolish i. of his heart;	17:20

IMAGINE
can you i. to yourselves that	Al 5:16
Or do ye i. to yourselves that	5:17
can ye i. yourselves brought	5:18
the people i. up in their hearts,	He 16:22
ye need not i. in your hearts	3Ne 29: 3

IMAGINED
ye have i. up unto yourselves	Mrm 9:10
have ye i. up unto yourselves	9:10
i. up unto yourselves a god	9:15

IMAGINING
I. up some vain thing in their	3Ne 2: 2

IMITATE
seeking earnestly to i. that	Abr 1:26

IMMANUEL
and shall call his name I.	2Ne 17:14
the breadth of thy land, O I.	18: 8
eternal praise to the King I.,	DC 128:22

IMMATERIAL
There is no such thing as i. matter.	DC 131: 7

IMMEDIATE
which bringeth i. destruction.	Mos 7:31
of the i. goodness of God,	25:10
mercy upon all their i. connections,	DC 109:70
and their i. connections,	109:71
and all their i. connections,	109:72
where i. appeal cannot be made	134:11

IMMEDIATELY
I. after my father left	2Ne 25:10
ye do, he doth i. bless you;	Mos 2:24
sent a message i. unto them,	Al 15: 4
went i., obeying the message	15: 5

IMMORTALITY

And he, i., seeing the contention	Al 19:31
was i. published throughout	30:57
about, his face i. towards him,	32: 6
i. shall the great plan of	34:31
Adam had put forth his hand i.,	42: 5
cause the death of the king i.	51:34
I i. gave orders that my men	57:24
he i. sent an epistle to Pahoran,	59: 3
Moroni i. caused that provisions	62:12
he i. sent forth Lehi with an	He 1:28
i. returned to the Nephites to	5:17
i. when the judge had been	9: 6
abroad among the people i.,	3Ne 19: 2
i. after I had learned these	Mro 8: 7
judgment shall i. follow,	DC 82:11
i. there shall appear a great	88:93
and i. after shall the curtain of	88:95
to transmit, i., a copy of	102:26
Let a conference be held i.;	118: 1
they will i. begin to exercise	121:39
that you are now called i. to	124: 2
by me, and i. unloosed my bands;	Abr 1:15
i. after the tribulation of those	JS 1:33
I was seized upon by some	2:15
i. a personage appeared at	2:30
as i. around his person.	2:32
gather i. around the person	2:43
almost i. after the heavenly	2:47
I. after my marriage, I left	2:58
i. after my arrival there	2:62
I. on our coming up out of	2:73

IMMENSITY
God to fill the i. of space.—	DC 88:12

IMMERSE
shall ye i. them in the water,	3Ne 11:26
Then shall he i. him or her	DC 20:74

IMMERSED
i. therein in order to answer to	DC 128:12
to be i. in the water and	128:12

IMMERSION
of baptism by i. for the	DC 13: 1
and of baptism by i. for the	JS 2:69
Baptism by i. for the	AoF 4

IMMENSE
were slain with an i. slaughter.	Al 49:21

IMMORTAL
men become incorruptible, and i.,	2Ne 9:13
as they have become i.,	9:15
my i. spirit may join the choirs	Mos 2:28
his i. soul to a lively sense of	2:38
body is raised to an i. body,	Al 11:45
whole becoming spiritual and i.,	11:45
from this mortal to an i. state	12:20
their souls, yea, their i. souls,	He 3:30
body of flesh into an i. state,	3Ne 28:15
whether they were mortal or i.,	28:17
sanctified, i., and eternal state.	DC 77: 1
presence and into his i. rest.	121:32
in its sanctified and i. state,	130: 9
world to come, even i. glory;	Mses 6:59
peaceable things of i. glory;	6:61

IMMORTALITY
my mortal shall put on i.,	En 1:27
this mortal shall put on i.,	Mos 16:10
this mortal body raised in i.,	Al 5:15
this mortality to a state of i.,	12:12
this mortal does not put on i.,	40: 2
mortality raised to i.,	41: 4
from mortality to i.;	3Ne 28: 8
cleansed from mortality to i.—	28:36
that your mortal must put on i.,	Mrm 6:21
be raised in i. unto eternal life,	DC 29:43
with honor, and glory, and i.,	75: 5
thou shalt have a crown of i.,	81: 6
crown you with honor, i., and	124:55
Herein is glory and honor, and i.	128:12

IMMORTALITY

salvation, and honor, and i.,	DC 128:23
the i. and eternal life of man.	Mses 1:39

IMMOVABLE
firm and steadfast, and i.	1 Ne 2:10
that ye should be steadfast and i.,	Mos 5:15
i. in keeping the commandments	Al 1:25
and also they were i. because	He 5:34
firm, and steadfast, and i.,	3 Ne 6:14
a determination that is fixed, i.,	DC 88:133

IMMUTABLE
with an i. covenant that	DC 98: 3
promise i. and unchangeable,	104: 2

IMPART
nor i. unto him of my substance	Mos 4:17
ye ought to i. of the substance	4:21
ye should i. of your substance	4:26
should i. of their substance,	18:27
he should i. more abundantly;	18:27
should i. of their substance	18:28
should i. to the support of	21:17
did i. much consolation to	27:33
might i. the word of God to	28: 1
they did i. the word of God,	Al 1:20
to i. the word of God unto	1:26
they did i. of their substance,	1:27
I will i. unto thee of my food:	8:20
they shall not i. only according	12: 9
they did i. the word of God,	16:14
and i. of your substance,	34:28
will i. unto you of my Spirit,	DC 11:13
i. it freely to the printing of	19:26
I. a portion of thy property,	19:34
thou hast to i. unto them,	42:30
as ye i. of your substance	42:31
shall i. to the eastern brethren;	48: 2
i. of the money which I have	60:10
let him i. all the money which	63:43
all the money which he can i.,	63:43
learn to i. one to another as	88:123
and i. not his portion,	104:18
do not i. of their substance,	105: 3

IMPARTED
had i. unto them the word of God	Al 1:26
i. the word of God unto them,	17:18
since he i. his word unto us	24:15
the word which he has i. unto me,	36:26
which were i. for the support of	54: 2

IMPARTETH
he i. his word by angels unto	Al 32:23

IMPARTIALLY
the evidences and pleadings i.,	DC 102:20

IMPARTING
i. to one another both	Mos 18:29
as i. their substance to the poor	Al 4:13

IMPEACH
gospel that all the world cannot i.;	DC 135: 7

IMPEACHED
testimony that cannot be i.,	DC 68:23

IMPEDE
i. the progress of this people	Al 60:30

IMPEDED
march that it could not be i.	3 Ne 7:13

IMPENETRABLE
and how blind and i. are	Mos 8:20

IMPENITENT
became more hardened and i.,	Al 47:36
and i. and grossly wicked,	He 6: 2

IMPERATIVE
an i. duty that we owe to God,	DC 123: 7

468

INASMUCH

it is an i. duty that we owe	DC 123: 9
it is an i. duty that we owe	123:11

IMPERFECTION
me not because of mine i.,	Mrm 9:31
my father, because of his i.,	9:31
had no i. in our record.	9:33

IMPERFECTIONS
of the i. which are in it,	Mrm 8:12
made manifest unto you our i.,	9:31
and his i. you have known;	DC 67: 5
for my weakness and i.;	JS 2:29

IMPORTANCE
Wherefore, how great the i. to	2 Ne 2: 8
is of more i. than they all—	Al 7: 7
a character of sufficient i.	JS 2:23

IMPORTANT
a history of all the i. things	DC 69: 3
i. difficulties which might arise	102: 2
most i. business of the church,	107:78
many great and i. things	AoF 9

IMPORTUNE
continue to i. for redress,	DC 101:76
Let them i. at the feet of	101:86
let them i. at the feet of the	101:87
let them i. at the feet of the	101:88

IMPOSITIONS
and nefarious and murderous i.	DC 123: 5

IMPOSSIBLE
it is i. that man should find out	Jac 4: 8
i. for the people of Limhi to	Mos 22: 2
it is i. for him to deny his word.	Al 11:34
i. that ye should be ignorant of	34: 2
i. that he could overpower them	52:17
i. for the Nephites to obtain	He 4:19
we know that this is i.,	8: 6
it was i. for the robbers to lay	3 Ne 4:18
i. for the tongue to describe,	Mrm 4:11
render it i. to be otherwise—	DC 107:28
i. for a man to be saved in	131: 6
i. for a person young as I was,	JS 2: 8

IMPRESSIONS
so deep were the i. made on	JS 2:46

IMPROVE
if we do not i. our time while	Al 34:33
man may i. upon his talent,	DC 82:18

IMPROVING
by i. upon the properties	DC 104:68

IMPURE
can rolling waters remain i.?	DC 121:33

IN: *see in the APPENDIX.*

INALIENABLE
their inherent and i. rights	DC 134: 5

INASMUCH
i. as ye shall keep my	1 Ne 2:20
i. as thy brethren shall rebel	2:21
i. as thou shalt keep my	2:22
I. as thy seed shall keep my	4:14
i. as ye shall keep my	17:13
i. as those whom the Lord God	2 Ne 1: 9
I. as ye shall keep my	1:20
i. as ye will not keep my	1:20
i. as he shall make intercession	2: 9
I. as ye shall keep my	4: 4
i. as ye will not keep my	4: 4
i. as they will not hearken	5:20
i. as they will not remember me,	5:25
i. as it shall be expedient,	25:30
I. as ye will keep my	Jar 1: 9
I. as ye will not keep my	Om 1: 6

INASMUCH

i. as it was possible.	Al	1:32
I. as ye shall keep my		9:13
I. as ye will not keep my		9:13
i. as the Lamanites have not kept		9:14
i. as ye shall keep the		36: 1
i. as ye shall keep the		36:30
i. as ye will not keep the		36:30
i. as ye shall keep the		38: 1
i. as ye will not keep the		38: 1
I. as ye are not guilty of the		43:46
i. as they shall keep my		50:20
i. as they will not keep the		50:20
i. as they did repent they did	He	4:15
i. as there were dissenters that		11:25
and i. as they did the Lord	Eth	11: 8
i. as they erred it might be	DC	1:25
i. as they sought wisdom		1:26
i. as they sinned they might		1:27
i. as they were humble they		1:28
i. as the knowledge of a Savior		3:16
i. as they receive thy teachings		28: 8
And i. as ye do not write,		35:23
i. as my people shall assemble		39:15
i. as they do repent and		39:18
i. as he keepeth my		41: 8
i. as ye believe on my name		42: 1
i. as ye shall find them that		42: 8
i. as ye impart of your		42:31
i. as ye do it unto the least		42:38
i. as they break not my laws		42:52
i. as ye do this, glory shall		43:10
I. as ye do it not, it shall		43:10
that i. as they are faithful,		44: 2
and i. as they do repent,		45:64
given him, i. as he is faithful,		47: 4
And i. as ye have lands,		48: 2
And i. as ye have not lands,		48: 3
and i. as ye have received me,		50:43
i. as they are faithful unto me,		52: 4
also, i. as they are faithful,		52: 5
i. as they are not faithful,		52: 6
i. as my disciples are enabled		57: 5
i. as can be done in		57: 6
And i. as men do good they		58:28
i. as the inhabitants of the		58:48
i. as there is land obtained,		58:54
i. as ye do these things with		59:15
that i. as ye do this,		59:16
i. as they are faithful they shall		61:10
i. as they are commanded to		61:24
the wicked, i. as it is given;		61:33
i. as they do this they shall		61:34
And i. as you have humbled		61:37
i. as he obeyeth mine		64: 5
i. as you have turned away		66: 1
i. as you can send, send;		66: 6
i. as you strip yourselves from		67:10
i. as he is found guilty before		68:23
i. as parents have children in		68:25
i. as they are appointed to		68:30
i. as they receive more than		70: 7
i. as they become heirs		70: 8
i. as they have not sinned.		70:17
i. as ye are faithful		71: 7
i. as they have wherewith to		72:11
And, i. as it is practicable,		73: 4
and i. as they do this, I will		75:11
and i. as they are faithful,		75:13
i. as your brethren are willing		75:25
And i. as he is faithful, I will		79: 3
i. as you desire a companion,		80: 1
i. as thou art faithful in		81: 3
that i. as you have forgiven		82: 1
i. as ye keep not my sayings,		82: 4
i. as his wants are just.—		82:17
i. as you sin not.		82:20
i. as you receive these things;		84:60
that i. as they have families,		84:103
i. as any man drinketh wine		89: 5
i. as she is faithful,		90:31
and i. as you are faithful		92: 2
and i. as you keep my sayings		93:52
i. as he keepeth my		96: 6
i. as he continueth to abide	DC	97: 4
i. as my people build a house		97:15
i. as ye do this the Holy Ghost		100: 8
and i. as they keep my		100:14
i. as they gather together		101:58
i. as they are willing to be		101:63
i. as they bring forth fruit		101:100
i. as they hearken from this		103: 5
i. as they keep not my		103: 8
i. as they are not the saviors		103:10
i. as mine enemies come		103:24
i. as those whom I		104: 2
i. as they were not faithful		104: 3
i. as some of my servants		104: 4
i. as any man belonging to		104: 5
i. as you are found		104: 8
I. as ye are cut off for		104: 9
i. as he will be humble before		104:23
And i. as he is faithful,		104:25
And i. as they are faithful,		104:31
And, i. as they are faithful,		104:33
And i. as he is faithful,		104:35
i. as it shall be made known		104:36
And i. as he is faithful,		104:38
And i. as he is faithful		104:42
i. as he is faithful,		104:46
i. as you are diligent and		104:80
i. as ye are humble and		104:82
I. as you obtain a chance to		104:84
i. as they are faithful and		105:12
i. as there are those who have		105:18
i. as my servant Joseph shall		105:21
i. as they follow the counsel		105:37
up i. as he will humble himself		106: 7
i. as there are other bishops		107:75
i. as there is not satisfaction		107:78
i. as a President of the		107:82
But i. as they will repent,		109:53
i. as thou hast abased thyself		112: 3
I. as they shall humble		112:22
i. as there are those among you		114: 2
i. as they pursue me without		127: 1
i. as their pretensions are all		127: 1
i. as it is out of my power to do		127:10
i. as you have inquired of my		132: 1
I. as laws have been enacted		OD
I. as thy children are conceived	Mses	6:55
i. as ye were born into the		6:59
i. as they will repent in the day		7:39

INCESSANT
tumult were so great and i.   JS 2: 9

INCLINED
let thine ear be i.;   DC 121: 4

INCLUDING
i. the Levitical Priesthood.   DC 107: 1
even twelve i. himself, to testify   114: 1

INCOMINGS
your i. may be in the name of   DC 88:120
i. may be in the name of the Lord,   109: 9
That all the i. of thy people,   109:17

INCOMPREHENSIBLE
their afflictions, and their i. joy,   Al 28: 8

INCORRECT
mix and believe in i. traditions   Al 3: 8
the i. tradition of their fathers;   37: 9

INCORRECTNESS
i. of the traditions of their   Al 9:17
of the i. of the traditions of   26:24

INCORRUPTIBLE
all men become i., and immortal,   2Ne 9:13
must soon become i. bodies;   Mrm 6:21

INCORRUPTION
death, nor corruption nor i.,   2Ne 2:11
corruption could not put on i.   9: 7

INCORRUPTION 470 INFEST

this corruption shall put on i.,	Mos	16:10	by the fire of mine i. will I	DC 35:14
and this corruption raised in i.,	Al	5:15	the wrath of mine i. is full.	43:26
corruption does not put on i.,		40: 2	know mine arm and mine i.,	56: 1
immortality, corruption to i.—		41: 4	and of judgement, and of i.;	56:16
			and i., and chastening hand of	87: 6
INCREASE			wrath and i. upon the people.	88:88
their anger did i. against me,	2Ne	5: 2	the i. of the Lord is kindled	97:24
Of the i. of government and		19: 7	all wrath and i. from you,	98:22
And the meek also shall i.,		27:30	thine i. shall be turned away;	98:47
one half of the i. of our flocks	Mos	7:22	let fall the sword of mine i.	101:10
began to i. in riches,		24: 7	Mine i. is soon to be poured	101:11
would not this i. your faith?	Al	32:29	and thine i. fall upon them,	109:52
of your fields, that they may i.		34:25	works, bring cursings, wrath, i.,	124:48
his armies, which did i. daily		50:12	judgment, wrath, and i.,	124:52
thus seeing our forces i. daily,		56:29	the fiery i. of the wrath of God to	Mses 7: 1
out their days and i. their seed,	He	7:24	the fire of mine i. is kindled	7:34
that the contentions did i.,		11: 1		
did still i. and wax strong,		11:32	**INDIVIDUAL**	
yea, in the i. of their fields,		12: 2	four beasts limited to i. beasts,	DC 77: 3
began to i. in great degree,	3Ne	1:28	are limited to four i. beasts,	77: 3
That faith also might i. in	DC	1:21	a Urim and Thummim to each i.	130:10
For Zion must i. in beauty,		82:14	as will secure to each i. the	134: 2
more sacred unto me than his i.,		117:13	and the i. rights of its members,	134: 9
forth afterwards an i. of love		121:43		
he cannot have an i.		131: 4	**INDIVIDUALLY**	
which continued to i.;	JS	2:22	church collectively and not i.—	DC 1:30
which continued to i. until		2:30		
			INDIVIDUALS	
INCREASED			of the church, or any i. of it	DC 42:33
the action, and i. the joy—	2Ne	19: 3	the i. who are to stand up	102:17
			the church and not i.,	105: 2
INCULCATE			naming also some three i.	128: 3
to i. or encourage polygamy;	DC	OD	regulating our interests as i.	134: 6
INCUMBRANCES			**INDOLENCE**	
i. that are upon the house	DC	96: 9	giving way to i., and all manner	Al 47:36
INCUR			**INDOLENT**	
may not i. the displeasure of	2Ne	1:22	Thus they were a very i. people,	Al 17:15
i. the vengeance of a just God	DC	3: 4		
			INDUCED	
INCURRED			I have been i. to write this	JS 2: 1
and i. the displeasure of God	Mos	1:17		
			INDULGE	
INDEBTED			and i. themselves somewhat in	Jac 1:15
for which ye are i. unto him.	Mos	2:23	did i. themselves in sorceries,	Al 1:32
And ye are still i. unto him,		2:24		
i. to your heavenly Father,		2:34	**INDUSTRIOUS**	
			did cause my people to be i.,	2Ne 5:17
INDEED			yea, they were i., and did labor	Mos 23: 5
Hear ye i., but they understood	2Ne	16: 9	began to be a very i. people;	Al 23:18
see ye i., but they perceived not.		16: 9	And they were exceedingly i.,	Eth 10:22
or made, neither i. can be.	DC	93:29		
therefore ye are free i.;		98: 8	**INDUSTRY**	
mine house, even stewards i.		104:57	they had obtained by their i.;	Al 4: 6
I., the whole district of country	JS	2: 5	much riches by the hand of my i.	10: 4
i. did I behold the plates,		2:52		
i., we may say that we follow	AoF	13	**INEQUALITY**	
			that this i. should be no more	Mos 29:32
INDEPENDENCE			saw great i. among the people,	Al 4:12
the place which is now called I.	DC	57: 3	and seeing all their i.,	4:15
should be lands purchased in I.,		58:37	there was no i. among them;	16:16
			how great the i. of man is	28:13
INDEPENDENT			a great i. in all the land,	3Ne 6:14
i. above all other creatures	DC	78:14		
All truth is i. in that sphere		93:30	**INEXPRESSIBLE**	
			did rack my soul with i. horror.	Al 36:14
INDEPENDENTLY				
to act in the office of bishop i.,	DC	107:76	**INFANCY**	
			perisheth not that dieth in his i.;	Mos 3:18
INDIFFERENCE			against me, almost in my i.?	JS 2:20
i. concerning the freedom of	Al	59:13		
			INFANT	
INDIGENT			and the i. perisheth not that	Mos 3:18
of the i. circumstances of	JS	2:46	in their i. state, innocent	DC 93:38
			an i. shall not die until he is	101:30
INDIGNATION				
in their hate is their i.	2Ne	20: 5	**INFERIOR**	
and the i. shall cease,		20:25	pertaining to an i. kingdom,	DC 130: 9
and the weapons of his i.,		23: 5		
fiery i. of the wrath of God	Al	40:14	**INFEST**	
the cup of mine i. is full;	DC	29:17	mountains, who did i. the land;	3Ne 1:27
			did i. the land, insomuch	Mrm 1:18

INFESTED

INFESTED
i., by times or at seasons, by — Mos 18: 4
i. by wild and ravenous beasts. — Al 2:37
robbers who i. the mountains — He 11:31

INFINITE
been brought by his i. goodness — 2Ne 1:10
it must needs be an i. atonement— 9: 7
save it should be an i. atonement 9: 7
the atonement, which is i. 25:16
through the i. goodness of God, — Mos 5: 3
the Lord saw fit in his i. mercy 28: 4
be an i. and eternal sacrifice. — Al 34:10
is short of an i. atonement 34:12
Son of God, yea, i. and eternal. 34:14
Lord in his great i. goodness — He 12: 1
his i. goodness and grace, — Mro 8: 3
heaven, who is i. and eternal, — DC 20:17
are one god, i. and eternal, 20:28

INFINITY
an i. of fulness, from everlasting — DC 109:77

INFIRM
For I am i., and such wickedness — Al 31:30

INFIRMITIES
subject to all manner of i. — Mos 2:11
he will take upon him their i., — Al 7:12
his people according to their i. 7:12
that I may bear with mine i. 31:30
of their sicknesses and their i., — 3Ne 7:22
laws thou shalt bear their i. — DC 42:52

INFLAME
until night, and wine i. them! — 2Ne 15:11

INFLICT
the Lord seeth fit to i. upon him, — Mos 3:19
and i. the wounds of death in — Al 44: 7
or to i. any physical punishment — DC 134:10

INFLICTED
which were i. on the church by — Mos 27: 1
could be i. by their brethren, — Al 27:29
hanving i. death upon all those 62:11
where personal abuse is i. or — DC 134:11

INFLICTETH
and the law i. the punishment; — Al 42:22

INFLICTING
unto the i. of the punishment — 2Ne 2:10

INFLUENCE
No power or i. can or ought — DC 121:41
i. shall cast thee into trouble, 122: 4
by the i. of that spirit 123: 7
mingle religious i. with civil 134: 9
nor to meddle with or i. them 134:12
Let every man use all his i. 136:10
to use my i. with the members OD
an astonishing i. over me — JS 2:15
i. of my wife's father's family 2:75

INFLUENCED
not be i. by any other motive — JS 2:46

INFORM
to i. their king, Amalickiah, — Al 49:25

INFORMATION
the same i. of the Nephites, — Al 47:36
i. in relation to many subjects, — DC 128: 1

INFORMED
i. the messengers of Moroni, — Al 43:24
they had been i. by their spies, 56:35
he i. me of great judgments — JS 2:45
was again i. that the time 2:53
I i. him that part of the plates 2:65

INFORMING
i. her that the king had — Al 47:32

INFRINGE
i. upon the rights and liberties — DC 134: 4

INFRINGED
right of property or character i., — DC 134:11

INFUSED
had i. such joy into his soul, — Al 19: 6

INHABIT
who should i. the isles of the sea, — 1Ne 19:10

INHABITANT
and fair cities without i. — 2Ne 15: 9
the cities be wasted without i., 16:11
and shout, thou i. of Zion; 22: 6

INHABITANTS
be destroyed, and the i. thereof; — 1Ne 1:13
over all the i. of the earth; 1:14
be too narrow by reason of the i.; 21:19
unto the i. of the earth, — 2Ne 2: 8
And now, O i. of Jerusalem, 15: 3
a snare to the i. of Jerusalem. 18:14
and the i. of Samaria, that say 19: 9
and I have put down the i. 20:13
the i. of Gebim gather 20:31
visit the i. of the world; 28:16
if the i. of the earth shall repent 28:17
the i. who were in the land of — Al 50: 9
came upon the i. of the city, — He 1:19
because of the many i. who 3: 5
the i. thereof were drowned. — 3Ne 8: 9
and the i. thereof were slain, 8:14
the i. thereof who had not fallen 8:20
among all the i. of the earth, 9: 1
wo unto the i. of the whole 9: 2
with fire, and the i. thereof. 9: 3
the i. thereof to be drowned. 9: 4
with earth, and the i. thereof, 9: 5
i. thereof to be buried up in 9: 6
of Onihah and the i. thereof, 9: 7
of Mocum and the i. thereof, 9: 7
Jerusalem and the i. thereof; 9: 7
the i. thereof have I buried up 9: 8
with fire, and the i. thereof, 9:10
the i. thereof began to hide up — Mrm 1:18
the i. of the city Teancum. 4: 3
and did drive the i. forth 4:14
taking all the i. with them, 4:22
destroy the i. of our land. 5: 4
i. thereof were not gathered 5: 5
an account of those ancient i. — Eth 1: 1
as the i. of the land have 2:11
all the i. of the earth which 3:25
the i. thereof shall pass away, 4: 9
the i. began to be destroyed 9:30
northward was covered with i. 10:21
the i. thereof, blessed are they, 13:11
swept off the i. of the earth, 14:27
unto you, O i. of the earth. — DC 1: 6
unto the i. of the earth, 1: 8
fall upon the i. of the earth. 1:13
come upon the i. of the earth, 1:17
unto you, O i. of the earth: 1:34
come unto the i. of the earth 5: 5
among the i. of the earth, 5:19
i. thereof are consumed away 5:19
shall pass upon the i. thereof, 19: 3
take hold of the i. thereof, 29:18
call upon the i. of the earth. 43:28
call upon the i. to repent, 45:64
the i. of Zion are terrible; 45:70
the i. of the earth will repent. 58:48
whilst the i. on either side 61: 3
unto the i. of the earth, 62: 5
from the i. of the earth. 63:32
unto the i. of the earth; 63:37

INHABITANTS 472 INHERITANCE

the i. of Zion shall judge all	DC 64:38	they cannot i. that place which	Eth	12:34
the i. thereof may receive it,	65: 5	i. the kingdom of heaven.	DC	6:37
be a law unto the i. of Zion,	68:26	shall i. the kingdom of heaven.		10:55
the i. of Zion shall also observe	68:29	for they shall i. eternal life.		50: 5
the i. of Zion also shall	68:30	and shall i. eternal life.		51:19
pleased with the i. of Zion,	68:31	generations shall i. the earth		56:20
hearken, O ye i. of Zion,	70: 1	that live shall i. the earth,		59: 2
consecrated unto the i. of Zion,	70: 8	and shall not i. the land.		64:35
Call upon the i. of the earth,	71: 4	i. the mansions prepared		72: 4
and rejoice ye i. thereof,	76: 1	wise steward shall i. all things.		78:22
the i. thereof are begotten	76:24	meek of the earth shall i. it.		88:17
the i. of the telestial world,	76:109	must i. another kingdom,		88:21
against the i. of the earth;	82: 6	and the righteous shall i. it.		88:26
i. of the earth shall mourn;	87: 6	and another shall not i. it;		101:101
shall the i. of the earth be	87: 6	not resurrected, but i. the same		129: 3
and the i. thereof—	88:61	cannot, therefore, i. my glory;		132:18
prepare ye, O i. of the earth;	88:92	and shall i. thrones, kingdoms,		132:19
gospel unto the i. thereof,	99: 1	not i. them out of the world,		132:39
judge among the i. of Zion,	107:74	nowise i. the kingdom of God,	Mses	6:57
upon the i. of the earth,	109:38			
driven by the i. of Jackson	109:47	INHERITANCE		
i. and founders of this city;	111: 9	and the land of his i.,	1Ne	2: 4
let not the i. of the earth	112: 5	leave the land of their i.,		2:11
upon the i. of the earth,	112:24	the land of our father's i.,		3:16
prepared for the i. thereof.	124:83	down to the land of our i.,		3:22
unto the i. of Warsaw,	124:88	forth from the land of our i.,		5: 2
unto the i. of Carthage,	124:88	possess again the land of their i.		10: 3
unto the i. of Burlington,	124:88	and obtain the land for their i.;		13:15
unto the i. of Madison,	124:88	should have for the land of their i.;		13:30
unto the i. of the earth.	124:89	possessions and the land of our i.;		17:21
warn the i. of the earth	124:106	together to the lands of their i.;		22:12
a Urim and Thummim to the i.	130: 9	a land for the i. of my seed.	2Ne	1: 5
and hear, O ye i. of the earth.	133:16	would be no place for an i.		1: 8
O i. of the earth,	133:36	take away the land of their i.;		1: 9
he beheld also the i. thereof,	Mses 1:28	most precious land, for thine i.		3: 2
were i. on the face thereof.	1:29	and the i. of thy seed		3: 2
this earth, and the i. thereof,	1:35	again to the lands of their i.		6:11
this earth, and the i. thereof,	1:36	home to the lands of their i.,		9: 2
of Hanannihah, and all the i.	7: 9	unto the lands of their i.		10: 7
unto Enoch all the i. of the	7:21	forth to the lands of their i.		10: 8
wo be unto the i. of the earth.	7:25	shall be a land of thine i.,		10:10
and many of the i. thereof died.	8: 4	for the land of their i.;		10:19
upon the i. of Jerusalem,	JS 1:18	out of the land of our i.;		10:20
an account of the former i.	2:34	again to the land of their i.		25:11
the Savior to the ancient i.;	2:34	shall possess the land of your i.,	Jac	3: 4
		whatsoever place of our i.	Jar	1: 7
INHABITED		possess the land of their i.	Om	1:27
the earth that it should be i.;	1Ne 17:36	out of all the lands of their i.	WM	1:14
they are i. also by our brethren.	2Ne 10:21	the land of our fathers' first i.,	Mos	9: 1
It shall never be i., neither	23:20	while in the land of their first i.,		10:13
had i. the land Bountiful,	Al 22:33	I grant an i. at my right hand.	Al	5:58
who had before i. the land	He 3: 6	which was the land of their i.		21:18
i. by the people of king Jacob,	3Ne 9: 9	the place of their fathers' first i.,		22:28
shall Jerusalem be i. again	20:46	unto our brethren for an i.		27:22
the desolate cities to be i.	22: 3	unto them lands for their i.;		35: 9
		their i. in the land of Jershon,		35:14
INHERENT		they gave them lands for their i.		43:12
their i. and inalienable rights	DC 134: 5	is the land of our first i.;		54:12
		our land, the land of our first i.		54:13
INHERIT		returned to the place of his i.;		62:42
cause to i. the desolate heritages;	1Ne 21: 8	this is the land of your i.;	3Ne	15:13
for thou shall i. the land	2Ne 4:11	this people this land for their i.		16:16
they shall i. the kingdom of God,	9:18	unto you this land, for your i.		20:14
to i. this land, which was	Mos 7: 9	of their fathers for their i.,		20:29
to i. the land of his fathers,	7:21	Jerusalem for the land of their i.		20:33
to i. the land of our fathers,	9: 3	and it shall be the land of their i.		20:46
did i. the land of our fathers	10: 3	have given this land for their i.		21:22
nowise i. the kingdom of God.	27:26	home to the land of their i.		21:28
that we may live and i. the land,	29:32	to the lands of their i.,		29: 1
i. the kingdom of heaven.	Al 5:51	possession of the lands of our i.	Mrm	2:27
i. the kingdom of heaven;	7:14	get the lands of our i. divided.		2:28
nowise i. the kingdom of God.	9:12	to return to the land of your i.;		3:17
can i. the kingdom of heaven;	11:37	of Israel, to the land of their i.,		5:14
ye i. the kingdom of heaven?	11:37	we may receive it for our i.	Eth	1:38
they may i. the land Jershon;	27:24	I shall give you for your i.;		2:15
nowise i. the kingdom of God.	39: 9	obtain the land of their first i.;		7:16
can i. the kingdom of God;	40:26	again to the land of his i.		9:13
to i. the kingdom of God,	41: 4	or he cannot receive an i. in		12:32
to i. the kingdom of the devil,	41: 4	it shall be a land of their i.;		13: 8
land northward to i. the land.	He 3: 3	receiving the land for their i.,		13:21
who shall i. the kingdom of God.	3Ne 11:33	shalt receive an i. in Zion.	DC	25: 2
in nowise i. the kingdom of God.	11:38	unto you for the land of your i.,		38:19
for they shall i. the earth.	12: 5	have it for the land of your i.,		38:20
thy seed shall i. the Gentiles	22: 3	the i. of your children forever,		38:20

INHERITANCE | 473 | INIQUITY

be given unto them for an i.;	DC 45:58
that ye may purchase an i.	45:65
to purchase land for an i.,	48: 4
right and this i. in the church,	51: 4
unto them the lnad of your i.	52: 5
which is the land of your i.,	52:42
planted in the land of your i.	55: 5
even in lands for their i.	56:13
obtain it for an everlasting i.	57: 5
divide unto the saints their i.,	57: 7
need to plant them in their i.	57: 8
and plant them in their i.	57:15
unto this land to receive an i.;	58:36
that he may receive his i.	58:38
and receive his i. in the land;	58:40
to receive their i. in this land,	58:44
to purchase lands for an i.	58:51
lest they receive none i.,	58:53
and shall receive an i. upon	63:20
there is none i. for you.	63:29
few shall stand to receive an i.	63:31
receive an i. in this world,	63:48
receive an i. before the Lord,	63:49
an i. in the land of Zion.	64:30
and for raiment; for an i.;	70:16
answereth all things, for an i.,	72:17
those who receive not their i.	85: 3
find none i. in that day,	85: 9
not find an i. among the saints	85:11
and receive their i. and be	88:107
receive an i. from the hand of	90:30
ye shall have an i. with me—	93:45
Hyrum Smith receive his i.	94:13
goodly land, to possess thine i.;	99: 7
out from the land of their i.—	101: 1
in exchange for his former i.,	104:24
in which he lives, and the i.,	104:34
which pertains to that i.,	104:34
the i. upon which his father	104:43
I have reserved an i. for	104:45
from the lands of their i.,	109:47
take up their i. in the same,	125: 4

INHERITANCES

they may remain upon their i.	DC 83: 3
wherewith to give them i.	83: 5
receive i. legally from the	85: 1
after receiving their i.	85: 2
the i. of the saints whose	85: 7
Jared Carter receive their i.—	94:14
the benefit of those who seek i.,	96: 3
they polluted their i.	101: 6
return, and come to their i.,	101:18
return to the lands of their i.,	103:11
if they pollute their i.	103:14
if they pollute their i.	103:14

INHERITED

who had before i. the land.	He 3: 5
i. lies, upon the hearts of the	DC 123: 7

INIQUITIES

and this because of your i.?	1Ne 3:29
they should repent of their i.;	18:15
boldly concerning your i.	2Ne 1:26
grieveth because of mine i.	4:17
save they shall repent of their i.	5:22
for your i. have ye sold	7: 1
a knowledge of their i.	9:33
I shook your i. from my soul,	9:44
because of priestcrafts and i.,	10: 5
Wherefore, because of their i.,	10: 6
for the i. of their fathers,	24:21
to generation according to their i.;	25: 9
reject him, because of their i.,	25:12
For none of these i. come of	26:33
greater i. than the Lamanites,	Jac 2:35
behold, it is because of our i.	Mos 7:20
because of the i. of their fathers,	10:12
visiting the i. of my people.	11:22
will I visit them in their i.	12: 1
because of their i., shall be	12: 2
this will I do because of their i.	12: 7

and this because of thine i.	Mos 12:12
ye shall be smitten for your i.,	12:31
the truth concerning your i.	13: 7
the i. of the fathers upon	13:13
for the sins and i. of his people,	13:28
he was bruised for our i.;	14: 5
laid on him the i. of us all.	14: 6
for he shall bear their i.	14:11
they being warned of their i.	16:12
diseases because of your i.	17:16
repented of his sins and i.,	18: 1
of the i. of his father,	19:17
and turn from our i.?	20:21
their cry because of their i.;	21:15
many sins and i. against God;	21:30
they have been taken in divers i.	26:11
they do not repent of their i.	26:11
to do after the manner of his i.	27: 8
of soul because of their i.,	28: 4
the i. and abominations of	28:15
and also because of their i.	29:18
these people commit sins and i.	29:30
caused by the i. of their kings;	29:31
their i. are answered upon the	29:31
all his i. and abominations,	29:36
i. which cannot be enumerated—	29:36
against them concerning their i.	Al 8:25
did wax more gross in their i.	8:28
you that ye shall live in your i.,	9:19
doth the Lord judge of your i.;	10:20
exceeding sore because of his i.;	15: 5
of their i. and their traditions,	19:14
afflict them because of their i.;	19:27
because of the i. of this people.	31:33
did remember all my sins and i.,	36:13
in fine so great had been my i.,	36:14
their hearts in sin and i.,	37:10
unto them concerning their i.;	37:30
that ye refrain from your i.;	39:12
and all manner of i.;	45:12
live and wax strong in your i.	60:31
do not repent of their sins and i.,	60:33
unto them concerning their i.,	He 4:14
all these i. did come unto	6:32
And they did grow in their i.	6:33
That I may tell you of your i.?	7:13
which is because of your i.!	7:14
unto us concerning our i.	8: 8
us as he knoweth of our i.;	8: 8
and all manner of i.—	10: 3
Because of thine i. thou shalt	12:20
Because of thine i. thou shalt	12:21
murders, and all manner of i.	13:22
and this because of your i.	13:23
testifieth of your sins and i.,	13:26
Behold, our i. are great.	13:37
do await you because of your i.,	14:11
in the days of their i. hath	15: 3
except ye repent of all your i.,	3Ne 3:15
the sins and i. of the people,	6:20
to hide their i. and their	9: 5
every one of you from his i.;	20:26
their i. upon their own heads,	20:28
they repented hot of their i.,	Mrm 5: 2
repent of all your sins and i.,	7: 5
and all manner of i.;	8:36
not continue in your i. until	Eth 2:11
the people did repent of their i.	7:26
they began to repent of their i.	9:34
except they repented of their i.	11:12
their i. shall be spoken upon	DC 1: 3
because of their i. and their	3:18
they weep because of their i.;	45:53
turned away from your i.,	66: 1
fill up the measure of their i.,	103: 3
will slay me, because of mine i.,	Mses 5:39

INIQUITOUS

ye cannot dethrone an i. king	Mos 29:21

INIQUITY

unto the people concerning their i.	1Ne 1:hd
and they were ripe in i.;	17:35

INIQUITY 474 INJUSTICE

straitened them because of their i.	1 Ne	17:41
Ye are swift to do i. but		17:45
and smite us because of our i.,		18:10
and the i. of my brethren,		18:18
the world, because of their i.,		19: 9
and to do all manner of i.;		22:23
if so, it shall be because of i.;	2 Ne	1: 7
for if i. shall abound cursed		1: 7
save it shall be i. among them,		1:31
cursing, because of their i.		5:21
that draw i. with cords of vanity,		15:18
and thine i. is taken away,		16: 7
and the wicked for their i.;		23:11
among the Jews because of i.,		25: 9
they will be drunken with i.		27: 1
behold, all ye that doeth i.,		27: 4
he covered because of your i.		27: 5
that watch for i. are cut off;		27:31
that they are fully ripe in i.		28:16
he would rid you from this i.	Jac	2:16
This people begin to wax in i.;		2:23
because of the i. of their fathers;		3: 7
save it be for the cause of i.;	En	1:10
in vain, and all because of i.	Mos	7:24
labor exceedingly to support i.		11: 6
ye have studied and taught i.		13:11
quick to do i., and slow to		13:29
taken upon himself their i. and		15: 9
the i. which Abinadi had testified		17: 2
the i. of king Noah and his priests;		23: 9
been brought into i. by them;		23:12
were bound with the bands of i.		23:12
and also from the bonds of i.,		23:13
stood and testified of their i.		26: 9
those that had been taken in i.,		26:34
and repent of their i.,		26:36
of bitterness and bonds of i.		27:29
of the i. of their fathers;		28: 2
of their i. of their fathers;		29:14
murdering, nor any manner of i.;		29:14
whosoever has committed i.,		29:15
how much i. doth one wicked		29:17
behold, he has his friends in i.,		29:22
of the people doth choose i.,		29:27
from one piece of i. to another,	Al	4:11
wo unto all ye workers of i.;		5:32
O ye workers of i.;		5:37
of this people should choose i.,		10:19
harden his heart and will do i.,		12:35
therefore your i. provoketh him		12:36
his people had waxed strong in i.		13:17
had been slain because of his i.		15: 3
been spent in the grossest i.;		26:24
that we destroy them and their i.		26:25
i. after the manner of Korihor.		30:58
because of the i. of the people.		31: 1
to know of i. among his people;		31: 2
and i. shall be among this people?		31:30
because of the i. of this people.		31:31
grieved for the i. of his people,		35:15
hatred against sin and i.		37:32
i. ye brought upon the Zoramites;		39:11
this because of their own i.,		40:13
and in the bonds of i.;		41:18
before this great i. shall come.		45:12
And now, because of i., this		45:14
yea, how quick to do i.,		46: 8
of God, yea, and resisting i.		48:16
because of the i. of the people,		49: 3
thus because of i. amongst		53: 9
it is because of your i. that		60:28
your i. is for the cause of		60:32
been the cause of this great i.;		61: 4
will put an end to this great i.		61:18
because of the i. of those who		62: 2
dissensions, and all manner of i.		62:40
the people because of their i.,	He	4:14
because of their i. the church		4:23
weary because of their i.;		5: 4
this great i. had come upon		7: 6
and slow to be led to do i.;		7: 7
neighbor, and do all manner of i.		7:21
the people because of their i.,		11:34
they began to wax strong in i.		11:36

and how quick to do i.,	He	12: 4
do all manner of that which is i.;		12: 5
because of the i. of him who		12:18
be unto him that will do i.,		12:22
do all manner of i. unto them,		13:24
Do this, and there is no i.;		13:27
the land because of your i.		13:30
for happiness in doing i.,		13:38
whosoever doeth i., doeth it unto		14:30
i. of the tradition of their fathers.		15: 4
notwithstanding their i.—		15:10
began to be more hardened in i.,		16:12
Satan did stir them up to do i.		16:22
began to fear because of their i.	3 Ne	1:18
year also passed away in i.		2:10
and this because of their i.		2:19
the cause of this i. of the		6:15
the people to do all manner of i.,		6:15
the people to do all manner of i.;		6:16
i. he desired they should—		6:17
all this i. had come upon the		7: 5
so great i. upon the people,		7: 9
cleansed every whit from his i.—		8: 1
it is because of their i. and		9: 2
depart from me, ye that work i.		14:23
among them because of their i.;		15:19
it is because of their i. that they		15:19
it is because of their i. that they		15:20
in unbelief because of i.;		21: 5
exceedingly because of i.,	4 Ne	1:28
and to do all manner of i.		1:34
because of the i. of the people.	Mrm	1:13
of the land, because of their i.		1:16
began to repent of their i.,		2:10
bitterness and in the bonds of i.		8:31
when they are ripened in i.	Eth	2: 9
not until the fulness of i. among		2:10
smitten us because of our i.,		3: 3
that they shall repent of their i.,		4: 6
all manner of i. according to		9:10
when they were ripened in i.;		9:20
began to repent of their i.;		11: 8
do all manner of i. in his days,		11:10
a mighty man among them in i.,		11:15
because of the i. of the people,		14: 1
people repented not of their i.;		15: 6
should be no i. among them;	Mro	6: 7
whoso was found to commit i.,		6: 7
and rejoiceth not in i. but		7:45
and in the bonds of i.,		8:14
despair cometh because of i.		10:22
of the i. of their fathers,	DC	3:18
been hidden because of i.		6:27
stirreth them up to i. against		10:20
them away to do i.,		10:29
the world is ripening in i.;		18: 6
there is no i. in the church,		20:54
blessed, not because of your i.,		38:14
he or she do any manner of i.,		42:87
Purge ye out the i. which is		43:11
cold, and i. shall abound.		45:27
they that have watched for i.		45:50
when the cup of their i. is full.		101:11
groans under the weight of its i.		123: 7
i. and transgression of my holy		124:50
And because i. shall abound,	JS	1:10
because i. shall abound,		1:30

INJURE
have a mind to i. one another,	Mos	4:13

INJURED
should not be i. by his brother,	He	6:22

INJURIES
striving to repair all the i.	Mos	27:35

INJURIES
striving to repair all the i.	Mos	27:35
both of character and personal i.,	DC	123: 2

INJUSTICE
it is i. that the sinner should	Al	42: 1
might not bring upon him i.,		55:19

INJUSTICE

to prevent insult or i.	DC 102:15
and prevent insult and in.	102:17

INMOST

wish from the i. part of my heart,	Al 13:27

INNER

upon the i. bank of the ditch;	Al 53: 4
into the i. part of the wall.	62:21
length thereof, in the i. court.	DC 94: 4
length thereof, in the i. court;	94:11
in length, in the i. court thereof.	95:15
the lower part of the i. court	95:16
the higher part of the i. court	95:17
became quickened in the i. man.	Mses 6:65

INNOCENCE

have remained in a state of i.,	2Ne 2:23

INNOCENT

slay me ye will shed i. blood,	Mos 17:10
blood of the i. shall stand as a	Al 14:11
being an i. man, his blood would	20:18
that I should shed i. blood;	20:19
it be the shedding of i. blood	39: 5
declare unto you that he is i.	He 9:30
Every spirit of man was i.	DC 93:38
infant state, i. before God.	93:38
that the i. among you may not	104: 7
thy servants have been i.	109:31
cries of their i. ones to ascend	109:49
whereby to shed i. blood,	132:19
whereby to shed i. blood,	132:19
wherein they shed i. blood,	132:26
wherein ye shed i. blood,	132:27
is i. and hath not broken her vow,	132:44
placed for the protection of the i.	134: 6
I shall die i.,	135: 4
They were i. of any crime,	135: 7
i. blood on the floor of Carthage	135: 7
their *i. blood* on the escutcheon	135: 7
I. blood on the banner of liberty,	135: 7
and their *i. blood*, with the	135: 7
the i. blood of all the martyrs	135: 7
and they have shed i. blood,	136:36

INNUMERABLE

with an enemy which was i.	Al 58: 8
together an i. army of men,	He 1:14
an i. company of angels,	DC 76:67
they were as i. as the stars in	76:109
continue as i. as the stars;	132:30
and i. are they unto man;	Mses 1:35

INQUIRE

save a man should i. of the Lord;	1Ne 15: 3
that he did i. of the Lord,	16:24
to i. concerning their brethren.	Mos 7: 2
that I might i. of you,	7:11
to i. concerning our brethren,	7:13
Zeezrom began to i. of them	Al 12: 8
did i. concerning the place where	16:20
I will go and i. of the Lord,	27: 7
I. of the Lord, and if he saith	27:10
And now I would i. what	40: 7
that he should i. of the Lord	43:23
did not i. of them concerning	57:17
we did i. of Gid concerning	57:28
the five who were sent to i.	He 9:12
Go and i. of the Lord whether	Eth 1:38
And if thou wilt i., if thou shalt	DC 6:11
you are left to i. for yourself	30: 3
the president may i. and	102:23
i. diligently concerning the	111: 9
ends of the earth shall i. after	122: 1
other things to i. of him:	Mses 1:18
in going to i. of the Lord	JS 2:18
to pray and i. of the Lord	2:68

INQUIRED

Have ye i. of the Lord?	1Ne 15: 8
as I i. of the Lord,	Jac 2:11
the king i. of him to know if	Mos 8: 6

INSOMUCH

he went and i. of the Lord what	Mos 26:13
because thou hast i. of me	26:19
Mosiah went and i. of the Lord	28: 6
Alma i. of the Lord concerning	Al 16: 6
And the king i. of Ammon if	17:22
king Lamoni i. of his servants,	18: 8
Ammon went and i. of the Lord,	27:11
I have i. diligently of God	40: 3
I have i. diligently of the Lord	40: 9
that they i. among the people,	He 9:12
the judges i. of them to know,	9:13
I have i. of the Lord, and he	3Ne 28:37
I i. of the Lord concerning	Mro 8: 7
for thou hast i. of me,	DC 6:14
as often as thou hast i.,	6:14
that thou hast i. of me and	6:15
that inasmuch as you have i.	132: 1
mother i. what the matter was.	JS 2:20

INQUIRERS

and put all i. after truth in	JS 2: 1

INQUIRIES

had come to make i. of me.	JS 2:66

INQUIRY

watchful and careful, with all i.,	DC 42:76

INSEPARABLY

and element, i. connected,	DC 93:33

INSECTS

and i. shall pester their land also,	Mos 12: 6

INSENSIBILITY

nor misery, neither sense nor i.	2Ne 2:11

INSEPARABLY

rights of the priesthood are i.	DC 121:36

INSIST

but I will i. that ye shall	Al 22: 3

INSOMUCH

i. that he thrust us out,	1Ne 3:25
i. that could preserve the	5:21
i. that we did speak unto him	7: 4
i. that they took their journey	7: 5
i. that they have driven him out	7:14
i. that they did soften their hearts;	7:19
i. that they did bow down before	7:20
i. that they who had commenced	8:23
i. that Satan hath great power	13:29
i. that I will bring forth unto	13:34
i. that there were wars and	14:15
i. that I had joy and great hopes	16: 5
i. that we could obtain no food.	16:21
i. that he was brought down into	16:25
i. that I did obtain food for our	16:31
i. that the Lord did bless us	16:39
i. that they did rejoice over me,	17:19
i. that my frame has no strength.	17:47
i. that they were confounded	17:52
i. that they began to dance,	18: 9
i. that I could not move,	18:12
i. that there arose a great storm,	18:13
i. that they loosed me.	18:20
i. that they did seek to take	2Ne 5: 2
i. as they have become	9:15
i. that we truly can command in	Jac 4: 6
i. that he did lead away many	7: 3
i. that I did confound him	7: 8
i. that he fell to the earth.	7:15
i. that the power of God came	7:21
i. that king Benjamin did drive	Om 1:24
i. that many of the Nephites	Al 2:17
i. that there were slain of the	2:19
i. that he slew Amlici with the	2:31
i. that they could not be	8:31
i. that it has not been found in	12:13
i. that they fled many ways.	17:27
i. that they began to be	17:36
i. that they began to be	17:37

INSOMUCH — INSPIRED

i. that they brought many to	Al	21:17	i. that the Israelites, who were	He	8:11
i. that his whole household were		22:23	i. that they fell to the earth;		9: 4
i. that they began to rebel against		24: 2	i. that we fell to the earth;		9:14
i. that they would not that he		24: 2	i. that they did confound them.		9:18
i. that I verily believed that		30:53	i. that the five were set at liberty,		9:38
i. that they were gathered		43:51	i. that they divided hither and		10: 1
i. that they were determined to		46: 2	i. that they were divided against		10:18
i. that the king of the		47: 1	i. that there were wars		11: 1
i. that in the latter end of the		48: 2	i. that they have become extinct,		11:10
i. that he had gathered		48: 3	i. that it did bring forth her fruit		11:17
i. that they were highly favored		48:20	i. that they did put an end to		11:23
i. that the Lamanites were		49:11	i. that they did defy the whole		11:32
i. that they were slain with		49:21	i. that in the night before he		14: 3
i. that their wounds were upon		49:24	i. that it shall appear unto		14: 3
i. that the people of Morianton		50:26	i. that ye shall fall to the earth.		14: 7
i. that he feared not to come		51:11	i. that they could not hit him		16: 2
i. that as they did lift their		51:18	i. that they went away unto		16: 3
i. that they did gain advantage		51:31	i. that they began to be hard	3Ne	2: 1
i. that they did slay them even		51:32	i. that he did blind their eyes		2: 2
i. that they had obtained		53: 8	i. that they did drive them back		2:17
i. that they did rob them of		54:17	i. that they were about to be		2:19
i. that they were all armed;		55:16	i. that they did repent of all		3:25
i. that we should not suffer		56: 8	i. that they could raise grain,		4: 6
i. that when they saw the army		56:37	i. that there never was known		4:11
i. that the whole army of the		56:52	i. that they did fall back		4:12
i. that they were compelled to		56:54	i. that the robbers were about to		4:20
i. that we did slay upwards of		57:14	i. that none did escape who		5: 4
i. that he did speak peace to		58:11	i. as the children of Lehi have		5:22
i. that they were not discovered		58:19	i. that the church began to be		6:14
i. that they did destroy them		58:21	i. that in the thirtieth year he		6:14
i. that we did arrive before them		58:27	i. that the more righteous part of		7: 7
i. that they did flee into the		58:29	i. that in some degree they had		7:14
i. that we have obtained those		58:33	i. that it did shake the whole		8: 6
i. that even one soul has not		58:39	i. that they were found in		8:18
i. that he might with ease		59: 3	i. that the inhabitants thereof		8:20
i. that many have fought and		60: 9	i. that soon after the ascension		10:18
i. that the blood of thousands		60:10	i. that there was no part of		11: 3
i. that ye can have no more		60:30	i. that they did bathe his feet		17:10
i. that they have risen up in		61: 3	i. did they send forth unto the		19: 3
i. that those who have risen		61: 7	i. that by his power they were		28:20
i. that they do fear us and		61: 7	i. that Satan could have no		28:39
i. that they did come to battle.		62: 7	i. that they did heal the sick,	4Ne	1: 5
i. that they did flee out by		62:24	i. that they did build cities		1: 7
i. that they were relieved from		62:29	i. that they were spread upon		1:23
i. that they were all in one		62:33	i. that they did receive all		1:27
i. that the Lamanites were		62:34	i. that the Lord did take away	Mrm	1:13
i. that he considered that		62:35	i. that the inhabitants thereof		1:18
i. that he did find the king;		62:36	i. that they did frighten my		2: 3
i. that they did pursue Teancum,		62:36	i. that they did not flee from		2:24
i. that they did slay them with		62:38	i. that they did return to		3: 7
i. that they did humble		62:41	i. that the Lamanites did take		4: 2
i. that the Lord did bless them,		62:51	i. that they did beat again the		4:15
i. that by sending him forth he	He	1:16	i. that the Lamanites did not		4:20
i. that they did take possession		1:20	i. that they did raise an army	Eth	8: 5
against the wall, i. that he died.		1:21	i. that he desired her to wife.		8:11
i. that he was about to go forth		1:22	strong, i. that they became		9:16
i. that they began to retreat		1:29	i. that Riplakish was killed,		10: 8
i. that it became an exceedingly		1:30	pestilences, i. that there was		11: 7
i. that they were in the power of		1:32	i. that in the third year he		13:23
i. that they came to large		3: 4	i. that thou shalt weep for the	DC	42:45
i. that they began to cover the		3: 8	i. that ye shall obtain power		44: 4
i. that he did prosper in the		3:20	i. that the wicked will not		45:67
i. that there were thousands who		3:24	i. that he seemed to be like		107:43
i. that there was much bloodshed.		4: 1	i. that they shall not discover		111: 4
i. that they would not hearken		4: 3	i. that Haran, my brother, died;	Abr	2: 1
i. that in the fifty and eighth		4: 5	i., that, if possible, they shall	JS	1:22
i. that they were wicked even		4:22			
i. that they could not be governed		5: 3	**INSPIRATION**		
i. that they did confound many		5:17	Which was given by i.,	DC	20:10
i. that they came forth and did		5:17	to write by the spirit of i.;	Mses	6: 5
i. that there were eight thousand		5:19			
i. that they durst not lay their		5:23	**INSPIRE**		
i. that the more part of the		5:50	i. the hearts of the Lamanites	Al	48: 1
i. that their righteousness did		6: 1	he did i. their hearts against		48: 2
i. that they did reject the		6: 2	God does i. men and call	DC	20:11
i. that the Nephites did go into		6: 7			
i. that they did unite with those		6:21	**INSPIRED**		
i. that they had become		6:31	they were i. by the Zoramites	Al	43:44
i. that a more part of it had		6:32	were i. by a better cause,		43:45
i. that this band of robbers was		6:37	i. their hearts with these		43:48
i. that they did trample under		6:39	being i. by his wickedness		50:35
i. that he could not stay among		7: 3	began to be men i. from heaven	3Ne	6:20
i. that the remainder of them		8:10	to serve him, is i. of God.	Mro	7:13

INSPIRED

commandments which i. him;	DC 20: 7
i. by the gift of the Holy Ghost,	20:26
Being i. of the Holy Ghost to	21: 2
Him have I i. to move the	21: 7

INSTANCE
For i., Jesus said: *Handle me*	DC 129: 2

INSTANCES
in many i. they do err	2Ne 28:14
ways of the Lord in very many i.;	Al 31:11
has proved unto you, in many i.,	34: 6
small means in many i. doth	37: 6
by my spirit in many i.,	DC 18: 2
they err in many i. because	33: 4

INSTANT
It shall be at an i., suddenly—	2Ne 26:18
away by a whirlwind, in an i.,	Abr 2: 7
and in an i., as it were,	JS 2:44
the i. that I arrived there.	2:50

INSTANTLY
when, i. I saw, as it were,	JS 2:43

INSTEAD
i. of sweet smell there shall be	2Ne 13:24
i. of a girdle, a rent;	13:24
i. of well set hair, baldness;	13:24
i. of a stomacher, a girding	13:24
burning i. of beauty.	13:24
i. of consoling and healing	Jac 2: 9
i. of feasting upon the pleasing	2: 9
i. of filling up their ditches by	Al 49:22
we, i. of being Lamanites, were	57:10
i. of taking up their swords	60:16
i. of gathering you, except ye will	He 7:19
i. of laying up for yourselves	8:25
a cursing i. of a blessing.	DC 24: 4
a cursing i. of a blessing.	24: 6
a cursing i. of a blessing,	24:15
the gospel, i. of any others.	107:38
For i. of blessings, ye, by	124:48
i. of the counsel which I have	124:84
another seed, i. of Abel, whom	Mses 6: 2
I. of quoting the first verse as	JS 2:36

INSTITUTED
of the washing of feet i.	DC 88:139
was i. in the days of Adam,	107:41
was i. from before the	124:33
Which ordinance is i. for	124:134
which quorum is i. for	124:137
Which quorum is i. for	124:139
ordinance was i. to form a	128:12
the baptismal font was i. as	128:13
as were i. from before the	132: 5
i. for the fulness of my glory;	132: 6
governments were i. of God	134: 1
that religion is i. of God;	134: 4
human laws being i. for the	134: 6

INSTITUTION
agreeable to the i. of heaven;	DC 107:33

INSTRUCT
i. me, that I should build a ship?	1Ne 17:51
shall i. and edify each other,	DC 43: 8

INSTRUCTED
believe that I was i. of the Lord.	1Ne 17:18
men are i. sufficiently that	2Ne 2: 5
i. me that I should not walk	18:11
having been i. in the same	Al 47:36
sought wisdom they might be i.;	DC 1:26
i. in the law of my church,	43: 9
i. more perfectly in theory,	88:78

INSTRUCTION
be kept for the i. of my people,	1Ne 19: 3
having the same i. and the	Al 47:36
after the manner of his i.	3Ne 3:26
hast received in of my Spirit.	DC 6:14
are given of me for your i.;	33:16
children also may receive i.	55: 4
for their i. in all things	88:127
for a place of i. for all those	97:13
received i. and intelligence	JS 2:54

INSTRUCTIONS
the manner of the i. of Moroni.	Al 49: 8
according to the i. of the Lord.	Eth 2:16
and give him thine i.;	DC 66: 8
diligently for further i. at	124:88
obey the i. which I am	132: 3
other wise documents and i.	135: 3
by my i., taken down	OD
peace, and desiring to receive i.,	Abr 1: 2

INSTRUCTOR
i. of every artificer in brass and	Mses 5:46

INSTRUMENT
an i. in the hands of God,	2Ne 1:24
an i. in the hands of God,	3:24
has made me an i. in his hands	Mos 23:10
an i. in the hands of God in	Al 1: 8
I may be an i. in thy hands	2:30
might be an i. in the hands of God	17: 9
make an i. of thee in my hands	17:11
be an i. in the hands of God	29: 9
forth an i. for his work;	3Ne 22:16

INSTRUMENTALITY
benefit of Zion, through your i.	DC 111: 2
through the i. of my servants.	112: 1

INSTRUMENTS
were i. in the hands of God	Mos 27:36
made i. in the hands of God	Al 26: 3
and we have been i. in his hands	26:15
been i. in the hands of God	35:14

INSULT
to prevent i. or injustice.	DC 102:15
prevent i. and injustice.	102:17

INSURRECTIONS
I will stir up i. among you,	Al 60:27

INTEGRITY
because of the i. of his heart,	DC 124:15
because of the i. of his heart;	124:20

INTELLIGENCE
For i. cleaveth unto	DC 88:40
intelligence cleaveth unto i.;	88:40
i., or the light of truth, was not	93:29
act for itself, as all i. also;	93:30
The glory of God is i.,	93:36
Whatever principle of i. we	130:18
gains more knowledge and i.	130:19
i. from him at each of our	JS 2:54

INTELLIGENCES
all the i. thine eyes have seen	Abr 3:21
midst of all the i. thou hast seen.	3:21
the i. that were organized before	3:22

INTELLIGENT
one shall be more i. than the other,	Abr 3:18
one is more i. than the other,	3:18
one being more i. than the other;	3:19
there shall be another more i.	3:19
thy God, I am more i. than they all.	3:19

INTENT
For the fulness of mine i. is that	1Ne 6: 4
with real i., repenting of your sins,	2Ne 31:13
seek them for the i. to do good—	Jac 2:19
For, for this i. have we written	4: 4
for this i. we keep the law of	4: 5
for the i. of the benefit of	Jar 1: 2
the i. for which it was given;	1:11

INTENT 　　　　　　　　　　 INVIOLATE

INTENT
i. to destroy the church of God.	Al	2: 4
aware of the i. of the Amlicites,		2:12
the thought and i. of our hearts?		21: 6
not with the i. to destroy		26:26
but with the i. that perhaps		26:26
being the i. of this last sacrifice,		34:15
And Moroni, perceiving their i.,		43:48
it was their i. to slay us before		56:37
for this i. have I come up upon	He	14:11
to the i. that ye might believe		14:12
to the i. that they might believe		14:28
to the i. that there should be no		14:28
this to the i. that whosoever		14:29
for this i. hath the Lord		15: 4
to the i. that they might believe;		16: 5
the i. that they might not believe	3Ne	1:22
the i. that they may be brought		26: 8
and for this i. shall they go—	Mrm	5:14
for the i. that ye may believe		7: 9
he hath written the i. thereof.		8: 5
sought forgiveness, with real i.,	Mro	6: 8
he shall do it with real i.		7: 6
and not with real i. of heart;		7: 9
for this i. I have written this		8: 6
a sincere heart, with real i.,		10: 4
for this i. have I sent them.	DC	60: 9
for this i. was it made		88:20
for this i. are they sanctified.		88:20

INTENTION
knew the i. of the Lamanites,	Al	43:29
their i. to destroy their brethren,		43:29
it was not Amalickiah's i. to		47: 8
it was his i. to gain favor with		47: 8
I hereby declare my i. to	DC	OD
I started with the i. of going	JS	2:48
the true meaning and i. of		2:74

INTENTIONS
also concerning their i. to flee	Al	50:31
And their i. of mobbing us	JS	2:75

INTENTS
the thoughts and i. of his heart?	Mos	5:13
the thoughts and i. of his heart;	Al	12: 7
the thoughts and i. of the heart;		18:32
and the i. of thy heart.	DC	6:16
thoughts and i. of the heart.		33: 1
thoughts and i. of their hearts,		88:109

INTERCESSION
i. for all the children of men;	2Ne	2: 9
because of the i. for all,		2:10
made i. for the transgressors.	Mos	14:12
make i. for the children of men—		15: 8

INTERCOURSE
i. one with another, to buy and	He	6: 8

INTEREST
hath no i. in the kingdom of God.	Mos	4:18
seeking the i. of his neighbor,	DC	82:19
one-tenth of all their i.		119: 4
for an i. in that house		124:78
with his i. support the cause		124:89
let him do if he will have an i.;		124:112
to secure the public i.;		134: 5

INTERESTS
regulating our i. as individuals	DC 134: 6

INTERFERE
i. in prescribing rules of worship	DC 134: 4
to i. with bond-servants,	134:12

INTERFERENCE
such i. we believe to be	DC 134:12

INTERIOR
to the Secretary of the I.,	DC	OD

INTERPOLATIONS
are i. by the hands of men.	DC 91: 2

INTERPOSITION
the i. of their all-wise Creator,	Mos 29:19

INTERPRET
and he did i. the engravings	Om	1:20
know if he could i. languages,	Mos	8: 6
that is able to i. the language		8:11
he could i. such engravings;		21:28
that no one can i. them;	Eth	3:22

INTERPRETATION
of God unto the i. thereof—	T Pg
The i. thereof by the gift of	T Pg
To know the i. thereof—	1Ne 11:11
tongues, and the i. of tongues;	Mrm	9: 7
means for the i. thereof.		9:34
which, by i., is a honey bee;	Eth	2: 3
I should seal up the i. thereof;		4: 5
by i., is large, or to exceed		15: 8
to another, the i. of languages	Mro 10:16
is given the i. of tongues.	DC	46:25
which is by i., the creator		95: 7
tongues as of fire, and the i.		109:36
healing, i. of tongues,	AoF	7

INTERPRETED
which, being i., is many waters.	1Ne 17: 5
who i. the writing which was	Al	10: 2
Rabbanah, which is, being i.,		18:13
which, being i., is the holy stand.		31:21
which is, being i., a compass;		37:38

INTERPRETERS
And the things are called i.,	Mos	8:13
these i. were doubtless prepared		8:19
all the records, and also the i.,		28:20
and that ye preserve these i.	Al	37:21
these i. were prepared that		37:24
wherefore I have sealed up the i.,	Eth	4: 5

INTERPRETING
and in the gift of i. languages,	Om	1:25
for the purpose of i. languages;	Mos 28:14

INTERRUPT
to i. their rejoicing?	Al	30:22

INTERRUPTION
work of translation without i.;	JS	2:75

INTERVENED
the space of time which i.	JS	2:28

INTERVIEWS
our i. must have occupied	JS	2:47
from him at each of our i.,		2:54

INTO: see in the *APPENDIX*.

INTOLERABLE
so i. that I was under the	JS	2:61

INTRIGUE
some i. amongst the Nephites,	Al	53: 8
and i. among themselves		53: 9

INTRIGUES
all the i. of the Lamanites,	Al	55:27

INTRODUCED
has been i. among this people.	Al	1:12

INVENT
of weapons which we could i.,	Mos	9:16

INVENTED
stratagem that could be i.	JS	2:60

INVIGORATED
and your minds may be i.	DC 88:124

INVIOLATE
laws are framed and held i.	DC 134: 2

INVITATION 479 ISHMAEL

INVITATION
sendeth an i. unto all men,	Al	5:33
I speak by way of i., saying:		5:62

INVITE
to i. them forth to battle.	Eth	14:28
and i. all to come unto Christ.	DC	20:59

INVITED
which all nations shall be i.	DC	58: 9

INVITETH
he i. them all to come unto him	2Ne	26:33
and i. and enticeth to sin,	Mro	7:12
i. and enticeth to do good		7:13
i. and enticeth to do good,		7:13
every thing which i. to do good,		7:16

INWARD
the i. vessel shall be cleansed	Al	60:23
have first cleansed our i. vessel,		60:24

INWARDLY
but i. they are ravening wolves.	3Ne	14:15

IOWA
the saints in the Territory of I.?	DC	125: 1

IRAD
And unto Enoch was born I.,	Mses	5:43
And I. begat Mahujael, and other		5:43
and I., the son of Enoch, having		5:49

IRON
And I beheld a rod of i.,	1Ne	8:19
which came along by the rod of i.,		8:20
hold of the end of the rod of i.;		8:24
darkness, clinging to the rod of i.,		8:24
hold of the end of the rod of i.;		8:30
holding fast to the rod of i.,		8:30
rod of i., which my father had		11:25
yoketh them with a yoke of i.,		13: 5
the rod of i. which our father saw,		15:23
thy neck is an i. sinew,		20: 4
in all manner of wood, and of i.,	2Ne	5:15
the thickets of the forests with i.,		20:34
and also in i. and copper,	Jar	1: 8
and of their brass and their i.;	Mos	11: 3
gold, and of silver, and of i.,		11: 8
yea, I will make thy horn i.,	3Ne	20:19
did make gold, and silver, and i.,	Eth	10:23
of gold, and of silver, and of i.,		10:23
It is an i. yoke,	DC	123: 8
murdered under its i. hand;		123: 9
And with i., with copper,		124:27
of every artificer in brass and i.	Mses	5:46

IRREANTUM
the sea, which we called I.,	1Ne	17: 5

IRRELIGIOUS
of men, both religious and i.,	JS	2:27

IRREVOCABLY
There is a law, i. decreed	DC	130:20

IS: *see in the APPENDIX.*

ISAAC: *see also GALLAND, Isaac, HALE, Isaac, and MORLEY, Isaac.*
and the God of I., and the God	1Ne	6: 4
even Abraham, I., and Jacob;		17:40
the God of Abraham, and of I.,		19:10
of God in offering up his son I.,	Jac	4: 5
of Abraham, and I., and Jacob;	Mos	7:19
of Abraham and I. and of Jacob.		23:23
Abraham, with I., and with Jacob,	Al	5:24
with Abraham, I., and Jacob,		7:25
the God of I., and the God of		29:11
the God of I., and the God of		36: 2
sit down with Abraham, and I.,	He	3:30
of Abraham, and the God of I.,	3Ne	4:30
of Abraham, and the God of I.,	Mrm	9:11
with Joseph and Jacob, and I.,	DC	27:10
Joseph, and Jacob, and I.,		98:32
servants Abraham, I., and Jacob,		132: 1
commanded to offer his son I.;		132:36
as I. also and Jacob		132:37
offering of Abraham of his son I.		132:50
with Abraham, I., and Jacob,		133:55
God of Abraham and of I. and		136:21

ISABEL
Lamanites, after the harlot I.	Al	39: 3

ISAIAH
rehearse unto them the words of I.,	1Ne	15:20
was written by the prophet I.;		19:23
I will read you the words of I.	2Ne	6: 4
they which I. spake concerning		6: 5
which have been spoken by I.		6: 5
write more of the words of I.,		11: 2
I write some of the words of I.,		11: 8
The word that I., the son of		12: 1
Then said the Lord unto I.:		17: 3
which I. the son of Amoz did see.		23: 1
been spoken by the mouth of I.		25: 1
I. spake many things which		25: 1
words of I. are not plain unto		25: 4
delighteth in the words of I.,		25: 5
all that which I. hath spoken,		25: 6
prophecies of I. shall be fulfilled		25: 7
Yea, even doth not I. say:	Mos	14: 1
be led, yea, even as I. said,		15: 6
and also I., and Jeremiah,	He	8:20
the prophet I. shall be fulfilled,	3Ne	16:17
Jonas, and Zedekiah, and I.—		19: 4
words of I. should be fulfilled—		20:11
for great are the words of I.		23: 1
Search the prophecies of I.	Mrm	8:23
some of I., and some of Enoch;	DC	76:100
verses of the 11th chapter of I.?		113: 1
verse of the 11th chapter of I.,		113: 3
is meant by the command in I.,		113: 7
what people had I. reference to?		113: 7
the eleventh chapter of I.,	JS	2:40

ISHMAEL
take *the daughters of I. to wife.*	1Ne	1:hd
and bring down I. and his family		7: 2
we went up unto the house of I.,		7: 4
gain favor in the sight of I.,		7: 4
Lord did soften the heart of I.,		7: 5
and two of the daughters of I.,		7: 6
and the two sons of I.,		7: 6
their father, I., and his wife,		7: 6
one of the daughters of I.,		7:19
and one of the sons of I.,		7:19
and all the house of I.		7:22
one of the daughters of I.		16: 7
took of the daughters of I.		16: 7
took the eldest daughter of I.		16: 7
sons of I. did begin to murmur		16:20
the sons of I. and our wives.		16:27
I. died, and was buried in the place		16:34
the daughters of I. did mourn		16:35
and also unto the sons of I.:		16:37
the sons of I. and also their wives		18: 9
and also unto him		18:17
sons who are the sons of I.,	2Ne	1:28
he spake unto the sons of I.,		4:10
the sons of I. were angry with me		4:13
and also the sons of I.,	Al	3: 7
Giddonah, who was the son of I.,		10: 2
Ammon went to the land of I.,		17:19
being called after the sons of I.,		17:19
as Ammon entered the land of I.,		17:20
who was over the land of I.,		17:21
and he was a descendant of I.		17:21
and Lemuel, and the sons of I.,		18:38
with him to the land of I.,		20:14
will I return to the land of I.,		20:15
land of Middoni to the land of I.,		21:18
synagogues built in the land of I.;		21:20
people who were in the land of I.,		21:21
land save it were the land of I.;		22: 1

ISHMAEL / ISRAEL

he has gone to the land of I.,	Al	22: 4
who were in the land of I.;		23: 9
they came to the land of I.		24: 5
over to dwell in the land of I.		25:13
and Lemuel, and the sons of I.,		43:13
Lamanites, Lemuelites, and I.	Jac	1:13
the Lemuelites and the I.,	Al	47:35
and Lemuelites, and I.;	4Ne	1:38
and the Lemuelites and the I.	Mrm	1: 8
the I. were called Lamanites,		1: 9
and the Lemuelites, and the I.,	DC	3:18

ISHMAELITISH

sons of Ishmael, and I. women.	Al	3: 7

ISLANDS

and from the i. of the sea.	2Ne	21:11
wild beasts of the i. shall cry		23:22
and in the i. of the sea,		29:11
are upon the i. of the sea,	DC	1: 1
and upon the i. of the sea—		88:94
unto the i. of the sea;		133: 8
and upon the i. of the sea,		133:20
the i. shall become one land.		133:23

ISLE

we are upon an i. of the sea.	2Ne	10:20

ISLES

should inhabit the i. of the sea,	1Ne	19:10
kings of the i. of the sea		19:12
he remember the i. of the sea;		19:16
Listen, O i., unto me,		21: 1
I heard them, O i. of the sea,		21: 8
and fro upon the i. of the sea;		22: 4
The i. shall wait upon me,	2Ne	8: 5
dispersion, from the i. of the sea,		10: 8
who are upon the i. of the sea;		10:21
as it says i., there must needs be		10:21
who are upon the i. of the sea;		29: 7

ISRAEL

a remnant of the house of I.;	T Pg	
the remnant of the House of I.	T Pg	
gave thanks unto the God of I.	1Ne	5: 9
given thanks unto the God of I.,		5:10
concerning the house of I.,		10:12
after the house of I. should		10:14
remnants of the house of I.,		10:14
the house of I. hath gathered		11:35
judge the twelve tribes of I.;		12: 9
ye are of the house of I.		12: 9
hath made unto the house of I.;		13:23
hath made unto the house of I.;		13:23
remnant of the house of I.		13:33
remnant of the house of I.—		13:34
numbered among the house of I.;		14: 2
the house of I. shall no more be		14: 2
unto the house of I.;		14: 5
unto the house of I.?		14: 8
who are of the house of I.		14:17
unto the house of I.		14:26
the house of I. was compared		15:12
broken off from the house of I.,		15:12
not a branch of the house of I.?		15:12
they are of the house of I.,		15:14
again among the house of I.;		15:16
or of the house of I.		15:17
of all the house of I.,		15:18
or of the house of I.;		15:20
who were the children of I.,		17:23
children of I. were in bondage;		17:25
children of I. might quench		17:29
even the very God of I.		19: 7
those who are of the house of I.		19:10
shall visit all the house of I.		19:11
they crucify the God of I.,		19:13
and glory of the God of I.		19:13
despised the Holy One of I.,		19:14
against the Holy One of I.,		19:15
who are of the house of I.		19:16
unto all the house of I.,		19:19
remnant of the house of I.,		19:24

unto all the house of I.,	1Ne	19:24
called by the name of I.,		20: 1
mention of the God of I.,		20: 1
themselves upon the God of I.,		20: 2
O Jacob, and I. my called,		20:12
Redeemer, the Holy One of I.;		20:17
O ye house of I.,		21: 1
my people, O house of I.		21: 1
Thou art my servant, O I.,		21: 3
though I. be not gathered,		21: 5
to restore the preserved of I.		21: 6
the Lord, the Redeemer of I.,		21: 7
then, O house of I.,		21:12
not forget thee, O house of I.		21:15
house of I., sooner or later,		22: 3
because of the Holy One of I.;		22: 5
who are of the house of I.		22: 6
after all the house of I.		22: 7
unto all the house of I.,		22: 9
who are of the house of I.		22:11
Redeemer, the Mighty One of I.		22:12
against thee, O house of I.,		22:14
against the Holy One of I.		22:18
was the Holy One of I.;		22:21
and the Holy One of I.		22:24
and the Holy One of I.		22:26
in the Holy One of I.		22:28
will reject the Holy One of I.,	2Ne	1:10
of the Holy One of I.		3: 2
branch unto the house of I.;		3: 5
my people, O house of I.		3: 9
restoring thee, O house of I.,		3:13
restoration unto the house of I.,		3:24
concerning all the house of I.;		6: 5
ye are of the house of I.		6: 5
ye are of the house of I.		6: 5
Lord God, the Holy One of I.,		6: 9
necks against the Holy One of I.,		6:10
judgments of the Holy One of I.		6:10
Lord is God, the Holy One of I.		6:15
O house of I., is my hand shortened		7: 2
unto thee, O house of I.		7: 4
with all the house of I.—		9: 1
our God, the Holy One of I.,		9:11
resurrection of the Holy One of I.		9:12
seat of the Holy One of I.;		9:15
saints of the Holy One of I.,		9:18
believed in the Holy One of I.,		9:19
our God, the Holy One of I.!		9:19
faith in the Holy One of I.		9:23
Lord God, the Holy One of I.,		9:24
mercies of the Holy One of I.		9:25
which is the Holy One of I.		9:26
greatness of the Holy One of I.		9:40
is the Holy One of I.;		9:41
the God of I. did witness that		9:44
come unto the Holy One of I.,		9:51
branch unto the house of I.		9:53
numbered among the house of I.		10:18
from the house of I.,		10:22
them that are escaped of I.		14: 2
of Hosts is the house of I.,		15: 7
counsel of the Holy One of I.		15:19
word of the Holy One of I.		15:24
the son of Remaliah, king of I.,		17: 1
offense to both the houses of I.,		18:14
for signs and for wonders in I.		18:18
and it hath lighted upon I.		19: 8
and they shall devour I.		19:12
will the Lord cut off from I.		19:14
the light of I. shall be for a fire,		20:17
that day, that the remnant of I.,		20:20
upon the Lord, the Holy One of I.,		20:20
though my people I. be as the		20:22
shall assemble the outcasts of I.,		21:12
like as it was to I. in the day		21:16
great is the Holy One of I.		22: 6
and will yet choose I.,		24: 1
the house of I. shall possess them,		24: 2
which are of the house of I.,		25: 4
that brought I. up out of the land		25:20
and Christ is the Holy One of I.;		25:29
rejoice in the Holy One of I.		27:30
and shall fear the God of I.		27:34

ISRAEL

a remnant of the house of I.	2 Ne	28: 2
of God, the Holy One of I.;		28: 5
which are of the house of I.;		29: 1
which are of the house of I.;		29: 2
other tribes of the house of I.,		29:12
words of the lost tribes of I.;		29:13
the lost tribes of I.		29:13
which are of the house of I.,		29:14
who are of the house of I.,		29:14
Son, who is the Holy One of I.		30: 2
praises unto the Holy One of I.		31:13
who are of the house of I.,		33:13
while the children of I. were in	Jac	1: 7
he spake unto the house of I.,		5: 1
Hearken, O ye house of I.,		5: 2
I will liken thee, O house of I.,		5: 3
concerning the house of I.,		6: 1
he remembereth the house of I.,		6: 4
unto God, the Holy One of I.,	Om	1:25
Christ, who is the Holy One of I.,		1:26
who brought the children of I.	Mos	7:19
as numerous as the hosts of I.		8: 8
a law given to the children of I.,		13:29
are a branch of the tree of I.,	Al	26:36
yea, who are of the house of I.,	3 Ne	10: 4
O ye people of the house of I.,		10: 5
O ye people of the house of I.,		10: 5
house of I. whom I have spared,		10: 6
But if not, O house of I.,		10: 7
know that I am the God of I.,		11:14
covenanted with my people I.;		15: 5
other tribes of the house of I.,		15:15
all the people of the house of I.		16: 5
unbelief of you, O house of I.,		16: 7
who are of the house of I.;		16: 8
who are of the house of I.,		16: 8
who are of the house of I.,		16: 9
who are of the house of I.		16: 9
unto my people, O house of I.,		16:11
show unto thee, O house of I.,		16:12
unto you, O house of I.,		16:12
among my people, O house of I.		16:13
who are of the house of I.,		16:14
suffer my people, O house of I.,		16:15
foot of my people, O house of I.		16:15
myself unto the lost tribes of I.,		17: 4
of the people of the house of I.,		17:14
a remnant of the house of I.		20:10
unto his people, O house of I.		20:12
my people, O house of I.		20:21
and ye are of the house of I.;		20:25
of my people, O house of I.,		20:27
God of I. shall be your rearward.		20:42
my people, O house of I.,		21: 1
with his people, O house of I.;		21: 4
among my people, O house of I.;		21: 6
who are of the house of I.		21: 7
among my people, O house of I.;		21:20
also as many of the house of I.		21:23
Redeemer, the Holy One of I.—		22: 5
which are of the house of I.;		23: 2
unto him in Horeb for all I.,		25: 4
all the scattered tribes of I.,		28:29
made with the children of I.,		29: 1
coming the children of I.		29: 2
his people of the house of I.		29: 3
the remnant of the house of I.;		29: 8
hath made unto the house of I.		29: 9
who are of the house of I.		30: 2
and also unto you, house of I.,	Mrm	3:17
unto you, twelve tribes of I.,		3:18
even among all the house of I.,		4:12
have care for the house of I.,		5:10
the calamity of the house of I.;		5:11
the Jews, or all the house of I.,		5:14
and unto all the house of I.		5:20
ye remnant of the house of I.;		7: 1
that ye are of the house of I.		7: 2
who are the house of I.,		8:21
made unto the house of I.—		8:21
hath made with the house of I.;		9:37
Come unto me, O ye house of I.,	Eth	4:14
unto your fathers, O house of I.	Eth	4:15
also concerning the house of I.,		13: 5
be built unto the house of I.		13: 5
who were of the house of I.		13:10
made unto thee, O house of I.,	Mro	10:31
brought the children of I.	DC	8: 3
Gentiles unto the house of I.		14:10
and also the house of I.		18: 6
judge the whole house of I.,		29:12
I. shall be saved in mine own		35:25
God, the Mighty One of I.;		36: 1
for I. shall be saved,		38:33
which are of the house of I.		39:11
who are of the house of I.		42:39
restoration of the scattered I.		45:17
and the stone of I.		50:44
appointed to be a judge in I.,		58:17
do like unto the children of I.,		61:25
over the twelve tribes of I.;		77: 9
gather together the tribes of I.		77: 9
out of all the tribes of I.—		77:11
to gather the tribes of I.;		77:14
taught to the children of I. in		84:23
among the children of I.		84:27
hath redeemed his people, I.,		84:99
a savior unto my people I.		86:11
by them, as the children of I.,		89:21
and of the nations of I.,		90: 8
all mine I., shall be saved.		101:12
Moses led the children of I.		103:16
For ye are the children of I.,		103:17
until the army of I. becomes		105:26
hold the armies of I. guiltless		105:30
And also to be a judge in I.,		107:72
to sit as a judge in I.		107:76
to thy name, O Lord God of I.,		109: 1
all the scattered remnants of I.,		109:67
converted and redeemed with I.,		109:70
the keys of the gathering of I.		110:11
and the redemption of I.		113: 8
remnants of I. in their scattered		113:10
upon the tribes of I.,		133:34
concerning the Camp of I.		136: 1
who led the children of I. out		136:22
to save my people I.		136:22
from bondage, even I. my chosen.	Mses	1:26
was not before sent upon I.,	JS	1:18
shall be sent again upon I.		1:18
in the literal gathering of I.	AoF	10

ISRAELITES

the I., who were our fathers,	He	8:11

ISRAEL'S

for I. God is their God,	DC	127: 3

ISSUE

position to i. the Manifesto	DC	OD

IT: *see in the APPENDIX.*

ITEMS

concerning the i. in addition	DC	68:13

ITES

Lamanites, nor any manner of i.;	4 Ne	1:17

ITS

and i. numbers were few,	1 Ne	14:12
Bountiful, because of i. much fruit		17: 5
Bountiful, because of i. much fruit.		17: 6
in the end of i. creation.	2 Ne	2:12
to crumble to i. mother earth,		9: 7
shall deliver up i. dead;		9:11
shall deliver up i. dead;		9:12
must deliver up i. captive		9:12
must deliver up i. captive		9:12
every sort according to i. number.	Jac	5:31
will I cast away into i. own place.		5:77
mortal frame to i. mother earth.	Mos	2:26
deny justice when it has i. claim.		15:27
received i. name from the king,		18: 4

ITS

church began to fail in i. progress.	Al	4:10
reunited again in i. perfect form;		11:43
be restored to i. proper frame,		11:43
be restored to i. perfect frame,		11:44
destroy, because of i. greatness.		16: 9
being preached in i. purity		16:21
lost from i. body in a strange land;		26:36
not guilty because of i. parents.		30:25
yea, and i. motion, yea, and also		30:44
forth unto i. own likeness.		32:31
no thought for i. nourishment,		32:38
try the experiment of i. goodness.		34: 4
fathers, by following i. course,		37:45
joint shall be restored to i. body;		40:23
should be restored to i. body,		41: 2
thing to i. natural frame—		41: 4
in a state opposite to i. nature?		41:12
been prepared in i. strangth.		55:13
of the sun and also of i. setting;	He	14: 4
according to i. proper order;	3Ne	1:19
if the salt shall lose i. savor		12:13
salt that hath lost i. savor,		16:15
because of i. exceeding height,	Eth	3: 1
answer the end of i. creation;	DC	49:16
will hasten the city in i. time,		52:43
shall bring forth in i. strength.		59: 3
have I blessed it, in i. time,		61:17
in i. sanctified, immortal, and		77: 1
years of i. continuance,		77: 6
or i. temporal existence.		77: 6
filled the measure of i. creation,		88:19
filleth the measure of i. creation,		88:25
justice continueth i. course		88:40
its course and claimeth i. own;		88:40
every kingdom in i. hour,		88:61
in its hour, and in i. time,		88:61
in its time, and in i. season,		88:61
will hasten my work in i. time.		88:73
salt of the earth lose i. savor,		101:40
in i. true light before the council;		102:16
as salt that has lost i. savor,		103:10
of heaven and i. righteousness,		106: 3
must be agreed to i. decisions,		107:27
Priesthood and i. counselors		107:79
i. wealth pertaining to gold		111: 4
slanderer cease i. perverseness.		112: 9
river in i. decreed course,		121:33
under the weight of i. iniquity,		123: 7
murdered under i. iron hand;		123: 9
earth, in i. sanctified and		130: 9
the moon shall withhold i. light,		133:49
in i. spiritual privileges,		134: 9
individual rights of i. members,		134: 9
to enter into i. practice,		OD
for all flesh had corrupted i. way	Mses	8:29
according to i. times and seasons	Abr	3: 4
therefore the reckoning of i. time		3: 5
many as to i. number of days,		3: 5
a longer time as to i. reckoning		3: 7
in itself yieldeth i. own likeness		4:11
forth grass from i. own seed,		4:12
forth herb from i. own seed,		4:12
forth the tree from i. own seed,		4:12
upon the earth after i. kind;		4:25
is equal with Kolob in i.	Fac	2: 4
and in i. measuring of time.		2: 2
borrow i. light from Kolob		2: 5
This planet received i. power		2: 5
earth in i. four quarters.		2: 6
When i. branches are yet tender,	JS	1:38
to militate against i. character		2: 1
and i. progress in the world—		2: 1
light ahd made i. appearance.		2:43
receive i. paradisiacal glory.	AoF	10

ITSELF

which sheddeth i. abroad in the	1Ne	11:22
the body is restored to i. again,	2Ne	9:13
the ax boast i. against him that		20:15
saw magnify i. against him that		20:15
if the rod should shake i. against		20:15
if the staff should lift up i. as if		20:15

482

body should be restored to i.	Al	41: 2
thought for the things of i.	3Ne	13:34
that which is now exalted of i.	DC	49:10
thought for the things of i.		84:84
seeketh to become a law unto i.,		88:35
has placed it, to act for i.,		93:30
enough to make hell i. shudder,		123:10
and press i. upon my feelings		128: 1
whose seed should be in i.	Mses	2:11
whose seed should be in i.,		2:12
whose seed in i. yieldeth its own	Abr	4:11
only bring forth the same in i.,		4:12
which had already manifested i.	JS	2:74

JABAL

Adah bare J.; he was the father	Mses	5:45

JACKSON

can be purchased in J. county,	DC	101:71
all the lands in J. county		105:28
inhabitants of H. county, Missouri,		109:47
house unto my name, in J. county,		124:51

JACOB

JACOB: see also SCOTT, Jacob.

Joseph who was the son of J.	1Ne	5:14
he might preserve his father, J.,		5:14
the God of Isaac, and the God of J.,		6: 4
even Abraham, Isaac, and J.;		17:40
the elder was called J.		18: 7
J. and Joseph also, being young,		18:19
the God of J., yieldeth himself,		19:10
hear this, O house of J.,		20: 1
Hearken unto me, O J., and Israel		20:12
hath redeemed his servant J.		20:20
to bring J. again to him—		21: 5
to raise up the tribes of J.,		21: 6
Redeemer, the Mighty One of J.		21:26
And now, J., I speak unto you:	2Ne	2: 1
Nevertheless, J., my firstborn		2: 2
J. and Joseph, my younger		5: 6
I, Nephi, did consecrate J.		5:26
The words of J., the brother of		6: 1
I, J., having been called of God,		6: 2
now I, J., would speak somewhat		6: 8
Redeemer, the Mighty One of J.		6:18
now I, J., speak unto you again,		10: 1
now, J. spake many more things		11: 1
my brother, J., also has seen him		11: 3
to the house of the God of J.;		12: 3
O house of J., come ye		12: 5
thy people, the house of J.,		12: 6
his face from the house of J.,		18:17
The Lord sent his word unto J.		19: 8
are escaped of the house of J.,		20:20
yea, even the remnant of J.,		20:21
the Lord will have mercy on J.,		24: 1
shall cleave to the house of J.		24: 1
concerning the house of J.:		27:33
J. shall not now be ashamed,		27:33
sanctify the Holy One of J.,		27:34
of the words of my brother J.		31: 1
THE BOOK OF J.	Jac	:hd
gave me, J., a commandment		1: 1
gave me, J., a commandment		1: 2
I J., take it upon me to fulfil		1: 8
But I, J., shall not hereafter		1:14
I, J., spoke unto them these words		1:17
For I, J., and my brother Joseph		1:18
which J., the brother of Nephi,		2: 1
I, J., according to the		2: 2
J., get thou up into the temple		2:11
I, J., would speak unto you		3: 1
I, J., spake many more things		3:12
plates are called the plates of J.,		3:14
I, J., having ministered much unto		4: 1
I J., am led on by the Spirit unto		4:15
that I, J., had faith in Christ		7: 3
Brother J., I have sought much		7: 6
when I, J., had spoken these words,		7:15
thing was pleasing unto me, J.,		7:22
that I, J., began to be old;		7:26
I, J., saw that I must soon go		7:27

JACOB

from J. down to the reign of	WM	1: 3
of Abraham, and Isaac, and J.;	Mos	7:19
of Abraham and Isaac and of J.		23:23
who consisted of Nephi, J., and	Al	3: 6
Abraham, with Isaac, and with J.,		5:24
with Abraham, Isaac, and J.,		7:25
God of Isaac, and the God of J.,		29:11
God of Isaac, and the God of J.,		36: 2
are a remnant of the seed of J.,		46:23
let us remember the words of J.,		46:24
this was the language of J.		46:26
their leader, whose name was J.,		52:20
behold, J., who was a Zoramite,		52:20
and told it unto J., their leader.		52:22
J., being their leader, being also		52:33
J. was determined to slay them		52:34
was wounded and J. was killed.		52:35
Abraham, and Isaac, and with J.,	He	3:30
God of Isaac, and the God of J.,	3Ne	4:30
he hath blessed the house of J.,		5:21
all the remnant of the house of J.,		5:24
with all the house of J.,		5:25
covenanted with the house of J.		5:25
restoring all the house of J.		5:25
a man whom they did call J.;		7: 9
J. seeing that their enemies were		7:12
Gadiomnah, and the city of J.,		9: 8
inhabited by the people of king J.,		9: 9
who are descendants of J.,		10: 4
our father J. also testified		10:17
a remnant of the house of J.,		20:16
which I made with your father J.;		20:22
a remnant of the house of J.,		21: 2
people who are a remnant of J.		21:12
among this the remnant of J.,		21:22
my people, the remnant of J.,		21:23
ye sons of J. are not consumed.		24: 6
the remnant of the house of J.	4Ne	1:49
remnant of the house of J.;	Mrm	5:12
a remnant of the seed of J.		5:24
are a remnant of the seed of J.;		7:10
of Isaac, and the God of J.;		9:11
a branch of the house of J.;	DC	10:60
And also with Joseph and J.,		27:10
J. shall flourish in the		49:24
which are a remnant of J.,		52: 2
and thy fathers, Joseph, and J.,		98:32
thy servants, the sons of J.,		109:58
a great love for the children of J.,		109:61
mercy upon the children of J.,		109:62
cause that the remnants of J.,		109:65
to thee, O Mighty God of J.—		109:68
servants Abraham, Isaac, and J.,		132: 1
J. did none other things than		132:37
with Abraham, Isaac, and J.,		133:55
Abraham and of Isaac and of J.		136:21

JACOBITES

they were called Nephites, J.,	Jac	1:13
J., and Josephites, and Zoramites;	4Ne	1:36
J., and Josephites, and Zoramites.		1:37
of the Nephites and the J. and	Mrm	1: 8
to the Nephites, and the J.,	DC	3:17

JACOBUGATH

And behold, that great city J.,	3Ne	9: 9

JACOM

they were called J., and Gilgah,	Eth	6:14

JAH-OH-EH

called by the Egyptians J.	Fac	2: 1

JAIL

They were shot in Carthage j.,	DC	135: 1
confined in j. by the conspiracy		135: 7
blood on the floor of Carthage j.		135: 7

JAMES: *see also* COVILL, *James; and* FOSTER, *James.*

him and for thy brother J.;	DC	7: 7
with Peter, and J., and John,		27:12
say unto you, my servant J.,		39: 7
The voice of Peter, J., and John		128:20
day reading the Epistle of J.,	JS	2:11
else I must do as J. directs,		2:13
the testimony of J. to be true—		2:26
direction of Peter, J. and John,		2:72

JAMES, George

also J. be ordained a priest.	DC	52:38

JANUARY

On the 18th of J., 1827, we	JS	2:57

JAPHETH

years old, and begat J.;	Mses	8:12
of her who was the mother of J.,		8:12
three sons, Shem, Ham, and J.		8:27

JAQUES, Vienna

that my handmaid J. should	DC	90:28

JARED: *see also* CARTER, *Jared.*

a record of the people of J.,	T Pg	
of Orihah, who was the son of J.;	Eth	1:32
Which J. came forth with his		1:33
the brother of J. being a large		1:34
J., his brother, said unto him:		1:34
the brother of J. did cry unto		1:35
Lord had compassion upon J.;		1:35
not confound the language of J.;		1:35
J. and his brother were not		1:35
Then J. said unto his brother:		1:36
the brother of J. did cry unto		1:37
J. spake again unto his brother,		1:38
the brother of J. did cry unto		1:39
been spoken by the mouth of J.		1:39
Lord did hear the brother of J.,		1:40
J. thy brother and his family;		1:41
friends of J. and their families.		1:41
J. and his brother, and their		2: 1
and also the friends of J. and		2: 1
talked with the brother of J.;		2: 4
the brother of J. saw him not.		2: 4
his wrath unto the brother of J.,		2: 8
bring J. and his brethren forth		2:13
came again unto the brother of J.,		2:14
Lord talk with the brother of J.,		2:14
the brother of J. repented of		2:15
the brother of J. did go to work,		2:16
the brother of J. cried unto		2:18
said unto the brother of J.:		2:20
that the brother of J. did so,		2:21
Lord said untothe brother of J.:		2:23
that the brother of J.,		3: 1
the brother of J. had said these		3: 6
off the eyes of the brother of J.,		3: 6
the brother of J. fell down		3: 6
saw that the brother of J. had fallen		3: 7
Lord said unto the brother of J.:		3:21
showed unto the brother of J. all		3:25
commanded the brother of J.		4: 1
which the brother of J. saw;		4: 4
manifest unto the brother of J.		4:14
even as the brother of J. did,		4: 7
which the brother of J. saw,		4: 7
the record of J. and his brother.		6: 1
the brother of J. had carried up		6: 2
the brother of J. came down		6: 2
the brother of J. did sing praises		6: 9
And J. had four sons;		6:14
the brother of J. also begat		6:15
the friends of J. and his brother		6:16
the brother of J. began to be old,		6:19
wherefore he said unto J.:		6:19
the daughters of the brother of J.		6:20
of sons and daughters of J.		6:20
J. said unto them:		6:23
But J. said unto his brother:		6:24
firstborn of the brother of J.;		6:25
that neither would the sons of J.,		6:27
J. died, and his brother also.		6:29
the saying of the brother of J.		7: 5
And Omer begat J.;		8: 1
J. begat sons and daughters.		8: 1
J. rebelled against his father,		8: 2
the doings of J. their brother,		8: 5

JARED 484 JERUSALEM

army and gave battle unto J.	Eth	8: 5
they had slain the army of J.		8: 6
J. became exceeding sorrowful		8: 7
daughter of J. being exceeding		8: 8
the daughter of J. was exceeding		8: 9
when J. had sent for Akish,		8:11
the daughter of J. danced before		8:11
that he said unto J.:		8:11
And J. said unto him:		8:12
gathered in unto the house of J.		8:13
it was the daughter of J. who		8:17
J. put it into the heart of Akish;		8:17
save it were J. and his family.		9: 3
that J. was anointed king over		9: 4
J. was murdered upon his		9: 6
in bringing J. and his brother		10: 2
descendant of the brother of J.		11:17
of these was the brother of J.;		12:20
sight of the brother of J.,		12:20
after the brother of J. had		12:21
the brother of J. had obtained		12:21
like unto the brother of J.,		12:24
the brother of J. said unto		12:30
the account of the people of J.,	Mro	1: 1
given to the brother of J.	DC	17: 1
was two hundred years old		107:47
J., Enoch, and Methuselah,		107:53
sixty-five years, and begat J.;	Mses	6:20
lived, after he begat J.,		6:20
And J. lived one hundred and		6:21
and J. lived, after he begat Enoch,		6:21
J. taught Enoch in all the ways		6:21
of J. were nine hundred and		6:24

JAREDITES

it will be like unto the J.,	Mro	9:23

JAROM

THE BOOK OF J.	Jar	1:hd
behold, I, J., write a few words		1: 1
And I, J., do not write more,		1:14
being commanded by my father, J.,	Om	1: 1

JARRINGS

there were j., and contentions,	DC	101: 6

JASHON

came even to the land of J.,	Mrm	2:16
the city of J. was near the		2:17

JAVELIN

quiver, and the dart, and the j.,	Jar	1: 8
and put a j. to his heart;	Al	51:34
and he did cast a j. at him,		62:36

JAWS

if the very j. of hell shall gape	DC	122: 7

JEALOUS

their God, and am a j. God,	Mos	11:22
I the Lord thy God am a j. God,		13:13
Akish began to be j. of his son,	Eth	9: 7

JEALOUSIES

as you strip yourselves from j.	DC	67:10

JEBERECHIAH

and Zechariah the son of J.	2Ne	18: 2

JEHOVA

My name is J., and I know	Abr	2: 8

JEHOVAH

for the Lord J. is my strength	2Ne	22: 2
the pleasing bar of the great J.,	Mro	10:34
O J., have mercy upon	DC	109:34
But deliver thou, O J.,		109:42
from thy house, O J., to bear		109:56
how he has covenanted with J.,		109:68
even the voice of J., saying:		110: 3
to the decrees of the great J.		128: 9
my name is J., and I have	Abr	1:16

JEOPARDIZING

thereby j. the lives of men;	DC	134:12

JEOPARDY

in j. of either life or limb,	DC	134:10

JEREMIAH

spoken by the mouth of J.	1Ne	5:13
J. have they cast into prison.		7:14
and also Isaiah, and J.,	He	8:20
(J. being that same prophet who		8:20
according to the words of J.		8:20
Kumen, and Kumenonhi, and J.,	3Ne	19: 4

JEREMY

Elihu under the hand of J.;	DC	84: 9
J. under the hand of Gad;		84:10

JERSHON

we will give up the land of J.,	Al	27:22
this land J. is the land which		27:22
between the land J. and the land		27:23
our brethren in the land J.;		27:23
they may inherit the land J.;		27:24
went down into the land of J.,		27:26
possession of the land of J.,		27:26
established in the land of J.,		28: 1
established in the land of J.,		28: 1
set round about the land of J.,		28: 1
the brethren in the land of J.		28: 8
established in the land of J.		30: 1
went over to the land of J.		30:19
was south of the land of J.,		31: 3
came over into the land of J.		35: 1
came over into the land of J.		35: 2
over also into the land of J.		35: 6
of Ammon who were in J.,		35: 8
departed out of the land of J.,		35:13
and gave place in the land of J.		35:13
inheritance in the land of J.,		35:14
their armies in the land of J.		43: 4
meet them in the land of J.		43:15
Lamanites in the borders of J.,		43:18
Nephites in the borders of J.;		43:22
of his army in the land of J.,		43:25
from Haran by the way of J.,	Abr	2:16
built an altar in the land of J.,		2:17
we passed from J. through the		2:18

JERUSALEM

depart out of the land of J.,	1Ne	1:hd
returneth to the land of J.		1:hd
Lehi, having dwelt at J. in all		1: 4
city J. must be destroyed.		1: 4
returned to his own house at J.;		1: 7
Wo, unto J., for I have seen		1:13
did my father read concerning J.—		1:13
concerning the destruction of J.,		1:18
out of the land of J.,		2:11
J., that great city, could be		2:13
unto the Jews who were at J.,		2:13
thy brethren shall return to J.		3: 2
to go up to the land of J.		3: 9
come up to the land of J.,		3:10
that J. must be destroyed,		3:17
ye shall go up to J. again,		3:29
Let us go up again unto J.,		4: 1
came without the walls of J.		4: 4
return to the city of J.		4:30
tarried at J., and had perished		5: 4
up to the land of J.,		5: 6
return unto the land of J.,		7: 2
wilderness to go up to J.		7: 3
return unto the land of J.		7: 7
concerning the destruction of J.;		7:13
concerning the destruction of J.		7:13
if ye will return unto J.		7:15
even that great city J.,		10: 3
time that my father left J.,		10: 4
beheld the great city of J.,		11:13
out of the land of J.,		16:35
to return again to J.		16:36

JERUSALEM

out of the land of J.	1 Ne	17:14
out of the land of J.,		17:20
before they came out of J.		17:20
who were in the land of J.		17:22
brought from the land of J.		18:24
the time my father left J.		19: 8
for those who are at J.,		19:13
for those who are at J.;		19:20
of those who are at J.		22: 4
them out of the land of J.	2 Ne	1: 1
flee out of the land of J.		1: 3
I know that J. is destroyed;		1: 4
and had we remained in J.		1: 4
out of the land of J.		1: 9
from the time that we left J.;		1:24
out of the land of J.,		1:30
from the time we left J.		5:28
that those who were at J.,		6: 8
Awake, awake, stand up, O J.,		8:17
on thy beautiful garments, O J.,		8:24
arise, sit down, O J.;		8:25
show himself unto those at J.,		9: 5
at J. will stiffen their necks		10: 5
saw concerning Judah and J.:		12: 1
the word of the Lord from J.		12: 3
away from J., and from Judah,		13: 1
For J. is ruined,		13: 8
left in Zion and remain in J.		14: 3
written among the living in J.		14: 3
shall have purged the blood of J.		14: 4
And now, O inhabitants of J.,		15: 3
went up toward J. to war		17: 1
a snare to the inhabitants of J.		18:14
images did excel them of J.		20:10
so do to J. and to her idols?		20:11
upon Mount Zion and upon J.,		20:12
daughter of Zion, the hill of J.		20:32
the time that I came out from J.		25: 4
for I came out from J.,		25: 5
I, of myself, have dwelt at J.,		25: 6
after my father left J.;		25:10
and possess the land of J.;		25:11
behold, J. shall be destroyed		25:14
the time that my father left J.;		25:19
how that we came out from J.,		30: 4
from the time that Lehi left J.;	Jac	1: 1
people forth out of the land of J.,		2:25
of my people in the land of J.,		2:31
I have led out of the land of J.,		2:32
wanderers, cast out from J.,		7:26
time that our father Lehi left J.	En	1:25
led them out of the land of J.	Om	1: 6
of Zarahemla came out from J.		1:15
from the time they left J.	Mos	1: 6
brought out of the land of J.;		1:11
them out of the land of J.,		2: 4
the time our father, Lehi, left J.;		2:34
from the time that Lehi left J.		6: 4
fathers out of the land of J.,		7:20
driven out of the land of J.		10:12
together ye waste places of J.;		12:23
his people, he hath redeemed J.;		12:23
together, ye waste places of J.;		15:30
his people, he hath redeemed J.		15:30
from the time that Lehi left J.		28:20
years from the time Lehi left J.		29:46
brought out of the land of J.,	Al	3:11
shall be born of Mary, at J.		7:10
Lehi, was brought out of J. by		9: 9
of God out of the land of J.,		9:22
who came out of the land of J.,		10: 3
of the Jews who were at J.;		11: 4
that their father, Lehi, left J.		18:36
from the time that Lehi left J.		18:38
called by the Lamanites, J.,		21: 1
a great city, which was called J.		21: 2
Aaron came to the city of J.,		21: 4
our fathers out of the land of J.?		22: 9
and who were in the land of J.,		24: 1
from the time Lehi left J.;		28: 2
fathers out of the land of J.		36:29
pressed and brought out of J.		54:23
who came out of the land of J.;	He	5: 6
first came out of the land of J.,		7: 7
testified of the destruction of J.)		8:20
we know that J. was destroyed		8:20
dispute that J. was destroyed?		8:21
driven out of the land of J.?		8:21
father Lehi was driven out of J.		8:22
as unto them who shall be at J.?		16:18
land as well as in the land of J.?		16:19
Lehi, who came out of J.	3 Ne	1:hd
from the time that Lehi left J.;		1: 1
the departure of Lehi out of J.		1: 2
passed away since Lehi left J.		2: 6
people of Lehi since he left J.		4:11
from the time that Lehi left J.,		5:15
our fathers out of the land of J.,		5:20
city of J. and the inhabitants		9: 7
of Israel, ye that dwell at J.,		10: 5
father Lehi brought out of J.?		10:17
tell it unto your brethren at J.		15:14
land, neither of the land of J.,		16: 1
if it so be that my people at J.,		16: 4
together, ye waste places of J.;		16:19
people, he hath redeemed J.		16:19
done unto your brethren at J.,		17: 8
and it shall be a New J.		20:22
which is the land of J.,		20:29
again, and give unto them J.		20:33
together, ye waste places of J.;		20:34
his people, he hath redeemed J.		20:34
on thy beautiful garments, O J.,		20:36
arise, sit down, O J.;		20:37
then shall J. be inhabited again		20:46
shall be called the New J.		21:23
of the land, unto the New J.		21:24
Father hath led away out of J.		21:26
shall the offering of Judah and J.		24: 4
the Jews at J. sought to kill	4 Ne	1:31
be his disciples in the land of J.	Mrm	3:18
Jesus chose in the land of J.		3:19
was the place of the New J.,	Eth	13: 3
he spake concerning a New J.		13: 4
J. from whence Lehi should		13: 5
it could not be a new J. for		13: 5
that a New J. should be built		13: 6
of Joseph out of the land of J.,		13: 7
like unto the J. of old;		13: 8
And then cometh the New J.;		13:10
then also cometh the J. of old;		13:11
and arise from the dust, O J.;	Mro	10:31
people of the destruction of J.;	DC	5:20
with me in my ministry at J.,		29:12
who journeyed from J. in the		33: 8
the New J. shall be prepared,		42: 9
building up of the New J.		42:35
where the New J. shall be built.		42:62
both here and in the New J.		42:67
this temple which is in J.,		45:18
I have told you concerning J.;		45:24
it shall be called the New J.,		45:66
and have built the city of J.		77:15
shall be the city of New J.		84: 2
the city New J. shall be built		84: 4
even as mine apostles at J.		95: 9
that J., from this hour, may		109:62
in her stakes, and in J.,		124:36
who be of Judah flee unto J.,		133:13
and he shall speak from J.,		133:21
land of J. and the land of		133:24
upon the holy city, the New J.;		133:56
shall be called Zion, a New J.	Mses	7:62
concerning the destruction of J.,	JS	1:12
and upon the inhabitants of J.,		1:18
days which shall come upon J.,		1:21

JESSE: *see also BAKER, Jesse.*

a rod out of the stem of J.,	2 Ne	21: 1
there shall be a root of J.,		21:10
Who is the Stem of J. spoken of	DC	113: 1
should come of the Stem of J.?		113: 3
who is partly a descendant of J.		113: 4
What is the root of J. spoken of		113: 5
it is a descendant of J., as well as		113: 6

JESUS

JESUS		
that J. is the CHRIST,	T Pg	
his name shall be J. Christ,	2Ne	25:19
save it be this J. Christ,		25:20
the Jews, that J. is the very Christ,		26:12
also that J. is the Christ,		26:12
And the gospel of J. Christ shall		30: 5
to the knowledge of J. Christ,		30: 5
can we follow J. save we shall		31:10
it speaketh of J., and persuadeth		33: 4
I glory in my J., for he hath		33: 6
can command in the name of J.	Jac	4: 6
And he shall be called J. Christ,	Mos	3: 8
and faith on the Lord J. Christ.		3:12
for we believe in J. Christ,		4: 2
faith which they had in J. Christ		4: 3
and deliverance of J. Christ	Al	4:14
of God, which is in Christ J.;		5:44
I know that J. Christ shall come,		5:48
to the testimony of J. Christ,		6: 8
and deliverance of J. Christ;		9:28
O blessed J., who has saved me		19:29
the coming of one J. Christ,		36:17
O J., thou Son of God, have mercy		36:18
in J. Christ their Redeemer.		37: 9
and faith on the Lord J. Christ;		37:33
their faith on the Lord J. Christ.		37:33
unto the Lord J. Christ for mercy,		38: 8
Believest thou in J. Christ,		45: 4
J. Christ shall manifest himself		45:10
redeemed by the Lord J. Christ;		46:39
believe on the name of J. Christ,	He	3:28
the atoning blood of J. Christ,		5: 9
faith on the Lord J. Christ,		13: 6
of the coming of J. Christ,		14:12
I am a disciple of J. Christ,	3Ne	5:13
God and my Savior J. Christ,		5:20
Redeemer, who is J. Christ,		5:26
the prophets who testified of J.		7:10
faith on the Lord J. Christ.		7:16
his faith on the Lord J. Christ		7:18
And in the name of J. did he		7:19
the people, in the name of J.		7:20
which was in J. Christ,		7:21
many miracles in the name of J.;		8: 1
do a miracle in the name of J.		8: 1
I am J. Christ the Son of God.		9:15
unto the Lord J. Christ,		10:10
J. Christ did show himself unto		11:hd
conversing about this J. Christ,		11: 2
Behold, I am J. Christ, whom		11:10
when J. had spoken these words		11:12
did fall down at the feet of J.,		11:17
authority given me of J. Christ,		11:25
when J. had spoken these words		12: 1
when J. had spoken these words		13:25
when J. had spoken these words		14: 1
when J. had ended these sayings		15: 1
when J. had said these words		15: 2
when J. had spoken these words,		15:11
when J. had spoken these words		17: 1
that when J. had thus spoken,		17: 5
and J. stood in the midst;		17:12
and J. stood in the midst,		17:13
J. groaned within himself,		17:14
heard J. speak to the Father;		17:16
we both saw and heard J. speak;		17:17
J. had made an end of praying		17:18
that J. spake unto them,		17:19
J. commanded his disciples that		18: 1
done this, J. said unto them:		18:10
when J. had spoken these words		18:17
when J. had spoken these words,		18:26
when J. had made an end of these		18:36
when J. had touched them all,		18:38
that they could not see J.		18:38
J. had ascended into heaven,		19: 1
that the multitude had seen J.,		19: 2
was noised abroad concerning J.;		19: 3
where J. should show himself		19: 3
disciples whom J. had chosen—		19: 6
the Father in the name of J.		19: 6
Father also in the name of J.		19: 7
words which J. had spoken—	3Ne	19: 8
words which J. had spoken—		19: 8
to the Father in the name of J.		19: 8
all those whom J. had chosen.		19:12
J. came and stood in the midst		19:15
and they did pray unto J.,		19:18
J. departed out of the midst of		19:19
when J. had thus prayed unto		19:24
J. blessed them as they did pray		19:25
and also the garments of J.;		19:25
And J. said unto them:		19:26
when J. had spoken these words		19:30
they were white, even as J.		19:30
J. had made an end of praying		19:35
one voice, and gave glory to J.,		20: 9
they had all given glory unto J.,		20:10
in me, that I am J. Christ,		20:31
in my words, who am J. Christ,		21:11
when J. had said these words		23: 6
And J. said unto them:		23:11
J. commanded that it should be		23:13
when J. had expounded all the		23:14
when J. had told these things		26: 1
which J. did truly teach unto		26: 6
words which J. hath spoken.		26: 8
disciples whom J. had chosen		26:17
were baptized in the name of J.		26:17
even as J. had commanded them.		26:20
baptized in the name of J.		26:21
disciples of J. were journeying		27: 1
were baptizing in the name of J.,		27: 1
And J. again showed himself		27: 2
J. came and stood in the midst		27: 2
when J. had ended these sayings		27:33
when J. had said these words,		28: 1
when J. had spoken these words,		28:12
according to the word of J.		28:23
of them unto J. many souls,		28:29
unto the Father in the name of J.		28:30
hearken unto the words of J.,		28:34
receiveth not the words of J.		28:34
no miracle wrought by J. Christ;		29: 7
hear the words of J. Christ,		30: 1
THE DISCIPLES OF J. CHRIST	4Ne	1:hd
the disciples of J. had formed		1: 1
were baptized in the name of J.;		1: 1
wrought by the disciples of J.,		1: 5
save it were in the name of J.		1: 5
among the disciples of J.		1:13
the disciples of J., whom he had		1:14
over the disciples of J. who did		1:30
at Jerusalem sought to kill J.,		1:31
smite upon the people of J.;		1:34
the people of J. did not smite		1:34
were the three disciples of J.		1:37
save it were the disciples of J.		1:46
and knew of the goodness of J.	Mrm	1:15
come unto J. with broken hearts		2:14
our Lord and Savior J. Christ.		3:14
whom J. chose to be his disciples		3:18
twelve whom J. chose in this		3:19
other twelve whom J. chose in		3:19
believe the gospel of J. Christ,		3:21
that J., whom they slew, was		3:21
been clasped in the arms of J.		5:11
persuaded that J. is the Christ,		5:14
could ye have rejected that J.,		6:17
and believe in J. Christ, that he		7: 5
be baptized in the name of J.,		7: 8
save it be the disciples of J.,		8:10
J. Christ hath shown you unto		8:35
and the holiness of J. Christ,		9: 5
the Father in the name of J.,		9: 6
the fall of man came J. Christ,		9:12
because of J. Christ came the		9:12
which came by J. Christ,		9:13
that J. Christ did not many		9:18
thus said J. Christ, the Son of		9:22
ask the Father in the name of J.		9:27
do it in the name of J. Christ,		9:29
may the Lord J. Christ grant		9:37
faith on the name of J. Christ.		9:37
of the land, who is J. Christ,	Eth	2:12

JESUS

Behold, I am J. Christ.	Eth	3:14
J. showed himself unto this		3:17
and he saw the finger of J.,		3:19
therefore he saw J.; and he did		3:20
saith J. Christ, the Son of God,		4: 7
greater things, saith J. Christ;		4: 8
the Father in the name of J.,		5: 5
yea, even J. Christ.		12:22
ye know that I have seen J.,		12:39
commend you to seek this J.		12:41
and also the Lord J. Christ,		12:41
In the name of J. Christ I	Mro	3: 3
of sins through J. Christ,		3: 3
the name of thy Son, J. Christ,		4: 3
the name of thy Son, J. Christ,		5: 2
in remembrance of the Lord J.		6: 6
and our Lord J. Christ,		7: 2
that J. is the Christ,		7:44
followers of his Son, J. Christ;		7:48
your Lord J. Christ hath been		8: 2
the name of his Holy Child, J.,		8: 3
and our Lord J. Christ,		9:26
upon the merits of J. Christ,	DC	3:20
I am J. Christ, the Son of God.		6:21
I am J. Christ, the Son of God.		10:57
in the power of J. Christ,		11:10
I am J. Christ, the Son of God.		11:28
I am J. Christ, the Son of the		14: 9
to the words of J. Christ,		15: 1
to the words of J. Christ,		16: 1
I, J. Christ, your Lord and		17: 9
my name, which is J. Christ,		18:22
J. Christ is the name which is		18:23
I, J. Christ, your Lord and		18:33
in the name of J. Christ;		18:41
I, J. Christ, your Lord and		18:47
I am J. Christ; I came by		19:24
our Lord and Savior J. Christ		20: 1
an apostle of J. Christ,		20: 2
an apostle of J. Christ,		20: 3
our Lord and Savior J. Christ,		20: 4
of the gospel of J. Christ		20: 9
on the name of J. Christ,		20:29
our Lord and Savior J. Christ		20:30
our Lord and Savior J. Christ		20:31
them the name of J. Christ,		20:37
in the name of J. Christ,		20:70
has the authority from J. Christ		20:73
commissioned of J. Christ,		20:73
remembrance of the Lord J.;		20:75
name of thy Son, J. Christ,		20:77
name of thy Son, J. Christ,		20:79
an apostle of J. Christ,		21: 1
grace of your Lord J. Christ,		21: 1
J. was crucified by sinful men		21: 9
Listen to the voice of J. Christ,		27: 1
Listen to the voice of J. Christ,		29: 1
but of me, even J. Christ,		31:13
even J. Christ your Redeemer;		34: 1
I am J. Christ, the Son of God,		35: 2
I am J. Christ, the Son of God;		36: 8
your God, even J. Christ,		38: 1
Great I AM, even J. Christ—		39: 1
J. Christ the Son of the living		42: 1
I am J. Christ, the Savior of		43:34
I am J. that was crucified.		45:52
that J. Christ is the Son of God,		46:13
on the name of the Lord J.,		49:12
in the name of J. Christ,		49:13
Behold, I am J. Christ,		49:28
through J. Christ, his Son.		50:27
you will in the name of J.		50:29
of the Father in the name of J.;		50:31
unto you, I am J. Christ,		51:20
I am J. Christ, the Son of God,		52:44
in the name of J. Christ,		55: 2
and in the name of J. Christ		59: 5
even J. Christ, your advocate,		62: 1
and Omega, even J. Christ.		63:60
your Redeemer, even J. Christ.		66:13
record of me, even J. Christ,		68: 6
not the gospel of J. Christ.		74: 2
the atonement of J. Christ;		74: 7

JEWS

of J. Christ, who is the Son,	DC	76:14
came into the world, even J.,		76:41
received the testimony of J.,		76:51
J. the mediator of the new		76:69
testimony of J. in the flesh,		76:74
valiant in the testimony of J.;		76:79
neither the testimony of J.		76:82
neither the testimony of J.,		76:101
saith your Lord, even J. Christ.		79: 4
your Redeemer, even J. Christ.		80: 5
and Omega, even J. Christ.		81: 7
A revelation of J. Christ unto		84: 1
even the Spirit of J. Christ.		84:45
through J. Christ his Son.—		88: 5
the name of the Lord J. Christ,		88:133
for the revelation of J. Christ.		90:11
even J. Christ your Lord.		95:17
J. the mediator of the new covenant.		107:19
proclamation of the gospel of J.		107:35
in the name of J. Christ, the Son		109: 4
of my Church of J. Christ of		115: 3
The Church of J. Christ of		115: 4
for the gospel of J. Christ.		121:29
seer of the Church of J. Christ		127:12
by the revelation of J. Christ,		128: 8
of this Church of J. Christ		128:21
J. said: *Handle me and see,*		129: 2
wise and true God, and J. Christ,		132:24
has done more, save J. only,		135: 3
for the religion of J. Christ,		135: 7
of the Church of J. Christ of		136: 2
Moses to J. and his apostles,		136:37
from J. and his apostles to		136:37
of the Chruch of J. Christ of		OD
of the Church of J. Christ of		OD
of the Church of J. Christ of		OD
which is J. Christ, the only name	Mses	6:52
Son of Man, even J. Christ,		6:57
Only Begotten, even J. Christ,		7:50
baptized in the name of J. Christ,		8:24
And J. went out, and departed	JS	1: 2
And J. said unto them:		1: 3
And J. left them, and went		1: 4
And J. answered, and said unto		1: 5
of the Church of J. Christ of		2: 1
Father, and in His Son, J. Christ,	AoF	1
Faith in the Lord J. Christ;		4

JETHRO

hand of his father-in-law, J.;	DC	84: 6
J. received it under the hand		84: 7

JEW

and also to J. and Gentile—		T Pg
convincing of the J. and Gentile		T Pg
out of the mouth of a J.	1Ne	13:23
forth from the mouth of a J.;		13:24
forth from the mouth of a J.		13:24
forth from the mouth of the J.,		13:38
out of the mouth of the J.;		14:23
out of the mouth of the J.,		14:23
out of the mouth of the J.,		14:23
J. and Gentile, both bond and	2Ne	10:16
alike unto God, both J. and Gentile.		26:33
I have charity for the J.—		33: 8
I say J., because I mean them		33: 8
my beloved brethren, and also J.,		33:10
both unto Gentile and unto J.;	DC	18:26
that soon it may go to the J.,		19:27
between J. and Gentile;		57: 4

JEWELS

The rings, and nose j.;		2Ne 13:21
that day when I make up my j.;		3Ne 24:17
when I shall make up my j.,		DC 60: 4
shall come to make up my j.		101: 3

JEWISH

be raised up to the J. nation		DC 77:15

JEWS

after the record of the J.	1Ne	1:hd
consists of the learning of the J.		1: 2

JEWS   488   JOHNSON

the J. did mock him because of	1Ne	1:19	and to prophesy to the J.	DC 77:15
when the J. heard these things		1:20	overthrow the kingdom of the J.,	84:28
they were like unto the J. who		2:13	they shall turn unto the J.	90: 9
Laban hath the record of the J.		3: 3	the hearts of the J. unto the	98:17
concerning the elders of the J.,		4:22	and the prophets unto the J.;	98:17
concerning the elders of the J.,		4:27	and secondly unto the J.	107:33
that the J. might not know		4:36	the Gentiles and then to the J.;	107:34
to obtain the record of the J.		5: 6	the Gentiles and then unto the J.	107:35
record of the J. from the beginning,		5:12	and also unto the J.	107:97
spake unto them concerning the J.—		10: 2	but also unto the J.;	112: 4
raise up among the J.—		10: 4	and then upon the J.	133: 8
should be preached among the J.,		10:11	of the temple, and the J.;	JS 1: 4
dwindling of the J. in unbelief.		10:11	be great tribulation on the J.,	1:18
is a record of the J.,		13:23	unto you concerning the J.;	1:21
go forth from the J. in purity		13:25		
from the J. unto the Gentiles,		13:26	JOB	
also the J. who were scattered		13:39	Thou art not yet as J.;	DC 121:10
unto the J. and also unto the		13:42	as they did J.	121:10
unto the J. and also unto the		13:42		
Gentiles and also unto the J.,		13:42	JOEL	
shall be rejected of the J.,		15:17	quoted the second chapter of J.,	JS 2:41
the restoration of the J.		15:19		
ther estoration of the J.,		15:20	JOHN: *see also BENNETT, John C.; CARTER,*	
the J. also sought to take away		17:44	*John S.; CORRILL, John; GOULD, John;*	
That he has spoken unto the J.,	2Ne	9: 2	*HICKS, John A.; JOHNSON, John;*	
should come among the J.,		10: 3	*MURDOCK, John; PAGE, John E.; SMITH,*	
of prophesying among the J.		25: 1	*John; SNIDER, John; TAYLOR, John; and*	
concerning the manner of the J.;		25: 2	*WHITMER, John.*	
hath beheld the things of the J.,		25: 5	the apostle of the Lamb was J.,	1Ne 14:27
the J. do understand the things		25: 5	J., my beloved, who was with me	3Ne 28: 6
which were spoken unto the J.		25: 5	to be written by my servant J.	Eth 4:16
the manner of the things of the J.		25: 5	J., my beloved, what desirest	DC 7: 1
after the manner of the J.;		25: 6	Hearken, my servant J., and	15: 1
hath come to pass among the J.,		25: 6	to the revelations of J.,	20:35
hath been destroyed among the J.		25: 9	also J. the son of Zacharias,	27: 7
the J. shall be scattered among		25:15	and his name should be J.,	27: 7
the J. shall be scattered by other		25:15	Which J. I have sent unto	27: 8
who should be rejected of the J.		25:18	Peter, and James, and J.,	27:12
the convincing of the J., that		26:12	I say unto you, my servant J.,	30: 9
the Gentiles and also the J.,		27: 1	wast sent forth, even as J.,	35: 4
it shall proceed forth from the J.,		29: 4	that my servant J. should write	47: 1
thank they the J. for the Bible		29: 4	by the mouth of my servant J.,	61:14
labors, and the pains of the J.,		29: 4	verse of the fifth chapter of J.,	76:15
have ye remembered the J.		29: 5	some of Christ and some of J.,	76:100
a Bible save it were by the J.?		29: 6	sea of glass spoken of by J.,	77: 1
behold, I shall speak unto the J.		29:12	used by the Revelator. J.,	77: 2
the J. shall have the words of		29:13	beasts, which were shown to J.,	77: 5
shall have the words of the J.;		29:13	twenty elders, spoken of by J.?	77: 5
the Nephites and the J. shall have		29:13	these elders whom J. saw,	77: 5
words of the Nephites and the J.		29:13	by the book which J. saw,	77: 6
as many of the J. as will not		30: 2	book which was eaten by J.,	77:14
concerning the J. and the Gentiles,		30: 3	until J., whom God raised	84:27
they are descendants of the J.		30: 4	recorded in the testimony of J.	88: 3
the J. which are scattered also		30: 7	And J. saw and bore record of	93: 6
and respect the words of the J.,		33:14	I, J., bear record that I beheld	93:11
the J. were a stiffnecked people;	Jac	4:14	I, J., saw that he received not	93:12
that by the stumbling of the J.		4:15	I, J., bear record, and lo,	93:15
upon which the J. can build.		4:16	And I, J., bear record that	93:16
contained the record of the J.	Om	1:14	the fulness of the record of J.	93:18
after the manner of the J.	Al	11: 4	and J. bore record of me,	93:26
after the manner of the J.;		11: 4	remember that J. the Revelator	128: 6
built after the manner of the J.		16:13	The voice of Peter, James, and J.	128:20
I never seen among all the J.;	3Ne	19:35	J. 14:23—The appearing of the	130: 3
that I was lifted up by the J.,		28: 6	to Elijah, and from Elijah to J.,	133:55
They will also be among the J.,		28:28	under the alter that J. saw,	135: 7
and the J. shall know them not.		28:28	said that his name was J.,	JS 2:72
spurn, nor make game of the J.,		29: 8	that is called J. the Baptist	2:72
as the J. at Jerusalem sought	4Ne	1:31	direction of Peter, James and J.,	2:72
also that the J., the covenant	Mrm	3:21		
unto the unbelieving of the J.;		5:14	JOHN'S	
restoring the J., or all the		5:14	of J. testimony concerning me.	DC 88:141
and that he was slain by the J.,		7: 5	the fulness of J. record is	93: 6
unto the Gentiles from the J.,		7: 8		
is had among the J.—	Eth	1: 3	JOHNSON, Aaron	
through the testimony of the J.,	DC	3:16	J. be ordained unto this calling	DC 124:132
the Gentiles and to the J. also;		20: 9		
lo, lo! to the J. also.		21:12	JOHNSON, John	
this generation of J. shall not		45:21	that my servant Zombre [J.]	DC 96: 6
then shall the J. look upon me		45:51	Joseph Coe, J., Martin Harris,	102: 1
was had among all the J.		74: 2	6, Sylvester Smith; 7, J.;	102:34
for it was had among the J.;		74: 6	Zombre [J.] obtained in exchange	104:24
			let my servant Zombre [J.] have	104:34

JOHNSON 489 JOSEPH

JOHNSON, Luke
also unto my servant J.,   DC 68: 7
my servant J. go with him,   75: 9
Hyde, Sylvester Smith, and J.,   102: 3
3, Samuel H. Smith; 4, J.;   102:34

JOHNSON, Lyman
and unto my servant J.,   DC 68: 7
I say unto my servant J.,   75:14

JOIN
unto them that j. house to house,   2Ne 15: 8
and j. his enemies together;   19:11
j. the choirs above in singing   Mos 2:28
his brethren did j. the Lamanites,   23:35
they did j. the churches of God;   25:23
neither would they j. the church.   26: 4
j. in fasting and mighty prayer   Al 6: 6
did j. themselves to the people of   25:13
did j. the army of Moroni,   55:24
I did j. my two thousand sons,   56:10
had come to j. their brethren,   57: 6
to j. the people of Ammon   62:27
did j. the people of Ammon,   62:29
j. themselves unto the church   He 3:24
and to j. with them in their   6:38
to j. those Gadianton robbers.   3Ne 1:29
j. the inhabitants of the city   Mrm 4: 3
them that would not j. them.   Eth 14:27
j. what sect they pleased;   JS 2: 6
that I might know which to j.   2:18
and which I should j.   2:18
that I must j. none of them,   2:19
forbade me to j. with any of   2:20
duty to j. with any of them,   2:26
to j. any of the religious sects   2:28

JOINED
one that is j. to the wicked   2Ne 23:15
strangers shall be j. with them,   24: 1
Thou shalt not be j. with them   24:20
would have gladly j. with them,   Mos 21:31
and j. Mosiah's people,   22:13
the Amlicites have j. them;   Al 2:24
were j. to the church of God;   4: 4
j. that day by more than the   24:26
who j. the people of the Lord,   24:29
and j. the people of Ammon.   47:29
j. upon the borders of Lehi;   50:25
and j. them to my stripling   56:57
come over and j. the Lamanites   59: 6
and j. the army of Moroni.   59: 8
he hath j. an alliance with him;   61: 8
until they were j. by dissenters,   3Ne 7:12
are j. together in this order;   DC 78: 8
because they are not j. by me,   132:18
four of them j. that church,   JS 2: 7

JOINING
away j. the borders of Mormon.   Al 21: 1
them by j. the Lamanites.   48:24
j. the borders of Aaron and   50:14
lot which is set off j. the house,   DC 104:28

JOINS
which j. the land Bountiful,   Al 27:22

JOINT
both limb and j. shall be restored   Al 11:43
limb and j. shall be restored   40:23
neither in body, limb, nor j.;   DC 84:80

JOINTS
all my j. are weak,   1Ne 19:20
of both j. and marrow;   DC 6: 2
of both j. and marrow;   11: 2
of both j. and marrow;   12: 2
of both j. and marrow;   14: 2
the dividing asunder of the j.   33: 1

JONAS
also his son, whose name was J.,   3Ne 19: 4
Jeremiah, and Shemnon, and J.,   19: 4

JONEAM
J. had fallen with his ten   Mrm 6:14

JORDAN
baptize in Bethabara, beyond J.;   1Ne 10: 9
they had crossed the river J.   17:32
the way of the Red Sea beyond J.   2Ne 19: 1
as we had fled to the city of J.;   Mrm 5: 3

JOSEPH: *see also COE, Joseph; KNIGHT, Joseph; SMITH, Joseph; SMITH, Joseph, Jun.; SMITH, Joseph, Sen.; SMITH'S, Joseph, Sen.; WAKEFIELD, Joseph; and YOUNG, Joseph.*
that he was a descendant of J.;   1Ne 5:14
that J. who was the son of Jacob,   5:14
Laban also was a descendant of J.,   5:16
that we are a descendant of J.   6: 2
called Jacob and the younger J.   18: 7
Jacob and J. also, being young,   18:19
I speak unto you, J., my last-born.   2Ne 3: 1
And now, J., my last-born,   3: 3
and I am a descendant of J.   3: 4
of the Lord which he made unto J.   3: 4
Wherefore, J. truly saw our day.   3: 5
For J. truly testified,   3: 6
Yea, J. truly said: 3: 7
And thus prophesied J.,   3:14
Yea, thus prophesied J.:   3:16
And now, behold, my son J.,   3:22
And now, blessed art thou, J.   3:25
hath spoken, concerning J.,   4: 1
concerning the prophecies of J.,   4: 3
Jacob and J., my younger brethren,   5: 6
Nephi, did consecrate Jacob and J.,   5:26
promise may be fulfilled unto J.,   25:21
For I, Jacob, and my brother J.   Jac 1:18
from the fruit of the loins of J.   2:25
Nephi, Jacob, and J., and Sam,   Al 3: 6
J. who was sold into Egypt   10: 3
are a remnant of the seed of J.,   46:23
our liberty as a remnant of J.   46:24
of the remnant of the coat of J.   46:24
the remainder of the seed of J.   46:24
what the remnant of the seed of J.,   46:27
been merciful unto the seed of J.   3Ne 5:21
a remnant of the seed of J.   5:23
a remnant of the seed of J.   10:17
we a remnant of the seed of J.?   10:17
a remnant of the house of J.   15:12
the remnant of the seed of J.,   Eth 13: 6
as J. brought his father down   13: 7
a remnant of the seed of J.   13: 7
be merciful unto the seed of J.   13: 7
merciful unto the father of J.   13: 7
the remnant of the house of J.   13: 8
the remnant of the seed of J.,   13:10
Behold, thou art J., and thou   DC 3: 9
not believe you, my servant J.,   5: 7
unto you, my servant J.,   5: 9
command you, my servant J.,   5:21
speak unto you, my servant J.,   5:23
command you, my servant J.,   5:29
behold, I say into thee J.,   5:30
stand by my servant J.,   6:18
translate, even as my servant J.   6:25
and also unto my servant J.,   6:28
is to write for my servant J.   9: 4
servant J. sufficient strength,   9:12
eternal life; and his name is J.   18: 8
speak a few words unto you, J.;   23: 5
And also with J. and Jacob,   27:10
and my servant J. shall be   28:10
by the hand of my servant J.,   35:17
and assist you, my servant J.,   47: 1
the city of Enoch [J.],   78: 4
heathen nations, the house of J.,   90:10
he is a descendant of Seth [J.]   96: 7
and thy fathers, J., and Jacob,   98:32
my friends Sidney and J.,   100: 1
spokesman unto my servant J.   100: 9
as my servant J. shall appoint   105:21
rebel not against my servant J.;   112:15

JOSEPH — 490 — JOURNEYED

in all places where my servant J.,	DC 112:17
Ephraim, or of the house of J.,	113: 4
of Jesse, as well as of J.,	113: 6
let not my servant J.,	115:13
servant J. and his counselors,	115:16
be manifested unto my servant J.,	115:18
one as my servant J. shall show	124:22
show unto my servant J. all	124:42
let my servant J. and his house	124:56
even so I say unto my servant J.:	124:58
let my servant J. and his seed	124:59
let my servant J. pay stock into	124:72
J. cannot pay over fifteen thousand	124:72
the work that my servant J. shall	124:79
the counsel of my servant J.,	124:89
as counselor unto my servant J.,	124:91
as well as my servant J.;	124:94
also with my servant J.;	124:95
receive counsel from my servant J.,	124:95
let my servant J. tarry at home,	124:102
be counselor unto my servant J.,	124:103
in which my servant J. resides.	124:105
Let him assist my servant J.,	124:107
Law assist my servant J.,	124:107
unto the counsel of my servant J.,	124:112
build a house for my servant J.,	124:115
counsel of my servants J. and	124:118
J. to be a presiding elder over	124:125
unto them by my servant J.,	125: 2
J., my son, if thou livest until	130:15
the Lord unto you my servant J.,	132: 1
my servant J. to holt this power	132: 7
loins ye are, namely, my servant J.—	132:30
I gave unto thee, my servant J.,	132:40
I reveal it unto you, my servant J.,	132:44
I say unto you, my servant J.,	132:48
been given unto my servant J.,	132:52
J. that he shall be made ruler	132:53
and cleave unto my servant J.,	132:54
servant J. do all things for her,	132:55
handmaid forgive my servant J.	132:56
let not my servant J. put his	132:57
servant J.; for I will justify him;	132:60
J. leaped from the window,	135: 1
When J. went to Carthage	135: 4

JOSEPHITES

were called Nephites, Jacobites, J.,	Jac 1:13
Jacobites, and J., and Zoramites;	4Ne 1:36
Jacobites, and J., and Zoramites.	1:37
the J. and the Zoramites;	Mrm 1: 8
and the Jacobites, and the J.,	DC 3:17

JOSH

of Laman, and the city of J.,	3Ne 9:10
and J., had fallen with their ten	Mrm 6:14

JOSHUA

forth and came to the land of J.,	Mrm 2: 6

JOSIAH: *see BUTTERFIELD, Josiah, and STOAL, Josiah.*

JOT

all fulfilled, every j. and tittle,	Al 34:13
one j. or tittle should not pass	3Ne 1:25
one j. nor one tittle hath not	12:18

JOTHAM

the days of Ahaz the son of J.,	2Ne 17: 1

JOURNEY

three days' j. into the wilderness	1Ne 1:hd
took our j. in the wilderness,	3: 9
they took their j. with us	7: 5
on our j. towards the tent of	7:21
take his j. into the wilderness.	16: 9
again take our j., traveling nearly	16:33
again take our j. in the wilderness;	17: 1
and did j. in the wilderness	2Ne 5: 7
took their j. again into the	Om 1:29
nor progress in their j.,	Mos 1:17
from the labors of their j.;	7:16

take a j. into the wilderness,	Mos 8: 7
on our j. into the wilderness	9: 3
of their j. in the wilderness.	10:13
and they pursued their j.	22:12
And they fled eight days' j.	23: 3
their j. into the wilderness.	24:24
their j. into the wilderness	28: 9
j. over into the land of Melek,	Al 8: 3
and traveled three days' j.	8: 6
took his j. towards the city which	8:13
j. towards the land of Middoni.	20:28
Aaron took his j. towards the	21: 1
distance of a day and a half's j.	22:32
did not progress in their j.;	37:41
and took their j. round about in	43:22
being a day's j. for a Nephite,	He 4: 7
thy j. among the Lamanites.	DC 28:14
your j. with your brother	30: 5
and he shall j. with you;	35:22
take their j. as soon as	52: 3
and j. to the land of Missouri.	52: 3
take their j. speedily;	52: 7
their j. unto the same place	52: 8
And let them j. from thence	52: 9
take their j. also,	52:22
Ezra Booth take their j.,	52:23
take their j. with my servants	52:24
Whitlock also take their j.,	52:25
and Orson Pratt take their j.,	52:26
their j. unto this same land,	52:27
Jacob Scott also take their j.	52:28
Coltrin also take their j.	52:29
Smith also take their j.	52:30
Carter also take their j.	52:31
ordained, and also take their j.	52:32
let all these take their j. unto	52:33
neither j. in another's track.	52:33
their j. into the eastern lands;	52:35
take your j. with my servants	53: 5
and take your j., and appoint	54: 7
thus you shall take your j.	54: 8
take your j. with my servants	55: 5
also take his j. with them.	55: 6
shall take up his j. speedily	56: 5
concerning your j. unto the land	60: 5
and take your j. speedily	60: 5
take their j. for Cincinnati;	60: 6
take their j. from St. Louis,	60: 8
let them take their j. in haste	61: 9
should take their j. in haste—	61:21
let them take their j. in haste.	61:21
come upon the waters to j.,	61:23
they shall j. by land,	61:24
as they are commanded to j.	61:24
of the camp of the Lord, to j.	61:29
And from thence let them j.	61:32
let them j. and declare the	61:33
And let them j. together,	61:35
And now continue your j.	62: 4
take his j. up unto the land of	63:39
Samuel W. Smith take their j.	75:13
they shall also take their j. into	75:14
also shall take their j. unto	75:15
let them take their j. also into	75:17
Yea, let all those take their j.,	75:18
Sidney Rigdon go on his j.,	93:51
continue your j. and let your	100:12
Parley P. Pratt j. with my	103:37
Lyman Wight j. with my	103:38
Hyrum Smith j. with my	103:39
Orson Hyde j. with my servant	103:40
with your coming this j.,	111: 1
j. from the land of Kirtland,	117: 1
and those who j. with them,	136: 2
and other necessaries for the j.,	136: 5
to assist us on our j.	JS 2:61

JOURNEYED

j. unto the tent of our father.	1Ne 4:38
while we j. in the wilderness	5: 6
with us, as we j. in the wilderness	5:22
that as we j. in the wilderness,	7: 6
fire, as we j. in the wilderness;	17:12

JOURNEYED — 491 — JOY

promise, as we j. in the wilderness,	1Ne 18:25
after we had j. for the space of	2Ne 5: 7
And they j. in the wilderness,	Om 1:16
j. many days in the wilderness,	Al 17: 9
j. from Jerusalem in the	DC 33: 8
pass that Enoch j. in the land,	Mses 6:26
as he j., the Spirit of God	6:26
I j. from the land of Cainan,	6:42
as we j. from Haran by the way of	Abr 2:16
Abraham, j., going on still	2:21

JOURNEYING

fatigued, because of their j.,	1Ne 16:19
that while he was j. thither,	Al 8:14
was j. to see a very near kindred,	10: 7
was j. from the land of Gideon	17: 1
j. towards the land of Zarahemla.	17: 1
and Lamoni were j. thither,	20: 8
as the disciples of Jesus were j.	3Ne 27: 1
And after you have don j.,	DC 54: 9
come not in j. upon them,	61:18
while j. unto their homes;	61:23
way for the j. of my saints;	61:24
and he met Adam in j. to the	107:45
as I was j., and stood upon	Mses 7: 2

JOURNEYINGS

bear their j. without murmurings.	1Ne 17: 2
and also our j. in the wilderness,	19: 1
His j. in the wilderness,	2Ne 1:hd
which attended them in their j.,	Al 17: 5
Now these were their j.:	17: 6
all the j. of their fathers in	18:37
their j. in the land of Nephi.	28: 8
And in all his j. let him	DC 124:106
seen your labor and toil in j.	126: 2
the Camp of Israel in their j.	136: 1

JOURNEYS

thus they took their several j.	Al 17:18

JOVIAL

associated with j. company, etc.,	JS 2:28

JOY

behold, he was filled with j.,	1Ne 5: 1
behold their j. was full,	5: 7
my woul with exceeding great j.;	8:12
peace, yea, tidings of great j.,	13:37
I had j. and great hopes of them,	16: 5
food, how great was their j.!	16:32
unto their great j. and salvation,	19:11
that my soul might have j. in you,	2Ne 1:21
having no j., for they knew no	2:23
men are, that they might have j.	2:25
J. and gladness shall be found	8: 3
everlasting j. and holiness	8:11
they shall obtain gladness and j.;	8:11
their j. shall be full forever.	9:18
the nation, and increased the j.—	19: 3
they j. before thee according to the	19: 3
according to the j. in harvest,	19: 3
have no j. in their young men,	19:17
with j. shall ye draw water out of	22: 3
and their j. shall be in the Lord,	27:30
learn with j. and not with sorrow,	Jac 4: 3
may have j. again in the fruit of	5:60
ye shall have j. in the fruit which	5:71
ye shall have j. with me because	5:75
life, and the j. of the saints,	En 1: 3
the glad tidings of great j.	Mos 3: 3
they may also be filled with j.	3: 4
rejoice with exceeding great j.,	3:13
and they were filled with j.,	4: 3
causeth such exceeding great j.	4:11
hearts should be filled with j.,	4:20
so exceeding great was your j.	4:20
with such exceeding great j.	5: 4
Break forth into j.;	12:23
Break forth into j.,	15:30
they clapped their hands for j.	18:11
filled with exceeding great j.	21:24
Limhi was again filled with j.	21:28
Mosiah received them with j.;	Mos 22:14
did also receive them with j.	24:25
were filled with exceeding great j.	25: 8
Now this did cause much j. in	Al 2: 8
filled with great j. because of	4:14
exceeding great j. of knowing	7: 4
I shall also have j. over you;	7: 5
my j. over you should come by	7: 5
my j. cometh over them after	7: 5
I have spoken, great is my j.	7:17
may have glad tidings of great j.;	13:22
might receive the word with j.,	16:17
hear with great j. and gladness.	16:20
and what added more to his j.,	17: 2
was swolled within him with j.;	17:29
had infused such j. into his soul,	19: 6
and he sunk again with j.;	19:13
he was also overpowered with h.;	19:14
her hands, being filled with j.,	19:30
that I may be filled with j.,	22:15
that I receive this great j.	22:15
thy j. doth carry thee away unto	26:10
but behold, my j. is full, yea,	26:11
yea, my heart is brim with j.,	26:11
we will rejoice, for our j. is full;	26:16
our j. would be full if perhaps	26:30
yea, and my j. is carried away,	26:35
my light, my j. and my salvation,	26:36
Now this is my j., and my great	26:37
the j. of Ammon was so great	27:17
up in the j. of his God,	27:17
Now was not this exceeding j.?	27:18
this is j. which none receiveth	27:18
the j. of Alma in meeting his	27:19
also the j. of Aaron, of Omner,	27:19
their j. was not that to exceed	27:19
it did cause great j. among them.	27:26
and their incomprehensible j.,	28: 8
j. because of the light of Christ	28:14
j. or remorse of conscience.	29: 5
and this is my j.	29: 9
then is my soul filled with j.;	29:10
in the which my j. is full.	29:13
I do not j. in my own success	29:14
but my j. is more full because of	29:14
as it were, so great is my j.	29:16
in the j. of our brethren?	30:34
causes such j. in their hearts?	30:35
swallowed up in the j. of Christ.	31:38
and he beheld with great j.;	32: 6
afflictions, for in thee is my j.;	33:11
light, through the j. of his Son.	33:23
And oh, what j., and what	36:20
yea, my soul was filled with j.,	36:20
exquisite and sweet as was my j.	36:21
to taste of the exceeding j.	36:24
doth give me exceeding great j.	36:25
that I shall have great j. in you,	38: 2
I have had great j. in thee	38: 3
God with exceeding great j.	45: 1
my soul hath j. in my son,	46:25
whose soul did j. in the liberty	48:11
they received him with j.;	55: 9
in which we may have great j.	56: 9
them great hopes and much j.	56:17
But behold, to my great j.,	56:56
I was filled with exceeding j.	57:36
I do not j. in your great	61: 2
who do j. in your afflictions,	61: 3
I do j. in receiving your epistle,	61:19
filled with exceeding great j.	62: 1
peace and exceeding great j.	He 3:32
continual peace and great j.	3:32
filling their souls with j.	3:35
they were filled with that j.	5:44
of the church did have great j.	6: 3
another, and did have great j.	6: 3
did also have great j. and peace,	6:14
would my soul have had j.	7: 8
them glad tidings of great j.;	16:14
your j. and your faith concerning	3Ne 1: 6
loud voice, because of their j.,	4: 9
hearts were swollen with j.,	4:33

JOY — 492 — JUDGE

mourning was turned into j.,	3Ne 10:10	Let us go up against J.		2Ne 17: 6
For ye shall have great j. and	12:12	that Ephraim departed from J.,		17:17
Break forth into j., sing	16:19	And he shall pass through J.;		18: 8
the j. which filled our souls at	17:17	together shall be against J.		19:21
great was the j. of the multitude	17:18	together the dispersed of J.		21:12
And now behold, my j. is full.	17:20	the adversaries of J. shall be		21:13
shall they break forth into j.—	20:34	Ephraim shall not envy J.,		21:13
they have j. in their works for	27:11	and J. shall not vex Ephraim.		21:13
now, behold, my j. is great,	27:30	that Zedekiah, king of J., was	OM	1:15
in them I have fulness of j.	27:31	*of Zedekiah, the king of J.*	3Ne	1:hd
cause ye shall have fulness of j.;	28:10	Then shall the offering of J.		24: 4
yea, your j. shall be full,	28:10	children of J. may begin to return	DC 109:64
hath given me fulness of j.;	28:10	let them who be of J. flee unto		133:13
But behold this my j. was vain,	Mrm 2:13	And they also of the tribe of J.,		133:35
and did shed tears of j. before	Eth 6:12			
j. in the fruit of your labors	DC 6:31	**JUDEA**		
ye both j. in that which ye	7: 8	young men to the city of J.,	Al	56: 9
shall fill your soul with j.;	11:13	I arrived at the city of J.,		56:15
his j. in the soul that repenteth!	18:13	not come against the city of J.,		56:18
great shall be your j. with him	18:15	march back to the city of J.		56:57
if your j. will be great with one	18:16	provisions and send them to J.,		57:11
how great will be your j. if you	18:16	let them who are in J. flee into	JS	1:13
declare glad tidings of great j.	31: 3			
that which bringeth j., that	42:61	**JUDGE**		
with songs of everlasting j.	45:71	shall j. the twelve tribes of Israel;	1Ne 12: 9
enter into the j. of his Lord,	51:19	thou beholdest shall j. thy seed.		12:10
with j. and with rejoicing.	52:43	j. him to be a thing of naught;		19: 9
that thy j. may be full.	59:13	mine arm shall j. the people.	2Ne	8: 5
with songs of everlasting j.	66:11	he shall j. among the nations,		12: 4
enter into the j. of these things.	70:18	the j., and the prophet,		13: 2
be filled with j. and gladness;	75:21	and standeth to j. the people.		13:13
glad tidings of great j.,	79: 1	men of Judah, j., I pray you,		15: 3
the j. of my countenance.	88:52	not j. after the sight of his eyes,		21: 3
with the j. of my countenance.	88:53	righteousness shall he j. the poor,		21: 4
receive a fulness of j.;	93:33	shall j. them at the last day,		25:18
cannot receive a fulness of j.	93:34	I will j. the world, every man		29:11
with songs of everlasting j.,	101:18	shall the Lord God j. the poor,		30: 9
this world your j. is not full,	101:36	j. ye—for Christ will show unto		33:11
but in me your j. is full.	101:36	he standeth to j. the world;	Mos	3:10
was j. in heaven when my servant	106: 6	And if ye j. the man who		4:22
with songs of everlasting j.;	109:39	j. them according to their crimes.		26:11
eternal j. for all our sufferings.	109:76	Behold, I j. them not;		26:12
and thy saints shout aloud for j.	109:80	j. according to the sins which		26:29
with a loud voice, and with great j.,	124:88	might j. the people of that church		26:33
cry aloud and spare not, with j.	124:101	appoint judges, to j. this people		29:11
glad tidings of great j.	128:19	that will j. this people according		29:11
Let the mountains shout for j.	128:23	and j. this people according to		29:13
and ye solid rocks weep for j.!	128:23	they do not j. you according to		29:28
all the sons of God shout for j.!	128:23	they may be judged of a higher j.		29:28
filled with songs of everlasting j.	133:33	do not j. righteous judgments,		29:29
and in this life I shall have j.,	Mses 5:10	they shall j. your higher judges,		29:29
and the j. of our redemption,	5:11	to j. them according to the law		29:39
forth with songs of everlasting j.	7:53	to j. them according to the law;		29:41
and received a fulness of j.;	7:67	to be the first chief j.,		29:42
		he did j. righteous judgments;		29:43
JOYED		Alma was the first and chief j.		29:44
that I could have j. with him in	He 7: 7	*Chief J. over the people of*	Al	1:hd
		Alma, the first and chief J.		1:hd
JOYFUL		Alma, being the chief j. and the		2:16
and be j., O earth;	1Ne 21:13	and he was appointed chief j.;		4:17
to hear the j. news declared	Al 13:25	to j. and to govern the people.		4:17
behold, this was a j. meeting.	27:16	thou art not the chief j. over us.		8:12
that your souls may be j.	DC 136:29	the Lord j. of your iniquities;		10:20
		every man who was a j. of the law,		11: 1
JOYOUS		labored to j. those who were		11: 1
and the most j. to the soul.	1Ne 11:23	he was complained of to the j.;		11: 2
		and the j. executed authority,		11: 2
JUBAL		And the j. received for his wages		11: 3
and his brother's name was J.	Mses 5:45	before the chief j. of the land.		14: 4
		before the chief j. of the land.		14: 5
JUDAH		the chief j. of the land came and		14:14
the reign of Zedekiah, king of J.	1Ne 1: 4	And the j. smote them again		14:15
the reign of Zedekiah, king of J.;	5:12	Now this j. was after the order		14:16
forth out of the waters of J.,	20: 1	that the j. stood before them,		14:19
the fruit of the loins of J.	2Ne 3:12	the j. also smote them again on		14:20
the fruit of the loins of J.,	3:12	ye stand again and j. this people,		14:20
concerning J. and Jerusalem:	12: 1	the chief j. over the land of		14:23
away from Jerusalem, and from J.,	13: 1	the chief j. stood before them,		14:24
J. is fallen, because their tongues	13: 8	the chief j., and the lawyers,		14:27
men of J., judge, I pray you,	15: 3	went and told the chief j.		27:20
the men of J. his pleasant plant;	15: 7	the chief j. sent a proclamation		27:21
the son of Uzziah, king of J.,	17: 1	also the chief j. over the land.		30:21

JUDGE

the chief j. saw hardness of	Al	30:29
the chief j. who was governor		30:29
before Alma and the chief j.,		30:51
now when the chief j. saw this,		30:51
was sent forth by the chief j.		30:57
Now of this thing ye must j.		32:20
suppose that I mean to j. you only		32:24
deal justly, j. righteously,		41:14
Nephihah, the second chief j.,		50:37
he was appointed chief j.		50:39
ordinance to j. righteously,		50:39
the chief j. Pahoran;		51: 2
he should no longer be chief j.		51: 4
Pahoran should remain chief j.		51: 6
concerning the chief j., Pahoran.		51:12
were so wroth with the chief j.,		51:13
is the chief j. and the governor		60: 1
to be chief j. and a governor	He	1: 5
to be a chief j. and a governor		1:13
Pacumeni, who was the chief j.,		1:21
did murder the chief j. Cezoram,		6:19
behold, your j. is murdered,		8:27
concerning the chief j. be true,		9: 2
the chief j. had fallen to the earth,		9: 3
spoken concerning the chief j.		9: 4
the j. had been murdered—		9: 6
they who have murdered the j.,		9: 8
abroad that the j. was slain,		9: 9
chief j. who had been slain.		9:10
chief j. whether he was dead?		9:12
with some one to slay the j.,		9:16
the true murderer of this j.		9:17
murder Seezoram, our chief j.		9:23
the true murderer of our chief j.		9:41
the death of the chief j.,		10:13
that Lachoneus was the chief j.	3Ne	1: 1
as also was the chief j.		3:19
and the j., Lachoneus, and		6: 6
Now there was no lawyer nor j.		6:22
and brought up before the j.		6:26
murder the chief j. of the land.		7: 1
J. not, that ye be not judged.		14: 1
For with what judgment ye j.,		14: 2
I shall stand to j. the world.		27:16
not smite, neither shall he j.;	Mrm	8:20
so be that I do not speak, j. ye;	Eth	4:10
authority for these things, j. ye;		5: 6
I j. these things of you	Mro	7: 4
do not j. that which is evil to		7:14
it is given unto you to j.,		7:15
and the way to j. is as plain,		7:15
show unto you the way to j.;		7:16
the light by which ye may j.,		7:18
that ye do not j. wrongfully;		7:18
that same judgment which ye j.		7:18
I j. better things of you,		7:39
I j. that ye have faith in Christ		7:39
the Eternal J. of both quick		10:34
cannot always j. the righteous,	DC	10:37
walk humbly, to j. righteously;		11:12
j. the whole house of Israel,		29:12
appointed to be a j. in Israel,		58:17
And to j. his people by the		58:18
let God j. between me and		64:11
like unto a j. sitting on a hill,		64:37
high place, to j. the nations,		64:37
j. all things pertaining to Zion.		64:38
even the bishop, who is a j.,		64:40
before the j. of my people.		68:33
A certificate from the j.		72:17
and Christ are the j. of all.		76:68
and j. all things, and shall		77:12
the woman and the unjust j.,		101:81
a j. which feared not God,		101:82
importune at the feet of the j.;		101:86
And also to be a j. in Israel,		107:72
Thus shall he be a j.,		107:74
common j. among the inhabitants		107:74
to sit as a j. in Israel.		107:76
J. ye for yourselves.		127: 2
can j. between thee and God;	Mses	1:15
I can j. between him and thee.		1:18
even Jesus Christ, a righteous J.,		6:57

JUDGED

God was j. of the world;	1Ne	11:32
thy seed shall be j. of them;		12: 9
they must be j. of their works,		15:32
God, to be j. of their works;		15:33
and our father hath j. them,		17:22
in the presence of him to be j.	2Ne	2:10
then must they be j. according		9:15
all men shall be j. of their works,		9:44
shall be j. of them according		25:22
and be j. according to their works,		28:23
and their brethren shall be j.	WM	1:11
I shall stand to be j. of God	Mos	2:27
and hath j. of thy righteousness,		3: 4
whereof they shall be j.,		3:24
my people should be j. of him,		11:27
of God or j. of this man?		12:13
ye have j. me that I am mad.		13: 4
the bar of God, to be j. of him		16:10
into thy hands to be j.		26:12
and j. those that had been		26:34
men shall stand to be j. of him,		27:31
that a man should be j. of God		29:12
may be j. according to the laws		29:25
they may be j. of a higher judge.		29:28
brought before him to be j.,	Al	1: 2
to be j. according to the crimes		1:10
to be j. according to the deeds		5:15
might be j. according to the law,		10:13
brought before them to be j.		11: 1
j. the man according to the law		11: 2
be j. according to their works,		11:41
to be j. according to their works,		11:44
to be j. according to their works?		12: 8
to be j. according to our works.		12:12
to stand before him to be j.,		24:15
j. according to their crimes,		30:11
j. at the last and judgment day,		33:22
my God, to be j. of my deeds.		36:15
be j. according to their works.		40:21
be j. according to their works;		41: 3
be j. according to their works,		42:23
to be j. of the crime which	3Ne	6:26
Judge not, that ye be not j.		14: 1
ye judge, ye shall be j.;		14: 2
God, to be j. of their works,		26: 4
to be j. of their works,		27:14
be j. according to their works.		27:15
written, shall this people be j.,		27:25
be written shall the world be j.		27:26
be j. according to your works	Mrm	3:18
be j. by the twelve whom		3:19
j. by the other twelve whom		3:19
stand to be j. of your works,		3:20
j. according to your works;		6:21
rashly shall be j. rashly again;		8:19
ye judge ye shall also be j.	Mro	7:18
by them shall the world be j.,	DC	20:13
be j. according to men in the		76:73
be j. according to their works,		76:111
j. according to men in the flesh.		88:99
spirits of men who are to be j.,		88:100
dead were j. out of those things		128: 6
dead were j. out of those things		128: 7
of the books shall your dead be j.,		128: 8
j. his people wisely and justly	Abr	1:26

JUDGES

nevertheless, let us appoint j.,	Mos	29:11
we will appoint wise men to be j.,		29:11
by the voice of this people, j.,		29:25
And now if ye have j., and they		29:28
If your higher j. do not judge		29:29
j. should be gathered together,		29:29
they shall judge your higher j.,		29:29
concerning who should be their j.,		29:39
did appoint j. to rule over them,		29:41
commenced the reign of the j.		29:44
account of the reign of the J.,	Al	1:hd
first year of the reign of the j.		1: 1
fifth year of the reign of the j.		1:33
and they were laid before the j.		2: 6
fifth year of the reign of the j.		3:25
fifth year of the reign of the j.		3:27

JUDGES

sixth year of the reign of the j.	Al	4: 1
seventh year of the reign of the j.		4: 5
seventh year of the reign of the j.		4: 5
eighth year of the reign of the j.,		4: 6
eighth year of the reign of the j.,		4: 9
eighth year of the reign of the j.;		4:10
ninth year of the reign of the j.		4:20
ninth year of the reign of the j.		8: 2
tenth year of the reign of the j.		8: 3
tenth year of the reign of the j.		10: 6
might deliver them to their j.		10:13
crimes of the people before the j.		10:14
of your lawyers and your j.		10:27
against our lawyers, and our j.		10:29
who were appointed to be j.,		11: 1
until the reign of the j.,		11: 4
also against their lawyers and j.		14: 2
their lawyers and j. of the land,		14: 5
there came many lawyers, and j.,		14:18
tenth year of the reign of the j.		14:23
tenth year of the reign of the j.		15:19
year of the reign of the j.		16: 1
the eleventh year of the j.,		16: 9
year of the reign of the j.		16:12
year of the reign of the j.		16:21
in the first year of the j.;		17: 6
year of the reign of the j.		28: 7
year of the reign of the j.		28: 9
year of the reign of the j.		30: 2
year of the reign of the j.		30: 4
year of the reign of the j.,		30: 5
of the reign of the j. until now,		30:32
year of the reign of the j.		35:12
year of the reign of the j.;		35:13
for behold, they are their own j.,		41: 7
year of the reign of the j.		43: 3
of the reign of the j. over		44:24
of the reign of the j. over		45: 2
of the reign of the j. over		45:20
the lower j. of the land,		46: 4
was appointed by the chief j.		46:34
year of the reign of the j.		46:37
year of the reign of the j.		48: 2
year of the reign of the j. over		49:29
year of the reign of the j.,		50: 1
year of the reign of the j. over		50:17
year of the reign of the j.		50:23
year of the reign of the j.		50:24
year of the reign of the j.,		50:25
year of the reign of the j. over		50:35
year of the reign of the j. over		51: 1
year of the reign of the j.;		51:12
year of the reign of the j. over		51:37
year of the reign of the j. over		52: 1
year of the reign of the j.		52:14
year of the reign of the j.		52:15
year of the reign of the j. over		52:18
year of the reign of the j. over		53:23
twenty and ninth year of the j.,		54: 1
year of the reign of the j. over		55:35
year of the reign of the j.		56: 1
year of the reign of the j.		57: 5
year of the reign of the j. over		59: 1
year of the reign of the j. over		62:11
year of the reign of the j. over		62:12
year of the reign of the j. over		62:39
And their j., and their chief		62:47
and their chief j. were chosen.		62:47
year of the reign of the j.		62:52
year of the reign of the j. over		63: 1
year of the reign of the j.		63: 3
year of the reign of the j.,		63: 4
year of the reign of the j.,		63:10
year of the reign of the j. over		63:16
fortieth year of the reign of the j.	He	1: 1
fortieth year of the reign of the j.;		1:13
year of the reign of the j. that		1:14
year of the reign of the j.,		1:34
year of the reign of the j.,		2: 1
year of the reign of the j. over		2:12
year of the reign of the j.,		3: 1
year of the reign of the j.		3:18

JUDGMENT

year of the reign of the j. over	He	3:22
year of the reign of the j.,		3:23
year of the reign of the j.		3:32
year of the reign of the j.		3:33
year of the reign of the j.,		3:37
year of the reign of the j.,		4: 4
year of the reign of the j.		4: 5
years of the reign of the j.		4: 8
year of the reign of the j.,		4: 9
year of the reign of the j.		4:10
year of the reign of the j.		4:17
year of the reign of the j.,		4:18
year of the reign of the j.		6: 1
year of the reign of the j.,		6:15
year of the reign of the j. over		6:32
year of the reign of the j. over		6:41
year of the reign of the j. over		7: 1
there were men who were j.,		8: 1
those j. were angry with him		8: 4
those j. who were at the garden		9:11
the j. desired that they		9:13
the j. inquired of them to know		9:13
the j. did expound the matter		9:16
they did rebuke the j. in the words		9:18
year of the reign of the j. over		10:19
year of the reign of the j.		11: 1
their chief j. and their leaders,		11: 8
the j. did say unto Nephi,		11: 9
year of the reign of the j. over		11:24
year of the reign of the j. over		11:29
year of the reign of the j.		11:35
year of the reign of the j. over		16: 9
year of the reign of the j.,		16:10
year of the reign of the j.		16:11
year of the reign of the j.		16:12
year of the reign of the j.		16:13
year of the reign of the j. over		16:24
angry were chiefly the chief j.,	3Ne	6:21
put to death secretly by the j.,		6:23
against these j. who had		6:25
those j. had many friends		6:27
unite with the kindreds of those j.		6:27
ye shall be j. of this people,		27:27
shall be j. of that house,	DC	75:21
to have other bishops or j. in		107:74
the decision of the bishop or j.,		107:78

JUDGETH

he j., and his judgment is just;	Mos	3:18
the same that j. rashly shall	Mrm	8:19
but let God rule him that j.,	DC	58:20

JUDGING

j. every man according to his	DC	19: 3

JUDGMENT

at the j.-seat of Christ.	T Pg	
thou shalt be brought into j.	1Ne	10:20
unclean before the j.-seat of God;		10:21
of the house of Israel in great j.		13:33
after I have visited them in j.,		13:34
knew that ye were lacking in j.;		17:19
surely my j. is with the Lord,		21: 4
shall execute j. in righteousness.		22:21
I will give j. unto him in	2Ne	3:17
I will make my j. to rest		9: 7
the first j. which came upon man		9: 7
must appear before the j.-seat of		9:15
and then cometh the j.,		9:15
according to the holy j. of God.		9:15
him at the great and j. day.		9:22
righteous, even the day of j.,		9:46
The Lord will enter into j. with		13:14
thereof by the spirit of j.		14: 4
and he looked for j.,		15: 7
of Hosts shall be exalted in j.,		15:16
and to establish it with j.		19: 7
To turn away the needy from j.,		20: 2
many souls spotless at his j.-seat.		33: 7
brought against you at the j. bar;		33:15
the Lord did visit them in great j.;	Om	1: 7
that a righteous j. might come	Mos	3:10

JUDGMENT

he judgeth, and his h. is just;	Mos	3:18
against this people, at the j. day;		3:24
taken from prison and from j.;		14: 8
j. of an everlasting punishment		27:31
the reign of Alma in the j.-seat,	Al	1: 2
he sat in the j.-seat to judge		4:17
the j.-seat unto Nephihah.		4:18
up the j.-seat to Nephihah,		4:20
wholly confined to the j.-seat,		7: 1
the j.-seat hath been given to		7: 2
up the j. seat unto Nephihah;		8:12
for them in the day of j.		9:15
they must come to j., even		12:27
even that same j. of which we		12:27
save it were in the j.-seat;		30:33
be judged at the last and j. day,		33:22
ye shall have a righteous j.		41:14
having filled the j.-seat with		50:37
appointed to fill the j.-seat,		50:39
be dethroned from the j.-seat		51: 5
Pahoran retained the j.-seat,		51: 7
j. may come upon the wicked;		60:13
in j. against the Lamanites,		60:32
take away the j.-seat from		61: 4
save only to retain my j.-seat		61: 9
driven Pahoran from the j.-seat,		62: 2
was restored to his j.-seat.		62: 8
Pahoran did return to his j.-seat;		62:44
who should have the j.-seat	He	1: 2
did contend for the j.-seat,		1: 3
did contend for the j.-seat;		1: 4
he could not obtain the j.-seat,		1: 6
even to the j.-seat of Pahoran,		1: 9
as he sat upon the j.-seat.		1: 9
was no one to fill the j.-seat;		2: 1
who should fill the j.-seat.		2: 1
was appointed to fill the j.-seat,		2: 2
would place him in the j.-seat		2: 5
he went forth towards the j.-seat		2: 6
conduct him to the j.-seat		2: 7
Let us go forth unto the j.-seat.		2: 8
were going forth unto the j.-seat,		2: 9
Helaman did fill the j.-seat		3:20
did fill the j.-seat with justice		3:37
Nephi delivered up the j.-seat		5: 1
and he yielded up the j.-seat,		5: 4
as he sat upon the j.-seat.		6:15
his son, while in the j.-seat;		6:19
robbers filling the j.-seats—		7: 1
wrath against the day of j.		8:25
yea, go ye in unto the j.-seat,		8:27
who seeketh to sit in the j.-seat.		8:27
among them ran to the j.-seat;		9: 1
and came in unto the j.-seat,		9: 3
unto the place of the j.-seat—		9: 7
and came to the place of the j.,		9:14
a righteous j. might come upon		14:29
did destroy upon the j. seat,	3Ne	7: 1
in danger of the j. of God;		12:21
shall be in danger of his j.		12:22
For with what j. ye judge,		14: 2
that shall rise against thee in j.		22:17
I will come near to you to j.;		24: 5
according to the j. which I		27:27
before the j.-seat of Christ;		28:31
by them, before that j. day.		28:32
until the j. day of Christ;		28:40
that he may not execute h.		29: 9
before the j. seat of Christ	Mrm	3:20
before the j. seat of Christ.		3:22
before the j.-seat of Christ		6:21
to stand before his j.-seat.		7: 6
before him at the j. day		7: 7
be well with you in the day of j.		7:10
for j. is mine, saith the Lord,		8:20
cometh the j. of the Holy One		9:14
Orihah did execute j. upon	Eth	7: 1
and he was also mighty in j.		7: 8
execute j. in righteousness;		7:11
Shule did execute j. against		7:24
did execute j. in righteousness		7:27
did execute j. in righteousness		9:21
did execute j. in wickedness		11:14
God would execute j. against		11:20

495 JUDGMENTS

before the j. seat of Christ,	Eth	12:38
with that same j. which ye	Mro	7:18
you at the j.-seat of Christ.		8:21
that God will stay his hand in j.		9:14
Come out in j., O God,		9:15
in j. upon Idumea, or the world.	DC	1:36
has depended upon his own j.		3:13
condemnation in the day of j.		10:23
and the last great day of j.,		19: 3
until the j. of the great day,		38: 5
thinking I will stay my hand in j.		39:16
I will stay mine hand in j.		39:18
your souls in the day of j.		41:12
trump, and by the voice of j.,		43:25
will I come upon the earth in j.,		43:29
until they come before me in j.		43:33
I will bring them to j.		50: 6
send forth j. unto victory.		52:11
the day of visitation, and of j.,		56:16
or sitteth upon the j. seat.		58:20
they made to be used, with j.,		59:20
against them in the day of j.		60:15
you to do according to j.		62: 8
lest j. shall come upon them		63:15
require of them in the day of j.		70: 4
in the day of j. you shall be		75:21
for the heathen in the day of j.,		75:22
justice and j. are the penalty		82: 4
j. shall immediately follow,		82:11
Leave j. alone with me,		82:23
j. to be poured out upon		84:58
of a j. which is to come.		84:87
hour of their j. is nigh,		84:115
by mercy, justice, nor j.,		88:35
j. goeth before the face of him		88:40
hour of j. which is to come;		88:84
for the j. of our God is come.		88:92
the hour of his j. is come.		88:104
to be used with j. and skill.		89: 8
I shall bring them unto j.		97: 2
brought into j. before me,		98:28
and lo, I come quickly to j.,		99: 5
his own sins in the day of j.		101:78
Execute j. and justice for		105:25
to sit in j. upon transgressors		107:72
dominion, truth, justice, j.,		109:77
and I have in reserve a swift j.		121:24
And I will answer j., wrath,		124:52
upon the world with a curse to j.;		133: 2
for the hour of his j. is come.		133:38
brought j. upon all people;		133:50
meet before the j.-seat of Christ,		135: 5
mercy, truth, justice, and j.	Mses	6:61
until the j. of the great day.		7:57
of justice and j. in his hand.	Fac	3: 1

JUDGMENTS

great and terrible j. of the Lord.	1Ne	12: 5
kept the statutes and j. of the Lord,		17:22
the j. of God were upon them,		18:15
the j. of him that is just	2Ne	1:10
and the j. of the Lord;		1:16
we did observe to keep the j.,		5:10
the j. of the Holy One of Israel		6:10
Holy, holy are thy j., O Lord		9:46
they may know the j. of God,		25: 3
concerning the j. of God,		25: 6
his j. must speedily come	Jac	2:14
the j. and the power of God,	En	1:23
upon them according to his j.,	Om	1:22
and did observe his j.	Mos	6: 6
before God that his j. are just.		16: 1
j. of God would come upon him.		17:11
the j. of God are always just,		29:12
the j. of man are not always just.		29:12
the j. of God will come upon you;		29:27
judges do not judge righteous j.,		29:29
and he did judge righteous j.;		29:43
believed that it was the j. of God	Al	4: 3
contrary to the statutes, and j.,		8:17
that all his j. are just;		12:15
the j. which he shall exercise		14:11
lest the same j. would come		30:57

JUDGMENTS

turned thy j. away from me,	Al	33:11
Thou hast turned away thy j.		33:13
thus the j. of God did come		37:30
the j. of God should come upon		58: 9
keep his statutes, and his j.,		58:40
the j. of God will come upon		60:14
to keep the statutes and the j.,		3:20
the j. of god did stare them		4:23
all the j. will come upon us		8: 8
I may know concerning the j.		8:12
the j. which Nephi had spoken		9: 5
hear and know of the j. of God		14:11
and his statutes and his j.		15: 5
also the j. of the Father	3Ne	16: 9
with the statutes and j.		25: 4
the j. of God will overtake	Mrm	4: 5
the j. of the Lord which should		5: 2
I revoke not the j. which I	DC	19: 5
all my j. are not given unto		29:30
according to their j. hereafter.		61:22
sore j. fall upon your heads.		82: 2
the j. which are on the land;		88:79
Talk not of j., neither boast		105:24
by the j. which thou wilt send		109:30
those j. thou art about to send,		109:38
not thy j. fall upon that city.		109:40
that thou wilt pour out thy j.,		109:45
and my j. may be kept thereon,		119: 6
and your statutes and j.,		124:39
and j. upon your own heads,		124:48
as in their own j. are best		134: 5
lest j. come upon you,		136:42
fear for the j. of the Almighty	Mses	7:66
great j. which were coming	JS	2:45
these grievous j. would come		2:45

JUDGMENT-SEAT: see *JUDGMENT* and *SEAT*.

JUDGMENT-SEATS: see *JUDGMENT* and *SEATS*.

JULY

on the fourth day of J. next;	DC	115:10

JUN.: see *SMITH, Joseph, Jun.*; and *WHITMER, Peter, Jun.*

JUNE

on the 27th of J., 1844,	DC	135: 1
in Utah since last J.,		OD

JUST

which he shall write are j. and true;	1Ne	14:23
the judgments of him that is j.	2Ne	1:10
the displeasure of a j. God upon		1:22
unto my God: Thy ways are j.		26: 7
aside the j. for a thing of naught.		27:32
aside the j. for a thing of naught		28:16
my father that he was a j. man—	En	1: 1
to his judgments, which are j.;	Om	1:22
king Benjamin to be a j. man		1:25
j. men to be their teachers,	Mos	2: 4
also a j. man to be their king,		2: 4
in singing the praises of a j. God.		2:28
therefore, they are j. and true.		2:35
judgeth, and his judgment is j.;		3:18
of that which is j. and true.		4:12
for his punishments are j.—		4:17
more j. will be your condemnation		4:22
and your condemnation if j.		4:25
God that his judgments are j.		16: 1
he himself being a j. man.		19:17
have j. men to be your kings		23: 8
except they were j. men.		23:17
punishment is j. upon them;		27:31
judgments of God are always j.,		29:12
of man are not always j.		29:12
have j. men to be your kings,		29:13
because all men are not j.		29:16
who were j. and holy men.	Al	3: 6
against our laws which are j.,		10:24
both the j. and the unjust,		12: 8

JUSTICE

that all his judgments are j.;	Al	12:15
that he is j. in all his works,		12:15
known unto j. and holy men,		13:26
upon them in his wrath may be j.;		14:11
of that which is j. and true;		18:34
for I know that they are j. men		20:15
the firm decree of a j. God,		29: 4
to that which is j. and true.		29: 8
to do that which was j.—		31: 5
behold will our law, which is j.,		34:11
For j. as surely as this director		37:45
Behold, it is requisite and j.,		41: 2
j. for that which is just;		41:13
just for that which is j.;		41:13
God might be a perfect, j. God,		42:15
affixed, and a j. law given,		42:18
we see how merciful and j. are		50:19
it was not a j. cause that had		55: 1
that there was a j. God,		57:26
it should be j. in us to go		61:19
And he was a j. man, and he did		63: 2
the governor, was a j. man,	3Ne	3:12
to be a j. and a true record;		5:18
it was a j. man who did keep		8: 1
give unto you, which shall be j.		27:27
to dwell with a holy and j. God,	Mrm	9: 4
thing is good is j. and true;	Mro	10: 6
the vengeance of a j. God	DC	3: 4
according to that which is j.		11:23
is j. and true;		20:30
is j. and true,		20:31
his sons and saith I am j.?		38:26
to receive a j. remuneration		42:72
or a j. remuneration for all		42:73
a j., and a wise steward		51:19
by the testimony of the j.,		58:18
in the resurrection of the j.,		76:17
in the resurrection of the j.—		76:50
all those who are j. and true.		76:53
in the resurrection of the j.		76:65
who are j. men made perfect		76:69
inasmuch as his wants are j.—		82:17
as a j. measure unto you.		98:24
to j. and holy principles;		101:77
witnesses or Apostles j. named.		107:26
have a j. recompense of wages		124:121
mete out a j. recompense of reward		127: 3
the record shall be j. as holy,		128: 4
answer the ordinance j. the same		128: 4
the spirits of j. men made perfect,		129: 3
the spirit of a j. man made perfect		129: 6
for a j. man to deceive;		129: 7
We do not believe it j. to mingle		134: 9
believe it. to preach the gospel		134:12
and also thou art j.; thou art	Mses	7:30
for Noah was a j. man,		8:27
j. at this moment of great	JS	2:16
dark, except j. around him;		2:43
what I had j. experienced;		2:47
and was j. leaving the house,		2:64

JUSTICE

of the j. of the Eternal God,	1Ne	12:18
according to the j. of God,		14: 4
the j. of God did also divide		15:30
to be cast out because of that j.		15:35
and the mercy, and the j. of God.	2Ne	2:12
greatness and j. of our God!		9:17
satisfieth the demands of his j.		9:26
when j. shall be administered unto		9:46
in his grace, and in his j.,		11: 5
it with judgment and with j.		19: 7
and send down j. upon those who	Jac	3: 1
counseleth in wisdom, and in j.,		4:10
according to the power of j.,		6:10
for j. cannot be denied,		6:10
the demands of divine j. do	Mos	2:38
which j. could no more deny		3:26
power, and j., and mercy of him		5:15
standing betwixt them and h.;		15: 9
and satisfied the demands of j.		15: 9
for he cannot deny j. when		15:27
with equity and j. in my hands.	Al	10:21

JUSTICE

redeemed according to God's j.;		
for the works of j. could not be	Al	12:18
the sword of his j. fall upon us,		12:32
did not exercise his j. upon us,		26:19
of mercy, which overpowereth j.,		26:20
can satisfy the demands of j.,		34:15
whole law of the damands of j.;		34:16
requisite with the j. of God;		34:16
requisite with the j. of God		41: 2
have j. restored unto you again;		41: 3
concerning the j. of God		41:14
Therefore, according to j.,		42: 1
it should destroy the work of j.		42:13
Now the work of j. could not be		42:13
and they were in the grasp of j.;		42:13
yea, the j. of God, which		42:14
to appease the demands of j.,		42:14
if men sinned what could j. do,		42:15
j. claimeth the creature and		42:21
works of j. would be destroyed,		42:22
according to the law and j.		42:22
j. exerciseth all his demands,		42:23
ye suppose that mercy can rob j.?		42:24
deny the j. of God no more.		42:25
by denying he j. of God;		42:30
let hte j. of God, and his mercy,		42:30
the j. of the cause in which they		42:30
and to bring the wicked to j.		46:29
concerning the j. of God,		50:39
his j. and judgment may come		54: 6
sword of j. doth hang over you;		60:13
were requisite with the j. of God,		60:29
with j. and equity;		61:12
with j. and equity;	He	3:20
not be governed by the law nor j.,		3:37
no j. unto the children of men;		5: 3
the sword of j. hangeth over		7: 4
the sword of j. falleth upon		13: 5
laws according to equity and j.		13: 5
murder from the grasp of j.,	3Ne	6: 4
the sword of my j. shall hang		6:29
to the mercy, and the j.,		20:20
because of the j. of the Father.		26: 5
of the j. of an offended God,		27:17
the sword of his j. is in his right		28:35
shall come out in j. against you—		29: 4
according to his j. and mercy.	Mrm	5:24
of the j. of the Eternal God		6:22
he did do j. unto the people,	Eth	8:23
not exempt from the j. of God.		10:11
and j. and judgment are the	DC	10:28
mercy, J., grace and truth,		82: 4
neither by mercy, j., nor		84:102
j. continueth its course and		88:35
speak according to equity and j.		88:40
Execute judgment and j. for		102:16
from the j. and the laws of God,		105:25
might, dominion, truth, j.,		107:84
the least shadow or coloring of j.		109:77
the law in equity and j.		127: 1
have a right in j. to deprive		134: 3
to wisdom, mercy, truth, j.,		134: 7
naught but peace, j., and truth	Mses	6:61
of j. and judgment in his hand.		7:31
	Fac	3: 1

JUSTIFIABLE

mankind, and is j. before me.	DC	98: 5

JUSTIFICATION

j. through the grace of our Lord	DC	20:30
your God, for j. before me.		98:38

JUSTIFIED

and the righteous have I j.,	1Ne	16: 2
And by the law no flesh is j.;	2Ne	2: 5
and in this are ye j.?	DC	50:15
Edward Partridge is not j.;		50:39
unto you that ye are not j.,		63:19
be j. in the eyes of the law,		64:13
then ye are j. in saying that		67: 7
those conditions are not j.		88:39
that I may be j. when I shall		97: 2
to his works thou art j.;		98:31

497

in thine hands and thou art j.	DC	98:31
j. my servants Abraham, Isaac,		132: 1
then is he j.;		132:61
therefore is he j.		132:62
that all men are j. in defending		134:11
by the Spirit ye are j.,	Mses	6:60

JUSTIFIETH

the Lord is near, and he j. me.	2Ne	7: 8
do ye suppose that God j. you	Jac	2:14
sinner, and j. him not at all.	Al	41:15

JUSTIFY

Who j. the wicked for reward,	2Ne	15:23
he will j. in committing a little		28: 8
my righteous servant j. many;	Mos	14:11
I, the Lord, j. you, and	DC	98: 6
j. them in going out to battle		98:36
will not commit sin, and I will j.		132:59
servant Joseph; for I will j. him;		132:60
do not j. sedition nor conspiracy.		134: 7
all thy words will I j.;	Mses	6:34

JUSTLY

deal j., judge righteously,	Al	41:14
we do j. ascribe it to the		57:26
every man dealing j., one with	3Ne	26:19
did deal j. one with another.	4Ne	1: 2
yea, to do j., to walk humbly,	DC	11:12
is j. entitled to a re-hearing,		102:33
judged his people wisely and j.	Abr	1:26

KAE-E-VANRASH

through the medium of K.,	Fac	2: 5

KEEP

as ye shall k. my commandments,	1Ne	2:20
as thou shalt k. my commandments,		2:22
thy seed shall k. my commandments,		4:14
could not k. the commandments		4:15
bace them to k. the commandments		8:38
ye do not k. the commandments		15:10
remember to k. his commandments		15:25
to k. the commandments		16: 4
of men k. the commandments		17: 3
that ye shall k. my commandments;		17:13
as ye shall k. my commandments		17:13
did strive to k. the commandments		17:15
shall k. his commandments,	2Ne	1: 9
shall k. his commandments		1: 9
as ye shall k. my commandments		1:20
will not k. my commandments		1:20
if ye shall k. my commandments		1:32
ye shall k. the commandments		3: 2
as ye shall k. my commandments		4: 4
will not k. my commandments		4: 4
did observe to k. the judgments,		5:10
we k. the law of Moses,		25:24
yet we k. the law because of		25:25
ye must k. the performances		25:30
ye shall k. the commandments		30: 1
willing to k. the commandments		31:10
willing to k. the commandments		31:14
should k. his commandments	Jac	2:21
shall k. my commandments,		2:29
commandment they observe to k.;		3: 6
intent we k. the law of Moses,		4: 5
and they did k. the root and		5:73
and k. not the law of Moses		7: 7
to k. them in the fear of the Lord.	En	1:23
would k. them from going down		1:23
observed to k. the law of Moses	Jar	1: 5
as ye will k. my commandments		1: 9
did not k. the commandments,		1:10
will not k. my commandments,	Om	1: 6
this manner we k. the records,		1: 9
k. the commandments of God,	Mos	1: 7
k. the commandments of God,		2: 4
ye should k. the commandments		2:13
you is to k. his commandments;		2:22
if ye would k. his commandments		2:22
if ye do k. his commandments		2:22
if ye shall k. the commandments		2:31

KEEP

k. the commandments of God.	Mos 2:41	k. the commandments of God;	He	5: 6
to his neighbor, and k. him?	5:14	they did begin to k. his statutes		6:34
with God to k. his commandments	6: 1	k. the commandments of God,		7: 7
and did k. his commandments	6: 6	and to k. my commandments.		10: 4
and k. them from falling into	10: 2	k. the commandments of God,		13: 1
he did not k. the commandments	11: 2	observe to k. his commandments		15: 5
about the land to k. them off;	11:17	they can k. us in ignorance,		16:20
law of Moses why do ye not k. it?	12:29	will k. us down to be servants		16:21
if ye k. the commandments	12:33	thus will they k. us in ignorance		16:21
if ye k. the commandments	12:33	his son Nephi did k. the records	3Ne	1: 3
and k. my commandments.	13:14	into a covenant to k. the peace,		6: 3
the sabbath day, to k. it holy.	13:16	to k. the commandments of		6:14
for to k. these commandments?	13:25	just man who did k. the record—		8: 1
ye should k. the law of Moses	13:27	ye shall k. my commandments,		12:20
to k. the law of Moses.	13:27	therefore k. my commandments.		15:10
to k. them in remembrance of	13:30	ye shall k. my commandments,		18:14
and would not k. them;	15:26	k. these sayings which I have		18:33
and k. his commandments,	18:10	Ammaron, did k. the record	4Ne	1:47
the sabbath day, and k. it holy,	18:23	no man could k. that which was	Mrm	2:10
he might k. the people of Limhi	19:28	king Mosiah k. them,	Eth	4: 1
and k. his commandments.	21:31	to k. them in darkness,		8:16
and k. his commandments.	21:32	place whither he would k. it,		14: 1
would not k. their promise;	23:37	k. his commandments which	Mro	4: 3
that they should k. their record,	24: 6	to k. them in the right way,		6: 4
k. the commandments of God.	27:33	k. them continually watchful		6: 4
he should k. and preserve them,	28:20	k. you through the endurance of		8: 3
also k. a record of the people,	28:20	he will k. my commandments,	DC	5:28
he did k. his commandments,	29:43	k. my commandments, and seek		6: 6
him to k. his commandments,	Al 7:15	k. my commandments, and		6: 9
and k. your garments spotless,	7:25	k. my commandments, and ye		6:37
ye shall k. my commandments,	9:13	and k. my commandments.		8: 5
will not k. my commandments	9:13	k. my commandments but		10:56
to k. his commandments	25:14	k. my commandments, and seek		11: 6
they did k. the law of Moses;	25:15	K. my commandments, and		11: 9
should k. the law of Moses as yet,	25:15	K. my commandments;		11:18
k. those outward performances	25:15	to k. my commandments,		11:20
to k. the commandments	30: 3	k. my commandments, and seek		12: 6
taught to k. the law of Moses	30: 3	K. my commandments in all		14: 6
to k. them in ignorance, that	30:23	if you k. my commandments		14: 7
and ye k. them down, even as	30:27	must k. my commandments		18:43
k. the commandments of God,	31: 9	you k. not my commandments		18:46
k. the commandments of God	36: 1	k. the commandments which		19:13
k. the commandments of God	36:30	k. his commandments which		20:77
k. the commandments of God	36:30	K. my commandments		25:15
ye k. a record of this people,	37: 2	and covenants to k. them.		33:14
and k. all these things sacred	37: 2	K. all the commandments		35:24
ye will k. my commandments	37:13	and k. my commandments.		42: 1
ye k. not his commandments	37:13	and k. all my commandments.		42:29
which he will k. and preserve	37:14	to k. all the commandments		42:78
k. the commandments of God,	37:16	K. all my commandments.		43:35
that ye k. them, that the	37:21	be enabled to k. my laws;		44: 5
ye shall k. from this people,	37:27	k. these things from going		45:72
ye shall k. these secret plans of	37:29	and k. all my commandments,		46: 9
k. the commandments of God.	37:35	and k. a regular history,		47: 1
k. the commandments of God	38: 1	to k. the church record and		47: 3
k. the commandments of God	38: 1	and k. my commandments,		56: 2
way, to k. the tree of life—	42: 2	appointed to k. my storehouse;		58:24
support, and k., and preserve us,	44: 4	k. thyself unspotted from		59: 9
Will ye k. my commandments?	45: 6	not to k. my commandments.		63:22
I will k. thy commandments	45: 7	K. these sayings, for they are		66:11
k. the commandments of God,	46:23	Sabbath day to k. it holy.		68:29
a covenant to k. the peace—	46:31	k. my commandments;		71:11
k. the commandments of God,	48:25	To k. the Lord's storehouse;		72:10
should k. his commandments	48:25	as ye k. not my sayings,		82: 4
shall k. my commandments	50:20	appointed, to k. a history,		85: 1
will not k. the commandments	50:20	to k. and do these sayings,		89:18
covenanting to k. the peace	50:36	k. slothfulness and uncleanness		90:18
to k. the peace and the freedom	50:39	if you k. my commandments		93:20
k. the commandments of God	53:21	as you k. my sayings		93:52
Let us k. of our wine till we go	55:10	If you k. my commandments		95:11
k. and protect all the prisoners	55:27	k. not my commandments.		95:12
to k. them from the armies of	56:57	as they k. my commandments		100:14
k. guards, that the Lamanites	57: 9	and k. his commandments.		100:17
employ all our force to k. them,	57:13	k. not my commandments,		103: 8
do observe to k. his statutes,	58:40	to k. the commandments		103:29
k. you continually in his	58:41	among you to k. the treasury,		104:61
easier to k. the city from falling	59: 9	appointed to k. the treasury,		104:67
k. the commandments of my God;	60:34	will k. our moneys.		105: 8
to k. the commandments of	63: 2	if my people will k. my		110: 8
he did observe to k. the statutes,	He 3:20	house also, to k. and preserve it		117:16
k. the commandments of God,	3:37	observe not this law, to k. it		119: 6

KEEP 499 KEPT

come here essaying to k. my	DC 124:85
love me, k. my commandments;	124:87
my will and k. my commandments	125: 2
and promise to k. all the	136: 2
and k. all your pledges one with	136:20
K. yourselves from evil	136:21
Eden, to dress it, and to k. it.	Mses 3:15
to k. the way of the tree of life.	4:31
Tarry ye here and k. the tents,	6:38
cause, to k. the commandment,	6:42
water ye k. the commandment;	6:60
k. the commandments of God,	Abr 1: 2
they who k. their first estate	3:26
they who k. not their first	3:26
those who k. their first estate;	3:26
they who k. their second estate	3:26
of Eden, to dress it and to k. it.	5:11
strict charges to k. them safe,	JS 2:60
we were forced to k. secret	2:74

KEEPER
the k. of the gate is the Holy One	2Ne 9:41
And Abel was a k. of sheep,	Mses 5:17
Am I my brothers k.?	5:34

KEEPERS
and they were k. of cattle;	Mses 5:45
places, saying unto the tent-k.	6:38

KEEPEST
God of Israel, who k. covenant	DC 109: 1

KEEPETH
and he k. his guards about him;	Mos 29:22
k. the commandments of God	Al 7:16
he k. my commandments.	DC 41: 8
that k. my commandments,	58: 2
he that k. the laws of God	58:21
and k. it with slothfulness,	58:29
that k. my commandments	63:23
who k. the Lord's storehouse,	70:11
and k. my commandments,	93: 1
he k. my commandments.	93:27
that k. his commandments	93:28
he k. my commandments	96: 6

KEEPING
in k. the commandments	1Ne 2:10
in k. the commandments	3:16
in k. the commandments	3:21
in k. the commandments	4: 1
in k. the commandments	4:34
in k. my commandments,	15:11
k. in the most fertile parts	16:14
in k. his commandments.	2Ne 31: 7
in k. this commandment,	Jac 3: 6
in k. my commandments.	En 1:10
in k. the commandments	Mos 1:11
in k. his commandments,	4: 6
in k. the commandments	10:13
and k. his commandments.	23:14
in k. the commandments of God,	Al 1:25
walked, k. yourselves blameless	5:27
in k. the commandments of God	7:23
in k. the commandments of God	8:15
for k. the commandments of God.	21:23
k. the commandments of God	37:20
in k. his commandments;	38: 2
k. the commandments of God?	39: 1
k. the commandments of God	48:15
k. the commandments of God,	48:16
in k. the commandments of	50:22
k. the commandments of God,	He 5:14
firm in k. the commandments	DC 5:22
in k. my commandments,	5:35
k. the commandments of God,	6:20
in k. my commandments	18: 8
in k. my commandments,	30: 8
by k. the commandments	76:52
k. all former commandments	92: 2
in k. my commandments,	104:42
faithful in k. all my words	136:37
Be diligent in k. all my	136:42

KEPT
his fathers had k. the records.	1Ne 5:16
father had k. the commandments	5:20
in the record which has been k.	6: 1
k. back by that abominable church,	13:32
k. back by that abominable church,	13:34
they k. the statutes and judgments	17:22
should be k. for the instruction	19: 3
k. for the knowledge of my people.	19: 5
be k. as yet from the knowledge	2Ne 1: 8
be k. from all other nations,	1: 9
who hath k. the commandments	1:24
I, Nephi, had k. the records	5:29
things which I write shall be k.	25:21
the book shall be k. from them.	27: 8
was sealed shall be k. in the book	27:10
and have k. my commandments,	Jac 5:75
being k. on the other plates of	7:26
that our genealogy may be k.	Jar 1: 1
k. them from being destroyed	1:12
that they may be k. according	1:15
and I have not k. the statutes	Om 1: 2
I had k. these plates according	1: 3
and k. and preserved them from	1: 6
which have been k. and preserved	Mos 1: 5
and have been k. and preserved	2:11
and has k. and preserved you,	2:20
ye have k. my commandments,	2:31
have been k. from falling into	2:31
has k. and preserved his people	7:20
that have k. the commandments	15:22
the people of Limhi k. together	21:18
which he had k. and preserved	28:11
they have been k. and preserved	28:15
and all the things which he had k.,	28:20
of God and k. them, were called	Al 3:11
is they who have k. the records	3:12
have not k. the commandments	9:14
k. and preserved until now;	9:22
and k. in prison for many days,	20:30
that they may be k. bright,	24:15
that they may be k. bright,	24:16
k. his holy commandments.	36:13
things sacred which I have k.,	37: 2
even as I have k. them;	37: 2
a wise purpose that they are k.	37: 2
should be k. and handed down	37: 4
and be k. and preserved by	37: 4
if they are k. they must retain	37: 5
which he has k. sacred, and also	37:14
are many mysteries which are k.,	40: 3
Helaman, which he k. in his days.	45:hd
those records which have been k.?	45: 2
had k. the commandments of God	49:27
k. them down by the seashore,	51:25
But he k. his men round about,	52: 6
he k. thus preparing for war	52: 7
been k. from taking up arms	53:11
that we k. spies out round about,	56:22
and k. them from falling from	58:39
these things were to be k. sacred,	63:13
k. sufficient guards in the land	He 1:18
records k. of the proceedings of	3:13
been k. chiefly by the Nephites.	3:15
the records which had been k.,	3Ne 1: 2
things which had been k. sacred	1: 2
have k. his commandments	5:22
which ye shall write shall be k.	16: 4
forth the record which ye have k.	23: 7
and have not k. them.	24: 7
that we have k. his ordinance	24:14
he that k. this last record,	4Ne 1:19
(and he k. it upon the plates	1:19
his son Amos k. it in his stead;	1:19
k. it upon the plates of Nephi	1:19
he k. it eighty and four years,	1:20
his son Amos k. the record	1:21
k. it upon the plates of Nephi;	1:21
could not be k. from beholding	Eth 3:19
not be k. from within the veil,	3:20
k. up by the power of the devil	8:16
k. him upon little or no food	9: 7
not be k. from within the veil,	12:19
no longer be k. without the veil.	12:21

KEPT

k. the hilt of his sword in his	Eth	14: 2
have been k. back because of	DC	6:26
be k. in a book by one of		20:82
be a record k. among you;		21: 1
and k. my commandments,		29:12
I k. in chains of darkness		38: 5
I cause the wicked to be k.,		38: 6
I have k. in store a blessing		39:15
ye shall see that my law is k.		41: 4
k. to administer to those who		42:33
shall be k. in my storehouse,		42:34
that they may be k. until all		44: 6
k. in the hands of the bishop.		51:13
k. and blessed with much fruit.		52:34
they who have k. the covenant		54: 6
law shall be k. on this land.		58:19
and have not k. them.		63:13
come, and hath k. the faith,		63:50
for they k. not the law,		64:15
spirits of men k. in prison,		76:73
be k. by the consecrations of		83: 6
the system may be k. perfect.		84:110
is their genealogy to be k.,		85: 4
not k. the commandments		93:44
not k. the commandments,		93:47
k. the enemy from breaking		101:54
not k. the commandment,		104: 4
a seal shall be k. upon it that		104:66
my judgments may be k. thereon,		119: 6
k. from the truth because they		123:12
k. workways with the wind		123:16
things which have been k. hid		124:41
records which are k. on the earth.		128: 7
is the record which is k. in heaven;		128: 7
the records which they have k.		128: 8
k. a proper and faithful record		128: 9
k. hid from the wise and prudent,		128:18
commanded to be k. from the world		133:60
they k. not the commandments of	Mses	5:52
a book of remembrance was k.,		6: 5
genealogy was k. of the children of		6: 8
have not k. the commandments,		6:28
have I k. even unto this day,	Abr	1:31
and k. not his first estate;		3:28
still I k. myself aloof from	JS	2: 8

KEY

the k. of the mysteries of	DC	84:19
the k. of the knowledge of God.		84:19
the k. of the ministering of		84:26
consist in the k. of knowledge.		128:14
The new name is the k. word.		130:11
holding the k. of power	Fac	2: 2
also the grand K.-words of the		2: 3
which is the grand K., or,		2: 5
K.-words of the Priesthood?		2: 7

KEYS

servant of Laban who had the k.	1Ne	4:20
the k. of this gift, which shall	DC	6:28
and the k. of this ministry		7: 7
the k. of the ministering of		13: 1
the k. of the record of the		27: 5
the k. of bringing to pass the		27: 6
the k. of the power of turning		27: 9
the k. of your ministry and of		27:12
the k. of my kingdom,		27:13
the k. of the mysteries,		28: 7
the k. of the mystery of those		35:18
by the k. which I have given		35:25
the k. of the church have been		42:69
the k. of the mysteries of		64: 5
The k. of the kingdom of God		65: 2
the k. or authority of the same.		68:17
hold the k. of this priesthood,		68:18
unto him the k. of salvation		78:16
given the k. of the kingdom,		81: 2
bear the k. of the kingdom		90: 2
the k. of this kingdom shall		90: 3
the k. of this last kingdom;		90: 6
the k. of the school of the		90: 7
the k. of which kingdom have		97:14
holds the k. or authority of		107:15
to hold the k. of this priesthood,	DC	107:16
k. of all the spiritual blessings		107:18
k. of the ministering of angels,		107:20
being sent out, holding the k.,		107:35
hold the k. of that priesthood.		107:70
to the k. of this ministry,		107:76
k. of the gathering of Israel		110:11
k. of this dispensation are		110:16
k. which I have given unto him,		112:15
to hold the k. of my kingdom,		112:16
the k. of the dispensation,		112:32
and the k. of the kingdom,		113: 6
k. of this kingdom and ministry.		115:19
k. of the holy priesthood ordained,		124:34
k. of the patriarchal blessings		124:92
k. whereby he may ask and		124:95
k. by which he may ask and		124:97
ye may hold the k. thereof,		124:123
Twelve hold the k. to open up		124:128
the k. thereof, for helps and		124:143
the k. of the kingdom of heaven:		128:10
him to whom these k. are given		128:11
the k. of the kingdom,		128:14
together of dispensations, and k.,		128:18
posessing the k. of the kingdom,		128:20
their rights, their k., their honors,		128:21
These are three grand k.		129: 9
on whom this power and the k.		132: 7
and the k. of this priesthood;		132:19
who had the k. of this power;		132:39
k. and power of the priesthood		132:45
I have endowed him with the k.		132:59
who holds the k. of this power,		132:64
the k. of the sealing ordinances,		OD
the k. of the ministering of	JS	2:69
held the k. of the Priesthood		2:72

KEY WORDS: *see KEY and WORDS.*

KIB

And Shule was the son of K.	Eth	1:31
And K. was the son of Orihah,		1:32
he also begat K. in his old age.		7: 3
that K. reigned in his stead;		7: 3
and K. begat Corihor.		7: 3
that K. dwelt in captivity,		7: 7
K. begat Shule in his old age,		7: 7
restored it unto his father K.		7: 9

KICK

to k. against the pricks,	DC	121:38

KID

leopard shall lie down with the k.,	2Ne	21: 6
leopard shall lie down with the k.,		30:12

KILL

the Spirit that I should k. Laban;	1Ne	4:10
I will k. thy root with famine,	2Ne	24:30
And they that k. the prophets,		26: 5
and they sought to k. him.	Mos	10:15
Thou shalt not k.		13:21
to battle against us and k. us,	Al	58:15
adultery, and steal, and k.,	He	7: 5
did k. many and did carry away		11:33
before you, that thou shalt not k.,	3Ne	12:21
whosoever shall k. shall be in		12:21
and did seek to k. them,	4Ne	1:31
at Jerusalem sought to k. Jesus,		1:31
and they sought to k. Ether,	Eth	13:22
Thou shalt not k.; and he	DC	42:18
again, I say, Thou shalt not k.;		42:19
persons among you shall k.		42:79
and they will k. one another.		45:33
neither commit adultery, nor k.,		59: 6
it was written: Thou shalt not k.		132:36
any finding him should k. him.	Mses	5:40
k. you, but they will save her	Abr	2:23
to be afflicted, and shall k. you,	JS	1: 7

KILLED

and k. the prophets,	Jac	4:14
came upon them and k. them,	Mos	11:17

KILLED 501 KINDRED

if their chief leader was k.,	Al 47:17
was wounded and Jacob was k.	52:35
of your brethren have been k.	60:12
and had not k. the prophets,	He 13:33
not k. and stoned the prophets,	3Ne 8:25
my father also was k. by them,	Mrm 8: 3
insomuch that Riplakish was k.,	Eth 10: 8
For they k. the prophets,	DC 136:36
they were k. upon this altar,	Abr 1:11

KILLETH
the murderer who deliberately k.,	2Ne 9:35
but he that k. shall die.	DC 42:19

KILLS
he that k. shall not have	DC 42:18

KIM
And Levi was the son of K.	Eth 1:21
K. was the son of Morianton.	1:22
great age, and then he begat K.;	10:13
K. did reign in the stead of	10:13
K. did not reign in righteousness,	10:13

KIMBALL, Heber C.
They are K., Parley P. Pratt,	DC 124:129

KIMNOR
send for Akish, the son of K.;	Eth 8:10

KIND
all manner of seeds of every k.,	1Ne 8: 1
both of grain of every k.,	8: 1
the seeds of fruit of every k.	8: 1
we did take seed of every k.	16:11
beasts in the forests of every k.,	18:25
herds, and animals of every k.	2Ne 5:11
and every k. of sin,	Jac 3:12
all manner of cattle of every k.,	En 1:21
all manner of tools of every k.	Jar 1: 8
riches which we have of every k.?	Mos 4:19
even all our grain of every k.,	7:22
ruins of buildings of every k.,	8: 8
weapons of war made of every k.,	10: 1
all manner of fruit of every k.	10: 4
yea, and cloth of every k.,	10: 5
herds, and fatlings of every k.	Al 1:29
of weapons of war, of every k.,	2:12
of weapons of war of every k.;	2:14
and temptations of every k.;	7:11
all manner of diseases of every k.;	9:22
a measure of every k. of grain.	11: 7
of wild animals of every k.,	22:31
trials and troubles of every k.,	36:27
great afflictions of every k.	56:16
of weapons of war of every k.,	60: 2
manner of afflictions of every k.	60: 3
flocks and herds of every k.;	62:29
all manner of shields of every k.	He 1:14
and many records of every k.,	3:15
of precious ore of every k.;	6:11
linen and cloth of every k.	6:13
of precious things of every k.	12: 2
weapons of war of every k.,	3Ne 3:26
cattle, and flocks of every k.,	4: 4
of all their grain of every k.,	6: 2
male and female, of every k.;	Eth 1:41
seed of the earth of every k.;	1:41
male and female, of every k.	2: 1
of the land, seeds of every k.	2: 3
charity suffereth long, and is k.,	Mro 7:45
and pestilences of every k.,	DC 43:25
is a welding link of some k.	128:18
yielding fruit, after his k.,	Mses 2:11
herb yielding seed after his k.,	2:12
should be in itself, after his k.,	2:12
forth abundantly, after their k.,	2:21
every winged fowl after his k.;	2:21
the living creature after his k.,	2:24
beasts of the earth after their k.,	2:24
of the earth after their k.,	2:25
and cattle after their k.,	2:25
upon the earth after his k.;	2:25

thou art merciful and k. forever;	Mses 7:30
tree yielding fruit, after his k.,	Abr 4:11
yielding seed after his k.;	4:12
the same in itself, after his k.;	4:12
forth abundantly after their k.;	4:21
every winged fowl after their k.	4:21
the living creature after his k.	4:24
beasts of the earth after their k.;	4:24
forth the beasts after their k.,	4:25
and cattle after their k.,	4:25
upon the earth after its k.;	4:25
together in some k. of cement.	JS 2:52

KINDLE
Behold all ye that k. fire,	2Ne 7:11
and shall k. in the thickets	19:18
he shall k. a burning like the	20:16
k. a flame of unquenchable fire	Mrm 9: 5

KINDLED
in the sparks which ye have k.	2Ne 7:11
is the anger of the Lord k.	15:25
the anger of the Lord shall be k.	26: 6
is already k. against you;	He 13:30
neither could there be fire k.	3Ne 8:21
And the anger of the Lord is k.,	DC 1:13
anger is k. against them.	5: 8
mine anger is k. against the	56: 1
against none is his wrath k.,	59:21
mine anger is k. against them.	60: 2
him whose anger is k. against	61:31
him whose anger is k. against	63: 2
anger was k. against them,	84:24
indignation of the Lord is k.	97:24
thine anger be k. against them;	109:27
may thine anger be k.,	109:52
anger be k. against;	121: 5
fierce anger is k. against them;	Mses 6:27
indignation is k. against them;	7:34
fierce anger is k. against them.	7:34
anger is k. against the sons of men,	8:15

KINDLETH
the anger of God k. against	DC 82: 6

KINDLY
sent up k. unto the bishop	DC 99: 6
and to have treated me k.,	JS 2:28

KINDNESS
because of his loving k.	1Ne 19: 9
with everlasting k. will I have	3Ne 22: 8
my k. shall not depart from thee,	22:10
brotherly k., godliness, charity,	DC 4: 6
brotherly k. and charity;	107:30
By k., and pure knowledge,	121:42
the loving k. of their Lord,	133:52
and according to his loving k.,	133:52

KINDRED
nation k., tongue and people	1Ne 19:17
nation, k., tongue, and people	2Ne 26:13
to every k., nation, and tongue,	Mos 3:13
nation, k., tongue, and people.	3:20
brethren, my k. and my people,	4: 4
nation, k., tongue, and people.	15:28
nation, k., tongue or people;	16: 1
journeying to see a very near k.,	Al 9:20
even all my k. hath he blessed,	10:11
and also by his father and his k.;	15:16
mourning for their k. who had	28: 5
mourning for the loss of their k.,	28:11
truly mourn for the loss of their k.,	28:12
nation, k., tongue and people,	37: 4
nation, k., tongue, and people,	45:16
family and his k. and friends;	3Ne 7: 2
to his family, k. and friends;	7:14
howling for the loss of their k.	10: 2
the loss of their k. and friends.	10: 8
administered it unto his k.	Eth 8:17
nation, k., tongue, or people	DC 10:51
to every nation, k., tongue,	77: 8

KINDRED 502 KING

of every nation, k., tongue,	DC 77:11
nation, k., tongue, or people,	98:33
the k. of the earth be blessed.	124:58
preached unto every nation, and k.,	133:37
k., and from thy father's house,	Abr 2: 3

KINDREDS

all nations, k., tongues, and people	1Ne 5:18
all nations, k., tongues, and people,	11:36
all k., tongues, and people,	13:40
all nations, k., tongues, and people.	14:11
the nations and k. of the earth.	14:15
all the k. of the earth be blessed.	15:18
all the k. of the earth be blessed.	22: 9
all the k. of the earth cannot	22:10
all nations, k., tongues, and people	22:28
all nations, k., tongues, and people,	2Ne 30: 8
nations, k., tongues and people,	Mos 27:25
I have many k. and friends,	Al 10: 4
judges had many friends and k.;	3Ne 6:27
unite with the k. of those judges	6:27
had much family and many k.	7: 4
the friends and k. of those who	7: 6
all the k. of the earth be blessed.	20:25
the k. of the earth be blessed—	20:27
when all people, and all k.,	26: 4
nations, k., tongues and people,	28:29
nations, k., tongues and people.	DC 7: 3
nations, k., tongues and people.	42:58
nations, k., tongues, and people;	88:103
abroad among all nations, k.,	112: 1
concerning the k. of the earth,	124:58
all nationa, k., and tongues,	JS 2:33

KINDS

there are all k. of bad fruit;	Jac 5:32
thirst, and all k. of afflictions;	Al 20:29
who did work all k. of ore	He 6:11
also many other k. of animals	Eth 9:18
to another, all k. of tongues;	Mro 10:15
and of divers k. of tongues.	10:16
workmen sent forth of all k.	DC 58:54
are two k. of beings in heaven,	129: 1
left to all k. of temptations;	JS 2:28
mingling with all k. of society,	2:28

KING

the reign of Zedekiah, k. of Judah,	1Ne 1: 4
the reign of Zedekiah, k. of Judah;	5:12
he has thought to make himself a k.	16:38
would that I should be their k.	2Ne 5:18
that they should have no k.;	5:18
unto whom ye look as a k.	6: 2
that raiseth up a k. against me	10:14
I, the Lord, the k. of heaven,	10:14
king of heaven, will be their k.,	10:14
In the year that k. Uzziah died,	16: 1
seen the K., the Lord of Hosts.	16: 5
the son of Uzziah, k. of Judah,	17: 1
that Rezin, k. of Syria,	17: 1
the son of Remaliah, k. of Israel,	17: 1
and set a k. in the midst of it,	17: 6
from Judah, the k. of Assyria.	17:17
by the k. of Assyria,	17:20
away before the k. of Assyria.	18: 4
many, even the k. of Assyria	18: 7
curse their k. and their God,	18:21
stout heart of the k. of Assyria,	20:12
against the k. of Babylon,	24: 4
In the year that k. Ahaz died	24:28
to be a k. and a ruler over	Jac 1: 9
under the reign of the second k.,	1:15
Mosiah, who was made k. over	Om 1:12
that Zedekiah, k. of Judah, was	1:15
was appointed to be their k.	1:19
seen, in the days of k. Benjamin,	1:24
that k. Benjamin did drive them	1:24
knowing k. Benjamin to be a	1:25
to the reign of this k. Benjamin,	WM 1: 3
to the reign of this k. Benjamin,	1: 3
into the hands of k. Benjamin,	1:10
until the days of k. Benjamin.	1:10
handed down from k. Benjamin,	WM 1:11
concerning this k. Benjamin—	1:12
k. Benjamin gathered together	1:13
k. Benjamin, with the assistance	1:16
k. Benjamin was a holy man,	1:17
k. Benjamin, by laboring with	1:18
who belonged to k. Benjamin,	Mos 1: 1
k. Benjamin had continual	1: 1
things did k. Benjamin teach	1: 8
after k. Benjamin had made an	1: 9
thou art a k. and a ruler over	1:10
after k. Benjamin had made an	1:15
which k. Benjamin should speak	2: 1
also a just man to be their k.,	2: 4
which k. Benjamin should speak	2: 6
k. Benjamin could not teach	2: 7
a ruler and a k. over this people;	2:11
ye have called me your k.; and if	2:18
if I, whom ye call your k., do	2:18
also, if I, whom ye call your k.,	2:19
ought to thank your heavenly K.!	2:19
even I, whom ye call your k.,	2:26
be your teacher, nor your k.;	2:29
is a k. and a ruler over you.	2:30
when k. Benjamin had made an	4: 1
which k. Benjamin had spoken	4: 3
k. Benjamin again opened his	4: 4
when k. Benjamin had thus spoken	5: 1
things which our k. has spoken	5: 4
k. Benjamin desired of them;	5: 6
when k. Benjamin had made an	6: 1
a ruler and a k. over his people,	6: 3
k. Benjamin lived three years and	6: 5
k. Mosiah did walk in the ways	6: 6
And k. Mosiah did cause his	6: 7
after k. Mosiah had had	7: 1
k. Mosiah granted that sixteen	7: 2
they met the k. of the people	7: 7
were again brought before the k.,	7: 8
and they stood before the k.,	7: 8
a k. by the voice of the people.	7: 9
and bowed himself before the k.;	7:12
O k., I am very thankful before	7:12
to the k. of the Lamanites.	7:15
k. Limhi commanded his guards	7:16
k. Limhi sent a proclamation	7:17
Zeniff, who was made k. over	7:21
and craftiness of k. Laman,	7:21
into a treaty with k. Zeniff,	7:21
to the k. of the Lamanites,	7:22
the k. of the Lamanites doth exact	7:22
after k. Limhi had made an end	8: 1
which k. Benjamin had taught	8: 3
to the people of k. Limhi,	8: 3
k. Limhi dismissed the multitude,	8: 4
the k. inquired of him to know if	8: 6
And the k. said unto him:	8: 7
I can assuredly tell thee, O k.,	8:13
the k. of the people who are in	8:14
And the k. said that a seer is	8:15
the k. rejoiced exceedingly,	8:19
into the city, in unto the k.,	9: 5
of the disposition of the k.,	9: 5
And I went in unto the k.,	9: 6
the craftiness of k. Laman,	9:10
k. Laman began to grow uneasy,	9:11
k. Laman began to stir up his	9:13
k. Laman died, and his son	10: 2
has k. Laman, by his cunning,	10:18
which k. Noah had put upon his	11: 6
and flattering words of the k.	11: 7
k. Noah built many elegant and	11: 8
k. Noah sent guards round about	11:17
k. Noah sent his armies against	11:18
of the wickedness of their k.	11:19
when k. Noah had heard of the	11:27
And k. Noah hardened his heart	11:29
the life of k. Noah shall be	12: 3
carried him bound before the k.,	12: 9
and said unto the k.:	12: 9
And now, O k., what great evil	12:13

KING

And now, O k., behold, we are	Mos 12:14
and thou, O k., hast not sinned;	12:14
k. Noah caused that Abinadi	12:17
that they said unto the k.:	12:18
the k. commanded that he should	12:18
when the k. had heard these	13: 1
the people of k. Noah durst not	13: 5
the k. commanded that the	17: 1
he began to plead with the k.	17: 2
But the k. was more wroth,	17: 3
the k. caused that his guards	17: 5
k. Noah was about to release	17:11
saying: He has reviled the k.	17:12
the k. was stirred up in anger	17:12
from the servants of k. Noah,	18: 1
come to the knowledge of the k.	18: 3
received its name from the k.,	18: 4
from the searches of the k.	18: 5
come to the knowledge of the k.	18:31
the k., having discovered a	18:32
were discovered unto the k.	18:32
the k. said that Alma was	18:33
the army of the k. returned,	19: 1
the forces of the k. were small,	19: 2
out threatenings against the k.,	19: 3
and an enemy to the k.,	19: 4
that he would slay the k.	19: 4
that he fought with the k.;	19: 5
when the k. saw that he was	19: 5
upon the tower to slay the k.,	19: 6
the k. cast his eyes round about	19: 6
And now the k. cried out in	19: 7
And now the k. was not so	19: 8
the k. commanded the people	19: 9
the k. commanded them that all	19:11
they would deliver up k. Noah	19:15
to the k. of the Lamanites	19:15
was one of the sons of the k.	19:16
secretly, to search for the k.	19:18
all save the k. and his priests.	19:18
the k. commanded that	19:20
and they were angry with the k.,	19:20
that they had slain the k.,	19:23
what they had done to the k.	19:24
the k. of the Lamanites made an	19:25
Limhi, being the son of the k.,	19:26
unto the k. of the Lamanites	19:26
the k. of the Lamanites had	19:28
k. Limhi did have continual peace	19:29
And now the priests of k. Noah,	20: 3
yea, even the k. himself went	20: 7
found the k. of the Lamanites	20:12
here is the k. of the Lamanites;	20:13
And now the k. said:	20:15
went forth and said unto the k.:	20:17
and tell the k. of these things,	20:19
except the k. doth pacify them	20:20
And now let us pacify the k.,	20:22
Limhi told the k. all the things	20:23
the k. was pacified towards	20:24
that they followed the k.,	20:25
the k. of the Lamanites did bow	20:25
and returned with their k.	20:26
the oath which their k. had made	21: 3
began to murmur with the k.	21: 6
And they did afflict the k.	21: 6
k. Limhi commanded that every	21:17
the k. himself did not trust his	21:19
the k. having been without the	21:23
Now k. Limhi had sent, previous	21:25
k. Mosiah had a gift from God,	21:28
k. Noah and his priests had	21:30
k. Limhi had also entered into	21:32
k. Limhi and many of his people	21:33
and k. Limhi and his people,	21:36
Ammon and k. Limhi began to	22: 1
forth and stood before the k.	22: 3
Now O k., thou hast hitherto	22: 3
And now O k., if thou hast	22: 4
the k. granted unto him that	22: 5
the k. hearkened unto the words	22: 9
k. Limhi caused that his people	22:10
wine which k. Limhi did send	22:10
people of k. Limhi did depart	Mos 22:11
by the people of k. Noah.	23:hd
the armies of k. Noah would	23: 1
before the armies of k. Noah.	23: 1
the people of k. Noah could not	23: 2
that Alma should be their k.,	23: 6
that we should have a k.;	23: 7
that ye should have a k.	23: 7
be well for you to have a k.	23: 8
remember the iniquity of k. Noah	23: 9
have been oppressed by k. Noah,	23:12
even out of the hands of k. Noah	23:13
no man to be a k. over you.	23:13
after the people of k. Limhi,	23:30
found those priests of k. Noah,	23:31
the k. of the Lamanites had	23:39
a k. and a ruler over his people,	23:39
will of the k. of the Lamanites.	23:39
eyes of the k. of the Lamanites;	24: 1
the k. of the Lamanites granted	24: 1
the k. of the Lamanites had	24: 2
name of the k. of the Lamanites	24: 3
he was called k. Laman.	24: 3
he was k. over a numerous people.	24: 3
was driven out before the k.,	24: 9
for he was subject to k. Laman,	24: 9
k. Mosiah did also receive them	24:25
k. Mosiah caused that all the	25: 1
k. Limhi was desirous that he	25:17
k. Mosiah granted unto Alma that	26: 1
the words of k. Benjamin,	26: 1
k. Mosiah had given Alma the	26: 8
should be brought before the k.	26:10
And he said unto the k.:	26:11
But k. Mosiah said unto Alma:	26:12
the case before their k., Mosiah.	27: 1
k. Mosiah sent a proclamation	27: 2
of God, or even the k.—	27:10
under the reign of k. Mosiah,	27:35
returned to their father, the k.,	28: 1
k. Mosiah went and inquired of	28: 6
k. Mosiah had no one to confer	28:10
after k. Mosiah had done these	28:20
concerning who should be their k.	29: 1
Aaron thy son should be our k.	29: 2
therefore the k. could not	29: 3
k. Mosiah sent again among	29: 4
for ye are desirous to have a k.	29: 5
Therefore I will be your k.	29:11
a k. or kings to rule over you.	29:16
doth one wicked k. cause	29:17
Yea, remember k. Noah,	29:18
cannot dethrone an iniquitous k.	29:21
an unrighteous k. doth pervert	29:23
and that ye have no k.;	29:30
did k. Mosiah write unto them,	29:33
and troubles of a righteous k.,	29:33
of the people to their k.;	29:33
unrighteous k. to rule over them;	29:35
after k. Mosiah had sent these	29:37
relinquished their desires for a k.,	29:38
k. Mosiah having gone the way of	Al 1: 1
given us by Mosiah, our last k.;	1:14
Amlici to be k. over the people.	2: 2
was not made k. over the people.	2: 7
consecrate Amlici to be their k.	2: 9
when Amlici was made k. over them	2:10
with the k. of the Lamanites;	2:32
the k. of the Lamanites fled	2:32
of the k. of the Lamanites	2:33
hands of the people of k. Noah,	5: 4
glory of the K. of all the earth;	5:50
and also the K. of heaven shall	5:50
Mosiah say, who was our last k.,	10:19
been established by k. Mosiah.	11: 4
was a k. over the land of Salem;	13:17
for he was the k. of Salem;	13:18
and carry them before the k.;	17:20
the pleasure of the k. to slay them,	17:20
Ammon was carried before the k.	17:21
the k. inquired of Ammon if it	17:22
k. Lamoni was much pleased	17:24
became a servant to k. Lamoni.	17:25

KING

in the service of the k. three days,	Al	17:26
and the servants of the k. were		17:27
and the servants of the k.,		17:27
the servants of the k. began to		17:28
Now the k. will slay us, as he has		17:28
restoring these flocks unto the k.,		17:29
preserve the flocks unto the k.		17:31
did head the flocks of the k.,		17:32
to scatter the flocks of the k.		17:35
them to the pasture of the k.,		17:39
and then went in unto the k.,		17:39
they were carried in unto the k.		17:39
k. Lamoni caused that his		18: 1
And they answered the k.,		18: 3
be slain by the enemies of the k.;		18: 3
that he is a friend to the k.		18: 3
And now, O k., we do not		18: 3
when the k. heard these words,		18: 4
that k. Lamoni inquired of his		18: 8
Now the k. had commanded		18: 9
who was k. over all the land.		18: 9
when k. Lamoni heard that		18:10
horses and the chariots for the k.		18:12
he went in unto the k.,		18:12
the countenance of the k. was		18:12
powerful or great k.,		18:13
the k. desireth thee to stay.		18:13
turned himself unto the k.,		18:14
I should do for thee, O k.?		18:14
And the k. answered him not for		18:14
But the k. answered him not.		18:15
perceived the thoughts of the k.		18:16
when the k. had heard these		18:18
k. Lamoni did open his mouth,		18:18
And the k. said: How knowest		18:20
And the k. answered him, and		18:23
And k. Lamoni said: Is it above		18:31
And k. Lamoni said: I believe		18:33
unto the k. and to his servants)		18:37
and expounded them to the k.,		18:40
the k. believed all his words.		18:40
k. Lamoni was under the power of		19: 6
he went in to see the k.		19: 7
and he saw the k., and he knew		19: 7
when the servants of the k. had		19:15
they who had stood before the k.		19:15
queen, and the k., and Ammon		19:17
unto the house of the k.		19:18
they beheld the k., and the queen,		19:18
or upon the k. and his house,		19:19
The k. hath brought this evil		19:20
which belonged to the k.,		19:21
defending the flocks of the k.		19:21
she took the k., Lamoni, by the		19:30
k. Lamoni desired that Ammon		20: 1
behold, the k. will seek thy life;		20: 2
the k. of the land of Middoni,		20: 4
I may flatter the k. of the land,		20: 4
there I will plead with the k. that		20: 7
who was k. over all the land.		20: 8
when the k. saw that Ammon		20:21
Now the k., fearing he should		20:23
upon the old k. according to		20:24
the k. began to rejoice because		20:25
For the k. was greatly astonished		20:27
in the eyes of the k. of the land;		20:28
k. Lamoni would not suffer that		21:19
from the oppressions of the k.,		21:21
under the reign of k. Lamoni.		21:22
unto the people of k. Lamoni;		21:23
even to the house of the k.		22: 1
and bowed himself before the k.,		22: 2
Behold, O k., we are the brethren		22: 2
now, O k., if thou wilt spare		22: 3
And he said unto them:		22: 3
And Aaron said unto the k.:		22: 4
Now the k. said unto them:		22: 5
And he said: I know that		22: 7
as thou livest, O k., there is a God.		22: 8
And the k. said: Is God		22: 9
the k. would believe his words,		22:12
the scriptures unto the k.—		22:12
all these things unto the k.		22:14
things unto him, the k. said:	Al	22:15
the k. did bow down before the		22:17
when the k. had said these words,		22:18
that had happened unto the k.		22:19
And she came in unto the k.;		22:19
servants, or the servants of the k.,		22:19
and raised the k. from the earth,		22:22
And the k. stood forth,		22:23
the k. stood forth among them		22:25
when the k. saw that the people		22:26
the k. sent a proclamation		22:27
the k. of the Lamanites sent a		23: 1
k. had been converted unto		23: 3
when the k. had sent forth this		23: 3
the k. and those who were		23:16
the k. consulted with Aaron		23:16
began to rebel against their k.,		24: 2
not that he should be their k.;		24: 2
the k. conferred the kingdom upon		24: 3
the k. died in that selfsame year		24: 4
their k. commanded them that		24: 6
when the k. had made an end of		24:17
the purpose of destroying the k.,		24:20
and they said unto the k.:		27: 4
But the k. said unto them:		27: 6
And the k. said unto him:		27: 8
But the k. said unto him:		27:10
Ammon went and told the k.		27:13
was desirous to be a k.;		46: 4
that he should be their k.;		46: 4
and establish him to be their k.		46: 5
the k. of the Lamanites sent		47: 1
they feared to displease the k.,		47: 2
the commandments of the k.		47: 2
the k. was wroth because of		47: 3
dethrone the k. of the Lamanites.		47: 4
who were in favor of the k.;		47: 5
appointed a man to be a k.		47: 6
to the commandments of the k.;		47: 8
and dethrone the k. and take		47: 8
k. had given him command,		47:13
to the commands of the k.		47:16
designs in dethroning the k.		47:16
And the k. came out to meet him		47:21
as the k. came out to meet him		47:22
should go forth to meet the k.		47:22
bowed themselves before the k.,		47:22
that the k. put forth his hand		47:23
he stabbed the k. to the heart;		47:24
Now the servants of the k. fled;		47:25
the servants of the k. have		47:26
what had happened to the k.;		47:27
found the k. lying in his gore,		47:27
Whosoever loved the k., let him		47:27
that all they who loved the k.,		47:28
after the servants of the k.		47:28
when the servants of the k. saw		47:29
heard that the k. was slain—		47:32
that the k. had been slain by		47:32
concerning the death of the k.		47:33
same servant that slew the k.,		47:34
that the k. was slain by his own		47:34
concerning the death of the k.		47:34
yea, he was acknowledged k.		47:35
made k. over the Lamanites,		48: 2
if k. Amalickiah had come down		49:10
to inform their k., Amalickiah,		49:25
were called k.-men, for they		51: 5
to establish a k. over the land.		51: 5
also put the k.-men to silence,		51: 7
men who were called k.-men		51:13
should go against those k.-men,		51:17
put an end to those k.-men,		51:21
by the appellation of k.-men;		51:21
privily into the tent of the k.,		51:34
he did cause the death of the k.		51:34
appointed k. over the people;		52: 3
thus k. Ammoron, the brother of		52: 3
the brother of k. Amalickiah,		52: 3
the k. (Ammoron) had departed		52:12
I am Ammoron, the k. of the		54:16
one of the servants of the k.		55: 5
epistle from Ammoron, the k.,		57: 1

KING

I sent an epistle unto the k.,	Al 57: 2
were it not for these k.-men,	60:16
which those k.-men had over us;	60:16
yea, even those k.-men.	60:17
have appointed a k. over them,	61: 8
unto the k. of the Lamanites,	61: 8
be placed k. over this people	61: 8
was the k. of those dissenters	62: 6
k.-men who had been taken	62: 9
men of Pachus and those k.-men,	62: 9
the k. of the Lamanites, was	62:33
that he did find the k.;	62:36
the k. did awake his servant	62:36
the k. of the Lamanites, whose	He 1:16
go unto the k. of the Lamanites.	4: 2
which k. Benjamin spake unto	5: 9
Zedekiah, the k. of Judah.	3Ne 1:hd
Mosiah, who was k. over the	2: 5
to establish a k. over the land,	6:30
establish k. over the land;	7: 1
And they did call him their k.;	7:10
became a k. over this wicked	7:10
he being the k. of the band,	7:12
by the people of k. Jacob,	9: 9
the Lamanites had a k., and his	Mrm 2: 9
the k. of the Lamanites sent an	3: 4
unto the k. of the Lamanites,	6: 2
the k. of the Lamanites did	6: 3
did k. Mosiah keep them,	Eth 1: 1
one of his sons to be a k.	6:22
that they may have a k.	6:24
out from among our sons a k.,	6:24
refused and would not be their k.	6:25
constrain no man to be their k.	6:25
Orihah was anointed to be k.	6:27
of Moron where the k. dwelt,	7: 5
of Moron, where the k. dwelt,	7: 6
rebelled against Shule, the k.,	7:15
gave battle unto Shule the k.,	7:16
he became a k. over that part	7:16
battle again unto Shule, the k.;	7:17
and he took Shule, the k.,	7:17
power any more over Shule the k.,	7:19
under the reign of Shule the k.	7:19
k. Shule did execute judgment	7:24
the head of my father, the k.	8:10
the head of my father, the k.	8:12
Jared was anointed k. over	9: 4
he anointed Emer to be k.	9:14
he had anointed Emer to be k.	9:15
to the commandment of the k.,	9:29
and did establish himself k.	10: 9
he had established himself k.	10:10
did anoint him to be their k.	10:10
he did make war against the k.	10:15
Corom, whom he anointed k.	10:16
to battle against the k., Amgid,	10:32
Coriantumr was k. over all the	12: 1
to the reign of k. Benjamin,	DC 10:41
ye shall have no k. nor ruler,	38:21
for I will be your k. and	38:21
they persecuted their k.	45:53
and he will be their k. and	45:59
praise to the K. Immanuel,	128:22
the wonders of your Eternal K.!	128:23
I am Messiah, the K. of Zion,	Mses 7:53
the god of Pharaoh, k. of Egypt,	Abr 1: 6
priest of Pharaoh, the k. of Egypt,	1: 8
that of Pharaoh, k. of Egypt.	1:13
the god of Pharaoh, k. of Egypt;	1:17
signifies k. by royal blood.	1:20
this k. of Egypt was a descendant	1:21
by the politeness of the k.,	Fac 3: 1
K. Pharaoh, whose name	3: 2
of Pharaoh, K. of Egypt,	3: 4
his defense before K. Agrippa,	JS 2:24

KINGDOM

the everlasting k. of the Lamb;	1Ne 13:37
cannot dwell in the k. of God;	15:33
if so, the k. of God must be filthy	15:33
the k. of God is not filthy,	1Ne 15:34
enter into the k. of God;	15:34
is to dwell in the k. of God,	15:35
But it is the k. of the devil,	22:22
which k. is established among	22:22
who belong to the k. of the devil	22:23
reign over you in his own k.	2Ne 2:29
they shall inherit the k. of God,	9:18
cannot be saved in the k. of God.	9:23
into the eternal k. of God,	10:25
and upon his k. to order it,	19: 7
shall be saved in the k. of God.	25:13
shall be saved in the k. of God.	28: 8
the k. of the devil must shake,	28:19
can be saved in the k. of God.	31:21
if not all, may be saved in his k.	33:12
we knew of Christ and his k.,	Jac 1: 6
seek ye for the k. of God.	2:18
shall be saved in the k. of God.	6: 4
the k. upon one of his sons.	Mos 1: 9
concerning all the affairs of the k.	1:15
hath no interest in the k. of God.	4:18
all the charges concerning the k.,	6: 3
again began to establish the k.	10: 1
the k. upon one of my sons;	10:22
conferred the k. upon Noah,	11: 1
had changed the affairs of the k.	11: 4
are the heirs of the k. of God.	15:11
things pertaining to the k. of God.	18:18
having the k. conferred upon him	19:26
Limhi began to establish the k.	19:27
did have continual peace in his k.	19:29
the k. had been conferred upon	25:13
in nowise inherit the k. of God.	27:26
had no one to confer the k. upon,	28:10
who would accept of the k.	28:10
could not confer the k. upon him;	29: 3
Aaron take upon him the k.;	29: 3
willing to take upon them the k.	29: 3
whom the k. doth rightly belong	29: 6
will not take upon him the k.	29: 6
to whom the k. doth belong,	29: 7
and claim his right to the k.,	29: 9
to sit down in the k. of God,	Al 5:24
have place in the k. of heaven;	5:25
children of the k. of the devil.	5:25
the k. of heaven is soon at hand,	5:28
the k. of heaven is soon at hand;	5:50
nowise inherit the k. of heaven.	5:51
the k. of heaven is at hand,	7: 9
inherit the k. of heaven;	7:14
which leads to the k. of God;	7:19
be received into the k. of God;	7:21
in the k. of heaven	7:25
nowise inherit the k. of God.	9:12
the k. of heaven is nigh at hand;	9:25
he was about to deliver up the k.,	10:19
for the k. of heaven is at hand.	10:20
can inherit the k. of heaven;	11:37
ye inherit the k. of heaven?	11:37
more concerning the k. of God.	12: 8
rejected their rights to the k.	17:hd
having refused the k. which	17: 6
of his tarrying in his own k.,	20:12
wilt ask, even to half of the k.	20:23
that Lamoni may retain his k.,	20:24
son Lamoni should retain his k.,	20:26
that my son may retain his k.	20:26
may come unto me, in my k.;	20:27
yea, I will forsake my k., that I	22:15
conferred the k. upon his son,	24: 3
sit down in the k. of God;	29:17
righteous shall sit down in his k.,	34:36
at the last day into his k.,	38:15
nowise inherit the k. of God.	39: 9
shine forth in the k. of God.	40:25
thing can inherit the k. of God;	40:26
to inherit the k. of God,	41: 4
to inherit the k. of the devil,	41: 4
establish a k. unto themselves	43:29
and take possession of the k.	47: 8
servants, he obtained the k.;	47:35

KINGDOM

Amalickiah had obtained the k.	Al 48: 1
of God in the k. of heaven,	He 3:30
for the k. of heaven is at hand;	5:32
build up unto themselves a k.,	3Ne 7:12
for of such is the k. of God.	9:22
who shall inherit the k. of God.	11:33
in nowise inherit the k. of God.	11:38
for theirs is the k. of heaven.	12: 3
for theirs is the k. of heaven.	12:10
case enter into the k. of heaven.	12:20
For thine is the k., and the	13:13
seek ye first the k. of God	13:33
shall enter into the k. of heaven;	14:21
thing can enter into his k.;	27:19
come unto thee in thy k.	28: 2
ye shall come unto me in my k.;	28: 3
blessed in the k. of my Father.	28: 8
sit down in the k. of my Father;	28:10
into the k. of the Father	28:40
and heirs to the k. of God.	4Ne 1:17
in the presence of God in his k.,	Mrm 7: 7
in the k. prepared for him	Eth 4:19
be received into the k. of God.	5: 5
which means he obtained the k.	7: 9
bestowed upon him the k.;	7:10
he did spread his k. upon all	7:11
Shule gave him power in his k.	7:13
upon his throne in his own k.	7:18
did build up his k. in his stead;	7:19
the k. of Shule, and the kingdom	7:20
the k. of Cohor, the son of Noah.	7:20
Nimrod gave up the k. of Cohor	7:22
do in the k. of Shule according	7:22
he had gained the half of the k.	8: 2
he had gained the half of the k.	8: 3
give up the k. unto his father.	8: 6
because of the loss of the k.,	8: 7
he had set his heart upon the k.	8: 7
redeem the k. unto her father.	8: 8
did overthrow the k. of Omer.	9: 1
nearly all the people of the k.,	9:12
he did build up a righteous k.;	10: 2
did obtain unto himself the k.	10:15
had obtained unto himself the k.	10:16
the k. was taken away from him.	10:30
drew away the half of the k.	10:32
reigned over the half of the k.	10:32
over the remainder of the k.	10:32
sought again to destroy the k.	10:33
Ahah, his son, did obtain the k.;	11:10
of Ahah, did obtain the k.;	11:11
overthrow the half of the k.;	11:15
did maintain the half of the k.	11:15
and did obtain the k. again	11:16
Moron and obtain the k.;	11:18
that they might obtain the k.	13:18
Lord would give unto him his k.	13:20
and did obtain the k. again	13:24
and obtained unto himself the k.;	14:10
he would give up the k. for	15: 4
but that he would take the k.,	15:18
I am saved in the k. of God.	15:34
rest our souls in the k. of God.	Mro 9: 6
be saved in the k. of God;	10:21
ye be saved in the k. of God	10:21
be saved in the k. of God;	10:26
salvation in the k. of God.	DC 6: 3
be saved in the k. of God,	6:13
inherit the k. of heaven.	6:37
speedily come unto me in my k.	7: 4
shall inherit the k. of heaven.	10:55
build up the k. of the devil—	10:56
salvation in the k. of God.	11: 3
seek the k. of God, and all	11:23
salvation in the k. of God.	12: 3
salvation in the k. of God.	14: 3
in the k. of my Father.	15: 6
in the k. of my Father.	16: 6
in the k. of my Father!	18:15
into the k. of my Father,	18:16
place in the k. of my Father.	18:25
unto the k. of my Father.	18:44
saved in the k. of my Father.	18:46
be saved in the k. of God.	DC 20:29
sons and daughters in my k.	25: 1
in this my Father's k. which	27: 4
committed the keys of my k.,	27:13
good will to give you the k.	29: 5
the k. of heaven is at hand;	33:10
the k. is yours until I come.	35:27
the peaceable things of the k.;	36: 2
Behold, the k. is yours,	38: 9
fear not, for the k. is yours.	38:15
the peaceable things of the k.	39: 6
The k. of heaven is at hand;	39:19
to the children of the k.	41: 6
the k. of heaven is at hand.	42: 7
know the mysteries of the k.,	42:65
for unto you the k., or in	42:69
glory shall be added to the k.	43:10
ye desire the glories of the k.,	43:12
desire the mysteries of the k.,	43:13
whom the k. has been given;	45: 1
are earnestly seeking the k.—	46: 5
earnestly seeking after the k.,	46: 6
the k. is given you of the Father,	50:35
they shall see the k. of God	56:18
greater in the k. of heaven.	58: 2
laws of the k. which are given	58:18
blessings of the k. are yours.	61:37
Behold, the k. is yours,	62: 9
give the mysteries of my k.,	63:23
I have given unto you the k.	64: 4
of the mysteries of the k.	64: 5
The keys of the k. of God are	65: 2
that his k. may go forth upon	65: 5
to meet the k. of God which	65: 5
may the k. of God go forth,	65: 6
the k. of heaven may come,	65: 6
according to the laws of the k.	70: 8
gospel, the things of the k.,	71: 1
to whom the k. and power	72: 1
gospel and the things of the k.	72:14
addition to the laws of the k.,	72:24
the hidden mysteries of my k.	76: 7
all things pertaining to my k.	76: 7
to take the k. of our God	76:28
crown over the k. of our God.	76:79
he shall deliver up the k.,	76:107
and the mysteries of his k.	76:114
The k. is yours and the	78:18
have given the keys of the k.,	81: 2
For even yet the k. is yours,	82:24
of the mysteries of the k.,	84:19
overthrow the k. of the Jews,	84:28
and the church and k., and	84:34
receiveth my Father's k.;	84:38
meet for their Father's k.;	84:58
the children of the k. pollute	84:59
not come into my Father's k.	84:74
whom the k. has been given—	84:76
preach this gospel of the k.,	84:80
proclaim this gospel of the k.	84:86
the glory of the celestial k.;	88: 8
bodies who are of the celestial k.	88:20
must inherit another k.,	88:21
even that of a terrestrial k.	88:21
or that of a telestial k.	88:21
abide the law of a celestial k.	88:22
abide the law of a terrestrial k.	88:23
abide the law of a telestial k.	88:24
not meet for a k. of glory.	88:24
abide a k. which is not a	88:24
which is not a k. of glory.	88:24
abideth the law of a celestial k.,	88:25
in the which there is no k.;	88:37
there is no k. in which	88:37
either a greater or a lesser k.	88:37
unto every k. is given	88:38
every k. in its hour, and in	88:61
first laborers in this last k.	88:70
first laborers in this last k.,	88:74
another the doctrine of the k.	88:77
pertain unto the k. of God,	88:78
that bear the keys of the k.	90: 2
which k. is coming forth for	90: 2

KINGDOM 507 KIRTLAND

the keys of this k. shall never	DC 90: 3	of the coming of the k. army;	Mos 18:34
holding the keys of this last k.;	90: 6	he being the k. captain,	20:17
unfold the mysteries of the k.;	90:14	had been one of the k. priests,	24: 9
affairs of this church and k.	90:16	can they scatter the k. flocks	Al 18: 3
pertaining to the church and k.	94: 3	And one of the k. servants said	18:13
pertaining to the k. of God	97:14	in unto him into the k. palace,	22: 2
the keys of which k. have been	97:14	had seen the cause of the k. fall,	22:20
little child, receiveth my k.;	99: 3	one of the k. principal waiters,	Fac 3: 5
things of my k. on the earth.	100:11	Astronomy, in the k. court.	3: 6
mine house, a ruler in my k.	101:61		
come in the k. of my Father	101:65	KINGS	
and works meet for my k.	101:100	an account of the reign of the k.,	1 Ne 9: 4
and organize my k. upon	103:35	the more part of the reign of k.	9: 4
church and k. on the earth,	104:59	of the k. of the isles of the sea	19:12
by the law of the celestial k.;	105: 4	K. shall see and arise,	21: 7
of the law of the celestial k.;	105: 5	k. shall be thy nursing fathers,	21:23
the k. of Zion is in very deed	105:32	k. shall be thy nursing fathers,	2 Ne 6: 7
very deed the k. of our God	105:32	Yea, the k. of the Gentiles shall be	10: 9
seeking diligently the k.	106: 3	shall be no k. upon the land,	10:11
mysteries of the k. of heaven,	107:19	shall be forsaken of both her k.	17:16
the k., which thou hast set up	109:72	Are not my princes altogether k.?	20: 8
chosen to hold the keys of my k.,	112:16	thrones all the k. of the nations.	24: 9
to unlock the door of the k.	112:17	All the k. of the nations,	24:18
to open the door of my k.	112:21	according to the reigns of the k.	Jac 1: 9
and the keys of the k.,	113: 6	according to the reigns of the k.;	1:11
have I given the keys of this k.	115:19	according to the reigns of the k.	1:14
to open up the authority of my k.	124:128	and the reigns of their k.	3:13
give unto thee the keys of the k.	128:10	our k. and our leaders were	Jar 1: 7
the keys of the k.,	128:14	according to the writings of the k.,	1:14
as possessing the keys of the k.,	128:20	upon plates which is had by the k.,	Om 1:11
things pertaining to an inferior k.,	130: 9	had been handed down by the k.,	WM 1:10
who come into the celestial k.,	130:11	have just men to be your k.	Mos 23: 8
but that is the end of his k.,	131: 4	appointed k. over all these lands.	24: 2
prepare a throne for you in the k.	132:49	could have just men to be your k.,	29:13
is not worthy of my k.	136:31	ye could have men for your k.	29:13
you have received my k.	136:41	always have k. to rule over you.	29:13
in nowise inherit the k. of God,	Mses 6:57	a king or k. to rule over you.	29:16
born again into the k. of heaven,	6:59	caused by the iniquities of their k.;	29:31
established his k. and judged him	Abr 1:26	upon the heads of their k.	29:31
not have glory in the same k.	3:26	thus ended the reign of the k.	29:47
since the beginning of their k.	JS 1:18	their k. to be powerful;	Al 18:13
and k. against kingdom;	1:29	those who were in favor of k.	51: 8
and kingdom against k.;	1:29	and they sought to be k.;	51: 8
this Gospel of the K. shall be	1:31	but shall be subject unto k.	3 Ne 6:30
and an annoyer of his k.;	2:20	the k. shall shut their mouths	20:45
than that of building his k.;	2:46	that k. shall shut their mouths;	21: 8
his k. was to be conducted	2:54	and before k. and rulers	DC 1:23
pertaining to the K. of God.	AoF 9	they who are priests and k.,	76:56
		Remember the k., the princes,	109:55
KINGDOMS		be made to all the k. of the world,	124: 3
and beheld many nations and k.	1 Ne 13: 1	know my will concerning those k.	124: 5
I behold many nations and k.	13: 2	Awake, O k. of the earth!	124:11
these are the nations and k.	13: 3	in sending my word to the k. and	124:16
founded the k. of the idols,	2 Ne 20:10	solemn proclamation unto the k.	124:107
noise of the k. of nations	23: 4	believe in being subject to k.,	AoF 12
And Babylon, the glory of k.,	23:19		
to tremble, that did shake k.?	24:16	KINS	
and there were two k.,	Eth 7:20	from all thy k.-folk, into a	Abr 1:16
did obtian k. and great glory?	8: 9		
be made rulers over many k.,	DC 78:15	KINSFOLK	
and the k. of the world, in all	84:82	and my father and my k.;	Al 10:11
I will rend their k.;	84:118	slain in battle, and all my k.,	Mrm 8: 5
All k. have a law given;	88:36	unto the house of Jared all his k.,	Eth 8:13
And there are many k.;	88:37		
what shall I liken these k.,	88:46	KINS-FOLK: see KINS and FOLK.	
Behold, all these are k.,	88:47		
will liken these k. unto a man	88:51	KIRTLAND	
I will liken all these k.,	88:61	let my disciples in K. arrange	DC 63:38
also of countries and of k.—	88:79	a strong hold in the land of K.,	64:21
and of countries, and of k.,	93:53	and in the land of Shinehah [K.];	82:12
until the k. of the world are	103: 7	the land of Shinehah [K.]	82:13
the k. of the world shall	103: 8	high priests, assembled in K.,	89: 1
the k. of this world may be	105:32	of Zion, here in the land of K.,	94: 1
k., principalities, and powers.	128:23	who are in the church at K.;	98:19
or all k. of a lower order,	130: 9	in the land of Shinehah [K.].	104:21
pertaining to a higher order of k.	130:10	in the land of Shinehah [K.].	104:40
and shall inherit thrones, k.,	132:19	the City of Shinehah [K.].	104:48
spring all the k. of the earth	Mses 8: 3	unto my name in the land of K.	105:33
		to thy name in this place [K.].	109: 2
KING-MEN: see KING and MEN.		journey from the land of K.,	117: 1
		properties of K. be turned out	117: 5
KING'S		my servants in the land of K.	117:16
were surrounded by the k. guard,	Mos 7: 7	even unto K.;	124:83
		I, the Lord, will build up K.,	124:83

KISH

KISH
And Lib was the son of K.	Eth	1:18
And K. was the son of Corom.		1:19
and K. reigned in his stead.		10:17
that K. passed away also,		10:18

KISHKUMEN
behold, they sent forth one K.,	He	1: 9
so speedy was the flight of K. that		1:10
that K. had murdered Pahoran.		1:11
K. was not known among the		1:12
And K. and his band, who had		1:12
K., who had murdered Pahoran,		2: 3
the leader of the band of K.		2: 4
did flatter them, and also K.,		2: 5
K. sought to destroy Helaman.		2: 5
he met K., and he gave unto him		2: 7
K. made known unto him the		2: 7
had known all the heart of K.,		2: 8
of Helaman said unto K.:		2: 8
this did please K. exceedingly,		2: 9
did stab K. even to the heart,		2: 9
found that K. did not return		2:11
formed by K. and Gadianton.		6:18
given by Gadianton and K.		6:24
city of Gad, and the city of K.,	3Ne	9:10

KISS
the Lord and did k. his feet.	3Ne	11:19
the multitude did k. his feet.		17:10
upon our necks, and we will k.	Mses	7:63

KLI-FLOS-IS-ES
through the medium of k.,	Fac	2: 5

KNEE
Yea, every k. shall bow, and	Mos	27:31
these all shall bow the k.,	DC	76:110
and every k. shall bow,		88:104

KNEEL
should k. down upon the ground.	3Ne	17:13
k. down upon the face of the		19: 6
k. down again upon the earth,		19:16
should k. down upon the earth.		19:16
did k. down with the church,	Mro	4: 2
he shall k. with the church	DC	20:76

KNEELED
and I k. down before my Maker,	En	1: 4
I k. down and began to offer	JS	2:15

KNEES
he fell upon his k., and began to	Al	19:14
down before the Lord, upon his k.;		22:17
and strengthen the feeble k.	DC	81: 5
prayer upon his k. before God,		88:131

KNELT
they had k. upon the ground,	3Ne	17:14
himself also k. upon the earth;		17:15
they k. again and prayed to the		19: 8
had all k. down upon the earth,		19:17

KNEW
because they k. not the dealings	1Ne	2:12
he k. that I had been blessed of		3: 8
For he k. that Jerusalem must be		3:17
I also k. that he had sought to		4:11
I also k. that the law was		4:16
I k. that the Lord had delivered		4:17
he k. that he was a descendant		5:14
for I k. that it was desirable		8:12
they k. not whither they should		8:14
I k. that it was the Spirit of		11:11
k. they must unavoidably come		15: 4
k. that I had spoken hard things		16: 2
k. that ye could not construct		17:19
k. that ye were lacking in judgment;		17:19
k. not whither they should steer		18:13
I k. not at the time when I made		19: 2
I k. that thou are obstinate,		20: 4

KNEW

shouldst say – Behold I k. them.	1Ne	20: 7
I k. that thou wouldst deal		20: 8
no joy, for they k. no misery;	2Ne	2:23
doing no good, for they k. no sin.		2:23
for I k. their hatred towards me		5:14
wherefore, we k. of Christ	Jac	1: 6
may know that we k. of Christ,		4: 4
I k. that it was a poor spot of		5:22
I k. that all the fruit of the		5:42
k. that God could not lie;	En	1: 6
k. it would be according to		1:17
they k. not the course they should	Mos	7:.4
Lamanites k. nothing concerning		10:11
in disguise, that they k. him not,		12: 1
for he k. concerning the iniquity		17: 2
they k. not whither they had fled.		21:31
nevertheless they k. not God;		24: 5
For Amulon k. Alma, that he		24: 9
For they k. not what to think;		25: 8
shall they that never k. me come		26:25
unto them that I never k. them;		26:27
they k. that there was nothing save		27:18
he k. that it was the power of God.		27:20
they k. that according to their law	Al	2: 3
k. not that they were fulfilling		3:18
souls of those who k. not God.		6: 6
for they k. not that the earth		9: 3
Now they k. not that God could		9: 5
I k. concerning these things,		10: 6
they k. not that Amulek could		10:17
that they k. the thoughts and		12: 7
also k. concerning the blindness of		14: 6
k. not that the Lord had promised		17:35
for he k. not what he should say		18:14
for he k. that king Lamoni was		19: 6
k. that the dark veil of unbelief		19: 6
he k. that this had overcome		19: 6
and he k. that he was not dead.		19: 7
k. that it was the power of God;		19:17
I also k. that there was a God.		30:52
which they k. nothing about.		31:22
For they k. that if they should		43:10
they also k. the extreme hatred		43:11
as Moroni k. the intention of		43:29
for he k. that he would stir up		46:30
he k. that Amalickiah would do		46:30
For they k. not that Moroni		49:13
k. not whether to go or to strike.		52:36
because he k. that Ammoron had		55: 1
yea. he k. that Ammoron knew		55: 1
k. that it was not a just cause		55: 1
we k. in those cities they were		56:23
overtaken by Antipus we k. not,		56:43
do not doubt our mothers k. it.		56:48
strength unto us, we k. not;		58: 9
k. that Teancum was dead		62:37
not only k. of these things,	He	8:18
the people k. nothing concerning		9: 8
who k. concerning the true		11:23
they k. that the great plan of	3Ne	1:16
they k. that the prophets had		1:18
they k. that it was the day that		1:19
they k. it was because of their		4:33
they k. that it must needs be		5: 1
they k. that it must be expedient		5: 2
they k. that it must needs be		5: 2
no one k. it save it were himself		5:20
for they k. the will of God		6:18
Holy Ghost, and they k. it not.		9:20
I never k. you; depart from me,		14:23
I k. not whether they were		28:36
k. of the goodness of Jesus.	Mrm	1:15
I k. the judgments of the Lord		5: 2
I k. not that the Lord had	Eth	3: 8
he k. that it was the finger of		3:19
for he k., nothing doubting.		3:19
he k. that the Lord could show		3:26
of time, and ye k. it not;	DC	38:13
they k. no law shall have		45:54
hidden things which no man k.,		101:33
for he k. not the mine of God,	Mses	4: 6
they k. that they had been naked.		4:13

KNEW 509 KNOW

KNEW
Adam k. his wife, and she bare	Mses 5: 2
Adam k. Eve his wife, and she	5:16
Satan k. this, and it pleased	5:21
Cain k. his wife, and she conceived	5:42
and they k. every man his brother.	5:51
Adam k. his wife again, and she	6: 2
Enoch k., and looked upon their	7:41
k. not until the flood came,	JS 1:43
had seen a vision, he k. he had,	2:24
yet he k., and would know to	2:24
I k. it, and I knew that	2:25
and I k. that God knew it,	2:25
and I knew that God k. it,	2:25
I k. that by so doing I would	2:25
that I k. the place again when	2:42
I k. the place the instant that	2:50

KNEWEST
heardest not; yea, thou k. not;	1Ne 20: 8
come, and thou k. it not.	DC 35: 4

KNIGHT, Joseph
I manifest unto you, K., by	DC 23: 6

KNIGHT, Newel
And let my servants K. and	DC 52:32
say unto you, my servant K.,	54: 2
Selah J. Griffin and K.,	56: 6
let my servant K. remain with	56: 7
Thomas Grover, K., David Dort,	124:132

KNIGHT, Vinson
concerning my servant K.,	DC 124:74
I give unto you K.,	124:141

KNIT
having their hearts k. together	Mos 18:21

KNOCK
ye ask not, neither do ye k.;	2Ne 32: 4
k., and it shall be opened unto	3Ne 14: 7
k., and it shall be opened unto	27:29
k., and it shall be opened	DC 4: 7
if you will k. it shall be	6: 5
if you will k. it shall be	11: 5
if you will k. it shall be	12: 5
if you will k. it shall be	14: 5
k. and it shall be opened	49:26
k., and it shall be opened	66: 9
k. and it shall be opened	75:27
k., and it shall be opened	88:63

KNOCKETH
whoso k., to him will he open;	2Ne 9:42
to him that k., it shall be	3Ne 14: 8
unto him that k., it shall be	27:29

KNOW
that they may k. the covenants	T Pg
I k. that the record which I make	1Ne 1: 3
I would that ye should k.,	1:18
to k. of the mysteries of God,	2:16
for I k. that the Lord giveth no	3: 7
K. ye not that the Lord hath	3:29
behold ye k. that this is true;	4: 3
ye also k. that an angel hath	4: 3
the Jews might not k. concerning	4:36
I k. that I am a visionary man;	5: 4
I k. that the Lord will deliver my	5: 5
I k. of a surety that the Lord	5: 8
I also k. of a surety that the Lord	5: 8
I would that ye might k.,	7: 1
ye shall k. at some future period	7:13
which purpose I k. not.	9: 5
one among you whom ye k. not;	10: 8
see, and hear, and k. of these things,	10:17
to k. the things that my father had	11: 1
To k. the interpretation thereof—	11:11
I k. that he loveth his children;	11:17
I do not k. the meaning of all	11:17
I said unto him: I k. not.	13:22
desiring to k. of them the cause	15: 6
our seed k. that they are of the	1Ne 15:14
then shall they k. and come to the	15:14
they may k. how to come unto him	15:14
we k. that he lies unto us;	16:38
ye shall k. that it is by me	17:13
shall k. that I, the Lord, am God;	17:14
we k. that the people who were	17:22
we k. that they are a righteous	17:22
ye k. that the children of Israel	17:25
ye k. that they were laden with	17:25
ye k. that it must needs be	17:25
ye k. that Moses was commanded	17:26
ye k. that by his word the waters	17:26
ye k. that the Egyptians were	17:27
ye also k. that they were fed	17:28
ye also k. that Moses, by his word	17:29
ye k. that they were led forth	17:42
I k. not but they are at this day	17:43
I k. that the day must surely come	17:43
ye also k. that by the power of	17:46
ye k. that by his word he can	17:46
they may k. that I am the Lord	17:53
We k. of a surety that the Lord	17:55
for we k. that it is the power of	17:55
be that we k. concerning them	19:21
might k. concerning the doings of	19:22
and thou didst not k. them.	20: 6
thou shalt k. that I am the Lord;	21:23
all flesh shall k. that I, the Lord,	21:26
we k. that they have been led away.	22: 4
should k. that all the kindreds of	22:10
k. that the Lord is their Savior	22:12
his sheep, and they k. him;	22:25
I k. that Jerusalem is destroyed;	2Ne 1: 4
I k. that he hath not sought for	1:25
I k. that thou art a true friend	1:30
I k. that thou art redeemed,	2: 3
that they k. good from evil.	2: 5
that they may k. that there is no	2: 8
for I k. their faith.	3:19
I k. that if ye are brought up	4: 5
I k. in whom I have trusted.	4:19
I k. that cursed is he that	4:34
I k. that God will give liberally	4:35
if my people desire to k. the	5:33
ye k. that I have spoken unto you	6: 2
ye yourselves k. that it ever has	6: 3
thou shalt k. that I am the Lord;	6: 7
shall k. that the Lord is God,	6:15
all flesh shall k. that I the Lord	6:18
I should k. how to speak	7: 4
I k. that I shall not be ashamed.	7: 7
ye that k. righteousness,	8: 7
that ye might k. concerning the	9: 1
For I k. that ye have searched	9: 4
to k. of things to come;	9: 4
I k. that ye know that our flesh	9: 4
ye k. that our flesh must waste	9: 4
I k. that ye know that in	9: 5
ye k. that in the body he shall	9: 5
supposing they k. of themselves,	9:28
I k. that the words of truth are	9:40
ye shall k. at the last day,	9:44
but I k. my guilt; I transgressed	9:46
and k. that he be their God.	10: 4
and come, that we may k. it.	15:19
that he may k. to refuse the evil	17:15
child shall k. to refuse the evil	17:16
And all the people shall k.,	19: 9
for they k. not concerning the	25: 1
may k. the judgments of God,	25: 3
I k. that the Jews do understand	25: 5
I k. concerning the regions round	25: 6
I k. that no man can err;	25: 7
men shall k. of a surety,	25: 7
for I k. that they shall be of	25: 8
for we k. that it is by grace that	25:23
our children may k. to what source	25:26
children may k. the deadness of	25:27
and k. for what end the law was	25:27
I k. that it shall come to pass;	26:10
that I k. all their works.	27:27

KNOW

I k. that they must surely come	2Ne	28: 1
K. ye not that they are more		29: 7
K. ye not that I, the Lord your		29: 7
K. ye not that the testimony of		29: 8
of our seed k. concerning us,		30: 4
they shall k. that it is a blessing		30: 6
write but a few things, which I k.		31: 1
K. ye not that he was holy?		31: 7
I k. that if ye shall follow the Son,		31:13
I k. by this that unless a man shall		31:16
that ye might k. the gate by which		31:17
ye would k. that ye must pray;		32: 8
and I k. that he will hear my cry.		33: 3
And I k. that the Lord God will		33: 4
and ye shall k. that I have been		33:11
ye yourselves k. that I have	Jac	2: 3
and k. that by the help of the		2: 5
ye k. that these commandments		2:34
we k. that the things which we		4: 1
may k. that we knew of Christ,		4: 4
we may k. that it is by his grace,		4: 7
ye yourselves k. that he counseleth		4:10
I k. that the roots are good,		5:36
K. ye not that if ye will do		6: 9
and also k. that thou goest about		7: 6
but I k. that there is no Christ,		7: 9
I k. if there should be no		7:12
in the which ye k. so much.		7:13
for I k. that in him I shall rest.	En	1:27
ye should k. that I fought much	Om	1: 2
and I k. of no revelation save		1:11
yea, and I also k. that	WM	1: 4
I k. they will be choice unto		1: 6
now, I do not k. all things;		1: 7
I k. that they will be		1:11
might k. concerning the prophecies	Mos	1: 2
who k. nothing concerning these		1: 5
and we can k. of their surety		1: 6
that ye may k. that I can		2:15
desiring to k. of his people		5: 1
also, we k. of their surety		5: 2
for he shall k. the name by which		5: 9
and k. the voice by which ye		5:12
if ye k. not the name by which ye		5:14
k. the commandments of God,		6: 3
to k. concerning the people		7: 1
now, I desire to k. the cause		7:10
Now, I k. of a surety that my		7:14
to k. if he could interpret		8: 6
desirous to k. the cause of their		8:12
a seer can k. of things which		8:17
might k. of the disposition of		9: 5
that I might k. if I might go in		9: 5
they shall k. that I am the Lord		11:22
he shall k. that I am the Lord.		12: 3
and yet desire to k. of me what		12:25
K. ye not that I speak the truth?		12:30
Yea, ye k. that I speak the truth;		12:30
what k. ye concerning the law of		12:31
k. if ye keep the commandments		12:33
that ye may k. of their surety		17: 9
did k. the thoughts of their hearts.		24:12
for I k. of the covenant which		24:13
that ye may k. of a surety		24:14
Alma did not k. concerning them;		26: 9
if they k. me they shall come		26:24
shall they k. that I am the Lord		26:26
and k. of the goodness and glory		27:22
and this I k., because I was		27:27
to k. concerning those people who		28:12
people should k. the things which		28:19
to k. their will concerning who		29: 1
that he might k. of their plans and	Al	2:21
ye will k. at that day that ye		5:21
that I k. of these things myself?		5:45
I do k. that these things whereof		5:45
that I k. of their surety?		5:45
I might k. these things of myself.		5:46
k. of myself that they are true;		5:46
I k. of myself that whatsoever		5:48
I k. that Jesus Christ shall come,		5:48
that he hath given me to k.,		7: 4
as to this thing I do not k.;		7: 8
but this much I do k., that the	Al	7: 8
he may k. according to the flesh		7:12
yea, I k. that ye believe them;		7:17
that I k. that ye believe them		7:17
Behold, we k. that thou art Alma;		8:11
we k. that thou art high priest		8:11
we k. that because we are not of		8:12
we k. that thou hast no power		8:12
I k. that thou art a holy prophet		8:20
I k. that thou wilt be a		8:20
to k. of the incorrectness of		9:17
come in a time when you k. not,		9:18
among all those who k. me;		10: 4
yet I would not k.; therefore		10: 6
wherefore I k. he is a holy man		10: 9
I k. that the things whereof he		10:10
Amulek could k. of their designs.		10:17
Now we k. that this man is a		10:28
knowing even as we k. now,		11:43
that we k. that thy plan was		12: 4
that they might k. of these things		12: 7
that he might k. more concerning		12: 8
to k. the mysteries of God;		12: 9
to k. the mysteries of God		12:10
of God until he k. them in full.		12:10
until they k. nothing concerning		12:11
k. concerning the things whereof		12:28
seeing we k. these things, and		12:37
k. in what manner to know		13: 2
cometh, we k. not how soon.		13:25
K. ye not that I have power to		14:19
multitudes to k. the cause of it;		14:29
to k. whether the Lord would that		16: 5
they might k. the word of God.		17: 2
to k. of the plan of redemption.		17:16
k. anything concerning the Lord;		17:35
Great Spirit or a man, we k. not;		18: 3
but this much we do k., that he		18: 3
k. that he is a friend to the king.		18: 3
for we k. he cannot be slain.		18: 3
I k. that it is the Great Spirit;		18: 4
k. that this is the Great Spirit,		18:11
I k. that thou art more powerful		18:21
I do not k. what that meaneth.		18:25
but I do not k. the heavens.		18:29
and desired to k. what she would		19: 3
I k., in the strength of the Lord		20: 4
for I k. that they are just men		20:15
I k. that if I should slay my son,		20:19
k. concerning the things which		21: 8
I desire to k. the cause why he		22: 3
I k. that the Amalekites say that		22: 7
give away all my sins to k. thee,		22:18
to believe and to k. the truth,		24:19
and we k. that they are blessed,		24:22
Yea, I k. that I am nothing;		26:12
to k. the mysteries of God;		26:22
we k. that they have gone to		26:34
and exult in the hope, and even k.,		28:12
for I k. that he granteth unto		29: 4
yea, I k. that he allotteth unto		29: 4
and I k. that good and evil have		29: 5
seeing that I k. these things,		29: 6
I k. that which the Lord hath		29: 9
I surely do k. that the Lord did		29:11
For no man can k. of anything		30:13
How do ye k. of their surety?		30:15
Behold, ye cannot k. of things		30:15
ye cannot k. that there shall be		30:15
ye do not k. that they are true.		30:24
ye do not k. that there shall be		30:26
I k. there is a God,		30:39
Behold, I k. that thou believest,		30:42
ye do not k. that there is a God;		30:48
I k. that I am dumb, for I		30:52
and I k. that nothing save it were		30:52
to k. of iniquity among his people;		31: 2
being brought to k. the word,		32:16
or even compelled to k., before		32:16
then we shall k. of a surety;		32:17
as ye have desired to k. of me		32:24
Ye cannot k. of their surety		32:26
needs k. that the seed is good.		32:33

KNOW

and this because ye k., for ye	Al	32:34
ye k. that the word hath swelled		32:34
ye also k. that it hath sprouted		32:34
ye must k. that it is good;		32:35
to k. if the seed was good.		32:36
desiring to k. whether they		33: 1
yea, I k. that these things were		34: 2
I do k. that Christ shall come		34: 8
And this I k., because the Lord		34:36
let the people k. concerning		35: 5
I do k. that whosoever shall put		36: 3
ye think that I k. of myself—		36: 4
they do k. of these things		36:26
which I have spoken, as I do k.;		36:26
And I k. that he will raise me		36:28
for ye ought to k. as I do know,		36:30
ye ought to know as I do k., that		36:30
and ye ought to k. also, that		36:30
that they shall k. of the mysteries		37: 4
people, that they k. them not,		37:27
For I k. that thou wast in bonds;		38: 4
I also k. that thou wast stoned		38: 4
that I k. these things of myself,		38: 6
K. ye not, my son, that these		39: 5
and ye k. that ye deny it,		39: 6
of God that I might k.—		40: 3
me to k. that this is the case—		40: 5
diligently of the Lord to k.;		40: 9
this is the thing of which I do k.		40: 9
then shall they k. that God		40:10
would k. whither they had gone.		43:22
that he might k. when the camp		43:28
Ye k. that ye are in our hands,		44: 1
which we k. that we shall break,		44: 8
his death or burial we k. not of.		45:18
Behold, this we k., that he was		45:19
for this cause we k. nothing		45:19
the Lamanites did not k. that		52:29
we k. not such a being;		54:21
we k. not but that he hath made		54:21
I k. the place where the		55: 3
ue also k. concerning the		56: 6
we k. not but they have halted		56:43
we do not k. the cause that		58:34
k. why we have not received		58:34
k. but what ye are unsuccessful;		58:35
for we k. that they are more		58:36
ye yourselves k. that ye have		60: 2
we desire to k. the cause of		60: 6
we desire to k. the cause of your		60: 6
For we k. not but what ye		60:18
We k. not but what ye are		60:18
Ye k. that ye transgress		60:33
ye do k. that ye do trample		60:33
whither she did go we k. not.		63: 8
no one should k. his wickedness.	He	2: 3
ye may k. how that it is said,		5: 6
that they might k. the cause of		7:11
of myself that I k. these things;		7:29
I k. that these things are true		7:29
now we k. that this is impossible,		8: 6
we k. that he has testifies aright		8: 8
may k. concerning the judgments		8:12
now I would that ye should k.,		8:19
k. that Jerusalem was destroyed		8:20
now, seeing ye k. these things		8:24
now we will k. of a surety		9: 2
ye say ye have sent, we k. not;		9:12
the judges inquired of them to k.,		9:13
we k. not who has done it;		9:15
only this much we k., we ran		9:15
we k. that this Nephi must have		9:16
do ye k. how long the Lord		9:21
might k. concerning this thing;		9:23
I did k. of the wickedness and		9:23
Do we not k. that it is the blood		9:32
we k. that thou art guilty.		9:34
I, Nephi, k. nothing concerning		9:36
ye k. that I am an honest man,		9:36
he could not k. of all things.		9:41
we k. that thou art a man of God,		11: 8
and I k. that thou wilt, even at		11:14

511

KNOW

shall k. of the rising of the sun	He	14: 4
shall k. of a surety that there		14: 4
k. of the judgments of God		14:11
k. the conditions of repentance;		14:11
ye might k. of the coming of		14:12
might k. of the signs of his coming,		14:12
ye k. at this time are solid,		14:21
that ye might k. good from evil,		14:31
behold, ye do k. of yourselves,		15: 7
k. of the wicked and abominable		15: 7
ye k. of yourselves are firm and		15: 8
ye k. also that they have buried		15: 9
k. that the Christ must shortly		16: 4
they might k. and remember at		16: 5
but behold, we k. that all these		16:16
k. that this is a wicked tradition,		16:20
distant, a land which we k. not;		16:20
k. that their faith had not been	3Ne	1: 8
began to k. that the Son of God		1:17
works thereof I k. to be good;		3: 9
I k. the record which I make		5:18
shall they k. their Redeemer,		5:26
k. concerning the ministry of		7:15
and we k. our record to be true,		8: 1
k. that they were carried away.		8:16
ye may k. that I am the God		11:14
did k. of a surety and have		11:15
have seen me and k. that I am.		12: 1
and that ye k. that I am.		12: 2
k. what thy right hand doeth;		13: 3
k. how to give good gifts unto		14:11
shall k. them by their fruits.		14:16
by their fruits ye shall k. them.		14:20
iniquity that they k. not of you.		15:19
that they k. not of them.		15:20
tribes whom they k. not of,		16: 4
they k. that their record is true		17:25
ye k. that a man is unworthy		18:29
for behold I k. my sheep,		18:31
ye k. not but what they will		18:32
my people shall k. my name;		20:39
they shall k. that I am he		20:39
that ye may k. the time when		21: 1
may k. concerning this people		21: 2
and k. of the true points of my		21: 6
shall begin to k. these things—		21: 7
k. that the work of the Father		21: 7
ye k. the things that ye must do		27:21
k. ye that ye shall be judges		27:27
I k. your thoughts, and ye have		28: 6
of their transfiguration, I k. not;		28:17
But this much I k., according		28:18
the Gentiles shall k. them not.		28:27
and the Jews shall k. them not.		28:28
k. that these things must surely		28:33
ye may k. that the covenant		29: 1
ye may k. that the words of		29: 2
would that ye should k. that	4Ne	1:23
professed to k. the Christ,		1:27
I k. that I shall be lifted up	Mrm	2:19
k. that they were preparing		3: 4
may k. that ye must all stand		3:20
k. from whence their blessings		5:10
I k. that such will sorrow for		5:11
K. ye not that ye are in the		5:23
K. ye not that he hath all power,		5:23
k. of the things of their fathers;		7: 1
K. ye that ye are of the house of		7: 2
K. ye that ye must come unto		7: 3
K. ye that ye must lay down		7: 4
K. ye that ye must come to the		7: 5
will k. concerning your fathers,		7: 9
ye will also k. that ye are a		7:10
they will slay me, I k. not.		8: 3
suffer that I may live I k. not.		8: 5
none that do k. the true God		8:10
k. of greater things than these.		8:12
But behold, we k. no fault;		8:17
unto me, and I k. your doing.		8:35
I k. that ye do walk in the		8:36
k. not the God in whom they		9:20
I k. that ye shall hear my words.		9:30

KNOW

ye may k. the decrees of God—	Eth	2:11
we k. that thou art holy and		3: 2
And I k., O Lord, that thou hast		3: 4
We k. that thou art able to		3: 5
I k. that thou speakest the truth,		3:12
might k. that he was God,		3:18
k. that it is I that speaketh,		4:10
and he shall k. and bear record.		4:11
k. that these things are true;		4:11
then shall ye k. that the Father		4:15
ye shall k. that the time is at		4:16
ye may k. that the work of		4:17
they shall k. of a surety that		5: 3
shall k. that I have authority		5: 6
that we may k. of them what		6:19
I k. that thou workest unto		12:29
I k. that this love which thou		12:34
I k. by this thing which thou		12:35
where all men shall k. that my		12:38
then shall ye k. that I have		12:39
we k. the manner to be true;	Mro	4: 1
by their works ye shall k. them;		7: 5
ye may k. good from evil;		7:15
k. with a perfect knowledge,		7:15
he may k. good from evil;		7:16
k. with a perfect knowledge		7:16
k. with a perfect knowledge		7:17
ye k. the light by which ye		7:18
that ye may k. good from evil;		7:19
I k. that it is solemn mockery		8: 9
I k. that God is not a partial		8:18
ye may k. that I am yet alive;		9: 1
I k. that they must perish		9:22
k. that many of our brethren		9:24
I would that they should k.		10: 1
may k. the truth of all things.		10: 5
And ye may k. that he is,		10: 7
that ye shall k. that I lie not,		10:27
k. that the day speedily cometh;	DC	1:35
k. the promises of the Lord,		3:20
k. of a surety that these things		5:12
k. of a surety that they are true,		5:25
thou shalt k. mysteries which		6:11
that thou mayest k. that thou		6:15
that thou mayest k. that there		6:16
that you might k. concerning		6:22
may k. the mysteries of God,		8:11
And then shall ye k., or by		11:14
or by this shall you k.,		11:14
may k. of a surety my doctrine.		11:16
to k. that which would be of		15: 4
to k. that which would be of		16: 4
have desired to k. of me,		18: 1
you k. that they are true.		18: 2
if you k. that they are true,		18: 3
if they k. not the name by		18:25
my voice, and k. my words.		18:36
their works you shall k. them.		18:38
to k. even as mine apostles.		19: 8
how sore you k. not,		19:15
how exquisite you k. not,		19:15
how hard to bear you k. not.		19:15
they must not k. these things,		19:22
we k. that there is a God in		20:17
we k. that all men must repent		20:29
we k. that justification		20:30
we k. also, that sanctification		20:31
we k. that these things are		20:35
and his diligence I k.,		21: 1
they could not k. the sweet.—		29:39
will believe and k. the truth		31: 2
see me and k. that I am;		38: 8
ye k. not the hearts of men		38:29
upon thy works and I k. thee.		39: 7
my coming, and shall k. me.		39:23
k. how to govern my church		41: 3
thou mayest k. the mysteries		42:61
given to k. the mysteries of		42:65
it is not given to k. them.		42:65
this ye shall k. assuredly—		43: 3
you may k. they are not of me.		43: 6
k. how to act and direct		43: 8
on earth, nor ever shall k.,		43:33

KNOW

ye k. that the end of the world	DC 45:22
ye k. that the heavens and	45:22
k. that the promises which	45:35
they k. that the hour is nigh.	45:38
behold me and k. that I am,	45:46
they k. that I am the Lord;	45:52
to k. any further concerning	45:60
they may not k. your works	45:72
That when they shall k. it,	45:73
to k. that Jesus Christ is the	46:13
to k. the differences of	46:15
to k. the diversities of	46:16
shall be given to k. the place,	48: 5
desire to k. the truth in part,	49: 2
shall they k. until he comes.	49: 7
holy men that ye k. not of.	49: 8
ye cannot understand and k.,	50:21
that you may k. the truth,	50:25
But k. this, it shall be given	50:30
may k. that it is not of God.	50:31
see me, and k. that I am.	50:45
shall k. the spirits in all cases	52:19
and they shall k. mine arm	56: 1
that the earth may k. that	58: 8
By this ye may k. if a man	58:43
all men shall k. what it is that	60: 4
the Spirit to k. all his ways;	61:27
flesh shall k. that I am God.	63: 6
and whose hearts I k.,	67: 1
this you also k.	67: 5
do not k. that they are true;	67: 7
For ye k. that there is no	67: 9
see me and k. that I am—	67:10
shall see and k. that which	67:14
to k. the signs of the times,	68:11
k. concerning my church;	69: 3
and k. this, that in the day of	75:21
k. his will concerning you.—	75:23
of eternity shall they k.,	76: 8
all those who k. my power,	76:31
and k. as they are known,	76:94
believe, and k. to be true.	80: 2
by this you may k. they are	84:50
by this you may k. the righteous	84:53
by this you may k. my disciples.	84:91
Until all shall k. me,	84:98
shall see it, and k. that I am,	84:119
ye k. that ye have seen me,	88:50
see my face and k. that I am;	93: 1
and k. how to worship,	93:19
and k. what you worship,	93:19
whereby ye may k. how to act	96: 1
who k. their hearts are honest,	97: 8
thou mayest k. the certainty	100:11
be still and k. that I am God.	101:16
may k. my will concerning	101:43
may hear and k. that which	101:94
that you may k. how to act	103: 1
and k. more perfectly concerning	105:10
may k. that this is thy work,	109:23
We k. that thou hast spoken	109:45
ends of the earth may k. that we,	109:57
and k. that thou art God.	109:70
by this ye may k. that the great	110:16
I k. thy heart, and have heard thy	112:11
who have professed to k. my name	112:26
eyes see and k. all their works,	121:24
he may k. that thy faithfulness	121:44
k. thou, my son, that all these	122: 7
they k. not where to find it—	123:12
darkness, wherein we k. them;	123:13
You k., brethren, that a very	123:16
to k. my will concerning those	124: 5
to k. my will concerning them,	124:73
It is sufficient to k., in this case,	128:18
grand keys whereby you may k.	129: 9
praying very earnestly to k.	130:14
have inquired of my hand to k.	132: 1
neither do ye k. me.	132:22
then shall ye k. me,	132:23
to k. the only wise and true God,	132:24
for ye k. neither the day nor	133:11
men shall k. that my garments	135: 5

KNOW 513 KNOWING

present with me, for I k. them all.	Mses	1: 6
cause I k. that man is nothing,		1:10
for they are mine and I k. them.		1:35
This I k. now is bone of my		3:23
God doth k. that in the day ye eat		4:11
as one of us to k. good and evil;		4:28
I k. not, save the Lord		5: 6
is the Lord that I should k. him?		5:16
this that thy father may not k. it;		5:29
I k. not. Am I my brother's		5:34
nevertheless we k. them, and		6:45
the first of all we k., even Adam.		6:45
they may k. to prize the good.		6:55
unto them to k. good from evil;		6:56
as thou art God, and I k. thee,		7:59
shall k. that all flesh shall die;		8:17
k. the end from the beginning;	Abr	2: 8
to k. the times of reckoning, and		3: 6
k. the set time of all the stars		3:10
k. that I am he of whom it is	JS	1: 1
you k. that summer is nigh		1:38
they shall k. that he is near,		1:39
for you k. not at what hour		1:46
But k. this, if the good man		1:47
is it, and how shall I k. it?		2:10
for how to act I did not k.,		2:12
then had, I would never k.;		2:12
to k. which of all the sects was		2:18
that I might k. which to join.		2:18
would k. to his latest breath,		2:24
that I might k. of my state		2:29

KNOWEST

thou k. that I believe all	1Ne	11: 5
K. thou the condescension of God?		11:16
K. thou the meaning of the tree		11:21
K. thou the meaning of the book?		13:21
also k. concerning the covenants		14: 5
thou k. the greatness of God;	2Ne	2: 2
thou k. that this spot of ground	Jac	5:23
thing which thou k. to be true?		7:14
K. thou of any one that can	Mos	8:12
K. thou that the righteous yieldeth	Al	11:23
thou k. that there is a God,		11:24
How k. thou these things?		11:30
How k. thou the thoughts of		18:20
How k. thou the thought and		21: 6
How k. thou that we have cause		21: 6
How k. thou that we are not a		21: 6
that thou k. any such thing.		21: 8
that thou k. of things to come,		21: 8
Thou k. that we do not glut		30:32
k. that we receive no gain?		30:35
k. that the Lord did deliver thee.		38: 4
k. concerning all these things—		56: 4
Because thou k. these things	Eth	3:13
thou k. the wickedness of this	Mro	9:20
thou k. that they are without		9:20
thou k. that thou hast inquired	DC	6:15
that k. thy thoughts and the		6:16
Thou k. my laws concerning		42:28
k. thou we have done this work		109: 5
thou k., O Lord, that thy		109:31
Thou k., O Lord, that they		109:48
k. that thou hast a great love		109:61
strange land which thou k. not of;	Abr	1:16

KNOWETH

the Lord k. all things	1Ne	9: 6
whither they are none of us k.,		22: 4
wisdom of him who k. all things.	2Ne	2:24
of our God! For he k. all things,		9:20
Who seeth us, and who k. us?		27:27
And no man k. of his ways	Jac	4: 8
for no man k. of such things;		7: 7
but the Lord k. all things	WM	1: 7
k. that ye are eternally indebted	Mos	2:34
k. that he rebelleth against God!		3:12
how k. a man the master whom		5:13
who k. but what my son, to whom		29: 7
k. not when the time shall come;	Al	5:29
Now the Spirit k. all things;		7:13

is there that k. these things?	Al	26:21
there is none that k. these things,		26:21
he that k. not good from evil		29: 5
but he that k. good and evil,		29: 5
for if a man k. a thing he hath		32:18
no cause to believe, for he k. it.		32:18
is he that k. the will of God		32:19
And who k. but what they will be		37:10
that no one k. them save God		40: 3
but God k. the time which is		40: 4
for God k. all these things;		40: 5
God k. all the times which are		40:10
who k. but what the remnant of		46:27
he k. as well all things which shall	He	8: 8
us as he k. of our iniquities;		8: 8
and whither he went, no man k.;	3Ne	1: 3
whither they went no man k.		8:16
your Father k. what things ye		13: 8
your heavenly Father k. that ye		13:32
k. whither he hath taken them.		17: 4
Father of heaven, k. your state;	Mrm	6:22
no one k. the end of the war.		8: 8
the face of the land no man k.		8:10
nevertheless God k. all things;		8:17
And he k. their prayers,		8:24
And he k. their faith,		8:24
k. not the gospel of Christ;		9: 8
the Lord k. the things which		9:34
other people k. our language;		9:34
who k. but the Lord will carry	Eth	1:38
told you things which no man k.	DC	6:24
tell you that which no man k.		15: 3
tell you that which no man k.		16: 3
no man k. where the city Zion		28: 9
Holy Ghost, that k. all things.		35:19
The same which k. all things,		38: 2
day or the hour no man k.;		39:21
the Comforter k. all things,		42:17
their end no man k. on earth,		43:33
hour and the day no man k.,		49: 7
who k. the weakness of man		62: 1
k. that you have need of		84:83
in truth and k. all things.		93:28
God k. all these things,		127: 2
which no man k. save he		130:11
not broken her vow, and whe k. it,		132:44
that which k. all things, and	Mses	6:61
of that day, and hour, no one k.;	JS	1:40

KNOWING

led by the Spirit, not k. beforehand	1Ne	4: 6
he k. that his master, Laban, had		4:22
k. the great and marvelous works	2Ne	1:10
shall be as God k. good and evil.		2:18
free forever, k. good from evil;		2:26
by k. the deadness of the law,		25:27
he k. that I, Jacob, had faith	Jac	7: 3
k. my father that he was a	En	1: 1
I k. that the Lord God was able		1:15
k. king benjamin to be a just	Om	1:25
my fathers k. that many of them	WM	1: 4
not k. the mysteries of God.	Mos	1: 3
have died not k. the will of God		3:11
devilish, k. evil from good,		16: 3
k. that they are established	Al	7: 4
k. even as we know now,		11:43
as Gods, k. good from evil,		12:31
k. that Alma was high priest over		16: 5
k. the hardness of the hearts of		22:22
as God, k. good and evil;		42: 3
k. of the prophecies of Alma,		43:23
k. that it was the only desire		43:30
k. that it was easier to keep the		59: 9
k. of their exceeding great		62:19
lest by k. these things and	He	14:19
k. of their unconquerable spirit,	3Ne	3: 4
k. of their everlasting hatred		3: 4
k. of their weakness because of		4:24
k. the mercies and the	Mrm	2:12
k. that these things must surely		5: 8
k. it to be the last struggle of		6: 6
For behold, God k. all things,	Mro	7:22

KNOWING 514 KNOWLEDGE

I the Lord, k. the calamity	DC 1:17	brought to the k. of the truth,	Al 23: 6
seeing and k. for themselves;	76:117	come to the k. of the truth,	23:15
a man's k. that he is sealed	131: 5	brought to the k. of the truth;	24:27
be as gods, k. good and evil.	Mses 4:11	and have had great k. of things	24:30
k. that if any person needed	JS 2:12	to thek. of the truth?	26:24
		the k. of what had happened	30:57
KNOWINGLY		faith is not to have a perfect k.	32:21
suffer any one k. to partake	3Ne 18:28	that it was not a perfect k.—	32:26
		more than faith is a perfect k.	32:26
KNOWLEDGE		hath not grown up to a perfect k.	32:29
having had a great k. of	1Ne 1: 1	now, behold, is your k. perfect?	32:34
I make it according to my k.	1: 3	your k. is perfect in that thing,	32:34
come to the k. of the true	10:14	this light is your k. perfect?	32:35
come to the k. of their forefathers,	15:14	the k. which I have is of God.	36:26
also to the k. of the gospel	15:14	them to the k. of their God	37: 8
come to the k. of their Redeemer	15:14	them to the k. of the Lord	37: 9
kept for the k. of my people.	19: 5	to the k. of their Redeemer?	37:10
lost from the k. of those who	22: 4	to the k. of the truth;	37:19
from the k. of other nations;	2Ne 1: 8	against the light and k. of God,	39: 6
having a k. of the creation	1:10	sin against so great light and k.,	45:12
them to the k. of the covenants	3: 7	in the same k. of the Lrod,	47:36
them to the k. of their fathers	3:12	had a perfect k. of his fraud;	55: 1
also to the k. of my covenants,	3:12	a k. of those plans which had been	He 2: 6
he hath given me k. by visions	4:23	in the k. of their God;	6:34
come to the k. of their Redeemer,	6:11	not sinned against that great k.	7:24
living souls, having a perfect k.	9:13	unto our k. the true murderer	9:41
that our k. shall be perfect.	9:13	God hath given unto you a k.	14:30
have a perfect k. of all our guilt,	9:14	brethren to the k. of the truth;	15: 6
a perfect k. of their enjoyment,	9:14	are brought to the k. of the truth,	15: 7
for a k. of their iniquities shall	9:33	again to the k. of the truth—	15:11
the true k. of their Redeemer.	10: 2	shall be brought to the true k.,	15:13
great k. concerning these things,	10:20	is the k. of their Redeemer,	15:13
captivity, because they have no k.;	15:13	brought to a k. of their error	3Ne 1:25
child shall not have k. to cry,	18: 4	me and my people so much k.	5:20
the spirit of k. and of the	21: 2	to the k. of the Lord their God.	5:23
shall be full of the k. of the Lord,	21: 9	unto the k. of the covenant	5:25
unto the k. of their fathers,	30: 5	the k. of their death came not	6:23
also to the k. of Jesus Christ,	30: 5	they may receive a k. of you	16: 4
shall be full of the k. of the Lord	30:15	may be brought to a k. of me,	16: 4
for they will not search k.,	32: 7	k. of the fulness of my gospel.	16:12
nor understand great k., when	32: 7	brought to the k. of the Lord	20:13
a small degree of k. concerning	Jac 4: 2	a k. of these things must come	Mrm 5: 9
attain to a perfect k. of him,	4:12	come to the k. of your fathers,	7: 5
attain to the k. of a resurrection	4:12	unto the k. of the people;	8:16
a perfect k. of the language of	7: 4	this record according to our k.,	9:32
Lamanites to the k. of the truth;	7:24	restoration to the k. of Christ,	9:36
according to the best of my k.,	7:26	of the k. of this man	Eth 3:19
again come to the k. of God,	WM 1: 8	having this perfect k. of God,	3:20
according to the k. and the	1: 9	the k. which is hid up	4:13
contrary to his own k.	Mos 2:33	ye may know with a perfect k.,	Mro 7:15
the k. of the Savior shall spread	3:20	ye may know with a perfect k.	7:16
the k. of the goodness of God	4: 5	ye may know with a perfect k.	7:17
to a k. of the goodness of God,	4: 6	And after rejecting so great a k.,	8:29
to the k. of the glory of God,	4:11	the k. which I have received	9: 7
the k. of the glory of him that	4:12	he may teach the word of k. by	10:10
in the k. of that which is just	4:12	receive k. from time to time.	DC 1:28
has brought us to this great k.,	5: 4	the k. of a Savior has come	3:16
a k. of a remnant of the people	8:12	shall the k. of a Savior come	3:16
a k. of this very people who	8:12	to the k. of the Lamanites,	3:18
had a k. of the land of Nephi,	9: 1	come to the k. of their fathers,	3:20
by his k. shall my righteous	14:11	Remember faith, virtue, k.,	4: 6
not come to the k. of the king.	18: 3	many to the k. of the truth,	6:11
having the k. of God, that they	18:26	a k. of whatsoever things you	8: 1
to the k. of their Redeemer;	18:30	a k. concerning the engravings	8: 1
not come to the k. of the king.	18:31	shall have k. concerning it.	8: 9
you to a k. of his truth.	23:10	k. from all those ancient records	8:11
brought to the k. of the truth;	27:14	bring to the k. of the people	10:40
many to the k. of the truth,	27:36	to the k. of my people.	10:52
to the k. of their Redeemer.	27:36	come to a k. of this work.	20:13
to the k. of the Lord their God,	28: 2	whoso having k., have I not	29:49
nevertheless it gave them much k.,	28:18	k. upon knowledge, that thou	42:61
and so much k. given unto them	Al 9:19	knowledge upon k., that thou	42:61
contrary to the light and k.	9:23	another is given the word of k.,	46:18
and Amulek had a k. of him,	12: 7	taught to be wise and to have k.	46:18
and the k. of this went forth	15:11	and in the k. of the truth.	50:40
strong in the k. of the truth;	17: 2	to the k. which they receive	58:56
many to the k. of the truth;	17: 4	have sought in your hearts k.	67: 5
to the k. of the truth,	17: 9	may the more easily obtain k.—	69: 7
to the k. of the baseness of	17: 9	unto the elders until further k.,	73: 5
to a k. of that which is just	18:34	representation of light and k.,	77: 4
giveth me k., and also power	18:35	that is, they are full of k.;	77: 4
many to the k. of the truth;	21:17	the key of the k. of God.	84:19
brought to the k. of the Lord,	23: 5	filled with the k. of the Lord,	84:98

KNOWLEDGE   515   KNOWN

and a k. also of countries	DC 88:79
and great treasures of k.,	89:19
truth is k. of things as they	93:24
and to obtain a k. of history,	93:53
that my k. and glory may	101:25
and in faith, and virtue, and k.,	107:30
unfruitful in the k. of the Lord.	107:31
k. of them by the Spirit of Truth;	107:71
come to a k. of the truth,	109:67
God shall give unto you k. by	121:26
pouring down k. from heaven	121:33
By kindness, and pure k.,	121:42
gathering up a k. of all the facts,	123: 1
all who have k. of antiquities,	124:26
a k. of said bishopric is given	124:141
k. of the general character	128: 4
die without a k. of the gospel.	128: 5
in obtaining a k. of facts	128:11
which consist in the key of k.	128:14
k. of God descend upon them.	128:19
And if a person gains more k.	130:19
this matter was without my k.	OD
also the tree of k. of good and evil.	Mses 3: 9
the tree of the k. of good and evil,	3:17
and I gave unto them their k.,	7:32
to be one who possessed great k.,	Abr 1: 2
possess a greater k., and to be a	1: 2
you may have a k. of this altar	1:12
a k. of the beginning of the	1:31
the tree of k. of good and evil.	5: 9
the tree of k. of good and evil,	5:13

KNOWN

making k. unto him the things	1Ne 2:17
not have k. the goodness of God,	5: 4
was able to make them k. unto me,	11: 1
shall make k. the plain and precious	13:40
shall make k. to all kindreds,	13:40
shall be made k. in the records	13:41
the Lord did make them k. unto me.	14:29
maketh no such thing k. unto us.	15: 9
things shall be made k. unto you.	15:11
purposes are k. unto the Lord.	19: 3
all things made k. unto the prophets,	22: 2
the making k. of the covenants	22: 9
to make these things k. unto	2Ne 2: 8
this is k. in all the earth.	22: 5
of all nations shall be made k.;	30:16
made k. unto the children of men.	30:16
for you that ye had not k. me.	31:14
it maketh k. unto them of	33: 4
wherefore, ye make k. them before;	Jac 2:34
not since k. concerning them.	Om 1:30
after ye have k. and have been	Mos 2:36
are made k. unto me by an angel	3: 2
or if ye have k. of his goodness	4:11
if ye had k. me ye would not	7:13
and things which are not k. shall	8:17
shall be made k. by them,	8:17
things shall be made k. by them	8:17
which otherwise could not be k.	8:17
k. the commandments of God,	15:26
having made it k. to his people,	23: 1
they durst not lie, if it were k.,	Al 1:17
any wickedness if it were k.;	1:33
have k. the ways of righteousness	5:37
made k. unto me by the Holy	5:46
it has been made k. unto you,	7:20
had all things made k. unto them,	9:20
never have k. much of the ways of	10: 5
never had k. much of these things;	10: 5
angel hath made them k. unto me.	11:31
made k. unto us by his Spirit;	12: 3
made k. unto them the plan of	12:30
made k. unto them according to	12:30
made k. unto them the plan of	12:32
made k. unto us in plain terms,	13:23
made k. unto just and holy men,	13:26
made k. unto them concerning	18:39
Lord did he make k. unto them.	18:39
have made it k. unto me that thou	19: 4
and never having made it k.,	19:17
by making k. unto the people	19:17
making it k. unto the people.	19:17

thou make thyself k. unto me,	Al 22:18
made these things k. unto us	24:14
made these things k. unto us	24:14
might be made k. unto us as	24:14
they had never k. these things.	24:30
made k. unto them all these	27:25
such an one as never had been k.	28: 2
who never has been seen or k.,	30:28
hast made it k. unto us that	31:16
thou hast made it k. unto them	31:29
that he should make k. unto you	34: 3
should not have k. these things;	36: 5
made these things k. unto me,	36: 5
not yet fully made k. unto me;	37:11
which purpose is k. unto God;	37:12
darkness and made k. unto us.	37:26
shall ye make k. unto them;	37:29
maketh these things k. unto me;	38: 6
should not have k. these things.	38: 6
why these things should be k.	39:17
be made k. unto this people	39:18
made k. unto me by an angel,	40:11
the Lamanites been k. to fight	43:43
unto thee ye shall not make k.,	45: 9
unto thee shall not be made k.,	45: 9
would make it k. unto them	48:16
which never had been k. among	49: 8
that there were not any k. by	51:21
had made k. unto the queen	52:12
now ye have k. that these were	56: 3
never were men k. to have fought	56:56
make it k. unto all his people,	59: 2
k. unto God were all their cries,	60:10
Kishkumen was not k. among	He 1:12
Kishkumen made k. unto him the	2: 7
of Helaman had k. all the heart	2: 8
which at that time were not k.	3:23
should not be k. unto the world.	6:27
God has made them k. unto me,	7:29
and make k. unto us the true	9:17
made k. unto them beforehand,	16: 5
k. unto the children of men	3Ne 1:14
it was made k. unto them that	1:25
there never was k. so great a	4:11
an one as never had been k.	8: 5
such as never had been k. in	8: 7
shall be made k. unto them.	16: 7
be made k. unto the Gentiles	21: 2
shall be made k. unto them	21: 3
shall their works be k. unto men.	27:25
things must surely be made k.,	Mrm 5: 8
k. of God that wickedness will	5:12
make all things k. unto you.	8:12
Akish made k. unto them,	Eth 8:14
it hath been made k. unto me	8:20
an one as never had been k.	11: 7
I make not myself k. to the	Mro 1: 1
they erred it might be made k.;	DC 1:25
these things k. unto all flesh;	1:34
made k. unto future generations;	5: 5
Make not thy gift k. unto any	6:12
if you had k. this you could	9:10
all things k. unto the world	10:37
gospel should be made k. also,	10:49
which purpose is k. in me;	18: 8
a church where they are not k.,	20:84
Make k. thy calling unto the	23: 2
strength such as is not k.	24:12
be made k. what ye shall do.	26: 1
so great as you never have k.	39:10
a blessing such as is not k.	39:15
it is k. to the church that he	42:11
all these things shall be made k.;	45:60
will make k. unto you what I	52: 2
shall be made k. unto them	52: 4
made k. unto them the land	52: 5
should be made k. unto you,	53: 1
be made k. in a time to come,	53: 6
The residue shall be made k.	55: 6
shall be made k. by the Spirit	58:50
be made k. from time to time,	58:55
talent that it may not be k.	60:13
shall be made k. concerning	60:17
their works shall be made k.	97: 6

KNOWN / LABOR

KNOWN

as it shall be made k. to him	DC	104:36
Let thy habitation be k. in Zion,		112: 6
my name and have not k. me,		112:26
Thy days are k., and thy years		122: 9
of kingdoms will be made k.;		130:10
k. unto you all things in due time.		132:45
things might be k. among you,		133:36
thy name k. to thine adversaries,		133:42
the regions which are not k.,		133:46
name of which shall not be k.	Mses	1:42
never should have k. good and		5:11
they made all things k. unto		5:12
having k. their secret, began to		5:49
God hath made k. unto our		6:50
my name shall be k. in the	Abr	1:19
as they were made k. unto the		1:31
k. in what watch the thief would	JS	1:47
was it k. that I had them,		2:60

KNOWS

is not anything save he k. it.	2Ne	9:20
behold, he k. all thy thoughts,	Al	12: 3
Great Spirit, who k. all things?		18:18
he k. all the thoughts and		18:32
when this time cometh no one k.;		40: 4
of that which he k. and	DC	58:59
nor their torment, no man k.;		76:45
no man k. it except him to		76:90
as it is made k. unto them		61:22
make k. my will unto you,		63:22
I will make it k. unto you,		63:22
are made k. unto them,		64:17
be made k. unto my disciples,		64:19
and prophets shall be k.		64:39
make k. his wonderful works		65: 4
and his language you have k.,		67: 5
his imperfections you have k.;		67: 5
it shall be made k. unto you.		71: 2
made k. by the commandments		72: 7
making k. the duty of the bishop		72: 9
it shall be made k. unto them,		73: 2
be made k. from on high,		75:27
will I make k. unto them		76: 7
make k. unto them the secrets		76:10
and know as they are k.,		76:94
capable to make them k.,		76:116

KOKAUBEAM

K., which signifies stars, or all	Abr	3:13
Kolob is the greatest of all the K.		3:16

KOKOB

said unto me: K., which is star.	Abr	3:13

KOLOB

the name of the great one is K.,	Abr	3: 3
that K. was after the manner		3: 4
according to the reckoning of K.		3: 4
until thou come nigh unto K.,		3: 9
which K. is after the reckoning of		3: 9
K. is set nigh unto the throne of		3: 9
K. is the greatest of all the		3:16
which was after the time of K.;		5:13
K., signifying the first	Fac	2: 1
One day in K. is equal		2: 1
Stands next to K., called		2: 2
which is equal with K. in		2: 4
its light from K.		2: 5
from the revolutions of K.		2: 5

KORASH

and the god of K., and the god of	Abr	1: 6
Mahmackrah, K., and also a god		1:13
and the god of K., and the god of		1:17
Manmackrah, K., and Pharaoh.	Fac	1: 4
The idolatrous god of K.		1: 8

KORIHOR

Anti-Christ, whose name was K.,	Al	30:12
And K. said unto him:		30:23
And K. answered him, Yea.		30:36
And now K. said unto Alma:		30:43
Now K. said unto him:		30:48
K. was struck dumb, that he	Al	30:50
and wrote unto K., saying:		30:51
K. put forth his hand and wrote,		30:52
the curse was not taken off of K.;		30:56
of what had happened unto K.		30:57
had believed in the words of K.		30:57
of the wickedness of K.;		30:58
iniquity after the manner of K.		30:58
K. did go about from house to		30:58
that after the end of K.,		31: 1

KUMEN

Mathonihah, his brother, and K.,	3Ne	19: 4

KUMENONHI

Kumen, and K., and Jeremiah,	3Ne	19: 4

LABAN

behold, L. hath the record	1Ne	3: 3
go unto the house of L.,		3: 4
go in unto the house of L.		3:11
went in unto the house of L.,		3:11
he desired of L. the records		3:12
L. was angry, and thrust him out		3:13
told the things which L. had done,		3:14
again unto the house of L.		3:23
we went in unto L., and desired		3:24
when L. saw our property,		3:25
did flee before the servants of L.,		3:26
and it fell into the hands of L.		3:26
servants of L. did not overtake us,		3:27
will deliver L. into your hands.		3:29
will deliver L. into our hands?		3:31
then why not mightier than L.		4: 1
destroy L., even as the Egyptians.		4: 3
forth towards the house of L.		4: 5
came near unto the house of L.		4: 7
I found that it was L.		4: 8
Spirit that I should kill L.;		4:10
had delivered L. into my hands		4:17
took L. by the hair of the head,		4:18
I took the garments of L.		4:19
forth unto the treasury of L.		4:20
forth towards the treasury of L.,		4:20
the servant of L. who had the keys		4:20
commanded him in the voice of L.,		4:20
supposed me to be his master, L.,		4:21
he knowing that his master, L., had		4:22
unto him as if it had been L.		4:23
and that I was truly that L. whom		4:26
for they supposed it was L.,		4:28
servant of L. beheld my brethren		4:30
I did seize upon the servant of L.,		4:31
the servant of L., and departed		4:38
my sons out of the hands of L.		5: 5
them out of the hands of L.,		5: 8
L. also was a descendant of Joseph,		5:16
us out of the hands of L.,		7:11
thou art the servant of L.;	2Ne	1:30
Nephi, did take the sword of L.,		5:14
having wielded the sword of L.	Jac	1:10
own arm, with the sword of L.	WM	1:13
and also, the sword of L.,	Mos	1:16
breastplate, the sword of L.,	DC	17: 1

LABOR

desirous that they might not l.,	1Ne	17:18
the l. which they had to perform		17:41
neither should they withhold their l.		17:49
and to l. with their hands.	2Ne	5:17
your l. for that which cannot		9:51
For we l. diligently to write,		25:23
in Zion shall l. for Zion;		26:31
if they l. for money they shall		26:31
that ye are beginning to l. in sin,	Jac	2: 5
and we l. diligently to engraven		4: 3
that we may l. in the vineyard.		5:15
down into the vineyard to l.		5:16
we may l. again in the vineyard.		5:29
notwithstanding all our l.;		5:32
that we may l. diligently		5:61
let us go to and l. with our might		5:62
Go to, and l. in the vineyard,		5:71

LABOR

and if ye l. with your might	Jac	5:71
did go and l. with their mights;		5:72
the teachers, did l. diligently,	Jar	1:11
your king, do l. to serve you,	Mos	2:18
not ye to l. to serve one another?		2:18
thus did the people l. exceedingly		11: 6
Six days shalt thou l., and do all		13:17
should l. with their own hands		18:24
for their l. they were to receive the		18:26
and did l. exceedingly.		23: 5
should l. with their own hands		27: 5
ought not to l. with their hands,	Al	1: 3
when the priests left their l. to		1:26
they did all l., every man according		1:26
and also much l. in the spirit,		17: 5
that they might not l. for them		17:14
l. abundantly with their hands.		24:18
yea, all the day long did ye l.;		26: 5
to l. in the vineyards of the Lord;		28:14
as even one senine for my l.;		30:33
it profit us to l. in the church		30:34
that after much l. among them,		32: 2
there can be no l. performed.		34:33
a man who did l. exceedingly		48:12
did cause the Lamanites to l.		53: 4
to cause the Lamanites to l.,		53: 5
to guard them while at their l.;		53: 5
commence a l. in strengthening		55:25
did begin to l. exceedingly,		62:29
l. exceedingly all that night,	3Ne	19: 3
that they should l. continually	Eth	10: 6
whoso refused to l. he did cause		10: 6
that ye should l. diligently,	Mro	8: 6
hardness, let us l. diligently;		9: 6
for if we should cease to l.,		9: 6
for we have a l. to perform		9: 6
l. more than you have strength	DC	10: 4
l. all your days in crying		18:15
those who l. in my vineyard		21: 9
your l. shall be at your brother		30:10
your whole l. shall be in Zion,		30:11
with the l. of his hands,		38:40
called to l. in my vineyard,		39:13
Wherefore l. ye, labor ye in		43:28
l. ye in my vineyard for the		43:28
let them l. in the vineyard;		50:38
Let them l. with their families,		52:36
let them l. with their own		52:39
to your l. in my vineyard.		53: 6
not l. with your own hands!		56:17
to l. for the saints of God.		58:54
and l. with his own hands,		58:60
will l. while it is called today.		64:25
as they are appointed to l.,		68:30
l. ye in my vineyard.		71: 4
who l. in spiritual things,		72:14
but l. with your might.—		75: 3
and let him l. in the church.		75:28
and l. in his own calling,		84:109
Go ye and l. in the field,		88:52
tarry ye, and l. diligently,		88:84
l. in the vineyard of necessity		107:96
l. diligently to build a house		115:10
from that time forth l. diligently		115:12
in your l. in sending my word		124:16
If ye l. with all your might,		124:44
l. with his own hands that he		124:112
I have seen your l. and toil		126: 2
Eve, also, his wife, did l. with him.	Mses	5: 1
maintenance by his daily l.,	JS	2:23
by continuous l. were enabled		2:55

LABORED

Then I said, I have l. in vain,	1Ne	21: 4
Wherefore we l. diligently	Jac	1: 7
and having l. in all his days		1:10
the Lord of the vineyard l. also		5:72
And thus they l., with all		5:74
are they who have l. diligently		6: 3
And he l. diligently that he might		7: 3
prayed and l. with all diligence,	En	1:12
have l. with mine own hands	Mos	2:14

have l. with all the power and	Mos	29:14
the disadvantages they l. under,		29:35
Alma l. much in the spirit,	Al	8:10
the time which they l. to judge		11: 1
Behold, they have l. exceedingly,		29:15
for behold I have l. even from		30:32
have l. abundantly to build		32: 5
I have l. without ceasing, that		36:24
had l. with so much diligence		51:14

LABORER

not suffer the l. in Zion to perish.	2Ne	26:30
But the l. in Zion shall labor		26:31
receive the reward of the l.	DC	23: 7
the l. is worthy of his hire.		31: 5
wear the garments of the l.		42:42
steward and as a faithful l.;		72:17
the l. is worthy of his hire.		84:79
for the l. is worthy of his hire.		106: 3

LABORERS

did Alma and his fellow l. do	Mos	26:38
my fellow l. who are with me—	Al	31:32
shall call l. into my vineyard.	DC	33: 3
faithful l. into my vineyard,		39:17
first l. in this last kingdom.		88:70
first l. in this last kingdom,		88:74

LABORING

by l. with our might	Jac	1:19
ye have been diligent in l. with me		5:75
by l. with all the might of	WM	1:18
l. with their own hands for their	Mos	27: 4
commence l. in digging a ditch	Al	53: 3
I am l. with them continually;	Mro	9: 4
while he is l. in my vineyard,	DC	104:20
l. under the extreme difficulties	JS	2:11
who was l. along with me,		2:48
of l. with our hands,		2:55

LABORS

the l., and the pains of the Jews,	2Ne	29: 4
But our l. were vain;	En	1:20
from the l. of their journey;	Mos	7:16
with the l. of our hands;		9:12
left their l. to hear the word	Al	1:26
again diligently unto their l.;		1:26
the l. which he had performed.		8: 1
forth and see the fruits of our l.;		26:31
those who are the fruit of their l.		29:17
with the l. of their hands,		30:27
glutting on the l. of the people.		30:31
upon the l. of this people;		30:32
l. which I have performed		30:33
for our l. in the church,		30:34
for men to perform their l.		34:32
great joy in the fruit of my l.;		36:25
partake of the fruits of their l.		40:26
was caused by the l. and heat		51:33
while they should perform their l.		53: 1
the Lamanites had, by their l.,		55:33
they might have, with their l.,	3Ne	6: 3
have joy in the fruit of your l.	DC	6:31
in temporal l. thou shalt not		24: 9
performing your l. on the land,		26: 1
in the l. of the church;		41: 9
shall rest from all their l.,		59: 2
unto you to rest from your l.,		59:10
their l. even now are wanted		61:32
also shall remember their l.,		68:30
And the l. of the faithful who		72:14
or churches, in which he l.,		72:19
rest from all their l. here,		124:86
wages for all their l. which they		124:121
l. shall be accounted unto them		124:122
the necessary l. of the day;	JS	2:48

LACHONEUS

that L. was the chief judge	3Ne	1: 1
L., the governor of the land,		3: 1
L., most noble and chief governor		3: 2
a pity unto me, most noble L.,		3: 3

LACHONEUS 518 LAMAN

write this epistle unto you, L.,	3Ne	3:10
when L. received this epistle		3:11
L., the governor, was a just man,		3:12
the words and prophecies of L.		3:16
according to the words of L.		3:16
L. did appoint chief captains		3:17
proclamation of L. had gone		3:22
L. did cause that they should		3:24
which had been spoken by L.,		3:25
Gidgiddoni, and the judge, L.,		6: 6
now it was in the days of L.,		6:19
of Lachoneus, the son of L.,		6:19
L. did fill the seat of his father		6:19

LACK
If any of you l. wisdom,	JS	2:11

LACKED
to them that l. wisdom,	JS	2:13
a man who l. wisdom might		2:26

LACKETH
he that l. wisdom, let him	DC	42:68

LACKING
knew that ye were l. in judgment;	1Ne	17:19

LAD
favor in thy sight, and am but a l.,	Mses	6:31

LADDERS
cords and l., to be let down	Al	62:21
their strong cords and their l.;		62:23

LADEN
l. with tasks, which were grievous	1Ne	17:25
that ye should not be l. with taxes,	Mos	2:14
you shall be l. with sheaves	DC	31: 5
you shall be l. with sheaves		33: 9
shall be l. with many sheaves,		75: 5

LADY
and thou art an elect l.,	DC	25: 3

LAID
l. the foundation of the earth,	1Ne	20:13
and l. the foundations of the earth,	2Ne	8:13
hast l. thy body as the ground		8:23
flesh must have l. down to rot		9: 7
And he l. it upon my mouth,		16: 7
he hath l. up his carriages.		20:28
Since thou art l. down no feller		24: 8
after he is l. in a sepulchre		25:13
shall have l. siege against them		26:15
and I have l. up unto myself	Jac	5:31
to have l. up fruit thereof against		5:46
which hath been l. for you?		6: 8
he l. a tax of one fifth part	Mos	11: 3
hath l. on him the iniquities of		14: 6
they l. and watched them;		20: 4
l. wait for them in the fields		20: 8
therefore they l. wait for them.		21:21
burdens which were l. upon Alma		24:15
Alma l. the case before their king,		27: 1
until he was l. before his father.		27:19
they were l. before the judges.	Al	2: 6
Behold, the ax is l. at the root		5:52
is beginning to be l. by the		10:27
which he has l. to catch this		12: 6
are l. under a strict command		12: 9
was l. from the foundation of		12:25
was a plan of redemption l.,		12:25
plan of redemption which was l.)		12:33
and l. before him the records and		18:36
his wife, and l. him upon a bed;		18:43
for he has been l. upon his bed		19: 5
they that l. down the weapons of		23:13
of these have l. down their lives,		26:34
are l. low in the earth,		28:11
are l. down by ancient priests,		30:23
scriptures are l. before thee,		30:44
l. it upon the point of his sword,		44:13
he l. the plan in his heart to		47: 4
lest there was a plan l. to lead		58:24

of those plans which had been l.	He	2: 6
that they l. hold on them,		9: 9
doctrine which had been l. down		11:22
shall be many mountains l. low,		14:23
of destruction which they had l.	3Ne	1:16
which they had l. up in store.		4:18
such I have l. down my life,		9:22
records, and l. them before him,		23: 8
as was l. before mine eyes;	Mrm	5: 8
the Father hath l. up for you,	Eth	4:14
as he l. his hands upon them—	Mro	2: 1
as many as they l. their hands,		2: 3
they l. their hands upon them,		3: 2
thus he has l. a cunning plan,	DC	10:23
body which was l. down for you,		27: 2
a great work l. up in store,		38:33
shall be l. before the bishop of		42:31
they are l. before the bishop of		42:32
l. the foundation of the earth,		45: 1
shall be l. low of power.		49:10
l. my hands upon the nations,		84:96
ax is l. at the root of the trees;		97: 7
sell the lots that are l. off for		104:36
the lot which is l. off for the		104:43
which I have l. before you,		104:86
l. before him according to the		107:72
l. the burden of all the churches		112:18
on whom there is l. much power.		113: 4
no man l. hands on him;	Mses	6:39
he l. it, an host of men hath he		6:44
and was l. under the water,		6:64
the priests l. violence upon me,	Abr	1:12
were l. two stones crossways	JS	2:52
having l. his hands upon us,		2:68
I l. my hands upon his head		2:71
he l. his hands on me and		2:71
l. open to our understandings,		2:74

LAISH
cause it to be heard unto L.,	2Ne	20:30

LAKE
as a l. of fire and brimstone,	2Ne	9:16
that l. of fire and brimstone,		9:19
the l. of fire and brimstone,		9:26
even a l. of fire and brimstone,		28:23
into that l. of fire and brimstone	Jac	3:11
into that l. of fire and brimstone,		6:10
which l. of fire and brimstone is		6:10
is as a l. of fire and brimstone,	Mos	3:27
be as a l. of fire and brimstone,	Al	12:17
into a l. of fire and brimstone?		14:14
that l. which burneth with fire	DC	63:17
go away into the l. of fire and		76:36
purposes, from Salt L. City,		OD
in Salt L. City, in the Spring		OD
Salt L. City, Utah, October 6,		OD

LAMAH
And L. had fallen with his	Mrm	6:14

LAMAN
L., Lemuel, Sam, and Nephi.	1Ne	1:hd
who were L., Lemuel and Sam.		2: 5
called the name of the river, L.,		2: 8
he spake unto L., saying:		2: 9
the stiffneckedness of L. and Lemuel;		2:11
L. and Lemuel, being the eldest,		2:12
L. and Lemuel would not hearken		2:18
the lot fell upon L.;		3:11
L. went in unto the house of		3:11
L. fled out of his presence,		3:14
L. was angry with me,		3:28
hearkened unto the words of L.		3:28
L. and Lemuel did speak many		3:28
L. and Lemuel again began to murmur,		3:31
when L. saw me he was exceedingly		4:28
L. and Lemuel, and two of the		7: 6
unto L. and unto Lemuel:		7: 8
behold, L. and Lemuel, I fear		8: 4
desirous that L. and Lemuel should		8:17
L. and Lemuel partook not of the		8:35
exceedingly feared for L. and Lemuel;		8:36
wilderness, across the river L.		16:12
L. and Lemuel and the sons of		16:20

LAMAN   519   LAMANITES

L. said unto Lemuel and also	1Ne 16:37	pay tribute to the king of the L.	Mos	7:15
L. stir up their hearts to anger.	16:38	pay tribute to the king of the L.,		7:22
L. and Lemuel did take me and	18:11	king of the L. doth exact of us,		7:22
now my son, L., and also Lemuel	2Ne 1:28	out of the hands of the L.		9:hd
he called the children of L.,	4: 3	been sent as a spy among the L.		9: 1
to the sons and daughters of L.,	4: 8	a numerous host of L. came		9:14
unto the sons and daughters of L.;	4: 9	forth against the L. to battle.		9:16
L. and Lemuel and the sons of	4:13	forth to battle against the L.;		9:17
cunning and craftiness of king L.,	Mos 7:21	we did go forth against the L.,		9:18
and the craftiness of king L.,	9:10	against the time the L. should		10: 1
king L. began to grow uneasy,	9:11	that the L. might not come upon		10: 2
king L. began to stir up his people	9:13	to go to battle against the L.,		10: 9
king L. died, and his son began	10: 6	go up to battle against the L.;		10:10
king L., by his cunning, and lying	10:18	go up to battle against the L.		10:10
king of the Lamanites was L.,	24: 3	the L. knew nothing concerning		10:11
therefore he was called king L.	24: 3	unto my people concerning the L.,		10:19
for he was subject to king L.,	24: 9	which was possessed by the L.;		11:12
upon them, yea, upon L. and	Al 3: 7	the L. began to come in upon		11:16
the rebellions of L. and Lemuel,	18:38	the L. came upon them and		11:17
descendants of L. and Lemuel.	24:29	thus the L. began to destroy them,		11:17
L. and Lemuel, and the sons of	43:13	stand against thousands of the L.;		11:19
who was a descendant of L.	55: 4	the army of the L. were within the		19: 6
found one, whose name was L.;	55: 5	spare me, for the L. are upon us,		19: 7
that L. and a small number of	55: 6	they should flee before the L.,		19: 9
therefore Moroni appointed L.	55: 7	the L. did pursue them,		19:10
L. went to the guards who were	55: 8	and flee before the L.		19:11
But L. said unto them:	55:10	stand forth and plead with the L.		19:13
And L. said unto them:	55:12	the L. had compassion on them,		19:14
when L. and his men saw that	55:15	the L. did spare their lives,		19:15
these were descendants of L.,	56: 3	Moah into the hands of the L.,		19:15
And behold, the city of L.,	3Ne 9:10	pay tribute to the king of the L.		19:15
		the L. had granted unto them		19:22
LAMANITE		by paying a tribute to the L.		19:22
the support of the L. prisoners	Al 54: 2	the king of the L. made an oath		19:25
behold now, I am a bold L.;	54:24	made oath unto the king of the L.		19:26
Fear not; behold, I am a L.	55: 8	the king of the L. set guards		19:28
given to some of the L. prisoners.	55:31	that the L. did not molest them		19:29
if their wine would poison a L.	55:32	where the daughters of the L. did		20: 1
Samuel, a L., prophesies	He 7:hd	discovered the daughters of the L.,		20: 4
prophecy of Samuel, the L.,	13:hd	of the daughters of the L.		20: 5
one Samuel, a L., came into the	13: 2	when the L. found that their		20: 6
I, Samuel, a L., do speak the	13: 5	when the L. had come up,		20: 9
Samuel, the L. did prophesy	14: 1	to drive the L. before them;		20:11
because I am a L., and have	14:10	not half so numerous as the L.		20:11
the words of Samuel, the L.,	16: 1	they found the king of the L.		20:12
were spoken by Samuel, the L.	3Ne 1: 5	here is the king of the L.;		20:13
by the prophet Samuel, the L.	8: 3	stolen the daughters of the L.?		20:18
my servant Samuel, the L., that	23: 9	without arms to meet the L.		20:25
Abinadi, and also Samuel the L.	Mrm 1:19	that they did meet the L.;		20:25
		the king of the L. did bow		20:25
LAMANITES		when the L. saw the people of		20:26
and also of the L.—	T Pg	the L. began again to be stirred		21: 2
Written to the L., who are a	T Pg	for the L. had surrounded them		21: 5
the people who were now called L.	2Ne 5:14	and went forth against the L.		21: 7
the people which were not L.	Jac 1:13	that the L. did beat them,		21: 8
Zoramites, L., Lemuelites,	1:13	a great fear of the L. had come		21:10
but I shall call them L. that	1:14	of Limhi to anger against the L.;		21:11
greater iniquities than the L.,	2:35	to soften the hearts of the L.		21:15
and the L., which are not filthy	3: 3	fall into the hands of the L.		21:19
Behold, the L. your brethren,	3: 5	had stolen the daughters of the L.,		21:20
to reclaim and restore the L.	7:24	disturbance between the L. and		21:22
for my brethren, the L.	En 1:11	out of the hands of the L.		21:36
the L. should not be destroyed,	1:13	for the L. being so numerous,		22: 2
at some future day unto the L.,	1:13	with our brethren, the L.		22: 3
bring them forth unto the L.	1:16	The L., or the guards of		22: 6
diligently to restore the L. unto	1:20	or the guards of the L.,		22: 6
wars between the Nephites and L.	1:24	the last tribute of wine to the L.,		22: 7
benefit of our brethren the L.	Jar 1: 2	the tribute of wine to the L.;		22:10
and the L. also.	1: 6	when the L. had found that the		22:15
wherefore, we withstood the L.	1: 7	an army of the L. was in the		23:25
being prepared to meet the L.,	1: 9	of the appearance of the L.		23:26
the hands of their enemies, the L.	Om 1: 2	soften the hearts of the L.,		23:28
people, the Nephites, and the L.;	1:10	did soften the hearts of the L.		23:29
taken the lives of many of the L.	1:10	the L. took possession of the		23:29
between the Nephites and the L.	1:24	Now the armies of the L., which		23:30
the armies of the L. came down	WM 1:13	that Amulon did plead with the L.;		23:33
slain many thousands of the L.	1:14	were the daughters of the L.,		23:33
they did contend against the L.	1:14	the L. had compassion on Amulon		23:34
dissensions away unto the L.,	1:16	and his brethren did join the L.		23:35
like unto our brethren, the L.,	Mos 1: 5	the L. promised unto Alma and		23:36
fallen into the hands of the L.,	1:14	the L. would not keep their		23:37
we are in bondage to the L.,	7:15	the king of the L. had granted		23:39
or out of the hands of the L.,	7:15	to the will of the king of the L.		23:39

LAMANITES

in the eyes of the king of the L.;	Mos 24: 1
the king of the L. granted unto	24: 1
the L. had taken possession of	24: 2
king of the L. had appointed	24: 2
the king of the L. was Laman,	24: 3
among all the people of the L.	24: 4
the L. began to increase in	24: 7
a deep sleep to come upon the L.,	24:19
for the L. have awakened and	24:23
I will stop the L. in this valley	24:23
as there were of the L.;	25: 3
who had been slain by the L.	25: 9
out of the hands of the L.	25:10
when they thought upon the L.,	25:11
to wife the daughters of the L.,	25:12
of God to their brethren, the L.—	28: 1
let his sons go up among the L.	28: 6
thy sons out of the hands of the L.	28: 7
to preach the word among the L.;	28: 9
between the Nephites and the L.,	Al 1:hd
saw a numerous host of the L.;	2:24
the L. and the Amlicites, being	2:27
the L. and the Amlicites did fall	2:28
with the king of the L.;	2:32
but the king of the L. fled back	2:32
the guards of the king of the L.	2:33
of the L. who had been slain	2:34
to cross and contend with the L.	2:34
the L. and the Amlicites began to	2:35
the L. and the Amlicites who had	3: 3
after the manner of the L.;	3: 4
their heads like unto the L.	3: 4
heads of the L. were shorn;	3: 5
the skins of the L. were dark,	3: 6
his seed with that of the L.	3: 9
himself to be led away by the L.	3:10
believe in the tradition of the L.,	3:11
and also of the people of the L.	3:12
Behold, the L. have I cursed,	3:14
by the L. and the Amlicites,	3:20
another army of the L. came in	3:20
battle at this time against the L.;	3:22
went up and slew many of the L.,	3:23
foot and destroyed by the L.	4: 2
bondage by the hands of the L.	5: 5
that inasmuch as the L. have not	9:14
the L. have been cut off from his	9:14
which are extended to the L.;	9:16
for the L. shall be sent upon you;	9:18
L. might destroy all his people	9:19
far more tolerable for the L. than	9:23
of the Lord are extended to the L.,	9:24
the armies of the L. had come in	16: 2
had been taken captive by the L.	16: 5
the L. will cross the river Sidon	16: 6
have been taken captive by the L.	16: 6
came upon the armies of the L.,	16: 8
the L. were scattered and driven	16: 8
had been taken captive by the L.,	16: 8
the L. having been driven out of	16: 9
the L. did not come again to war	16:12
of Nephi to preach to the L.;	17:hd
of fourteen years among the L.,	17: 4
the word of God unto the L.	17: 8
their brethren, the L.,	17: 9
Go forth among the L.,	17:11
courage to go forth unto the L.	17:12
borders of the land of the L.,	17:13
of Ishmael, who also became L.	17:19
the L. took him and bound him,	17:20
to dwell in the land among the L.,	17:22
according to the custom of the L.	17:25
the L. drive their flocks hither,	17:26
a certain number of the L., who	17:27
it was the practice of the L. to	18: 7
after the manner of the L.,	18:43
to his prayers upon the L.,	19:14
so many of their brethren, the L.	19:27
did commence among the L.;	19:36
and their brethren, to the L.	21:hd
the borders of the land of the L.,	21: 1
called by the L., Jerusalem,	21: 1
the L. and the Amalekites and the	21: 2
Now the L. of themselves were	Al 21: 3
cause the L. that they should	21: 3
or in every assembly of the L.	21:16
the L. and the Nephites divided.	22:27
the more idle part of the L.	22:28
there were many L. on the east	22:29
were nearly surrounded by the L.;	22:29
hemmed in the L. on the south,	22:33
L. could have no more possessions	22:34
the L. were an enemy to them,	22:34
the king of the L. sent a	23: 1
among the L., to preach and to	23: 4
as many of the L. as believed in	23: 6
The people of the L. who were	23: 9
the people of the L. who were	23:10
the people of the L. who were	23:11
the people of the L. who were	23:12
the names of the cities of the L.	23:13
of war; and they were all L.	23:13
and also the hearts of the L.	23:14
named all the cities of the L.	23:15
and were no more called L.	23:17
and the Amulonites and the L.	24: 1
the L. began to make preparations	24: 4
saw the preparations of the L.	24: 5
defend themselves against the L.	24: 5
these L. were brought to believe	24:19
the L., made preparations for war,	24:20
the L. began to fall upon them,	24:21
the L. saw that their brethren	24:23
when the L. saw this they did	24:24
number of those of the L. who	24:28
those L. were more angry because	25: 1
among the L. who were slain	25: 4
power and authority over the L.,	25: 5
many of the L. should perish	25: 5
L. began to hunt the seed of	25: 8
hunted at this day by the L.	25: 9
for they were driven by the L.,	25:12
when the L. saw that they could	25:13
they had had among the L.,	25:17
brethren, the L., were in darkness,	26: 3
unto our brethren, the L.,	26:23
L. to the knowledge of the truth?	26:24
ye can convince the L. of the	26:24
Go amongst thy brethren, the L.,	26:27
those L. who had gone to war	27: 1
who do stir up the L. to anger	27:12
among their brethren, the L.	27:20
the armies of the L. had followed	28: 1
thousands of the L. were slain	28: 2
the L. were driven and scattered,	28: 3
between the Nephites and the L.;	28: 9
after the L. were driven out of	30: 1
who were once the people of the L.	30:19
wilderness was full of the L.	31: 3
into a correspondence with the L.,	31: 4
they began to mix with the L.	35:10
L. began to make preparations	35:11
with the armies of the L.	35:13
betwixt the L. and the Nephites,	35:13
so many thousands of the L. of	37: 9
of many thousands of the L.	37:19
among the borders of the L.,	39: 3
between the Nephites and the L.,	43: 3
that the Zoramites became L.;	43: 4
the L. were coming upon them;	43: 4
the L. came with their thousands;	43: 5
disposition than the L. were,	43: 6
chief captains over the L.,	43: 6
stir up the L. to anger against	43: 8
fall into the hands of the L.,	43:10
the L. would destroy.	43:10
the extreme hatred of the L.	43:11
fall into the hands of the L.	43:11
alone, to withstand against the L.,	43:13
armies of the L. had gathered	43:15
he met the L. in the borders	43:18
when the armies of the L. saw	43:19
defend themselves against the L.	43:23
armies of the L. were marching	43:24
the L. should come into that land	43:25
to battle against the L.,	43:26

LAMANITES — 521 — LAMANITES

the time of the coming of the L.	Al 43:26
camp of the L. should come.	43:28
knew the intention of the L.,	43:29
which course the L. were to take.	43:30
the L. came up on the north of	43:34
as the L. had passed the hill riplah	43:35
and encircled the L. about on	43:35
L., when they saw the Nephites,	43:36
dreadful on the part of the L.,	43:37
from the strokes of the L.,	43:38
the work of death among the L.	43:38
the L. became frightened,	43:39
Moroni and his army met the L.	43:41
the L. did flee again before them,	43:42
the L. did fight exceedingly;	43:43
never had the L. been known	43:43
thus the L. did smite in their	43:44
Nephites contending with the L.,	43:47
and the anger of the L.,	43:48
that they turned upon the L.,	43:49
against the L. with power;	43:50
the L. began to flee before them;	43:50
the L. were more numerous,	43:51
of the stubbornness of the L.;	44:17
the L. did contend with their	44:17
the weapons of war from the L.;	44:20
on the Nephites and on the L.	44:21
be numbered among the L.,	45:14
and them shall the L. pursue	45:14
of their wars with the L.	45:21
which they had had over the L.,	46: 7
L. should have any more	46:30
would stir up the L. to anger	46:30
land of Nephi among the L.,	47: 1
and did stir up the L. to anger	47: 1
that the king of the L. sent a	47: 1
to dethrone the king of the L.	47: 4
command of those parts of the L.	47: 5
for thither had all the L. fled;	47: 5
favor with the armies of the L.,	47: 8
was the custom among the L.,	47:17
the L. appointed Amalickiah to	47:19
as was the custom with the L.,	47:23
among all the people of the L.,	47:35
who were composed of the L.,	47:35
and ferocious than the L.—	47:36
in with the traditions of the L.;	47:36
to inspire the hearts of the L.	48: 1
appoint men to speak unto the L.	48: 1
been made king over the L.,	48: 2
the Nephites as well as the L.	48: 2
hardened the hearts of the L.	48: 3
with their brethren, the L.,	48:21
space of many years with the L.,	48:22
to take up arms against the L.,	48:23
destroy them by joining the L.	48:24
the armies of the L. were seen	49: 1
arrows and the stones of the L.;	49: 2
the L. had destroyed it once	49: 3
the L. could not cast their stones	49: 4
the chief captains of the L. were	49: 5
leaders of the L. had supposed,	49: 6
they were prepared for the L.,	49: 8
the L. or the Amalickiahites,	49: 9
he would have caused the L. to	49:10
the L. were disappointed in their	49:11
fought with the L. in the valley	49:16
when the L. had found that Lehi	49:17
the L. could not get into their	49:18
themselves against the L.	49:20
the captains of the L. brought	49:21
the L. did attempt to destroy	49:23
thousand of the L. were slain;	49:23
exposed to the arrows of the L.	49:24
when the L. saw that their	49:25
his people against the L.;	50: 1
stones and the arrows of the L.	50: 4
all the L. who were in the east	50: 7
Moroni had driven all the L. out	50: 7
off all the strongholds of the L.	50:11
between the Nephites and the L.,	50:11
strength and the power of the L.	50:12
line of the possessions of the L.	Al 50:13
unbelief, and mingle with the L.	50:22
the hearts of the people of the L.	51: 9
down, at the head of the L.	51:12
that the L. were coming down	51:13
that the L. were coming into	51:14
prepare for war against the L.,	51:22
the L. had come into the land	51:22
to receive the L. to battle.	51:24
not suffer the L. to go against	51:25
thus had the L. obtained,	51:27
afforded strongholds for the L.	51:27
exceed the L. in their strength	51:31
did gain advantage over the L.	51:31
lest the L. had awakened and	51:36
when the L. awoke on the first	52: 1
when the L. saw this they	52: 2
that the L. were determined to	52: 5
the L. had taken many prisoners,	52: 8
retain all the prisoners of the L.	52: 8
those whom the L. had taken.	52: 8
lest the L. should obtain that	52: 9
opportunity to scourge the L.	52:10
fallen into the hands of the L.	52:10
the L. are upon us in the borders	52:11
with his army against the L.;	52:17
to cause the L. to come out	52:19
embassies to the army of the L.,	52:20
he might decoy the L. out of	52:21
when the guards of the L. had	52:22
the armies of the L. did march	52:23
armies of the L. coming out	52:23
when the L. saw that he began	52:24
was thus leading away the L.	52:24
meet the L. when they should	52:26
the L. did pursue Teancum	52:27
the chief captains of the L. had	52:28
the L. did not know that Moroni	52:29
before the L. had retreated	52:31
the L. were wearied because of	52:31
he led the L. forth to battle	52:33
did not give way before the L.	52:34
the L. in the rear delivered up	52:36
when the L. had heard these	52:38
over the prisoners of the L.,	53: 1
after the L. had finished burying	53: 3
they did cause the L. to labor	53: 4
did guard the prisoners of the L.;	53: 5
to cause the L. to labor,	53: 5
make an attack upon the L.	53: 5
greatest of the armies of the L.,	53: 6
of the strongest holds of the L.	53: 6
attempt a battle with the L. in	53: 7
to guard against the L.,	53: 7
the armies of the L., on the west	53: 8
who in the beginning, were L.;	53:10
the L. had taken many women	54: 3
of the Nephites from the L.	54: 3
Ammoron, the king of the L.;	54:16
place where the L. do guard my	55: 3
when the L. heard these words	55: 9
the L. were in a deep sleep	55:16
But had they awakened the L.,	55:18
he would not fall upon the L.	55:19
surround the armies of the L.	55:21
when the L. awoke in the	55:22
that he did cause the L.,	55:25
all the intrigues of the L.,	55:27
Many times did the L. attempt	55:29
the L. had, by their labors,	55:33
army had been reduced by the L.	56:10
the L. had also retained many	56:12
the L. have obtained possession	56:13
when the L. saw that Antipus	56:18
desirous that the L. should come	56:21
watch the movements of the L.,	56:22
the L., thus seeing our forces	56:29
the L. began to grow uneasy	56:30
the strongest army of the L.;	56:34
the most powerful army of the L.;	56:36
the L. were pursuing us.	56:39
we saw the L. upon us,	56:41

LAMANITES

these L. who had pursued us.	Al	56:49
to fall into the hands of the L.;		56:50
began to give way before the L.		56:51
that the L. took courage,		56:52
thus were the L. pursuing them		56:52
the whole army of the L. halted		56:52
the L. had turned them about,		56:53
again upon the rear of the L.		56:53
thousand, did surround the L.,		56:54
power did they fall upon the L.,		56:56
did the L. deliver themselves up		56:56
from the armies of the L.,		56:57
the L. could not come upon us		57: 9
And we, instead of being L.,		57:10
the L. being cut off from		57:11
the L. began to lose all hopes of		57:12
which we had taken from the L.		57:15
the L. were upon us, and they		57:17
they were firm before the L.,		57:19
about to give way before the L.,		57:20
was they who did beat the L.;		57:22
that after the L. had fled,		57:24
and also the dead of the L.,		57:28
out to watch the camp of the L.		57:30
the armies of the L. are		57:31
the L. were also receiving great		58: 5
the L. were sallying forth against		58: 6
with all our might against the L.,		58:13
when the L. saw that we were		58:14
the L. should come out to battle.		58:17
the L. did come out with their		58:18
the L. did follow after us with		58:19
were not discovered by the L.		58:19
when the L. had passed by,		58:20
did cut off the spies of the L.		58:20
the L. did suffer their whole		58:22
when the L. saw that they were		58:24
the chief captains of the L. had		58:25
morrow we were beyond the L.,		58:27
the armies of the L. did arrive		58:29
the armies of the L. did flee out		58:30
which had been taken by the L.,		58:31
and carried off by the L.		58:31
the L. have fled to the land of		58:38
that which the L. have taken		58:41
cities which the L. had taken		59: 4
to go against the L. to battle,		59: 5
were attacked by the L.		59: 5
come over and joined the L.		59: 6
falling into the hands of the L.		59: 9
the success of the L. over them.		59:12
and send forth against the L.,		60: 2
the L. are coming upon us,		60:17
we contend no more with the L.		60:24
out in judgment against the L.,		60:32
written unto the king of the L.,		61: 8
enable the L. to conquer the		61: 8
shall be conquered under the L.		61: 8
not shed the blood of the L. if		61:10
fortify the land against the L.		62:13
to overthrow the L. in that		62:14
a large body of men of the L.,		62:15
the L. should come out to battle		62:19
the L., knowing of their exceeding		62:19
the L. did camp with their army.		62:20
where the L. did not camp		62:22
when the L. awoke and saw		62:24
many of the L. who were slain.		62:26
many of the L. that were		62:27
all the prisoners of the L. did		62:29
from all the prisoners of the L.		62:29
reduce the armies of the L.		62:30
when the L. saw that Moroni		62:31
the L. fled from Lehi and		62:32
the armies of the L. were all		62:33
Ammoron, the king of the L.,		62:33
the L. were encircled about		62:34
the L. also were weary because		62:35
war between them and the L.,		62:35
go forth into the camp of the L.,		62:36
and came upon the L.,		62:38
between the Nephites and the L.		62:41
were most exposed to the L.,		62:42
had gone forth unto the L.;	Al	63:14
of the L. are converted.	He	1:hd
the righteousness of the L.,		1:hd
L. had gathered together an		1:14
Therefore, the king of the L., whose		1:16
that the L. durst not come into		1:18
that the L. durst not come into		1:26
L. were not frightened according		1:27
the L. could not retreat either way,		1:31
plunged the L. into the midst of		1:32
the L. did yield themselves into		1:32
L. who had been taken prisoners		1:33
between the Nephites and the L.,		2: 1
of Ammon, who were L. by birth,		3:12
the account of the L. and of		3:14
mixed with the L. until they are		3:16
ferocious, yea, even becoming L.		3:16
did go unto the king of the L.		4: 2
to stir up the L. to war against		4: 3
the L. were exceedingly afraid,		4: 3
from the Nephites unto the L.;		4: 4
they did fortify against the L.,		4: 7
help of a numerous army of the L.,		4: 8
fallen into the hands of the L.		4: 9
land of Nephi, among the L.—		4:12
smitten, and driven before the L.,		4:13
no more possessions over the L.		4:18
so numerous were the L. that		4:19
greatness of the number of the L.		4:20
wicked even like unto the L.		4:22
like unto their brethren, the L.,		4:24
and they saw that the L. were		4:25
saw that the strength of the L.		4:26
of Zarahemla, among the L.		5:16
and Lehi did preach unto the L.		5:18
the great astonishment of the L.,		5:19
eight thousand of the L. who were		5:19
taken by an army of the L.		5:21
L. durst not lay their hands		5:25
that were in the prison were L.		5:27
the L. could not flee because of		5:34
that the L. said unto him:		5:40
part of the L. were convinced		5:50
the L. had become, the more part		6: 1
of the conversion of the L.,		6: 3
many of the L. did come down		6: 4
many of the L. did go into		6: 6
among the Nephites or the L.		6: 7
the L. did also go whithersoever		6: 8
whether it were among the L. or		6: 8
rich, both the L. and the Nephites;		6: 9
the more wicked part of the L.		6:18
when the L. found that there were		6:20
L. began to grow exceedingly in		6:34
pour out his Spirit upon the L.,		6:36
L. did hunt the band of robbers		6:37
destroyed from among the L.		6:37
better for the L. than for you		7:23
even among the L. as well as		11: 6
both the Nephites and the L., did		11:21
before gone over unto the L.,		11:24
themselves the name of L.,		11:24
were real descendants of the L.,		11:24
also among the people of the L.		11:27
the Nephites and also of the L.;		11:32
the L. did observe strictly to keep		13: 1
the L. hath he hated because their		15: 4
the L., again to the knowledge of		15:11
extended to our brethren, the L.;		15:12
the Nephites and also of the L.,		16:15
of much sorrow among the L.;	3Ne	1:29
thus were the L. afflicted also,		1:30
both the Nephites and the L.,		2:11
the L. who had become converted		2:12
those L. who had united with		2:14
of the Nephites and of the L.,		3:14
who were desirous to remain L.,		6: 3
it were among a few of the L.		6:14
the Holy Ghost, even as the L.,		9:20
those who had been called L.,		10:18
both Nephites and L.,	4Ne	1: 2
neither were there L., nor any		1:17
taken upon them the name of L.;		1:20

LAMANITES   LAMB

there began to be L. again in	4Ne	1:20
those who were called by the L.—		1:36
rejected the gospel were called L.,		1:38
as the L. were taught to hate		1:39
like unto their brethren, the L.		1:43
the people of Nephi and the L.		1:45
between the Nephites, and the L.	Mrm	1: 8
the L. and the Lemuelites and		1: 9
the Ishmaelites were called L.,		1: 9
parties were Nephites and L.		1: 9
the Nephites did beat the L.		1:11
the L. withdrew their design,		1:12
robbers, who were among the L.,		1:18
between the Nephites and the L.		2: 1
Nephites, against the L.;		2: 2
the L. did come upon us with		2: 3
defend ourselves against the L.		2: 4
the L. did come upon us and		2: 4
filled with robbers and with L.;		2: 8
and also on the part of the L.;		2: 8
And now, the L. had a king,		2: 9
did begin to flee before the L.;		2:16
stand boldly before the L.		2:23
did not flee from before the L.,		2:24
we did go forth against the L.		2:27
we made a treaty with the L.		2:28
the L. did give unto us the land		2:29
give unto the L. all the land		2:29
the L. did not come to battle		3: 1
king of the L. sent an epistle		3: 4
might stop the armies of the L.,		3: 6
the L. did come down to the		3: 7
armies to battle against the L.,		4: 1
a fresh army of the L. did		4: 2
the L. did take possession of		4: 2
Nephites went up unto the L.		4: 4
L. could have had no power		4: 4
the L. did make preparations		4: 6
the L. did come against the		4: 7
saw that they had driven the L.		4: 8
both the Nephites and the L.		4: 9
the L. came again upon the		4:10
of the Nephites and of the L.;		4:11
the L. did take possession		4:13
the L. had sacrificed their		4:15
did go against the L. with		4:15
that they did beat again the L.,		4:15
the L. did not come again		4:16
gain no power over the L.,		4:18
the L. did come down against		4:19
they did stand against the L.		4:20
the L. did not beat them until		4:20
the L. were about to overthrow		4:23
the L. did come against us as		5: 3
were destroyed by the L.,		5: 5
the L. did come again against		5: 6
which hath been among the L.,		5:15
we did march forth before the L.		6: 1
epistle unto the king of the L.,		6: 2
the king of the L. did grant		6: 3
to gain advantage over the L.		6: 4
to fall into the hands of the L.,		6: 6
the L. would destroy them)		6: 6
behold the armies of the L.		6: 7
when the L. had returned		6:11
had dissented over unto the L.,		6:15
hunted by the L., until they		8: 2
the L. have hunted my people,		8: 7
L. are at war one with another;		8: 8
there are none save it be the L.		8: 9
there is none save it be the L.,	Eth	4: 3
and they are had among the L.		8:20
wrought the change upon the L.,		12:14
great a miracle among the L.		12:15
make not myself known to the L.	Mro	1: 1
worth unto my brethren, the L.,		1: 4
go not out soon against the L.		8:27
had a sore battle with the L.		9: 2
lest the L. shall destroy this		9: 3
the L. have many prisoners,		9: 7
great abomination of the L.,		9: 9
many of the daughters of the L.		9: 9
the L. did not carry away,		9:16
armies of the L. are betwixt	Mro	9:17
doth exceed that of the L.		9:20
have dissented over unto the L.,		9:24
write unto my brethren, the L.;		10: 1
come to the knowledge of the L.,	DC	3:18
L. might come to the knowledge		3:20
come unto their brethren the L.,		10:48
and also all that had become L.		10:48
of whom the L. are a remnant,		19:27
that you shall go unto the L.		28: 8
be on the borders by the L.		28: 9
take thy journey among the L.		28:14
my church among the L.;		30: 6
the wilderness among the L.		32: 2
L. shall blossom as the rose.		49:24
unto the borders of the L.		54: 8
LAMANITES'		
flight was swifter than the L.	Mrm	5: 7
whose flight did not exceed the L.		5: 7
LAMANITISH		
as he was with the L. servants	Al	17:26
were one of the L. women,		19:16
LAMB		
had baptized the L. of God,	1Ne	10:10
Behold the L. of God,		11:21
the L. of God went forth		11:27
beheld the L. of God going		11:31
healed by the power of the L.		11:31
and beheld the L. of God, that		11:32
against the apostles of the L.;		11:34
the twelve apostles of the L.		11:35
the twelve apostles of the L.		11:36
the L. of God descending out		12: 6
the twelve disciples of the L.,		12: 8
the twelve apostles of the L.?		12: 9
because of their faith in the L.		12:10
like unto the L. of God.		12:11
white in the blood of the L.		12:11
Messiah who is the L. of God,		12:18
the truth which is in the L.		13:24
the twelve apostles of the L.,		13:26
away from the gospel of the L.		13:26
which is the book of the L. of God.		13:28
plainness which is in the L.		13:29
away out of the gospel of the L.,		13:29
parts of the gospel of the L.		13:32
Wherefore saith the L. of God:		13:33
Behold, saith the L. of God,		13:34
parts of the gospel of the L.		13:34
saith the L.—I will be merciful		13:34
plain and precious, saith the L.		13:34
For, behold, saith the L.:		13:35
by the gift and power of the L.		13:35
written my gospel, saith the L.,		13:36
the everlasting kingdom of the L.;		13:37
the book of the L. of God,		13:38
forth by the power of the L.,		13:39
the twelve apostles of the L.,		13:39
the twelve apostles of the L.,		13:40
the L. of God is the Son of the		13:40
established by the mouth of the L.;		13:41
words of the L. shall be made known		13:41
the twelve apostles of the L.;		13:41
hearken unto the L. of God		14: 1
hearts against the L. of God,		14: 2
destruction, saith the L. of God;		14: 3
hearts against the L. of God.		14: 6
cometh, saith the L. of God,		14: 7
the church of the L. of God,		14:10
the church of the L. of God,		14:10
the church of the L. of God,		14:12
the church of the L., who were the		14:12
to fight against the L. of God.		14:13
the power of the L. of God,		14:14
saints of the church of the L.,		14:14
the twelve apostles of the L.		14:20
this apostle of the L. shall write		14:24
the apostle of the L. of God		14:25
the truth which is in the L.,		14:26
the name of the apostle of the L.		14:27

LAMB

wolf also shall dwell with the l.,	2Ne 21: 6
shall the wolf dwell with the l.;	30:12
that whould baptize the L. of God,	31: 4
if the L. of God, he being holy,	31: 5
wherein the L. of God did fulfil	31: 6
out of the mouth of the L. of God,	33:14
brought as a l. to the slaughter,	Mos 14: 7
may have faith on the L. of God,	Al 7:14
through the blood of the L.	13:11
white through the blood of the L.	34:36
followers of God and the L.	He 6: 5
had a l.-skin about their loins,	3Ne 4: 7
as a child with a suckling l.,	28:22
even as a child with a l.;	4Ne 1:33
stand before the L. of God—	Mrm 9: 2
or can ye behold the L. of God?	9: 3
by the blood of the L.,	9: 6
through the blood of the L.;	Eth 13:10
washed in the blood of the L.;	13:11
unto the marriage of the L.,	DC 58:11
ye the supper of the L.,	65: 3
worshiping God, and the L.,	76:21
glory of the L., who was slain,	76:39
the Lord, even Christ the L.,	76:85
to God and the L. be glory,	76:119
The L. of God hath overcome	88:106
upon the throne, even the L.	88:115
Hosanna to God and the L.!	109:79
wolves for the blood of the l.;	122: 6
L. shall stand upon Mount Zion,	133:18
shall be in the presence of the L.	133:55
stand on the right hand of the L.,	133:56
they shall sing the song of the L.,	133:56
going like a l. to the slaughter;	135: 4
L. is slain from the foundation	Mses 7:47

LAMB'S

written in the L. Book of Life,	DC 132:19

LAMBS

Then shall the l. feed after their	2Ne 15:17

LAMB-SKIN: see LAMB and SKIN.

LAME

causing the l. to walk,	Mos 3: 5
Have ye any that are l.,	3Ne 17: 7
and their afflicted, and their l.,	17: 9
healed all their sick, and their l.,	26:15
and cause the l. to walk,	4Ne 1: 5
to speak, and the l. to walk.	DC 35: 9
The l. who hath faith to leap	42:51
the poor, the l., and the blind,	58:11

LAMECH

L. was thirty-two years old	DC 107:51
And Methusael begat L.	Mses 5:43
L. took unto himself two wives;	5:44
And L. said unto his wives, Adah	5:47
Hear my voice, ye wives of L.,	5:47
L. shall be seventy and seven fold;	5:48
L. having entered into a covenant	5:49
L., being angry, slew him,	5:50
the Lord cursed L., and his house,	5:52
L. had spoken the secret unto	5:53
L. was despised, and cast out,	5:54
eighty-seven years, and begat L.;	8: 5
after he begat L., seven hundred	8: 6
And L. lived one hundred and	8: 8
L. lived, after he begat Noah,	8:10
days of L. were seven hundred and	8:11

LAMENT

And her gates shall l. and mourn;	2Ne 13:26
And then shall ye l., and say:	He 13:32
then shall they l. because they	DC 45:53

LAMENTATION

to our great sorrow and l.,	Mos 9:19
there was a great mourning and l.	21: 9
was a great mourning and l.	Al 28: 4
sorrow and l. of the righteous.	He 6:33
because of my mourning and l.	7:15

to be a mourning and a l.	Mrm 2:11
when I, Mormon, saw their l.	2:12
they took up a howling and a l.	Eth 15:16
l. in the day of visitation,	DC 56:16
of weeping, of mourning, and of l.;	112:24

LAMENTATIONS

cause for l. among the people,	Al 4:13
and their l. into the praise and	3Ne 10:10
their cries, their howlings and l.,	Eth 15:16

LAMENTED

been a cause to have been l.)	Al 50:30

LAMENTING

greatly l. his loss.	Al 18:43
they did cease l. and howling	3Ne 10: 2

LAMONI

and his name was L.;	Al 17:21
king L. was much pleased with	17:24
became a servant to king L.	17:25
to watch the flocks of L.,	17:25
king L. caused that his servants	18: 1
Now this was the tradition of L.,	18: 5
L. began to fear exceedingly,	18: 5
king L. inquired of his servants,	18: 8
by the father of L., who was	18: 9
when king L. heard that Ammon	18:10
king L. did open his mouth,	18:18
yet harmless, he said unto L.:	18:22
And king L. said: Is it above	18:31
And king L. said: I believe	18:33
king L. was under the power of	19: 6
all the servants of L. had fallen	19:17
took the king, L., by the hand,	19:30
also did all the servants of L.;	19:33
king L. desired that Ammon	20: 1
had heard this, he said unto L.:	20: 3
Now L. said unto Ammon:	20: 4
Now L. said unto him:	20: 4
Now when L. had heard this he	20: 6
Ammon and L. were journeying	20: 8
they met the father of L.,	20: 8
the father of L. said unto him:	20: 9
L. rehearsed unto him whither	20:11
when L. had rehearsed unto him	20:13
L., thou art going to deliver these	20:13
the father of L. commanded him	20:14
But L. said unto him:	20:15
that L. may retain his kingdom,	20:24
great love he had for his son L.,	20:26
that my son L. should retain his	20:26
had been spoken by his son L.,	20:27
Ammon and L. proceeded on	20:28
L. found favor in the eyes of	20:28
delivered by L. and Ammon.	20:30
delivered by the hand of L. and	21:14
Ammon and L. returned from	21:18
king L. would not suffer that	21:19
was under the reign of king L.	21:22
preach unto the people of king L.;	21:23
thus teaching the people of L.	22: 1
and he was the father of L.	22: 1
to teach the people of L.	22: 4
might hold a council with L.	24: 5

LAMPS

your l. trimmed and burning,	DC 33:17

LAND

out of the l. of Jerusalem,	1Ne 1:hd
to the l. of Jerusalem	1:hd
into the promised l.,	1:hd
the l. of his inheritance,	2: 4
out of the l. of Jerusalem,	2:11
the l. of their inheritance,	2:11
be led to a l. of promise;	2:20
a l. which I have prepared for you;	2:20
a l. which is choice above all	2:20
up to the l. of Jerusalem.	3: 9
up to the l. of Jerusalem,	3:10
the l. of our father's inheritance,	3:16

LAND   LAND

if my father should dwell in the l.	1Ne	3:18
commanded to flee out of the l.,		3:18
be that he flee out of the l.		3:18
down to the l. of our inheritance,		3:22
shall prosper in the l. of promise.		4:14
forth from the l. of our inheritance,		5: 2
I have obtained a l. of promise,		5: 5
up to the l. of Jerusalem,		5: 6
out of the l. of Egypt,		5:15
towards the l. of promise.		5:22
in the l. of promise.		7: 1
unto the l. of Jerusalem,		7: 2
unto the l. of Jerusalem.		7: 7
shall obtain the l. of promise;		7:13
have driven him out of the l.		7:14
go up to the l., and remember		7:15
the l. of their inheritance.		10: 3
into the l. of promise,		10:13
beheld the l. of promise;		12: 1
wars and contentions in the l.;		12: 3
on the face of the l. of promise;		12: 4
upon the face of the l.		12:20
who were in the promised l.		13:12
upon the l. of promise;		13:14
obtain the l. for their inheritance;		13:15
upon the waters, and upon the l.		13:17
they did prosper in the l.;		13:20
upon the face of the l.		13:30
which is the l. that the Lord		13:30
for the l. of their inheritance;		13:30
upon the promised l. forever;		14: 2
out of the l. of Jerusalem,		16:35
the l. which we called Bountiful,		17: 5
had been in the l. of Bountiful		17: 7
be led towards the promised l.;		17:13
have arrived in the promised l.,		17:14
out of the l. of Jerusalem.		17:14
out of the l. of Jerusalem.		17:20
the l. of our inheritance;		17:21
in the l. of Jerusalem		17:22
the children of the l.,		17:32
the children of this l.,		17:33
who were in the l. of promise,		17:33
Lord did curse the l. against them,		17:35
and curseth the l. unto them		17:38
them out of the l. of Egypt.		17:40
into the l. of promise.		17:42
in the l. which the Lord thy God		17:55
towards the promised l.		18: 8
towards the promised l.		18:22
arrive at the promised l.;		18:23
went forth upon the l.,		18:23
we did call it the promised l.		18:23
from the l. of Jerusalem.		18:24
find upon the l. of promise,		18:25
people, who should possess the l.,		19: 3
and these from the l. of Sinim.		21:12
the l. of thy destruction,		21:19
even upon the face of this l.;		22: 7
them out of the l. of Jerusalem.	2Ne	1: 1
them concerning the l. of promise,		1: 3
flee out of the l. of Jerusalem.		1: 3
we have obtained a l. of promise,		1: 5
a l. which is choice above all		1: 5
a l. which the Lord God hath		1: 5
a l. for the inheritance of		1: 5
hath covenanted this l. unto me,		1: 5
shall none come into this l. save		1: 6
this l. is consecrated unto him		1: 7
it shall be a l. of liberty unto		1: 7
cursed shall be the l. for their sakes,		1: 7
wisdom that this l. should be kept		1: 8
nations would overrun the l.,		1: 8
bring out of the l. of Jerusalem		1: 9
prosper upon the face of this l.;		1: 9
may possess this l. unto themselves.		1: 9
blessed upon the face of this l.,		1: 9
away the l. of their inheritance;		1: 9
into this precious l. of promise—		1:10
ye shall prosper in the l.; but		1:20
us forth into the l. of promise;		1:24
brought out of the l. of Jerusalem,		1:30
long upon the face of this l.;	2Ne	1:31
upon the face of this l. forever.		1:31
the Lord hath consecrated this l.		1:32
consecrate also unto thee this l.,		3: 2
which is a most precious l.,		3: 2
thy people out of the l. of Egypt.		3:10
ye shall prosper in the l.;		4: 4
for thou shall inherit the l.		4:11
and to multiply in the l.		5:13
were not to be found upon the l.,		5:16
teachers over the l. of my people.		5:26
But behold, this l., said God,		10:10
shall be a l. of thine inheritance,		10:10
shall be blessed upon the l.		10:10
this l. shall be a land of liberty		10:11
a l. of liberty unto the Gentiles,		10:11
there shall be no kings upon the l.,		10:11
And I will fortify this l. against		10:12
I will consecrate this l.		10:19
for the l. of their inheritance;		10:19
for it is a choice l., saith God		10:19
out of the l. of our inheritance,		10:20
we have been led to a better l.,		10:20
Their l. is also full of silver		12: 7
their l. is also full of horses,		12: 7
Their l. is also full of idols;		12: 8
and if they look unto the l.,		15:30
and the l. be utterly desolate;		16:11
forsaking in the midst of the l.		16:12
the l. that hou abhorrest shall		17:16
that is in the l. of Assyria.		17:18
eat that is left in the l.		17:22
all thel. shall become briers and		17:24
shall fill the breadth of thy l.,		18: 8
afflicted the l. of Zebulun,		19: 1
and the l. of Naphtali,		19: 1
in the l. of the shadow of death,		19: 2
Lord of Hosts is the l. darkened,		19:19
even determined in all the l.		20:23
came up out of the l. of Egypt.		21:16
to destroy the whole l.		23: 5
fierce anger, to lay the l. desolate;		23: 9
flee every one into his own l.		23:14
and set them in their own l.;		24: 1
the l. of the Lord shall be for		24: 2
because thou hast destroyed thy l.		24:20
they do not rise, nor possess the l.,		24:21
will bring the Assyrian in my l.,		24:25
possess the l. of Jerusalem,		25:11
again to the l. of thie inheritance.		25:11
Israel up out of the l. of Egypt,		25:20
those who shall come upon this l.		27: 1
gather in upon the face of the l.;		30: 7
in the which this l.,	Jac	2:12
which is a l. of promise unto you		2:12
forth out of the l. of Jerusalem,		2:25
cursed be the l. for their sakes.		2:29
my people in the l. of Jerusalem,		2:31
led out of the l. of Jerusalem,		2:32
the l. is cursed for your sakes;		3: 3
possess the l. of your inheritance,		3: 4
in all the l. of the vineyard.		5:21
parts of the l. of my vineyard.		5:43
out of all the l. of my vineyard;		5:69
I have given unto them this l.,	En	1:10
this land, and it is a holy l.;		1:10
the people of Nephi did till the l.,		1:21
them off from the face of the l.	Jar	1: 3
had waxed strong in the l.		1: 5
And the laws of the l. were		1: 5
upon much of the face of the l.,		1: 6
spread upon the face of the l.,		1: 8
ye shall prosper in the l.		1: 9
from off the face of the l.		1:10
destroyed upon the face of the l.;		1:12
them out of the l. of Jerusalem	Om	1: 6
ye shall not prosper in the l.		1: 6
king over the l. of Zarahemla;		1:12
flee out of the l. of Nephi,		1:12
depart out of the l. with him,		1:12
they departed out of the l.		1:13
until they came down into the l.		1:13
is called the l. of Zarahemla.		1:13

LAND

the l. where Mosiah discovered	Om	1:16
scattered in the l. northward.		1:22
out of the l. of Zarahemla.		1:24
to return to the l. of Nephi;		1:27
possess the l. of their inheritance.		1:27
again to the l. of Zarahemla.		1:28
down out of the l. of Nephi,	WM	1:13
were many holy men in the l.,		1:17
once more establish peace in the l.		1:18
in all the l. of Zarahemla,	Mos	1: 1
that ye may prosper in the l.		1: 7
throughout all this l.		1:10
of Mosiah who dwell in the l.,		1:10
brought out of the l. of Jerusalem;		1:11
were in the l. of Zarahemla		1:18
throughout all the l.,		2: 1
together throughout all the l.,		2: 1
and waxed great in the l.		2: 2
them out of the l. of Jerusalem,		2: 4
peace in the l. of Zarahemla,		2: 4
ye should prosper in the l.;		2:22
ye shall prosper in the l.,		2:31
dwell in the l. of Lehi-Nehpi,		7: 1
they left the l. of Zarahemla;		7: 1
go up to the l. of Lehi-Nephi		7: 2
to go up to the l. of Lehi-Nephi;		7: 4
which is north of the l. of Shilom,		7: 5
went down into the l. of Nephi.		7: 6
who were in the l. of Nephi,		7: 7
and in the l. of Shilom;		7: 7
up out of the l. of Zarahemla		7: 9
of Zarahemla to inherit this l.,		7: 9
which was the l. of their fathers,		7: 9
up out of the l. of Zarahemla		7:13
Zeniff brought up out of that l.		7:13
who were in the l. of Zarahemla		7:14
Israel out of the l. of Egypt,		7:19
out of the l. of Jerusalem,		7:20
to inherit the l. of his fathers,		7:21
possessions of a part of the l.,		7:21
and the l. round about—		7:21
who were in the l. of Zarahemla.		8: 2
Zeniff went up out of the l.		8: 2
himself came up out of the l.		8: 2
they left the l. of Zarahemla,		8: 5
might find the l. of Zarahemla,		8: 7
and found not the l. of Zarahemla		8: 8
but returned to this l., having		8: 8
having traveled in a l. among		8: 8
discovered a l. which was covered		8: 8
a l. which had been peopled with		8: 8
there is no one in the l. that		8:11
who are in the l. of Zarahemla		8:14
they left the l. of Zarahemla		9:hd
a knowledge of the l. of Nephi,		9: 1
or of the l. of our fathers' first		9: 1
spared, the l. of Zarahemla,		9: 2
to inherit the l. of our fathers,		9: 3
desirous to go up to possess the l.,		9: 3
the wilderness to go up to the l.;		9: 3
near to the l. of our fathers.		9: 4
and possess the l. in peace.		9: 5
possess the l. of Lehi-Nephi,		9: 6
and the l. of Shilom.		9: 6
should depart out of the l.,		9: 7
I and my people went into the l.		9: 7
to multiply and prosper in the l.		9: 9
that he yielded up the l. that		9:10
that after we had dwelt in the l.		9:11
people should wax strong in the l.,		9:11
wars and contentions in the l.		9:13
of my reign in the l. of Nephi,		9:14
on the south of the l. of Shilom,		9:14
we had driven them out of our l.		9:18
began to possess the l. in peace.		10: 1
I set guards round about the l.,		10: 2
did inherit the l. of our fathers		10: 3
thus we did prosper in the l.—		10: 5
have continual peace in the l.		10: 5
round about the l. of Shemlon,		10: 7
the north of the l. of Shilom,		10: 8
driven out of the l. of Jerusalem		10:12
in the l. of their first inheritance,		10:13

had arrived in the promised l.,	Mos	10:15
this my people up into this l.,		10:18
suffered these many years in the l.		10:18
drive them agin out of our l.;		10:20
we returned again to our own l.,		10:21
and overlook the l. of Shilom,		11:12
and also the l. of Shemlon,		11:12
look over all the l. round about.		11:12
to be built in the l. Shilom;		11:13
on the hill north of the l. Shilom,		11:13
the time they fled out of the l.;		11:13
vineyards round about in the l.;		11:15
sent guards round about the l.		11:17
many of their flocks out of the l.;		11:17
insects shall pester their l. also,		12: 6
nations which shall possess the l.;		12: 8
forth upon the face of the l.		12:12
thou hast prospered in the l.,		12:15
thee out of the l. of Egypt,		12:34
thy days may be long upon the l.		13:20
cut off of the l. of the living;		14: 8
being in the borders of the l.		18: 4
were done in the borders of the l.,		18:31
towards the l. of Shemlon,		19: 6
within the borders of the l.		19: 6
them back to the l. of Nephi,		19:15
that they might possess the l.,		19:15
would return to the l. of Nephi,		19:19
to return to the l. of Nephi,		19:22
that they might possess the l.		19:22
they returned to the l. of Nephi,		19:24
set guards round about the l.,		19:28
keep the people of Limhi in the l.,		19:28
they went up to the l. of Nephi,		20: 7
their king in peace to their own l.		20:26
to dwell in the l. again in peace.		21: 1
the borders of the l. round about.		21: 2
to drive them out of their l.		21: 7
a great many widows in the l.,		21:10
to prosper by degrees in the l.,		21:16
watch the l. round about,		21:20
into the l. of Nephi by night,		21:21
his brethren came into the l.		21:22
come from the l. of Zarahemla,		21:24
search for the l. of Zarahemla;		21:25
find a l. which had been peopled;		21:26
a l. which was covered with dry		21:26
a l. which had been peopled and		21:26
it to be the l. of Zarahemla,		21:26
returned to the l. of Nephi,		21:26
arrived in the borders of the l.		21:26
none in the l. that had authority		21:33
travel around the l. of Shilom.		22: 8
round about the l. of Shilom		22:11
towards the l. of Zarahemla,		22:11
arrived in the l. of Zarahemla,		22:13
departed out of the l. by night,		22:15
And they came to a l., yea,		23: 4
a very beautiful and pleasant l.,		23: 4
a l. of pure water.		23: 4
to prosper exceedingly in the l.;		23:19
and they called the l. Helam.		23:19
exceedingly in the l. of Helam;		23:20
they were in the l. of Helam,		23:25
while tilling the l. round about,		23:25
was in the borders of the l.		23:25
possession of the l. of Helam.		23:29
begun to possess the l. of Amulon		23:31
in search of the l. of Nephi when		23:35
they discovered the l. of Helam,		23:35
way which led to the l. of Nephi		23:36
way that led to the l. of Nephi		23:37
round about the l. of Helam,		23:37
of them went to the l. of Nephi;		23:38
returned to the l. of Helam,		23:38
who had been left in the l.		23:38
who were in the l. of Helam;		23:39
who were in the l. of Shemlon,		24: 1
and in the l. of Shilom,		24: 1
and in the l. of Amulon.		24: 1
in every l. which was possessed		24: 4
and this people out of this l.,		24:23

LAND

therefore get thee out of this l.,	Mos	24:23
arrived in the l. of Zarahemla;		24:25
they left the l. of Zarahemla		25: 5
they left the l. of Zarahemla		25: 6
his people who tarried in the l.		25: 7
all the l. of Zarahemla;		25:19
in the l. of Zarahemla.		25:23
blessed, and prospered in the l.		25:24
a proclamation throughout the l.		27: 2
to be much peace agin in the l.;		27: 6
villages in all quarters of the l.		27: 6
thy fathers in the l. of Helam,		27:16
and in the l. of Nephi;		27:16
round about through all the l.,		27:32
all the l. of Zarahemla,		27:35
go up to the l. of Nephi that		28: 1
no more contentions in all the l.		28: 2
might go up to the l. of Nephi.		28: 5
who should possess the l.		28:15
sent out throughout all the l.,		29: 1
gone up to the l. of Nephi,		29: 3
establish peace throughout the l.,		29:14
he has hitherto visited this l.		29:27
should be no more in this l.,		29:32
I desire that this l. be a land of		29:32
that this land be a l. of liberty,		29:32
we may live and inherit the l.,		29:32
remains upon the face of the l.		29:32
chance throughout the l.;		29:38
in bodies throughout the l.,		29:39
had established peace in the l.,		29:40
they did throughout all the l.		29:41
continual peace through the l.		29:43
all the l. of Zarahemla.		29:44
of priestcraft through the l.;	Al	1:16
together throughout all the l.,		2: 5
ran by the l. of Zarahemla,		2:15
in the l. of Minon, above the		2:24
Minon, above the l. of Zarahemla,		2:24
in the course of the l. of Nephi,		2:24
are upon our brethren in that l.;		2:25
beyond the borders of the l.;		2:36
out of the l. of Jerusalem,		3:11
fought in the l. of Zarahemla,		3:20
sent to drive them out of their l.		3:21
out of the borders of their l.		3:23
began to establish peace in the l.,		3:24
nor wars in the l. of Zarahemla;		4: 1
cities and villages throughout the l.		5:hd
first in the l. of Zarahemla,		5: 1
from thence throughout all the l.		5: 1
to establish a church in the l.		5: 3
the l. which was called the		5: 3
was called the l. of Mormon;		5: 3
and we were brought into this l.,		5: 5
of God throughout this l. also.		5: 5
every one that dwelleth in the l.;		5:49
is the l. of our forefathers,		7:10
from the l. of Gideon,		8: 1
done in the l. of Zarahemla,		8: 1
journey over into the l. of Melek,		8: 3
the people in the l. of Melek,		8: 4
throughout all the l. of Melek.		8: 4
all the borders of the l. which		8: 5
baptized throughout all the l.;		8: 5
on the north of the l. of Melek;		8: 6
was with the l. of Ammonihah.		8: 7
in many parts of the l.,		8:11
speedily to the l. of Ammonihah.		8:18
church of God throughout the l.		8:23
and I was in this l. and they		8:24
my back towards this l. forever.		8:24
were in the l. of Ammonihah.		9:hd
ye shall prosper in the l.?		9:13
of their transgressions in the l.		9:14
prolong their existence in the l.		9:16
shall not be prolonged in the l.,		9:18
of God out of the l. of Jerusalem,		9:22
were in the l. of Ammonihah,		10: 1
came out of the l. of Jerusalem,		10: 3
righteous, who are now in the l.,		10:22
was a king over the l. of Salem;		13:17
peace in the l. in his days;		13:18
being wanderers in a strange l.;	Al	13:23
unto many at this time in our l.;		13:24
before the chief judge of the l.		14: 4
lawyers and judges of the l.,		14: 5
all the people that were in the l.;		14: 5
before the chief judge of the l.		14: 5
the chief judge of the l. came and		14:14
judge over the l. of Ammonihah		14:23
out even into the l. of Sidom;		15: 1
out of the l. of Ammonihah,		15: 1
were in the l. of Sidom,		15: 4
throughout all the l. of Sidom.		15:11
a church in the l. of Sidom,		15:13
priests and teachers in the l.,		15:13
were in the l. of Ammonihah,		15:15
were in the l. of Ammonihah,		15:16
over to the l. of Ammonihah		15:18
peace in the l. of Zarahemla,		16: 1
of war heard throughout the l.		16: 1
into the borders of the l.,		16: 2
army to drive them out of the l.,		16: 3
the borders of the l. of Manti.		16: 6
having been driven out of the l.,		16: 9
possess the l. of Ammonihah		16:11
continual peace in all the l.		16:12
the word throughout all the l.		16:15
became general throughout the l.,		16:15
his Spirit on all the face of the l.		16:16
established throughout all the l.—		16:21
in its purity in all the l.,		16:21
and went up to the l. of Nephi		17:hd
from the l. of Gideon southward,		17: 1
away to the l. of Manti,		17: 1
towards the l. of Zarahemla.		17: 1
out of the l. of Zarahemla,		17: 7
to go up to the l. of Nephi,		17: 8
of the l. of the Lamanites,		17:13
journeys throughout the l.		17:18
went to the l. of Ishmael,		17:19
the l. being called after the		17:19
entered the l. of Ishmael,		17:20
or to cast them out of his l.,		17:20
who was over the l. of Ishmael;		17:21
in the l. among the Lamanites,		17:22
were scattered unto their own l.,		18: 7
him forth to the l. of Nephi;		18: 9
appointed at the l. of Nephi,		18: 9
who was king over all the l.		18: 9
Nephite should remain in the l.		19:19
established a church in that l.,		20: 1
go with him to the l. of Nephi,		20: 1
not go up to the l. of Nephi,		20: 2
shalt go to the l. of Middoni;		20: 2
go with thee to the l. of Middoni,		20: 4
the king of the l. of Middoni,		20: 4
I go to the l. of Middoni,		20: 4
I may flatter the king of the l.,		20: 4
in prison in the l. of Middoni.		20: 5
down to the l. of Middoni,		20: 7
who was king over all the l.		20: 8
not go to the l. of Middoni,		20:14
with him to the l. of Ishmael.		20:14
I return to the l. of Ishmael,		20:15
but I go to the l. of Middoni		20:15
towards the l. of Middoni.		20:28
the eyes of the king of the l.;		20:28
arrived in the l. of Middoni.		20:30
of the l. of the Lamanites,		21: 1
the l. which was called by the		21: 1
the l. of their fathers' nativity;		21: 1
over into the l. of Middoni.		21:12
fled out of the l. of Middoni		21:13
returned from the l. of Middoni		21:18
of Middoni to the l. of Ishmael,		21:18
was the l. of their inheritance.		21:18
built in the l. of Ishmael;		21:20
who were in the l. of Ishmael,		21:21
and in all the l. round about.		21:21
if it were in the l. which was		21:22
from the l. of Middoni		22: 1
by the Spirit to the l. of Nephi,		22: 1
king which was over all the l.		22: 1
save it were the l. of Ishmael;		22: 1

LAND 528 LAND

he has gone to the l. of Ishmael,	Al 22: 4	possession of the l. of Jershon;	Al	27:26
out of the l. of Jerusalem?	22: 9	established in the l. of Jershon,		28: 1
proclamation throughout all the l.,	22:27	established in the l. of Jershon,		28: 1
his people who were in all his l.,	22:27	round about the l. of Jershon,		28: 1
from the l. of Zarahemla	22:27	about the l. of Zarahemla;		28: 1
the north by the l. of Zarahemla,	22:27	among all the people in the l.		28: 2
the west, in the l. of Nephi;	22:28	returned again to their l.		28: 3
west of the l. of Zarahemla,	22:28	heard throughout all the l.,		28: 4
on the west in the l. of Nephi,	22:28	journeyings in the l. of Nephi,		28: 8
all the northern parts of the l.	22:29	their sufferings in the l.,		28: 8
l. which they called Bountiful.	22:29	brethren in the l. of Jershon.		28: 8
l. which they called Desolation,	22:30	have been up to the l. of Nehpi.		29:14
the l. which had been peopled	22:30	established in the l. of Jershon,		30: 1
the l. on the northward was	22:31	were driven out of the l.,		30: 1
the l. on the southward was	22:31	buried by the people of the l.—		30: 1
had come from the l. northward	22:31	peace throughout all the l.		30: 2
and the l. Desolation,	22:32	a man into the l. of Zarahemla,		30: 6
and thus the l. of Nephi and the	22:32	over to the l. of Jershon also,		30:19
and the l. of Zarahemla were	22:32	be carried out of the l.		30:21
there being a small neck of l.	22:32	over into the l. of Gideon,		30:21
between the l. northward	22:32	also the chief judge over the l.		30:21
and the l. southward.	22:32	him to the l. of Zarahemla,		30:29
had inhabited the l. Bountiful,	22:33	who was governor over all the l.		30:29
not overrun the l. northward.	22:33	as he did in the l. of Gideon;		30:30
only in the l. of Nephi,	22:34	many travels round about the l.		30:32
should be, in any part of their l.	23: 1	published throughout all the l.;		30:57
proclamation throughout the l.	23: 3	judge to all the people in the l.,		30:57
go forth throughout all the l.,	23: 3	l. which they called Antionum,		31: 3
and teachers throughout the l.	23: 4	east of the l. of Zarahemla,		31: 3
who were in the l. of Ishmeal;	23: 9	south of the l. of Jershon,		31: 3
who were in the l. of Middoni;	23:10	into the l. to preach the word		31:11
who were in the l. of Shilom,	23:12	when they had come into the l.,		31:12
who were in the l. of Shemlon,	23:12	over into the l. of Jershon.		35: 1
the l. wheresoever they dwelt,	23:14	over into the l. of Jershon.		35: 2
who were in the l. of Amulon,	24: 1	together throughout all the l.		35: 4
and also in the l. of Helam,	24: 1	brethren were cast out of the l.;		35: 6
who were in the l. of Jerusalem,	24: 1	over also into the l. of Jershon.		35: 6
in fine, in all the l. round about,	24: 1	they should cast out of their l.		35: 8
came forth to the l. of Midian,	24: 5	over from them into their l.		35: 8
they came to the l. of Ishmael	24: 5	out of the l. of Jershon,		35:13
and came up to the l. of Nephi	24:20	came over into the l. of Melek,		35:13
of Anti-Nephi-Lehi out of the l.	24:20	gave place in the l. of Jershon		35:13
borders of the l. of Zarahemla,	25: 2	returned to the l. of Zarahemla,		35:14
were in the l. of Ammonihah,	25: 2	were driven out of their l.;		35:14
preached to them in their l.;	25: 6	inheritance in the l. of Jershon,		35:14
returned again to their own l.;	25:13	ye shall prosper in the l.		36: 1
to dwell in the l. of Ishmael	25:13	his power into the promised l.;		36:28
of Ishmael and the l. of Nephi,	25:13	out of the l. of Jerusalem;		36:29
from the l. of Zarahemla	26: 1	of God ye shall prosper in the l.;		36:30
up out of the l. of Zarahemla,	26: 9	ye shall prosper in the l.—		37:13
we have wrought in this l.,	26:12	that shall hereafter possess the l.		37:25
in the l. of Zarahemla,	26:23	there is a curse upon all this l.,		37:28
we go up to the l. of Nephi,	26:23	cursed be the l. forever and ever		37:31
and their iniquity out of the l.,	26:25	straight course to the promised l.		37:44
been so great love in all the l.?	26:33	its course, to the promised l.,		37:45
lost from its body in a strange l.;	26:36	into a far better l. of promise.		37:45
of us, wanderers in a strange l.	26:36	of God ye shall prosper in the l.;		38: 1
whatsoever l. they may be in;	26:37	go over into the l. of Siron,		39: 3
again to the l. of Nephi.	27: 1	their armies in the l. of Jershon.		43: 4
go down to the l. of Zarahemla	27: 5	came into the l. of Antionum,		43: 5
otherwise we will perish in the l.	27:10	which is the l. of the Zoramites;		43: 5
Get this people out of this l.,	27:12	together in the l. of Antionum,		43:15
therefore get thee out of this l.;	27:12	meet them in the l. of Jershon.		43:15
and departed out of the l.,	27:14	out of the l. of Antionum		43:22
divided the l. of Nephi from	27:14	come into the l. of Manti		43:22
from the l. of Zarahemla,	27:14	and take possession of the l.;		43:22
over near the borders of the l.	27:14	over into the l. of Manti,		43:24
forth into the l. of Zarahemla,	27:15	his army in the l. of Jershon,		43:25
that ye shall come into their l.	27:15	should come into that l. and		43:25
was going forth into the l.,	27:16	over into the l. of Manti.		43:25
back to the l. of Zarahemla;	27:20	people in that quarter of the l.		43:26
unto them in the l. of Nephi,	27:20	unto themselves over all the l.;		43:29
throughout all the l.,	27:21	the borders of the l. Manti.		43:32
will give up the l. of Jershon,	27:22	towards the l. of Manti.		43:42
which joins the l. Bountiful,	27:22	shall prosper thee in this l.		45: 8
the south of the l. Bountiful;	27:22	Cursed shall be the l., yea,		45:16
and this l. Jershon is the land	27:22	yea, this l., unto every nation,		45:16
the l. which we will give unto	27:22	the blessing of God upon the l.,		45:16
between the l. Jershon and the	27:23	out of the l. Zarahemla,		45:18
land Jershon and the l. Nephi,	27:23	as if to go into the l. of Melek.		45:18
our brethren in the l. Jershon;	27:23	the church again in all the land,		45:22
may inherit the l. Jershon;	27:24	city throughout all the l.		45:22
down into the l. of Jershon,	27:26	teachers throughout all the l.,		45:22

LAND

the lower judges of the l.,	Al 46: 4
had sent upon the face of the l.	46:10
remain to possess the l.—	46:13
the freedom of the l. might	46:16
he named all the l. which was	46:17
south of the l. Desolation,	46:17
and in fine, all the l. both on	46:17
A chosen l. and the land of	46:17
and the l. of liberty.	46:17
maintain this title upon the l.,	46:20
brethren in the l. northward,	46:22
forth in all the parts of the l.	46:28
departed into the l. of Nephi	46:29
back into the l. of Zarahemla.	46:33
tower which was in all the l.,	46:36
to have peace again in the l.;	46:37
did maintain peace in the l.	46:37
were very frequent in the l.—	46:40
went up in the l. of Nephi	47: 1
throughout all his l., among	47: 1
to the l. of Nephi, to the city	47:20
over into the l. of Zarahemla	47:29
king throughout all the l.,	47:35
also to reign over all the l.,	48: 2
all the people who were in the l.,	48: 2
toward the l. of Zarahemla	48: 6
yea, all round about the l.	48: 8
did fortify and strengthen the l.	48: 9
would prosper them in the l.,	48:15
would prosper them in the l.;	48:15
they should prosper in the l.	48:25
towards the l. of Ammonihah.	49: 1
down out of the l. of Nephi,	49:10
towards the l. of Noah,	49:12
for every city in all the l.	49:13
forward to the l. of Noah	49:13
been the weakest part of the l.,	49:15
returned to the l. of Nephi,	49:25
throughout all the l. which	50: 1
about every city in all the l.	50: 6
south of the l. of Zarahemla.	50: 7
And the l. of Nephi did run in	50: 8
were in the l. of Zarahemla	50: 9
and in the l. round about	50: 9
the seashore, and possess the l.	50: 9
between the l. of Zarahemla and	50:11
and the l. of Nephi,	50:11
possessing all the l. northward,	50:11
the l. which was northward of	50:11
northward of the l. Bountiful,	50:11
the name of the city, or the l.,	50:14
and were strong in the l.	50:18
they shall prosper in the l.	50:20
concerning the l. of Lehi,	50:25
and the l. of Morianton,	50:25
possessed the l. of Morianton	50:26
claim a part of the l. of Lehi;	50:26
who possessed the l. of Lehi	50:27
to the l. which was northward,	50:29
of the l. which was northward.	50:29
to flee into the l. northward.	50:31
who were in the l. Bountiful,	50:32
of those parts of the l.,	50:32
flight into the l. northward.	50:33
borders of the l. Desolation;	50:34
the sea into the l. northward,	50:34
restored to the l. of Morianton,	50:36
an entire peace in the l.,	51: 2
be chief judge over the l.;	51: 4
to establish a king over the l.	51: 5
remain chief judge over the l.	51: 6
soldiers from all parts of his l.,	51: 9
down to the l. of Zarahemla.	51:11
coming into the borders of the l.,	51:14
unto the governor of the l.,	51:15
come into the l. of Moroni,	51:22
the borders of the l. Bountiful,	51:28
possession of the l. Bountiful,	51:30
and also the l. northward.	51:30
borders of the l. Bountiful;	51:32
marching into the l. northward,	52: 2
those parts of the l. which they	52: 5
should fortify the l. Bountiful,	52: 9
led into the land northward,	Al 52: 9
that quarter of the l.,	52:10
upon us in the borders of the l.	52:11
out of the l. of Zarahemla,	52:12
forces to that part of the l.,	52:13
and the west borders of the l.,	52:15
towards the l. Bountiful,	52:15
his army at the l. of Bountiful,	52:18
forth into the l. Bountiful.	52:39
back into the l. Bountiful;	53: 3
a ditch round about the l.,	53: 3
Lamanites in the l. of Nephi;	53: 6
their cities in that part of the l.	53: 8
down into the l. of Zarahemla,	53:10
down into the l. of Zarahemla;	53:12
protect the l. unto the laying	53:17
borders of the l. on the south	53:22
or the l. of your possessions,	54: 6
which is the l. of Nephi.	54: 6
follow you even into your own l.,	54:12
the l. of our first inheritance;	54:12
yea, and we will seek our l.,	54:13
the l. of our first inheritance.	54:13
people in that quarter of the l.	56: 1
warfare in this part of the l.	56: 2
down out of the l. of Nephi—	56: 3
the people of that part of the l.	56: 9
at this time in the l. of Nephi;	56:12
The l. of Manti, or the city of	56:14
us from the l. of Zarahemla.	56:28
them to the l. of Zarahemla,	56:57
from the l. of Zarahemla,	57: 6
and from the l. round about,	57: 6
to the l. of Zarahemla.	57:11
down to the l. of Zarahemla;	57:15
down to the l. of Zarahemla;	57:15
down to the l. of Zarahemla;	57:16
down to the l. of Zarahemla	57:16
to guard them down to the l.	57:28
down to the l. of Zarahemla	57:29
maintaining those parts of the l.	57:30
from the l. of Zarahemla	58: 3
embassy to the governor of our l.,	58: 3
from the l. of Zarahemla.	58: 4
of God should come upon our l.,	58: 4
towards the l. of Zarahemla.	58: 9
towards the l. of Zarahemla,	58:23
way towards the l. of Manti.	58:24
out of all this quarter of the l.	58:26
women and children out of the l.	58:30
forces into that quarter of the l.;	58:30
have fled to the l. of Nephi.	58:35
in all the l. round about	58:38
maintain that part of the l.	59: 2
epistle to the l. of Zarahemla,	59: 3
to flee from the l. of Manti,	59: 4
and from the l. round about,	59: 6
Lamanites in this part of the l.	59: 6
again to the governor of the l.,	59: 6
and the governor over the l.,	60: 1
they should come into our l.	60: 1
about in the borders of the l.	60: 2
to maintain this part of our l.,	60:22
even in the l. of Zarahemla,	60:25
the chief governor of this l.,	60:30
fled to the l. of Gideon,	61: 2
throughout this part of the l.;	61: 5
have got possession of the l.,	61: 6
the remainder of the l.,	61: 8
they would stay in their own l.	61: 8
the war in that part of the l.,	61:10
march towards the l. of Gideon.	61:15
march towards the l. of Gideon.	62: 3
he came to the l. of Gideon;	62: 4
out of the l. of Zarahemla	62: 6
had taken possession of the l.	62: 6
armies into the l. of Zarahemla,	62: 7
peace to the l. of Zarahemla,	62:11
preserving that part of the l.	62:12
this was done to fortify the l.	62:13
of men in the l. of Zarahemla,	62:14
towards the l. of Nephihah,	62:14
were marching towards the l.,	62:15

LAND 530 LAND

towards the l. of Nephihah.	Al 62:18	the l. south was called Lehi	He	6:10
fled into the l. of Moroni,	62:25	the l. north was called Mulek,		6:10
forth from the l. of Nephihah	62:30	bring Mulek into the l. north,		6:10
of Nephihah to the l. of Lehi.	62:30	and Lehi into the l. south.		6:10
they came to the l. of Moroni	62:32	exceedingly strong in the l.		6:12
one body in the l. of Moroni.	62:33	from that tower into this l.;		6:28
borders of the l. of Moroni,	62:34	over all the face of the l.,		6:28
did drive them out of the l.;	62:38	all the l. of the Nephites,		6:38
fortified those parts of the l.	62:42	returned to the l. of Zarahemla		7: 1
of God throughout all the l.	62:46	from the l. northward.		7: 1
began to prosper again in the l.,	62:48	who were in the l. northward,		7: 2
exceeding strong again in the l.	62:48	again unto the l. of his nativity.		7: 3
wax strong and prosper in the l.	62:51	power and authority of the l.;		7: 4
out of the l. of Zarahemla	63: 4	out of the l. of Jerusalem,		7: 7
the l. which was northward.	63: 4	joyed with him in the promised l.;		7: 7
the borders of the l. Bountiful,	63: 5	are in the l. of our possession,		7:22
Bountiful, by the l. Desolation,	63: 5	out of the l. of Jerusalem?		8:21
led into the l. northward.	63: 5	about upon the face of the l.,		10:12
out again to the l. northward.	63: 7	were wars throughout all the l.		11: 1
forth into the l. northward.	63: 9	let there be a famine in the l.,		11: 4
to the l. northward in a ship,	63:10	was a great famine upon the l.,		11: 5
who had gone forth into that l.	63:10	the more wicked parts of the l.		11: 6
of men throughout all the l.,	63:12	this famine may cease in this l.		11:12
to the l. of Zarahemla to battle	He 1:17	the l. was filled with rejoicing;		11:18
guards in the l. of Zarahemla;	1:18	began to prosper again in the l.,		11:20
the strongest hold in all the l.,	1:22	cover the whole face of the l.,		11:20
to go forth against all the l.	1:22	throughout the face of all the l.;		11:21
not tarry in the l. of Zarahemla,	1:23	exceeding great peace in the l.;		11:21
obtain the north parts of the l.	1:23	people upon all the face of the l.		11:32
was in the center of the l.,	1:24	did visit many parts of the l.		11:33
through the center of the l.	1:25	came into the l. of Zarahemla,		13: 2
not come into the center of the l.,	1:26	about to return to his own l.		13: 2
come into the center of the l.,	1:27	which are in the l. round about,		13:16
the most capital parts of the l.,	1:27	curse shall come upon the l.,		13:17
should come to the l. Bountiful	1:28	people's sake who are upon the l.,		13:17
they came to the l. Bountiful,	1:29	of the great curse of the l.,		13:18
towards the l. of Zarahemla,	1:29	because of the curse of the l.		13:19
depart out of the l. in peace.	1:33	a curse should come upon the l.,		13:23
took their flight out of the l.,	2:11	he hath cursed the l. because		13:30
out of the l. of Zarahemla,	3: 3	because of the curse of the l.		13:35
forth unto the l. northward	3: 3	for behold the l. is cursed,		13:36
northward to inherit the l.	3: 3	O ye people of the l., that ye		13:39
forth into all parts of the l.,	3: 5	no light upon the face of this l.,		14:20
who had before inherited the l.	3: 5	to pass upon all the face of this l.		14:28
no part of the l. was desolate,	3: 6	will he not show himself in this l.		16:19
who had before inhabited the l.	3: 6	as well as in the l. of Jerusalem?		16:19
timber upon the face of the l.,	3: 7	but in a l. which is far distant,		16:20
go forth from the l. southward	3: 8	distant, a l. which we know not;		16:20
to the l. northward,	3: 8	upon all the face of the l.,		16:22
who were in the l. northward	3: 9	upon all the face of the l.		16:23
spring up upon the face of the l.	3: 9	and the governor over the l.	3Ne	1: 1
scarce in the l. northward,	3:10	out of the l. of Zarahemla,		1: 2
people in the l. northward that	3:11	Then he departed out of the l.,		1: 3
did also go forth into this l.	3:12	great uproar throughout the l.;		1: 7
still great contention in the l.,	3:19	both in the l. north and in		1:17
that he did prosper in the l.	3:20	land north and in the l. south,		1:17
peace established in the l.,	3:23	again to have peace in the l.		1:23
the more settled parts of the l.,	3:23	who did infest the l.;		1:27
were not destroyed out of the l.	3:23	who did remain in the l.		1:28
And l. their souls, yea, their	3:30	do great wickedness in the l.		2: 3
rejoicing in the l. of Zarahemla,	3:31	return to the l. of Zarahemla,		2: 9
in all the l. which was possessed	3:31	nowhere be found in all the l.		2: 9
and their prosperity in the l.;	3:36	throughout all the l.;		2:11
slain and driven out of the l.,	4: 2	and carnage throughout the l.,		2:11
possession of the l. of Zarahemla;	4: 5	the governor of the l.,		3: 1
even unto the l. which was near	4: 5	and chief governor of the l.,		3: 2
which was near the l. Bountiful.	4: 5	of the l. of the Nephites,		3:11
even into the l. of Bountiful;	4: 6	substance, save it were their l.,		3:13
which was in the l. southward.	4: 8	throughout all the face of the l.,		3:22
obtaining many parts of the l.;	4: 9	the l. which was appointed was		3:23
away into the l. of Nephi,	4:12	was the l. of Zarahemla and		3:23
came out of the l. of Jerusalem;	5:16	and the l. Bountiful,		3:23
who were in the l. southward;	5:16	between the l. Bountiful and		3:23
thence into the l. of Zarahemla,	5:16	Bountiful and the l. Desolation.		3:23
were in the l. of Zarahemla	5:19	themselves together in this l.		3:24
thence to go to the l. of Nephi.	5:20	together in the l. southward,		3:24
into the l. of Zarahemla,	6: 4	was upon the l. northward.		3:24
did go into the l. northward;	6: 6	and they did dwell in one l.,		3:25
went into the l. northward.	6: 6	which were in the l. south and		4: 1
there was peace in all the l.,	6: 7	which were in the l. north,		4: 1
into whatsoever part of the l.	6: 7	from off the face of the l.;		4: 4
metals, both in the l. south and	6: 9	upon the face of the l.		4: 6
land south and in the l. north.	6: 9	the furthermost parts of the l.		4:23

LAND

called after the l. of Mormon	3Ne	5:12	were many churches in the l.;	4Ne 1:27
the l. in which Alma did		5:12	spread over all the face of the l.;	1:46
out of the l. of Jerusalem,		5:20	go to the l. Antum, unto a hill	Mrm 1: 3
whom he brought out of that l.)		5:20	father into the l. southward,	1: 6
both on the l. northward and		6: 2	even to the l. of Zarahemla.	1: 6
and on the l. southward.		6: 2	face of the l. had become covered	1: 7
did establish peace in all the l.		6: 3	there was peace settled in the l.;	1:12
there was great order in the l.;		6: 4	upon the face of the whole l.,	1:13
nothing in all the l. to hinder		6: 5	were taken away out of the l.,	1:16
this great peace in the l.		6: 6	the l. was cursed for their sake.	1:17
city to city, and from l. to land,		6: 8	the Lamanites, did infest the l.,	1:18
city to city, and from land to l.,		6: 8	the Lord had cursed the l.,	1:18
were many merchants in the l.,		6:11	upon all the face of the l.,	1:19
a great inequality in all the l.,		6:14	us forth out of the l. of David.	2: 5
church was broken up in all the l.		6:14	and came to the l. of Joshua,	2: 6
among the people in all the l.,		6:20	the l. was filled with robbers	2: 8
signed by the governor of the l.		6:22	throughout all the face of the l.,	2: 8
not unto the governor of the l.		6:23	throughout all the face of the l.	2: 8
contrary to the laws of the l.,		6:24	the witchcraft which was in the l.	2:10
from the governor of the l.—		6:24	and a lamentation in all the l.	2:11
up unto the l. of Zarahemla,		6:25	as dung upon the face of the l.	2:15
to the governor of the l.,		6:25	came even to the l. of Jashon,	2:16
to establish a king over the l.,		6:30	near the l. where Ammaron	2:17
l. should no more be at liberty		6:30	the l. which was called Shem.	2:20
establish a king over the l.;		7: 1	give unto us the l. northward,	2:29
murder the chief judge of the l.		7: 1	led into the l. southward.	2:29
destroy the government of the l.		7: 2	Lamanites all the l. southward.	2:29
a great contention in the l.,		7: 7	together at the l. Desolation,	3: 5
the northernmost part of the l.,		7:12	which led into the l. southward.	3: 5
degree they had peace in the l.;		7:14	them off from the face of the l.	3:10
three days over the face of the l.		8: 3	to the l. of your inheritance;	3:17
had been known in all the l.		8: 5	disciples in the l. of Jerusalem.	3:18
had been known in all the l.		8: 7	whom Jesus chose in this l.;	3:19
destruction in the l. southward.		8:11	chose in the l. of Jerusalem.	3:19
destruction in the l. northward;		8:12	out of the l. Desolation.	4: 1
face of the l. was changed,		8:12	again to the l. of Desolation.	4: 2
cracks, upon all the face of the l.		8:18	fought in the l. Desolation.	4:19
darkness upon the face of the l.		8:19	were about to overthrow the l.,	4:23
upon all the face of the l.,		8:20	the inhabitants of our l.	5: 4
were upon the face of the l.		8:22	to the l. of their inheritance,	5:14
upon all the face of this l.,		9: 1	might have received in the l.,	5:19
and the government of the l.;		9: 9	Gentiles who shall possess the l.	5:19
I caused to come upon this l.,		9:12	people unto the l. of Cumorah,	6: 2
the people of the l. did hear		10: 1	forth to the l. of Cumorah,	6: 4
there was silence in the l.		10: 1	it was in a l. of many waters,	6: 4
there was silence in all the l. for		10: 2	people unto the l. of Cumorah.	6: 5
from off the face of the l.,		10: 9	in one to the l. of Cumorah,	6: 6
together in the l. Bountiful,		11:hd	slew them to molder upon the l.,	6:15
which was in the l. Bountiful;		11: 1	this l. is one continual round of	8: 8
is the l. of your inheritance;		15:13	do exist upon the face of the l.	8: 9
hath led away out of the l.		15:15	who did tarry in the l. until	8:10
sheep which are not of this l.,		16: 1	they be upon the face of the l.	8:10
neither of the l. of Jerusalem.		16: 1	who have possessed this l.,	8:23
parts of that l. round about		16: 1	saints who have dwelt in the l.	9:36
forth upon the face of this l.,		16: 8	will drive us out of the l.,	Eth 1:38
this l. for their inheritance.		16:16	if he will drive us out of the l.,	1:38
I should give unto you this l.,		20:14	a l. which is choice above all	1:38
people will I establish in this l.,		20:22	a l. which is choice above all	1:42
scourge unto the people of this l.		20:28	was upon the face of the l.,	2: 3
the l. of their fathers for their		20:29	even unto the l. of promise,	2: 7
which is the l. of Jerusalem,		20:29	possess this l. of promise,	2: 8
promised l. unto them forever,		20:29	decrees of God concerning this l.,	2: 9
for the l. of their inheritance.		20:33	that it is a l. of promise;	2: 9
be the l. of their inheritance.		20:46	a l. which is choice above all	2:10
be established in this l.,		21: 4	among the children of the l.,	2:10
I will cut off the cities of thy l.,		21:15	as the inhabitants of the l.	2:11
off witchcrafts out of thy l.,		21:16	Behold, this is a choice l.,	2:12
this l. for their inheritance;		21:22	but serve the God of the l.,	2:12
upon all the face of the l.,		21:24	the l. which I shall give you	2:15
to the l. of their inheritance.		21:28	it shall be a l. choice above all	2:15
for ye shall be a delightsome l.,		24:12	upon all the face of the l.	4:17
forth upon the face of the l.,		28:18	waters, towards the promised l.;	6: 5
people upon the face of the l.;		28:23	to blow towards the promised l.	6: 8
upon all the face of the l.,	4Ne	1: 2	And they did l. upon the shore	6:12
continued to be peace in the l.		1: 4	the shore of the promised l.	6:12
them exceedingly in the l.;		1: 7	the shores of the promised l.	6:12
all the people, in all the l.;		1:13	down upon the face of the l.,	6:12
was no contention in the l.,		1:15	forth upon the face of the l.,	6:13
was no contention in all the l.		1:18	they came to the promised l.;	6:16
there was still peace in the l.,		1:20	spread upon the face of the l.,	6:18
to be Lamanites again in the l.		1:20	they did wax strong in the l.	6:18
spread upon all the face of the l.,		1:23	execute judgment upon the l.	7: 1

LAND 532 LAND

and dwelt in the l. of Nehor;	Eth 7: 4	
came up unto the l. of Moron	7: 5	
Now the l. of Moron,	7: 6	
l. which is called Desolation	7: 6	
upon all the face of the l.,	7:11	
the l. of their first inheritance;	7:16	
a king over that part of the l.	7:16	
bringing a curse upon the l.,	7:23	
a law throughout all the l.,	7:25	
began to prosper again in the l.	7:26	
great deep into the promised l.;	7:27	
and dwelt in the l. of Heth.	8: 2	
he should depart out of the l.;	9: 3	
Omer departed out of the l.	9: 3	
and fled out of the l.,	9: 9	
to the l. of his inheritance.	9:13	
he saw peace in the l. for the	9:15	
take the curse from off the l.,	9:16	
out his blessings upon this l.,	9:20	
whoso should possess the l.	9:20	
and he saw peace in the l.;	9:22	
over all the face of the l.,	9:26	
upon the face of the l.,	9:26	
came prophets in the l. again,	9:28	
a curse upon the face of the l.;	9:28	
to be a great dearth upon the l.,	9:30	
also upon the face of the l.,	9:31	
towards the l. southward,	9:31	
which fled into the l. southward.	9:32	
cities upon the face of the l.,	10: 4	
spread over all the face of the l.	10: 4	
began to be war again in the l.,	10: 8	
were driven out of the l.	10: 8	
did gain power over all the l.,	10: 9	
himself king over all the l.	10: 9	
war against the king of the l.;	10:15	
people did prosper in the l.;	10:16	
did go into the l. southward,	10:19	
food for the people of the l.,	10:19	
the l. was covered with animals	10:19	
city by the narrow neck of l.,	10:20	
where the sea divides the l.	10:20	
did preserve the l. southward	10:21	
whole face of the l. northward	10:21	
a l. that was choice above all	10:28	
began to be robbers in the l.;	10:33	
exceeding great war in all the l.	11: 4	
great calamity in all the l.,	11: 6	
curse should come upon the l.,	11: 6	
of earth upon the face of the l.	11: 6	
and contentions in all the l.,	11: 7	
people to possess the l.,	11:21	
was king over all the l.	12: 1	
from off the face of this l.	13: 2	
it became a choice l. above all	13: 2	
a chosen l. of the Lord;	13: 2	
a New Jerusalem upon this l.	13: 4	
should be built upon this l.,	13: 6	
down into the l. of Egypt,	13: 7	
out of the l. of Jerusalem,	13: 7	
shall be built upon this l.;	13: 8	
be a l. of their inheritance;	13: 8	
another people receiving the l.	13:21	
a war upon all the face of the l.,	13:25	
upon all the face of the l.	13:26	
people upon the face of the l.	13:31	
a great curse upon all the l.	14: 1	
great was the curse upon the l.	14: 1	
came forth to the l. of Moron,	14: 6	
came up unto the l. of Moron,	14:11	
that quarter of the l. whither	14:15	
fear of Shiz throughout all the l.;	14:18	
went forth throughout the l.—	14:18	
throughout the face of the l.	14:19	
whole face of the l. was covered	14:21	
strewed upon the face of the l.,	14:22	
forth upon the face of the l.,	14:23	
upon all the face of thel.;	14:23	
they fled to the l. of Corihor,	14:27	
upon all the face of the l.,	15:12	
were upon the face of the l.,	15:14	
in this part of the l. they are	Mro 8:28	
upon all the face of this l.	9:19	
nations should possess this l.;	DC 10:49	
leave a blessing upon this l.	10:50	
believe in this gospel in this l.	10:50	
performing your labors on the l.,	26: 1	
place upon the face of this l.,	29: 8	
shall be a great work in the l.,	35: 7	
riches, even a l. of promise,	38:18	
a l. flowing with milk and	38:18	
for the l. of your inheritance,	38:19	
for the l. of your inheritance,	38:20	
hearts of men in your own l.	38:29	
according to the laws of the l.;	42:79	
according to the laws of the l.	42:79	
up unto the law of the l.	42:84	
up unto the law of the l.	42:85	
up unto the law of the l.	42:86	
sickness shall cover the l.	45:31	
a l. of peace, a city of refuge,	45:66	
may be enabled to purchase l.	48: 4	
according to the laws of the l.,	51: 6	
them this l. for a little season,	51:16	
let them act upon this l.	51:17	
the l. which I will consecrate	52: 2	
and journey to the l. of Missouri.	52: 3	
the l. of your inheritance.	52: 5	
for Satan is abroad in the l.,	52:14	
by the way unto this same l.	52:22	
by the way unto this same l.	52:23	
by the way unto this same l.	52:25	
even unto this same l.	52:26	
their journey unto this same l.,	52:27	
upon the l. of Missouri,	52:42	
which is the l. of your inheritance,	52:42	
is now the l. of your enemies.	52:42	
go to now and flee the l.,	54: 7	
unto the l. of Missouri,	54: 8	
in the l. of your inheritance	55: 5	
speedily to the l. of Missouri,	56: 5	
to the l. which I have appointed.	56: 7	
no divisions made upon the l.,	56: 9	
still to go to the l. of Missouri;	56: 9	
him again in the l. of Missouri,	56:12	
my commandments, in this l.,	57: 1	
land, which is the l. of Missouri,	57: 1	
the l. which I have appointed	57: 1	
this is the l. of promise,	57: 2	
the l. should be purchased	57: 6	
to buy l. in all the regions	57: 6	
be planted in the l. of Zion,	57:14	
commanded to come to this l.,	57:15	
and also concerning this l.	58: 1	
and in bearing record of the l.	58: 7	
unto him his mission in this l.	58:14	
law shall be kept on this l.	58:19	
man break the laws of the l.,	58:21	
to break the laws of the l.	58:21	
this l. is the land of his residence,	58:24	
this land is the l. of his residence,	58:24	
the l. of the residence ot him	58:24	
bring their families to this l.,	58:25	
directions concerning this l.	58:34	
cometh unto this l. to receive	58:36	
receive his inheritance in the l.;	58:40	
receive their inheritance in this l.,	58:44	
not appointed to stay in this l.,	58:46	
a description of the l. of Zion,	58:50	
inasmuch as there is l. obtained,	58:54	
of all kinds unto this l.,	58:54	
consecrate and dedicate this l.,	58:57	
unto them in their own l.,	58:58	
let no man return from this l.	58:59	
who are coming to this l.,	58:61	
hold a conference upon this l.	58:61	
who have come up unto this l.	59: 1	
stand upon the l. of Zion,	59: 3	
to the l. from whence they came;	60: 1	
the l. from whence you came.	60: 5	
who are to come unto this l.	60:12	
come up unto the l. of Zion,	60:14	
able to go up to the l. of Zion	61:16	
in the beginning cursed the l.,	61:17	
they go by water or by l.;	61:22	
they shall journey by l.,	61:24	

LAND

and go up unto the l. of Zion;	DC 61:24
whether upon the l. or upon	61:28
gone up unto the l. of Zion;	62: 2
yourselves upon the l. of Zion;	62: 4
together in the l. of Missouri.	62: 6
together unto the l. of Zion,	63:24
Behold, the l. of Zion—	63:25
the l. of Zion shall not be	63:29
assembled upon the l. of Zion;	63:36
dispose of the l., that he may	63:39
journey up unto the l. of Zion,	63:39
be sent up unto the l. of Zion,	63:40
shall go up unto the l. of Zion,	63:41
be sent up unto the l. of Zion.	63:43
treasures unto the l. of Zion	63:48
to his agency in the l. of Zion;	64:18
strong hold in the l. of Kirtland,	64:21
open heart up to the l. of Zion;	64:22
shall go up unto the l. of Zion.	64:26
inheritance in the l. of Zion.	64:30
eat the good of the l. of Zion	64:34
cut off out of the l. of Zion,	64:35
and shall not inherit the l.	64:35
proclaim my gospel from l. to	66: 5
my gospel from land to l.,	66: 5
not up unto the l. of Zion as yet;	66: 6
people to people, and from l. to	68: 1
to people, and from land to l.,	68: 1
sayings unto the l. of Zion.	68:32
shall carry unto the l. of Zion,	69: 1
stewardships to the l. of Zion;	69: 5
the l. of Zion shall be a seat	69: 6
shall grow up on the l. of Zion,	69: 8
in whatsoever l. they shall be	72:23
shall go up unto the l. of Zion	72:26
in the l. of their fathers.	77:15
this place and in the l. of Zion.—	78: 3
in the l. of the living,	81: 3
both in the l. of Zion, and in	82:12
in the l. of Shinehah [Kirtland];	82:12
consecrated the l. of Shinehah	82:13
according to the laws of the l.	83: 3
kingdom pollute my holy l.?	84:59
remnants who are left of the l.	87: 5
judgments which are on the l.;	88:79
he shall stand forth upon the l.	88:110
and go up unto the l. of Zion,	90:28
go up unto the l. of Zion,	90:30
Zion, here in the l. of Kirtland.	94: 1
your brethren in the l. of Zion,	97: 1
over the school in the l. of Zion	97: 4
which is planted in a goodly l.,	97: 9
built unto me in the l. of Zion,	97:10
concerning the laws of the l.,	98: 4
that law of the l. which is	98: 5
the constitutional law of the l.;	98: 6
go up also unto the goodly l.,	99: 7
found about in this eastern l.	100: 3
from the l. of their inheritance—	101: 1
nobleman had a spot of l.,	101:44
upon this very choice piece of l.,	101:44
may overlook the l. round about,	101:45
unto the l. of my vineyard,	101:56
get ye straightway unto my l.;	101:57
of mine house and possess the l.	101:58
the l. which I have appointed	101:70
appointed to be the l. of Zion,	101:70
the l. which can be purchased	101:71
the Constitution of this l.,	101:80
redeemed the l. by the shedding	101:80
been scattered on the l. of Zion;	103: 1
restoration to the l. of Zion,	103:13
ye shall possess the goodly l.	103:20
together unto the l. of Zion,	103:22
the l. which I have bought	103:22
to drive you from my goodly l.,	103:24
consecrated the l. of their brethren,	103:24
return to the l. of their brethren,	103:30
to go up unto the l. of Zion	103:30
not go up unto the l. of Zion	103:34
up with you unto the l. of Zion.	103:34
upon the consecrated l.,	103:35
which dwell in the l. of Shinehah	104:21
the lot of l. which my servant	DC 104:24
in the l. of Shinehah [Kirtland].	104:40
my name in the l. of Kirtland.	105:33
the l. of Freedom and the regions	106: 1
church of Christ in the l. of Zion,	107:59
mercy upon the rulers of our l.;	109:54
namely, the Constitution of our l.,	109:54
tribes from the l. of the north.	110:11
together upon the l. of Zion,	115: 6
holy and consecrated l. unto me;	115: 7
journey from the l. of Kirtland,	117: 1
or the l. where Adam dwelt,	117: 8
up hither unto the l. of my people,	117: 9
to the l. of Adam-Ondi-Ahman,	117:11
speedily, unto the l. of Zion;	117:14
my servants in the l. of Kirtland	117:16
for a season in the l. of Zion,	118: 2
who gather unto the l. of Zion	119: 5
sanctify the l. of Zion unto me,	119: 6
shall not be a l. of Zion unto you.	119: 6
or to the seas, or to the dry l.,	121:30
thou art in perils by l. or by sea;	122: 5
build a house in the l. of promise,	124:38
been slain in the l. of Missouri,	124:54
because of the sickness of the l.	124:87
sickness of the l. shall redound	124:87
l. opposite the city of Nauvoo,	125: 3
my church, upon the l. of Zion,	133: 4
Go ye forth unto the l. of Zion,	133: 9
the sea, and upon the l. of Zion.	133:20
the islands shall become one l.;	133:23
And the l. of Jerusalem	133:24
l. of Zion shall be turned back	133:24
shall no longer be a thirsty l.	133:29
be ready to go to a l. of peace.	136:16
of Israel out of the l. of Egypt;	136:22
forbidden by the law of the l.	OD
and each l. was called earth,	Mses 1:29
Let there be dry l., and it was so.	2: 9
I, God, called the dry l. Earth;	2:10
the whole l. of Havilah,	3:11
And the gold of that l. was good,	3:12
the whole l. of Ethiopia.	3:13
to divide two and two in the l.,	5: 3
to till the l., and to tend flocks,	5: 3
brethren dwelt in the l. of Nod,	5:41
in the l. upon the footstool of God.	6: 9
upon all the face of the l.	6:15
of God came out from the l.,	6:17
and dwelt in a l. of promise,	6:17
that Enoch journeyed in the l.,	6:26
came the saying abroad in the l.:	6:36
that Enoch went forth in the l.,	6:37
is a strange thing in the l.;	6:38
came out from the l. of Cainan,	6:41
of Cainan, the l. of my fathers,	6:41
l. of righteousness unto this day.	6:41
journeyed from the l. of Cainan,	6:42
shall divide themselves in the l.,	7: 7
l. shall be barren and unfruitful,	7: 7
curse the l. with much heat,	7: 8
and I beheld the l. of Sharon,	7: 9
of Sharon, and the l. of Enoch,	7: 9
of Enoch, and the l. of Omner,	7: 9
of Omner, and the l. of Heni,	7: 9
of Heni, and the l. of Shem,	7: 9
of Shem, and the l. of Haner,	7: 9
and the l. of Hanannihah,	7: 9
a l. out of the depth of the sea,	7:14
upon the l. which came up out	7:14
giants of the l., also, stood afar	7:15
And the Lord blessed the l.,	7:17
forth a great famine into the l.,	8: 4
In the l. of the Chaldeans,	Abr 1: 1
was built in the l. of Chaldea,	1: 8
l. which thou knowest not of;	1:16
in the l. of Ur, of Chaldea.	1:20
of the gods of the l., and utterly	1:20
was preserved in the l.	1:22
l. of Egypt being first discovered	1:23
the l. it was under water,	1:24
preserved the curse in the l.	1:24
concerning the l. of Chaldea,	1:29

LAND   534   LANDS

there should be a famine in the l.	Abr	1:29	yea, and also all the l., even unto	He	4: 5
throughout all the l. of Chaldea,		1:30	possession of almost all their l.		4:13
famine to wax sore in the l. of Ur,		2: 1	and the one-half of all their l.		4:16
father, yet lived in the l. of Ur,		2: 1	the remainder of their l.,		4:19
unto a l. that I will show thee.		2: 3	the l. of their possession.		5:52
Therefore I left the l. of Ur,		2: 4	manner of gold in both these l.,		6:11
to go into the l. of Canaan;		2: 4	your l. shall be taken from you,		7:28
l. which we denominated Haran.		2: 4	back even into their own l.		11:29
in a strange l. which I will give		2: 6	the mountains unto their own l.,		11:31
in the way to the l. of Canaan,		2:15	wall, and did flee out of their l.,		16: 7
to come to the l. of Canaan.		2:16	drive them back out of their l.	3Ne	2:17
built an altar in the l. of Jershon,		2:17	your cities, your l., and		3: 6
through the l. unto the place of		2:18	ye will deliver up your l.		3:10
of the l. of the Canaanites,		2:18	destroy them in their own l.		3:20
the l. of this idolatrous nation.		2:18	ourselves in the center of our l.,		3:21
Unto thy seed will I give this l.		2:19	to take possession of the l.,		4: 1
of a famine in the l.;		2:21	of all the l. which had been		4: 1
the Gods prounounced the dry l.,		4:10	l. which had been deserted by		4: 2
			had left their l. desolate,		4: 3
LANDING			people of Nephi from their l.,		4:16
being the place of their first l.	Al	22:30	of the earth unto their own l..		5:26
			did all return to their own l.		6: 1
LANDS			they did return to their own l.		6: 2
choice above all other l.	1Ne	2:20	l., according to their numbers,		6: 3
choice above all other l.,		13:30	to the l. of their inheritance,		29: 1
the righteous into precious l.,		17:38	in all the l. round about.	4Ne	1: 1
doings of the Lord in other l.,		19:22	taken possession of the l. of	Mrm	2:27
to the l. of their inheritance;		22:12	get the l. of our inheritance		2:28
which is choice above all other l.;	2Ne	1: 5	preparing their l. and their arms		3: 1
them the l. of their possessions,		1:11	get possession of any of our l.;		3: 6
again to the l. of their inheritance.		6:11	return to their own l. again.		3: 7
home to the l. of their inheritance,		9: 2	and drive them out of their l.		4:15
in all their l. of promise.		9: 2	whatsoever l. we had passed by,		5: 5
unto the l. of their inheritance.		10: 7	vapors of smoke in foreign l.;		8:29
forth to the l. of their inheritance.		10: 8	above all the l. of the earth.	Eth	1:42
God unto me, above all other l.,		10:19	was choice above all other l.,		2: 7
shall return to their l. of promise.		24: 2	which is choice above all other l.;		2:10
those who shall be upon other l.,		27: 1	great sea which divideth the l.		2:13
upon all the l. of the earth,		27: 1	a land choice above all other l.		2:15
unto the l. of their possessions,		29:14	overthrow the freedom of all l.,		8:25
yea, and in all the l. of my people,	Jac	2:31	was choice above all other l.;		9:20
swept them away out of our l.,	Jar	1: 7	that was choice above all l.,		10:28
of all the l. of their inheritance.	WM	1:14	choice land above all other l.,		13: 2
their flocks, and tilling their l.,	Mos	9:14	property, yea, even part of thy l.,	DC	19:34
taken possession of all these l.;		24: 2	the purpose of purchasing l.		42:35
appointed kings over all these l.		24: 2	Ye hear of wars in foreign l.;		45:63
they all returned to their l.,	Al	3: 1	hear of wars in your own l.;		45:63
and upon your houses and l.,		7:27	out from the eastern l.,		45:64
people of Nephi to call their l.,		8: 7	And inasmuch as ye have l.,		48: 2
to possess their own l.		16: 8	inasmuch as ye have not l.,		48: 3
and their l. remained desolate.		16:11	be appointed to purhcase the l.,		48: 6
them l. for their inheritance;		35: 9	their journey into the eastern l.;		52:35
they have l. for their inheritance		35:14	even in l. for their inheritance.		56:13
wives, and children, and their l.		35:14	disciples are enabled to buy l.		57: 5
Nephites was to support their l.,		43: 9	he may obtain money to buy l.		57: 8
them l. for their inheritance.		43:12	the l. of the heritage of God		58:17
to defent their l. and their		43:26	l. purchased in Independence,		58:37
the Nephites to preserve their l.,		43:30	moneys to purchase l. in Zion.		58:49
and their families, and their l.,		43:47	purchase l. for an inheritance		58:51
yea, the thoughts of their l.,		43:48	let the privileges of the l. be		58:55
liberty which binds us to our l.		44: 5	that you should purchase the l.,		63:27
to their houses and their l.		44:23	Go unto the eastern l.,		66: 7
and the borders of their l.;		48: 8	for houses and for l.,		70:16
support their liberty, their l.,		48:10	purchase l. with money,		101:70
wilderness into their own l.,		50: 7	send them to purchase these l.		101:73
which was north of the l. of		50: 9	may buy l. and gather together		101:74
off the l. of their possessions,		50:12	to the l. of their inheritances,		103:11
upon the l. of their possession.		50:12	their moneys, and purchase l.,		103:23
were also restored to their l.		50:36	even from your own l.		103:24
Morianton concerning their l.,		51: 1	in houses, or in l., or in cattle,		104:68
should take possession of their l.		52:13	l. which I have consecrated		105:15
your armies into your own l.,		54: 6	all the l. in Jackson county		105:28
with your armies to your own l.		54: 7	that these l. should be purchased;		105:29
will retain our cities and our l.;		54:10	after these l. are purchased,		105:30
might retain our cities, and our l.,		58:10	taking possession of their own l.,		105:30
enemies, and to maintain our l.,		58:12	from the l. of their inheritance,		109:47
given us victory over those l.,		58:33	may begin to return to the l.		109:64
obtained those cities and those l.,		58:33	shall spread to foreign l.;		110:10
are in the possession of our l.;		58:38	take his family unto the eastern l.,		124:83
those l. which were lost.		59: 1	his family unto the eastern l.,		124:108
taking possession of our l.,		60:17	and all ye seas and dry l. tell		128:23
back again to their own l.,		63:15	houses and l., wives and children,		132:55
come into the heart of their l.	He	1:18	send forth unto foreign l.;		133: 8
			And he beheld many l.; and each	Mses	1:29

LANESHINE

LANESHINE
for the L. house [printing office] — DC 104:28
the L. house [printing office] — 104:29

LANGUAGE
confounded the l. of the people, — T Pg
in the l. of my father, — 1Ne 1: 2
the l. of the Egyptians. — 1: 2
was the l. of my father — 1:15
the l. of our fathers; — 3:19
after this manner of l. — 3:21
after this manner of l. — 5: 3
after this manner of l. — 5: 6
after this manner of l. — 5: 8
after this manner of l. — 10:15
after this manner of l. — 17:22
unto men according to their l., — 2Ne 31: 3
of the l. of the people; — Jac 7: 4
for he taught me in his l., — En 1: 1
their l. had become corrupted; — Om 1:17
they should be taught in his l. — 1:18
were taught in the l. of Mosiah, — 1:18
confounded the l. of the people; — 1:22
in all the l. of his fathers, — Mos 1: 2
in the l. of the Egyptians — 1: 4
that is able to interpret the l. — 8:11
should be translated into our l.; — 8:12
in all the l. of the Nephites, — 9: 1
the l. of Nephi began to be — 24: 4
confounded the l. of the people — 28:17
in the l. of him who hath — Al 5:61
attempt to address you in my l. — 7: 1
remember that this was their l. — 26:24
behold, this was the l. of Jacob. — 46:26
shall be your l. in those days. — He 13:37
which, according to our l., we — 3Ne 5:18
other people knoweth our l.; — Mrm 9:34
confounded the l. of the people, — Eth 1:33
not confound the l. of Jared; — 1:35
he confound not their l. — 1:36
a l. that they cannot be read. — 3:22
the l. which ye shall write — 3:24
telleth another in mine own l., — 12:39
after the manner of their l., — DC 1:24
give your l. to exhortation — 23: 7
whose l. is meek and — 52:16
and his l. you have known, — 67: 5
might express beyond his l.; — 67: 5
own tongue, and in his own l., — 90:11
used l. which appeared to — OD
was recorded, in the l. of Adam, — Mses 6: 5
l. which was pure and undefiled. — 6: 6
and it is given in our own l. — 6:46
for, in the l. of Adam, — 6:57
the l. which God had given him. — 7:13

LANGUAGES
in the gift of interpreting l., — Om 1:25
to know if he could interpret l., — Mos 8: 6
the purpose of interpreting l.; — 28:14
the interpretation of l. and — Mro 10:16
with all good books, and with l., — DC 90:15

LARGE
They come to the l. waters. — 1Ne 1:hd
They cross the l. waters — 1:hd
nevertheless being l. in stature, — 2:16
being a man l. in stature, — 4:31
beheld a l. and spacious field. — 8: 9
unto a l. and spacious field, — 8:20
in a l. and spacious building, — 11:35
the l. and spacious building, — 12:18
a l. stone brought unto him — Om 1:20
for there was a l. number who — 1:27
brought breastplates, which are l., — Mos 8:10
assembled together in l. bodies. — 25:15
building l. cities and villages in — 27: 6
became a l. and wealthy people. — 27: 7
a man who was l., and was noted — Al 1: 2
a l. portion of their substance — 43:13
was a l. and a strong man; — 46: 3

covered with l. bodies of water, — Al 50:29
had sent a l. number of men to — 52: 7
together a l. number of men, — 52:12
leaving a l. body of men in the — 62:14
march with a l. body of men — 62:14
they took a l. body of men of — 62:15
there was a l. company of men, — 63: 4
him an exceedingly l. ship, — 63: 5
he was a l. and a mighty man. — He 1:15
did march forth with a l. army, — 1:23
they came to l. bodies of water — 3: 4
which are particular and very l., — 3:13
I being young, was l. in stature; — Mrm 2: 1
plates had been sufficiently l. — 9:33
being a l. and mighty man, — Eth 1:34
which, by interpretation, is l., — 15: 8
they were l. and mighty men — 15:26
all l. branches of the church, — DC 107:39
l. ship is benefited very much — 123:16

LARGER
are written upon the l. plates, — Jac 3:13

LASCIVIOUSNESS
them against fornication and l., — Jac 3:12
adultery, and all manner of l., — Al 16:18
the works of darkness, and l., — 45:12
indolence, and all manner of l.; — 47:36
murders, nor any manner of l.; — 4Ne 1:16

LASHED
have burdens l. upon their backs; — Mos 12: 5

LAST
lifted up at the l. day, — 1Ne 13:37
These l. records, which thou hast — 13:40
the l. shall be first, and the first — 13:42
first, and the first shall be l. — 13:42
lifted up at the l. day; — 16: 2
and I am also the l. — 20:12
ye shall be saved at the l. day. — 22:31
of the law at the great and l. day, — 2Ne 2:26
in the l. days of my probation; — 2:30
unto you, Joseph, my l.-born. — 3: 1
And now, Joseph, my l.-born — 3: 3
shall smite them at the l. day. — 9:33
ye shall know at the l. day, — 9:44
in the l. night the angel spake — 10: 3
in the l. days when the mountain — 12: 2
worth unto them in the l. days; — 25: 8
shall judge them at the l. day, — 25:18
unto you concerning the l. days; — 26:14
But, behold, in the l. days, — 27: 1
and at l. we shall be saved — 28: 8
they are his words, at the l. day; — 33:11
kingdom at that great and l. day. — 33:12
shall condemn you at the l. day. — 33:14
be found spotless at the l. day. — Jac 1:19
upon your heads at the l. day, — 3:10
the great, and the l., and the only — 4:16
Look hither and behold the l. — 5:25
and the second and also the l.; — 5:39
And the wild fruit of the l. had — 5:40
this l., whose branch hath — 5:43
labor with our might this l. time, — 5:62
for the l. time that I shall prune — 5:62
begin at the l. that they may be — 5:63
and taht the first may be l., — 5:63
old and young, the first and the l.; — 5:63
and the l. and the first, — 5:63
once again for the l. time. — 5:63
once more, for the l. time, — 5:64
so that these l. grafts shall grow, — 5:64
is the l. time that I shall nourish — 5:71
for this l. time have we nourished — 5:75
for the l. time have I nourished — 5:76
is the day, yea, even the l. time, — 6: 2
I saw the l. which he wrote, — Om 1: 9
be judged at the great and l. day, — WM 1:11
the l. words which king Benjamin — Mos 8: 3
against you at the l. day. — 17:10

LAST 536 LASTS

and pay the l. tribute of wine	Mos 22: 7	concerning the l. days;	DC 27: 6
shall be lifted up at the l. day.	23:22	of the gospel for the l. times;	27:13
I will not receive at the l. day.	26:28	that the first shall be l.,	29:30
the l. words which the angel spake	27:17	and that the l. shall be first	29:30
Yea, even at the l. day, when	27:31	which is the l. of my work.	29:32
should be saved at the l. day,	Al 1: 4	death which is the l. death,	29:41
given us by Mosiah, our l. king;	1:14	the l. time that I shall call	33: 3
Yea, and at the l., if he can,	5:59	sent forth in these l. days,	39:11
and it shall be at the l. day,	7:21	may be pruned for the l. time.	39:17
at l. be brought to sit down with	7:25	my vineyard for the l. time—	43:28
Mosiah say, who was our l. king,	10:19	for the l. time call upon the	43:28
and the end, the first and the l.;	11:39	and chosen in these l. days,	52: 1
in the l. provocation as well as	12:36	will lift them up at the l. day.	52:44
the l. death, as well as the first.	12:36	raised up in these l. days.	53: 1
may be lifted up at the l. day	13:29	in the l. days, by the mouth of	61:14
against them at the l. day.	14:11	in the l. days have I blessed it,	61:17
the same words, even until the l.;	14:25	not to be mocked in the l. days.	63:58
when the l. had spoken unto them	14:25	for his saints in these l. days,	64:30
ye shall be cast off at the l. day?	22: 6	the land of Zion in these l. days.	64:34
may not be cast off at the l. day?	22:15	my church in these l. days	64:37
and be saved at the l. day.	22:18	to be revealed in the l. days,	66: 2
to our God at the l. day,	24:15	shall be lifted up at the l. day.	75:16
never used them, at the l. day;	24:16	and be lifted up at the l. day,	75:22
by the storm at the l. day,	26: 6	this is the testimony, l. of all,	76:22
raise them up at the l. day.	26: 7	the devil until the l. resurrection,	76:85
his children at the l. day,	30:60	L. of all, these all are they who	76:102
at the l. and judgment day,	33:22	the Jewish nation in the l. days,	77:15
be a great and l. sacrifice;	34:10	established in the l. days	84: 2
be a great and l. sacrifice;	34:13	of abomination in the l. days.	84:117
to that great and l. sacrifice;	34:14	behold, in the l. days, even now	86: 4
that great and l. sacrifice will	34:14	the first, and so on unto the l.,	88:59
the intent of this l. sacrifice,	34:15	and from the l. unto the first,	88:59
his subjects at the l. day;	34:39	and from the first unto the l.;	88:59
shall be lifted up at the l. day.	36: 3	the great and l. promise	88:69
will raise me up at the l. day,	36:28	first laborers in this l. kingdom.	88:70
shall be lifted up at the l. day.	37:37	first laborers in this l. kingdom,	88:74
shall be lifted up at the l. day.	38: 5	this great and l. promise,	88:75
at the l. day into his kingdom,	38:15	the Gentiles for the l. time,	88:84
against you at the l. day,	39: 8	until that great and l. day,	88:102
at the l. day, be restored unto	41: 3	of all saints in the l. days.—	89: 2
but in the l. day it shall be	42:27	conspiring men in the l. days,	89: 4
this war did l. all that year;	He 11: 2	is coming forth for the l. time.	90: 2
and third year it did also l.	11: 2	the keys of this l. kingdom;	90: 6
in the great and l. day there are	12:25	my vineyard for the l. time,	95: 4
did l. for about the space of	3Ne 8:19	upon them his l. blessing.	107:53
l. for the space of three days	8:23	prophets, concerning the l. days.	109:23
him will I raise up at the l. day.	15: 1	the wicked, in the l. days—	109:45
even unto the great and l. day,	26: 4	I am the first and the l.;	110: 4
shall ye be called at the l. day.	27: 5	for the l. days and for the last time,	112:30
same shall be saved at the l. day.	27: 6	for the last days and for the l. time,	112:30
spotless before me at the l. day,	27:20	l. of all, being sent down from	112:32
shall be lifted up at the l. day.	27:22	of my people in the l. days.	113: 6
not receive them at the l. day;	28:34	God should call in the l. days,	113: 8
shall take place at the l. day;	28:39	my church be called in the l. days,	115: 4
he that kept this l. record,	4Ne 1:19	to be revealed in the l. times,	121:27
I shall be lifted up at the l. day.	Mrm 2:19	l. effort which is enjoined on	123: 6
the l. struggle of my people,	6: 6	to be revealed in the l. days,	128:17
will uphold such at the l. day.	8:31	Malachi says, l. chapter, verses 5th	128:17
at that great and l. day.	9: 6	to hold this power in the l. days,	132: 7
I that speaketh at the l. day.	Eth 4:10	arm is stretched out in the l. days,	136:22
unto my name at the l. day,	4:19	contracted in Utah since l. June	OD
against the world at the l. day.	5: 4	by the court of l. resort,	OD
stand before God at the l. day.	5: 6	even so will I come in the l. days,	Mses 7:60
and did l. for the space of	10: 9	of the Son of Man, in the l. days,	7:65
who were first, who shall be l.;	13:12	the l. pertaining to the	Fac 2: 1
and there are they who were l.,	13:12	in the l. days, two shall be in	JS 1:44
the l. words which are written by	15:34	l. chapter of the same prophecy,	2:36
and great glory at the l. day,	Mro 7:35	twenty-eighty verse to the l.	2:41
will he, so long as time shall l.,	7:36	be conducted in the l. days.	2:54
possessed of it at the l. day,	7:47		
I have chosen in these l. days.	DC 1: 4	LAST-BORN: see LAST and BORN.	
before God at the l. day.	4: 2		
be lifted up at the l. day.	5:35	LASTED	
shall be lifted up at the l. day.	9:14	the thunder and the lightning l.,	He 14:27
these l. commandments of mine,	17: 8	which l. for the space of many	Eth 9:12
shall be lifted up at the l. day.	17: 8		
they be called at the l. day;	18:24	LASTING	
the l. great day of judgment,	19: 3	cause of this great and l. war	Al 62:35
great and the l. commandment	19:32	great and l. had been the war,	Eth 14:21
of Christ in these l. days,	20: 1		
church since the l. conference;	20:82	LASTS	
have caused this l. covenant	22: 3	and reap while the day l.,	DC 6: 3
yea, even for the l. time;	24:19	and reap while the day l.,	11: 3

LASTS

and reap while the day l.,	DC	12: 3
and reap while the day l.,		14: 3

LATCHET

whose shoe's l. I am not worthy	1Ne	10: 8
the l. of their shoes be broken;	2Ne	15:27

LATE

until it is everlastingly too l.,	He	13:38

LATER

sooner or l., will be scattered	1Ne	22: 3
but let it be sooner or l., in it I	Al	13:25

LATEST

posterity unto the l. generation.	DC	107:56
would know to his l. breath,	JS	2:24

LATTER

in the l. days, when our seed	1Ne	15:13
should be fulfilled in the l. days;		15:18
of the Jews in the l. days.		15:19
manifest unto them in the l. days,	2Ne	3: 5
of their fathers in the l. days,		3:12
the l. end of the seventeenth	Al	30: 6
the l. end of the nineteenth		48: 2
the l. end of the nineteenth		48:21
the l. end of the twenty and		52:18
and ninth year, in the l. end,		58:38
the l. end of the forty and	He	3:22
that in the l. times the promises		15:12
in the l. end of the year,	3Ne	3:22
the l. end of the eighteenth year		4: 1
in the l. day shall the truth		16: 7
from the decision of the l.	DC	102:31
The l. can only be called in		102:32
Jesus Christ of L.-day Saints,		115: 3
Jesus Christ of L.-day Saints.		115: 4
the heads of the L.-day Saints.		121:33
of Jesus Christ of L.-day Saints.		127:12
of Jesus Christ of L.-day Saints!		128:21
a people, and as L.-day Saints,		128:24
l., through the providence of God,		135: 2
thousands of the L.-day Saints,		135: 3
of Jesus Christ of L.-day Saints,		132: 2
my advice to the L.-day Saints		OD
of Jesus Christ of L.-day Saints.		OD
of Jesus Christ of L.-day Saints,		OD
Jesus Christ of L.-day saints,	JS	2: 1

LAUGHED

and they l. us to scorn?	Al	26:23
that have l. shall see their folly.	DC	45:49
up and l., and his angels rejoiced.	Mses	7:26

LAUGHETH

devil l., and his angels rejoice,	3Ne	9: 2

LAUGHTER

not with much l., for this is	DC	59:15
excess of l. far from you.		88:69
light speeches, from all l.,		88:121

LAUNCHED

and l. it forth into the west sea,	Al	63: 5

LAW

according to the l. of Moses,	1Ne	4:15
save they should have the l.		4:15
the l. was engraven upon the		4:16
according to the l. of Moses;		17:22
And the l. is given unto men.	2Ne	2: 5
by the l. no flesh is justified;		2: 5
or, by the l. men are cut off.		2: 5
by the temporal l. they were cut		2: 5
by the spiritual l. they perish		2: 5
to answer the ends of the l.,		2: 7
the ends of the l. be answered.		2: 7
the ends of the l. which the Holy		2:10
if ye shall say there is no l.,		2:13
be by the punishment of the l.		2:26
But I will write unto him my l.,	2Ne	3:17
according to the l. of Moses.		5:10
a l. shall proceed from me,		8: 4
in whose heart I have written my l.,		8: 7
and his l. must be fulfilled.		9:17
Wherefore, he has given a l.;		9:25
where there is no l. given there		9:25
those who have not thel. given		9:26
wo unto him that has the l. given,		9:27
I transgressed thy l.,		9:46
hath the l. of Moses been given;		11: 4
out of Zion shall go forth the l.,		12: 3
have cast away the l. of the Lord		15:24
seal the l. among my disciples.		18:16
To the l. and to the testimony;		18:20
we keep the l. of Moses,		25:24
until the l. shall be fulfilled.		25:24
For, for this end was the l. given;		25:25
the l. hath become dead unto us,		25:25
yet we keep the l. because of the		25:25
we speak concerning the l.		25:27
may know the deadness of the l.;		25:27
knowing the deadness of the l.,		25:27
for what end the l. was given.		25:27
after the l. is fulfilled in Christ,		25:27
when the l. ought to be done away.		25:27
also deny the prophets and the l.		25:28
until the l. shall be fulfilled		25:30
shall be the l. which ye shall do.		26: 1
intent we keep the l. of Moses,	Jac	4: 5
and keep not the l. of Moses		7: 7
and convert the l. of Moses into		7: 7
observed to keep the l. of Moses	Jar	1: 5
teaching the l. of Moses,		1:11
according to the l. of Moses;	Mos	2: 3
having transgressed the l. of God		2:33
he appointed unto them a l., even		3:14
a law, even the l. of Moses.		3:14
the l. of Moses availeth nothing		3:15
We teach the l. of Moses.		12:28
If ye teach the l. of Moses why		12:29
that ye teach the l. of Moses.		12:31
ye concerning the l. of Moses?		12:31
salvation come by the l. of Moses?		12:31
did come by the l. of Moses.		12:32
cometh by the l. of Moses,		13:27
keep the l. of Moses as yet;		13:27
to keep the l. of Moses.		13:27
doth not come by the l. alone;		13:28
notwithstanding the l. of Moses.		13:28
that there should be a l. given		13:29
yea, even a very strict l.;		13:29
there was a l. given them, yea,		13:30
yea, a l. of performances and		13:30
a l. which they were to observe		13:30
did they understand the l.?		13:32
did not all understand the l.;		13:32
if ye teach the l. of Moses,		16:14
neither the l. of Moses;		24: 5
this people according to our l.;		29:11
the l. which has been given to		29:15
ye observe and make it your l.—		29:26
to the l. which has been given,		29:28
the l. which had been given them;		29:39
judge them according to the l.;		29:41
the l. which has been given us	Al	1:14
this people must abide by the l.		1:14
if it were known, for fear of the l.,		1:17
the l. could have no power on		1:17
durst not steal, for fear of the l.,		1:18
a strict l. among the people of		1:21
the l. was in force upon		1:32
thus exercising the l. upon them,		1:33
executed according to the l.—		2: 1
knew that according to their l.		2: 3
be judged according to the l.,		10:13
to administer the l. at their		10:14
have I testified against your l.?		10:26
I have spoken against your l.;		10:26
have spoken in favor of your l.,		10:26
he hath spoken against our l.		10:28
it was in the l. of Mosiah that		11: 1

LAW

man who was a judge of the l.,	Al	11: 1	by faith was the l. of Moses	Eth 12:11
according to the l. and the		11: 2	answered the ends of the l.,	Mro 7:28
to the l. which was given.		11: 3	the l. of circumcision is done	8: 8
and had reviled against their l.		14: 2	all they that are without the l.	8:22
they had reviled against the l.,		14: 5	on all them that have no l.;	8:22
people, and condemn our l.?		14:20	under the curse of a broken l.	8:24
they did keep the l. of Moses;		25:15	gate by the l. of Moses,	DC 22: 2
they should keep the l. of Moses		25:15	whosoever shall go to l. with	24:17
notwithstanding the l. of Moses,		25:15	shall be cursed by the l.	24:17
the l. of Moses was a type of		25:15	a l. which was temporal;	29:34
salvation came by the l. of Moses;		25:16	I will give unto you my l.;	38:32
but the l. of Moses did serve to		25:16	faith ye shall receive my l.,	41: 3
against the l. of our brethren,		27: 9	ye shall see that my l. is kept.	41: 4
according to the l. of Moses;		30: 3	He that receiveth my l. and	41: 5
taught to keep the l. of Moses		30: 3	obey the l. which I shall give	42: 2
was no l. against a man's belief;		30: 7	in my scriptures for a l.,	42:59
that there should be a l. which		30: 7	be my l. to govern my church;	42:59
there was no l. to punish him.		30: 9	according to the l. of God.	42:81
a l. that men should be judged		30:11	up unto the l. of the land,	42:84
no l. against a man's belief;		30:11	up unto the l. of the land.	42:85
(and the l. could have no hold		30:12	up unto the l. of the land.	42:86
received only according to l.		30:33	be delivered up unto the l.,	42:87
according to the l. of Moses.		31: 9	delivered up unto the l. of God.	42:91
behold will our l., which is just,		34:11	for a l. unto my church,	43: 2
the l. requireth the life of him		34:12	And this shall be a l. unto you,	43: 5
shall the l. of Moses be fulfilled;		34:13	act upon the points of my l.	43: 8
is the whole meaning of the l.,		34:14	in the l. of my church,	43: 9
is exposed to the whole l.		34:16	my l. which ye have received.	44: 6
could he sin if there was no l.?		42:17	they that knew no l. shall have	45:54
How could there be a l. save		42:17	my l. shall be kept on this	58:19
affixed, and a just l. given,		42:18	this is a l. unto every man	58:36
Now, if there was no l. given—		42:19	according as the l. directs.	58:36
if there was no l. given against		42:20	to the l. and the prophets;	59:22
And if there was no l. given,		42:21	justified in the eyes of the l.,	64:13
But there is a l. given, and a		42:22	for they kept not the l.,	64:15
creature and executeth the l.,		42:22	a l. unto the inhabitants of Zion,	68:26
the l. inflicteth the punishment;		42:22	none are exempt from this l.	70:10
according to the l. and justice.		42:23	to the l. which has been given,	72: 9
few particular points of the l.		51: 2	according to the l. every man	72:15
nor suffer the l. to be altered;		51: 3	the l. of circumcision was had	74: 2
concerning the altering of the l.		51: 3	concerning the l. of circumcision,	74: 3
that the l. should be altered		51: 4	subject to the l. of Moses,	74: 3
that the l. should be altered		51: 5	of Moses, which l. was fulfilled.	74: 3
their trial, according to the l.,		62: 9	subjection to the l. of Moses,	74: 4
executed according to the l.;		62: 9	except the l. of Moses should	74: 5
this l. should be strictly observed		62:10	they who died without l.;	76:72
executed according to the l.		62:10	which is affixed unto my l.	82: 4
were made concerning the l.		62:47	under the hand of his father-in-l.,	84: 6
be executed according to the l.	He	2:10	the l. of carnal commandments,	84:27
could not be governed by the l.		5: 3	consecration, agreeable to his l.,	85: 3
this people and against our l.?		8: 2	in the book of the l. of God,	85: 5
the corruptness of their l.;		8: 3	in the book of the l. of God;	85: 7
according to the l. of Moses.		13: 1	written in the book of the l.,	85:11
according to the l. of Moses.		15: 5	the l. by which all things are	88:13
to observe the l. of Moses.	3Ne	1:24	are not sanctified through the l.	88:21
that the l. was not yet fulfilled,		1:25	unto you, even the l. of Christ,	88:21
and punished according to the l.		5: 5	the l. of a celestial kingdom	88:22
death, not according to the l.		6:25	the l. of a terrestrial kingdom	88:23
according to the l. which had		6:26	the l. of a telestial kingdom	88:24
to be tried according to the l.		6:27	the l. of a celestial kingdom	88:25
administered according to the l.		6:29	and transgresseth not the l.—	88:25
they did set at defiance the l.		6:30	that which is governed by l. is	88:34
in me is the l. of Moses fulfilled.		9:17	by law is also preserved by l.	88:34
that I am come to destroy the l.		12:17	That which breaketh a l., and	88:35
not passed away from the l.,		12:18	a law, and abideth not by l.,	88:35
I have given you the l. and the		12:19	to become a l. unto itself,	88:35
before you, and the l. is fulfilled.		12:19	cannot be sanctified by l.,	88:35
any man will sue thee at the l.		12:40	All kingdoms have a l. given;	88:36
which were under the l.,		12:46	every kingdom is given a l.;	88:38
this is the l. and the prophets.		14:12	unto every l. there are certain	88:38
concerning the l. of Moses;		15: 2	hath given a l. unto all things,	88:42
unto you that the l. is fulfilled		15: 4	doctrine, in the l. of the gospel,	88:78
I am he that gave the l.,		15: 5	to bind up the l. and seal up the	88:84
the l. in me is fulfilled,		15: 5	that l. of the land which is	98: 5
I have come to fulfil the l.;		15: 5	in befriending that l. which is	98: 6
the l. which was given unto		15: 8	the constitutional l. of the land;	98: 6
I am the l., and the light.		15: 9	as pertaining to l. of man,	98: 7
is the l. and the prophets,		15:10	the l. also maketh you free.	98: 8
Remember ye the l. of Moses,		25: 4	this is the l. I gave unto	98:32
ordinances of the l. of Moses;	4Ne	1:12	this is the l. that I gave unto	98:33
he did execute a l. throughout	Eth	7:26	according to the l. of heaven,	102: 4
the life of his father-in-l.;		9: 5	to the l. of my gospel,	104:18
the head of his father-in-l.,		9: 5	the l. of the celestial kingdom;	105: 4

LAW 539 LAWS

the l. of the celestial kingdom;	DC 105: 5	the l. which have been given you	Mos 29:25
and justice for us according to l.,	105:25	he had established l., and	Al 1: 1
given concerning Zion and her l.	105:34	were obliged to abide by the l.	1: 1
they may seal up the l.,	109:38	power to enact l. according to	4:16
thy servants to seal up the l.,	109:46	to the l. which had been given,	4:16
a standing l. unto them forever,	119: 4	against our l. which are just,	10:24
and shall ovserve this l.,	119: 5	ye do transgress the l. of God,	60:33
if my people observe not this l.,	119: 6	their feet the l. of Mosiah,	He 4:22
and by this l. sanctify the land	119: 6	their l. had become corrupted,	4:22
a l. on earth and in heaven,	128: 9	their l. and their governments	5: 2
There is a l., irrevocably decreed	130:20	the l. had become corrupted.	5: 2
it is by obedience to that l.	130:21	to the l. of their country	6:23
those who have this l. revealed	132: 3	and also the l. of their God.	6:23
abide the l. which was appointed	132: 5	to the l. of their country,	6:24
must and shall abide the l.,	132: 6	to the l. of their wickedness,	6:24
the conditions of this l. are these:	132: 7	formed their l. according to	3Ne 6: 4
saith the Lord, except it be by l.,	132:11	contrary to the l. of the land,	6:24
or by my word, which is my l.,	132:12	leaders did establish their l.,	7:11
they are not bound by any l. when	132:15	were not united as to their l.,	7:14
these angels did not abide my l.,	132:17	they did establish very strict l.	7:14
by my word, which is my l.,	132:18	that ye have ever abused his l.?	Mrm 9: 3
wife by my word, which is my l.,	132:19	and the l. of God,	DC 3: 6
except ye abide my l. ye cannot	132:21	to the l. of our country,	20: 1
Receive ye, therefore, my l.	132:24	transgression of these holy l.,	20:20
neither do they abide in my l.	132:25	ye shall have no l. but my laws	38:22
and he that abideth not this l.	132:27	no laws but my l. when I come,	38:22
the l. of my Holy Priesthood,	132:28	appointed unto him in my l.	41:10
by this l. is the continuation of the	132:31	knowest my l. concerning	42:28
ye into my l. and ye shall be saved.	132:32	as they break not my l.	42:52
But if ye enter not into my l.	132:33	Ye shall observe the l. which	42:66
Because this was the l.;	132:34	according to the l. of the land;	42:79
and he abode in my l.;	132:37	according to the l. of the land.	42:79
my word and according to my l.,	132:48	according to the l. of man;	44: 4
if she abide not in my l.	132:54	be enabled to keep my l.;	44: 5
as touching the l. of the priesthood,	132:58	according to the l. and	48: 6
and according to my l. and	132:59	organized according to my l.;	51: 2
to the l. of the priesthood—	132:61	according to the l. and	51: 4
virgins given unto him by this l.,	132:62	according to the l. of the land.	51: 6
unto her the l. of my priesthood,	132:64	themselves according to my l.	51:15
who receive and abide in my l.	132:64	according to the l. of the	58:18
if she receive not this l.,	132:65	break the l. of the land,	58:21
is exempt from the l. of Sarah,	132:65	he that keepeth the l. of God	58:21
unto Abraham according to the l.	132:65	to break the l. of the land.	58:21
And now, as pertaining to this l.,	132:66	the l. which ye have received	58:23
testimony and bound up the l.,	133:72	are the l. of the church,	58:23
as will administer the l. in equity	134: 3	is said in my l., or forbidden,	64:27
we do not believe that human l.	134: 4	according to the l. of the	70: 8
men should appeal to the civil l.	134:11	to the l. of the kingdom,	72:24
pretended requirements of the l.,	135: 4	according to the l. of the Lord.	82:15
forbidden by the l. of the land.	OD	to the l. of my church,	82:21
have given unto you another l.	Mses 6:56	to the l. of the church	83: 1
honoring, and sustaining the l.	AoF 12	according to the l. of the land.	83: 3
		of l. of God and man,	93:53
LAW, WILLIAM: *see also WILLIAM.*		concerning the l. of the land,	98: 4
L. pay stock into that house,	DC 124:82	the l. and constitution of	101:77
S. also receive the keys	124:97	the l. and commandments	103:35
L. assist my servant Joseph,	124:107	the l. of consecration which	105:29
Joseph, and Hyrum, and L.,	124:118	become sugject unto her l.	105:32
and my servant L.,	124:126	l. respecting church business—	107:59
		before him according to the l.,	107:72
LAWFUL		according to the l. of the church.	107:79
the l. captives delivered?	1Ne 21:24	from the justice and the l. of God,	107:84
or the l. captive delivered?	2Ne 6:16	organized according to thy l.,	109:15
which are not l. to be written.	3Ne 26:18	all their glories, l., and set times,	121:31
it is l. that he should have	DC 49:16	transgression of my holy l.	124:50
are not l. for man to utter;	76:115	both in making l. and	134: 1
For ye are l. heirs, according	86: 9	l. are framed and held inviolate	134: 2
it shall be l. in me,	132:65	to enforce the l. of the same;	134: 3
		by the l. of such governments;	134: 5
LAWGIVER		have a right to enact such l.	134: 5
for I am your l., and what	DC 38:22	to the l. all men own respect	134: 6
will be their king and their l.	45:59	human l. being instituted for	134: 6
not offend him who is your l.—	64:13	and divine l. given of heaven,	134: 6
		are bound to enact l. for the	134: 7
LAWS		and reverence are shown to the l.	134: 7
And the l. of the land were	Jar 1: 5	by the l. of that government	134: 8
that they transgress the l. of God,	Mos 4:14	bringing offenders against good l.	134: 8
would establish the l. of God,	29:13	where such l. exist as will protect	134:11
he teareth up the l. of those who	29:22	appeal cannot be made to the l.,	134:11
And he enacteth l., and sendeth	29:23	as l. have been enacted by	OD
l. after the manner of his own	29:23	which l. have been pronounced	OD
whosoever doth not obey his l.	29:23	to submit to those l.,	OD
		by obedience to the l. and	AoF 3

LAWYER 540 LAYING

LAWYER

there was no l. nor judge nor	3Ne	6:22

LAWYERS

who were l., who were hired or	Al	10:14
these l. were learned in all the		10:15
ye l. and hypocrites, for ye are		10:17
wise l. whom we have selected.		10:24
the unrighteousness of your l.		10:27
he has reviled against our l.,		10:29
the l. put it into their hearts that		10:30
the object of these l. was to		10:32
also against their l. and judges.		14: 2
their l. and judges of the land,		14: 5
there came many l., and judges,		14:18
teachers and their l. went in		14:23
and the chief judge, and the l.,		14:27
many l., and many officers.	3Ne	6:11
had been high priests and l.;		6:21
those who were l. were angry		6:21
almost all the l. and the		6:27

LAY

they did l. their hands upon me,	1Ne	7:16
sought to l. hands upon me;		7:19
forth to l. their hands upon me		17:48
whoso shall l. his hands upon me		17:48
durst they l. their hands upon me		17:52
whose limbs ye must soon l. down	2Ne	1:14
and l. the foundations of the earth,		8:16
remember him, and l. aside our sins,		10:20
And I will l. it waste;		15: 6
roar, and l. hold of the prey,		15:29
shall l. their hand upon Edom		21:14
anger, to l. the land desolate;		23: 9
will l. down the haughtiness of		23:11
l. a snare for him that reproveth		27:32
that I may l. up fruit thereof	Jac	5:13
behold, I shall l. up much fruit,		5:18
I shall l. up against the season,		5:18
I may l. up of the fruit thereof		5:19
and l. it up against the season,		5:20
and l. it up against the season,		5:23
canst l. it up against the season.		5:27
must l. up fruit against the season,		5:29
which I shall l. up unto myself		5:71
will I l. up of the fruit of my		5:76
I will l. up unto mine own self		5:76
and their bones l. scattered in	Om	1:22
to l. their hands on him;	Mos	13: 2
if ye l. your hands upon me,		13: 3
durst not l. their hands on him,		13: 5
l. not this thing to your charge.		20:17
yea, can ye l. aside these things,	Al	5:53
and l. aside every sin,		7:15
forth to l. their hands on me;		9: 7
sought to l. their hands upon me,		9:32
also Zeezrom l. sick at Sidom,		15: 3
and he l. as if he were dead		18:43
his body and l. it in a sepulchre,		19: 1
l. prostrate upon the earth,		19:17
and they all l. there as though		19:18
saw him l. as if he were dead,		22:19
durst not l. their hands on Aaron		22:20
not l. their hands on Ammon,		23: 1
not l. their hands on them		23: 2
they did l. down the weapons of		23: 7
which l. nearly bordering upon		31: 3
neither must ye l. aside your		32:36
not suffer to l. down their lives,		48:24
which would l. a foundation for		50:32
if ye will l. down your arms,		54:18
shall l. down their weapons		54:18
he began again to l. a plan that		59: 4
did l. wait to destroy Helaman	He	2: 3
l. hold upon the word of God,		3:29
l. up for yourselves a treasure		5: 8
not l. their hands upon them		5:23
not l. their hands upon them;		5:25
ye cannot l. your hands on us		5:26
l. down their weapons of war,		5:51
l. their own lands upon him,		8: 4
did not l. their hands on him;	He	8: 4
seek to l. their hands upon him		10:15
Behold, we l. a tool here and on		13:34
forth to l. their hands on him,		16: 7
and did l. waste so many cities,	3Ne	2:11
l. siege round about the people		4:16
to l. siege sufficiently long to		4:18
L. not up for yourselves treasures		13:19
But l. up for yourselves		13:20
l. thy stones with fair colors,		22:11
l. thy foundations with sapphires.		22:11
and silver did they l. up in store	4Ne	1:46
city Teancum l. in the borders	Mrm	4: 3
the country which l. before us,		5: 4
and blood l. upon the face of		6:15
l. down your weapons of war,		7: 4
l. hold upon the gospel of Christ,		7: 8
they shall l. hands on the sick		9:24
And they did also l. snares	Eth	2: 2
did l. that upon men's shoulders		10: 5
if a man should l. his tool or		14: 1
Coriantumr did l. siege to		14: 5
whom ye shall l. your hands,	Mro	2: 2
l. hold upon every good thing,		7:19
l. hold upon every good thing?		7:20
may l. hold on every good thing.		7:21
l. hold upon every good thing;		7:25
l. hold upon every good gift,		10:30
l. the foundation of this church,	DC	1:30
to l. up treasures for yourself		6:27
has sought to l. a cunning plan,		10:12
the sacrament, or l. on hands;		20:58
to l. their hands upon them		20:70
to l. the foundation thereof,		21:12
shall l. their hands upon you		24:16
he shall l. his hands upon thee,		25: 8
l. aside the things of this world,		25:10
I will l. my hand upon you		36: 2
Wherefore l. to with your might		39:17
ye shall l. your hands,		39:23
and l. their hands upon them		42:44
l. the case before the church,		42:81
to l. the foundation of the city;		48: 6
you shall l. your hands,		55: 3
that you may l. it to heart,		58: 5
L. your hands upon the sick,		66: 9
l. all things before the bishop		72:15
not l. any sin to your charge;		82: 7
to l. down their lives for my sake		101:35
to l. down his life for my sake;		103:27
to l. down his life for my sake		103:28
and l. waste mine enemies;		105:15
l. down their weapons of bloodshed,		109:66
poisonous serpent cannot l. hold		124:99
l. aside all his hard speeches;		124:116
called to l. the foundation of Zion;		124:118
Which foundation he did l.,		136:38
I l. musing on the singularity	JS	2:44
I l. overwhelmed in astonishment		2:46
l. the plates, deposited in a		2:51
The box in which they l.		2:52
on these stones l. the plates		2:52
as far as in them l.		2:75

LAYETH

Messiah, who l. down his life	2Ne	2: 8
that he l. down his own life		26:24
the same l. up in store that	DC	4: 4
l. down his life in my cause,		98:13
l. down his life for my sake		103:27

LAYING

and l. down of contentions,	2Ne	3:12
by l. on his hands according to	Al	6: 1
l. the foundation of the devil;		10:17
for ye are l. traps and snares to		10:17
Ye are l. plans to pervert the		10:18
l. the fall of man before him,		22:13
plan of redemption, (l. it aside)		42:11
unto the l. down of their lives;		53:17
l. aside the commandments of	He	7: 4
l. up for yourselves treasures		8:25

LAYING

unto the l. down of thy life	Eth	12:33
l. on of hands for the baptism of	DC	20:41
by the l. on of the hands,		20:43
by the l. on of the hands of		20:68
continue in l. on of the hands		24: 9
by the l. on of the hands,		33:15
by the l. on of the hands,		35: 6
by the l. on of the hands of		49:14
and the l. on of the hands by		52:10
Spirit by the l. on of hands;		53: 3
Spirit by the l. on of hands;		55: 1
not stayed from l. hold upon		56:17
honored in l. the foundation,		58: 7
in l. his moneys before the		58:35
ye are l. the foundation of		64:33
by the l. on of the hands,		68:25
receive the l. on of the hands.		68:27
Spirit by the l. on of the hands		76:52
a work of l. out and preparing		94: 1
yet l. the foundation thereof,		101:47
by the l. on of the hands.		107:67
l. the foundation of my house.		115:11
l. of the foundation of Zion		119: 2
l. stones together in some kind	JS	2:52
not the power of l. on hands		2:70
L. on of hands for the gift of	AoF	4
and by the l. on of hands,		5

LAZINESS

they were supported in their l.,	Mos	11: 6

LAZY

a l. and an idolatrous people;	Mos	9:12

LEAD

he might l. away the souls of men	1Ne	14: 3
to l. them away to destruction.		15:24
perhaps, that he may l. us away		16:38
should l. them out of bondage?		17:24
according to his word he did l. them;		17:31
hath mercy on them shall l. them,		21:10
they who l. thee cause thee to err	2Ne	13:12
and a little child shall l. them.		21: 6
and a little child shall l. them.		30:12
they shall not l. away captive	Jac	2:33
God will l. away the righteous		3: 4
that he might l. away the hearts		7: 3
that he did l. away many haerts;		7: 3
he took the l. of their journey	Mos	10:13
l. astray the people of the Lord,		27:10
l. away the people of the church;	Al	1: 7
to l. them to war against their		2:14
l. those who were unbelievers on		4:11
l. them to believe in my words.		17:29
which l. you away into a belief		30:16
And may ye l. away this people		30:27
again l. away the hearts of		30:55
tendency to l. the people to do		31: 5
doth l. their hearts to wander		31:19
he did not l. them away after		31:22
to l. away your heart again		39:11
lest they l. away the hearts of		39:12
ye l. away the hearts of no more		39:13
would l. to the overthrow of		50:32
did l. away the most powerful		56:36
could l. them out of the city		58: 1
to l. them on to destruction;		58:24
l. the man of Christ in a straight	He	3:29
he did venture to l. them forth		4:16
l. away and deceive the hearts	3Ne	2: 2
l. them away to believe that		2: 2
Satan did l. away the hearts of		6:16
And l. us not into temptation,		13:12
l. their souls to destruction.	DC	10:22
to take the l. of all meetings.		20:44
he is to take the l. of meetings		20:49
he is to take the l. of meetings		20:56
I will l. them whithersoever		38:33
cheer, for I will l. you along.		78:18
who shall l. them like as Moses		103:16
are appointed to l. my people,		105: 7
God shall l. thee by the hand,		112:10
have appointed to l. my people,		124:45

to l. them captive at his will,	Mses	4: 4
I will l. thee by my hand, and I	Abr	1:18

LEADER

their l. being a strong and mighty	Om	1:28
and he was also their l.	Mos	7: 3
the l. of those priests was Amulon.		23:32
he slew none save it were their l.	Al	17:38
that Zoram, who was their l.,		31: 1
name of Zerahemnah was their l.		43: 5
Now, the l. of the Nephites,		43:16
their chief l. and commander;		43:44
the l. of those who were wroth		46: 3
be a king and a l. over them,		47: 6
desiring that the l. of those who		47:10
a second l. over the whole army.		47:13
if their chief l. was killed,		47:17
to appoint the second l. to		47:17
second leader to be their chief l.		47:17
Amalickiah to be their l. and		47:19
their l., whose name was Jacob,		52:20
and told it unto Jacob, their l.		52:22
Jacob, being their l., being also		52:33
that Helaman should be their l.		53:19
I am a l. of the people of the		54:14
would that I should be their l.;		56: 5
appointed a l. over the people		56: 9
appoint Coriantumr to be their l.,	He	1:17
the l. of the band of Kishkumen.		2: 4
l. and the governor of this band	3Ne	3: 1
unto themselves another l.,		4:17
And their l., Zemnarihah, was		4:28
a chief or a l. over them;		7: 3
me that I should be their l.,	Mrm	2: 1
or the l. of their armies.		2: 1
and a l. of this people,		3:11
whom you will to be your l.,	DC	54: 7

LEADERS

For the l. of this people cause	2Ne	19:16
our kings and our l. were mighty	Jar	1: 7
murmur, and complain to their l.	Mos	27: 1
rulers and l. over his people,	Al	2:14
were their chief captains and l.,		43:44
the l. of the Lamanites had		49: 6
of their l. who were not slain		51:19
and many of his l., because		56:51
because of the fall of their l.,		56:51
their chief judges and their l.,	He	11: 8
those who had been appointed l.,	3Ne	6: 6
became tribes and l. of tribes.		7: 3
their l. did establish their laws,		7:11
were their chiefs and their l.		7:14
l. of churches and teachers	Mrm	8:28
be your counselors and your l.,	DC	112:30
l. of the Church have taught,		OD

LEADETH

and l. them away into broad roads,	1Ne	12:17
And he l. away the righteous		17:38
who l. thee by the way thou		20:17
and he l. them by the neck	2Ne	26:22
l. them away carefully down to		28:21
l. them to faith on the Lord.	He	15: 7
the way, which l. to destruction,	3Ne	14:13
is the way, which l. unto life,		14:14
same that l. men to all good;	Eth	4:12
this thing l. into captivity.		6:23
l. them along until he draggeth	DC	10:26
Spirit which l. to do good—		11:12
way that l. unto the exaltation		132:22
the way that l. to the deaths;		132:25

LEADING

l. them by day and giving light	1Ne	17:30
l. away the hearts of many,	Al	30:18
l. away many women, and also		30:18
l. away the people after the silly		30:31
l. away the hearts of this people,		30:45
l. the hearts of the people to		31: 1
thus l. away the Lamanites		52:24
l. away the hearts of the people,	3Ne	2: 3
l. them away by fair promises	Eth	8:17
the l. of the ten tribes from	DC	110:11

LEADS
path which l. to eternal life; 2Ne 31:18
straight path which l. to life, 33: 9
which l. to the kingdom of God; Al 7:19
narrow is the way that l. to life, 3Ne 27:33
the way which l. to death, 27:33

LEAF
and turned down the l. upon it: DC 135: 4

LEAH
And a l. is the half of a shiblum. Al 11:17

LEANED
when Coriantumr had l. upon Eth 15:30
as I l. up to the fireplace, JS 2:20

LEANNESS
send among his fat ones, l.; 2Ne 20:16

LEAP
The lame who hath faith to l. DC 42:51
who hath faith to leap shall l. 42:51

LEAPED
Zeezrom l. upon his feet, and Al 15:11
Joseph l. from the window, DC 135: 1

LEARN
that ye may l. and glorify the name 2Ne 6: 4
neither shall they l. war any more. 12: 4
unto my people, that they may l. 25: 4
that murmured shall l. doctrine. 27:35
for they shall l. wisdom; 28:30
that they may l. with joy Jac 4: 3
things that ye may l. wisdom; Mos 2:17
that ye may l. that when ye are 2:17
he was desirous to l. them. Al 20:27
and that ye may l. wisdom; 32:12
that ye should l. wisdom; 32:12
hear my words and l. of me; 36: 3
and l. wisdom in thy youth; 37:35
yea, l. in thy youth to keep the 37:35
this that ye may l. wisdom, 38: 9
that ye may l. of me that there 38: 9
ye may l. to be more wise than Mrm 9:31
L. of me, and listen to my words; DC 19:23
declare my gospel and l. of me, 32: 1
l. the parable of the fig-tree, 35:16
I would that ye should l. that 53: 7
and l. of me what I will 58: 1
l. that he who doeth the works 59:23
l. to impart one to another 88:123
the churches, and study and l., 90:15
to l. wisdom and to find truth. 97: 1
that you may l. my will 105: 1
until they l. obedience, 105: 6
now let every man l. his duty, 107:99
they do not l. this one lesson— 121:35
l. that the storm is fully blown 127: 1
him that is ignorant l. wisdom 136:32
l. who performed the ceremony; OD
l. a parable of the fig-tree— JS 1:38

LEARNED
the manner which was l. by men, 1Ne 18: 2
given me the tongue of the l., 2Ne 7: 4
mine ear to hear as the l. 7: 4
When they are l. they think they 9:28
But to be l. is good if 9:29
and the wise, and the l., 9:42
he may show them unto the l., 27:15
And the l. shall say: Bring 27:15
Then shall the l. say: 27:18
to him that is not l.; 27:19
the man that is not l. shall say: 27:19
shall say: I am not l. 27:19
The l. shall not read them, 27:20
the wisdom of their wise and l. 27:26
O the wise, and the l., 28:15
And he was l., that he had a Jac 7: 4
l. in all the arts and cunning Al 10:15
l. of the faithfulness of Ammon Al 18: 2
confound the wise and the l. 32:23
I began to be l. somewhat Mrm 1: 2
For, if I have l. the truth, Mro 8: 5
I had l. these things of you 8: 7
First, the rich and the l., DC 58:10
have not l. to be obedient 105: 3
We have l. by sad experience 121:39
"I have l. for myself that JS 2:20

LEARNER
the teacher any better than the l.; Al 1:26

LEARNING
in all the l. of my father; 1Ne 1: 1
consists of the l. of the Jews 1: 2
might be for our profit and l. 19:23
things for your profit and l.; 2Ne 2:14
for the l. and the profit of 4:15
puffed up because of their l., 9:42
own wisdom and their own l., 26:20
they shall teach with their l., 28: 4
in l. from the mouth of Ammon Mos 21:28
riches and their chances for l., 3Ne 6:12
great l. because of their riches. 6:12
manner of the l. of my people) Mrm 1: 2
given to writing, and to l. much. DC 25: 8
you for your profit and l. 46: 1
seek l. even by study 88:118
a house of l., a house of glory, 88:119
seek l. even by study and 109: 7
a house of faith, a house of l., 109: 8
they may seek l. even by study, 109:14

LEARNS
and he that l. not his duty DC 107:100

LEAST
to excuse yourself in the l. point Al 42:30
with the l. degree of allowance. 45:16
not in the l. aright before him; He 7: 4
did doubt in the l. the words of 3Ne 5: 1
with the l. degree of allowance; DC 1:31
the l. degree you have tasted 19:20
ye do it unto the l. of these, 42:38
notwithstanding he is the l. 50:26
the l. that is among them, 67: 6
from the l. unto the greatest, 84:98
hath seen any or the l. of these 88:47
l. shadow or coloring of justice 127: 1
influence them in the l. to cause 134:12
or, at l., to make the people JS 2: 9
at l. I knew that by so doing 2:25
visit, without the l. variation; 2:45

LEATHERN
with a l. girdle about their loins. Mos 10: 8

LEAVE
to l. the land of their inheritance, 1Ne 2:11
obliged to l. behind our property, 3:26
they might l. me in the wilderness 7:16
might l. this world with gladness 2Ne 1:21
I l. unto you a blessing, 1:28
save I should l. a blessing upon 4: 5
I l. my blessing upon you, 4: 6
I l. unto you the same blessing 4: 9
and where will ye l. your glory? 20: 3
they shall l. a record behind them, Mos 12: 8
all the men should l. their wives 19:11
were many that would not l. them, 19:12
taken l. of their father, Mosiah, Al 17: 6
and Himni he did l. in the church 31: 6
of Antiparah did l. the city, 57: 4
I will l. a part of my freemen 60:25
I will l. the strength and the 60:25
l. the remainder in the charge 61:15
l. them neither root nor branch. 3Ne 25: 1
the remainder shall ye l. in Mrm 1: 4
did l. a blessing upon this land DC 10:50
L. thy house and home, except 19:36
shall l. a cursing instead of 24:15

LEAVE

Thou shalt not l. this place until	DC	28:10
to l. his merchandise and to		41: 9
can be made to l. their homes,		52: 3
shall l. the place, and shall		56:10
after they l. the canal		61:24
l. your blessing upon that		75:19
L. judgment alone with me,		82:23
I l. these sayings with you		88:62
l. the residue in mine hand.		101:71
and l. the residue in my hands.		103:40
take l. of my saints in the city of		118: 5
to l. your family as in times past,		126: 1
to l. the place for a short season,		127: 1
l. them neither root nor branch.		133:64
man l. his father and his mother,	Mses	3:24
shall a man l. his father and	Abr	5:18
l. them neither root nor branch.	JS	2:37

LEAVES

in them when they cast their l.;	2Ne	16:13
and their l. are yet tender,	DC	45:37
they sewed fig-l. together	Mses	4:13
and it begins to put forth l.,	JS	1:38

LEAVING

l. none to reign in his stead;	Al	1: 1
l. a part of his army in the land		43:25
l. men in every city to maintain		51:25
l. the remainder to maintain		56:33
l. a large body of men in the		62:14
went their ways, l. Nephi alone,	He	10: 1
l. the bodies of both men,	Eth	14:22
I wrote to you previous to my l.	DC	128: 7
necessity of l. Manchester,	JS	2:61
and was just l. the house,		2:64

LEBANON

come upon all the cedars of L.,	2Ne	12:13
L. shall fall by a mighty one.		20:34
and also the cedars of L.,		24: 8
L. shall be turned into a		27:28

LED

had l. them out of the land	1Ne	2:11
shall be l. to a land of promise;		2:20
And I was l. by the Spirit,		4: 6
thou hast l. us forth from the land		5: 2
they were also l. out of captivity		5:15
l. to the tree by which I stood.		8:19
l. by the head of the fountain,		8:20
the path which l. unto the tree		8:21
in the path which l. to the tree.		8:22
we should be l. with one accord		10:13
l. to the fountain of living waters,		11:25
father saw, that l. to the tree?		15:23
directions of the ball, which l. us		16:16
and after he has l. us away,		16:38
be l. towards the promised land;		17:13
it is by me that ye are l.		17:13
l. away by the foolish imaginations		17:20
he hath l. us out of the land		17:20
and hath l. us away because we would		17:22
would have been l. away out		17:23
would have been l. out of bondage,		17:24
notwithstanding they being l.,		17:30
l. forth by his matchless power		17:42
shall be l. away into captivity.		17:43
fathers, who were l. out of Egypt,		19:10
he l. them through the deserts;		20:21
all the tribes have been l. away;		22: 4
that they have been l. away.		22: 4
since they have been l. away,		22: 5
the righteous must be l. up		22:24
should be l. out of other countries	2Ne	1: 5
and are l. according to the will		1:18
hath l. me through mine afflictions		4:20
we have been l. to a better land,		10:20
behold, the Lord God has l. away		10:22
and they that are l. of them are		19:16
they are l., that in many instances		28:14
of Israel, which I have l. away,		29:12
I have l. this people forth out of	Jac	2:25

which I have l. out of the land	Jac	2:32
I, Jacob, am l. on by the Spirit		4:15
have l. away much of this people		7: 7
they were l. by their evil nature	En	1:20
after he had l. them out of	Om	1: 6
they were l. by many preachings		1:13
were l. by the power of his arm,		1:13
or director, which l. our fathers	Mos	1:16
that thereby they might be l.,		1:16
shall be l., yea, even as Isaiah said,		15: 6
Yea, even so he shall be l.,		15: 7
being l. by Ammon and his		22:11
the way which l. to the land of		23:36
the way that l. to the land of		23:37
he l. their way in the wilderness.		24:20
therefore he l. many of the people		27: 8
to be l. away by the Lamanites	Al	3:10
l. by him through the wilderness?		9: 9
by the devil, and l. by his will		12:11
and thus be l. by the Holy Spirit,		13:28
were l. by the Spirit of the Lord,		21:16
was l. by the spirit to the land of		22: 1
being l. by a man whose name		30:59
not be l. away after the foolish		31:17
not be l. away by the temptation		34:39
l. them away unto destruction;		36:14
he l. them by his power into		36:28
not yourself to be l. away		39:11
l. captive by the will of the devil.		40:13
was l. by a man whose name was		43:35
and he l. his army forth and		43:35
l. by the flatteries of Amalickiah,		46: 5
they were l. away by Amalickiah		46: 6
to be l. away by the evil one.		46: 8
he l. away the hearts of many		46:10
l. by a man whose name was		50:28
l. by the sea into the land		50:34
l. by a man whose name was		50:35
l. into the land northward,		52: 9
he l. the Lamanites forth		52:33
be l. away into the wilderness.		58:22
have l. away the hearts of many		61: 4
l. into the land northward.		63: 5
And they were l. by a man	He	1:15
being who l. on the people		6:28
slow to be l. to do iniquity;		7: 7
which l. to the chief market,		7:10
gate by which l. the highway.		7:10
l. by foolish and blind guides?		13:29
l. to believe the holy scriptures,		15: 7
were l. by way by some who were	3Ne	1:29
which l. from city to city,		6: 8
whom the Father hath l. away		15:15
ye be l. away captive by him.		18:15
himself to be l. into temptation.		18:25
which the Father hath l. away		21:26
they are l. away captive by him		27:32
they were l. by many priests	4Ne	1:34
l. into the land southward.	Mrm	2:29
l. into the land southward.		3: 5
I had l. them, notwithstanding		3:12
I had l. them many times to		3:12
were l. even by God the Father.		5:17
they are l. about by Satan,		5:18
being l. in the front by me.		6:11
who were l. by my son Moroni.		6:11
of the Holy Ghost l. them	Eth	12: 4
they are l. by the Holy Ghost,	Mro	6: 4
l. at any time by the Comforter	DC	20:45
I have given shall they be l.,		28: 4
be l. by him to the land which		35:25
as Moses l. the children of Israel.		56: 7
must needs be l. out of bondage		103:16
as your fathers were l. at the		103:17
in this city, as you shall be l.,		103:18
l. in paths where the poisonous		111: 3
he who l. the children of Israel		124:99
that he l. the people of God,		136:22
was l. away by their idolatry;	Mses	7:13
I was l. to say in my heart:	Abr	1:27
l. me into divers temptations,	JS	2:25
		2:28

LEES

LEES
of wine on the l. well refined,	DC	58: 8

LEFT
And he l. his house,	1Ne	2: 4
he l. gold and silver, and all		3:16
that my father l. Jerusalem,		10: 4
time my father l. Jerusalem.		19: 8
Behold, I was l. alone;		21:21
from the time that we l. Jerusalem;	2Ne	1:24
blessing which I l. unto the sons		4: 9
from the time we l. Jerusalem.		5:28
they that are l. in Zion		14: 3
eat that is l. in the land.		17:22
and he shall eat on the l. hand		19:20
as one gathereth eggs that are l.		20:14
his people which shall be l.,		21:11
his people which shall be l.,		21:16
after my father l. Jerusalem;		25:10
time that my father l. Jerusalem;		25:19
I am l. to mourn because of		32: 7
the time that Lehi l. Jerusalem;	Jac	1: 1
that our father Lehi l. Jerusalem.	En	1:25
from the time they l. Jerusalem	Mos	1: 6
time our father, Lehi, l. Jerusalem;		2:34
himself on the l. hand of God.		5:10
not found on the l. hand of God,		5:12
the time that Lehi l. Jerusalem.		6: 4
they l. the land of Zarahemla		7: 1
they l. the land of Zarahemla,		8: 5
they l. the land of Zarahemla		9:hd
And the rest l. their wives		19:12
wounded and l. upon the ground,		20:12
their dead, and they have l. him;		20:13
secret pass on the l. of the camp		22: 7
who had been l. in the land.		23:38
they l. the land of Zarahemla		25: 5
they l. the land of Zarahemla		25: 6
the time that Lehi l. Jerusalem.		28:20
from the time Lehi l. Jerusalem.		29:46
when the priests l. their labor	Al	1:26
the people also l. their labors		1:26
turning from the right to the l.,		7:20
being l. to choose good or evil;		13: 3
in one day it was l. desolate;		16:10
was l. to the pleasure of the king		17:20
their father, Lehi, l. Jerusalem.		18:36
the time that Lehi l. Jerusalem		18:38
to the right hand or to the l.,		24:23
the time Lehi l. Jerusalem;		28: 2
had l. them and had gone to		48:24
those whom he had l.		52:13
had been l. to protect the city,		52:25
l. to protect the city Bountiful.		52:27
turn to the right nor to the l.,		56:37
turn to the right nor to the l.		56:40
I turn to the right nor to the l.		56:40
right and the others on the l.;		58:17
who were l. to guard the city,		58:21
were l. in their own strength;	He	4:13
shall be l. unto you desolate.		15: 1
down and shall be l. to perish.		15: 2
the time that Lehi l. Jerusalem;	3Ne	1: 1
away since Lehi l. Jerusalem.		2: 6
cities which had been l. desolate.		4: 1
had l. their lands desolate,		4: 3
of Lehi since he l. Jerusalem.		4:11
time that Lehi l. Jerusalem,		5:15
and the places were l. desolate.		8:14
let not thy l. hand know what thy		13: 3
on the right hand and on the l.,		22: 3
hand of the Lord unto the l.,		29: 9
yea, we were l. to ourselves,	Mrm	2:26
l. by the hands of those		6:15
into pits and l. them to perish.	Eth	9:29
was none l. to bury the dead,		14:22
l. them to wander whithersoever	Mro	9:16
to the right hand nor to the l.,	DC	3: 2
who are found on my l. hand.		19: 5
the wicked on my l. hand will I		29:27
are l. to inquire for yourself		30: 3
let them be l. or rented as		38:37
have l. their companions for		42:75

LEHI

shall not be l. one stone upon	DC	45:20
which is l. unto this people		51: 8
on your right hand and on your l.,		84:88
be l. unto them desolate.		84:115
remnants who are l. of the land		87: 5
they are l. without excuse,		88:82
men may be l. without excuse;		101:93
be l. to pollute mine heritage,		105:15
not one of them is l. to stand by		121:15
is aware, he is l. unto himself,		121:38
nation may be l. without excuse		123: 6
may be l. also without excuse—		124: 7
refuge for those who shall be l.		124:10
I have l. my affairs with agents		127: 1
to you in my letter before I l.		128: 1
I was l. thus, without being able		130:16
l. a fame and name that cannot		135: 3
have l. a witness of my name?		136:40
and Moses was l. unto himself.	Mses	1: 9
and as he was l. unto himself,		1: 9
Therefore I l. the land of Ur,	Abr	2: 4
down, and I. unto you desolate.	JS	1: 2
there shall not be l. here, upon		1: 3
And Jesus l. them, and went		1: 4
shall be taken, and the other l.;		1:44
shall be taken, and the other l.;		1:45
l. the State of Vermont, and		2: 3
I was l. to all kinds of		2:28
but the fear soon l. me.		2:32
the room was again l. dark,		2:43
was l. as it had been before		2:43
I was again l. to ponder on		2:47
I l. the field, and went to		2:50
I l. Mr. Stoal's, and went to		2:58
I l. him and went to		2:65

LEGAL
a l. right to the bishopric,	DC	68:16
has a l. right to this office,		68:18
No man has a l. right to this		107:16
l. right to the presidency of this		107:76

LEGALLY
they are not l. authorized to	DC	68:20
and receive inheritances l.		85: 1

LEGS
and the ornaments of the l.,	2Ne	13:20
their wounds were upon their l.,	Al	49:24
his feet naked, as were his l.,	JS	2:31

LEHI
An account of L. and his wife	1Ne	1:hd
The Lord warns L. to depart		1:hd
(my father, L., having dwelt at		1: 4
my father, L., as he went forth		1: 5
things unto my father, L.,		1:18
Blessed art thou L., because		2: 1
did my father, L., comfort my mother,		5: 6
my father, L., took the records		5:10
my father, L., also found upon		5:14
thus my father, L., did discover		5:16
after my father, L., had made an end		7: 1
meet for him, L., that he should		7: 1
my father, L., had said many things		18:17
An account of the death of L.	2Ne	1:hd
our father, L., also spake many		1: 1
Wherefore, I, L., prophesy		1: 6
Wherefore, I, L., have obtained		1: 9
And I, L., according to the things		2:17
after my father, L., had spoken		4:12
the time that L. left Jerusalem	Jac	1: 1
were given to our father, L.;		2:34
that our father L. left Jerusalem	En	1:25
that our father, L., could have	Mos	1: 4
time our father, L., left Jerusalem;		2:34
the time that L. left Jerusalem.		6: 4
the time that L. left Jerusalem.		28:20
from the time L. left Jerusalem.		29:46
our father, L., was brought out	Al	9: 9
words which he spake unto L.,		9:13
of Nephi, who was the son of L.,		10: 3

LEHI

and he had two sons, L. and Aha)—	Al	16: 5
their father, L., left Jerusalem.		18:36
the time that L. left Jerusalem		18:38
from the time L. left Jerusalem;		28: 2
I saw, even as our father L. saw,		36:22
led by a man whose name was L.,		43:35
to contend with the army of L.		43:36
were pursued by L. and his men;		43:40
driven by L. into the waters of		43:40
And L. retained his armies upon		43:40
on the east were the men of L.		43:52
the men of L. on the east of the		43:53
among the children of L.		49: 8
Moroni had appointed L. to be		49:16
that same L. who fought with		49:16
that L. commanded the city		49:17
for they feared L. exceedingly;		49:17
which they called L.,		50:15
which he spake unto L., saying:		50:19
concerning the land of L.,		50:25
joined upon the borders of L.;		50:25
claim a part of the land of L.;		50:26
who possessed the land of L.		50:27
that the people of L. had fled to		50:28
them and the people of L.;		50:36
between the people of L. and		51: 1
also the people of the city of L.		51:24
Nephihah, and the city of L.,		51:26
and then they were met by L.		52:27
beheld L. with his army coming		52:28
before L. should overtake		52:28
and the men of L. were fresh.		52:28
all they feared was L. and his		52:29
L. was not desirous to overtake		52:30
and the men of L. on the other,		52:31
L. pressed upon their rear with		52:36
to the city of Mulek with L.,		53: 2
of the city and gave it unto L.		53: 2
L. was a man who had been		53: 2
the eldest son of our father L.;		56: 3
and the city of L. and the		59: 5
remainder in the charge of L.		61:15
food to send forth unto L. and		61:18
See that ye strengthen L. and		61:21
gave L. and Teancum command		62: 3
armies of L. and teacum.		62:13
of Nephihah to the land of L.		62:30
were met by L. and Teancum;		62:32
fled from L. and Teancum,		62:32
Moroni and L. and Teancum did		62:34
when L. and Moroni knew that		62:37
sent forth L. with an army	He	1:28
unto the youngest, the name of L.		3:21
also Nephi and L., who were		4:14
and his brother L. also, all the		5: 4
L. did preach unto the Lamanites		5:18
and L. did proceed from thence		5:20
Nephi and L. were encircled about		5:23
Nephi and L. were not burned;		5:23
Nephi and L. did stand forth		5:26
the faces of Nephi and L.;		5:36
behold the faces of Nephi and L.		5:37
Nephi and L. were in the midst		5:44
Nephi and L. went into the land		6: 6
land south was called L.		6:10
and L. into the land south.		6:10
L. was driven out of Jerusalem		8:22
behold, L., his brother, was not		11:19
Nephi and L., and many of their		11:23
Nephi who was the son of L.,	3Ne	1:hd
the time that L. left Jerusalem.		1: 1
departure of L. out of Jerusalem.		1: 2
since L. left Jerusalem.		2: 6
among all the people of L. since		4:11
the time that L. left Jerusalem,		5:15
and a pure descendant of L.		5:20
as the children of L. have kept		5:22
which our father L. brought out		10:17
among all the children of L.,	Mrm	4:12
it was the faith of Nephi and L.	Eth	12:14
from whence L. should come—		13: 5
to L. while in the wilderness,	DC	17: 1

LEHI-NEPHI

to dwell in the land of L.,	Mos	7: 1
or in the city of L.;		7: 1
go up to the land of L. to		7: 2
go up to the land of L.;		7: 4
or even the city of L.,		7:21
might possess the land of L.,		9: 6
the walls of the city of L.,		9: 8

LEHONTI

whose name was L., that he	Al	47:10
when L. received the message		47:11
came to pass that L. would not;		47:11
could not get L. to come down		47:12
fourth time his message unto L.,		47:12
when L. had come down with		47:13
L. came down with his men		47:14
surrounded by the armies of L.		47:14
poison by degrees to L.,		47:18
when L. was dead, the Lamanites		47:19

LEHONTI'S

the mount, neartly to L. camp;	Al	47:12
deliver them up into L. hands,		47:13

LEMAN

Sidney, and Parley, and L.;	DC	49: 1
my servant L. shall be ordained		49: 4

LEMUEL

Laman, L., Sam, and Nephi.	1Ne	1:hd
who were Laman, L., and Sam.		2: 5
And he also spake unto L.:		2:10
stiffneckedness of Laman and L.;		2:11
Laman and L., being the eldest,		2:12
unto them in the valley of L.,		2:14
Laman and L. would not hearken		2:18
and also was L., for he hearkened		3:28
L. did speak many hard words		3:28
L. again began to murmur,		3:31
frightened, and also L. and Sam.		4:28
and L., and two of the daughters		7: 6
yea, even unto Laman and unto L.:		7: 8
Laman and L., I fear exceedingly		8: 4
that Laman and L. should come		8:17
and L. partook not of the fruit,		8:35
feared for Laman and L.;		8:36
tent, in the valley of L.,		9: 1
tent, in the valley of L.,		10:16
the valley which he called L.		16: 6
Laman and L. and the sons		16:20
And Laman said unto L. and also		16:37
Laman and L. did take me		18:11
now my son, Laman, and also L.	2Ne	1:28
the sons and daughters of L.		4: 8
Laman and L. and the sons of		4:13
them, yea, upon Laman and L.,	Al	3: 7
the rebellions of Laman and L.,		18:38
of Shemlon, and in the city of L.,		23:12
descendants of Laman and L.		24:29
a compound of Laman and L.,		43:13

LEMUELITES

Lamanites, L., and Ishmaelites.	Jac	1:13
the L. and the Ishmaelites,	Al	47:35
were called Lamanites, and L.,	4Ne	1:38
and the Lamanites and the L.	Mrm	1: 8
L. and the Ishmaelites were		1: 9
of the Lamanites, and the L.	DC	3:18

LEND

and l. an ear unto my counsel,	2Ne	28:30
not borrow neither would he l.;	Eth	14: 2

LENDING

day to day, by l. you breath,	Mos	2:21

LENGTH

At l. their provisions did arrive,	Al	57:10
the exceeding great l. of the war		62:41
the exceeding great l. of the war;		62:41
the l. thereof was the length of	Eth	2:17

LENGTH

thereof was the l. of a tree;	Eth	2:17
and in the l. thereof,	DC	94: 4
width thereof and the l. thereof,		94:11
let it be sixty-five feet in l.,		95:15
At l. I came to the conclusion	JS	2:13
at l. came to the determination		2:13
At l. the time arrived for		2:59

LENGTHEN

I shall l. out mine arm unto	2Ne	28:32
yea, he will l. out their days	He	7:24
go beck, that it l. out the day		12:14
l. thy cords and strengthen thy	3Ne	22: 2

LENGTHENED

their time was l., according to	2Ne	2:21
mine arm is l. out all the day		28:32

LEOPARD

the l. shall lie down with the kid,	2Ne	21: 6
the l. shall lie down with the kid,		30:12

LEPROUS

blind, or halt, or maimed, or l.,	3Ne	17: 7

LESS

l. than the dust of the earth.	Mos	4: 2
or l. concerning these things?		13:33
were no l. serviceable unto the	Al	48:19
are l. than the dust of the earth.	He	12: 7
to be l. and less astonished at	3Ne	2: 1
l. astonished at a sign or a		2: 1
declare more or l. than this,		11:40
shall do more or l. than these		18:13
declareth more or l. than this,	DC	10:68
whatsoever is more or l. than this		93:25
whatsoever is more or l. than this,		98: 7
whatsoever is l. than these		98:10
years shall not be numbered l.;		122: 9
not receive l. than fifty dollars		124:64
that which is more or l. than this		124:120

LESSER

and the treading of l. cattle.	2Ne	17:25
the l. part began to breathe out	Mos	19: 3
for the l. part of the people to		29:26
the value of the l. numbers of	Al	11:14
same receiveth the l. portion		12:10
to them is given the l. portion		12:11
and the l. part walking more	He	16:10
a l. part of the things which he	3Ne	26: 8
to officiate in all the l. offices	DC	68:19
which glory is that of the l.,		76:81
And the l. priesthood continued,		84:26
belonging to the l. priesthood,		84:30
ordained unto the l. priesthood,		84:107
elders, and also the l. priests;		84:111
as well as the l. priesthood,		85:11
a greater or a l. kingdom.		88:37
Why it is called the l. priesthood		107:14
to officiate in all the l. offices,		107:17
power and authority of the l.,		107:20
and the l. light to rule the night,	Mses	2:16
and the l. light was the moon;		2:16
The planet which is the l. light,	Abr	3: 5
l. than that which is to rule the		3: 5
and the set time of the l. light		3: 6
the set time of the l. light is		3: 7
the l. light to rule the night;		4:16
with the l. light they set the stars		4:16

LESSON

that they do not learn this one l.—	DC	121:35

LEST

l. they should pursue us	1Ne	4:36
l. they should be cast off		8:36
l. ye shall be cast off		17:47
l. they should wither before me,		17:52
l. the Lord should be angry		18:10
l. they should be drowned		18:13
for fear l. thou shouldst say—		20: 5
unto thee, l. thou shouldst say—		20: 7
l. for the hardness of your hearts	2Ne	1:17
l. he shall suffer again;		1:25
l. by any means the people who		5:14
l. they see with their eyes,		16:10
trembleth l. he shall fall.		28:28
l. by any means he should swear	Jac	1: 7
l. the roots thereof should be too		5:65
I fear l. I have committed the		7:19
fear l. my case shall be awful;		7:19
l. there shall arise contentions	Mos	2:32
l. he should look for that		8:13
l. by any means my people should		9:11
l. our first parents should enter	Al	12:21
with fear l. he had done wrong		18: 5
l. there should some evil come		22:21
feared l. that a multitude should		22:22
l. they overrun us and destroy		26:25
l. they should commit sin;		27:23
l. they should offend their		30:28
l. the same judgments would		30:57
l. ye become sinners like unto		34:40
l. perhaps I should be destroyed,		36:11
l. peradventure they should fall		37:27
l. they lead away the hearts of		39:12
l. he should put forth his hand,		42: 3
l. by any means a part of the		43:25
l. they should lose their lives.		47: 2
l. the army of Moroni should		50:28
l. the Lamanites had awakened		51:36
l. the Lamanites should obtain		52: 9
l. perhaps they should not obtain		52:28
l. by so doing they should lose		53:15
l. they should not be sufficiently		56:24
l. they should be surrounded;		56:40
l. they should overtake me,		56:40
l. they should overpower the		56:46
fearing l. there were many of		56:55
l. by any means the judgments		58: 9
l. there was a plan laid to lead		58:24
l. that he should be destroyed;	He	2:11
l. they should be overpowered,		4:20
fear l. they should be burned.		5:23
l. they should be a means of		6:25
l. they should cry out against		8: 4
l. all the judgments which Nephi		9: 5
l. all the words which thou hast		11: 8
l. by knowing these things and		14:19
l. by any means they should sin;		15: 9
l. by any means those things	3Ne	1: 7
l. the Nephites should come upon		4: 6
l. at any time he shall get thee,		12:25
l. they trample them under their		14: 6
l. ye be tempted by the devil,		18:15
l. ye enter into temptation;		18:18
l. I come and smite the earth		25: 6
l. he shall come out in justice	Mrm	5:24
l. a remnant of the seed of		5:24
aware l. he shall be in danger of		8:17
beware l. he commandeth this		8:18
I feared l. he should smite me;	Eth	3: 8
l. they should be destroyed,		12: 3
I fear l. the Gentiles shall		12:25
l. they should destroy me.	Mro	1: 1
I fear l. the Spirit hath ceased		8:28
I fear l. the Lamanites shall		9: 3
I fear l. the Spirit of the Lord		9: 4
unto God l. he should smite me.		9:21
l. I smite you by the rod of	DC	19:15
repent, l. I humble you with		19:20
l. you suffer these punishments		19:20
these things l. they perish.		19:22
l. they fall into temptation;		20:33
l. thou shouldst enter into		23: 1
l. perils shall come upon you.		29: 3
l. you enter into temptation		31:12
l. the wickedness of men		38:30
l. ye become as the Nephites		38:39
l. ye be found among the wicked.		43:19
l. death shall overtake you;		45: 2
beware l. ye are deceived;		46: 8
l. there shall be any among you		46:27
l. he do that which is not in		50: 9
l. you be seized therewith.		50:33

LEST 547 LIBERTY

l. your enemies come upon you;	DC 54: 7	that same l. who beguiled our	Eth	8:25
let him take heed l. he fall.	58:15	that same l. who hath caused		8:25
do this l. they receive none	58:53	who was a l. from the beginning.	DC	93:25
presence, l. thou provoke them,	60:15			
l. their faith fail and they are	61:18	**LIARS**		
l. judgment shall come upon	63:15	the law, for l. were punished;	Al	1:17
l. there should be confusion,	63:24	and the unbelieving, and all l.,	DC	63:17
l. sore judgments fall upon your	82: 2	And l. and hypocrites shall be		64:39
l. you destroy the wheat also.	86: 6	These are they who are l.,		76:103
l. they are accounted as a	90: 5			
l. that wicked one have power	93:49	**LIB**		
l. I come and smite the whole	98:17	Hearthom was the son of L.	Eth	1:17
l. the enemy should come upon	101:53	And L. was the son of Kish.		1:18
l. by her continual coming	101:84	and L. reigned in his stead.		10:18
l. the whole earth be smitten	110:15	L. also did that which was good		10:19
l. the blood of this generation be	112:33	in the days of L. the poisonous		10:19
l. he esteem thee to be his enemy;	121:43	And L. also himself became a		10:19
l. I come and smite the earth with	128:17	that L. did live many years		10:29
l. an enemy come and destroy	132:57	and his name was L.;		14:10
look back l. sudden destruction	133:15	L. was a man of great stature,		14:10
thy neighbor, l. he condemn thee.	136:25	that in the first year of L.,		14:11
l. judgments come upon you,	136:42	and gave battle unto L.		14:11
neither shall ye touch it, l. ye die.	Mses 4: 9	that he fought with L.,		14:12
now l. he put forth his hand	4:28	L. did smite upon his arm		14:12
l. any finding him should kill	5:40	did press forward upon L.,		14:12
the sons of men, l. he should die.	5:54	and L. gave battle unto him		14:13
Repent, l. I come out and	7:10	L. did smite the army of		14:14
		that L. did pursue him until		14:15
LET: *see in the APPENDIX.*		with him as he fled before L.		14:15
		he gave battle unto L.,		14:16
LETTER		the brother of L. did come		14:16
a l. certifying that they are	DC 20:84	the army of the brother of L.		14:16
if the member receiving the l.	20:84	name of the brother of L. was		14:17
by l. or some other way.	44: 1			
the l. of the gospel,	107:20	**LIBELOUS**		
now close my l. for the present,	127:11	l. publications that are afloat;	DC	123: 4
As I stated to you in my l.	128: 1	l. histories that are published,		123: 5
it was declared in my former l.	128: 2			
the revelation contained in the l.	128: 7	**LIBERAL**		
		therefore they were l. to all,	Al	1:30
LETTING		the word of God was l. unto all,		6: 5
l. the guilty and the wicked go	He 7: 5			
		LIBERALLY		
LEVEL		God will give l. to him that	2Ne	4:35
and l. them with the earth,	Al 51:17	and I will give him l. and	DC	42:68
and the l. roads were spoiled,	3Ne 8:13	ask of God, who giveth l.;		46: 7
		that giveth to all men l.,	JS	2:11
LEVELED		wisdom, and would give l.,		2:13
hewn down and l. to the earth.	Al 51:18			
		LIBERATE		
LEVER		and to l. the captive,	Jac	2:19
I obtained a l., which I got	JS 2:52			
		LIBERATED		
LEVI: *see also HANCOCK, Levi W.*		all the prisoners should be l.,	Al	55:24
he shall purify the sons of L.,	3Ne 24: 3	the five were l. on the day of	He	9:18
And Corom was the son of L.	Eth 1:20			
And L. was the son of Kim.	1:21	**LIBERTIES**		
and in his old age he begat L.;	10:14	country, their rights and their l.;	Al	43:26
L. did serve in captivity after	10:15	for their homes and their l.,		43:45
until the sons of L. do offer	DC 13: 1	to infringe upon the rights and l.	DC	134: 4
your sacrifices by the sons of L.	124:39			
and he shall purify the sons of L.,	128:24	**LIBERTY**		
until the sons of L. do offer	JS 2:69	shall be a land of l. unto them;	2Ne	1: 7
		free to choose l. and eternal life,		2:27
LEVITICAL		a land of l. unto the Gentiles,		10:11
including the L. Priesthood.	DC 107: 1	ye should stand fast in this l.	Mos	23:13
the Aaronic or L. Priesthood.	107: 6	unto them their lives and their l.		23:36
priest (of the L. order),	107:10	that this land be a land of l.,		29:32
		the l. which had been granted		29:39
LEVITY		may destroy the l. of thy people,	Al	8:17
But I was guilty of l., and	JS 2:28	the l. of worshiping the Lord		21:22
		privileges, yea, and also their l.,		43: 9
LIAHONA		preserve their lands, and their l.,		43:30
or our fathers called it L.,	Al 37:38	thoughts of their lands, their l.,		43:48
		for their l. and their freedom		43:49
LIAR		that l. which binds us to our		44: 5
Wo unto the l., for he shall be	2Ne 9:34	destroy the foundation of l.		46:10
except ye make our Creator a l.	Al 5:25	(and he called it the title of l.)		46:13
he is a l. from the beginning,	5:25	the blessings of l. to rest upon		46:13
whosoever denieth this is a l.	5:39	chosen land, and the land of l.		46:17
have been void, making God a l.,	12:23	let us preserve our l. as a		46:24
who is one of the children of a l.?	20:10	desirous to maintain their l.,		46:28
Nephites, who are sons of a l.	20:13	he caused the title of l. to be		46:36

LIBERTY / LIFE

planted the standard of l.	Al 46:36	they l. in wait to deceive,	DC 123:12
preparing to support their l.,	48:10	do all things that l. in our power;	123:17
whose soul did joy in the l. and	48:11	ye shall l. down in sorrow.	133:70
lead to the overthrow of their l.	50:32		
also many of the people of l.,	51: 7	LIED	
and also with the people of l.,	51:13	for I have l. unto God;	Jac 7:19
arms and support the cause of l.	51:17	I have thus l. unto God	7:19
yielded to the standard of l.,	51:20	this man has l. concerning you,	Mos 12:14
the title of l. upon their towers,	51:20	for he hath l. unto us;	Al 10:28
fight for the l. of the Nephites,	53:17	hast l. before God unto me.	11:25
never would give up their l.,	53:17	Behold thou hast l., for thou	11:36
upon the l. of their fathers	56:47	thou hast not l. unto men only	12: 3
children, and the cause of our l.	58:12	only but thou hast l. unto God;	12: 3
they stand fast in that l.	58:40	that Amulek had l. unto them,	14: 2
and the l. of my people.	61: 9	that he has l. in his words,	DC 10:18
standeth fast in that l. in the	61: 9	they will say that you have l.	10:31
those who stand fast in that l.	61:21		
he did raise the standard of l.	62: 4	LIES	
yea, a true friend to l.;	62:37	we know that he l. unto us;	1Ne 16:38
to destroy the l. of the people.	He 1: 8	devil, who is the father of all l.,	2Ne 2:18
that the five were set at l.,	9:38	to remain with the father of l.,	9: 9
and their freedom and their l.	3Ne 2:12	the prophet that teacheth l.,	19:15
suppose to be your right and l.;	3: 2	devil, who is the father of all l.;	Eth 8:25
a god, in the defence of your l.,	3: 2	inherited l., upon the hearts of	DC 123: 7
murder no more were set at l.	5: 4	the devil, the father of all l.,	Mses 4: 4
land should no more be at l.	6:30	shalt be the father of his l.;	5:24
the l. wherewith ye are	DC 88:86		
innocent blood on the banner of l.,	135: 7	LIEST	
		yea, when thou l. down at night	Al 37:37
LIBNAH			
of Elkenah, and the god of L.,	Abr 1: 6	LIETH	
before the gods of Elkenah, L.,	1:13	but it l. in a straight course	2Ne 9:41
of Elkenah, and the god of L.,	1:17	speaketh the truth and l. not.	Jac 4:13
the gods of Elkenah, L.,	Fac 1: 4	murdered, and he l. in his blood;	He 8:27
The idolatrous god of L.	1: 6	and he l. not, but fulfilleth all	3Ne 27:18
		unto him that l. to deceive	DC 10:28
LICENSE		that another l. to deceive,	10:28
shall entitle him to a l.,	DC 20:64	he that l. and will not repent	42:21
Sidney Gilbert obtain a l.—	57: 9	wherefore the world l. in sin.	49:20
		and my power l. beneath.	63:59
LICENSES		the whole world l. in sin,	84:49
their l. from other elders,	DC 20:63	thy path l. among the mountains,	112: 7
		is much which l. in futurity,	123:15
LICK		sin l. at the door, and Satan	Mses 5:23
and l. up the dust of thy feet;	1Ne 21:23		
and l. up the dust of thy feet;	2Ne 6: 7	LIFE	
shall l. up the dust of their feet;	6:13	they seek to destroy his l.	1Ne 1:hd
		an account of mine own l.	1:17
LIE		and they also sought his l.,	1:20
down to l. low in the dust;	1Ne 18:18	they seek to take away thy l.	2: 1
ye shall l. down in sorrow.	2Ne 7:11	to take away the l. of my father.	2:13
they l. at the head of all the	8:20	sought to take away mine own l.;	4:11
leopard shall l. down with the kid,	21: 6	we would spare his l.	4:32
young ones shall l. down together;	21: 7	to take away the l. of my father,	7:14
beasts of the desert shall l. there;	23:21	they sought to take away my l.,	7:16
all of them, l. in glory,	24:18	striving to take away my l.	7:19
the needy shall l. down in safety;	24:30	or to the tree of l.;	11:25
that they should not l.;	26:32	the tree of l. was a representation	11:25
yea, l. a little, take the advantage	28: 8	unto peace and l. eternal, or	14: 7
leopard shall l. down with the kid,	30:12	representation of the tree of l.	15:22
young ones shall l. down together;	30:13	the wicked from the tree of l.,	15:28
knew that God could not l.;	En 1: 6	and also from that tree of l.,	15:36
about to l. down in my grave;	Om 1:30	sought to take away his l.;	17:44
Nevertheless, they durst not l.,	Al 1:17	sought to take away his l.;	17:44
that ye can l. unto the Lord	5:17	ye sought to take away his l.;	2Ne 1:24
to l. and to deceive this people	12: 4	Messiah, who layeth down his l.	2: 8
they would l. down and perish,	24:23	remain as dead, having no l.	2:11
at night l. down unto the Lord,	37:37	in opposition to the tree of l.;	2:15
deny them except ye shall l.,	He 8:24	to choose liberty and eternal l.,	2:27
the earth, and did l. in his blood.	9: 3	his words, and choose eternal l.,	2:28
a God of truth, and canst not l.	Eth 3:12	did seek to take away my l.	5: 2
and to plunder, and to l.,	8:16	did seek to take away my l.	5: 4
words of Christ; and I l. not.	Mro 10:26	they sought to take away my l.	5:19
ye shall know that I l. not,	10:27	passed from this first death unto l.,	9:15
that l. in wait to destroy thee	DC 5:33	spiritually-minded is l. eternal.	9:39
Deceive and l. in wait to catch,	10:25	death or the way of eternal l.	10:23
it is no sin to l. that they may	10:25	unto that l. which is in Christ,	25:27
they may catch a man in a l.,	10:25	that he layeth down his own l.	26:24
Thou shalt not l.;	42:21	path which leads to eternal l.;	31:18
And if he or she shall l.,	42:86	Ye shall have eternal l.	31:20
the faithful and cannot l.	62: 6	to the end, which is l. eternal.	33: 4
loveth and maketh a l.,	63:17	straight path which leads to l.,	33: 9
whosoever loves and makes a l.	76:103	until ye shall obtain eternal l.	Jac 6:11

LIFE

speak concerning eternal l.,	En	1: 3
even unto the end of his l.,	Mos	4: 6
mean the l. of the mortal body—		4: 6
to whom also your l. belongeth;		4:22
salvation and eternal l.,		5:15
and sought to take away his l.;		11:26
the l. of king Noah shall be		12: 3
prophesieth evil concerning thy l.,		12:10
thy l. shall be as a garment in a		12:10
thus they have eternal l.		15:23
resurrection, or have eternal l.,		15:24
children also have eternal l.		15:25
the light and the l. of the world;		16: 9
and also a l. which is endless,		16: 9
to the resurrection of endless l.		16:11
that ye may have eternal l.—		18: 9
may he grant unto you eternal l.,		18:13
as he was about his own l.;		19: 8
Gideon did spare his l.		19: 8
that thou shalt have eternal l.;		26:20
and they shall have eternal l.;		28: 7
all men should have eternal l.	Al	1: 4
have mercy and spare my l.,		2:30
such an one hath not eternal l.		5:28
of the fruit of the tree of l.;		5:34
bread and the waters of l. freely;		5:34
shall be written in the book of l.,		5:58
of the fruit of the tree of l.		5:62
he shall have eternal l., according		7:16
tolerable for them in this l.		9:15
they that shall have eternal l.,		11:40
even from the first death unto l.,		11:45
of the fruit of the tree of l.,		12:21
of the fruit of the tree of l.		12:23
this l. became a probationary		12:24
partaken of the tree of l.		12:26
that ye shall receive eternal l.;		13:29
the light of everlasting l.		19: 6
behold, the king will seek thy l.;		20: 2
Ammon that he would spare his l.		20:21
king, fearing he should lose his l.,		20:23
began to rejoice because of his l.		20:25
that I may have this eternal l.		22:15
even to take the l. of their enemy;		26:32
for this is my l. and my light,		26:36
of the light of Christ unto l.		28:14
it be unto death or unto l.;		29: 4
desireth good or evil, l. or death,		29: 5
man fared in this l. according		30:17
pluck of the fruit of the tree of l.		32:40
springing up unto everlasting l.		32:41
up in you unto everlasting l.		33:23
take the l. of his brother?		34:11
the l. of him who hath murdered;		34:12
this l. is the time for men to		34:32
the day of this l. is the day for		34:32
for after this day of l., which is		34:33
improve our time while in this l.,		34:33
the time that ye go out of this l.,		34:34
the l. and the light of the world.		38: 9
to that God who gave them l.		40:11
if their works were good in this l.,		41: 3
way, to keep the tree of l.—		42: 2
and take also of the tree of l.,		42: 3
and partaken of the tree of l.,		42: 5
were cut off from the tree of l.		42: 6
as the l. of the soul should be,		42:16
eternal also as the l. of the soul.		42:16
of the waters of l. freely;		42:27
the desires which ye have for l.,		44: 6
blood for blood, yea, l. for life;		54:12
blood for blood, yea, life for l.;		54:12
presious gift of eternal l.,	He	5: 8
unto l. which is eternal.		8:15
we will grant unto thee thy l. if		9:20
and seek to destroy my l.		9:24
hast not sought thine own l.,		10: 4
good shall have everlasting l.;		12:26
the same shall have everlasting l.		14: 8
ye might choose l. or death;		14:31
they might have everlasting l.	3Ne	5:13
unto me ye shall have eternal l.		9:14
the light and the l. of the world.		9:18
such I have laid down my l.,		9:22
the light and the l. of the world;		11:11
take no thought for your l.,		13:25
Is not the l. more than meat,		13:25
the way, which leadeth unto l.,		14:14
to the end will I give eternal l.		15: 9
the l. of my servant shall be in		21:10
resurrection of everlasting l.;		26: 5
is the way that leads to l.,		27:33
did not put an end to my l.	Mrm	6:10
with that which hath no l.,		8:39
I am the light, and the l.,	Eth	4:12
they did grant unto him his l.		8: 6
the same should lose his l.		8:14
Akish sought the l. of his		9: 5
unto the laying down of thy l.		12:33
of his property and his own l.		14: 2
and became as if he had no l.		15:32
for the safety of mine own l.	Mro	1: 3
to be raised unto l. eternal,		7:41
God with that he will spare thy l.,		9:22
of his glory and of eternal l.,		9:25
I grant unto you eternal l.,	DC	5:22
he that hath eternal l. is rich.		6: 7
might have eternal l.;		10:50
partake of the waters of l.		10:66
the l. and light of the world,		10:70
he that hath eternal l. is rich.		11: 7
the l. and the light of the world.		11:28
the light and the l. of the world,		12: 9
you shall have eternal l.,		14: 7
shall be blessed unto eternal l.;		18: 8
nor seek thy neighbor's l.		19:25
even unto the end of thy l.		19:32
receive a crown of eternal l.;		20:14
should have eternal l.,		20:26
I will preserve thy l.,		25: 2
my right hand unto eternal l.;		29:27
in immortality unto eternal l.,		29:43
shall be blessed unto eternal l.		30: 8
The light and the l. of the world,		34: 2
world that he gave his own l.,		34: 3
The light and the l. of the world;		39: 2
that which bringeth l. eternal.		42:61
and the riches of eternal l.,		43:25
me and have everlasting l.		45: 5
light and the l. of the world—		45: 7
I power to obtain eternal l.		45: 8
they also might have eternal l.		46:14
endure whether in l. or in death,		50: 5
for they shall inherit eternal l.		50: 5
cut off, either in l. or in death,		50: 8
the l. and the light, the Spirit		50:27
and shall inherit eternal l.		51:19
whether in l. or in death;		58: 2
eternal l. in the world to come.		59:23
whether in l. or in death.		61:39
and preserveth in l. them whom		63: 3
springing up unto everlasting l.		63:23
that they might have l. and be		66: 2
have a crown of eternal l.		66:12
to seal them up unto eternal l.		68:12
immortality, and eternal l.		75: 5
are theirs, whether l. or death,		76:59
to save l. and to destroy;		77: 8
the heavens, to the seal upto l.,		77: 8
beginning of days or end of l.		78:16
eternal l. in the mansions		81: 6
heed to the words of eternal l.		84:43
minds continually the words of l.,		84:85
And also their manner of l.,		85: 2
your l. and the priesthood have		86:10
I give unto you of eternal l.,		88: 4
which giveth l. to all things,		88:13
of beasts, of the staff of l.,		89:14
and in him was the l. of men		93: 9
I give a promise of eternal l.		96: 6
And whoso layeth down his l.		98:13
find it again, even l. eternal.		98:13
words of wisdom and eternal l.		98:20
if he has sought thy l., and		98:31

LIFE 550 LIFTED

and thy l. is endangered by him,	DC 98:31	causing them to l. up their heads	Al	30:18
his l. shall be as the age of	101:30	they may not l. up their heads,		30:23
neither the l. of the body;	101:37	they did l. their weapons of war		51:18
and for the l. of the soul.	101:37	they did l. their eyes to heaven;	He	5:36
and ye shall have eternal l.	101:38	Yea, ye will l. him up, and ye		13:28
the garners to possess eternal l.,	101:65	not l. their swords against them,		15: 9
to lay down his l. for my sake;	103:27	L. up your head and be of good	3Ne	1:13
whoso layeth down his l. for	103:27	and did l. their cries to the Lord		4: 8
to lay down his l. for my sake	103:28	watchmen shall l. up the voice;		16:18
he shall be cursed in his l.,	104: 5	their watchmen l. up their voice,		20:32
honor, immortality, and eternal l.	124:55	not l. themselves up in the	Mrm	8:36
common lot all the days of my l.;	127: 2	but may Christ l. thee up,	Mro	9:25
which is the book of l.;	128: 6	l. up thy heart and rejoice,	DC	25:13
which was the book of l.;	128: 7	l. up your hearts and rejoice,		27:15
book which was the book of l.	128: 7	L. up your hearts and be glad,		29: 5
immortality and eternal l.—	128:12	L. up your heart and rejoice,		31: 3
immortality and eternal l.;	128:23	to l. up your voices as with		33: 2
we attain unto in this l.,	130:18	To l. up your voice as with the		34: 6
intelligence in this l. through	130:19	l. up your voice and spare not,		34:10
he is sealed up unto eternal l.,	131: 5	L. up your hearts and be glad,		35:26
written in the Lamb's Book of L.,	132:19	ye shall l. up your voices by		42:16
shall be given eternal l.	133:62	L. up your hearts and rejoice,		42:69
and the protection of l.	134: 2	shall l. up their hands against		42:81
on the right of property or l.,	134:10	L. up your voices and spare not.		43:20
in jeopardy of either l. or limb,	134:10	do l. up my voice and call		43:21
with their situations in this l.,	134:12	men shall l. up their voices		45:32
In l. they were not divided,	135: 3	also l. up his voice in meetings,		47: 2
immortality and eternal l. of man.	Mses 1:39	l. them up at the last day.		52:44
moving creature that hath l.,	2:20	let them l. up their voice		60: 7
the earth, wherein I grant l.,	2:30	they shall l. up their voices		61:31
into his nostrils the breath of l.;	3: 7	l. a warning voice unto the		63:37
planted the tree of l. also in the	3: 9	if any man l. his voice against		71:10
into them the breath of l.,	3:19	l. up the hands which hang		81: 5
thou eat all the days of thy l.;	4:20	and shall l. up their voice,		84:98
thou eat of it all the days of thy l.	4:23	first l. a standard of peace		98:34
and partake also of the tree of l.,	4:28	l. up your voices unto this people;		100: 5
to keep the way of the tree of l.	4:31	Rigdon shall l. up his voice in		103:29
and in this l. I shall have joy,	5:10	l. up his eyes in hell, being in		104:18
eternal l. which God giveth	5:11	And l. up an ensign of peace,		105:39
words of eternal l. in this world	6:59	and l. up his voice and warn the		106: 2
eternal l. in the world to come,	6:59	will l. him up inasmuch as he will		106: 7
be sanctified and have eternal l.?	7:45	l. up your heads and rejoice.		110: 5
sought Noah to take away his l.;	8:18	Cursed are all those that shall l.		121:16
for they have sought his l.	8:26	let him l. up his voice long and		124:75
endeavored to take away my l.	Abr 1: 7	he shall l. up his voice again		124:104
me up and take away my l.,	1:15	l. up his voice as with the sound		124:106
my son, to take away thy l.	1:17	L. up your heart, and be glad;	Mses	7:44
against me, to take away my l.	1:30			
of salvation, even of l. eternal.	2:11	LIFTED		
the moving creatures that have l.;	4:20	he was l. up upon the cross	1Ne	11:33
behold, we will give them l.,	4:30	been l. up by the power of God		13:30
into his nostrils the breath of l.,	5: 7	shall be l. up at the last day,		13:37
the tree of l., also, in the midst	5: 9	should be l. up at the last day;		16: 2
It was the first time in my l.	JS 2:14	l. unto exceeding rudeness.		18: 9
a very early period of my l.,	2:20	hands of wicked men, to be l. up,		19:10
my circumstances in l. such as	2:22	the Lord has l. up his hand		22: 6
my common vocations in l.	2:27	upon every one who is l. up,	2Ne	12:12
		for they are high and l. up;		12:13
LIFT		all the nations which are l. up,		12:14
L. up thine eyes round about	1Ne 21:18	upon a throne, high and l. up,		16: 1
I will l. up mine hand to the	21:22	l. up in the pride of their eyes,		26:20
I will l. up my voice unto thee;	2Ne 4:35	and their churches are l. up;		28:12
will l. up mine hand to the Gentiles,	6: 6	to be l. up somewhat in pride.	Jac	1:16
L. up your eyes to the heavens,	8: 6	ye are l. up in the pride of your		2:13
and l. up your heads forever,	9: 3	l. up in the pride of their hearts.	Mos	11: 5
may l. up their hearts and rejoice	11: 8	l. up in the pride of their hearts;		11:19
shall not l. up sword against	12: 4	l. up their voices against him,		17:12
And he will l. up an ensign	15:26	shall be l. up at the last day.		23:22
itself against them that l. it up,	20:15	l. their voices in the praises of		24:22
as if the staff should l. up itself	20:15	l. up in the pride of his heart	Al	1: 6
shall l. up his staff against thee,	20:24	being l. up in the pride of		1:32
shall he l. it up after the manner	20:26	l. up in the pride of their eyes,		4: 6
L. up the voice, O daughter	20:30	l. up in the pride of their eyes,		4: 8
L. ye up a banner upon the	23: 2	l. up in the pride of their hearts—		6: 3
l. up your heads and receive	Jac 3: 2	l. up in the pride of your hearts;		7: 6
l. up your hearts and be	Mos 7:18	may be l. up at the last day		13:29
l. up your heads, and rejoice,	7:19	that l. his club to smite Ammon,		17:37
watchmen shall l. up the voice;	12:22	arms as were l. against him,		17:38
watchmen shall l. up their voice;	15:29	as he l. the sword to smite him,		19:22
L. up your heads and be of	24:13	who l. the sword to slay Ammon,		19:24
l. up their heads and rejoice;	Al 1: 4	whose arms were l. to slay them.		24:25
l. up thy head and rejoice,	8:15	were l. up unto great boasting,		31:25

LIFTED

he l. up his voice to heaven,	Al	31:26
shall be l. up at the last day.		36: 3
shall be l. up at the last day.		37:37
shall be l. up at the last day.		38: 5
that ye are not l. up unto pride;		38:11
proud, being l. up in their hearts,		45:24
were not l. up in the pride of		62:49
And they were l. up in pride,	He	3:34
be l. up one above another;		6:17
l. you up beyond that which is		7:26
as he l. up the brazen serpent		8:14
shall he be l. up who should come.		8:14
how quick to be l. up in pride;		12: 5
and some were l. up unto pride	3Ne	6:10
Some were l. up in pride, and		6:13
shall be l. up in the pride of		16:10
be l. up upon thine adversaries,		20:17
be l. up upon their adversaries,		21:13
might be l. up upon the cross;		27:14
had been l. up upon the cross,		27:14
as I have been l. up by men		27:14
men be l. up by the Father,		27:14
for this cause have I been l. up;		27:15
ye shall be l. up at the last day.		27:22
that I was l. up by the Jews,		28: 6
those who were l. up in pride,	4Ne	1:24
I shall be l. up at the last day.	Mrm	2:19
be l. up in the pride of their		8:28
should be l. up upon the cross;	Eth	4: 1
l. up to dwell in the kingdom		4:19
shalt be l. up at the last day.	DC	5:35
shall be l. up at the last day.		9:14
shall be l. up at the last day.		17: 8
have l. thee up out of thine		24: 1
I am he who was l. up.		45:52
shall be l. up at the last day.		75:16
and be l. up at the last day.		75:22
and l. their voice on high.		84: 1
that Moses l. up his eyes unto	Mses	1:24
and Enoch was high and l. up,		7:24
The Righteous is l. up, and the		7:47
the Son of Man l. up on the cross,		7:55
man was l. up in the imagination		8:22
they l. up their hands upon me,	Abr	1:15
l. up my voice unto the Lord my		1:15
destroy him who hath l. up		1:17

LIFTING

like the l. up of smoke.	2Ne	19:18
l. themselves up with their pride,	Al	4:12
as if talking or l. their voices	He	5:36
l. up thy heart for gladness?	DC	19:39
ever l. up your heart unto me		30: 6
l. up your voices as with the		42: 6
l. up holy hands upon them.		60: 7
L. up your voices as with the		75: 4
the exaltation or l. up of Zion.		124: 9

LIGHT

be your l. in the wilderness;	1Ne	17:13
giving l. them by night,		17:30
It is a l. thing that thou		21: 6
give thee for a l. to the Gentiles,		21: 6
of them out of darkness unto l.—	2Ne	3: 5
walketh in darkness and hath no l.?		7:10
walk in the l. of your fire		7:11
to rest for a l. for the people.		8: 4
nigh unto an angel of l.,		9: 9
and I will be a l. unto them		10:14
let us walk in the l. of the Lord;		12: 5
that put darkness for l.,		15:20
and l. for darkness,		15:20
the l. is darkened in the heavens		15:30
because there is no l. in them.		18:20
in darkness have seen a great l.;		19: 2
upon them hath the l. shined.		19: 2
the l. of Israel shall be for		20:17
thereof shall not give their l.;		23:10
shall not cause her l. to shine.		23:10
works of darkness rather than l.,		26:10
set themselves up for a l. unto		26:29
shall be made manifest in the l.;		30:17
giveth l. unto the understanding;		31: 3

551

LIGHT

ye are not brought into the l.,	2Ne	32: 4
towards you in the l. of the day,	Jac	6: 5
hidden things shall come to l.,	Mos	8:17
He is the l. and the life of the		16: 9
yea, a l. that is endless,		16: 9
burdens, that they may be l.;		18: 8
were made l.; yea, the Lord did		24:15
behold the marvelous l. of God.		27:29
by the l. of the everlasting word;	Al	5: 7
after having had so much l.		9:19
transgress contrary to the l. and		9:23
and the l. which did light up		19: 6
light which did l. up his mind,		19: 6
was the l. of the glory of God,		19: 6
a marvelous l. of his goodness—		19: 6
yea, this l. had infused such joy		19: 6
that the l. of everlasting life		19: 6
behold the marvelous l. of God!		26: 3
them into his everlasting l.,		26:15
for this is my life and my l.,		26:36
joy because of the l. of Christ		28:14
unto you, yea, because it is l.;		32:35
and whatsoever is l., is good,		32:35
after ye have tasted this l. is		32:35
that your burdens may be l.,		33:23
what marvelous l. I did behold;		36:20
shine forth in darkness unto l.,		37:23
forth out of darkness unto l.		37:25
I will bring to l. all their secrets		37:25
is the life and the l. of the world.		38: 9
the l. and knowledge of God,		39: 6
shall sin against so great l.		45:12
the l. of the morning came		56:41
ye choose darkness rather than l.?	He	14:20
refuse to give his l. unto you;		14:20
no l. upon the face of this land,		14:20
as l. as though it was mid-day.	3Ne	1:19
And there could be no l.,		8:21
there could not be any l. at all;		8:21
And there was not any l. seen,		8:22
that there was no l. seen;		8:23
I am the l. and the life of		9:18
I am the l. and the life of the		11:11
to be the l. of this people.		12:14
do men l. a candle and put it		12:15
it giveth l. to all that are in the		12:15
Therefore let your l. so shine before		12:16
The l. of the body is the eye;		13:22
whole body shall be full of l.		13:22
the l. that is in thee be darkness,		13:23
Behold, I am the law, and the l.		15: 9
ye are a l. unto this people,		15:12
Behold I am the l.; I have set		18:16
hold up your l. that it may		18:24
I am the l. which ye shall hold		18:24
the l. of his countenance did		19:25
whoso shall bring it to l.,	Mrm	8:14
can have power to bring it to l.		8:15
that shall bring this thing to l.;		8:16
brought out of darkness unto l.,		8:16
and they were l. upon the water,	Eth	2:16
O Lord, in them there is no l.;		2:19
behold there is no l. in them.		2:22
ye may have l. in your vessels?		2:23
shall not go by the l. of fire.		2:23
that ye may have l. when ye are		2:25
that we may have l. while we		3: 4
in me shall all mankind have l.,		3:14
I am the l., and the life, and		4:12
they did give l. unto the vessels.		6: 2
give l. unto men, women, and		6: 3
they did have l. continually,		6:10
the l. by which ye may judge,	Mro	7:18
which l. is the light of Christ,		7:18
which light is the l. of Christ,		7:18
diligently to the l. of Christ		7:19
the l. which he has received;	DC	1:33
I am the l. which shineth in		6:21
you assist in bringing to l.,		6:27
shall bring to l. this ministry;		6:28
love darkness rather than l.,		10:21
I am the l. which shineth in		10:58
to l. their marvelous works,		10:61

LIGHT

also bring to l. my gospel	DC	10:62
bring to l. the true points of		10:62
the life and l. of the world,		10:70
I am the l. which shineth in		11:11
bringing to l. those things		11:19
the life and the l. of the world.		11:28
the l. and the life of the world,		12: 9
a l. which cannot be hid in		14: 9
love darkness rather than l.,		29:45
The l. and the life of the world,		34: 2
a l. which shineth in darkness		34: 2
The l. and the life of the world;		39: 2
a l. which shineth in darkness		39: 2
l. and the life of the world—		45: 7
a l. that shineth in darkness		45: 7
to be a l. to the world,		45: 9
a l. shall break forth among		45:28
for they perceive not the l.,		45:29
l. shall begin to break forth,		45:36
That which is of God is l.;		50:24
and he that receiveth l.,		50:24
in God, receiveth more l.;		50:24
that l. groweth brighter and		50:24
the life and the l., the Spirit		50:27
in this l. ye shall hold them		58:23
are a representation of l.		77: 4
who sins against the greater l.		82: 3
whatsoever is truth is l.,		84:45
and whatsoever is l. is Spirit,		84:45
the Spirit giveth l. to every man		84:46
clothed with l. for a covering,		85: 7
a l. unto the Gentiles,		86:11
all things, the l. of truth;		88: 6
This is the l. of Christ.		88: 7
the sun, and the l. of the sun,		88: 7
and is the l. of the moon,		88: 8
also the l. of the stars,		88: 9
And the l. which shineth,		88:11
shineth, which giveth you l.,		88:11
the same l. that quickeneth		88:11
Which l. proceedeth forth from		88:12
The l. which is in all things,		88:13
l. cleaveth unto light;		88:40
light cleaveth unto l.;		88:40
they give l. to each other in		88:44
the sun giveth his l. by day,		88:45
the moon giveth her l. by night,		88:45
and the stars also give their l.,		88:45
The l. shineth in darkness,		88:49
I am the true l. that is in you,		88:50
the l. of the countenance of		88:56
the l. of the countenance of		88:58
bodies shall be filled with l.,		88:67
that body which is filled with l.		88:67
and shall refuse to give l.;		88:87
cease from all your l. speeches,		88:121
all your pride and l.-mindedness,		88:121
are accounted as a l. thing,		90: 5
the true l. that lighteth every		93: 2
The l. and the Redeemer of		93: 9
the life of men and the l. of men.		93: 9
receiveth truth and l.,		93:28
Intelligence, or the l. of truth,		93:29
and they receive not the l.		93:31
whose spirit receiveth not the l.		93:32
or, in other words, l. and truth.		93:36
L. and truth forsake that		93:37
and taketh away that		93:39
your children in l. and truth.		93:40
taught your children l. and truth,		93:42
in its true l. before the council;		102:16
any additional l. is shown		102:21
in case no additional l. is given,		102:22
set to be a l. unto the world,		103: 9
you may be the children of l.,		106: 5
witness and a l. unto the church		106: 8
that thy l. may be a standard		115: 5
in bringing to l. all the hidden		123:13
heed to the l. and glory of Zion,		124: 6
may come to the l. of truth,		124: 9
he appeared as an angel of l.!		128:20
If it be the devil as an angel of l.,		129: 8
the moon shall withhold its l.,		133:49

l, God, said: Let there be l.;	Mses	2: 3
there be light; and there was l.		2: 3
And I, God, saw the l.;		2: 4
and that l. was good.		2: 4
divided the l. from the darkness.		2: 4
And I, God, called the l. Day;		2: 5
heaven to give l. upon the earth;		2:15
the greater l. to rule the day,		2:16
and the lesser l. to rule the night,		2:16
and the greater l. was the sun,		2:16
and the lesser l. was the moon;		2:16
heaven to give l. upon the earth.		2:17
divide the l. from the darkness;		2:18
planet which is the lesser l.,	Abr	3: 5
greater l. which is set to rule		3: 6
lesser l. which is set to rule		3: 6
the set time of the lesser l. is		3: 7
the stars that are set to give l.,		3:10
(the Gods) said: Let there be l.;		4: 3
be light; and there was l.		4: 3
(the Gods) comprehended the l.,		4: 4
divided the l., or caused it		4: 4
the Gods called the l. day,		4: 5
to give l. upon the earth;		4:15
the greater l. to rule the day,		4:16
the lesser l. to rule the night;		4:16
lesser l. they set the stars also;		4:16
to give l. upon the earth,		4:17
to divide the l. from the darkness.		4:17
eternal l. upon his head;	Fac	2: 3
borrow its l. from Kolob		2: 5
receiving l. from the revolutions		2: 5
the l. of the morning cometh	JS	1:26
the moon shall not give her l.,		1:33
I saw a pillar of l. exactly		2:16
When the l. rested upon me		2:17
who stood above me in the l.,		2:18
When the l. had departed,		2:20
vision he had when he saw a l.,		2:24
he had both seen a l. and heard		2:24
I had actually seen a l.,		2:25
in the midst of that l. I saw		2:25
a l. appearing in my room,		2:30
The room was exceedingly l.,		2:32
I saw the l. in the room begin		2:43
before this heavenly l. had		2:43
surrounded by l. as before.		2:49
descended in a cloud of l.,		2:68

LIGHTED
and it hath l. upon Israel.	2Ne	19: 8
was again beginning to get l.,	JS	2:44

LIGHTER
room was l. than at noonday,	JS	2:30

LIGHTETH
true light that l. every man	DC	93: 2

LIGHTLY
when at first he l. afflicted	2Ne	19: 1
save it were l., concerning the	Jac	1: 2
treated l. the things you have	DC	84:54
they esteemed l. my counsel;		101: 8
that cannot be l. passed over,		128:15
my communication not only l.,	JS	2:21

LIGHT-MINDEDNESS: see *LIGHT* and *MINDEDNESS*.

LIGHTNESS
the l. of a fowl upon the water.	Eth	2:16

LIGHTNING
thunder and the l. lasted,	He	14:27
whose countenance was as l.,	DC	20: 6
smitten by the vivid shaft of l.		85: 8
the fierce and vivid l. also,		87: 6
his countenance truly like l.	JS	2:32

LIGHTNINGS
I saw l., and I heard thunderings,	1Ne	12: 4
and the l. of his power,		19:11
visited with thunderings, and l.,	2Ne	26: 6

LIGHTNINGS 553 LIKE

there shall be thunderings and l.	He	14:21
should be thunderings and l.		14:26
there were exceeding sharp l.,	3Ne	8: 7
and the thunderings and the l.,		8:12
and the thunderings, and the l.,		8:17
when the thunderings, and the l.,		8:19
when the l. shall streak forth	DC	43:22
and by the voice of l.,		43:25
thunderings, and the voice of l.,		88:90

LIGHTS

shall be great l. in heaven,	He	14: 3
above, from the Father of l.	DC	67: 9
Let there be l. in the firmament	Mses	2:14
them be for l. in the firmament		2:15
I, God, made two great l.;		2:16
signifies stars, or all the great l.,	Abr	3:13
the Gods organized the l. in the		4:14
organized them to be for l. in		4:15
Gods organized the two great l.,		4:16

LIKE

thou mightest be l. unto this river,	1Ne	2: 9
thou mightest be l. unto this valley,		2:10
they were l. unto the Jews		2:13
against him l. unto my brothers.		2:16
let us be strong l. unto Moses,		4: 2
should be a free man l. unto us		4:33
compared l. unto an olive-tree,		10:12
it was l. unto the tree which		11: 8
l. unto the building which my		11:35
l. unto the Lamb of God.		12:11
beautiful, l. unto my people		13:15
l. unto the engravings which are		13:23
l. unto the brightness of a		15:30
strong, yea, even l. unto the men;		17: 2
thou art l. unto our father,		17:20
our brother is l. unto him.		17:22
and ye are l. unto them.		17:44
l. unto the voice of thunder,		17:45
offspring of thy bowels l. the gravel		20:19
made my mouth l. a sharp sword;		21: 2
God raise up unto you, l. unto me;		22:20
be miserable l. unto himself.	2Ne	2:27
he shall be great l. unto Moses,		3: 9
And he shall be l. unto me;		3:15
the land l. unto thy brother Nephi.		4:11
shalt be even l. unto thy brother,		4:11
and thy seed l. unto his seed;		4:11
built l. unto Solomon's temple.		5:16
was l. unto the temple of Solomon;		5:16
they had become l. unto a flint;		5:21
have I set my face l. a flint,		7: 7
make her wilderness l. Eden,		8: 3
her desert l. the garden of the		8: 3
shall vanish away l. smoke,		8: 6
shall wax old l. a garment;		8: 6
therein shall die in l. manner.		8: 6
shall eat them up l. a garment,		8: 8
worm shall eat them l. wool.		8: 8
who shall be made l. unto grass?		8:12
must have become l. unto him,		9: 9
in misery, l. unto himself,		9: 9
a perfect knowledge l. unto us		9:13
commandments of God, l. unto us,		9:27
shall be l. unto a father to them;		10:18
soothsayers l. the Philistines,		12: 6
and round tires l. the moon;		13:18
hoofs shall be counted l. flint		15:28
and their wheels l. a whirlwind,		15:28
their roaring l. a lion.		15:28
They shall roar l. young lions;		15:29
l. the roaring of the sea;		15:30
l. the lifting up of smoke.		19:18
down l. the mire of the streets.		20: 6
the inhabitants l. a valiant man;		20:13
burning l. the burning of a fire.		20:16
the lion shall eat straw l. the ox.		21: 7
from Assyria, l. as it was to Israel		21:16
mountains l. as of a great people,		23: 4
Art thou become l. unto us?		24:10
I will be l. the Most High.		24:14
l. an abominable branch,		24:19

unto the Jews l. unto them,	2Ne	25: 5
the one l. unto the other,		26:28
or l. unto a thirsty man		27: 3
one nation l. unto another?		29: 8
one nation l. unto another.		29: 8
the lion shall eat straw l. the ox.		30:13
give the Holy Ghost, l. unto me;		31:12
in writing, l. unto speaking;		33: 1
such as l. unto David of old	Jac	1:15
of your brethren l. unto yourselves,		2:17
they may be rich l. unto you.		2:17
shall do l. unto them of old.		2:26
whoredoms, l. unto them of old,		2:33
which are not filthy l. unto you,		3: 3
l. unto a tame olive-tree,		5: 3
was l. unto the natural fruit.		5:17
this tree l. unto the others.		5:25
l. unto the wild olive-tree,		5:46
they became l. unto one body;		5:74
even l. as it was in the beginning.		5:75
l. as it were unto us a dream,		7:26
for their faith was l. unto thine.	En	1:18
have been l. unto our brethren,	Mos	1: 5
weak l. unto their brethren;		1:13
But I am l. as yourselves,		2:11
which is l. an unquenchable fire,		2:38
be driven before l. a dumb ass.		12: 5
we, l. sheep, have gone astray;		14: 6
they fought l. lions for their prey.		20:10
and l. dragons did they fight.		20:11
and suffered in the l. manner;		21:12
because I was l. to be cast off.		27:27
heads l. unto the Lamanites.	Al	3: 4
of dilemma l. your brethren,		7:18
in the l. manner as he was,		25:12
ye become sinners l. unto them;		34:40
yea, they did fight l. dragons,		43:44
and shall become l. unto them,		45:14
ever would be, l. unto Moroni,		48:17
he was a man l. unto Ammon,		48:18
themselves l. unto their brethren,		51:21
he was a man l. unto Moroni,		53: 2
even l. unto the Lamanites.	He	4:22
weak, l. unto their brethren,		4:24
yea, even l. unto a valley.		12:10
laid low, l. unto a valley,		14:23
white l. unto the Nephites;	3Ne	2:15
that ye may be l. unto us—		3: 7
l. the dog to his vomit,		7: 8
or l. the sow to her wallowing in		7: 8
not ye therefore l. unto them,		13: 8
was not arrayed l. one of these.		13:29
of your brethren, l. unto me;		20:23
For he is l. a refiner's fire,		24: 2
refiner's fire, and l. fuller's soap.		24: 2
l. a transfiguration of them,		28:15
l. unto the son of perdition,		29: 7
vain l. unto their brethren,	4Ne	1:43
wicked one l. unto another.		1:45
weak l. unto our brethren.	Mrm	2:26
l. unto the lightness of a fowl	Eth	2:16
would hold water l. unto a dish;		2:17
thereof was tight l. unto a dish;		2:17
were tight l. unto a dish;		2:17
was tight l. unto a dish;		2:17
shut, was tight l. unto a dish.		2:17
l. unto flesh and blood;		3: 6
vessels being tight l. unto a dish,		6: 7
tight l. unto the ark of Noah;		6: 7
l. unto the rest of the earth;		10:17
l. unto the brother of Jared,		12:24
l. unto the Jerusalem of old,		13: 8
they shall be l. unto the old		13: 9
appear we shall be l. him,	Mro	7:48
their flesh l. unto wild beasts,		9:10
how can a people l. this, that		9:11
how can a people l. this,		9:13
will be l. unto the Jaredites,		9:23
l. as one crying from the dead,		10:27
and the same gift l. unto him;	DC	17: 7
he is l. unto Nathanael of old,		41:11
my word l. unto angels of God.		42: 6
l. unto a parable which I		45:36

LIKE

l. unto mine apostle of old,	DC	49:11
seek ye a living l. unto men,		54: 9
l. as it was in ancient days,		58:17
nor do anything l. unto it.		59: 6
l. unto the children of Israel,		61:25
l. unto a judge sitting on a hill,		64:37
that shall make one l. unto it,		67: 7
ye cannot make one l. unto it,		67: 8
are not arrayed l. one of these.		84:82
l. as a tree that is smitten by		85: 8
l. unto the pattern which I		97:10
shall lead them l. as Moses		103:16
be l. unto his father in all things,		107:43
office of a teacher, in l. manner,		107:62
and to be l. unto Moses—		107:91
of pure gold, in color l. amber.		110: 2
was white l. the pure snow;		110: 3
prowl around thee l. wolves		122: 6
l. unto my servant Edward		124:21
and I feel, l. Paul, to glory in		127: 2
For he is l. a refiner's fire,		128:24
and l. fuller's soap;		128:24
that he is a man l. ourselves.		130: 1
not reside on a planet l. this earth.		130: 6
on a globe l. a sea of glass and fire,		130: 7
will be made l. unto a crystal		130: 9
the earth shall be l. as it was in		133:24
garments l. him that treadeth		133:48
l. most of the Lord's anointed		135: 3
going l. a lamb to the slaughter;		135: 4
l. a woman that is taken in travail;		136:35
natural strength l. unto man;	Mses	1:10
will raise up another l. unto thee;		1:41
being angry, slew him, not l. unto		5:50
l. unto his brother Abel.		6: 3
yea, millions of earths l. this,		7:30
which are l. unto men of old,		8:21
a god l. unto that of Pharaoh,	Abr	1:13
thy seed after thee, l. unto these;		3:14
them that was l. unto God,		3:24
answered l. unto the Son of Man:		3:27
since, that I felt much l. Paul,	JS	2:24
countenance truly l. lightning.		2:32

LIKEN

I did l. all scriptures unto us,	1Ne	19:23
and l. them unto yourselves,		19:24
I will l. his words unto my people,	2Ne	11: 2
and ye may l. them unto you		11: 8
I will l. thee O house of Israel,	Jac	5: 3
I will l. him unto a wise man,	3Ne	14:24
what shall I l. these kingdoms,	DC	88:46
I will l. these kingdoms unto		88:51
I will l. all these kingdoms,		88:61
unto what shall I l. the children		101:81
I will l. them unto the		101:81
Thus will I l. the children of		101:85

LIKENED

it is l. unto their being nourished	1Ne	22: 8
they may be l. unto you,	2Ne	6: 5
which may be l. unto you,		6: 5
he l. them unto a tame olive-tree,	Jac	6: 1
shall be l. unto a foolish man,	3Ne	14:26
to whom I l. the servant	DC	103:21

LIKENESS

or any l. of any thing in heaven	Mos	12:36
or any l. of things which are		13:12
bringeth forth unto its own l.	Al	32:31
and in the l. of the same body	Eth	3:17
image is in the l. of the world,	DC	1:16
own image and in his own l.,		20:18
l. of that which is temporal;		77: 2
l. of that which is spiritual;		77: 2
of man in the l. of his person,		77: 2
his l. was the express likeness		107:43
the express l. of his father,		107:43
to answer to the l. of the dead,		128:12
l. of the resurrection of the dead		128:12
being in l. of the dead.		128:12
that all things may have their l.,		128:13

LIMHI

man in our image, after our l.;	Mses	2:26
in the l. of God made he him;		6: 8
and begat a son in his own l.,		6:10
behold, all things have their l.,		6:63
seed in itself yieldeth its own l.	Abr	4:11
man in our image, after our l.;		4:26

LIKEWISE

ye shall all l. perish;	2Ne	30: 1
others, and said unto them l.;	3Ne	11:22
l. also is it counted evil unto	Mro	7: 9
village or city ye enter, do l.	DC	84:93
or an hundred, let him do l.;		104:69
to have them do l.		OD
l. shall mine elect be gathered	JS	1:27
So l., mine elect, when they		1:39

LILIES

Consider the l. of the field how	3Ne	13:28
consider the l. of the field,	DC	84:82

LIMB

both l. and joint shall be restored	Al	11:43
and every l, and joint shall be		40:23
neither in body, l., nor joint;	DC	84:80
in jeopardy of either life or l.,		134:10

LIMBS

whose l. ye must soon lay down	2Ne	1:14
l. might receive their strength—	Mos	27:22
the l. of Alma received their		27:23
neither had I the use of my l.	Al	36:10
my l. did receive their strength		36:23

LIMHAH

L. had fallen with his ten	Mrm	6:14

LIMHER

and Amnor, and Manti, and L.;	Al	2:22

LIMHI

I am L., the son of Noah,	Mos	7: 9
after L. had heard the words of		7:14
king L. commanded his guards		7:16
king L. sent a proclamation		7:17
after king L. had made an end		8: 1
them to the poeple of king L.,		8: 3
king L. dismissed the multitude,		8: 4
captive, whose name was L.		19:16
L. was desirous that his father		19:17
L. was not ignorant of the		19:17
also L., being the son of the king,		19:26
L. began to establish the		19:27
keep the people of L. in the land,		19:28
king L. did have continual peace		19:29
were angry with the people of L.,		20: 6
thought it was the people of L.		20: 6
to destroy the people of L.		20: 7
L. had discovered them from the		20: 8
the people of L. began to		20: 9
the people of L. began to drive		20:11
and brought him before L.,		20:13
But L. said unto them:		20:14
And L. said unto him:		20:14
L. had heard nothing concerning		20:16
L. told the king all the things		20:23
in behalf of the people of L.		20:25
the Lamanites saw the people of L.,		20:26
L. and his people returned to		21: 1
which their king had made unto L.;		21: 3
among the people of L.,		21: 9
the people of L. to anger against		21:11
king L. commanded that every		21:17
the people of L. kept together		21:18
Lamanites and the people of L.,		21:22
king L. had sent, previous to the		21:25
L. was again filled with joy in		21:28
king L. had also entered into a		21:32
king L. and many of his people		21:33
and king L. and his people,		21:36
Ammon and king L. began to		22: 1
impossible for the people of L. to		22: 2

LIMHI

king L. caused that his people	Mos 22:10
which king L. did send unto them.	22:10
the people of king L. did depart	22:11
been found by the people of L.	22:14
the people of L. had departed out	22:15
after the people of king L.,	23:30
he did exhort the people of L.	25:16
king L. was desirous that he	25:17
been found by the people of L.,	28:11
delivered to him by the hand of L.;	28:11
the people of L. out of bondage.	Al 1: 8
were cast by the servants of L.	He 5:21
were found by the people of L.,	Eth 1: 2
the people of L. did find them.	15:33

LIMITED

l. to individual beasts,	DC 77: 3
l. to four individual beasts,	77: 3
circumstances were very l.,	JS 2:55

LIMNAH

shum of gold, and a l. of gold.	Al 11: 5
a l. of gold was the value of	11:10

LINE

l. upon line, precept upon precept,	2Ne 28:30
line upon l., precept upon precept,	28:30
a Nephite, on the l. Bountiful and	Al 22:32
the l. between the Nephites and	50:11
by the l. of the possessions of	50:13
the l. which they had fortified	He 4: 7
the l. which was between the	3Ne 3:23
the l. running directly between	DC 57: 4
give unto the faithful l. upon	98:12
unto the faithful line upon l.	98:12
giving l. upon line, precept upon	128:21
line upon l., precept upon precept;	128:21

LINEAGE

time they can prove their l.,	DC 68:21
through the l. of his fathers,	84:14
through the l. of their fathers;	84:15
the l. of your fathers.—	86: 8
through you and your l. until	86:10
came down by l. in the following	107:41
she, Zion, has a right to by l.;	113: 8
Pharaoh, being of that l. by	Abr 1:27

LINEN

and scarlets, and fine-twined l.,	1Ne 13: 7
scarlets, and the fine-twined l.,	13: 8
The glasses, and the fine l.,	2Ne 13:23
and work all manner of fine l.,	Mos 10: 5
of silk and fine-twined l.,	Al 1:29
silks, and their fine-twined l.,	4: 6
of fine-twined l. and cloth of	He 6:13
grain, and of silks, and of fine l.,	Eth 9:17
have silks, and fine-twined l.;	10:24

LINGER

and my soul l. in the valley of	2Ne 4:26

LINK

is a welding l. of some kind	DC 128:18

LION

their roaring like a l.	2Ne 15:28
the young l. and fatling together;	21: 6
the l. shall eat straw like the ox.	21: 7
the young l., and the fatling,	30:12
the l. shall eat straw like the ox.	30:13
as a l. among the beasts of	3Ne 20:16
a young l. among the flocks of	20:16
as a l. among the beasts of	21:12
a young l. among the flocks of	21:12
shall go forth among you as a l.,	Mrm 5:24
enemies than the fierce l.,	DC 122: 4

LIONS

They shall roar like young l.;	2Ne 15:29
fought like l. for their prey.	Mos 20:10
with her young from two l.;	Al 14:29
the roar of the l. was heard out	Mses 7:13

LIPS

I am a man of unclean l.;	2Ne 16: 5
midst of a people of unclean l.;	16: 5
Lo, this has touched thy l.;	16: 7
with the breath of his l. shall he	21: 4
and with their l. do honor me,	27:25
with the breath of his l. shall he	30: 9
let the unbelieving hold their l.,	DC 63: 6
they take my name in their l.—	63:61
draw near to me with their l.,	JS 2:19

LIQUORS

thus they did try all their l.	Al 55:32

LIST

and ye l. to obey the evil spirit,	Mos 2:32
With a l. of the names of	DC 20:82
a regular l. of all the names of	20:82
wages of whom they l. to obey.	29:45
and will do whatsoever I l.,	98:21

LISTED

the spirit which they l. to obey,	Al 3:26
Son of Man even as they l.;	DC 49: 6

LISTEN

L., O isles, unto me,	1Ne 21: 1
O that ye would l. unto the word	Jac 2:16
that thou wouldst l. to my words	Mos 22: 4
L. to the words of Christ, your	Mro 8: 8
L. unto them and give heed, or	8:21
the islands of the sea, l. together.	DC 1: 1
l. to the words of Jesus Christ,	15: 1
l. to the words of Jesus Christ,	16: 1
of me, and l. to my words;	19:23
L. to the voice of Jesus Christ,	27: 1
L. to the voice of Jesus Christ,	29: 1
L. to the voice of the Lord	35: 1
l. to the voice of him who is	39: 1
L. to him who is the	45: 3
and ye elders l. together,	45: 6
and l., you that call yourselves	63: 1
l. to the voice of the Lord,	72: 1
l. to the counsel of him who	78: 2
L. to the voice of him who	81: 1
and let all l. unto his sayings,	88:122
l. to the counsel which I shall	100: 2
L., ye elders of my church	133:16
and ye elders l. together;	136:41

LISTENED

thou hast hitherto l. to my words	Mos 22: 4
Cain was wroth, and l. not	Mses 5:26

LISTETH

him who l. to obey that spirit,	Mos 2:33
for if he l. to obey him,	2:33
he l. to obey the evil spirit,	2:37
wages of him whom he l. to obey,	Al 3:27
the enemy l. to carry them.	26: 6

LIT

life was l. up in his soul,	Al 19: 6

LITERAL

be l. descendants of Aaron.	DC 68:15
be l. descendants of Aaron	68:16
except he be a l. descendant	68:18
no l. descendant of Aaron	68:19
a l. descendant of Aaron,	68:20
he be a l. descendant of Aaron.	107:16
when no l. descendant of Aaron	107:17
belongs to the l. descendants	107:40
is a l. descendant of Aaron;	107:69
is a l. descendant of Aaron	107:70
is not a l. descendant of Aaron,	107:73
But a l. descendant of Aaron,	107:76
l. seed, or the seed of the body)	Abr 2:11
We believe in the l. gathering	AoF 10

LITERARY

the l. concerns of my church	DC 72:20
celebrated for his l. attainments.	JS 2:64

LITTLE

the head thereof a l. way off;	1Ne	8:14
Behold, thou art l.;	2Ne	3:25
For yet a very l. while,		20:25
and a l. child shall lead them.		21: 6
it is yet a very l. while		27:28
justify in committing a l. sin;		28: 8
yea, lie a l.,		28: 8
here a l. and there a little;		28:30
here a little and there a l.;		28:30
and a l. child shall lead them.		30:12
cannot write but a l. of my words,	Jac	4: 1
began to put forth somewhat a l.,		5: 6
and nourish it a l. longer,		5:27
Spare it a l. longer.		5:50
Yea, I will spare it a l. longer,		5:51
must needs be that I write a l.;	Jar	1: 2
except it be your l. children	Mos	2:34
ye young men, and you l. children		2:40
that l. children could sin		3:16
and become as l. children,		3:18
except it be l. children,		3:21
except it were l. children,		6: 2
l. children also have eternal life.		15:25
and of him that had but l.,		18:27
but l. should be required;		18:27
being l. children at the time		26: 1
l. children do have words given	Al	32:23
the many l. dissensions and		45:21
this l. force which I brought		56:17
perhaps destroyed our l. army;		56:19
march forth with my l. sons to		56:30
had gone forth with my l. army,		56:33
that my l. sons should fall into		56:39
my l. band of two thousand		57: 6
a l. before they were to receive		57: 8
my l. band of two thousand		57:19
this did profit us but l.;		58: 5
your country and your l. ones,		60:29
save it were a l. pride which	He	3: 1
did cause some l. dissensions		3: 1
there being but l. timber upon		3: 7
but l. alteration in the affairs of		16:12
cometh unto me as a l. child,	3Ne	9:22
repent, and become as a l. child,		11:37
and become as a l. child,		11:38
if ye are not of l. faith.		13:30
to tarry a l. longer with them.		17: 5
l. children should be brought.		17:11
they brought their l. children		17:12
and he took their l. children,		17:21
Behold your l. ones.		17:23
encircled those l. ones about,		17:24
went a l. way off from them		19:19
went a l. way off and bowed		19:27
that he went again a l. way off		19:31
In a l. wrath I hid my face from		22: 8
and kept him upon l. or no food	Eth	9: 7
that we could write but l.,		12:24
his sword, that he rested a l.,		15:30
the baptism of your l. children.	Mro	8: 5
wherefore, l. children are whole,		8: 8
ye should baptize l. children.		8: 9
themselves as their l. children,		8:10
be saved with their l. children.		8:10
l. children need no repentance,		8:11
l. children are alive in Christ,		8:12
how many l. children have died		8:12
if l. children could not be		8:13
that l. children need baptism		8:14
l. children with a perfect love;		8:17
L. children cannot repent;		8:19
saith that l. children need baptism		8:20
all l. children are alive in Christ,		8:22
no water, save a l., do they give		9: 8
you must wait yet a l. while,	DC	5:17
Therefore, fear not, l. flock;		6:34
Wait a l. longer, until you		11:16
the earth but for a l. season;		29:22
l. children are redeemed from		29:46
unto Satan to tempt l. children,		29:47
your family, yea, your l. ones;	DC	31: 2
from them only for a l. time,		31: 6
Fear not, l. flock, the kingdom		35:27
shall go forth for a l. season,		42: 5
only reign for a l. season,		43:31
Behold, ye are l. children		50:40
Fear not, l. children, for you		50:41
this land for a l. season,		51:16
l. children also may receive		55: 4
after a l., if it so be that they		61:22
be of good cheer, l. children;		61:36
whether it be l. or much,		63:40
the store, yet for a l. season.		63:42
saith that l. children are unholy;		74: 6
But l. children are holy,		74: 7
the l. book which was eaten by		77:14
unto you, ye are l. children,		78:17
a l. while and ye shall see it,		84:119
have received, for a l. season.		88:71
shall be loosed for a l. season,		88:111
who receiveth you as a l. child,		99: 3
she is chastened for a l. season.		100:13
be chastened for a l. season		103: 4
should wait for a l. season,		105: 9
should wait for a l. season,		105:13
let them tarry for a l. season,		105:21
of all the churches for a l. season.		112:18
they have offended my l. ones		121:19
soon as they get a l. authority,		121:39
here a l., and there a little;		128:21
here a little, and there a l.;		128:21
the l. one become a strong nation,		133:58
a l. over fourteen years of age,	JS	2:23
arms also, a l. above the wrist;		2:31
his legs, a l. above the ankles.		2:31
though with a l. variation from		2:36
with a l. exertion raised it up.		2:52

LITTLENESS

all his l. of soul before me,	DC	117:11

LIVE

As the Lord liveth, and as we l..	1Ne	3:15
as the Lord liveth, and as I l.,		4:32
while we did l. upon raw meat		17: 2
And as I l., saith the Lord,		21:18
having a l. coal in his hand,	2Ne	16: 6
that ye should l. in peace	Mos	2:20
that ye may l. and move and do		2:21
but to l. peaceably, and to render		4:13
who l. without God in the world,		27:31
as the Lord sees fit that we may l.		29:32
ye shall l. in your iniquities,	Al	9:19
of the tree of life, and l. forever?		12:21
that they should l. forever.		12:21
would look upon it might l.		33:19
And many did look and l.		33:19
that ye l. in thanksgiving daily,		34:38
if they would look they might l.;		37:46
if we will look we may l. forever.		37:46
see that ye look to God and l.		37:47
of life, and eat and l. forever,		42: 5
l. unto the Lord their God,		48:10
that ye shall l. and wax strong		60:31
look upon that serpent should l.,	He	8:15
might l., even unto that life		8:15
fourth generation who shall l.,		13:10
to the end, and ye shall l.;	3Ne	15: 9
ye shall l. to behold all the doings		28: 7
suffer that I may l. I know not.	Mrm	8: 5
Shez did l. to an exceeding old	Eth	10: 4
And Morianton did l. to an		10:13
and he did l. to a good old age,		10:16
that Lib did l. many years,		10:29
he should only l. to see the		13:21
that I may l. and bring souls	DC	7: 2
but surely must, as I l.,		29:21
your family shall l.		31: 5
as I l. I will that he shall		32: 1
in which to l. and translate.		41: 7
should l. as seemeth him good,		41: 8
and if they l. they shall live		42:44

LIVE

they live they shall l. unto me.	DC 42:44
Thou shalt l. together in love,	42:45
Ye saints arise and l.;	43:18
to the ears of all that l.,	43:21
their voices unto all that l.,	43:22
things were made which l.,	45: 1
unto me and your souls shall l.,	45:46
places to l. for the present time.	48: 3
those that l. shall inherit	59: 2
God, even the Father, and l.	84:22
For you shall l. by every word	84:44
and they l. not again until the	88:101
ye shall l. after the manner of	95:13
ye shall l. by every word which	98:11
of the nation in which you l.,	124: 3
If they l. here let them live unto	124:86
they live here let them l. unto me;	124:86
tree of life, and eat and l. forever,	Mses 4:28
As I l., even so will I come in the	7:60
thy sister, and thy soul shall l.	Abr 2:24
my soul shall l. because of thee.	2:25
After I went to l. with him,	JS 2:56

LIVED

l. after the manner of happiness.	2Ne 5:27
and I have l. to see his death;	Om 1:23
And king Benjamin l. three years	Mos 6: 5
l. to fulfil the commandments	29:45
Lamanites l. in the wilderness,	Al 22:28
of life, he would have l. forever,	42: 5
after we have l. unto the age	3Ne 28: 2
he l. four years, and he saw	Eth 9:22
he l. until he was an hundred	9:24
Heth l. in captivity all his days.	10:31
And he l. to a good old age,	11: 4
Esaias also l. in the days of	DC 84:13
than any other man that ever l.	135: 3
He l. great, and he died great	135: 3
They l. for glory;	135: 6
Adam l. one hundred and thirty	Mses 6:10
all the days that Adam l. were	6:12
Seth l. one hundred and five	6:13
And Seth l., after he begat Enos,	6:14
Enos l. ninety years, and begat	6:17
Enos l., after he begat Cainan,	6:18
Cainan l. seventy years, and begat	6:19
and Cainan l. after he begat	6:19
Mahalaleel l., sixty-five years, and	6:20
Mahalaleel l., after he begat	6:20
And Jared l. one hundred and	6:21
Jared l., after he begat Enoch,	6:21
Enoch l. sixty-five years, and	6:25
Methuselah l. one hundred and	8: 5
Methuselah l., after he begat Lamech,	8: 6
Lamech l. one hundred and	8: 8
Lamech l., after he begat Noah,	8:10
father, yet l. in the land of Ur,	Abr 2: 1
was in the place where we l.	JS 2: 5
who l. in Chenango county,	2:56

LIVELY

to a l. sense of his own guilt,	Mos 2:38
be a l. member in this order;	DC 92: 2

LIVES

sought to take away their l. also.	1Ne 4:28
mercies of God in sparing their l.,	2Ne 1: 2
and also our l. passed away like	Jac 7:26
the l. of many of the Lamanites	Om 1:10
and granted unto you your l.,	Mos 2:23
you are dependent for your l.	4:21
even unto the end of your l.,	4:30
obedient unto the end of your l.	5: 8
doth exact of us, or our l.	7:22
the most part of your l.	13:11
the Lamanites did spare their l.,	19:15
But they fought for their l.,	20:11
than that we should lose our l.;	20:22
would grant unto them their l.	23:36
of the l. of this people.	Al 10: 5
at this time to preserve your l.,	18: 4
if thou wilt spare our l., we will	22: 3
for I will grant unto you your l.,	22: 3

557

they would give up their own l.;	Al 24:18
they had rather sacrifice their l.	26:32
of these have laid down their l.;	26:34
of many thousand l.;	28:10
blood, but we will spare your l.,	44: 6
spare the remainder of their l.,	44:19
lest they should lose their l.	47: 2
it were to preserve their l.	48:14
not suffer to lay down their l.,	48:24
unto the laying down of their l.;	53:17
than they did upon their l.;	56:47
should put an end to their l.,	57:15
have fought and bled out their l.	60: 9
sparing their l., and delivering	He 12: 2
sought all the days of your l. for	13:38
unto them, all the days of our l.	16:21
for the safety of their l. and their	3Ne 2:12
with the sword for their l.	Mrm 2:14
did struggle for their l. without	5: 2
the sake of the l. of the people.	Eth 15: 4
would spare the l. of the people.	15: 5
and spare the l. of the people.	15:18
were about to flee for their l.;	15:28
secret chambers seeketh your l.	DC 38:28
the place upon which he l.	56: 8
we give of him: That he l.!	76:22
and mission in all your l.,	90:16
the place where he now l.;	90:20
given their l. for my name	101:15
lay down their l. for my sake	101:35
escape my wrath in your l.	104: 8
the house in which he l.,	104:34
wear out our l. in bringing to	123:13
and continuation of the l.,	132:22
This is eternal l.—to know the	132:24
crowns of eternal l. in the eternal	132:55
jeopardizing the l. of men;	134:12

LIVEST

For as sure as thou l., behold,	Al 19:13
as thou l., O king, there is a God.	22: 8
Joseph, my son, if thou l. until	DC 130:15

LIVETH

As the Lord l., and as we live,	1Ne 3:15
as the Lord l., and as I live,	4:32
And assuredly, as the Lord l.,	2Ne 9:16
And as the Lord God l. that	25:20
and as the Lord God l.,	25:20
For assuredly as the Lord l.	27:31
as the Lord l. ye will be saved.	Om 1:26
the Redeemer l. and cometh	Al 7: 7
as the Lord l., even so has he sent	10:10
And as sure as the Lord l.,	23: 6
I say unto you, as the Lord l.,	23: 6
therefore as the Lord l., ye	44:11
as the Lord l., our armies shall	54:10
for as the Lord l., if a prophet	He 13:26
as surely as the Lord l. shall	15:17
As the Lord l., except ye repent	3Ne 3:15
as the Lord l., if we do this	3:21
And as surely as the Lord l.,	5:24
as the Lord l., so shall it be.	5:26
the Lord l. he will remember	Mrm 8:23
as sure as Christ l. he spake	Mro 7:26
assuredly as the Lord l.,	DC 8: 1
as your Lord and your God l.	17: 6
he that l. in righteousness	43:32
he that l. when the Lord shall	63:50
have appointed, while he l.,	64: 5
he who l., I am he who was slain;	110: 4
For as I, the Lord God, l., even	Mses 4:30

LIVING

to the fountain of l. waters,	1Ne 11:25
against the true and l. God.	17:30
and they are l. souls,	2Ne 9:13
the pains of every l. creature,	9:21
among l. in Jerusalem—	14: 3
for the l. to hear from the dead?	18:19
example of the Son of the l. God,	31:16
he spent his time in riotous l.	Mos 11:14
cut off out of the land of the l.;	14: 8

LIVING   558   LOINS

trust in the true and l. God.	Al 5:13	Behold, and l., I will take care of	DC 88:72
do worship the true and l. God,	7: 6	and l., the Bridegroom cometh;	88:92
should deny the true and l. God,	11:25	and l., I will come quickly,	88:126
sayest there is a true and l. God?	11:26	and l., they shall turn unto	90: 9
Yea, there is a true and l. God.	11:27	and l., the heavens were opened,	93:15
every l. soul of the Ammonihahites	16: 9	and l., vengeance cometh	97:22
in truth, the true and the l. God,	43:10	behold, and l., I come quickly	99: 5
was not a l. soul among all the	3Ne 5: 1	and l., I have much people in	100: 3
Christ, the Son of the l. God,	30: 1	and l., I am with you even	100:12
Christ, the Son of the l. God;	Mrm 5:14	and l., I am with you even	105:41
ye will serve the true and l. God.	9:28	l., I am with you to bless you	108: 8
Christ, the Son of the l. God;	9:29	l., I shall triumph over all my	127: 2
the only true and l. church	DC 1:30	l., I am the Lord thy God,	132: 2
Christ, the Son of the l. God,	14: 9	l., I am with him,	132:57
the only l. and true God,	20:19	l., this shall be their cry,	133: 9
and depart from the l. God;	20:32	l., the Bridegroom cometh;	133:10
Christ the Son of the l. God	42: 1	l., there are none to deliver you;	133:71
and their companions are l.,	42:75	And l., I am with thee, even	Mses 1:26
ear to the voice of the l. God;	50: 1	l., the heavens I saw, and the Lord	6:42
seek ye a l. like unto men,	54: 9	l., a great people which dwelt in	7: 5
Christ, the Son of the l. God.	55: 2	l., Zion, in process of time, was	7:21
as the Spirit of the l. God	61:28	l., all the nations of the earth	7:23
be in him a well of l. water,	63:23	say unto you, L., here is Christ,	JS 1:21
by the Spirit of the l. God,	68: 1	some crying, "L., here!" and	2: 5
I am the Son of the l. God,	68: 6	"Lo, here!" and others, "L., there!"	2: 5
Christ the Son of the l. God,	68:25		
to the church of the l. God;	70:10	LOADING	
unto the city of the l. God,	76:66	into the ship, with all our l.	1Ne 18: 6
given the seal of the l. God	77: 9		
gospel in the land of the l.,	81: 3	LOAN	
of the church of the l. God,	82:18	by l. as shall be agreed by	DC 104:53
his trump in the ears of all l.,	88:108	obtain a chance to l. money	104:84
as well for the dead as for the l.	128:11	l. enough to deliver yourself	104:84
where the l. are wont to assemble,	128:13		
to show forth the l. and the dead,	128:13	LOATHSOME	
in relation to the dead and the l.	128:15	and l., and a filthy people,	1Ne 12:23
gladness for the l. and the dead;	128:19	shall be l. unto thy people,	2Ne 5:22
come forth pools of l. water;	133:29	a filthy, and a l. people,	Mrm 5:15
every l. creature that moveth,	Mses 2:21		
the l. creature after his kind,	2:24	LOCATE	
every l. thing that moveth upon	2:28	Let him come and l. his family	DC 124:105
of life; and man became a l. soul,	3: 7	the Lord shall l. a stake of Zion.	136:10
And it became also a l. soul.	3: 9		
and they were also l. souls;	3:19	LOCATED	
Adam called every l. creature,	3:19	or l. high priests abroad	DC 102:29
she was the mother of all l.;	4:26		
their heads, and by the l. God,	5:29	LODGE	
were created and became l. souls	6: 9	may come from afar to l. therein;	DC 124:23
and so became of dust a l. soul,	6:59		
every l. creature that moveth,	Abr 4:21	LODGING	
the l. creature after his kind,	4:24	have taken up their l. at Geba;	2Ne 20:29
over every l. thing that moveth	4:28		
life, and man became a l. soul.	5: 7	LOFTINESS	
Adam called every l. creature,	5:20	the l. of man shall be bowed	2Ne 12:17
		Is not the l. of thy vineyard—	Jac 5:48
LO			
and l., these from the north	1Ne 21:12	LOFTY	
L., this has touched thy lips;	2Ne 16: 7	the l. looks of man shall be	2Ne 12:11
And l., he shall suffer	Mos 3: 7	upon the proud and l.,	12:12
And l., he cometh unto his own,	3: 9	the eyes of the l. shall be humbled.	15:15
behold, and l., the Lord is God,	DC 1:39		
and l., he that thrusteth in his	4: 4	LOINS	
thus saith the Lord God, l., lo!	21:12	gird on his armor about my l.	1Ne 4:19
God, lo, l.! to the Jews also.	21:12	the sword girded about my l.	4:21
for, l., I am with thee, even unto	24: 8	thou art the fruit of my l.;	2Ne 3: 4
l., I am with him to the end.	24:10	out of the fruit of his l.	3: 5
the end, and l., I am with you.	31:13	unto the fruit of my l.	3: 6
your backs, for l., I am with you.	33: 9	out of the fruit of thy l.	3: 7
And l., if the world receive	57:12	among the fruit of thy l.	3: 7
and l., I am with the faithful	62: 9	a work for the fruit of thy l.,	3: 7
l., your enemies are upon you,	63:31	out of the fruit of thy l.;	3:11
Hearken, and l., a voice as of	65: 1	unto the seed of thy l.—	3:11
and l., mine eyes are upon you,	67: 2	the fruit of thy l. shall write;	3:12
and l., this is an ensample unto	68: 2	the fruit of the l. of Judah	3:12
l., I will be with them even	75:13	written by the fruit of thy l.,	3:12
and l., I am with them also,	75:14	by the fruit of the l. of Judah,	3:12
and l., he is fallen! is fallen,	76:27	peace among the fruit of thy l.,	3:12
l., this is the end of the vision	76:49	of the Lord, of the fruit of my l.,	3:14
and l., these are they who are of	76:71	unto the fruit of thy l.;	3:18
and l., we saw the glory and	76:109	writing of the fruit of thy l.,	3:18
and l., it must needs be that	78: 3	unto the fruit of thy l.;	3:18
and l., these are the words of	81: 7	spokesman of thy l. shall declare	3:18
and l., the tares are bound in	86: 7	unto the fruit of thy l.	3:19

LOINS

as if the fruit of thy l. had	2Ne 3:19
who are the fruit of thy l.;	3:21
the girdle of their l. be loosed,	15:27
shall be the girdle of his l.,	21: 5
shall be the girdle of his l.,	30:11
from the fruit of the l. of Joseph.	Jac 2:25
a short skin girdle about their l.	En 1:20
a leathern girdle about their l.	Mos 10: 8
which was girded about their l.,	Al 3: 5
which was girded about their l.;	43:20
girded on his armor about his l.;	46:13
their armor girded about their l.,	46:21
had a lamb-skin about their l.,	3Ne 4: 7
rejoice, and gird up your l.,	DC 27:15
your l. girt about with truth,	27:16
and I will gird up their l.,	35:14
gird up your l. and I will	36: 8
gird up your l. and be prepared.	38: 9
gird up your l. lest ye be	43:19
Gird up your l. and be watchful	61:38
and faithfulness upon his l.,	63:37
Gird up your l. and be sober.	73: 6
gird up your l. and be faithful,	75:22
Therefore, gird up your l.,	106: 5
gird up thy l. for the work.	112: 7
Arise and gird up your l.,	112:14
his seed, and of the fruit of his l.—	132:30
from whose l. ye are,	132:30
my people may gird up their l.,	Mses 7:62
should be of the fruit of his l.	8: 2
that from his l. should spring all	8: 3
directly from the l. of Ham.	Abr 1:11
descendant from the l. of Ham,	1:21

LONESOME

being a l. and a solemn people,	Jac 7:26

LONG

that thy days may be l. in the	1Ne 17:55
I did praise him all the day l.;	18:16
loving kindness and his l.-suffering	19: 9
l. upon the face of this land;	2Ne 1:31
in from their l. dispersion,	10: 8
Then said I: Lord, how l.?	16:11
as l. as the earth should stand.	25:21
as l. as the earth shall stand;	25:22
is lengthened out all the day l.,	28:32
of men ехеnо more, for a l. time.	30:18
that a l. time passed away,	Jac 5:15
this l. time have I nourished it,	5:20
I have nourished it this l. time,	5:22
I have nourished it this l. time,	5:23
I have nourished it this l. time,	5:25
that a l. time had passed away,	5:29
this l. time have we nourished this	5:31
so l. as it shall bring forth evil	5:35
mine hand almost all the day l.,	5:47
for a l. time will I lay up of the	5:76
own self of the fruit, for a l. time,	5:76
hands unto them all the day l.;	6: 4
good word of God all the day l.,	6: 7
all the day l. did I cry unto him;	En 1: 4
l. strugglings for my brethren,	1:11
exhorting with all l.-suffering	Jar 1:11
his patience, and his l.-suffering	Mos 4: 6
and his goodness and l.-suffering	4:11
how l. doth he suffer with his	8:20
they shall howl all the day l.	12: 4
days may be l. upon the land	13:20
even all the day l. did they cry unto	21:14
exhorting them with l.-suffering	27:33
so l. as the Lord sees fit that we	29:32
even as l. as any of our posterity	29:32
and l.-suffering towards them?	Al 5: 6
full of patience and l.-suffering;	7:23
and his l.-suffering towards us,	9:11
earth l. before this period of time,	9:11
patience, mercy, and l.-suffering,	9:26
full of love and all l.-suffering;	13:28
How l. shall we suffer these	14:26
ye shall be patient in l.-suffering	17:11
yea, all the day l. did ye labor;	26: 5
and of his l.-suffering towards	26:16

559

O, how l., O Lord, wilt thou	Al 31:26
O Lord God, how l. wilt thou	31:30
and patience, and l.-suffering,	32:43
and my soul did l. to be there.	36:22
thy patience and thy l.-suffering	38: 3
be known so l. beforehand.	39:17
desired to do evil all the day l.	41: 5
his mercy, and his l.-suffering	42:30
so l. as we are faithful unto	44: 4
so l. as there should a band of	46:13
not l. after their dissensions	47:36
so l. as there were any who	48:25
they did not l. maintain an	51: 2
because of their l. march.	52:31
weary, because of their l. march	56:50
the Lord had blessed them so l.	He 6:17
how l. the Lord your God will	9:21
how l. will ye suppose that the	13:29
how l. will ye suffer yourselves	13:29
how l. will ye choose darkness	13:29
to lay siege sufficiently l.	3Ne 4:18
so l. as they shall call on the	4:30
up for the space of a l. time	6:17
in, from their l. dispersion,	21: 1
the l.-suffering of the Lord,	Mrm 2:12
unto my God all the day l.	3:12
how l. the Lord will suffer that	8: 5
l. dispersed covenant people of	8:15
this l. time ye have cried unto	Eth 1:43
praise the Lord all the day l.;	6: 9
so l. had been the scene of	14:21
will he, so l. as time shall last,	Mro 7:36
And charity suffereth l., and is	7:45
and his mercy and l.-suffering,	9:25
as l. as the world shall stand,	10:19
sound both l. and loud,	DC 29:13
of a trump, both l. and loud,	34: 6
shall sound both l. and loud,	43:18
voice of mercy all the day l.,	43:25
the l. absence of your spirits	45:17
his trump both l. and loud,	88:94
And consulted for a l. time,	101:48
which is forty rods l. and	104:43
so l. as he is in full fellowship,	104:75
meekness and l. suffering,	107:30
how l. wilt thou suffer this people	109:49
upon the mountains for a l. time,	109:61
and humility, and l.-suffering,	118: 3
How l. shall thy hand be stayed,	121: 2
how l. shall they suffer these	121: 3
How l. can rolling waters	121:33
only by persuasion, by l.-suffering,	121:41
so l. as they repent not, and	124:50
so l. as they repent not, and	124:52
so l. as he and his heirs shall hold	124:69
let him lift up his voice l. and	124:75
with her so l. as he is in the world	132:15
so l. as they were in the world;	132:30
so l. as a regard and reverence	134: 7

LONGER

my soul! No l. droop in sin.	2Ne 4:28
and nourish it a little l.,	Jac 5:27
Spare it a little l.	5:50
Yea, I will spare it a little l.,	5:51
that I can no l. be your teacher,	Mos 2:29
we shall no l. be in subjection to	7:18
could no l. follow their tracks;	22:16
no l. be called by the names of	25:12
pursue the Amlicites no l.	Al 2:20
harden not your hearts any l.;	34:31
he should no l. be chief judge	51: 4
and I will suffer them no l.,	He 13: 8
to tarry a little l. with them.	3Ne 17: 5
ye need not any l. spurn at the	29: 4
Lord no l. worketh by revelation,	29: 6
and ye need not any l. hiss,	29: 8
will not suffer their cries any l.	Mrm 8:41
Then will ye l. deny the Christ,	9: 3
and he had faith no l., for	Eth 3:19
no l. be kept without the veil.	12:21
any l. enforce my commands.	Mro 9:18
I dwell no l. upon this horrible	9:20

LONGER / LOOKED

Wait a little l., until you shall	DC 11:16
run about l. as a blind guide?	19:40
he shall mourn for her no l.;	21: 8
he standeth no l. in the office	63:56
is bound and time is no l.	84:100
there shall be time no l.;	88:110
cease to sleep l. than is needful;	88:124
you shall no l. be bound as	104:47
thy hiding place no l. be covered;	121: 4
and shall no l. stay themselves;	133:26
shall no l. be a thirsty land.	133:29
of the lesser light is a l. time	Abr 3: 7
reckoning of time shall be l. still;	3: 8

LONG-SUFFERING: see LONG and SUFFERING.

LOOK

the Spirit said unto me: L.!	1 Ne 11: 8
he said unto me: L.!	11:12
as if to l. upon him,	11:12
the angel spake unto me, saying: L.!	11:19
he said unto me: L.!	11:24
angel said unto me again: L.	11:26
spake unto me again, saying: L.!	11:30
spake unto me again, saying: L.!	11:31
spake unto me again, saying: L.!	11:32
the angel said unto me: L.,	12: 1
the angel said unto me: L.!	12:11
the angel spake unto me, saying: L.!	13: 1
he said unto me: L.,	14: 9
the angel spake unto me, saying: L.!	14:18
they did not l. unto the Lord	15: 3
L. upon the ball, and behold	16:26
had to perform was to l.;	17:41
I did l. unto my God,	18:16
should l. to the great Mediator,	2 Ne 2:28
unto whom ye l. as a king	6: 2
L. unto the rock from whence ye	8: 1
L. unto Abraham, your father,	8: 2
and l. upon the earth beneath;	8: 6
and ye l. upon me as a teacher,	9:48
and if they l. unto the land,	15:30
and I will l. for him.	18:17
and their God, and l. upward.	18:21
they shall l. unto the earth	18:22
shall narrowly l. upon thee,	24:16
and l. not forward any more	25:16
not l. forward any more for a	25:18
and l. forward with steadfastness	25:24
may l. for a remission of their sins.	25:26
may l. forward unto that life	25:27
but l. forward unto Christ	26: 8
L. unto God with firmness of	Jac 3: 1
and l. upon them that they may	4: 3
Behold, l. here; behold the tree.	5:16
L. hither; behold I have planted	5:23
L. hither, and behold another	5:24
L. hither and behold the last.	5:25
to l. forward unto the Messiah,	Jar 1:11
he has wherewith that he can l.,	Mos 8:13
no man can l. in them except he	8:13
he should l. for that he ought not	8:13
is commanded to l. in them	8:13
l. over all the land round about.	11:12
but that they should l. forward	18:21
wise and l. forward to these things,	29:10
did not l. upon him as a tyrant	29:40
l. forward with an eye of faith,	Al 5:15
can ye l. up to God at that day	5:19
I say unto you, can you l. up,	5:19
l. forward for the remission of	7: 6
not dare to l. up to our God;	12:14
in what manner to l. forward	13: 2
could not l. upon sin save it	13:12
l. forward on the Son of God,	13:16
they might l. forward to him for	13:16
shall we l. when we are damned?	14:21
did l. forward to the coming of	25:15
we can l. forth and see the fruits	26:31
l. upon shedding the blood of	27:28
they never did l. upon death with	27:28
Why do ye l. for a Christ?	30:13

Ye l. forward and say that ye	Al 30:16
durst not l. up with boldness,	30:27
that whosoever would l. upon it	33:19
And many did l. and live.	33:19
hardened that they would not l.,	33:20
the reason they would not l. is	33:20
if they would l. they might live;	37:46
if we will l. we may live forever.	37:46
see that ye l. to God and live.	37:47
to l. to the Lord your God,	38: 2
Lord cannot l. upon sin with	45:16
will l. upon you as guiltless	60:23
that they might turn and l.	He 5:37
them that they did turn and l.;	5:37
as should l. upon that serpent	8:15
l. upon the Son of God with	8:15
shall he tremble, and shall l. pale,	9:33
to l. with great earnestness for	3 Ne 8: 3
did l. steadfastly towards heaven,	11: 5
L. unto me, and endure to the	15: 9
and did l. steadfastly upon him	17: 5
l. ye unto the revelations of	Mrm 8:33
O Lord, l. upon me in pity,	Eth 3: 3
I the Lord cannot l. upon sin	DC 1:31
L. unto me in every thought;	6:36
l. not for a Messiah to come	19:27
l. to the poor and the needy,	38:35
Ye l. and behold the fig-trees,	45:37
And then they shall l. for me,	45:44
the Jews l. upon me and say:	45:51
for the angels to l. upon;	62: 3
things that ye must l. for;	63:53
not l. back lest sudden destruction	133:15
things they l. not for.	133:43
wherefore l., and I will show thee	Mses 1: 1
I could not l. upon God,	1:14
l. upon thee in the natural man.	1:14
L., and I will show unto thee the	7: 4
L.; and I looked towards the	7: 6
L.; and I looked, and I beheld	7: 9
your heart, and be glad; and l.	7:44
L., and he looked and beheld the	7:55
is a very fair woman to l. upon;	Abr 2:22

LOOKED

And I l. to behold from whence	1 Ne 8:14
I l. and beheld a tree;	11: 8
I l. as if to look upon him,	11:12
I l. and beheld the great city	11:13
I l. and beheld the virgin	11:20
I l., and I beheld the Son	11:24
I l. and beheld the Redeemer	11:27
I l., and I beheld the heavens	11:30
I l., and beheld the Lamb	11:31
I l., and beheld the Lamb	11:32
I l. and beheld the land	12: 1
I l., and beheld three	12:11
I l. and beheld the people	12:15
I l. and beheld many nations	13: 1
I l. and beheld many waters;	13:10
I l. and beheld a man	13:12
I l. and beheld the whore	14:11
I l. and beheld a man,	14:19
he l. that it should bring forth	2 Ne 15: 2
I l. that it should bring forth	15: 4
he l. for judgment, and behold,	15: 7
the Lord of the vineyard l. and	Jac 5:17
and have l. forward to that day	Mos 15:11
have l. up to you for protection,	Al 60: 8
l. forward, and have rejoiced	He 8:22
he l. upon the twelve whom he	3 Ne 13:25
he l. round about again on the	17: 1
And as they l. to behold they	17:24
they l. upon me as thou I	Mrm 5: 1
I have l. upon thee and thy	DC 35: 3
l. upon the wide expanse of	38: 1
I have l. upon thy works	39: 7
have l. upon the long absence	45:17
the Lord, have l. upon you,	50: 4
it came to pass that Moses l.,	Mses 1: 8
pass that Moses l. upon Satan	1:13
and I l. towards the north,	7: 6

LOOKED 561 LORD

LOOKED
I l., and I beheld the land of	Mses	7: 9
he l. up and laughed, and his		7:26
l. upon the residue of the people,		7:28
and l. upon their wickedness,		7:41
it came to pass that Enoch l.;		7:45
that Enoch l. upon the earth;		7:48
he l. and beheld the Son of Man		7:55
And God l. upon the earth,		8:29
having l. around me, and	JS	2:15
When I first l. upon him,		2:32
I l. up, and beheld the same		2:49
I l. in, and there indeed did		2:52

LOOKEST
when thou l. upon the face of	DC	109:53

LOOKETH
Yea, and he l. down upon all the	Al	18:32
that whosoever l. on a woman,	3Ne	12:28
and l. upon his sons and saith	DC	38:26
l. upon a woman to lust		42:23
he that l. on a woman to lust		63:16
day when he l. not for him,	JS	1:53

LOOKING
came by l. beyond the mark,	Jac	4:14
L. forward to that day, thus	Al	4:14
l. forward with an eye of faith		32:40
l. forward to the fruit thereof,		32:41
a state of awful, fearful l. for		40:14
be l. forth for the time of	DC	35:15
be l. forth for the signs of		39:23
be l. forth for the great day		45:39
l. forth for the heavens to		49:23
l. forth for the coming of		61:38
l. forth with fear, in torment,	Mses	7: 1
be l. forth for the time of my		7:62
l. forth with fear for the		7:66
my back, l. up into heaven.	JS	2:20

LOOKS
lofty l. of man shall be humbled,	2Ne	12:11
and the glory of his high l.		20:12
great power, which l. small unto	Eth	3: 5

LOOSE
nevertheless they did not l. me.	1Ne	18:13
my brethren that they would l. me.		18:19
Yet I will not l. his tongue,	2Ne	3:17
l. thyself from the bands of thy		8:25
l. yourselves from the pains of	Jac	3:11
he may l. the bands of death	Al	7:12
shall l. the bands of this temporal		11:42
whatsoever ye shall l. on earth	He	10: 7
l. thyself from the bands of thy	3Ne	20:37
and he did l. their tongues,		26:14
strong, no man can l. them;	DC	88:94
whatsoever he shall l. on earth		124:93
whatsoever you l. on earth,		127: 7
and whatsoever you l. on earth		128: 8
whatsoever thou shalt l. on earth		128:10
He had on a l. robe of most	JS	2:31

LOOSED
bands were l. from off my hands	1Ne	7:18
they came unto me, and l. the bands		18:15
insomuch that they l. me.		18:20
after they had l. me,		18:21
he cannot be l. for the space of		22:26
hastened, that he may be l.,	2Ne	8:14
the girdle of their loins be l.,		15:27
the earth save it shall be l.		30:17
and their bands were l.;	Mos	7: 8
them about, were they l.?	Al	5: 9
Yea, they were l., and their		5: 9
l. from the bands of death,		5:10
they were l. from their bands;		14:28
that his bands should be l.;		17:24
he l. from the pains of hell;		26:13
has l. our brethren from the		26:14
on earth shall be l. in heaven;	He	10: 7
he l. their tongues that they	3Ne	26:14
l. from this eternal band of	Mrm	9:13

LOOSING
then shall your tongue be l.;	DC	11:21
is opened and thy tongue l.;		23: 3
and your tongue shall be l.,		31: 3
when he is l. again he shall		43:31
shall not be l. for the space of		88:110
he shall be l. for a little season,		88:111
neither shall the seal be l.		104:64
on earth shall be l. in heaven.		124:93
may be l. in heaven;		127: 7
on earth shall be l. in heaven.		128: 8
on earth shall be l. in heaven.		128:10

LOOSING
the l. of the bands of death;	Al	11:41
Zion l. herself from the bands	DC	113: 9

LOP
shall l. the bough with terror;	2Ne	20:33

LORD
and hid up unto the L.,		T Pg
and his up unto the L.,		T Pg
at the time the L. confounded		T Pg
great things the L. hath done		T Pg
know the covenants of the L.,		T Pg
The L. warns Lehi to depart	1Ne	1:hd
been highly favored of the L.		1: 1
prayed unto the L., yea, even		1: 5
as he prayed unto the L.,		1: 6
filled with the Spirit of the L.		1:12
exclaim many things unto the L.;		1:14
marvelous are thy works, O L.		1:14
which the L. had shown unto him.		1:15
after the L. had shown so many		1:18
the tender mercies of the L. are		1:20
the L. spake unto my father,		2: 1
the L. commanded my father,		2: 2
obedient unto the word of the L.,		2: 3
he did as the L. commanded him.		2: 3
and made an offering unto the L.,		2: 7
gave thanks unto the L. our God.		2: 7
the commandments of the L.!		2:10
wherefore, I did cry unto the L.;		2:16
the L. had manifested unto me		2:17
I cried unto the L. for them.		2:18
the L. spake unto me, saying:		2:19
off from the presence of the L.		2:21
returned from speaking with the L.,		3: 1
the L. hath commanded me that		3: 2
the L. hath commanded me that		3: 4
it is a commandment of the L.		3: 5
thou shalt be favored of the L.		3: 6
things which the L. hath commanded,		3: 7
for I know that the L. giveth no		3: 7
that I had been blessed of the L.		3: 8
As the L. liveth, and as we live,		3:15
which the l. hath commanded us.		3:15
the commandments of the L.;		3:16
the commandments of the L.		3:16
an angel of the L. came		3:29
the L. hath chosen him to be		3:29
the L. will deliver Laban into		3:29
the L. will deliver Laban into		3:31
the commandments of the L.;		4: 1
the L. is able to deliver us,		4: 3
the L. hath delivered him into		4:11
the commandments of the L.;		4:11
the L. hath delivered him into		4:12
the L. slayeth the wicked to bring		4:13
I remembered the words of the L.		4:14
the commandments of the L.		4:15
the L. had delivered Laban into		4:17
received much strength of the L.,		4:31
as the L. liveth, and as I live,		4:32
Surely the L. hath commanded us		4:34
the commandments of the L.?		4:34
the L. will deliver my sons		5: 5
the L. hath commanded my husband		5: 8
the L. hath protected my sons,		5: 8
which the L. hath commanded		5: 8
and burnt offerings unto the L.;		5: 9
preserved by the hand of the L.,		5:14
wherewith the L. had commanded		5:20

which the L. had commanded us,	1 Ne	5:21
the commandments of the L.		5:21
it was wisdom in the L. that		5:22
the L. spake unto him again,		7: 1
might raise up seed unto the L.		7: 1
the L. commanded him that I,		7: 2
unto him the words of the L.		7: 4
the L. did soften the heart of		7: 5
unto the word of the l.?		7: 9
ye have seen an angel of the L.?		7:10
great things the L. hath done		7:11
the L. is able to do all things		7:12
word of the L. shall be fulfilled		7:13
things which the L. hath spoken		7:13
the Spirit of the L. ceaseth soon		7:14
Spirit of the L. constraineth me		7:15
I prayed unto the L., saying:		7:17
O L., according to my faith		7:17
would pray unto the L. their God		7:21
had done praying unto the L.		7:21
they did give thanks unto the L.		7:22
I have reason to rejoice in the L.		8: 3
I began to pray unto the L.		8: 8
after I had prayed unto the L.		8: 9
cast off from the presence of the L.		8:36
perhaps the L. would be merciful		8:37
the commandments of the L.;		8:38
a commandment of the L.		9: 3
the L. hath commanded me to		9: 5
But the L. knoweth all things		9: 6
to the own due time of the L.,		10: 3
a prophet would the L. God raise		10: 4
to prepare the way of the L.—		10: 7
Prepare ye the way of the L.,		10: 8
fulfilling of the word of the L.,		10:13
their L. and their Redeemer.		10:14
the course of the L. is one eternal		10:19
L. was able to make things known		11: 1
away in the Spirit of the L.,		11: 1
Hosanna to the L., the most high		11: 6
that it was the Spirit of the L.;		11:11
twelve called by the angel of the L.		11:34
angel of the L. spake unto me		11:35
angel of the L. spake unto me		11:36
terrible judgments of the L.		12: 5
I beheld the Spirit of the L.,		13:15
humble themselves before the L.;		13:16
the power of the L. was with them.		13:16
contains the covenants of the L.,		13:23
contain the covenants of the L.,		13:23
angel of the L. said unto me:		13:24
plainness of the gospel of the L.,		13:24
also many covenants of the L.		13:26
pervert the right ways of the L.,		13:27
is the land that the L. God hath		13:30
the L. God will not suffer that		13:30
Neither will the L. God suffer		13:32
angel of the L. spake unto me,		13:34
the covenants of the L. unto		14: 5
the covenant people of the L.,		14:14
for the L. God hath ordained the		14:25
in the own due time of the L.,		14:26
angel of the L. did make them		14:29
man should inquire of the L.;		15: 3
they did not look unto the L.		15: 3
Have ye inquired of the L.?		15: 8
We have not; for the l. maketh		15: 9
the commandments of the L.?		15:10
things which the L. hath said?		15:11
by the Spirit of the L. which was		15:12
the covenant people of the L.;		15:14
that the L. may show his power		15:17
covenant the L. made to our		15:18
humble themselves before the L.		15:20
heed unto the word of the L.;		15:25
the commandments of the L.		16: 4
humble themselves before the L.;		16: 5
the commandments of the L.		16: 8
Nephi, had been blessed of the L.		16: 8
the L. spake unto my father		16: 9
which the L. had given unto us;		16:11
began to murmur against the L.		16:20
they did murmur against the L.		16:20
unto complaining against the L.	1 Ne	16:22
he did inquire of the L.,		16:24
the voice of the L. came unto		16:25
of his murmuring against the L.,		16:25
the voice of the L. said unto him:		16:26
concerning the ways of the L.;		16:29
the L. can bring about great things.		16:29
humble themselves before the L.,		16:32
the L. has talked with him,		16:38
the L. was with us,		16:39
the voice of the L. came and did		16:39
chastened by the voice of the L.		16:39
the L. did bless us again		16:39
the blessings of the L. upon us,		17: 2
things were prepared of the L.		17: 5
voice of the L. came unto me,		17: 7
and cried unto the L.		17: 7
the L. spake unto me, saying:		17: 8
I said: L., whither shall I go		17: 9
the L. told me whither I should		17:10
the L. had not hitherto suffered		17:12
the L. said also that:		17:14
shall know that I, the L., am God;		17:14
I, the L., did deliver you from		17:14
the commandments of the L.,		17:15
I was instructed of the L.		17:18
and judgments of the L.,		17:22
unto the words of the L.?		17:23
if the L. had not commanded		17:24
Moses was commanded of the L.		17:26
the L. their God, their Redeemer,		17:30
the L. esteemeth all flesh in one;		17:35
the L. did curse the land against		17:35
the L. hath created the earth that		17:36
the L. straitened them because of		17:41
the L. commanded my father		17:44
but slow to remember the L.		17:45
if the L. has such great power,		17:51
the L. said unto me:		17:53
I will shock them, saith the L.,		17:53
they may know that I am the L.		17:53
but the L. did shake them,		17:54
surety that the L. is with thee,		17:55
power of the L. that has shaken us.		17:55
wherefore, worship the L. thy God,		17:55
which the L. thy God shall give thee.		17:55
they did worship the L.,		18: 1
the L. did show me from time		18: 1
the manner which the L. had shown		18: 2
and I did pray oft unto the L.;		18: 3
the L. showed unto me great things.		18: 3
according to the word of the L.,		18: 4
themselves again before the L.		18: 4
the voice of the L. came unto my		18: 5
which the L. had commanded us,		18: 6
lest the L. should be angry with		18:10
the L. did suffer it that he might		18:11
which had been prepared of the L.,		18:12
I did not murmur against the L.		18:16
I prayed unto the L.;		18:21
the L. commanded me,		19: 1
should be commanded of the L.		19: 2
purposes are known unto the L.		19: 3
further commandments of the L.		19: 4
The L. God surely shall visit		19:11
will I gather in, saith the L.,		19:16
shall see the salvation of the L.		19:17
remember the L. their Redeemer.		19:18
for had not the L. been merciful,		19:20
concerning the doings of the L.		19:22
believe in the L. their Redeemer		19:23
swear by the name of the L.,		20: 1
the God of Israel, who is the L.		20: 2
the L. of Hosts is his name.		20: 2
The L. hath loved him;		20:14
Also, saith the L.; I the Lord,		20:15
I the L., Yea, I have spoken;		20:15
the L. God, and his Spirit, hath		20:16
thus saith the L., thy Redeemer,		20:17
the L. thy God who teacheth thee		20:17
the L. hath redeemed his servant		20:20
saith the L., unto the wicked.		20:22
the L. hath called me from		21: 1

LORD

surely my judgment is with the L.,	1Ne	21: 4
And now, saith the L.–		21: 5
glorious in the eyes of the L.,		21: 5
Thus saith the L., the Redeemer		21: 7
because of the L. that is faithful.		21: 7
Thus saith the L.:		21: 8
the L. hath comforted his people,		21:13
The L. hath forsaken me,		21:14
and my L. hath forgotten me–		21:14
as I live, saith the L.,		21:18
Thus saith the L. God:		21:22
shalt know that I am the L.;		21:23
But thus saith the L.,		21:25
know that I, the L., am they Savior		21:26
the L. has lifted up his hand		22: 6
thus are the covenants of the L.		22: 6
the L. God will raise up a mighty		22: 7
the L. God will proceed to do a		22: 8
the L. God will proceed to make		22:11
know that the L. is their Savior		22:12
to ensnare the people of the L.		22:14
perverted the right ways of the L.,		22:14
the L. will surely prepare a way		22:20
A prophet shall the L. your God		22:20
The L. warns Nephi to depart	2Ne	1:hd
how great things the L. had done		1: 1
how merciful the L. had been		1: 3
a land which the L. God hath		1: 5
the L. hath covenanted this land		1: 5
countries by the hand of the L.		1: 5
be brought by the hand of the L.		1: 6
whom the L. God shall bring out		1: 9
blessings from the hand of the L.–		1:10
and marvelous works of the L.		1:10
the L. hath redeemed my soul from		1:15
and the judgments of the L.;		1:16
the L. your God should come out		1:17
and a favored people of the L.		1:19
but it was the Spirit of the L.		1:27
keep the commandments of the L.,		1:32
the L. hath consecrated this land		1:32
the L. God gave unto man that		2:16
commandments which the L. God		2:21
may the L. consecrate also unto		3: 2
may the L. bless thee forever,		3: 3
great were the covenants of the L.		3: 4
he obtained a promise of the L.,		3: 5
the L. God would rise up a		3: 5
in the covenants of the L.		3: 5
shall the L. my God raise up,		3: 6
Thus saith the L. unto me:		3: 7
my word only, saith the L.,		3:11
of my covenants, saith the L.		3:12
O house of Israel, saith the L.		3:13
that seer will the L. bless;		3:14
which I have obtained of the L.,		3:14
which the L. shall bring forth		3:15
by the power of the L. shall		3:15
for the L. hath said unto me,		3:16
And the L. hath said:		3:17
And the L. said unto me also:		3:18
For the L. God hath said that:		4: 4
the L. God will not suffer that		4: 7
Spirit of the L. which was in him,		4:12
of the admonitions of the L.		4:13
delighteth in the things of the L.;		4:16
the great goodness of the L.,		4:17
if the L. in his condescension		4:26
cry unto the L., and say:		4:30
O L., I will praise thee forever;		4:30
O L., wilt thou redeem my soul?		4:31
O L., wilt thou not shut the		4:32
O L., wilt thou encircle me around		4:33
O L., wilt thou make a way for mine		4:33
O L., I have trusted in thee,		4:34
cry much unto the L. my God,		5: 1
the L. did warn me, that I,		5: 5
and the commandments of the L.		5:10
And the L. was with us;		5:11
by the hand of the L.,		5:12
the words of the L. had been		5:19
to the commandments of the L.,		5:19
the word of the L. was fulfilled		5:20
off from the presence of the L.	2Ne	5:20
the L. God did cause a skin of		5:21
And thus saith the L. God:		5:22
the L. spake it, and it was done.		5:23
And the L. God said unto me:		5:25
the L. God said unto me:		5:30
to the commandments of the L.,		5:31
Thus saith the L. God:		6: 6
shalt know that I am the L.;		6: 7
the L. has shown me that		6: 8
the L. has shown unto me that		6: 9
L. God, the Holy One of Israel,		6: 9
the L. will be merciful unto them,		6:11
the L. God will fulfil his covenants		6:12
the covenant people of the L.		6:13
the people of the L. shall not		6:13
the people of the L. are they who		6:13
shall know that the L. is God,		6:15
But thus saith the L.:		6:17
For thus saith the L.:		6:17
know that I the L. am thy Savior		6:18
Yea, for thus saith the L.:		7: 1
For thus saith the L.:		7: 1
The L. God hath given me the		7: 4
The L. God hath opened mine ear,		7: 5
For the L. God will help me,		7: 7
And the L. is near,		7: 8
For the L. God will help me.		7: 9
is among you that feareth the L.,		7:10
For the L. shall comfort Zion,		8: 3
desert like the garden of the L.		8: 3
O arm of the L.;		8: 9
the redeemed of the L. shall		8:11
And forgettest the L. thy maker,		8:13
But I am the L. thy God,		8:15
the L. of Hosts is my name.		8:15
hast drunk at the hand of the L.		8:17
are full of the fury of the L.,		8:20
Thus saith thy L., the Lord		8:22
the L. and thy God pleadeth the		8:22
concerning the covenants of the L.		9: 1
blessings which the L. God shall		9: 3
off from the presence of the L.		9: 6
And assuredly, as the L. liveth,		9:16
for the L. God hath spoken it,		9:16
L. God, the Holy One of Israel,		9:24
come unto the L., the Holy One.		9:41
for the L. God is his name.		9:41
judgments, O L. God Almighty–		9:46
how great the covenants of the L.,		9:53
behold, thus saith the L. God:		10: 7
the promises of the L. are great		10: 9
I, the L., the king of heaven,		10:14
the L. has made the sea our path,		10:20
great are the promises of the L.		10:21
For behold, the L. God has led		10:22
the L. remembereth all them		10:22
in the covenants of the L.		11: 5
go up to the mountain of the L.,		12: 3
the word of the L. from Jerusalem.		12: 3
let us walk in the light of the L.;		12: 5
O L., thou hast forsaken thy people,		12: 6
in the dust, for the fear of the L.		12:10
the L. alone shall be exalted		12:11
the day of the L. of Hosts		12:12
the day of the L. shall come		12:13
the L. alone shall be exalted		12:17
for the fear of the L. shall come		12:19
for the fear of the L. shall come		12:21
the L., the Lord of Hosts, doth		13: 1
the L. of Hosts, doth take away		13: 1
doings have been against the L.,		13: 8
The L. standeth up to plead,		13:13
The L. will enter into judgment		13:14
saith the L. God of Hosts.		13:15
Moreover, the L. saith:		13:16
the L. will smite with a scab		13:17
the L. will discover their secret		13:17
In that day the L. will take		13:18
the branch of the L. be beautiful		14: 2
When the L. shall have washed		14: 4
And the L. will create upon		14: 5
the vineyard of the L. of Hosts		15: 7

LORD 564 LORD

In mine ears, said the L. of Hosts,	2Ne 15: 9
they regard not the work of the L.,	15:12
the L. of Hosts shall be exalted	15:16
the law of the L. of Hosts,	15:24
is the anger of the L. kindled	15:25
I saw also the L. sitting upon a	16: 1
Holy, holy, holy, is the L. of Hosts;	16: 3
seen the King, the L. of Hosts.	16: 5
Also I heard the voice of the L.,	16: 8
Then said I: L., how long?	16:11
And the L. have removed men	16:12
Then said the L. unto Isaiah:	17: 3
Thus saith the L. God:	17: 7
Moreover, the L. spake again unto	17:10
thee a sign of the L. thy God;	17:11
neither will I tempt the L.	17:12
the L. himself shall give you a	17:14
The L. shall bring upon thee,	17:17
in that day that the L. shall hiss	17:18
shall the L. shave with a razor	17:20
the word of the L. said unto me:	18: 1
Then said the L. to me:	18: 3
The L. spake also unto me again,	18: 5
the L. bringeth up upon them the	18: 7
For the L. spake thus to me	18:11
Sanctify the L. of Hosts himself,	18:13
And I will wait upon the L.,	18:17
children whom the L. hath given	18:18
in Israel from the L. of Hosts,	18:18
The zeal of the L. of Hosts	19: 7
The L. sent his word unto Jacob	19: 8
the L. shall set up the adversaries	19:11
do they seek the L. of Hosts.	19:13
will the L. cut off from Israel	19:14
the L. shall have no joy in	19:17
the wrath of the L. of Hosts	19:19
when the L. hath performed his	20:12
shall the L., the Lord of Hosts,	20:16
the L. of Hosts, send among his	20:16
the L., the Holy One of Israel,	20:20
the L. God of Hosts shall make	20:23
thus saith the L. God of Hosts;	20:24
the L. of Hosts shall stir up a	20:26
the L., the Lord of Hosts shall	20:33
the L. of Hosts shall lop the bough	20:33
the Spirit of the L. shall rest	21: 2
and of the fear of the L.	21: 2
in the fear of the L.;	21: 3
be full of the knowledge of the L.,	21: 9
the L. shall set his hand again	21:11
the L. shall utterly destroy the	21:15
O L., I will praise thee;	22: 1
the L. JEHOVAH is my strength	22: 2
Praise the L., call upon his name,	22: 2
Sing unto the L.; for he hath	22: 5
the L. of Hosts mustereth the hosts	23: 4
the L., and the weapons of his	23: 5
for the day of the L. is at hand;	23: 6
the day of the L. cometh,	23: 9
in the wrath of the L. of Hosts,	23:13
the L. will have mercy on Jacob,	24: 1
the land of the L. shall be for	24: 2
the L. shall give thee rest,	24: 3
The L. hath broken the staff	24: 5
saith the L. of Hosts,	24:22
son, and nephew, saith the L.	24:22
destruction, saith the L. of Hosts.	24:23
The L. of Hosts hath sworn,	24:24
For the L. of Hosts hath purposed,	24:27
That the L. hath founded Zion,	24:32
them by the prophets of the L.	25: 9
the L. God hath scourged them by	25:16
the L. will set his hand again	25:17
And as the L. God liveth that	25:20
and as the L. God liveth,	25:20
hath the L. God promised unto	25:21
saith the L. of Hosts,	26: 4
saith the L. of Hosts;	26: 5
anger of the L. shall be kindled	26: 6
saith the L. of Hosts.	26: 6
before the presence of the L.;	26: 7
the Spirit of the L. will not always	26:11
the days when the L. God shall	2Ne 26:14
after the L. God shall have	26:15
the L. God will give unto him	26:16
For thus saith the L. God:	26:17
yea, thus saith the L. God:	26:18
L. God worketh not in darkness.	26:23
hath the L. commanded any that	26:28
the L. hath forbidden this thing;	26:30
the L. hath given a	26:30
the L. God hath commanded	26:32
the name of the L. their God	26:32
these iniquities come of the L.;	26:33
visited of the L. of Hosts,	27: 2
the L. hath poured out upon you	27: 5
the L. God shall bring forth unto	27: 6
until the own due time of the L.,	27:10
the L. God hath said that the	27:13
the L. God will proceed to bring	27:14
the L. God shall say unto him	27:15
the L. God will deliver again	27:19
shall the L. God say unto him:	27:20
the L. shall say unto him	27:24
to hide their counsel from the L.!	27:27
saith the L. of Hosts,	27:27
behold, saith the L. of Hosts:	27:28
and their joy shall be in the L.,	27:30
For assuredly as the L. liveth	27:31
Therefore, thus saith the L.,	27:33
built up, and not unto the L.,	28: 3
churches, and not unto the L.—	28: 3
the L. and the Redeemer hath done	28: 5
wrought by the hand of the L.,	28: 6
to hide their counsels from the L.;	28: 9
and pervert the right way of the L.,	28:15
saith the L. God Almighty,	28:15
the L. God will speedily visit	28:16
destroyed, saith the L. of Hosts.	28:17
behold, thus saith the L. God:	28:30
saith the L. God of Hosts!	28:32
unto them, saith the L. God,	28:32
saith the L. God of Hosts.	28:32
But thus saith the L. God:	29: 4
I the L. have not forgotten my	29: 5
I, the L. your God, have created	29: 7
are the covenant people of the L.;	30: 2
for the L. covenanteth with	30: 2
sealed up again unto the L.,	30: 3
the L. God shall commence his	30: 8
shall the L. God judge the poor,	30: 9
the L. God shall cause a great	30:10
be full of the knowledge of the L.	30:15
doth the L. God work among	31: 3
For the L. God giveth light unto	31: 3
prophet which the L. showed unto	31: 4
by following your L.	31:13
your L. and your Redeemer	31:17
perform any thing unto the L.	32: 9
the L. God will consecrate my	33: 4
thus hath the L. commanded me,	33:15
mine errand from the L.	Jac 1:17
magnify our office unto the L.,	1:19
obedient unto the word of the L.,	2: 4
behold, as I inquired of the L.,	2:11
For behold, thus saith the L.:	2:23
before me, saith the L.	2:24
Wherefore, thus saith the L.,	2:25
I the L. God will not suffer that	2:26
hearken to the word of the L.:	2:27
For I, the L. God, delight in	2:28
thus saith the L. of Hosts.	2:28
saith the L. of Hosts,	2:29
if I will, saith the L. of Hosts,	2:30
I, the L., have seen the sorrow,	2:31
saith the L. of Hosts.	2:32
saith the L. of Hosts.	2:32
saith the L. of Hosts.	2:33
and the L. God will lead away	3: 4
the commandment of the L.,	3: 5
the L. God will not destroy them,	3: 6
the L. God showeth us our	4: 7
marvelous are the works of the L.	4: 8
seek not to counsel the L.,	4:10

LORD

words of me, a prophet of the L.	Jac	5: 2
For behold, thus saith the L.,		5: 3
saith the L. of the vineyard,		5: 8
servant of the L. of the vineyard		5:10
the word of the L. of the vineyard,		5:10
the L. of the vineyard caused		5:11
the L. of the vineyard went his		5:14
the L. of the vineyard said unto		5:15
the L. of the vineyard, and also		5:16
the L. of the vineyard looked		5:17
the L. of the vineyard said unto		5:19
the L. of the vineyard said unto		5:22
the L. of the vineyard said unto		5:23
the L. of the vineyard said again		5:24
the L. of the vineyard said unto		5:26
the L. of the vineyard and the		5:28
servant of the L. of the vineyard		5:28
the L. of the vineyard said unto		5:29
the L. of the vineyard and the		5:30
the L. of the vineyard did taste		5:31
And the L. of the vineyard said:		5:31
the L. of the vineyard said unto		5:33
the L. of the vineyard said unto		5:35
the L. of the vineyard said unto		5:38
the L. of the vineyard wept,		5:41
the L. of the vineyard said unto		5:49
said unto the L. of the vineyard:		5:50
And the L. said:		5:51
the L. of the vineyard said unto		5:57
the L. of the vineyard sent his		5:70
as the l. had commanded him,		5:70
the L. of the vineyard said unto		5:71
the L. of the vineyard labored		5:72
of the L. of the vineyard		5:72
of the L. of the vineyard,		5:74
the L. had preserved unto himself		5:74
the L. of the vineyard had		5:74
when the L. of the vineyard saw		5:75
servants of the L. shall go forth		6: 2
I had heard the voice of the L.		7: 5
the L. God poured in his Spirit		7: 8
And thy will, O L., be done,		7:14
power of the L. came upon him,		7:15
nurture and admonition of the L.—	En	1: 1
And I said: L., how is it done?		1: 7
voice of the L. came into my mind		1:10
began to be unshaken in the L.;		1:11
diligence, the L. said unto me:		1:12
that the L. God would preserve a		1:13
that the L. God was able to		1:15
And the L. said unto me:		1:18
keep them in the fear of the L.		1:23
the sabbath day holy unto the L.	Jar	1: 5
mighty men in the faith of the L.;		1: 7
the people the ways of the L.;		1: 7
the word of the L. was verified,		1: 9
prophets of the L. did threaten		1:10
and the commandments of the L.	Om	1: 2
For the L. would not suffer,		1: 6
Wherefore, the L. did visit them in		1: 7
he being warned of the L. that		1:12
hearken unto the voice of the L.		1:12
as the L. had commanded him.		1:13
hearken unto the voice of the L.;		1:13
the L. had sent the people of		1:14
brought by the hand of the L.		1:16
at the time the L. confounded		1:22
the severity of the L. fell upon		1:22
to be a just man before the L.,		1:25
is good save it comes from the L.;		1:25
as the L. liveth ye will be saved.		1:26
workings of the Spirit of the L.	WM	1: 7
but the L. knoweth all things		1: 7
And in the strength of the L.		1:14
them by the hand of the L.	Mos	1: 2
promises which the L. made unto		1: 7
the L. our God hath given us.		1:10
which the L. God hath brought		1:11
the commandments of the L.		1:11
highly favored people of the L.		1:13
that the L. will deliver them up,		1:13
was prepared by the hand of the L.		1:16

give thanks to the L. their God,	Mos	2: 4
suffered by the hand of the L. that		2:11
the L. hath granted unto me.		2:11
keep the commandments of the L.,		2:13
but the L. God doth support me,		2:30
was commanded them of the L.;		2:35
from the Spirit of the L.,		2:36
the L. has no place in him,		2:37
shrink from the presence of the L.,		2:38
for the L. hath spoken it.		2:41
the L. hath heard thy prayers,		3: 4
the L. Omnipotent who reigneth,		3: 5
and faith on the L. Jesus Christ.		3:12
And the L. God hath sent his		3:13
Yet the L. God saw that his		3:14
of Christ, the L. Omnipotent.		3:17
of Christ, the L. Omnipotent.		3:18
the atonement of Christ the L.,		3:19
all things which the L. seeth fit		3:19
name of the L. God Omnipotent.		3:21
the L. thy God hath commanded		3:22
the L. God hath commanded me.		3:23
And thus saith the L.:		3:24
shrink from the presence of the L.		3:25
Thus hath the L. commanded me.		3:27
unto him by the angel of the L.,		4: 1
the fear of the L. had come upon		4: 1
the Spirit of the L. came upon them,		4: 3
that should put his trust in the L.,		4: 6
which the L. can comprehend.		4: 9
calling on the name of the L.		4:11
concerning the coming of our L.,		4:30
the Spirit of the L. Omnipotent,		5: 2
Christ, the L. God Omnipotent,		5:15
did walk in the ways of the L.,		6: 6
the L. would not have suffered that		5:25
a prophet of the L. have they		7:26
For behold, the L. hath said:		7:29
the promise of the L. is fulfilled,		7:32
But if ye will turn to the L.		7:33
marvelous are the works of the L.,		8:20
slow to remember the L. our God.		9: 3
in the strength of the L. did we		9:17
did cry mightily to the L. that		9:17
did go up in the strength of the L.		10:10
knew nothing concerning the L.,		10:11
nor the strength of the L.,		10:11
the commandments of the L.—		10:13
therefore he was favored of the L.,		10:13
for the L. heard his prayers and		10:13
not the dealings of the L.;		10:14
their hearts against the L.		10:14
as the L. had commanded him,		10:16
putting their trust in the L.;		10:19
And may the L. bless my people.		10:22
abominable in the sight of the L.		11: 2
Behold, thus saith the L.,		11:20
thus saith the L.—		11:20
and turn unto the L. their God,		11:21
that I am the L. their God,		11:22
and turn unto the L. their God,		11:23
it be the L. the Almighty God.		11:23
cry mightily to the L. their God,		11:25
and thus saith the L., and thus		11:25
but the L. delivered him out of		11:26
or who is the L., that shall bring		11:27
heart against the word of the L.,		11:29
Thus has the L. commanded me,		12: 1
And the L. said unto me:		12: 2
Thus saith the L., it shall come		12: 2
he shall know that I am the L.		12: 3
pretended the L. hath spoken it.		12:12
the L. shall bring again Zion;		12:22
for the L. hath comforted his		12:23
The L. hath made bare his holy		12:24
perverting the ways of the L.!		12:26
perverted the ways of the L.		12:26
that the L. has cause to send me		12:29
which the L. delivered unto Moses		12:33
I am the L. thy God, who hath		12:34
which the L. sent me to deliver;		13: 3
the Spirit of the L. was upon him;		13: 5

LORD

Sinai while speaking with the L.	Mos 13: 5	the L. hath heard the prayers of	Mos 27:14
for I the L. thy God am a jealous	13:13	had beheld an angel of the L.;	27:18
name of the L. thy God in vain;	13:15	what the L. had done for his son,	27:21
the L. will not hold him guiltless	13:15	to pray to the L. their God that	27:22
the sabbath of the L. thy God,	13:18	have been redeemed of the L.;	27:24
in six days the L. made heaven	13:19	And the L. said unto me:	27:25
the L. blessed the sabbath day,	13:19	the L. in mercy hath seen fit to	27:28
which the L. thy God giveth thee.	13:20	unto the people that the L. reigneth.	27:37
the L. would not have caused me	13:26	the knowledge of the L. their God,	28: 2
to remember the L. their God;	13:29	to rejoice in the L. their God,	28: 2
is the arm of the l. revealed?	14: 1	the L. their God had given them.	28: 2
the L. hath laid on him the	14: 6	the Spirit of the L. work upon	28: 4
it pleased the L. to bruise him;	14:10	the L. saw fit in his infinite mercy	28: 4
the pleasure of the L. shall	14:10	went and inquired of the L. if	28: 6
concerning the coming of the L.—	15:11	And the L. said unto Mosiah:	28: 7
the L. would redeem his people,	15:11	preserved by the hand of the L.,	28:15
even the L., who has redeemed	15:18	the L. confounded the language	28:17
And thus the L. bringeth about	15:24	perverting the way of the L.,	29: 7
life, being redeemed by the L.	15:24	thus doth the L. work with his	29:20
for the L. redeemeth none such	15:26	given them by the hand of the L.	29:25
the L. hath redeemed none such;	15:27	these things in the fear of the L.;	29:30
neither can the L. redeem such;	15:27	so long as the L. sees fit that we	29:32
the salvation of the L. shall be	15:28	did walk in the ways of the L.,	29:43
Yea, L., thy watchmen shall lift	15:29	for the L. had created all men,	Al 1: 4
the L. shall bring again Zion.	15:29	the L. did strengthen the hand of	2:18
for the L. hath comforted his	15:30	by the hand of the L.,	2:28
The L. hath made bare his holy	15:31	the L. did hear their cries,	2:28
shall see the salvation of the L.;	16: 1	O L., have mercy and spare my	2:30
hearken unto the voice of the L.;	16: 2	the L. God set a mark upon	3: 7
the L. redeemeth them not.	16: 2	the L. God might preserve his	3: 8
having never called upon the L.	16:12	promises of the L. unto Nephi	3:17
cometh through Christ the L.,	16:15	the Spirit of the L. did not fail	4:15
salvation of the L. their God.	17:15	again the L. did deliver them	5: 5
redemption, and faith on the L.	18: 7	that ye hear the voice of the L.,	5:16
baptized in the name of the L.,	18:10	can lie unto the L. in that day,	5:17
O L., pour out thy Spirit upon	18:12	L., our works have been righteous	5:17
the Spirit of the L. was upon him,	18:13	for the L. God hath spoken it!	5:32
may the Spirit of the L. be poured	18:13	true; for the L. God hath made	5:46
repentance and faith on the L.,	18:20	the L. in much mercy hath	7: 2
give thanks to the L. their God.	18:23	the L. God hath power to do all	7: 8
to worship the L. their God,	18:25	and prepare the way of the L.,	7: 9
to hear the word of the L.	18:32	And may the L. bless you,	7:25
Alma and the people of the L.	18:34	an angel of the L. appeared unto	8:14
in vain for the people of the L.	19: 1	the L. God will destroy them.	8:16
hearken unto the words of the L.,	20:21	thy people, (for thus saith the L.)	8:17
word of the L. might be fulfilled.	21: 4	message from the angel of the L.	8:18
the L. was slow to hear their	21:15	Repent ye, for thus saith the L.,	8:29
the L. did hear their cries,	21:15	that the L. might show forth	8:31
the L. did not see fit to deliver	21:15	which the L. had given them.	8:32
waiting upon the Spirit of the L.	21:34	off from the presence of the L.	9:13
Alma and the people of the L.,	23:hd	off from the presence of the L.	9:14
having been warned of the L.	23: 1	the word of the L. has been verified	9:14
And the L. did strengthen them,	23: 2	the L. will be merciful unto	9:16
have a king; for thus saith the L.:	23: 7	for the L. will be merciful unto	9:17
abominable in the sight of the L.,	23: 9	to the fierce anger of the L.	9:18
the L. did hear my cries,	23:10	unto them of the L. their God;	9:19
the L. seeth fit to chasten his	23:21	highly favored people of the L.;	9:20
but the L. their God,	23:23	unto by the voice of the L.;	9:21
remember the L. their God	23:27	Jerusalem, by the hand of the L.;	9:22
and began to cry unto the L.	23:28	from the hand of the L.,	9:23
that the L. did soften the hearts of	23:29	promises of the L. are extended	9:24
concerning the L. their God,	24: 5	has not the L. expressly promised	9:24
their voices to the L. their God,	24:12	the L. has sent his angel to visit	9:25
the voice of the L. came to them	24:13	prepare the way of the L.,	9:28
I, the L. God, do visit my people	24:14	the L. did not suffer them that	9:33
yea, the L. did strengthen them	24:15	much of the ways of the L.,	10: 5
patience to all the will of the L.	24:15	an angel of the L. appeared unto	10: 7
the voice of the L. came unto	24:16	shalt feed a prophet of the L.;	10: 7
the L. caused a deep sleep to come	24:19	the blessing of the L. shall rest	10: 7
except it were the L. their God.	24:21	unto you, that as the L. liveth,	10:10
now the L. said unto Alma:	24:23	the blessing of the L. hath rested	10:11
repentance and faith on the L.	25:15	well doth the L. judge of your	10:20
was the L. that did deliver them.	25:16	will not the L. stay his hand;	10:23
the L. did pour out his Spirit	25:24	according to the Spirit of the L.,	11:22
not call upon the L. their God.	26: 4	contrary to the Spirit of the L.	11:22
he went and inquired of the L.	26:13	not enter into the rest of the L.;	12:36
the voice of the L. came to him,	26:14	we provoke not the L. our God	12:37
know that I am the L. their God,	26:26	when the L. God gave these	13: 1
according to the word of the L.	26:34	the L. God ordained priests,	13: 1
the L. did visit them and prosper	27: 7	into the rest of the L. their God.	13:12
lead astray the people of the L.,	27:10	enter into the rest of the L.	13:16
the angel of the L. appeared	27:11	the voice of the L., by the mouth	13:22
For the L. hath said:	27:13	humble yourselves before the L.,	13:28

LORD   567   LORD

Having faith on the L.;	Al 13:29		the L. doth counsel in wisdom,	Al 29: 8
And may the L. grant unto you	13:30		which the L. hath commanded	29: 9
the L. receiveth them up unto	14:11		which the L. hath commanded	29: 9
according to the will of the L.	14:13		and coming to the L. their God,	29:10
the L. will destroy this people	14:24		what the L. has done for me,	29:10
suffer these great afflictions, O L.?	14:26		that the L. did deliver them out	29:11
O L., give us strength according	14:26		the L. God, the God of Abraham,	29:11
the L. had granted unto them	14:28		keep the commandments of the L.;	30: 3
Alma cried unto the L., saying:	15:10		perverting the ways of the L.?	30:22
O L. our God, have mercy on	15:10		be unto thee even as the L. will.	30:55
baptized Zeezrom unto the L.;	15:12		all converted again unto the L.;	30:58
to baptize unto the L. whosoever	15:13		perverteth the ways of the L.,	30:60
and strengthened him in the L.	15:18		perverting the ways of the L.,	31: 1
whether the L. would that they	16: 5		did pervert the ways of the L.	31:11
that Alma inquired of the L.	16: 6		they did call the day of the L.;	31:12
the L. will deliver unto thee	16: 6		O, how long, O L., wilt thou	31:26
the L. did pour out his Spirit on	16:16		O L., how long wilt thou	31:30
into the rest of the L. their God.	16:17		O L., wilt thou give me strength,	31:30
the L. pouring out his blessings	16:21		O L., my heart is exceeding	31:31
were still his brethren in the L.;	17: 2		O L., wilt thou grant unto me	31:31
the L. would grant unto them a	17: 9		O L., wilt thou comfort my soul,	31:32
the L. did visit them with his	17:10		all these wilt thou comfort, O L.	31:32
the L. said unto them also:	17:11		O L., wilt thou grant unto us	31:34
trusting in the L. that they	17:13		Behold, O L., their souls are	31:35
the promises of the L. were	17:15		give unto us, O L., power and	31:35
the L. had promised Mosiah that	17:35		And the L., provided for them that	31:38
anything concerning the L.;	17:35		ye will resist the Spirit of the L.,	32:28
and all the works of the L.	18:39		I did turn unto my closet, O L.,	33: 7
he began to cry unto the L.	18:41		Thou art angry, O L., with this	33:16
O L., have mercy; according	18:41		for the L. God hath spoken it.	34: 8
the Spirit of the L. poured out	19:14		when you do not cry unto the L.,	34:27
for the fear of the L. had come	19:15		therefore, the Spirit of the L. hath	34:35
did call on the name of the L.,	19:16		the L. hath said he dwelleth not	34:36
been converted unto the L. for	19:16		fear of the L. came upon us.	36: 7
been converted to the L.,	19:17		the L. doth give me exceeding	36:25
the L. had said unto Mosiah,	19:23		preserved by the hand of the L.	37: 4
Mosiah trusted him unto the L.	19:23		the L. God doth work by means	37: 7
and were converted unto the L.	19:31		the L. doth confound the wise	37: 7
work of the L. did commence	19:36		knowledge of the L. their God,	37: 9
the L. did begin to pour out his	19:36		which the L. doth command you,	37:16
voice of the L. came to Ammon	20: 2		appeal unto the L. for all things	37:16
in the strength of the L. thou	20: 4		the L. saw that his people began	37:22
from the ground to the L. his God,	20:18		therefore the L. said, if they did	37:22
were led by the Spirit of the L.,	21:16		And he said: I will prepare	37:23
that the L. began to bless them,	21:17		all the prophets of the L. who	37:30
of worshiping the L. their God	21:22		did cry unto the L. their God	37:30
the Spirit of the L. has called	22: 4		faith on the L. Jesus Christ;	37:33
concerning the Spirit of the L.?	22: 5		faith on the L. Jesus Christ.	37:33
before the L., upon his knees;	22:17		let all thy doings be unto the L.,	37:36
were converted unto the L.	22:23		thou goest let it be in the L.;	37:36
had been converted unto the L.,	23: 3		thoughts be directed unto the L.;	37:36
to the knowledge of the L.,	23: 5		be placed upon the L. forever.	37:36
And as sure as the L. liveth,	23: 6		Counsel with the L. in all thy	37:37
I say unto you, as the L. liveth,	23: 6		at night lie down unto the L.,	37:37
and were converted unto the L.,	23: 6		compass; and the L. prepared it.	37:38
who were converted unto the L.	23: 8		to look to the L. your God,	38: 2
were converted unto the L.;	23:13		because the L. was with thee;	38: 4
who had been converted unto the L.	24: 6		that the L. did deliver thee.	38: 4
to call on the name of the L.	24:21		the L. in his great mercy sent his	38: 7
the L. worketh in many ways to	24:27		cry out unto the L. Jesus Christ	38: 8
who joined the people of the L.,	24:29		O L., forgive my unworthiness,	38:14
fathers, and to believe in the L.,	25: 6		And may the L. bless your soul,	38:15
they did walk in the ways of the L.,	25:14		in the sight of the L.;	39: 5
the L. had granted unto them	25:17		the Spirit of the L. doth say	39:12
they are in the hands of the L.	26: 7		turn to the L. with all your mind,	39:13
yea, we will glory in the L.	26:16		for the L. to send his angel to	39:19
can glory too much in the L.?	26:16		inquired diligently of the L.	40: 9
behold, the L. comforted us,	26:27		nor portion of the Spirit of the L.;	40:13
together this people of the L.,	27: 5		that are redeemed of the L.;	41: 7
I will go and inquire of the L.,	27: 7		after the L. God sent our first	42: 2
Yea, if the L. saith unto us go,	27: 7		the L. God placed cherubim and	42: 3
Inquire of the L., and if he saith	27: 8		from the presence of the L.;	42: 7
went and inquired of the L.,	27:10		cut off from the presence of the L.,	42: 9
and the L. said unto him:	27:11		cut off from the presence of the L.	42:11
which the L. had said unto him.	27:13		that he should inquire of the L.	43:23
yea, all the people of the L.	27:14		word of the L. came unto Alma,	43:24
a highly favored people of the L.	27:30		for the L. had said unto them,	43:46
now may the L., the Redeemer	28: 8		And again, the L. has said that:	43:47
to the promises of the L.,	28:11		one voice unto the L. their God,	43:49
to the promises of the L.,	28:12		unto the L. for their freedom,	43:50
labor in the vineyards of the L.;	28:14		ye behold that the L. is with us;	44: 3
which the L. hath allotted	29: 3		never will the l. suffer that we	44: 4
For behold, the L. doth grant	29: 8		as the L. liveth, ye shall not	44:11

LORD

the L. had again delivered them	Al	45: 1
thanks unto the L. their God;		45: 1
and the L. shall prosper thee		45: 8
called the disciples of the L.;		45:14
Thus saith the L. God—		45:16
the L. cannot look upon sin		45:16
or buried by the hand of the L.,		45:19
the L. took Moses unto himself;		45:19
by the hand of the L.		46: 7
men do forget the L. their God,		46: 8
forth in the strength of the L.,		46:20
that the L. God may bless them.		46:20
not forsake the L. their God;		46:21
the L. should rend them even as		46:21
redeemed by the L. Jesus Christ;		46:39
the same knowledge of the L.,		47:36
forgetting the L. their God.		47:36
faithful unto the L. their God.		48: 7
might live unto the L. their God,		48:10
the L. would deliver them;		48:16
were highly favored of the L.,		48:20
for the promise of the L. was,		48:25
did thank the L. their God,		49:28
just are all the dealings of the L.,		50:19
off from the presence of the L.		50:20
the commandments of the L.		50:22
to worship the L. their God,		50:39
had been converted unto the L.;		53:10
against the people of the L.,		54: 4
But, as the L. liveth, our armies		54:10
to remember the L. their God		55:31
as well in the L. as in the		56: 2
thus were we favored of the L.;		56:19
the L. our God did visit us with		58:11
and the L. has supported them,		58:39
to remember the L. their God		58:40
may the L. our God, who has		58:41
the L. suffereth the righteous to		60:13
into the rest of the L. their God.		60:13
them in the strength of the L.,		60:16
of the L. your God?		60:20
that the L. will still deliver us,		60:21
means which the L. has provided		60:21
the L. will not suffer that ye		60:31
can you suppose that the L. will		60:32
Behold, the L. saith unto me:		60:33
them in the strength of the L.,		61:18
except they repent the L. hath		61:20
Lehi and Teancum in the L.;		61:21
baptized unto the L. their God.		62:45
to remember the L. their God;		62:49
things the L. had done for them,		62:50
did pray unto the L. their God		62:51
that the L. did bless them,		62:51
of the L. his God;		63: 2
began to grow up unto the L.	He	3:21
the work of the L. did prosper		3:26
may see that the L. is merciful		3:27
the L. commanded him to give		4:22
the Spirit of the L. did no more		4:24
the Spirit of the L. doth not dwell		4:24
the L. did cease to preserve them		4:25
cleave unto the L. their God,		4:25
that the L. surely should come		5:10
the L. did bring Mulek into		6:10
the L. had blessed them so long		6:17
the Spirit of the L. began to		6:35
the L. began to pour out his		6:36
unto the words of the L.—		7: 7
turn ye turn ye unto the L. your God.		7:17
the L. will not grant unto you		7:22
For behold, thus saith the l.;		7:23
therefore the L. will be merciful		7:24
the L. God has made them known		7:29
the L. your God will suffer you		9:21
which the L. had shown unto him.		10: 2
thus saith the L. God, who is		10:11
when the L. had spoken these		10:12
word of the L. which had been		10:12
hearken unto the words of the L.		10:13
unto them the word of the L.,		10:14
thus saith the L., ye shall be		10:14
Nephi did cry unto the L.,		11: 3
O L. do not suffer that this	He	11: 4
but O L., rather let there be a		11: 4
remembrance of the L. their God,		11: 4
to remember the L. their God;		11: 7
cry unto the L. our God that he		11: 8
he cried again unto the L.,		11: 9
O L., behold this people repenteth;		11:10
Now, O L., because of this their		11:11
O L., wilt thou turn away		11:12
O L., wilt thou hearken unto me,		11:13
O L., thou didst hearken unto my		11:14
Yea, O L., and thou seest that		11:15
O L., wilt thou turn away thine		11:16
if so, O L., thou canst bless them		11:16
the L. did turn away his anger		11:17
remembrance of the L. their God.		11:34
again to forget the L. their God.		11:36
that the L. in his great infinite		12: 1
and do forget the L. their God,		12: 2
the L. doth chasten his people		12: 3
to remember the L. their God,		12: 5
desire that the L. their God,		12: 6
earth, and the L. shall say—		12:18
And if the L. shall say—		12:19
if the L. shall say unto a man—		12:20
And if the L. shall say—		12:21
the voice of the L. their God;		12:23
off from the presence of the L.:		12:25
voice of the L. came unto him,		13: 3
things the L. put into his heart.		13: 4
do speak the words of the L.		13: 5
and faith on the L. Jesus Christ,		13: 6
angel of the L. hath declared it		13: 7
Therefore, thus saith the L.;		13: 8
except ye repent, saith the L.;		13:10
and return unto the L. your God		13:11
away mine anger, saith the L.;		13:11
thus saith the L., blessed are		13:11
for I perceive, saith the L., that		13:12
hearts against me, saith the L.		13:12
the time cometh, saith the L.,		13:14
the land, saith the L. of Hosts,		13:17
saith the L. of Hosts, yea, our		13:18
and shall hide it up unto the L.		13:18
For I will, saith the L., that they		13:19
they be smitten, saith the L.		13:20
the words which the L. saith;		13:21
not remember the L. your God		13:22
not to thank the L. your God		13:22
are not drawn out unto the L.,		13:22
the L. God caused that a curse		13:23
for as the L. liveth, if a prophet		13:26
unto you the word of the L.,		13:26
that the L. will suffer you?		13:29
the anger of the L. is already		13:30
poverty ye shall cry unto the L.;		13:32
that day, saith the L. of Hosts.		13:32
had remembered the L. our God		13:33
that the word of the L. came		13:36
O L., canst thou not turn away		13:37
anger of the L. be turned away		13:39
hath the L. commanded me,		14: 9
and prepare the way of the L.		14: 9
which the L. hath commanded		14:10
into the presence of the L.		14:15
off from the presence of the L.,		14:16
back into the presence of the L.		14:17
been a chosen people of the L.;		15: 3
hath the L. prolonged their days,		15: 4
leadeth them to faith on the L.,		15: 7
behold, the L. shall bless them		15:10
the L. shall prolong their days,		15:11
the promises of the L. have been		15:12
the L. shall be merciful unto them.		15:12
Therefore, saith the L.:		15:16
again unto me, saith the L.		15:16
And now behold, saith the L.,		15:17
destroy them, saith the L.,		15:17
as surely as the L. liveth shall		15:17
shall these things be, saith the L.		15:17
might be baptized unto the L.		16: 1
Spirit of the L. was with him,		16: 2
among the people of the L.,		16:23

LORD 569 LORD

that he cried mightily unto the L.,	3Ne	1:12
voice of the L. came unto him,		1:12
day that the L. should be born,		1:19
and were converted unto the L.		1:22
become converted unto the L.		2:12
cry unto the L. for strength		3:12
As the L. liveth, except ye		3:15
iniquities, and cry unto the L.,		3:15
Pray unto the L., and let us go		3:20
The L. forbid; for if we should		3:21
the L. would deliver us into their		3:21
therefore as the L. liveth, if we		3:21
prayers unto the L. their God,		3:25
their cries to the L. their God,		4: 8
in the strength of the L. they did		4:10
May the L. preserve his people		4:29
name of the L. God Almighty,		4:32
knowledge of the L. their God.		5:23
And as surely as the L. liveth,		5:24
as the L. liveth so shall it be.		5:26
the commandments of the L.		6:14
which the L. would make for his		6:20
condemned the prophets of the L.		6:25
against the people of the L.,		6:29
turned from the L. their God,		7:14
and also the voice of the L.,		7:15
faith on the L. Jesus Christ.		7:16
his faith on the L. Jesus Christ		7:18
who were converted unto the L.;		7:21
unto the L. Jesus Christ,		10:10
the L. spake unto them saying:		11:13
and bowed himself before the L.		11:19
the L. commanded him that he		11:20
And the L. said unto him:		11:21
And again the L. called others,		11:22
perform unto the L. thine oaths;		12:33
that saith unto me, L., Lord,		14:21
that saith unto me, Lord, L.,		14:21
L., Lord, have we not prophesied		14:22
L., have we not prophesied in thy		14:22
the L. shall bring again Zion.		16:18
the L. hath comforted his		16:19
The L. hath made bare his holy		16:20
calling him their L. and their		19:18
knowledge of the L. their God,		20:13
consecrate their gain unto the L.,		20:19
their substance unto the L. of		20:19
shall the L. your God raise up		20:23
For thus saith the L.:		20:38
that bear the vessels of the L.		20:41
for the L. will go before you,		20:42
of the married wife, saith the L.		22: 1
the L. of Hosts is his name;		22: 5
the L. hath called thee as a		22: 6
saith the L. thy Redeemer.		22: 8
saith the L. that hath mercy on		22:10
children shall be taught of the L.;		22:13
of the servants of the L.,		22:17
is of me, saith the L.		22:17
Yea, L., Samuel did prophesy		23:10
and the L. whom ye seek shall		24: 1
come, saith the L. of Hosts.		24: 1
offer unto the L. an offering		24: 3
Jerusalem be pleasant unto the L.,		24: 4
fear not me, saith the L. of Hosts.		24: 5
For I am the L., I change not;		24: 6
unto you, saith the L. of Hosts.		24: 7
herewith, saith the L. of Hosts,		24:10
the fields, saith the L. of Hosts.		24:11
land, saith the L. of Hosts.		24:12
stout against me, saith the L.		24:13
mournfully before the L. of Hosts?		24:14
Then they that feared the L.		24:16
the L. hearkened and heard;		24:16
for them that feared the L.,		24:16
be mine, saith the L. of Hosts,		24:17
them up, saith the L. of Hosts,		25: 1
do this, saith the L. of Hosts.		25: 3
and dreadful day of the L.;		25: 5
but the L. forbade it, saying:		26:11
been commanded me of the L.		26:12
the L. truly did teach the people,		26:13
L., we will that thou wouldst tell	3Ne	27: 3
And the L. said unto them:		27: 4
they were converted unto the L.,		28:23
but the L. forbade;		28:25
when the L. seeth fit in his		28:29
those whom the L. hath chosen,		28:36
I wrote, I have inquired of the L.,		28:37
that when the L. shall see fit,		29: 1
know that the words of the L.,		29: 2
that the L. delays his coming		29: 2
the L. will remember his covenant		29: 3
spurn at the doings of the L.,		29: 4
spurneth at the doings of the L.;		29: 5
deny the revelations of the L.,		29: 6
the L. no longer worketh by		29: 6
L. remembereth his covenant		29: 8
turn the right hand of the L.		29: 9
were all converted unto the L.,	4Ne	1: 2
And the L. did prosper them		1: 7
promises which the L. had made		1:11
from their L. and their God,		1:12
and to hear the word of the L.		1:12
For the L. did bless them in		1:18
he did hide them up unto the L.		1:49
and the promises of the L.		1:49
hid up the records unto the L.,	Mrm	1: 2
have I deposited unto the L.		1: 3
the L. did take away his		1:13
there were no gifts from the L.,		1:14
therefore I was visited of the L.,		1:15
the L. had cursed the land,		1:18
and their sorrow before the L.,		2:12
and the long-suffering of the L.,		2:12
the L. would not always suffer		2:13
deposited the records unto the L.,		2:17
the strength of the L. was not		2:26
Spirit of the L. did not abide		2:26
that the L. did say unto me:		3: 2
was the L. that had spared them,		3: 3
hearts against the L. their God.		3: 3
our L. and Savior Jesus Christ,		3:14
the voice of the L. came unto me		3:14
as the L. had commanded me;		3:16
the covenant people of the L.,		3:21
according to the words of the L.,		4:12
had his up unto the L.		4:23
I knew the judgments of the L.		5: 2
Gentiles, who the L. hath said		5: 9
are to be his up unto the L.		5:12
to the commandment of the L.,		5:13
the L. their God hath given		5:14
the Spirit of the L. hath already		5:16
the L. hath reserved their		5:19
the L. remember the covenant		5:20
also the L. will remember the		5:21
been commanded of the L.		6: 6
to me by the hand of the L.,		6: 6
departed from the ways of the L.!		6:17
how long the L. will suffer that		8: 5
coming of our L. and Savior.		8: 6
it is the hand of the L. which		8: 8
the L. would not suffer them to		8:10
hideth up this record unto the L.;		8:14
of the commandment of the L.		8:14
to light, him will the L. bless.		8:14
covenant people of the L.		8:15
that which is forbidden of the L.		8:18
shall be smitten again, of the L.		8:19
judgment is mine, saith the L.,		8:20
strifes against the work of the L.,		8:21
the covenant people of the L.		8:21
will destroy the work of the L.,		8:21
the L. will not remember his		8:21
purposes of the L. shall roll on,		8:22
dust will they cry unto the L.;		8:23
and as the L. liveth he will		8:23
the L. should suffer to bring		8:25
shall, for the L. hath spoken it;		8:26
they come, by the hand of the L.,		8:26
of saints shall cry unto the L.,		8:27
for the L. will uphold such at		8:31
the L. hath shown unto me		8:34

LORD

should mourn before the L.,	Mrm	8:40	the L. commanded him that	Eth 3:28
orphans to mourn before the L.,		8:40	until the L. should show them	3:28
cry unto the L. from the ground,		8:40	the L. commanded the brother of	4: 1
when the L. shall come,		9: 2	from the presence of the L.,	4: 1
unbelieving, turn ye unto the L.;		9: 6	the L. hath commanded me	4: 5
back into the presence of the L.;		9:13	to the commandment of the L.	4: 5
stand against the works of the L.?		9:26	For the L. said unto me:	4: 6
the almighty power of the L.?		9:26	and become clean before the L.,	4: 6
will despise the works of the L.?		9:26	exercise faith in me, saith the L.,	4: 7
despisers of the works of the L.,		9:26	contend against the word of the L.,	4: 8
hearken unto the words of the L.;		9:27	after the L. had prepared the	6: 2
come unto the L. with all your		9:27	the L. caused stones to shine	6: 3
the L. knoweth the things which		9:34	unto the L. their God.	6: 4
may the L. Jesus Christ grant		9:37	the L. God caused that there	6: 5
destroyed by the hand of the L.	Eth	1: 1	they did cry unto the L.,	6: 7
the L. confounded the language		1:33	did sing praises unto the L.;	6: 9
according to the word of the L.		1:33	did sing praises unto the L.,	6: 9
a man highly favored of the L.,		1:34	praise the L. all the day long;	6: 9
Cry unto the L., that he will		1:34	did not cease to praise the L.	6: 9
of Jared did cry unto the L.,		1:35	humble themselves before the L.,	6:12
the L. had compassion upon		1:35	shed tears of joy before the L.,	6:12
Cry again unto the L.,		1:36	to walk humbly before the L.;	6:17
of Jared did cry unto the L.,		1:37	did walk humbly before the L.,	6:30
the L. had compassion upon		1:37	how great things the L. had done	6:30
inquire of the L. whether he		1:38	how great things the L. had done	6:30
but the L. will carry us forth		1:38	who were sent from the L.,	7:23
let us be faithful unto the L.,		1:38	the L. did spare them,	7:26
of Jared did cry unto the L.		1:39	things that the L. had done	7:27
the L. did hear the brother of		1:40	the L. worketh not in secret	8:19
the L. came down and talked		2: 4	the L. will not suffer that	8:22
the L. commanded them that		2: 5	the L. commandeth you,	8:24
that the L. did go before them,		2: 5	the L. was merciful into Omer,	9: 2
continually by the hand of the L.		2: 6	warned Omer in a dream	9: 3
the L. would not suffer that		2: 7	the L. began again to take the	9:16
which the L. God had preserved		2: 7	the L. did pour out his blessings	9:20
the L. did bring Jared and his		2:13	should possess it unto the L.,	9:20
the L. came again unto the		2:14	for upon such, saith the L.:	9:20
the L. talk with the brother of		2:14	must prepare the way of the L.	9:28
to call upon the name of the L.		2:14	the L. did cause the serpents	9:33
did call upon the name of the L.		2:15	iniquities and cry unto the L.	9:34
And the L. said unto him:		2:15	sufficiently before the L.	9:35
off from the presence of the L.		2:15	the L. did show forth his power	9:35
And the L. said:		2:16	what the L. had done in	10: 2
to the instructions of the L.		2:16	did walk in the ways of the L.;	10: 2
of Jared cried unto the L.,		2:18	was right in the sight of the L.,	10: 5
O L., I have performed the		2:18	off from the presence of the L.	10:11
And behold, O L., in them		2:19	he was not favored of the L.	10:13
the L. said unto the brother of		2:20	was right in the sight of the L.	10:16
as the L. had commanded.		2:21	was good in the sight of the L.	10:17
he cried again unto the L.		2:22	was good in the sight of the L.	10:19
O L., behold I have done even		2:22	prospered by the hand of the L.	10:28
Behold, O L., wilt thou suffer		2:22	for the L. had spoken it.	10:28
the L. said unto the brother of		2:23	repent, and turn unto the L.,	11: 1
and cried again unto the L.,		3: 1	not unto the voice of the L.,	11: 7
O L., thou hast said that we		3: 2	the L. did have mercy on them.	11: 8
Now behold, O L., and do not		3: 2	the L. would utterly destroy them	11:12
nevertheless, O L., thou hast		3: 2	which was wicked before the L.	11:14
O L., thou hast smitten us		3: 3	the L. God would execute	11:20
O L., look upon me in pity,		3: 3	that the L. God would send or	11:21
And I know, O L., that thou		3: 4	Ether was a prophet of the L.;	12: 2
therefore touch these stones, O L.,		3: 4	because of the Spirit of the L.	12: 2
O L., thou canst do this.		3: 5	had beheld the finger of the L.,	12:21
the L. stretched forth his hand		3: 6	the L. could not withhold	12:21
he saw the finger of the L.;		3: 6	the L. hath commanded me,	12:22
of Jared fell down before the L.,		3: 6	L., the Gentiles will mock at	12:23
the L. saw that the brother of		3: 7	L. thou hast made us mighty	12:23
and the L. said unto him:		3: 7	the L. spake unto me, saying:	12:26
And he saith unto the L.:		3: 8	O L., thy righteous will be done,	12:29
I saw the finger of the L.,		3: 8	that I prayed unto the L. that	12:36
that the L. had flesh and blood.		3: 8	that the L. said unto me:	12:37
And the L. said unto him:		3: 9	and also the L. Jesus Christ,	12:41
Nay; L., show thyself unto me.		3:10	a chosen land of the L.;	13: 2
And the L. said unto him:		3:11	the L. would have that all men	13: 2
Yea, L., I know that thou		3:12	the holy sanctuary of the L.	13: 3
the L. showed himself unto him,		3:13	a holy city unto the L.,	13: 5
the L. had showed unto him.		3:18	become a holy city of the L.;	13: 5
that it was the finger of the L.;		3:19	the L. brought a remnant of	13: 7
the L. said unto the brother of		3:21	build up a holy city unto the L.,	13: 8
the L. had said these words,		3:25	the word of the L. came to	13:20
the L. could not withhold		3:26	L. would give unto him	13:20
the L. could show him all things.		3:26	the word of the L. which came	14:24
And the L. said unto him:		3:27	the L. did visit them in the fulness	14:25

LORD 571 LORD

hide up the records unto the L.,	Eth	15:11	saith the L. of Hosts,	DC	29: 9
the Spirit of the L. had ceased		15:19	I the L. God will send forth		29:18
And the L. spake unto Ether,		15:33	I, the L. God, caused that he		29:41
the words of the L. had all		15:33	I, the L. God, gave unto Adam		29:42
whether the L. will that I be		15:34	until I, the L. God, should		29:42
will of the L. in the flesh,		15:34	thus did I, the L. God, appoint		29:43
according to the will of the L.	Mro	1: 4	to the voice of the L. your God,		33: 1
remembrance of the L. Jesus.		6: 6	prepare ye the way of the L.,		33:10
and our L. Jesus Christ,		7: 2	the L. God, shall say unto you,		34: 1
enter into the rest of the L.,		7: 3	preparing the way of the L.		34: 6
unto the chosen vessels of the L.,		7:31	for the L. God hath spoken;		34:10
the L. God prepareth the way		7:32	your L. and your Redeemer.		34:12
your L. Jesus Christ hath been		8: 2	the voice of the L. your God,		35: 1
inquired of the L. concerning		8: 7	Thus saith the L. God,		36: 1
the word of the L. came to me		8: 7	Thus saith the L. your God,		38: 1
Redeemer, your L. and your God.		8: 8	no curse when the L. cometh;		38:18
pervert the ways of the L.		8:16	that bear the vessels of the L.		38:42
the Spirit of the L. hath ceased		9: 4	saith the L. and your God,		41: 1
and our L. Jesus Christ,		9:26	day of the L. is nigh at hand.		43:17
how merciful the L. hath been		10: 3	the L. shall utter his voice		43:18
the L. God will say unto you:		10:27	for the great day of the L.;		43:20
the voice of the L. is unto all	DC	1: 2	for the great day of the L.?		43:21
for I the L. have commanded		1: 5	the great day of the L. is come?		43:22
what I the L. have decreed in		1: 7	the L. shall utter his voice		43:23
the L. shall come to recompense		1:10	the words of the L. your God.		43:27
the voice of the L. is unto the		1:11	thus saith the L. unto you my		44: 1
to come, for the L. is nigh;		1:12	I, the L., had spoken these words		45:34
the anger of the L. is kindled,		1:13	the great day of the L. to come,		45:39
the arm of the L. shall be		1:14	the day of the L. shall come,		45:42
will not hear the voice of the L.,		1:14	the arm of the L. shall fall,		45:45
seek not the L. to establish		1:16	shall the arm of the L. fall		45:47
I the L., knowing the calamity		1:17	shall the L. set his foot upon		45:48
speak in the name of God the L.,		1:20	the L. shall utter his voice,		45:49
I, the L., am well pleased,		1:30	they know that I am the L.;		45:52
I the L. cannot look upon sin		1:31	the L. shall be in their midst,		45:59
the commandments of the L.		1:32	I, the L., have said, gather		45:64
saith the L. of hosts.		1:33	the glory of the L. shall be		45:67
I the L. am willing to make		1:34	and the terror of the L. also		45:67
the L. shall have power over		1:36	For when the L. shall appear		45:74
What I the L. have spoken,		1:38	because of the terror of the L.,		45:75
behold, and lo, the L. is God,		1:39	be pleasing unto the same L.,		46:15
and dreadful day of the L.		2: 1	according as the L. will,		46:15
chosen to do the work of the L.,		3: 9	Thus saith the L.; for I am		49: 5
whom the L. has suffered to		3:18	I, the L. God, have spoken it;		49: 7
the promises of the L. might be		3:19	on the name of the L. Jesus,		49:12
know the promises of the L.,		3:20	great day of the L. shall come,		49:24
I, the L., am God, and have		5: 2	I, the L., have looked upon		50: 4
which the L. hath shown unto		5:25	thus saith the L., I will bring		50: 6
And I the L. command him,		5:26	saith the L., by the Spirit,		50:10
And the L. said unto me:		7: 1	will I, the L., reason with you		50:12
L., give unto me power over		7: 2	I the L. ask you this question—		50:13
And the L. said unto me:		7: 3	unto me, saith the L. your God,		51: 1
the L. said unto Peter:		7: 4	until I, the L., shall provide		51:16
assuredly as the L. liveth,		8: 1	enter into the joy of his L.,		51:19
to tempt the L. thy God,		10:15	thus saith the L. unto the		52: 1
to tempt the L. thy God.		10:29	I, the L., will make known unto		52: 2
your L. and your God.		10:70	For thus saith the L.,		52:11
again an offering unto the L.		13: 1	I, the L., will hasten the city		52:43
your L. and your Redeemer.		15: 1	unto you, of the L. your God,		53: 1
your L. and your Redeemer.		16: 1	which I, the L., have raised up		53: 1
talked with the L. face to face,		17: 1	I, the L., who was crucified for		53: 2
as your L. and your God liveth		17: 6	Behold, thus saith the L.,		54: 1
Christ, your L. and your God,		17: 9	Behold, thus saith the L., unto		55: 1
the L. your Redeemer suffered		18:11	even the L. of the whole earth,		55: 1
Christ, your L. and your God,		18:33	name, saith the L. your God;		56: 1
Christ, your L. and your God,		18:47	Behold, I, the L., command;		56: 3
Alpha and Omega, Christ the L.;		19: 1	Wherefore I, the L., command		56: 4
be the name of the L. God!		19:37	of the rebellious, saith the L.		56: 4
our L. and Savior Jesus Christ		20: 1	saith the L. God of hosts;		56:10
our L. and Savior Jesus Christ,		20: 4	I, the L., will pay it unto him		56:12
For the L. God has spoken it;		20:16	thus saith the L. unto my		56:14
our L. and Savior Jesus Christ		20:30	For behold, the L. shall come,		56:19
of our L. and Savior Jesus Christ		20:31	saith the L. your God,		57: 1
And the L. God has spoken it;		20:36	thus saith the L. your God,		57: 3
walking in holiness before the L.		20:69	supper of the house of the L.,		58: 9
remembrance of the L. Jesus;		20:75	partake of the supper of the L.,		58:11
grace of your L. Jesus Christ,		21: 1	I, the L., have spoken it.		58:12
the year of your L. eighteen		21: 3	I that made man, saith the L.,		58:30
the L. God will disperse the		21: 6	Who am I, saith the L.,		58:31
For thus saith the L. God:		21: 7	This is not the work of the L.,		58:33
thus saith the L. God, lo, lo!		21:12	I, the L., am not well pleased		58:41
the voice of the L. your God,		25: 1	I, the L., remember them no		58:42
voice of Jesus Christ, your L.,		27: 1	appointed unto them of the L.		58:44

LORD 572 LORD

the L. willeth that the disciples	DC 58:52
for the temple, unto the L.	58:57
blessed, saith the L., are they	59: 1
Thou shalt love the L. thy God	59: 5
shalt thank the L. thy God	59: 7
a sacrifice unto the L. thy God	59: 8
thy brethren, and before the L.	59:12
I, the L., have spoken it,	59:24
Behold, thus saith the L. unto	60: 1
I, the L., rule in the heavens	60: 4
thus saith the L. unto you,	61: 2
for I, the L., forgive sins,	61: 2
I, the L., have decreed in	61: 5
I, the L., will be with them.	61:10
I, the L., will reason with you	61:13
I, the L., in the beginning	61:14
as I, the L., in the beginning	61:17
I, the L., have decreed,	61:19
I, the L., was angry with you	61:20
I, the L., have appointed a way	61:24
saints of the camp of Israel,	61:29
saith the L. your God, even	62: 1
I, the L., have brought you	62: 6
I, the L., promise the faithful	62: 6
I, the L., am willing, if any	62: 7
it from the hand of the L.,	62: 7
yourselves the people of the L.,	63: 1
and hear the word of the L.	63: 1
I, the L., utter my voice,	63: 5
I, the L., am not pleased with	63:12
I, the L., have said that the	63:17
I, the L., say unto you that	63:19
is the will of the L. your God	63:24
I, the L., hold it in mine own	63:25
I, the L., render unto Caesar	63:26
I the L. will that you should	63:27
I, the L., am angry with the	63:32
I, the L., am with them,	63:34
I, the L., have decreed all	63:36
I, the L., will give unto my	63:41
the dead that die in the L.,	63:49
when the L. shall come,	63:49
an inheritance before the L.,	63:49
liveth when the L. shall come	63:50
after the manner of the L.,	63:53
I, the L., am not pleased with	63:55
is not acceptable unto the L.,	63:56
and if the L. receive it not,	63:56
I, the L., am not to be mocked	63:58
who use the name of the L.,	63:62
I, the L., will own them;	63:63
thus saith the L. your God	64: 1
I, the L., forgive sins unto	64: 7
condemned before the L.;	64: 9
I, the L., will forgive whom	64:10
I, the L., was angry with him	64:15
I, the L., withheld my Spirit.	64:16
for I, the L., will to retain	64:21
I, the L., will not hold any	64:22
I, the L., require the hearts of	64:22
after the manner of the L.—	64:24
for I am the L. of Hosts;	64:24
that the L. should take	64:28
according to the will of the L.	64:29
I, the L., declare unto you,	64:31
the L. requireth the heart and	64:34
I, the L., have made my	64:37
the glory of the L. shall be	64:41
The L. hath spoken it.	64:43
Prepare ye the way of the L.,	65: 1
Prepare ye the way of the L.,	65: 3
Pray unto the L., call upon	65: 4
Call upon the L., that his	65: 5
thus saith the L. unto my	66: 1
saith the L. your Redeemer,	66: 1
in my sight, saith the L.,	66: 3
the L. will show them unto you.	66: 3
I, the L., will show unto you	66: 4
I, the L., will go with you.	66: 8
till I, the L., shall send you.	66: 9
thus saith the L. your God,	66:13
I, the L., give unto you a	67: 4
shall be the will of the L.,	68: 4
shall be the mind of the L.,	DC 68: 4
shall be the word of the L.,	68: 4
shall be the voice of the L.,	68: 4
promise of the L. unto you,	68: 5
for I the L. am with you,	68: 6
This is the word of the L.	68: 7
in the due time of the L.,	68:14
by revelation from the L.	68:21
walk uprightly before the L.	68:28
in remembrance before the L.	68:30
I, the L., am not well pleased	68:31
not his prayers before the L.	68:33
saith the L. your God,	69: 1
I, the L., will that my servant,	69: 2
hear the word of the L. which	70: 1
thus saith the L. unto them—	70: 2
I, the L., have appointed them,	70: 3
this is what the L. requires	70: 9
as I, the L., have appointed	70: 9
I, the L., shall place them,	70:16
I, the L., shall send them.	70:16
I, the L., am merciful and	70:18
thus saith the L. unto you	71: 1
strong reasons against the L.	71: 8
thus saith the L. unto you—	71: 9
listen to the voice of the L.,	72: 1
For verily thus saith the L.,	72: 1
for it is required of the L.,	72: 3
the will of the L. your God,	72: 8
The word of the L., in addition	72: 9
the L. shall put into his hands.	72:13
For verily, thus saith the L.,	73: 1
and Sidney Rigdon, saith the L.,	73: 3
not of the L., but of himself,	74: 5
your L. and your God—	75: 1
which I, the L., chasten him	75: 7
Calling on the name of the L.	75:10
is the will of the L. your God	75:12
verily thus saith the L.,	75:13
thus saith the L. unto you,	75:23
I, the L., give unto you this	75:25
for the L. is God, and besode	76: 1
For thus saith the L.—	76: 5
I, the L., am merciful and	76: 5
in the year of our L. one	76:11
the L. had appointed unto us,	76:15
the L. touched the eyes of	76:19
and the glory of the L. shone	76:19
the L. commanded us that we	76:28
the voice of the L. unto us;	76:30
Thus saith the L. concerning	76:31
in the due time of the L.,	76:38
I, the L., show it by vision	76:47
that the L. commanded us	76:80
until the L., even Christ the	76:85
And heard the voice of the L.	76:110
are the works of the L.,	76:114
the L. God sanctify the earth,	77:12
The L. spake unto Enoch	78: 1
unto me, saith the L. your God,	78: 1
before me, saith the L. God.	78: 2
verily thus saith the L.,	78: 8
saith the L. God, the Holy	78:15
and fear not, saith your L.,	79: 4
thus saith the L. unto you	80: 1
the word of the L. your God,	81: 1
the glory of him who is your L.	81: 4
even so I, the L., forgive you.	82: 1
I, the L., will not lay any sin	82: 7
return, saith the L. your God.	82: 7
I, the L., am bound when ye	82:10
according to the laws of the L.	82:15
Verily, thus saith the L.,	83: 1
the word of the L. concerning	84: 2
appointed by the finger of the L.,	84: 3
whom the L. was well pleased.	84: 3
this is the word of the L.,	84: 4
house shall be built unto the L.,	84: 5
be even the glory of the L.,	84: 5
the L. confirmed a priesthood	84:18
therefore, the L. in his wrath,	84:24
which the L. in his wrath caused	84:27
straight the way of the L.	84:28

LORD 573 LORD

for the coming of the L.,	DC 84:28	be stayed until the L. come;	DC 97:23
sacrifice in the house of the L.,	84:31	indignation of the L. is kindled	97:24
shall be built unto the L.	84:31	I, the L., have accepted of	97:27
filled with the glory of the L.,	84:32	ever, saith the L. your God.	97:28
receive me, saith the L.;	84:35	Waiting patiently on the L.,	98: 2
the word of the L. is truth,	84:45	the ears of the L. of Sabaoth,	98: 2
with the knowledge of the L.,	84:98	the L. hath sworn and decreed	98: 2
The L. hath brought again Zion;	84:99	my name's glory, saith the L.	98: 3
The L. hath redeemed his	84:99	I, the L., justify you,	98: 6
The L. hath redeemed his	84:100	I, the L. God, make you free,	98: 8
The L. hath gathered all	84:100	in my heart, saith the L.,	98:14
The L. hath brought down	84:100	I, the L., am not well pleased	98:19
The L. hath brought up Zion	84:100	I, the L., will chasten them	98:21
as the L. shall direct them,	84:103	I, the L., will turn away all	98:22
with you saith the L. Almighty,	84:118	I, the L., commanded them.	98:33
I, the L., have put forth my	84:119	these testimonies before the L.;	98:35
of God, saith the L. of Hosts.	85: 5	I, the L., would give unto	98:36
I, the L. God, will send one	85: 7	I, the L., would fight their	98:37
as the L. speaketh, he will	85:10	people, saith the L. your God,	98:38
thus saith the L. unto you	86: 1	testimonies before the L.;	98:44
while the L. is beginning to	86: 4	I the L., will avenge thee of	98:45
angels are crying unto the L.	86: 5	turn to the L. their God,	98:47
But the L. saith unto them,	86: 6	upon them, saith the L. thy God,	98:48
thus saith the L. unto you,	86: 8	as a testimony before the L.	98:48
the L. hath said it.	86:11	thus saith the L. unto my	99: 1
thus saith the L. concerning	87: 1	thus saith the L. unto you,	100: 1
ears of the L. of Sabaoth,	87: 7	I, the L., have suffered you to	100: 4
until the day of the L. come;	87: 8	call upon the name of the L.,	100:17
it cometh quickly, saith the L.	87: 8	I, the L., have suffered the	101: 2
thus saith the L. unto you	88: 1	the voice of the L. their God;	101: 7
this is pleasing unto your L.,	88: 2	the L. their God is slow to	101: 7
the ears of the L. of Sabaoth,	88: 2	day when the L. shall come,	101:32
And the l. of the field went	88:56	And seek the face of the L.	101:38
of the countenance of his l.	88:56	as their l. commanded them,	101:46
of the countenance of their l.,	88:58	need hath my l. of this tower?	101:47
as his l. had commanded him,	88:60	need hath my l. of this tower,	101:48
his l. might be glorified in his,	88:60	the commandments of their l.	101:50
in him, and he in his l.,	88:60	the l. of the vineyard, called	101:52
in their traveling call on the L.,	88:71	And the l. of the vineyard said	101:55
the mouth of the L. shall name,	88:84	the servant said unto his l.:	101:59
the mouth of the L. shall call	88:85	his l. commanded him;	101:62
be clean, until the L. comes.	88:86	then will the L. arise and come	101:89
face of the L. shall be unveiled;	88:95	and obtain the mind of the L.	102:23
may be in the name of the L.;	88:120	I, the L. their God, shall give	103: 5
may be in the name of the L.;	88:120	I, the L. their God, shall speak	103: 7
may be in the name of the L.,	88:120	the L. of the vineyard spake	103:21
the name of the L. Jesus Christ,	88:133	I, the L., have decreed in	104: 5
doings in the house of the L.,	88:137	I, the L., am not to be mocked	104: 6
thus saith the L. unto you:	89: 4	I, the L., have promised unto	104: 7
I, the L., have ordained for	89:12	that I, the L., should make	104:13
I, the L., give unto them a	89:21	I, the L., stretched out the	104:14
Thus saith the L., verily, verily	90: 1	that I, the L., have decreed	104:16
arm of the L. shall be revealed	90:10	I, the L., confer upon my	104:22
mouth of the L. shall name.	90:20	the sacred treasury of the L.;	104:66
mouth of the L. shall name.	90:21	and consecrated unto the L.	104:66
the storehouse of the L. may	90:23	the coming of the L. draweth nigh,	106: 4
I, the L., will contend with	90:36	in the knowledge of the L.	107:31
I, the L., have spoken it.	90:37	to officiate in the name of the L.,	107:33
thus saith the L. unto you	91: 1	are to act in the name of the L.,	107:34
Verily, thus saith the L.,	92: 1	should be the chosen of the L.,	107:42
Verily, thus saith the L.:	93: 1	saw the L., and he walked with	107:49
stand rebuked before the L.;	93:47	And the L. appeared unto them,	107:54
the acceptable year of the L.	93:51	L. administered comfort unto Adam,	107:55
shall be dedicated unto the L.	94: 6	unto you, saith the L. of Hosts,	107:60
wholly dedicated unto the L.	94: 7	no more before the L.;	107:80
wholly dedicated unto the L.	94:12	thus saith the L. unto you,	108: 1
which I, the L. God, have given	94:15	Thanks be to thy name, O L. God	109: 1
thus saith the L. unto you	95: 1	And now thou beholdest, O L.,	109: 3
the ears of the L. of Sabaoth,	95: 7	we ask thee, O L., to accept of	109: 4
unto me, saith your L.;	95:10	may be in the name of the L.,	109: 9
and the mind of the L.—	95:13	may be in the name of the L.,	109: 9
desires unto me, saith your L.	95:16	may be in the name of the L.,	109: 9
even Jesus Christ your L.	95:17	may be in the name of the L.;	109:17
for I, the L., show mercy	97: 2	may be in the name of the L.;	109:18
I, the L., am well pleased	97: 3	may be in the name of the L.,	109:19
I, the L., am willing to show	97: 6	knowest, O L., that thy servants	109:31
I, the L., have spoken it.	97: 7	Break it off, O L.;	109:33
I, the L., shall command—	97: 8	O L., we delight not in the	109:43
I, the L., will cause them to	97: 9	Thy will be done, O L., and not	109:44
which I, the L., require at	97:12	O L., deliver thy people from the	109:46
me in the name of the L.,	97:15	break off, O L., this yoke of	109:47
and the hand of the L. is there;	97:19	Thou knowest, O L., that they	109:48
verily, thus saith the L.,	97:21	O L., how long wilt thou suffer this	109:49

LORD 574 LORD

mercy, O L., upon the wicked mob, DC	109:50
make bare thine arm, O L.,	109:51
mercy, O L., upon all the nations	109:54
Now these words, O L., we have	109:60
O L., remember thy servant,	109:68
Have mercy, O L., upon his wife	109:69
Remember, O L., the presidents	109:71
Remember all thy church, O L.,	109:72
that we may ever be with the L.;	109:75
O L. God Almighty, hear us	109:77
O hear, O hear, O hear us, O L.	109:78
We saw the L. standing upon	110: 2
dreadful day of the L. come—	110:14
dreadful day of the L. is near,	110:16
L. your God, am not displeased	111: 1
Verily thus saith the L. unto you	112: 1
I, the L., was not well pleased.	112: 2
the L., have a great work for thee	112: 6
the L. thy God shall lead thee by	112:10
I, the L., will feel after them,	112:13
face of the earth, saith the L.	112:24
shall it go forth, saith the L.;	112:25
those among you, saith the L.,	112:26
midst of my house, saith the L.	112:26
church in this place, saith the L.	112:27
thus saith the L.: It is Christ.	113: 2
thus saith the L.: It is a servant	113: 4
thus saith the L., it is a descendant	113: 6
exhorted to return to the L.	113:10
promise of the L. is that he will	113:10
thus saith the L.: It is wisdom	114: 1
thus saith the L., that inasmuch	114: 2
thus saith the L. unto you	115: 1
thus saith the L. unto my servant	117: 1
before I, the L., send again the	117: 1
not tarry, for I, the L.,	117: 2
desires, before me, saith the L.;	117: 4
property unto me? saith the L.	117: 4
turned out for debts, saith the L.	117: 5
Let them go, saith the L.,	117: 5
remain in your hands, saith the L.	117: 5
forth in abundance? saith the L.	117: 7
before me, saith the L.,	117:11
unto my people, saith the L.,	117:11
name but in deed, saith the L.	117:11
forever and ever, saith the L.	117:12
of my Church, saith the L.;	117:13
than his increase, saith the L.	117:13
saith the L., for the benefit of my	117:14
remember the L. their God,	117:16
mine own due time, saith the L.	117:16
saith the L.: Let a conference	118: 1
I, the L., give unto them	118: 3
of my house, saith the L.	118: 5
the L., I require all their surplus	119: 1
my holy priesthood, saith the L.	119: 4
saith the L., the time is now come	120: 1
own voice unto them, saith the L.	120: 1
O L., how long shall they suffer	121: 3
O L. God Almighty, maker of	121: 4
against mine anointed, saith the L.,	121:16
not sinned before me, saith the L.,	121:16
testify against them, saith the L.	121:23
the Spirit of the L. is grieved;	121:37
thus saith the L. unto you,	124: 1
I, the L., love him because of	124:15
is right before, me saith the L.	124:15
mine if he do this, saith the L.	124:17
has to my testimony I, the L., love him.	124:20
the poor of my people, saith the L.	124:21
contemplate the word of the L.;	124:23
or the L. your God will not dwell	124:24
with your dead, saith the L. your	124:32
acceptable unto me, saith the L.	124:35
expect at my hands, saith the L.	124:47
you practise before, me saith the L.	124:48
and hate me, saith the L. God.	124:50
saith the L. your God.	124:51
hate me, saith the L. your God.	124:52
saith the L. your God.	124:53
For I am the L. your God,	124:54
land of Missouri, saith the L.	124:54
forever and ever, saith the L.	DC 124:59
do my will, saith the L. your God.	124:69
out of their place, saith the L.	124:71
for I, the L., am God, and	124:71
can any other man, saith the L.	124:72
for he shall be mine, saith the L.	124:75
forgive all his sins, saith the L.	124:76
I, the L., love him for the work	124:78
I, the L., will build up Kirtland,	124:83
I, the L., have a scourge	124:83
my general conference, saith the L.	124:88
and ever, saith the L. your God.	124:101
I, the L. your God, will heal	124:104
saith the L. your God	124:119
and not blessings, saith the L.	124:120
for their support, saith the L.;	124:122
calling, saith the L. your God.	124:135
priests of my church, saith the L.	124:136
to my church, saith the L.	124:137
presiding, saith the L. your God.	124:140
my name, saith the L. your God.	124:145
What is the will of the L.	125: 1
thus saith the L., I say	125: 2
I have appointed, saith the L.	125: 4
verily thus saith the L. unto you:	126: 1
Forasmuch as the L. has revealed	127: 1
for the L. God hath spoken it.	127: 2
And again, verily thus saith the L.:	127: 4
lose your reward, saith the L. of Hosts.	127: 4
thus saith the L. unto you	127: 6
may testify of a truty, saith the L.;	127: 6
priesthood, saith the L. of Hosts.	127: 8
generation, saith the L. of Hosts.	127: 9
I will write the word of the L.	127:10
myself your servant in the L.,	127:12
a record of a truth before the L.	128: 2
the L. ordained and prepared	128: 5
L. has given a dispensation of the	128: 9
in the name of the L.,	128: 9
second man is the L. from heaven.	128:14
great and dreadful day of the L.:	128:17
A voice of the L. in the wilderness	128:20
the trees of the field praise the L.;	128:23
the great day of the L. is at hand;	128:24
that they may offer unto the L.	128:24
offer unto the L. an offering in	128:24
are continually before the L.	130: 7
prophesy, in the name of the L.	130:12
thus saith the L. unto you	132: 1
I, the L., justified my servants	132: 1
lo, I am the L. thy God,	132: 2
he shall be damned, saith the L.	132: 6
house of order, saith the L. God,	132: 8
accept of an offering, saith the L.,	132: 9
I appoint unto you, saith the L.,	132:11
I am the L. thy God;	132:12
which is my law, saith the L.	132:12
or by my word, saith the L.,	132:13
saith the L. your God.	132:13
not joined by me, saith the L.,	132:18
house of order, saith the L. God.	132:18
redemption, saith the L. God.	132:26
everlasting covenant, saith the L.	132:27
but shall be damned, saith the L.	132:27
I am the L. thy God,	132:28
by my word, saith the L.,	132:29
for I, the L., commanded it.	132:35
them unto another, saith the L.	132:39
I am the L. thy God,	132:40
by my word, saith the L.,	132:46
you curse I will curse, saith the L.;	132:47
for I, the L., am thy God.	132:47
and with my power, saith the L.,	132:48
For I am the L. thy God,	132:49
for I did it, saith the L.,	132:51
be destroyed, saith the L. God.	132:52
For I am the L. thy God,	132:53
she shall be destroyed, saith the L.;	132:54
for I am the L. thy God,	132:54
I, the L. thy God, will bless her,	132:56
for I am the L. thy God,	132:57
saith the L. your God.	132:60

destroyed saith the L. your God;	DC 132:64	
L. his God, will give unto him,	132:65	
church, saith the L. your God,	133: 1	
word of the L. concerning you.—	133: 1	
L. who shall suddenly come to	133: 2	
L. who shall come down upon the	133: 2	
that bear the vessels of the L.	133: 5	
call upon the name of the L.	133: 6	
the voice of the L. is unto you:	133: 7	
voice of the L. unto all people:	133: 9	
for the great day of the L.	133:10	
saith the L., let not your flight	133:15	
and hear the voice of the L.;	133:16	
L. God hath sent forth the angel	133:17	
Prepare ye the way of the L.,	133:17	
L., even the Savior, shall stand	133:25	
in remembrance before the L.;	133:26	
hands of the servants of the L.,	133:32	
in holiness before the L.,	133:35	
saith the L., that these things	133:36	
Calling upon the name of the L.	133:40	
for the presence of the L. shall	133:41	
O L., thou shalt come down	133:42	
L. shall be red in his apparel,	133:48	
the loving kindness of their L.,	133:52	
the L. sent forth the fulness of	133:57	
the L. shall thrash the nations	133:59	
to the mind and will of the L.,	133:61	
sanctifieth himself before the L.	133:62	
hearken not to the voice of the L.	133:63	
shall burn them up, saith the L.	133:64	
shall be the answer of the L.	133:65	
the L. your God hath spoken it.	133:74	
exclaiming: O L. my God!	135: 1	
the Prophet and Seer of the L.,	135: 3	
that I prayed unto the L.	135: 5	
to pass that the L. said unto me:	135: 5	
will cry unto the L. of Hosts	135: 7	
The Word and Will of the L.	136: 1	
and statutes of the L. our God.	136: 2	
in all the ordinances of the L.	136: 4	
ears of the L. against this people.	136: 8	
of the L. concerning his people.	136: 9	
where the L. shall locate a stake	136:10	
take the name of the L. in vain,	136:21	
for I am the L. your God,	136:21	
the free gift of the L. thy God,	136:27	
praise the L. with singing,	136:28	
call on the L. thy God with	136:29	
calling upon the L. his God,	136:32	
I am the L. God Almighty, and	Mses 1: 3	
glory of the L. was upon Moses,	1:31	
the L. God said unto Moses:	1:31	
that Moses spake unto the L.,	1:36	
And the L. God spake unto Moses,	1:37	
that the L. spake unto Moses,	2: 1	
L. God, made the heaven and the	3: 4	
the L. God, created all things,	3: 5	
I, the L. God, had not caused	3: 5	
L. God, had created all the children	3: 5	
L. God, spake, and there went	3: 6	
L. God, formed man from the dust	3: 7	
the L. God, planted a garden	3: 8	
the L. God, to grow every tree,	3: 9	
L. God, planted the tree of life	3: 9	
L. God, caused a river to go out	3:10	
L. God, called the name of the	3:11	
the L. God, created much gold;	3:11	
L. God, took the man, and put	3:15	
the L. God, commanded the man,	3:16	
L. God, said unto mine Only	3:18	
L. God, formed every beast of	3:19	
L. God, caused a deep sleep to	3:21	
the L. God, had taken from man,	3:22	
L. God, spake unto Moses, Saying:	4: 1	
I, the L. God, had given him,	4: 3	
which I, the L. God, had made.	4: 5	
heard the voice of the L. God,	4:14	
from the presence of the L. God	4:14	
I, the L. God, called unto Adam,	4:15	
I, the L. God, said unto Adam:	4:17	
the L. God, said unto the woman:	4:19	
the L. God, said unto the serpent;	Mses 4:20	
Unto the woman, I the L. God.	4:22	
unto Adam, I, the L. God, said:	4:23	
for thus have I, the L. God, called	4:26	
the L. God, make coats of skins,	4:27	
the L. God, said unto mine Only	4:28	
L. God, will send him forth	4:29	
For as I, the L. God, liveth,	4:30	
the L. God, had driven them out,	5: 1	
as I the L. had commanded him.	5: 1	
called upon the name of the L.,	5: 4	
they heard the voice of the L.	5: 4	
should worship the L. their God,	5: 5	
for an offering unto the L.	5: 5	
the commandments of the L.	5: 5	
an angel of the L. appeared	5: 6	
offer sacrifices unto the L.?	5: 6	
save the L. commanded me.	5: 6	
L. God called upon men by the	5:14	
have gotten a man from the L.;	5:16	
Who is the L. that I should	5:16	
unto the voice of the L.	5:17	
Make an offering unto the L.	5:18	
ground an offering unto the L.	5:19	
And the L. had respect unto Abel,	5:20	
And the L. said unto Cain:	5:22	
any more to the voice of the L.,	5:26	
walked in holiness before the L.	5:26	
his wife mourned before the L.,	5:27	
L. said unto Cain: Where is Abel,	5:34	
L. said: What hast thou done?	5:35	
Cain said unto the L.: Satan	5:38	
this day from the face of the L.,	5:39	
things are not hid from the L.	5:39	
And I the L. said unto him:	5:40	
I the L. set a mark upon Cain,	5:40	
out from the presence of the L.,	5:41	
Wherefore the L. cursed Lamech,	5:52	
call upon the name of the L.,	6: 4	
the Lord, and the L. blessed them;	6: 4	
saith the L.: I am angry with	6:27	
to the earth, before the L.,	6:31	
spake before the L., Saying:	6:31	
L. said unto Enoch: Go forth	6:32	
serve the L. God who made you.	6:33	
L. spake unto Enoch, and said	6:35	
A seer hath the L. raised up	6:36	
the L. spake with me, and gave me	6:42	
The L. which spake with me,	6:43	
father Adam spake unto the L.,	6:53	
And the L. said unto Adam:	6:53	
the L. spake unto Adam, saying:	6:55	
the L. had spoken with Adam,	6:64	
that Adam cried unto the L.,	6:64	
away by the Spirit of the L.,	6:64	
unto the L., there came a voice	7: 2	
I saw the L.; and he stood	7: 4	
And again the L. said unto me:	7: 6	
the L. said unto me: Prophesy;	7: 7	
the L. shall curse the land with	7: 8	
it came to pass that the L. said	7: 9	
the L. said unto me: Go to this	7:10	
and he spake the word of the L.,	7:13	
the L. came and dwelt with his	7:16	
fear of the L. was upon all	7:17	
great was the glory of the L.,	7:17	
And the L. blessed the land,	7:17	
the L. called his people ZION,	7:18	
that Enoch talked with the L.;	7:20	
he said unto the L.: Surely Zion	7:20	
L. said unto Enoch: Zion have I	7:20	
that the L. showed unto Enoch	7:21	
the L. said unto Enoch: Behold	7:21	
And Enoch said unto the L.:	7:29	
The L. said unto Enoch: Behold	7:32	
that the L. spake unto Enoch,	7:41	
and that the L. smiled upon it,	7:43	
but the L. said unto Enoch:	7:44	
he cried unto the L., saying:	7:45	
When shall the day of the L. come?	7:45	
the L. said: It shall be in the	7:46	
he wept, and cried unto the L.,	7:49	

LORD — LOSS

L., wilt thou not have compassion	Mses	7:49
continued his cry unto the L.,		7:50
I ask thee, O L., in the name of		7:50
And the L. could not withhold;		7:51
L. said: Blessed is he through		7:53
that Enoch cried unto the L.,		7:54
the L. said unto Enoch: Look,		7:55
Enoch wept and cried unto the L.,		7:58
he called unto the L., saying:		7:59
L. said unto Enoch: As I live,		7:60
L. said unto Enoch: Then shalt		7:63
And the L. showed Enoch all things,		7:67
the covenants of the L. might be		8: 2
the L. cursed the earth with a		8: 4
ground which the L. hath cursed.		8: 9
his sons hearkened unto the L.,		8:13
L. said unto Noah: The daughters		8:15
the L. said unto Noah: My spirit		8:17
but the L. was with Noah,		8:18
the power of the L. was upon him.		8:18
L. ordained Noah after his own		8:19
heart was pained that the L. had		8:25
L. said: I will destroy man		8:26
found grace in the eyes of the L.;		8:27
commandments which the L. their	Abr	1: 5
up my voice unto the L. my God,		1:15
and the L. hearkened and heard,		1:15
the L. broke down the altar of		1:20
the L. my God preserved in		1:31
the L. God caused the famine to		2: 1
the L. had said unto me: Abraham,		2: 3
brother's son, prayed unto the L.,		2: 6
the L. appeared unto me, and		2: 6
I am the L. thy God; I dwell		2: 7
after the L. had withdrawn		2:12
departed as the L. had said unto		2:14
and made an offering unto the L.,		2:17
and called on the L. devoutly,		2:18
the L. appeared unto me in answer		2:19
which I had built unto the L.,		2:20
I built another altar unto the L.,		2:20
again upon the name of the L.		2:20
into Egypt, the L. said unto me:		2:22
my wife, all that the L. had said		2:25
L. my God had given unto me,		3: 1
the L. said unto me: These are		3: 3
near unto me, for I am the L.		3: 3
L. said unto me, by the Urim		3: 4
was after the manner of the L.,		3: 4
was a day unto the L.,		3: 4
the L. said unto me: The planet		3: 5
L. said unto me: Now, Abraham,		3: 6
I, Abraham, talked with the L.,		3:11
the night time when the L. spake		3:14
the L. said unto me: Abraham, I		3:15
there is nothing that the L. thy		3:17
L. said unto me: These two facts		3:19
I am the L. thy God, I am more		3:19
The L. thy God sent his angel to		3:20
Now the L. had shown unto me,		3:22
do all things whatsoever the L.		3:25
the L. said: Whom shall I send?		3:27
the L. said: I will send the first.		3:27
then the L. said: Let us go down.		4: 1
The angel of the L.,	Fac	1: 1
he had built unto the L.		2: 2
in the own due time of the L.		2:12
cometh in the name of the L.,	JS	1: 1
pray ye the L. that your		1:17
what hour your l. doth come.		1:46
whom his l. hath made ruler		1:49
is that servant whom his l.,		1:50
My l. delayeth his coming,		1:51
The l. of that servant shall		1:53
was born in the year of our L.		2: 3
going to inquire of the L.		2:18
burn them, saith the L. of Hosts,		2:37
great and dreadful day of the L.		2:38
what the L. was going to do,		2:54
inquire of the L. respecting		2:68
praying and calling upon the L.,		2:68
again an offering unto the L.		2:69
Faith in the L. Jesus Christ;	AoF	4

LORD'S		
the mountain of the L. house	2Ne	12: 2
Behold, I, I am the L.;		28: 3
others shall say: I, I am the L.;		28: 3
that on this, the L. day,	DC	59:12
ye are on the L. errand;		64:29
of the Lord is the L. business.		64:29
who keepeth the L. storehouse,		70:11
this part of the L. vineyard.		72: 2
To keep the L. storehouse;		72:10
be cast into the L. storehouse,		82:18
upon the L. storehouse,		83: 5
Mount Zion in the L. house,		84:32
It is the duty of the L. clerk,		85: 1
The L. scourge shall pass		97:23
the threshold of the L. house		109:13
the mountains of the L. house.		133:13
and for the L. errand		133:58
like most of the L. anointed		135: 3
is the reckoning of the L. time,	Abr	3: 4
the reckoning of the L. time;		3: 9
that it was after the L. time,		5:13

LORENZO: see SNOW, Lorenzo.

LOSE		
l. their way, that they wandered	1Ne	8:23
that I should l. this tree;	Jac	5: 7
that I should l. this tree;		5:11
that I should l. this tree		5:13
that I should l. this tree.		5:32
grieveth me that I should l. them.		5:46
that I should l. the trees of my		5:51
I l. the trees of my vineyard.		5:65
that I should l. the trees of my		5:66
than that we should l. our lives;	Mos	20:22
perhaps thou souldst l. thy soul.	Al	20:18
fearing he should l. his life, said:		20:23
lest they should l. their lives.		47: 2
doing they should l. their souls;		53:15
they did l. many prisoners.		55:29
began to l. all hopes of succor;		57:12
slippery that we should l. them;	He	13:33
but if the salt shall l. its savor	3Ne	12:13
Akish desired should l. his head;	Eth	8:14
the same should l. his life.		8:14
temptation and l. your reward.	DC	31:12
in nowise l. their reward.		58:28
shall in nowise l. his crown;		75:28
breaketh it shall l. his office		78:12
shall in nowise l. his reward.		84:90
salt of the earth l. its savor,		101:40
you shall in nowise l. your reward,		127: 4

LOSS		
because of the l. of my bow,	1Ne	16:18
because of the l. of my bow,		16:21
because of the l. of their father,		16:35
the l. of the slain of my people!	2Ne	26: 7
back again, suffering much l.	Mos	21:11
for the l. of their brethren,	Al	4: 2
the l. of their flocks and herds,		4: 2
for the l. of their fields of grain,		4: 2
greatly lamenting his l.		18:43
after having suffered much l. and		25: 6
Amalekites, because of their l.,		27: 2
for the l. of their kindred,		28:11
mourn for the l. of their kindred,		28:12
l. on the part of the Nephites		31: 4
swords and the l. of blood,		43:38
even to the l. of his blood.		48:13
concerning their great l.		49:25
notwithstanding their great l.,		51:11
we had suffered great l.		57:23
fainted because of the l. of blood;		57:25
that we have suffered so much l.		60:28
without the l. of one soul;		62:26
own lands, suffering great l.		63:15
this great l. of the Nephites,	He	4:11
for the l. of their kindred	3Ne	10: 2
of the l. of their kindred and		10: 8
are fallen, and I mourn your l.	Mrm	6:18
of the l. of the kingdom,	Eth	8: 7

LOSS 577 LOVE

Now the l. of men, women and	Eth 14:31	and l. where he now resides,	DC 104:39
fainted with the l. of blood.	15: 9	the l. and building on which	104:39
the l. of the slain of their people;	15:16	the l. which is on the corner	104:39
the l. of the slain of their people.	15:17	also the l. on which the Shule	104:39
they fainted with the l. of blood.	15:27	the l. which is laid off for the	104:43
had fainted with the l. of blood.	15:29	have been my common l.	127: 2
for the l. of them that die,	DC 42:45	and I took L., my brother's son,	Abr 2: 4
		and L., my brother's son, prayed	2: 6
LOST		Arise, and take L. with thee;	2: 6
they wandered off and were l.	1Ne 8:23	said unto me, and L. with me;	2:14
into forbidden paths and were l.	8:28	I was in Ur, in Chaldea, and L.,	2:15
many were l. from his view,	8:32		
in a l. and in a fallen state,	10: 6	LOTS	
that they perish and are l.	12:17	we cast l.—who of us should go	1Ne 3:11
their bows having l. their springs,	16:21	on the first and second l. on	DC 94:14
after thou hast l. the first,	21:20	again, let it be divided into l.,	96: 3
seeing I have l. my children,	21:21	to cast l. by numbers,	102:12
are many who are already l.	22: 4	proceeded to cast l. or ballot,	102:34
unto all men that were l.,	2Ne 2:21	those l. which have been named	104:34
from their l. and fallen state.	25:17	sell the l. that are laid off	104:36
the words of the l. tribes of Israel;	29:13		
the l. tribes of Israel shall have the	29:13	LOUD	
l. the confidence of your children,	Jac 2:35	did say unto them with a l. voice	1Ne 8:15
made all mankind must be l.	7:12	the Spirit cried with a l. voice,	11: 6
they were l. in the wilderness	Mos 8: 8	and cried with a l. voice, saying:	Al 19:29
Thus all mankind were l.;	16: 4	and cry with a l. voice, saying:	31:14
would have been endlessly l.	16: 4	saying unto them with a l. voice:	44:13
from their l. and fallen state.	16: 4	and crying with a l. voice, saying:	46:19
they were l. in the wilderness	21:25	and cried with a l. voice,	He 13: 4
they were l. in the wilderness.	22:16	began to shout with a l. voice,	3Ne 4: 9
had been l. in the wilderness	23:30	and did cry with a l. voice,	4:28
ye are a l. and a fallen people.	Al 9:30	voice, neither was it a l. voice;	11: 3
they were a l. and a fallen people	9:32	truth, even with a l. voice,	DC 19:37
as a hair of their heads be l.;	11:44	shall sound both long and l.,	29:13
became a l. and fallen people.	12:22	of a trump, both long and l.,	34: 6
not one soul of them had been l.	16: 8	shall declare it with a l. voice,	36: 3
were the most l. of all mankind)	24:11	crying with a l. voice,	39:19
and has been l. from its body	26:36	shall sound both long and l.,	43:18
better that thy soul should be l.	30:47	against that spirit with a l. voice	50:32
yea, all are fallen and are l.,	34: 9	declare my word with l. voices,	60: 7
a hair of the head shall not be l.;	40:23	of the gospel, with a l. voice,	84:114
and man became l. forever,	42: 6	crying with a l. voice,	88:92
save they had l. much blood.	52: 4	his trump both long and l.,	88:94
the cities which they had l.—	52:15	distinctly, with l. speech.	88:129
those lands which were l.	59: 1	upon them with l. proclamation,	124: 7
the city of Nephihah was l.	59:11	him lift up his voice long and l.,	124:75
the righteous are l. because	60:13	everlasting gospel with a l. voice,	124:88
until they had l. possession of	He 4:13	go forth, saying with a l. voice:	133:38
as salt that hath l. its savor,	3Ne 16:15	Satan cried with a l. voice, and	Mses 1:19
myself unto the l. tribes of Israel,	17: 4	that Satan cried with a l. voice,	1:22
are not l. unto the Father,	17: 4	cried with a l. voice, testifying	6:37
even the tribes which have been l.,	21:26	and he heard a l. voice saying:	7:25
for none of them are l.	27:30	And he heard a l. voice;	7:56
and none of them are l.;	27:31		
Coriantumr, having l. his blood,	Eth 14:30	LOUDER	
we have l. a great number of	Mro 9: 2	a voice l. than that which	DC 38:30
and they have l. their love,	9: 5		
that thou hast l. thy privileges	DC 3:14	LOUIS	
of your head shall not be l.,	9:14	the place which is called St. L.	DC 60: 5
wicked man, you have l. them.	10: 1	take their journey from St. L.,	60: 8
l. your gift at the same time	10: 2		
hair, neither mote, shall be l.,	29:25	LOVE	
hath given me shall be l.	50:42	it is the l. of God, which	1Ne 11:22
l. their husbands or fathers;	83: 1	representation of the l. of God;	11:25
as salt that has l. its savor,	103:10	representation of the l. of God.	11:25
to that power which she had l.	113: 8	eternally in the arms of his l.	2Ne 1:15
restore again that which was l.	124:28	He hath filled me with his l.,	4:21
find that which thy neighbor has l.,	136:26	for they l. the truth and are not	9:40
that one soul shall not be l.,	Mses 4: 1	have charity, which charity is l.	26:30
entirely l. in a strife of words	JS 2: 6	and a l. of God and of all men.	31:20
		and feast upon his l.;	Jac 3: 2
LOT		their husbands l. their wives,	3: 7
the l. fell upon Laman;	1Ne 3:11	and their wives l. their husbands;	3: 7
it was their l. to have fallen into	Al 20:30	and their wives l. their children;	3: 7
upon a l. which is not far	DC 57: 3	the l. of God was restored again	7:23
beginning at the temple l.,	84: 3	with l. towards God and all men.	Mos 2: 4
arrange by l. the inheritances	85: 7	meek, humble, patient, full of l.,	3:19
let the first l. on the south be	94: 3	and have tasted of his l.,	4:11
the second l. on the south shall	94:10	and be filled with the l. of God,	4:12
And on the third l. shall my	94:13	will teach them to l. one another,	4:15
the l. of Tahhanes [the tannery]	104:20	unto thousands of them that l. me	13:14
the l. of land which my servant	104:24	and in l. one towards another.	18:21
have the l. which is set off	104:28	l. his neighbor as himself,	23:15
which is l. number one,	104:28	wax strong in l. towards Mosiah;	29:40
the l. upon which his father	104:28	and they did sing redeeming l.	Al 5: 9

LOVE — LOWLY

to sing the song of redeeming l.,	Al 5:26	that all they who l. the king,	Al	47:28
submissive, patient, full of l.	13:28	the people of Nephi hath he l.,	He	15: 3
having the l. of God always in	13:29	had l. them, according to	Mrm	3:12
l. he had for his son Lamoni,	20:26	said that thou hast l. the world,	Eth	12:33
brought to sing redeeming l.,	26:13	as many as have l. me and	DC	29:12
the matchless bounty of his l.;	26:15	Who so l. the world that he		34: 3
their l. towards their brethren	26:31	Son whom the Father l.		76:25
their l. towards their brethren.	26:32	and I have l. you—		95: 1
been so great l. in all the land?	26:33	and they l. Satan more than God.	Mses	5:13
their l. and of their hatred to sin.	26:34	And Cain l. Satan more than God.		5:18
that ye may be filled with l.;	38:12	and they l. Satan more than God.		5:28
the pity and the exceeding l.	53:11			
for the cause of your l. of glory	60:32	**LOVELY**		
that thou shalt l. thy neighbor	3Ne 12:43	virtuous, l., or of good report	AoF	13
say unto you, l. your enemies,	12:44			
for they l. to pray, standing in	13: 5	**LOVES**		
hate the one and l. the other,	13:24	whosoever l. and makes a lie.	DC 76:103	
the l. of God which did dwell	4Ne 1:15			
according to the l. of God which	Mrm 3:12	**LOVEST**		
For behold, ye do l. money,	8:37	thou l. that lucre more than him.	Al	11:24
more than ye l. the poor and	8:37	If thou l. me thou shalt	DC	42:29
this l. which thou hast had for	Eth 12:34			
unto my brethren whom I l.,	12:38	**LOVETH**		
to l. God, and to serve him,	Mro 7:13	I know that he l. his children;	1Ne	11:17
charity is the pure l. of Christ,	7:47	he l. those who will have him		17:40
ye may be filled with this l.,	7:48	for he l. the world,	2Ne	26:24
perfect l. casteth out all fear.	8:16	he l. our souls as well as he	Al	24:14
charity, which is everlasting l.;	8:17	as well as he l. our children;		24:14
I l. little children with a	8:17	them because he l. them.	He	15: 3
little children with a perfect l.;	8:17	whosoever l. and maketh a lie,	DC	63:17
with hope and perfect l.,	8:26	virtue l. virtue; light cleaveth		88:40
which l. endureth by diligence	8:26	he l. that which is right		124:15
and they have lost their l.,	9: 5			
and l. God with all your might,	10:32	**LOVING**		
faith, hope, charity and l.,	DC 4: 5	because of his l. kindness	1Ne	19: 9
encircle thee in the arms of my l.	6:20	the l. kindness of their Lord,	DC 133:52	
l. darkness rather than light,	10:21	and according to his l. kindness,		133:52
shall be humble and full of l.,	12: 8			
they should l. and serve him,	20:19	**LOW**		
all those who l. and serve God	20:31	brought down to lie l. in the dust;	1Ne	18:18
l. darkness rather than light,	29:45	who must be brought l. in the dust;		22:23
Thou shalt l. thy wife with all	42:22	walk in the path of the l. valley,	2Ne	4:32
Thou shalt live together in l.,	42:45	and he shall be brought l.		12:12
the l. of men shall wax cole,	45:27	of men shall be made l.;		12:17
the benefit of those who l. me	46: 9	been brought down l. in the dust,		26:15
Thou shalt l. the Lord thy	59: 5	speech shall be l. out of the dust,		26:16
Thou shalt l. thy neighbor	59: 6	very l. with a burning fever;	Al	15: 5
bestows on those who l. him,	76:116	are laid l. in the earth,		28:11
See that ye l. one another;	88:123	be many mountains laid l.,	He	14:23
grace of God in the bonds of l.,	88:133	shall be laid l. of power.	DC	49:10
brethren in Zion, in l. greeting,	90:32	the mountains to be made l.,		49:23
Lord unto you whom I l.,	95: 1	the rich, the high and the l.,		58:47
whom I l. I also chasten	95: 1	in that the rich are made l.		104:16
the l. of the Father shall not	95:12	high ones shall be brought l.,		112: 8
great l. for the children of Jacob,	109:61	many l. ones shall be exalted.		112: 8
Be not partial towards them in l.	112:11			
let thy l. be for them as for	112:11	**LOWER**		
let thy l. abound unto all men,	112:11	small number of your l. judges	Mos	29:29
and unto all who l. my name.	112:11	the l. judges of the land,	Al	46: 4
and l. to have others suffer,	121:13	a l. court and a higher court,	DC	94: 5
and meekness, and by l. unfeigned;	121:41	shall be a l. and a higher court.		94:11
an increase of l. toward him	121:43	the l. part of the inner court		95:16
I, the Lord, l. him because of	124:15	or all kingdoms of a l. order,		130: 9
And for his l. he shall be great,	124:17			
for the l. which he has to	124:20	**LOWLINESS**		
I, the Lord, l. him.	124:20	diligently, with l. of heart.	1Ne	2:19
l. him for the work he hath done,	124:78	ye are brought to a l. of heart;	Al	32:12
l. me, keep my commandments;	124:87	meekness, and l. of heart;	Mro	8:26
in his l., and in his pity,	133:53	of meekness and l. of heart		8:26
also unto my brethren whom I l.,	135: 5	before you in all l. of heart	DC	42:74
that they should l. one another,	Mses 7:33	and l. of heart, meekness and		107:30
the l. of many shall wax cole,	JS 1:10	will do this in all l. of heart,		118: 3
the l. of many shall wax cold;	1:30			
the great l. which the converts	2: 6	**LOWLY**		
		behold that ye are l. in heart;	Al	32: 8
LOVED		and to be meek and l. in heart;		37:33
Behold, he l. our fathers,	1Ne 17:40	but to be meek and l. in heart;		37:34
The Lord hath l. him;	20:14	shall be meek, and l. of heart.	Mro	7:43
The people having l. Nephi	Jac 1:10	save the meek and l. in heart;		7:44
and they l. murder	Jar 1: 6	a man be meek and l. in heart,		7:44
l. the vain things of the world,	Al 1:16	and be meek and l. of heart.	DC	32: 1
Whosoever l. the king, let him	47:27			

LUCIFER 579 MADE

LUCIFER
O L., son of the morning!	2Ne 24:12
was L., a son of the morning.	DC 76:26

LUCRE
l. which doth corrupt the soul;	Mos 29:40
thou lovest that l. more than him.	Al 11:24

LUCY: see also SMITH, Lucy.
Sophronia, Catherine, and L.	2: 4
church, namely, my mother, L.;	2: 7

LUKE: see JOHNSON, Luke.

LULL
l. them away into carnal security,	2Ne 28:21

LURAM
and also L. and Emron;	Mro 9: 2

LURKETH
for their reward l. beneath,	DC 58:33

LUST
he did l. after it, insomuch	1Ne 3:25
on a woman, to l. after her,	3Ne 12:28
upon a woman to l. after her	DC 42:23
on a woman to l. after her,	63:16

LUSTER
l. was above that of the sun	1Ne 1: 9
his face shone with exceeding l.,	Mos 13: 5

LUSTFUL
from all your l. desires,	DC 88:121
and l. and covetous desires	101: 6

LUSTS
those who seek the l. of the flesh	1Ne 22:23
more after the l. of your eyes,	Al 39: 9
ye may consume it on your l.,	Mrm 9:28
may consume it upon their l.	DC 46: 9

LYING
by his cunning, and l. craftiness,	Mos 10:18
speak l. and vain words to his people.	11:11
l., thieving, robbing, committing	Al 1:32
had caught him in his l.	12: 1
taken in thy l. and craftiness,	12: 3
among the people by his l. words;	14: 6
thou art possessed with a l. spirit,	30:42
by thy l. and by thy flattering	30:47
and found the king l. in his gore,	47:27
murdering, plundering, l., stealing,	He 4:12
murders, and robbing, and l..	Mrm 8:31
the l. in wait to destroy thee,	DC 5:32
that by l. they may say they	10:13
in l. against those words.	10:31
neither l., backbiting, nor evil	20:54
for the temple is l. westward,	57: 3
also every tract l. westward,	57: 4
which are l. before you.	67: 4
who have spread l. reports abroad,	109:29
subject that is l. before us,	128:11
I found myself l. on my back,	JS 2:20

LYINGS
against all l., and deceivings,	Al 16:18
by their cunning and their l.,	20:13
l. sent forth among the people.	3Ne 1:22
but notwithstanding these l.	1:22
by their l. and their flattering	1:29
be filled with all manner of l.,	16:10
l., and deceivings, and envyings,	21:19
of your l. and deceivings,	30: 2
tumults, nor whoredoms, nor l.,	4Ne 1:16
that there may be an end to l. and	DC 109:30

LYMAN: see also JOHNSON, Lyman; SHERMAN, Lyman; and WIGHT, Lyman.
the Lord unto you, my servant L.:	DC 108: 1
servant George, and my servant L.,	124:22

LYMAN, Amasa
I give unto him L. and Noah	DC 124:136
let my servants L. and George A.	136:14

MACHINERY
in buildings, and in m.,	Jar 1: 8

MACK
previous to her marriage, was M.,	JS 2: 4

MACK, Solomon
Mack, daughter of M.);	JS 2: 4

MAD
we to do with him, for he is m.	Mos 13: 1
ye have judged me that I am m.	13: 4
others said he was m.;	JS 2:24

MADE
upon plates which I have m.	1Ne 1:17
and m. an offering unto the Lord,	2: 7
thou shalt be m. a ruler	2:22
he also m. an oath unto us	4:35
when Zoram had m. an oath unto	4:37
had m. an end of prophesying	7: 1
had m. an end of speaking	10: 2
garments are m. white in his blood.	12:10
These are m. white in the blood	12:11
which he hath m. unto the	13:23
which he hath m. unto the	13:23
shall be m. known in the records	13:41
which he hath m. to his people	14:17
things shall be m. known unto you.	15:11
covenant the Lord m. to our	15:18
had m. an end of speaking	16: 1
bow, which was m. of fine steel;	16:18
after I had m. a bellows,	17:11
the covenants which he had m.;	17:40
rough places to be m. smooth,	17:46
upon the plates which I m.	19: 1
at the time when I m. them	19: 2
transpired before I m. these plates	19: 2
m. mention upon the first plates.	19: 2
after I had m. these plates	19: 3
which he m. to their fathers.	19:15
hath m. mention of my name.	21: 1
he hath m. my mouth like a	21: 2
and m. me a polished shaft;	21: 2
they that m. thee waste	21:17
Spirit are all things m. known	22: 2
Nephi, had m. an end of teaching	2Ne 1: 1
which he m. unto Joseph.	3: 4
Messiah should be m. manifest	3: 5
which I have m. with thy fathers.	3: 7
he shall be m. strong,	3:13
which I m. unto thy fathers.	3:21
father had m. an end of speaking	4: 3
father had m. an end of speaking	4: 8
father had m. an end of speaking	4:10
after he had m. an end of speaking	4:11
upon my plates, which I had m.,	5:29
and m. these plates upon which	5:31
which he has m. unto his children;	6:12
hath m. the depths of the sea	8:10
who shall be m. like unto grass?	8:12
have m. unto the children of men,	10:15
have m. unto the children of men,	10:17
the Lord has m. the sea our path,	10:20
which he hath m. to our fathers;	11: 5
which their own fingers have m.	12: 8
of men shall be m. low;	12:17
which he hath m. for himself	12:20
and also m. a wine-press therein;	15: 2
wherein thou wast m. to serve.	24: 3
that m. the earth to tremble,	24:16
m. the world as a wilderness,	24:17
have m. mention unto my children	25: 6
and wer are m. alive in Christ	25:25
the work say of him that m. it,	27:27
him that made it, he m. me not?	27:27
have m. unto the children of men,	29: 1
which I have m. unto thee,	29: 2

MADE 580 MADE

all nations shall be m. known;	2Ne 30:16	Ammon had m. ready the horses	Al	18:12
all things shall be m. known	30:16	he also m. known unto them		18:39
save it shall be m. manifest	30:17	a sepulchre, which they had m.		19: 1
the promise which he hath m.,	31:18	h. made it known unto me that		19: 4
will be m. strong unto them;	33: 4	and never having m. it known,		19:17
had been m. manifest unto us	Jac 1: 5	when I m. a feast unto my sons,		20: 9
were m. by the hand of Nephi.	3:14	m. these things known unto us		24:14
it has been m. manifest unto me,	7:12	m. these things known unto us		24:14
also has been m. manifest unto me	7:12	of salvation might be m. knosn		24:14
there should be no atonement m.	7:12	and our swords are m. bright,		24:15
thy faith hath m. thee whole.	En 1: 8	and has m. us clean thereby.		24:15
the covenant which he had m.;	1:17	when the king had m. an end of		24:17
Mosiah, who was m. king over	Om 1:12	m. preparations for war,		24:20
after I had m. an abridgment	WM 1: 3	have been m. instruments in the		26: 3
promises which the Lord m. unto	Mos 1: 7	and m. known unto them all		27:25
king Benjamin had m. an end of	1: 9	there could be no atonement m.		30:17
king Benjamin had m. an end of	1:15	also thou hast m. it known		31:16
had m. a proclamation throughout	2: 1	say that thou hast m. it known		31:29
m. known unto me by an angel	3: 2	that an atonement should be m.;		34: 9
king Benjamin had m. an end of	4: 1	there must be an atonement m.,		34: 9
the covenant which ye have m.	5: 6	it is expedient should be m.		34: 9
the covenant which ye have m.	5: 7	m. white through the blood of		34:36
under this head ye are m. free,	5: 8	had m. an end of these words,		35: 1
whereby ye can be m. free.	5: 8	m. these things known unto me,		36: 5
king Benjamin had m. an end of	6: 3	not yet fully m. known unto me;		37:11
of the oath which they had m.,	6: 3	his promises which he has m.		37:17
was m. a king by the voice of	7: 9	be m. manifest unto this people;		37:21
an effectual struggle to be m.	7:18	be m. manifest unto this people;		37:21
who was m. king over this people,	7:21	and m. known unto us.		37:26
king Limhi had m. an end of	8: 1	be m. known unto this people		39:18
shall secret things be m. manifest,	8:17	m. known unto me by an angel,		40:11
shall be m. known by them,	8:17	an atonement should be m.;		42:15
shall be m. known by them	8:17	they m. preparations for war;		43: 4
when Ammon had m. an end of	8:19	had m. an end of speaking		44:10
weapons of war m. of every kind,	10: 1	unto thee shall not be m. known,		45: 9
and m. wine in abundance;	11:15	that a regulation should be m.		45:21
Lord hath m. bare his holy arm	12:24	was the covenant which they m.,		46:22
the Lord m. heaven and earth,	13:19	they had m. their escape—		47:32
after Abinadi had m. an end of	13:25	m. king over the Lamanites,		48: 2
he m. his grave with the wicked,	14: 9	promise which he m. was rash;		51:10
and m. intercession for our	14:12	m. preparations and were ready		51:24
his soul has been m. an offering	15:10	had m. known unto the queen		52:12
which he hath m. for his people,	15:19	Teancum m. preparations to		52:17
Lord hath m. bare his holy arm	15:31	the oath which they had m.		53:14
there was no redemption m.,	16: 5	he hath m. us as well as you.		54:21
king of the Lamanites m. an oath	19:25	that a search should be m.		55: 4
m. oath unto the king of the	19:26	m. them more desirous to drink		55:10
the oath that I m. unto you;	20:14	covenant which their fathers m.,		56: 6
oath which ye m. unto my people?	20:14	the covenant which they had m.		56: 7
search to be m. among his people.	20:16	covenant which they had m.,		56: 8
oath which we have m. unto him;	20:22	God has m. them free;		58:40
the oath which their king had m.	21: 3	redeemed us and m. us free,		58:41
having m. it known to his people,	23: 1	the covenant which I have m.		60:34
m. me an instrument in his hands	23:10	the which God hath m. us free.		61: 9
wherewith ye have been m. free,	23:13	God hath m. them free.		61:21
the covenant which ye have m.	24:13	a regulation should be m. again		62:44
were m. light; yea, the Lord did	24:15	regulations were m. concerning		62:47
when Mosiah had m. an end of	25: 7	Kishkumen m. known unto him	He 2: 7
when Mosiah had m. an end of	25:14	Lord God has m. them known		7:29
and had m. an end of speaking to	25:17	which thou hast m. with him.		9:20
by the laws which he had m.	Al 1: 1	and your destruction is m. sure;		13:32
was not m. king over the people.	2: 7	and your destruction is m. sure;		13:38
Amlici was m. king over them	2:10	and he hath m. you free.		14:30
cleansed and m. white through	5:27	they have been m. free.		15: 8
they are m. known unto me by	5:46	m. known unto them beforehand,		16: 5
God hath m. them manifest	5:46	which I have m. known unto	3Ne 1:14
Alma had m. an end of speaking	6: 1	it was m. known unto them that		1:25
Alma had m. these regulations	6: 7	oaths which Giddianhi had m.,		4:12
it has been m. known unto you,	7:20	which had been m. among them,		4:24
all things m. known unto them,	9:20	I have m. my record of these		5:10
An angel hath m. them known	11:31	plates which I have m.		5:11
there had been no redemption m.,	11:41	cast up, and many roads m.,		6: 8
thoughts are m. known unto us by	12: 3	no mistake m. by this man in		8: 2
there had been no redemption m.;	12:18	and m. hills and valleys in the		9: 8
m. an end of speaking these words,	12:19	covenant which I have m. with		15: 8
m. known unto them the plan of	12:30	which the Father hath m. unto		16: 5
and this he m. known unto them	12:30	shall be m. known unto them.		16: 7
m. known unto them the plan of	12:32	covenant which I have m. unto		16:11
having their garments m. white,	13:12	The Lord hath m. bare his holy		16:20
great many, who were m. pure	13:12	Jesus had m. an end of praying		17:18
more particularly m. mention.	13:19	m. an end of these sayings,		18:36
m. known unto us in plain terms,	13:23	Jesus had m. an end of praying		19:35
m. known unto just and holy men,	13:26	Father hath m. unto his people,		20:12
had m. an end of speaking unto	14: 1	of the covenant which I m.		20:22

MADE 581 MADE

the covenant which the Father m.	3Ne 20:25
which he m. with Abraham,	20:27
covenant which I have m. with	20:29
The Father hath m. bare his	20:35
m. known unto the Gentiles	21: 2
shall be m. known unto them	21: 3
covenant which he hath m. unto	21: 7
greater things be m. manifest	26: 9
he hath m. it manifest unto me	28:37
which the Father hath m. with	29: 1
covenant which he hath m. unto	29: 3
the covenant which he hath m.	29: 9
but they were all m. free,	4Ne 1: 3
promises which the Lord had m.	1:11
m. a treaty with the Lamanites	Mrm 2:28
repent of the oath which I had m.	5: 1
things must surely be m. known,	5: 8
which he m. unto Abraham and	5:20
I m. this record out of the	6: 6
my father hath m. this record,	8: 5
his covenant which he hath m.	8:21
the covenant which he hath m.	8:23
hath m. manifest unto you our	9:31
the covenant which he hath m.	9:37
have m. the barges according	Eth 2:18
that they should be m. manifest.	4: 2
greater things m. manifest than	4: 4
those which were m. manifest	4: 4
shall be m. manifest unto you	4:14
the covenant which he m.	4:15
shall be m. manifest in very deed.	4:16
and m. swords out of steel for	7: 9
Akish m. known unto them,	8:14
it hath been m. known unto me	8:20
Lord thou hast m. us mighty	12:23
not m. us mighty in writing;	12:23
thou hast m. all this people	12:23
thou hast m. us that we could	12:24
not m. us mighty in writing	12:24
m. our words powerful and great,	12:25
thy garments shall be m. clean.	12:37
thou shalt be m. strong,	12:37
the covenant which God m. with	13:11
he m. the remainder of this	13:14
m. an end of abridging the	Mro 1: 1
m. unto the children of men,	7:31
the covenants which he hath m.	7:32
had been no redemption m.	7:38
which he hath m. unto thee,	10:31
it might be m. known;	DC 1:25
they might be m. strong,	1:28
promises m. to the fathers,	2: 2
promises which were m. to you,	3: 5
sacred promises which were m.	3:13
which he m. to his people;	3:19
shall be m. known unto future	5: 9
then shall you be m. rich.	6: 7
strength, whereby it is m. up?	9:12
gospel should be m. known also,	10:49
then shall you be m. rich.	11: 7
covenants which thou hast m.	25:13
be m. known what you shall do.	26: 1
except it is m. new among you;	27: 4
m. manifest in the eyes of	35: 7
m. all nations drink of the wine	35:11
heaven, before the world was m.;	38: 1
spake, and the world was m.,	38: 3
and the rich have I m.,	38:16
And I have m. the earth rich,	38:17
be m. accountable unto me,	42:32
words of that God who m. you.	43:23
who m. the heavens and all	45: 1
all things were m. which live,	45: 1
the promises that I have m.	45:16
promises which have been m.	45:35
these things shall be m. known;	45:60
creation before the world was m.	49:17
the mountains to be m. low,	49:23
hereafter shall be m. strong.	50:16
all things shall be m. sure,	51: 6
soon as preparations can be m.	52: 3
shall be m. known unto them	52: 4
m. known unto them the land	52: 5
be m. ruler over many things.	DC 52:13
shall be m. strong,	52:17
should be m. known unto you,	53: 1
be m. known in a time to come,	53: 6
covenant which they m. unto me	54: 4
The residue shall be m. known	55: 6
no divisions m. upon the land,	56: 9
Who am I that m. man,	58:30
shall be m. known by the Spirit	58:50
be m. known from time to time,	58:55
are m. for the benefit and the	59:18
were they m. to be used,	59:20
There be a craft m.,	60: 5
shall be m. known concerning	60:17
as it is m. known unto them	61:22
folly shall be m. manifest,	63:15
are m. known unto them,	64:17
m. known unto my disciples,	64:19
have m. my church in these	64:37
be m. partakers of the glories	66: 2
be m. strong in every place;	66: 8
shall be m. known unto you.	71: 2
shame shall be m. manifest.	71: 7
shall be m. known by the	72: 7
shall be m. known unto them,	73: 2
be m. known from on high,	75:27
he m. war and overcame,	76:30
been m. partakers thereof,	76:31
before the worlds were m.	76:39
into his power and m. by him;	76:42
who are m. partakers thereof;	76:46
who are just men m. perfect	76:69
God m. the world in six days,	77:12
and be m. rulers over many	78:15
shall be m. glorious;	78:19
earth be m. to feel the wrath,	87: 6
m. a full end of all nations;	87: 6
thereof by which it was m.	88: 7
thereof by which it was m.;	88: 8
thereof by which they were m.;	88: 9
redemption which is m. for you	88:14
for, for this intent was it m.	88:20
and he was m. glad with	88:56
the decree which God hath m.	88:61
last promise which I have m.	88:69
which I have m. un to you,	88:75
wherewith ye are m. free;	88:86
that m. all nations drink of	88:94
her bands are m. strong,	88:94
who m. all nations drink of	88:105
and be m. equal with him.	88:107
God m. for the use of man	89:15
and m. flesh my tabernacle,	93: 4
the world was m. by him,	93: 9
The worlds were m. by him;	93:10
by him; men were m. by him;	93:10
all things were m. by him,	93:10
truth, was not created or m.,	93:29
of Zion be m. strong.	96: 1
promise m. unto his fathers—	96: 7
their works shall be m. known.	97: 6
the earth, by which it was m.,	101:33
then ye could have m. ready	101:54
and their bands m. strong,	101:66
no such decision had been m.	102:27
which I have m. and prepared	104:13
in that the rich are m. low.	104:16
abundance which I have m.,	104:18
it shall be m. known to him	104:36
which ye have m. unto me	104:55
every decision m. by either of	107:27
are to be m. in all righteousness,	107:30
is m. in unrighteousness,	107:32
to whom the promises were m.	107:40
which you have m. and do make,	108: 3
which thou hast m. unto us,	109:11
the rough places m. smooth;	109:74
whom I have m. counselors for	112:20
beginning be m. on the fourth day	115:10
Have I not m. the earth?	117: 6
he shall be m. a merchant	117:14
m. to bow down with grief,	123: 7
which you have m.;	124: 1

proclamation shall be m. to all the	DC 124: 3	the promises m. to the fathers,	JS	2:39
that spot that it shall be m. holy.	124:44	light had m. its appearance.		2:43
he shall be m. ruler over many;	124:113	impressions m. on my mind,		2:46
contract which he has m. with	124:115	I m. an attempt to take them		2:53
the record they have m. is true.	128: 4			
and m. a record of the same	128: 4	MADEST		
which are truly m. out,	128:14	thou m. him that the things	Eth	12:24
without us cannot be m. perfect—	128:15	and by what thou m. them?	Mses	1:30
without our dead be m. perfect.	128:15			
them cannot be m. perfect;	128:18	MADISON		
they without us be m. perfect.	128:18	also unto the inhabitants of M.,	DC 124:88	
can they nor we be m. perfect	128:18			
spirits of just men m. perfect,	129: 3	MADMENAH		
the spirit of a just man m. perfect	129: 6	M. is removed;	2Ne 20:31	
be m. like unto crystal and will	130: 9			
of kingdoms will be m. known.	130:10	MAGAZINES		
or expectations, that are not m.	132: 7	And all that are in the m.,	DC 123: 5	
contracts that are not m. unto	132: 7			
that is not m. in my name?	132: 9	MAGGOTS		
promise was m. unto Abraham;	132:31	shall cause m. to come in	DC 29:18	
which he m. unto Abraham.	132:33			
he shall be m. ruler over many.	132:44	MAGIC		
be m. ruler over many things;	132:53	the murderers, and the m. art,	Mrm 2:10	
worship him that m. heaven, and	133:39			
that men might be m. partakers	133:57	MAGICS		
immediate appeal cannot be m. to	134:11	and witchcrafts, and m.;	Mrm 1:19	
Hyrum had m. ready to go—	135: 4			
thou shalt be m. strong,	135: 5	MAGISTRATE		
his folly shall be m. manifest.	136:19	the civil m. should restrain crime,	DC 134: 4	
be m. stronger than many waters;	Mses 1:25			
For mine own purpose have I m.	1:31	MAGISTRATES		
m. the firmament and divided	2: 7	require civil officers and m. to	DC 134: 3	
things which I had m. were good.	2:10	and m. as such, being placed for	134: 6	
things which I had m. were good;	2:12	kings, presidents, rulers, and m.,	AoF	12
I, God, m. two great lights;	2:16			
m. even according to my word.	2:16	MAGNA CHARTA		
things which I had m. were good;	2:18	and on the m. of the United States,	DC 135: 7	
m. the beasts of the earth after	2:25			
God, saw everything that I had m.,	2:31	MAGNIFY		
which I had m. were very good;	2:31	the saw m. itself against him	2Ne 20:15	
and all things which I had m.;	3: 2	my heart doth m. his holy name.	25:13	
things which I had m. were finished,	3: 2	And we did m. our office unto	Jac	1:19
which I, God, had created and m.	3: 3	to m. mine office with soberness,	2: 2	
m. the heaven and the earth;	3: 4	shall m. to the eyes of men	Eth	3:24
and m. according to my word.	3: 7	M. thine office; and after thou	DC	24: 3
m. I, the Lord God, to grow	3: 9	wherewith to m. thine office,	24: 9	
had taken from man, m. I a woman,	3:22	and thou shalt m. thine office,	66:11	
which I, the Lord God, had m.	4: 5	to m. the calling whereunto	88:80	
together and m. themselves aprons.	4:13	I will m. my name upon all	132:64	
they m. all things known unto	5:12			
the sons of men whom he had m.;	5:56	MAGNIFYING		
in the likeness of God m. he him;	6: 8	and the m. their calling,	DC 84:33	
serve the Lord God who m. you.	6:33			
heavens he m. ; the earth is his	6:44	MAHAH		
we are m. partakers of misery	6:48	and Gilgah, and M., and Orihah.	Eth	6:14
God hath m. known unto our	6:50			
I m. the world, and men before	6:51	MAHALALEEL		
which I have m., and so became	6:59	M. and Pelagoram [Sidney	DC 82:11	
and m. to bear record of me,	6:63	M. was four hundred and ninety-six	107:46	
all the creations which I have m.;	7:36	he called Seth, Enos, Cainan, M.,	107:53	
thou hast m. me, and given unto	7:59	seventy years, and begat M.;	Mses	6:19
oath which I have m. unto you	7:60	Cainan lived after he begat M.	6:19	
all the creations which I have m.;	7:64	M. lived sixty-five years, and begat	6:20	
be fulfilled, which he m. to Enoch;	8: 2	and M. lived, after he begat Jared,	6:20	
may have all things m. manifest;	8:24	days of M. were eight hundred and	6:20	
pained that the Lord had m.	8:25			
and that I have m. them;	8:26	MAHAN		
the priest m. an offering unto	Abr 1: 9	M., the master of this great secret,	Mses	5:31
m. after the form of a bedstead,	1:13	Cain was called Master M.,	5:31	
were m. known unto the fathers,	1:31	wherin he became Master M.,	5:49	
and m. an offering unto the Lord,	2:17			
works which his hands had m.;	3:11	MAHEMSON		
things which his hands had m.,	3:12	and M. [Martin Harris],	DC 82:11	
that he m. the greater star;	3:18	let my servant M. [Martin Harris]	104:24	
works which my hands have m.,	3:21	let my servant M. [Martin Harris]	104:26	
of the ground m. the Gods to	5: 9			
Is m. to represent God,	Fac 2: 3	MAHER-SHALAL-HASH-BAZ		
m. ruler over his household,	JS 1:49	it with a man's pen, concerning M.	2Ne 18: 1	
I had m. such an attempt,	2:14	call his name, M.	18: 3	
never as yet m. the attempt to	2:14			
when he m. his defense before	2:24	MAHIJAH		
could be m. to appear so	2:31	whose name was M., and said	Mses	6:40

MAHMACKRAH — MAKE

MAHMACKRAH
of Libnah. and the god of M.,　Abr　1: 6
the gods of Elkenah, Libnah, M.,　　1:13
god of Libnah, and the god of M.,　　1:17
the gods of Elkenah, Libnah, M.,　Fac　1: 4
The idolatrous god of M.　　1: 7

MAHUJAEL
Irad begat M., and other　Mses　5:43
M. begat Methusael, and other　　5:43

MAHUJAH
and stood upon the place M.,　Mses　7: 2

MAID
man-servant, nor thy m.-servant,　Mos　13:18
man-servant, nor his m.-servant,　　13:24
with one of his m. servants,　Al　50:30
to wife, in his old age, a young m.,　Eth　9:24

MAID-SERVANT: see *MAID and SERVANT.*

MAIL
and send it to you by m.,　DC 127:10

MAIMED
lame, or blind, or halt, or m.,　3Ne 17: 7

MAIN
the m. top thereof began to perish.　Jac　5: 6
will pluck off those m. branches　　5: 7
that you should tarry, for the m.,　DC 111: 8

MAINSPRING
the very m. of all corruption,　DC 123: 7

MAINTAIN
that we may m. our armies.　Al　27:24
whosoever will m. this title　　46:20
that they will m. their rights,　　46:20
desirous to m. their liberty,　　46:28
might m. a free government,　　46:35
they did m. peace in the land　　46:37
did also m. order in the church;　　46:38
might m. that which was called　　48:10
and m. the cause of God all his　　50:39
did not long m. an entire peace　　51: 2
covenanted to m. their rights　　51: 6
to m. the cause of freedom.　　51: 7
leaving men in every city to m.　　51:25
people should m. those cities,　　52: 4
determined to m. those cities　　52: 5
we will m. our religion and the　　54:10
to m. and to obtain their rights　　54:24
also m. all the ground and　　55:27
by night to m. their cities;　　56:16
to m. those cities which they had　　56:20
determined to m. those cities　　56:26
the remainder to m. the city,　　56:33
still determined to m. the city;　　57:11
and to m. our lands, and our　　58:12
m. so great a number of cities　　58:32
might with ease m. that part of　　59: 3
of the people to m. that city,　　59: 9
they would easily m. that city.　　59: 9
to m. those places which he had　　59:10
to m. this part of our land,　　60:25
to m. the city of Zarahemla,　　61: 8
armies should m. those parts　He　1:26
and also to m. their rights,　3Ne　2:12
again, and we did m. the city.　Mrm　5: 4
did m. the half of the kingdom　Eth　11:15

MAINTAINED
other cities which were m. by　Mrm　5: 4
should be m. for the rights　DC 101:77
m. by virtue of the priesthood,　　121:41
character which ought to be m.　JS　2:28

MAINTAINING
in m. that quarter of the land,　Al　52:10
the m. those parts of the land　　58: 3
his armies in m. those parts　He　4:19

m. that which ye suppose to be　3Ne　3: 2
in m. rights and privileges.　DC　98: 5

MAINTENANCE
the m. of the sacred word of God,　Al　44: 5
which m. he supposeth will　　61: 8
on their husbands for their m.,　DC　83: 2
upon their parents for their m.　　83: 4
of obtaining a scanty m. by　JS　2:23
to get a comfortable m.　　2:55

MAJESTY
and the glory of his m. shall　2Ne 12:10
and the glory of his m. shall　　12:19
and the m. of his glory shall　　12:21
might, m., power, and dominion.　Al　5:50
in his might, m., and cominion,　　12:15
of the glorious m. on high,　DC 20:16
moving in his m. and power.　　88:47
may roll on in great power and m.,　　109:59
with glory, honor, power, m.,　　109:77
their honors, their m. and glory,　　128:21

MAJOR: see *ASHLEY, Major N.*

MAJORITY
the m. of the council having　DC 102:22
A m. may form a quorum　　107:28

MAKE
I m. a record of my proceedings　1Ne　1: 1
I m. a record in the language　　1: 2
the record which I m. is true;　　1: 3
and I m. it with mine own hand;　　1: 3
I m. it according to my knowledge.　　1: 3
do not m. a full account of the　　1:16
I shall m. a full account.　　1:16
m. an account of my proceedings,　　1:17
I m. an abridgment of the　　1:17
I m. an account of mine own life.　　1:17
of their faith, to m. them mighty　　1:20
was desirable to m. one happy.　　8:10
upon which I m. a full account　　9: 2
upon which I m. a full account　　9: 2
that I should m. these plates　　9: 3
commanded me to m. these plates　　9: 5
and m. his paths straight;　　10: 8
and should m. himself manifest,　　10:11
able to m. them known unto me,　　11: 1
m. known the plain and precious　　13:40
shall m. known to all kindreds,　　13:40
Lord did m. them known unto me.　　14:29
now I m. an end of speaking　　14:30
did m. out of wood a bow,　　16:23
thought to m. himself a king　　16:38
that I may m. tools to construct　　17: 9
ore, that I might m. tools.　　17:10
I, Nephi, did m. a bellows　　17:11
together that I might m. fire.　　17:11
that we should m. much fire,　　17:12
will m. thy food become sweet,　　17:12
I did m. tools of the ore　　17:16
he did m. them mighty unto the　　17:32
began to m. themselves merry,　　18: 9
wherefore I did m. plates of ore　　19: 1
of the Lord to m. these plates;　　19: 2
did m. a record upon the other　　19: 4
and m. mention of the God of　　20: 1
he shall m. his way prosperous.　　20:15
I will m. all my mountains　　21:11
Thy children shall m. haste　　21:17
he shall m. bare his arm　　22:10
proceed to m. bare his arm　　22:11
And now I, Nephi, m. an end;　　22:29
to m. these things known unto the　2Ne　2: 8
he shall m. intercession for all　　2: 9
I will m. him great in mine eyes;　　3: 8
not m. him mighty in speaking.　　3:17
I will m. a spokesman for him.　　3:17
I will m. for him a spokesman.　　3:18
of their words will I m. strong　　3:21
Wilt thou m. me that I may shake　　4:31
wilt thou m. a way for mine escape　　4:33
Wilt thou m. my path straight　　4:33

MAKE 584 MAKE

did m. many swords, lest by any	2Ne	5:14
M. other plates; and thou shalt		5:30
I m. their rivers a wilderness		7: 2
I m. sackcloth their covering.		7: 3
he will m. her wilderness like		8: 3
I will m. my judgment to rest		8: 4
m. me not a ruler of the people.		13: 7
That say: Let him m. speed,		15:19
M. the heart of this people fat,		16:10
and m. their ears heavy,		16:10
let us m. a breach therein for us,		17: 6
of Hosts shall m. a consumption,		20:23
m. him of quick understanding		21: 3
and m. men go over dry shod.		21:15
m. mention that his name is		22: 4
I will m. a man more precious		23:12
the shepherds m. their fold there.		23:20
I will also m. it a possession		24:23
that m. a man an offender for		27:32
I must m. an end of my sayings.		30:18
m. an end of my prophesying		31: 1
And now I m. an end of speaking	Jac	2:22
And I m. an end of speaking		3:14
and m. a mock of the great plan		6: 8
And I m. an end of my writing		7:27
And I m. an end.	Om	1: 3
And I m. an end.		1: 9
And I m. an end.		1:11
And I m. an end of my speaking.		1:30
and I m. it according to the	WM	1: 9
ye should m. a proclamation	Mos	1:10
should m. slaves one of another,		2:13
should m. a treaty with them;		9: 2
m. unto thee any graven image,		12:36
m. unto thee any graven image,		13:12
which God himself shall m. for the		13:28
m. his soul an offering for sin		14:10
the Son power to m. intercession		15: 8
and to m. themselves merry.		20: 1
will m. himself manifest unto all.		27:30
that which will m. for the peace of		29:10
ye observe and m. it your law—		29:26
to m. war with the Nephites.	Al	2:15
and except we m. haste they		2:25
except ye m. our Creator a liar		5:25
doth m. a mock of his brother,		5:30
angel to m. these things manifest		10:10
crime which they could m. appear		10:13
they might m. him cross his words,		10:16
I will m. an instrument of thee		17:11
did he m. known unto them.		18:39
should m. ready his horses and		20: 6
thou m. thyself known unto me,		22:18
began to m. preparations for war		24: 4
not even m. any preparations		24: 6
m. use of that which is their own		30:28
not m. any reply to his words;		30:29
that he should m. known unto you		34: 3
began to m. preparations for war		35:11
which he shall m. unto you,		37:17
shall ye m. known unto them;		37:29
unto thee ye shall not m. known;		45: 9
m. them rulers over the people.		46: 5
if he would m. him (Amalickiah)		47:13
God would m. it known unto		48:16
to m. an attack upon the city		52:16
to m. an attack upon the city		52:17
m. an attack upon the Lamanites.		53: 5
Moroni to m. preparations to		55:33
to m. an attack upon them in		56:21
to m. an attack upon other		56:22
they would m. their escape;		56:40
began to m. preparations to go		57: 3
began to m. preparations to		58:15
m. it known unto all his people,		59: 2
do not m. use of the means		60:21
and did m. all manner of cloth,	He	6:13
and m. known unto us the true		9:17
shall m. as if he were astonished;		9:30
I will m. thee mighty in word		10: 5
these robbers did m. great havoc,		11:27
they did m. a great uproar	3Ne	1: 7
that they should m. weapons of		3:26

I do m. the record on plates	3Ne	5:11
m. a record of these things		5:14
I do m. my record from the		5:16
I do m. a record of the things		5:17
I know the record which I m.		5:18
now I m. an end of my saying,		5:19
Lord would m. for his people,		6:20
I m. an end of my sayings.		10:19
not m. one hair black or white;		12:36
I will m. my people with whom		20:19
yea, I will m. thy horn iron,		20:19
and I will m. thy hoofs brass.		20:19
shall m. them mighty above all,		20:27
m. the desolate cities to be		22: 3
will m. thy windows of agates,		22:12
day when I m. up my jewels;		24:17
m. an end of my sayings,		26:12
Mormon, m. an end of speaking		28:24
nor m. game of the Jews,		29: 8
now I, Mormon, m. a record of	Mrm	1: 1
and m. preparations to defend		2: 4
did m. a record according to		2:17
I did m. a full account of all		2:18
I did forbear to m. a full account		2:18
Lamanites did m. preparations		4: 6
I would m. all things known		8:12
I m. an end of speaking		8:13
thou shalt m. a hole in the top,	Eth	2:20
I could not m. a full account		3:17
did m. him serve in captivity;		8: 3
he did m. war against the king		10:15
and they did m. gold, and silver,		10:23
did m. all manner of tools		10:25
did m. all manner of tools		10:26
did m. all manner of weapons		10:27
m. them sure and steadfast,		12: 4
I m. weak things become strong		12:27
I m. not myself known to the	Mro	1: 1
to m. manifest concerning the		7:22
to m. these things known unto	DC	1:34
M. not thy gift known unto any		6:12
will m. him as flaming fire		7: 6
I will m. thee to minister for		7: 7
to m. all things known unto		10:37
M. known thy calling unto		23: 2
m. a selection of sacred hymns,		25:11
and m. his paths straight;		33:10
m. the ears of all tingle that		43:22
to m. a commencement to lay		48: 6
will m. known unto you what		52: 2
And now I m. an end of		56:20
and the agent m. preparations		57:15
I shall m. up my jewels,		60: 4
For I am able to m. you holy,		60: 7
I would m. known my will		63:22
I will m. it known unto you,		63:22
and he shall m. another;		63:56
Lord, m. his paths straight.		65: 1
m. ready for the bridegroom.		65: 3
m. known his wonderful works		65: 4
that shall m. one like unto it,		67: 7
cannot m. one like unto it,		67: 8
I m. an end of my sayings.		72:23
will I m. known unto them		76: 7
will I m. known unto them		76:10
capable to m. them known,		76:116
m. unto yourselves friends with		82:22
to m. straight the way of		84:28
m. use of it for their benefit,		84:103
you to m. appointments,		84:107
that I may m. you clean;		88:74
of the vine, of your own m.		89: 6
on his journey, and m. haste,		93:51
Williams m. haste also,		93:52
I, the Lord God, m. you free,		98: 8
come to m. up my jewels.		101: 3
to m. the case clear to the		102:23
m. every man accountable,		104:13
m. use of the stewardship		104:63
m. a proclamation of peace		105:39
m. proposals for peace unto		105:40
in order to m. their decisions of		107:27
which you have made and do m.,		108: 3

MAKE 585 MAN

m. a display of thy testimony	DC 109:49
m. bare thine arm, O Lord,	109:51
m. a disposition of his	114: 1
I not m. solitary places to bud	117: 7
are enough to m. hell itself shudder,	123:10
to m. a solemn proclaimation of	124: 2
the oath which I m. unto you,	124:47
this I m. an example unto you,	124:53
that he might m. a record of	128: 2
m. a covenant with her for time	132:18
m. known unto you all things	132:45
I m. a way for your escape,	132:50
and m. her heart to rejoice.	132:56
he shall m. bare his holy arm	133: 3
and m. his paths straight,	133:17
come down to m. thy name known	133:42
I m. the rivers a wilderness;	133:68
and m. sackcloth their covering.	133:69
thou shalt m. diligent search	136:26
Let us m. man in our image,	Mses 2:26
I will m. an help meet for him.	3:18
a tree to be desired m. her wise,	4:12
m. coats of skins, and clothed	4:27
M. an offering unto the Lord.	5:18
to m. of thee a minister to bear my	Abr 2: 6
I will m. of thee a great nation,	2: 9
and m. thy name great among us	2: 9
said: These I will m. my rulers;	3:23
we will m. an earth whereon	3:24
Let us m. an help meet for the	5:14
m. him ruler over all his goods.	JS 1:50
to m. the people think they	2: 9
the woods to m. the attempt.	2:14
to m. a boy of no consequence	2:22
could not m. it otherwise;	2:24
not m. him think or believe	2:24
to m. me deny what I have	2:25
come to m. inquiries of me.	2:66

MAKER
And forgettest the Lord thy m.,	2Ne 8:13
have spoken the words of your M.	9:40
before the presence of my M.	Jac 2: 6
and I kneeled down before my M.,	En 1: 4
by their everlasting M., that	He 1:11
For thy m., thy husband,	3Ne 22: 5
on the things of me, your M.,	DC 30: 2
Lord God Almighty, m. of heaven,	121: 4
to be answered by man to his M.	134: 6

MAKES
until he m. reconciliation.	DC 46: 4
he m. them equal in power,	76:95
whosoever loves and m. a lie.	76:103

MAKETH
Lord m. no such thing known	1Ne 15: 9
trust in man or m. flesh his arm.	2Ne 4:34
trust in man, or m. flesh his arm,	28:31
it m. known unto them of their	33: 4
which m. manifest unto the	Jar 1: 4
which m. these things known	Al 38: 6
he m. his sun to rise on the	3Ne 12:45
m. an anchor to the souls of men,	Eth 12: 4
loveth and m. a lie,	DC 63:17
he m. war with the saints of	76:29
it m. my bones to quake	85: 6
quake while it m. manifest,	85: 6
m. all nations to drink of	86: 3
and the law also m. you free.	98: 8
things, which m. alive all things;	Mses 6:61

MAKING
m. known unto him the things	1Ne 2:17
an account of my m. these plates	19: 5
the m. known of the covenants	22: 9
m. a tinkling with their feet—	2Ne 13:16
m. all manner of tools of every	Jar 1: 8
the record which I have been m.	WM 1: 1
m. in the whole, about four	Mos 6: 4
m. in the whole, five hundred	29:46
ye are m. his paths straight.	Al 7:19
have been void, m. God a liar,	12:23

by m. known unto the people	Al 19:17
m. it known unto the people.	19:17
did not stop m. preparations for	50: 1
m. regulations to prepare for war	51:22
as if m. preparations for war;	52: 6
m. fortifications to guard against	53: 7
m. preparations to come out	58:16
m. preparations to go against the	59: 5
m. a mock of that which was	He 4:12
m., in the whole, three hundred	Mrm 3: 4
and m. a history of all the	DC 69: 3
m. known the duty of the	72: 9
m. him four hundred and	107:49
in m. a solemn proclamation	124:107
m. laws and administering them,	134: 1
In m. this confession, no one	JS 2:28

MALACHI
the Father had given unto M.,	3Ne 24: 1
Thus said the Father unto M.—	24: 1
spoken of by the mouth of M.—	DC 110:14
for M. says, last chapter,	128:17
was written by the prophet M.:	133:64
part of the third chapter of M.;	JS 2:36

MALE
old and young, both m. and female;	1Ne 8:27
bond and free, both m. and female,	2Ne 10:16
bond and free, m. and female;	26:33
bond and free, both m. and female,	Al 1:30
bond and free, both m. and female,	11:44
thy flocks, both m. and female,	Eth 1:41
gathered together, m. and female,	2: 1
he created man, m. and female,	DC 20:18
m. and female created I them.	Mses 2:27
m. and female, created he them,	6: 9
to form they him, m. and female	Abr 4:27

MALICE
envyings, and strifes, and m.	2Ne 26:21
that they should not have m.;	26:32
strife, and m., and persecutions,	Al 4: 9
and strifes, and m., and revilings,	16:18
envyings, strifes, m.,	He 13:22
unto envying, and strifes, and m.,	Mrm 8:36

MALIGNANT
guilty of any great or m. sins.	JS 2:28

MAMMON
Ye cannot serve God and M.	3Ne 13:24
the m. of unrighteousness,	DC 82:22

MAN
because he was a visionary m.,	1Ne 2:11
Behold, he is a mighty m.,	3:31
I beheld a m., and he had	4: 7
have I shed the blood of m.	4:10
better then one m. should perish	4:13
being a m. large in stature,	4:31
should be a free m. like unto us	4:33
him that he was a visionary m.;	5: 2
I know that I am a visionary m.;	5: 4
I saw m., and he was dressed	8: 5
remember, O m., for all thy	10:20
behold a m. descending	11: 7
unto him as a m. speaketh,	11:11
he was in the form of a m.;	11:11
as a m. speaketh with another.	11:11
a m. among the Gentiles,	13:12
down and wrought upon the m.;	13:12
beheld a m., and he was dressed	14:19
save a m. should inquire of the	15: 3
were expedient for m. to receive,	17:30
as a m., into the hands of wicked	19:10
to him whom m. despiseth,	21: 7
that a m. must be obedient	22:30
is prepared from the fall of m.,	2Ne 2: 4
eternal purposes in the end of m.,	2:15
God gave unto m. that he should	2:16
Wherefore, m. could not act for	2:16
which are expedient unto m.	2:27
O wretched m. that I am!	4:17

MAN 586 MAN

yea, even too great for m.;	2 Ne	4:25
he that putteth his trust in m.		4:34
when I came, there was no m.;		7: 2
he afraid of m., who shall die,		8:12
the son of m., who shall be made		8:12
become subject unto m. in the flesh,		9: 5
must needs come unto m. by		9: 6
and because m. became fallen		9: 6
first judgment which came upon m.		9: 7
the way for m. is narrow, but it lieth		9:41
beginning of the world, unto m.,		11: 4
the mean m. boweth not down,		12: 9
the great m. humbleth himself not,		12: 9
lofty looks of m. shall be humbled,		12:11
the loftiness of m. shall be bowed		12:17
a m. shall cast his idols of silver,		12:20
Cease ye from m., whose breath is		12:22
The mighty m. and the man of		13: 2
the m. of war, the judge and the		13: 2
of fifty, and the honorable m.,		13: 3
a m. shall take hold of his brother		13: 6
women shall take hold of one m.,		14: 1
the mean m. shall be brought down,		15:15
the mighty m. shall be humbled,		15:15
because I am a m. of unclean lips;		16: 5
and the houses without m.,		16:11
a m. shall nourish a young cow		17:21
no m. shall spare his brother.		19:19
every m. the flesh of his own arm—		19:20
the inhabitants like a valiant m.;		20:13
I will make a m. more precious		23:12
even a m. than the golden wedge		23:12
as a sheep that no m. taketh up;		23:14
every m. turn to his own people,		23:14
the m. that made the earth to		24:16
I know that no m. can err;		25: 7
spoken, whereby m. can be saved.		25:20
to teach any m. the right way;		25:28
Lord will not always strive with m.		26:11
the Spirit ceaseth to strive with m.		26:11
unto a hungry m. which dreameth,		27: 3
unto a thirsty m. which dreameth,		27: 3
book shall be delivered unto a m.,		27: 9
book shall be delivered unto the m.		27:12
And the m. shall say: I cannot		27:17
the m. that is not learned shall		27:19
they that make a m. an offender		27:32
he that putteth his trust in m.,		28:31
shall it be until the end of m.,		29: 9
every m. according to their works,		29:11
unless a m. shall endure to the		31:16
whereby m. can be saved in		31:21
which teacheth a m. to pray		32: 8
teacheth not a m. to pray,		32: 8
when a m. speaketh by the power		33: 1
no m. will be angry at the words		33: 5
a m. who seeketh to overthrow	Jac	1:hd
he anointed a m. to be a king		1: 9
there shall not any m. among you		2:27
that m. should find out all his		4: 8
And no m. knoweth of his ways		4: 8
m. came upon the face of the		4: 9
and to speak and m. was created,		4: 9
which a m. took and nourished		5: 3
a m. among the people of Nephi,		7: 1
no m. knoweth of such things;		7: 7
to the words of this wicked m.		7:23
my father that he was a just m.—	En	1: 1
I of myself am a wicked m.,	Om	1: 2
to be a just m. before the Lord,		1:25
being a strong and mighty m.,		1:28
and a stiffnecked m.,		1:28
king Benjamin was a holy m.,	WM	1:17
also a just m. to be their king,	Mos	2: 4
every m. according to his family,		2: 5
every m. having his tent with		2: 6
myself am more than a mortal m.		2:10
that the m. that doeth this,		2:37
if that m. repenteth not,		2:38
mercy hath no claim on that m.;		2:39
even more than m. can suffer,		3: 7
they shall consider him a m.,		3: 9
the natural m. is an enemy to God,	Mos	3:19
and putteth off the natural m.		3:19
every m. according to his works,		3:24
is the m. who receiveth salvation,		4: 7
whereby m. can be saved except		4: 8
that m. doth not comprehend all		4: 9
render to every m. according to		4:13
The m. has brought upon himself		4:17
But I say unto you, O m.,		4:18
the m. who putteth up his petition		4:22
I say unto you, wo be unto that m.,		4:23
every m. according to that which		4:26
that a m. should run faster than		4:27
O m., remember, and perish not.		4:30
For how knoweth a m. the		5:13
doth a m. take an ass which		5:14
being a strong and mighty m.,		7: 3
yea, a chosen m. of God, who		7:26
take upon him the image of m.,		7:27
image after which m. was created		7:27
m. was created after the image of		7:27
a m. that can translate the		8:13
no m. can look in them except he		8:13
the m. that is commanded to do		8:14
which is greater can no m. have,		8:16
power of God, which no m. can;		8:16
a m. may have great power given		8:16
m., through faith, might work		8:18
austere and a blood-thirsty m.		9: 2
every m. according to his age.		10: 9
a m. among them whose name		11:20
we have brought a m. before thee		12: 9
of God or judged of this m.?		12:13
this m. has lied concerning you,		12:14
Behold, here is the m.,		12:16
nor thy daughter, thy m.-servant,		13:18
neighbor's wife, nor his m.-servant,		13:24
could not any m. be saved except		13:32
and take upon him the form of m.,		13:34
a m. of sorrows, and acquainted		14: 3
and he was a young m.,		17: 2
a m. among them whose name		19: 4
and he being a strong m.		19: 4
he himself being a just m.		19:17
that every m. should impart to		21:17
one m. shall not think himself		23: 7
ye trust no m. to be a king		23:13
except he be a m. of God,		23:14
every m. should love his neighbor		23:15
that every m. should esteem his		27: 4
very wicked and an idolatrous m.		27: 8
And he was a m. of many words,		27: 8
that a m. should be judged of God		29:12
be judged of God than of m.,		29:12
of m. are not always just.		29:12
and every m. may enjoy his rights		29:32
that every m. might bear his part.		29:34
that every m. should have an		29:38
every m. expressed a willingness		29:38
him more than any other m.;		29:40
was a m. brought before him	Al	1: 2
a m. who was large, and was noted		1: 2
he met a m. who belonged to the		1: 7
but the m. withstood him,		1: 7
the name of the m. was Gideon;		1: 8
the m. who slew him was taken by		1:10
shed the blood of a righteous m.,		1:13
a m. who has done much good		1:13
power on any m. for his belief.		1:17
any m., belonging to the church,		1:21
labor, every m. according to his		1:26
every m. according to that		1:27
every m. suffering according to		1:33
a certain m., being called Amlici,		2: 1
he being a very cunning m.,		2: 1
a wise m. as to the wisdom of		2: 1
order of the m. that slew Gideon		2: 1
he, being a wicked m., would		2: 4
every m. according to his mind,		2: 5
that Alma, being a m. of God,		2:30
so doth every m. that is cursed		3:19
every m. receiveth wages of him		3:27

MAN 587 MAN

And he selected a wise m. who	Al 4:16	was appointed unto m. to die—	Al	42: 6
there can no m. be saved except	5:21	and m. became lost forever,		42: 6
if a m. bringeth forth good	5:41	yea, they became fallen m.		42: 6
yea, the sins of every m. who	5:48	that m. should be reclaimed		42: 8
being called after the m. who	6: 7	m. had brought upon himself		42:12
hungered, and he said to a m.:	8:19	how could a m. repent except		42:17
And the m. said unto him:	8:20	remorse of conscience unto m.		42:18
thou art the m. whom an angel	8:20	if a m. murdered he should		42:19
the m. received him into his	8:21	a m. by the name of Zerahemnah		43: 5
and the m. was called Amulek;	8:21	the m. who had been appointed		43:16
that any m. could slay them;	8:31	by a m. whose name was Lehi,		43:35
believe the testimony of one m.,	9: 2	a m. fell among the Nephites,		43:38
no more authority than one m.	9: 6	know, that he was a righteous m.;		45:19
also a m. of no small reputation	10: 4	was a large and a strong m.;		46: 3
a holy m., who is a chosen man	10: 7	one very wicked m. can cause		46: 9
who is a chosen m. of God;	10: 7	he was a m. of cunning device		46:10
I found the m. whom the angel	10: 8	a m. of many flattering words,		46:10
and behold it was this same m.	10: 8	Moroni being a m. who was		46:34
said unto me he is a holy m.;	10: 9	a very subtle m. to do evil		47: 4
I know he is a holy m. because it	10: 9	had appointed a m. to be a king		47: 6
This m. doth revile against our	10:24	was a strong and amighty m.;		48:11
this m. is a child of the devil,	10:28	a m. of a perfect understanding;		48:11
that every m. who was judge of	11: 1	a m. that did not delight in		48:11
Now if a m. owed another,	11: 2	a m. whose soul did joy in the		48:11
that the m. should be brought	11: 2	a m. whose heart did swell with		48:12
he judged the m. according to	11: 2	a m. who did labor exceedingly		48:12
thus the m. was compelled to pay	11: 2	a m. who was firm in the faith		48:13
Now Zeezrom was a m. who was	11:21	he was a m. like unto Ammon,		48:18
every m. that believeth on his	12:15	built up to the height of a m.,		50: 2
that m. should rise from the dead	12:20	a m. whose name was Morianton,		50:28
there was a space granted unto m.	12:24	being a m. of much passion,		50:30
these things should come unto m.,	12:28	a m. whose name was Teancum,		50:35
expedient that m. should know	12:28	every m. of Teancum did exceed		51:31
our God, have mercy on this m.,	15:10	Lehi was a m. who had been		53: 2
forth among them, every m. alone,	17:17	he was a m. like unto Moroni,		53: 2
every m. that lifted his club to	17:37	deliver up a m. and his wife		54:11
Surely, this is more than a m.	18: 2	a m. who was a descendant of		55: 4
he be the Great Spirit or a m.,	18: 3	a m. who had fought valiantly		62:37
that a m. has such great power,	18: 3	And he was a just m., and he did		63: 2
Where is this m. that has such	18: 8	being an exceedingly curious m.,		63: 5
has been so faithful as this m.;	18:10	this m. built other ships.		63: 7
I am a m., and am thy servant;	18:17	that no m. could overtake him.	He	1:10
I am a m.; and man in the	18:34	tell no m. that Kishkimen had		1:11
m. in the beginning was created	18:34	a m. whose name was Coriantumr;		1:15
things concerning the fall of m.,	18:36	he was a large and a mighty m.		1:15
that the m. had fallen dead,	19:24	Coriantumr, being a mighty m.,		1:16
thy son, he being an innocent m.,	20:18	and behold the m. of Christ in a		3:29
And the m. said unto him:	21: 8	their strength, even m. for man.		4:26
created m. after his own image,	22:12	their strength, even man for m.		4:26
of transgression, m. had fallen.	22:12	a m. whose name was Cezoram.		5: 1
laying the fall of m. before him,	22:13	means whereby m. can be saved,		5: 9
And since m. had fallen he could	22:14	which cannot be uttered by m.;		5:33
there was not a wicked m. slain	24:27	this m. did cry unto the		5:37
what natural m. is ther that	26:21	And they said unto the m.:		5:38
how great the inequality of m. is	28:13	the beginning of m. even down to		6:29
But behold, I am a m., and do	29: 3	Why do ye not seize upon this m.		8: 1
there came a m. into the land of	30: 6	Why seest thou this m., and		8: 2
if a m. desired to serve God,	30: 9	suffer this m. to revile against us?		8: 5
a m. was punished only for the	30:11	Let this m. alone, for he is a		8: 7
For no m. can know of anything	30:13	alone, for he is a good m.,		8: 7
but every m. fared in this life	30:17	God gave power unto one m.,		8:11
every m. prospered according	30:17	gave unto this m. such power,		8:12
every m. conquered according	30:17	were spoken by this m., Moses,		8:13
whatsoever a m. did was no crime.	30:17	whether this m. be a prophet		9: 2
when a m. was dead, that was the	30:18	Now, as for the murder of this m.,		9:15
this m. went over to the land of	30:19	raise himself to be a great m.,		9:16
a m. whose name was Zoram—	30:59	behold, we will detect this m.,		9:17
every m. did go forth and offer	31:20	who is this m. that hath done this		9:20
they did offer up, every m., the	31:22	say that I have agreed with a m.		9:23
for a m. sometimes, if he is	32:13	say that I have agreed with a m.		9:24
for if a m. knoweth a thing he	32:18	ye know that I am an honest m.,		9:36
every m. according to his work.	32:20	know that thou art a m. of God,		11: 8
yea, not a sacrifice of m.,	34:10	a great prophet, and a m. of God,		11:18
is not any m. that can sacrifice	34:11	it appeareth unto m. that the sun		12:15
if a m. murdereth, behold will	34:11	if a m. hide up a treasure in		12:18
being a very wicked m., sent over	35: 8	that no m. shall find thee from		12:19
there cannot any m. work after	37:39	no m. getteth it hence forth and		12:19
or means whereby m. can be saved,	38: 9	if the Lord shall say unto a m.—		12:20
which are appointed unto m.	40:10	save he be a righteous m. and		13:18
the soul of m. should be restored	41: 2	if a m. shall come among you		13:19
he drew out the m., and he placed	42: 2	if a m. shall come among you		13:27
that the m. had become as God,	42: 3	appear unto m. as if it was day.		14: 3
a time granted unto m. to repent,	42: 4	whither he went, no m. knoweth;	3Ne	1: 3

MAN 588 MAN

the governor, was a just m.,	3Ne	3:12	every m. kept the hilt of his	Eth	14: 2
even as this m. hath been felled		4:29	Lib was a m. of great stature,		14:10
every m., with his family, his		6: 1	more than any other m. among		14:10
any m. should be put to death		6:24	a man who is drunken with wine;		15:22
every m. according to his family		7: 2	a m. being evil cannot do that	Mro	7: 6
no m. among them save he had		7: 4	if a m. being evil giveth a gift,		7: 8
a m. whom they did call Jacob;		7: 9	is it counted evil unto a m.,		7: 9
every m. according to his family,		7:14	a m. being evil cannot do that		7:10
just m. who did keep the record—		8: 1	a m. being a servant of the devil		7:11
any m. who could do a miracle in		8: 1	of Christ is given to every m.,		7:16
no mistake made by this m.		8: 2	persuadeth no m. to do good,		7:17
they went no m. knoweth,		8:16	be one m. upon the face thereof		7:36
they saw a M. descending out		11: 8	For no m. can be saved,		7:38
if any m. will sue thee at the		12:40	and awful is the state of m.,		7:38
No m. can serve two masters;		13:24	if a m. have faith he must		7:42
Or what m. is there of you,		14: 9	if a m. be meek and lowly in		7:44
I will liken him unto a wase m.,		14:24	I fear not what m. can do;		8:16
be likened unto a foolish m.,		14:26	I am but a m., and I have but		9:18
can there be written by any m.,		17:17	I have but the strength of a m.,		9:18
and hear, every m. for himself;		17:25	come unto every m. severally,		10:17
ye shall not forbid any m.		18:22	which were written by this m.,		10:27
that a m. is unworthy to eat		18:29	to recompense unto every m.	DC	1:10
every m. did take his wife and		19: 1	measure to every m. according		1:10
neither can be written by m.		19:32	has measured to his fellow m.		1:10
can they be uttered by m.		19:34	every m. walketh in his own way,		1:16
as a m. gathereth his sheaves		20:18	m. should not counsel his		1:19
so marred, more than any m.,		20:44	not counsel his fellow m.,		1:19
although a m. shall declare it		21: 9	every m. might speak in the		1:20
Will a m. rob God?		24: 8	shall not always strive with m.,		1:33
as a m. spareth his own son		24:17	although a m. may have many		3: 4
and raised a m. from the dead,		26:15	have feared m. more than God.		3: 7
should not any m. write them.		26:16	into the hands of a wicked m.		3:12
every m. dealing justly, one with		26:19	m. that desires the witness.—		5:23
be called in the name of a m.		27: 8	the power of God and not of m.		5:25
then it be the church of a m.;		27: 8	things which no m. knoweth		6:24
wherein no m. can work.		27:33	into the hands of a wicked m.,		10: 1
we have lived unto the age of m.,		28: 2	even the m. in whom you have		10: 6
unto whatsoever m. it seemeth		28:30	I said that he is a wicked m.,		10: 7
every m. did deal justly one	4Ne	1: 2	they may catch a m. in a lie,		10:25
no m. could keep that which	Mrm	2:10	that which no m. knoweth save		15: 3
to behold the ways of m.		2:18	that which no m. knoweth save		16: 3
or for m. to write a perfect		4:11	given whereby m. can be saved;		18:23
m. must be raised to stand		7: 6	are not of men nor of m.,		18:34
face of the land no m. knoweth.		8:10	they are of men and not of m.;		18:34
faults they be the faults of a m.		8:17	judging every m. according to		19: 3
m. shall not smite, neither shall		8:20	every m. must repent or suffer,		19: 4
by Adam came the fall of m.		9:12	And that he created m.,		20:18
because of the fall of m. came		9:12	m. became sensual and devilish,		20:20
came the redemption of m.		9:12	and became fallen m.		20:20
because of the redemption of m.,		9:13	that m. may fall from grace		20:32
m. was created of the dust of		9:17	although a m. should be		22: 2
being a large and mighty m.,	Eth	1:34	no m. knoweth where the city		28: 9
a m. highly favored of the Lord,		1:34	neither any m. nor the children		29:34
where there never had m. been.		2: 5	appoint unto m. the days of		29:43
will not always strive with m.;		2:15	that you have feared m. and		30: 1
thou wilt for the benefit of m.;		3: 4	not fearing what m. can do,		30:11
and it was as the finger of a m.,		3: 6	words are not of m. nor of men,		31:13
never has m. come before me with		3: 9	every m. which will embrace it		36: 7
have I showed myself unto m.		3:15	let every m. choose for himself		37: 4
never has m. believed in me		3:15	every m. esteem his brother as		38:24
m. have I created after the		3:16	every m. esteem his brother as		38:25
showed himself unto this m.		3:17	For what m. among you having		38:26
that this m. might know that		3:18	every m., both elder, priest,		38:40
of the knowledge of this m.		3:19	voice, every m. to his neighbor,		38:41
and heard, and show it to no m.		3:21	or the hour no m. knoweth;		39:21
constrain no m. to be their king.		6:25	every m. shall be made		42:32
mighty as to the strength of a m.;		7: 8	that every m. who has need		42:33
will that m. should shed blood,		8:19	And if any m. or woman shall		42:80
from the beginning of m.		8:19	if a m. or woman shall rob		42:84
caused m. to commit murder		8:25	if I, who am a m., do lift up my		43:21
were useful for the food of m.		9:18	end no m. knoweth on earth,		43:33
all of which were useful unto m.,		9:19	according to the laws of m.;		44: 4
arose a mighty m. among them		11:15	of the coming of the Son of M.		45:39
there arose another mighty m.;		11:17	every m. that will not take		45:68
unto the overpowering of m.		12:24	to every m. is given a gift by		46:11
hast prepared a house for m.,		12:32	to every m. to profit withal.		46:16
in which m. might have a more		12:32	every m. according to his family,		48: 6
wherefore m. must hope,		12:32	have done unto the Son of M.		49: 6
even as a m. telleth another in		12:39	and the day no m. knoweth,		49: 7
from the beginning of m.;		13: 2	is ordained of God unto m.		49:15
every m. with his band fighting		13:25	filled with the measure of m.,		49:17
if a m. should lay his tool or		14: 1	m. should not eat the same,		49:18
every m. did cleave unto that		14: 2	ordained for the use of m.		49:19

that one m. should possess	DC 49:20
wo be unto m. that sheddeth	49:21
the Son of M. cometh not in	49:22
neither of a m. traveling on	49:22
to and fro as a drunken m.,	49:23
let every m. beware lest he do	50: 9
as a m. reasoneth one with	50:11
when a m. reasoneth he is	50:12
he is understood of m.,	50:12
because he reasoneth as a m.;	50:12
no m. is possessor of all things	50:28
let no m. hinder them doing	50:38
every m. equal according to	51: 3
shall appoint a m. his portion,	51: 4
let every m. deal honestly,	51: 9
and one m. shall not build upon	52:33
he shall reward every m.,	56:19
Let no m. think he is ruler;	58:20
Let no m. break the laws of	58:21
Who an I that made m.,	58:30
this is a law unto every m.	58:36
if a m. repenteth of his sins—	58:43
let no m. return from this land	58:59
behold the Son of M. cometh.	58:65
benefit and the use of m.,	59:18
all these things unto m.;	59:20
in nothing doth m. offend God,	59:21
because of the fear of m.	60: 2
the coming of the Son of M.,	61:38
knoweth the weakness of m.	62: 1
without faith no m. pleaseth	63:11
fear shall come upon every m.;	63:33
And that every m. should take	63:37
to him to die at the age of m.	63:50
the coming of the Son of M.	63:53
the coming of the Son of M.,	64:23
committed unto m. on the earth,	65: 2
the Son of M. shall come down	65: 5
For no m. has seen God at	67:11
can any natural m. abide the	67:12
the coming of the Son of M.;	68:11
No m. has a legal right to	68:18
every m. in his stewardship,	70: 9
hereafter appoint unto any m.	70: 9
if any m. lift his voice against	71:10
the m. who shall be appointed	72: 8
every m. that cometh up to	72:15
rendereth every m. acceptable,	72:17
that every man who is obliged to	75:28
Let every m. be diligent in	75:29
entered into the heart of m.	76:10
the voice of the Son of M.,	76:16
nor their torment, no m. knows;	76:45
will be revealed unto m.,	76:46
neither any m. except those	76:48
let no m. glory in man,	76:61
let no man glory in m.,	76:61
no m. knows it except him	76:90
every m. shall receive according	76:111
not lawful for m. to utter;	76:115
Neither is m. capable to make	76:116
of God, the happiness of m.,	77: 2
the spirit of m. in the likeness	77: 2
formed m. out of the dust of	77:12
complete the salvation of m.,	77:12
to the salvation of m.,	78: 4
appoint every m. his portion.	78:21
every m. according to his wants	82:17
every m. may improve upon	82:18
every m. may gain other talents,	82:18
Every m. seeking the interest	82:19
Adam, who was the first m.—	84:16
no m. can see the face of God,	84:22
Spirit giveth light to every m.	84:46
the spirit enlighteneth every m.	84:46
if any m. shall administer	84:71
And any m. that shall go	84:80
shall be meted unto every m.	84:85
let no m. among you,	84:86
return not again unto that m.	84:92
that every m. who goes forth	84:103
if any m. shall give unto any	84:105
And if any m. among you	84:106
let every m. stand in his own	DC 84:109
While that m., who was called	85: 8
the body are the soul of m.	88:15
For what doth it profit a m.	88:33
with God, but not with m.	88:44
any m. who hath seen any or	88:47
unto a m. having a field,	88:51
their Lord, every m. in his hour,	88:58
Every m. in his own order,	88:60
every m. who hath been warned	88:81
to and fro as a drunken m.;	88:87
strong, no m. can loose them;	88:94
every m. may have an equal	88:122
as any m. drinketh wine or	89: 5
belly, and is not good for m.,	89: 8
nature, and use of m.—	89:10
ordained for the use of m.	89:12
is ordained for the use of m.	89:14
not only for m. but for the	89:14
hath God made for the use of m.	89:15
is good for the food of m.;	89:16
Nevertheless, wheat for m.,	89:17
every m. shall hear the fulness	90:11
a m. who has got riches in	90:22
a m. of God, and of strong	90:22
light that lighteth every m.	93: 2
And no m. receiveth a fulness	93:27
M. was also in the beginning	93:29
here is the agency of m.,	93:31
is the condemnation of m.;	93:31
every m. whose spirit receiveth	93:32
For m. is spirit.	93:33
m. cannot receive a fulness of	93:34
m. is the tabernacle of God,	93:35
Every spirit of m. was innocent	93:38
redeemed m. from the fall,	93:38
of laws of God and m.,	93:53
as pertaining to law of m.,	98: 7
both of m., or of the beasts	101:24
in that day the enmity of m.,	101:26
whatsoever any m. shall ask,	101:27
have power to tempt any m.	101:28
hidden things which no m. knew,	101:33
reward every m. according	101:65
every m. may act in doctrine	101:78
every m. may be accountable	101:78
any m. should be in bondage	101:79
not God, neither regarded m.	101:82
I fear not God, nor regard m.,	101:84
every m. is to speak according	102:16
raise up unto my people a m.,	103:16
is the m. to whom I likened	103:21
Let no m. be afraid to lay	103:27
inasmuch as any m. belonging	104: 5
that if any m. among you,	104:10
every m. his stewardship;	104:11
every m. may give an account	104:12
make every m. accountable,	104:13
if any m. shall take of the	104:18
no m. among you shall call it	104:62
if any m. among you obtain	104:69
that any m. among you say	104:72
No m. has a legal right to this	107:16
he (Seth) was a perfect m.,	107:43
now let every m. learn his duty,	107:99
that the Son of M. might have a	109: 5
art the m. whom I have chosen	112:16
recompense every m. according as	112:34
let no m. despise my servant	117:15
a time appointed for every m.,	121:25
when every m. shall enter into	121:32
As well might m. stretch forth his	121:33
or the authority of that m.	121:37
The Son of M. hath descended	122: 8
fear not what m. can do,	122: 9
no m. count them as small things;	123:15
Let no m. desprise my servant	124:21
be a delightful habitation for m.,	124:60
from any one m. for stock in	124:64
dollars stock from any one m.	124:65
share of stock from any one m.	124:66
be permitted to receive any m.,	124:67
neither can any other m.,	124:72

MAN 590 MANCHESTER

Let no m. go from this place who	DC 124:85
no m. pay stock to the quorum	124:119
let every m. who pays stock bear	124:122
his priesthood no m. taketh from	124:130
no m. taketh his priesthood,	124:132
as the envy and wrath of m. have	127: 2
to any m. by actual revelation,	128: 9
The first m. is of the earth, earthy;	128:14
second m. is the Lord from heaven.	128:14
spirit of a just m. made perfect	129: 6
of heaven for a just m. to deceive;	129: 7
that he is a m. like ourselves.	130: 1
which no m. knoweth save he	130:11
to the coming of the Son of M.	130:12
of the coming of the Son of M.,	130:14
see the face of the Son of M.;	130:15
the coming of the Son of M. will	130:17
m. may receive the Holy Ghost,	130:23
a m. must enter into this order of	131: 2
impossible for a m. to be saved in	131: 6
no m. shall come unto the Father	132:12
m. marry him a wife in the world,	132:15
if a m. marry a wife, and make a	132:18
if a m. marry a wife by my word,	132:19
if a m. marry a wife according	132:26
m. receiveth a wife in the new and	132:41
and if she by with another m.,	132:41
and she be with another m.,	132:42
if a m. be called of my Father,	132:59
if any m. espouse a virgin,	132:61
and have vowed to no other m.,	132:61
another m., she has committed	132:63
if any m. have a wife,	132:64
let every m. call upon the name	133: 6
and hath committed it unto m.,	133:36
no m. among you received me,	133:66
of God for the benefit of m.;	134: 1
every m. should be honored in his	134: 6
between m. and man;	134: 6
between m. and m.;	134: 6
to be answered by m. to his Maker.	134: 6
exclaiming: *I am a dead m.!*	135: 1
than any other m. that ever lived	135: 3
Let every m. use all his influence	136:10
m. shall seek to build up himself,	136:19
only m. on the earth at the	OD
no m. can behold all my works,	Mses 1: 5
no m. can behold all my glory,	1: 5
natural strength like unto m.;	1:10
cause I know that m. is nothing,	1:10
Moses, son of m., worship me.	1:12
look upon thee in the natural m.	1:14
first m. of all men have I called	1:34
innumerable are they unto m.;	1:35
cannot be numbered unto m.;	1:37
immortality and eternal life of m.	1:39
Let us make m. in our image,	2:26
created m. in mine own image,	2:27
said unto m.: Behold, I have	2:29
not yet a m. to till the ground;	3: 5
m. from the dust of the ground,	3: 7
and m. became a living soul,	3: 7
upon the earth, the first m. also;	3: 7
I put the m. whom I had formed.	3: 8
is pleasant to the sight of m.;	3: 9
of man; and m. could behold it.	3: 9
which I prepared for the use of m.;	3: 9
m. saw that it was good for food.	3: 9
took the m., and put him into	3:15
God, commanded the m. saying:	3:16
that the m. should be along;	3:18
taken from m., made I a woman,	3:22
and brought her unto the m.	3:22
because she was taken out of m.	3:23
a m. leave his father and his	3:24
both naked, the m. and his wife,	3:25
to destroy the agency of m.	4: 3
m. said: The woman thou gavest	4:18
the m. is become as one of us to	4:28
So I drove out the m., and I	4:31
See thou show them unto no m.,	4:32
have gotten a m. from the Lord;	5:16
have slain a m. to my wounding,	5:47

and a young m. to my hurt.	Mses 5:47
they knew every m. his brother.	5:51
In the day that God created m.,	6: 8
and no m. shall pierce thee.	6:32
a wild m. hath come among us.	6:38
no m. laid hands on him; for fear	6:39
And there came a m. unto him,	6:40
M. of Holiness is his name,	6:57
Only Begotten is the Son of M.,	6:57
became quickened in the inner m.	6:65
as a m. talketh one with another,	7: 4
the Father, and of the Son of M.;	7:24
were it possible that m. could	7:30
Eden, gave I unto m. his agency;	7:32
M. of Holiness is my name;	7:35
M. of Counsel is my name;	7:35
of the coming of the Son of M.,	7:47
When the Son of M. cometh in	7:54
beheld the Son of M. lifted up on	7:55
at the right hand of the Son of M.,	7:56
Enoch beheld the Son of M. ascend	7:59
of the coming of the Son of M.,	7:65
shall not always strive with m.,	8:17
every m. was lifted up in the	8:22
that the Lord had made m. on	8:25
I will destroy m. whom I have	8:26
of the earth, both m. and beast,	8:26
for Noah was a just m., and	8:27
on the first m., who is Adam,	Abr 1: 3
Pharaoh, being a righteous m.,	1:26
as one m. talketh with another;	3:11
answered like unto the Son of M.:	3:27
Let us go down and form m. in	4:26
Gods went down to organize m. in	4:27
had not formed a m. to till the	5: 5
Gods formed m. from the dust	5: 7
life, and m. became a living soul.	5: 7
Eden, and there they put the m.,	5: 8
the Gods took the m. and put	5:11
And the Gods commanded the m.,	5:12
make an help meet for the m.,	5:14
not good that the m. should be	5:14
the Gods had taken from m.,	5:16
and brought her unto the m.	5:16
because she was taken out of m.;	5:17
shall a m. leave his father and	5:18
both naked, the m. and his wife,	5:19
heed that no m. deceive you;	JS 1: 5
if any m. shall say unto you,	1:21
the coming of the Son of M. be.	1:26
of the Son of M. in heaven,	1:36
see the Son of M. coming in	1:36
for the Son of M. shall come,	1:37
the coming of the Son of M.;	1:41
the coming of the Son of M. be.	1:43
if the good m. of the house had	1:47
think not, the Son of M. cometh.	1:48
more power to the heart of m.	2:12
a m. who lacked wisdom might	2:26
how the young m. found out	2:64
a m. must be called of God,	AoF 5

MANAGE

and m. the affairs of this war.	Al 60: 1
to m. them and the concerns	DC 70: 5
To m. the affairs of the poor,	82:12

MANAGEMENT

to the m. of the creature;	Al 30:17
altered the m. of affairs	49:11
the sole m. of the government,	He 6:39

MANAGING

benefit of m. the concerns of	DC 82:17

MANASSEH

M., Ephraim; and Ephraim,	2Ne 19:21
Ephraim, M.; they together shall	19:21
who was a descendant of M., who	Al 10: 3

MANCHESTER

in Colesville, Fayette, and M.,	DC 24: 3
moved with his family into M.	JS 2: 3

MANCHESTER   591   MANKIND

year after our removal to M.,	JS	2: 5
Convenient to the village of M.,		2:51
under the necessity of leaving M.,		2:61

MANFULLY
they shall fight m. for me;	DC	35:14

MANGLED
were m. by dogs and wild beasts	Al	16:10

MANIFEST
and should make himself m.,	1 Ne	10:11
that he should m. himself unto		10:17
I will m. myself unto thy seed,		13:35
shall m. himself unto all nations,		13:42
shall m. himself unto the Gentiles		13:42
he shall m. himself unto them		14: 1
they were m. unto the prophet		22: 2
should be made m. unto them	2Ne	3: 5
should m. himself unto them		6: 9
and after he should m. himself		6: 9
he will m. himself unto them in		6:14
shall m. himself unto them in the		25:12
it shall be made m. in the light;		30:17
until after he shall m. himself		32: 6
and when he shall m. himself		32: 6
had been made m. unto us	Jac	1: 5
it has been made m. unto me,		7:12
also has been made m. unto me		7:12
shall m. himself in the flesh;	En	1: 8
m. unto the children of men,	Jar	1: 4
shall secret things be made m.,	Mos	8:17
will make himself m. unto all.		27:30
m. unto me by his Holy Spirit;	Al	5:46
make these things m. unto me;		10:10
did m. unto the people that I		36:23
be made m. unto this people;		37:21
be made m. unto this people;		37:21
Christ shall m. himself unto them,		45:10
he did m. himself unto them,	He	8:23
did truly m. unto the people	3Ne	7:22
truly m. himself unto them—		10:18
not m. myself unto them save		15:23
the greater things be made m.		26: 9
he hath made it m. unto me		28:37
to m. unto the world the things	Mrm	3:16
doth the Spirit m. unto me;		3:20
that he hath made m. unto you		9:31
that they should be made m.	Eth	4: 2
were greater things made m.		4: 4
m. unto the brother of Jared.		4: 4
then will I m. unto them		4: 7
it shall be made m. unto you		4:14
shall be made m. in very deed.		4:16
thus didst thou m. thyself unto		12:31
make m. concerning the coming	Mro	7:22
m. things unto the children of		7:24
m. the word of God unto me;		8: 9
m. the truth of it unto you,		10: 4
truly m. by their works that	DC	20:37
shall m. before the church,		20:69
I m. unto you, Joseph Knight,		23: 6
m. in the eyes of all people.		35: 7
their folly shall be made m.,		63:15
their shame shall be made m.		71: 7
the power of godliness is m.		84:20
power of godliness is not m.		84:21
to quake while it maketh m.,		85: 6
works of him were plainly m.		93: 5
from the beginning is plainly m.		93:31
they can m. it, and the case		102:20
it is m. before the council of		104:74
shall be m. unto my servant,		105:36
a place to m. himself to his		109: 5
I will m. myself to my people		110: 7
they shall be m.		121:28
they are truly m. from heaven—		123:13
m. unto him the truth of all		124:97
all things for their glory are m.,		130: 7
be m. to those who dwell on it;		130: 9
and his folly shall be made m.		136:19
ye may have all things made m.;	Mses	8:24

MANIFESTATION
by the m. of the Spirit of God.	Al	5:47
m. of the Spirit which is in me.		7:17
with the m. of my Spirit;	DC	5:16
spoken by the m. of my Spirit.		8: 1
for a m. of my blessings upon		70:15
the power and m. of the Spirit,		76:118
and also for a m. to me,	JS	2:29
in obtaining a divine m.,		2:29

MANIFESTATIONS
and the m. of his Spirit,	Mos	5: 3
according to the m. of the Spirit	Mrm	3:16
with the m. of my Spirit,	Eth	4:11
the m. of the Spirit of God	Mro	10: 8
the m. of my blessings upon	DC	21: 8
m. of the Spirit may be given to		46:16
through the m. of the Spirit.		70:13
m. of the Spirit shall be withheld.		70:14

MANIFESTED
m. plainly of the ocming of a	1 Ne	1:19
m. unto me by his Holy Spirit.		2:17
after he has m. himself unto the		13:42
the Messiah shall be m. in body		15:13
and hath m. himself unto his	2Ne	25:14
these things are m. unto us	Jac	4:13
any time m. myself unto them.	3Ne	16: 2
shall be m. unto the Gentiles,		16: 4
hath been m. by the things	Eth	2:12
I have m. unto you, by my Spirit	DC	18: 2
it was truly m. unto this		20: 5
that if you behold a spirit m.		50:31
shall be m. by the Comforter,		90:14
be m. unto my servant Joseph,		115:18
m. by the respective clergy,	JS	2: 6
which had already m. itself		2:74

MANIFESTETH
And that he m. himself unto all	2Ne	26:13
before that he m. himself in the flesh.	Jac	4:11
Holy Ghost, which m. all things	DC	18:18
m. that Jesus was crucified by		21: 9
for the Spirit m. truth;		91: 4

MANIFESTING
m. himself unto all nations—	T Pg	
m. boldly concerning your	2Ne	1:26

MANIFESTO
to issue the M. which has	DC	OD

MANKIND
all m. were in a lost and in a	1 Ne	10: 6
he sought also the misery of all m.	2Ne	2:18
which is infinite for all m.—		25:16
all m. must be lost.	Jac	7:12
for all m., which ever were since	Mos	4: 7
all m. must have perished.		15:19
of all m. becoming carnal,		16: 3
Thus all m. were lost;		16: 4
Marvel not that all m., yea,		27:25
that all m. should be saved	Al	1: 4
all m. became a lost and fallen		12:22
see that death comes upon m.,		12:24
and he shall redeem all m. who		19:13
to redeem m. from their sins?		21: 7
could be no redemption for m.		21: 9
we were the most lost of all m.)		24:11
all m. must unavoicably perish;		34: 9
fall had brought upon all m.		42: 9
that m. should be reclaimed		42: 9
we see that all m. were fallen,		42:14
and redeemeth all m. from the	He	14:16
for all m., by the fall of Adam		14:16
of Christ redeemeth m., yea,		14:17
mankind, yea, even all m.,		14:17
In me shall all m. have light,	Eth	3:14
privileges, belongs to all m.,	DC	98: 5
thy son, and I will redeem all m.,	Mses	4: 1
and all m., even as many as will.		5: 9
all m. may be saved, by obedience	AoF	3

MANNA 592 MANNER

MANNA
know that they were fed with m.	1Ne	17:28
and fed them with m. that they	Mos	7:19

MANNER
after this m. was the language	1Ne	1:15
silver, and all m. of riches.		3:16
after this m. of language		3:21
after this m. of language		5: 3
after this m. of language		5: 6
after this m. of language		5: 8
gathered together all m. of seeds		8: 1
their m. of dress was exceeding		8:27
after this m. of language		10:15
after the m. of the flesh.		11:18
afflicted with all m. of diseases,		11:31
after the m. of wars and		12: 3
and all m. of tumultuous noises;		12: 4
and all m. of abominations,		12:23
and all m. of precious clothing;		13: 7
after this m. did my brother		16:38
after the m. which I shall show thee,		17: 8
after the m. which thou hast		17: 9
after this m. of language		17:22
after what m. I should work		18: 1
after the m. which was learned		18: 2
the ship after the m. of men;		18: 2
after the m. which the Lord had		18: 2
it was not after the m. of men.		18: 2
and all m. of wild animals,		18:25
And we did find all m. of ore,		18:25
after this m. has the prophet		19:24
and to do all m. of iniquity;		22:23
after this m. did my father of old	2Ne	3:22
after the m. of it did make many		5:14
and to work in all m. of wood,		5:15
after the m. of the temple of		5:16
the m. of the construction was like		5:16
lived after the m. of happiness.		5:27
after the m. of his holy order,		6: 2
dwell therein shall die in like m.		8: 6
and all m. of secret works of		9: 9
shall the lambs feed after their m.,		15:17
after the m. of Egypt.		20:24
lift it up after the m. of Egypt.		20:26
the m. of prophesying among the		25: 1
concerning the m. of the Jews;		25: 2
after the m. of the things of the		25: 5
after the m. of the Jews;		25: 6
and all m. of destructions—		26: 6
and all m. of abominations—		27: 1
which shall teach after this m.,		28: 9
for after this m. doth the Lord		31: 3
and for all m. of precious ores,	Jac	2:12
after this m. did Sherem contend		7: 7
and raise all m. of grain,	En	1:21
and flocks of all m. of cattle		1:21
And after this m. do I write		1:23
making all m. of tools	Jar	1: 8
after this m. did they teach		1:11
after the m. of wars,		1:13
after this m. we keep the records,	Om	1: 9
subject to all m. of infirmities	Mos	2:11
nor any m. of riches of you;		2:12
commit any m. of wickedness,		2:13
and curing all m. of diseases.		3: 5
yea, even with all m. of seeds,		9: 9
and with seeds of all m. of fruits;		9: 9
and with all m. of weapons		9:16
and raise all m. of grain,		10: 4
and all m. of fruit of every kind.		10: 4
and work all m. of fine linen,		10: 5
and all m. of wickedness.		11: 2
and of all m. of precious things,		11: 8
should work all m. of fine work		11:10
be afflicted with all m. of diseases		17:16
after this m. he did baptize every		18:16
and suffered in the like m.;		21:12
delighting in all m. of wickedness		24: 7
after the m. he did his brethren		25:18
suffering all m. of afflictions,		26:38
after the m. of his iniquities		27: 8
seer, after the m. of old times.		28:16
nor any m. of iniquity;	Mos	29:14
the m. of his own wickedness;		29:23
whoredoms and all m. of iniquities		29:36
delivered from all m. of bondage;		29:40
after the m. of his preaching.	Al	1: 6
afflict them with all m. of words,		1:20
and all m. of good homely cloth.		1:29
and all m. of wickedness;		1:32
with all m. of weapons of war,		2:12
with all m. of weapons of war		2:14
after the m. of the Lamanites;		3: 4
and all m. of precious things,		4: 6
and suffering all m. of afflictions,		4:13
with blood and all m. of filthiness?		5:22
guilty of all m. of wickedness?		5:23
I am called to speak after this m.,		5:44
all m. of diseases of every kind;		9:22
they are rich in all m. of things—		9:22
reckon after the m. of the Jews		11: 4
after the m. of the Jews?		11: 4
and all m. of disturbances and		11:20
in a m. that thereby the people		13: 2
know in what m. to look forward		13: 2
And this is the m. after which		13: 3
they were ordained after this m.—		13: 8
ordinances were given after this m.,		13:16
were full of all m. of wickedness;		13:17
all m. of such things did they say		14:22
built after the m. of the Jews.		16:13
and all m. of lasciviousness,		16:18
after the m. of the Lamanites,		18:43
with all m. of wild animals		22:31
commit any m. of wickedness.		23: 3
to death, in the like m. as he was,		25:12
have suffered all m. of afflictions,		26:30
aggravating and distressing m.		27:29
and after this m. did he preach,		30:12
he did go on in the same m. as		30:30
iniquity after the m. of Korihor.		30:58
after a m. which Alma and his		31:12
offered up thanks after this m.,		31:23
to offer up thanks after their m.		31:23
and upon all m. of fine goods.		31:24
should suffer no m. of afflictions,		31:38
even until ye believe in a m. that		32:27
in what m. they should begin		33: 1
beast, neither of any m. of fowl;		34:10
ye bear with all m. of afflictions;		34:40
yea, and in all m. of afflictions;		36:27
after the m. of so curious a		37:39
which is spoken of in this m.,		40:17
and all m. of weapons of war.		43:18
and all m. of iniquities;		45:12
and all m. of lasciviousness;		47:36
in a m. which never had been		49: 8
after the m. of the instructions		49: 8
their m. of preparation for war.		49: 9
one in a particular m. which		50:15
in a m. to overthrow the free		51: 5
after the m. of the fortifications		51:27
after this m. were they driven.		51:32
from their support after this m.,		57:11
all m. of weapons of war		60: 2
all m. of afflictions of every kind.		60: 3
should suffer all m. of afflictions,		60:17
raising all m. of grain,		62:29
all m. of iniquity among the		62:40
and from all m. of afflictions and		62:50
a m. that they all could not be	He	1:12
all m. of shields of every kind.		1:14
in this m. they did fall upon them		1:24
and all m. of their buildings.		3: 9
and all m. of abominations		3:14
the m. of their conversion,		6: 4
and of all m. of precious metals,		6: 9
there was all m. of gold in both		6:11
and did make all m. of cloth,		6:13
and all m. of wickedness,		6:23
and do all m. of iniquity.		7:21
and all m. of iniquities—		10: 3
and in all m. of precious things		12: 2
and with all m. of pestilence,		12: 3
all m. of that which is iniquity;		12: 5

murders, and all m. of iniquities.	He	13:22
do all m. of iniquity unto them,		13:24
all m. of ways to destroy him;		13:26
after the m. of his instruction.	3Ne	3:26
about after the m. of robbers;		4: 7
and all m. of afflictions,		6:13
people to do all m. of iniquity,		6:15
people to do all m. of iniquity;		6:16
and their m. of government,		7:14
after this m. shall ye baptize in		11:27
say all m. of evil against you		12:11
After this m. therefore pray ye:		13: 9
be filled with all m. of lyings,		16:10
mischiefs, and all m. of hypocrisy,		16:10
or that are afflicted in any m.?		17: 7
that were afflicted in any m.;		17: 9
after this m. do they bear record:		17:16
done all m. of cures among them,		26:15
what m. of men ought ye to be?		27:27
all m. of miracles did they work	4Ne	1: 5
nor any m. of lasciviousness;		1:16
Lamanites, nor any m. of -ites;		1:17
apparel, and all m. of fine pearls,		1:24
receive all m. of wickedness,		1:27
and to do all m. of iniquity.		1:34
with all m. of precious things.		1:41
did traffic in all m. of traffic.		1:46
after the m. of the learning of	Mrm	1: 2
they are written after this m.,		5:12
with all m. of weapons of war.		6: 9
and all m. of abominations;		8:31
and all m. of iniquities;		8:36
according to our m. of speech.		9:32
all m. of that which was upon	Eth	2: 3
after the m. of barges which		2:16
after the m. which they had built,		2:16
built after a m. that they were		2:17
after the m. and in the likeness		3:17
had prepared all m. of food,		6: 4
commit all m. of wickedness		8:16
do not write the m. of their oaths		8:20
do all m. of iniquity according		9:10
Having all m. of fruit, and of		9:17
And also all m. of cattle,		9:18
all m. of fine workmanship		10: 7
they did work in all m. of ore,		10:23
brass and all m. of metals;		10:23
did work all m. of fine work.		10:23
they did work all m. of cloth,		10:24
they did make all m. of tools		10:25
they did make all m. of tools		10:26
make all m. of weapons of war.		10:27
they did work all m. of work		10:27
oaths after the m. of the ancients,		10:33
do all m. of iniquity in his days,		11:10
after the m. by which he brought		11:21
all m. of wickedness upon		13:26
clothed after the m. of war—		15:15
a m. that the people of Limhi		15:33
The m. which the disciples.	Mro	3: 1
after this m. did they ordain		3: 4
The m. of their elders and priests		4: 1
we know the m. to be true;		4: 1
The m. of administering the		5: 1
after the m. of the workings of		6: 9
after this m. did he speak		7: 1
this m. doth the devil work,		7:17
after this m. bringeth to pass		7:32
this m. did the Holy Ghost		8: 9
ways of the Lord after this m.,		8:16
murder them in a most cruel m.,		9:10
after the m. of their language,	DC	1:24
dealt with you after this m.		9: 6
concerning the m. of baptism—		20:37
in the following m. unto all		20:72
this m. shall he administer it—		20:76
The m. of administering the		20:78
in a m. which shall speak in		38:30
or she do any m. of iniquity,		42:87
after the m. of the Lord,		63:53
after the m. of the Lord—		64:24
after the m. of his burial,		76:51
And also their m. of life,		85: 2
not after the m. of the world,	DC	95:13
live after the m. of the world;		95:13
be built after the m. which		95:14
appointed after the same m. that		102:10
after the m. of the foregoing,		102:24
but are full of all m. of evil,		105: 3
by lineage in the following m.:		107:41
the office of a teacher, in like m.,		107:62
in a m. that we may be		109:11
with all m. of false accusations;		122: 6
in a prompt and proper m.,		127: 1
and in an especial m.		128:17
and all m. of blasphemies,		132:26
in a brutal m. and		135: 1
in a savage m. with four balls,		135: 2
in the most solemn m., declare		OD
with Satan, after the m. of Cain,	Mses	5:49
the cross, after the m. of men;		7:55
after the m. of the Egyptians.	Abr	1: 9
after the m. of the Egyptians.		1:11
which m. of the figures is called		1:14
after the m. of the government		1:25
was after the m. of the Lord,		3: 4
after his m. of reckoning,		3: 4
in a m. to create in them a	JS	2:23
all m. of evil against me falsely		2:25
a proper and affectionate m.		2:28
in what m. his kingdom was		2:54
in a m. which we never could		2:74

MAN'S
and write in it with a m. pen,	2Ne	18: 1
every m. heart shall melt;		23: 7
this m. name was Nephihah,	Al	4:17
used for the shedding of m. blood,		24:17
for the shedding of m. blood;		24:18
no law against a m. belief;		30: 7
no law against a m. belief;		30:11
the m. name was Aminadab.	He	5:39
and the Son dwell in a m. heart	DC	130: 3
prophet's time, and m. time,		130: 4
flesh and bones as tangible as m.;		130:22
m. knowing that he is sealed up		131: 5
a m. hand was against his own	Mses	6:15
his spirit (that is, the m. spirit),	Abr	5: 7

MAN-SERVANT: see MAN and SERVANT.

MANSIONS
for you in the m. of my Father.	En	1:27
among the m. of thy Father,	Eth	12:32
in the m. of thy Father.		12:34
in the m. of my Father.		12:37
crown in the m. of the Father,	DC	59: 2
to inherit the m. prepared		72: 4
the m. which are prepared;		76:111
the m. which I have prepared		81: 6
Father's house are many m.,		98:18
in the m. of my Father.		106: 8
prepared in the m. of my Father.		135: 5

MANTI
him upon the top of the hill M.,	Al	1:15
Zeram, and Amnor, and M.,		2:22
the borders of the land of M.		16: 6
away beyond the borders of M.		16: 7
away to the land of M.,		17: 1
through the borders of M.,		22:27
might come into the land of M.		43:22
come over into the land of M.,		43:24
over into the land of M.		43:25
into the borders of the land M.		43:32
them, towards the land of M.;		43:42
The land of M., or the city of		56:14
land of Manti, or the city of M.,		56:14
driven back to the city of M.		57:22
was to obtain the city of M.;		58: 1
who were in the city of M.;		58:13
concerning the city of M.		58:25
way towards the land of M.		58:26
before them at the city of M.		58:27
take possession of the city of M.		58:28
are with me in the city of M.;		58:39
to flee from the land of M.,		59: 6

MANTLE

MANTLE
bond of charity, as with a m.. DC 88:125

MANTLES
and the m., and the wimples, 2Ne 13:22

MANY
and having seen m. afflictions	1Ne	1: 1
there came m. prophets,		1: 4
and m. things did my father read		1:13
m. should perish by the sword,		1:13
m. should be carried away captive		1:13
seen m. great and marvelous things,		1:14
exclaim m. things unto the Lord;		1:14
for he hath written m. things		1:16
also hath written m. things which		1:16
shown so m. marvelous things		1:18
they did murmur in m. things		2:11
did speak m. hard words unto us,		3:28
he spake unto me m. times		4:27
m. prophecies which have been		5:13
And he prophesied m. things		5:19
m. of their seed, will be saved.		8: 3
traveled for the space of m. hours		8: 8
m. of whom were pressing forward,		8:21
m. were drowned in the depths		8:32
m. were lost from his view,		8:32
as m. as heeded them, had fallen		8:34
dream or vision, which were m.,		8:36
prophesied unto them of m. things,		8:38
also a great m. more things,		9: 1
m. be carried away captive		10: 3
m. more things which I do not write		10:15
as m. of them as were expedient		10:15
I saw m. fall down at his feet		11:24
in number as m. as the sand		12: 1
I beheld m. generations pass away,		12: 3
and I beheld m. cities,		12: 3
I saw m. cities that they were sunk;		12: 4
I saw m. that they were burned		12: 4
I saw m. that did tumble		12: 4
saw m. of the fourth generation		12:12
I saw m. generations pass away,		12:21
beheld m. nations and kingdoms.		13: 1
behold m. nations and kingdoms.		13: 2
and I saw m. harlots.		13: 7
beheld m. waters; and they divided		13:10
of my brethren by the m. waters;		13:12
went forth upon the m. waters,		13:12
out of captivity, upon the m. waters.		13:13
I beheld m. multitudes of the		13:14
containeth m. of the prophecies		13:23
of brass, save there are not so m.;		13:23
m. parts which are plain and most		13:26
also m. covenants of the Lord		13:26
there are m. plain and precious		13:28
even across the m. waters		13:29
the m. plain and precious things		13:29
an exceeding great m. do stumble,		13:29
they shall write m. things which		13:35
and she sat upon m. waters;		14:11
the whore who sat upon m. waters;		14:12
also m. things which have been.		14:21
are m. things which thou hast seen;		14:24
spake m. great things unto them,		15: 3
for the space of m. years,		15:13
m. generations after the Messiah		15:13
speak m. words unto my brethren,		15:20
travel for the space of m. days,		16:15
traveled for the space of m. days,		16:17
I did say m. things unto them		16:24
traveled for the space of m. days		16:33
worketh m. things by his cunning		16:38
did spaek m. words unto them,		16:39
sojourn for the space of m. years,		17: 4
being interpreted, is m. waters.		17: 5
we had suffered m. afflictions		17: 6
for the space of m. days,		17: 7
in the wilderness for these m. years;		17:20
these m. years we have suffered		17:21
there were m. who perished.		17:41
and has wrought so m. miracles		17:51
said m. things unto my brethren,	1Ne	17:52
even for the space of m. days,		17:52
the wind for the space of m. days,		18: 9
had said m. things unto them,		18:17
sailed for the space of m. days		18:23
m. of mine own prophecies have I		19: 1
m. of the kings of the isles		19:12
did show unto m. concerning us;		19:21
I did read m. things to them,		19:22
I did read m. things unto them		19:23
there are m. who are already lost		22: 1
loosed for the space of m. years;		22:26
also spake m. things unto them—	2Ne	1: 1
m. nations would overrun the		1: 8
for the space of m. generations;		1:18
after m. generations have gone by		3:20
wrote, there are not m. greater.		4: 2
not m. days after his death,		4:13
I had spoken m. things unto them,		4:14
m. of which sayings are written upon		4:14
and m. of the scriptures which are		4:15
for the space of m. days.		5: 7
for the space of m. days		5: 7
of it did make m. swords,		5:14
not built of so m. precious things;		5:16
shalt engraven m. things upon them		5:30
unto you exceeding m. things.		6: 2
there are m. things which have		6: 5
m. shall be afflicted in the flesh,		6:11
have searched much, m. of you,		9: 4
that m. of our children shall perish		10: 2
God will be merciful unto m.;		10: 2
Jacob spake m. more things to my		11: 1
m. people shall go and say, Come		12: 3
and shall rebuke m. people:		12: 4
truth m. houses shall be desolate,		15: 9
and m., even the king of Assyria		18: 7
And m. among them shall stumble		18:15
Isaiah spake m. things which were		25: 1
were hard for m. of my people		25: 1
taught them m. things concerning		25: 2
unto as m. as will believe on his		25:14
for the space of m. generations,		25:16
m. generations shall pass away,		26: 2
m. of the fourth generation shall		26: 9
they have built up m. churches;		26:20
there are m. churches built up		26:21
in the mouth of as m. witnesses as		27:14
there shall be m. which shall say:		28: 7
shall also be m. which shall say:		28: 8
shall be m. which shall teach		28: 9
that in m. instances they do err		28:14
there shall be m.—at that day		29: 1
m. of the Gentiles shall say:		29: 3
that I may prove unto m. that I		29: 9
as m. of the Gentiles as will		30: 2
as m. of the Jews as will not repent		30: 2
shall be m. which shall believe		30: 3
m. generations shall not pass away		30: 6
as m. as shall believe in Christ		30: 7
are m. that harden their hearts		33: 2
they cast m. things away		33: 2
that I shall meet m. souls spotless		33: 7
that m. of us, if not all, may be		33:12
And we also had m. revelations,	Jac	1: 6
desiring m. wives and concubines,		1:15
children, m. of whose feelings are		2: 7
that m. of you have begun to		2:12
you have obtained m. riches;		2:13
had m. wives and concubines,		2:24
m. hearts died, pierced with		2:35
I, Jacob, spake m. more things		3:12
but m. of their proceedings are		3:13
m. hundred years before his coming;		4: 4
and we have m. revelations		4: 6
delivered unto them m. things		4:14
after m. days it began to put forth		5: 6
I take away m. of these young		5: 8
but as m. as will not harden		6: 4
after so m. have spoken		6: 8
And he preached m. things which		7: 2
that he did lead away m. hearts;		7: 3

MANY 595 MANY

notwithstanding the m. revelations	Jac	7: 5
the m. things which I had seen		7: 5
shall come m. hundred years hence.		7: 7
nourished for the space of m. days.		7:15
m. means were devised to reclaim		7:24
that m. of my brethren may		7:27
And m. years pass away before he	En	1: 8
unto him with m. long strugglings		1:11
And m. of them did eat nothing		1:20
wild goats, and also m. horses.		1:21
exceeding m. prophets among us.		1:22
there are m. among us who have	Jar	1: 4
who have m. revelations,		1: 4
as m. as are not stiffnecked		1: 4
they came m. times against us,		1: 7
and we had m. seasons of peace;	Om	1: 3
we had m. seasons of serious war		1: 3
the lives of m. of the Lamanites		1:10
as m. as would hearken unto		1:12
as m. as would hearken unto		1:13
they were led by m. preachings		1:13
Nevertheless, they had had m. wars		1:17
And it is m. hundred years after	WM	1: 2
also m. of the words of Nephi;		1: 3
m. of them have been fulfilled;		1: 4
m. things as have been prophesied		1: 4
as m. as go beyond this day must		1: 4
m. thousands of the Lamanites.		1:14
m. dissensions away unto the		1:16
there was m. holy men in the land,		1:17
m. more things did king Benjamin	Mos	1: 8
so m. that they did not number		2: 2
m. signs, and wonders, and types,		3:15
so m. that I cannot number them.		4:29
therefore they wandered m. days		7: 4
for they had suffered m. things;		7:16
notwithstanding our m. strugglings,		7:18
m. more things did he do for them.		7:19
m. of our brethren have been slain,		7:24
of m. things which are to come,		7:26
m. more things did they do which		7:28
for he spake m. things unto them		8: 1
for the space of m. days,		8: 8
in a land among m. waters,		8: 8
as m. as were desirous to go up		9: 3
after m. days' wandering in the		9: 4
for m. years, yea, for the space of		10: 3
we have suffered these m. years		10:18
so m. that we did not number		10:20
had m. wives and concubines.		11: 2
m. elegant and spacious buildings;		11: 8
caused m. buildings to be built		11:13
and drove m. of their flocks out		11:17
m. things did Abinadi prophesy		12: 8
my righteous servant justify m.;		14:11
and he bore the sins of m.,		14:12
working m. mighty miracles		15: 6
he being concealed for m. days		17: 4
shall cause that m. shall suffer		17:15
as m. as would hear his word		18: 3
And m. did believe his words.		18: 3
as m. as did believe him did go		18: 4
as m. as believed him went		18: 6
after m. days there were a		18: 7
m. that would not leave them,		19:12
after m. days the Lamanites		21: 2
and slew m. of them.		21: 8
a great m. widows in the land,		21:10
and m. of their precious things;		21:21
not m. days before the coming of		21:26
so m. of their brethren had been		21:29
commit so m. sins and iniquities		21:30
and also m. of his people,		21:32
king Limhi and m. of his people		21:33
hearkened unto my words m. times		22: 3
being m. days in the wilderness		22:13
m. things which were abominable		23: 9
so m. of you to a knowledge of		23:10
lost in the wilderness for m. days.		23:30
so m. of the children of Nephi,		25: 2
or so m. of those who were		25: 2
not so m. of the people of Nephi		25: 3
even shed m. tears of sorrow.	Mos	25: 9
had taught the people m. things,		25:17
as m. as he did baptize did belong		25:18
because there were so m. people		25:20
there being m. churches they were		25:22
were m. of the rising generation		26: 1
that they did deceive m. with their		26: 6
cause them to commit m. sins;		26: 6
were m. witnesses against them;		26: 9
here are m. whom we have		26:11
receiving m., and baptizing many.		26:37
receiving many, and baptizing m.		26:37
And he was a man of m. words,		27: 8
he led m. of the people to do after		27: 8
being smitten by m. of them.		27:32
bringing m. to the knowledge of		27:36
did plead with their father m. days		28: 5
for m. shall believe on their words,		28: 7
destroy the souls of m. people.		29: 7
the sins of m. people have been		29:31
m. more things did king Mosiah		29:33
m. did believe on his words,	Al	1: 5
so m. that they began to support		1: 5
being stricken with m. years,		1: 9
m. who loved the vain things of		1:16
there were m. among them who		1:22
hearts of m. were hardened,		1:24
And also m. withdrew themselves		1:24
that m. of the Nephites did fall		2:17
that m. died in the wilderness		2:38
Now m. women and children had		3: 2
and also m. of their flocks		3: 2
and also m. of their fields of grain		3: 2
And now as m. of the Lamanites		3: 3
depths of the sea, and they are m.		3: 3
not m. days after the battle		3:20
and slew m. of the Lamanites,		3:23
m. were baptized in the waters		4: 4
and because of their m. flocks		4: 6
yea, and to m. of the people whom		4: 7
m. of them were sorely grieved		4: 7
have fasted and prayed m. days		5:46
having m. sheep doth not watch		5:59
there be m. things to come;		7: 7
the people of Gideon m. things		8: 1
established in m. parts of the land,		8:11
for I had fasted m. days.		8:26
And Alma tarried m. days with		8:27
how m. times he delivered our		9:10
m. promises which are extended		9:16
and m. of them will be saved,		9:17
revelation, and also m. gifts,		9:21
who have received so m. blessings		9:23
his angel to visit m. of his people,		9:25
And not m. days hence the Son		9:26
I have m. kindreds and friends,		10: 4
for I was called m. times and I		10: 6
for he has fasted m. days		10: 7
It is given unto m. to know the		12: 9
there were m. who were ordained		13:10
and there were m., exceeding great		13:12
were many, exceeding great m.,		13:12
there were m. before him,		13:19
also there were m. afterwards,		13:19
declaring it unto m. at this time		13:24
Alma spake m. more words		13:31
m. of them did believe on his		14: 1
m. such things did the people		14: 5
came m. lawyers, and judges,		14:18
questioned them about m. words;		14:18
And m. came forth also, and		14:20
And m. such things did they say		14:21
And m. such things, yea, all		14:22
they did mock them for m. days.		14:22
had thus suffered for m. days,		14:23
and m. of their teachers and		14:23
great sin, and his m. other sins,		15: 3
they were m.; for they did		15:14
after m. days their dead bodies		16:11
of Ammonihah for m. years.		16:11
as m. as would hear their words,		16:14
also m. more who had been		16:15

m. of the people did inquire	Al 16:20
m. to the knowledge of the truth;	17: 4
m. were brought before the altar	17: 4
for they had m. afflictions;	17: 5
m. days in the wilderness,	17: 9
unto the salvation of m. souls.	17:11
m. of whom did worship idols,	17:15
insomuch that they fled m. ways.	17:27
he smote off as m. of their arms	17:38
For he had slain m. of them	18: 6
they might drive away m.	18: 7
do m. mighty works in his name;	19: 4
unto the Lord for m. years,	19:16
were m. among them who said	19:25
destroyed so m. of their brethren,	19:27
speaking m. words which were	19:30
as m. as heard his words believed,	19:31
m. among them who would not	19:32
m. did declare unto the people	19:34
m. that did believe in their words;	19:35
and as m. as did believe were	19:35
and kept in prison for m. days,	20:30
for m. of the Amalekites and the	21: 4
And they contended with m.	21:11
did preach the word unto m.,	21:12
cast into prison suffered m. things,	21:14
m. to the knowledge of the truth;	21:17
they did convince m. of their sins,	21:17
he did teach them m. things.	21:21
the queen and m. of the servants.	22:23
were m. Lamanites on the east	22:29
so sure as m. as believed,	23: 6
or as m. as were brought to	23: 6
as m. of the Lamanites as	23: 6
Aaron and m. of their priests,	23:16
and of the m. murders which we	24: 9
forgiven us of those our m. sins	24:10
and the m. murders which we	24:11
were m. whose hearts had swollen	24:24
the Lord worketh in m. ways	24:27
who slew so m. of their brethren	24:28
m. battles with the Nephites,	25: 3
that m. of the Lamanites should	25: 5
For m. of them, after having	25: 6
much loss and so m. afflictions,	25: 6
there were m. of them converted	25: 6
that m. of their brethren should	25: 8
that m. should suffer death by	25:11
cause to be put to death,	25:12
m. of them came over to dwell in	25:13
how m. of them are brought to	26: 3
m. mighty miracles we have	26:12
how m. thousands of our	26:13
say unto you, Nay, they are m.;	26:31
how m. of these have laid down	26:34
m. struggles to destroy them,	27: 1
because of the m. murders and	27: 6
the m. murders and sins which we	27: 8
on account of their m. murders	27:23
of m. thousand lives;	28:10
the bodies of m. thousands are	28:11
the bodies of m. thousands are	28:11
and m. thousands are mourning	28:11
While m. thousands of them	28:12
when I see m. of my brethren	29:10
m. more such things did he say	30:17
leading away the hearts of m.,	30:18
yea, leading away m. women,	30:18
wise than m. of the Nephites;	30:20
notwithstanding my m. travels	30:32
notwithstanding the m. labors	30:33
means of bringing m. souls down	30:47
of the Lord in very m. instances;	31:11
and m. of them are their brethren;	31:35
Yea, there are m. who do say:	32:17
words given unto them m. times	32:23
And m. did look and live.	33:19
m. who were so hardened that	33:20
proved unto you, in m. instances,	34: 6
have received so m. witnesses,	34:30
ye have had so m. witnesses,	34:33
for the m. mercies and blessings	34:38
out of the land; and they were m.;	35: 6
m. threatenings against them.	Al 35: 9
bringing m. of the Zoramites to	35:14
and as m. as were brought to	35:14
had murdered m. of his children,	36:14
up by the memory of my m. sins,	36:17
m. have been born of God,	36:26
small means in m. instances doth	37: 6
about the salvation of m. souls.	37: 7
and convinced m. of the error of	37: 8
convinced so m. thousands of	37: 9
of bringing m. thousands of them,	37:10
and also m. thousands of our	37:10
restoration of m. thousands of	37:19
also m. other miracles wrought	37:40
did steal away the hearts of m.;	39: 4
away the hearts of m. people	39:12
are m. mysteries which are kept,	40: 3
m. of the Nephites were slain	43:44
in two m. of their head plates,	43:44
did pierce m. of their breastplates,	43:44
did smite off m. of their arms;	43:44
Now there were m., when they	44:15
m. came forth and threw down	44:15
as m. as entered into a covenant	44:15
and the m. little dissensions and	45:21
as m. as would not hearken to	46: 1
there were m. in the church who	46: 7
a man of m. flattering words,	46:10
away the hearts of m. people	46:10
by his brethren into m. pieces;	46:23
that there were m. who died,	46:39
of the m. plants and roots	46:40
were m. who died with old age;	46:41
the m. privileges and blessings	48:12
cease for the space of m. years	48:22
sending so m. of their brethren	48:23
m. of which were very severe.	49:24
to build m. cities on the north,	50:15
also m. of the people of liberty,	51: 7
m. thousands who had been slain	51:11
did drive them, slaying m.	51:23
taking possession of m. cities,	51:26
so m. cities, by their numberless	51:27
before them and slaying m.	51:28
had taken m. prisoners,	52: 8
and m. of the chief captains held	52:19
were m. slain on both sides;	52:35
there were m. that would not;	52:39
m. afflictions and tribulations	53:13
they had m. sons, who had not	53:16
as m. as were able to take up	53:16
taken m. women and children,	54: 3
as m. prisoners of the Nephites	54: 3
have breathed out m. threatenings	54:19
as m. as were able to use a	55:17
M. times did the Lamanites	55:29
they did lose m. prisoners.	55:29
m. times did they attempt to	55:30
had also retained m. prisoners,	56:12
of so m. of our valiant men:	56:13
brought unto us m. provisions	56:27
and m. of his leaders, because	56:51
lest there were m. of them slain.	56:55
about the city for m. nights;	57: 9
which they attempted m. times;	57: 9
as m. times as they attempted	57: 9
not m. days had passed away	57:12
who had not received m. wounds.	57:25
of the Lamanites, who were m.,	57:28
to day, and also m. provisions;	58: 5
for the space of m. months,	58: 7
carried with them m. women and	58:30
they have received m. wounds;	58:40
m. have fought and bled out their	60: 9
because so m. of your brethren	60:12
there are m. who have fallen by	60:12
m. times we have been delivered	60:20
led away the hearts of m. people,	61: 4
as m. men as it were possible	61: 5
and slew m. of them, and took	62:15
forth against them, and slew m.,	62:25
and surrounded m. others,	62:25

MANY 597 MANY

m. of the Lamanites who were	Al 62:26	
m. of the Lamanites that were	62:27	
that as m. as were desirous,	62:28	
having taken m. prisoners,	62:30	
regained m. of the Nephites who	62:30	
m. exceedingly sore afflictions.	62:37	
for the space of m. years.	62:39	
m. had become hardened,	62:41	
m. were softened because of	62:41	
of so m. wars and contentions	62:44	
m. people of their wickedness,	62:45	
m. of the Nephites who did enter	63: 6	
and also m. women and children;	63: 6	
m. more people did enter into it;	63: 7	
were m. people who went forth	63: 9	
of m. holy prophets,	He 1:hd	
m. of the Lamanites are	1:hd	
sons of Pahoran, (for he had m.)	1: 4	
but as m. as were found were	1:12	
taking possession of m. cities	1:27	
many cities and of m. strongholds.	1:27	
yea, m. were slain, and among	1:30	
was exceeding expert in m. words,	2: 4	
contention and m. dissensions;	3: 3	
great m. who departed out of	3: 3	
bodies of water and m. rivers.	3: 4	
because of the m. inhabitants	3: 5	
that they might build m. cities,	3:11	
were m. of the people of Ammon,	3:12	
now there are m. records kept	3:13	
by m. of this people, which are	3:13	
there are m. books and many	3:15	
and m. records of every kind,	3:15	
so m. the blessings which were	3:25	
m. souls, yea, even tens of	3:26	
of m. of their brethren.	3:34	
m. dissensions in the church,	4: 1	
obtaining m. parts of the land;	4: 9	
yea, they regained m. cities	4: 9	
Moronihah did preach m. things	4: 9	
preach m. things unto the people,	4:14	
prophesy m. things unto them	4:14	
in the space of not m. years.	4:26	
he did teach them m. things	5:13	
also m. things which are written.	5:13	
confound m. of those dissenters	5:17	
prison m. days without food,	5:22	
as m. as were convinced did	5:51	
were m. of the Nephites who had	6: 2	
m. of the Lamanites did come	6: 4	
m. did preach with exceedingly	6: 5	
bringing down m. of them into	6: 5	
m. of the Lamanites did go into	6: 6	
did raise m. flocks and herds,	6:12	
flocks and herds, yea, m. fatlings.	6:12	
m. prophecies concerning that	6:14	
m., even among the Nephites, of	6:18	
in the space of not m. years,	6:32	
prophesy m. things unto them;	7: 2	
in the space of not m. years;	7: 6	
yea, m. things did Nephi speak	8: 3	
And behold they are m., and he	8: 8	
And as m. as should look upon	8:15	
even so as m. as should look	8:15	
m. before the days of Abraham	8:18	
m. thousand years before his	8:18	
m. prophets that have testified	8:19	
so m. evidences which ye have	8:24	
and m. of their brethren who	11:23	
having m. revelations daily,	11:23	
in the space of not m. years,	11:26	
of robbers, and did destroy m.;	11:30	
did visit m. parts of the land,	11:33	
did kill m., and did carry away	11:33	
his people with m. afflictions,	12: 3	
out the day for m. hours—	12:14	
did preach, m. days, repentance	13: 2	
shall suffer m. things and shall	13: 6	
saith the Lord, that there are m.,	13:12	
did prophesy a great m. more	14: 1	
m. signs and wonders in heaven.	14: 6	
for the space of m. hours,	14:21	
be m. mountains laid low	14:23	
m. places which are now called	14:23	
m. highways shall be broken up,	14:24	
m. cities shall become desolate.	14:24	
And m. graves shall be opened,	14:25	
shall yield up m. of their dead;	14:25	
m. saints shall appear unto many.	14:25	
many saints shall appear unto m.	14:25	
for the space of m. hours.	14:26	
that m. shall see greater things	14:28	
there are m. who do add to	15: 6	
as m. of them as are brought to	15: 7	
as m. as have come to this,	15: 8	
Zenos, and m. other prophets,	15:11	
m. afflictions which they shall	15:12	
the m. mighty works which	15:17	
m. who heard the words of	16: 1	
as m. as believed on his word	16: 1	
as m. as there were who did not	16: 2	
and also m. shot arrows at him	16: 2	
were m. more who did believe	16: 3	
as m. as believed on the words of	16: 5	
guessed right, among so m.;	16:16	
m. more things did the people	16:22	
the m. miracles which they did,	16:23	
And there were m., who had not	3Ne 1:16	
of these things for m. years,	1:18	
also m. others, baptizing unto	1:23	
they did commit m. murders,	1:27	
m. dissenters of the Nephites	1:28	
they had m. children who did	1:29	
and did slay so m. of the people,	2:11	
and did lay waste so m. cities,	2:11	
m. contentions and dissensions,	2:18	
robbers did gain m. advantages	2:18	
in a state of m. afflictions;	2:19	
stand against so m. brave men	3: 3	
because of the m. wrongs which	3: 4	
a great m. thousand people who	3:24	
m. thousands who did yield	4:27	
unto the gushing out of m. tears,	4:33	
m. signs which had been given,	5: 2	
as m. as would repent of their	5: 4	
as m. as there were who did not	5: 5	
as m. as were found breathing out	5: 5	
and so m. murders committed.	5: 6	
there had m. things transpired	5: 8	
was done among so m. people	5: 8	
nevertheless there are m. things	5:18	
there were m. cities built anew,	6: 7	
there were m. old cities repaired.	6: 7	
there were m. highways cast up,	6: 8	
and m. roads made, which led	6: 8	
were m. merchants in the land,	6:11	
and also m. lawyers, and m. officers.	6:11	
many lawyers, and m. officers.	6:11	
m. of the people who were	6:21	
were m. of those who testified of	6:23	
had m. friends and kindreds;	6:27	
and m. kindreds and friends;	7: 4	
there would be m. dissenters)	7:12	
minister m. things unto them;	7:17	
did also do m. more miracles,	7:20	
as m. as were converted did	7:21	
as m. as had devils cast out	7:22	
were m. in the commencement of	7:26	
he truly did m. miracles in the	8: 1	
so m. signs had been given.	8: 4	
m. smooth places became rough.	8:13	
m. great and notable cities were	8:14	
sunk, and m. were burned,	8:14	
m. were shaken till the buildings	8:14	
were m. of them who were slain.	8:15	
m. great destructions have I	9:12	
as m. as have received me,	9:17	
as m. as shall believe on my	9:17	
land for the space of m. hours;	10: 1	
land for the space of m. hours.	10: 2	
of m. of the holy prophets.	10:14	
m. have testified of these things	10:15	
m. there be who go in thereat;	14:13	
M. will say to me in that day:	14:22	
done m. wonderful works?	14:22	
as m. as have not been fulfilled	15: 6	

MANY 598 MANY

as m. as could come for the	3Ne 17:10
the people that there were m.,	19: 3
they did not multiply m. words,	19:24
midst of them who shall be m.;	20:16
shalt beat in pieces m. people;	20:19
as m. as have spoken, have	20:24
As m. were astonished at thee—	20:44
So shall he sprinkle m. nations;	20:45
as m. of the house of Israel as	21:23
m. there be that testify of these	23: 5
m. saints who should arise from	23: 9
and should appear unto m.,	23: 9
m. saints did arise and appear	23:11
did arise and appear unto m.	23:11
as m. as did come unto them;	26:17
as m. as were baptized in the	26:17
And m. of them saw and heard	26:18
m. there by that travel therein,	27:33
as m. to the church as would	28:18
as m. as were baptized did	28:18
out of them unto Jesus m. souls,	28:29
as m. as did come unto them,	4Ne 1: 1
m. cities which had been sunk,	1: 9
also m. of that generation	1:14
were m. churches in the land;	1:27
m. churches which professed to	1:27
m. miracles which were wrought	1:29
m. priests and false prophets	1:34
to build up m. churches,	1:34
and did slay m. of them.	Mrm 1:11
had led them m. times to battle,	3:12
and did slay m. of the Nephites,	4: 2
and did take m. prisoners.	4: 2
and did take m. prisoners both	4:14
and it was in a land of m. waters,	6: 4
there shall be m. who will say,	8:31
did not m. mighty miracles?	9:18
m. mighty miracles wrought by	9:18
which they did cross m. waters,	Eth 2: 6
for these m. years we have been	3: 3
because of the m. great works	3:18
they were m. times buried in	6: 6
encompassed about by m. waters	6: 7
therefore they began to be m.	6:16
whose days were exceeding m.	7: 1
Corihor drew away m. people	7: 4
begat m. sons and daughters.	7:12
Corihor repented of the m. evils	7:13
had m. sons and daughters.	7:14
brethren and m. of the people.	7:15
that he did flatter m. people,	8: 2
and traveled m. days,	9: 3
lasted for the space of m. years,	9:12
having seen exceeding m. days,	9:15
also m. other kinds of animals	9:18
he begat m. sons and daughters;	9:21
and did build m. mighty cities,	9:23
and did poison m. people.	9:31
m. of them which did perish	9:32
his father did build up m. cities	10: 4
have m. wives and concubines,	10: 5
did build m. spacious buildings.	10: 5
and he did build m. prisons,	10: 6
after the space of m. years,	10: 9
he gained power over m. cities;	10: 9
last for the space of m. years;	10: 9
because of his m. whoredoms;	10:11
Morianton built up m. cities,	10:12
he begat m. sons and daughters;	10:17
and after he had seen m. days	10:17
that Lib did live m. years,	10:29
he served m. years in captivity,	10:30
fought for the space of m. years,	10:32
the days of Com m. prophets,	11: 1
prophesied unto Com m. things;	11: 3
also m. famines and pestilences.	11: 7
Ethem there came m. prophets,	11:12
half of the kingdom for m. years.	11:15
there also came m. prophets,	11:20
And there were m. whose faith	12:19
for there were m. who rose up,	13:15
m. people who were slain by	13:18
m. thousands fell by the sword.	14: 4
and he did overthrow m. cities,	Eth 14:17
he gave him m. deep wounds;	14:30
on as m. as they laid their	Mro 2: 3
how m. little children have died	8:12
Lamanites have m. prisoners,	9: 7
m. of the daughters of the	9: 9
m. widows and their daughters	9:16
and m. old women do faint by	9:16
as m. as have fled to the army	9:17
that m. of our brethren have	9:24
m. more will also dissent over	9:24
gifts of God, for they are m.;	10: 8
man may have m. revelations,	DC 3: 4
power to do m. mighty works,	3: 4
there are m. that lie in wait to	5:33
bring m. to the knowledge of	6:11
it has told you m. things;	8: 6
there are m. things engraven	10:45
m. there were that understood	10:59
that as m. as receive me,	11:30
m. times you have desired of	15: 4
m. times you have desired of	16: 4
by my Spirit in m. instances,	18: 2
should bring m. souls unto me!	18:16
as m. as repent and are	18:22
convincing of m. of their sins,	18:44
as m. as shall hereafter come	20:13
as m. as would believe and	20:25
as m. as were before he came,	20:26
for thou shalt have m.;	24: 8
as m. as will hearken to my	29: 2
as m. as have loved me and	29:12
even as m. as would believe;	29:43
had m. afflictions because of	31: 2
and they err in m. instances	33: 4
as m. as will believe in me,	33: 6
as m. as would believe might	34: 3
as m. as will believe on my	35: 2
as m. as shall come before my	36: 5
as m. as have believed in	38: 4
But to as m. as received me,	39: 4
as m. as will receive me,	39: 4
hast rejected me m. times	39: 9
as m. as ye shall baptize with	39:23
thy brother or sister offend m.,	42:90
shall be chastened before m.	42:90
And m. shall be converted,	44: 4
but unto as m. as received me	45: 8
I power to do m. miracles,	45: 8
places, and m. desolations;	45:33
not m. years hence ye shall	45:63
for there are m. gifts,	46:11
there are m. spirits which are	50: 2
as m. of my servants as are	50:38
be made ruler over m. things.	52:13
and as m. as will go may go,	56: 7
you have m. things to do and	56:14
and do m. things of their	58:27
not yet come, for m. years,	58:44
m. dangers upon the waters,	61: 4
m. destructions upon the	61: 5
m. have turned away from	63:13
m. who observe not to keep	63:22
and not a day of m. words.	63:58
m. there be who are under	63:62
as m. as believe on my name.	66: 1
Tarry not m. days in this place;	66: 6
and push m. people to Zion	66:11
of as m. as the Father shall	68:12
John Whitmer travel m. times	69: 7
been faithful over m. things,	70:17
be laden with m. sheaves,	75: 5
the things of m. generations.	76: 8
after the m. testimonies which	76:22
show it by vision unto m.,	76:47
as m. as will come to the church	77:11
rulers over m. kingdoms,	78:15
also m. whom I have called	84:32
shall do m. wonderful works,	84:66
death and misery of m. souls;	87: 1
after m. days, slaves shall rise	87: 4
And there are m. kingdoms;	88:37
as m. as the mouth of the Lord	88:84

MANY 599 MARCH

For not m. days hence and	DC	88:87
who sitteth upon m. waters,		88:94
as m. as will believe;		90: 8
not well pleased with m. things;		90:35
have m. things to repent of.		90:35
There are m. things contained		91: 1
There are m. things contained		91: 2
m. things that are not right		93:43
m. who have been ordained		95: 5
m. of whom are truly humble		97: 1
Father's house are m. mansions,		98:18
m. who are in the church at		98:19
the children of Zion, even m.,		101:41
after m. days all things were		101:62
there are m. who will say:		105: 8
and not m. years hence they		105:15
as m. as have come up hither,		105:20
have power after m. days		105:37
benefit of Zion, and m. people in		111: 2
and among m. nations.		112: 7
by thy word m. high ones shall		112: 8
by thy word m. low ones shall		112: 8
in love above m. others,		112:11
and he shall be a ruler over m.		117:10
And not m. years hence,		121:15
there be one God or m. gods,		121:28
m. called, but few are chosen.		121:34
m. are called, but few are chosen.		121:40
For there are m. yet on the earth		123:12
m. of them for your good,		124: 9
there are m. things with which		124:84
he shall be made ruler over m.;		124:113
For I am about to restore m.		127: 8
as well as m. other things.		127:10
in relation to m. subjects,		128: 1
I have m. things to say to you		128:25
having m. wives and concubines—		132: 1
m. there are that go in thereat,		132:25
from Hagar sprang m. people.		132:34
David also received m. wives and		132:38
as also m. others of my servants,		132:38
for he shall be made ruler over m.		132:44
shall be made ruler over m. things;		132:53
are m. things pertaining thereunto.		132:58
voice as the voice of m. waters,		133:22
unto m. that dwell on the earth.		133:36
and m. other wise documents and		135: 3
gathered m. thousands of the		135: 3
decide how m. can go next spring;		136: 7
M. have marveled because of		136:39
it was for the space of m. hours	Mses	1:10
be made stronger than m. waters;		1:25
he beheld m. lands; and each land		1:29
have I called Adam, which is m.		1:34
m. worlds that have passed away		1:35
And there are m. that now stand,		1:35
The heavens, they are m., and		1:37
take m. of them from the book		1:41
among as m. as shall believe.		1:41
as m. as would not hearken		4: 4
had drawn away m. after him,)		4: 6
first of all women, which are m.		4:26
after m. days an angel of the		5: 6
all mankind, even as m. as will.		5: 9
as m. as believed in the Son,		5:15
as m. as believed not and		5:15
his wife and m. of his brethren		5:41
also begat m. sons and daughters.		5:42
unto as m. as called upon God		6: 5
he begat m. sons and daughters;		6:11
and begat m. sons and daughters.		6:14
begat m. sons and daughters.		6:18
And for these m. generations,		6:28
m. have believed and become		7: 1
m. have believed not, and have		7: 1
for the space of m. generations.		7: 4
and the Holy Ghost fell on m.,		7:27
m. of the spirits as were in prison		7:57
m. of the inhabitants thereof		8: 4
and to be a father of m. nations,	Abr	1: 2
there were m. flocks in Haran;		2: 5
as m. as receive this Gospel		2:10
there were m. great ones which		3: 2
not so m. as to its number of	Abr	3: 5
hands had made, which were m.;		3:12
m. of the noble and great ones;		3:22
that day, m. followed after him.		3:28
For m. shall come in my name,	JS	1: 6
and shall deceive m.;		1: 6
then shall m. be offended,		1: 8
m. false prophets shall arise,		1: 9
shall arise, and shall deceive m.;		1: 9
the love of m. shall wax cold;		1:10
the love of m. shall wax cold;		1:30
Owing to the m. reports which		2: 1
m. other things did he say unto		2:20
fell into m. foolish errors,		2:28
He quoted m. other passages		2:41
offered m. explanations which		2:41
prophesied m. things which		2:73
m. other things connected with		2:73
m. great and important things	AoF	9
we have endured m. things,		13
MAR		
neither whale that could m. them;	Eth	6:10
MARCH		
that his armies should m. forth	Al	47:27
they would m. thither to battle;		49:15
did m. forth against them;		51:18
begun his m. towards the land		52:15
m. forth with his army against		52:17
and m. down near the seashore;		52:22
did m. forth against Teancum,		52:23
should m. forth into the city,		52:24
were wearied because of their m.,		52:28
wearied because of their long m.		52:31
being in their course of m.,		52:34
compelled to m. with their		52:39
Helaman did m. at the head of		53:22
I, Helaman, did m. at the head		56: 9
Neither durst they m. down		56:25
m. forth with my little sons to		56:30
to m. near the city of Antiparah,		56:31
we did m. forth, as if with		56:32
Antipus did m. forth with a part		56:33
he did not m. forth until I		56:33
their m. in a straight course		56:37
did speed the m. of his army.		56:38
therefore we did continue our m.,		56:39
took our m. into the wilderness.		56:39
because of their long m. in so		56:50
by the speed of their m.—		56:51
took our m. back to the city		56:57
took our m. with speed towards		57:34
were weary because of their m.;		58:25
m. forward by another way		58:26
And because of this our m. in		58:27
ye can upon your m. hither,		61:17
took his m. towards the land		62: 3
he could in all his m. towards		62: 4
men he could in all his m.,		62: 6
m. with a large body of men		62:14
they pursued their m. towards the		62:18
that his men should m. forth		62:22
should m. forth against them,		62:25
of the greatness of the m.;		62:35
m. down to the land of Zarahemla	He	1:17
that Coriantumr did m. forth at		1:19
and their m. was with such		1:19
m. forth with his whole army		1:20
did m. forth with a large army,		1:23
therefore he did m. forth		1:24
this m. of Coriantumr through		1:25
and did m. forth by thousands	3Ne	3:22
m. into the furthermost parts		4:23
their m. beyond the robbers,		4:25
when the robbers began their m.,		4:25
so speedy was their m. that it		7:13
also m. forward against the city	Mrm	4:14
m. forth before the Lamanites.		6: 1
m. forth to the land of Cumorah,		6: 4
brother of Shared did m. forth	Eth	14: 5
but they did m. forth from		14:22
they did m. forth one against		15:15

MARCHED

MARCHED
m. away beyond the borders of	Al	16: 7
m. over into the land of Manti.		43:25
and m. out into the wilderness,		46:31
m. forth into the wilderness,		46:32
Amalickiah m. with his armies		47:20
and m. towards the land of Noah,		49:12
m. forward to the land of Noah		49:13
m. to the borders of the land		51:28
m. forth against the Nephites		52:12
by night, m. in the wilderness,		52:22
while he m. with the remainder		52:26
were m. back into the land		53: 3
their army and m. against us.		56:35
Moroni m. forth on the morrow,		62:38
we m. forth and came to the land	Mrm	2: 6

MARCHING
m. round about in the wilderness,	Al	43:24
was m. forth with his numerous		51:30
in m. into the land northward		52: 2
m. towards the city of Cumeni;		57:31
m. towards the land of Zarahemla,		58:24
they were m. towards the land,		62:15
m. through the most capital parts	He	1:27
m. out by day and by night,	3Ne	4:21
Lamanites m. towards them;	Mrm	6: 7

MARK
came by looking beyond the m.,	Jac	4:14
the m. which was set upon their	Al	3: 6
Lord God set a m. upon them,		3: 7
and there was a m. set upon him.		3:10
they also had m. set upon them;		3:13
they set the m. upon themselves,		3:13
a m. of red upon their foreheads.		3:13
and I will set a m. on them		3:14
I will set a m. upon him that		3:15
I will set a m. upon him that		3:16
m. themselves in their foreheads;		3:18
I the Lord set a m. upon Cain,	Mses	5:40

MARKED
they had m. themselves with red	Al	3: 4

MARKET
which led to the chief m.,	He	7:10

MARKS, William
saith the Lord unto my servant M.,	DC	117: 1
M. be faithful		117:10
be ordained by my servant M.,		124:79
Let my servant M. pay stock		124:80

MARRED
his visage was so m., more than	3Ne	20:44
shall be m. because of them.		21:10

MARRIAGE
were married, and given in m.,	4Ne	1:11
for m. is ordained of God unto	DC	49:15
in unto the m. of the Lamb,		58:11
and everlasting covenant of m.];		131: 2
and m. are not of force when		132:15
neither marry nor are given in m.;		132:16
not teaching polygamy or plural m.,		OD
allege that the m. was performed		OD
contracting any m. forbidden		OD
and marrying and giving in m.?	Mses	8:21
marrying and giving in m.;	JS	1:42
(whose name, previous to her m.,		2: 4
Immediately after my m., I left		2:58

MARRIAGES
allege that plural m. are still	DC	OD
m. have been contracted in		OD
or any other number of plural m.		OD
by Congress forbidding plural m.,		OD
declaration concerning plural m.		OD

MARRIED
than the children of the m. wife,	3Ne	22: 1
And they were m., and given	4Ne	1:11
such among you if they are m.;	DC	42:76
And if they are not m.,		42:77
we were m., while I was yet	JS	2:57
much opposed to our being m.		2:58
m. at the house of Squire Tarbill,		2:58

MARROW
asunder of both joints and m.;	DC	6: 2
asunder of both joints and m.;		11: 2
asunder of both joints and m.;		12: 2
asunder of both joints and m.;		14: 2
asunder of the joints and m.,		33: 1
navel and m. to their bones;		89:18

MARRY
shall m. her who is divorced	3Ne	12:32
whoso forbiddeth to m. is no	DC	49:15
man m. him a wife in the world,		132:15
m. her not by me nor by my word,		132:15
out of the world they neither m.		132:16
if a man m. a wife, and make a		132:18
if a man m. a wife by my word,		132:19
m. a wife according to my word,		132:26

MARRYING
and m. and giving in marriage?	Mses	8:21
m. and giving in marriage;	JS	1:42

MARSH, Thomas B.: *see also THOMAS.*
let my servant M. and my	DC	52:22
servants M. and Ezra Thayre,		56: 5
Ezra Thayre and my servant M.;		75:31

MARSHAL
the land will m. themselves.	DC	87: 5

MARSHALED
m. and disciplined for war.	DC	87: 4

MARTIN: *see HARRIS, Martin.*

MARTYRDOM
them forth to the place of m.,	Al	14: 9
Now this m. caused that many		25: 8
announce the m. of Joseph Smith	DC	135: 1

MARTYRS
classed among the m. of religion,	DC	135: 6
the innocent blood of all the m.		135: 7

MARVEL
m. not that I tell you these things;	Jac	4:12
M. not that all mankind, yea,	Mos	27:25
and they began to m. again	Al	19:24
you m. why these things should		39:17
bidden to go forth and m. not,	He	5:49
yourselves together, and do m.;		7:15
yea, and ye have great need to m.;		7:15
yea, ye ought to m. because		7:15
M. not that I said unto you that	3Ne	15: 3
M. not that I said unto you:	DC	10:35
m. not that I have called him		18: 8
m. not, for the hour cometh		27: 5
Now this caused us to m.,		76:18
Therefore, m. not at these things,		136:37

MARVELED
heard these words, he m. again,	Al	18:18
when they saw it they greatly m.,		22:23
They doubted and m. also		59:12
were some among them who m.,	3Ne	15: 2
m. because of his death;	DC	136:39
he greatly m. and wondered.	Mses	1: 8

MARVELING
and they were m. and	3Ne	11: 1
m. greatly at what had been	JS	2:44

MARVELINGS

MARVELINGS
is it this that causeth thy m.?	Al	18:16
is it, that thy m. are so great?		18:17

MARVELOUS
seen many great and m. things,	1Ne	1:14
Great and m. are thy works,		1:14
had shown so many m. things		1:18
a great and a m. work among		14: 7
proceed to do a m. work among		22: 8
great and m. works of the Lord	2Ne	1:10
showing me his great and m. works,		4:17
to do a m. work and a wonder		25:17
proceed to do a m. work among		27:26
yea, a m. work and a wonder,		27:26
proceed to do a m. work among		29: 1
and m. are the works of the Lord.	Jac	4: 8
by his matchless and m. power,	Mos	1:13
how m. are the works of the Lord,		8:20
I behold the m. light of God.		27:29
that God could do such m. works,	Al	9: 5
truth of such great and m. things?		9: 6
his mysteries and m. power		10: 5
his mysteries and his m. power;		10: 5
was a m. light of his goodness—		19: 6
to behold the m. light of God!		26: 3
doing this great and m. work.		26:15
and what m. light I did behold;		36:20
it did show unto them m. works.		37:41
and then those m. works ceased,		37:41
be preserved by his m. power.		57:26
has shown unto you this m. thing,	He	5:26
did speak unto them m. words		5:33
they could speak forth m. words.		5:45
prophesy such m. things unto us.		9: 2
great and m. works cannot come		16:16
believe in some great and m. thing		16:20
so great and m. were the words	3Ne	3:16
of some, would be great and m.;		5: 8
the great and m. change which		11: 1
so great and m. things as we		17:16
so great and m. things as we		17:17
so great and m. were the words		19:34
shall be a great and a m. work		21: 9
fathers great and m. things,		26:14
their mouths and utter m. things;		26:16
great and m. works shall be		28:31
a great and m. work wrought		28:32
of all the m. works of Christ,		28:33
there were great and m. works	4Ne	1: 5
the m. works which were wrought	Mrm	7: 9
great and m. is the destruction		8: 7
great and m. things concerning		8:34
things that God hath wrought m.		9:16
comprehend the m. woks of God?		9:16
the great and m. things which	Eth	4:15
prophesied of great and m. things,		11:20
did prophesy great and m. things		12: 5
great and m. were the prophecies		13:13
a m. work is about to come	DC	4: 1
A great and m. work is		6: 1
which are great and m.;		6:11
your hands, and do m. works;		8: 8
bring to light their m. works,		10:61
A great and m. work is		11: 1
A great and m. work is		12: 1
A great and m. work is		14: 1
I will work a m. work among		18:44
his wisdom, m. are his ways,		76: 2
m. are the works of the Lord,		76:114
not understand his m. workings;		121:12
had such m. power as I had	JS	2:16

MARY
his mother shall be called M.	Mos	3: 8
he shall be born of M.,	Al	7:10

MASS
more part of it is one solid m.,	He	14:21

MASSACRE
slay and m. them according to	Al	49: 7

MASSACRED
be m. by the barbarous cruelty	Al	48:13

MASTER
he supposed me to be his m.,	1Ne	4:21
he knowing that his m., Laban,		4:22
the m. of the vineyard went forth,	Jac	5: 4
the m. of the vineyard saw it,		5: 7
the servant said unto his m.:		5:16
whither the m. had hid the		5:20
the servant said unto his m.:		5:21
the servant said unto his m.:		5:34
the servant said unto his m.:		5:48
the devil, who is the m. of sin,	Mos	4:14
the m. whom he has not served,		5:13
the m. will not suffer his house	DC	104:86
the m. of this great secret,	Mses	5:31
Cain was called M. Mahan,		5:31
wherein he became M. Mahan,		5:49
m. of that great secret which		5:49
M., show us concerning the	JS	1: 2

MASTERS
and put task-m. over them.	Mos	24: 9
task-m. were in a profound sleep.		24:19
No man can serve two m.,	3Ne	13:24
shall rise up against their m.,	DC	87: 4
to the will and wish of their m.,		134:12

MATCHLESS
led forth by his m. power	1Ne	17:42
by his m. and marvelous power,	Mos	1:13
and preserved by his m. power,		2:11
his m. power, and his wisdom,		4: 6
had not been for his m. power,	Al	9:11
with the m. bounty of his love;		26:15
his m. power in delivering them		49:28
by his miraculous and m. power,	He	4:25

MATERIALS
and we will take of these m.,	Abr	3:24

MATHONI
and also M., and Mathonihah,	3Ne	19: 4

MATHONIHAH
Mathoni, and M., his brother,	3Ne	19: 4

MATTER
heard nothing concerning this m.;	Mos	20:16
of the people concerning this m.		22: 1
he should do concerning this m.,		26:13
to their leaders concerning the m.,		27: 1
in their voices concerning the m.;	Al	2: 6
Now I need not rehearse the m.;		13:20
of the Lord concerning the m.		16: 6
they had seen concerning the m.		18: 1
unto the people concerning the m.:		24: 7
all things concerning the m.,		50:31
warm dispute concerning the m.,		51: 4
this m. of their contention was		51: 7
But behold these things m. not.		54:22
a very serious m. to determine		57:16
I say much concerning this m.?		60:18
them to know, concerning the m.,	He	9:13
expound the m. unto the people,		9:36
know nothing concerning the m.		9:36
the people concerning this m.,	3Ne	27: 3
of the Lord concerning the m.	Mro	8: 7
any more concerning this m.	DC	5:29
your mind concerning that m.?		6:23
the world concerning the m.		10:37
unto you concerning this m.;		19:32
no more concerning this m.		59:22
wearying me concerning this m.		90:33
how to act concerning this m.,		96: 1
heed that ye see to this m.,		96: 4
counsel him concerning this m.,		105:22
views in relation to this m.,		128: 2
in relation to this m., it would		128: 3
and grand secret of the whole m.,		128:11
trouble me no more on this m.		130:15

MATTER

no such thing as immaterial m.	DC 131: 7
spirit is m., but it is more fine	131: 7
we shall see that it is all m.	131: 8
answer thee as touching this m.	132: 2
whatever was done in this m.	OD
inquired what the m. was.	JS 2:20
rehearsed the whole m. to him.	2:50

MATTERETH

And it m. not to me that	1 Ne 6: 3
it m. not that if it so be	Jac 5: 8
it m. not unto thee;	5:13
forth from the dead, it m. not;	Al 40: 5
appointed for men to rise it m.;	40: 8
die at once, and this m.;	40: 8
But behold, it m. not—	58:37
censured me, but it m. not;	61: 9
and whither I go it m. not.	Mrm 8: 4
Do this, or do that, and it m. not,	8:31
it m. not unto thee,	Eth 12:37
it m. not, if it so be that	15:34
it m. not what ye shall eat or	DC 27: 2
you good, it m. not unto me,	60: 5
And it m. not unto me,	61:22
you good, it m. not unto me;	62: 5
it m. not unto me whether	63:40
east or to the west, it m. not,	80: 3
not charity it m. not unto thee,	135: 5

MATTERS

then it m. not whither I go.	Mos 13: 9
if ye speak against it, it m. not.	Al 5:58
church, concerning church m.,	DC 30: 7
difficult cases of church m.;	102:28
upon controversies in spiritual m.	107:80
and neglect the more weighty m.?	117: 8

MATTHEW

for the precedent, M. 16:18, 19;	DC 128:10

MATTOCK

that shall be digged with the m.,	2 Ne 17:25

MAY

that they m. know the covenants	T Pg
that ye m. be found spotless	T Pg
that they m. accomplish the thing	1 Ne 3: 7
that we m. preserve unto our	3:19
that we m. preserve unto them	3:20
that I m. write of the things	6: 3
that I m. persuade men to come	6: 4
that I m. burst these bands	7:17
that they m. know how to come	15:14
that the Lord m. show his power	15:17
that he m. deceive our eyes,	16:38
that he m. lead us away	16:38
that he m. do with us according	16:38
that I m. carry thy people	17: 8
that I m. find ore to molten,	17: 9
that I m. make tools to construct	17: 9
that they m. know that I am the	17:53
that thy days m. be long in the	17:55
the more sacred things m. be kept	19: 5
that ye m. have hope as well as	19:24
they m. forget, yet will I not	21:15
give place to me that I m. dwell.	21:20
that they m. possess this land	2 Ne 1: 9
that ye m. not come down into	1:21
That ye m. not be cursed with a	1:22
that ye m. not incur the	1:22
that they m. know that there is no	2: 8
that he m. bring to pass the	2: 8
that he m. redeem the children	2:26
that he m. reign over you in his	2:29
m. the Lord consecrate also unto	3: 2
m. the Lord bless thee forever,	3: 3
that the cursing m. be taken	4: 6
that I m. shake at the appearance	4:31
M. the gates of hell be shut	4:32
that I m. walk in the path of	4:32
that I m. be strict in the plain	4:32
that we m. not be afflicted more	5: 3
that I m. learn and glorify	6: 4
they m. be likened unto you,	6: 5

which m. be likened unto you,	2 Ne 6: 5
hasteneth, that he m. be loosed,	8:14
that I m. plant the heavens	8:16
Bow down, that we m. go over—	8:23
these things that ye m. rejoice,	9: 3
world that he m. save all men if	9:21
that ye m. not shrink with awful	9:46
that ye m. not remember your	9:46
that they m. come to that which will	10: 2
that my covenants m. be fulfilled	10:15
m. God raise you from death by	10:25
that ye m. be received into the	10:25
that ye m. praise him through grace	10:25
m. lift up their hearts and rejoice	11: 8
and ye m. liken them unto you	11: 8
that they m. be placed alone in	15: 8
that they m. follow strong drink,	15:11
hasten his work, that we m. see it;	15:19
and come, that we m. know it.	15:19
that he m. know to refuse the evil	17:15
that widows m. be their prey,	20: 2
that they m. rob the fatherless!	20: 2
that a child m. write them.	20:19
that they m. go into the gates of	23: 2
m. know the judgments of God,	25: 3
unto my people, that they m. learn.	25: 4
that the promise m. be fulfilled	25:21
children m. know to what source	25:26
they m. look for a remission of	25:26
children m. know the deadness of	25:27
m. look forward unto that life which	25:27
that he m. whisper concerning	26:16
learning, that they m. get gain	26:20
that he m. draw all men unto	26:24
the world, that they m. get gain	26:29
the Lord, that they m. come forth;	27:10
he m. show them unto the learned,	27:15
that I m. preserve the words	27:22
that I m. remember my covenants	29: 1
that I m. set my hand again	29: 1
that I m. remember the promises	29: 2
that I m. prove unto many that	29: 9
m. be for the welfare of thy soul.	32: 9
not all, m. be saved in his kingdom	33:12
that they m. be rich like unto	Jac 2:17
ye m., if your minds are firm,	3: 2
ye m., because of your filthiness,	3:10
shake yourselves that ye m. awake	3:11
that ye m. not become angels to	3:11
that they m. learn with joy	4: 3
that they m. know that we knew	4: 4
that we m. know that it is by his	4: 7
and ye m. obtain a resurrection,	4:11
hath done it, that they m. stumble.	4:14
that it m. become the head of	4:17
that perhaps it m. shoot forth	5: 4
the fire that they m. be burned.	5: 7
I m. preserve the fruit thereof	5: 8
that they m. not cumber the	5: 9
that I m. preserve unto myself	5:13
that I m. lay up fruit thereof	5:13
that we m. labor in the vineyard.	5:15
that I m. lay up of the fruit	5:19
that I m. preserve it unto mine	5:20
that I m. preserve it unto mine	5:23
that perhaps it m. bring forth good	5:27
that we m. labor again in the	5:29
that I m. preserve again good	5:33
that it m. be cast into the fire,	5:37
that the tree m. not perish,	5:53
that, perhaps, I m. preserve unto	5:53
that I m. preserve them also	5:54
that I m. preserve the roots also	5:54
perhaps they m. bring forth good	5:54
I m. yet have glory in the fruit	5:54
the roots thereof m. take strength	5:59
the good m. overcome the evil.	5:59
m. bring forth again good fruit;	5:60
that I m. have joy again in the	5:60
that I m. rejoice exceedingly	5:60
that we m. labor diligently	5:61
that we m. prepare the way,	5:61
that I m. bring forth again	5:61
that they m. be first,	5:63

MAY 603 MAY

and that the first m. be last,	Jac	5:63
that all m. be nourished once		5:63
way for them, that they m. grow.		5:64
the top m. be equal in strength,		5:66
my brethren m. read my words.		7:27
that our genealogy m. be kept.	Jar	1: 1
that they m. be kept according		1:15
But m. God grant that he may	WM	1: 2
that he m. survive them, that he		1: 2
that he m. write somewhat		1: 2
some day it m. profit them.		1: 2
that they m. once again come to		1: 8
that they m. once again be a		1: 8
that they m. be preserved		1:11
that ye m. profit thereby;	Mos	1: 7
that ye m. prosper in the land		1: 7
they m. be gathered together;		1:10
they m. be distinguished above all		1:11
open your ears that ye m. hear,		2: 9
hearts that ye m. understand,		2: 9
mysteries of God m. be unfolded		2: 9
these things that ye m. know that		2:15
things that ye m. learn wisdom;		2:17
that ye m. learn that when ye are		2:17
breath, that ye m. live and move		2:21
m. join the choirs above in singing		2:28
that it m. have no place in you		2:36
that ye m. be blessed, prospered,		2:36
m. dwell with God in a state of		2:41
they m. also be filled with joy.		3: 4
m. receive forgiveness of our sins,		4: 2
and our hearts m. be purified;		4: 2
that ye m. hear and understand		4: 4
substance that he m. not suffer,		4:17
ye m. walk guiltless before God—		4:26
things whereby ye m. commit sin;		4:29
we m. not bring upon ourselves a		5: 5
we m. not drink out of the cup of		5: 5
God Omnipotent, m. seal you his,		5:15
that you m. be brought to heaven,		5:15
ye m. have everlasting salvation		5:15
a man m. have great power given		8:16
that they m. destroy them;		10:18
And m. the Lord bless my people.		10:22
Abinadi hither, that I m. slay him,		11:28
this will I do that I m. discover		12: 8
hither that we m. question him;		12:18
that thy days m. be long upon		13:20
that ye m. know of their surety		17: 9
burdens, that they m. be light;		18: 8
in all places that ye m. be in,		18: 8
that ye m. be redeemed of God,		18: 9
that ye m. have eternal life—		18: 9
that he m. pour out his Spirit		18: 9
that he m. do this work with		18:10
m. the Spirit of the Lord be poured		18:12
m. he grant unto you eternal life,		18:13
him hither that I m. see him.		18:13
that he m. tell his people that		20:14
they m. be pacified towards us;		20:19
m. drive them into the wilderness		20:19
ye m. stand as witnesses for me		22: 14
ye m. know of a surety that I,		24:14
that their prayers m. be answered,		24:14
they m. foresee that he will come,		27:16
that ye m. be judged according		27:30
they m. be judged of a higher judge.		29:25
every man m. enjoy his rights		29:28
we m. live and inherit the land,		29:32
that I m. be an instrument in thy	Al	29:32
their seed m. be separated from		2:30
that I m. have mercy upon them.		3:14
that they m. be cursed also.		3:14
the word of God m. be fulfilled,		3:15
that ye m. not be destroyed.		5:57
that ye also m. be partakers of		5:60
he m. loose the bands of death		5:62
his bowels m. be filled with mercy,		7:12
he m. know according to the flesh		7:12
ye m. be washed from your sins,		7:14
ye m. have faith on the Lamb		7:14
ye m. walk blameless before him,		7:22
m. walk after the holy order of		7:22
And m. the Lord bless you.	Al	7:25
that ve m. at last be brought to		7:25
m. the peace of God rest upon you,		7:27
that they m. destroy the liberty		8:17
that ye m. not be destroyed,		9:25
that he m. have power over you,		10:25
ye m. also enter into that rest.		13:13
what I have said m. suffice.		13:20
m. have glad tidings of great joy;		13:22
that we m. understand, that we		13:23
of our fathers m. be fulfilled,		13:26
that ye m. not be tempted above		13:28
m. be lifted up at the last day		13:29
And m. the Lord grant unto you		13:30
ye m. not bring down his wrath		13:30
that ye m. not be bound down by		13:30
m. not suffer the second death.		13:30
suffer that they m. do this thing,		14:11
m. do this thing unto them,		14:11
upon them in his wrath m. be just;		14:11
ye m. show forth good examples		17:11
that they m. have water—		17:26
that I m. win the hearts of		17:29
that I m. lead them to believe in		17:29
m. be brought to a knowledge of		18:34
and I go that I m. deliver them.		20: 3
I m. flatter the king of the land,		20: 4
that they m., by their cunning		20:13
again m. rob us of our property.		20:13
m. release the brethren of Ammon,		20:15
m. be cast out of prison.		20:22
m. be cast out of prison.		20:24
Lamoni m. retain his kingdom.		20:24
m. do according to his own desires		20:24
my son m. retain his kingdom		20:26
m. be cast out of prison,		20:27
thy brethren m. come unto me,		20:27
that they m. assemble themselves		22: 7
that I m. have this eternal life		22:15
that I m. be born of God,		22:15
that I m. be filled with joy,		22:15
m. not be cast off at the last day?		22:15
that I m. receive this great joy.		22:15
I m. be raised from the dead,		22:18
that they m. be kept bright,		24:15
that they m. be kept bright,		24:16
whatsoever land they m. be in;		26:37
that we m. protect our brethren in		27:23
they m. inherit the land Jershon;		27:24
that we m. maintain our armies.		27:24
And now m. the Lord, the		28: 8
perhaps I m. be an instrument		29: 9
not m. God grant unto these,		29:17
they m. sit down in the kingdom		29:17
that they m. go no more out,		29:17
that they m. praise him forever.		29:17
And m. God grant that it may		29:17
that it m. be done according		29:17
they m. not lift up their heads,		30:23
that ye m. glut yourselves with		30:27
that we m. have rejoicings in		30:34
that it m. have no place in you;		30:42
m. destroy the children of God.		30:42
that I m. be convinced that		30:43
that thy soul m. be destroyed.		30:46
that we m. not be led away after		31:17
that I m. bear with mine		31:30
unto me that I m. have strength,		31:31
that I m. suffer with patience		31:31
that they m. have strength,		31:33
that they m. bear their afflictions		31:33
that we m. have success in		31:34
we m. bring these, our brethren,		31:35
that ye m. be humble, and that ye		32:12
and that ye m. learn wisdom;		32:12
seed m. be planted in your heart,		32:28
with great care, that it m. get root,		32:37
that it m. grow up, and bring forth		32:37
that it m. take root in you,		32:42
And then m. God grant unto you		33:23
that your burdens m. be light,		33:23
that ye m. try the experiment of		34: 4
that they m. have faith unto		34:15

Therefore m. God grant unto you,	Al 34:17	that ye m. thrust your hands	3Ne 11:14
ye m. begin to exercise your faith	34:17	also that ye m. feel the prints of	11:14
that ye m. prosper in them.	34:24	that ye m. know that I am the	11:14
fields, that they m. increase.	34:25	m. baptize you with water;	12: 1
whatsoever place ye m. be in,	34:38	they m. see your good works	12:16
that ye m. not be led away by	34:39	That ye m. be the children of	12:45
that he m. not overpower you,	34:39	that they m. have glory of men.	13: 2
ye m. not become his subjects	34:39	That thine alms m. be in secret;	13: 4
Now ye m. suppose that this is	37: 6	that they m. be seen of men.	13: 5
And it m. suffice if I only say	37:12	that they m. appear unto men	13:16
that he m. show forth his power	37:14	that there m. be one fold and	16: 3
that he m. sift you as chaff	37:15	they m. receive a knowledge of	16: 4
m. be made manifest unto this	37:21	m. be brought in, or may be	16: 4
m. be made manifest unto this	37:21	m. be brought to a knowledge of	16: 4
that I m. discover unto my people	37:23	name, that ye m. understand,	17: 3
that I m. discover unto them the	37:23	ye m. witness unto the Father	18:11
he m. watch over you in your sleep;	37:37	that he m. sift you as wheat.	18:18
if we will look we m. live forever.	37:46	and your children m. be blessed.	18:21
this that ye m. learn wisdom,	38: 9	that they m. come unto you	18:22
that ye m. learn of me that there	38: 9	that it m. shine unto the world.	18:24
that ye m. be filled with love;	38:12	I m. fulfil other commandments	18:27
And m. the Lord bless your soul,	38:15	he m. not destroy my people,	18:31
they m. prepare the minds of	39:16	that they m. believe in me,	19:23
it m. be termed a resurrection,	40:15	that I m. be in them as thou,	19:23
m. walk therein and be saved.	41: 8	art in me, that we m. be one.	19:23
m. come and partake of the	42:27	that they m. be purified in me,	19:28
of mercy m. have claim upon them.	42:31	that they m. be purified in me,	19:29
And m. God grant unto you even	42:31	that I m. be in them as thou,	19:29
that ye m. become extinct;	44: 7	art in me, that we m. be one,	19:29
m. depart into the wilderness;	44: 8	that I m. be glorified in them.	19:29
that the Lord God m. bless them.	46:20	that ye m. know the time when	21: 1
he m. cast us at the feet of our	46:22	m. know concerning this people	21: 2
servants that they m. be slain.	47:27	of the Father m. be fulfilled	21: 4
I m. expect you will do it again.	54: 8	that he m. show forth his power	21: 6
that I m. preserve my food for	54:20	that they m. repent and come	21: 6
of your wine, that we m. drink;	55: 9	they m. be numbered among	21: 6
You m. do according to your	55:12	they m. know that the work of	21: 7
in which we m. have great joy.	56: 9	that they m. build a city,	21:23
we m. console ourselves in	56:11	that they m. be gathered in,	21:24
you m. well suppose that this	56:17	whereby they m. come unto me,	21:27
Moroni, m. the Lord our God,	58:41	that they m. call on the Father in	21:27
yea, and m. he favor this people,	58:41	his people m. be gathered home	21:28
even that ye m. have success in	58:41	But who m. abide the day of	24: 2
m. come upon the wicked;	60:13	they m. offer unto the Lord	24: 3
that he m. support those parts of	60:24	there m. be meat in my house;	24:10
that we m. also recover the	60:24	that they m. be brought again	26: 8
that I m. preserve the rights	61: 9	they m. be judged according to	27:15
we m. retain our freedom,	61:14	that ye m. be sanctified by the	27:20
that we m. rejoice in the great	61:14	ye m. stand spotless before me	27:20
that they m. not perish until ye	61:16	m. have an end, that we may	28: 2
that we m. obtain more food to	61:18	we m. speedily come unto thee in	28: 2
Thus we m. see that the Lord is	He 3:27	their desire m. be fulfilled,	28:29
m. lay hold upon the word of God,	3:29	ye m. know that the covenant	29: 1
names ye m. remember them;	5: 6	ye m. know that the words of	29: 2
them ye m. remember their works;	5: 6	he m. not execute judgment	29: 9
ye m. know how that it is said,	5: 6	ye m. receive a remission of	30: 2
that it m. be said of you, and also	5: 7	m. be numbered with my people	30: 2
that ye m. not do these things	5: 8	that ye m. know that ye must	Mrm 3:20
do these things that ye m. boast,	5: 8	that ye m. believe the gospel of	3:21
ye m. do these things to lay up	5: 8	that they m. come forth in his	5:12
that ye m. have that precious gift	5: 8	that they m. be persuaded that	5:14
of darkness m. be removed	5:40	that the Father m. bring about,	5:14
I m. tell you of your iniquities?	7:13	the seed of this people m. more	5:15
he m. be condemned according	8: 1	if it so be that God m. give unto	7: 1
no power whereby I m. know	8:12	that they m. know of the things	7: 1
this famine m. cease in this land.	11:12	intent that ye m. believe that;	7: 9
and cause that it m. be done	11:13	Lord will suffer that I m. live	8: 5
that she m. bring forth her fruit,	11:13	perhaps ye m. be found spotless,	9: 6
and we m. see at the very time	12: 2	ye m. consume it on your lusts,	9:28
m. God grant, in his great fulness,	12:24	that ye m. learn to be more wise	9:31
ye m. have a remission of them	14:13	that we m. rid our garments of	9:35
must die that salvation m. come;	14:15	m. the Lord Jesus Christ grant	9:37
thereby men m. be brought into	14:15	that their prayers m. be answered	9:37
they m. bring the remainder of	15: 6	m. God the Father remember	9:37
they m. have guessed right,	16:16	and m. he bless them forever,	9:37
that ye m. be like unto us—	3Ne 3: 7	he m. get the full account.	Eth 1: 4
my people m. recover their rights	3:10	we m. not understand our words.	1:34
that we m. fall upon the robbers	3:20	it m. be that he will turn away	1:36
M. the Lord preserve his people	4:29	that we m. receive it for our	1:38
m. cause to be felled to the earth	4:29	ye m. know the decrees of God—	2:11
M. the God of Abraham, and the	4:30	that ye m. repent, and not	2:11
converted, that I m. heal you?	9:13	m. not bring down the fulness	2:11

MAY

that ye m. not perish in the flood.	Eth	2:20	that they m. destroy him.	DC 10:25
should do that ye m. have light		2:23	the work m. not come forth in	10:33
for you that ye m. have light		2:25	that you m. be preserved.	10:35
we m. receive according to our		3: 2	tongue, or people they m. be.	10:51
they m. shine forth in darkness;		3: 4	that I m. establish my gospel,	10:63
that we m. have light while we		3: 4	m. not be so much contention;	10:63
they m. become sanctified in me,		4: 7	Yea, if they will come, they m.,	10:66
ye m. know that the work of		4:17	he m. treasure up for his soul	11: 3
in order that ye m. translate;		5: 1	you m. know of a surety	11:16
ye m. be privileged that ye may		5: 2	m. assist in bringing to light	11:19
that ye m. show the plates unto		5: 2	he m. treasure up for his soul	12: 3
that we m. number them,		6:19	he m. treasure up for his soul	14: 3
that we m. know of them what		6:19	you m. stand as a witness of	14: 8
that they m. have a king.		6:24	that you m. declare repentance	14: 8
ye m. repent of your sins,		8:23	you m. bring souls unto me,	15: 6
that evil m. be done away,		8:26	you m. rest with them in the	15: 6
the time m. come that Satan		8:26	you m. bring souls unto me,	16: 6
that Satan m. have no power		8:26	you m. rest with them in the	16: 6
that they m. be persuaded to		8:26	m. not be destroyed,	17: 4
m. come unto the fountain of		8:26	I m. bring about my righteous	17: 4
ye m. also have hope, and be		12: 9	they m. come unto repentance,	18:44
that they m. be humble;		12:27	m. come unto the kingdom of	18:44
m. be and abide in you forever.		12:41	that you m. enter into my rest.	19: 9
perhaps they m. be of worth	Mro	1: 4	that soon it m. go to the Jew,	19:27
they m. eat in remembrance of		4: 3	that they m. believe the gospel,	19:27
m. always have his Spirit to be		4: 3	that man m. fall from grace	20:32
they m. do it in remembrance		5: 2	he m. also ordain other priests,	20:48
that they m. witness unto thee,		5: 2	m. take a certificate from him	20:64
they m. have his Spirit to be		5: 2	m. receive it from a conference.	20:64
ye m. know good from evil;		7:15	m. have the privilege of	20:66
ye m. know with a perfect		7:15	that a vote m. be called.	20:66
he m. know good from evil;		7:16	all things m. be done in order.	20:68
ye m. know with a perfect		7:16	there m. be works and faith	20:69
ye m. know with a perfect		7:17	they m. eat in remembrance	20:77
the light by which ye m. judge,		7:18	m. always have his Spirit to	20:77
ye m. know good from evil;		7:19	m. do it in remembrance	20:79
m. lay hold on every good thing.		7:21	they m. witness unto thee,	20:79
they m. bear testimony of him.		7:31	they m. have his Spirit to be	20:79
of men m. have faith in Christ,		7:32	m. be kept in a book by one	20:82
m. have place in their hearts,		7:32	their names m. be blotted out	20:83
faith in me, that ye m. be saved.		7:34	m. take a letter certifying	20:84
ye m. be filled with this love,		7:48	which certificate m. be signed by	20:84
m. become the sons of God;		7:48	it m. be signed by the teachers	20:84
that we m. have this hope;		7:48	you m. receive the reward of	23: 7
we m. be purified even as		7:48	that I m. send my servant,	25: 6
repentance m. come unto them.		8:28	whole earth m. not be smitten	27: 9
ye m. know that I am yet alive;		9: 1	that ye m. be able to withstand	27:15
we m. conquer the enemy of all		9: 6	that ye m. be able to stand.	27:15
I trust that I m. see thee soon;		9:24	with me, that we m. be one.	29:13
m. not the things which I have		9:25	you m. naturally understand;	29:33
but m. Christ lift thee up,		9:25	unto you that ye m. understand;	29:33
m. his sufferings and death,		9:25	great things m. be required at	29:48
m. the grace of God the Father,		9:26	that I m. unfold the same to	32: 4
m. know the truth of all things.		10: 5	you m. be ready at the coming	33:17
And ye m. know that he is,		10: 7	they m. become the sons of God,	35: 2
m. teach the word of wisdom;		10: 9	one in me, that we m. be one.	35: 2
m. teach the word of knowledge		10:10	m. be ordained and sent forth,	36: 7
he m. work mighty miracles;		10:12	tares that they m. be burned;	38:12
he m. prophesy concerning all		10:13	it m. rejoice upon the hills	39:13
house of Israel, m. be fulfilled.		10:31	it m. be pruned for the last time.	39:17
ye m. be perfect in Christ;		10:32	that ye m. know how to govern	41: 3
that all that will hear m. hear:	DC	1:11	that ye m. be gathered in one,	42: 9
man m. have many revelations,		3: 4	that ye m. be my people and	42: 9
that they m. believe the gospel		3:20	has need m. be amply supplied	42:33
ye m. stand blameless before		4: 2	covenant people m. be gathered	42:36
power that they m. behold		5:13	all things m. be done according	42:55
that they days m. be prolonged,		5:33	as m. be thought best or	42:72
he m. treasure up for his soul		6: 3	m. be dealt with according to	42:81
he m. be for the word's sake.		6:18	that he or she m. be ashamed.	42:91
that I m. live and bring souls		7: 2	m. have opportunity to confess	42:92
m. know the mysteries of God,		8:11	that the church m. not speak	42:92
you m. translate and receive		8:11	that you m. not be deceived,	43: 6
that you m. assist to translate.		9: 2	you m. know they are not of me.	43: 6
that you m. come off conqueror;		10: 5	that ye m. know how to act and	43: 8
that you m. conquer Satan,		10: 5	that I m. reserve unto myself	43:14
that you m. escape the hands of		10: 5	ye m. give even as I have spoken.	43:16
he m. destroy this work;		10:12	m. not have power over you;	44: 5
they m. say they have caught		10:13	that you m. be preserved in all	44: 5
that we m. not be ashamed in		10:19	m. be enabled to keep my laws;	44: 5
we m. get glory of the world.		10:19	that every bond m. be broken	44: 5
that he m. lead their souls to		10:22	that they m. be kept until all	44: 6
to catch that ye m. destroy;		10:25	until all things m. be done	44: 6
they m. catch a man in a lie,		10:25	that they m. come unto me	45: 5

MAY

MAY 606 MAY

ye m. know that the promises	DC 45:35
that ye m. now translate it,	45:61
that ye m. be prepared for the	45:61
ye m. purchase an inheritance	45:65
ye m. accomplish this work	45:72
they m. not know your works	45:72
they m. consider these things.	45:73
that fear m. seize upon them,	45:74
that ye m. not be seduced by	46: 7
and that ye m. not be deceived	46: 8
that all m. be benefited that	46: 9
m. consume it upon their lusts.	46: 9
that all m. be profited thereby.	46:12
m. be given to every man to	46:16
that all m. be taught to be wise	46:18
unto some it m. be given to have	46:29
that there m. be a head	46:29
member m. be profited thereby.	46:29
in time ye m. be enabled to	48: 4
that he m. reason with them,	49: 4
that ye m. understand,	50:10
that you m. understand.	50:12
that you m. know the truth,	50:25
you m. chase darkness from	50:25
m. know that it is not of God.	50:31
therefore that ye m. be ready.	50:46
that ye m. be one, even as I	51: 9
that ye m. not be deceived;	52:14
the prophecied m. be fulfilled.	52:36
also m. receive instruction	55: 4
that you m. be planted in the	55: 5
as many as will go m. go,	56: 7
m. be rewarded again according	56:12
that they m. obtain it for	57: 5
he m. sell goods without fraud,	57: 8
he m. obtain money to buy	57: 8
he m. obtain whatsoever things	57: 8
things the disciples m. need	57: 8
that he m. send goods also unto	57: 9
my gospel m. be preached unto	57:10
all things m. be right before me,	57:13
that you m. lay it to heart,	58: 5
that the earth m. know that	58: 8
he m. receive his inheritance	58:38
ye m. know if a man repenteth	58:43
that thy fasting m. be perfect	59:13
that thy joy m. be full.	59:13
talent that it m. not be known.	60:13
that they m. fill their mission,	61: 9
m. partake the fatness thereof.	61:17
that you m. abide the day of	61:39
you m. return to bear record,	62: 5
you m. have advantage of	63:27
m. have claim on the world,	63:27
they m. not be stirred up unto	63:27
that he m. be prepared in the	63:39
that such m. receive a more	63:66
do that God m. be glorified—	64:13
that ye m. be justified in	64:13
that ye m. not offend him who	64:13
m. be made known unto my	64:19
m. not be tempted above that	64:20
that thereby I m. save some.	64:21
they m. obtain an inheritance	64:30
that his kingdom m. go forth	65: 5
inhabitants thereof m. receive it,	65: 5
m. the kingdom of God go	65: 6
kingdom of heaven m. come,	65: 6
thine enemies m. be subdued;	65: 6
he m. officiate in the office of	68:19
they m. claim their anointing	68:21
he m. the more easily obtain	69: 7
this also m. be consecrated to	72:12
he m. render himself and his	72:19
revelations m. be published,	72:21
they also m. obtain funds which	72:21
also m. render themselves	72:22
m. be able to bear his presence	76:118
salvation m. be unto you in that	78: 2
you m. be equal in the bonds	78: 5
whereby you m. accomplish	78:13
church m. stand independent	78:14
you m. come up unto the crown	78:15
you m. understand my will	82: 8
how you m. act before me,	DC 82: 9
that it m. turn to you for	82: 9
every man m. improve upon	82:18
man m. gain other talents,	82:18
m. remain upon their inheritances	83: 3
by this you m. know they are	84:50
And by this you m. know the	84:53
That they m. bring forth fruit	84:58
the testimony m. go from you	84:62
m. receive the Holy Ghost,	84:74
this you m. know my disciples	84:91
that it m. be consecrated for	84:104
he m. be edified in all meekness,	84:106
he m. become strong also.	84:106
that all m. be edified together,	84:110
the system m. be kept perfect.	84:110
that he m. tithe his people,	85: 3
be had where it m. be found on	85: 4
it m. abide in your hearts,	88: 3
that it m. be prepared for	88:18
m. possess it forever and	88:20
that ve m. understand?	88:46
that I m. make you clean;	88:74
I m. testify unto your Father,	88:75
that I m. fulfil this promise,	88:75
that you m. be instructed more	88:78
ye m. be prepared in all things	88:80
that you m. be perfected in	88:84
their souls m. escape the wrath	88:85
that he m. gather together his	88:111
m. be in the name of the Lord;	88:120
m. be in the name of the Lord,	88:120
m. be in the name of the Lord,	88:120
that all m. be edified of all,	88:122
man m. have an equal privilege.	88:122
that ye m. not be weary;	88:124
your minds m. be invigorated.	88:124
always, that ye m. not faint,	88:126
m. hear his words carefully	88:129
that he m. be an example—	88:130
it m. become a sanctuary,	88:137
thereby they m. be perfected in	90: 8
they m. receive the word,	90: 9
the word m. go forth unto	90: 9
he m. be enabled to discharge	90:23
m. not be brought into disrepute	90:23
the money m. be consecrated	90:29
she m. settle down in peace	90:31
that you m. understand and	93:19
you m. come unto the Father	93:19
they m. do the work which	94:15
that their sins m. be forgiven,	95: 1
that I m. bring to pass my	95: 4
that I m. pour out my Spirit	95: 4
whereby ye m. know how to act	96: 1
he m. assist in bringing forth	96: 8
that he m. dwell therein.	96: 9
that I m. show unto you my will	97: 1
I m. be justified when I shall	97: 2
there m. be a house built unto	97:12
That they m. be perfected in	97:14
that you m. be found worthy.	98:14
knowledge and glory m. dwell	101:25
ye m. possess your souls,	101:38
that you m. know my will	101:43
m. overlook the land round about,	101:45
olive-trees m. not be broken	101:45
I m. come with the residue	101:58
of my saints m. continue,	101:64
that I m. built them up unto	101:64
the wheat m. be secured in	101:65
that they m. be burned with	101:66
they m. buy lands and gather	101:74
this way they m. establish Zion.	101:74
every man m. act in doctrine	101:78
every man m. be accountable	101:78
that their ears m. be opened	101:92
I m. be merciful unto them,	101:92
that these things m. not come	101:92
that all men m. be left without	101:93
wise men and rulers m. hear	101:94
I m. proceed to bring to pass	101:95
that men m. discern between	101:95

MAY 607 MAY

whom they m. consider worthy	DC 102: 7
the president m. inquire and	102:23
m. appeal to the high council	102:27
such case, as m. be appealed,	102:33
that you m. know how to act	103: 1
you m. obtain three hundred.	103:32
ye m. obtain one hundred.	103:33
Smith, Jun.] m. go with you,	103:35
m. not be concemned with	104: 7
among you m. not escape;	104: 7
every m. m. give an account	104:12
it m. be holy and consecrated	104:66
that you m. learn my will	105: 1
they themselves m. be prepared,	105:10
my people m. be taught more	105:10
you m. rest in peace and safety,	105:25
you m. find favor in the eyes of	105:26
enemies that m. be upon them,	105:30
it m. become fair as the sun,	105:31
her banners m. be terrible unto	105:31
m. be constrained to	105:32
that you m. be the children of	106: 5
assurance wherewith he m. stand;	106: 8
m. officiate in the office of bishop	107:17
A majority m. form a quorum	107:28
it m. be brought before a	107:32
m. be set apart unto the ministering	107:71
all things m. be done in order	107:84
notwithstanding they m. hold	107:98
incomings m. be in the name of	109: 9
outgoings m. be in the name of	109: 9
salutations m. be in the name of	109: 9
that it m. be done to thine honor	109:10
that we m. be found worthy,	109:11
thy glory m. rest down upon thy	109:12
m. be sanctified and consecrated	109:12
holy presence m. be continually in	109:12
Lord's house m. feel thy power,	109:13
m. be taught words of wisdom	109:14
m. seek learning even by study,	109:14
that they m. grow up in thee,	109:15
house m. be a house of prayer,	109:16
m. be in the name of the Lord;	109:17
m. be in the name of the Lord;	109:18
m. be in the name of the Lord,	109:19
they m. speedily repent and return	109:21
that thy servants m. go forth	109:22
that thy name m. be upon them,	109:22
they m. bear exceedingly great and	109:23
m. know that this is thy work,	109:23
that they m. be delivered from	109:28
their works m. be brought to naught,	109:30
that there m. be an end to lyings	109:30
that we m. rise up in the midst of	109:33
they m. seal up the law,	109:38
that thy people m. not faint	109:38
they m. gather out of that city	109:39
that they m. come forth to Zion,	109:39
that they m. be prepared against	109:46
that they m. cease to spoil,	109:50
that they m. repent of their sins,	109:50
cause of thy people m. not fail	109:52
m. thine anger be kindled,	109:52
that they m. be wasted away,	109:52
m. those principles, which were so	109:54
That their hearts m. be softened	109:56
that their prejudices m. give way	109:56
and thy people m. obtain favor	109:56
all the ends of the earth m. know	109:57
m. gather out the righteous	109:58
gathering of thy people m. roll on	109:59
that thy work m. be cut short	109:59
m. begin to be redeemed;	109:62
bondage m. begin to be broken	109:63
of Judah m. begin to return	109:64
they m. lay down their weapons	109:66
And m. all the scattered remnants	109:67
they m. be exalted in thy presence,	109:69
their prejudices m. be broken up	109:70
that they m. be converted	109:70
thy right hand m. exalt them,	109:71
their names m. be perpetuated	109:71
m. become a great mountain and fill	109:72
That thy church m. come forth	DC 109:73
that thy glory m. fill the earth;	109:74
we m. ever be with the Lord;	109:75
That our garments m. be pure,	109:76
that we m. be clothed upon with	109:76
that we m. mingle our voices with	109:79
by this ye m. know that the great	110:16
This place you m. obtain by hire.	111: 9
that they m. receive my word.	112:19
that he m. perform a mission	114: 1
that thy light m. be a standard	115: 5
her stakes, m. be for a defense,	115: 6
saints, that they m. worship me.	115: 8
judgments m. be kept thereon,	119: 6
that it m. be most holy,	119: 6
that they m. not understand his	121:12
that he m. prove them also	121:12
m. come upon themselves to the	121:13
That they m. be disappointed	121:14
and their hopes m. be cut off;	121:14
That they m. be conferred	121:37
That he m. know that thy	121:44
That we m. not only publish	123: 6
nation m. be left without excuse	123: 6
and then m. we stand still,	123:17
m. be left also without excuse—	124: 7
that I m. visit them in the day	124: 8
that ye m. find grace in their eyes,	124: 9
that they m. come to the light	124: 9
I m. receive him unto myself,	124:19
he m. be trusted because of	124:20
he m. receive the consecrations of	124:21
that he m. administer blessings	124:21
that strangers m. come from afar	124:23
the weary traveler m. find health	124:23
that will come, m. come,	124:26
that he m. come to and restore	124:28
m. be baptized for those who	124:29
you m. receive honor and glory.	124:34
that I m. reveal mine ordinances	124:40
that you m. prove yourselves	124:55
that I m. bless you, and crown	124:55
that he m. contemplate the glory	124:60
he m. receive also the counsel	124:61
whereby they m. receive stock	124:63
Hyrum m. take the office of	124:91
unto him that he m. be a prophet,	124:94
m. act in concert also with	124:95
whereby he m. ask and receive,	124:95
Hyrum m. bear record of the	124:96
his name m. be had in honorable	124:96
by which he m. ask and receive	124:97
he m. obtain the confidence of	124:112
that he m. be exalted.	124:114
that ye m. hold the keys thereof,	124:123
ye m. not fall notwithstanding	124:124
hour of temptation that m. come	124:124
these m. constitute a quorum	124:126
another m. be appointed unto	124:130
another m. be appointed unto	124:132
m. travel also if they choose,	124:135
they m. preside over the quorum	124:136
nevertheless they m. travel,	124:140
that they m. be prepared for	125: 2
as the case m. require, or as	127: 1
as the circumstances m. admit of.	127: 1
as you m. choose to call it.	127: 2
that they m. testify of a truth,	127: 6
it m. be recorded in heaven;	127: 7
on earth m. be bound in heaven;	127: 7
on earth m. be loosed in heaven;	127: 7
they m. be put in the archives	127: 9
is that you all m. be saved.	127:12
every word m. be established.	128: 3
You m. think this order of things	128: 5
it m. be recorded in heaven.	128: 7
It m. seem to some to be a very	128: 9
all things m. have their likeness,	128:13
m. accord one with another—	128:13
m. offer unto the Lord an offering	128:24
you m. therefore detect him.	129: 8
grand keys whereby you m. know	129: 9
It m. probably arise through the	130:13

man m. receive the Holy Ghost,	DC 130:23	I m. them from whence I came.	2Ne 33: 8
and it m. descend upon him and	130:23	I m. the life of the mortal body—	Mos 4: 6
He m. enter into the other,	131: 4	I m. all you who deny the beggar,	4:24
(M. 17th, 1843.)	131: 5	know of me what these things m.?	12:25
whatsoever they m. be,	132:13	I m. all the holy prophets ever	15:13
they m. bear the souls of men;	132:63	I m, those who were lifted up	Al 6: 3
that he m. be glorified.	132:63	What does this m. which Amulek	12: 8
the borders of my people m. be	133: 9	What does the scripture m.,	12:21
her stakes m. be strengthened,	133: 9	or what all these things could m.	19:24
that Zion m. go forth unto the	133: 9	suppose that I m. to judge you	32:24
that they m. be ready to go	136:16	For I do not m. that ye all of you	32:25
that your souls m. be joyful.	136:29	I do not m. the end of the book	He 2:14
that they m. be prepared to	136:31	but I m. the end of the book of	2:14
that his eyes m. be opened	136:32	what do all these things m.,	5:38
may be opened that he m. see,	136:32	I m. them who are now alive or	3Ne 27:31
his ears opened that he m. hear;	136:32	is what the scriptures m.	DC 74: 7
To Whom it m. Concern:	OD		
fowl which m. fly above the	Mses 2:20	**MEANETH**	
We m. eat of the fruit of the	4: 8	the things which our father m.	1Ne 15:13
he m. not reject his words.	5:16	this is what our father m.;	15:17
that thy father m. not know it;	5:29	he m. that it will not come	15:17
that I m. murder and get gain.	5:31	he m. that it shall come by way	15:17
they m. know to prize the good.	6:55	What m. this thing which	15:21
and thus m. all become my sons.	6:68	What m. the tree which he saw?	15:21
they that mourn m. be sanctified	7:45	What m. the rod of iron	15:23
sanctify me, that I m. rest,	7:48	What m. the river of water	15:26
people m. gird up their loins,	7:62	What m. these things which	22: 1
m. have all things made manifest;	8:24	and it m. us in the days to come,	22: 6
that you m. have a knowledge	Abr 1:12	it m. that the time cometh	22: 7
you m. have an understanding of	1:14	Howbeit he m. not so,	2Ne 20: 7
m. be well with me for thy sake,	2:25	What m. the words which are	Mos 12:20
that ye m. declare all these words.	3:15	I do not know what that m.	Al 18:25
then it m. be that a planet or a	3:17	suppose that this is what it m.	40:17
planet or a star m. exist above it;	3:17	it m. that reuniting of the soul	40:18
an earth whereon these m. dwell;	3:24		
the fowl, that they m. fly above	4:20	**MEANING**	
being the second day of M.,	JS 2:60	not know the m. of all things.	1Ne 11:17
the ensuing month (M., 1829),	2:68	Knowest thou the m. of the tree	11:21
the fifteenth day of M., 1829,	2:72	Knowest thou the m. of the book?	13:21
all mankind m. be saved, by	AoF 3	understood the m. of those things,	Al 33:20
how, where, or what they m.	11	this is the whole m. of the law,	34:14
we m. say that we follow the	13	is the m. of the word restoration	41:12
		the m. of the word restoration is	41:13
MAYEST		m. the church, thou shalt give	DC 21: 4
that thou m. be my salvation	1Ne 21: 6	[m. the new and everlasting	131: 2
That thou m. say to the prisoners:	21: 9	the true m. and intention of	JS 2:74
unto thee that thou m. rejoice;	Mos 3: 4		
thou m. declare unto thy people,	3: 4	**MEANS**	
thou m. do with him as seemeth	12:16	by small m. the Lord can	1Ne 16:29
thou m. judge them according to	26:11	m. whereby they can accomplish	17: 3
Thou m. speak boldly, and tell	Al 18:20	he did provide m. for us	17: 3
m. bring souls unto repentance,	42:31	lest by any m. the people who	2Ne 5:14
thou m. no more be confounded,	Mro 10:31	lest by any m. he should swear	Jac 1: 7
then thou m. translate again.	DC 5:30	I do not, by any m., get shaken	4:18
thou m. accomplish the thing	5:34	many m. were devised to reclaim	7:24
thou m. find out mysteries,	6:11	and by any m. be destroyed,	En 1:13
thou m. bring many to the	6:11	nor any other way nor m.	Mos 3:17
thou m. know that thou hast	6:15	this is the m. whereby	4: 8
thou m. know that there is none	6:16	for there are divers ways and m.,	4:29
unto the church, thou m. do it.	28: 4	Thus God has provided a m.	8:18
thou m. know the mysteries	42:61	lest by any m. my people should	9:11
thou m. more fully keep thyself	59: 9	by some m. fall into the hands of	21:19
m. be glorified in heaven	65: 6	that by some m. they might	21:20
thou m. go up also unto the	99: 7	by the m. of those two stones	28:13
that thou m. be a spokesman	100:11	be the m. of saving some soul;	Al 26:30
thou m. know the certainty	100:11	could be the m. of saving some.	26:30
That thou m. be my servant	112:17	the m. of bringing many souls	30:47
that thou m. be a wise steward;	136:27	it would be the m. of great loss	31: 4
of the garden thou m. freely eat,	Mses 3:16	and bringeth about m. unto men	34:15
thou m. choose for thyself,	3:17	small m. in many instances doth	37: 6
hast fallen thou m. be redeemed,	5: 9	the Lord God doth work by m.	37: 7
of the garden thou m. freely eat,	Abr 5:12	by very small m. the Lord doth	37: 7
		the m. of bringing many thousands	37:10
ME: *see in the APPENDIX.*		miracles were worked by small m.	37:41
		no other way or m. whereby	38: 9
MEAN		there was no m. to reclaim men	42:12
Doth this thing m. the torment	1Ne 15:31	lest by any m. a part of the	43:25
or doth it m. the final state	15:31	sorry to be the m. of sending	48:23
the m. man boweth not down,	2Ne 12: 9	had now, by the m. of Moroni,	49:14
What m. ye? Ye beat my	13:15	they might by some m. flatter	52:19
the m. man shall be brought down,	15:15	lest by any m. the judgments	58: 9
Yea, what do the Gentiles m.?	29: 4	Gid and Teomner by this m. had	58:23

MEANS

do not make use of the m. which	Al 60:21
by the m. of their strong cords	62:23
no other way nor m. whereby	He 5: 9
use every m. in their power	6:20
a m. of bringing down the	6:25
lest by any m. they should sin;	15: 9
lest by any m. those things	3Ne 1: 7
thou shalt by no m. come out	12:26
be the m. of bringing salvation	18:32
m. for the interpretation thereof.	Mrm 9:34
by which m. he obtained the	Eth 7: 9
by which m. they drew away	9:11
m. whereby thou mayest	DC 5:34
you shall be the m. of doing	6: 8
ask me to tell you by that m.,	8: 9
by the m. of the Urim and	10: 1
strength and m. provided to	10: 4
the m. of doing much good	11: 8
m. which were before prepared,	20: 8
the m. I have appointed,	64: 5
until I shall send m. unto you	104:80
and without compulsory m.	121:46
or by the m. of their own agents,	128: 8
more sure word of prophecy m.	131: 5
has been the m. of publishing	135: 3
and by m. of the Urim and	JS 2:62

MEANT

m. by the chains of hell.	Al 12:11
now this is what he m., that many	25:11
and wist not what it m.,	3Ne 11: 8
is m. by the command in Isaiah.	DC 113: 7
the Egyptians m. it to signify	Fac 1:12

MEANTIME

In the m. we were forced	JS 2:74

MEASURE

and opened her mouth without m.;	2Ne 15:14
they were desirous beyond m.	Mos 28:12
yea, exceedingly, beyond m.	29:40
did they m. after the manner of	Al 11: 4
their reckoning and their m.,	11: 4
and either for a m. of barley,	11: 7
for a m. of every kind of grain,	11: 7
shiblon for half a m. of barley.	11:15
they were astonished beyond all m.	31:19
they were filled up in a m. with	49:22
astonished beyond m.	He 3:25
and with what m. ye mete, it	3Ne 14: 2
upon the wicked without m.—	DC 1: 9
m. to every man according to	1:10
according to the m. which he	1:10
filled with the m. of man,	49:17
blessed even above m.,	58:61
filled the m. of its creation,	88:19
filleth the m. of its creation,	88:25
as a just m. unto you.	98:24
to be poured out without m.	101:11
pour out my wrath without m.	103: 2
the m. of their iniquities,	103: 3
pour out thy judgments, without m.;	109:45
I will bless thee above m.,	Abr 2: 9

MEASURED

and time only is m. unto men.	Al 40: 8
it shall be m. to you again.	3Ne 14: 2
he has m. to his fellow man.	DC 1:10

MEASUREMENT

pertaining to the m. of time.	Fac 2: 1
m. according to celestial time,	2: 1
to the m. of this earth,	2: 1

MEASURING

m. of the time of Oliblish,	Fac 2: 4
revolution and in its m. of time.	2: 4

MEAT

while we did live upon raw m.	1Ne 17: 2
fruits and m. from the wilderness,	18: 6
eat nothing save it was raw m.;	En 1:20
he brought forth bread and m.	Al 8:21
that ye shall become m. for dogs	He 7:19
had nothing save it were m. for	3Ne 4:19
which m. they did obtain in the	4:19
Is not the life more than m.,	13:25
there may be m. in my house;	24:10
For they cannot bear m. now,	DC 19:22
both in money and in m.,	51:13
to you it shall be for m.	Mses 2:29
be given every clean herb for m.;	2:30
will give it; it shall be for their m.	Abr 4:29
to them every green herb for m.,	4:30
to give them m. in due season?	JS 1:49

MEATS

forbiddeth to abstain from m.,	DC 49:18

MEDDLE

nor to m. with or influence them	DC 134:12

MEDES

will stir up the M. against them,	2Ne 23:17

MEDIATION

through the great m. of all men,	2Ne 2:27

MEDIATOR

ye should look to the great M.,	2Ne 2:28
through Jesus the m. of	DC 76:69
Jesus the m. of the new covenant.	107:19

MEDITATED

we m. upon these things,	DC 76:19

MEDITATION

when, in the midst of my m.,	JS 2:44

MEDIUM

through the m. of mine anointed,	DC 132: 7
through the m. of Kae-e-vanrash,	Fac 2: 5
through the m. of Kli-flos-is-es,	2: 5

MEEK

and they persecute the m.,	2Ne 9:30
equity for the m. of the earth;	21: 4
the m. also shall increase,	27:30
and they persecute the m.	28:13
equity for the m. of the earth.	30: 9
submissive, m., humble, patient,	Mos 3:19
becoming humble, m., submissive,	Al 13:28
and to be m. and lowly in heart;	37:33
but to be m. and lowly in heart;	37:34
backs upon the poor and the m.,	He 6:39
And blessed are the m., for they	3Ne 12: 5
my grace is sufficient for the m.,	Eth 12:26
save he shall be m., and lowly	Mro 7:43
save the m. and lowly in heart;	7:44
a man be m. and lowly in heart,	7:44
canst thou be humble and m.,	DC 19:41
and be m. and lowly of heart.	32: 1
the poor and the m. shall have	35:15
whose language is m. and	52:16
not sufficiently m. before me.	58:41
the poor and the m. of the earth	88:17
show mercy unto all the m.,	97: 2
all the poor and m. of the earth;	109:72

MEEKNESS

faith in Christ because of your m.;	Mro 7:39
the remission of sins bringeth m.,	8:26
because of m. and lowliness	8:26
walk in the m. of my Spirit,	DC 19:23
words, in the spirit of m.	25: 5
Continue in the spirit of m.,	25:14
Govern your house in m.,	31: 9
neighbor, in mildness and in m.	38:41
desire in their hearts, in m.,	63:57
that he may be edified in all m.,	84:106
of heart, in the spirit of m.,	100: 7
m. and long suffering, and in	107:30
in all lowliness of heart, in m.	118: 3
by gentleness and m., and by love	121:41
be written in the spirit of m.	124: 4
spirit of m., confessing me	124:18

MEET 610 MELT

MEET
it was not m. for him, Lehi,	1Ne	7: 1
out of this time to m. their God;		18:18
Go forth now to m. Ahaz,	2Ne	17: 3
to m. thee at thy coming;		24: 9
that I shall m. many souls spotless		33: 7
farewell, until I shall m. you	Jac	6:13
prepared to m. the Lamanites,	Jar	1: 9
Let us go forth to m. my people,	Mos	20:24
arms to m. the Lamanites.		20:25
they did m. the Lamanites;		20:25
they did prepare to m. them;	Al	2:12
prepared to m. the Amlicites		2:13
ye are not prepared to m. God.		5:28
which are m. for repentance—		5:54
which are m. for repentance		9:30
forth fruit m. for repentance.		12:15
a time to prepare to m. God;		12:24
forth fruit m. for repentance,		13:13
behold there shall ye m. them,		16: 6
Lord that they should m. again		17:13
And when Ammon did m. them		20:29
they went out to m. them,		24:21
for men to prepare to m. God;		34:32
were prepared to m. them in		43:15
he was prepared to m. them.		43:33
And the king came out to meet him		47:21
as the king came out to m. him		47:22
should go forth to m. the king		47:22
unprepared to m. their God.		48:23
did m. the people of Morianton;		50:35
to m. them upon the plains		52:20
to m. them upon the plains.		52:20
to m. the Lamanites when they		52:26
should m. Moroni and his army.		52:30
not sufficiently strong to m. them;		56:23
did m. the spies of our armies,		57:30
we were prepared to m. them,		58:29
and did m. the men of Pachus,		62: 7
they were prepared to m. them;	3Ne	4:10
behold, ye shall m. together oft;		18:22
when ye shall m. together,		18:22
armies, and did m. them again,	Mrm	2:26
And there will I m. thee,	Eth	1:42
m. before the judgment-seat of		12:38
and they did m. in great anger,		13:27
did m. in the valley of Gilgal;		13:27
m. that they were worthy of it.	Mro	6: 1
the church did m. together oft,		6: 5
did m. together oft to partake		6: 6
unto you, or shall m. you again.		8:30
to m. you before the pleasing		10:34
it is m. unto you to know even	DC	19: 8
the church m. together often;		20:55
are to m. in conference once in		20:61
the church m. together often		20:75
it is not m. that the things		41: 6
it is m. that my servant Joseph		41: 7
it is m. that my servant Sidney		41: 8
forth to m. me in the cloud.		45:45
it is not m. that I should		58:26
it is not m. that my servants,		64:26
to m. the kingdom of God		65: 5
call upon them to m. you		71: 7
fruit m. for their Father's		84:58
not m. for a kingdom of glory.		88:24
go ye out to m. him.		88:92
and be caught up to m. him.		88:96
shall be caught up to m. him		88:97
are first caught up to m. him;		88:98
neither m. in the sight of your		89: 5
that it is m. in mine eyes that		90:30
works m. for my kingdom		101:100
caught up in the cloud to m. thee,		109:75
that which was m. in mine eyes,		121:16
go forth to m. the Bridegroom;		133:10
go ye out to m. him.		133:10
go ye, out to m. him.		133:19
thou shalt m. him who rejoiceth		133:44
m. before the judgment-seat of		135: 5
I will make an help m. for him.	Mses	3:18
was not found an help m. for him.		3:20
and all thy city m. them there,		7:63
us make an help m. for the man,	Abr	5:14
we will form an help m. for him.		5:14
was found an help m. for him.		5:21
he would there m. with me,	JS	2:53

MEETING
thus without m. any resistance,	Al	24:22
behold, this was a joyful m.		27:16
joy of Alma in m. his brethren		27:19
of m. them upon fair grounds,		52:21
m. together oft both to pray	4Ne	1:12
And it shall be done in a m.,	DC	42:89
let a conference m. be called;		58:58
hold a m. and rejoice together,		62: 4

MEETINGS
their m. were conducted by the	Mro	6: 9
And to take the lead of all m.	DC	20:44
elders are to conduct the m.		20:45
to take the lead of m. when		20:49
the lead of m. in the absence of		20:56
all m. as they are directed and		46: 2
out from your public m.,		46: 3
out of your sacrament m.;		46: 4
any out of your sacrament m.		46: 5
concerning your confirmation m.,		46: 6
also lift up his voice in m.,		47: 2
attended their several m. as	JS	2: 8

MELCHIZEDEK
as the people in the days of M.,	Al	13:14
M. to whom Abraham paid tithes;		13:15
M. was a king over the land of		13:17
M. having exercised mighty faith,		13:18
and M. did establish peace in		13:18
of the M. Priesthood,	DC	68:15
priest of the M. Priesthood		68:19
of the M. Priesthood.		68:19
Most High, after the order of M.,		76:57
the priesthood from M.,		84:14
priesthoods, namely, the M. and		107: 1
first is called the M. Priesthood		107: 2
M. was such a great high priest.		107: 2
called that priesthood after M.,		107: 4
or the M. Priesthood.		107: 4
one is the M. Priesthood,		107: 6
under the priesthood of M.		107: 7
M. Priesthood holds the right		107: 8
Priesthood, after the order of M.,		107: 9
the order of the M. Priesthood		107:10
the greater, or the M. Priesthood,		107:14
high priest of the M. Priesthood		107:17
Presidency of the M. Priesthood.		107:17
the higher, or M. Priesthood,		107:18
Of the M. Priesthood, three		107:22
ordained after the order of M.,		107:29
that is, after the order of M.,		107:71
Priesthood after the order of M.		107:73
Priesthood, after the order of M.,		107:76
which is after the order of M.,		124:123
M., Abraham, and all to whom	Fac	2: 3
keys of the Priesthood of M.,	JS	2:72

MELEK
journey over into the land of M.,	Al	8: 3
the people in the land of M.		8: 4
throughout all the land of M.		8: 4
he had finished his work at M.		8: 6
on the north of the land of M.;		8: 6
and Zeezrom, who were at M.;		31: 6
came over into the land of M.,		35:13
as if to go into the land of M.		45:18

MELODY
thanksgiving and the voice of m.	2Ne	8: 3

MELT
every man's heart shall m.;	2Ne	23: 7
should m. with fervent heat,	3Ne	26: 3
and the elements shall m. with	Mrm	9: 2
shall m. with fervent heat;	DC	101:25
their prospects shall m. away as		121:11

MELTETH

as the hoar frost m. before the DC 121:11

MELTING

be as the m. fire that burneth, DC 133:41

MEMBER

And visit the house of each m.,	DC 20:47
And visit the house of each m.,	20:51
Every m. of the church of	20:70
Any m. of the church of Christ	20:80
if the m. receiving the letter	20:84
priest, teacher, and also m.,	38:40
that every m. may be profited	46:29
stand as a m. in the church,	58:60
the body hath need of every m.,	84:110
a lively m. in this order;	92: 2
become a m. of the order,	96: 8
teacher, deacon, and m.	107:10
every m. in each quorum must	107:27

MEMBERS

m. of the church of Christ—	DC 20:38
that all the m. do their duty.	20:55
The duty of the m. after they	20:68
the m. shall manifest before	20:69
of the names of the several m.	20:82
All m. removing from the church	20:84
m. and in good standing,	20:84
stewardships, even as the m.	42:70
unto the church, not to the m.,	42:89
residue of both elders and m.	57:16
the m. of the church—	72:24
the lesser priesthood, or the m.,	85:11
four priests, and thirteen m.	102: 5
and the individual rights of its m.,	134: 9
have a right to deal with their m.	134:10
to use my influence with the m.	OD

MEMORIAL

alms have come up as a m. DC 112: 1

MEMORIALS

and your m. for your sacrifices DC 124:39

MEMORY

fathers, according to his m.;	Om	1:18
up by the m. of my many sins,	Al	36:17
by the m. of my sins no more.		36:19
enlarged the m. of this people,		37: 8
In m. of our God, our religion,		46:12
according to my m.;	Eth	5: 1

MEN

they are the mistakes of m.;	T Pg	
unto the children of m., save he	1Ne	3: 7
may persuade m. to come unto		6: 4
of worth unto the children of m.		6: 6
his will, for the children of m.		7:12
his works among the children of m.;		9: 6
himself unto the children of m.		10:17
and the way is prepared for all m.		10:18
in the hearts of the children of m.;		11:22
going forth among the children of m.;		11:24
descending upon the children of m.;		11:30
going forth among the children of m.		11:31
the hearts of the children of m.,		12:17
and the pride of the children of m.		12:18
the hearts of the children of m.		13:27
understanding of the children of m.,		13:29
all m. must come unto him,		13:40
lead away the souls of m.		14: 3
digged for the destruction of m.		14: 3
work among the children of m.;		14: 7
to the understanding of all m.		14:23
wickedness of the children of m.		15: 4
in body unto the children of m.,		15:13
the final state of the souls of m.		15:35
strong, yea, even like unto the m.;		17: 2
if it so be that the children of m.		17: 3
miracles among the children of m.,		17:51
manner which was learned by m.,		18: 2
after the manner of m.;		18: 2
not after the manner of m.	1Ne	18: 2
which were for the use of m.		18:25
excuse myself because of other m.,		19: 6
the things which some m. esteem		19: 7
God of Israel do m. trample under		19: 7
towards the children of m.		19: 9
into the hands of wicked m.,		19:10
shall come upon the children of m.		22: 2
and shall be hated of all m.		22: 5
the hearts of the children of m.;		22:15
out upon all the children of m.;		22:16
and it cometh unto m. according		22:18
up among the children of m.,		22:22
creation of the earth, and all m.,	2Ne	1:10
which bind the children of m.,		1:13
the dust, my sons, and be m.,		1:21
cometh to bring salvation unto m.		2: 3
m. are instructed sufficiently		2: 5
And the law is given unto m.		2: 5
or, by the law m. are cut off.		2: 5
for all the children of m.;		2: 9
all m. come unto God;		2:10
the days of the children of m.		2:21
gave unto the children of m.		2:21
that all m. must repent;		2:21
for he showed unto all m.		2:21
Adam fell that m. might be;		2:25
m. are, that they might have joy.		2:25
he may redeem the children of m.		2:26
m. are free according to the flesh;		2:27
the great mediation of all m.,		2:27
that all m. might be miserable		2:27
unto the children of m.		4:26
hath visited m. in so much mercy,		4:26
fear ye not the reproach of m.,		8: 7
in the flesh, and die for all m.,		9: 5
that all m. might become subject		9: 5
as death hath passed upon all m.,		9: 6
and stirreth up the children of m.		9: 9
the spirits of m. will be restored		9:12
and all m. become incorruptible,		9:13
when all m. shall have passed		9:15
world that he may save all m. if		9:21
he suffereth the pains of all m.,		9:21
both m., women, and children,		9:21
resurrection might pass upon all m.,		9:22
And he commandeth all m. that		9:23
frailties, and the foolishness of m.!		9:28
when all m. shall be judged of		9:44
unto the children of m.;		9:53
have made unto the children of m.,		10:15
have made unto the children of m.,		10:17
have all m. that dwell thereon		10:19
should come all m. must perish.		11: 6
hearts and rejoice for all m.		11: 8
them unto you and unto all m.		11: 8
the haughtiness of m. shall be		12:11
the haughtiness of m. shall be		12:17
Thy m. shall fall by the sword		13:25
of Jerusalem, and m. of Judah,		15: 3
m. of Judah his pleasant plant;		15: 7
their honorable m. are famished,		15:13
and m. of strength to mingle		15:22
Lord have removed m. far away,		16:12
a small thing for you to weary m.,		17:13
with bows shall m. come thither,		17:24
as m. rejoice when they divide		19: 3
have no joy in their young m.,		19:17
and make m. go over dry shod.		21:15
also dash the young m. to pieces,		23:18
m. shall know of a surety,		25: 7
of worth unto the children of m.,		25: 8
wonder among the children of m.		25:17
wonders, among the children of m.		26:13
things forth unto the children of m.		26:14
he may draw all m. unto him.		26:24
he hath given it free for all m.;		26:27
persuade all m. to repentance.		26:27
all m. are privileged the one like		26:28
priestcrafts are that m. preach		26:29
that all m. should have charity,		26:30
that m. should not murder;		26:32
good among the children of m.;		26:33

MEN

be plain unto the children of m.;	2Ne	26:33
revealed unto the children of m.		27:11
been among the children of m.,		27:11
his word unto the children of m.;		27:13
will show unto the children of m.		27:21
all things unto the children of m.		27:22
work not among the children of m.		27:23
is taught by the precepts of m.—		27:25
will show unto the children of m.		27:28
the poor among m. shall rejoice		27:30
worth unto the children of m.,		28: 2
he hath given his power unto m.;		28: 5
are taught by the precepts of m.		28:14
in the hearts of the children of m.,		28:20
unto the precepts of m.,		28:26
will give unto the children of m.		28:30
hearken unto the precepts of m.,		28:31
have made unto the children of m.,		29: 1
your God, have created all m.,		29: 7
my word unto the children of m.,		29: 7
For I command all m.,		29:11
known unto the children of m.		30:16
revealed unto the children of m.		30:18
the hearts of the children of m.		30:18
work among the children of m.		31: 3
he speaketh unto m. according		31: 3
showeth unto the children of m.		31: 7
showeth unto the children of m.		31: 9
he said unto the children of m.:		31:10
and a love of God and of all m.		31:20
and the stiffneckedness of m.;		32: 7
the hearts of the children of m.		33: 1
they teach all m. that they should		33:10
persuade all m. not to rebel	Jac	1: 8
that all m. would believe in Christ,		1: 8
against the m. of my people,		2:32
unto the children of m.,		4: 7
to the understanding of m.;		4:13
manifest unto the children of m.,	Jar	1: 4
were mighty m. in the faith		1: 7
all m. to come unto God,	Om	1:25
were many holy m. in the land,	WM	1:17
become m. of understanding;	Mos	1: 2
just m. to be their teachers,		2: 4
with love towards God and all m.		2: 4
O, all ye old m., and also ye		2:40
and also ye young m., and you little		2:40
among the children of m.,		3: 5
and shall go forth amongst m.,		3: 5
in the hearts of the children of m.		3: 6
come unto the children of m.		3: 9
come upon the children of m.		3:10
among all the children of m.,		3:13
come unto the children of m.,		3:17
m. drink damnation to their own		3:18
down among the children of m.		4: 2
towards the children of m.;		4: 6
that sixteen of their strong m.		7: 2
down among the children of m.,		7:27
was covered with bones of m.,		8: 8
mysteries to the children of m.		8:19
of the children of m.;		8:20
with four of my m. into the city,		9: 5
that the m. should till the ground,		10: 4
m. armed with bows, and with		10: 8
my old m. that could bear arms,		10: 9
all my young m. that were able		10: 9
people, as to the strength of m.		10:11
and shall be driven by m.,		12: 2
down among the children of m.,		13:34
He is despised and rejected of m.,		14: 3
down among the children of m.,		15: 1
miracles among the children of m.,		15: 6
intercession for the children of m.—		15: 8
towards the children of m.;		15: 9
down among the children of m.;		17: 8
the m. should leave their wives		19:11
sent m. into the wilderness		19:18
and they met the m. of Gideon.		19:22
And the m. of Gideon told them		19:22
the people told the m. of Gideon		19:23
more than there was of m.;		21:17
a small number of m. to search		21:25
have just m. to be your kings	Mos	23: 8
except they were just m.		23:17
all their m. and all their women		24:22
be an equality among all m.;		27: 3
yea, m. and women, all nations,		27:25
all m. shall stand to be judged		27:31
will appoint wise m. to be judges,		29:11
have just m. to be your kings,		29:13
ye could have m. for your kings		29:13
because all m. are not just		29:16
all cases among the children of m.,		29:20
for the Lord had created all m.,	Al	1: 4
and had also redeemed all m.;		1: 4
all m. should have eternal life.		1: 4
Amlici did arm his m. with all		2:14
they who went out with their m.		2:22
trodden down by the hosts of m.		3: 2
who were just and holy m.		3: 6
an invitation unto all m.,		5:33
forth among all the children of m.		5:50
that all m. shall reap a reward of		9:28
it was those m. who sought to		10:14
thou hast not lied unto m. only		12: 3
doth grant unto the children of m.,		12: 9
merciful unto the children of m.,		12:15
unto m. that they must die;		12:27
caused m. to behold of his glory.		12:29
therefore God conversed with m.,		12:30
gave commandments unto m.,		12:31
But God did call on m.,		12:33
unto the children of m.,		13: 6
the hearts of the children of m.		13:24
known unto just and holy m.,		13:26
these m. are spotless before God.		14: 7
sent m. to cast stones at them.		14: 7
the minds of the children of m.,		16:16
m. of a sound understanding		17: 2
by the wickedness of these m.		17:28
those m. again stood to scatter		17:33
m. who do scatter our flocks.		17:33
one of their m. could slay him		17:35
down upon all the children of m.:		18:32
were also rebuked by those m.		19:21
for I know that they are just m.		20:15
that God will save all m.		21: 6
that we should slay these m.,		22:20
testimony to God, and also to m.,		24:18
towards the children of m.?		26:16
m. that had so great reason to		26:35
towards God, and also towards m.;		27:27
the Lord, the Redeemer of all m.,		28: 8
to ensnare the hearts of m.		28:13
the great call of diligence of m.		28:14
and destruction among m.,		28:14
unto m. according to their desire,		29: 4
unto m. according to their wills,		29: 4
and evil have come before all m.;		29: 5
bring m. on to unequal grounds.		30: 7
m. should be judged according to		30:11
all m. were on equal grounds.		30:11
atonement made for the sins of m.,		30:17
away many women, and also m.,		30:18
among the children of m.?		31:26
for they are despised of all m.		32: 5
his word by angels unto m.,		32:23
not only m. but women also.		32:23
to be heard of thee and not of m.,		33: 8
all m. shall stand before him,		33:22
come among the children of m.,		34: 8
bringeth about means unto m.		34:15
and is trodden under foot of m.		34:29
for m. to prepare to meet God;		34:32
for m. to perform their labors.		34:32
that they pray to be heard of m.,		38:13
that m. shall come forth from the		40: 5
what becometh of the souls of m.		40: 7
one time appointed for m. to rise		40: 8
time only is measured unto m.		40: 8
there is a time appointed unto m.		40: 9
what becometh of the souls of m.		40: 9
the spirits of all m., as soon as		40:11
yea, the spirits of all m., whether		40:11
m. should be judged according to		41: 3

MEN 613 MEN

all m. that are in a state of nature,	Al 41:11	I numbered those young m. who	Al	56:55
reclaim m. from this fallen state,	42:12	never were m. known to have		56:56
of m. in this probationary state,	42:13	a part of those m. who were not		56:57
repentance could not come unto m.	42:16	the number of six thousand m.,		57: 6
m. would not be afraid to sin.	42:20	we selected a part of our m.,		57:16
if m. sinned what could justice do,	42:21	and also a numerous army of m.		57:17
m. into the presence of God;	42:23	those m. whom we sent with the		57:18
and the redemption of m., and	42:26	those m. who had been selected		57:22
sent certain m. unto him,	43:23	my m. who had been wounded		57:24
pursued by Lehi and his m.;	43:40	taken care of our wounded m.,		57:28
when the m. of Moroni saw the	43:48	our m. to the maintaining those		58: 3
on the east were the m. of Lehi.	43:52	by an army of two thousand m.		58: 8
saw the m. of Lehi on the east	43:53	Gid, with a small number of m.,		58:16
commanded his m. that they	43:54	and a small number of m.		58:16
not desire to be m. of blood.	44: 1	Gid and his m. were on the right		58:17
I will command my m. that they	44: 7	I caused that my m., those who		58:18
the children of m. do forget the	46: 8	that my m. should not sleep,		58:26
place among the children of m.	46: 9	those m. who came up unto us		58:34
with a small number of his m.,	46:33	send more m. to our assistance;		58:36
to which m. were subject by the	46:40	should cause m. to be gathered		59: 3
surround those m. in their camps	47:13	be m. sent to the city Nephihah,		59: 9
Lehonti came down with his m.	47:14	appointed to gather together m.,		60: 2
surrounded the m. of Amalickiah,	47:14	that myself, and also my m.,		60: 3
he delivered his m., contrary to	47:16	and also Helaman and his m.,		60: 3
he did appoint m. to speak unto	48: 1	were it not for these king-m.,		60:16
place the greater number of m.;	48: 9	those king-m. had over us;		60:16
if all m. had been, and were,	48:17	yea, even those king-m.		60:17
the hearts of the children of m.	48:17	also m. to strengthen our armies?		60:19
for they were all m. of God.	48:18	send forth food and m. unto us,		60:24
all m. whosoever would hearken	48:19	your provisions and of your m.,		60:34
captain over the m. of that city;	49:16	as many m. as it were possible		61: 5
a body of their strongest m.,	49:20	speedily with a few of your m.,		61:15
words unto the children of m.;	50:19	took a small number of m.,		62: 3
were called king-m., for they	51: 5	whatsoever m. he could in all		62: 6
also put the king m. to silence.	51: 7	stronger than the m. of Pachus,		62: 6
when the m. who were called	51:13	and did meet the m. of Pachus,		62: 7
men who were called king-m.	51:13	his m. were taken prisoners,		62: 8
should go against those king-m.,	51:17	the m. of Pachus received their		62: 9
fight against the m. of Moroni	51:18	king-m. who had been taken		62: 9
put an end to those king-m.,	51:21	those m. of Pachus and those		62: 9
by the appellation of king-m.;	51:21	of Pachus and those king-m.,		62: 9
leaving m. in every city to	51:25	an army of six thousand m.		62:12
repulsed by Teancum and his m.,	51:31	that an army of six thousand m.,		62:13
Teancum and his m. did pitch	51:32	leaving a large body of m. in the		62:14
and behold, his m. were asleep,	51:35	march with a large body of m.		62:14
But he kept his m. round about,	52: 6	body of m. of the Lamanites,		62:15
had sent a large number of m. to	52: 7	his m. should march forth and		62:22
together a large number of m.,	52:12	that his m. should march forth		62:25
might assist Teancum with his m.	52:15	was a large company of m.,		63: 4
take a small number of m.,	52:22	thousand and four hundred m.,		63: 4
and the m. of Lehi were fresh.	52:28	forth among the children of m.		63:12
they feared was Lehi and his m.	52:29	an innumerable army of m.,	He	1:14
the m. of Moroni on one hand,	52:31	both m., women, and children,		1:27
and the m. of Lehi on the other,	52:31	if m. build they cannot fall.		5:12
Moroni commanded his m. that	52:32	with whom these m. do converse?		5:38
Moroni and his m. were more	52:34	the hearts of the children of m.		6:30
with such fury with his strong m.,	52:36	no justice unto the children of m.;		7: 4
commanded their m. that they	52:38	there were certain m. passing by		7:11
Moroni placed m. over them to	53: 1	to get gain, to be praised of m.,		7:21
did employ his m. in preparing	53: 7	there were m. who were judges,		8: 1
two thousand of those young m.,	53:18	seeketh to destroy the souls of m.		8:28
And they were all young m.,	53:20	certain m. who were among		9: 1
they were m. who were true at	53:20	they saw those five m. who had		9: 7
were m. of truth and soberness,	53:21	These m. are they who have		9: 8
my food for my m. of war;	54:20	the destruction of those wicked m.		11:11
should be made among his m.,	55: 4	they sent an army of strong m.		11:28
and a small number of his m.	55: 6	the hearts of the children of m.;		12: 1
that a small number of m.	55: 7	do good, are the children of m.;		12: 4
when Laman and his m. saw that	55:15	nothingness of the children of m.;		12: 7
Moroni had prepared his m. with	55:16	cause, that m. might be saved,		12:22
caused the m. who were with him	55:21	that m. might be brought unto		12:24
of the sons of those m. whom	56: 3	that all m. might be saved.		12:25
thousand of these young m.	56: 5	thereby m. may be brought into		14:15
of these two thousand young m.	56: 9	among the children of m.—		14:28
slain a vast number of our m.,	56:10	And angels did appear unto m.,		16:14
of so many of our valiant m.:	56:13	did appear unto men, wise m.,		16:14
Antipus and his m. toiling with	56:15	known unto the children of m.	3Ne	1:14
there were sent two thousand m.	56:28	that is was wrought by m. and		2: 2
prepared with ten thousand m.,	56:28	and their young m. and their		2:16
but I said unto my m.:	56:43	stand against so many brave m.		3: 3
therefore the m. of Antipus,	56:51	there began to be m. inspired		6:20
they gathered together their m.	56:53	but few righteous m. among them.		7: 7

MEN

of Nephi, m. unto this ministry,	3Ne	7:25
he stirreth up the hearts of m.		11:29
stir up the hearts of m. with anger,		11:30
all m., everywhere, to repent		11:32
when m. shall revile you and		12:11
to be trodden under foot of m.		12:13
do m. light a candle and put it		12:15
ye do not your alms before m.		13: 1
that they may have glory of m.		13: 2
that they may be seen of m.		13: 5
if ye forgive m. their trespasses		13:14
ye forgive not m. their trespasses		13:15
may appear unto m. to fast.		13:16
thou appear not unto m. to fast,		13:18
would that m. should do to you,		14:12
Do m. gather grapes of thorns,		14:16
can the hearts of m. conceive so		17:17
of m., women, and children.		17:25
form more than the sons of m.—		20:44
is built upon the works of m.,		27:11
I might draw all m. unto me,		27:14
as I have been lifted up by m.		27:14
m. be lifted up by the Father,		27:14
I will draw all m. unto me,		27:15
hath given unto the children of m.		27:18
their works be known unto m.		27:25
manner of m. ought ye to be?		27:27
Father unto the children of m.,		28: 7
bring the souls of m. unto me,		28: 9
Ghost unto the children of m.,		28:11
been trempled under feet of m.,		28:35
work among the children of m.;	4Ne	1: 5
together a great number of m.,	Mrm	1:11
the hearts of the children of m.		4: 5
to harrow up the souls of m.		5: 8
that my m. were hewn down,		6:10
wherein all m. are redeemed,		9:13
all m. shall be awakened by the		9:13
miracles among the children of m.		9:20
among the children of m. until	Eth	1: 3
unto the understanding of m.		3: 5
even all m. were created in the		3:15
magnify to the eyes of m.		3:24
due time unto the children of m.		3:27
them unto the children of m.		3:28
to come unto the children of m.		4: 1
for it persuadeth m. to do good.		4:11
thing persuadeth m. to do good		4:12
same that leadeth m. to all good;		4:12
to give light unto m., women, and		6: 3
hath hardened the hearts of m.		8:25
the hearts of the children of m.,		8:26
together a small number of m.,		9: 9
an anchor to the souls of m.,		12: 4
because of the faith of m. he		12: 8
no faith among the children of m.		12:12
if m. come unto me I will show		12:27
I give unto m. weakness that		12:27
my grace is sufficient for all m.		12:27
workest unto the children of m.		12:29
thou workest after m. have faith.		12:30
a place for the children of m.		12:33
hast had for the children of m.		12:34
except m. shall have charity		12:34
all m. shall know that my		12:38
all m. should serve him who dwell		13: 2
rose up, who were mighty m.,		13:15
of both m., women, and children		14:22
loss of m , women and children		14:31
slain two millions of mighty m.,		15: 2
both m. women and children		15:15
they were large and mighty m.		15:26
as to the strength of m.		15:26
when the m. of Coriantumr had		15:28
Shiz arose, and also his m.,		15:28
and callings of God unto m.;	Mro	3: 4
walk with the children of m.		7: 4
thing persuadeth m. to do evil,		7:17
minister unto the children of m.,		7:22
things unto the children of m.,		7:24
otherwise m. were fallen,		7:24
m. began to exercise faith in		7:25
m. also were saved by faith in		7:26
hath upon the children of m.?	Mro	7:27
the cause of the children of m.;		7:28
minister unto the children of m.		7:29
to call m. unto repentance,		7:31
made unto the children of m.,		7:31
the way among the children of m.,		7:31
the residue of m. may have faith		7:32
made unto the children of m.		7:32
appear unto the children of m.?		7:36
appear and minister unto m.;		7:37
wo be unto the children of m.,		7:37
great number of our choice m.		9: 2
were m., women, and children.		9: 7
been unto the children of m.,		10: 3
the faith of the children of m.,		10: 7
of the Spirit of God unto m.,		10: 8
unbelief of the children of m.		10:19
wo be unto the children of m.		10:25
and whose eyes are upon all m.;	DC	1: 1
of the Lord is unto all m.,		1: 2
all m. shall know that the day		1:35
frustrated, but the work of m.;		3: 3
on in the persuasions of m.		3: 6
m. set at naught the counsels		3: 7
up and become as other m.,		3:11
forth among the children of m.		4: 1
words unto the children of m.		5: 6
persuasions of m. no more;		5:21
forth unto the children of m.		6: 1
a greater work yet among m.		7: 5
wicked m. have taken them		10: 8
to destroy the souls of m.		10:27
forth among the children of m.		11: 1
God unto the convincing of m.,		11:21
forth among the children of m.,		11:22
forth among the children of m.,		11:22
grant unto the children of m.		11:22
forth among the children of m.		12: 1
forth unto the children of m.		14: 1
unto the children of m.		17: 4
purposes unto the children of m.		17: 9
the children of m. are stirred up		18: 6
I command all m. everywhere		18: 9
he suffered the pain of all m.,		18:11
that all m. might repent and		18:11
he might bring all m. unto him,		18:12
expedient unto the children of m.		18:18
all m. must take upon them		18:24
and gifts of God unto m.;		18:32
These words are not of m. nor		18:34
all m. must repent and be		18:42
and not only m., but women,		18:42
work among the children of m.,		18:44
the hearts of the children of m.,		19: 7
unto the children of m.		19:19
God does inspire m. and call		20:11
know that all m. must repent		20:29
was crucified by sinful m.		21: 9
as is not known among m.		24:12
righteousness with m. on earth		29:11
wailing among the hosts of m.;		29:15
and m. again begin to deny		29:22
both m. and beasts, the fowls		29:24
judgments are not given unto m.;		29:30
any man nor the children of m.;		29:34
tempt the children of m.,		29:39
words are not of man nor of m.,		31:13
forth unto the children of m.;		35:10
I unto you concerning all m.—		36: 4
among the children of m.,		38:11
know not the hearts of m. in		38:29
the wickedness of m. reveal		38:30
certain m. among them shall		38:34
when m. are endowed with		38:38
known among the children of m.,		39:15
m. shall go forth into all		39:15
shall teach them unto all m.;		42:58
to teach the children of m.		43:15
as with me in days of old,		45:10
sought for by all holy m.,		45:12
as unto m. in days of old.		45:15
the love of m. shall wax cold,		45:27
because of the precepts of m.		45:29

MEN 615 MEN

m. standing in that generation,	DC 45:31	and afflicted by wicked m.;	DC 109:48
m. shall lift up their voices	45:32	form acquaintance with m. in	111: 3
m. will harden their hearts	45:33	name among the children of m.	112: 6
hearts of the children of m.	45:55	let thy love abound unto all m.,	112:11
or the commandments of m.;	46: 7	let m. be appointed to supply	118: 1
for some are of m., and others	46: 7	and aspire to the honors of m.,	121:35
conditions of the children of m.	46:15	upon the souls of the children of m.,	121:37
to be certain m. appointed,	48: 5	and disposition of almost all m.,	121:39
I will that all m. shall repent,	49: 8	be full of charity towards all m.,	121:45
holy m. that ye know not of.	49: 8	what are the m. going to do	122: 6
seek ye a living like unto m.,	54: 9	by the subtle craftiness of m.,	123:12
Wo unto you rich m.,	56:16	m. whom I have appointed,	124:46
Wo unto you poor m.,	56:17	to any of the sons of m. to do a	124:49
m. should be anxiously engaged	58:27	sons of m. go with all their	124:49
And inasmuch as m. do good	58:28	at the hands of those sons of m.,	124:49
I command and m. obey not;	58:32	may obtain the confidence of m.	124:112
disciples and the children of m.	58:52	righteous m. that were before you.	127: 4
all m. shall know what it is	60: 4	and appointment of those m. by	128: 4
as with m. in days of old.	61:13	or any set of m., this power	128: 9
by faith, not by the will of m.,	63:10	m. did in authority, in the name	128: 9
and not for the good of m.	63:12	salvation of the children of m.,	128:11
old m. shall die; but they shall	63:51	the spirits of just m. made perfect,	129: 3
let all m. beware how they	63:61	have an end when m. are dead.	132: 7
is required to forgive all m.	64:10	whether it be ordained of m.,	132:13
hearts of the children of m.	64:22	not remain after m. are dead,	132:13
whose voice is unto m.—	65: 1	they may bear the souls of m.;	132:63
forth unto the children of m.,	66: 2	for he calleth upon all m.,	133:16
who are just m. made perfect	76:69	all m. everywhere to repent.	133:16
spirits of m. kept in prison,	76:73	have not m. heard nor perceived	133:45
according to m. in the flesh;	76:73	m. might be made partakers of	133:57
are honorable m. of the earth,	76:75	holds m. accountable for their acts	134: 1
blinded by the craftiness of m.	76:75	and that m. are amenable to him,	134: 4
not minifest unto m. in the flesh;	84:21	to bind the consciences of m.,	134: 4
m. shall fall upon the ground	88:89	all m. are bound to sustain and	134: 5
according to m. in the flesh.	88:99	to the laws all m. owe respect	134: 6
spirits of m. who are to be judged,	88:100	their tendency to evil among m.,	134: 8
and reveal the secret acts of m.,	88:108	all m. should step forward and	134: 8
and reveal the secret acts of m.,	88:109	society has authority to try m.	134:10
of conspiring m. in the last days,	89: 4	m. should appeal to the civil law	134:11
interpolations by the hands of m.	91: 2	all m. are justified in defending	134:11
and dwelt among the sons of m.	93: 4	jeopardizing the lives of m.;	134:12
and in him was the life of m.	93: 9	salvation of m. in this world,	135: 3
life of men, and the light of m.	93: 9	the benefit of the children of m.;	135: 3
m. were made by him;	93:10	towards God, and towards all m.	135: 4
m. became again in their infant	93:38	*m. shall know that my garments*	135: 5
from the children of m.,	93:39	of traitors and wicked m.;	135: 7
my word to the children of m.	96: 4	will touch the hearts of honest m.	135: 7
go forth unto the hcildren of m.,	96: 5	of able bodied and expert m.,	136: 7
the hearts of the children of m.	96: 5	all the children of m. which	Mses 1: 8
my word unto the children of m.	96: 8	not had among the children of m.	1:23
honest m. and wise men should be	98:10	of all m. have I called Adam,	1:34
m. should be sought for diligently,	98:10	the children of m. shall esteem	1:41
good m. and wise men ye should	98:10	again among the children of m.—	1:41
m. ye should observe to uphold;	98:10	known among the children of m.	1:42
if m. will smite you, or your	98:23	created all the children of m.;	3: 5
not be confounded before m.;	100: 5	to deceive and to blind m.,	4: 4
When m. are called unto mine	101:39	m. began from that time forth to	5:13
of the earth and the savor of m.;	101:39	Lord God called upon m. by the	5:14
are called to be the savor of m.,	101:40	spread among all the sons of m.	5:52
trodden under the feet of m.	101:40	And it was among the sons of m.,	5:53
are my warriors, my young m.,	101:55	among the daughters of m. these	5:53
let honorable m. be appointed,	101:73	came not among the sons of m.,	5:54
be appointed, even wise m.,	101:73	prevail among all the sons of m.	5:55
by the hands of wise m. whom	101:80	the sons of m. whom he had made;	5:56
for m. ought always to pray	101:81	then began these m. to call upon	6: 4
all m. may be left without excuse;	101:93	children of m. were numerous	6:15
That wise m. and rulers may hear	101:94	had great dominion among m.,	6:15
that m. may discern between the	101:95	called upon all m., everywhere,	6:23
and to be the saviors of m.;	103: 9	taught unto the children of m.	6:23
as they are not the saviors of m.,	103:10	all m. were offended because	6:37
and trodden under foot of m.	103:10	an host of m. hath he brought in	6:44
young m. and the middle aged—	103:22	come among the children of m.,	6:49
the churches send up wise m.	103:23	m. have become carnal, sensual,	6:49
but m. do not always do my will.	103:31	unto our fathers that all m. must	6:50
and for the salvation of m.	104: 1	m. before they were in the flesh.	6:51
given unto the children of m.	104:17	shall come unto the children of m.,	6:52
my warriors, my young m.,	105:16	m. must repent and be baptized	6:53
And to have sent wise m.,	105:28	all m., everywhere, must repent,	6:57
himself from the crafts of m.	106: 6	the plan of salvation unto all m.,	6:62
and were righteous and holy m.	107:29	the doings of the children of m.;	7:41
administered to the children of m.,	109: 4	Wo, wo is me, the mother of m.;	7:48
and as all m. sin	109:34	the cross, after the manner of m.;	7:55
the destruction of our fellow m.;	109:43	be among the children of m.,	7:61

MEN

also the resurrection of all m.;	Mses	7:62
m. began to multiply on the		8:14
of m. saw that those daughters		8:14
is kindled against the sons of m.,		8:15
if m. do not repent, I will send		8:17
Gospel unto the children of m.,		8:19
called upon the children of m.		8:20
ourselves the daughters of m.!		8:21
and the same are mighty m.,		8:21
which are like unto m. of old,		8:21
men of old, m. of great renown.		8:21
the wickedness of m. had become		8:22
these strange gods, m., women,	Abr	1: 8
say unto one, I say unto all m.;	JS	1:46
and so unacquainted with m.		2: 8
that giveth to all m. liberally,		2:11
the commandments of m.,		2:19
yet m. of high standing would		2:22
the hands of all classes of m.,		2:27
of the children of m.		2:73
that m. will be punished for their	AoF	2
allow all m. the same privilege,		11
and in doing good to all m.;		13

MEND

they did not m. their ways.	He	11:36
he repent and m. his ways.	DC	75:29

MEN'S

lay that upon m. shoulders	Eth	10: 5
and m. hearts shall fail them,	DC	45:26
according to m. faith it shall		52:20
hold upon other m. goods,		56:17
surely, m. hearts shall fail;		88:91
and m. hearts failing them,	Mses	7:66

MENTION

made m. upon the first plates.	1Ne	19: 2
make m. of the God of Israel,		20: 1
hath he made m. of my name.		21: 1
make m. that his name is exalted.	2Ne	22: 4
have made m. unto my children		25: 6
have more particularly made m.	Al	13:19
shall m. the loving kindness of	DC	133:52

MENTIONED

other purposes, as before m.	DC	42:71
trumpets, m. in the 8th chapter		77:12
as m. in the 10th chapter of		77:14
three presidents previously m.		107:24
those names which I have m.,		124:144
white stone m. in Revelation		130:10
before m. religious excitement;	JS	2:21
on the evening of the above-m.		2:29
which cannot be m. here.		2:41
found m. in the translation of		2:68

MERCANTILE

the Ozondah [m. establishment]	DC	104:39
the Ozondah [m. establishment],		104:39
the Ozondah [m. establishment]		104:40
whole Ozondah [m. establishment],		104:41

MERCHANDISE

leave his m. and to spend all	DC	41: 9
make a disposition of his m.,		114: 1

MERCHANT

be made a m. unto my name,	DC	117:14

MERCHANTS

were many m. in the land,	3Ne	6:11

MERCIES

the tender m. of the Lord	1Ne	1:20
the multitude of his tender m.		8: 8
the m. of God in sparing their	2Ne	1: 2
the m. of the Holy One of Israel		9:25
relying upon the m. of those	Al	24:25
upon the m. of the world—		26:28
not upon the m. of the world		26:28
alone but upon the m. of God.		26:28
rely upon the m. of our brethren.		27: 9

MERCY

will not understand thy m.	Al	33:16
for the many m. and blessings		34:38
because of the m. of the Father	3Ne	16: 9
with great m. will I gather thee.		22: 7
knowing the m. and the	Mrm	2:12
the multitude of his tender m.	Eth	6:12
to deny the pure m. of God	Mro	8:19
denieth the m. of Christ,		8:20
denying the m. of Christ,		8:23
suiting his m. according to	DC	46:15

MERCIFUL

and, because thou art m.,	1Ne	1:14
perhaps the Lord would be m.		8:37
I will be m. unto the Gentiles,		13:33
I will be m. unto the Gentiles		13:34
for had not the Lord been m.,		19:20
hos m. the Lord had been in	2Ne	1: 3
he will be m. unto you		4: 7
the Lord will be m. unto them,		6:11
the m. plan of the great Creator,		9: 6
God will be m. unto many;		10: 2
seeing that our m. God has given		10:20
for I will be m. unto my people,		23:22
I will be m. unto them, saith the		28:32
but will be m. unto them;	Jac	3: 6
how m. is our God unto us.		6: 4
God is exceeding m. unto them,	Jar	1: 3
he had been m. unto them,	Mos	24:21
the Lord will be m. unto them	Al	9:16
the Lord will be m. unto all who		9:17
is m. unto the children of men,		12:15
Oh, how m. is our God!		24:15
our God would have been so m.		26:17
and he is a m. Being, even unto		26:35
then do I remember his m. arm		29:10
God is m. unto all who believe		32:22
Thou are m., O God, for thou		33: 4
thou wast m. when I prayed		33: 4
and thou wast m. unto me when		33: 5
thou art m. unto thy children		33: 8
thou hast been m. unto me,		33: 9
thou hast been thus m. unto me,		33:11
m. for that which is merciful.		41:13
merciful for that which is m.		41:13
that you are m. unto your brethren;		41:14
just God, and a m. God also.		42:15
thus we see how m. and just are		50:19
we may see that the Lord is m.	He	3:27
the Lord will be m. unto them;		7:24
the Lord shall be m. unto them.		15:12
been m. unto the seed of Joseph.	3Ne	5:21
And blessed are the m., for		12: 7
supposing that he would be m.	Mrm	2:12
thou hast been m. unto us.	Eth	3: 3
the Lord was m. unto Omer,		9: 2
be m. unto the seed of Joesph		13: 7
m. unto the father of Joseph		13: 7
how m. the Lord hath been unto	Mro	3:10
But remember, God is m.;	DC	3:10
will be m. unto your weakness.		38:14
I will be m. unto you;		50:16
m. unto those who confess		61: 2
I will be m. unto you,		64: 4
am m. and will bless them,		70:18
I, the Lord, am m. and		76: 5
that I may be m. unto them,		101:92
thou art gracious and m.,		109:53
Be m. unto thy servant,	Mses	1:36
thou art m. and kind forever;		7:30

MERCIFULLY

Zion, for I will deal m. with her.	DC	111: 6

MERCY

thy power, and goodness, and m.	1Ne	1:14
that he would have m. on me,		8: 8
for he that hath m. on them		21:10
will have m. upon his afflicted.		21:13
the merits, and m., and grace	2Ne	2: 8
the m., and the justice of God.		2:12
hath visited men in so much m.,		4:26
wisdom of God, his m. and grace!		9: 8

MERCY

greatness of the m. of our God,	2Ne	9:19
greatness. and his grace and m.,		9:53
in his justice, and power, and m.		11: 5
shall have m. on their fatherless		19:17
Lord will have m. on Jacob,		24: 1
and in justice, and in great m.,	Jac	4:10
while his arm of m. is extended		6: 5
m. hath no claim on that man;	Mos	2:39
m. could have claim on them no		3:26
O have m., and apply the		4: 2
m. of him who created all things,		5:15
showing m. unto thousands of		13:14
having the bowels of m.;		15: 9
the arms of m. were extended		16:12
the arms of m. were extended		16:12
the Lord in m. hath seen fit to		27:28
saw fit in his infinite m.		28: 4
extending the arm of m. towards		29:20
O Lord, have m. and spare my life,	Al	2:30
that I may have m. upon them.		3:14
by the m. and power of God.		5: 4
his m. and long-suffering towards		5: 6
the arms of m. are extended		5:33
full of grace, and m., and truth.		5:48
and the Lord in much m. hath		7: 2
his bowels may be filled with m.,		7:12
his matchless power, and his m.,		9:11
patience, m., and long-suffering,		9:26
then will I have m. upon you,		12:33
he shall have claim on m.		12:34
our God, have m. on this man,		15:10
saying: O Lord, have m.;		18:41
according to thy abundant m.		18:41
God, have m. on this people!		19:29
the great God has had m. on us,		24:14
in his m. he doth visit us by his		24:14
of his great power, and of his m.,		26:16
in his great m. hath brought us		26:20
bowels of m. are over all the earth.		26:37
whosoever repenteth shall find m.;		32:13
he that findeth m. and endureth		32:13
to bring about the bowels of m.,		34:15
m. can satisfy the demands of		34:16
that he would have m. upon you;		34:17
Yea, cry unto him for m.;		34:18
thou Son of God, have m. on me,		36:18
the Lord in his great m. sent his		38: 7
unto the Lord Jesus Christ for m.,		38: 8
remember my brethren in m.—		38:14
ye shall have m. restored unto		41:14
m. could not take effect except		42:13
the plan of m. could not be brought		42:15
to bring about the plan of m.,		42:15
what could justice do, or m. either,		42:21
which repentance m. claimeth;		42:22
and m. claimeth the penitent,		42:23
and m. cometh because of the		42:23
m. claimeth all which is her own;		42:24
suppose that m. can rob justice?		42:25
let the justice of God, and his m.,		42:30
the great plan of m. may have claim		42:31
of the Nephites, pleading for m.		55:23
goodness and his m. towards them,	He	12: 6
mine arm of m. is extended	3Ne	9:14
merciful, for they shall obtian m.		12: 7
my bowels are filled with m.		17: 7
will I have m. on thee,		22: 8
the Lord that hath m. on thee.		22:10
according to the m., and the		26: 5
for whom there was no m.,		29: 7
according to his justice and m.	Mrm	6:22
the Lord did have m. on them.	Eth	11: 8
his rights of m. which he hath	Mro	7:27
alive in him because of his m.		8:19
are without order and without m.		9:18
and his m. and long-suffering,		9:25
through the m. of God,	DC	1:29
whose arm of m. hath atoned		29: 1
the voice of m. all the day long,		43:25
for they shall obtain m.		54: 6
our God; for he is full of m.,		84:102
by law, neither by m.,		88:35
m. hath compassion on mercy		88:40
on m. and claimeth her own;	DC	88:40
Lord, show m. unto all the meek,		97: 2
the Lord, am willing to show m.;		97: 6
are they, for they shall obtain m.		99: 3
of wrath I will remember m.		101: 9
for I will have m. on him;		106: 7
and showest m. unto thy servants		109: 1
have m. upon this people, and		109:34
m., O Lord, upon the wicked mob,		109:50
m., O Lord, upon all the antions		109:54
m. upon the rulers of our land;		109:54
m. upon the children of Jacob,		109:62
m., O Lord, upon his wife and		109:69
Have m. upon all their immediate		109:70
truth, justice, judgment, m.,		109:77
myself to my people in m.		110: 7
A voice of m. from heaven;		128:19
m., truth, justice, and judgment.	Mses	6:61
and m. shall go begore thy face		7:31
m. upon Noah and his seed,		7:50

MERELY

by m. casting about your eyes	Al	33:21

MERIDIAN

he came in the m. of time,	DC	20:26
which came in the m. of time		39: 3
should come in the m. of time,	Mses	5:57
shall come in the m. of time.		6:57
shall come in the m. of time.		6:62
It shall be in the m. of time,		7:46

MERIT

do m. any thanks from you,	Mos	2:19
could not m. anything of himself;	Al	22:14

MERITS

the m., and mercy, and grace	2Ne	2: 8
the m. of him who is mighty		31:19
through the m. of his Son.	Al	24:10
remission of them through his m.	He	14:13
alone upon the m. of Christ,	Mro	6: 4
upon the m. of Jesus Christ,	DC	3:20

MERRY

wives began to make themselves m.,	1Ne	18: 9
shall say: Eat, drink, and be m.,	2Ne	28: 7
shall say: Eat, drink, and be m.;		28: 8
and to make themselves m.	Mos	20: 5
they did drink and were m.,	Al	55:14
If thou art m., praise the Lord	DC	136:28

MESSAGE

for I have not delivered the m.	Mos	13: 3
therefore I finish my m.		13: 7
But I finish my m.; and then		13: 9
receivedst thy first m. from him.	Al	8:15
after Alma had received his m.		8:18
sent a m. immediately unto them,		15: 4
obeying the m. which he had sent		15: 5
delivered the m. unto Moroni.		43:24
when Lehonti received the m.		47:11
fourth time his m. unto Lehonti,		47:12
the queen had received this m.		47:33
saying he has a m. from God	DC	129: 4
but he will still deliver his m.		129: 7

MESSENGER

Behold, I will send my m.,	3Ne	24: 1
even the m. of the covenant,		24: 1
to be a m. before my face	DC	45: 9
even the m. of salvation—		93: 8
When a m. comes saying		129: 4
that he was a m. sent from	JS	2:33
to me by this extraordinary m.;		2:44
the same heavenly m. was again		2:44
the same m. at my bedside,		2:46
the heavenly m. had ascended		2:47
same m. standing over my head,		2:49
do as commanded by the m.		2:50
where the m. had told me		2:50
breastplate, as stated by the m.		2:52
but was forbidden by the m.,		2:53

MESSENGER / MIDDONI

MESSENGER

I found the same m. there,	JS 2:54
heavenly m. delivered them up	2:59
until he, the m., should call	2:59
that the m. had said that	2:60
the m. called for them,	2:60
a m. from heaven descended	2:68
The m. who visited us on this	2:72
under the hand of this m.,	2:72

MESSENGERS

answer the m. of the nations?	2Ne 24:32
informed the m. of Moroni,	Al 43:24
those m. went and delivered	43:24
And send ye swift m.,	DC 124:26
swift messengers, yea, chosen m.,	124:26

MESSIAH

plainly of the coming of a M.,	1Ne 1:19
a M., or, in other words, a Savior	10: 4
this M., of whom he had spoken,	10: 5
who should come before the M.,	10: 7
that he should baptize the M.	10: 9
after he had baptized the M.	10:10
after they had slain the M.,	10:11
to the knowledge of the true M.,	10:14
and the Son of God was the M.	10:17
the M. who is the Lamb of God,	12:18
after the M. shall be manifested	15:13
the fulness of the gospel of the M.	15:13
the true M., their Redeemer	2Ne 1:10
in and through the Holy M.;	2: 6
mercy, and grace of the Holy M.,	2: 8
the M. cometh in the fulness of	2:26
not the M., but a branch which	3: 5
the M. should be made manifest	3: 5
still wait for the coming of the M.	6:13
the M. will set himself again	6:14
the M. hath risen from the dead,	25:14
forward any more for another M.,	25:16
convincing them of the ture M.,	25:18
any more for a M. to come,	25:18
save it should be a false M.	25:18
there is save one M. spoken of	25:18
that M. is he who should be	25:18
the M. cometh in six hundred	25:19
And after the M. shall come	26: 3
to look forward unto the M.,	Jar 1:11
concerning the coming of the M.,	Mos 13:33
concerning the coming of the M.	He 8:13
in the name of M. I confer	DC 13: 1
look not for a M. to come	19:27
believe in the M..	109:67
whose seed M. shall come;	Mses 7:53
I am M., the King of Zion,	7:53
servants, in the name of M.,	JS 2:69

MET

they m. the king of the people	Mos 7: 7
m. the people in the wilderness,	19:18
and they m. the men of Gideon.	19:22
he m. a man who belonged to the	Al 1: 7
were m. on every hand, and slain	2:37
the first army m. the Amlicites.	3:20
he m. with the sons of Mosiah	17: 1
they m. the father of Lamoni,	20: 8
Ammon m. all his brethren;	24: 5
he and his brethren m. Alma,	27:16
he m. the Lamanites in the	43:18
and his army m. the Lamanites	43:41
m. again by the armies of Moroni.	43:42
that they were m. by Teancum,	51:29
he m. with a disappointment by	51:31
m. by Lehi and a small army,	52:27
time they were m. in the front.	56:23
m. by Lehi and Teancum;	62:32
he m. Kishkumen, and he gave	He 2: 7
m. by the armies of the Nephites	3Ne 4:25
and he m. Adam in journeying to	DC 107:45
m. with a great affliction by	JS 2:56

METALS

and of all manner of precious m.,	He 6: 9
and brass, and all manner of m.;	Eth 10:23

METE

and with what measure ye m.,	3Ne 14: 2
he will m. out a just recompense	DC 127: 3

METED

shall be m. unto every man.	DC 84:85
being m. out as a just measure	98:24

METHODIST

contending for the M. faith,	JS 2: 5
somewhat partial to the M. sect,	2: 8
with one of the M. preachers,	2:21

METHODISTS

It commenced with the M.,	JS 2: 5
against the Baptists and M.,	2: 9
M. in their turn were	2: 9

METHOUGHT

m. I saw in my dream,	1Ne 8: 4
Yea, m. I saw, even as our	Al 36:22

METHUSAEL

Mahujael begat M., and other	Mses 5:43
And M. begat Lamech.	5:43

METHUSELAH

M. was one hundred years old	DC 107:50
ordained under the hand of M.	107:52
Mahalaleel, Jared, Enoch, and M.,	107:53
years, and begat M.	Mses 6:25
came to pass that M., the son	8: 2
came to pass that M. prophesied	8: 3
M. lived one hundred and	8: 5
M. lived, after he begat Lamech,	8: 6
days of M. were nine hundred	8: 7

MICAH: see WELTON, Micah B.

MICHAEL

And also with M., or Adam,	DC 27:11
M., mine archangel, shall sound	29:26
hath appointed m. your prince,	78:16
And M., the seventh angel,	88:112
battle against M. and his armies.	88:113
For M. shall fight their battles,	88:115
and called him M., the prince,	107:54
The voice of M.	128:20
the voice of M., the archangel;	128:21
from M. or Adam down to	128:21

MICHMASH

at M. he hath laid up his carriages.	2Ne 20:28

MID

morning, m.-day, and evening.	Al 34:21
as light as though it was m.-day.	3Ne 1:19

MID-DAY: see MID and DAY.

MIDDLE

the aged, and also the m. aged,	Al 5:49
and they that are of m. age also	DC 101:55
young men and the m. aged—	103:22
young men, and m.-aged,	105:16
thick and rounding in the m.	JS 2:51
the m. part of it was visible	2:51

MIDDLE-AGED: see MIDDLE and AGED.

MIDDONI

thou shalt go to the land of M.;	Al 20: 2
brethren are in prison at M.,	20: 3
will go with thee to the land of M.;	20: 4
for the king of the land of M.,	20: 4
therefore I go to the land of M.,	20: 4
are in prison in the land of M.	20: 5
thee down to the land of M.,	20: 7
should not go to the land of M.,	20:14
but I go to the land of M.	20:15
journey towards the land of M.	20:28
had arrived in the land of M.;	20:30
came over into the land of M.	21:12

MIDDONI — MIGHT

MIDDONI

fled out of the land of M. unto	Al 21:13
returned from the land of M. to	21:18
he departed from the land of M.	22: 1
come up out of M. with thee.	22: 3
who were in the land of M.;	23:10

MIDIAN

according to the slaughter of M.	2Ne 20:26
they came forth to the land of M.,	24: 5

MIDST

descending out of the m. of heaven,	1Ne 1: 9
of Jerusalem from the m. thereof	2Ne 14: 4
and built a tower in the m. of it,	15: 2
alone in the m. of the earth!	15: 8
were torn in the m. of the streets.	15:25
I dwell in the m. of a people of	16: 5
forsaking in the m. of the land.	16:12
and set a king in the m. of it,	17: 6
One of Israel in the m. of thee.	22: 6
of my hands, in the m. of him,	27:34
and a throne in the m. thereof,	Mos 11: 9
they were in the m. of darkness;	Al 5: 7
forth in the m. of the multitude,	22:26
in the m. of thy congregations.	33: 9
into the m. of his soldiers.	44:12
in the m. of Gid and Teomner,	58:19
into the m. of the Nephites,	He 1:32
as standing in the m. of fire	5:23
and Lehi were in the m. of them;	5:44
as if in the m. of a flaming fire,	5:44
was standing in the m. of them.	10: 1
away out of the m. of them.	10:16
and stood in the m. of them;	3Ne 11: 8
and Jesus stood in the m.;	17:12
and Jesus stood in the m.,	17:13
as it were in the m. of fire;	17:24
stood in the m. of the multitude.	19: 4
Jesus came and stood in the m.	19:15
departed out of the m. of them,	19:19
ye shall be in the m. of this people;	20:16
be in the m. of this people;	20:22
even I will be in the m. of you.	20:22
go ye out of the m. of her;	20:41
in the m. of them as a lion	21:12
thy horses out of the m. of thee,	21:14
images out of the m. of thee,	21:17
groves out of the m. of thee;	21:18
and I also will be in the m.	21:25
Jesus came and stood in the m.	27: 2
and I fell wounded in the m.;	Mrm 6:10
had fallen, and he also in the m.	6:13
as a whale in the m. of the sea;	Eth 2:24
and shall reign in their m.,	DC 1:36
will I be in the m. of them—	6:32
even so am I in the m. of you.	6:32
be glad, for I am in your m.,	29: 5
with them and be in their m.;	32: 3
I am in your m. and ye cannot	38: 7
the Lord shall be in their m.,	45:59
and I will be in your m.,	49:27
Wherefore, I am in your m.,	50:44
for I am in your m.,	61:36
he took Moses out of their m.,	84:25
he stands in the m. of his people.	84:101
who is in the m. of all things.	88:13
in the m. of the power of God.	88:45
cause groanings in the m. of her,	88:89
fly through the m. of heaven,	88:92
in the m. of the pillar of heaven—	88:97
flying through the m. of heaven,	88:103
in the m. of persecution and	99: 1
in the m. of mine house,	101:61
preside in the m. of my people,	103:35
Adam stood up in the m. of the	107:56
may rise up in the m. of this	109:33
in the m. of my house,	112:26
Let him preside in the m. of my	117:10
ordained in the m. of the Council	121:32
terrible in the m. of thine enemies	122: 4
and loud, in the m. of the people,	124:75
honored in the m. of his house,	124:76
from the m. of wickedness,	133:14

crying through the m. of heaven,	DC 133:17
stand in the m. of his people,	133:25
up in the m. of the great deep.	133:27
flying through the m. of heaven,	133:36
be a firmament in the m. of the	Mses 2: 6
also in the m. of the garden,	3: 9
beholdest in the m. of the garden,	4: 9
and he dwelt in the m. of Zion;	7:69
I dwell in the m. of them all;	Abr 3:21
in the m. of all the intelligences	3:21
and he stood in the m. of them,	3:23
expanse in the m. of the waters,	4: 6
the tree of life, also, in the m.	5: 9
In the m. of this war of words	JS 2:10
in the m. of that light I saw	2:25
in the m. of my meditation,	2:44
in the m. of our afflictions	2:61

MIGHT

that they m. not be destroyed—	T Pg
life, that they m. take it away.	1Ne 1:20
that they m. be faithful in	3:21
that he m. obtain our property.	3:25
would that I m. not slay him.	4:10
that I m. obtain the records	4:17
that the Jews m. not know	4:36
that he m. preserve his father,	5:14
now I would that ye m. know,	7: 1
that they m. raise up seed	7: 1
that they m. leave me in the	7:16
that perhaps I m. discover	8:13
that perhaps I m. see them.	8:17
that they m. obtain the path	8:21
that I m. see, and hear, and know	10:17
that they m. pervert the right ways	13:27
that they m. blind the eyes	13:27
that he m. lead away the souls	14: 3
that ye m. walk uprightly before	16: 3
that we m. carry into the	16:11
that we m. again rest ourselves	16:17
that we m. tarry for the space	16:33
that we m. not perish.	17: 5
ore, that I m. make tools.	17:10
that I m. have wherewith to blow	17:11
together that I m. make fire.	17:11
that they m. not labor,	17:18
which time we m. have enjoyed	17:21
and we m. have been happy.	17:21
Israel m. quench their thirst.	17:29
a way that they m. be healed;	17:41
that he m. show forth his power,	18:11
that I m. engraven upon them	19: 1
that perhaps I m. persuade them	19:18
that they m. know concerning the	19:22
that I m. more fully persuade them	19:23
that it m. be for our profit	19:23
and m., and power, and great glory.	22:24
that these things m. not come	2Ne 1:19
but that ye m. be a choice and	1:19
that my soul m. have joy in you,	1:21
that my heart m. leave this world	1:21
that I m. not be brought down with	1:21
that they m. repent while in	2:21
Adam fell that men m. be;	2:25
men are, that they m. have joy.	2:25
that all men m. be miserable like	2:27
that they m. not be enticing unto	5:21
that ye m. know concerning the	9: 1
that all men m. become subject	9: 5
that the resurrection m. pass upon	9:22
that all m. stand before him at	9:22
the spirit of counsel and m.,	21: 2
all your m., mind, and strength,	25:29
that ye m. know the gate by	31:17
that we m. persuade them to come	Jac 1: 7
that they m. enter into his rest,	1: 7
by laboring with our m.	1:19
their blood m. not come upon	1:19
that I m. rid my garments of	2: 2
that I m. declare unto you	2: 2
that I m. testify unto you	2: 6
that I m. raise up unto me a	2:25
stone upon which they m. build	4:15

MIGHT

that perhaps I m. preserve the roots	Jac	5:11
I m. preserve them unto myself,		5:11
that I m. plant this tree		5:44
may labor diligently with our m.		5:61
labor with our m. this last time,		5:62
in the vineyard, with your m.		5:71
and if ye labor with your m.		5:71
that he m. overthrow the doctrine		7: 2
that he m. lead away the hearts		7: 3
that he m. come unto me.		7: 3
that I m. speak unto you;		7: 6
with all their m., trusting in the		7:25
that it m. be brought forth	En	1:13
perhaps, they m. be brought		1:13
with all the m. of his body	WM	1:18
m. become men of understanding;	Mos	1: 2
m. know concerning the prophecies		1: 2
that we m. read and understand		1: 5
that thereby they m. be led,		1:16
m. gather themselves together,		1:18
they m. go up to the temple		2: 1
that they m. offer sacrifice		2: 3
they m. give thanks to the Lord		2: 4
that they m. rejoice and be filled		2: 4
they m. remain in their tents		2: 6
his people m. hear the words		2: 7
they m. also receive his words.		2: 8
all the m., mind and strength		2:11
own hands that I m. serve you,		2:14
these things that I m. boast,		2:15
that thereby I m. accuse you;		2:15
that I m. be found blameless,		2:27
that I m. rid my garments of		2:28
that I m. go down in peace,		2:28
that I m. declare unto you that		2:29
that ye m. understand,		2:40
that salvation m. come unto the		3: 9
that a righteous judgment m. come		3:10
m. receive remission of their sins,		3:13
salvation m. come to him that		4: 6
that thereby he m. win the prize;		4:27
thereby they m. hear and know		6: 3
he m. not become burdensome		6: 7
that he m. do according to		6: 7
m. go up to the land of Lehi-Nephi		7: 2
that I m. inquire of you,		7:11
that thereby they m. eat, and		7:16
they m. gather themselves		7:17
manna that they m. not perish		7:19
so that they m. understand		8: 3
Ammon, that he m. read them.		8: 5
m. find the land of Zarahemla,		8: 7
we m. appeal unto our brethren		8: 7
faith, with mighty miracles;		8:18
that Im. spy out their forces,		9: 1
that our army m. come upon them		9: 1
I m. know of the disposition of		9: 5
that I m. know if I might go in		9: 5
know if I m. go in with my people		9: 5
I m. possess the land of Lehi-Nephi,		9: 6
the land that we m. possess it.		9: 7
up the land that we m. possess it.		9:10
that they m. glut themselves with		9:12
that they m. feast themselves upon		9:12
and we did go forth in his m.;		9:18
that thereby I m. have weapons		10: 1
the Lamanites m. not come upon		10: 2
that we m. clothe our nakedness;		10: 5
I m. discover their preparations,		10: 7
that I m. guard against them,		10: 7
they m. not come upon my people		10: 7
to go to battle with their m.,		10:19
that they m. rest their bodies		11:11
that he m. stir up my people to		11:28
that he m. hold a council with them		12:17
that they m. cross him, that		12:19
m. have wherewith to accuse him;		12:19
suffer that he m. depart in peace.		17: 2
that they m. slay him.		17: 3
him up that he m. be slain.		17:12
that it m. not come to the		18: 3
that they m. wax strong in		18:26
that they m. teach with power		18:26

that they m. not come to the	Mos	18:31
that they m. possess the land,		19:15
that they m. possess the land		19:22
that he m. keep the people of		19:28
that they m. not depart into		19:28
word of the Lord m. be fulfilled.		21: 4
that they m. not perish with		21:17
that he m. be some means fall		21:19
they m. take those priests that		21:20
that they m. punish them;		21:21
that they m. have the voice of		22: 1
unto him that he m. speak.		22: 5
that they m. write one to another.		24: 6
m. be called the children of Nephi		25:12
desirous that he m. be baptized;		25:17
that they m. be baptized also.		25:17
that he m. establish churches		25:19
that he m. have them,		26:33
m. judge the people of that church		26:33
of his servants m. be answered		27:14
they m. witness what the Lord had		27:21
mouth of Alma, that he m. speak,		27:22
limbs m. receive their strength—		27:22
eyes of the people m. be opened		27:22
grant unto them that they m.,		28: 1
that they m. preach the things		28: 1
they m. impart the word of God		28: 1
m. bring them to the knowledge of		28: 2
they m. cure them of their hatred		28: 2
they m. also be brought to rejoice		28: 2
m. become friendly to one another,		28: 2
m. go up to the land of Nephi.		28: 5
they m. go and do according to		28: 8
that every man m. bear his part.		29:34
that they m. lift up their heads	Al	1: 4
that he m. lead away the people of		1: 7
that he m. subject them to him.		2:10
that he m. know of their plans		2:21
whereby he m. guard himself		2:21
that he m. preserve his people from		2:21
his people m. have room to cross		2:34
did pursue them with their m.,		2:36
that their seed m. be distinguished		3: 8
God m. preserve his people,		3: 8
they m. not mix and believe in		3: 8
that they m. reap their rewards		3:26
he m. have power to enact laws		4:16
he himself m. go forth among		4:19
he m. preach the word of God		4:19
that he m. pull down, by		4:19
no way that he m. reclaim them		4:19
I m. know these things of myself.		5:46
in his m., majesty, power, and		5:50
that the word m. be fulfilled		7:11
he m. take upon him the sins of		7:13
m. blot out their transgressions		7:13
I m. awaken you to a sense of		7:22
m. baptize them unto repentance.		8:10
Lord m. show forth his power		8:31
m. destroy all his people who are		9:19
that they m. not be destroyed;		9:22
that they m. cast me into prison.		9:32
they m. catch them in their words,		10:13
they m. find witness against them,		10:13
m. deliver them to their judges		10:13
m. be judged according to the law,		10:13
they m. be slain or cast into prison,		10:13
m. be skillful in their profession.		10:15
they m. make him cross his words,		10:16
that they m. have more employ,		11:20
they m. get money according to		11:20
m. destroy that which was good;		11:21
he m. bring you into subjection		12: 6
he m. encircle you about with		12: 6
he m. chain you down to		12: 6
that they m. know of these things		12: 7
that he m. know more concerning		12: 8
in his m., majesty, and dominion,		12:15
unto man in which he m. repent;		12:24
people m. know in what manner		13: 2
m. have had as great privilege as		13: 4
they also m. enter into his rest—		13: 6
the people m. look forward on		13:16

MIGHT

that they m. look forward to him	Al 13:16
that they m. enter into the rest	13:16
to God that it m. be in my day;	13:25
m. destroy Alma and Amulek;	14: 2
fire also, that they m. be burned	14: 8
they m. witness the destruction	14: 9
from them that they m. hunger,	14:22
and water that they m. thirst;	14:22
m. be delivered from Satan,	15:17
That they m. not be hardened	16:17
that they m. not be unbelieving,	16:17
that they m. receive the word	16:17
they m. enter into the rest of	16:17
they m. know the word of God.	17: 2
m. provide food for themselves	17: 7
that they m. be an instrument in	17: 9
that they m. not labor for them	17:14
m. bring them unto repentance;	17:16
they m. bring them to know of	17:16
that I m. not slay you as I did	18: 4
m. drive away many that were	18: 7
the name of the Lord, in their m.,	19:16
that he m. let it fall upon Ammon,	19:22
she m. raise her from the ground;	19:29
he m. show him unto his father.	20: 1
he m. smite him to the earth.	20:16
he m. reign over the people who	21:21
m. have the liberty of worshiping	21:22
m. slay Aaron and his brethren.	22:21
that they m. not overrun the land	22:33
also that they m. have a country	22:34
a country whither they m. flee,	22:34
And thus they m. go forth	23: 3
of God m. have no obstruction,	23: 3
that it m. go forth throughout all	23: 3
that his people m. be convinced	23: 3
that they m. be convinced that	23: 3
desirous that they m. have a name,	23:16
thereby they m. be distinguished	23:16
that they m. be distinguished.	23:16
that they m. hold a council with	24: 5
that we m. repent of these things,	24:10
unto us that we m. not perish;	24:14
of salvation m. be made known	24:14
sickle, and did reap with your m.,	26: 5
we m. save some few of their souls.	26:26
perhaps we m. be the means of	26:30
that I m. go forth and speak with	29: 1
that there m. not be more	29: 2
he m. be brought before Alma,	30:29
the curse m. be taken from him.	30:54
they m. not enter into temptation.	31:10
whatsoever circumstances they m.	32:25
that ye m. try the experiment	32:36
that they m. obtain this fruit	33: 1
would look upon it m. live.	33:19
your eyes that ye m. be healed,	33:21
your eyes, that ye m. perish?	33:21
that they m. contend with the	35:13
that he m. give unto them every	35:16
that I m. not be brought to	36:15
that I m. bring souls unto	36:24
that I m. bring them to taste of	36:24
they m. also be born of God,	36:24
that he m. show forth his power	37:18
word of God m. be fulfilled,	37:24
this people m. not be destroyed.	37:28
if they would look they m. live;	37:46
all your mind, m., and strength;	39:13
salvation m. come unto them,	39:16
of God that I m. know—	40: 3
that God m. be a perfect, just God,	42:15
he m. preserve their hatred	43: 7
m. bring them into subjection	43: 7
m. usurp great power over them,	43: 8
m. gain power over the Nephites	43: 8
that they m. preserve them from	43: 9
that they m. preserve their rights	43: 9
that they m. worship God	43: 9
m. come into the land of Manti	43:22
m. come over into the land of	43:24
that they m. commence an attack	43:24
that he m. know when the camp	Al 43:28
they m. establish a kingdom	43:29
that we m. shed your blood for	44: 2
that he m. slay Moroni;	44:12
with their swords and their m.	44:17
of the land m. be favored.	46:16
that all m. see the writing	46:19
that he m. obtain his purposes.	46:30
m. maintain a free government,	46:35
m. place himself at their head	47: 8
that they m. not be destroyed.	47:15
he m. accomplish his designs	47:16
that they m. live unto the Lord	48:10
they m. maintain that which was	48:10
that they m. take effect,	49: 4
m. obtain a pass to their armies,	49:22
they m. have an equal chance	49:22
that they m. secure their armies	50:10
m. take possession of the land	51:30
he m. take again by stratagem	52:10
that he m. assist Teancum with	52:15
m. receive strength to his army.	52:17
m. be some means flatter them	52:19
m. gain advantage over them	52:19
he m. decoy the Lamanites out	52:21
he m. find a man who was a	55: 4
m. not bring upon him injustice,	55:19
m. destroy them with poison or	55:30
toiling with their m. to fortify	56:15
m. have perhaps destroyed our	56:19
that they m. not pass us by night	56:22
pursuing them, with their m.,	56:37
that they m. not be surrounded	56:37
they m. catch us in their snare;	56:43
that we m. assist our brethren	57:34
that we m. not all perish;	57:36
we m. receive more strength	58: 3
that we m. retain our cities,	58:10
we did go forth with all our m.	58:13
they m. discover the number	58:14
overtake us that they m. slay us;	58:19
that they m. rejoice also.	59: 2
that he m. with ease maintain	59: 3
he m. obtain the remainder of	59: 4
while it m. have otherwise been	60: 5
that ye m. have succored them,	60: 8
m. have sent armies unto them	60: 8
they m. not come into bondage.	62: 5
that he m. spend the remainder	62:43
they m. pitch battle against	He 1:15
that he m. obtain the north parts	1:23
that he m. murder Helaman.	2: 7
they m. be executed according to	2:10
that in time they m. have timber	3: 9
that they m. build many cities,	3:11
unto them that they m. speak,	5:18
them that they m. slay them.	5:22
that they m. turn and look.	5:37
that they m. be lifted up	6:17
to plunder, that they m. get gain.	6:17
that they m. distinguish a brother	6:22
they m. murder, and plunder,	6:23
high that they m. get to heaven.	6:28
that they m. get gain and glory	7: 5
that they m. the more easily	7: 5
that they m. know the cause of	7:11
that I m. pour out my soul unto	7:14
that ye m. get gold and silver.	7:21
having a contrite spirit, m. live,	8:15
they ran in their m., and came	9: 3
then he m. declare it unto us,	9:16
he m. convert us unto his faith,	9:16
m. raise himself to be a great man,	9:16
ways that they m. cross him,	9:19
they m. accuse him to death—	9:19
m. know concerning this thing;	9:23
that they m. cast him into prison.	10:15
pestilence of the sword m. cease;	11:14
this cause, that men m. be saved,	12:22
m. be brought unto repentance	12:24
they m. be restored unto grace	12:24
would that all men m. be saved.	12:25

MIGHT

that ye m. have glad tidings;	He 13: 7	
that ye m. hear and know of	14:11	
that ye m. know the conditions	14:11	
ye m. know of the coming of	14:12	
that ye m. know of the signs	14:12	
that ye m. believe on his name.	14:12	
the intent that they m. believe	14:28	
will believe m. be saved,	14:29	
judgment m. come upon them;	14:29	
that ye m. know good from evil.	14:31	
ye m. choose life or death;	14:31	
that they m. be baptized unto	16: 1	
m. know that the Christ must	16: 4	
they m. know and remember at	16: 5	
the intent that they m. believe;	16: 5	
that he m. harden the hearts of	16:22	
been spoken m. not come to pass.	3Ne 1: 7	
they m. know that their faith	1: 8	
they m. not believe in those	1:22	
exert themselves in their m.	3:16	
m. subsist for the space of seven	4: 4	
they m. have everlasting life.	5:13	
they m. have, with their labors,	6: 3	
that he m. know concerning	7:15	
m. be hid from before my face,	9:11	
m. not cry unto me from the	9:11	
that they m. drink of it.	18: 8	
that ye m. feel and see;	18:25	
m. be on the morrow in the place	19: 3	
that these things m. come forth	21: 4	
I m. be lifted up upon the cross;	27:14	
that I m. draw all men unto me,	27:14	
ye m. bring the souls of men	28: 9	
that thereby salvation m. come?	28:35	
that they m. not taste of death	28:38	
they m. not suffer pain nor	28:38	
that they m. come again unto	4Ne 1:49	
did fortify the city with our m.;	Mrm 2: 4	
that we m. get them together in	2: 7	
that they m. not be destroyed.	2:17	
m. save them from destruction.	2:21	
that we m. stop the armies of	3: 6	
they m. not get possession of any	3: 6	
that they m. take possession of	4: 7	
they went forth in their own m.,	4: 8	
ye m. not have too great sorrow	5: 9	
they m. have been clasped in	5:11	
which they m. have received in	5:19	
we m. gather together our people	6: 2	
that ye m. bring damnation upon	8:33	
man m. know that he was God,	Eth 3:18	
that they m. not cross the great	6: 3	
they m. subsist upon the water,	6: 4	
m. fall by the poisonous serpents.	9:33	
that they m. get gain.	10:22	
they m. clothe themselves	10:24	
m. with surety hope for	12: 4	
others m. be partakers of	12: 8	
they m. hope for those things	12: 8	
man m. have a more excellent	12:32	
that they m. have charity.	12:36	
that he m. be merciful unto the	13: 7	
that they m. obtain the kingdom.	13:18	
m. slay him with his own sword,	15: 5	
that they m. get all who were	15:14	
they m. receive all the strength	15:14	
that they m. be destroyed;	15:19	
they contended in their m.	15:24	
that they m. be remembered	Mro 6: 4	
all your m., mind and strength,	10:32	
all this that it m. be fulfilled,	DC 1:18	
every man m. speak in the name	1:20	
faith also m. increase in	1:21	
covenant m. be established;	1:22	
my gospel m. be proclaimed	1:23	
they m. come to understanding.	1:24	
they erred it m. be made known;	1:25	
wisdom they m. be instructed,	1:26	
sinned they m. be chastened,	1:27	
chastened, that they m. repent;	1:27	
they m. be made strong,	1:28	
m. have power to translate	1:29	
m. have power to lay the	1:30	
of the Lord m. be fulfilled,	DC 3:19	
the Lamanites m. come to the	3:20	
they m. know the promises of	3:20	
repentance they m. be saved.	3:20	
with all your heart, m., mind	4: 2	
thrusteth in his sickle with his m.,	4: 4	
thrust in his sickle with his m.,	6: 3	
that you m. know concerning	6:22	
that he m. bring souls unto me,	7: 4	
desired that he m. do more,	7: 5	
they m. preach in their days,	10:48	
m. come unto their brethren	10:48	
m. have eternal life;	10:50	
that it m. be free unto all of	10:51	
thrust in his sickle with his m.,	11: 3	
all your m., mind and strength.	11:20	
thrust in his sickle with his m.,	12: 3	
give heed with your m.,	12: 9	
thrust in his sickle with his m.,	14: 3	
I m. bring about my righteous	17: 9	
all men m. repent and come	18:11	
he m. bring all men unto him,	18:12	
I m. subdue all things unto	19: 2	
m. work upon the hearts of	19: 7	
that they m. not suffer if they	19:16	
I m. not drink the bitter cup,	19:18	
you m. be an elder unto this	21:11	
the scriptures m. be fulfilled;	24:14	
that all things m. be revealed	25: 9	
you m. be called and ordained	27: 8	
m. be raised in immortality	29:43	
reap with all your m., mind,	33: 7	
m. become the sons of God.	34: 3	
ye m. escape the power of	38:31	
member, go to with his m.,	38:40	
lay to with your m. and call	39:17	
that thyself m. be glorified;	45: 4	
Lord, and the power of his m.	45:75	
they also m. have eternal life	46:14	
the earth m. answer the end	49:16	
And that it m. be filled with	49:17	
that he m. have in abundance.	49:19	
that he m. overthrow you.	50: 3	
that you m. be obedient,	58: 6	
your hearts m. be prepared	58: 6	
you m. be honored in laying	58: 7	
a feast of fat things m. be	58: 8	
the testimony m. go forth from	58:13	
all thy m., mind, and strength;	59: 5	
that ye m. bear record;	61: 4	
your sins, that you m. be one,	61: 8	
m. not perish in wickedness;	61: 8	
the promise m. be fulfilled,	62: 6	
that they m. have life and	66: 2	
that you m. express beyond his	67: 5	
children m. remain without	74: 6	
the tradition m. be done away,	74: 6	
be idle but labor with your m.—	75: 3	
that you m. know his will	75:23	
through him all m. be saved	76:42	
m. be washed and cleansed	76:52	
m. be judged according to	76:73	
glory, and in power, and in m.,	76:91	
equal in power, and in m.,	76:95	
in glory, and in m., and in	76:114	
they m. behold the face of God;	84:23	
and honor, and power, and m.,	84:102	
that he m. be in all and	88: 6	
which they m. have received.	88:32	
that he m. visit the second also,	88:57	
his lord m. be glorified in him,	88:60	
that they all m. be glorified.	88:60	
that they m. receive the gospel,	88:99	
crowned with the glory of his m.,	88:107	
mourning m. come up into the	95: 7	
sworn by the power of his m.	97:20	
all their m., mind, and strength,	98:47	
the prophets m. be fulfilled.	101:19	
M. not this money be given to	101:49	
as the case m. require.	102: 1	
difficulties which m. arise in	102: 2	
that they m. fill up the measure	103: 3	
that their cup m. be full;	103: 3	

MIGHT 623 MIGHTY

m. be chastened for a little	DC 103: 4
they m. have been redeemed	105: 2
Son of Man m. have a place to	109: 5
power, majesty, m., dominion,	109:77
with their m., built this house	110: 6
m. bring them into bondage	121:18
As well m. man stretch forth his	121:33
that I m. show forth my wisdom	124: 1
ordinances m. be revealed which	124:38
If ye labor with all your m.,	124:44
sons of men go with all their m.	124:49
that he m. make a record of	128: 2
one principle m. accord with	128:12
I m. have rendered a plainer	128:18
m. require an offering at your	132:51
things m. be known among you,	133:36
mountains m. flow down at thy	133:40
that men m. be made partakers	133:57
that they m. have charity.	135: 5
let them go to with their m.,	136: 6
that he m. be honored	136:39
and the wicked m. be condemned.	136:39
ye m. be sanctified from all sin,	Mses 6:59
m. never more be covered by	7:50
covenants of the Lord m. be	8: 2
that they m. slay me also,	Abr 1:12
that they m. offer me up and	1:15
the famine m. be turned away	2:17
house, that they m. not perish.	2:17
they m. bring forth great whales,	4:21
and not upbraid, I m. venture.	JS 2:13
that I m. know which to join.	2:18
lacked wisdom m. ask of God,	2:26
that I m. know of my state	2:29

MIGHTEST

thou m. be like unto this river,	1Ne 2: 9
thou m. be like unto this valley,	2:10
that thou m. be brought to the	Mos 27:14
thou m. have cause to destroy me.	Al 11:25
thou m. set them against us,	12: 4
that thou m. take it again	Eth 12:33
thou m. speedily come unto me	DC 7: 4

MIGHTIER

he is m. than all the earth.	1Ne 4: 1
then why not m. than Laban	4: 1
and he is m. than I,	10: 8
cried the m. unto them, saying:	Al 10:25
one of them is m. than us all?	22:20

MIGHTILY

people did cry m. to the Lord	Mos 9:17
and cry m. to the Lord their God,	11:25
they did cry m. from day to day,	21:10
and they did cry m. to God;	21:14
that they began to cry m. to God.	24:10
because they cried m. unto him	29:20
having prayed m. to him that he	Al 2:28
contend m., one with another.	2:29
forth and cry m. unto this people,	9:25
yea, and cry m. against them	14:11
and the earth shook m.,	14:27
the earth, and cried m., saying:	22:17
cried m. unto Moroni, promising	44:19
and he prayed m. unto his God	46:13
cried m. to his God in behalf of	3Ne 1:11
that he cried m. unto the Lord,	1:12
cry m. unto the Father in the	Mrm 9: 6

MIGHTS

did go and labor with their m.;	Jac 5:72
their m., minds, and strength.	DC 20:31

MIGHTY

their faith, to make them m.	1Ne 1:20
Behold, he is a m. man,	3:31
he did make them m. unto the	17:32
shall the prey be taken from the m.,	21:24
captives of the m. shall be taken	21:25
Redeemer, the M. One of Jacob.	21:26
God will raise up a m. nation	22: 7
Redeemer, the M. One of Israel.	22:12
not make him m. in speaking.	2Ne 3:17
shall rise up one m. among them,	2Ne 3:24
faith, to work m. wonders,	3:24
bold in m. prayer before him;	4:24
the prey be taken from the m.,	6:16
Even the captives of the m. shall	6:17
for the M. God shall deliver his	6:17
Redeemer, the M. One of Jacob.	6:18
For should the m. miracles be	10: 6
The m. man, and the man of war,	13: 2
and thy m. in the war.	13:25
and the m. man shall be humbled,	15:15
Wo unto the m. to drink wine,	15:22
Wonderful, Counselor, The M. God,	19: 6
remnant of Jacob, unto the m. God.	20:21
Lebanon shall fall by a m. one.	20:34
with his m. wind he shall shake	21:15
I have also called my m. ones,	23: 3
working m. miracles, signs, and	26:13
merits of him who is m. to save.	31:19
neither am I m. in writing, like	33: 1
I cried unto him in m. prayer	En 1: 4
were m. men in the faith	Jar 1: 7
being a strong and m. man,	Om 1:28
amongst men, working m. miracles,	Mos 3: 5
has wrought a m. change in us,	5: 2
he being a strong and m. man,	7: 3
faith, might work m. miracles;	8:18
and go forth in m. power upon	13:34
after working many m. miracles	15: 6
he did show forth his m. power	23:24
there was a m. change wrought	Al 5:12
and a m. change was also wrought	5:13
Have ye experienced this m. change	5:14
crieth unto me with a m. voice,	5:51
join in fasting and m. prayer	6: 6
who is m. to save and to	7:14
with God in m. prayer,	8:10
having exercised m. faith,	13:18
and cried with a m. voice, saying:	13:21
with m. power he did sling stones	17:36
do many m. works in his name;	19: 4
many m. miracles we have wrought	26:12
with m. threatenings to destroy	26:18
for mercy; for he is m. to save.	34:18
was a strong and a m. man;	48:11
with such m. power did they fall	56:56
and he was a large and a m. man.	He 1:15
Coriantumr, being a m. man,	1:16
shall send forth his m. winds,	5:12
when all his hail and his m. storm	5:12
make thee m. in word and in deed,	10: 5
had the m. works been shown	15:15
the many m. works which I	15:17
shall make them m. above all,	3Ne 20:27
united in m. prayer and fasting.	27: 1
there were m. miracles wrought	4Ne 1:13
doing m. miracles among them.	1:30
did not many m. miracles?	Mrm 9:18
were many m. miracles wrought	9:18
being a large and m. man,	Eth 1:34
being called after the m. hunter)	2: 1
m. as to the strength of a man;	7: 8
he was also m. in judgment.	7: 8
and did build many m. cities,	9:23
did cast up m. heaps of earth	10:23
there arose a m. man among them	11:15
there arose another m. man;	11:17
hast made us m. in word	12:23
hast not made us m. in writing;	12:23
hast not made us m. in writing	12:24
were m. even as thou art,	12:24
who rose up, who were m. men,	13:15
slain two millions of m. men,	15: 2
And they were large and m. men	15:26
in my name, in m. prayer;	Mro 2: 2
that he may work m. miracles;	10:12
break down the m. and strong	DC 1:19
power to do many m. works,	3: 4
himself in m. prayer and faith	5:24
of Zion in m. power for good,	21: 7
vineyard with a m. glessing,	21: 9
vineyard with a m. pruning,	24:19
and call upon me in m. prayer.	29: 2

MIGHTY   624   MINDS

Lord God, the M. One of Israel;	DC 36: 1
by faith, unto m. works,	63:11
who is m. and powerful,	65: 1
will send one m. and strong,	85: 7
and the m. works of God	88:108
and the m. works of God	88:109
power to be m. in testimony.	100:10
m. in expounding all scriptures,	100:11
boast of faith nor of m. works,	105:24
as with a rushing m. wind,	109:37
O M. God of Jacob—	109:68
send forth the power of his m. arm.	123: 6
upon the m. ocean, even the	133:20
in righteousness, m. to save.	133:47
and the same are m. men,	Mses 8:21

MIGRON
come to Aiath, he is passed to M.;   2Ne 20:28

MILCAH
my brother, took M. to wife,   Abr 2: 2

MILD
with herbs and m. food,	DC 42:43
animals, and for m. drinks,	89:17

MILDNESS
it was a still voice of perfect m.,	He 5:30
the m. of the voice, behold	5:31
in m. and in meekness.	DC 38:41

MILE
shall compel thee to go a m.,   3Ne 12:41

MILES, Daniel
Josiah Butterfield, M.,   DC 124:138

MILITATE
to m. against its character as   JS 2: 1

MILK
buy wine and m. without money	2Ne 9:50
for the abundance of m. they shall	17:22
buy m. and honey, without money	26:25
but m. they must receive;	DC 19:22
flowing with m. and honey,	38:18

MILL
Two shall be grinding at the m.,   JS 1:45

MILLENNIUM
For the great M., of which	DC 43:30
referred to the beginning of the m.	130:16

MILLER, George: see also GEORGE.
my servant M. is without guile;	DC 124:20
I say unto you, let my servant M.,	124:62
I say unto you, if my servant M.,	124:70

MILLIONS
nearly two m. of his people,	Eth 15: 2
slain two m. of mighty men,	15: 2
yea, m. of earths like this,	Mses 7:30

MILLSTONE
a m. had been hanged about   DC 121:22

MINCING
walking and m. as they go,   2Ne 13:16

MIND
so much was him m. swallowed up	1Ne 15:27	
and be determined in one m.	2Ne 1:21	
all your might, m., and strength,		25:29
unto God with firmness of m.,	Jac	3: 1
voice of the Lord came into my m.	En	1:10
of infirmities in body and m.;	Mos	2:11
all the might, m. and strength		2:11
have a m. to injure one another,		4:13
serve him with all diligence of m.,		7:33
every man according to his m.,	Al	2: 5
the great tribulations of his m.		15: 3
other sins, did harrow up his m.		15: 3
his m. also was exceeding sore	Al	15: 5
much, both in body and in m.,		17: 5
was being cast away from his m.,		19: 6
light which did light up his m.,		19: 6
been somewhat troubled in m.		22: 3
is the effect of a frenzied m.;		30:16
were pleasing unto the carnal m.;		30:53
your m. doth begin to expand.		32:34
unto you to prepare your m.;		34: 3
not of the carnal m. but of God.		36: 4
as my m. caught hold upon this		36:18
all your m., might, and strength;		39:13
I will ease your m. somewhat		39:17
thy m. is worried concerning the		40: 1
that thy m. has been worried also		41: 1
more which doth worry your m.,		42: 1
being somewhat of a sober m.,	Mrm	1:15
of heart, and blindness of m.,	Eth	4:15
of strong faith and a firm m.	Mro	7:30
rest in your m. forever.		9:25
all your might, m. and strength,		10:32
heart, might, m. and strength,	DC	4: 2
and I did enlighten thy m.;		6:15
cast your m. upon the night		6:22
I not speak peace to your m.		6:23
I will tell you in your m. and		8: 2
must study it out in your m.;		9: 8
and your m. became darkened.		10: 2
which shall enlighten your m.,		11:13
your might, m. and strength.		11:20
your m. has been on the things		30: 2
your might, m., and strength.		33: 7
one heart and with one m.,		45:65
thy might, m., and strength,		59: 5
the heart and a willing m.;		64:34
the carnal neither natural m.,		67:10
neither after the carnal m.		67:12
shall be the m. of the Lord,		68: 4
shall not be weary in m.,		84:80
and the m. of the Lord—		95:13
all their might, m., and strength.		98:47
and obtain the m. of the Lord		102:23
subject seems to occupy my m.,		128: 1
this according to the m. and will		133:61
for he knew not the m. of God,	Mses	4: 6
were of one heart and one m.,		7:18
to disabuse the public m.,	JS	2: 1
my m. was called up to serious		2: 8
my m. became somewhat partial		2: 8
My m. at times was greatly		2: 9
"Never m., all is well—		2:20
excite the public m. against me,		2:22
had now got my m. satisfied		2:26
the vision was opened to my m.		2:42
impressions made on my m.,		2:46

MINDED
to be carnally-m. is death,	2Ne 9:39
to be spiritually-m. is life eternal.	9:39
high-m. governors of the nation	DC 124: 3

MINDEDNESS
all your pride and light-m.,	DC 88:121
admonished in all your high-m.	90:17

MINDFUL
who has been m. of this people,	Al	26:36
who has been m. of us,		26:36
that God is m. of every people,		26:37
Christ hath been m. of you,	Mro	8: 2
I am m. of you always in my		8: 3

MINDS
and so blind in your m., that ye	1Ne	7: 8
the blindness of their m. unto their		14: 7
and blinded their m., and reviled		17:30
your souls if your m. were pure?	2Ne	9:47
and wound their delicate m.	Jac	2: 9
for ye may, if your m. are firm,		3: 2
and the blindness of their m.,	Jar	1: 3
and your m. that the mysteries	Mos	2: 9
according to the m. and the	Al	11: 4
I would cite your m. forward		13: 1

MINDS 625 MINE

hearts and blindness of their m.,	Al	13: 4
concerning the blindness of the m.,		14: 6
the m. of the children of men,		16:16
this was the m. of the people;		17: 6
this derangement of your m. comes		30:16
upon the m. of the people than		31: 5
question which is in your m. is		34: 5
privily the m. of all the people.		35: 5
out the m. of all the people,		35: 6
this people, to prepare their m.;		39:16
prepare the m. of their children		39:16
being fixed in their m. with a		47: 6
Lamanites and blinded their m.,		48: 3
preparing the m. of the people		48: 7
young, and their m. are firm,		57:27
their hearts, and blind in their m.,	3Ne	2: 1
according to the m. of those who		7:14
and the blindness of their m.—		7:16
prepare your m. for the morrow,		17: 3
and the blindness of their m.	Eth	15:19
their mights, m., and strength.	DC	20:31
all having corrupt m.		33: 4
of eternity rest upon your m.		43:34
always retain in your m.		46:10
Let not your m. turn back;		67:14
your m. in times past have been		84:54
remain steadfast in your m.		84:61
up in your m. continually		84:85
your m. become single to God,		88:68
your m. may be invigorated.		88:124
clear to the m. of the council,		102:23
be taken away out of their m.		104:81
The veil was taken from our m.,		110: 1
darkness the m. of the people,		112:23
and to blind their m.,		121:12
m. were pointed to by the angels,		121:27
Our m. being now enlightened,	JS	2:74

MINE

and I make it with m. own hand;	1Ne	1: 3
I have made with m. own hands;		1:17
I make an account of m. own life.		1:17
sought to take away m. own life;		4:11
put them upon m. own body;		4:19
the fulness of m. intent is		6: 4
ye are m. elder brethren,		7: 8
I cast m. eyes towards the head		8:17
plates of Nephi, after m. own name;		9: 2
to proceed with m. account,		10: 1
for me in m. other book.		10:15
as I sat pondering in m. heart		11: 1
forth unto them, in m. own power,		13:34
m. afflictions were great above all,		15: 5
also m. ankles were much swollen,		18:15
the Lord because of m. afflictions.		18:16
also many of m. own prophecies		19: 1
say — M. idol hath done them.		20: 5
name's sake will I defer m. anger,		20: 9
For m. own sake, yea, for mine		20:11
for m. own sake will I do this,		20:11
M. hand hath also laid the		20:13
lift up m. hand to the Gentiles,		21:22
in the wilderness of m. afflictions;	2Ne	3: 3
the wilderness of m. afflictions,		3: 3
I will make him great in m. eyes;		3: 8
by the finger of m. own hand;		3:17
are written upon m. other plates;		4:14
are written upon m. other plates.		4:14
grieveth because of m. iniquities.		4:17
hath led me through m. afflictions		4:20
He hath confounded m. enemies,		4:22
m. eyes have beheld great things,		4:25
slacken, because of m. afflictions?		4:26
am I angry because of m. enemy?		4:27
again because of m. enemies.		4:29
strength because of m. afflictions.		4:29
me out of the hands of m. enemies?		4:31
wilt thou make a way for m. escape		4:33
mine escapt before m. enemies!		4:33
but the ways of m. enemy.		4:33
my rock and m. everlasting God.		4:35
and Sam, m. elder brother and		5: 6

be pleased with m. engravings	2Ne	5:32
they must search m. other plates.		5:33
Yea, m. anxiety is great for you;		6: 3
lift up m. hand to the Gentiles,		6: 6
He waketh m. ear to hear as the		7: 4
The Lord God hath opened m. ear,		7: 5
Who is m. adversary?		7: 8
This shall ye have of m. hand—		7:11
and m. arm shall judge the people.		8: 5
and on m. arm shall they trust.		8: 5
thee in the shadow of m. hand,		8:16
and my transgressions are m.;		9:46
In m. ears, said the Lord of Hosts,		15: 9
for m. eyes have seen the King,		16: 5
O Assyrian, the rod of m. anger,		20: 5
and m. anger in their destruction.		20:25
for m. anger is not upon them		23: 3
m. eyes hath beheld the things of		25: 5
I proceed with m. own prophecy,		25: 7
the words unto m. own people;		25: 8
I am able to do m. own work;		27:20
them forth in m. own due time;		27:21
I am able to do m. own work.		27:21
I shall see fit in m. own wisdom		27:22
lengthen out m. arm unto them		28:32
for m. arm is lengthened out all		28:32
Jews, m. ancient covenant people.		29: 4
Jews, m. ancient covenant people?		29: 5
according to m. own pleasure.		29: 9
the Spirit stoppeth m. utterance,		32: 7
m. eyes water my pillow by night,		33: 3
obtained m. errand from the Lord.	Jac	1:17
magnify m. office with soberness,		2: 2
by the power of m. arm,		2:25
the season, unto m. own self.		5:18
the season, unto m. own self.		5:19
may preserve it unto m. own self;		5:20
may preserve it unto m. own self.		5:23
the season, unto m. own self.		5:29
fruit thereof unto m. own self?		5:33
and for m. own purpose I have		5:36
the season, unto m. own self.		5:46
Have I slackened m. hand, that I		5:47
and I have stretched forth m. hand		5:47
roots thereof for m. own purpose.		5:53
them also for m. own purpose,		5:54
the roots also unto m. own self,		5:54
of my vineyard unto m. own self		5:76
I will lay up unto m. own self		5:76
will, O Lord, be done, and not m.		7:14
and supplication for m. own soul;	En	1: 4
out of m. own mouth that	Mos	1:10
have labored with m. own hands		2:14
I, myself, with m. own hands,		9:19
I will visit them in m. anger.		11:20
they be called; and they are m.		26:18
will visit this people in m. anger;	Al	8:29
behold, he hath blessed m. house,		10:11
through m. Only Begotten Son;		12:33
through m. Only Begotten Son,		12:34
must not stretch forth m. hand;		14:11
have the wish of m. heart,		29: 1
m. own hands for my support,		30:32
I may bear with m. infirmities.		31:30
those who were m. enemies,		33: 3
been despised by m. enemies;		33:10
and wast angry with m. enemies,		33:10
hear me because of m. afflictions		33:11
unto thee in all m. afflictions,		33:11
not grant unto me m. epistle,		55: 3
with me, yea, those sons of m.,		56:17
And Ammoron refused m. epistle,		57: 3
now, behold, I close m. epistle.		58:41
I direct m. epistle to Pahoran,		60: 1
And except ye grant m. epistle,		60:25
And thus I close m. epistle.		60:36
And now I close m. epistle to		61:21
now I return again to m. account;	He	3:17
in the presence of m. angels,		10: 6
I will turn away m. anger,		13:11
sealing it with m. own hand,	3Ne	3: 5
I have made with m. own hands.		5:11

MINE 626 MINE

I have seen with m. own eyes.	3Ne 5:17
m. arm of mercy is extended	9:14
whoso heareth these sayings of m.	14:24
that heareth these sayings of m.	14:26
remembereth these sayings of m.	15: 1
together in m. own due time,	20:29
gone away from m. ordinances,	24: 7
And they shall be m., saith the	24:17
before m. eyes ever since I have	Mrm 2:18
Vengeance is m., and I will	3:15
to go up against m. enemies;	3:16
as was laid before m. eyes;	5: 8
judgment is m., saith the Lord,	8:20
and vengeance is m. also,	8:20
not because of m. imperfection,	9:31
And I take m. account from	Eth 1: 2
created after m. own image?	3:15
beginning after m. own image.	3:15
show them in m. own due time	3:27
another in m. own language,	12:39
for the safety of m. own life.	Mro 1: 3
give it, for thus do m. apostles.	2: 2
Behold, this is m. authority,	DC 1: 6
strayed from m. ordinances,	1:15
broken m. everlasting covenant;	1:15
m. everlasting covenant might be	1:22
whether by m. own voice or	1:38
m. anger is kindled against	5: 8
same that came unto m. own,	6:21
and m. own received me not,	6:21
I came unto m. own,	10:57
and m. own received me not.	10:57
same who came unto m. own	11:29
and m. own received me not;	11:29
m. arm is over all the earth.	15: 2
m. arm is over all the earth.	16: 2
last commandments of m.,	17: 8
called m. unto m. own purpose,	18: 8
even as unto Paul m. apostle,	18: 9
to know even as m. apostles.	19: 8
as if from m. own mouth,	21: 5
Oliver Cowdery m. apostle;	21:10
your words, in m. own due time.	24:16
have sent m. angels to commit	27:16
the gathering of m. elect;	29: 7
for m. elect hear my voice	29: 7
was spoken by m. apostles	29:10
that m. apostles, the Twelve	29:12
cup of m. indignation is full;	29:17
the workmanship of m. hand.	29:25
Michael, m. archangel, shall	29:26
I declared from m. own mouth	29:29
name of m. Only Begotten Son.	29:42
through m. Only Begotten;	29:46
according to m. own pleasure,	29:48
even so will I gather m. elect	33: 6
and m. arm is not shortened;	35: 8
by the fire of m. indignation	35:14
as they are in m. own bosom,	35:20
the salvation of m. own elect;	35:20
be saved in m. own due time;	35:25
are present before m. eyes;	38: 2
of Enoch into m. own bosom;	38: 4
in m. own name, by the virtue	38: 4
that m. eyes are upon you,	38: 7
I made, and all flesh is m.,	38:16
are not one ye are not m.	38:27
the riches of the earth are m.	38:39
meridian of time unto m. own,	39: 3
and m. own received me not;	39: 3
will stay m. hand in judgment.	39:18
unto you in m. own due time	42:62
of angels, and by m. own voice,	43:25
wrath of m. indignation is full.	43:26
in m. own due time will I come	43:29
I came unto m. own, and mine	45: 8
m. own received me not;	45: 8
I have sent m. everlasting	45: 9
sent m. Only Begotten Son	49: 5
m. everlasting covenant,	49: 9
like unto m. apostle of old,	49:11
now hearing these words of m.	50:36
little children, for you are m.,	50:41
of me if he obey m. ordinances.	DC 52:15
if he obey m. ordinances.	52:16
upon you m. ordination,	53: 3
m. anger is kindled against the	56: 1
and they shall know m. arm	56: 1
mine arm and m. indignation,	56: 1
cut off in m. own due time,	56: 3
for m. anger is kindled against	60: 2
a portion unto m. elders who	60:10
this whole company of m. elders	61: 3
have decreed in m. anger	61: 5
all flesh is in m. hand,	61: 6
today m. anger is turned away.	61:20
m. eyes are upon those who	62: 2
was shown unto m. apostles	63:21
hold it in m. own hands;	63:25
will I send m. angels to pluck	63:54
for this once, for m. own glory,	64: 3
as he obeyeth m. ordinances,	64: 5
m. everlasting covenant,	66: 2
and lo, m. eyes are upon you,	67: 2
and the earth are in m. hands,	67: 2
of eternity are m. to give.	67: 2
worthy, in m. own due time,	67:14
in m. own due time.	71:10
in m. own due time for the	82:13
for it is m. and I will repay.	82:23
m. own voice out of the heavens;	84:42
m. angels charge concerning you.	84:42
And as I said unto m. apostles,	84:63
for you are m. apostles,	84:63
as I said unto m. apostles	84:64
and m. angels round about you,	84:88
proclaim m. everlasting gospel,	84:103
the way that m. apostles,	84:108
that m. house shall be polluted	88:134
And let m. aged servant, Joseph	90:20
especially m. aged servant Joseph	90:25
rewarded in m. own due time.	90:29
it is meet in m. eyes that she	90:30
over Zion in m. own due time.	90:32
a committee to build m. houses,	94:15
the building of m. house;	95: 3
to prepare m. apostles to prune	95: 4
even as m. apostles at Jerusalem.	95: 9
for the school of m. apostles,	95:17
design to build m. holy house.	96: 2
is necessary to benefit m. order,	96: 4
and all m. ancient prophets	98:32
that I gave unto m. ancients,	98:33
to proclaim m. everlasting gospel	99: 1
they are in m. hands,	100: 1
they shall be m. in that day	101: 3
the sword of m. indignation	101:10
M. indignation is soon to be	101:11
all m. Israel, shall be saved.	101:12
for all flesh is in m. hands;	101:16
to m. everlasting gospel,	101:22
called unto m. everlasting gospel,	101:39
that m. olive-trees may not be	101:45
all the strength of m. house,	101:55
who are the strength of m. house,	101:55
my vineyard; for it is m.;	101:56
down the walls of m. enemies;	101:57
avenge me of m. enemies,	101:58
with the residue of m. house	101:58
in the midst of m. house,	101:61
leave the residue in m. hand.	101:71
Avenge me of m. adversary.	101:83
into the hands of m. enemies.	101:96
be polluted by m. enemies,	101:97
by the hands of m. enemies,	103: 2
in m. own time.	103: 2
to prevail against m. enemies	103: 6
m. angel shall go up before	103:19
M. angels shall go up before	103:20
as m. enemies come against you	103:24
ye shall avenge me of m. enemies.	103:25
in avenging me of m. enemies,	103:26
and all things therein are m.	104:14
my saints, for all things are m.	104:15
needs be done in m. own way;	104:16
all these properties are m.,	104:55

MINE 627 MINISTERED

And if the properties are m.,	DC	104:56
to be stewards over m. house,		104:57
all these things are m.,		104:86
the redemption of m. afflicted		105: 1
that m. elders should wait for		105: 9
until m. elders are endowed		105:11
that m. elders should wait for		105:13
and lay waste m. enemies;		105:15
be left to pollute m. heritage,		105:15
down the towers of m. enemies,		105:16
the strength of m. house have		105:17
and Baneemy [m. elders]		105:27
down the towers of m. enemies		105:30
avenging me of m. enemies		105:30
remembered with the first of m. elders,		108: 4
with the rest of m. elders		108: 4
unto them with m. own voice,		110: 8
m. house also, to keep and preserve		117:16
in m. own due time,		117:16
For the building of m. house,		119: 2
and by m. own voice unto them,		120: 1
the heel against m. anointed,		121:16
that which was meet in m. eyes,		121:16
from the ordinances of m. house.		121:19
m. eyes see and know all their		121:24
and he shall be great in m. eyes;		124:13
for he shall be m. if he do this,		124:17
blessed and holy is he, for he is m.		124:19
the consecrations of m. house,		124:21
that I may reveal m. ordinances		124:40
they pollute m. holy grounds,		124:46
m. holy ordinances, and charters,		124:46
for he shall be m., saith the Lord.		124:75
order of m. Only Begotten Son.		124:123
traveling high council, m. apostles,		124:139
through the medium of m. anointed,		132: 7
m. house is a house of order,		132: 8
according to m. appointment,		132:26
unto m. handmaid, Emma Smith,		132:51
let m. handmaid, Emma Smith,		132:52
And I command m. handmaid,		132:54
let m. handmaid forgive		132:56
by m. own voice, and by the voice		132:59
I have sent forth m. angel		133:36
did tread upon them in m. anger,		133:51
day when I came unto m. own,		133:66
be redeemed in m. own due time,		136:18
for they are in m. hands		136:30
I did call upon by m. angels,		136:37
m. voice out of the heavens,		136:37
the workmanship of m. hands;	Mses	1: 4
similitude of m. Only Begotten;		1: 6
m. Only Begotten is and shall be		1: 6
m. own eyes have beheld God;		1:11
the similitude of m. Only Begotten.		1:16
in the name of m. Only Begotten,		1:17
For m. own purpose have I made		1:31
which is m. Only Begotten Son,		1:32
I also created them for m. own		1:33
which is m. Only Begotten.		1:33
for they are m. and I know them.		1:35
unto me, for they are m.		1:37
by m. Only Begotten I created		2: 1
God, said unto m. Only Begotten,		2:26
created man in m. own image,		2:27
in the image of m. Only Begotten		2:27
said unto m. Only Begotten,		3:18
the name of m. Only Begotten,		4: 1
give unto him m. own power;		4: 3
the power of m. Only Begotten,		4: 3
God, said unto m. Only Begotten:		4:28
thou didst accept and not m.;		5:38
slay me, because of m. iniquities,		5:39
the name of m. Only Begotten Son,		6:52
the blood of m. Only Begotten;		6:59
the blood of m. Only Begotten,		6:62
Enoch: Behold m. abode forever.		7:21
the workmanship of m. own hands,		7:32
m. indignation is kindled against		7:34
I can stretch forth m. hands and		7:36
m. eye can pierce them also,		7:36
the workmanship of m. hands		7:36
the workmanship of m. hands;		7:37

all the workmanship of m. hands.	Mses	7:40
testimony of m. Only Begotten;		7:62
to gather out m. elect from the		7:62
And there shall be m. abode,		7:64
m. anger is kindled against the		8:15
I sought for m. appointment	Abr	1: 4
God preserved in m. own hands;		1:31
he put his hand upon m. eyes,		3:12
they multiplied before m. eyes,		3:12
shall m. elect be gathered	JS	1:27
I speak for m. elect's sake;		1:29
m. elect, when they shall see		1:39
than this did at this time to m.		2:12
heard something of a silver m.		2:56
if possible, to discover the m.		2:56
hands, to dig for the silver m.,		2:56
or through any neglect of m.,		2:59

MINGLE

of strength to m. strong drink;	2Ne	15:22
whosoever did m. his seed with	Al	3: 9
and m. with the Lamanites.		50:22
m. themselves among the people,	He	1:12
that we may m. our voices	DC	109:79
not believe it just to m. religious		134: 9

MINGLED

shall not be m. with the names of	Al	5:57

MINGLETH

that m. his seed with thy brethren,	Al	3:15

MINGLING

m. with all kinds of society,	JS	2:28

MINISTER

and they did m. unto them.	1Ne	11:30
chosen to m. unto thy seed.		12: 8
which I shall m. unto them,		13:35
whom he shall m. in the flesh;	2Ne	2: 4
to be your teacher nor your m.,	Mos	23:14
and began to m. unto them.	Al	22:23
And he did m. unto them,		22:23
his brethren did m. unto them.		35: 7
and did m. unto the people,	He	5:50
did m. many things unto them;	3Ne	7:17
Nephi did m. with power and		7:17
angels did m. unto him daily.		7:18
and did m. unto them;		11:hd
from among you to m. unto you,		12: 1
chosen to m. unto this people.		13:25
whither I have been to m.		16: 1
the angels did m. unto them.		17:24
unworthily, when ye shall m. it;		18:28
but ye shall m. unto him and		18:30
m. unto him of my flesh and		18:30
such shall ye continue to m.;		18:32
of heaven and did m. unto them.		19:14
and should m. unto them.		23: 9
he did m. unto them?		23:11
he did teach and m. unto the		26:14
and did m. one to another;		26:19
m. upon the face of the earth;		28:16
did not m. of the things which		28:16
and did m. unto all the people,		28:18
m. unto all the scattered tribes of		28:29
and he did m. unto him.	Eth	3:20
the elder or priest did m. it—	Mro	4: 1
to m. unto the children of men,		7:22
to m. unto the children of men.		7:29
to m. according to the word of		7:30
angels appear and m. unto men;		7:37
he shall m. for those who	DC	7: 6
will make thee to m. for him		7: 7
to m. even according to the first;		68:14
appointed to m. for them,		76:88
angels who m. to this earth		130: 5
to m. for those who are worthy		132:16
of thee a m. to bear my name	Abr	2: 6

MINISTERED

which was m. unto their fathers	1Ne	15:14
that angels have m. unto him.		16:38

MINISTERED 628 MIRACLES

came down and m. unto me.	2Ne 4:24	also in thy m. in proclaiming	DC 81: 3
having m. much unto my people	Jac 4: 1	of God in the church unto the m.,	84:86
and they had m. unto me.	7: 5	you may be perfected in you m.	88:84
of heaven and m. unto them.	He 5:48	called to the m. in the church,	88:127
that he had m. unto them,	3Ne 19: 2	may be perfected in their m.	90: 8
arose and m. unto the people.	19: 7	that you continue in the m.	90:12
had m. those same words which	19: 8	of the m. of the presidency,	94: 3
in the midst and m. unto them.	19:15	called to the work of the m.	97:13
and they have m. unto me.	28:26	the understanding of thier m.,	97:14
and they have m. unto us.	Mrm 8:11	shall be set apart unto this m.,	107:74
And he m. unto him even as	Eth 3:18	to the keys of this m.,	107:76
as he m. unto the Nephites;	3:18	keys of this kingdom and m.	115:19
gospel which was m. unto them,	DC 10:62	for the work of the m.	124:143
God m. unto him by an holy	20: 6	through thy m. my name shall	Abr 1:19
and he m. not unto them,	Mses 5:52	their hands they shall bear this m.	2: 9

MINISTERING		MINON	
he went forth m. unto the people,	1Ne 11:28	in the land of M., above the land	Al 2:24
and the m. of angels.	Jac 7:17		
and in the m. of angels,	Om 1:25	MINUTES	
unto them, and m. unto them;	3Ne 10:19	and in their seasons, in their m.,	DC 88:44
were m. unto the disciples,	19:15	qualified for taking accurate m.;	128: 3
Wherefore, by the m. of angels,	Mro 7:25		
of angels and m. spirits;	10:14	MIRACLE	
as flaming fire and a m. angel;	DC 7: 6	there is a m. wrought by the hand	2Ne 28: 6
the keys of the m. of angels,	13: 1	therefore they had this m.,	Al 37:40
others by the m. of angels,	20:10	notwithstanding that great m.	He 10:13
voice of God, or the m. of angels.	20:35	do a m. in the name of Jesus	3Ne 8: 1
and by the m. of angels,	43:25	no m. wrought by Jesus Christ;	29: 7
now, neither the m. of angels;	67:13	shall say that it was not a m.	Mrm 9:17
to be m. spirits for them;	76:88	God can do no m. among them;	Eth 12:12
the key of the m. of angels	84:26	great a m. among the Lamanites.	12:15
the keys of the m. of angels,	107:20		
unto the m. of temporal things,	107:71	MIRACLES	
which angels are m. servants,	132:16	and has wrought so many m.	1Ne 17:51
mine angels, my m. servants,	136:37	should the mighty m. be wrought	2Ne 10: 4
thing now as m. of angels,	JS 2:65	mighty m., signs, and wonders,	26:13
the keys of the m. of angels,	2:69	the power and m. of God,	26:20
		and I am a God of m.;	27:23
MINISTERS		he is not a God of m.	28: 6
the twelve m. of thy seed shall	1Ne 12: 9	amongst men, working mighty m.,	Mos 3: 5
these twelve m. whom thou	12:10	faith, might work mighty m.;	8:18
standing m. unto the church.	DC 84:111	after working many mighty m.	15: 6
to ordain evangelical m.,	107:39	of God working m. in them—	Al 23: 6
seventy are to be traveling m.,	107:97	many mighty m. we have wrought	26:12
anointing of thy m. be sealed	109:35	also many other m. wrought	37:40
is instituted for standing m.;	124:137	because those m. were worked by	37:41
ordained to be standing m. to	124:137	working m. among the people,	He 16: 4
		the many m. which they did,	16:23
MINISTRATION		and greater m. wrought among	3Ne 1: 4
through the m. of the terrestrial;	DC 76:86	he did also do many more m.,	7:20
through the m. of the celestial.	76:87	do some m. among the people.	7:22
		many m. in the name of Jesus;	8: 1
MINISTRY		show unto them so great m.,	19:35
HIS REIGN AND M.	1Ne 1:hd	all manner of m. did they work	4Ne 1: 5
engraven of the m. of my people.	9: 3	nothing did they work m. save	1: 5
are for the more part of the m.;	9: 4	there were mighty m. wrought	1:13
proceedings, and my reign and m.;	10: 1	many m. which were wrought	1:29
the m. and the prophecies,	19: 3	doing mighty m. among them.	1:30
for thou didst forsake the m.,	Al 39: 3	notwithstanding all these m.,	1:31
shouldst have tended to the m.	39: 4	the work of m. and of healing	Mrm 1:13
the m. unto which ye were called,	39:16	said that m. are done away;	8:26
concerning the m. of Christ,	3Ne 7:15	a god who is not a God of m.	9:10
men unto this m., that all such	7:25	will show unto you a God of m.,	9:11
account of his m. shall be given	10:19	a god who can do no m.,	9:15
me and been with me in my m.,	16: 4	not ceased to be a God of m.	9:15
that our m., wherein thou hast	28: 2	word hath m. been wrought?	9:17
who was with me in my m.,	28: 6	did not many mighty m.?	9:18
the office of their m. is to call	Mro 7:31	were many mighty m. wrought	9:18
soon after my calling to the m.	8: 1	if there were m. wrought then,	9:19
and hath called you to his m.,	8: 2	God ceased to be a God of m.	9:19
shall bring to light this m.;	DC 6:28	not to be God, and is a God of m.	9:19
this part of my gospel and m.,	6:29	reason why he ceaseth to do m.	9:20
power and the keys of this m.	7: 7	even all they who wrought m.	Eth 12:16
of Mormon, and to my m.;	24: 1	at any time hath any wrought m.	12:18
and bear the keys of your m.	27:12	have m. ceased because Christ	Mro 7:27
with me in my m. at Jerusalem,	29:12	brethren, have m. ceased?	7:29
the m. whereunto you have	30: 2	has the day of m. ceased?	7:35
attend to the m. in the church,	30: 4	by faith that m. are wrought;	7:37
have been ordained unto this m.,	67:10	that he may work mighty m.;	10:12
shall be set apart for this m.	68:22	Require not m., except I shall	DC 24:13
Harris be united in the m.;	75:30	I will show m., signs, and	35: 8
faithful in the work of the m.	77: 5	gave I power to do many m.,	45: 8
		is given the working of m..	46:21

MIRACULOUS — MOBBING

MIRACULOUS
by the m. power of God	Al	9:hd
fought with such m. strength;		56:56
ascribe it to the m. power of God,		57:26
by his m. and matchless power,	He	4:25
m. directors which were given	DC	17: 1

MIRACULOUSLY
so m. prospered in regaining.	Al	59: 3

MIRE
down like the m. of the streets.	2Ne	20: 6
sow to her wallowing in the m.	3Ne	7: 8

MISCHIEF
become an idle people, full of m.	2Ne	5:24

MISCHIEFS
lyings, and of deceits, and of m.,	3Ne	16:10

MISERABLE
and become m. forever.	2Ne	2: 5
and had become m. forever,		2:18
might be m. like unto himself.		2:27
they would have been forever m.,	Al	12:26
their souls were m., being cut off		42:11
ye would be more m. to dwell	Mrm	9: 4

MISERY
the eternal gulf of m. and woe.	2Ne	1:13
neither holiness nor m.,		2:11
incorruption, happiness nor m.,		2:11
there be no punishment nor m.		2:13
sought also the m. of all mankind.		2:18
no joy, for they knew no m.;		2:23
of lies, in m., like unto himself;		9: 9
that I am a prey to his awful m.		9:46
state of m. and endless torment,	Mos	3:25
has brought upon himself his m.;		4:17
eternal happiness or eternal m.,	Al	3:26
a state of endless m. and woe.		9:11
everlasting gulf of death and m.,		26:20
and this state of m. of the soul,		40:15
consignation to happiness or m.,		40:15
consignation to happiness or m.		40:17
the soul in happiness or in m.		40:21
or to endless m. to inherit the		41: 4
be consigned to a state of m.		42: 1
and also their destruction and m.		42:26
that everlasting gulf of m.	He	3:29
the gulf of m. and endless wo,		5:12
everlasting m. and endless wo?		7:16
to a state of endless m.,		12:26
than that m. which never dies—	Mrm	8:38
And m. thou shalt receive if	DC	19:33
the depth, and the m. thereof,		76:48
death and m. of many souls;		87: 1
made partakers of m. and woe.	Mses	6:48
and m. shall be their doom;		7:37
their wickedness, and their m.,		7:41

MISSING
that their daughters had been m.,	Mos	20: 6

MISSION
the hour of your m. is come;	DC	31: 3
unto him his m. in this land.		58:14
his m. is given unto him,		58:16
whoso standeth in this m.		58:17
haste upon their errand and m.		61: 7
that they may fill their m.,		61: 9
so be that they fill their m.,		61:22
your m. is not yet full.		62: 2
whose m. is appointed unto them		68: 2
Verily this is a m. for a season,		71: 3
to understand that it was a m.,		77:14
the m. with which I have		88:80
shall be your business and m.		90:16
that he may perform a m. unto		114: 1
a m. in store for my servant		124:102
has sealed his m. and his works		135: 3

MISSIONS
the conference, their several m.	DC	73: 2

MISSOURI
which shall be held in M.,	DC	52: 2
and journey to the land of M.		52: 3
rejoice upon the land of M.,		52:42
westward, unto the land of M.,		54: 8
speedily to the land of M.,		56: 5
still to go to the land of M.;		56: 9
unto him again in the land of M.,		56:12
this land, which is the land of M.,		57: 1
rejoice together in the land of M.		62: 6
boundaries of the State of M.,		84: 3
inhabitants of Jackson county, M.,		109:47
stop the M. river in its decreed		121:33
in Jackson county, M.,		124:51
been slain in the land of M.,		124:54
both in M. and this State,		127: 1

MIST
there arose a m. of darkness;	1Ne	8:23
an exceeding great m. of darkness,		8:23
through the m. of darkness,		8:24
I saw a m. of darkness on the		12: 4
went up a m. from the earth,	Mses	3: 6
went up a m. from the earth,	Abr	5: 6

MISTAKE
I m., for I have seen much of	Al	10: 5
if there was no m. made by	3Ne	8: 2

MISTAKES
they are the m. of men;	T Pg	

MISTRESS
and also her m., the queen,	Al	19:17

MISTS
And the m. of darkness are the	1Ne	12:17
great were the m. of darkness	3Ne	8:22

MISUNDERSTAND
unto you, that ye cannot m.	2Ne	25:28

MITCHELL
I left him and went to Dr. M.,	JS	2:65

MIX
not m. and believe in incorrect	Al	3: 8
began to m. with the Lamanites		35:10

MIXED
and m. with the Lamanites until	He	3:16

MIXETH
of him that m. with their seed;	2Ne	5:23

MIXTURE
destroy the m. of thy seed,	1Ne	13:30
without m. upon the whole earth.	DC	115: 6
were a m. of all the seed of Adam	Mses	7:22

M'LELLIN, William E.: *see also WILLIAM.*
the Lord unto my servant M.—	DC	66: 1
and unto my servant M.,		68: 7
verily I say unto my servant M.,		75: 6
pleased with my servant M.,		90:35

MOAB
lay their hand upon Edom and M.;	2Ne	21:14

MOB
O Lord, upon the wicked m.,	DC	109:50
by an armed m.-painted black—		135: 1

MOBBED
been threatened with being m.,	JS	2:75

MOBBING
And their intentions of m. us	JS	2:75

MOBS

MOBS
and who were opposed to m., JS 2:75

MOCK
the Jews did m. him because of 1Ne 1:19
and make a m. of the great plan Jac 6: 8
doth make a m. of his brother, Al 5:30
they did m. them for many days. 14:22
with him, and began to m. him; 21:10
a m. of that which was sacred, He 4:12
do m. them, and cast stones 13:24
prophets, and did m. them. Eth 7:24
Gentiles will m. at these things, 12:23
Gentiles shall m. at our words. 12:25
Fools m., but they shall mourn; 12:26

MOCKED
but suffereth himself to be m., Mos 15: 5
we have been cast out, and m., Al 26:29
am not to be m. in the last days. DC 63:58
I, the Lord, am not to be m. 104: 6
am God, and cannot be m. in 124:71

MOCKER
And calamity shall cover the m., DC 45:50

MOCKERY
that it is solemn m. before God, Mro 8: 9
But it is m. before God, 8:23

MOCKING
they were in the attitude of m. 1Ne 8:27

MOCUM
and the city of M. and the 3Ne 9: 7

MOISTURE
hold of the m. of the root thereof, Jac 5:18

MOLDER
slew them to m. upon the land, Mrm 6:15

MOLDERING
thousands are m. in heaps upon Al 28:11
which are now m. in corruption Mrm 6:21

MOLES
to the m. and to the bats; 2Ne 12:20

MOLEST
there shall be none to m. them, 2Ne 1: 9
the Lamanites did not m. them Mos 19:29

MOLTEN
that I may find ore to m., 1Ne 17: 9
which I did m. out of the rock. 17:16
my m. image hath commanded 20: 5
did m. out of a rock sixteen small Eth 3: 1
which I have m. out of the rock. 3: 3
and he did m. out of the hill, 7: 9

MOMENT
you from one m. to another— Mos 2:21
a small m. have I forsaken thee, 3Ne 22: 7
I hid my face from thee for a m., 22: 8
be given thee in the very m. DC 24: 6
very hour, yea, in the very m., 100: 6
shall be but a small m.; 121: 7
and but for a small m. 122: 4
at the very m. when I was ready JS 2:16
just at this m. of great alarm, 2:16

MONARCHY
for they were not fighting for m. Al 43:45

MONEY
he that hath no m., come buy 2Ne 9:50
without m. and without price. 9:50
m. for that which is of no worth, 9:51
without m. and without price. 26:25
for if they labor for m. they shall 26:31
to support him and give him m. Al 1: 5
without m. and without price. Al 1:20
that they might get m. according 11:20
unpunished because of their m.; He 7: 5
saying, Behold here is m.; 9:20
shall be redeemed without m. 3Ne 20:38
for your m. you shall be forgiven Mrm 8:32
For behold, ye do love m., 8:37
sons of Akish did offer them m., Eth 9:11
and for shoes and for m., DC 24:18
save all the m. that ye can, 48: 8
m. which is left unto this people— 51: 8
take the m. to provide food 51: 8
could receive m. of this church, 51:11
things both in m. and in meat, 51:13
the m. which he has paid, 56:10
must needs pay the m., 56:12
that he may obtain m. to 57: 8
the m. which I have given him, 60:10
all the m. which he can impart, 63:43
clothe you, and give you m. 84:89
clothes you, or gives you m., 84:90
and receive m. by gift, 84:103
have not families, who receive m., 84:104
receive m. to bear her expenses, 90:28
the m. may be consecrated unto 90:29
Might not his m. be given to 101:49
I have bought it with m. 101:56
purchase all the lands with m., 101:70
which can be purchased for m., 101:70
which I have bought with m. 103:22
chance to loan m. by hundreds, 104:84
to overthrow the m. changers in 117:16
of my having been a m.-digger. JS 2:56

MONEY-DIGGER: see *MONEY* and *DIGGER*.

MONEYS
and to pay m. for you. DC 54: 7
appointed him, to receive m., 57: 6
laying his m. before the bishop 58:35
shall do with his m. according 58:36
receive m. to purchase lands 58:49
all the churches to obtain m., 58:51
all the m. which can be spared, 63:40
obtaining m. even as I have 63:46
the commandments and the m. 69: 1
gather together all their m.; 101:72
up wise men with their m., 103:23
devote his m. for the 104:26
And all m. that you receive 104:68
as fast as you receive m., 104:68
unto Zion, and will keep our m. 105: 8
purchased with their m., 105:30
stock into their hands, in m., 124:70
they receive the real value of m., 124:70

MONSTER
from the grasp of this awful m.; 2Ne 9:10
yea, that m., death and hell, 9:10
from that awful m. the devil, 9:19
are delivered from that awful m., 9:26
saying when he was a m., Al 19:26
no m. of the sea could break Eth 6:10

MONTH
the fourth day of this seventh m., Al 10: 6
the twelfth day, in the tenth m., 14:23
on the fifth day of the second m., 16: 1
second m. in the eleventh year, 16: 1
in the eleventh m. of the 49: 1
on the tenth day of the m., 49: 1
the first morning of the first m., 52: 1
on the second day in the first m., 56: 1
in the second m. of this year, 56:27
the third day of the seventh m. 56:42
that on the morrow m. I will 3Ne 3: 8
and it was in the sixth m., 4: 7
commenced in this the sixth m.; 4:11
in the first m., on the fourth 8: 5
on the fourth day of the m., 8: 5
in the fourth m. and on the DC 20: 1
on the sixth day of the m. 20: 1

MONTH 631 MORE

in the fourth m., and on the	DC	21: 3
on the sixth day of the m.		21: 3
In the m. of October, 1825,	JS	2:56
to work for nearly a m.,		2:56
in the m. of December, and the		2:62
Sometime in this m. of February,		2:63
the ensuing m. (May, 1829),		2:68

MONTHS

for the space of many m.,	Al	58: 7
in conference once in three m.,	DC	20:61
in their weeks, in their m.,		88:44
thirty-four years and four m.,		107:44
all the appointed days, m.,		121:31
all the days of their days, m., and		121:31
its number of days, and of m.,	Abr	3: 5

MOON

cauls, and round tires like the m.;	2Ne	13:18
the m. shall not cause her light to		23:10
and also the m. and the stars;	He	14:20
neither the sun, nor the m.,	3Ne	8:22
clear as the m., and fair as	DC	5:14
the m. shall be turned into		29:14
the m. be turned into blood;		34: 9
and the m. be turned into blood,		45:42
as that of the m. differs from		76:71
as the m. differs from the sun.		76:78
glory of the m. in the firmament.		76:81
as the glory of the m. is one.		76:97
As also he is in the m.,		88: 8
and is the light of the m.,		88: 8
the m. giveth her light by night,		88:45
the m. shall be bathed in blood;		88:87
as the sun, and clear as the m.,		105:31
and shine forth fair as the m.,		109:73
or to the sun, m., or stars—		121:30
And let the sun, m., and the morning		128:23
the m. shall withhold its light,		133:49
and the lesser light was the m.;	Mses	2:16
the m. to rule over the night,		2:18
unto me: Olea, which is the m.	Abr	3:13
and the m. be above the earth,		3:17
as also Floeese or the M.,	Fac	2: 5
the m. shall not give her light,	JS	1:33

MOONS

with them for the space of nine m.	Om	1:21

MORAL

according to the m. agency	DC	101:78

MORE

and my sons are no m.,	1Ne	5: 2
they be dimmed any m. by time.		5:19
also a great many m. things,		9: 1
for the m. part of the ministry;		9: 4
for the m. part of the reign of kings		9: 4
many m. things which I do not write		10:15
no m. brought down into captivity;		14: 2
Israel shall no m. be confounded,		14: 2
they should no m. be confounded,		15:20
m. than we are able to bear.		16: 1
which led us in the m. fertile parts		16:16
fathers would have been m. choice than		17:34
murmur no m. against their father;		17:49
the m. part of all our proceedings		19: 2
m. particularly made mention upon		19: 2
the m. plain and precious parts		19: 3
that the m. sacred things may be		19: 5
m. especially given unto those		19:10
they no m. turn aside their hearts		19:15
I might m. fully persuade them		19:23
they shall be smitten no m.,		21:13
the m. part of all the tribes		22: 4
Satan shall have no m. power		22:15
a few m. days and I go the way	2Ne	1:14
Rebel no m. against your brother,		1:24
a m. history part are written		4:14
give place no m. for the enemy of		4:28
that we may not be afflicted m.		5: 3
m. particular part of the history		5:33
thou shalt no m. drink it again.		8:22
there shall no m. come into thee	2Ne	8:24
to its mother earth, to rise no m.		9: 7
if the flesh should rise no m. our		9: 8
became the devil, to rise no m.		9: 8
I would speak unto you m.;		9:54
who are the m. wicked part of		10: 3
there must needs be m. than this,		10:21
spake many m. things to my people		11: 1
write m. of the words of Isaiah,		11: 2
God sendeth m. witnesses,		11: 3
neither shall they learn war any m.		12: 4
What could have been done m. to		15: 4
did m. grievously afflict by the		19: 1
shall no m. again stay upon him		20:20
make a man m. precious than		23:12
and look not forward any m. for		25:16
they need not look forward any m.		25:18
have received, and we need no m.!		28:27
need no m. of the word of God,		28:29
that receiveth I will give m.;		28:30
and there cannot be any m. Bible.		29: 3
Bible, and we need no m. Bible.		29: 6
there are m. nations than one?		29: 7
ye shall receive m. of my word?		29: 8
have not caused m. to be written.		29:10
that ye are m. righteous than		30: 1
somewhat m. concerning the Jews		30: 3
of men no m., for a long time.		30:18
then, how much m. need have we,		31: 5
there will be no m. doctrine given		32: 6
And now I, Nephi, cannot say m.;	Jac	2: 3
weighed down with much m. desire		2:13
have obtained m. abundantly		3: 5
are m. righteous than you;		3: 9
that ye revile no m. against them		3:12
many m. things unto the people		5:41
What could I have done m. for		5:47
what could I have done m. in		5:49
What could I have done m. for		5:64
once m., for the last time,		5:75
his vineyard was no m. corrupt,		5:75
my vineyard is no m. corrupted,		6:12
O be wise; what can I say m.?		7:20
he could say no m., and he		7:23
hearkened no m. to the words of		
For what could I write m. than	Jar	1: 2
they were exceeding m. numerous		1: 6
And I, Jarom, do not write m.,		1:14
and the m. wicked part of the	Om	1: 5
did once m. establish peace	WM	1:18
no m. contention in all the land	Mos	1: 1
many m. things did king Benjamin		1: 8
he will no m. preserve them		1:13
myself am m. than a mortal man,		2:10
for I have somewhat m. to speak		3: 1
even m. than man can suffer,		3: 7
then are they found no m. blameless		3:22
whence they can no m. return;		3:25
which justice could no m. deny		3:26
have claim on them no m. forever.		3:26
m. just will be your condemnation		4:22
have no m. disposition to do evil,		5: 2
they should no m. bind Ammon		7:16
many m. things did he do for them.		7:19
and many m. things did they do		7:28
Nephi was m. faithful in keeping		10:13
therefore, I say no m.		10:22
when it shall no m. be expedient		13:27
m. or less concerning these things?		13:33
that there can be no m. death.		16: 9
But the king was m. wroth,		17: 3
pour out his Spirit m. abundantly		18:10
if he have m. abundantly he		18:27
should impart m. abundantly;		18:27
to raise grain m. abundantly,		21:16
m. than there was of men;		21:17
that there was no m. disturbance		21:22
and he also sent m. wine, as a		22:10
they became m. numerous.		26: 5
seek to destroy the church no m.,		27:16
and my soul is pained no m.		27:29
should be no m. contentions		28: 2
this inequality should be no m.		29:32

m. things did king Mosiah write	Mos	29:33
esteem him m. than any other		29:40
no m. among the people of God.	Al	1:24
far m. wealthy than those who		1:31
they became m. still, and durst not		1:33
shall no m. be called thy seed;		3:17
being troubled no m. for a time		3:24
to establish the church m. fully;		4: 4
m. importance than they all—		7: 7
of heaven to go no m. out.		7:25
wax m. gross in their iniquities.		8:28
no m. authority than one man		9: 6
it shall be m. tolerable for them		9:15
and even m. tolerable for them		9:15
m. tolerable for the Lamanites		9:23
there was m. than one witness		10:12
were m. angry with Amulek,		10:24
that they might have m. employ,		11:20
lovest that lucre m. than him.		11:24
Is there m. than one God?		11:28
life, that they can die no m.;		11:45
that they can no m. see corruption.		11:45
began to tremble m. exceedingly,		12: 7
for he was convinced m. and more		12: 7
more and m. of the power of God;		12: 7
that he might know m. concerning		12: 8
seeing there is no m. corruption.		12:18
people began to be m. astonished;		12:19
have m. particularly made mention.		13:19
many m. words unto the people,		13:31
the m. part of them were desirous		14: 2
Alma and Amulek were no m.;		15: 3
many m. who had been chosen		16:15
and what added m. to his moy,		17: 2
Surely, this is m. than a man.		18: 2
his chariots he was m. astonished,		18:10
art m. powerful than all they;		18:21
they had no m. desire to do evil.		19:33
and I will govern him no m.—		20:26
into the hands of a m. hardened		20:30
and a m. stiffnecked people;		20:30
the m. idle part of the Lamanites		22:28
no m. possession on the north,		22:33
could have no m. possessions		22:34
did not fight against God any m.,		23: 7
and were no m. called Lamanites.		23:17
of God did no m. follow them.		23:18
let us stain our swords no m.		24:12
can no m. be washed bright		24:13
were joined that day by m. than		24:26
m. than a thousand brought to		24:27
they become m. hardened, and		24:30
those Lamanites were m. angry		25: 1
they did no m. attempt to slay		25: 1
there might not be m. sorrow		29: 2
why should I desire m. than to		29: 6
but my joy is m. full because of		29:14
that they may go no m. out,		29:17
many m. such things did he say		30:17
they were m. wise than many of		30:20
never open thy mouth any m.,		30:47
not deceive this people any m.,		30:47
ye shall not m. have utterance.		30:49
and now will ye dispute m.?		30:51
had m. powerful effect upon the		31: 5
and m. especially by our priests;		32: 5
say no m. to the other multitude;		32: 7
m. blessed who truly humble		32:14
much m. blessed than they who		32:15
how much m. cursed is he that		32:19
any m. than faith is a perfect		32:26
can no m. than desire to believe,		32:27
his kingdom, to go no m. out;		34:36
no m. deny the coming of Christ;		34:37
no m. against the Holy Ghost,		34:38
after the m. popular part of the		35: 3
seek no m. to destroy the church		36: 9
angel spake m. things unto me,		36:11
seek no m. to destroy the church		36:11
to the earth and I did hear no m.		36:11
could remember my pains no m.;		36:19
by the memory of my sins no m.		36:19
somewhat m. to say unto thee	Al	39: 1
no m. after the lusts of your eyes,		39: 9
the hearts of no m. to do wickedly;		39:13
somewhat m. I would say		40: 1
m. than one time appointed for		40: 8
one m. offense against your God		41: 9
m. fully condemneth the sinner,		41:15
m. which doth worry your mind,		42: 1
these things trouble you no m.,		42:29
deny the justice of God no m.		42:30
no m. concerning their preaching,		43: 2
of a m. wicked and murderous		43: 6
it was m. dreadful on the part of		43:37
the m. vital parts of the body,		43:38
the m. vital parts of the body		43:38
the Lamanites were m. numerous,		43:51
by m. than double the number of		43:51
to contend m. powerfully		44:16
shall no m. be numbered among		45:13
that he was never heard of m.;		45:18
of Moroni were m. numerous		46:29
should have any m. strength;		46:30
the m. part of them would not,		47: 2
m. hardened and impenitent,		47:36
m. wild, wicked and ferocious		47:36
and m. than a thousand of		49:23
and his men were m. powerful;		52:34
exceeded m. than the number of		52:40
m. than those who had been slain		52:40
the m. part of all his battles;		53: 2
did no m. attempt a battle with		53: 7
they never would shed blood m.;		53:11
if ye seek to destroy us m.		54:13
and shall be at war no m.		54:18
he was m. angry, because he		55: 1
that he shall have any m. power		55: 2
m. desirous to drink of the wine;		55:10
they took of it m. freely;		55:13
that we should not suffer m.		56: 6
did think m. upon the liberty of		56:47
not any m. than sufficient for		57:15
m. numerous than was our army		58: 2
we might receive m. strength		58: 3
not send m. strength unto us,		58: 9
does not grant us m. strength;		58:34
send m. men to our assistance;		58:36
they are m. numerous than that		58:36
stirred yourselves m. diligently		60:10
no m. with the Lamanites until		60:24
have no m. power to impede		60:30
obtain m. food to send forth		61:18
no m. take up their weapons		62:16
was once m. peace established		62:42
many m. people did enter into it;		63: 7
they were never heard of m.		63: 8
m. of this Gadianton shall be	He	2:12
are no m. called the Nephites,		3:16
the m. settled parts of the land,		3:23
holy fathers, to go no m. out.		3:30
the m. humble part of the people		3:34
obtain no m. possessions over		4:18
to obtain m. power over them;		4:19
Lord did no m. preserve them;		4:24
m. numerous than they,		4:25
m. numerous than they who		5: 2
somewhat m. to desire of you,		5: 8
seek no m. to destroy my		5:29
seek no m. to destroy my		5:32
the m. part of the Lamanites		5:50
the m. part of them, a righteous		6: 1
they were m. numerous among		6:18
among the m. wicked part of		6:18
of the m. part of the Nephites,		6:21
the m. part of them had turned		6:31
a m. part of it had come unto		6:32
the m. wicked part of them,		6:37
at the m. wicked part of them,		6:38
the m. part of the righteous		6:38
the m. easily commit adultery,		7: 5
to one m. than the other, save		7:23
they are m. righteous than you,		7:24
to speak m. unto them saying:		8:11

MORE 633 MORE

deny no m. that he has done this	He	9:35
the m. wicked parts of the land.		11: 6
did no m. seek to destroy Nephi,		11:18
and the m. part of the people,		11:21
and m. especially their women		11:33
even the m. part of this great city,		13:12
shall find them again no m.,		13:18
prophesy a great many m. things		14: 1
five years m. cometh, and behold,		14: 2
the m. part of it is one solid mass,		14:21
the m. part of them are in the path		15: 5
m. part of them are doing this,		15: 6
m. who did believe on his words,		16: 3
m. part of them did not believe		16: 6
he was never heard of m.		16: 8
m. part of the people remaining		16:10
m. circumspectly before God.		16:10
to be m. hardened in iniquity,		16:12
do m. and more of that which was		16:12
m. of that which was contrary		16:12
m. things did the people imagine		16:22
began to be fulfilled m. fully;	3Ne	1: 4
the m. part of the people did		1:22
no m. expedient to observe the		1:24
any m. signs or wonders given;		2: 3
that they would murder no m.		5: 4
should no m. be at liberty but		6:30
m. righteous part of the people		7: 7
the m. part of the people had		7: 8
their enemies were m. numerous		7:12
did also do many m. miracles,		7:20
the m. part of the year did pass		7:26
there was a m. great and		8:12
shall not come any m. unto me		9: 5
not come up any m. unto me		9: 7
not come up any m. unto me		9: 8
not come up unto me any m.		9: 9
ye were m. righteous than they,		9:13
no m. the shedding of blood;		9:19
m. righteous part of the people		10:12
declare m. or less than this,		11:40
m. blessed are they who shall		12: 2
cometh of m. than these is evil.		12:37
Is not the life m. than meat,		13:25
how much m. shall your Father		14:11
to say no m. of the Father		15:18
shall do m. or less than these		18:13
there shall no m. come into thee		20:36
was so marred, m. than any man,		20:44
form m. than the sons of men—		20:44
shalt have no m. soothsayers;		21:16
no m. worship the works of thy		21:17
for m. are the children of the		22: 1
of thy widowhood any m.		22: 4
should no m. go over the earth,		22: 9
the m. part of the things which		26: 7
whence they can no m. return,		27:17
Therefore, m. blessed are they, for		28: 7
of the Father to go no m. out,		28:40
did not walk any m. after the	4Ne	1:12
substance no m. common		1:25
deny the m. parts of his gospel,		1:27
the m. wicked part of the people		1:40
exceedingly m. numerous than		1:40
m. especially among the people of	Mrm	2:11
ten years m. had passed away.		3: 1
that I would no m. assist them;		5: 1
m. fully believe his gospel,		5:15
ten m. who did fall by the sword,		6:15
delight no m. in the shedding of		7: 4
even until they are no m.;		8: 7
I say no m. concerning them,		8: 9
m. than ye love the poor and		8:37
would be m. miserable to dwell		9: 4
be m. wise than we have been.		9:31
but thou shalt not sin any m.,	Eth	2:15
Sawest thou m. than this?		3: 9
they did not gain power any m.		7:19
no m. wars in the days of Shule;		7:27
away the m. part of the people		9:11
and m. especially the elephants		9:19
they should pursue them no m.,		9:33
a people m. blessed than were		10:28
m. prospered by the hand of	Eth	10:28
prepared a m. excellent way;		12:11
might have a m. excellent hope;		12:32
who shall have m. abundantly.		12:35
they shall no m. be confounded,		13: 8
And I was about to write m.,		13:13
m. than any other man among		14:10
not to have written m.,	Mro	1: 1
I write a few m. things,		1: 4
not to have written any m.;		1: 4
but I write a few m. things,		1: 4
many m. will also dissent over		9:24
m. than four hundred and twenty		10: 1
mayest no m. be confounded,		10:31
have feared man m. than God,	DC	3: 7
other men, and have no m. gift.		3:11
walk m. uprightly before me,		5:21
the persuasions of men no m.;		5:21
he shall say no m. unto them		5:26
that he shall do no m.,		5:29
trouble me any m. concerning		5:29
translated a few m. pages		5:30
thou shalt have no m. gift,		5:31
can do no m. unto you than		6:29
go your ways and sin no m.;		6:35
desired that he might do m.,		7: 5
or labor m. than you have		10: 4
a m. particular account was		10:39
m. particular concerning the		10:40
declareth m. or less than this,		10:68
m. express than other scriptures,		19: 7
m. than if you should obtain		19:38
one or m. or their teachers		20:81
go thy way and sin no m.		24: 2
remember to sin no m.,		29: 3
now I declare no m. unto you		29:50
m. than on the things of me,		30: 2
m. blessed are you because you		34: 5
no m. be confounded at all.		35:25
that ye should translate any m.		37: 1
m. especially in Colesville;		37: 2
in eternity, no m. to pass away.		38:20
forsaketh it, and doeth it no m.,		42:25
m. than is necessary for their		42:33
elders of the church, two or m.,		42:44
m. especially for those that have		42:45
m. than that which would be for		42:55
two elders of the church, or m.,		42:80
are m. than two witnesses		42:80
in God, receiveth m. light;		50:24
which are m. than is needful		51:13
the Lord, remember them no m.		58:42
m. fully keep thyself unspotted		59: 9
trouble me no m. concerning this		59:22
if they are no m. faithful		60: 3
and m. especially hereafter;		61: 4
now are wanted m. abundantly		61:32
a m. exceeding and eternal		63:66
m. easily obtain knowledge.—		69: 7
they receive m. than is needful		70: 7
Yea, even m. abundantly,		70:13
shall be given m. abundantly,		71: 6
give no m. unto you at this time.		73: 6
be m. tolerable for the heathen		75:22
even than an hundred fold, yea, m.		78:19
go your ways and sin no m.;		82: 7
m. perfectly in theory,		88:78
over the saints any m. at all.		88:114
they shall not any m. see death.		88:116
whatsoever is m. or less than		93:25
give m. earnest heed unto your		93:48
see that they are m. diligent		93:50
unto you no m. at this time.		94:17
and if she sin no m.		97:27
whatsoever is m. or less than		98: 7
that he come no m. upon you,		98:28
hold it no m. as a testimony		98:39
shall no m. come upon them,		98:48
brought any m. as a testimony		98:48
is found no m. room for them;		101:21
no m. to be thrown down,		101:75
and if m. difficult, six;		102:14
in no case shall m. than six be		102:14

MORE 634 MORMON

no m. to be thrown down.	DC 103:13	the people of M. brought back.	Al 50:36
may be taught m. perfectly,	105:10	were restored to the land of M.,	50:36
know m. perfectly concerning	105:10	of Lehi and the people of M.	51: 1
be had in remembrance no m.	107:80	city of Lehi, and the city of M.,	51:26
and resist no m. my voice.	108: 2	by Teancum, who had slain M.	51:29
And arise up and be m. careful	108: 3	to attack the city M.;	55:33
the m. ancient inhabitants and	111: 9	fortified the city M. until it	55:33
there are m. treasures than one	111:10	city of Lehi and the city of M.,	59: 5
in debt any m. for the building of	115:13	And Kim was the son of M.	Eth 1:22
neglect the m. weighty matters?	117: 8	And M. was a descendant of	1:23
his sacrifice shall be m. sacred	117:13	M., (he being a descendant of	10: 9
thy voice shall be m. terrible	122: 4	that M. built up many cities,	10:12
to require that work no m. at	124:49	M. did live to an exceeding great	10:13
that which is m. or less than this	124:120		
is no m. required at your hand	126: 1	MORIANTUM	
for the want of m. time;	127:11	exceed that of our people in M.	Mro 9: 9
trouble me no m. on this matter.	130:15		
And if a person gains m. knowledge	130:19	MORLEY, Isaac	
The m. sure word of prophecy	131: 5	And again, let my servant M.	DC 52:23
but it is m. fine or pure,	131: 7	and also my servant M.,	64:15
those who are worthy of a far m.,	132:16	I have forgiven my servant M.	64:16
I will reveal m. unto you,	132:66	my servant M. may not be	64:20
has done m., save Jesus only,	135: 3		
So no m. at present. Amen	136:42	MORMON	
that forty or m. such marriages	OD	THE BOOK OF M.	T Pg
now the serpant was m. subtle	Mses 4: 5	Written by THE HAND OF M.	T Pg
and they loved Satan m. than God.	5:13	THE WORDS OF M.	WM 1:hd
Cain loved Satan m. than God.	5:18	And now I, M., being about to	1: 1
listened not any m. to the	5:26	And now I, M., proceed to	1: 9
they loved Satan m. than God.	5:28	And I, M., pray to God that	1:11
might never m. be covered by	7:50	to a place which was called M.,	Mos 18: 4
for it moveth in order m. slow;	Abr 3: 5	in M. a fountain of pure water,	18: 5
one shall be m. intelligent than the	3:18	together at the place of M.,	18: 7
one is m. intelligent than the	3:18	Behold, here are the waters of M.	18: 8
one being m. intelligent than the	3:19	went forth to the place of M.;	18:16
shall be another m. intelligent	3:19	baptized in athe waters of M.,	18:16
I am m. intelligent than they all.	3:19	that all this was done in M.,	18:30
were m. pretended than real;	JS 2: 6	yea, by the waters of M.,	18:30
m. power to the heart of man	2:12	that was near the waters of M.;	18:30
unless I could get m. wisdom	2:12	yea, the place of M.,	18:30
would never be any m. of them.	2:21	of Mormon, the waters of M.,	18:30
The persecution became m. bitter	2:60	of Mormon, the forest of M.,	18:30
m. so than any he had before	2:64	his brethren in the waters of M.;	25:18
their m. mysterious passages	2:74	baptized in the waters of M.	26:15
		which was called the land of M.;	Al 5: 3
MOREH		his brethren in the waters of M.	5: 3
was situated in the plains of M.,	Abr 2:18	away joining the borders of M.	21: 1
sacrifice there in the plains of M.,	2:18	And behold, I am called M.,	3Ne 5:12
		being called after the land of M.	5:12
MOREOVER		I am M., and a pure descendant	5:20
M., the Lord saith:	2Ne 13:16	I, M., do write the things which	26:12
M., the Lord spake again unto	17:10	I M., make an end of my sayings,	26:12
M., the word of the Lord said	18: 1	I M., make an end of speaking	28:24
And m., I shall give this people	Mos 1:11	I, M., would that ye should	4Ne 1:23
Yea, and m. I say unto you,	1:13	THE BOOK OF M.	Mrm 1:hd
And m., he also gave him charge	1:16	now I, M., make a record of	1: 1
And m., I say unto you that	2:29	and call it the Book of M.	1: 1
And m., I would desire that	2:41	I, M., being a descendant of	1: 5
And m., I say unto you, that	3:17	(and my father's name was M.)	1: 5
And m., I say unto you, that	3:20	I, M., saw their lamentation	2:12
And m., I say unto you, that	13:28	I, M., did utterly refuse from	3:11
And m., have ye sufficiently	Al 5: 6	I, M., seeing that the Lamanites	4:23
And m., I say unto you that it	5:47	I, M., did not desire to harrow up	5: 8
And m. they did say:	26:25	I, M., wrote an epistle unto	6: 2
And m., I would ask, do ye	32:11	I, M., began to be old;	6: 6
m. to be held in office at the head	He 7: 5	the record of my father, M.	8: 1
m., that they might the more	7: 5	I am the son of M., and my	8:13
M., when ye fast be not as the	3Ne 13:16	M. did hide up the records unto	Eth 15:11
		of the words of my father M.,	Mro 7: 1
MORIANCUMER		now I, M., speak unto you,	7: 2
called the name of the place M.;	Eth 2:13	An epistle of my father M.,	8: 1
and the land of M., which	Al 50:25	The second epistle of M. to his	9:hd
who possessed the land of M.	50:26	power of God, the Book of M.	DC 1:29
the people of M. took up arms	50:26	the printing of the Book of M.,	19:26
that when the people of M.,	50:28	to translate the Book of M.,	20: 8
by a man whose name was M.,	50:28	chosen to write the Book of M.,	24: 1
M. put it into their hearts that	50:29	you to reveal the Book of M.,	27: 5
M. being a man of much passion,	50:30	the Book of M. and the holy	33:16
would hearken to the words of M.	50:32	in the Bible and the Book of M.,	42:12
to head the people of M.,	50:33	covenant, even the Book of M.	84:57
did meet the people of M.;	50:35	believer in the Book of M.,	124:119
stubborn were the people of M.,	50:35	of this book and the Book of M.,	135: 1
slay M. and defeat his army,	50:35	has brought forth the Book of M.,	135: 3

MORMON 635 MORONI

of Ether, in the Book of M.,	DC	135: 4
reminded that the Book of M.,		135: 6
to translate the Book of M.,	JS	2:67
we also believe the Book of M.	AoF	8

MORMONISM
a broad seal affixed to "M."	DC	135: 7

MORNING
as my father arose in the m.,	1Ne	16:10
weary he waketh m. by morning.	2Ne	7: 4
weary he waketh morning by m.		7: 4
that rise up early in the m.,		15:11
heaven, O Lucifer, son of the m.!		24:12
And in the m. the Lord caused	Mos	24:19
both m., mid-day, and evening.	Al	34:21
and when thou risest in the m.		37:37
the first m. of the first month,		52: 1
the Lamanites awoke in the m.	Al	55:22
that before the dawn of the m.,		56:39
when the light of the m. came		56:41
was in the m. of the third day		56:42
when the m. came they were		62:23
the sun did rise in the m. again,	3Ne	1:19
And it was in the m., and the		10: 9
For he did cry from the m.,	Eth	12: 3
was Lucifer, a son of the m.	DC	76:26
is fallen, even a son of the m.!		76:27
in coming up hither this m.		108: 1
Contend thou, therefore, m. by		112: 5
thou, therefore, morning by m.;		112: 5
and the m. stars sing together,		128:23
but I am calm as a summer's m.;		135: 4
same m., after Hyrum had		135: 4
and the m. were the first day.	Mses	2: 5
and the m. were the second day.		2: 8
and the m. were the third day.		2:13
and the m. were the fourth day.		2:19
and the m. were the fifth day.		2:23
and the m. were the sixth day.		2:31
the evening until m. they called	Abr	4: 5
the m. until the evening they called		4: 5
evening until m. that they called		4: 8
m. until evening that they called		4: 8
evening until the m. they called		4:13
m. until the evening they called		4:13
until m. that it was night;		4:19
m. until evening that it was day;		4:19
until m. that they called night;		4:23
m. until evening that they called		4:23
evening until m. they called		4:31
m. until evening that they called		4:31
the light of the m. cometh out	JS	1:26
It was on the m. of a beautiful,		2:14

MORON
Coriantor was the son of M.	Eth	1: 7
And M. was the son of Ethem.		1: 8
came up unto the land of M.		7: 5
Now the land of M., where		7: 6
him away captive into M.		7:17
all his days; and he begat M.		11:14
that M. did reign in his stead;		11:14
M. did that which was wicked		11:14
iniquity, and gave battle unto M.,		11:15
that M. did overthrow him,		11:16
that he did overthrow M.		11:18
M. dwelt in captivity all the		11:18
came forth to the land of M.,		14: 6
came up unto the land of M.,		14:11

MORONI
Sealed by the hand of M.,	T Pg	
into the hands of my son M.,	WM	1: 1
and his name was M.;	Al	43:16
And M. took all the command,		43:17
the people of Nephi, or that M.,		43:19
that the armies of M. would know		43:22
M. sent spies into the wilderness		43:23
M., also, knowing of the		43:23
informed the messengers of M.,		43:24
delivered the message unto M.		43:24
Now M., leaving a part of his army	Al	43:25
M. caused that his army should		43:27
And M. placed spies round about,		43:28
as M. knew the intention of the		43:29
the army of M. was concealed.		43:34
that M. and his army met the		43:41
met again by the armies of M.		43:42
when the men of M. saw the		43:48
And M., perceiving their intent,		43:48
armies of M. encircled them		43:52
the armies of M. on the west of		43:53
Now M., when he saw their terror,		43:54
And M. said unto Zerahemnah:		44: 1
his bow into the hands of M.,		44: 8
M. returned the sword and the		44:10
when M. had said these words,		44:12
and he was angry with M.,		44:12
forward that he might slay M.;		44:12
weapons of war at the feet of M.;		44:15
And now M. was angry,		44:17
soldier of M. had prophesied.		44:18
cried mightily unto M.,		44:19
M. caused that the work of death		44:20
of the Nephites, or M.,		44:23
when M., who was the chief		46:11
M. prayed that the cause of the		46:16
when M. had said these words,		46:19
when M. had proclaimed these		46:21
their garments at the feet of M.,		46:22
M. said unto them:		46:23
when M. had said these words		46:28
the people of M. were more		46:29
M. thought it was not expedient		46:30
M. thought it was expedient that		46:31
up into the hands of M.		46:33
M. being a man who was		46:34
thus M. planted the standard of		46:36
M., on the other hand, had been		48: 7
M. was a strong and a mighty		48:11
and this was the faith of M.,		48:16
ever would be, like unto M.,		48:17
unto the people than was M.;		48:19
M. had stationed an army by		49: 2
of the instructions of M.		49: 8
M. had altered the management		49:11
knew not that M. had fortified,		49:13
had now, by the means of M.,		49:14
this was wisdom in M.;		49:15
M. had appointed Lehi to be chief		49:16
he did curse God, and also M.,		49:27
M. had kept the commandments		49:27
that M. did not stop making		50: 1
Thus M. did prepare strongholds		50: 6
M. caused that his armies should		50: 7
M. had driven all the Lamanites		50: 9
Thus M., with his armies,		50:12
called the name of the city M.;		50:13
a city between the city of M.		50:14
the borders of Aaron and M.;		50:14
of Nephi, than in the days of M.,		50:23
of Lehi fled to the camp of M.,		50:27
of Lehi had fled to the camp of M.,		50:28
lest the army of M. should come		50:28
came over to the camp of M.,		50:31
told M. all things concerning		50:31
M., feared that they would		50:32
Therefore M. sent an army,		50:33
the army which was sent by M.,		50:35
and returned to the camp of M.		50:35
sworn to drink the blood of M.		51: 9
when M. saw this, and also saw		51:14
give him (M.) power to compel		51:15
M. commanded that his army		51:17
to fight against the men of M.		51:18
M. put an end to those king-men,		51:21
while M. was thus breaking down		51:22
had come into the land of M.,		51:22
strong in the city of M.,		51:23
who fled out of the city of M.		51:24
of the fortifications of M.;		51:27
until M. had sent a large number		52: 7
M. also sent orders unto him that		52: 8

MORONI 636 MORROW

And M. also sent unto him,	Al 52:10	M., after he had obtained	Al	62:30
by the command of M.—	52:15	did strengthen the army of M.		62:30
to wait for the coming of M.,	52:17	M. went forth from the land of		62:30
M. did arrive with his army at	52:18	that M. was coming against them,		62:31
M. and Teancum and many of	52:19	and fled before the army of M.		62:31
M., having no hopes of meeting	52:21	M. and his army did pursue them		62:32
and M. and his army, by night,	52:22	they came to the land of M.		62:32
M. commanded that a part of	52:24	in one body in the land of M.		62:33
thus M. had obtained possession	52:26	M. and Lehi and Teancum did		62:34
that M. had been in their rear	52:29	the borders of the land of M.,		62:34
should meet M. and his army.	52:30	M. knew that Teancum was dead		62:37
by the men of M. on one hand,	52:31	M. marched forth on the morrow,		62:38
M. commanded his men that	52:32	after M. had fortified those parts		62:42
with exceeding fury against M.	52:33	M. yielded up the command of		62:43
M. being in their course of	52:34	came to pass that M. died also.		63: 3
M. and his men were more	52:34	the city of M. did sink into the	3Ne	8: 9
and M. was wounded and Jacob	52:35	that great city M. have I		9: 4
Now M. seeing their confusion,	52:37	which I gave unto my son M.	Mrm	6: 6
weapons of war at the feet of M.,	52:38	(among whom was my son M.)		6:11
M. placed men over them to	53: 1	who were led by my son M.		6:12
M. went to the city of Mulek	53: 2	I, M., do finish the record of		8: 1
a man who had been with M.	53: 2	Behold, I am M.; and were it		8:12
and he was a man like unto M.,	53: 2	now I, M., proceed to give	Eth	1: 1
Teancum, by the orders of M.,	53: 3	as I, M., said I could not make		3:17
M. was compelled to cause the	53: 5	I, M., have written the words		5: 1
M. had thus gained a victory over	53: 6	I, M., proceed to give the record		6: 1
in the absence of M. on account	53: 8	I, M., do not write the manner of		8:20
Ammoron sent unto M. desiring	54: 1	I, M., am commanded to write		8:26
M. felt to rejoice exceedingly	54: 2	I, M., proceed with my record.		9: 1
among all the prisoners of M.,	54: 3	I, M., would speak somewhat		12: 6
prisoners whom M. had taken;	54: 3	I, M., having heard these words,		12:29
M. resolved upon a stratagem to	54: 3	I, M., bid farewell unto the		12:38
had brought an epistle to M.	54: 4	I, M., proceed to finish my		13: 1
I am M.; I am a leader of	54:14	THE BOOK OF M.	Mro	1:hd
wrote another epistle unto M.,	54:15	I, M., after having made an end		1: 1
and I close my epistle to M.	54:24	I, M., will not deny the Christ;		1: 3
when M. had received this epistle	55: 1	I, M., write a few of the words		7: 1
when M. had said these words,	55: 4	father Mormon, written to me, M.;		8: 1
M. caused that Laman and a	55: 6	My beloved son, M., I rejoice		8: 2
M. appointed Laman and caused	55: 7	*epistle of Mormon to his son, M.*		9:hd
they returned to M. and told	55:15	Now I, M., write somewhat as		10: 1
according to the design of M.	55:16	with M., whom I have sent	DC	27: 5
M. had prepared his men with	55:16	M., an angel from heaven,		128:20
when M. had armed all those	55:17	and that his name was M.;	JS	2:33
this was not the desire of M.;	55:19			
behold, this was the desire of M.	55:24	MORONIHAH		
they did join the army of M.,	55:24	of his son, whose name was M.;	Al	62:43
it was expedient for M. to make	55:33	to war against the people of M.,		63:15
M. received an epistle from	56: 1	or against the army of M.,		63:15
My dearly beloved brother, M.,	56: 2	gave M. great advantage over	He	1:25
my beloved brother M., that never	56:45	M. had supposed that the		1:26
now, my beloved brother, M.,	58:41	M. had caused that their strong-		1:26
after M. had received and had	59: 1	when M. had discovered this,		1:28
when M. had sent this epistle to	59: 4	that M. did head them in their		1:30
M. was thus making preparations	59: 5	M. took possession of the city of		1:33
together from the city of M.	59: 5	M. had established again peace		2: 1
even and joined the army of M.	59: 8	and the armies of M. were driven		4: 6
M. had supposed that there	59: 9	M. did succeed with his armies		4: 9
M. saw that the city of Nephihah	59:11	M. did preach many things unto		4:14
that M. was angry with the	59:13	when M. saw that they did repent		4:16
behold, I, M., am constrained,	60:34	that M. could obtain no more		4:18
I am M., your chief captain.	60:36	M. did employ all his armies in		4:19
after M. had sent his epistle unto	61: 1	carried up upon the city of M.	3Ne	8:10
do send these words unto M.,	61: 2	buried up in that great city M.		8:25
Behold, I say unto you, M., that I	61: 2	that great city M. have I		9: 5
my beloved brother, I, M., let us	61:14	and M., and Antionum, and	Mrm	6:14
now, M., I do joy in receiving	61:19			
epistle to my beloved brother, M.	61:21	MORONI'S		
when M. had received this epistle	62: 1	one of M. soldiers smote it	Al	44:12
M. took a small number of men,	62: 3			
when M. had gathered together	62: 6	MORROW		
M. and Pahoran went down with	62: 7	on the m. he should take his	1Ne	16: 9
M. and Pahoran having restored	62:11	on the m., after we had		18: 6
M. immediately caused that	62:12	on the m. I will declare unto you	2Ne	9:54
M. and Pahoran, leaving a large	62:14	up into the temple on the m.,	Jac	2:11
Now M. was desirous that the	62:19	Gather together on the m.,		7:16
M. went forth in the darkness	62:20	on the m. the multitude were		7:17
now M. returned to his army,	62:21	for on the m. I shall proclaim	Mos	1:10
M. caused that his men should	62:22	on the m. they started to go up,		7: 3
the armies of M. were within	62:24	on the m. I will cause that		7:14
M. saw that they were fleeing	62:25	on the m. that king Limhi sent		7:17
of them fled into the land of M.,	62:25	for on the m. I will deliver you		24:16
had M. and Pahoran obtained	62:26			

MORROW

on the m. they returned into	Al	2:23
but came again on the m ;		14:20
on the m. he shall rise again;		19: 8
even until that time on the m.		19:11
on the m. he entered the city		47:31
thus, on the m., when the guards		52:22
that on the m. they did return.		57:17
on the m. , that when the		58:14
on the m. we were beyond the		58:27
Moroni marched forth on the m.,		62:38
that on the m. the people did	He	9:10
tool here and on the m. it is gone;		13:34
on the m. come I into the world,	3Ne	1:13
the m. month I will command		3: 8
on the m., when the robbers		4:25
therefore no thought for the m.,		13:34
the m. shall take thought for the		13:34
prepare your minds for the m.,		17: 3
also show himself on the m.		19: 2
that they might be on the m.		19: 3
on the m., when the multitude		19: 4
on the m. that the multitude		26:16
did behold on the m., when the	Mrm	6:11
upon the m., he could not find it,	Eth	14: 1
the m. they did come to battle.		15: 8
on the m. they did go again to		15:17
on the m. they fought even until		15:21
on the m. they fought again;		15:23
on the m. they fought again,		15:24
prepared for death on the m.		15:26
on the m. he did overtake them;		15:29
take ye no thought for the m.,	DC	84:81
let the m. take thought for		84:84

MORTAL

my m. shall put on immortality,	En	1:27
myself am more than a m. man.	Mos	2:10
about to yield up this m. frame		2:26
I mean the life of the m. body—		4: 6
this m. shall put on immortality,		16:10
you are dead as to the m. body;		18:13
m. body raised in immortality,	Al	5:15
have been done in the m. body?		5:15
his dwelling in his m. tabernacle;		7: 8
the death of the m. body,		11:45
the resurrection of the m. body.		11:45
this m. body is raised to an		11:45
from this m. to an immortal state		12:20
m. does not put on immortality,		40: 2
are departed from this m. body,		40:11
they were m. or immortal,	3Ne	28:17
your m. must put on immortality,	Mrm	6:21

MORTALITY

raised from this m. to a state of	Al	12:12
m. raised to immortality,		41: 4
an eye from m. to immortality;	3Ne	28: 8
from m. to immortality—		28:36

MOSES

let us be strong like unto M.;	1Ne	4: 2
according to the law of M.,		4:15
did contain the five books of M.,		5:11
according to the law of M.;		17:22
if the Lord had not commanded M.		17:24
ye know that M. was commanded		17:26
ye also know that M., by his word		17:29
and reviled against M.		17:30
they did revile against M.,		17:42
were written in the book of M.;		19:23
fulfilling of the words of M.,		22:20
this prophet of whom M. spake		22:21
he shall be great like unto M.,	2Ne	3: 9
M. will I raise up, to deliver		3:10
as I am sure of the promise of M.;		3:16
hath said: I will raise up a M.;		3:17
according to the law of M.		5:10
hath the law of M. been given;		11: 4
and gave unto M. power that he		25:20
in Christ, we keep the law of M.,		25:24
fulfilled which was given unto M.		25:30
intent we keep the law of M.,	Jac	4: 5
and keep not the law of M.		7: 7
and convert the law of M. into	Jac	7: 7
observed to keep the law of M.	Jar	1: 5
teaching the law of M.,		1:11
according to the law of M.	Mos	2: 3
them a law, even the law of M.		3:14
that the law of M. availeth nothing		3:15
We teach the law of M.		12:28
If ye teach the law of M. why do ye		12:29
said that ye teach the law of M.		12:31
know ye concerning the law of M.?		12:31
salvation come by the law of M.?		12:31
did come by the law of M.		12:32
which the Lord delivered unto M.		12:33
salvation cometh by the law of M.		13:27
keep the law of M. as yet;		13:27
expedient to keep the law of M.		13:27
notwithstanding the law of M.		13:28
did not M. prophesy unto them		13:33
if ye teach the law of M., also		16:14
their God, neither the law of M.;		24: 5
and they did keep the law of M.;	Al	25:15
should keep the law of M. as yet,		25:15
notwithstanding the law of M.,		25:15
the law of M. was a type of his		25:15
salvation came by the law of M.;		25:16
but the law of M. did serve to		25:16
according to the law of M.;		30: 3
taught to keep the law of M.		30: 3
according to the law of M.		31: 9
Behold, he was spoken of by M.;		33:19
also he has appealed unto M.,		34: 7
shall the law of M. be fulfilled;		34:13
hand of the Lord, even as M.		45:19
the Lord took M. unto himself;		45:19
power unto one man, even M.,	He	8:11
were spoken by this man, M.,		8:13
M. did not only testify of these		8:16
according to the law of M.		13: 1
according to the law of M.		15: 5
to observe the law of M.	3Ne	1:24
in me is the law of M. fulfilled.		9:17
would concerning the law of M.;		15: 2
fulfilled that was given unto M.		15: 4
law which was given unto M.		15: 8
I am he of whom M. spake,		20:23
shall be done even as M. said)		21:11
Remember ye the law of M.,		25: 4
ordinances of the law of M.;	4Ne	1:12
faith was the law of M. given.	Eth	12:11
the spirit by which M. brought	DC	8: 3
strait gate by the law of M.,		22: 2
he receiveth them even as M.		28: 2
become subject to the law of M.,		74: 3
in subjection to the law of M.,		74: 4
except the law of M. should be		74: 5
some of John, and some of M.,		76:100
And the sons of M., according		84: 6
this M. plainly taught to the		84:23
he took M. out of their midst,		84:25
concerning the sons of M.—		84:31
for the sons of M. and also the		84:31
And the sons of M. and of		84:32
They become the sons of M.		84:34
like as M. led the children of		103:16
and to be like unto M.—		107:91
and M. appeared before us,		110:11
for this cause I commanded M.,		124:38
as also M., David, and Solomon,		132: 1
Solomon, and M. my servants,		132:38
M. also, and they who were before		133:54
And from M. to Elijah,		133:55
was written by the prophet M.,		133:63
from Abraham to M.,		136:37
M. to Jesus and his apostles,		136:37
which he spake unto M. at a	Mses	1: 1
at a time when M. was caught up		1: 1
the glory of God was upon M.;		1: 2
M. could endure his presence.		1: 2
And God spake unto M., saying:		1: 3
And I have a work for thee M.,		1: 6
I show unto thee, M., my son;		1: 7
it came to pass that M. looked,		1: 8
and M. beheld the world and the		1: 8

MOSES 638 MOST

of God withdrew from M.,	Mses	1: 9
that his glory was not upon M.;		1: 9
and M. was left unto himself.		1: 9
many hours before M. did again		1:10
when M. had said these words		1:12
M., son of man, worship me.		1:12
M. looked upon Satan and said:		1:13
M. said: I will not cease to call		1:18
when M. had said these words,		1:19
M. began to fear exceedingly;		1:20
M. received strength, and called		1:21
even from the presence of M.,		1:22
of this thing M. bore record;		1:23
departed from the presence of M.,		1:24
that M. lifted up his eyes		1:24
Blessed art thou M., for I, the		1:25
M. cast his eyes and beheld		1:27
that M. called upon God,		1:30
glory of the Lord was upon M.,		1:31
M. stood in the presence of God,		1:31
the Lord God said unto M.:		1:31
that M. spake unto the Lord,		1:36
the Lord God spake unto M.,		1:37
M., my son, I will speak unto thee		1:40
spoken unto M. in the mount,		1:42
pass that the Lord spake unto M.,		2: 1
I, the Lord God, spake unto M.,		4: 1
I spake unto my servant M.,		4:32
according to the prophecy of M.,	JS	1:55

MOSES'

even as M. did while in the mount	Mos	13: 5
church be called in M. name	3Ne	27: 8
name then it be M. church;		27: 8

MOSIAH

M., who was made king over	Om	1:12
the people of M. with the plates		1:14
M. discovered that the people of		1:15
land where M. discovered them;		1:16
the time that M. discovered them,		1:17
and M., nor the people of		1:17
nor the people of M., could		1:17
M. caused that they should be		1:18
were taught in the language of M.,		1:18
people of Zarahemla, and of M.,		1:19
M. was appointed to be their		1:19
in the days of M., there was a		1:20
was born in the days of M.;		1:23
THE BOOK OF M.	Mos	1:hd
M., and Helorum, and Helaman.		1: 2
he had M. brought before him;		1:10
the people of M. who dwell in		1:10
M. went and did as his father had		1:18
after M. had done as his father		2: 1
that my son M. is a king and a		2:30
was spoken of by my father M.		2:32
and had consecrated his son M.		6: 3
M. began to reign in his father's		6: 4
king M. did walk in the ways of		6: 6
king M. did cause his people that		6: 7
king M. had had continual peace		7: 1
king M. granted that sixteen of		7: 2
king M. had a gift from God,		21:28
that M. received them with joy;		22:14
king M. did also receive them		24:25
king M. caused that all the people		25: 1
M. did read, and caused to be read,		25: 5
when M. had made an end of		25: 7
when M. had made an end of		25:14
king M. granted unto Alma that		25:19
in the reign of M. they were not		26: 5
king M. had given Alma that		26: 8
But king M. said unto Alma:		26:12
laid the case before their king, M.		27: 1
M. consulted with his priests.		27: 1
king M. sent a proclamation		27: 2
the sons of M. were numbered		27: 8
secretly with the sons of M.		27:10
of them were the sons of M.;		27:34
the names of the sons of M.		27:34
were under the reign of king M.,		27:35
after the sons of M. had done		28: 1
king M. went and inquired of	Mos	28: 6
And the Lord said unto M.:		28: 7
M. granted that they might go		28: 8
king M. had no one to confer the		28:10
after M. had finished translating		28:17
cause the people of M. to mourn		28:18
after king M. had done these		28:20
when M. had done this he sent		29: 1
any of the sons of M. willing		29: 3
king M. sent again among the		29: 4
more things did king M. write		29:33
after king M. had sent these things		29:37
did wax strong in love towards M.;		29:40
M. died also, in the thirty and		29:46
king M. having gone the way of	Al	1: 1
given us by M., our last king;		1:14
Yea, well did M. say,		10:19
it was in the law of M. that		11: 1
been established by king M.		11: 4
An account of the sons of M.,		17:hd
he met with the sons of M.		17: 1
these sons of M. were with Alma		17: 2
taken leave of their father, M.,		17: 6
that the hearts of the sons of M.,		17:12
the sons of M. had undertaken		17:16
the Lord had promised M. that		17:35
the Lord had said unto M.,		19:23
M. trusted him unto the Lord.		19:23
went about with the sons of M.,		36: 6
like unto Ammon, the son of M.,		48:18
and even the other sons of M.		48:18
Alma, and also the words of M.;	He	4:21
under their feet the laws of M.,		4:22
away since the days of M.,	3Ne	2: 5
cause did king M. keep them,	Eth	4: 1

MOSIAH'S

and joined M. people, and became	Mos	22:13

MOST

was of the m. precious steel.	1Ne	4: 9
I beheld that it was m. sweet,		8:11
to the Lord, the m. high God;		11: 6
in the Son of the m. high God;		11: 6
A virgin, m. beautiful and fair		11:15
m. desirable above all things.		11:22
and the m. joyous to the soul.		11:23
a church which is m. abominable		13: 5
church, which is m. abominable		13:26
which are plain and m. precious;		13:26
the plain and m. precious parts		13:32
the m. plain and precious parts		13:34
plain and pure, and m. precious		14:23
whose fruit is m. precious		15:36
m. desirable above all other fruits;		15:36
keeping in the m. fertile parts		16:14
land, which is a m. precious land,	2Ne	3: 2
I will be like the M. High.		24:14
I considered to be m. precious;	Jac	1: 2
seed, doth abound m. plentifully.		2:12
smiled upon you m. pleasingly,		2:13
whose fruit is m. bitter,		5:52
those which are m. bitter;		5:57
the m. precious above all other		5:61
which was m. precious unto him		5:74
iniquity the m. part of your lives.	Mos	13:11
of the m. expert among them,	Al	10:31
were the m. lost of all mankind)		24:11
for he is the M. High God,		26:14
in the m. aggravating and		27:29
fruit thereof, which is m. precious,		32:42
the m. bitter pain and anguish		38: 8
m. abominable above all sins		39: 5
by all that is m. dear unto us—		44: 5
m. acquainted with the strength		48: 5
and his fathers to be m. sacred;		50:38
the m. dangerous circumstances.		53: 9
yea, the m. numerous.		56:34
lead away the m. powerful army		56:36
and sixty fought m. desperately;		57:19
m. exposed to the Lamanites,		62:42
the m. capital parts of the land,	He	1:27

MOST

save it were the m. believing part	He	16:15
m. noble and chief governor of	3Ne	3: 2
unto me, m. noble Lachoneus,		3: 3
Hosanna to the M. High God.		4:32
God Almighty, the M. High God.		4:32
the name of the M. High God!		11:17
for that which they m. desired;		19: 9
through his m. beloved, his great	Mrm	5:14
combination is m. abominable	Eth	8:18
which was m. dear and precious	Mro	9: 9
in a m. cruel manner,		9:10
broken the m. sacred promises	DC	3:13
which would be of the m. worth		15: 4
which will be of the m. worth		15: 6
which would be of the m. worth		16: 4
which will be of the m. worth		16: 6
unto the m. holy faith.		21: 2
the name of the m. high God.		36: 3
the name of the M. High God.		39:19
the saints of the M. High God;		45:66
heard and m. assuredly believe,		52:36
knows and m. assuredly believes.		58:59
devotions unto the M. High;		59:10
thy sacraments unto the M. High,		59:12
a sacrament unto the M. High.		62: 4
that is the m. wise among you;		67: 6
are priests of the M. High,		76:57
be servants of the M. High;		76:112
the saints of the M. High,		82:13
among the saints of the M. High;		85:11
uplifted hands unto the M. High.		88:120
your m. holy desires unto me,		95:16
is the m. expedient in me,		96: 5
Things m. precious, things that are		101:34
called on the m. difficult cases of		102:28
m. important business of the church,		107:78
the m. difficult cases of the church,		107:78
uplifted hands unto the M. High—		109: 9
hands, uplifted to the M. High;		109:19
and it shall be called m. holy,		115: 7
that it may be m. holy,		119: 6
the m. damning hand of murder,		123: 7
for the M. High to dwell therein.		124:27
your oracles in your m. holy places		124:39
this m. glorious of all subjects		128:17
and that too m. holy,		132: 7
like the of the Lord's anointed		135: 3
in the m. solemn manner, declare		OD
m. decided against the Baptists	JS	2: 9
the m. popular sects of the day,		2:23
of the m. bitter persecution		2:23
robe of m. exquisite whiteness.		2:31
the m. elevated of any in		2:51
the m. strenuous exertions were		2:60

MOSTLY

it is m. translated correctly;	DC	91: 1

MOTE

why beholdest thou the m. that	3Ne	14: 3
Let me pull the m. out of thine		14: 4
to cast the m. out of thy brother's		14: 5
And not one hair, neither m.,	DC	29:25

MOTH

and the m. shall eat them up.	2Ne	7: 9
For the m. shall eat them up		8: 8
where m. and rust doth corrupt,	3Ne	13:19
m. nor rust doth corrupt,		13:20
for that which m. doth corrupt		27:32

MOTHER

family, which consisted of my m.,	1Ne	2: 5
my m., Sariah, was exceeding glad,		5: 1
m. complained against my father.		5: 3
my father, Lehi, comfort my m.,		5: 6
and my m. was comforted.		5: 7
her m., and one of the sons of		7:19
I beheld your m., Sariah,		8:14
is the m. of the Son of God,		11:18
their m. Gentiles were gathered		13:17
which is the m. of harlots,		13:34

MOUNT

which is the m. of abominations,	1Ne	14: 9
which is the m. of abominations;		14:10
the great m. of abominations did		14:13
belonged to the m. of abominations,		14:16
is upon the m. of harlots;		14:16
poured out upon the m. of harlots,		14:17
honor thy father and thy m.,		17:55
the afflictions of their m.;		18:19
from the bowels of my m.		21: 1
sorrow did thy m. bear thee.	2Ne	3: 1
is your m. put away.		7: 1
and to crumble to its m. earth,		9: 7
to cry, My father, and my m.,		18: 4
the branches of their m. tree,	Jac	5:54
and grafted into their m. tree.		5:56
branches again into their m. tree,		5:60
the roots of their m. tree,		5:60
this mortal frame to its m. earth.	Mos	2:26
and his m. shall be called Mary.		3: 8
Honor thy father and thy m.,		13:20
and to return to their m. earth.	Mrm	6:15
church, the m. of abominations,	DC	88:94
the society of thy father and m.		122: 6
man leave his father and his m.,	Mses	3:24
she was the m. of all living;		4:26
Wo, wo is me, the m. of men;		7:48
her who was the m. of Japheth,		8:12
man leave his father and his m.,	Abr	5:18
my m., Lucy Smith (whose	JS	2: 4
church, namely, my m., Lucy;		2: 7
m. inquired what the matter was.		2:20
I then said to my m.,		2:20

MOTHER'S

the bill of your m. divorcement?	2Ne	7: 1
Holy Ghost from his m. womb.	DC	84:27

MOTHERS

their queens thy nursing m.;	1Ne	21:23
and their queens thy nursing m.;	2Ne	6: 7
queens shall become nursing m.;		10: 9
had been taught by their m.,	Al	56:47
unto me the words of their m.,		56:48
do not doubt you m. knew it.		56:48
that their m. had taught them.		57:21
then would our m. and our fair	3Ne	8:25
ye fathers and m., ye husbands	Mrm	6:19
of fathers and m., brothers and	DC	132:55

MOTION

yea, and its m., yea, and also	Al	30:44
the foregoing m. was unanimous.	DC	OD

MOTIONS

when you feel these swelling m.,	Al	32:28

MOTIVE

be influenced by any other m.	JS	2:46

MOUNT

did go into the m. oft,	1Ne	18: 3
every dwelling-place of M. Zion,	2Ne	14: 5
Hosts, which dwelleth in M. Zion.		18:18
and they shall m. up like the		19:18
his whole work upon M. Zion		20:12
the m. of the daughter of Zion,		20:32
upon the m. of the congregation,		24:13
laid siege against them with a m.,		26:15
be that fight against M. Zions.		27: 3
unto Moses in the m. of Sinai,	Mos	12:33
while in the m. of Sinai,		13: 5
the m. which was called Antipas.	Al	47: 7
which was near the m. Antipas.		47: 9
embassy into the m. Antipas.		47:10
those who were upon the m.,		47:10
come down to the foot of the m.,		47:10
not go down to the foot of the m..		47:11
to come down off from the m.,		47:12
he went up into the m.,		47:12
went forth unto the m.,	Eth	3: 1
which they called the m. Shelem,		3: 1
hands upon the top of the m.,		3: 1

MOUNT   640   MOURNING

to go down out of the m. from	Eth	4: 1
had carried up into the m.,		6: 2
came down out of the m.,		6: 2
brother of Jared upon the m.,	DC	17: 1
loud, even as upon M. Sinai,		29:13
set his foot upon this m.,		45:48
unto mine apostles upon the m.;		63:21
who are come unto M. Zion,		76:66
saints to stand upon M. Zion,		84: 2
M. Zion in the Lord's house,		84:32
m. up in the imagination of his		124:99
shall stand upon M. Zion,.		133:18
stand upon the m. of Olivet,		133:20
he shall stand upon M. Zion,		133:56
spoken unto Moses in the m.,	Mses	1:42
and get ye upon the m. Simeon.		7: 2
I turned and went up on the m.;		7: 3
as I stood upon the m., I beheld		7: 3
and went upon the M. of Olives.	JS	1: 4
he sat upon the M. of Olives,		1: 4

MOUNTAIN

into an exceeding high m.,	1Ne	11: 1
up into the top of the m.,		16:30
and get thee into the m..		17: 7
and went up into the m.,		17: 7
when the m. of the Lord's house	2Ne	12: 2
let us go up to the m. of the Lord,		12: 3
nor destroy in all my holy m.,		21: 9
up a banner upon the high m.,		23: 2
nor destroy in all my holy m.;		30:15
if ye shall say unto this m.,	He	10: 9
Behold, if he say unto this m.—		12:17
the city there became a great m..	3Ne	8:10
the m. waves shall dash upon	Eth	2:24
the m. waves which broke upon		6: 6
said unto the m. Zerin, Remove—		12:30
out of the m. without hands	DC	65: 2
become a great m. and fill the		109:72
into an exceedingly high m.,	Mses	1: 1
unto a m. on the east of Bethel,	Abr	2:20

MOUNTAINS

I saw m. tumbling into pieces;	1Ne	12: 4
how beautiful upon the m.		13:37
by m. which shall be carried up.		19:11
I will make all my m. a way,		21:11
break forth into singing, O m.;		21:13
away upon exceeding high m..	2Ne	4:25
established in the top of the m.,		12: 2
And upon all the high m.,		12:14
noise of the multitude in the m.		23: 4
upon my m. tread him under foot;		24:25
and m. shall cover them,		26: 5
the very trees obey us, or the m.,	Jac	4: 6
How beautiful upon the m. are	Mos	12:21
O how beautiful upon the m. were		15:15
how beautiful upon the m. are		15:16
how beautiful upon the m. are		15:17
O how beautiful upon the m. are		15:18
and the m. to fall upon us	Al	12:14
would retreat back into the m.,	He	11:25
the wilderness and upon the m.		11:28
and out of the m. unto their own		11:31
robbers who infested the m.		11:31
and the m. tremble and quake.		12: 9
there shall be many m. laid low,		14:23
valleys which shall become m.,		14:23
robbers, who dwelt upon the m.,	3Ne	1:27
out of their lands into the m.		2:17
and let us go up upon the m.		3:20
from the hills, and out of the m.,		4: 1
How beautiful upon the m. are		20:40
For the m. shall depart and		22:10
his name could they remove m.;	Mrm	8:24
yea, publish it upon the m.,	DC	19:29
and for the m. to be made low,		49:23
and rejoice upon the m.,		49:25
upon the m. for a long time,		109:61
cause the m. to flow down		109:74
thy path lieth among the m.,		112: 7
and the beasts of the m.?		117: 6

the m. of Adam-Ondi-Ahman,	DC	117: 8
lift up his voice again on the m.,		124:104
How beautiful upon the m. are		128:19
Let the m. shout for joy,		128:23
the m. of the Lord's house.		133:13
which shall break down the m.,		133:22
that the m. might flow down		133:40
m. flow down at thy presence,		133:44
and the m. shall flee before you,	Mses	6:34
earth trembled, and the m. fled,		7:13
were blessed upon the m.,		7:17
tears as the rain upon the m.?		7:28
I say to the m.—Depart hence —	Abr	2: 7
are in Judea flee into the m.;	JS	1:13

MOURN

the daughters of Ishmael did m.	1Ne	16:35
And her gates shall lament and m.;	2Ne	13:26
and I am left to m. because of the		32: 7
wherefore, we did m. out our days.	Jac	7:26
how great reason we have to m..	Mos	7:23
the reasons which we have to m.;		7:24
Yea, and are willing to m. with		18: 9
to mourn with those that m.;		18: 9
did m. for the death of Abinadi;		21:30
they did m. for their departure,		21:31
cause the people of Mosiah to m.		28:18
that every soul had cause to m.;	Al	4: 3
same have cause to wail and m..		5:36
thousands of others truly m. for		28:12
for which cause we have to m..		56:10
he did also m. exceedingly		62: 9
together to m. and to fast,	He	9:10
ought to begin to howl and m.,		9:22
shall have great cause to m.		15: 2
they were heard to cry and m.,	3Ne	8:25
blessed are all they that m.,		12: 4
ye are fallen, and I m. your loss.	Mrm	6:18
and cause that widows should m.		8:40
and also orphans to m. before		8:40
Fools mock, but they shall m.;	Eth	12:26
he shall m. for her no longer;	DC	21: 8
nations of the earth shall m.,		45:49
inhabitants of the earth shall m.;		87: 6
while all the wicked shall m..		97:21
the wicked rule the people m..		98: 9
that all they that m. may be	Mses	7:45
when Enoch heard the earth m.,		7:49
all the tribes of the earth m.;	JS	1:36

MOURNED

truly had m. because of us.	1Ne	5: 1
and his daughters m. over him,	Al	18:43
the prophets m. and withdrew	Eth	11:13
his soul m. and refused to be		15: 3
And all they who have m.	DC	101:14
his wife m. before the Lord,	Mses	5:27
and all the creations of God m.;		7:56

MOURNFULLY

walked m. before the Lord of	3Ne	24:14

MOURNING

sorrow and m. shall flee away.	2Ne	8:11
m. of the daughters of my people	Jac	2:31
And now there was a great m.	Mos	21: 9
the widow m. for her husband.		21: 9
the daughter m. for their father,		21: 9
had been the cause of so much m.	Al	19:14
great m. and lamentation heard		28: 4
widows m. for their husbands,		28: 5
of fathers m. for their sons,		28: 5
thus the cry of m. was heard		28: 5
m. for their kindred who had		28: 5
m. for the loss of their kindred,		28:11
the days of fasting, and m.,		30: 2
know the cause of so great m.	He	7:11
And because of my m. and		7:15
and there was great m. and	3Ne	8:23
and the m., and the weeping,		10:10
their m. was turned into joy,		10:10
Thus there began to be a m.	Mrm	2:11

MOURNING 641 MOVED

their lamentation and their m.	Mrm	2:12
and your m. might come up	DC	95: 7
weeping, of m., and of lamentation;		112:24
there was great m. in Chaldea,	Abr	1:20

MOURNINGS
their howlings, and their m.,	Eth	15:17

MOUTH
in the borders near the m. thereof.	1Ne	2: 8
by the m. of all the holy prophets,		3:20
been spoken by the m. of Jeremiah		5:13
out of the m. of a Jew.		13:23
forth from the m. of a Jew;		13:24
forth from the m. of a law		13:24
forth from the m. of a Jew,		13:38
established by the m. of the Lamb;		13:41
out of the m. of the Jew;		14:23
out of the m. of the Jew,		14:23
out of the m. of the Jew,		14:23
they went forth out of my m.,		20: 3
made my m. like a sharp sword;		21: 2
which opened his m. to utterance	2Ne	1:27
shall proceed forth out of my m.		3:21
him with the strength of my m.		7: 8
I have put my words in thy m.,		8:16
by the m. of his holy prophets,		9: 2
they have gone forth out of his m.,		9:17
opened her m. without measure;		15:14
And he laid it upon my m.,		16: 7
shall devour Israel with open m.		19:12
and every m. speaketh folly.		19:17
or opened the m., or peeped.		20:14
the earth with the rod of his m.,		21: 4
been spoken by the m. of Isaiah.		25: 1
in the m. of as many witnesses		27:14
draw near unto me with their m.,		27:25
should proceed forth out of my m.		29: 2
the earth with the rod of his m.;		30: 9
out of the m. of the Lamb of God,		33:14
out of mine own m. that thou	Mos	1:10
opened his m. and began to speak		4: 4
was spoken by the m. of the angel.		4:11
yet he opened not his m.;		14: 7
is dumb so he opened not his m.		14: 7
neither was any deceit in his m.		14: 9
is dumb, so he opened not his m.		15: 6
has opened his m. to prophesy,		15:13
by the m. of the holy prophets.		18:19
learning from the m. of Ammon		21:28
to him by the m. of Alma.		25:21
that he could not open his m.;		27:19
hewould open the m. of Alma,		27:22
delivered by the m. of Abinadi?	Al	5:11
my language; yea, by my own m.,		7: 1
unto you by the words of my m.,		7: 1
he opened his m. and began to		12: 1
by the m. of angels, doth		13:22
unto us by the m. of angels,		13:25
holy men, by the m. of angels,		13:26
king Lamoni did open his m.		18:18
heard from the m. of Ammon;		19:31
shalt never open thy m. any more,		30:47
by the m. of his holy angel,		36: 5
that I could not open my m.,		36:10
he opened his m. and said unto	He	7:13
by the m. of my holy prophets.	3Ne	1:13
did open his m. unto them again,		14: 1
but my m. was shut, and I was	Mrm	1:16
been spoken by the m. of Jared.	Eth	1:39
have gone forth out of my m.,		2:24
in the m. of three witnesses shall		5: 4
by the m. of all the prophets,		15: 3
unto prophets, by his own m.,	Mro	7:23
forth out of the m. of God,		7:25
the m. of the everlasting God;		10:28
in the m. of two or three	DC	6:28
smite you by the rod of my m.,		19:15
as if from mine own m.,		21: 5
he shall open his m. and		24:12
the m. of all the holy prophets		27: 6

must open thy m. at all times,	DC	28:16
the m. of Ezekiel the prophet,		29:21
I declared from mine own m.		29:29
have gone forth out of my m.		29:30
shall open your m. to declare		30: 5
open your m. in my cause,		30:11
by the m. of two witnesses;		42:81
by the m. of my servants,		43:25
by the m. of my servants,		43:30
from the m. of my servant,		50:36
from the m. of the city of		58:13
by the m. of my servant Joseph		60:17
by the m. of my servant John,		61:14
by the m. of his prophets,		84: 2
forth from the m. of God.		84:44
whose m. shall utter words,		85: 7
the m. of the Lord shall name,		88:84
the m. of the Lord shall call		88:85
the m. of the Lord shall name.		90:20
the m. of the Lord shall name.		90:21
forth out of the m. of God.		98:11
by the m. of thy prophets		109:45
by the m. of Malachi—		110:14
jaws of hell shall gape open the m.		122: 7
the m. of two or three witnesses		128: 3
he spake by the m. of the serpent.)	Mses	4: 7
out of my m. they must be fulfilled.		4:30
went forth out of the m. of God		5:15
earth which hath opened her m.		5:36
of the world, from my own m.,		6:30
Open thy m., and it shall be filled,		6:32

MOUTHS
and their m. had been shut,	WM	1:15
spoken by the m. of their fathers,	Mos	1: 2
that your m. should be stopped		4:20
they cry unto thee with their m.,	Al	31:27
spoken by the m. of the prophets.		40:22
by the m. of the prophets—		40:24
they durst not open their m.,	3Ne	11: 8
the kings shall shut their m.		20:45
that kings shall shut their m.;		21: 8
even babes did open their m.		26:16
by the m. of my disciples,	DC	1: 4
Open your m. and they shall		33: 8
open your m. and spare not,		33: 9
open your m. and they shall		33:10
by the m. of my prophets		42:39
the m. of the prophets shall not		58: 8
for they will not open their m.,		60: 2
shall not open their m. in the		61:30
that you should open your m.		71: 1
the m. of all the holy prophets		86:10
by the m. of the prophets,		109:23
by the m. of thy prophets.		109:41
and by the m. of my servants,	Mses	6:30

MOVE
insomuch that I could not m.,	1Ne	18:12
that ye may live and m. and do	Mos	2:21
that he could not m. his hands;		27:19
which m. in their regular form	Al	30:44
if he say unto the earth—M.—	He	12:13
to m. the cause of Zion in	DC	21: 7
live, and m., and have a being.		45: 1
of power, to m., to act, etc.		77: 4
all things, by which they m. in		88:42
but he will not m.,		129: 7
"I m. that, recognizing		OD

MOVED
And the posts of the door m. at	2Ne	16: 4
And his heart was m.,		17: 2
as the trees of the wood are m.		17: 2
have m. the borders of the people,		20:13
there was none that m. the wing,		20:14
Hell from beneath is m. for thee		24: 9
they were m. with compassion	Al	27: 4
and m. forth toward the land		48: 6
they were m. with compassion		53:13
unto the earth—Move—it is m.	He	12:13

MOVED 642 MUCH

had faith it would not have m.;	Eth	12:30	hath visited men in so m. mercy,	2Ne 4:26
holy places, and shall not be m.;	DC	45:32	Nephi, did cry m. unto the Lord	5: 1
are m. upon by the Holy Ghost.		68: 3	have had m. trial because of him;	5: 3
when m. upon by the Holy Ghost		68: 4	know that ye have searched m.,	9: 4
break, neither can it be m.		84:40	then, how m. more need have we,	31: 5
in holy places, and be not m.,		87: 8	as m. as it were possible,	Jac 1: 4
neither be m. out of her place,		97:19	and the spirit of m. prophecy;	1: 6
not be m. out of her place,		101:17	they also began to search m. gold	1:16
thy bowels be m. with compassion		121: 3	weighed down with m. more desire	2: 3
thy bowels m. with compassion		121: 4	must use so m. boldness of speech	2: 7
when m. upon by the Holy Ghost;		121:43	how m. better are you than they,	3: 7
not be m. out of their place,		124:45	ministered m. unto my people	4: 1
shall be m. out of their place,		124:71	hath brought forth m. strength;	5:18
shall be m. upon by my Spirit,		124:88	because of the m. strength	5:18
Spirit m. upon the face of the	Mses	2: 2	behold, I shall lay up m. fruit,	5:18
was m. upon by the Holy Ghost,		6: 8	not brought forth m. fruit	5:19
and m. to Palmyra, Ontario	JS	2: 3	that it had brought forth m. fruit.	5:20
he m. with his family into		2: 3	and it hath brought forth m. fruit.	5:20
			that it hath brought forth m. fruit.	5:22
MOVEMENT			and it hath brought forth m. fruit;	5:23
discovered a m. among the people,	Mos	18:32	against the season m. fruit.	5:31
			it hath brought forth m. fruit,	5:32
MOVEMENTS			and because of their m. strength	5:36
watch to m. of the Lamanites,	Al	56:22	it hath brought forth m. evil fruit;	5:37
			hath brought forth so m. evil fruit	5:37
MOVETH			he sought m. opportunity that	7: 3
the dust of the earth m. hither	He	12: 8	he could use m. flattery,	7: 4
for surely it is the earth that m.		12:15	flattery, and m. power of speech,	7: 4
every living creature that m.,	Mses	2:21	I have sought m. opportunity	7: 6
thing that m. upon the earth.		2:28	know that thou goest about m.,	7: 6
for it m. in order more slow;	Abr	3: 5	ye have led away m. of this people	7: 7
every living creature that m.,		4:21	in the which ye know so m.	7:13
every living thing that m. upon		4:28	that m. should be done among	Jar 1: 3
			upon m. of the face of the land,	1: 6
MOVING			for the space of m. of the time.	1:13
be m. swiftly upon the waters,	DC	61: 3	that I fought m. with the sword	Om 1: 2
seen God m. in his majesty		88:47	I saw m. war and contention	1:10
the m. creature that hath life,	Mses	2:20	a serious war and m. bloodshed	1:24
the m. creatures that have life;	Abr	4:20	obtain m. advantage over them;	1:24
			there having been m. contention	WM 1:16
MR.			and they did use m. sharpness	1:17
to board with a M. Isaac Hale,	JS	2:57	as m. as the dust of the earth;	Mos 2:25
in the service of M. Stoal.		2:57	how m. more just will be your	4:22
my marriage, I left M. Stoal's,		2:58	But this m. I can tell you,	4:30
M. Harris was a resident of		2:61	so m. that they did shed blood	7:25
aforementioned M. Martin Harris		2:63	by the shedding of m. blood;	9: 2
M. Anthon called me back,		2:64	But this m. I tell you,	13:10
after the arrival of M. Cowdery		2:67	was not so m. concerned about	19: 8
			to the shedding of so m. blood.	20:22
MUCH			back again, suffering m. loss.	21:11
and he saw and heard m.;	1Ne	1: 6	as m. as it was possible,	21:18
having received m. strength		4:31	after m. tribulation, the Lord	23:10
m. spake my father concerning this		10: 8	and they were m. frightened	23:26
my father spake m. concerning		10:12	were in sickness, in m. want;	27: 5
m. of my gospel, which shall be		13:34	And there began to be m. peace	27: 6
I, Nephi, spake m. unto them		15:19	and did speak m. flattery	27: 8
and so m. was his mind swallowed		15:27	causing m. dissension among	27: 9
and being m. fatigued, because of		16:19	for he has prayed with m. faith	27:14
suffer m. for the want of food.		16:19	wandering through m. tribulation,	27:28
did speak m. unto my brethren,		16:22	word of God in m. tribulation,	27:32
wandered m. in the wilderness,		16:35	they did impart m. consolation	27:33
and we have suffered m. affliction,		16:35	with long-suffering and m. travail	27:33
and wade through m. affliction		17: 1	they suffered m. anguish of soul	28: 4
because of its m. fruit		17: 5	suffering m. and fearing that	28: 4
afflictions and m. difficulty,		17: 6	it gave them m. knowledge,	28:18
so m. that we cannot write them		17: 6	cause of shedding m. blood	29: 7
because of its m. fruit.		17: 6	also this people to commit m. sin.	29: 9
that we should make m. fire,		17:12	how m. iniquity doth one wicked	29:17
m. fruits and meat from the		18: 6	save it be through m. contention,	29:21
and to speak with m. rudeness,		18: 9	and the shedding of m. blood.	29:21
speak to them with m. soberness,		18:10	and was noted for his m. strength.	Al 1: 2
did treat me with m. harshness;		18:11	so m. that many did believe on	1: 5
also mine ankles were m. swollen,		18:15	for himself with m. boldness.	1:11
did breathe out m. threatenings		18:17	done m. good among this people;	1:13
and having suffered m. grief		18:17	of m. affliction to the church;	1:23
of their grief and m. sorrow,		18:18	cause of m. trial with the church.	1:23
having need of m. nourishment,		18:19	m. peace among the people of	1:33
and he hath suffered m. sorrow	2Ne	1:24	drawn away m. people after him;	2: 2
suffered afflictions and m. sorrow,		2: 1	even so m. that they began to be	2: 2
tongue, that he shall speak m.,		3:17	having m. dispute and	2: 5
among them, who shall do m. good,		3:24	did cause m. joy in the hearts	2: 8
bringing to pass m. restoration		3:24	did slay them with m. slaughter,	2:19

MUCH 643 MULEK

and struck with m. fear, saying:	Al	2:23	and so m. difficulty in the	He	1:18
being exercised with m. faith,		2:30	neither was there m. contention		3: 2
cause of m. affliction to Alma,		4: 7	yea, there was m. contention		3: 3
having had m. business that I		7: 1	did send forth m. by the way of		3:10
and the Lord in m. mercy hath		7: 2	to wade through m. affliction.		3:34
great hopes and m. desire that		7: 3	that there was m. bloodshed.		4: 1
by the cause of so m. afflictions		7: 5	yea, m. preaching and many		6:14
through m. affliction and sorrow.		7: 5	only this m. we know, we ran		9:15
not in a state of so m. unbelief		7: 6	who doth prophesy so m. evil		9:27
but this m. I do know, that		7: 8	being m. cast down because of		10: 3
Spirit hath said this m. unto me,		7: 9	there began to be m. strife.		11:23
that I had m. desire that ye		7:18	also visited with m. destruction.		11:30
Alma labored m. in the spirit,		8:10	and they were m. disturbed,		16:22
wading through m. tribulation		8:14	did do m. slaughter among	3Ne	1:27
after having had so m. light		9:19	did cause m. sorrow unto those		1:28
so much light and so m. knowledge		9:19	also a cause of m. sorrow among		1:29
I have also acquired m. riches		10: 4	m. preaching and prophesying		2:10
have known m. of the ways of		10: 5	spread so m. death and carnage		2:11
had known m. of these things;		10: 5	weary because of his m. fighting		4:14
I have seen m. of his mysteries		10: 5	because of their m. provision		4:18
having m. business to do		10:31	which there was so m. wickedness,		5: 6
not so m. as a hair of their		11:44	and my people so much knowledge		5:20
been m. peace in the land of		16: 1	save he had m. family and		7: 4
given themselves to m. prayer,		17: 3	be heard for their m. speaking.		13: 7
had m. success in bringing many		17: 4	Are ye not m. better than they?		13:26
they did suffer m., both in body		17: 5	how m. more shall your Father		14:11
and also m. labor in the spirit.		17: 5	This m. did the Father command		15:16
and they fasted m. and prayed		17: 9	But this m. I know, according		28:18
and prayed m. that the Lord		17: 9	people as m. as it were possible,	Mrm	2:21
was m. pleased with Ammon,		17:24	hath my father so m. sorrow?	Eth	8: 9
rushed forth with m. swiftness		17:32	Com did fight against them m.;		10:34
but this m. we do know, that he		18: 3	cause the shedding of m. blood;		11:10
been the cause of so m. mourning		19:14	that they could speak m.,		12:23
it has been as m. as we could do		24:15	sons of Coriantumr fought m.		13:19
after having suffered m. loss and		25: 6	fought much and bled m.		13:19
can glory too m. in the Lord?		26:16	delight is in so m. abomination—	Mro	9:13
can say too m. of his great power,		26:16	be pierced with m. sorrow;	DC	1: 3
a time of m. fasting and prayer.		28: 6	the means of doing m. good in		6: 8
and hath given me m. success,		29:13	which contain m. of my gospel,		6:26
and have brought forth m. fruit;		29:15	may not be so m. contention;		10:63
here he did not have m. success,		30:21	the means of doing m. good		11: 8
so m. as even one senine for		30:33	to writing, and to learning m.		25: 8
even until I had m. success,		30:53	by m. prayer and faith,		26: 2
after m. labor among them,		32: 2	they pray unto me in m. faith.		37: 2
m. more blessed than they who		32:15	call upon me in m. faith,		39:16
how m. more cursed is he that		32:19	as m. as is sufficient for		42:32
with m. care it will get root,		32:37	kept and blessed with m. fruit.		52:34
so m. faith as even to plant the		34: 4	shall follow after m. tribulation.		58: 3
as m. as ye shall put your trust in		38: 5	after m. tribulation come the		58: 4
even so m. ye shall be delivered		38: 5	shall be crowned with m. glory;		58: 4
wisdom, nor of your m. strength.		38:11	bring to pass m. righteousness;		58:27
give so m. heed unto my words as		39: 2	not with m. laughter,		59:15
but this m. I say, that there		40:21	whether it be little or m.,		63:40
so m. greater than the Nephites.		43:21	of him unto whom m. is given		82: 3
did fast m. and pray much,		45: 1	much is given m. is required;		82: 3
did fast much and pray m.,		45: 1	that yieldeth m. precious fruit		97: 9
did they have m. peace and		46:38	I have m. people in this place,		100: 3
but not so m. so with fevers,		46:40	For after m. tribulation,		103:12
their m. reluctance.		48:22	as m. in one region as can be,		105:24
being a man of m. passion,		50:30	m. treasure in this city for you,		111: 2
fell upon her and beat her m.		50:30	temptations, and m. tribulation,		112:13
which caused m. rejoicing among		51: 7	on whom there is laid m. power.		113: 4
had labored with so m. diligence		51:14	hearts are set so m. upon the		121:35
because of their m. fatigue,		51:33	is m. which lieth in futurity,		123:15
save they had lost m. blood.		52: 4	large ship is benefited very m.		123:16
as m. as was in his power,		52:10	which will cause m. bloodshed		130:12
as m. as it was in their power,		52:13	he will have so m. the advantage		130:19
they fled in m. confusion, lest		52:28	Lord God, created m. gold;	Mses	3:11
being m. confused, knew not		52:36	shall curse the land with m. heat,		7: 8
them great hopes and m. joy.		56:17	since, that I felt m. like Paul,	JS	2:24
so m. more numerous than was		58: 2	m. opposed to our being married.		2:58
traveled m. in the wilderness		58:23			
who caused so m. bloodshed		60:16	**MUFFLERS**		
the cause of so m. bloodshed		60:16	and the bracelets, and the m.;	2Ne	13:19
why should I say m. concerning		60:18			
we have suffered so m. loss.		60:28	**MULEK**		
of so m. war and bloodshed,		62:35	who was a descendant of M.,	Mos	25: 2
yea, and so m. famine.		62:35	city of Gid, and the city of M.,	Al	51:26
word of God with m. power		62:45	all their army into the city of M.,		52: 2
sail forth with m. provisions,		63: 6	an attack upon the city of M.,		52:16
they also took m. provisions,		63: 7	an attack upon the city of M.,		52:17
because of so m. contention	He	1:18	and take again the city of M.		52:19

MULEK 644 MULTITUDE

MULEK (cont.)
which protected the city of M.,	Al	52:20
on the west of the city M.;		52:22
possession of the city M. with		52:26
should not obtain the city M.		52:28
way through to the city of M.		52:34
Moroni went to the city of M.		53: 2
possession of the city of M.,		53: 6
the city of Gid to the city of M.;	He	5:15
and the land north was called M.,		6:10
the Lord did bring M. into the		6:10
not slain, all except it were M.?		8:21

MULES
to ride upon horses, or upon m.,	DC	62: 7

MULOKI
thy brother Aaron, and also M.	Al	20: 2
the preaching of Aaron, and M.,		21:hd
there he found M. preaching the		21:11

MULTIPLICITY
with a m. of blessings,	DC	97: 5
multiply a m. of blessings		97:28
with a m. of blessings;		104: 2
even a m. of blessings.		104:33
a m. of blessings upon him.		104:38
even a m. of blessings.		104:42
even a m. of blessings.		104:46
with a m. of blessings;		124:13
with a m. of blessings,		124:90

MULTIPLIED
Thou hast m. the nation,	2Ne	19: 3
And we m. exceedingly,	Jar	1: 8
for they had m. exceedingly	Mos	2: 2
know that the people had m.,	4Ne	1:23
abundance is m. unto them	DC	70:13
and they m. before mine eyes,	Abr	3:12

MULTIPLY
and to m. in the land.	2Ne	5:13
and we did begin to m. and prosper	Mos	9: 9
that they did m. and prosper		23:20
they did multiply and were strong	Al	50:18
to m. and to wax exceeding strong		62:48
that they did m. and spread,	He	3: 8
did m. and wax exceedingly		6:12
and began to m. and spread,		11:20
they did not m. many words,	3Ne	19:24
and did m. exceedingly fast,	4Ne	1:10
this church did m. exceedingly		1:28
and to m. and to till the earth;	Eth	6:18
they shall m. and wax strong,	DC	45:58
and m. a multiplicity of		97:28
I will m. blessings upon him,		104:23
I will m. blessings upon him		104:25
and m. blessings upon them.		104:31
I will m. blessings upon them		104:33
I will m. blessings upon him.		104:35
I will m. a multiplicity of		104:38
I will m. blessings upon him		104:42
I will m. blessings upon the		104:46
bless him and m. him and give		132:55
God, will bless her, and m. her,		132:56
to m. and replenish the earth,		132:63
and m., and fill the waters	Mses	2:22
and let fowl m. in the earth;		2:22
m., and replenish the earth,		2:28
I will greatly m. thy sorrow		4:22
began to m. and to replenish		5: 2
to m. on the face of the earth,		8:14
I will m. thee, and thy seed	Abr	3:14
cause them to be fruitful and m.,		4:22
cause the fowl to m. in the		4:22
cause them to be fruitful and m.,		4:28

MULTITUDE
the m. of his tender mercies.	1Ne	8: 8
great was the m. that did		8:33
the m. of the earth was gathered		11:35
and their m. dried up with thirst.	2Ne	15:13
and their glory, and their m.,		15:14
noise of the m. in the mountains	2Ne	23: 4
the m. of their terrible ones		26:18
shall the m. of all the nations be		27: 3
the m. were gathered together;	Jac	7:17
when the m. had witnessed		7:21
For the m. being so great	Mos	2: 7
because of the greatness of the m.;		2: 8
cast his eyes round about on the m.,		4: 1
he dismissed the m.,		6: 3
should stand up before the m.,		8: 2
that king Limhi dismissed the m.,		8: 4
that a m. should be gathered		27:21
for the m. was great,	Al	12: 2
And there came a m.,		19:18
when the m. beheld that		19:24
caused the m. to be gathered		19:28
which was among the m.		19:28
a m. should assemble themselves		22:22
was a m. gathered together		22:24
stand forth in the midst of the m.,		22:26
there came a great m. unto him,		32: 4
did say no more to the other m.;		32: 7
withdrew themselves from the m.		35: 1
this man did cry unto the m.,	He	5:37
knew nothing concerning the m.		9: 8
bound and brought before the m.,		9:19
from m. to multitude, declaring		10:17
from multitude to m., declaring		10:17
the m. were gathered together	3Ne	11:hd
great m. gathered together,		11: 1
the eyes of the whole m. were		11: 8
the whole m. fell to the earth;		11:12
that the m. went forth,		11:15
(for Nephi was among the m.)		11:18
forth his hand unto the m.,		12: 1
he turned again to the m.,		14: 1
his eyes round about on the m.,		15: 1
round about again on the m.,		17: 1
round about again on the m.		17: 5
all the m., with one accord, did		17: 9
as many as could come for the m.		17:10
the m. gave way till they		17:12
he commanded the m. that they		17:13
and the m. did bear record		17:15
so great was the joy of the m.		17:18
and the m. bare record of it,		17:21
And he spake unto the m.,		17:23
And the m. did see and hear		17:25
commanded the m. that they		18: 2
that they should give unto the m.		18: 4
And when the m. had eaten		18: 5
should also give unto the m.		18: 8
and they gave unto the m.,		18: 9
he turned again unto the m.		18:17
the m. heard not the words		18:37
and overshadowed the m.		18:38
into heaven, the m. did disperse,		19: 1
that the m. had seen Jesus,		19: 2
on the morrow unto the m.		19: 2
should show himself unto the m.		19: 3
the m. was gathered together,		19: 4
stood in the midst of the m.		19: 4
the m. was so great that they		19: 5
the twelve did teach the m.;		19: 6
the m. should kneel down upon		19: 6
and the m. followed them.		19:10
and the m. did witness it,		19:14
that he spake unto the m.,		19:16
And the m. did hear and do		19:33
he commanded the m. that they		20: 1
bread, and gave unto the m.		20: 4
when they had given unto the m.		20: 5
that they should give unto the m.		20: 5
the disciples, neither by the m.,		20: 6
the m. had all eaten and drunk,		20: 9
he expounded them unto the m.;		26: 1
unto the children of the m. of		26:14
the m. gathered themselves		26:16
the m. of the promises which	4Ne	1:11
disciples, in the hearing of the m.:	Mrm	9:22
of the m. of his tender mercies	Eth	6:12
and the m. heard it not, but	Mro	2: 3
a m. of nations shall come	DC	107:55

MULTITUDES

saw other m. pressing forward;	1 Ne	8:30
saw other m. feeling their way		8:31
and the m. were gathered		11:28
And I beheld m. of people		11:31
I saw the m. of the earth,		11:34
and I beheld m. of people,		12: 1
I beheld m. gathered together		12: 2
I saw m. who had fallen		12: 5
I saw m. of the earth		12:13
my seed gathered together in m.		12:15
and they went forth in m.		12:20
them gathered together in m.;		12:21
many m. of the Gentiles		13:14
did gather together m. upon		14:13
came running together by m.	Al	14:29
the people came together in m.	He	7:11
he beheld the m. of people who		7:12
but did return unto the m.		10:12
great m. united themselves to	JS	2: 5
m. were on the alert continually		2:60

MUNICIPALS

and endowment of all her m.,	DC	124:39

MURDER

secret combinations of m.	2 Ne	9: 9
yea, the foundation of m.,		26:22
commanded that men should not m.;		26:32
and they loved m.	Jar	1: 6
nor that ye should m., or plunder,	Mos	2:13
and that they should m. them,		10:17
neither durst they rob, nor m.,	Al	1:18
and that they ought not to m.,		23: 3
afraid he would die if he should m.?		42:19
ye have sought to m. us,		54:13
not delight in m. or bloodshed,		55:19
secret work of m. and of robbery;	He	2: 4
that he might m. Helaman.		2: 7
how that it was his object to m.,		2: 8
who belonged to his band to m.,		2: 8
did m. the chief judge Cezoram,		6:19
thus they might m., and plunder,		6:23
if he would m. his brother Abel		6:27
of darkness, and of secret m.;		6:29
works of darkness and secret m.,		6:30
for the which ye do m., and		7:21
raising the cry of m. among		9: 6
Now, as for the m. of this man,		9:15
is this man that hath done this m.?		9:20
that he should m. Seezoram,		9:23
more that he had done this m.		9:35
did commit m. and plunder;		11:25
were to plunder and rob and m.	3 Ne	4: 5
that they would m. no more		5: 4
those who were guilty of m.		6:29
m. the chief judge of the land.		7: 1
is one continual round of m.	Mrm	8: 8
to gain power, and to m.,	Eth	8:16
commit m. from the beginning;		8:25
m. them in a most cruel manner,	Mro	9:10
my people, and drive, and m.,	DC	121:23
the most damning hand of m.,		123: 7
commit no m. whereby to shed		132:19
commit no m. whereby to shed		132:19
commit no m. wherein they shed		132:26
ye commit m. wherein ye shed		132:27
that m., treason, robbery, theft,		134: 8
that I may m. and get gain.	Mses	5:31
have they devised m., and		6:28

MURDERED

for he that m. was punished unto	Al	1:18
But if he m. he was punished		30:10
the life of him who hath m.;		34:12
I had m. many of his children,		36:14
they m. all the prophets of the		37:30
the blood of those whom they m.		37:30
if a man m. he should die—		42:19
of Amalickiah whom ye have m.		54:16
my brother whom ye have m.,		54:22
king who was m. by Amalickiah.	Al	55: 5
and m. Pahoran as he sat upon	He	1: 9
that Kishkumen had m. Pahoran.		1:11
at the time that he m. Pahoran.		1:12
Kishkumen, who had m. Pahoran,		2: 3
been m., plundered, and hunted,		3:16
Cezoram was m. by an unknown		6:15
in his stead, was also m.		6:15
and behold, your judge is m.,		8:27
he hath been m. by his brother,		8:27
when the judge had been m. —		9: 6
are they who have m. the judge,		9: 8
the which ye have m. Seezoram,		9:27
Have ye m. your brother?		9:29
of those who m. the prophets.	3 Ne	7: 6
that they have m. the prophets,	Eth	8:25
Jared was m. upon his throne,		9: 6
his high priest m. him as he		14: 9
m. him in a secret pass,		14:10
been m. under its iron hand;	DC	123: 9
HE WAS M. IN COLD BLOOD."		135: 4

MURDERER

Wo unto the m. who deliberately	2 Ne	9:35
make known unto us the true m.	He	9:17
that he himself was the very m.,		9:38
the true m. of our chief judge.		9:41
who was a m. from the beginning.	Eth	8:15

MURDERERS

ye are m. in your hearts	1 Ne	17:44
they not testify that ye are m.,	Al	5:23
upon those who were their m.;		37:30
awaits to receive such m. as thou		54: 7
band of robbers and secret m.,	He	2:10
those m. and plunderers were a		6:18
called Gadianton's robbers and m.		6:18
and that the m. had been taken		9: 9
there are five who are the m.,		9:12
no robbers, nor m.,	4 Ne	1:17
and the robbers, and the m.,	Mrm	2:10
or into the hands of m.,	DC	122: 7

MURDERETH

Now, if a man m., behold will	Al	34:11
whosoever m. against the light		39: 6

MURDERING

stealing, nor plundering, nor m.,	Mos	29:14
committing whoredoms, and m.,	Al	1:32
stealing, robbing, plundering, m.,		16:18
delighted in m. the Nephites,		17:14
sought to obtain these things by m.		17:14
m. thousands of your brethren —		60: 7
and they are m. our people		60:17
m., plundering, lying, stealing,	He	4:12

MURDERINGS

their m., and their plunderings,	Al	50:21
their m., and their plunderings,	He	10: 3

MURDEROUS

more wicked and m. disposition	Al	43: 6
withdraw your m. purposes,		54: 7
m. combinations shall get above	Eth	8:23
nefarious and m. impositions	DC	123: 5

MURDERS

and of m., and of abominations.	2 Ne	10:15
this people, because of their m.?	Al	18: 2
m. which we have committed.		24: 9
and m. which we have committed,		24:10
m. which we have committed,		24:11
the m. which they had committed;		24:25
because of the many m. and sins		27: 6
the many m. and sins which we		27: 8
on account of their many m. and		27:23
yea, all their m., and robbings,		37:21
secret m. and abominations;		37:22
only their wickedness and their m.		37:29
and abominations and m.;		37:29

MURDERS

abominations and their m.	Al 37:29
had been m., and contentions,	62:40
their wickedness, and their m.,	He 3:14
they began to commit secret m.,	6:17
should not suffer for their m.,	6:21
with them in their secret m.	6:38
ripening, because of your m. and	8:26
strifes, malice, persecutions and m.,	13:22
they did commit many m.,	3Ne 1:27
those secret m. in their hearts,	5: 5
and so many m. committed.	5: 6
secret m. and combinations;	9: 9
all manner of hypocrisy, and m.,	16:10
your idolatries, and of your m.,	30: 2
whoredoms, nor lyings, nor m.,	4Ne 1:16
there shall be m., and robbing,	Mrm 8:31
forsake their m. and wickedness.	Eth 11: 1

MURDOCK, John

And also my servant M.,	DC 52: 8
the Lord unto my servant M. —	99: 1

MURMUR

they did m. in many things	1Ne 2:11
did m. against their father.	2:12
did m. because they dnew not	2:12
behold thy brothers m., saying	3: 5
again began to m., saying:	3:31
and did still continue to m.;	4: 4
then ye would not m. because	16: 3
did begin to m. exceedingly,	16:20
and also my father began to m.	16:20
they did m. against the Lord.	16:20
they did m. against my father,	16:35
they did m. against my father,	16:36
they began to m. against me,	17:17
my brethren m. and complain	17:22
that they should m. no more	17:49
I did not m. against the Lord	18:16
Yea, they did m. against me,	2Ne 5: 3
Wherefore m. ye, because that	29: 8
began to m. with the king	Mos 21: 6
began to m., and complain	27: 1
servants of the king began to m.,	Al 17:28
began to m. among themselves;	19:19
if so, we do not desire to m.	58:35
we would not m. nor complain.	60: 4
is it that the people should m.	3Ne 27: 4
Do not m., my son, for it is	DC 9: 6
M. not because of the things	25: 4

MURMURED

because thou hast not m.	1Ne 3: 6
And ye have m. because he	2Ne 1:26
wouds which they m. against me.	5: 4
they that m. shall learn doctrine.	27:35

MURMURING

chastened because of his m.	1Ne 16:25

MURMURINGS

their journeyings without m.	1Ne 17: 2
also all the m. of the people	Mos 29:33
to be great m. among them	Al 22:24
chasten him for the m. of his	DC 75: 7

MUSIC

the Lord with singing, with m.,	DC 136:28

MUSING

I lay m. on the singularity	JS 2:44

MUST

the people that they m. repent,	1Ne 1: 4
city Jerusalem m. be destroyed.	1: 4
that Jerusalem m. be destroyed,	3:17
it m. needs be that he flee	3:18
of Jerusalem m. be fulfilled.	7:13
I m. speak somewhat of the things	10: 1
it m. needs be that we should	10:13
ye m. be cast off forever.	10:21
all men m. come unto him, or	13:40
they m. come according to the	1Ne 13:41
whoso repenteth not m. perish.	14: 5
knew they m. unavoidably come	15: 4
they m. be judged of their works,	15:32
they m. be cast off also, as to	15:33
they m. be brought to stand	15:33
they m. needs be filthy;	15:33
it m. needs be that they cannot	15:33
kingdom of God m. be filthy also.	15:33
there m. needs be a place of filthiness	15:34
we m. perish in the wilderness	16:35
of God m. be fulfilled.	17: 3
it m. needs be a good thing	17:25
the day m. surely come that	17:43
that they m. be destroyed,	17:43
and that they m. perish	18:15
all these things m. surely come,	19:12
the rocks of the earth m. rend;	19:12
it m. needs be that we know	19:21
cometh that they m. be burned.	22:15
the fulness of his wrath m. come,	22:17
these things m. shortly come;	22:18
and vapor of smoke m. come;	22:18
and it m. needs be upon	22:18
for the time surely m. come	22:19
are those who m. be brought low	22:23
they are those who m. be consumed	22:23
the righteous m. be led up as	22:24
the Holy One of Israel m. reign	22:24
all these things m. come according	22:27
a man m. be obedient to the	22:30
whose limbs ye m. soon lay down	2Ne 1:14
we m. have perished with hunger	1:24
And it m. needs be that	1:27
power of God m. be with him,	1:27
commanding you that ye m. obey.	1:27
For it m. needs be,	2:11
m. needs be a compound in one;	2:11
body it m. needs remain as dead,	2:11
it m. needs have been created for	2:12
thing m. needs destroy the wisdom	2:12
all things m. have vanished away.	2:13
it m. needs be that there was	2:15
m. needs suppose that an angel	2:17
that all men m. repent;	2:21
created m. have remained in	2:22
they m. have remained forever,	2:22
they m. search mine other plates.	5:33
that our flesh m. waste away	9: 4
m. needs be a power of resurrection,	9: 6
the resurrection m. needs come	9: 6
it m. needs be an infinite	9: 7
m. needs have remained to an	9: 7
this flesh m. have laid down	9: 7
our spirits m. become subject to	9: 8
our spirits m. have become like	9: 9
and hell m. deliver up their dead,	9:12
and hell m. deliver up its captive	9:12
grave m. deliver up its captive	9:12
of God m. deliver up the spirits	9:13
they m. appear before the	9:15
and then m. they be judged	9:15
and his law m. be fulfilled.	9:17
all men that they m. repent,	9:23
to the end, they m. be damned;	9:24
it m. needs be expedient that	9:48
it m. needs be expedient that	10: 3
I m. needs destroy the secret works	10:15
there m. needs be more than	10:21
should come all men m. perish.	11: 6
it m. needs be expedient that	25:16
ye m. bow down before him,	25:29
ye m. keep the performances	25:30
but I m. cry unto my God: thy	26: 7
therefore they m. go down to hell.	26:10
it m. needs be that the Gentiles	26:12
that they m. surely come to pass.	28: 1
whore of all the earth, m. tumble	28:18
and great m. be the fall thereof.	28:18
kingdom of the devil m. shake,	28:19
m. needs be stirred up unto	28:19

MUST

m. stand before the throne of God,	2Ne	28:23
from whence they m. go into the		28:23
that he m. destroy the wicked		30:10
I m. make an end of my sayings.		30:18
which I know m. surely come		31: 1
a few words which I m. speak		31: 2
Wherefore, ye m. press forward		31:20
but m. perish in the dark.		32: 4
it grieveth me that I m. speak		32: 8
ye would know that ye m. pray;		32: 8
him that he m. not pray.		32: 8
unto you that ye m. pray always,		32: 9
ye m. not perform any thing		32: 9
commanded me, and I m. obey.		33:15
and he saw that he m. soon die;	Jac	1: 9
I m. use so much boldness of		2: 7
I m. do according to the strict		2:10
I m. tell you the truth according to		2:11
his judgments m. speedily come		2:14
I m. speak unto you concerning		2:22
we write upon plates m. remain;		4: 1
save it be upon plates m. perish		4: 2
they m. needs fall; for God hath		4:14
I m. lay up fruit against the		5:29
which are ripened, that m. perish,		5:58
m. surely come to pass.		6: 1
that ye m. be hewn down		6: 7
ye m. go away into that lake of		6:10
all mankind m. be lost.		7:12
I m. soon go down to my grave;		7:27
I m. soon go down to my grave,	En	1:26
that I m. preach and prophesy		1:26
it m. needs be that I write a	Jar	1: 2
m. surely come to pass —	WM	1: 4
we m. have suffered in ignorance,	Mos	1: 3
he saw that he m. very soon go		1: 9
they m. have fallen into the hands		1:14
that ye m. repent of your sins		4:10
all things m. be done in order.		4:27
end of your lives, ye m. perish.		4:30
m. be called by some other name;		5:10
I m. fulfill the commandments		13: 4
they m. unavoidably perish,		13:28
all mankind m. have perished.		15:19
them towards us we m. perish.		20:20
m. be born again; yea, born of		27:25
be the case, they m. be cast off;		27:27
m. unavoidably remain in bondage		29:19
this people m. abide by the law.	Al	1:14
such things m. be established by		2: 3
his garments m. be purified until		5:21
Behold ye m. prepare quickly;		5:28
m. repent or he cannot be saved!		5:31
m. receive his wages of him;		5:42
m. repent and be born again.		5:49
the word of God m. be fulfilled.		5:58
say unto you that ye m. repent,		7:14
unto them that they m. go forth		9:25
we m. come forth and stand		12:15
unto men that they m. die;		12:27
they m. come to judgment,		12:27
I m. not stretch forth mine hand;		14:11
things which m. shortly come;		16:19
that they m. keep those outward		25:15
that they m. speedily repent,		30:57
m. go forth and stand upon the		31:14
that ye m. not worship God only		32:11
Now of this thing ye m. judge.		32:20
It m. needs be that this is a		32:28
then you m. needs say that the		32:30
ye m. needs know that the seed		32:33
ye m. know that it is good;		32:35
neither m. ye lay aside your		32:36
said m. be planted in their hearts;		33: 1
ye m. believe what Zenos said;		33:13
there m. be an atonement made,		34: 9
mankind m. unavoidably perish;		34: 9
m. perish except it be through		34: 9
it m. be an infinite and eternal		34:10
ye m. pour out your souls in your		34:26
they m. retain their brightness;		37: 5
you m. appeal unto the Lord		37:16
whatsoever ye m. do with them)	Al	37:16
I m. stop the work of destruction		38: 7
there m. needs be a space betwixt		40: 6
in him, as we m. needs suppose.		46:41
even if it m. be by the sword.		60:35
they m. unavoidably perish.	He	4:25
ye m. build your foundation;		5:12
You m. repent, and cry unto the		5:41
Nephi m. have agreed with some		9:16
he surely m. die that salvation		14:15
the Christ m. shortly come —		16: 4
of things which m. shortly come,		16: 5
Son of God m. shortly appear;	3Ne	1:17
it m. be fulfilled in every whit;		1:25
them that it m. be fulfilled;		1:25
it m. needs be that they must		5: 1
be that they m. be fulfilled.		5: 1
it m. be expedient that Christ		5: 2
it m. needs be that all things		5: 2
I say unto you, ye m. repent,		11:37
I say unto you, ye m. repent,		11:38
them also I m. bring, and they		15:17
them also I m. bring, and they		15:21
ye m. watch and pray always,		18:15
ye m. watch and pray always		18:18
Therefore ye m. always pray unto		18:19
then I m. go unto my Father		18:27
it m. needs be that he must		23: 2
he m. speak also to the Gentiles.		23: 2
m. take upon you the name of		27: 5
ye know the things that ye m. do		27:21
all people m. surely stand		28:31
that these things m. surely come.		28:33
that there m. needs be a change		28:37
be that they m. taste of death;		28:37
know that ye m. all stand before	Mrm	3:20
ye m. stand to be judged of your		3:20
things m. surely be made known,		5: 8
which are hid m. be revealed		5: 8
m. come unto the remnant of		5: 9
mortal m. put on immortality,		6:21
m. soon become incorruptible		6:21
then ye m. stand before the		6:21
ye m. come unto repentance,		7: 3
ye m. lay down your weapons		7: 4
ye m. come to the knowledge		7: 5
man m. be raised to stand		7: 6
all these things m. be fulfilled.		8:33
that which m. shortly come,		8:34
we m. be encompassed about	Eth	3: 2
that we m. call upon thee,		3: 2
m. soon go down to the grave;		6:19
that they m. prepare the way of		9:28
people saw that they m. perish		9:34
it m. needs be that some had		12: 7
wherefore man m. hope, or he		12:32
faith he m. needs have hope;	Mro	7:42
he m. needs have charity;		7:44
he m. needs have charity.		7:44
of all, for all things m. fail —		7:46
they m. repent and be baptized,		8:10
m. have gone to an endless hell.		8:13
he m. go down to hell.		8:14
the other m. perish because		8:15
they m. perish soon, unto the		8:29
for I know that they m. perish		9:22
Wherefore, there m. be faith;		10:20
and if there m. be faith there		10:20
be faith there m. also be hope;		10:20
and if there m. be hope there		10:20
hope there m. also be charity.		10:20
ye m. needs be in despair;		10:22
he m. fall and incur the	DC	3: 4
you m. wait yet a little while,		5:17
you m. study it out in your mind;		9: 8
you m. ask me if it be right,		9: 8
I m. bring forth the fulness of		14:10
you m. rely upon my word,		17: 1
it m. needs be that the children		18: 6
all men m. take upon them		18:24
you m. perform it according to		18:30
m. walk uprightly before me		18:31

MUST

you m. preach unto the world,	DC 18:41
You m. repent and be	18:41
For all men m. repent and be	18:42
you m. keep my commandments	18:43
every man m. repent or suffer,	19: 4
they m. suffer even as I;	19:17
but milk they m. receive,	19:22
they m. not know these things,	19:22
all men m. repent and believe	20:29
you m. take up your cross,	23: 6
you m. pray vocally before	23: 6
all things m. be done in order,	28:13
thou m. open thy mouth at	28:16
by mine apostles m. be fulfilled;	29:10
not come to pass but surely m.,	29:21
it m. needs be that the devil	29:39
it m. needs be that the riches	38:39
ye m. visit the poor and the	44: 6
m. needs flee unto Zion	45:68
m. be done in the name of Christ,	46:31
ye m. give thanks unto God	46:32
ye m. practise virtue and	46:33
it m. needs be necessary that	48: 3
It m. needs be necessary that	48: 4
before me and m. needs repent.	49: 2
ye m. grow in grace and in the	50:40
it m. needs be that he receive	51: 1
it m. needs be that they be	51: 2
Thayre m. repent of his pride,	56: 8
m. needs pay the money,	56:12
m. go forth from this place into	58:64
the gospel m. be preached unto	58:64
things that ye m. look for;	63:53
and m. be spoken with care,	63:64
But all things m. come to pass	64:32
m. be designated by this	68:20
m. be done away from among	68:32
m. lay all things before	72:15
m. give an account of his	72:16
m. needs be sent unto the world	75:24
who, as it is written, m. come	77:14
it m. needs be that there be	78: 3
you m. prepare yourselves by	78: 7
For Zion m. increase in beauty,	82:14
her borders m. be enlarged;	82:14
her stakes m. be strengthened;	82:14
Zion m. arise and put on her	82:14
it m. be preached unto them,	84:76
and m. needs remain through	86:10
it m. needs be sanctified from	88:18
m. inherit another kingdom,	88:21
he m. abide a kingdom which	88:24
they m. remain filthy still.	88:35
which m. shortly come to pass;	88:79
m. needs stand rebuked before	93:47
Your family m. needs repent	93:48
it m. be done according to	94: 2
ye m. needs be chastened and	95: 2
that m. needs be chastened,	97: 6
m. needs be chastened and tried,	101: 4
they m. needs be chastened –	101:41
my word m. needs be fulfilled.	101:64
I m. gather together my people,	101:65
said unto you m. needs be,	101:93
of Zion m. needs come by	103:15
m. needs be led out of bondage	103:17
it m. needs be done in mine	104:16
people m. needs be chastened	105: 6
obedience, if it m. needs be,	105: 6
m. be by the unanimous voice of	107:27
m. be agreed to its decisions,	107:27
m. needs be presiding elders to	107:60
m. needs be that one be appointed	107:65
a bishop m. be chosen from the	107:69
But thy word m. be fulfilled.	109:44
if it m. needs be, for their support,	124:122
books spoken of m. be the books	128: 7
a man m. enter into this order	131: 2
unto them m. obey the same.	132: 3
m. and shall abide the law,	132: 6
My people m. be tried in all things,	136:31

out of my mouth they m. be	Mses 4:30
wherefore they m. be fulfilled.	5:15
our fathers that all men m. repent.	6:50
Why is it that men m. repent	6:53
all men, everywhere, m. repent,	6:57
even so ye m. be born again	6:59
told you m. come to pass;	JS 1:23
I m. either remain in darkness	2:13
I m. do as James directs,	2:13
that I m. join none of them,	2:19
I m. have no other object in	2:46
m. not be influenced by any	2:46
interviews m. have occupied	2:47
a man m. be called of God,	AoF 5

MUSTERETH

m. the hosts of the battle.	2Ne 23: 4

MUTTER

unto wizards that peep and m. –	2Ne 18:19

MY: *see in the APPENDIX.*

MYSELF

I beheld m. that I was in a	1Ne 8: 7
I will manifest m. unto thy seed,	13:35
I did arm m. with a bow	16:23
not that I would excuse m.	19: 6
to the flesh, I would excuse m.	19: 6
of m., have dwelt at Jerusalem,	2Ne 25: 6
preserve the fruit thereof unto m.;	Jac 5: 8
I might preserve them unto m.,	5:11
preserve unto m. the natural	5:13
thereof against the season, unto m.;	5:13
I have laid up unto m. against	5:31
may preserve unto m. the roots	5:53
which I shall lay up unto m.	5:71
the good will I preserve unto m.,	5:77
I of m. am a wicked man,	Om 1: 2
think that I of m. am more than	Mos 2:10
even I, m., have labored with	2:14
when I, m., was with my guards	7:10
And I, m., with mine own hands,	9:19
I have suffered m. that I have	17: 9
and I m. was caught in a snare,	23: 9
for I am unworthy to glory of m.	23:11
even I m. have labored with	29:14
that I know of these things m.?	Al 5:45
I might know these things of m.	5:46
know of m. that they are true;	5:46
that I know of m. that whatsoever	5:48
as for m., to me he doth not stink.	19: 5
therefore I will not boast of m.,	26:12
I do not glory of m., but I glory	29: 9
I will testify unto you of m.	34: 8
ye think that I know of m. –	36: 4
not of any worthiness of m.	36: 5
that I know these things of m.,	38: 6
that m., and also my men, and	60: 3
that these things shall be, of m.,	He 7:29
it is not of m. that I know	7:29
of my saying, which is of m.,	3Ne 5:19
not manifest m. unto them save	15:23
manifested m. unto them.	16: 2
I go to show m. unto them.	16: 3
show m. unto the lost tribes of	17: 4
declare unto you hereafter of m.,	21: 2
therefore I show m. unto you.	Eth 3:13
have I showed m. unto man	3:15
m. known to the Lamanites	Mro 1: 1
spoken, and I excuse not m.;	DC 1:38
subdue all things unto m. –	19: 2
suffering caused m., even God,	19:18
I will reveal m. from heaven	29:11
unto m. my works have no end,	29:33
and I m. will go with them	32: 3
reserve unto m. a pure people	43:14
and were received unto m. –	45:12
which I have reserved unto m.,	49: 8
whom I shall reserve unto m.,	63:39
These things I say not of m.;	85:10

MYSELF 649 NAME

quickly, and receive you unto m.	DC 88:126
raise up unto m. a pure people,	100:16
which I have reserved unto m.	104:68
I cannot receive her unto m.	105: 5
will manifest m. to my people	110: 7
I may receive him unto m.,	124:19
Patten I have taken unto m.,	124:130
Brunson I have taken unto m.;	124:132
I subscribe m. your servant in	127:12
and I took him to m.	136:38
that I was naked, and I hid m.	Mses 4:16
not of m., but through thine	7:59
m. a follower of righteousness,	Abr 1: 2
chronology running back from m.	1:28
in relation both to m. and	JS 2: 1
Hyrum, m., Samuel Harrison,	2: 4
still I kept m. aloof from all	2: 8
I often said to m.:	2:10
and finding m. alone, I kneeled	2:15
abandon m. to destruction —	2:16
I found m. delivered from the	2:17
did I get possession of m.,	2:18
When I came to m. again,	2:20
I found m. lying on my back,	2:20
"I have learned for m. that	2:20
cause of great sorrow to m.	2:23
I betook m. to prayer and	2:29
father's family, and about m.	2:61

MYSTERIES

the goodness and the m. of God,	1Ne 1: 1
desires to know of the m. of God,	2:16
the m. of God shall be unfolded	10:19
the depths of the m. of him;	Jac 4: 8
not knowing the m. of God.	Mos 1: 3
read and understand of his m.,	1: 5
the m. of God may be unfolded	2: 9
purpose of unfolding all such m.	8:19
and his m. and marvelous power.	Al 10: 5
his m. and his marvelous power;	10: 5
many to know the m. of God.	12: 9
unto him to know the m. of God	12:10
know nothing concerning his m.;	12:11
given to know the m. of God;	26:22
visions and their pretended m.,	30:28
of the m. contained thereon.	37: 4
these m. are not yet fully made	37:11
the m. and the works of darkness,	37:21
are many m. which are kept,	40: 3
m. of God shall be unfolded	DC 6: 7
inquire, thou shalt know m.	6:11
that thou mayest find out m.,	6:11
you may know the m. of God,	8:11
the m. of God shall be unfolded	11: 7
given him the keys of the m.,	28: 7
the m. and peaceable things —	42:61
know the m. of the kingdom,	42:65
desire the m. of the kingdom,	43:13
give the m. of my kingdom,	63:23
keys of the m. of the kingdom	64: 5
expounding the m. thereof	71: 1
to them will I reveal all m.,	76: 7
the hidden m. of my kingdom	76: 7
and the m. of his kingdom	76:114
the revealed will, m., and the	77: 6
of the m. of the kingdom,	84:19
unfold the m. of the kingdom;	90:14
expounding all scriptures and m.	97: 5
m. of the kingdom of heaven,	107:19

MYSTERIOUS

and the m. arts of the evil one,	He 16:21
and for what cause it seems m.,	DC 127: 2
more m. passages revealed	JS 2:74

MYSTERY

I will unfold this m. unto you;	Jac 4:18
a great m. is contained within	Mos 8:19
Now, I unfold unto you a m.;	Al 40: 3
m. which we cannot understand,	He 16:21
unfold unto them this great m.;	DC 10:64
I will explain unto you this m.,	19: 8
the m. of godliness, how great	19:10
keys of the m. of those things	DC 35:18
And now I show unto you a m.,	38:13

NAAMAH

sister of Tubal Cain was called N.	Mses 5:46

NAHOM

in the place which was called N.	1Ne 16:34

NAILS

the prints of the n. in my hands	3Ne 11:14
the prints of the n. in his hands	11:15
the n. in my hands	DC 6:37

NAKED

to do good—to clothe the n.;	Jac 2:19
that they go hungry, or n.;	Mos 4:14
the hungry, clothing the n.,	4:26
heads shaved that they were n.;	10: 8
yea, and to every needy, n. soul.	18:28
not send away any who were n.,	Al 1:30
n., save it were skin which was	3: 5
backs upon the needy and the n.	4:12
their clothes that they were n.;	14:22
for behold they were n., and	20:29
turn away the needy, and the n.,	34:28
and they were n., save it were a	43:20
yea, all were n., save it were	43:20
their n. skins and their bare	44:18
their clothing from the n.,	He 4:12
and the needy, and the n.,	Mrm 8:39
they were both n., the man and	Mses 3:25
they knew that they had been n.	4:13
because I beheld that I was n.,	4:16
Who told thee thou wast n.?	4:17
they were both n., the man and	Abr 5:19
His hands were n., and his arms	JS 2:31
so, also, were his feet n., as were	2:31

NAKEDNESS

our uncleanness, and our n.;	2Ne 9:14
that we might clothe our n.;	Mos 10: 5
their n. was exposed to the	Al 43:37
thick garments to cover their n.	49: 6
of every kind, to clothe their n.	He 6:13
to see your n. before God,	Mrm 9: 5
clothe themselves from their n.	Eth 10:24

NAME

called the n. of the river, Laman,	1Ne 2: 8
Zoram was the n. of the servant;	4:35
I have given the n. of Nephi;	9: 2
plates of Nephi, after mine own n.;	9: 2
the n. of the apostle of the Lamb	14:27
did call the n. of the place Shazer.	16:13
In the n. of the Almighty God,	17:48
who are called by the n. of Israel,	20: 1
who swear by the n. of the Lord,	20: 1
yea, the Lord of Hosts is his n.	20: 2
not suffer my n. to be polluted,	20:11
his n. should not have been	20:19
hath he made mention of my n.	21: 1
his n. shall be called after me;	2Ne 3:15
be after the n. of his father.	3:15
call the n. of the place Nephi;	5: 8
and glorify the n. of your God.	6: 4
the Lord of Hosts is my n.	8:15
repent, and be baptized in his n.,	9:23
repent and believe in his n.,	9:24
and be baptized in his n.,	9:24
for the Lord God is his n.	9:41
praise the holy n. of my God.	9:49
and give thanks unto his holy n.	9:52
unto me that this should be his n.—	10: 3
only let us be called by thy n.	14: 1
and shall call his n. Immanuel.	17:14
his n., Maher-shalal-hash-baz.	18: 3
his n. shall be called, Wonderful,	19: 6
Praise the Lord, call upon his n.,	22: 4
mention that his n. is exalted.	22: 4
cut off from Babylon for his n.	24:22
those who shall believe on his n.	25:13
my heart doth magnify his holy n.	25:13

NAME

as many as will believe on his n.,	2Ne 25:14
and worship the Father in his n.,	25:16
his n. shall be Jesus Christ,	25:19
none other n. given under heaven	25:20
not take the n. of the Lord	26:32
they shall sanctify my n.,	27:34
baptized in the n. of my Beloved	31:11
He that is baptized in my n.,	31:12
take upon you the n. of Christ,	31:13
way nor n. given under heaven	31:21
the Father in the n. of Christ,	32: 9
the Father in the n. of Christ	33:12
retain in remembrance his n.	Jac 1:11
be of whatever n. they would.	1:11
and worshiped the Father in his n.,	4: 5
we worship the Father in his n.	4: 5
can command in the n. of Jesus	4: 6
whose n. was Sherem.	7: 1
blessed be the n. of my God	En 1: 1
shall receive in the n. of Christ,	1:15
I shall give this people a n.,	Mos 1:11
a n. that never shall be blotted out,	1:12
even through faith on his n.;	3: 9
there shall be no other n. given	3:17
in and through the n. of Christ,	3:17
and faith on the n. of the Lord	3:21
calling on the n. of the Lord	4:11
ye have been calling on his n.,	4:20
changed through faith on his n.;	5: 7
is no other n. given whereby	5: 8
take upon you the n. of Christ,	5: 8
the n. by which he is called;	5: 9
be called by the n. of Christ.	5: 9
take upon him the n. of Christ	5:10
must be called by some other n.;	5:10
the n. that I said I should give	5:11
that the n. be not blotted out	5:11
name written always in your hearts,	5:12
the n. by which he shall call you.	5:12
the n. by which ye are called.	5:14
upon them the n. of Christ.	6: 2
them whose n. was Abinadi;	11:20
not take the n. of the Lord thy	13:15
that taketh his n. in vain.	13:15
among them whose n. was Alma,	17: 2
received its n. from the king,	18: 4
baptized in the n. of the Lord,	18:10
them whose n. was Gideon,	19: 4
captive, whose n. was Limhi.	19:16
the n. of the leader of those priests	23:32
the n. of the king of the Lamanites,	24: 3
called after the n. of his father;	24: 3
themselves the n. of Nephi,	25:12
take upon them the n. of Christ,	25:23
who are willing to bear my n.;	26:18
for in my n. shall they be called;	26:18
serve me and go forth in my n.,	26:20
receive shall believe in my n.;	26:22
in my n. are they called;	26:24
the n. of the man was Gideon;	Al 1: 8
and his n. was Nehor;	1:15
upon them the n. of Christ.	1:19
distinguished by the n. of Amlici,	2:11
this man's n. was Nephihah,	4:17
in his own n. he doth call you,	5:38
which is the n. of Christ;	5:38
to the n. by which ye are called,	5:38
steadfastly believeth on his n.	5:48
And blessed be the n. of God,	7: 4
after the n. of him who first	8: 7
unto all who call on his n.	9:17
through faith on his n.	9:27
whose n. was Zeezrom.	10:31
of those who believe on his n.;	11:40
man that believeth on his n.	12:15
that time forth to call on his n.;	12:30
call on men, in the n. of his Son,	12:33
the Lord, and call on his holy n.,	13:28
(and his n. was Zoram, and he	16: 5
to call on his n. and confess	17: 4
and his n. was Lamoni;	17:21
do many mighty works in his n.;	Al 19: 4
Blessed be the n. of God,	19:12
mankind who believe on his n.	19:13
did call on the n. of the Lord,	19:16
women, whose n. was Abish,	19:16
will repent and believe on his n.	19:36
whose n. is Antiomno,	20: 4
whosoever would believe on his n.	22:13
and call on his n. in faith,	22:16
desirous that they might have a n.,	23:16
the n. that they should take upon	23:16
and they were called by this n.	23:17
the n. of Anti-Nephi-Lehi,	24: 1
called his n. Anti-Nephi-Lehi.	24: 3
to call on the n. of the Lord;	24:21
Blessed be the n. of our God;	26: 8
let us give thanks to his holy n.,	26: 8
we will praise his n. forever.	26:12
will repent and believe on his n.	26:35
Yea, blessed is the n. of my God,	26:36
blessed be the n. of my God,	26:36
by that n. ever after.	27:26
Anti-Christ, whose n. was Korihor,	30:12
the high priest's n. was Giddonah.	30:23
and I say, that in the n. of God,	30:49
by a man whose n. was Zoram—	30:59
and his n. was Helaman;	31: 7
unto all who believe on his n.;	32:22
those who shall believe on his n.;	34:15
ye begin to call upon his holy n.,	34:17
upon you the n. of Christ;	34:38
a man by the n. of Zerahemnah	43: 5
and his n. was Moroni;	43:16
led by a man whose n. was Lehi,	43:35
the n. of that all-powerful God,	44: 5
and his n. was Amalickiah.	46: 1
gladly, the n. of Christ, or	46:15
take upon us the n. of Christ,	46:18
take upon them the n. of Christ,	46:21
whose n. was Lehonti,	47:10
called the n. of the city Moroni;	50:13
they called the n. of the city,	50:14
a man whose n. was Morianton,	50:28
a man whose n. was Teancum,	50:35
Now behold, his n. was Pahoran.	50:40
upon them the n. of freemen;	51: 6
and his n. was Ammoron;	52: 3
their leader, whose n. was Jacob,	52:20
one, whose n. was Laman;	55: 5
blessed is the n. of our God;	57:35
son, whose n. was Moronihah;	62:43
called after the n. of his father.	63:11
a man whose n. was Coriantumr;	He 1:15
whose n. was Tubaloth, who was	1:16
unto the eldest the n. of Nephi,	3:21
unto the youngest, the n. of Lehi.	3:21
hearts, call upon his holy n.	3:27
believe on the n. of Jesus Christ,	3:28
a man whose n. was Cezoram.	5: 1
the man's n. was Aminadab.	5:39
themselves the n. of Lamanites,	11:24
those who shall believe on his n.	14: 2
that ye might believe on his n.	14:12
And if ye believe on his n.	14:13
and his n. was Gidgiddoni.	3Ne 3:18
whose n. was Zemnarihah;	4:17
call on the n. of their God	4:30
Blessed be the n. of the Lord	4:32
in the n. of Jesus did he cast	7:19
the people, in the n. of Jesus.	7:20
many miracles in the n. of Jesus;	8: 1
do a miracle in the n. of Jesus	8: 1
hath the Father glorified his n.	9:15
many as shall believe on my n.,	9:17
in whom I have glorified my n.—	11: 7
the n. of the Most High God!	11:17
desireth to be baptized in my n.,	11:23
in my n. shall ye baptize them.	11:23
ye shall say, calling them by n.,	11:24
you in the n. of the Father, and	11:25
manner shall ye baptize in my n.;	11:27

NAME 651 NAME

child, and be baptized in my n.,	3Ne	11:37
and be baptized in my n.,		11:38
art in heaven, hallowed be thy n.		13: 9
have we not prophesied in thy n.,		14:22
in thy n. have cast out devils,		14:22
and in thy n. done many		14:22
do not ask the Father in my n.,		16: 4
and ask of the Father, in my n.,		17: 3
believe and be baptized in my n.		18: 5
and are baptized in my n.;		18:11
repent and are baptized in my n.		18:16
pray unto the Father in my n.;		18:19
shall ask the Father in my n.,		18:20
unto the Father, always in my n.,		18:21
them unto the Father, in my n.		18:23
him unto the Father, in my n.;		18:30
and is baptized in my n.,		18:30
dead, whose n. was Timothy,		19: 4
also his son, whose n. was Jonas,		19: 4
the Father in the n. of Jesus.		19: 6
Father also in the n. of Jesus.		19: 7
the Father in the n. of Jesus.		19: 8
pray unto the Father in my n.		20:31
that my people shall know my n.;		20:39
and be baptized in my n.		21: 6
may call on the Father in my n.		21:27
the Lord of Hosts is his n.;		22: 5
should glorify his n. in me		23: 9
and that thought upon his n.		24:16
But unto you that fear my n.,		25: 2
baptized in the n. of Jesus		26:17
baptized in the n. of Jesus		26:21
baptizing in the n. of Jesus,		27: 1
praying unto the Father in his n.;		27: 2
tell us the n. whereby we shall		27: 3
upon you the n. of Christ,		27: 5
name of Christ, which is my n.?		27: 5
by this n. shall ye be called at		27: 5
whoso taketh upon him my n.,		27: 6
shall do, ye shall do it in my n.;		27: 7
ye shall call the church in my n.		27: 7
call upon the Father in my n.		27: 7
save it be called in my n.?		27: 8
church be called in Moses' n.		27: 8
it be called in the n. of a man		27: 8
but if it be called in my n.		27: 8
things ye do call, in my n.;		27: 9
if it be in my n. the Father		'27: 9
and is baptized in my n.		27:16
and be baptized in my n.,		27:20
ye shall ask the Father in my n.		27:28
the Father in the n. of Jesus		28:30
and be baptized in my n.,		30: 2
baptized in the n. of Jesus;	4Ne	1: 1
save it were in the n. of Jesus.		1: 5
them not of the Lamanites;		1:20
my father's n. was Mormon)	Mrm	1: 5
a king, and his n. was Aaron;		2: 9
be baptized in the n. of Jesus,		7: 8
in his n. could they remove		8:24
in his n. could they cause the		8:24
upon you the n. of Christ?		8:38
the Father in the n. of Jesus,		9: 6
the Father in the n. of Christ		9:21
in my n. shall they cast out		9:24
shall believe in my n.,		9:25
ask the Father in the n. of Jesus		9:27
do it in the n. of Jesus Christ,		9:29
faith on the n. of Jesus Christ.		9:37
n. of the valley was Nimrod,	Eth	2: 1
they called the n. of the place		2:13
call upon the n. of the Lord.		2:14
did call upon the n. of the Lord		2:15
they who shall believe on my n.;		3:14
glorify my n. in the flesh;		3:21
call upon the Father in my n.,		4:15
and be baptized in my n.;		4:18
them that believe in my n.		4:18
is found faithful unto my n.		4:19
the Father in the n. of Jesus,		5: 5
and his n. was Pagag.		6:25
was one whose n. was Noah.		7:14
(and his n. was Nimrah)	Eth	9: 8
eldest son, whose n. was Shez,		10: 3
glorified the n. of the Father,		12: 8
and did speak in thy n.,		12:31
of Shared, whose n. was Gilead,		14: 8
and his n. was Lib;		14:10
the n. of the brother of Lib		14:17
And he called them by n., saying:	Mro	2: 2
call on the Father in my n.,		2: 2
and in my n. shall ye give it,		2: 2
the Father in the n. of Christ,		3: 3
In the n. of Jesus Christ I		3: 3
of faith on his n. to the end.		3: 3
the Father in the n. of Christ,		4: 2
the n. of thy Son, Jesus Christ,		4: 3
upon them the n. of thy Son,		4: 3
the n. of thy Son, Jesus Christ,		5: 2
upon them the n. of Christ,		6: 3
were saved by faith in his n.;		7:26
shall ask the Father in my n.,		7:26
and be baptized in my n.,		7:34
they shall have faith in his n.;		7:38
the n. of his Holy Child, Jesus,		8: 3
endurance of faith on his n.		8: 3
Father, in the n. of Christ,		10: 4
might speak in the n. of God	DC	1:20
glorified through faith in his n.,		3:20
gathered together in my n.,		6:32
works, which they did in my n.;		10:61
to them that believe on my n.		11:30
servants, in the n. of Messiah		13: 1
shall ask the Father in my n.,		14: 8
and his n. is Joseph.		18: 8
Ask the Father in my n.,		18:18
upon you the n. of Christ,		18:21
and are baptized in my n.		18:22
Jesus Christ is the n. which is		18:23
there is none other n. given		18:23
n. which is given of the Father,		18:24
in that n. shall they be called		18:24
the n. by which they are called,		18:25
shall take upon them my n.;		18:27
to take upon them my n. with		18:27
to take upon them my n. with		18:28
of me to baptize in my n.,		18:29
worship the Father in my n.		18:40
in the n. of Jesus Christ;		18:41
for Endless is my n.,		19:10
Joseph Smith, Jun., in my n.;		19:13
be the n. of the Lord God!		19:37
and be baptized in his holy n.,		20:25
on the n. of Jesus Christ,		20:29
worship the Father in his n.,		20:29
in faith on his n. to the end,		20:29
be rendered to his holy n.,		20:36
the n. of Jesus Christ,		20:37
in the n. of Jesus Christ,		20:70
and bless them in his n.		20:70
say, calling him or her by n.:		20:73
in the n. of the Father, and		20:73
ask thee in the n. of thy Son,		20:77
upon them the n. of thy Son,		20:77
ask thee in the n. of thy Son,		20:79
of Christ, bearing my n.—		21:11
calling upon God in my n.,		24: 5
bearing my n. before the world,		24:10
they receive you not in my n.,		24:15
command to be smitten in my n.;		24:16
and his n. should be John,		27: 7
especial witnesses of my n.,		27:12
the n. of mine Only Begotten		29:42
many as will believe on my n.,		35: 2
all those who believe on my n.		35: 8
shall ask it in my n. in faith,		35: 9
the n. of the most high God.		36: 3
as have believed in my n.,		38: 4
in mine own n., by the virtue		38: 4
your sins, calling on my n.,		39:10
the n. of the Most High God.		39:19
that have professed my n.,		41: 1
yourselves together in my n.,		42: 1
as ye believe on my n.		42: 1

NAME

asked the Father in my n.,	DC 42: 3
ye shall go forth in my n.,	42: 4
two by two, in my n.,	42: 6
their hands upon them in my n.;	42:44
brethren that believe on my n.,	45: 5
them that believed on my n.	45: 8
must be done in the n. of Christ,	46:31
apostle of old, whose n. was Peter:	49:11
on the n. of the Lord Jesus,	49:12
be baptized in the n. of Jesus	49:13
in the church that profess my n.	50: 4
in the n. of Jesus and it shall	50:29
of the Father in the n. of Jesus;	50:31
baptism in the n. of Jesus Christ,	55: 2
O ye people who profess my n.,	56: 1
in the n. of Jesus Christ thou	59: 5
they take my n. in their lips—	63:61
who use the n. of the Lord,	63:62
call upon his holy n.,	65: 4
of as many as believe on my n.	66: 1
in the n. of the Father, and of	68: 8
Calling on the n. of the Lord for	75:10
and believed on his n. and were	76:51
buried in the water in his n.,	76:51
call upon my n. for revelations,	82: 4
In my n. they shall do many	84:66
In my n. they shall cast out	84:67
In my n. they shall heal	84:68
In my n. they shall open	84:69
not baptized in water in my n.,	84:74
ye ask the Father in my n.	88:64
the mouth of the Lord shall n.,	88:84
swear in the n. of him who	88:110
may be in the n. of the Lord;	88:120
may be in the n. of the Lord;	88:120
may be in the n. of the Lord,	88:120
the n. of the Lord Jesus Christ,	88:133
the mouth of the Lord shall n.	90:20
the mouth of the Lord shall n.	90:21
unto me, and calleth on my n.,	93: 1
come into the Father in my n.,	93:19
unto me in the n. of the Lord,	97:15
that ye warn him in my n.,	98:28
thing ye declare in my n.,	100: 7
call upon the n. of the Lord,	100:17
given their lives for my n.	101:15
all they who call on my n.,	101:22
suffer persecution for my n.,	101:35
build them up unto my n.	101:64
call themselves after my n.,	101:75
call themselves after my n.;	101:97
in the n. and for the church	102: 5
to act in the n. of the church.	102: 8
call themselves after my n.	103: 4
names, and in their own n.;	104:49
their business in their own n.,	104:49
your business in your won n.,	104:50
and consecrate it unto my n.	104:60
faithful and call upon my n.,	104:82
and to blaspheme my n. upon	105:15
to be built unto my n. in	105:33
the n. of the Supreme Being,	107: 4
too frequent repetition of his n.,	107: 4
witnesses of the n. of Christ	107:23
to officiate in the n. of the Lord,	107:33
are to act in the n. of the Lord,	107:34
Thanks be to thy n., O Lord	109: 1
to build a house to thy n.	109: 2
in the n. of Jesus Christ,	109: 4
in whose n. alone salvation can	109: 4
to build a house to thy n.,	109: 5
may be in the n. of the Lord,	109: 9
may be in the n. of the Lord,	109: 9
may be in the n. of the Lord,	109: 9
may be in the n. of the Lord;	109:17
may be in the n. of the Lord;	109:18
may be in the n. of the Lord,	109:19
that thy n. may be upon them,	109:22
honorably hold a n. and standing	109:24
thy n. shall be put in this house;	109:26
in bearing record of thy n.,	109:31
to bear testimony of thy n.;	DC 109:56
to build a holy city to thy n.,	109:58
which we have built unto thy n.;	109:78
this church, to put upon it thy n.	109:79
built this house to my n.	110: 6
house, and my n. shall be here;	110: 7
to bear testimony of my n.	112: 1
thou shalt bear record of my n.,	112: 4
in publishing my n. among	112: 6
and unto all who love my n.	112:11
faithful before me unto my n.	112:12
place ye shall proclaim my n.	112:19
whosoever ye shall send in my n.,	112:21
who have professed to know my n.	112:26
testify of my n. and bear glad	114: 1
among you who deny my n.,	114: 2
to build a house unto my n.;	115:10
building of a house unto my n.;	115:13
let a house be built unto my n.	115:14
not in n. but in deed,	117:11
his n. shall be had in	117:12
be made a merchant unto my n.,	117:14
and bear record of my n.	118: 4
will rejoice in thy n. forever.	121: 6
the earth shall inquire after thy n.,	122: 1
honor to himself and unto my n.	124:18
build a house unto my n.,	124:22
if it be built unto my n.,	124:24
and build a house to my n.,	124:27
which you have built to my n.?	124:37
to build unto my holy n.	124:39
this house be built unto my n.,	124:40
if you build a house unto my n.,	124:47
of men to do a work unto my n.,	124:49
up a city and a house unto my n.,	124:51
you again to build a house to my n.,	124:55
let it be built unto my n.,	124:56
let my n. be named upon it,	124:56
let the n. of that house be called	124:60
his n. may be had in	124:96
bear record of my n. in all	124:139
you build it unto my n.,	124:145
who call themselves by my n.	125: 2
and build up cities unto my n.,	125: 2
build up a city unto my n.	125: 3
n. of Zarahemla be named upon	125: 3
and toil in journeyings for my n.	126: 2
authority, in the n. of the Lord,	128: 9
the eternal creations declare his n.	128:23
whereon is a new n. written,	130:11
the new n. is the key word.	130:11
in the n. of the Lord God,	130:12
that is not made in my n.?	132: 9
or powers, or things of n.,	132:13
you bind on earth, in my n. and	132:46
if he do anything in my n.,	132:59
I will magnify my n. upon all	132:64
call upon the n. of the Lord.	133: 6
having his father's n. written	133:18
Calling upon the n. of the Lord	133:40
come down to make thy n. known	133:42
fame and n. that cannot be slain.	135: 3
take the n. of the Lord in vain,	136:21
I have left a witness of my n.?	136:40
Almighty, and Endless is my n.;	Mses 1: 3
Blessed be the n. of my God,	1:15
in the n. of mine Only Begotten,	1:17
In the n. of the Only Begotten,	1:21
And calling upon the n. of God,	1:25
n. of which shall not be known	1:42
called the n. of the first Pison,	3:11
n. of the second river was called	3:13
n. of the third river was Hiddekel;	3:14
that should be the n. thereof.	3:19
in the n. of mine Only Begotten,	4: 1
And Adam called his wife's n. Eve,	4:26
called upon the n. of the Lord,	5: 4
thou doest in the n. of the Son,	5: 8
upon God in the n. of the Son	5: 8
saying: Blessed be the n. of God,	5:10
and Eve blessed the n. of God,	5:12

he called the n. of the city	Mses 5:42	your good, and to my n. glory.	DC	98: 3
after the n. of his son, Enoch.	5:42	in my cause, for my n. sake,		98:13
the n. of one being Adah,	5:44	them sharply for my n. sake,		112:12
and the n. of the other, Zillah.	5:44	made counselors for my n. sake		112:20
and his brothers n. was Jubal,	5:45	of all nations, for my n. sake;	JS	1: 7
and he called his n. Seth.	6: 2			
Adam glorified the n. of God;	6: 2	NAMES		
and he called his n. Enos.	6: 3	distinguish them by these n.,	Jac	1:14
call upon the n. of the Lord,	6: 4	he called their n. Mosiah, and	Mos	1: 2
and called their n. Adam,	6: 9	take the n. of all those who		6: 1
image, and called his n. Seth.	6:10	their n. were Amaleki, Helem,		7: 6
whose n. was Mahijah,	6:40	called by the n. of their fathers,		25:12
the n. of mine Only Begotten Son,	6:52	and their n. were blotted out.		26:36
only n. which shall be given	6:52	their n. were Ammon, and		27:34
asking all things in his n.,	6:52	the n. of the sons of Mosiah.		27:34
Man of Holiness is his n.,	6:57	and their n. were blotted out,	Al	1:24
and the n. of his Only Begotten	6:57	their n. shall be blotted out,		5:57
baptize in the n. of the Father,	7:11	the n. of the wicked shall not be		5:57
Man of Holiness is my n.;	7:35	among the n. of the righteous,		5:57
Man of Counsel is my n.;	7:35	The n. of the wicked shall not be		5:57
Endless and Eternal is my n.,	7:35	mingled with the n. of my people;		5:57
the n. of thine Only Begotten,	7:50	the n. of the righteous shall be		5:58
the n. of thine Only Begotten,	7:59	their n. were blotted out,		6: 3
he called his n. Noah, saying:	8: 9	that their n. were not numbered		6: 3
in the n. of Jesus Christ,	8:24	the n. of the different pieces of		11: 4
behold, my n. is Jehovah,	Abr 1:16	the n. are given by the Nephites,		11: 4
to put upon thee my n., even	1:18	n. of the cities of the Lamanites		23:13
my n. shall be known in the	1:19	their n. Anti-Nephi-Lehies;		23:17
of thee a minister to bear my n. in	2: 6	the n. of those whom he took		31: 7
My n. is Jehovah, and I know	2: 8	these are the n. of those who		31: 7
and make thy n. great among all	2: 9	their n. who did contend for	He	1: 3
will bless them through thy n.;	2:10	the n. of our first parents who		5: 6
shall be called after thy n.,	2:10	that when you remember your n.		5: 6
again upon the n. of the Lord.	2:20	the n. of the disciples whom	3Ne	19: 4
the n. of the great one is Kolob,	3: 3	I was about to write the n.		28:25
that should be the n. thereof.	5:20	and their n. were taken,	Mro	6: 4
Pharoah, whose n. is given	Fac 3: 2	their n. were blotted out,		6: 7
cometh in the n. of the Lord,	JS 1: 1	a list of the n. of the several	DC	20:82
For many which come in my n.,	1: 6	all the n. of the whole church		20:82
(whose n., previous to her	2: 4	their n. may be blotted out		20:83
spake unto me, calling me by n.	2:17	the general church record of n.		20:83
He called me by n., and said	2:33	who have given your n. to go		75: 2
and that his n. was Moroni;	2:33	who have given your n. that		75:23
my n. should be had for good	2:33	whose n. are written in heaven,		76:68
unto me, calling me by n.	2:49	have their n. enrolled with		85: 3
by the n. of Josiah Stoal,	2:56	Their n. shall not be found,		85: 5
by the n. of Martin Harris,	2:61	neither the n. of the fathers,		85: 5
servants, in the n. of Messiah,	2:69	nor the n. of the children		85: 5
said that his n. was John,	2:72	the saints whose n. are found,		85: 7
		and the n. of their fathers,		85: 7
NAMED		whose n. are not found written		85:11
n. all the cities of the Lamanites	Al 23:15	of the n. of the sanctified,		88: 2
he n. all the land which was	46:17	be organized in their own n.,		104:49
of the above n. Presidency.	DC 68:21	own name, and in their own n.;		104:49
place which is n. among you,	96: 2	own name, and in your own n.		104:50
upon the house n. among you,	96: 9	by giving your n. by common		104:85
The above-n. councilors were	102: 2	that their n. may be perpetuated		109:71
the above-n. councilors were	102: 5	And also the n. of all persons		123: 3
of the above-n. councilors,	102: 6	and approve of those n. which		124:144
of the above-n. councilors,	102: 8	giving the date, and n.,		128: 3
been n. for my servant Olihah	104:34	henceforward their n. will be		135: 6
witnesses for my servant just n.	107:26	age to age shall their n. go		135: 6
let my name be n. upon it,	124:56	Adam gave n. to all cattle, and	Mses	3:20
of Zarahemla be n. upon it.	125: 3	And Adam gave n. to all cattle,	Abr	5:21
son, whom he had n. Cainan.	Mses 6:17			
		NAMING		
NAMELY		n. also some three individuals	DC	128: 3
the following was the result, n.:	DC 102:34			
two priesthoods, n.,	107: 1	NAPHTALI		
n., the Constitution of our	109:54	Zebulun, and the land of N.,	2Ne	19: 1
N., Samuel Bent, Henry G.	124:132			
n., the baptism for the dead;	128:17	NARROW		
kinds of beings in heaven, n.:	129: 1	beheld a straight and n. path,	1Ne	8:20
n., my servant Joseph—	132:30	even now be too n. by reason		21:19
consisting of eleven souls, n.,	JS 2: 4	the way for man is n.,	2Ne	9:41
n., my mother, Lucy;	2: 7	are ye in this straight and n. path		31:18
		into this straight and n. path,		31:19
NAME'S		and enter into the n. gate,		33: 9
for my n. sake will I defer mine	1Ne 20: 9	continue in the way which is n.,	Jac	6:11
persecuted for my n. sake,	3Ne 12:10	by a n. strip of wilderness,	Al	22:27
altogether for my n. glory,	DC 19: 7	n. pass which led by the sea		50:34
your good, and his n. glory.	21: 6	secure the n. pass which led		52: 9

NARROW 654 NATIONS

by the n. neck which led into	Al 63: 5	
a straight and n. course across	He 3:29	
and n. is the way, which leadeth	3Ne 14:14	
n. is the way that leads to life,	27:33	
to the n. passage which led into	Mrm 2:29	
by the n. pass which led into	3: 5	
city by the n. neck of land,	Eth 10:20	
strait is the gate, and n. the way	DC 132:22	

NARROWLY
shall n. look upon thee, — 2Ne 24:16

NARROWNESS
and the n. of the gate, — 2Ne 31: 9

NASHVILLE
as well as in the city of N., — DC 125: 4

NATHAN
by the hand of N., my servant — DC 132:39

NATHANAEL
for he is like unto N. of old, — DC 41:11

NATION

than that a n. should dwindle	1Ne 4:13	
he raiseth up a righteous n.,	17:37	
every n. kindred, tongue, and	19:17	
to him whom the n. abhorreth,	21: 7	
God will raise up a mighty n.	22: 7	
every n. which shall war	22:14	
give ear unto me, O my n.;	2Ne 8: 4	
there is none other n. on earth	10: 3	
n. shall not lift up sword against	12: 4	
shall not lift up sword against n.,	12: 4	
Thou hast multiplied the n.,	19: 3	
him against a hypocritical n.,	20: 6	
yea, unto every n., kindred,	26:13	
one n. like unto another?	29: 8	
one n. like unto another.	29: 8	
to every kindred, n., and tongue,	Mos 3:13	
n., kindred, tongue, and people.	3:20	
n., kindred, tongue, and people.	15:28	
n., kindred, tongue, and people	16: 1	
n., kindred, tongue, or people;	Al 9:20	
of their own n. and tongue,	29: 8	
should go forth unto every n.,	37: 4	
every n. that shall hereafter	37:25	
unto every n., kindred, tongue,	45:16	
robbed me, even this whole n.	3Ne 24: 9	
shall go with thee, a great n.	Eth 1:43	
the n. which I will raise up	1:43	
whatsoever n. shall possess it	2: 9	
whatsoever n. shall possess it	2:12	
whatsoever n. shall uphold such	8:22	
they shall spread over the n.,	8:22	
Behold, the pride of this n., or	Mro 8:27	
whatsoever n., kindred, tongue,	DC 10:51	
out of every n. under heaven;	45:69	
out of every n. under heaven.	64:42	
to every n., kindred, tongue,	77: 8	
of every n., kindred, tongue,	77:11	
raised up to the Jewish n.	77:15	
even the n. of Great Britain,	87: 3	
out unto battle against any n.,	98:33	
if any n., tongue, or people	98:34	
unto that people, n., or tongue;	98:34	
that n., tongue, or people.	98:36	
and in his fury vex the n.;	101:89	
door of my kingdom unto any n.	112:21	
n. may be left without excuse	123: 6	
high-minded governors of the n.	124: 3	
shall be preached unto every n.,	133:37	
the little one become a strong n.,	133:58	
the reader in every n. will be	135: 6	
the n. that has driven you out.	136:34	
I will make of thee a great n.,	Abr 2: 9	
into the land of this idolatrous n.	2:18	
for n. shall rise against nation,	JS 1:29	
for nation shall rise against n.,	1:29	

NATIONS

manifesting himself unto all n.	T Pg	
unto all n., kindreds, tongues,	1Ne 5:18	
the destruction of all n., kindreds,	11:36	
and beheld many n. and kingdoms.	13: 1	
I behold many n. and kingdoms.	13: 2	
These are the n. and kingdoms	13: 3	
among the n. of the Gentiles	13: 4	
of the hands of all other n.	13:19	
unto all the n. of the Gentiles;	13:29	
unto all the n. of the Gentiles,	13:29	
power of God above all other n.,	13:30	
shall manifest himself unto all n.,	13:42	
among all n., kindreds, tongues,	14:11	
among all the n. of the Gentiles,	14:13	
the n. and kindreds of the earth.	14:15	
among all the n. which belonged	14:16	
destroyeth the n. of the wicked.	17:37	
and be hated among all n.	19:14	
and also among all n.	22: 3	
shall be scattered among all n.	22: 5	
his arm in the eyes of the n.	22:10	
arm in the eyes of all the n.,	22:11	
all n., kindreds, tongues, and	22:28	
from the knowledge of other n.;	2Ne 1: 8	
n. would overrun the land,	1: 8	
shall be kept from all other n.,	1: 9	
will bring other n. unto them,	1:11	
be wrought among other n.,	10: 4	
shall be scattered among all n.	10: 6	
n. of the Gentiles shall be great	10: 8	
this land against all other n.	10:12	
and all n. shall flow unto it.	12: 2	
And he shall judge among the n.,	12: 4	
Hosts soon cometh upon all n.,	12:12	
the n. which are lifted up,	12:14	
will lift up an ensign to the n.	15:26	
beyond Jordan in Galilee of the n.	19: 1	
destroy and cut off n. not a few.	20: 7	
shall set up an ensign for the n.,	21:12	
of n. gathered together,	23: 4	
he that ruled the n. in anger,	24: 6	
thrones all the kings of the n.	24: 9	
which did weaken the n.!	24:12	
All the kings of the n.,	24:18	
that is stretched out upon all n.	24:26	
answer the messengers of the n.?	24:32	
God, that they come upon all n.,	25: 3	
shall be scattered among all n.:	25:15	
Jews shall be scattered by other n.	25:15	
hath scourged them by other n.	25:16	
power that he should heal the n.	25:20	
the n. who shall possess them	25:22	
behold all the n. of the Gentiles	27: 1	
all the n. that fight against Zion,	27: 3	
the multitude of all the n. be	27: 3	
that there are more n. than one?	29: 7	
upon all the n. of the earth?	29: 7	
testimony of two n. is a witness	29: 8	
the two n. shall run together	29: 8	
the two n. shall run together	29: 8	
speak unto all n. of the earth	29:12	
his work among all n., kindreds,	30: 8	
the things of all n. shall be made	30:16	
I will preserve them for other n.	Mos 12: 8	
of this people to other n.	12: 8	
holy arm in the eyes of all the n.,	12:24	
holy arm in the eyes of all the n.;	15:31	
n., kindreds, tongues and people,	27:25	
angels, doth declare it unto all n.;	Al 13:22	
the Lord doth grant unto all n.,	29: 8	
of their hearts above all n.,	3Ne 16:10	
arm in the eye of all the n.;	16:20	
upon all the n. of the Gentiles.	20:20	
arm in the eyes of all the n.;	20:35	
So shall he sprinkle many n.;	20:45	
with the Father, among all n.,	21:28	
And they shall go out from all n.;	21:29	
all n. shall call you blessed,	24:12	
all n. and tongues shall stand	26: 4	

NATIONS   655   NATURE

unto all n., kindreds, tongues	3Ne 28:29
all other n. under heaven,	Eth 2:12
the freedom of all lands, n.,	8:25
prophesy before n., kindreds,	DC 7: 3
other n. should possess this land;	10:49
for all n. shall tremble.	34: 8
all n. drink of the wine of	35:11
thrash the n. by the power of	35:13
gospel among the n.—	36: 5
shall go forth among all n.,	38:33
shall go forth into all n.	39:15
hand in judgment upon the n.,	39:16
taught unto all n., kindreds,	42:58
shall say to the sleeping n.:	43:18
Call upon the n. to repent,	43:20
Hearken, O ye n. of the earth,	43:23
O, ye n. of the earth,	43:24
and scattered among all n.	45:19
be scattered among all n.;	45:24
of the Lord fall upon the n.	45:47
the n. of the earth shall	45:49
heathen n. be redeemed,	45:54
out from among all n.,	45:71
all n. shall be afraid because	45:75
the n. of the earth shall bow	49:10
forth deceiving the n.—	52:14
and of wrath upon the n.	56: 1
all n. shall be invited.	58: 9
a high place, to judge the n.	64:37
n. of the earth shall tremble	64:43
over the n. of the earth,	77:11
have laid my hands upon the n.,	84:96
maketh all n. to drink of	86: 3
will be poured out upon all n.,	87: 2
States will call on other n.,	87: 3
shall also call upon other n.,	87: 3
themselves against other n.;	87: 3
shall be poured out upon all n.	87: 3
hath made a full end of all n.;	87: 6
and the perplexities of the n.,	88:79
that made all n. drink of	88:94
and all n. shall hear it.	88:94
midst of heaven, unto all n.,	88:103
all n. drink of the wine of	88:105
Zion, and of the n. of Israel,	90: 8
power in convincing the n.,	90:10
the nations, the heathen n.,	90:10
And the n. of the earth	97:19
without measure upon all n.;	101:11
which are soon to befall the n.	101:98
may be terrible unto all n.;	105:31
the affairs of the same in all n.,	107:33
the affairs of the same in all n.,	107:34
a multitude of n. shall come of	107:55
to travel among all n.,	107:98
upon all the n. of the earth,	109:54
to send it abroad among all n.,	112: 1
and among many n.	112: 7
the Twelve, abroad among all n.—	112:16
may be a standard for the n.;	115: 5
armies of the n. of the earth?	117: 6
to all the n. of the earth	124: 3
upon all the n. that forget God,	133: 2
arm in the eyes of all the n.,	133: 3
gather ye out from among the n.,	133: 7
unto the n. which are afar off;	133: 8
call upon all n., first upon the	133: 8
Go ye out from among the n.,	133:14
n. shall tremble at thy presence.—	133:42
the Lord shall thrash the n.	133:59
interests as individuals and n.,	134: 6
to preach the gospel to the n.	134:12
hearts of honest men among all n.;	135: 7
n. feared greatly, so powerful	Mses 7:13
fear of the Lord was upon all n.,	7:17
n. of the earth were before	7:23
always be found among all n.,	7:52
and to be a father of many n.,	Abr 1: 2
make thy name great among all n.,	2: 9
and Priesthood unto all n.;	2: 9
and ye shall be hated of all n.,	JS 1: 7
for a witness unto all n.,	1:31
for good and evil among all n.,	2:33

NATIVE

my n. cheery temperament.	JS 2:28

NATIVITY

the land of their fathers' n.;	Al 21: 1
again unto the land of his n.	He 7: 3

NATURAL

the n. branches of the olive-tree,	1Ne 10:14
the n. branches of the olive-tree,	15: 7
the grafting in of the n. branches	15:13
a n. branch of the olive-tree,	15:16
the n. branches of the tree;	Jac 5:13
the n. branches of the tame	5:14
was like unto the n. fruit.	5:17
the n. branches of the tree	5:19
the n. branches of the tree,	5:20
whose n. branches had been broken	5:30
if the n. branches have also	5:38
the fruit of the n. branches had	5:39
the n. branches of the tree	5:52
the n. branches of the tree	5:54
that they took from the n. tree	5:55
and grafted in unto the n. trees,	5:55
also took of the n. trees	5:56
I have preserved the n. branches	5:60
I have grafted in the n. branches	5:60
bring forth again the n. fruit,	5:61
which n. fruit is good and	5:61
and bring forth the n. fruit,	5:64
the branches of the n. tree	5:67
I graft in again into the n. tree;	5:67
the branches of the n. tree	5:68
the n. branches of the tree;	5:68
they shall bring forth the n. fruit,	5:68
began to be the n. fruit again	5:73
the n. branches began to grow	5:73
had become again the n. fruit;	5:74
unto himself the n. fruit,	5:74
I have preserved the n. fruit,	5:75
brought unto me again the n. fruit,	5:75
the n. man is an enemy to God,	Mos 3:19
and putteth off the n. man	3:19
had overcome his n. frame,	Al 19: 6
what n. man is there that	26:21
every thing to its n. frame—	41: 4
to take a thing of a n. state and	41:12
they are not n. nor temporal,	DC 29:35
by his n. death he might be	29:43
behold with your n. eyes,	58: 3
the carnal neither n. mind,	67:10
can any n. man abide	67:12
same body which was a n. body;	88:28
but that which is n.;	128:14
again receive his n. strength	Mses 1:10
not my n., but my spiritual	1:11
n. eyes could not have beheld;	1:11
look upon thee in the n. man.	1:14
were not visible to the n. eye;	6:36

NATURALLY

that you may n. understand;	DC 29:33
before they were n. upon the	Mses 3: 5
to grow every tree, n.,	3: 9

NATURE

The God of n. suffers.	1Ne 19:12
and they were led by their evil n.	En 1:20
as in Adam, or by n., they fall,	Mos 3:16
that persists in his own carnal n.,	16: 5
all men that are in a state of n.,	Al 41:11
gone contrary to the n. of God;	41:11
contrary to the n. of happiness.	41:11
in a state opposite to its n.?	41:12
sensual, and devilish, by n.,	42:10
by the n. of the climate—	46:40
contrary to the n. of that	He 13:38
n., and use of man.—	DC 89:10
it is the n. and disposition of	121:39
has become a second n. to me;	127: 2
n. of this ordinance consists in	128: 8
according to the n. of the offense;	134: 8

NATURE / NEAREST

NATURE (cont.)
and the foibles of human n.;	JS	2:28
such was never in my n.		2:28

NATURES
our n. have become evil	Eth	3: 2

NAUGHT
and he shall be as n. before the	1Ne	17:48
others set at n. and trample		19: 7
they set him at n.,		19: 7
judge him to be a thing of n.;		19: 9
have spent my strength for n.		21: 4
have been created for a thing of n.;	2Ne	2:12
together, and it shall come to n.;		18:10
and they sell themselves for n.;		26:10
the terrible one is brought to n.,		27:31
aside the just for a thing of n.		27:32
aside the just for a thing of n.		28:16
and esteem them as things of n.		33: 2
set at n. the commandments of	He	4:21
they do set at n. his counsels,		12: 6
Ye have sold yourselves for n.,	3Ne	20:38
be counted as n. among them—	Mrm	5: 9
but they esteemed him as n.,	Eth	13:13
setteth at n. the atonement of	Mro	8:20
neither can they come to n.	DC	3: 1
sets at n. the counsels of God;		3: 4
set at n. the counsels of God,		3: 7
set at n. the counsels of God,		3:13
preach n. but repentance,		19:21
the prudent shall come to n.		76: 9
their works may be brought to n.,		109:30
shall esteem my words as n.	Mses	1:41
n. but peace, justice, and truth		7:31

NAUVOO
that house be called N. House;	DC	124:60
even the city of N.		124:109
for boarding, even the N. House,		124:111
of the quorum of the N. House,		124:117
to the quorum of the N. House		124:119
let the quorum of the N. House		124:121
do in building the N. House;		124:121
land opposite the city of N.,		125: 3
or in the city of N.,		125: 4

NAVEL
shall receive health in their n.	DC	89:18

NAY
Behold, I say unto you, N.	1Ne	17:33
I say unto you, N.		17:34
Behold, I say unto you, N.;	2Ne	26:25
Behold, I say unto you, N.		26:26
Behold, I say unto you, N.;		26:27
Behold I say unto you, N.;		26:28
N.; but ye have cursed them,		29: 5
Behold, I say unto you, N.;		31:19
N., I have nourished it,	Jac	2:14
I answer you, N.		5:47
N.; he has poured out his spirit	Mos	2:25
I say unto you, N.,		4:20
I say unto you, N., ye have not.		5:14
I say unto you, N., ye have not.		12:37
I say unto you, N.; for if ye		12:37
I say unto you, N., they did not		13:26
Behold, I say unto you, N.,	Al	13:32
I say unto you, N.;		5: 8
I say unto you, N.,		5:25
I say unto you, N., thou knowest		9:19
N., but I will be thy servant.		11:24
N., they would not even make		17:25
Behold, I say unto you, N.,		24: 6
I say unto you, Nay, they are		24:13
Behold, I say unto you, N.,		26:31
And he answered, N.		26:33
Behold, I say unto you, N.;		30:38
Behold I say unto you, N.;		32:18
I say unto you, N.		32:36
N., ye cannot say this; for that		34:11
Behold, I say unto you, N.;		34:34
		40:18

I say unto you, N.;	Al	42:25
n., not amongst all the Nephites.		56:45
Behold I say unto you, N.		60:23
behold, he shall say unto you, N.	He	9:28
N., but on a candlestick, and it	3Ne	12:15
Verily, verily, I say unto you, N.		12:26
Yea, yea; N., nay;		12:37
Nay, n.; for whatsoever cometh		12:37
Behold I say unto you, N.;	Mrm	9:15
N.; Lord, show thyself unto me.	Eth	3:10
Behold I say unto you, N.;	Mro	7:29
Behold I say unto you, N.;		7:37
Verily, I say unto you, N.	DC	84:59
Verily I say unto you, N.;		132:35

NAZARETH
I beheld the city of N.;	1Ne	11:13
and in the city of N.		11:13

NEAR
n. the shore of the Red Sea;	1Ne	2: 5
the borders n. the mouth thereof.		2: 8
came n. unto the house of Laban		4: 7
it was n. the tree of which I was		8:13
in the borders n. the Red Sea.		16:14
they were brought n. even to be		18:18
they were n. to be cast with sorrow		18:18
Come ye n. unto me;		20:16
And the Lord is n.,	2Ne	7: 8
Let him come n. me,		7: 8
My righteousness is n.;		8: 5
and her time is n. to come,		23:22
draw n. unto me with their mouth,		27:25
For behold, the time draweth n.,	Jac	5:29
so bold as to come n. the walls	Mos	7:10
n. to the land of our fathers.		9: 4
he built a tower n. the temple;		11:12
being n. the water a thicket		18: 5
was n. the waters of Mormon;		18:30
tower which was n. the temple.		19: 5
to see a very n. kindred,	Al	10: 7
over n. the borders of the land,		27:14
n. the bank of the river Sidon,		43:27
which was n. the mount Antipas.		47: 9
approach n. the walls of the city.		50: 5
march down n. the seashore;		52:22
came n. the city Bountiful,		52:27
march n. the city of Antiparah;		56:31
and came n. the city Antiparah.		56:33
which was n. to the city.		58:13
wilderness which was n. the city,		58:14
Lamanites did arrive n. the city,		58:29
which is n. the city of Nephihah.		62:18
did pierce him n. the heart.		62:36
which was n. the land Bountiful.	He	4: 5
durst they come n. unto them		5:25
was also n. unto the garden gate		7:10
for it shall not come n. thee.	3Ne	22:14
And I will come n. to you		24: 5
city of Jashon was n. the land	Mrm	2:17
was also n. the city Desolation.		4: 3
was n. the land which is called	Eth	7: 6
was n. the hill Comnor;		14:28
pitched his tents n. unto them;		15: 8
call upon me while I am n.—	DC	88:62
Draw n. unto me and I will		88:63
and I will draw n. unto you;		88:63
dreadful day of the Lord is n.,		110:16
n. the close of the twelfth chapter		135: 4
was come n. to enter into Egypt,	Abr	2:22
great ones which were n. unto it;		3: 2
Kolob, because it is n. unto me,		3: 3
come n. unto the throne of God.		3:10
creation n. to the celestial	Fac	2: 2
they shall know that he is n.,	JS	1:39
"they draw n. to me with		2:19

NEARER
borders which are n. the Red Sea;	1Ne	2: 5

NEAREST
was n. unto the throne of God;	Abr	3: 2

NEAREST 657 NEEDEST

seen, because it is n. unto me.	Abr	3:16
n. to the celestial, or the	Fac	2: 1

NEARLY

n. a south-southeast direction,	1Ne	16:13
n. the same course as in the		16:33
n. eastward from that time forth.		17: 1
wicked, yea, n. unto ripeness;		17:43
n. surrounded by the Lamanites;	Al	22:29
were n. surrounded by water,		22:32
n. bordering upon the seashore,		31: 3
as numerous, n., as were the		43:14
n. the end of the nineteenth		46:37
mount, n. to Lehonti's camp;		47:12
people had n. all become wicked;	3Ne	7: 7
n. all the people of the kingdom,	Eth	9:12
n. two millions of his people,		15: 2
to work for n. a month,	JS	2:56

NEAS

wheat and of barley, and with n.,	Mos	9: 9

NEAT

yet they were n. and comely.	Al	1:27

NECESSARIES

and other n. for the journey,	DC	136: 5

NECESSARILY

ye are n. brought to be humble.	Al	32:12
that all governments n. require	DC	134: 3

NECESSARY

is n. that ye should learn wisdom;	Al	32:12
Is it not as n. that the plan of		39:18
the shedding of blood if it were n.;		48:14
is n. to be done at the time.	DC	20:62
than is n. for their support		42:33
n. that the bishop be present		42:82
It is n. that ye should remain		48: 1
needs be n. that they have		48: 3
It must needs be n. that ye		48: 4
it is n. and expedient in me		71: 1
n. appendages belonging unto		84:29
n. appendages belonging to		84:30
is n. to benefit mine order,		96: 4
n. to call such a council or not.		102:29
all things n. shall be added		106: 3
n. to have other bishops or		107:74
For their salvation is n. and		128:15
is n. in the ushering in of the		128:18
to the n. labors of the day;	JS	2:48

NECESSITIES

for their n. and their wants,	DC	70: 7

NECESSITY

of n. they feel after me.	DC	101: 8
Of n. there are presidents,		107:21
the labor in the vineyard of n.		107:96
the n. of obtaining a scanty	JS	2:23
under the n. of laboring with		2:55
under the n. of taking her		2:58
I was under the n. of leaving		2:61

NECK

and thy n. is an iron sinew,	1Ne	20: 4
thyself from the bands of thy n.,	2Ne	8:25
he shall reach even to the n.;		18: 8
and his yoke from off thy n.,		20:27
and he leadeth them by the n.		26:22
there being a small n. of land	Al	22:32
by the narrow n. which led		63: 5
thyself from the bands of thy n.,	3Ne	20:37
city by the narrow n. of land,	Eth	10:20
herself from the bands of her n.;	DC	113: 9
bands of her n. are the curses		113:10
His head and n. were also bare.	JS	2:31

NECKS

stiffened their n. against the Holy	2Ne	6:10
will stiffen their n. against him,		10: 5
and walk with stretched forth n.		13:16
and the stiffness of their n.	2Ne	25:12
They wear stiff n. and high heads;		28:14
and wear stiff n. and high heads	Jac	2:13
and the stiffness of their n.;	Jar	1: 3
break it off from the n. of thy	DC	109:33
and stiffen not their n. against me,		112:13
had been hanged about their n.,		121:22
and we will fall upon their n.,	Mses	7:63
they shall fall upon our n.,		7:63

NEED

an oath, that he n. not fear;	1Ne	4:33
ye have n. that I, your younger		7: 8
having n. of much nourishment,		18:19
the righteous n. not fear;		22:17
the righteous n. not fear,		22:22
they who n. fear, and tremble,		22:23
ye n. not suppose that I and my		22:31
they n. not look forward any more	2Ne	25:18
they n. not harden their hearts		25:27
received, and we n. no more!		28:27
we n. no more of the word of God,		28:29
and we n. no more Bible,		29: 6
ye n. not suppose that I cannot		29: 9
ye n. not suppose that it contains		29:10
neither n. ye suppose that I have		29:10
ye n. not suppose that the Gentiles		30: 1
should have n. to be baptized by		31: 5
then, how much more n. have we,		31: 5
that stand in n. of your succor;	Mos	4:16
unto him that standeth in n.;		4:16
those that stand in n. of comfort,		18: 9
to those priests that stood in n.,		18:28
they n. not fear nor tremble,	Al	1: 4
whatsoever they stood in n.—		1:29
as to those who stood in n.		1:30
who stood in n. of their succor,		4:13
whatsoever things ye stand in n.,		7:23
I n. not rehearse the matter;		13:20
to those who stand in n.—		34:28
ye stand in n. to be nourished by		39:10
I n. not rehearse unto you		56: 4
ye n. not suppose that the		60:13
and ye have great n. to marvel;	He	7:15
what things ye have n. of	3Ne	13: 8
ye have n. of all these things.		13:32
ye n. not say that the Lord		29: 2
ye n. not imagine in your hearts		29: 3
ye n. not any longer spurn at		29: 8
and ye n. not any longer hiss,		29: 8
ye n. not suppose that ye can		29: 9
no one n. say they shall not	Mrm	8:26
things soever ye shall stand in n.		9:27
the whole n. no physician, but	Mro	8: 8
little children n. no repentance,		8:11
that little children n. baptism		8:14
that little children n. baptism		8:20
to my church n. not fear,	DC	10:55
you n. not suppose that you are		11:15
every man who has n. may be		42:33
wasteth flesh and hath no n.		49:21
things the disciples may n.		57: 8
no n. to break the laws of		58:21
And also he hath n. to repent,		58:41
you have n. of all these things.		84:83
it hath no n. of the feet;		84:109
body hath n. of every member,		84:110
hath n. to be chastened,		93:50
what n. hath my lord of this		101:47
What n. hath my lord of this		101:48
there is no n. of these things.		101:49
I have n. of this to help me		104:72
when they n. assistance,		107:38
no one n. suppose me guilty	JS	2:28

NEEDED

if it were n., I would guard thee	Al	18:21
Joseph tarry at home, for he is n.	DC	124:102
person n. wisdom from God,	JS	2:12

NEEDEST

what thou n. for food and for	DC	24:18
And thou n. not fear, for thy		25: 9

NEEDETH

NEEDETH
he n. to accomplish the work	DC	43:13

NEEDFUL
more than is n. for the wants	DC	51:13
it is not n. for this whole		61: 3
that which is n. for clothing.		61:11
that which is not n. with him,		61:12
than is n. for their necessities		70: 7
prepare every n. thing,		88:119
cease to sleep longer than is n.;		88:124
not n. that the Apocrypha		91: 3
it is not n. that it should be		91: 6
prepare every n. thing,		109: 8
prepared to obtain every n. thing;		109:15
it was n. that he should seal		136:39
n. for me to obtain another	Abr	1: 1

NEEDS
it must n. be that he flee	1Ne	3:18
it must n. be that we should		10:13
they must n. be filthy;		15:33
it must n. be that they		15:33
there must n. be a place of		15:34
it must n. be a good thing		17:25
it must n. be that we know		19:21
it must n. be upon the		22:18
And it must n. be that the	2Ne	1:27
For it must n. be, that there is		2:11
things must n. be a compound		2:11
it must n. remain as dead,		2:11
it must n. have been created for		2:12
must n. destroy the wisdom of		2:12
it must n. be that there was		2:15
must n. suppose that an angel		2:17
there must n. be a power of		9: 6
the resurrection must n. come unto		9: 6
it must n. be an infinite		9: 7
must n. have remained to an		9: 7
it must n. be expedient that		9:48
it must n. be expedient that		10: 3
must n. destroy the secret works		10:15
there must n. be more than this,		10:21
it must n. be expedient that		25:16
it must n. be that the Gentiles		26:12
must n. be stirred up unto		28:19
they must n. fall; for God hath	Jac	4:14
it must n. be that I write a	Jar	1: 2
according to their n. and	Mos	18:29
It must n. be that this is a good	Al	32:28
you must n. say that the seed is		32:30
ye must n. know that the seed is		32:33
there must n. be a space betwixt		40: 6
as we must n. suppose.		46:41
it must n. be that they must be	3Ne	5: 1
it must n. be that all things		5: 2
it must n. be that he must		23: 2
must n. be a change wrought		28:37
it n. be that they must taste of		28:37
it must n. be that some had	Eth	12: 7
faith he must n. have hope;	Mro	7:42
he must n. have charity;		7:44
he must n. have charity.		7:44
hope ye must n. be in despair;		10:22
it must n. be that the children	DC	18: 6
it must n. be that the devil		29:39
it must n. be that the riches		38:39
must n. flee unto Zion for		45:68
it must n. be necessary that		48: 3
It must n. be necessary that		48: 4
before me and must n. repent.		49: 2
it must n. be that he receive		51: 1
it must n. be that they be		51: 2
and his wants and n.		51: 3
must n. pay the money,		56:12
must n. be sent unto the		75:24
it must n. be that there be		78: 3
to his wants and his n.,		82:17
must n. remain through you		86:10
it must n. be sanctified from		88:18
and must n. stand rebuked		93:47
Your family must n. repent		93:48
ye must n. be chastened	DC	95: 2
that must n. be chastened,		97: 6
must n. be chastened and tried,		101: 4
they must n. be chastened—		101:41
my word must n. be fulfilled.		101:64
have said unto you must n. be,		101:93
Zion must n. come by power;		103:15
n. be led out of bondage		103:17
But it must n. be done in mine		104:16
people must n. be chastened		105: 6
obedience, if it must n. be,		105: 6
must n. be presiding elders		107:60
must n. be that one be appointed		107:65
if it must n. be, for their support,		124:122

NEEDY
turn away the n. from judgement,	2Ne	20: 2
the n. shall lie down in safety;		24:30
yea, and to every n., naked soul.	Mos	18:28
to the poor, and the n., and the	Al	1:27
turning their backs upon the n.		4:12
substance to the poor and the n.,		4:13
backs upon the poor, and the n.,		5:55
if ye turn away the n.,		34:28
than ye love the poor and the n.,	Mrm	8:37
suffer the hungry, and the n.,		8:39
look to the poor and the n.,	DC	38:35
to the poor and the n.,		42:34
poor and the n. of my church,		42:37
visit the poor and the n.		44: 6
poor and n. of my church;		51: 5
the poor and the n.,		52:40
the church, to the poor and n.		72:12
unto the poor and the n.,		104:18
all the poor, the n., and afflicted		109:55
the cause of the poor and the n.;		124:75

NEFARIOUS
n. and murderous impositions	DC	123: 5

NEGLECT
But if ye n. the tree, and take	Al	32:38
great has been your n. towards us.		60: 5
of this exceeding great n.;		60: 6
of your exceeding great n.		60: 9
great n. towards their brethren,		60:14
n. the more weighty matters?	DC	117: 8
or through any n. of mine,	JS	2:59

NEGLECTED
but behold, ye have n. them	Al	60:10
Or is it that ye have n. us		60:19

NEHOR
and his name was N.;	Al	1:15
who was slain by the hand of N.		2:20
who was slain by the hand of N.		6: 7
after the order and faith of N.,		14:16
who were of the profession of N.;		14:18
they were of the profession of N.,		15:15
they were of the profession of N.,		16:11
or who were of the order of N.,		24:29
and dwelt in the land of N.;	Eth	7: 4
he returned to the city N.		7: 9
N., my brother, took Milcah to	Abr	2: 2

NEHORS
it was called Desolation of N.;	Al	16:11
after the order of the N.;		21: 4
were after the order of the N.		21: 4
were after the order of the N.		24:28

NEIGHBOR
and every one by his n.;	2Ne	13: 5
dig a pit for thy n.;		28: 8
which have afflicted your n.,	Jac	2:20
among you borroweth of his n.	Mos	4:28
cause thy n. to commit sin also.		4:28
an ass which belongeth to his n.,		5:14
bear false witness against thy n.		13:23
should love his n. as himself,		23:15
should esteem his n. as himself,		27: 4

NEIGHBOR

false witness against your n.,	He	7:21
that thou shalt love thy n. and	3Ne	12:43
voice, every man to his n.,	DC	38:41
shalt not speak evil of thy n.,		42:27
take his sword against his n.		45:68
love thy n. as thyself.		59: 6
seeking the interest of his n.,		82:19
hath been warned to warn his n.		88:81
If thou borrowest of thy n.,		136:25
Go straightway and tell thy n.,		136:25
find that which thy n. has lost,		136:26

NEIGHBORHOOD

the n. in which my servant Joseph	DC	124:105
most elevated of any in the n.	JS	2:51
the n. where my father resided,		2:66
manifested itself in the n.		2:74

NEIGHBORING

with my little sons to a n. city,	Al	56:30
carrying provisions to a n. city.		56:30

NEIGHBOR'S

shalt not covet thy n. house,	Mos	13:24
thou shalt not covet thy n. wife		13:24
nor anything that is thy n.		13:24
forgiveth not his n. trespasses		26:31
shalt not covet thy n. wife;	DC	19:25
nor seek thy n. life.		19:25

NEITHER

N. did they believe that	1Ne	2:13
n. should they be dimmed		5:19
n. at any time shall I give		6: 1
N. will he suffer that		13:31
N. will the Lord God suffer		13:32
n. should they be scattered		15:20
n. could the temptations		15:24
n. would they believe that I		17:18
n. should they withhold their		17:49
n. durst they lay their hands upon		17:52
n. did I build the ship after		18: 2
n. shall the heat nor the sun		21:10
n. wickedness, neither holiness	2Ne	2:11
wickedness, n. holiness nor misery,		2:11
nor misery, n. good nor bad.		2:11
having no life n. death,		2:11
n. sense nor insensibility.		2:11
we are not, n. the earth;		2:13
n. to act nor to be acted upon;		2:13
rebellious, n. turned away back.		7: 5
n. be ye afraid of their revilings.		8: 7
n. that taketh her by the hand,		8:18
perisheth not, n. can be corrupted.		9:51
n. shall they learn war any more.		12: 4
n. is there any end of their		12: 7
n. is there any end of their		12: 7
there is n. bread nor clothing;		13: 7
n. consider the operation of his		15:12
n. shall the girdle of their loins be		15:27
fear not, n. be faint-hearted		17: 4
n. shall it come to pass.		17: 7
n. will I tempt the Lord.		17:12
n. fear the fear,		18:12
n. do they seek the Lord of Hosts.		19:13
n. shall have mercy on their		19:17
n. doth his heart think so;		20: 7
n. reprove after the hearing of his		21: 3
n. shall it be dwelt in from		23:20
n. shall the Arabian		23:20
n. shall the shepherds make their		23:20
n. shall he deliver the book.		27:10
n. shall his face now wax pale.		27:33
n. shall it be until the end of man,		29: 9
n. from that time henceforth and		29: 9
n. need ye suppose that I have		29:10
n. can I write but a few of the		31: 1
ye ask not, n. do ye knock;		32: 4
n. am I mighty in writing,		33: 1
n. shall ye revile against them	Jac	3: 9
not with sorrow, n. with contempt,		4: 3
there is no Christ, n. has been,		7: 9
n. did they blaspheme.	Jar	1: 5
has been written, n. prophecy;	Om	1:11
N. have I suffered that ye should	Mos	2:13
n. do I tell these things that		2:15
n. are there any conditions		4: 8
n. will ye suffer that they		4:14
n. do they desire that she should		8:20
n. will I deliver them out of their		11:25
n. have I told you that which		13: 3
n. was any deceit in his mouth.		14: 9
yea, n. can the Lord redeem such;		15:27
n. did the brethren of Amulon		24: 5
n. the law of Moses;		24: 5
n. could they all hear the word		25:20
n. did they believe concerning		26: 2
n. would they join the church.		26: 4
n. would Aaron take upon him		29: 3
n. were any of the sons of		29: 3
n. should we have any right to		29: 8
n. had he delighted in the		29:40
n. durst they rob, nor murder,	Al	1:18
n. was the teacher any better		1:26
n. doth he vary from that which		7:20
n. hath he a shadow of turning		7:20
n. can filthiness or anything		7:21
n. was it possible that any man		8:31
n. did they measure after the		11: 4
n. has God saved them because		14:15
n. did they know anything		17:35
n. can they scatter the king's		18: 3
n. will I return to the land of		20:15
n. do we believe that thy fathers		21: 8
n. should they spit upon them,		23: 2
n. should they cast stones at		23: 2
n. against any of their brethren.		23: 7
n. were any of the Amulonites;		23:14
n. would they turn aside to the		24:23
n. shall they be harrowed up by		26: 6
n. shall they be driven with fierce		26: 6
n. were the dead of the Nephites		30: 2
n. has any of my brethren, save		30:33
n. would they observe the		31:10
hunger not, n. should they thirst;		31:38
n. must ye lay aside your faith,		32:36
n. is it because the fruit thereof		32:39
hunger not, n. shall he thirst.		32:42
not a sacrifice of man, n. of beast,		34:10
n. of any manner of fowl;		34:10
n. had I the use of my limbs.		36:10
of the first offense, n. the second,		43:46
n. do we desire to bring any one		44: 2
n. could they come upon them		49: 4
know not such a being; n. do ye;		54:21
n. durst they with a part, lest		56:24
N. durst they march down against		56:25
n. durst they cross the head of		56:25
n. did Antipus overtake them;		56:38
n. would I turn to the right nor		56:40
n. was there one soul among them		57:25
n. do those men who came up		58:34
n. were they slow to remember		62:49
n. on the north, nor on the south,	He	1:31
n. was there much contention		3: 2
n. durst they come near unto		5:25
n. was it a voice of a great		5:30
n. did it take hold upon the walls		5:44
marvel not, n. should they doubt.		5:49
their stones n. with their arrows.		16: 2
n. did they come again in the	3Ne	4:15
n. candles, neither torches;		8:21
neither candles, n. torches;		8:21
n. could there be fire kindled		8:21
was not any light seen, n. fire,		8:22
n. the sun, nor the moon, nor		8:22
n. were they fallen upon and		10:13
n. were they overpowered by		10:13
n. was it a loud voice;		11: 3
n. shall there be disputations		11:28
n. by heaven, for it is God's		12:34
N. shalt thou swear by the head,		12:36
n. will your Father forgive your		13:15
n. moth nor rust doth corrupt,		13:20

NEITHER

they sow not, n. do they reap	3Ne	13:26
they toil not, n. do they spin;		13:28
n. cast ye your pearls before		14: 6
n. a corrupt tree bring forth good		14:18
N. at any time hath the Father		15:15
n. of the land of Jerusalem,		16: 1
n. in any parts of that land		16: 1
n. have I at any time		16: 2
never seen, n. hath the ear heard,		17:16
n. can there be written by any		17:17
n. can the hearts of men conceive		17:17
n. can be written by man the		19:32
n. can they be uttered by man.		19:34
n. have they heard so great		19:36
had been no bread, n. wine,		20: 6
disciples, n. by the multitude;		20: 6
n. be thou confounded, for thou		22: 4
n. shall the covenant of my		22:10
n. shall your vine cast her fruit		24:11
leave them n. root nor branch.		25: 1
n. sorrow save it be for the sins		28: 9
n. was it given unto them power		28:14
n. were there Lamanites, nor	4Ne	1:17
shall not smite, n. shall he judge;	Mrm	8:20
n. wild beasts nor poisonous		8:24
n. shadow of changing?		9: 9
n. my father, because of his		9:31
n. them who have written before		9:31
n. shall ye take fire with you,	Eth	2:23
n. whale that could mar them;		6:10
that n. would the sons of Jared,		6:27
n. doth he will that man should		8:19
n. at any time hath any		12:18
n. his fair sons nor daughters;		13:17
n. the fair sons and daughters		13:17
n. the fair sons and daughters		13:17
repented not, n. his household,		13:22
his household, n. the people;		13:22
not borrow n. would he lend;		14: 2
N. did they receive any unto	Mro	6: 2
n. will he give a good gift.		7:10
n. can a good fountain bring		7:11
no, not one; n. do his angels;		7:17
n. do they who subject		7:17
n. have angels ceased to		7:29
need no repentance, no baptism.		8:11
hath n. faith, hope, no charity;		8:14
n. a changeable being;		8:18
sparing none, n. old nor young;		9:19
cannot tell, n. can it be written.		9:19
n. can ye be saved in the		10:21
n. can ye if ye have no hope.		10:21
n. ear that shall not hear,	DC	1: 2
n. heart that shall not be		1: 2
n. the voice of his servants,		1:14
n. give heed to the words of		1:14
n. trust in the arm of flesh—		1:19
n. can they come to naught.		3: 1
n. doth he turn to the right		3: 2
n. doth he vary from that which		3: 2
n. of you have I condemned.		9:12
n. keep my commandments		10:56
n. adding to, nor diminishing		20:35
n. hardness with each other,		20:54
n. lying, backbiting, nor evil		20:54
n. teachers nor deacons have		20:58
n. by your dead works.		22: 2
nor purse nor scrip, n. staves,		24:18
neither staves, n. two coats.		24:18
not purchase wine n. strong drink		27: 3
n. shall anything be appointed		28:12
one hair, n. mote, shall be lost,		29:25
works have no end, n. beginning;		29:33
n. any man, nor the children of		29:34
n. Adam, your father, whom I		29:34
temporal, n. carnal nor sensual.		29:35
n. your hearts of unbelief;		38:14
n. the angels in heaven, nor		49: 7
n. of a man traveling on		49:22
n. with boasting nor rejoicing,		50:33
n. journey in another's track.		52:33
n. commit adultery, nor kill,		59: 6
not to excess, n. by extortion.		59:20
n. shalt thou bury thy talent	DC	60:13
n. in wrath nor with strife.		60:14
the law, n. the commandment;		64:15
the carnal n. natural mind,		67:10
N. can any natural man abide		67:12
of God, n. after the carnal mind.		67:12
n. the ministering of angels;		67:13
them not, n. take therefrom.		68:34
the church, n. unto the world;		70: 6
n. the bishop, neither the agent		70:11
n. the agent who keepeth the		70:11
n. he who is appointed in		70:11
not tarry, n. be idle but labor		75: 3
n. are there any who can stay		76: 3
n. the place thereof, nor		76:45
N. was it revealed, neither is		76:46
n. is, neither will be		76:46
n. will be revealed unto man,		76:46
n. any man except those who		76:48
n. the testimony of Jesus.		76:82
n. the testimony of Jesus,		76:101
of Jesus, n. the prophets,		76:101
n. the everlasting covenant		76:101
N. is man capable to make them		76:116
Hurt not the earth, n. the sea,		77: 9
break, n. can it be moved.		84:40
n. speak them before the		84:73
purse or scrip, n. two coats.		84:78
weary in mind, n. darkened,		84:80
n. in body, limb, nor joint;		84:80
shall not go hungry, n. athirst.		84:80
they toil not, n. do they spin		84:82
N. take ye thought beforehand		84:85
N. is their genealogy to be kept		85: 4
n. the names of the fathers,		85: 5
n. rejoices in him who is the		88:33
by law, n. by mercy, justice,		88:35
n. again, until the end of the		88:101
behold it is not good, n. meet in		89: 5
for the body, n. for the belly,		89: 8
world, n. in the world to come;		90: 3
nor ashamed, n. confounded;		90:17
n. with my servant Sidney		90:35
or made, n. indeed can be.		93:29
n. be moved out of her place,		97:19
against them, n. seek revenge,		98:23
upon you, n. upon your family,		98:28
n. the second nor the third		98:35
n. shall there be any other place		101:20
n. the life of the body;		101:37
not God, n. regarded man.		101:82
n. shall the seal be loosed		104:64
n. boast of faith nor of mighty		105:24
the Twelve, n. to the Seventy,		107:98
n. my servant Sidney,		115:13
n. my servant Hyrum,		115:13
n. charge thee with transgression,		121:10
n. fulfil the promises which ye		124:47
n. can any other man,		124:72
n. let his heart faint;		124:75
n. can we without our dead be		128:15
n. can they without us be		128:18
N. can they nor we be made		128:18
n. in nor after the resurrection,		132:13
they n. marry nor are given in		132:16
is not valid n. of force when they		132:18
saith the Lord, n. by my word;		132:18
n. do ye know me.		132:22
n. do they abide in my law.		132:25
ye know n. the day nor the hour.		133:11
the ear, n. hath any eye seen,		133:45
leave them n. root nor branch.		133:64
n. my power to deliver.		133:67
n. preach the gospel to, nor		134:12
end to my works, n. to my words	Mses	1:38
n. in the water, neither in the		3: 5
in the water, n. in the air;		3: 5
n. shall ye touch it, lest ye die.		4: 9
voice of the Lord, n. to Abel,		5:26
N. let him who is in the field	JS	1:15
n. on the Sabbath day;		1:17
not deny it, n. dared I do it;		2:25
leave them n. root nor branch.		2:37

NEITHER 661 NEPHI

n. the breastplate with the Urim	JS 2:42
not yet arrived, n. would it,	2:53

NEPHEW

and remnant, and son, and n.,	2Ne 24:22

NEPHI

THE PLATES OF N.	T Pg
record of the people of N.,	T Pg
THE FIRST BOOK OF N.	1Ne 1:hd
Lamen, Lemuel, Sam, and N.	1:hd
N. taketh his brethren	1:hd
according to the account of N.;	1:hd
I, N., wrote this record.	1:hd
I, N., having been born of	1: 1
I, N., do not make a full account	1:16
I, N., will show unto you	1:20
I, N., being exceeding young,	2:16
Blessed art thou, N., because	2:19
I, N., returned from speaking	3: 1
I, N., said unto my father:	3: 7
I, N., and my brethren took our	3: 9
I, N., crept into the city	4: 5
when I, N., had heard these words,	4:14
I, N., being a man large in	4:31
I, N., do not give the genealogy	6: 1
I, N., and my brethren, should	7: 2
I, N., did again, with my brethren,	7: 3
me, N., and Sam, and their father,	7: 6
I, N., being grieved for the	7: 8
when I, N., had spoken these words	7:16
rejoice in the Lord because of N.	8: 3
mother, Sariah, and Sam, and N.;	8:14
I, N., do not speak all the	8:29
I have given the name of N.;	9: 2
they are called the plates of N.,	9: 2
also are called the plates of N.	9: 2
I, N., proceed to give an account	10: 1
I, N., having heard all the words	10:17
I, N., was desirous also that	10:17
blessed art thou, N., because	11: 6
N., what beholdest thou?	11:14
I, N., saw that he was lifted	11:33
I, N., also saw many of the fourth	12:12
I, N., beheld that the Gentiles	13:16
I, N., beheld that the Gentiles	13:19
I, N., beheld that they did prosper	13:20
I, N., beheld it;	13:23
the angel spake unto me, N.,	14: 5
I, N., beheld the power of	14:14
I, N., heard and bear record,	14:27
I, N., am forbidden that	14:28
after I, N., had been carried	15: 1
I, N., was grieved because of	15: 4
I, N., spake much unto them	15:19
I, N., did exhort them to give heed	15:25
after I, N., had made an end of	16: 1
I, N., did exhort my brethren,	16: 4
I, N., took one of the daughters	16: 7
I, N., had been blessed of the Lord	16: 8
I, N., went forth to slay food,	16:18
I, N., having been afflicted with	16:21
I, N., did speak much unto my	16:22
I, N., did make out of wood a bow,	16:23
I, N., beheld the pointers which	16:28
I, N., did go forth up into the	16:30
and also our brother N.,	16:37
I, N., had been in the land of	17: 7
I, N., did make a bellows	17:11
I, N., did strive to keep the	17:15
I, N., was exceeding sorrowful	17:19
I, N., spake unto them, saying:	17:23
I, N., said unto them that	17:49
I, N., said many things unto my	17:52
I, N., did not work the timbers	18: 2
I, N., did go into the mount oft,	18: 3
I, N., began to fear exceedingly	18:10
I, N., began to speak to them	18:10
I, N., did guide the ship,	18:22
I, N., received a commandment	19: 1
I, N., did make a record upon	19: 4
I, N., have written these things	19:18
I, N., did teach my brethren	1Ne 19:22
I, N., had read these things	22: 1
I, N., said unto them:	22: 2
I, N., declare unto you,	22:21
I, N., say unto you that	22:27
I, N., make an end;	22:29
THE SECOND BOOK OF N.	2Ne 1:hd
The Lord warns N. to depart	1:hd
I, N., had made an end of teaching	1: 1
hearken unto the voice of N.	1:28
art a true friend unto my son, N.,	1:30
dwell safely with thy brother, N.	2: 3
unto the words of thy brother, N.;	3:25
And now, I, N., speak concerning	4: 1
the land like unto thy brother N.	4:11
For I, N., was constrained to	4:14
I, N., did cry much unto the	5: 1
that I, N., should depart from them	5: 5
that I, N., did take my family,	5: 6
call the name of the place N.;	5: 8
wherefore, we did call it N.	5: 8
call themselves the people of N.	5: 9
I, N., had also brought the records	5:12
I, N., did take the sword of Laban,	5:14
And I, N., did build a temple;	5:16
I, N., did cause my people to be	5:17
But I, N., was desirous that they	5:18
I, N., did consecrate Jacob and	5:26
I, N., had kept the records upon	5:29
I, N., to be obedient to the	5:31
of Jacob, the brother of N.,	6: 1
he spake unto the propIe of N.:	6: 1
consecrated by my brother N.,	6: 2
I, N., write more of the words of	11: 2
Now I, N., do speak somewhat	25: 1
I, N., have not taught them many	25: 1
I, N., have not taught my children	25: 6
For I, N., have seen it,	26: 7
which I have made unto thee, N.,	29: 2
I, N., would not suffer that ye	30: 1
And now I, N., make an end of	31: 1
And now I, N., cannot say more;	32: 7
I, N., cannot write all the things	33: 1
I, N., have written what I have	33: 3
THE BROTHER OF N.	Jac 1:hd
the history of the people of N.	1:hd
wherefore, N. gave me, Jacob,	1: 1
which are called the people of N.	1: 2
commandment of my brother N.	1: 8
Now N. began to be old,	1: 9
people having loved N. exceedingly,	1:10
called by the people, second N.,	1:11
Nephi, third N., and so forth,	1:11
And it came to pass that N. died.	1:12
seed to destroy the people of N.,	1:14
and those who are friendly to N.	1:14
call Nephites, or the people of N.,	1:14
the people of N., under the reign	1:15
this people, by the hand of N.	1:18
which Jacob, the brother of N.,	2: 1
spake unto the people of N.,	2: 1
of Nephi, after the death of N.:	2: 1
things unto the people of N.	3:12
were made by the hand of N.	3:14
a man among the people of N.,	7: 1
the people of N. did fortify against	7:25
kept on the other plates of N.,	7:26
my brother N. had commanded	7:27
about among the people of N.	En 1:19
the people of N. did seek diligently	1:20
the people of N. did till the land,	1:21
the people of N. had waxed	Jar 1: 5
did threaten the people of N.,	1:10
go to the other plates of N.	1:14
should flee out of the land of N.,	Om 1:12
to return to the land of N.;	1:27
abridgment from the plates of N.,	WM 1: 3
also many of the words of N.	1: 3
shall take from the plates of N.;	1: 5
which I take from the plates of N.;	1: 9
came down out of the land of N.,	1:13
And behold, also the plates of N.,	Mos 1: 6

NEPHI

and also the plates of N.;	Mos 1:16	unto them in the land of N.,	Al 27:20
went down into the land of N.	7: 6	the land Jershon and the land N.,	27:23
who were in the land of N.,	7: 7	they were among the people of N.,	27:27
a knowledge of the land of N.,	9: 1	slaughter among the people of N.;	28: 3
of my reign in the land of N.,	9:14	the people of N. returned again	28: 3
even into the city of N.,	9:15	among all the people of N.—	28: 4
N. was more faithful in keeping	10:13	the judges over the people of N.;	28: 7
towards the children of N.	10:17	their journeyings in the land of N.,	28: 8
a resort for the children of N.	11:13	have been up to the land of N.	29:14
he also being a descendant of N.	17: 2	the judges over the people of N.)	30: 2
them back to the land of N.,	19:15	the judges over the people of N.	30: 4
would return to the land of N.,	19:19	the judges over the people of N.	35:12
about to return to the land of N.,	19:22	done, upon the plates of N.,	37: 2
they returned to the land of N.,	19:24	saw that the people of N., or	43:19
to return to the city of N.,	20: 3	the judges over the people of N.	44:24
they went up to the land of N.	20: 7	written upon the plates of N.	44:24
people returned to the city of N.,	21: 1	*account of the people of N.*,	45:hd
returned again to the city of N.	21:12	the people of N. were	45: 1
come into the land of N. by night,	21:21	the judges over the people of N.,	45: 2
returned to the land of N.,	21:26	even until the people of N. shall	45:11
in search of the land of N.	23:35	among the people of N.,	45:13
way which led to the land of N.	23:36	among the people of N.	45:13
way that led to the land of N.	23:37	the judges over the people of N.,	45:20
of them went to the land of N.;	23:38	possessed by the people of N.	45:22
the language of N. began to	24: 4	were the affairs of the people of N.	46: 7
so many of the children of N.,	25: 2	departed into the land of N.	46:29
who were descendants of N.,	25: 2	and went up in the land of N.	47: 1
so many of the people of N.	25: 3	anger against the people of N.,	47: 1
the people of N. were assembled	25: 4	to the land of N., to the city of	47:20
upon themselves the name of N.	25:12	land of Nephi, to the city of N.,	47:20
might be called the children of N.	25:12	he entered the city N. with	47:31
those who were descendants of N.	25:13	from the reign of N. down to the	47:35
and in the land of N.;	27:16	against the people of N.	48: 1
go up to the land of N. that they	28: 1	down out of the land of N.,	49:10
might go up to the land of N.	28: 5	returned to the land of N.,	49:25
and also the plates of N.,	28:11	the people of N. did thank the	49:28
gone up to the land of N.,	29: 3	the judges over the people of N.	49:29
of the kings over the people of N.;	29:47	the land of N. did run in a	50: 8
Judge over the people of N.,	Al 1:hd	Zarahemla and the land of N.,	50:11
judges over the people of N.,	1: 1	were the people of N. in the	50:17
peace among the people of N.	1:33	the judges over the people of N.	50:17
governor of the people of N.,	2:16	been verified to the people of N.;	50:21
in the course of the land of N.,	2:24	time among the people of N.,	50:23
the people of N. took their tents,	2:26	of Nephi, since the days of N.,	50:23
who consisted of N., Jacob, and	3: 6	peace among the people of N.,	50:25
the Nephites, or the people of N.,	3:11	among the people of N.,	50:32
the words which he said to N.:	3:14	the judges over the people of N.	50:35
the promises of the Lord unto N.	3:17	people of N. had peace restored	50:37
came in upon the people of N.,	3:20	year, over the people of N.	50:40
the judges over the people of N.,	4: 1	the judges over the people of N.,	51: 1
the judges over the people of N.;	4: 5	to be among the people of N.;	51: 9
or among the people of N.,	4:19	the judges over the people of N.;	51:37
the judges over the people of N.,	4:20	the judges over the people of N.	52: 1
which was in the borders of N.;	5: 3	the judges over the people of N.	52:14
the judges over the people of N.	8: 2	the judges over the people of N.	52:18
the judges over the people of N.,	8: 3	beloved by all the people of N.	53: 2
the custom of the people of N.	8: 7	the Lamanites in the land of N.;	53: 6
who are called the people of N.,	9:19	the judges over the people of N.	53:23
Aminadi was a descendant of N.,	10: 3	which is the land of N.	54: 6
the judges over the people of N.)	14:23	a war against the people of N.	55: 1
the judges over the people of N.	15:19	the judges over the people of N.	55:35
the judges over the people of N.	16: 1	down out of the land of N.—	56: 3
the judges over the people of N.	16:12	at this time in the land of N.;	56:12
did the people of N. have	16:12	we, the people of N., the people	56:54
the judges over the people of N.	16:21	have fled to the land of N.	58:38
and went up to the land of N.	17:hd	the judges over the people of N.,	59: 1
to go up to the land of N.	17: 8	the judges over the people of N.;	62:11
him forth to the land of N.;	18: 9	the judges over the people of N.	62:12
feast appointed at the land of N.,	18: 9	the judges over the people of N.;	62:39
hast had upon the people of N.,	18:41	of iniquity among the people of N.;	62:40
go with him to the land of N.,	20: 1	among the people of N.	62:42
shalt not go up to the land of N.,	20: 2	people of N. began to prosper	62:48
led by the Spirit to the land of N.,	22: 1	the judges over the people of N.	62:52
on the west, in the land of N.;	22:28	the judges over the people of N.,	63: 1
on the west in the land of N.,	22:28	the judges over the people of N.	63:16
and thus the land of N. and the	22:32	the judges over the people of N.,	He 1: 1
possessions only in the land of N.,	22:34	governor over the people of N.	1: 5
who were in the city of N.;	23:11	known among the people of N.,	1:12
and came up to the land of N.	24:20	the judges over the people of N.	2:12
of Ishmael and the land of N.,	25:13	destruction of the people of N.	2:13
we go up to the land of N.,	26:23	mean the end of the book of N.,	2:14
returned again to the land of N.	27: 1	contention among the people of N.	3: 1
which divided the land of N. from	27:14	among the people of N.	3:17

NEPHI

unto the eldest the name of N.,	He 3:21
the judges over the people of N.	3:22
N. began to reign in his stead.	3:37
away into the land of N.,	4:12
and also N. and Lehi, who were	4:14
N. delivered up the judgment-seat	5: 1
N. had become weary because of	5: 4
among all the people of N.,	5:14
forth among all the people of N.	5:16
N. and Lehi did preach unto the	5:18
N. and Lehi did proceed from	5:20
thence to go to the land of N.	5:20
N. and Lehi were encircled about	5:23
N. and Lehi were not burned;	5:23
N. and Lehi did stand forth	5:26
the faces of N. and Lehi;	5:36
behold the faces of N. and Lehi.	5:37
N. and Lehi were in the midst of	5:44
and also N. and Lehi went into	6: 6
the judges over the people of N.	6:32
the judges over the people of N.	6:41
THE PROPHECY OF N.,	7:hd
God threatens the people of N.	7:hd
God smiteth the people of N.	7:hd
N., the son of Helaman, returned	7: 1
and when N. saw it, his heart was	7: 6
when my father N. first came out	7: 7
which was in the garden of N.,	7:10
N. had bowed himself upon the	7:10
saw N. as he was pouring out	7:11
when N. arose he beheld the	7:12
when N. had said these words,	8: 1
N. had spoken unto them	8: 3
many things did N. speak which	8: 3
the people to anger against N.,	8: 7
who sought to destroy N.	8:10
N. also testified of these things,	8:22
when N. had spoken these words,	9: 1
the words which N. had spoken	9: 4
judgments which N. had spoken	9: 5
together at the garden of N.;	9: 8
who were at the garden of N.,	9:11
things even as N. had testified,	9:14
according to the words of N.	9:15
and did cry out against N.,	9:16
we know that this N. must have	9:16
they had spoken against N.,	9:18
caused that N. should be taken	9:19
But N. said unto them:	9:21
Has N., the pretended prophet,	9:27
that I, N., know nothing	9:36
even according as N. had said	9:37
set at liberty, and also was N.	9:38
believed on the words of N.;	9:39
who said that N. was a prophet.	9:40
their ways, leaving N. alone,	10: 1
N. went his way towards his	10: 2
Blessed art thou, N., for those	10: 4
thou art N., and I am God.	10: 6
had spoken these words unto N.,	10:12
miracle which N. had done in	10:13
N. did declare unto them the word	10:14
when N. had declared unto them	10:15
the judges over the people of N.	10:19
land among all the people of N.	11: 1
N. did cry unto the Lord, saying:	11: 3
according to the words of N.	11: 5
land, among all the people of N.	11: 5
to remember the words of N.	11: 7
that they would say unto N.:	11: 8
that the judges did say unto N.,	11: 9
when N. saw that the people had	11: 9
did no more seek to destroy N.,	11:18
people of N. began to prosper	11:20
N. and Lehi, and many of their	11:23
the judges over the people of N.,	11:24
dissenters from the people of N.,	11:24
among the people of N.,	11:27
the judges over the people of N.	11:29
who are called the people of N.	15: 3
the people of N. hath he loved,	15: 3
went forth and sought for N.;	He 16: 1
away unto N. to be baptized.	16: 3
behold, N. was baptizing, and	16: 4
the judges over the people of N.	16: 9
the judges over the people of N.	16:24
THE BOOK OF N.	3Ne 1:hd
THE SON OF N., WHO WAS	1:hd
being a descendant of N. who	1:hd
N., the son of Helaman, had	1: 2
giving charge unto his son N.,	1: 2
his son N. did keep the records	1: 3
when N., the son of Nephi, saw	1:10
son of N., saw this wickedness	1:10
the words which came unto N.	1:15
N. went forth among the people,	1:23
And N., who was the father of	2: 9
N., who was the father of N.,	2: 9
robbers and the people of N.	2:17
the people of N. did gain some	2:17
forth against the people of N.;	2:18
wickedness of the people of N.	2:18
round about the people of N.;	4:16
should cut off the people of N.	4:16
true account was given by N.	5: 9
according to the record of N.,	5:10
were called the plates of N.	5:10
the affairs of the people of N.	7:13
N.—having been visited by	7:15
N. did minister with power	7:17
N. did cry unto the people in	7:23
there were ordained of N., men	7:25
people of N. who were spared,	10:18
himself unto the people of N.,	11:hd
together, of the people of N.,	11: 1
to pass that he spake unto N.	11:18
N. was among the multitude)	11:18
And N. arose and went forth,	11:19
had spoken these words unto N.,	12: 1
N. and his brother whom he had	19: 4
N. went down into the water and	19:11
to pass that he said unto N.:	23: 7
when N. had brought forth the	23: 8
N. remembered that this thing	23:12
the plates of N. do contain the	26: 7
engraven upon the plates of N.,	26:11
forth among all the people of N.,	28:23
THE BOOK OF N.	4Ne 1:hd
WHO IS THE SON OF N.	1:hd
account of the people of N.,	1:hd
the people of N. did wax strong,	1:10
N., he that kept this last record,	1:19
kept it upon the plates of N.)	1:19
he kept it upon the plates of N.	1:19
kept it upon the plates of N.;	1:21
also written in the book of N.;	1:21
taught to hate the children of N.	1:39
who were called the people of N.	1:43
both the people of N. and the	1:45
ye shall take the plates of N.	Mrm 1: 4
shall engrave on the plates of N.	1: 4
being a descendant of N.,	1: 5
the people of N. appointed me	2: 1
especially among the people of N.	2:11
and taken the plates of N.,	2:17
upon the plates of N. I did	2:18
people of N. again were hunted	2:20
record out of the plates of N.,	6: 6
father was a descendant of N.	8:13
destruction of the people of N.	Eth 8:21
was the faith of N. and Lehi	12:14
engraven upon the plates of N.;	DC 10:38
things upon the plates of N.	10:39
engraven upon the plates of N.	10:40
which are on the plates of N.,	10:41
publish it as the record of N.;	10:42
abridgment of the account of N.	10:44
engraven upon the plates of N.	10:45
part of the engravings of N.,	10:45
become even as N. of old,	33: 8
law and I gave unto my servant N.,	98:32

NEPHIHAH

NEPHIHAH
Now this man's name was N.,	Al	4:17
the judgment-seat unto N.		4:18
up the judgment-seat to N.,		4:20
up the judgment-seat unto N.;		8:12
the city, or the land, N.		50:14
N., the second chief judge, died,		50:37
the son of N. was appointed to		50:39
came to the city of N.;		51:24
against the city of N. to battle,		51:25
of many cities, the city of N., and		51:26
of Sidon, over to the city of N.		56:25
the people of N., who were		59: 5
forth against the people of N.,		59: 7
remainder of the people of N.		59: 8
be men sent to the city		59: 9
that the city of N. was lost		59:11
towards the land of N.,		62:14
march towards the land of N.		62:18
they had come to the city of N.,		62:18
their tents in the plains of N.,		62:18
which is near the city of N.		62:18
possession of the city of N.		62:26
possession of the city of N.,		62:30
from the land of N. to the land		62:30

NEPHI'S
N. brethren rebel against him.	1Ne	1:hd
N. brethren rebel against him.	2Ne	1:hd

NEPHITE
I am a N., and I know that thou	Al	8:20
Ammon, and behold, he was a N.		19:18
the N. should remain in the land.		19:19
art thou going with this N.,		20:10
day and a half's journey for a N.		22:32
who was a N. by birth,		49:25
it would also poison a N.;		55:32
being a day's journey for a N.,	He	4: 7
who was a N. by birth,		5:35
put to death every N. that will	Mro	1: 2

NEPHITES
I shall also speak unto the N.	2Ne	29:12
shall have the words of the N.,		29:13
the N. shall have the words of the		29:13
the N. and the Jews shall have		29:13
words of the N. and the Jews.		29:13
were not Lamanites were N.;	Jac	1:13
nevertheless, they were called N.,		1:13
call N., or the people of Nephi,		1:14
welfare of my brethren, the N.;	En	1: 9
my people, the N., should fall into		1:13
a record of my people, the N.		1:13
between the N. and Lamanites		1:24
numerous than were they of the N.;	Jar	1: 6
many times against us, the N.,		1: 7
to preserve my people, the N.,	Om	1: 2
the more wicked part of the N.		1: 5
the N., and the Lamanites;		1:10
the N. and the Lamanites.		1:24
behold, the N. did obtain		1:24
destruction of my people, the N.	WM	1: 1
that we be slaves to the N. than	Mos	7:15
in all the language of the N.,		9: 1
which he did receive from the N.		19:28
up in anger against the N.,		21: 2
afflictions of the N. were great,		21: 5
among those who were called N.		25:12
were numbered with the N.,		25:13
of their hatred towards the N.,		28: 2
people who were called the N.;		29:44
of a war between the N.	Al	1:hd
the remainder were called N.,		2:11
the people of the N. were aware		2:12
began to make war with the N.		2:15
Amlicites did contend with the N.		2:17
many of the N. did fall before		2:17
strengthen the hand of the N.,		2:18
the N. did pursue the Amlicites		2:19
and there were slain of the N.		2:19
the N. did pitch their tents		2:20
returned into the camp of the N.	Al	2:23
the N. being strengthened by the		2:28
they fled before the N. towards		2:36
the N. did pursue them with		2:36
the N. who were not slain by		3: 1
were distinguished from the N.,		3: 4
kept them, were called the N.,		3:11
the names are given by the N.,		11: 4
before the N. could raise a		16: 3
the N. were desirous to obtain		16: 4
captain over the armies of the N.,		16: 5
come again to war against the N.		16:12
among all the people of the N.		16:15
delighted in murdering the N.,		17:14
their custom to bind all the N.		17:20
among all the people of the N.		19:10
so much mourning among the N.,		19:14
sent from the N. to torment them.		19:26
had always attended the N.,		19:27
thou art going to deliver these N.,		20:13
Lamanites and the N. divided.		22:27
whither the N. had driven them.		22:29
the N. were nearly surrounded by		22:29
the N. had taken possession of		22:29
the N. had inhabited the land		22:33
thus the N. in their wisdom,		22:33
Now this was wisdom in the N.—		22:34
believe in the traditions of the N.;		23: 5
they were friendly with the N.;		23:18
sent these our brethren, the N.,		24: 7
with these brethren, the N.		24: 8
swore vengeance upon the N.;		25: 1
had many battles with the N.,		25: 3
slain by the hands of the N.;		25: 4
gave great power unto the N.;		25: 6
could not overpower the N.		25:13
has not, even among the N.		26:33
had gone to war against the N.		27: 1
not seek revenge from the N.,		27: 2
Zarahemla to our brethren the N.,		27: 5
Behold, the N. will destroy us,		27: 6
called by the N. the people		27:26
the armies of the N. were set		28: 1
and contentions among the N.,		28: 9
wars between the N. and the		28: 9
dead of the N. numbered		30: 2
more wise than many of the N.;		30:20
separated themselves from the N.		30:59
of the Zoramites from the N.		31: 2
the N. greatly feared that the		31: 4
great loss on the part of the N.		31: 4
were dissenters from the N.;		31: 8
Ammon, and also against the N.		35:11
Jershon for the armies of the N.,		35:13
betwixt the Lamanites and the N.,		35:13
our stiffnecked brethren, the N.,		37:10
wars between the N. and		43: 3
the people of the N. saw the		43: 4
their hatred towards the N.,		43: 7
to anger against the N.;		43: 8
he might gain power over the N.		43: 8
the design of the N. was to		43: 9
the N. would not suffer that		43:12
unto the N. a large portion		43:13
thus the N. were compelled,		43:13
who had dissented from the N.,		43:13
numerous, nearly, as were the N.;		43:14
the N. were obliged to contend		43:14
the armies of the N. were		43:15
Now, the leader of the N., or		43:16
be the chief captain over the N.—		43:16
of all the armies of the N.—		43:16
captain over the armies of the N.		43:17
afraid of the armies of the N.		43:21
so much greater than the N.		43:21
durst not come against the N.		43:22
whither the armies of the N.		43:23
desire of the N. to preserve		43:30
when they saw the N. coming		43:36
to the heavy blows of the N.		43:37
a man fell among the N., by		43:38
thus the N. did carry on the		43:38

many of the N. were slain by	Al	43:44
the N. were inspired by a better		43:45
this cause were the N. contending		43:47
double the number of the N.;		43:51
were encircled about by the N.,		43:53
more powerfully against the N.		44:16
to the sharp swords of the N.;		44:18
before the swords of the N.;		44:18
both on the N. and on the		44:21
And the armies of the N., or of		44:23
that this very people, the N.,		45:10
of the armies of the N.,		46:11
his will with the armies of the N.,		46:34
which was possessed by the N.;		46:36
standard of liberty among the N.		46:36
to go to battle against the N.		47: 1
to go to battle against the N.		47: 2
subjected to go against the N.		47: 6
to go against the N. to battle.		47:21
they had taken from the N.		47:23
and all the dissenters of the N..		47:35
the same information of the N.,		47:36
from their towers, against the N.		48: 1
inspire their hearts against the N.,		48: 2
the N. as well as the Lamanites.		48: 2
to go to battle against the N.		48: 3
to overpower the N. and		48: 4
with the strength of the N.,		48: 5
the armies of the N., and		48: 8
which was possessed by the N.		48: 9
the N. were taught to defend		48:14
rejoice over the blood of the N.,		48:25
N. had dug up a ridge of		49: 4
because of the wisdom of the N.		49: 5
to have attacked the N. at		49:10
captains durst not attack the N.		49:11
of affairs among the N.,		49:11
for them to come against the N.		49:12
thus were the N. prepared to		49:19
began to contend with the N.,		49:21
not obtain power over the N. by		49:22
Thus the N. had all power over		49:23
did attempt to destroy the N.		49:23
not a single soul of the N. which		49:23
not obtained his desire over the N.;		49:26
which was possessed by the N.		50: 1
the line between the N. and		50:11
the N. possessing all the land		50:11
the N. began the foundation of		50:13
against the people of the N.,		51: 9
to come to battle against the N.		51:10
slain by the hand of the N.;		51:11
the N. were not sufficiently strong		51:23
driving the N. before them and		51:28
marched forth against the N.		52:12
endeavoring to harass the N.,		52:13
they should also harass the N.		52:13
were the N. in those dangerous		52:14
they were surrounded by the N.,		52:31
yea, and also the dead of the N.		53: 1
and also the dead of the N.,		53: 3
of some intrigue amongst the N.,		53: 8
gained some ground over the N.,		53: 8
since been protected by the N.		53:10
had been protected by the N.		53:12
tribulations which the N. bore		53:13
and they called themselves N.		53:16
to fight for the liberty of the N.,		53:17
fight in all cases to protect the N.		53:17
been a disadvantage to the N.,		53:19
as many prisoners of the N.		54: 3
a leader of the people of the N.		54:14
either to the subjecting the N. to		54:20
guards who were over the N.		55: 6
the N. were guarded in the city		55: 7
the guards who were over the N.,		55: 8
we have escaped from the N.,		55: 8
till we go against the N. to		55:10
us to go against the N.		55:11
the N. could have slain them.		55:18
armed those prisoners of the N.		55:20
they were surrounded by the N.		55:22
the N. had power over them;		55:23
that they should fight with the N.:	Al	55:23
cast them at the feet of the N.,		55:23
be liberated, who were N.;		55:24
N. began again to be victorious,		55:28
administer of their wine to the N.,		55:30
N. were not slow to remember		55:31
nay, not amongst all the N.		56:45
of being Lamanites, were N.;		57:10
that the N. were weary because of		58:25
weapons of war against the N.		62:16
thus were the N. relieved from		62:29
having regained many of the N.		62:30
the N. and the Lamanites also		62:35
at that time against the N.		62:38
of the war between the N. and the		62:41
many of the N. who did enter		63: 6
up again to anger against the N.		63:14
An account of the N.	He	1:hd
abominations of the N.,		1:hd
among the people of the N.		1: 1
pitch battle against the N.		1:15
a dissenter from among the N.;		1:15
could stand against the N.,		1:16
should gain power over the N.—		1:16
to battle against the N.		1:17
no time for the N. to gather		1:19
that the N. had fled before them,		1:22
greatness of the number of the N.		1:25
on every hand by the N.		1:31
into the midst of the N.,		1:32
they were in the power of the N.,		1:32
into the hands of the N.		1:32
peace between the N. and the		2: 1
of the Lamanites and of the N.,		3:14
have been kept chiefly by the N.		3:15
generation to another by the N.,		3:16
they are no more called the N.,		3:16
among the people of the N.		3:22
which was possessed by the N.		3:31
Lamanites to war against the N.;		4: 3
who went up from the N. unto		4: 4
up to anger against the N.;		4: 4
down against the N. to battle,		4: 5
the N. and the armies of		4: 6
thus those dissenters of the N.,		4: 8
all the possession of the N.		4: 8
Now this great loss of the N.,		4:11
for the N. to obtain more power		4:19
the N. were in great fear,		4:20
who had gone over from the N.,		5:17
immediately returned to the N.		5:17
and N. who were dissenters.		5:27
they did yield up unto the N.		5:52
did exceed that of the N.		6: 1
there were many of the N. who		6: 2
declare unto the people of the N.		6: 4
N. did go into whatsoever part		6: 7
whether among the N. or the		6: 7
the Lamanites or among the N.;		6: 8
both the Lamanites and the N.;		6: 9
were many, even among the N.,		6:18
of the more part of the N.,		6:21
hold upon the hearts of the N.;		6:31
N. did begin to dwindle in unbelief,		6:34
began to withdraw from the N.,		6:35
that the N. did build them up		6:38
overspread all the land of the N.,		6:38
Lamanite, prophesies unto the N.		7:hd
judges over the people of the N.,		7: 1
iniquity had come upon the N.,		7: 6
some of the N. who believed on		9:39
of the people of the N.,		10: 3
as well as among the N.,		11: 6
both the N. and the Lamanites,		11:21
defy the whole armies of the N.,		11:32
the Lamanite, to the N.		13:hd
the N. did still remain in		13: 1
the hearts of the people of the N.,		13: 8
which are possessed by the N.,		13:16
through the preaching of the N.:		15: 4
concerning the people of the N.:		15:17
heard of more among the N.;		16: 8
both of the N. and also of the		16:15

NEPHITES

were many dissenters of the N.	3Ne	1:28
unto those N. who did remain		1:28
king over the people of the N.		2:5
the N. began to reckon their		2:8
both the N. and the Lamanites,		2:11
unite with their brethren, the N.,		2:12
the N. were threatened with		2:13
who had united with the N.		2:14
were numbered among the N.;		2:14
became white like unto the N.;		2:15
were numbered among the N.;		2:16
Nephites, and were called N.		2:16
Go down upon the N. and		3:3
possession of the land of the N.,		3:11
the N. and of the Lamanites,		3:14
were numbered among the N.,		3:14
over all the armies of the N.,		3:17
of the armies of the N. was		3:18
the custom among all the N.		3:19
people who were called N.,		3:24
had been deserted by the N.,		4:1
had been deserted by the N.,		4:2
the N. had left their lands		4:3
up in open battle against the N.;		4:4
and the N. being in one body,		4:4
go up to battle against the N.		4:5
the N. should come upon them		4:6
go up to battle against the N.		4:6
the armies of the N., when they		4:8
that the N. had fallen with		4:9
the N. did not fear them;		4:10
behold, the N. did beat them,		4:12
the armies of the N. did return		4:15
this was an advantage to the N.;		4:18
to have any effect upon the N.,		4:18
the N. were continually		4:21
met by the armies of the N.		4:25
up prisoners unto the N.,		4:27
among all the people of the N.		5:1
people of the N. did all return		6:1
both N. and Lamanites,	4Ne	1:2
people who were called the N.,		1:36
were called N., and Jacobites,		1:37
to be a war between the N.,	Mrm	1:8
who consisted of the N. and		1:8
this war was between the N., and		1:8
parties were N. and Lamanites.		1:9
the N. had gathered together		1:11
the N. did beat the Lamanites		1:11
a war again between the N. and		2:1
the head of an army of the N.,		2:2
on the part of the N. and also		2:8
the N. began to repent of their		2:10
the N. did begin to flee before		2:16
had employed my people, the N.,		3:1
my people, the N., had done,		3:9
the N. did go up with their		4:1
the armies of the N. were driven		4:2
and did slay many of the N.,		4:2
the armies of the N. went up		4:4
and driven back by the N.		4:8
when the N. saw that they had		4:8
both the N. and the Lamanites.		4:9
again upon the N. to battle;		4:10
the N. repented not of the evil		4:10
of the N. and of the Lamanites;		4:11
exceed the number of the N.		4:13
the N. being angry because the		4:15
not come again against the N.		4:16
did come down against the N.		4:17
did the N. gain no power over		4:18
the which they did beat the N.		4:19
N. were driven and slaughtered		4:21
the N. did again flee from before		4:22
I did go forth among the N.,		5:1
were maintained by the N.,		5:4
did tread the people of the N.		5:6
destruction of my people, the N.		6:1
the N. who had escaped into		8:2
hunted my people, the N.,		8:7
destruction of my people, the N.		8:7
showed himself unto the N.	Eth	3:17
as he ministered unto the N.;		3:18

NEVER

is called Desolation by the N.	Eth	7:6
where the N. were destroyed,		9:3
was called by the N. Zarahemla.		9:31
or the people of the N., hath	Mro	8:27
received the record of the N.,	DC	1:29
to the N., and the Jacobites.		3:17
to destroy their brethren the N.,		3:18
ye become as the N. of old.		38:39

NEST

hand hath found as a n. the riches	2Ne	20:14

NET

as a wild bull in a n.,	2Ne	8:20

NETHERMOST

in the n. part of my vineyard,	Jac	5:13
in the n. parts of the vineyard,		5:14
to the n. part of the vineyard,		5:19
into the n. parts of the vineyard,		5:38
into the n. parts of the vineyard.		5:39
in the n. parts of my vineyard,		5:52

NEUM

according to the words of N.,	1Ne	19:10

NEVER

N. at any time have I shed	1Ne	4:10
plates of brass should n. perish;		5:19
which I n. had before seen,		11:1
I n. had before set my foot.		11:1
they would n. perish;		15:24
they shall n. be brought down into	2Ne	1:7
It shall n. be inhabited,		23:20
evildoers shall n. be renowned.		24:20
and n. hath any of them been		25:9
that his seed n. perish		25:21
whom thou hast n. before heard	En	1:8
name that n. shall be blotted out,	Mos	1:12
he n. doth vary from that which		2:22
endure a n.-ending torment.		2:39
a state of n.-ending happiness.		2:41
ourselves a n.-ending torment,		5:5
that n. should be blotted out,		5:11
that can n. be darkened;		16:9
having n. called upon the Lord		16:12
then shall they that n. knew me		26:25
unto them that I n. knew them;		26:27
I n. have known much of the ways	Al	10:5
I said I n. had known much of		10:5
with their bodies, n. to be divided;		11:45
state that the soul can n. die?		12:20
and n. having made it known,		19:17
unto the Lord, n. did fall away.		23:6
that we have n. used them,		24:16
that they n. would use weapons		24:18
they had n. known these things.		24:30
which n. have been revealed;		26:22
there n. were men that had so		26:35
they n. could be prevailed upon		27:28
they n. did look upon death with		27:28
as n. had been known among all		28:2
a state of n.-ending happiness.		28:12
a being who n. has been seen		30:28
who n. was nor ever will be.		30:28
I have n. received so much as		30:33
n. open thy mouth any more,		30:47
and his brethren had n. beheld;		31:12
n. speaking of their God again		31:23
n. pluck of the fruit of the tree		32:40
to n. be weary of good works,		37:34
and n., until I did cry out unto		38:8
wickedness n. was happiness.		41:10
Therefore, as the soul could n. die,		42:9
n. had the Lamanites been known		43:43
n. will the Lord suffer that we		44:4
they n. would come to war again		44:19
that he was n. heard of more;		45:18
taught n. to give an offense,		48:14
n. to raise the sword except it		48:14
the devil would n. have power		48:17
their wars n. did cease for the		48:22
a manner which n. had been		49:8
there n. was a happier time		50:23

NEVER

that they n. would shed blood	Al 53:11
n. would give up their liberty,	53:17
as they n. had hitherto been a	53:19
n. had I seen so great courage,	56:45
Now they n. had fought, yet they	56:47
yea, n. were men known to have	56:56
that they were n. heard of more.	63: 8
such an one as ye n. have beheld;	He 14: 5
n. would again have dwindled	15:15
he was n. heard of more among	16: 8
there n. was known so great	3Ne 4:11
an one as n. had been known	8: 5
such as n. had been known in	8: 7
I n. knew you; depart from me,	14:23
The eye hath n. seen, neither hath	17:16
great faith have I n. seen among	19:35
soul shall n. hunger nor thirst,	20: 8
for ye shall n. taste of death;	28: 7
n. endure the pains of death;	28: 8
who were n. to taste of death,	28:25
n. had been so great wickedness	Mrm 4:12
than that misery which n. dies-	8:38
were there n. had man been.	Eth 2: 5
n. has man come before me with	3: 9
n. have I showed myself unto	3:15
n. has man believed in me as	3:15
n. were greater things made	4: 4
the wind did n. cease to blow	6: 8
n. could be a people more	10:28
such an one as n. had been upon	11: 6
such an one as n. had been known	11: 7
nothing, for charity n. faileth.	Mro 7:46
spiritual, n. will be done away,	10:19
n. be taken again from the earth,	DC 13: 1
n. at any time have I declared	29:29
if they n. should have bitter	29:39
so great as you n. have known.	39:10
that this house shall n. fall.	45:18
n. to cast any one out from	46: 3
upon this rock shall n. fall.	50:44
the same, and his years n. fail.	76: 4
them n. to have been born;	76:32
shall n. be taken from you,	90: 3
shall n. be brought any more	98:48
which they have n. considered;	101:94
they shall n. cease to prevail	103: 7
thy people shall n. be turned	122: 3
things which n. have been revealed	128:18
servant and n. deviating friend,	128:25
is n. but one on the earth at	132: 7
but n. control conscience;	134: 4
n. suppress the freedom of the	134: 4
also my words, for they n. cease.	Mses 1: 4
which thing I n. had supposed.	1:10
we n. should have had seed,	5:11
n. should have known good and	5:11
earth might n. more be covered	7:50
climeth up by me shall n. fall;	7:53
N. did any passage of scripture	JS 2:12
I then had, I would n. know;	2:12
had n. as yet made the attempt	2:14
n. before felt in any being—	2:16
"N. mind, all is well—	2:20
would n. be any more of them.	2:21
such was n. in my nature.	2:28
which time I had n. seen him.	2:66
n. be taken again from the earth	2:69
we n. could attain to previously,	2:74

NEVER-ENDING: see *NEVER* and *ENDING*.

NEVERTHELESS

n., having been highly favored	1Ne 1: 1
n. being large in stature,	2:16
n. they did follow me up	4: 4
N. I went forth,	4: 7
N., I have received a	9: 3
n., I knew that it was the	11:11
n., I do not know the meaning	11:17
n., they contain the covenants	13:23
N., thou beholdest that the	13:30
n., I beheld that the church	14:12
n., ye know that they were led	17:42
n., the Lord did suffer it that	1Ne 18:11
n. they did not loose me.	18:13
N., I did look unto my God,	18:16
N., I do not write anything upon	19: 6
N., when that day cometh,	19:15
N., they call themselves of	20: 2
N., for my name's sake will	20: 9
N., after they shall be nursed	22: 6
n., ye sought to take away his life;	2Ne 1:24
n., thou hast been brought out of	1:30
N., Jacob, my firstborn in the	2: 2
broken off, n., to be remembered	3: 5
N., notwithstanding the great	4:17
n., I know in whom I have trusted.	4:19
n., I did for them according to	5:18
N., I speak unto you again;	6: 3
N., the Lord has shown unto me	6: 9
n., the Lord will be merciful	6:11
n., in our bodies we shall see	9: 4
N., God will be merciful unto	10: 2
n., I will soften the hearts of	10:18
n., we have been driven out of	10:20
n. only these things have I caused	11: 1
N., God sendeth more witnesses,	11: 3
N., the dimness shall not be such	19: 1
n. they are plain unto all those	25: 4
n., in the days that the prophecies	25: 7
n., they hardened their hearts;	25:10
n., they put down the power	26:20
and be merry; n., fear God—	28: 8
n., they are led, that in many	28:14
n., I will be merciful unto them,	28:32
n., they were called Nephites,	Jac 1:13
n. they are cursed with a sore	3: 3
N., the Lord God showeth us	4: 7
N., I know that the roots are good,	5:36
N., not my will be done;	7:14
n., God is exceeding merciful	Jar 1: 3
n., he did spare the righteous	Om 1: 7
N., they had had many wars	1:17
N., after many days' wandering	Mos 9: 4
n., Gideon did spare his life.	19: 8
n., Limhi was not ignorant of	19:17
n. the Lord did hear their cries,	21:15
N., they did find a land which had	21:26
n. they did prolong the time;	21:35
N., if it were possible that ye	23: 8
N., after much tribulation,	23:10
N., in this I do not glory,	23:11
N. the Lord seeth fit to chasten	23:21
N.— whosoever putteth his trust	23:22
n. he should have no power to	23:39
n. they knew not God;	24: 5
n., he became a very wicked	27: 8
N. he cried again, saying:	27:13
N., after wandering through	27:28
n. they suffered much anguish of	28: 4
n. it gave them much knowledge,	28:18
n., let us appoint judges,	29:11
n. he had established laws,	Al 1: 1
N., this did not put an end to	1:16
N., they durst not lie, if it were	1:17
N., there were many among them	1:22
n., they were steadfast and	1:25
n., the law was put in force upon	1:32
N. the Lord did strengthen the	2:18
N., the Nephites being	2:28
n. they had not shorn their heads	3: 4
n. they had come out in open	3:18
n. the Spirit of the Lord did not	4:15
n., their souls were illuminated	5: 7
n. have gone astray, as sheep	5:37
N. the children of God were	6: 6
n. I do not desire that my joy	7: 5
n. the Son of God suffereth	7:13
N. Alma labored much in the	8:10
N., they hardened their hearts,	8:11
n. they did not exercise their	8:31
N. I say unto you, that it shall	9:15
n. a part of his words are	9:34
N., after all this, I never have	10: 5
N., I did harden my heart, for I	10: 6
N., there were some among them	10:13

NEVERTHELESS

n. they are laid under a strict	Al 12: 9	N., he that repents and does	DC	1:32
n. there was a space granted unto	12:24	N., my work shall go forth,		3:16
N., after many days their dead	16:11	n., it is not expedient that you		9:10
N. they departed out of the land	17: 7	N., it is now restored unto you		10: 3
n. they were angry because of	17:36	N., it is not written that		19: 6
n., Lamoni began to fear	18: 5	N., glory be to the Father,		19:19
n., whatsoever thou desirest of me	18:21	N., thou are not excusable in		24: 2
n. I believe that it shall be	19: 9	n., go thy way and sin no more.		24: 2
n., it were better that he should	20:17	N., I will bless you and your		31: 2
n. they were patient in all their	20:29	N., thou hast seen great sorrow,		39: 9
N., Aaron and a certain number of	21:13	N. ye are commanded never		46: 3
n. the Nephites had taken	22:29	n., if any have trespassed,		46: 4
n., the Lamanites were driven	28: 3	n., I will be merciful unto you;		50:16
N., there was no law against a	30:11	n. let him repent and he shall		50:39
n. it hath not grown up to a	32:29	N. thy vows shall be offered up		59:11
N., because those miracles were	37:41	N., I suffered it that ye might		61: 4
n., there are many mysteries	40: 3	N., all flesh is in mine hand,		61: 6
N., the Nephites were inspired by	43:45	N., I would not suffer that ye		61: 8
n., they were driven insomuch	43:51	N., unto whom is given power		61:27
n., my soul hath joy in my son,	46:25	N., ye are blessed, for the		62: 3
n., it is strange to relate,	47:36	N., I give commandments,		63:13
N., they could not suffer to lay	48:24	N., he that endureth in faith		63:20
n. their chief captains had sworn	49:17	N., I, the Lord, render unto		63:26
N., he had refused Alma to	50:38	n., I, the Lord am with them,		63:34
N., they did not long maintain	51: 2	N., let him impart all the		63:43
n., he did prepare himself and	51:10	n., it is appointed to him to die		63:50
N., I will grant to exchange	54:20	N., he has sinned; but verily		64: 7
N., we may console ourselves in	56:11	n. I have forgiven my servant		64:16
n., we did resolve to send them	57:16	N., let my servant John		69: 7
n., we had suffered great loss.	57:23	N., inasmuch as they receive		70: 7
n., according to the goodness of	57:25	N., in your temporal things		70:14
n. we could not come to battle	58: 6	n., I forgive him and say unto		75: 8
n. they stand fast in that	58:40	N., I, the Lord, show it by vision		76:47
n. for the righteous' sake, yea,	62:40	n., be of good cheer, for I will		78:18
N., these things were to be kept	63:13	N., there are those among you		82: 2
N., it came to pass that Pahoran	He 1: 5	N., search diligently and		84:94
n. the people who went forth	3: 7	N., let the bishop go unto		84:114
N. Helaman did fill the	3:20	n., they shall return again to		88:32
N. they did fast and pray oft,	3:35	n., he who came unto his own		88:48
N., Nephi and Lehi were not	5:23	n., the day shall come when		88:49
N., the people of the church did	6: 3	n., they are to be used		89:12
n., they durst not lay their own	8: 4	N., wheat for man, and corn for		89:17
n., if this thing which he has said	9: 2	N., through you shall the oracles		90: 4
N., they did rebuke the judges in	9:18	N., I am not well pleased with		90:35
N., they cause that Nephi should	9:19	N., my servants sinned a very		95:10
n., he shall declare unto you that	9:30	N., there are those that must		97: 6
n. the night shall not be	14: 4	N., Zion shall escape if she		97:25
N., the people began to harden	16:15	N., let it be read this once to		97:27
n., the people of Nephi did gain	3Ne 2:17	N., when the wicked rule the		98: 9
n., they cannot all be written in	5: 8	N., thine enemy is in thine hands;		98:31
n. there are many things which,	5:18	n. thou shalt forgive him.		98:41
n. they were enemies;	7:11	n. thou shalt forgive him.		98:42
n. they had come to an	7:14	N., as I have said unto you in		101:68
n., their hearts were turned	7:14	N., I do not say they shall not		101:100
n., all these great and terrible	8:19	N., if they pollute their		103:14
n., and notwithstanding it being	11: 3	N. a bishop must be chosen from		107:69
N., ye shall not cast him out	18:30	N., a high priest, that is, after		107:71
N., ye shall not cast him out of	18:32	N., inasmuch as thou hast		112: 3
n. they did not cease to pray.	19:26	n., I, the Lord, will build up		124:83
N., so great and marvelous were	19:34	n. they may travel, yet they are		124:137
N., when they shall have received	20:28	But n., deep water is what		127: 2
n. they did not minister of the	28:16	N., in all ages of the world,		128: 9
N., and notwithstanding all these	4Ne 1:31	n., it was written: Thou shalt		132:36
N., the people did harden their	1:34	N., calling upon God, he received	Mses	1:20
N. they would struggle with the	Mrm 2:14	n., all things were before created		3: 7
n., I know that I shall be lifted	2:19	n., thou mayest choose for thyself,		3:17
n. the strength of the Lord was	2:26	n., we know them, and cannot deny,		6:45
n., it was without faith, because	3:12	n., they hearkened not.		8:24
n. God knoweth all things;	8:17	it was n. a fact that I had	JS	2:24
N., I will bring you up again out	Eth 2:24			
n., O Lord, thou hast given us a	3: 2	NEW		
n., thou hast been merciful unto	3: 3	a n. writing, which was plain	1Ne	16:29
n. Kib begat Shule in his old	7: 7	I have showed thee n. things		20: 6
n. they did not gain power any	7:19	and can speak with a n. tongue,	2Ne	31:14
N., the Lord was merciful unto	9: 2	consecrated n. ones in their stead,	Mos	11: 5
n., in his old age he begat	9:14	thus they become n. creatures;		27:26
n., there were some which fled	9:32	bringing n. forces into that city,	Al	55:34
n., Shez was smitten by the hand	10: 3	also n. supplies of provisions.		55:34
n., he did not prevail against	10:34	a n. supply of provisions and		57:17
n., the army of Coriantumr did	14:12	also a n. supply of provisions.		58: 3
n., the brother of Lib did	14:16	there shall a n. star arise,	He	14: 5
N., Shiz did not cease to pursue	14:24	also that a n. star did appear,	3Ne	1:21
n., they conquered not, and	15:17	and all things have become n.		12:47

that all things had become n.	3Ne	15: 2
that all things had become n.		15: 3
and it shall be a N. Jerusalem.		20:22
shall be called the N. Jerusalem.		21:23
land, in unto the N. Jerusalem.		21:24
shall speak with n. tongues;	Mrm	9:24
the place of the N. Jerusalem,	Eth	13: 3
a N. Jerusalem upon this land.		13: 4
it could not be a n. Jerusalem		13: 5
a N. Jerusalem should be built		13: 6
And there shall be a n. heaven		13: 9
a new heaven and a n. earth;		13: 9
and all things have become n.		13: 9
then cometh the N. Jerusalem;		13:10
is a n. and an everlasting	DC	22: 1
except it is made n. among you;		27: 4
there shall be a n. heaven		29:23
a new heaven and a n. earth.		29:23
and all things shall become n.,		29:24
the city of the N. Jerusalem		42: 9
building up of the N. Jerusalem		42:35
the N. Jerusalem shall be built.		42:62
here and in the N. Jerusalem.		42:67
until the N. Testament be		45:60
be called the N. Jerusalem,		45:66
and give a n. commandment		56: 5
and all things become n.,		63:49
unto him a n. commission		75: 7
and a n. commandment,		75: 7
mediator of the n. covenant,		76:69
unto you a n. commandment,		82: 8
be the city of N. Jerusalem.		84: 2
the city N. Jerusalem shall be		84: 4
remember the n. covenant,		84:57
voice together sing this n. song,		84:98
go unto the city of N. York,		84:114
and all things shall become n.,		101:25
to Cainhannoch [N. York]		104:81
the mediator of the n. covenant.		107:19
publish the n. translation of my		124:89
whereon is a n. name written,		130:11
The n. name is the key word.		130:11
the n. and everlasting covenant		131: 2
a n. and an everlasting covenant;		132: 4
the n. and everlasting covenant,		132: 6
the n. and everlasting covenant		132:19
the n. and everlasting covenant		132:26
my n. and everlasting covenant,		132:27
in the n. and everlasting covenant,		132:41
the n. and everlasting covenant,		132:42
the holy city, the N. Jerusalem;		133:56
be called Zion, a N. Jerusalem,	Mses	7:62
in the State of N. York,	JS	2: 3
as they stand in our N. Testament.		2:40
Ontario county, N. York.		2:51
county, State of N. York.		2:56
Chenango county, N. York.		2:58
county, in the State of N. York,		2:61
them to the city of N. York.		2:63
went to the city of N. York,		2:64
the Baptist in the N. Testament,		2:72

NEWEL: *see KNIGHT, Newel; and WHITNEY, Newel K.*

NEWLY
we will n. arrange the affairs of	Mos	29:11

NEWS
the joyful n. declared unto us	Al	13:25

NEXT
to be the n. best place for them	Al	49:12
our n. object was to obtain the		58: 1
to hold the n. conference;	DC	26: 1
time until the n. conference,		52: 2
a mission unto me n. spring,		114: 1
on the fourth day of July n.;		115:10
n. spring let them depart to go		118: 4
the twenty-sixth day of April n.,		118: 5
in the n. resurrection;		132:19

how many can go n. spring;	DC	136: 7
Stands n. to Kolob, called	Fac	2: 2
which is the n. grand governing		2: 2
quoted the n. verse differently:	JS	2:39

NICOLAITANE
be ashamed of the N. band	DC	117:11

NIGH
n. unto an angel of light,	2Ne	9: 9
the Holy One of Israel draw n.		15:19
and it well n. consumeth me		26: 7
and the end draweth n.	Jac	5:47
for behold the end draweth n.,		5:62
for the end draweth n.		5:64
for the end is n. at hand,		5:71
repenting n. unto death,	Mos	27:28
kingdom of heaven is n. at hand;	Al	9:25
for the day of salvation draweth n.;		13:21
is to come, for the Lord is n.;	DC	1:12
is not yet, but is n. at hand,		1:35
For the hour is n. and the day		29: 9
For the hour is n., and that		29:10
my coming, for it is n. at hand—		35:15
even now already summer is n.		35:16
your redemption draweth n.		35:26
day of the Lord is n. at hand.		43:17
that summer is now n. at hand;		45:37
they know that the hour is n.		45:38
I say unto you, they are n.,		45:63
which time is n. at hand—		49: 6
is not yet, but is n. at hand.		58: 4
well-n. ripened for destruction.		61:31
they are now n. at hand,		63:53
hour of their judgment is n.,		84:115
they were n. unto cursing.		104: 3
which is n. at hand.		104:59
coming of the Lord draweth n.,		106: 4
for the hour of his coming is n.—		133:17
until thou come n. unto Kolob,	Abr	3: 9
Kolob is set n. unto the throne of		3: 9
that summer is n. at hand;	JS	1:38

NIGHT
And it was by n.;	1Ne	4: 5
had been out by n. among them.		4:22
Lord spake unto my father by n.,		16: 9
giving light unto them by n.,		17:30
by visions in the n.-time.	2Ne	4:23
thanks unto his holy name by n.		9:52
last n. the angel spake unto me		10: 3
the shining of a flaming fire by n.;		14: 5
drink, that continue until n.,		15:11
be as a dream of a n. vision;		27: 3
mine eyes water my pillow by n.,		33: 3
when the n. came I did still raise	En	1: 4
in one day and a n. we did slay	Mos	9:18
into the land of Nephi by n.,		21:21
the Lamanites, by n. are drunken;		22: 6
them into the wilderness by n.		22: 6
depart by n. into the wilderness		22:11
departed out of the land by n.,		22:15
in the n.-time gathered their		24:18
all the n.-time were they gathering		24:18
did pitch their tents for the n.	Al	2:20
then cometh the n. of darkness		34:33
yea, when thou liest down at n.		37:37
of evil when the n. cometh.		41: 5
from that endless n. of darkness;		41: 7
when it was n. he sent a secret		47:10
with his army in the n.-time,		47:13
that when the n. had come,		51:33
stole forth and went out by n.,		51:33
Moroni and his army, by n.,		52:22
this was done in the n.-time,		55:22
to encircle them about by n.,		55:29
and toiled by n. to maintain		56:16
not pass us by n. nor by day		56:22
But behold, it was n.; therefore		56:38
therefore we did camp for the n.		56:38
surround, by n., the city Cumeni,		57: 8

NIGHT / NINETY-SIX

come upon us by n. and slay us,	Al	57: 9
about to enter the city by n.		57:10
it was n. and they did pitch		58:25
when it was n., I caused that my		58:26
this our march in the n.-time,		58:27
And when the n. came, Moroni		62:20
forth in the darkness of the n.,		62:20
all let down into the city by n.,		62:23
thus they did encamp for the n.		62:35
any stratagem in the n.-time,		62:35
having been out by n.,	He	2: 6
that in the n. before he cometh		14: 3
be one day and a n. and a day,		14: 4
one day and there were no n.;		14: 4
there shall be two days and a n.;		14: 4
the n. shall not be darkened;		14: 4
shall be the n. before he is born.		14: 4
day and that n. and that day	3Ne	1: 8
one day as if there were no n.,		1: 8
on this n. shall the sign be given,		1:13
this n. shall the sign be given.		1:14
no darkness when the n. came.		1:15
no darkness in all that n.,		1:19
from the robbers day and n.		3:14
marching out by day and by n.,		4:21
upon them by n. and by day.		4:22
out his armies in the n.-time,		4:24
this did they do in the n.-time,		4:25
with all diligence day and n.		5: 3
even all the n. it was noised		19: 3
labor exceedingly all that n.,		19: 3
therein, until the n. cometh,		27:33
when the n. came, they did not	Eth	6: 9
into the house of Noah by n.		7:18
did give battle unto him by n.		8: 5
by n. he went forth viewing		13:13
came upon the people, by n.		13:14
out of the wilderness by n.,		14: 5
troubled by day and by n.,		14:23
when it was n. they were weary,		15:16
when the n. came again they did		15:17
when the n. came they slept upon		15:20
fought even until the n. came.		15:21
And when the n. came they were		15:22
when the n. came they had all		15:23
slept upon their swords that n.,		15:24
when the n. came there were		15:25
daylight is from the dark n.	Mro	7:15
the n. that you cried unto me	DC	6:22
of a trump, both day and n.		24:12
generation as a thief in the n.,		45:19
crying unto the Lord day and n.,		86: 5
the moon giveth her light by n.,		88:45
pass over by n. and by day,		97:23
And the enemy came by n.,		101:51
as a thief in the n.—		106: 4
when the n. cometh let not the		112: 5
dwell in his presence day and n.		133:35
the name of the Lord day and n.,		133:40
song of the Lamb, day and n.		133:56
and the darkness, I called N.;	Mses	2: 5
to divide the day from the n.,		2:14
and the lesser light to rule the n.,		2:16
the moon to rule over the n.,		2:18
even the n., is above or greater	Abr	3: 5
which is set to rule the n.		3: 6
the n. time when the Lord spake		3:14
and the darkness they called N.		4: 5
until morning they called n.;		4: 5
that which they called day and n.		4: 5
until morning that they called n.;		4: 8
time that they called n. and day.		4: 8
until the morning they called n.;		4:13
to divide the day from the n.;		4:14
the lesser light to rule the n.;		4:16
over the day and over the n.,		4:17
until morning that it was n.;		4:19
morning that they called n.;		4:23
until morning they called n.;		4:31
retired to my bed for the n.,	JS	2:29
occupied the whole of that n.		2:47
related to me the previous n.,		2:49

NIGHTS		
space of two days and two n.,	Mos	27:23
space of two days and two n.;	Al	18:43
that after two days and two n.		19: 1
space of two days and two n.;		19: 5
of three days and three n.		36:10
for three days and for three n.		36:16
was three days and three n. in		38: 8
about the city for many n.;		57: 9

NIGHT-TIME: *see NIGHT and TIME.*

NIMRAH		
(and his name was N.)	Eth	9: 8
N. gathered together a small		9: 9

NIMROD		
the name of the valley was N.,	Eth	2: 1
down into the valley of N.		2: 4
had a son who was called N.;		7:22
N. gave up the kingdom of Cohor		7:22

NINE		
hundred and seventy and n. years	En	1:25
for the space of n. moons.	Om	1:21
two hundred and seventy-n. of	Mos	9:19
five hundred and n. years from		29:46
six hundred and n. years had	3Ne	2: 6
n. years had passed away from		2: 7
n. years had passed away.		2: 8
until forth and n. years had	4Ne	1: 6
until fifty and n. years had		1: 6
and seventy and n. years passed	Mrm	5: 5
he reigned forty and n. years,	Eth	9:25
and n. of the people of Shiz.		15:23
n. high priests, seventeen elders,	DC	102: 5
at the age of sixty-n. years,		107:42
n. hundred and thirty years,	Mses	6:12
n. hundred and twelve years,		6:16
were n. hundred and five years,		6:18
were n. hundred and ten years,		6:19
n. hundred and sixty-two years,		6:24
n. hundred and sixty-nine years,		8: 7
nine hundred and sixty-n. years,		8: 7

NINETEENTH		
in the n. year of the reign of	Al	45: 2
commencement of the n. year		45:20
nearly the end of the n. year		46:37
the latter end of the n. year		48: 2
in the latter end of the n. year,		48:21
the eleventh month of the n. year,		49: 1
thus ended the n. year of		49:29
in the n. year Giddianhi found	3Ne	4: 5
this n. year did pass away,		4:15
the best blood of the n. century	DC	135: 6

NINETIETH		
in the n. year of the reign of	He	16:13
thus ended the n. year of		16:24

NINETY		
the n. and first year had passed	3Ne	1: 1
of the n. and second year,		1: 4
the n. and second year did		1:26
the n. and third year did also		1:27
in the n. and fourth year they		1:28
the n. and fifth year also,		2: 1
away the n. and sixth year;		2: 4
also the n. and seventh year;		2: 4
also the n. and eighth year;		2: 4
also the n. and ninth year;		2: 4
hundred and n. and four years	4Ne	1:21
four hundred and n.-six years	DC	107:46
to preside over n.-six elders,		107:89
Enos lived n. years, and begat	Mses	6:17
eight hundred and n.-five years,		6:20
five hundred and n.-five years.		8:10

NINETY-FIVE: *see NINETY and FIVE.*

NINETY-SIX: *see NINETY and SIX.*

NINTH

commencement of the n. year,	Al	4:11
commencement of the n. year		4:20
n. year of the reign of the judges		8: 2
twenty and n. year of the judges,		54: 1
thus ended the twenty and n. year		55:35
of the twenty and n. year,		57: 6
this is the twenty and n. year,		58:38
in the thirty and n. year of		63:10
thus ended the thirty and n. year		63:16
in the forty and n. year of the	He	3:23
of the forty and n. year;		3:32
the fifty and eighth and n. years		4: 8
in the sixty and n. year of the		7: 1
in the seventy and n. year		11:23
in the eighty and n. year of		16:12
also the ninety and n. year;	3Ne	2: 4
in the twenty and n. year		6:10
and also the thirty and n.,	4Ne	1: 6
till the seventy and n. year		1:14
hundred and forty and n. year	Mrm	2:28
came to the twenty-n. verse	DC	76:15
n. number of the *Times and*	Fac	3: 3

NO: *see in the APPENDIX.*

NOAH: *see also, PACKARD, Noah.*

I am Limhi, the son of N.,	Mos	7: 9
conferred the kingdom upon N.,		11: 1
N. began to reign in his stead;		11: 1
the taxes which king N. had put		11: 6
king N. built many elegant and		11: 8
king N. sent guards round about		11:17
king N. sent his armies against		11:18
when king N. had heard of the		11:27
king N. hardened his heart against		11:29
the life of king N. shall be valued		12: 3
king N. caused that Abinadi		12:17
the people of king N. durst not lay		13: 5
king N. was about to release		17:11
fled from the servants of king N.,		18: 1
they would deliver up king N.		19:15
the priests of king N., being		20: 3
supposing them to be priests of N.		21:23
had they been the priests of N. he		21:23
king N. and his priests had		21:30
by the people of king N.		23:hd
the armies of king N. would come		23: 1
before the armies of king n.		23: 1
the people of king N. could not		23: 2
iniquity of king N. and his priests;		23: 9
have been oppressed by king N.,		23:12
even out of the hands of king N.		23:13
found those priests ot king N.,		23:31
Yea, remember king N.,		29:18
the hands of the people of king N.,	Al	5: 4
were the people in the days of N.,		10:22
some around the borders of N.,		16: 3
who were the priests of N.,		25: 4
he said unto the priests of N.		25:12
descendants of the priests of N.		43:13
marched towards the land of N.,		49:12
marched forward to the land of N.		49:13
the city of N., which had		49:14
the city of N. had hitherto been		49:15
this, the waters of N. unto me,	3Ne	22: 9
the waters of N. should no more		22: 9
tight like unto the ark of N.;	Eth	6: 7
was one whose name was N.		7:14
that N. rebelled against Shule,		7:15
into the house of N. by night		7:18
the son of N. did build up his		7:19
kingdom of Cohor, the son of N.		7:20
Cohor, the son of N., caused		7:21
of his fathers, even till N.;	DC	84:14
And from N. till Enoch,		84:15
N. was ten years old when he		107:52
N. also, and they who were		133:54
Enoch also saw N., and his family;	Mses	7:42
sons of N. should be saved with		7:42
Enoch saw that N. built an ark;		7:43
from N., he beheld all the families		7:45
not bless the children of N.?	Mses	7:49
have mercy upon N. and his seed,		7:50
call upon the children of N.;		7:51
concerning the children of N.;		7:60
covenanted with Enoch that N.		8: 2
of the earth (through N.),		8: 3
he called his name N., saying:		8: 9
Lamech lived, after he begat N.,		8:10
N. was four hundred and fifty		8:12
N. and his sons hearkened unto		8:13
And the Lord said unto N.:		8:15
it came to pass that N. prophesied,		8:16
And the Lord said unto N.:		8:17
sought N. to take away his life;		8:18
but the Lord was with N.,		8:18
the Lord ordained N. after his		8:19
N. called upon the children of men		8:20
not unto the words of N.		8:21
N. continued his preaching unto		8:23
it repented N., and his heart was		8:25
repenteth N. that I have created		8:26
N. found grace in the eyes of the		8:27
N. was a just man, and perfect		8:27
And God said unto N.:		8:30
As it was with N. so shall it be	Abr	1:19
reign of Adam, and also of N.,		1:26
would fain claim it from N.,		1:27
of Eden, as also to Seth, N.,	Fac	2: 3
as it was in the days of N.,	JS	1:41
that N. entered into the ark		1:42

NOB

shall he remain at N. that day;	2Ne	20:32

NOBILITY

down their pride and their n.	Al	51:17
down their pride and their n.,		51:18
who professed the blood of n.;		51:21

NOBLE

most n. and chief governor of	3Ne	3: 2
unto me, most n. Lachoneus,		3: 3
your n. spirit in the field of battle.		3: 5
learned, the wise and the n.;	DC	58:10
and the wise, and the n.,		122: 2
many of the n. and great ones;	Abr	3:22

NOBLEMAN

A certain n. had a spot of land,	DC	101:44
servants of the n. went		101:46
the servants of the n. arose		101:51
the n., the lord of the vineyard,		101:52

NOBLES

may go into the gates of the n.	2Ne	23: 2
the kings, the princes, the n.,	DC	109:55

NOBLY

so honorably and n. defended,	DC	109:54

NOD

brethren dwelt in the land of N.,	Mses	5:41

NOISE

the warrior is with confused n.,	2Ne	19: 5
The n. of the multitude in the		23: 4
tumultuous n. of the kingdoms		23: 4
the n. of thy viols is not heard;		24:11
with a great n., and with storm,		27: 2
people having heard a great n.	Al	14:29
a voice of a great tumultuous n.,	He	5:30

NOISED

was n. abroad among the people	3Ne	19: 2
was n. abroad concerning Jesus;		19: 3

NOISES

all manner of tumultuous n.;	1Ne	12: 4
tumultuous n. did pass away.	3Ne	10: 9

NOMINATION

filled by the n. of the president	DC	102: 8

NONE

n. of us knoweth,	1Ne	22: 4
shall n. come into this land save	2Ne	1: 6
there shall be n. to molest them,		1: 9
unto n. else can the ends of the		2: 7
And I have n. other object save		2:30
he shall do n. other work, save		3: 8
and n. will he destroy that believe		6:14
yea, there was n. to answer,		7: 2
And n. to guide her among all		8:18
and there is n. other way save		9:41
is n. other nation on earth that		10: 3
n. shall be weary nor stumble		15:26
N. shall slumber nor sleep;		15:27
away safe, and n. shall deliver.		15:29
there was n. that moved the wing,		20:14
is persecuted, and n. hindereth.		24: 6
and n. shall be alone in his		24:31
and there is n. other people that		25: 5
there is n. other name given		25:20
he commandeth n. that they		26:24
the other, and n. are forbidden.		26:28
they should do n. of these things:		26:32
For n. of these iniquities come		26:33
denieth n. that come unto him,		26:33
the eyes of n. shall behold it		27:12
n. other which shall view it, save		27:13
I am no devil, for there is n.—		28:22
Lord covenanteth with n. save		30: 2
n. other way nor name given		31:21
for n. of these can I hope except		33: 9
and concubines he shall have n.;	Jac	2:27
concubines they should have n.,		3: 5
there is n. of it which is good.		5:32
n. of the prophets have written,		7:11
For salvation cometh to n. such	Mos	3:12
n. shall be found blameless before		3:21
And there is n. other salvation		4: 8
n. shall deliver them, except		11:23
for the Lord redeemeth n. such		15:26
For salvation cometh to n. such;		15:27
the Lord hath redeemed n. such;		15:27
but there was n. in the land that		21:33
n. received authority to preach		23:17
and n. were consecrated except		23:17
and n. could deliver them but		23:23
and n. could deliver them except		24:21
had been conferred upon n. but		25:13
leaving n. to reign in his stead;	Al	1: 1
n. were deprived of the privilege		6: 5
and salvation cometh to n. else.		11:40
have been void, taking n. effect.		12:26
afterwards, but n. were baptized.		13:19
slew n. save it were their leader		17:38
were n. who were Amalekites		24:29
is n. that knoweth these things,		26:21
this is joy which n. receiveth		27:18
say unto you that ye have n.,		30:40
and n. shall have passed away.		34:13
and n. could deliver them except		36: 2
n. but the truly penitent are		42:24
n. other have they spared alive.		56:12
n. other power can operate		60:25
n. hideth up their treasures unto	He	13:19
n. shall redeem it because of		13:19
n. did escape who were not	3Ne	5: 4
were n. who were brought unto		7:24
were n. righteous among them,		9:11
will accept n. of your sacrifices		9:19
suffer n. of these things to		12:29
that n. of you should go away,		18:25
n. of them that have seen so		19:36
in pieces, and n. can deliver.		20:16
in pieces, and n. can deliver.		21:12
for n. of them are lost.		27:30
and n. of them are lost;		27:31
n. that were righteous save	4Ne	1:46
and there is n. to deliver.	Mrm	5:24
ore I have n., for I am alone.		8: 5
n. save it be the Lamanites and		8: 9
n. that do know the true God		8:10
n. can have power to bring it		8:15
of the Lord, and n. can stay it;	Mrm	8:26
there are n. save a few only		8:36
n. other people knoweth our		9:34
And there shall be n. greater	Eth	1:43
is n. save it be the Lamanites,		4: 3
good cometh of n. save it be of		4:12
were n. of the fair sons and		13:17
there was n. to restrain them.		13:31
was n. left to bury the dead,		14:22
n. were received unto baptism	Mro	6: 3
for God receiveth n. such.		7: 9
n. is acceptable before God,		7:44
sparing n., neither old nor		9:19
n. that doeth good among you,		10:25
men, and there is n. to excape;	DC	1: 2
and n. shall stay them,		1: 5
to n. else will I grant this		5:14
n. else save God that knowest		6:16
there is n. other name given		18:23
partake of n. except it is made		27: 4
commandments, and n. else.		29:12
n. have I appointed to be his		30: 7
is n. which doeth good save		33: 4
are n. that doeth good except		35:12
there is n. else with whom I am		38:10
shalt cleave unto her and n. else.		42:22
ye receive n. such among you if		42:76
n. other appointed unto you		43: 3
n. else shall be appointed unto		43: 4
n. of them that my Father		50:42
saying n. other things than		52: 9
declaring n. other things than		52:36
become void and of n. effect.		54: 4
they receive n. inheritance,		58:53
thou shalt do n. other thing,		59:13
against n. is his wrath kindled		59:21
n. is able to go up to the land		61:16
there is n. inheritance for you.		63:29
n. are exempt from this law		70:10
of his doings n. can find out.		76: 2
and n. doeth good, for all have		82: 6
shall find n. inheritance in that day,		85: 9
n. of these things shall come		97:27
there is n. other place appointed		101:20
n. shall be exempted from the		107:84
did n. other things than that		132:37
did n. other things than that		132:37
in n. of these things did he sin		132:39
servant Joseph, and to n. else.		132:54
and n. were with me;		133:50
there was n. of you to answer;		133:67
there are n. to deliver you;		133:71
n. other people shall dwell there	Mses	7: 7
should of their flesh be saved;	JS	1:20
that I must join n. of them,		2:19

NOON

that of the sun at n.-day.	1Ne	1: 9
walking in darkness at n.-day.	DC	95: 6

NOONDAY

room was lighter than at n.,	JS	2:30

NOON-DAY: see NOON and DAY.

NOR

n. touch me with their fingers,	1Ne	17:52
not in truth n. in righteousness.		20: 1
n. destroyed from before me.		20:19
They shall not hunger n. thirst,		21:10
the heat n. the sun smite them;		21:10
n. to take away the land of	2Ne	1: 9
not sought for power n. authority		1:25
neither holiness n. misery.		2:11
neither good n. bad.		2:11
n. corruption nor incorruption,		2:11
nor corruption n. incorruption,		2:11
happiness n. misery,		2:11
neither sense nor insensibility.		2:11
be no righteousness n. happiness		2:13
be no punishment n. misery.		2:13
to act n. to be acted upon;		2:13

NOR 673 NOR

n. that his bread should fail.	2Ne	8:14
n. your labor for that which		9:51
there is neither bread n. clothing;		13: 7
it shall not be pruned n. digged;		15: 6
be weary n. stumble among them.		15:26
None shall slumber n. sleep;		15:27
n. the latchet of their shoes be		15:27
fear ye their fear, n. be afraid.		18:12
They shall not hurt n. destroy		21: 9
n. shall they delight in it.		23:17
do not rise, n. possess the land,		24:21
n. fill the face of the world with		24:21
They shall not hurt n. destroy		30:15
none other way n. name given		31:21
n. understand great knowledge,		32: 7
neither has been, n. ever will be.	Jac	7: 9
have written, n. prophesied, save		7:11
hast never before heard n. seen.	En	1: 8
prophesying, n. of my revelations.	Jar	1: 2
n. the people of Mosiah,	Om	1:17
they did not prosper n. progress	Mos	1:17
and have not sought gold n. silver		2:12
n. any manner of riches of you;		2:12
n. that ye should make slaves		2:13
n. that ye should murder, or		2:13
n. even have I suffered that ye		2:13
be your teacher, n. your king;		2:29
n. any other way nor means		3:17
n. means whereby salvation can		3:17
n. impart unto him of my		4:17
n. repent of the thing which		4:22
bind Ammon n. his brethren,		7:16
n. the strength of the Lord,		10:11
thyself unto them, n. serve them;		13:13
thou, n. thy son, nor thy		13:18
n. thy daughter, thy man-servant,		13:18
n. thy maid-servant, nor thy		13:18
n. thy cattle, nor thy stranger		13:18
n. thy stranger that is within thy		13:18
n. his man-servant, nor his		13:24
n. his maid-servant, nor his ox,		13:24
n. his ox, nor his ass,		13:24
n. his ass, nor anything that is		13:24
n. anything that is thy neighbor's.		13:24
he hath no form n. comeliness;		14: 2
n. seek to destroy them.		19:29
your teaches n. your minister,		23:14
n. did they teach them the words		24: 5
let no pride n. haughtiness		27: 4
be no wars n. contentions,		29:14
no stealing, n. plundering,		29:14
n. murdering, nor any manner		29:14
n. any manner of iniquity;		29:14
they need not fear n. tremble,	Al	1: 4
neither durst they rob, n. murder,		1:18
there were no contentions n. wars		4: 1
been no wars n. contentions for		16: 1
n. either of their brethren who		23: 1
spit upon them, n. smite them,		23: 2
n. cast them out of their		23: 2
synagogues, n. scourge them;		23: 2
not to murder, n. to plunder,		23: 3
nor to plunder, n. to steal,		23: 3
n. to commit adultery, nor to		23: 3
n. to commit any manner of		23: 3
strength, n. in my own wisdom;		26:11
who never was n. ever will be.		30:28
wisdom, n. of your much strength.		38:11
n. the vain things of this world;		39:14
they have no part n. portion of		40:13
with breastplates, n. shields—		43:21
fighting for monarchy n. power		43:45
n. suffer the law to be altered;		51: 3
not a woman n. a child among		54: 3
not pass us by night n. by day		56:22
turn to the right n. to the left,		56:37
turn to the right n. to the left		56:40
turn to the right n. to the left		56:40
would not murmur n. complain.		60: 4
your power n. your authority,		60:28
on the north, n. on the south,	He	1:31
nor on the south, n. on the east,		1:31
nor on the east. n. on the west.		1:31
governed by the law n. justice,	He	5: 3
no other way n. means whereby		5: 9
anger, to wars, n. to bloodshed;		6:17
n. by those who did belong to his		6:22
were no wild beasts n. game in	3Ne	4: 2
there was no lawyer n. judge		6:22
lawyer nor judge n. high priest		6:22
neither fire, n. glimmer, neither		8:22
neither the sun, n. the moon,		8:22
sun, nor the moon, n. the stars,		8:22
one jot n. one tittle hath not		12:18
N. by the earth, for it is his		12:35
moth n. rust doth corrupt,		13:20
do not break through n. steal.		13:20
n. yet for your body, what ye		13:25
do they reap n. gather into barns;		13:26
shall never hunger n. thirst,		20: 8
out with haste n. go by flight;		20:42
go out in haste, n. go by flight,		21:29
leave them neither root n. branch.		25: 1
might not suffer pain n. sorrow		28:38
not any longer hiss, n. spurn,		29: 8
spurn, n. make game of the Jews,		29: 8
Jews, n. any of the remnant of		29: 8
were no envyings, n. strifes,	4Ne	1:16
nor strifes, n. tumults, nor		1:16
n. whoredoms, nor lyings, nor		1:16
n. lyings, nor murders, nor any		1:16
n. murders, nor any manner of		1:16
n. any manner of lasciviousness;		1:16
were no robbers, n. murderers,		1:17
n. any manner of -ites;		1:17
hold them, n. retain them again.	Mrm	1:18
n. even among all the house of		4:12
not friends n. whither to go;		8: 5
wild beasts n. poisonous serpents,		8:24
are no revelations, n. prophecies,		9: 7
prophecies, n. gifts, nor healing,		9: 7
n. healing, nor speaking with		9: 7
n. speaking with tongues, and		9: 7
his fair sons n. daughters;	Eth	13:17
neither faith, hope, n. charity;	Mro	8:14
none, neither old n. young;		9:19
evil gift, n. the unclean thing.		10:30
to the right hand n. to the left,	DC	3: 2
n. trouble me any more		5:29
n. the spirit of prophecy,		11:25
are not of men n. of man,		18:34
n. seek thy neighbor's life.		19:25
adding to, n. diminishing from		20:35
backbiting, n. evil speaking;		20:54
neither teachers n. deacons have		20:58
shalt take no purse n. scrip,		24:18
any man, n. the children of men;		29:34
are not natural n. temporal,		29:35
neither carnal n. sensual.		29:35
words are not of man n. of men,		31:13
ye shall have no king n. ruler,		38:21
n. in the world to come.		42:18
neighbor, n. do him any harm.		42:27
n. wear the garments of the		42:42
on earth, n. ever shall know,		43:33
n. shall they know until he		49: 7
with boasting n. rejoicing,		50:33
idolatry n. wickedness practised.		52:39
be no in haste, n. by flight;		58:56
neither commit adultery, n. kill,		59: 6
n. do anything like unto it.		59: 6
neither in wrath n. with strife.		60:14
will of men, n. as they please,		63:10
eye hath not seen, n. ear heard,		76:10
n. yet entered into the heart		76:10
n. in the world to come.—		76:34
place thereof, n. their torment,		76:45
neither the sea, n. the trees,		77: 9
world n. in the world to come.		84:41
neither in body, limb, n. joint;		84:80
n. the names of the children		85: 5
by mercy, justice, n. judgment.		88:35
world, n. in the world to come.		93:52
the second time, the third time,		98:35
gathering be in haste, n. by flight;		101:68
fear not God, n. regard man,		101:84

be called his, n. any part of it.	DC	104:70
of faith n. of mighty works,		105:24
n. their posterity after them		121:21
cannot be controlled n. handled		121:36
n. unto the voice of these men		124:46
n. under fifty dollars;		124:72
n. his seed be found begging bread.		124:90
can they n. we be made perfect		128:18
in n. after the resurrection,		132:13
her not by me n. by my word,		132:15
they neither marry n. are given in		132:16
be forgiven in the world n. out		132:27
neither the day n. the hour.		133:11
have not men heard n. perceived		133:45
leave them neither root n. branch.		133:64
n. dictate forms for public or		134: 4
not justify sedition n. conspiracy.		134: 7
n. baptize them contrary to the		134:12
n. to meddle with or influence		134:12
n. permitting any person to enter		OD
n. believe on his Only Begotten	Mses	5:57
n. ever shall be sent again upon	JS	1:18
n. do I believe that any earthly		2:31
leave them neither root n. branch.		2:37
n. ever before had thought of.		2:74

NORTH

these from the n. and from	1Ne	21:12
in the sides of the n.;	2Ne	24:13
shall come from the n. a smoke,		24:31
and in the n., and in the south,		29:11
which is n. of the land of Shilom,	Mos	7: 5
the hill which was n. of Shilom,		7:16
the n. of the land of Shilom,		10: 8
the hill n. of the land Shilom,		11:13
yea, on the n. and on the south,		27: 6
wilderness which was west and n.,	Al	2:36
on the west, and on the n.,		2:37
on the n. of the land of Melek;		8: 6
wilderness which was on the n.		22:27
on the n., even until they came		22:29
no more possession on the n.,		22:33
came up on the n. of the hill,		43:34
on the n. and on the south—		46:17
which was n. of the lands of		50: 9
to build many cities on the n.,		50:15
in the n. by the borders of		50:15
obtain the n. parts of the land.	He	1:23
neither on the n., nor on the		1:31
from the sea south to the sea n.,		3: 8
to defend their n. country.		4: 7
land south and in the land n.		6: 9
land n. was called Mulek		6:10
bring Mulek into the land n.,		6:10
both in the n. and in the south;		6:12
both in the n. and in the south.		6:12
both in the land n. and in the	3Ne	1:17
and which were in the land n.,		4: 1
both on the n. and on the south,		6: 2
from the south and from the n.;		20:13
retreat towards the n. countries.	Mrm	2: 3
upon the face of this n. country.	Eth	1: 1
to be fruit in the n. countries,		9:35
and from the n. countries,		13:11
to the n. and to the south.	DC	42:63
from the n. and from the south,		44: 1
or to the n., or to the south.		75:26
to the n. or to the south,		80: 3
and second lots on the n.		94:14
tribes from the land of the n.		110:11
the east, and the west, and the n.,		125: 4
driven back into the n. countries,		133:23
they who are in the n. countries		133:26
the n., and I beheld the people of	Mses	7: 6

NORTHERN

of all the n. parts of the land	Al	22:29
against the N. States,	DC	87: 3

NORTHERNMOST

into the n. part of the land,	3Ne	7:12

NORTHROP

you, my servants Ezra and N.,	DC	33: 1

NORTHWARD

bones lay scattered in the land n.	Om	1:22
it being so far n. that it	Al	22:30
on the n. was called Desolation,		22:31
come from the land n. for food.		22:31
land n. and the land southward.		22:32
might not overrun the land n.,		22:33
as our brethren in the land n.,		46:22
possessing all the land n.,		50:11
was n. of the land Bountiful,		50:11
flee to the land which was n.,		50:29
of the land which was n.		50:29
to flee into the land n.		50:31
stop their flight into the land n.		50:33
led by the sea into the land n.,		50:34
Bountiful, and also the land n.		51:30
in marching into the land n.,		52: 2
pass which led into the land n.,		52: 9
retreat down by the seashore, n.		52:23
other cities which were on the n.		56:22
we did flee before them, n.		56:36
into the land which was n.		63: 4
neck which led into the land n.		63: 5
and they took their course n.		63: 6
and set out again to the land n.		63: 7
who went forth into the land n.		63: 9
forth to the land n. in a ship,		63:10
and went forth unto the land n.	He	3: 3
land southward to the land n.,		3: 8
people who were in the land n.		3: 9
exceeding scarce in the land n.,		3:10
enable the people in the land n.		3:11
did go into the land n.;		6: 6
and Lehi went into the land n.,		6: 6
of Zarahemla from the land n.		7: 1
people who were in the land n.,		7: 2
both on the n. and on the		11:20
which was upon the land n.	3Ne	3:24
furthermost parts of the land n.		4:23
both on the land n. and on		6: 2
destruction in the land n.;		8:12
n. to the land which was called	Mrm	2:20
did give unto us the land n.,		2:29
down into the valley which is n.	Eth	1:42
into the valley which was n.,		2: 1
the whole face of the land n.		10:21

NOSE

The rings, and n. jewels;	2Ne	13:21

NOSTRILS

man, whose breath is in his n.;	2Ne	12:22
into his n. the breath of life;	Mses	3: 7
and breathed into his n. the	Abr	5: 7

NOT: *see in the APPENDIX.*

NOTABLE

great and n. cities were sunk,	3Ne	8:14
unto the great and n. cities	DC	84:117

NOTED

and was n. for his much strength.	Al	1: 2

NOTHING

and took n. with him,	1Ne	2: 4
n. save it were the power of God,		18:20
n., save it shall be iniquity	2Ne	1:31
should have charity they were n.		26:30
he doeth n. save it be plain		26:33
There is n. which is secret save it		30:17
there is n. which is sealed upon		30:17
and it profiteth me n.,	Jac	5:32
The tree profiteth me n.,		5:35
the roots thereof profit me n.		5:35
of my vineyard are good for n.		5:42
did eat n. save it was raw meat;	En	1:20
n. save it was exceeding harshness,		1:23

there was n. short of these things,	En	1:23
there is n. which is good save	Om	1:25
know n. concerning these things,	Mos	1: 5
there should n. come upon you		2:14
the law of Moses availeth n. except		3:15
people had heard n. from them		7: 1
knew n. concerning the Lord,		10:11
they should teach n. save it were		18:19
they should preach n. save it were		18:20
heard n. concerning this matter;		20:16
for there was n. preached in all		25:22
and n. shall overthrow it,		27:13
was n. save the power of God		27:18
I shall say n. which is contrary	Al	11:22
know n. concerning his mysteries;		12:11
and Amulek answered him n.;		14:17
but they answered them n.		14:18
to speak; but they answered n.		14:19
Yea, I know that I am n.;		26:12
n. save it were the power of God		30:52
which they knew n. about.		31:22
n. which is short of an infinite		34:12
is vain, and availeth you n.,		34:28
n. so exquisite and so bitter as		36:21
n. so exquisite and sweet as was		36:21
we know n. concerning his death		45:19
do n. and he would deliver you?		60:11
and n. did he speak which was	He	8: 3
heaven, where n. doth corrupt,		8:25
n. can come which is unclean,		8:25
the people knew n. concerning		9: 8
I, Nephi, know n. concerning		9:36
n. can save this people save it		13: 6
they had n. save it were meat	3Ne	4:19
n. in all the land to hinder the		6: 5
shall be thenceforth good for n.,		12:13
good for n. but to be cast out		16:15
n. varying from the words		19: 8
n. upon earth so white as		19:25
n. entereth into his rest save it		27:19
in n. did they work miracles	4Ne	1: 5
believeth in Christ, doubting n.,	Mrm	9:21
believe in my name, doubting n.,		9:25
for he knew, n. doubting.	Eth	3:19
real intent it profitteth him n.	Mro	7: 6
yea, and it profitteth him n.,		7: 9
if he have not charity he is n.;		7:44
if ye have not charity, ye are n.,		7:46
unto such baptism availeth n.—		8:22
n. that is good denieth the		10: 6
Say n. but repentance unto	DC	6: 9
without faith you can do n.;		8:10
Say n. but repentance unto		11: 9
and charity, you can do n.		18:19
times it availeth him n.,		22: 2
n. shall prevail against them.		32: 3
in n. doth man offend God,		59:21
good for n. only to be cast out		101:40
good for n. but to be cast out		103:10
n. shall be withheld,		121:28
if he pays n. into their hands		124:68
but he hath n. in me.		127:11
in n. did they sin save		132:38
n. in my teachings to the		OD
this cause I know that man is n.,	Mses	1:10
is n. that the Lord thy God shall	Abr	3:17

NOTHINGNESS

you to a sense of your n.,	Mos	4: 5
your own n., and his goodness		4:11
O how great is the n. of the	He	12: 7

NOTICE

pass by you, and n. them not?	Mrm	8:39
take n. sufficient to excite the	JS	2:22

NOTIFIED

n. of their appointment.	DC	118: 6

NOTION

is an old sectarian n.,	DC	130: 3

NOTWITHSTANDING

n. we had suffered many afflictions	1Ne	17: 6
n. they being led,		17:30
n. he hath done all this,		20:22
n. our afflictions, we have	2Ne	1: 5
n. the great goodness of the Lord,		4:17
n. they have been carried away		25:11
n. we believe in Christ,		25:24
are given, n. all persecution—		26: 8
for, n. the pains of my soul,		26:10
n. I shall lengthen out mine arm		28:32
But n. he being holy, he showeth		31: 7
these things, n. my weakness.		33:11
n. the greatness of the task,	Jac	2:10
n., n. all our labor;		5:32
n. all the care which we have		5:46
n. the many revelations		7: 5
n. our many strugglings, which	Mos	7:18
perish, n. the law of Moses.		13:28
n. there being many churches		25:22
But n. all this, they did impart		27:33
n. all their persecutions.	Al	1:28
n. they were so numerous that		2:35
n. a shepherd hath called		5:37
n. the promises of the Lord		17:15
N. they believed in a Great Spirit		18: 5
But n. this, king Lamoni did		18:18
But n. the law of Moses, they		25:15
n. my many travels round about		30:32
And n. the many labors which I		30:33
n. their number being so much		43:21
n. the preaching of Helaman		46: 6
n. their exceeding great care over		46: 6
n. their great victory which		46: 7
n. their peace amongst		48:21
n. their much reluctance.		48:22
but n. their great loss,		51:11
n. all the intrigues of the		55:27
n. the Lamanites being cut off		57:11
n. the enormity of our numbers,		57:13
n. that which we had taken		57:15
n. the weakness of our armies,		58:37
n. their riches, or their strength,		62:49
n. the greatness of the number	He	1:25
And n. the mildness of the voice,		5:31
n. so many evidences which		8:24
behold, n. that great miracle		10:13
n. his greatness and his		12: 6
their days, n. their iniquity—		15:10
and n. the many afflictions which		15:12
n. they shall be driven to and		15:12
n. the many mighty works		15:17
n. the signs and the wonders		16:23
n. these lyings and deceivings	3Ne	1:22
n. the much preaching and		2:10
n. the threatenings and the oaths		4:12
n. they were not a righteous		7:11
n. so many signs had been		8: 4
n. it being a small voice it did		11: 3
n. they have come forth upon		16: 8
and n. all these miracles,	4Ne	1:31
And n. I being young,	Mrm	2: 1
but n. all our fortifications		2: 4
and n. the great destruction		2: 8
n. their wickedness I had led		3:12
n. they had sworn unto him to	Eth	9:10
n. their hardness, let us labor	Mro	9: 6
n. this great abomination of the		9: 9
But n. those things which are	DC	46: 2
n. he is the least and the		50:26
n. the tribulation which shall		78:14
n. it shall die, it shall be		88:26
For n. they die, they also		88:27
I say unto you, n. their sins,		101: 9
n. her children are scattered.		101:17
n. the vanity of his heart, I will		106: 7
n. he was bowed down with age,		107:56
n. they may hold as high and		107:98
n. your follies.		111: 1
n. the hour of temptation that		124:124
n. the Pharoahs would fain claim	Abr	1:27

NOTWITHSTANDING / NUMBER

one is more intelligent than	Abr	3:18
n. the great love which the	JS	2: 6

NOURISH
he doth n. them, and strengthen	1Ne	17: 3
a man shall n. a young cow	2Ne	17:21
and dig about it, and n. it,	Jac	5: 4
and n. it, according to my words.		5:12
and n. it a little longer,		5:27
did n. all the fruit of the vineyard.		5:28
we will n. again the trees		5:58
time that I shall n. my vineyard;		5:71
to n. and prune his vineyard;		6: 2
and did n. them with things	Mos	23:18
Let us n. it with great care,	Al	32:37
if ye n. it with much care it		32:37
and ye will not n. the tree,		32:39
if ye will not n. the word,		32:40
But if ye will n. the word,		32:41
n. the tree as it beginneth to grow,		32:41
even so n. it by your faith.		33:23
and they did n. them, and did		35: 9

NOURISHED
their being n. by the Gentiles	1Ne	22: 8
took and n. in his vineyard;	Jac	5: 3
and n. it according to his word.		5: 5
digged about, and pruned, and n.,		5:11
this long time have I n. it,		5:20
I have n. it this long time,		5:22
I have n. it this long time,		5:23
behold that I have n. it also,		5:24
and I have n. it this long time,		5:25
behold I have n. this tree like		5:25
this long time have we n. this tree,		5:31
they have n. the roots,		5:34
mine hand, that I have not n. it?		5:47
Nay, I have n. it,		5:47
that all may be n. once again		5:63
time have we n. my vineyard;		5:75
time have I n. my vineyard,		5:76
been n. by the good word of God		6: 7
was n. for the space of many days.		7:15
sick, or that had not been n.;	Al	1:30
in need to be n. by your brothers.		39:10
her wings, and have n. you.	3Ne	10: 4
n. by the good word of God,	Mro	6: 4
be n. with all tenderness,	DC	42:43

NOURISHING
patience with the word in n. it,	Al	32:42

NOURISHMENT
and n. from the true vine?	1Ne	15:15
having need of much n.,		18:19
and take no thought for its n.,	Al	32:38

NOVEMBER
(who died N. 19th, 1824,	JS	2: 4

NOW: *see in the APPENDIX.*

NOWHERE
they could n. be found	He	2:11
could n. be found in all the land.	3Ne	2: 9

NOWISE
do this ye shall in n. be cast out.	2Ne	25:29
n. inherit the kingdom of God.	Mos	27:26
ye can in n. inherit the kingdom	Al	5:51
n. inherit the kingdom of God.		9:12
can in n. inherit the kingdom		39: 9
ye will in n. be delivered out	3Ne	3:15
ye can in n. receive these things.		11:37
in n. inherit the kingdom of God.		11:38
the end, ye will in n. be cast out.	Mrm	9:29
ye can in n. be saved in the	Mro	10:21
in n. deny the power of God.		10:32
or they can in n. be saved;	DC	33:12
shall in n. lose their reward.		58:28
shall in n. lose his crown;		75:28
shall in n. lose his reward.		84:90
you shall in n. lose your reward,		127: 4

can in n. enter into my glory,	DC	132:27
n. inherit the kingdom of God,	Mses	6:57

NUMBER
how great a n. had testified	1Ne	10: 5
in n. as many as the sand		12: 1
even that I did not n. them.		12: 3
every sort according to its n.	Jac	5:31
concerning a certain n. who went	Om	1:27
there was a large n. who were		1:27
took others to a considerable n.,		1:29
And there were a great n.,	Mos	2: 2
many that they did not n. them;		2: 2
so many that I cannot n. them.		4:29
the greater n. of our army was		9: 2
many that we did not n. them.		10:20
he did not send a sufficient n.,		11:17
a goodly n. gathered together		18: 7
in n. about two hundred and		18:16
priest to every fifty of their n.		18:18
in n. about four hundred and		18:35
a small n. of them gathered		20: 2
among the n. of their dead;		20:12
there was a great n. of women,		21:17
of the greatness of their n.		21:17
a small n. of men to search for		21:25
he did n. among the people of		26:35
they took a small n. with them		28: 1
a small n. of your lower judges		29:29
now the n. of the slain were	Al	3: 1
of the greatness of their n.—		3: 1
Now this is their n., according		11:18
for a certain n. of years,		16: 1
a certain n. of the Lamanites,		17:27
and they were in n. not a few.		17:34
he slew a certain n. of them		17:36
they were not few in n.;		17:37
the n. which he had slain of		19:21
a certain n. of his brethren were		21:13
the n. who had been slain;		24:26
Now the greatest n. of those of		24:28
the greatest n. of whom were		24:28
behold the n. of your sheaves!		26: 5
their n. being so much greater		43:21
double the n. of the Nephites;		43:51
the n. of their dead was not		44:21
because of the greatness of the n.;		44:21
the n. of their dead was		44:21
with a small n. of his men,		46:33
greatness of the n. of his people,		48: 4
did place the greater n. of men;		48: 9
seeing the enormity of their n.,		52: 5
large n. of men to strengthen		52: 7
together a large n. of men,		52:12
should take a small n. of men		52:22
the n. of prisoners who were		52:40
exceeded more than the n. of		52:40
obtained possession of a n. of		53: 8
and a small n. of his men		55: 6
that a small n. of men		55: 7
had slain a vast n. of our men,		56:10
the n. of six thousand men,		57: 6
greater n. of them were slain;		57:33
that they might discover the n.		58:14
Gid, with a small n. of men,		58:16
Teomner and a small n. of men		58:16
maintain so great a n. of cities		58:32
Moroni took a small n. of men,		62: 3
in n. about four thousand who		62:17
the greatness of the n. of the	He	1:25
and among the n. who were slain		1:30
of the greatness of the n. of		4:20
a certain n. of the dissenters		11:24
also a certain n. who were real		11:24
having so great a n., and having	3Ne	4: 4
not so strong in n. as the		7:11
the n. of them who had been		12: 1
in n. about two thousand and		17:25
yea, an exceeding great n.,		19: 3
together a great n. of men,	Mrm	1:11
exceed the n. of thirty thousand.		1:11
this same year a n. of battles,		1:11
and did slay a great n. of them,		3: 8

NUMBER

this because their n. did exceed	Mrm 4:13
exceed the n. of the Nephites.	4:13
of the greatness of their n.	4:17
the n. of the vessels which had	Eth 3: 1
in n. about twenty and two	6:16
people that we may n. them,	6:19
the n. of the sons and the	6:20
the n. of sons and daughters	6:20
that they did n. their people;	6:21
together a small n. of men,	9: 9
a great n. of our choice men.	Mro 9: 2
The n. composing the council,	DC 102: 5
commencing with n. one and	102:12
so in succession to n. twelve.	102:12
to appoint one of their own n.	102:25
to the n. of five hundred of the	103:30
which is lot n. one, and also	104:28
chosen out of the n. of the	107:93
ye could not n. them.	132:30
a sufficient n. of able-bodied	136: 7
other n. of plural marriages	OD
worlds without n. have I	Mses 1:33
n. the particles of the earth,	7:30
to the n. of thy creations;	7:30
not so many as to its n. of days,	Abr 3: 5
thou canst count the n. of sands,	3:14
so shall be the n. of thy seeds.	3:14
ninth n. of the *Times and*	Fac 3: 3
a considerable n. of them,	JS 2:62

NUMBERED

shall be n. among the seed	1Ne 14: 2
shall be n. among the house	14: 2
thy seed shall be n. with his seed;	2Ne 4:11
n. among the house of Israel.	10:18
them who shall be n. among thy seed,	10:19
was n. with the transgressors;	Mos 14:12
be n. with those of the first	18: 9
be n. among those who were	25:12
were n. with the Nephites,	25:13
not be n. among my people;	26:32
not n. among the people of	26:36
were n. among the unbelievers;	27: 8
sons of Alma was n. among them,	27: 8
that they could not be n.	Al 2:35
number of the slain were not n.,	3: 1
shall not be n. among the	5:57
their names were not n. among	6: 3
also n. among the people who	27:27
Now their dead were not n.	30: 2
the dead of the Nephites n.—	30: 2
number of their dead was not n.	44:21
n. among the people of Nephi,	45:13
n. among the people of Nephi.	45:13
be n. among the Lamanites,	45:14
I n. those young men who had	56:55
and be n. among his sheep.	He 15:13
were n. among the Nephites;	3Ne 2:14
were n. among the Nephites,	2:16
were n. among the Nephites,	3:14
ye are n. among those whom	15:24
shall be n. among my sheep,	16: 3
shall be n. among my people,	16:13
shall not be n. among my people,	18:31
know my sheep, and they are n.	18:31
may be n. among my people,	21: 6
be n. among this the remnant of	21:22
be n. with my people who are	30: 2
they were not n. because of	Mrm 4:17
ye are n. among the people of	7:10
and after that they had n. them,	Eth 6:21
are n. among the remnant of	13:10
were n. among the people of	Mro 6: 4
n. among the people of Christ.	6: 7
be n. among the people of his	7:39
thy years shall not be n. less;	DC 122: 9
but all things are n. unto me,	Mses 1:35
they cannot be n. unto man;	1:37
but they are n. unto me,	1:37
to pass that they n. the days;	Abr 4:13
day; and they n. the sixth time.	4:31

NUMBERETH

and he n. his sheep,	1Ne 22:25
yea, he n. his people,	Al 26:37

NUMBERLESS

surrounded with n. concourses	1Ne 1: 8
I saw n. concourses of people,	8:21
with n. concourses of angels,	Al 36:22
many cities, by their n. hosts,	51:27
n. as the sand upon the sea shore.	Mses 1:28

NUMBERS

and its n. were few, because of	1Ne 14:12
upon his people, upon small n.,	Mos 11:16
captains, according to their n.	Al 2:13
lesser n. of their reckoning—	11:14
into the wilderness with their n.	17: 8
of the greatness of their n.;	30: 2
of the greatness of their n.,	49: 6
supposing by their n. to	52:23
of the smallness of his n.	52:23
the enormity of our n.,	57:13
they would break out in great n.,	57:14
not strong, according to our n.,	58:15
the greatness of their n.,	62:19
daily an addition to their n.,	He 11:25
exceeding greatness of the n. of	11:31
who do add to their n. daily.	15: 6
lands, according to their n.,	3Ne 6: 3
so great were their n. that	Mrm 5: 6
of the greatness of their n.	6: 8
councilors to cast lots by n.,	DC 102:12
councilors who draw even n.,	102:17
n. were great, even numberless	Mses 1:28
stars represented by n. 22 and	Fac 2: 5
can find out these n.,	2:11

NUMERICAL

a n. figure, in Egyptian	Fac 2: 4

NUMEROUS

which now began to be n.,	Jac 3:13
they were exceeding more n.	Jar 1: 6
they had become exceeding n.	Om 1:17
as n. as the hosts of Israel.	Mos 8: 8
a n. host of Lamanites came	9:14
with their n. hosts, men armed	10: 8
not half so n. as the Lamanites.	20:11
they come with their n. hosts;	20:20
for the Lamanites being so n.,	22: 2
And he was king over a n. people.	24: 3
yea, they were not half so n.	25: 3
half so n. as the people of God;	26: 5
brethren they became more n.	26: 5
the people began to be very n.,	27: 6
saw a n. host of the Lamanites;	Al 2:24
being n. almost, as it were	2:27
notwithstanding they were so n.	2:35
sent up a n. army against them;	3:23
those descendants were as n.,	43:14
the Lamanites were more n.,	43:51
more n. than the Amalickiahites—	46:29
gathered together a n. host	48: 3
marching forth with his n. army	51:30
the Lamanites; yea, the most n.	56:34
our prisoners were so n. that,	57:13
and also a n. army of men.	57:17
more n. than was our army	58: 2
destroy us with their n. hosts,	58:15
did come out with their n. army	58:18
we know that they are more n.	58:36
And thus being exceeding n.,	59: 7
their armies were so n. that	59: 8
have risen up are exceeding n.	61: 3
they came down with a n. army	63:15
forth at the head of his n. host,	He 1:19
of a n. army of the Lamanites,	4: 8
so n. were the Lamanites that	4:19
exceedingly more n. than they,	4:25
they who chose evil were more n.	5: 2
more n. among the more wicked	6:18

NUMEROUS

robbers had become so n.,	3Ne 2:11
enemies were more n. than	7:12
exceedingly more n. than	4Ne 1:40
the people were as n. almost,	Mrm 1: 7
had become exceeding n.	Eth 7:11
the children of men were n.	Mses 6:15
people of Canaan, which are n.,	7: 7

NURSED
shall be n. by the Gentiles,	1Ne 22: 6

NURSING
kings shall be thy n. fathers,	1Ne 21:23
their queens thy n. mothers;	21:23
kings shall be thy n. fathers,	2Ne 6: 7
and their queens thy n. mothers;	6: 7
shall be n. fathers unto them,	10: 9
queens shall become n. mothers;	10: 9

NURTURE
n. and admonition of the Lord—	En 1: 1

O: *see in the APPENDIX.*

OAK
as an o. whose substance is in	2Ne 16:13

OAKS
and upon all the o. of Bashan;	2Ne 12:13

OATH
with an o., that he need not fear;	1Ne 4:33
he also made an o. unto us	4:35
Zoram had made an o. unto us,	4:37
of the o. which they had made,	Mos 6: 3
Lamanites made an o. unto them,	19:25
o. unto the king of the Lamanites	19:26
the o. that I made unto you;	20:14
the o. which ye made unto my	20:14
I have broken the o. because thy	20:15
fulfil the o. which we have made	20:22
and I swear unto you with an o.	20:24
the o. which their king had made	21: 3
ourselves to take an o. unto you,	Al 44: 8
except ye depart with an o. that	44:11
sworn with an o. to defend	48:13
took an o. that they would	49:13
sworn with an o. to attack	49:17
swearing with an o. that he	49:27
with an o. and sacred ordinance	50:39
because of their o. they had	53:11
they had taken an o. that they	53:11
according to their o. they	53:11
the o. which they had made.	53:14
because of the fulfilling the o.	56: 8
if ye will do this, with an o.,	3Ne 3: 8
I swear unto you that ye	3: 8
did repent of the o. which I had	Mrm 5: 1
sworn by the o. of the ancients,	Eth 9: 5
to the o. and covenant which	DC 84:39
receive this o. and covenant	84:40
I will not perform the o. which	124:47
and sware unto him with an o.,	Mses 7:51
to fulfil the o. which I have made	7:60

OATH'S
but he slew him for the o. sake.	Mses 5:50

OATHS
you that ye retain all their o.,	Al 37:27
keep these secret plans of their o.	37:29
into their covenants and their o.,	He 6:21
these secret o. and covenants	6:25
those secret o. and covenants	6:26
down their plots, and their o.,	6:30
o. which Giddianhi had made,	3Ne 4:12
perform unto the Lord thine o.;	12:33
to build up the secret o. and	4Ne 1:42
the o. which were given by	Eth 8:15
to administer these o. unto	8:16
of their o. and combinations,	8:20
and administered o. after the	10:33

contracts, bonds, obligations, o.,	DC 132: 7
by their o., they have brought	Mses 6:29

OATS
the ox, and o. for the horse,	DC 89:17

OBEDIENCE
promised o. unto the commands.	Jac 7:27
in o. to the commandments,	DC 89:18
chastened until they learn o.,	105: 6
through his diligence and o.	130:19
it is by o. to that law upon	130:21
in o. to that which I have told	132:50
by o to the laws and ordinances	AoF 3

OBEDIENT
o. unto the word of the Lord,	1Ne 2: 3
o. to the commandments of God.	22:30
shall be o. to the commandments,	22:31
to be o. to the commandments	2Ne 5:31
that he would be o. unto him	31: 7
o. unto the word of the Lord,	Jac 2: 4
o. unto the commands of God	4: 5
to be o. to his commandments	Mos 5: 5
be o. unto the end of your lives.	5: 8
was o. unto his commands,	Al 47: 3
favor of those who were not o.;	47: 5
o. unto the things which I	DC 28: 3
that you might be o., and	58: 6
the willing and o. shall eat	64:34
have not learned to be o. to	105: 3
was o. unto the commandments	Mses 5: 5
God giveth unto all the o.	5:11
behold, they shall be very o.	Abr 4:31

OBEDIENTLY
and they serve him o., and he	DC 38:26

OBEY
I did o. the voice of the Spirit,	1Ne 4:18
commanding you that ye must o.	2Ne 1:27
children of Ammon shall o. them.	21:14
commanded me, and I must o.	33:15
and the very trees o. us,	Jac 4: 6
they did o. the commandments	5:72
and ye list to obey the evil spirit,	Mos 2:32
him who listeth to o. that spirit;	2:33
for if he listeth to o. him,	2:33
he listeth to o. the evil spirit,	2:37
whosoever doth not o. his laws	29:23
the spirit which they listed to o.,	Al 3:26
of him whom he listeth to o.	3:27
more part of them would not, o.	47: 2
did o. and observe to perform	57:21
wages of whom they list to o.	DC 29:45
that he would o. my word.	40: 1
hearken and heard.	42: 2
of me if he o. mine ordinances.	52:15
if he o. mine ordinances.	52:16
he that will not o. shall	56: 3
o. the former commandment	56: 8
And ye o. not the truth,	56:15
I command and men o. not;	58:32
o. not his commandments	59:21
Foster will o. my voice,	124:115
o. the instructions which I am	132: 3
must o. the same	132: 3
and ye shall o. my voice;	132:53
for they shall o. thy command	Mses 1:25
the Gods saw they would o.	Abr 4:25

OBEYED
that I o. the voice of the angel,	Al 10: 8
who have o. my gospel;	DC 59: 3
my voice, and it shall be o.	63: 5
because you have o. my voice	108: 1
ye o. not my voice when I called	133:71
the Gods saw that they were o.	Abr 4:10
the Gods saw that they were o.	4:12
they had ordered until they o.	4:18
Gods saw that they would be o.,	4:21
I o.; I returned to my father	JS 2:50

OBEYETH

OBEYETH
that o. the voice of his servant,	2Ne 7:10
as he o. mine ordinances.	DC 64: 5
on my name, and o. my voice,	93: 1

OBEYING
o. the message which he had	Al 15: 5
in o., honoring, and sustaining	AoF 12

OBEYS
o. not my commandments?	DC 58:30
the sea, and it o. my voice;	Abr 2: 7

OBJECT
I have none other o. save it be	2Ne 2:30
the o. of these lawyers was to	Al 10:32
our next o. was to obtain the	58: 1
unto him the o. of his desire,	He 2: 7
that it was his o. to murder,	2: 8
the o. of all those who belonged	2: 8
My o. in going to inquire of	JS 2:18
must have no other o. in view	2:46

OBLATIONS
thou shalt offer thine o.	DC 59:12

OBLIGATIONS
covenants, contracts, bonds, o.,	DC 132: 7

OBLIGED
o. to leave behind our property,	1Ne 3:26
were o. to abide by the laws	Al 1: 1
were o. to contend with their	43:14
were o. to maintain the cause	51: 7
were o. to employ all our force	57:13
were o. to flee before them;	59: 8
they were again o. to return out	He 11:31
who is o. to provide for his	DC 75:28

OBSCURE
and though I was an o. boy,	JS 2:22
strange it was that an o. boy,	2:23

OBSCURITY
they shall be brought out of o.	1Ne 22:12
and come forth out of o.,	2Ne 1:23
the blind shall see out of o.	27:29
to bring it forth out of o.	DC 1:30

OBSERVANCE
wherefore, because of this o.,	Jac 3: 6

OBSERVE
remember to o. the statutes	2Ne 1:16
we did o. to keep the judgments,	5:10
say unto you shall ye o. to do.	32: 6
commandment they o. to keep;	Jac 3: 6
o. the commandments of God,	Mos 4:30
and did o. his judgments	6: 6
should o. to do all these things	13:25
a law which they were to o.	13:30
they should o. the sabbath day,	18:23
therefore this shall ye o. and	29:26
that ye o. to do the words which	Al 5:61
did o. to keep his commandments	25:14
did o. to keep the commandments	30: 3
o. to keep his commandments	31: 9
would they o. the performances	31:10
o. to perform every word of	57:21
do o. to keep his statutes,	58:40
did o. to do good continually,	63: 2
he did o. to keep the statutes,	He 3:20
Lamanites did o. strictly to keep	13: 1
do o. to keep his commandments	15: 5
repent, and o. to do my will,	15:17
to o. the law of Moses.	3Ne 1:24
this shall ye always o. to do,	18: 6
sober child, and art quick to o.;	Mrm 1: 2
strict to o. that there should	Mro 6: 7
they shall o. the covenants	DC 42:13
all this ye shall o. to do as	42:15
thou shalt o. all these things,	42:65
Ye shall o. the laws which ye	42:66
o. to keep all the commandments	DC 42:78
who o. not to keep my	63:22
also o. the Sabbath day	68:29
things which he shall o. and	69: 3
to o. their covenants by sacrifice—	97: 8
if she o. to do all things	97:25
But if she o. not to do	97:26
should o. to do all things	98: 4
wise men ye should o. to uphold;	98:10
and o. the words of wisdom	98:20
o. all things whatsoever I	98:21
if ye o. to do whatsoever I	98:22
o. the commandment which I	101:69
o. to have all things prepared	101:72
to o. all the words which I,	103: 7
hearken not to o. all my words,	103: 8
shall o. this law, or they shall	119: 5
if my people o. not this law,	119: 6

OBSERVED
o. to keep the law of Moses	Jar 1: 5
this shall be o. from this time	Mos 26:32
o. the steadiness of thy brother,	Al 39: 1
this law should be strictly o.	62:10
the things that ye have o.	Mrm 1: 3
all the things that ye have o.	1: 4
and o. the commandment,	DC 54: 6

OBSERVETH
that o. not his prayers	DC 68:33

OBSERVING
in o. the ordinances of God,	Al 30: 3
henceforth in o. your vows,	DC 108: 3

OBSTINATE
I knew that thou art o.,	1Ne 20: 4

OBSTRUCTION
word of God might have no o.,	Al 23: 3

OBTAIN
that we should o. these records,	1Ne 3:19
that he might o. our property.	3:25
that I might o. the records	4:17
to o. the record of the Jews.	5: 6
that we should o. the record?	7:11
we shall o. the land of promise;	7:13
that they might o. the path	8:21
o. the land for their inheritance;	13:15
o. food for our families.	16:17
for we did o. no food.	16:18
that we could o. no food.	16:21
Whither shall I go to o. food?	16:23
did o. food for our families.	16:31
they should o. these things.	19:19
they shall o. gladness and joy;	2Ne 8:11
ye shall o. riches, if ye seek them;	Jac 2:19
all these witnesses we o. a hope,	4: 6
and ye may o. a resurrection.	4:11
until ye shall o. eternal life.	6:11
Nephites did o. much advantage	Om 1:24
they o. possession of our city,	Al 2:25
did not o. the outer door of the	14:27
to o. those who had been carried	16: 4
they sought to o. these things by	17:14
that they might o. this fruit	33: 1
easy for him to o. forgiveness;	39: 6
easy for him to o. a forgiveness.	39: 6
that he might o. his purposes.	46:30
not o. power over the Nephites	49:22
might o. a pass to their armies,	49:22
would o. possession of those	50:32
Lamanites did o. that point	52: 9
should not o. the city Mulek	52:28
to o. as many prisoners of the	54: 3
maintain and to o. their rights	54:24
was to o. the city of Manti;	58: 1
might o. the remainder of	59: 4
may o. more food to send forth	61:18
could not o. the judgment-seat.	He 1: 6
that he might o. the north parts	1:23
could o. no more possessions	4:18

OBTAIN

to o. the remainder of their	He	4:19
to o. more power over them;		4:19
they did o. the sole management		6:39
for that which ye could not o.;		13:38
to plunder and to o. food,	3Ne	4: 4
they did o. in the wilderness;		4:19
merciful, for they shall o. mercy.		12: 7
he did o. the land of their first	Eth	7:16
did o. kingdoms and great		8: 9
he did o. all his fine work,		10: 7
did o. unto himself the kingdom.		10:15
his son, did o. the kingdom;		11:10
of Ahah, did o. the kingdom;		11:11
and did o. the kingdom again.		11:16
Moron and o. the kingdom;		11:18
that they might o. the kingdom.		13:18
did o. the kingdom again unto		13:24
first seek to o. my word,	DC	11:21
you shall o. a view of them,		17: 2
should o. treasures of earth		19:38
o. power to organize yourselves		44: 4
I power to o. eternal life.		45: 8
that ye o. all that ye can		48: 4
for they shall o. mercy.		54: 6
may o. it for an everlasting		57: 5
o. money to buy lands for		57: 8
he may o. whatsoever things		57: 8
Sidney Gilbert o. a license—		57: 9
let him o. whatsoever he can		57:12
can o. in righteousness,		57:12
the churches to o. moneys,		58:51
they may o. an inheritance		64:30
not fail, that they shall o. it.		64:31
more easily o. knowledge—		69: 7
that they also may o. funds		72:21
ye o. places for your families,		75:25
o. places for their families,		75:26
they o. not the crown over		76:79
diligently to o. an agent,		90:22
shall o. benefit therefrom;		91: 5
and to o. a knowledge of history,		93:53
are such, for they shall o.;		97: 2
are they, for they shall o. mercy.		99: 3
and o. the mind of the Lord by		102:23
if you cannot o. five hundred,		103:32
you may o. three hundred.		103:32
if ye cannot o. three hundred,		103:33
ye may o. one hundred.		103:33
among you o. five talents		104:69
or if he o. ten, or twenty,		104:69
o. this blessing by your diligence		104:79
o. a chance to load money by		104:84
to o. every needful thing;		109:15
may o. favor in the sight of all;		109:56
This place you may o. by hire.		111: 9
may o. the confidence of men.		124:112
when we o. any blessing from		130:21
And in order to o. the highest,		131: 2
if he does not, he cannot o. it.		131: 3
o. another place of residence;	Abr	1: 1
might ask of God, and o.,	JS	2:26

OBTAINED

I have o. a land of promise,	1Ne	5: 5
we had o. the records		5:21
beheld that I had o. food,		16:32
of promise which they had o.—	2Ne	1: 3
we have o. a land of promise,		1: 5
I, Lehi, have o. a promise,		1: 9
he o. a promise of the Lord,		3: 5
which I have o. of the Lord,		3:14
and the devil hath o. me,		9:46
the promises which we have o.		10: 2
and o. the witnesses which		27:22
Have ye o. a Bible save it were		29: 6
o. mine errand from the Lord.	Jac	1:17
that you have o. many riches;		2:13
of you have o. more abundantly		2:13
after ye have o. a hope in Christ		2:19
and o. a good hope of glory in		4:11
which he o. by the taxation of	Mos	11:13
they had o. by their industry;	Al	4: 6

servants, he o. the kingdom;	Al	47:35
Amalickiah had o. the kingdom		48: 1
had not o. his desire over the		49:26
And thus had the Lamanites o.,		51:27
which they had o. possession		52: 5
Moroni had o. possession of		52:26
had o. possession of the city		53: 6
o. possession of a number of		53: 8
But he had o. his desires;		55:20
Lamanites have o. possession		56:13
would have o. their purpose.		56:50
o. possession of their strongholds.		58:23
o. those cities and those lands,		58:33
o. the possession of the city of		62:26
o. possession of the city of		62:30
that he had o. the possession of	He	1:22
o., through disguise, a knowledge		2: 6
had o. all the possession of the		4: 8
which means he o. the kingdom	Eth	7: 9
o. the head of his father-in-law,		9: 5
had o. unto himself the kingdom		10:16
o. power over the remainder of		10:32
three disciples o. a promise		12:17
they o. not the promise until		12:17
which word he had o. by faith.		12:20
of Jared had o. by faith,		12:21
have o. the promise that		12:22
o. unto himself the kingdom;		14:10
o. a sufficient hope by which ye	Mro	7: 3
have o. all which I shall grant	DC	11:22
after that you have o. faith,		17: 3
But o. a promise that they		45:14
let there be one o. for my		52:41
inasmuch as there is land o.,		58:54
not be o. but by purchase		63:29
until they have o. companies		103:30
have o. to the number of five		103:30
until you have o. a hundred		103:34
[John Johnson] o. in exchange		104:24
time that they should be o.	JS	2:42
I o. a lever, which I got fixed		2:52

OBTAINEST

if thou o. more than that	DC	42:55

OBTAINING

unto their o. power over it.	1Ne	17:35
thus been o. power by fraud	Al	48: 7
designs in o. the city Cumeni.		57:12
success in o. the possession of		58:41
o. those lands which were lost.		59: 1
succeeded in o. possession of	He	4: 5
in o. many parts of the land;		4: 9
o. moneys even as I have	DC	63:46
o. all things which shall be for		69: 8
for the o. of heavenly things.		78: 5
be equal in o. heavenly things;		78: 6
o. these two priesthoods		84:33
in o. revelations;		94: 3
in o. the fulfilment of these		103:40
consists in o. the powers		128:11
in o. a knowledge of facts		128:11
of o. a scanty maintenance by	JS	2:23
in o. a divine manifestation,		2:29
should come for o. the plates.		2:53
time arrived for o. the plates,		2:59

OBVIATE

To o. this difficulty, there can	DC	128: 3

OCCASION

assist the elder if o. requires.	DC	20:52
by the deacons, if o. requires.		20:57
have sought o. against him		64: 6
sought o. against one another		64: 8
as often as o. would permit.	JS	2: 8
I took o. to give him an		2:21
who visited us on this o. and		2:72

OCCASIONED

o. by the speed of their march—	Al	56:51

OCCUPIED
have o. the whole of that night. JS 2:47

OCCUPY
they shall no o. these plates 1 Ne 6: 6
subject seems to o. my mind, DC 128: 1

OCCUR
any vacancy shall o. by the death, DC 102: 8

OCCURRENCE
consequence of this alleged o. DC OD

OCEAN
and upon the mighty o., DC 133:20

O'CLOCK
June, 1844, about five o. p.m., DC 135: 1

OCTOBER
Salt Lake City, Utah O. 6, 1890. DC OD
In the month of O., 1825, I hired JS 2:56

OF: see in the APPENDIX.

OFF
that they are not cast o. forever—	T Pg	
o. from the presence of the Lord	1 Ne	2:21
and I smote o. his head		4:18
after I had smitten o. his head		4:19
loosed from o. my hands and feet,		7:18
the head thereof a little way o.;		8:14
they wandered o. and were lost.		8:23
feared lest they should be cast o.		8:36
to them, and not cast them o.;		8:37
whose branches should be broken o.		10:12
ye must be cast o. forever.		10:21
it passed from o. the face of the		12: 5
broken o. from the house of Israel,		15:12
they must be cast o. also, as to		15:33
lest ye shall be cast o. forever.		17:47
branch who have been broken o.;		19:24
from whom ye have been broken o.;		19:24
that I cut thee not o.		20: 9
name should not have been cut o.		20:19
all ye that are broken o.		21: 1
all ye that are broken o.,		21: 1
against Zion shall be cut o.		22:19
cut o. from among the people.		22:20
and shake o. the awful chains	2 Ne	1:13
be cut o. and destroyed forever;		1:17
be cut o. from my presence.		1:20
Shake o. the chains with which		1:23
by the law men are cut o.		2: 5
the temporal law they were cut o.;		2: 5
which was to be broken o.,		3: 5
be cut o. from my presence.		4: 4
be cut o. from the presence of		5:20
were cut o. from his presence.		5:20
or have I cast thee o. forever?		7: 1
to them that plucked o. the hair.		7: 6
were cut o. from the presence of		9: 6
Behold, I take o. my garments,		9:44
shake o. the chains of him that		9:45
for we are not cast o.;		10:20
them who have been broken o.,		10:22
with the tongs from o. the altar;		16: 6
will the Lord cut o. from Israel		19:14
and cut o. nations not a few.		20: 7
taken away from o. thy shoulder,		20:27
and his yoke from o. thy neck,		20:27
of Judah shall be cut o.;		21:13
cut o. from Babylon the name,		24:22
his seed depart from o. them,		24:25
depart from o. their shoulders.		24:25
watch for iniquity are cut o.;		27:31
will not repent shall be cast o.;		30: 2
will pluck o. those main branches	Jac	5: 7
and these which I have plucked o.		5: 9
Pluck o. the branches that have		5:26
natural branches had been broken o.,		5:30
branches began to be plucked o.		5:73
and has not as yet swept them o.	Jar	1: 3
from o. the face of the land.		1:10
and putteth o. the natural man	Mos	3:19
and to take o. their flocks,		9:14
about the land to keep them o.;		11:17
them from o. the face of the earth;		12: 8
he was cut o. out of the land of		14: 8
and carried o. their grain and		21:21
if thou wilt of thyself be cast o.		27:16
be the case, they must be cast o.;		27:27
because I was like to be cast o.		27:27
they should be cast o. forever.		28: 4
cut o. from the face of the earth	Al	9:11
you from o. the face of the earth;		9:12
o. from the presence of the Lord.		9:13
o. from the presence of the Lord.		9:14
been cut o. from his presence,		9:14
from o. the face of the earth?		9:24
my words, and cast o. your sins,		13:27
he smote o. their arms with his		17:37
smote o. as many of their arms		17:38
when he had driven them afar o.,		17:39
arms which had been smitten o.		17:39
and smote o. the arms of others,		18:16
smote o. the arms of my brethren		18:20
ye shall be cast o. at the last day?		22: 6
may not be cast o. at the last day?		22:15
ye have put o. the Spirit of God		30:42
was not taken o. of Korihor;		30:56
shall be cut o. from his presence.		36:30
shall be cut o. from his presence.		37:13
from o. the face of the earth.		37:22
from o. the face of the earth;		37:25
shall be cast o. from his presence.		38: 1
were cut o. from the tree of life		42: 6
o. from the face of the earth—		42: 6
were cut o. both temporally and		42: 7
cut o. from the presence of		42: 9
being cut o. from the presence of		42:11
to be cut o. from his presence.		42:14
did smite o. many of their arms;		43:44
that he took o. his scalp and it		44:12
who smote o. the scalp of		44:13
up the scalp from o. the ground		44:13
cut o. the people of Amalickiah,		46:30
cut o. the course of Amalickiah		46:31
come down o. from the mount,		47:12
they were swept o. by the stones		49:22
he cut o. all the strongholds of		50:11
did seek to cut o. the strength		50:12
Lamanites from o. the lands of		50:12
be cut o. from the presence of		50:20
from o. the face of the earth.		54:12
being cut o. from their support		57:11
cut them o. from their support		58:15
cut o. the spies of the Lamanites		58:20
when they had cut them o.,		58:21
and carried o. by the Lamanites.		58:31
to destroy them o. the face of	He	6:20
from o. the face of the earth.		7:28
be cut o. from my presence—		12:21
be cast o. from the presence of		12:25
o. from the presence of the Lord,		14:16
they are cut o. again as to things		14:18
from o. the face of the land;	3 Ne	4: 4
cut o. the people of Nephi		4:16
cut them o. from all their		4:16
cutting them o. by thousands		4:21
cut o. the way of their retreat,		4:24
cut o. in their places of retreat.		4:26
from o. the face of the land,		10: 9
and went a little way o. from		19:19
went a little way o. and bowed		19:27
that he went again a little way o.		19:31
all thine enemies shall be cut o.		20:17
be cut o. from among the people.		20:23
be cut o. from among my people		21:11
all their enemies shall be cut o.		21:13
cut o. thy horses out of the midst		21:14
I will cut o. the cities of thy land,		21:15
I will cut o. witchcrafts out of		21:16
graven images I will also cut o.,		21:17

OFF 682 OFFERING

I cut o. from among my people,	3Ne 21:20
cut them o. from the face of	Mrm 3:10
cut o. from the face of the earth.	3:15
but began to be swept o. by them	4:18
strongholds did cut them o.	5: 4
or they should be swept o. when	Eth 2: 8
or they should be swept o. when	2: 9
serve God or shall be swept o.;	2:10
the land, that they are swept o.	2:10
be cut o. from the presence of	2:15
veil was taken from o. the eyes	3: 6
take the curse from o. the land,	9:16
was cut o. from the presence of	10:11
from o. the face of the earth	11:12
from o. the face of this land	13: 2
swept o. the inhabitants before	14:27
he smote o. the head of Shiz.	15:30
had smitten o. the head of Shiz,	15:31
be cut o. while in the thought,	Mro 8:14
cut o. from among the people;	DC 1:14
from o. the face of the earth;	5:33
you may come o. conqueror;	10: 5
casting o. the dust of your feet	24:15
shall fall from o. their bones,	29:19
not for me shall be cut o.	45:44
shall stand afar o. and tremble.	45:74
detected and shall be cut o.,	50: 8
who are cut o. from my church,	50: 8
otherwise, they will be cut o.	51: 2
faithful, they shall be cut o.,	52: 6
cut o. in mine own due time,	56: 3
be cut o. out of my church,	56:10
shake o. the dust of thy feet	60:15
otherwise they shall be cut o.	63:63
be cut o. out of the land of	64:35
my church who are afar o.,	70: 1
shake o. the dust of your feet	75:20
have been cut o. from the church,	85:11
a fig that falleth from o. a fig-tree.	88:87
I will not utterly cast them o.;	101: 9
hideth the earth, shall be taken o.,	101:23
enemy while he was yet afar o.;	101:54
in his time, will cut o. those wicked,	101:90
as ye are cut o. for transgression,	104: 9
which is set o. joining the house,	104:28
lots that are laid o. for the	104:36
the lot which is laid o. for the	104:43
Break it o., O Lord;	109:33
break it o. from the necks of	109:33
break o., O Lord, this yoke of	109:47
may begin to be broken o. from	109:63
and their hopes may be cut o.;	121:14
the nations which are afar o.;	133: 8
cut o. from among the people	133:63
and their eyes cannot see afar o.;	Mses 6:27
that they feel and stood afar o.,	7:14
of the land, also, stood afar o.;	7:15
all flesh from o. the earth.	8:30
cut o. from among the people;	JS 1:55
when the converts began to file o.,	2: 6
I am well enough o."	2:20
cut o. from among the people,"	2:40
of mine, I should be cut o.;	2:59
the characters o. the plates,	2:62
I had drawn o. the plates,	2:63

OFFEND

going, for he feared to o. him.	Al 20:11
they should o. their priests,	30:28
o. some unknown being, who	30:28
thy brother or sister o. thee,	DC 42:88
thy brother or sister o. many,	42:90
And if any one o. openly,	42:91
If any shall o. in secret,	42:92
in nothing doth man o. God,	59:21
ye may not o. him who is	64:13
by so doing I would o. God,	JS 2:25

OFFENDED

they began to be o. because of	Al 35:15
of the justice of an o. God,	3Ne 28:35
or her whom he or she has o.,	DC 42:92
have o. my little ones	121:19

men were o. because of him.	Mses 6:37
And then shall many be o.,	JS 1: 8

OFFENDER

make a man an o. for a word,	2Ne 27:32

OFFENDERS

they themselves are the o.,	DC 42:75
bringing o. against good laws	134: 8

OFFENSE

a rock of o. to both the houses	2Ne 18:14
one more o. against your God	Al 41: 9
ye are not guilty of the first o.,	43:46
also taught never to give an o.,	48:14
him by whom this o. cometh;	DC 54: 5
according to the nature of the o.;	134: 8
in which the o. is committed;	134: 8
I have a conscience void of o.	135: 4

OFFENSIVE

o. in the sight of God.	JS 2:28

OFFER

did o. sacrifice and burnt offerings	1Ne 5: 9
did o. sacrifice and burnt offerings	7:22
and o. your whole souls as	Om 1:26
that they might o. sacrifice	Mos 2: 3
and o. up the same prayers.	Al 31:20
from this stand they did o. up,	31:22
o. up thanks after their manner.	31:23
ye shall o. up unto me no more	3Ne 9:19
shall o. for a sacrifice unto me	9:20
o. unto the Lord an offering in	24: 3
did o. them up as sacrifices	Mrm 4:14
sons of Akish did o. them money,	Eth 9:11
of Levi do o. again an offering	DC 13: 1
o. a sacrifice unto the Lord	59: 8
and o. up thy sacraments	59: 9
thou shalt o. thine oblations	59:12
and o. a sacrament unto the	62: 4
shall o. an acceptable offering	84:31
Let him o. himself in prayer	88:131
to o. up your sacraments before	89: 5
commanded to o. up his only son.	101: 4
if he will o. unto me an acceptable	124:104
may o. unto the Lord an offering	128:24
o. unto the Lord an offering in	128:24
o. him your hand and request	129: 4
he will o. you his hand,	129: 8
was commanded to o. his son Isaac;	132:36
commanded you to o. unto her;	132:51
o. the firstlings of their flocks,	Mses 5: 5
Why dost thou o. sacrifices unto	5: 6
to o. up upon the alter which was	Abr 1: 8
child did the priest of Pharaoh o.	1:10
o. me up and take away my life,	1:15
o. up Abraham as a sacrifice.	Fac 1: 3
to o. up the desire of my heart	JS 2:15
of Levi do o. again an offering	2:69

OFFERED

o. up thanks after this manner,	Al 31:23
thy vows shall be o. up	DC 59:11
which was o. unto you;	67: 3
Lorenzo Snow o. the following:	OD
but o. an acceptable sacrifice,	Mses 6: 3
priest had o. upon this altar	Abr 1:11
virgins were o. up because	1:11
I o. sacrifice there in the plains	2:18
he o. sacrifice upon an altar,	Fac 2: 2
and o. many explanations which	JS 2:41
o. and promised us protection	2:75

OFFERETH

he o. himself a sacrifice for sin,	2Ne 2: 7
for if he o. a gift, or prayeth	Mro 7: 6

OFFERING

and made an o. unto the Lord,	1Ne 2: 7
in o. up his son Isaac,	Jac 4: 5
whole souls as an o. unto him,	Om 1:26
shalt make his soul an o. for sin	Mos 14:10

soul has been made an o. for sin	Mos 15:10	and ordained to that o.,	DC 107:22
Lord an o. in righteousness.	3Ne 24: 3	who are of the o. of an elder;	107:60
Then shall the o. of Judah and	24: 4	who are of the o. of a priest;	107:61
again an o. unto the Lord	DC 13: 1	who are of the o. of a teacher,	107:62
shall offer an acceptable o.	84:31	the o. of a bishop is not equal	107:68
unto me for your sacracrament o.,	95:16	for the o. of a bishop is in	107:68
o. up of your most holy desires	95:16	they shall act in the same o.	107:75
whose o. I have accepted,	96: 6	to act in the o. of bishop	107:76
Lord, have accepted of her o.;	97:27	president over the o. of a deacon	107:85
not accept the o. of peace,	98:35	over the o. of the teachers	107:86
and will accept their o.;	105:19	the duties of their o.,	107:86
I am well pleased with your o.	124: 1	teach them the duties of their o.,	107:87
offer unto me an acceptable o.,	124:104	president over the o. of elders	107:89
for your o. is acceptable to me.	126: 1	of the o. of the High Priesthood	107:91
the Lord an o. in righteousness.	128:24	to act in the o. in which he	107:99
the Lord an o. in righteousness;	128:24	I seal upon his head the o. of a	124:21
Will I accept of an o.,	132: 9	may take the o. of Priesthood	124:91
as I accepted the o. of Abraham	132:50	and stand in the o. of his calling,	124:103
require an o. at your hand,	132:51	this is the o. of their calling,	124:135
flocks, for an o. unto the Lord.	Mses 5: 5		
Make an o. unto the Lord.	5:18	**OFFICERS**	
ground an o. unto the Lord.	5:19	and sent forth o. that the man	Al 11: 2
respect unto Abel, and to his o.;	5:20	and delivered them to the o. to	14:17
But unto Cain, and to his o.,	5:21	him up into the hands of the o.,	30:29
for his o. thou didst accept	5:38	many lawyers, and many o.	3Ne 6:11
in o. up their children unto	Abr 1: 7	for all the o. of the church,	DC 88:127
o. unto these strange gods, men,	1: 8	are presidents, or presiding o.	107:21
priest made an o. unto the god	1: 9	thus differing from other o. in the	107:23
Even the thank-o. of a child did	1:10	thus differing from other o. in the	107:25
and made an o. unto the Lord,	2:17	all the other o. of the church,	107:58
offer again an o. unto the Lord	JS 2:69	Whereas other o. of the church,	107:98
		o. belonging to my Priesthood,	124:123
OFFERINGS		require civil o. and magistrates to	134: 3
did offer sacrifice and burnt o.	1Ne 5: 9		
did offer sacrifice and burnt o.	7:22	**OFFICES**	
might offer sacrifice and burnt o.	Mos 2: 3	to officiate in all the lesser o.	DC 68:19
burnt o. shall be sone away,	3Ne 9:19	the o. of elder and bishop are	84:29
your sacrifices and your burnt o.	9:19	the o. of teacher and deacon are	84:30
robbed thee? In tithes and o.	24: 8	all their several callings and o.;	97:13
but to accept of their o.	DC 124:49	would fill their o. according to	102: 4
this cause have I accepted the o.	124:51	All other authorities or o.	107: 5
and I will accept of his o.,	124:75	authority over all the o. in the	107: 8
be unto me as the o. of Cain,	124:75	a right to officiate in all the o. in	107: 9
		a right to officiate in all these o.	107:12
OFFICE		to officiate in all the lesser o.,	107:17
And we did magnify our o. unto	Jac 1:19	are ordained to the several o.	107:21
to magnify mine o. with soberness,	2: 2	and responsible o. in the church.	107:98
diligent in the o. of my calling;	2: 3	above o. I have given unto you,	124:143
conferred the o. upon him,	Mos 29:42	that you should fill all these o.	124:144
the o. of being high priest over	Al 4:18	prepare rooms for all these o. in	124:145
he retained the o. of high priest	4:18		
the o. of the high priesthood	13:18	**OFFICIAL**	
to be held in o. at the head of	He 7: 5	O. DECLARATION	DC OD
the o. of their ministry is to	Mro 7:31		
to any o. in this church,	DC 20:65	**OFFICIALLY**	
Magnify thine o.; and after	24: 3	o. notified of their appointment.	DC 118: 6
wherewith to magnify thine o.,	24: 9		
the o. of thy calling shall be for	25: 5	**OFFICIATE**	
to the o. wherewith I have	38:23	authority to o. in all the lesser	DC 68:19
in the o. whereunto I have	42:10	may o. in the office of bishop	68:19
have appointed to another o.	47: 3	to o. in their priesthood.	68:20
as are ordained unto this o.,	50:38	a right to o. in all the offices	107: 9
stand fast in the o. whereunto	54: 2	right to o. in their own standing,	107:10
stand in the o. to which I have	57: 6	An elder has a right to o. in	107:11
stand in the o. to which I have	57: 7	a right to o. in all these offices	107:12
stand in the o. to which I have	58:40	to o. in all the lesser offices,	107:17
in the o. to which I have	63:56	may o. in the office of bishop	107:17
thou shalt magnify thine o.,	66:11	to o. in the name of the Lord,	107:33
has a legal right to this o.,	68:18		
officiate in the o. of bishop	68:19	**OFFSPRING**	
breaketh it shall lose his o.	78:12	the o. of thy bowels like the	1Ne 20:19
the o. which I have appointed	81: 3	bosom of thy wife, and of thine o.,	DC 122: 6
stand in the o. which I have	81: 5		
every man stand in his own o.,	84:109	**OFT**	
act in that o. according to	102: 4	did go into the mount o.,	1Ne 18: 3
removal from o. for transgression,	102: 8	did pray o. unto the Lord;	18: 3
according to the dignity of his o.	102:10	gather themselves together o.,	Al 6: 6
the Laneshine house [printing o.],	104:28	they did fast and pray o.	He 3:35
the Laneshine house [printing o.],	104:29	how o. have I gathered you as a	3Ne 10: 4
The o. of an elder comes under	107: 7	how o. would I have gathered you	10: 5
and also in the o. of an elder,	107:10	how o. would I have gathered you	10: 5
has a legal right to this o.,	107:16	how o. will I gather you as a	10: 6
may officiate in the o. of bishop	107:17	behold, ye shall meet together o.;	18:22

OFT 684 OLD

OFT

be that they come unto you o.	3Ne	18:23
did show himself unto them o.,		26:13
did break bread o., and bless it,		26:13
and in meeting together o.	4Ne	1:12
the chruch did meet together o.,	Mro	6: 5
did meet together o. to partake		6: 6
But as o. as they repented and		6: 8
how o. you have transgressed	DC	3: 6
How o. have I called upon you		43:25
as o. as thine enemy repenteth		98:40

OFTEN

had o. heard my father speak	En	1: 3
as o. as it was in their power,	Mos	18:25
and as o. as my people repent		26:30
that feared the Lord spake o.	3Ne	24:16
as o. as thou hast inquired	DC	6:14
the church meet together o.,		20:55
the church meet together o.		20:75
how o. would I have gathered		43:24
o. times it maketh my bones		85: 6
and speak o. one to another,		133: 6
they had o. been proved before,		135: 7
were deep and o. poignant,	JS	2: 8
o. as occasion would permit.		2: 8
I o. said to myself:		2:10
and o. has since, how very		2:23
was o. the cause of great sorrow		2:23
I o. felt condemned for my		2:29

OGATH

in a place which was called O.	Eth	15:10

OH

O., how merciful is our God!	Al	24:15
O. then, why did he not consign		26:19
O., my soul, almost as it were,		26:20
O., thought I, that I could be		36:15
And o., what joy, and what		36:20
O., remember, and take it upon		39: 9
O., that I could have had my	He	7: 7
O., this unbelieving and	DC	5: 8
O., remember these words, and		8: 5

OHIO

until ye shall go to the O.,	DC	37: 1
assemble together at the O.,		37: 3
that ye should go to the O.;		38:32
thou art called to go to the O.		39:14
assemble themselves at the O.,		39:15
the people in O. call upon me		39:16
church, unto the church in O.,		58:49
or unto the bishop in O.,		84:104

OIL

and burning, and o. with you,	DC	33:17

OLAHA

on the plains of O. Shinehah,	DC	117: 8

OLD

as with the prophets of o.,	1Ne	1:20
with people, both o. and young,		8:27
as well in times of o. as		10:17
these times as in times of o.,		10:19
as well in times of o. as		10:19
even did they err of o.;		19: 6
even as he had prophets of o.,		19:20
show unto the prophets of o.		19:21
in other lands, among people of o.		19:22
that o. serpent, who is the devil,	2Ne	2:18
did my father of o. prophesy.		3:22
which was in him, he waxed o.		4:12
all they shall wax o. as a garment,		7: 6
earth shall wax o. like a garment;		8: 6
even as in times of o.,		26:22
Now Nephi began to be o.,	Jac	1: 9
such as like unto David of o.		1:15
shall do like unto them of o.		2:26
whoredoms, like unto them of o.,		2:33
also spake them unto prophets of o.		4:13
waxed o., and began to decay.		5: 3
the trees, both o. and young,		5:63

that I, Jacob, began to be o.;	Jac	7:26
that I began to be o.,	En	1:25
that I began to be o.;	Om	1:25
he waxed o., and he saw that he	Mos	1: 9
And ye behold that I am o., and am		2:26
O, all ye o. men, and also ye		2:40
my o. men that could bear arms,		10: 9
even I, in my o. age, did go up		10:10
I, being o., did confer the		10:22
yea, even that o. serpent that		16: 3
after the manner of o. times.		28:16
being eighty and two years o.,		29:45
being sixty and three years o.;		29:46
both o. and young, both bond and	Al	1:30
both o. and young, both bond and		5:49
both o. and young, both bond and		11:44
he had wrought upon the o. king		20:24
what Zenos, the prophet of o.,		33: 3
have been written by them of o.?		33:12
that a second prophet of o. has		33:17
was only twenty and five years o.		43:17
were many who died with o. age;		46:41
even as they did of o. time.	He	13:24
in the days of our fathers of o.,		13:25
there were many o. cities repaired.	3Ne	6: 7
which was given by them of o.,		6:28
been said by them of o. time,		12:21
it is written by them of o. time,		12:27
things which were of o. time,		12:46
O. things are done away, and all		12:47
that o. things had passed away,		15: 2
that o. things had passed away,		15: 3
that o. things have passed away,		15: 7
as in the days of o., and as in		24: 4
are seventy and two years o.		28: 3
about twenty and four years o.	Mrm	1: 3
that I, being eleven years o.,		1: 6
I, Mormon, began to be o.;		6: 6
and begin as in times of o.,		9:27
brother of Jared began to be o.,	Eth	6:19
also begat Kib in his o. age.		7: 3
was thirty and two years o.		7: 4
until he became exceeding o.;		7: 7
Kib begat Shule in his o. age.		7: 7
sons and daughters in his o. age.		7:26
account concerning them of o.,		8: 9
were given by them of o.		8:15
to search up these things of o.;		8:17
combination, even as they of o.;		8:18
that Omer began to be o.;		9:14
in his o. age he begat Emer;		9:14
even until he was exceeding o.		9:23
an hundred and two years o.		9:24
took to wife, in his o. age,		9:24
and forty and two years o.		9:24
the secret plans again of o.,		9:26
live to an exceeding o. age;		10: 4
in his o. age he begat Levi;		10:14
he did live to a good o. age,		10:16
and they adopted the o. plans,		10:33
And he lived to a good o. age,		11: 4
that they of o. were called after		12:10
it had been in a time of o.;		13: 5
like unto the Jerusalem of o.;		13: 8
they shall be like unto the o.		13: 9
save he o. have passed away,		13: 9
also cometh the Jerusalem of o.;		13:11
many o. women do faint by the	Mro	9:16
none, neither o. nor young;		9:19
which waxeth o. and shall perish	DC	1:16
the engravings of o. records,		8: 1
was had by the prophets of o.		17: 2
as well as in generations of o.;		20:11
all o. covenants have I caused		22: 1
unto me, even as in days of o.		22: 3
all o. things shall pass away,		29:24
become even as Nephi of o.,		33: 8
even as the apostles of o.		35: 6
become as the Nephites of o.		38:39
he is like unto Nathanael of o.,		41:11
to repent, both o. and young,		43:20
as with men in days of o.,		45:10
as unto men in days of o.		45:15

like unto mine apostle of o.,	DC	49:11
as with men in days of o.		61:13
and o. things shall pass away,		63:49
grow up until they become o.;		63:51
o. men shall die; but they shall		63:51
My disciples, in days of o.,		64: 8
and apostles in days of o.		66: 2
the hands, when eight years o.,		68:25
their sins when eight years o.,		68:27
my kingdom from days of o.,		76: 7
beheld Satan, that o. serpent,		76:28
at the time he was eight days o.		84:28
take the o. and cast it unto the		84:105
shall be bound, that o. serpent,		88:110
shall not die until he is o.;		101:30
He was eighty-seven years o.		107:45
years and seven days o. when he		107:46
Jared was two hundred years o.		107:47
Enoch was twenty-five years o.		107:48
four hundred and thirty years o.		107:49
was one hundred years o. when		107:50
Lamech was thirty-two years o.		107:51
Noah was ten years o. when he		107:52
chamber of o. Father Whitmer,		128:21
is an o. sectarian notion,		130: 3
until thou art eighty-five years o.,		130:15
carried them all the days of o.;		133:53
forty-four years o. in February,		135: 6
four hundred and fifty years o.,	Mses	8:12
was five hundred years o.		8:12
which are like unto men of o.,		8:21
was sixty and two years o. when	Abr	2:14
prophecies of the O. Testament.	JS	2:36
an o. gentleman by the name		2:56
prevailed with the o. gentleman		2:56

OLEA
unto me: O., which is the moon.	Abr	3:13

OLIBLISH
called by the Egyptians O.,	Fac	2: 2
measuring of the time of O.,		2: 4

OLIHAH
Horan and O. [Oliver Cowdery],	DC	82:11
my servant O. [Oliver Cowdery]		104:28
and O. [Oliver Cowdery]		104:29
servant O. [Oliver Cowdery].		104:34

OLIMLAH
O., a slave belonging to	Fac	3: 6

OLISHEM
at the head of the plain of O.	Abr	1:10

OLIVE
compared like unto an o.-tree,	1Ne	10:12
the natural branches of the o.-tree,		10:14
the natural branches of the o.-tree,		15: 7
was compared unto an o.-tree,		15:12
a natural branch of the o.-tree,		15:16
olive-tree, into the true o.-tree.		15:16
like unto a tame o.-tree,	Jac	5: 3
saw that his o.-tree began to decay;		5: 4
the branches from a wild o.-tree,		5: 7
the branches of the wild o.-tree,		5: 9
the branches of the wild o.-tree.		5:10
branches of the tame o.-tree		5:14
wild o. branches had been grafted;		5:17
the branches of the wild o.-tree		5:34
become like unto the wild o.-tree,		5:46
likened them unto a tame o.-tree,		6: 1
land, and plant twelve o.-trees;	DC	101:44
o.-trees may not be broken		101:45
and planted the o.-trees,		101:46
and broke down the o.-trees.		101:51

OLIVER: see also COWDERY, Oliver; and GRANGER, Oliver.
Behold, thou art O., and I	DC	6:20
I speak unto you, O., a few		23: 1
thy brother O. shall continue		24:10
I say unto thee, O., that it	DC	28: 1
journey with your brother O.:		30: 5

OLIVES
went upon the Mount of O.	JS	1: 4
he sat upon the Mount of O.,		1: 4

OLIVET
stand upon the mount of O.,	DC	133:20

OLIVE-TREE: see OLIVE and TREE.

OMEGA
I am Alpha and O., the	3Ne	9:18
Alpha and O., Christ the Lord;	DC	19: 1
your God, even Alpha and O.,		35: 1
Great I AM, Alpha and O.,		38: 1
that I am Alpha and O.,		45: 7
the Lord, even Alpha and O.,		54: 1
everlasting, even Alpha and O.,		61: 1
Behold, I am Alpha and O.,		63:60
Behold, I am Alpha and O.,		68:35
my Spirit, even Alpha and O.,		75: 1
the words of Alpha and O.,		81: 7
I am Alpha and O.,		84:120
I am Alpha and O.		112:34
Behold, I am Alpha and O.,		132:66

OMEGUS
Alphus; or, in other words, O.;	DC	95:17

OMER
And Emer was the son of O.	Eth	1:29
And O. was the son of Shule.		1:30
he begat O., and Omer reigned		8: 1
and O. reigned in his stead.		8: 1
And O. begat Jared;		8: 1
in the days of the reigns of O		8: 4
now O. was a friend to Akish;		8:11
overthrow the kingdom of O.		9: 1
the Lord was merciful unto O.,		9: 2
the Lord warned O. in a dream		9: 3
O. departed out of the land with		9: 3
came over and dwelt with o.		9: 9
who fled with the house of O.		9:12
O. was restored again to the		9:13
that O. began to be old;		9:14

OMNER
and Aaron, and O., and Himni,	Mos	27:34
and Aaron, O. and Himni,	Al	22:35
on Ammon, or Aaron, or O.,		23: 1
Ammon, and Aaron, and O., and		25:17
and also the joy of Aaron, of O.,		27:19
took Ammon, and Aaron, and O.;		31: 6
yea, Ammon, and Aaron, and O.,		31:32
Morianton, and the city of O.,		51:26
of Enoch, and the land of O.,	Mses	7: 9

OMNI
into the hands of my son O.,	Jar	1:15
THE BOOK OF O.	Om	1:hd
I, O., being commanded by my		1: 1

OMNIPOTENT
the Lord O. who reigneth,	Mos	3: 5
the name of Christ, the Lord O.		3:17
blood of Christ, the Lord O.		3:18
on the name of the Lord God O.		3:21
of the Spirit of the Lord O.,		5: 2
that Christ, the Lord God O.,		5:15

ON: see in the APPENDIX.

ONCE
have o. brought forth good fruit	Jac	5:42
o. again for the last time.		5:63
o. more, for the last time,		5:64
away the bad thereof all at o.,		5:65
only this o. will I prune my		5:69
that they may o again come to	WM	1: 8
that they may o. again be a		1: 8

ONCE

did o. more establish peace in	WM	1:18
by those who were o. his friends	Al	15:16
have been o. enlightened by		24:30
o. the people of the Lamanites.		30:19
worship God only o. in a week?		32:11
when it o. has had place in you,		39: 6
for all do not die at o., and		40: 8
spoken shall all be reunited at o.,		40:19
who were o. their brethren,		48:24
Lamanites had destroyed it o.		49: 3
was o. more peace established		62:42
o. belonged to the church of God	He	5:35
when they are o. enlightened,		15:10
were o. a delightsome people,	Mrm	5:17
conference o. in three months,	DC	20:61
for this o., for mine own glory,		64: 3
not all be spokesmen at o.;		88:122
let it be read this o. to her ears,		97:27
smite you, or your families, o.,		98:23
shall be delivered this o. out of		104:83
put into your hands, this o.,		104:85
you this privilege, this o.;		104:86
that o. were put upon him		124:95
I was o. praying very earnestly		130:14

ONE: *see in the APPENDIX*.

ONE-HALF: *see ONE and HALF*.

ONES

the only o. that have testified,	1Ne	22:31
O ye wicked o., enter into the	2Ne	12:10
the waste places of the fat o.		15:17
send among his fat o., leanness;		20:16
high o. of stature shall be hewn		20:33
young o. shall lie down together;		21: 7
commanded my sanctified o.,		23: 3
I have also called my mighty o.,		23: 3
all the chief o. of the earth;		24: 9
the multitude of their terrible o.		26:18
young o. shall lie down together;		30:13
consecrated new o. in their stead,	Mos	11: 5
are not they the o. who have		20:18
to catch the holy o. of God.	Al	10:17
not the o.ly o. who have spoken		33:18
your country and your little o.,		60:29
gone hence, who were the holy o.,	3Ne	5:14
Behold your little o.		17:23
encircled those little o. about,		17:24
O ye fair o., how could ye have	Mrm	6:17
O ye fair o., how could ye have		6:17
husbands and wives, ye fair o.,		6:19
down the mighty and strong o.,	DC	1:19
your family, yea, your little o.;		31: 2
fear because of her terrible o.		64:43
the only o. on whom the		76:37
the only o. who shall not be		76:38
and plead with her strong o.,		90:36
the cries of their innocent o. to		109:49
and the great o. of the earth,		109:55
and afflicted o. of the earth;		109:55
all their sick and afflicted o.,		109:72
let these, thine anointed o.,		109:80
by thy word many high o. shall		112: 8
many low o. shall be exalted.		112: 8
they have offended my little o.		121:19
there were many great o. which	Abr	3: 2
These are the governing o.;		3: 3
many of the noble and great o.;		3:22
the great o. of the most popular	JS	2:23

ONE-TENTH: *see ONE and TENTH*.

ONIDAH

unto the people upon the hill O.,	Al	32: 4
the place which was called O.,		47: 5
therefore they fled to O.,		47: 5

ONIHAH

city of O. and the inhabitants	3Ne	9: 7

ONITAH

who were the daughters of O.,	Abr	1:11

ONLY

there are save two churches o.;	1Ne	14:10
must be destroyed, save a few o.,		17:43
and not o. unto the Gentiles		22: 9
the o. ones that have testified,		22:31
to the bringing forth my word o.,	2Ne	3:11
o. in and through the grace of		10:24
o. these things have I caused to be		11: 1
o. let us be called by thy name		14: 1
the O. Begotten of the Father,		25:12
the o. and true doctrine of the		31:21
and not o. we ourselves had	Jac	4: 4
of God and his O. Begotten Son.		4: 5
of Christ, his O. Begotten Son,		4:11
and the o. sure foundation,		4:16
o. a part of the tree hath		5:25
o. this once will I prune my		5:69
I have o. been in the service of	Mos	2:16
are o. in the service of your God.		2:17
o. in and through the name of		3:17
o. through repentance and faith		3:21
o. according to the words		3:22
o. a few of them have I written		8: 1
that o. in and through Christ ye		16:13
o. he did not bury himself		18:15
are not o. guilty of priestcraft,	Al	1:12
the o. Begotten of the Father,		5:48
of the O. Begotten of the Father,		9:26
and it was o. thy desire that I		11:25
thou hast not lied unto men o.		12: 3
o. according to the portion of his		12: 9
through mine O. Begotten Son;		12:33
through mine O. Begotten Son,		12:34
of the O. Begotten Son, who was		13: 5
the O. Begotten of the Father,		13: 9
And now we o. wait to hear the		13:25
desired of him was his o. desire.		19: 7
it was o. the distance of a day		22:32
o. in the land of Nephi,		22:34
were not converted, save o. one;		23:14
punished o. for the crimes which		30:11
received o. according to law		30:33
none, save it be your word o.		30:40
would o. admit one person.		31:13
save it be in your synagogues o.?		32:10
worship God o. once in a week?		32:11
than he that o. believeth, or only		32:19
or only hath cause to believe,		32:19
not o. men but women also.		32:23
judge you o. according to that		32:24
ye have o. exercised your faith		32:36
not the o. ones who have spoken		33:18
o. unto him that has faith unto		34:16
it may suffice if I o. say they are		37:12
and o. their wickedness and their		37:29
saved, o. in and through Christ.		38: 9
time o. is measured unto men.		40: 8
o. on conditions of repentance		42:13
and o. let your sins trouble you,		42:29
was o. twenty and five years old		43:17
they had o. their swords and		43:20
the o. desire of the Nephites		43:30
o. sought to defend ourselves.		54:13
this saying o. made them more		55:10
o. deliver up our prisoners on		57: 2
army, save a few guards o.,		58:22
o. to retain my judgment-seat		61: 9
o. through the atoning blood of	He	5: 9
ye not o. deny my words, but ye		8:13
Moses did not o. testify of		8:16
Abraham not o. knew of these		8:18
and o. this much we know,		9:15
not o. in this record but also	Mrm	7: 8
save a few o. who do not lift		8:36
serve him, the true and o. God,	Eth	2: 8
And o. a few have I written,		12:40
he should o. live to see the		13:21
o. a few years have passed away,	Mro	9:12
o. according to the unbelief of		10:19
the o. true and living church	DC	1:30
Behold, they have o. got a part,		10:44
the o. doctrine which is in me.		10:62
and not o. men, but women,		18:42

ONLY		
the o. living and true God,	DC	20:19
the o. being whom they should		20:19
God gave his O. Begotten Son,		20:21
Not o. those who believed		20:26
he is o. to preach, teach,		20:50
name of mine O. Begotten Son.		29:42
through mine O. Begotten;		29:46
from them o. for a little time,		31: 6
o. reign for a little season,		43:31
the o. people that shall not		45:69
sent mine O. Begotten Son		49: 5
o. have claim on that portion		51: 5
he o. is saved who endureth		53: 7
o. as it shall be appointed		58:44
o. let thy food be prepared with		59:13
o. let my servant Reynolds		61:35
o. be faithful, and declare glad		62: 5
showeth no signs, o. in wrath		63:11
through his O. Begotten Son,		76:13
the O. Begotten of the Father—		76:23
against the O. Begotten Son		76:25
denied the O. Begotten Son		76:35
And the o. ones on whom		76:37
the o. ones who shall not be		76:38
of the O. Begotten Son.		76:57
for they are o. to be seen		76:116
and not for your sakes o.,		84:48
not o. to say, but to do		84:57
will not o. shake the earth,		84:118
o. in assembling yourselves		89: 5
used, o. in times of winter,		89:13
not o. for man but for the		89:14
of man o. in times of famine		89:15
of the O. Begotten of the Father,		93:11
to offer up his o. son.		101: 4
for nothing o. to be cast out		101:40
those o. whom I have appointed		101:55
two o. of the councilors shall		102:13
o. to be called on the most		102:28
can o. be called in question		102:32
of Zion, o. on this wise—		104:47
not bound o. up to this hour		104:53
unto them, o. on this wise,		104:53
o. by the voice of the order,		104:64
o. by the voice and common		104:71
not o. to the people that have		105:38
not o. in his own place, but in the		106: 2
distinguished from him o. by his		107:43
not o. unto the Gentiles, but		112: 4
o. upon the principles of		121:36
o. by persuasion, by long-suffering,		121:41
That we may not o. publish to		123: 6
not o. to our own wives and		123: 9
who are o. kept from the truth		123:12
o. in the days of your poverty,		124:30
o. in that house.		124:70
o. in that house,		124:71
o. in that house,		124:71
order of mine O. Begotten Son.		124:123
it is o. to answer the will of God,		128: 5
not o. this, but those things		128:18
that is the o. way he can appear—		129: 6
o. it will be coupled with eternal		130: 2
can o. be discerned by purer eyes;		131: 7
to know the o. wise and true God,		132:24
amenable to him, and to him o.,		132: 4
They can o. excommunicate		134:10
were the o. persons in the room		135: 2
has done more, save Jesus o.,		135: 3
were o. confined in jail by the		135: 7
o. in that I have left a witness		136:40
o. man on the earth at the		OD
similitude of mine O. Begotten;	Mses	1: 6
mine O. Begotten is and shall be		1: 6
the similitude of his O. Begotten;		1:13
God, for him o. shalt thou serve.		1:15
the similitude of mine O. Begotten.		1:16
in the name of mine O. Begotten,		1:17
the O. Begotten, worship me.		1:19
this one God o. will I worship,		1:20
In the name of the O. Begotten,		1:21
which is mine O. Begotten Son,		1:32
which is mine O. Begotten.	Mses	1:33
But o. an account of this earth,		1:35
by mine O. Begotten I created		2: 1
God, said unto mine O. Begotten,		2:26
in the image of mine O. Begotten		2:27
God, said unto mine O. Begotten,		3:18
in the name of mine O. Begotten,		4: 1
by the power of mine O. Begotten,		4: 3
God, said unto mine O. Begotten:		4:28
the sacrifice of the O. Begotten		5: 7
am the O. Begotten of the Father		5: 9
nor believe on his O. Begotten Son,		5:57
the name of mine O. Begotten,		6:52
the o. name which shall be given		6:52
O. Begotten is the Son of Man,		6:57
the blood of mine O. Begotten;		6:59
the blood of mine O. Begotten,		6:62
in the name of thine O. Begotten,		7:50
in the name of thine O. Begotten;		7:59
testimony of mine O. Begotten;		7:62
heart, being o. evil continually.		8:22
whose seed could o. bring forth the	Abr	4:12
o. the beginning of the sorrows	JS	1:19
in heaven, but my father o.		1:40
communication not o. lightly,		2:21
o. between fourteen and		2:22
Not o. was his robe exceedingly		2:32
o. to those to whom I should		2:42
were o. counteracted by		2:75
ONTARIO		
to Palmyra, O. (now Wayne)	JS	2: 3
in the same county of O.—		2: 3
village of Manchester, O. county,		2:51
ONTI		
ezrom of silver, and an o. of silver.	Al	11: 6
an o. was as great as them all.		11:13
ONTIES		
here are six o. of silver,	Al	11:22
Behold these six o., which are		11:25
ONYX		
was boellium and the o. stone.	Mses	3:12
OPEN		
that he saw the heavens o.,	1Ne	1: 8
that I saw the heavens o.;		11:14
I beheld the heavens o.,		11:27
I beheld the heavens o. again,		11:30
And I saw the heavens o.,		12: 6
whoso knocketh, to him will he o.;	2Ne	9:42
he will not o. unto them.		9:42
shall devour Israel with o. mouth.		19:12
o. your ears that ye may hear,	Mos	2: 9
out in o. rebellion against God;		2:37
that he could not o. his mouth;		27:19
he would o. the mouth of Alma,		27:22
out in o. rebellion against God;	Al	3:18
king Lamoni did o. his mouth,		18:18
Aaron began to o. the scriptures		21: 9
they did o. a correspondence		23:18
never o. thy mouth any more,		30:47
that I could not o. my mouth,		36:10
the gate of heaven is o. unto all,	He	3:28
behold, they saw the heavens o.;		5:48
it were to come up in o. battle	3Ne	4: 4
and did o. their ears to hear it;		11: 5
they durst not o. their mouths,		11: 8
the gates of hell stand o. to		11:40
and did o. his mouth unto them		14: 1
and they saw the heavens o.,		17:24
hell are ready o. to receive them.		18:13
and their hearts were o. and		19:33
o. you the windows of heaven,		24:10
even babes did o. their mouths		26:16
hewn down in o. rebellion against	Mrm	2:15
Jesus, who stood with o. arms		6:17
he shall o. his mouth and	DC	24:12
must o. thy mouth at all times,		28:16
o. your mouth to declare my		30: 5

OPEN

o. your mouth in my cause,	DC 30:11
will o. the hearts of the people,	31: 7
o. ye your ears and hearken to	33: 1
O. your mouths and they shall	33: 8
o. your mouths and spare not,	33: 9
o. your mouths and they shall	33:10
men should o. their hearts,	58:52
will not o. their mouths,	60: 2
shall not o. their mouths in	61:30
o. your hearts and give ear	63: 1
that shall go with an o. heart	64:22
you should o. your mouths in	71: 1
are willing to o. their hearts.	75:25
and put him to an o. shame.	76:35
shall o. the eyes of the blind.	84:69
to o. the door by the proclamation	107:35
to o. the door of my kingdom	112:21
the very jaws of hell shall gape o.	122: 7
as the door shall be open to him	124:115
the keys to o. up the authority	124:128
in the o. firmament of heaven.	Mses 2:20
O. thy mouth, and it shall be	6:32
beheld the heavens o., and I was	7: 3
in the o. expanse of heaven.	Abr 4:20
but this robe, as it was o.,	JS 2:31
a conduit o. right up into	2:43
laid o. to our understandings,	2:74

OPENED

time thine ear was not o.;	1Ne 20: 8
which o. his mouth to utterance	2Ne 1:27
The Lord God hath o. mine ear,	7: 5
o. her mouth without measure;	15:14
or o. the mouth, or peeped.	20:14
and o. not the house of his	24:17
Benjamin again o. his mouth	Mos 4: 4
yet he o. not his mouth;	14: 7
is dumb so he o. not his mouth.	14: 7
is dumb, so he o. not his mouth.	15: 6
has o. his mouth to prophesy,	15:13
the eyes of the people might be o.	27:22
o. his mouth and began to speak	Al 12: 1
we have o. a correspondence	24: 8
he o. his mouth and said unto	He 7:13
And many graves shall be o.,	14:25
and it shall be o. unto you.	3Ne 14: 7
him that knocketh, it shall be o.	14: 8
and o. the eyes of their blind	26:15
and it shall be o. unto you;	27:29
him that knocketh, it shall be o.	27:29
behold, the heavens were o.,	28:13
the heavens are o. and are shut;	Eth 4: 9
and it shall be o. unto you.	DC 4: 7
knock it shall be o. unto you.	6: 5
knock it shall be o. unto you.	11: 5
knock it shall be o. unto you.	12: 5
knock it shall be o. unto you.	14: 5
thy heart shall be o. to preach	23: 2
and thy heart is o.,	23: 3
for their graves shall be o.,	29:26
and it shall be o. unto you.	49:26
and it shall be o. unto you.	66: 9
and it shall be o. unto them,	75:27
of the Spirit our eyes were o.	76:12
and they were o.,	76:19
knock, and it shall be o.	88:63
for their graves shall be o.;	88:97
and lo, the heavens were o.,	93:15
an effectual door shall be o.	100: 3
that their ears may be o.	101:92
the heavens o. unto them,	107:19
eyes of our understanding were o.	110: 1
heavens were again o. unto us;	110:11
door shall be o. unto you,	112:19
an effectual door shall be o.	118: 3
and the books were o.;	128: 6
and another book was o.,	128: 6
that the books were o.;	128: 7
and another book was o.,	128: 7
graves of the saints shall be o.;	133:56
that his eyes may be o. that	136:32
his ears o. that he may hear;	136:32
then your eyes shall be o.,	Mses 4:11

688

OPPRESSED

the eyes of them both were o.,	Mses 4:13
my transgression my eyes are o.,	5:10
earth which hath o. her mouth	5:36
the vision was o. to my mind	JS 2:42
been o. by the Spaniards in	2:56

OPENING

by the o. of the earth,	1Ne 19:11
that by o. this correspondence	Al 24: 9
o. of the earth to receive them,	3Ne 10:14
or the o. of the sixth seal,	DC 77:10
the o. of the seventh seal,	77:13

OPENLY

himself shall reward thee o.	3Ne 13: 4
in secret, shall reward thee o.	13: 6
in secret, shall reward thee o.	13:18
And if any one offend o.,	DC 42:91
she shall be rebuked o.,	42:91

OPERATE

power can o. against them—	Al 60:25

OPERATION

consider the o. of his hands.	2Ne 15:12

OPERATIONS

know the diversities of o.,	DC 46:16

OPHIR

man than the golden wedge of O.	2Ne 23:12

OPINION

I give it as my o., that	Al 40:20

OPINIONS

unless their religious o.	DC 134: 4
proscribe them in their o.	134: 7
such religious o. do not	134: 7
words and a contest about o.	JS 2: 6
war of words and tumult of o.,	2:10

OPPORTUNITY

he sought much o. that he might	Jac 7: 3
I have sought much o. that I	7: 6
and supposing that this o.,	Al 19:17
would seek every o. to scourge	52:10
have o. to confess in secret	DC 42:92
otherwise, as we could get o.	JS 2:55

OPPOSE

they durst not o. but were obliged	Al 51: 7
slay every one who did o. them,	He 1:20

OPPOSED

death unto all those who o. them.	Al 57:19
much o. to our being married.	JS 2:58
me, and who were o. to mobs,	2:75

OPPOSITE

it in a state o. to its nature?	Al 41:12
affixed o. to the plan of happiness,	42:16
land o. the city of Nauvoo,	DC 125: 3

OPPOSITION

in o. to that of the happiness	2Ne 2:10
there is an o. in all things,	2:11
needs be that there was an o.:	2:15
forbidden fruit in o. to the	2:15
Why the o. and persecution that	JS 2:20

OPPRESS

feed them that o. thee with	1Ne 21:26
I will feed them that o. thee,	2Ne 6:18
that o. the hireling in his wages,	3Ne 24: 5

OPPRESSED

shall be o., every one by another	2Ne 13: 5
should be o. and afflicted?	Mos 13:35
He was o., and he was afflicted,	14: 7
ye have been o. by king Noah,	23:12
that they have been greatly o.	DC 109:48

OPPRESSION

OPPRESSION
- for judgment, and behold, o.; 2 Ne 15: 7
- because of their o. to the poor, He 4:12
- thou shalt be far from o. for 3 Ne 22:14
- and be redeemed from o., DC 109:67
- o., supported and urged on 123: 7
- of their enemies, and by o., 124:53

OPPRESSIONS
- free from the o. of the king, Al 21:21
- these wrongs and unlawful o., DC 121: 3
- that have had a hand in their o., 123: 3

OPPRESSOR
- because of the fury of the o., 2 Ne 8:13
- And where is the fury of the o.? 8:13
- of his shoulder, the rod of his o. 19: 4
- How hath the o. ceased, 24: 4
- to appoint the portion of the o. DC 124: 8

OPPRESSORS
- children are their o., 2 Ne 13:12
- they shall rule over their o. 24: 2
- upon the heads of all their o. DC 127: 3

OR: *see in the APPENDIX.*

ORACLES
- o. be given to another, DC 90: 4
- they who receive the o. of God, 90: 5
- o. in your most holy places 124:39
- the o. for the whole church. 124:126

ORATOR
- artificer, and the eloquent o. 2 Ne 13: 3

ORCHARDS
- houses, or for barns, or for o., DC 59:17

ORDAIN
- did he o. to preach unto them, Mos 18:18
- gave him power to o. priests 25:19
- I o. you to be a priest, Mro 3: 3
- I o. you to be a teacher, 3: 3
- they o. priests and teachers, 3: 4
- whom I shall call and o., DC 5:11
- to o. priests and teachers; 18:32
- to o. other elders, priests, 20:39
- he may also o. other priests, 20:48
- o. you unto the first priesthood 27: 8
- as God shall appoint and o. 46:27
- and o. unto this power. 95:14
- shall o. him unto this blessing, 96: 9
- will o. you unto this calling, 100: 9
- to o. evangelical ministers, 107:39
- to o. and set in order all the 107:58

ORDAINED
- they were o. of God and chosen. 1 Ne 12: 7
- the Lord God hath o. the apostle 14:25
- been called of God, and o. 2 Ne 6: 2
- authority from God, and o. priests; Mos 18:18
- the priests whom he had o. 18:24
- he o. priests and elders, by laying Al 6: 1
- that the Lord God o. priests, 13: 1
- o. after the order of his Son, 13: 2
- manner after which they were o.— 13: 3
- and o. unto the high priesthood 13: 6
- they were o. after this manner— 13: 8
- and o. with a holy ordinance, 13: 8
- there were many who were o. and 13:10
- o. by the holy order of God, 49:30
- there were o. of Nephi, men 3 Ne 7:25
- shall one be o. among you, 18: 5
- disciples o. in their stead; 4 Ne 1:14
- o. priests and teachers— Mro 3: 1
- they o. them by the power of 3: 4
- hereafter you shall be o. and DC 5: 6
- for ye are not yet o.— 5:17
- they are they who are o. of me 18:29
- you are they who are o. of me 18:32
- o. an apostle of Jesus Christ, 20: 1
- and o. under his hand; 20: 3
- be o. according to the gifts 20:60

689

ORDAINED

- be o. by the power of the Holy DC 20:60
- who is o. by a priest, 20:64
- No person is to be o. to any 20:65
- is to be o. by the direction 20:67
- that he should be o. by you, 21:10
- all those whom thou hast o., 24:19
- thou shalt be o. under his hand 25: 7
- called and o. even as Aaron; 27: 8
- by whom I have o. you and 27:12
- be o. and sent forth to preach 36: 5
- may be o. and sent forth, 36: 7
- o. a bishop unto the church, 41: 9
- o. by some one who has 42:11
- o. by the heads of the church. 42:11
- he that is o. of me shall 43: 7
- o. as I have told you before, 43: 7
- my servant Leman shall be o. 49: 4
- not o. of God, for marriage is 49:15
- for marriage is o. of God 49:15
- eat the same, is not o. of God; 49:18
- o. for the use of man for food 49:19
- unto what were ye o.? 50:13
- he that is o. of me and sent 50:17
- We that is o. of God and sent 50:26
- things which are not o. of him— 50:35
- as are o. unto this office, 50:38
- and Selah J. Griffin both be o., 52:32
- Jared Carter be o. a priest, 52:38
- George James be o. a priest. 52:38
- thou shalt be o. by the hand 55: 2
- you shall be o. to assist 55: 4
- let him be o. as an agent 63:45
- let him be o. unto this power; 63:45
- let them be o. unto this power. 63:57
- have been o. unto this ministry, 67:10
- were o. unto this priesthood, 68: 2
- set apart and o. unto this power, 68:19
- and o. under the hands of this 68:20
- and o. them to be stewards 70: 3
- and o. unto this power. 72: 8
- who has been o. unto the church 72: 9
- which were o. of the Father, 76:13
- are o. unto this condemnation. 76:48
- o. and sealed unto this power; 76:52
- o. unto the holy order of God, 77:11
- are o. out of every nation, 77:11
- are o. unto the high priesthood 78: 1
- who has o. you from on high, 78: 2
- wherewith he has been o., 79: 1
- was o. by the angel of God 84:28
- o. unto the lesser priesthood, 84:107
- wholesome herbs God hath o. 89:10
- have o. for the use of man 89:12
- grain is o. for the use of man 89:14
- those who are o. unto this power, 90:11
- are many who have been o. 95: 5
- shall be o. unto this blessing. 104:61
- o. a presiding high priest over 106: 1
- is called and set apart and o. unto 107:17
- o. to the several offices in these 107:21
- appointed and o. to that office, 107:22
- who were o. after the order of 107:29
- o. by Adam at the age of 107:42
- Enos was o. at the age of 107:44
- o. by the hand of Adam, 107:46
- o. under the hand of Adam; 107:47
- o. under the hand of Adam. 107:48
- was o. under the hand of Seth. 107:50
- o. under the hand of Methuselah. 107:51
- o. to the High Priesthood 107:52
- the blessings which thou hast o. 107:73
- o. through the instrumentality 109:21
- According to that which was o. 112: 1
- the keys of the holy priesthood o., 121:32
- For it is o. that in Zion, 124:34
- are o. by the ordinance of my 124:36
- o. by my servant William Marks, 124:39
- the counsel which I have o., 124:79
- o., and anointed, as counselor 124:84
- o. unto this calling in his stead— 124:91
- be o. for standing presidents, 124:132
- o. to be standing ministers to 124:135
- o. from before the foundation 124:137
- 127: 2

ORDAINED

the Lord o. and prepared	DC 128: 5
hath o., before the world was,	128:22
as I and my Father o. unto you,	132:11
whether it be o. of men,	132:13
as was o. by me and my Father	132:28
Lord o. Noah after his own order,	Mses 8:19
be o. to administer the same;	Abr 1: 2
upon us, he o. us, saying:	JS 2:68
and o. him to the Aaronic	2:71
o. me to the same Priesthood—	2:71
were o. under the hand of this	2:72

ORDAINING

may have the privilege of o.,	DC 20:66

ORDAINS

which is in the one who o. him.	DC 20:60

ORDER

after the manner of his holy o.,	2Ne 6: 2
upon his kingdom to o. it,	19: 7
things are done in wisdom and o.;	Mos 4:27
all things must be done in o.	4:27
after the o. of the man that	Al 2: 1
priesthood of the holy o. of God,	4:20
according to the holy o. of God,	5:hd
according to the holy o. of God,	5:44
is the o. after which I am called,	5:49
do walk after the holy o. of God,	5:54
according to the o. of God,	6: 1
to establish the o. of the church	6: 4
holy o. by which he was called.	6: 8
walk after the holy o. of God,	7:22
established the o. of the church,	8: 1
according to the holy o. of God,	8: 4
ordained priests, after his holy o.,	13: 1
which was after the o. of his Son,	13: 1
after the o. of his Son,	13: 2
priesthood of the holy o. of God,	13: 6
being after the o. of his Son,	13: 7
which o. was from the	13: 7
the high priesthood of the holy o.,	13: 8
forever, after the o. of the Son,	13: 9
holy o. of this high priesthood,	13:10
were called after this holy o.,	13:11
this same o. which I have spoken,	13:14
it being a type of his o., or it being	13:16
type of his order, or it being his o.,	13:16
according to the holy o. of God,	13:18
after the o. and faith of Nehor,	14:16
in o. to defend thy flocks	18:16
after the o. of the Nehors;	21: 4
were after the o. of the Nehors.	21: 4
after the o. of the Nehors.	24:28
who were of the o. of Nehor,	24:29
be restored to their proper o.	41: 2
be restored to their proper o.,	41: 4
after the holy o. of God	43: 2
also maintain o. in the church;	46:38
by the holy o. of God,	49:30
were called by the holy o. of God,	He 8:18
even after the o. of his Son;	8:18
again, according to its proper o.;	3Ne 1:19
there was great o. in the land;	6: 4
in o. that ye may translate;	Eth 5: 1
called after the holy o. of God.	12:10
They are without o. and without	Mro 9:18
all things may be done in o.	DC 20:68
all things must be done in o.,	28:13
in o. that every member may	46:29
all these things be done in o.;	58:55
after the o. of Melchizedek,	76:57
was after the o. of Enoch,	76:57
after the o. of the Only	76:57
in their destined o. or sphere	77: 3
unto the holy o. of God,	77:11
and o. unto my church,	78: 4
joined together in this o.;	78: 8
This o. I have appointed to	82:20
an everlasting o. unto you,	82:20
is after the holiest o. of God.	84:18
set in o. the house of God,	85: 7

ORDERED

in o. to defend themselves	DC 87: 3
Every man in his own o.,	88:60
a house of o., a house of God;	88:119
the o. of the house prepared	88:127
the o. of the house of the	88:128
the o. and will of God in the	89: 2
And set in o. the churches,	90:15
set in o. all the affairs of this	90:16
Set in o. your houses;	90:18
I give unto the united o.,	92: 1
ye shall receive him into the o.	92: 1
be a lively member in this o.;	92: 2
set in o. your own house,	93:43
first set in o. thy house.	93:44
and set in o. his family,	93:50
to the o. of the priesthood,	94: 6
necessary to benefit mine o.,	96: 4
become a member of the o.,	96: 8
in o. that all things be prepared	101:69
which belong to the o.	104: 1
established, to be a united o.,	104: 1
everlasting o. for the benefit	104: 1
as any man belonging to the o.	104: 5
any man among you, of the o.,	104:10
the properties of the o.—	104:19
to the counsel of the o.,	104:21
united consent or voice of the o.,	104:21
to the counsel of the o.,	104:36
and by the voice of the o.	104:36
o. which I have established	104:40
longer be bound as a united o.	104:47
United O. of the Stake of Zion,	104:48
United O. of the City of Zion.	104:48
dissolved as a united o.	104:53
agreed by this o. in council,	104:53
only by the voice of the o.,	104:64
common consent of the o.	104:71
common consent of the o.—	104:72
before the council of the o.	104:74
council and voice of the o.	104:76
council and voice of the o.,	104:77
after the O. of the Son of God.	107: 3
after the o. of Melchizedek,	107: 9
after the o. of the Melchizedek	107:10
priest (of the Levitical o.),	107:10
in o. to make their decisions	107:27
after the o. of Melchizedek,	107:29
The o. of this priesthood was	107:40
This o. was instituted in the days	107:41
to ordain and set in o. all the	107:58
after the o. of Melchizedek,	107:71
after the o. of Melchizedek.	107:73
after the o. of Melchizedek,	107:76
that all things may be done in o.	107:84
showing the o. of the Seventy,	107:93
a house of glory, a house of o.,	109: 8
will o. all things for your good,	111:11
is after the o. of Melchizedek,	124:123
the o. of mine Only Begotten Son.	124:123
all the records be had in o.,	127: 9
think this o. of things to be	128: 5
in o. to answer to the likeness	128:12
is contrary to the o. of heaven	129: 7
or all kingdoms of a lower o.,	130: 9
to a higher o. of kingdoms	130:10
And in o. to obtain the highest,	131: 2
into this o. of the priesthood	131: 2
mine house is a house of o.,	132: 8
for my house is a house of o.,	132:18
after the o. of him who was	Mses 6:67
ordained Noah after his own o.,	8:19
o. established by the fathers	Abr 1:26
which belong to the same o.	3: 3
for it moveth in o. more slow;	3: 5
this is in o. because it standeth	3: 5
which belong to the same o. as that	3: 9
in o. to have everybody	JS 2: 6
in o., if possible, to discover	2:56

ORDERED

Antipus o. that I should march	Al 56:30
Gods o. the expanse, so that it	Abr 4: 7

ORDERED

and it was so, even as they o.	Abr	4: 7
Gods o., saying: Let the waters		4: 9
dry; and it was so as they o.;		4: 9
and it was so, even as they o.		4:11
those things which they had o.		4:18

ORDERS

Moroni also sent o. unto him	Al	52: 8
he also sent o. unto him that		52: 9
Teancum had received o. to make		52:16
Teancum, by the o. of Moroni,		53: 3
by the o. of Ammoron to not		56:18
I immediately gave o. that my		57:24
do they represent classes or o.?	DC	77: 3

ORDINANCE

and ordained with a holy o.,	Al	13: 8
which calling, and o.,		13: 8
with an oath and sacred o. to		50:39
This being an o. unto you,	DC	21:11
it was a mission, and an o.,		77:14
the o. of the washing of feet,		88:139
the o. of the washing of feet		88:139
the o. of washing feet		88:140
this o. belongeth to my house,		124:30
o. of baptizing for the dead		124:33
by the o. of my holy house,		124:39
Which o. is instituted for		124:134
answer the o. just the same		128: 4
by conforming to the o. and		128: 5
nature of this o. consists in		128: 8
o. which God has prepared for		128: 8
The o. of baptism by water,		128:12
this o. was instituted to form		128:12
the o. of baptism for the dead,		128:12
unto Adam, by an holy o.,	Mses	5:59

ORDINANCES

the performances and o. of God	2Ne	25:30
law of performances and of o.,	Mos	13:30
these o. were given after this	Al	13:16
strict in observing the o. of God,		30: 3
foolish o. and performances		30:23
ye are gone away from mine o.,	3Ne	24: 7
that we have kept his o. and		24:14
and o. of the law of Moses;	4Ne	1:12
they have strayed from mine o.,	DC	1:15
of me if he obey mine o.		52:15
is of God if he obey mine o.		52:16
these are the first o. which		53: 6
as he obeyeth mine o.		64: 5
in the o. thereof,		84:20
And without the o. thereof,		84:21
in administering outward o.		107:14
to administer in outward o.,		107:20
comes the administering of o.		107:67
from the o. of mine house.		121:19
o. might be revealed which		124:38
that I may reveal mine o. therein		124:40
mine holy o., and charters,		124:46
o. in their own *propria persona,*		128: 8
walk in all the o. of the Lord.		136: 4
the keys of the sealing o.,		OD
the laws and o. of the Gospel.	AoF	3
the first principles and o. of		4
administer in the o. thereof.		5

ORDINARY

no common or o. case is	DC	102:28

ORDINATION

Take upon you mine o.,	DC	53: 3
was called by his o. to		68: 1
in the power of the o.		79: 1
when he received his o.		107:45
and receive right by o.		108: 4

ORE

shall I go that I may find o.	1Ne	17: 9
whither I should go to find o.,		17:10
I did make tools of the o.		17:16
we did find all manner of o.,		18:25

691

ORIHAH

I did make plates of o.	1Ne	19: 1
it was engraven on plates of o.	Mos	21:27
or precious o. of every kind;	He	6:11
who did work all kinds of o. and		6:11
o. I have none, for I am alone.	Mrm	8: 5
did work in all manner of o.,	Eth	10:23
mighty heaps of earth to get o.,		10:23

OREB

of Midian at the rock of O.;	2Ne	20:26

ORES

and of silver, and of precious o.,	2Ne	5:15
for all manner of precious o.,	Jac	2:12

ORGAN

such as handle the harp and o.	Mses	5:45

ORGANIZATION

there be an o. of my people,	DC	78: 3
the o. of the said Church.	JS	2: 2
the same o. that existed in	AoF	6

ORGANIZE

to o. yourselves according to	DC	44: 4
how to o. this people.		51: 1
to prepare and o. yourselves		78:11
together, and o. yourselves,		88:74
O. yourselves; prepare every		88:119
proceeded to o. the high council		102: 1
o. a council after the manner		102:24
and o. my kingdom upon		103:35
ye shall o. yourselves and		104:11
you to o. yourselves,		104:58
O. yourselves; prepare every		109: 8
o. themselves, and appoint one of		124:62
and Erastus Snow o. a company.		136:12
Wilford Woodruff o. a company.		136:13
George A. Smith o. a company.		136:14
the Gods went down to o. man	Abr	4:27
that we have said, and o. them;		4:31

ORGANIZED

it being regularly o. and	DC	20: 1
a regularly o. branch of the		20:65
Which church was o. and		21: 3
that they be o. according to		51: 2
any of her stakes which are o.,		68:25
any of her stakes which are o.		68:26
I have commanded to be o.;		90: 7
o. agreeable to the		92: 1
of Christ is regularly o.,		102:12
to be o. and established,		104: 1
After you are o., you shall		104:48
brethren, after they are o.,		104:48
shall be o. in their own names,		104:49
be o. according to thy laws,		109:15
let the Twelve be o.;		118: 1
be o. into companies,		136: 2
companies be o. with captains		136: 3
companies are o. let them go to		136: 3
were o. before the world was;		136: 6
the Gods, o. and formed the	Abr	3:22
the Gods o. the earth to bring		4: 1
the Gods o. the lights in the		4:12
o. them to be for signs and		4:14
o. them to be for lights in the		4:15
the Gods o. the two great lights,		4:16
the Gods o. the earth to bring		4:25
all these things shall be thus o.		4:30

ORGANIZING

a privilege of o. themselves	DC	51:15

ORIGINAL

of God hath atoned for o. guilt,	Mses	6:54

ORIHAH

And Kib was the son of O.,	Eth	1:32
and Gilgah, and Mahah, and O.		6:14
O. was anointed to be king		6:27
O. did walk humbly before		6:30
O. did execute judgment upon		7: 1

ORNAMENT

with them all, as with an o.,	1 Ne 21:18
he did o. with pure gold;	Mos 11:11

ORNAMENTED

he o. them with fine work of	Mos 11: 8
and was o. with gold and silver	11: 9
things which they are o. with;	Al 31:28

ORNAMENTS

the bravery of their tinkling o.,	2 Ne 13:18
and the o. of the legs,	13:20
bracelets, and their o. of gold,	Al 31:28

ORPHANS

o. to mourn before the Lord,	Mrm 8:40
and o. shall be provided for,	DC 83: 6

ORSON: see also HYDE, Orson, and PRATT, ORSON.

My son O., hearken and hear and	DC 34: 1

OTHER

or in o. words, I, Nephi,	1 Ne 1:hd
choice above all o. lands,	2:20
wife, and his three o. daughters.	7: 6
or, in o. words I have seen	8: 2
desirable above all o. fruit.	8:12
desirable above all o. fruit.	8:15
on the o. side of the river	8:26
he saw o. multitudes pressing	8:30
he also saw o. multitudes	8:31
Upon the o. plates should be	9: 4
the o. plates are for the more	9: 4
or, in o. words, a Savior	10: 4
expedient for me in mine o. book.	10:15
Jerusalem, and also o. cities.	11:13
fair above all o. virgins.	11:15
to battle, one against the o.,	12: 2
abominable above all o. churches,	13: 5
it wrought upon o. Gentiles;	13:13
of the hands of all o. nations.	13:19
abominable above all o. churches;	13:26
power of God above all o. nations,	13:30
is choice above all o. lands,	13:30
I beheld o. books, which came	13:39
on the one hand or on the o.—	14: 7
the o. is the church of the devil;	14:10
his mind swallowed up in o. things	15:27
desirable above all o. fruits;	15:36
and also for o. wise purposes,	19: 3
a record upon the o. plates,	19: 4
myself because of o. men,	19: 6
but I would speak in o. words—	19: 7
doings of the Lord in o. lands,	19:22
which is choice above all o. lands,	2 Ne 1: 5
who should be led out of o. countries	1: 5
from the knowledge of o. nations;	1: 8
they shall be kept from all o. nations,	1: 9
he will bring o. nations unto them,	1:11
one being sweet and the o. bitter.	2:15
was inticed by the one or the o.	2:16
I have none o. object save it be	2:30
he shall do none o. work,	3: 8
are written upon mine o. plates.	4:14
are written upon mine o. plates.	4:14
said unto me: Make o. plates;	5:30
they must search mine o. plates.	5:33
will be restored one to the o.;	9:12
For on the o. hand,	9:13
there is none o. way save it be	9:41
there is none o. nation on earth	10: 3
be wrought among o. nations	10: 4
this land against all o. nations.	10:12
God unto me, above all o. lands,	10:19
and there is none o. people that	25: 5
Jews shall be scattered by o. nations.	25:15
hath scourged them by o. nations	25:16
there is none o. name given under	25:20
the one like unto the o.,	26:28
those who shall be upon o. lands,	27: 1
none o. which shall view it, save	27:13
when the one shall say unto the o.:	2 Ne 28: 3
the o. tribes of the house of Israel,	29:12
there is none o. way nor name	31:21
be engraven upon his o. plates,	Jac 1: 3
as precious in his sight as the o.	2:21
and the o. part of the tree hath	5:25
above all o. parts of the land of	5:43
most precious above all o. fruit.	5:61
and brought o. servants;	5:70
kept on the o. plates of Nephi,	7:26
go to the o. plates of Nephi;	Jar 1:14
and put them with the o. plates,	WM 1:10
there shall be no o. name given	Mos 3:17
nor any o. way nor means	3:17
there is none o. salvation save	4: 8
there is no o. head whereby	5: 8
There is no o. name given	5: 8
must be called by some o. name;	5:10
or in o. words, he said that	7:27
which were above all the o. seats,	11:11
will preserve them for o. nations	12: 8
of this people to o. nations.	12: 8
shalt have no o. God before me.	12:35
him more than any o. man;	29:40
been favored above every o.	Al 9:20
or in o. words, being without	13: 7
great sin, and his many o. sins,	15: 3
he was set among o. servants to	17:25
say no more to the o. multitude;	32: 7
or rather, in o. words, blessed is he	32:16
one hand even as it is on the o.;	32:20
that on the o. hand, there can be	36:21
also many o. miracles wrought	37:40
no o. way or means whereby man	38: 9
or, I would say, in o. words, that	40: 2
or in o. words, their resurrection	40:19
on one hand, the o. on the other—	41: 4
on one hand, the other on the o.—	41: 4
and the o. to evil according to	41: 5
And so it is on the o. hand.	41: 6
While on the o. hand, there was	43:38
on the o. side of the river	43:41
blessed him, and also his o. sons;	45:15
or, in o. words, if they should	46:21
Moroni, on the o. hand, had been	48: 7
or in o. words, if they were	48:15
and even the o. sons of Mosiah,	48:18
forts of security by any o. way	49:18
to enter the fort by any o. way,	49:19
on the o. hand, there was not	49:23
on the o. hand, the people of	49:28
by stratagem or some o. way	52:10
and the men of Lehi on the o.,	52:31
they were beloved by each o.,	53: 2
none o. have they spared alive.	56:12
make an attack upon our o. cities	56:22
and fled to their o. cities,	57: 4
that none o. power can operate	60:25
this man built o. ships.	63: 7
one o. ship also did sail forth;	63: 8
that there is no o. way nor means	He 5: 9
on the o. hand, that the Nephites	6:38
to one more than the o., save it	7:23
the o. words which he has spoken	9: 2
Zenos, and many o. prophets,	15:11
Or in o. words, yield yourselves	3 Ne 3: 7
or in o. words, the resurrection	6:20
cheek, turn to him the o. also;	12:39
hate the one and love the o.,	13:24
to the one and despise the o.	13:24
concerning the o. tribes of the	15:15
o. sheep I have which are not of	15:17
the o. tribes hath the Father	15:20
O. sheep I have which are not of	15:21
I have o. sheep which are not	16: 1
o. tribes whom they know not of,	16: 4
I may fulfil o. commandments	18:27
o. scriptures I would that ye	23: 6
and the o. on the other hand,	26: 5
and the other on the o. hand,	26: 5
there were o. disciples ordained	4 Ne 1:14
shall be judged by the o. twelve	Mrm 3:19

shall have o. witness besides him	Mrm	3:21
there were also o. cities which were		5: 4
none o. people knoweth our		9:34
was choice above all o. lands,	Eth	2: 7
is choice above all o. lands;		2:10
all o. nations under heaven,		2:12
land choice above all o. lands.		2:15
that Akish begat o. sons,		9:10
also many o. kinds of animals		9:18
was choice above all o. lands;		9:20
also begat o. sons and daughters.		9:25
choice land choice above all o. lands,		13: 2
more than any o. man among		14:10
the o. must perish because he	Mro	8:15
and become as o. men,	DC	3:11
pretend to no o. gift until		5: 4
grant unto you no o. gift until		5: 4
Behold, there is no o. power,		8: 7
behold, o. records have I,		9: 2
or, in o. words, if he bringeth		10:17
that o. nations should possess		10:49
O. sheep have I which are not		10:59
that I had o. sheep, and that		10:60
is none o. name given whereby		18:23
more express than o. scriptures,		19: 7
white above all o. whiteness;		20: 6
to ordain o. elders, priests,		20:39
he may also ordain o. priests,		20:48
neither hardness with each o.,		20:54
their licenses from o. elders,		20:63
the o. elders shall appoint		20:82
pretend to no o. revelation;		32: 4
sit thou here; and to the o.:		38:26
church, or in o. words, unto me—		42:37
or in o. words, the keys of the		42:69
the poor, and for o. purposes,		42:71
or in o. words, if they shall		42:74
none o. appointed unto you		43: 3
shall instruct and edify each o.,		43: 8
by letter or some o. way.		44: 1
of truth or some o. way?		50:17
And if it be by some o. way		50:18
of truth or some o. way?		50:19
If it be by some o. way it is not		50:20
in o. places, in all churches.		51:18
saying none o. things than		52: 9
declaring none o. things than		52:36
hold upon o. men's goods,		56:17
or, in o. words, him that		58:20
And o. directions concerning		58:38
thou shalt do none o. thing,		59:13
in o. words that thy joy may		59:13
or in o. words rejoicing and		59:14
or in o. words they shall not		61:23
or in o. words, the store, yet		63:42
o. bishops to be set apart		68:14
every o. creature which God		77: 2
Or in o. words, the city of		78: 4
Or, in o. words, let my servant		78: 9
above all o. creatures beneath		78:14
Or, in o. words, I give unto		82: 9
in o. words, you are to have		82:17
every man may gain o. talents,		82:18
in o. words upon the Lord's		83: 5
States will call on o. nations,		87: 3
shall also call upon o. nations,		87: 3
themselves against o. nations;		87: 3
which o. Comforter is the same		88: 3
they give light to each o. in		88:44
in o. words, those who are		88:127
mild drinks, as also o. grain.		89:17
in o. words, light and truth.		93:36
in o. words, I will call you		93:45
or, in o. words, Alphus;		95:17
or, in o. words, Omegus;		95:17
give unto him o. commandments.		97: 4
in o. words, all mine Israel,		101:12
there is none o. place appointed		101:20
there be any o. place appointed		101:20
o. places which I will appoint		101:21
power to appoint o. high priests,		102: 7
assisted by two o. presidents,		102:10
o. presidents have power to		102:11
in o. words, shall break the	DC	104: 5
in o. words, if any man among		104:69
All o. authorities or offices in		107: 5
the o. is the Aaronic or Levitical		107: 6
thus differing from o. officers in		107:23
thus differing from o. officers in		107:25
or validity one with the o.—		107:27
and set in order all the o. officers		107:58
Or, in o. words, the		107:66
necessary to have o. bishops or		107:74
as there are o. bishops appointed		107:75
power to call o. high priests,		107:79
are to choose o. seventy		107:95
And also o. seventy, until		107:96
Whereas o. officers of the church,		107:98
o. stakes besides this one which		109:59
o. places should be appointed for		115:18
of the Eternal God of all o. gods		121:32
stock to any o. purpose,		124:70
neither can any o. man,		124:72
o. is to preside over the churches		124:140
the o. has no responsibility of		124:140
as well as many o. things.		127:10
these o. records can be handed,		128: 4
o. words, taking a different view		128: 8
might accord with the o.;		128:12
welding link of some kind or o.		128:18
upon some subject or o.—		128:18
He may enter into the o., but		131: 4
fulfilling, among o. things, the		132:34
Jacob did none o. things than		132:37
they did none o. things than		132:37
and have vowed to no o. man,		132:61
from one end of heaven to the o.		133: 7
than any o. man that ever lived		135: 3
and many o. wise documents and		135: 3
and o. necessaries for the journey,		136: 5
forty or any o. number of		OD
Temples or in any o. place		OD
I have o. things to inquire of	Mses	1:18
Irad, and o. sons and daughters.		5:43
begat Mahujael, and o. sons and		5:43
begat Methusael, and o. sons and		5:43
and the name of the o., Zillah.		5:44
none o. people shall dwell there		7: 7
and we will kiss each o.;		7:63
and there be one above the o.,	Abr	3:16
be two things, one above the o.,		3:17
be more intelligent than the o.,		3:18
is more intelligent than the o.,		3:18
more intelligent than the o.;		3:19
pertaining to o. planets;	Fac	2: 2
in o. words, the governing		2: 5
fifteen o. fixed planets or		2: 5
one end of heaven to the o.	JS	1:37
shall be taken, and the o. left;		1:44
shall be taken, and the o. left;		1:45
On the o. hand, the Baptists		2: 9
and said, pointing to the o.—		2:17
many o. things did he say		2:20
no o. clothing on but this robe,		2:31
o. passages of scripture,		2:41
no o. object in view in getting		2:46
be influenced by any o. motive		2:46
attempting to work as at o. times,		2:48
and the o. things with them.		2:52
many o. things connected with		2:73
OTHER'S		
rejoiced in each o. safety;	Al	53: 2
OTHERS		
saw twelve o. following him,	1Ne	1:10
I beheld o. pressing forward,		8:24
beheld twelve o. following him,		11:29
Holy Ghost fell upon twelve o.;		12: 7
And also o. who have been,		14:26
o. set at naught and trample		19: 7
and o. with the thunderings		19:11
and the o. shall say:	2Ne	28: 3
And o. will he pacify, and lull		28:21
behold, o. he flattereth away,		28:22
this tree like unto the o.	Jac	5:25

OTHERS   694   OURSELVES

that they also took o.	Om	1:29
up with their pride, despising o.,	Al	4:12
while o. were abasing themselves,		4:13
while o. would reject the Spirit		13: 4
o. captive into the wilderness.		16: 3
and smote off the arms of o.,		18:16
but o. say that he is dead		19: 5
And o. rebuked them, saying:		19:20
and o. said he was sent by the		19:25
But o. rebuked them all, saying		19:26
thousands of o. truly mourn		28:12
ye that he should afflict o.,		30:51
unto thee, while o. shall perish.		31:28
right and the o. on the left;		58:17
and surrounded many o.,		62:25
and they succeeded with those o.	He	4: 4
And there were o. who said:		9:41
and did carry away o. captive		11:33
also many o., baptizing unto	3Ne	1:23
o. did receive great learning		6:12
o. were exceedingly humble;		6:13
o. would receive railing and		6:13
And again the Lord called o.,		11:22
with some o. and their families,	Eth	1:33
thereby o. might be partakers		12: 8
gave commandments to o.,	DC	1:18
o. who are called to declare my		18:26
and is confirmed to o. by the		20:10
are of men, and o. of devils.		46: 7
To o. it is given to believe		46:14
to o. it is given to have faith		46:20
to o. it is given to prophesy;		46:22
to o. the discerning of spirits.		46:23
and o. remain with you that		63:14
o. shall be planted in their		64:40
servant Oliver Cowdery and o.		69: 4
o. with whom the Lord was		84: 3
o. have many things to repent		90:35
the gospel, instead of any o.		107:38
in love above many o.,		112:11
in company with o.,		114: 1
o. shall be planted in their stead		114: 2
they are willing to bring upon o.,		121:13
and love to have o. suffer,		121:13
my servant John Snider, and o.,		124:22
o. also who wish to know my will		124:73
as also many o. of my servants,		132:38
o. of the prophets who had the		132:39
upon the rights and liberties of o.;		134: 4
"Lo, here!" and o., "Lo, there!"	JS	2: 5
tenets and disprove all o.		2: 9
o. said he was mad;		2:24

OTHERWISE

o. their blood would come upon	Jac	1:19
o. they shall hearken unto these		2:30
o. ye are condemned;	Mos	4:25
which o. could not be known.		8:17
Or o., can ye imagine yourselves	Al	5:18
o. I will smite thee to the earth.		20:24
o. we will perish in the land.		27:10
o., justice claimeth the creature		42:22
o., we will retain our swords,		44: 8
it might have o. been if ye		60: 5
o. ye have no reward of your	3Ne	13: 1
O. they should be destroyed,	Eth	13:21
o. men were fallen, and there	Mro	7:24
either a stewardship or o.,	DC	42:72
o. he shall not prosper.		49: 4
if o., they will be cut off.		51: 2
shall provide for them o.,		51:16
O. he shall receive the money		56:10
o. there is none inheritance		63:29
o. they shall be cut off.		63:63
o., a greater condemnation.		63:66
o., think not of thy property.		66: 6
o. they are not legally		68:20
o. the abundance of the		70:14
O. he shall not be accepted		72:18
O. he who shall go up unto		72:26
O. Satan seeketh to turn their		78:10
o. there remaineth a scourge		84:58

o. ye could not abound.	DC	88:50
o. there is no existence.		93:30
o. whatsoever is less than		98:10
O. thou shalt continue		99: 8
o. ye are no stewards.		104:56
by common consent or o.,		104:85
o. I cannot receive her unto		105: 5
o. we will not go up unto		105: 8
render it impossible to be o.—		107:28
o. there can be no appeal		107:32
And if it cannot be o.,		109:52
o., their labors shall be accounted		124:122
or o., as the case may require,		127: 1
heaven could not make it o.;	JS	2:24
make him think or believe o.		2:24
o. I could not get them.		2:46
hiring out by day's work and o.,		2:55
that we would ever be o.—		2:61

OUGHT

look unto the Lord as they o.	1Ne	15: 3
when the law o. to be done away.	2Ne	25:27
which ye o. not to have done.	Jac	2:34
the Lord as I o. to have done.	Om	1: 2
then o. not ye to labor to serve	Mos	2:18
O how you o. to thank your		2:19
O then, how ye o. to impart of		4:21
he should look for that he o. not		8:13
you o. to tremble before God.		12:30
before God, for ye o. to tremble;		15:26
Therefore o. ye not to tremble?		15:27
And now, o. ye not to tremble		16:13
that these things o. not to be;		29:34
that these things o. not to be,		29:36
teacher o. to become popular;	Al	1: 3
o. not to labor with their hands,		1: 3
o. to be supported by the people.		1: 3
and ye o. to be beloved, and ye		9:30
ye o. to bring forth words which		9:30
these things o. not so to be—		16:18
o. to be placed in the sepulchre;		19: 5
and that they o. not to murder,		23: 3
for I o. to be content with the		29: 3
I o. not to harrow up in my		29: 4
ye o. to search the scriptures;		33: 2
o. to retain in remembrance,		36:29
for ye o. to know as I do know,		36:30
and ye o. to know also, that		36:30
for ye o. to be beloved;		60:10
ye o. to have stirred yourselves		60:10
yea, ye o. to marvel because	He	7:15
O ye o. to begin to howl and		9:22
ye o. to search these things.	3Ne	23: 1
manner of men o. ye to be?		27:27
this thing o. not to be;	Mro	8:24
ask for that which you o. not.	DC	8:10
on me for strength as you o.		30: 1
ye o. to forgive one another;		64: 9
ye o. to say in your hearts—		64:11
These things o. not to be,		68:32
O. ye not to have done even as		101:53
for men o. always to pray		101:81
No power or influence can or o.		121:41
O. not to be revealed by	Fac	2: 9
o. to have been my friends	JS	2:28
which o. to be maintained by		2:28

OUR: *see in the APPENDIX.*

OURS
will be done, O Lord, and not o.	DC	109:44

OURSELVES
and we hid o. in the	1Ne	3:27
that we might again rest o.		16:17
and not only we o. had a hope	Jac	4: 4
And we, o., also, through the	Mos	5: 3
upon o. a never-ending torment,		5: 5
we do assemble o. together	Al	21: 6
that we do not glut o. upon the		30:32
not suffer o. to take an oath		44: 8
it shall be o. if we do not		46:27

OURSELVES   695   OVER

we have only sought to defend o.	Al	54:13
may console o. in this point,		56:11
had prepared our city and o.		56:20
we should suppose o. unwise,		57: 2
to defend o. and our country		58: 8
war which broke out among o.;		60:16
so much bloodshed among o.;		60:16
we were contending among o.,		60:16
of so much bloodshed among o.;		60:16
subject o. to the yoke of		61:12
subject o. to our enemies,		61:13
if we will yield o. unto them,	He	16:21
will prepare o. in the center	3Ne	3:21
make preparations to defend o.	Mrm	2: 4
we were left to o., that the Spirit		2:26
to o., to our wives and children,	DC 123: 7	
see that he is a man like o.		130: 1
not taken unto o. the daughters	Mses	8:21

OUT: *see in the APPENDIX.*

OUTCASTS
shall assemble the o. of Israel,	2Ne	21:12
together an army of o.,	Eth	10: 9

OUTER
obtain the o. door of the prison;	Al	14:27
shall be cast out into o. darkness;		40:13
shall the o. vessel be cleansed also.		60:23
Even in o. darkness,	DC 101:91	
shall go away into o. darkness,		133:73

OUTGOINGS
your o. may be in the name of	DC	88:120
your o. may be in the name of		109: 9
o. from this house may be in		109:18

OUTWARD
keep those o. performances	Al	25:15
off from all their o. privileges,	3Ne	4:16
in administering o. ordinances.	DC 107:14	
administer in o. ordinances,		107:20

OVEN
and tomorrow is cast into the o.,	3Ne	13:30
cometh that shall burn as an o.,		25: 1
cometh that shall burn as an o.,	DC 133:64	
cometh that shall burn as an o.,	JS	2:37

OVER
o. all the inhabitants of the earth;	1Ne	1:14
o. all those whom he hath chosen,		1:20
and a teacher o. thy brethren.		2:22
shall have no power o. thy seed		2:23
chosen him to be a ruler o. you,		3:29
for he is God o. all the earth,		11: 6
Satan hath great power o. them.		13:29
and one Shepherd o. all the earth.		13:41
she had dominion o. all the earth,		14:11
himself a king and a ruler o. us,		16:38
that they did rejoice o. me,		17:19
unto their obtaining power o. it.		17:35
brother shall be a ruler o. us.		18:10
power o. the hearts of the		22:15
up to get power o. the flesh,		22:23
power o. the hearts of the people,		22:26
power and authority o. you;	2Ne	1:25
for power nor authority o. you,		1:25
reign o. you in his own kingdom.		2:29
younger brother thinks to rule o. us;		5: 3
brethren, to rule o. this people.		5: 3
teachers o. the land of my people.		5:26
a way for the ransomed to pass o.?		8:10
Bow down, that we may go o.—		8:23
as the street to them that went o.		8:23
and babes shall rule o. them.		13: 4
and women rule o. them.		13:12
come up o. all his channels,		18: 7
and go o. all his banks.		18: 7
he shall overflow and go o.,		18: 8
They are gone o. the passage;		20:29
shall shake his hand o. the river,		21:15
and make men go o. dry shod.	2Ne	21:15
they shall rule o. their oppressors.		24: 2
shall have power o. the hearts of		30:18
a king and a ruler o. his people	Jac	1: 9
in great mercy, o. all his works.		4:10
king o. the land of Zarahemla;	Om	1:12
obtain much advantage o. them;		1:24
and he did reign o. his people in	WM	1:17
a king and a ruler o. this people,	Mos	1:10
a ruler and a king o. this people;		2:11
is a king and a ruler o. you.		2:30
shall have no power o. you.		2:31
a ruler and a king o. his people,		6: 3
who was made king o. this people,		7:21
he being o.-zealous to inherit		7:21
that she should rule o. them!		8:20
yet, I being o.-zealous to inherit		9: 3
look o. all the land round about.		11:12
which is run o. by the beasts		12:11
having gained the victory o. death;		15: 8
and hath power o. the dead;		15:20
and the devil has power o. them;		16: 3
the devil hath all power o. him.		16: 5
and exercise authority o. them;		21: 3
no man to be a king o. you.		23:13
they did watch o. their people,		23:18
o. Alma and his brethren.		23:37
a king and a ruler o. his people,		23:39
appointed teachers o. his people,		24: 1
even o. the people who were in		24: 1
appointed kings o. all these lands.		24: 2
was king o. a numerous people.		24: 3
o. Alma and his brethren,		24: 8
he exercised authority o. them,		24: 9
and put task-masters o. them.		24: 9
and he put guards o. them		24:11
and teachers o. every church.		25:19
the authority o. the church.		26: 8
do who were o. the church,		26:38
to exercise his power o. them.		27: 9
always have kings to rule o. you.		29:13
a king or kings to rule o. you.		29:16
unrighteous king to rule o. them;		29:35
appoint judges to rule o. them,		29:41
kings o. the people of Nephi;		29:47
Judge o. the people of Nephi,	Al	1:hd
High Priest o. the Church.		1:hd
the judges o. the people of Nephi,		1: 1
Amlici to be king o. the people.		2: 2
was not made king o. the people.		2: 7
when Amlici was made king o. them		2:10
rulers and leaders o. his people,		2:14
the judges o. the people of Nephi,		4: 1
priest o. the people of the church,		4: 4
the judges o. the people of Nephi;		4: 5
priests, and elders o. the church;		4: 7
of being high priest o. the church,		4:18
the judges o. the people of Nephi,		4:20
a high priest o. the church of God,		5: 3
sheep doth not watch o. them,		5:59
preside and watch o. the church.		6: 1
and went o. upon the east of		6: 7
that I shall also have joy o. you;		7: 5
my joy o. you should come by		7: 5
my joy cometh o. them after		7: 5
the judges o. the people of Nephi.		8: 2
the judges o. the people of Nephi,		8: 3
journey o. into the land of Melek,		8: 3
art high priest o. the church		8:11
that thou hast no power o. us;		8:12
thou art not the chief judge o. us.		8:12
high priest o. the church of God		8:23
that he may have power o. you,		10:25
was a king o. the land of Salem;		13:17
the judges o. the people of Nephi)		14:23
judge o. the land of Ammonihah		14:23
came o. to the land of Zarahemla,		15:18
the judges o. the people of Nephi.		15:19
the judges o. the people of Nephi,		16: 1
o. the armies of the Nephites,		16: 5
was high priest o. the church,		16: 5
sons crossed o. the river Sidon,		16: 7

the judges o. the people of Nephi.	Al	16:12
got the victory o. the devil,		16:21
the judges o. the people of Nephi.		16:21
who was o. the land of Ishmael;		17:21
who was king o. all the land.		18: 9
his daughters mourned o. him,		18:43
watched o. the bed of her husband,		19:11
who was king o. all the land.		20: 8
and came o. to a village which		21:11
over into the land of Middoni.		21:12
And he did rejoice o. them,		21:21
that he might reign o. the people		21:21
king which was o. all the land		22: 1
went o. into the borders of the		25: 2
and authority o. the Lamanites,		25: 5
came o. to dwell in the land of		25:13
o. that everlasting gulf of death		26:20
of mercy are o. all the earth.		26:37
o. near the borders of the land.		27:14
o. in the place of which has been		27:16
by the victory of Christ o. it.		27:28
the judges o. the people of Nephi;		28: 7
the judges o. the people of Nephi)		30: 2
the judges o. the people of Nephi.		30: 4
o. to the land of Jershon also,		30:19
was a high priest o. that people.		30:20
o. into the land of Gideon,		30:21
also the chief judge o. the land.		30:21
power and authority o. them,		30:23
who was governor o. all the land.		30:29
the devil has power o. you,		30:42
fields, yea, o. all your flocks.		34:20
houses, yea, o. all your household,		34:21
him o. the crops of your fields,		34:24
Cry o. the flocks of your fields,		34:25
devil hath all power o. you;		34:35
came o. into the land of Jershon.		35: 1
came o. into the land of Jershon.		35: 2
o. also into the land of Jershon.		35: 6
o. unto the people of Ammon		35: 8
came o. from them into their land.		35: 8
Zoramites that came o. unto		35: 9
the judges o. the people of Nephi.		35:12
came o. into the land of Melek,		35:13
in wisdom o. all his works,		37:12
may watch o. you in your sleep;		37:37
go o. into the land of Siron,		39: 3
chief captains o. the Lamanites,		43: 6
usurp great power o. them,		43: 8
gain power o. the Nephites by		43: 8
chief captain o. the Nephites—		43:16
o. the armies of the Nephites.		43:17
come o. into the land of Manti,		43:24
o. into the land of Manti.		43:25
unto themselves o. all the land;		43:29
a part o. into the valley,		43:31
that we have gained power o. you,		44: 5
have power o. this people;		44: 7
judges o. the people of Nephi.		44:24
the judges o. the people of Nephi,		45: 2
the judges o. the people of Nephi,		45:20
all the land, o. all the churches.		45:22
and teachers o. the churches		45:23
make them rulers o. the people.		46: 5
great care o. the church,		46: 6
were high priests o. the church.		46: 6
they had had o. the Lamanites,		46: 7
to exercise authority o. them.		46:34
a king and a leader o. them,		47: 6
o. whom the king had given		47:13
second leader o. the whole army.		47:13
o. into the land of Zarahemla		47:29
made king o. the Lamanites,		48: 2
also to reign o. all the land,		48: 2
be chief captains o. his armies.		48: 5
never have power o. the hearts of		48:17
should rejoice o. the blood of		48:25
captain o. the men of that city;		49:16
by casting o. stones and arrows		49:19
obtain power o. the Nephites by		49:22
had all power o. their enemies;		49:26
his desire o. the Nephites;		49:29
judges o. the people of Nephi.		49:29
judges o. the people of Nephi.	Al	50:17
came o. to the camp of Moroni,		50:31
judges o. the people of Nephi.		50:35
and governor o. the people,		50:39
year, o. the people of Nephi.		50:40
judges o. the people of Nephi,		51: 1
be chief judge o. the land;		51: 4
to establish a king o. the land.		51: 5
remain chief judge o. the land		51: 6
and authority o. the people.		51: 8
advantage o. the Lamanites.		51:31
judges o. the people of Nephi;		51:37
judges o. the people of Nephi,		52: 1
appointed king o. the people;		52: 3
judges o. the people of Nephi.		52:14
judges o. the people of Nephi.		52:18
might gain advantage o. them		52:19
did set guards o. the prisoners		53: 1
men o. them to guard them		53: 1
a victory o. one of the greatest		53: 6
some ground o. the Nephites,		53: 8
judges o. the people of Nephi.		53:23
which doth hang o. you except		54: 6
who were o. the Nephites.		55: 6
who were o. the Nephites,		55: 8
Nephites had power o. them;		55:23
judges o. the people of Nephi.		55:35
a leader o. the people of that		56: 9
o. to the city of Nephihah.		56:25
them charge o. our prisoners		57:16
chief captain o. the band who		57:29
given us victory o. those lands,		58:33
judges o. the people of Nephi,		59: 1
come o. and joined the Lamanites		59: 6
of the Lamanites o. them.		59:12
and the governor o. the land,		60: 1
have gained no power o. us.		60:15
which those king-men had o. us;		60:16
of justice doth hand o. you;		60:29
the chief captain o. the army.		61: 2
have appointed a king o. them,		61: 8
be placed king o. this people		61: 8
command o. the remainder of		62: 3
judges o. the people of Nephi;		62:11
judges o. the people of Nephi,		62:12
down o. the walls of the city.		62:36
judges o. the people of Nephi;		62:39
judges o. the people of Nephi,		62:52
judges o. the people of Nephi,		63: 1
judges o. the people of Nephi.		63:16
judges o. the people of Nephi,	He	1: 1
governor o. the people of Nephi.		1: 5
and a governor o. the people,		1:13
gain power o. the Nephites—		1:16
great advantage o. them,		1:25
judges o. the people of Nephi.		2:12
judges o. the people of Nephi.		3:22
possessions o. the Lamanites.		4:18
to obtain more power o. them;		4:19
it shall have no power o. you		5:12
had gone o. from the Nephites,		5:17
o. all the face of the land,		6:28
judges o. the people of Nephi.		6:32
judges o. the people of Nephi.		6:41
o. the people of the Nephites,		7: 1
enemies can have no power o. us.		8: 6
shall have power o. this people,		10: 6
judges o. the people of Nephi.		10:19
judges o. the people of Nephi,		11:24
gone o. unto the Lamanites,		11:24
judges o. the people of Nephi.		11:29
should rule and reign o. them;		12: 6
come o. and fall upon that city,		12:17
of justice hangeth o. this people;		13: 5
judges o. the people of Nephi.		16: 9
judges o. the people of Nephi.		16:24
and the governor o. the land.	3Ne	1: 1
began to rejoice o. their brethren,		1: 6
who was king o. the people of		2: 5
gain many advantages o. them.		2:18
destruction did hang o. them,		2:19
captains o. all the armies of		3:17
to establish a king o. the land,		6:30

OVER

not establish a king o. the land;	3Ne 7: 1	also to preside o. Zion in	DC 90:32
a chief or a leader o. them;	7: 3	and the angels rejoice o. them.	90:34
a king o. this wicked band;	7:10	one hath power, as yet, o. you,	93:42
days o. the face of the land.	8: 3	to preside o. the school in	97: 4
shall not have power o. you;	16:12	Lord's scourge shall pass o.	97:23
shall hang o. them at that day;	20:20	are in authority o. you—	101:76
should have no more go o. the earth,	22: 9	preside o. the council of	102:10
could have no power o. them,	28:39	to preside o. the council	102:11
o. the disciples of Jesus who	4Ne 1:30	to preside o. such councel	102:25
o. all the face of the land;	1:46	o. unto the buffetings of	104:10
which hung o. my people,	Mrm 2: 8	steward o. earthly blessings,	104:13
have had no power o. them.	4: 4	to be stewards o. mine house,	104:57
gain no power o. the Lamanites,	4:18	high priest o. my church,	106: 1
advantage o. the Lamanites.	6: 4	authority o. all the offices in	107: 8
dissented o. unto the Lamanites,	6:15	thou art a prince o. them forever.	107:55
gained the victory o. the grave;	7: 5	elders to preside o. those who	107:60
of vengeance hangeth o. you;	8:41	priests to preside o. those who	107:61
of his tender mercies o. them.	Eth 6:12	teachers to preside o. those	107:62
their sons to be a king o. them.	6:22	the High Priesthood to preside o.	107:65
anointed to be king o. the people.	6:27	the Presiding High Priest o. the	107:66
went o. and dwelt in the land of	7: 4	handed o. and carried up unto the	107:78
a king o. that part of the land.	7:16	duty of a president o. the office	107:85
gain power any more o. Shule	7:19	is to preside o. twelve deacons,	107:85
they shall spread o. the nation,	8:22	duty of the president o. the office	107:86
came o. and passed by the hill	9: 3	is to preside o. twenty-four of the	107:86
came o. by the place where the	9: 3	duty of the president o. the	107:87
was anointed king o. the people,	9: 4	to preside o. forty-eight priests,	107:87
came o. and dwelt with Omer.	9: 9	duty of the president o. the	107:89
o. all the face of the land,	9:26	to preside o. ninety-six elders,	107:89
spread o. all the face of the land.	10: 4	is to preside o. the whole church,	107:91
he gained power o. many cities;	10: 9	presidents to preside o. them,	107:93
he did gain power o. all the land,	10: 9	presidents is to preside o. the six;	107:94
himself king o. all the land.	10: 9	and are to preside o. them;	107:95
he reigned o. the half of the	10:32	angels have charge o. them;	109:22
Com gained power o. Amgid,	10:32	rise up and prevail o. thy people	109:26
power o. the remainder of	10:32	reports abroad, o. the world,	109:29
reign o. the people all his days.	11:10	that you shall have power o. it,	111: 4
was king o. all the land.	12: 1	and my hand shall be o. him;	112:15
o. the hearts of the people;	15:19	be faithful o. a few things,	117:10
that it hath no power o. them;	Mro 8: 8	and he shall be a ruler o. many.	117:10
dissented o. unto the Lamanites,	9:24	depart to go o. the great waters,	118: 4
will also dissent o. unto them;	9:24	thou shalt triumph o. all thy foes.	121: 8
power o. his own dominion.	DC 1:35	be a president o. their quorum	124:62
shall have power o. his saints,	1:36	receive o. fifteen thousand dollars	124:65
have no power o. them except	5: 3	o. fifteen thousand dollars stock	124:72
give unto me power o. death,	7: 2	he shall be made ruler o. many;	124:113
asking to translate it o. again.	10:15	presiding elder o. all my church,	124:125
for mine arm is o. all the earth.	15: 2	a president o. the Twelve	124:127
for mine arm is o. all the earth.	16: 2	be a president o. a quorum of	124:133
and watch o. the church;	20:42	or servants o. different stakes	124:134
to watch o. the church always,	20:53	may preside o. the quorum of	124:136
to preside o. the conference by	28:10	preside o. the quorum of elders,	124:137
to those who were set o. you,	30: 2	preside o. the quorum of seventies;	124:138
counselor o. him in the church,	30: 7	other is to preside o. the churches	124:140
watch o. him that his faith fail	35:19	to preside o. the bishopric;	124:141
your king and watch o. you.	38:21	that the storm is fully blown o.,	127: 1
a steward o. his own property,	42:32	triumph o. all my enemies.	127: 2
may not have power o. you;	44: 5	o. their own signatures,	128: 4
ordain to watch o. the church	46:27	that cannot be lightly passed o.,	128:15
unto you, power o. that spirit;	50:32	he shall be made ruler o. many.	132:44
be made ruler o. many things.	52:13	be made ruler o. many things,	132:53
the elders watch o. the churches,	52:39	been faithful o. a few things,	132:53
and they rejoice o. you,	62: 3	and shall reign o. all flesh.	133:25
I am o. all, and in all,	63:59	the Lord, who ruleth o. all flesh.	133:61
presidency o. this priesthood,	68:17	were delivered o. unto darkness.	133:72
stewards o. the revelations and	70: 3	and your enemies triumph o. you,	136:42
stewardship o. temporal things.	70:11	the church o. which I preside	OD
been faithful o. many things,	70:17	And then to rule o. the day,	Mses 2:18
be handed o. unto the bishop	72: 6	and the moon to rule o. the night,	2:18
and handed o. to the bishop	72:13	dominion o. the fishes of the sea,	2:26
as stewards o. the literary	72:20	and o. the fowl of the air,	2:26
for the heavens wept o. him—	76:26	fowl of the air, and o. the cattle,	2:26
reign on the earth o. his people.	76:63	the cattle, and o. all the earth,	2:26
o. the kingdom of our God.	76:79	and o. every creeping thing that	2:26
power o. the four parts of	77: 8	dominion o. the fish of the sea,	2:28
o. the twelve tribes of Israel;	77: 9	of the air, and o. the fowl of the air,	2:28
o. the nations of the earth,	77:11	and o. every living thing that	2:28
o. the buffetings of Satan	78:12	husband, and he shall rule o. thee.	4:22
made rulers o. many kingdoms,	78:15	have dominion o. all the beasts	5: 1
o. to the buffetings of Satan	82:21	And thou shalt rule o. him;	5:23
to watch o. the church,	84:111	whole heavens shall weep o. them,	7:37
and the angels rejoice o. you;	88: 2	soul, and wept o. his brethren,	7:44
not have power o. the saints	88:114	and my power shall be o. thee	Abr 1:18
o. the affairs of the church	90:13	I stretch my hand o. the sea, and	2: 7

therefore my hand shall be o. thee. Abr 2: 8
o. all the intelligences thine eyes 3:21
to rule o. the day and over the 4:17
over the day and o. the night, 4:17
dominion o. the fish of the sea, 4:26
and o. the fowl of the air, 4:26
of the air, and o. the cattle, 4:26
the cattle, and o. all the earth, 4:26
and o. every creeping thing that 4:26
dominion o. the fish of the sea, 4:28
and o. the fowl of the air, 4:28
o. every living thing that moveth 4:28
the firmament o. our heads; Fac 1:12
made ruler o. his household, JS 1:49
make him ruler o. all his goods. 1:50
astonishing influence o. me 2:15
of light exactly o. my head, 2:16
of a little o. fourteen years 2:23
rehearse or repeat o. again to 2:46
messenger standing o. my head, 2:49

OVERANXIETY
because of my o. for you. Jac 4:18

OVERBEARANCE
Use boldness, but not o.; Al 38:12

OVERCAME
whom he made war and o., DC 76:30
power which entirely o. me, JS 2:15

OVERCOME
being o. with the Spirit 1Ne 1: 7
being o. with the Spirit, 1: 8
that they had o. my seed; 12:20
I was o. because of my afflictions, 15: 5
wild branches have o. the roots Jac 5:37
had o. that part of the tree 5:40
they have o. the good branch 5:45
branches thereof o. the roots 5:48
branches have o. the roots thereof, 5:48
that the good may o. the evil. 5:59
until the good shall o. the bad, 5:66
they were o. that they fell to 7:21
this had o. his natural frame, Al 19: 6
the multitude that they were o. 3Ne 17:18
and the enemy shall not o. DC 38: 9
the same are o. of the world. 50: 8
accusation, that ye be not o., 50:33
and power to o. all things 50:35
and I have o. the world, 50:41
he that is o. and bringeth 52:18
through faith they shall o., 61: 9
my will, the same shall o., 63:20
endureth shall o. the world. 63:47
remain to o. through patience, 63:66
that ye should o. the world; 64: 2
is faithful shall o. all things, 75:16
and ye shall o. all things, 75:22
to be o., and to deny the truth 76:31
And who o. by faith, 76:53
And they shall o. all things. 76:60
I have o. and have trodden 76:107
The Lamb of God hath o. and 88:106
o. him who seeketh the throne 88:115
steadfast and is not o., JS 1:11
but he that shall not be o., 1:30

OVERCOMES
and chasten her until she o. DC 90:36

OVERFLOW
he shall o. and go over, 2Ne 18: 8
shall o. with righteousness. 20:22

OVERFLOWING
they shall see an o. scourge; DC 45:31

OVERLOOK
and o. the land of Shilom, Mos 11:12
may o. the land round about, DC 101:45

OVERLOOKED
that o. those works of pickets, Al 50: 4

OVERPOWER
did o. the people of my seed. 1Ne 12:19
darts of the adversary o. them 15:24
that they could not o. them Mos 9:11
saw that he was about to o. him, 19: 5
they could not o. the Nephites Al 25:13
devil, that he may not o. you, 34:39
to o. the Nephites and to bring 48: 4
o. and subject their brethren to 49: 7
impossible that he could o. them 52:17
to o. Teancum because of 52:23
that we could o. them; 56:23
should o. the army of Antipus. 56:46
as they were about to o. us. 57:18
the people could not o. them; 3Ne 1:27
thinketh to o. your testimony DC 10:33

OVERPOWERED
down, being o. by the Spirit. Al 19:13
and he was also o. with joy; 19:14
sleep had o. them because 51:33
o. by the persuasions of Helaman 53:14
great fear, lest they should be He 4:20
o. by the vapor of smoke and 3Ne 10:13

OVERPOWERETH
bowels of mercy, which o. justice, Al 34:15

OVERPOWERING
unto the o. of man to read Eth 12:24

OVERRUN
many nations would o. the land, 2Ne 1: 8
and have o. the roots thereof; Jac 5:37
might not o. the land northward. Al 22:33
lest they o. us and destroy us. 26:25

OVERSHADOW
of darkness which did o. them; He 5:34

OVERSHADOWED
who shall be o. and conceive Al 7:10
were o. with a cloud of darkness, He 5:28
of darkness, which had o. them, 5:31
and o. the multitude that 3Ne 18:38
while they were o. he 18:39

OVERSHADOWING
may be removed from o. us? He 5:40
shall be removed from o. you. 5:41
was dispersed from o. them, 5:43

OVERSPREAD
o. all the land of the Nephites, He 6:38

OVERTAKE
servants of Laban did not o. us, 1Ne 3:27
did pursue them, and did o. them, Mos 19:10
not o. them to destroy them. 23: 2
before Lehi should be o. Al 52:28
not desirous to o. them till they 52:30
before Antipus should o. them, 56:37
therefore they did not o. us, 56:38
neither did Antipus o. them; 56:38
the left lest they should o. me, 56:40
fled and we could not o. them, 57:34
exceedingly desirous to o. us 58:19
that no man could o. him. He 1:10
cause that it shall soon o. you. 3Ne 29: 4
of God will o. the wicked; Mrm 4: 5
on the morrow he did o. them; Eth 15:29
lest death shall o. you; DC 45: 2
shall not o. you as a thief. 106: 5

OVERTAKEN
they fled, all that were not o., Mos 9:15
o. by Antipus we knew not, Al 56:43

OVERTAKEN 699 OWN

armies of Antipus had o. them,	Al	56:49
he was o. and slain.	3Ne	4:14
or being o. in a fault,	DC	20:80

OVERTAKETH
and it o. the world as a thief	DC 106: 4

OVERTHREW
God o. Sodom and Gomorrah.	2Ne 23:19

OVERTHROW
to o. the doctrine of Christ.	Jac	1:hd
might o. the doctrine of Christ.		7: 2
and nothing shall o. it, save	Mos	27:13
lead to the o. of their liberty.	Al	50:32
to o. the free government		51: 5
our o. and utter destruction.		58: 9
o. the Lamanites in that city.		62:14
Gadianton did prove the o.,	He	2:13
were about to o. the land,	Mrm	4:23
to your o. and destruction	Eth	8:23
seeketh to o. the freedom of		8:25
did o. the kingdom of Omer.		9: 1
did o. the half of the kingdom;		11:15
that Moron did o. him,		11:16
he did o. Moron and obtain		11:18
and he did o. many cities,		14:17
that he might o. you.	DC	50: 3
will not o. the wicked,		64:21
o. the kingdom of the Jews,		84:28
to o. the money changers		117:16

OVERWHELMED
I lay o. in astonishment at	JS	2:46

OVER-ZEALOUS: see OVER and ZEALOUS.

OWE
not pay that which he did o.,	Al	11: 2
support which we o. to our wives		44: 5
to which we o. all our happiness;		44: 5
whom we o. this great victory;		57:22
imperative duty that we o. to God,	DC	123: 7
an imperative duty that we o.,		123: 9
we o. to all the rising generation,		123:11
to the laws all men o. respect		134: 6

OWED
Now if a man o. another,	Al	11: 2
compelled to pay that which he o.,		11: 2
which they o. their God;		43:46

OWING
O. to the many reports which	JS	2: 1
o. to the distinctness of the		2:50
O. to my continuing to assert		2:58
o. to a spirit of persecution		2:74

OWLS
and o. shall dwell there,	2Ne 23:21

OWN
I make it with mine o. hand;	1Ne	1: 3
to his o. house at Jerusalem;		1: 7
I have made with mine o. hands,		1:17
I make an account of mine o. life.		1:17
sought to take away mine o. life;		4:11
off his head with his o. sword.		4:18
off his head with his o. sword		4:19
and put them upon mine o. body;		4:19
of Nephi, after mine o. name;		9: 2
to the o. due time of the Lord,		10: 3
forth unto them, in mine o. power,		13:34
in the o. due time of the Lord,		14:26
also many of mine o. prophecies		19: 1
For mine o. sake, yea, for		20:11
for mine o. sake will I do this,		20:11
oppress thee with their o. flesh;		21:26
drunken with their o. blood		21:26
shall turn upon their o. heads;		22:13
the sword of their o. hands shall		22:13
shall fall upon their o. heads,		22:13
be drunken with their o. blood.		22:13
and your o. eternal welfare.	2Ne	1:25
over you in his o. kingdom.		2:29
by the finger of mine o. hand;		3:17
oppress thee, with their o. flesh;		6:18
be drunken with their o. blood		6:18
in the fulness of his o. time.		11: 7
the work of their o. hands,		12: 8
which their o. fingers have made.		12: 8
We will eat our o. bread,		14: 1
and wear our o. apparel;		14: 1
Wo unto the wise in their o. eyes		15:21
and prudent in their o. sight!		15:21
the flesh of his o. arm—		19:20
every man turn to his o. people,		23:14
flee every one into his o. land.		23:14
and set them in their o. land;		24: 1
one of them in his o. house.		24:18
I proceed with mine o. prophecy,		25: 7
the words unto mine o. people;		25: 8
unto themselves their o. wisdom		26:20
wisdom and their o. learning,		26:20
that he layeth doen his o. life		26:24
until the o. due time of the Lord,		27:10
I am able to do mine o. work;		27:20
them forth in mine o. due time;		27:21
I am able to do mine o. work.		27:21
I shall see fit in mine o. wisdom		27:22
these things upon your o. heads;		29: 5
according to mine o. pleasure,		29: 9
of the people upon our o. heads	Jac	1:19
shall remember your o. filthiness,		3: 9
the season, unto mine o. self.		5:18
the season, unto mine o. self.		5:19
may preserve it unto mine o. self;		5:20
may preserve it unto mine o. self.		5:23
the season, unto mine o. self.		5:29
fruit thereof unto mine o. self?		5:33
and for mine o. purpose I have		5:36
the season, unto mine o. self.		5:46
thereof for mine o. purpose.		5:53
them also for mine o. purpose,		5:54
the roots also unto mine o. self,		5:54
of my vineyard unto mine o. self		5:76
I will lay up unto mine o. self		5:76
will I cast away into its o. place.		5:77
be cast out into their o. place!		6: 3
and supplication for mine o. soul;	En	1: 4
with sorrow upon their o. heads.		1:10
the Lamanites in his o. due time.		1:16
that he wrote it with his o. hand;	Om	1: 9
and I, with my o. sword, have		1:10
contentions among his o. people.	WM	1:12
with the strength of his o. arm,		1:13
out of mine o. mouth that thou	Mos	1:10
have labored with mine o. hands		2:14
do according to your o. will,		2:21
damnation to his o. soul;		2:33
contrary to his o. knowledge.		2:33
to a lively sense of his o. guilt,		2:38
And lo, he cometh unto his o.,		3: 9
drink damnation to their o. souls		3:18
to an awful view of their o. guilt		3:25
damnation to their o. souls.		3:25
in their o. carnal state,		4: 2
of God, and your o. nothingness,		4:11
their families, to their o. houses.		6: 3
to his o. will and pleasure,		7:33
every one unto his o. house.		8: 4
with mine o. hands, did help to		9:19
depended upon their o. strength.		10:11
we returned again to our o. land,		10:21
after the desires of his o. heart.		11: 2
did boast in their o. strength,		11:19
turned every one to his o. way;		14: 6
persists in his o. carnal nature,		16: 5
their o. carnal wills and desires;		16:12
labor with their o. hands		18:24
of his o. free will and good		18:28
as he was about his o. life;		19: 8
in peace to their o. land.		20:26
it were among their o. brethren.		24: 7
laboring with their o. hands		27: 4
labor with their o. hands		27: 5

OWN

with their o. eyes they had	Mos	27:18
manner of his o. wickedness;		29:23
answered upon their o. heads.		29:30
to answer for his o. sins.		29:38
were not proud in their o. eyes,	Al	1:20
up in the pride of their o. eyes;		1:32
himself his o. condemnation.		3:19
believe according to their o. will		4: 8
according to his o. record,		5: 2
in his o. name he doth call you,		5:38
according to his o. record.		7:hd
by my o. mouth, seeing that it is		7: 1
yea, he returned to his o. house		8: 1
the hands of their o. brethren?		9:10
return to thine o. house, for thou		10: 7
be governed by their o. voices—		10:19
shall be to your o. destruction.		13:20
a consciousness of his o. guilt;		14: 6
and took him to his o. house,		15:18
to possess their o. lands.		16: 8
for them with their o. hands.		17:14
scattered unto their o. land,		18: 7
his tarrying in his o. kingdom,		20:12
do according to his o. desires		20:24
created man after his o. image,		22:12
would give up their o. lives;		24:18
returned again to their o. land;		25:13
I do not boast in my o. strength,		26:11
strength, nor in my o. wisdom;		26:11
even to his o. house.		27:20
of their o. nation and tongue,		29: 8
not joy in my o. success alone,		29:14
according to your o. desires;		30:27
use of that which is their o.		30:28
mine o. hands for my support		30:32
to build with our o. hands;		32: 5
bringeth forth unto its o. likeness.		32:31
that can sacrifice his o. blood		34:11
them according to his o. record.		35:16
not boast in your o. wisdom,		38:11
because of their o. iniquity,		40:13
behold, they are their o. judges,		41: 7
to follow after their o. will.		42: 7
becasue of his o. disobedience;		42:12
mercy claimeth all which is her o.;		42:24
they grew rich in their o. eyes,		45:24
upon us by our o. transgressions.		46:18
was slain by his o. servants;		47:34
wilderness into their o. lands,		50: 7
the lands of their o. possessions,		50: 9
contentions among his o. people,		51:22
again privily to his o. camp,		51:35
was dead in his o. tent;		52: 1
to build with their o. hands.		53: 5
for the support of his o. people;		54: 2
he also desired his o. people		54: 2
your armies into your o. lands,		54: 6
with your armies to your o. lands.		54: 7
you even into your o. land,		54:12
than sufficient for our o. people,		57:15
those lands, which were our o.		58:33
they would stay in their o. land.		61:10
among their o. people,		62:11
he retired to his o. house		62:43
back again to their o. lands,		63:15
boastings in their o. strength,	He	4:13
were left in their o. strength;		4:13
and did turn into their o. ways,		6:31
do according to their o. wills—		7: 5
not lay their o. hands upon him,		8: 4
his way towards his o. house,		10: 2
hast not sought thine o. life,		10: 4
did not go unto his o. house,		10:12
back even into their o. lands.		11:29
mountains unto their o. lands,		11:31
about to return to his o. land.		13: 2
the pride of your o. hearts;		13:27
their o. condemnation.		14:29
yea, even unto his o. country,		16: 7
prophesy among his o. people.		16: 7
depend upon their o. strength		16:15
and upon their o. wisdom,		16:15
cannot witness with our o. eyes		16:20
Behold, I come unto my o.,	3Ne	1:14
sealing it with mine o. hand,		3: 5
destroy them in their o. lands.		3:20
have made with mine o. hands.		5:11
I have seen with mine o. eyes.		5:17
be fulfilled in his o. due time,		5:25
the earth unto their o. lands,		5:26
did all return to their o. lands		6: 1
they did return to their o. lands		6: 2
I came unto my o., and my own		9:16
and my o. received me not.		9:16
the beam that is in thine o. eye?		14: 3
behold, a beam is in thine o. eye?		14: 4
the beam out of thine o. eye;		14: 5
and did return to his o. home.		19: 1
iniquities upon their o. heads,		20:28
together in mine o. due time,		20:29
as a man spareth his o. son that		24:17
show forth his o. words in it.		27:10
their words upon their o. heads.		27:32
could keep that which was his o.,	Mrm	2:10
return to their o. lands again.		3: 7
to boast in their o. strength,		3: 9
they went forth in their o. might,		4: 8
come forth in his o. due time.		5:12
and work out your o. salvation		9:27
are created after mine o. image?	Eth	3:15
beginning after mine o. image.		3:15
I will cause in my o. due time		3:24
show them in mine o. due time		3:27
his throne in his o. kingdom.		7:18
he slew him with his o. sword;		9:27
another in mine o. language,		12:39
cleave unto that which was his o.,		14: 2
of his property and his o. life		14: 2
slay him with his o. sword,		15: 5
for the safety of mine o. life.	Mro	1: 3
prophets, by his o. mouth,		7:23
puffed up, seeketh not her o.,		7:45
every man walketh in his o. way,	DC	1:16
after the image of his o. God,		1:16
have power over his o. dominion.		1:35
whether by mine o. voice or by		1:38
he boasts in his o. strength,		3: 4
after the dictates of his o. will		3: 4
depended upon his o. judgment		3:13
and boasted in his o. wisdom.		3:13
same that came unto mine o.,		6:21
and mine o. received me not.		6:21
themselves in their o. snare.		10:26
I came unto mine o., and		10:57
and mine o. received me not.		10:57
same who came unto mine o.		11:29
and mine o. received me not;		11:29
called him unto mine o. purpose,		18: 8
not covet thine o. property,		19:26
turn to their o. condemnation—		20:15
after his o. image and in his		20:18
and in his o. likeness, created		20:18
as if from mine o. mouth,		21: 5
in mine o. due time.		24:16
will I be ashamed to o. before		29:27
I declared from mine o. mouth		29:29
according to mine o. pleasure,		29:48
world that he gave his o. life,		34: 3
as they are in mine o. bosom,		35:20
the salvation of mine o. elect;		35:20
be saved in mine o. due time;		35:25
of Enoch into mine o. bosom;		38: 4
in mine o. name, by the virtue		38: 4
hearts of men in your o. land.		38:29
meridian of time unto mine o.,		39: 3
and mine o. received me not;		39: 3
a steward over his o. property,		42:32
of the work of thine o. hands;		42:40
unto you in mine o. due time		42:62
of angels, and by mine o. voice,		43:25
in mine o. due time will I come		43:29
I came unto mine o.,		45: 8
and mine o. received me not;		45: 8
hear of wars in your o. lands.		45:63
unto himself for his o. wants,		51:14
labor with their o. hands		52:39

cut off in mine o. due time,	DC	56: 3
seek to counsel in your o. ways.		56:14
not labor with your o. hands!		56:17
to the counsel of his o. will,		58:20
things of their o. free will,		58:27
unto them in their o. land,		58:58
and labor with his o. hands,		58:60
Who buildeth up at his o. will		63: 4
Lord, hold it in mine o. hands;		63:25
things are in his o. hands,		63:44
and I, the Lord, will o. them;		63:63
for this once, for mine o. glory,		64: 3
worthy, in mine o. due time,		67:14
in mine o. due time.		71:10
to provide for his o. family,		75:28
the shedding of his o. blood.		76:69
according to his o. words,		76:111
his own works, his o. dominion,		76:111
the Father hath in his o. hands		78:17
[Kirtland] in mine o. due time		82:13
by mine o. voice out of the		84:42
every man stand in his o. office,		84:109
and labor in his o. calling;		84:109
return again to their o. place,		88:32
mercy and claimeth her o.;		88:40
its course and claimeth its o.;		88:40
he who came unto his o. was		88:48
Every man in his o. order,		88:60
and it shall be in his o. time,		88:68
own time, and in his o. way,		88:68
and according to his o. will.		88:68
sins are upon their o. heads.		88:82
cast away into their o. place,		88:114
of the vine, of your o. make.		89: 6
of the gospel in his o. tongue,		90:11
tongue, and in his o. language,		90:11
rewarded in mine o. due time.		90:29
over Zion in mine o. due time.		90:32
set in order your o. house,		93:43
Yet I will o. them, and they		101: 3
be accountable for his o. sins		101:78
appoint one of their o. number		102:25
measure in mine o. time.		103: 2
even from your o. lands after		103:24
needs be done in mine o. way;		104:16
organized in their o. names,		104:49
names, and in their o. name;		104:49
their business in their o. name,		104:49
name, and in their o. names;		104:49
your business in your o. name,		104:50
name, and in your o. names.		104:50
among you shall call it his o.,		104:62
among you say that it is his o.;		104:70
possession of their o. lands,		105:30
not only in his o. place, but		106: 2
to officiate in their o. standing,		107:10
unto them with mine o. voice,		110: 8
in mine o. due time,		117:16
and by mine o. voice unto them,		120: 1
take them in their o. craftiness;		121:12
not only to our o. wives and		123: 9
by your o. works, bring cursings,		124:48
judgments upon your o. heads,		124:48
by their o. free will and act,		124:69
and labor with his o. hands		124:112
for my o. safety and the safety of		127: 1
over their o. signatures,		128: 4
with his o. statement that he		128: 4
according to their o. words,		128: 8
in their o. *propria persona*,		128: 8
or by the means of their o. agents,		128: 8
as was Aaron, by mine o. voice,		132:59
be turned back into their o. place,		133:24
day when I came unto mine o.,		133:66
as in their o. judgments are best		134: 5
his works with his o. blood;		135: 3
be redeemed in mine o. due time.		136:18
mine o. voice out of the heavens,		136:37
mine o. eyes have beheld God;	Mses	1:11
For mine o. purpose have I		1:31
Also created them for mine o.		1:33
God, created man in mine o. image,		2:27
give unto him mine o. power;	Mses	4: 3
and by his o. voice, and by the		5:58
image of his o. body, male and		6: 9
and begat a son in his o. likeness,		6:10
own likeness, after his o. image,		6:10
hand was against his o. brother,		6:15
which he called after his o. son,		6:17
their o. counsels in the dark;		6:28
in their o. abominations have		6:28
from my o. mouth, from the		6:30
and it is given in our o. language.		6:46
father Adam by his o. voice,		6:51
hast taken Zion to thine o. bosom,		7:31
the workmanship of mine o. hands,		7:32
and they hate their o. blood;		7:33
and held it in his o. hand;		7:43
of myself, but through thine o. grace;		7:59
received it up into his o. bosom;		7:69
ordained Noah after his o. order,		8:19
God preserved in mine o. hands;	Abr	1:31
whose seed in itself yieldeth its o.		4:11
bring forth grass from its o. seed,		4:12
bring forth herb from its o. seed,		4:12
forth the tree from its o. seed,		4:12
to organize man in their o. image,		4:27
the o. due time of the Lord.	Fac	2:12
to establish their o. tenets	JS	2: 9
I refer to his o. account of		2:63
be punished for their o. sins,	AoF	2
the dictates of our o. conscience,		11

OX

both the cow and the o., and the	1Ne	18:25
the lion shall eat straw like the o.	2Ne	21: 7
the lion shall eat straw like the o.		30:13
nor his o., nor his ass, not	Mos	13:24
for man, and corn for the o.,	DC	89:17

OXEN

shall be for the sending forth of o.,	2Ne	17:25
also all manner of cattle, of o.,	Eth	9:18

OZONDAH

the O. [mercantile establishment]	DC	104:39
the O. [mercantile establishment],		104:39
the O. [mercantile establishment]		104:40
O. [mercantile establishment],		104:41

PAANCHI

Pahoran, P., and Pacumeni.	He	1: 3
P., and that part of the people that		1: 7

PACE

and withdrew a p. from them.	Al	44: 1
to withdraw a p. from them,		55:21

PACHUS

stronger than the men of P.,	Al	62: 6
and did meet the men of P.,		62: 7
P. was slain and his men were		62: 8
men of P. received their trial,		62: 9
yea, those men of P. and those		62: 9

PACIFIED

they were p. and did humble	1Ne	15:20
that they may be p. towards us;	Mos	20:19
king was p. towards his people;		20:24
and were p. towards them,		20:26
they were p. towards Aaron	Al	22:25
saw that the people were p.,		22:26

PACIFY

And others will he p., and lull	2Ne	28:21
except the king doth p. them	Mos	20:20
And now let us p. the king,		20:22

PACKARD, Noah

Amasa Lyman and P. for	DC	124:136

PACUMENI

Pahoran, Paanchi, and P.	He	1: 3
P., when he saw that he could not		1: 6

PACUMENI

P. was appointed, according to	He	1:13
P., who was the chief judge, did		1:21
And thus ended the days of P.		1:21

PAGAG

of Jared; and his name was P.	Eth	6:25
they chose all the brothers of P.,		6:26

PAGE, Hiram

thou shalt take thy brother, P.,	DC	28:11

PAGE, John E.

and also my servant P.,	DC	118: 6
William Smith, John Taylor, P.,		124:129

PAGES

hast translated a few more p.	DC	5:30

PAHORAN

Now behold, his name was P.	Al	50:40
P. did fill the seat of his father,		50:40
concerning the chief judge P.;		51: 2
But behold, P. would not alter		51: 3
that P. should be dethroned		51: 5
that P. should remain chief judge		51: 6
P. retained the judgment-seat,		51: 7
among the brethren of P. and		51: 7
concerning the chief judge, P.		51:12
immediately sent an epistle to P.,		59: 3
governor of the land, who was P.,		60: 1
I direct mine epistle to P.,		60: 1
he received an epistle from P.,		61: 1
I, P., who am the chief governor		61: 2
I, P., do not seek for power,		61: 9
because of the faithfulness of P.,		62: 1
driven P. from the judgment-seat,		62: 2
according to the desire of P.,		62: 3
uniting his forces with those of P.		62: 6
Moroni and P. went down with		62: 7
and P. was restored to his		62: 8
and P. having restored peace		62:11
Moroni and P. leaving a large		62:14
P. obtained the possession of		62:26
P. did return to his judgment-seat;		62:44
P. had died, and gone the way of	He	1: 2
brethren, who were the sons of P.		1: 2
P., Paanchi, and Pacumeni.		1: 3
these are not all the sons of P.,		1: 4
P. was appointed by the voice of		1: 5
even to the judgment-seat of P.,		1: 9
murdered P. as he sat upon		1: 9
pursued by the servants of P.;		1:10
that Kishkumen had murdered P.		1:11
at the time that he murdered P.		1:12
in the stead of his brother P.;		1:13
Kishkumen, who had murdered P.,		2: 3

PAID

and therefore he hath p. you.	Mos	2:24
to whom Abraham p. tithes;	Al	13:15
our father Abraham p. tithes of		13:15
hast p. the uttermost senine.	3Ne	12:26
the money which he has p.,	DC	56:10

PAIN

O the p., and the anguish of my	2Ne	26: 7
fill his breast with guilt, and p.,	Mos	2:38
temptations, and p. of body,		3: 7
filled with p. and anguish for		25:11
with great anxiety even unto p.,	Al	13:27
this people doth p. my soul.		31:30
joy as exceeding as was my p.!		36:20
in the most bitter p. and anguish		38: 8
ye shall not have p. while ye	3Ne	28: 9
might not suffer p. nor sorrow		28:38
he suffered the p. of all men,	DC	18:11
to tremble because of p.,		19:18
after their p. shall be sanctified		133:35

PAINED

and my heart is p.;	1Ne	17:47
and my soul is p. no more.	Mos	27:29

702

PARADISE

in the fire, he also was p.;	Al	14:10
to reign, and all eternity is p.,	DC	38:12
I am p., I am weary, because	Mses	7:48
his heart was p. that the Lord		8:25

PAINS

he suffereth the p. of all men,	2Ne	9:21
the p. of every living creature,		9:21
notwithstanding the p. of my soul,		26:10
and the p. of the Jews,		29: 4
yourselves from the p. of hell	Jac	3:11
even the p. of death by fire;	Mos	17:15
I suffer, the p. of death by fire.		17:18
suffering p. and afflictions and	Al	7:11
will take upon him the p. and		7:11
encircled about by the p. of hell.		14: 6
the p. of the women and children		14:10
he loosed from the p. of hell;		26:13
tormented with the p. of hell;		36:13
with the p. of a damned soul.		36:16
could remember my p. no more;		36:19
and so bitter as were my p.		36:21
never endure the p. of death;	3Ne	28: 8

PAINTED

by an armed mob—p. black—	DC	135: 1

PALACE

he also built him a spacious p.,	Mos	11: 9
in unto him into the king's p.,	Al	22: 2
is after the similitude of a p.	DC	124: 2

PALACES

dragons in their pleasant p.;	2Ne	23:22

PALE

neither shall his face now wax p.	2Ne	27:33
he tremble, and shall look p.,	He	9:33
and to stand aghast and p.,	DC	123:10

PALENESS

Because of this fear and this p.	He	9:34

PALESTINA

Rejoice not thou, whole P.,	2Ne	24:29
thou, whole P., art dissolved;		24:31

PALMS

thee upon the p. of my hands;	1Ne	21:16
with p. in our hands,	DC	109:76

PALMYRA

P., Ontario (now Wayne) county,	JS	2: 3
after my father's arrival in P.,		2: 3
was a resident of P. township,		2:61
certifying to the people of P.		2:64

PALSY

the very devil to tremble and p.	DC	123:10

PANGS

p. and sorrows shall take hold	2Ne	23: 8

PARABLE

shall learn the p. of the fig-tree,	DC	35:16
I have given unto you as a p.,		38:27
a p. which I will show you—		45:36
shall the p. be fulfilled which		45:56
the p. of the wheat and of		86: 1
unto this p. I will liken all		88:61
now, I will show unto you a p.,		101:43
to the p. of the wheat and		101:65
unto the p. of the woman		101:81
in the p. which I have given		103:21
And now I show unto you a p.	JS	1:27
Now learn a p. of the fig-tree—		1:38

PARADISIACAL

and receive its p. glory	AoF	10

PARADISE

the p. of God must deliver up	2Ne	9:13

PARADISE

of happiness, which is called p.,	Al	40:12
as well as the righteous in p.,		40:14
had all gone to the p. of God,	4Ne	1:14
soon go to rest in the p. of God,	Mro	10:34
heaven, the p. of God,	DC	77: 2
were then in the p. of God.		77: 5

PARAGRAPH

he read the following p.,	DC	135: 4

PARALLEL

being on a p., the one on the	3Ne	26: 5

PARCHED

the p. ground shall no longer be a	DC	133:29

PARDONED

up unto me, and are not p.,	DC	56:14

PARENT

with all the feeling of a tender p.,	1Ne	8:37
hear the words of a trembling p.,	2Ne	1:14
of the transgression of a p.	Al	30:25

PARENTS

having been born of goodly p.,	1Ne	1: 1
and Eve, who were our first p.;		5:11
my p. being stricken in years,		18:17
after he had created our first p.,	2Ne	2:15
of the transgression of their p.		2:21
upon the heads of your p.		4: 6
being who beguiled our first p.,		9: 9
contempt, concerning their first p.	Jac	4: 3
And his first p. came out from	Om	1:22
that did beguile our first p.,	Mos	16: 3
lest our first p. should enter	Al	12:21
possible that our first p. could		12:26
is not guilty because of its p.		30:25
Lord God sent our first p. forth		42: 2
that our first p. were cut off		42: 7
the names of our first p. who	He	5: 6
entice our first p. to partake		6:26
liar who beguiled our first p.,	Eth	8:25
teach p. that they must repent	Mro	8:10
as p. have children in Zion,	DC	68:25
sin be upon the heads of the p.		68:25
have claim upon their p.		83: 4
if their p. have not wherewith		83: 5
of the p. cannot be answered upon	Mses	6:54

PARLEY: *see also* PRATT. Parley P.

Sidney, and P., and Leman;	DC	49: 1
my servants Sidney and P.,		49: 3

PART

in this p. of my record;	1Ne	6: 1
for the more p. of the ministry;		9: 4
for the more p. of the reign of kings		9: 4
but a small part of the things		14:28
the more p. of all our proceedings		19: 2
the more p. of all the tribes		22: 4
and I have chosen the good p.,	2Ne	2:30
a more history p. are written		4:14
more particular p. of the history		5:33
the more wicked p. of the world;		10: 3
is in the uttermost p. of Egypt,		17:18
a hundredth p. of the proceedings	Jac	3:13
the nethermost p. of my vineyard,		5:13
the nethermost p. of the vineyard,		5:19
and only a p. of the tree hath		5:25
and the other p. of the tree hath		5:25
had overcome that p. of the tree		5:40
a p. thereof brought forth good		5:45
a p. thereof brought forth wild		5:45
more wicked p. of the Nephites	Om	1: 5
I cannot write the hundredth p.	WM	1: 5
possessions of a p. of the land,	Mos	7:21
one fifth p. of all they possessed,		11: 3
a fifth p. of their gold and of		11: 3
and a fifth p. of their ziff, and of		11: 3
and a fifth p. of their fatlings;		11: 3
also a fifth p. of all their grain.		11: 3
the most p. of your lives.		13:11

PART

have p. in the first resurrection:	Mos	15:24
have a p. in the first resurrection,		15:24
no p. in the first resurrection.		15:26
And the lesser p. began to		19: 3
and a p. of them returned to		23:38
as though it would p. asunder.		27:18
draw away a p. of this people		29: 7
for the lesser p. of the people to		29:26
every man might bear his p.		29:34
was that p. of the wilderness	Al	2:37
a part of his words are written in		9:34
one-tenth p. of all he possessed.		13:15
from the inmost p. of my heart,		13:27
But the more p. of them were		14: 2
the more idle p. of the Lamanites		22:28
a p. of which had come from		22:31
should be, in any part of their land.		23: 1
that p. of the land wheresoever		23:14
say the smallest p. which I feel.		26:16
loss on the part of the Nephites.		31: 4
more popular p. of the Zoramites		35: 3
no p. nor portion of the Spirit of		40:13
every p. of the body should be		41: 2
upon the weaker p. of the people.		43:24
leaving a p. of his army in the		43:25
p. of the Lamanites should come		43:25
the remaining p. of his army		43:25
brought a p. over into the valley,		43:31
where a p. of the army of Moroni		43:34
on the p. of the Lamanites,		43:37
they were the greater p. of them		46: 4
the rent p. of his garment		46:19
had written upon the rent p.,		46:19
a p. of the remnant of the coat		46:24
that p. of his seed which shall		46:25
the more p. of them would not,		47: 2
that p. of his army which was		47: 3
that it was in p. rebuilt;		49: 3
been the weakest p. of the land,		49:15
claim a p. of the land of Lehi;		50:26
a p. of the people who desired		51: 2
draw away a p. of their forces		52:13
forces to that p. of the land,		52:13
commanded that a p. of his army		52:24
Mulek with a p. of his army,		52:26
the more p. of all his battles;		53: 2
their cities in that p. of the land.		53: 8
warfare in this p. of the land.		56: 2
people of that p. of the land.		56: 9
neither durst they with a p.,		56:24
forth with a p. of his army,		56:33
a p. of those men who were not		56:57
or with a p. of our strong force,		57: 8
we selected a p. of our men,		57:16
in that p. where he was,		59: 2
maintain that p. of the land		59: 3
Lamanites in this p. of the land.		59: 6
I will leave a p. of my freemen		60:25
to maintain this p. of our land,		60:25
throughout this p. of the land;		61: 6
the war in that p. of the land,		61:15
preserving that p. of the land.		62:12
spy out in what p. of the city		62:20
into the inner p. of the wall.		62:21
down into that p. of the city,		62:22
that p. of the people that were	He	1: 7
no p. of the land was desolate,		3: 6
hundredth p. of the proceedings		3:14
more humble p. of the people		3:34
And the rebellious p. were slain		4: 2
the more p. of the Lamanites		5:50
had become, the more p. of them,		6: 1
whatsoever p. of the land		6: 7
more wicked p. of the Lamanites.		6:18
of the more p. of the Nephites,		6:21
the more p. of them had turned		6:31
a more p. of it had come unto		6:32
the more wicked p. of them,		6:37
the more wicked p. of them,		6:38
the more p. of the righteous		6:38
and the more p. of the people,		11:21
the more p. of this great city,		13:12
more p. of it is one solid mass,		14:21

PART 704 PARTICULAR

more p. of them are in the path of	He	15: 5	partake of the fruit of the tree	Al	5:34
more p. of them are doing this,		15: 6	should enter and p. of the fruit		12:21
more p. of them did not believe		16: 6	consigned to p. of the fruits of		40:26
more p. of the people remaining		16:10	he should not p. of the fruit		42: 3
and the lesser p. walking more		16:10	p. of the waters of life freely;		42:27
the most believing p. of them,		16:15	they would not p. of their wine,		55:31
more p. of the people did believe,	3Ne	1:22	to p. of the forbidden fruit—	He	6:26
contain even a hundredth p. of		5: 8	their works and p. of their spoils,		6:38
more righteous p. of the people		7: 7	to p. of my flesh and blood	3Ne	18:28
more p. of the people had turned		7: 8	p. not of the sacrament of Christ	Mrm	9:29
northernmost p. of the land,		7:12	souls of all those who p. of it;	Mro	4: 3
a p. of them would not suffice,		7:17	oft to p. of bread and wine,		6: 6
the more p. of the year did pass		7:26	p. of the waters of life freely.	DC	10:66
more righteous p. of the people		10:12	often to p. of bread and wine		20:75
no p. of their frame that it did		11: 3	souls of all those who p. of it,		20:77
a hundredth p. of the things		26: 6	when ye p. of the sacrament,		27: 2
the more p. of the things which		26: 7	you shall p. of none except		27: 4
a lesser p. of the things which		26: 8	let him not p. until he makes		46: 4
a small p. of the people who had	4Ne	1:20	p. of the supper of the Lord,		58:11
the more wicked p. of the people		1:40	may p. the fatness thereof.		61:17
the wicked p. of the people		1:42	shall they p. of all this glory.		101:35
on the p. of the Nephites and	Mrm	2: 8	she stay herself and p. not of		132:51
also on the p. of the Lamanites;		2: 8	hand and p. also of the tree of life,	Mses	4:28
that the first p. of theis record,	Eth	1: 3			
a p. of the account I give,		1: 5	PARTAKEN		
a king over that p. of the land.		7:16	after they had p. of the fruit	1Ne	8:25
away the more p. of the people		9:11	had p. of the forbidden fruit	2Ne	2:19
slew a p. of the army of		14: 5	for Adam to have p. of the fruit	Al	12:23
a p. of them fled to the army		14:20	and p. of the tree of life		12:26
a p. of them fled to the army of		14:20	and p. of the tree of life,		42: 5
the hundredth p. I have not		15:33			
in this p. of the land they are	Mro	8:28	PARTAKER		
that p. of the provisions which		9:16	and a p. of the blessings of	DC	96: 7
and this p. of my gospel and	DC	6:29	the loins of Ham, and was a p.	Abr	1:21
Behold, they have only got a p.,		10:44			
this first p. of the engravings		10:45	PARTAKERS		
bring this p. of my gospel to		10:52	p. of the fruit of the tree of life	Al	5:62
that p. which I have commanded		17: 6	and p of the heavenly gift.	4Ne	1: 3
yea, even p. of thy lands,		19:34	be p. of the heavenly gift,	Eth	12: 8
third p. of the hosts of heaven		29:36	have hope, and be p. of the gift,		12: 9
shall have p. in the first		45:54	p. of the fulfilling of the		13:11
to know the truth in p.,		49: 2	all alike and p. of salvation.	Mro	8:17
not suffer that ye should p.		61: 8	be made p. of the glories	DC	66: 2
that ye should p.		61: 9	have been made p. thereof,		76:31
shall have their p. in that lake		63:17	who are made p. thereof.		76:46
shall not have p. in the first		63:18	p. of the glory of the same,		93:22
this p. of the Lord's vineyard.		72: 2	might be made p. of the glories		133:57
in this p. of my vineyard		72: 5	made p. of misery and woe.	Mses	6:48
in this p. of my vineyard.		72: 5			
in this p. of the vineyard,		72: 9	PARTAKING		
in this p. of the vineyard;		72:10	of which I was p. the fruit.	1Ne	8:13
in this p. of the vineyard		72:16	and were p. of the fruit.		8:27
in this p. of the vineyard—		72:16	those that were p. of the fruit		8:33
in this p. of the vineyard,		72:17	his p. of the forbidden fruit;	Mos	3:26
in this p. of the vineyard		72:19	by the p. of the forbidden fruit;	Al	12:22
who shall have p. in the first		76:64	to their p. of the sacrament	DC	20:68
their p. in that prison which		88:99	after p. of bread and wine,		88:141
the lower p. of the inner court		95:16			
the higher p. of the inner court		95:17	PARTED		
call it his own, or any p. of it,		104:62	and they p. hither and thither,	He	8:11
be called his, nor any p. of it.		104:70	from thence it was p., and	Mses	3:10
shall not any p. of it be used,		104:71	p. and became into four heads.	Abr	5:10
He first quoted p. of the third	JS	2:36			
so that the middle p. of it		2:51	PARTIAL		
a thousandth p. of them,		2:61	if not so, God is a p. God,	Mro	8:12
p. of the plates were sealed,		2:65	know that God is not a p. God,		8:18
			Be not p. towards them in love	DC	112:11
PARTAKE			somewhat p. to the Methodist	JS	2: 8
did go forth and p. of the fruit	1Ne	8:11			
my family should p. of it also;		8:12	PARTICLE		
unto me, and p. of the fruit,		8:15	and exercise a p. of faith,	Al	32:27
and p. of the fruit also.		8:16	there was not a p. of it which	Mses	1:27
come and p. of the fruit also;		8:17			
unto me and p. of the fruit.		8:18	PARTICLES		
and p. of the fruit of the tree.		8:24	could number the p. of the earth,	Mses	7:30
P. of the forbidden fruit,	2Ne	2:18			
they shall not p. of his salvation.		26:24	PARTICULAR		
should not p. of his salvation?		26:27	I am p. to give a full account	1Ne	6: 3
should not p. of his goodness?		26:28	the more p. part of the history	2Ne	5:33
unto him and p. of his goodness;		26:33	his word unto them in every p.	Al	25:17
not p. of the goodness of God,		33:14	one in a p. manner which		50:15
and p. of the goodness of God,	Jac	1: 7	that a few p. points of the law		51: 2
and p. of his salvation,	Om	1:26	which are p. and very large,	He	3:13

PARTICULAR   705   PASS

a more p. account was given	DC	10:39	maintaining those p. of the land	Al 58: 3
more p. concerning the things		10:40	in whatsoever p. they should	60: 2
let him be very p. and precise		128: 3	support those p. of our country	60:24
this order of things to be very p.;		128: 5	of our possessions in these p.,	60:24
			fortified those p. of the land	62:42
PARTICULARLY			save it were those p. which had	63:12
more p. made mention upon the	1Ne	19: 2	obtain the north p. of the land.	He 1:23
unto them will I speak p.,	2Ne	25: 8	maintain those p. round about	1:26
have more p. made mention.	Al	13:19	the most capital p. of the land,	1:27
they testified p. concerning us,	3Ne	10:16	forth into all p. of the land,	3: 5
			whatever p. it had not been	3: 5
PARTIES			more settled p. of the land,	3:23
and two p. were Nephites and	Mrm	1: 9	obtaining many p. of the land;	4: 9
to the satisfaction of the p.	DC	102: 2	those p. which he had taken.	4:19
when the p. or either of them		102:24	the more wicked p. of the land.	11: 6
Should the p. or either of them		102:27	did visit many p. of the land,	11:33
all sects, p., and denominations,		123:12	the furthermost p. of the land	3Ne 4:23
p. allege that the marriage		OD	neither in any p. of that land	16: 1
to the different religious p.,	JS	2: 5	deny the more p. of his gospel,	4Ne 1:27
myself aloof from all these p.,		2: 8	those p. of my scriptures which	DC 6:27
Who of all these p. are right;		2:10	those p. of my scripture of	8: 1
of these p. of religionists,		2:11	those p. of my gospel which	10:46
			preached my gospel in those p.,	37: 2
PARTLY			unto the church in these p.	38:34
who is p. a descendant of Jesse	DC	113: 4	uttermost p. of the earth—	58:64
			over the four p. of the earth,	77: 8
PARTNERS			from the four p. of the earth,	110:11
and p. of all our substance.	3Ne	3: 7	shall not discover your secret p.;	111: 4
PARTOOK			**PARTY**	
And as I partook of the fruit	1Ne	8:12	some to one p. and some to	JS 2: 6
p. of the fruit of the tree.		8:30		
Laman and Lemuel p. not		8:35	**PASS**	
I p. and finished my	DC	19:19	For it came to p.	1Ne 1: 4
and he p. of the forbidden fruit		29:40	Wherefore it came to p.	1: 5
			And it came to p.	1: 6
PARTRIDGE, Edward: *see also EDWARD.*			And it came to p. that	1: 7
I have called my servant P.;	DC	41: 9	And it came to p. that	1: 9
my servant P. shall stand		42:10	And it came to p. that	1:12
my servant P. is not justified;		50:39	And it came to p. that	1:14
will speak unto my servant P.,		51: 1	And it came to p. that	1:19
let my servant P., and those		51: 3	For behold, it came to p. that	2: 1
And let my servant P., when		51: 4	And it came to p. that	2: 2
example unto my servant P.,		51:18	And it came to p. that	2: 3
let my servants P. and Martin		52:24	And it came to p. that	2: 4
and Sidney Rigdon and P.		52:41	And it came to p. that	2: 6
Let my servant P. stand in		57: 7	And it came to p. that	2: 7
have selected my servant P.,		58:14	And it came to p. that	2: 8
concerning my servant P.,		58:24	And it came to p. that	2:14
let my servant P. direct the		58:62	And it came to p. that	2:16
And let my servant P. impart		60:10	And it came to p. that	2:17
And also my servant P.,		64:17	And it came to p. that	2:19
servant P., and his counselors;		115: 2	And it came to p. that	3: 1
and also my servant P.,		124:19	And it came to p. that	3: 2
like unto my servant P.,		124:21	And it came to p. that	3: 7
			And it came to p. that	3: 8
PARTS			And it came to p. that	3:10
many p. which are plain	1Ne	13:26	And it came to p. that	3:11
precious p. of the gospel		13:32	And behold, it came to p. that	3:13
precious p. of the gospel		13:34	And it came to p. that	3:21
fertile p. of the wilderness,		16:14	And it came to p. that	3:22
fertile p. of the wilderness.		16:16	And it came to p. that	3:24
plain and precious p. of them,		19: 3	And it came to p. that	3:25
from the four p. of the earth;	2Ne	10: 8	And it came to p. that	3:26
Lord will discover their secret p.		13:17	And it came to p. that	3:27
the nethermost p. of the vineyard,	Jac	5:14	And it came to p. that	3:28
the nethermost p. of the vineyard,		5:38	And it came to p.	3:29
the nethermost p. of the vineyard.		5:39	And it came to p. that	4: 1
above all other p. of the land of		5:43	And it came to p. that	4:10
the nethermost p. of my vineyard,		5:52	And it came to p. that	4:12
established in many p. of the land,	Al	8:11	And it came to p. that	4:28
unto us in all p. of our vineyard.		13:23	And it came to p. that	4:29
of all the northern p. of the land		22:29	And it came to p. that	4:30
the more vital p. of the body,		43:38	And it came to p. that	4:32
the more vital p. of the body		43:38	And it came to p. that	4:35
forth in all the p. of the land		46:28	And it came to p. that	4:37
of those p. of the Lamanites		47: 5	And it came to p. that	4:38
the weakest p. of their cities;		48: 5	And it came to p. that	5: 1
of those p. of the land,		50:32	And it had come to p. that	5: 4
soldiers from all p. of his land,		51: 9	And it came to p. that	5: 9
those p. of the land which they		52: 5	And it came to p. that	5:14
of those p. which were within		55:20	And it came to p. that	5:20

PASS

it came to p. that	1 Ne	7: 1	must unavoidably come to p.	1 Ne	15: 4
And it came to p. that		7: 2	And it came to p. that		15: 5
And it came to p. that		7: 3	And it came to p. that		15: 6
And it came to p. that		7: 4	will not come to p. until		15:17
And it came to p. that		7: 5	And it came to p. that		15:19
And it came to p. that		7: 6	And it came to p. that		15:20
And it came to p. in		7: 7	And it came to p. that		15:21
And it came to p. that		7:16	And it came to p. that		15:32
And it came to p. that		7:16	And now it came to p. that		16: 1
But it came to p. that		7:17	And it came to p. that		16: 2
And it came to p. that		7:18	And it came to p. that		16: 4
And it came to p. that		7:19	And it came to p. that		16: 5
And it came to p. that		7:20	And it came to p. that		16: 7
And it came to p. that		7:21	And it came to p. that		16: 9
And it came to p. that		7:21	And it came to p. that		16:10
And it came to p. that		7:22	And it came to p. that		16:11
And it came to p. that		8: 1	And it came to p. that		16:12
And it came to p. that		8: 2	And it came to p. that		16:13
And it came to p. that		8: 5	And it came to p. that		16:14
And it came to p. that		8: 6	And it came to p. that		16:15
And it came to p. that		8: 7	And it came to p. that		16:18
And it came to p. after		8: 9	And it came to p. that		16:19
And it came to p. that		8:10	And it came to p. that		16:20
And it came to p. that		8:11	Now it came to p. that		16:21
And it came to p. that		8:15	And it came to p. that		16:22
And it came to p. that		8:16	And it came to p. that		16:23
And it came to p. that		8:17	And it came to p. that		16:24
And it came to p. that		8:18	And it came to p. that		16:25
And it came to p. that		8:22	And it came to p. that		16:26
And it came to p. that		8:23	And it came to p. that		16:27
And it came to p. that		8:24	And it came to p. that		16:28
And it came to p. that		8:32	And it came to p. that		16:30
And it came to p. after		8:36	And it came to p. that		16:31
For behold, it came to p.		10: 2	And it came to p. that		16:32
And it came to p. after		10:11	And it came to p. that		16:32
And it came to p. after		10:17	And it came to p. that		16:33
For it came to p. after		11: 1	And it came to p. that		16:34
And it came to p. that		11: 8	And it came to p. that		16:35
And it came to p. after		11: 9	And it came to p. that		16:39
And it came to p. that		11:12	And it came to p. that		17: 1
And it came to p. that		11:13	And it came to p. that		17: 6
And it came to p. that		11:14	And it came to p. that		17: 7
And it came to p. that		11:19	And it came to p. that		17: 7
And it came to p. that		11:25	And it came to p. that		17: 8
And it came to p. that		11:29	And it came to p. that		17:10
And it came to p. that		11:30	And it came to p. that		17:11
And it came to p. that		11:32	And it came to p. that		17:16
And it came to p. that		11:36	And now it came to p.		17:19
And it came to p. that		12: 1	And it came to p. that		17:23
And it came to p. that		12: 2	And it came to p. that		17:31
And it came to p. that		12: 3	the earth that it shall p. away;		17:46
Many generations p. away,		12: 3	And now it came to p. that		17:48
And it came to p. that		12: 4	And it came to p. that		17:49
And it came to p. after		12: 5	And it came to p. that		17:52
three generations p. away		12:11	And it came to p. that		17:53
And it came to p. that		12:13	And it came to p. that		17:54
And it came to p. that		12:15	And it came to p. that		18: 1
And it came to p. that		12:20	And it came to p. that		18: 4
many generations p. away.		12:21	And it came to p. that		18: 5
And it came to p. that		12:23	And it came to p. that		18: 6
And it came to p. that		13: 1	And it came to p. after		18: 8
And it came to p. that		13: 4	And it came to p. that		18:11
And it came to p. that		13: 6	And it came to p. that		18:12
And it came to p. that		13:10	And it came to p. that		18:15
And it came to p. that		13:11	And it came to p. after		18:21
And it came to p. that		13:13	And it came to p. that		18:21
And it came to p. that		13:14	And it came to p. that		18:22
And it came to p. that		13:16	And it came to p. that		18:23
And it came to p. that		13:20	And it came to p. that		18:24
And it came to p. that		13:34	And it came to p. that		18:24
And it came to p. that		13:38	And it came to p. that		18:25
And it shall come to p.,		14: 1	And it came to p. that		19: 1
And it came to p. that		14: 5	Now it came to p. that		19:22
And it came to p. that		14: 8	and it came to p. that		19:22
And it came to p. that		14: 9	before it came to p. I showed		20: 5
And it came to p. that		14:11	And now it came to p. that		22: 1
And it came to p. that		14:12	which shall come to p. according		22: 1
And it came to p. that		14:13	And it shall come to p. that		22:20
And it came to p. that		14:14	And now it came to p. that	2 Ne	1: 1
And it came to p. that		14:15	may bring to p. the resurrection		2: 8
And it came to p. that		14:18	could not be brought to p.,		2:11
And it came to p. that		15: 1	And it shall come to p. that		3:20
And it came to p. that		15: 2	bringing to p. much restoration		3:24

PASS

And it came to p. that	2Ne	4: 8
And it came to p. that		4:10
And it came to p. after		4:12
And it came to p. that		4:12
And it came to p. that		4:13
Behold, it came to p. that		5: 1
And it came to p. that		5: 5
Wherefore, it came to p. that		5: 6
And it came to p. that		5:13
And it came to p. that		5:17
And it came to p. that		5:18
And it came to p. that		5:26
And it came to p. that		5:27
And it came to p. that		5:30
way for the ransomed to p. over?		8:10
And it shall come to p. that		9:15
word, which cannot p. away,		9:16
resurrection might p. upon all men,		9:22
And it shall come to p. that		10: 8
And it shall come to p. in		12: 2
And it shall come to p. that		12:11
And it shall come to p.,		13:24
And it shall come to p.,		14: 3
And it shall come to p. in		17: 1
neither shall it come to p.		17: 7
And it shall come to p. in		17:18
And it shall come to p. in		17:21
And it shall come to p.,		17:22
And it shall come to p. in		17:23
And he shall p. through Judah;		18: 8
And they shall p. through it		18:21
and it shall come to p. that		18:21
Wherefore it shall come to p.		20:12
And it shall come to p. in		20:20
And it shall come to p. in		20:27
And it shall come to p. in		21:11
And it shall come to p. in		24: 3
And it shall come to p. in		24: 4
so shall it come to p.;		24:24
hath come to p. among the Jews,		25: 6
times when they shall come to p.		25: 7
behold it shall come to p. that		25:14
many generations shall p. away,		26: 2
I know that it shall come to p.;		26:10
And it shall come to p.,		26:19
And it shall come to p. that		27: 6
behold, it shall come to p. that		27:15
Wherefore it shall come to p.,		27:19
And again it shall come to p. that		27:24
that they must surely come to p.		28: 1
For it shall come to p. in		28: 3
And it shall come to p. that		29:13
And it shall come to p. that		29:14
generations shall not p. away		30: 6
And it shall come to p. that		30: 7
And it shall come to p. that		30: 8
I know must surely come to p.;		31: 1
For behold, it came to p. that	Jac	1: 1
And it came to p. that		1:12
And now it came to p. that		1:15
Now behold, it came to p. that		4: 1
And it came to p. that		5: 4
And it came to p. that		5: 5
And it came to p. that		5: 6
And it came to p. that		5: 7
And it came to p. that		5:10
And it came to p. that		5:14
And it came to p. that		5:15
And it came to p. that		5:16
And it came to p. that		5:16
And it came to p. that		5:17
And it came to p. that		5:19
And it came to p. that		5:20
And it came to p. that		5:21
And it came to p. that		5:23
And it came to p. that		5:24
And it came to p. that		5:26
And it came to p. that		5:28
And it came to p. that		5:29
And it came to p. that		5:30
And it came to p. that		5:31
And it came to p. that		5:35

And it came to p. that	Jac	5:38
And it came to p. that		5:39
And it came to p. that		5:39
And it came to p. that		5:41
And it came to p. that		5:48
And it came to p. that		5:49
And it came to p. that		5:55
And it came to p. that		5:70
And it came to p. that		5:72
And it came to p. that		5:75
must surely come to p.		6: 1
And now it came to p. after		7: 1
And it came to p. that		7: 2
And it came to p. that		7: 6
And it came to p. that		7:13
And it came to p. that		7:15
And it came to p. that		7:15
And it came to p. that		7:16
And it came to p. that		7:17
And it came to p. that		7:20
And it came to p. that		7:23
And it came to p. that		7:24
And it came to p. that		7:26
Behold, it came to p. that	En	1: 1
And many years p. away		1: 8
Now, it came to p. that		1: 9
And it came to p. that		1:12
And now it came to p. that		1:19
And it came to p. that		1:21
And it came to p. that		1:25
And it came to p. that	Jar	1: 7
And it came to p. that		1:10
And it came to p. that		1:12
And it came to p. that		1:13
Behold, it came to p. that	Om	1: 1
And it came to p. that		1: 3
Behold, it came to p. that		1: 5
And it came to p. that		1: 8
Behold, it came to p. that		1:10
And it came to p. that		1:13
Behold, it came to p. that		1:15
But it came to p. that		1:18
And it came to p. that		1:18
And it came to p. that		1:19
And it came to p. in the days		1:20
And it came to p. that		1:25
And it came to p. that		1:29
must surely come to p.—	WM	1: 4
Wherefore, it came to p. that		1:10
And it came to p. also that		1:13
And it came to p. that		1:14
And it came to p. that		1:15
behold, it came to p. that		1:16
And it came to p. that	Mos	1: 2
And it came to p. that		1: 9
And it came to p. that		1:15
And now, it came to p. that		1:18
And it came to p. that		2: 1
And it came to p. that		2: 5
And it came to p. that		2: 8
And now, it came to p. that		4: 1
And it came to p. that		4: 3
And now, it came to p. that		5: 1
And it shall come to p. that		5: 9
And now it shall come to p.,		5:10
And it came to p. that		6: 2
And again, it came to p. that		6: 3
And it came to p. that		6: 6
And now, it came to p. that		7: 1
And it came to p. that		7: 2
And it came to p. that		7: 3
And it came to p. when		7: 8
And now, it came to p. that		7:14
And now, it came to p.		7:17
And it came to p. that		7:18
And it came to p. that		8: 1
And it came to p. that		8: 4
And it came to p. that		8: 5
And it came to p. that		9: 5
Therefore it came to p.,		9:11
Therefore it came to p. that		9:13
Yea, and it came to p. that		9:15
And it came to p. that		9:16

PASS

And it came to p. that	Mos 10: 1	And it came to p. that	Mos 21:33
And it came to p. that	10: 3	And now it came to p. that	22: 1
And it came to p. that	10: 6	And it came to p. that	22: 2
And it came to p. that	10: 8	Now it came to p. that	22: 3
And it came to p. that	10: 9	Behold the back p., through	22: 6
And it came to p. that	10:10	will p. through the secret pass	22: 7
And it came to p. that	10:10	secret p. on the left of the camp	22: 7
And it came to p. that	10:20	And it came to p. that	22: 9
And it came to p. that	10:21	And it came to p. that	22:11
And now it came to p. that	11: 1	And it came to p. that	22:14
And it came to p. that	11: 8	And now it came to p. when	22:15
And it came to p. that	11:12	And it came to p. that	23:17
And it came to p. that	11:13	And it came to p. that	23:19
And it came to p. that	11:14	And it came to p. that	23:20
And it came to p. that	11:15	And it came to p. that	23:24
And it came to p. that	11:16	For behold, it came to p. that	23:25
And it came to p. that	11:18	Now it came to p. that	23:26
And it came to p. that	11:20	And it came to p. that	23:29
And it shall come to p. that	11:22	And it came to p. that	23:33
And it shall come to p. that	11:23	And it came to p. that	23:36
Yea, and it shall come to p. that	11:24	And it came to p. that	24: 1
Now it came to p. that	11:26	And now it came to p. that	24: 8
And it came to p. that	12: 1	And it came to p. that	24:10
it shall come to p. that	12: 2	And it came to p. that	24:13
And it shall come to p. that	12: 3	And now it came to p. that	24:15
And it shall come to p. that	12: 4	And it came to p. that	24:16
And it shall come to p. that	12: 6	Now it came to p. that	24:18
And it shall come to p. that	12: 8	And it came to p. that	24:24
And it came to p. that	12: 9	And it came to p. that	25: 5
And it came to p. that	12:17	And it came to p. that	25:12
And it came to p. that	12:18	And now it came to p. that	25:14
And it came to p. that	12:20	And it came to p. that	25:17
And it shall come to p. that	12:31	And it came to p. that	25:19
Now it came to p. after	13: 5	And it came to p. that	25:23
And it came to p. that	13:25	Now it came to p. that	26: 1
Bring to p. the resurrection of	13:35	For it came to p. that	26: 6
Bringeth to p. the resurrection	15:20	And it came to p. that	26: 7
And now, it came to p. that	16: 1	And it came to p. that	26: 9
And now it came to p. that	17: 1	And it came to p. that	26:14
And it came to p. that	17: 5	And it shall come to p. that	26:25
And it came to p. that	17:13	And it came to p. when	26:33
so shall it come to p. that	17:15	And it came to p. that	26:34
And it will come to p. that	17:16	And it came to p. that	26:37
And now, it came to p. that	18: 1	And now it came to p. that	27: 1
which was to be brought to p.	18: 2	And it came to p. that	27: 2
And it came to p. that	18: 4	And now it came to p. that	27:10
And it came to p. that	18: 6	And now it came to p. that	27:17
And it came to p. after	18: 7	And it came to p. after	27:23
And it came to p. that	18: 8	And now it came to p. that	27:32
And now it came to p. that	18:12	Now it came to p. that	28: 1
And it came to p. that	18:17	And it came to p. that	28: 5
And it came to p. that	18:18	And it came to p. that	28: 8
And now it came to p. that	18:30	And it came to p. that	29: 2
But behold, it came to p. that	18:32	And now it came to p.,	29:37
And it came to p. that	18:34	Therefore, it came to p. that	29:39
And it came to p. that	19: 1	And it came to p. that	29:41
And it came to p. that	19: 5	And it came to p. that	29:42
And it came to p. that	19:10	And now it came to p. that	29:43
Now it came to p. that	19:11	And now it came to p. that	29:45
And it came to p. that	19:13	And it came to p. that	29:46
And it came to p. that	19:14	Now it came to p. that	Al 1: 1
And it came to p. that	19:18	And it came to p. that	1: 2
And it came to p. that	19:18	And it came to p. that	1: 5
And it came to p. that	19:22	And it came to p. as he was	1: 7
And it came to p. that	19:24	And it came to p. that	1:11
And it came to p. that	19:25	And it came to p. that	1:15
And it came to p. that	19:27	But it came to p. that	1:19
And it came to p. that	20: 2	And it came to p. that	1:33
And it came to p. that	20: 6	And it came to p. in the	2: 1
And it came to p. that	20: 9	And it came to p. that	2: 5
And it came to p. that	20:10	And it came to p. that	2: 7
And it came to p. that	20:11	And it came to p. that	2: 9
And it came to p. that	20:12	And it came to p. that	2:14
And it came to p. that	20:24	And it came to p. that	2:15
And it came to p. that	20:25	And it came to p. that	2:19
And it came to p. that	20:25	And it came to p. that	2:20
And it came to p. that	21: 1	And it came to p. that	2:23
And it came to p. that	21: 2	And it came to p. that	2:26
And it came to p. that	21: 6	And it came to p. that	2:29
And it came to p. that	21: 8	And it came to p. that	2:30
And it came to p. that	21:11	And it came to p. that	2:35
And it came to p. that	21:16	And it came to p. that	2:38
And it came to p. that	21:22	And it came to p. that	3: 1

PASS

And it came to p. that	Al 3: 9	And it came to p. that	Al 19:16
And it came to p. that	3:11	And it came to p. that	19:24
Now it came to p. that	3:20	And it came to p. that	19:25
And it came to p. that	3:21	And it came to p. that	19:29
Now it came to p. in the	4: 1	And it came to p. that	19:33
And it came to p. in the	4: 5	And it came to p. that	19:35
And it came to p. in the	4: 6	And it came to p. that	20: 1
And it came to p. in the	4:11	Now it came to p. that	20: 3
And now it came to p. that	4:15	And it came to p. that	20: 8
Now it came to p. that	5: 1	And it came to p. that	20:11
And now it came to p. that	6: 1	And it came to p. that	20:28
And it came to p. that	6: 2	And it came to p. that	21: 4
And it also came to p. that	6: 3	And it came to p. as he	21:10
And now it came to p. that	6: 7	And it came to p. that	21:12
And now it came to p. that	8: 1	And it came to p. that	21:17
And it came to p. in the	8: 3	And it came to p. that	21:18
And it came to p. that	8: 5	and it came to p. that	21:23
And it came to p. that	8: 8	And it came to p. that	22: 2
And it came to p. that	8:14	And it came to p. that	22:12
it came to p. while	8:14	And it came to p. that	22:15
Now it came to p. that	8:18	And it came to p. that	22:17
And it came to p. that	8:21	And it came to p. that	22:19
And it came to p. that	8:22	And it came to p. that	22:26
And it came to p. that	8:28	And it came to p. that	22:27
And it came to p. that	8:32	And it came to p. that	22:33
it came to p. as I began	9: 1	Behold, now it came to p. that	23: 1
that the earth should p. away?	9: 2	And now it came to p. that	23: 4
that the earth should p. away.	9: 3	And now it came to p. that	23:16
Now it came to p. that	9:31	And it came to p. that	23:17
But it came to p. that	9:33	And it came to p. that	24: 1
And it came to p. that	9:34	And now it came to p. that	24:17
And it came to p. that	10: 8	And it came to p. that	24:20
And it came to p. that	10:16	And it came to p. that	24:25
But it came to p. as they	10:17	And it came to p. that	24:26
And now it came to p. that	10:24	And behold, now it came to p.	25: 1
And now it came to p. that	10:28	And it came to p. that	25: 7
And it came to p. that	10:30	of Abinadi were brought to p.,	25: 9
Now it came to p. that	12:19	And it came to p. that	25:13
bring to p. the resurrection of	12:25	And it came to p. that	26:10
And now it came to p. that	13:21	Now it came to p. that	27: 1
And it came to p. after	14: 1	And it came to p. that	27: 2
But it came to p. that	14: 4	And it came to p. that	27:11
And it came to p. that	14: 6	And now it came to p. that	27:13
And it came to p. that	14: 7	And it came to p. that	27:15
And it came to p. that	14: 9	And it came to p. that	27:16
Now it came to p. that	14:14	And now it came to p. that	27:20
And it came to p. that	14:17	And it came to p. that	27:21
And it came to p. that	14:19	And it came to p. that	27:22
And it came to p. that	14:20	Now, it came to p. that	27:25
And it came to p. after	14:23	And it came to p. that	27:26
And it came to p. that	14:25	And now it came to p. that	28: 1
And it came to p. that	14:27	brought to p. the destruction of	28:10
And it came to p. that	15: 1	brought to p. an awful scene of	28:10
And it came to p. that	15: 5	Behold, now it came to p. that	30: 1
And it came to p. that	15: 6	but it came to p. after	30: 2
And it came to p. that	15:14	And it came to p. in	30: 5
And it came to p. that	15:16	But it came to p. in	30: 6
And it came to p. in the	16: 1	And it came to p. that	30:21
And now it came to p.,	16: 3	And it came to p. that	30:22
Now it came to p. that	16: 4	And it came to p. that	30:30
And it came to p. that	16: 6	And now it came to p. that	30:46
And it came to p. that	16: 7	And it came to p. that	30:56
And now it came to p. that	17: 1	And it came to p. that	30:58
And it came to p. that	17: 9	And it came to p. that	30:59
And it came to p. that	17:10	Now it came to p. that	31: 1
And it came to p. that	17:12	Now it came to p. that	31:19
And it came to p. when	17:13	Now it came to p. that	31:36
And it came to p. that	17:24	And it came to p. that	32: 1
And it came to p. that	17:25	And it came to p. that	32: 2
And it came to p. that	17:31	bring to p. the resurrection,	33:22
And it came to p. that	17:32	And now it came to p. that	34: 1
And it came to p. that	18: 1	Now it came to p. that	35: 1
And it came to p. that	18: 8	And it came to p. that	35: 3
And it came to p. that	18:12	And it came to p. that	35: 6
And it came to p. that	18:15	And it came to p. that	35: 7
And it came to p. that	18:16	And it came to p. that	36:10
And it came to p. that	18:40	And it came to p. that	36:17
And it came to p. that	18:43	are great things brought to p.;	37: 6
And it came to p. that	19: 1	And it came to p. that	38: 8
And it came to p. that	19: 3	Behold, he bringeth to p. the	40: 3
And it came to p. that	19:11	And then shall it come to p.,	40:12
And it came to p. that	19:12	And then shall it come to p.,	40:13

their resurrection cometh to p.	Al 40:19
bringeth to p. the resurrection	42:23
And now it came to p. that	43: 1
For behold, it came to p. that	43: 4
And it came to p. that	43: 5
And it came to p. as	43:15
And it came to p. that	43:18
Behold, now it came to p. that	43:22
But it came to p., as	43:23
And it came to p. that	43:24
And it came to p. that	43:27
And it came to p. that	43:34
And it came to p. that	43:36
And it came to p. that	43:39
And it came to p. that	43:41
And it came to p. that	43:48
And it came to p. that	43:49
And now it came to p. that	44: 1
And it came to p. that	44: 8
Now it came to p. that	44:13
And it came to p. that	44:16
And it came to p. that	44:17
And it came to p. that	44:20
Behold, now it came to p. that	44:22
And it came to p. in the	45: 1
shall not all p. away before	45: 2
And now it came to p. that	45:12
And it came to p. that	45:15
And now it came to p. in	45:18
And it came to p. that	45:20
And now it came to p. that	45:22
And it came to p. that	45:23
And now it came to p. that	46: 1
And it came to p. that	46:11
And it came to p. that	46:12
And it came to p. that	46:17
And now it came to p. that	46:21
And it came to p. that	46:28
and it came to p. that	46:29
And it came to p. that	46:31
And it came to p. that	46:32
And it came to p. that	46:33
And it came to p. also,	46:35
And it came to p. that	46:36
And it came to p. that	46:39
And now it came to p. that	47: 2
And it came to p. that	47: 2
And behold, it came to p. that	47: 3
And it came to p. that	47: 7
And it came to p. that	47: 9
And it came to p. that	47:10
And it came to p. that	47:11
And it came to p. that	47:11
And it came to p. that	47:11
And it came to p. that	47:12
And it came to p. that	47:13
And it came to p. that	47:14
And it came to p. that	47:15
And it came to p. that	47:16
And it came to p. that	47:18
And it came to p. that	47:20
And it came to p. that	47:23
And it came to p. that	47:24
And it came to p. that	47:27
And it came to p. that	47:28
And it came to p. on the	47:31
And now it came to p. that	47:32
And it came to p. that	47:34
And it came to p. that	47:35
And now it came to p. that,	48: 1
And it came to p. that	48: 6
Now it came to p. that	48: 7
And now it came to p. in the	49: 1
And it came to p. that	49: 9
And now behold it came to p.,	49:17
And it came to p. that	49:21
over the Nephites by the p.,	49:22
obtain a p. to their armies,	49:22
the Lamanites through the p.,	49:24
And it came to p.,	49:25
And it came to p. that	49:25
And it came to p. that	49:26
And it came to p.,	49:28
And now it came to p. that	Al 50: 1
And it came to p. that	50: 7
And it came to p. that	50: 9
And it came to p. that	50:13
And it came to p. that	50:24
And it came to p. that	50:25
And it came to p. that	50:28
And it came to p. that	50:31
And it came to p. that	50:34
by the narrow p. which led by	50:34
And it came to p. that	50:35
And it came to p. that	50:37
Behold, it came to p. that	50:39
And now it came to p. in the	51: 1
And it came to p. that	51: 5
And it came to p. that	51: 7
And it came to p. that	51: 7
And it came to p. that	51:13
And it came to p. that	51:14
And it came to p. that	51:15
And it came to p. that	51:16
And it came to p. that	51:17
And it came to p. that	51:18
And it came to p. that	51:19
Behold, it came to p. that	51:22
And it came to p. that	51:23
And it came to p. that	51:23
But it came to p. that	51:25
And it came to p. that	51:28
But it came to p. that	51:29
And it came to p. that	51:30
And it came to p. that	51:32
And it came to p. that	51:32
And it came to p. that	51:33
And it came to p. that	51:34
And now, it came to p. in the	52: 1
And it came to p. that	52: 3
And it came to p. that	52: 4
And it came to p. that	52: 7
secure the narrow p. which led	52: 9
But behold, it came to p. in the	52:15
And it came to p. that	52:16
And it came to p. that	52:17
And it came to p. that	52:18
And it came to p. they sent	52:20
And it came to p. that	52:21
And it came to p. that	52:23
And it came to p. that	52:24
And it came to p. that	52:27
And it came to p. that	52:31
And it came to p. that	52:33
And it came to p. that	52:35
And it came to p. that	52:38
And it came to p. that	53: 1
And it came to p. that	53: 3
And it came to p. that	53: 6
And it came to p. that	53: 7
And now it came to p. that	53: 8
But it came to p. that	53:13
But behold, it came to p.	53:16
And now it came to p. that	53:22
And now it came to p. in the	54: 1
And it came to p. that	54: 2
Now it came to p. that	54:15
Now it came to p. that	55: 1
And now it came to p. that	55: 4
And it came to p. that	55: 5
And it came to p. that	55:13
And it came to p. they did	55:14
And it came to p. that	55:25
And it came to p. that	55:26
And it came to p. that	55:27
And it came to p. that	55:28
And now it came to p. that	55:33
And now it came to p. in the	56: 1
And now it came to p. that	56:18
they might not p. us by night	56:22
if they should p. by us,	56:23
They durst not p. by us with	56:24
And now it came to p. in the	56:27
And it came to p. that	56:32
And it came to p. that	56:33

And it came to p. that	Al	56:35	And it came to p. that	Al	63: 8
And it came to p. that		56:36	And it came to p. that		63: 9
And it came to p. that		56:39	And it came to p. in the		63:10
And it came to p. that		56:41	And it came to p. also in		63:14
But it came to p. that		56:42	And now behold, it came to p.	He	1: 1
And it came to p. that		56:49	Nevertheless, it came to p. that		1: 5
And it came to p. that		56:52	And it came to p. that		1: 6
And now it came to p. that		56:54	And it came to p. as he		1: 8
And now it came to p. that		56:55	And it came to p. in the		1:14
And now it came to p. that		57: 1	And it came to p. that		1:18
And it came to p. that		57: 6	But it came to p. that		1:19
And it came to p. that		57: 7	And it came to p. that		1:21
And it came to p. that		57: 9	And it came to p. that		1:21
And it came to p. that		57:12	And it came to p. that		1:30
But it came to p. that		57:13	And it came to p. that		1:33
But it came to p. that		57:17	And it came to p. in the		2: 1
And it came to p. that		57:18	And it came to p. that		2: 2
And it came to p. that		57:24	And it came to p. as he		2: 6
And it came to p. that		57:25	And it came to p. that		2: 7
And now it came to p. that		57:28	And it came to p. that		2:10
And it came to p. that		57:30	And now it came to p. in		3: 1
And it came to p. that		57:32	And it came to p. in the		3: 3
And it came to p. because		57:33	And it came to p. that		3: 8
And it came to p. that		57:33	And it came to p. as		3:10
Now it came to p. that		57:36	And it came to p. that		3:12
And behold, now it came to p.		58: 1	And it came to p. that		3:19
And it came to p. that		58: 4	And it came to p. that		3:21
And it came to p. that		58: 4	And it came to p. that		3:22
And it came to p. that		58: 7	And it came to p. in the		3:23
But it came to p. that		58: 8	And it came to p. that		3:24
Yea, and it came to p. that		58:11	And it came to p. that		3:26
And it came to p. that		58:14	And it came to p. that		3:32
And it came to p. that		58:15	And it came to p. that		3:36
And it came to p. that		58:18	And it came to p. in the		3:37
And it came to p. that		58:19	And it came to p. that		3:37
p. by in the midst of Gid and		58:19	And it came to p. in the		4: 1
And it came to p. that		58:20	And it came to p. that		4: 3
And it came to p. that		58:21	But it came to p. in the		4: 4
And it came to p. that		58:23	And it came to p. in the		4: 9
And it came to p. that		58:23	And it came to p. in the		4:10
Now it came to p. that		58:26	And it came to p. that		4:15
And thus it came to p.,		58:28	And it came to p. in the		4:18
And it came to p. that		58:29	And it came to p.,		4:20
Yea, and it came to p. that		58:30	And it came to p. that		5: 1
Now it came to p. in the		59: 1	And it came to p. that		5: 4
And it came to p. that		59: 3	And it came to p. that		5:13
And it came to p. when		59: 4	And it came to p. that		5:17
And it came to p. that		59: 5	And it came to p. that		5:18
And it came to p. that		59:13	And it came to p. that		5:20
And it came to p. that		60: 1	And it came to p. that		5:21
Behold, now it came to p. that		61: 1	And it came to p. that		5:23
And now it came to p. that		62: 1	And it came to p. that		5:26
And it came to p. that		62: 3	And it came to p. that		5:28
And it came to p. that		62: 5	And it came to p. that		5:29
And it came to p. that		62: 7	And it came to p. when		5:30
And it came to p. in the		62:12	And it came to p. that		5:32
And it came to p. that		62:13	And it came to p. that		5:34
And it came to p. that		62:14	And it came to p. that		5:36
And it came to p. that		62:15	And it came to p. that		5:37
And it came to p. after		62:16	And it came to p. that		5:40
And it came to p. that		62:18	And it came to p. that		5:42
And it came to p. that		62:18	And it came to p. that		5:43
And it came to p. that		62:21	And it came to p. that		5:46
And it came to p. that		62:22	And it came to p. that		5:50
And it came to p. that		62:23	And it came to p. that		5:52
that they did flee out by the p.		62:24	And it came to p. that		6: 1
Now it came to p. that		62:27	And it came to p. that		6: 4
And it came to p. that		62:28	And it came to p. that		6: 6
Now it came to p. that		62:30	And it came to p. that		6: 8
And it came to p. that		62:31	And it came to p. that		6: 9
And it came to p. that		62:32	and fourth year did p. away		6:13
And it came to p. that		62:34	And it came to p. that		6:15
And it came to p. that		62:36	And it came to p. that		6:15
Now it came to p. that		62:37	And now it had come to p.		6:18
Now it came to p. that		62:38	And now it came to p. that		6:20
And it came to p. that		62:42	And it came to p. that		6:22
And it came to p. that		62:46	And it came to p. that		6:32
And it came to p. that		62:52	And it came to p. that		6:37
And it came to p. in the		63: 1	And it came to p. on		6:38
And it came to p. that		63: 3	And it came to p. that		6:41
And it came to p. that		63: 4	Behold, now it came to p. in		7: 1
And it came to p. that		63: 5	And behold, now it came to p.		7:10
And it came to p. that		63: 8	And it came to p. that		7:11

PASS

And it came to p. that	He 7:13	
And now it came to p. that	8: 1	
And it came to p. that	8: 7	
will surely come to p. except	8: 7	
And it came to p. that	8:10	
Behold, now it came to p. that	9: 1	
And it came to p. that	9: 3	
And it came to p. that	9: 9	
And it came to p. that	9:10	
And it came to p. that	9:12	
And it came to p. that	9:13	
And now it came to p. that	9:16	
And it came to p. that	9:18	
And it came to p. that	9:37	
And it came to p. that	10: 1	
And it came to p. that	10: 2	
And it came to p. as he	10: 3	
and it came to p. as he	10: 3	
this people, it shall come to p.	10:10	
And behold, now it came to p.	10:12	
And it came to p. that	10:15	
And it came to p. that	10:17	
And it came to p. that	10:18	
And now it came to p. in	11: 1	
And it came to p. that	11: 3	
And it came to p. that	11: 7	
And it came to p. that	11: 9	
And it came to p. that	11: 9	
And it came to p. that	11:17	
And it came to p. that	11:17	
And thus it did come to p.	11:20	
And it came to p. that	11:21	
But it came to p. that	11:23	
And it came to p. that	11:24	
And it came to p. that	11:28	
But behold, it came to p. that	11:29	
And it came to p. in the	11:30	
And it came to p. that	11:32	
And it came to p. in the	11:37	
And now it came to p. in the	13: 1	
And it came to p. that	13: 2	
And it came to p. that	13: 2	
And it came to p. that	13: 4	
hundred years p. not away	13: 5	
four hundred years shall not p.	13: 9	
And it shall come to p.,	13:18	
And now it came to p. that	14: 1	
And it shall come to p. that	14: 7	
And it shall come to p. that	14: 8	
to bring to p. the resurrection	14:15	
bringeth to p. the resurrection,	14:16	
bringeth to p. the condition of	14:18	
these wonders should come to p.	14:28	
And now, it came to p. that	16: 1	
But it came to p. in the	16:13	
works cannot come to p.,	16:16	
thing which should come to p.,	16:20	
Now it came to p. that	3Ne 1: 1	
And it came to p. that	1: 4	
And it came to p. that	1: 7	
spoken might not come to p.	1: 7	
Now it came to p. that	1: 9	
the sign should come to p.	1: 9	
Now it came to p. that	1:10	
And it came to p. that	1:11	
And it came to p. that	1:12	
And it came to p. that	1:15	
And it came to p. that	1:19	
And it came to p. that	1:19	
And it had come to p.,	1:20	
And it came to p. also that	1:21	
And it came to p. that	1:22	
And it came to p. that	1:23	
But it came to p. that	1:25	
jot or tittle should not p. away	1:25	
and second year did p. away,	1:26	
the signs which did come to p.,	1:26	
And it came to p. that	1:27	
year did also p. away in peace,	1:27	
And it came to p. that	1:28	
And it came to p. that	2: 1	
And it came to p. that	2: 3	
And thus did p. away the	2: 4	

And it came to p. that	3Ne 2:10	
And it came to p. in the	2:11	
And it came to p. that	2:13	
And it came to p. in the	2:14	
And now it came to p. that	2:17	
And now it came to p. when	3: 1	
And it came to p. that	3:11	
And it came to p. in the	3:17	
And it came to p. that	3:22	
eighteenth year did p. away.	4: 1	
And it came to p. that	4: 4	
And it came to p. that	4: 5	
And it came to p. that	4: 7	
And it came to p. that	4: 8	
And it came to p. that	4: 9	
And it came to p. that	4:13	
And it came to p. that	4:14	
And it came to p. that	4:15	
nineteenth year did p. away,	4:15	
And it came to p. that	4:20	
And it came to p. that	4:23	
And it came to p. that	4:31	
which had come to p. already	5: 2	
all things should come to p.	5: 2	
And now it came to p. that	5: 4	
And now it came to p. that	6: 1	
And it came to p. that	6: 2	
And it came to p. that	6: 7	
But it came to p. in the	6:10	
Now it came to p. that	6:26	
Now it came to p. that	6:27	
And it came to p. that	7:11	
And it came to p. in the	7:14	
And it came to p. that	7:15	
And it came to p. that	7:18	
And it came to p. that	7:21	
and first year did p. away,	7:21	
part of the year did p. away.	7:26	
And now it came to p. that	8: 1	
And now it came to p.,	8: 2	
And it came to p. in the	8: 5	
And it came to p. that	8:19	
And it came to p. that	8:20	
And it came to p. that	8:23	
And it came to p. that	9: 1	
And now behold, it came to p.	10: 1	
And it came to p. that	10: 3	
And now it came to p. that	10: 8	
And it came to p. that	10: 9	
did the three days p. away.	10: 9	
tumultuous noises did p. away.	10: 9	
And it came to p. that	10:18	
And now it came to p. that	11: 1	
And it came to p. that	11: 3	
And it came to p., as they	11: 4	
And it came to p. that	11: 8	
And it came to p. that	11: 9	
And it came to p. that	11:12	
And it came to p. that	11:13	
And it came to p. that	11:15	
And it came to p. that	11:18	
And now it came to p. that	12: 1	
And now it came to p. that	13:25	
And now it came to p. that	14: 1	
And it came to p. that	15: 1	
And it came to p. that	15: 2	
And now it came to p. that	15:11	
Behold, now it came to p. that	17: 1	
And it came to p. that	17: 5	
And it came to p. that	17: 9	
And it came to p. that	17:11	
And it came to p. that	17:13	
And it came to p. that	17:14	
And it came to p. that	17:18	
And it came to p. that	17:19	
And it came to p. that	18: 1	
And it came to p. that	18: 8	
And it came to p. that	18: 9	
And it came to p. that	18:17	
And now it came to p. that	18:26	
And it came to p. that	18:36	
And it came to p. that	18:38	

PASS 713 PASS

And now it came to p. that	3Ne 19: 1	And it came to p. that	Mrm 2: 3
And it came to p. that	19: 4	And it came to p. that	2: 4
and it came to p. that	19: 4	And it came to p. that	2: 4
And it came to p. that	19: 7	And it came to p. that	2: 7
And it came to p. that	19:11	And it came to p. that	2: 9
And it came to p. when they	19:13	And it came to p. that	2:10
And it came to p. that	19:15	And it came to p. that	2:12
And it came to p. that	19:16	And it came to p. that	2:15
And it came to p. that	19:17	And it came to p. that	2:16
And it came to p. that	19:19	And it came to p. that	2:20
And it came to p. that	19:24	And it came to p. that	2:20
And it came to p. that	19:25	And it came to p. that	2:21
And it came to p. that	19:31	And it came to p. in the	2:22
And it came to p. that	19:35	And it came to p. that	2:23
And it came to p. that	20: 1	And it came to p. that	2:25
And it came to p. that	20: 3	And it came to p. that	2:25
And it came to p. that	20:10	And it came to p. that	2:26
And it shall come to p.,	20:20	And it came to p. that	3: 1
And it shall come to p. that	20:21	And it came to p. that	3: 2
And it shall come to p. that	20:23	And it came to p. that	3: 4
And it shall come to p. that	20:30	And it came to p. that	3: 5
then shall be brought to p.	20:36	by the narrow p. which led into	3: 5
And when these things come to p.	21: 7	And it came to p. that	3: 7
it shall come to p. that kings	21: 8	and it came to p. that	3: 7
Therefore it shall come to p.	21:11	And it came to p. that	3:11
it shall come to p. in that day,	21:14	And it came to p. that	3:16
it shall come to p. that all	21:19	And now it came to p. that	4: 1
For it shall come to p.,	21:20	And it came to p. that	4: 2
that which is written come to p.:	22: 1	And it came to p. that	4: 6
And now it came to p. that	23: 6	And it came to p. in the	4: 7
And it came to p. that	23: 7	And it came to p. that	4: 8
And it came to p. that	23:12	And it came to p. that	4:10
And it came to p. that	23:13	And it came to p. that	4:13
And now it came to p. that	23:14	And it came to p. that	4:15
And it came to p. that	24: 1	And it came to p. that	4:19
And it came to p. that	24: 1	And it came to p. that	4:22
And now it came to p. that	26: 1	And it came to p. that	5: 1
and the earth should p. away;	26: 3	And it came to p. that	5: 3
And it came to p. that	26:14	And it came to p. that	5: 4
And it came to p. that	26:15	And it came to p. that	5: 5
Behold, it came to p. on	26:16	And it came to p. that	5: 6
And it came to p. that	26:17	And it came to p. that	5: 7
And it came to p. that	26:20	But behold, it shall come to p.	5:20
And it came to p. that	27: 1	And it came to p. that	6: 1
it came to p. that the disciples	27: 1	And it came to p. that	6: 3
And it shall come to p.,	27:16	And it came to p. that	6: 4
And it came to p. that	27:33	And it came to p. that	6: 6
And it came to p. when	28: 1	And it came to p. that	6: 7
And it came to p. that	28:12	And it came to p. that	6: 8
But it came to p. that	28:16	And it came to p. that	6: 9
And it came to p. that	28:23	And it came to p. that	6:10
And it shall come to p.,	28:29	And it came to p. that	6:15
And it came to p. that	4Ne 1: 1	bringeth to p. the resurrection	7: 6
And it came to p. in the	1: 2	brought to p. the redemption	7: 7
And it came to p. that	1: 4	And now it came to p. that	8: 2
thirty and eighth year p. away,	1: 6	and the afflicted to p. by you,	8:39
And now, behold, it came to p.	1:10	bringeth to p. the resurrection,	9:13
And it came to p. that	1:13	bringeth to p. a redemption	9:13
And it came to p. that	1:14	And it came to p. that	Eth 1:35
And it came to p. that	1:15	And it came to p. that	1:37
And it came to p. that	1:19	And it came to p. that	1:38
And it came to p. that	1:21	And it came to p. that	1:39
And it came to p. that	1:22	And it came to p. that	1:40
And it came to p. that	1:27	And it came to p. that	2: 1
And now it came to p. in this	1:35	And it came to p. that	2: 4
And it came to p. that	1:36	And it came to p. that	2: 5
And it came to p. that	1:38	And it came to p. that	2: 5
And it came to p. that	1:40	And it came to p. that	2: 6
and fifty years p. away,	1:41	it came to p. that the Lord	2:13
And it came to p. that	1:42	And it came to p. at the	2:14
And it came to p. that	1:45	And it came to p. that	2:16
And it came to p. that	1:46	And it came to p. that	2:18
And it came to p. that	1:47	And it came to p. that	2:21
And it came to p. that	1:48	And it came to p. that	3: 1
And it came to p. that	Mrm 1: 6	And it came to p. that	3: 6
And it came to p. in this	1: 8	And it came to p. that	3:21
And it came to p. that	1:10	And it came to p. that	3:28
And it came to p. that	1:11	thereof shall p. away,	4: 9
And it came to p. that	1:11	For it came to p. after the	6: 2
And it came to p. that	1:12	And it came to p. that	6: 4
And it came to p. in that	1:19	and it came to p. that	6: 4
And it came to p. that	2: 1	And it came to p. that	6: 5
Therefore it came to p. that	2: 2	And it came to p. that	6: 6

PASS

And it came to p. that	Eth	6: 7	all this came to p. in the days	Eth	11: 7
And it came to p. that		6: 8	And it came to p. that		11: 9
And it came to p. that		6:13	And it came to p. that		11:10
And it came to p. that		6:18	And it came to p. that		11:12
And it came to p. that		6:21	And it came to p. that		11:13
And it came to p. that		6:22	And it came to p. that		11:14
And it came to p. that		6:25	And it came to p. that		11:14
And it came to p. that		6:25	And it came to p. that		11:15
And it came to p. that		6:26	And it came to p. that		11:16
And it came to p. that		6:27	And it came to p. that		11:17
And it came to p. that		6:29	And it came to p. that		11:18
And it came to p. that		6:30	And it came to p. that		11:19
And it came to p. that		7: 1	And it came to p. that		11:23
And it came to p. that		7: 3	And it came to p. that		12: 1
brought to p. the saying of		7: 3	And it came to p. that		12: 5
And it came to p. that		7: 5	And it came to p. that		12:36
And it came to p. that		7: 7	And it came to p. that		12:37
And it came to p. that		7: 8	when the earth shall p. away.		13: 8
And it came to p. that		7:11	bringeth to p. the scripture		13:12
And it came to p. that		7:12	And it came to p. that		13:15
And it came to p. that		7:14	Wherefore, it came to p. that		13:18
And it came to p. that		7:15	And it came to p. that		13:19
And it came to p. as he		7:17	And it came to p. that		13:22
And it came to p. that		7:18	And it came to p. that		13:23
And it came to p. that		7:24	And it came to p. that		13:27
And it came to p. that		7:24	And it came to p. that		13:28
And it came to p. that		7:26	And it came to p. that		13:28
And it came to p. that		8: 1	And it came to p. that		13:29
And it came to p. that		8: 2	And it came to p. that		14: 4
And it came to p. that		8: 4	And it came to p. that		14: 5
And it came to p. that		8: 5	And it came to p. that		14: 7
And it came to p. that		8: 6	And it came to p. that		14: 9
And it came to p. that		8: 6	And it came to p. that		14:10
And it came to p. that		8: 9	murdered him in a secret p.,		14:10
And it came to p. that		8:11	And it came to p. that		14:11
And it came to p. that		8:13	And it came to p. that		14:12
And it came to p. that		8:14	And it came to p. that		14:13
And it came to p. that		8:15	And it came to p. that		14:14
And it came to p. that		8:18	And it came to p. that		14:15
For it cometh to p. that		8:25	And it came to p. that .		14:17
bringeth to p. the destruction		8:25	And it came to p. that		14:19
behold, it came to p. that		9: 1	And it came to p. that		14:26
And it came to p. that		9: 4	And it came to p. that		14:29
And it came to p. that		9: 5	And it came to p. that		14:29
And it came to p. that		9: 7	And it came to p. that		14:30
And it came to p. that		9: 9	And it came to p. when		15: 1
And it came to p. that		9:10	And it came to p. that		15: 4
And it came to p. that		9:14	And it came to p. that		15: 5
And it came to p. that		9:15	And it came to p. that		15: 6
And it came to p. that		9:23	And it came to p. that		15: 8
And it came to p. that		9:23	And it came to p. that		15: 9
And it came to p. that		9:24	And it came to p. that		15:10
And it came to p. that		9:24	And it came to p. that		15:11
And it came to p. that		9:25	And it came to p. that		15:12
And it came to p. that		9:27	And it came to p. that		15:13
And it came to p. that		9:29	And it came to p. that		15:15
And it came to p. that		9:30	And it came to p. that		15:16
And it came to p. that		9:31	And it came to p. that		15:17
And it came to p. that		9:32	And it came to p. that		15:18
And it came to p. that		9:33	And it came to p. that		15:20
that the people could not p.,		9:33	And it came to p. that		15:24
whoso should attempt to p.		9:33	And it came to p. that		15:26
And it came to p. that		9:34	And it came to p. that		15:27
And it came to p. that		9:35	And it came to p. that		15:28
And it came to p. that		10: 1	And it came to p. that		15:29
And it came to p. that		10: 2	And it came to p. that		15:30
And it came to p. that		10: 4	And it came to p. that		15:31
And it came to p. that		10: 5	And it came to p. that		15:32
And it came to p. that		10: 7	bringeth to p. the Father,	Mro	7:32
And it came to p. after the		10: 9	heavens and the earth p. away,	DC	1:38
And it came to p. that		10:12	my word shall not p. away,		1:38
And it came to p. that		10:13	And it shall come to p., that		14: 8
And it came to p. that		10:15	I shall p. upon the inhabitants		19: 3
And it came to p. that		10:17	the judgments which I shall p.,		19: 5
many days he did p. away,		10:17	And it shall come to p. that		24:16
And it came to p. that		10:18	bringing to p. the restoration of		27: 6
And it came to p. that		10:19	bring to p. the gathering of		29: 7
And it came to p. that		10:29	spoke so shall it come to p.;		29:10
And it came to p. that		10:30	And it shall come to p.,		29:17
And it came to p. that		10:32	And it shall come to p. that		29:20
And it came to p. that		11: 2	not come to p. but surely must,		29:21
And it came to p. that		11: 5	be consumed and p. away,		29:23

PASS 715 PASSED

all old things shall p. away,	DC	29:24
before the earth shall p. away,		29:26
And it came to p. that		29:36
Wherefore, it came to p. that		29:40
And it shall come to p. that		35: 7
to bring to p. even your		38:13
eternity, no more to p. away.		38:20
And it shall come to p. that		39:12
And again, it shall come to p.		39:23
And it shall come to p.,		42:10
And it shall come to p.,		42:32
And it shall come to p.,		42:37
For it shall come to p.,		42:39
And it shall come to p. that		42:46
And again, it shall come to p.		42:48
And behold, it shall come to p.		42:63
And it shall come to p.,		42:79
the earth shall p. away so as		43:32
And it shall come to p.,		44: 2
And it shall come to p. that		44: 3
And it shall come to p.,		45:21
of Jews shall not p. away		45:21
them shall come to p.		45:21
and the earth shall p. away;		45:22
shall not p. away until all		45:23
that shall not p. until they		45:31
these things shall come to p.,		45:35
And it shall come to p. that		45:39
And it shall come to p. among		45:68
And it shall come to p. that		45:71
And it shall come to p. that		46:28
Wherefore, it shall come to p.,		50:31
heaven and the earth p. away,		56:11
these words shall not p. away,		56:11
bring to p. much righteousness;		58:27
And it shall come to p.,		60: 3
and old things shall p. away,		63:49
But all things must come to p.		64:32
For it shall come to p. that		64:38
And it came to p. that		74: 3
And it came to p. that		74: 4
generation shall not all p. away		84: 5
brought to p. by the faith		84:99
And it shall come to p. that		85: 7
that will shortly come to p.,		87: 1
And it shall come to p.,		87: 4
And it shall come to p. also		87: 5
brought to p. the resurrection		88:14
must shortly come to p.;		88:79
destroying angel shall p. by		89:21
For it shall come to p. in		90:11
to bring to p. my work,		90:26
It shall come to p. that every		93: 1
And it shall come to p.,		93:18
bring to p. my strange act,		95: 4
Lord's scourge shall p. over		97:23
I have said, it shall come to p.		101:10
to bring to p. my act,		101:95
brought to p. unto you through		103:36
cannot be brought to p. until		105:11
it shall come to p. in due time		111: 4
it shall come to p. that all those		119: 5
called to p. through tribulation;		122: 5
bounds are set, they cannot p.		122: 9
it shall come to p. that if you		124:47
which I am called to p. through,		127: 2
by whom they cannot p.;		132:18
and they shall p. by the angels,		132:19
And it came to p. that I prayed		135: 5
And it came to p. that the Lord said		135: 5
it came to p. that Moses looked,	Mses	1: 8
it came to p. that it was for the		1:10
it came to p. that when Moses had		1:12
it came to p. that Moses looked		1:13
it came to p. that Moses began		1:20
it came to p. that Satan cried		1:22
it came to p. that when Satan		1:24
it came to p., as the voice was		1:27
it came to p. that Moses called		1:30
it came to p. that Moses spake		1:36
And as one earth shall p. away,		1:38
to bring to p. the immortality and		1:39
it came to p. that the Lord		2: 1
And it came to p. that after I,	Mses	5: 1
it came to p. that Cain brought		5:19
it came to p. that Cain took		5:28
it came to p. that while they were		5:32
it shall come to p., that he that		5:39
it came to p. that all the days		6:24
came to p. that Enoch journeyed		6:26
it came to p. that Enoch went		6:37
it came to p. when they heard		6:39
it came to p., as I journeyed		6:42
it came to p., when the Lord had		6:64
came to p. that Enoch continued		7: 1
it came to p. that I turned and		7: 3
it came to p. that I beheld in		7: 5
it came to p. that the Lord said		7: 9
came to p. that Enoch continued		7:12
it came to p. in his days, that he		7:19
it came to p. that Enoch talked		7:20
came to p. that the Lord showed		7:21
it came to p. that the God of		7:28
it came to p. that the Lord spake		7:41
it came to p. that Enoch looked;		7:45
it came to p. that Enoch Looked		7:48
came to p. that Enoch continued		7:50
it came to p. that Enoch cried		7:54
it came to p. that Enoch saw		7:65
came to p. that Zion was not,		7:69
it came to p. that Methuselah,		8: 2
it came to p. that Methuselah		8: 3
it came to p. that Methuselah		8: 5
came to p. that Noah prophesied,		8:16
it came to p. that Noah called		8:20
came to p. that Noah continued		8:23
And it came to p. that the priest	Abr	1: 9
it came to p. that the priests		1:12
it came to p. that I, Abraham,		2: 2
it came to p. when I was come		2:22
it shall come to p., when the		2:23
it came to p. that I, Abraham,		2:25
it came to p. that from the evening		4: 5
it came to p. that it was from		4: 8
it came to p. that it was from		4: 8
came to p. that they numbered		4:13
it came to p., from the morning		4:13
it came to p. that it was from		4:19
it came to p. that it was from		4:19
it came to p. that it was from		4:23
it came to p. that it was from		4:23
it came to p. that it was from		4:31
it came to p. that it was from		4:31
told you must come to p.;	JS	1:23
shall not p. away until all I		1:34
heaven and earth shall p. away;		1:35
yet my words shall not p.,		1:35
should shortly come to p.		2:73
PASSAGE		
They are gone over the p.;	2Ne	20:29
even to the narrow p. which led	Mrm	2:29
Never did any p. of scripture	JS	2:12
PASSAGES		
understood the same p. of	JS	2:12
many o. p. of scripture,		2:41
more mysterious p. revealed		2:74
PASSED		
the vapor of darkness, that it p.	1Ne	12: 5
fourth generation who p. away		12:12
they p. through on dry ground.		17:26
And thirty years had p. away	2Ne	5:28
that forty years had p. away,		5:34
as death hath p. upon all men,		9: 6
shall have p. from this first death		9:15
he is p. to Migron;		20:28
generations shall have p. away,		26: 9
generation shall have p. away		26: 9
when these things have p. away		26:10
fifty and five years had p. away	Jac	1: 1
that a long time p. away,		5:15
that a long time had p. away,		5:29
after some years had p. away,		7: 1
that the time p. away with us,		7:26

PASSED

also our lives p. away like as	Jac	7:26
had p. away from the time that	En	1:25
two hundred years had p. away,	Jar	1: 5
and eight years had p. away—		1:13
seventy and six years had p. away,	Om	1: 3
eighty and two years had p. away,		1: 3
and twenty years had p. away,		1: 5
and none shall have p. away.	Al	34:13
had p. the hill Riplah,		43:35
not many days had p. away		57:12
when the Lamanites had p. by,		58:20
or when the army had p. by,		58:20
what I have spoken had p.	He	3:17
thus p. away the sixty and fifth		6:14
ninety and first year had p. away	3Ne	1: 1
thus p. away the ninety and fifth		2: 1
an hundred years had p. away		2: 5
and nine years had p. away		2: 6
And nine years had p. away		2: 7
nine years had p. away.		2: 8
thus p. away the tenth year		2:10
eleventh year also p. away in		2:10
thirteenth year had p. away		2:13
twenty and second year p. away,		5: 7
twenty and five years p. away.		5: 7
sixth and seventh years p. away,		6: 4
thus p. away the twenty and		6: 9
thus six years had not p. away		7: 8
Thus p. away the thirty and		7:23
and third year had p. away;		8: 2
hath not p. away from the law,		12:18
that old things had p. away,		15: 2
that old things had p. away,		15: 3
that old things have p. away,		15: 7
thirty and fourth year p. away,	4Ne	1: 1
and seventh year p. away also,		1: 4
and nine years had p. away,		1: 6
and nine years had p. away.		1: 6
seventy and first year p. away,		1:14
and ninth year had p. away;		1:14
an hundred years had p. away,		1:14
that generation had p. away.		1:14
and ten years had p. away;		1:18
from Christ had p. away;		1:18
two hundred years had p. away;		1:22
generation had all p. away		1:22
and ten years had p. away		1:27
and thirty years had p. away.		1:34
and four years had p. away,		1:40
hundred years had p. away,		1:45
and five years had p. away,		1:47
twenty years had p. away.		1:48
twenty and six years had p. away.	Mrm	2: 2
and thirty years had p. away.		2: 9
day of grace was p. with them,		2:15
forty and four years had p. away.		2:15
and ninth year had p. away.		2:28
until ten years more had p.		3: 1
after this tenth year had p. away,		3: 4
and sixth year had p. away,		4:10
whatsoever lands we had p. by,		5: 5
seventy and nine years p. away.		5: 5
and four years had p. away,		6: 5
they p. by me that they did not		6:10
four hundred years have p. away		8: 6
have all these things p., of which		9:15
and p. by the hill of Shim,	Eth	9: 3
that Kish p. away also,		10:18
old save the old have p. away,		13: 9
only a few years have p. away,	Mro	9:12
and twenty years have p. away		10: 1
Things which have p.,	DC	101:33
sentence of death p. upon thee;		122: 7
that cannot be lightly p. over,		128:15
many worlds that have p. away	Mses	1:35
then we p. from Jershon through	Abr	2:18

PASSETH

as one generation p. to another	2Ne	1:12
shall be as chaff that p. away—		26:18

PASSING

there were certain men p. by	He	7:11

PASSION

being a man of much p.,	Al	50:30

PASSIONS

also see that ye bridle all your p.,	Al	38:12

PAST

but ye were p. feeling,	1Ne	17:45
can know of things which are p.,	Mos	8:17
your days of probation are p.;	He	13:38
the time was p. for the words to	3Ne	1: 5
Behold the time is p., and		1: 6
without principle, and p. feeling;	Mro	9:20
you feared, and the time is p.,	DC	9:11
not the summer shall be p.,		45: 2
The harvest is p., the summer		56:16
your minds in times p. have		84:54
to leave your family as in times p.,		126: 1
are manifest, p., present, and future,		130: 7
June or during the p. year,		OD

PASTORS

of the wickedness of the p.	1Ne	21: 1
apostles, prophets, p., teachers,	AoF	6

PASTURE

in him they shall find p.	1Ne	22:25
them to the p. of the king,	Al	17:39

PASTURES

their p. shall be in all high places.	1Ne	21: 9

PATH

beheld a straight and narrow p.,	1Ne	8:20
that they might obtain the p.		8:21
in the p. which led to the tree.		8:22
who had commenced in the p.		8:23
walk in the p. of the low valley,	2Ne	4:32
wilt thou make my p. straight		4:33
the Lord has made the sea our p.,		10:20
the straightness of the p.,		31: 9
in this straight and narrow p.		31:18
into this straight and narrow p.,		31:19
and walk in the straight p.		33: 9
and continue in the p. until		33: 9
ye are in the p. which leads to	Al	7:19
of them are in the p. of their duty,	He	15: 5
thy p. lieth among the mountains,	DC	112: 7

PATHROS

and from Egypt, and from P.,	2Ne	21:11

PATHS

fell away into forbidden p.	1Ne	8:28
and make his p. straight;		10: 8
walk in the p. of righteousness.		16: 5
that his p. are righteous.	2Ne	9:41
and we will walk in his p.;		12: 3
and destroy the way of thy p.		13:12
to guide you in wisdom's p.	Mos	2:36
the Lord, and walk in his p.,	Al	7: 9
ye are in the p. of righteousness;		7:19
ye are making his p. straight.		7:19
he cannot walk in crooked p.;		7:20
and his p. are straight, and his		37:12
how slow to walk in wisdom's p.!	He	12: 5
doth not walk in crooked p.,	DC	3: 2
therefore his p. are straight,		3: 2
and walk in the p. of virtue		25: 2
and make his p. straight;		33:10
the Lord, make his p. straight.		65: 1
p. were the poisonous serpent		124:99
and make his p. straight,		133:17

PATIENCE

and his wisdom, and his p.,	Mos	4: 6
he trieth their p. and their faith.		23:21
did submit cheerfully and with p.		24:15
great was their faith and their p.		24:16
they bore with p. the persecution	Al	1:25
full of p. and long-suffering;		7:23
full of p., mercy, and		9:26
bear with p. thine afflictions,		26:27

PATIENCE

suffer with p. these afflictions	Al	31:31
with great diligence, and with p.,		32:41
and your p. with the word		32:42
faith, and your diligence, and p.,		32:43
exhorted you unto faith and to p.–		34: 3
I would exhort you to have p.,		34:40
But that ye have p., and bear		34:41
thy p. and thy long-suffering		38: 3
bear all these things with p.		38: 4
their p. in their tribulations–		60:26
knowledge, temperance, p.,	DC	4: 6
have p., faith, hope and charity.		6:19
in all p. and faith.		21: 5
remain to overcome through p.,		63:66
continue in p. until ye are		67:13
that in p. ye may possess		101:38
virtue, and knowledge, temperance, p.,		107:30
and your perseverance, and p.,		127: 4

PATIENT

meek, humble, p., full of love,	Mos	3:19
humble, meek, submissive, p.,	Al	13:28
yet ye shall be p. in long-suffering		17:11
they were p. in all their sufferings.		20:29
have been p. in our sufferings,		26:28
Be p.; be sober; be temperate;	DC	6:19
Be p., my son, for it is wisdom		9: 3
be p. until you shall accomplish		11:19
Be p. in afflictions, for thou		24: 8
Be p. in afflictions, revile not		31: 9
be p. in tribulation until I come;		54:10
Be p. in affliction.		66: 9

PATIENTLY

Waiting p. on the Lord,	DC	98: 2
ye bear it p. and revile not		98:23
But if ye bear it not p.,		98:24
your enemy, and bear it p.,		98:25
third time, and ye bear it p.,		98:26
Wait p. until the solemn assembly		108: 4
await p. and diligently for		124:88

PATRIARCH

the office of Priesthood and P.,	DC	124:91
Hyrum Smith to be a p. unto you,		124:124
and Hyrum Smith the P.		135: 1

PATRIARCHAL

the keys of the p. blessings	DC	124:92
of Ham, which was p.	Abr	1:25
in the days of the first p. reign,		1:26

PATRIARCHS

records of the fathers, even the p.,	Abr	1:31

PATTEN, David

even as I did my servant P.,	DC	124:19
P. I have taken unto myself;		124:130

PATTEN, David W.

It is wisdom in my servant P.,	DC	114: 1

PATTERN

do even according to this p.	DC	24:19
unto you a p. in all things,		52:14
even according to this p.,		52:18
by this p. ye shall know		52:19
even according to the p. which		63:21
be a p. unto the elders until		73: 5
according to the p. given in		88:141
to the p. which I have given		94: 2
to the p. which shall be given		94: 5
to the p. which shall be given		94: 6
to the p. in all things as		94:12
the p. which I have given you.		97:10
according to the foregoing p.,		102:12
to the former p. written,		102:27
according to the p. which I will		115:14
according to the p. which I shall		115:15
according to the p. which I shall		115:16
according to the p. given by the	Mses	6:46

PAUL

even as unto P. mine apostle,	DC	18: 9
these are they who are of P.,		76:99
feel, like P., to glory in tribulation;		127: 2
as P. hath declared,		128:13
as P. says concerning the fathers–		128:15
give you another quotation of P.,		128:16
since, that I felt much like P.,	JS	2:24
follow the admonition of P.–	AoF	13

PAVED

was a p. work of pure gold,	DC	110: 2

PAVILION

where is the p. that covereth	DC	121: 1
let thy p. be taken up;		121: 4

PAY

than to p. tribute to the king of	Mos	7:15
we at this time do p. tribute to		7:22
should p. tribute to the king of		19:15
should p. tribute unto him,		19:26
and p the last tribute of wine		22: 7
not p. that which he did owe,	Al	11: 2
compelled to p. that which he owed,		11: 2
can ye p. even one senine?	3Ne	12:26
whoso was not able to p. taxes	Eth	10: 6
P. the debt thou hast contracted	DC	19:35
thou shalt p. for that which		42:54
let them p. unto this church		51:11
and to p. moneys for you.		54: 7
must needs p. the money,		56:12
I, the Lord, will pay it unto him		56:12
and to p. thy devotions unto		59:10
and p. as seemeth him good.		64:28
who shall p. for that which		72:11
as they have wherewith to p.;		72:11
who hath not wherewith to p.		72:13
p. the debt out of that which		72:13
you shall p. all your debts.		104:78
I will give you power to p. them.		111: 5
been tithed shall p. one-tenth		119: 4
except the same shall p. his stock		124:67
if any p. stock into their hands it		124:69
let my servant Joseph p. stock into		124:72
p. over fifteen thousand dollars		124:72
p. stock into that house,		124:80
p. stock into that house,		124:81
p. stock into that house,		124:82
p. stock into the hands of those		124:111
p. stock also into the hands of the		124:117
no man p. stock to the quorum		124:119

PAYING

p. a tribute to the Lamanites	Mos	19:22

PAYS

the amount of stock he p. into	DC	124:68
if he p. nothing into their hands		124:68
let every man who p. stock		124:122

PEACE

and whoso shall publish p.,	1Ne	13:37
the convincing of them unto p.		14: 7
then had thy p. been as a river,		20:18
there is no p., saith the Lord,		20:22
and establishing p. among the fruit	2Ne	3:12
destroy my p. and afflict my soul?		4:27
Father, The Prince of P.		19: 6
increase of government and p.		19: 7
and they shall have p. with him,		26: 9
p. and the love of God was	Jac	7:23
and we had many seasons of p.;	Om	1: 3
once more establish p. in the land.	WM	1:18
king Benjamin had continual p.	Mos	1: 1
had established p. in the land of		2: 4
live in p. one with another–		2:20
that I might go down in p.–		2:28
and having p. of conscience,		4: 3
king Mosiah had had continual p.		7: 1
people and possess the land in p.		9: 5

PEACE 718 PEKAH

began to possess the land in p.	Mos 10: 1
have continual p. in the land	10: 5
that publisheth p.; that bringeth	12:21
the chastisement of our p. was	14: 5
are they who have published p.,	15:14
those that are still publishing p.!	15:16
who shall hereafter publish p.,	15:17
tidings, that is the founder of p.,	15:18
suffer that he might depart in p.	17: 2
to establish p. among his people.	19:27
king Limhi did have continual p.	19:29
returned with their king in p.	20:26
to dwell in the land again in p.	21: 1
and they began again to have p.	26:37
nor haughtiness disturb their p.;	27: 4
to be much p. again in the land;	27: 6
For they did publish p.;	27:37
will make for the p. of this people.	29:10
establish p. throughout the land,	29:14
he had established p. in the land,	29:40
was continual p. through the land.	29:43
began to have continual p. again,	Al 1:28
p. among the people of Nephi	1:33
began to establish p. in the land,	3:24
was continual p. in all that time.	4: 5
may the p. of God rest upon you,	7:27
establish p. in the land in his days;	13:18
he was called the prince of p.,	13:18
much p. in the land of Zarahemla,	16: 1
have continual p. in all the land.	16:12
they buried their weapons of p.,	24:19
buried the weapons of war, for p.	24:19
there began to be continual p.	30: 2
the judges, there was continual p.	30: 5
and I did find p. to my soul.	38: 8
his kingdom, to sit down in p.	38:15
a state of rest, a state of p., where	40:12
depart with a covenant of p.	44:14
entered into a covenant of p.	44:15
into a covenant with him of p.	44:20
religion, and freedom, and our p.,	46:12
into a covenant to keep the p.—	46:31
to have p. again in the land;	46:37
they did maintain p. in the land	46:37
have much p. and rejoicing	46:38
the Lamanites, as a token of p.,	47:23
and their children, and their p.,	48:10
their p. amongst themselves,	48:21
was continual p. among them,	49:30
of the judges also ended in p.;	50:24
p. among the people of Nephi	50:25
their covenanting to keep the p.	50:36
had p. restored unto them,	50:37
keep the p. and the freedom of	50:39
having established p. between	51: 1
the twenty and fifth year in p.;	51: 1
not long maintain an entire p.	51: 2
subjecting them to p. and	51:22
them until they shall sue for p.	55: 3
he did speak p. to our souls,	58:11
restored p. to the land of	62:11
once more p. established among	62:42
the remainder of his days in p.	62:43
should depart out of the land in p.	He 1:33
p. between the Nephites and the	2: 1
p. established in the land,	3:23
was p. and exceeding great joy	3:32
was continual p. and great joy	3:32
there was p. also, save it were	3:33
and second year ended in p. also,	3:36
P., peace be unto you,	5:47
p. be unto you, because of your	5:47
there was p. in all the land,	6: 7
fourth year did pass away in p.	6:13
did also have great joy and p.,	6:14
and sixth year did end in p.	11:21
and seventh year began in p.;	11:21
exceeding great p. in the land;	11:21
also they had p. in the seventy and	11:22
again to have p. in the land.	3Ne 1:23
year did also pass away in p.,	1:27
into a covenant to keep the p.,	6: 3
did establish p. in all the land.	6: 3
had established this great p.	6: 6
the people had continual p.	3Ne 6: 9
had enjoyed p. but a few years.	6:16
degree they had p. in the land;	7:14
destroy the p. of my people	9: 9
unto them, that publisheth p.;	20:40
shall be the p. of thy children.	22:13
continued to be p. in the land.	4Ne 1: 4
there was still p. in the land,	1:20
there was p. settled in the land;	Mrm 1:12
p. did remain for the space of	1:12
saw p. in the land for the space	Eth 9:15
and he saw p. in the land;	9:22
in his day; and he died in p.	9:22
brought p. again unto his father.	10: 3
when p. shall be taken from	DC 1:35
Did I not speak p. to your	6:23
hold your p. until I shall see	10:37
hold your p.; appeal unto my	11:18
But now hold your p.;	11:22
and you shall have p. in me.	19:23
preparation of the gospel of p.,	27:16
hold thy p. concerning them,	42:57
if ye have slept in p. blessed	45:46
New Jerusalem, a land of p.,	45:66
reward, even p. in this world,	59:23
P. be with you; my blessings	82:23
grace and truth, and p.,	84:102
the bond of perfectness and p.	88:125
That she may settle down in p.	90:31
renounce war and proclaim p.,	98:16
first lift a standard of p.	98:34
not accept the offering of p.,	98:35
In the day of their p.	101: 8
seeing this is a time of p.?	101:48
you may rest in p. and safety,	105:25
I say unto you, sue for p.,	105:38
And lift up an ensign of p.,	105:39
make a proclamation of p. unto	105:39
make proposals for p. unto	105:40
let thy p. and thy salvation be	109:39
by the p. and power of my Spirit.	111: 8
My son, p. be unto thy soul;	121: 7
no government can exist in p.,	134: 2
as without them p. and harmony	134: 6
and the breach of the general p.,	134: 8
for the public p. and tranquility	134: 8
dangerous to the p. of every	134:12
be ready to go to a land of p.	136:16
naught but p., justice, and truth	Mses 7:31
happiness and p. and rest for me,	Abr 1: 2
of many nations, a prince of p.,	1: 2
servant rise up and depart in p.	2:13

PEACEABLE

are the p. followers of Christ,	Mro 7: 3
p. walk with the children of men.	7: 4
the p. things of the kingdom;	DC 36: 2
the p. things of the kingdom.	39: 6
the mysteries and p. things—	42:61
p. things of immortal glory;	Mses 6:61

PEACEABLY

injure one another, but to live p.,	Mos 4:13

PEACEMAKERS

And blessed are all the p.,	3Ne 12: 9

PEAKED

and the ends thereof were p.;	Eth 2:17

PEARLS

cast ye your p. before swine,	3Ne 14: 6
and all manner of fine p.,	4Ne 1:24
the p. to be cast before swine.	DC 41: 6

PEEP

unto wizards that p. and mutter—	2Ne 18:19

PEEPED

or opened the mouth, or p.	2Ne 20:14

PEKAH

and P. the son of Remaliah,	2Ne 17: 1

PELAGORAM 719 PEOPLE

PELAGORAM
my servant P.[Sidney Rigdon],	DC	78: 9
and P. [Sidney Rigdon],		82:11
my servant P. [Sidney Rigdon]		104:20
my servant P. [Sidney Rigdon]		104:22

PEN
and write in it with a man's p.,	2Ne	18: 1

PENALTY
p. thereof being a second death,	Al	12:32
the p. which is affixed unto	DC	82: 4

PENETRATE
the storm cannot p. to them;	Al	26: 6

PENETRATED
heart that shall not be p.	DC	1: 2
ear be p. with their cries?		121: 2

PENITENT
these things, save it be the p.	Al	26:21
save it be the truly p. and		27:18
many of my brethren truly p.,		29:10
he beheld, who were truly p.,		32: 7
and mercy claimeth the p.,		42:23
none but the truly p. are saved.		42:24
were humble and p. before God.	3Ne	6:13

PENNSYLVANIA
county, State of P.;	JS	2:56
county, in the State of P.		2:61
the place of my destination in P.;		2:62

PENTECOST
as upon those on the day of P.;	DC	109:36

PEOPLE
the record of the p. of Nephi,	T Pg	
a record of the p. of Jared,	T Pg	
confounded the language of the p.,	T Pg	
he prophesieth unto the p.	1Ne	1:hd
prophets, prophesying unto the p.		1: 4
his heart, in behalf of his p.		1: 5
he went forth among the p.,		1:18
and declared unto this p.		2: 1
of the wickedness of the p.		3:17
nations, kindreds, tongues, and p.		5:18
numberless concourses of p.,		8:21
And it was filled with p.,		8:27
account of the history of my p.;		9: 2
I make a full account of my p.		9: 2
engraven of the ministry of my p.		9: 3
wars and contentions of my p.;		9: 4
wars and contentions of my p.		9: 4
went forth ministering unto the p.,		11:28
And I beheld multitudes of p.		11:31
that he was taken by the p.;		11:32
nations, kindreds, tongues, and p.,		11:36
and I beheld multitudes of p.,		12: 1
with the sword among my p.		12: 2
and beheld the p. of my seed		12:15
did overpower the p. of my seed.		12:19
the p. of the seed of my brethren		12:20
loathsome, and a filthy p.,		12:23
fair and beautiful, like unto my p.		13:15
to all kindreds, tongues, and p.,		13:40
and they shall be a blessed p.		14: 2
nations, kindreds, tongues, and p.		14:11
the covenant p. of the Lord,		14:14
which he hath made to his p.		14:17
of the destructions of my p.,		15: 5
the covenant p. of the Lord;		15:14
carry thy p. across these waters.		17: 8
that the p. who were in the land		17:22
of Jerusalem were a righteous p.;		17:22
know that they are a righteous p.;		17:22
this p. had rejected every word		17:35
upon them the record of my p.		19: 1
kept for the instruction of my p.,		19: 3
and destructions of my p.		19: 4
commanded my p. what they		19: 4
kept for the knowledge of my p.;		19: 5
they shall be scourged by all p.,	1Ne	19:13
and all the p. who are of the		19:16
nation, kindred, tongue and p.		19:17
written these things unto my p.,		19:18
in other lands, among p. of old.		19:22
wickedness of the pastors of my p.;		21: 1
scattered abroad, who are of my p.,		21: 1
and hearken ye p. from far;		21: 1
servant for a covenant of the p.,		21: 8
the Lord hath comforted his p.,		21:13
and set up my standard to the p.;		21:22
to ensnare the p. of the Lord.		22:14
surely prepare a way for his p.,		22:20
shall be cut off from among the p.		22:20
of the righteousness of his p.,		22:26
no power over the hearts of the p.,		22:26
nations, kindreds, tongues, and p.		22:28
and a favored p. of the Lord.	2Ne	1:19
up unto you, to deliver my p.,		3: 9
will I raise up, to deliver thy p.		3:10
shall commence among all my p.,		3:13
shall bring my p. unto salvation.		3:15
elder brethren, to rule over this p.		5: 3
my p. would that we should call		5: 8
call themselves the p. of Nephi.		5: 9
the p. who were now called		5:14
and those who were called my p.		5:14
did teach my p. to build buildings,		5:15
cause my p. to be industrious,		5:17
might not be enticing unto my p.		5:21
shall be loathsome unto thy p.,		5:22
they did become an idle p.,		5:24
teachers over the land of my p.		5:26
I had made, of my p. thus far.		5:29
for the profit of thy p.		5:30
And if my p. are pleased with		5:32
And if my p. desire to know		5:33
part of the history of my p.		5:33
he spake unto the p. of Nephi:		6: 1
and set up my standard to the p.;		6: 6
the covenant p. of the Lord shall		6:13
and the p. of the Lord shall not		6:13
the p. of the Lord are they who		6:13
God shall deliver his covenant p.		6:17
Hearken unto me, my p.;		8: 4
to rest for a light for the p.		8: 4
and mine arm shall judge the p.		8: 5
the p. in whose heart I have		8: 7
Zion: Behold, thou art my p.		8:16
God pleadeth the cause of his p.;		8:22
spake many more things to my p.		11: 1
I will liken his words unto my p.,		11: 2
proving unto my p. the truth of		11: 4
in proving unto my p. that save		11: 6
whoso of my p. shall see these		11: 8
many p. shall go and say,		12: 3
and shall rebuke many p.:		12: 4
O Lord, thou hast forsaken thy p.,		12: 6
are lifted up, and upon every p.;		12:14
And the p. shall be oppressed,		13: 5
make me not a ruler of the p.		13: 7
And my p., children are their		13:12
O my p., they who lead thee		13:12
and standeth to judge the p.		13:13
with the ancients of his p.		13:14
Ye beat my p. to pieces,		13:15
my p. are gone into captivity,		15:13
of the Lord kindled against his p.,		15:25
midst of a p. of unclean lips;		16: 5
Go and tell this p.—Hear ye		16: 9
Make the heart of this p. fat,		16:10
heart of his p., as the trees		17: 2
be broken that it be not a p.		17: 8
bring upon thee, and upon thy p.,		17:17
as this p. refuseth the waters		18: 6
Associate yourselves, O ye p.,		18: 9
not walk in the way of this p.,		18:11
to all to whom this p. shall say,		18:12
should not a p. seek unto their		18:19
The p. that walked in darkness		19: 2
And all the p. shall know,		19: 9
For the p. turneth not unto		19:13
the leaders of this p. cause them		19:16

PEOPLE 720 PEOPLE

the p. shall be as the fuel of the	2Ne 19:19	unto me, I will command my p.;	Jac	2:30
the right from the poor of my p.,	20: 2	of the daughters of my p.		2:31
and against the p. of my wrath	20: 6	yea, and in all the lands of my p.,		2:31
I have moved the borders of the p.,	20:13	of the fair daughters of this p.,		2:32
found as a nest the riches of the p.;	20:14	unto me against the men of my p.,		2:32
though thy p. Israel be as	20:22	captive the daughters of my p.		2:33
O my p. that dwellest in Zion,	20:24	they shall become a blessed p.		3: 6
shall stand for an ensign of the p.;	21:10	things unto the p. of Nephi,		3:12
to recover the remnant of his p.	21:11	of the proceedings of this p.,		3:13
for the remnant of his p.	21:16	much unto my p. in word,		4: 1
declare his doings among the p.,	22: 4	the Jews were a stiffnecked p.;		4:14
like as of a great p.,	23: 4	the second time to recover his p.,		6: 2
every man turn to his own p.,	23:14	a stiffnecked and a gainsaying p.;		6: 4
I will be merciful unto my p.,	23:22	a man among the p. of Nephi,		7: 1
And the p. shall take them	24: 2	he began to preach among the p.,		7: 2
He who smote the p. in wrath	24: 6	which were flattering unto the p.;		7: 2
destroyed thy land and slain thy p.;	24:20	lead away the hearts of the p.,		7: 3
the poor of his p. shall trust in it.	24:32	of the language of the p.;		7: 4
for many of my p. to understand;	25: 1	ye have led away much of this p.		7: 7
Wherefore, I write unto my p.,	25: 3	that he said unto the p.:		7:16
Wherefore, hearken, O my p.,	25: 4	I desire to speak unto the p.		7:16
delighteth in plainness unto my p.,	25: 4	was restored again among the p.;		7:23
is none other p. that understand	25: 5	the p. of Nephi did fortify		7:25
the words unto mine own p.;	25: 8	the record of this p. being kept		7:26
manifested himself unto his p.,	25:14	being a lonesome and a solemn p.,		7:26
God and the p. of his church.	25:14	so be, that my p., the Nephites,	En	1:13
the second time to restore his p.	25:17	a record of my p., the Nephites;		1:13
which should deceive the p.;	25:18	went about among the p. of Nephi,		1:19
And now behold, my p.,	25:28	the p. of Nephi did seek diligently		1:20
ye are a stiffnecked p.;	25:28	ferocious, and a blood-thirsty p.,		1:20
and contentions among my p.	26: 2	the p. of Nephi did till the land,		1:21
shall be signs given unto my p.	26: 3	the p. were a stiffnecked people,		1:22
the loss of the slain of my p.!	26: 7	the people were a stiffnecked p.,		1:22
destruction cometh unto my p.;	26:10	preach and prophesy unto this p.,		1:26
nation, kindred, tongue, and p.,	26:13	should be done among this p.,	Jar	1: 3
and he hath commanded his p.	26:27	the p. of Nephi had waxed strong		1: 5
and abominations of the p.	27: 8	they taught the p. the ways of		1: 7
as this p. draw near unto me with	27:25	did threaten the p. of Nephi,		1:10
a marvelous work among this p.,	27:26	long-suffering the p. to diligence;		1:11
and they say unto the p.:	28: 5	with the sword to preserve my p.,	Om	1: 2
the second time to recover my p.,	29: 1	and contention between my p.,		1:10
for a standard unto my p.,	29: 2	the record of this p. is		1:11
Jews, mine ancient covenant p.	29: 4	And they discovered a p., who		1:14
Jews, mine ancient covenant p.?	29: 5	were called the p. of Zarahemla.		1:14
the Lord have not forgotten my p.	29: 5	among the p. of Zarahemla;		1:14
my p., which are of the house of	29:14	Lord had sent the p. of Mosiah		1:14
my word and against my p.,	29:14	the p. of Zarahemla came out		1:15
are the covenant p. of the Lord;	30: 2	Mosiah, nor the p. of Mosiah,		1:17
be a white and delightsome p.	30: 6	the p. of Zarahemla, and of		1:19
shall also become a delightsome p.	30: 7	and the slain of his p.		1:21
nations, kindreds, tongues, and p.,	30: 8	discovered by the p. of Zarahemla;		1:21
about the restoration of his p.	30: 8	the language of the p.;		1:22
a great division among the p.,	30:10	almost all the destruction of my p.,	WM	1: 1
and he will spare his p.,	30:10	the entire destruction of my p.		1: 2
which were taught among my p.;	33: 1	part of the things of my p.		1: 5
and especially unto my p.	33: 3	once again be a delightsome p.		1: 8
my prayers for the gain of my p.	33: 4	my p. and their brethren shall		1:11
I have charity for my p.,	33: 7	contentions among his own p.		1:12
history of the p. of Nephi.	Jac 1:hd	to battle against his p.		1:13
concerning the history of this p.	1: 2	and teachers among the p.,		1:16
which are called the p. of Nephi.	1: 2	prophets who were among his p.—		1:16
the history of his p. should be	1: 3	reign over his p. in righteousness;		1:17
and for the sake of our p.	1: 4	of the stiffneckedness of the p.—		1:17
unto us concerning our p.,	1: 5	all the p. who belonged to king	Mos	1: 1
labored diligently among our p.,	1: 7	all this land among all this p.,		1:10
to be a king and a ruler over his p.	1: 9	or the p. of Zarahemla,		1:10
The p. having loved Nephi	1:10	and the p. of Mosiah who dwell		1:10
the p. were desirous to retain	1:11	I shall proclaim unto this my p.		1:10
called by the p., second Nephi,	1:11	a king and a ruler over this p.,		1:10
thus they were called by the p.,	1:11	I shall give this p. a name,		1:11
the p. which were not Lamanites	1:13	distinguished above all the p.		1:11
seek to destroy the p. of Nephi,	1:14	they have been a diligent p. in		1:11
call Nephites, or the p. of Nephi,	1:14	highly favored p. of the Lord		1:13
the p. of Nephi, under the reign	1:15	a wicked and an adulterous p.,		1:13
priests and teachers of this p.,	1:18	and proclaimed unto all the p.		1:18
answering the sins of the p. upon	1:19	that the p. gathered themselves		2: 1
spake unto the p. of Nephi,	2:11	his p. might hear the words		2: 7
which I shall give thee unto this p.	2:11	speak to his p. from the tower		2: 8
This p. begin to wax in iniquity;	2:23	yet I have been chosen by this p.,		2:11
I have led this p. forth out of	2:25	a ruler and a king over this p.;		2:11
that this p. shall do like unto	2:26	But, O my p., beware lest there		2:32
Wherefore this p. shall keep my	2:29	thou mayest declare unto thy p.,		3: 4

the abominations of his p.	Mos	3: 7
God saw that his p. were a		3:14
were a stiffnecked p.,		3:14
nation, kindred, tongue, and p.		3:20
have taught thy p. the things		3:22
bright testimony against this p.,		3:24
brethren, my kindred and my p.,		4: 4
had thus spoken to his p.,		5: 1
desiring to know of his p. if		5: 1
finished speaking to the p.,		6: 1
a ruler and a king over his p.,		6: 3
priests to teach the p.,		6: 3
Mosiah did cause his p. that		6: 7
become burdensome to his p.,		6: 7
no contention among all his p.		6: 7
concerning the p. who went up		7: 1
for his p. had heard nothing from		7: 1
they met the king of the p. who		7: 7
a king by the voice of the p.		7: 9
will cause that my p. shall rejoice		7:14
a proclamation among all his p.,		7:17
O ye, my p., lift up your heads		7:18
preserved his p. even until now;		7:20
who was made king over this p.,		7:21
bringing this p. into subjection		7:22
if this p. had not fallen into		7:25
I will not succor my p. in the		7:29
If my p. shall sow filthiness they		7:30
If my p. shall sow filthiness they		7:31
made an end of speaking to his p.,		8: 1
he told his p. all the things		8: 1
to the p. of king Limhi,		8: 3
contained the record of his p.		8: 5
for the afflictions of my p.,		8: 7
forty and three of my p. should		8: 7
a p. who were as numerous as		8: 8
the p. who have been destroyed,		8:12
a knowledge of this very p.		8:12
the king of the p. who are in		8:14
long doth he suffer with his p.;		8:20
An account of his p., from the		9:hd
if I might go in with my p. and		9: 5
that his p. should depart out of		9: 7
I and my p. went into the land		9: 7
to bring my p. into bondage,		9:10
my p. should wax strong in the		9:11
a lazy and an idolatrous p.;		9:12
Laman began to stir up his p.		9:13
should contend with my p.;		9:13
my p. were watering and feeding		9:14
I and my p. did go forth against		9:16
I and my p. did cry mightily		9:17
I might have weapons for my p.		10: 1
up again to war against my p.		10: 1
and thus I did guard my p.		10: 2
And he began to stir his p. up		10: 6
up in rebellion against my p.;		10: 6
come up to battle against my p.		10: 6
they might not come upon my p.		10: 7
the women and children of my p.		10: 9
Yet they were a strong p.,		10:11
ferocious, and a blood-thirsty p.,		10:12
the ruling of the p. out of their		10:15
this my p. up into this land,		10:18
told all these things unto my p.		10:19
my p. again began to pursue their		10:21
And may the Lord bless my p.		10:22
did cause his p. to commit sin,		11: 2
king Noah had put upon his p.;		11: 6
thus did the p. labor exceedingly		11: 6
speak lying and vain words to his p.		11:11
obtained by the taxation of his p.		11:13
a wine-bibber, and also his p.		11:15
began to come in upon his p.,		11:16
Go forth, and say unto this p.,		11:20
Wo be unto this p., for I have		11:20
visiting the iniquities of my p.		11:22
except this p. repent and turn		11:23
Abinadi had spoken unto the p.,		11:27
my p. should be judged of him,		11:27
upon my p. such great affliction?		11:27
he might stir up my p. to anger		11:28
raise contentions among my p.;		11:28
the eyes of the p. were blinded;	Mos	11:29
go and prophesy unto this my p.,		12: 1
that I will smite this my p. with		12: 4
the abominations of this p. to		12: 8
Abinadi prophesy against this p.		12: 8
prophesied evil concerning thy p.,		12: 9
great sins have thy p. committed,		12:13
the Lord hath comforted his p.,		12:23
and pretend to teach this p.,		12:25
what teach ye this p.?		12:27
and cause this p. to commit sin,		12:29
me to prophesy against this p.,		12:29
even a great evil against this p.?		12:29
have ye taught this p. that they		12:37
the p. of king Noah durst not lay		13: 5
Have ye taught this p. that they		13:25
prophesy evil concerning this p.		13:26
for the sins and iniquities of his p.,		13:28
for they were a stiffnecked p.,		13:29
that God should redeem his p.?		13:33
for the transgressions of my p.		14: 8
of men, and shall redeem his p.		15: 1
cast out, and disowned by his p.		15: 5
the Lord would redeem his p.		15:11
Lord, who has redeemed his p.;		15:18
granted salvation unto his p.;		15:18
which he hath made for his p.,		15:19
nation, kindred, tongue, and p.		15:28
the Lord hath comforted his p.,		15:30
nation, kindred, tongue, and p.		16: 1
that God redeemed his p. from		16: 4
evil concerning me and my p.		17: 8
unto you concerning this p.,		17: 9
upon those that destroy his p.		17:19
about privately among the p.,		18: 1
and the redemption of the p.,		18: 2
of God, and to be called his p.,		18: 8
when the p. had heard these		18:11
Lord, who had redeemed his p.		18:20
together to teach the p.,		18:25
were not to depend upon the p.		18:26
the p. of the church should impart		18:27
a movement among the p.,		18:32
Alma was stirring up the p. to		18:33
Alma and the p. of the Lord		18:34
in vain for the p. of the Lord.		19: 1
among the remainder of the p.		19: 2
yea, they will destroy my p.		19: 7
so much concerned about his p.		19: 8
the king commanded the p. that		19: 9
met the p. in the wilderness,		19:18
the p. told the men of Gideon		19:23
his p. should not slay them.		19:25
conferred upon him by the p.,		19:26
that his p. should pay tribute		19:26
to establish peace among his p.		19:27
keep the p. of Limhi in the land,		19:28
that the p. would slay them,		20: 3
were angry with the p. of Limhi,		20: 6
thought it was the p. of Limhi.		20: 6
king himself went before his p.;		20: 7
to destroy the p. of Limhi.		20: 7
he gathered his p. together,		20: 8
the p. of Limhi began to fall		20: 9
the p. of Limhi began to drive		20:11
so speedy was the flight of his p.		20:12
come up to war against my p.?		20:14
my p. have not broken the oath		20:14
oath which ye made unto my p.?		20:14
because thy p. did carry away		20:15
away the daughters of my p.;		20:15
in my anger I did cause my p.		20:15
come up to war against thy p.		20:15
I will search among my p. and		20:16
a search to be made among his p.		20:16
forbear, and do not search this p.,		20:17
whom this p. sought to destroy?		20:18
that he may tell his p. that		20:19
king was pacified towards his p.;		20:24
Let us go forth to meet my p.,		20:24
with an oath that my p. shall		20:24
my people shall not slay thy p.		20:24
in behalf of the p. of Limhi.		20:25

PEOPLE 722 PEOPLE

the Lamanites saw the p. of Limhi,	Mos 20:26	might judge the p. of that church	Mos	26:33
Limhi and his p. returned to the	21: 1	among the p. of the church;		26:35
the p. began to murmur with	21: 6	among the p. of the church,		26:36
among the p. of Limhi,	21: 9	the p. began to be very		27: 6
remainder of the p. of Limhi	21:11	became a large and wealthy p.		27: 7
Now the p. of Limhi kept	21:18	speak much flattery to the p.;		27: 8
he caused that his p. should	21:20	he led many of the p. to do after		27: 8
Lamanites and the p. of Limhi,	21:22	stealing away the hearts of the p.;		27: 9
a record of the p. whose bones	21:27	much dissension among the p.;		27: 9
the p. to commit so many sins	21:30	lead astray the p. of the Lord,		27:10
and the p. that went with him,	21:30	is the transgression of my p.		27:13
and also many of his p.,	21:32	hath heard the prayers of his p.,		27:14
king Limhi and many of his p.	21:33	eyes of the p. might be opened		27:22
the study of Ammon and his p.,	21:36	nations, kindreds, tongues and p.,		27:25
and king Limhi and his p.,	21:36	this time forward to teach the p.,		27:32
Limhi began to consult with the p.	22: 1	publishing to all the p. the things		27:32
the p. should gather themselves	22: 1	the p. who were under the reign		27:35
the voice of the p. concerning	22: 1	and they did declare unto the p.		27:37
impossible for the p. of Limhi	22: 2	been found by the p. of Limhi,		28:11
deliver this p. out of bondage.	22: 4	of the great anxiety of his p.;		28:12
proclamation among all this p.	22: 6	those p. who had been destroyed.		28:12
his p. should gather their flocks	22:10	and abominations of his p.;		28:15
the p. of king Limhi did depart	22:11	of the p. who were destroyed,		28:17
and joined Mosiah's p., and	22:13	the language of the p.		28:17
been found by the p. of Limhi.	22:14	cause the p. of Mosiah to mourn		28:18
the p. of Limhi had departed	22:15	that all p. should know the things		28:19
Alma and the p. of the Lord,	23:hd	also keep a record of the p.,		28:20
by the p. of king Noah.	23:hd	all the land, among all the p.,		29: 1
having made it known to his p.,	23: 1	the voice of the p. came, saying:		29: 2
the p. of king Noah could not	23: 2	Mosiah sent again among the p.;		29: 4
the p. were desirous that Alma	23: 6	word sent he among the p.		29: 4
for he was beloved by his p.	23: 6	O ye my p., or my brethren,		29: 5
hands of king Noah and his p.,	23:13	and draw away a part of this p.		29: 7
Thus did Alma teach his p.,	23:15	destroy the souls of many p.		29: 7
they did watch over their p.,	23:18	also this p. to commit much sin.		29: 9
Lord seeth fit to chasten his p.;	23:21	will make for the peace of this p.		29:10
and thus it was with this p.	23:22	to judge this p. according to		29:11
after the p. of king Limhi,	23:30	arrange the affairs of this p.,		29:11
a king and a ruler over his p.,	23:39	that will judge this p. according to		29:11
appointed teachers over his p.,	24: 1	and judge this p. according to		29:13
over the p. who were in the land	24: 1	father Benjamin did for this p.—		29:13
he was king over a numerous p.	24: 3	and abominations of his p.		29:18
which was possessed by his p.;	24: 4	sendeth them forth among his p.,		29:23
all the p. of the Lamanites.	24: 4	you by the voice of this p.,		29:25
a p. friendly one with another;	24: 5	the voice of the p. desireth		29:26
to be a cunning and a wise p.,	24: 7	the lesser part of the p. to desire		29:26
yea, a very cunning p.,	24: 7	business by the voice of the p.		29:26
Alma and his p. did not raise	24:12	the voice of the p. doth choose		29:27
and I will covenant with my p.	24:13	according to the voice of the p.		29:29
do visit my p. in their afflictions.	24:14	that if these p. commit sins		29:30
Thou shalt go before this p.,	24:17	the sins of many p. have been		29:31
deliver this p. out of bondage.	24:17	especially among this my p.;		29:32
Alma and his p. in the night-time	24:18	all the travails of soul for their p.,		29:33
Alma and his p. departed into	24:20	all the murmurings of the p. to		29:33
thou and this p. out of this land,	24:23	should come upon all the p.,		29:34
no further in pursuit of his p.	24:23	these things forth among the p.,		29:37
all the p. should be gathered	25: 1	he had granted unto his p. that		29:40
were of the p. of Zarahemla,	25: 2	p. who were called the Nephites;		29:44
not so many of the p. of Nephi	25: 3	the kings over the p. of Nephi;		29:47
and of the p. of Zarahemla	25: 3	*Chief Judge over the p. of Nephi,*	Al	1:hd
the p. of Nephi were assembled	25: 4	*and contentions among the p.*		1:hd
also all the p. of Zarahemla,	25: 4	the judges over the p. of Nephi,		1: 1
the records of Zeniff to his p.;	25: 5	they were acknowledged by the p.;		1: 1
the records of the p. of Zeniff,	25: 5	had gone about among the p.		1: 3
his p. who tarried in the land	25: 7	declaring unto the p. that every		1: 3
all the p. of Zarahemla were	25:13	ought to be supported by the p.		1: 3
speaking and reading to the p.,	25:14	And he also testified unto the p. that		1: 4
Alma should also speak to the p.	25:14	lead away the p. of the church;		1: 7
unto the p. repentance and	25:15	in delivering the p. of Limhi out		1: 8
he did exhort the p. of Limhi	25:16	was taken by the p. of the church,		1:10
had taught the p. many things	25:17	been introduced among this p.		1:12
and all his p. were desirous	25:17	to be enforced among this p.		1:12
because there were so many p.	25:20	done much good among this p.;		1:13
they were called the p. of God.	25:24	been acknowledged by this p.;		1:14
the time he spake unto his p.;	26: 1	this p. must abide by the law.		1:14
a separate p. as to their faith,	26: 4	that what he had taught to the p.		1:15
so numerous as the p. of God;	26: 5	law among the p. of the church		1:21
the p. stood and testified of	26: 9	no more among the p. of God.		1:24
a church among this p.;	26:17	the word of God unto the p.,		1:26
and they shall be my p.	26:17	the p. also left their labors to		1:26
Yea, blessed is this p. who are	26:18	peace among the p. of Nephi		1:33
as often as my p. repent will I	26:30	to be a contention among the p.;		2: 1
not be numbered among my p.;	26:32	drawn away much p. after him;		2: 2

Amlici to be king over the p.	Al	2: 2
alarming to the p. of the church,		2: 3
by the voice of the p.		2: 3
should gain the voice of the p.,		2: 4
that the p. assembled themselves		2: 5
the voice of the p. came against		2: 7
he was not made king over the p.		2: 7
Now the p. of Amlici were		2:11
Nephites, or the p. of God.		2:11
the p. of the Nephites were aware		2:12
rulers and leaders over his p.,		2:14
the governor of the p. of Nephi,		2:16
therefore he went up with his p.,		2:16
that his p. should pitch their tents		2:20
his p. from being destroyed.		2:21
the p. of Nephi took their tents,		2:26
to save and preserve this p.		2:30
his p. might have room to cross		2:34
Lord God might preserve his p.,		3: 8
the Nephites, or the p. of Nephi,		3:11
records which are true of their p.,		3:12
also of the p. of the Lamanites.		3:12
came in upon the p. of Nephi,		3:20
the judges over the p. of Nephi,		4: 1
But the p. were afflicted, yea,		4: 2
priest over the p. of the church,		4: 4
the judges over the p. of Nephi;		4: 5
the p. of the church began to wax		4: 6
to many of the p. whom Alma had		4: 7
had begun to be among their p.		4: 7
the p. of the church began to be		4: 8
among the p. of the church,		4: 9
on the destruction of the p.		4:11
great inequality among the p.,		4:12
for lamentations among the p.,		4:13
them by the remainder of his p.,		4:15
according to the voice of the p.		4:16
and the crimes of the p.		4:16
to judge and to govern the p.		4:17
might go forth among his p.,		4:19
or among the p. of Nephi, that		4:19
which were among his p.,		4:19
the judges over the p. of Nephi,		4:20
delivered to the p. in their cities		5:hd
the word of God unto the p.,		5: 1
words which he spake to the p.		5: 2
the hands of the p. of king Noah,		5: 4
redeem his p. from their sins?		5:21
to redeem his p. from their sins?		5:27
to stand and testify unto this p.		5:44
Go forth and say unto this p.—		5:51
mingled with the names of my p.;		5:57
unto the p. of the church,		6: 1
to redeem his p. from their sins,		6: 8
he delivered to the p. in Gideon,		7:hd
liveth and cometh among his p.		7: 7
cry unto this p., saying—		7: 9
and the sicknesses of his p.		7:11
bands of death which bind his p.;		7:12
how to succor his p. according		7:12
take upon him the sins of his p.,		7:13
having taught the p. of Gideon		8: 1
the judges over the p. of Nephi.		8: 2
the judges over the p. of Nephi,		8: 3
the p. in the land of Melek		8: 4
teach the p. throughout all the		8: 4
the p. came to him throughout		8: 5
the custom of the p. of Nephi to		8: 7
upon the hearts of the p. of		8: 9
pour out his Spirit upon the p.		8:10
Now when the p. had said this,		8:13
the wickedness of the p. who were		8:14
again unto the p. of the city;		8:16
may destroy the liberty of thy p.,		8:17
which he has given unto his p.		8:17
the owrd of God among all this p.,		8:24
again and prophesy unto this p.,		8:25
he began to preach unto the p.		8:27
the p. did wax more gross in their		8:28
forth and prophesy unto this p.,		8:29
I will visit this p. in mine anger;		8:29
and also Amulek, among the p.,		8:30
and to prophesy unto the p.,	Al	8:32
were declared unto the p.		9:hd
and preach again unto this p.,		9: 1
the p. who were in the city of		9: 1
hard-hearted and a stiffnecked p.		9: 5
than one man among his p.,		9: 6
your iniquities, to destroy his p.		9:19
might destroy all his p. who are		9:19
who are called the p. of Nephi,		9:19
a highly favored p. of the Lord;		9:20
nation, kindred, tongue, or p.;		9:20
if this p. who have received so		9:23
his angel to visit many of his p.,		9:25
cry mightily unto this p., saying:		9:25
quick to hear the cries of his p.		9:26
of the angel, crying unto the p.		9:29
that ye are a lost and a fallen p.		9:30
the p. were wroth with me because		9:31
hard-hearted and a stiffnecked p.		9:31
they were a lost and a fallen p.		9:32
Amulek preached unto the p. who		10: 1
of the lives of this p.		10: 5
because of the sins of this p.,		10: 7
the p. began to be astonished,		10:12
hired or appointed by the p.		10:14
crimes of the p. before the judges.		10:14
the arts and cunning of the p.;		10:15
to the utter destruction of this p.		10:18
this p. should be governed by		10:19
this p. should choose iniquity,		10:19
this p. should fall into		10:19
well doth he cry unto this p.,		10:20
I will come down among my p.,		10:21
were the p. in the days of Noah,		10:22
the p. were more angry with		10:24
of the destruction of this p. is		10:27
the p. cried out against him,		10:28
business to do among the p.		10:31
be cast out from among the p.		11: 2
and the circumstances of the p.,		11: 4
they did stir up the p. to riotings,		11:20
they did stir up the p. against		11:20
Shall he save his p. in their sins?		11:34
Now Zeezrom said unto the p.:		11:35
but he shall not save his p—		11:35
shall not save his p. in their sins.		11:36
into the world to redeem his p.;		11:40
the p. began again to be		11:46
heard by the p. round about,		12: 2
for to lie and to deceive this p.		12: 4
which he has laid to catch this p.,		12: 6
the p. began to be more		12:19
became a lost and fallen p.		12:22
to teach these things unto the p.		13: 1
that thereby the p. might know		13: 2
the p. in the days of Melchizedek,		13:14
the p. might look forward on the		13:16
his p. had waxed strong in iniquity		13:17
preach repentance unto his p.		13:18
glad tidings among all his p.,		13:22
many more words unto the p.,		13:31
an end of speaking unto the p.		14: 1
the p. went forth and witnessed		14: 5
all the p. that were in the land;		14: 5
should send his Son among the p.,		14: 5
such things did the p. testify		14: 5
which he had caused among the p.		14: 6
he began to cry unto the p.,		14: 7
that the p. may do this thing		14:11
ye preach again unto this p.,		14:14
not answer the words of this p.?		14:19
ye stand again and judge this p.,		14:20
the judges over the p. of Nephi)		14:23
the Lord will destroy this p.		14:24
when the p. saw this, they began		14:26
the p. having heard a great noise		14:29
the p. who had departed out of		15: 1
great astonishment of all the p.;		15:11
time forth to preach unto the p.		15:12
But as to the p. that were in		15:15
hard-hearted and a stiffnecked p.;		15:15
seeing that the p. were checked		15:17

PEOPLE

the judges over the p. of Nephi.	Al	15:19
the judges over the p. of Nephi,		16: 1
slay the p. and destroy the city.		16: 2
destroyed the p. who were in the		16: 3
p. of Ammonihah were destroyed;		16: 9
the p. did not go in to possess		16:11
the judges over the p. of Nephi.		16:12
the p. of Nephi have continual		16:12
preaching repentance to the p.		16:13
among all the p. of the Nephites.		16:15
who did go forth among the p.		16:18
And many of the p. did inquire		16:20
the p. did hear with great joy		16:20
out his blessings upon the p.—		16:21
the judges over the p. of Nephi.		16:21
also this was the minds of the p.;		17: 6
a hardened and a ferocious p.,		17:14
p. who delighted in murdering		17:14
they were a very indolent p.,		17:15
the Lamanites, or among his p.		17:22
dwell among this p. for a time;		17:23
great punishments upon this p.,		18: 2
to scatter the flocks of the p.,		18: 7
to teach these things unto this p.,		18:34
the holy scriptures of the p.,		18:36
hast had upon the p. of Nephi,		18:41
have upon me, and my p.		18:41
among all the p. of the Nephites.		19:10
or among all the p. of God		19:14
by making known unto the p.		19:17
making it known unto the p.		19:17
the p. began to murmur among		19:19
God, have mercy on this p.!		19:29
the contention among his p.,		19:31
unto the p. the selfsame thing—		19:33
many did declare unto the p.		19:34
and they became a righteous p.,		19:35
extended to all p. who will repent		19:36
unto my sons, and unto my p.?		20: 9
and a more stiffnecked p.,		20:30
and the p. of Amulon had built		21: 2
synagogues to preach unto the p.,		21: 5
are not this p. as good as thy		21: 5
this people as good as thy p.?		21: 5
that we are not a righteous p.?		21: 6
the p. would harden their hearts,		21:12
and he caused that his p., or the		21:20
the p. who were under his reign,		21:20
were a p. who were under him,		21:21
and that they were a free p.,		21:21
that he might reign over the p.		21:21
preach unto the p. of king Lamoni;		21:23
thus teaching the p. of Lamoni		22: 1
to teach the p. of Lamoni.		22: 4
they should go and call the p.,		22:21
hardness of the hearts of the p.,		22:22
saw that the p. were pacified,		22:26
all his p. who were in all his land,		22:27
by the p. of Zarahemla,		22:30
a proclamation among all his p.,		23: 1
throughout all the land unto his p.,		23: 3
that his p. might be convinced		23: 3
For they became a righteous p.;		23: 7
The p. of the Lamanites		23: 9
also of the p. of the Lamanites		23:10
also of the p. of the Lamanites		23:11
also of the p. of the Lamanites		23:12
to be a very industrious p.;		23:18
against the p. of Anti-Nephi-Lehi.		24: 2
for war against the p. of God.		24: 4
the p. who had been converted		24: 6
words which he said unto the p.		24: 7
I thank my God, my beloved p.,		24: 7
the p. were assembled together,		24:17
the p. of Anti-Nephi-Lehi out		24:20
when the p. saw that they were		24:21
that the p. of God were joined		24:26
had been slain were righteous p.,		24:26
ways to the salvation of his p.		24:27
who joined the p. of the Lord,		24:29
after a p. have been once		24:30
slay the p. of Anti-Nephi-Lehi		25: 1
upon the p. who were in the land		25: 2

join themselves to the p. of God,	Al	25:13
were the p. of Anti-Nephi-Lehi.		25:13
they began to be a righteous p.;		25:14
as stiffnecked a p. as they are;		26:24
who has been mindful of this p.,		26:36
that God is mindful of every p,.		26:37
yea, he numbereth his p., and his		26:37
began to stir up the p. in anger		27: 2
the p. of Anti-Nephi-Lehi;		27: 2
this p. again refused to take		27: 3
together this p. of the Lord,		27: 5
Get this p. out of this land,		27:12
are this p. in this generation,		27:12
they gathered together all their p.,		27:14
yea, all the p. of the Lord,		27:14
desiring the voice of the p.		27:21
were the p. of Anti-Nephi-Lehi.		27:21
the voice of the p. came, saying:		27:22
to the p. of Anti-Nephi-Lehi,		27:25
the Nephites the p. of Ammon;		27:26
they were among the p. of Nephi,		27:27
p. who were of the church of God.		27:27
were a zealous and beloved p.,		27:30
a highly favored p. of the Lord.		27:30
that after the p. of Ammon were		28: 1
had been known among all the p.		28: 2
slaughter among the p. of Nephi;		28: 3
the p. of Nephi returned again		28: 3
among all the p. of Nephi—		28: 4
the judges over the p. of Nephi;		28: 7
cry repentance unto every p.!		29: 1
to preach the word unto this p.,		29:13
after the p. of Ammon were		30: 1
were buried by the p. of the land—		30: 1
the judges over the p. of Nephi)		30: 2
the p. did observe to keep the		30: 3
the p. did have no disturbance		30: 4
the judges over the p. of Nephi.		30: 4
he began to preach unto the p.		30: 6
began to preach unto the p. that		30:12
things among the p. of Ammon		30:19
were once the p. of the Lamanites.		30:19
was a high priest over that p.		30:20
Why do ye teach this p. that		30:22
I do not teach this p. to bind		30:23
Ye say that this p. is a free		30:24
say that this people is a free p.		30:24
Ye say that this p. is a guilty		30:25
is a guilty and a fallen p.,		30:25
thus ye lead away this p. after		30:27
leading away the p. after the silly		30:31
of glutting on the labors of the p.		30:31
upon the labors of this p.;		30:32
the word of God unto my p.		30:32
that we preach unto this p. to		30:35
thou that we deceive this p.,		30:35
away the hearts of this p.,		30:45
not deceive this p. any more.		30:47
Go and reclaim this p., for they		30:53
lead away the hearts of this p.;		30:55
judge to all the p. in the land,		30:57
as he went forth among the p.,		30:59
p. who had separated themselves		30:59
the hearts of the p. to bow down		31: 1
because of the iniquity of the p.		31: 1
to know of iniquity among his p.;		31: 2
tendency to lead the p. to do		31: 5
upon the minds of the p. than		31: 5
we are a chosen and a holy p.,		31:18
after the p. had all offered up		31:23
were a wicked and a perverse p.;		31:24
for we are a chosen p. unto thee,		31:28
iniquity shall be among this p.?		31:30
wickedness among this p. doth		31:30
of the iniquity of this p.		31:31
of the iniquities of this p.		31:33
the word of God unto the p.,		32: 1
success among the poor class of p.;		32: 2
unto the p. upon the hill Onidah,		32: 4
art angry, O Lord, with this p.,		33:16
the p. would not understand his		33:17
that he will come to redeem his p.,		33:22
him the transgressions of his p.,		34: 8

PEOPLE

throughout all the land all the p.,	Al 35: 4	would spare the p. of the city;	Al 47:33
not let the p. know concerning	35: 5	all the p. of the Lamanites,	47:35
privily the minds of all the p.	35: 5	against the p. of Nephi;	48: 1
out the minds of all the p.,	35: 6	all the p. who were in the land,	48: 2
the p. of the Zoramites were	35: 8	of the number of his p.,	48: 4
angry with the p. of Ammon	35: 8	preparing the minds of the p.	48: 7
sent over unto the p. of Ammon	35: 8	which he bestowed upon his p.;	48:12
the p. of Ammon did not fear	35: 9	the welfare and safety of his p.	48:12
anger against the p. of Ammon,	35:10	to defend his p., his rights,	48:13
war against the p. of Ammon,	35:11	doing good, in preserving his p.,	48:16
the judges over the p. of Nephi.	35:12	no less serviceable unto the p.	48:19
the p. of Ammon departed out of	35:13	the p. did humble themselves	48:20
grieved for the iniquity of his p.,	35:15	because of the iniquity of the p.,	49: 3
among all the p. in every city,	35:15	care not for the blood of his p.	49:10
the hearts of the p. began to wax	35:15	would destroy the p. of that city.	49:13
my father prophesy unto the p.	36:17	exceedingly angry with his p.,	49:26
did manifest unto the p. that	36:23	preparing for the safety of his p.	49:27
that ye keep a record of this p.,	37: 2	the p. of Nephi did thank the	49:28
nation, kindred, tongue, and p.,	37: 4	the judges over the p. of Nephi.	49:29
enlarged the memory of this p.,	37: 8	forth to preach among the p.	49:30
those p. who have been destroyed,	37:21	to defend his p. against the	50: 1
be made manifest unto this p.;	37:21	secure their armies and their p.	50:10
be made manifest unto this p.;	37:21	were the p. of Nephi in the	50:17
his p. began to work in darkness,	37:22	the judges over the p. of Nephi.	50:17
discover unto my p. who serve me,	37:23	verified to the p. of Nephi;	50:21
ye shall keep from this p.,	37:27	time among the p. of Nephi,	50:23
this p. might not be destroyed.	37:28	peace among the p. of Nephi	50:25
and their covenants from this p.,	37:29	the p. who possessed the land	50:26
these p. were destroyed on	37:29	the p. of Morianton took up	50:26
not those secret plans unto this p.,	37:32	the p. who possessed the land	50:27
Go unto this p. and declare the	37:47	that when the p. of Morianton,	50:28
among the p. of the Zoramites.	38: 3	that the p. of Lehi had fled to	50:28
work of destruction among his p.;	38: 7	the p. who were in the land	50:32
and teach the word unto this p.	38:15	Morianton and unite with his p.,	50:32
among the p. of the Zoramites.	39: 2	among the p. of Nephi,	50:32
hearts of many p. to destruction;	39:12	to head the p. of Morianton,	50:33
tidings of salvation unto his p.	39:15	did meet the p. of Morianton;	50:35
these glad tidings unto this p.,	39:16	were the p. of Morianton,	50:35
be made known unto this p.	39:18	the judges over the p. of Nephi.	50:35
to preach the word unto this p.	42:31	thus were the p. of Morianton	50:36
did go forth among the p.,	43: 1	between them and the p. of Lehi;	50:36
the p. of the Nephites saw that	43: 4	p. of Nephi had peace restored	50:37
the p. of Anti-Nephi-Lehi,	43:11	judge and governor over the p.,	50:39
were called the p. of Ammon—	43:11	and the freedom of the p.,	50:39
the p. of Ammon did give unto	43:13	over the p. of Nephi.	50:40
his p. were armed with swords,	43:18	judges over the p. of Nephi,	51: 1
saw that the p. of Nephi, or	43:19	between the p. of Lehi and	51: 1
prepared his p. with breastplates	43:19	and the p. of Morianton	51: 1
upon the weaker part of the p.	43:24	be a contention among the p.	51: 2
all the p. in that quarter of	43:26	a part of the p. who desired	51: 2
shall have power over this p.;	44: 7	was settled by the voice of the p.	51: 7
he commanded his p. that they	44:17	the voice of the p. came in favor	51: 7
and also his p. with them,	44:19	also many of the p. of liberty,	51: 7
should cease again among the p.	44:20	power and authority over the p.	51: 8
the judges over the p. of Nephi	44:24	to be among the p. of Nephi;	51: 9
account of the p. of Nephi,	45:hd	hearts of the p. of the Lamanites	51: 9
p. of Nephi were exceedingly	45: 1	against the p. of the Nephites,	51: 9
judges over the p. of Nephi,	45: 2	and also with the p. of liberty,	51:13
I perceive that this very p.,	45:10	of the stubborness of those p.	51:14
the p. of Nephi shall become	45:11	with the voice of the p.,	51:15
among the p. of Nephi,	45:13	and dissensions among the p.;	51:16
among the p. of Nephi.	45:13	according to the voice of the p.	51:16
nation, kindred, tongue, and p.,	45:16	and the pride of those p. who	51:21
judges over the p. of Nephi,	45:20	contentions among his own p.,	51:22
went forth among the p. to	45:20	also the p. of the city of Lehi	51:24
which had been among the p.,	45:21	had headed his p. in his flight.	51:29
possessed by the p. of Nephi.	45:22	the judges over the p. of Nephi;	51:37
those p. who were wroth with	46: 4	the judges over the p. of Nephi,	52: 1
make them rulers over the p.	46: 5	appointed king over the p.;	52: 3
the affairs of the p. of Nephi	46: 7	that his p. should maintain	52: 4
led away the hearts of many p.	46:10	the judges over the p. of Nephi.	52:14
he went forth among the p.,	46:19	the judges over the p. of Nephi.	52:18
the p. came running together	46:21	beloved by all the p. of Nephi.	53: 2
all the p. who were desirous to	46:28	concerning the p. of Ammon,	53:10
the p. of Moroni were more	46:29	support of the p. in the borders	53:22
his p. were doubtful concerning	46:29	the judges over the p. of Nephi.	53:23
took those of his p. who would	46:29	for the support of his own p.;	54: 2
to cut off the p. of Amalickiah,	46:30	he also desired his own p. for	54: 2
judges and the voice of the p.,	46:34	ye have waged against my p.,	54: 5
anger against the p. of Nephi,	47: 1	fought against the p. of the Lord,	54: 8
all his land, among all his p.,	47: 1	in my anger, and also my p.;	54:13
and joined the p. of Ammon.	47:29	leader of the p. of the Nephites.	54:14
gained the hearts of the p.	47:30	that my p. shall lay down their	54:18

PEOPLE

against me and my p.;	Al	54:19	no contention among the p.	He 3: 2
a war against the p. of Nephi.		55: 1	the p. who had before inhabited	3: 6
the Lamanites do guard my p.		55: 3	the p. who went forth became	3: 7
delighted in the saving of his p.		55:19	the p. who were in the land	3: 9
the judges over the p. of Nephi.		55:35	the p. in the land northward	3:11
stating the affairs of the p. in		56: 1	were many of the p. of Ammon,	3:12
the p. of that part of the land.		56: 9	kept of the proceedings of this p.,	3:13
not be surrounded by our p.		56:37	this people, by many of this p.,	3:13
when the p. of Antipus saw that		56:53	part of the proceedings of this p.,	3:14
we, the p. of Nephi, the people		56:54	among the p. of Nephi.	3:17
the p. of Antipus, and I with my		56:54	among the p. of the Nephites,	3:22
the p. of Antiparah did leave		57: 4	the judges over the p. of Nephi.	3:22
than sufficient for our own p.,		57:15	were poured out upon the p.,	3:25
yea, and will destroy our p.		57:31	but into the hearts of the p. who	3:33
concerning the affairs of our p.		58: 4	p. to suffer great persecutions,	3:34
for the support of our p.		58:10	gotten into the hearts of the p.;	3:36
sons of the p. of Ammon,		58:39	also a contention among the p.,	4: 1
yea, and may he favor this p.,		58:41	preach many things unto the p.	4:14
the judges over the p. of Nephi,		59: 1	preach many things unto the p.	4:14
make it known unto all his p.,		59: 2	they had been a stiffnecked p.,	4:21
the p. of Nephihah, who were		59: 5	him to give unto the p.;	4:22
against the p. of Nephihah,		59: 7	they had become a wicked p.,	4:22
remainder of the p. of Nephihah		59: 8	established by the voice of the p.,	5: 2
to the assistance of the p. to		59: 9	they were a stiffnecked p.,	5: 3
of the wickedness of the p.,		59:11	declare unto the p. these words.	5: 6
of the wickedness of the p.,		59:12	king Benjamin spake unto his p.;	5: 9
who have been chosen by this p.		60: 1	should come to redeem his p.,	5:10
the slaughter among our p.;		60: 5	among all the p. of Nephi,	5:14
had for the welfare of this p.;		60: 9	forth among all the p. of Nephi	5:16
and the freedom of this p.;		60:10	and did minister unto the p.,	5:50
of God will come upon this p.,		60:14	more part of them, a righteous p.,	6: 1
murdering our p. with the sword,		60:17	the p. of the church did have	6: 3
impede the progress of this p.		60:30	unto the p. of the Nephites	6: 4
to destroy his righteous p.		60:31	northward, to preach unto the p.	6: 6
those of my p. who are freemen,		61: 3	appointed by the p. in his stead,	6:15
led away the hearts of many p.,		61: 4	the p. began to grow exceedingly	6:16
be placed king over this p.		61: 8	down the p. unto destruction.	6:25
and the liberty of my p.		61: 9	put it into the hearts of the p.	6:28
the judges over the p. of Nephi;		62:11	same being who led on the p.	6:28
Zarahemla, among their own p.,		62:11	until he dragged the p. down to	6:28
the judges over the p. of Nephi,		62:12	the judges over the p. of Nephi.	6:32
dwell with the p. of Ammon,		62:17	the judges over the p. of Nephi.	6:41
to join the p. of Ammon		62:27	God threatens the p. of Nephi	7:hd
of Ammon and become a free p.		62:27	God smiteth the p. of Nephi	7:hd
did join the p. of Ammon,		62:29	over the p. of the Nephites,	7: 1
the judges over the p. of Nephi;		62:39	had been forth among the p.,	7: 2
iniquity among the p. of Nephi;		62:40	the p. in a state of such awful	7: 4
among the p. of Nephi.		62:42	were his p. easy to be entreated,	7: 7
him again to preach unto the p.		62:44	told the p. what they had seen,	7:11
unto the convincing of many p.		62:45	p. came together in multitudes	7:11
the p. of Nephi began to prosper		62:48	for the wickedness of the p.	7:11
the judges over the p. of Nephi.		62:52	he beheld the multitudes of p.	7:12
the judges over the p. of Nephi.		63: 1	against him, saying unto the p.:	8: 1
many more p. did enter into it;		63: 7	revile against this p. and against	8: 2
many p. who went forth into		63: 9	for they feared the p. lest they	8: 4
the p. who had gone forth into		63:10	Therefore they did cry unto the p.,	8: 5
against the p. of Moronihah,		63:15	he doth condemn all this p.,	8: 5
the judges over the p. of Nephi.		63:16	did stir up the p. to anger	8: 7
the judges over the p. of Nephi,	He	1: 1	those p. who sought to destroy	8:10
among the p. of the Nephites.		1: 1	it should be shown unto the p.,	8:18
did also cause the p. to contend:		1: 3	spoken should come upon the p.;	9: 5
cause three divisions among the p.		1: 4	servants ran and told the p.,	9: 6
appointed by the voice of the p.		1: 5	people did gather themselves together	9: 7
governor over the p. of Nephi.		1: 5	the p. knew nothing concerning	9: 8
did unite with the voice of the p.		1: 6	the p. did assemble themselves	9:10
Paanchi, and that part of the p.		1: 7	that they inquired among the p.,	9:12
about to flatter away those p.		1: 7	expound the matter unto the p.,	9:16
according to the voice of the p.,		1: 8	blind, and ye stiffnecked p.,	9:21
to destroy the liberty of the p.		1: 8	so much evil concerning this p.,	9:27
those p. who were desirous that		1: 9	there were some among the p.,	9:40
not known among the p. of Nephi,		1:12	arose a division among the p.,	10: 1
mingle themselves among the p.,		1:12	of the wickedness of the p.	10: 3
according to the voice of the p.,		1:13	have given unto thee, unto this p.	10: 4
judge and a governor over the p.,		1:13	ye shall have power over this p.	10: 6
slaying the p. with a great		1:27	to the wickedness of this p.	10: 6
contention again among the p.		2: 1	ye have power among this p.	10: 7
by the voice of the p.		2: 2	say that God shall smite this p.,	10:10
and authority among the p.;		2: 5	go and declare unto this p.,	10:11
the judges over the p. of Nephi.		2:12	sent it forth among all the p.	10:17
destruction of the p. of Nephi.		2:13	the judges over the p. of Nephi.	10:19
contention among the p. of Nephi		3: 1	land among all the p. of Nephi.	11: 1
little dissensions among the p.,		3: 1	that this p. shall be destroyed	11: 4

PEOPLE

land, among all the p. of Nephi.	He 11: 5	
the p. saw that they were about	11: 7	
And the p. began to plead with	11: 8	
the p. had repented and did	11: 9	
Lord, behold this p. repenteth;	11:10	
If this p. repent I will spare	11:14	
turn away his anger from the p.,	11:17	
the p. did rejoice and glorify God,	11:18	
the p. of Nephi began to prosper	11:20	
and the more part of the p.,	11:21	
they did preach unto the p.,	11:23	
the judges over the p. of Nephi,	11:24	
dissenters from the p. of Nephi,	11:24	
among the p. of Nephi,	11:27	
among the p. of the Lamanites.	11:27	
the judges over the p. of Nephi.	11:29	
great fear to come unto the p.	11:32	
evil, which came unto the p.	11:34	
when he doth prosper his p.,	12: 2	
welfare and happiness of his p.;	12: 2	
the Lord doth chasten his p. with	12: 3	
and began to preach unto the p.	13: 2	
repentance unto the p.,	13: 2	
again, and prophesy unto the p.	13: 3	
and prophesied unto the p.	13: 4	
into my heart to say unto this p.	13: 5	
of justice hangeth over this p.;	13: 5	
of justice falleth upon this p.	13: 5	
destruction awaiteth this p.,	13: 6	
it surely cometh unto this p.,	13: 6	
nothing can save this p. save	13: 6	
and shall be slain for his p.	13: 6	
hearts of the p. of the Nephites,	13: 8	
Behold ye, the p. of this great	13:21	
Yea, wo unto this p., because of	13:24	
hardened and ye stiffnecked p.,	13:29	
O ye p. of the land, that ye	13:39	
Cry unto this p., repent and	14: 9	
wo unto this p. who are called	15: 3	
who are called the p. of Nephi	15: 3	
have been a chosen p. of the Lord;	15: 3	
the p. of Nephi hath he loved,	15: 3	
the p. of the Nephites;	15:17	
crying repentance unto the p.,	16: 4	
working miracles among the p.,	16: 4	
to prophesy among his own p.	16: 7	
thus were the affairs of the p.	16: 8	
the judges over the p. of Nephi.	16: 9	
more part of the p. remaining	16:10	
alteration in the affairs of the p.,	16:12	
the p. began to be more hardened	16:12	
great signs given unto the p.,	16:13	
p. began to harden their hearts,	16:15	
more things did the p. imagine	16:22	
harden the hearts of the p.	16:22	
wrought among the p. of the Lord,	16:23	
hold upon the hearts of the p.	16:23	
the judges over the p. of Nephi.	16:24	
stead, yea, the record of this p.	3Ne 1: 3	
miracles wrought among the p.	1: 4	
the p. who believed began to be	1: 7	
saw this wickedness of his p.,	1:10	
to his God in behalf of his p.,	1:11	
the p. began to be astonished	1:15	
all the p. upon the face of the	1:17	
lyings sent forth among the p.,	1:22	
part of the p. did believe,	1:22	
Nephi went forth among the p.,	1:23	
the p. began again to have peace	1:23	
bringing glad tidings unto the p.	1:26	
the p. could not overpower	1:27	
do much slaughter among the p.	1:27	
p. began to forget those signs	2: 1	
deceive the hearts of the p.;	2: 2	
possession of the hearts of the p.	2: 2	
the p. began to wax strong in	2: 3	
leading away the hearts of the p.,	2: 3	
over the p. of the Nephites.	2: 5	
p. did still remain in wickedness,	2:10	
and did slay so many of the p.,	2:11	
expedient that all the p.,	2:11	
robbers and the p. of Nephi	2:17	
the p. of Nephi did gain some	2:17	
forth against the p. of Nephi;	3Ne 2:18	
wickedness of the p. of Nephi,	2:18	
thus were the p. in a state of	2:19	
also the firmness of your p.,	3: 2	
would yield up unto this my p.,	3: 6	
my p. may recover their rights	3:10	
also of threatening the p.	3:11	
his p. should cry unto the Lord	3:12	
proclamation among all the p.,	3:13	
fear to come upon all the p.;	3:16	
the p. said unto Gidgiddoni:	3:20	
a great many thousand p. who	3:24	
among all the p. of Lehi since	4:11	
round about the p. of Nephi;	4:16	
should cut off the p. of Nephi	4:16	
desire of the p. of Zemnarihah	4:22	
did give command unto his p.	4:23	
May the Lord preserve his p. in	4:29	
protect this p. in righteousness,	4:30	
among all the p. of the Nephites	5: 1	
was done among so many p.	5: 8	
all the proceedings of this p.;	5: 9	
the church among the p.,	5:12	
declare his word among his p.,	5:13	
given me and my p. so much	5:20	
the p. of the Nephites did all	6: 1	
hinder the p. from prospering	6: 5	
and the p. had continual peace.	6: 9	
some disputings among the p.;	6:10	
p. began to be distinguished by	6:12	
cause of this iniquity of the p.	6:15	
the stirring up of the p. to do	6:15	
lead away the hearts of the p.	6:16	
p. having been delivered up	6:17	
and did govern the p. that year.	6:19	
among the p. in all the land,	6:20	
the sins and iniquities of the p.,	6:20	
the Lord would make for his p.,	6:20	
the p. who were exceeding angry	6:21	
which had been given by the p.	6:26	
against the p. of the Lord,	6:29	
the p. were divided one against	7: 2	
iniquity had come upon the p.	7: 5	
more righteous part of the p.	7: 7	
more part of the p. had turned	7: 8	
so great iniquity upon the p.,	7: 9	
number as the tribes of the p.,	7:11	
they were not a righteous p.,	7:11	
he commanded his p. that they	7:12	
with the tribes of the p.;	7:12	
forth out of the reach of the p.	7:13	
the affairs of the p. of Nephi.	7:13	
and suffered death by the p.	7:19	
the p. saw it, and did witness	7:20	
miracles, in the sight of the p.	7:20	
signify unto the p. that they	7:21	
manifest unto the p. that they	7:22	
some miracles among the p.	7:22	
And Nephi did cry unto the p.	7:23	
before God, and unto the p.,	7:25	
the p. began to look with great	8: 3	
and disputations among the p.,	8: 4	
and weeping among all the p.	8:23	
were the groanings of the p.,	8:23	
thus were the howlings of the p.	8:25	
Wo, wo, wo unto this p.;	9: 2	
sons and daughters of my p.;	9: 2	
inhabited by the p. of king Jacob,	9: 9	
did destroy the peace of my p.	9: 9	
upon this land, and upon this p.,	9:12	
all the p. of the land did hear	10: 1	
the astonishment of the p.	10: 2	
came a voice again unto the p.	10: 3	
and all the p. did hear,	10: 3	
O ye p. of these great cities	10: 4	
O ye p. of the house of Israel,	10: 5	
O ye p. of the house of Israwl,	10: 5	
the p. had heard these words,	10: 8	
of the p. who were spared alive	10:10	
more righteous part of the p.	10:12	
p. of Nephi who were spared,	10:18	
himself unto the p. of Nephi,	11:hd
together, of the p. of Nephi,	11: 1	

PEOPLE

his hand and spake unto the p.,	3Ne 11: 9
that ye shall baptize this p.	11:21
Therefore, go forth unto this p.,	11:41
you to be the light of this p.	12:14
light so shine before this p.,	12:16
chosen to minister unto this p.	13:25
covenanted with my p. Israel;	15: 5
which I have made with my p.	15: 8
and ye are a light unto this p.,	15:12
so be that my p. at Jerusalem,	16: 4
all the p. of the house of Israel.	16: 5
scattered my p. who are of	16: 8
my p. who are of the house of	16: 8
of the Father upon my p. who	16: 9
p. who are of the house of Israel	16: 9
all the p. of the whole earth,	16:10
which I have made unto my p.,	16:11
be numbered among my p.,	16:13
And I will not suffer my p.,	16:14
suffer my p., O house of Israel,	16:15
trodden under foot of my p.,	16:15
give unto this p. this land for	16:16
the Lord hath comforted his p.,	16:19
of the wickedness of the p. of	17:14
it unto the p. of my church,	18: 5
among my p. who do repent	18:16
not be numbered among my p.,	18:31
that he may not destroy my p.,	18:31
was noised abroad among the p.	19: 2
did they send forth unto the p.	19: 3
arose and ministered unto the p.	19: 7
commanded me concerning this p.,	20:10
Father hath made unto his p.,	20:12
they have scattered my p.—	20:15
I will gather my p. together	20:18
because of the iniquity of the p.	20:19
I will make my p. with whom	20:19
shalt beat in pieces many p.;	20:21
that I will establish my p.,	20:22
this p. will I establish in this	20:22
shall be cut off from among this p.;	20:23
be cut off from among the p.	20:27
unto the scattering of my p.,	20:28
scourge unto the p. of this land.	20:29
which I have made with my p.;	20:34
Father hath comforted his p.,	20:39
my p. shall know my name;	20:46
hath covenanted with his p.	20:46
be inhabited again with my p.,	21: 1
from their long dispersion, my p.,	21: 2
may know concerning this p.	21: 2
concerning this my p. who shall	21: 4
and be set up as a free p. by	21: 4
hath covenanted with his p.,	21: 6
be numbered among my p.,	21: 7
which he hath made unto the p.	21:11
be cut off from among my p.	21:12
p. who are a remnant of Jacob	21:20
will I cut off from among my p.,	21:23
And they shall assist my p.,	21:24
then shall they assist my p.	21:26
among the remnant of this p.	21:26
among all the dispersed of my p.,	21:27
among all the dispersed of my p.,	21:28
his p. may be gathered home	22:10
shall the covenant of my p. be	23: 2
all things concerning my p.	23: 9
he should testify unto this p.,	26: 4
when all p., and all kindreds,	26: 6
did truly teach unto the p.;	26: 7
things which he taught the p.	26: 8
things which he taught the p.;	26: 8
be brought again unto this p.,	26:11
I will try the faith of my p.	26:13
the Lord truly did teach the p.,	26:14
he had revealed unto the p.;	27: 3
are disputations among the p.	27: 4
that the p. should murmur and	27:24
Write the works of this p.,	27:25
written, shall this p. be judged,	27:27
ye shall be judges of this p.,	28:18
and did minister unto all the p.,	28:23
among all the p. of Nephi,	28:23
all p. upon the face of the land;	

the p. of that generation were	3Ne 28:23
kindreds, tongues and p.,	28:29
all p. must surely stand before	28:31
his p. of the house of Israel.	29: 3
numbered with my p. who are	30: 2
An account of the p. of Nephi,	4Ne 1:hd
the p. were all converted unto	1: 2
the p. of Nephi did wax strong,	1:10
fair and delightsome p.	1:10
no contention among all the p.,	1:13
dwell in the hearts of the p.	1:15
there could not be a happier p.	1:16
among all the p. who had been	1:16
a small part of the p. who had	1:20
that the p. had multiplied,	1:23
the p. did harden their hearts,	1:31
the p. did harden their hearts,	1:34
smite upon the p. of Jesus;	1:34
the p. of Jesus did not smite	1:34
a great division among the p.	1:35
arose a p. who were called the	1:36
thus were the affairs of the p.	1:40
the more wicked part of the p.	1:40
than were the p. of God.	1:40
the wicked part of the p. began	1:42
the p. who were called the	1:43
who were called the p. of Nephi	1:43
both the p. of Nephi and the	1:45
p. did still remain in wickedness)	1:47
manner of the learning of my p.)	Mrm 1: 2
observed concerning this p.;	1: 3
engravings concerning this p.	1: 3
observed concerning this p.	1: 4
and the p. were as numerous	1: 7
because of the iniquity of the p.	1:13
endeavor to preach unto this p.,	1:16
the p. of Nephi appointed me	2: 1
that we did gather in our p.	2: 7
which hung over my p.,	2: 8
especially among the p. of Nephi.	2:11
again become a righteous p.	2:12
the p. of Nephi again were	2:20
we did gather in our p. as much	2:21
that I did speak unto my p.,	2:23
the great calamity of my p.,	2:27
I had employed my p.,	3: 1
Cry unto this p.—Repent ye,	3: 2
And I did cry unto this p.,	3: 3
I did cause my p. that they	3: 5
my p., the Nephites, had done,	3: 9
and a leader of this p.,	3:11
because this p. repented not	3:15
also unto the remnant of this p.,	3:19
the covenant p. of the Lord,	3:21
carnage which was among the p.,	4:11
the Lord, as was among this p.	4:12
tread the p. of the Nephites	5: 6
come unto the remnant of these p.,	5: 9
hath said should scatter this p.,	5: 9
this p. should be counted as	5: 9
of the wickedness of this p.	5: 9
for the destruction of this p.;	5:11
that this p. had not repented	5:11
seed of this p. may more fully	5:15
for this p. shall be scattered,	5:15
dark, a filthy, and a loathsome p.,	5:15
were once a delightsome p.,	5:17
destruction of my p., the Nephites.	6: 1
gather together our p. unto the	6: 2
all the remainder of our p. unto	6: 5
gathered in all our p. in one	6: 6
to be the last struggle of my p.,	6: 6
my p., with their wives and	6: 7
fall upon my p. with the sword,	6: 9
hewn down all my p. save	6:11
survived the dead of our p.,	6:11
my p. who were hewn down,	6:11
my p. who were led by my son	6:12
even all my p., save it were	6:15
because of the slain of my p.,	6:16
unto the remnant of this p.	7: 1
numbered among the p. of the	7:10
tale of the destruction of my p.	8: 3

PEOPLE

Lamanites have hunted my p.,	Mrm 8: 7
is the destruction of my p.,	8: 7
wickedness of the p. was so great	8:10
them to remain with the p.;	8:10
of speaking concerning this p.	8:13
covenant p. of the Lord.	8:15
unto the knowledge of the p.;	8:16
the covenant p. of the Lord who	8:21
and perverse and stiffnecked p.,	8:33
other p. knoweth our language;	9:34
were found by the p. of Limhi,	1: 2
the language of the p.,	1:33
the p. were scattered.	1:33
preserved for a righteous p.	2: 7
prepared the vessels for my p.,	2:22
thine anger from this thy p.,	3: 3
of the world to redeem my p.	3:14
appear unto my p. in the flesh.	3:16
should show himself unto his p.	4: 1
had showed himself unto his p.	4: 2
in the eyes of all the p.	4:16
Let us gather together our p.	6:19
the p. were gathered together.	6:20
that they did number their p.;	6:21
the p. desired of them that	6:22
the p. would that his father	6:25
anointed to be king over the p.	6:27
and the p. began to prosper;	6:28
taught his p. how great things	6:30
drew away many p. after him.	7: 4
his p. under Corihor his son,	7: 7
the p. had become exceeding	7:11
brethren and many of the p.	7:15
the p. who were under the reign	7:19
that his p. should give battle	7:21
came prophets among the p.,	7:23
wickedness and idolatry of the p.	7:23
the p. did revile against the	7:24
by this cause the p. were brought	7:25
because the p. did repent of	7:26
that he did flatter many p.,	8: 2
these oaths unto the p.,	8:16
that they are had among all p.,	8:20
caused the destruction of this p.	8:21
destruction of the p. of Nephi.	8:21
the destruction of all p.	8:25
was anointed king over the p.,	9: 4
giving audience to his p.	9: 5
the hearts of all the p.;	9: 6
they won the hearts of the p.,	9:10
the p. of Akish were desirous	9:11
more part of the p. after them.	9:11
all the p. of the kingdom,	9:12
that which was good unto his p.	9:23
the p. had spread again over all	9:26
the p. believed not the words of	9:29
land, and did poison many p.	9:31
that the p. could not pass,	9:33
the p. did follow the course of	9:34
when the p. saw that they must	9:34
the p. began to revive again,	9:35
to build up again a broken p.	10: 1
the p. began again to spread	10: 4
afflict the p. with his whoredoms	10: 7
the p. did rise up in rebellion	10: 8
and gave battle unto the p.;	10: 9
he did ease the burden of the p.,	10:10
gain favor in the eyes of the p.	10:10
he did do justice unto the p.,	10:11
the p. became exceeding rich	10:12
the p. did prosper in the land;	10:16
food for the p. of the land,	10:19
could be a p. more blessed	10:28
the destruction of that great p.	11: 1
prophets were rejected by the p.,	11: 2
the p. sought to destroy them.	11: 2
of the destruction of the p.	11: 5
the land, and also upon the p.,	11: 6
the p. began to repent of	11: 8
reign over the p. all his days.	11:10
prophesied again unto the p.;	11:12
the p. hardened their hearts,	Eth 11:13
withdrew from among the p.	11:13
arose a rebellion among the p.,	11:15
cried repentance unto the p.,	11:20
another p. to possess the land,	11:21
began to prophesy unto the p.,	12: 2
exhorting the p. to believe in	12: 3
marvelous things unto the p.,	12: 5
hast made all this p. that they	12:23
the destruction of the p. of	13: 1
which should come upon the p.	13:13
which came upon the p.,	13:14
was cast out from among the p.	13:15
a great war among the p.,	13:15
many p. who were slain by	13:18
his kingdom and spare the p.—	13:20
another p. receiving the land	13:21
his household, neither the p.;	13:22
p. upon the face of the land	13:31
because of the iniquity of the p.,	14: 1
any other man among all the p.	14:10
had taken all the p. with him	14:15
the p. began to flock together	14:19
p. became troubled by day	14:23
the p. began to be frightened,	14:27
Shiz commanded his p. that	14:31
nearly two millions of his p.,	15: 2
that he would spare the p.,	15: 4
the sake of the lives of the p.	15: 4
would spare the lives of the p.	15: 5
the p. repented not of their	15: 6
the p. of Coriantumr were	15: 6
anger against the p. of Shiz;	15: 6
the p. of Shiz were stirred up	15: 6
against the p. of Coriantumr;	15: 6
the p. of Shiz did give battle	15: 6
unto the p. of Coriantumr.	15: 6
fled again before the p. of Shiz.	15: 7
p. upon all the face of the land,	15:12
behold all the doings of the p.;	15:13
the p. who were for Coriantumr	15:13
the p. who were for Shiz were	15:13
gathering together the p.,	15:14
the loss of the slain of their p.;	15:16
the loss of the slain of their p.	15:17
and spare the lives of the p.	15:18
power over the hearts of the p.;	15:19
of the p. of Coriantumr,	15:23
and nine of the p. of Shiz.	15:23
and two of the p. of Shiz,	15:25
of the p. of Coriantumr.	15:25
the p. of Limhi did find them.	15:33
the account of the p. of Jared,	Mro 1: 1
the p. of the church of Christ;	6: 4
numbered among the p. of Christ.	6: 7
did he speak unto the p.,	7: 1
among the p. of his church.	7:39
or the p. of the Nephites,	8:27
Lamanites shall destroy this p.;	9: 3
the sufferings of this p.	9: 7
that of our o. in Moriantum.	9: 9
how can a p. like this, that are	9:11
a civil and a delightsome p.)	9:12
how can a p. like this, whose	9:13
Wo unto this p.	9:15
O the depravity of my p.!	9:18
the wickedness of this p.;	9:20
the return of his p. unto him,	9:22
Hearken, O ye p. of My church,	DC 1: 1
Hearken ye p. from afar;	1: 1
of warning shall be unto all p.,	1: 4
fear and tremble, O ye p.,	1: 7
cut off from among the p.;	1:14
of a Savior come unto my p.—	3:16
which he made to his p.;	3:19
as I also told the p. of the	5:20
unto the p. of this generation:	5:25
of the wickedness of the p.;	6:26
nations, kindreds, tongues and p.	7: 3
will harden the hearts of the p.	10:32
to the knowledge of the p.	10:40
should come forth unto this p.	10:46

PEOPLE

nation, kindred, tongue, or p.	DC 10:51	come and reign with my p.	DC 84:119
to the knowledge of my p.	10:52	that he may tithe his p.,	85: 3
I will show unto this p. that	10:60	enrolled with the p. of God.	85: 3
stir up the hearts of the p. to	10:63	a savior unto my p. Israel.	86:11
repentance unto this p.,	15: 6	out to testify and warn the p.,	88:81
repentance unto this p.,	16: 6	and indignation upon the p.	88:88
cry repentance unto this p.	18:14	for fear shall come upon all p.	88:91
crying repentance unto this p.,	18:15	and all p. shall see it together.	88:93
among every p. that thou shalt	19:29	kindreds, tongues, and p.;	88:103
contains a record of a fallen p.,	20: 9	of his trump. saying to all p.,	88:104
Who will gather his p. even as	29: 2	languages, tongues, and p.	90:15
will open the hearts of the p.,	31: 7	before the eyes of the p.	90:23
manifest in the eyes of all p.	35: 7	by the tithing of my p.	97:11
and you shall be a free p.,	38:22	as my p. build a house unto	97:15
unto me a righteous p.,	38:31	report thereof shall vex all p.;	97:23
shall be the richest of all p.,	38:39	that my p. should observe	98: 4
sent forth to recover my p.,	39:11	the wicked rule the p. mourn.	98: 9
as my p. shall assemble	39:15	nation, kindred, tongue, or p.,	98:33
the p. in Ohio call upon me	39:16	or p. should proclaim war	98:34
Hearken and hear, O ye my p.,	41: 1	standard of peace unto that p.,	98:34
that ye may be my p. and I	42: 9	if that p. did not accept the	98:35
That my covenant p. may be	42:36	that nation, tongue, or p.	98:36
do for the salvation of my p.	42:36	is an ensample unto all p.,	98:38
unto the poor of my p. who are	42:39	I have much p. in this p.,	100: 3
nations, kindreds, tongues and p.	42:58	lift up your voices unto this p.;	100: 5
reserve unto myself a pure p.	43:14	a spokesman unto this p.;	100: 9
and my p. shall be redeemed	43:29	up unto myself a pure p.,	100:16
preach repentance unto the p.	44: 3	indignation in behalf of my p.;	101:10
enemy seeketh to destroy my p.	44: 5	I must gather together my p.,	101:65
O ye p. of my church,	45: 1	and constitution of the p.,	101:77
O ye p. of my church,	45: 6	have appointed unto my p.,	101:96
to be a standard for my p.,	45: 9	against me, and against my p.,	101:98
this p. shall be destroyed	45:19	that my p. should claim,	101:99
the only p. that shall not be	45:69	which my p. shall realize,	103: 5
this work in the eyes of the p.,	45:72	raise up unto my p. a man,	103:16
O ye p. of my church;	46: 1	preside in the midst of my p.,	103:35
that ye go among this p.,	49:11	prepare my p. for the time	104:59
how to organize this p.	51: 1	redemption of mine afflicted p.—	105: 1
unto this p. their portions,	51: 3	for the transgressions of my p.,	105: 2
that which belongs to this p.	51: 7	And my p. must needs be	105: 6
be appointed unto this p.	51: 7	are appointed to lead my p.,	105: 7
which is left unto this p.—	51: 8	the transgressions of my p.,	105: 9
appointed unto this p.,	51: 8	that my p. may be taught	105:10
to the wants of this p.	51: 8	for the redemption of my p.,	105:16
and be alike among this p.,	51: 9	let all my p. who dwell in	105:23
which belongeth to this p.	51:10	with the feelings of the p.;	105:24
for the wants of this p.,	51:13	you are saying unto the p.:	105:25
I grant unto this p. a privilege	51:15	find favor in the eyes of the p.,	105:26
consecrate unto my p.,	52: 2	soften the hearts of the p.,	105:27
O ye p. who profess my	56: 1	the p. that have smitten you,	105:38
the stiffneckedness of my p.	56: 6	smitten you, but also to all p.;	105:38
saith the Lord unto my p.—	56:14	up his voice and warn the p.,	106: 2
send goods also unto the p.,	57: 9	to manifest himself to his p.	109: 5
judge his p. by the testimony	58:18	we ask thee to assist us, thy p.,	109:10
shall push the p. together	58:45	thou hast made unto us, thy p.,	109:11
unto God against that p.,	61:31	glory may rest down upon thy p.,	109:12
a p. who are well nigh	61:31	that all p. who shall enter upon	109:13
Hearken, O ye p., and open	63: 1	That all the incomings of thy p.,	109:17
yourselves the p. of the Lord,	63: 1	And when thy p. transgress,	109:21
them in the eyes of the p.,	63:15	establish the p. that shall worship,	109:24
day for the tithing of my p.,	64:23	rise up and prevail over thy p.	109:26
be an ensign unto the p.,	64:42	if any p. shall rise against this	109:27
wonderful works among the p.	65: 4	people shall rise against this p.,	109:27
in every place, unto every p.,	66: 7	smite this p. thou wilt smite them;	109:28
reasoning with the p.	66: 7	thou wilt fight for thy p.	109:28
and push many p. to Zion	66:11	lyings and slanders against thy p.	109:30
living God, from p. to people,	68: 1	Jehovah, have mercy upon this p.,	109:34
people to p., and from	68: 1	the transgressions of thy p.,	109:34
before the judge of my p.	68:33	be poured out upon thy p.,	109:36
and all ye p. of my church	70: 1	that thy p. may not faint	109:38
great contention among the p.	74: 3	the p. of that city receive	109:39
reign on the earth over his p.	76:63	the p. of that city receive not	109:41
nation, kindred, tongue, and p.;	77: 8	deliver thy p. from the calamity	109:46
nation, kindred, tongue, and p.,	77:11	wilt thou suffer this p. to bear	109:49
be an organization of my p.,	78: 3	mob, who have driven thy p.,	109:50
for the poor of my p.,	78: 3	didst appoint a Zion unto thy p.	109:51
for the restoration of his p.,	84: 2	cause of thy p. may not fail	109:52
diligently to sanctify his p.	84:23	great ones of the earth, and all p.,	109:55
Lord before the face of his p.,	84:28	p. may obtain favor in the sight	109:56
Lord hath redeemed his p.,	84:99	gathering of thy p. may roll on	109:59
Lord hath redeemed his p.;	84:100	let the hearts of all my p. rejoice,	110: 6
stands in the midst of his p.	84:101	manifest myself to my p. in mercy	110: 7
warn the p. of those cities	84:114	p. will keep my commandments,	110: 8

PEOPLE — PERFECT

upon the heads of my p.	DC 110:10
and many p. in this city	111: 2
nations, kindreds, tongues, and p.,	112: 1
gross darkness the minds of the p.,	112:23
gathering of my p. in the last days.	113: 6
what p. had Isaiah reference to?	113: 7
unto all the elders and p. of	115: 3
let my p. labor diligently to build	115:10
if my p. build it not according	115:15
if my p. do build it according	115:16
accept it at the hands of my p.	115:16
will sanctify him before the p.;	115:19
shall come to visit his p.,	116: 1
hither unto the land of my p.,	117: 9
preside in the midst of my p.	117:10
with the blessings of my p.	117:10
and be a bishop unto my p.,	117:11
for the benefit of my p.	117:14
the blessings of my p. be on him	117:15
beginning of the tithing of my p.	119: 3
if my p. observe not this law,	119: 6
the wrongs of thy p. and of	121: 2
all those that discomfort my p.,	121:23
p. shall never be turned against	122: 3
by the p. of this State;	123: 1
have been practised upon this p.—	123: 5
shall be the safety of my p.,	124:10
your silver, to the help of my p.,	124:11
to the kings and p.,	124:16
the heads of the poor of my p.,	124:21
p. are always commanded to	124:39
ordinances therein unto my p.;	124:40
if my p. will hearken unto	124:45
I have appointed to lead my p.,	124:45
in the midst of the p.,	124:75
calf for the worship of my p.	124:84
upon the heads of all my p.,	124:92
and remain with my p.,	124:104
and the safety of this p.	127: 1
therefore, as a church and a p.,	128:24
from Hagar sprang many p.,	132:34
O ye p. of my church,	133: 1
prepare ye, O my p.;	133: 4
O ye p. of my church,	133: 4
the voice of the Lord unto all p.:	133: 9
borders of my p. may be enlarged,	133: 9
the cry go forth among all p.:	133:10
voice shall be heard among all p.;	133:21
shall stand in the midst of his p.,	133:25
and kindred, and tongue, and p.	133:37
brought judgment upon all p.;	133:50
be cut off from among the p.	133:63
and upheld by the voice of the p.	134: 3
in the eyes of God and his p.,	135: 3
Let all the p. of the Church	136: 2
ears of the Lord against this p.	136: 8
of the Lord concerning his p.	136: 9
to remove this p. to the p.ace	136:10
last days, to save my p. Israel.	136:22
My p. must be tried in all things,	136:31
hearken, O ye p. of my church;	136:41
shalt deliver my p. from bondage,	Mses 1:26
the residue of the p. of God	6:17
in the land, among the p.;	6:26
prophesy unto this p., and say unto	6:27
I am angry with this p., and my	6:27
but a lad, and all the p. hate me;	6:31
Say unto this p.: Choose ye	6:33
the Lord raised up unto his p.	6:36
forth in the land, among the p.,	6:37
the p. trembled, and could not	6:47
the saying abroad among the p.,	6:54
prophesy, saying unto the p.,	7: 2
great p. which dwelt in tents,	7: 5
which were the p. of Shum.	7: 5
and I beheld the p. of Canaan,	7: 6
Behold the p. of Canaan,	7: 7
array against the p. of Shum,	7: 7
and the p. of Canaan shall divide	7: 7
none other p. shall dwell there,	7: 7
dwell there but the p. of Canaan;	7: 7
they were despised among all p.	7: 8
Go to this p., and say unto	7:10
continued to call upon all the p.,	Mses 7:12
save it were the p. of Canaan,	7:12
Enoch, that he led the p. of God,	7:13
the enemies of the p. of God,	7:14
all p. that fought against God;	7:15
Lord came and dwelt with his p.,	7:16
the Lord, which was upon his p.	7:17
the Lord called his p. ZION,	7:18
righteousness unto the p. of God.	7:19
residue of the p. have I cursed.	7:20
also beheld the residue of the p.	7:22
upon the residue of the p.,	7:28
but my p. will I preserve;	7:61
my p. may gird up their loins,	7:62
and all his p. walked with God,	7:69
his preaching unto the p., saying:	8:23
judged his p. wisely and justly	Abr 1:26
be cut off from among the p.;	JS 1:55
and division amongst the p.,	2: 5
make the p. think they were	2: 9
evil spoken of among all p.	2:33
be cut off from among the p.,"	2:40
certifying to the p. of Palmyra	2:64

PEOPLED
a land which had been p. with	Mos 8: 8
find a land which had been p.;	21:26
yea, a land which had been p. and	21:26
been p. and been destroyed,	Al 22:30

PEOPLE'S
because of the p. sake who are	He 13:17

PERADVENTURE
lest p. they should fall into	Al 37:27
that p. you may obtain three	DC 103:32
p. ye may obtain one hundred.	103:33
p. my servant Baurak Ale	103:35

PERCEIVE
I p. that ye ponder still	2Ne 32: 8
for I p. by the workings of	Jac 4.15
Yea, and I p. that it cuts you to	Mos 13: 7
for I p. that they are not	13:11
I p. that ye have studied and	13:11
I p. that ye are in the paths of	Al 7:19
I p. that ye are in the path	7:19
I p. that ye are making his paths	7:19
I p. that it has been made known	7:20
I p. that thy mind is worried	40: 1
And I p. that thy mind has been	41: 1
I p. there is somewhat more	42: 1
I p. this very people,	45:10
for I p., saith the Lord, that	He 13:12
I p. that ye are weak,	3Ne 17: 2
For I p. that ye desire that	17: 8
I p. that thou art a sober child,	Mrm 1: 2
for they p. not the light,	DC 45:29

PERCEIVED
see ye indeed, but they p. not.	2Ne 16: 9
he p. their thoughts, and he said	Al 10:17
he p. the thoughts of the king.	18:16
he p. that there were some	3Ne 15: 2
heard nor p. by the ear,	DC 133:45

PERCEIVING
Moroni, p. their intent, sent forth	Al 43:48

PERDITION
by him even as was the son of p.;	3Ne 27:32
become like unto the son of p.,	29: 7
And was called P., for the	DC 76:26
they who are the sons of p.,	76:32
except those sons of p. who	76:43
of his lies; thou shalt be called P.;	Mses 5:24

PERFECT
having a p. knowledge like unto	2Ne 9:13
that our knowledge shall be p.	9:13
a p. knowledge of all our guilt,	9:14
p. knowledge of their enjoyment,	9:14
having p. faith in the Holy One	9:23
having a p. brightness of hope,	31:20

PERFECT

attain to a p. knowledge of him,	Jac 4:12
a p. knowledge of the language	7: 4
yea, a p. remembrance of all	Al 5:18
be reunited again in its p. form;	11:43
shall be restored to its p. frame,	11:44
is not to have a p. knowledge	32:21
that it was not a p. knowledge—	32:26
than faith is a p. knowledge.	32:26
not grown up to a p. knowledge.	32:29
behold, is your knowledge p.?	32:34
your knowledge is p. in that thing,	32:34
this light is your knowledge p.?	32:35
to their proper and p. frame.	40:23
that God might be a p., just God,	42:15
a man of a p. understanding;	48:11
with p. uprightness before God.	50:37
had a p. knowledge of his fraud;	55: 1
was a still voice of p. mildness,	He 5:30
I would that ye should be p.	3Ne 12:48
Father who is in heaven is p.	12:48
man to write a p. description of	Mrm 4:11
this p. knowledge of God,	Eth 3:20
may know with a p. knowledge,	Mro 7:15
a p. knowledge it is of God.	7:16
p. knowledge it is of the devil;	7:17
for p. love casteth out all fear.	8:16
little children with a p. love;	8:17
filleth with hope and p. love,	8:26
grace ye may be p. in Christ;	10:32
the grace of God ye are p. in Christ,	10:32
the grace of God are p. in Christ,	10:33
and brighter until the p. day.	DC 50:24
that thy fasting may be p.,	59:13
who are just men made p.	76:69
wrought out this p. atonement	76:69
that the system may be kept p.	84:110
Because he (Seth) was a p. man,	107:43
without us cannot be made p.—	128:15
without our dead be made p.	128:15
without them cannot be made p.;	128:18
can they without us be made p.	128:18
they nor we be made p. without	128:18
and complete and p. union,	128:18
the spirits of just men made p.,	129: 3
the spirit of a just man made p.	129: 6
man, and p. in his generation;	Mses 8:27

PERFECTED

unto Christ, and be p. in him,	Mro 10:32
your redemption shall be p.;	DC 45:46
in patience until ye are p.	67:13
and shall have p. his work;	76:106
p. and sanctified by the same.	88:34
may be p. in your ministry	88:84
may be p. in their ministry	90: 8
be p. in the understanding of	97:14

PERFECTING

and the p. of my saints.	DC 124:143

PERFECTION

of their surety at first, unto p.,	Al 32:26

PERFECTLY

and of copper, and are p. sound.	Mos 8:10
were p. honest and upright	Al 27:27
more p. in theory,	DC 88:78
may be taught more p.,	105:10
know more p. concerning	105:10

PERFECTNESS

remember your awful guilt in p.,	2Ne 9:46
is the bond of p. and peace.	DC 88:125

PERFORM

the labor which they had to p.	1Ne 17:41
the Lord of Hosts will p. this.	2Ne 19: 7
ye must not p. any thing unto	32: 9
desire more than to p. the work	Al 29: 6
day for men to p. their labors.	34:32
while they should p. their labors.	53: 1
to p. every word of command	57:21
p. unto the Lord thine oaths;	3Ne 12:33
we have a labor to p. whilst	Mro 9: 6
p. with soberness the work	DC 6:35
p. it according to the words	18:30
p. the duties of his calling,	20:64
p. my work, my strange work,	101:95
he may p. a mission unto me	114: 1
p. them in a house which you	124:37
I will not p. the oath which	124:47
all they have to p. that work,	124:49

PERFORMANCE

consecrate thy p. unto thee,	2Ne 32: 9
that thy p. may be for the welfare	32: 9

PERFORMANCES

keep the p. and ordinances of God	2Ne 25:30
a law of p. and of ordinances,	Mos 13:30
must keep those outward p.	Al 25:15
the foolish ordinances and p.	30:23
observe the p. of the church,	31:10
after the p. and ordinances of	4Ne 1:12
obligations, oaths, vows, p.,	DC 132: 7

PERFORMED

the Lord hath p. his whole work	2Ne 20:12
from the labors which he had p.	Al 8: 1
I have p. in the church,	30:33
wherein there can be no labor p.	34:33
I have p. the work which thou	Eth 2:18
that the marriage was p. in	DC OD
to learn who p. the ceremony;	OD

PERFORMING

to p. your labors on the land,	DC 26: 1
hinder them from p. that work,	124:49

PERHAPS

p. I might discover my family	1Ne 8:13
that p. I might see them.	8:17
that p. the Lord would be	8:37
thinking, p., that he may lead us	16:38
that p. I might persuade them	19:18
that p. it may shoot forth	Jac 5: 4
that p. I might preserve the roots	5:11
that p. it may bring forth good	5:27
that, p., I may preserve unto	5:53
p. they may bring forth good fruit	5:54
that, p., the roots thereof may	5:59
that, p., the trees of my	5:60
and, p., that I may rejoice	5:60
that, p., they might be brought	En 1:13
p. some day it may profit them.	WM 1: 2
P. thou shalt say: The man has	Mos 4:17
p. thou shalt cause thy neighbor	4:28
p., they will give us a knowledge	8:12
p., they will give us a knowledge	8:12
That p. they might bring them	28: 2
that p. they might cure them of	28: 2
p. been consigned to a state of	Al 9:11
Behold, p. they will burn us also.	14:12
p. they might bring them unto	17:16
that p. they might bring them to	17:16
yea, and p. until the day I die.	17:23
that p. she might raise her from	19:29
and p. thou wouldst lose thy soul.	20:18
for p., if we should stain our	24:13
p. we might save some few of	26:26
p. we might be the means of	26:30
if p. we could be the means of	26:30
that p. I may be an instrument	29: 9
lest p. I should be destroyed,	36:11
p. he would have caused them	49:10
p. he might take again by	52:10
lest p. they should not obtain	52:28
p. he might find a man who	55: 4
p. destroyed our lettle army;	56:19
and p. they will repent and turn	He 11: 4
that p. we might save them	Mrm 2:21
p. ye may be found spotless,	9: 6
p. they may be of worth unto	Mro 1: 4
p. a committee can be appointed	DC 123: 4

PERILS

lest p. shall come upon you.	DC	29: 3
art in p. among false brethren;		122: 5
art in p. among robbers;		122: 5
if thou art in p. by land or by sea;		122: 5
as for the p. which I am called to		127: 2

PERIOD

ye shall know at some future p.	1 Ne	7:13
at this p. of time when I am	Mos	2:28
earth long before this p. of time,	Al	9:11
at some p. of time they will be		9:17
no time for their trials at this p.		51:19
became now at this p. of time		53:19
circumstances at this p. of time.		58: 5
all of them are at this p. of time		58:31
this p. when the sign was given,	3 Ne	2: 8
during that p. been solemnized	DC	OD
at a very early p. of my life,	JS	2:20

PERISH

many should p. by the sword,	1 Ne	1:13
unto thee that they shall p.!		1:14
to p. in the wilderness.		2:11
behold, he would also p.		3:18
It is better that one man should p.		4:13
dwindle and p. in unbelief.		4:13
and we p. in the wilderness.		5: 2
plates of brass should never p.;		5:19
ye shall also p. with them.		7:15
that if ye go ye will also p.;		7:15
that they p. and are lost.		12:17
that whoso repenteth not must p.		14: 5
How is it that ye will p.,		15:10
fast unto it, they would never p.;		15:24
we must p. in the wilderness		16:35
with food, that we did not p.		16:39
of the Lord that we might not p.		17: 5
upon them, and that they must p.		18:15
shall wander in the flesh, and p.,		19:14
behold, the righteous shall not p.;		22:19
voice of Nephi ye shall not p.	2 Ne	1:28
they p. from that which is good,		2: 5
God will not suffer that ye saw p.;		4: 7
and shall not be suffered to p.,		6:11
And they shall p.		9:28
their treasure shall p. with them		9:30
will not hear; for they shall p.		9:31
will not see; for they shall p. also.		9:32
our children shall p. in the flesh		10: 2
fighteth against Zion shall p.,		10:13
up a king against me shall p.,		10:14
both male and female, shall p.;		10:16
should come all men must p.		11: 6
unto the wicked, for they shall p.;		13:11
but the wicked shall p.		23:22
his seed should never p. as long as		25:21
unto the wicked, for they shall p.;		26: 3
they p. because they cast out		26: 3
they are they which shall not p.		26: 8
suffer the laborer in Zion to p.		26:30
they labor for money they shall p.		26:31
for whoso doeth them shall p.		26:32
of their wise and learned shall p.		27:26
ripe in iniquity they shall p.		28:16
they be stirred up to anger, and p.;		28:19
ye shall all likewise p.;		30: 1
but must p. in the dark.		32: 4
must p. and vanish away;	Jac	4: 2
tender branches, and it p. not.		5: 4
the main top thereof began to p.		5: 6
that the root of this tree will p.,		5: 8
roots thereof that they p. not,		5:11
that it beginneth to p.;		5:37
will I do that the tree may not p.,		5:53
which are ripened, that must p.,		5:58
and the graft thereof shall p.,		5:65
righteous that they should not p.,	Om	1: 7
in vain, and turn him out to p.	Mos	4:16
your substance that he p. not,		4:22
his substance shall p. with him;		4:23
the end of your lives, ye must p.		4:30

O man, remember, and p. not.	Mos	4:30
might not p. in the wilderness;		7:19
he ought not and he should p.		8:13
that they must unavoidably p.,		13:28
rather stay and p. with them.		19:12
and also p. with them.		19:19
has done this thing shall p.		20:16
them towards us we must p.		20:20
they might not p. with hunger;		21:17
that any human soul should p.;		28: 3
righteousness rather than to p.	Al	13:10
except we repent we shall p.		21: 6
unto us that we might not p.;		24:14
that they would lie down and p.,		24:23
Lamanites should p. by fire		25: 5
otherwise we will p. in the land.		27:10
out of this land, that they p. not;		27:12
unto thee, while others shall p.		31:28
about your eyes that ye might p.?		33:21
mankind must unavoidably p.;		34: 9
and must p. except it be through		34: 9
and we will p. or conquer.		44: 8
of the seed of Joseph shall p.,		46:24
which shall p. as his garment,		46:27
or to p. by the sword,		50:22
not one soul of them who did p.;		57:25
that we might not all p.;		57:36
about to p. for the want of food.		58: 7
were about to p. with hunger,		60: 9
that we should p. with hunger;		60:35
that they may not p. until ye		61:16
they must unavoidably p.	He	4:25
except ye repent ye shall p.;		7:28
that they did p. by thousands		11: 6
were about to p. by famine,		11: 7
down and shall be left to p.		15: 2
were about to p. with hunger.	3 Ne	4:20
for ye shall wonder and p.	Mrm	9:26
also we shall p., for in them	Eth	2:19
therefore we shall p.		2:19
that ye may not p. in the flood.		2:20
into pits and left them to p.		9:29
which did p. by the way;		9:32
people saw that they must p.		9:34
that they should p. not,		13: 7
that he should p. not.		13: 7
or he would p. by the sword.		15:28
and the other must p. because	Mro	8:15
they shall p. except they repent.		8:16
they must p. soon, unto the		8:29
I know that they must p. except		9:22
if they p. it will be like unto		9:23
And if it so be that they p.,		9:24
if thou art spared and I shall p.		9:24
and shall p. in Babylon, even	DC	1:16
know these things, lest they p.		19:22
shall not p. by the waters.		61: 6
might not p. in wickedness;		61: 8
disciples, that they p. not.		64:19
wisdom of the wise shall p.,		76: 9
houses and their barns shall p.,		121:20
are upon shall p. in the floods;	Mses	7:38
house, that they might not p.	Abr	2:17

PERISHED

we had p. in the wilderness;	1 Ne	5: 2
tarried at Jerusalem and had p.		5: 4
there were many who p.		17:41
I should have p. also.		19:20
Jerusalem we should also have p.	2 Ne	1: 4
we must have p. with hunger		1:24
the tree thereof would have p.	Jac	5:18
they are alive and they have not p.;		5:34
swords, the hilts thereof have p.,	Mos	8:11
all mankind must have p.		15:19
those that have p. in their sins		15:26
would not look therefore they p.	Al	33:20
their oath they would have p.;		53:11
for Heth had p. by the famine,	Eth	10: 1
more, but I have not as yet p.;	Mro	1: 1
and have p. in their sins,	Mses	7: 1

PERISHETH

PERISHETH
feast upon that which p. not,	2Ne	9:51
the infant p. not that dieth in	Mos	3:18
which he hath done he p. forever,		4:18
whosoever p., perisheth unto	He	14:30
perisheth, p. unto himself;		14:30
up in store that he p. not,	DC	4: 4

PERISHING
household from p. with famine.	1Ne	5:14
very act of p. under the sword—	Al	24:23
side are p. in unbelief.	DC	61: 3

PERMANENT
for a p. and everlasting	DC	78: 4

PERMIT
as soon as time will p.	DC	58:52
as your circumstances shall p.,		84:117
as often as occasion would p.	JS	2: 8

PERMITTED
were p., or rather commanded,	Mos	7: 8
Ye are p. to speak.		7:11
saw that he was p. to speak,		7:12
yet alive, and am p. to speak;		7:12
been p. to come unto you,	Al	7: 1
they were not p. to enter into		32: 3
ye are p. to act for yourselves;	He	14:30
that I am p. to speak unto you	Mro	7: 2
that thou shalt be p. to see.	DC	19:29
not be p. to dwell thereon.		101:99
no unclean thing shall be p. to		109:20
p. to receive fifteen thousand		124:64
shall not be p. to receive over		124:65
shall not be p. to receive under		124:66
shall not be p. to receive		124:67
and be p. to enter into my glory.		132: 4

PERMITTING
nor p. any person to enter into	DC	OD

PERPETUATED
that their names may be p. and	DC	109:71

PERPLEXITIES
and the p. of the nations	DC	88:79

PERSECUTE
and they p. the meek,	2Ne	9:30
and they p. the meek		28:13
and p. your brethren because ye	Jac	2:13
his brethren, and began to p. him,	Mos	24: 8
children should p. their children.		24: 8
not any unbeliever p. any of		27: 2
p. those that did belong to the	Al	1:19
did p. them, and afflict them		1:20
p. those that did not belong to		1:21
began to p. those that did not		4: 8
men shall revile you and p.,	3Ne	12:11
despitefully use you and p. you;		12:44
p. the true church of Christ,	4Ne	1:29
to p. the saints, and to fight	DC	121:38
and if they p. you,		127: 4
all united to p. me.	JS	2:22
should p. him unto death,		2:24
Why p. me for telling the truth?		2:25

PERSECUTED
the nations in anger, is p.,	2Ne	24: 6
and p. him because ye were proud	Jac	2:20
being p. by all those who did not	Mos	26:38
greatly p. by those who were		27:32
are p. for my name's sake,	3Ne	12:10
so p. they the prophets who		12:12
because they p. their king.	DC	45:53
who have been afflicted, and p.,		101: 1
so p. they the prophets and		127: 4
though I was hated and p. for	JS	2:25
and p. by those who ought to		2:28

PERSECUTEST
why p. thou the church of God?	Mos	27:13

PERSECUTETH
that p. the saints of God	DC	88:94

PERSECUTING
and while they were p. me,	JS	2:25

PERSECUTION
are given, notwithstanding all p.—	2Ne	26: 8
be no p. among themselves.	Al	1:21
they bore with patience the p.		1:25
persist in the p. of your brethren,		5:54
p. of many of their brethren.	He	3:34
would receive railing and p.	3Ne	6:13
the fear of p. and the cares of	DC	40: 2
the midst of p. and wickedness.		99: 1
who suffer p. for my name,		101:35
and p. that arose against me,	JS	2:20
and was the cause of great p.,		2:22
and create a bitter p.;		2:22
most bitter p. and reviling.		2:23
all the p. under heaven could		2:24
all the time suffering severe p.		2:27
p. still followed me,		2:58
The p. became more bitter and		2:60
The p., however, became so		2:61
the p. so heavy upon us that		2:61
owing to a spirit of p. which		2:74

PERSECUTIONS
the p. which were inflicted on	Mos	27: 1
should be no p. among them,		27: 3
notwithstanding all their p.	Al	1:28
and strife, and malice, and p.,		4: 9
p. which were heaped upon them		4:15
or that heapeth upon him p.?		5:30
of the p. to suffer great p.,	He	3:34
strifes, malice, p. and murders,		13:22
yea, even unto great p.;	3Ne	6:10
and strifes, and malice, and p.,	Mrm	8:36
and all his afflictions and p.—	DC	109:68

PERSECUTOR
the great p. of the church,	DC	86: 3

PERSEVERANCE
let your diligence, and your p.,	DC	127: 4

PERSIST
and if ye p. in these things	Jac	2:14
will ye still p. in the wearing of	Al	5:53
will ye p. in supposing that ye		5:54
will ye p. in the persecution of		5:54
will you p. in turning your backs		5:55
ye that will p. in your wickedness,		5:56
that if ye p. in your wickedness		9:18

PERSISTED
p. in their wickedness continually.	Mrm	4:10

PERSISTS
that p. in his own carnal nature,	Mos	16: 5

PERSON
not trust his p. without the walls	Mos	21:19
thereof would only admit one p.	Al	31:13
No p. is to be ordained to any	DC	20:65
The p. who is called of God		20:73
with the p. who has presented		20:73
every p. who belongeth to this		42:78
man in the likeness of his p.,		77: 2
There is not any p. belonging to		107:81
And if a p. gains more knowledge		130:19
nor permitting any p. to		OD
for a p. young as I was,	JS	2: 8
if any p. needed wisdom from		2:12
but his whole p. was glorious		2:32
as immediately around his p.		2:32
not show them to any p.;		2:42
around the p. of him who had		2:43

PERSONA
in their own *propria p.*,	DC	128: 8

PERSONAGE

PERSONAGE
but is a p. of Spirit. — DC 130:22
the P. who addressed me said — JS 2:19
a p. appeared at my bedside, — 2:30

PERSONAGES
who are resurrected p., — DC 129: 1
rested upon me I saw two P., — JS 2:17
than I asked the P. who stood — 2:18
midst of that light I saw two P., — 2:25

PERSONAL
both of character and p. injuries, — DC 123: 2
in that verse, is a p. appearance; — 130: 3
were p. abuse is inflicted or — 134:11

PERSONALLY
p. acquainted with the elder or — DC 20:84
Christ will reign p. upon the — AoF 10

PERSONS
having no respect to p. as to — Al 1:30
without any respect of p., — 16:14
God, and a respecter to p.; — Mro 8:12
For I am no respecter of p., — DC 1:35
except to those p. to whom — 5: 3
and I am no respecter of p. — 38:16
that whatever p. among you, — 42:74
that any p. have left their — 42:75
if any p. among you shall kill — 42:79
also the names of all p. that — 123: 3
and encroachments of all p. — 134:11
of from 150 to 200 p. — 135: 1
were the only p. in the room — 135: 2
and designing p., in relation — JS 2: 1

PERSUADE
of language did I p. my brethren, — 1Ne 3:21
that I may p. men to come unto — 6: 4
that perhaps I might p. them — 19:18
that I might more fully p. them — 19:23
to write, to p. our children, — 2Ne 25:23
should p. all men to repentance. — 26:27
might p. them to come unto — Jac 1: 7
could p. all men not to rebel — 1: 8
could p. all ye ends of the earth — Mrm 3:22
to p. to believe in Christ, — Mro 7:16

PERSUADED
shall be p. to believe in Christ, — 2Ne 25:16
be p. that Jesus is the Christ, — Mrm 5:14
may be p. to do good continually, — Eth 8:26
have been p. by those whom — DC 30: 2

PERSUADETH
for it p. them to do good; — 2Ne 33: 4
and p. them to believe in him, — 33: 4
for it p. men to do good. — Eth 4:11
thing p. men to do good — 4:12
thing p. men to do evil, — Mro 7:17
he p. no man to do good, — 7:17

PERSUADING
p. them to look forward unto — Jar 1:11

PERSUASION
only by p., by long-suffering, — DC 121:41

PERSUASIONS
away after the p. of Amlici; — Al 2: 3
by the p. of Helaman and — 53:14
have gone on in the p. of men. — DC 3: 6
to the p. of men no more. — 5:21

PERTAIN
p. unto the kingdom of God, — DC 88:78
all things that p. unto it. — 104:29
that p. to the dispensation of — 124:41

PERTAINING
which are p. to righteousness; — 1Ne 15:33
p. to things both temporal and — 22: 3
as p. to the things of this world. — Mos 4:23

735

PERVERTING

things p. to the kingdom of God. — Mos 18:18
with things p. to righteousness. — 23:18
things p. unto righteousness, — Al 5:42
things p. unto righteousness. — 12:16
things p. unto righteousness; — 12:32
things p. to righteousness. — 21:23
of things p. to righteousness, — 24:30
the things p. unto righteousness. — 35:16
p. to things of righteousness; — 40:26
to things p. to righteousness. — He 11:19
to things p. to righteousness. — 14:18
of the things p. to Christ — 3Ne 6:23
p. unto things of righteousness, — DC 11:14
judge all things p. to Zion. — 64:38
all things p. to my kingdom. — 76: 7
all things p. to the bishopric — 82:12
p. to those who do not belong — 90:25
all things p. to the church — 94: 3
p. to the kingdom of God on — 97:14
And as p. to law of man, — 98: 7
p. to the things of my kingdom — 100:11
and principle p. to futurity, — 101:78
all things p. to Zion. — 105:37
its wealth p. to gold and silver — 111: 4
as p. to the Twelve, — 112:16
in futurity, p. to the saints, — 123:15
all things p. to this house, — 124:42
as p. to my boarding house — 124:56
as p. to the price thereof. — 124:121
p. to the priesthood; — 127: 8
as p. to our salvation. — 128:15
things p. to an inferior kingdom, — 130: 9
things p. to a higher order of — 130:10
as p. to the new and everlasting — 132: 6
there are many things p. thereunto. — 132:58
p. to the law of the priesthood— — 132:61
as p. to these things, — 132:64
And now, as p. to this law, — 132:66
but cursed him as p. to the — Abr 1:26
p. to the measurement of time, — Fac 2: 1
also p. to other planets; — 2: 2
p. to the Kingdom of God. — AoF 9

PERTAINS
which p. to that inheritance, — DC 104:34

PERVERSE
O ye wicked and p. generation, — Al 9: 8
O ye wicked and p. generation, — 10:17
O ye wicked and p. generation, — 10:25
were a wicked and a p. people; — 31:24
wicked and ye p. generation; — He 13:29
and p. and stiffnecked people, — Mrm 8:33
a crooked and p. generation. — DC 33: 2
a crooked and p. generation, — 34: 6

PERVERSENESS
of the slanderer cease its p. — DC 112: 9

PERVERSION
have become strong in their p.; — Mro 9:19

PERVERT
might p. the right ways of the — 1Ne 13:27
and p. the right way of the Lord, — 2Ne 28:15
they p. the right way of God, — Jac 7: 7
p. the ways of all righteousness. — Mos 29:23
to p. the ways of the righteous; — Al 10:18
they did p. the ways of the Lord — 31:11
shall p. the ways of the Lord — Mro 8:16

PERVERTED
hath p. the right ways of the Lord, — 1Ne 22:14
have p. the ways of the Lord. — Mos 12:26

PERVERTETH
him who p. the ways of the Lord; — Al 30:60

PERVERTING
you for p. the ways of the Lord; — Mos 12:26
and p. the way of the Lord, — 29: 7
go about p. the ways of the Lord? — Al 30:22
were p. the ways of the Lord, — 31: 1

PESTER
insects shall p. their land also, — Mos 12: 6

PESTILENCE
and by bloodsheds, and by p., — 2Ne 6:15
yea, with famine and with p.; — Mos 12: 4
shall be smitten with a great p.— — 12: 7
famine, and by p., and the sword. — Al 10:22
and by p., and by the sword; — 10:23
the people of Nephi with p.; — He 7:hd
earth with famine, and with p., — 10: 6
the p. of the sword might cease; — 11:14
and the p. and destruction — 11:15
famine and with all manner of p., — 12: 3
and with famine and with p. — 13: 9
confusion, which bringeth p. — DC 63:24
with sore affliction, with p., — 97:26
by famine, sword, and p.; — JS 2:45

PESTILENCES
famines, p., and bloodsheds shall — 2Ne 10: 6
then shall they see wars and p., — Al 45:11
and also many famines and p., — Eth 11: 7
famines and p. of every kind, — DC 43:25
there shall be famines, and p., — JS 1:29

PETER: *see also HAWS, Peter; and WHITMER, Peter, Jun.*
this cause the Lord said unto P.; — DC 7: 4
I say unto thee, P., this was a — 7: 5
Hearken, my servant P., and — 16: 1
And also with P., and James, — 27:12
Behold, I say unto you, P., — 30: 5
of old, whose name was P.: — 49:11
That thou art P., and upon this — 128:10
The voice of P. James, and John — 128:20
under the direction of P., James — JS 2:72

PETERSON, Ziba
And P. also shall go with them; — DC 32: 3
has been bestowed upon P. — 58:60

PETITION
putteth up his p. to you in vain, — Mos 4:16
who putteth up his p. to you — 4:22
and yet ye put up no p., — 4:22
he sent a p., with the voice — Al 51:15
according to thy p., — DC 90: 1

PETITIONS
sent in their voices with their p. — Al 51: 3
hear us in these our p., — DC 109:77
answer these p., and accept — 109:78

PHARAOH
and the armies of P. did follow — 1Ne 4: 2
who were the armies of P. — 17:27
people, as I did the heart of P., — DC 105:27
and the God of P., king of Egypt; — Abr 1: 6
was also the priest of P. — 1: 7
was the custom of the priest of P., — 1: 8
an offering unto the god of P., — 1: 9
did the priest of P. offer upon — 1:10
also a god like unto that of P., — 1:13
the God of P., king of Egypt; — 1:17
and also in the court of P.; — 1:20
P. signifies king by royal blood. — 1:20
established by P., the eldest son — 1:25
P., being a righteous man, — 1:26
Now, P., being of that lineage by — 1:27
Mahmackrah, Korash, and P. — Fac 1: 4
The idolatrous god of P. — 1: 9
King P., whose name is — 3: 2
Prince of P., King of Egypt, — 3: 4

PHARAOH'S
sitting upon P. throne, — Fac 3: 1

PHARAOHS
the P. would fain claim it from — Abr 1:27

PHELPS, William W.: *see also WILLIAM.*
let my servant P. be planted — DC 57:11
let my servant P. stand in the — DC 58:40
my servant P. be in haste — 61: 7
Sidney Gilbert and P. take — 61: 9
also unto my servant P., — 70: 1

PHILIP: *see BURROUGHS', Philip.*

PHILISTINES
unto soothsayers like the P., — 2Ne 12: 6
Syrians before and the P. behind; — 19:12
upon the shoulders of the P. — 21:14

PHYSICAL
any p. punishment upon them. — DC 134:10

PHYSICIAN
the whole need no p., but they — Mro 8: 8
be a p. unto the church, — DC 31:10

PICKETS
should be a frame of p. built — Al 50: 3
overlooked those works of p., — 50: 4

PICTURES
and upon all pleasant p. — 2Ne 12:16

PIECE
from one p. of iniquity to another, — Al 4:11
he took a p. thereof, and wrote — 46:12
this very choice p. of land, — DC 101:44

PIECES
I saw mountains tumbling into p.; — 1Ne 12: 4
Ye beat my people to p., — 2Ne 13:15
and ye shall be broken in p.; — 18: 9
and ye shall be broken in p.; — 18: 9
and ye shall be broken in p. — 18: 9
also shall be dashed to p. — 23:16
also dash the young men to p., — 23:18
upon them and crush them to p. — 26: 5
of the different p. of their gold, — Al 11: 4
by his brethren into many p.; — 46:23
treadeth down and teareth in p., — 3Ne 20:16
shalt beat in p. many p.; — 20:19
treadeth down and teareth in p., — 21:12
as a lion, and tear you in p., — Mrm 5:24
for they will be dashed in p.; — Eth 2:23
he took it and tore it to p., — JS 2:65

PIERCE
daggers placed to p. their souls — Jac 2: 9
show you that he can p. you, — 2:15
did p. many of their breastplates, — Al 43:44
which did p. him near the heart. — 62:36
it did p. even to the very soul— — He 5:30
it did p. them that did hear — 3Ne 11: 3
it did p. them to the very soul, — 11: 3
let thine eye p.; — DC 121: 4
thee, and no man shall p. thee. — Mses 6:32
and mine eye can p. them also, — 7:36

PIERCED
hearts died, p. with deep wounds. — Jac 2:35
behold they were p. and smitten, — Al 44:18
be p. with much sorrow; — DC 1: 3
the wounds which p. my side, — 6:37

PIERCETH
through and p. all things, — DC 85: 6

PIERCING
the p. eye of the Almighty God. — Jac 2:10

PILGRIMS
strangers and p. on the earth; — DC 45:13

PILLAR
there came a p. of fire — 1Ne 1: 6
encircled about with a p. of fire, — He 5:24
yea every soul, by a p. of fire. — 5:43
of my coming in a p. of fire, — DC 29:12
the midst of the p. of heaven— — 88:97
I saw a p. of light exactly over — JS 2:16

PILLARS

PILLARS
represent the p. of heaven, — Fac 1:11

PILLOW
mine eyes water my p. by night, — 2Ne 33: 3

PINE
the fir-tree, and the p.-tree, — DC 124:26

PINE-TREE: see PINE and TREE.

PINS
the wimples, and the crisping-p.; — 2Ne 13:22

PIONEERS
to go as p. to prepare for — DC 136: 7

PIPE
and the viol, the tabret, and p., — 2Ne 15:12

PISON
called the name of the first P., — Mses 3:11

PIT
great p., which hath been digged — 1Ne 14: 3
great p. which hath been digged — 14: 3
fall into the p. which they digged — 22:14
the p. from whence ye are digged. — 2Ne 8: 1
that he should not die in the p., — 8:14
to hell, to the sides of the p., — 24:15
go down to the stones of the p.; — 24:19
dig a p. for thy neighbor; — 28: 8
he who diggeth a p. for them — DC 109:25
if thou shouldst be cast into the p., — 122: 7

PITCH
and we did p. our tents again; — 1Ne 16:13
we did p. our tents for the space — 16:17
we did p. our tents again, — 16:33
we did p. our tents by the — 17: 6
and did p. our tents; — 18:23
of many days we did p. our tents. — 2Ne 5: 7
shall the Arabian p. tent there; — 23:20
p. their tents in the valley of — Al 2:20
did p. their tents for the night. — 2:20
to p. their tents in the valley — 47: 9
did p. their tents in the borders — 51:32
did p. his tents in the borders — 51:32
and we did p. our tents by the — 58:13
and they did p. their tents, — 58:25
did p. their tents in the plains — 62:18
p. battle against the Nephites. — He 1:15
we did p. our tents around about — Mrm 6: 4
did p. their tents in a place — Eth 15:10
did p. their tents by the hill — 15:11

PITCHED
he p. his tent in a valley — 1Ne 2: 6
they p. their tents round about, — Mos 2: 6
they p. their tents round about — 2: 6
and there they p. their tents. — 7: 5
we p. our tents in the place where — 9: 4
And they p. their tents, — 23: 5
they p. their tents in a valley, — 24:20
where they had p. their tents, — Al 27:25
where we had first p. our tents — 58:17
to the sea they p. their tents; — Eth 2:13
and there he p. his tent, — 9: 3
they p. their tents in the valley — 14:28
Coriantumr p. his tents in — 14:28
these waters they p. their tents; — 15: 8
Shiz also p. his tents near — 15: 8
of Bethel, and p. my tent there; — Abr 2:20

PITCHING
p. their tents by the way. — DC 61:25

PITS
dig p. sufficient to hold them. — 3Ne 28:20
some of them they cast into p. — Eth 9:29

PITY
shall have no p. on the fruit of — 2Ne 23:18

PLACE

the p. and the exceeding love — Al 53:11
And it seemeth a p. unto me, — 3Ne 3: 3
O Lord, look upon me in p., — Eth 3: 3
and in his love, and in his p., — DC 133:53

PLACE
They call the p. Bountiful. — 1Ne 1:hd
thou shalt have p. with us. — 4:34
be a p. of filthiness prepared — 15:34
And there is a p. prepared, — 15:35
call the name of the p. Shazer. — 16:13
wilderness, to the p. of Shazer. — 16:14
the p. which was called Nahom. — 16:34
and we called the p. Bountiful, — 17: 6
The p. is too strait for me; — 21:20
give p. to me that I may dwell. — 21:20
would be no p. for an inheritance. — 2Ne 1: 8
the evil one have p. in my heart — 4:27
give p. no more for the enemy of — 4:28
Wilt thou not p. a stumbling block — 4:33
call the name of the p. Nephi; — 5: 8
every dwelling-p. of Mount Zion, — 14: 5
and for a p. of refuge, — 14: 6
till there can be no p., — 15: 8
in that day, every p. shall be, — 17:23
earth shall remove out of her p., — 23:13
and bring them to their p.; — 24: 2
must go into the p. prepared for — 28:23
save in the first p. ye shall pray — 32: 9
that it hath no p. in them; — 33: 2
these will I p. in the nethermost — Jac 5:13
will I cast away into its own p. — 5:77
be cast out into their own p.! — 6: 3
I soon go to the p. of my rest, — En 1:27
there is a p. prepared for you — 1:27
whatsoever p. of our inheritance. — Jar 1: 7
And now, in the first p., he hath — Mos 2:23
that it may have no p. in you — 2:36
the Lord has no p. in him, — 2:37
in the p. where our brethren were — 9: 4
I did p. them in their ranks, — 10: 9
a p. which was called Mormon, — 18: 4
together at the p. of Mormon, — 18: 7
went forth to the p. of Mormon; — 18:16
yea, the p. of Mormon, — 18:30
Now there was a p. in Shemlon — 20: 1
a p. which they called Amulon; — 23:31
a p. at my right hand. — 26:23
a p. eternally at my right hand. — 26:24
same p. where the first army met — Al 3:20
a p. to sit down in the kingdom — 5:24
p. in the kingdom of heaven; — 5:25
in the first p. being left to — 13: 3
in the first p. they were on the — 13: 5
forth to the p. of martyrdom, — 14: 9
the p. where the Son of God — 16:20
their flocks to the p. of water, — 17:26
their flocks to this p. of water, — 17:27
them back unto the p. of water; — 17:31
together again to the p. of water. — 17:32
their flocks at the p. of water; — 18: 6
The heavens is a p. where God dwells — 18:30
house to house and from p. — 20:30
and from place to p. — 20:30
in whatsoever p. they were in — 21:22
in the p. of their fathers' first — 22:28
being the p. of their first landing. — 22:30
in whatsoever p. they should be, — 23: 1
and to p. another in his stead, — 24:20
be gathered together in their p., — 26: 6
the p. of which has been spoken; — 27:16
that it may have no p. in you; — 30:42
For they had a p. built up in the — 31:13
a p. for standing, which was high — 31:13
Now the p. was called by them — 31:21
have no p. to worship our God; — 32: 5
he desireth, in the first p., that — 32:22
give p. for a portion of my words. — 32:27
if ye give p., that a seed may — 32:28
from you, and hath no p. in you, — 34:35
whatsoever p. ye may be in, — 34:38
gave p. in the land of Jershon for — 35:13
when it once has had p. in you, — 39: 6

PLACE

and p. it in an unnatural state,	Al	41:12
to p. it in a state opposite to		41:12
wicked man can cause to take p.		46: 9
the p. which was called Onidah,		47: 5
to Onidah, to the p. of arms.		47: 5
might p. himself at their head		47: 8
queen, unto the p. where she sat;		47:34
did p. the greater number of men;		48: 9
it was by their p. of entrance,		49: 4
to be the next best p. for them		49:12
which had hitherto been a weak p.,		49:14
come into their p. of security		49:20
security by the p. of entrance;		49:20
armies before the p. of entrance,		49:21
to get into their p. of security;		49:21
a contention which took p.		50:25
a union took p. between them		50:36
that he hath gone to such a p.?		54:22
the p. where the Lamanites do		55: 3
determined to conquer in this p.		56:17
we had no p. for our prisoners,		56:57
that same p. where we had first		58:17
in whatsoever p. he did enter,		62: 4
with a cord, from p. to place,		62:36
with a cord, from place to p.,		62:36
to the p. of his inheritance;		62:42
p. him in the judgment-seat	He	2: 5
lead them forth from p. to place,		4:16
lead them forth from place to p.,		4:16
that ye shall have no p. in them;		7:22
that we shall have no p. in them.		8: 5
unto the p. of the judgment-seat—		9: 7
came to the p. of the judgment,		9:14
there shall be no p. for refuge;		15: 2
abroad, having no p. for refuge,		15:12
it were their land, unto one p.	3Ne	3:13
the p. which had been appointed		3:22
that this siege should take p.		4:17
did p. his armies in the way of		4:24
of that which hath taken p.		5:15
to land, and from p. to place.		6: 8
to land, and from place to p.		6: 8
did p. at their head a man		7: 9
in the p. of the city there became		8:10
one p. they were heard to cry,		8:24
in another p. they were heard to		8:25
change which had taken p.		11: 1
in the p. where Jesus should		19: 3
things shall be about to take p.—		21: 1
Enlarge the p. of thy tent,		22: 2
to that which shall take p. at		28:39
leave in the p. where they are;	Mrm	1: 4
And there we did p. our armies,		3: 6
to city and from p. to place,		8: 7
to city and from place to p.,		8: 7
the name of the p. Moriancumer;	Eth	2:13
by the p. where the Nephites		9: 3
a p. which was called Ablom,		9: 3
by the p. where the sea divides		10:20
a p. at the right hand of God,		12: 4
the p. which thou hast prepared.		12:32
a p. for the children of men.		12:33
that p. which thou hast prepared		12:34
the p. which I have prepared		12:37
the p. of the New Jerusalem,		13: 3
the p. in whither he would keep it,		14: 1
a p. which was called Ogath.		15:10
had built for the p. of worship.	Mro	7: 1
may have p. in their hearts,		7:32
come to the p. where thou art	DC	6:14
have p. in the kingdom of		18:25
and upon every high p.,		19:29
whatsoever p. ye shall enter,		24:15
Thou shalt not leave this p.		28:10
gathered in unto one p. upon		29: 8
there is a p. prepared for them		29:38
beginning, which p. is hell.		29:38
I will prepare a p. for them.		31: 6
forth to the p. which I have		38:35
from this p. ye shall go forth		42: 8
in the p. of thy stewardship.		42:53
be gathered unto this p.;		45:43
have no p. in the hearts of	DC	45:55
a p. of safety for the saints		45:66
The p. is not yet to be revealed;		48: 5
shall be given to know the p.,		48: 5
the p. which I have appointed.		49:25
their journey unto the same p.		52: 8
take their journey unto one p.,		52:33
the p. which shall be appointed		53: 4
until I prepare a p. for you.		54: 9
the p. upon which he lives.		56: 8
paid and shall leave the p.,		56:10
and the p. for the city of Zion.		57: 2
the p. which is now called		57: 3
is the center p.;		57: 3
plant himself in this p.,		57: 8
Phelps be planted in this p.,		57:11
whatsoever p. I shall appoint		57:13
for the p. of the storehouse,		58:37
from this p. into all the world,		58:64
the p. which is called St. Louis.		60: 5
in this p. let them lift up		60: 7
in that they shall lift up		61:31
which remaineth in this p.,		64:26
on a hill, or in a high p.,		64:37
Tarry not many days in this p.;		66: 6
bear testimony in every p.,		66: 7
be made strong in every p.;		66: 8
a p. to receive and do all these		69: 6
many times from p. to place,		69: 7
from place to p., and from		69: 7
I, the Lord, shall p. them,		70:16
shall not have p. in the church,		75:29
neither the p. thereof,		76:45
living God, the heavenly p.,		76:66
both in this p. and in the		78: 3
a p. in the celestial world,		78: 7
countries, from p. to place,		79: 1
from place to p., and from		79: 1
the saints, beginning at this p.,		84: 4
even the p. of the temple,		84: 4
whatsoever p. ye cannot go		84:62
nations, beginning at this p.		87: 2
return again to their own p.,		88:32
Tarry ye, tarry ye in this p.,		88:70
cast away into their own p.,		88:114
be found standing in his p.,		88:128
in a p. that the congregation		88:129
shall not have p. among you;		88:134
let there be a p. provided,		90:19
upon the p. where he now lives;		90:20
be removed out of her p.		90:37
or be removed out of their p.		93:48
and remove you out of your p.		93:49
be removed out of their p.		93:50
the p. which is named among		96: 2
For a p. of thanksgiving		97:13
for a p. of instruction for all		97:13
neither be moved out of her p.,		97:19
I have prepared a p. for you,		98:18
I have much people in this p.,		100: 3
you to come unto this p.;		100: 4
not be moved out of her p.,		101:17
is none other p. appointed		101:20
any other p. appointed than		101:20
forth out of his hiding p.,		101:89
in the p. of absent councilors.		102: 7
the p. where he now resides,		104:20
p. upon which he now dwells.		104:27
yourselves a p. for a treasury,		104:60
shall be removed out of his p.,		104:77
not only in his own p.,		106: 2
to the p. Shedolamak.		107:45
in this p. [Kirtland].		109: 2
have a p. to manifest himself to		109: 5
thy house, a p. of thy holiness.		109:13
And from this p. they may bear		109:23
Tarry in this p., and in the		111: 7
And the p. where it is my will		111: 8
This p. you may obtain by hire.		111: 9
whatsoever p. ye shall proclaim		112:19
the affairs of my chruch in this p.,		112:27
it is the p. where Adam shall		116: 1

PLACE 739 PLAGUES

the p. of those who are fallen.	DC 118: 1
that covereth thy hiding p.?	121: 1
thy hiding p. no longer be covered;	121: 4
call him forth from his hiding p.;	123: 6
upon the p. which he shall show	124:22
For there is not a p. found	124:28
the p. whereon it shall be built.	124:42
shall build it on the p. where	124:43
not be moved out of their p.	124:45
a house to my name, even in this p.,	124:55
and his house have p. therein,	124:56
have p. in that house,	124:59
resting-p. for the weary traveler,	124:60
shall be moved out of their p.,	124:71
Let no man go from this p. who	124:85
wisdom in me to leave the p.	127: 1
in my letter before I left my p.,	128: 1
previous to my leaving my p.—	128: 7
was commanded to be in a p.	128:13
and glories should take p.,	128:18
The p. where god resides is	130: 8
be turned back into their own p.,	133:24
in the p. which I have prepared	135: 5
to remove this p. to the p.	136:10
or in any other p. in the	OD
be gathered together unto one p.,	Mses 2: 9
and stood upon the p. Mahujah,	7: 2
and had not p. among them.	7:22
unto a p. which I shall prepare,	7:62
to obtain another p. of residence;	Abr 1: 1
the land unto the p. of Sechem;	2:18
arose from the p. of the altar	2:20
be gathered together unto one p.,	4: 9
or the p. where God resides;	Fac 2: 2
you shall stand in the holy p.;	JS 1:12
was in the p. where we lived	2: 5
After I had retired to the p.	2:15
I could see the p. where the	2:42
I knew the p. again when I	2:42
and went to the p. where the	2:50
I knew the p. the instant that	2:50
I should come to that p.	2:53
a Mr. Isaac Hale, of that p.;	2:57
to the p. where they were	2:59
reach the p. of my destination	2:62
Martin Harris came to our p.,	2:63
For what took p. relative to	2:63
the p. where he found them.	2:64

PLACED

that they may be p. alone in	2Ne 15: 8
daggers p. to pierce their souls	Jac 2: 9
he p. his heart upon his riches,	Mos 11:14
God p. cherubim and a flaming	Al 12:21
or being p. in a state to act	12:31
ought to be p. in the sepulchre;	19: 5
be p. upon the Lord forever.	37:36
he p. at the east end of the	42: 2
the Lord God p. cherubim and	42: 3
Moroni p. spies round about,	43:28
having p. his army according to	43:33
he also p. armies on the south,	50:10
Moroni p. men over them to	53: 1
p. in the most dangerous	53: 9
p. to protect the city Cumeni.	57: 7
p. you in a situation that ye	60: 8
he shall be p. king over this	61: 8
that they should be p. in power	He 2: 5
circumstances they should be p.,	6:21
be p. as guards round about	3Ne 3:14
and p. him upon his throne	Eth 7:18
p. himself upon the throne of	14: 6
and p. upon the head of	DC 52:37
in which God has p. it,	93:30
of those who are p. as rulers	101:76
which shall be p. upon it,	104:64
a seal shall be p. upon it;	104:67
being p. for the protection of the	134: 6
p. at the east of the Garden of	Mses 4:31

PLACES

the rough p. to be made smooth,	1Ne 17:46
and smooth p. shall be broken up.	1Ne 17:46
pastures shall be in all high p.	21: 9
thy waste and thy desolate p.,	21:19
he will comfort all her waste p.;	2Ne 8: 3
the waste p. of the fat ones shall	15:17
ye waste p. of Jerusalem;	Mos 12:23
ye waste p. of Jerusalem;	15:30
in all p. that ye may be in,	18: 9
came forth out of their secret p.	20: 5
upon them from their waiting p.,	20: 9
your closets, and your secret p.,	Al 34:26
and their p. of resort, and the	48: 5
small forts, or p. of resort;	48: 8
in preparing their p. of security.	49: 5
disappointed in their p. of retreat	49:11
p. of security to be built upon	50: 4
and preparing p. of resort.	52: 6
did rise up from their secret p.,	58:20
those p. which he had recovered.	59:10
to build up their waste p.,	He 11:20
the wilderness and secret p.,	11:25
p. which are now called valleys	14:23
their holds and their secret p.	3Ne 1:27
and into their secret p.	2:17
strongholds, and their secret p.,	4: 1
again to their p. of security.	4:15
cut off in their p. of retreat.	4:26
many smooth p. became rough.	8:13
and the p. were left desolate.	8:14
and valleys in the p. thereof;	9: 8
the p. of your dwellings shall	10: 7
ye waste p. of Jerusalem;	16:19
or your p. of worship, for	18:32
ye waste p. of Jerusalem;	20:34
and earthquakes in divers p.	Mrm 8:30
your friends, and in all p.	DC 23: 6
And at all times, and in all p.,	24:12
shall stand in holy p.,	45:32
earthquakes also in divers p.,	45:33
in your p. of abode,	48: 1
that they have p. to live	48: 3
rough p. to become smooth—	49:23
in other p., in all churches.	51:18
of the truth in all p.,	58:47
obtain p. for your families,	75:25
obtain p. for their families,	75:26
stand ye in holy p.,	87: 8
in the secret p. by the way	99: 4
build up the waste p. of Zion—	101:18
other p. which I will appoint	101:21
together, and stand in holy p.;	101:22
unto my name upon holy p.;	101:64
the p. which I have appointed.	101:67
and establish her waste p.,	101:75
build up the waste p. of Zion.	103:11
the p. of thine appointment,	109:39
the rough p. made smooth;	109:74
The door of the kingdom in all p.	112:17
other p. should be appointed for	115:18
make solitary p. to bud and	117: 7
be appointed to fill the p. of	118: 6
those p. which I have appointed	124:36
be the p. for your baptisms for	124:36
oracles in your most holy p.	124:39
unto the p. which I shall appoint	125: 2
at sundry times, and in divers p.,	128:21
shall be hurled from their p.	133:49
upon the hills and the high p.,	Mses 6:37
to hear him, upon the high p.,	6:38
upon the high p., and did flourish.	7:17
and earthquakes, in divers p.	JS 1:29

PLACING

p. themselves in a state,	Al 12:31
because of the p. of our words;	Eth 12:25

PLAGUE

and with famine, and p.,	DC 87: 6
pestilence, with p., with sword,	97:26

PLAGUES

And p. shall go forth,	DC 84:97

PLAIN

PLAIN
many parts which are p.	1Ne 13:26
many p. and precious things	13:28
after these p. and precious things	13:29
the many p. and precious things	13:29
were p. unto the understanding	13:29
the p. and most precious parts	13:32
the most p. and precious parts	13:34
which shall be p. and precious,	13:34
which shall be p. and precious;	13:35
make known the p. and precious	13:40
p. and pure, and most precious	14:23
writings, which was p. to be read,	16:29
the more p. and precious parts	19: 3
because he hath been p. unto you.	2Ne 1:26
I may be strict in the p. road!	4:32
Would I be p. unto you	9:47
of Isaiah are not p. unto you,	25: 4
they are p. unto all those that	25: 4
he doeth nothing save it be p.	26:33
even as p. as word can be.	32: 7
made known unto us in p. terms,	Al 13:23
that he told me in p. humility,	Eth 12:39
and the way to judge is as p.,	Mro 7:15
let all thy garments be p.,	DC 42:40
sufficiently p. to suit my purpose	128:18
at the head of the p. of Olishem.	Abr 1:10

PLAINER
rendered a p. translation to this,	DC 128:18

PLAINLY
manifested p. of the coming	1Ne 1:19
spoken p. that ye cannot err.	2Ne 25:20
I have spoken p. unto you,	25:28
I shall speak unto you p.,	31: 2
are manifested unto us p.,	Jac 4:13
and he spake p. unto them	7:17
And he spake p. unto them,	7:18
I have spoken p. unto you	Mos 2:40
I have spoken unto you p. that	Al 5:43
And Amulek hath spoken p.	12:12
because they had testified so p.	14: 3
And thus we can p. discern,	24:30
because he spake p. unto them	He 8: 4
I will show it p. as I showed it	DC 45:16
this Moses p. taught to the	84:23
works of him were p. manifest.	93: 5
is p. manifest unto them,	93:31
before the council of the order p.	104:74
Tell us p. who thou art, and	Mses 6:40

PLAINNESS
contained the p. of the gospel	1Ne 13:24
the p. which is in the Lamb	13:29
according to the p. of the truth	2Ne 9:47
according to the p. which hath	25: 4
my soul delighteth in p.	25: 4
own prophecy, according to my p.;	25: 7
to the p. of my prophesying.	31: 2
For my soul delighteth in p.;	31: 3
when it is given unto them in p.,	32: 7
according to the p. of the truth;	33: 5
I glory in p.; I glory in truth;	33: 6
to the p. of the word of God.	Jac 2:11
and they despised the words of p.,	4:14
for God hath taken away his p.	4:14
exceeding great p. of speech,	En 1:23
because of the p. of his words	Al 14: 2
reasoning in p. and simplicity—	DC 133:57

PLAINS
and I saw the p. of the earth,	1Ne 12: 4
to meet them upon the p.	Al 52:20
army to meet them upon the p.	52:20
tents in the p. of Nephihah,	62:18
battle against them. upon the p.;	62:19
he came to the p. of Heshlon.	Eth 13:28
him battle again upon the p.;	13:29
until he came to the p. of Agosh.	14:15
had come to the p. of Agosh	14:16
and on the p. of Olaha Shinehah,	DC 117: 8

PLANS

was situated in the p. of Moreh.	Abr 2:18
sacrifice there in the p. of Moreh,	2:18

PLAN
merciful p. of the great Creator,	2Ne 9: 6
O how great the p. of our God!	9:13
O that cunning p. of the evil one!	9:28
and eternal p. of deliverance	11: 5
of the great p. of redemption,	Jac 6: 8
they revealed the p. of salvation?	Jar 1: 2
thy p. was a very subtle plan,	Al 12: 4
subtle p., as to the subtlety of	12: 4
this was a p. of thine adversary,	12: 5
not been for the p. of redemption,	12:25
there was a p. of redemption laid,	12:25
the p. of redemption would have	12:26
unto them the p. of redemption,	12:30
unto them the p. of redemption,	12:32
on such the p. of redemption could	12:32
(this being the p. of redemption	12:33
to know of the p. of redemption.	17:16
unto them the p. of redemption,	18:39
and also the p. of redemption,	22:13
that the p. of salvation might be	24:14
and the p. of redemption, that	29: 2
the great p. of the Eternal God	34: 9
and eternal p. of redemption.	34:16
shall the great p. of redemption	34:31
the p. of redemption should be	39:18
the p. of restoration is requisite	41: 2
the great p. of salvation would	42: 5
destroy the great p. of happiness.	42: 8
were not for the p. of redemption,	42:11
the p. of redemption could not	42:13
the p. of mercy could not be	42:15
bring about the p. of mercy,	42:15
opposite to the p. of happiness,	42:16
great p. of mercy may have claim	42:31
he laid the p. in his heart to	47: 4
have carried this p. into effect,	50:30
he resolved upon a p. that he	52:21
was a p. laid to lead them on	58:24
to lay a p. that he might obtain	59: 4
(and this was their secret p.,	He 2: 8
the great p. of destruction which	3Ne 1:16
thought to devise a plan whereby	Eth 8: 8
has sought to lay a cunning p.,	DC 10:12
thus he has laid a cunning p.,	10:23
This is the p. of salvation unto all	Mses 6:62
obeyed, and that their p. was good.	Abr 4:21

PLANET
to the p. on which they reside?	DC 130: 4
angels do not reside on a p. like	130: 6
The p. which is the lesser light,	Abr 3: 5
another p. whose reckoning of time	3: 8
the time of one p. above another,	3: 9
a p. or a star may exist above it;	3:17
This p. receives its power	Fac 2: 5

PLANETS
all the p. which move in their	Al 30:44
the earth and all the p.	DC 88:43
also of the p., and of the stars,	Abr 1:31
govern all those p. which belong	3: 9
pertaining to other p.;	Fac 2: 2
one of the governing p. also,	2: 5
fifteen other fixed p. or	2: 5

PLANS
that he might know of their p.	Al 2:21
laying p. to pervert the ways of	10:18
cunning p. which he hath devised	28:13
ye shall keep these secret p.	37:29
trust not those secret p. unto	37:32
a knowledge of those p. which	He 2: 6
their p. of awful wickedness,	6:30
have concealed their secret p.	11:10
all the secret p. of Gadianton;	11:26
by their secret p. did obtain	Eth 8: 9
to embrace the secret p. again	9:26

PLANS 741 PLATES

and they adopted the old p.,	Eth	10:33
their secret p. of wickedness,		13:15

PLANT

and we began to p. seeds;	1 Ne	18:24
that I may p. the heavens	2 Ne	8:16
the men of Judah his pleasant p.;		15: 7
comest thou hither to p. this tree,	Jac	5:21
I did p. in a good spot of		5:43
that I might p. this tree in the		5:44
up before him as a tender p.,	Mos	14: 2
to p. the seed that ye might try	Al	32:36
or how they should p. the seed,		33: 1
shall p. this word in your hearts,		33:23
to p. the word in your hearts,		34: 4
he shall p. in the hearts of	DC	2: 2
another will I p. in his stead.		35:18
p. himself in this p.,		57: 8
may need to p. them in their		57: 8
p. them in their inheritance.		57:15
and p. twelve olive-trees;		101:44
they shall p. vineyards, and they		101:101
every p. of the field before it	Mses	3: 5
concerning every p. of the field	Abr	5: 5
And he shall p. in the hearts	JS	2:39

PLANTED

and p. it with the choicest vine,	2 Ne	15: 2
I have p. another branch of the	Jac	5:23
branch also, which I have p.;		5:24
this have I p. in a good spot of		5:25
of these which I have p. in the		5:52
branches of the tree which I p.		5:54
he p. vineyards round about	Mos	11:15
a seed may be p. in your heart,	Al	32:28
the experiment, and p. the seed,		32:33
said must be p. in their hearts;		33: 1
thus Moroni p. the standard of		46:36
you may be p. in the land of	DC	55: 5
Phelps be p. in this p.,		57:11
be p. in the land of Zion,		57:14
shall be p. in their stead.		64:40
which is p. in a goodly land,		97: 9
and p. the olive-trees,		101:46
after ye had p. the vineyard,		101:53
others shall be p. in their stead		114: 2
stake which I have p. to be a		124: 2
P a garden eastward in Eden,	Mses	3: 8
I, the Lord God, p. the tree of life		3: 9
And the Gods p. a garden,	Abr	5: 8

PLANTS

of the many p. and roots which	Al	46:40
set to be as p. of renown,	DC	124:61

PLATE

he fastened on his head p.,	Al	46:13

PLATES

HAND OF MORMON UPON P.	T Pg	
FROM THE P. OF NEPHI	T Pg	
upon p. which I have made	1 Ne	1:17
engraven upon p. of brass.		3: 3
engraven upon the p. of brass,		3:12
engraven upon the p. of brass.		3:24
which were upon the p. of brass,		4:16
we took the p. of brass		4:24
engraven upon the p. of brass,		4:38
found upon the p. of brass		5:10
these p. of brass should go forth		5:14
p. of brass never perish;		5:18
I give it after upon these p.		5:19
cannot be written upon these p.,		6: 1
shall not occupy these p. with		6: 3
cannot be written upon these p.		6: 6
I have spoken concerning these p.,		9: 1
they are not the p. upon which		9: 2
for the p. upon which I make		9: 2
they are called the p. of Nephi,		9: 2
these p. also are called		9: 2
also are called the p. of Nephi.		9: 2
that I should make these p.,		9: 3
Upon the other p. should be	1 Ne	9: 4
these p. are for the more part of		9: 4
other p. are for the more part of		9: 4
commanded me to make these p.		9: 5
to give an account upon these p.		10: 1
which are upon the p. of brass,		13:23
wherefore I did make p. of ore		19: 1
And upon the p. which I made		19: 1
of the Lord to make these p.;		19: 2
those p. of which I have spoken;		19: 2
transpired before I made these p.		19: 2
made mention upon the first p.		19: 2
And after I had made these p.		19: 3
should be written upon these p.;		19: 3
a record upon the other p.,		19: 4
these p. should be handed down		19: 4
an account of my making these p.		19: 5
do not write anything upon p. save		19: 6
written upon the p. of brass.		19:21
engraven upon the p. of brass,		19:22
engraven upon the p. of brass,		22: 1
written upon the p. of brass		22:30
are written upon the p. of brass.	2 Ne	4: 2
are written upon mine other p.;		4:14
are written upon mine other p.		4:14
engraven upon the p. of brass.		4:15
I do not write upon these p. all		5: 4
engraven upon the p. of brass;		5:12
had kept the records upon my p.,		5:29
said unto me: Make other p.;		5:30
went and made these p.		5:31
engravings which are upon these p.		5:32
they must search mine other p.		5:33
concerning the small p.,	Jac	1: 2
that I should write upon these p.		1: 3
be engraven upon his other p.,		1: 3
that I should preserve these p.		1: 4
the heads of them upon these p.,		3:13
cannot be written upon these p.;		3:13
are written upon the larger p.,		3:14
These p. are called the plates of		3:14
plates are called the p. of Jacob,		4: 1
of engraving our words upon p.)		4: 1
the things which we write upon p.		4: 2
upon anything save it be upon p.		4: 2
can write a few words upon p.,		4: 3
to engraven these words upon p.,		7:26
kept on the other p. of Nephi;		7:27
unto my son Enos: Take these p.		7:27
end of my writing upon these p.,	Jar	1: 2
And as these p. are small,		1:14
write more, for the p. are small.		1:14
can go to the other p. of Nephi;		1:15
deliver these p. into the hands of	Om	1: 1
write somewhat upon these p.,		1: 3
and I had kept these p.		1: 8
I did deliver the p. unto me		1:11
this people is engraven upon p.		1:14
of Mosiah with the p. of brass		1:18
written, but not in these p.		1:25
I shall deliver up these p. unto		1:30
and these p. are full.	WM	1: 3
abridgment from the p. of Nephi,		1: 3
and I found these p., which		1: 4
things which are upon these p.		1: 5
shall take from the p. of Nephi;		1: 6
behold, I shall take these p.,		1: 9
I take from the p. of Nephi;		1:10
delivered up these p. into the hands		1:10
and put them with the other p.,	Mos	1: 3
engraven on the p. of brass,		1: 3
were it not for these p.,		1: 4
were for the help of these p.;		1: 6
behold, also the p. of Nephi,		1:16
engraven on the p. of brass;		1:16
and also the p. of Nephi;		8: 5
the p. which contained the record		8: 9
have brought twenty-four p.		8:11
engravings that are on the p.		8:19
is contained within these p.,		10:16
engraven on the p. of brass,		21:27
it was engraven on p. of ore.		28:11
engraven on the p. of brass,		

PLATES

and also the p. of Nephi,	Mos 28:11
which were on the p. of gold	28:11
he took the p. of brass,	28:20
have done, upon the p. of Nephi,	Al 37: 2
And these p. of brass, which	37: 3
all the p. which do contain that	37: 5
do contain, which are on these p.,	37: 9
concerning those twenty-four p.,	37:21
arm-shields, and their head-p.;	43:38
in two many of their head-p.,	43:44
written upon the p. of Nephi.	44:24
breastplates, and their head-p.,	49:24
with arrows, and with head-p.,	He 1:14
concerning the p. of brass,	3Ne 1: 2
and they had head-p. upon them;	4: 7
engraven on the p. which were	5:10
were called the p. of Nephi.	5:10
on p. which I have made with	5:11
written upon the p. of brass	10:17
the p. of Nephi do contain the	26: 7
engraven upon the p. of Nephi,	26:11
kept it upon the p. of Nephi)	4Ne 1:19
he kept it upon the p. of Nephi	1:19
kept it upon the p. of Nephi;	1:21
ye shall take the p. of Nephi	Mrm 1: 4
engrave on the p. of Nephi	1: 4
and taken the p. of Nephi,	2:17
upon the p. of Nephi I did	2:18
upon these p. I did forbear	2:18
record out of the p. of Nephi,	6: 6
save it were these few p.	6: 6
also if I had room upon the p.,	8: 5
the p. thereof are of no worth,	8:14
And if our p. had been	9:33
from the twenty and four p.	Eth 1: 2
but they are had upon the p.;	1: 4
I have written upon these p.	4: 4
that ye may show the p. unto	5: 2
and breastplates, and head-p.,	15:15
purpose are these p. preserved,	DC 3:19
got the p. of which you have	5: 1
a gift to translate the p.;	5: 4
engraven upon the p. of Nephi;	10:38
things upon the p. of Nephi.	10:39
engraven upon the p. of Nephi	10:40
which are on the p. of Nephi,	10:41
engraven upon the p. of Nephi	10:45
you shall have a view of the p.,	17: 1
deposited, written upon gold p.,	JS 2:34
deposited with the p.;	2:35
when I got those p. of which	2:42
with me about the p.,	2:42
where the p. were deposited,	2:42
get the p. for the purpose of	2:46
object in view in getting the p.	2:46
me the p. were deposited;	2:50
lay the p., deposited in a	2:51
indeed did I behold the p.,	2:52
on these stones lay the p. and	2:52
come for obtaining the p.	2:53
arrived for obtaining the p.,	2:59
the characters off the p.	2:62
which I had drawn off the p.,	2:63
that there were gold p. in the	2:64
if I would bring the p. to him	2:65
that part of the p. were sealed,	2:65
of my having received the p.,	2:66
in the translation of the p.	2:68

PLAY

shall p. on the hole of the asp,	2Ne 21: 8
shall p. on the hole of the asp,	30:14
they did p. with the beasts as	3Ne 28:22
p. with the wild beasts even as	4Ne 1:33

PLEAD

did p. with my brethren,	1Ne 7:19
did p. with me that I would	7:20
The Lord standeth up to p.,	2Ne 13:13
and he will p. your cause,	Jac 3: 1
he began to p. with the king	Mos 17: 2
and p. with the Lamanites that	19:13

PLEASED

did p. in behalf of the people	Mos 20:25
did p. with the Lamanites;	23:33
to p. with their brethren,	23:33
they did p. with their father	28: 5
And he began to p. for them	Al 14: 7
there I will p. with the king that	20: 7
he began to p. with Ammon	20:21
they p. with the queen saying:	22:20
they p. with Amalickiah that	47:15
the people began to p. with	He 11: 8
he p. with them that they would	Eth 8: 6
and p. with her strong ones,	DC 90:36
we p. before thee for a full and	109:32
to p. the cause of the poor and	124:75
chosen hath p. before my face.	Mses 7:39

PLEADED

p. for himself with much boldness.	Al 1:11
have I p. before the Father	DC 38: 4

PLEADETH

God p. the cause of his people;	2Ne 8:22

PLEADING

of the Nephites, p. for mercy.	Al 55:23
is p. your cause before him—	DC 45: 3

PLEADINGS

hearing the evidences and p.	DC 102:20

PLEASANT

and upon all p. pictures.	2Ne 12:16
the men of Judah his p. plant;	15: 7
and dragons in their p. palaces;	23:22
a very beautiful and p. land,	Mos 23: 4
and it was p. to their taste,	Al 55:13
unto them, yea, a p. voice,	He 5:46
and all thy borders of p. stones.	3Ne 22:12
Jerusalem be p. unto the Lord,	24: 4
that is p. to the sight of man;	Mses 3: 9
that it became p. to the eyes,	4:12
every tree that is p. to the sight	Abr 5: 9

PLEASE

and they p. themselves in	2Ne 12: 6
Now this did p. Kishkumen	He 2: 9
before him, and I will p. him,	Eth 8:10
both to p. the eye and to	DC 59:18
the will of men, nor as they p.,	63:10
should not take when he p.,	64:28

PLEASED

if my people are p. with the	2Ne 5:32
will be p. with mine engravings	5:32
Yet it p. the Lord to bruise him;	Mos 14:10
Lamoni was much p. with Ammon,	Al 17:24
Son, in whom I am well p.,	3Ne 11: 7
before him that she p. him,	Eth 8:11
which I, the Lord, am well p.,	DC 1:30
none else with whom I am well p.;	38:10
in whom thou wast well p.;	45: 4
in whom I am well p.,	50:37
in whom I am well p.,	51: 3
am not well p. with him,	58:41
with some I am not well p.,	60: 2
with whom I am well p.,	61:35
is angry he is not well p.;	63:11
I, the Lord, am not p. with	63:12
I, the Lord, am not p. with	63:55
I, the Lord, am not well p. with	68:31
whom the Lord was well p.	84: 3
not well p. with many things;	90:35
I am not well p. with my	90:35
well p. that there should be	97: 3
not well p. with many who are	98:19
which I, the Lord, was not well p.	112: 2
I am well p. with your offering	124: 1
for I am well p. with him,	124:12
things with which I am not p.,	124:84
Satan knew this, and it p. him.	Mses 5:21
as they were p. to call it,	JS 2: 6
let them join what sect they p.;	2: 6

PLEASES

PLEASES
destroyeth when he p., — DC 63: 4

PLEASETH
And it p. God that he hath — DC 59:20
it p. me, that you have come — 60: 1
without faith no man p. God; — 63:11

PLEASING
which are p. unto the world — 1Ne 6: 5
things which are p. unto God — 6: 5
that which is p. unto God. — 2Ne 5:32
which thing is p. unto God; — Jac 2: 7
to hear the p. word of God, — 2: 8
upon the p. word of God — 2: 9
and receive the p. word of God, — 3: 2
before the p. bar of God, — 6:13
this thing was p. unto me, Jacob, — 7:22
p. me, because of the prophecies — WM 1: 4
were in the carnal mind; — Al 30:53
the p. bar of the great — Mro 10:34
which is p. unto me, — DC 25:11
be p. unto the same Lord, — 46:15
before me as is p. unto me. — 55: 4
which are not p. in my sight, — 66: 3
this is p. unto your Lord, — 88: 2
And it is p. unto me that — 89:13

PLEASINGLY
hath smiled upon you most p., — Jac 2:13

PLEASURE
according to his will and p. — 1Ne 16:38
he will do his p. on Babylon, — 20:14
according to his will and p. — 2Ne 10:22
according to the will and p. of — 25:22
according to mine own p. — 29: 9
according to his will and p.? — Jac 4: 9
according to his will and p. — 5:14
then shall I see his face with p., — En 1:27
according to his own will and p., — Mos 7:33
the p. of the Lord shall prosper — 14:10
according to their own will and p. — Al 4: 8
it was left to the p. of the king — 17:20
according to his will and p. — 17:20
slay him according to their p., — 17:35
them according to their p. — 49: 7
according to their p. — 50: 5
Bountiful, according to their p. — 50:11
according to mine own p., — DC 29:48
have p. in unrighteousness. — 56:15
up at his own will and p.; — 63: 4
the good p. of my will — 76: 7
and I will do my p. with them. — 136:30

PLEASURES
according to their wills and p., — Al 12:31

PLEDGE
And p. the properties which — DC 104:85

PLEDGED
as p. by the governor, — DC 135: 7

PLEDGES
and keep all your p. — DC 136:20

PLENTIFULLY
your seed, doth abound most p. — Jac 2:12

PLENTY
our women did give p. of suck — 1Ne 17: 2
had also a p. of provisions — Al 57: 6
have an exceeding p. of gold, — He 6: 9

PLOT
being who did p. with Cain, — He 6:27
p. with Cain and his followers — 6:27

PLOTS
know of their plans and their p., — Al 2:21
and doth hand down their p., — He 6:30

PLOW
beat their swords into p.-shares, — 2Ne 12: 4
both to p. and to sow, to reap — Eth 10:25

PLOW-SHARES: *see PLOW and SHARES.*

PLUCK
go and p. the branches from a — Jac 5: 7
will p. off those main branches — 5: 7
P. off the branches that have not — 5:26
let us p. from the tree those — 5:52
P. not the wild branches from — 5:57
we will p. from the trees those — 5:58
and ye p. it up and cast it out. — Al 32:38
ye can never p. of the fruit of — 32:40
ye shall p. the fruit thereof, — 32:42
I will p. up thy groves out of — 3Ne 21:18
to p. out the wicked and — DC 63:54
p. not up the tares while — 86: 6

PLUCKED
to them that p. off the hair. — 2Ne 7: 6
and these which I have p. off — Jac 5: 9
and because I p. not the branches — 5:45
wild branches began to be p. off — 5:73
wherefore they shall be p. out. — DC 64:36

PLUNDER
nor that ye should murder, or p., — Mos 2:13
they should rob and p. them, — 10:17
all manner of wickedness and p., — 24: 7
a practice of p. among them. — Al 18: 7
ought not to murder, nor to p., — 23: 3
murders, and to rob and to p., — He 6:17
thus they might murder, and p., — 6:23
do murder, and p., and steal, — 7:21
they did commit murder and p.; — 11:25
robbers to p. and to obtain food, — 3Ne 4: 4
were to p. and rob and murder. — 4: 5
and to murder, and to p., and — Eth 8:16

PLUNDERED
been murdered, p., and hunted, — He 3:16

PLUNDERERS
those murderers and p. were a — He 6:18

PLUNDERING
no stealing, nor p., nor — Mos 29:14
and the stealing, and the p., — 29:36
stealing, robbing, p., murdering, — Al 16:18
and robbing and p. them; — 17:14
these things by murdering and p., — 17:14
and their robbings, and their p., — He 3:14
murdering, p., lying, stealing, — 4:12

PLUNDERINGS
and robbings, and their p., — Al 37:21
their murderings, and their p., — 50:21
for their murders, and their p., — He 6:21
their murderings, and their p., — 10: 3

PLUNGED
p. the Lamanites into the midst — He 1:32

PLURAL
allege that p. marriages are still — DC OD
teaching polygamy or p. marriage, — OD
any other number of p. marriages — OD
by Congress forbidding p. marriages, — OD
declaration concerning p. marriages — OD

P.M.
June, 1844, about five o'clock p., — DC 135: 1

POCKET
and put it into my p., — JS 2:64
accordingly took it out of my p. — 2:65

POIGNANT
were deep and often p., — JS 2: 8

POINT

POINT
they did p. the finger of scorn	1Ne	8:33
those spindles should p. the way	Al	37:40
will p. to you a straight course to		37:44
p. unto them a straight course to		37:44
to excuse yourself in the least p.		42:30
laid it upon the p. of his sword,		44:13
that he should not gain the p.,		46:29
Lamanites should abtain that p.		52: 9
may console ourselves in this p.,		56:11
Joseph shall p. out to them,	DC	124:79
thou standest in p. of reckoning,	Abr	3: 5

POINTED
the one p. the way whither we	1Ne	16:10
yea, the sharp p. arrow,	Jar	1: 8
minds were p. to by the angels,	DC	121:27

POINTERS
the p. which were in the ball,	1Ne	16:28

POINTING
mocking and p. their fingers	1Ne	8:27
p. to the covenant which should		15:18
it p. our souls to him;	Jac	4: 5
p. to that great and last sacrifice;	Al	34:14
and said, p. to the other—	JS	2:17

POINTS
and the very p. of his doctrine,	1Ne	15:14
upon those p. of doctrine,	Al	41: 9
a few particular p. of the law		51: 2
concerning the p. of doctrine	He	11:22
the true p. of doctrine,		11:23
the p. of my doctrine,	3Ne	11:28
of the true p. of my doctrine,		21: 6
the true p. of my doctrine,	DC	10:62
the p. of my doctrine;		10:63
to act upon the p. of my law		43: 8

POISON
and the effect thereof is p.	Mos	7:30
should administer p. by degrees	Al	47:18
they might destroy them with p.		55:30
no p. should be administered		55:32
wine would p. a Lamanite		55:32
it would also p. a Nephite;		55:32
and did p. many p.	Eth	9:31
administer p. unto them	DC	84:71
the p. of a serpent shall not		84:72
administer unto him deadly p.;		124:98

POISONOUS
been bitten by the p. serpents,	2Ne	25:20
wild beasts nor p. serpents,	Mrm	8:24
there came forth p. serpents	Eth	9:31
to flee before the p. serpents,		9:31
might fall by the p. serpents.		9:33
the p. serpents were destroyed.		10:19
and against p. serpents,	DC	24:13
in paths where the p. serpent		124:99

POISONS
serpents, and against deadly p.;	DC	24:13

POLE
fastened it upon the end of a p.	Al	46:12
took the p., which had on the end		46:13

POLISHED
and made me a p. shaft;	1Ne	21: 2
p. with the refinement which is	DC	124: 2

POLITENESS
by the p. of the king,	Fac	3: 1

POLITICAL
been sent for p. purposes,	DC	OD

POLLUTE
p. my holy land?	DC	84:59
if they p. their inheritances		103:14
if they p. their inheritances.		103:14

POOR

be left to p. mine heritage,	DC	105:15
to come into thy house to p. it;		109:20
and do not p. this holy house.		110: 8
they p. mine holy grounds,		124:46

POLLUTED
not suffer my name to be p.,	1Ne	20:11
of their sinful and p. state,	Mos	25:11
awful, sinful, and p. state?	Al	26:17
have become p. because of	Mrm	8:36
why have ye p. the holy church		8:38
house shall be p. by him.	DC	88:134
they p. their inheritances.		101: 6
be p. by mine enemies,		101:97

POLLUTION
suffer any p. to come upon it.	DC	124:24

POLLUTIONS
there shall be great p. upon	Mrm	8:31
O ye p., ye hypocrites,		8:38

POLYGAMY
of the practice of p.—	DC	OD
We are not teaching p. or		OD
inculcate or encourage p.;		OD

POMP
and their multitude, and their p.,	2Ne	15:14
Thy p. is brought down to the		24:11

PONDER
that ye p. somewhat in your hearts	2Ne	32: 1
ye p. these things in your hearts?		32: 1
that ye p. still in your hearts;		32: 8
p. upon the things which I have	3Ne	17: 3
and p. it in your hearts.	Mro	10: 3
p. upon the things which you	DC	30: 3
with you to p. in your hearts,		88:62
p. the warning in their hearts		88:71
left to p. on the strangeness	JS	2:47

PONDERETH
and my heart p. them,	2Ne	4:15
my heart p. continually upon		4:16

PONDERING
as I sat p. in mine heart	1Ne	11: 1
p. upon the things which the Lord	He	10: 2
as he was thus p.—being much		10: 3
as he was thus p. in his heart,		10: 3

POOL
of the conduit of the upper p.	2Ne	17: 3

POOLS
for the bittern, and p. of water;	2Ne	24:23
come forth p. of living water;	DC	133:29

POOR
they are rich they despise the p.,	2Ne	9:30
the spoil of the p. in your houses.		13:14
and grind the faces of the p.,		13:15
right from the p. of my people,		20: 2
unto Laish, O p. Anathoth.		20:30
shall he judge the p.,		21: 4
the first-born of the p. shall feed,		24:30
the p. of his people shall trust		24:32
and grind upon the face of the p.		26:20
the p. among men shall rejoice		27:30
They rob the p. because of their		28:13
they rob the p. because of their		28:13
the meek and the p. in heart,		28:13
shall the Lord God judge the p.,		30: 9
that it was a p. spot of ground;	Jac	5:22
And again, I say unto the p.,	Mos	4:24
of your substance to the p.,		4:26
to the p., and the needy,	Al	1:27
imparting their substance to the p.		4:13
in turning your backs upon the p.,		5:55
among the p. class of people;		32: 2
therefore they were p.; yea,		32: 3
p. as to things of the world;		32: 3
and also they were p. in heart.		32: 3

POOR

of whom were p. in heart,	Al 32: 4
but they did receive all the p. of	35: 9
of their oppression to the p.,	He 4:12
turn their backs upon the p.	6:39
blessed are the p. in spirit who	3Ne 12: 3
ye should do alms unto the p.;	13: 1
there were not rich and p.,	4Ne 1: 3
more than ye love the p. and	Mrm 8:37
the p. and the meek shall have	DC 35:15
the p. have complained before	38:16
look to the p. and the needy,	38:35
thou wilt remember the p.,	42:30
of your substance unto the p.,	42:31
to administer to the p. and	42:34
has consecrated unto the p.	42:37
unto the p. of my people who	42:39
for the good of the p., and for	42:71
that ye must visit the p. and	44: 6
for the p. and needy of my	51: 5
the p. and the needy,	52:40
give your substance to the p.,	56:16
Wo unto you p. men, whose	56:17
But blessed are the p. who are	56:18
and the p. shall rejoice;	56:19
might be prepared for the p.;	58: 8
then shall the p., the lame,	58:11
the low, and the p. to repent.	58:47
church, to the p. and needy.	72:12
for the p. of my people,	78: 3
manage the affairs of the p.,	82:12
provided for, as also the p.	83: 6
the old and cast it unto the p.,	84:105
searching after the p. to	84:112
the p. and the meek of the earth	88:17
that the p. shall be exalted,	104:16
unto the p. and the needy,	104:18
to the p. and afflicted among	105: 3
all the p., the needy, and afflicted	109:55
all the p. and meek of the earth;	109:72
blessings upon the heads of the p.	124:21
to plead the cause of the p. and	124:75
support the cause of the p.,	124:89
in taking the p., the widows,	136: 8
and there was no p. among them.	Mses 7:18
being very p., and the	JS 2:61

POORER
of ground was p. than the first.	Jac 5:23

POOREST
it was the p. spot in all the land	Jac 5:21

POPULAR
become p. in the eyes of the world,	1Ne 22:23
and teacher ought to become p.;	Al 1: 3
the more p. part of the Zoramites	35: 3
of the most p. sects of the day,	JS 2:23

PORE
blood cometh from every p.,	Mos 3: 7
and to bleed at every p.,	DC 19:18

PORTION
divide him a p. with the great,	Mos 14:12
the p. of his word which he doth	Al 12: 9
the lesser p. of the word;	12:10
the greater p. of the word,	12:10
the lesser p. of the word	12:11
grant unto them a p. of his Spirit	17: 9
a p. of that Spirit dwelleth in me,	18:35
he has given us a p. of his Spirit	24: 8
give us a p. of their substance	27:24
give place for a p. of my words.	32:27
nor p. of the Spirit of the Lord;	40:13
a large p. of their substance	43:13
Impart a p. of thy property,	DC 19:34
he shall appoint a man his p.,	51: 4
shall secure unto him his p.,	51: 4
have power to claim that p.	51: 5
on that p. that is deeded	51: 5
a p. unto mine elders who are	60:10
that p. of Spirit and power	71: 1
and appoint every man his p.	78:21

that p. that shall be meted	DC 84:85
their p. shall be appointed them	85: 9
by a p. of the celestial glory	88:29
a p. of the terrestrial glory	88:30
by a p. of the telestial glory	88:31
that p. that is necessary to	96: 4
appoint them their p. among	101:90
made, and impart not his p.,	104:18
appoint the p. of the oppressor	124: 8
not appropriate any p. of that	124:70
appropriate any p. of that stock	124:71
and received his p.;	132:39
shall appoint him his p. with	JS 1:54

PORTIONS
unto this people their p.,	DC 51: 3

POSITION
by virtue of his p.	DC OD

POSSESS
should p. again the land of their	1Ne 10: 3
that they should p. it.	17:36
people, who should p. the land,	19: 3
that they may p. this land unto	2Ne 1: 9
the house of Israel shall p. them,	24: 2
they do not rise, nor p. the land,	24:21
and p. the land of Jerusalem;	25:11
the nations who shall p. them	25:22
they shall p. the land of your	Jac 3: 4
to p. the land of their inheritance.	Om 1:27
your whole soul has power to p.,	Mos 2:20
one half of all we have or p.	7:22
he should p. the power of God,	8:16
desirous to go up to p. the land,	9: 3
and p. the land in peace.	9: 5
might p. the land of Lehi-Nephi,	9: 6
the land that we might p. it.	9: 7
the land that we might p. it.	9:10
began to p. the land in peace.	10: 1
nations which shall p. the land;	12: 8
that they might p. the land,	19:15
that they might p. the land	19:22
begun to p. the land of Amulon	23:31
creature who should p. the land	28:15
and herds, and all that you p.,	Al 7:27
to p. their own lands.	16: 8
to p. the land of Ammonihah	16:11
I will give up all that I p.,	22:15
spirit which doth p. your bodies	34:34
have power to p. your body in	34:34
that shall hereafter p. the land.	37:25
remain to p. the land—	46:13
by the seashore, and p. the land.	50: 9
p. the cities which he had taken,	52:13
Gentiles who shall p. the land.	Mrm 5:19
should p. this land of promise,	Eth 2: 8
whatsoever nation shall p. it	2: 9
that doth p. it shall serve God	2:10
whatsoever nation shall p. it	2:12
that whoso should p. the land	9:20
should p. it unto the Lord,	9:20
another people to p. the land,	11:21
nations should p. this land,	DC 10:49
ye shall p. it again in eternity,	38:20
that one man should p. that	49:20
to p. it from generation to	69: 8
may p. it forever and ever;	88:20
land, to p. thine inheritance;	99: 7
patience ye may p. your souls,	101:38
of mine house and p. the land.	101:58
the garners to p. eternal life,	101:65
to p. it forever and ever.	103: 7
ye shall p. the goodly land.	103:20
my saints should p. them	105:29
to p. a greater knowledge, and to	Abr 1: 2

POSSESSED
with all the faculty which I p.,	1Ne 15:25
tax of one fifth part of all they p.,	Mos 11: 3
which was p. by the Lamanites;	11:12
even one half of all they p.,	19:15
of one half of all they p.	19:22

POSSESSED

even one half of all they p.	Mos 19:26
was p. by Alma and his brethren.	23:35
land which was p. by his people;	24: 4
and faculties which I have p.;	29:14
name of him who first p. them;	Al 8: 7
of one tenth part of all he p.	13:15
Art thou also p. with the devil?	14: 7
thou art p. with a sying spirit,	30:42
was p. by the people of Nephi.	45:22
which was p. by the Nephites;	46:36
which was p. by the Nephites.	48: 9
which was p. by the Nephites.	50: 1
who p. the land of Morianton	50:26
people who p. the land of Lehi	50:27
are the cities which they p.	56:15
which was p. by the Nephites.	He 3:31
which are p. by the Nephites,	13:16
who have p. this land, shall	Mrm 8:23
whoso is found p. of it at	Mro 7:47
one who p. great knowledge,	Abr 1: 2

POSSESSING

p. all the land northward,	Al 50:11
as p. the keys of the kingdom,	DC 128:20

POSSESSION

I will also make it a p. for	2Ne 24:23
took p. of the land of Helam.	Mos 23:29
taken p. of all these lands;	24: 2
they obtain p. of our city,	Al 2:25
the Nephites had taken p. of	22:29
have no more p. on the north,	22:33
took p. of the land of Jershon;	27:26
and take p. of their house—	40:13
of Manti and take p. of the land;	43:22
that land and take p. of the city,	43:25
and take p. of the kingdom.	47: 8
and took p. of the city.	47:31
power upon the lands of their p.	50:12
take p. of the land which was	50:29
p. of those parts of the land,	50:32
to take p. of those records	50:38
Amalickiah took p. of the city,	51:23
p. of all their fortifications.	51:23
taking p. of many cities,	51:26
take p. of the land Bountiful,	51:30
which they had obtained p. of;	52: 5
should take p. of their lands	52:13
into the city, and take p. of it.	52:24
obtained p. of the city Mulek	52:26
p. of the city of Mulek,	53: 6
p. of a number of their cities in	53: 8
to gain p. of those parts which	55:20
and took p. of the city,	55:24
the Lamanites have obtained p.	56:13
other cities, which they had p. of,	57: 4
and did take p. of the city.	58:21
obtained p. of their strongholds.	58:23
take p. of the city of Manti	58:28
at this period of time in our p.;	58:31
we are in the p. of our lands;	58:38
success in obtaining the p. of	58:41
upon us, taking p. of our lands,	60:17
They have got p. of the land,	61: 8
p. of the city of Zarahemla,	61:18
and had taken p. of the land.	62: 6
the p. of the city of Nephihah	62:26
p. of the city of Nephihah,	62:30
Shiblon took p. of those sacred	63: 1
were in the p. of Helaman	63:12
did take p. of the whole city.	He 1:20
in p. of the city of Zarahemla,	1:22
the p. of the strongest hold in	1:22
taking p. of many cities and of	1:27
took p. of the city of Zarahemla	1:33
p. of the land of Zarahemla;	4: 5
the p. of the Nephites which was	4: 8
lost p. of almost all their lands.	4:13
Nephites the lands of their p.	5:52
which are in the land of our p.,	7:22
get p. of the hearts of the people	3Ne 2: 2
p. of the land of the Nephites,	3:11
to take p. of the lands,	4: 1
p. of all the lands which had	3Ne 4: 1
and we did take p. of the city,	Mrm 2: 4
again taken p. of the lands of	2:27
not get p. of any of our lands;	3: 6
take p. of the city Desolation,	4: 2
take p. of the city Teancum also.	4: 7
p. again of the city Desolation.	4: 8
take p. of the city Desolation,	4:13
taking p. of their own lands,	DC 105:30
after thee for an everlasting p.,	Abr 2: 6
after truth in p. of the facts,	JS 2: 1
as I have such facts in my p.	2: 1
therefore, did I get p. of myself,	2:18
the p. and use of these stones	2:35

POSSESSIONS

we might have enjoyed our p.	1Ne 17:21
from them the lands of their p.,	2Ne 1:11
home unto the lands of their p.;	29:14
the p. of a part of the land,	Mos 7:21
more p. only in the land of Nephi,	Al 22:34
of the lands of their own p.,	50: 9
south, in the borders of their p.,	50:10
from off the lands of their p.,	50:12
line of the p. of the Lamanites.	50:13
own lands, or the land of your p.,	54: 6
we had regained of our p.;	58: 3
cities, and our lands, and our p.,	58:10
maintain our lands, and our p.,	58:12
number of cities and so great p.	58:32
obtain the remainder of those p.	59: 4
recover the remainder of our p.	60:24
even the half of all their p.	He 4:10
more p. over the Lamanites.	4:18
cities, your lands, and your p.,	3Ne 3: 6
up your lands and your p.,	3:10
to their own lands and their p.,	6: 2
their store and their p. here;	DC 64:26

POSSESSOR

he is p. of all things;	DC 50:27
no man is p. of all things except	50:28

POSSIBILITY

there is a p. that man may	DC 20:32

POSSIBLE

How is it p. that the Lord will	1Ne 3:31
whatsoever things were p. for us,	2Ne 5: 7
upon them as much as it were p.,	Jac 1: 4
how is it p. that these,	4:17
if it were p., they would destroy	En 1:14
For it were not p. that our father,	Mos 1: 4
if it were p. that little children	3:16
in a body as much as it was p.,	21:18
if it were p. that ye could always	23: 8
if it were p. that you could	29:13
inasmuch as it was p.	Al 1:32
if it were p. that Amlici should	2: 4
neither was it p. that any man	8:31
if it were p. that they could fall	9:19
there was no p. chance that they	12:21
if it had been p. for Adam to	12:23
if it were p. that our first parents	12:26
bring, if it were p., their brethren,	17: 9
and retake it if it were p.	52:16
from the Lamanites as it were p.	54: 3
if it were p. to put an end to	56:29
with as many men as it were p.	61: 5
not p. that they could disbelieve	3Ne 7:18
our people as fast as it were p.,	Mrm 2: 7
before it was p. to stop them	2:16
our people as much as it were p.,	2:21
were it p., I would make all	8:12
all the strength which it was p.	Eth 15:14
how is it p. that ye can lay	Mro 7:20
if it were p. that you should	DC 5: 7
if it were p. that other nations	10:49
to this land, as soon as p.,	57:15
provided, as soon as it is p.,	90:19
were it p. that man could	Mses 7:30
if p., they shall deceive the very	JS 1:22

POSSIBLE 747 POWER

POSSIBLE

If p. to discover the mine.	JS	2:56
to get them from me if p.		2:60

POSSIBLY

as soon as he p. can,	DC 114: 1

POSTERITY

as long as any of our p. remains	Mos	29:32
his p. should be the chosen of	DC	107:42
with the residue of his p. who		107:53
befall his p. unto the latest		107:56
they and their p. shall be swept		121:15
nor their p. after them		121:21
be put upon the head of his p.		124:57
names go down to p. as gems for		135: 6
the p. of all the sons of Noah	Mses	7:42
for the benefit of my p. that shall	Abr	1:31

POSTS

And the p. of the door moved	2Ne	16: 4

POTIPHAR'S

by the hill called P. Hill,	Abr	1:10
P. Hill was in the land of Ur,		1:20

POTTER'S

shall be esteemed as the p. clay.	2Ne	27:27

POUR

I did p. out my whole soul	En	1: 9
that he may p. out his Spirit	Mos	18:10
O Lord, p. out thy Spirit upon		18:12
did p. out their hearts to him;		24:12
the Lord did p. out his Spirit		25:24
that he would p. out his Spirit	Al	8:10
the Lord did p. out his Spirit on		16:16
began to p. out his soul in prayer		19:14
to p. out his Spirit upon them;		19:36
ye must p. out your souls in your		34:26
we did p. out our souls in prayer		58:10
Lord began to p. out his Spirit	He	6:36
that I might p. out my soul		7:14
and p. you out a blessing that	3Ne	24:10
the Lord did p. out his blessings	Eth	9:20
p. out the fulness of my wrath.		9:20
I will p. out my Spirit upon you,	DC	19:38
which I will p. out upon you,		27:18
I will p. out my Spirit upon		44: 2
I may p. out my Spirit upon		95: 4
I will p. out my wrath		103: 2
thou wilt p. out thy judgments		109:45

POURED

the wrath of God was p. out	1Ne	14:15
the wrath of God is p. out		14:17
the wrath of God shall be p. out		22:16
the Lord hath p. out upon you	2Ne	27: 5
the Lord God p. in his Spirit	Jac	7: 8
has p. out his Spirit upon you,	Mos	4:20
hath p. out his soul unto death;		14:12
Spirit of the Lord be p. out upon		18:13
they p. out their thanks to God		24:21
he had p. out his whole soul		26:14
the Spirit of the Lord p. out	Al	19:14
he had p. out his soul to God,		46:17
the blessings which were p. out	He	3:25
great blessings p. out upon	3Ne	10:18
p. out in prayer unto my God	Mrm	3:12
wrath of God shall be p. out	DC	1: 9
be p. out from time to time,		5:19
be p. forth upon their heads.		39:15
judgment to be p. out upon		84:58
that war will be p. out upon		87: 2
war shall be p. out upon all		87: 3
to be p. out without measure		101:11
blessing to be p. out upon		105:12
ordained to be p. out upon those		109:21
gift of tongues be p. out upon		109:36
blessings which shall be p. out		110: 9
blessing which shall be p. out		110:10
wrath when it shall be p. out		115: 6
wrath of God to be p. out upon	Mses	7: 1

POURING

the Lord p. out his blessings	Al	16:21
was p. out his soul unto God	He	7:11
the p. out of the Holy Ghost	3Ne	20:27
p. down knowledge from heaven	DC	121:33

POVERTY

their p. as to the things of	Al	32: 4
of all men because of their p.,		32: 5
out because of our exceeding p.;		32: 5
because of your exceeding p.,		32:12
because of their exceeding p.		32:15
out because of your exceeding p.,		34:40
in the days of your p. ye cannot	He	13:31
in the days of your p. ye shall		13:32
were ignorant because of their p.,	3Ne	6:12
out of our p. we have given	DC	109: 5
only in the days of your p.,		124:30

POWDER

to pieces and grind them to p.	2Ne	26: 5

POWER

by the gift and p. of God	TPg	
thy p., and goodness, and mercy	1Ne	1:14
unto the p. of deliverance.		1:20
with p., being filled with the		2:14
shall have no p. over thy seed		2:23
by the Spirit and p. of God,		3:20
given them p. whereby they could		5: 8
for behold, he hath all p. unto		9: 6
spake by the p. of the Holy Ghost,		10:17
which p. he received by faith		10:17
by the p. of the Holy Ghost		10:17
by the p. of the Holy Ghost		10:19
in p. and great glory;		11:28
healed by the p. of the Lamb		11:31
the p. of the Lord was with them.		13:16
the p. of God was with them,		13:18
delivered by the p. of God		13:19
Satan hath great p. over them.		13:29
lifted up by the p. of God		13:30
unto them, in mine own p.,		13:34
by the gift and p. of the Lamb.		13:35
and the p. of the Holy Ghost;		13:37
forth by the p. of the Lamb,		13:39
in word, and also in p.,		14: 1
the p. of the Lamb of God,		14:14
with the p. of God in great glory.		14:14
may show his p. unto the Gentiles,		15:17
according to the p. of God		17:29
unto their obtaining p. over it.		17:35
led forth by his matchless p.		17:42
by the p. of his almighty word		17:46
I am filled with the p. of God,		17:48
as naught before the p. of God.		17:48
if the Lord has such great p.,		17:51
that it is the p. of the Lord		17:55
by what p. they had been brought		18: 9
that he might show forth his p.,		18:11
save it were the p. of God,		18:20
and the lightnings of his p.,		19:11
p. and glory of the God of Israel.		19:13
have no more p. over the hearts		22:15
preserve the righteous by his p.,		22:17
built up to get p. over the hearts		22:23
and might, and p., and great glory.		22:24
Satan has no p.;		22:26
he hath no p. over the hearts		22:26
p. given them to do all things	2Ne	1:10
and he will give unto them p.,		1:11
that he sought p. and authority		1:25
not sought for p. nor authority		1:25
sharpness of the p. of the word		1:26
the p. of God must be with him,		1:27
again by the p. of the Spirit,		2: 8
and also the p., and the mercy,		2:12
the captivity and p. of the devil;		2:27
spirit of the devil p. to captivate,		2:29
in the spirit of p., unto the bringing		3: 5
give p. to bring forth my word		3:11

POWER

by the p. of the Lord shall bring	2Ne 3:15
I will give p. unto him in a rod;	3:17
to that which was in my p.	5:18
manifest himself unto them in p.	6:14
or have I no p. to deliver?	7: 2
must needs be a p. of resurrection,	9: 6
it is by the p. of the resurrection	9:12
they are delivered by the p. of him.	9:25
death by the p. of the resurrection,	10:25
death by the p. of the atonement,	10:25
in his justice, and p., and mercy	11: 5
and gave unto Moses p. that he	25:20
and also gave him p. that he	25:20
by the p. of the Holy Ghost;	26:13
God will give unto him p.,	26:16
the p. and miracles of God,	26:20
shall be sealed by the p. of God,	27:10
shall be read by the p. of Christ;	27:11
shall behold it, by the p. of God,	27:12
And they deny the p. of God,	28: 5
he hath given his p. unto men;	28: 5
and denieth the p. of God,	28:26
by the p. of the Holy Ghost.	28:31
shall have p. over the hearts of	30:18
by the p. of the Holy Ghost;	32: 3
by the p. of the Holy Ghost	33: 1
the p. of the Holy Ghost carrieth	33: 1
unto you, with p. and great glory,	33:11
by the p. of mine arm,	Jac 2:25
we have p. to do these things.	4: 7
behold, by the p. of his word	4: 9
created by the p. of his word.	4: 9
to the p. of the resurrection	4:11
shall go forth in his p.,	6: 2
the p. of God, and the gift of the	6: 8
that the p. of the redemption	6: 9
according to the p. of justice,	6:10
flattery, and much p. of speech,	7: 4
according to the p. of the devil.	7: 4
by the p. of the Holy Ghost;	7:12
by this p. of the Holy Ghost,	7:13
he has p., both in heaven and in	7:14
the p. of the Lord came upon	7:15
and the p. of the Holy Ghost,	7:17
deceived by the p. of the devil.	7:18
the p. of God came down upon	7:21
sought by the p. of their arms	7:24
by the p. of his holy arm,	En 1:13
the judgments and the p. of God,	1:23
wrought upon by the p. of God	1:26
were led by the p. of his arm,	Om 1:13
by the gift and p. of God.	1:20
and the p. of his redemption.	1:26
speak the word of God with p.	WM 1:17
his matchless and marvelous p.,	Mos 1:13
preserved by his matchless p.,	2:11
your whole soul has p. to possess,	2:20
enemies shall have no p. over you.	2:31
that with p., the Lord Omnipotent	3: 5
his matchless p., and his wisdom,	4: 6
he has all wisdom, and all p.,	4: 9
through the wisdom, and p.,	5:15
he should possess the p. of God,	8:16
have great p. given him from God.	8:16
he spake with p. and authority	13: 6
ye have not p. to slay me,	13: 7
go forth in mighty p. upon	13:34
conceived by the p. of God;	15: 3
giving the Son p. to make	15: 8
and hath p. over the dead;	15:20
and the devil has p. over them;	16: 3
the devil hath all p. over him.	16: 5
through the p., and sufferings,	18: 2
by the p. and authority of God	18:17
also, as often as it was in their p.,	18:25
with p. and authority from God.	18:26
the strength and p. of God,	21:30
been delivered by the p. of God	23:13
forth his mighty p. unto them,	23:24
no p. to do anything contrary to	23:39
and his p. in delivering Alma	25:10
gave him p. to ordain priests	25:19
to exercise his p. over them.	27: 9
of the p. and authority of God,	Mos 27:14
can ye dispute the p. of God?	27:15
was nothing save the p. of God	27:18
knew that it was the p. of God.	27:20
with all the p. and faculties	29:14
doth the Lord work with his p.	29:20
no p. on any man for his belief.	Al 1:17
according to the will and p. and	4:14
and gave him p. according to	4:16
that he might have p. to enact laws	4:16
p. and authority from God	5: 3
Noah, by the mercy and p. of God.	5: 4
of bondage by the p. of his word;	5: 5
might, majesty, p., and dominion.	5:50
the Lord God hath p. to do all	7: 8
by the p. of the Holy Ghost,	7:10
to the p. of his deliverance;	7:13
that thou hast no p. over us;	8:12
And they had p. given unto them,	8:31
they did not exercise their p. until	8:31
might show forth his p. in them.	8:31
p. which the Lord had given them.	8:32
p. of God which was in them,	9:hd
had not been for his matchless p.,	9:11
the p. and deliverance of Jesus	9:28
the p. and captivation of the devil.	9:28
his mysteries and marvelous p.	10: 5
his mysteries and his marvelous p.;	10: 5
that he may have p. over you,	10:25
he hath exercised his p. in thee.	12: 5
to the p. of his captivity.	12: 6
more and more of the p. of God;	12: 7
for p. was given unto them that	12: 7
and in his p., and in his might,	12:15
he has all p. to save every man	12:15
to the p. and captivity of Satan,	12:17
of redemption could have no p.,	12:32
the p. of God which is in us,	14:10
ye see that ye had not p. to save	14:15
that I have p. to deliver you up	14:19
If ye have such great p. why do	14:20
If ye have the p. of God deliver	14:24
the p. of God was upon Alma	14:25
Lord had granted unto them p.,	14:28
and of their p. of deliverance;	15: 2
the p. of Christ unto salvation?	15: 6
ascribing all the p. of Alma and	15:15
with p. and authority of God.	17: 3
by the p. of their words many were	17: 4
to the word and p. of God	17:17
I will show forth my p. unto these	17:29
or the p. which is in me,	17:29
with mighty p. he did sling stones	17:36
began to be astonished at his p.;	17:36
also of his great p. in contending	18: 2
that a man has such great p.,	18: 3
this man that has such great p.?	18: 8
also tell me by what p. ye slew	18:20
by what p. I do these things?	18:22
and also p. according to my faith	18:35
hast p. to do many mighty words	19: 4
Lamoni was under the p. of God;	19: 6
concerning the great p. of Ammon.	19:15
knew that it was the p. of God;	19:17
them to believe in the p. of God,	19:17
be the cause of this great p.,	19:24
the p. of God working miracles	23: 6
usurped the p. and authority	25: 5
gave great p. unto the Nephites;	25: 6
the p. of his word which is in us,	26:13
can say too much of his great p.,	26:16
through the p. and wisdom of God	26:29
for he has all p., all wisdom,	26:35
and the p. of the devil,	28:13
usurp p. and authority over them,	30:23
but the devil has p. over you,	30:42
show unto me that he hath p.,	30:43
thou convinced of the p. of God?	30:51
save it were the p. of God could	30:52
give unto us, O Lord, p. and	31:35
against the p. of your enemies.	34:22
have p. to possess your body in	34:34
the devil hath all p. over you;	34:35

POWER

and he led them by his p. into	Al 36:28
has also, by his everlasting p.,	36:29
that he may show forth his p.	37:14
away from you by the p. of God,	37:15
no p. of earth or hell can take	37:16
that he might show forth his p.	37:18
he hath shown forth his p. in	37:19
he will also still show forth his p.	37:19
according to the p. of God,	37:28
wrought by the p. of God,	37:40
the p. and resurrection of Christ,	41: 2
might usurp great p. over them,	43: 8
might gain p. over the Nephites	43: 8
not fighting for monarchy nor p.	43:45
against the Lamanites with p.;	43:50
we might shed your blood for p.;	44: 2
that we have gained p. over you,	44: 5
shall have p. over this people;	44: 7
and they were seeking for p.	46: 4
he had p. according to his will	46:34
obtaining p. by fraud and deceit,	48: 7
the devil would never have p.	48:17
not obtain p. over the Nephites	49:22
had all p. over their enemies;	49:23
because of his matchless p. in	49:28
and the p. of the Lamanites	50:12
have no p. upon the lands of	50:12
by those who sought p. and	51: 8
give him (Moroni) p. to compel	51:15
should have p. to harass them	52: 9
as much as was in his p.,	52:10
as much as it was in their p.,	52:13
according to the p. of their armies.	52:13
by the p. and word of God,	53:10
more p. than what he hath got.	55: 2
p. to gain possession of those	55:20
the Nephites had p. over them;	55:23
mighty p. did they fall upon	56:56
to the miraculous p. of God,	57:26
preserved by his marvelous p.	57:26
could have gained no p. over us.	60:15
the desire of p. and authority	60:16
seeking for p. and authority,	60:17
that none other p. can operate	60:25
to usurp p. and authority	60:27
behold I do not fear you p.	60:28
can have no more p. to impede	60:30
I seek not for p., but to pull	60:36
I, Pahoran, do not seek for p.,	61: 9
give unto them p. to conduct the	61:15
word of God with much p.	62:45
gain p. over the Nephites—	He 1: 6
were in the p. of the Nephites,	1:32
be placed in p. and authority	2: 5
and to rob, and to gain p.,	2: 8
to obtain more p. over them;	4:19
his miraculous and matchless p.,	4:25
he hath p. given unto him from	5:11
unto the p. of the Redeemer,	5:11
it shall have no p. over you	5:12
they did preach with great p.,	5:17
such great p. and authority,	5:18
for they had p. and authority,	5:18
there was p. given unto them	5:37
preach with exceedingly great p.	6: 5
did use every means in their p.	6:20
usurped the p. and authority	7: 4
enemies can have no p. over us.	8: 6
that God gave p. unto one man,	8:11
God gave unto this man such p.,	8:12
that he hath given unto me no p.	8:12
had such great p. given unto him,	8:13
given unto me by the p. of God.	9:36
ye shall have p. over this people,	10: 6
Behold, I give unto you p.,	10: 7
ye have p. among this people.	10: 7
the p. of God was with him,	10:16
having great p. and authority	11:18
by the p. of his voice they are	12:10
by the p. of his voice doth	12:11
yea, by the p. of his voice, do	12:12
because of the p. of the devil	16: 6
men and by the p. of the devil,	3Ne 2: 2
to slay them because of p.	3Ne 4:29
Satan had great p., unto the	6:15
tempting them to seek for p.,	6:15
have p. to condemn any one to	6:22
they had p. from the governor	6:24
themselves unto the p. of Satan.	7: 5
having had p. given unto him	7:15
Nephi did minister with p. and	7:17
he had greater p. than they,	7:18
angry with him because of his p.;	7:20
by the p. and Spirit of God,	7:21
I give unto you p. that ye shall	11:21
gave unto them p. to baptize.	11:22
p. and authority to baptize.	12: 1
I have given p. that they may	12: 1
thine is the kingdom, and the p.,	13:13
shall not have p. over you;	16:12
to him will I give p. that he	18: 5
he gave them p. to give the	18:37
and by the p. of the Holy Ghost	21: 2
people by the p. of the Father,	21: 4
forth his p. unto the Gentiles,	21: 6
give unto him p. that he shall	21:11
shall the p. of heaven come	21:25
shown forth his p. unto them,	26:15
according to the p. of the Father	27:15
p. that they could utter the things	28:14
by his p. they were delivered	28:20
of the convincing p. of God	28:29
Satan could have no p. over them,	28:39
or by the p. of the Holy Ghost!	29: 6
and because of the p. of Satan	4Ne 1:28
did exercise p. and authority	1:30
by the p. of the word of God,	1:30
the p. of the evil one was wrought	Mrm 1:19
come upon us with exceeding great p.	2: 3
could have had no p. over them.	4: 4
gain no p. over the Lamanites,	4:18
ye stand before the p. of God,	5:22
Know ye not that he hath all p.,	5:23
by the p. of the Father he hath	7: 5
were wrought by the p. of God	7: 9
none can have p. to bring it	8:15
shall be done by the p. of God.	8:16
by the p. of his word did they	8:24
because of the p. of his word.	8:24
the p. of God shall be denied,	8:28
be awakened by the p. of God	9:13
by the p. of his word man was	9:17
by the p. of his word have	9:17
the almighty p. of the Lord?	9:26
the same will have p. that he	Eth 1: 4
O Lord, that thou hast all p.,	3: 4
art able to show forth great p.,	3: 5
be shown by the p. of God;	5: 3
be shown forth the p. of God	5: 4
Shule gave him p. in his kingdom.	7:13
not gain p. any more over Shule	7:19
which gave p. unto the prophets	7:25
them of old who also sought p.,	8:15
kept up by the p. of the devil	8:16
to help such as sought p.	8:16
as sought power to gain p.,	8:16
to get p. and gain,	8:22
are built up to get p. and gain—	8:23
Satan may have no p. upon the	8:26
as Akish was desirous for p.;	9:11
the Lord did show forth his p.	9:35
he gained p. over many cities;	10: 9
he did gain p. over all the land,	10: 9
Com gained p. over Amgid,	10:32
p. over the remainder of the	10:32
was built up to get p. and gain;	11:15
to possess the land, by his p.,	11:21
thyself unto them in great p.	12:31
Satan had full p. over the hearts	15:19
done this ye shall have p. that	Mro 2: 2
by the p. of the Holy Ghost,	3: 4
by the p. of the Holy Ghost,	6: 4
by the p. of the Holy Ghost;	6: 9
the p. of the Holy Ghost led	6: 9
by the p. and gift of Christ;	7:16
according to the p. thereof;	7:32

POWER

shall have p. to do whatsoever	Mro	7:33
p. and great glory at the last day,		7:35
the p. of the Holy Ghost		7:36
and the p. of his resurrection,		7:41
by the p. of the Holy Ghost		7:44
by the p. of the Holy Ghost,		8: 7
that it hath no p. over them;		8: 8
and the p. of his redemption.		8:20
the p. of redemption cometh		8:22
and the p. of his Holy Spirit,		8:23
put down all p. and authority		8:28
on the right hand of his p.,		9:26
by the p. of the Holy Ghost.		10: 4
by the p. of the Holy Ghost		10: 5
by the p. of the Holy Ghost;		10: 7
ye deny not the p. of God;		10: 7
he worketh by p., according to		10: 7
that the p. and gifts of God		10:24
work by the p. and gifts of God.		10:25
in nowise deny the p. of God.		10:32
in Christ, and deny not his p.,		10:33
to them is p. given to seal	DC	1: 8
might have p. to translate		1:29
mercy of God, by the p. of God,		1:29
p. to lay the foundation of		1:30
the devil shall have p. over his		1:35
the Lord shall have p. over his		1:36
p. to do many mighty words,		3: 4
sight and p. to translate,		3:12
have no p. over them except		5: 3
I will give them p. that they		5:13
none else will I grant this p.,		5:14
the p. of God and not of man.		5:25
unto me by the p. of God;		5:26
give unto me p. over death,		7: 2
you three I will give this p.		7: 7
Behold, there is no other p.,		8: 7
save the p. of God, that can		8: 7
no p. shall be able to take it		8: 8
give unto you p. that you may		9: 2
which you had p. given unto you		10: 1
has given him p. to translate;		10:16
he will also give him p. again;		10:16
if God giveth him p. again,		10:17
no gift, and that he has no p.;		10:18
believing in the p. of Jesus		11:10
my p. which speaketh unto thee;		11:10
by my p. I give these words		11:11
yea, the p. of God unto the		11:21
p. to become the sons of God,		11:30
with sharpness and with p.,		15: 2
with sharpness and with p.,		16: 2
of them, by the p. of God;		17: 3
my p. that he has sent them,		17: 5
have received the same p.,		17: 7
to the p. of the Holy Ghost		18:32
by my p. you can read them		18:35
and save it were by my p.		18:35
by the p. of my Spirit have		18:47
Retaining all p., even to the		19: 3
it is by my almighty p. that you		19:14
you with my almighty p.;		19:20
And gave him p. from on high,		20: 8
to reign with almighty p.		20:24
gift and p. of the Holy Ghost,		20:35
honor, p. and glory be rendered		20:36
by the p. of the Holy Ghost,		20:60
of Zion in mighty p. for good,		21: 7
the p. of turning the hearts of		27: 9
with p. and authority unto		28: 3
with p. and great glory,		29:11
for they have no p.		29:29
created by the word of my p.,		29:30
which is the p. of my Spirit.		29:30
by the p. of my Spirit created I		29:31
thine honor, which is my p.;		29:36
p. is not given unto Satan to		29:47
to build up my church		30: 6
the p. of my Spirit quickeneth		33:16
with p. and great glory.		34: 7
by the p. of the Holy Ghost.		34:10
nations by the p. of my Spirit;		35:13
escape the p. of the enemy,	DC	38:31
endowed with p. from on high;		38:32
and no p. shall stay my hand.		38:33
endowed with p. from on high		38:38
gave I p. to become my sons;		39: 4
p. to become my sons.		39: 4
that p. shall rest upon thee;		39:12
given by the p. of the Spirit		42: 5
go forth in the p. of my Spirit,		42: 6
have p. to become my sons;		42:52
he shall not have p. except		43: 4
by the p. of my Spirit;		43:15
ye shall be endowed with p.,		43:16
p. to organize yourselves		44: 5
may not have p. over you;		44: 5
gave I p. to do many		45: 8
gave I p. to obtain eternal life.		45: 8
clothed with p. and great glory;		45:44
and the p. of his might.		45:75
his p. on the right hand of		49: 6
shall be laid low of p.		49:10
has given the adversary p.;		50: 7
light, the Spirit and the p.,		50:27
unto you, p. over that spirit;		50:32
p. to overcome all things		50:35
not have p. to claim that		51: 5
that trembleth under my p.		52:17
p. to give the Holy Spirit.		55: 3
coming in p. and great glory		56:18
cometh the day of my p.;		58:11
the p. is in them, wherein they		58:28
bespeaketh the p. of God.		60: 1
voice of him who has all p.,		61: 1
p. to command the waters,		61:27
p. that he shall be enabled to		63:41
be ordained unto this p.;		63:45
them be ordained unto this p.		63:57
and my p. lieth beneath.		63:59
is the honor p. and glory,		65: 6
the p. of God unto salvation.		68: 4
given p. to seal them up unto		68:12
and ordained unto this p.;		68:19
portion of Spirit and p. which		71: 1
more abundantly, even p.		71: 6
kingdom and p. have been given.		72: 1
and ordained unto this p.		72: 8
by my p. will I make known		76:10
By the p. of the Spirit our eyes		76:12
all those who know my p.,		76:31
through the p. of the devil		76:31
the truth and defy my p.—		76:31
second death shall have any p.;		76:37
the Father had put into his p.		76:42
and sealed unto this p.;		76:52
even in glory, and in p.,		76:91
he makes them equal in p.,		76:95
to sit on the throne of his p.		76:108
by the p. of the Holy Spirit,		76:116
the p. and manifestation of		76:118
are a representation of p.,		77: 4
given p. over the four parts		77: 8
p. to shut up the heavens,		77: 8
given p. over the nations of		77:11
he hath not put into his p.,		77:12
in the p. of the ordination		79: 1
the p. of godliness is manifest.		84:20
the p. of godliness is not		84:21
eight days old unto this p.,		84:28
in whose hand is given all p.		84:28
not have p. to harm them.		84:72
preach the gospel in my p.;		84:77
and honor, and p., and might,		84:102
holding the scepter of p. in		85: 7
the p. thereof by which it was		88: 7
the p. thereof by which it was		88: 8
the p. thereof by which it was		88: 9
earth also, and the p. thereof,		88:10
the p. of God who sitteth		88:13
the p. by which it is quickened,		88:26
in the midst of the p. of God.		88:45
moving in his majesty and p.		88:47
not have p. over the saints		88:114

POWER — PRACTICABLE

Lord shall be revealed in p.	DC 90:10
who are ordained unto this p.,	90:11
And he received all p., both in	93:17
and that wicked one hath p.,	93:42
lest that wicked one have p.	93:49
chosen with p. from on high;	95: 8
you shall have p. to build it.	95:11
appoint and ordain unto this p.	95:14
sworn by the p. of his might	97:20
have p. to declare my word	99: 2
for in me there is all p.	100: 1
I will give unto him p. to	100:10
I will give unto thee p. to	100:11
not have p. to tempt any man.	101:28
cannot have p. to act without	102: 6
shall have p. to appoint	102: 7
he has p. to preside over	102:11
have p. to preside in his stead,	102:11
having p. to determine the	102:22
have p. to call and organize	102:24
have p. to appoint one of	102:25
have p. to say whether it is	102:29
p. to determine whether	102:33
of Zion must needs come by p.;	103:15
be led out of bondage by p.,	103:17
And I now give unto you p.	104:10
not have p. to bring evil	104:10
endowed with p. from on high.	105:11
have p. after many days	105:37
p. and authority over all the	107: 8
and has p. in administering	107:14
set apart and ordained unto this p.	107:17
p. and authority of the higher,	107:18
p. and authority of the lesser,	107:20
equal in authority and p. to the	107:24
decisions of the same p. or validity	107:27
have p. to call other high priests,	107:79
counselors shall have p. to decide	107:79
may feel thy p.,	109:13
from this house armed with thy p.,	109:22
p. to rise up and prevail over thy	109:26
by thy p., that we may rise up	109:33
with p. from on high.	109:35
roll on in great p. and majesty,	109:59
with glory, honor, p., majesty,	109:77
help us by the p. of thy Spirit,	109:79
that you shall have p. over it,	111: 4
I will give you p. to pay them.	111: 5
by the peace and p. of my Spirit,	111: 8
p. to open the door of my	112:21
is the p. of this priesthood given,	112:30
Which p. you hold, in connection	112:31
on whom there is laid much p.	113: 4
hold the p. of priesthood to bring	113: 8
also to return to that p. which	113: 8
What p. shall stay the heavens?	121:33
No p. or influence can or ought	121:41
send forth the p. of his mighty arm.	123: 6
do all things that lie in our p.;	123:17
and by the p. of the Holy Ghost,	124: 4
as it is out of my p. to do so,	127:10
consists in the p. of the priesthood,	128: 8
a p. which records or binds	128: 9
this p. has always been given.	128: 9
is the sealing and binding p.,	128:14
and the p. of their priesthood,	128:21
through the p. of the Holy Priesthood.	131: 5
on the earth to hold this p.	132: 7
my servant Joseph to hold this p.	132: 7
p. and the keys of this priesthood	132:18
and appointed unto this p.,	132:19
whom I have appointed this p.,	132:20
be gods, because they have all p.,	132:39
who had the keys of this p.;	132:44
then shall you have p.,	132:44
by the p. of my Holy Priesthood,	132:45
keys and p. of the priesthood,	132:48
and with my p., saith the Lord,	132:59
keys of the p. of this priesthood,	132:64
who holds the keys of this p.,	133:59
nations by the p. of his Spirit.	133:67
neither my p. to deliver.	
by the gift and p. of God,	DC 135: 3
not have p. to stop my work.	136:17
he shall have no p.,	136:19
And by the word of my p.,	Mses 1:32
away by the word of my p.	1:35
this I did by the word of my p.,	2: 5
give unto him mine own p.;	4: 3
by the p. of mine Only Begotten,	4: 3
of secret works, seeking for p.	6:15
hath all p. according to wisdom,	6:61
great was the p. of the language	7:13
p. of Satan was upon all the face	7:24
the p. of the Lord was upon him.	8:18
and my p. shall be over thee.	Abr 1:18
holding the key of p. also,	Fac 2: 2
clothed with p. and authority;	2: 3
the governing p., which	2: 5
receives its p. through	2: 5
with p. and great glory;	JS 1:36
with more p. to the heart of man	2:12
I was seized upon by some p.	2:15
out of the p. of this enemy	2:16
to the p. of some actual being	2:16
had such marvelous p. as I had	2:16
but they deny the p. thereof."	2:19
had not the p. of laying on hands	2:70

POWERFUL

so p. was the Spirit of God;	1Ne 17:52
the all-p. Creator of heaven and	Jac 2: 5
that they began to be very p.;	Al 2: 2
interpreted, p. or great king,	18:13
considering their kings to be p.;	18:13
thou art more p. than all they;	18:21
more p. effect upon the minds of	31: 5
for God is p. to the fulfilling of	37:16
in the name of that all-p. God,	44: 5
and his men were more p.;	52:34
most p. army of the Lamanites;	56:36
word of God, which is quick and p.,	He 3:29
we are p., and our cities great,	8: 6
made our words p. and great,	Eth 12:25
word, which is quick and p.,	DC 6: 2
my word, which is quick and p.,	11: 2
my word, which is quick and p.,	12: 2
my word, which is quick and p.,	14: 2
whose word is quick and p.	27: 1
whose word is quick and p.,	33: 1
on high, who is mighty and p.,	65: 1
so p. was the word of Enoch,	Mses 7:13

POWERFULLY

more p. against the Nephites.	Al 44:16

POWERS

the very p. of hell would have	Al 48:17
the p. of heaven shall be in the	3Ne 20:22
my glory with the p. of heaven.	28: 7
p. of the earth could not hold	28:39
the Nephites with all their p.;	Mrm 4:17
disperse the p. of darkness	DC 24: 1
delivered from the p. of Satan	38:11
the p. of darkness prevail upon	58:22
be subject to the p. that be,	84:119
to exert the p. of heaven;	121:29
dominions, principalities and p.,	121:36
connected with the p. of heaven,	121:36
that the p. of heaven cannot be	128:11
consists in obtaining the p. of	128:18
of dispensations, and keys, and p.,	128:23
kingdoms, principalities and p.!	132:13
by thrones, or principalities, or p.,	132:19
kingdoms, principalities, and p.,	Mses 7:27
caught up by the p. of heaven	JS 1:33
p. of heaven shall be shaken.	1:36
the p. of the heavens shall be	2: 9
all the p. of both reason and	2:16
exerting all my p. to call upon	2:20
the p. of darkness combine	

PRACTICABLE

inasmuch as it is p., to preach	DC 73: 4

PRACTICE 752 PRAY

PRACTICE: *see also PRACTISE.*
it was the p. of the Lamanites	Al	18: 7
a p. of plunder among them.		18: 7
of the p. of polygamy—	DC	OD
to enter into its p.,		OD

PRACTICES
somewhat in wicked p.,	Jac	1:15

PRACTISE: *see also PRACTICE.*
p. virtue and holiness before me.	DC	38:24
must p. virtue and holiness		46:33
which you p. before me,		124:48

PRACTISED
no idolatry nor wickedness p.	DC	52:39
have been p. upon this p.—		123: 5

PRAIRIES
every tract bordering by the p.,	DC	57: 5

PRAISE
also for the p. of the world	1Ne	13: 9
give p. unto their everlasting		15:15
I did p. him all the day long;		18:16
for my p. will I refrain from		20: 9
O Lord, I will p. thee forever;	2Ne	4:30
I will p. the holy name of my God.		9:49
may p. him through grace divine.		10:25
O Lord, I will p. thee;		22: 1
P. the Lord, call upon his name,		22: 4
may get gain and p. of the world;		26:29
render all the thanks and p.	Mos	2:20
they shall sing to his p. forever.		18:30
let us sing to his p., yea, let	Al	26: 8
for which we will p. his name		26:12
have reason to p. him forever,		26:14
yea, we will p. our God forever.		26:16
that they may p. him forever,		29:17
yea, and I will p. him forever,		36:28
p. because of your firmness,	3Ne	3: 2
the p. and thanksgiving unto the		10:10
because of the p. of the world?	Mrm	8:38
p. the Lord all the day long;	Eth	6: 9
did not cease to p. the Lord.		6: 9
fruits of p. and wisdom,	DC	52:17
he seeketh the p. of the world.		58:39
with acclamations of p.,		109:79
forth anthems of eternal p. to		128:22
the trees of the field p. the Lord;		128:23
p. the Lord with singing,		136:28
a prayer of p. and thanksgiving.		136:28

PRAISED
and p. God even in the very act of	Al	24:23
and to be p. for their wisdom.		38:13
is to get gain, to be p. of men,	He	7:21

PRAISES
shout p. unto the Holy One	2Ne	31:13
in singing the p. of a just God.	Mos	2:28
their voices in the p. of their God.		24:22
to sing ceaseless p. with the	Mrm	7: 7
they did sing p. unto the Lord;	Eth	6: 9
the brother of Jared did sing p.		6: 9

PRAISEWORTHY
lovely, or of good report or p.,	AoF	13

PRAISING
of singing and p. their God.	1Ne	1: 8
father in the p. of his God;		1:15
of singing and p. their God;	Al	36:22
in singing, and p. their God	3Ne	4:31

PRATT, Orson: *see also ORSON.*
Parley P. Pratt and P. take	DC	52:26
and unto my servant P.,		75:14
journey with my servant P.,		103:40
P., Orson Hyde, William Smith,		124:129
servants P. and Wilford Woodruff		136:13

PRATT, Parley P.: *see also PARLEY.*
now concerning my servant P.,	DC	32: 1
and my servant P. go forth	DC	50:37
And let my servants P. and		52:26
and also with my servant P.,		97: 3
is my will that my servant P.		103:30
Let my servant P. journey with		103:37
They are Heber C. Kimball, P.,		124:129

PRAY
that they would p. unto the Lord	1Ne	7:21
I began to p. unto the Lord		8: 8
I did p. oft unto the Lord;		18: 3
I p. the God of my salvation that	2Ne	9:44
p. unto him continually by day,		9:52
judge, I p. you, betwixt me and		15: 3
saying: Read this, I p. thee.		27:15
Spirit which teacheth a man to p.		32: 8
ye would know that ye must p.;		32: 8
spirit teacheth not a man to p.,		32: 8
teacheth him that he must not p.		32: 8
ye must p. always, and not faint;		32: 9
ye shall p. unto the Father in		32: 9
I p. continually for them by day,		33: 3
I p. the Father in the name of		33:12
p. unto him with exceeding faith,	Jac	3: 1
And I, Mormon, p. to God that	WM	1:11
I p. that ye should awake to	Mos	2:40
I p. thee forbear, and do not		20:17
being commanded of God to p.		26:39
and to p. to the Lord their God		27:22
and watch and p. continually,	Al	13:28
that Alma should p. unto God,		30:54
Do not p. as the Zoramites do,		38:13
that they p. to be heard of men,		38:13
did fast much and p. much,		45: 1
did p. unto the Lord their God		62:51
they did fast and p. oft,	He	3:35
I p. that the anger of the Lord		13:39
P. unto the Lord, and let us go	3Ne	3:20
p. for them who despitefully use		12:44
they love to p., standing in the		13: 5
p. to thy Father who is in		13: 6
But when ye p., use not vain		13: 7
After this manner therefore p. ye:		13: 9
time we heard him p. for us		17:17
ye must watch and p. always,		18:15
even so shall ye p. in my church,		18:16
watch and p. always lest ye		18:18
always p. unto the Father in		18:19
P. in your families unto the		18:21
But ye shall p. for them,		18:23
p. for them unto the Father,		18:23
shall p. for him unto the Father,		18:30
and should p. unto the Father		19: 6
disciples did p. unto the Father		19: 7
they did p. for that which they		19: 9
his disciples that they should p.		19:17
And behold, they began to p.;		19:18
and they did p. unto Jesus,		19:18
I p. thee that thou wilt give		19:21
them, and they p. unto me;		19:22
they p. unto me because I am		19:22
Father, I p. unto thee for them,		19:23
without ceasing, to p. unto him;		19:24
unto them what they should p.,		19:24
as they did p. unto him;		19:25
Jesus said unto them: P. on;		19:26
they did not cease to p.		19:26
I p. for them, and also for them		19:28
Father, I p. not for the world,		19:29
behold they did p. steadfastly,		19:30
that they should cease to p.,		20: 1
not cease to p. in their hearts.		20: 1
and shall p. unto the Father in		20:31
p. unto the Father in the name of		28:30
both to p. and to hear the	4Ne	1:12
p. to the Father in the name of	Mro	4: 2
oft, to fast and to p.,		6: 5
preach, or to exhort, or to p.,		6: 9
if he shall p. and not with real		7: 9
p. unto the Father with all		7:48
P. for them, my son, that		8:28
I p. unto God that he will		9:22
P. always, that you may come off	DC	10: 5

PRAY

p. vocally as well as in thy heart;	DC	19:28
P. always, and I will pour out		19:38
church take heed and p. always,		20:33
to p. vocally and in secret		20:47
to p. vocally and in secret		20:51
p. vocally before the world		23: 6
P. always, lest you enter into		31:12
p. always that I may unfold		32: 4
they p. unto me in much faith.		37: 2
shall p. for and lay their hands		42:44
P. always that you enter not		61:39
P. unto the Lord, call upon		65: 4
teach their children to p.,		68:28
P. always, that ye may not faint,		88:126
Search diligently, p. always,		90:24
p. always lest that wicked one		93:49
at home, and p. always,		93:50
always to p. and not to faint,		101:81
P. ye, therefore, that their ears		101:92
p. earnestly that peradventure		103:35
p. for thy brethren of the Twelve.		112:12
Tell me, I p. thee, why these	Mses	1:30
I p. thee, show me these things.		7:54
say unto them, I p. thee,	Abr	2:25
p. ye the Lord that your flight	JS	1:17
made the attempt to p. vocally.		2:14
to p. and inquire of the Lord		2:68

PRAYED

as he went forth p. unto the Lord,	1Ne	1: 5
as he p. unto the Lord,		1: 6
I p. unto the Lord, saying:		7:17
after I had p. unto the Lord		8: 9
I p. unto the Lord;		18:21
and after I had p. the winds		18:21
I p. unto him with many long	En	1:11
after I had p. and labored with		1:12
for he has p. with much faith	Mos	27:14
after they had fasted and p.		27:23
having p. mightily to him that	Al	2:28
I have fasted and p. many days		5:46
they fasted much and p. much		17: 9
and this because he p. in faith.		31:38
merciful when I p. concerning		33: 4
O Lord, and p. unto thee,		33: 7
he p. mightily unto his God		46:13
Moroni p. that the cause of		46:16
behold he p. unto the Father,	3Ne	17:15
which he p. cannot be written,		17:15
and p. unto the Father for them.		17:21
as I have p. among you even		18:16
that I have p. unto the Father,		18:24
knelt again and p. to the Father		19: 8
And when they had thus p.		19:10
when Jesus had thus p. unto		19:24
he p. again unto the Father,		19:27
way off and p. unto the Father;		19:31
speak the words which he p.,		19:32
by man the words which he p.		19:32
hearts the words which he p.		19:33
were the words which he p.		19:34
I p. unto the Lord that he	Eth	12:36
After they had p. unto the Father	Mro	3: 2
that I p. unto the Lord	DC	135: 5
and Lot, my brother's son, p.	Abr	2: 6
p. that the famine might be		2:17

PRAYER

bold in mighty p. before him;	2Ne	4:24
my cry and answered my p.	Jac	7:22
I cried unto him in mighty p.	En	1: 4
And my p. to God is concerning	WM	1: 8
and join in fasting and mighty p.	Al	6: 6
wrestling with God in mighty p.,		8:10
had given themselves to much p.,		17: 3
to pour out his soul in p. and		19:14
a time of much fasting and p.		28: 6
even that he hath heard my p.;		29:10
fasting, and mourning, and p.,		30: 2
in p. and supplication to God		31:10
the selfsame p. unto God,		31:22
was according to the p. of Alma;		31:38

753 PRAYERS

said concerning p. or worship?	Al	33: 3
for thou hast heard my p., even		33: 4
I did cry unto thee in my p.,		33: 5
thou dist hear me in my p.		33: 6
and continue in p. unto him.		34:19
drawn out in p. unto him		34:27
behold, your p. is vain, and		34:28
be watchful unto p. continually,		34:39
pour out our souls in p. to God,		58:10
united in mighty p. and fasting.	3Ne	27: 1
continuing in fasting and p.,	4Ne	1:12
poured out in p. unto my God	Mrm	3:12
in my name, in mighty p.;	Mro	2: 2
continually watchful unto p.,		6: 4
endureth by diligence unto p.,		8:26
himself in mighty p. and faith,	DC	5:24
upon the Father in solemn p.,		20:76
the righteous is a p. unto me,		25:12
by much p. and faith, for all		26: 2
the church, by the p. of faith.		28:13
and call upon me in mighty p.		29: 2
united in p. according to my		29: 6
heart unto me in p. and faith,		30: 6
by the p. of your faith ye shall		41: 3
unto you by the p. of faith;		42:14
before me by the p. of faith.		43:12
with p. and thanksgiving,		46: 7
through the p. of faith.		52: 9
desire it through the p. of faith,		58:44
thou shalt go to the house of p.		59: 9
Verily, this is fasting and p.,		59:14
other words, rejoicing and p.		59:14
receive the Spirit through p.;		63:64
taught through p. by the Spirit.		63:65
in p. always, vocally and in thy		81: 3
solemnity and the spirit of p.,		84:61
that ye shall continue in p.		88:76
a house, even a house of p.,		88:119
Let him offer himself in p.		88:131
with this same p. and covenant,		88:135
ye are called to do this by p.		88:137
is to be commenced with p.;		88:141
and by your p. of faith with		93:51
according to the p. of faith;		93:52
After p. the conference		102:34
humility and the p. of faith.		104:79
and exercise the p. of faith,		104:80
faith, and p. of the church,		107:22
a house, even a house of p.,		109: 8
this house may be a house of p.,		109:16
my p. to God is that you all		127:12
a p. of praise and thanksgiving.		136:28
to p. and supplication to	JS	2:29

PRAYERFUL

faithful, and p., and humble	DC	105:23

PRAYERS

my wife with her tears and p.,	1Ne	18:19
because of the p. of the faithful;	2Ne	6:11
and the p. of the faithful shall be		26:15
consecrate my p. for the gain of		33: 4
For the Lord hath heard thy p.,	Mos	3: 4
our cries and did answer our p.;		9:18
for the Lord heard his p.		10:13
I will not hear their p., neither		11:25
my cries, and did answer my p.,		23:10
hath heard the p. of his people,		27:14
also the p. of his servant, Alma,		27:14
that the p. of his servants might be		27:14
that their p. may be answered,		27:16
desires, and their faith, and p.,	Al	9:20
his people and to answer their p.		9:26
if it were not for the p. of		10:22
it is by the p. of the righteous		10:23
poured out according to his p.		19:14
unto them according to their p.,		25:17
and his sons had heard these p.,		31:19
forth and offer up the same p.		31:20
of the p. of the righteous,		62:40
their p. unto the Lord their God,	3Ne	3:25
the p. of those who have		5:14

.

PRAYERS 754 PREACH

the Lord will remember the p.	Mrm 5:21	he began to p. unto the people.	Al 8:27
And he knoweth their p.,	8:24	they went forth and began to p.	8:32
their p. were also in behalf of	8:25	and p. again unto this people,	9: 1
according to the p. of all the	9:36	as I began to p. unto them,	9: 1
that their p. may be answered	9:37	although he should p. unto us	9: 2
mindful of you always in my p.,	Mro 8: 3	and began to p. unto them also.	9:34
desired in their p. should come	DC 10:46	p. repentance unto his people.	13:18
to their faith in their p.;	10:47	p. again unto this people,	14:14
their faith in their p. was that	10:49	began from that time forth to p.	15:12
upon this land in their p.,	10:50	to p. the word throughout all	16:15
to their faith in their p.	10:52	did p. against all lyings, and	16:18
and his p. I have heard.	21: 7	*to p. to the Lamanites;*	17:hd
I have heard thy p., and	35: 3	to p. the word of God unto	17: 8
for I have heard your p.,	38:16	to p. the word of God to a wild	17:14
things because of your p.;	38:30	began to p. to the Amalekites.	21: 4
that I have heard your p.;	53: 1	p. to them in their synagogues,	21: 4
whose p. I have heard,	67: 1	synagogues to p. unto the people,	21: 5
he that observeth not his p.	68:33	they did p. the word unto many,	21:12
alms of your p. have come up	88: 2	Ammon did p. unto the people of	21:23
for thy p. and the prayers of	90: 1	should p. the word unto them.	22:26
the p. of thy brethren have	90: 1	go forth and p. the word	23: 3
and whose p. I have heard,	96: 6	to p. and to teach the word	23: 4
for your p. have entered into	98: 2	Nephites, unto us to p. unto us,	24: 7
slow to hearken unto their p.,	101: 7	to p. unto our brethren, the	26:23
faithfulness, and p. of faith.	103:36	to p. the word unto this people,	29:13
I have heard their p., and will	105:19	he began to p. unto the people	30: 6
your conversation, in all your p.,	108: 7	began to p. unto the people that	30:12
I have heard thy p.;	112: 1	And after this manner did he p.,	30:12
and give thee answer to thy p.	112:10	And thus he did p. unto them,	30:18
have heard thy p. concerning	112:11	to p. these things among the	30:19
Your p. are acceptable before me;	124: 2	and began to p. unto them also;	30:21
unto me in answer to my p.,	Abr 2:19	that we p. unto this people to	30:35
		to p. unto them the word.	31: 7
PRAYEST		to p. the word unto them.	31:11
when thou p. thou shalt not do	3Ne 13: 5	and began to p. the word of God	32: 1
when thou p., enter into thy	13: 6	did p. the word in their streets.	32: 1
		P. unto them repentance, and	37:33
PRAYETH		are called of God to p. the word	42:31
p. continually without ceasing—	Al 26:22	for they did p. the word of God,	48:19
offereth a gift, or p. unto God,	Mro 7: 6	forth to p. among the people.	49:30
Wherefore he that p.,	DC 52:15	take upon him again to p. unto	62:44
		Moronihah did p. many things	He 4:14
PRAYING		did p. many things unto the	4:14
And after they had done p.	1Ne 7:21	upon him to p. the word of God	5: 4
and continue in fasting and p.,	Om 1:26	they did p. with great power,	5:17
watching and p. continually,	Al 15:17	that Nephi and Lehi did p. unto	5:18
an end of p. unto the Father,	3Ne 17:18	many did p. with exceedingly	6: 5
Jesus had made an end of p.	19:35	northward, to p. unto the people.	6: 6
they were p. unto the Father	27: 2	and they did p. the word of God	6:37
p. unto God the Father in	Mro 8: 3	p. the word of God unto them,	7: 2
be faithful, p. always,	DC 33:17	they did p. unto the people,	11:23
P. always that they faint not;	75:11	and began to p. unto the people.	13: 2
and your fasting, and your p.,	95:16	did p., many days, repentance	13: 2
unto thee p. thy forgiveness,	98:39	to p. and to prophesy among his	16: 7
p. earnestly on the subject,	130:13	it were a few that began to p.,	3Ne 1:24
p. very earnestly to know	130:14	did p. unto them repentance	7:23
p. and calling upon the Lord,	JS 2:68	and did p. the gospel of Christ	28:23
		endeavor to p. unto this people,	Mrm 1:16
PREACH		was forbidden that I should p.	1:16
my father did p. unto them.	1Ne 8:37	was forbidden to p. unto them,	1:17
rejoice in Christ, we p. of Christ,	2Ne 25:26	p. the gospel to every creature;	9:22
and p. up unto themselves their	26:20	to p. repentance and remission	Mro 3: 3
priestcrafts are that men p. and	26:29	whether to p., or to exhort,	6: 9
those who p. false doctrines,	28:15	that they might p. in their days,	DC 10:48
began to p. among the people,	Jac 7: 2	that you are called to p. until	11:15
that I must p. and prophesy unto	En 1:26	to p. my gospel unto every	18:28
did p. unto them repentance.	Mos 18: 7	And you must p. unto the world,	18:41
did he ordain to p. unto them,	18:18	p. naught but repentance,	19:21
should p. nothing save it were	18:20	p., exhort, declare the truth,	19:37
thus he commanded them to p.	18:22	The priest's duty is to p.,	20:46
authority to p. or to teach except	23:17	he is only to p., teach,	20:50
that they might p. the things	28: 1	shall be opened to p. the truth	23: 2
the Lamanites to p. the word.	28: 6	called to p. before the world.	23: 4
to go up to p. the word among	28: 9	and p. my gospel unto them;	28: 8
to p. to those who believed on	Al 1: 7	to p. from this time forth,	31: 4
to p. according to their belief;	1:17	called of me to p. my gospel—	34: 5
that he might p. the word of God	4:19	thou shalt p. my gospel and	35:23
to p. unto my beloved brethren,	5:49	you are called to p. my gospel	36: 1
p. unto all, both old and young,	5:49	to p. the everlasting gospel	36: 5
he began to p. the word of God	8: 8	p. the fulness of my gospel,	39:11
and p. again unto the people of	8:16	to go forth to p. my gospel,	42:11
of the city; yea, p. unto them.	8:16	p. repentance unto the people.	44: 3
been called to p. the word of God	8:24	you shall go and p. my gospel	49: 1

PREACH

to p. the gospel unto them.	DC	49: 3
p. my gospel by the Spirit,		50:14
to p. the word of truth by the		50:17
doth he p. it by the Spirit of		50:17
thus let them p. by the way		52:10
p. by the way unto this		52:25
journey, and p. by the way,		52:26
same land, and p. by the way.		52:27
to p. faith and repentance		53: 3
to p. repentance and remission		55: 2
let them p. the gospel in		58:46
Let them p. by the way,		58:47
p. the word, not in haste,		60: 8
been sent to p. my gospel		60:13
p. the gospel to every creature,		68: 8
p. in the regions round about		73: 4
p. the gospel to every creature		80: 1
go ye and p. my gospel,		80: 3
to p. the gospel in my power;		84:77
p. this gospel of the kingdom,		84:80
p. my everlasting gospel,		106: 2
The Seventy are also called to p.		107:25
have right to p. my gospel,		108: 6
p. my gospel unto every creature		112:28
Let the residue continue to p.		118: 3
We believe it just to p. the gospel		134:12
neither p. the gospel to, nor		134:12
in authority to p. the Gospel	AoF	5

PREACHED

after he had p. unto them,	1Ne	8:38
should be p. among the Jews,		10:11
And he p. many things which	Jac	7: 2
p. in all the churches except	Mos	25:22
he p. the word unto your fathers,	Al	5:13
are the words which Amulek p.		10: 1
and the word of God being p.		16:21
Aaron and his brethren had p.		25: 6
the word of God p. unto them.		31: 8
after they had p. the word unto		35: 2
which had been p. unto them,		35: 3
except that they p. the word,		43: 2
p. after the holy order of God		43: 2
cause the word of God to be p.	3Ne	5: 4
fulness of my gospel shall be p.		20:30
be p. among the remnant of		21:26
have the gospel p. unto them,	DC	35:15
p. my gospel in those parts,		37: 2
it is p. by the Spirit of truth?		50:21
be p. unto those who sit in		57:10
be p. unto every creature,		58:64
for this cause p. the apostles		63:52
and p. the gospel unto them,		76:73
it must be p. unto them,		84:76
shall be p. unto every nation,		133:37
the Gospel began to be p.,	Mses	5:58
the Gospel p., and a decree		5:59
shall be p. in all the world,	JS	1:31

PREACHER

for the p. was no better than	Al	1:26
And the first p. of this church	DC	21:12

PREACHERS

and false p. and teachers	WM	1:16
they were p. of righteousness,	Mses	6:23
with one of the Methodist p.,	JS	2:21

PREACHETH

that p. and he that receiveth,	DC	50:22

PREACHING

The words of his p. unto	Jac	1:hd
if there were p. which was sacred,		1: 4
p. that which ye call the gospel,		7: 6
p. and prophesying of wars,	En	1:23
p. unto the people repentance	Mos	25:15
every priest p. the word		25:21
p. the word of God in much		27:32
p. to them that which he termed	Al	1: 3
church after the manner of his p.		1: 6
went forth p. false doctrines;		1:16
with tongues, and the gift of p.,		9:21

PRECIOUS

Amulek went forth p. repentance	Al	16:13
An account of the p. of Aaron,		21:hd
he found Muloki p. the word		21:11
p. the word of God in every		21:16
go forth p. the word of God,		23: 1
through the p. of Ammon and		23: 6
Lamanites as believed in their p.,		23: 6
the p. of the word had a great		31: 5
say no more concerning their p.,		43: 2
p. of Helaman and his brethren,		46: 6
their p., and their prophecies,	He	3:14
and all the p. and prophesying		6: 2
much p. and many prophecies		6:14
through the p. of the Nephites;		15: 4
and prophesying, and p.,		16: 4
notwithstanding the much p.	3Ne	2:10
p. and testifying boldly of the		6:20
be converted through their p.		15:22
p. the things which they had		27: 1
as would believe in their p.;		28:18
of the scriptures, and to p.,	DC	26: 1
let your p. be the warning		38:41
p. my gospel, two by two, in		42: 6
thence p. the word by the way,		52: 9
p. the word by the way unto		52:22
p. the word by the way unto		52:23
p. the gospel by the way,		58:63
P. and expounding, writing,		69: 8
should continue p. the gospel,		73: 1
and for your p., and your		95:16
to fill the several calls for p.		107:38
continue in p. for Zion,		124:18
continued his p. in righteousness	Mses	7:19
Noah continued his p. unto		8:23

PREACHINGS

and they were led by many p.	Om	1:13

PRECARIOUS

exceedingly p. and dangerous,	Al	46: 7

PRECEDENT

for the p., Matthew 16:18,19:	DC	128:10

PRECEEDED

which had p. forth from	1Ne	13:38

PRECEPT

unto us, and hear ye our p.;	2Ne	28: 5
Behold, hearken ye unto my p.;		28: 6
line upon line, p. upon precept,		28:30
line upon line, precept upon p.,		28:30
line upon line, p. upon precept;	DC	98:12
line upon line, precept upon p.,		98:12
line upon line, p. upon precept;		128:21
line upon line, precept upon p.;		128:21

PRECEPTS

is taught by the p. of men –	2Ne	27:25
are taught by the p. of men.		28:14
hearkeneth unto the p. of men,		28:26
those who hearken unto my p.,		28:30
hearken unto the p. of men,		28:31
save their p. shall be given by		28:31
because of the p. of men.	DC	45:29
the p. and commandments		103: 4

PRECIOUS

and his silver, and his p. things,	1Ne	2: 4
their silver, and their p. things,		2:11
our silver, and our p. things.		3:22
silver, and all our p. things.		3:24
was of the most p. steel.		4: 9
the tree which is p. above all.		11: 9
all manner of p. clothing;		13: 7
the p. clothing, and the harlots,		13: 8
which are plain and most p.;		13:26
many plain and p. things		13:28
these plain and p. things were		13:29
the many plain and p. things		13:29
the plain and most p. parts		13:32
the most plain and p. parts		13:34
gospel, which shall be plain and p.,		13:34

PRECIOUS 756 PREPARE

PRECIOUS

which shall be plain and p.;	1 Ne	13:35
make known the plain and p. things		13:40
p. and easy to the understanding		14:23
whose fruit is most p. and most		15:36
away the righteous into p. lands,		17:38
more plain and p. parts of them,		19: 3
into this p. land of promise—	2 Ne	1:10
land, which is a most p. land,		3: 2
gold, and of silver, and of p. ores,		5:15
not built of so many p. things;		5:16
a man more p. than fine gold;		23:12
which I considered to be most p.;	Jac	1: 2
and for all manner of p. ores,		2:12
one being is as p. in his sight as		2:21
most p. above all other fruit.		5:61
which was most p. unto him		5:74
and in silver, and in p. things,	Jar	1: 8
and of all manner of p. things,	Mos	11: 8
and silver and with p. things.		11: 9
and all their p. things,		19:15
and many of their p. things;		21:21
and silver, and their p. things,		22:12
and of silver, and of p. things,	Al	1:29
and all manner of p. things,		4: 6
a virgin, a p. and chosen vessel,		7:10
and silver, and his p. things,		15:16
gold and silver, and p. stones;		17:14
and all their p. things which		31:28
Behold, O Lord, their souls are p.,		31:35
the fruit thereof, which is most p.,		32:42
soul at this time as p. unto God as		39:17
that p. gift of eternal life,	He	5: 8
and of all manner of p. metals,		6: 9
and of p. ore of every kind;		6:11
and in all manner of p. things		12: 2
silver, and all their p. things,	3 Ne	6: 2
with all manner of p. things.	4 Ne	1:41
and of silver, and of p. things;	Eth	9:17
dear and p. above all things.	Mro	9: 9
that yieldeth much p. fruit.	DC	97: 9
Things most p., things that are		101:34
their souls are p. before thee;		109:43
your silver, and your p. stones,		124:26
with all the p. trees of the earth;		124:26
all your p. things of the earth;		124:27

PRECISE

p. in taking the whole proceedings,	DC	128: 3

PRECISELY

agreeing p. with the doctrine	DC	128: 7
p. as they stand in our	JS	2:40
p. in one year from that time,		2:53

PREDICATED

which all blessings are p.—	DC	130:20
to that law upon which it is p.		130:21

PREDICTED

p. whatsoever should befall his	DC	107:56

PREFACE

my p. unto the book of my	DC	1: 6

PREJUDICE

had excited a great deal of p.	JS	2:22

PREJUDICES

that their p. may give way	DC	109:56
that their p. may be broken up		109:70

PREPARATION

were in a p. to hear the word.	Al	32: 6
called Antipas, in p. to battle.		47: 7
at their manner of p. for war.		49: 9
the p. of the gospel of peace,	DC	27:16
this is the p. wherewith I		78:13
the p. wherewith I design to		95: 4
p. that the Lord ordained		128: 5

PREPARATIONS

javelin, and all p. for war.	Jar	1: 8

PREPARE

that I might discover their p.,	Mos	10: 7
even all their p. for war		20: 8
began to make p. for war	Al	24: 4
saw the p. of the Lamanites		24: 5
not even make any p. for war;		24: 6
Lamanites, made p. for war,		24:20
began to make p. for war		35:11
therefore they made p. for war;		43: 4
not stop making p. for war,		50: 1
made p. and were ready to		51:24
as if making p. for war;		52: 6
Teancum made p. to make an		52:17
p. to attack the city Morianton;		55:33
make p. to go against the city		57: 3
make p. to come out against us		58:15
making p. to come out against us,		58:16
making p. to go against the		59: 5
make p. to defend ourselves	Mrm	2: 4
make p. to come against the		4: 6
I partook and finished my p.	DC	19:19
as soon as p. can be made		52: 3
make p. for those families		57:15

PREPARATORY

miserable, having no p. state;	Al	12:26
a p. redemption for such.		13: 3
it became a p. state.		42:10
yea, this p. state; for except		42:13
of angels and the p. gospel;	DC	84:26
foundation, and a p. work,		115: 9

PREPARE

save he shall p. a way for them	1 Ne	3: 7
to p. the way of the Lord—		10: 7
P. ye the way of the Lord,		10: 8
should p. the way before him.		11:27
I will p. the way before you,		17:13
the Lord will surely p. a way		22:20
P. your souls for that glorious day	2 Ne	9:46
P. slaughter for his children for		24:21
that we may p. the way,	Jac	5:61
shall ye p. the way for them,		5:64
they began to p. for war,	Mos	10: 6
they did p. to meet them;	Al	2:12
Behold ye must p. quickly;		5:28
would that he should p. quickly,		5:29
and p. the way of the Lord,		7: 9
p. ye the way of the Lord,		9:28
a time to p. to meet God;		12:24
a time to p. for that endless state		12:24
to p. the minds of the children of		16:16
to p. their hearts to receive the		16:16
should p. his horses and chariots,		18: 9
unto you to p. your mind;		34: 3
time for men to p. to meet God;		34:32
is given us to p. for eternity,		34:33
I will p. unto my servant		37:23
this people, to p. their minds;		39:16
may p. the minds of their children		39:16
became a state for them to p.;		42:10
to flee, or to p. for war,		48:15
Thus Moroni did p. strongholds		50: 6
did p. himself and his armies		51:10
making regulations to p. for war		51:22
should p. in haste strong cords		62:21
and p. the way of the Lord.	He	14: 9
will p. ourselves in the center	3 Ne	3:21
p. your minds for the morrow,		17: 3
p. the way whereby they may		21:27
he shall p. the way before me,		24: 1
to p. to return to the land of	Mrm	3:17
repent and p. to stand before		3:22
and they did also p. a vessel,	Eth	2: 2
I p. you against these things;		2:25
save I p. you against the waves		2:25
what will ye that I should p.		2:25
p. them that they may shine		3: 4
must p. the way of the Lord		9:28
to p. a place for the children of		12:33
to p. the way among the	Mro	7:31
P. ye, prepare ye for that which	DC	1:12
p. ye for that which is to come,		1:12

PREPARE 757 PREPARE

to p. their hearts and be	DC	29: 8
and I will p. a place for them.		31: 6
p. them against the time when		31: 8
p. ye the way of the Lord,		33:10
John, to p. the way before me,		35: 4
to p. and accomplish the things		38:40
P. yourselves for the great day		43:20
p. for the great day of the Lord?		43:21
to p. the way before me.		45: 9
until I p. a place for you.		54: 9
P. ye the way of the Lord,		65: 1
P. ye the way of the Lord,		65: 3
p. ye the supper of the Lamb,		65: 3
and p. the way for the		71: 4
you must p. yourselves by		78: 7
to p. and organize yourselves		78:11
wherewith I p. you,		78:13
to p. them for the coming of		84:28
and to p. the way,		84:107
to p. them against the day of		85: 3
p. yourselves, and sanctify		88:74
to p. the saints for the hour of		88:84
P. ye, prepare ye, O inhabitants		88:92
p. ye, O inhabitants of the		88:92
p. every needful thing;		88:119
I p. a way for their deliverance		95: 1
I design to p. mine apostles		95: 4
And p. for the revelation		101:23
to p. my people for the time		104:59
p. for yourselves a place for		104:60
p. every needful thing,		109: 8
p. the hearts of thy saints		109:38
shall send them to p. a way		124:139
p. rooms for all these offices		124:145
p. thy heart to receive and obey		132: 3
and p. a throne for you in		132:49
p. ye, prepare ye, O my people;		133: 4
prepare ye, p. ye, O my people;		133: 4
P. yourselves for the great day		133:10
P. ye the way of the Lord,		133:17
p. ye for the coming of the		133:19
To p. the weak for those things		133:58
to p. for those who are to tarry.		136: 6
to p. for putting in spring crops.		136: 7
Let each company p. houses,		136: 9
unto a place which I shall p.,	Mses	7:62
Let us p. the earth to bring forth	Abr	4:11
Let us p. the waters to bring forth		4:20

PREPARED

a land which I have p. for you;	1Ne	2:20
and the way is p. for all men		10:18
was p. for the wicked.		15:29
p. for that which is filthy.		15:34
And there is a place p.,		15:35
these things were p. of the Lord		17: 5
he p. a way that they might		17:41
after we had p. all things,		18: 6
the compass, which had been p.		18:12
And the way is p. from the fall	2Ne	2: 4
ball, or compass, which was p.		5:12
into everlasting fire; p. for them;		9:16
kingdom of God, which was p.		9:18
yea, that happiness which is p.		9:43
go into the place p. for them,		28:23
there is a place p. for you in	En	1:27
being p. to meet the Lamanites,	Jar	1: 9
p. by the hand of the Lord	Mos	1:16
atonement which has been p.		4: 6
the atonement which was p.		4: 7
p. for the purpose of unfolding		8:19
was p. from the foundation of		15:19
Christ, whom he has p. from		18:13
p. for the devil and his angels.		26:27
were p. from the beginning,		28:14
were p. to meet the Amlicites	Al	2:13
ye are not p. to meet God.		5:28
that such an one is not p.;		5:29
unto such an one, for he is not p.,		5:31
p. from the foundation of the		12:30
is p. according to his word.		12:37
p. from the foundation of the		13: 3
holy calling which was p. with,		13: 3
p. from the foundation of the	Al	13: 5
Only Begotten Son, who was p.—		13: 5
p. from eternity to all eternity,		13: 7
p. from the foundation of the		18:39
to the feast which he had p.		20:12
p. from the foundation of the		22:13
these interpreters were p. that		37:24
a compass; and the Lord p. it.		37:38
it was p. to show unto our		37:39
for so was it p. for them,		37:46
The way is p., and if we will		37:46
the way is p. that whosoever		41: 8
p. from the foundation of the		42:26
Nephites were p. to meet them		43:15
p. his people with breastplates		43:19
was not p. with any such thing;		43:20
they were p. against the time of		43:26
desire, he was p. to meet them.		43:33
plants and roots which God had p.		46:40
also p. themselves with shields,		49: 6
p. themselves with garments of		49: 6
being thus p. they supposed		49: 7
they were p. for them, in a		49: 8
they were p. for the Lamanites,		49: 8
thus were the Nephites p. to		49:19
Thus they were p., yea, a body		49:20
thus were they p. to defend		49:20
they were p. that they could		50: 5
we are p. to receive you;		54: 9
having been p. in its strength.		55:13
Moroni had p. his men with		55:16
p. our city and ourselves for		56:20
were p. with ten thousand men,		56:28
that we were p. to meet them,		58:29
which is p. to engulf the wicked—	He	3:29
of robbers had p. for battle,	3Ne	4: 1
they were p. to meet them;		4:10
p. means for the interpretation	Mrm	9:34
and I have p. the vessels for	Eth	2:22
of the vessels which had been p.		3: 1
in the vessels which we have p.,		3: 4
I am he who was p. from		3:14
in the kingdom p. for him		4:19
the Lord had p. the stones		6: 2
into the vessels which were p.,		6: 2
had p. all manner of food,		6: 4
p. a way that thereby others		12: 8
God p. a more excellent way;		12:11
thou hast p. a house for man,		12:32
in the place which thou hast p.		12:32
that place which thou hast p.		12:34
in the place which I have p.		12:37
p. a way for their everlasting		14:25
and p. for death on the morrow.		15:26
means which were before p.,	DC	20: 8
be p. in all things against the		29: 8
p. for the devil and his angels.		29:28
p. for them from the beginning,		29:38
and p. thee for a greater work.		35: 3
gird up your loins and be p.		38: 9
if ye are p. ye shall not fear.		38:30
have p. thee for a greater work.		39:11
the New Jerusalem shall be p.,		42: 9
be p. for the things to come.		45:61
that your hearts might be p.		58: 6
a feast of fat things might be p.		58: 8
the house of the Lord, well p.,		58: 9
p. for the great day to come.		58:11
which I have p. for them.		59: 2
thy food be p. with singleness		59:13
may be p. in the coming spring		63:39
be p. for the days to come,		65: 5
the mansions p. for him		72: 4
in the mansions which are p.;		76:111
things which are p. for them.		78:10
up unto the crown p. for you,		78:15
own hands and p. for you;		78:17
the mansions which I have p.		81: 6
be p. for the celestial glory;		88:18
ye may be p. in all things		88:80
prison which is p. for them,		88:99
p. for the presidency of		88:127
house which shall be p. for him.		88:128

and I have p. a place for you;	DC 98:18	they did cease to flee from my p.	1Ne 4:29
let all things be p. before you.	101:68	cast off from the p. of the Lord.	8:36
all things be p. before you,	101:69	he had gone from before my p.	11:12
have all things p. before you.	101:72	ye shall be cut off from my p.	2Ne 1:20
made and p. for my creatures.	104:13	can dwell in the p. of God,	2: 8
I p. all things, and have given	104:17	they stand in the p. of him to be	2:10
shall be another treasury p.,	104:67	ye shall be cut off from my p.	4: 4
That they themselves may be p.,	105:10	cut off from the p. of the Lord.	5:20
have p. a great endowment	105:12	they were cut off from his p.	5:20
I have p. a blessing and	105:18	cut off from the p. of the Lord.	9: 6
I have p. a crown for him in the	106: 8	before the p. of the Eternal God,	9: 8
p. to obtain every needful thing;	109:15	be shut out from the p. of our God,	9: 9
be p. against the day of burning.	109:46	me before the p. of the Lord;	26: 7
a scourge p. for the inhabitants	124:83	shame before the p. of my Maker,	Jac 2: 6
that they may be p. for that	125: 2	in the p. of the pure in heart,	2:10
p. before the foundation of the	128: 5	shrink from the p. of the Lord,	Mos 2:38
ordinance which God has p. for	128: 8	shrink from the p. of the Lord	3:25
all things be p. before you;	133:15	cut off from the p. of the Lord.	Al 9:13
p. for him that waiteth for thee.	133:45	cut off from the p. of the Lord.	9:14
p. in the mansions of my Father.	135: 5	have been cut off from his p.,	9:14
may be p. to receive the glory	136:31	fall upon us to hide us from his p.	12:14
which I p. for the use of man;	Mses 3: 9	and fled from the p. of Alma	14:29
was p. from before the foundation	5:57	did flee from the p. of Alma	14:29
and a hell I have p. for them,	6:29	was about to return out of his p.	18:12
a prison have I p. for them.	7:38	was done in the p. of the queen	22:23
the Gods p. the waters that	Abr 4:21	coming into the p. of my God	36:14
the Gods p. the earth to bring	4:24	to stand in the p. of my God,	36:15
God had p. them for the	JS 2:35	ye shall be cut off from his p.	36:30
		ye shall be cut off from his p.	37:13
PREPARETH		ye shall be cast off from his p.	38: 1
he p. a way to accomplish	1Ne 9: 6	from the p. of the Lord;	42: 7
who p. a way for our escape	2Ne 9:10	off from the p. of the Lord,	42: 9
the Lord God p. the way that	Mro 7:32	cut off from the p. of the Lord.	42:11
Son Ahman, who p. all things	DC 78:20	forever to be cut off from his p.	42:14
		back men into the p. of God;	42:23
PREPARING		they are restored into his p.,	42:23
in p. the way for the fulfilling	1Ne 14:17	cut off from the p. of God.	50:20
already p. to come against us;	Mos 20:19	keep you continually in his p.;	58:41
p. the hearts of the children of	Al 13:24	unto thee in the p. of mine angels,	He 10: 6
that Ammon was p. his horses	18:10	thou shalt be cut off from my p.—	12:21
been p. the minds of the people	48: 7	cast off from the p. of the Lord;	12:25
thus he was p. to support	48:10	brought into the p. of the Lord.	14:15
in p. their places of security.	49: 5	cut off from the p. of the Lord,	14:16
p. for the safety of his people.	49:27	back into the p. of the Lord.	14:17
and p. for war with all diligence;	51: 9	to dwell in the p. of God in	Mrm 7: 7
was p. to defend himself	52: 6	back into the p. of the Lord;	9:13
and p. places of resort.	52: 6	cut off from the p. of the Lord.	Eth 2:15
that he kept thus p. for war	52: 7	ye are brought back into my p.;	3:13
employ his men in p. for war,	53: 7	from the p. of the Lord,	4: 1
they were all that year p. for war.	He 4: 4	cut off from the p. of the Lord.	10:11
in p. the way whereby his	3Ne 21:28	Garden of Eden, from my p.,	DC 29:41
in p. their lands and their arms	Mrm 3: 1	in the p. of all the hosts of	38:11
they were p. to come again to	3: 4	not in their p., lest thou	60:15
p. the way of the Lord for his	DC 34: 6	from the p. of my Father	63:34
p. the way before my face for	39:20	man abide the p. of God,	67:34
p. and finishing of his word,	77:12	to abide the p. of God now,	67:13
the p. of the way before the	77:12	in authority in the p. of God,	76:25
p. a beginning and foundation	94: 1	down from the p. of God	76:25
in p. the churches to keep	103:29	shall dwell in the p. of God	76:62
While p. to start—	JS 2:61	receive of the p. of the Son,	76:77
		They who dwell in his p. are	76:94
PRESBYTERIAN		they may be able to bear his p.	76:118
Methodist faith, some for the P.,	JS 2: 5	and could not endure his p.;	84:24
proselyted to the P. faith,	2: 7	forth from the p. of God	88:12
		even with the p. of God	88:19
PRESBYTERIANISM		and my p. shall be there.	94: 8
myself that P. is not true."	JS 2:20	my p. shall not come into it.	94: 9
		and my p. shall be there,	97:16
PRESBYTERIANS		up before you, but not my p.	103:19
The P. were most decided against	JS 2: 9	up before you and also my p.,	103:20
		And my p. shall be with you	103:26
PRESCRIBED		the communion and p. of God	107:19
grievousness which they have p.;	2Ne 20: 1	and that thy holy p. may be	109:12
		that they may be exalted in thy p.,	109:69
PRESCRIBING		mountains to flow down at thy p.,	109:74
interfere in p. rules of worship	DC 134: 4	shall enter into his eternal p.	121:32
p. rules on spiritual concerns,	134: 6	wax strong in the p. of God;	121:45
		they reside in the p. of God,	130: 7
PRESENCE		the ice shall flow down at their p.	133:26
cut off from the p. of the Lord.	1Ne 2:21	shall tremble at their p.	133:31
and thrust him out from his p.;	3:13	to dwell in his p. day and night,	133:35
But Laman fled out of his p.,	3:14	might flow down at thy p.	133:40
they fled from before my p.;	4:28	for the p. of the Lord shall	133:41

PRESENCE 759 PRESERVED

nations shall tremble at thy p.—	DC 133:42	the p. of the lives of this people	Al	10: 5
mountains flow down at thy p.,	133:44	their p. was astonishing to our		57:26
shall be the glory of his p.	133:49			
the angel of his p. saved them;	133:53	**PRESERVE**		
shall be in the p. of the Lamb.	133:55	we may p. unto our children	1 Ne	3:19
Moses could endure his p.	Mses 1: 2	that we may p. unto them		3:20
p. of God withdrew from Moses,	1: 9	that he might p. his father,		5:14
withered and died in his p.;	1:11	we could p. the commandments		5:21
even from the p. of Moses,	1:22	and I will p. thee,		21: 8
departed from the p. of Moses,	1:24	he will p. the righteous		22:17
Moses stood in the p. of God,	1:31	I will p. thy seed forever.	2 Ne	3:16
hide themselves from the p. of	4:14	but that he would p. them;		9:53
they were shut out from his p.	5: 4	that I may p. the words which		27:22
shut out from the p. of the Lord,	5:41	and that I should p. these plates	Jac	1: 3
sent forth from the p. of God,	5:58	I may p. the fruit thereof		5: 8
could not stand in his p.	6:47	that perhaps I might p. the roots		5:11
shut out from the p. of God.	6:49	I might p. them unto myself,		5:11
can dwell there, or dwell in his p.;	6:57	that I may p. unto myself		5:13
angel of his p. stood by me,	Abr 1:15	may p. it unto mine own self;		5:20
from the p. of God to me,	JS 2:33	may p. it unto mine own self.		5:23
		that I may p. again good fruit		5:33
PRESENT		should do something for it to p. it.		5:37
even down unto this p. time.	1 Ne 3:20	and these I had hoped to p.,		5:46
at the p. our strugglings were	En 1:14	I may p. unto myself the roots		5:53
ignorance, even at this p. time,	Mos 1: 3	that I may p. them also for		5:54
even down to this p. time.	1: 4	that I may p. the roots also		5:54
more wine, as a p. unto them;	22:10	the good will I p. unto myself,		5:77
down to the p. time.	Al 18:38	would p. a record of my people,	En	1:13
handed down even to the p. time.	23: 5	God was able to p. our records,		1:15
even down to the p. day;	36:29	that he would p. the records;		1:16
of Nephi down to the p. time.	47:35	to p. our genealogy—	Om	1: 1
even down until the p. time.	3 Ne 5:15	with the sword to p. my people,		1: 2
speak unto you as if ye were p.,	Mrm 8:35	and he will no more p. them	Mos	1:13
translate at this p. time.	DC 9: 3	will p. them for other nations		12: 8
when there is no elder p.;	20:49	that he should keep and p. them,		28:20
But when there is an elder p.,	20:50	p. his people from being destroyed.	Al	2:21
all things are p. before mine	38: 2	to save and p. this people.		2:30
that the bishop be p. also.	42:82	the Lord God might p. his people,		3: 8
should remain for the p. time	48: 1	and thus we will p. the flocks		17:31
let them buy for the p. time	48: 3	at this time to p. your lives,		18: 4
places to live for the p. time.	48: 3	generation, for I will p. them.		27:12
your natural eyes, for the p. time,	58: 3	which he will keep and p. for		37:14
life or death, or things p.,	76:59	that ye p. these interpreters.		37:21
and p. it unto the Father,	76:107	that he might p. their hatred		43: 7
you who are p. this day,	84:42	might p. them from the hands		43: 9
appointed successors are p.	102: 6	that they might p. their rights		43: 9
council are to p. the case,	102:16	of the Nephites to p. their lands,		43:30
when the high priest is not p.	107:11	support, and keep, and p. us,		44: 4
there are no higher authorities p.	107:12	Yea, let us p. our liberty as		46:24
and p. the whole concatenation	123: 5	it were to p. their lives.		48:14
but p. them to the heads of	123: 6	with so much diligence to p.;		51:14
I now close my letter for the p.,	127:11	that I may p. my food for		54:20
recorder to be p. at all times,	128: 3	p. the rights and the liberty of		61: 9
three individuals that are p.,	128: 3	of the Lord did no more p. them;	He	4:24
if there be any p., who can	128: 3	the Lord did cease to p. them		4:25
days of Adam even to the p. time.	128:18	protect and p. one another		6:21
or Adam down to the p. time,	128:21	May the Lord p. his people in	3 Ne	4:29
and let us p. in his holy temple,	128:24	they did p. the land southward	Eth	10:21
but shall now close for the p.,	128:25	I will p. thy life, and thou	DC	25: 2
their glory are manifest, past, p.,	130: 7	indignation will I p. them.		35:14
let this suffice for the p.	132:66	in life them whom he will p.;		63: 3
So no more at p.	136:42	thus shall ye p. the avails of		104:65
on the earth at the p. time	OD	to keep and p. it holy,		117:16
all things are p. with me, for I	Mses 1: 6	but my people will I p.;	Mses	7:61
of the earth to the p. time,	Abr 1: 3	all my endeavors to p. them,	JS	2:59
which I hold unto this p. time.	1:28			
revealed at the p. time.	Fac 2: 9	**PRESERVED**		
to give at the p. time.	2:12	p. by the hand of the Lord,	1 Ne	5:14
I shall p. the various events	JS 2: 2	same God who had p. them.		5:15
or as they at p. exist,	2: 2	p. in the wilderness by him,		19:10
		to restore the p. of Israel.		21: 6
PRESENTED		and the righteous be p.,		22:17
be p. as the first-fruits of Christ	Jac 4:11	he hath p. me upon the waters	2 Ne	4:20
when p. to an elder, shall	DC 20:64	kept and p., and handed down		25:21
who has p. himself or herself	20:73	own purpose I have p. them;	Jac	5:36
to be p. unto all the churches	58:51	I have p. the natural branches		5:60
which you have p. before me,	78: 2	p. the roots of their mother tree,		5:60
p. the characters which had	JS 2:64	that I have p. the roots		5:60
		the Lord had p. unto himself that		5:74
PRESERVATION		p. unto himself the natural fruit,		5:74
his arm in the p. of our fathers	Mos 1:14	and I have p. the natural fruit,		5:75

PRESERVED

and p. them from falling into	Om	1: 6
p. from this time henceforth.	WM	1:11
I know that they will be p.;		1:11
kept and p. by the hand of God,	Mos	1: 5
he has hitherto p. our fathers.		1:13
and p. by his matchless power,		2:11
and has kept and p. you,		2:20
be blessed, prospered, and p.–		2:36
I suffered that ye should be p.,		7:11
has kept and p. his people		7:20
things which he had kept and p.		28:11
and p. by the hand of the Lord,		28:15
p. them from being destroyed,	Al	9:10
been kept and p. until now;		9:22
and p. by the hand of the Lord		37: 4
that these things should be p.;		37: 8
they are p. for a wise purpose,		37:12
therefore they shall be p.		37:19
your cunning that has p. you		44: 9
your shields that have p. you.		44: 9
of the coat of Joseph was p.		46:24
garment of my son hath been p.,		46:24
of the seed of my son be p.		46:24
little army; but thus were we p.		56:19
be p. by his marvelous power.		57:26
which the Lord God had p.	Eth	2: 7
very purpose are these plates p.,	DC	3:19
the world, that you may be p.		10:35
See that all things are p.;		38:38
and they shall be p. in safety;		42:56
you may be p. in all things;		44: 5
they are faithful they shall be p.,		61:10
faithful among you should be p.		62: 6
also p. by law and perfected		88:34
be p. unto the end of the earth;		107:42
and p. by thy fostering hand.		109:69
blood of the Canaanites was p.	Abr	1:22
that race which p. the curse		1:24
my God p. in mine own hands;		1:31

PRESERVETH

and p. in life them whom he	DC	63: 3

PRESERVING

and is p. you from day to day,	Mos	2:21
of Ammon in p. his flocks,	Al	18: 2
doing good, in p. his people,		48:16
assist our brethren in p. the city.		57:34
of the goodness of God in p. us,		57:36
to assist him in p. that part of		62:12
in p. them from falling into	3Ne	4:31
in p. them from famine.	Eth	9:35
be diligent in p. what thou hast,	DC	136:27

PRESIDE

to p. and watch over the church.	Al	6: 1
to p. over the conference by	DC	28:10
p. over the affairs of the church		90:13
all your lives, to p. in council,		90:16
called you also to p. over Zion		90:32
to p. over the school in		97: 4
should p. over the council of		102:10
power to p. over the council		102:11
power to p. in his stead,		102:11
to p. over such council for		102:25
p. in the midst of my people,		103:35
elders to p. over those who are		107:60
priests to p. over those who are		107:61
teachers to p. over those who		107:62
High Priesthood to p. over the		107:65
is to p. over twelve deacons,		107:85
p. over twenty-four of the teachers,		107:86
is to p. over forty-eight priests,		107:87
is to p. over ninety-six elders,		107:89
is to p. over the whole church,		107:91
seven presidents to p. over them,		107:93
presidents is to p. over the six;		107:94
and are to p. over them;		107:95
Let him p. in the midst of my		117:10
p. over the quorum of high priests		124:136
p. over the quorum of elders,		124:137
to p. over the quorum of seventies;		124:138
other is to p. over the churches		124:140
to p. over the bishopric;	DC	124:141
of the Church over which I p.		OD

PRESIDENCY

is appointed to him by the p.	DC	48: 6
be appointed by the First P.		68:15
firstborn holds the right of the p.		68:17
under the hands of the First P.		68:19
be designated by this P.,		68:20
under the hands of this P.,		68:20
hands of the above named P.		68:21
save it be before the First P.		68:22
is found guilty before this P.,		68:23
the P of the High Priesthood:		81: 2
for the p. of the school of		88:127
of the p. of the school:		88:128
continue in the ministry and p.		90:12
building of a house for the p.,		94: 3
for the word of the p.,		94: 3
work of the ministry of the p.,		94: 3
Lord for the work of the p.		94: 7
of the First P. of the Church.		102:26
of the First P. of the Church,		102:27
of the First P. of the Church		102:33
holds the right of p.,		107: 8
The P. of the High Priesthood,		107: 9
under the direction of the p.,		107:10
The bishopric is the p. of this		107:15
P. of the Melchizedek Priesthood.		107:17
quorum of the P. of the Church.		107:22
of the P. of the Church,		107:33
to the quorum of the p.,		107:36
right to the p. of this priesthood,		107:76
the P. of the High Priesthood.		107:78
the P. of the council of the		107:79
the P. of the High Priesthood		107:79
This p. is a distinct one		107:90
receiveth those, the First P.,		112:20
Twelve, and those, the First P.,		112:30
which I shall show unto their p.,		115:15
I shall show unto their p.,		115:16
redemption of the First P.		117:13
debts of the P. of my Church.		119: 2
composed of the First P. of my		120: 1
that of the P. of my Church;		124:84
a quorum and First P.,		124:126
the grand P. in Heaven;	Fac	3: 1

PRESIDENT

Every p. of the high priesthood	DC	20:67
that is appointed to be p.,		88:128
they shall salute the p. or		88:135
be administered by the p.,		88:140
importune at the feet of the p.;		101:88
And if the p. heed them not,		101:89
by the nomination of the p.		102: 8
The p. of the church, who is		102: 9
is also the p. of the council,		102: 9
the p. shall give a decision		102:19
error in the decision of the p.,		102:20
the p. may inquire and		102:23
that the p. or presidents of		102:33
P. of the High Priesthood of		107:65
where a P. of the High Priesthood,		107:76
as a P. of the High Priesthood		107:82
duty of a p. over the office of		107:85
duty of the p. over the office of		107:86
the duty of the p. over the		107:87
This p. is to be a bishop;		107:88
duty of the p. over the office of		107:89
duty of the P. of the office of		107:91
seventh p. of these presidents		107:94
to the honorable p.-elect,		124: 3
appoint one of them to be a p.		124:62
Brigham Young to be a p. over		124:127
Don C. Smith to be a p. over		124:133
and the p. of the teachers and		124:142
also the p. of the deacons and		124:142
also the p. of the stake and		124:142
a p. and his two counselors		136: 3
as P. of the Church of		OD
P. of the Church of Jesus Christ		OD
P. Lorenzo Snow offered		OD
Wilford Woodruff as the P. of		OD

PRESIDENT-ELECT

PRESIDENT-ELECT: see PRESIDENT and ELECT.

PRESIDENTS
and one or three p. as the	DC 102: 1
were acknowledged p. by	102: 3
of the president or p.,	102: 8
assisted by two other p.,	102:10
the other p. have power to	102:11
president or p. of the seat	102:33
Of necessity there are p., or	107:21
three p. previously mentioned.	107:24
decisions of a quorum of three p.	107:29
seven p. to preside over them,	107:93
the seventh president of these p.	107:94
these seven p. are to choose	107:95
Remember, O Lord, the p.,	109:71
all the p. of thy church,	109:71
be appointed standing p.	124:134
be ordained for standing p.;	124:135
with their captains and p.,	136: 7
p., and captains of hundreds,	136:15
in being subject to kings, p.,	AoF 12

PRESIDING
But the p. elders, traveling	DC 20:66
high priesthood (or p. elder),	20:67
or p. elder of the church.	88:140
ordained a p. high priest over	106: 1
are presidents, or p. officers	107:21
three P. High Priests, chosen	107:22
a Traveling P. High Council,	107:33
there must needs be p. elders	107:60
the P. High Priest over the	107:66
a p. elder over all my church,	124:125
one has the responsibility of p.	124:140
has no responsibility of p.,	124:140

PRESS
did p. forward through the mist	1 Ne 8:24
they did p. their way forward,	8:30
and also made a wine-p. therein;	2Ne 15: 2
Wherefore, ye must p. forward	31:20
Wherefore, if ye shall p. forward,	31:20
did p. forward upon Lib,	Eth 14:12
did p. upon the armies of Shiz	15:10
trodden the wine-p. alone,	DC 76:107
the wine-p. of the fierceness	76:107
trodden the wine-p. alone,	88:106
the wine-p. of the fierceness of	88:106
and p. itself upon my feelings	128: 1
I have trodden the wine p. alone,	133:50
P. dispatches having been sent	OD

PRESSED
Lehi p. upon their rear with such	Al 52:36
Zoram, whom your fathers p.	54:23

PRESSES
he built wine-p., and made wine	Mos 11:15

PRESSING
many of whom were p. forward,	1 Ne 8:21
I beheld others p. forward,	8:24
other multitudes p. forward;	8:30

PRETEND
and p. to teach this people,	Mos 12:25
you should p. to no other gift	DC 5: 4
p. to no other revelation;	32: 4

PRETENDED
they p. to preach according to	Al 1:17
visions and their p. mysteries,	30:28
Amalickiah p. to be wroth,	47:27
Has Nephi, the p. prophet, who	He 9:27
which you have p. to translate.	DC 10:13
that you have p. to translate,	10:31
p. requirements of the law,	135: 4
were more p. than real;	JS 2: 6

PRETENDETH
he p. the Lord hath spoken it.	Mos 12:12

PRETENSIONS
p. are all founded in falsehood	DC 127: 1

PREVAIL
but could not p. against it.	2Ne 17: 1
the gates of hell shall not p.	3Ne 11:39
wickedness did p. upon the	Mrm 1:13
he did not p. against them.	Eth 10:34
upon my rock, they cannot p.	DC 6:34
hell shall not p. against them.	10:69
hell shall not p. against you;	17: 8
hell shall not p. against you.	18: 5
hell shall not p. against you;	21: 6
nothing shall p. against them.	32: 3
hell shall not p. against you.	33:13
of darkness p. upon the earth,	38:11
shall not p. against you.	98:22
to p. against mine enemies	103: 6
they shall never cease to p.	103: 7
world shall p. against them.	103: 8
rise up and p. over thy people	109:26
gates of hell shall not p. against	128:10
the works of darkness began to p.	Mses 5:55

PREVAILED
they never could be p. upon to	Al 27:28
a famine p. throughout all the	Abr 1:30
I p. with the old gentleman	JS 2:56

PREVALENT
Hence arose the very p. story of	JS 2:56

PREVENT
to p. insult or injustice.	DC 102:15
and p. insult and injustice.	102:17

PREVIOUS
p. to the coming of Ammon,	Mos 21:25
p. to the time of the watering of	Al 18: 9
p. to their partaking of the	DC 20:68
was blessed by him three years p.	107:42
Three years p. to the death of	107:53
p. to my leaving my place—	128: 7
p. to the coming of the Son of Man	130:12
millennium or to some p. appearing,	130:16
days p. to his assassination,	135: 4
(whose name, p. to her marriage,	JS 2: 4
related to me the p. night,	2:49
had, p. to my hiring to him,	2:56

PREVIOUSLY
the commandment p. given,	DC 92: 1
which they have p. purchased	105:30
three presidents p. mentioned.	107:24
I had p. designed to go,	JS 2:15
manifestation, as I p. had one.	2:29
we never could attain to p.,	2:74

PREY
shall the p. be taken from	1 Ne 21:24
the p. of the terrible shall	21:25
in the wilderness for beasts of p.	2Ne 5:24
the p. be taken from the mighty,	6:16
the p. of the terrible shall be	6:17
that I am a p. to his awful misery.	9:46
roar, and lay hold of the p.,	15:29
that widows may be their p.,	20: 2
take the spoil, and to take the p.,	20: 6
feeding upon beasts of p.;	En 1:20
fought like lions for their p.	Mos 20:10
become an easy p. for them.	Al 49: 3
a p. to the worms of the flesh.	Eth 14:22
enemies shall become a p. unto	DC 133:28

PRICE
without money and without p.	2Ne 9:50
without money and without p.	26:25
without money and without p.	Al 1:20
as pertaining to the p. thereof.	DC 124:121

PRICK
did p. their hearts with the word,	Jar 1:12

PRICKS

PRICKS
to kick against the p.,	DC 121:38

PRIDE
building was the p. of the world;	1 Ne	11:36
the p. of the children of men.		12:18
because of the p. of my seed,		12:19
in the p. and stoutness of heart:	2 Ne	19: 9
for the reward of their p.		26:10
lifted up in the p. of their eyes,		26:20
Because of p., and because of		28:12
because of p. they are puffed up.		28:12
in their p. they are puffed up.		28:13
because of p., and wickedness,		28:14
puffed up in the p. of their hearts,		28:15
to be lifted up somewhat in p.	Jac	1:16
lifted up in the p. of your hearts,		2:13
and let not this p. of your hearts		2:16
spoken unto you concerning p.;		2:20
unto you concerning this p.		2:22
up in the p. of their hearts.	Mos	11: 5
up in the p. of their hearts;		11:19
should let no p. nor haughtiness		27: 4
son should turn again to his p.		29: 9
be lifted up in the p. of his heart,	Al	1: 6
lifted up in the p. of their own eyes;		1:32
lifted up in the p. of their eyes,		4: 6
lifted up in the p. of their eyes,		4: 8
malice, and persecutions, and p.,		4: 9
to exceed the p. of those who		4: 9
lifting themselves up with their p.,		4:12
all the p. and craftiness and all		4:19
Behold, are ye stripped of p.?		5:28
puffed up in the p. of your hearts;		5:53
up in the p. of their hearts—		6: 3
lifted up in the p. of your hearts;		7: 6
as to the p. of their hearts,		15:17
unto great boasting, in their p.		31:25
are swallowed up in their p.		31:27
that ye are not lifted up unto p.;		38:11
to pull down their p. and their		51:17
they did pull down their p.		51:18
and the p. of those people who		51:21
up in the p. of their eyes;		62:49
save it were a little p. which was	He	3: 1
save it were the p. which began		3:33
And they were lifted up in p.,		3:34
it were the exceeding great p.		3:36
because of the p. of their hearts,		4:12
that p. which ye have suffered to		7:26
stronger and stronger in their p.,		11:37
how quick to be lifted up in p.,		12: 5
but they do swell with great p.,		13:22
after the p. of your own hearts;		13:27
walk after the p. of your eyes,		13:27
the people remaining in their p.		16:10
and some were lifted up into p.	3 Ne	6:10
Some were lifted up in p., and		6:13
the puffing them up with p.,		6:15
up in the p. of their hearts		16:10
those who were lifted up in p.,	4 Ne	1:24
up in the p. of their hearts;	Mrm	8:28
rise in the p. of their hearts,		8:28
do walk in the p. of your hearts;		8:36
up in the p. of their hearts,		8:36
because of the p. of your hearts.		8:36
the p. of this nation, or the	Mro	8:27
But beware of p., lest thou	DC	23: 1
of meekness, and beware of p.		25:14
beware of p., lest ye become		38:39
because of p. and the cares of		39: 9
Thayre must repent of his p.,		56: 8
your p. and light-mindedness,		88:121
your high mindedness and p.,		90:17
p. of their hearts,		98:20
gratify our p., our vain ambition,		121:37

PRIEST
witnesses to record, Uriah the p.,	2 Ne	18: 2
even one p. to every fifty of	Mos	18:18
now, Alma was their high p.,		23:16
and every p. preaching the word	Mos	25:21
Alma, who was the high p.		26: 7
he being also the high p.,		29:42
the High P. over the Church.	Al	1:hd
every p. and teacher ought to		1: 3
when the p. had imparted unto		1:26
and the p., not esteeming himself		1:26
the high p. over the people		4: 4
of being high p. over the church,		4:18
retained the office of high p.		4:18
Alma, the High P. according to		5:hd
to be a high p. over the church		5: 3
thou art high p. over the church		8:11
am the high p. over the church		8:23
also a high p. after this same order		13:14
Alma was high p. over the church,		16: 5
Ammon, who was a high p.		30:20
and carried before the high p.,		30:21
that the high p. said unto him:		30:22
when the high p. and the chief		30:29
lawyer nor judge nor high p.	3 Ne	6:22
his high p. murdered him as	Eth	14: 9
I ordain you to be a p.,	Mro	3: 3
elder or p. did minister it—		4: 1
the p. is to assist the elder if	DC	20:52
the absence of the elder of p.—		20:56
Every elder, p., teacher, or		20:60
Each p., teacher, or deacon,		20:64
who is ordained by a p., may		20:64
high councilor, and high p.,		20:67
And the elder or p. shall		20:76
send by the hand of some p.;		20:82
be signed by any elder or p.		20:84
acquainted with the elder or p.,		20:84
both elder, p., teacher, and		38:40
Jared Carter be ordained a p.,		52:38
George James be ordained a p.		52:38
as a high p. of the Melchizedek		68:19
no bishop or high p. who shall		68:22
be a high p. in my church,		81: 1
unto the children of the p.,		85:12
ordained a presiding high p.		106: 1
was such a great high p.		107: 2
p. (of the Levitical order),		107:10
when the high p. is not present.		107:11
The high p. and elder are to		107:12
But as a high p. of the		107:17
those who are of the office of a p.;		107:61
and from teacher to p.,		107:63
and from p. to elder,		107:63
the Presiding High P. over		107:66
a high p., that is, after the order		107:71
a rightful heir, a High P.,	Abr	1: 2
by the hand of the p. of Elkenah.		1: 7
The p. of Elkenah was also the		1: 7
was also the p. of Pharoah.		1: 7
the custom of the p. of Pharoah,		1: 8
the p. made an offering unto the		1: 9
child did the p. of Pharoah offer		1:10
this p. had offered upon this		1:11
and smote the p. that he died;		1:20
after the p. of Elkenah was		1:29
the hands of the p. of Elkenah.		3:20
The idolatrous p. of Elkenah	Fac	1: 3
p. contending against priest,	JS	2: 6
priest contending against p.,		2: 6

PRIESTCRAFT
p. has been introduced among	Al	1:12
thou are not only guilty of p.,		1:12
were p. to be enforced among		1:12
an end to the spreading of p.		1:16

PRIESTCRAFTS
because of p. and iniquities,	2 Ne	10: 5
that there shall be no p.;		26:29
p. are that men preach and set		26:29
hypocrisy, and murders, and p.,	3 Ne	16:10
and envyings, and strifes, and p.,		21:19
of your murders, and your p.,		30: 2
in many instances because of p.,	DC	33: 4

PRIESTHOOD

PRIESTHOOD		
the high p. of the holy order of	Al	4:20
the high p. of the holy order of		13: 6
This high p. being after the order		13: 7
the high p. of the holy order,		13: 8
calling, and ordinance, and high p.,		13: 8
the holy order of this high p.,		13:10
who also took upon him the high p.		13:14
the office of the high p.		13:18
I will reveal unto you the P.,	DC	2: 1
I confer the P. of Aaron, which		13: 1
Every president of the high p.		20:67
to ordain you unto the first p.		27: 8
were ordained unto this p.,		68: 2
of the Melchizedek P.,		68:15
of the presidency over this p.,		68:17
to hold the keys of this p.,		68:18
priest of the Melchizedek P.		68:19
of the Melchizedek P.		68:19
authorized to officiate in their p.		68:20
concerning their right of the p.		68:21
are ordained unto the high p.		78: 1
the Presidency of the High P.:		81: 2
according to the Holy P.		84: 6
Abraham received the p. from		84:14
who received the p. by the		84:16
Which p. continueth in the		84:17
the Lord confirmed a p. also		84:18
which p. also continueth and		84:18
the p. which is after the holiest		84:18
greater p. administereth		84:19
and the authority of the p.,		84:21
midst, and the holy p. also;		84:25
And the lesser p. continued,		84:26
which p. holdeth the key of		84:26
belonging unto the high p.		84:29
belonging to the lesser p.,		84:30
which p. was confirmed upon		84:30
all they who receive this p.		84:35
which belongeth to the p.		84:39
all those who receive the p.,		84:40
who come not unto this p.		84:42
ordained unto the lesser p.,		84:107
they who are of the high p.,		85:11
church, as well as the lesser p.,		85:11
whom the p. hath continued		86: 8
and the p. have remained,		86:10
and through this p., a savior		86:11
to the order of the p.,		94: 6
including the Levitical P.		107: 1
is called the Melchizedek P.		107: 2
Holy P., after the Order of the		107: 3
called that p. after Melchizedek,		107: 4
or the Melchizedek P.		107: 4
are appendages to this p.		107: 5
one is the Melchizedek P.,		107: 6
is the Aaronic or Levitical P.		107: 6
under the p. of Melchizedek.		107: 7
Melchizedek P. holds the right of		107: 8
The Presidency of the High P.,		107: 9
order of the Melchizedek P.		107:10
The second p. is called the		107:13
called the P. of Aaron,		107:13
Why it is called the lesser p.		107:14
greater, or the Melchizedek P.,		107:14
is the presidency of this p.		107:15
to hold the keys of this p.,		107:16
high priest of the Melchizedek P.		107:17
Presidency of the Melchizedek P.		107:17
the higher, or Melchizedek P.,		107:18
of the lesser, or Aaronic P.,		107:20
Of the Melchizedek P.,		107:22
order of this p. was confirmed		107:40
Then comes the High P.,		107:64
one be appointed of the High P.		107:65
to preside over the p.,		107:65
President of the High P. of the		107:65
over the High P. of the Church.		107:66
must be chosen from the High P.,		107:69
cannot hold the keys of that p.		107:70
has been ordained to the High P.		107:73
right to the presidency of this p.,		107:76
where a President of the High P.,		107:76

763

the Presidency of the High P.	DC	107:78
of the council of the High P.		107:79
the Presidency of the High P.		107:79
as a President of the High P.		107:82
counselors of the High P.;		107:82
president over the P. of Aaron		107:87
is one of the duties of this p.		107:88
of the office of the High P.		107:91
is the power of this p. given,		112:30
unto whom rightly belongs the p.,		113: 6
power of p. to bring again Zion,		113: 8
is to put on the authority of the p.		113: 8
foundation of Zion and for the p.,		119: 2
for my holy p., saith the Lord.		119: 4
shall not have right to the p.,		121:21
rights of the p. are inseparably		121:36
Amen to the p. or		121:37
maintained by virtue of the p.,		121:41
doctrine of the p. shall distil		121:45
and the p. shall remain with thee;		122: 9
even the fulness of the p.		124:28
keys of the holy p. ordained,		124:34
this house, and the p. thereof,		124:42
office of P. and Patriarch,		124:91
and glory, and honor, and p.,		124:95
priesthood, and gifts of the p.,		124:95
the officers belonging to my P.,		124:123
P. which is after the order of		124:123
his p. no man taketh from him;		124:130
no man taketh his p.,		124:132
be appointed unto the same p.		124:132
which p. is to preside over the		124:137
pertaining to the p.,		127: 8
consists in the power of the p.,		128: 8
has given a dispensation of the p.		128: 9
the powers of the Holy P.		128:11
fixed on the restoration of the p.,		128:17
and the power of their p.;		128:21
enter into this order of the p.		131: 2
through the power of the Holy P.		131: 5
of this p. are conferred),		132: 7
this power and the keys of this p.;		132:19
unto thee the law of my Holy P.,		132:28
by the power of my Holy P.,		132:44
the keys and power of the p.,		132:45
as touching the law of the p.,		132:58
the keys of the power of this p.,		132:59
pertaining to the law of the p.—		132:61
unto her the law of my p.,		132:64
Now this same P., which was in	Mses	6: 7
mine appointment unto the P.	Abr	1: 4
name, even the P. of thy father,		1:18
him as pertaining to the P.		1:26
he could not have the right of P.,		1:27
concerning the right of P.,		1:31
shall bear this ministry and P.		2: 9
and in thee (that is, in thy P.)		2:11
and in thy seed (that is, thy P).		2:11
Key-words of the Holy P.,	Fac	2: 3
to whom the p. was revealed.		2: 3
Key-words of the P.;		2: 7
head, representing the P., as		3: 1
I will reveal unto you the P.,	JS	2:38
I confer the P. of Aaron,		2:69
this Aaronic P. had not the		2:70
ordained him to the Aaronic P.,		2:71
ordained me to the same P.—		2:71
and conferred this p. upon us,		2:72
keys of the P. of Melchizedek,		2:72
which P., he said, would in due		2:72
of having received the P.		2:74
PRIESTHOODS		
the obtaining these two p.	DC	84:33
are, in the church, two p.,		107: 1
several offices in these two p.		107:21
PRIEST'S		
the high p. name was Giddonah.	Al	30:23
the p. duty is to preach,	DC	20:46
PRIESTS		
that they should be p. and teachers	2Ne	5:26

PRIESTS

PRIESTS — PRINCIPLE

their p. shall contend one with	2Ne 28: 4
been consecrated p. and teachers	Jac 1:18
and the p., and the teachers,	Jar 1:11
and also had appointed p.	Mos 6: 3
and also his p., and their wives	11: 4
he put down all the p. that	11: 5
words of the king and p.;	11: 7
were set apart for the high p.,	11:11
his p. spend their time with	11:14
wickedness of their king and p.	11:19
the p. should gather themselves	12:17
Are you p., and pretend to	12:25
these words, he said unto his p.:	13: 1
that the p. should take him	17: 1
having counseled with his p.,	17: 6
the p. lifted up their voices	17:12
authority from God, ordained p.;	18:18
the p. whom he had ordained	18:24
the p. were not to depend upon	18:26
to those p. that stood in need,	18:28
all save the king and his p.	19:18
about to take the p. also	19:21
and his p. had fled from them	19:23
And now the p. of king Noah,	20: 3
remember the p. of thy father,	20:18
and the p. that had fled into	20:23
they might take those p. that	21:20
supposing them to be p. of Noah	21:23
had they been the p. of Noah	21:23
king Noah and his p. had caused	21:30
iniquity of king Noah and his p.;	23: 9
in bondage to him and his p.,	23:12
he consecrated all their p. and	23:17
found those p. of king Noah,	23:31
leader of those p. was Amulon.	23:32
had been one of the king's p.,	24: 9
gave him power to ordain p.	25:19
every church having their p.	25:21
they were brought before the p.,	26: 7
up unto the p. by the teachers;	26: 7
the p. brought them before Alma,	26: 7
Mosiah consulted with his p.	27: 1
all their p. and teachers should	27: 5
that the p. should assemble	27:22
when the p. left their labor to	Al 1:26
to be teachers, and p., and elders	4: 7
he ordained p. and elders,	6: 1
the Lord God ordained p.,	13: 1
those p. were ordained after	13: 2
Thus they become high p. forever,	13: 9
and became high p. of God;	13:10
many lawyers, and judges, and p.,	14:18
the lawyers, and p., and teachers,	14:27
and consecrated p. and teachers	15:13
Now those p. who did go forth	16:18
consecrating p. and teachers	23: 4
with Aaron and many of their p.,	23:16
who were the p. of Noah,	25: 4
concerning the seed of the p. who	25: 9
he said unto the p. of Noah	25:12
which are laid down by ancient p.,	30:23
lest they should offend their p.,	30:28
against the p. and teachers,	30:31
and more especially by our p.;	32: 5
their rulers and their p. and	35: 5
descendants of the p. of Noah.	43:13
did appoint p. and teachers	45:22
had appointed p. and teachers	45:23
were high p. over the church.	46: 6
Helaman and the high p. did	46:38
the high p. and the teachers	He 3:25
had been high p. and lawyers;	3Ne 6:21
all the lawyers and the high p.,	6:27
many p. and false prophets	4Ne 1:34
ordained p. and teachers—	Mro 3: 1
they ordain p. and teachers,	3: 4
elders and p. administering the	4: 1
elders, p., and teachers were	6: 1
to ordain p. and teachers;	DC 18:32
The duty of the elders, p.,	20:38
to ordain other elders, p.,	20:39
he may also ordain other p.,	20:48
high councilors, high p.,	20:66
The elders or p. are to have	DC 20:68
the elders, p. and teachers of	42:12
two of the elders, or high p.,	42:31
The p. and teachers shall have	42:70
the elders or high p. who are	42:71
be high p. who are worthy,	68:15
the high p. of my church,	72: 1
they who are p. and kings,	76:56
are p. of the Most High,	76:57
who are sealed are high p.,	77:11
apostles, even God's high p.;	84:63
the high p. should travel,	84:111
the elders, and also the lesser p.;	84:111
beginning at the high p.,	88:127
benefit of the council of high p.,	89: 1
council of twenty-four high p.	102: 1
to consist of twelve high p.,	102: 1
high p., were chosen to be	102: 3
nine high p., seventeen elders,	102: 5
four p., and thirteen members.	102: 5
to appoint other high p.,	102: 7
of a general council of high p.,	102: 8
The high p., when abroad,	102:24
the said council of high p.	102:25
This council of high p. abroad	102:28
or located high p. abroad	102:29
traveling high p. abroad,	102:30
High p. after the order of	107:10
three Presiding High P.,	107:22
Methuselah, who were all high p.,	107:53
p. to preside over those who are	107:61
have power to call other high p.,	107:79
is to preside over forty-eight p.,	107:87
over a quorum of high p.;	124:133
over the quorum of high p.	124:136
and his counselors for p.,	124:142
the p. laid violence upon me,	Abr 1:12
by the idolatrous p.,	Fac 1: 4
good feelings of both the p. and	JS 2: 6

PRIMITIVE
that existed in the P. Church,	AoF 6

PRINCE
Father, The P. of Peace.	2Ne 19: 6
he was called the p. of peace,	Al 13:18
the father of all, the p. of all,	DC 27:11
appointed Michael your p.,	78:16
Michael, the p., the archangel.	107:54
thou art a p. over them forever.	107:55
the p. of this world cometh,	127:11
father of many nations, a p. of	Abr 1: 2
P. of Pharaoh, King of Egypt,	Fac 3: 4
slave belonging to the p.	3: 6

PRINCES
p. also shall worship,	1Ne 21: 7
children unto them to be their p.,	2Ne 13: 4
his people and the p. thereof;	13:14
Are not my p. altogether kings?	20: 8
Remember the kings, the p.,	DC 109:55

PRINCIPAL
one of the king's p. waiters,	Fac 3: 5

PRINCIPALITIES
All thrones and dominions, p. and	DC 121:29
kingdoms, p., and powers!	128:23
ordained of men, by thrones, or p.,	132:13
inherit thrones, kingdoms, p., and	132:19

PRINCIPLE
knowest that they are without p.,	Mro 9:20
more perfectly in theory, in p.,	DC 88:78
Given for a p. with promise,	89: 3
in theory, in p., and in doctrine,	97:14
supporting that p. of freedom	98: 5
may act in doctrine and p.	101:78
respecting doctrine or p.,	102:23
the p. agreeing precisely with the	128: 7
one p. might accord with the other;	128:12
Whatever p. of intelligence we	130:18
touching the p. and doctrine of	132: 1

PRINCIPLES

teach the p. of my gospel,	DC 42:12
according to just and holy p.;	101:77
the p. of the law of the celestial	105: 5
may those p., which were so	109:54
upon the p. of righteousness.	121:36
p. in relation to the dead and the	128:15
upon the p. of Astronomy,	Fac 3: 6
the first p. and ordinances of	AoF 4

PRINT

even to shinelah [p.] my words,	DC 104:58

PRINTER

hast contracted with the p.	DC 19:35
is a p. unto the church.	57:11

PRINTING

the p. of the Book of Mormon,	DC 19:26
Cowdery to do the work of p.,	55: 4
and also for the house of the p.	58:37
revelations and the p. thereof,	84:104
the p. of the translation of my	94:10
thereof, for the work of the p.,	94:12
the Laneshine house [p. office],	104:28
the Laneshine house [p. office]	104:29
shineland [p.] these sacred things	104:63

PRINTS

ye may feel the p. of the nails	3Ne 11:14
and did feel the p. of the nails	11:15
the p. of the nails in my hands	DC 6:37

PRISON

Jeremiah have they cast into p.	1Ne 7:14
and were committed to p.	Mos 7: 7
when they had been in p. two days	7: 8
Abinadi should be cast into p.;	12:17
taken from p. and from judgment;	14: 8
bound him and cast him into p.	17: 5
and bound, and cast into p.	21:23
bound in bands and cast into p.	Al 8:31
And also they are cast into p.,	9:hd
that they might cast me into p.	9:32
at that time and cast me into p.	9:33
they might be slain or cast into p.,	10:13
to the officers to be cast into p.	14:17
had been cast into p. three days,	14:18
came in unto the p. to see them,	14:18
strong cords, and confined in p.	14:22
lawyers went in unto the p.	14:23
obtain the outer door of the p.;	14:27
walls of the p. were rent in twain,	14:27
Amulek came forth out of the p.,	14:28
came forth out of the p.;	14:28
the p. had fallen to the earth,	14:28
coming forth out of the p.,	14:29
captivity, or to cast them into p.,	17:20
Muloki and Ammah are in p.	20: 2
brethren are in p. at Middoni,	20: 3
will cast thy brethren out of p.	20: 4
thee that thy brethren were in p.?	20: 4
are in p. in the land of Middoni.	20: 5
will cast thy brethren out of p.	20: 7
brethren may be cast out of p.	20:22
brethren may be cast out of p.,	20:24
brethren may be cast out of p.,	20:27
were brought forth out of p.	20:28
they were taken and cast into p.,	20:30
and kept in p. for many days,	20:30
were taken and cast into p.,	21:13
who were cast into p. suffered	21:14
for the first time out of p.;	21:15
thou hast delivered out of p.	22: 2
bind them, or to cast them into p.;	23: 2
with strong cords, and cast into p.;	26:29
God has delivered me from p.,	36:27
we be cast into p., or be sold,	46:23
were taken and cast into p.,	51:19
been taken and cast into p.;	62: 9
were taken, and were cast into p.,	He 1:22
the Lamanites and cast into p.;	5:21
that same p. in which Ammon	He 5:21
into p. many days without food,	5:22
forth into the p. to take them	5:22
and the walls of the p. did shake	5:27
they that were in the p. were	5:27
the walls of the p. trembled	5:31
hold upon the walls of the p.;	5:44
them and cast them into p.	9: 9
been taken and were cast into p.	9: 9
whom we have cast into p.	9:12
behold they cast us into p.	9:14
converted while they were in p.	9:39
that they might cast him into p.	10:15
not take him to cast him into p.,	10:16
did cast their prisoners into p.,	3Ne 5: 4
and thou shalt be cast into p.	12:25
while ye are in p. can ye pay	12:26
they were cast into p. by them	28:19
and they did cast them into p.;	4Ne 1:30
broke down the door of the p.	Eth 7:18
therefore he shut him up in p.,	9: 7
unto taxes he did cast into p.;	10: 6
pay taxes he did cast into p.;	10: 6
he did cause to be refined in p.,	10: 7
did cause to be wrought in p.	10: 7
the p. to tumble to the earth.	12:13
the spirits of men kept in p.,	DC 76:73
in that p. which is prepared	88:99
and thou be dragged to p.,	122: 6
to redeem them out of their p.,	128:22
a p. have I prepared for them.	Mses 7:38
the spirits as were in p. came forth	7:57

PRISONER

wife and his children, for one p.;	Al 54:11

PRISONERS

That thou mayest say to the p.:	1Ne 21: 9
they shall bow down under the p.,	2Ne 20: 4
opened not the house of his p.?	24:17
his army, and took them p.,	Al 50:35
all the p. who fell into his hands;	52: 8
Lamanites had taken many p.,	52: 8
retain all the p. of the Lamanites	52: 8
number of p. who were taken	52:40
over the p. of the Lamanites,	53: 1
guard the p. of the Lamanites;	53: 5
a stronghold to retain his p.	53: 6
that he would exchange p.	54: 1
for the support of the Lamanite p.	54: 2
among all the p. of Moroni,	54: 3
the p. whom Moroni had taken;	54: 3
as many p. of the Nephites	54: 3
I will not exchange p., save	54:11
grant to exchange p. according to	54:20
not exchange p. with Ammoron	55: 3
whom they have taken p.;	55: 3
cast in weapons of war unto the p.,	55:16
Moroni had armed all those p.;	55:17
armed those p. of the Nephites	55:20
that their p. were armed within.	55:22
He took them p. of war,	55:24
all the p. should be liberated,	55:24
Lamanites, whom he had taken p.,	55:25
p. should be taken to the city	55:26
all the p. whom they had taken,	55:27
attempts they did lose many p.	55:29
given to some of the Lamanite p.	55:31
had also retained many p.,	56:12
also themselves as p. of war.	56:54
themselves up as p. of war.	56:56
as we had no place for our p.,	56:57
deliver up those p. of war whom	57: 1
by delivering up the p. for	57: 2
deliver up our p. on exchange.	57: 2
for he would not exchange p.;	57: 3
our p. to the land of Zarahemla.	57:11
our p. were so numerous that,	57:13
themselves p. of war.	57:14
concerning these p. of war;	57:16
gave them charge over our p.	57:16
inquire of them concerning the p.;	57:17

PRISONERS — PROCEEDETH

PRISONERS
men whom we sent with the p.	Al 57:18
been selected to convey the p.,	57:22
inquire of Gid concerning the p.	57:28
land of Zarahemla with our p.	57:30
our p. did hear their cries,	57:32
those who have been taken p.	58:31
and his men were taken p.,	62: 8
many others, and took them p.;	62:25
of the Lamanites that were p.	62:27
the p. of the Lamanites did join	62:29
from all the p. of the Lamanites.	62:29
having taken many p., which	62:30
Nephites who had been taken p.,	62:30
Lamanites who had been taken p.	He 1:33
who did yield themselves up p.	3Ne 4:27
they had taken all the robbers p.;	5: 4
did cast their p. into prison,	5: 4
Nephites, and did take many p.	Mrm 4: 2
take many p. both women and	4:14
the Lamanites have many p.	Mro 9: 7
Lamanites have they taken p.;	9: 9
for the p. shall go free.	DC 128:22

PRISONS
and from bonds, and from p.,	Al 62:50
the p. could not hold them,	3Ne 28:19
the p. were rent in twain,	4Ne 1:30
cause p. to tumble to the earth;	Mrm 8:24
and he did build many p.,	Eth 10: 6

PRIVATE
in public as well as in p.	DC 19:28
both in public and in p.;	71: 7
thy heart, in public and in p.,	81: 3
forms for public or p. devotion;	134: 4

PRIVATELY
went about p. among the people,	Mos 18: 1
And he taught them p., that it	18: 3
the disciples came unto him p.,	JS 1: 4

PRIVATION
and we have suffered every p.;	Al 26:28

PRIVILEGE
deprived of the p. of assembling	Al 6: 5
as great p. as their brethren.	13: 4
to serve God, it was his p.;	30: 9
in God it was his p. to serve him;	30: 9
in the great p. of our church,	61:14
taken away this p. from you.	DC 9: 5
may have the p. of ordaining,	20:66
a p. of organizing themselves	51:15
say unto you that it is your p.,	67:10
this p. of seeing and knowing	76:117
every man may have an equal p.	88:122
it is his p. to be assisted by	102:10
a p. of speaking for themselves	102:18
from bondage, it is your p.	104:84
I give unto you this p.,	104:86
p. of receiving the mysteries	107:19
to deprive citizens of this p.,	134: 7
We claim the p. of worshiping	AoF 11
and allow all man the same p.,	11

PRIVILEGED
but all men are p. the one like	2Ne 26:28
be p. to come upon them as	Al 49: 6
ye may be p. that ye may	Eth 5: 2
are p. to go up unto Zion—	DC 72:24

PRIVILEGES
may enjoy his rights and p. alike,	Mos 29:32
their rights and p. of the church;	Al 2: 4
not enjoy their rights and p.	30:27
preserve their rights and their p.,	43: 9
the many p. and blessings which	48:12
grant unto them their sacred p.	50:39
rights and the p. of their religion	51: 6
reclaim their rights and their p.	55:28
and the p. of their church and	3Ne 2:12
off from all their outward p.,	4:16
hast lost thy p. for a season—	DC 3:14

PRIVILY
let the p. of the lands be	DC 58:55
in maintaining rights and p.,	98: 5
proscribed in its spiritual p.,	134: 9

PRIVILY
they sought to put them away p.	Al 14: 3
they found out p. the minds of	35: 5
Teancum stole p. into the tent	51:34
again p. to his own camp,	51:35

PRIZE
that thereby he might win the p.;	Mos 4:27
they may know to p. the good.	Mses 6:55

PROBABILITY
no p. that we would ever be	JS 2:61

PROBABLY
p. arise through the slave question,	DC 130:13

PROBATION
in the days of your p.,	1Ne 10:21
the body in the days of p.,	15:31
body in their days of p.	15:32
state became a state of p.,	2Ne 2:21
in the last days of my p.;	2:30
that wasteth the days of his p.,	9:27
until the end of the day of p.	33: 9
behold, your days of p. are past;	He 13:38
Be wise in the days of your p.;	Mrm 9:28
unto man the days of his p.—	DC 29:43

PROBATIONARY
this life became a p. state;	Al 12:24
unto man to repent, yea, a p. time,	42: 4
this p. state became a state for	42:10
of men in this p. state,	42:13

PROCEED
I, Nephi, p. to give an account	1Ne 10: 1
to p. with mine account,	10: 1
I p. according to that which	19: 5
will p. to do a marvelous work	22: 8
will p. to make bare his arm	22:11
shall p. forth out of my mouth	2Ne 3:21
for a law shall p. from me,	8: 4
I p. with mine own prophecy,	25: 7
he will p. to do a marvelous work	25:17
will p. to bring forth the words	27:14
I will p. to do a marvelous word	27:26
I shall p. to do a marvelous word	29: 1
should p. forth out of my mouth	29: 2
it shall p. forth from the Jews,	29: 4
shall p. forth out of the mouth of	33:14
now I, Mormon, p. to finish	WM 1: 9
and Lehi did p. from thence	He 5:20
p. to give my account of the	3Ne 5:19
p. to write the things which	26:12
p. to give an account of those	Eth 1: 1
now I p. with my record;	2:13
p. to give the record of Jared	6: 1
I, Moroni, p. with my record.	9: 1
p. to finish my record	13: 1
shall p. forth out of the mouth	Mro 10:28
That I may p. to bring to	DC 101:95
if you p. to do the things	104:86

PROCEEDED
the book p. forth from the	1Ne 13:24
when it p. forth from the	13:24
p. out of the mouth of the Jew,	14:23
p. out of the mouth of the Jew,	14:23
and Lamoni p. on their journey	Al 20:28
every word which p. forth out	Mro 7:25
p. to organize the high council	DC 102: 1
then p. to cast lots or ballot,	102:34

PROCEEDETH
p. out of the mouth of a Jew.	1Ne 13:23
p. that which is great.	DC 64:33
by every word that p. forth	84:44
Which light p. forth from the	88:12
every word which p. forth	98:11

PROCEEDING

PROCEEDING
p. out of the mouth of the Jew; 1Ne 14:23

PROCEEDINGS
a record of my p. in my days. 1Ne 1: 1
account of my p., in my days. 1:17
of my p., and my reign 10: 1
the more part of all our p. 19: 2
part of the p. of this people, Jac 3:13
many of their p. are written 3:13
give an account of their p. Mos 28: 9
many records kept of the p. of He 3:13
part of the p. of this people, 3:14
contain all the p. of this people; 3Ne 5: 9
immediately, a copy of their p., DC 102:26
precise in taking the whole p., 128: 3
from all unlawful p., JS 2:75

PROCESS
your destruction in p. of time, DC 38:13
in p. of time it came to pass Mses 5:19
Zion, in p. of time, was taken 7:21
In p. of time my mind became JS 2: 8

PROCLAIM
I shall p. unto this my people Mos 1:10
p. these things unto the world; DC 1:18
time forth to p. my gospel, 30: 9
p. against that spirit with a 50:32
that you should p. my gospel 66: 5
to p. the everlasting gospel, 68: 1
p. unto the world in the 71: 2
to go forth to p. my gospel, 75: 2
p. the things which I have 75: 9
p. the things which I have 75:13
countries, and p. my gospel, 75:15
p. the gospel unto the world. 75:24
goeth forth to p. this gospel 84:86
to p. mine everlasting gospel, 84:103
p. the acceptable year of 93:51
renounce war and p. peace, 98:16
should p. war against them, 98:34
to p. mine everlasting gospel 99: 1
go out and p. thy word 109:38
whatsoever place ye shall p. 112:19
and p. my everlasting gospel 124:88

PROCLAIMED
and p. unto all the people who Mos 1:18
Moroni had p. these words, Al 46:21
might be p. by the weak and DC 1:23
and hast p. my word, 60:14
about where it has not been p. 66: 5
everlasting gospel shall be p. 109:29

PROCLAIMING
return, p. my word among DC 60:14
mouths in p. my gospel, 71: 1
p. the truth according to the 75: 4
p. glad tidings of great joy, 79: 1
in p. the gospel in the land 81: 3
shalt continue p. my gospel 99: 8
moneys for the p. of my words, 104:26
hear from heaven, p. in our ears, 128:23

PROCLAMATION
a p. throughout all this land Mos 1:10
a p. throughout all the land, 2: 1
sent a p. among all his people, 7:17
send a p. among all this people 22: 6
sent a p. throughout the land 27: 2
the king sent a p. throughout Al 22:27
king of the Lamanites sent a p. 23: 1
he sent his p. throughout 23: 3
the king had sent forth this p., 23: 4
the chief judge sent a p. 27:21
the p. was sent forth by the 30:57
a p. throughout all his land, 47: 1
when the p. had gone forth 47: 2
I have sent a p. throughout 61: 6
there was a p. sent abroad He 9: 9
he sent a p. among all the 3Ne 3:13
the p. of Lachoneus had gone 3:22

PROFOUND

and make a p. of peace DC 105:39
to open the door by the p. of the 107:35
make a solemn p. of my gospel, 124: 2
p. shall be made to all the kings 124: 3
upon them with loud p., and with 124: 7
help you to write this p., 124:12
in making a solemn p. unto 124:107

PROCRASTINATE
p. the day of your repentance; Al 13:27
p. the day of your repentance 34:33

PROCRASTINATED
if ye have p. the day of your Al 34:35
p. the day of your salvation He 13:38

PROFANED
And they p. not; neither did they Jar 1: 5

PROFESS
And then will I p. unto them: 3Ne 14:23
in the church that p. my name. DC 50: 4
ye people who p. my name, 56: 1

PROFESSED
ye that have p. to have known Al 5:37
who p. the blood of nobility; 51:21
p. to belong to the church of He 3:33
p. to belong to the church of 4:11
which p. to know the Christ, 4Ne 1:27
that have p. my name, DC 41: 1
who have p. to know my name 112:26

PROFESSING
p. and yet be not of God. DC 46:27

PROFESSION
they might be skillful in their p. Al 10:15
who were of the p. of Nehor; 14:18
for they were of the p. of Nehor, 15:15
for they were of the p. of Nehor, 16:11

PROFESSOR
P. Charles Anthon, a gentleman JS 2:64
P. Anthon stated that the 2:64
sanctioned what P. Anthon had 2:65

PROFESSORS
those p. were all corrupt; JS 2:19
against me among p. of religion, 2:22
and this, too, by p. of religion. 2:75

PROFIT
might be for our p. and learning. 1Ne 19:23
who teacheth thee to p., 20:17
things for your p. and learning; 2Ne 2:14
learning and the p. of my children. 4:15
my sight, for the p. of thy people. 5:30
the roots thereof. p. me nothing Jac 5:35
some day it may p. them. WM 1: 2
diligently, that ye may p. thereby; Mos 1: 7
what doth it p. us to labor in the Al 30:34
behold, this did p. us but little; 58: 5
what doth it p. that we have 3Ne 24:14
of God unto men, to p. them. Mro 10: 8
for your p. and learning. DC 46: 1
to every man to p. withal, 46:16
for your p. and for salvation. 84:73
For what doth it p. a man if 88:33

PROFITED
that all may be p. thereby. DC 46:12
every member may be p. thereby. 46:29

PROFITETH
foolishness and it p. them not. 2Ne 9:28
and it p. me nothing, Jac 5:32
The tree p. me nothing, 5:35
real intent it p. him nothing. Mro 7: 6
yea, and it p. him nothing, 7: 9

PROFOUND
task-masters were in a p. sleep. Mos 24:19
things were done in a p. silence. Al 55:17

PROGRESS — PROMISES

PROGRESS
prosper nor p. in their journey,	Mos	1:17
the church began to fail in its p.	Al	4:10
did not p. in their journey;		37:41
impede the p. of this people		60:30
the rise and p. of the Church	JS	2: 1
and its p. in the world—		2: 1

PROLONG
he shall p. his days,	Mos	14:10
they did p. the time;		21:35
p. their existence in the land.	Al	9:16
bless them and p. their days,	He	15:10
the Lord shall p. their days,		15:11

PROLONGED
of the children of men were p.,	2Ne	2:21
and her day shall not be p.		23:22
days shall not be p. in the land,	Al	9:18
hath the lord p. their days.	He	15: 4
cause, that thy days may be p.,	DC	5:33

PROMISE
shall be led to a land of p.;	1Ne	2:20
shall prosper in the land of p.		4:14
I have obtained a land of p.,		5: 5
towards the land of p.		5:22
unto the Lord in the land of p.		7: 1
we shall obtain the land of p.;		7:13
one accord into the land of p.,		10:13
and beheld the land of p.;		12: 1
on the face of the land of p.;		12: 4
Gentiles upon the land of p.;		13:14
who were in the land of p.,		17:33
power into the land of p.		17:42
did find upon the land of p.,		18:25
them concerning the land of p.,	2Ne	1: 3
we have obtained a land of p.,		1: 5
I, Lehi, have obtained a p., that		1: 9
into this precious land of p.—		1:10
us forth into the land of p.;		1:24
he obtained a p. of the Lord,		3: 5
this p., which I have obtained		3:14
I am sure of the fulfilling of this p.;		3:14
as I am sure of the p. of Moses;		3:16
in all their lands of p.		9: 2
shall return to their lands of p.		24: 2
that the p. may be fulfilled		25:21
unto the fulfilling of the p.		31:18
which is a land of p. unto you	Jac	2:12
the p. of the Lord is fulfilled,	Mos	7:32
would not keep their p.;		23:37
into a far better land of p.	Al	37:45
for the p. of the Lord was, if		48:25
his p. which he made was rash;		51:10
this p. is unto all, even unto	Mrm	9:21
even unto the land of p.,	Eth	2: 7
should possess this land of p.,		2: 8
this land, that it is a land of p.;		2: 9
a p. that they should not taste		12:17
they obtained not the p. until		12:17
the p. which the brother of		12:21
my fathers have obtained the p.		12:22
faith in him according to the p.	Mro	7:41
gave p. that he should have a	DC	27: 7
greater riches, even a land of p.,		38:18
But obtained a p. that they		45:14
Wherefore, this is the land of p.,		57: 2
that the p. might be fulfilled,		62: 6
p. the faithful and cannot lie.		62: 6
a p. I give unto you that have		67:10
the p. of the Lord unto you,		68: 5
sealed by the Holy Spirit of p.,		76:53
do not what I say, ye have no p.		82:10
even the Holy Spirit of p.;		88: 3
This Comforter is the p. which		88: 4
Remember the great and last p.		88:69
that I may fulfil this p.,		88:75
this great and last p.,		88:75
Given for a principle with p.,		89: 3
I, the Lord, give unto them a p.,		89:21
this is the p. of the Father		95: 9
whom I give a p. of eternal life	DC	96: 6
the p. made unto his fathers—		96: 7
he giveth this p. unto you,		98: 3
And I give unto you this p.,		100: 8
With p. immutable and		104: 2
I give unto you a p.,		104:83
the p. is, if these things abound		107:31
received the p. of God by his		107:42
this is the p. of the Father unto		108: 5
the p. of the Lord is that he will		113:10
give unto them a p. that I will		118: 3
completely claim that p. which		123: 6
to build a house in the land of p.,		124:38
even the Holy Spirit of p.,		124:124
sealed by the Holy Spirit of p.,		132: 7
sealed by the Holy Spirit of p.,		132:18
unto them by the Holy Spirit of p.,		132:19
sealed by the Holy Spirit of p.,		132:26
This p. is yours also, because ye		132:31
p. was made unto Abraham;		132:31
receive the p. of my Father,		132:33
fulfil the p. which was given by		132:63
with a covenant and p. to keep		136: 2
Shulon, and dwelt in a land of p.,	Mses	6:17
for I give unto thee a p. that	Abr	2:11

PROMISED
large waters into the p. land,	1Ne	1:hd
he p. that he would go down		4:35
who were in the p. land.		13:12
a blessed people upon the p. land		14: 2
shall be led towards the p. land;		17:13
ye have arrived in the p. land,		17:14
the wind towards the p. land.		18: 8
sailed again towards the p. land.		18:22
we did arrive at the p. land;		18:23
and we did call it the p. land.		18:23
he has p. unto us that our seed	2Ne	9:53
hath the Lord God p. unto me		25:21
witnesses which I have p. unto		27:22
and he p. obedience unto the	Jac	7:27
and he has p. you that if ye	Mos	10:15
they had arrived in the p. land.		23:36
the Lamanites p. unto Alma and	Al	9:24
for has not the Lord expressly p.		17:35
the Lord had p. Mosiah that he		36:28
by his power into the p. land;		37:18
For he p. unto them that he		37:44
a straight course to the p. land.		37:45
its course, to the p. land,	He	7: 7
joyed with him in the p. land;	3Ne	20:29
the p. land unto them forever,	Eth	6: 5
the waters, towards the p. land;		6: 8
to blow towards the p. land		6:12
upon the shore of the p. land.		6:12
upon the shores of the p. land		6:16
they came to the p. land;		7:27
the great deep into the p. land;	DC	49:10
that which I have p. I have		58:31
have p. and have not fulfilled?		88: 3
that I p. unto my disciples,		103:13
have p. after your tribulations,		104: 7
have p. unto you a crown of	JS	2:75
and p. us protection from		

PROMISES
the p. which we have obtained are	2Ne	10: 2
are p. unto us according to the		10: 2
the p. of the Lord are great unto		10: 9
For I will fulfil my p. which		10:17
But great are the p. of the Lord		10:21
that I may remember the p.		29: 2
the p. which the Lord made unto	Mos	1: 7
and his fair p., deceived me,		10:18
these were the p. of the Lord	Al	3:17
many p. which are extended to		9:16
the p. of the Lord are extended to		9:24
p. of the Lord were extended		17:15
according to the p. of the Lord,		28:11
according to the p. of the Lord,		28:12
For he will fulfil all his p.		37:17
for he has fulfilled his p. which		37:17

PROMISES PROPHECY

these p. have been verified to	Al	50:21
the p. of the Lord have been	He	15:12
the p. which the Lord had made	4Ne	1:11
and the p. of the Lord.		1:49
until all his p. shall be fulfilled,	Mrm	8:22
leading them away by fair p.	Eth	8:17
p. which are in them shall all	DC	1:37
the p. made to the fathers,		2: 2
the p. which were made to you,		3: 5
most sacred p. which were		3:13
the p. of the Lord might be		3:19
might know the p. of the Lord,		3:20
by whom the p. remain;		27:10
to fulfil the p. that I have made		45:16
the p. which have been made		45:35
his p. are not fulfilled.		58:33
to whom the p. were made.		107:40
to secure a fulfilment of the p.		109:11
neither fulfil the p. which ye		124:47
Abraham received p. concerning		132:30
fulfilling, among other things, the p.		132:34
according to the p., and		132:37
the p. made to the fathers,	JS	2:39

PROMISING
p. that he would covenant and	Al	44:19

PROMOTE
wilt p. the glory of him who is	DC	81: 4

PROMOTING
p. this extraordinary scene of	JS	2: 6

PROMPT
will transact all business in a p.	DC	127: 1
religious opinions p. them to		134: 4

PROMPTLY
he has been p. reproved.	DC	OD

PROMULGATE
and there p. my gospel,	DC	118: 4

PRONOUNCED
there is a wo p. upon him who	Mos	2:33
shall be p. upon the wicked	DC	29:41
laws have been p. constitutional		OD
the Gods p. the dry land, earth;	Abr	4:10
the waters, p. they, great waters;		4:10

PROPER
shall be restored to its p. frame,	Al	11:43
to their p. and perfect frame.		40:23
should be restored to their p. order.		41: 2
shall be restored to their p. order,		41: 4
again, according to its p. order;	3Ne	1:19
to be guided in a right and p. way	DC	101:63
in a prompt and p. manner,		127: 1
kept a p. and faithful record of		128: 9
a p. and affectionate manner	JS	2:28

PROPERTIES
consecrate of thy p. for	DC	42:30
the consecration of the p. of		42:32
be p. in the hands of the church,		42:33
to have equal claims on the p.,		82:17
of all those who consecrate p.,		85: 1
the p. which belong to the order		104: 1
concerning the p. of the order—		104:19
all these p. are mine,		104:55
And if the p. are mine,		104:56
be improving upon the p.		104:68
And pledge the p. which		104:85
Let the p. of Kirtland be		117: 5
be tithed of their surplus p.,		119: 5
in moneys, or in p. wherein		124:70

PROPERTY
when Laban saw our p.,	1Ne	3:25
that he might obtain our p.		3:25
obliged to leave behind our p.,		3:26
he also had taken away our p.		4:11

and deliver up their p.,	Mos	19:15
they again may rob us of our p.	Al	20:13
regained the one-half of their p.	He	4:16
of your liberty, and your p.,	3Ne	3: 2
in the defence of his p. and	Eth	14: 2
shalt not covet thine own p.,	DC	19:26
destruction of thyself and p.		19:33
Impart a portion of thy p.,		19:34
affairs of the p. of this church.		38:36
a stewart over his own p.,		42:32
the p. which is consecrated to		42:71
otherwise, think not of thy p.		66: 6
become the common p. of		82:18
for what is p. unto me?		117: 4
I require all their surplus p. to		119: 1
the p. and amount of damages		123: 2
injuries, as well as real p.;		123: 2
in due time, by turning out p.,		127: 1
put his p. out of his hands,		132:57
the right and control of p.,		134: 2
on the right of p. or life,		134:10
right of p. or character infringed,		134:11
themselves, their friends, and p.,		134:11
to the dividend of their p.,		136: 8
use all his influence and p. to		136:10

PROPHECIES
the p. of the holy prophets,	1Ne	5:13
many p. which have been spoken		5:13
the p. of the holy prophets;		13:23
and the p. of my father;		19: 1
and also many of mine own p.		19: 1
that the ministry and the p.,		19: 3
Nephi, speak concerning the p.	2Ne	4: 1
And the p. which he wrote,		4: 2
concerning the p. of Joseph,		4: 3
that the p. of Isaiah shall be		25: 7
we write according to our p.,		25:26
the p. of the coming of Christ;	WM	1: 4
the p. which had been spoken	Mos	1: 2
the records which contain the p.		2:34
and explaining the p. and		27:35
were taught the records and p.	Al	23: 5
against the p. which had been		30: 6
these things which ye call p.,		30:14
all the p. of the holy prophets?		30:22
that those ancient p. are true.		30:24
knowing of the p. of Alma,		43:23
the p. concerning that which is		58:40
p. of many holy prophets,	He	1:hd
their preaching, and their p.,		3:14
to remember the p. of Alma		4:21
much preaching and many p.		6:14
yea, the p. of the holy prophets,		15: 7
the p. of the prophets began to	3Ne	1: 4
words and p. of Lachoneus		3:16
not unto the fulfilling of the p.		10:14
according to.the p. and the	4Ne	1:49
Search the p. of Isaiah.	Mrm	8:23
there are no revelations, nor p.,		9: 7
marvelous were the p. of Ether;	Eth	13:13
the p. which had been spoken		13:21
p. which were spoken by	Mro	8:29
unto the fulfilling of the p.		10:28
the p. and promises which are	DC	1:37
that the p. may be fulfilled.		52:36
the p. of the Old Testament.	JS	2:36

PROPHECY
and also by the spirit of p.	TPg	
are filled with the spirit of p.	2Ne	25: 4
But I give unto you a p.,		25: 4
I proceed with mine own p.,		25: 7
and according to my p. they		25:10
and the spirit of much p.;	Jac	1: 6
and the spirit of p.;		4: 6
behold, this is my p.—		6: 1
has been written, neither p.;	Om	1:11
to the words of the spirit of p.;	Al	3:27
come according to the spirit of p.;		4:13
to the spirit of revelation and p.		4:20
so according to the spirit of p.		5:47

PROPHECY 770 PROPHET

and according to the spirit of p.	Al	6: 8
to the spirit of revelation and p.;		8:24
and having the spirit of p.,		9:21
come, according to the spirit of p.		10:12
according to the spirit of p.		12: 7
was according to the spirit of p.		13:26
heard that he had the spirit of p.,		16: 5
therefore they had the spirit of p.,		17: 3
the spirit of revelation and of p.,		23: 6
relying upon the spirit of p.,		25:16
I tell you by the spirit of p.,		37:15
according to the spirit of p. and		43: 2
even until the p. is fulfilled;		45: 9
this p. shall be fulfilled.		45:14
denying the spirit of p. and	He	4:12
to disbelieve in the spirit of p.		4:23
THE P. OF NEPHI,		7:hd
come, according to his p.?		8:20
The p. of Samuel, the		13:hd
And this is according to the p.,		15:13
the p. of all the holy prophets.	3Ne	1:26
spirit of revelation and also p.;		3:19
worketh by revelation, or by p.,		29: 6
revelation, nor the spirit of p.,	DC	11:25
from the p. of his book,		20:35
The more sure word of p.		131: 5
revelation and the spirit of p.,		131: 5
Now this p. Adam spake, as he	Mses	6: 8
according to the p. of Moses,	JS	1:55
last chapter of the same p.,		2:36
I also had the spirit of p.,		2:73
must be called of God, by p.,	AoF	5
believe in the gift of tongues, p.,		7

PROPHESIED

written many things which he p.	1Ne	1:16
he p. many things concerning		5:19
preached unto them, and also p.		8:38
these things have been p.		22: 5
And thus p. Joseph, saying:	2Ne	3:14
Yea, thus p. Joseph:		3:16
behold, he truly p. concerning		4: 2
And he p. concerning us,		4: 2
the prophets have written, nor p.,	Jac	7:11
as many things as have been p.	WM	1: 4
and p. of many things which are	Mos	7:26
who has p. evil concerning thy		12: 9
and he has p. in vain.		12:14
even all the prophets who have p.		13:33
the holy prophets who have p.		15:11
which he p. against us—		20:21
has been p. by our fathers,	Al	37: 4
as the soldier of Moroni had p.		44:18
p. unto the people whatsoever	He	13: 4
it had been p. among them	3Ne	11:12
have we not p. in thy name,		14:22
been p. by Samuel the prophet;	Mrm	2:10
p. of the destruction of that	Eth	11: 1
they p. unto to Com many things;		11: 3
who p. of the destruction of		11: 5
and p. again unto the people;		11:12
p. of great and marvelous things,		11:20
p. in all his days, and taught	Mses	6:13
of God; wherefore Enos p. also.		6:13
spake and p., and called upon		6:23
I p., saying: Behold the people		7: 7
Methuselah p. that from his loins		8: 3
Noah p., and taught the things of		8:16
p. many things which should	JS	2:73
I p. concerning the rise of		2:73

PROPHESIES

Samuel, a Lamanite, p. unto the	He	7:hd

PROPHESIETH

he p. unto the people	1Ne	1:hd
Behold, my brethren, he that p.,	Jac	4:13
also p. evil concerning thy life,	Mos	12:10
to behold the seer, for he p.,	Mses	6:38

PROPHESY

began to p. and to declare	1Ne	1:18
began to p. concerning his seed—		5:17

did my father p. and speak	1Ne	10:15
Wherefore, I, Lehi, p. according	2Ne	1: 6
manner did my father of old p.		3:22
Wherefore I shall p. according		25: 4
delighteth to p. concerning him,		25:13
preach of Christ, we p. of Christ,		25:26
behold, I p. unto you concerning		26:14
now, I would p. somewhat more		30: 3
let him p. to the understanding	Jac	4:13
said unto you that I would p.,		6: 1
preach and p. unto this people,	En	1:26
we could p. of all things.	Mos	5: 3
and began to p., saying:		11:20
began to p. among them, saying:		12: 1
go and p. unto this my people,		12: 1
Stretch forth thy hand and p.		12: 2
Abinadi p. against this people.		12: 8
to send me to p. against this people,		12:29
to p. evil concerning this people.		13:26
did not Moses p. unto them		13:33
that has opened his mouth to p.,		15:13
again and p. unto this people,	Al	8:25
go forth and p. unto this people,		8:29
preach and p. unto the people,		8:32
p. that this great city should be		9: 4
also to have heard my father p.		36:17
somewhat to p. unto thee;		45: 9
what I p. unto thee ye shall		45: 9
what I p. unto thee shall not		45: 9
did p. many things unto them	He	4:14
did p. many things unto them;		7: 2
to p. such marvelous things unto		9: 2
doth p. so much evil concerning		9:27
p. unto the people whatsoever		13: 3
p. a great many more things		14: 1
should p. these things unto you;		14: 9
and to p. among his own people.		16: 7
Samuel did p. according to	3Ne	23:10
they did p. that the Lord	Eth	11:12
began to p. unto the people,		12: 2
that Ether did p. great and		12: 5
and p. unto Coriantumr that,		13:20
may p. concerning all things;	Mro	10:13
and shalt p. before nations,	DC	7: 3
therefore p., and it shall be		34:10
shall be given unto him to p.;		35:23
and p. as seemeth me good;		42:16
I will speak unto you and p.,		45:15
to others it is given to p.;		46:22
and to p. to the Jews after		77:15
I p., in the name of the Lord		130:12
p. concerning all the families	Mses	5:10
Enoch, my son, p. unto this		6:27
Enoch began to p., saying		7: 2
And the Lord said unto me: P.;		7: 7

PROPHESYING

there came many prophets, p.	1Ne	1: 4
Lehi, had made an end of p.		7: 1
manner of p. among the Jews.	2Ne	25: 1
I, Nephi, make an end of my p.		31: 1
to the plainness of my p.		31: 2
revelation which was great, or p.,	Jac	1: 4
am led on by the Spirit unto p.;		4:15
p. of things to come,	En	1:19
preaching and p. of wars,		1:23
not write the things of my p.,	Jar	1: 2
and believe in p.,	Om	1:25
to understand the spirit of p.,	Mos	12:25
and all the preaching and p.	He	6: 2
Nephi was baptizing, and p.,		16: 4
p. which was sent among them;	3Ne	2:10
p. that the wickedness and	Eth	7:23

PROPHESYINGS

led by many preachings and p.	Om	1:13
these plates, which contain these p.	WM	1: 6

PROPHET

a p. would the Lord God raise up	1Ne	10: 4
a p. who should come before		10: 7
the p. who should prepare the way		11:27

PROPHET — PROPHETS

or from one p. to another,	1 Ne 19: 4
for thus spake the p.:	19:11
saith the p. Zenos.	19:12
saith the p., they shall	19:13
saith the p., and have	19:14
saith the p., that they	19:15
the words of the p. Zenos,	19:16
saith the p.;	19:17
written by the p. Isaiah;	19:23
Hear ye the words of the p.,	19:24
hear ye the words of the p.,	19:24
this manner has the p. written.	19:24
they were manifest unto the p.	22: 2
For behold, saith the p.,	22:15
for thus saith the p.,	22:17
A p. shall the Lord your God raise	22:20
all those who will not hear that p.	22:20
this p. of whom Moses spake	22:21
according to the words of the p.	22:23
according to the words of the p.	2 Ne 2:30
they of whom the p. has written;	6:12
for this cause the p. has written	6:12
according to the words of the p.,	6:14
man of war, the judge, and the p.,	13: 2
and the p. that teacheth lies,	19:15
unto you concerning that p.	31: 4
read the words of the p. Zenos,	Jac 5: 1
the words of me, a p. of the Lord.	5: 2
things which this p. Zenos spake,	6: 1
a p. of the Lord have they slain;	Mos 7:26
that a seer is greater than a p.	8:15
a seer is a revelator and a p. also;	8:16
And was he not a holy p.?	Al 5:11
that thou art a holy p. of God,	8:20
thou shalt feed a p. of the Lord;	10: 7
that thou art a p. of a holy God,	19: 4
Zenos, the p. of old, has said	33: 3
a second p. of old has testified	33:17
if he had not been a p. he could	He 8: 9
the p. Zenos did testify boldly	8:19
(Jeremiah being that same p.	8:20
surety whether this man be a p.	9: 2
we do not believe that he is a p.;	9: 2
chosen of God, and a p.	9:16
Has Nephi, the pretended p., who	9:27
who said that Nephi was a p.	9:40
did esteem him as a great p.,	11:18
if a p. come among you	13:26
you will say that he is a false p.,	13:26
and say that he is a p.	13:27
and also by the p. Zenos,	15:11
had been given by Samuel the p.	3 Ne 1: 9
Gidgiddoni was a great p.	3:19
been given by the p. Samuel,	8: 3
the p. Zenos did testify of these	10:16
words of the p. Isaiah shall be	16:17
a p. shall the Lord your God	20:23
soul who will not hear that p.	20:23
I will send you Elijah the p.	25: 5
prophesied by Samuel the p.;	Mrm 2:10
Ether was a p. of the Lord;	Eth 12: 2
by the hand of Elijah the p.,	DC 2: 1
called a seer, a translator, a p.,	21: 1
by the mouth of Ezekiel the p.	29:21
a revelator, a translator, and a p.,	107:92
for Elijah the p., who was taken	110:13
as spoken of by Daniel the p.	116: 1
unto him that he may be a p.,	124:94
a revelator, a seer, and p.	124:125
p. and seer of the Church of	127:12
I will send you Elijah the p.	128:17
was written by the p. Moses,	133:63
was written by the p. Malachi:	133:64
martyrdom of Joseph Smith the P.	135: 1
Joseph Smith, the P. and Seer	135: 3
spoken of by Daniel the p.	JS 1:12
spoken of by Daniel the p.,	1:32
by the hand of Elijah the p.	2:38
said that that p. was Christ;	2:40

PROPHETESS

And I went unto the p.;	2 Ne 18: 3

PROPHET'S

God's time, angel's time, p. time,	DC 130: 4

PROPHETS

came many p., prophesying	1 Ne 1: 4
as with the p. of old,	1:20
according to the words of the p.	2:13
have rejected the words of the p.	3:18
by the mouth of all the holy p.,	3:20
the prophecies of the holy p.,	5:13
they have rejected the p.,	7:14
he also spake concerning the p.,	10: 5
hearken unto the words of the p.,	13:23
that the records of the p.	13:39
even as he had p. of old,	19:20
did show unto the p. of old	19:21
all things made known unto the p.,	22: 2
by the mouth of his holy p.,	2 Ne 9: 2
do understand the things of the p.,	25: 5
it were foretold them by the p.	25: 9
one Messiah spoken of by the p.,	25:18
according to the words of the p.,	25:19
according to the words of the p.,	25:19
denying him ye also deny the p.	25:28
because they cast out the p.,	26: 3
And they that kill the p.,	26: 5
hearken unto the words of the p.,	26: 8
and ye have rejected the p.;	27: 5
but also all the holy p. which	Jac 4: 4
Wherefore, we search the p.,	4: 6
also spake them unto p. of old.	4:13
of plainness, and killed the p.,	4:14
Will ye reject the words of the p.;	6: 8
none of the p. have written,	7:11
exceeding many p. among us.	En 1:22
the p. of the Lord did threaten	Jar 1:10
the p., and the priests,	1:11
this small account of the p.,	WM 1: 3
after there had been false p.,	1:16
with the assistance of the holy p.	1:16
and also the p., did once more	1:18
been spoken by the holy p.,	Mos 2:34
God hath sent his holy p. among	3:13
also holy p. spake unto them	3:15
all the p. who have prophesied	13:33
has heard the words of the p.,	15:11
holy p. who have prophesied	15:11
Yea, and are not the p., every	15:13
I mean all the holy p.	15:13
the resurrection of all the p.,	15:22
by the mouth of the holy p.	18:19
Jacob, and also all the holy p.,	Al 5:24
Isaac, and Jacob, and the holy p.	7:25
which had been spoken by the p.,	18:36
that they are just men and holy p.	20:15
which had been spoken by the p.,	30: 6
are handed down by holy p.,	30:14
all the prophecies of the holy p.?	30:22
and also all the holy p.?	30:44
murdered all the p. of the Lord	37:30
spoken by the mouths of the p.	40:22
spoken by the mouths of the p.—	40:24
prophecies of many holy p.,	He 1:hd
but also the holy p.,	8:16
been many p. that have testified	8:19
had been laid down by the p.	11:22
that ye do cast out the p.,	13:24
we would not have slain the p.;	13:25
and had not killed the p.,	13:33
the prophecies of the holy p.,	15: 7
Zenos, and many other p.,	15:11
the words of the p. began to be	16:13
the prophecies of the p. began	3 Ne 1: 4
by the mouth of my holy p.	1:13
not believed the words of the p.,	1:16
believed in the words of the p.	1:16
the p. had testified of these	1:18
according to the words of the p.	1:20
of the prophecy of all the holy p.	1:26
which was spoken of by the p.,	2: 7
the words of all the holy p. who	5: 1
according to the words of the p.;	5: 2

PROPHETS   772   PROSPER

condemned the p. of the Lord	3Ne 6:25	For they killed the p., and them	DC	136:36
of those who murdered the p.	7: 6	of whom it is written by the p.,	JS	1: 1
the p. who testified of Jesus.	7:10	And many false p. shall arise,		1: 9
they did stone the p. and did	7:14	arise false Christs, and false p.,		1:22
not killed and stoned the p.,	8:25	apostles, p., pastors, teachers,	AoF	6
blood of the p. and the saints	9: 5			
blood of the p. and the saints	9: 7	PROPORTION		
blood of the p. and the saints	9: 8	in p. to the amount of stock	DC	124:68
blood of the p. and the saints	9: 9	bear his p. of their wages,		124:122
wickedness in casting out the p.,	9:10	each company bear an equal p.,		136: 8
blood of the p. and the saints	9:11			
which had been spoken by the p.	10:11	PROPOSALS		
it was they who received the p.	10:12	And make p. for peace	DC	105:40
prophecies of many of the holy p.	10:14			
whom the p. testified shall come	11:10	PROPOSED		
whom it was written by the p.,	11:15	to the conditions which I have p.	Al	44: 1
so persecuted they the p. who	12:12			
come to destroy the law or the p.	12:17	PROPRIA		
for this is the law and the p.	14:12	in their own p. persona,	DC	128: 8
Beware of false p., who come	14:15			
Behold, I do not destroy the p.,	15: 6	PROPRIETY		
And this is the law and the p.,	15:10	p. of all the saints gathering	DC	123: 1
all the p. from Samuel and	20:24			
ye are the children of the p.;	20:25	PROSCRIBE		
Search the p., for many there	23: 5	or p. them in their opinions,	DC	134: 7
have been spoken by the holy p.,	29: 2			
by many priests and false p.	4Ne 1:34	PROSCRIBED		
came p. among the people,	Eth 7:23	p. in its spiritual privileges,	DC	134: 9
people did revile against the p.,	7:24			
who did revile against the p.	7:24	PROSECUTIONS		
gave power unto the p. that	7:25	in the getting up of their p.	DC	127: 1
that they have murdered the p.,	8:25			
came p. in the land again,	9:28	PROSELYTED		
believed not the words of the p.,	9:29	p. to the Presbyterian faith,	JS	2: 7
in the days of Com many p.,	11: 1			
the p. were rejected by the	11: 2	PROSPECTS		
all the p. who prophesied	11: 5	their p. shall melt away	DC	121:11
of Ethem there came many p.,	11:12			
the p. mourned and withdrew	11:13	PROSPER		
there also came many p.,	11:20	ye shall p., and shall be led	1Ne	2:20
reject all the words of the p.,	11:22	they shall p. in the land		4:14
this Jesus of whom the p. and	12:41	they did p. and obtain		13:15
by the mouth of all the p.,	15: 3	that they did p. in the land;		13:20
God also declared unto p.,	Mro 7:23	p. upon the face of this land;	2Ne	1: 9
which were spoken by the p.,	8:29	ye shall p. in the land;		1:20
words of the p. and apostles,	DC 1:14	ye shall p. in the land;		4: 4
which was written by the p.—	1:18	and we did p. exceedingly;		5:11
which my holy p., yea, and	10:46	we began to p. exceedingly,		5:13
was had by the p. of old.	17: 2	they did not p. against us.	Jar	1: 9
in the words of the holy p.,	20:26	ye shall p. in the land.		1: 9
by the mouth of all the holy p.	27: 6	ye shall not p. in the land.	Om	1: 6
call on the holy p. to prove	35:23	that ye may p. in the land	Mos	1: 7
I spake by the mouths of my p.	42:39	they did not p. nor progress		1:17
p. and apostles have written,	52: 9	ye should p. in the land;		2:22
than the p. and apostles,	52:36	he doth bless you and p. you.		2:22
mouths of the p. shall not fail;	58: 8	ye shall p. in the land,		2:31
are given by the p. of God.	58:18	up their ways that they p. not;		7:29
to the law and the p.;	59:22	to multiply and p. in the land.		9: 9
apostles and p. shall be known.	64:39	thus we did p. in the land—		10: 5
written by the p. and apostles	66: 2	and thou shalt also p.		12:15
neither the p., neither the	76:101	the pleasure of the Lord shall p.		14:10
two p. that are to be raised up	77:15	they began to p. by degrees in		21:16
spoken by the mouth of his p.,	84: 2	they began to p. exceedingly		23:19
by the mouths of all the holy p.	86:10	did multiply and p. exceedingly		23:20
of the school of the p.,	88:127	p. exceedingly in the affairs of		26:37
in the school of the p.	88:136	the Lord did visit them and p. them,		27: 7
in the school of the p.,	88:137	And thus they did p. and become	Al	1:31
keys of the school of the p.,	90: 7	ye shall p. in the land?		9:13
the translation of the p.,	90:13	fields, that ye may p. in them.		34:24
arose in the school of the p.;	95:10	of God ye shall p. in the land.		36: 1
hearts of the Jews unto the p.,	98:17	of God ye shall p. in the land;		36:30
and the p. unto the Jews;	98:17	ye shall p. in the land—		37:13
mine ancient p. and apostles.	98:32	they did not p.; even so it is		37:43
that the p. might be fulfilled.	101:19	of God ye shall p. in the land;		38: 1
spoken by the mouths of the p.,	109:23	Lord shall p. thee in this land.		45: 8
spoken by the mouths of thy p.	109:41	God would p. them in the land,		48:15
spoken by the mouth of thy p.	109:45	he would p. them in the land;		48:15
so persecuted they the p. and	127: 4	they should p. in the land.		48:25
a quotation from one of the p.,	128:17	And they did p. exceedingly,		50:18
declaring the fulfilment of the p.—	128:20	they shall p. in the land.		50:20
others of the p. who had the	132:39	began to p. again in the land,		62:48
and their p. shall hear his voice,	133:26	wax strong and p. in the land.		62:51
the p. who were before him;	133:54	that he did p. in the land.	He	3:20

PROSPER

that the work of the Lord did p.	He	3:26
therefore they did not p., but		4:13
did repent they did begin to p.		4:15
began to p. again in the land,		11:20
doth bless and p. those who put		12: 1
time when he doth p. his people,		12: 2
And they began again to p. and	3Ne	6: 4
is formed against thee shall p.;		22:17
Lord did p. them exceedingly	4Ne	1: 7
and the people began to p.;	Eth	6:28
p. exceedingly and wax great.		7:19
began to p. again in the land.		7:26
house of Emer did p. exceedingly		9:16
the people did p. in the land;		10:16
you, and you shall p.	DC	9:13
otherwise he shall not p.		49: 4
is formed against you shall p.;		71: 9
do these things she shall p.,		97:18
formed against them shall p.;		109:25

PROSPERED

and have p., and have been kept	Mos	2:31
that ye may be blessed, p., and		2:36
and thou hast p. in the land,		12:15
were blessed, and p. in the land.		25:24
have been p. until they are rich	Al	9:22
every man p. according to		30:17
miraculously p. in regaining.		59: 3
hath blessed them and p. them	3Ne	5:22
they were blessed and p. until	4Ne	1:18
more p. by the hand of the Lord.	Eth	10:28

PROSPERETH

yea, Zion p., all is well—	2Ne	28:21

PROSPERING

people from p. continually,	3Ne	6: 5

PROSPERITY

his seed, that they dwell in p.	2Ne	1:31
shall harm or disturb their p.		1:31
to the p. of the church of God;	Mos	27: 9
exceeding great p. in the church	Al	49:30
or their strength, or their p.,		62:49
there was exceeding great p.	He	3:24
great was the p. of the church,		3:25
riches and their p. in the land;		3:36
and their exceedingly great p.		12: 2
because of their p. in Christ.	4Ne	1:23

PROSPEROUS

he shall make his way p.	1Ne	20:15
thus, in their p. circumstances,	Al	1:30
in these p. circumstances were		50:17

PROSTRATE

Ammon lay p. upon the earth,	Al	19:17
their servants p. upon the earth,		19:18
did p. himself upon the earth,		22:17

PROSTRATED

and p. themselves before them	Al	24:21

PROTECT

that we may p. our brethren in	Al	27:23
established armies to p. the south		52:15
who had been left to p. the city,		52:25
left to p. the city Bountiful.		52:27
to p. the land unto the laying		53:17
p. the Nephites and themselves		53:17
keep and p. all the prisoners		55:27
placed to p. the city Cumeni.		57: 7
p. and preserve one another	He	6:21
p. this people in righteousness,	3Ne	4:30
where such laws exist as will p.	DC	134:11

PROTECTED

the Lord hath p. my sons,	1Ne	5: 8
which p. the city of Mulek,	Al	52:20
since been p. by the Nephites.		53:10
had been p. by the Nephites.		53:12
while p. in their inherent and	DC	134: 5
unbecoming every citizen thus p.,	DC	134: 5
for them, they should be p.	JS	2:59

PROTECTION

and did call upon me for p.	Mos	9:15
because of the assurance of p.	Al	50:12
sought p. in their fortifications.		52: 2
have looked up to you for p.,		60: 8
and did supplicate him for p.;	3Ne	4:10
on the name of their God for p.		4:30
and they fled unto Com for p.,	Eth	11: 2
the rights and p. of all flesh,	DC	101:77
and the p. of life.		134: 2
placed for the p. of the innocent		134: 6
laws for the p. of all citizens		134: 7
promised us p. from all	JS	2:75

PROTECTOR

whom ye look as a king or a p.,	2Ne	6: 2
having been a great p. for them,	Jac	1:10

PROUD

the p. and they who do wickedly	1Ne	22:15
yea, upon the p. and lofty,	2Ne	12:12
the arrogancy of the p. to cease,		23:11
that is p. shall be thrust through;		23:15
Wherefore, all those who are p.,		26: 4
ye were p. in your hearts,	Jac	2:20
they were not p. in their own eyes,	Al	1:20
among them who began to be p.,		1:22
of the church began to wax p.,		4: 6
But they grew p., being lifted up		45:24
And now we call the p. happy;	3Ne	24:15
all the p., yea, and all that do		25: 1
began to be p. in their hearts,	4Ne	1:43
all the p. and they that do	DC	29: 9
shalt not be p. in thy heart;		42:40
all the p. and they that do		64:24
humbling the rich and the p.		84:112
all the p., yea, and all that do		133:64
all the p., yea, and all that do	JS	2:37

PROUDLY

the child shall behave himself p.	2Ne	13: 5

PROVE

to p. unto them that my words	2Ne	11: 3
I do this that I may p. unto many		29: 9
would p. their entire destruction.	Al	1:12
which would p. their destruction.		3: 8
to p. that these things are true.		34: 7
Gadianton did p. the overthrow,	He	2:13
he was brought to p. that he		9:38
to p. by the scriptures that it	3Ne	24:10
and p. me now herewith, saith		24:10
that thou wilt p. them,	Eth	12:35
holy prophets to p. his words,	DC	35:23
they can p. their lineage,		68:21
send you out to p. the world,		84:79
try you and p. you herewith.		98:12
that I will p. you in all things,		98:14
that he may p. them also		121:12
you may p. yourselves unto me		124:55
when he shall p. himself faithful		124:113
to p. you all, as I did Abraham,		132:51
we will p. them herewith, to see	Abr	3:25
sophistry to p. their errors,	JS	2: 9
destined to p. a disturber and		2:20

PROVED

that my brother has p. unto you,	Al	34: 6
p. them in the field of battle,	3Ne	3: 4
be p. according to the laws of	DC	42:79
as it shall be p. by the Spirit		57:13
hypocrites shall be p. by them,		64:39
as they had often been p. before,		135: 7

PROVEN

p. their destruction except	Mro	8:27

PROVERB

take up this p. against the king	2Ne	24: 4

PROVETH

PROVETH
and he p. all his words	2Ne 11: 3

PROVIDE
strengthen them, and p. means	1Ne 17: 3
he did p. means for us while	17: 3
they might p. food for themselves	Al 17: 7
I will p. means whereby	DC 5:34
p. for him food and raiment,	43:13
money to p. food and raiment,	51: 8
shall p. for them otherwise,	51:16
And thus p. for my saints,	57:10
set you to p. for his saints	64:30
to p. for his own family,	75:28
let him p., and he shall in	75:28
my purpose to p. for my saints,	104:15
decreed to p. for my saints,	104:16
that I will p. for their families;	118: 3
Let each company p. themselves	136: 5

PROVIDED
Thus God has p. a means that	Mos 8:18
the Lord p. for them that they	Al 31:38
which the Lord has p. for us?	60:21
and means p. to enable you	DC 10: 4
p. he is called and set apart	68:19
and orphans shall be p. for,	83: 6
unto you, let there be a place p.,	90:19
those things that are p. for you,	90:26
until your children are p. for,	99: 6
p. he is called and set apart	107:17
p. that such dealings be for	134:10

PROVIDENCE
the hand of p. hath smiled upon	Jac 2:13
That through my p.,	DC 78:14
through the p. of God, escaped,	135: 2
family (under Divine p.)	JS 2:75

PROVIDING
and p. food for their armies.	Al 53: 7

PROVING
in p. unto my people the truth of	2Ne 11: 4
in p. unto my people that save	11: 6
P. to the world that the holy	DC 20:11

PROVISION
because of their much p.	3Ne 4:18

PROVISIONS
save it were his family, and p.,	1Ne 2: 4
all the remainder of our p.	16:11
p. according to that which	18: 6
and had taken with us our p.	18: 8
and also their p. with them,	Mos 22:12
the p. which were imparted for	Al 54: 2
and also new supplies of p.	55:34
was brought unto us many p.	56:27
men, and p. for them,	56:28
and p. arrive for our support,	56:29
an end to our receiving p.	56:29
carrying p. to a neighboring city.	56:30
did march forth, as if with our p.;	56:32
we received a supply of p.,	57: 6
plenty of p. brought unto us.	57: 6
were to receive a supply of p.	57: 8
At length their p. did arrive,	57:10
we did take them and their p.	57:10
that we should take those p. and	57:11
our p. were not any more	57:15
their support a new supply of p.	57:17
and also a new supply of p.	58: 3
wait to receive p. and strength	58: 4
day to day, and also many p.;	58: 5
withheld your p. from them,	60: 9
send speedily unto me of your p.	60:34
they have withheld our p.,	61: 4
have sent a few p. unto them,	61:16
caused that p. should be sent,	62:12
took the p. and their weapons	62:15
and did sail forth with much p.,	63: 6
and they also took much p.,	63: 7
carry forth p. unto the people	Al 63:10
reserved for themselves p.,	3Ne 4: 4
Because of the scantiness of p.	4:19
had not eaten up all their p.,	6: 2
that part of the p. which	Mro 9:16
with all the teams, wagons, p.,	DC 136: 5

PROVOCATION
as in the p. in the days of	Jac 1: 7
upon you as in the first p.,	Al 12:36
the last p. as well as the first,	12:36

PROVOKE
to p. the eyes of his glory.	2Ne 13: 8
God, to p. him to anger,	Jac 1: 8
that we p. not the Lord our God	Al 12:37
presence, lest thou p. them,	DC 60:15

PROVOKED
ye have p. him to anger	He 7:18
not her own, is not easily p.,	Mro 7:45

PROVOKETH
therefore your iniquity p. him	Al 12:36

PROWL
enemies p. around thee like wolves	DC 122: 6

PRUDENCE
all these to be used with p.	DC 89:11
in all wisdom and p., over all	Abr 3:21

PRUDENT
things of the wise and the p. shall	2Ne 9:43
and the p., and the ancient;	13: 2
and p. in their own sight!	15:21
done these things; for I am p.;	20:13
the understanding of their p. shall	27:26
the understanding of the p. shall	DC 76: 9
kept hid from the wise and p.,	128:18

PRUDENTLY
Behold, my servant shall deal p.;	3Ne 20:43

PRUNE
I will p. it, and dig about it,	Jac 5: 4
Let us p. it, and dig about it,	5:27
that I shall p. my vineyard.	5:62
dig about them, and p. them,	5:64
this once will I p. my vineyard.	5:69
to nourish and p. his vineyard;	6: 2
called to p. my vineyard	DC 24:19
and to p. my vineyard.	75: 2
mine apostles to p. my vineyard	95: 4

PRUNED
it shall not be p. nor digged;	2Ne 15: 6
he p. it, and digged about it,	Jac 5: 5
should be digged about, and p.,	5:11
digged about it, and I have p. it,	5:47
and p. it, and dug about it,	5:76
it may be p. for the last time.	DC 39:17

PRUNING
and their spears into p.-hooks—	2Ne 12: 4
my vineyard with a mighty p.,	DC 24:19

PRUNING-HOOKS: see *PRUNING* and *HOOKS.*

PUBLIC
in p. as well as in private.	DC 19:28
for the p. benefit of the church,	42:35
out from your p. meetings,	46: 3
both in p. and in private;	71: 7
heart, in p. and in private,	81: 3
forms for p. or private devotion;	134: 4
to secure the p. interest;	134: 5
for the p. peace and tranquility	134: 8
also that in p. discourses	OD
to disabuse the p. mind,	JS 2: 1
excite the p. mind against me,	2:22

PUBLICATIONS 775 PURCHASED

PUBLICATIONS
to gather up the libelous p. — DC 123: 4

PUBLICLY
I now p. declare that — DC OD

PUBLISH
and whoso shall p. peace, — 1Ne 13:37
who shall hereafter p. peace, — Mos 15:17
For they did p. peace; — 27:37
they did p. good tidings of good; — 27:37
given them to p. unto you, — DC 1: 6
behold, they will p. this, — 10:32
p. it as the record of Nephi; — 10:42
yea, p. it upon the mountains, — 19:29
land of Zion, to p. my word. — 118: 2
not only p. to all the world, — 123: 6
p. the new translation of my — 124:89

PUBLISHED
are they who have p. peace, — Mos 15:14
who have p. salvation; — 15:14
p. throughout all the land; — Al 30:57
That the revelations may be p., — DC 72:21
the libelous histories that are p., — 123: 5
which have been widely p., — OD

PUBLISHETH
good tidings; that p. peace; — Mos 12:21
that p. salvation; that saith unto — 12:21
tidings unto them, that p. peace; — 3Ne 20:40
them of good, that p. salvation; — 20:40

PUBLISHING
of those that are still p. peace! — Mos 15:16
p. to all the people the things — 27:32
p. all the things which they had — 27:35
p. my name among the children — DC 112: 6
has been the means of p. it — 135: 3

PUFFED
p. up because of their learning, — 2Ne 9:42
shall be p. up in their hearts, — 28: 9
because of pride they are p. up. — 28:12
in their pride they are p. up. — 28:13
p. up in the pride of their hearts, — 28:15
ye that are p. up in the vain things — Al 5:37
p. up in the pride of your hearts; — 5:53
while they are p. up, even to — 31:27
envieth not, and is not p. up, — Mro 7:45

PUFFING
the p. them up with pride, — 3Ne 6:15

PULL
he might p. down, by the word — Al 4:19
to p. down his wrath upon us — 12:37
to p. down their pride and — 51:17
they did p. down their pride — 51:18
ye will p. down the wrath of — 54: 9
for power, but to p. it down. — 60:36
Let me p. the mote out of thine — 3Ne 14: 4

PULLING
by p. down the banks of earth, — Al 49:22

PULPIT
upon the breastwork of the p., — DC 110: 2

PULSIPHER, Ezra
Herriman, P., Levi Hancock, — DC 124:138

PUNISH
I will p. the fruit of the stout — 2Ne 20:12
I will p. the world for evil, — 23:11
that they might p. them; — Mos 21:21
there was no law to p. him. — Al 30: 9
p. guilt, but never suppress the — DC 134: 4

PUNISHED
they p. according to their crimes; — WM 1:15
been p. according to their crimes; — WM 1:16
him have I p. according to — Mos 29:15
for liars were p.; therefore — Al 1:17
fear of the law, for such were p.; — 1:18
that murdered was p. unto death. — 1:18
murdered he was p. unto death; — 30:10
if he robbed he was also p.; — 30:10
and if he stole he was also p.; — 30:10
adultery he was also p.; — 30:10
all this wickedness they were p. — 30:10
a man was p. only for the crimes — 30:11
and p. according to the law. — 3Ne 5: 5
wicked that the wicked are p.; — Mrm 4: 5
and should be p. accordingly; — DC 134: 5
crime should be p. according to — 134: 8
should be p. according to their — 134: 8
men will be p. for their own sins, — AoF 2

PUNISHMENT
unto the inflicting of the p. — 2Ne 2:10
which p. that is affixed is in — 2:10
there be no p. nor misery. — 2:13
save it be by the p. of the law — 2:26
is no law given there is no p.; — 9:25
and where there is no p. there is — 9:25
and of eternity, and of eternal p. — Jac 7:18
for his wages an everlasting p., — Mos 2:33
the judgment of an everlasting p. — 27:31
of God in the p. of the sinner; — Al 42: 1
unto men except there were a p., — 42:16
be a law save there was a p.? — 42:17
Now, there was a p. affixed, — 42:18
is a law given, and a p. affixed, — 42:22
and the law inflicteth the p.; — 42:22
the p. which is given from my — DC 19:10
from my hand is endless p., — 19:11
Eternal p. is God's punishment. — 19:11
Eternal punishment is God's p. — 19:11
Endless p. is God's punishment. — 19:12
Endless punishment is God's p. — 19:12
go away into everlasting p., — 76:44
punishment, which is endless p., — 76:44
is eternal p., to reign with — 76:44
and the p. of the guilty; — 134: 6
offenders against good laws to p. — 134: 8
any physical p. upon them. — 134:10
my p. is greater than I can bear. — Mses 5:38

PUNISHMENTS
for his p. are just— — Mos 4:17
such great p. upon this people, — Al 18: 2
p. of which I have spoken, — DC 19:20

PUNY
might man stretch forth his p. arm — DC 121:33

PURCHASE
not p. wine neither strong drink — DC 27: 3
that ye may p. an inheritance — 45:65
p. land for an inheritance, — 48: 4
appointed to p. the lands, — 48: 6
moneys to p. lands in Zion. — 58:49
to p. lands for an inheritance — 58:51
to p. this whole region of — 58:52
that you should p. the lands, — 63:27
but by p. or by blood, — 63:29
And if by p., behold you are — 63:30
to p. all the lands with money, — 101:70
send them to p. these lands. — 101:73
their moneys, and p. lands — 103:23

PURCHASED
should be p. by the saints, — DC 57: 4
lands p. in Independence, — 58:37
which can be p. for money — 101:70
which can be p. in Jackson — 101:71
county that can be p., — 105:28
that these lands should be p.; — 105:29
and after they are p. that — 105:29
And after these lands are p., — 105:30
which they have previously p. — 105:30

PURCHASING 776 PURPOSE

PURCHASING
for the purpose of p. lands for	DC	42:35
the p. of all the lands in		105:28

PURE
the hilt thereof was of p. gold,	1Ne	4: 9
which were written were plain and p.,		14:23
your souls if your minds were p.?	2Ne	9:47
with p. hearts and clean hands,		25:16
in the presence of the p. in heart,	Jac	2:10
unto you that are p. in heart.		3: 1
O all ye that are p. in heart,		3: 2
unto you that are not p. in heart,		3: 3
and they are of p. gold.	Mos	8: 9
he did ornament with p. gold;		11:11
a fountain of p. water,		18: 5
a land of p. water.		23: 4
down in p. testimony against them.	Al	4:19
with a p. heart and clean hands?		5:19
and are spotless, p. and white?		5:24
p. and spotless before God,		13:12
great many, who were made p.		13:12
and p. above all that is pure;		32:42
and pure above all that is p.;		32:42
and a p. descendant of Lehi.	3Ne	5:20
blessed are all the p. in heart,		12: 8
may be found spotless, p., fair,	Mrm	9: 6
charity is the p. love of Christ,	Mro	7:47
be purified even as he is p.		7:48
p. mercies of God unto them,		8:19
whose garments were p. and	DC	20: 6
be purified, even as I am p.		35:21
his heart is p. before me,		41:11
and they are p. before me,		41:12
reserve unto myself a p. people		43:14
the poor who are p. in heart,		56:18
even with water, p. water,		84:92
p. wine of the grape of the vine,		89: 6
in a goodly land, by a p. stream,		97: 9
and all the p. in heart		97:16
THE P. IN HEART;		97:21
raise up unto myself a p. people,		100:16
that remain, and are p. in heart,		101:18
That our garments may be p.,		109:76
was a paved work of p. gold,		110: 2
his head was white like the p. snow;		110: 3
and thine eye, yea thy p. eye,		121: 2
By kindness, and p. knowledge,		121:42
While the p. in heart, and the wise,		122: 2
and to all the p. in heart—		123:11
who have been p. in heart,		124:54
matter, but it is more fine or p.,		131: 7
are virtuous and p. before me;		132:52
and those who are not p.,		132:52
and have said they were p.,		132:52
if ye do this with a p. heart,		136:11
for ye are not yet p.;		136:37
a language which was p. and	Mses	6: 6

PURER
can only be discerned by p. eyes;	DC	131: 7

PURGE
and p. them as gold and silver,	3Ne	24: 3
P. ye out the iniquity which is	DC	43:11
and p. them as gold and silver,		128:24

PURGED
have p. the blood of Jeruslaem	2Ne	14: 4
is taken away, and thy sin p.		16: 7

PURIFIED
and our hearts may be p.;	Mos	4: 2
his garments must be p. until	Al	5:21
p. those whom I have chosen,	3Ne	19:28
that they may be p. in me,		19:28
even as they are p. in me.		19:28
that they may be p. in me,		19:29
that we may be p. even as he	Mro	7:48
they shall be p., even as I	DC	35:21
he that is not p. shall not		38: 8
be p. and cleansed from all sin.		50:28
are p. and cleansed from all sin,		50:29
when our bodies are p. we shall		131: 8

PURIFIER
sit as a refiner and p. of silver;	3Ne	24: 3
as a refiner and p. of silver,	DC	128:24

PURIFY
he shall p. the sons of Levi,	3Ne	24: 3
and p. themselves before him;	DC	76:116
p. your hearts, and cleanse		88:74
But p. your hearts before me;		112:28
and he shall p. the sons of Levi,		128:24
to p. the vineyard of corruption.		135: 6

PURIFYING
to the p. and the sanctification	He	3:35

PURITY
go forth from the Jews in p.	1Ne	13:25
to come forth in their p.,		14:26
being clothed with p.,	2Ne	9:14
preached in its p. in all the land,	Al	16:21

PURPOSE
these plates, for the special p.	1Ne	9: 3
these plates for a wise p. in him,		9: 5
in him, which p. I know not.		9: 5
there would have been no p. in	2Ne	2:12
This is the p. that is purposed		24:26
for the p. of convincing them		25:18
the Son, with full p. of heart,		31:13
and for mine own p. I have	Jac	5:36
roots thereof for mine own p.		5:53
them also for mine own p.,		5:54
and come with full p. of heart,		6: 5
And I do this for a wise p.;	WM	1: 7
for the sole p. of bringing this	Mos	7:22
to the Lord with full p. of heart,		7:33
for the p. of unfolding all such		8:19
for this p. have I come to convince		27:14
for the p. of interpreting		28:14
it was for the sole p. to get gain,	Al	11:20
this is for the p. of preparing the		13:24
for the p. of burying their dead.		19: 1
for the p. of destroying the		24:20
for a wise p. that they are kept.		37: 2
they are preserved for a wise p.,		37:12
which p. is known unto God;		37:12
preserve for a wise p. in him,		37:14
these things for a wise p. in him,		37:18
one p. hath he fulfilled,		37:19
save he will withdraw his p.,		55: 2
for that p. that we should come		56:43
would have obtained their p.		56:50
unto me with full p. of heart.	3Ne	10: 6
unto me with full p. of heart,		12:24
unto me with full p. of heart,		18:32
his great and eternal p.,	Mrm	5:14
for this very p. are these plates	DC	3:19
until my p. is fulfilled in this;		5: 4
Joseph, for a wise p. in me,		5: 9
you do with full p. of heart,		17: 1
called him unto mine own p.,		18: 8
which p. is known in me;		18: 8
my name with full p. of heart.		18:27
my name with full p. of heart,		18:28
and set apart for that p.		42:31
for the p. of purchasing lands		42:35
and this for a wise p. in me.		61:30
the p. of bringing forth my word		96: 4
for the p. of subduing the		96: 5
the p. and the end thereof—		101:33
for this p. have I established		101:80
I raised up unto this very p.,		101:80
the p. of settling important		102: 2
priests, convened for that p.,		102: 8
my p. to provide for my saints,		104:15
for this p. I have commanded		104:58
For the p. of building up my		104:59
the p. of shineland [printing]		104:63
the p. of building that house		124:62
of that stock to any other p.,		124:70
instituted for the p. of qualifying		124:134
to suit my p. as it stands.		128:18
p. of regulating our interests		134: 6
For mine own p. have I made	Mses	1:31

PURPOSE

created them for mine own p.;	Mses	1:33
the p. of translating the book.	JS	2:35
for the p. of getting rich.		2:46
was resorted to for that p.		2:60

PURPOSED

as I have p., so shall it stand—	2Ne	24:24
that is p. upon the whole earth;		24:26
For the Lord of Hosts hath p.,		24:27
for I have p. to take thee away	Abr	2: 6

PURPOSES

to bring forth his righteous p.	1Ne	4:13
and also for other wise p., which		19: 3
p. are known unto the Lord.		19: 3
wisdom of God and his eternal p.,	2Ne	2:12
to bring about his eternal p.		2:15
about his great and eternal p.;	Al	37: 7
about his great and eternal p.,		42:26
do that he might obtain his p.		46:30
withdraw your murderous p.,		54: 7
except you withdraw you p.,		54: 9
For the eternal p. of the Lord	Mrm	8:22
and the p. of God cannot be	DC	3: 1
bring about my righteous p.		17: 4
bring about my righteous p.		17: 9
of the poor, and for other p.,		42:71
His p. fail not, neither are		76: 3
for sacred and holy p.		104:65
myself for holy and sacred p.,		104:68
sent for political p.,		OD

PURSE

shalt take no p. nor scrip	DC	24:18
them not to have p. or scrip,		84:78
from this hour take p. or scrip,		84:86

PURSUE

lest they should p. us	1Ne	4:36
that the Lamanites did p. them,	Mos	19:10
into the wilderness to p. them;		22:15
have awakened and do p. thee;		24:23
the Nephites did p. the Amlicites	Al	2:19
could p. the Amlicites no longer		2:20
and the Nephites did p. them		2:36
them shall the Lamanites p.		45:14
and p. his servants that they		47:27
the Lamanites did p. Teancum		52:27
they did not p. us far before		56:42
courage, and began to p. them;		56:52
did p. them from city to city,		62:32
that they did p. Teancum,		62:36
that his armies should p. them	3Ne	4:13
did p. them and did slay them,		4:13
did p. them with our armies,	Mrm	2:26
they should p. them no more,	Eth	9:33
did p. him until he came to		13:28
did p. him to the wilderness		14: 3
Lib did p. him until he came		14:15
did not cease to p. Coriantumr;		14:24
Shiz did p. Coriantumr eastward,		14:26
p. the armies of Coriantumr;		14:31
Wherefore, he did p. them,		15:29
as they p. me without a cause,	DC	127: 1
to p. my common vocations in	JS	2:27

PURSUED

And Gideon p. after him and	Mos	19: 6
and they p. their journey.		22:12
after they had p. them two days,		22:16
were p. by Lehi and his men;	Al	43:40
p. after the servants of the king.		47:28
the army which p. after them		47:30
having p. after them in vain;		47:30
he had p. them with his army,		47:32
and p. them with vigor.		52:24
p. their march in a straight		56:37
these Lamanites who had p. us.		56:49
p. their march towards the land		62:18
p. by the servants of Pahoran;	He	1:10
boldness, was p. as he fled;	3Ne	4:14
they were p. until they came	Mrm	2:16

PURSUING

saw an army p. after them,	Al	47:29
who were p. them in vain,		52:24
the army of Antipus p. them,		56:37
the Lamanites were p. us.		56:39
were the Lamanites p. them		56:52

PURSUIT

no further in p. of this people.	Mos	24:23
return from the p. of Teancum.	Al	52:26
were again in the p. of me;	DC	127: 1

PUSH

shall p. the people together	DC	58:45
and p. many people to Zion		66:11

PUT

and p. them upon mine own body;	1Ne	4:19
we did p. forth into the sea		18: 8
did p. all our seeds into the earth,		18:24
p. on the armor of righteousness,	2Ne	1:23
not p. my trust in the arm of flesh;		4:34
Have I p. thee away, or have I		7: 1
To whom have I p. thee away,		7: 1
is your mother p. away.		7: 1
P. on strength, O arm of the		8: 9
have p. my words in thy mouth,		8:16
But I will p. it into the hand of		8:23
awake, p. on thy strength, O Zion;		8:24
p. on thy beautiful garments,		8:24
could not p. on incorruption,		9: 7
that p. darkness for light,		15:20
that p. bitter for sweet,		15:20
I have p. down the inhabitants		20:13
child shall p. his hand on the		21: 8
they p. down the power and		26:20
child shall p. his hand on the		30:14
it began to p. forth somewhat	Jac	5: 6
mortal shall p. on immortality,	En	1:27
and p. them with the remainder of	WM	1: 6
and p. them with the other plates,		1:10
should p. his trust in the Lord,	Mos	4: 6
and yet ye p. up no petition,		4:22
should have p. you to death.		7:11
rejoice, and p. your trust in God,		7:19
they did p. him to death;		7:28
and p. your trust in him,		7:33
For he p. down all the priests		11: 5
Noah had p. upon his people;		11: 6
he hath p. him to grief;		14:10
mortal shall p. on immortality,		16:10
that he should be p. to death.		17: 1
thou shalt be p. to death unless		17: 8
having been p. to death because		17:20
also and p. them to death,		19:21
let us p. a stop to the shedding of		20:22
began to p. heavy burdens upon		21: 3
and p. on their armor, and went		21: 7
that they should be p. to death.		21:23
and p. tasks upon them,		24: 9
and p. task-masters over them.		24: 9
and he p. guards over them to		24:11
upon God they should be p. to death.		24:11
which are p. upon your shoulders,		24:14
them that p. their trust in him.		29:20
this did not p. an end to the	Al	1:16
the law was p. in force upon		1:32
to p. them in force according to		4:16
p. their trust in the true and		5:13
the lawyers p. it into their hearts		10:30
which I shall p. unto you?		11:21
sought to p. them away privily.		14: 3
p. forth their hands to touch him		19:24
he p. forth his hand and raised		22:22
that they should be p. to death,		25: 7
cause many to be p. to death,		25:12
ye have p. off the spirit of God		30:42
he p. forth his hand and wrote		30:51
And Korihor p. forth his hand		30:52

PUT — QUANTITY

this p. an end to the iniquity	Al 30:58
or what they should p. on.	31:37
shall p. their trust in God shall	36: 3
and I do p. my trust in him,	36:27
as ye shall p. your trust in God	38: 5
does not p. on immortality,	40: 2
does not p. on incorruption—	40: 2
lest he should p. forth his hand,	42: 3
p. forth his hand immediately,	42: 5
and p. Amalickiah to death;	46:30
he caused to be p. to death;	46:35
the king p. forth his hand to	47:23
Morianton p. it into their	50:29
also p. the king-men to silence,	51: 7
or to p. them to death.	51:15
to p. an end to such contentions	51:16
p. an end to those king-men,	51:21
he p. an end to the stubbornness	51:21
and p. a javelin to his heart;	51:34
to p. an end to our receiving	56:29
or to p. them to death.	57:13
should p. an end to their lives,	57:15
they do p. their trust in God	57:27
we should p. our trust in him,	61:13
p. an end to this great iniquity,	61:18
fight against it, were p. to death.	62: 9
p. into the heart of Gadianton	He 6:26
p. it into the hearts of the people	6:28
who p. it into the heart of	6:29
did p. an end to their strife	11:23
a stop p. to this work of	11:28
those who p. their trust in him.	12: 1
things the Lord p. into his heart.	13: 4
which he doth p. into my heart;	13: 5
hath p. it into my heart to say	13: 5
should be p. to death except the	3Ne 1: 9
p. up their prayers unto the Lord	3:25
did p. an end to all those wicked,	5: 6
p. to death secretly by the judges,	6:23
any man should be p. to death	6:24
and p. it under a bushel?	12:15
whosoever shall p. away his wife,	12:31
whosoever shall p. away his wife,	12:32
your body, what ye shall p. on.	13:25
and p. on thy strength, O Zion;	20:36
p. on thy beautiful garments,	20:36
thou shalt not be p. to shame;	22: 4
which have been p. up unto him	Mrm 5:21
did not p. an end to my life.	6:10
mortal must p. on immortality,	6:21
he did p. forth the stones into	Eth 6: 2
was about to p. him to death,	7:18
p. it into his heart to search	8:17
Jared p. it into the heart of	8:17
he did cause to be p. to death.	10: 6
should be p. to death;	11: 5
when God p. forth his finger	12:20
they p. to death every Nephite	Mro 1: 2
p. down all power and authority	8:28
p. on thy beautiful garments,	10:31
Satan hath p. it into thy	DC 10:10
he hath p. into their hearts to	10:13
he has p. it into their hearts to	10:15
p. your trust in this Spirit	11:12
p. away their companions for	42:74
I have p. into your hands by	43:15
p. all enemies under his feet,	49: 6
p. into the hands of the bishop,	58:51
the Lord shall p. into his hands.	72:13
and p. him to an open shame.	76:35
the Father had p. into his power	76:42
hath not p. into his power,	77:12
p. on her beautiful garments.	82:14
have p. forth my hand to	84:119
that I shall p. into your hearts,	100: 5
I have p. into your hands,	104:85
that thou hast p. forth thy hand,	109:23
thy name shall be p. in this house;	109:26
P. upon thy servants the	109:38
that has been p. upon them.	109:47
to p. upon it thy name.	109:79
P. on thy strength, O Zion—	113: 7
and to p. on her strength is to	113: 8
is to p. on the authority of the	DC 113: 8
property to be p. into the hands	119: 1
and abuses p. upon them by the	123: 1
have I p. upon his head,	124:57
that his blessing shall also be p.	124:57
let him p. stock into that house	124:74
p. stock into that house as	124:77
p. stock into that house;	124:78
William p. his trust in me,	124:87
that once were p. upon him	124:95
that they may be p. in the archives	127: 9
my servant hath p. upon them,	132:19
p. his property out of his hands,	132:57
and two shall p. their tens of	133:58
to p. them in jeopardy of either	134:10
I p. the man whom I had formed.	Mses 3: 8
p. him into the Garden of Eden,	3:15
Satan p. it into the heart of	4: 6
will p. enmity between thee and	4:21
lest he p. forth his hand and	4:28
cursing which I will p. upon thee,	5:25
to p. upon thee my name,	Abr 1:18
he p. his hand upon mine eyes,	3:12
man's spirit), and p. it into him;	5: 7
Eden, and there they p. the man,	5: 8
spirit they had p. into the body	5: 8
p. him in the Garden of Eden,	5:11
it begins to p. forth leaves,	JS 1:38
have been p. in circulation	2: 1
p. all inquirers after truth	2: 1
I was p. to board with a Mr.	2:57
and p. it into my pocket,	2:64

PUTTETH

cursed is he that p. his trust in	2Ne 4:34
cursed is he that p. his trust in	4:34
Cursed is he that p. his trust in	28:31
and p. off the natural man	Mos 3:19
the beggar p. up his petition	4:16
the man who p. up his petition	4:22
whosoever p. his trust in him	23:22
for Satan p. it into their hearts	DC 63:28
that p. forth his hand to	85: 8

PUTTING

p. their trust in the Lord;	Mos 10:19
and p. trust in dead works.	Mro 8:23
prepare for p. in spring crops.	DC 136: 7

QUAKE

did q. and tremble exceedingly.	1Ne 1: 6
need fear, and tremble, and q.;	22:23
unto the causing of them to q.	2Ne 4:22
and they shall q., and tremble,	Mos 27:31
did cause them to q. and tremble.	28: 3
therefore they did q., and had	He 9: 5
the mountains tremble and q.	12: 9
frame that it did not cause to q.;	3Ne 11: 3
and all the earth shall q.;	DC 29:13
it maketh my bones to q.	85: 6

QUAKING

because of the q. thereof.	1Ne 12: 4
great q. of the whole earth;	3Ne 8:12
and the q. of the earth.	8:17

QUAKINGS

the q. of the earth did cease—	3Ne 8:19

QUALIFIED

q. for taking accurate minutes;	DC 128: 3

QUALIFY

of God, q. him for the work.	DC 4: 5

QUALIFYING

instituted for the purpose of q.	DC 124:134

QUALITIES

because of the excellent q. of	Al 46:40

QUANTITY

with a sufficient q. of food,	Al 62:13

QUARREL

QUARREL
fight and q. one with another, Mos 4:14

QUARRELINGS
their q. and their contentions, Al 50:21

QUARTER
people in that q. of the land Al 43:26
maintaining that q. of the land,. 52:10
scourge the Lamanites in that q., 52:10
people in that q. of the land. 56: 1
flee out of all this q. of the land. 58:30
forces into that q. of the land; 58:35
that q. where there never had Eth 2: 5
that q. of the land whither 14:15

QUARTERS
from the four q. of the earth. 1Ne 19:16
from the four q. of the earth; 22:25
villages in all q. of the land. Mos 27: 6
from the four q. of the earth 3Ne 5:24
from the four q. of the earth 5:26
from the four q. of the earth; 16: 5
from the four q. of the earth, Eth 13:11
from the four q. of the earth, DC 33: 6
from the four q. of the earth. 45:46
to the four q. of the earth; 135: 3
from the four q. of the earth, Mses 7:62
earth in its four q. Fac 2: 6
from the four q. of the earth. JS 1:27

QUEEN
the q. having heard of the fame of Al 19: 2
and went in unto the king, 19: 3
what the q. desired of him was 19: 7
as the q. had desired him; 19: 7
And he said unto the q.: 19: 8
and the q. also sunk down, 19:13
and also her mistress, the q., 19:17
they beheld the king, and the q., 19:18
and took the q. by the hand, 19:29
his servants ran and told the q. 22:19
they plead with the q. saying: 22:20
when the q. saw the fear of the 22:21
saw the determination of the q., 22:22
done in the presence of the q. 22:23
of the commandment of the q., 22:24
the q., when she had heard that 47:32
had sent an embassy to the q. 47:32
the q. had received this message 47:33
with him, and went in unto the q., 47:34
they satisfied the q. concerning 47:34
sought the favor of the q., 47:35
and had made known unto the q. 52:12

QUEENS
their q. thy nursing mothers; 1Ne 21:23
and their q. thy nursing mothers; 2Ne 6: 7
q. shall become nursing mothers; 10: 9

QUENCH
of Israel might q. their thirst. 1Ne 17:29
and q. the Holy Spirit, Jac 6: 8
q. all the fiery darts of the DC 27:17

QUENCHED
dieth not, and the fire is not q., DC 76:44

QUESTION
him hither that we may q. him; Mos 12:18
And they began to q. him, 12:19
them who thought to q. them, Al 10:13
that they began to q. Amulek, 10:16
as they began to q. him, he 10:17
this Zeezrom began to q. Amulek, 11:21
great q. which is in your minds 34: 5
began to q. him in divers ways He 9:19
I the Lord ask you this q.— DC 50:13
answer this q. yourselves; 50:16
Q: What is the sea of glass 77: 1
Q: What are we to understand 77: 2
Q: Are the four beasts limited 77: 3
Q: What are we to understand 77: 4

QUICKLY

Q: What are we to understand DC 77: 5
Q: What are we to understand 77: 6
Q: What are we to understand 77: 7
Q: What are we to understand 77: 8
Q: What are we to understand 77: 9
Q: What time are the things 77:10
Q: What are we to understand 77:11
Q: What are we to understand 77:12
Q: When are the things to be 77:13
Q: What are we to understand 77:14
Q: What is to be understood 77:15
called in q. by the general 102:32
In answer to the q.— 130: 4
arise through the slave q. 130:13
all confidence in settling the q. JS 2:12

QUESTIONED
q. them about many words; Al 14:18

QUESTIONS
that they should answer the q. Mos 7: 8
and withstood all their q., 12:19
withstand them in all their q., 12:19
Will ye answer me a few q. which Al 11:21
Will ye answer the q. which I 11:21
Q. by Elias Higbee: DC 113: 7

QUICK
shall make him of q. understanding 2Ne 21: 3
q. to do iniquity, and slow to Mos 13:29
q. to hear the cries of his people Al 9:26
how q. the children of men do 46: 8
how q. to do iniquity, and to 46: 8
of God, which is q. and powerful, He 3:29
they were q. to hearken unto 7: 7
and how q. to do iniquity, 12: 4
how q. to hearken unto the 12: 4
how q. to be lifted up in pride; 12: 5
how q. to boast, and do all 12: 5
q. return from righteousness 3Ne 7:15
child, and art q. to observe; Mrm 1: 2
Judge of both q. and dead. Mro 10:34
word, which is q. and powerful, DC 6: 2
word, which is q. and powerful, 11: 2
word, which is q. and powerful, 12: 2
word, which is q. and powerful, 14: 2
whose word is q. and powerful. 27: 1
whose word is q. and powerful, 33: 1

QUICKENED
except q. by the Spirit of God. DC 67:11
shall die, it shall be q. again, 88:26
the power by which it is q., 88:26
by which your bodies are q. 88:28
Ye who are q. by a portion 88:29
they who are q. by a portion 88:30
they who are q. by a portion 88:31
they who remain shall also be q.; 88:32
being q. in him and by him. 88:49
shall be q. and be caught up 88:96
and became q. in the inner man. Mses 6:65

QUICKENETH
of my Spirit q. all things. DC 33:16
that q. your understandings; 88:11
that q. all things, 88:17
which q. all things, which maketh Mses 6:61

QUICKLY
Behold ye must prepare q.; Al 5:28
would that he should prepare q., 5:29
would ye not behold q., or 33:21
Agree with thine adversary q. 3Ne 12:25
unto you, that I come q. DC 33:18
I say unto you, I come q. 34:12
Behold, I come q. 35:27
Behold, I come q. 39:24
and behold, I come q., 41: 4
Jesus Christ, and I come q. 49:28
Jesus Christ, who cometh q., 51:20
and, behold, I come q., 54:10
and Omega, and I come q. 68:35
for behold, it cometh q., 87: 8

QUICKLY 780 RAISE

Behold, and lo, I will come q., DC 88:126
and lo, I come q. to judgment, 99: 5
until I come, for I come q.; 112:34

QUIET
Take heed, and be q.; fear not, 2Ne 17: 4
whole earth is at rest, and is q.; 24: 7

QUITE
q. unconscious of anything. JS 2:48

QUIVER
in his q. hath he hid me; 1Ne 21: 2
and the q., and the dart, Jar 1: 8

QUORUM
form a q. of the Presidency of DC 107:22
they form a q., equal in authority 107:24
they form a q., equal in authority 107:26
every member in each q. must 107:27
A majority may form a q. 107:28
of a q. of three presidents 107:29
form a q. equal in authority 107:36
to the q. of the presidency, 107:36
form a q. equal in authority 107:37
to be a president over their q. 124:62
of the q. of the Nauvoo House, 124:117
to the q. of the Nauvoo House 124:119
let the q. of the Nauvoo House 124:121
that these may constitute a q. 124:126
over a q. of high priests; 124:133
over the q. of high priests 124:136
preside over the q. of elders, 124:137
which q. in instituted for 124:137
preside over the q. of seventies; 124:138
Which q. is instituted for 124:139
The difference between this q. 124:140
this quorum and the q. of elders 124:140

QUORUMS
made by either of these q. must DC 107:27
The decisions of these q., 107:30
decision of these q. is made in 107:32
assembly of the several q., 107:32

QUOTATION
You will discover in this q. that DC 128: 7
give you another q. of Paul, 128:16
in connection with this q. I will 128:17
I will give you a q. from 128:17

QUOTED
He first q. part of the third chapter JS 2:36
he q. also the fourth or last 2:36
in our books, he q. it thus: 2:36
he q. the fifth verse thus: 2:38
q. the next verse differently: 2:39
he q. the eleventh chapter of 2:40
He q. also the third chapter 2:40
He also q. the second chapter 2:41
He q. many other passages 2:41

QUOTING
commenced q. the prophecies of JS 2:36
Instead of q. the first verse as 2:36

RABBANAH
R., which is, being interpreted, Al 18:13
R., the king desireth thee to stay. 18:13

RACA
shall say to his brother, R., 3Ne 12:22

RACE
r. which preserved the curse in Abr 1:24

RACK
did r. my soul with inexpressible Al 36:14

RACKED
was r. with eternal torment; Mos 27:29
have r. with hatred against us, Al 26: 9
I was r. with eternal torment, 36:12

degree and r. with all my sins. Al 36:12
and for three nights was I r., 36:16
as I was thus r. with torment, 36:17
r. with a consciousness of guilt Mrm 9: 3

RAGE
shall he r. in the hearts of 2Ne 28:20
and hell shall r. against thee; DC 122: 1

RAGED
men, and r. in their hearts; Mses 6:15

RAGGED
and into the tops of the r. rocks, 2Ne 12:21

RAGING
this r. deep in darkness; Eth 3: 3

RAGS
Be thou clothed in r. and sit DC 38:26

RAHAB
Art thou not he that hath cut R., 2Ne 8: 9

RAHLEENOS
is called by the Chaldeans R., Abr 1:14

RAILING
some did return r. for railing, 3Ne 6:13
some did return railing for r., 6:13
would receive r. and persecution 6:13
Not with r. accusation, DC 50:33

RAIMENT
we have, for both food and r., Mos 4:19
than meat, and the body than r.? 3Ne 13:25
And why take ye thought for r.? 13:28
thou needest for food and for r., DC 24:18
provide for him food and r., 43:13
use of man for food and for r., 49:19
money to provide food and r., 51: 8
whether for food or for r., 59:17
Yea, for food and for r., 59:19
For food and for r.; for an 70:16
and stained all my r.; 133:51

RAIN
a covert from storm and from r. 2Ne 14: 6
command the clouds that they r. 15: 6
clouds that they rain no r. upon it. 15: 6
send forth r. upon the face of He 11:13
caused that r. should fall upon 11:17
And the r. descended, and the 3Ne 14:25
And the r. descended, and the 14:27
when the r. descends, and the 18:13
no r. upon the face of the earth. Eth 9:30
he did send r. upon the face of 9:35
had not caused it to r. upon the Mses 3: 5
shed forth their tears as the r. 7:28
the Gods had not caused it to r. Abr 5: 5

RAINS
also the r. and the floods have Eth 2:24
winds blow, and the r. descend, DC 90: 5

RAISE
that they might r. up seed 1Ne 7: 1
prophet would the Lord God r. up 10: 4
to r. up the tribes of Jacob, 21: 6
God will r. up a mighty nation 22: 7
shall the Lord your God r. up 22:20
seer shall the Lord my God r. up, 2Ne 3: 6
A choice seer will I r. up out of 3: 7
whom I have said I would r. up 3: 9
And Moses will I r. up, 3:10
But a seer will I r. up out of the 3:11
I will r. up a Moses; 3:17
I will r. up unto the fruit of thy 3:18
we began to r. flocks, and herds, 5:11
shall r. up unto the Gentiles. 10:11
may God r. you from death 10:25
the serpent which he did r. up 25:20
that I might r. up unto me a Jac 2:25

RAISE 781 RATHER

r. up seed unto me, I will	Jac	2:30
I did still r. my voice high	En	1: 4
and r. all manner of grain,		1:21
and r. all manner of grain and	Mos	10: 4
r. contentions among my people;		11:28
to r. grain more abundantly,		21:16
not r. their voices to the Lord		24:12
they did r. their voices and give		25:10
Nephites could r. a sufficient army	Al	16: 3
she might r. her from the ground;		19:29
will r. them up at the last day.		26: 7
he will r. me up at the last day,		36:28
put forth his hand to r. them,		47:23
never to r. the sword except it		48:14
did r. the standard of liberty		62: 4
They did r. grain in abundance,	He	6:12
they did r. many flocks and herds,		6:12
r. himself to be a great man,		9:16
that they could r. grain,	3Ne	4: 6
brother did he r. from the dead,		7:19
him will I r. up at the last day.		15: 1
shall the Lord your God r. up		20:23
heal the sick, and r. the dead,	4Ne	1: 5
and r. up unto me of thy seed,	Eth	1:43
I will r. up unto me of thy seed,		1:43
that they did r. an army and		8: 5
and will r. up elders and send	DC	88:72
r. up unto myself a pure people,		100:16
will r. up unto my people a man,		103:16
will that he should r. the dead,		124:100
will r. up another like unto thee;	Mses	1:41

RAISED

it hath r. up from their thrones	2Ne	24: 9
and r. forts against them;		26:15
They are r. to dwell with God	Mos	15:23
mortal body r. in immortality,	Al	5:15
this corruption r. in incorruption,		5:15
be r. from this temporal death,		11:42
body is r. to an immortal body,		11:45
being r. from this mortality to		12:12
But Ammon r. his sword, and		20:22
that I may be r. from the dead,		22:18
and r. the king from the earth,		22:22
r. to dwell at the right hand of		28:12
type was r. up in the wilderness		33:19
mortality r. to immortality,		41: 4
r. to endless happiness to inherit		41: 4
The one r. to happiness		41: 5
but as he r. his sword, behold,		44:12
had r. the first from the ground,		47:24
servants of Amalickiah r. a cry,		47:25
for he had r. up in rebellion	He	1: 8
and r. contentions among them;		8: 7
this mountain—Be thou r. up,		12:17
whom he had r. from the dead,	3Ne	19: 4
having r. me up unto you first,		20:26
and r. a man from the dead,		26:15
man must be r. to stand before	Mrm	7: 6
Shiz r. upon his hands and fell;	Eth	15:31
to be r. unto life eternal,	Mro	7:41
he might be r. in immortality	DC	29:43
which I, the Lord, have r. up		53: 1
be r. up to the Jewish nation		77:15
John, whom God r. up,		84:27
of wise men whom I r. up		101:80
unto this end have I r. you up,		124: 1
the Lord r. up unto his people.	Mses	6:36
with a little exertion r. it up.	JS	2:52

RAISETH

he r. up a righteous nation,	1Ne	17:37
For he that r. up a king	2Ne	10:14

RAISING

as healing the sick, r. the dead,	Mos	3: 5
the r. of the spirit or the soul	Al	40:15
r. all manner of grain, and		62:29
r. the cry of murder among	He	9: 6
and in r. grain, and in flocks,	Eth	10:12
and fields for r. grain,	DC	136: 9

RAMAH

pitch their tents by the hill R.;	Eth	15:11

RAMATH

R. is afraid;	2Ne	20:29

RAMEUPTOM

the place was called by them R.,	Al	31:21

RAN

a river of water; and it r. along,	1Ne	8:13
and r. and got upon the tower	Mos	19: 5
r. by the land of Zarahemla,	Al	2:15
she r. forth from house to house,		19:17
servants r. and told the queen		22:19
which r. from the sea east even to		22:27
they r. and told it unto Jacob,		52:22
they r. to the city and fell upon		58:21
And he r. and told Helaman all	He	2: 9
and they r. and told the people		7:11
r. to the judgment-seat;		9: 1
that they r. in their might,		9: 3
servants r. and told the people,		9: 6
We r. and came to the place		9:14
we r. and came according as ye		9:15

RANKS

and I did place them in their r.,	Mos	10: 9
began to be distinguished by r.,	3Ne	6:12

RANSOM

as a r. for those whom the	Al	52: 8

RANSOMED

a way for the r. to pass over?	2Ne	8:10

RAPHAEL

the voice of Gabriel, and of R.,	DC	128:21

RASCALITY

concatenation of diabolical r.	DC	123: 5

RASH

promise which he made was r.;	Al	51:10

RASHLY

the same that judgeth r. shall	Mrm	8:19
rashly shall be judged r. again;		8:19

RATHER

works of darkness r. than light,	2Ne	26:10
were permitted, or r. commanded,	Mos	7: 8
or, r., shall secret things be made		8:17
r. stay and perish with them.		19:12
caused, or I did acknowledge,	Al	1:15
the ground, or r. the bank,		2:34
would r. suffer that the Lamanites		9:19
righteousness r. than to perish;		13:10
r. he did administer unto them,		17:18
r. than shed the blood of their		24:18
r. than take away from a brother		24:18
r. than spend their days in		24:18
unto death r. than commit sin;		24:19
they had r. sacrifice their lives		26:32
or r., if he believed in God		30: 9
or r., in other words, blessed is		32:16
would ye r. harden your hearts		33:21
or r. led them away unto		36:14
but r. say: O Lord, forgive my		38:14
but r. return unto them, and		39:13
or r. that salvation might come		39:16
they chose evil works r. than good;		40:13
or r. Moroni, feared that they		50:32
r. than be smitten down to the the		51:20
r. by the power and word of God,		53:10
r. which thy brother hath waged		54: 5
O Lord, r. let there be a famine	He	11: 4
ye choose darkness r. than light?		13:29
r. than that they should visit	3Ne	3: 6
r. have commanded that ye		18:25
r. the sorrowing of the damned,	Mrm	2:13

RATHER

but r. give thanks unto God	Mrm 9:31
love darkness r. than light,	DC 10:21
love darkness r. than light,	29:45
but r. let him glory in God,	76:61
but r. be ordained for	124:135

RATIONS
shall receive wine for our r.,	Al 55:11

RAUKEEYANG
R., signifying expanse, or	Fac 1:12
Hebrew word R., signifying	2: 4

RAVENING
but inwardly they are r. wolves.	3Ne 14:15

RAVENOUS
infested by wild and r. beasts.	Al 2:37
no r. wolf to enter among you,	5:60

RAVISHED
shall be spoiled and their wives r.	2Ne 23:16

RAW
while we did live upon r. meat	1Ne 17: 2
eat nothing save it was r. meat;	En 1:20

RAYS
the burning r. of the rising sun;	DC 121:11

RAZOR
shall the Lord shave with a r.	2Ne 17:20

REACH
he shall r. even to the neck;	2Ne 18: 8
forth out of the r. of the people.	3Ne 7:13
understanding r. to heaven;	DC 76: 9
was I enabled to r. the place of	JS 2:62
high that it r. the heavens.	En 1: 4
until they had r. the wilderness,	Al 2:37

READ
and bade him that he should r.	1Ne 1:11
as he r., he was filled with the	1:12
And he r., saying:	1:13
and many things did my father r.	1:13
when my father had r. and seen	1:14
the things which he r. in the book,	1:19
writing, which was plain to be r.,	16:29
I did r. many things to them,	19:22
I did r. many things unto them	19:23
I did r. unto them that which	19:23
after I, Nephi, had r. these things	22: 1
these things which ye have r.?	22: 1
the things of which I have r.	22: 3
to the things which I have r.,	2Ne 2:17
I will r. you the words of Isaiah.	6: 4
the words which I shall r. are they	6: 5
I have r. these things that ye	9: 1
shall be r. upon the house tops;	27:11
shall be r. by the power of Christ;	27:11
saying: R. this, I pray thee.	27:15
the book, and I will r. them.	27:15
the learned say: I cannot r. it.	27:18
The learned shall not r. them,	27:20
thou shalt r. the words which	27:20
when thou hast r. the words which	27:22
the words which thou hast not r.,	27:22
unto him that shall r. the words	27:24
have r. the words of the prophet	Jac 5: 1
my brethren may r. my words.	7:27
he could r. these engravings,	Mos 1: 4
we might r. and understand of	1: 5
Ammon, that he might r. them.	8: 5
as Ammon had r. the record,	8: 6
I r. unto you the remainder of	13:11
Mosiah did r., and caused to be	25: 5
caused to be r., the records of	25: 5
he r. the records of the people	25: 5
he also r. the account of Alma	25: 6
remember to have r. what Zenos,	Al 33: 3
ask if ye have r. the scriptures?	33:14
desiring that he should r. it,	Al 51:15
and had r. Helamna's epistle,	59: 1
have ye not r. that God gave	He 8:11
we r. that in the great and last	12:25
Have they not r. the scriptures,	3Ne 27: 5
yea, he has not r. the scriptures;	Mrm 9: 8
For do we not r. that God is	9: 9
a language that they cannot be r.	Eth 3:22
Hath he not r. the record which	8: 9
overpowering of man to r. them.	12:24
when ye shall r. these things,	Mro 10: 3
in God that ye should r. them,	10: 3
they r. contrary from that	DC 10:11
can r. them one to another;	18:35
canst thou r. this without	19:39
let it be r. this once to her ears,	97:27
he r. the following paragraph,	135: 4
Manifesto which has been r.	OD
children were taught to r. and	Mses 6: 6
'I cannot r. a sealed book.'	JS 2:65

READER
and to the r. I bid farewell,	Jac 7:27
and the r. in every nation will	DC 135: 6

READETH
whoso r., let him understand;	3Ne 10:14
whoso r. let him understand—	DC 57: 9
whoso r., let him understand	71: 5
whoso r. it, let him understand,	91: 4
whoso r. let him understand.	JS 1:12

READINESS
his armies should stand in r.,	Al 51:36

READING
made an end of r. the records,	Mos 25: 7
speaking and r. to the people,	25:14
r. the scriptures unto the king—	Al 22:12
r. the Epistle of James, first	JS 2:11

READS
and fifth verse, which r.:	JS 2:11
the way it r. in our Bibles.	2:36
verse as it r. in our books,	2:36

READY
as if he were r. to destroy?	2Ne 8:13
Ammon had made r. the horses	Al 18:12
should make r. his horses and	20: 6
r. to receive the Lamanites to	51:24
was r. to give them battle on	52: 1
are r. open to receive them.	3Ne 18:13
may be r. at the coming of	DC 33:17
r. to receive the fulness of	35:12
therefore, that ye may be r.	50:46
make r. for the Bridegroom.	65: 3
who are r. and waiting to be	86: 5
therefore, she is r. to be burned.	88:94
and then ye could have made r.	101:54
Hyrum had made r. to go—	135: 4
may be r. to go to a land of peace	136:16
but would have been r.	JS 1:47
Therefore be ye also r., for in	1:48
I was r. to sink into despair	2:16

REAL
but with r. intent, repenting of	2Ne 31:13
O then, is not this r.?	Al 32:35
r. descendants of the Lamanites,	He 11:24
forgiveness, with r. intent,	Mro 6: 8
he shall do it with r. intent	7: 6
and not with r. intent of heart;	7: 9
a sincere heart, with r. intent,	10: 4
injuries, as well as r. property;	DC 123: 2
receive the r. value of moneys,	124:70
were more pretended than r.;	JS 2: 6

REALITY
to an awful r. of these things?	2Ne 9:47
not destroy the r. of his vision.	JS 2:24
they did in r. speak to me;	2:25

REALIZE 783 REBELLION

REALIZE
they did not r. that it was the	Mrm	3: 3
that r. and know from whence		5:10
decree which my people shall r.,	DC	103: 5

REALLY
speaketh of things as they r. are,	Jac	4:13
and of things as they r. will be;		4:13

REAP
and we did r. again in abundance.	2Ne	5:11
they shall r. destruction;		26:10
they shall r. the chaff thereof	Mos	7:30
they shall r. the east wind,		7:31
r. their rewards according to	Al	3:26
to r. eternal happiness or		3:26
shall r. a reward of their works,		9:28
shall r. the salvation of their souls,		9:28
shall r. the damnation of their souls,		9:28
and did r. with your might,		26: 5
shall r. the rewards of your faith,		32:43
neither do they r. nor gather	3Ne	13:26
and to sow, to r. and to hoe,	Eth	10:25
therefore, whoso desireth to r.,	DC	6: 3
and r. while the day lasts,		6: 3
will thrust in his sickle and r.,		6: 4
that shall ye also r.;		6:33
also r. good for your reward.		6:33
whoso desireth to r. let him		11: 3
and r. while the day lasts,		11: 3
will thrust in his sickle and r.,		11: 4
have thrust in their sickle to r.		11:27
whoso desireth to r. let him		12: 3
and r. while the day lasts,		12: 3
will thrust in his sickle and r.		12: 4
whoso desireth to r. let him		14: 3
and r. while the day lasts,		14: 3
will thrust in his sickle and r.,		14: 4
to r. in the field which is white		31: 4
r. with all your might, mind		33: 7
command to r. down the earth,		38:12
sent forth to r. down the fields;		86: 5
r. eternal joy for all our sufferings.		109:76

REAR
about on the east in their r.	Al	43:35
coming upon them in their r.,		43:36
that Moroni had been in their r.		52:29
Lehi pressed upon their r. with		52:36
the Lamanites in the r.		52:36
to fall upon them in their r.,		56:23
thus bring them up in the r.		56:23
Helaman came upon their r.		56:52
upon the r. of the Lamanites.		56:53
in their front and in their r.	3Ne	4:25

REARED
shall be r. in this generation.	DC	84: 4

REARWARD
God of Israel shall be your r.	3Ne	20:42
and I will be their r.		21:29
go before you and be your r.;	DC	49:27

REASON
I have r. to rejoice in the Lord	1Ne	8: 3
for I have r. to suppose that they,		8: 3
narrow by r. of the inhabitants;		21:19
come unto man by r. of the fall;	2Ne	9: 6
fall came by r. of transgression;		9: 6
how great r. we have to mourn.	Mos	7:23
we have no r. to doubt but	Al	24:26
how great r. have we to rejoice?;		26: 1
have we not great r. to rejoice?		26:13
we have r. to praise him forever,		26:14
Now have we not r. to rejoice?		26:35
had so great r. to rejoice as we,		26:35
because they have r. to fear,		28:11
we see the great r. of sorrow,		28:14
the r. they would not look is		33:20
which we have r. to suppose hath	He	5: 8
And they began to r. and		16:17
I have r. to bless my God	3Ne	5:20
the r. why he ceaseth to do	Mrm	9:20
this is the r. that thou hast lost	DC	3:14
r. as with men in days of old,		45:10
hearken and I will r. with you,		45:15
that he may r. with them,		49: 4
and let us r. together,		50:10
Let us r. even as a man		50:11
will I, the Lord, r. with you		50:12
I, the Lord, will r. with you		61:13
the r. that ye did not receive.		67: 3
by r. of transgression cometh	Mses	6:59
powers of both r. and sophistry	JS	2: 9
the r. why I had received		2:60

REASONABLE
it is not r. that such a being as	He	16:18

REASONABLY
which can be r. construeed	DC	OD

REASONETH
as a man r. one with another	DC	50:11
Now, when a man r. he is		50:12
because he r. as a man;		50:12

REASONING
show unto you my strong r.	DC	45:10
synagogues, r. with the people.		66: 7
r. with and expounding all		68: 1
r. in plainness and simplicity—		133:57
is r. upon the principles	Fac	3: 6

REASONS
the r. which we have to mourn;	Mos	7:24
bring forth their strong r.	DC	71: 8

REBEL
Nephi's brethren r. against him.	1Ne	1:hd
wherefore, I did not r. abainst him		2:16
thy brethren shall r. against thee,		2:21
day that they shall r. against me,		2:23
except they shall r. against me		2:23
so be that they r. against me,		2:24
their families, did r. against us;		7: 6
Nephi's brethren r. against him.	2Ne	1:hd
R. no more against your brother,		1:24
all men not to r. against God,	Jac	1: 8
none such that r. against him	Mos	15:26
whosoever doth r. against him		29:23
that if ye will r. against him that	Al	9:24
began to r. against their king,		24: 2
they did wilfully r. against God.	3Ne	6:18
wilfully r. against the gospel of	4Ne	1:38
was Shez, did r. against him;	Eth	10: 3
r. not against my servant Joseph;	DC	112:15

REBELLED
have wilfully r. against God,	Mos	15:26
that I had r. against my God,	Al	36:13
had r. against their country		62: 2
and r. against your holy God;	He	8:25
wilfully r. against their God;	Mrm	1:16
he r. against his father,	Eth	7: 4
that Noah r. against Shule,		7:15
Jared r. against his father,		8: 2
of Shiblom r. against him,		11: 4
for he r. against me, saying,	DC	29:36
r. against the Only Begotten		76:25
the devil, who r. against God,		76:28
that Satan r. against me,	Mses	4: 3
wives, and they r. against him,		5:53
unto Seth, and he r. not,		6: 3

REBELLETH
knoweth that he r. against God!	Mos	3:12

REBELLING
going about r. against God,	Mos	27:11
I went on r. against God,	Al	10: 6

REBELLION
in the which r., they were	1Ne	7: 7
out in open r. against God;	Mos	2:37

REBELLION 784 RECEIVE

up in r. against my people;	Mos 10: 6	Bible which they r. from them?	2Ne 29: 4	
of sin and r. against God,	16: 5	that ye shall r. more of my word?	29: 8	
up the people to r. against him;	18:33	then shall ye r. the Holy Ghost;	31:13	
their r. against their brethren,	Al 3: 6	entered in by the way ye should r.	31:18	
come out in open r. against God;	3:18	and r. the Holy Ghost,	32: 5	
lay down the weapons of their r.,	23: 7	and r. the pleasing word of God,	Jac 3: 2	
laid down the weapons of their r.,	23:13	r. them with thankful hearts,	4: 3	
they did rise up in r. against us.	57:32	believing that ye shall r.	En 1:15	
because of their r. we did cause	57:33	the name of Christ, ye shall r. it.	1:15	
have risen up in r. against me,	61: 3	they might also r. his words.	Mos 2: 8	
have risen up in r. against us	61: 7	the blind to r. their sight,	3: 5	
if they would not rise up in r.	61:11	might r. remission of their sins,	3:13	
up in r. against their brethren.	He 1: 7	may r. forgiveness of our sins,	4: 2	
for he had raised up in r. and	1: 8	faith, believing that ye shall r.,	4:21	
in open r. against their God,	Mrm 2:15	O God, r. my soul.	17:19	
the people did rise up in r.	Eth 10: 8	they were to r. the grace of God,	18:26	
his brother did rise up in r.	10:14	the tribute which he did r.	19:28	
arose in r. among the people,	11:15	did also r. them with joy.	24:25	
for their r. against you	DC 84:76	him shall ye r. into the church,	26:21	
at the r. of South Carolina,	87: 1	and him will I also r.	26:21	
r. are unbecoming every citizen	134: 5	whomsoever ye r. shall believe	26:22	
		shall ye not r. into my church,	26:28	
REBELLIONS		I will not r. at the last day.	26:28	
unto them concerning their r.	2Ne 1: 2	limbs might r. their strength—	27:22	
the r. of Laman and Lemuel,	Al 18:38	Repent, and I will r. you.	Al 5:33	
their r. did he relate unto them;	18:38	must r. his wages of him;	5:42	
such as r. and dissensions,	61:14	for whatsoever things ye do r.	7:23	
in Thompson, and their r.	DC 56: 6	said in a vision: Thou shalt r.	8:20	
of bloodshed, and cease their r.	109:66	and they would not r. me, but	8:24	
		thou shalt r. him into thy house	10: 7	
REBELLIOUS		Thou shalt r. into thy house—	10: 8	
and I was not r.,	2Ne 7: 5	r. wages according to the time	11: 1	
the p. part were slain and driven	He 4: 2	the children of men to r. his word	13:24	
the r. shall be pierced with	DC 1: 3	hope that ye shall r. eternal life;	13:29	
heaven, the unbelieving and r.;	1: 8	their hearts to r. the word which	16:16	
anger is kindled against the r.,	56: 1	they might r. the word with joy,	16:17	
upon the heads of the r.,	56: 4	out of my breast, and r. his Spirit,	22:15	
against the wicked and r.;	63: 2	that I may r. this great joy	22:15	
let the r. fear and tremble;	63: 6	believing that ye shall r.,	22:16	
And the r. shall be cut off	64:35	then shalt thou r. the hope which	22:16	
the r. are not of the blood of	64:36	if we do not r. anything for our	30:34	
		knowest that we r. no gain?	30:35	
REBUILT		the Holy Ghost, but that ye r. it,	34:38	
behold, the city had been r.,	Al 49: 2	but they did r. all the poor of	35: 9	
city of Ammonihah had been r.	49: 3	limbs did r. their strength again,	36:23	
yea, that it was in part r.;	49: 3	did I r. a remission of my sons.	38: 8	
		and r. you at the last day into	38:15	
REBUKE		then shall ye r. your reward;	41:14	
at my r. I dry up the sea,	2Ne 7: 2	to r. the Lamanites to battle.	51:24	
the r. of thy God.	8:20	he might r. strength to his army.	52:17	
and shall r. many people:	12: 4	awaits to r. such murderers as	54: 7	
went forth and began to r. them,	Al 19:31	we are prepared to r. you;	54: 9	
they did r. the judges in He	9:18	shall r. wine for our rations,	55:11	
I will r. the devourer for	3Ne 24:11	to r. a supply of provisions.	57: 8	
Thy voice shall be a r. unto	DC 112: 9	r. more strength from the land	58: 3	
at thy r. let the tongue of	112: 9	to r. provisions and strength	58: 4	
at my r. I dry up the sea.	133:68	that we did r. food, which was	58: 8	
		the assistance which we did r.,	58: 8	
REBUKED		behold ye would not r. me.	He 13: 7	
And others r. them, saying:	Al 19:20	ye will r. him, and say that he	13:27	
they were also r. by those men	19:21	of the Lord they did r. them.	3Ne 4:10	
But others r. them all, saying	19:26	and others did r. great learning	6:12	
his brother Aaron r. him, saying:	26:10	while others would r. railing	6:13	
he or she shall be r. openly,	DC 42:91	will come, him will I r.;	9:14	
he or she shall be r. in secret,	42:92	as a little child, him will I r.,	9:22	
needs stand r. before the Lord;	93:47	opening of the earth to r. them,	10:14	
and stand r. before my face;	95: 2	ye can in nowise r. these things.	11:37	
		of hell stand open to r. such	11:40	
RECALL		shall r. a remission of their sins.	12: 2	
unless thou wilt r. all the words	Mos 17: 8	of heart, and I will r. you.	12:24	
I will not r. the words which	17: 9	they may r. a knowledge of you	16: 4	
and I will not r. my words,	17:10	hell are ready open to r. them.	18:13	
he would r. the things which he	29: 9	right, believing that ye shall r.,	18:20	
I cannot r. the words which	Al 44:11	my name, then shall ye r. him,	18:30	
		the blessing which they shall r.,	20:15	
RECEDED		not be room enough to r. it.	24:10	
after the waters had r. from	Eth 13: 2	Therefore, ask, and ye shall r.;	27:29	
		baptized did r. the Holy Ghost.	28:18	
RECEIVE		will not r. them at the last day;	28:34	
believing that ye shall r.,	1Ne 15:11	were to r. a greater change,	28:40	
will they not r. the strength	15:15	r. a remission of your sins,	30: 2	
which were expedient for man to r.,	17:30	did also r. the Holy Ghost.	4Ne 1: 1	
shall r. hereafter these things	2Ne 25: 3	the blind to r. their sight,	1: 5	

RECEIVE   785   RECEIVE

did r. all manner of wickedness,	4Ne 1:27	which ye shall hereafter r.	DC	48: 6
did they await to r. them.	Mrm 6: 7	r. the gift of the Holy Ghost,		49:14
stood with open arms to r. you!	6:17	ask and ye shall r.;		49:26
may r. it for our inheritance.	Eth 1:38	doth he r. it by the Spirit of		50:19
shalt unstop the hole and r. air.	2:20	and you r. not that Spirit,		50:31
may r. according to our desires.	3: 2	accounted of God worthy to r.		50:34
when ye shall r. this record	4:17	which ye shall hereafter r.—		50:35
ye r. no witness until after the	12: 6	r. directions how to organize		51: 1
or he cannot r. an inheritance	12:32	and r. alike, that ye may be		51: 9
Coriantumr should r. a burial	13:21	would r. money of this church,		51:11
r. great strength to his army.	14: 7	ordinances which you shall r.;		53: 6
might r. all the strength which	15:14	may r. instruction before me		55: 4
was possible that they could r.	15:14	he shall r. the money which		56:10
did they r. any unto baptism	Mro 6: 2	those of whom he shall r.		56:12
faith believing that ye shall r.,	7:26	that which they do they shall r.,		56:13
that ye shall r. these things,	10: 3	will r. wisdom here is wisdom.		57: 3
when ye shall r. these things,	10: 4	to r. moneys, to be an agent		57: 6
r. knowledge from time to time.	DC 1:28	if the world r. his writings—		57:12
Ask, and ye shall r.;	4: 7	and r. that which is to follow.		58: 5
r. this same testimony among	5:14	and they r. not the blessing.		58:32
r. a witness from my hand,	5:32	land to r. an inheritance;		58:36
will r. of me you shall r.;	6: 5	that he may r. his inheritance		58:38
also r. admonition of him.	6:19	r. his inheritance in the land;		58:40
shall you r. a knowledge of	8: 1	r. their inheritance in this land,		58:44
r. a knowledge concerning the	8: 1	to r. moneys to purchase lands		58:49
r. knowledge from all those	8:11	lest they r. none inheritance,		58:53
will ask of me you shall r.;	11: 5	the knowledge which they r.		58:56
in me that you shall r.	11:14	r. a crown in the mansions of		59: 2
that as many as r. me,	11:30	they shall r. for their reward		59: 3
will ask of me you shall r.;	12: 5	shall r. his reward, even peace		59:23
will ask of me you shall r.;	14: 5	against those who r. thee not,		60:15
you shall r. the Holy Ghost,	14: 8	he shall r. this blessing,		62: 7
faith believing that you shall r.,	18:18	if he r. it from the hand of		62: 7
meat now, but milk they must r.;	19:22	and shall r. an inheritance upon		63:20
misery thou shalt r. if thou	19:33	stand to r. an inheritance.		63:31
And those who r. it in faith,	20:14	whom I have appointed to r.		63:40
shall r. a crown of eternal life;	20:14	r. an inheritance in this world,		63:48
elders are to r. their licenses	20:63	shall r. an inheritance before		63:49
may r. it from a conference.	20:64	and if the Lord r. it not,		63:56
For his word ye shall r.,	21: 5	r. the Spirit through prayer;		63:64
r. the reward of the laborer.	23: 7	may r. a more exceeding and		63:66
But if they r. thee not,	24: 4	r. my will concerning you.		64: 1
they r. you not in my name,	24:15	inhabitants thereof may r. it,		65: 5
all those who r. my gospel	25: 1	Ask, and ye shall r.;		66: 9
r. an inheritance in Zion,	25: 2	should r. the blessing which		67: 3
thou shalt r. the Holy Ghost,	25: 8	the reason that ye did not r.		67: 3
of righteousness thou shalt r.	25:15	r. the laying on of the hands.		68:27
all things you shall r. by faith.	26: 2	r. counsel and assistnace from		69: 4
to r. commandments and	28: 2	to r. and do all these things.		69: 6
as they r. thy teachings	28: 8	r. more than is needful for		70: 7
therefore ye r. these things;	29: 3	him understand and r. also;		71: 5
to my command, ye shall r.	29: 6	to r. the funds of the church		72:10
to r. a crown of righteousness,	29:13	pay for that which they r.,		72:11
they r. their wages of whom	29:45	house ye enter, and they r. you,		75:19
people, and they will r. you.	31: 7	ye enter, and they r. you not,		75:20
world, for they will not r. you.	31:10	them ask and they shall r.,		75:27
they shall r. the Holy Ghost	35: 6	and r. the Holy Spirit by the		76:52
the blind to r. their sight,	35: 9	are they who r. of his glory,		76:76
to r. the fulness of my gospel,	35:12	r. of the presence of the Son,		76:77
and you shall r. my Spirit,	36: 2	who r. not of his fulness in		76:86
unto as many as will r. me,	39: 4	also the telestial r. it of the		76:88
and you shall r. my Spirit,	39:10	r. according to his own works,		76:111
r. the fulness of my gospel,	39:18	if you will r. it, this is Elias		77: 9
r. the gift of the Holy Ghost,	39:23	r. the greater condemnation.		82: 3
your faith ye shall r. my law,	41: 3	they who r. this priesthood		84:35
in my name, even so ye shall r.	42: 3	receive this priesthood r. me,		84:35
shall find them that will r. you	42: 8	those who r. the priesthood,		84:40
and if ye r. not the Spirit	42:14	r. this oath and covenant of		84:40
and r. according to his wants.	42:33	inasmuch as you r. these things;		84:60
shall not r. again that which	42:37	shall r. the Holy Ghost.		84:64
thou shalt r. of thy brother.	42:54	they may r. the Holy Ghost,		84:74
thou shalt r. revelation upon	42:61	and r. money by gift,		84:103
hereafter r. church covenants,	42:67	who r. money, send it up unto		84:104
to r. a just remuneration for	42:72	and r. inheritances legally		85: 1
also, shall r. his support,	42:73	who r. not their inheritance		85: 3
ye r. none such among you if	42:76	to r. his will concerning you:		88: 1
or ye shall not r. them.	42:77	shall r. the same body which		88:28
to r. commandments and	43: 2	even ye shall r. your bodies,		88:28
to r. commandments and	43: 3	shall then r. of the same,		88:29
ye r. not the teachings of any	43: 5	shall then r. of the same,		88:30
and shall r. through him whom	43: 7	shall then r. of the same,		88:31
But they r. it not;	45:29	which they are willing to r.,		88:32
in Spirit shall r. in Spirit;	46:28	and he r. not the gift?		88:33

RECEIVE 786 RECEIVED

ask, and ye shall r.;	DC 88:63	RECEIVED		
that they might r. the gospel,	88:99	r. much strength of the Lord,	1Ne	4:31
and r. their inheritance and	88:107	I have r. a commandment		9: 3
quickly, and r. you unto myself.	88:126	had r. the fulness of the Gospel,		10:14
I r. you to fellowship,	88:133	which power he r. by faith on		10:17
ye shall not r. any among you	88:138	after I had r. strength		15: 6
shall r. health in their navel	89:18	I, Nephi, r. a commandment		19: 3
who r. the oracles of God,	90: 5	have r. so great blessings	2Ne	1:10
they may r. the word,	90: 9	be r. into the eternal kingdom		10:25
r. revelations to unfold the	90:14	unto him that saith: We have r.,		28:27
Vienna Jaques should r. money	90:28	We have r. the word of God,		28:29
and r. an inheritance from	90:30	and have r. the baptism of fire		31:14
ye shall r. him into the order.	92: 1	and ye have r. the holy Ghost,		31:18
r. the fulness of the record of	93:18	after ye had r. the Holy Ghost		32: 2
in due time r. of his fulness.	93:19	which I have r. from God,	Jac	2: 9
you shall r. of his fulness,	93:20	before I r. a remission of	En	1: 2
you shall r. grace for grace.	93:20	they are r. into heaven,	Mos	2:41
and they r. not the light.	93:31	r. a remission of their sins,		4: 3
r. a fulness of joy;	93:33	r. a remission of your sins,		4:11
cannot r. a fulness of joy.	93:34	covet that which ye have not r.		4:25
Smith r. his inheritance.	94:13	having r. its name from the king,		18: 4
Carter r. their inheritances—	94:14	having r. a wound has fallen		20:13
my will; ask and ye shall r.;	103:31	Mosiah r. them with joy;		22:14
unto you, ask and ye shall r.;	103:35	and he also r. their records,		22:14
And all moneys that you r.	104:68	none r. authority to preach or to		23:17
as fast as you r. moneys,	104:68	of Alma r. their strength,		27:23
I cannot r. her unto myself.	105: 5	Have ye r. his image in your	Al	5:14
should r. their endowment	105:33	and were r. into the church.		6: 2
the counsel which they r.,	105:37	be r. into the kingdom of God;		7:21
to r. counsel of him whom	108: 1	after which ye have been r.		7:22
r. right by ordination with the rest	108: 4	after Alma had r. his message		8:18
r. a fulness of the Holy Ghost,	109:15	the man r. him into his house;		8:21
of that city r. their testimony,	109:39	who have r. so many blessings		9:23
that city r. not the testimony	109:41	And the judge r. for his wages		11: 3
as fast as ye are able to r. them.	111:11	they r. their wages according to		11:20
that they may r. my word.	112:19	and r. the office of the		13:18
and r. their bishopric.	114: 2	which he had r. from his father,		18: 5
shall not fail if he r. counsel.	124:16	I have never r. so much as even		30:33
I may r. him unto myself,	124:19	have r. only according to law		30:33
that he may r. the consecrations	124:21	Alma having r. tidings that the		31: 1
that you may r. honor and glory.	124:34	ye have r. so many witnesses,		34:30
wherein you r. conversations,	124:39	are r. into a state of happiness,		40:12
That he may r. also the counsel	124:61	weapons of war, which he had r.,		44:10
may r. stock for the building	124:63	has also r. Alma in the spirit,		45:19
shall not r. less than fifty dollars	124:64	when Lehonti r. the message		47:11
permitted to r. fifteen thousand	124:64	the queen had r. this message		47:33
not be permitted to r. over	124:65	Teancum had r. orders to make		52:16
not be permitted to r. under	124:66	when he had r. this epistle,		54:15
not be permitted to r. any man,	124:67	when Moroni had r. this epistle		55: 1
he shall r. stock in that house;	124:68	they r. him with joy;		55: 9
not r. any stock in that house.	124:68	Moroni r. an epistle from		56: 1
r. any stock into their hands,	124:70	Antipus had r. a greater		56:18
r. the real value of moneys,	124:70	I r. an epistle from Ammoron,		57: 1
shall r. counsel from my servant	124:95	we r. a supply of provisions,		57: 6
keys whereby he may ask and r.,	124:95	who had not r. many wounds.		57:25
also r. the keys by which	124:97	our small force which we had r.,		58:12
may ask and r. blessings;	124:97	we have not r. greater strength.		58:34
and he shall r. of my Spirit,	124:97	they have r. many wounds;		58:40
r. the oracles for the whole church.	124:126	after Moroni had r. and had		59: 1
Shadrach Roundy, if he will r. it,	124:141	he r. an epistle from Pahoran,		61: 1
A man may r. the Holy Ghost,	130:23	these are the words which he r.:		61: 1
prepare his heart to r. and obey	132: 3	when Moroni had r. this epistle		62: 1
Or will I r. at your hands	132:10	men of Pachus r. their trial,		62: 9
ye r. me not in the world	132:22	the evidences which they had r.	He	5:50
But if ye r. me in the world,	132:23	great knowledge which ye have r.;		7:24
and shall r. your exaltation;	132:23	evidences which ye have r.;		8:24
R. ye, therefore, my law.	132:24	yea, even if ye have r. all things,		8:24
because they r. me not,	132:25	r. an epistle from the leader	3Ne	3: 1
ye cannot r. the promise of	132:33	when Lachoneus r. this epistle		3:11
r. all those that have been	132:52	of those that had r. no wrong,		3:11
who r. and abide in my law.	132:64	and r. a remission of their sins.		7:25
if she r. not this law,	132:65	my own, and my own r. me not.		9:16
for him to r. all things	132:65	And as many as have r. me,		9:17
be prepared to r. the glory	136:31	it was they who r. the prophets		10:12
again r. his natural strength	Mses 1:10	and r. power and authority		12: 1
to r. thy brother's blood	5:36	I have r. a commandment of		16: 3
shall r. the gift of the Holy Ghost,	6:52	r. the fulness of my gospel,		20:28
will r. them into our bosom,	7:63	unto them which they had r.,		23: 6
ye shall r. the Holy Ghost,	8:24	when they shall have r. this,		26: 9
and desiring to r. instructions,	Abr 1: 2	into a furnace and r. no harm.		28:21
for as many as r. this Gospel	2:10	suckling lamb, and r. no harm.		28:22
and r. its paradisiacal glory.	AoF 10	r. into the kingdom of the Father		28:40

RECEIVED 787 RECEIVETH

they had r. from their Lord	4Ne	1:12
commandment which I have r.,	Mrm	5: 9
commandment which I have r.;		5:13
they might have r. in the land,		5:19
the two stones which he had r.,	Eth	3:28
be r. into the kingdom of God.		5: 5
even that which they have r.,		12:35
r. great strength to his army,		14: 8
when Shiz had r. his epistle		15: 5
had r. sufficient strength that		15:28
none were r. unto baptism save	Mro	6: 3
they had been r. unto baptism,		6: 4
which I have r. from Amoron,		9: 7
after having r. the record of	DC	1:29
even the light which he has r.;		1:33
record that you have r. of me;		5: 1
hast r. instruction of my Spirit.		6:14
and mine own r. me not.		6:21
behold, you have r. a witness;		6:24
have you not r. a witness?		6:24
destroy that which they have r.,		10:52
and mine own r. me not.		10:57
deny that which you have r.,		10:62
and mine own r. me not;		11:29
you have r. the same power,		17: 7
after that you have r. this,		18:43
after that you have r. this,		18:46
which you have r. by the hand		19:13
that you have r. them;		19:14
had r. a remission of his sins,		20: 5
have r. of the Spirit of Christ		20:37
shall be r. by baptism into		20:37
after they are r. by baptism. –		20:68
No one can be r. into the church		20:71
priesthood which you have r.,		27: 8
the things which you have r.		30: 3
they r. not the Holy Ghost;		35: 5
and mine own r. me not;		39: 3
But to as many as r. me,		39: 4
he r. the word with gladness,		40: 2
he has r. these testimonies		42:32
he has r. by consecration,		42:32
until ye have r. them in full.		42:57
the things which thou hast r.,		42:59
the laws which ye have r.		42:66
ye have r. a commandment		43: 2
revelations which you have r.		43: 7
by that which ye have r.,		43: 9
the kingdom which ye have r.,		43:10
even that which ye have r.		43:10
unto them that have r. him,		43:14
to my law which ye have r.		44: 6
own, and mine own r. me not;		45: 8
but unto as many as r. me		45: 8
earth, and were r. unto myself –		45:12
wise and have r. the truth,		45:57
which ye have r., and which		48: 6
my gospel which ye have r.,		49: 1
received, even as ye have r. it,		49: 1
that which he has r. of them,		49: 4
And then r. ye spirits which		50:15
and r. them to be of God;		50:15
these things which ye have r.,		50:35
inasmuch as ye have r. me,		50:43
laws which ye have r. from		58:23
the fulness ye have not yet r.		63:21
his heart, and r. not counsel,		63:55
and have r. my truths,		66: 1
be r. as a wise steward and		72:17
Father, and r. of his fulness;		76:20
Holy Spirit after having r. it,		76:35
who r. the testimony of Jesus,		76:51
who have r. of his fulness,		76:56
r. the fulness of the Father,		76:71
Who r. not the testimony of		76:74
the flesh, but afterwards r. it.		76:74
who r. not the gospel of Christ,		76:82
r. of his fulness and of his grace;		76:94
But r. not the gospel, neither		76:101
Firstborn, and r. into the cloud.		76:102
which he r. under the hand of		84: 6
Jethro r. it under the hand		84: 7
Caleb r. it under the hand		84: 8
Esaias r. it under the hand		84:12
Abraham r. the priesthood	DC	84:14
r. it through the lineage of		84:14
who r. the priesthood by		84:16
covenant after he hath r. it,		84:41
priesthood which ye have r.,		84:42
lightly the things you have r. –		84:54
unto all who have not r. it.		84:75
that which they might have r.		88:32
thus they all r. the light of		88:58
which they have r.,		88:71
who have r. their part in that		88:99
be r. by the ordinance of		88:139
world and r. of my Father,		93: 5
he r. not of the fulness at		93:12
first, but r. grace for grace;		93:12
r. not of the fulness at first,		93:13
grace, until he r. a fulness;		93:13
r. not of the fulness at the first.		93:14
r. a fulness of the glory of		93:16
And he r. all power, both in		93:17
He r. a fulness of truth,		93:26
r. the promise of God by his		107:42
when he r. his ordination.		107:45
every creature who has not r. it;		112:28
who have r. a dispensation		112:31
dispensation, which ye have r.,		112:32
in the gospel which we have r.?		128:19
it cannot be r. there,		132:18
after ye have r. my		132:27
Abraham r. all things, whatsoever		132:29
whatsoever he r., by revelation		132:29
Abraham r. promises		132:30
Abraham r. concubines,		132:37
David also r. many wives and		132:38
things which they r. not of me.		132:38
and r. his portion;		132:39
no man among you r. me,		133:66
sent unto you ye r. them not.		133:71
and both r. four balls.		135: 1
you have r. my kingdom.		136:41
calling upon God, he r. strength,	Mses	1:20
Moses r. strength, and called		1:21
and r. a fulness of joy;		7:67
God r. it up into his own bosom;		7:69
commandments which I had r.	JS	2:49
r. instruction and intelligence		2:54
I had r. such strict charges		2:60
of my having r. the plates,		2:66
of having r. the Priesthood		2:74
RECEIVEDST		
r. thy first message from him.	Al	8:15
RECEIVES		
at the time he r. stock;	DC	124:67
to each individual who r. one,		130:10
this planet r. its power	Fac	2: 5
RECEIVETH		
r. it with gladness;	2Ne	28:28
for unto him that r. I will give		28:30
for he for his wages an	Mos	2:33
this is the man who r. salvation,		4: 7
every man r. wages of him whom	Al	3:27
for his wages he r. death,		5:42
the same r. the lesser portion		12:10
Lord r. them up unto himself,		14:11
this is joy which none r. save		27:18
For every one that asketh, r.;	3Ne	14: 8
for he that asketh, r.;		27:29
r. not the words of Jesus		28:34
he hath sent r. not him;		28:34
And whoso r. this record,	Mrm	8:12
for God r. none such.	Mro	7: 9
give unto you as he r. them,	DC	21: 4
he r. them even as Moses.		28: 2
he that r. my gospel receiveth		39: 5
that receiveth my gospel r. me;		39: 5
he that r. not my gospel		39: 5
not my gospel r. not me.		39: 5
he that r. these things		39:22
that receiveth these things r. me;		39:22
He that r. my law and doeth		41: 5
saith he r. it and doeth it not,		41: 5

RECEIVETH		788		RECORD	
that r. him shall be saved,	DC 49: 5	according to the r. of Kolob.	Abr	3: 4
r. him not shall be damned—	49: 5	which thou standest in point of r.,		3: 5
he that r. the word of truth,	50:19	the r. of its time is not so many		3: 5
that r. the word by the Spirit	50:21	unto thee to know the times of r.,		3: 6
r. it as it is preached by	50:21	is a longer time as to its r.		3: 7
that preacheth and he that r.,	50:22	than the r. of the time of the		3: 7
and he that r. light,	50:24	whose r. of time shall be longer		3: 8
in God, r. more light;	50:24	there shall be the r. of the time		3: 9
He that r. of God, let him	50:34	is after the r. of the Lord's time;		3: 9
wherefore he r. no reward.	58:26	not appointed unto Adam his r.		5:13
and r. a commandment with	58:29			
unto him that r. it shall be	71: 6	RECLAIM		
And he who r. all things with	78:19	to r. and restore the Lamanites	Jac	7:24
For he that r. my servants	84:36	no way that he might r. them	Al	4:19
receiveth my servants r. me;	84:36	Go and r. this people, for they		30:53
And he that r. me receiveth	84:37	to r. men from this fallen state,		42:12
receiveth me r. my Father;	84:37	r. their rights and their privileges.		55:28
And he that r. my Father	84:38			
r. my Father's kingdom;	84:38	RECLAIMED		
And whoso r. not my voice	84:52	be r. from this temporal death,	Al	42: 8
And whoso r. you, there I	84:88	be r. from this spiritual death.		42: 9
Whoso r. you receiveth me;	84:89	but behold such shall be r.;	DC	50: 7
Whoso receiveth you r. me;	84:89	manner to have r. me—	JS	2:28
He that r. you not,	84:92			
wisdom r. wisdom; truth	88:40	RECOGNIZING		
whoso r. not by the Spirit,	91: 6	r. Wilford Woodruff as the	DC	OD
And no man r. a fulness	93:27			
r. truth and light, until he	93:28	RECOLLECT		
whose spirit r. not the light	93:32	The first thing that I can r.	JS	2:49
And who r. you receiveth	99: 2			
who receiveth you r. me;	99: 2	RECOLLECTION		
who r. you as a little child,	99: 3	a bright r. of all our guilt.	Al	11:43
little child, r. my kingdom;	99: 3			
Whosoever r. my word receiveth	112:20	RECOLLECTS		
receiveth my word r. me,	112:20	any one who r. my youth,	JS	2:28
and whosoever r. me,	112:20			
receiveth me, r. those,	112:20	RECOMMENCE		
save he that r. it.	130:11	let them r. laying the	DC 115:11
he that r. a fulness thereof	132: 6			
if a man r. a wife	132:41	RECOMMEND		
		I cannot r. them unto God lest	Mro	9:21
RECEIVING		my son, I r. thee unto God,		9:22
r. many, and baptizing many.	Mos 26:37	a r. from the church.	DC	52:41
upon his feet, r. his strength.	Al 22:22			
an end to our r. provisions	56:29	RECOMMENDED		
were also r. great strength from	58: 5	r. by the church or churches,	DC	72:19
and r. strength from day to day,	59: 7	r. and authorized by you,		112:21
I do joy in r. your epistle,	61:19			
r. daily an addition to their	He 11:25	RECOMPENSE		
they came forth r. no harm.	4Ne 1:32	r. unto every man according to	DC	1:10
from among them, r. no harm.	1:33	and his r. shall be with him,		56:19
another people r. the land	Eth 13:21	to r. every man according as		112:34
if the member r. the letter is	DC 20:84	have a just r. of wages for		124:121
r. mine everlasting covenant,	66: 2	will mete out a just r. of reward		127: 3
after r. their inheritances.	85: 2			
the privilege of r. the mysteries	107:19	RECONCILE		
r. light from the revelations	Fac 2: 5	r. yourselves to the will of God,	2Ne 10:24
RECENT		RECONCILED		
in their r. report to the	DC OD	after ye are r. unto God,	2Ne 10:24
		and to be r. to God;		25:23
RECEPTION		they shall be r. unto Christ,		33: 9
the r. and safety of the brethren	Al 28: 8	brethren, be r. unto him	Jac	4:11
by the r. of the Holy Ghost,	3Ne 27:20	and first be r. to thy brother,	3Ne 12:24
and the r. of the Holy Spirit	DC 53: 3	or first confess thou shalt be r.	DC	42:88
and a r. of the Holy Spirit	55: 1			
		RECONCILIATION		
RECKON		not partake until he makes r.	DC	46: 4
did not r. after the manner of	Al 11: 4			
Nephites began to r. their time	3Ne 2: 8	RECORD		
		it is an abridgment of the r.	T Pg	
RECKONED		which is a r. of the people of	T Pg	
he shall be r. in the house of	DC 104:45	*after the r. of the Jews.*	1Ne	1:hd
		I, Nephi, wrote this r.		1:hd
RECKONING		I make a r. of my proceedings		1: 1
altered their r. and their measure,	Al 11: 4	I make a r. in the language		1: 2
Now the r. is thus—	11: 5	the r. which I make is true;		1: 3
of the lesser numbers of their r.—	11:14	abridgment of the r. of my father,		1:17
number, according to their r.	11:18	abridged the r. of my father		1:17
this man in the r. of our time,	3Ne 8: 2	Laban hath the r. of the Jews		3: 3
Is not the r. of God's time,	DC 130: 4	to obtain the r. of the Jews.		5: 6
the Lord, after his manner of r.,	Abr 3: 4	And also a r. of the Jews		5:12
This is the r. of the Lord's time,	3: 4	fathers in this part of my r.;		6: 1

RECORD

it is given in the r. which	1 Ne	6: 1
that we should obtain the r.?		7:11
bear r. that he had baptized		10:10
bear r. that it is the Son of God.		11: 7
and I saw and bear r.		11:32
I saw and bear r., that		11:36
I also saw and bear r. that		12: 7
of whom the Holy Ghost beareth r.,		12:18
beholdest is a r. of the Jews,		13:23
it is a r. like unto the		13:23
whom the twelve apostles bear r.;		13:24
they bear r. according to the		13:24
bear r. that the name of the		14:27
And I bear r. that I saw		14:29
upon them the r. of my people.		19: 1
engraven the r. of my father,		19: 1
wherefore, the r. of my father,		19: 2
make a r. upon the other plates,		19: 4
unto me faithful witnesses to r.,	2 Ne	18: 2
the r. of this people being kept	Jac	7:26
wherefore, I conclude this r.,		7:26
preserve a r. of my people,	En	1:13
And I bear r. that the people of		1:20
the r. of this people is engraven	Om	1:11
contained the r. of the Jews.		1:14
being about to deliver up the r.	WM	1: 1
to finish my r. upon them,		1: 5
remainder of my r. I shall take		1: 5
with the remainder of my r.,		1: 6
proceed to finish out my r.,		1: 9
contained the r. of his people	Mos	8: 5
as soon as Ammon had read the r.,		8: 6
THE R. OF ZENIFF.—		9:hd
shall leave a r. behind them,		12: 8
they brought a r. with them,		21:27
a r. of the people whose bones		21:27
that they should keep their r.,		24: 6
also keep a r. of the people,		28:20
according to the r. of Alma,	Al	1:hd
according to his own r., saying:		5: 2
according to his own r.		7:hd
according to the r. of Alma.		9:hd
according to the r. of Alma.		17:hd
them according to his own r.		35:16
that ye keep a r. of this people,		37: 2
And thus ended the r. of Alma,		44:24
according to the r. of Helaman,		45:hd
return in our r. to Amalickiah		47: 1
according to the r. of Helaman	He	1:hd
Yea, did he not bear r. that		8:14
according to the r. of Helaman		16:25
yea, the r. of this people.	3 Ne	1: 3
have made my r. of these things		5:10
according to the r. of Nephi,		5:10
I do make the r. on plates		5:11
should make a r. of these things		5:14
a small r. of that which hath		5:15
make my r. from the accounts		5:16
I do make a r. of the things		5:17
I know the r. which I make		5:18
make to be a just and a true r.;		5:18
that according to our r.,		8: 1
and we know our r. to be true,		8: 1
just man who did keep the r.—		8: 1
know of a surety and did bear r.,		11:15
and I bear r. of the Father,		11:32
and the Father beareth r. of me,		11:32
beareth r. of the Father and me;		11:32
and I bear r. that the Father		11:32
I bear r. of it from the Father;		11:35
will the Father bear r. of me,		11:35
will the Father bear r. of me,		11:36
Holy Ghost will bear r. unto him		11:36
and the multitude did bear r.		17:15
this manner do they bear r.:		17:16
the multitude bare r. of it,		17:21
did see and hear and bear r.,		17:25
they know that their r. is true		17:25
therefore they did not bear r.;		18:37
the disciples bare r. that he		18:37
hereafter that this r. is true.		18:37
the disciples saw and did bear r.		18:39
did witness it, and did bear r.;	3 Ne	19:14
did hear and do bear r.;		19:33
Bring forth the r. which ye		23: 7
the Holy Ghost beareth r. of		28:11
according to the r. which hath		28:18
of Nephi, according to his r.	4 Ne	1:hd
Nephi, he that kept this last r.,		1:19
Amos kept the r. in his stead;		1:21
did keep the r. in his stead.		1:47
the end of the r. of Ammaron.		1:49
I, Mormon, make a r. of the	Mrm	1: 1
a r. according to the words of		2:17
now I finish my r. concerning		6: 1
therefore I made this r. out of		6: 6
not only in this r. but also in		7: 8
the r. which shall come unto		7: 8
which r. shall come from the		7: 8
do finish the r. of my father,		8: 1
my father hath made this r.,		8: 5
And whoso receiveth this r.,		8:12
the same who hideth up this r.		8:14
the r. thereof is of great worth;		8:14
have written this r. according to		9:32
had no imperfection in our r.		9:33
that the first part of this r.,	Eth	1: 3
that wrote this r. was Ether,		1: 6
now I proceed with my r.,		2:13
and he shall know and bear r.		4:11
when ye shall receive this r.—		4:17
and the Holy Ghost bear r.—		5: 4
the r. of Jared and his brother.		6: 1
the r. which our fathers brought		8: 9
I, Moroni, proceed with my r.		9: 1
we have seen in this r. that one		12:20
which beareth r. of them,		12:41
Moroni, proceed to finish my r.		13: 1
made the remainder of this r.,		13:14
and he finished his r.;		15:33
received the r. of the Nephites,	DC	1:29
and the Spirit beareth r.,		1:39
the r. is true, and the truth		1:39
you have testified and borne r.		5: 1
until you have finished this r.,		9: 1
publish it as the r. of Nephi;		10:42
contains a r. of a fallen people,		20: 9
which beareth r. of the Father		20:27
the general church r. of names.		20:83
shall be a r. kept among you;		21: 1
the r. of the stick of Ephraim;		27: 5
and beareth r. of the Father		42:17
to keep the church r. and		47: 3
in bearing r. of the land upon		58: 7
except he hear r. by the way,		58:59
bearing r. of the things which		58:63
and the Spirit beareth r.		59:24
that ye might bear r.;		61: 4
you may return to bear r.,		62: 5
bear r. that they are true.		67: 8
and ye shall bear r. of me,		68: 6
as the Father shall bear r.,		68:12
of the earth, and bear r.,		71: 4
things shall be had on r.,		72: 6
Of whom we bear r.;		76:14
the r. which we bear is the		76:14
we heard the voice bearing r.		76:23
this we saw also, and bear r.,		76:25
heavens bore r. unto us—		76:40
And again we bear r.—		76:50
general church r. of all things		85: 1
John saw and bore r. of		93: 6
the fulness of John's r. is		93: 6
And he bore r., saying:		93: 7
I, John, bear r. that I beheld		93:11
And I, John, bear r., and lo,		93:15
John, bear r. that he received		93:16
the fulness of the r. of John.		93:18
John bore r. of me, saying:		93:26
shall be shed forth in bearing r.		100: 8
in bearing r. of thy name,		109:31
thou shalt bear r. of my name,		112: 4
and bear r. of my name.		118: 4

RECORD 790 RECOVERED

Hyrum may bear r. of the	DC 124:96	these r. should be translated	Mos 8:12
to bear r. of my name in all	124:139	from whence these r. came;	8:12
he might make a r. of a truth	128: 2	a man that can translate the r.;	8:13
certifying in his r. that he saw	128: 3	all r. that are of ancient date;	8:13
that the r. they have made is true.	128: 4	the r. which were engraven on	10:16
enter the r. on the general	128: 4	and he also received their r.,	22:14
the r. shall be just as holy,	128: 4	also the r. which had been	22:14
made a r. of the same on the	128: 4	the r. of Zeniff to his people;	25: 5
contained the r. of their works,	128: 7	the r. of the people of Zeniff,	25: 5
is the r. which is kept in heaven;	128: 7	made an end of reading the r.,	25: 7
whatsoever you r. on earth shall	128: 8	Therefore he took the r. which	28:11
whatsoever you do not r. on earth	128: 8	the r. which were on the plates	28:11
kept a proper and faithful r. of	128: 9	finished translating these r.,	28:17
witnesses to bear r. of the book!	128:20	yea, all the r., and also the	28:20
of this thing Moses bore r.;	Mses 1:23	those r. which were brought out	Al 3:11
which beareth r. of the Father and	1:24	it is they who have kept the r.	3:12
which beareth r. of the Father and	5: 9	they also brought forth their r.	14: 8
the r. of heaven, the Comforter;	6:61	r. which were cast in with them,	14:14
and made to bear r. of me,	6:63	the r. and the holy scriptures	18:36
all things bear r. of me.	6:63	unto them all the r. and scriptures	18:38
This is the r. of the Father, and	6:66	were taught the r. and prophecies	23: 5
which beareth r. of the Father	7:11	command you that ye take the r.	37: 1
and Enoch bore r. of it, saying:	7:28	have the r. of the holy scriptures	37: 3
at the commencement of this r.	Abr 1:12	things that these r. do contain,	37: 9
some of these things upon this r.,	1:31	these r. and their words brought	37: 9
		those r. which have been kept?	45: 2
RECORDED		to take possession of those r.	50:38
r. in heaven for the angels to	DC 62: 3	according to the r. of Helaman,	He 1:hd
r. in the second chapter and	85:12	according to the r. of his sons,	1:hd
r. in the book of the names of	88: 2	many r. kept of the proceedings	3:13
r. in the testimony of John.	88: 3	books and many r. of every kind,	3:15
and are r. with this seal and	98: 2	the r. which were delivered	6:26
it may be r. in heaven;	127: 7	all the r. which had been kept,	3Ne 1: 2
find r. in Revelation 20:12—	128: 6	his son Nephi did keep the r.	1: 3
it may be r. in heaven.	128: 7	who had the charge of the r.,	2: 9
on earth shall be r. in heaven,	128: 8	there are r. which do contain	5: 9
shall not be r. in heaven;	128: 8	Nephi had brought forth the r.,	23: 8
kept in the which was r.,	Mses 6: 5	up the r. which were sacred—	4Ne 1:48
		all the sacred r. which had	1:48
RECORDER		that Ammaron hid up the r.	Mrm 1: 2
let there be a r.	DC 127: 6	Ammaron had deposited the r.	2:17
to you concerning a r.	128: 2	r. which Ammaron hid up	4:23
that there should be a r.,	128: 2	r. which had been handed down	6: 6
r. to be present at all times,	128: 3	r. which had been entrusted to	6: 6
there can be a r. appointed	128: 3	and hide up the r. in the earth;	8: 4
let there be a general r.,	128: 4	Mormon did hide up the r.	Eth 15:11
Then the general church r. can	128: 4	I have sacred r. that I would	Mro 9:24
		And I seal up these r., after I	10: 2
RECORDINGS		which contain these r.—	DC 3:19
That in all your r. it may be	DC 127: 7	there are r. which contain	6:26
that in all your r. it may be	128: 7	the engravings of old r.,	8: 1
		r. which have been hid up,	8:11
RECORDS		then, behold, other r. have I,	9: 2
seek the r., and bring them down	1Ne 3: 4	be found on any of the r. or	85: 4
he desired of Laban the r.	3:12	let all the r. be had in order,	127: 9
not that he should have the r.	3:13	to whom these other r. can be	128: 4
that we should obtain these r.,	3:19	statement and r. to be true,	128: 4
that he would give unto us the r.	3:24	refer to the r. which are kept	128: 7
that I might obtain the r.	4:17	according to the r. which they have	128: 8
my father, Lehi, took the r.	5:10	a power which r. or binds	128: 9
and his fathers had kept the r.	5:16	And as are r. on the earth	128:14
And we had obtained the r.	5:21	so also are the r. in heaven.	128:14
the r. of the prophets and of	13:39	containing the r. of our dead,	128:24
These last r., which thou hast	13:40	r. have come into my hands,	Abr 1:28
made known in the r. of thy seed,	13:41	But the r. of the fathers, even	1:31
as well as in the r. of the twelve	13:41		
Nephi, had also brought the r.	2Ne 5:12	RECOVER	
I, Nephi, had kept the r.	5:29	the second time to r. them;	2Ne 6:14
would destroy our r. and us,	En 1:14	the second time to r. the remnant	21:11
God was able to preserve our r.,	1:15	the second time to r. my people,	29: 1
that he would preserve the r.;	1:16	and have not sought to r. them.	29: 5
the r. of our wars are engraven,	Jar 1:14	the second time to r. his people,	Jac 6: 2
after this manner we keep the r.,	Om 1: 9	may also r. the remainder of	Al 60:24
had brought no r. with them;	1:17	my people may r. their rights	3Ne 3:10
I deliver these r. into the hands	WM 1: 2	on the sick and they shall r.;	Mrm 9:24
I searched among the r. which	1: 3	sent forth to r. my people,	DC 39:11
other plates, which contained r.	1:10	the sick, and they shall r.	66: 9
taught them concerning the r.	Mos 1: 3		
plates, which contain these r.	1: 3	RECOVERED	
and also that these r. are true.	1: 6	those places which he had r.	Al 59:10
of Nephi, which contain the r.	1: 6	were r. from our astonishment,	He 9:14
gave him charge concerning the r.	1:16	when Coriantumr had r. of	Eth 15: 1
been taught concerning the r.	2:34	four balls, but has since r.;	DC 135: 2

RECOVERING

RECOVERING
but soon r. in some degree,	JS	2:20

RED
near the shore of the R. Sea;	1Ne	2: 5
which are nearer the R. Sea;		2: 5
it emptied into the R. Sea;		2: 8
the fountain of the R. Sea,		2: 9
the waters of the R. Sea		4: 2
in the waters of the R. Sea.		4: 2
the borders near the R. Sea.		16:14
the waters of the R. Sea		17:26
were drowned in the R. Sea,		17:27
afflict by the way of the R. Sea	2Ne	19: 1
through the R. Sea on dry ground,	Mos	7:19
had marked themselves with r.	Al	3: 4
mark of r. upon their foreheads.		3:13
up the Egyptians in the R. Sea;		36:28
upon the waters of the R. Sea,	He	8:11
of Israel through the R. Sea	DC	8: 3
on the borders of the R. Sea.		17: 1
Lord shall be r. in his apparel,		133:48

REDEEM
he may r. the children of men	2Ne	2:26
O Lord, wilt thou r. my soul?		4:31
shortened at all that it cannot r.,		7: 2
that God should r. his people?	Mos	13:33
and shall r. his people.		15: 1
the Lord would r. his people,		15:11
to r. them from their		15:12
neither can the Lord r. such;		15:27
to r. his people from their sons.	Al	5:21
to r. his people from their sins?		5:27
to r. his people from their sins,		6: 8
to r. those who will be baptized		9:27
into the world to r. his people;		11:40
and he shall r. all mankind who		19:13
to r. mankind from their sins?		21: 7
that he will come to r. his people,		33:22
that he cometh to r. the world.	He	5: 9
should come to r. his people,		5:10
not come to r. them in their sons,		5:10
but to r. them from their sons.		5:10
to r. them from their sons		5:11
and none shall r. it because of		13:19
to r. all those who shall believe		14: 2
of the world to r. my people.	Eth	3:14
she could r. the kingdom unto		8: 8
things, and shall r. all things,	DC	77:12
and r. my vineyard;		101:56
an abundance, to r. Zion,		101:75
r. that which thou didst appoint		109:51
r. them out of their prison;		128:22
that I could not r.,		133:67
I will r. all mankind, that one	Mses	4: 1

REDEEMED
hath r. his servant Jacob.	1Ne	20:20
Lord hath r. my soul from hell;	2Ne	1:15
I know that thou art r.,		2: 3
that they are r. from the fall		2:26
the r. of the Lord shall return,		8:11
saith the Lord, who r. Abraham,		27:33
he hath r. my soul from hell.		33: 6
he hath r. Jeruslaem;	Mos	12:23
having r. them, and satisfied		15: 9
the Lord, who has r. his people;		15:18
with God who has r. them;		15:23
life, being r. by the Lord.		15:24
the Lord hath r. none such;		15:27
he hath r. Jerusalem.		15:30
that God r. his people from		16: 4
that ye may be r. of God,		18: 9
the Lord, who had r. his people		18:20
but they would not be r.		26:26
and have been r. of the Lord;		27:24
righteousness, being r. of God,		27:25
r. from the gall of bitterness		27:29
all men, and had also r. all men;	Al	1: 4
they cannot be r. according to		12:18
that are r. of the Lord;		41: 7
were r. by the Lord Jesus Christ;		46:39
who has r. us and made us free,	Al	58:41
that they were r. by him;	He	8:23
people, he hath r. Jerusalem.	3Ne	16:19
their God, who hath r. them.		20:13
people, he hath r. Jerusalem.		20:34
shall be r. without money.		20:38
this is wherein all men are r.,	Mrm	9:13
being r. and loosed from this		9:13
ye are r. from the fall;	Eth	3:13
be r. from their spiritual fall,	DC	29:44
little children are r. from the		29:46
and my people shall be r.		43:29
the heathen nations be r.,		45:54
r. in the due time of the Lord,		76:38
are they who shall not be r.		76:85
hath r. his people, Israel,		84:99
Lord hath r. his people;		84:100
having r. man from the fall,		93:38
Zion shall be r., although		100:13
r. the land by the shedding of		101:80
have been r. even now.		105: 2
may begin to be r.;		109:62
and be r. from oppression,		109:67
converted and r. with Israel,		109:70
the year of my r. is come;		133:52
and in his pity, he r. them,		133:53
Zion shall be r. in mine own		136:18
hast fallen thou mayest be r.,	Mses	5: 9

REDEEMER
or this R. of the world.	1Ne	10: 5
they should rely on this R.		10: 6
their Lord and their R.		10:14
and beheld the R. of the world,		11:27
of the Gospel of their R.		15:14
to the knowledge of their R.		15:14
their R., going before them,		17:30
remember the Lord their R.		19:18
believe in the Lord their R.		19:23
thus saith the Lord, thy R.,		20:17
Thus saith the Lord, the R.		21: 7
am thy Savior and thy R.,		21:26
is their Savior and their R.,		22:12
Messiah, their R. and their God,	2Ne	1:10
of the righteousness of thy R.;		2: 3
come to the knowledge of their R.,		6:11
thy R., the Mighty One of Jacob.		6:18
the true knowledge of their R.		10: 2
for he verily saw my R.,		11: 2
the R. hath done his work,		28: 5
Lord and your R. should do;		31:17
my rest, which is with my R.;	En	1:27
to the knowledge of their R.;	Mos	18:30
their God, that I am their R.;		26:26
I rejected my R., and denied		27:30
to the knowledge of their R.		27:36
the R. liveth and cometh among	Al	7: 7
behold, I have seen my R.;		19:13
the Lord, the R. of all men,		28: 8
rejoice in Jesus Christ their R.		37: 9
to the knowledge of their R.?		37:10
the cause of our R. and our God.		61:14
bringeth unto the power of the R.,	He	5:11
it is upon the rock of our R.,		5:12
which is the knowledge of their R.,		15:13
then shall they know their R.,	3Ne	5:26
the Lord Jesus Christ, their R.		10:10
to a knowledge of me, their R.		16: 4
thy R., the Holy One of Israel—		22: 5
on thee, saith the Lord thy R.		22: 8
to the words of Chrsit, your R.,	Mro	8: 8
who is your God and your R.,	DC	8: 1
your R., your Lord and your God.		10:70
Christ, your Lord and your R.		15: 1
Christ, your Lord and your R.		16: 1
the Lord your R. suffered death		18:11
and your God, and your R.,		18:47
the end, the R. of the world.		19: 1
Lord, your God, and your R.,		27: 1
the voice of Jesus Christ, your R.,		29: 1
even Jesus Christ, your R.,		31:13
even Jesus Christ your R.;		34: 1
I am your Lord and your R.		34:12

REDEEMER — REFLECTED

REDEEMER
truths, saith the Lord your R.,	DC	66: 1
the Lord your God, your R.,		66:13
of the Lord your God, your R.		72: 8
commanded you, saith your R.,		78:20
your R., even Jesus Christ.		80: 5
light and the R. of the world;		93: 9

REDEEMETH
for the Lord r. none such	Mos	15:26
the Lord r. them not.		16: 2
and r. all mankind from the first	He	14:16
of Christ r. mankind,		14:17

REDEEMING
and they did sing r. love.	Al	5: 9
have felt to sing the song of r. love,		5:26
they are brought to sing r. love,		26:13

REDEMPTION
also the r. of the world.	1 Ne	1:19
r. cometh in and through the	2 Ne	2: 6
a mock of the great plan of r.,	Jac	6: 8
that the power of the r. and the		6: 9
and the power of his r.	Om	1:26
of God, yea, the r. of Christ;	WM	1: 8
were through the r. of God.	Mos	13:32
For were it not for the r.		15:19
though there was no r. made,		16: 5
there could have been no r.		16: 6
r. cometh through Christ		16:15
and the r. of the people,		18: 2
r., and faith on the Lord.		18: 7
through the r. of Christ,		18:13
exercise faith in the r. of him	Al	5:15
as though there had been no r.		11:41
as though there had been no r.		12:18
had not been for the plan of r.,		12:25
but there was a plan of r. laid,		12:25
thus the plan of r. would have		12:26
known unto them the plan of r.,		12:30
known unto them the plan of r.,		12:32
on such the plan of r. could have		12:32
the plan of r. which was laid)		12:33
to look forward to his Son for r.		13: 2
a preparatory r. for such.		13: 3
thou believest in the r. of Christ		15: 8
them to know of the plan of r.		17:16
unto them the plan of r.,		18:39
there could be no r. for mankind		21: 9
and also the plan of r., which		22:13
and my r. from everlasting wo.		26:36
repentance and the plan of r.,		29: 2
r. cometh through the Son of		34: 7
the great and eternal plan of r.		34:16
the great plan of r. be brought		34:31
plan of r. should be made known		39:18
if it were not for the plan of r.,		42:11
the plan of r. could not be		42:13
the salvation and the r. of men,		42:26
even r. should come unto them.	He	8:18
the r. which the Lord would make	3 Ne	6:20
behold, by me r. cometh,		9:17
to bring r. unto the people,		9:21
he hath brought to pass the r.	Mrm	7: 7
of Jesus Christ came the r.		9:12
And because of the r. of man,		9:13
a r. from an endless sleep,		9:13
there have been no r. made.	Mro	7:38
of him and the power of his r.		8:20
the power of r. cometh on		8:22
r., through faith on the name of	DC	29:42
be glad, your r. draweth nigh.		35:26
the day of r. shall come,		45:17
your r. shall be perfected;		45:46
world for the r. of the world,		49: 5
of Satan until the day of r.		78:12
of Satan until the day of r.		82:21
through the r. which is made		88:14
the dead is the r. of the soul.		88:16
And the r. of the soul is		88:17
then cometh the r. of those		88:99
concerning the r. of Zion.		101:43
importune for redress, and r.,		101:76
and r. of your brethren,		103: 1
your r., and the redemption	DC	103:13
and the r. of your brethren,		103:13
the r. of Zion must needs		103:15
so shall the r. of Zion be.		103:18
restoration and r. of Zion.		103:29
of Satan until the day of r.		104: 9
the r. of mine afflicted people—		105: 1
season for the r. of Zion—		105: 9
season, for the r. of Zion.		105:13
for the r. of my people,		105:16
and fulfilled, after her r.		105:34
and the r. of Israel;		113: 8
the r. of the First Presidency		117:13
are sealed up unto the day of r.,		124:124
of Satan unto the day of r.,		132:26
joy of our r., and the eternal	Mses	5:11
the righteous, the hour of their r.;		7:67

REDOUBLED
it has been r. by those who	Al	60:32
and your works be r.,	DC	127: 4

REDOUND
the land shall r. to your glory.	DC	124:87

REDRESS
continue to importune for r.,	DC	101:76
law, and r. us of our wrongs.		105:25
r. of all wrongs and grievances,		134:11

REDUCE
r. the armies of the Lamanites	Al	62:30

REDUCED
were small, having been r.,	Mos	19: 2
had been r. by the Lamanites	Al	56:10

REED
shall wither even as a dried r.;	1 Ne	17:48

REEL
shall tremble, and r. to and fro	DC	45:48
to tremble and to r. to and fro		49:23
tremble and r. to and fro		88:87

REFER
r. to the records which are kept	DC	128: 7
will r. you to the representation	Abr	1:12
I r. to his own account of	JS	2:63

REFERENCE
what people had Isaiah r. to?	DC	113: 7
He had r. to those whom		113: 8

REFERRED
decide whether this coming r. to	DC	130:16

REFERRING
r. to Abraham, as given	Fac	3: 3

REFINE
all kinds of ore and did r. it;	He	6:11

REFINED
For, behold, I have r. thee,	1 Ne	20:10
he did cause to be r. in prison,	Eth	10: 7
of wine on the lees well r.,	DC	58: 8

REFINEMENT
be polished with the r. which	DC	124: 2

REFINER
as a r. and purifier of silver;	3 Ne	24: 3
sit as a r. and purifier of silver,	DC	128:24

REFINER'S
For he is like a r. fire, and like	3 Ne	24: 2
For he is like a r. fire,	DC	128:24

REFINERS
dross, which the r. do cast out,	Al	34:29

REFLECTED
I r. on it again and again,	JS	2:12

REFLECTION 793 REHEARSED

REFLECTION
mind was called up to serious r.	JS	2: 8
It caused me serious r. then,		2:23

REFORMED
called among us the r. Egyptian,	Mrm	9:32

REFRAIN
for my praise will I r. from	1Ne	20: 9
see that ye r. from idleness.	Al	38:12
that ye r. from your iniquities;		39:12
henceforth, and r. from sin,	DC	82: 2
r. from contracting any		OD

REFUGE
and for a place of r.,	2Ne	14: 6
there shall be no place for r.;	He	15: 2
abroad, having no place for r.,		15:12
a land of peace, a city of r.,	DC	45:66
and for a r. from the storm,		115: 6
r. for those who shall be left		124:10
which I have appointed for r.,		124:36
seek to find safety and r. out		124:109

REFUSE
that he may know to r. the evil	2Ne	17:15
child shall know to r. the evil		17:16
darkened and r. to give his light	He	14:20
r. from this time forth to be	Mrm	3:11
the stars shall r. their shining,	DC	34: 9
and shall r. to give light;		88:87
Abraham, however, did not r.,		132:36
I will r. to be comforted; but	Mses	7:44

REFUSED
having r. the kingdom which	Al	17: 6
again r. to take their arms,		27: 3
had r. Alma to take possession		50:38
and they r. to take up arms,		51:13
And Ammoron r. mine epistle,		57: 3
wife of youth, when thou wast r.,	3Ne	22: 6
I utterly r. to go up against	Mrm	3:16
he r. and would not be their	Eth	6:25
whoso r. to labor he did cause		10: 6
and r. to be comforted.		15: 3
utterly r. to hearken to my voice;	Abr	1: 5

REFUSETH
as this people r. the waters of	2Ne	18: 6

REGAINED
of the land which we had r.	Al	58: 3
of our country which he has r.,		60:24
having r. many of the Nephites		62:30
yea, they r. many cities which	He	4: 9
r. the one-half of their property		4:16

REGAINING
so miraculously prospered in r.	Al	59: 3
succeeded in r. even the half	He	4:10

REGARD
they r. not the work of the Lord,	2Ne	15:12
which shall not r. silver and gold,		23:17
fear not God, nor r. man,	DC	101:84
a r. and reverence are shown to		134: 7

REGARDED
not God, neither r. man.	DC	101:82

REGION
all the r. round about Sidom,	Al	15:14
in all the r. round about,		16:15
and in that r. round about,	DC	30:10
up my church in every r.—		42: 8
in the r. and shadow of death.		57:10
this whole r. of country,		58:52
the r. round about the land		101:70
stay in the r. round,		105:20
as much in one r. as can be,		105:20
the sects in that r. of country.	JS	2: 5

REGIONS
concerning the r. round about;	2Ne	25: 6
Middoni unto the r. round about.	Al	21:13
who were in all the r. round about,		22:27
and in all the r. round about,	He	3:31
throughout all the r. round about		5:50
and in the r. round about.	DC	30: 4
forth into the r. westward;		42: 8
forth into the r. round about,		44: 3
time in those r. round about,		48: 3
in the r. round about them;		52:39
journey into the r. westward,		54: 8
in all the r. round about,		57: 6
gospel in the r. round about;		58:46
in those r. round about where		66: 5
world in the r. round about,		71: 2
churches in the r. round about,		73: 1
to preach in the r. round about		73: 4
down to the r. of darkness.		77: 8
in the r. round about;		100: 3
opened in the r. round about		100: 3
who dwell in the r. round about		105:23
the land of Freedom and the r.		106: 1
Tarry in this place, and in the r.		111: 7
for stakes in the r. round about,		115:18
go forth unto the r. round about.		133: 9
from the r. which are not known,		133:46

REGULAR
which move in their r. form	Al	30:44
a r. list of all the names of	DC	20:82
that they are r. members and		20:84
write and keep a r. history,		47: 1

REGULARLY
it being r. organized and	DC	20: 1
a r. organized branch of the		20:65
has been r. ordained by the		42:11
their r. appointed successors		102: 6
of Christ is r. organized,		102:12

REGULATE
r. all the affairs of the church;	Mos	26:37
r. all the affairs of the same	DC	107:33

REGULATING
r. and establishing the affairs of	DC	78: 3
r. all the affairs of the same		107:34
r. our interests as individuals		134: 6

REGULATION
a r. should be made throughout	Al	45:21
that a r. should be made again		62:44

REGULATIONS
when Alma had made these r. he	Al	6: 7
making r. to prepare for war		51:22
r. were made concerning the law.		62:47
the r. of the government were	3Ne	7: 6
according to the rules and r. of	DC	134:10

RE-HEARING
and the case shall have a r.	DC	102:20
And if, after a careful r.,		102:21
have a r., which case shall		102:27
is justly entitled to a r.,		102:33

REHEARSE
I did r. unto them the words	1Ne	15:20
and r. unto them all that had	Mos	8: 2
Now I need not r. the matter;	Al	13:20
Now I need not r. unto you		56: 4
r. or repeat over again to me	JS	2:46

REHEARSED
he also r. unto them the last	Mos	8: 3
they r. unto his father all that		27:20
and r. and laid before him the	Al	18:36
And he also r. unto them		18:37
he also r. unto them concerning		18:38
Lamoni r. unto him whither he		20:11

REHEARSED

when Lamoni had r. unto him all	Al	20:13
they r. unto me the words of		56:48
r. the whole matter to him.	JS	2:50

REIGN
HIS R. AND MINISTRY

HIS R. AND MINISTRY	1Ne	1:hd
the r. of Zedekiah, king of Judah,		1: 4
the r. of Zedekiah, king of Judah;		5:12
of the r. of Zedekiah;		5:13
account of the r. of the kings,		9: 4
the more part of the r. of kings		9: 4
and my r. and ministry;		10: 1
and the Holy One of Israel must r.		22:24
to hell, that he may r. over you	2Ne	2:29
And whoso should r. in his stead	Jac	1:11
under the r. of the second king,		1:15
to the r. of this king Behjamin,	WM	1: 3
to the r. of this king Benjamin,		1: 3
and he did r. over his people in		1:17
began to r. in his father's stead.	Mos	6: 4
began to r. in the thirtieth year		6: 4
of my r. in the land of Nephi,		9:14
his son began to r. in his stead.		10: 6
Noah began to r. in his stead;		11: 1
And now in the r. of Mosiah		26: 5
under the r. of king Mosiah,		27:35
commenced the r. of the judges		29:44
the thirty and third year of his r.,		29:46
thus ended the r. of the kings		29:47
An account of the r. of the Judges,	Al	1:hd
first year of the r. of the judges		1: 1
leaving none to r. in his stead;		1: 1
the first year of the r. of Alma		1: 2
second year of the r. of Alma,		1:23
fifth year of the r. of the judges.		1:33
of the fifth year of their r.		2: 1
fifth year of the r. of the judges.		3:25
fifth year of the r. of the judges.		3:27
sixth year of the r. of the judges		4: 1
year of the r. of the judges,		4: 5
year of the r. of the judges		4: 5
year of the r. of the judges,		4: 6
year of the r. of the judges,		4: 9
year of the r. of the judges;		4:10
year of the r. of the judges		4:20
to another, to r. in my stead;		7: 2
ninth year of the r. of the judges		8: 2
tenth year of the r. of the judges		8: 3
tenth year of the r. of the judges.		10: 6
until the r. of the judges,		11: 4
and he did r. under his father.		13:18
tenth year of the r. of the judges		14:23
tenth year of the r. of the judges		15:19
year of the r. of the judges		16: 1
year of the r. of the judges		16:12
year of the r. of the judges		16:21
people who were under his r.,		21:20
that he might r. over the people		21:21
under the r. of king Lamoni.		21:22
of the r. of the judges over the		28: 7
of the r. of the judges is ended.		28: 9
of the r. of the judges over the		30: 2
of the r. of the judges over the		30: 4
year of the r. of the judges,		30: 5
of the r. of the judges until now,		30:32
of the r. of the judges over the		35:12
year of the r. of the judges;		35:13
year of the r. of the judges.		43: 3
year of the r. of the judges over		44:24
year of the r. of the judges over		45: 2
year of the r. of the judges over		45:20
year of the r. of the judges.		46:37
from the r. of Nephi down to		47:35
year of the r. of the judges,		48: 2
also to r. over all the land,		48: 2
year of the r. of the judges over		49:29
year of the r. of the judges,		50: 1
year of the r. of the judges over		50:17
year of the r. of the judges.		50:23
year of the r. of the judges,		50:24
year of the r. of the judges,		50:25
year of the r. of the judges over		50:35

REIGN

commence his r. in the end of	Al	50:40
year of the r. of the judges over		51: 1
year of the r. of the judges;		51:12
year of the r. of the judges over		51:37
year of the r. of the judges over		52: 1
appointed to r. in his stead.		52: 3
year of the r. of the judges over		52:14
year of the r. of the judges,		52:15
year of the r. of the judges over		52:18
year of the r. of the judges over		53:23
year of the r. of the judges over		55:35
year of the r. of the judges,		56: 1
year of the r. of the judges.		57: 5
year of the r. of the judges over		59: 1
year of the r. of the judges over		62:11
year of the r. of the judges over		62:12
year of the r. of the judges over		62:39
year of the r. of the judges over		62:52
year of the r. of the judges over		63: 1
year of the r. of the judges.		63: 3
year of the r. of the judges,		63: 4
year of the r. of the judges,		63:10
year of the r. of the judges over		63:16
year of the r. of the judges over	He	1: 1
to r. in the stead of his brother		1:13
year of the r. of the judges;		1:13
year of the r. of the judges,		1:14
year of the r. of the judges.		1:34
year of the r. of the judges,		2: 1
year of the r. of the judges over		2:12
year of the r. of the judges		3: 1
year of the r. of the judges		3:18
year of the r. of the judges over		3:22
year of the r. of the judges,		3:23
year of the r. of the judges.		3:32
year of the r. of the judges,		3:33
year of the r. of the judges,		3:37
Nephi began to r. in his stead.		3:37
year of the r. of the judges,		4: 4
year of the r. of the judges		4: 5
years of the r. of the judges.		4: 8
year of the r. of the judges		4: 9
year of the r. of the judges		4:10
year of the r. of the judges,		4:17
year of the r. of the judges		4:18
year of the r. of the judges		6: 1
year of the r. of the judges,		6:15
year of the r. of the judges over		6:32
year of the r. of the judges over		6:41
year of the r. of the judges over		7: 1
year of the r. of the judges over		10:19
year of the r. of the judges		11: 1
year of the r. of the judges over		11:24
year of the r. of the judges over		11:29
year of the r. of the judges.		11:35
should rule and r. over them;		12: 6
year of the r. of the judges over		16: 9
year of the r. of the judges,		16:10
year of the r. of the judges.		16:11
year of the r. of the judges.		16:12
year of the r. of the judges,		16:13
year of the r. of the judges over		16:24
of the r. of Zedekiah,	3Ne	1:hd
And he began to r., and the	Eth	6:28
to r. in the stead of his father.		7:10
who were under the r. of Shule		7:19
And also in the r. of Shule		7:23
to be king to r. in his stead.		9:14
that Emer did r. in his stead,		9:15
under the r. of Emer;		9:16
Coriantum to r. in his stead.		9:21
Coriantum to r. in his stead		9:22
and he did r. in his stead.		9:27
exceeding rich under his r.,		10:12
Kim did r. in the stead of		10:13
and he did r. eight years,		10:13
did not r. in righteousness,		10:13
he did r. over the people all		11:10
that Moron did r. in his stead;		11:14
and shall r. in their midst,	DC	1:36
to the r. of king Benjamin,		10:41
to r. with almighty power		20:24

REIGN 795 REJOICE

for abominations shall not r. DC 29:21
Which causeth silence to r., 38:12
and shall r. with me on earth. 43:29
only r. for a little season, 43:31
and will r. till he descends 49: 6
reigns whose right it is to r., 58:22
r. with the devil and his angels 76:44
of heaven to r. on the earth 76:63
power to r. forever and ever. 76:108
come and r. with my people. 84:119
even Satan, sitteth to r.— 86: 3
and shall r. over all flesh. 133:25
days of the first patriarchal r., Abr 1:26
even in the r. of Adam, and 1:26
r. personally upon the earth; AoF 10

REIGNED
who have r. in righteousness Mos 29:22
that Kib r. in his stead; Eth 7: 3
and Omer r. in his stead. 8: 1
and Akish r. in his stead. 9: 6
and Com r. in his stead; 9:25
he r. forty and nine years, 9:25
and Riplakish r. in his stead. 10: 4
when he had r. for the space of 10: 8
and Kish r. in his stead. 10:17
and Lib r. in his stead. 10:18
Hearthrom r. in the stead of his 10:30
when Hearthom had r. twenty 10:30
he r. over the half of the 10:32
and Shiblom r. in his stead. 11: 4
darkness r. upon the face of the Abr 4: 2

REIGNETH
and the Holy One of Israel r. 1Ne 22:26
his son, r. in his stead. Om 1:23
the Lord Omnipotent who r., Mos 3: 5
that saith unto Zion, Thy God r.; 12:21
and said unto Zion: Thy God r.! 15:14
shall be broken, and the Son r., 15:20
unto the people that the Lord r. 27:37
unto Zion: Thy God r.! 3Ne 20:40
and now r. in the heavens, DC 49: 6
dominions, and darkness r.; 82: 5
Behold, thy God r.! 128:19

REIGNS
according to the r. of the kings. Jac 1: 9
according to the r. of the kings; 1:11
according to the r. of the kings. 1:14
and the r. of their kings. 3:13
in the days of the r. of Omer Eth 8: 4
until he r. whose right it is DC 58:22
r. upon his throne forever 76:92

REINS
faithfulness the girdle of his r. 2Ne 21: 5
faithfulness the girdle of his r. 30:11

REJECT
will r. the Holy One of Israel, 2Ne 1:10
they will r. him, because of 25:12
they will r. the stone upon which Jac 4:15
Behold, will ye r. these words? 6: 8
ye r. the words of the prophets; 6: 8
and will ye r. all the words 6: 8
others would r. the Spirit of God Al 13: 4
they did r. the word of God He 6: 2
And they did r. all his words, 7: 3
r. the fulness of my gospel, 3Ne 16:10
they did r. all the words of Eth 11:22
unto you, if they r. my words, DC 6:29
But if they r. not my words, 6:31
hearts in unbelief, and r. it, 20:15
caused him to r. the word. 40: 2
if they do r. these things. 84:114
For if they do r. these things 84:115
r. my servants and my testimony 124: 8
for no one can r. this covenant 132: 4
he may not r. his words. Mses 5:16

REJECTED
have r. the words of the prophets. 1Ne 3:18

behold, they have r. the prophets, 1Ne 7:14
that he shall be r. of the Jews, 15:17
wicked are r. from the righteous, 15:36
people had r. every word of God, 17:35
Messiah, who was r. by them; 2Ne 25:18
he who should be r. of the Jews. 25:18
and ye have r. the prophets; 27: 5
for they have r. them, 27:20
having r. the sure foundation, Jac 4:17
He is despised and r. of men; Mos 14: 3
I r. my Redeemer, and denied 27:30
the same were r., and their Al 6: 3
he being r. by those who were 15:16
r. their rights to the kingdom 17:hd
as ye have r. these things, 54: 8
of that God whom you have r. 54: 9
God whom ye say we have r., 54:21
for ye have r. all these things, He 8:24
Behold, ye have r. the truth, 8:25
they who r. the gospel were 4Ne 1:38
could ye have r. that Jesus, Mrm 6:17
have r. the gospel of Christ; Eth 4: 3
prophets were r. by the people, 11: 2
they r. all the words of Ether; 13: 2
thou hast r. me many times DC 39: 9
shall be r. of my Father 99: 4
ye shall be r. as a church, 124:32
cannot be r. by any court 135: 7
Thy brethren have r. you 136:34
for he r. the greater counsel Mses 5:25

REJECTETH
unto him that r. the word of God! 2Ne 27:14
village or city that r. you, DC 84:94
village or city that r. you, 84:95
And whoso r. you shall be 99: 4

REJECTING
r. signs and wonders, 1Ne 19:13
after r. so great a knowledge, Mro 8:29

REJOICE
for his soul did r., 1Ne 1:15
in the which things I do r.; 5: 5
they did r. exceedingly, 5: 9
I have reason to r. in the Lord 8: 3
at that day will they do r. 15:15
that they did r. over me, 17:19
And when I desire to r., 2Ne 4:19
R., O my heart, and give place 4:28
R., O my heart, and cry unto 4:30
my soul will r. in thee, my God, 4:30
you these things that ye may r., 9: 3
Let your hearts r. 9:52
may lift up their hearts and r. 11: 8
r. in Rezin and Remaliah's son; 18: 6
as men r. when they divide 19: 3
them that r. in my highness. 23: 3
Yea, the fir-trees r. at thee, 24: 8
R. not thou, whole Palestina, 24:29
we talk of Christ, we r. in Christ, 25:26
and the poor among men shall r. 27:30
And then shall they r.; 30: 6
my heart would r. exceedingly Jac 2:22
Now in this thing we do r.; 4: 3
perhaps, that I may r. exceedingly 5:60
And I r. in the day when En 1:27
Zarahemla did r. exceedingly, Om 1:14
that they might r. and be filled Mos 2: 4
has caused that ye should r., 2:20
unto thee that thou mayest r.; 3: 4
and r. with exceeding great joy, 3:13
if ye do this ye shall always r., 4:12
whereby we do r. with such 5: 4
And now, I will r.; 7:14
that my people shall r. also. 7:14
lift up your heads, and r., 7:19
yea, and Ammon also did r. 21:28
also be brought to r. in the Lord 28: 2
in the which they did r. 28:18
might lift up their heads and r.; Al 1: 4
and my soul doth exceedingly r., 7:26
therefore, lift up thy head and r., 8:15

REJOICE 796 RELIEF

REJOICE		
for thou hast great cause to r.;	Al	8:15
be sooner or later, in it I will r.		13:25
Alma did r. exceedingly to see		17: 2
began to r. because of his life.		20:25
And he did r. over them,		21:21
his heart began to r., and he said:		22: 8
brethren did r. exceedingly,		25:17
how great reason have we to r.;		26: 1
Behold, thousands of them do r.,		26: 4
with joy, and I will r. in my God.		26:11
have we not great reason to r.?		26:13
yea, we will r., for our joy is		26:16
Now have we not reason to r.?		26:35
had so great reason to r. as we,		26:35
yet they r. and exult in the hope,		28:12
and to r. in Jesus Christ their		37: 9
should r. over the blood of		48:25
to r. exceedingly at this request,		54: 2
Antipus did r. exceedingly;		56:10
he was, that they might r. also.		59: 2
r. in the greatness of your heart.		61: 9
may r. in the great privilege of		61:14
and did r. one with another,	He	6: 3
filled with gladness and did r.		8:17
people did r. and glorify God,		11:18
began to r. over their brethren,	3Ne	1: 6
And they did r. and cry again		4:30
devil laugheth, and his angels r.,		9: 2
my heart did begin to r.	Mrm	2:12
and did r. and glory in his day;	Eth	9:22
I r. exceedingly that your Lord	Mro	8: 2
lift up thy heart and r.,	DC	25:13
lift up your hearts and r.,		27:15
Lift up your heart and r.,		31: 3
and Zion shall r. upon the hills		35:24
that it may r. upon the hills		39:13
Lift up your hearts and r.,		42:69
and r. upon the mountains,		49:25
both are edified and r. together.		50:22
let him r. that he is		50:34
r. upon the land of Missouri,		52:42
man, and the poor shall r.;		56:19
and they r. over you,		62: 3
hold a meeting and r. together,		62: 4
be preserved and r. together		62: 6
and r. ye inhabitants thereof,		76: 1
and the angels r. over you;		88: 2
and the angels r. over them.		90:34
let Zion r., for this is Zion—		97:21
therefore, let Zion r., while		97:21
yea, r. evermore, and in		98: 1
journey and let your hearts r.;		100:12
and r. before thee.		109:67
lift up your heads and r.		110: 5
Let the hearts of your brethren r.,		110: 6
the hearts of all my people r.,		110: 6
tens of thousands shall greatly r.		110: 9
servants will r. in thy name		121: 6
Let his family r. and turn		124:76
Let all the saints r.,		127: 3
Let your hearts r.,		128:22
and make her heart to r.		132:56

REJOICED		
we were exceedingly r. when	1Ne	17: 6
and have r. in it above that of	En	1:26
the king r. exceedingly,	Mos	8:19
and his father r., for he knew		27:20
they were exceedingly r. because		29:39
of Nephi were exceedingly r.,	Al	45: 1
they r. in each other's safety;		53: 2
r. because of the welfare, yea,		59: 1
r. in his day which is to come.	He	8:22
and laughed, and his angels r.	Mses	7:26
and his soul r., saying:		7:47
r. in the God of our salvation.	JS	2:73

REJOICES		
he r. not in that which is	DC	88:33
neither r. in him who is		88:33

REJOICETH		
he that r., shall descend into	2Ne	15:14

yea, and even the Father r.,	3Ne	27:30
and r. not in iniquity but	Mro	7:45
in iniquity but r. in the truth,		7:45
shalt meet him who r.	DC	133:44

REJOICING		
was great r. among the people	Om	1:14
they returned r. in their spoil.	Mos	11:18
came forth out of the water r.,		18:16
returned to the land of Nephi, r.,		19:24
of sorrow, and also of r.—	Al	28:14
no Christ, to interrupt their r.?		30:22
peace and r. in the church.		46:38
they went out of the world r.		46:39
much r. among the brethren		51: 7
r. in the land of Zarahemla,	He	3:31
of the land was filled with r.;		11:18
loud voice, with a sound of r.,	DC	19:37
canst thou read this without r.		19:39
his days of r. are come unto		21: 8
my gospel with the sound of		28:16
my gospel with the sound of r.,		29: 4
neither with boasting nor r.,		50:33
faithful with joy and with r.		52:43
otherwords, r. and prayer.		59:14
and go on your way r.		84:105
and spare not, with joy and r.,		124:101

REJOICINGS		
and great were their r.	Mos	23:24
r. in the joy of our brethren?	Al	30:34
their great r. which they had		46: 7

RELATE		
to r. that tale to their wives	Mos	9: 2
rebellions did he r. unto them;	Al	18:38
nevertheless, it is strange to r.,		47:36
r. a thousandth part of them,	JS	2:61

RELATED		
And they r. unto them all that	Al	15: 2
also r. unto them his conversion,		27:25
r. the account of the vision	JS	2:24
again r. the very same things		2:45
Having r. these things, he		2:45
He then again r. unto me all		2:49
as he r. them to me after		2:63
r. to him the circumstances of		2:66

RELATION		
in r. to the baptism for your dead.	DC	127: 5
give you information in r. to		128: 1
views in r. to this matter,		128: 2
Now, in r. to this matter,		128: 3
very subject in r. to the dead,		128: 6
r. to the salvation of the children		128:11
the earth in r. to your dead,		128:14
principles in r. to the dead		128:15
in r. to the baptism for the dead,		128:16
for their acts in r. to them,		124: 1
in r. to this subject,	Fac	1:12
in r. to the rise and progress	JS	2: 1
in r. both to myself and		2: 1
events in r. to this Church,		2: 1

RELATIONSHIP		
was instituted to form a r. with	DC	128:12

RELATIVE		
r. to him and the characters,	JS	2:63

RELEASE		
king Noah was about to r. him,	Mos	17:11
may r. the brethren of Ammon,	Al	20:15
that I would r. thy brethren,		20:26
R. thyself from bondage.	DC	19:35

RELIED		
have not r. on me for strength	DC	30: 1

RELIEF		
and administer r. to the sick	Jac	2:19
and administering to their r.,	Mos	4:26

RELIEF — 797 — REMAINDER

ye do administer unto our r., Al 60:30
administer to their r. that DC 38:35
and administer to their r., 44: 6
made to the laws, and r. afforded. 134:11

RELIEVED
r. from a great burthen; Al 62:29
r. from all the prisoners of the 62:29

RELIGION
and their rights, and their r. Al 43:47
angry with us because of our r. 44: 2
done unto us because of our r. 44: 3
and unto our faith, and our r.; 44: 4
by our faith, by our r., and 44: 5
In memory of our God, our r., 46:12
their rights, and their r., 46:20
and his country, and his r., 48:13
and the privileges of their r. 51: 6
we will maintain our r. and the 54:10
that r. is instituted of God; DC 134: 4
classed among the martyrs of r.; 135: 6
ambassador for the r. of Jesus 135: 7
on the subject of r. JS 2: 5
for the teachers of r. of the 2:12
with him on the subject of r., 2:21
me among professors of r., 2:22
this, too, by professors of r. 2:75

RELIGIONISTS
contests of these parties of r., JS 2:11

RELIGIOUS
unless their r. opinions prompt DC 134: 4
exercise of their r. belief; 134: 7
such r. opinions do not justify 134: 7
mingle r. influence with civil 134: 9
one r. society is fostered and 134: 9
r. societies have a right to deal 134:10
r. society has authority to try 134:10
to the different r. parties, JS 2: 5
scene of r. feeling, 2: 6
mentioned r. excitement; 2:21
men, both r. and irreligious, 2:27
any of the r. sects of the day, 2:28

RELINQUISHED
they r. their desires for a king, Mos 29:38

RELUCTANCE
notwithstanding their much r. Al 48:22

RELUCTANTLY
compelled r. to contend with Al 48:21

RELY
they should r. on this Redeemer. 1Ne 10: 6
go down and r. upon the mercies Al 27: 9
r. upon the merits of Jesus DC 3:20
you must r. upon my word, 17: 1
you r. upon the things which 18: 3

RELYING
r. wholly upon the merits of him 2Ne 31:19
r. upon the mercies of those Al 24:25
r. upon the spirit of prophecy, 25:16
r. upon the mercies of the world— 26:28
r. alone upon the merits of Mro 6: 4

REMAIN
forever r. in that awful state 1Ne 13:32
it must needs r. as dead, 2Ne 2:11
to r. with the father of lies, 9: 9
and r. in their sins. 9:38
left in Zion and r. in Jerusalem 14: 3
As yet shall he r. at Nob 20:32
we write upon plates must r.; Jac 4: 1
they might r. in their tents Mos 2: 6
that ye r. from day to day; 4:24
in your hearts ye r. guiltless, 4:25
r. in bondage until now. 29:19
filthy shall r. in his filthiness. Al 7:21

for you, if ye r. in your sins, Al 9:15
to r. in their state of ignorance; 9:16
the wicked r. as though there 11:41
Nephite should r. in the land. 19:19
and ye shall r. here until we 27:15
thus they r. in this state, 40:14
should a band of Christians r. 46:13
Pahoran should r. chief judge 51: 6
did still r. in wickedness, He 13: 1
Nephites who did r. in the land. 3Ne 1:28
did still r. in wickedness, 2:10
were desirous to r. Lamanites, 6: 3
in this state they were to r. 28:40
did still r. in wickedness) 4Ne 1:47
peace did r. for the space of Mrm 1:12
But I did r. among them, 1:17
I even r. alone to write 8: 3
them to r. with the people; 8:10
cause you to r. in your awful state Eth 4:15
did r. in captivity all his days; 10:14
daughters who r. in Sherrizah; Mro 9:16
by whom the promises r.; DC 27:10
he shall r. unto them that have 43:14
shall r. until the times of 45:25
should r. for the present time 48: 1
Newel Knight r. with them; 56: 7
These things r. with you to 62: 8
and others r. with you that 63:14
These things r. to overcome 63:66
spare any that r. in Babylon. 64:24
There r. hereafter, in the due 68:14
for their benefit while they r., 70:15
might r. without circumcision; 74: 6
may r. upon their inheritances 83: 3
And they shall r. under this 84:57
r. steadfast in your minds 84:61
all shall know me, who r., 84:98
must needs r. through you 86:10
they who r. shall also be 88:32
they must r. filthy still. 88:35
those who are to r. until that 88:102
end, who shall r. filthy still. 88:102
Rigdon, r. where he now resides 90:21
They that r., and are pure in 101:18
anything r. that is not finished. 115:12
let it r. in your hands, 117: 5
r. for a season in the land of Zion, 118: 2
can rolling waters r. impure? 121:33
priesthood shall r. with thee; 122: 9
and r. with my people, 124:104
not r. after men are dead, 132:13
whatsoever things r. are by me; 132:14
but r. separately and singly, 132:17
for those who are to r. behind 136: 9
r. in the flesh on the earth. Mses 1: 5
commandest that she should r. 4:18
I must either r. in darkness JS 2:13

REMAINDER
write the r. of these things; 1Ne 14:21
the r. shalt thou see. 14:24
write the r. of the things 14:28
and all the r. of our provisions 16:11
unto you the r. of my words. 2Ne 9:54
which r. of my record I shall WM 1: 5
them with the r. of my record, 1: 6
peace all the r. of his days. Mos 1: 1
understand the r. of my words 4: 4
all the r. of our days, 5: 5
the r. of the commandments of 13:11
among the r. of the people. 19: 2
the r. of the people of Limhi 21:11
the r. of them went to the land of 23:38
your king the r. of my days; 29:11
and the r. were called Nephites, Al 2:11
and drove the r. of them out 3:23
upon them by the r. of his people, 4:15
and the r. of them fled out of 21:13
the r., having fled into the east 25: 5
the r. he concealed in the west 43:32
stir up the r. of his soldiers 44:16
spare the r. of their lives, 44:19

the r. of the seed of Joseph	Al 46:24	REMALIAH		
the r. were delivered up into	46:33	the son of R., king of Israel,	2Ne	17: 1
the r. of those dissenters, rather	51:20	and of the son of R.		17: 4
while he marched with the r.	52:26	Syria, Ephraim, and the son of R.,		17: 5
the r. of them, being much	52:36			
leaving the r. to maintain the	56:33	REMALIAH'S		
the r. I took and joined them	56:57	and the head of Samaria is R. son.	2Ne	17: 9
the r. of our army were about to	57:20	and rejoice in Rezin and R. son;		18: 6
the r. of them broke through	57:33			
with the r. of my army,	58:17	REMARKABLE		
the r. of those possessions and	59: 4	of a r. vision of her father—	Al	19:16
the r. of the people of Nephihah	59: 8			
the r. of our possessions in	60:24	REMARKS		
conquer the r. of the land,	61: 8	the case have finished their r.	DC	102:18
leave the r. in the charge of	61:15			
over the r. of his army,	62: 3	REMEMBER		
the r. of them fled into the	62:25	r. the words which I speak	1Ne	7:15
spend the r. of his days in peace.	62:43	Therefore r., O man,		10:20
r. of the forty and ninth year;	He 3:32	Do ye not r. the things		15:11
obtain the r. of their lands,	4:19	r. to keep his commandments		15:25
of God all the r. of his days,	5: 4	slow to r. the Lord your God.		17:45
Lehi also, all the r. of his days;	5: 4	then will he r. the covenants		19:15
that the r. of them did fear.	8:10	then will he r. the isles		19:16
bring the r. of their brethren to	15: 6	that they would r. the Lord		19:18
and the r. of them were slain.	3Ne 4:27	I would that ye would r.;	2Ne	1:12
and the r., yea, even almost	6:27	that ye should r. to observe		1:16
the r. shall ye leave in the	Mrm 1: 4	R. the words of thy dying father.		3:25
And the r. did flee and join	4: 3	inasmuch as they will not r. me,		5:25
all the r. of our people unto	6: 5	r. the awfulness in transgressing		9:39
even all the r. of his days.	Eth 10:30	R., to be carnally minded is		9:39
over the r. of the kingdom.	10:32	R. the greatness of the Holy One		9:40
in all the r. of his days.	11: 3	R. that his paths are righteous.		9:41
all the r. of his days;	11:18	my beloved brethren, r. my words.		9:44
made the r. of this record,	13:14	ye may not r. your awful guilt		9:46
finishing of the r. of the work	DC 10: 3	r. the words which I have spoken		9:51
all the r. of this work does	10:46	r. the words of your God;		9:52
The r. I will show unto you	124:102	let us r. him, and lay aside our		10:20
the r. were reserved in chains	Mses 7:57	r. that ye are free to act for		10:23
together the r. of his elect	JS 1:37	r., after ye are reconciled unto		10:24
		that I may r. my covenants		29: 1
REMAINED		that I may r. the promises		29: 2
and had we r. in Jerusalem	2Ne 1: 4	that I would r. your seed;		29: 2
but he would have r. in the garden	2:22	Do they r. the travels,		29: 4
must have r. in the same state	2:22	and that I r. those who are upon		29: 7
they must have r. forever,	2:22	I r. one nation like unto another;		29: 8
have r. in a state of innocence,	2:23	that I would r. his seed forever.		29:14
must needs have r. to an endless	9: 7	I would that ye should r. that		31: 4
and r. so ever after, even in	Mos 26: 4	Do ye not r. that I said		32: 2
they yet r. a hard-hearted and a	Al 15:15	ye shall r. your own filthiness,	Jac	3: 9
and their lands r. desolate.	16:11	and r. that their filthiness came		3: 9
I r., with the remainder of my	58:17	ye shall r. your children,		3:10
there were some cities which r.;	3Ne 8:15	and also, r. that ye may,		3:10
life and the priesthood have r.,	DC 86:10	do ye not r. to have read the words		5: 1
they r. safe in my hands,	JS 2:60	I would that ye should r. that	Mos	1: 3
		r. that these sayings are true,		1: 6
REMAINETH		r. to search them diligently,		1: 7
and r. and dieth in his sins,	Mos 2:33	O r., remember that these		2:41
r. and dieth an enemy to God,	2:38	r. that these things are true;		2:41
there r. an effectual struggle	7:18	so I would that ye should r.,		4:11
r. in his fallen state	16: 5	And I would that ye should r.,		4:28
But whosoever r., and is not	Al 45:14	now, O man, r., and perish not.		4:30
it r. in me to do according as	DC 29:50	And I would that ye should r. also,		5:11
it r. with me to do with him	40: 3	r. to retain the name written		5:12
it r. with me to do hereafter.	61:28	slow to r. the Lord our God.		9: 3
this there r. condemnation.	63:64	now, ye r. that I said unto you:		13:12
there r. in him the greater sin.	64: 9	R. the sabbath day, to keep it		13:16
church, which r. in this place,	64:26	slow to r. the Lord their God;		13:29
there r. a scourge and	84:58	But r. that he that persists in		16: 5
the field r. to be burned.	86: 7	and r. that only in and through		16:13
whatsoever r., let it remain in	117: 5	For do ye not r. the priests of		20:18
Here is wisdom and it r. in me.	Mses 1:31	But r. the iniquity of king Noah		23: 9
for it r. in the sphere in which	3: 9	should r. the Lord their God		23:27
he that r. steadfast and is	JS 1:11	should r. that it was the Lord that		25:16
		r. the captivity of thy fathers		27:16
REMAINING		r. how great things he has done		27:16
took the r. part of his army	Al 43:25	r. king Noah, his wickedness and		29:18
be even a spark of freedom r.,	60:27	Behold, and r., the Holy One	Al	5:52
the people r. in their pride and	He 16:10	same what r. that I say unto him,		7:16
But should the r. councilors,	DC 102:20	will r. that I have said unto him,		7:16
		Do ye not r. that our father,		9: 9
REMAINS		Do ye not r. that they were all		9: 9
long as any of our posterity r.	Mos 29:32	do ye not r. the words which		9:13

REMEMBER

Now I would that ye should r.,	Al 9:14
should r. these things against him.	10:30
See that ye r. these things;	11:35
I would that ye should r. that	12: 5
I would that ye should r. that	13: 1
doth r. all my commandments	18:10
Now do ye r., my brethren, that	26:23
r. that this was their language.	26:24
then do I r. what the Lord has	29:10
then do I r. his merciful arm	29:10
and I also r. the captivity of	29:11
and I would that ye should r.,	32:22
Do ye r. to have read what	33: 3
if ye do not r. to be charitable,	34:29
that ye should r. these things,	34:37
I did r. all my sins and iniquities,	36:13
I could r. my pains no more;	36:19
O r., remember, my son Helaman,	37:13
O remember, r., my son Helaman,	37:13
And now r., my son, that God	37:14
r. the words which I have	37:32
O, r., my son, and learn wisdom	37:35
I would that ye should r., that	38: 5
and r. my brethren in mercy—	38:14
Oh, r., and take it upon you,	39: 9
And now r., my son, if it were	42:11
r. to keep the commandments	46:23
let us r. the words of Jacob,	46:24
But r., inasmuch as they will	50:20
slow to r. the Lord their God	55:31
I did r. the words which they	57:21
to r. the Lord their God	58:40
ye should r. that God has	60:23
slow to r. the Lord their God;	62:49
they did r. how great things	62:50
to r. the prophecies of Alma,	He 4:21
r. to keep the commandments of	5: 6
that when you r. your names	5: 6
your names ye may r. them;	5: 6
and when ye r. them ye may	5: 6
them ye may r. their works;	5: 6
when ye r. their works ye may	5: 6
O r., remember, my sons	5: 9
remember, r., my sons, the words	5: 9
r. that there is no other way nor	5: 9
r. that he cometh to redeem	5: 9
r. also the words which Amulek	5:10
now, my sons, r., remember that	5:12
r. that it is upon the rock of	5:12
And they did r. his words;	5:14
and they began to r. the Lord	11: 7
began to r. the words of Nephi.	11: 7
pestilence, they will not r. him.	12: 3
slow are they to r. the Lord	12: 5
Ye do not r. the Lord your	13:22
ye do always r. your riches,	13:22
now r., remember, my brethren,	14:30
r., my brethren, that whosoever	14:30
and r. at the time of their coming	16: 5
I would have you to r. also,	3Ne 7:24
R. the words which I have spoken.	13:25
then will I r. my covenant	16:11
but I will r. my covenant	16:12
the Father that ye do always r. me.	18: 7
if ye do always r. me ye	18: 7
Father that ye do always r. me.	18:11
if ye do always r. me ye	18:11
Ye r. that I spake unto you,	20:11
I will r. the covenant which	20:29
shalt not r. the reproach of	22: 4
shalt not r. the reproach of	22: 4
R. ye the law of Moses, my	25: 4
r. the things that I have told	27:12
the Lord will r. his covenant	29: 3
I would that ye should r.	Mrm 1: 3
will the Lord r. the covenant	5:20
the Lord will r. the prayers	5:21
the Lord will not r. his covenant	8:21
he will r. the covenant which	8:23
may God the Father r. the	9:37
r. that my Spirit will not always	Eth 2:15
R., when ye see these things,	4:16
r. how great things the Lord	6:30
Shez did r. the destruction	10: 2
I also r. that thou hast said	Eth 12:32
I r. that thou hast said that	12:33
he began to r. the words which	15: 1
he began to r. the words which	15: 3
thy Son, and always r. him,	Mro 4: 3
that they do always r. him,	5: 2
For I r. the word of God, which	7: 5
r. how merciful the Lord hath	10: 3
r. that every good gift cometh	10:18
r. that he is the same	10:19
exhort you to r. these things;	10:27
R., remember that it is not the	DC 3: 3
r. that it is not the work of God	3: 3
r. also the promises which were	3: 5
But r., God is merciful;	3:10
R. faith, virtue, knowledge,	4: 6
R. it is sacred and cometh from	6:10
Oh, r. these words, and keep	8: 5
R., this is your gift.	8: 5
R. that without faith you can	8:10
you r. it was said in those	10:39
r. the words of him who is the	10:70
R. the worth of souls is great	18:10
and always r. him and keep	20:77
that they do always r. him,	20:79
but r. to sin no more,	29: 3
r. that all my judgments are	29:30
r. that they shall have faith in	33:12
ye shall r. the church articles	33:14
behold, thou wilt r. the poor,	42:30
for r. that he hath no	42:79
would that ye should always r.,	46:10
And r. in all things the poor	52:40
R. this, which I tell you before,	58: 5
the Lord, r. them no more.	58:42
But r. that on this, the Lord's	59:12
R. that that which cometh from	63:64
Zion also shall r. their labors,	68:30
and r. the new covenant,	84:57
R. the great and last promise	88:69
all saints who r. to keep and	89:18
r. the covenant wherewith ye	90:24
day of wrath I will r. mercy.	101: 9
We ask thee, Holy Father, to r.	109:47
R. the kings, the princes,	109:55
O Lord, thy servant, Joseph	109:68
R., O Lord, the presidents,	109:71
R. all thy church, O Lord,	109:72
I r. my servant Oliver Granger;	117:12
r. the Lord their God,	117:16
R. thy suffering saints, O our God;	121: 6
r. that his stewardship will I	124:14
I want you to r. that	128: 6
r. that I forbid it, for in the	Mses 3:17

REMEMBERED

I r. the words of the Lord	1Ne 4:14
they shall be r. again among	15:16
and he r. the covenants which	17:40
to be r. in the covenants of	2Ne 29: 5
Gentiles, have ye r. the Jews,	29: 5
have r. all these things,	Mos 1: 4
that they r. no more among	Al 1:24
I have always r. the captivity	29:12
I r. also to have heard my father	36:17
they r. that which we had	58: 1
For they r. the words which	He 5: 5
O that we had r. the Lord our God	13:33
they r. that it had been	3Ne 11:12
Nephi r. that this thing had	23:12
I r. the things which Ammaron	Mrm 1: 5
because he r. not to call upon	Eth 2:14
the Father hath r. the covenant	4:15
he r. the great things that the	7:27
he r. what the Lord had done	10: 2
might be r. and nourished by	Mro 6: 4
be r. with the first of mine elders,	DC 108: 4
let him be r. for an interest	124:78

REMEMBEREST

Thou r. the twelve apostles	1Ne 12: 9
R. thou the covenants of the Father	14: 8
r. that thy brother hath aught	3Ne 12:23

REMEMBERETH

REMEMBERETH
the Lord r. all them who have	2Ne 10:22
wherefore he r. us also.	10:22
and he r. the heathen;	26:33
for he r. the house of Israel,	Jac 6: 4
he r. every creature of his creating,	Mos 27:30
whoso r. these sayings of mine	3Ne 15: 1
the Lord r. his covenant unto	29: 8
who r. thee in thy ways.	DC 133:44

REMEMBERING
unto the r. of my covenant	2Ne 3:21
in r. the captivity of our fathers;	Al 36: 2
r. unto the Father my body	DC 27: 2
r. for what they are given;	46: 8

REMEMBRANCE
to stir them up in the ways of r.	1Ne 2:24
to stir them up in r. of me;	2Ne 5:25
to retain in r. his name.	Jac 1:11
them up in r. of their duty.	Mos 1:17
to a r. of the awful situation of	2:40
retain in r., the greatness of God,	4:11
stir them up in r. of the oath	6: 3
to a r. of the deliverance of	9:17
to keep them in r. of God	13:30
awakened to a r. of their duty.	Al 4: 3
stir them up in r. of their duty,	4:19
retained in r. the captivity of	5: 6
in r. his mercy and long-suffering	5: 6
in r. that he has delivered their	5: 6
having a r. of all your guilt,	5:18
perfect r. of all your wickedness,	5:18
a r. that ye have set at defiance	5:18
stirred up in r. of the words	25: 6
retained in r. their captivity;	36:29
ye also ought to retain in r.,	36:29
stir him up in r. of the Lord	He 11: 4
in r. of the Lord their God.	11:34
shall ye do in r. of my body,	3Ne 18: 7
shall do it in r. of my blood,	18:11
a book of r. was written	24:16
in r. of the body of thy Son,	Mro 4: 3
in r. of the blood of thy Son,	5: 2
in r. of the Lord Jesus.	6: 6
in the r. of the Lord Jesus;	DC 20:75
eat in r. of the body of	20:77
in r. of the blood of thy Son,	20:79
had in r. before the Lord.	68:30
r. before the judge of my people.	68:33
written in the book of r.	85: 9
r. of the everlasting covenant.	88:131
r. of the everlasting covenant,	88:133
had in r. no more before the Lord;	107:80
r. before the common council of	107:82
and had in everlasting r.	109:71
his name shall be had in sacred r.	117:12
name may be had in honorable r.	124:96
to be held in r. from	127: 9
come in r. before the Lord;	133:26
And a book of r. was kept,	Mses 6: 5
For a book of r. we have written	6:46

REMINDED
reader in every nation will be r.	DC 135: 6

REMINDING
continually r. them of death,	En 1:23

REMISSION
may look for a r. of their sins.	2Ne 25:26
then cometh a r. of your sins	31:17
I received a r. of my sins.	En 1: 2
might receive r. of their sins,	Mos 3:13
received a r. of their sins,	4: 3
received a r. of your sins,	4:11
retain a r. of your sins;	4:12
begging for a r. of your sins.	4:20
retaining a r. of your sins	4:26
for a r. of their sins,	15:11
thus retaining a r. of their sins;	Al 4:14
forward for the r. of your sins,	7: 6
unto a r. of his sins;	12:34

REMNANT

to him for a r. of their sins,	Al 13:16
that ye see a r. of your sins.	30:16
did I receive a r. of my sins.	38: 8
ye may have a r. of them	He 14:13
there was a great r. of sins.	3Ne 1:23
repentance and r. of sins	7:16
them repentance and r. of sins.	7:23
and received a r. of their sins.	7:25
shall receive a r. of their sins.	12: 2
may receive a r. of your sins,	30: 2
r. of sins through Jesus Christ,	Mro 3: 3
unto the r. of sins.	8:11
bringeth r. of sins;	8:25
r. of sins bringeth meekness,	8:26
unto the r. of your sins,	10:33
immersion for the r. of sins;	DC 13: 1
and r. of sins by baptism,	19:31
had received a r. of his sins,	20: 5
unto the r. of their sins,	20:37
come unto the r. of his sins,	21: 8
for the r. of sins unto the	21: 9
was shed for the r. of your sins.	27: 2
for a r. of your sins;	33:11
for the r. of sins;	49:13
and repentance and r. of sins,	53: 3
shall have a r. of your sins	55: 1
repentance and r. of sins	55: 2
for the r. of their sins	68:27
baptism, and the r. of sins,	84:27
by water for the r. of sins,	84:64
for the r. of their sins,	84:74
repentance for the r. of sins,	107:20
baptism for the r. of sins,	JS 2:68
immersion for the r. of sins;	2:69
immersion for the r. of sins;	AoF 4

REMIT
whosesoever sins you r. on earth	DC 132:46

REMITTED
be r. eternally in the heavens;	DC 132:46

REMNANT
a r. of the house of Israel	T Pg
the r. of the House of Israel	T Pg
the r. of the house of Israel	1Ne 13:33
the r. of the house of Israel—	13:34
and this r. of whom I speak	13:34
the r. of the seed of my brethren,	13:38
the r. of the seed of my brethren.	13:38
the r. of the seed of my brethren,	13:39
Gentiles unto the r. of our seed—	15:13
shall the r. of our seed know	15:14
a r. of the house of Israel,	19:24
the r. of Israel, and such as are	2Ne 20:20
The r. shall return,	20:21
yea, even the r. of Jacob,	20:21
yet a r. of them shall return,	20:22
to recover the r. of his people	21:11
highway for the r. of his people	21:16
the r. of those that are slain,	24:19
the name, and r., and son,	24:22
and he shall slay thy r.	24:30
a r. of the house of Israel.	28: 2
forth unto the r. of our seed.	30: 3
then shall the r. of our seed know	30: 4
knowledge of a r. of the people	Mos 8:12
follow the r. of the Amlicites,	Al 2:21
the r. of the children of Amulon	25: 7
we are a r. of the seed of Jacob;	46:23
are a r. of the seed of Joseph,	46:23
our liberty as a r. of Joseph;	46:24
the r. of the coat of Joseph	46:24
as this r. of garment of my son	46:24
so shall a r. of the seed of	46:24
even as the r. of his garment.	46:24
the r. of the seed of Joseph,	46:27
a r. of the seed of Joseph to	3Ne 5:23
all the r. of the seed of Jacob,	5:24
who are r. of their seed.	10:16
a r. of the seed of Joseph	10:17
we a r. of the seed of Joseph?	10:17
a r. of the house of Joseph.	15:12
the r. of their seed, who shall	16: 4

REMNANT / REPAIR

REMNANT
are a r. of the house of Israel	3Ne 20:10
are a r. of the house of Jacob,	20:16
are a r. of the house of Jacob,	21: 2
them unto a r. of your seed,	21: 4
my people who are a r. of Jacob	21:12
among this the r. of Jacob,	21:22
my people, the r. of Jacob,	21:23
among the r. of this people.	21:26
of the r. of the house of Israel;	29: 8
the r. of the house of Jacob	4Ne 1:49
also unto the r. of this people,	Mrm 3:19
come unto the r. of these people,	5: 9
the r. of the house of Jacob;	5:12
lest a r. of the seed of Jacob	5:24
unto the r. of this people	7: 1
ye r. of the house of Israel;	7: 1
ye are a r. of the seed of Jacob;	7:10
the r. of the seed of Joseph,	Eth 13: 6
a r. of the seed of Joseph out	13: 7
the r. of the house of Joseph	13: 8
the r. of the seed of Joseph,	13:10
whom the Lamanites are a r.,	DC 19:27
shall a r. be scattered among	45:24
the r. shall be gathered unto	45:43
which are a r. of Jacob,	52: 2
a r. of his seed should always be	Mses 7:52

REMNANTS
the r. of the house of Israel,	1Ne 10:14
And then shall the r.,	3Ne 20:13
the r. who are left of the land	DC 87: 5
cause that the r. of Jacob,	109:65
all the scattered r. of Israel,	109:67
scattered r. are exhorted to	113:10
r. of Israel in their scattered	113:10

REMORSE
souls filled with guilt and r.,	Al 5:18
or death, joy or r. of conscience.	29: 5
r. of conscience unto man.	42:18

REMOVAL
r. from office for transgression,	DC 102: 8
or r. from the bounds of this	102: 8
after our r. to Manchester	JS 2: 5

REMOVE
earth shall r. out of her place,	2Ne 23:13
to r. the cause of diseases,	Al 46:40
could they r. mountains;	Mrm 8:24
unto the mountain Zerin, R.–	Eth 12:30
and r. you out of your place.	DC 93:49
in Zion, and r. not thy house;	112: 6
let him not r. his family unto	124:108
to r. this people to the place where	136:10

REMOVED
the Lord have r. men far away,	2Ne 16:12
Madmenah is r.;	20:31
but have r. their hearts far	27:25
cloud of darkness may be r.	He 5:40
the cloud of darkness shall be r.	5:41
shall depart and the hills be r.	3Ne 22:10
covenant of my people be r.,	22:10
and it was r.	Eth 12:30
should be r. from among you;	Mro 8: 6
not be r. out of her place.	DC 90:37
or be r. out of their place.	93:48
shall be r. out of their place.	93:50
shall be r. out of his place,	104:77
r. from thence unto a mountain	Abr 2:20
Having r. the earth, I obtained	JS 2:52

REMOVING
a captive, and r. to and fro?	1Ne 21:21
All members r. from the	DC 20:84

REMUNERATION
a just r. for all their services,	DC 42:72
a just r. for all his services	42:73

REND
the rocks of the earth must r.;	1Ne 19:12

the Lord should r. them even	Al 46:21
smite and r. and turn their backs	He 6:39
and the rocks did cease to r.,	3Ne 10: 9
and turn again and r. you.	14: 6
ye shall r. that veil of unbelief	Eth 4:15
they did r. the air exceedingly.	15:16
did r. the air with their cries,	15:17
I will r. their kingdoms;	DC 84:118
that thou wouldst r. the heavens,	133:40

RENDER
if you should r. all the thanks	Mos 2:20
to r. to him all that you have	2:34
to r. to every man according to	4:13
r. unto Caesar the things which	DC 63:26
r. an account of his stewardship,	72: 3
shall r. an account of their	72: 5
r. himself and his accounts	72:19
may r. themselves approved	72:22
when circumstances r. it	107:28
as to r. me entirely unable.	JS 2:48

RENDERED
if ye had r. unto our armies	Al 60: 5
r. desolate and without timber,	He 3: 5
glory be r. to his holy name,	DC 20:36
have r. a plainer translation	128:18

RENDERETH
r. every man acceptable,	DC 72:17

RENDING
r. their garments in token, or as	Al 46:21

RENEWED
these cities could not be r.	4Ne 1: 9
the covenant which he has r.	DC 84:48
that the earth will be r. and	AoF 10

RENEWING
unto the r. of their bodies.	DC 84:33

RENOUNCE
r. war and proclaim peace,	DC 98:16

RENOWN
have set to be as plants of r.,	DC 124:61
men of old, men of great r.	Mses 8:21

RENOWNED
of evildoers shall never be r.	2Ne 24:20

RENT
earth and the rocks, that they r.;	1Ne 12: 4
my soul is r. with anguish because	17:47
and instead of a girdle, a r.;	2Ne 13:24
walls of the prison were r.	Al 14:27
that he r. his coat; and he took	46:12
on the end thereof his r. coat,	46:13
waving the r. part of his garment	46:19
he had written upon the r. part,	46:19
as they had r. their garments.	46:21
whose coat was r. by his brethren	46:23
shall be r. by our brethren,	46:23
this temple it shall be r. in twain,	He 10: 8
Yea, they shall be r. in twain,	14:22
the rocks were r. in twain;	3Ne 8:18
them, for they were r. in twain.	28:19
the prisons were r. in twain,	4Ne 1:30
And my soul was r. with anguish,	Mrm 6:16
of darkness shall soon be r.,	DC 38: 8
the veil shall be r. and you shall	67:10
a loud voice, and r. upon the earth,	Mses 1:19
groaned; and the rocks were r.;	7:56

RENTED
let them be left or r. as	DC 38:37

REPAIR
and to r. the walls of the city,	Mos 9: 8
striving to r. all the injuries	27:35
r. unto them the many murders	Al 27: 8
to r. unto them the wrongs which	He 5:17

REPAIRED

REPAIRED
there were many old cities r. — 3Ne 6: 7

REPAY
Vengeance is mine, and I will r.; — Mrm 3:15
is mine also, and I will r. — 8:20
for it is mine and I will r. — DC 82:23
do not r. fourfold for the stock — 124:71
if thou canst not r. then go — 136:25

REPEAT
I heard a voice r. the following: — DC 130:14
rehearse or r. over again to me — JS 2:46

REPENT
unto the people that they must r., — 1Ne 1: 4
if it so be that they r. and come — 10:18
if the Gentiles r. it shall be well — 14: 5
did turn away their anger, and did r. — 16:39
perish save that they should r. — 18:15
if it so be that they will r. — 22:28
they might r. while in the flesh; — 2Ne 2:21
that all men must r.; — 2:21
they shall r. of their iniquities. — 5:22
if it so be that they shall r. — 6:12
they must r., and be baptized — 9:23
if they will not r. and believe in — 9:24
they would r., and know that he — 10: 4
shall r. of their wickedness — 28:17
if they will r. and come unto me; — 28:32
as many of the Gentiles as will r. — 30: 2
as many of the Jews as will not r. — 30: 2
save it be with them that r. — 30: 2
R. ye, repent ye, and be — 31:11
r. ye, and be baptized in the — 31:11
except ye r. the land is cursed — Jac 3: 3
except ye r. they shall possess — 3: 4
unless ye shall r. of your sins — 3: 8
that ye would r., and come — 6: 5
r. ye, and enter in at the strait — 6:11
that ye must r. of your sins — Mos 4:10
the same hath great cause to r.; — 4:18
nor r. of the thing which thou — 4:22
and except they r. I will — 11:20
And except they r. and turn to — 11:21
that except this people r. and — 11:23
except they r. in sackcloth and — 11:25
he did not r. of his evil doings. — 11:29
except they r. I will utterly — 12: 8
come upon thee except thou r., — 12:12
and they were commanded to r. — 16:12
and yet they would not r. — 16:12
tremble and r. of your sins, — 16:13
do not r. of their iniquities; — 26:11
as my people r. will I forgive — 26:30
whosoever will not r. of his sins — 26:32
sins and r. of their iniquity, — 26:36
except they r. of their wickedness — Al 3:14
he must r. or he cannot be saved! — 5:31
r., repent, for the Lord God — 5:32
r., for the Lord God hath — 5:32
R., and I will receive you. — 5:33
they must r. and be born again. — 5:49
R., all ye ends of the earth, — 5:50
R., for except ye repent ye can in — 5:51
except ye r. ye can in nowise — 5:51
except they speedily r. — 5:56
did not r. of their wickedness — 6: 3
R. ye, and prepare the way of the — 7: 9
I say unto you that ye must r., — 7:14
ye are willing to r. of your sins — 7:15
except they r. the Lord God will — 8:16
R. ye, for thus saith the Lord, — 8:29
except ye r. I will visit this people — 8:29
that he commandeth you to r.; — 9:12
except ye r., ye can in nowise — 9:12
he has commanded you to r., or — 9:12
this life than for you, except ye r. — 9:15
and if ye r. not they shall come — 9:18
R. ye, for the kingdom of heaven — 9:25
R. ye, repent, for the kingdom of — 10:20
r., for the kingdom of heaven is at — 10:20

802

REPENT

time is soon at hand except ye r. — Al 10:23
unto man in which he might r.; — 12:24
If ye will r., and harden not your — 12:33
let us r., and harden not our — 12:37
to r. and work righteousness — 13:10
And behold, they did r.; — 13:18
Now is the time to r., for the — 13:21
to r., and to search the scriptures. — 14: 1
will r. and believe on his name. — 19:36
except we r. we shall perish. — 21: 6
thou that we have cause to r.? — 21: 6
If ye will r. ye shall be saved, — 22: 6
and if ye will not r., ye shall be — 22: 6
yea, if thou wilt r. of all thy sins, — 22:16
Lamanites in which they did r. — 23:15
that we might r. of these things, — 24:10
to r. of all our sins and — 24:11
to r. sufficiently before God — 24:11
will r. and believe on his name. — 26:35
r. and come unto our God, — 29: 2
that they must speedily r., — 30:57
r. and harden not your hearts, — 34:31
to that awful crisis, that I will r., — 34:34
if they did not r. they should — 37:22
except they r. I will destroy — 37:25
we see that they did not r.; — 37:26
they r. before they are fully ripe. — 37:31
except ye r. they will stand as — 39: 8
ye should r. and forsake your sins, — 39: 9
a time granted unto man to r., — 42: 4
a time to r. and serve God. — 42: 4
how could a man r. except he — 42:17
except ye r. and withdraw your — 54: 6
except ye r. and withdraw your — 54: 7
except ye do r. of that which — 60:24
not r. of their sins and iniquities, — 60:33
except they r. the Lord hath — 61:20
cause them to r. of their sins — 62:45
if they did not r. of their sins. — He 4:14
they did r., and inasmuch as — 4:15
inasmuch as they did r. they did — 4:15
Moronihah saw that they did r. — 4:16
R. ye, repent ye, and seek — 5:29
r. ye, and seek no more to — 5:29
R. ye, repent ye, for the kingdom — 5:32
r. ye, for the kingdom of heaven — 5:32
You must r., and cry unto the — 5:41
destruction except they r. of — 7:hd
they r. and turn unto him. — 7:hd
O r. ye, repent ye! — 7:17
O repent ye, r. ye! — 7:17
except ye will r., behold, — 7:19
unto you except ye shall r. — 7:22
For if ye will not r., behold, — 7:22
unto those who r. of their sins, — 7:23
than for you except ye shall r. — 7:23
destroyed except thou shalt r. — 7:24
except ye r. ye shall perish; — 7:28
surely shall come to pass except we r.; — 8: 7
shall come upon you except ye r.? — 8:12
except ye r. it will come unto — 8:26
await you, except ye shall r. — 9:22
Except ye r. ye shall be smitten, — 10:11
destruction if they did not r. — 10:12
Except ye r., thus saith the Lord, — 10:14
perhaps they will r. and turn — 11: 4
If this people r. I will spare them. — 11:14
blessed are they who will r. — 12:23
except they r. I will take away — 13: 8
this shall surely come except ye r., — 13:10
But if ye will r. and return unto — 13:11
blessed are they who will r. and — 13:11
But blessed are they who will r., — 13:13
that ye would r. and be saved. — 13:39
r. and prepare the way of the — 14: 9
ye will r. of all your sins, — 14:13
Therefore r. ye, repent ye, — 14:19
r. ye, lest by knowing these — 14:19
except ye shall r. your houses — 15: 1
except ye r., your women shall — 15: 2
of Nephi except they shall r., — 15: 3
them than for you except ye r. — 15:14

REPENT

If they will not r., and observe	He 15:17		R. ye, repent ye, for the	DC 42: 7
except ye r. of all your	3Ne 3:15		r. ye, for the kingdom of	42: 7
that they did r. of all their sins;	3:25		he that stealeth and will not r.	42:20
many as would r. of their sins	5: 4		he that lieth and will not r.	42:21
whole earth except they shall r.;	9: 2		they shall r. of all their sins or	42:77
unto me, and r. of your sins,	9:13		Call upon the nations to r.,	43:20
therefore r., and come unto	9:22		voice and call upon you to r.,	43:21
if ye will r. and return unto	10: 6		R., and prepare for the great	43:21
to r. and believe in me.	11:32		R. ye, for the great day of the	43:22
I say unto you, ye must r.,	11:37		call upon the inhabitants to r.,	45:64
ye must r., and be baptized in	11:38		and inasmuch as they do r.,	45:64
that shall r. of your sins,	12:19		before me and must needs r.	49: 2
But if the Gentiles will r. and	16:13		I will that all men shall r.,	49: 8
ye always do to those who r.	18:11		R. and be baptized in the name	49:13
among my people who do r.	18:16		r. of all your sins;	49:26
But if he r. not he shall not	18:31		let him r. and he shall be	50:39
but what they will return and r.,	18:32		let them r. of all their sins,	54: 3
that if the Gentiles do not r.	20:15		Thayre must r. of his pride,	56: 8
except they r. it shall fall upon	20:20		many things to do and to r. of;	56:14
may r. and come unto me	21: 6		But if he r. not of his sins,	58:15
the Gentiles except they r.;	21:14		And let him r. of his sins,	58:39
whosoever will not r. and come	21:20		And also he hath need to r.,	58:41
if they will r. and hearken unto	21:22		and the low, and the poor to r.	58:47
R., all ye ends of the earth,	27:20		inhabitants of the earth will r.	58:48
and r. of your evil doings,	30: 2		such beware and r. speedily,	63:15
and did truly r. of their sins,	4Ne 1: 1		let the church r. of their sins,	63:63
they did not r. of their evil	Mrm 2: 8		and they r. of the evil,	64:17
the Nephites began to r. of	2:10		r., therefore, of those things	66: 3
R. ye, and come unto me,	3: 2		if he r. he shall be forgiven,	68:24
r. and prepare to stand before	3:22		except he r. and mend his	75:29
did r. of the oath which I had	5: 1		until they r. and remember	84:57
except ye shall r. and turn	5:22		r. of their former evil works;	84:76
r. ye, and humble yourselves	5:24		brethren in Zion begin to r.,	90:34
r. of all your sins and iniquities,	7: 5		have many things to r. of.	90:35
Therefore r., and be baptized	7: 8		Your family must needs r.	93:48
that ye may r., and not	Eth 2:11		if they do not r. and	98:21
they shall r. of their iniquity,	4: 6		your enemy if he r. not,	98:27
r. all ye ends of the earth,	4:18		he r. and come unto thee	98:39
And if it so be that they r.	5: 5		and r. not the first time,	98:41
be destroyed if they did not r.	7:23		the second time, and r. not,	98:42
people did r. of their iniquities	7:26		the third time, and r. not,	98:43
thereby ye may r. of your sins,	8:23		until he r. and reward thee	98:44
be destroyed if they did not r.	9:28		But if the children shall r.,	98:47
began to r. of their iniquities	9:34		speedily r. and return unto thee,	109:21
people except they should r.,	11: 1		if they will not r.,	109:29
should r. of their wickedness.	11: 6		that they may r. of their sins	109:50
began to r. of their iniquity;	11: 8		But inasmuch as they will r.,	109:53
and except they should r.	11:20		Let them r. of all their sins,	117: 4
Coriantumr that, if he would r.,	13:20		so long as they r. not,	124:50
He began to r. of the evil	15: 3		as they r. not, and hate me,	124:52
R. all ye ends of the earth,	Mro 7:34		And let him r. of all his folly,	124:116
must r. and be baptized,	8:10		all men everywhere to r.	133:16
shall perish except they r.	8:16		be great unless they speedily r.,	136:35
Little children cannot r.;	8:19		shalt r. and call upon God	Mses 5: 8
no condemnation, cannot r.;	8:22		them that they should r.;	5:14
except they should r.	8:27		put upon thee, except thou r.	5:25
they do not r., and Satan	9: 3		and called upon his sons to r.	6: 1
they r. and return unto him.	9:22		upon all men, everywhere, to r.;	6:23
chastened, that they might r.;	DC 1:27		R.—for thus saith the Lord:	6:27
r. of that which thou hast done	3:10		prepared for them, if they r. not;	6:29
if they r. not, until the earth	5:19		our fathers that all men must r.	6:50
to r. and walk more uprightly	5:21		and r., of all thy transgressions,	6:52
all men everywhere to r.,	18: 9		Why is it that men must r. and	6:53
all men might r. and come	18:11		that all men, everywhere, must r.,	6:57
as many as r. and are	18:22		R., lest I come out and	7:10
must r. and be baptized,	18:41		were the people of Canaan, to r.;	7:12
men must r. and be baptized,	18:42		as they will r. in the day that	7:39
every man must r. or suffer,	19: 4		if men do not r., I will send in	8:17
Wherefore, I command you to r.,	19:13		of men that they should r.;	8:20
Therefore I command you to r.—	19:15		Believe and r. of your sins	8:24
r., lest I smite you by the rod	19:15			
not suffer if they would r.;	19:16		**REPENTANCE**	
if they would not r. they must	19:17		even r. unto their brethren,	2Ne 3:20
I command you again to r.,	19:20		should persuade all men to r.	26:27
all men must r. and believe on	20:29		must needs be stirred up unto r.,	28:19
manner unto all those who r.—	20:72		gate by which ye should enter is r.	31:17
the wicked, for they will not r.	29:17		stirring them up unto r.	Jar 1:12
fall, because they r. not;	29:44		except it be through r. and	Mos 3:12
have I not commanded to r.?	29:49		only through r. and faith on	3:21
R., repent, and prepare ye the	33:10		and did preach unto them r.,	18: 7
r., and prepare ye the way of	33:10		preach nothing save it were r.	18:20
Yea, r. and be baptized,	33:11		which caused me sore r.;	23: 9
inasmuch as they do r. and	39:18		preaching unto the people r.	25:15

REPENTANCE 804 REPENTETH

except it were r. and faith	Mos 25:22	little children need no r.,	Mro	8:11
shall be baptized unto r.	26:22	baptism is unto r. to the		8:11
this because of their sincere r.,	29:19	r. is unto them that are under		8:24
works which are meet for r.—	Al 5:54	first fruits of r. is baptism;		8:25
Come and be baptized unto r.,	5:62	that r. may come unto them.		8:28
were baptized unto r.,	6: 2	through their r. they might be	DC	3:20
come and be baptized unto r.,	7:14	Say nothing but r. unto this		6: 9
he might baptize them unto r.	8:10	Say nothing but r. unto this		11: 9
who will be baptized unto r.,	9:27	angels, and of the gospel of r.,		13: 1
forth works which are meet for r.,	9:30	declare r. unto this generation.		14: 8
bringeth forth fruit meet for r.	12:15	declare r. unto this people,		15: 6
according to their faith and r.	12:30	declare r. unto this people,		16: 6
of their exceeding faith and r.,	13:10	of men are stirred up unto r.,		18: 6
and bring forth fruit meet for r.,	13:13	unto him, on conditions of r.		18:12
did preach r. unto his people.	13:18	you are called to cry r. unto		18:14
the day of your r.;	13:27	in crying r. unto this people,		18:15
may the Lord grant unto you r.,	13:30	that they may come unto r.,		18:44
not believe in the r. of their sins.	15:15	that you preach naught but r.,		19:21
forth preaching r. to the people	16:13	declare r. and faith on the		19:31
them on the conditions of r.	17:15	before God, and is capable of r.		20:71
they might bring them unto r.;	17:16	angels to declare unto them r.		29:42
faith and r., and so forth;	22:14	cry r. unto a crooked and		34: 6
to bring thousands of souls to r.,	26:22	baptize by water unto r.,		35: 5
to bring these our brethren to r.	26:22	Crying r., saying:		36: 6
their sore r. which they had,	27:23	r. and baptism by water,		39: 6
and cry r. unto every people!	29: 1	and preach r. unto the people.		44: 3
r. and the plan of redemption,	29: 2	to preach faith and r. and		53: 3
of God to bring some soul to r.;	29: 9	to preach r. and remission of		55: 2
to be humble, seeketh r.;	32:13	meekness, to warn sinners to r.,		63:57
they may have faith unto r.	34:15	understand the doctrine of r.,		68:25
he that exercises no faith unto r.	34:16	gospel of r. and of baptism,		84:27
unto him that has faith unto r.	34:16	baptism of r. for the remission		107:20
to exercise your faith unto r.,	34:17	if r. is to be found;		109:50
forth and bring fruit unto r.	34:30	*angels, and of the gospel of r.,*	JS	2:69
day of your r. until the end;	34:33	second, R.; third, Baptism	AoF	4
of your r. even until death,	34:35			
many of the Zoramites to r.;	35:14	REPENTED		
as many as were brought to r.	35:14	they r. of the thing which they had	1Ne	18:20
I might bring souls unto r.;	36:24	After ye have r. of your sins,	2Ne	31:14
their words brought them unto r.;	37: 9	have r. not of their evil doings;	Mos	12: 1
Preach unto them r., and faith	37:33	r. of his sins and iniquities,		18: 1
of God, having no space for r.;	42: 5	whosoever r. of their sins		26:35
only on conditions of r. of men	42:13	said he, I have r. of my sins,		27:24
r. could not come unto men except	42:16	who r. of their sins were	Al	6: 2
and a r. granted;	42:22	and they r. not of their sins,		15:15
which r. mercy claimeth;	42:22	for behold, he has r. of his sins;		20:17
shall bring you down unto r.	42:29	for they r. of the things which		24:24
thou mayest bring souls unto r.,	42:31	If he hath r. of his sins,		41: 6
they did baptize unto r. all	48:19	do evil, and has not r. in his days,		42:28
of God, being baptized unto r.	49:30	saw that the people had r.	He	11: 9
and were baptized unto r.	He 3:24	thou seest that they have r.,		11:15
from their sins because of r.:	5:11	O that I had r., and had not killed		13:33
tidings of the conditions of r.,	5:11	O that we had r. in the day		13:36
sins and were baptized unto r.,	5:17	that they had r. and received	3Ne	7:25
round about baptized unto r.,	5:19	O that we had r. before this		8:24
did exhort them to faith and r.	6: 4	O that we had r. before this		8:25
be saved, hath r. been declared.	12:22	they have r. not of their sins.	Mrm	3:13
men might be brought unto r.	12:24	and because this people r. not		3:15
he did preach, many days, r.	13: 2	the Nephites r. not of the evil		4:10
save it be r. and faith on	13: 6	they r. not of their iniquities,		5: 2
might know the conditions of r.;	14:11	that this people had not r.		5:11
to pass the condition of r.,	14:18	O that ye had r. before this		6:22
faith on the Lord, and unto r.,	15: 7	the brother of Jared r. of the	Eth	2:15
and r. bringeth a change of heart	15: 7	Corihor of the many evils		7:13
crying r. unto the people,	16: 4	except they r. of their iniquities.		11:12
many others, baptizing unto r.,	3Ne 1:23	But he r. not, neither his		13:17
knew it was because of their r.	4:33	whole earth who r. of their sins.		13:17
r. and remission of sins through	7:16	that Coriantumr r. not,		13:22
he did preach unto them r.	7:23	people r. not of their iniquity;		15: 6
none who were brought unto r.	7:24	they truly r. of all their sins.	Mro	6: 2
that were baptized unto r.	7:26	and if they r. not, and		6: 7
and the r. of all their sins,	27:19	as oft as they r. and sought		6: 8
their sorrowing was not unto r.,	Mrm 2:13	have truly r. of all their sins,	DC	20:37
unto them a chance for r.	3: 3	he who has r. of his sins,		58:42
that ye must come unto r.,	7: 3	r. of their sins, should be saved;	Mses	5:15
the people were brought unto r.	Eth 7:25	and r. not, should be damned;		5:15
again, crying r. unto them—	9:28	it r. Noah, and his heart		8:25
cried r. unto the people,	11:20	he r. of the evil which he had	Abr	1:30
to believe in God unto r.	12: 3			
r. and remission of sins	Mro 3: 3	REPENTETH		
ministry is to call men unto r.,	7:31	that whoso r. not must perish.	1Ne	14: 5
righteous but sinners to r.;	8: 8	Therefore if that man r. not,	Mos	2:38
r. and baptism unto those who	8:10	except he r. of that which		4:18

REPENTETH

r. in the sincerity of his heart,	Mos 26:29
Therefore, whosoever r., and	Al 12:34
he that r. and exerciseth faith,	26:22
whosoever r. shall find mercy;	32:13
himself, and r. of his sins,	32:15
O Lord, behold this people r.;	He 11:10
but wo unto him that r. not.	13:11
whosoever r. the same is not	14:18
whosoever r. not is hewn	14:18
whoso r. and cometh unto	3Ne 9:22
that whoso r. of his sins	11:23
if it so be that he r. and is	18:30
and r. and is baptized,	23: 5
whoso r. and is baptized in	27:16
whosoever r. and cometh unto	DC 10:67
is his joy in the soul that r.!	18:13
committeth adultery, and r. not,	42:24
he that sinneth and r. not	42:28
that he that sinneth and r. not	42:37
know if a man r. of his sins—	58:43
him that r. not of his sins,	64:12
and as oft as thine enemy r.	98:40
found a transgressor and r. not	104:10
unto him that r. and sanctifieth	133:62
it r. Noah that I have created	Mses 8:26

REPENTING

with real intent, r. of your sins,	2Ne 31:13
r. nigh unto death,	Mos 27:28
came r. and confessing their sins.	He 16: 5
But after r., and humbling	DC 20: 6

REPENTS

when he says that he r.,	Mos 26:31
he that r. and does the	DC 1:32
And he that r. not, from him	1:33
if he r. not he shall be cast out.	42:23
and r. with all his heart,	42:25

REPETITION

to avoid the too frequent r. of	DC 107: 4

REPETITIONS

when ye pray, use not vain r.,	3Ne 13: 7

REPLENISH

to multiply and r. the earth,	DC 132:63
multiply, and r. the earth,	Mses 2:28
to multiply, and to r. the earth.	5: 2
and multiply and r. the earth,	Abr 4:28

REPLENISHED

they be r. from the east,	2Ne 12: 6

REPLIED

I r., "Never mind, all is well—	JS 2:20
He r. to me that it was of	2:50
He r., 'I cannot read a sealed	2:65

REPLY

not make any r. to his words;	Al 30:29

REPORT

Who hath believed our r.,	Mos 14: 1
and the r. thereof shall vex	DC 97:23
r. to the Secretary of the	OD
or of good r. or praiseworthy,	AoF 13

REPORTED

one case has been r.,	DC OD

REPORTS

who have spread lying r. abroad,	DC 109:29
the many r. which have been	JS 2: 1

REPRESENT

do they r. classes or orders?	DC 77: 3
to r. the glory of the classes of	77: 3
Designed to r. the pillars	Fac 1:11
Is made to r. God, sitting	2: 3

REPRESENTATION

are a r. of the love of God;	1Ne 11:25

was a r. of the love of God.	1Ne 11:25
was a r. of the tree of life.	15:22
it was a r. of that awful hell,	15:29
a r. of things both temporal and	15:32
eyes are a r. of light and	DC 77: 4
wings are a r. of power,	77: 4
r. at the commencement of this	Abr 1:12

REPRESENTED

stars r. by numbers 22 and 23,	Fac 2: 5
as r. by the characters above	3: 5

REPRESENTING

r. also the grand Key-words	Fac 2: 3
upon his head, r. the Priesthood,	3: 1

REPRESENTS

R. this earth in its four	Fac 2: 6
R. God sitting upon his	2: 7

REPROACH

fear ye not the r. of men,	2Ne 8: 7
by thy name to take away our r.	14: 1
remember the r. of thy youth,	3Ne 22: 4
the r. of thy widowhood	22: 4

REPROACHFULLY

not speak r. of him or her.	DC 42:92

REPROVE

neither r. after the hearing of	2Ne 21: 3
and r. with equity for the meek	21: 4
and r. with equity for the meek	30: 9
send you out to r. the world	DC 84:87

REPROVED

toward him whom thou hast r.,	DC 121:43
he has been promptly r.	OD

REPROVETH

for him that r. in the gate,	2Ne 27:32

REPROVING

r. the world in righteousness	DC 84:117
R. betimes with sharpness,	121:43

REPUBLIC

by the voice of the people if a r.,	DC 134: 3

REPUGNANT

r. to the commandments of God.	Mos 29:36

REPULSED

r. by Teancum and his men,	Al 51.31
they were r. and driven back	Mrm 4: 8

REPUTATION

I am also a man of no small r.	Al 10: 4

REQUEST

go and do according to their r.	Mos 28: 8
to rejoice exceedingly at this r.,	Al 54: 2
prisoners according to your r.,	54:20
or either of them shall r. it.	DC 102:24
r. him to shake hands with you.	129: 4

REQUESTED

for I had r. it of my Father	Jac 7:22
have I told you that which ye r.	Mos 13: 3

REQUIRE

he doth r. that ye should do as	Mos 2:24
I will r. this at their hands,	DC 10:23
R. not miracles, except I shall	24:13
I, the Lord, r. the hearts of	64:22
stewardship will I r. of them	70: 4
sacrifice which I, the Lord, r.	97:12
presidents as the case might r.	102: 1
and the things which I r.	105:10
I do not r. at their hands	105:14
I r. all their surplus property	119: 1
stewardship will I r. at his hands.	124:14

REQUIRE

to r. that work no more | DC 124:49
as the case may r., | 127: 1
might r. an offering at your hand, | 132:51
sacrifice which I r. at his hands | 132:60
necessarily r. civil officers | 134: 3

REQUIRED
thing which I have r. of them; | 1Ne 3: 5
I have not r. it of them, | 3: 5
have also r. of me this thing; | En 1:18
but little, but little should be r.; | Mos 18:27
r. of you by them who desire it, | DC 24:14
labors on the land, such as is r., | 26: 1
r. at the hand of their fathers. | 29:48
that is not, of him it is not r. | 60:11
it is r. to forgive all men. | 64:10
for it is r. of the Lord, | 72: 3
you and r. of you. | 78: 7
whom much is given much is r.; | 82: 3
which I r. at their hands, | 105: 3
the union r. by the law of | 105: 4
blood of this generation be r. at | 112:33
no more r. at your hand to | 126: 1
done what was r. at my hand, | JS 2:60
what was r. at my hand. | 2:60

REQUIREMENTS
to the pretended r. of the law, | 135: 4

REQUIRES
all that he r. of you is | Mos 2:22
assist the elder if occasion r. | DC 20:52
by the deacons, if occasion r. | 20:57
the Lord r. of every man in | 70: 9
one to another as the gospel r. | 88:123
the sum which he r. to help | 104:73
the vineyard of necessity r. it. | 107:96

REQUIRETH
the law r. the life of him who | Al 34:12
the Lord r. the heart and a | DC 64:34

REQUISITE
it is not r. that a man should | Mos 4:27
is r. with the justice of God; | Al 41: 2
it is r. that all things should be | 41: 2
Behold, it is r. and just, | 41: 2
it is r. with the justice of God | 41: 3
were r. with the justice of God, | 61:12

RESCUED
I was r. by the shedding of | Mos 9: 2

RESERVE
that he would r. these things for | Al 37:18
r. unto myself a pure people | DC 43:14
let him also r. unto himself | 51:14
whom I shall r. unto myself, | 63:39
I have in r. a swift judgment | 121:24
in r. for the fulness of their glory; | 121:27

RESERVED
r. for themselves provisions, | 3Ne 4: 4
the Lord hath r. their blessings, | Mrm 5:19
I have r. those things which I | DC 5: 9
a city r. until a day of | 45:12
which I have r. unto myself, | 49: 8
the ground which has been r. | 104:34
I have r. an inheritance | 104:45
which I have r. unto myself | 104:68
r. unto the finishing and the end | 121:32
were r. in chains of darkness | Mses 7:57

RESIDE
from the church were they r., | DC 20:84
to the planet on which they r.? | 130: 4
angels do not r. on a planet like | 130: 6
they r. in the presence of God, | 130: 7
governments in which they r., | 134: 5

RESIDED
neighborhood where my father r., | JS 2:66

RESIDENCE
this land is the land of his r., | DC 58:24
the r. of him whom I have | 58:24
at the r. of my father, | Abr 1: 1
to obtain another place of r.; | 1: 1
celestial, or the r. of God. | Fac 2: 1

RESIDENT
a r. of Palmyra township, | JS 2:61

RESIDES
remain where he now r. until | DC 90:21
him the place where he now r., | 104:20
lot upon which his father r. | 104:28
and lot where he now r., | 104:39
upon which his father now r.; | 104:43
in which my servant Joseph r. | 124:105
The place where God r. is | 130: 8
the place where God r.; | Fac 2: 2

RESIDUE
the r. of men may have faith in | Mro 7:32
the r. of the wicked have I | DC 38: 5
a r. to be consecrated unto | 42:33
the r. shall be kept in my | 42:34
Let the r. of the elders watch | 52:39
the r. shall be made known | 53: 6
The r. shall be made known | 55: 6
unto the r. of both elders and | 57:16
concerning the r. of the elders | 58:44
accomplish the r. of the work | 58:58
the r. as shall be ruled by | 58:58
Let the r. of the elders of | 58:61
let the r. take their journey | 60: 8
the r. who are to come unto | 60:12
The r. hereafter. | 60:17
let the r. take that which is | 61:11
And now, concerning the r., | 61:33
until the r. of the church, | 64:26
And the r. of the money may | 90:29
And to the r. of the school, | 97: 6
together the r. of my servants, | 101:55
come with the r. of mine house | 101:58
leave the r. in mine hand. | 101:71
leave the r. in my hands. | 103:40
with the r. of his posterity who | 107:53
Let the r. continue to preach | 118: 3
the r. of the people of God | Mses 6:17
the r. of the people have I cursed. | 7:20
beheld the r. of the people which | 7:22
looked upon the r. of the people, | 7:28
upon the r. of the wicked the | 7:43

RESIST
will still r. the spirit of the truth, | Al 30:46
ye will r. the Spirit of the Lord, | 32:28
behold, we will r. wickedness | 61:10
Moroni, let us r. evil, and | 61:14
we cannot r. with our words, | 61:14
let us r. them with our swords, | 61:14
that ye shall not r. evil, | 3Ne 12:39
and r. no more my voice. | DC 108: 2

RESISTANCE
And thus without meeting any r., | Al 24:22

RESISTING
of God, yea, and r. iniquity. | Al 48:16

RESOLUTION
their minds with a determined r. | Al 47: 6

RESOLVE
we did r. to send them down | Al 57:16
did not r. upon any stratagem | 62:35

RESOLVED
he r. upon a plan that he might | Al 52:21
Moroni r. upon a stratagem to | 54: 3
R.: that the president or | DC 102:33

RESOLVING
r. by stratagem to destroy us; | Al 58: 6

RESORT

RESORT
a r. for the children of Nephi	Mos 11:13
Nephites, and their places of r.,	Al 48: 5
small forts, or places of r.;	48: 8
about and preparing places of r.	52: 6
by the court of last r.,	DC OD

RESORTED
and Alma r. thither,	Mos 18: 5
was r. to for that purpose.	JS 2:60

RESPECT
and r. the words of the Jews,	2Ne 33:14
having no r. to persons	Al 1:30
without any r. of persons,	16:14
But out of r. or reverence to	DC 107: 4
to the laws all men owe r.	134: 6
And the Lord had r. unto Abel,	Mses 5:20
and to his offering, he had not r.	5:21

RESPECTABILITY
of New York, and a farmer of r.	JS 2:61

RESPECTER
and a r. to persons;	Mro 8:12
For I am no r. of persons,	DC 1:35
and I am no r. of persons.	38:16
sons, and is no r. of them,	38:26

RESPECTING
r. the members of the church—	DC 72:24
r. doctrine or principle,	102:23
church laws r. church business—	107:59
r. what the Lord was going to	JS 2:54
r. both the characters and	2:65
inquire of the Lord r. baptism	2:68

RESPECTIVE
and uphold the r. governments in	DC 134: 5
manifested by the r. clergy,	JS 2: 6

RESPECTS
of the general peace, in all r.,	DC 134: 8

RESPONSIBILITY
taking upon us the r.,	Jac 1:19
according to the r. which I	2: 2
not under the r. to travel	DC 107:98
the one has the r. of presiding	124:140
has no r. of presiding,	124:140

RESPONSIBLE
high and r. offices in the church.	DC 107:98
that I should be r. for them;	JS 2:59

REST
that we might again r. ourselves	1Ne 16:17
that is just shall r. upon them.	2Ne 1:10
and it shall r. upon him.	1:29
my judgment to r. for a light	8: 4
and shall r. all of them in the	17:19
the r. of the trees of his forest	20:19
of the Lord shall r. upon him,	21: 2
and his r. shall be glorious.	21:10
the Lord shall give thee r.,	24: 3
The whole earth is at r.,	24: 7
that they might enter into his r.,	Jac 1: 7
wherefore my soul did r.	En 1:17
I soon go to the place of my r.,	1:27
I know that in him I shall r.	1:27
r. themselves from the labors of	Mos 7:16
that they might r. their bodies	11:11
And the r. left their wives	19:12
may the peace of God r. upon you,	Al 7:27
to r. himself from the labors which	8: 1
shall r. upon thee and thy house.	10: 7
and these shall enter into my r.	12:34
that he shall not enter into my r.	12:35
not enter into the r. of the Lord;	12:36
let us enter into the r. of God,	12:37
also might enter into his r.—	13: 6
into the r. of the Lord their God.	13:12
ye may also enter into that r.	13:13
enter into the r. of the Lord.	Al 13:16
last day and enter into his r.	13:29
into the r. of the Lord their God.	16:17
one day r. from all your afflictions.	34:41
and the r. of the brethren, after	35: 2
for such shall find r. to their souls.	37:34
is called paradise, a state of r.,	40:12
shall r. from all their troubles	40:12
Alma, also, himself, could not r.,	43: 1
liberty to r. upon his brethren,	46:13
entered into the r. of their God.	57:36
the r. of the Lord their God.	60:13
nothing entereth into his r. save	3Ne 27:19
and with me ye shall find r.	28: 3
like unto the r. of the earth;	Eth 10:17
enter into the r. of the Lord,	Mro 7: 3
ye shall r. with him in heaven.	7: 3
r. our souls in the kingdom of	9: 6
r. in your mind forever.	9:25
to r. in the paradise of God,	10:34
that you may r. with them in	DC 15: 6
that you may r. with them in	16: 6
that you may enter into my r.	19: 9
that power shall r. upon thee;	39:12
of eternity r. upon your minds.	43:34
shall find r. to their souls.	54:10
shall r. from all their labors,	59: 2
you to r. from your labors,	59:10
all the r. shall be brought forth	76:39
and a cloud shall r. upon it,	84: 5
should not enter into his r.	84:24
which r. is the fulness of his	84:24
you, the r. of my servants,	84:117
these are the r. of the dead;	88:101
my glory shall r. upon it;	97:15
and his r. shall be glorious.	101:31
you may r. in peace and safety,	105:25
let your soul be at r. concerning	108: 2
with the r. of mine elders whom	108: 4
That thy glory may r. down upon	109:12
and into his immortal r.	121:32
they shall r. from all their labors	124:86
When shall I r., and be cleansed	Mses 7:48
Creator sanctify me, that I may r.,	7:48
in the flesh, shall the earth r.?	7:54
saying: When shall the earth r.?	7:58
shall come that the earth shall r.,	7:61
thousand years the earth shall r.	7:64
happiness and peace and r. for me,	Abr 1: 2
we will r. on the seventh time	5: 2
the seventh time they would r.	5: 3
took me, with the r. of his hands,	JS 2:56

RESTED
of the Lord hath r. upon us	Al 10:11
his sword, that he r. a little,	Eth 15:30
I r. on the seventh day from all	Mses 3: 2
in it I had r. from all my work	3: 3
When the light r. upon me	JS 2:17

RESTETH
this condemnation r. upon the	DC 84:56

RESTING
r. place for the weary traveler,	DC 124:60

RESTING-PLACE: *see RESTING and PLACE.*

RESTORATION
concerning the r. of the Jews	1Ne 15:19
concerning the r. of the Jews,	15:20
the bringing to pass much r.	2Ne 3:24
about the r. of his people	30: 8
bringeth about the r. of these;	Mos 15:24
Now, this r. shall come to all,	Al 11:44
to the r. of many thousands	37:19
this bringeth about the r. of	40:22
this is the r. of which has been	40:24
the r. of which has been spoken;	41: 1
the plan of r. is requisite with	41: 2
it has been spoken concerning r.,	41:10
is the meaning of the word r.	41:12
the meaning of the word r. is to	41:13

RESTORATION 808 RESURRECTION

RESTORATION (cont.)

word r. more fully condemneth	Al 41:15
according to the r. of God.	42:28
the r. of our brethren,	He 15:11
their r. to the lands of their	3Ne 29: 1
their r. to the knowledge of	Mrm 9:36
to pass the r. of all things	DC 27: 6
the r. of the scattered Israel.	45:17
last days, at the time of the r.,	77:15
days for the r. of his people,	84: 2
until the r. of all things	86:10
their r. to the land of Zion,	103:13
the r. and redemption of Zion.	103:29
on the r. of the priesthood,	128:17
in the r. of the Ten Tribes;	AoF 10

RESTORE

and to r. the preserved of Israel.	1Ne 21: 6
the second time to r. his people	2Ne 25:17
to reclaim and r. the Lamanites	Jac 7:24
to r. the Lamanites unto	En 1:20
of Israel and r. all things.	DC 77: 9
must come and r. all things.	77:14
and r. four-fold for all their	98:47
and r. again that which was lost	124:28
I am about to r. many things to	127: 8
and r. all things.	132:40
wherein I r. all things,	132:45
r. that which thou hast borrowed;	136:25

RESTORED

and after they were r. they	1Ne 15:20
shall be r. to the true church	2Ne 9: 2
and the spirits of men will be r.	9:12
the body is r. to itself again,	9:13
they are r. to that God who	9:26
and our children shall be r.,	10: 2
they shall be r. in the flesh,	10: 7
shall be r. again to the land of	25:11
be r. unto the knowledge of	30: 5
was r. again among the people;	Jac 7:23
shall be r. to its proper frame,	Al 11:43
shall be r. to its perfect frame,	11:44
The soul shall be r. to the body,	40:23
and joint shall be r. to its body;	40:23
shall be r. to their proper and	40:23
should be r. to their proper order.	41: 2
of man should be r. to its body,	41: 2
the body should be r. to itself.	41: 2
be r. unto that which is good.	41: 3
shall be r. unto them for evil.	41: 4
shall be r. to their proper order,	41: 4
be r. from sin to happiness.	41:10
have mercy r. unto you again;	41:14
have justice r. unto you again;	41:14
judgment r. unto you again;	41:14
return unto you again, and be r.;	41:15
they are r. into his presence,	42:23
be r. unto him according to	42:27
r. to the land of Morianton,	50:36
they were also r. to their lands.	50:36
of Nephi had peace r. unto them,	50:37
was r. to his judgment-seat.	62: 8
having r. peace to the land of	62:11
be r. unto grace for grace,	He 12:24
be r. unto that which is good,	14:31
that which is good r. unto you;	14:31
that which is evil r. unto you.	14:31
and r. it unto his father Kib.	Eth 7: 9
Omer was r. again to the	9:13
which had been r. unto them.	10:12
it is now r. unto you again;	DC 10: 3
r. to the blessings which	109:21

RESTORING

unto the r. thee, O house of	2Ne 3:13
in r. them to the true faith.	En 1:14
in r. these flocks unto the king,	Al 17:29
r. all the house of Jacob unto the	3Ne 5:25
in r. the Jews, or all the house	Mrm 5:14

RESTRAIN

is in God, which he could not r.,	2Ne 1:26

and there was none to r. them.	Eth 13:31
civil magistrate should r. crime,	DC 134: 4

RESTRAINED

for he could not be r. because	Eth 12: 2

RESULT

and the following was the r.,	DC 102:34

RESUME

r. the subject of the baptism	DC 128: 1

RESURRECTED

who are r. personages,	DC 129: 1
they who are not r., but inherit	129: 3

RESURRECTION

that he may bring to pass the r.	2Ne 2: 8
there must needs be a power of r.,	9: 6
r. must needs come unto man by	9: 6
the r. of the Holy One of Israel.	9:12
the r. might pass upon all men,	9:22
from death by the power of the r.,	10:25
and also of his death and r.;	26: 3
and ye may obtain a r.,	Jac 4:11
according to the power of the r.	4:11
to attain to the knowledge of a r.	4:12
the r., which is in Christ,	6: 9
he should bring to pass the r.	Mos 13:35
he bringeth to pass the r. of	15:20
And there cometh a r., even	15:21
even a first r.; yea, even	15:21
a r. of those that have been,	15:21
even until the r. of Christ—	15:21
now, the r. of all the prophets,	15:22
shall come forth in the first r.;	15:22
therefore, they are the first r.	15:22
who have part in the first r.;	15:24
have a part in the first r.,	15:24
that have no part in the first r.	15:26
there could have been no r.	16: 7
But there is a r., therefore	16: 8
to the r. of endless life	16:11
to the r. of endless damnation,	16:11
concerning the r. of the dead,	18: 2
and death of Christ, and his r.	18: 2
with those of the first r.,	18: 9
concerning the r. of the dead,	26: 2
because of the r. of the dead,	Al 4:14
the r. of the mortal body.	11:45
concerning the r. of the dead,	12: 8
is after the r. of the dead.	12:24
have been no r. of the dead;	12:25
to pass the r. of the dead,	12:25
and also the r. of the dead.	16:19
appear unto them after his r.,	16:20
concerning the r. of the dead,	21: 9
and views of Christ and the r.;	27:28
which shall bring to pass the r.,	33:22
concerning the r. of the dead.	40: 1
that there is no r.—	40: 2
he bringeth to pass the r. of the	40: 3
my son, the r. is not yet.	40: 3
that is concerning the r.	40: 3
of death and the time of the r.	40: 6
to the time appointed for the r.?	40: 7
the time of death and the r.	40: 9
soul between death and the r.—	40:11
paradise, until the time of their r.	40:14
misery of the soul, before the r.,	40:15
was a first r.	40:15
I admit it may be termed a r.,	40:15
spoken, that there is a first r.,	40:16
a r. of all those who have been,	40:16
to the r. of Christ from the dead.	40:16
do not suppose that this first r.,	40:17
the r. of the souls and their	40:17
Adam down to the r. of Christ.	40:18
their r. cometh to pass before	40:19
before the r. of those who die	40:19
who die after the r. of Christ.	40:19
I do not say that their r. cometh	40:20

RESURRECTION

cometh at the r. of Christ;	Al 40:20
righteous, at the r. of Christ,	40:20
whether it be at his r. or after,	40:21
a space between death and the r.	40:21
to the power and r. of Christ,	41: 2
to pass the r. of the dead;	42:23
the r. of the dead bringeth back	42:23
bring to pass the r. of the dead,	He 14:15
this death bringeth to pass the r.,	14:16
r. of Christ redeemeth mankind,	14:17
in other words, the r. of Christ;	3Ne 6:20
to the r. of everlasting life;	26: 5
evil, to the r. of damnation;	26: 5
he bringeth to pass the r. of	Mrm 7: 6
of Christ bringeth to pass the r.,	9:13
Christ and the power of his r.,	Mro 7:41
have not hope of a glorious r.	DC 42:45
shall have part in the first r.;	45:54
not have part in the first r.	63:18
the world the r. of the dead.	63:52
of the r. of the dead,	76:16
good in the r. of the just,	76:17
evil in the r. of the unjust—	76:17
forth by the r. of the dead,	76:39
forth in the r. of the just—	76:50
shall have part in the first r.	76:64
forth in the r. of the just.	76:65
from the devil until the last r.,	76:85
pass the r. from the dead.	88:14
And the r. from the dead is	88:16
likeness of the r. of the dead	128:12
it will rise with us in the r.	130:18
or force in and after the r.	132: 7
neither in nor after the r.,	132:13
Ye shall come forth in the first r.;	132:19
and if it be after the first r.,	132:19
in the next r.;	132:19
shall come forth in the first r.,	132:26
who were with Christ in his r.	133:55
of mine Only Begotten; his r.	Mses 7:62
yea, and also the r. of all men;	7:62

RETAIN

to r. in remembrance his name.	Jac 1:11
and always r. in remembrance,	Mos 4:11
r. a remission of your sins;	4:12
to r. the name written always in	5:12
in thy heart to r. them from me;	Al 11:25
or to r. them in captivity,	17:20
Lamoni may r. his kingdom,	20:24
Lamoni should r. his kingdom,	20:26
that my son may r. his kingdom	20:26
Nay, let us r. our swords that	24:13
they did r. a hope through faith,	25:16
ought to r. in remembrance,	36:29
they must r. their brightness;	37: 5
and they will r. their brightness;	37: 5
you that ye r. all their oaths,	37:27
otherwise we will r. our swords,	44: 8
should r. all the prisoners who	52: 8
should r. all the prisoners of	52: 8
a stronghold to r. his prisoners.	53: 6
will r. our cities and our lands;	54:10
that we might r. our cities,	58:10
only to r. my judgment-seat	61: 9
that we may r. our freedom,	61:14
your poverty ye cannot r. them.	He 13:31
not hold them, nor r. them	Mrm 1:18
and always r. in your minds	DC 46:10
he shall not r. the gift,	51: 5
Newel K. Whitney r. his store,	63:42
to r. a strong hold in the land	64:21
sins you r. on earth shall be	132:46

RETAINED

but he r. the office of high priest	Al 4:18
sufficiently r. in remembrance	5: 6
sufficiently r. in remembrance	5: 6
sufficiently r. in remembrance	5: 6
have always r. in remembrance	36:29
Lehi r. his armies upon the	43:40
Zerahemnah r. his sword,	44:12
Pahoran r. the judgment-seat,	51: 7
had also r. many prisoners,	Al 56:12
And we r. our city Cumeni,	57:23
he r. all his force to maintain	59:10
as if he had r. the gift;	Mro 7: 8
translated, which you have r.;	DC 10:41
on earth shall be r. in heaven.	132:46

RETAINING

of r. a remission of your sins	Mos 4:26
thus r. a remission of their sins;	Al 4:14
r. from them their rights of	3Ne 3:10
R. all power, even to the	DC 19: 3

RETAKE

and r. it if it were possible.	Al 52:16
Lamanites than to r. it from them,	59: 9

RETAKEN

advantage which they had r.	Al 55:27

RETAKING

in r. the cities which they	Al 52:15

RETIRE

r. to thy bed early, that ye	DC 88:124

RETIRED

and he r. to his own house	Al 62:43
weary, and r. to their camps;	Eth 15:16
after they had r. to their camps	15:16
I r. to the woods to make	JS 2:14
After I had r. to the place where	2:15
after I had r. to my bed for	2:29

RETREAT

disappointed in their places of r.	Al 49:11
to r. down by the seashore,	52:23
should r. into the wilderness.	58:18
to r. into the wilderness again,	58:24
began to r. back towards	He 1:29
did head them in their r.,	1:30
could not r. either way,	1:31
r. back into the mountains,	11:25
did cut off the way of their r.,	3Ne 4:24
his armies in the way of their r.	4:24
also cut off in their places of retreat.	4:26
r. towards the north countries.	Mrm 2: 3
possible to stop them in their r.	2:16

RETREATED

they r. into the wilderness,	Al 49:12
and r. with all their army into	52: 2
before the Lamanites had r. far	52:31

RETREATS

because of their r. and their	Al 58: 6

RETURN

thy brethren shall r. to Jerusalem.	1Ne 3: 2
were about to r. unto my father	3:14
and r. to the city of Jerusalem.	4:30
r. unto the land of Jerusalem.	7: 2
to r. unto the land of Jerusalem.	7: 7
if ye will r. unto Jerusalem	7:15
r. again, yea, even be brought back	10: 3
we did r. again to our families	16:14
r. without food to our families,	16:19
r. to our tents, bearing the beasts	16:32
to r. again to Jerusalem.	16:36
from whence no traveler can r.;	2Ne 1:14
unto me that they should r. again.	6: 9
the redeemed of the Lord shall r.,	8:11
for they shall r. to God,	9:38
they shall r., and shall be eaten,	16:13
The remnant shall r.,	20:21
yet a remnant of them shall r.;	20:22
shall r. to their lands of promise.	24: 2
they shall r. again, and possess	25:11
I will r. all these things upon	29: 5
to r. to the land of Nephi;	Om 1:27
from whence they can no more r.;	Mos 3:25
r. the thing that he borroweth,	4:28
caused that they should r.	8: 4

RETURN

would r. to the land of Nephi,	Mos	19:19
them that they should not r.;		19:20
about to r. to the land of Nephi,		19:22
to r. to the city of Nephi,		20: 3
durst not r. to their wives and		20: 3
we will r. again to the Amlicites,	Al	3:13
r. to the city of Ammonihah,		8:16
Amulek, r. to thine own house,		10: 7
about to r. out of his presence.		18:12
that he should r. with him		20:14
will I r. to the land of Ishmael,		20:15
will r. to the account of Aaron		22: 1
r. again to the account of		22:35
ye shall remain here until we r.;		27:15
that I will r. to my God.		34:34
but rather r. unto them,		39:13
send out shall r. unto you again,		41:15
I r. to an account of the wars		43: 3
will not r. again against us		44:11
Now we will r. in our record to		47: 1
r. from the pursuit of Teancum.		52:26
r. with your armies to your own		54: 7
I did r. with my two thousand		56:49
that on the morrow they did r.		57:17
they should not r. to the city.		58:20
they did not r. at that time		62:38
did r. to his judgment-seat;		62:44
And the first ship did also r.,		63: 7
found that Kishkumen did not r.	He	2:11
now I r. again to mine account;		3:17
but did r. unto the multitudes		10:12
to r. out of the wilderness		11:31
was about to r. to his own land.		13: 2
that he should r. again,		13: 3
and r. unto the Lord your God		13:11
they shall r. again unto me,		15:16
not r. to the land of Zarahemla,	3Ne	2: 9
the armies of the Nephites did r.		4:15
Nephites did all r. to their own		6: 1
they did r. to their own lands		6: 2
some did r. railing for railing,		6:13
quick r. from righteousness		7:15
will ye not now r. unto me,		9:13
repent and r. unto me with full		10: 6
will repent and r. unto me,		16:13
what they will r. and repent,		18:32
and did r. to his own home.		19: 1
I will r. their iniquities upon		20:28
R. unto me and I will return unto		24: 7
unto me and I will r. unto you,		24: 7
Wherein shall we r.?		24: 7
Then shall ye r. and discern		24:18
from whence there is no r.		27:11
whence they can no more r.,		27:17
my sorrow did r. unto me	Mrm	2:15
did r. to their own lands again.		3: 7
r. to the land of your inheritance;		3:17
and to r. to their mother earth.		6:15
sorrows cannot bring your r.		6:20
witness the r. of his people	Mro	9:22
they repent and r. unto him.		9:22
go, until the time thou shalt r.,	DC	28:15
own mouth that they should r.,		29:29
servant Oliver Cowdery shall r.		37: 3
of the Spirit when they shall r.		42: 5
let them r. to their homes.		58:46
and Joseph Smith, Jun., r.,		58:58
let no man r. from this land		58:59
And let them also r., preaching		58:63
to r. speedily to the land from		60: 1
until they r. to the churches		60: 8
who are commanded to r.;		60:10
r. it by the way of the agent;		60:11
thou shalt speedily r.,		60:14
until they r. to their homes,		61:35
you may r. to bear record,		62: 5
shall r. upon his business,		64:18
R. not till I, the Lord, shall send		66: 9
shall the former sins r.,		82:10
r. not again unto that man.		84:92
r. again to their own place,		88:32
and are pure in heart, shall r.,		101:18
shall r. to the lands of their		103:11
should not r. to the land of	DC	103:30
speedily repent and r. unto thee,		109:21
children of Judah may begin to r.		109:64
also to r. to that power which		113: 8
remnants are exhorted to r. to		113:10
then I will r. to you again.		127: 1
thou shalt r. unto the ground—	Mses	4:25
and unto dust shalt thou r.		4:25
even so my words cannot r. void,		4:30
my Chosen shall r. unto me,		7:39
not r. to take anything out	JS	1:14
r. back to take his clothes;		1:15
them to me after his r.,		2:63

RETURNED

he r. to his own house at	1Ne	1: 7
r. from speaking with the Lord,		3: 1
when we had r. to the tent of		5: 7
I r. to the tent of my father.		15: 1
they r. again to the land of	Om	1:28
and they r., every one, according	Mos	6: 3
but r. to this land, having		8: 8
and we r., those of us that were		9: 2
we r. again to our own land,		10:21
they r. rejoicing in their spoil.		11:18
the army of the king r.,		19: 1
they r. to the land of Nephi,		19:24
r. with their king in peace		20:26
people r. to the city of Nephi,		21: 1
r. again to the city of Nephi.		21:12
r. to the land of Nephi, having		21:26
of them r. to the land of Helam,		23:38
until they r. again.		25: 5
until the time they r. again.		25: 6
and r. to their father, the king,		28: 1
they all r. again diligently unto	Al	1:26
r. into the camp of the Nephites		2:23
they all r. to their lands,		3: 1
then they r. again and began		3:24
Alma r. from the land of		8: 1
r. to his own house at Zarahemla		8: 1
he r. speedily to the land of		8:18
and r. towards my house.		10: 8
Alma r. and said unto them:		16: 6
he r. and they watered their flocks		17:39
and r. them to the pasture of		17:39
Ammon and Lamoni r.		21:18
they r. again to their own land;		25:13
r. again to the land of Nephi.		27: 1
he r. to the people of		27:25
of Nephi r. again to their land.		28: 3
they r. to their homes, never		31:23
r. to the land of Zarahemla,		35:14
Moroni r. the sword and the		44:10
r. and came to their houses and		44:23
r., having pursued after them in		47:30
they r. to the land of Nephi,		49:25
and r. to the camp of Moroni.		50:35
r. again privily to his own camp,		51:35
r. again to the city Bountiful,		52:17
they r. to Moroni and told		55:15
not r. with my two thousand		56:50
they r. in season to save us		57:17
And now Moroni r. to his army,		62:21
r. to the city of Zarahemla;		62:42
Helaman r. to the place of his		62:42
immediately r. to the Nephites	He	5:17
r. to the land of Zarahemla from		7: 1
but r. again unto the land of his		7: 3
when the Lamanites had r. unto	Mrm	6:11
he r. to the city Nehor and	Eth	7: 9
wherefore, they r. to their camp.		14:31
I r. to my father in the field,	JS	2:50

RETURNETH

r. to the land of Jerusalem	1Ne	1:hd

RETURNING

always r. thanks unto God	Al	7:23
children are r. to their homes,		58:31

REUNITE

spirit and body shall again r.,	Mro	10:34

REUNITED
spirit and the body shall be r.	Al	11:43
shall all be r. at once,		40:19
the souls and the bodies are r.,		40:20
dead shall come forth, and be r.,		40:21

REUNITING
it meaneth the r. of the soul with	Al	40:18

REVEAL
they r. all things from the	2Ne	27:10
to r. all things unto the		27:22
it shall be given to r. things	Al	26:22
should r. unto the world of	He	6:24
will r. unto you the Priesthood,	DC	2: 1
to r. the Book of Mormon,		27: 5
my word which I r. unto you,		27:18
I will r. myself from heaven		29:11
r. these things unto you by		38:30
them will I r. all mysteries,		76: 7
and r. the secret acts of men,		88:108
and r. the secret acts of men,		88:109
he shall r. all things—		101:32
r. not the things which I have		105:23
that I may r. mine ordinances		124:40
I deign to r. unto my church		124:41
I r. unto you a new and an		132: 4
knoweth it, and I r. it unto you,		132:44
I will r. more unto you,		132:66
I r. unto you concerning this	Mses	2: 1
to r. it unto the sons of Adam;		5:49
will r. unto you the Priesthood,	JS	2:38
all that He does now r.,	AoF	9
He will yet r. many great and		9

REVEALED
and all things shall be r. unto	2Ne	27:11
which is secret save it shall be r.;		30:17
all things which have been r. unto		30:18
of men shall at that day be r.,		30:18
save it be r. unto him;	Jac	4: 8
they r. the plan of salvation;	Jar	1: 2
by then shall all things be r.,	Mos	8:17
whom is the arm of the Lord r.?		14: 1
it has thus been r. unto me,	Al	5:47
that he should be r. unto them.		25:15
things which never have been r.;		26:22
greater than he had r. unto	3Ne	26:14
things which are hid must be r.	Mrm	5: 8
and their secret acts shall be r.	DC	1: 3
the arm of the Lord shall be r.;		1:14
things might be r. unto them,		25: 9
things which I r. unto them;		27:12
I say unto you that it is not r.,		28: 9
have been r. to my servant,		31: 4
be r. unto you from on high,		42: 9
which is hereafter to be r.—		42:35
be r. unto you in mine own		42:62
The place is not yet to be r.;		48: 5
place, or to them it shall be r.		48: 5
things which are r. unto them.		58:63
that hereafter shall be r.		63:14
are to be r. in the last days,		66: 2
after the Father has r. him.		76:43
Neither was it r., neither is,		76:46
neither will be r. unto man,		76:46
him to whom God has r. it.		76:90
it contains the r. will,		77: 6
the arm of the Lord shall be r.		90:10
record is hereafter to be r.		93: 6
which I have r. unto them,		105:23
in me that they should be r.		105:23
not been r. since the world was		121:26
to be r. in the last times,		121:27
shall be r. and set forth upon		121:29
shall be r. in the days of the		121:31
of God, and for his arm to be r.		123:17
my testimony which I have r.		124: 8
those ordinances might be r.		124:38
as the Lord has r. unto me		127: 1
glories to be r. in the last days,		128:17
be r. from the days of Adam		128:18
things which never have been r.	DC	128:18
shall be r. unto babes and		128:18
the book to be r.		128:20
this law r. unto them		132: 3
the glories which were to be r.,		133:57
And God r. himself unto Seth,	Mses	6: 3
as r. from God to	Fac	2: 2
as r. to Adam in the		2: 3
whom the priesthood was r.		2: 3
writings that cannot be r.		2: 8
Ought not to be r.		2: 9
an angel of God had r. it	JS	2:64
more mysterious passages r.		2:74
We believe all that God has r.,	AoF	9

REVEALING
r. through the heavens the	Fac	2: 7

REVELATION
spirit of prophecy and of r.—	TPg	
in the book shall be a r. from God,	2Ne	27: 7
the r. which was sealed shall		27:10
or r. which was great,	Jac	1: 4
and I know of no r. save	Om	1:11
to the spirit of r. and prophecy.	Al	4:20
the spirit of r. which is in me.		5:46
the r. of the truth of the word		6: 8
to the spirit of r. and prophecy;		8:24
prophecy, and the spirit of r.,		9:21
prophecy, and the spirit of r.,		17: 3
according to the spirit of r. and		23: 6
to the spirit of prophecy and r.;		43: 2
spirit of r. which is in me,		45:10
the spirit of prophecy and of r.,	He	4:12
prophecy and in the spirit of r.;		4:23
one that had the spirit of r. and	3Ne	3:19
the Lord no longer worketh by r.,		29: 6
behold, this is the spirit of r.;	DC	8: 3
Deny not the spirit of r.,		11:25
A r. I give unto you concerning		25: 2
and pretend to no other r.		32: 4
ask, thou shalt receive r. upon		42:61
shalt receive revelation upon r.,		42:61
by commandment or by r.		64:12
by r. from the Lord under		68:21
chapter, and 6th verse of the R.?		77: 1
chapter and 1st verse of R.?		77: 8
R. 7th chapter and 2nd verse?		77: 9
in the 8th chapter of R.?		77:12
in the 9th chapter of R.?		77:13
in the 10th chapter of R.?		77:14
in the eleventh chapter of R.?		77:15
A r. of Jesus Christ unto his		84: 1
And this r. unto you and		84:75
but by r. and the word of		89: 2
this word of wisdom by r.		89: 4
for the r. of Jesus Christ.		90:11
a r. and commandment		92: 1
for the r. which is to come,		101:23
of Joseph Smith, Jun., by r.,		102: 1
council was appointed by r.		102: 2
is appointed by r.,		102: 9
the mind of the Lord by r.		102:23
a r. and commandment,		103: 1
be designated unto them by r.—		107:39
agreeable to the r. which says:		107:58
And as thou hast said in a r.,		109: 6
speak to them, or give them r.		113:10
I wrote a few words of r. to you		128: 2
will find recorded in R. 20:12—		128: 6
the r. contained in the letter		128: 7
by the r. of Jesus Christ,		128: 8
to any man by actual r.,		128: 9
white stone mentioned in R. 2:17,		130:10
by r. and the spirit of prophecy,		131: 5
by r. and commandment		132: 7
by r. and commandment,		132:29
prophecy, r., visions, healing,	AoF	7

REVELATIONS
the warnings and the r. of God;	2Ne	5: 6
And we also had many r.,	Jac	1: 6

REVELATIONS / REWARD

and we have many r.	Jac	4: 6
despise not the r. of God.		4: 8
notwithstanding the many r.		7: 5
my prophesying, nor of my r.	Jar	1: 2
among us who have many r.,		1: 4
in prophesying, and in r.,	Om	1:25
contain these prophesyings and r.,	WM	1: 6
having many r. daily,	He	11:23
shall deny the r. of the Lord,	3Ne	29: 6
look ye unto the r. of God;	Mrm	8:33
you who deny the r. of God,		9: 7
done away, that there are no r.,		9: 7
unfolding unto them all my r.,	Eth	4: 7
my r. which I have caused to		4:16
a man may have many r.,	DC	3: 4
according to the r. of John,		20:35
the r. of God which shall come		20:35
commandments and r. of God.		20:45
the r. and commandments which		28: 1
receive commandments and r.		28: 2
the commandments and the r.,		28: 3
and the r. which are sealed,		28: 7
have r., but write them not		28: 8
receive commandments and r.		43: 2
receive commandments and r.		43: 3
that shall come before you as r.		43: 5
teach those r. which you have		43: 7
according to the r. and		52:17
and with r. in their time—		59: 4
the r. and commandments		70: 3
for the commandments and r.		71: 4
the r. may be published,		72:21
the r. and commandments		75: 4
Ye call upon my name for r.,		82: 4
the bringing forth of the r.		84:104
receive r. to unfold the		90:14
the presidency, in obtaining r.;		94: 3
r. which I have given unto you,		104:58
in the r. given unto us;		109:11
concerning the r. and		109:60
for the beginning of the r. and		124:39
the r. I have given unto you,		124:119
has brought forth the r. and		135: 3
no such things as visions or r.	JS	2:21

REVELATOR

a seer is a r. and a prophet also;	Mos	8:16
expressions, used by the R.,	DC	77: 2
he shall be a r. unto thee,		100:11
to be a seer, a r., a translator,		107:92
seer, and a r. unto my church,		124:94
to be a translator, a r., a seer,		124:125
John the R. was contemplating		128: 6

REVENGE

that they would seek r.,	Mos	19:19
saw that they could not seek r.	Al	27: 2
blood and r. continually.	Mro	9: 5
seeking for blood and r.		9:23
against them, neither seek r.,	DC	98:23

REVERENCE

r. him because of his greatness.	Al	47:22
all things bow in humble r.,	DC	76:93
respect or r. to the name		107: 4
who shall r. thee in thy house.		109:21
and r. are shown to the laws		134: 7

REVILE

and they did r. against Moses,	1Ne	17:42
ye will r. against the truth;	2Ne	9:40
and r. against that which is good,		28:16
that ye r. no more against them	Jac	3: 9
neither shall ye r. against them		3: 9
This man doth r. against our laws	Al	10:24
to r. us and to cast us out—		12: 4
he would r. even against God,		30:29
did r. against the priests and		30:31
that ye do not r. against those		34:40
hearest him r. against this	He	8: 2
suffer this man to r. against us?		8: 5
they did r. against him,		10:15
and would not turn and r. again,	3Ne	6:13
men shall r. you and persecute,		12:11
did r. against the prophets,	Eth	7:24
who did r. against the prophets.		7:24
r. not against those that revile.	DC	31: 9
revile not against those that r.		31: 9
and r. not against them,		98:23
you r. not against your enemy,		98:25

REVILED

r. against Moses and against	1Ne	17:30
saying: He has r. the king.	Mos	17:12
and r. him, and spit upon him,	Al	8:13
he has r. against our lawyers,		10:29
and had r. against their law		14: 2
that they had r. against the law,		14: 5
but they r. him, saying:		14: 7
and he was ridiculed and r.	JS	2:24

REVILERS

in me, reviling not against r.	DC	19:30

REVILING

in me, r. not against revilers.	DC	19:30
most bitter persecution and r.	JS	2:23
they were persecuting me, r. me,		2:25

REVILINGS

neither be ye afraid of their r.	2Ne	8: 7
and r., and stealing, robbing,	Al	16:18

REVIVE

and the people began to r.	Eth	9:35

REVOKE

I r. not the judgments which	DC	19: 5
I, the Lord, command and r.,		56: 4
I r. the commandment which		56: 5
I r. the commandment which		56: 6
I r. and they receive not		58:32
and I r. not the decree.		61:19
I r. the commission which I		75: 6

REVOLTED

who had r. from the church	4Ne	1:20

REVOLUTION

one complete r. throughout all	Mrm	2: 8
one r. was a day unto	Abr	3: 4
equal with Kolob in its r.	Fac	2: 4

REVOLUTIONS

All the times of their r.,	DC	121:31
and seasons in the r. thereof;	Abr	3: 4
the sun in their annual r.	Fac	2: 5
light from the r. of Kolob,		2: 5

REWARD

the r. of their hands shall be	2Ne	13:11
Who justify the wicked for r.,		15:23
for the r. of their pride		26:10
men shall reap a r. of their works,	Al	9:28
great evil thou shalt have thy r.		11:25
and how great shall be their r.!		29:15
so shall he have his r. of evil		41: 5
then shall ye receive your r.;		41:14
great shall be your r. in heaven;	3Ne	12:12
ye have no r. of your Father		13: 1
unto you, they have their r.		13: 2
himself shall r. thee openly.		13: 4
unto you, they have their r.		13: 5
in secret, shall r. thee openly.		13: 6
unto you, they have their r.		13:16
in secret, shall r. thee openly.		13:18
shall also reap good for your r.	DC	6:33
and great shall be your r.		14:11
receive the r. of the laborer.		23: 7
into temptation and lose your r.		31:12
and great shall be thy r.;		42:65
and my r. is with me,		54:10
and he shall r. every man,		56:19
the r. of the same is greater		58: 2

REWARD

wherefore he receiveth no r.	DC 58:26
shall in nowise lose their r.	58:28
for their r. lurketh beneath,	58:33
they shall receive for their r.	59: 3
righteousness shall receive his r.,	59:23
also a r. in the world to come.	63:48
r. thee according to thy deeds.	64:11
for a r. of their diligence	70:15
Great shall be their r. and	76: 6
shall in nowise lose his r.	84:90
your r. shall be an hundred-fold.	98:25
r. shall be doubled unto you	98:26
repent and r. thee four-fold	98:44
to r. every man according	101:65
and my r. is with me to	112:34
his r. shall not fail if he receive	124:16
mete out a just recompense of r.	127: 3
you shall in nowise lose your r.,	127: 4
there is a r. in heaven.	127: 4
and glory is their eternal r.	135: 6

REWARDED

have r. evil unto themselves!	2Ne 13: 9
shall be r. unto righteousness.	Al 41: 6
have good r. unto you again.	41:14
may be r. again according to	DC 56:12
be r. in mine own due time.	90:29
seek revenge, ye shall be r.;	98:23
be r. for thy righteousness;	98:30

REWARDEST

if thou r. him according	DC 98:31

REWARDETH

he r. you no good thing.	Al 34:39

REWARDS

their r. according to their works,	Al 3:26
shall reap the r. of your faith,	32:43

REYNOLDS: see CAHOON, Reynolds.

REZIN

that R., king of Syria,	2Ne 17: 1
the fierce anger of R. with Syria,	17: 4
and the head of Damascus, R.;	17: 8
rejoice in R. and Remaliah's son;	18: 6
the adversaries of R. against him,	19:11

RIB

the r. which I, the Lord God, had	Mses 3:22
the r. which the Gods had taken	Abr 5:16

RIBS

I took one of his r. and closed up	Mses 3:21
and they took one of his r.,	Abr 5:15

RICH

wo unto the r., who are rich as to	2Ne 9:30
r. as to the things of the world.	9:30
because they are r. they despise	9:30
the learned, and they that are r.,	9:42
and the r., that are puffed up in	28:15
they may be r. like unto you.	Jac 2:17
became exceeding r. in gold,	Jar 1: 8
r. as pertaining to the things of	Mos 4:23
and with the r. in his death;	14: 9
they began to be exceeding r.,	Al 1:29
are r. in all manner of things—	9:22
they grew r. in their own eyes,	45:24
they became exceedingly r.;	50:18
they began to grow exceeding r.	62:48
that they became exceeding r.,	He 6: 9
and thus they did become r.	6:11
there were not r. and poor,	4Ne 1: 3
they had become exceeding r.,	1:23
they became exceedingly r.	Eth 6:28
they became exceeding r.—	9:16
the people became exceeding r.	10:12
and then shall you be made r.	DC 6: 7
he that hath eternal life is r.	6: 7
and then shall you be made r.	11: 7
he that hath eternal life is r.	11: 7

RICHES

and the r. have I made,	DC 38:16
And I have made the earth r.,	38:17
Wo unto you r. men, that will	56:16
First, the r. and the learned,	58:10
and call upon the r., the high	58:47
humbling the r. and the proud.	84:112
in that the r. are made low.	104:16
bring forth their r. treasures unto	133:30
for the purpose of getting r.	JS 2:46

RICH, Charles C.

R., Thomas Grover, Newel	DC 124:132

RICHARDS, Willard

R., be appointed to fill the places	DC 118: 6
Wilford Woodruff, R., George A.	129:129
Taylor and R., two of the Twelve	135: 2

RICHER

the r. blessings upon the head of	DC 133:34

RICHES

silver, and all manner of r.,	1Ne 3:16
and their wisdom, and their r.—	2Ne 9:42
before the r. of Damascus	18: 4
found as a nest the r. of the people;	20:14
that you have obtained many r.;	Jac 2:13
But before ye seek for r.,	2:18
shall obtain r., if ye seek them;	2:19
nor any manner of r. of you;	Mos 2:12
r. which we have of every kind?	4:19
and thus he did do with the r.	11:13
he placed his heart upon his r.,	11:14
do ye set your hearts upon r.?	12:29
began to increase in r.,	24: 7
he had not exacted r. of them,	29:40
did for the sake of r. and honor.	Al 1:16
did not set their hearts upon r.?	1:30
because of their exceeding r.,	4: 6
and to set their hearts upon r.	4: 8
things of the world, upon your r.?	5:53
have not set your hearts upon r.	7: 6
and I have also acquired much r.	10: 4
and their hearts were set upon r.,	17:14
Seek not after r. nor the vain	39:14
of their exceeding great r.;	45:24
But notwithstanding their r., or	62:49
of their exceeding great r.	He 3:36
because of their exceeding r.,	4:12
so long with the r. of the world	6:17
set their hearts upon their r.;	6:17
set your hearts upon the r. and	7:21
of your exceeding great r.!	7:26
they have set their hearts upon r.;	13:20
set their hearts upon their r.,	13:20
ye are cursed because of your r.,	13:21
also are your r. cursed because	13:21
ye do always remember your r.,	13:22
the land, and also upon your r.,	13:23
cometh that he curseth your r.,	13:31
in the day that he gave us our r.,	13:33
behold, our r. are gone from us.	13:33
because of their exceeding great r.,	3Ne 6:10
according to their r. and their	6:12
great learning because of their r.	6:12
power, and authority, and r.,	6:15
because of their exceeding r.,	4Ne 1:43
because of his exceeding r.,	Eth 10: 3
Seek not for r. but for wisdom,	DC 6: 7
Seek not for r. but for wisdom;	11: 7
to give unto you greater r.,	38:18
And if ye seek the r. which	38:39
ye shall have the r. of eternity;	38:39
the r. of the earth are mine to	38:39
of the r. of those who embrace	42:39
honor and the r. of eternal life,	43:25
gather up your r. that ye	45:65
your r. will canker your souls;	56:16
the r. of eternity are mine	67: 2
ernestly the r. of eternity,	68:31
the r. of eternity are yours.	78:18
who has got r. in store—	90:22

RICHEST

RICHEST
ye shall be the r. of all people, — DC 38:39

RID
and am r. of your blood. — 2Ne 9:44
might r. my garments of your sins, — Jac 2: 2
would r. you from this iniquity — 2:16
r. my garments of your blood, — Mos 2:28
can get r. of the justice of — 3Ne 28:35
may r. our garments of the blood — Mrm 9:35
they shall r. their garments, — DC 61:34

RIDE
you desire to r. upon horses, — DC 62: 7

RIDETH
the destroyer r. upon the face — DC 61:19

RIDGE
had dug up a r. of earth — Al 49: 4

RIDGES
upon the top of these r. of earth — Al 50: 2

RIDICULED
and he was r. and reviled. — JS 2:24

RIGDON, Sidney: *see also SIDNEY.*
by the hand of my servant R., — DC 36: 2
come before my servants R. and — 36: 5
my servant R. should live as — 41: 8
Joseph Smith, Jun., and R. — 42: 1
and R. take their journey — 52: 3
journey with my servants R. and — 52:24
and R. and Edward Partridge — 52:41
Joseph Smith, Jun., and R. — 53: 5
Joseph Smith, Jun., and R., — 55: 5
I give unto my servant R. — 58:50
let my servant R. consecrate — 58:57
after that let my servants R. — 58:58
from thence let my servants, R., — 60: 6
made known concerning R. — 60:17
concerning my servants, R., — 61:23
say unto you, my servants, R., — 61:30
pleased with my servant R.; — 63:55
and R., seek them a home, — 63:65
and also unto my servant R., — 70: 1
Joseph Smith, Jun., and R., — 71: 1
Joseph Smith, Jun., and R., — 73: 3
We, Joseph Smith, Jun., and R., — 76:11
and my servant Pelagoram [R.], — 78: 9
Mahalaleel and Pelagoram [R.], — 82:11
I say unto thy brethren, — 90: 6
let my counselor, even R., remain — 90:21
I say unto my servant R., — 93:44
let my servant R. go on — 93:51
Joseph Smith, Jun., R. and — 102: 3
my servant R. shall lift up — 103:29
journey with my servant R. — 103:38
Let my servant Pelagoram [R.] — 104:20
upon my servant Pelagoram [R.] — 104:22
and also my servant R., — 115: 1
for counselors my servant R. — 124:126

RIGGS, Burr
Ashley, and my servant R., — DC 75:17

RIGHT
pervert the r. ways of the Lord, — 1Ne 13:27
r. hand hath spanned the heavens. — 20:13
perverted the r. ways of the Lord. — 22:14
he shall snatch on the r. hand — 2Ne 19:20
take away the r. from the poor — 20: 2
to teach any man the r. way; — 25:28
the r. way is to believe in Christ — 25:28
the r. way is to believe in Christ, — 25:29
and pervert the r. way of the Lord, — 28:15
they pervert the r. way of God, — Jac 7: 7
law of Moses which is the r. way; — 7: 7
whatsoever ye ask that is r., — Mos 4:21
be found at the r. hand of God, — 5: 9
the end a place at my r. hand. — 26:23
a place eternally at my r. hand. — 26:24

we have no r. to destroy my son, — Mos 29: 8
we have any r. to destroy another — 29: 8
claim his r. to the kingdom, — 29: 9
contrary to that which is r.; — 29:26
to desire that which is not r.; — 29:26
an inheritance at my r. hand. — Al 5:58
of turning from the r. to the left, — 7:20
or from that which is r. to — 7:20
that whatsoever they did was r.; — 18: 5
which is r., that will I do. — 18:17
aside to the r. hand or to the left, — 24:23
to dwell at the r. hand of God, — 28:12
of their r. to the government — 54:17
not turn to the r. nor to the left, — 56:37
not turn to the r. nor to the left — 56:40
turn to the r. nor to the left — 56:40
Gid and his men were on the r. — 58:17
and it was according to his r. — He 1:13
he did do that which was r. — 3:20
souls, at the r. hand of God — 3:30
guessed r., among so many; — 16:16
to be your r. and liberty; — 3Ne 3: 2
in that which ye believe to be r., — 3: 5
shall smite thee on thy r. cheek, — 12:39
know what thy r. hand doeth; — 13: 3
Father in my name, which is r., — 18:20
shalt break forth on the r. hand — 22: 3
of his justice is in his r. hand; — 29: 4
can turn the r. hand of the Lord — 29: 9
and depart from the r. way, — Mrm 9:20
did not do that which was r. — Eth 10: 5
he did that which was r. in the — 10:16
a place at the r. hand of God, — 12: 4
hilt of his sword in his r. hand, — 14: 2
to keep them in the r. way, — Mro 6: 4
down on the r. hand of God, — 7:27
on the r. hand of his power, — 9:26
to the r. hand nor to the left, — DC 3: 2
you must ask me if it be r., — 9: 8
if it is r. I will cause that your — 9: 8
you shall feel that it is r. — 9: 8
if it be not r. you shall have — 9: 9
on the r. hand of the Father, — 20:24
shall stand at my r. hand at — 29:12
shall be gathered on my r. hand — 29:27
thine heart is now r. before me — 39: 8
James Covill was r. before me, — 40: 1
have all things r. before me. — 41: 3
for they are not r. before me — 49: 2
on the r. hand of his glory, — 49: 6
this r. and this inheritance — 51: 4
all things may be r. before me, — 57:13
reigns whose r. it is to reign, — 58:22
at the r. hand of my Father, — 66:12
a legal r. to the bishopric, — 68:16
the r. of the presidency over — 68:17
has a legal r. to this office, — 68:18
their r. of the priesthood — 68:21
on the r. hand of the Father, — 76:20
even on the r. hand of God; — 76:23
I will be on your r. hand — 84:88
that are not r. in your house. — 93:43
guided in a r. and proper way — 101:63
it is not r. that any man — 101:79
a r. to one-half of the council, — 102:15
crown of glory at my r. hand. — 104: 7
holds the r. of presidency, — 107: 8
a r. to officiate in all the offices — 107: 9
a r. to officiate in their own — 107:10
An elder has a r. to officiate — 107:11
a r. to officiate in all these offices — 107:12
No man has a legal r. to this office, — 107:16
of Aaron has a legal r. to the — 107:76
receive r. by ordination — 108: 4
that you shall have r. to preach — 108: 6
that thy r. hand may exalt them, — 109:71
she, Zion, has a r. to by lineage; — 113: 8
not have r. to the priesthood, — 121:21
he loveth that which is r. — 124:15
with Abraham at his r. hand, — 124:19
by blessing and also by r.; — 124:91
shadow or coloring of justice or r. — 127: 1

stand on the r. hand of the Lamb.	DC 133:56
the r. and control of property,	134: 2
human law has a r. to interfere in	134: 4
governments have a r. to enact	134: 5
and governments have a r.,	134: 7
a r. in justice to deprive citizens	134: 7
religious societies have a r. to	134:10
on the r. of property or life,	134:10
the r. of property or character	134:11
not believe it r. to interfere with	134:12
crowned at the r. hand of the Son	Mses 7:56
stood on the r. hand of God;	7:57
given unto me a r. to thy throne,	7:59
and the r. whereunto I should be	Abr 1: 2
the r. belonging to the fathers.	1: 2
even the r. of the firstborn,	1: 3
not have the r. of the Priesthood,	1:27
concerning the r. of Priesthood,	1:31
this r. shall continue in thee,	2:11
as we have any r. to give	Fac 1:12
on the r. hand of God.	JS 1: 1
who was r. and who was wrong.	2: 8
Who of all these parties are r.;	2:10
If any one of them be r.,	2:10
which of all the sects was r.,	2:18
which of all the sects was r.–	2:18
a conduit open r. up into	2:43

RIGHTEOUS

to bring forth his r. purposes.	1Ne 4:13
And, behold, they are r. forever;	12:10
divide the wicked from the r.;	15:30
wicked are rejected from the r.,	15:36
and the r. have I justified	16: 2
if ye were r. and were willing	16: 3
of Jerusalem were a r. people;	17:22
we know that they are a r. people;	17:22
do ye suppose that they were r.?	17:33
than they if they had been r.?	17:34
he that is r. is favored of God.	17:35
he raiseth up a r. nation,	17:37
And he leadeth away the r. into	17:38
the wicked shall destroy the r.	22:16
will preserve the r. by his power,	22:17
and the r. be preserved,	22:17
Wherefore, the r. need not fear;	22:17
the r. shall not perish;	22:19
And the r. need not fear,	22:22
the r. must be led up as calves	22:24
but unto the r. it shall be blessed	2Ne 1: 7
would rise up a r. branch unto	3: 5
deliver up the spirits of the r.,	9:13
deliver up the body of the r.;	9:13
the r. shall have a perfect	9:14
they who are r. shall be righteous	9:16
who are righteous shall be r. still,	9:16
But, behold, the r., the saints of	9:18
but the r. fear them not,	9:40
Remember that his paths are r.	9:41
shall be administered unto the r.,	9:46
shall become a r. branch unto	9:53
concerning this r. branch of which	10: 1
Say unto the r. that it is well	13:10
away the righteousness of the r.	15:23
behold, the r. that hearken unto	26: 8
words of the r. shall be written,	26:15
suppose that ye are more r.	30: 1
raise up unto me a r. branch	Jac 2:25
away the r. out from among you.	3: 4
are more r. than you;	3: 5
nevertheless, he did spare the r.	Om 1: 7
a r. judgment might come upon	Mos 3:10
ye have made is a r. covenant.	5: 6
my r. servant justify many;	14:11
do not judge r. judgments,	29:29
trials and troubles of a r. king,	29:33
and he did judge r. judgments;	29:43
hast shed the blood of a r. man,	Al 1:13
our works have been r. works	5:17
among the names of the r.,	5:57
For the names of the r. shall be	5:58
numbered among those of the r.	6: 3
if they have been r. they shall	9:28

to pervert the ways of the r.,	Al 10:18
were not for the prayers of the r.,	10:22
it is by the prayers of the r.	10:23
if ye will cast out the r.	10:23
the r. yieldeth to no such	11:23
both the wicked and the r.;	11:44
and they became a r. people,	19:35
that we are not a r. people;	21: 6
For they became a r. people;	23: 7
had been slain were r. people,	24:26
they began to be a r. people;	25:14
hearts of the r. doth he dwell;	34:36
the r. shall sit down in his	34:36
the spirits of those who are r.	40:12
as well as the r. in paradise,	40:14
the wicked as well as the r.,	40:19
the bodies are reunited, of the r.,	40:20
then shall the r. shine forth in	40:25
r. for that which is righteous;	41:13
righteous for that which is r.;	41:13
ye shall have a r. judgment	41:14
we know, that he was a r. man;	45:19
Lord suffereth the r. to be slain	60:13
suppose that the r. are lost	60:13
to destroy his r. people.	60:31
because of the prayers of the r.,	62:40
more part of them, a r. people,	He 6: 1
sorrow and lamentation of the r.	6:33
seduced the more part of the r.	6:38
Condemning the r. because of	7: 5
they are more r. than you,	7:24
because of those who are r.	13:12
if it were not for the r. who are	13:13
that when ye shall cast out the r.	13:14
save he be a r. man and shall	13:18
treasures unto me save it be the r.;	13:19
a r. judgment might come upon	14:29
more r. part of the people had	3Ne 7: 7
but few r. men among them.	7: 7
they were not a r. people,	7:11
there were none r. among them,	9:11
ye were more r. than they,	9:13
the more r. part of the people	10:12
between the r. and the wicked,	24:18
were none that were r. save	4Ne 1:46
would again become a r. people.	Mrm 2:12
the prayers of the r., which	5:21
and if it so be that ye are r.,	6:21
he that is r. shall be righteous	9:14
is righteous shall be r. still;	9:14
had preserved for a r. people.	Eth 2: 7
did build up a r. kingdom;	10: 2
O Lord, thy r. will be done,	12:29
not to call the r. but sinners	Mro 8: 8
shall not show it unto the r.;	DC 10:36
you cannot always judge the r.,	10:37
tell the wicked from the r.,	10:37
may bring about my r. purposes	17: 4
bring about my r. purposes	17: 9
the song of the r. is a prayer	25:12
the r. shall be gathered upon	29:27
gathered unto me a r. people,	38:31
the r. shall be gathered out	45:71
entire separation of the r. and	63:54
that which is r. cometh down	67: 9
know the r. from the wicked,	84:53
and the r. shall inherit it.	88:26
between the r. and the wicked,	101:95
and were r. and holy men.	107:29
of his posterity who were r.,	107:53
gather out of that city the r.,	109:39
gather out the r. to build a	109:58
and r. men that were before you.	127: 4
warn the r. to save themselves	134:12
even Jesus Christ, a r. Judge,	Mses 6:57
When shall the blood of the r. be	7:45
The R. is lifted up, and the Lamb	7:47
and he saw the day of the r.	7:67
Pharaoh, being a r. man,	Abr 1:26

RIGHTEOUS'

blessed the earth for the r. sake.	Al 45:15
face of the land for the r. sake.	46:10

nevertheless for the r. sake,	Al	62:40
it is for the r. sake that it is	He	13:14

RIGHTEOUSLY

deal justly, judge r., and do	Al	41:14
and sacred ordinance to judge r.,		50:39
to walk humbly, to judge r.;	DC	11:12

RIGHTEOUSNESS

into the fountain of all r.!	1Ne	2: 9
three generations pass away in r.;		12:11
generation who passed away in r.		12:12
and they were armed with r.		14:14
which are pertaining to r.;		15:33
would walk in the paths of r.		16: 5
because of their r.,		19:11
they swear not in truth nor in r.		20: 1
thy r. as the waves of the sea.		20:18
he shall execute judgment in r.		22:21
because of the r. of his people,		22:26
the people, for they dwell in r.,		22:26
for his ways are r. forever.	2Ne	1:19
put on the armor of r.		1:23
of the r. of thy Redeemer;		2: 3
r. could not be brought to pass,		2:11
ye shall also say there is no r.		2:13
And if there be no r. there be		2:13
if there be no r. nor happiness		2:13
thou not shut the gates of thy r.		4:32
me around in the robe of thy r.!		4:33
my God, the rock of my r.		4:35
ye that follow after r.		8: 1
My r. is near;		8: 5
my r. shall not be abolished.		8: 6
unto me, ye that know r.,		8: 7
But my r. shall be forever,		8: 8
of their enjoyment, and their r.,		9:14
yea, even with the robe of r.		9:14
and my heart delighteth in r.;		9:49
for r., but behold, a cry.		15: 7
is holy shall be sanctified in r.		15:16
take away the r. of the righteous		15:23
decreed shall overflow with r.		20:22
with r. shall he judge the poor,		21: 4
r. shall be the girdle of his loins,		21: 5
the Son of r. shall appear		26: 9
shall have passed away in r.		26: 9
with r. shall the Lord God judge		30: 9
r. shall be the girdle of his loins,		30:11
baptized by water, to fulfil all r.,		31: 5
the Lamb of God did fulfil all r.		31: 6
it is sanctified unto us for r.,	Jac	4: 5
he did reign over his people in r.;	WM	1:17
becometh an enemy to all r.;	Mos	2:37
and hath judged of thy r.,		3: 4
he being an enemy to all r.		4:14
with things pertaining to r.		23:18
and fallen state, to a state of r.,		27:25
of those who have reigned in r.		29:22
doth pervert the ways of all r.		29:23
works have been the works of r.	Al	5:16
and bring forth works of r.,		5:35
doeth not the works of r.,		5:36
to have known the ways of r.		5:37
as to things pertaining unto r.,		5:42
again in the way of his r.		7: 4
that ye are in the paths of r.;		7:19
die as to things pertaining unto r.		12:16
as to things pertaining unto r.;		12:32
and their r. before God,		13:10
choosing to repent and work r.		13:10
things of God, and of his r.		19:34
concerning things pertaining to r.		21:23
of things pertaining to r.,		24:30
for he doth work r. forever.		26: 8
devil, who is an enemy to all r.		34:23
the things pertaining unto r.		35:16
he is the work of truth and r.		38: 9
things pertaining to things of r.;		40:26
and desired r. until the end		41: 6
so he shall be rewarded unto r.		41: 6
of the r. of the Lamanites,	He	1:hd
their r., and their wickedness,		3:14
their r. did exceed that of the	He	6: 1
had turned out of the way of r.,		6:31
the righteous because of their r.;		7: 5
joy in the r. of my brethren.		7: 8
as to things pertaining to r.		11:19
that r. which is in our great and		13:38
as to things pertaining to r.		14:18
decrease as to their faith and r.,	3Ne	1:30
Lord preserve his people in r.		4:29
protect this people in r.,		4:30
devil, to combine against all r.		6:28
people had turned from their r.,		7: 8
from r. unto their wickedness		7:15
do hunger and thirst after r.,		12: 6
the kingdom of God and his r.,		13:33
In r. shalt thou be established;		22:14
their r. is of me, saith the Lord.		22:17
unto the Lord an offering in r.		24: 3
shall the Son of R. arise with		25: 2
judgment upon the land in r.	Eth	7: 1
he did execute judgment in r.;		7:11
he did execute judgment in r.		7:27
come unto the fountain of all r.		8:26
Emer did execute judgment in r.		9:21
he even saw the Son of R.,		9:22
that Kim did not reign in r.,		10:13
the fountain of all r.		12:28
is not counted unto him for r.	Mro	7: 7
may conquer the enemy of all r.,		9: 6
not the Lord to establish his r.,	DC	1:16
are pertaining unto things of r.,		11:14
an offering unto the Lord in r.		13: 1
receive it in faith, and work r.,		20:14
a crown of r. thou shalt		25:15
having on the breastplate of r.,		27:16
dwell in r. with men on earth		29:11
being clothed with robes of r.,		29:12
in me, to receive a crown of r.,		29:13
he that liveth in r. shall be		43:32
until a day of r. shall come—		45:12
obtain all that ye can in r.,		48: 4
not in truth and r. before me.		50: 9
I will cut my work short in r.,		52:11
inasmuch as can be done in r.,		57: 6
he can obtain in r.,		57:12
and bring to pass much r.;		58:27
unto the Lord thy God in r.		59: 8
vows shall be offered up in r.		59:11
he who doeth the works of r.		59:23
should take r. in his hands		63:37
honor those who serve me in r.		76: 5
shall be cut short in r.—		84:97
reproving the world in r.		84:117
shalt be rewarded for thy r.;		98:30
people, that will serve me in r.;		100:16
kingdom of heaven and its r.,		106: 3
are to be made in all r.,		107:30
according to truth and r.		107:84
thy work may be cut short in r.		109:59
clothed upon with robes of r.,		109:76
only upon the principles of r.		121:36
an unchanging scepter of r.		121:46
because of thy r.;		122: 4
unto the Lord an offering in r.		128:24
unto the Lord an offering in r.;		128:24
it was accounted unto him for r.		132:36
it was accounted unto him for r.,		132:37
who rejoiceth and worketh r.,		133:44
I am he who spake in r.,		133:47
And they were preachers of r.,	Mses	6:23
a land of r. unto this day.		6:41
his people, and they dwelt in r.		7:16
and one mind, and dwelt in r.;		7:18
continued his preaching in r.		7:19
r. for a season abide upon my		7:48
And r. will I send down out of		7:62
r. and truth will I cause to		7:62
to dwell on the earth in r. for		7:65
been myself a follower of r.,	Abr	1: 2
to be a greater follower of r.,		1: 2
having turned from their r.,		1: 5
to this Church, in truth and r.,	JS	2: 2
offering unto the Lord in r.		2:69

RIGHTFUL

RIGHTFUL
became a r. heir, a High Priest,	Abr 1: 2

RIGHTLY
whom the kingdom doth r. belong	Mos 29: 6
when it r. belonged unto them.	Al 54:17
the government doth r. belong,	54:18
and r. belongs to the literal	DC 107:40
whom r. belongs the priesthood,	113: 6

RIGHTS
and every man may enjoy his r.	Mos 29:32
would deprive them of their r.	Al 2: 4
rejected their r. to the kingdom	17:hd
not enjoy their r. and privileges.	30:27
that they might preserve their r.	43: 9
their r. and their liberties;	43:26
and their r., and their religion.	43:47
that they will maintain their r.,	46:20
people, his r., and his country,	48:13
covenanted to maintain their r.	51: 6
maintain and to obtain their r.	54:24
their r. and their privileges.	55:28
preserve the r. and the liberty	61: 9
and also to maintain their r.,	3Ne 2:12
recover their r. and government,	3:10
from them their r. of government,	3:10
and the r. of their country;	6:30
his r. of mercy which he hath	Mro 7:27
maintaining r. and privileges,	DC 98: 5
r. and protection of all flesh,	101:77
That the r. of the priesthood are	121:36
their r., their keys, their honors,	128:21
infringe upon the r. and liberties	134: 4
and inalienable r. by the laws of	134: 5
the individual r. of its members,	134: 9

RILLS
ye r., flow down with gladness.	DC 128:23

RIMS
fastened into the two r. of a bow.	Mos 28:13

RINGLETS
and their r., and their bracelets,	Al 31:28

RINGS
and the tablets, and the ear-r.;	2Ne 13:20
The r., and nose jewels;	13:21

RIOTINGS
they did stir up the people to r.,	Al 11:20

RIOTOUS
and he spent his time in r. living	Mos 11:14

RIPE
and they were r. in iniquity;	1Ne 17:35
in that day that they are fully r.	2Ne 28:16
which, when it is fully r.,	Mos 12:12
they would be r. for destruction.	Al 10:19
Behold, the field was r., and	26: 5
when they are fully r.;	37:28
repent before they are fully r.	37:31
wickedly, when they are fully r.;	45:16
shall ye be r. for destruction;	He 13:14
ye will sin until ye are fully r.	Eth 2:15
at hand when the earth is r.;	DC 29: 9
until the harvest is fully r.;	86: 7

RIPENED
and it will soon become r.,	Jac 5:37
those branches which are r.,	5:58
when they are r. in iniquity.	Eth 2: 9
when they were r. in iniquity;	9:20
well-nigh r. for destruction.	DC 61:31

RIPENESS
wicked, yea, nearly unto r.;	1Ne 17:43

RIPENING
they were r. for destruction,	He 5: 2
and r. for an everlasting	6:40

RISEN

Yea, even at this time ye are r.,	He 8:26
were r. again for destruction.	11:37
the world is r. in iniquity;	DC 18: 6

RIPLAH
and on the south of the hill R.;	Al 43:31
Lamanites had passed the hill R.,	43:35

RIPLAKISH
was a descendant of R.	Eth 1:23
And R. was the son of Shez.	1:24
old age; and he begat R.	10: 4
and R. reigned in his stead.	10: 4
R. did not do that which was right	10: 5
insomuch that R. was killed,	10: 8
(he being a descendant of R.)	10: 9

RIPLIANCUM
he came to the waters of R.,	Eth 15: 8

RISE
slain he should r. from the dead,	1Ne 10:11
being the first that should r.	2Ne 2: 8
would r. up a righteous branch	3: 5
shall r. up one mighty among them,	3:24
to its mother earth, to r. no more.	9: 7
if the flesh should r. no more	9: 8
became the devil, to r. no more.	9: 8
Wo unto them that r. up early	15:11
do not r., nor possess the land,	24:21
For I will r. up against them,	24:22
he shall r. from the dead,	25:13
And he shall r. the third day	Mos 3:10
would r. contentions among you.	29: 7
that all shall r. from the dead	Al 11:41
that all shall r. from the dead,	12: 8
that man should r. from the dead	12:20
on the morrow he shall r. again;	19: 8
had appointed that he should r.	19:11
r. up in great swelling words	30:31
he shall r. again from the dead,	33:22
that all shall r. from the dead.	40: 5
time appointed for men to r.	40: 8
that they shall r. from the dead;	40: 9
time cometh when all shall r.,	40:10
did r. up in rebellion against us.	57:32
r. up from their secret places,	58:20
would not r. up in rebellion	61:11
to r. up in rebellion against their	He 1: 7
the time that he shall r. again	14:20
sun did r. in the morning again,	3Ne 1:19
maketh his sun to r. on the evil	12:45
shall r. against thee in judgment	22:17
r. in the pride of their hearts,	Mrm 8:28
Who will r. up against the	9:26
people did r. up in rebellion	Eth 10: 8
brother did r. up in rebellion	10:14
disputations r. among you.	Mro 8: 4
The r. of the Church of Christ	DC 20: 1
they shall r. from the dead	63:49
slaves shall r. up against their	87: 4
die, they also shall r.	88:27
have power to r. up and prevail	109:26
if any people shall r. against this	109:27
that we may r. up in thy might	109:33
when he falls he shall r. again,	117:13
the dead, if the dead r. not at all?	128:16
will r. with us in the resurrection.	130:18
and shall r. up and bless thee,	Abr 2:10
let thy servant r. up and depart	2:13
nation shall r. against nation,	JS 1:29
r. and progress of the Church	2: 1
concerning the r. of this Church,	2:73

RISEN
Messiah hath r. from the dead,	2Ne 25:14
after Christ shall have r. from	26: 1
And if Christ had not r. from	Mos 16: 7
r. up in rebellion against me,	Al 61: 3
and those who have r. up are	61: 3
have r. up in rebellion against us	61: 7
of the Father he hath r. again,	Mrm 7: 5
after he had r. from the dead;	Eth 12: 7
hath r. again from the dead,	DC 18:12

RISEST

RISEST
when thou r. in the morning let — Al 37:37

RISING
and r. again he said: O king, — Mos 7:12
were many of the r. generation — 26: 1
aged, and the r. generation; — Al 5:49
r. up in great contentions, — He 4:12
shall know of the r. of the sun — 14: 4
wickedness of the r. generation. — 3Ne 1:30
the beginning of the r. up and — DC 5:14
and for the r. generations — 69: 8
the burning rays of the r. sun; — 121:11
we owe to all the r. generation, — 123:11

RISK
do not r. one more offense — Al 41: 9

RISKED
have hitherto r. to commit sin. — Al 41: 9

RITES
for their r. of worship and — Al 43:45
and by our r. of worship, — 44: 5

RIVER
by the side of a r. of water. — 1Ne 2: 6
called the name of the r., Laman, — 2: 8
the waters of the r. emptied into — 2: 9
thou mightest be like unto this r., — 2: 9
I beheld a r. of water; — 8:13
eyes towards the head of the r., — 8:17
extended along the bank of the r., — 8:19
beheld, on the other side of the r. — 8:26
even the r. of which he spake; — 12:16
What meaneth the r. of water — 15:26
wilderness, across the r. Laman. — 16:12
they had crossed the r. Jordan — 17:32
then had thy peace been as a r., — 20:18
by them beyond the r., — 2Ne 17:20
upon them the waters of the r., — 18: 7
shall shake his hand over the r., — 21:15
which was east of the r. Sidon, — Al 2:15
they were crossing the r. Sidon, — 2:27
on the west of the r. Sidon, — 2:34
the west side of the r. Sidon. — 2:34
they had all crossed the r. Sidon — 2:35
upon the bank of the r. Sidon — 3: 3
upon the east of the r. Sidon, — 6: 7
on the west of the r. Sidon. — 8: 3
Lamanites will cross the r. Sidon — 16: 6
on the east of the r. Sidon, — 16: 6
sons crossed over the r. Sidon, — 16: 7
on the east side of the r. Sidon. — 16: 7
by the head of the r. Sidon, — 22:27
at the head of the r. Sidon, — 22:29
away by the head of the r. Sidon, — 43:22
near the bank of the r. Sidon, — 43:27
on the west of the r. Sidon — 43:27
on the west of the r. Sidon, — 43:32
began to cross the r. Sidon, — 43:35
to flee towards the r. Sidon. — 43:39
upon the bank of the r. Sidon — 43:40
the other side of the r. Sidon — 43:41
upon the bank by the r. Sidon. — 43:51
yea, even on both sides of the r., — 43:52
Lehi on the east of the r. Sidon, — 43:53
on the west of the r. Sidon, — 43:53
on the east of the r. Sidon. — 49:16
by the head of the r. Sidon— — 50:11
Missouri r. in its decreed course, — DC 121:33
on the Susquehanna r., declaring — 128:20
a r. to go out of Eden to water the — Mses 3:10
of the second r. was called Gihon; — 3:13
name of the third r. was Hiddekel; — 3:14
the fourth r. was the Euphrates. — 3:14
There was a r. running out of Eden, — Abr 5:10

RIVERS
I make their r. a wilderness — 2Ne 7: 2
large bodies of water and many r. — He 3: 4
was in a land of many waters, r., — Mrm 6: 4
And ye r., and brooks, and rills, — DC 128:23
I make the r. a wilderness; — 133:68
r. shall turn from their course; — Mses 6:34
the r. of water were turned out of — 7:13

RIVETED
which hath so strongly r. the — DC 123: 7

ROAD
I may be strict in the plain r.! — 2Ne 4:32

ROADS
his view, wandering in strange r. — 1Ne 8:32
leadeth them away into broad r., — 12:17
cast up, and many r. made, — 3Ne 6: 8
and the level r. were spoiled, — 8:13

ROAR
They shall r. like young lions; — 2Ne 15:29
they shall r., and lay hold of the — 15:29
that day they shall r. against them — 15:30
the r. of the lions was heard out — Mses 7:13

ROARED
the Lord thy God, whose waves r.; — 2Ne 8:15

ROARING
their r. like a lion. — 2Ne 15:28
like the r. of the sea; — 15:30

ROB
that they may r. the fatherless! — 2Ne 20: 2
They r. the poor because of their — 28:13
they r. the poor because of their — 28:13
they should r. and plunder them, — Mos 10:17
neither durst they r., nor murder, — Al 1:18
again may r. us of our property. — 20:13
suppose that mercy can r. justice? — 42:25
did r. them of their right to — 54:17
to murder, and to r., and to gain, — He 2: 8
and to r. and to plunder, — 6:17
to plunder and r. and murder. — 3Ne 4: 5
Will a man r. God? — 24: 8
if a man or woman shall r., — DC 42:84

ROBBED
and have r. their treasures, — 2Ne 20:13
for they said that he r. them. — Mos 10:16
Behold, he r. our fathers; — Al 20:13
if he r. he was also punished; — 30:10
Yet ye have r. me. — 3Ne 24: 8
Wherein have we r. thee? — 24: 8
with a curse, for ye have r. me, — 24: 9

ROBBER
thou art a r., and I will slay thee. — 1Ne 3:13
the people as a thief and a r. — Al 11: 2
Gadianton the r. had established — He 3:23
and the threatenings of a r.; — 3Ne 3:12
was the end of Giddianhi the r. — 4:14
was smitten by the hand of a r., — Eth 10: 3

ROBBERS
forth to take this band of r. — He 2:10
Gadianton's r. and murderers. — 6:18
that there were r. among them — 6:20
did unite with those bands of r., — 6:21
Lamanites did hunt the band of r. — 6:37
band of r. was utterly destroyed — 6:37
those Gadianton r. filling the — 7: 4
this secret band of r. who did — 11: 2
an exceeding great band of r.; — 11:26
they became r. of Gadianton. — 11:26
these r. did make great havoc, — 11:27
to search out this band of r., — 11:28
forth against this band of r., — 11:30
of the numbers of those r. who — 11:31
And the r. did still increase — 11:32
it were for the Gadianton r., — 3Ne 1:27
to join those Gadianton r. — 1:29

ROBBERS / RODS

ROBBERS (cont.)

Gadianton r. had become so	3Ne 2:11
arms against those Gadianton r.,	2:12
between the r. and the people	2:17
gain some advantage of the r.,	2:17
r. did gain many advantages over	2:18
the governor of this band of r.;	3:1
wicked and abominable r.	3:11
Giddianhi, the governor of the r.,	3:12
that the r. should come down	3:12
and to guard them from the r.	3:14
the hands of those Gadianton r.	3:15
that the r. should come down	3:17
that we may fall upon the r.	3:20
those armies of r. had prepared	4:1
there was no game for the r.	4:2
the r. could not exist save it	4:3
no chance for the r. to plunder	4:4
they did hope to destroy the r.	4:4
about after the manner of r.;	4:7
r. did not come again to battle;	4:15
r. to lay siege sufficiently long	4:18
of provisions among the r.—	4:19
the r. were about to perish with	4:20
on their march beyond the r.,	4:25
when the r. began their march,	4:25
the r. who were on the south	4:26
had taken all the r. prisoners,	5:4
those r. who had entered into	6:3
There were no r., nor murderers,	4Ne 1:17
the r. of Gadianton did spread	1:46
And these Gadianton r., who	Mrm 1:18
the land was filled with r. and	2:8
for the thieves, and the r., and	2:10
and the r. of Gadianton,	2:27
and the r. of Gadianton,	2:28
save it be the Lamanites and r.	8:9
there began to be r. in the land;	Eth 10:33
And there were r., and in fine,	13:26
if thou art in perils among r.;	DC 122:5

ROBBERY

secret work of murder and of r.;	He 2:4
that murder, treason, r., theft,	DC 134:8

ROBBING

lying, thieving, r., committing	Al 1:32
stealing, r., plundering, murdering,	16:18
and r. and plundering them;	17:14
be murders, and r., and lying,	Mrm 8:31

ROBBINGS

yea, all their murders, and r.,	Al 37:21
and their murders, and their r.,	He 3:14

ROBE

he was dressed in a white r.;	1Ne 8:5
he was dressed in a white r.	14:19
in the r. of thy righteousness!	2Ne 4:33
even with the r. of righteousness.	9:14
and he was clothed in a white r.;	3Ne 11:8
without even a hole in his r.	DC 135:2
He had on a loose r. of most	JS 2:31
no other clothing on but this r.,	2:31
was his r. exceedingly white,	2:32

ROBERT: *see FOSTER, Robert D.; and THOMPSON, Robert B.*

ROBES

clothed with r. of righteousness,	DC 29:12
clothed in r. and sit thou here;	38:26
with r. of righteousness,	109:76

ROCK

and dwelt upon a r. before him;	1Ne 1:6
ourselves in the cavity of a r.	3:27
and my r. and my salvation.	13:36
their r. and their salvation?	15:15
I did molten out of the r.	17:16
which was in him, smote the r.,	17:29
the waters to flow out of the r.	20:21
he clave the r. also and the waters	20:21
and the r. of my salvation.	2Ne 4:30
the r. of my righteousness.	2Ne 4:35
my r. and mine everlasting God.	4:35
the r. from whence ye are hewn,	8:1
who is the r. of your salvation.	9:45
wicked ones, enter into the r.,	12:10
and for a r. of offense to both the	18:14
of Midian at the r. of Oreb;	20:26
that he should smite the r.	25:20
he that is built upon the r.	28:28
God and r. of their salvation;	Jac 7:25
is upon the r. of our Redeemer,	He 5:12
the r. upon which ye are built,	5:12
do the foundations r., even to	12:12
upon this buildeth upon my r.,	3Ne 11:39
and is not built upon my r.;	11:40
who built his house upon a r.—	14:24
for it was founded upon a r.	14:25
for ye are built upon my r.	18:12
these are not built upon my r.,	18:13
and did molten out of a r.	Eth 3:1
I have molten out of the r.	3:3
hid himself in the cavity of a r.	13:13
he dwelt in the cavity of a r.	13:14
dwelt in the cavity of a r.,	13:18
again in the cavity of the r.	13:22
for if ye are built upon my r.,	DC 6:34
him will I establish upon my r.,	10:69
you shall have my word, my r.,	11:16
Build upon my r., which is my	11:24
church, my gospel, and my r.	18:4
of my gospel and my r.,	18:5
gospel before you, and my r.,	18:17
upon this r. I will build my	33:13
yea, upon this r. ye are built,	33:13
He that buildeth upon this r.	50:44
upon this r. I will build my	128:10
of Zion, the R. of Heaven,	Mses 7:53
was our covering and our r.	Abr 2:16

ROCKS

I saw the earth and the r.,	1Ne 12:4
the r. of the earth must rend;	19:12
shall go into the holes of the r.,	2Ne 12:19
To go into the clefts of the r.,	12:21
into the tops of the ragged r.,	12:21
and in the holes of the r.,	17:19
if we could command the r.	Al 12:14
the r. which are upon the face of	He 14:21
the r. were rent in twain;	3Ne 8:18
and the r. did cease to rend,	10:9
and ye solid r. weep for joy!	DC 128:23
and they shall smite the r.,	133:26
the r. were rent; and the saints	Mses 7:56

ROD

they did smite us even with a r.	1Ne 3:28
as they smote us with a r.,	3:29
your younger brother with a r.?	3:29
And I beheld a r. of iron,	8:19
which came along by the r. of iron,	8:20
hold of the end of the r. of iron,	8:24
darkness, clinging to the r. of iron,	8:24
hold of the end of the r. of iron;	8:30
holding fast to the r. of iron,	8:30
the r. of iron, which my father had	11:25
What meaneth the r. of iron	15:23
in the wilderness with his r.;	17:41
will give power unto him in a r.;	2Ne 3:17
the r. of his oppressor.	19:4
O Assyrian, the r. of mine anger,	20:5
As if the r. should shake itself	20:15
he shall smite thee with a r.,	20:24
and as his r. was upon the sea	20:26
forth a r. out of the stem of Jesse,	21:1
the earth with the r. of his mouth,	21:4
the r. of him that smote thee is	24:29
the earth with the r. of his mouth;	30:9
smite you by the r. of my mouth,	DC 19:15
What is the r. spoken of in the	113:3

RODS

which is forty r. long and	DC 104:43

ROE

it shall be as the chased r., 2Ne 23:14

ROLFE, Samuel
R. and his counselors for priests, DC 124:142

ROLL
Take thee a great r., and write in it 2Ne 18: 1
purposes of the Lord shall r. on, Mrm 8:22
thence shall the gospel r. forth DC 65: 2
without hands shall r. forth, 65: 2
as they r. upon their wings 88:45
gathering of thy people may r. on 109:59

ROLLED
and garments r. in blood; 2Ne 19: 5
the earth shall be r. together Mrm 5:23
the earth shall be r. together 9: 2
is unfolded after it is r. up, DC 88:95

ROLLING
How long can r. waters DC 121:33

ROLLS
The earth r. upon her wings, DC 88:45

ROOM
r. that I may write of the things 1Ne 6: 3
his people might have r. to cross Al 2:34
not be r. enough to receive it. 3Ne 24:10
if I had r. upon the plates, Mrm 8: 5
found no more r. for them; DC 101:21
not r. enough on the mountains 117: 8
in the r. of my servant Hyrum, 124:91
were the only persons in the r. 135: 2
a light appearing in my r., JS 2:30
until the r. was lighter than 2:30
The r. was exceedingly light, 2:32
I saw the light in the r. begin 2:43
until the r. was again left dark, 2:43
the r. was left as it had been 2:43
my r. was again beginning to 2:44

ROOMS
that ye should prepare r. for DC124:145

ROOT
their r. shall be rottenness, 2Ne 15:24
there shall be a r. of Jesse, 21:10
out of the serpent's r. shall come 24:29
I will kill thy r. with famine, 24:30
the r. of this tree will perish, Jac 5: 8
of the moisture of the r. thereof, 5:18
the r. thereof hath brought forth 5:18
of the much strength of the r. 5:18
that the r. and the top may be equal 5:48
the r. and the top thereof equal, 5:73
and as a r. out of dry ground; Mos 14: 2
ax is laid at the r. of the tree; Al 5:52
with great care, that it may get r., 32:37
with much care it will get r., 32:37
behold it will not get any r.; 32:38
it hath no r. it withers away, 32:38
fruit thereof, it shall take r.; 32:41
that it may take r. in you, 43:42
leave them neither r. nor branch. 3Ne 25: 1
laid at the r. of the trees; DC 97: 7
wasted away, both r. and branch, 109:52
What is the r. of Jesse 113: 5
leave them neither r. nor branch. 133:64
leave them neither r. nor branch. JS 2:37

ROOTED
wicked spirit r. out of my breast, Al 22:15

ROOTS
a branch shall grow out of his r. 2Ne 21: 1
perhaps I might preserve the r. Jac 5:11
they have nourished the r., 5:34
the r. thereof profit me nothing 5:35
I know that the r. are good, 5:36
and have overrun the r. thereof; 5:37
have overcome the r. thereof 5:37
overcome the r. which are good? Jac 5:48
have overcome the r. thereof, 5:48
faster than the strength of the r., 5:48
may preserve unto myself the r. 5:53
the r. of the natural branches of 5:54
that I may preserve the r. also 5:54
the r. thereof may take strength 5:59
branches and the r. thereof, 5:60
the r. of their mother tree, 5:60
that I have preserved the r. 5:60
lest the r. thereof should be too 5:65
of Israel, both r. and branches; 6: 4
r. which God had prepared Al 46:40

ROPE
and sin as it were with a cart r. 2Ne 15:18

ROSE
they r. and stood upon their feet. Al 14:25
there were many who r. up, Eth 13:15
and r. again the third day; DC 20:23
shall blossom as the r. 49:24
they r. up and blessed Adam, 107:54
r. up against Abel, his brother, Mses 5:32

ROT
flesh must have laid down to r. 2Ne 9: 7

ROTTENNESS
their root shall be r., 2Ne 15:24

ROUGH
the r. places to be made smooth, 1Ne 17:46
many smooth places became r. 3Ne 8:13
r. places to become smooth— DC 49:23
the r. places made smooth; 109:74

ROUND
And as I cast my eyes r. about, 1Ne 8:13
I also cast my eyes r. about, 8:26
course of the Lord is one eternal r. 10:19
a r. ball of curious workmanship; 16:10
Lift up thine eyes r. about 21:18
and r. tires like the moon; 2Ne 13:18
concerning the regions r. about; 25: 6
have camped against them r. about, 26:15
they pitched their tents r. about, Mos 2: 5
their tents r. about the temple, 2: 6
that he cast his eyes r. about on 4: 1
and the land r. about— 7:21
I set guards r. about the land, 10: 2
my spies out r. about the land 10: 7
look over all the land r. about. 11:12
vineyards r. about in the land; 11:15
sent guards r. about the land 11:17
cast his eyes r. about towards 19: 6
set guards r. about the land, 19:28
the borders of the land r. about. 21: 2
should watch the land r. about, 21:20
went r. about the land of Shilom 22:11
while tilling the land r. about, 23:25
set guards r. about the land 23:37
throughout the land r. about 27: 2
traveling r. about through all 27:32
his course is one eternal r. Al 7:20
heard by the people r. about; 12: 2
all the region r. about Sidom, 15:14
in all the region r. about, 16:15
flocks r. about that they flee not; 17:33
unto the regions r. about. 21:13
and in all the land r. about. 21:21
were in all the regions r. about, 22:27
and r. about on the borders 22:27
r. about on the wilderness side; 22:29
and the wilderness r. about. 22:34
in fine, in all the land r. about, 24: 1
r. about the land of Jershon, 28: 1
in all the borders r. about 28: 1
many travels r. about the land 30:32
and his course is one eternal r. 37:12
and took their journey r. about 43:22
were marching r. about in the 43:24
Moroni placed spies r. about, 43:28

ROUND 821 RULER

up banks of earth r. about	Al	48: 8
r. about their cities and the		48: 8
yea, all r. about the land,		48: 8
a ridge of earth r. about them,		49: 4
city in all the land r. about;		49:13
which had been dug r. about,		49:18
heaps of earth r. about all the		50: 1
of a man, r. about the cities.		50: 2
built upon the timbers r. about;		50: 3
r. about every city in all the land.		50: 6
and in the land r. about		50: 9
But he kept his men r. about,		52: 6
by casting up walls r. about		52: 6
strengthen the cities r. about,		52:10
digging a ditch r. about the land,		53: 3
the city of Bountiful r. about		53: 4
r. about the city Gid.		55:25
that we kept spies out r. about,		56:22
and from the land r. about,		57: 6
we did camp r. about the city		57: 9
sent out their spies r. about us		58:14
in all the land r. about in		59: 2
and from the land r. about,		59: 6
there are thousands r. about in		60:22
r. about in the borders of the		62:34
would attack the cities r. about	He	1:26
maintain those parts r. about		1:26
Lehi with an army r. about		1:28
and in all the regions r. about		3:31
land of Zarahemla and r. about		5:19
all the regions r. about		5:50
great cities which are r. about,		7:22
which are in the land r. about,		13:16
should be built r. about them,	3Ne	3:14
guards r. about to watch them,		3:14
to lay siege r. about the people		4:16
r. about the temple which was		11: 1
they cast their eyes r. about,		11: 3
he cast his eyes r. about on		15: 1
any parts of that land r. about		16: 1
he looked r. about again on		17: 1
he cast his eyes r. about again		17: 5
upon the ground r. about him,		17:12
in all the lands r. about.	4Ne	1: 1
is one continual r. of murder	Mrm	8: 8
in all the countries r. about	Eth	9:35
and his course is one eternal r.	DC	3: 2
and in the regions r. about.		30: 4
and in that region r. about,		30:10
whose course is one eternal r.,		35: 1
forth into the regions r. about,		44: 3
in those regions r. about,		48: 3
in the regions r. about them;		52:39
land in all the regions r. about,		57: 6
gospel in the regions r. about;		58:46
yea, in those regions r. about,		66: 5
world in the regions r. about,		71: 2
churches in the regions r. about,		73: 1
preach in the regions r. about		73: 4
glory of the Lord shone r. about.		76:19
encompasseth them r. about.		76:29
and mine angels r. about you,		84:88
also should travel r. about		84:112
all things are r. about him;		88:41
and is r. about all things;		88:41
in the regions r. about;		100: 3
opened in the regions r. about		100: 3
set watchmen r. about them,		101:45
may overlook the land r. about,		101:45
and built a hedge r. about,		101:46
and built the hedge r. about,		101:53
in the region r. about the land		101:70
and the counties r. about,		101:71
stay in the region r. about,		105:20
dwell in the regions r. about		105:23
the adjoining counties r. about.		105:28
and the regions r. about;		106: 1
thy glory be r. about them,		109:22
and in the regions r. about;		111: 7
for stakes in the regions r. about,		115:18
forth unto the regions r. about.		133: 9

ROUNDING
think and r. in the middle	JS	2:51

ROUNDY, Shadrach
R., if he will receive it,	DC	124:141

ROYAL
one of the r. descent directly	Abr	1:11
Pharaoh signifies king by r. blood.		1:20

RUDENESS
and to speak with much r.,	1Ne	18: 9
lifted up unto exceeding r.		18: 9
because of the r. of thy brethren.	2Ne	2: 1

RUGGLES: see EAMES, Ruggles.

RUIN
not this r. come under thy hand—	2Ne	13: 6
not to an imaginary r., but to	JS	2:16

RUINED
For Jerusalem is r.,	2Ne	13: 8
for the salvation of a r. world;	DC	135: 6

RUINS
also covered with r. of buildings	Mos	8: 8

RULE
brother thinks to r. over us;	2Ne	5: 3
brethren, to r. over this people.		5: 3
and babes shall r. over them.		13: 4
and women r. over them.		13:12
they shall r. over their oppressors.		24: 2
that I r. in the heavens above		29: 7
that she should r. over them!	Mos	8:20
always have kings to r. over you.		29:13
a king or kings to r. over you.		29:16
unrighteous king to r. over them;		29:35
appoint judges to r. over them,		29:41
r. and do according to their wills,	He	7: 5
should r. and reign over them;		12: 6
let God r. him that judgeth,	DC	58:20
Lord, r. in the heavens above,		60: 4
when the wicked r. the		98: 9
the greater light to r. the day,	Mses	2:16
the lesser light to r. the night,		2:16
And the sun to r. over the day,		2:18
and the moon to r. over the night,		2:18
and he shall r. over thee.		4:22
And thou shalt r. over him;		5:23
than that which is to r. the day,	Abr	3: 5
light which is set to r. the day,		3: 6
light which is set to r. the night.		3: 6
for I r. in the heavens above,		3:21
the greater light to r. the day,		4:16
the lesser light to r. the night;		4:16
r. over the day and over the		4:17

RULED
he that r. the nations in anger,	2Ne	24: 6
shall be r. by the conferences.	DC	58:58

RULER
a r. and a teacher over thy brethren.	1Ne	2:22
chosen him to be a r. over you,		3:29
taken it upon him to be our r.		16:37
to make himself a king and a r.		16:38
brother shall be a r. over us.		18:10
we will not have him to be our r.;	2Ne	5: 3
that I should be their r.		5:19
Wherefore, I had been their r.		5:19
Thou hast clothing, be thou our r.,		13: 6
make me not a r. of the people.		13: 7
be a king and a r. over his people	Jac	1: 9
a king and a r. over this people,	Mos	1:10
a r. and a king over this people;		2:11
is a king and a r. over you.		2:30
a r. and a king over his people,		6: 3
that our r. should make a treaty		9: 2
a king and a r. over his people,		23:39
son should be our king and our r.		29: 2

RULER 822 SACRED

RULER
who was a chief r. among them,	Al 12:20
the chief r. of the Zoramites,	35: 8
ye shall have no king nor r.,	DC 38:21
will be your r. when I come;	41: 4
be made r. over many things.	52:13
Let no man think he is r.;	58:20
a r. in my kingdom.	101:61
and he shall be a r. over many.	117:10
he shall be made r. over many;	124:113
for he shall be made r. over many.	132:44
be made r. over many things;	132:53
made r. over his household,	JS 1:49
make him r. over all his goods.	1:50

RULERS
to servant of r.:	1Ne 21: 7
the scepters of the r.	2Ne 24: 5
your r., and the seers hath he	27: 5
also appointed r. and leaders	Al 2:14
those r. who were the remnant	25: 7
their r. and their priests and	35: 5
make them r. over the people.	46: 5
world, and before kings and r.	DC 1:23
made r. over many kingdoms,	78:15
of those who are placed as r.	101:76
wise men and r. may hear	101:94
mercy upon the r. of our land;	109:54
r. and magistrates as such,	134: 6
We believe that r., states, and	134: 7
These I will make my r.;	Abr 3:23
subject to kings, presidents r.,	AoF 12

RULES
in prescribing r. of worship	DC 134: 4
prescribing r. on spiritual concerns,	134: 6
r. and regulations of such societies;	134:10

RULETH
He r. high in the heavens,	1Ne 17:39
the Lord, who r. over all flesh.	DC 133:61

RULING
had taken the r. of the people	Mos 10:15

RUMOR
r. with her thousand tongues	JS 2:61

RUMORS
wars, and r. of wars,	1Ne 12: 2
I saw wars and r. of wars	12:21
in wars and r. of wars	12:21
there were wars and r. of wars	14:15
to be wars and r. of wars	14:16
shall have wars, and r. of wars;	2Ne 25:12
spreading r. and contentions upon	He 16:22
be heard of wars, r. of wars,	Mrm 8:30
of wars and r. of wars,	DC 45:26
hear of wars, and r. of wars;	JS 1:23
hear of wars, and r. of wars.	1:28

RUN
the two nations shall r. together	2Ne 29: 8
the two nations shall r. together	29: 8
r. faster than he has strength.	Mos 4:27
which is r. over by the beasts	12:11
he was r. upon and trodden	Al 30:59
the land of Nephi did r. in a	50: 8
in a body r. upon our swords,	57:33
Do not r. faster or labor more	DC 10: 4
Or canst thou r. about longer	19:40
and all wild animals that r. or	89:14
And shall r. and not be weary,	89:20

RUNNING
r. into the fountain of all	1Ne 2: 9
came r. together by multitudes	Al 14:29
r. from the east towards the	22:27
the people came r. together	46:21
r. by the head of the river	50:11
the line r. directly between	DC 57: 4
chronology r. back from myself	Abr 1:28
There was a river r. out of Eden,	5:10

RUSH
branch and r. in one day.	2Ne 19:14
of Giddianhi did r. upon them	3Ne 4:10

RUSHED
r. forth with much swiftness	Al 17:32
and he r. forward that he might	44:12

RUSHING
filled, as with a r. mighty wind,	DC 109:37
sound of the r. of great waters,	110: 3

RUST
thereof were cankered with r.;	Mos 8:11
where moth and r. doth corrupt,	3Ne 13:19
moth nor r. doth corrupt,	13:20

RYDER, Simonds
and placed upon the head of R.	DC 52:37

RYE
and r. for the fowls and for	DC 89:17

SABAOTH
into the ears of the Lord of S.,	DC 87: 7
into the ears of the Lord of S.,	88: 2
into the ears of the Lord of S.,	95: 7
into the ears of the Lord of S.,	98: 2

SABBATH
the s. day holy unto the Lord.	Jar 1: 5
Remember the s. day, to keep it	Mos 13:16
the s. of the Lord thy God,	13:18
the Lord blessed the s. day,	13:19
they should observe the s. day,	18:23
shall all observe the S. day	DC 68:29
on the following S.,	127:10
winter, neither on the S. day;	JS 1:17

SACKCLOTH
and I make s. their covering.	2Ne 7: 3
a stomacher, a girding of s.;	13:24
they repent in s. and ashes,	Mos 11:25
and did humble themselves in s.,	He 11: 9
and make s. their covering.	DC 133:69

SACRAMENT
the s. of Christ unworthily;	Mrm 9:29
baptize, and administer the s.,	DC 20:46
to baptize, administer the s.,	20:58
to their partaking of the s.,	20:68
when ye partake of the s.,	27: 2
out of your s. meetings;	46: 4
any out of your s. meetings	46: 5
offer a s. unto the Most High.	62: 4
unto me for your s. offering,	95:16

SACRAMENTS
and offer up thy s. upon my	DC 59: 9
thy s. unto the Most High,	59:12
offer up your s. before him.	89: 5

SACRED
that the more s. things may be	1Ne 19: 5
save it be that I think it be s.	19: 6
there were preaching which was s.,	Jac 1: 4
and keep all these things s.	Al 37: 2
with these things, which are s.,	37:14
sacred, which he has kept s.,	37:14
these things which are s. shall	37:15
do with these things which are s.	37:16
ye take care of these s. things,	37:47
by the s. support which we owe	44: 5
of the s. word of God,	44: 5
Alma and his fathers to be most s.;	50:38
s. ordinance to judge righteously,	50:39
unto them their s. privileges to	50:39
possession of those s. things	63: 1
Shiblon to confer those s. things,	63:11
these things were to be kept s.,	63:13
a mock of that which was s.,	He 4:12

SACRED

things which had been kept s.	3Ne	1: 2
did administer that which was s.	4Ne	1:27
up the records which were s.—		1:48
all the s. records which had		1:48
to generation, which were s.—		1:48
the s. engravings concerning	Mrm	1: 3
by our fathers, which were s.,		6: 6
unto the Lord, which were s.	Eth	15:11
I have s. records that I would	Mro	9:24
deliveredst up that which was s.	DC	3:12
broken the most s. promises		3:13
Remember it is s. and cometh		6:10
Trifle not with s. things.		6:12
have been hid up, that are s.;		8:11
cannot write that which is s.		9: 9
them up, yea, that which was s.,		10: 9
make a selection of s. hymns,		25:11
which cometh from above is s.,		63:64
and all the s. things shall be		104:62
exclusive of the s. things,		104:63
[printing] these s. things		104:63
the avails of the s. things		104:64
the s. things in the treasury,		104:65
for s. and holy purposes.		104:65
the s. treasury of the Lord;		104:66
be the holy and s. writings,		104:68
for holy and s. purposes,		104:68
shall be had in s. remembrance		117:12
his sacrifice shall be more s.		117:13
s. the freedom of conscience.		134: 5

SACRIFICE

did offer s. and burnt offerings	1Ne	5: 9
did offer s. and burnt offerings		7:22
he offereth himself a s. for sin,	2Ne	2: 7
that they might offer s. and	Mos	2: 3
they had rather s. their lives than	Al	26:32
should be a great and last s.;		34:10
not a s. of man, neither of beast,		34:10
for it shall not be a human s.;		34:10
be an infinite and eternal s.		34:10
man that can s. his own blood		34:11
should be a great and last s.;		34:13
pointing to that great and last s.;		34:14
last s. will be the Son of God,		34:14
this being the intent of this last s.,		34:15
shall offer for a s. unto me	3Ne	9:20
offer a s. unto the Lord thy	DC	59: 8
and verily it is a day of s.,		64:23
an acceptable offering and s.		84:31
observe their covenants by s.—		97: 8
every s. which I, the Lord,		97: 8
this is the tithing and the s.		97:12
for his s. shall be more sacred		117:13
by covenant and s.		132:51
for he shall do the s. which		132:60
of the s. of the Only Begotten	Mses	5: 7
but offered an acceptable s.		6: 3
turned their hearts to the s. of	Abr	1: 7
I offered s. there in the plains		2:18
offer up Abraham as a s.	Fac	1: 3
The altar for s. by the		1: 4
as he offered s. upon an altar,		2: 2

SACRIFICED

s. their women and their children,	Mrm	4:15
and their children were again s.		4:21

SACRIFICES

your s. and your burnt offerings	3Ne	9:19
I will accept none of your s.		9:19
and did offer them up as s.	Mrm	4:14
and your memorials for your s.	DC	124:39
I have seen your s.,		132:50
have seen your s. in obedience		132:50
Why dost thou offer s. unto the	Mses	5: 6

SAD

hypocrites, of a s. countenance,	3Ne	13:16
the s. tale of the destruction of	Mrm	8: 3
have learned by s. experience	DC	121:39

SAFE

and shall carry away s.,	2Ne	15:29
build and have s. foundation.	Jac	4:15
no flesh shall be s. upon the	DC	61:15
strict charges to keep them s.,	JS	2:60
they remained s. in my hands,		2:60

SAFELY

shall dwell s. in the Holy One	1Ne	22:28
they shall dwell s. forever.	2Ne	1: 9
shalt dwell s. with thy brother,		2: 3

SAFETY

and on whom ye depend for s.,	2Ne	6: 2
the needy shall lie down in s.;		24:30
reception and s. of the brethren	Al	28: 8
encircles them in the arms of s.,		34:16
the welfare and s. of his people.		48:12
preparing for the s. of his people.		49:27
they rejoiced in each other's s.;		53: 2
for the s. of their country;		62:10
for the s. of their lives and	3Ne	2:12
for the s. of mine own life.	Mro	1: 3
they shall be preserved in s.;	DC	42:56
a place of s. for the saints of		45:66
needs flee unto Zion for s.		45:68
you may rest in peace and s.,		105:25
shall be the s. of my people,		124:10
traveler may find health and s.		124:23
seek to find s. and refuge		124:109
for my own s. and the safety of		127: 1
and the s. of this people.		127: 1
for the good and s. of society.		134: 1
Zion shall dwell in s. forever.	Mses	7:20

SAID

in a dream, and s. unto him:	1Ne	2: 1
And this they s. he had done		2:11
I, Nephi, s. unto my father:		3: 7
Wherefore, he s. unto him:		3:13
But behold I s. unto them		3:15
but I s. in my heart:		4:10
the Spirit s. unto me again:		4:11
the Spirit s. unto me again:		4:12
Wherefore, he s. that these		5:19
when I had s. these words,		7:18
of the fruit, s. my father.		8:35
he s. unto us, because		8:36
And my father s. he should		10: 9
and he also s. he should		10: 9
Wherefore, he s. it must		10:13
And the Spirit s. unto me:		11: 2
And I s.: I desire to		11: 3
And the Spirit s. unto me:		11: 4
And I s.: Yea, thou knowest		11: 5
the Spirit s. unto me: Look!		11: 8
I s. unto the Spirit:		11: 9
And he s. unto me:		11:10
And I s. unto him:		11:11
he s. unto me: Look!		11:12
and he s. unto me: Nephi,		11:14
And I s. unto him:		11:15
And he s. unto me:		11:16
And I s. unto him:		11:17
And he s. unto me:		11:18
And the angel s. unto me:		11:21
And after he had s. these words,		11:24
he s. unto me: Look!		11:24
the angel s. unto me again:		11:26
the angel s. unto me:		12: 1
And he s. unto me:		12: 9
And the angel s. unto me:		12:11
And the angel s. unto me:		12:11
And the angel s. unto me:		12:14
And the angel s. unto me:		12:22
And the angel s. unto me:		13: 2
And I s.: I behold		13: 2
And he s. unto me:		13: 3
And the angel s. unto me:		13: 5
the angel s. unto me:		13:11
And the angel s. unto me:		13:21
And I s. unto him:		13:22

SAID 824 SAID

And he s.: Behold	1 Ne	13:23	and he s.: I will prune it,	Jac 5: 4
and he s. unto me:		13:23	and he s. unto his servant:	5: 7
the angel of the Lord s. unto me:		13:24	the Lord of the vineyard s. unto	5:15
he s. unto me:		14: 8	the servant s. unto his master:	5:16
I s. unto him, Yea.		14: 8	And he s. unto the servant:	5:18
he s. unto me:		14: 9	the Lord of the vineyard s. unto	5:19
And he s. unto me:		14:10	and he s. unto the servant:	5:20
And the angel s. unto me:		14:20	And he s. unto the servant:	5:20
And they s.: Behold,		15: 7	for behold, s. he, this long time	5:20
And I s. unto them:		15: 8	the servant s. unto his master:	5:21
And they s. unto me:		15: 9	the Lord of the vineyard s. unto	5:22
Behold, I s. unto them:		15:10	wherefore, I s. unto thee,	5:22
things which the Lord hath s.?		15:11	the Lord of the vineyard s. unto	5:23
And I s. unto them:		15:22	the Lord of the vineyard s. again	5:24
And they s. unto me:		15:23	And he s. unto the servant:	5:25
And I s. unto them that		15:24	the Lord of the vineyard s. unto	5:26
And they s. unto me:		15:26	behold, the servant s. unto him:	5:27
And I s. unto them that		15:27	the Lord of the vineyard s. unto	5:29
And I s. unto them that		15:28	the Lord of the vineyard s.:	5:31
And I s. unto them that		15:29	the Lord of the vineyard s. unto	5:33
which the angel s. unto me		15:29	the servant s. unto his master:	5:34
And I s. unto them that		15:30	the Lord of the vineyard s. unto	5:35
And they s. unto me:		15:31	the Lord of the vineyard s. unto	5:38
I s. unto them that		15:32	wept, and s. unto the servant:	5:41
behold they s. unto me:		16: 1	the servant s. unto his master:	5:48
I s. unto them that		16: 2	the Lord of the vineyard s. unto	5:49
all these things were s. and done		16: 6	the servant s. unto the Lord of	5:50
And I s. unto my father:		16:23	And the Lord s.: Yea, I will	5:51
voice of the Lord s. unto him		16:26	the Lord of the vineyard s. unto	5:57
And Laman s. unto Lemuel		16:37	according to that which I have s.	5:57
And I s.: Lord, whither		17: 9	the Lord of the vineyard s. unto	5:71
for he s.: I will make		17:12	his servants, and s. unto them:	5:75
and the Lord s. also that:		17:14	as I s. unto you that I would	6: 1
I, Nephi, s. unto them that		17:49	And I s. unto him: Deniest thou	7: 9
And I s. unto them:		17:50	And he s.: If there should be	7: 9
I, Nephi, s. many things unto		17:52	And I s. unto him: Believest	7:10
the Lord s. unto me:		17:53	And he s.: Yea.	7:10
And now, they s.: We know		17:55	And I s. unto him: Then	7:11
my father, Lehi, had s. many things		18:17	he s. unto me: Show me a sign	7:13
And s. unto me:		21: 3	And I s. unto him: What am I	7:14
Then I s., I have		21: 4	that he s. unto the people:	7:16
And he s.: It is a		21: 6	And he s.: I fear lest I have	7:19
But, behold, Zion hath s.:		21:14	s. that I believed the scriptures;	7:19
came unto me and s. unto me:		22: 1	when he had s. these words	7:20
And I, Nephi, s. unto them:		22: 2	wherefore, I s. unto my son Enos:	7:27
For, behold, s. he,	2 Ne	1: 4	And I s.: Lord, how is it done?	En 1: 7
But, s. he, notwithstanding		1: 5	And he s. unto me:	1: 8
And he hath s. that:		1:20	according as I have s.:	1:10
Wherefore, he s. unto Eve,		2:18	the Lord s. unto me:	1:12
wherefore he s.: Partake		2:18	for he had s. unto me:	1:15
Yea, Joseph truly s.:		3: 7	And the Lord s. unto me:	1:18
whom I have s. I would raise up		3: 9	because I s. unto you that I had	Mos 2:16
for the Lord hath s. unto me,		3:16	vary from that which he hath s.;	2:22
And the Lord hath s.:		3:17	Therefore, as I s. unto you that	2:27
And the Lord s. unto me also:		3:18	And he s. unto me: Awake;	3: 2
and s. unto them: Behold,		4: 3	And he s. unto me: Awake, and	3: 3
For the Lord God hath s. that:		4: 4	say unto you as I have s. before,	4:11
And the Lord God s. unto me:		5:25	and therefore he s. unto them:	5: 6
the Lord God s. unto me:		5:30	the name that I s. I should	5:11
who have s. to thy soul:		8:23	And he s. unto them: Behold,	7: 9
Wherefore, as I s. unto you,		10: 3	and rising again he s.:	7:12
this land, s. God, shall be a		10:10	he was exceeding glad, and s.:	7:14
by the words of three, God hath s.,		11: 3	And because he s. unto them	7:27
In mine ears, s. the Lord of Hosts,		15: 9	and s. that he should take	7:27
And one cried unto another, and s.:		16: 3	or in other words, he s. that	7:27
Then s. I: Wo is unto me!		16: 5	And now, because he s. this,	7:28
laid it upon my mouth, and s.:		16: 7	For behold, the Lord hath s.:	7:29
Then I s.: Here am I;		16: 8	And the king s. unto him:	8: 7
And he s.: Go and tell this		16: 9	things that they had s. are true	8: 9
Then s. I: Lord, how long?		16:11	Therefore I s. unto thee:	8:11
And he s.: Until the cities be		16:11	Now Ammon s. unto him:	8:13
Then s. the Lord unto Isaiah:		17: 3	And the king s. that a seer	8:15
But Ahaz s.: I will not ask,		17:12	And Ammon s. that a seer	8:16
And he s.: Hear ye now,		17:13	because they s. that he	10:15
the word of the Lord s. unto me:		18: 1	for they s. that he robbed them.	10:16
Then s. the Lord to me:		18: 3	he was also wroth; and he s.:	11:27
For thou hast s. in thy heart:		24:13	for he has s. these things that	11:28
for the Lord God hath s. that		27:13	And the Lord s. unto me:	12: 2
he s. unto the children of men:		31:10	and s. unto the king:	12: 9
And the Father s.:		31:11	that they s. unto the king:	12:18
remember that I s. unto you		32: 2	one of them s. unto him:	12:20
wherefore, I s. unto you,		32: 3	And now Abinadi s. unto them:	12:25
For he s. that the history of his	Jac	1: 3	And they s.: We teach the	12:28

And again he s. unto them:	Mos	12:29
for ye have s. that ye teach		12:31
And they answered and s. that		12:32
But now Abinadi s. unto them:		12:33
Now Abinadi s. unto them,		12:37
he s. unto his priests:		13: 1
and s. unto them:		13: 2
ye remember that I s. unto you:		13:12
that he s. unto them:		13:25
And now ye have s. that		13:27
Have they not s. that God		13:34
Yea, and have they not s. also		13:35
And now Abinadi s. unto them:		15: 1
yea, even as Isaiah s., as a		15: 6
and s. unto Zion: Thy God		15:14
stretched forth his hand and s.:		16: 1
And he s. unto him:		17: 7
For thou hast s. that God		17: 8
Now Abinadi s. unto him:		17: 9
when Abinadi had s. these words,		17:20
that he s. unto them:		18: 8
And when he had s. these words,		18:13
Lord was upon him, and he s.:		18:13
And after Alma had s. these		18:14
And this he s. unto them,		18:29
And now the king s. that		18:33
brought him before Limhi, and s.:		20:13
But Limhi s. unto them:		20:14
And Limhi s. unto him:		20:14
And now the king s.:		20:15
therefore he s.: I will search		20:16
weht forth and s. unto the king:		20:17
and he s. unto them:		20:24
before the king, and s. unto him:		22: 3
And Gideon s. unto him:		22: 5
But he s. unto them:		23: 7
And he s. unto Alma:		24:17
now the Lord s. unto Alma:		24:23
not believe what had been s.		26: 2
And he s. unto the king:		26:11
But king Mosiah s. unto Alma:		26:12
And as I s. unto you,		27:11
For the Lord hath s.:		27:13
And again, the angel s.:		27:14
For, s. he, I have repented		27:24
And the Lord s. unto me:		27:25
And the Lord s. unto Mosiah:		28: 7
And now, as I s. unto you,		28:20
recall the things which he had s.,		29: 9
But Alma s. unto him:	Al	1:12
when Alma had s. these words		2:31
the words which he s. to Nephi:		3:14
the Spirit hath not s. unto me that		7: 8
the Spirit hath s. this much unto		7: 9
that I have s. unto him, he		7:16
For as I s. unto you from the		7:18
vary from that which he hath s.;		7:20
I have s. these things unto you		7:22
Now when the people had s. this,		8:13
hungered, and he s. to a man:		8:19
And the man s. unto him:		8:20
whom an angel s. in a vision:		8:20
was filled he s. unto Amulek:		8:23
And they s. also: We will not		9: 4
And they s.: Who is God, that		9: 6
And again it is s. that:		9:13
because I s. unto them that they		9:31
And also because I s. unto them		9:32
I s. I never had known much of		10: 5
appeared unto me and s.:		10: 7
man whom the angel s. unto me:		10: 8
And the angel s. unto me he is		10: 9
it was s. by an angel of God.		10: 9
and he s. unto them:		10:17
therefore, he s. unto Amulek:		11:21
And Amulek s. unto him:		11:22
And Zeezrom s. unto him:		11:22
Now Amulek s.: O thou child of		11:23
And Zeezrom s. unto him:		11:26
And Amulek s.: Yea, there		11:27
Now Zeezrom s.: Is there more		11:28
Now Zeezrom s. unto him again:		11:30
And he s.: An angel hath made		11:31

And Zeezrom s. again: Who is he	Al	11:32
And he s. unto him, Yea.		11:33
And Zeezrom s. again: Shall he		11:34
Amulek answered and s. unto him:		11:34
Now Zeezrom s. unto the people:		11:35
for he s. there is but one God;		11:35
because I s. he shall not save his		11:36
he hath s. that no unclean thing		11:37
And Amulek s. unto him:		11:39
And he s. unto Alma:		12: 8
came forth and s. unto him:		12:20
What is this that thou hast s.,		12:20
Now Alma s. unto him:		12:22
making God a liar, for he s.:		12:23
Now, as I s. concerning		13:10
what I have s. may suffice.		13:20
when Alma had s. these words		13:21
they also s. that Amulek had lied		14: 2
was pained; and he s. unto Alma:		14:10
But Alma s. unto him:		14:11
Now Amulek s. unto Alma:		14:12
And Alma s.: Be it according		14:13
their cheeks, and s. unto them:		14:14
judge stood before them, and s.:		14:19
and smote them again, and s.		14:24
Alma s. unto him, taking him by		15: 6
And he answered and s.:		15: 7
And Alma s.: If thou		15: 8
And he s.: Yea, I believe		15: 9
when Alma had s. these words,		15:11
Now as I s., Alma having seen		15:18
Alma returned and s. unto them:		16: 6
they s. God could not destroy,		16: 9
with his Spirit, and s. unto them:		17:10
the Lord s. unto them also:		17:11
And Ammon s. unto him:		17:23
But Ammon s. unto him: Nay,		17:25
for, s. he, I will show forth my		17:29
Ammon s. unto his brethren:		17:33
astonished exceedingly, and s.:		18: 2
they answered the king, and s.:		18: 3
he s. unto them: Now I know		18: 4
And they s. unto him:		18: 9
the king's servants s. unto him,		18:13
and thus he s. unto him:		18:13
unto the king, and s. unto him:		18:14
Ammon s. unto him again:		18:15
And he s. unto him:		18:16
open his mouth, and s. unto him:		18:18
Ammon answered and s. unto him:		18:19
And the king s.: How knowest		18:20
harmless, he s. unto Lamoni:		18:22
the king answered him, and s.:		18:23
with boldness, and s. unto him:		18:24
he answered, and s. unto him:		18:25
And then Ammon s.:		18:26
And he s., Yea.		18:27
And Ammon s.: This is God.		18:28
And Ammon s. unto him again:		18:28
And he s.: Yea, I believe that		18:29
And Ammon s. unto him:		18:30
And king Lamoni s.: Is it above		18:31
And Ammon s.: Yea, and he		18:32
And king Lamoni s.: I believe		18:33
Ammon s. unto him: I am a		18:34
when Ammon had s. these words,		18:36
after he had s. all these things,		18:40
And now, when he had s. this,		18:42
And she s. unto him:		19: 4
And he s. unto the queen:		19: 8
And Ammon s. unto her:		19: 9
And she s. unto him:		19: 9
be according as thou hast s.		19: 9
And Ammon s. unto her:		19:10
his hand unto the woman, and s.:		19:12
Now, when he had s. these words,		19:13
for the Lord had s. unto Mosiah,		19:23
who s. that Ammon was the		19:25
and others s. he was sent by the		19:25
some who s. that Ammon was		19:27
and they s. that it was this Great		19:27
And when she had s. this,		19:30
heard this, he s. unto Lamoni:		20: 3

SAID

Now Lamoni s. unto Ammon:	Al 20: 4
Now Lamoni s. unto him:	20: 4
And Ammon s. unto him:	20: 5
it be God; and he s. unto me—	20: 5
And he s. unto Ammon:	20: 7
the father of Lamoni s. unto him:	20: 9
And he also s.: Whither art thou	20:10
father was angry with him, and s.:	20:13
But Lamoni s. unto him:	20:15
But Ammon stood forth and s.	20:17
when Ammon had s. these words	20:19
Ammon raised his sword, and s.	20:22
fearing he should lose his life, s.:	20:23
to his desire, he s. unto him:	20:24
when Ammon had s. these words,	20:25
astonished exceedingly, and s.:	20:26
Now Aaron s. unto him:	21: 7
And the man s. unto him:	21: 8
before the king, and s. unto him:	22: 2
And the king s. unto them:	22: 3
And Aaron s. unto the king:	22: 4
Now the king s. unto them:	22: 5
What is this that ye have s.	22: 5
what is this that Ammon s.—	22: 6
Aaron answered him and s.	22: 7
And the king s.: I know that	22: 7
heart began to rejoice, and he s.:	22: 8
And the king s.: Is God	22: 9
And Aaron s. unto him:	22:10
And he s.: Yea, I believe	22:11
the king s.: What shall I do	22:15
Behold, s. he, I will give up all	22:15
But Aaron s. unto him:	22:16
when Aaron had s. these words,	22:17
when the king had s. these words,	22:18
and s. unto him: Stand.	22:22
now I, after having s. this,	22:35
which he s. unto the people	24: 7
which he s. concerning the seed	25: 9
For he s. unto them:	25:10
And he s. unto the priests	25:12
when Ammon had s. these words,	26:10
But Ammon s. unto him:	26:11
that we s. unto our brethren in	26:23
For they s. unto us:	26:24
the Lord comforted us, and s.:	26:27
and they s. unto the king:	27: 4
But the king s. unto them:	27: 6
And Ammon s.: I will go and	27: 7
And the king s. unto him:	27: 8
But Ammon s. unto him:	27: 9
But the king s. unto him:	27:10
and the Lord s. unto him:	27:11
which the Lord had s. unto him.	27:13
that Ammon s. unto them:	27:15
the high priest s. unto him:	30:23
And Korihor s. unto him:	30:23
Now Alma s. unto him:	30:32
And then Alma s. unto him:	30:37
Now Alma s. unto him:	30:39
And now Korihor s. unto Alma:	30:43
But Alma s. unto him:	30:44
And he s.: Yea, I will deny,	30:45
that Alma s. unto him:	30:46
Now Korihor s. unto him:	30:48
Now Alma s. unto him:	30:49
when Alma had s. these words,	30:50
of an angel and s.	30:53
And he s. unto me: There is	30:53
Now when he had s. this,	30:54
But Alma s. unto him:	30:55
when Alma had s. these words,	31:36
among them s. unto him:	32: 5
truly penitent, and s. unto them:	32: 7
Behold thy brother hath s.,	32: 9
And now, as I s. unto you,	32:14
now as I s. concerning faith—	32:21
Now, as I s. concerning faith,	32:26
which he s. must be planted in	33: 1
And Alma s. unto them:	33: 2
ye have s. that ye could not	33: 2
s. concerning prayer or worship?	33: 3
For he s.: Thou are merciful,	33: 4

And now Alma s. unto them:	Al 33:12
ye must believe what Zenos s.;	33:13
for, behold he s.: Thou hast	33:13
For behold, he s.: Thou art	33:16
now, as I s. unto you before,	34:33
the Lord hath s. he dwelleth not	34:36
has also s. that the righteous	34:36
behold, the voice s. unto me:	36: 8
And he s. unto me: If thou	36: 9
And he s.: If ye will keep	37:13
therefore the Lord s., if they	37:22
And the Lord s.: I will prepare	37:23
even as I s. unto Helaman,	38: 1
than what I s. unto thy brother;	39: 1
for the Lord had s. unto them,	43:46
again, the Lord has s. that:	43:47
And Moroni s. unto Zerahemnah:	44: 1
of Moroni, and s. unto him:	44: 8
when Moroni had s. these words,	44:12
son Helaman and s. unto him:	45: 2
And Helaman s. unto him:	45: 3
And Alma s. again: Believest	45: 4
And he s.: Yea, I believe all	45: 5
And Alma s. unto him again:	45: 6
And he s.: Yea, I will keep	45: 7
Then Alma s. unto him:	45: 8
after Alma had s. these things	45:15
And he s.: Thus saith the Lord	45:16
as I have s. so shall it be:	45:16
when Alma had s. these words	45:17
And he s.: Surely God shall not	46:18
when Moroni had s. these words,	46:19
Moroni s. unto them:	46:23
he s.—Even as this remnant	46:24
when Moroni had s. these words	46:28
pretended to be wroth, and s.:	47:27
and they s. also: They have	47:34
But, as I have s., in the latter	48:21
I s. that the city of Ammonihah	49: 3
And he also s. unto him,	52:11
their confusion, he s. unto them:	52:37
And he s.: Behold, I will not	55: 2
when Moroni had s. these words,	55: 4
with joy; and they s. unto him:	55: 9
But Laman s. unto them:	55:10
For, s. they: We are weary,	55:11
And Laman s. unto them:	55:12
but I s. unto my men:	56:43
even so they s. unto me:	56:46
the words which they s. unto me	57:21
words which Gid s. unto me:	57:30
God has s. that the inward	60:23
But ye have s., except they	61:20
of Helaman s. unto Kishkumen:	He 2: 8
ye may know how that it is s.,	5: 6
that it may be s. of you, and also	5: 7
has been s. and written of them.	5: 7
for he s. unto him that the Lord	5:10
when they had s. these words,	5:27
And they s. unto the man:	5:38
And Aminadab s. unto them:	5:39
the Lamanites s. unto him:	5:40
And Aminadab s. unto them:	5:41
he opened his mouth and s.	7:13
when Nephi had s. these words,	8: 1
and they s. among themselves,	9: 1
if this thing which he has s.	9: 2
they s. among themselves:	9: 8
And they answered and s.:	9:12
But Nephi s. unto them:	9:21
even according as Nephi had s.	9:37
words which he had s. were true;	9:37
who s. that Nephi was a prophet.	9:40
And there were others who s.:	9:41
hearken unto my words when I s.,	11:14
thy words which thou hast s.	11:16
And he s. unto them: Behold,	13: 5
And behold, he s. unto them:	14: 2
yea, he hath s. unto me:	14: 9
as I s. unto you concerning	14:20
for he s. unto me that there	14:26
And he s. unto me that while	14:27
And the angel s. unto me that	14:28

SAID 827 SAID

Yea, he s. unto them:	3Ne	3:15
the people s. unto Gidgiddoni:		3:20
it was s. by some that the time		8:19
and it s. unto them:		11: 6
And the Lord s. unto him:		11:21
and s. unto them likewise;		11:22
And he s. unto them:		11:22
hath been s. by them of old time,		12:21
had chosen, and s. unto them:		13:25
multitude, and s. unto them:		15: 1
when Jesus had s. these words		15: 2
And he s. unto them:		15: 3
Marvel not that I s. unto you		15: 3
because I s. unto you that old		15: 7
he s. unto those twelve whom		15:11
that ye are they of whom I s.:		15:21
I s. they shall hear my voice;		15:23
multitude, and he s. unto them:		17: 1
upon the things which I have s.,		17: 3
And he s. unto them:		17: 6
groaned within himself, and s.:		17:14
when he had s. these words,		17:15
and he s. unto them:		17:20
when he had s. these words,		17:21
the multitude, and s. unto them:		17:23
he s. unto the disciples:		18: 5
that when he s. these words,		18: 8
done this, Jesus s. unto them:		18:10
the multitude and s. unto them:		18:17
had chosen, and s. unto them:		18:26
himself to the earth, and he s.:		19:19
And Jesus s. unto them:		19:26
the disciples, and s. unto them:		19:35
And he s. unto them:		20: 8
unto Jesus he s. unto them:		20:10
and s. that when the words of		20:11
shall be done even as Moses s.)		21:11
when Jesus had s. these words		23: 6
he s. unto them again,		23: 6
had received, he s. unto them:		23: 6
that he s. unto Nephi:		23: 7
cast his eyes upon them and s.:		23: 8
And he s. unto them:		23: 9
his disciples answered him and s.:		23:10
And Jesus s. unto them:		23:11
Thus s. the Father unto		24: 1
Ye have s.: It is vain		24:14
midst of them, and s. unto them:		27: 2
And they s. unto him:		27: 3
And the Lord s. unto them:		27: 4
he s. unto his disciples:		27:33
when Jesus had s. these words,		28: 1
And he s. unto them:		28: 3
the three, and s. unto them:		28: 4
And he s. unto the first:		28: 6
and Ammaron s. unto me:	Mrm	1: 2
the Lord hath s. should scatter		5: 9
it shall be s. that miracles are		8:26
For behold, thus s. Jesus Christ,		9:22
Jared, his brother, s. unto him:	Eth	1:34
Then Jared s. unto his brother:		1:36
upon him, and s. unto him:		1:40
And the Lord s. unto him:		2:15
And the Lord s.:		2:16
And the Lord s. unto the		2:20
And the Lord s. unto the		2:23
thou hast s. that we must be		3: 2
of Jared had s. these words,		3: 6
and the Lord s. unto him:		3: 7
And the Lord s. unto him:		3: 9
And the Lord s. unto him:		3:11
when he had s. these words,		3:13
showed himself unto him, and s.:		3:13
as I, Moroni, s. I could not		3:17
the Lord s. unto the brother of		3:21
the Lord had s. these words,		3:25
he had s. unto him in times		3:26
And the Lord s. unto him:		3:27
For the Lord s. unto me:		4: 6
wherefore he s. unto you:		6:19
the brother of Jared s. unto them:		6:23
Jared s. unto his brother:		6:24
And therefore he s. unto them:	Eth	6:24
her father, and s. unto him:		8: 9
that he s. unto Jared:		8:11
And Jared s. unto him:		8:12
his kinsfolk, and s. unto them:		8:13
And I s. unto him:		12:23
And when I had s. this,		12:26
was comforted, and s.:		12:29
the brother of Jared s. unto		12:30
thou hast s. that thou hast		12:32
I remember that thou hast s.		12:33
this thing which thou hast s.,		12:35
that the Lord s. unto me:		12:37
unto Ether, and s. unto him:		15:33
their hands upon them, and s.:	Mro	3: 2
they took the cup, and s.:		5: 1
God hath s. a man being evil		7: 6
of which I s. I would speak;		7:21
And Christ hath s.:		7:33
And he hath s.: Repent all		7:34
Christ truly s. unto our fathers:		10:23
vary from that which he hath s.,	DC	3: 2
spake unto you, s. unto you:		5: 2
Yea, for this cause I have s.:		5:34
as I s. unto my disciples,		6:32
And the Lord s. unto me:		7: 1
And I s. unto him:		7: 2
And the Lord s. unto me:		7: 3
cause the Lord s. unto Peter:		7: 4
I s. that he is a wicked man,		10: 7
Marvel not that I s. unto		10:35
for I s., show it not unto the		10:35
it was s. in those writings that		10:39
And I s. unto them, that		10:47
And for this cause have I s.:		10:53
I am he who s.—		10:59
as s. conferences shall direct or		20:61
s. conferences are to do whatever		20:62
to that which I have s.		42:55
And I s. unto them:		45:35
Wherefore I, the Lord, have s.,		45:64
it shall be s. among the wicked:		45:70
And thus, even as I have s.,		52:42
it shall be s. in days to come		61:16
unto you, as I have s. before,		63:16
I, the Lord, have s. that		63:17
that as I s. that I would make		63:22
Behold, it is s. in my laws,		64:27
it is not s. at any time that		64:28
Concerning whom I have s.		76:34
as I s. concerning the sons		84:31
And as I s. unto mine apostles,		84:63
as I s. unto mine apostles		84:64
The Lord hath s. it.		86:11
And he s. unto the first:		88:52
And he s. unto the second:		88:53
all things whatsoever I have s.		98:21
and even as I have s., it shall		101:10
and he s. unto his servants:		101:44
servants, and s. unto them,		101:52
the lord of the vineyard s.		101:55
the servant s. unto his lord:		101:59
And he s. unto his servant:		101:60
as I have s. unto you in a		101:68
afterward he s. within		101:84
What I have s. unto you		101:93
the s. council of high priests		102:25
shall be the duty of s. council		102:26
with the decision of s. council,		102:27
as I have s. unto you in a		103:12
as I s. unto your fathers:		103:19
Therefore, as I s. unto you,		103:35
only on this wise, as I s.,		104:53
sacred things as I have s.		104:63
for, as I s. in a former,		105:14
unto Adam, and s. unto him:		107:55
as thou hast s. in a revelation,		109: 6
also by faith, as thou hast s.;		109:14
stood before us, and s.:		110:13
s. he, it is the place where		116: 1
as I s. unto Abraham concerning		124:58
as I have before s. unto you.		124:107

SAID

even as I have s.	DC124:108
a knowledge of s. bishopric is	124:141
as the Savior s., the prince of this	127:11
Jesus s.: *Handle me and see,*	129: 2
and it shall be s. unto them	132:19
not pure, and have s. they were	132:52
for her, even as he hath s.;	132:55
And it shall be s.: Who is this	133:46
he s.: "I am going like a lamb	135: 4
IT SHALL YET BE S. OF ME—	135: 4
shall it be s. to the slaughter?	135: 4
to pass that the Lord s. unto me:	135: 5
he s. unto himself: Now, for this	Mses 1:10
when Moses had s. these words,	1:12
Moses looked upon Satan and s.:	1:13
God s. unto me: Worship God,	1:15
God s. unto me: Thou art after the	1:16
again Moses s.: I will not cease	1:18
now, when Moses had s. these words,	1:19
the Lord God s. unto Moses:	1:31
I, God, s.: Let there be light;	2: 3
God, s.: Let there be a firmament	2: 6
I s.: Let it divide the waters	2: 6
God, s.: Let the waters under the	2: 9
I, God, s.: Let there be dry land;	2: 9
s.: Let the earth bring forth	2:11
God, s.: Let there be lights in the	2:14
s.: Let the waters bring forth	2:20
s.: Let the earth bring forth the	2:24
God, s. unto mine Only Begotten,	2:26
s.: Let them have dominion over	2:26
s. unto them: Be fruitful, and	2:28
God, s. unto man: Behold, I have	2:29
s. unto mine Only Begotten,	3:18
Adam s.: This I know now is	3:23
s. unto me—Father, thy will be	4: 2
And he s. unto the woman: Yea,	4: 7
God s.—Ye shall not eat of every	4: 7
the woman s. unto the serpent:	4: 8
God hath s.—Ye shall not eat	4: 9
And the serpent s. unto the woman:	4:10
unto Adam, and s. unto him:	4:15
And he s.: I heard thy voice in	4:16
And I, the Lord God, s. unto Adam:	4:17
man s.: The woman thou gavest	4:18
the Lord God, s. unto the woman:	4:19
woman s.: The serpent beguiled	4:19
the Lord God, s. unto the serpent:	4:20
the woman, I, the Lord God, s.:	4:22
unto Adam, I, the Lord God, s.:	4:23
God, s. unto mine Only Begotten:	4:28
Adam s. unto him: I know not,	5: 6
conceived and bare Cain, and s.:	5:16
And the Lord s. unto Cain:	5:22
And it shall be s. in time to come—	5:25
Satan s. unto Cain: Swear unto me	5:29
And Cain s.: Truly I am Mahan,	5:31
s. unto Cain: Where is Abel,	5:34
And he s.: I know not.	5:34
Lord s.: What hast thou done?	5:35
Cain s. unto the Lord: Satan	5:38
And I the Lord s. unto him:	5:40
And Lamech s. unto his wives,	5:47
for he s.: God hath appointed me	6: 2
Lord s. unto Enoch: Go forth and	6:32
unto Enoch, and s. unto him:	6:35
was Mahijah, and s. unto him:	6:40
he s. unto them: I came out	6:41
he s. unto them: Because that	6:48
he also s. unto him: If thou wilt	6:52
and s.: Why is it that men must	6:53
And the Lord s. unto Adam: Behold	6:53
and he s. unto me: Look,	7: 4
And again the Lord s. unto me:	7: 6
the Lord s. unto me: Prophesy,	7: 7
that the Lord s. unto me: Look;	7: 9
the Lord s. unto me: Go to this	7:10
s. unto the Lord: Surely Zion shall	7:20
Lord s. unto Enoch: Zion have I	7:20
Lord s. unto Enoch: Behold mine	7:21
And Enoch s. unto the Lord:	7:29
Lord s. unto Enoch: Behold these	7:32
And unto thy brethren have I s.,	7:33
wept over his brethren, and s.	Mses 7:44
but the Lord s. unto Enoch:	7:44
s.: It shall be in the meridian of	7:46
Lord s.: Blessed is he through	7:53
Lord s. unto Enoch: Look, and	7:55
Lord s. unto Enoch: As I live,	7:60
Lord s. unto Enoch: Then shalt	7:63
And the Lord s. unto Noah:	8:15
Lord s. unto Noah: My spirit	8:17
the Lord s.: I will destroy man	8:26
And God s. unto Noah:	8:30
s. unto me concerning the land	Abr 1:29
Now the Lord had s. unto me:	2: 3
Lord appeared unto me, and s.	2: 6
I s. in my heart: Thy servant has	2:12
departed as the Lord had s.	2:14
s. unto me: Unto thy seed will	2:19
Lord s. unto me: Behold, Sarai,	2:22
all that the Lord had s. unto me—	2:25
the Lord s. unto me: These are the	3: 3
the Lord s. unto me, by the Urim	3: 4
the Lord s. unto me: The planet	3: 5
Lord s. unto me: Now, Abraham,	3: 6
he s. unto me: My son, my son,	3:12
he s. unto me: This is Shinehah,	3:13
he s. unto me: Kokob, which is	3:13
he s. unto me: Olea, which is	3:13
he s. unto me: Kokaubeam,	3:13
the Lord s. unto me: Abraham,	3:15
the Lord s. unto me: These two	3:19
in the midst of them, and he s.:	3:23
he s. unto me: Abraham, thou art	3:23
he s. unto those who were with him:	3:24
the Lord s.: Whom shall I send?	3:27
and s.: Here am I, send me.	3:27
the Lord s.: I will send the first.	3:27
then the Lord s.: Let us go down.	4: 1
(the Gods) s.: Let there be light;	4: 3
the Gods also s.: Let there be an	4: 6
the Gods s.: Let us prepare the	4:11
the Gods s.: Let us prepare the	4:20
the Gods s.: We will bless them,	4:22
and it was so, as they had s.	4:24
counsel among themselves and s.:	4:26
the Gods s.: We will bless them.	4:28
the Gods s.: We will cause them	4:28
the Gods s.: Behold, we will give	4:29
Gods s.: We will do everything	4:31
do everything that we have s.,	4:31
the Gods s. among themselves:	5: 2
had s. concerning every plant	5: 5
Adam s.: Let us make an help	5:14
Adam s.: This was bone of my	5:17
is s. by the Egyptians to be	Fac 2: 5
of the temple, as thou hast s.—	JS 1: 3
And Jesus s. unto them:	1: 3
s. concerning the destruction	1: 4
answered, and s. unto them:	1: 5
And, as I s. before,	1:36
organization of the s. Church.	2: 2
I often s. to myself:	2:10
and s., pointing to the other—	2:17
s. that all their creeds were an	2:19
I then s. to my mother,	2:20
some s. he was dishonest,	2:24
others s. he was mad;	2:24
s. unto me that he was a	2:33
He s. there was a book deposited,	2:34
He also s. that the fulness of	2:34
He s. that that prophet was	2:40
He also s. that this was not	2:41
the messenger had s. that	2:60
he s. that they were Egyptian,	2:64
he s. they were true characters.	2:64
"He then s. to me,	2:65
what Professor Anthon had s.	2:65
He s. this Aaronic Priesthood	2:70
s. that his name was John,	2:72
which Priesthood, he s., would	2:72

SAIDST

Thou s. unto me—Behold these	Al 11:25
unto my words, for thou s. that:	He 11:14

SAIL

SAIL
s. forth with much provisions,	Al	63: 6
other ship also did s. forth;		63: 8
the waves, without s. or anchor,	Mrm	5:18

SAILED
we s. again towards the	1 Ne	18:22
after we had s. for the space		18:23

SAINT
and becometh a s. through the	Mos	3:19
the place which is called S. Louis.	DC	60: 5
take their journey from S. Louis,		60: 8

SAINTS
which slayeth the s. of God,	1 Ne	13: 5
they destroy the s. of God,		13: 9
who were the s. of God,		14:12
the s. of the church of the Lamb,		14:14
and also from the s. of God.		15:28
the s. of the Holy One of Israel,	2 Ne	9:18
For he delivereth his s. from		9:19
which is prepared for the s.		9:43
cast out the prophets, and the s.,		26: 3
the cry of the blood of the s.		26: 3
that kill the prophets, and the s.,		26: 5
And the blood of the s. shall cry		28:10
eternal life, and the joy of the s.,	En	1: 3
many s. shall appear unto many.	He	14:25
blood of the prophets and the s.	3 Ne	9: 5
blood of the prophets and the s.		9: 7
blood of the prophets and the s.		9: 8
blood of the prophets and the s.		9: 9
blood of the prophets and the s.		9:11
not shed the blood of the s.,		10:12
many s. who should arise from		23: 9
many s. did arise and appear		23:11
those s. who have gone before	Mrm	8:23
when the blood of s. shall cry		8:27
he avengeth the blood of the s.		8:41
to the prayers of all the s.		9:36
suffer that the blood of his s.,	Eth	8:22
all the s. shall dwell with God.	Mro	8:26
shall have power over his s.,	DC	1:36
Ye s. arise and live;		43:18
the s. that have slept shall		45:45
the s. shall come forth from		45:46
a place of safety for the s.		45:66
for the gathering of the s.		57: 1
be purchased by the s.,		57: 4
unto the s. their inheritance,		57: 7
lands for the good of the s.,		57: 8
And thus provide for my s.,		57:10
for the good of the s.		57:12
to labor for the s. of God.		58:54
in its time, for the use of my s.,		61:17
for the journeying of my s.;		61:24
is given the course for the s.,		61:29
the s. of the camp of the Lord,		61:29
your God concerning his s.,		63:24
the s. also shall hardly escape;		63:34
my s. should be assembled		63:36
set you to provide for his s.		64:30
war with the s. of God,		76:29
not be gathered with the s.,		76:102
with the s. which are in Zion;		78: 9
of the s. of the Most High,		82:13
for the gathering of his s.		84: 2
by the gathering of the s.,		84: 4
the inheritances of the s.		85: 7
the s. of the Most High;		85:11
That the cry of the s., and		87: 7
and of the blood of the s.,		87: 7
prepare the s. for the hour of		88:84
persecuteth the s. of God,		88:94
s. that are upon the earth,		88:96
and the s. shall be filled with		88:107
not have power over the s.		88:114
and also the s. in Zion—		89: 1
the temporal salvation of all s.		89: 2
weak and the weakest of all s.,		89: 3
who are or can be called s.		89: 3
all s. who remember to keep		89:18
of thanksgiving for all s.,		97:13
of the gathering of my s.—	DC	101:20
gathering together of my s.		101:64
of the gathering of my s.;		101:70
the earth is given unto the s.,		103: 7
purpose to provide for my s.,		104:15
decreed to provide for my s.,		104:16
up of the city of my s.,		104:36
their substance, as becometh s.,		105: 3
gathering together of my s.		105:15
my s. should possess them		105:29
prepare the hearts of thy s.		109:38
and thy s. shout aloud for joy.		109:80
of Jesus Christ of Latter-day S.,		115: 3
of Jesus Christ of Latter-day S.		115: 4
the gathering together of my s.,		115: 8
speedily by the gathering of my s.;		115:17
Let them take leave of my s.		118: 5
Remember thy suffering s.,		121: 6
the heads of the Latter-day S.		121:33
to persecute the s., and to fight		121:38
s. gathering up a knowledge		123: 1
in futurity, pertaining to the s.,		123:15
let all my s. come from afar.		124:25
my s., may be baptized for		124:29
I command you, all ye my s.,		124:31
and the perfecting of my s.		124:143
the s. in the Territory of Iowa?		125: 1
and are essaying to be my s.,		125: 2
Let all the s. rejoice,		127: 3
I will say to all the s.,		127:10
of Jesus Christ of Latter-day S.		127:12
of Jesus Christ of Latter-day S.!		128:21
as Latter-day S., offer unto the Lord		128:24
graves of the s. shall be opened;		133:56
thousands of the Latter-day S.,		135: 3
of Jesus Christ of Latter-day S.,		136: 2
teach this, my will, to the s.,		136:16
of Jesus Christ of Latter-day S.,		OD
my advice to the Latter-day S.		OD
of Jesus Christ of Latter-day S.		OD
of Jesus Christ of Latter-day S.,		OD
the s. arose, and were crowned	Mses	7:56
Jesus Christ of Latter-day S.,	JS	2: 1

SAITH
Wherefore s. the Lamb of God:	1 Ne	13:33
Behold, s. the Lamb of God,		13:34
s. the Lamb—I will be		13:34
and precious, s. the Lamb.		13:34
For, behold, s. the Lamb:		13:35
my gospel, s. the Lamb,		13:36
s. the Lamb of God;		14: 3
s. the Lamb of God.		14: 7
shock them, s. the Lord,		17:53
come, s. the prophet Zenos.		19:12
at Jerusalem, s. the prophet,		19:13
hearts aside, s. the prophet,		19:14
day cometh, s. the prophet,		19:15
gather in, s. the Lord,		19:16
of the Lord, s. the prophet;		19:17
Also, s. the Lord;		20:15
And thus s. the Lord,		20:17
s. the Lord, unto the wicked.		20:22
And now, s. the Lord—		21: 5
Thus s. the Lord,		21: 7
Thus s. the Lord:		21: 8
And as I live, s. the Lord,		21:18
Thus s. the Lord God:		21:22
But thus s. the Lord,		21:25
For behold, s. the prophet,		22:15
for thus s. the prophet		22:17
Thus s. the Lord unto me:	2 Ne	3: 7
s. the Lord, but to the		3:11
of my covenants, s. the Lord.		3:12
O house of Israel, s. the Lord.		3:13
And thus s. the Lord God:		5:22
Thus s. the Lord God:		6: 6
for thus s. the angel,		6:11
But thus s. the Lord:		6:17
For thus s. the Lord:		6:17
Yea, for thus s. the Lord:		7: 1
For thus s. the Lord:		7: 1
Thus s. thy Lord, the Lord and		8:22

SAITH

behold, thus s. the Lord God:	2Ne	10: 7
great in the eyes of me, s. God,		10: 8
against Zion shall perish, s. God.		10:13
are against me, s. our God.		10:16
thus s. our God:		10:18
s. God unto me:		10:19
they shall worship me, s. God.		10:19
s. the Lord God of Hosts.		13:15
Moreover, the Lord s.:		13:16
Thus s. the Lord God:		17: 7
For he s.: Are not my		20: 8
For he s.: By the strength		20:13
thus s. the Lord God of Hosts;		20:24
s. the Lord of Hosts,		24:22
and son, and nephew, s. the Lord.		24:22
s. the Lord of Hosts.		24:23
s. the Lord of Hosts,		26: 4
s. the Lord of Hosts;		26: 5
s. the Lord of Hosts.		26: 6
For thus s. the Lord God:		26:17
yea, thus s. the Lord God:		26:18
but he s.: Come unto me all		26:25
s. the Lord of Hosts,		27:27
behold, s. the Lord of Hosts:		27:28
Therefore, thus s. the Lord,		27:33
s. the Lord God Almighty,		28:15
s. the Lord of Hosts.		28:17
and he s. unto them:		28:22
him that s.: We have received,		28:27
behold, thus s. the Lord God:		28:30
s. the Lord God of Hosts!		28:32
s. the Lord God,		28:32
s. the Lord God of Hosts.		28:32
But thus s. the Lord God:		29: 4
behold, thus s. the Father:		31:20
For behold, thus s. the Lord:	Jac	2:23
abominable before me, s. the Lord.		2:24
Wherefore, thus s. the Lord,		2:25
thus s. the Lord of Hosts.		2:28
s. the Lord of Hosts,		2:29
s. the Lord of Hosts,		2:30
s. the Lord of Hosts,		2:32
s. the Lord of Hosts,		2:32
s. the Lord of Hosts.		2:33
For behold, thus s. the Lord,		5: 3
s. the Lord of the vineyard,		5: 8
And thus s. the Lord:	Mos	3:24
And again, he s.: If my people		7:30
And again he s.: If my people		7:31
Behold, thus s. the Lord,		11:20
this people, thus s. the Lord—		11:20
and thus s. the Lord, and thus		11:25
saying: Thus s. the Lord,		12: 2
and s. that God will destroy them.		12: 9
and s. that thy life shall be as a		12:10
he s. that thou shalt be as a stalk,		12:11
he s. thou shalt be as the blossoms		12:12
And he s. all this shall come		12:12
that s. unto Zion, Thy God		12:21
for thus s. the Lord: Ye shall		23: 7
and he s.: Repent, and I will	Al	5:33
Yea, he s.: Come unto me and		5:34
Yea, he s. the Spirit:		5:50
I say unto you, that the Spirit s.:		5:50
And also the spirit s. unto me,		5:51
the Spirit s.: Behold, the ax is		5:52
may be fulfilled, which s.:		5:57
word might be fulfilled which s.		7:11
for the Spirit s. if ye are not		7:14
(for thus s. the Lord)		8:17
Repent ye, for thus s. the Lord,		8:29
yet he s. that the Son of God		11:35
Now Amulek s. again unto him:		11:36
Now Zeezrom s. again unto him:		11:38
the scripture mean, which s. that		12:21
Yea, if the Lord s. unto us go,		27: 8
and if he s. unto us go, we will go;		27:10
For thus s. the scripture:		30: 8
Thus s. the Lord God—		45:16
the scriptures s. the Lord took		45:19
but he s. unto them:		55: 8
Behold, the Lord s. unto me:		60:33
For behold, thus s. the Lord:	He	7:23
and those things which he s.		8: 7
that thus s. the Lord God,		10:11
thus s. the Lord, ye shall be		10:14
Therefore, thus s. the Lord:		13: 8
except ye repent, s. the Lord;		13:10
away mine anger, s. the Lord;		13:11
yea, thus s. the Lord, blessed		13:11
for I perceive, s. the Lord,		13:12
hearts against me, s. the Lord.		13:12
the time cometh, s. the Lord		13:14
the land, s. the Lord of Hosts,		13:17
s. the Lord of Hosts, yea,		13:18
For I will, s. the Lord, that they		13:19
they be smitten, s. the Lord.		13:20
the words which the Lord s.:		13:21
he s. that ye are cursed because		13:21
you and he s. that all is well,		13:28
that day, s. the Lord of Hosts.		13:32
Therefore, s. the Lord:		15:16
again unto me, s. the Lord.		15:16
And now behold, s. the Lord,		15:17
destroy them, s. the Lord,		15:17
shall these things be, s. the Lord.		15:17
But Gidgiddoni s. unto them:	3Ne	3:21
Not every one that s. unto me,		14:21
belief in me, s. the Father,		16: 7
But wo, s. the Father, unto		16: 8
behold, s. the Father, I will bring		16:10
return unto me, s. the Father,		16:13
tread them down, s. the Father.		16:14
shall come to pass, s. the Father,		20:20
fall upon them, s. the Father,		20:20
their won heads, s. the Father.		20:28
unto them forever, s. the Father.		20:29
For thus s. the Lord:		20:38
that s. unto Zion: Thy God		20:40
pass in that day, s. the Father,		21:14
come to pass, s. the Father,		21:20
go before them, s. the Father,		21:29
of the married wife, s. the Lord.		22: 1
thou wast refused, s. thy God.		22: 6
s. the Lord thy Redeemer.		22: 8
s. the Lord that hath mercy on		22:10
is of me, s. the Lord.		22:17
shall come, s. the Lord of Hosts.		24: 1
fear not me, s. the Lord of Hosts.		24: 5
unto you, s. the Lord of Hosts.		24: 7
herewith, s. the Lord of Hosts,		24:10
the fields, s. the Lord of Hosts.		24:11
land, s. the Lord of Hosts.		24:12
stout against me, s. the Lord.		24:13
be mine, s. the Lord of Hosts,		24:17
them up, s. the Lord of Hosts,		25: 1
do this, s. the Lord of Hosts.		25: 3
And he s.: These scriptures,		26: 2
he truly s. that no one shall	Mrm	8:14
And he that s.: Show unto		8:18
judgment is mine, s. the Lord,		8:20
And he s. unto the Lord:	Eth	3: 8
exercise faith in me, s. the Lord,		4: 7
my revelations, s. Jesus Christ,		4: 7
no greater things, s. Jesus Christ;		4: 8
for upon such, s. the Lord:		9:20
pass the scripture which s.,		13:12
which s. by their works ye shall	Mro	7: 5
he that s. that little children		8:20
s. the voice of him who dwells	DC	1: 1
s. the Lord of Hosts.		1:33
Yea, he s. unto them:		10:25
because Satan s. unto them:		10:29
For thus s. the Lord God:		21: 7
yea, and thus s. the Lord God,		21:12
what he s. to thee thou shalt		28:10
s. the Lord of Hosts,		29: 9
Thus s. the Lord God,		36: 1
Thus s. the Lord your God,		38: 1
and he s. unto the one:		38:26
his sons and s. I am just?		38:26
my voice, which s. unto thee:		39:10
s. the Lord and your God,		41: 1
he that s. he receiveth it and		41: 5

SAITH

thus s. the Lord unto you	DC 44: 1
Thus s. the Lord; for I am	49: 5
for, thus s. the Lord, I will	50: 6
And now come, s. the Lord,	50:10
unto me, s. the Lord your God,	51: 1
Behold, thus s. the Lord unto	52: 1
For thus s. the Lord, I will	52:11
Behold, thus s. the Lord,	54: 1
Behold, thus s. the Lord unto	55: 1
s. the Lord your God;	56: 1
of the rebellious, s. the Lord.	56: 4
s. the Lord God of hosts;	56:10
Behold, thus s. the Lord	56:14
s. the Lord your God,	57: 1
thus s. the Lord your God,	57: 3
I that made man, s. the Lord,	58:30
Who am I, s. the Lord,	58:31
blessed, s. the Lord, are they	59: 1
Behold, thus s. the Lord unto	60: 1
thus s. the Lord unto you,	61: 2
s. the Lord your God,	62: 1
Behold, thus s. the Lord your	64: 1
as the scripture s. unto you,	64:12
thus s. the Lord unto me	66: 1
s. the Lord your Redeemer,	66: 1
in my sight, s. the Lord,	66: 3
thus s. the Lord your God,	66:13
s. the Lord your God,	69: 1
thus s. the Lord unto them—	70: 2
thus s. the Lord unto you	71: 1
thus s. the Lord unto you—	71: 9
For verily thus s. the Lord,	72: 2
For verily, thus s. the Lord,	73: 1
s. the Lord, it is expedient	73: 3
which s. that little children are	74: 6
verily thus s. the Lord,	75:13
thus s. the Lord unto you,	75:23
For thus s. the Lord—	76: 5
Thus s. the Lord concerning	76:31
s. the Lord your God,	78: 1
before me, s. the Lord.	78: 2
now, verily thus s. the Lord,	78: 8
s. the Lord God,	78:15
s. your Redeemer, even the Son	78:20
s. your Lord, even Jesus Christ.	79: 4
thus s. the Lord unto you	80: 1
return, s. the Lord your God.	82: 7
Verily, thus s. the Lord,	83: 1
receive me, s. the Lord;	84:35
with you s. the Lord Almighty,	84:118
of the law of God, s. the Lord of	85: 5
thus s. the still small voice,	85: 6
thus s. the Lord unto you	86: 1
But the Lord s. unto them,	86: 6
thus s. the Lord unto you,	86: 8
thus s. the Lord concerning	87: 1
cometh quickly, s. the Lord.	87: 8
thus s. the Lord unto you	88: 1
thus s. the Lord unto you:	89: 4
Thus s. the Lord, verily,	90: 1
thus s. the Lord unto you	91: 1
Verily, thus s. the Lord,	92: 1
Verily, thus s. the Lord:	93: 1
thus s. the Lord unto you	95: 1
unto me, s. your Lord:	95:10
desires unto me, s. your Lord.	95:16
apostles, s. Son Ahman;	95:17
verily, thus s. the Lord,	97:21
ever, s. the Lord your God	97:28
my name's glory, s. the Lord.	98: 3
in my heart, s. the Lord,	98:14
s. the Lord your God,	98:38
s. the Lord thy God,	98:48
Behold, thus s. the Lord	99: 1
thus s. the Lord unto you,	100: 1
Which s., or teacheth, to	101:70
and not to faint, which s.—	101:81
and the wicked, s. your God.	101:95
s. the Lord of Hosts,	107:60
thus s. the Lord unto you,	108: 1
thus s. the Lord unto you	112: 1
the face of the earth, s. the Lord.	112:24
shall it go forth, s. the Lord;	112:25
s. the Lord, who have professed	DC 112:26
midst of my house, s. the Lord.	112:26
church in this place, s. the Lord.	112:27
thus s. the Lord: It is Christ.	113: 2
thus s. the Lord: It is a servant	113: 4
thus s. the Lord, it is a descendant	113: 6
s.: Put on thy strength, O Zion—	113: 7
thus s. the Lord: It is wisdom in	114: 1
thus s. the Lord, that inasmuch as	114: 2
thus s. the Lord unto you,	115: 1
thus s. the Lord unto my servant	117: 1
desires, before me, s. the Lord;	117: 4
property me? s. the Lord.	117: 4
turned out for debts, s. the Lord.	117: 5
Let them go, s. the Lord,	117: 5
remain in your hands, s. the Lord.	117: 5
forth in abundance? s. the Lord.	117: 7
of soul before me, s. the Lord,	117:11
unto my people, s. the Lord,	117:11
name but in deed, s. the Lord.	117:11
forever and ever, s. the Lord.	117:12
of my Church, s. the Lord;	117:13
than his increase, s. the Lord.	117:13
unto my name, s. the Lord,	117:14
in mine own due time, s. the Lord.	117:16
s. the Lord: Let a conference be	118: 1
of my house, s. the Lord.	118: 5
thus s. the Lord, I require all	119: 1
my holy priesthood, s. the Lord.	119: 4
s. the Lord, the time is now	120: 1
voice unto them, s. the Lord.	120: 1
swept from under heaven, s. God,	121:15
mine anointed, s. the Lord,	121:16
sinned before me, s. the Lord,	121:16
s. the Lord of Hosts;	121:23
thus s. the Lord unto you,	124: 1
is right before me, s. the Lord.	124:15
if he do this, s. the Lord.	124:17
the poor of my people, s. the Lord.	124:21
with your dead, s. the Lord	124:32
acceptable unto me, s. the Lord.	124:35
expect at my hands, s. the Lord.	124:47
practise before me, s. the Lord.	124:48
and hate me, s. the Lord God.	124:50
by their enemies, s. the Lord	124:51
hate me, s. the Lord your God.	124:52
s. the Lord your God.	124:53
land of Missouri, s. the Lord.	124:54
forever and ever, s. the Lord.	124:59
my will, s. the Lord your God.	124:69
their place, s. the Lord God;	124:71
can any other man, s. the Lord.	124:72
for he shall be mine, s. the Lord.	124:75
forgive all his sins, s. the Lord.	124:76
general conference, s. the Lord.	124:88
and ever, s. the Lord your God.	124:101
unto you, s. the Lord your God;	124:119
not blessings, s. the Lord your God.	124:120
for their support, s. the Lord;	124:122
their calling, s. the Lord your God.	124:135
of my church, s. the Lord.	124:136
to my church, s. the Lord.	124:137
presiding, s. the Lord your God.	124:140
my name, s. the Lord your God.	124:145
thus s. the Lord, I say unto you,	125: 2
I have appointed, s. the Lord.	125: 4
verily thus s. the Lord unto you:	126: 1
thus s. the Lord: Let the work	127: 4
your reward, s. the Lord of Hosts.	127: 4
s. the Lord unto you concerning	127: 6
may testify of a truth, s. the Lord;	127: 6
priesthood, s. the Lord of Hosts.	127: 8
s. the Lord of Hosts.	127: 9
s. the Lord unto you my servant	132: 1
shall be damned, s. the Lord God.	132: 6
house of order, s. the Lord God,	132: 8
of an offering, s. the Lord,	132: 9
I appoint unto you, s. the Lord,	132:11
which is my law, s. the Lord.	132:12
by me or by my word, s. the Lord,	132:13
resurrection, s. the Lord your God.	132:13
not joined by me, s. the Lord,	132:18
house of order, s. the Lord God.	132:18

SAITH 832 SALVATION

of redemption, s. the Lord God, DC 132:26
everlasting covenant, s. the Lord 132:27
but shall be damned, s. the Lord. 132:27
by my word, s. the Lord, 132:29
them unto another, s. the Lord. 132:39
and by my word, s. the Lord, 132:46
you curse I will curse, s. the Lord; 132:47
with my power, s. the Lord, 132:48
for I did it, s. the Lord, 132:51
be destroyed, s. the Lord God. 132:52
she shall be destroyed, s. the Lord; 132:54
s. the Lord your God. 132:60
destroyed, s. the Lord your God; 132:64
my church, s. the Lord your God, 133: 1
s. the Lord, let not your flight 133:15
s. the Lord, that these things 133:36
burn them up, s. the Lord of hosts, 133:64
Repent—for thus s. the Lord: Mses 6:27
for he s.—I am Messiah, 7:53
burn them, s. the Lord of Hosts, JS 2:37

SAKE
Nevertheless, for my name's s. 1Ne 20: 9
For mine own s., yea, for mine 20:11
for mine own s. will I do this, 20:11
for Christ's s., and for the sake of Jac 1: 4
and for the s. of our people. 1: 4
for the s. of these things which Mos 4:26
for the s. of retaining a remission 4:26
did for the s. of riches and honor. Al 1:16
of afflictions, for Christ's s., 4:13
for the s. of glutting on the 30:31
wast stoned for the word's s.; 38: 4
the earth for the righteous' s. 45:15
of the land for the righteous' s. 46:10
for the righteous' s., yea, 62:40
it is for the righteous' s. that He 13:14
because of the people's s. who 13:17
persecuted for my name's s., 3Ne 12:10
against you falsely, for my s.; 12:11
for my s. shall the Father work 21: 9
against thee shall fall for thy s. 22:15
will bless the church for my s. 27: 7
the land was cursed for their s. Mrm 1:17
for the s. of the lives of the Eth 15: 4
he may be for the word's s. DC 6:18
for the s. of adultery, 42:75
servant Oliver Cowdery's s. 69: 1
for the s. of the whole world. 84:48
servants for the world's s., 93:46
are their servants for my s.— 93:46
my cause, for my name's s., 98:13
lay down their lives for my s. 101:35
to lay down his life for my s. 103:27
layeth down his life for my s. 103:27
to lay down his life for my s. 103:28
them sharply for my name's s., 112:12
for my name's s. unto you 112:20
shall be the ground for thy s.; Mses 4:23
for the s. of getting gain, but 5:50
but he slew him for the oath's s. 5:50
may be well with me for thy s., Abr 2:25
all nations, for my name's s.; JS 1: 7
for the elect's s., according to 1:20
unto you for the elect's s.; 1:23
I speak for mine elect's s.; 1:29

SAKES
unto them for their s. 1Ne 17:38
cursed shall be the land for their s., 2Ne 1: 7
I speak unto you for your s., 6: 4
or cursed be the land for their s. Jac 2:29
the land is cursed for your s.; 3: 3
go unto the Father for your s. 3Ne 18:35
the devourer for your s., 24:11
the enemy and for your s. DC 37: 1
confirmed upon you for your s., 84:48
and not for your s. only, 84:48

SALEM
was a king over the land of S.; Al 13:17
of peace, for he was the king of S.; 13:18

SALLY
fearful, and began to s. forth, Al 56:29
and to s. forth from the hills, 3Ne 4: 1

SALLYING
Lamanites were s. forth against Al 58: 6

SALT
you to be the s. of the earth; 3Ne 12:13
but if the s. shall lose its savor 12:13
The s. shall be thenceforth good 12:13
as s. that hath lost its savor, 16:15
as the s. of the earth and DC 101:39
if that s. of the earth lose its 101:40
as s. that has lost its savor, 103:10
purposes, from S. Lake City, OD
in S. Lake City, in the Spring OD
S. Lake City, Utah, October 6, OD

SALTED
wherewith shall the earth be s.? 3Ne 12:13

SALUTATION
found unworthy of this s. DC 88:134
you for a s. to one another 88:136

SALUTATIONS
your s. may be in the name of DC 88:120
all your s. may be in the name of 109: 9
their s. may be in the name of 109:19

SALUTE
s. his brother or brethren with DC 88:132
I s. you in the name of the 88:133
shall s. the president or teacher 88:135

SALVATION
and my rock and my s. 1Ne 13:36
their rock and their s.? 15:15
unto their great joy and s., 19:11
shall see the s. of the Lord, 19:17
that thou mayest be my s. 21: 6
and in a day of s. have I 21: 8
he cometh to bring s. unto men. 2Ne 2: 3
and s. is free. 2: 4
shall bring my people unto s. 3:15
my God, and the rock of my s. 4:30
my s. is gone forth, 8: 5
But my s. shall be forever, 8: 6
my s. from generation to generation. 8: 8
I pray the God of my s. that 9:44
God who is the rock of your s. 9:45
Behold, God is my s.; 22: 2
he also has become my s. 22: 2
draw water out of the wells of s. 22: 3
they shall not partake of his s. 26:24
they should not partake of his s.? 26:27
in bringing forth s. unto the 29: 4
plainly, for the s. of our souls. Jac 4:13
the God and rock of their s.; 7:25
they might be brought unto s.— En 1:13
they revealed the plan of s.? Jar 1: 2
and partake of his s., Om 1:26
that s. might come unto the Mos 3: 9
For s. cometh to none such 3:12
means whereby s. can come 3:17
and believe that s. was, and is, 3:18
thereby s. might come to him 4: 6
this is the man who receiveth s., 4: 7
is the means whereby s. cometh. 4: 8
there is none other s. save 4: 8
name given whereby s. cometh; 5: 8
everlasting s. and eternal life, 5:15
of good; that publisheth s.; 12:21
shall see the s. of our God? 12:24
doth s. come by the law of Moses? 12:31
s. did come by the law of Moses. 12:32
s. cometh by the law of Moses. 13:27
s. doth not come by the law alone; 13:28
of good, who have published s.; 15:14
granted s. unto his people; 15:18
not having s. declared unto 15:24

SALVATION

For s. cometh to none such;	Mos	15:27
that the s. of the Lord shall be		15:28
shall see the s. of our God.		15:31
all shall see the s. of the Lord;		16: 1
in the s. of the Lord their God.		17:15
that s. should be declared to		28: 3
grounds had they to hope for s.?	Al	5:10
shall reap the s. of their souls,		9:28
and s. cometh to none else.		11:40
for the day of s. draweth nigh;		13:21
in the power of Christ unto s.?		15: 6
unto the s. of many souls.		17:11
plan of s. might be made known		24:14
ways to the s. of his people.		24:27
that s. came by the law of Moses;		25:16
through faith, unto eternal s.,		25:16
light, yea, into everlasting s.;		26:15
even to the s. of our souls.		26:20
a merciful Being, even unto s.,		26:35
and my light, my joy and my s.,		26:36
be unto s. or unto destruction.		29: 4
that the word is in Christ unto s.		34: 6
he shall bring s. to all those		34:15
the time and the day of your s.;		34:31
work out your s. with fear		34:37
the s. of many souls.		37: 7
God unto the s. of their souls.		37: 8
glad tidings of s. unto his people.		39:15
that s. might come unto them,		39:16
plan of s. would have been		42: 5
And thus cometh about the s.		42:26
unto the s. of their souls.	He	5:11
the day of your s. until it is		13:38
must die that s. may come;		14:15
s. hath come unto them through		15: 4
unto the s. of our souls.	3Ne	5:20
earth shall see the s. of God.		16:20
means of bringing s. unto them.		18:32
shall see the s. of the Father;		20:35
them of good, that publisheth s.;		20:40
that thereby s. might come?		28:35
work out your own s. with fear	Mrm	9:27
all alike and partakers of s.	Mro	8:17
but bringeth s. to his soul;	DC	4: 4
s. in the kingdom of God.		6: 3
no gift greater than the gift of s.		6:13
those who shall be heirs of s.		7: 6
s. in the kingdom of God.		11: 3
s. in the kingdom of God.		12: 3
s. in the kingdom of God.		14: 3
and my rock, and my s.		18:17
And take the helmet of s.,		27:18
to the s. of mine own elect;		35:20
for your s. I give unto you		38:16
I do for the s. of my people.		42:36
saved you with an everlasting s.,		43:25
grow up without sin unto s.		45:58
considering the end of your s.,		46: 7
see signs, but not unto s.		63: 7
and for the s. of souls,		64: 3
and the power of God unto s.		68: 4
for they shall be heirs of s.		76:88
and complete the s. of man,		77:12
s. may be unto you in that thing		78: 2
espoused, to the s. of man,		78: 4
given unto him the keys of s.		78:16
may turn to you for your s.		82: 9
for your profit and for s.		84:73
the temporal s. of all saints		89: 2
ministry for the s. of Zion,		90: 8
of the gospel of their s.		90:10
even the messenger of s.—		93: 8
the Lord, and the gospel of s.,		93:51
all this for the s. of Zion.		93:53
unto me for the s. of Zion—		97:12
be her s. and her high tower.		97:20
in me for the s. of souls.		100: 4
and proper way for their s.—		101:63
the s. and redemption of your		103: 1
and for the s. of men until		104: 1
to be done for your s.,		104:51
and also for their s.,		104:51
in whose name alone s. can be	DC	109: 4
thy peace and thy s. be upon		109:39
anointed ones, be clothed with s.,		109:80
to see the s. of God,		123:17
for the s. of the dead who		128: 5
which God has prepared for their s.		128: 8
in relation to the s. of the		128:11
as pertaining to our s.		128:15
their s. is necessary and essential		128:15
necessary and essential to our s.,		128:15
glory, and s., and honor,		128:23
shall see the s. of their God.		133: 3
for the s. of men in this world,		135: 3
for the s. of a ruined world;		135: 6
s. shall come unto the children of	Mses	6:52
This is the plan of s. unto all men,		6:62
be saved with a temporal s.;		7:42
which are the blessings of s.,	Abr	2:11
and our rock and our s.,		2:16
rejoiced in the God of our s.	JS	2:73

SAM

Laman, Lemuel, S., and Nephi.	1Ne	1:hd
who were Laman, Lemuel, and S.		2: 5
And I spake unto S.,		2:17
and also Lemuel and S.		4:28
against me, Nephi, and S.,		7: 6
because of Nephi and also of S.;		8: 3
mother, Sariah, and S., and Nephi;		8:14
Laman, and also Lemuel and S.,	2Ne	1:28
he spake unto Sam, saying:		4:11
and S., mine elder brother and his		5: 6
Jacob, and Joseph, and S.,	Al	3: 6

SAMARIA

the head of Ephraim is S.,	2Ne	17: 9
the head of S. is Remaliah's son.		17: 9
the spoil of S. shall be taken away		18: 4
the inhabitants of S., that say		19: 9
Is not S. as Damascus?		20: 9
them of Jerusalem and of S.;		20:10
I have done unto S. and her idols,		20:11

SAME

and in that s. year	1Ne	1: 4
s. God who had preserved them.		5:15
For he is the s. yesterday,		10:18
following the s. direction,		16:14
traveling nearly the s. course		16:33
Spirit is the s., yesterday, today,	2Ne	2: 4
the s. state in which they were		2:22
I leave unto you the s. blessing		4: 9
cursed you even with the s. cursing.		5:23
In the s. day shall the Lord		17:20
that I am the s. yesterday, today,		27:23
I speak the s. words unto one		29: 8
that I am the s. yesterday, today,		29: 9
to the end, the s. shall be saved.		31:15
in the s. book with my brother;	Om	1: 9
the s. drinketh damnation to	Mos	2:33
the s. cometh out in open		2:37
the s. might receive remission of		3:13
the s. hath great cause to repent;		4:18
all depend upon the s. Being,		4:19
that s. God has brought our		7:20
in them, the s. is called seer.		8:13
the s. shall be lifted up at the		23:22
the s. shall ye not receive into		26:28
the s. hath brought himself under		26:31
the s. shall not be numbered		26:32
the s. were not numbered among		26:36
bring the s. curse upon his seed.	Al	3: 9
in the s. place where the first		3:20
the s. have cause to wail and		5:36
the s. becometh a child of the		5:41
the s. were rejected, and their		6: 3
the s. will remember that I say		7:16
and it was the s. Aminadi who		10: 2
and behold it was this s. man		10: 8
the s. receiveth the lesser		12:10
even that s. judgment of which		12:27
on the s. standing with their		13: 5

SAME

a high priest after this s. order	Al 13:14
it was this s. Melchizedek	13:15
smote them, saying the s. words,	14:25
that s. God who delivered	29:12
that s. God did establish his	29:13
that s. God hath called me by a	29:13
he did go on in the s. manner	30:30
lest the s. judgments would	30:57
thou art the s. yesterday, today,	31:17
and offer up the s. prayers.	31:20
to the end the s. shall be saved.	32:13
the end, the s. shall be blessed—	32:15
that s. spirit which doth possess	34:34
that s. spirit will have power to	34:34
the s. is not compelled to come;	42:27
s. servant that slew the king,	47:34
having the s. instruction and	47:36
the s. information of the Nephites,	47:36
the s. knowledge of the Lord,	47:36
that s. Lehi who fought with	49:16
they also began in that s. year	50:15
in the s. year that the people of	50:37
at the s. time that they had	51:12
men that they should do the s.	52:38
the s. who had brought an epistle	54: 4
at the s. time they were met in	56:23
in that s. place where we had	58:17
even back by the s. way which	58:24
in this s. year they came down	63:15
this s. year there was exceeding	He 3:24
in this s. year, behold, Nephi	5: 1
that s. prison in which Ammon	5:21
that in the s. year, that his son,	6:15
by that s. being who did entice	6:26
that s. being who did plot with	6:27
that s. being who put it into	6:28
s. being who led on the people	6:28
that s. being who put it into	6:29
that s. prophet who testified of	8:20
to their strife in that s. year.	11:23
in that s. year they were driven	11:29
the s. shall have everlasting life.	14: 8
the s. is not hewn down and cast	14:18
this s. year were they brought	3Ne 1:25
in this s. year, yea, the thirtieth	7: 1
among them in that s. year,	7:16
baptized, the s. shall be saved;	11:33
doctrine, the s. cometh of evil,	11:40
those s. words which Jesus had	19: 8
baptized, the s. shall be saved.	23: 5
the s. shall be saved at the last	27: 6
the s. is he that is also hewn	27:17
they did have in this s. year	Mrm 1:11
in that s. year there began to	2: 1
the s. shall know of greater	8:12
I am the s. who hideth up	8:14
the s. that judgeth rashly shall	8:19
the s. is in danger to be hewn	8:21
God is the s. yesterday, today,	9: 9
it is that s. God who created	9:11
the s. will have power that he	Eth 1: 4
in the likeness of the s. body	3:17
the s. that leadeth men to all	4:12
the s. should lose his life.	8:14
that s. liar who beguiled our	8:25
that s. liar who hath caused	8:25
in that s. year in which he was	13:15
that s. hill where my father	15:11
the s. as if he had retained	Mro 7: 8
with that s. judgment which	7:18
the s. today and tomorrow,	10: 7
and they come from the s. God.	10: 8
the s. God who worketh all	10: 8
of knowledge by the s. Spirit;	10:10
of healing by the s. Spirit;	10:11
he is the s. yesterday, today,	10:19
voice of my servants, it is the s.	DC 1:38
the s. layeth up in store that	4: 4
to receive this s. testimony	5:14
the s. is called of God.	6: 4
I am the s. that came unto	6:21
I am the s. that spake unto	8:12
lost your gift at the s. time,	10: 2
bringeth forth the s. words,	DC 10:17
behold we have the s. with us,	10:17
should bring forth the s. words	10:31
unto me, the s. is my church.	10:67
the s. is not of me, but is	10:68
the s. is called of God.	11: 4
I am the s. who came unto	11:29
the s. is called of God.	12: 4
the s. is called of God.	14: 4
have received the s. power,	17: 7
same power, and the s. faith,	17: 7
and the s. gift like unto him;	17: 7
called even with that s. calling	18: 9
the end, the s. shall be saved.	18:22
he is the s. God yesterday,	20:12
the s. unchangeable God,	20:17
organized branch of the s.,	20:65
the s. things which I revealed	27:12
that s. death which is the	29:41
the s. to their understanding.	32: 4
the s. today as yesterday,	35: 1
the s. which has made all nations	35:11
the s. which looked upon the	38: 1
The s. which knoweth all things,	38: 2
I am the s. which spake,	38: 3
I am the s. which have taken	38: 4
The s. which came in the	39: 3
doeth it, the s. is my disciple;	41: 5
the s. is not my disciple,	41: 5
be pleasing unto the s. Lord,	46:15
man should not eat the s.,	49:18
the s. are overcome of the	50: 8
the s. is appointed to be	50:26
their journey unto the s. place	52: 8
the s. is accepted of me if he	52:15
the s. is of God if he obey	52:16
by the way unto this s. land.	52:22
by the way unto this s. land.	52:23
by the way unto this s. land.	52:25
even unto this s. land.	52:26
their journey unto this s. land,	52:27
the s. shall be kept and blessed	52:34
the s. is not my disciple.	52:40
the s. shall not be saved.	56: 2
the reward of the s. is greater	58: 2
the s. is a slothful and not	58:26
slothfulness, the s. is damned.	58:29
of his sins, the s. is forgiven,	58:42
my will, the s. shall overcome,	63:20
the s. shall be in him a well	63:23
keys or authority of the s.	68:17
the s. is worthy of his hire,	70:12
eternity to eternity he is the s.,	76: 4
spoken of in the s. verse?	77: 2
and the s. will feed you,	84:89
the s. that I promised unto	88: 3
the s. light that quickeneth	88:11
receive the s. body which was	88:28
shall then receive of the s.,	88:29
shall then receive of the s.,	88:30
shall then receive of the s.,	88:31
perfected and sanctified by the s.	88:34
this s. prayer and covenant,	88:135
saying Amen, in token of the s.	88:135
partakers of the glory of the s.,	93:22
appointed after the s. manner	102:10
sanction the s. by their vote.	102:19
power to determine the s.	102:22
the keys or authority of the s.	107:15
by the unanimous voice of the s.;	107:27
of the s. power or validity	107:27
not entitled to the s. blessings	107:29
the affairs of the s. in all nations,	107:33
the affairs of the s. in all nations,	107:34
From the s. comes the	107:67
they shall act in the s. office.	107:75
shall fall into the s. himself;	109:25
the time of the writing of the s.;	124: 4
for which the s. was instituted	124:33
exept the s. shall pay his stock	124:67
be crowned with the s. blessing,	124:95
be appointed unto the s. calling.	124:130
the s. priesthood in his stead;	124:132

SAME

their inheritance in the s.,	DC 125: 4	they may become s. in me,	Eth	4: 7
when called upon certify to the s.,	128: 3	then are ye s. in Christ by	Mro	10:33
just the s. as if he had seen	128: 4	those who are s. take heed also.	DC	20:34
made a record of the s. on the	128: 4	of my gospel, and become s.,		39:18
and faithful record of the s.,	128: 9	be s. by that which ye have		43: 9
but inherit the s. glory.	129: 3	husband is s. by the wife,		74: 1
that s. sociality which exists	130: 2	wife is s. by the husband;		74: 1
unto them must obey the s.	132: 3	being s. through the atonement		74: 7
to enforce the laws of the s.;	134: 3	who are s. before his throne,		76:21
at the s. time, however,	134: 5	It is the earth, in its s.,		77: 1
laws exist as will protect the s.;	134:11	finished his work, and s. it,		77:12
The s. morning, after Hyrum	135: 4	are s. by the spirit unto the		84:33
of the s. he greatly marveled and	Mses 1: 8	book of the names of the s.,		88: 2
the s. that compasseth the whole	3:13	s. from all unrighteousness,		88:18
s. which was from the beginning,	4: 1	and for this intent are they s.		88:20
Now this s. Priesthood, which	6: 7	not s. through the law which		88:21
the s. is the God of heaven,	6:43	Wherefore, it shall be s.;		88:26
and the s. are mighty men,	8:21	perfected and s. by the same.		88:34
ordained to administer the s.;	Abr 1: 2	in sin, cannot be s. by law,		88:35
belong to the s. order as that	3: 3	the glory of God, and the s.;		88:116
belong to the s. order as that	3: 9	but deny me, cannot be s.		101: 5
not have glory in the s. kingdom	3:26	and let it be s. before me,		105:31
only bring forth the s. in itself,	4:12	are chosen; and they shall be s.;		105:36
overcome, the s. shall be saved.	JS 1:11	be s. and consecrated to be holy,		109:12
overcome, the s. shall be saved.	1:30	that thou hast s. it,		109:13
in the s. county of Ontario—	2: 3	in its s. and immortal state,		130: 9
the s. passages of scripture	2:12	after their pain shall be s. in		133:35
chapter of the s. prophecy,	2:36	to posterity as gems for the s.		135: 6
the s. heavenly messenger was	2:44	the seventh day, and s. it;	Mses	3: 3
again related the very s. things	2:45	ye might be s. from all sin,		6:59
the s. messenger at my bedside,	2:46	and by the blood ye are s.;		6:60
to me the s. things as before;	2:46	may be s. and have eternal life?		7:45
the s. messenger standing over	2:49	themselves to form; and s. it.	Abr	5: 3
I found the s. messenger there,	2:54			
the s. heavenly messenger	2:59	SANCTIFIETH		
me to the s. Priesthood—	2:71	s. himself before the Lord	DC 133:62	
the s. that is called John the	2:72			
the s. organization that existed	AoF 6	SANCTIFY		
allow all men the s. privilege,	11	S. the Lord of Hosts himself,	2Ne 18:13	
		they shall s. my name.		27:34
SAMUEL: *see also* BENT, Samuel; ROLFE, Samuel; SMITH, Samuel H.; and WILLIAMS, Samuel.		and s. the Holy One of Jacob,		27:34
		to bless and s. this bread to	Mro	4: 3
		to bless and s. this wine to the		5: 2
S., a Lamanite, prophesies	He 7:hd	s. this bread to the souls of	DC	20:77
prophecy of S., the Lamanite,	13:hd	s. this wine to the souls of		20:79
there was one S., a Lamanite,	13: 2	s. yourselves before me;		43:11
Behold, I, S., a Lamanite,	13: 5	S. yourselves and ye shall be		43:16
S., the Lamanite, did prophesy	14: 1	the world, and to s. the world,		76:41
the words of S., the Lamanite,	16: 1	the Lord God s. the earth,		77:12
did not believe in the words of S.	16: 2	to s. his people that they		84:23
as believed on the words of S.	16: 5	s. yourselves that your minds		88:68
did not believe in the words of S.;	16: 6	yourselves, and s. yourselves;		88:74
spoken by S., the Lamanite.	3Ne 1: 5	I will s. him before the people;		115:19
words of S. are not fulfilled;	1: 6	s. the land of Zion unto me,		119: 6
had been given by S. the prophet.	1: 9	O my people; s. yourselves;		133: 4
the prophet S., the Lamanite,	8: 3	When will my Creator s. me,	Mses	7:48
and all the prophets from S.	20:24			
my servant S., the Lamanite,	23: 9	SANCTION		
S. did prophesy according to	23:10	to s. the same by their vote.	DC 102:19	
and also S. the Lamanite.	Mrm 1:19			
prophesied by S. the prophet;	2:10	SANCTIONED		
speak a few words unto you, S.;	DC 23: 4	s. by the voice of a general	DC 102: 8	
		who s. what Professor Anthon	JS	2:65
SAMUEL HARRISON (Smith): *see also* SMITH, Samuel H.				
Hyrum, myself, S., William,	JS 2: 4	SANCTUARIES		
my brothers Hyrum and S.;	2: 7	because of their fine s.;	2Ne 28:13	
		themselves together at their s.	Al	15:17
SANCTIFICATION		in their temples, and in their s.,		16:13
which s. cometh because of	He 3:35	Behold, we have built s.,		21: 6
and the s. of their hearts,	3:35	them that they should build s.,		22: 7
s. through the grace of our Lord	DC 20:31	also their temples, and their s.		23: 2
and to the s. of the church.	100:15	and their synagogues, and their s.,	He	3: 9
		and of synagogues and their s.,		3:14
SANCTIFIED				
shall be s. in righteousness.	2Ne 15:16	SANCTUARY		
I have commanded my s. ones,	23: 3	And he shall be for a s.;	2Ne 18:14	
is s. unto us for righteousness,	Jac 4: 5	and the holy s. of the Lord.	Eth 13: 3	
been s. by the Holy Spirit,	Al 5:54	that it may become a s.,	DC 88:137	
after this holy order, and were s.,	13:11			
being s. by the Holy Ghost,	13:12	SAND		
may be s. by the reception of	3Ne 27:20	as many as the s. of the sea.	1Ne 12: 1	
and they were s. in the flesh,	28:39	seed also had been as the s.;		20:19
		Israel be as the s. of the sea,	2Ne 20:22	

SAND

who built his house upon the s.—	3Ne 14:26
as it were the s. of the sea.	Mrm 1: 7
or as the s. upon the seashore;	DC 76:109
count the s. upon the seashore	132:30
numberless as the s. upon the sea	Mses 1:28

SANDS

as it were, as the s. of the sea,	Al 2:27
thou canst count the number of s.,	Abr 3:14

SANDY

that is built upon a s. foundation	2Ne 28:28
buildeth upon a s. foundation,	3Ne 11:40
are built upon a s. foundation;	18:13

SAPPHIRES

and lay thy foundations with s.	3Ne 22:11

SARAH

and unto S., she that bare you;	2Ne 8: 2
S. gave Hagar to Abraham to wife.	DC 132:34
he is exempt from the law of S.,	132:65
I, Abraham, took S. to	

SARAI

I, Abraham, took S. to wife,	Abr 2: 2
and his wife, and S. my wife,	2: 4
I took S., whom I took to wife	2:15
S., thy wife, is a very fair woman	2:22
I, Abraham, told S. my wife,	2:25

SARIAH

Lehi and his wife S.,	1Ne 1:hd
consisted of my mother, S., and	2: 5
and also my mother, S., was	5: 1
Lehi, comfort my mother, S.,	5: 6
I beheld your mother, S.,	8:14

SAT

with him as he s. in his house.	1Ne 3:11
as I s. pondering in mine heart	11: 1
and she s. upon many waters;	14:11
whore who s. upon many waters;	14:12
and he s. in the judgment-seat	Al 4:17
he s. down upon the ground,	34: 1
unto the place where she s.;	47:34
as he s. upon the judgment-seat.	He 1: 9
as he s. upon the judgment-seat.	6:15
as he s. upon his throne,	Eth 9: 5
as he s. upon his throne.	14: 9
s. down on the right hand of	Mro 7:27
of a dove, and s. upon him,	DC 93:15
he s. upon the Mount of Olives,	JS 1: 4

SATAN

S. hath great power over them.	1Ne 13:29
S. shall have no more power	22:15
S. has no power;	22:26
S. shall have power over the	2Ne 30:18
Now S. had gotten great hold	Al 8: 9
why hath S. got such great hold	10:25
to the power and captivity of S.,	12:17
they might be delivered from S.,	15:17
for S. has great hold on the	27:12
ye shall be delivered up unto S.,	37:15
S. did stir up the hearts of	He 6:21
S. did stir them up to do iniquity	16:22
S. did get great hold upon the	16:23
forth among the people, by S.,	3Ne 1:22
thus did S. get possession of	2: 2
and S. did go about, leading	2: 3
S. had great power, unto the	6:15
S. did lead away the hearts of	6:16
themselves unto the power of S.	7: 5
for S. desireth to have you,	18:18
S. could have no power over	28:39
and because of the power of S.	4Ne 1:28
behold, they are led about by S.,	Mrm 5:18
that S. may have no power	Eth 8:26
S. had full power over the hearts	15:19
S. stirreth them up continually	Mro 9: 3
that you may conquer S.,	DC 10: 5
the hands of the servants of S.	10: 5
S. hath put it into their hearts	DC 10:10
that S. shall accomplish his evil	10:14
S. has great hold upon their	10:20
S. stirreth them up, that he	10:22
because S. saith unto them:	10:29
S. will harden the hearts of	10:32
S. thinketh to overpower your	10:33
S. doth stir up the hearts of	10:63
even to the destroying of S.	19: 3
delivered from the powers of S.	24: 1
and that S. deceiveth him;	28:11
power is not given unto S. to	29:47
S. shall tremble and Zion shall	35:24
straightway S. tempted him;	40: 2
For S. shall be bound,	43:31
And S. shall be bound, that he	45:55
S. hath sought to deceive you,	50: 3
S. desireth to sift him as chaff.	52:12
for S. is abroad in the land,	52:14
S. putteth it into their hearts	63:28
S. seeketh to destroy his soul;	64:17
we beheld S., that old serpent,	76:28
S. seeketh to turn their hearts	78:10
over to the buffetings of S.	78:12
over to the buffetings of S.	82:21
And S. is bound and time is	84:100
the enemy, even S., sitteth to	86: 3
and S. shall be bound,	88:110
S. shall not have power to	101:28
escape the buffetings of S.	104: 9
over unto the buffetings of S.;	104:10
delivered unto the buffetings of S.	132:26
for S. seeketh to destroy;	132:57
S. came tempting him, saying:	Mses 1:12
Moses looked upon S. and said:	1:13
Get thee hence, S.; deceive me	1:16
Depart hence, S.	1:18
S. cried with a loud voice, and	1:19
Depart from me, S., for this one	1:20
now S. began to tremble, and the	1:21
Only Begotten, depart hence, S.	1:21
that S. cried with a loud voice,	1:22
that when S. had departed from	1:24
S., whom thou hast commanded	4: 1
because that S. rebelled against	4: 3
he became S., yea, even the devil,	4: 4
S. put it into the heart of the	4: 6
S. came among them, saying:	5:13
and they loved S. more than God.	5:13
And Cain loved S. more than God.	5:18
And S. commanded him, saying:	5:18
S. knew this, and it pleased him.	5:21
and S. desireth to have thee;	5:23
and they loved S. more than God.	5:28
S. said unto Cain: Swear unto	5:29
S. sware unto Cain that he would	5:30
S. tempted me because of my	5:38
into a covenant with S.,	5:49
administered unto Cain by S.;	5:49
that had covenanted with S.;	5:52
S. had great dominion among men,	6:15
Behold S. hath come among the	6:49
the power of S. was upon all the	7:24
he beheld S.; and he had a great	7:26
S. shall be their father, and misery	7:37
that S. would try to tempt me	JS 2:46

SATISFACTION

to the s. of the parties.	DC 102: 2
is not s. upon the decision	107:78

SATISFIED

and they shall not be s.;	2Ne 19:20
of his soul, and shall be s.; by	Mos 14:11
and s. the demands of justice.	15: 9
they s. the queen concerning	Al 47:34
And your hearts are not s.	DC 56:15
and whose bellies are not s.,	56:17
I had now got my mind s. so	JS 2:26

SATISFIETH

the atonement s. the demands	2Ne 9:26

SATISFY

labor for that which cannot s.	2Ne	9:51
can s. the demands of justice,	Al	34:16

SATYRS

and s. shall dance there.	2Ne	23:21

SAUL

Gibeah of S. is fled.	2Ne	20:29

SAVAGE

their wild and s. condition	DC	109:65
was wounded in a s. manner		135:2

SAVE

s. it were his family, and provisions,	1Ne	2:4
s. he shall prepare a way for		3:7
s. they should have the law.		4:15
s. they should rely on this		10:6
s. there are not so many;		13:23
s. it be the casting of it into		14:3
there are s. two churches only;		14:10
s. a man should inquire of the		15:3
suffered all things, s. it were death;		17:20
s. it were by his word.		17:31
destroyed, s. a few only,		17:43
perish s. that they should repent		18:15
s. it were the power of God,		18:20
s. it be that I think it be sacred.		19:6
and I will s. thy children.		21:25
s. that we know that they have		22:4
s. they shall be brought by the	2Ne	1:6
nothing, s. it shall be iniquity		1:31
s. it be through the merits,		2:8
s. it should be that he was		2:16
s. it be by the punishment of		2:26
s. it be the everlasting welfare		2:30
s. the work which I shall command		3:8
s. I should leave a blessing upon		4:5
s. it were not built of so many		5:16
s. they shall repent of their		5:22
Thy sons have fainted, s. these two;		8:20
s. it should be an infinite		9:7
s. it be that our knowledge shall		9:13
is not anything s. he knows it.		9:20
that he may s. all men if		9:21
s. it be by the gate;		9:41
s. they shall cast these things		9:42
s. Christ should come all men		11:6
s. it be that they are taught		25:5
s. it were foretold them by		25:9
s. it be those which are carried		25:10
s. it should be a false Messiah		25:18
there is s. one Messiah spoken of		25:18
s. it be this Jesus Christ,		25:20
s. it be for the benefit of		26:24
s. it be plain unto the children of		26:33
s. it be that three witnesses shall		27:12
which shall view it, s. it be a few		27:13
s. it be according to their faith.		27:23
have all gone astray s. it be a few,		28:14
s. their precepts shall be given		28:31
a Bible s. it were by the laws?		29:6
s. it be with them that repent		30:2
s. they shall be a white and		30:6
s. it shall be revealed;		30:17
s. it shall be made manifest in		30:17
s. it shall be loosed.		30:17
s. it be a few words which I		31:2
s. we shall be willing to keep		31:10
s. it were by the word of Christ		31:19
merits of him who is mighty to s.		31:19
s. it were by the Holy Ghost?		32:2
s. in the first place ye shall pray		32:9
s. he shall be of the spirit of		33:5
s. it were lightly, concerning	Jac	1:2
have s. it be one wife;		2:27
s. I shall visit them with a sore		2:33
have s. it were one wife,		3:5
anything s. it be upon plates		4:2
s. it be revealed unto him;		4:8
s. it were these, had become		5:42
nothing s. it be to be hewn		5:42
s. it be those which are most	Jac	5:57
s. they have spoken concerning		7:11
s. it be for the cause of iniquity;	En	1:10
eat nothing s. it was raw meat;		1:20
s. it was exceeding harshness,		1:23
s. that which has been written,	Om	1:11
s. it comes from the Lord;		1:25
they were all slain, s. fifty,		1:28
s. this which hath been spoken of;	Mos	4:8
nothing s. it were the things which		18:19
nothing s. it were repentance and		18:20
all s. the king and his priests.		19:18
all cases s. it were in sickness,		27:5
s. it is the transgression of my		27:13
nothing s. the power of God		27:18
s. it be through much contention,		29:21
to s. and preserve this people.	Al	2:30
s. it were skin which was girded		3:5
s. it were in bearing down in		4:19
and that he will s. you?		5:17
who is mighty to s. and to		7:14
Shall he s. his people in their sins?		11:34
but he shall not s. his people—		11:35
not s. his people in their sins.		11:36
he cannot s. them in their sins;		11:37
he has all power to s. every man		12:15
s. it were with abhorrence;		13:12
but he should not s. them;		14:5
and s. them from the flames.		14:10
ye had not power to s. those who		14:15
s. it were Alma and Amulek,		14:28
slew none s. it were their leader		17:38
have had no witness s. thy word,		19:9
s. it were one of the		19:16
No one hath told me, s. it be God;		20:5
believe that God will s. all men.		21:6
s. it were through the death		21:9
s. it were the land of Ishmael;		22:1
were not converted, s. only one;		23:14
these things, s. it be the penitent.		26:21
might s. some few of their souls.		26:26
angels sent from God to s. them		27:4
s. it be the truly penitent		27:18
s. it were in the judgment-seat;		30:33
s. it were to declare the truth,		30:34
none, s. it be your word only.		30:40
s. it were the power of God		30:52
s. it were swallowed up in the joy		31:38
s. it be in your synagogues only?		32:10
mercy; for he is mighty to s.		34:18
s. it be the shedding of innocent		39:5
knoweth them s. God himself.		40:3
a law s. there was a punishment?		42:17
s. it were a skin which was		43:20
s. it were the Zoramites and		43:20
s. it be a few who shall be		45:14
s. it was by their place of		49:4
other way s. by the entrance,		49:18
s. it were by the entrance,		49:18
s. they had lost much blood.		52:4
s. it be on conditions that ye		54:11
s. he will withdraw his purpose,		55:2
s. they had first given to some of		55:31
to s. us from falling into		57:17
army, s. a few guards only,		58:22
s. it be those who have been		58:31
s. only to retain my		61:9
s. it were Teancum;		62:35
s. it were those parts which had		63:12
s. it were in small bodies;	He	1:24
s. it were a little pride which		3:1
desolate, s. it were for timber		3:6
all s. it were the secret		3:23
s. it were the pride which began		3:33
s. it were the exceeding great		3:36
s. it were to their destruction.		5:3
s. it be unto those who repent of		7:23
s. it were given unto me by the		9:36
s. it were a few contentions		11:22
s. the sword of justice falleth		13:5
nothing can s. this people save		13:6
s. it be repentance and faith on		13:6
s. he be a righteous man		13:18

SAVE | 838 | SAVED

unto me s. it be the righteous;	He 13:19	waters, s. it be upon the canal,	DC 61:23
s. it were the people began to be	16:12	to journey, s. upon the canal.	61:23
s. it were the most believing part	16:15	that thereby I may s. some.	64:21
s. it were a few that began to	3Ne 1:24	s. it be before the First	68:22
s. it were for the Gadianton	1:27	to s. life and to destroy;	77: 8
s. it were they had wronged	3:11	s. he is clean from the blood	88:138
substance, s. it were their land,	3:13	s. I, the Lord, commanded	98:33
(s. it were in their times of	3:19	s. those only whom I have	101:55
s. it were in the wilderness.	4: 2	all s. the ground which has	104:34
s. it were in the wilderness,	4: 3	s. it be the holy and sacred	104:68
s. it were to come up in open	4: 4	warn them to s. themselves from	109:41
s. it were to plunder and rob	4: 5	will s. all those of your brethren	124:54
had nothing s. it were meat for	4:19	which no man knoweth s. he that	130:11
no one knew it s. it were himself	5:20	in nothing did they sin s. in	132:38
s. it were among a few of the	6:14	sin against me s. in the case of Uriah	132:39
s. their condemnation was	6:22	in righteousness, mighty to s.	133:47
s. he had much family and	7: 4	warn the righteous to s. themselves	134:12
s. it were their leaders did	7:11	has done more, s. Jesus only,	135: 3
s. he were cleansed every whit	8: 1	last days, to s. my people Israel.	136:22
s. they know that they were	8:16	s. the Lord commanded me.	Mses 5: 6
to s. the world from sin.	9:21	s. it were the people of Canaan,	7:12
s. it were by the Holy Ghost.	15:23	of Adam s. it was the seed of Cain,	7:22
s. it be called in my name?	27: 8	kill you, but they will s. her	Abr 2:23
s. it be those who have washed	27:19		
s. it be those which are	27:23	**SAVED**	
they all spake, s. it were three,	28: 2	and the God of Jacob and be s.	1Ne 6: 4
sorrow. s. it be for the sins of	28: 9	many of their seed, will be s.	8: 3
s. it were the three who were	28:12	be s. in the everlasting kingdom	13:37
sorrow s. it were for the sins of	28:38	unto him, or they cannot be s.	13:40
s. it were in the name of Jesus.	4Ne 1: 5	to come unto him and be s.	15:14
s. it were the three who	1:14	they shall be s., even if it so be	22:17
s. it were a small part of	1:20	ye shall be s. at the last day.	22:31
passed away. s. it were a few.	1:22	they that believe in him shall be s.	2Ne 2: 9
s. it were the disciples of Jesus.	1:46	they shall be s.;	6:12
might s. them from destruction.	Mrm 2:21	they cannot be s. in the kingdom	9:23
s. it were these few plates	6: 6	the grace of God that ye are s.	10:24
s. it were twenty and four of	6:11	shall be s. in the kingdom of God.	25:13
s. it were those twenty and four	6:15	whereby man can be s.	25:20
s. it be that God shall command	7: 4	that it is by grace that we are s.	25:23
none s. it be the Lamanites	8: 9	stripes, and at last we shall be s.	28: 8
s. it be the disciples of Jesus,	8:10	to the end, the same shall be s.	31:15
s. it be given him of God;	8:15	of the living God, he cannot be s.	31:16
none s. a few only who do not	8:36	whereby man can be s. in the	31:21
s. it is the air which is in them;	Eth 2:19	many of us, if not all, may be s.	33:12
s. I prepare you against the	2:25	be s. in the kingdom of God.	Jac 6: 4
none s. it be the Lamanites,	4: 3	as the Lord liveth ye will be s.	Om 1:26
cometh of none s. it be of me.	4:12	could sin they could not be s.;	Mos 3:16
Jared, even all s. it were one;	6:27	whereby man can be s. except	4: 8
s. it were Jared and his family.	9: 3	of God ye shall be s.;	12:33
all, s. it were thirty souls,	9:12	go, if it so be that I am s.	13: 9
household s. it were Shiz—	10: 1	could not any man be s. except	13:32
s. the old have passed away,	13: 9	and through Christ ye can be s.?	16:13
household s. it were himself.	13:21	should be s. at the last day,	Al 1: 4
s. it were Coriantumr.	13:21	I say unto you that they are s.	5: 9
not been slain, s. it was Ether.	15:12	on what conditions are they s.?	5:10
s. it were fifty and two of	15:23	therefore they were s.	5:13
s. it were Coriantumr and Shiz,	15:29	can ye think of being s. when	5:20
s. they brought forth fruit meet	Mro 6: 1	at that day that ye cannot be s.;	5:21
baptism s. they came forth with	6: 2	there can no man be s. except	5:21
s. they took upon them the name	6: 3	must repent or he cannot be s.!	5:31
s. they shall have faith in his	7:38	and many of them will be s.,	9:17
faith, s. ye shall have hope?	7:40	having been s. from famine,	9:22
and hope, s. he shall be meek,	7:43	therefore, how can ye be s.,	11:37
s. the meek and lowly in heart;	7:44	ye cannot be s. in your sins.	11:37
no water, s. a little, do they	9: 8	neither has God s. them	14:15
s. that which is good;	9:19	who has s. me from an awful hell!	19:29
any s. it be those who are of	DC 6:12	thy soul could not be s.	20:17
none else s. God that knowest	6:16	If ye will repent ye shall be s.,	22: 6
power, s. the power of God,	8: 7	and be s. at the last day.	22:18
no thought s. it was to ask me.	9: 7	go to our God and shall be s.	24:16
s. it be given you from me.	9: 9	to doubt but what they were s.	24:26
knoweth s. me and thee alone—	15: 3	elected us that we shall be s.,	31:17
knoweth s. me and thee alone—	16: 3	to the end the same shall be s.	32:13
s. it be one soul unto me,	18:15	or means whereby man can be s.,	38: 9
s. it be the church of the devil.	18:20	may walk therein and be s.	41: 8
s. it were by my power	18:35	but the truly penitent are s.	42:24
all s. the support of thy family.	19:34	have s. thousands of them from	60: 8
doeth good s. it be a few;	33: 4	means whereby man can be s.,	He 5: 9
S. yourselves from this	36: 6	do iniquity, and he cannot be s.;	12:22
S. yourselves. Be ye clean that	38:42	this cause, that men might be s.,	12:22
s. all the money that ye can,	48: 4	for these are they that shall be s.	12:23
s. it be by the shedding of blood.	58:53	I would that all men might be s.	12:25
s. those who confess not his	59:21	who are righteous that it is s.;	13:12

SAVED   839   SAW

that ye would repent and be s.	He 13:39
will believe might be s.,	14:29
ye ends of the earth, and be s.	3Ne 9:22
part of the people who were s.,	10:12
baptized, the same shall be s.;	11:33
come unto me and be ye s.;	12:20
is baptized, the same shall be s.	23: 5
same shall be s. at the last day.	27: 6
repentance, or ye cannot be s.	Mrm 7: 3
and is baptized shall be s.,	9:23
and is baptized shall be s.;	Eth 4:18
of all righteousness and be s.	8:26
if it so be that I am s. in the	15:34
men also were s. by faith in	Mro 7:26
faith in me, that ye may be s.	7:34
upon the face thereof to be s.?	7:36
no man can be s., according	7:38
be s. with their little children.	8:10
could not be s. without baptism,	8:13
in Christ that thou wilt be s.;	9:22
be s. in the kingdom of God;	10:21
ye be s. in the kingdom of God	10:21
be s. in the kingdom of God;	10:26
repentance they might be s.	DC 3:20
be s. in the kingdom of God,	6:13
the end, the same shall be s.	18:22
given whereby man can be s.;	18:23
cannot be s. in the kingdom of	18:46
faith to the end, should be s.—	20:25
cannot be s. in the kingdom of	20:29
or they can in nowise be s.;	33:12
Israel shall be s. in mine own	35:25
in store, for Israel shall be s.,	38:33
to these things shall be s.,	42:60
and would have s. you with	43:25
ended, and your souls not s.	45: 2
that receiveth him shall be s.,	49: 5
he only is s. who endureth	53: 7
the same shall not be s.	56: 2
ended, and my soul is not s.!	56:16
and is baptized shall be s.,	68: 9
through him all might be s.	76:42
commandments they shall be s.	100:14
commandments, shall be s.	100:17
all mine Israel, shall be s.	101:12
and s. my vineyard from the	101:54
and is baptized shall be s.,	112:29
is that you all may be s.	127:12
for a man to be s. in ignorance.	131: 6
in their s. condition,	132:17
into my law and ye shall be s.	132:32
angel of his presence s. them;	133:53
of their sins, should be s.;	Mses 5:15
be s. with a temporal salvation;	7:42
overcome, the same shall be s.	JS 1:11
should none of their flesh be s.;	1:20
overcome, the same shall be s.	1:30
all mankind may be s., by	AoF 3

SAVES
s. all the works of his hands,	DC 76:43
he s. all except them—	76:44

SAVETH
that God s. one child because	Mro 8:15

SAVING
be the means of s. some soul;	Al 26:30
could be the means of s. some.	26:30
s. of his people from destruction;	55:19
s. for the cause of fornication,	3Ne 12:32

SAVIOR
other words, a S. of the world.	1Ne 10: 4
and the S. of the world;	13:40
that I, the Lord, am thy S.	21:26
that the Lord is their S.	22:12
know that I the Lord am thy S.	2Ne 6:18
following your Lord and your S.	31:13
knowledge of the S. shall spread	Mos 3:20
God and my S. Jesus Christ,	3Ne 5:20
our Lord and S. Jesus Christ,	Mrm 3:14
following the example of our S.,	Mrm 7:10
the coming of our Lord and S.	8: 6
as the words of our S. himself.	Mro 8:29
even the S. of the world;	DC 1:20
the knowledge of a S. has come	3:16
the knowledge of a S. come	3:16
repentance and faith on the S.,	19:31
Yea, come unto me thy S.	19:41
of our Lord and S. Jesus Christ	20: 1
our Lord and S. Jesus Christ,	20: 4
our Lord and S. Jesus Christ	20:30
our Lord and S. Jesus Christ	20:31
God, the S. of the world;	42: 1
Christ, the S. of the world.	43:34
Redeemer, the S. of the world,	66: 1
and beside him there is no S.	76: 1
a s. unto my people Israel.	86:11
as the S. said, the prince of this	127:11
When the S. shall appear	130: 1
And the Lord, even the S.,	133:25
Begotten is and shall be the S.,	Mses 1: 6
as delivered by the S. to the	JS 2:34

SAVIORS
and to be the s. of men;	DC 103: 9
as they are not the s. of men,	103:10

SAVOR
but if the salt shall lose its s.	3Ne 12:13
as salt that hath lost its s.,	16:15
the earth and the s. of men;	DC 101:39
called to be the s. of men;	101:40
salt of the earth lose its s.,	104:40
as salt that has lost its s.,	103:10

SAW
and he s. and heard much;	1Ne 1: 6
the thing which he s. and heard	1: 6
he s. the heavens open,	1: 8
he thought he s. God sitting upon	1: 8
he s. one descending out of	1: 9
And he also s. twelve others	1:10
things which he s. in visions	1:16
the things which he s. and heard,	1:19
when my father s. that the waters	2: 9
when Laban s. our property,	3:25
and I s. that the blade thereof	4: 9
I s. the servant of Laban	4:20
when Laman s. me he was	4:28
when my father s. all these things,	5:17
me-thought I s. in my dream,	8: 4
I s. a man, and he was dressed in	8: 5
I s. the head thereof a little way	8:14
I s. them, but they would not	8:18
I s. numberless concourses of	8:21
he s. other multitudes pressing	8:30
he also s. other multitudes feeling	8:31
things which he s. in a vision,	8:36
things which he s. in a vision,	10:17
the things which my father s.	11: 3
that thy father s. the tree	11: 4
I s. him not; for he had gone	11:12
I saw I s. the heavens open;	11:14
the tree which thy father s.?	11:21
I s. many fall down at his feet	11:24
before my face, and I s. them not.	11:29
I s. angels descending upon the	11:30
and I s. and bear record.	11:32
I, Nephi, s. that he was lifted up	11:33
I s. the multitudes of the earth,	11:34
the building which my father s.	11:35
I s. and bear record, that the	11:36
I s. a mist of darkness on the	12: 4
and I s. lightnings, and I heard	12: 4
I s. the earth and the rocks,	12: 4
and I s. mountains tumbling	12: 4
I s. the plains of the earth,	12: 4
and I s. many cities that they	12: 4
I s. many that they were burned	12: 4
I s. many that did tumble to the	12: 4
after I s. these things, I saw	12: 5
I s. the vapor of darkness,	12: 5

SAW   840   SAW

I s. multitudes who had fallen	1 Ne 12: 5
And I s. the heavens open,	12: 6
And I also s. and bear record	12: 7
And I, Nephi, also s. many of	12:12
I s. the multitudes of the earth	12:13
filthy water which thy father s.;	12:16
building, which thy father s.,	12:18
I beheld and s. that the seed of	12:19
I beheld, and s. the people of	12:20
And I s. them gathered	12:21
I s. wars and rumors of wars	12:21
I s. many generations pass away.	12:21
I s. among the nations of the	13: 4
I s. the devil that he was the	13: 6
And I also s. gold, and silver,	13: 7
and I s. many harlots.	13: 7
of the great whore whom I s.	14:12
of the things which I s. and heard;	14:28
small part of the things which I s.	14:28
I s. the things which my father	14:29
the things which my father s.,	14:29
concerning the things which I s.	14:30
if all the things which I s.	14:30
which our father s. in a dream?	15:21
meaneth the tree which he s.?	15:21
rod of iron which our father s.,	15:23
river of water which our father s.?	15:26
the water which my father s.	15:27
our father also s. that the justice	15:30
when my brethren s. that I was	17:17
now when they s. that I began	17:19
when they s. that they were about	18:20
Wherefore, Joseph truly s. our	2 Ne 3: 5
for he verily s. my Redeemer,	11: 2
that Isaiah, the son of Amoz, s.	12: 1
I s. also the Lord sitting upon	16: 1
Shall the s. magnify itself	20:15
he s. that he must soon die;	Jac 1: 9
he s. that his olive-tree began to	5: 4
the master of the vineyard s. it,	5: 7
the Lord of the vineyard s. that	5:75
I, Jacob, s. that I must soon go	7:27
I s. wars between the Nephites	En 1:24
And I s. that I must soon go down	1:26
I s. the last which he wrote,	Om 1: 9
I s. much war and contention	1:10
and he s. that he must very soon	Mos 1: 9
the Lord God s. that his people	3:14
when Ammon s. that he was	7:12
when I s. that which was good	9: 1
when the king s. that he was	19: 5
Lamanites s. the people of Limhi,	20:26
the Lord s. fit in his infinite	28: 4
we s. a numerous host of the	Al 2:24
wickedness which they s. had	4: 7
For they s. and beheld with	4: 8
Alma s. the wickedness of the	4:11
he s. also that the example of the	4:11
Yea, the s. great inequality	4:12
he s. that it was expedient that	12:28
when Amulek s. the pains of the	14:10
and when the people s. this, they	14:26
when they s. Alma and Amulek	14:29
and when s. them he	15: 5
when Ammon s. this his heart	17:29
when he s. the afflictions of those	17:30
he s. that the countenance of the	18:12
and he s. the king, and he knew	19: 7
when she s. that all the servants	19:17
they also s. Ammon, and behold,	19:18
and when she s. the contention	19:28
when the king s. that Ammon	20:21
Now when Ammon s. that he had	20:24
when he s. that Ammon had no	20:26
when he also s. the great love he	20:26
when he s. that they would not	21:11
they s. that the people would	21:12
when Aaron s. that the king	22:12
when she s. him lay as if he were	22:19
when the queen s. the fear of the	22:21
when Aaron s. the determination	22:22
And when they s. it they greatly	22:23
when the king s. that the people	22:26
s. the preparations of the	Al 24: 5
when the people s. that they	24:21
when the Lamanites s. that their	24:23
when the Lamanites s. this they	24:24
when the Lamanites s. that they	25:13
when they s. that they could not	27: 2
s. this work of destruction	27: 4
s. this great work of destruction,	27: 4
s. the hardness of his heart,	30:29
when they s. that he would	30:29
when the chief judge s. this,	30:51
when Alma s. this his heart was	31:24
he s. that they were a wicked	31:24
he s. that their hearts were set	31:24
he also s. that their hearts were	31:25
I s. that I had rebelled against	36:13
Yea, methought I s., even as our	36:22
I saw, even as our father Lehi s.,	36:22
the Lord s. that his people began	37:22
when they s. your conduct they	39:11
s. that the Lamanites were	43: 4
s. that the people of Nephi,	43:19
when they s. the Nephites	43:36
s. the fierceness and the anger	43:48
s. the men of Lehi on the east	43:53
Moroni, when he s. their terror,	43:54
s. the scalp which was upon	44:15
when he s. that they were all	44:19
he s. that a part of the remnant	46:24
when Amalickiah s. that the	46:29
he also s. that his people were	46:29
s. that they were surrounded,	47:15
s. an army pursuing after them,	47:29
s. that their chief captains	49:25
that when Moroni s. this,	51:14
also s. that the Lamanites were	51:14
s. that Teancum was ready to	52: 1
when the Lamanites s. this	52: 2
Teancum s. that the Lamanites	52: 5
he s. that it was impossible that	52:17
as Teancum s. the armies of	52:23
when the Lamanites s. that he	52:24
that when they s. the danger,	53:13
they s. him coming and they	55: 8
s. that they were all drunken,	55:15
thus they s. that the Nephites	55:23
when they s. our afflictions	56: 7
s. that Anitpus had received a	56:18
when we s. that the Lamanites	56:30
when they s. the army of Antipus	56:37
we s. the Lamanites upon us,	56:41
the people of Antipus s. that the	56:53
when the Lamanites s. that we	58:14
they s. that we were not strong,	58:15
we s. that they were making	58:16
the Lamanites s. that they were	58:24
s. that we were prepared to	58:29
s. that the city of Nephihah was	59:11
saw that the armies of Moroni	62:24
s. that they were fleeing before	62:25
s. that Moroni was coming	62:31
when he s. that he could not	He 1: 6
s. that he was condemned unto	1: 9
when Coriantumr s. that he was	1:22
and s. that the Nephites had fled	1:22
when Moronihah s. that they did	4:16
they s. that they had been a	4:21
and they s. that their laws had	4:22
s. that they had become weak,	4:24
they s. that the Lamanites were	4:25
they s. that the strength of the	4:26
when they s. that they were	5:24
For they s. that the Lamanites	5:25
s. through the cloud of darkness	5:36
s. that the cloud of darkness	5:43
s. that they were encircled	5:43
they s. the heavens open;	5:48
who s. and heard these things;	5:49
when Nephi s. it, his heart was	7: 6
s. Nephi as he was pouring out	7:11
Abraham s. of his coming,	8:17
when they s. this they were	9: 4
when they s. they believed,	9: 5

SAW 841 SAY

they s. those five men who had	He	9: 7	woman s. that the tree was good	Mses	4:12
when we s. all things even as		9:14	unto them, and they s. him not;		5: 4
s. that they were about to perish		11: 7	heavens I s., and the Lord spake		6:42
s. that the people had repented		11: 9	I s. the Lord; and he stood		7: 4
Now when they s. this,		16: 3	he s. angels descending out of		7:25
s. that they could not hit him		16: 6	Enoch also s. Noah, and his		7:42
s. this wickedness of his people,	3Ne	1:10	Enoch s. that Noah built an ark;		7:43
when they s. the appearance of		4: 8	as Enoch s. this, he had bitterness		7:44
the armies of Giddianhi s. this		4: 9	Enoch s. the day of the coming of		7:47
And the people s. it, and did		7:20	Enoch s. the day of the coming of		7:65
they s. a Man descending		11: 8	he s. great tribulations among the		7:66
as we s. and heard Jesus speak		17:16	s. the sea, that it was troubled,		7:66
both s. and heard Jesus speak;		17:17	he s. the day of the righteous,		7:67
and they s. the heavens open,		17:24	s. that those daughters were fair,		8:14
they s. angels descending out		17:24	s. that the wickedness of men had		8:22
disciples s. and did bear record		18:39	s. that it was needful for me to	Abr	1: 1
whom they both s. and heard.		20: 9	I s. the stars, that they were		3: 2
s. and heard these children;		26:16	I s. those things which his hands		3:12
s. and heard unspeakable things,		26:18	s. these souls that they were good,		3:23
s. and heard unspeakable things.		28:13	and he s. that they were good;		3:23
things which they s. and heard;		28:14	the Gods s. that they were obeyed.		4:10
s. their lamentation and their	Mrm	2:12	the Gods s. that they were obeyed.		4:12
I s. that the day of grace was		2:15	s. that they would be obeyed,		4:21
I s. thousands of them hewn		2:15	the Gods s. they would obey.		4:25
things which I s. and heard,		3:16	s. that it was after the Lord's		5:13
him whom they s. and heard,		3:21	I s. a pillar of light exactly	JS	2:16
when the Nephites s. that they		4: 8	I s. two Personages, whose		2:17
the brother of Jared s. him not.	Eth	2: 4	he had when he s. a light,		2:24
and he s. the finger of the Lord;		3: 6	that light I s. two Personages,		2:25
the Lord s. that the brother of		3: 7	I s. the light in the room begin		2:43
I s. the finger of the Lord,		3: 8	when, instantly I s., as it were,		2:43
and he s. the finger of Jesus,		3:19	was there I first s. my wife		2:57
when he s., he fell with fear;		3:19			
therefore he s. Jesus; and he did		3:20	SAWEST		
which the brother of Jared s.;		4: 4	S. thou more than this?	Eth	3: 9
which the brother of Jared s.,		4: 7			
s. that he must soon go down		6:19	SAY		
he s. peace in the land for the		9:15	For it sufficeth me to s. that	1Ne	6: 2
and he s. peace in the land;		9:22	Now behold, I s. unto you that		7:15
s. the Son of Righteousness,		9:22	and I also did s. unto them		8:15
people s. that they must perish		9:34	Behold, I s. unto you,		15:12
because they s. them not.		12: 5	Behold, I s. unto you,		15:16
but truly s. with their eyes		12:19	But behold, I s. unto you,		15:34
Ether s. the days of Christ,		13: 4	and s.: Thou speakest hard		16: 3
He s. that there had been slain		15: 2	for I did s. many things unto		16:24
s. them that they were fulfilled		15: 3	Behold, I s. unto you, Nay.		17:33
when Coriantumr s. that he was		15: 7	I s. unto you, Nay.		17:34
who is the Son whom we s.	DC	76:14	that I should s. unto this water,		17:50
And s. the holy angels,		76:21	if I should s. it, it would be done.		17:50
For we s. him, even on the		76:23	I s., trample under their feet		19: 7
we s. also, and bear record,		76:25	for fear lest thou shouldst s.—		20: 5
And we s. a vision of the		76:30	unto thee, lest thou shouldst s.—		20: 7
for we s. and heard,		76:50	s. ye: The Lord hath redeemed		20:20
we s. the terrestrial world,		76:71	That thou mayest s. to the		21: 9
which we s. of the terrestrial,		76:80	shall again in thine ears s.:		21:20
we s. the glory of the telestial,		76:81	Then shalt thou s. in thine heart:		21:21
we s., in the heavenly vision,		76:89	my brethren, I s. unto you,		22:18
we s. the glory of the terrestrial		76:91	whatsoever he shall s. unto you.		22:20
we s. the glory of the celestial,		76:92	now behold, I, Nephi, s. unto you		22:27
and lo, we s. the glory and		76:109	behold, I s., if the day shall	2Ne	1:10
end of the vision which we s.,		76:113	Ye s. that he hath used sharpness;		1:26
these elders whom John s.,		77: 5	ye s. that he hath been angry		1:26
by the book which John s.,		77: 6	if ye shall s. there is no law,		2:13
John s. and bore record of		93: 6	ye shall also s. there is no sin.		2:13
I s. his glory, that he was in		93: 7	If ye shall s. there is no sin,		2:13
I, John, s. that he received not		93:12	also s. there is no righteousness.		2:13
he s. the Lord, and he walked with		107:49	and cry unto the Lord, and s.:		4:30
We s. the Lord standing upon the		110: 2	But it sufficeth me to s.,		5: 4
certifying in his record that he s.		128: 3	And it sufficeth me to s. that		5:34
And I s. the dead, small and great,		128: 6	and s. unto Zion: Behold,		8:16
under the alter that John s.,		135: 7	Do not s. that I have spoken		9:40
And he s. God face to face,	Mses	1: 2	many people shall go and s.,		12: 3
fear, he s. the bitterness of hell.		1:20	and shall s.: Thou hast		13: 6
And I, God, s. the light;		2: 4	S. unto the righteous that it		13:10
I, God, s. that all things which		2:10	That s.: Let him make speed,		15:19
I, God, s. that all things which		2:12	And s. unto him: Take heed,		17: 4
s. that all things which I had		2:18	S. ye not, a confederacy,		18:12
I, God, s. that all things which		2:21	all to whom this people shall s.,		18:12
s. that all these things were good.		2:25	when they shall s. unto you:		18:19
God, s. everything that I had made,		2:31	that s. in the pride and stoutness		19: 9
I, God, s. that they were good;		3: 2	And in that day thou shalt s.:		22: 1
man s. that it was good for food.		3: 9	And in that day shall ye s.:		22: 4

SAY 842 SAY

and s.: How hath the oppressor	2Ne 24: 4	now, if ye s. this in your hearts	Mos	4:25
they shall speak and s. unto thee:	24:10	ye s. that your hearts are changed		5: 7
shall consider thee, and shall s.:	24:16	I s. unto you, I would that ye		5:12
yea, behold I s. unto you,	25:20	I s. unto you, Nay;		5:14
And now behold, I s. unto you	25:29	I s. unto you, that even so shall		5:14
For behold, I s. unto you	26: 2	Yea, I s. unto you, great are		7:24
beloved brethren, I s. unto you	26:23	And I s. unto thee again:		8:12
Behold, I s. unto you, Nay;	26:25	therefore, I s. no more.		10:22
Behold, I s. unto you, Nay.	26:26	Go forth, and s. unto this people,		11:20
Behold I s. unto you, Nay;	26:27	I s. unto you, wo be unto you		12:26
Behold I s. unto you, Nay;	26:28	by the law of Moses? What s. ye?		12:31
the Lord God shall s. unto him	27:15	I s. unto, Nay, ye have not.		12:37
And the learned shall s.:	27:15	I s. unto you, Nay, ye have not.		12:37
and to get gain will they s. this,	27:16	I s. unto you, Nay; for if ye		13:26
And the man shall s.: I cannot	27:17	I s. unto you that it is expedient		13:27
Then shall the learned s.:	27:18	but I s. unto you, that the time		13:27
man that is not learned shall s.:	27:19	And moreover, I s. unto you,		13:28
shall the Lord God s. unto him:	27:20	And now I s. unto you that it		13:29
the Lord shall s. unto him	27:24	But behold, I s. unto you,		13:31
and they s.: Who seeth us,	27:27	I s. unto you, Nay, they did not		13:32
And they also s.: Surely,	27:27	Yea, even doth not Isaiah s.:		14: 1
shall the work s. of him that	27:27	And now I s. unto you, who		15:10
shall the thing framed s. of him	27:27	Behold, I s. unto you, that		15:10
when the one shall s. unto the other:	28: 3	And now what s. ye?		15:10
and the others shall s.:	28: 3	Behold I s. unto you, that		15:11
thus shall every one s. that hath	28: 3	I s. unto you, that all those		15:11
and they s. unto the people:	28: 5	I s. unto you, that these are		15:11
if they shall s. there is a miracle	28: 6	I s. unto you that they are his		15:13
there shall be many which shall s.:	28: 7	I s. unto you, this is not all.		15:18
shall also be many which shall s.:	28: 8	I s. unto you, were it not for this,		15:19
and s. that is of no worth!	28:16	And now I s. unto you that		15:28
they will s.: All is well in Zion;	28:21	I s. unto you, I will not recall		17: 9
Wo be unto him that shall s.:	28:29	Now I s. unto you, if this be		18:10
and from them that shall s.,	28:30	therefore I s. unto you it is not		23: 7
many of the Gentiles shall s.:	29: 3	And now I s. unto you, ye have		23:12
Thou fool, that shall s.:	29: 6	Therefore I s. unto you, that		26:28
For behold, I s. unto you that	30: 2	Therefore I s. unto you, Go;		26:29
Behold, I s. unto you, Nay;	31:19	for verily I s. unto you, he that		26:31
For behold, again I s. unto you	32: 5	Now I s. unto you, Go;		26:32
things which he shall s. unto you	32: 6	Now I s. unto thee: Go,		27:16
now I, Nephi, cannot s. more;	32: 7	And now I s. unto thee, Alma,		27:16
But behold, I s. unto you	32: 9	I s. unto you, unless this be		27:27
I s. Jew, because I mean them	33: 8	Now I s. unto you let us be		29: 8
Behold, I s. unto you, Nay.	Jac 2:14	I s. unto you, if this could		29:13
what s. ye of it?	2:20	Now I s. unto you, that		29:16
Behold, I s., is not this the	5:48	now I s. unto you, ye cannot		29:21
O be wise; what can I s. more?	6:12	And now behold I s. unto you,		29:24
a being which ye s. shall come	7: 7	For behold I s. unto you, the sins		29:31
Behold, I s. unto you that none of	7:11	And again, I s. he that	Al	3:17
he could s. no more, and he	7:20	behold, I s. unto you that he		5: 3
I s. there was nothing short of	En 1:23	And I s. unto you, they		5: 4
and he will s. unto me:	1:27	yea, I s. unto you, they were in		5: 5
I s. unto you, Yea;	Jar 1: 2	And now behold, I s. unto you,		5: 6
I s. unto you, my sons,	Mos 1: 5	Behold, I s. unto you, Nay,		5: 8
moreover I s. unto you,	1:13	I s. unto you, Yea, they were		5: 9
For I s. unto you, that if	1:14	And I s. unto you that they are		6: 9
I s. unto you that as I have	2:12	Behold I s. unto you that this is		5:12
Behold, I s. unto you that	2:16	I s. unto you, can you imagine		5:16
I s. unto you, my brethren,	2:20	unto the Lord in that day, and say—		5:17
I s. unto you that if ye should	2:21	I s. unto you, can ye look up,		5:19
I s., if ye should serve him	2:21	I s. unto you, can you look up,		5:19
can ye s. aught of yourselves?	2:25	I s. unto you, can ye think of		5:20
Ye cannot s. that ye are even as	2:25	I s. unto you, ye will know at		5:21
I s. unto you that I have	2:28	I s. unto you, Nay; except ye		5:25
And moreover, I s. unto you that	2:29	And now behold, I s. unto you,		5:26
I s. unto you, that there are	2:34	Could ye s., if ye were called to die		5:27
And now, I s. unto you,	2:36	I s. unto you, if ye are not ye are		5:28
I s. unto you, that the man	2:37	Behold, I s., is there one among		5:29
And now I s. unto you,	2:39	I s. unto you that such an one is		5:29
and s. that he hath a devil,	3: 9	And again I s. unto you, is there		5:30
I s. unto you they are blessed;	3:16	Behold, I s. unto you, that the		5:38
And moreover, I s. unto you,	3:17	Behold, I s. unto you, that the		5:39
And moreover, I s. unto you,	3:20	Behold, I s. unto you, whosoever		5:39
I s. unto you, if ye have	4: 6	For I s. unto you that		5:40
I s., that this is the man who	4: 7	Behold, I s. unto you they are		5:46
And again I s. unto you as I	4:11	And moreover, I s. unto you that		5:47
And behold, I s. unto you that if	4:12	I s. unto you, that I know of		5:48
Perhaps thou shalt s.:	4:17	whatsoever I shall s. unto you,		5:48
But I s. unto you, O man,	4:18	and I s. unto you, that I know		5:48
I s. unto you, wo be unto that	4:23	And now I s. unto you that		5:49
and now, I s. these things unto	4:23	yea, I s. unto you the aged,		5:49
And again, I s. unto the poor,	4:24	beloved brethren, I s. unto you,		5:50
I would that ye s. in your hearts	4:24	Go forth and s. unto this people—		5:51

SAY

And again I s. unto you,	Al	5:52
beloved brethren, I s. unto you,		5:53
I s. unto you that these are they		5:56
And now I s. unto you, all you		5:57
what have ye to s. against this?		5:58
I s. unto you, if ye speak		5:58
And now I s. unto you that the		5:60
For behold, I s. unto you there		7: 7
Behold, I do not s. that he will		7: 8
Now I s. unto you that ye must		7:14
Yea, I s. unto you come and fear		7:15
will remember that I s. unto him,		7:16
Behold, I s. unto you, yea,		7:17
therefore I s. unto you the time		7:21
Yea, s. unto them, except they		8:16
also s. unto my servant Amulek,		8:29
Behold, now I s. unto you that		9:12
Nevertheless I s. unto you, that		9:15
But behold, I s. unto you that if		9:18
I s. unto you, Nay; he would		9:19
And now behold I s. unto you,		9:23
I s. unto you that if this be the		9:23
for behold I s. unto you, that as		10:10
Yea, well did Mosiah s., who was		10:19
yea, well did he s. that if the time		10:19
And now I s. unto you that well		10:20
Yea, and I s. unto you that if it		10:22
ye s. that I have spoken against		10:26
And now behold, I s. unto you,		10:27
for I shall s. nothing which is		11:22
I s. unto you, Nay, thou knowest		11:24
I s. unto you he shall not, for it is		11:34
And I s. unto you again that he		11:37
I s. unto you that this mortal		11:45
remember that what I s. unto		12: 5
what I say unto thee I s. unto all		12: 5
And behold I s. unto you all that		12: 6
And now behold, I s. unto you		12:16
Then, I s. unto you, they shall be		12:18
And now behold, I s. unto you		12:23
brethren, behold I s. unto you,		12:36
What s. ye for yourselves?		14:15
things did they s. unto them,		14:21
things did they s. unto them:		14:22
he knew not what he should s.		18:14
I s. unto you, what is it, that		18:17
and some s. that he is not dead,		19: 5
but others s. that he is dead		19: 5
I s. unto thee, woman, there has		19:10
Amalekites s. that there is a God,		22: 7
yea, I s. unto you, as the Lord		23: 6
Behold, I s. unto you, Nay,		24:13
to his brethren, which s. thus:		26: 1
Behold I s. unto you, how great		26: 1
who can s. too much of his		26:16
Behold, I s. unto you, I cannot		26:16
I cannot s. the smallest part		26:16
I s. unto you, there is none that		26:21
And moreover they did s.:		26:25
I s. unto you, Nay, they are		26:31
And now behold I s. unto you,		26:33
Behold, I s. unto you, Nay,		26:33
Yea, I s. unto you, there		26:35
yea, I s., blessed be the		26:36
and if he s. unto us, go down		27: 7
which ye s. are handed down by		30:14
Ye look forward and s. that ye		30:16
many more such things did he s.		30:17
Ye s. that this people is a free		30:24
Behold, I s. they are in		30:24
Ye s. that those ancient		30:24
Behold, I s. that ye do not		30:24
Ye s. that this people is a		30:25
Behold, I s. that a child is		30:25
ye also s. that Christ shall come.		30:26
But behold, I s. that ye do not		30:26
And ye s. also that he shall be		30:26
being, who they s. is God—		30:28
For behold, I s. unto you, I know		30:39
I s. unto you that ye have		30:40
Will ye s., show unto me a		30:44
and I s. also, that ye do not		30:48
and I s., that in the name of God,		30:49
me that which I should s.	Al	30:53
yet they cry unto thee and s.—		31:28
Yea, and they s. that thou hast		31:29
Therefore he did s. no more to		32: 7
Behold I s. unto you, do ye		32:10
I s. unto you, it is well that		32:12
Yea, there are many who do s.:		32:17
Behold, I s. unto you, Nay;		32:18
Behold, I s. unto you that it is		32:20
now, behold, I s. unto you,		32:22
begin to s. within yourselves—		32:28
I s. unto you, Yea; nevertheless		32:29
needs s. that the seed is good;		32:30
I s. unto you, Yea; for every		32:31
I s. unto you, Yea, because it is		32:35
Behold I s. unto you, Nay;		32:36
beginneth to grow ye will s.		32:37
But behold, I s. unto you, if ye		33: 2
Behold, I s. unto you, that I		34: 8
I s. unto you, Nay.		34:11
beloved brethren, I s. unto you,		34:28
I s. unto you, if ye do not any		34:28
Ye cannot s., when ye are		34:34
Nay, ye cannot s. this;		34:34
Now, behold, I s. unto you,		36: 5
Yea, I s. unto you, my son,		36:21
and again I s. unto you, my son,		36:21
but behold I s. unto you,		37: 6
Yea, I s. unto you, were it not		37: 9
And it may suffice if I only s. they		37:12
I have somewhat to s. concerning		37:38
And now I s., is there not a type		37:45
for I s. unto you, even as I		38: 1
I s. unto you, my son, that I		38: 3
Do not s,: O God, I thank thee		38:14
but rather s.: O Lord, forgive		38:14
somewhat more to s. unto thee		39: 1
yea, I s. unto you, my son, that		39: 6
of the Lord doth s. unto me:		39:12
I would s. somewhat unto you		39:15
Behold, I s. unto you, that it is		39:15
Behold, I s. unto you, is not a		39:17
more I would s. unto thee;		40: 1
Behold, I s. unto you, that there		40: 2
or, I would s., in other words,		40: 2
Behold, I s. unto you, Nay;		40:18
well as the righteous, I do not s.:		40:19
that I s. that they all come forth;		40:19
Now, my son, I do not s. that		40:20
or after, I do not s.;		40:21
but this much I s., that there		40:21
my son, I have somewhat to s.		41: 1
I s. unto thee, my son, that		41: 2
Behold, I s. unto you, wickedness		41:10
or I would s., in a carnal state,		41:11
I s. unto you, Nay; not one whit.		42:25
Now we shall s. no more		43: 2
write the words which I shall s.		45: 9
yea, I s. unto you, that because		45:12
yea, I s. unto you, that from that		45:12
Yea, verily, verily I s. unto you,		48:17
I s. unto you, yea, that it was in		49: 3
have somewhat to s. concerning		53:10
whom ye s. we have rejected,		54:21
Therefore what s. ye, my sons,		56:44
And now I s. unto you,		56:45
somewhat to s. unto them		60: 2
I s. unto you that myself,		60: 3
I s. unto you if ye have		60:12
for I s. unto you, there are		60:12
And now behold, I s. unto you,		60:14
But why should I s. much		60:18
Behold I s. unto you, Nay.		60:23
Behold, I s. unto you, Moroni,		61: 2
I do not s. that these things shall	He	7:29
s. that he hath given unto me no		8:12
Yea, and behold I s. unto you,		8:18
Will ye s. that the sons of		8:21
the five whom ye s. ye have sent,		9:12
ye s. that I have agreed with a		9:23
But behold, I s. unto you, that		9:23
ye s. that I have agreed with a		9:24
Behold I s. unto you:		9:26

SAY

of Seezoram, and s. unto him—	He	9:26
he shall s. unto you, Nay.		9:28
And ye shall s. unto him:		9:29
fear, and wist not what to s.		9:30
ye have seen this, ye shall s.:		9:32
And then shall ye s.:		9:34
And then shall he s. unto you,		9:36
if ye shall s. unto this temple		10: 8
And if ye shall s. unto this		10: 9
if ye shall s. that God shall smite		10:10
that they would s. unto Nephi:		11: 8
the judges did s. unto Nephi,		11: 9
if he s. unto the earth—Move—		12:13
Yea, if he s. unto the earth—		12:14
also, if he s. unto the waters of		12:16
if he s. unto this mountain—		12:17
earth, and the Lord shall s.—		12:18
And if the Lord shall s.—		12:19
behold, if the Lord shall s. unto		12:20
And if the Lord shall s.—		12:21
unto him to whom he shall s. this,		12:22
fulfilling the words which s.:		12:26
hath put it into my heart to s.		13: 5
And now when ye talk, ye s.:		13:25
will s. that he is a false prophet,		13:26
come among you and shall s.:		13:27
yea, he will s.: Walk after the		13:27
come among you and s. this,		13:27
and s. that he is a prophet.		13:27
And then shall ye lament, and s.:		13:32
Yea, in that day ye shall s.:		13:33
Yea, I s. unto you, that the more		15: 6
Yea, I s. unto you, that in the		15:12
Therefore I s. unto you,		15:14
began to s. that the time was	3Ne	1: 5
Yea, verily I s. unto you, if ye		9:14
Behold, I s. unto you,		10:15
Verily I s. unto you, that whoso		11:23
the words which ye shall s.,		11:24
verily I s. unto you, that		11:27
verily, verily I s. unto you,		11:29
verily, verily, I s. unto you,		11:31
Verily, verily, I s. unto you,		11:35
And again I s. unto you,		11:37
And again I s. unto you,		11:38
Verily, verily, I s. unto you,		11:39
s. all manner of evil against you		12:11
Verily, verily, I s. unto you,		12:13
Verily, verily, I s. unto you,		12:14
For verily I s. unto you,		12:18
for verily I s. unto you,		12:20
But I s. unto you, that		12:22
whosoever shall s. to his brother,		12:22
and whosoever shall s.,		12:22
Verily, verily, I s. unto thee,		12:26
Verily, verily, I s. unto you, Nay.		12:26
But I s. unto you, that		12:28
Verily, verily, I s. unto you,		12:32
verily, verily, I s. unto you,		12:34
But I s. unto you, that ye shall		12:39
But behold I s. unto you, love		12:44
Verily, verily, I s. that I would		13: 1
Verily I s. unto you, they have		13: 2
Verily I s. unto you, they have		13: 5
Verily I s. unto you, they have		13:16
Therefore I s. unto you, take no		13:25
And yet I s. unto you,		13:29
Verily, verily, I s. unto you,		14: 1
how wilt thou s. to thy brother:		14: 4
Many will s. to me in that		14:22
Behold, I s. unto you that		15: 4
verily I s. unto you, shall		15: 6
I was commanded to s. no more		15:18
verily, I s. unto you that the		15:19
verily, I s. unto you again that		15:20
And verily I s. unto you, that		15:21
verily, verily, I s. unto you		16: 1
verily, verily, I s. unto you, that		16: 9
that I should s. unto you:		16:10
Verily, verily, I s. unto you,		16:16
Isaiah shall be fulfilled, which s.:		16:17
Verily, verily, I s. unto you,		18:15
verily, verily, I s. unto you,	He	18:18
verily, verily, I s. unto you,		18:27
Verily I s. unto you, there are		19:36
verily, verily, I s. unto you,		20:12
And I s. unto you, that if the		20:15
whatsoever he shall s. unto you.		20:23
Verily I s. unto you, yea, and		20:24
Verily, verily, I s. unto you,		20:39
And then shall they s.:		20:40
Verily, verily, I s. unto you,		20:46
And verily I s. unto you,		21: 1
for verily I s. unto you that		21: 2
Verily, verily, I s. unto you,		21: 3
Verily I s. unto you, at that day		21:26
now, behold, I s. unto you,		23: 1
Verily I s. unto you, I		23: 9
But ye s.: Wherein shall we		24: 7
But ye s.: Wherein have we		24: 8
Yet ye s.: What have we		24:13
Verily, verily, I s. unto you, why		27: 4
which s. ye must take upon you		27: 5
Verily I s. unto you, that ye are		27: 9
verily I s. unto you they have		27:11
Verily, verily, I s. unto you,		27:21
Verily I s. unto you, even as I		27:27
And verily I s. unto you,		27:28
And now behold, I s. unto you		29: 1
ye need not s. that the Lord		29: 2
that shall s. the Lord no longer		29: 6
wo unto him that shall s. at		29: 7
that the Lord did s. unto me:	Mrm	3: 2
I s. no more concerning them,		8: 9
the house of Israel, and shall s.:		8:21
behold I s. unto you, that those		8:23
no one need s. they shall not		8:26
there shall be many who will s.,		8:31
churches built up that shall s.:		8:32
will ye s. that there is no God?		9: 2
I s. unto you that ye would be		9: 4
and s. that they are done away,		9: 7
Behold I s. unto you, he that		9: 8
Behold I s. unto you, Nay;		9:15
Who shall s. that it was not		9:17
who shall s. that Jesus Christ		9:18
And behold, I s. unto you he		9:19
I s. unto you that whoso		9:21
it sufficeth me to s. that Jesus	Eth	3:17
me to wife, then shall ye s.:		8:10
Behold I s. unto you, Nay;	Mro	7:29
Behold I s. unto you, Nay;		7:37
Behold I s. unto you that ye		7:41
behold I s. unto you that he		7:43
Behold I s. unto you that this		8:10
Behold I s. unto you, that he		8:14
the Lord God will s. unto you:		10:27
upon all men; yea, verily I s.:	DC	1: 1
And verily I s. unto you,		1: 8
again, verily I s. unto you,		1:34
Behold, I s. unto you, that as		5: 1
this shall you s. unto him—		5: 2
Verily, I s. unto you, that woe		5: 5
Behold, verily I s. unto you,		5: 9
Behold, I s. unto him, he exalts		5:24
then he shall s. unto the people		5:25
he shall s. no more unto them		5:26
these things, except he shall s.:		5:26
are the words which he shall s.		5:26
behold, I s. unto him, he shall		5:28
that you shall s. unto him,		5:29
I s. unto thee Joseph,		5:30
behold, I s. unto you, keep		6: 6
Verily, verily, I s. unto you,		6: 8
S. nothing but repentance unto		6: 9
Verily, verily, I s. unto thee,		6:14
Verily, verily, I s. unto you,		6:22
Verily, verily, I s. unto you,		6:26
Verily, verily, I s. unto you,		6:29
Verily, verily, I s. unto you, that		6:32
Verily, verily, I s. unto thee,		7: 3
I s. unto thee, Peter, this was		7: 5
Verily I s. unto you, ye shall		7: 8
verily, verily, I s. unto you,		8: 1

Behold, I s. unto you, my son,	DC 9: 1
But, behold, I s. unto you,	9: 8
Now, behold, I s. unto you,	10: 1
And behold, I s. unto you,	10:11
they may s. they have caught	10:13
Verily, I s. unto you,	10:14
behold, they s. and think in	10:16
we will s. that he has lied in	10:18
Verily, verily, I s. unto you,	10:20
Verily, verily, I s. unto you,	10:28
Behold, I s. unto you,	10:30
they will s. that you have lied	10:31
I do not s. that you shall not	10:36
therefore I s. unto you, hold	10:37
And now, verily I s. unto you,	10:38
I do not s. this to destroy my	10:54
I s. this to build up my church;	10:54
verily, verily, I s. unto you,	10:56
behold, I s. unto you, keep	11: 6
Verily, verily, I s. unto you,	11: 8
S. nothing but repentance unto	11: 9
verily, verily, I s. unto thee,	11:12
Verily, verily, I s. unto you,	11:13
verily, verily, I s. unto you,	11:30
behold, I s. unto you, keep	12: 6
now, behold, I s. unto you,	15: 6
now, behold, I s. unto you,	16: 6
Behold, I s. unto you, that you	17: 1
and shall s., calling him or her	20:73
shall take the cup also, and s.:	20:78
Behold, I s. unto you, that all	22: 1
he can s. enough in my cause;	24:10
for verily I s. unto you,	25: 1
And verily I s. unto thee that	25:10
verily, verily, I s. unto you,	25:16
Behold, I s. unto you that you	26: 1
For, behold, I s. unto you,	27: 2
Behold, I s. unto thee, Oliver,	28: 1
verily, verily, I s. unto thee,	28: 2
behold, I s. unto you that you	28: 8
And now, behold, I s. unto you	28: 9
Behold, I s. unto you that it	28: 9
verily, verily, I s. unto you,	29: 3
Verily, I s. unto you that ye	29: 4
verily, verily, I s. unto you,	29:12
But, behold, I s. unto you that	29:14
verily, verily, I s. unto you	29:22
behold, verily I s. unto you,	29:26
Wherefore I will s. unto them—	29:28
now, behold, I s. unto you,	29:29
verily I s. unto you that all	29:34
the wicked when I shall s.:	29:41
But, behold, I s. unto you that I,	29:42
But behold, I s. unto you,	29:46
And, again, I s. unto you,	29:49
Behold, I s. unto you, David,	30: 1
Behold, I s. unto you, Peter,	30: 5
I s. unto you, my servant John,	30: 9
Behold, verily I s. unto you,	31: 6
Behold, I s. unto you that you	31:10
behold, I s. unto him that	32: 1
I s. unto you, my servants	33: 1
verily, verily, I s. unto you	33: 2
verily, verily, I s. unto you,	33: 5
verily, verily, I s. unto you,	33: 7
verily, verily, I s. unto you,	33:12
verily, verily, I s. unto you,	33:18
the Lord God, shall s. unto you,	34: 1
verily, verily, I s. unto you,	34: 7
verily, verily, I s. unto you,	34:12
verily, verily, I s. unto my	35: 3
And now I s. unto you, tarry	35:22
Behold, I s. unto you, my	36: 1
Behold, I s. unto you that it is	37: 1
And again, I s. unto you that	37: 2
verily, I s., even as many as	38: 4
verily, I s. unto you, ye are	38: 7
Verily I s. unto you, ye are	38:10
But, verily I s. unto you that	38:21
But, verily I s. unto you,	38:23
And again I s. unto you,	38:25
I s. unto you, be one;	38:27
And again, I s. unto you that	38:28

you s. that there will soon be	DC 38:29
And again, I s. unto you, I give	38:40
verily, verily, I s. unto you,	39: 5
now, behold, I s. unto you,	39: 7
And verily I s. unto thee,	39: 8
verily, verily, I s. unto thee,	39:14
verily, verily, I s. unto you,	39:16
Behold, verily I s. unto you,	40: 1
Again I s. unto you, hearken	42: 2
For verily I s., as ye have	42: 3
Behold, verily I s. unto you,	42: 4
And again, I s. unto you,	42:10
Again I s. unto you, that it	42:11
And again, I s., thou shalt	42:19
Behold, verily I s. unto you,	42:74
And again, I s. unto you,	42:76
verily, verily, I s. unto you,	43: 2
verily, verily, I s. unto you,	43: 4
For verily I s. unto you,	43: 7
And again, I s. unto you,	43:13
Again I s., hearken ye elders	43:15
shall s. to the sleeping nations:	43:18
what will ye s. when the day	43:21
Behold, verily I s. unto you,	43:27
Behold, I s. unto you, that ye	44: 6
And again I s. hearken unto	45: 2
For verily I s. unto you that	45: 7
ye s. is the God of Enoch,	45:11
your enemies s. that this house	45:18
But, verily I s. unto you,	45:19
Ye s. that ye know that the	45:22
ye s. also that ye know that	45:22
And in this ye s. truly,	45:23
they shall s. that Christ delayeth	45:26
ye s. when they begin to shoot	45:37
the Jews look upon me and s.:	45:51
for I will s. unto them:	45:52
verily I s. unto you, they shall	45:57
And now, behold, I s. unto you,	45:60
For verily I s. unto you,	45:62
I s. unto you, they are nigh,	45:63
And now I s. unto you,	45:72
for verily I s. unto you that	46: 1
And again I s. unto you,	46: 5
And again, I s. unto you,	46: 6
For verily I s. unto you,	46: 9
again, verily I s. unto you,	46:10
again, verily I s. unto you,	46:17
And again, I s. unto you,	46:31
Again, verily I s. unto you,	47: 2
And again, I s. unto you that	47: 3
behold, verily I s. unto you,	49: 1
Behold, I s. unto you,	49: 2
Wherefore, I s. unto you that	49: 9
this people, and s. unto them,	49:11
again, verily I s. unto you,	49:15
again, verily I s. unto you,	49:22
Behold, I s. unto you,	49:26
Behold, verily I s. unto you,	50: 2
Behold, verily I s. unto you,	50: 7
Verily I s. unto you,	50:17
again, verily I s. unto you,	50:25
I s. it that you may know	50:25
behold, verily I s. unto you,	50:36
Verily, I s. unto you,	51:20
Wherefore, verily I s. unto you,	52: 3
again, verily I s. unto you,	52: 7
again, verily I s. unto you,	52:22
Yea, verily I s., let all these	52:33
And again, I s. unto you,	52:35
again, verily I s. unto you,	52:38
Behold, I s. unto you,	53: 1
again, verily I s. unto you,	53: 5
verily, verily, I s. unto you,	54: 2
behold, I s. unto you, seek ye	54: 9
again, verily I s. unto you,	55: 5
again, verily I s. unto you,	56: 8
again, verily I s. unto you,	57: 8
again, verily I s. unto you,	57:11
For verily I s. unto you,	58: 2
Behold, verily I s. unto you,	58: 6
For verily I s. unto you,	58:19
Verily I s., men should be	58:27

SAY

Then they s. in their hearts:	DC 58:33	not the head s. unto the feet	DC 84:109
verily, I s. concerning	58:44	And verily I s. unto you,	84:117
behold, verily I s. unto you,	58:52	These things I s. not of myself;	85:10
Verily I s., that inasmuch	59:16	Behold, verily I s., the field	86: 2
But verily I s. unto you,	61: 3	Behold, verily I s. unto you,	86: 5
verily I s., it behooveth me	61: 9	Now, verily I s. unto you,	88:14
that what I s. unto one	61:18	again, verily I s. unto you,	88:25
I say unto one I s. unto all,	61:18	again, verily I s. unto you,	88:34
again I s. unto you, let them	61:21	again, verily I s. unto you,	88:42
again, verily I s. unto you,	61:30	I s. unto you, he hath seen	88:48
now, verily I s. unto you,	61:36	again, verily I s. unto you,	88:62
and what I s. unto one	61:36	Verily, I s. unto you, let those	88:85
I say unto one I s. unto all,	61:36	verily I s. unto you,	88:117
Yea, verily, I s., hear the word	63: 2	Behold, verily, I s. unto you,	88:136
verily I s., let the wicked take	63: 6	again, verily I s. unto you,	89:10
Verily, I s. unto you,	63: 8	verily I s. unto you my son,	90: 1
And verily I s. unto you,	63:16	Verily I s. unto you,	90: 3
Verily I s., that they shall	63:18	verily I s. unto thy brethren,	90: 6
I, the Lord, s. unto you that	63:19	now, verily I s. unto you,	90:12
now, verily I s. unto you,	63:22	Now, verily I s. unto you,	90:19
Verily I s., let him be	63:45	again, verily I s. unto you,	90:28
behold, verily I s. unto you,	63:55	Verily I s. unto you, that it is	90:30
again, verily I s. unto you,	63:57	behold, verily I s. unto you,	90:32
behold, verily I s., that many	63:62	s. unto your brethren in Zion,	90:32
For verily I s. unto you,	64: 2	Behold, I s. unto you that	90:34
but verily I s., for this once,	64: 3	But verily I s. unto you,	90:36
but verily I s. unto you,	64: 7	Verily, I s. unto you,	91: 3
Wherefore, I s. unto you,	64: 9	What I s. unto one I say	92: 1
ye ought to s. in your hearts—	64:11	I say unto one I s. unto all.	92: 1
Verily I s., for this cause	64:14	again, I s. unto you my servant	92: 2
And now, verily I s. that it is	64:18	therefore, I s. unto you,	93:20
And again, I s. unto you,	64:20	And now, verily I s. unto you,	93:21
for verily I s., tomorrow all	64:24	But verily I s. unto you,	93:41
verily I s. that the rebellious	64:36	Verily, I s. unto my servant	93:44
For, behold, I s. unto you	64:41	Verily, I s. unto my servant	93:45
Verily I s. unto you, blessed	66: 2	verily I s. unto Joseph Smith,	93:47
Verily I s. unto you, my servant	66: 3	What I s. unto one I say	93:49
Behold, verily I s. unto you,	66: 5	I say unto one I s. unto all;	93:49
behold, verily I s. unto you	67: 3	I s. unto you, my friends,	93:51
again, verily I s. unto you	67:10	And, verily I s. unto you,	93:53
Verily I s. unto you, proclaim	71: 2	again, verily I s. unto you,	94: 1
Verily I s. unto you, the elders	72: 5	Verily I s. unto you, that it	94: 4
And now, verily I s. unto you,	72: 8	again, verily I s. unto you,	94:10
And now, verily I s. unto you,	72:16	behold, verily I s. unto you,	95: 5
And now, verily I s. unto you,	72:19	Yea, verily I s. unto you,	95: 8
Now, verily I s. unto you	73: 3	Verily I s. unto you, it is	95:11
Verily, verily, I s. unto you,	75: 1	Behold, I s. unto you,	96: 1
Behold, I s. unto you that it is	75: 3	behold, verily I s. unto you,	96: 5
verily I s. unto my servant	75: 6	again, verily I s. unto you,	96: 6
I forgive him and s. unto him	75: 8	Verily I s. unto you, it is	96: 8
verily I s. unto my servant	75:14	Verily I s. unto you	97: 1
again, I s. unto my servant	75:15	Verily, verily I s. unto you,	97: 2
again I s. unto my servant	75:17	I s. unto you, concerning	97: 3
Behold, I s. unto you,	75:24	Verily I s. unto you,	97: 8
again, verily I s. unto you,	75:28	Verily I s. unto you, that it is	97:10
of whom I s. that it had been	76:32	shall honor her and shall s.:	97:19
who s. they are some of one	76:100	Verily I s. unto you	98: 1
For verily I s. unto you,	78: 3	verily I s. unto you concerning	98: 4
Verily, verily I s. unto you,	78:17	Verily I s. unto you, that I,	98:21
Verily I s. unto you,	79: 1	And again I s. unto you,	98:22
Verily, verily I s. unto you	81: 1	now, verily I s. unto you,	98:28
Verily, verily I s. unto you	82: 1	again, verily I s. unto you,	98:39
but verily I s. unto you,	82: 2	now, verily I s. unto you,	99: 6
what I s. unto one I say	82: 5	Therefore, verily I s. unto you,	100: 5
I say unto one I s. unto all:	82: 5	moment, what ye shall s.	100: 6
now, verily I s. unto you,	82: 7	things whatsoever ye shall s.	100: 8
And again, I s. unto you,	82: 8	Verily I s. unto you,	101: 1
bound when ye do what I s.;	82:10	Behold, I s. unto you, there were	101: 6
but when ye do not what I s.,	82:10	Verily I s. unto you,	101: 9
verily I s. unto you,	82:11	that is to s. in the earth,	101:31
yea, verily I s. unto you,	82:14	Yea, verily I s. unto you,	101:32
And now, verily I s. unto you,	82:22	began to s. among themselves:	101:47
not only to s., but to do	84:57	Again, verily I s. unto you,	101:63
Verily, I s. unto you, Nay.	84:59	Now, verily I s. unto you,	101:72
I s. unto you who now hear	84:60	And again I s. unto you,	101:76
apostles, even so I s. unto you,	84:63	And again, I s. unto you,	101:96
apostles I s. unto you again,	84:64	I do not s. they shall not	101:100
Verily, verily, I s. unto you,	84:74	have power to s. whether it	102:29
But, verily I s. unto all those	84:76	Verily I s. unto you,	103: 1
And again I s. unto you,	84:77	But verily I s. unto you,	103: 5
beforehand what ye shall s.;	84:85	But verily I s. unto you,	103:11
Wo, I s. again, unto that house,	84:95	Behold, I s. unto you,	103:15
verily, verily, I s. unto you,	84:103	for I s. not unto you as I	103:19

SAY 847 SAYING

Reference	Citation	Reference	Citation
But I s. unto you:	DC 103:20	I s. unto you, Samuel Rolfe and	DC124:142
Verily, verily I s. unto you,	103:21	I s. unto you, if those who call	125: 2
s. unto the strength of my	103:22	I would s. to all those with whom	127: 1
But verily I s. unto you,	103:34	I will s. to all the saints, that I	127:10
Verily I s. unto you,	104: 1	And I s. also unto thee, that thou	128:10
And now, verily I s. unto you,	104:19	that s. unto Zion: Behold,	128:19
But, verily I s. unto you,	104:57	I s., how glorious is the voice	128:23
let not any among you s. that	104:70	I have many things to s. to you	128:25
among you s. to the treasurer:	104:72	s. unto you, that the conditions	132: 7
again, verily I s. unto you,	104:78	I s. unto you, if a man marry	132:18
Verily I s. unto you who have	105: 1	I s. unto you, if a man marry	132:19
Behold, I s. unto you,	105: 2	I s. unto you, except ye abide	132:21
there are many who will s.:	105: 8	I s. unto you, if a man marry	132:26
to s. unto the strength of	105:16	Verily I s. unto you, Nay;	132:35
now, verily I s. unto you,	105:20	I s. unto you, if a man receiveth	132:41
I s. unto you, my friends,	105:26	I s. unto you, that whatsoever	132:46
Verily I s. unto you,	105:33	I s., whomsoever you bless	132:47
And again I s. unto you,	105:38	I s. unto you, my servant Joseph,	132:48
verily I s. unto you, the coming of	106: 4	I s. unto you: A commandment	132:51
verily I s. unto you, there was joy in	106: 6	I s., let mine handmaid forgive	132:56
I s. unto you, saith the Lord of	107:60	I s., let not my servant Joseph	132:57
I s. unto you, the most important	107:78	I s. unto you, if any man have	132:64
I s. unto you, the duty of a	107:85	I s. unto you, I will reveal more	132:66
Help thy servants to s.,	109:44	I s. unto you again, the time	133: 7
I s. unto you, there have been	112: 2	he shall s.: I am he who spake	133:47
I s. unto you, and what I say	112:14	I s. unto you, that these are the	Mses 3: 4
and what I s. unto you, I say	112:14	prophesy unto this people, and s.	6:27
unto you, I s. unto all the Twelve:	112:14	S. unto this people: Choose ye	6:33
I s. unto you, I am with him,	112:15	I s. unto you: This is the plan of	6:62
I s. unto you, my servant Thomas,	112:16	s. unto them—Repent, lest I come	7:10
I s. unto you, that whosoever ye	112:21	I s. to the mountains—Depart	Abr 2: 7
I s. unto you, darkness covereth	112:23	(that is to s., the literal seed,	2:11
I s. unto you, the keys of the	112:32	they will s.—She is his wife;	2:23
I s. unto you, behold how great	112:33	Let her s. unto the Egyptians,	2:24
I s. unto you all: Arise and	115: 5	s. unto them, I pray thee	2:25
I s. unto you, let not my servant	115:13	For I s. unto you, that ye	JS 1: 1
I s. unto you, it is my will that	115:17	the prophets, until ye shall s.:	1: 1
I s. unto you, I remember my	117:12	Verily I s. unto you, there shall	1: 3
I s. unto him that his name shall	117:12	if any man shall s. unto you,	1:21
I s. unto you, let all my servants	117:16	if they shall s. unto you:	1:25
I s. unto you, it shall come to	119: 5	I s. unto you, this generation,	1:34
I s. unto you, if my people	119: 6	And what I s. unto one,	1:46
I s. unto you, it shall not be a land	119: 6	unto one, I s. unto all men;	1:46
shall s., My father, my father,	122: 6	verily I s. unto you, he shall	1:50
in answer to them I s. unto you,	124: 2	servant shall s. in his heart:	1:51
I s. unto you, let my servant	124:12	other things did he s. unto me,	2:20
I s. unto you, blessed is my	124:15	I was led to s. in my heart:	2:25
I s. unto you that it is my will	124:18	which, I am sorry to s., led me	2:28
I s. unto you, my servant	124:20	we may s. that we follow the	AoF 13
I therefore s. unto you, I seal	124:21		
I s. unto you, let all my saints	124:25	SAYEST	
s. unto them: Come ye, with all	124:26	Thou s. there is a true and living	Al 11:26
I s. unto you, that after you have	124:33	thou s. that I spake as though	11:36
I s. unto you, how shall your	124:37	Thou also s., except we repent we	21: 6
s. unto you, that your anointings	124:39	And if now thou s. there is a God,	22: 7
I s. unto you, let this house be	124:40	Then why s. thou that we preach	30:35
I s. unto you, they shall not be	124:45		
do not do the things that I s.,	124:47	SAYING	
I s. unto you, that when I give a	124:49	And he read, s.:	1Ne 1:13
I s. unto you, I command you	124:55	he spake unto Laman, s.:	2: 9
I s. unto you, as pertaining to	124:56	the Lord spake unto me, s.:	2:19
even so I s. unto my servant	124:58	he spake unto me, s.:	3: 2
I s. unto you, let my servant	124:62	thy brothers murmur, s.	3: 5
I s. unto you, if my servant	124:70	he spake unto them, s.:	3:29
I s. unto you, let my servant	124:72	again began to murmur, s.:	3:31
I s. unto you concerning my	124:74	I spake unto my brethren, s.:	4: 1
I s. unto you, let my servant	124:77	unto me in the wilderness, s.	4:14
I s. unto you, let my servant	124:91	I also spake unto him, s.:	4:34
in the very hour, what he shall s.	124:97	that he was a visionary man; s.:	5: 2
I s. unto you, I have a mission	124:102	my father spake unto her, s.:	5: 4
I s. unto you, if my servant	124:103	And she spake, s.:	5: 8
I s. unto you, even now, if he	124:110	the Lord spake unto him again, s.	7: 1
I s. unto you, let my servant	124:111	therefore I spake unto them, s.,	7: 8
I s. unto you, if my servant	124:115	I prayed unto the Lord, s.:	7:17
I s. unto you, let no man pay	124:119	he spake unto us, s.:	8: 2
I s. unto you, let the quorum of	124:121	Spirit cried with a loud voice, s.:	11: 6
I s. unto you, I now give unto	124:123	the angel spake unto me, s.:	11:19
I s. unto you, another may be	124:130	And I answered him, s.:	11:22
I s. unto you, I give unto you	124:131	And he spake unto me, s.:	11:23
I s. unto you, let my servant	124:132	the angel spake unto me again, s.	11:30
I s. unto you, I give unto you	124:137	And he spake unto me again, s.:	11:31
I s. unto you, I give unto you	124:141	the angel spake unto me again, s.:	11:32

Lord spake unto me again, s.:	1 Ne	11:35
Lord spake unto me again, s.:		11:36
And the angel spake unto me, s.:		12: 8
And the angel spake unto me, s.:		12:16
the angel spake unto me, s.:		13: 1
And the angel spake unto me, s.:		13: 8
of the Lord spake unto me, s.:		13:34
And the angel spake unto me, s.:		13:40
angel spake unto me, Nephi, s.:		14: 5
the angel spake unto me, s.:		14:16
the angel spake unto me, s.:		14:18
made to our father Abraham, s.:		15:18
they did speak unto me again, s.:		15:21
s.: Our father is dead;		16:35
voice of the Lord came unto me, s.:		17: 7
the Lord spake unto me, s.:		17: 8
began to murmur against me, s.:		17:17
they did rejoice over me, s.:		17:19
I, Nephi, spake unto them, s.:		17:23
I spake unto them, s.:		17:48
but I would not suffer them, s.:		17:55
they were angry with me, s.:		18:10
Wherefore I spake unto them, s.:		19:24
of heaven unto Abraham, s.:		22: 9
words of Moses, which he spake, s.:		22:20
For Joseph truly testified, s.:	2 Ne	3: 6
And thus prophesied Joseph, s.:		3:14
And he spake unto them, s.:		4: 9
he spake unto Sam, s.:		4:11
they did murmur against me, s.:		5: 3
which he spake unto me, s. that:		5:20
In that day shall he swear, s.:		13: 7
shall take hold of one man, s.:		14: 1
I heard the voice of the Lord, s.:		16: 8
it was told the house of David, s.:		17: 2
taken evil counsel against thee, s.:		17: 5
Lord spake again unto Ahaz, s.:		17:10
Lord spake also unto me again, s.:		18: 5
walk in the way of this people, s.:		18:11
also the cedars of Lebanon, s.:		24: 8
Lord of Hosts hath sworn, s.:		24:24
Behold, doth he cry unto any, s.:		26:25
show them unto the learned, s.:		27:15
voice of the Son came unto me, s.:		31:12
the voice of the Son unto me, s.:		31:14
heard a voice from the Father, s.:		31:15
thus came the word unto me, s.:	Jac	2:11
spake unto the house of Israel, s.:		5: 1
s. unto his servant:		5:11
this wise did he speak unto me, s.:		7: 6
by s. that the time passed away		7:26
there came a voice unto me, s.:	En	1: 5
came into my mind again, s.:		1:10
spake unto our fathers, s. that:	Jar	1: 9
he spake unto our fathers, s.	Om	1: 6
s.: My sons, I would that	Mos	1: 3
which he spake unto him, s.:		1:10
and caused to be written, s.:		2: 9
cried aloud with one voice, s.:		4: 2
began to speak unto them, s.:		4: 4
they all cried with one voice, s.:		5: 2
spake unto them in this wise, s.:		7:18
and gave thanks to God, s.:		8:19
s. that their fifty could stand		11:19
and began to prophesy, s.:		11:20
thus hath he commanded me, s.,		11:20
to prophesy among them, s.:		12: 1
the Lord commanded me, s.—		12: 1
forth thy hand and prophesy, s.:		12: 2
been taught by our fathers, s.:		12:20
Moses in the mount of Sinai, s.:		12:33
and he continued his words, s.:		13: 6
and began to accuse him, s.:		17:12
scorch him, he cried unto them, s.:		17:14
forth in the water, and cried, s.:		18:12
in the anguish of his soul, s.:		19: 7
to them in their afflictions, s.:		24:13
Lord came unto them again, s.:		24:16
voice of the Lord came to him, s.:		26:14
Nevertheless he cried again, s.:		27:13
the voice of the people came, s.:		29: 2
the words that were written, s.:		29: 4
and struck with much fear, s.:	Al	2:23
with much faith, cried, s.:	Al	2:30
according to his own record, s.:		5: 2
voice of the Lord, s. unto you,		5:16
unto me with a mighty voice, s.:		5:51
I speak by way of invitation, s.:		5:62
hath said this much unto me, s.:		7: 9
Cry unto this people, s.—		7: 9
they hardened their hearts, s.		8:11
of the Lord appeared unto him, s.:		8:14
And the word came to Alma, s.:		8:29
prophesy unto this people, s.—		8:29
began to contend with me, s.:		9: 1
did boldly testify unto them s.:		9: 7
which he spake unto Lehi, s.		9:13
cry mightily unto this people, s.:		9:25
in the land of Ammonihah, s.:		10: 1
and they cried out, s.:		10:24
cried the mightier unto them, s.:		10:25
people cried out against him, s.:		10:28
began to question Amulek, s.:		11:21
these things unto him, s.:		12: 9
s.: If ye will repent,		12:33
and cried with a mighty voice, s.:		13:21
he began to cry unto the people, s.:		14: 7
but they reviled him, s.:		14: 7
forth also, and smote them, s.:		14:20
spitting upon them, sna s.:		14:21
smote them, s. the same words,		14:25
And Alma cried, s.: How long		14:26
Alma cried unto the Lord, s.:		15:10
of the king began to murmur, s.:		17:28
began to weep exceedingly, s.:		17:28
flattered them by his words, s.:		17:31
Lamoni inquired of his servants, s.:		18: 8
of the faithfulness of Ammon, s.:		18:10
he began to cry unto the Lord, s.:		18:41
some s. that it was a great evil		19:19
And others rebuked them, s.:		19:20
But others rebuked them all, s.		19:26
and cried with a loud voice, s.:		19:29
of the Lord came to Ammon s.:		20: 2
unto him, he answered him, s.:		20:19
began to contend with him, s.:		21: 5
the earth, and cried mightily, s.:		22:17
and they plead with the queen s.:		22:20
his brother Aaron rebuked him, s.:		26:10
the voice of the people came, s.:		27:22
this manner did he preach, s.:		30:12
hand and wrote unto Korihor, s.:		30:51
put forth his hand and wrote, s.:		30:52
and cry with a loud voice, s.:		31:14
his voice to heaven, and cried, s.:		31:26
arose and began to teach them, s.:		34: 1
be fulfilled, which he spake, s.:		37:24
received, unto Zerahemnah, s.:		44:10
s. unto them with a loud voice:		44:13
the s. went abroad in the church		45:19
and crying with a loud voice, s.:		46:19
at the feet of Moroni, s.:		46:22
of Amalickiah raised a cry, s.:		47:25
which he spake unto Lehi, s.:		50:19
he wrote unto Ammoron, s.:		54: 4
are the words which he wrote, s.:		54:15
this s. only made them more		55:10
are the words which he wrote, s.:		56: 2
the words of their mothers, s.:		56:48
And they cried unto us, s.—		57:31
the words which he wrote, s.:		60: 1
began to speak unto them, s.:	He	5:26
above the cloud of darkness, s.:		5:29
behold the voice came again, s.:		5:32
as if it were a whisper, s.:		5:46
against him, s. unto the people:		8: 1
they did cry unto the people, s.:		8: 5
to speak more unto them s.:		8:11
inquired among the people, s.:		9:12
them all that they had done, s.:		9:13
did cry out against Nephi, s.:		9:16
S. unto him: Thou art		9:20
s., Behold here is money;		9:20
a voice came unto him s.:		10: 3
them the word of the Lord, s.:		10:14
Nephi did cry unto the Lord, s.:		11: 3

SAYING

he cried again unto the Lord, s.:	He	11: 9
they cried unto their captains, s.:		16: 6
and upon their own wisdom, s.:		16:15
contend among themselves, s.:		16:17
to rejoice over their brethren, s.:	3Ne	1: 6
of the Lord came unto him, s.:		1:12
the words which were written, s.:		3: 1
and did cry with a loud voice, s.:		4:28
and cry again with one voice, s.:		4:30
And now I make an end of my s.,		5:19
they were heard to cry, s.:		8:24
were heard to cry and mourn, s.:		8:25
did hear, and did witness of it, s.:		10: 3
and spake unto the people, s.:		11: 9
the Lord spake unto them s.:		11:13
did cry out with one accord, s.:		11:16
say, calling them by name, s.:		11:24
and cried unto them, s.:		12: 1
Therefore take no thought, s.,		13:31
his mouth unto them again, s.:		14: 1
they understood not the s. that		15: 2
prayed again unto the Father, s.:		19:27
am he of whom Moses spake, s.:		20:23
your fathers, s. unto Abraham:		20:25
which he made with Abraham, s.:		20:27
which he did tell unto them, s.:		24: 1
but the Lord forbade it, s.:		26:11
one by one, s. unto them:		28: 1
all spake, save it were three, s.:		28: 2
me that I should write, s.:		30: 1
of the Lord came unto me s.:	Mrm	3:14
again unto his brother, s.:	Eth	1:38
of Jared cried unto the Lord, s.:		2:18
cried again unto the Lord s.:		2:22
cried again unto the Lord, s.:		3: 1
the s. of the brother of Jared		7: 5
s. unto them that by faith all		12: 3
the Lord spake unto me, s.:		12:26
And he called them by name, s.:	Mro	2: 2
Father in the name of Christ, s.:		4: 2
these words unto our fathers, s.:		7:26
wise did he write unto me, s.:		8: 1
the power of the Holy Ghost, s.:		8: 7
must preach unto the world, s.:	DC	18:41
Father in solemn prayer, s.:		20:76
for he rebelled against me, s.,		29:36
and they shall be filled, s.:		33:10
declare it with a loud voice, s.:		36: 3
Crying repentance, s.:		36: 6
crying with a loud voice, s.:		39:19
baptizing with water, s.:		42: 7
both bond and free, s.:		43:20
the ears of all that live, s.—		43:21
that hear, s. these words—		43:22
his voice out of heaven, s.:		43:23
S.: Father, behold the		45: 4
and spake unto them, s.:		45:16
S.: I, the Lord, will make		52: 2
s. none other things than		52: 9
a commandment, s. thus:		59: 5
in s. that ye do not know that		67: 7
And we heard the voice, s.:		76:49
unto the Father, spotless, s.:		76:107
the voice of the Lord s.:		76:110
the everlasting gospel, s.:		77: 9
Enoch [Joseph Smith, Jun.], s.:		78: 1
sing this new song, s.:		84:98
while it maketh manifest, s.:		85: 6
And also unto the third, s.:		88:54
sounding the trump of God, s.:		88:92
angel shall sound his trump, s.:		88:94
which is the fourth trump, s.:		88:102
of his trump, s. to all people,		88:104
hear the sound of the trump, s.:		88:104
which is the sixth angel, s.:		88:105
which is the seventh angel, s.:		88:106
or by s. Amen, in token of		88:135
And he bore record, s.:		93: 7
came a voice out of heaven s.:		93:15
and John bore record of me, s.:		93:26
long time, s. among themselves:		101:48
and she came unto him, s.:		101:83
while you are s. unto the people:		105:25
calling us thy friends, s.—	DC	109: 6
even the voice of Jehovah, s.:		110: 3
s. that in us and our seed		110:12
This is a faithful s.		128: 9
When a messenger comes s. he		129: 4
through the midst of heaven, s.:		133:17
go forth, s. with a loud voice:		133:38
s.: O that thou wouldst rend		133:40
And God spake unto Moses, s.:	Mses	1: 3
Satan came tempting him, s.:		1:12
out of the burning bush, s.:		1:17
commanded, s.: I am the Only		1:19
s.: Depart from me, Satan,		1:20
strength, and called upon God, s.:		1:21
and he heard a voice, s.:		1:25
Moses called upon God, s.:		1:30
Moses spake unto the Lord, s.:		1:36
Lord God spake unto Moses, s.:		1:37
the Lord spake unto Moses, s.:		2: 1
blessed them, s.: Be fruitful, and		2:22
God, commanded the man, s.:		3:16
Lord God, spake unto Moses, s.:		4: 1
he came before me, s.—Behold,		4: 1
of which I commanded thee, s.—		4:23
the Lord appeared unto Adam, s.:		5: 6
And then the angel spake, s.:		5: 7
s.: I am the Only Begotten of		5: 9
s.: Blessed be the name of God,		5:10
and was glad, s.: Were it not for		5:11
Satan came among them, s.:		5:13
and he commanded them, s.:		5:13
behold, Cain hearkened not, s.:		5:16
And Satan commanded him, s.:		5:18
s.: I am free; surely the flocks		5:33
s.: In the day that God created		6: 8
heard a voice from heaven, s.:		6:27
and spake before the Lord, s.:		6:31
came the s. abroad in the land:		6:36
s. unto the tent-keepers:		6:38
Enoch continued his speech, s.:		6:43
by his own voice, s.: I am God;		6:51
Hence came the s. abroad among		6:54
the Lord spake unto Adam, s.:		6:55
freely unto your children, s.:		6:58
heard a voice out of heaven, s.:		6:66
Enoch continued his speech, s.:		7: 1
Enoch began to prophesy, s.		7: 2
came a voice out of heaven, s.—		7: 2
and I prophesied, s.: Behold the		7: 7
and he heard a loud voice, s.:		7:25
and Enoch bore record of it, s.:		7:28
and he cried unto the Lord, s.:		7:45
flesh; and his soul rejoiced, s.:		7:47
voice from the bowels thereof, s.:		7:48
wept, and cried unto the Lord, s.:		7:49
continued his cry unto the Lord, s.:		7:50
Enoch cried unto the Lord, s.:		7:54
s.: When shall the earth rest?		7:58
and he called unto the Lord, s.:		7:59
went forth the s., ZION is FLED.		7:69
he called his name Noah, s.:		8: 9
they came up before him, s.:		8:23
his preaching unto the people, s.:		8:23
And the Gods ordered, s.:	Abr	4: 9
the Gods commanded the man, s.:		5:12
to him, for to hear him, s.:	JS	1: 2
came unto him privately, s.:		1: 4
shall come in my name, s.—		1: 6
to the prophecy of Moses, s.:		1:55
s. it was all of the devil,		2:21
for s. that I had seen a vision,		2:25
against me falsely for so s.,		2:25
s. that it was about to be		2:40
s. that I must have no other		2:46
s. that there was no such thing		2:65
upon us, he ordained us, s.:		2:68

SAYINGS

many of which s. are written upon	2Ne	4:14
I must make an end of my s.		30:18
remember that these s. are true,	Mos	1: 6
and the s. of our fathers		1: 6
had made an end of these s.		1:15
had made an end of these s.		13:25

SAYINGS

Abinadi had finished these s.,	Mos 17: 1
can ye withstand these s.;	Al 5:53
king had made an end of these s.,	24:17
Zerahemnah had heard these s.,	44: 8
of the land did hear these s.,	3Ne 10: 1
after these s. there was silence	10: 1
this time I make an end of my s.	10:19
whoso heareth these s. of mine	14:24
that heareth these s. of mine	14:26
when Jesus had ended these s.	15: 1
remembereth these s. of mine	15: 1
that ye shall write these s.	16: 4
these s. which ye shall write	16: 4
keep these s. which I have	18:33
had made an end of these s.,	18:36
Mormon, make an end of my s.,	26:12
when Jesus had ended these s.	27:33
that these s. shall come unto	29: 1
when ye shall see these s.	29: 4
Who can deny his s.?	Mrm 9:26
Keep these s., for they are	DC 66:11
carry these s. unto the land	68:32
These s. are true and faithful;	68:34
now I make an end of my s.	72:23
inasmuch as ye keep not my s.,	82: 4
I leave these s. with you	88:62
and let all listen unto his s.,	88:122
to keep and do these s.,	89:18
I give unto you these s.	93:19
more earnest heed unto your s.,	93:48
inasmuch as you keep my s.	93:52

SAYS

Now, he s. that the Lord has	1Ne 16:38
wherefore as it s. isles,	2Ne 10:21
when he s. that he repents,	Mos 26:31
And now he s. that he has not	Al 10:28
Behold what the scripture s.—	Mrm 8:20
to the revelation which s.:	DC 107:58
to the commandment which s.:	107:77
as Paul s. concerning the fathers—	128:15
for Malachi s., last chapter,	128:17

SCAB

smite with a s. the crown of the	2Ne 13:17

SCALES

their s. of darkness shall begin to	2Ne 30: 6

SCALP

that he took off his s. and it	Al 44:12
smote the s. of Zerahemnah,	44:13
took up the s. from off the	44:13
Even as this s. has fallen to	44:14
which is the s. of your chief,	44:14
the s. which was upon the sword,	44:15

SCANTINESS

Because of the s. of provisions	3Ne 4:19

SCANTY

obtaining a s. maintenance by	JS 2:23

SCARCE

as timber was exceeding s. in	He 3:10
wild game became s. in the	3Ne 4:20

SCARCELY

I had s. done so when	JS 2:15

SCARLETS

s., and fine-twined linen,	1Ne 13: 7
s., and the fine-twined linen,	13: 8

SCATHE

if the fire can s. a green tree	DC 135: 6

SCATTER

and began to s. abroad upon	Mos 27: 6
again stood to s. their flocks;	Al 17:33
these men who do s. our flocks.	17:33
stood to s. the flocks of the king.	17:35

can they s. the king's flocks	Al 18: 3
to s. the flocks of the people,	18: 7
he shall s. you forth that ye	He 7:19
hath said should s. this people,	Mrm 5: 9
tower, and s. their watchmen.	DC 101:57
and s. their watchmen;	105:16

SCATTERED

the people of Jared, who were s.	T Pg
s. upon all the face of the earth.	1Ne 10:12
s. upon all the face of the earth.	10:13
the house of Israel should be s.	10:14
they were s. before the Gentiles	13:14
s. upon all the face of the earth,	13:39
s. upon all the face of the earth;	14:14
after they are s. by the Gentiles;	15:17
neither should they be s. again.	15:20
broken off, that are s. abroad,	21: 1
s. upon all the face of the earth,	22: 3
they are s. to and fro upon the	22: 4
hereafter be s. and be confounded,	22: 5
they shall be s. among all nations	22: 5
all the house of Israel have been s.	22: 7
by them shall our seed be s.	22: 7
And after our seed is s.	22: 8
and he will cause them to be s.	2Ne 1:11
they shall be s., and smitten,	6:11
shall be s. among all nations.	10: 6
Jews shall be s. among all nations;	25:15
Jews shall be s. by other nations.	25:15
And after they have been s.,	25:16
the Jews which are s. also shall	30: 7
And they were s. upon much of	Jar 1: 6
and their bones lay s. in	Om 1:22
shall be driven and s. to and fro,	Mos 17:17
and they were s. abroad upon	28:17
until they were s. on the west,	Al 2:37
even to them that are s. abroad	13:22
and the Lamanites were s. and	16: 8
and s. the flocks of Ammon	17:27
and they s. them insomuch that	17:27
because their flocks were s. by	17:28
Behold, our flocks are s. already.	17:28
their brethren had s. their flocks	18: 6
their flocks s. they were slain.	18: 6
that were s. unto their own land,	18: 7
of my brethren that s. my flocks—	18:20
flocks s. at the waters of Sebus—	19:20
and s. the flocks which belonged	19:21
should be s. abroad and slain,	25:12
were slain and s. abroad.	28: 2
Lamanites were driven and s.,	28: 3
s. upon the face of the earth,	He 3:16
multitudes who were s. about	10:12
shall be smitten and s. abroad,	15:12
seed of Jacob, who are s. abroad	3Ne 5:24
who shall be s. forth upon the	16: 4
have s. my people who are of	16: 8
which shall be s. abroad upon	20:13
after they have s. my people—	20:15
people who shall be s. by them;	21: 2
s. upon all the face of the land,	21:24
unto all the s. tribes of Israel,	28:29
for this people shall be s.,	Mrm 5:15
driven and s. by the Gentiles;	5:20
driven and s. by the Gentiles,	5:20
they should be s. upon all the	Eth 1:33
of the Lord the people were s.	1:33
who were s. and gathered in	13:11
restoration of the s. Israel.	DC 45:17
and s. among all nations.	45:19
be s. among all nations;	45:24
And they that have been s.	101:13
her children are s.	101:17
have been s. by their enemies,	101:76
been s. on the land of Zion;	103: 1
brethren which have been s.	103:11
been s. upon the mountains	109:61
all the s. remnants of Israel,	109:67
s. remnants are exhorted	113:10
Israel in their s. condition	113:10
s. abroad in all the world;	115: 3

SCATTERED 851 SCRIPTURES

SCATTERED
all the nations of the earth s.	DC	124: 3
by those who are s. abroad,		124:35
different stakes s. abroad;		124:134

SCATTERETH
fleeth from the shepherd, and s.,	Mos	8:21

SCATTERING
unto the s. them to destruction.	1Ne	17:32
unto the s. of my people,	3Ne	20:27
and s. their watchmen,	DC	105:30

SCENE
How can we witness this awful s.?	Al	14:10
that by beholding this s. it		19:17
to pass an awful s. of bloodshed.		28:10
a continual s. of wickedness	Mrm	2:18
the horrible s. of the blood and		4:11
awful s. of blood and carnage		5: 8
the s. of bloodshed and carnage,	Eth	14:21
no longer upon this horrible s.	Mro	9:20
promoting this extraordinary s.	JS	2: 6
a s. of great confusion and		2: 6
on the singularity of the s.,		2:44

SCENT
so great was the s. thereof that	Al	16:11
the s. thereof went forth upon	Eth	14:23
because of the s. thereof.		14:23

SEPTER
holding the s. of power in	DC	85: 7
servant Warren bowed to my s.,		106: 6
thy s. an unchanging scepter		121:46
unchanging s. of righteousness		121:46
with the s. of justice and	Fac	3: 1

SCEPTERS
the s. of the rulers.	2Ne	24: 5

SCHOOL
of the s. of the prophets,	DC	88:127
of the presidency of the s.:		88:128
in the s. of the prophets.		88:136
in the s. of the prophets,		88:137
any among you into this s.		88:138
of the s. of the prophets,		90: 7
of the church and the s.;		90:13
in the s. of the prophets;		95:10
for the s. of mine apostles,		95:17
concerning the s. in Zion,		97: 3
there should be a s. in Zion,		97: 3
over the s. in the land of Zion		97: 4
to the edification of the s.,		97: 5
And to the residue of the s.,		97: 6
teaching s. in the neighborhood	JS	2:66
one of those who sent to the s.,		2:66

SCHOOLS
books for s. in this church,	DC	55: 4

SCOFFING
because of those that were s.	1Ne	8:28

SCORCH
when the flames began to s. him,	Mos	17:14

SCORCHED
to be s. with a burning heat.	Al	15: 3

SCORCHETH
heat of the sun cometh and s. it,	Al	32:38

SCORE
within three s. and five years shall	2Ne	17: 8

SCORN
did point the finger of s. at me	1Ne	8:33
and they laughed us to s.?	Al	26:23

SCORNER
and the s. is consumed,	2Ne	27:31
and the s. shall be consumed;	DC	45:50

SCORNFUL
that they began to be s.,	Al	4: 8

SCOTT, Jacob
and S. also take their journey.	DC	52:28

SCOURGE
they shall be a s. unto thy seed,	1Ne	2:24
they s. him, and he suffereth it;		19: 9
shall be a s. unto thy seed,	2Ne	5:25
they shall s. them even unto		5:25
should s. him and crucify him,		6: 9
shall stir up a s. for him		20:26
shall s. you even unto destruction.	Jac	3: 3
shall s. him, and shall crucify	Mos	3: 9
their synagogues, nor s. them;	Al	23: 2
opportunity to s. the Lamanites		52:10
shall be a s. unto the people	3Ne	20:28
a desolating s. shall go forth	DC	5:19
they shall see an overflowing s.;		45:31
there remaineth a s. and		84:58
s. them for their wickedness.		84:96
The Lord.s s. shall pass over		97:23
a s. prepared for the inhabitants		124:83

SCOURGED
they shall be s. by all people,	1Ne	19:13
hath s. them by other nations	2Ne	25:16
mocked, and s., and cast out,	Mos	15: 5
and s. his skin with faggots,		17:13
shall be s. from city to city,	DC	63:31

SCRIBE
and be unto him for a s.,	DC	25: 6
there is no one to be a s. for him,		25: 6
of thy counselor and s.,		90:19

SCRIP
shalt take no purse nor s.,	DC	24:18
shoes and for money, and for s.		24:18
them not to have purse or s.,		84:78
this hour take purse or s.,		84:86

SCRIPTURE
What does the s. mean, which	Al	12:21
For thus saith the s.:		30: 8
Behold what the s. says—	Mrm	8:20
to pass the s. which saith,	Eth	13:12
contain those parts of my s.	DC	8: 1
as the s. saith unto you,		64:12
by the Holy Ghost shall be s.,		68: 4
did any passage of s. come with	JS	2:12
passages of s. so differently		2:12
many other passages of s.,		2:41

SCRIPTURES
for I did liken all s. unto us,	1Ne	19:23
the s. which are engraven upon	2Ne	4:15
my soul delighteth in the s.,		4:15
they understand not the s.,	Jac	2:23
But behold, unto him the s.,		4:16
unto him: Believest thou the s.?		7:10
and said that I believed the s.;		7:19
and they searched the s.,		7:23
the prophecies and the s. to	Mos	27:35
to unfold the s. beyond that	Al	12: 1
Behold, the s. are before you;		13:20
to repent, and to search the s.		14: 1
which contained the holy s..		14: 8
had searched the s. diligently,		17: 2
and the holy s. of the people,		18:36
unto them all the records and s.		18:38
Aaron began to open the s. unto		21: 9
reading the s. unto the king—		22:12
did expound unto him the s.		22:13
The s. are laid before thee,		30:44
and ye ought to search the s.;		33: 2
Do ye believe those s. which		33:12
would ask if ye have read the s.?		33:14
holy s. testify of these things,		34:30
records of the holy s. upon them,		37: 5
behold, some have wrested the s.,		41: 1
the s. saith the Lord took		45:19

SCRIPTURES

are led to believe the holy s.,	He	15: 7
the s. began to be fulfilled.		16:14
to prove by the s. that it was	3Ne	1:24
having not understood the s.		1:24
the s. concerning my coming		9:16
thus far were the s. fulfilled		10:11
he that hath the s., let him		10:14
expounded all the s. unto them		23: 6
other s. I would that ye should		23: 6
had expounded all the s. in one,		23:14
These s., which ye had not with		26: 2
Have they not read the s.,		27: 5
if ye had all the s. which		28:33
yea, he has not read the s.;	Mrm	9: 8
those parts of my s. which	DC	6:27
they do wrest the s. and do		10:63
more express than other s.,		19: 7
that the holy s. are true,		20:11
written in those s. which have		20:21
of his book, the holy s.,		20:35
according to the s.;		20:41
faith agreeable to the holy s.—		20:69
be dealt with as the s. direct.		20:80
and expounding all s. unto		24: 5
office, and to expound all s.,		24: 9
that the s. might be fulfilled;		24:14
under his hand to expound s.,		25: 7
devoted to the studying of the s.,		26: 1
the holy s. are given of me for		33:16
and the s. shall be given,		35:20
the fulness of my s. is given,		42:15
these things are given in my s.;		42:28
my s. shall be given as I have		42:56
been given unto thee in my s.		42:59
expounding all s. unto them.		68: 1
thereof out of the s.,		71: 1
this is what the s. mean.		74: 7
hasten to translate my s.,		93:53
of the translation of my s.,		94:10
in expounding all s. and		97: 5
mighty in expounding all s.,		100:11
my words, the fulness of my s.,		104:58
have the s. laid open to our	JS	2:74

SCROLL

should be wrapt together as a s.,	3Ne	26: 3
shall be rolled together as a s.?	Mrm	5:23
shall be rolled together as a s.,		9: 2
as a s. is unfolded after it is	DC	88:95

SEA

near the shore of the Red S.;	1Ne	2: 5
which are nearer the Red S.;		2: 5
it emptied into the Red S.;		2: 8
the fountain of the Red S.,		2: 9
the waters of the Red S.		4: 2
in the waters of the Red S.		4: 2
as many as the sand of the s.,		12: 1
in the borders near the Red S.		16:14
the s., which we called Irreantum,		17: 5
the waters of the Red S.		17:26
were drowned in the Red S.,		17:27
into the depths of the s.;		17:48
we did put forth into the s.		18: 8
up in the depths of the s.;		18:10
they should be drowned in the s.;		18:13
up in the depths of the s.		18:15
up in the depths of the s.		18:20
should inhabit the isles of the s.,		19:10
the kings of the isles of the s.		19:12
remember the elses of the s.;		19:16
as the waves of the s.		20:18
heard thee, O isles of the s.,		21: 8
upon the isles of the s.;		22: 4
were not swallowed up in the s.	2Ne	1: 2
at my rebuke I dry up the s.,		7: 2
he who hath dried the s.,		8:10
made the depths of the s. away		8:10
from the isles of the s.,		10: 8
Lord has made the s. our path,		10:20
and we are upon an isle of the s.		10:20
who are upon the isles of the s.;		10:21
upon all the ships of the s.,		12:16
like the roaring of the s.;	2Ne	15:30
afflict by the way of the Red S.		19: 1
Israel be as the sand of the s.,		20:22
and as his rod was upon the s.		20:26
as the waters cover the s.		21: 9
and from the islands of the s.		21:11
the tongue of the Egyptian s.		21:15
who are upon the isles of the s.;		29: 7
and in the islands of the s.,		29:11
as the waters cover the s.		30:15
mountains, or the waves of the s.	Jac	4: 6
through the Red S. on dry ground,	Mos	7:19
also wronged while crossing the s.;		10:12
after they had crossed the s.,		10:13
made heaven and earth, and the s.,		13:19
it were, as the sands of the s.,	Al	2:27
bones are in the depths of the s.,		3: 3
was bordering even to the s.,		22:27
which ran from the s. east even to		22:27
the sea east even to the s. west,		22:27
from the east to the west s.;		22:32
from the east unto the west s.,		22:33
which is on the east by the s.,		27:22
up the Egyptians in the Red S.;		36:28
are buried in the depths of the s.		44:22
from the east s. to the west.		50: 8
of Nephi, from the west s.,		50:11
and it was by the east s.;		50:13
narrow pass which led by the s.		50:34
yea, by the s., on the west and		50:34
of the land by the west s.;		52:11
on the borders by the west s.		52:12
on the borders by the east s.,		52:13
of the Lamanites, on the west s.,		53: 8
land on the south by the west s.		53:22
launched it forth into the west s.,		63: 5
drowned in the depths of the s.		63: 8
from the s. south to the sea	He	3: 8
the sea south to the s. north,		3: 8
from the s. west to the sea east.		3: 8
from the sea west to the s. east.		3: 8
the west s., even unto the east;		4: 7
upon the waters of the Red S.,		8:11
from the s. west to the sea east.		11:20
from the sea west to the s. east.		11:20
sink into the depths of the s.,	3Ne	8: 9
be sunk in the depths of the s.,		9: 4
drowned in the depths of the s.;		10:13
as it were the sand of the s.	Mrm	1: 7
their dead were cast into the s.		3: 8
beyond the s. in the wilderness,	Eth	2: 7
forth even to that great s.		2:13
as they came to the s. they		2:13
a whale in the midst of the s.;		2:24
out of the depths of the s.;		2:24
you against the waves of the s.,		2:25
up in the depths of the s.?		2:25
light which we shall cross the s.		3: 4
and set forth into the s.,		6: 4
tossed upon the waves of the s.		6: 5
buried in the depths of the s.,		6: 6
and no monster of the s.		6:10
where the s. divides the land.		10:20
are upon the islands of the s.,	DC	1: 1
of Israel through the Red S.		8: 3
on the borders of the Red S.		17: 1
air, and the fishes of the s.;		29:24
drowned in the depth of the s.		54: 5
What is the s. of glass spoken		77: 1
not the earth, neither the s.,		77: 9
the voice of the waves of the s.		88:90
upon the islands of the s.—		88:94
upon the land and upon the s.,		88:110
heavens, or of the fish of the s.,		101:24
and also the fish of the s.,		117: 6
drowned in the depth of the s.		121:22
thou art in perils by land or by s.;		122: 5
on a globe like a s. of glass and fire,		130: 7
unto the islands of the s.		133: 8
and upon the islands of the s.,		133:20
s., and the fountains of waters—		133:39
at my rebuke I dry up the s.		133:68
as the sand upon the s. shore.	Mses	1:28

SEA   853   SEARCHES

of the waters, called I the S.; Mses 2:10
and fill the waters in the s.; 2:22
dominion over the fishes of the s., 2:26
dominion over the fish of the sea, 2:28
land of Canaan, by the s. east, 6:42
a land out of the depth of the s., 7:14
up out of the depth of the s. 7:14
saw the s., that it was troubled, 7:66
I stretch my hand over the s., Abr 2: 7
dominion over the fish of the s., 4:26
dominion over the fish of the s., 4:28

SEAL
s. the law among my disciples. 2Ne 18:16
then shalt thou s. up the book 27:22
For what I s. on earth, shall 33:15
God Omnipotent, may s. you his, Mos 5:15
the devil, and he doth s. you his; Al 34:35
whatsoever ye shall s. on earth He 10: 7
write them and shall s. them up, Eth 3:22
and ye shall s. them up also 3:23
these things and s. them up; 3:27
should s. up the two stones 3:28
me that I should s. them up; 4: 5
s. up the interpretation thereof; 4: 5
And I s. up these records, after Mro 10: 2
to s. both on earth and in DC 1: 8
to s. them up unto the day when 1: 9
to s. them up unto eternal life. 68:12
the first s. contains the things 77: 7
the heavens, to s. up unto life, 77: 8
given the s. of the living God 77: 9
or the opening of the sixth s. 77:10
the opening of the seventh s., 77:13
and s. up the testimony, 88:84
with this s. and testament— 98: 2
this shall be my s. and blessing 101:61
shall be a s. upon the treasury, 104:62
and a s. shall be upon it; 104:64
neither shall the s. be loosed 104:64
and a s. shall be kept upon it 104:66
a s. shall be placed upon it; 104:67
thy word they may s. up the law, 109:38
thy servants to s. up the laws, 109:46
God hath set his hand and s. 121:12
I s. upon his head the office of 124:21
that whatsoever you s. on earth 132:46
I s. upon you your exaltation, 132:49
To s. the testimony of this book 135: 1
a broad s. affixed to "Mormonism" 135: 7
s. his testimony with his blood, 136:39

SEALED
s. up, and his up unto the T Pg
S. by the hand of Moroni, T Pg
they are s. up to come forth 1Ne 14:26
written and s. up in a book, 2Ne 26:17
behold the book shall be s.; 27: 7
of the things which are s. up, 27: 8
the things which are s. shall not 27: 8
But the words which are s. he 27:10
For the book shall be s. by the 27:10
the revelation which was s. shall 27:10
words of the book which were s. 27:11
Take these words which are not s. 27:15
cannot bring the book, for it is s. 27:17
Touch not the things which are s., 27:21
and s. up again unto the Lord, 30: 3
which is s. upon the earth save 30:17
having s. the truth of his words Mos 17:20
on earth shall be s. in heaven; He 10: 7
I have s. up the interpreters, Eth 4: 5
the things which I have s. up; 5: 1
the revelations which are s., DC 28: 7
those things which have been s., 35:18
ordained and s. unto this power; 76:52
are s. by the Holy Spirit of 76:53
which was s. on the back 77: 6
seals with which it was s.? 77: 7
till we have s. the servants of 77: 9
who are s. are high priests, 77:11

he shall have s. all things, DC 77:12
anointing of thy ministers be a. 109:35
s. up unto the day of redemption, 124:124
he is s. up unto eternal life, 131: 5
s. by the Holy Spirit of promise, 132: 7
s. by the Holy Spirit of promise, 132:18
s. unto them by the Holy Spirit of 132:19
hath been s. upon their heads, 132:19
s. by the Holy Spirit of promise, 132:26
on earth shall be s. in heaven; 132:46
they s. up the testimony and 133:72
has s. his mission and his works 135: 3
that part of the plates were s., JS 2:65
'I cannot read a s. book.' 2:65

SEALING
s. it with mine own hand, 3Ne 3: 5
by s. the one hundred and DC 77:11
hold the s. blessings of my church, 124:124
is the s. and binding power, 128:14
the keys of the s. ordinances OD

SEALS
on the back with seven s.? DC 77: 6
the seven s. with which it was 77: 7

SEAMS
be found in s. and in cracks, He 14:22
and in s. and in cracks, 3Ne 8:18

SEANTUM
Go to the house of S., He 9:26

SEARCH
he did s. them from the beginning. 1Ne 5:10
they must s. mine other plates. 2Ne 5:33
for they will not s. knowledge, 32: 7
began to s. much gold and silver, Jac 1:16
of you have begun to s. for gold, 2:12
Wherefore, we s. the prophets, 4: 6
remember to s. them diligently, Mos 1: 7
secretly, to s. for the king and 19:18
I will s. among my people and 20:16
he caused a s. to be made 20:16
and do not s. this people, 20:17
to s. for the land of Zarahemla; 21:25
in s. of the land of Nephi 23:35
repent, and to s. the scriptures. Al 1: 1
in s. of their brethren, who 16: 5
let us go in s. of the flocks, 17:31
they went in s. of the flocks, 17:32
ye ought to s. the scriptures; 33: 2
caused that a s. should be made 55: 4
unto the judgment-seat and s.; He 8:27
did s. out all the secret plans 11:26
to s. out this band of robbers, 11:28
the scriptures, let him s. them, 3Ne 10:14
before you, therefore s. them— 20:11
ye ought to s. these things. 23: 1
ye s. these things diligently; 23: 1
S. the prophets, for many there 23: 5
S. the prophecies of Esaiah. Mrm 8:23
to s. up these things of old; Eth 8:17
s. diligently in the light of Mro 7:19
S. these commandments, for DC 1:37
you shall s. out the Twelve, 18:37
through all, and s. all things, 63:59
s. diligently and spare not; 84:94
let the bishop s. diligently to 90:22
S. diligently, pray always, and 90:24
s. till thou shalt deliver it 136:26

SEARCHED
s. them and found that they were 1Ne 5:21
know that ye have s. much, 2Ne 9: 4
and they s. the scriptures, Jac 7:23
I s. among the records which WM 1: 3
returned, having s. in vain Mos 19: 1
had s. the scriptures diligently, Al 17: 2

SEARCHES
from the s. of the king. Mos 18: 5

SEARCHING 854 SEAT

SEARCHING
he view me with his all-s. eye;	2Ne	9:44
the glance of his all-s. eye.	Mos	27:31
s. after the poor to administer	DC	84:112

SEAS
maker of heaven, earth, and s.,	DC	121: 4
set to the heavens or to the s.,		121:30
all ye s. and dry lands tell		128:23
and fill the waters in the s.	Abr	4:22

SEASHORE
we did pitch our tents by the s.;	1Ne	17: 6
rejoiced when we came to the s.;		17: 6
about on the borders of the s.,	Al	22:27
in the borders by the s.,		22:28
thus bordering along by the s.		22:28
Lamanites on the east by the s.,		22:29
nearly bordering upon the s.,		31: 3
even to the borders by the s.,		50: 9
north by the borders of the s.,		50:15
were on the borders by the s.		50:25
was in the borders by the s.		51:22
kept them down by the s.,		51:25
on the east borders by the s.		51:26
borders on the beach by the s.,		51:32
and march down near the s.;		52:22
began to retreat down by the s.,		52:23
beyond, in the borders by the s.		56:31
was in the borders by the s.		62:25
down upon the borders by the s.,		62:32
in the borders west by the s.	Mrm	2: 6
lay in the borders by the s.;		4: 3
and dwelt in tents upon the s.	Eth	2:13
was called Ablom, by the s.,		9: 3
fled to the borders upon the s.		14:12
battle unto him upon the s.		14:13
even to the borders of the s.,		14:26
or as the sand upon the s.;	DC	76:109
to count the s. upon the s.		132:30

SEASON
speak a word in s. unto thee,	2Ne	7: 4
thereof against the s., unto myself;	Jac	5:13
against the s., unto mine own self.		5:18
against the s., unto mine own self.		5:19
and lay it up against the s.,		5:20
and lay it up against the s.,		5:23
canst lay it up against the s.		5:27
against the s., unto mine own self.		5:29
myself against the s. much fruit.		5:31
against the s., unto mine own self.		5:46
and the s. speedily cometh;		5:71
the s., which speedily cometh;		5:76
then cometh the s. and the end;		5:77
they returned in s. to save us	Al	57:17
did arrive in s. to check them,		57:18
forth grain in the s. of grain;	He	11: 6
and her grain in the s. of grain.		11:13
her fruit in the s. of her fruit.		11:17
her grain in the s. of her grain.		11:17
have joy in their words for a s.,	3Ne	27:11
hast lost thy privileges for a s.—	DC	3:14
pages thou shalt stop for a s.,		5:30
the earth but for a little s.,		29:22
they shall go forth for a little s.,		42: 5
he shall only reign for a little s.,		43:31
them this land for a little s.,		51:16
of the earth, in the s. thereof,		59:18
the store, yet for a little s.		63:42
before the Lord in the s.,		68:33
also, for the space of a s.,		71: 2
Verily this is a mission for a s.,		71: 3
in his time, and in his s.—		88:58
in its time, and in its s.,		88:61
they have received, for a little s.		88:71
he shall be loosed for a little s.,		88:111
Every herb in the s. thereof,		89:11
every fruit in the s. thereof;		89:11
she is chastened for a little s.		100:13
be chastened for a little s.		103: 4
should wait for a little s.		105: 9
should wait for a little s.,		105:13
let them tarry for a little s.,	DC	105:21
of all the churches for a little s.		112:18
remain for a s. in the land of Zion,		118: 2
swift judgment in the s. thereof,		121:24
to leave the place for a short s.,		127: 1
are to remain behind this s.;		136: 9
righteousness for a s. abide	Mses	7:48
to give them meat in due s.?	JS	1:49
and farmed with him that s.		2:58
to board for a s. at his house,		2:66

SEASONS
and we had many s. of peace;	Om	1: 3
and we had many s. of serious war		1: 3
infested, by times or at s.,	Mos	18: 4
which at some s. of the year	Al	46:40
in their times and their s.;	DC	88:42
in their times and in their s.,		88:44
to change the times and s.,		121:12
for s., and for days, and for years;	Mses	2:14
according to its times and s. in	Abr	3: 4
them to be for signs and for s.,		4:14
number of the *Times and S.*	Fac	3: 3

SEAT
at the judgment-s. of Christ	T Pg	
before the judgment-s. of God;	1Ne	10:21
appear before the judgment-s.	2Ne	9:15
souls spotless at his judgment-s.		33: 7
reign of Alma in the judgment-s.,	Al	1: 2
and he sat in the judgment-s.		4:17
he delivered the judgment-s. unto		4:18
the judgment-s. to Nephihah,		4:20
confined to the judgment-s.,		7: 1
the judgment-s. hath been given		7: 2
the judgment-s. unto Nephihah,		8:12
save it were in the judgment-s.;		30:33
having filled the judgment-s.		50:37
appointed to fill the judgment-s.,		50:39
did fill the s. of his father,		50:40
dethroned from the judgment-s.		51: 5
Pahoran retained the judgment-s.,		51: 7
to take away the judgment-s.		61: 9
only to retain my judgment-s.		61: 9
Pahoran from the judgment-s.,		62: 2
was restored to his judgment-s.		62: 8
did return to his judgment-s.;		62:44
should have the judgment-s.	He	1: 2
contend for the judgment-s.		1: 3
contend for the judgment-s.;		1: 4
could not obtain the judgment-s.,		1: 6
to the judgment-s. of Pahoran,		1: 9
as he sat upon the judgment-s.		1: 9
no one to fill the judgment-s.;		2: 1
who should fill the judgment-s.		2: 1
appointed to fill the judgment-s.,		2: 2
place him in the judgment-s.		2: 5
forth towards the judgment-s.		2: 6
conduct him to the judgment-s.		2: 7
go forth unto the judgment-s.		2: 8
going forth unto the judgment-s.		2: 9
fill the judgment-s. with justice		3:20
fill the judgment-s. with justice		3:37
delivered up the judgment-s. to		5: 1
he yielded up the judgment-s.,		5: 4
as he sat upon the judgment-s.		6:15
son, while in the judgment-s.;		6:19
go ye in unto the judgment-s.,		8:27
seeketh to sit in the judgment-s.		8:27
them ran to the judgment-s.;		9: 1
came unto the judgment-s.;		9: 3
the place of the judgment-s.—		9: 7
Lachoneus did fill the s. of his	3Ne	6:19
destroy upon the judgment s.,		7: 1
before the judgment-s. of Christ;		28:31
before the judgment-s. of Christ,	Mrm	3:20
before the judgment-s. of Christ.		3:22
before the judgment-s. of Christ		6:21
stand before his judgment-s.		7: 6
before the judgment-s. of Christ,	Eth	12:38
at the judgment-s. of Christ.	Mro	8:21
sitteth upon the judgment-s.	DC	58:20
the land of Zion shall be a s.		69: 6

SEAT 855 SECRET

the s. of the First Presidency		DC 102:26
the s. of the First Presidency		102:27
the s. of the First Presidency		102:33
before the judgment s. of Christ,		135: 5

SEATS
The s. which were set apart for		Mos 11:11
which were above all the other s.,		11:11
robbers filling the judgment-s.—	He	7: 4

SEBUS
which was called the water of S.,	Al	17:26
who stood by the waters of S.;		17:34
to stand by the waters of S.		18: 7
scattered at the waters of S.		19:20
who had stood at the waters of S.		19:21
their brethren at the waters of S.,		19:21

SECHEM
the land unto the place of S.;	Abr	2:18

SECOND
THE S. BOOK OF NEPHI	2Ne	1:hd
and the daughters of my s. son;		4: 9
will set himself again the s. time		6:14
set his hand again the s. time		21:11
set his hand again the s. time		25:17
set my hand again the s. time		29: 1
called by the people, s. Nephi,	Jac	1:11
under the reign of the s. king,		1:15
brimstone which is the s. death.		3:11
yea, the first and the s. and		5:39
set his hand again the s. time		6: 2
forth a s. time into the water,	Mos	18:15
when the s. trump shall sound		26:25
s. year of the reign of Alma,	Al	1:23
cometh a death, even a s. death,		12:16
penalty thereof being a s. death,		12:32
in these his s. commandments		12:37
may not suffer the s. death.		13:30
on the fifth day of the s. month,		16: 1
the fifth day of the s. month		16: 1
a s. prophet of old has testified		33:17
shall be one time, or a s. time,		40: 5
of the first offense, neither the s.,		43:46
sent again the s. time,		47:11
a s. leader over the whole army.		47:13
to appoint the s. leader to		47:17
the twenty and s. year of the		50:24
Nephihah, the s. chief judge,		50:37
the s. day in the first month,		56: 1
in the s. month of this year,		56:27
in the forty and s. year of	He	2: 1
ended the forty and s. year of		2:12
the fifty and s. year ended in peace		3:36
in the sixty and s. year of		4:18
when the sixty and s. year of		6: 1
in the seventy and s. year of		11: 1
in the eighty and s. year		11:36
a spiritual death, yea, a s. death,		14:18
brought down unto this s. death.		14:19
of the ninety and s. year,	3Ne	1: 4
thus the ninety and s. year did		1:26
thus had the twenty and s. year		5: 7
the thirty and s. year also.		7:23
the s. time that he showed himself		26:15
and the forty and s.,	4Ne	1: 6
and the fifty and s.;		1: 6
also the seventy and s. year,		1:14
the s. generation had all		1:22
hundred and sixty and s. year	Mrm	3: 8
had come again the s. time.		4:20
when they had come the s. time,		4:21
in the s. year the word of	Eth	13:20
and they came the s. time,		14:29
were driven again the s. time.		14:29
The s. epistle of Mormon to his	Mro	9:hd
be the s. elder of this church,	DC	20: 3
of the Lord for his s. coming.		34: 6
brimstone, which is the s. death.		63:17
on whom the s. death shall		76:37
and the s. also of the		77: 7
of the s. thousand years,	DC	77: 7
recorded in the s. chapter and		85:12
sixty-first and s. verses of Ezra.		85:12
And he said unto the s.:		88:53
in the s. hour I will visit you		88:53
that he might visit the s. also,		88:57
sound, which is the s. trump;		88:99
the s. angel sound his trump,		88:109
in the s. thousand years—		88:109
the s. lot on the south shall		94:10
first and s. lots on the north		94:14
shall smite you the s. time,		98:25
the s. nor the third time,		98:35
on unto the s, and third time;		98:40
against thee the s. time,		98:42
The s. priesthood is called		107:13
has become a s. nature to me;		127: 2
the s. man is the Lord from heaven.		128:14
and if he espouse the s.,		132:61
and the morning were the s. day.	Mses	2: 8
name of the s. river was called		3:13
they who keep their s. estate	Abr	3:26
the s. was angry, and kept not		3:28
the s. time that they called		4: 8
the s. year after our removal to	JS	2: 5
twenty-s. and twenty-third		2:40
quoted the s. chapter of Joel,		2:41
On the twenty-s. day of		2:59
being the s. day of May,		2:60
and he (Oliver Cowdery) the s.		2:72
s., Repentance; third, Baptism	AoF	4

SECONDLY
And s., he doth require that	Mos	2:24
First spiritual, s. temporal,	DC	29:32
first temporal, and s. spiritual,		29:32
and s. unto the Jews.		107:33
S.: The spirits of just men		129: 3

SECRECY
by his brother by a garb of s.,	He	9: 6

SECRET
I have not spoken in s.;	1Ne	20:16
unto s. combinations of murder	2Ne	9: 9
manner of s. works of darkness.		9: 9
destroy the s. works of darkness,		10:15
Lord will discover their s. parts.		13:17
there are also s. combinations,		26:22
is nothing which is s. save		30:17
shall s. things be made manifest,	Mos	8:17
came forth out of their s. works,		20: 5
we will pass through the s. pass		22: 7
your closets, and your s. places,	Al	34:26
of darkness, and their s. works,		37:21
the s. works of those people		37:21
s. murders and abominations;		37:22
their s. works, their works of		37:23
unto light all their s. works		37:25
their s. abominations have been		37:26
in their s. abominations;		37:27
keep these s. plans of their oaths		37:29
of darkness and s. combinations.		37:30
of darkness and s. combinations,		37:31
those s. plans unto this people,		37:32
he sent a s. embassy into the		47:10
did rise up from their s. places,		58:20
carry on the s. work of murder	He	2: 4
(and this was their s. plan,		2: 8
band of robbers and s. murderers,		2:10
out of the land, by a s. way,		2:11
save it were the s. combinations		3:23
began to commit s. murders,		6:17
their signs, yea, their s. signs,		6:22
secret signs, and their s. words;		6:22
these s. oaths and covenants		6:25
those s. oaths and covenants did		6:26
of darkness, and of s. murder;		6:29
of darkness and s. murder;		6:30
with them in their s. murders		6:38
s. band which was established by		7:25
to the s. band of Gadianton,		8: 1

SECRET 856 SEE

their s. works of darkness;	He	8: 4
both belong to your s. band,		8:28
their s. works of darkness,		10: 3
it was this s. band of robbers		11: 2
have concealed their s. plans		11:10
the wilderness and s. places,		11:25
all the s. plans of Gadianton;		11:26
their holds and their s. places	3Ne	1:27
mountains and into their s. places.		2:17
acquainted with our s. works,		3: 7
this the s. society of Gadianton;		3: 9
strongholds, and their s. places,		4: 1
power and s. combinations,		4:29
those s. murders in their hearts,		5: 5
to all those wicked, and s.,		5: 6
because of the s. combination		7: 6
Now this s. combination,		7: 9
because of their s. murders		9: 9
That thine alms may be in s.;		13: 4
and thy Father who seeth in s.,		13: 4
pray to thy Father who is in s.;		13: 6
and thy Father, who seeth in s.,		13: 6
but unto thy Father, who is in s.;		13:18
and thy Father, who seeth in s.,		13:18
and of s. abominations;		16:10
and of your s. abominations,		30: 2
to build up the s. oaths	4Ne	1:42
because of s. combinations and	Mrm	8:27
build up your s. abominations		8:40
by their s. plans did obtain	Eth	8: 9
they formed a s. combination,		8:18
worketh not in s. combinations,		8:19
uphold such s. combinations,		8:22
because of this s. combination		8:24
the s. combinations of Akish		9: 1
of this wicked and s. society		9: 6
to embrace the s. plans again		9:26
because of that s. combination		11:15
because of their s. society and		11:22
their s. plans of wickedness,		13:15
sword of those s. combinations,		13:18
because of s. combinations.		14: 8
that one of the s. combinations		14:10
murdered him in a s. pass,		14:10
their s. acts shall be revealed.	DC	1: 3
before the world as well as in s.,		19:28
to pray vocally and in s. and		20:47
them to pray vocally and in s.		20:51
before the world as well as in s.,		23: 6
which is had in s. chambers,		38:13
the enemy in the s. chambers		38:28
and of s. combinations.		42:64
If any shall offend in s.,		42:92
he or she shall be rebuked in s.,		42:92
opportunity to confess in s. to		42:92
thou provoke them, but in s.;		60:15
and reveal the s. acts of men,		88:108
and reveal the s. acts of men,		88:109
in the s. places by the way		99: 4
not discover your s. parts;		111: 4
and of all their s. abominations,		117:11
and grand s. of the whole matter,		128:11
all these things were done in s.	Mses	5:30
the master of this great s.,		5:31
master of that great s. which was		5:49
Enoch, having known their s.,		5:49
there was a s. combination,		5:51
spoken the s. unto his wives,		5:53
death, because of s. works,		6:15
he is in the s. chambers;	JS	1:25
to keep s. the circumstances of		2:74

SECRETARY
to the S. of the Interior,	DC	OD

SECRETE
s. himself in the wilderness,	Al	58:16
s. themselves also in the		58:16

SECRETED
army should be s. in the valley	Al	43:27
they had thus s. themselves,		58:17

SECRETLY
men into the wilderness s.,	Mos	19:18
for he did go about s. with		27:10
put to death s. by the judges,	3Ne	6:23

SECRETS
all their s. and abominations,	Al	37:25
the s. of my will—	DC	76:10

SECT
join what s. they pleased;	JS	2: 6
partial to the Methodist s.,		2: 8

SECTARIAN
an old s. notion, and is false.	DC	130: 3
the s. world was concerned—	JS	2:26

SECTS
the earth among all s., parties,	DC	123:12
became general among all the s.	JS	2: 5
of religion of the different s.		2:12
which of all the s. was right,		2:18
which of all the s. was right—		2:18
common among all the s.—		2:22
most popular s. of the day,		2:23
to join any of the religious s.		2:28

SECULAR
to do his s. business as he shall	DC	84:113

SECURE
that they might s. their armies	Al	50:10
s. the narrow pass which led		52: 9
shall s. unto him his portion,	DC	51: 4
s. a fulfilment of the promises		109:11
as will s. to each individual		134: 2
to s. the public interest;		134: 5

SECURED
s. their grain and their flocks;	Mos	21:18
sowed thy fields and s. them,	DC	24: 3
wheat may be s. in the garners		101:65

SECURITY
this land for the s. of thy seed	2Ne	1:32
thy brethren, for thy s. forever,		3: 2
and lull them away into carnal s.,		28:21
in preparing their places of s.	Al	49: 5
fortified, or had built forts of s.,		49:13
could not get into their forts of s.		49:18
to come into their place of s.		49:20
to get into their place of s.;		49:21
caused places of s. to be built		50: 4
and ye are surrounded by s.,		60:19
return again to their places of s.	3Ne	4:15
diligence and for their s.;	DC	70:15

SEDITION
s. and rebellion are unbecoming	DC	134: 5
not justify s. nor conspiracy.		134: 7

SEDUCED
s. the more part of the righteous	He	6:38
may not be s. by evil spirits,	DC	46: 7

SEE
that perhaps I might s. them.	1Ne	8:17
these things did my father s.,		9: 1
that I might s., and hear,		10:17
he shall s. and write the		14:21
the remainder shalt thou s.		14:24
things which thou shalt s.		14:25
thus we s. that by small means		16:29
And thus we s. that the		17: 3
my brethren began to s. that		18:15
the earth shall s. the salvation		19:17
Kings shall s. and arise,		21: 7
in our bodies we shall s. God.	2Ne	9: 4
unto the blind that will not s.;		9:32
my people shall s. these words		11: 8
hasten his work, that we may s. it;		15:19
s. ye indeed, but they perceived not.		16: 9

lest they s. with their eyes,	2Ne	16:10
Isaiah the son of Amoz did s.		23: 1
They that s. thee shall narrowly		24:16
until I shall s. fit in mine own		27:22
the blind shall s. out of obscurity		27:29
they shall s. that the terrible one		27:31
then shall I s. his face with	En	1:27
and I have lived to s. his death;	Om	1:23
these things s. that ye do them.	Mos	4:10
And s. that all these things are		4:27
for they shall s. eye to eye		12:22
shall s. the salvation of our God?		12:24
Ye s. that ye have not power		13: 7
and when we shall s. him there		14: 2
for sin he shall s. his seed,		14:10
He shall s. the travail of his soul,		14:11
for sin he shall s. his seed.		15:10
for they shall s. eye to eye,		15:29
shall s. the salvation of our God.		15:31
shall s. the salvation of the Lord;		16: 1
and people shall s. eye to eye		16: 1
him hither that I may s. him.		20:14
the Lord did not s. fit to deliver		21:15
to s. and know of the goodness		27:22
Now I would that ye should s. that	Al	3:19
And s. that ye have faith, hope,		7:24
we s. that the word of the Lord		9:14
to s. a very near kindred,		10: 7
S. that ye remember these		11:35
they can no more s. corruption.		11:45
we s. that there was no possible		12:21
Now we s. that Adam did fall		12:22
and thus we s., that by his fall,		12:22
And we s. that death comes		12:24
ye s. that ye had not power to		14:15
in unto the prison to s. them,		14:18
exceedingly to s. his brethren;		17: 2
should go in and s. my husband,		19: 5
he went in to s. the king		19: 7
we s. that Ammon could not be		19:23
we s. that his arm is extended		19:36
I shall greatly desire to s. thee		20:27
And thus we s. that, when these		24:19
and thus we s. that they buried		24:19
thus we s. that the Lord worketh		24:27
and s. the fruits of our labors:		26:31
we s. that God is mindful of every		26:37
And thus we s. how great the		28:13
And thus we s. the great call of		28:14
and thus we s. the great reason		28:14
therefore we s. that the Lord		29: 8
when I s. many of my brethren		29:10
of things which ye do not s.;		30:15
ye s. a remission of your sins.		30:16
And thus we s. the end of him		30:60
and thus we s. that the devil		30:60
ye s. that a second prophet of old		33:17
we s. that they did not repent;		37:26
see that ye take care of these		37:47
s. that ye look to God and live.		37:47
S. that ye are not lifted up unto		38:11
s. that ye do not boast in your		38:11
s. that ye bridle all your passions,		38:12
s. that ye refrain from idleness.		38:12
s. that you are merciful unto your		41:14
we s. that the man had become		42: 3
And thus we s., that there was a		42: 4
ye s. by this that our first parents		42: 7
thus we s. they became subjects		42: 7
And thus we s. that all mankind		42:14
ye s. that ye cannot destroy		44: 3
ye s. that this is the true faith		44: 4
yea, ye s. that God will support,		44: 4
then we will s. who shall have		44: 7
we will s. who shall be brought		44: 7
and then shall they s. wars		45:11
we s. how quick the children of		46: 8
we also s. the great wickedness		46: 9
Yea, we s. that Amalickiah,		46:10
that all might s. the writing		46:19
behold, come and s.		47:26
and s. what had happened to		47:27
we s. how merciful and just are		50:19
we s. that these promises	Al	50:21
we shall s. that his promise		51:10
s. that ye fulfil the word of God.		60:35
S. that ye strengthen Lehi and		61:21
ye shall s. that this Gadianton	He	2:13
Thus we may s. that the Lord is		3:27
thus we s. that the gate of heaven		3:28
we s. that whosoever will may lay		3:29
thus we s. that the Nephites did		6:34
And thus we s. that the Spirit of		6:35
thus we s. that the Lord began		6:36
And thus we s. that they were in		6:40
and s. if ye will in this thing seek		9:25
yea, we can s. that the Lord in		12: 1
and we may s. at the very time		12: 2
thus we s. that except the Lord		12: 3
many shall s. greater things than		14:28
when they shall s. all these signs		15: 3
ye can s. that they fear to sin—		15: 9
ye can s. of yourselves that they		15:15
s. and behold if all these deaths	3Ne	10:14
and did s. with their eyes and		11:15
in heart, for they shall s. God.		12: 8
they may s. your good works		12:16
then shalt thou s. clearly to cast		14: 5
for they shall s. eye to eye		16:18
shall s. the salvation of God.		16:20
I s. that your faith is sufficient		17: 8
And the multitude did s. and		17:25
they all of them did s. and hear,		17:25
ye s. that I have prayed unto		18:24
ye s. that I have commanded		18:25
me, that ye might feel and s.;		18:25
that they could not s. Jesus.		18:38
for they shall s. eye to eye.		20:32
s. the salvation of the Father;		20:35
not been told them shall they s.;		20:45
not been told them shall they s.;		21: 8
that when the Lord shall s. fit,		29: 1
when ye shall s. these sayings		29: 4
he shall s. fit, in his wisdom.	Mrm	5:13
be brought to s. your nakedness		9: 5
S. that ye are not baptized		9:29
s. that ye partake not of the		9:29
but s. that ye do all things in		9:29
when ye s. these things, ye shall	Eth	4:16
authority when ye shall s. me,		5: 6
when ye shall s. these things		8:24
dispute not because ye s. not,		12: 6
only live to s. the fulfilling of		13:21
thus we s. that the Lord did		14:25
s. that ye do not judge	Mro	7:18
for we shall s. him as he is;		7:48
I shall perish and not s.;		9:24
trust that I may s. thee soon;		9:24
shall s. me at the bar of God;		10:27
there is no eye that shall not s.,	DC	1: 2
s. that ye serve him with all		4: 2
the things which he desires to s.		5:24
s. that ye are faithful and		10: 3
We will s. if God has given him		10:16
until I shall s. fit to make all		10:37
you shall both hear and s.,		14: 8
thou shalt be permitted to s.		19:29
shalt desire to s. thy family;		19:36
s. that there is no iniquity in		20:54
s. that the church meet together		20:55
s. that all the members do their		20:55
hear my voice, and shall s. me,		35:21
your midst and ye cannot s. me;		38: 7
soon cometh that ye shall s. me,		38: 8
S. that all things are preserved;		38:38
ye shall s. that my law is kept.		41: 4
To s. to all things as it shall be		41:10
He who hath faith to s. shall		42:49
who hath faith to see shall s.		42:49
find it and s. it in their flesh.		45:14
this temple which ye now s.		45:20
shall s. an overflowing scourge;		45:31
and ye s. them with your eyes,		45:37
they shall s. all these things,		45:38
they shall s. signs and wonders,		45:40
s. me in the clouds of heaven,		45:44

SEE

have laughed shall s. their folly.	DC 45:49
hear my voice and s. me,	50:45
they shall s. the kingdom of God	56:18
seeketh signs shall s. signs,	63: 7
s. me and know that I am—	67:10
s. and know that which was	67:14
so as to s. and understand	76:12
and they s. as they are seen,	76:94
no man can s. the face of God,	84:22
and shall s. eye to eye,	84:98
ye cannot s. it now, yet a little	84:119
a little while and ye shall s. it,	84:119
because you cannot s. him—	88:66
come that you shall s. him;	88:68
all people shall s. it together.	88:93
shall not any more s. death.	88:116
S. that ye love one another;	88:123
shall s. my face and know that	93: 1
s. that they are more diligent	93:50
heed that ye s. to this matter,	96: 4
shall come into it shall s. God.	97:16
shall s. to it that ye warn him	98:28
all flesh shall s. me together.	101:23
and now s. to it, that ye go	104:63
s. to it that ye trouble not	112:27
S. the 6th, 7th, and 8th verses.	113:10
eyes s. and know all their works,	121:24
to s. the salvation of God,	123:17
s. that all my debts are canceled	127: 1
Jesus said: *Handle me and s.*,	129: 2
flesh and bones, as ye s. me have.	129: 2
we shall s. him as he is.	130: 1
We shall s. that he is a man	130: 1
s. the face of the Son of Man;	130:15
should die and thus s. his face.	130:16
We cannot s. it; but when our	131: 8
we shall s. that it is all matter.	131: 8
s. the salvation of their God.	133: 3
may be opened that he may s.,	136:32
to s. what he would call them;	Mses 3:19
S. thou show them unto no man,	4:32
again in the flesh I shall s. God.	5:10
and their eyes cannot s. afar off;	6:27
wash them, and thou shalt s.	6:35
bosom, and they shall s. us;	7:63
when the Egyptians shall s. her,	Abr 2:23
s. that ye do on this wise:	2:23
exist, behold thine eyes s. it;	3: 6
I could not s. the end thereof.	3:12
to s. if they will do all things	3:25
to s. what he would call them;	5:20
ye shall not s. me henceforth	JS 1: 1
S. ye not all these things,	1: 3
shall s. the abomination of	1:12
s. that ye be not troubled,	1:23
s. the Son of Man coming in	1:36
they shall s. all these things,	1:39
that I could s. into his bosom.	2:31
that I could s. the place where	2:42
'Let me s. that certificate.'	2:65

SEED

shall have power over thy s.	1 Ne 2:23
shall be a scourge unto thy s.,	2:24
Inasmuch as thy s. shall keep	4:14
to prophesy concerning his s.—	5:17
and people who were of his s.	5:18
many things concerning his s.	5:19
give commandment unto my s.,	6: 6
prophesying concerning his s.,	7: 1
raise up s. unto the Lord	7: 1
they, and also many of their s.,	8: 3
behold thy s., and also the seed	12: 1
and also the s. of thy brethren.	12: 1
chosen to minister unto thy s.	12: 8
the twelve ministers of thy s.	12: 9
beholdest shall judge thy s.	12:10
Behold thy s., and also the s.	12:14
and also the s. of thy brethren.	12:14
and beheld the people of my s.	12:15
against the s. of my brethren;	12:15
the s. of my brethren did contend	12:19
did contend against my s.,	12:19
because of the pride of my s.,	1 Ne 12:19
the s. of my brethren did overpower	12:19
overpower the people of my s.	12:19
people of the s. of my brethren	12:20
that they had overcome my s.;	12:20
from the s. of my brethren.	13:10
upon the s. of thy brethren.	13:11
from the s. of my brethren	13:12
unto the s. of my brethren,	13:12
upon the s. of my brethren;	13:14
thy father that his s. should have	13:30
destroy the mixture of thy s.,	13:30
destroy the s. of thy brethren.	13:31
is the s. of thy father—	13:34
will manifest myself unto thy s.,	13:35
after thy s. shall be destroyed,	13:35
and also the s. of thy brethren,	13:35
remnant of the s. of thy brethren.	13:38
remnant of the s. of my brethren.	13:38
remnant of the s. of my brethren,	13:39
known in the records of thy s.,	13:41
among the s. of thy father;	14: 2
when our s. shall have dwindled	15:13
unto the remnant of our s.—	15:13
shall the remnant of our s. know	15:14
hath not spoken of our s. alone,	15:18
In thy s. shall all the kindreds	15:18
and we did take s. of every kind	16:11
Thy s. also had been as the sand;	20:19
by them shall our s. be scattered.	22: 7
And after our s. is scattered	22: 8
shall be of great worth unto our s.;	22: 8
In thy s. shall all the kindreds	22: 9
land for the inheritance of my s.	2 Ne 1: 5
thy s. shall be blessed with his	1:31
seed shall be blessed with his s.,	1:31
this land for the security of thy s.	1:32
of thy s. with the s. of my son.	1:32
and the inheritance of thy s.	3: 2
for thy s. shall not utterly be	3: 3
my word unto the s. of thy loins—	3:11
I will preserve thy s. forever.	3:16
for thy s. shall not be destroyed,	3:23
and unto the s. of thy brethren.	3:24
prophesied concerning all his s.	4: 2
you and unto your s. forever.	4: 7
in the end thy s. shall be blessed.	4: 9
Blessed art, thou and thy s.;	4:11
And thy s. shall be numbered with	4:11
shall be numbered with his s.;	4:11
and thy s. like unto his seed;	4:11
and thy seed like unto his s.;	4:11
for we did sow s.,	5:11
cursed shall be the s. of him	5:23
him that mixeth with their s.;	5:23
They shall be a scourge unto thy s.,	5:25
that our s. shall not utterly be	9:53
I will afflict thy s. by the hand	10:18
consecrate this land unto thy s.,	10:19
shall be numbered among thy s.,	10:19
the s. of a homer shall yield an	15:10
so the holy s. shall be the	16:13
the s. of evildoers shall never be	24:21
and handed down unto my s.	25:21
that his s. should never perish	25:21
After my s. and the s. of my	26:15
and the s. of my brethren shall	26:15
and especially unto our s.,	28: 2
that I would remember your s.;	29: 2
words of your s. should proceed	29: 2
out of my mouth unto your s.;	29: 2
that I would remember his s.	29:14
forth unto the remnant of our s.	30: 3
shall the remnant of our s. know	30: 4
and hand them down unto my s.,	Jac 1: 3
promise unto you and to your s.,	2:12
raise up s. unto me, I will	2:30
and, having not s., and knowing	Om 1:25
offering for sin he shall see his s.,	Mos 14:10
offering for sin he shall see his s.	15:10
And who shall be his s.?	15:10
say unto you, that these are his s.,	15:11
And now, are they not his s.?	15:12

SEED 859 SEEING

say unto you that they are his s.	Mos	15:13
thy s. shall cause that many		17:15
their s. might be distinguished	Al	3: 8
from the s. of their brethren,		3: 8
whosoever did mingle his s. with		3: 9
bring the same curse upon his s.		3: 9
their s. may be separated from		3:14
separated from thee and thy s.,		3:14
mingleth his s. with thy brethren,		3:15
fighteth against thee and thy s.		3:16
shall no more be called thy s.;		3:17
whomsoever shall be called thy s.,		3:17
Lord unto Nephi and to his s.		3:17
almost all the s. of Amulon		25: 4
began to hunt the s. of Amulon		25: 8
the s. of the priests who caused		25: 9
their s. should cause many to be		25:12
will compare the word unto a s.		32:28
place, that a s. may be planted		32:28
if it be a true s., or a good seed,		32:28
if it be a true seed, or a good s.,		32:28
needs be that this is a good s.,		32:28
as the s. swelleth, and sprouteth,		32:30
needs say that the s. is good;		32:30
are ye sure that this is a good s.?		32:31
every s. bringeth forth unto its		32:31
if a s. groweth it is good,		32:32
experiment, and planted the s.		32:33
needs know that the s. is good.		32:33
exercised your faith to plant the s.		32:36
to know if the s. was good.		32:36
not because the s. was not good,		32:39
or how they should plant the s.,		33: 1
or the s. of those who are now		45:13
a remnant of the s. of Jacob;		46:23
a remnant of the s. of Joseph,		46:23
a remnant of the s. of my son		46:24
remainder of the s. of Joseph		46:24
that part of his s. which shall		46:25
the remnant of the s. of Joseph,		46:27
their days and increase their s.,	He	7:24
the s. of Zedekiah are with us,		8:21
merciful unto the s. of Joseph	3Ne	5:21
a remnant of the s. of Joseph		5:23
the remnant of the s. of Jacob,		5:24
who are the remnant of their s.		10:16
a remnant of the s. of Joseph.		10:17
a remnant of the s. of Joseph?		10:17
the remnant of their s., who		16: 4
in thy s. shall all the kindreds		20:25
In thy s. shall all the kindreds		20:27
unto a remnant of your s.,		21: 4
from the Gentiles, unto your s.		21: 5
thy s. shall begin to know these		21: 7
thy s. shall inherit the Gentiles		22: 3
this I speak unto their s.,	Mrm	5:10
that the s. of this people may		5:15
a remnant of the s. of Jacob		5:24
a remnant of the s. of Jacob;		7:10
also of the s. of the earth of	Eth	1:41
will I bless thee and thy s.,		1:43
and raise up unto me of thy s.		1:43
and of the s. of thy brother,		1:43
I will raise up unto me of thy s.,		1:43
the remnant of the s. of Joseph,		13: 6
a remnant of the s. of Joseph		13: 7
merciful unto the s. of Joseph		13: 7
the remnant of the s. of Joseph		13:10
unto Adam and unto his s.,	DC	29:42
also upon Aaron and his s.		84:18
Aaron and the s. of Abraham,		84:34
were the sowers of the s.;		86: 2
and of the s. of Abraham,		103:17
him, and his s. after him;		104:22
for him and his s. after him;		104:24
upon him and his s. after him.		104:25
them and their s. after them.		104:32
them and their s. after them,		104:33
unto him and his s. after him.		104:37
upon him and his s. after him,		104:40
his agent, and his s. after him.		104:41
upon him and his s. after him,		104:42
conferred upon Aaron and his s.,	DC	107:13
descendants of the chosen s.,		107:40
in us and our s. all generations		110:12
In thee and in thy s. shall		124:58
Joseph and his s. after him have		124:59
for himself and his s. after him,		124:81
himself and his s. after him,		124:82
nor his s. be found begging bread.		124:90
promises concerning his s.,		132:30
as touching Abraham and his s.,		132:30
forth grass, the herb yielding s.,	Mses	2:11
fruit, whose s. should be in itself		2:11
herb yielding s. after his kind,		2:12
fruit, whose s. should be in itself,		2:12
given you every herb bearing s.,		2:29
be the fruit of a tree yielding s.;		2:29
between thy s. and her seed;		4:21
between thy s. and her s.;		4:21
we never should have had s.,		5:11
God hath appointed me another s.,		6: 2
a mixture of all the s. of Adam		7:22
save it was the s. of Cain,		7:22
for the s. of Cain were black,		7:22
mercy upon Noah and his s.,		7:50
that a remnant of his s. should		7:52
he through whose s. Messiah shall		7:53
unto the fathers concerning the s.	Abr	1: 4
give unto thy s. after thee for an		2: 6
a blessing unto thy s. after thee,		2: 9
and shall be accounted thy s.,		2:10
thy s. (that is, thy Priesthood),		2:11
thy s. after thee (that is to say,		2:11
(that is to say, the literal s.,		2:11
or the s. of the body)		2:11
Unto thy s. will I give this land.		2:19
multiply thee, and thy s. after		3:14
grass; the herb yielding s.;		4:11
whose s. in itself yieldeth its		4:11
bring forth grass from its own s.,		4:12
bring forth herb from its own s.,		4:12
yielding s. after his kind, and		4:12
forth the tree from its own s.,		4:12
whose s. could only bring forth		4:12
give them every herb bearing s.		4:29
the fruit of the tree yielding s.		4:29

SEEDS

all manner of s. of every kind,	1Ne	8: 1
and also of the s. of fruit		8: 1
with all our loading and our s.,		18: 6
we began to plant s.; yea we		18:24
put all our s. into the earth,		18:24
yea, even with all manner of s.,	Mos	9: 9
with s. of corn, and of wheat,		9: 9
with s. of all manner of fruits;		9: 9
of the land, s. of every kind.	Eth	2: 3
and a continuation of the s.	DC	132:19
to take teams, s., and farming		136: 7
shall be the number of thy s.	Abr	3:14

SEEING

s. I have lost my children,	1Ne	21:21
s. that our merciful God has given	2Ne	10:20
and s. all their inequality,	Al	4:15
s. no way that he might reclaim		4:19
s. that I have been permitted to		7: 1
s. that it is the first time that I		7: 1
s. that your hearts have been		9:30
s. that ye are a lost and a fallen		9:30
s. there was more than one		10:12
s. that the words of Amulek had		12: 1
s. that he began to tremble under		12: 1
s. that thou hast been taken in thy		12: 3
s. there is no more corruption.		12:18
s. we know these things,		12:37
s. a great check, yea, seeing		15:17
s. that the people were checked as		15:17
s. that they could not hit him		17:36
s. the Spirit of the Lord poured		19:14
s. the contention among his		19:31
s. that the Lord had granted unto		25:17
Now, s. that I know these things,		29: 6

s. that the holy scriptures testify	Al	34:30
s. that the hearts of the people		35:15
s. the enormity of their number,		52: 5
Now Moroni s. their confusion,		52:37
thus s. our forces increase daily,		56:29
And s. the people in a state of	He	7: 4
s. that he had gained favor in		8:10
s. ye know these things and		8:24
Jacob s. that their enemies were	3Ne	7:12
s. that the Lamanites were	Mrm	4:23
s. the sorrows of her father,	Eth	8: 8
s. that ye know the light by	Mro	7:18
s. that I, the Lord, have	DC	63:36
this privilege of s. and knowing		76:117
s. this is a time of peace?		101:48
canst weep, s. thou art holy,	Mses	7:29
weep, s. these shall suffer?		7:37

SEEK

they s. to destroy his life.	1Ne	1:hd
they s. to take away thy life.		2: 1
s. the records, and bring them		3: 4
all those who diligently s. him,		10:17
shall s. to bring forth my Zion		13:37
those who s. the lusts of the flesh		22:23
and they that s. to destroy him	2Ne	3:14
they did s. to take away my life.		5: 2
they did s. to take away my life.		5: 4
did s. in the wilderness for beasts		5:24
S. unto them that have familiar		18:19
not a people s. unto their God		18:19
do they s. the Lord of Hosts,		19:13
to it shall the Gentiles s.;		21:10
they s. to destroy the things of God.		26:17
they s. not the welfare of Zion.		26:29
that s. deep to hide their counsel		27:27
s. deep to hide their counsels		28: 9
Lamanites that s. to destroy	Jac	1:14
But before ye s. for riches,		2:18
s. ye for the kingdom of God.		2:18
shall obtain riches, if ye s. them;		2:19
s. them for the intent to do good—		2:19
for they s. to excuse themselves		2:23
those who s. your destruction.		3: 1
s. not to counsel the Lord,		4:10
people of Nephi did s. diligently	En	1:20
for they will not s. wisdom,	Mos	8:20
that they would s. revenge,		19:19
nor s. to destroy them.		19:29
s. to destroy the church no more,		27:16
behold, the king will s. thy life;	Al	20: 2
if our brethren s. to destroy us,		24:16
in vain to s. their destruction,		27: 1
they could not s. revenge from		27: 2
s. no more to destroy the		36: 9
s. no more to destroy the		36:11
S. not after riches nor the vain		39:14
and we will s. not your blood,		44: 6
s. to destroy the church of God,		46:10
did s. to cut off the strength and		50:12
s. every opportunity to scourge		52:10
if ye s. to destroy us more		54:13
we will s. to destroy you;		54:13
yea, and we will s. our land,		54:13
I will s. death among them		55: 3
I s. not for power, but to pull		60:36
I s. not for honor of the world,		60:36
I, Pahoran, do not s. for power,		61: 9
and s. no more to destroy my	He	5:29
and s. no more to destroy my		5:32
they began to s. to get gain		6:17
and s. to destroy my life.		9:24
will in this thing s. to destroy me.		9:25
s. to lay their hands upon him		10:15
did no more s. to destroy Nephi,		11:18
s. all manner of ways to destroy		13:26
with me and do s. to destroy me		14:10
all who shall s. to slay them	3Ne	4:29
tempting them to s. for power,		6:15
ye first the kingdom of God		13:33
s., and ye shall find;		14: 7
and the Lord whom ye s. shall		24: 1
and did s. to kill them,	4Ne	1:31
who did not s. his destruction.	Eth	9: 2
commend you to s. this Jesus		12:41
They s. not the Lord to establish	DC	1:16
s. to bring forth and establish		6: 6
S. not for riches but for wisdom,		6: 7
s. to bring forth and establish		11: 6
S. not for riches but for wisdom;		11: 7
S. not to declare my word,		11:21
but first s. to obtain my word,		11:21
s. the kingdom of God, and all		11:23
s. to bring forth and establish		12: 6
S. to bring forth and establish		14: 6
nor s. thy neighbor's life.		19:25
s. not to counsel your God.		22: 4
and s. for the things of a better.		25:10
if you s. it with all your hearts.		38:19
if ye s. the riches which it		38:39
for the Gentiles to s. to it,		45: 9
s. ye earnestly the best gifts,		46: 8
that s. or that ask of me,		46: 9
s. ye a living like unto men,		54: 9
because you s. to counsel in		56:14
those among you who s. signs,		63: 8
s. them a home, as they are		63:65
S. not to be cumbered.		66:10
s. ye out of the Book of		67: 6
they also s. not earnestly		68:31
s. me diligently and ye shall		88:63
s. ye diligently and teach one		88:118
s. ye out of the best books		88:118
s. learning, even by study and		88:118
of those who s. inheritances,		96: 3
he shall s. diligently to take		96: 9
s. diligently to turn the hearts		98:16
against them, neither s. revenge,		98:23
And s. the face of the Lord		101:38
s. diligently that peradventure		103:32
s. diligently that peradventure		103:33
s. ye diligently and teach		109: 7
s. ye out of the best books		109: 7
s. learning even by study and		109: 7
may s. learning even by study		109:14
shall s. counsel, and authority,		122: 2
it is not my will that he shall s.		124:109
if any man shall s. to build up		136:19
S. ye; and keep all your pledges		136:20
we s. after these things.	AoF	13

SEEKER

and humble s. of happiness.	Al	27:18

SEEKETH

he that diligently s. shall find;	1Ne	10:19
s. that all men might be miserable	2Ne	2:27
who s. to overthrow the doctrine	Jac	1:hd
to be humble, s. repentance;	Al	32:13
s. to sit in the judgment-seat.	He	8:27
s. to destroy the souls of men.		8:28
and he that s., findeth;	3Ne	14: 8
s. to overthrow the freedom of	Eth	8:25
not puffed up, s. not her own,	Mro	7:45
secret chambers s. your lives.	DC	38:28
enemy s. to destroy my people.		44: 5
and him that s. to do so;		46: 9
he s. the praise of the world.		58:39
with him, for he s. to excel,		58:41
he that s. signs shall see signs,		63: 7
Satan s. to destroy his soul;		64:17
Satan s. to turn their hearts		78:10
s. to become a law unto itself,		88:35
He that s. me early shall find		88:83
overcome him who s. the throne		88:115
for Satan s. to destroy;		132:57
build up himself, and s. not my		136:19

SEEKING

were continually s. to destroy us.	En	1:20
s. to destroy the church,	Mos	27:10
a tyrant who was s. for gain,		29:40
s. to destroy the church of God;	Al	36: 5
and they were s. for power.		46: 4
of those who are s. for power		60:17
yourselves are s. for authority.		60:18

SEEKING / SEEN

SEEKING (continued)

s. to hurl away your sould down	He	7:16
also s. to put down all power	Mro	8:28
s. for blood and revenge.		9:23
s. to destroy the souls of men.	DC	10:27
earnestly s. the kingdom—		46: 5
earnestly s. after the kingdom,		46: 6
Every man s. the interest		82:19
s. diligently to learn wisdom		97: 1
s. diligently the kingdom of		106: 3
of secret works, s. for power.	Mses	6:15
s. earnestly to imitate that	Abr	1:26

SEEM

for it did s. unto them like a	3Ne	28:15
as it shall s. good unto you.	DC	104:85
they s. but a small thing to me,		127: 2
may s. to some to be a very bold		128: 9
this will not s. very strange to	JS	2:28

SEEMED

he s. to be like unto his father	DC	107:43
of country s. affected by it,	JS	2: 5
It s. to enter with great force		2:12
it s. to me for a time as if		2:15

SEEMETH

many witnesses as s. him good	2Ne	27:14
do with him as s. thee good.	Mos	12:16
And it s. a pity unto me,	3Ne	3: 3
whatsoever man it s. them good.		28:30
it s. me that they have no fear	Mro	9: 5
write somewhat as s. me good;		10: 1
left or rented as s. them good.	DC	38:37
to do with him as s. me good.		40: 3
should live as s. him good,		41: 8
and prophesy as s. me good;		42:16
about, as s. them good,		48: 3
as I will, as s. me good.		52: 6
and revoke, as it s. me good;		56: 4
inheritance as s. him good;		58:38
as s. him good or as he shall		58:51
or bought, as s. you good,		60: 5
two by two, as s. them good,		61:35
two by two, as s. you good,		62: 5
please, and pay as s. him good.		64:28
them, for thus it s. me good.		84:103
do with them as s. me good;		100: 1
of that house, as s. him good;		124:72
into that house as s. him good,		124:77
into that house, as s. him good,		124:80
into that house, as s. him good,		124:81
and I will do as s. me good.	Mses	6:32

SEEMINGLY

the s. good feelings of both	JS	2: 6

SEEMS

for what cause it s. mysterious,	DC	127: 2
subject to occupy my mind,		128: 1
It s. as though the adversary	JS	2:20

SEEN

and having s. many afflictions	1Ne	1: 1
and the things which he had s.		1: 7
for I have s. thine abominations!		1:13
my father had read and s. many		1:14
of the things which he had s.,		1:15
which he had both s. and heard.		1:18
for if I had not s. the things		5: 4
have s. an angel of the Lord?		7:10
in other words, I have s. a vision.		8: 2
of the thing which I have s.		8: 3
the whiteness that I had ever s.		8:11
the things that my father had s.,		11: 1
which I never had before s.,		11: 1
the tree which my father had s.;		11: 8
after I had s. the tree,		11: 9
of iron, which my father had s.		11:25
the many waters which thou hast s.		13:29
whose formation thou hast s.		13:32
last records, which thou hast s.		13:40
many things which thou hast s.;		14:24
and s. all these things,		15: 1
of the things which I had s.,	1Ne	15: 4
Ye have s. an angel,		17:45
Thou hast s. and heard all this;		20: 6
I have s. a vision, in which I	2Ne	1: 4
things which I have s. and heard.		4:16
if I have s. so great things,		4:26
even as I have s. him.		11: 2
my brother, Jacob, also has s. him		11: 3
has seen him as I have s. him;		11: 3
for mine eyes have s. the King,		16: 5
in darkness have s. a great light;		19: 2
for I have s. his day,		25:13
For I, Nephi, have s. it,		26: 7
I have s. it; wherefore, I know		26:10
things which ye have s. me do.		31:12
I have s. that your Lord		31:17
I, the Lord, have s. the sorrow,	Jac	2:31
things which I had s. concerning		7: 5
for I truly had s. angels,		7: 5
unto me, for I have heard and s.;		7:12
hast never before heard nor s.	En	1: 8
things which I had heard and s.		1:19
And behold, I have s., in the days	Om	1:24
I have s. their abominations,	Mos	11:20
the Lord in mercy hath s. fit to		27:28
which they had heard and s.,		27:32
all the things which they had s.,		27:35
having s. the afflictions of the	Al	4:15
I have s. much of his mysteries		10: 5
after what ye have s., will ye		14:14
Alma having s. all these things,		15:18
had s. concerning the matter.		18: 1
to the things which they had s.,		18: 2
I have s. my Redeemer; and		19:13
had s. that they had fallen,		19:15
that they had s. angels and had		19:34
Hast thou s. an angel?		21: 5
the servants had s. the cause of		22:20
who never has been s. or known,		30:28
hope for things which are not s.,		32:21
and have s. eye to eye as I		36:26
seen eye to eye as I have s.;		36:26
I have s. an angel face to face,		38: 7
for ye have s. that they pray to		38:13
Lamanites were s. approaching		49: 1
never had I s. so great courage,		56:45
all the things which he had s.,	He	2: 9
which they had heard and s.,		5:50
told the people what they had s.,		7:11
when ye have s. this, ye shall say:		9:32
and wonders which they had s.;	3Ne	1:22
which they had heard and s.—		2: 1
I have s. with mine own eyes.		5:17
therefore having s. angels,		7:15
And there was not any light s.,		8:22
days that there was no light s.;		8:23
have s. me and know that I am.		12: 1
shall testify that ye have s. me,		12: 2
before men to be s. of them;		13: 1
that they may be s. of men.		13: 5
both heard my voice, and s. me;		15:24
they who have s. me and been		16: 4
The eye hath never s., neither		17:16
that which ye have s. me do.		18:24
that the multitude had s. Jesus,		19: 2
So great faith have I never s.		19:35
that have s. so great things as		19:36
so great things as ye have s.		19:36
which they had both heard and s.,		27: 1
works which ye have s. me do		27:21
that which ye have s. me do		27:21
which ye have s. and heard,		27:23
which they had heard and s.,		28:16
But behold, I have s. them,		28:26
which I have both s. and heard,	Mrm	1: 1
of the things which I have s.,		5: 9
my father and I have s. them,		8:11
thou hast s. that I shall take	Eth	3: 9
ye could not have s. my finger.		3: 9
which ye have s. and heard		3:21
which ye have s. and heard		3:21
write the things which he had s.;		4: 1
having s. exceeding many days,		9:15

SEEN — SELL

SEEN (cont.)

and after he had s. many days	Eth 10:17
are hoped for and not s.;	12: 6
things which they have not s.	12: 8
we have s. in this record that	12:20
thou hast s. thy weakness	12:37
ye know that I have s. Jesus,	12:39
I have s. the things which the	DC 5:25
for I have s. them, for they	5:25
I have s. them, and they have	5:26
have s. them with your eyes,	17: 3
testify that you have s. them,	17: 5
Joseph Smith, Jun., has s. them;	17: 5
my power that he has s. them,	17: 5
his weeping for Zion I have s.,	21: 8
things which thou hast not s.,	25: 4
thou hast s. great sorrow,	39: 9
s. abominations in the church	50: 4
which they have s. and heard	52:36
which he hath s. and heard	64:19
no man has s. God at any time	67:11
things which eye has not s.,	76:10
and they see as they are s.,	76:94
only to be s. and understood	76:116
any man who hath s. any or	88:47
s. God moving in his majesty	88:47
say unto you, he hath s. him;	88:48
ye know that ye have s. me,	88:50
would have s. the enemy	101:54
I have s. the work which he	124:17
I have s. your labor and toil in	126: 2
just the same as if he had s.	128: 4
I have s. your sacrifices,	132:50
I have s. your sacrifices in	132:50
neither hath any eye s.,	133:45
because thou hast s. thy weakness,	135: 5
Kokaubeam that thou hast s.,	Abr 3:16
eyes have s. from the beginning;	3:21
all the intelligences thou hast s.	3:21
it was s. that the seemingly	JS 2: 6
He had s. a vision, he knew	2:24
he had both s. a light and	2:24
I had actually s. a light, and	2:25
saying that I had s. a vision,	2:25
I have actually s. a vision;	2:25
deny what I have actually s.?	2:25
I had s. a vision; I knew it,	2:25
to affirm that I had s. a vision.	2:27
anything earthly I had ever s.;	2:31
what I had both s. and heard	2:46
assert that I had s. a vision,	2:58
than any he had before s.	2:64
which time I had never s. him.	2:66

SEER

A s. shall the Lord my God	2Ne 3: 6
who shall be a choice s. unto	3: 6
A choice s. will I raise up	3: 7
But a s. will I raise up	3:11
that s. will the Lord bless;	3:14
in them, the same is called s.	Mos 8:13
a s. is greater than a prophet.	8:15
a s. is a revelator and a prophet	8:16
But a s. can know of things	8:17
has these things is called s.,	28:16
shalt be called a s., a translator,	DC 21: 1
be a s., a revelator, a translator,	107:92
he may be a prophet, and a s.,	124:94
a revelator, a s., and prophet.	124:125
prophet and s. of the Church of	127:12
the Prophet and S. of the Lord,	135: 3
A s. hath the Lord raised up	Mses 6:36
we go yonder to behold the s.,	6:38

SEERS

the s. hath he covered because	2Ne 27: 5
stones were what constituted "s."	JS 2:35

SEES

so long as the Lord s. fit that we	Mos 29:32

SEEST

the virgin whom thou s.	1Ne 11:18
thou s. the foundation of a	13:26

thou s. that after the book hath	1Ne 13:28
thou s.—because of the many	13:29
thou s. that the Lord God will	13:30
behold, thou s. all these things—	14:16
and thou s. that thy thoughts are	Al 12: 3
And thou s. that we know	12: 4
Why s. thou this man,	He 8: 2
thou s. that they have repented,	11:15
thou s. that they believe in me	3Ne 19:22
S. thou that ye are created after	Eth 3:15

SEETH

Who s. us, and who knoweth us?	2Ne 27:27
But when he s. his children,	27:34
which the Lord s. fit to inflict	Mos 3:19
the Lord s. fit to chasten his	23:21
all that he s. fit that they should	Al 29: 8
and thy Father who s. in secret,	3Ne 13: 4
and thy Father, who s. in secret,	13: 6
and thy Father, who s. in secret,	13:18
when the Lord s. fit in his	28:29

SEEZORAM

man that he should murder S.,	He 9:23
Seantum, who is the brother of S.,	9:26
the which ye have murdered S.,	9:27

SEIZE

I did s. upon the servant of Laban,	1Ne 4:31
Why do ye not s. upon this man	He 8: 1
that fear may s. upon them,	DC 45:74

SEIZED

all that have been s. therewith	2Ne 28:23
lest you be s. therewith.	DC 50:33
I was s. upon by some power	JS 2:15
enemy which had s. upon me,	2:16

SELAH: see GRIFFIN, Selah J.

SELECT

to copy, and to correct, and s.,	DC 57:13

SELECTED

with these whom they had s.,	Mos 28: 1
And he s. a wise man who was	Al 4:16
wise lawyers whom we have s.	10:24
numbers which they had s.,	17: 8
we s. a part of our men,	57:16
s. to convey the prisoners,	57:22
have s. my servant Edward	DC 58:14

SELECTING

of s. and writing books for	DC 55: 4
writing, copying, s., and	69: 8

SELECTION

to make a s. of sacred hymns,	DC 25:11

SELF

the season, unto mine own s.	Jac 5:18
the season, unto mine own s.	5:19
preserve it unto mine own s.;	5:20
preserve it unto mine own s.	5:23
the season, unto mine own s.	5:29
fruit thereof unto mine own s.?	5:33
the season, unto mine own s.	5:46
the roots also unto mine own s.,	5:54
of my vineyard unto mine own s.	5:76
I will lay up unto mine own s. of	5:76

SELFISHNESS

of his pride, and of his s.,	DC 56: 8

SELFSAME

for the s. end hath he created	Jac 2:21
unto the people the s. thing—	Al 19:33
king died in that s. year that	24: 4
man, the s. prayer unto God,	31:22
in that s. hour that they cried	43:50

SELL

they s. themselves for naught;	2Ne 26:10

buy and to s., and to get gain,	He	6: 8
will s. me for silver and for gold,	3Ne	27:32
who s. yourselves for that	Mrm	8:38
and they did buy and s. and	Eth	10:22
may s. goods without fraud,	DC	57: 8
Williams should s. his farm,		64:21
Gilbert, should s. their store		64:26
Gilbert should s. my storehouse,		101:96
s. the lots that are laid off		104:36
and do not s. or convey the stock		124:69

SEN.: *see SMITH, Joseph, Sen.; and SMITH'S, Joseph, Sen.*

SEND

I will s. them forth unto all	2Ne	11: 2
I will s. their words forth unto		11: 3
Whom shall I s., and who will go		16: 8
Then I said: Here am I; s. me.		16: 8
will s. him against a hypocritical		20: 6
s. among his fat ones, leanness;		20:16
and s. down justice upon those	Jac	3: 1
he did not s. a sufficient number,	Mos	11:17
I will s. forth hail among them,		12: 6
that the Lord has cause to s. me		12:29
let us s. a proclamation among		22: 6
king Limhi did s. unto them.		22:10
he will s. his armies against them		29:23
they did not s. away any who	Al	1:30
s. his Son among the people,		14: 5
doth s. such great punishments		18: 2
for the Lord to s. his angel to		39:19
that which ye do s. out shall		41:15
will he not s. you there to dwell		54:22
provisions and s. them to Judea,		57:11
to s. them down to the land of		57:16
s. an embassy to the govenor		58: 4
not s. more strength unto us,		58: 9
s. more men to our assistance;		58:36
s. forth against the Lamanites,		60:24
and s. forth food and men		60:24
and s. speedily unto me of		60:34
do s. these words unto Moroni,		61: 2
more food to s. forth unto Lehi		61:18
Helaman did s. forth to take this	He	2:10
they did s. forth much by the		3:10
shall s. forth his mighty winds,		5:12
s. forth rain upon the face of		11:13
he did s. out his armies in the	3Ne	4:24
stoning those whom I did s.		9:10
I did s. down fire and destroy		9:11
they s. forth unto the people		19: 3
Behold, I will s. my messenger,		24: 1
will s. you Elijah the prophet		25: 5
let my father s. for Akish,	Eth	8:10
he did s. rain upon the face of		9:35
God would s. or bring forth		11:21
of three witnesses will I s. forth	DC	5:15
and s. forth in this work.		10:45
s. one or more of their teachers		20:81
s. by the hand of some priest;		20:82
I will s. upon them a cursing		24: 4
I will s. unto them a cursing		24: 6
that I may s. my servant,		25: 6
the Lord God will s. forth flies		29:18
s. forth angels to declare unto		29:42
s. them forth to the place which		38:35
I s. you, my servants Sidney		49: 3
that I will s. forth judgment		52:11
s. goods also unto the people,		57: 9
that day will I s. mine angels		63:54
but inasmuch as you can s., send;		66: 6
but inasmuch as you can send, s.;		66: 6
till I, the Lord, shall s. you.		66: 9
s. forth the accounts of		69: 5
I, the Lord, shall s. them.		70:16
And I will s. upon him		79: 2
place ye cannot go ye shall s.,		84:62
I s. you out to prove the		84:79
I s. you out to reprove the		84:87
that they should s. it unto them		84:103
s. it up unto the bishop in Zion,		84:104
s. them before you to make	DC	84:107
will s. one mighty and strong,		85: 7
I now s. upon you another		88: 3
up elders and s. unto them.		88:72
when I shall s. you again		88:80
and s. them to purchase these		101:73
the churches s. up wise men		103:23
until I shall s. means unto you		104:80
wheresoever I shall s. you,		108: 6
judgments which thou wilt s.		109:30
judgments thou art about to s.,		109:38
s. it abroad among all nations,		112: 1
s. forth my word unto the ends		112: 4
whithersoever they shall s. you,		112:19
whosoever ye shall s. in my name,		112:21
whithersoever ye shall s. them—		112:21
s. again the snows upon the earth.		117: 1
can s. forth the power of his mighty		123: 6
And s. ye swift messengers,		124:26
s. my word to every creature.		124:128
s. them to prepare a way		124:139
you to s. my word abroad,		126: 3
and s. it to you by mail,		127:10
I will s. you Elijah the prophet		128:17
S. forth the elders of my church		133: 8
s. forth unto foreign lands;		133: 8
here am I, s. me, I will be thy	Mses	4: 1
s. him forth from the Garden		4:29
will I s. in the floods upon them,		7:34
righteousness will I s. down out		7:62
truth will I s. forth out of the		7:62
I will s. in the floods upon them.		8:17
Thou didst s. thine angel to	Abr	2:13
the Lord said: Whom shall I s.?		3:27
Son of Man: Here am I, s. me.		3:27
and said: Here am I, s. me.		3:27
the Lord said: I will s. the first.		3:27
shall s. his angels before him	JS	1:37

SENDETH

God s. more witnesses,	2Ne	11: 3
s. them forth among his people,	Mos	29.23
he s. an invitation unto all	Al	5:33
Who is God, that s. no more		9: 6
he s. down his wrath upon you		12:36
He that s. up treasures unto	DC	63:48

SENDING

it shall be for the s. forth of oxen,	2Ne	17:25
s. so many of their brethren	Al	48:23
by s. him forth he should gain	He	1:16
labor in s. my word to the kings	DC	124:16

SENECA

of Fayette, S. county,	DC	128:20
in Fayette, S. county,		128:21

SENINE

a s. of gold for a day, or a	Al	11: 3
which is equal to a s. of gold;		11: 3
a s. of gold, a seon of gold,		11: 5
was equal to a s. of gold,		11: 7
was twice the value of a s.		11: 8
as even one s. for my labor;		30:33
thou hast paid the uttermost s.	3Ne	12:26
in prison can ye pay even one s.?		12:26

SENSE

neither s. nor insensibility.	2Ne	2:11
to a lively s. of his own guilt,	Mos	2:38
you to a s. of your nothingness,		4: 5
to a s. of your duty to God,	Al	7:22
a s. of your awful situation,	Eth	8:24
in one s. of the word,	DC	128:14

SENSUAL

becoming carnal, s., devilish,	Mos	16: 3
as they had become carnal, s.,	Al	42:10
man became s. and devilish,	DC	20:20
temporal, neither carnal nor s.		29:35
time forth to be carnal, s., and	Mses	5:13
men have become carnal, s., and		6:49

SENT

SENT		
and s. his servants to slay us,	1 Ne	3:25
he s. fiery flying serpents		17:41
and his Spirit, hath s. me.		20:16
I have s. him, the Lord thy God		20:17
my voice have I s. up on high;	2 Ne	4:24
The Lord s. his word unto Jacob		19: 8
of the vineyard s. his servant;	Jac	5:70
the Lord had s. the people of	Om	1:14
be written and s. forth among	Mos	2: 8
hath s. me to declare unto thee		3: 4
hath s. his holy prophets among		3:13
he s. among them, desiring to		5: 1
king Limhi s. a proclamation		7:17
having been s. as a spy among		9: 1
I had s. my spies out round about		10: 7
king Noah s. guards round about		11:17
king Noah s. his armies against		11:18
which the Lord s. me to deliver;		13: 3
and s. his servants after him		17: 3
s. his servants to watch them.		18:32
he s. his army to destroy them.		18:33
Gideon s. men into the wilderness		19:18
they s. their armies forth;		20: 7
Now king Limhi had s.,		21:25
he s. the tribute of wine to the		22:10
also s. more wine, as a present		22:10
s. an army into the wilderness		22:15
and he also s. forth their wives,		23:33
king Mosiah s. a proclamation		27: 2
And I am s. from God.		27:15
s. out throughout all the land,		29: 1
king Mosiah s. again among the		29: 4
word s. he among the people.		29: 4
after king Mosiah had s. these		29:37
Alma s. spies to follow the	Al	2:21
Now those whom he had s. out		2:22
and s. his guards to contend with		2:32
was an army s. to drive them out		3:21
But he s. up a numerous army		3:23
of souls s. to the eternal world,		3:26
judgments of God s. upon them		4: 3
I am s. to command thee that		8:16
Lamanites shall be s. upon you;		9:18
the Lord has s. his angel to visit		9:25
even so has he s. his angel to		10:10
and s. forth officers that the man		11: 2
he s. angels to converse with		12:29
s. men to cast stones at them.		14: 7
and he s. a message immediately		15: 4
the message which he had s.		15: 5
Art thou s. from God?		18:33
she s. and desired that he		19: 2
he was s. by the Great Spirit;		19:25
had been s. from the Nephites		19:26
was s. by the Great Spirit		19:27
the king s. a proclamation		22:27
s. a proclamation among all his		23: 1
Yea, he s. a decree among them,		23: 2
therefore he s. his proclamation		23: 3
had s. forth this proclamation,		23: 4
in goodness s. these our brethren,		24: 7
they were angels s. from God		27: 4
the chief judge s. a proclamation		27:21
and s. him to the land of		30:29
was s. forth by the chief judge		30:57
they s. forth unto him desiring		33: 1
And they s. and gathered together		35: 4
s. over unto the people of		35: 8
or s. to declare the word,		35:15
God s. his holy angel to stop us		36: 6
s. his angel to declare unto me		38: 7
God s. our first parents forth		42: 2
Moroni s. spies into the		43:23
s. certain men unto him,		43:23
s. forth and inspired their hearts		43:48
which blessing God had s. upon		46:10
also s. forth in all the parts of		46:28
s. a proclamation throughout		47: 1
he s. a secret embassy into		47:10
Amalickiah s. again the second		47:11
and he s. again the third time.		47:11
and he s. again the fourth time		47:12
Amalickiah had s. an embassy	Al	47:32
she s. unto Amalickiah,		47:33
and s. forth to preach among		49:30
Therefore Moroni s. an army,		50:33
army which was s. by Moroni.		50:35
those who had s. in their voices		51: 3
he s. a petition, with the		51:15
Moroni had s. a large number of		52: 7
Moroni also s. orders unto him		52: 8
he also s. orders unto him		52: 9
And Moroni also s. unto him,		52:10
they s. embassies to the army of		52:20
that Ammoron s. unto Moroni		54: 1
s. it by the servant of Ammoron,		54: 4
and he s. to the city God,		55:16
there were s. two thousand men		56:28
we s. them to the land of		56:57
I s. an epistle unto the king,		57: 2
Ammoron had s. to their support		57:17
whom we s. with the prisoners		57:18
who had been s. out to watch		57:30
s. out their spies round about		58:14
than that which they have s.		58:36
s. an epistle to Pahoran,		59: 3
when Moroni had s. this epistle		59: 4
men s. to the city Nephihah,		59: 9
might have s. armies unto		60: 8
not cause food to be s. unto us,		60:19
after Moroni had s. his epistle		61: 1
I have s. a proclamation		61: 6
I have s. a few provisions unto		61:16
that provisions should be s.,		62:12
should be s. unto Helaman,		62:12
be s. to the armies of Lehi and		62:13
they s. them to dwell with the		62:17
when they had s. them away		62:18
were written and s. forth		63:12
they s. forth one Kishkumen,	He	1: 9
he went unto those that s. him,		1:11
he immediately s. forth Lehi		1:28
when Helaman s. forth to take		2:11
therefore he hath s. his angels		5:11
servants whom I have s. unto you		5:29
was a proclamation s. abroad		9: 9
Where are the five who were s.		9:12
the five whom ye say ye have s.,		9:12
they were the five who were s.;		9:13
that I am s. unto you from God.		9:36
s. it forth among all the people.		10:17
they s. an army of strong men		11:28
I was s. unto you to declare it		13: 7
lyings s. forth among the people,	3 Ne	1:22
which was s. among them;		2:10
he s. a proclamation among all		3:13
from heaven and s. forth,		6:20
saints whom I s. among them		9:11
s. me to bless you in turning		20:26
Father, because my Father s. me.		27:13
my Father s. me that I might		27:14
hath chosen and s. among them;		28:34
words of those whom he hath s.		28:34
s. an epistle unto me,	Mrm	3: 4
and the floods have I s. forth	Eth	2:24
believe the Father who s. me.		4:12
who were s. from the Lord,		7:23
when Jared had s. for Akish,		8:11
s. forth by the power and gift of	Mro	7:16
he s. angels to minister unto the		7:22
whom I have s. unto you to	DC	27: 5
John I have s. unto you,		27: 8
whom I have s. unto you,		27:12
I have s. mine angels to commit		27:16
and desolation are s. forth upon		29: 8
be a great hailstorm s. forth		29:16
Behold thou wast s. forth,		35: 4
gospel, which I have s. forth		35:12
I have s. forth the fulness of		35:17
be ordained and s. forth to preach		36: 5
may be ordained and s. forth,		36: 7
from on high and s. forth,		38:38
gospel, which I have s. forth in		39:11
covenant which I have s. forth		39:11
my servants shall be s. forth to		42:63

Ye are not s. forth to be taught,	DC	43:15
s. mine everlasting covenant		45: 9
s. mine Only Begotten Son		49: 5
I have s. unto you mine		49: 9
s. forth to teach the truth.		50:14
s. forth to preach the word of		50:17
ordained of God and s. forth,		50:26
s. forth by the will of the		50:27
unto which I have s. you.		58: 1
this cause I have s. you—		58: 6
for this cause I have s. you		58:14
let there be workmen s. forth		58:54
for this intent have I s. them.		60: 9
been s. to preach my gospel		60:13
will of him who hath s. you.		60:16
s. up unto the land of Zion,		63:40
s. up unto the land of Zion.		63:43
of Zion, and shall be s. away,		64:35
one s. down from on high,		65: 1
s. forth unto the children of		66: 2
needs be s. unto the world		75:24
four angels s. forth from God,		77: 8
I have called and s. forth to		84:32
against you at the time I s. you.		84:76
waiting to be s. forth to reap		86: 5
and he s. forth his servants		88:51
I s. you out to testify and		88:81
To be s. greeting; not by		89: 2
I s. them forth to be chastened.		95:10
s. up kindly unto the bishop		99: 6
the destroyer I have s. forth		105:15
And to have s. wise men,		105:28
The Twelve being s. out, holding the		107:35
and that thou hast s. us;		109:57
that he [Elijah] should be s.,		110:14
First Presidency, whom I have s.,		112:20
s. down from heaven unto you.		112:32
Jesus Christ, whom he hath s.		132:24
by the voice of him that s. me,		132:59
God hath s. forth the angel		133:17
I have s. forth mine angel		133:36
the Lord s. forth the fulness of		133:57
and when they were s. unto you		133:71
has s. the fulness of the everlasting		135: 3
Spirit is s. forth into the world		136:33
them that were s. unto them;		136:36
been s. for political purposes,		OD
s. forth from the presence of God,	Mses	5:58
a decree s. forth, that it should		5:59
have s. forth in the beginning		6:30
as it shall be s. forth in the world,		6:30
he s. forth in an unalterable decree,		7:52
s. his angel to deliver thee from	Abr	3:20
was not before s. upon Israel,	JS	1:18
shall be s. again upon Israel.		1:18
s. from the presence of God		2:33
of those who s. to the school,		2:66

SENTENCE
s. of death passed upon thee;	DC	122: 7

SENUM
a s. of silver, which is equal to	Al	11: 3
A s. of silver, an amnor of		11: 6
A s. of silver was equal to a		11: 7
A shiblon is half of a s.;		11:15

SENUMS
of silver was as great as two s.	Al	11:11
of silver was as great as four s.		11:12

SEON
a s. of gold, a shum of gold,	Al	11: 5
the amount of a s. of gold was		11: 8
was twice the value of a s.		11: 9

SEPARATE
being s. one from another.	Mos	2: 5
s. people as to their faith,		26: 4
for or against Amlici, in s. bodies.	Al	2: 5
from the wicked, and be ye s.,		5:57
s. themselves one from another,		31:37
they did s. one from another	3Ne	7: 2

SEPARATED
who was s. from the seed of my	1Ne	13:12
which s. the wicked from the tree		15:28
be s. from thee and thy seed,	Al	3:14
they s. themselves and departed		17:13
Therefore they s. themselves		17:17
when Ammon and his brethren s.		21: 1
s. themselves from the Nephites		30:59
hast s. us from our brethren;		31:16
ye were s. from among them	3Ne	15:19
hath the Father s. from them;		15:20
should be s. into twelve bodies.		19: 5
Who were s. from the earth,	DC	45:12
be not s. until they return to		61:35
And when s., man cannot		93:34
s. himself from the crafts of men;		106: 6
in death they were not s.!		135: 3

SEPARATELY
them every one his charge, s.,	Al	35:16
but remain s. and singly,	DC	132:17

SEPARATION
to the s. of it from the body,	Al	29:16
the s. of the Zoramites from		31: 2
an entire s. of the righteous	DC	63:54

SEPTEMBER
is dated S. 24th, 1890,	DC	OD
until the twenty-first of S.,	JS	2:27
twenty-first of S., after I		2:29
the twenty-second day of S.,		2:59

SEPULCHRE
and to be buried in a s.,	1Ne	19:10
after he is laid in a s.	2Ne	25:13
take his body and lay it in a s.,	Al	19: 1
he ought to be placed in the s.;		19: 5

SERAPHIC
and all the s. hosts of heaven,	DC	38: 1

SERAPHIM
Above it stood the s.;	2Ne	16: 2
Then flew one of the s. unto me,		16: 6

SERAPHS
shining s. around thy throne,	DC	109:79

SERIOUS
and we had many seasons of s. war	Om	1: 3
many wars and s. contentions,		1:17
a s. war and much bloodshed		1:24
foundation for s. consequences	Al	50:32
it became a very s. matter to		57:16
began to be a s. difficulty	He	1: 1
there began to be a s. contention		1: 2
was called up to s. reflection	JS	2: 8
caused me s. reflection then,		2:23

SERPENT
even that old s., who is the devil,	2Ne	2:18
fruit shall be a fiery flying s.		24:29
would cast their eyes unto the s.		25:20
yea, even that old s. that did	Mos	16: 3
as he lifted up the brazen s.	He	8:14
look upon that s. should live.		8:15
ask a fish, will he give him a s.?	3Ne	14:10
we beheld Satan, that old s.,	DC	76:28
the poison of a s. shall not		84:72
shall be bound, that old s.,		88:110
poisonous s. cannot lay hold		124:99
now the s. was more subtle	Mses	4: 5
put it into the heart of the s.,		4: 6
spake by the mouth of the s.)		4: 7
the woman said unto the s.:		4: 8
And the s. said unto the woman:		4:10
s. beguiled me, and I did eat.		4:19
the Lord God, said unto the s.:		4:20

SERPENT'S
out of the s. root shall come	2Ne	24:29

SERPENTS

SERPENTS
he sent fiery flying s. among	1 Ne 17:41
been bitten by the poisonous s.,	2 Ne 25:20
wild beasts nor poisonous s.,	Mrm 8:24
they shall take up s.;	9:24
there came forth poisonous s.	Eth 9:31
flee before the poisonous s.,	9:31
the Lord did cause the s. that	9:33
might fall by the poisonous s.	9:33
the poisonous s. were destroyed.	10:19
and against poisonous s.,	DC 24:13
be ye as wise as s. and yet	111:11

SERVANT
behold, I saw the s. of Laban	1 Ne 4:20
when the s. of laban beheld	4:30
I did seize upon the s. of Laban,	4:31
Zoram was the name of the s.;	4:35
plates of brass and the s. of Laban,	4:38
hath redeemed his s. Jacob.	20:20
Thou art my s., O Israel,	21: 3
I should be his s., to bring	21: 5
that thou shouldst be my s. to	21: 6
to s. of rulers: Kings shall see	21: 7
give thee my s. for a covenant	21: 8
thou art the s. of Laban;	2 Ne 1:30
that obeyeth the voice of his s.,	7:10
and he employeth no s. there;	9:41
and he said unto his s.:	Jac 5: 7
the s. of the Lord of the	5:10
saying unto his s.:	5:11
of the vineyard said unto his s.:	5:15
and also the s., went down	5:16
the s. said unto his master:	5:16
And he said unto the s.:	5:18
of the vineyard said unto the s.:	5:19
and he said unto the s.:	5:20
And he said unto the s.:	5:20
the s. said unto his master:	5:21
of the vineyard said unto his s.:	5:23
said again unto his s.:	5:24
And he said unto the s.:	5:25
of the vineyard said unto the s.:	5:26
behold, the s. said unto him:	5:27
the s. of the Lord of the	5:28
of the vineyard said unto his s.:	5:29
and the s. went down into the	5:30
of the vineyard said unto the s.:	5:33
And the s. said unto his master:	5:34
of the vineyard said unto his s.:	5:35
of the vineyard said unto his s.:	5:38
wept, and said unto the s.:	5:41
the s. said unto his master:	5:48
of the vineyard said unto the s.:	5:49
the s. said unto the Lord of the	5:50
of the vineyard said unto the s.:	5:57
of the vineyard sent his s.;	5:70
and the s. went and did as the	5:70
nor thy daughter, thy man-s.,	Mos 13:18
man-servant, nor thy maid-s.	13:18
neighbor's wife, nor his man-s.,	13:24
his man-servant, nor his maid-s.,	13:24
my righteous s. justify many;	14:11
pour out thy Spirit upon thy s.,	18:12
himself an unworthy s.	21:33
me to be an unprofitable s.,	22: 4
and I will be thy s. and deliver	22: 4
words alone of my s. Abinadi.	26:15
Thou art my s.; and I covenant	26:20
also the prayers of his s., Alma,	27:14
ye give to an humble s. of God	Al 8:19
and also say unto my s. Amulek,	8:29
Nay, but I will be thy s.	17:25
Therefore Ammon became a s. to	17:25
there has not been any s. among	18:10
I am a man and am thy s.;	18:17
the woman s. who had caused	19:28
should serve him, or be his s.	21:19
prepare unto my s. Gazelem, a	37:23
the same s. that slew the king,	47:34
Teancum and his s. stole forth	51:33
sent it by the s. of Ammoron,	54: 4
did awake his s. before he died,	62:36

SERVANT

when the s. of Helaman had	He 2: 8
the s. of Helaman said unto	2: 8
but behold, the s. of Helaman,	2: 9
my s. shall deal prudently;	3 Ne 20:43
the life of my s. shall be in	21:10
I commanded my s. Samuel,	23: 9
ye the law of Moses, my s.,	25: 4
and do not be angry with thy s.	Eth 3: 2
to be written by my s. John	4:16
a man being a s. of the devil	Mro 7:11
he cannot be a s. of the devil.	7:11
upon my s. Joseph Smith, Jun.,	DC 1:17
even my s. Joseph Smith, Jun.,	1:29
as my s. Martin Harris has	5: 1
you, my s. Joseph Smith, Jun.,	5: 1
you, my s. Joseph Smith, Jun.,	5: 2
not believe you, my s. Joseph,	5: 7
unto you, my s. Joseph,	5: 9
command you, my s. Joseph,	5:21
speak unto you, my s. Joseph,	5:23
him, my s. Martin Harris,	5:26
command you, my s. Joseph,	5:29
my s. Martin Harris humbleth	5:32
stand by my s. Joseph,	6:18
translate, even as my s. Joseph.	6:25
and also unto my s. Joseph,	6:28
for my s., Joseph Smith, Jun.,	9: 1
is to write for my s. Joseph.	9: 4
my s. Joseph sufficient strength,	9:12
Hearken, my s. John, and listen	15: 1
Hearken, my s. Peter, and listen	16: 1
do that my s. Joseph Smith, Jun.,	17: 4
as my s. Joseph Smith, Jun.,	17: 5
you, my s. Oliver Cowdery,	18: 1
of my s. Joseph Smith, Jun.,	18: 7
of my s. Joseph Smith, Jun.,	19:13
unto my s., Joseph Smith, Jun.,	25: 5
send my s., Oliver Cowdery,	25: 6
my s. Joseph Smith, Jun.,	28: 2
my s. Joseph shall be appointed	28:10
I say unto you, my s. John,	30: 9
to my s., Joseph Smith, Jun.	31: 4
my s. Parley P. Pratt,	32: 1
verily, I say unto my s. Sidney,	35: 3
by the hand of my s. Joseph;	35:17
I say unto you, my s. Edward,	36: 1
hand of my s. Sidney Rigdon,	36: 2
that my s. Oliver Cowdery	37: 3
I say unto you, my s. James,	39: 7
heart of my s. James Covil	40: 1
that my s. Joseph Smith, Jun.,	41: 7
meet that my s. Sidney Rigdon	41: 8
called my s. Edward Partridge;	41: 9
my s. Edward Partridge shall	42:10
ye my s. Joseph Smith, Jun.,	43:12
that my s. John should write	47: 1
and assist you, my s. Joseph,	47: 1
my s. Leman shall be ordained	49: 4
he is the least and the s. of all.	50:26
mine from the mouth of my s.,	50:36
Let my s. Joseph Wakefield,	50:37
my s. Parley P. Pratt go forth	50:37
And also my s. John Corrill,	50:38
my s. Edward Partridge is not	50:39
unto my s. Edward Partridge,	51: 1
let my s. Edward Partridge,	51: 3
let my s. Edward Partridge,	51: 4
unto my s. Edward Partridge,	51:18
let my s. Lyman Wight and	52: 7
and my s. John Corrill take	52: 7
also my s. John Murdock,	52: 8
and my s. Hyrum Smith,	52: 8
let my s. Lyman Wight beware,	52:12
let my s. Thomas B. Marsh	52:22
and my s. Ezra Thayre take	52:22
let my s. Isaac Morley and	52:23
and my s. Ezra Booth take	52:23
for my s. Oliver Cowdery also.	52:41
unto you, my s. Sidney Gilbert,	53: 1
unto you, my s. Newel Knight,	54: 2
unto you, my s. William,	55: 1
of my s. Joseph Smith, Jun.,	55: 2
assist my s. Oliver Cowdery	55: 4

SERVANT

let my s. Joseph Coe also take	DC 55: 6
unto my s. Thomas,	56: 5
and my s. Selah J. Griffin shall	56: 5
let my s. Newel Knight	56: 7
my s. Ezra Thayre must	56: 8
if my s. Joseph Smith, Jun., must	56:12
let my s. Sidney Gilbert stand	57: 6
let my s. Edward Partridge stand	57: 7
let my s. Sidney Gilbert plant	57: 8
also let my s. Sidney Gilbert	57: 9
let my s. William W. Phelps	57:11
let my s. Oliver Cowdery assist	57:13
my s. Edward Partridge,	58:14
my s. Edward Partridge,	58:24
a slothful and not a wise s.;	58:26
my s. Martin Harris should be	58:35
concerning my s. Martin Harris	58:38
let my s. William W. Phelps	58:40
unto my s. Sidney Rigdon	58:50
And let my s. Sidney Rigdon	58:57
let my s. Edward Partridge direct	58:62
let my s. Edward Partridge	60:10
of my s. Joseph Smith, Jun.,	60:17
that my s. Sidney Gilbert and	61: 7
and my s. William W. Phelps	61: 7
Let my s. Sidney Gilbert take	61:12
by the mouth of my s. John,	61:14
let my s. Reynolds Cahoon,	61:35
and my s. Samuel H. Smith,	61:35
Let my s. Titus Billings,	63:39
unto my s. Joseph Smith, Jun.,	63:41
Let my s. Newel K. Whitney	63:42
with my s. Oliver Cowdery	63:46
with my s. Sidney Rigdon;	63:55
from my s. Joseph Smith, Jun.,	64: 5
who was my s. Ezra Booth,	64:15
and also my s. Isaac Morley,	64:15
forgiven my s. Isaac Morley.	64:16
also my s. Edward Partridge,	64:17
that my s. Sidney Gilbert,	64:18
my s. Isaac Morley may not	64:20
my s. Frederick G. Williams	64:21
my s. William E. M'Lellin—	66: 1
I say unto you, my s. William,	66: 3
Let my s. Samuel H. Smith go	66: 8
upon my s. Joseph Smith, Jun.,	67: 5
of my s. Joseph Smith, Jun.	67:14
My s., Orson Hyde, was called	68: 1
unto you, my s. Orson Hyde,	68: 7
also unto my s. Luke Johnson,	68: 7
unto my s. Lyman Johnson,	68: 7
my s. William E. M'Lellin,	68: 7
let my s. Oliver Cowdery carry	68:32
my s. Oliver Cowdery's sake.	69: 1
will that my s., John Whitmer,	69: 2
go with my s. Oliver Cowdery;	69: 2
from my s. Oliver Cowdery	69: 4
let my s. John Whitmer travel	69: 7
unto my s. Joseph Smith, Jun.,	70: 1
also unto my s. Martin Harris,	70: 1
unto my s. Oliver Cowdery,	70: 1
unto my s. John Whitmer,	70: 1
also unto my s. Sidney Rigdon,	70: 1
unto my s. William W. Phelps,	70: 1
my s. Newel K. Whitney is	72: 8
unto my s. William E. M'Lellin,	75: 6
let my s. Luke Johnson go	75: 9
let my s. Orson Hyde and	75:13
and my s. Samuel H. Smith	75:13
unto my s. Lyman Johnson,	75:14
and unto my s. Orson Pratt,	75:14
I say unto my s. Asa Dodds,	75:15
unto my s. Calves Wilson,	75:15
unto my s. Major N. Ashley,	75:17
and my s. Burr Riggs,	75:17
let my s. Simeon Carter and	75:30
and my s. Emer Harris be	75:30
And also my s. Ezra Thayre	75:31
and my s. Thomas B. Marsh;	75:31
Also my s. Hyrum Smith	75:32
and my s. Reynolds Cahoon;	75:32
also my s. Daniel Stanton	75:33
my s. Seymour Brunson;	DC 75:33
also my s. Sylvester Smith	75:34
and my s. Gideon Carter;	75:34
also my s. Ruggles Eames	75:35
and my s. Stephen Burnett;	75:35
also my s. Micah B. Welton	75:36
and also my s. Eden Smith.	75:36
let my s. Ahashdah (Newel K.	78: 9
and my s. Gazelam, or Enoch	78: 9
and my s. Pelagoram [Sidney	78: 9
my s. Jared Carter should go	79: 1
be glad, my s. Jared Carter,	79: 4
you my s. Stephen Burnett:	80: 1
unto you my s. Eden Smith.	80: 2
my s. Frederick G. Williams:	81: 1
unto my s. Joseph Smith, Jun.;	81: 1
my s. Gazelam [Joseph Smith],	82:11
unto his s. Joseph Smith, Jun.,	84: 1
mine aged s., Joseph Smith, Sen.,	90:20
aged s. Joseph Smith's, Sen.,	90:25
my s. William E. M'Lellin,	90:35
with my s. Sidney Gilbert;	90:35
my s. Shederlaomach	92: 1
unto you my s. Shederlaomach	92: 2
my s. Frederick G. Williams,	93:41
s. unto my s. Sidney Rigdon,	93:44
unto my s. Joseph Smith, Jun.,	93:45
My s. Newel K. Whitney also,	93:50
let my S. Sidney Rigdon go	93:51
my s. Hyrum Smith receive	94:13
let my s. Ahashdah [Newel K.	96: 2
my s. Zombre [John Johnson]	96: 6
also with my s. Parley P. Pratt,	97: 3
law I gave unto my s. Nephi,	98:32
unto my s. John Murdock—	99: 1
you, my s. Sidney, should be	100: 9
spokesman unto my s. Joseph.	100: 9
And the s. said unto his lord:	101:59
And he said unto his s.:	101:60
And his s. went straightway,	101:62
my s. Sidney Gilbert	101:96
my s. Baurak Ale [Joseph Smith,	103:21
the s. to whom the Lord of	103:21
my s. Baurak Ale [Joseph Smith,	103:22
my s. Sidney Rigdon shall lift	103:29
that my s. Parley P. Pratt and	103:30
my s. Lyman Wight should	103:30
my s. Baurak Ale [Joseph Smith,	103:35
Let my s. Parley P. Pratt	103:37
with my s. Joseph Smith, Jun.	103:37
Let my s. Lyman Wight	103:38
with my s. Sidney Rigdon.	103:38
Let my s. Hyrum Smith	103:39
my s. Frederick G. Williams.	103:39
Let my s. Orson Hyde	103:40
with my s. Orson Pratt,	103:40
my s. Joseph Smith, Jun.,	103:40
my s. Pelagoram [Sidney Rigdon]	104:20
my s. Pelagoram [Sidney Rigdon]	104:22
my s. Mahemson [Martin Harris]	104:24
my s. Zombre [John Johnson]	104:24
my s. Mahemson [Martin Harris]	104:26
my s. Gazelam [Joseph Smith,	104:26
my s. Shederlaomach [Frederick	104:27
my s. Olihah [Oliver Cowdery]	104:28
my s. Zombre [John Johnson]	104:34
my s. Olihah [Oliver Cowdery]	104:34
let my s. Ahashdah [Newel K.	104:39
unto my s. Ahashdah [Newel K.	104:40
unto my s. Ahashdah [N. K.	104:41
my s. Gazelam [Joseph Smith,	104:43
my s. Gazelam [Joseph Smith,	104:45
my s. Gazelam [Joseph Smith,	104:46
my s. Baurak Ale [Joseph Smith,	105:16
as my s. Joseph shall appoint	105:21
my s. Baurak Ale [Joseph Smith,	105:27
shall be manifest unto my s.,	105:36
It is my will that my s.	106: 1
was joy in heaven when my s.	106: 6
blessed is my s. Warren,	106: 7
Lord unto you, my s. Lyman:	108: 1
against thy s. or servants,	109:29

SERVANT

remember thy s. Joseph Smith,	DC 109:68
Lord unto you my s. Thomas:	112: 1
rebel not against my s. Joseph;	112:15
I say unto you, my s. Thomas,	112:16
be my s. to unlock the door	112:17
in all places where my s. Joseph,	112:17
Joseph, and my s. Sidney,	112:17
and my s. Hyrum, cannot come;	112:17
It is a s. in the hands of Christ,	113: 4
It is wisdom in my s. David	114: 1
my s. Joseph Smith, Jun.,	115: 1
and also my s. Sidney Rigdon,	115: 1
and also my s. Hyrum Smith,	115: 1
my s. Edward Partridge,	115: 2
let not my s. Joseph,	115:13
neither my s. Sidney,	115:13
neither my s. Hyrum,	115:13
my s. Joseph and his counselors,	115:16
manifested unto my s. Joseph,	115:18
unto my s. William Marks,	117: 1
unto my s. Newel K. Whitney,	117: 1
Let my s. William Marks be	117:10
Let my s. Newel K. Whitney	117:11
remember my s. Oliver Granger;	117:12
despise my s. Oliver Granger,	117:15
Let my s. Thomas remain for	118: 2
Let my s. John Taylor,	118: 6
also my s. John E. Page,	118: 6
and also my s. Wilford Woodruff,	118: 6
and also my s. Willard Richards,	118: 6
unto you, my s. Joseph Smith,	124: 1
let my s. Robert B. Thompson	124:12
blessed is my s. Hyrum Smith;	124:15
let my s. John C. Bennett help	124:16
even you my s. Joseph Smith,	124:16
that my s. Lyman Wight	124:18
even as I did my s. David Patten,	124:19
and also my s. Edward Partridge,	124:19
my aged s. Joseph Smith, Sen.,	124:19
s. George Miller is without guile;	124:20
like unto my s. Edward Partridge,	124:21
no man despise my s. George,	124:21
Let my s. George, and my	124:22
servant George, and my s. Lyman,	124:22
Lyman, and my s. John Snider,	124:22
one as my s. Joseph shall show	124:22
will show unto my s. Joseph	124:42
my s. Joseph and his house	124:56
even so I say unto my s. Joseph:	124:58
let my s. Joseph and his seed	124:59
let my s. George Miller,	124:62
and my s. Lyman Wight,	124:62
and my s. John Snider,	124:62
and my s. Peter Haws,	124:62
if my s. George Miller,	124:70
and my s. Lyman Wight,	124:70
and my s. John Snider,	124:70
and my s. Peter Haws,	124:70
let my s. Joseph pay stock into	124:72
my s. Joseph cannot pay over	124:72
my s. Vinson Knight,	124:74
my s. Hyrum put stock into	124:77
Let my s. Isaac Galland put stock	124:78
Let my s. Isaac Galland be	124:79
ordained by my s. William Marks,	124:79
to go with my s. Hyrum to	124:79
work that my s. Joseph shall	124:79
Let my s. William Marks pay	124:80
Let my s. Henry G. Sherwood	124:81
Let my s. William Law pay	124:82
with my s. Almon Babbitt,	124:84
my s. William put his trust in me,	124:87
my s. William go and proclaim	124:88
the counsel of my s. Joseph,	124:89
let my s. William be appointed,	124:91
counselor unto my s. Joseph,	124:91
in the room of my s. Hyrum,	124:91
that my s. Hyrum may take	124:91
as well as my s. Joseph;	124:94
also with my s. Joseph;	124:95
counsel from my s. Joseph,	124:95
was my s. Oliver Cowdery:	124:95
my s. Hyrum may bear record	124:96

SERVANTS

Let my s. William Law	DC 124:97
let my s. William Cry aloud and	124:101
in store for my s. William,	124:102
William, and my s. Hyrum,	124:102
my s. Joseph tarry at home,	124:102
if my s. Sidney will serve me	124:103
be counselor unto my s. Joseph,	124:103
in which my s. Joseph resides.	124:105
Let him assist my s. Joseph,	124:107
let my s. William Law assist	124:107
William Law assist my s. Joseph,	124:107
my s. Sidney will do my will,	124:108
let my s. Amos Davids pay stock	124:111
counsel of my s. Joseph,	124:112
my s. Robert D. Foster will obey	124:115
build a house for my s. Joseph,	124:115
I give unto you my s. Joseph	124:125
for counselors my s. Sidney Rigdon	124:126
and my s. William Law,	124:126
my s. Brigham Young to be	124:127
s. Aaron Johnson be ordained	124:132
unto them by my s. Joseph,	125: 2
Lord unto you: My s. Brigham,	126: 1
I subscribe myself your s. in the	127:12
I am, as ever, your humble s.	128:25
the Lord unto you my s. Joseph,	132: 1
appointed unto my s. Joseph	132: 7
whatsoever my s. hath put upon	132:19
ye are, namely, my s. Joseph—	132:30
by the hand of Nathan, my s.,	132:39
I gave unto thee, my s. Joseph,	132:40
reveal it unto you, my s. Joseph,	132:44
I say unto you, my s. Joseph,	132:48
been given unto my s. Joseph,	132:52
I give unto my s. Joseph that	132:53
and cleave unto my s. Joseph,	132:54
my s. Joseph do all things for her,	132:55
handmaid forgive my s. Joseph	132:56
not my s. Joseph put his property	132:57
the Lord thy God, and he is my s.;	132:57
therefore, set on my s. Joseph;	132:60
saying: Be merciful unto thy s.,	Mses 1:36
and then thy s. will be content.	1:36
I spake unto my s. Moses,	4:32
wherefore am I thy s.?	6:31
Thy s. has sought thee earnestly;	Abr 2:12
let thy s. rise up and depart	2:13
then, is a faithful and wise s.,	JS 1:49
Blessed is that s. whom his	1:50
if that evil s. shall say in his	1:51
The lord of that s. shall come	1:53

SERVANTS

and sent his s. to slay us,	1Ne 3:25
we did flee before the s. of Laban,	3:26
the s. of Laban did not overtake	3:27
shall be for s. and handmaids;	2Ne 24: 2
Wherefore, go to, and call s.,	Jac 5:61
and brought other s.;	5:70
that the s. did go and labor	5:72
he called up his s., and said unto	5:75
the s. of the Lord shall go forth	6: 2
yet ye would be unprofitable s.	Mos 2:21
and sent his s. after him	17: 3
fled from the s. of king Noah,	18: 1
sent his s. to watch them.	18:32
that the prayers of his s. might be	27:14
he was set among other s. to	Al 17:25
he was with the Lamanitish s.	17:26
Ammon and the s. of the king	17:27
of Ammon and the s. of the king,	17:27
the s. of the king began to	17:28
power unto these my fellow-s.,	17:29
the hearts of these my fellow-s.,	17:29
that his s. should stand forth	18: 1
had done wrong in slaying his s.	18: 5
king Lamoni inquired of his s.,	18: 8
the king had commanded his s.,	18: 9
any servant among all my s.	18:10
chariots for the king and his s.,	18:12
one of the king's s. said unto	18:13
I defended thy s. and thy flocks,	18:16
to defend thy flocks and thy s.;	18:16

SERVANTS 869 SERVANTS

was unto the king and to his s.)	Al 18:37	
his s. took him and carried him	18:43	
the s. of my husband have made it	19: 4	
thy word, and the word of our s.;	19: 9	
when the s. of the king had seen	19:15	
saw that all the s. of Lamoni	19:17	
their s. prostrate upon the earth,	19:18	
because he slew his s. who had	19:20	
also did all the s. of Lamoni;	19:33	
that his s. should make ready	20: 6	
spare our lives, we will be thy s.	22: 3	
not suffer that ye shall be my s.;	22: 3	
his s. ran and told the queen all	22:19	
that her s., or the servants of	22:19	
or the s. of the king, should	22:19	
Now the s. had seen the cause of	22:20	
the queen saw the fear of the s.	22:21	
And she commanded her s. that	22:21	
of the queen and many fo the s.	22:23	
thy s. shall dwell here below	31:26	
one of his s. should administer	47:18	
his s. should go forth to meet	47:22	
Now the s. of the king fled;	47:25	
s. of Amalickiah raised a cry,	47:25	
the s. of the king have stabbed	47:26	
pursue his s. that they may be	47:27	
pursued after the s. of the king.	47:28	
when the s. of the king saw an	47:29	
king had been slain by his s.,	47:32	
king was slain by his own s.;	47:34	
assistance of his cunning s.,	47:35	
angry with one of his maid s.,	50:30	
that he did not awake his s.	51:34	
one of the s. of the king who	55: 5	
pursued by the s. of Pahoran;	He 1:10	
behold one of the s. of Helaman,	2: 6	
were cast by the s. of Limhi.	5:21	
seek no more to destroy my s.	5:29	
seek no more to destroy my s.	5:32	
the s. ran and told the people,	9: 6	
down to be s. to their words,	16:21	
words, and also s. unto them,	16:21	
unto you, and to be your s.;	3Ne 12: 1	
heritage of the s. of the Lord,	22:17	
and the authority of my s.,	DC 1: 6	
neither the voice of his s.,	1:14	
unto my s. in their weakness,	1:24	
voice or by the voice of my s.,	1:38	
testimony of three of my s.,	5:11	
the hands of the s. of Satan	10: 5	
Upon you my fellow s., in the	13: 1	
my s., Joseph Smith, Jun., and	27: 8	
that he shall go with my s.,	32: 2	
my s. Ezra and Northrop,	33: 1	
my s. Sidney Rigdon and	36: 5	
excepting my s. Joseph Smith,	42: 4	
my s. shall be sent forth to	42:63	
upon you by the mouth of my s.,	43:25	
spoken by the mouth of my s.,	43:30	
saith the Lord unto you my s.,	44: 1	
my s. Sidney, and Parley,	49: 1	
my s. Sidney and Parley,	49: 3	
be taught him by you my s.;	49: 4	
as many of my s. as are	50:38	
let my s. Joseph Smith, Jun.,	52: 3	
let my s. Edward Partridge	52:24	
with my s. Sidney Rigdon and	52:24	
Let my s. David Whitmer	52:25	
let my s. Parley P. Pratt	52:26	
let my s. Solomon Hancock	52:27	
Let my s. Edson Fuller and	52:28	
Let my s. Levi W. Hancock	52:29	
Let my s. Reynolds Cahoon and	52:30	
Let my s. Wheeler Baldwin and	52:31	
let my s. Newel Knight and	52:32	
let my s. Joseph Wakefield	52:35	
let my s. Joseph Smith, Jun.,	52:41	
with my s. Joseph Smith, Jun.,	53: 5	
my s. Joseph Smith, Jun.,	55: 5	
unto my s. Thomas B. Marsh	56: 5	
my s. Selah J. Griffin and	56: 6	
let my s. Sidney Rigdon and	58:58	
let my s., Sidney Rigdon,	60: 6	
let my s. Sidney Gilbert	DC 61: 9	
concerning my s., Sidney	61:23	
my s., Sidney Rigdon, Joseph	61:30	
Let my s., Joseph Smith, Jun.,	63:65	
my s., Newel K, Whitney and	64:26	
the Lord unto you, O ye my s.	68: 5	
my s. who are abroad in the	69: 5	
I give unto my s. for their	70:15	
my s. Joseph Smith, Jun., and	71: 1	
let my s. who are appointed	72:20	
verily I say unto you my s.,	73: 3	
be s. of the Most High;	76:112	
have sealed the s. of our God	77: 9	
verily, I say unto you, my s.,	82: 1	
for my s. Alam and Ahashdah	82:11	
For he that receiveth my s.	84:36	
unto you, the rest of my s.,	84:117	
the Lord unto you my s.,	86: 1	
he sent forth his s. into	88:51	
I called you s. for the world's	93:46	
ye are their s. for my sake—	93:46	
let my s. Joseph Smith, Jun.,	93:52	
my s. Reynolds Cahoon and	94:14	
my s. sinned a very grievous	95:10	
my s. Orson Hyde and John	100:14	
and he said unto his s.:	101:44	
the s. of the nobleman went	101:46	
the s. of the nobleman arose	101:51	
called upon his s., and said	101:52	
said unto one of his s.:	101:55	
together the residue of my s.,	101:55	
middle age also among all my s.,	101:55	
some of my s. have not kept	104: 4	
And let my s. Shederlaomach	104:29	
assembly shall be called of my s.	108: 4	
and showest mercy unto thy s.	109: 1	
commanded thy s. to build	109: 2	
thy s. have done according to	109: 3	
of the hands of us, thy s.,	109: 4	
that thy s. may go forth from	109:22	
against thy servant or s.,	109:29	
that thy s. have been innocent	109:31	
off from the necks of thy s.,	109:33	
Put upon thy s. the testimony	109:38	
whatsoever city thy s. shall enter,	109:39	
whatsoever city thy s. shall enter,	109:41	
not the testimony of thy s.,	109:41	
s. warn them to save themselves	109:41	
thy s. from their hands,	109:42	
Help thy s. to say, with thy	109:44	
enable thy s. to seal up the law,	109:46	
when thy s. shall go out from	109:56	
earth may know that we, thy s.,	109:57	
thy s., the sons of Jacob,	109:58	
Yea, I will appear unto my s.,	110: 8	
which my s. have been endowed	110: 9	
through the instrumentality of my s.	112: 1	
And also unto my faithful s.	115: 3	
my s. in the land of Kirtland	117:16	
of thy people and of thy s.,	121: 2	
s. will rejoice in thy name	121: 6	
they are the s. of sin,	121:17	
swear falsely against my s.,	121:18	
if they reject my s. and	124: 8	
the voice of my s. whom I	124:45	
the counsel of my s. Joseph, and	124:118	
standing presidents or s.	124:134	
justified my s. Abraham, Isaac,	132: 1	
David and Solomon, my s.,	132: 1	
which angels are ministering s.,	132:16	
also Solomon and Moses my s.,	132:38	
as many others of my s.,	132:38	
the children of Ephraim, my s.	133:30	
by the hands of the s. of the Lord,	133:32	
the s. of God shall go forth,	133:38	
ye believed not my s.,	133:71	
to interfere with bond-s.;	134:12	
Let my s. Ezra T. Benson and	136:12	
And let my s. Orson Pratt and	136:13	
let my s. Amasa Lyman and	136:14	
my s. that have been appointed	136:16	
mine angels, my ministering s.,	136:37	
and by the mouths of my s.,	Mses 6:30	

SERVANTS

begin to smite his fellow-s.,	JS	1:52
Upon you my fellow s.,		2:69

SERVE
if it so be that they shall s. him	2Ne	1: 7
wherein thou wast made to s.		24: 3
to s. you with all the might,	Mos	2:11
own hands that I might s. you,		2:14
your king, do labor to s. you,		2:18
ye to labor to s. one another?		2:18
should s. him who has created you		2:21
s. him with all your whole souls		2:21
and s. the devil, who is the		4:14
and to s. one another.		4:15
s. him with all diligence of mind,		7:33
thyself unto them, nor s. them;		13:13
that ye will s. him and keep his		18:10
to s. him until you are dead as to		18:13
a covenant with God to s. him		21:31
to s. him and keep		21:32
that they were willing to s. God		21:35
and thou shalt s. me and go forth		26:20
suffer that Ammon should s. him,	Al	21:19
did s. to strengthen their faith		25:16
ye this day, whom ye will s.		30: 8
Now if a man desired to s. God,		30: 9
God it was his privilege to s. him;		30: 9
discover unto my people who s. me,		37:23
a time to repent and s. God.		42: 4
try again if they will s. thee?	He	11:16
did s. God with all diligence	3Ne	5: 3
No man can s. two masters;		13:24
Ye cannot s. God and Mammon		13:24
It is vain to s. God, and what		24:14
will s. the true and living God.	Mrm	9:28
s. him, the true and only God,	Eth	2: 8
shall possess it shall s. God,		2: 9
doth possess it shall s. God		2:10
if they will but s. the God of		2:12
did make him s. in captivity;		8: 3
Levi did s. in captivity after		10:15
all men should s. him who dwell		13: 2
to s. him to the end.	Mro	6: 3
and to love God, and to s. him,		7:13
and deny him, and s. not God,		7:17
see that ye s. him with all your	DC	4: 2
if ye have desires to s. God		4: 3
they should love and s. him,		20:19
who love and s. God with all		20:31
to s. him to the end,		20:37
and they s. him obediently,		38:26
lovest me thou shalt s. me		42:29
Jesus Christ thou shalt s. him.		59: 5
who s. me in righteousness		76: 5
that will s. me in righteousness;		100:16
if my servant Sidney will s. me		124:103
for him only shalt thou s.	Mses	1:15
to s. the Lord God who made you.		6:33

SERVED
unto you that I had s. you,	Mos	2:27
the master whom he has not s.,		5:13
he s. many years in captivity,	Eth	10:30

SERVETH
spareth his own son that s. him.	3Ne	24:17
between him the s. God and		24:18
God and him that s. him not.		24:18

SERVICE
be spent in the s. of thy God.	2Ne	2: 3
to spend my days in your s.,	Mos	2:12
had spent my days in your s.,		2:16
have only been in the s. of God.		2:16
in the s. of your fellow beings		2:17
are only in the s. of your God.		2:17
has spent his days in your s.,		2:19
yet has been in the s. of God,		2:19
they have been of s. to thee,		22: 4
in the s. of the king three days,	Al	17:26
that embark in the s. of God,	DC	4: 2
devote all thy s. in Zion;		24: 7

as clerks employed in his s.;	DC	57: 9
employed in the s. of Mr. Stoal.	JS	2:57

SERVICEABLE
no less s. unto the people than	Al	48:19

SERVICES
just remuneration for all their s.,	DC	42:72
for all his s. in the church.		42:73

SERVITUDE
human beings to be held in s.	DC	134:12

SET
and s. an example for you?	1Ne	7: 8
I never had before s. my foot.		11: 1
others s. at naught and trample		19: 7
they s. him at naught,		19: 7
and s. up my standard to the		21:22
and s. them up for a standard,		22: 6
s. up my standard to the people;	2Ne	6: 6
s. himself again the second time		6:14
have I s. my face like a flint,		7: 7
for they s. it aside, supposing		9:28
instead of well s. hair, baldness;		13:24
and s. a king in the midst of it,		17: 6
Lord shall s. up the adversaries		19:11
the Lord shall s. his hand again		21:11
s. up an ensign for the nations,		21:12
and s. them in their own land;		24: 1
the Lord will s. his hand again		25:17
and s. themselves up for a light		26:29
that I may s. my hand again		29: 1
having s. the example before them.		31: 9
that ye have s. before them;	Jac	3:10
that he shall s. his hand again		6: 2
I s. guards round about the land,	Mos	10: 2
were s. apart for the high priests,		11:11
do ye s. your hearts upon riches?		12:29
that was s. apart that they should		18:25
s. guards round about the land,		19:28
s. guards round about the land		23:37
not s. their hearts upon riches;	Al	1:30
the mark which was s. upon their		3: 6
Lord God s. a mark upon them,		3: 7
there was a mark s. upon him.		3:10
also had a mark s. upon them;		3:13
s. the mark upon themselves,		3:13
and I will s. a mark on them		3:14
I will s. a mark upon him that		3:15
I will s. a mark upon him that		3:16
to s. their hearts upon riches		4: 8
that ye have s. at defiance the		5:18
not s. your hearts upon riches;		7: 6
and meat and s. before Alma.		8:21
to s. my back towards this land		8:24
thou mightest s. them against us,		12: 4
their hearts were s. upon riches,		17:14
he was s. among other servants		17:25
we will s. our armies between the		27:23
the Nephites were s. round about		28: 1
their hearts were s. upon gold,		31:24
their hearts are s. upon them,		31:28
not s. a good example for these?		39: 9
did s. guards over the prisoners		53: 1
against us are s. at defiance,		61: 7
and s. out again to the land		63: 7
s. at naught the commandments	He	4:21
s. their hearts upon their riches;		6:17
s. your hearts upon the riches		7:21
that the five were s. at liberty,		9:38
to s. their hearts upon the vain		12: 4
they do s. at naught his counsels,		12: 6
have s. their hearts upon riches;		13:20
s. their hearts upon their riches,		13:20
have s. your hearts upon them,		13:21
day s. apart by the unbelievers,	3Ne	1: 9
no more were s. at liberty.		5: 4
did s. at defiance the law and		6:30
A city that is s. on a hill cannot		12:14
s. them down upon the ground		17:12
I have s. an example for you.		18:16
and be s. up as a free people by		21: 4

| SET | 871 | SEVENTH |

that work wickedness are s. up;	3Ne	24:15
which shall be s. before you,	Mrm	7: 8
and s. forth into the sea,	Eth	6: 4
s. their feet upon the shores of		6:12
for he had s. his heart upon		8: 7
men s. at naught the counsels	DC	3: 7
has s. at naught the counsels of		3:13
to those who were s. over you,		30: 2
and s. apart for that purpose.		42:31
then shall the Lord s. his foot		45:48
he hath s. you to provide for		64:30
which is s. up on the earth.		65: 5
be s. apart unto the church,		68:14
he is called and s. apart and		68:19
high priest who shall be s. apart		68:22
his feet, and s. him upon high,		78:16
s. in order the house of God,		85: 7
s. in order the churches,		90:15
and s. in order all the affairs of		90:16
S. in order your houses;		90:18
s. in order your own house,		93:43
first s. in order thy house.		93:44
and s. in order his family,		93:50
this stake that I have s. for		96: 1
s. watchmen round about them,		101:45
and s. watchmen, and began		101:46
s. watchmen upon the walls		101:53
s. a watchman upon the tower,		101:53
they were s. to be a light unto		103: 9
have the lot which is s. off		104:28
provided he is called and s. apart		107:17
I have s. thee to be at the head;		107:55
to ordain and s. in order all the		107:58
s. apart unto the ministering of		107:71
be s. apart unto this ministry,		107:74
which thou hast s. up without hands,		109:72
God hath s. his hand and seal to		121:12
revealed and s. forth upon all who		121:29
bounds s. to the heavens or to		121:30
all their glories, laws, and s. times,		121:31
hearts are s. so much upon the		121:35
for their bounds are s.,		122: 9
the s. time has come to favor her.		124: 6
s. to be as plants of renown,		124:61
or any s. of men,		128: 9
and the gods, which are s. there,		132:19
s. on my servant Joseph;		132:60
God, s. them in the firmament of	Mses	2:17
I the Lord s. a mark upon Cain,		5:40
their hearts were s. to do evil,	Abr	1: 6
I have s. this one to govern all		3: 3
of reckoning, and the s. time,		3: 6
the s. time of the earth upon		3: 6
the s. time of the greater light		3: 6
light which is s. to rule the day,		3: 6
the s. time of the lesser light		3: 6
which is s. to rule the night.		3: 6
the s. time of the lesser light is		3: 7
Kolob is s. nigh unto the throne		3: 9
know the s. time of all the stars		3:10
stars that are s. to give light,		3:10
with the lesser light they s. the		4:16
the Gods s. them in the expanse		4:17

SETH
And Ahah was the son of S.	Eth	1:10
And S. was the son of Shiblon.		1:11
S. was brought into captivity,		11: 9
is a descendant of S. [Joseph]	DC	96: 7
From Adam to S., who was		107:42
he (S.) was a perfect man,		107:43
was ordained under the hand of S.		107:51
he called S., Enos, Cainan,		107:53
son, and he called his name S.	Mses	6: 2
God revealed himself unto S.,		6: 3
image, and called his name S.		6:10
Adam, after he had begotten S.,		6:11
S. lived one hundred and five		6:13
S. lived, after he begat Enos,		6:14
days of S. were nine hundred		6:16
as also to S., Noah, Melchizedek,	Fac	2: 3

SETS
and s. at naught the counsels	DC	3: 4

SETTETH
s. at naught the atonement of	Mro	8:20
s. up a golden calf for the	DC	124:84

SETTING
s. your hearts upon the vain	Al	5:53
of the sun and also of its s.;	He	14: 4
s. forth clearly and	DC	84:117

SETTLE
begun to s. the affairs of their	Al	51:12
assist to s. all these things,	DC	28:14
That she may s. down in peace		90:31
to s. difficulties, when the parties		102:24
that he s. up all his business		114: 1
let them s. up their business		117: 1

SETTLED
was s. by the voice of the people.	Al	51: 7
which affairs were s. in the	He	3: 1
the more s. parts of the land,		3:23
there was peace s. in the land;	Mrm	1:12
could not be s. by the church	DC	102: 2
who afterward s. her sons in it;	Abr	1:24

SETTLING
of s. important difficulties	DC	102: 2
s. the question by an appeal	JS	2:12

SEVEN
s. women shall take hold of	2Ne	14: 1
shall smite it in the s. streams,		21:15
were s. churches in the land of	Mos	25:23
and slew s. of their brethren	Al	18:16
subsist for the space of s. years,	3Ne	4: 4
twenty and s. of the people of	Eth	15:25
belonged to the s. churches,	DC	77: 5
on the back with s. seals?		77: 6
during the s. thousand years		77: 6
by the s. seals with which		77: 7
the trumpets of the s. angels		77:12
him, until seventy times s.		98:40
without s. of the above named		102: 6
These s. shall have power to		102: 7
He was eighty-s. years old when		107:45
ninety-six years and s. days old		107:46
they should have s. presidents		107:93
these s. presidents are to choose		107:95
until s. times seventy,		107:96
shall be seventy and s. fold;	Mses	5:48
eight hundred and s. years, and		6:14
one hundred and eighty-s. years,		8: 5
s. hundred and eighty-two years,		8: 6
s. hundred and seventy-seven		8:11
seven hundred and seventy-s.		8:11
eight hundred and twenty-s.,	JS	2:59

SEVENFOLD
shall be taken on him s.	Mses	5:40
If Cain shall be avenged s.,		5:48

SEVENTEEN
nine high priests, s. elders,	DC	102: 5

SEVENTEENTH
s. year of the reign of the judges,	Al	30: 5
the latter end of the s. year,		30: 6
And thus ended the s. year		35:12
came to pass in the s. year,	3Ne	3:22

SEVENTH
But the s. day, the sabbath of	Mos	13:18
in the s. year of the reign of	Al	4: 5
endeth the s. year of the reign of		4: 5
the fourth day of this s. month,		10: 6
in the twenty and s. year of		52:15
of the twenty and s. year of		52:18
of the twenty and s. year		56:20

SEVENTH SHAKE

the third day of the s. month,	Al	56:42
in the thirty and s. year of		63: 4
thus ended the thirty and s. year,		63: 6
even in the forty and s. year,	He	3:19
in the fifty and s. year they did		4: 5
of the sixty and s. year		6:16
in the sixty and s. year of the		6:32
the seventy and s. year began in		11:21
ended the seventy and s. year,		11:21
also the eighty and s. year of		16:10
and also the ninety and s. year;	3Ne	2: 4
the twenty and sixth and s. years		6: 4
the thirty and s. year passed	4Ne	1: 4
and twenty and s. year	Mrm	2: 3
hundred and sixty and s. year,		4:15
years, and so on until the s.	DC	77: 7
on the s. day he finished his		77:12
of the s. thousand years		77:12
of the s. thousand years—		77:12
after the opening of the s. seal,		77:13
which is the s. angel, saying:		88:106
until the s. angel shall sound		88:110
Michael, the s. angel, even		88:112
s. president of these presidents		107:94
on the s. day I, God, ended	Mses	3: 2
and I rested on the s. day		3: 2
And I, God blessed the s. day,		3: 3
the s. time we will end our work,	Abr	5: 2
we will rest on the s. time		5: 2
concluded upon the s. time,		5: 3
the s. time they would rest		5: 3

SEVENTIES
to preside over the quorum of s.;	DC	124:138

SEVENTY
hundred and s. and nine years	En	1:25
two hundred and s. and six	Om	1: 3
four hundred and s.-six years	Mos	6: 4
two hundred and s.-nine of our		9:19
thus ended the s. and first year	He	10:19
in the s. and second year of		11: 1
in the s. and third year it did		11: 2
thus in the s. and fourth year		11: 5
continue in the s. and fifth year,		11: 6
that in the s. and sixth year		11:17
the s. and sixth year did end		11:21
the s. and seventh year began		11:21
ended the s. and seventh year,		11:21
peace in the s. and eighth year,		11:22
And in the s. and ninth year		11:23
ye are s. and two years old	3Ne	28: 3
the s. and first year passed	4Ne	1:14
also the s. and second year,		1:14
till the s. and ninth year had		1:14
hundred and s. and fifth year.	Mrm	4:16
hundred and s. and nine years		5: 5
forgive him, until s. times seven.	DC	98:40
The S. are also called to preach		107:25
The S. are to act in the name		107:34
high council to call upon the S.,		107:38
distinct one from that of the s.,		107:90
showing the order of the S.,		107:93
chosen out of the number of the s.;		107:93
other s. besides the first		107:95
besides the first s. to whom		107:95
also other s., until seven		107:96
until seven times s.,		107:96
s. are to be traveling ministers,		107:97
the Twelve, neither to the S.,		107:98
Lamech shall be s. and seven fold;	Mses	5:48
Cainan lived s. years, and begat		6:19
seven hundred and s.-seven		8:11

SEVENTY-NINE: *see SEVENTY and NINE.*

SEVENTY-SEVEN: *see SEVENTY and SEVEN.*

SEVENTY-SIX: *see SEVENTY and SIX.*

SEVERAL
according to their s. stations,	Al	17:18
thus they took their s. journeys		17:18
The s. elders composing this	DC	20:61
be the duty of the s. churches,		20:81
to attend the s. conferences		20:81
the names of the s. members		20:82
one place, in their s. courses,		52:33
conference, their s. missions.		73: 2
in your s. stewardships—		82:11
shall permit, in your s. callings,		84:117
their s. callings and offices;		97:13
ordained to the s. offices in		107:21
assembly of the s. quorums,		107:32
to fill the s. calls for preaching		107:38
I attend their s. meetings	JS	2: 8

SEVERALLY
they come unto every man s.,	Mro	10:17
s. as they are appointed,	DC	107:63

SEVERE
many of which were very s.	Al	49:24
suffering s. persecution at	JS	2:27
more bitter and s. than before.		2:60

SEVERED
s. from the ordinances of mine	DC	121:19

SEVERITY
the s. of the Lord fell upon	Om	1:22

SEWED
they s. fig leaves together and	Mses	4:13

SEYMOUR: *see BRUNSON, Seymour.*

SHACKLES
chains, and s., and fetters of hell.	DC	123: 8

SHADOW
in the s. of his hand hath he hid	1Ne	21: 2
thee in the s. of mine hand,	2Ne	8:16
for a s. in the daytime		14: 6
in the land of the s. of death,		19: 2
a type and a s. of things which	Mos	13:10
it is a s. of those things which		16:14
neither hath he a s. of turning	Al	7:20
things are not without a s.;		37:43
neither s. of changing?	Mrm	9: 9
in whom there is s. of changing,		9:10
in the region and s. of death.	DC	57:10
least s. or coloring of justice		127: 1

SHADOWS
and wonders, and types, and s.	Mos	3:15

SHADRACH: *see ROUNDY, Shadrach.*

SHAFT
and made me a polished s.;	1Ne	21: 2
shall fall by the s. of death,	DC	85: 8
by the vivid s. of lightning.		85: 8

SHAFTS
yea, his s. in the whirlwind,	He	5:12

SHAGREEL
and also unto the god of S.,	Abr	1: 9
Now the god of S. was the sun.		1: 9

SHAKE
until their frames did s. before	1Ne	2:14
which cause the earth to s.		17:45
but the Lord did s. them,		17:54
and s. off the awful chains	2Ne	1:13
S. off the chains with which ye		1:23
may s. at the appearance of sin?		4:31
S. thyself from the dust;		8:25
and I s. them before you;		9:44
s. off the chains of him that		9:45
he ariseth to s. terribly the earth.		12:19
he ariseth to s. terribly the earth.		12:21
As if the rod should s. itself		20:15
he shall s. his hand against		20:32
shall s. his hand over the river,		21:15

SHAKE

s. the hand, that they may go	2Ne 23: 2
I will s. the heavens.	23:13
that did s. kingdoms?	24:16
kingdom of the devil must s.,	28:19
s. yourselves that ye may awake	Jac 3:11
had hope to s. me from the faith,	7: 5
which caused the earth to s.	Mos 27:11
doth not my voice s. the earth?	27:15
that could s. the earth and cause	27:18
with a voice to s. the earth,	Al 29: 1
the walls of the prison did s.	He 5:27
his voice doth the whole earth s.;	12:11
the earth shall s. and tremble;	14:21
that it did s. the whole earth	3Ne 8: 6
S. thyself from the dust;	20:37
could they cause the earth to s.;	Mrm 8:24
at my word the earth shall s.;	Eth 4: 9
to tremble and s. to the center.	DC 10:56
and cause the heavens to s. for	21: 6
heavens to s. for your good,	35:24
that which shall s. the earth;	38:30
the heavens shall s. and the	43:18
the heavens also shall s.	45:48
And s. off the dust of thy feet	60:15
s. off the dust of your feet	75:20
I will not only s. the earth,	84:118
and request him to s. hands	129: 4
Ask him to s. hands with you,	129: 7
when you ask him to s. hands	129: 8
and the heavens shall s., and also	Mses 7:61

SHAKEN

of the Lord that has s. us.	1Ne 17:55
they love the truth and are not s.	2Ne 9:40
get s. from my firmness	Jac 4:18
wherefore, I could not be s.	7: 5
would have been s. forever;	Al 48:17
voice of him who had s. the earth;	He 5:42
many were s. till the buildings	3Ne 8:14
for the heavens to be s.,	DC 49:23
not by me shall be s. and	132:14
powers of heaven shall be s.	JS 1:33
of the heavens shall be s.,	1:36

SHAKERS

have received it, unto the s.	DC 49: 1

SHAKETH

itself against him that s. it?	2Ne 20:15

SHALEMANASSEH

and S. and Mahemson	DC 82:11

SHALL: *see in the APPENDIX.*

SHALLOW

were covered with a s. covering.	Al 16:11

SHALT: *see in the APPENDIX.*

SHAME

I hid not my face from s.	2Ne 7: 6
and despised the s. of it,	9:18
and bear the s. of the world;	Jac 1: 8
and causeth me to shrink with s.	2: 6
stand with s. and awful guilt	6: 9
acknowledge to our everlasting s.	Al 12:15
for thou shalt not be put to s.;	3Ne 22: 4
shalt forget the s. of thy youth,	22: 4
and it shall turn to their s.	DC 10:23
their s. shall be made manifest.	71: 7
and put him to an open s.	76:35
to bring to s. and confusion,	109:29
the sun shall hide his face in s.,	133:49

SHARE

for a s. of stock in that house,	DC 124:64
a s. of stock from any one man	124:66

SHARED

that there arose up S.,	Eth 13:23
in the fourth year, did beat S.,	13:24
was exceedingly angry with S.,	13:27
S. fought against him for the	13:28
S. gave him battle again upon	13:29
Coriantumr gave S. battle	13:30
he beat S. and slew him.	13:30
S. wounded Coriantumr in his	13:31
and after the death of S.,	14: 3
there arose the brother of S.	14: 3
the brother of S. did give battle	14: 4
the brother of S. did march	14: 5
the brother of S., whose name	14: 8

SHARES

beat their swords into plow-s.,	2Ne 12: 4

SHARON

and I beheld the land of S.,	Mses 7: 9
the town of S., Windsor county,	JS 2: 3

SHARP

made my mouth like a s. sword;	1Ne 21: 2
Whose arrows shall be s.,	2Ne 15:28
yea, the s. pointed arrow,	Jar 1: 8
to be exceeding s. among them.	Al 19:28
the s. swords of the Nephites;	44:18
were exceeding s. lightnings,	3Ne 8: 7

SHARPER

s. than a two-edged sword,	DC 6: 2
s. than a two-edged sword,	11: 2
s. than a two-edged sword,	12: 2
s. than a two-edged sword,	14: 2
s. than a two-edged sword,	33: 1

SHARPLY

he began to contend with him s.,	Al 1: 7
Admonish them s. for my	DC 112:12

SHARPNESS

Ye say that he hath used s.;	2Ne 1:26
his s. was the sharpness of	1:26
the s. of the power of the word	1:26
and they did use much s.	WM 1:17
speak the word of God with s.	Mro 9: 4
when I use no s. they harden	9: 4
I speak unto you with s. and	DC 15: 2
I speak unto you with s. and	16: 2
Reproving betimes with s.,	121:43

SHAUMAHYEEM

to the Hebrew word, S.	Fac 1:12

SHAUMAU

to signify S., to be high	Fac 1:12

SHAVE

shall the Lord s. with a razor that	2Ne 17:20

SHAVED

and they had their heads s.	Mos 10: 8

SHAVEN

and their heads s.;	En 1:20

SHAZER

call the name of the place S.	1Ne 16:13
the wilderness, to the place of S.	16:14

SHE

s. truly had mourned because of us.	1Ne 5: 1
For s. had supposed that we had	5: 2
s. also had complained against my	5: 2
And s. spake, saying: Now I	5: 8
manner of language did s. speak.	5: 8
s. was exceedingly fair and white.	11:13
s. was carried away in the Spirit;	11:19
after s. had been carried away	11:19
s. is the whore of all the earth.	14:10
and s. sat upon many waters;	14:11
s. had dominion over all the earth,	14:11
that s. should not have compassion	21:15
and unto Sarah, s. that bare you;	2Ne 8: 2
the sons s. hath brought forth;	8:18
all the sons s. hath brought up.	8:18

SHE 874 SHED

and s. shall be desolate,	2Ne 13:26	
and s. conceived and bare a son.	18: 3	
that s. should rule over them!	Mos 8:20	
s. being a virgin, a precious	Al 7:10	
s. sent and desired that he	19: 2	
what s. would that he should do.	19: 3	
And s. said unto him:	19: 4	
And s. said unto him:	19: 9	
s. watched over the bed of her	19:11	
s. having been converted unto	19:16	
when s. saw that all the servants	19:17	
s. knew that it was the power of	19:17	
s. ran forth from house to house,	19:17	
when s. saw the contention which	19:28	
s. was exceeding sorrowful,	19:28	
s. went and took the queen by	19:29	
that perhaps s. might raise her	19:29	
as soon as s. touched her hand	19:29	
s. arose and stood upon her feet,	19:29	
And when s. had said this,	19:30	
s. clasped her hands, being filled	19:30	
when s. had done this, she took	19:30	
s. took the king, Lamoni, by the	19:30	
And s. came in unto the king;	22:19	
when s. saw him lay as if he were	22:19	
s. was angry with them, and	22:19	
s. also began to fear exceedingly,	22:21	
s. commanded her servants that	22:21	
Yea, s. did steal away the hearts	39: 4	
when s. had heard that the king	47:32	
s. sent unto Amalickiah,	47:33	
s. also desired him that he	47:33	
s. also desired him that he	47:33	
unto the place where s. sat;	47:34	
that s. fled, and came over to	50:31	
whither s. did go we know not.	63: 8	
that s. may bring forth her fruit,	He 11:13	
and even as s. is, so are they.	Mrm 5:18	
plan whereby s. could redeem	Eth 8: 8	
that s. did talk with her father,	8: 9	
before him that s. pleased him,	8:11	
he or s. shall be tried before	DC 42:80	
he or s. shall be condemned by	42:81	
he or s. shall be delivered up	42:84	
And if he or s. shall steal,	42:85	
he or s. shall be delivered up	42:85	
And if he or s. shall lie,	42:86	
he or s. shall be delivered up	42:86	
And if he or s. do any manner	42:87	
he or s. shall be delivered up	42:87	
if he or s. confess thou shalt be	42:88	
if he or s. confess not thou	42:89	
he or s. shall be chastened before	42:90	
or s. shall be rebuked openly,	42:91	
that he or s. may be ashamed.	42:91	
And if he or s. confess not,	42:91	
he or s. shall be delivered up	42:91	
or s. shall be rebuked in secret,	42:92	
or s. may have opportunity to	42:92	
her whom he or s. has offended,	42:92	
s. shall be an ensign unto	64:42	
s. is clothed with the glory of	84:101	
s. who sitteth upon many	88:94	
s. is the tares of the earth;	88:94	
s. is bound in bundles;	88:94	
s. is ready to be burned.	88:94	
S. is fallen who made all nations	88:105	
s. is fallen, is fallen!	88:105	
and s. be rewarded in mine own	90:29	
s. should go up unto the land	90:30	
s. may settle down in peace	90:31	
inasmuch as s. is faithful,	90:31	
chasten her until s. overcomes	90:36	
s. shall not be removed out	90:37	
do these things s. shall prosper,	97:18	
if s. observe to do all things	97:25	
But if s. observe not to do	97:26	
and if s. sin no more none of	97:27	
although s. is chastened for	100:13	
and s. came unto him, saying:	101:83	
continual coming s. weary me.	101:84	
which s., Zion, has a right to	113: 8	
to that power which s. had lost.	113: 8	
is in the world and s. with him,	DC 132:15	
he or s. shall commit any sin or	132:26	
And why did s. do it?	132:34	
and if s. be with another man,	132:41	
s. hath committed adultery	132:41	
If s. be not in the new and	132:42	
and s. be with another man,	132:42	
s. has committed adultery,	132:42	
s. hath not committed adultery,	132:44	
her vow, and s. knoweth it,	132:44	
s. stay herself and partake not	132:51	
But if s. will not abide this	132:54	
s. shall be destroyed,	132:54	
if s. abide not in my law.	132:54	
But if s. will not abide this	132:55	
then shall s. be forgiven	132:56	
s. has trespassed against me;	132:56	
after s. is espoused,	132:63	
s. has committed adultery,	132:63	
then shall s. believe and	132:64	
or s. shall be destroyed,	132:64	
if s. receive not this law,	132:65	
because s. did not believe and	132:65	
s. then becomes the transgressor;	132:65	
s. shall be called Woman, because	Mses 3:23	
because s. was taken out of man.	3:23	
s. took of the fruit thereof, and	4:12	
that s. should remain with me,	4:18	
s. gave me of the fruit of the tree	4:18	
s. was the mother of all living;	4:26	
and s. bare unto him sons and	5: 2	
and s. conceived and bare Cain,	5:16	
s. again conceived and bare his	5:17	
and s. conceived and bare Enoch,	5:42	
Zillah, s. also bare Tubal Cain,	5:46	
and s. bare a son, and he	6: 2	
they will.—S. is his wife;	Abr 2:23	
the Egyptians, s. is thy sister,	2:24	
now s. shall be called Woman,	5:17	
because s. was taken out of man;	5:17	

SHEARER
as a sheep before the s. is dumb, Mos 15: 6

SHEARERS
as a sheep before her s. is dumb Mos 14: 7

SHEARJASHUB
thou and S. thy son, 2Ne 17: 3

SHEATH
I drew it forth from the s. 1Ne 4: 9

SHEAVES

behold the number of your s.!	Al 26: 5
gatherethhis s. into the floor.	3Ne 20:18
and you shall be laden with s.	DC 31: 5
and you shall be laden with s.	33: 9
shall be laden with many s.,	75: 5
will crown him again with s.	79: 3

SHED

time have I s. the blood of man.	1Ne 4:10
did s. blood among themselves.	Mos 7:25
ye will s. innocent blood,	17:10
even s. many tears of sorrow.	25: 9
s. the blood of a righteous man,	Al 1:13
that I should s. innocent blood;	20:19
shall be s. for the atonement of	24:13
rather than s. the blood of	24:18
might s. your blood for power;	44: 2
they never would s. blood more;	53:11
their brethren to s. blood.	56: 6
We would not s. the blood of	61:10
We would not s. the blood of	61:11
who had not s. the blood of	3Ne 10:12
blood, which I have s. for you,	18:11
and did s. tears of joy before	Eth 6:12
will that man should s. blood,	8:19
which shall be s. by them,	8:22
thy Son, which was s. for them;	Mro 5: 2
which was s. for them;	DC 20:79
my blood which was s. for the	27: 2

SHED   875   SHERRIZAH

of thy Son which was s.,	DC 45: 4
you are forbidden to s. blood—	63:31
of God, that s. their blood—	88:94
s. forth upon them for the	90:11
the Holy Ghost shall be s. forth	100: 8
whereby to s. innocent blood,	132:19
whereby to s. innocent blood,	132:19
wherein they s. innocent blood,	132:26
wherein ye s. innocent blood,	132:27
they have s. innocent blood,	136:36
s. forth their tears as the rain	Mses 7:28
the blood of the Righteous be s.,	7:45

SHEDDETH

the love of God which s. itself	1Ne 11:22
wo be unto man that s. blood	49:21

SHEDDING

by the s. of much blood;	Mos 9: 2
s. of the blood of their brethren,	11:19
stop to the s. of so much blood.	20:22
be the cause of s. much blood	29: 7
and the s. of much blood.	29:21
delighted in the s. of blood;	29:40
used for the s. of man's blood;	Al 24:17
again for the s. of man's blood;	24:18
hearts delight in the s. of blood;	26:24
s. the blood of their brethren	27:28
be, a stop to the s. of blood;	34:13
it be the s. of innocent blood	39: 5
they should stop s. their blood.	43:54
even to the s. of blood if it	48:14
not in the s. of blood but in	48:16
not delight in the s. of blood;	48:23
had taken by the s. of blood;	52: 4
we will forbear s. your blood.	52:37
by the s. of the blood of so	56:13
Manti without the s. of blood.	58:28
without the s. of blood,	3Ne 3:10
me no more the s. of blood;	9:19
delighted in the s. of blood	Mrm 4:11
no more in the s. of blood,	7: 4
cause the s. of much blood;	Eth 11:10
face of the land were s. blood,	13:31
from the s. of blood to	14:22
of blood to the s. of blood,	14:22
the s. of the blood of Christ,	Mro 10:33
save it be by the s. of blood.	DC 58:53
and to the s. of blood.	63:28
through the s. of his own blood.	76:69
the land by the s. of blood.	101:80

SHEDERLAOMACH

S. [Frederick G. Williams],	DC 92: 1
S. [Frederick G. Williams],	92: 2
S. [Frederick G. Williams]	104:27
S. [Frederick G. Williams]	104:29

SHEDOLAMAK

in journeying to the place S.	DC 107:45

SHEDS

which the father s. forth	DC 76:53

SHEEP

and he numbereth his s.,	1Ne 22:25
and he shall feed his s.,	22:25
nourish a young cow and two s.;	2Ne 17:21
as a s. that no man taketh up;	23:14
we, like s., have gone astray;	Mos 14: 6
a s. before her shearers is dumb	14: 7
a s. before the shearer is dumb,	15: 6
and shalt gather together my s.	26:20
will hear my voice shall be my s.;	26:21
as s. having no shepherd.	Al 5:37
not the s. of the good shepherd.	5:38
not the s. of the good shepherd,	5:39
among you having many s.	5:59
into his fold, and ye are his s.;	5:60
even as a s. having no shepherd	25:12
and be numbered among his s.	He 15:13

other s. I have which are not	3Ne 15:17
Other s. I have which are not of	15:21
and ye are my s., and ye are	15:24
I have other s. which are not	16: 1
shall be numbered among my s.,	16: 3
people, for behold I know my s.,	18:31
young lion among the flocks of s.,	20:16
young lion among the flocks of s.,	21:12
of oxen, and cows, and of s.,	Eth 9:18
Other s. have I which are not	DC 10:59
people that I had other s.,	10:60
follow me, and feed my s.	112:14
And Abel was a keeper of s.,	Mses 5:17

SHEEP'S

come to you in s. clothing,	3Ne 14:15

SHELEM

which they called the mount S.,	Eth 3: 1

SHELF

his tool or his sword upon his s.,	Eth 14: 1

SHEM

the land which was called S.	Mrm 2:20
we did fortify the city of S.,	2:21
and S., and Josh, had fallen	6:14
of Heni, and the land of S.,	Mses 7: 9
he begat S. of her who was the	8:12
three sons, S., Ham, and Japheth.	8:27

SHEMLON

out round about the land of S.,	Mos 10: 7
and also the land of S.,	11:12
about towards the land of S.,	19: 6
there was a place in S. where	20: 1
who were in the land of S.,	24: 1
and who were in the land of S.,	Al 23:12

SHEMNON

Kumenonhi, and Jeremiah, and S.,	3Ne 19: 4

SHEOL

benighted dominion of S.—	DC 121: 4

SHEPHERD

and one S. over all the earth.	1Ne 13:41
there shall be one fold and one s.;	22:25
flock which fleeth from the s.,	Mos 8:21
astray, as sheep having no s.,	Al 5:37
a s. hath called after you and	5:37
the good s. doth call you;	5:38
unto the voice of the good s.,	5:38
are not the sheep of the good s.	5:38
are not the sheep of the good s.,	5:39
that the devil is your s., and ye	5:39
unto the voice of the good s.,	5:41
the voice of the good s.,	5:57
For what s. is there among you	5:59
the good s. doth call after you;	5:60
even as a sheep having no s. is	25:12
unto the voice of the good s.;	He 7:18
and their great and true s.,	15:13
shall be one fold, and one s.	3Ne 15:17
shall be one fold, and one s.	15:21
there may be one fold and one s.;	16: 3
they had Christ for their s.,	Mrm 5:17
midst, and I am the good s.,	DC 50:44

SHEPHERDS

shall the s. make their fold there.	2Ne 23:20

SHEREM

of Nephi, whose name was S.	Jac 7: 1
behold, I, S., declare unto you	7: 7
did S. contend against me.	7: 7

SHERRIZAH

they took from the tower of S.;	Mro 9: 7
daughters who remain in S.;	9:16
Lamanites are betwixt S. and	9:17

SHERWOOD

SHERWOOD, Henry G.
Let my servant S. pay stock — DC 124:81
Namely, Samuel Bent, S., — 124:132

SHEUM
and with neas, and with s., — Mos 9: 9

SHEZ
And Riplakish was the son of S. — Eth 1:24
And S. was the son of Heth. — 1:25
S., who was a descendant of
household save it were S.— — 10: 1
S. began to build up again — 10: 1
S. did remember the destruction — 10: 2
eldest son, whose name was S., — 10: 3
S. was smitten by the hand of — 10: 3
S. did live to an exceeding old — 10: 4

SHIBLOM
and S., and Shem, and Josh, — Mrm 6:14
good old age, and begat S.; — Eth 11: 4
and S. reigned in his stead. — 11: 4
the brother of S. rebelled — 11: 4
the brother of S. caused that — 11: 5
came to pass in the days of S. — 11: 7
that S. was slain, and Seth was — 11: 9

SHIBLON
A s. is half of a senum; — Al 11:15
a s. for half a measure of barley. — 11:15
And a shiblum is a half of a s. — 11:16
were S. and Corianton; — 31: 7
of Alma to his son, S. — 38:hd
And now my son, S., I would — 38: 5
unto them by Helaman, and S., — 49:30
S. took possession of those sacred — 63: 1
S. died also, and Corianton had — 63:10
for S. to confer those sacred — 63:11
Helaman, before the death of S. — 63:13
and also S., who was his son. — 63:17
And Seth was the son of S. — Eth 1:11
And S. was the son of Com. — 1:12

SHIBLONS
of gold is equal to three s. — Al 11:19

SHIBLUM
And a s. is a half of a shiblon. — Al 11:16
And a leah is the half of a s. — 11:17

SHIELD
to s. them from the arrows and — Al 49: 2
Taking the s. of faith wherewith — DC 27:17
and I will be their s. and — 35:14

SHIELDED
being s. from the more vital — Al 43:38
vital parts of the body being s. — 43:38
they were s. by their shields, — 49:24

SHIELDS
breastplates and with arm-s., — Al 43:19
also s. to defend their heads, — 43:19
armed with breastplates, nor s.— — 43:21
breastplates, and their arm-s., — 43:38
s. that have preserved you. — 44: 9
and his breastplate and his s., — 46:13
also prepared themselves with s., — 49: 6
they were shielded by their s., — 49:24
all manner of s. of every kind. — He 1:14
strong with armor, and with s., — 3Ne 3:26
having s., and breastplates, — Eth 15:15
their swords and with their s., — 15:24

SHILOAH
people refuseth.the waters of S. — 2Ne 18: 6

SHILOM
which is north of the land of S., — Mos 7: 5
of Nephi, and in the land of S.; — 7: 7
to the hill which was north of S., — 7:16
of Lehi-Nephi, and the city of S. — 7:21
Lehi-Nephi, and the land of S. — 9: 6
of Lehi-Nephi, and the city of S. — Mos 9: 8
on the south of the land of S., — 9:14
upon the north of the land of S., — 10: 8
and overlook the land of S., — 11:12
to be built in the land S.; — 11:13
on the hill north of the land of S. — 11:13
will travel around the land of S. — 22: 8
went round about the land of S. — 22:11
and in the land of S., — 24: 1
who were in the land of S., — Al 23:12
a hill which shall be called S.; — Mrm 1: 3
therefore I did go to the hill S., — 4:23
and passed by the hill of S., — Eth 9: 3

SHIMNILOM
of Lemuel, and in the city of S. — Al 23:12

SHINAR
and from Elam, and from S., — 2Ne 21:11

SHINE
shall not cause her light to s. — 2Ne 23:10
shall very soon s. forth among all — Al 5:50
which shall s. forth in darkness — 37:23
then shall the righteous s. forth — 40:25
behold, they did s. exceedingly, — He 5:36
Therefore let your light so s. before — 3Ne 12:16
that it may s. unto the world. — 18:24
countenance did s. upon them, — 19:25
it shall s. forth out of darkness, — Mrm 8:16
they may s. forth in darkness; — Eth 3: 4
s. forth unto us in the vessels — 3: 4
caused stones to s. in darkness, — 6: 3
and s. forth fair as the moon, — DC 109:73
Arise and s. forth, — 115: 5

SHINED
upon them hath the light s. — 2Ne 19: 2

SHINEHAH
in the land of S. [Kirtland]; — DC 82:12
have consecrated the land of S. — 82:13
in the land of S. [Kirtland]. — 104:21
stake in the land of S.[Kirtland]. — 104:40
Zion, the City of S. [Kirtland]. — 104:48
on the plains of Olaha S.; — 117: 8
And he said unto me; This is S. — Abr 3:13

SHINELAH
even to S. [print] my words, — DC 104:58

SHINELANE
s. [printing] these sacred things — DC 104:63

SHINETH
light which s. in darkness, — DC 6:21
light which s. in darkness, — 10:58
light which s. in darkness, — 11:11
a light which s. in darkness — 34: 2
a light which s. in darkness — 39: 2
a light that s. in darkness — 45: 7
Which truth s. This is — 88: 7
And the light which s., — 88:11
The light s. in darkness, — 88:49
and s. even unto the west, — JS 1:26

SHINING
and the s. of a flaming fire — 2Ne 14: 5
the stars shall refuse their s., — DC 34: 9
s. seraphs around thy throne, — 109:79

SHIP
and buildeth a s. — 1Ne 1:hd
Thou shalt construct a s., — 17: 8
make tools to construct the s. — 17: 9
that I was about to build a s., — 17:17
thinketh that he can build a s.; — 17:17
believe that I could build a s.; — 17:18
that ye could not construct a s., — 17:19
that I should build a s. — 17:49
that I should build a s.? — 17:51
work the timbers of the s. — 18: 1

SHIP / SHOULDST

SHIP
neither did I build the s. after	1 Ne 18: 2
after I had finished the s.,	18: 4
arise and go down into the s.	18: 5
we did go down into the s.,	18: 6
we did all go down into the s.,	18: 6
we had all gone down into the s.,	18: 8
whither they should steer the s.,	18:13
I, Nephi, did guide the s.,	18:22
him an exceedingly large s.,	Al 63: 5
And the first s. did also return,	63: 7
one other s. also did sail forth;	63: 8
to the land northward in a s.,	63:10
large s. is benefited very much	DC 123:16

SHIPPING
send forth much by the way of s.	He 3:10
s. and their building of ships,	3:14

SHIPS
upon all the s. of the sea,	2 Ne 12:16
upon all the s. of Tarshish,	12:16
this man built other s.	Al 63: 7
and their building of s.,	He 3:14

SHIZ
brother of Lib was called S.	Eth 14:17
S. pursued after Coriantumr,	14:17
fear of S. throughout all the land;	14:18
can stand before the army of S.?	14:18
fled to the army of S.,	14:20
S. did not cease to pursue	14:24
S. did pursue Coriantumr	14:26
there he gave battle unto S.	14:26
among the armies of S. that	14:27
trumpet unto the armies of S.	14:28
S. smote upon Coriantumr that	14:30
that S. commanded his people	14:31
he wrote an epistle unto S.,	15: 4
when S. had received his epistle	15: 5
anger against the people of S.;	15: 6
the people of S. were stirred up to	15: 6
the people of S. did give battle	15: 6
again before the people of S.	15: 7
S. also pitched his tents near	15: 8
did press upon the armies of S.	15:10
the people who were for S.	15:13
together to the army of S.	15:13
wrote again an epistle unto S.,	15:18
and nine of the people of S.	15:23
and two of the people of S.,	15:25
S. arose, and also his men,	15:28
save it were Coriantumr and S.,	15:29
S. had fainted with the loss of	15:29
he smote off the head of S.	15:30
he had smitten off the head of S.,	15:31
S. raised upon his hands and fell;	15:31

SHOCK
but I will s. them, saith the Lord,	1 Ne 17:53

SHOD
and make men go over dry s.	2 Ne 21:15
feet s. with the preparation of	DC 27:16
Let thy feet be s. also, for thou art	112: 7

SHOE'S
whose s. latchet I am not worthy	1 Ne 10: 8

SHOES
the latchet of their s. be broken;	2 Ne 15:27
and for s. and for money,	DC 24:18

SHONE
face s. with exceeding luster,	Mos 13: 5
of the Lord s. round about.	DC 76:19
his countenance s. above the	110: 3

SHOOK
that I s. your iniquities from	2 Ne 9:44
as thunder, which s. the earth;	Mos 27:18
and the earth s. mightily,	Al 14:27
and it s. the whole earth.	38: 7
words, the earth s. exceedingly,	He 5:27
behold the earth s. exceedingly,	He 5:31
that the earth s. again,	5:32
the earth s. as if it were about	5:33
to tremble, and the earth s.;	Mses 1:21
yearned; and all eternity s.	7:41

SHOOT
s. forth young and tender	Jac 5: 4
when they begin to s. forth,	DC 45:37

SHORE
borders near the s. of the Red Sea;	Ne 2: 5
upon the s. of the promised land.	Eth 6:12
as the sand upon the sea s.	Mses 1:28

SHORES
upon the s. of the promised land	Eth 6:12

SHORN
they had not s. their heads like	Al 3: 4
heads of the Lamanites were s.;	3: 5
and their heads were s., and	3 Ne 4: 7

SHORT
But, to be s. in writing,	1 Ne 8:30
a s. skin girdle about their loins	En 1:20
was nothing s. of these things,	1:23
s. of an infinite atonement	Al 34:12
march in so s. a space of time,	56:50
I will cut my work s. in	DC 52:11
be cut s. in righteousness—	84:97
that thy work may be cut s. in	109:59
leave the place for a s. season,	127: 1
In the s. space of twenty years,	135: 3

SHORTENED
is my hand s. at all that it cannot	2 Ne 7: 2
God, and mine arm is not s.;	DC 35: 8
yet my arm was not s. at all	133:67
except those days should be s.,	JS 1:20
those days shall be s.	1:20

SHORTER
a s. but true account was	3 Ne 5: 9

SHORTLY
these things must s. come;	1 Ne 22:18
forth things which must s. come;	Al 16:19
the Christ must s. come—	He 16: 4
of things which must s. come,	16: 5
the Son of God must s. appear;	3 Ne 1:17
that which must s. come,	Mrm 8:34
wars that will s. come to pass,	DC 87: 1
which must s. come to pass;	88:79
I s. after arose from my bed,	JS 2:48
which should s. come to pass.	2:73

SHOT
also many s. arrows at him as	He 16: 2
They were s. in Carthage jail,	DC 135: 1
Hyrum was s. first and fell	135: 1
was s. dead in the attempt,	135: 1
were both s. after they were dead,	135: 1

SHOULD: *see in the APPENDIX.*

SHOULDER
and the staff of his s.,	2 Ne 19: 4
government shall be upon his s.;	19: 6
be taken away from off thy s.,	20:27

SHOULDERS
shall be carried upon their s.	1 Ne 21:22
have been carried upon their s.,	22: 6
in their arms and upon their s.	22: 8
shall be carried upon their s.	2 Ne 6: 6
fly upon the s. of the Philistines	21:14
burden depart from off their s.	24:25
which are put upon your s.,	Mos 24:14
that upon men's s. which was	Eth 10: 5

SHOULDST
for fear lest thou s. say—	1 Ne 20: 5

SHOULDST

unto thee lest, thou s. say—	1 Ne 20: 7
way thou s. go, hath done it.	20:17
that thou s. be my servant	21: 6
that thou s. be afraid of man,	2 Ne 8:12
if thou s. prophesy that this	Al 9: 4
but if thou s. fall at this time,	20:17
is expedient that thou s. forbear;	20:18
for if thou s. slay thy son,	20:18
s. be the means of bringing many	30:47
Thou s. have tended to the	39: 4
thou s. enter into temptation.	DC 23: 1
that thou s. hold thy peace	42:57
if thou s. be cast into the pit.	122: 7
thee that thou s. not eat,	Mses 4:17
if so thou s. surely die?	4:17

SHOUT

Cry out and s., thou inhabitant	2 Ne 22: 6
and s. praises unto the Holy One	31:13
began to s. with a loud voice,	3 Ne 4: 9
and thy saints s. aloud for joy.	DC 109:80
Let the mountains s. for joy,	128:23
all the sons of God s. for joy!	128:23

SHOW

Which is to s. unto the remnant	T Pg
I, Nephi, will s. unto you that	1 Ne 1:20
that the Lord may s. his power	15:17
the manner which I shall s. thee,	17: 8
the Lord did s. me from time to	18: 1
that he might s. forth his power,	18:11
to s. unto me concerning them,	19:20
surely did s. unto the prophets	19:21
did s. unto many concerning us	19:21
I did s. them suddenly.	20: 3
that sit in darkness: S. yourselves.	21: 9
but he will s. that he hath not.	21:14
in the body he shall s. himself	2 Ne 9: 5
The s. of their countenance	13: 9
he shall s. himself unto you,	26: 1
he may s. them unto the learned,	27:15
I will s. unto the children of men	27:21
and I will s. unto the world	27:23
But behold, I will s. unto them,	27:27
I will s. unto the children of men	27:28
will s. unto them that fight against	29:14
it will s. unto you all things	32: 5
for Christ will s. unto you,	33:11
O that he would s. you that	Jac 2:15
S. me a sign by this power of	7:13
tempt God to s. unto thee a sign	7:14
I will s. unto you that they were	Mos 23:23
did s. forth his mighty power	23:24
if they would s. them the way	23:36
and s. unto your God that ye	Al 7:15
might s. forth his power in them.	8:31
ye may s. forth good examples	17:11
I will s. forth my power unto	17:29
he might s. him unto his father.	20: 1
If thou wilt s. me a sign,	30:43
s. unto me that he hath power,	30:43
Will ye say, S. unto me a sign,	30:44
except ye shall s. me a sign.	30:45
and except ye s. me a sign,	30:48
Alma should s. forth his sign?	30:51
others, to s. unto thee a sign?	30:51
s. unto us a sign from heaven,	32:17
that he may s. forth his power	37:14
that he might s. forth his power	37:18
also still s. forth his power	37:19
to s. unto our fathers the course	37:39
s. unto them marvelous works.	37:41
But I s. unto you one thing which	40: 3
I will s. unto you that we	57: 8
and s. unto me a true spirit of	60:25
I will not s. unto the wicked of	He 7:23
I will s. unto you another sign,	9:25
why will he not s. himself unto	16:18
why will he not s. himself in this	16:19
to s. unto the world that I will	3 Ne 1:13
I will s. unto you that they did	7: 1
they did s. forth signs also	7:22
I will s. unto you that the	10:18

SHOW

Jesus Christ did s. himself	3 Ne 11:hd
did he s. himself unto them.	11:hd
that Christ should s. himself	11:12
I go to s. myself unto them.	16: 3
I will s. unto thee, O house of	16:12
to s. myself unto the lost tribes	17: 4
desire that I should s. unto you	17: 8
I will s. unto you hereafter	18:37
also s. himself on the morrow	19: 2
where Jesus should s. himself	19: 3
I could not s. unto them so	19:35
that he may s. forth his power	21: 6
for I will s. unto them that	21:10
he did s. himself unto them oft,	26:13
Father s. forth his own works	27:10
they can s. themselves unto	28:30
S. unto me, or ye shall be	Mrm 8:18
I will s. unto you a God of	9:11
art able to s. forth great power,	Eth 3: 5
Nay; Lord, s. thyself unto me.	3:10
therefore I s. myself unto you.	3:13
and heard, and s. it to no man.	3:21
could s. unto him all things—	3:26
the Lord could s. him all things.	3:26
s. them in mine own due time	3:27
had received, and s. them not,	3:28
until the Lord should s. them	3:28
after Christ should s. himself	4: 1
will I s. no greater things,	4: 8
I will s. unto you the greater	4:13
that ye may s. the plates unto	5: 2
the Lord did s. forth his power	9:35
I would s. unto the world that	12: 6
I will s. unto them their	12:27
I will s. unto the Gentiles	12:28
I will s. unto them that faith,	12:28
thou didst s. thyself unto them	12:31
I s. unto you the way to judge;	Mro 7:16
and God will s. unto you,	7:35
And God shall s. unto you,	10:29
you should not s. them except	DC 5: 3
should s. them all these things	5: 7
whom I will s. these things,	5:11
I s. unto you wisdom,	10:34
s. it not unto the world until	10:34
s. it not unto the world—	10:35
said, s. it not unto the world,	10:35
not s. it unto the righteous;	10:36
I will s. unto them that my	10:43
I will s. unto this people that	10:60
shall s. these things unto them.	18:39
and s. not these things unto	19:21
and I will s. miracles, signs,	35: 8
now I s. unto you a mystery,	38:13
I will s. unto you my strong	45:10
s. unto you even my wisdom—	45:11
I will s. it plainly as I showed	45:16
I will s. unto you how the	45:17
parable which I will s. you—	45:36
the Lord will s. them unto you.	66: 1
I, the Lord, will s. unto you	66: 4
things to come will I s. them,	76: 8
s. it by vision unto many,	76:47
I shall s. unto three of you,	95:14
that I may s. unto you my will	97: 1
I, the Lord, s. mercy unto	97: 2
Lord, am willing to s. mercy;	97: 6
I will s. unto you a parable,	101:43
I will s. unto you wisdom	101:63
the pattern which I will s. unto	115:14
the pattern which I shall s. unto	115:15
the pattern which I shall s. unto	115:16
that I might s. forth my wisdom	124: 1
Joseph shall s. unto them,	124:22
place which he shall s. unto	124:22
will s. unto my servant Joseph	124:42
who shall s. unto him the keys	124:95
things which I shall s. unto him,	124:96
remainder I will s. unto you	124:102
to s. forth the living and the dead,	128:13
I will s. thee the workmanship	Mses 1: 4
this one thing I s. unto thee,	1: 7
and now I s. it unto thee.	1: 7

SHOW 879 SHULON

S. them not unto any except Mses 1:42
See thou s. them unto no man, 4:32
I will s. unto thee the world for 7: 4
I pray thee, s. me these things. 7:54
unto a land that I will s. thee. Abr 2: 3
behold I will s. you all these. 3:12
I s. these things unto thee 3:15
s. us concerning the buildings JS 1: 2
s. great signs and wonders, 1:22
now I s. unto you a parable. 1:27
not s. them to any person; 2:42
be commanded to s. them; 2:42

SHOWED
and s. all these things unto me. 1Ne 11:31
and s. himself unto them. 12: 6
the Lord s. unto me great things. 18: 3
of my mouth, and I s. them. 20: 3
before it came to pass I s. them 20: 5
I s. them for fear lest thou 20: 5
that I have s. thee new things 20: 6
for he s. unto all men that they 2Ne 2:21
which the Lord s. unto me, 31: 4
and shadows s. he unto them, Mos 3:15
he has s. unto you a sign; Al 30:51
because I s. unto you this sign He 9:24
which shall be s. unto them; 15: 3
the second time that he s. himself 3Ne 26:15
And Jesus again s. himself 27: 2
the Lord s. himself unto him, Eth 3:13
never have I s. myself unto man 3:15
Jesus s. himself unto this man 3:17
s. himself unto the Nephites. 3:17
which the Lord had s. unto him. 3:18
he s. unto the brother of Jared 3:25
Christ truly had s. himself 4: 2
by faith that Christ s. himself 12: 7
he s. not himself unto them 12: 7
s. himself not unto the world. 12: 7
he s. not himself until after 12:12
wherefore he s. him all things, 12:21
as I s. it unto my disciples DC 45:16
kingdom which he s. unto us, 76:114
the Lord s. unto Enoch all the Mses 7:21
the Lord s. Enoch all things, 7:67
I then s. him those which JS 2:64

SHOWEST
s. mercy unto thy servants who DC 109: 1

SHOWETH
he s. unto the children of men 2Ne 31: 7
it s. unto the children of men 31: 9
the Lord God s. us our weakness Jac 4: 7
Comforter, which s. all things, DC 39: 6
unto such he s. no signs, 63:11

SHOWING
in s. me his great and marvelous 2Ne 4:17
s. mercy unto thousands of them Mos 13:14
people, s. signs and wonders, He 16: 4
S. his body unto them, and 3Ne 10:19
s. one to another the great and 11: 1
s. themselves unto them of Mro 7:30
s. his body unto our fathers, 9:25
s. that he is the same God DC 20:12
s. forth the order and will of 89: 2
s. the order of the Seventy, 107:93
s. forth afterwards an increase of 121:43

SHOWN
which the Lord had s. unto him. 1Ne 1:15
after the Lord had s. so many 1:18
thou hast s. unto me the tree 11: 9
to them hath he s. all things, 14:26
which thou hast s. unto me? 17: 9
which the Lord had s. unto me; 18: 2
the Lord has s. me that those 2Ne 6: 8
the Lord has s. unto me that 6: 9
And he also has s. unto me that 6: 9
as it has been s. unto me that 10: 2
for this cause have they been s. 31:17
after Alma had s. them the way Mos 23:37

hath s. forth his power in them, Al 37:19
it is God that has s. unto you He 5:26
s. unto you that ye cannot lay 5:26
it should be s. unto the people, 8:18
which the Lord had s. unto him. 10: 2
mighty works been s. unto them 15:15
which have been s. unto you, 15:15
have great favors s. unto them, 3Ne 10:18
which I have s. unto you. 18: 7
s. forth his power unto them, 26:15
the Lord hath s. unto me Mrm 8:34
Christ hath s. you unto me, 8:35
it should be s. unto him; Eth 3:26
be s. by the power of God; 5: 3
be s. forth the power of God 5: 4
things should be s. unto you, 8:23
has s. himself unto the world, 12: 8
hath s. unto Joseph Smith, DC 5:25
they have been s. unto me by 5:25
they have been s. unto me by 5:26
be s. forth unto the children of 35:10
shall not anything be s. forth 35:11
for they shall be s. forth in 45:40
was s. unto mine apostles 63:21
beasts, which were s. to John, 77: 3
any additional light is s. upon 102:21
a regard and reverence are s. to 134: 7
Now the Lord had s. unto me, Abr 3:22
these things shall be s. forth, JS 1:34

SHOWS
and s. himself not approved DC 107:100

SHRINK
ye may not s. with awful fear; 2Ne 9:46
and causeth me to s. with shame Jac 2: 6
s. from the presence of the Lord Mos 2:38
s. from the presence of the Lord 3:25
and s. beneath the glance of 27:31
about to s. and flee from them. Al 43:48
not drink the bitter cup, and s.— DC 19:18

SHRUNK
I s. and would that I might not 1Ne 4:10

SHUDDER
enough to make hell itself s., DC 123:10

SHULE
And Omer was the son of S. Eth 1:30
And S. was the son of Kib. 1:31
Kib begat S. in his old age, 7: 7
S. was angry with his brother; 7: 8
S. waxed strong, and became 7: 8
of the thing which S. had done, 7:10
S. also begat many sons and 7:12
S. gave him power in his 7:13
that Noah rebelled against S., 7:15
gave battle unto S. the king, 7:16
battle again unto S., the king; 7:17
and he took S., the king, 7:17
the sons of S. crept into the 7:18
power any more over S. the king, 7:19
under the reign of S. the king 7:19
the kingdom of S., and the 7:20
people should give battle unto S. 7:21
S. did beat them and did slay 7:21
the kingdom of Cohor unto S., 7:22
did gain favor in the eyes of S.; 7:22
S. did bestow great favors upon 7:22
he did do in the kingdom of S. 7:22
And also in the reign of S. 7:23
king S. did execute judgment 7:24
S. begat sons and daughters in 7:26
no more wars in the days of S.; 7:27
which the S. [ashery] is situated. DC 104:39

SHULEM
S., one of the king's principal Fac 3: 5

SHULON
the land, which was called S., Mses 6:17

SHUM

SHUM
a seon of gold, a s. of gold,	Al	11: 5
And a s. of gold was twice		11: 9
and I beheld in the valley of S.,	Mses	7: 5
which were the people of S.		7: 5
array against the people of S.,		7: 7

SHURR
his tents in the valley of S.	Eth	14:28
the valley of S. was near the		14:28

SHUT
that he could not s. it.	2Ne	1:27
May the gates of hell be s.		4:32
wilt thou not s. the gates of		4:32
to be s. out from the presence of		9: 9
and s. their eyes lest they see		16:10
and their mouths had been s.,	WM	1:15
when thou hast s. thy door,	3Ne	13: 6
kings shall s. their mouths at		20:45
kings shall s. their mouths;		21: 8
my mouth was s., and I was	Mrm	1:16
the door thereof, when it was s.,	Eth	2:17
heavens are opened and are s.;		4: 9
therefore he s. him up in prison,		9: 7
straightway s. it up again;	DC	76:47
power to s. up the heavens,		77: 8
were s. out from his presence.	Mses	5: 4
Cain was s. out from the presence		5:41
s. out from the presence of God.		6:49
I will s. them up; a prison have		7:38

SICK
multitudes of people who were s.,	1Ne	11:31
down, yea, even upon their s.-beds.		18:17
relief to the s. and the afflicted.	Jac	2:19
miracles, such as healing the s.,	Mos	3: 5
visiting the s. and administering		4:26
and the s., and the afflicted;	Al	1:27
that were athirst, or that were s.,		1:30
those who were s. and afflicted.		4:12
also Zeezrom lay s. at Sidom,		15: 3
found him upon his bed, s.,		15: 5
visit not the s. and afflicted,		34:28
Have ye any that are s. among	3Ne	17: 7
did go forth with their s. and		17: 9
after having healed all their s.,		26:15
that they did heal the s.,	4Ne	1: 5
needy, the s. and the afflicted.	Mrm	8:37
and the s. and the afflicted to pass		8:39
they shall lay hands on the s.		9:24
physician, but they that are s.;	Mro	8: 8
casting out devils, healing the s.,	DC	24:13
devils; they shall heal the s.;		35: 9
whosoever among you are s.,		42:43
needy, the s. and the afflicted,		52:40
Lay your hands upon the s.,		66: 9
name they shall heal the s.;		84:68
for bruises and all s. cattle,		89: 8
with all their s. and afflicted		109:72
he shall heal the s., he shall cast		124:98

SICKEN
his heart again began to s.	Al	31: 1

SICKLE
for ye did thrust in the s., and	Al	26: 5
he that thrusteth in his s. with	DC	4: 4
let him thrust in his s. with		6: 3
whosoever will thrust in his s.		6: 4
let him thrust in his s. with		11: 3
whosoever will thrust in his s.		11: 4
have thrust in their s. to reap.		11:27
let him thrust in his s. with		12: 3
whosoever will thrust in his s.		12: 4
let him thrust in his s. with		14: 3
whosoever will thrust in his s.		14: 4
thrust in your s. with all		31: 5

SICKLES
wherefore, thrust in your s.,	DC	33: 7

SICKNESS
in all cases save it were in s.,	Mos	27: 5
saved from famine, and from s.,	Al	9:22
a desolating s. shall cover	DC	45:31
because of the s. of the land.		124:87
s. of the land shall redound to		124:87

SICKNESSES
pains and the s. of his people.	Al	7:11
and were healed of their s.	3Ne	7:22

SIDE
by the s. of a river of water.	1Ne	2: 6
on the other s. of the river		8:26
surrounded them on every s.	Mos	21: 5
on the back s. of the city.		22: 6
the west s. of the river Sidon.	Al	2:34
which was by the wilderness s.		8: 5
come in upon the wilderness s.,		16: 2
the east s. of the river Sidon.		16: 7
round about on the wilderness s.;		22:29
the other s. of the river Sidon,		43:41
to harass them on every s.		52: 9
our tents by the wilderness s.,		58:13
should hem them in on every s.,	3Ne	4:16
thrust your hands into my s.,		11:14
thrust their hands into his s.;		11:15
wounds which pierced my s.,	DC	6:37
of the hands by the water's s.		52:10
the inhabitants on either s.		61: 3
of justice or right on their s.		127: 1
On the west s. of this hill,	JS	2:51
in the middle on the upper s.,		2:51

SIDES
in the s. of the north;	2Ne	24:13
to hell, to the s. of the pit.		24:15
of death commenced on both s.,	Al	43:37
even on both s. of the river,		43:52
were many slain on both s.;		52:35
who had been slain on both s.		52:40
but they came up on all s. to lay	3Ne	4:16
thousands slain on both s.,	Mrm	4: 9
the s. thereof were tight like	Eth	2:17
women and children on both s.		14:31

SIDNEY: *see also* GILBERT, *Sidney; and* RIGDON, *Sidney.*
verily, I say unto my servant S.,	DC	35: 3
my servants S., and Parley,		49: 1
my servants S. and Parley,		49: 3
my friends S. and Joseph,		100: 1
my servant S., should be a		100: 9
Joseph, and my servant S.,		112:17
Joseph, neither my servant S.,		115:13
if my servant S. will serve me		124:103
If my servant S. will do my will,		124:108

SIDOM
came out even into the land of S.;	Al	15: 1
And also Zeezrom lay sick at S.,		15: 3
Amulek were in the land of S.,		15: 4
throughout all the land of S.		15:11
a church in the land of S.,		15:13
from all the region round about S.,		15:14
established the church at S.,		15:17

SIDON
which was east of the river S.,	Al	2:15
upon the hill east of S.		2:17
as they were crossing the river S.,		2:27
was on the west of the river S.,		2:34
been slain into the waters of S.,		2:34
on the west side of the river S.		2:34
they had all crossed the river S.		2:35
upon the bank of the river S.		3: 3
were cast into the waters of S.;		3: 3
baptized in the waters of S.		4: 4
upon the east of the river S.,		6: 7
on the west of the river S.,		8: 3
Lamanites will cross the river S.		16: 6

SIDON

on the east of the river S.,	Al	16: 6
sons crossed over the river S.,		16: 7
on the east side of the river S.		16: 7
by the head of the river S.,		22:27
at the head of the river S.,		22:29
by the head of the river S.,		43:22
near the bank of the river S.,		43:27
on the west of the river S.		43:27
on the west of the river S.,		43:32
began to cross the river S.,		43:35
to flee towards the river S.		43:39
by Lehi into the waters of S.,		43:40
they crossed the waters of S.		43:40
upon the bank of the river S.		43:40
the other side of the river S.,		43:41
fled even to the waters of S.		43:50
upon the bank by the river S.		43:51
Lehi on the east of the river S.,		43:53
on the west of the river S.,		43:53
their dead into the waters of S.,		44:22
on the east of the river S.		49:16
by the head of the river S.		50:11
durst they cross the head of S.,		56:25
Zarahemla, by the waters of S.	Mrm	1:10

SIEGE

shall have laid s. against them	2Ne	26:15
to lay s. round about the people	3Ne	4:16
that this s. should take place.		4:17
to lay s. sufficiently long to have		4:18
withdraw themselves from the s.,		4:23
Coriantumr did lay s. to the	Eth	14: 5

SIFT

that he may s. you as chaff	Al	37:15
that he may s. you as wheat.	3Ne	18:18
for Satan desireth to s. him	DC	52:12

SIGHT

gain favor in the s. of Ishmael,	1Ne	7: 4
which is great in the s. of God,	2Ne	3:24
upon them which are good in my s.,		5:30
and prudent in their own s.!		15:21
not judge after the s. of his eyes,		21: 3
as precious in his s. as the other.	Jac	2:21
in the s. of your great Creator?		3: 7
the blind to receive their s.,	Mos	3: 5
more blameless in the s. of God,		3:22
abominable in the s. of the Lord.		11: 2
abominable in the s. of the Lord,		23: 9
should do wrong in the s. of God.		26:13
in the s. of the Lord;	Al	39: 5
which was right in the s. of God	He	3:20
miracles, in the s. of the people,	3Ne	7:20
the blind to receive their s.,	4Ne	1: 5
withheld them not from his s.,	Eth	3:25
above all, in the s. of God;		8:18
was right in the s. of the Lord,		10: 5
was right in the s. of the Lord;		10:16
was good in the s. of the Lord		10:17
was good in the s. of the Lord.		10:19
the s. of the brother of Jared,		12:20
withhold anything from his s.;		12:21
s. and power to translate,	DC	3:12
souls is great in the s. of God;		18:10
the blind to receive their s.,		35: 9
are not pleasing in my s.,		66: 3
meet in the s. of your Father,		89: 5
be found worthy, in thy s.,		109:11
and find favor in thy s.,		109:21
may obtain favor in the s. of all;		109:56
that is pleasant to the s. of man;	Mses	3: 9
that I have found favor in thy s.,		6:31
tree that is pleasant to the s. and	Abr	5: 9
an abomination in his s.;	JS	2:19
offensive in the s. of God.		2:28

SIGN

shall be given unto thee for a s.,	1Ne	11: 7
should be a s. given of his death		19:10
Ask thee a s. of the Lord thy	2Ne	17:11
himself shall give you a s.—		17:14
show me a s. by this power of the	Jac	7:13
tempt God to show unto thee a s.		7:14

let that be a s. unto thee	Jac	7:14
If thou wilt show me a s.,	Al	30:43
Will ye say, Show unto me a s.,		30:44
except ye shall show me a s.		30:45
and except ye show me a s.,		30:48
This will I give unto thee for a s.,		30:49
Alma should show forth his s.?		30:51
others, to show unto thee a s.?		30:51
he has showed unto you a s.;		30:51
show unto us a s. from heaven,		32:17
and he gave unto him a s.;	He	2: 7
because I showed unto vou this s.		9:24
I will show unto you another s.,		9:25
Behold, I give unto you a s.;		14: 2
this will I give unto you for a s.		14: 3
this shall be unto you for a s.;		14: 4
this also shall be a s. unto you.		14: 5
again, another s. I give unto you,		14:14
unto you, yea, a s. of his death.		14:14
unto you concerning another s.,		14:20
another sign, a s. of his death,		14:20
except the s. should come to	3Ne	1: 9
this night shall the s. be given,		1:13
this night shall the s. be given.		1:14
the s. which had been given was		1:18
of the s. which had been given.		1:19
at a s. or a wonder from heaven,		2: 1
time when the s. was given,		2: 7
period when the s. was given,		2: 8
for the s. which had been given		8: 3
whom the s. had been given		11: 2
I give unto you a s., that ye may		21: 1
I will give unto you for a s.—		21: 2
it shall be a s. unto them,		21: 7
since the s. was given of the	Mro	10: 1
that ask and not for a s.	DC	46: 9
appear a great s. in heaven,		88:93
the s. of the Holy Ghost unto	Fac	2: 7
what is the s. of thy coming,	JS	1: 4
the s. of the Son of Man in		1:36

SIGNAL

the s. which had been given was	3Ne	1:16

SIGNALIZED

shall be s. unto you by the	DC	111: 8

SIGNATURES

certificates over their own s.,	DC	128: 4

SIGNED

s. by the governor of the land.	3Ne	6:22
may be s. by any elder or priest	DC	20:84
be s. by the teachers or deacons		20:84

SIGNIFIES

which s. hieroglyphics.	Abr	1:14
Pharaoh s. king by royal blood.		1:20
in the Chaldean s. Egypt,		1:23
which s. that which is forbidden.		1:23
Kokaubeam, which s. stars,		3:13
which celestial time s. one day	Fac	2: 1
S. Abraham in Egypt—		3: 3

SIGNIFY

did truly s. unto the people that	3Ne	7:21
meant it to s. Shaumau,	Fac	1:12

SIGNIFYING

Raukeeyang, s. expanse,	Fac	1:12
Kolob, s. the first creation,		2: 1
word Raukeeyang, s. expanse,		2: 4
in Egyptian s. one thousand;		2: 4

SIGNS

rejecting s. and wonders,	1Ne	19:13
are for s. and for wonders in	2Ne	18:18
shall be s. given unto my people		26: 3
for the s. which are given,		26: 8
mighty miracles, s., and wonders,		26:13
And many s., and wonders,	Mos	3:15
Thou hast had s. enough; will ye	Al	30:44
and all their s. and their wonders		37:27

SIGNS

that they did have their s.,	He	6:22
their signs, yea, their secret s.,		6:22
many s. and wonders in heaven.		14: 6
know of the s. of his coming,		14:12
they might believe that these s.		14:28
when they shall see all these s.		15: 3
people, showing s. and wonders,		16: 4
great s. given unto the people,		16:13
And notwithstanding the s. and		16:23
greater s. and greater miracles	3Ne	1: 4
might not believe in those s.		1:22
because of the s. which did come		1:26
to forget those s. and wonders		2: 1
any more s. or wonders given;		2: 3
many s. which had been given,		5: 2
and they did show forth s. also		7:22
so many s. had been given.		8: 4
these s. shall follow them	Mrm	9:24
s. shall follow them that believe	Eth	4:18
shall be greater s. in heaven	DC	29:14
show miracles, s., and wonders,		35: 8
forth for the s. of my coming,		39:23
the s. of my coming,		45:16
for the s. of the coming of		45:39
shall see s. and wonders,		45:40
s. following them that believe.		58:64
And he that seeketh s. shall		63: 7
that seeketh signs shall see s.,		63: 7
those among you who seek s.,		63: 8
behold, faith cometh not by s.,		63: 9
but s. follow those that believe.		63: 9
s. come by faith, not by the		63:10
Yea, s. come by faith,		63:11
unto such he showeth no s.,		63:11
sought after s. and wonders		63:12
be blest with s. following,		68:10
to know the s. of the times,		68:11
and the s. of the coming of		68:11
these s. shall follow them		84:65
And these s. shall follow him—		124:98
the night, and let them be for s.,	Mses	2:14
organized them to be for s. and	Abr	4:14
shall show great s. and wonders,	JS	1:22

SILENCE

also put the king-men to s.,	Al	51: 7
were done in a profound s.		55:17
there was s. in the land for the	3Ne	10: 1
there was s. in all the land for		10: 2
Which causeth s. to reign,	DC	38:12
there shall be s. in heaven for		88:95

SILENCED

of Amulek had s. Zeezrom,	Al	12: 1

SILENT

down in the cold and s. grave,	2Ne	1:14

SILK

of s. and fine-twined linen,	Al	1:29

SILKS

I also saw gold, and silver, and s.,	1Ne	13: 7
gold, and the silver, and the s.,		13: 8
exceeding riches, and their fine s.,	Al	4: 6
of fruit, and of grain, and of s.,	Eth	9:17
And they did have s., and		10:24

SILLY

the s. traditions of their fathers,	Al	30:31

SILVER

his s., and his precious things,	1Ne	2: 4
their s., and their precious things,		2:11
and s., and all manner of riches.		3:16
our s., and our precious things.		3:22
our s., and all our precious things.		3:24
I also saw gold, and s., and silks,		13: 7
Behold the gold, and the s.,		13: 8
ore, both of gold, and of s.,		18:25
of steel, and of gold, and of s.,	2Ne	5:15
Their land also is full of s.		12: 7
a man shall cast his idols of s.,		12:20
them, which shall not regard s.		23:17
to search much gold and s.,	Jac	1:16
to search much gold and s.,		2:12
rich in gold, and in s.,	Jar	1: 8
and have not sought gold nor s.	Mos	2:12
raiment, and for gold, and for s.,		4:19
part of their gold and of their s.,		11: 3
precious things, of gold, and of s.,		11: 8
ornamented with gold and s.		11: 9
one half of their gold, and their s.,		19:15
they had taken all their gold, and s.,		22:12
of grain, and of gold, and of s.,	Al	1:29
herds, and their gold and their s.,		4: 6
a senum of s., which is equal to		11: 3
of their gold, and of their s.,		11: 4
A senum of s., an amnor of		11: 6
an amnor of s., an ezrom of		11: 6
an ezrom of s., and an onti of		11: 6
of silver, and an onti of s.		11: 6
A senum of s. was equal to a		11: 7
an amnor of s. was as great as		11:11
an ezrom of s. was as great as		11:12
Behold, here are six onties of s.,		11:22
forsaken all his gold, and s.,		15:16
upon riches, or upon gold and s.,		17:14
were set upon gold, and upon s.,		31:24
exceeding plenty of gold, and of s.,	He	6: 9
and of s., and of precious ore		6:11
idols of their gold and their s.		6:31
that ye might get gold and s.		7:21
their herds, and in gold, and in s.,		12: 2
him of your gold, and of your s.,		13:28
and their gold, and their s.,	3Ne	6: 2
as a refiner and purifier of s.;		24: 3
and purge them as gold and s.,		24: 3
will sell me for s. and for gold,		27:32
gold and s. did they lay up	4Ne	1:46
linen, and of gold, and of s.,	Eth	9:17
in buildings, and in gold and s.		10:12
and they did make gold, and s.,		10:23
gold, and of s., and of iron,		10:23
wealth pertaining to gold and s.	DC	111: 4
with your gold and your s.,		124:11
with all your gold, and your s.,		124:26
sit as a refiner and purifier of s.,		128:24
and purge them as gold and s.,		128:24
were two stones in s. bows—	JS	2:35
heard something of a s. mine		2:56
to dig for the s. mine,		2:56

SILVERLINGS

thousand vines at a thousand s.,	2Ne	17:23

SIMEON: see also CARTER, Simeon.

and get ye upon the mount S.	Mses	7: 2

SIMILITUDE

a s. of God and his Only Begotten	Jac	4: 5
is after the s. of a palace.	DC	124: 2
instituted as a s. of the grave,		128:13
in the s. of mine Only Begotten;	Mses	1: 6
in the s. of his Only Begotten;		1:13
after the s. of mine Only Begotten.		1:16
This thing is a s. of the sacrifice		5: 7

SIMONDS: see RYDER, Simonds.

SIMPLE

that b. small and s. things are	Al	37: 6
by the weak and the s. unto	DC	1:23

SIMPLENESS

because of the s. of the way,	1Ne	17:41
according to the s. of their words.	2Ne	3:20

SIMPLICITY

reasoning in plainness and s.—	DC	133:57

SIN

offereth himself a sacrifice for s.,	2Ne	2: 7
ye shall also say there is no s.		2:13
If ye shall say there is no s.,		2:13
doing no good, for they knew no s.		2:23
And why should I yield to s.,		4:27
No longer droop in s.		4:28

SIN — SINCERITY

may shake at the appearance of s.?	2 Ne	4:31
the truth if ye were freed from s.?		9:47
I teach you the consequences of s.		9:48
Behold, my soul abhorreth s.,		9:49
their s. to be even as Sodom,		13: 9
s. as it were with a cart rope;		15:18
is taken away, and thy s. purged.		16: 7
justify in committing a little s.;		28: 8
it speaketh harshly against s.,		33: 5
ye are beginning to labor in s.,	Jac	2: 5
s. appeareth very abominable		2: 5
and every kind of s.,		3:12
committed the unpardonable s.,		7:19
that little children could s.	Mos	3:16
the devil, who is the master of s.,		4:14
or else thou shalt commit s.;		4:28
thy neighbor to commit s. also.		4:28
things whereby ye may commit s.;		4:29
did cause his people to commit s.,		11: 2
cause this people to commit s.,		12:29
make his soul an offering for s.		14:10
has been made an offering for s.		15:10
and goes on in the ways of s.		16: 5
those who committed s., that were		26: 6
this people to commit much s.		29: 9
fear not, and lay aside every s.	Al	7:15
could not look upon s. save it		13:12
And this great s., and his many		15: 3
death rather than commit s.;		24:19
away into s. and transgression,		24:30
and of their hatred to s.		26:34
lest they should commit s.;		27:23
is because of s. and transgression,		28:13
a man, and do s. in my wish;		29: 3
now hardening their hearts in s.		37:10
hatred against s. and iniquity.		37:32
is a s. which is unpardonable;		39: 6
have hitherto risked to commit s.		41: 9
be restored from s. to happiness.		41:10
man repent except he should s.?		42:17
How could he s. if there was no		42:17
there was no law given against s.		42:20
men would not be afraid to s.		42:20
no s. that he should defend		43:30
shall s. against so great light		45:12
the Lord cannot look upon s.		45:16
he who is the author of all s.	He	6:30
shall go on in this your way of s.?		9:21
lest by any means they should s.;		15: 9
can see that they fear to s.—		15: 9
they did not s. ignorantly,	3 Ne	6:18
to save the world from s.		9:21
shall s. against my gospel,		16:10
them to take happiness in s.	Mrm	2:13
but thou shalt not s. any more,	Eth	2:15
ye will s. until ye are fully ripe		2:15
and inviteth and enticeth to s.;	Mro	7:12
not capable of committing s.;		8: 8
and capable of committing s.;		8:10
I the Lord cannot look upon s.	DC	1:31
go your ways and s. no more;		6:35
it is no s. to lie that they may		10:25
uprightly before me and s. not.		18:31
go thy way and s. no more.		24: 2
remember to s. no more,		29: 3
Wherefore, they cannot s.,		29:47
death of him who did no s.,		45: 4
shall grow up without s. unto		45:58
for all are under s., except		49: 8
wherefore the world lieth in s.		49:20
purified and cleansed from all s.		50:28
purified and cleansed from all s.,		50:29
much laughter, for this is s.,		59:15
remaineth in him the greater s.		64: 9
the s. be upon the heads of		68:25
henceforth, and refrain from s.,		82: 2
not lay any s. to your charge;		82: 7
go your ways and s. no more;		82: 7
inasmuch as you s. not.		82:20
the whole world lieth in s.,		84:49
and under the bondage of s.		84:49
are under the bondage of s.,		84:50
me is under the bondage of s.		84:51
whole world groaneth under s.	DC	84:53
and willeth to abide in s.,		88:35
and altogether abideth in s.,		88:35
entangle not yourselves in s.,		88:86
against me a very grievous s.,		95: 3
have sinned a very grievous s.,		95: 6
sinned a very grievous s.;		95:10
and if she s. no more none of		97:27
and grievous s. against me,		101:98
and as all men s. forgive the		109:34
wise as serpents and yet without s.;		111:11
they are the servants of s.,		121:17
he or she shall commit any s.		132:26
in nothing did they s. save in		132:38
in none of these things did he s.		132:39
he will not commit s.,		132:59
s. lieth at the door, and Satan	Mses	5:23
thy children are conceived in s.,		6:55
s. conceiveth in their hearts, and		6:55
might be sanctified from all s.,		6:59

SINAI

unto Moses in the mount of S.,	Mos	12:33
did while in the mount of S.,		13: 5
loud, even as upon Mount S.,	DC	29:13

SINCE

s. the world began, even down	1 Ne	3:20
And s. they have been led away,		22: 5
S. thou art laid down no feller	2 Ne	24: 8
and I have not s. known	Om	1:30
ever were s. the fall of Adam,	Mos	4: 7
ever s. the world began—		13:33
ever s. the world began?		15:13
sins ever s. the world began,		15:26
now s. the coming of Ammon,		21:32
been ever s. the world began,	Al	7:25
And s. man had fallen he could		22:14
s. it has been all that we could do,		24:11
s. God hath taken away our		24:12
s. it has been as much as we could		24:15
s. he imparted his word unto us		24:15
rejoice as we, s. the world began;		26:35
s. the days of Nephi, than in		50:23
had ever s. been protected by		53:10
even s. the days of Abraham	He	8:19
s. the days of Mosiah,	3 Ne	2: 5
s. Lehi left Jerusalem.		2: 6
of Lehi s. he left Jerusalem.		4:11
s. the more part of the people		7: 8
s. I wrote, I have inquired of		28:37
ever s. I have been sufficient	Mrm	2:18
s. the coming of our Lord		8: 6
s. the sign was given of the	Mro	10:, 1
s. the coming of our Lord and	DC	20: 1
church s. the last conference;		20:82
prophets s. the world began,		27: 6
prophets s. the world began.		86:10
s. the world was until now;		121:26
s. I have been pursued by my		128: 1
For s. the beginning of the world		133:45
but has s. recovered;		135: 2
contracted in Utah s. last June		OD
s. the day that I created them	Mses	6:28
s. the beginning of their	JS	1:18
s. the organization of the		2: 2
then, and often has s.,		2:23
I have thought s., that I felt		2:24

SINCERE

because of their s. repentance,	Mos	29:19
if ye shall ask with a s. heart,	Mro	10: 4

SINCERELY

and humbling himself s.,	DC	20: 6
hath s. striven to do thy will.		109:68

SINCERITY

and ask in s. of heart that he	Mos	4:10
repenteth in the s. of his heart,		26:29
and we can witness of their s.,	Al	26:31
of mine afflictions and my s.;		33:11

SINCERITY

will, in the s. of their hearts. — He 3:27
faith, in the s. of his heart, — DC 5:24

SINEW

and thy neck is an iron s., — 1Ne 20: 4

SINFUL

of their s. and polluted state, — Mos 25:11
even in their carnal and s. state; — 26: 4
awful, s., and polluted state? — Al 26:17
Jesus was crucified by s. men — DC 21: 9

SING

they began to dance, and to s., — 1Ne 18: 9
S., O heavens; and be joyful, — 21:13
then will I s. to my well-beloved — 2Ne 15: 1
S. unto the Lord; for he hath done — 22: 5
the voice together shall they s.; — Mos 12:22
s. together ye waste places of — 12:23
the voice together shall they s.; — 15:29
s. together, ye waste places of — 15:30
for they shall s. to his praise — 18:30
themselves together to s., — 20: 1
together to s. and to dance. — 20: 2
and they did s. redeeming love. — Al 5: 9
to s. the song of redeeming love, — 5:26
let us s. to his praise, — 26: 8
brought to s. redeeming love, — 26:13
the voice together shall they s., — 3Ne 16:18
Break forth into joy, s. together, — 16:19
the voice together shall they s.; — 20:32
S. together, ye waste places of — 20:34
S., O barren, thou that didst — 22: 1
to s. ceaseless praises with the — Mrm 7: 7
did s. praises unto the Lord; — Eth 6: 9
brother of Jared did s. praises — 6: 9
pray, or to supplicate, or to s., — Mro 6: 9
voice together s. this new song, — DC 84:98
the morning stars s. together, — 128:23
shall s. the song of the Lamb, — 133:56

SINGING

of angels in the attitude of s. — 1Ne 1: 8
with a voice of s. declare ye, — 20:20
and break forth into s., — 21:13
and come with s. unto Zion; — 2Ne 8:11
they break forth into s. — 24: 7
in s. the praises of a just God. — Mos 2:28
the attitude of s. and praising — Al 36:22
did break forth, all as one, in s., — 3Ne 4:31
break forth into s., and cry — 22: 1
s. with songs of everlasting joy. — DC 45:71
s. Hosanna to God and the Lamb! — 109:79
Let the earth break forth into s. — 128:22
praise the Lord with s., — 136:28

SINGLE

not a s. soul of the Nephites — Al 49:23
if, therefore, thine eye be s., — 3Ne 13:22
with an eye s. to his glory, — Mrm 8:15
an eye s. to the glory of God, — DC 4: 5
with an eye s. to my glory— — 27: 2
with an eye s. to my glory, — 55: 1
with an eye s. to my glory, — 59: 1
an eye s. to the glory of God. — 82:19
if your eye be s. to my glory, — 88:67
your minds become s. to God, — 88:68

SINGLENESS

embrace it with s. of heart — DC 36: 7
be prepared with s. of heart — 59:13

SINGLY

but remain separately and s., — DC 132:17

SINGULARITY

musing on the s. of the scene, — JS 2:44

SINIM

and these from the land of S. — 1Ne 21:12

SINK

the city of Moroni did s. into — 3Ne 8: 9
I was ready to s. into despair — JS 2:16

SINNED

or who have ignorantly s. — Mos 3:11
and thou, O king, hast not s.; — 12:14
if men s. what could justice do, — Al 42:21
s. against that great knowledge — He 7:24
therefore in this ye have s., — 8:24
inasmuch as they s. they might — DC 1:27
those among you who have s.; — 64: 3
Nevertheless, he has s.; — 64: 7
who have not s. unto death. — 64: 7
Partridge, behold, he hath s., — 64:17
inasmuch as they have not s. — 70:17
And he s.; nevertheless, — 75: 8
you who have s. exceedingly; — 82: 2
yea, even all of you have s. — 82: 2
For ye have s. against me — 95: 3
have s. a very grievous s., — 95: 6
servants s. a very grievous s.; — 95:10
and cry they have s. — 121:16
when they have not s. before me, — 121:16

SINNER

more fully condemneth the s., — Al 41:15
God in the punishment of the s.; — 42: 1
the s. should be consigned to a — 42: 1
false prophet, and that he is a s., — He 13:26

SINNERS

he shall destroy the s. thereof — 2Ne 23: 9
they were the very vilest of s. — Mos 28: 4
ye become s. like unto them; — Al 34:40
but s. to repentance; — Mro 8: 8
ye s. stay and sleep until I — DC 43:18
to warn s. to repentance, — 63:57

SINNETH

he that s. and repenteth not — DC 42:28
he that s. and repenteth not — 42:37
but unto that soul who s. — 82: 7

SINS

take away the s. of the world — 1Ne 10:10
slain for the s. of the world. — 11:33
and did repent of their s., — 16:39
the s. which do so easily beset me. — 2Ne 4:18
heart groaneth because of my s.; — 4:19
unto all those who die in their s.; — 9:38
and remain in their s. — 9:38
brethren, turn away from your s.; — 9:45
and lay aside our s., — 10:20
for a remission of their s. — 25:26
take away the s. of the world. — 31: 4
real intent, repenting of your s., — 31:13
After ye have repented of your s., — 31:14
cometh a remission of your s. — 31:17
answering the s. of the people — Jac 1:19
might rid my garments of your s., — 2: 2
unless ye shall repent of your s. — 3: 8
s. be heaped upon your heads — 3:10
I received a remission of my s. — En 1: 2
Enos, thy s. are forgiven thee, — 1: 5
remaineth and dieth in his s., — Mos 2:33
atoneth for the s. of those who — 3:11
receive remission of their s., — 3:13
of Christ atoneth for their s. — 3:16
receive forgiveness of our s., — 4: 2
received a remission of their s., — 4: 3
that ye must repent of your s. — 4:10
received a remission of your s.; — 4:11
retain a remission of your s.; — 4:12
for a remission of your s. — 4:20
retaining a remission of your s. — 4:26
or what great s. have thy people — 12:13
the s. and iniquities of his people, — 13:28
and he bore the s. of many, — 14:12
for a remission of their s., — 15:11
are they whose s. he has borne; — 15:12
against him and die in their s.; — 15:26
those that have perished in their s. — 15:26
to tremble and repent of your s., — 16:13
repented of his s. and iniquities, — 18: 1
the people to commit so many s. — 21:30
cause them to commit many s.; — 26: 6

SINS

upon me the s. of the world;	Mos	26:23
the s. which he has committed;		26:29
confess his s. before thee and me,		26:29
will not repent of his s.		26:32
whosoever repented of their s.		26:35
that would not confess their s.		26:36
according to his s., or to the		26:39
the s. which he had committed,		26:39
I have repented of my s., and		27:24
confessing all their s., and		27:35
that if these people commit s.		29:30
the s. of many people have been		29:31
to answer for his own s.		29:38
retaining a remission of their s.;	Al	4:14
redeem his people from their s.		5:21
redeem his people from their s.?		5:27
take away the s. of the world,		5:48
yea, the s. of every man who		5:48
who repented of their s. were		6: 2
redeem his people from their s.,		6: 8
for the remission of your s., with		7: 6
upon him the s. of his people,		7:13
ye may be washed from your s.,		7:14
taketh away the s. of the world,		7:14
are willing to repent of your s.		7:15
for you, if ye remain in your s.,		9:15
fall into s. and transgressions,		9:19
because of the s. of this people,		10: 7
he save his people in their s.?		11:34
not save his people in their s.		11:36
he cannot save them in their s.;		11:37
ye cannot be saved in your s.		11:37
that whosoever dieth in his s.,		12:16
Son, unto a remission of his s.;		12:34
to him for a remission of their s.,		13:16
my words, and cast off your s.		13:27
great sin, and his many other s.,		15: 3
they repented not of their s.,		15:15
in the repentance of their s.		15:15
and confess their s. before him.		17: 4
behold, he has repented of his s.;		20:17
redeem mankind from their s.?		21: 7
did convince many of their s.,		21:17
death of Christ atone for their s.,		22:14
if thou wilt repent of all thy s.,		22:16
away all my s. to know thee,		22:18
have been convinced of our s.,		24: 9
forgiven us of those our many s.		24:10
to repent of all our s. and the		24:11
shed for the atonement of our s.		24:13
of the many murders and s.		27: 6
the many murders and s. which		27: 8
that ye see a remission of your s.		30:16
made for the s. of men,		30:17
slain for the s. of the world—		30:26
himself, and repenteth of his s.,		32:15
and die to atone for their s.;		33:22
atone for the s. of the world;		34: 8
will atone for the s. of another.		34:11
suffice for the s. of the world.		34:12
and racked with all my s.		36:12
remember all my s. and iniquities,		36:13
up by the memory of my many s.,		36:17
to atone for the s. of the world.		36:17
the memory of my s. no more.		36:19
did I receive a remission of my s.		38: 8
most abominable above all s.		39: 5
repent and forsake your s.,		39: 9
take away the s. of the world;		39:15
If he hath repented of his s.,		41: 6
atoneth for the s. of the world,		42:15
only let your s. trouble you,		42:29
least point because of your s.,		42:30
repent of their s. and iniquities,		60:33
cause them to repent of their s.		62:45
if they did not repent of their s.	He	4:14
come to redeem them in their s.,		5:10
but to redeem them from their s.		5:10
to redeem them from their s.		5:11
forth and did confess their s.		5:17
unto those who repent of their s.,		7:23
testifieth of your s. and iniquities,		13:26
name ye will repent of all your s.,	He	14:13
they confessed unto him their s.		16: 1
repenting and confessing their s.		16: 5
was a great remission of s.	3Ne	1:23
they did repent of all their s.;		3:25
they did forsake all their s.,		5: 3
as would repent of their s.		5: 4
and testifying boldly of the s.		6:20
repentance and remission of s.		7:16
repentance and remission of s.		7:23
received a remission of their s.		7:25
with fire because of their s.		9: 9
unto me, and repent of your s.,		9:13
upon me the s. of the world,		11:11
slain for the s. of the world.		11:14
whoso repenteth of his s.		11:23
receive a remission of their s.		12: 2
that ye shall repent of your s.,		12:19
the repentance of all their s.,		27:19
it be for the s. of the world;		28: 9
it were for the s. of the world.		28:38
receive a remission of your s.,		30: 2
and did truly repent of their s.,	4Ne	1: 1
sorrow for the s. of the world.		1:44
have repented not of their s.	Mrm	3:13
repent of all your s. and		7: 5
you shall be forgiven of your s.		8:32
and thy brethren of their s.;	Eth	2:15
thereby ye may repent of your s.,		8:23
who repented of their s.		13:17
repentance and remission of s.	Mro	3: 3
truly repented of all their s.		6: 2
unto the remission of s.		8:11
bringeth remission of s.;		8:25
the remission of s. bringeth		8:26
hide their s., and wickedness,		9:15
and die, for they die in their s.,		10:26
unto the remission of your s.,		10:33
for the remission of s.;	DC	13: 1
convincing of many of their s.,		18:44
and that you confess your s.,		19:20
remission of s. by baptism,		19:31
received a remission of his s.		20: 5
truly repented of all their s.,		20:37
unto the remission of their s.,		20:37
unto the remission of his s.,		21: 8
men for the s. of the world,		21: 9
for the remission of his s. unto		21: 9
thy s. are forgiven thee,		25: 3
shed for the remission of your s.		27: 2
mercy hath atoned for your s.;		29: 1
time your s. are forgiven you,		29: 3
and your s. are forgiven you,		31: 5
for a remission of your s.;		33:11
crucified for the s. of the world,		35: 2
and your s. are forgiven you,		36: 1
and wash away your s.,		39:10
they shall repent of all their s.		42:77
crucified for the s. of the world.		46:13
for the remission of s.;		49:13
repent of all your s.;		49:26
for your s. are forgiven you.		50:36
crucified for the s. of the world,		53: 2
repentance and remission of s.,		53: 3
crucified for the s. of the world—		54: 1
let them repent of all their s.,		54: 3
have a remission of your s.		55: 1
repentance and remission of s.		55: 2
your s. have come up unto me,		56:14
But if he repent not of his s.,		58:15
And let him repent of his s.,		58:39
who has repented of his s.,—		58:42
if a man repenteth of his s.—		58:43
chastened for all his s.;		58:60
confessing thy s. unto thy		59:12
and your s. are forgiven you.		60: 7
whose s. are now forgiven you,		61: 2
for I, the Lord, forgive s.,		61: 2
those who confess their s.		61: 2
were chastened for all your s.,		61: 8
and your s. are forgiven you.		62: 3
the church repent of their s.,		63:63

SINS

I have forgiven you your s.	DC	64: 3
I, the Lord, forgive s. unto		64: 7
those who confess their s.		64: 7
that repenteth not of his s.,		64:12
for the remission of their s.		68:27
to bear the s. of the world,		76:41
cleansed from all their s.,		76:52
he who s. against the greater		82: 3
shall the former s. return,		82: 7
that s. against this covenant,		82:21
baptism, and the remission of s.,		84:27
forgiveness of s. in this world		84:41
I will forgive you of your s.		84:61
water for the remission of s.,		84:64
for the remission of their s.,		84:74
their s. are upon their own		88:82
thy s. are forgiven thee,		90: 1
their s. are forgiven them also,		90: 6
soul who forsaketh his s.		93: 1
that their s. may be forgiven,		95: 1
they do not forsake their s.,		98:20
notwithstanding their s.,		101: 9
be accountable for his own s.		101:78
for the remission of s.,		107:20
Your s. are forgiven you,		108: 1
that they may repent of their s.		109:50
your s. are forgiven you;		110: 5
all thy s. are forgiven thee.		112: 3
be admonished for all their s.,		112:12
Let them repent of all their s.,		117: 4
we undertake to cover your s.,		121:37
for I will forgive all his s.,		124:76
and will forgive all his s.;		124:78
whosesoever s. you remit on earth		132:46
s. you retain on earth shall be		132:46
and will forgive all your s.;		132:50
and repented of their s., should be	Mses	5:15
wherein the s. of the parents cannot		6:54
and have perished in their s.,		7: 1
their s. shall be upon the heads		7:37
he suffereth for their s.;		7:39
repent of your s. and be baptized		8:24
of any great or malignant s.	JS	2:28
for forgiveness of all my s.		2:29
baptism for the remission of s.,		2:68
for the remission of s.;		2:69
be punished for their own s.,	AoF	2
for the remission of s.;		4

SIRON
go over into the land of S.,	Al	39: 3

SISTER
thy brother or s. offend thee,	DC	42:88
if thy brother or s. offend many,		42:90
the s. of Tubal Cain was called	Mses	5:46
unto the Egyptians, she is thy s.,	Abr	2:24
I pray thee, thou art my s.,		2:25
and my s. Sophronia.	JS	2: 7

SISTERS
younger brethren, and also my s.,	2Ne	5: 6
and mother and brethren and s.;	DC	122: 6
dearly beloved brethren and s.,		128:15
brothers and s., houses and lands,		132:55
my s., Sophronia, Catherine,	JS	2: 4

SIT
to them that s. in darkness:	1Ne	21: 9
s. down, O Jerusalem;	2Ne	8:25
and shall s. upon the ground.		13:26
I will s. also upon the mount of		24:13
to s. down in the kingdom of God,	Al	5:24
to s. down with Abraham,		7:25
s. down in the kingdom of God;		29:17
shall s. down in his kingdom,		34:36
his kingdom, to s. down in peace.		38:15
to s. upon your thrones in a		60: 1
ye could s. upon your thrones,		60:11
while we s. upon our thrones		60:21
will ye s. in idleness while ye are		60:22
who do also s. in idleness,		60:22
s. still and behold these things?		60:23
to s. down with Abraham, and	He	3:30
to s. in the judgment-seat.		8:27
they should s. themselves down	3Ne	18: 2
arise, s. down, O Jerusalem;		20:37
And he shall s. as a refiner and		24: 3
s. down in the kingdom of my		28:10
to s. down on the right hand of	DC	20:24
in robes and s. thou here;		38:26
in rags and s. thou there—		38:26
them that s. in darkness,		45:28
those who s. in darkness and in		57:10
to s. on the throne of his power		76:108
s. in council with the saints		78: 9
s. in judgment upon transgressors		107:72
to s. as a judge in Israel.		107:76
to s. in council with them,		107:85
to s. in council with them,		107:86
and s. in council with them,		107:87
and to s. in council with them,		107:89
the Ancient of Days shall s.,		116: 1
shall s. as a refiner and purifier of		128:24
and s. upon thrones,		132:37

SITS
who s. upon the throne forever	DC	76:110

SITTEST
where thou s. enthroned,	DC	109:77

SITTETH
s. on the right hand of his power,	Mro	9:26
or s. upon the judgment seat.	DC	58:20
enemy, even Satan, s. to reign—		86: 3
God who s. upon his throne,		88:13
him who s. upon the throne		88:40
who s. upon many waters,		88:94
him who s. upon the throne,		88:104
of him who s. upon the throne,		88:110
of him who s. upon the throne,		88:115
s. with Abraham at his right hand,		124:19
to him that s. upon the throne		124:101
and s. upon his throne.		132:29

SITTING
saw God s. upon his throne,	1Ne	1: 8
also the Lord s. upon a throne,	2Ne	16: 1
God s. upon his throne,	Al	36:22
unto the s. down in the place	Eth	12:37
like unto a judge s. on a hill,	DC	64:37
s. down in the place which I have		135: 5
God s. upon his throne,	Fac	2: 3
God s. upon his throne,		2: 7
s. upon Pharaoh's throne		3: 1

SITUATED
which the called Shule [ashery] is s.	DC	104:39
was s. in the plains of Moreh.	Abr	2:18

SITUATION
a remembrance of the awful s. of	Mos	2:40
have placed you in a s. that	Al	60: 8
to a sense of your awful s.,	Eth	8:24

SITUATIONS
dissatisfied with their s. in this	DC	134:12

SIX
s. hundred years from the time	1Ne	10: 4
in s. hundred years from the time		19: 8
seraphim; each one had s. wings;	2Ne	16: 2
cometh in s. hundred years		25:19
two hundred and seventy and s.	Om	1: 3
four hundred and seventy-s. years	Mos	6: 4
S. days shalt thou labor, and do		13:17
For in s. days the Lord made		13:19
s. thousand five hundred sixty	Al	2:19
here are s. onties of silver,		11:22
Behold these s. onties, which		11:25
s. of them had fallen by the sling,		17:38
the number of s. thousand men,		57: 6
an army of s. thousand men		62:12
an army of s. thousand men,		62:13
it was s. hundred years from	3Ne	1: 1

s. hundred and nine years had		3Ne 2: 6	also two hundred and s. years.		4Ne 1:41
s. years had not passed away		7: 8	three hundred and s. years		Mrm 3: 4
and twenty and s. years had		Mrm 2: 2	hundred and s. and first year		3: 7
made the world in s. days,		DC 77:12	hundred and s. and second year		3: 8
and s. elders, as they united		84: 1	hundred and s. and third year		4: 1
and if more difficult, s.;		102:14	hundred and s. and fourth year		4: 7
shall more than s. be appointed		102:14	hundred and s. and sixth year		4:10
was four hundred and ninety-s.		107:46	hundred and s. and seventh year,		4:15
to preside over ninety-s. elders,		107:89	in the space of s. and two years		Eth 9:16
is to preside over the s.;		107:94	s. and nine of the people of Shiz.		15:23
although but s. years of age,		122: 6	and s.-first and second verses of		DC 85:12
			by s.-five feet in the width		94: 4
SIXTEEN			by s.-five feet in the width		94:11
that s. of their strong men might		Mos 7: 2	let it be s.-five feet in length.		95:15
out of a rock s. small stones;		Eth 3: 1	at the age of s.-nine years,		107:42
			was s.-five and Adam blessed him.		107:48
SIXTEENTH			three hundred and s.-five years,		107:49
the s. year of the reign of		Al 30: 2	And Mahalaleel lived s.-five years,		Mses 6:20
no disturbance in all the s. year		30: 4	lived one hundred and s.-two years,		6:21
in the s. year from the coming		3Ne 3: 1	nine hundred and s.-two years,		6:24
in my s. year I did go forth		Mrm 2: 2	And Enoch lived s.-five years,		6:25
on the s. day of February,		DC 76:11	three hundred and s.-five years.		7:68
			nine hundred and s.-nine years,		8: 7
SIXTH			was s. and two years old when		Abr 2:14
in the s. year of the reign of		Al 4: 1			
in the twenty and s. year of		52: 1	SIXTY-FIRST: *see SIXTY and FIRST.*		
ending of the twenty and s. year		52:14			
But in the twenty and s. year,		56: 7	SIXTY FIVE: *see SIXTY and FIVE.*		
in the twenty and s. year,		56: 9			
ended the twenty and s. year.		56:20	SIXTY-NINE: *see SIXTY and NINE.*		
of the thirty and s. year of		63: 1			
thus ended the thirty and s. year		63: 3	SIXTY-TWO: *see SIXTY and TWO.*		
came to pass in the forty and s.,		He 3: 3			
The forty and s. year of the		3:18	**SIZE**		
in the fifty and s. year of		4: 4	of the good and the s. thereof;		Jac 5:65
in the sixty and s. year of the		6:15	the s. thereof shall be fifty and		DC 95:15
thus ended the sixty and s. year.		6:15	stands a hill of considerable s.,		JS 2:51
in the seventy and s. year		11:17	under a stone of considerable s.,		2:51
the seventy and s. year did end		11:21			
in the eighty and s. year,		13: 1	**SKILL**		
thus ended the eighty and s. year		16: 9	and their s. was in the bow,		En 1:20
away the ninety and s. year;		3Ne 2: 4	strength and in their s. of war,		Al 51:31
and it was in the s. month;		4: 7	used with judgment and s.		DC 89: 8
commenced in this the s. month;		4:11			
in the twenty and s. year,		6: 1	**SKILLFUL**		
twenty and s. and seventh years		6: 4	might be s. in their profession.		Al 10:15
in the thirty and s. year,		4Ne 1: 2			
hundred and forty and s. year		Mrm 2:22	**SKIN**		
hundred and sixty and s. year		4:10	God did cause a s. of blackness		2Ne 5:21
on the s. day of the month		DC 20: 1	a short s. girdle about their loins		En 1:20
on the s. day of the month		21: 3	and scourged his s. with faggots,		Mos 17:13
in the s. thousand years,		77:10	s. which was girded about their		Al 3: 5
or the opening of the s. seal.		77:10	a s. which was girded about		43:20
which is the s. angel, saying:		88:105	their s. became white like unto		3Ne 2:15
on the twenty-s. day of April		118: 5	had a lamb-s. about their loins,		4: 7
and the morning were the s. day.		Mses 2:31			
and they numbered the s. time.		Abr 4:31	**SKINS**		
			blow the fire, of the s. of beasts;		1Ne 17:11
SIXTIETH			which hath come upon their s.,		Jac 3: 5
in the s. year of the reign of		He 4: 9	their s. will be whiter than yours,		3: 8
			of the darkness of their s.;		3: 9
SIXTY			s. of the Lamanites were dark,		Al 3: 6
being s. and three years old;		Mos 29:46	their s. were worn exceedingly		20:29
five hundred s. and two souls.		Al 2:19	naked s. and their bare heads		44:18
s. of the sons of the Ammonites		57: 6	with garments of s., yea,		49: 6
band of two thousand and s.		57:19	coats of s., and clothed them.		Mses 4:27
those two thousand and s. were		57:20			
out of my two thousand and s.;		57:25	**SKIRTS**		
in the s. and first year of the		He 4:10	blood upon the s. of his cloak.		He 9:31
thus ended the s. and first year		4:17			
in the s. and second year of		4:18	**SLACKEN**		
when the s. and second year of		6: 1	my strength s., because of mine		2Ne 4:26
thus ended the s. and third year,		6: 6	Do not s. my strength because		4:29
thus the s. and fourth year did		6:13			
And in the s. and fifth year		6:14	**SLACKENED**		
passed away the s. and fifth year.		6:14	Have I s. mine hand, that		Jac 5:47
in the s. and sixth year of the		6:15			
thus ended the s. and sixth year.		6:15	**SLAIN**		
of the s. and seventh year		6:16	cast out, and stoned, and s.;		1Ne 1:20
in the s. and seventh year of		6:32	truly that Laban whom I had s.,		4:26
in the s. and eighth year also,		6:33	Laban, and that he had s. me		4:28
thus ended the s. and eighth year		6:41	after they had s. the Messiah,		10:11
in the s. and ninth year of		7: 1	and after he had been s.		10:11

SLAIN 888 SLAUGHTER

s. for the sins of the world.	1 Ne	11:33
And after he was s. I saw		11:34
my people before they were s.		13:15
had s. food for our families		16:14
bearing the beasts which I had s.;		16:32
have been s. and carried away	2 Ne	6: 8
and they shall fall under the s.		20: 4
remnant of those that are s.,		24:19
thy land and s. thy people;		24:20
the loss of the s. of my people!		26: 7
and the s. of his people.	Om	1:21
and they were all s., save fifty,		1:28
until they had s. many thousands	WM	1:14
of our brethren have been s.,	Mos	7:14
of the Lord have they s.;		7:26
commanded that I should be s.;		9: 2
place where our brethren were s.,		9: 4
of our brethren were s.		9:19
driven by men, and shall be s.;		12: 2
he shall be led, crucified, and s.,		15: 7
him up that he might be s.		17:12
wives and their children were s.,		19:19
that they had s. the king,		19:23
and their children were not s.;		19:24
those that were not s. returned		21:12
their number that had been s.		21:17
of their brethren had been s.;		21:29
who had been s. by the Lamanites		25: 9
therefore he was s. by the sword.	Al	1: 9
were s. of the Amlicites twelve		2:19
were s. of the Nephites six		2:19
who was s. by the hand of Nehor		2:20
our wives, and our children be s.		2:25
the Lamanites who had been s.		2:34
were met on every hand, and s.		2:37
the Nephites who were not s.		3: 1
buried those who had been s.—		3: 1
the number of the s. were not		3: 1
women and children had been s.		3: 2
the Amlicites who had been s.		3: 3
who was s. by the hand of Nehor		6: 7
might be s. or cast into prison,		10:13
were s. by the fall thereof.		14:27
were Alma and Amulek, was s.;		14:28
supposed that they had been s.		15: 3
profession of Nehor, who were s.;		16:11
because of the fear of being s.		17:29
of the s. of their brethren,		17:36
do know, that he cannot be s.		18: 3
for we know he cannot be s.		18: 3
For he had s. many of their		18: 6
their flocks scattered they were s.		18: 6
of the number which he had s.		19:21
whose brother had been s. with		19:22
see that Ammon could not be s.,		19:23
the number who had been s.;		24:26
been s. were righteous people,		24:26
a wicked man s. among them;		24:27
they had s. their brethren;		25: 1
which they were driven and s.		25: 3
the Lamanites who were s. were		25: 4
s. by the hands of the Nephites;		25: 4
should be scattered abroad and s.,		25:12
is driven and s. by wild beasts;		25:12
not suffer themselves to be s.		26:34
they suffered themselves to be s.		27: 3
of the Lamanites were s. and		28: 2
their kindred who had been s.		28: 5
be s. for the sins of the world—		30:26
many of the Nephites were s.		43:44
not suffer yourselves to be s.		43:46
into prison, or be sold, or be s.		46:23
his servants that they may be s.		47:27
had heard that the king was s.—		47:32
king had been s. by his servants,		47:32
king was s. by his own servants;		47:34
s. with an immense slaughter.		49:21
their chief captains were all s.;		49:23
of the Lamanites were s.;		49:23
of the Nephites which was s.		49:23
their chief captains were all s.		49:25
s. by the hand of the Nephites;		51:11
their leaders who were not s.		51:19
Teancum, who had s. Morianton	Al	51:29
were many s. on both sides;		52:35
all those who were not s.,		52:38
of those who had been s.,		52:40
who had been s. on both sides.		52:40
of the Nephites who were s.;		53: 1
Nephites could have l. them.		55:18
had s. a vast number of our men,		56:10
it is so if they are not s.		56:12
not stand against them, but be s.,		56:40
lest there were many of them s.		56:55
of those men who were not s.		56:57
of our brethren who were s.		57:26
greater number of them were s.;		57:33
souls of them who have been s.		57:36
even one soul has not been s.		58:39
suffereth the righteous to be s.		60:13
are lost because they are s.;		60:13
towards those who have been s.		60:14
Pachus was s. and his men		62: 8
thousand who had been s.		62:17
of the Lamanites who were s.		62:26
fled before them, and were s.,	He	1:22
of the Nephites who were s.		1:25
yea, many were s., and among the		1:30
among the number who were s.		1:30
Nephites, and he himself was s.,		1:32
hunted, and driven forth, and s.,		3:16
And the rebellious part were s.		4: 2
and trodden down, and s.,		4:20
for the which he was s.		8:19
the sons of Zedekiah were not s.,		8:21
abroad that the judge was s.,		9: 9
great chief judge who had been s.		9:10
and shall be s. for his people.		13: 6
would not have s. the prophets;		13:25
down and s. by their enemies.		15: 9
he was overtaken and s.	3 Ne	4:14
the remainder of them were s.		4:27
none did escape who were not s.,		5: 4
the inhabitants thereof were s.,		8:14
were many of them who were s.		8:15
because of the s. of the fair		9: 2
kindred which had been s.;		10: 2
were s. because they testified of		10:15
been s. for the sins of the world.		11:14
to be afflicted, and to be s.,		16: 9
their brethren who had been s.	Mrm	3: 9
thousands s. on both sides,		4: 9
because of the s. of my people,		6:16
and that he was s. by the Jews,		7: 5
father hath been s. in battle,		8: 5
they had s. the army of Jared	Eth	8: 6
of them who have been s.;		8:24
that Shiblom was s.,		11: 9
people who were s. by the sword		13:18
his brother, who had been s.,		14:24
been s. by the sword already		15: 2
s. two millions of mighty men,		15: 2
who had not been s., save		15:12
the loss of the s. of their people;		15:16
the loss of the s. of their people.		15:17
and children they have s.;	Mro	9: 8
life, even if you should be s.	DC	5:22
of the Lamb, who was s.,		76:39
was s. by the conspiracy of		84:16
I am he who was s.:		110: 4
s. in the land of Missouri,		124:54
and name that cannot be s.		135: 3
have s. a man to my wounding,	Mses	5:47
Lamb is s. from the foundation		7:47

SLANDERER

let the tongue of the s. cease	DC	112: 9

SLANDERS

may be an end to lyings and s.	DC	109:30

SLAUGHTER

according to the s. of Midian	2 Ne	20:26
Prepare s. for his children		24:21
we slew them with a great s.,	Mos	10:20
is brought as a lamb to the s.,		14: 7

SLAUGHTER

slew the Amlicites-with great s.,	Al	2:18
and did slay them with much s.,		2:19
tremendous s. among the people		28: 3
were slain with an immense s.		49:21
them with an exceeding great s.		59: 7
great has been the s. among		60: 5
did slay them with a great s.;		62:38
slaying the people with a great s.,	He	1:27
great s. which was among them,		4:11
do much s. among the people.	3Ne	1:27
terrible was the s. thereof,		4:11
never was known so great a s.		4:11
great s. which had been made		4:24
with an exceedingly great s.;	Mrm	4:21
going like a lamb to the s.;	DC	135: 4
shall it be said to the s.?		135: 4

SLAUGHTERED

the Nephites were driven and s.	Mrm	4:21

SLAUGHTERS

wars, and great s. with the sword	1Ne	12: 2

SLAVE

arise through the s. question.	DC	130:13
Olimlah, a s. belonging to the	Fac	3: 6

SLAVERY

brethren from bondage and s.;	Al	48:11

SLAVES

should make s. one of another,	Mos	2:13
and we will be their s.;		7:15
for it is better that we be s.		7:15
and we will be their s. until	Al	27: 8
should be any s. among them;		27: 9
not our s., but our brethren	3Ne	3: 7
s. shall rise up against their	DC	87: 4

SLAY

thou art a robber, and I will s. thee.	1Ne	3:13
and sent his servants to s. us,		3:25
he can s. fifty; then why not us?		3:31
and would that I might not s. him.		4:10
Spirit said unto me again: S. him,		4:12
into the wilderness to s. food		16:14
I, Nephi, went forth to s. food,		16:18
I did s. wild beasts,		16:31
let us s. our father, and also our		16:37
wherefore, now let us s. him,	2Ne	5: 3
of his lips shall he s. the wicked.		21: 4
and he shall s. thy remnant.		24:30
and stone them, and s. them;		26: 3
of his lips shall he s. the wicked.		30: 9
upon them and began to s. them,	Mos	9:14
we did s. three thousand and		9:18
we did s. them even until we had		9:18
and to s. them in their fields,		11:16
hither, that I may s. him,		11:28
therefore I will s. him.		11:28
with this fellow, and s. him;		13: 1
that ye have not power to s. me,		13: 7
him that they might s. him.		17: 3
And if ye s. me ye will shed		17:10
wrath that he would s. the king.		19: 4
get upon the tower to s. the king,		19: 6
them, and began to s. them.		19:10
that they would not s. them.		19:13
his people should not s. them.		19:25
that the people would s. them,		20: 3
places, and began to s. them.		20: 9
and now let us s. him.		20:13
Ye shall not s. him, but bring		20:14
my people shall not s. thy people.		20:24
Now they durst not s. them,		21: 3
And they began to s. the Amlicites	Al	2:17
did s. them with much slaughter,		2:19
with their might, and did s. them.		2:36
that any man could s. them;		8:31
and began to s. the people		16: 2
to s. them, or to retain them		17:20
Now the king will s. us, as he has		17:28
the king and he will not s. us.		17:31
one of their men could s. him	Al	17:35
came forth with clubs to s. him.		17:36
of those who sought to s. him;		17:39
those who sought to s. him,		18: 2
not s. you as I did your brethren.		18: 4
let it fall upon Ammon, to s. him;		19:22
who lifted the sword to s. Ammon,		19:24
him that he should s. Ammon		20:14
I will not s. Ammon, neither will		20:15
Behold, thou shalt not s. thy son;		20:17
for if thou shouldst s. thy son,		20:18
I know that if I should s. my son,		20:19
forth his hand to s. Ammon.		20:20
saw that Ammon could s. him,		20:21
should take them and s. them.		22:19
that we should s. these men,		22:20
might s. Aaron and his brethren.		22:21
began to s. them with the sword.		24:21
they did s. a thousand and five		24:22
whose arms were lifted to s. them.		24:25
attempt to s. the people of		25: 1
brethren and began to s. them;		25: 8
their brethren to s. them;		27:12
to fall upon them and to s. them.		43:41
yet we do not desire to s. you.		44: 1
that he might s. Moroni.		44:12
fall upon them and s. them.		44:17
that they began to s. them;		44:17
were determined to s. them.		46: 2
s. and massacre them		49: 7
and s. him who should attempt		50: 5
by the sword to s. them.		50:26
Teancum did s. Morianton		50:35
s. them even until it was dark.		51:32
Jacob was determined to s. them		52:34
it was their intent to s. us		56:37
would not s. our brethren if		56:46
began to s. them exceedingly,		56:52
the Lamanites, and did s. them;		56:54
come upon us by night and s. us,		57: 9
s. upwards of two thousand		57:14
overtake us that they might s. us;		58:19
and they did begin to s. them		59: 7
s. them with a great slaughter;		62:38
did s. every one who did oppose	He	1:20
them that they might s. them.		5:22
lay your hands on us to s. us.		5:26
with some one to s. the judge,		9:16
to s. one another with the sword.		10:18
stones at them, and do s. them,		13:24
and did s. so many of the people,	3Ne	2:11
shall spare not, but shall s. you,		3: 8
come upon them and s. them;		4: 6
pursue them and did s. them,		4:13
all who shall seek to s. them		4:29
and did s. many of them.	Mrm	1:11
did s. a great number of them,		3: 8
did s. many of the Nephites,		4: 2
And whether they will s. me,		8: 3
did beat them and did d. Cohor.	Eth	7:21
they were about to s. him also;		8: 6
that they would not s. him,		8: 6
s. both women and children,		14:17
might s. him with his own sword,		15: 5
that he would s. Coriantumr or		15:28
s. you and bring your soul to	DC	8: 4
the wicked shall s. the wicked,		63:33
of Israel, and not s. them.		89:21
that he that findeth me will s. me,	Mses	5:39
and shall s. them that they shall		7: 7
that they might s. me also,	Abr	1:12

SLAYETH

the Lord s. the wicked to bring	1Ne	4:13
which is the saints of God,		13: 5
s. thee, vengeance shall be taken	Mses	5:40

SLAYING

s. food by the way, with our bows	1Ne	16:15
done wrong in s. his servants;	Al	18: 5
they did forbear from s. them;		24:24
did drive them, s. many.		51:23

before them and s. many. Al 51:28
s. the people with a great He 1:27

SLEEP
awake; awake from a deep s., 2Ne 1:13
yea, even from the s. of hell, 1:13
None shall slumber nor s.; 15:27
out upon you the spirit of deep s. 27: 5
s. to come upon the Lamanites, Mos 24:19
were in a profound s. 24:19
awakened them out of a deep s., Al 5: 7
may watch over you in your s.; 37:37
s. had overpowered them 51:33
from the Nephites, and they s.; 55: 8
drunken, and were in a deep s., 55:15
were in a deep s. and drunken, 55:16
but we did s. upon our swords, 57: 9
that my men should not s., 58:26
redemption from an endless s., Mrm 9:13
from which s. all men shall be 9:13
and s. until I shall call again. DC 43:18
they shall not s. in the dust, 63:51
to s. longer than is needful; 88:124
And when he dies he shall not s., 101:31
a deep s. to fall upon Adam; Mses 3:21
caused a deep s. to fall upon Abr 5:15
that s. had fled from my eyes, JS 2:46

SLEEPETH
is not dead, but he s. in God, Al 19: 8

SLEEPING
shall say to the s. nations: DC 43:18

SLEPT
they s. upon their swords. Eth 15:20
they s. again upon their swords. 15:22
they s. upon their swords that 15:24
that they ate and s., 15:26
the saints that have s. shall DC 45:45
if ye have s. in peace blessed 45:46
who have s. in their graves 88:97
he s., and I took one of his ribs Mses 3:21
s., and they took one of his ribs, Abr 5:15

SLEW
s. them with a great slaughter, Mos 10:20
back, and s. many of them. 21: 8
the man who s. him was taken by Al 1:10
of the man that s. Gideon 2: 1
that they s. the Amlicites with 2:18
that he s. Amlici with the sword. 2:31
until he s. and drove them back. 2:33
and s. many of the Lamanites, 3:23
faith of Nehor, who s. Gideon. 14:16
thus he s. a certain number 17:36
s. none save it were their leader 17:38
and s. seven of their brethren 18:16
ye s. and smote off the arms of 18:20
because he s. his servants who 19:20
who s. so many of their brethren 24:28
same servant that s. the king, 47:34
s. all those who had been left 52:25
and s. many of them, and took 62:15
forth against them, and s. many, 62:25
pursue Teancum, and s. him. 62:36
that Jesus, whom they s., Mrm 3:21
the hands of those who s. them 6:15
of Noah by night and s. him, Eth 7:18
he s. him with his own sword; 9:27
be beat Shared and s. him. 13:30
s. a part of the army of 14: 5
Abel, his brother, and s. him. Mses 5:32
Lamech, being angry, s. him, 5:50
but he s. him for the oath's sake. 5:50
instead of Abel, whom Cain s. 6: 2

SLIGHT
if thou wilt s. these counsels, DC 19:33

SLING
with a s. and with stones. 1Ne 16:23
cast stones at them with his s.; Al 17:36
he did s. stones amongst them; 17:36
six of them had fallen by the s., 17:38
with the s. and with the sword, 18:16

SLINGS
and our stones and our s. 1Ne 16:15
and with clubs, and with s., Mos 9:16
and with stones, and with s.; 10: 8
and with stones, and with s., Al 2:12
and their stones, and their s., 3: 5
and their arrows, and their s.; 17: 7
arrows, their stones and their s.; 43:20
with their swords and their s., 49:20

SLIPPED
and they have s. away from us, He 13:35

SLIPPERY
your riches, that they become s., He 13:31
s. that we should lose them; 13:33
and all things are become s., 13:36
they became s., because the Mrm 1:18

SLOTHFUL
and be s., that ye would not Al 33:21
They were s., and forgot to 37:41
our fathers were s. to give heed 37:43
do not let us be s. because of 37:46
a s. and not a wise servant; DC 58:26
they became very s., and they 101:50
s. shall not be counted worthy 107:100

SLOTHFULNESS
because of their exceeding s., Al 60:14
the s. of our government, 60:14
heart, and keepeth it with s., DC 58:29
keep s. and uncleanness far 90:18

SLOW
but s. to remember the Lord your 1Ne 17:45
we were s. to remember the Lord Mos 9: 3
I will be s. to hear their cries; 11:24
and s. to remember the Lord 13:29
Lord was s. to hear their cry 21:15
not s. to remember the Lord Al 55:31
they s. to remember the Lord 62:49
and s. to be led to do iniquity; He 7: 7
iniquity, and how s. to do good, 12: 4
how s. are they to remember the 12: 5
how s. to walk in wisdom's paths! 12: 5
They were s. to hearken unto DC 101: 7
God is s. to hearken unto 101: 7
hate me; for I am s. of speech; Mses 6:31
for it moveth in order more s.; Abr 3: 5

SLUMBER
None shall s. nor sleep; 2Ne 15:27
awake from the s. of death; Jac 3:11
the inhabitants of the earth s., DC 112: 5

SLUMBERED
the words of them which have s. 2Ne 27: 6
the words of those who have s. 27: 9

SMALL
were s., because of the wickedness 1Ne 14:12
I have written but a s. part of 14:28
by s. means the Lord can bring 16:29
spoken unto you in a still s. voice, 17:45
a s. thing for you to weary men, 2Ne 17:13
concerning the s. plates, Jac 1: 1
a s. degree of knowledge 4: 2
which writing has been s.; 7:27
And as these plates are s., Jar 1: 2
write more, for the plates are s. 1:14
which contained this s. account WM 1: 3
his people, upon s. numbers, Mos 11:16
a thicket of s. trees, where 18: 5
the forces of the king were s., 19: 2
a s. number of them gathered 20: 2
a s. number of men to search 21:25

SMALL

took a l. number with them	Mos 28: 1
s. number of your lower judges	29:29
yea, even all their s. villages,	Al 8: 7
also a man of no s. reputation	10: 4
a s. neck of land between	22:32
that by s. and simple things are	37: 6
s. means in many instances doth	37: 6
by very s. means the Lord doth	37: 7
miracles were worked by s. means	37:41
with a s. number of his men,	46:33
and erecting s. forts, or places	48: 8
should take a s. number of men	52:22
met by Lehi and a s. army,	52:27
Laman and a s. number of his	55: 6
a s. number of men should	55: 7
out of the city by our s. bands.	58: 1
take courage with our s. force	58:12
Gid, with a s. number of men,	58:16
and a s. number of men should	58:16
our armies are s. to maintain	58:32
took a s. number of men,	62: 3
save it were in s. bodies;	He 1:24
began to cease, in a s. degree,	3:22
a s. record of that which hath	3Ne 5:15
it being a s. voice it did pierce	11: 3
For a s. moment have I forsaken	22: 7
unto them, both great and s.	26: 1
a s. part of the people who had	4Ne 1:20
I write a s. abridgment,	Mrm 5: 9
come forth, both s. and great,	9:13
And they were s., and they	Eth 2:16
out of a rock sixteen s. stones;	3: 1
great power, which looks s. unto	3: 5
together a s. number of men,	9: 9
out of s. things proceedeth	DC 64:33
thus saith the still s. voice,	85: 6
Let your families be s.,	90:25
shall be but a s. moment;	121: 7
and but for a s. moment	122: 4
no man count them as s. things;	123:15
s. helm in the time of a storm,	123:16
they seem but a s. thing to me,	127: 2
I saw the dead, s. and great,	128: 6
created no s. stir and division	JS 2: 5

SMALLEST

say the s. part which I feel.	Al 26:16
of which in the s., yea, even	DC 19:20

SMALLNESS

of the s. of his numbers.	Al 52:23

SMELL

instead of sweet s. there shall be	2Ne 13:24
raiment, for taste and for s.,	DC 59:19

SMILE

countenance did s. upon them,	3Ne 19:25
and he did s. upon them again;	19:30

SMILED

hath s. upon you most pleasingly,	Jac 2:13
heavens have s. upon her;	DC 84:101
ark; and that the Lord s. upon	Mses 7:43

SMITE

they did s. us even with a rod.	1Ne 3:28
why do ye s. your younger brother	3:29
I did s. two stones together that	17:11
of God, for God shall s. him.	17:48
and s. us because of our iniquity,	18:10
they s. him, and he suffereth it.	19: 9
shall the heat nor the sun s. them;	21:10
I will s. him with the strength of	2Ne 7: 8
shall s. them at the last day.	9:33
glory of his majesty shall s. thee.	12:10
glory of his majesty shall s. them,	12:19
majesty of his glory shall s. them,	12:21
the Lord will s. with a scab on	13:17
he shall s. thee with a rod,	20:24
shall s. the earth with the rod	21: 4
shall s. it in the seven streams,	21:15
power that he should s. the rock	25:20
shall s. the earth with the rod	30: 9
he can s. you to the dust!	Jac 2:15
but if God shall s. thee,	7:14
I will s. this my people with	Mos 12: 4
and it shall s. them;	12: 6
for God shall s. you if ye lay	13: 3
would s. them on their cheeks	21: 3
his sword and began to s. him,	Al 1: 9
s. one another with their fists.	1:22
that lifted his club to s. Ammon,	17:37
as he lifted the sword to s. him,	19:22
he might s. him to the earth.	20:16
I will s. thee except thou wilt	20:22
I will s. thee to the earth.	20:24
spit upon them, nor s. them,	23: 2
the sword or cimeter to s. them.	27:29
again, behold God shall s. thee,	30:47
for they did s. in two many of	43:44
did s. off many of their arms;	43:44
did s. in their fierce anger.	43:44
s. down all who should attempt	49:20
and s. you with the sword,	60:30
Coriantumr did s. him against	He 1:21
s. and rend and turn their backs	6:39
to s. upon the waters of the	8:11
shall s. the earth with famine,	10: 6
say that God shall s. this people,	10:10
shall s. thee on thy right cheek,	3Ne 12:39
and s. the earth with a curse.	25: 6
they did s. the earth with the	28:20
s. upon the people of Jesus;	4Ne 1:34
people of Jesus did not s. again.	1:34
man shall not s., neither shall	Mrm 8:20
I feared lest he should s. me;	Eth 3: 8
Lib did s. upon his arm that	14:12
Lib did s. the army of	14:14
unto God lest he should s. me.	Mro 9:21
lest I s. you by the rod of my	DC 19:15
I will s. them according to	24:16
s. the whole earth with a curse,	98:17
if men will s. you, or your	98:23
shall s. you the second time,	98:25
he shall s. you the third time,	98:26
if they shall s. this people	109:28
this people thou wilt s. them;	109:28
lest I come and s. the earth with	128:17
and they shall s. the rocks,	133:26
lest I come out and s. them with	Mses 7:10
begin to s. his fellow-servants,	JS 1:52

SMITER

I gave my back to the s.,	2Ne 7: 6

SMITETH

not unto him that s. them,	2Ne 19:13
God s. the people of Nephi	He 7:hd
he that s. shall be smitten	Mrm 8:19

SMITH

I have created the s. that	3Ne 22:16

SMITH, Don C.: *see also DON CARLOS.*

S. to be a president over a	DC 124:133

SMITH, Eden

and also my servant S.	DC 75:36
give unto you my servant S.	80: 2

SMITH, Emma

while I speak unto you, S.,	DC 25: 1
mine handmain, S., your wife,	132:51
S., receive all those that have	132:52
S., to abide and cleave unto	132:54

SMITH, George A.

Willard Richards, S.;	DC124:129
Lyman and S. organize a company.	136:14

SMITH, Hyrum: *see also HYRUM.*

Murdock, and my servant S.,	DC 52: 8
servants Sidney Rigdon and S.	52:24
Also my servant S. and my	75:32
shall my s. S. receive	94:13
Let my servant S. journey with	103:39
and also my servant S.	115: 1

SMITH 892 SMITTEN

SMITH, John — continued

blessed is my servant S.;	DC 124:15
S. to be a patriarch unto you,	124:124
and S. the Patriarch.	135: 1
S. was forty-four years old	135: 6

SMITH, John

S., Joseph Coe, John Johnson,	DC 102: 3
10, Joseph Smith, Sen.; 11, S.;	102:34

SMITH, Joseph: *see also JOSEPH.*

and my servant Gazelam [S.],	DC 82:11
Lord unto you, my servant S.,	124: 1
even you my servant S.,	124:16
of Latter-day Saints. S.	127:12
and never deviating friend, S.	128:25
martyrdom of S. the Prophet,	135: 1
S., the Prophet and Seer of	135: 3
S. was thirty-eight in December,	135: 6
from Jesus and his apostles to S.,	136:37
souls, namely, my father, S.;	JS 2: 4

SMITH, Joseph, Jun.: *see also JOSEPH.*

called upon my servant S.,	DC 1:17
my servant s., might have	1:29
my servant S., have got	5: 1
things unto you, my servant S.,	5: 2
the Lord hath shown unto S.,	5:25
to write for my servant S.,	9: 1
S., may not be destroyed,	17: 4
servant S., has seen them;	17: 5
by the hands of my servant S.,	18: 7
by the hand of my servant S.,	19:13
commandments were given to S.,	20: 2
a comfort unto my servant S.,	25: 5
you, my servants, S., and	27: 8
church excepting my servant S.,	28: 2
except it is his brother, S.	30: 7
been revealed to my servant, S.	31: 4
servants Sidney Rigdon and S.,	36: 5
my servant S., should have a	41: 7
excepting my servants S., and	42: 4
appoint ye my servant S., and uphold	43:12
let my servants S., and Sidney	52: 3
let my servants S., and Sidney	52:41
with my servants S., and Sidney	53: 5
by the hand of my servant S.,	55: 2
journey with my servants S.,	55: 5
if my servant S., must needs	56:12
Sidney Rigdon and S., return,	58:58
Sidney Rigdon, S., and	60: 6
the mouth of my servant S.,	60:17
my servants, Sidney Rigdon, S.,	61:23
my servants, Sidney Rigdon, S.,	61:30
will give unto my servant S.,	63:41
Let my servants, S., and Sidney	63:65
taken from my servant S.,	64: 5
have been upon my servant S.,	67: 5
the hands of my servant S.	67:14
I give unto my servant S.,	70: 1
unto you my servants S., and	71: 1
say unto my servants, S.,	73: 3
We, S., and Sidney Rigdon,	76:11
The Lord spake unto Enoch [S.],	78: 1
Gazelam, or Enoch [S.]	78: 9
counselor unto my servant S.:	81: 1
unto his servant S., and six	84: 1
dedicated by the hand of S.,	84: 3
I say unto my servant S.,	93:45
And now, verily I say unto S.—	93:47
And let my servants S., and	93:52
assembled at the house of S.,	102: 1
S., Sidney Rigdon and Frederick	102: 3
that they call my servant Baurak Ale [S.]	103:21
let my servant Baurak Ale [S.]	103:22
my servant Baurak Ale [S.] may	103:35
journey with my servant S.	103:37
servant S., shall counsel them,	103:40
Gazelam [S.] shall direct.	104:26
let my servant Gazelam [S.] have	104:43
house of my servant Gazelam [S.].	104:45
of my servant Gazelam [S.],	104:46
servant Baurak Ale [S.] to say	105:16
until my servant Baurak Ale [S.]	105:27
O Lord, remember thy servant S.,	DC 109:68
the Lord unto you, my servant S.,	115: 1

SMITH, Joseph, Sen.: *see also JOSEPH; and SMITH'S, Joseph, Sen.*

And let mine aged servant, S.,	DC 90:20
and S., John Smith, Joseph Coe,	102: 3
Hyde; 9, Jared Carter; 10, S.;	102:34
and also my aged servant S.,	124:19
My father, S., left the State	JS 2: 3

SMITH, Lucy: *see also LUCY.*

my mother, S. (whose name,	JS 2: 4

SMITH, Samuel H.: *see also SAMUEL.*

Reynolds Cahoon and S. also	DC 52:30
Cahoon, and my servant S.,	61:35
Let my servant S. go with	66: 8
Orson Hyde and my servant	75:13
Oliver Cowdery, S., Orson Hyde,	102: 3
Cowdery; 2, Joseph Coe; 3,	102:34
I give unto you Vinson Knight, S.,	124:141

SMITH, Sylvester

And also my servant S. and	DC 75:34
Hyde, S., and Luke Johnson,	102: 3
5, John S. Carter; 6, S.;	102:34

SMITH, William: *see also WILLIAM.*

orson Pratt, Orson Hyde, S.,	DC 124:129

SMITH'S, Joseph, Sen.: *see also JOSEPH; and SMITH, Joseph, Sen.*

especially mine aged servant S.,	DC 90:25

SMITING

by s. their arms with the edge of	Al 17:37
and s. their humble brethren	He 4:12

SMITTEN

after I had s. off his head	1Ne 4:19
before the Gentiles and were s.	13:14
and s. them by the hand of the	13:34
for they shall be s. no more;	21:13
cause them to be scattered and s.	2Ne 1:11
they shall be s. and afflicted.	6:10
they shall be scattered, and s.,	6:11
against them, and hath s. them;	15:25
shall have been s. by the Gentiles;	26:15
s. by the hand of the Gentiles.	26:19
they were s. with famine and	Mos 1:17
they are s. with sore afflictions?	7:28
and ye are s. and afflicted.	7:32
but we were s. with famine	9: 3
that they be s. by their enemies.	11:24
and shall be s. on the cheek;	12: 2
also be s. with the east wind;	12: 6
be s. with a great pestilence—	12: 7
shall be s. for your iniquities;	12:31
stricken, s. of God, and afflicted.	14: 4
ye shall be s. on every hand,	17:17
submitting themselves to be s.,	21:13
being s. by many of them.	27:32
then ye shall be s. by famine,	Al 10:23
the arms which had been s. off	17:39
cast them out, and had s. them,	20:30
were hunted, and they were s.	25:12
behold they were pierced and s.,	44:18
rather than be s. down to the	51:20
but were afflicted and s.,	He 4:13
and God has s. them that they	9: 8
Except ye repent ye shall be s.,	10:11
be s. even unto destruction.	10:14
the earth was s. that it was dry,	11: 6
and the whole earth was s.,	11: 6
were s. that they did perish by	11: 6
I will cause that they shall be s.;	13: 9
that day shall they be s.,	13:20
be s. and scattered abroad,	15:12
about to be s. down by it,	3Ne 2:19
the house of Israel to be s.,	16: 6
that they began to be s.;	Mrm 4: 4
Show unto me, or ye shall be s.—	8:18

SMITTEN

that smiteth shall be s. again,	Mrm 8:19
thou hast s. us because of our	Eth 3: 3
Shez was s. by the hand of	10: 3
had s. off the head of Shiz,	15:31
command to be s. in my name;	DC 24:16
may not be s. with a curse;	27: 9
as a tree that is s. by the	85: 8
driven and s. by the hands of	103: 2
the people that have s. you,	105:38
unto those who have s. you,	105:40
s. because of their transgression,	109:65
whole earth be s. with a curse—	110:15
the earth will be s. with a curse	128:18
of Elkenah was s. that he died,	Abr 1:29

SMOKE

and by s., and vapor of darkness,	1Ne 19:11
fire, and vapor of s. must come;	22:18
heavens shall vanish away like s.,	2Ne 8: 6
a cloud and s. by day	14: 5
and the house was filled with s.	16: 4
mount up like the lifting up of s.	19:18
shall come from the north a s.,	24:31
whose s. ascendeth up forever	Jac 6:10
whose s. ascendeth up forever	Mos 3:27
the vapor of s. and of darkness,	3Ne 10:13
destructions by fire, and by s.,	10:14
vapors of s. in foreign lands;	Mrm 8:29
and fire, and vapors of s.	DC 45:41

SMOKING

the two tails of these s. fire-brands,	2Ne 17: 4

SMOOTH

the rough places to be made s.,	1Ne 17:46
and s. places shall be broken up.	17:46
thou cast down and become s.,	He 10: 9
are broken up, and become s.,	12:10
many s. places became rough.	3Ne 8:13
rough places to become s.—	DC 49:23
the rough places made s.;	109:74

SMOTE

as they s. us with a rod,	1Ne 3:29
and I s. off his head with his	4:18
s. the rock, and there came forth	17:29
stay upon him that s. them,	2Ne 20:20
He who s. the people in wrath	24: 6
the rod of him that s. thee is	24:29
and he s. them with his hand	Al 14:14
And the judge s. them again	14:15
he s. them again, and delivered	14:17
the judge also s. them again	14:20
forth also, and s. them, saying:	14:20
before them, and s. them again,	14:24
they all went forth and s. them,	14:25
who s. upon Alma and Amulek,	14:27
s. off their arms with his sword;	17:37
he s. off as many of their arms	17:38
and s. off the arms of others,	18:16
and s. off the arms of my brethren	18:20
s. his arm that he could not use it.	20:20
and s. upon our cheeks;	26:29
s. it even to the earth,	44:12
he also s. Zerahemnah that he	44:12
s. off the scalp of Zerahemnah,	44:13
he s. upon him until he died;	Eth 14:16
Shiz s. upon Coriantumr with	14:30
he s. off the head of Shiz.	15:30
and s. the priest that he died;	Abr 1:20

SNARE

and a s. to the inhabitants of	2Ne 18:14
lay a s. for him that reproveth	27:32
I myself was caught in a s.,	Mos 23: 9
this was a s. of the adversary,	Al 12: 6
they might catch us in their s.;	56:43
themselves in their own s.	DC 10:26
shall come upon them as a s.,	63:15
bringeth a s. upon your souls.	90:17

SNARED

and be s., and be taken.	2Ne 18:15

SNARES

s. to catch the holy ones of God.	Al 10:17
could not be taken in their s.;	55:31
the s. and the wiles of the devil,	He 3:29
did also lay s. and catch fowls	Eth 2: 2
and they are caught in s.;	DC 61:18

SNATCH

he shall s. on the right hand	2Ne 19:20
to s. me out of an everlasting	Mos 27:28

SNATCHED

but I am s., and my soul is	Mos 27:29
to have s. us from our awful,	Al 26:17

SNIDER, John

S., and others, build a house	DC 124:22
S., and my servant Peter Haws,	124:62
S., and my servant Peter Haws,	124:70

SNOW

the whitness of the driven s.	DC 11: 8
head was white like the pure s.;	110: 3

SNOW, Erastus

Benson and S. organize a company,	DC 136:12

SNOW, Lorenzo

President S. offered the following:	DC OD

SNOWS

send again the s. upon the earth.	DC 117: 1

SO: *see in the APPENDIX.*

SOAP

refiner's fire, and like fuller's s.	3Ne 24: 2
refiner's fire, and like fuller's s.;	DC 128:24

SOBBINGS

and the s. of their hearts	Jac 2:35

SOBER

and declare the word, and be s.	Al 37:47
the word unto this people. Be s.	38:15
perceive that thou art a s. child,	Mrm 1: 2
being somewhat of a s. mind,	1:15
patient; be s.; be temperate;	DC 6:35
Be s. Keep all my	43:35
and be watchful and be s.,	61:38
Gird up your loins and be s.	73: 6

SOBERNESS

to speak to them with much s.;	1Ne 18:10
to magnify mine office with s.,	Jac 2: 2
I beseech of you in words of s.	6: 5
in the ways of truth and s.;	Mos 4:15
the word with truth and s.,	Al 42:31
they were men of truth and s.,	53:21
perform with s. the work which	DC 6:19
and speak the truth in s.	18:21

SOCIALITY

s. which exists among us here	DC 130: 2

SOCIETIES

religious s. have a right to	DC 134:10
rules and regulations of such s.;	134:10

SOCIETY

this the secret s. of Gadianton;	3Ne 3: 9
which s. and the works thereof	3: 9
of this wicked and secret s.	Eth 9: 6
because of their secret s. and	11:22
the s. of thy father and mother	DC 122: 6
for the good and safety of s.	134: 1
one religious s. is fostered and	134: 9
not believe that any religious s.	134:10
excommunicate them from their s.,	134:10
mingling with all kinds of s.,	JS 2:28

SOCKETS

and their eyes from their s.;	DC 29:19

SODOM   894   SOME

SODOM
declare their sin to be even as S.,	2Ne 13: 9
be as when God overthrew S.	23:19

SOEVER
for what things s. ye shall stand	Mrm 9:27

SOFTEN
did visit me, and did s. my heart	1Ne 2:16
Lord did s. the heart of Ishmael,	7: 5
that they did s. their hearts;	7:19
not s. the hearts of my brethren	18:19
destruction, could s. their hearts;	18:20
will s. the hearts of the Gentiles,	2Ne 10:18
to s. the hearts of the Lamanites	Mos 21:15
s. the hearts of the Lamanites,	23:28
s. the hearts of the Lamanites.	23:29
of his Spirit to s. our hearts,	Al 24: 8
I will s. the hearts of those	DC 104:80
I will s. the hearts of those	104:81
will s. the hearts of the people,	105:27
will visit and s. their hearts,	124: 9

SOFTENED
s. because of their afflictions,	Al 62:41
That their hearts may be s.	DC 109:56
heart shall be s. toward them,	121: 3
let thine heart be s.,	121: 4

SOFTENING
s. the hearts of their enemies that	He 12: 2

SOFTLY
the waters of Shiloah that go s.,	2Ne 18: 6

SOJOURN
while we did s. in the wilderness.	1Ne 17: 3
And we did s. for the space of	17: 4
down into Egypt, to s. there,	Abr 2:21

SOLD
of Jacob, who was s. into Egypt,	1Ne 5:14
of my creditors have I s. you?	2Ne 7: 1
Yea, to whom have I s. you?	7: 1
iniquities have ye s. yourselves,	7: 1
of Joseph who was s. into Egypt	Al 10: 3
we be cast into prison, or be s.,	46:23
have s. yourselves for naught,	3Ne 20:38
have farms that cannot be s.,	DC 38:37
that his farm should be s.	64:20
and let it not be s. until the	90:20
daughters of thy sons have s.	Mses 8:15

SOLDIER
that the s. who stood by,	Al 44:13
even as the s. of Moroni had	44:18

SOLDIERS
one of Moroni's s. smote it	Al 44:12
them into the midst of his s.	44:12
the remainder of his s. to anger,	44:16
s. from all parts of his land,	51: 9
his two thousand stripling s.,	53:22

SOLE
for the s. purpose of bringing this	Mos 7:22
was for the s. purpose to get gain,	Al 11:20
did obtain the s. management of	He 6:39

SOLEMN
being a lonesome and a s. people,	Jac 7:26
awful s. fear came upon them.	He 5:28
that it is s. mockery before God,	Mro 8: 9
upon the Father in s. prayer,	DC 20:76
and call a s. assembly,	88:70
friends, call your s. assembly,	88:117
should call your s. assembly,	95: 7
Wait patiently until the s. assembly	108: 4
Call your s. assembly,	109: 6
in calling our s. assembly,	109:10
a s. proclamation of my gospel,	124: 2
and your s. assemblies,	124:39
in making a s. proclamation	124:107
Call your s. assemblies,	DC 133: 6
in the most s. manner, declare	OD

SOLEMNITIES
let the s. of eternity rest	DC 43:34

SOLEMNITY
yea, a time of s., and a time	Al 28: 6
in s. and the spirit of prayer,	DC 84:61
in s. of heart, in the spirit of	100: 7
in order and in s. before him,	107:84

SOLEMNIZED
marriages are still being s.	DC OD
been s. in our Temples	OD

SOLES
ashes under the s. of your feet	3Ne 25: 3

SOLID
ye know at this time are s.,	He 14:21
the more part of it is one s. mass,	14:21
and ye s. rocks weep for joy!	DC 128:23

SOLITARY
s. places to bud and to blossom,	DC 117: 7

SOLOMON: see also HANCOCK, Solomon; HUMPHREY, Solomon; and MACK, Solomon.
the manner of the temple of S.	2Ne 5:16
was like unto the temple of S.;	5:16
and also S., his son.	Jac 1:15
concerning David, and S. his son.	2:23
David and S. truly had many	2:24
that even S., in all his glory,	3Ne 13:29
as also Moses, David, and S.,	DC 132: 1
also S. and Moses my servants,	132:38

SOLOMON'S
be built like unto S. temple.	2Ne 5:16

SOME
shall know at s. future period	1Ne 7:13
away into s. strange wilderness;	16:38
the things which s. men esteem	19: 7
s. with his voice, because of	19:11
I write s. of the words of Isaiah,	2Ne 11: 8
because s. of you have obtained	Jac 2:13
s. in one and some in another,	5:14
some in one and s. in another,	5:14
after s. years had passed away,	7: 1
be brought forth at s. future day	En 1:13
s. day it may profit them.	WM 1: 2
must be called by s. other name;	Mos 5:10
he might by s. means fall into	21:19
that by s. means they might take	21:20
s. lifting themselves up with	Al 4:12
And at s. period of time they will	9:17
there were s. among them who	10:13
s. around the borders of Noah,	16: 3
and s. say that he is not dead,	19: 5
s. saying that it was a great evil	19:19
And there were s. who said that	19:27
there should s. evil come upon her.	22:21
might save s. few of their souls.	26:26
be the means of saving s. soul;	26:30
could be the means of saving s.	26:30
to bring s. soul to repentance;	29: 9
offend s. unknown being, who	30:28
s. among you who would humble	32:25
s. that have understood that	40:15
s. have wrested the scriptures,	41: 1
were s. who died with fevers,	46:40
which at s. seasons of the year	46:40
by stratagem or s. other way	52:10
by s. means flatter them out of	52:19
on account of s. intrigue amongst	53: 8
s. ground over the Nephites	53: 8
to s. of the Lamanite prisoners.	55:31
fear that there is s. faction	58:36
s. dissenters who had gone forth	63:14
did cause s. little dissensions	He 3: 1

SOME	895			SON	
to s. being whom they beheld.	He	5:36	S. were contending for the	JS	2: 5
for there were s. who did cry out:		8: 7	s. for the Presbyterian, and		2: 5
gained favor in the eyes of s.,		8:10	and s. for the Baptist.		2: 5
must have agreed with s. one		9:16	s. to one party and some to		2: 6
s. of the Nephites who believed		9:39	one party and s. to another,		2: 6
there were s. also, who believed		9:39	I felt s. desire to be united		2: 8
there were s. among the people,		9:40	by s. power which entirely		2:15
who had s. years before gone over		11:24	to the power of s. actual being		2:16
there are s. who shall be cast out,		12:25	soon recovering in s. degree,		2:20
S. things they may have		16:16	S. few days after I had this		2:21
in s. great and marvelous thing		16:20	s. said he was dishonest, others		2:24
work s. great mystery which we		16:21	together in s. kind of cement.		2:52
there were s. who began to say	3Ne	1: 5	I translated s. of them,		2:62
away by s. who were Zoramites,		1:29			
Imagining up s. vain thing		2: 2	SOMETHING		
gain s. advantage of the robbers,		2:17	do s. for it to preserve it.	Jac	5:37
s. one that had the spirit of		3:19	humble servant of God s. to eat?	Al	8:19
which, in the eyes of s., would		5: 8	descovered s. to be wrong	JS	2:48
there began to be s. disputings		6:10	heard s. of a silver mine		2:56
s. were lifted up unto pride		6:10			
s. were ignorant because of their		6:12	SOMETIME		
S. were lifted up in pride,		6:13	S. in this month of February,	JS	2:63
s. did return railing for railing,		6:13			
in s. degree they had peace in		7:14	SOMETIMES		
s. miracles among the people.		7:22	a man s., if he is compelled	Al	32:13
were s. cities which remained;		8:15	s. associated with jovial	JS	2:28
were s. who were carried away		8:16	S. we were at home, and		2:55
it was said by s. that the time		8:19	were at home, and s. abroad,		2:55
s. among them who marveled,		15: 2			
bring forth s. bread and wine		18: 1	SOMEWHAT		
with s. others and their families,	Eth	1:33	therefore I was taught s. in all	1Ne	1: 1
s. of them they cast into pits		9:29	I must speak s. of the things of		10: 1
s. which fled into the land		9:32	Jacob, would speak s. concerning	2Ne	6: 8
that s. had faith in him,		12: 7	Nephi, do speak s. concerning		25: 1
the Lamanites, in s. future day,	Mro	1: 4	prophesy s. more concerning		30: 3
send by the hand of s. priests;	DC	20:82	ye ponder s. in your hearts		32: 1
their shining, and s. shall fall,		34: 9	indulge themselves s. in wicked	Jac	1:15
s. of you are guilty before me,		38:14	to be lifted up s. in pride.		1:16
by s. one who has authority,		42:11	it began to put forth s. a little,		5: 6
by letter or s. other way.		44: 1	write s. upon these plates,	Om	1: 1
for s. are of men, and others		46: 7	speak unto you s. concerning		1:12
To s. is given one, and to some		46:12	I would speak s. concerning		1:27
and to s. is given another,		46:12	may write s. concerning them,	WM	1: 2
To s. it is given by the Holy		46:13	and s. concerning Christ,		1: 2
to s. it is given by the Holy		46:15	I speak s. concerning that which		1: 3
given by the Holy Ghost to s.		46:16	he had s. of contentions among		1:12
to s. is given, by the Spirit		46:17	for I have s. more to speak	Mos	3: 1
to s. it is given to have faith		46:19	have been s. troubled in mind	Al	22: 3
to s. is given the working of		46:21	he hath spoken s. unto you		34: 3
to s. to speak with tongues;		46:24	I have s. to say concerning the		37:38
unto s. it may be given to		46:29	I have s. more to say unto thee		39: 1
who have deceived s.,		50: 7	I would say s. unto you		39:15
of truth or s. other way?		50:17	ease your mind s. on this subject.		39:17
if it be by s. other way it is		50:18	here is s. more I would say		40: 1
of truth or s. other way?		50:19	I have s. to say concerning the		41: 1
If it be s. other way it is not		50:20	I perceive there is s. more		42: 1
s. of whom are exceedingly		58:61	I have s. to prophesy unto		45: 9
with s. I am not well pleased,		60: 2	I have s. to say concerning		53:10
s. of whom have turned away		63:14	I have written unto you s.		54: 5
that thereby I may save s.		64:21	would tell you s. concerning		54: 6
they are s. of one and some of		76:100	have s. to tell you concerning		56: 2
of one and s. of another—		76:100	I have s. to say unto them		60: 2
s. of Christ and some of		76:100	I was s. worried concerning		61:19
of Christ and s. of John,		76:100	I have s. more to desire of you,	He	5: 8
and s. of Moses, and some		76:100	and I began to be learned s.	Mrm	1: 2
and s. of Elias, and some of		76:100	and being s. of a sober mind,		1:15
and s. of Esaias, and some of		76:100	did arouse them s. to vigor,		2:24
and s. of Isaiah, and some of		76:100	I would speak s. unto the		7: 1
of Isaiah and s. of Enoch;		76:100	would speak s. concerning these	Eth	12: 6
in s. things he hath not kept		93:44	I write s. of that which is	Mro	9: 1
repent and forsake s. things,		93:48	now I write s. concerning the		9: 7
as s. of my servants have not		104: 4	write s. a few things,		9:24
s. few things in thine heart		112: 2	write s. as seemeth me good;		10: 1
for s. good end, or bad,		127: 2	s. partial to the Methodist sect,	JS	2: 8
naming also s. three individuals		128: 3			
may seem to s. to be a very bold		128: 9	SON		
is a welding link of s. kind		128:18	Therefore go, my s.,	1Ne	3: 6
upon s. subject or other—		128:18	Joseph who was the s. of Jacob,		5:14
or to s. previous appearing,		130:16	by faith on the S. of God—		10:17
who hath appeared unto s. and		133:36	the S. of God was the Messiah		10:17
I shall endeavor to write s. of	Abr	1:31	because thou believest in the S.		11: 6
S. time in the second year after	JS	2: 5	record that it is the S. of God.		11: 7
s. crying, "Lo, here!"		2: 5	is the mother of the S. of God,		11:18

SON   896   SON

the S. of the Eternal Father!	1 Ne 11:21
and I beheld the S. of God	11:24
yea, the S. of the everlasting God	11:32
is the S. of the Eternal Father,	13:40
compassion on the s. of her womb?	21:15
And now my s., Laman, and also	2 Ne 1:28
friend unto my s., Nephi, forever.	1:30
of thy seed with the seed of my s.	1:32
And now, behold, my s. Joseph,	3:22
and the daughters of my second s.;	4: 9
and of the s. of man, who shall	8:12
word that Isaiah, the s. of Amoz,	12: 1
the days of Ahaz the s. of Jotham,	17: 1
Jotham, the s. of Uzziah, king of	17: 1
and Pekah the s. of Remaliah,	17: 1
thou and Shearjashub thy s.,	17: 3
and of the s. of Remaliah.	17: 4
Ephraim, and the s. of Remaliah,	17: 5
midst of it, yea, the s. of Tabeal.	17: 6
of Samaria is Remaliah's s.	17: 9
shall conceive, and shall bear a s.,	17:14
Zechariah the s. of Jeberechiah.	18: 2
and she conceived and bare a s.	18: 3
in Rezin and Remaliah's s.;	18: 6
unto us a s. is given;	19: 6
which Isaiah the s. of Amoz did	23: 1
O Lucifer, s. of the morning!	24:12
the name, and remnant, and s.,	24:22
believe in Christ, the S. of God,	25:16
Jesus Christ, the S. of God.	25:19
But the S. of righteousness shall	26: 9
that repent and believe in his S.,	30: 2
in the name of my Beloved S.	31:11
the voice of the S. came unto me,	31:12
if ye shall follow the S., with full	31:13
came the voice of the S. unto me,	31:14
the example of the S. of	31:16
of the Father and the S.;	31:18
witnesses of the Father and the S.,	31:18
of the Father, and of the S.,	31:21
and also Solomon, his s.	Jac 1:15
David, and Solomon his s.	2:23
in offering up his s. Isaac,	4: 5
of God and his Only Begotten S.	4: 5
of Christ, his Only Begotten S.,	4:11
wherefore, I said unto my s. Enos:	7:27
into the hands of my s. Omni,	Jar 1:15
them upon my s. Amaron.	Om 1: 3
Abinadom, am the s. of Chemish.	1:10
I am Amaleki, the s. of Abinadom.	1:12
and Benjamin, his s., reigneth	1:23
into the hands of my s. Moroni,	WM 1: 1
records into the hands of my s.;	1: 2
My s., I would that ye should	Mos 1:10
an end of these sayings to his s.,	1:15
that my s. Mosiah is a king	2:30
the commandments of my s.,	2:31
called Jesus Christ, the S. of God,	3: 8
in Jesus Christ, the S. of God,	4: 2
had consecrated his s. Mosiah	6: 3
I am Limhi, the s. of Noah,	7: 9
of Noah, who was the s. of Zeniff,	7: 9
his s. began to reign in his stead.	10: 6
thou, nor thy s., nor thy daughter,	13:18
he shall be called the S. of God,	15: 2
being the Father and the S.-	15: 2
and the S., because of the flesh;	15: 3
thus becoming the Father and S.-	15: 3
or the S. to the Father, being	15: 5
the will of the S. being swallowed	15: 7
giving the S. power to make	15: 8
be broken, and the S. reigneth,	15:20
Limhi, being the s. of the king,	19:26
the s. and the daughter mourning	21: 9
what the Lord had done for his s.,	27:21
Alma, who was the s. of Alma;	28:20
Aaron thy s. should be our king	29: 2
And who knoweth but what my s.,	29: 7
have no right to destroy my s.,	29: 8
And if my s. should turn again	29: 9
THE S. OF ALMA	Al 1:hd
was the s. of Alma the first,	1:hd
yea, the S., the Only Begotten of	5:48
the S. of God cometh in his glory,	Al 5:50
of Jesus Christ, the S. of God,	6: 8
and the S. of God cometh	7: 9
and bring forth a s., yea, even	7:10
a son, yea, even the S. of God.	7:10
the S. of God suffereth according	7:13
the S. of God shall come in his	9:26
I am the s. of Giddonah, who	10: 2
who was the s. of Ishmael, who	10: 2
of Nephi, who was the s. of Lehi,	10: 3
who was the s. of Joseph who was	10: 3
Is it the S. of God?	11:32
that the S. of God shall come,	11:35
Is the S. of God the very	11:38
before the bar of Christ the S.,	11:44
call on men, in the name of his S.,	12:33
through mine Only Begotten S.;	12:33
through mine Only Begotten S.,	12:34
was after the order of his S.,	13: 1
after the order of his S.,	13: 2
forward to his S. for redemption.	13: 2
of the Only Begotten S.,	13: 5
being after the order of his S.,	13: 7
forever, after the order of the S.,	13: 9
look forward on the S. of God,	13:16
send his S. among the people,	14: 5
the coming of the S. of God,	16:19
where the S. of God should come;	16:20
Behold, thou shalt not slay thy s.;	20:17
for if thou shouldst slay thy s.,	20:18
I know that if I should slay my s.,	20:19
love he had for his s. Lamoni.	20:26
that my s. Lamoni should retain	20:26
my s. may retain his kingdom	20:26
been spoken by his s. Lamoni,	20:27
that the S. of God shall come	21: 7
the kingdom upon his s.,	24: 3
through the merits of his S.	24:10
through the blood of the S. of	24:13
it is because of thy S. that thou	33:11
away from me, because of thy S.	33:11
thy judgments because of thy S.	33:13
ye disbelieve on the S. of God?	33:14
upon them because of thy S.	33:16
has testified of the S. of God,	33:17
spoken concerning the S. of God.	33:18
begin to believe in the S. of God,	33:22
be light, through the joy of his S.	33:23
by us to be the S. of God;	34: 2
the word be in the S. of God,	34: 5
cometh through the S. of God,	34: 7
sacrifice will be the S. of God,	34:14
of Alma to his s., Helaman.	36:hd
My s., give ear to my words;	36: 1
And now, O my s. Helaman,	36: 3
of one Jesus Christ, a S. of God,	36:17
O Jesus, thou S. of God, have	36:18
Yea, I say unto you, my s., that	36:21
and again I say unto you, my s.,	36:21
Yea, and now behold, O my s.,	36:25
But behold, my s., this is not all;	36:30
And now, my s. Helaman,	37: 1
remember, my s. Helaman, how	37:13
And now remember, my s.,	37:14
I command you, my s. Helaman,	37:20
And now, my s., these	37:24
And now, my s., we see that	37:26
And now, my s., I command	37:27
And now, my s., remember	37:32
O, remember, my s., and learn	37:35
And now, my s., I have	37:38
And now, my s., I would that ye	37:43
O my s., do not let us be	37:46
And now, my s., see that ye	37:47
And now, my s., farewell.	37:47
of Alma to his s., Shiblon.	38:hd
My s., give ear to my words,	38: 1
And now, my s., I trust that	38: 2
I say unto you, my s., that I	38: 3
And now my s., Shiblon, I would	38: 5
Now, my s., I would not that	38: 6
And now, my s., I have told	38: 9
Now go, my s., and teach the word	38:15

Be sober. My s., farewell.	Al	38:15
of Alma to his s., Corianton.		39:hd
And now, my s., I have		39: 1
And this is not all, my s.		39: 3
was no excuse for thee, my s.		39: 4
Know ye not, my s., that these		39: 5
yea, I say unto you, my s., that		39: 6
And now, my s., I would to God		39: 7
Now my s., I would that ye		39: 9
Behold, O my s., how great		39:11
therefore I command you, my s.,		39:12
And now, my s., I would say		39:15
And now, my s., this was the		39:16
Now my s., here is somewhat		40: 1
But behold, my s., the		40: 3
Now, my s., I do not say that		40:20
And now, my s., this is the		40:24
And now, my s., I have		41: 1
I say unto thee, my s., that the		41: 2
And now behold, my s., do not		41: 9
And now, my s., all men that are		41:11
O, my s., this is not the case;		41:13
Therefore, my s., see that you are		41:14
And now, my s., I perceive there		42: 1
Now behold, my s., I will		42: 2
And now remember, my s., if		42:11
Therefore, O my s., whosoever		42:27
And now, my s., I desire that ye		42:29
O my s., I desire that ye		42:30
And now, O my s., ye are called		42:31
And now, my s., go thy way,		42:31
Alma came unto his s. Helaman		45: 2
remnant of garment of my s.		46:24
remnant of the seed of my s.		46:24
my soul hath joy in my s.,		46:25
unto Ammon, the s. of Mosiah,		48:18
had conferred them upon his s.,		50:38
that the s. of Nephihah was		50:39
the eldest s. of our father Lehi;		56: 3
I am Helaman, the s. of Alma.		58:41
armies into the hands of his s.,		62:43
upon his s. of Helaman,		63:11
of Alma, and Helaman his s.,		63:17
also Shiblon, who was his s.		63:17
who was the s. of Helaman,	He	1:hd
who was the s. of Ammoron,		1:16
who was the s. of Helaman,		2: 2
Christ, who is the S. of God.		3:28
his eldest s. Nephi began to reign		3:37
who is Christ, the S. of God,		5:12
was after the s. of Zedekiah;		6:10
his s., who had been appointed		6:15
chief judge Cezoram, and his s.,		6:19
which Alma commanded his s.		6:25
NEPHI, THE S. OF HELAMAN.—		7:hd
that Nephi, the s. of Helaman,		7: 1
that the S. of God should come?		8:14
upon the S. of God with faith,		8:15
even after the order of his S.;		8:18
why not the S. of God come,		8:20
then cometh the S. of God to		14: 2
shall believe on the S. of God,		14: 8
of Jesus Christ, the S. of God,		14:12
if so, and he be the S. of God,		16:18
THE S. OF NEPHI, WHO	3Ne	1:hd
WAS THE S. OF HELAMAN		1:hd
was the s. of Helaman,		1:hd
who was the s. of Alma,		1:hd
who was the s. of Alma,		1:hd
who was the s. of Lehi,		1:hd
And Nephi, the s. of Helaman,		1: 2
giving charge unto his s. Nephi,		1: 2
Nephi, who was his eldest s.,		1: 2
his s. Nephi did keep the records		1: 3
when Nephi, the s. of Nephi,		1:10
of the Father and of the S.—		1:14
of the S. because of my flesh.		1:14
the S. of God must shortly appear;		1:17
of Jesus Christ, the S. of God.		5:13
is Jesus Christ, the S. of God;		5:26
Lachoneus, the s. of Lachoneus,		6:19
I am Jesus Christ the S. of God.		9:15
Behold my Beloved S., in whom	3Ne	11: 7
of the Father, and of the S.,		11:25
that the Father, and the S.,		11:27
if his s. ask bread, will give him		14: 9
his s., whose name was Jonas,		19: 4
am Jesus Christ, the S. of God,		20:31
and come unto my Beloved S.,		21:20
as a man spareth his own s.		24:17
shall the S. of Righteousness		25: 2
even as was the s. of perdition;		27:32
like unto the s. of perdition,		29: 7
Christ, the S. of the living God,		30: 1
WHO IS THE S. OF NEPHI—	4Ne	1:hd
his s. Amos kept it in his		1:19
his s. Amos kept the record		1:21
Christ, the S. of the living God;	Mrm	5:14
which I gave unto my s. Moroni.		6: 6
(among whom was my s. Moroni)		6:11
who were led by my s. Moroni.		6:12
that he is the S. of God, and that		7: 5
unto the Father, and unto the S.,		7: 7
I am the s. of Mormon, and my		8:13
even the Father and the S.;		9:12
said Jesus Christ, the S. of God,		9:22
Christ, the S. of the living God;		9:29
Coriantor was the s. of Moron.	Eth	1: 7
And Moron was the s. of Ethem.		1: 8
And Ethem was the s. of Ahah.		1: 9
And Ahah was the s. of Seth.		1:10
And Seth was the s. of Shiblon.		1:11
And Shiblon was the s. of Com.		1:12
Com was the s. of Coriantum.		1:13
was the s. of Amnigaddah.		1:14
Amnigaddah was the s. of Aaron.		1:15
who was the s. of Hearthom.		1:16
Hearthom was the s. of Lib.		1:17
And Lib was the s. of Kish.		1:18
And Kish was the s. of Corom.		1:19
And Corom was the s. of Levi.		1:20
And Levi was the s. of Kim.		1:21
Kim was the s. of Moriantom.		1:22
Riplakish was the s. of Shez.		1:24
And Shez was the s. of Heth.		1:25
And Heth was the s. of Com.		1:26
Com was the s. of Coriantum.		1:27
Coriantum was the s. of Emer.		1:28
And Emer was the s. of Omer.		1:29
And Omer was the s. of Shule.		1:30
And Shule was the s. of Kib.		1:31
And Kib was the s. of Orihah.		1:32
Orihah, who was the s. of Jared;		1:32
I am the Father and the S.		3:14
Jesus Christ, the S. of God,		4: 7
of which the Father, and the S.,		5: 4
his people under Corihor his s.,		7: 7
the s. of Noah did build up his		7:19
of Cohor, the s. of Noah.		7:20
Cohor, the s. of Noah, caused		7:21
a s. who was called Nimrod;		7:22
for Akish, the s. of Kimnor.		8:10
began to be jealous of his s.,		9: 7
saw the S. of Righteousness		9:22
And his eldest s., whose name		10: 3
Ahah, his s., did obtain the		11:10
in the gift of his S. hath God		12:11
first believed in the S. of God.		12:18
the name of thy S., Jesus Christ,	Mro	4: 3
of the body of thy S.,		4: 3
upon them the name of thy S.,		4: 3
the name of thy S., Jesus Christ,		5: 2
of the blood of thy S.,		5: 2
who are true followers of his S.,		7:48
My beloved s., Moroni,		8: 2
And now, my s., I speak unto		8: 4
And now, my s., I desire that		8: 6
wherefore, my beloved s., I		8: 9
Behold, my s., this thing ought		8:24
Behold, my s., I will write		8:27
Pray for them, my s., that		8:28
so great a knowledge, my s.,		8:29
Farewell, my s., until I shall		8:30
epistle of Mormon to his s., Moroni.		9:hd

SON 898 SONG

My beloved s., I write unto you	Mro	9: 1
And now behold, my s., I fear		9: 3
my beloved s., notwithstanding		9: 6
O my beloved s., how can a		9:11
But O my s., how can a people		9:13
And again, my s., there are		9:16
And now, my s., I dwell no		9:20
my s., I cannot recommend		9:21
behold, my s., I recommend		9:22
My s., be faithful in Christ;		9:25
I am Jesus Christ, the S. of God.	DC	6:21
Behold, I say unto you, my s.,		9: 1
Be patient, my s., for it is		9: 3
Do not murmur, my s., for it is		9: 6
am Jesus Christ, the S. of God.		10:57
Behold thou art Hyrum, my s.;		11:23
am Jesus Christ, the S. of God.		11:28
Christ, the S. of the living God,		14: 9
God gave his Only Begotten S.,		20:21
of the Father and of the S.;		20:27
Father, S., and Holy Ghost are		20:28
and of the S., and of the Holy		20:73
the name of thy S., Jesus Christ,		20:77
of the body of thy S.,		20:77
upon them the name of thy S.,		20:77
the name of thy S., Jesus Christ,		20:79
of the blood of thy S., which		20:79
also John the s. of Zacharias,		27: 7
promise that he should have a s.,		27: 7
name of mine Only Begotten S.		29:42
Thomas, my s., blessed are		31: 1
My s. Orson, hearken and hear		34: 1
Wherefore you are my s.;		34: 3
am Jesus Christ, the S. of God,		35: 2
am Jesus Christ, the S. of God;		36: 8
Christ the S. of the living God,		42: 1
of the Father and of the S.		42:17
behold the blood of thy S. which		45: 4
of the coming of the S. of Man.		45:39
I am the S. of God.		45:52
Jesus Christ is the S. of God,		46:13
sent mine Only Begotten S.		49: 5
have done unto the S. of Man		49: 6
the S. of Man cometh not in		49:22
through Jesus Christ, his S.		50:27
am Jesus Christ, the S. of God,		52:44
Christ, the S. of the living God.		55: 2
behold the S. of Man cometh.		58:65
the coming of the S. of Man,		61:38
the coming of the S. of Man.		63:53
the coming of the S. of Man,		64:23
the S. of Man shall come down		65: 5
I am the S. of the living God,		68: 6
of the Father, and of the S,		68: 8
the coming of the S. of Man;		68:11
descending from father to s.		68:21
Christ the S. of the living God,		68:25
through his Only Begotten S.,		76:13
of Jesus Christ, who is the S.,		76:14
the voice of the S. of Man,		76:16
we beheld the glory of the S.,		76:20
against the Only Begotten S.		76:25
the presence of God and the S.,		76:25
Lucifer, a s. of the morning.		76:26
fallen, even a s. of the morning!		76:27
denied the Only Begotten S.		76:35
deny the S. after the Father has		76:43
order of the Only Begotten S.		76:57
in prison, whom the S. visited,		76:73
receive of the presence of the S.,		76:77
Redeemer, even the S. Ahman,		78:20
through Jesus Christ his S.—		88: 5
verily I say unto you my s.,		90: 1
and the S. because I was in		93: 4
thus he was called the S. of God,		93:14
This is my beloved S.		93:15
apostles, saith S. Ahman;		95:17
to offer up his only s.		101: 4
after the Order of the S. of God		107: 3
handed down from father to s.,		107:40
Jesus Christ, in thy bosom,		109: 4
that the S. of Man might have a		109: 5
My s., peace be unto thy soul;		121: 7
thine elder s., although but six		122: 6
know thou, my s., that all these	DC	122: 7
The S. of Man hath descended		122: 8
order of mine Only Begotten S.		124:123
of the Father and the S.,		130: 3
and the S. dwell in a man's heart		130: 3
previous to the coming of the S. of		130:12
of the coming of the S. of Man,		130:14
Joseph, my s., if thou livest		130:15
see the face of the S. of Man;		130:15
the coming of the S. of Man will		130:17
tangible as man's; the S. also;		130:22
commanded to offer his s. Isaac.		132:36
the offering of Abraham of his s.		132:50
thou art my s.; wherefore look,	Mses	1: 4
a work for thee, Moses, my s.;		1: 6
I show unto thee, Moses, my s.;		1: 7
Moses, s. of man, worship me.		1:12
For behold, I am a s. of God,		1:13
record of the Father and the S.,		1:24
which is mine Only Begotten S.,		1:32
and by the S. I created them,		1:33
now, Moses, my s., I will speak		1:40
send me, I will be thy s., and I		4: 1
But behold, my Beloved S.,		4: 2
thou doest in the name of the S.,		5: 8
in the name of the S. forevermore.		5: 8
record of the Father and the S.,		5: 9
saying: I am also a s. of God;		5:13
as many as believed in the S.,		5:15
after the name of his s., Enoch.		5:42
and Irad, the s. of Enoch, having		5:49
believe on his Only Begotten S.,		5:57
s., and he called his name Seth.		6: 2
a s., and he called his name Enos.		6: 3
begat a s. in his own likeness,		6:10
taught his s. Enos in the ways		6:13
which he called after his own s.,		6:17
of Adam, who was the s. of God,		6:22
Enoch, my s., prophesy unto this		6:27
name of mine Only Begotten S.,		6:52
the S. of God hath atoned for		6:54
Only Begotten is the S. of Man,		6:57
record of the Father, and the S.,		6:66
thou art one in me, a s. of God;		6:68
name of the Father, and of the S.,		7:11
record of the Father and the S.		7:11
the Father, and of the S. of Man;		7:24
testimony of the Father and S.;		7:27
of the coming of the S. of Man,		7:47
S. of Man cometh in the flesh,		7:54
S. of Man lifted up on the cross,		7:55
at the right hand of the S. of Man,		7:56
Enoch beheld the S. of Man		7:59
day of the coming of the S. of Man,		7:65
the s. of Enoch, was not taken,		8: 2
eighty-two years, and begat a s.,		8: 8
This s. shall comfort us concerning		8: 9
of Jesus Christ, the S. of God,		8:24
against thee, Abraham, my s.,	Abr	1:17
eldest s. of Egypt, the daughter		1:25
and I took Lot, my brother's s.,		2: 4
Lot, my brother's s., prayed		2: 6
Lot, my brother's s., and all		2:15
he said unto me: My s., my son,		3:12
he said unto me: My son, my s.,		3:12
answered like unto the S. of Man:		3:27
the coming of the S. of Man be.	JS	1:26
sign of the S. of Man in heaven,		1:36
see the S. of Man coming in		1:36
for the S. of Man shall come,		1:37
the coming of the S. of Man;		1:41
the coming of the S. of Man be.		1:43
think not, the S. of Man cometh.		1:48
This is My Beloved S.	JS	2:17
and in His S., Jesus Christ,	AoF	1

SONG

a s. of my beloved,	2Ne	15: 1
is my strength and my s.;		22: 2
to sing the s. of redeeming love,	Al	5:26
delighteth in the s. of the heart;	DC	25:12
the s. of the righteous is a		25:12
sing this new s., saying:		84:98
shall sing the s. of the Lamb,		133:56

SONGS
with s. of everlasting joy.	DC 45:71
with s. of everlasting joy	66:11
with s. of everlasting joy,	101:18
with s. of everlasting joy;	109:39
filled with s. of everlasting joy.	133:33
forth with s. of everlasting joy.	Mses 7:53

SONS
his wife Sariah, and his four s.,	1Ne 1:hd
and my s. are no more,	5: 2
the Lord will deliver my s. out of	5: 5
the Lord hath protected my s.,	5: 8
s. should take daughters to wife,	7: 1
and the two s. of Ishmael	7: 6
and one of the s. of Ishmael,	7:19
and Lemuel and the s. of Ishmael	16:20
the s. of Ishmael and our wives.	16:27
and also unto the s. of Ishmael:	16:37
now, my father had begat two s.	18: 7
brethren and the s. of Ishmael	18: 9
and also unto the s. of Ishmael;	18:17
shall bring thy s. in their arms,	21:22
wherefore, my s., I would that ye	2Ne 1:12
O my s., that these things might	1:19
arise from the dust, my s.,	1:21
Awake, my s.; put on the armor of	1:23
my s. who are the sons of Ishmael,	1:28
my sons who are the s. of Ishmael,	1:28
And now, my s., I speak unto you	2:14
And now, my s., I would that ye	2:28
few words unto you all, my s.,	2:30
Laman, his s., and his daughters,	4: 3
behold, my s., and my daughters,	4: 3
s. and daughters of my first-born,	4: 3
behold, my s. and my daughters,	4: 5
the s. and daughters of Laman,	4: 8
the s. and daughters of Lemuel	4: 8
Behold, my s. and my daughters,	4: 9
who are the s. and the daughters of	4: 9
the s. and daughters of Laman;	4: 9
he spake unto the s. of Ishmael,	4:10
the s. of Ishmael were angry	4:13
shall bring thy s. in their arms,	6: 6
all the s. she hath brought forth;	8:18
all the s. she hath brought up.	8:18
These two s. are come unto thee,	8:19
Thy s. have fainted, save these two;	8:20
that he had three s.;	Mos 1: 2
My s., I would that ye should	1: 3
I say unto you, my s.,	1: 5
O my s., I would that ye should	1: 6
And now, my s., I would that ye	1: 7
did teach my son Benjamin teach his s.,	1: 8
made an end of teaching his s.,	1: 9
the kingdom upon one of his s.	1: 9
and his s., and his daughters,	2: 5
their s., and their daughters,	2: 5
his s., and his daughters;	5: 7
become his s. and his daughters.	5: 7
the kingdom upon one of my s.;	10:22
upon Noah, one of his s.;	11: 1
was one of the s. of the king	19:16
the s. of Mosiah were numbered	27: 8
and also one of the s. of Alma	27: 8
secretly with the s. of Mosiah	27:10
becoming his s. and daughters;	27:25
of them were the s. of Mosiah;	27:34
the names of the s. of Mosiah.	27:34
after the s. of Mosiah had done	28: 1
if he should let his s. go up	28: 6
and I will deliver thy s. out of	28: 7
not any of his s. who would	28:10
any of the s. of Mosiah willing	29: 3
and also the s. of Ishmael,	Al 3: 7
he had two s., Lehi and Aha)—	16: 5
now Zoram and his two s.,	16: 5
Zoram and his s. crossed over the	16: 7
account of the s. of Mosiah,	17:hd
he met with the s. of Mosiah	17: 1
these s. of Mosiah were with	17: 2
the hearts of the s. of Mosiah,	17:12
for which the s. of Mosiah had	Al 17:16
called after the s. of Ishmael,	17:19
deliver his s. out of their hands;	17:35
Lemuel, and the s. of Ishmael,	18:38
and his wife, and his s., and	18:43
when I made a feast unto my s.,	20: 9
Nephites, who are s. of a liar.	20:13
of fathers mourning for their s.,	28: 5
and he also took two of his s.	31: 6
the eldest of his s. he took not	31: 7
Alma and his brethren and his s.	31:19
Zeezrom and also my two s.—	31:32
and also the two s. of Alma	35:14
he caused that his s. should be	35:16
about with the s. of Mosiah,	36: 6
the s. of Alma did go forth	43: 1
Lemuel, and the s. of Ishmael,	43:13
blessed him, and also his other s.;	45:15
even the sister of Mosiah,	48:18
yea, and also Alma and his s.,	48:18
they had many s., who had not	53:16
two thousand of the s. of	56: 3
did join my two thousand s.,	56:10
are worthy to be called s.)	56:10
yea, those s. of mine, gave them	56:17
of those my two thousand s.	56:27
march forth with my little s.	56:30
that my little s. should fall into	56:39
Therefore what say ye, my s.,	56:44
I had ever called them my s.	56:46
of the s. of the Ammonites	57: 6
behold, it was these my s.,	57:22
s. of the people of Ammon,	58:39
according to the records of his s.,	He 1:hd
record of Helaman and his s.,	1:hd
who were the s. of Pahoran.	1: 2
are not all the s. of Pahoran.	1: 4
came to pass that he had two s.	3:21
who were the s. of Helaman,	4:14
Behold, my s., I desire that ye	5: 6
Therefore, my s., I would that ye	5: 7
And now my s., behold I have	5: 8
O remember, remember, my s.,	5: 9
And now, my s., remember,	5:12
Helaman taught to his s.;	5:13
s. of Zedekiah were not slain,	8:21
record of Helaman and his s.	16:25
s. and daughters of my people;	3Ne 9: 2
to become the s. of God;	9:17
form more than the s. of men—	20:44
he shall purify the s. of Levi,	24: 3
ye s. of Jacob are not consumed.	24: 6
O ye fair s. and daughters,	Mrm 6:19
become my s. and my daughters.	Eth 3:14
And Jared had four s.;	6:14
also begat s. and daughters.	6:15
also begat s. and daughters	6:16
the number of the s. and the	6:20
the number of s. and daughters	6:20
were twelve, he having four s.	6:20
one of their s. to be a king	6:22
out from among our s. a king,	6:24
neither would the s. of Jared,	6:27
he begat s. and daughters;	7: 2
were twenty and three s.	7: 2
and he begat s. and daughters.	7: 4
begat many s. and daughters.	7:12
had many s. and daughters.	7:14
And among the s. of Corihor	7:14
the s. of Shule crept into the	7:18
Shule begat s. and daughters	7:26
Jared begat s. and daughters	8: 1
that he begat s. and daughters	8: 4
to his s. and to his daughters	9: 2
also his s. and his daughters,	9: 3
that Akish begat other s.,	9:10
the s. of Akish did offer them	9:11
the s. of Akish and Akish	9:12
begat many s. and daughters;	9:21
and begat s. and daughters;	9:24
begat other s. and daughters.	9:25
and he begat s. and daughters.	10: 2

SONS 900 SOOTHSAYERS

and he begat s. and daughters	Eth	10:14
and begat s. and daughters;		10:16
begat many s. and daughters;		10:17
and begat s. and daughters;		10:29
his fair s. nor daughters;		13:17
fair s. and daughters of Cohor;		13:17
fair s. and daughters of Corihor;		13:17
the fair s. and daughters upon		13:17
the s. of Coriantumr fought		13:19
And the s. of Coriantumr,		13:24
they become the s. of God.	Mro	7:26
may become the s. of God;		7:48
Fear not to do good, my s.,	DC	6:33
to become the s. of God,		11:30
until the s. of Levi do offer		13: 1
are s. and daughters in my		25: 1
might become the s. of God.		34: 3
may become the s. of God,		35: 2
among you having twelve s.,		38:26
looketh upon his s. and saith		38:26
gave I power to become my s.;		39: 4
me, power to become my s.		39: 4
have power to become my s.;		42:52
and to become the s. of God;		45: 8
among the s. of Aaron;		68:16
s. and daughters unto God.		76:24
who are the s. of perdition,		76:32
except those s. of perdition		76:43
are gods, even the s. of God—		76:58
And the s. of Moses,		84: 6
upon Aaron and his s.		84:30
concerning the s. of Moses—		84:31
for the s. of Moses and also		84:31
and also the s. of Aaron shall		84:31
And the s. of Moses and of		84:32
Lord's house, whose s. are ye;		84:32
They become the s. of Moses		84:34
dwelt among the s. of men.		93: 4
thy servants, the s. of Jacob,		109:58
your sacrifices by the s. of Levi,		124:39
to any of the s. of men to do		124:49
and those s. of men go		124:49
at the hands of those s. of men,		124:49
all the s. of God shout for joy!		128:23
he shall purify the s. of Levi,		128:24
bare unto him s. and daughters,	Mses	5: 2
the s. and daughters of Adam		5: 3
they also begat s. and daughters.		5: 3
all things known unto their s.		5:12
also begat many s. and daughters.		5:42
and other s. and daughters.		5:43
and other s. and daughters.		5:43
and other s. and daughters.		5:43
to reveal it unto the s. of Adam;		5:49
spread among all the s. of men.		5:52
And it was among the s. of men,		5:53
came not among the s. of men,		5:54
prevail among all the s.		5:55
the s. of men whom he had made;		5:56
and called upon his s. to repent.		6: 1
begat many s. and daughters;		6:11
begat many s. and daughters.		6:14
begat many s. and daughters.		6:18
and begat s. and daughters.		6:19
and begat s. and daughters.		6:20
and begat s. and daughters.		6:21
genealogy of the s. of Adam,		6:22
and thus may all become my s.		6:68
and become the s. of God,		7: 1
which were the s. of Adam;		7:22
the s. of Noah should be saved		7:42
and begat s. and daughters;		8: 6
and begat s. and daughters;		8:10
And Noah and his s. hearkened		8:13
they were called the s. of God.		8:13
the s. of men saw that those		8:14
daughters of thy s. have sold		8:15
is kindled against the s. of men,		8:15
Behold, we are the s. of God;		8:21
with God, as did also his three s.,		8:27
who afterward settled her s. in it;	Abr	1:24
until the s. of Levi do offer	JS	2:69

SOON

the Lord ceaseth s. to strive with	1 Ne	7:14
for the day s. cometh that all the		22:15
For the time s. cometh that		22:16
whose limbs ye must s. lay down	2 Ne	1:14
day of the Lord of Hosts s. cometh		12:12
and he saw that he must s. die;	Jac	1: 9
and the end s. cometh;		5:29
and it will s. become ripened,		5:37
the time which will s. come.		5:71
after that the end s. cometh.		6: 2
I must s. go down to my grave;		7:27
I must s. go down to my grave,	En	1:26
I s. go to the place of my rest,		1:27
s. go the way of all the earth;	Mos	1: 9
as s. as Ammon had read the		8: 6
kingdom of heaven is s. at hand,	Al	5:28
kingdom of heaven is s. at hand;		5:50
shall very s. shine forth among		5:50
how s. ye have forgotten the		9: 8
have ye forgotten so s. how many		9:10
the time is s. at hand except		10:23
cometh, we know not how s.		13:25
as s. as she touched her hand		19:29
as s. as they are departed from		40:11
as s. as they were dead their		42:11
as s. as they had departed into		43:23
the time very s. cometh that		45:13
as s. as Amalickiah had		48: 1
shall s. be visited with death,		54:10
we s. accomplished our desire;		57: 8
s. after Moroni had sent his		61: 1
repent it will come unto you s.	He	8:26
that they s. became converted,	3 Ne	1:25
s. after the ascension of Christ		10:18
that it shall s. overtake you.		29: 4
the day s. cometh that your	Mrm	6:21
must s. become incorruptible		6:21
the time s. cometh that he		8:41
must s. go down to the grave;	Eth	6:19
s. after my calling to the	Mro	8: 1
out s. against the Lamanites.		8:27
they must perish s., unto the		8:29
trust that I may see thee s.;		9:24
I s. go to rest in the paradise		10:34
that s. it may go to the Jew,	DC	19:27
nigh and the day s. at hand		29: 9
the time is s. at hand that I		34: 7
the day s. cometh that ye shall		38: 8
of darkness shall s. be rent,		38: 8
there will s. be great wars in		38:29
as s. as preparations can be		52: 3
to this land, as s. as possible,		57:15
as s. as time will permit.		58:52
provided, as s. as it is possible,		90:19
indignation is s. to be poured		101:11
are s. to befall the nations.		101:98
as s. as he possible can,		114: 1
as s. as they get a little authority,		121:39
the flower thereof which s. falleth,		124: 7
s. became general among all	JS	2: 5
s. recovering in some degree,		2:20
I s. found, however, that my		2:22
afraid; but the fear s. left me.		2:32
but s. would come.		2:40
fulfilled, but was s. to be.		2:41
Gentiles was s. to come in.		2:41
I s. found out the reason		2:60
as s. as I had been baptized		2:73

SOONER

s. or later, will be scattered	1 Ne	22: 3
but let it be s. or later,	Al	13:25
not be any s. than that time.	DC	130:17
It no s. appeared than I found	JS	2:17
No s., therefore, did I get		2:18
no s. was it known that I had		2:60
No s. had I baptized Oliver		2:73

SOOTHSAYERS

and hearken unto s. like the	2 Ne	12: 6
and thou shalt have no more s.;	3 Ne	21:16

SOPHISTRY

SOPHISTRY
powers of both reason and s., JS 2: 9

SOPHRONIA
and my sisters, S., Catherine, JS 2: 4
and my sister S., 2: 7

SOCERER
the whoremonger, and the s., DC 63:17

SORCERERS
a swift witness against the s., 3Ne 24: 5
are they who are liars, and s., DC 76:103

SORCERIES
did indulge themselves in s., Al 1:32
there were s., and witchcrafts, Mrm 1:19

SORE
will curse them even with a s. curse, 1Ne 2:23
tempest began to be exceeding s., 18:14
not be cursed with a s. cursing; 2Ne 1:22
upon them, yea, even a s. cursing, 5:21
shall visit them with a s. curse, Jac 2:33
they are cursed with a s. cursing, 3: 3
with famine and s. afflictions, Mos 1:17
are smitten with s. afflictions? 7:28
with famine and s. afflictions, 9: 3
this my people with s. afflictions, 12: 4
the battle became exceeding s., 20:10
which caused me s. repentance; 23: 9
until it did become exceeding s., Al 15: 3
his mind also was exceeding s. 15: 5
became exceeding s. against them, 24: 2
because of their s. repentance 27:23
cause of s. affliction among us; 61: 4
many exceedingly s. afflictions. 62:37
sword but became s. by famine. He 11: 5
which had become exceedingly s. 3Ne 2:13
and did become exceedingly s.; 2:17
and they had a s. battle, Mrm 4: 2
an exceedingly s. battle fought 4:19
the war became exceeding s., Eth 10: 9
the battle became exceeding s. 13:27
the battle became exceeding s., 14: 4
the battle became exceeding s., 14:16
the battle became exceeding s. 14:29
fought an exceedingly s. battle, 15: 9
a s. battle with the Lamanites, Mro 9: 2
and your sufferings be s.— DC 19:15
how s. you know not, 19:15
lest s. judgments fall upon 82: 2
the Gentiles with a s. vexation. 87: 5
her works, with s. affliction, 97:26
is a very s. and grievous sin 101:98
s. and grievous chastisement, 103: 4
a very s. and grievous curse. 104: 4
cursed the earth with a s. curse, Mses 5:56
cursed the earth with a s. curse, 8: 4
caused the famine to wax s. in Abr 2: 1

SORELY
the king s. with their complaints; Mos 21: 6
many of them were s. grieved Al 4: 7
were afflicted and s. chastened. DC 64: 8
father was s. tormented because Abr 1:30

SORENESS
and great was the s. thereof. 1Ne 18:15

SORROW
down into the depths of s. 1Ne 16:25
Because of their grief and much s., 18:18
cast with s. into a watery grave. 18:18
hath been weighed down with s. 2Ne 1:17
with grief and s. to the grave, 1:21
suffered much s. because of you. 1:24
suffered afflictions and much s., 2: 1
in the days of my greatest s. did 3: 1
my soul linger in the valley of s., 4:26
ye shall lie down in s. 7:11
s. and mourning shall flee away. 8:11
behold, darkness and s., 15:30

shall give thee rest, from thy s., 2Ne 24: 3
I, the Lord, have seen the s., Jac 2:31
with joy and not with s., 4: 3
with s. upon their own heads. En 1:10
to our great s. and lamentation, Mos 9:19
his brethren were filled with s., 21:29
they were filled with s., 25: 9
and even shed many tears of s. 25: 9
yea, they were filled with s.; 28:18
and beheld with great s. that Al 4: 8
and s. which I have had for 7: 5
through much affliction and s. 7: 5
being weighed down with s., 8:14
was thus weighed down with s., 8:14
we see the great reason of s., 28:14
s. because of death and 28:14
that there might not be more s. 29: 2
cause of great s. to Alma 31: 2
carry us beyond this vale of s. 37:45
troubles and from all care, and s. 40:12
behold, this giveth my soul s.; 46:25
the great s. and lamentation of He 6:33
his heart was swollen with s. 7: 6
my soul shall be filled with s. 7: 9
of the exceeding s. of my heart, 7:14
much s. unto those Nephites 3Ne 1:28
much s. among the Lamanites; 1:29
neither s. save it be for the 28: 9
might not suffer pain nor s. 28:38
the disciples began to s. for 4Ne 1:44
and their s. before the Lord, Mrm 2:12
my s. did return unto me again, 2:15
my heart has been filled with s. 2:19
my heart did s. because of this 2:27
ye might not have too great s. 5: 9
such will s. for the calamity of 5:11
they will s. for the destruction 5:11
they will s. that this people 5:11
hath my father so much s.? Eth 8: 9
days, which were full of s. 9:15
and he began to s. in his heart; 15: 2
shall be pierced with much s.; DC 1: 3
thou hast seen great s., for 39: 9
there shall be no s. because 101:29
our hearts flow out with s. 109:48
made to bow down with grief, s., 123: 7
ye shall lie down in s. 133:70
calamity, even the days of s., 136:35
and their s. shall be great unless 136:35
I will greatly multiply thy s. Mses 4:22
s. thou shalt bring forth children, 4:22
in s. shalt thou eat of it all 4:23
cause of great s. to myself. JS 2:23

SORROWED
And they s. in their hearts, 3Ne 28: 5

SORROWETH
my heart s. because of my 2Ne 4:17
it s. me because of the fourth 3Ne 27:32

SORROWFUL
we began to be exceeding s., 1Ne 3:14
they were s., because of 7:20
and they were all exceeding s., 16:20
I, Nephi, was exceeding s. 17:19
they saw that I began to be s. 17:19
began to be very s.; Al 4:15
exceeding s., even unto tears. 19:28
meet them he was exceeding s., 20:29
surely this was a s. day; 28: 6
his heart was exceeding s. 31: 2
Lord, my heart is exceeding s.; 31:31
his heart was exceeding s. 35:15
was lost he was exceeding s., 59:11
dead they were exceeding s.; 62:37
them they were exceeding s., He 6:20
believed began to be very s.; 3Ne 1: 7
his heart was exceedingly s. 1:10
they were exceedingly s. because 3:26
Jared became exceeding s. Eth 8: 7
If thou art s., call on the Lord DC 136:29

SORROWING
for their s. was not unto	Mrm	2:13
rather the s. of the damned,		2:13

SORROWS
s. shall take hold of them;	2Ne	23: 8
a man of s., and acquainted with	Mos	14: 3
our griefs, and carried our s.;		14: 4
their s., and their afflictions,	Al	28: 8
my s. cannot bring your return.	Mrm	6:20
seeing the s. of her father,	Eth	8: 8
s. which shall come upon them.	JS	1:19

SORRY
who shall be s. for thee—	2Ne	8:19
they were s. to take up arms	Al	48:23
s. to be the means of sending		48:23
which, I am s. to say, led me	JS	2:28

SORT
every s. according to its number.	Jac	5:31

SORTS
all s. of fruit did cumber the tree.	Jac	5:30

SOUGHT
and they also s. his life,	1Ne	1:20
who s. to take away the life of		2:13
for thou hast s. me diligently,		2:19
he had s. to take away mine own		4:11
had s. to take away their lives		4:28
have s. to take away the life of		7:14
for they s. to take away my life,		7:16
and s. to lay hands upon me;		7:19
if ye have s. to do wickedly		10:21
Jews also s. to take away his life;		17:44
and ye also have s. to take away		17:44
ye s. to take away his life;	2Ne	1:24
accused him that he s. power		1:25
he hath not s. for power nor		1:25
he hath s. the glory of God,		1:25
having s. that which was evil		2:17
he s. also the misery of all mankind.		2:18
they s. to take away my life.		5:19
and have not s. to recover them.		29: 5
and s. for things that they could	Jac	4:14
he s. much opportunity that he		7: 3
I have s. much opportunity that		7: 6
they s. by the power of their		7:24
have not s. gold nor silver	Mos	2:12
and they s. to kill him.		10:15
and s. to take away his life;		11:26
they s. from that time forward		11:29
whom this people s. to destroy?		20:18
their brethren s. to destroy them,	Al	3: 7
and s. to lay their hands upon me,		9:32
those men who s. to destroy them,		10:14
they s. to put them away privily.		14: 3
yet they s. to obtain these things		17:14
of those who s. to slay him;		17:39
against those who s. to slay him,		18: 2
thou that hast s. to destroy him.		20:19
he s. to gain favor of those who		47: 5
Amalickiah s. the favor of the		47:35
he s. also to reign over all the		48: 2
and they s. to be kings;		51: 8
supported by those who s. power		51: 8
and s. protection in their		52: 2
ye have s. to murder us,		54:13
only s. to defend ourselves.		54:13
those who have s. to take away		61: 4
s. to destroy the liberty of the	He	1: 8
s. to destroy Helaman.		2: 5
people who s. to destroy Nephi		8:10
and hast not s. thine own life,		10: 4
own life, but hast s. my will,		10: 4
day we have s. them for battle.		13:34
who hath s. to destroy our souls.		13:37
have s. all the days of your lives		13:38
have s. for happiness in doing		13:38
went forth and s. for Nephi;		16: 1
at Jerusalem s. to kill Jesus,	4Ne	1:31
them of old who also s. power,	Eth	8:15
to help such as s. power	Eth	8:16
Akish s. the life of his		9: 5
s. again to destroy the kingdom.		10:33
the people s. to destroy them.		11: 2
s. to destroy Coriantumr by		13:15
them who s. to destroy him.		13:16
and they s. to kill Ether,		13:22
they repented and s. forgiveness,	Mro	6: 8
inasmuch as they s. wisdom	DC	1:26
they have s. to destroy you;		10: 6
trusted hath s. to destroy you.		10: 6
s. to take away the things		10: 7
has also s. to destroy your gift.		10: 7
devil has s. to lay a cunning plan,		10:12
a day which was s. for by all		45:12
Satan hath s. to deceive you,		50: 3
and they who have s. me early		54:10
have s. after signs and wonders		63:12
have s. occasion against him		64: 6
s. occasion against one another		64: 8
They s. evil in their hearts,		64:16
you have s. in your hearts		67: 5
and s. to take the kingdom of		76:28
s. diligently to sanctify his		84:23
men should be s. for diligently,		98:10
if he has s. thy life, and thy		98:31
should be s. for and upheld by		134: 3
s. to destroy the agency of man,	Mses	4: 3
and he s. also to beguile Eve,		4: 6
he s. to destroy the world.		4: 6
have s. their own counsels in		6:28
s. Noah to take away his life;		8:18
for they have s. his life.		8:26
s. for the blessings of the fathers,	Abr	1: 2
I s. for mine appointment unto		1: 4
Thy servant has s. thee earnestly;		2:12

SOUL
for his s. did rejoice,	1Ne	1:15
it filled my s. with exceeding		8:12
and the most joyous to the s.		11:23
not the destruction of the s.,		14: 3
with all the energies of my s.,		15:25
the final state of the s. after		15:31
unto them in the energy of my s.		16:24
my s. is rent with anguish		17:47
both to the body and s.,		19: 7
hath redeemed my s. from hell;	2Ne	1:15
this hath been the anxiety of my s.		1:16
that my s. might have joy		1:21
destruction of both s. and body.		1:22
thy s. shall be blessed,		2: 3
I write the things of my s.,		4:15
my s. delighteth in the scriptures,		4:15
my s. delighteth in the things of		4:16
my s. grieveth because of mine		4:17
my s. linger in the valley of		4:26
and afflict my s.?		4:27
Awake, my s.! No longer droop		4:28
no more for the enemy of my s.		4:28
yea, my s. will rejoice in thee,		4:30
O Lord, wilt thou redeem my s.?		4:31
who have said to thy s.:		8:23
shook your iniquities from my s.,		9:44
Behold, my s. abhorreth sin,		9:49
and let your s. delight in fatness.		9:51
my s. delighteth in his words.		11: 2
my s. delighteth in proving unto		11: 4
my s. delighteth in the covenants		11: 5
my s. delighteth in his grace,		11: 5
my s. delighteth in proving unto		11: 6
fruitful field, both s. and body;		20:18
my s. delighteth in plainness		25: 4
my s. delighteth in the words of		25: 5
my s. delighteth to prophesy		25:13
and strength, and your whole s.;		25:29
and the anguish of my s. for		26: 7
notwithstanding the pains of my s.,		26:10
and this grieveth my s.		26:11
he awaketh and his s. is empty;		27: 3
is faint, and his s. hath appetite;		27: 3
my s. delighteth in plainness;		31: 3
may be for the welfare of thy s.		32: 9

SOUL

he hath redeemed my s. from hell.	2Ne	33: 6
Yea, it grieveth my s.	Jac	2: 6
which healeth the wounded s.		2: 8
Wherefore, it burdeneth my s.		2: 9
arouse the faculties of your s.;		3:11
poured in his Spirit into my s.,		7: 8
And my s. hungered;	En	1: 4
and supplication for mine own s.;		1: 4
pour out my whole s. unto God		1: 9
wherefore my s. did rest.		1:17
and the faculty of his whole s.,	WM	1:18
whole s. has power to possess,	Mos	2:20
drinketh damnation to his own s.;		2:33
do awaken his immortal s. to a		2:38
was not one s., except it were		6: 2
make his s. an offering for sin		14:10
He shall see the travail of his s.,		14:11
poured out his s. unto death;		14:12
his s. has been made an offering		15:10
O God, receive my s.		17:19
yea, and to every needy, naked s.		18:28
cried out in the anguish of his s.,		19: 7
poured out his whole s. to God,		26:14
My s. hath been redeemed		27:29
My s. was racked with eternal		27:29
and my s. is pained no more.		27:29
that any human s. should perish;		28: 3
that any s. should endure		28: 3
they suffered much anguish of s.		28: 4
the travails of s. for their people,		29:33
lucre which doth corrupt the s.;		29:40
that every s. had cause to mourn;	Al	4: 3
I speak in the energy of my s.;		5:43
my s. doth exceedingly rejoice,		7:26
tribulation and anguish of s.,		8:14
state that the s. can never die?		12:20
his s. began to be harrowed up		14: 6
every s. within the walls thereof,		14:28
not one s. of them had been lost		16: 8
destroyed; yea, every living s.		16: 9
had infused such joy into his s.,		19: 6
life was lit up in his s.,		19: 6
to pour out his s. in prayer		19:14
thy s. could not be saved.		20:17
perhaps thou wouldst lose thy s.		20:18
not one s. among all the people		24: 6
Oh, my s., almost as it were,		26:20
be the means of saving some s.		26:30
I would declare unto every s.,		29: 2
to bring some s. to repentance;		29: 9
then is my s. filled with joy;		29:10
brethren my s. is carried away,		29:16
that thy s. may be destroyed.		30:46
better that thy s. should be lost		30:47
this people doth pain my s.		31:30
thou comfort my s. in Christ.		31:31
O Lord, wilt thou comfort my s.,		31:32
it beginneth to enlarge my s.;		32:28
for my s. was harrowed up to the		36:12
my s. with inexpressible horror.		36:14
become extinct both s. and body,		36:15
with the pains of a damned s.		36:16
my s. was filled with joy as		36:20
and my s. did long to be there.		36:22
bitter pain and anguish of s.;		38: 8
and I did find peace to my s.		38: 8
may the Lord bless your s.		38:15
crimes, to harrow up your s.,		39: 7
is not a s. at this time as		39:17
as a s. will be at the time of his		39:17
concerning the state of the s.		40:11
this state of misery of the s.,		40:15
raising of the spirit or the s.		40:15
reuniting of the s. with the body,		40:18
a state of the s. in happiness		40:21
be reunited, both s. and body,		40:21
The s. shall be restored to the		40:23
the body, and the body to the s.;		40:23
the s. of man should be restored		41: 2
as the s. could never die,		42: 9
as the life of the s. should be,		42:16
as eternal also as the life of the s.		42:16
had poured out his s. to God,		46:17

SOULS

behold, this giveth my s. sorrow;	Al	46:25
my s. hath joy in my son,		46:25
whose s. did joy in the liberty		48:11
not a single s. of the Nephites		49:23
his s. was filled with anger		51:14
had not one s. of them fallen		56:56
not one s. of them who did		57:25
one s. among them who had not		57:25
even one s. has not been slain.		58:39
yea, it grieves my s.		61: 2
My s. standeth fast in that		61: 9
without the loss of one s.;		62:26
it did pierce even to the very s.—	He	5:30
yea every s., by a pillar of fire.		5:43
did exclaim in the agony of his s.:		7: 6
then would my s. have had joy		7: 8
my s. shall be filled with sorrow		7: 9
was pouring out his s. unto God		7:11
pour out my s. unto my God,		7:14
did bring glad tidings to my s.		13: 7
not a living s. among all the	3Ne	5: 1
did pierce them to the very s.,		11: 3
drinketh damnation to his s.;		18:29
eateth of my body to his s.;		20: 8
drinketh of my blood to his s.;		20: 8
his s. shall never hunger nor		20: 8
every s. who will not hear that		20:23
my s. had been poured out in	Mrm	3:12
every s. who belongs to the		3:20
every s. was filled with terror		6: 8
my s. was rent with anguish,		6:16
every s. should be destroyed	Eth	13:21
and his s. mourned and refused		15: 3
but bringeth salvation to his s.;	DC	4: 4
he may treasure up for his s.		6: 3
and bring your s. to destruction.		8: 4
he may treasure up for his s.		11: 3
shall fill your s. with joy;		11:13
he may treasure up for his s.		12: 3
he may treasure up for his s.		14: 3
his joy in the s. that repenteth!		18:13
save it be one s. unto me,		18:15
joy will be great with one s.		18:16
my s. delighteth in the song of		25:12
thy s. delight in thy husband,		25:14
with all your s., from henceforth;		30:11
your sickle with all your s.,		31: 5
and marrow, s. and spirit;		33: 1
ended, and my s. is not saved!		56:16
body and to enliven the s.		59:19
able to cast the s. down to hell.		63: 4
Satan seeketh to destroy his s.;		64:17
but unto that s. who sinneth		82: 7
the s. that sins against this		82:21
every s. who believeth on		84:64
the body are the s. of man.		88:15
is the redemption of the s.		88:16
And the redemption of the s.		88:17
every s. who forsaketh his sins		93: 1
but care for the s., and for		101:37
and for the life of the s.		101:37
let your s. be at rest concerning		108: 2
all his littleness of s. before me,		117:11
My son, peace be unto thy s.;		121: 7
enlarge thy s. without hypocrisy,		121:42
distil upon thy s. as the dews		121:45
supress the freedom of the s.		134: 4
was not a s. which he beheld not;	Mses	1:28
and man became a living s.,		3: 7
And it became also a living s.		3: 9
that one s. shall not be lost,		4: 1
so became of dust a living s.,		6:59
saw this, he had bitterness of s.,		7:44
in the flesh, and his s. rejoiced,		7:47
is thy sister, and thy s. shall live.	Abr	2:24
my s. shall live because of thee.		2:25
and man became a living s.		5: 7

SOULS

might lead away the s. of men	1Ne	14: 3
final state of the s. of men		15:35
the everlasting welfare of your s.	2Ne	2:30
desirous for the welfare of your s.		6: 3

SOULS

and they are living s.,	2Ne	9:13
Prepare your s. for that glorious		9:46
Would I harrow up your s. if your		9:47
Wo unto their s., for they have		13:9
thus the devil cheateth their s.,		28:21
I shall meet many s. spotless		33:7
anxiety for the welfare of your s.	Jac	2:3
daggers placed to pierce their s.		2:9
of your hearts destroy your s.!		2:16
it pointing our s. to him;		4:5
for the salvation of our s.		4:13
and offer your whole s. as an	Om	1:26
serve him with all your whole s.	Mos	2:21
drink damnation to their own s.		3:18
drunk damnation to their own s.		3:25
exceeding great joy in your s.,		4:11
about two hundred and four s.;		18:16
about four hundred and fifty s.		18:35
anguish for the welfare of their s.		25:11
destroy the s. of many people.		29:7
five hundred thirty and two s.;	Al	2:19
five hundred sixty and two s.		2:19
and tens of thousands of s.		3:26
three thousand five hundred s.		4:5
has delivered their s. from hell?		5:6
their s. were illuminated by the		5:7
and their s. did expand,		5:9
with your s. filled with guilt		5:18
s. of those who knew not God.		6:6
reap the salvation of their s.,		9:28
reap the damnation of their s.,		9:28
everlasting destruction of your s.;		12:36
unto the salvation of many s.		17:11
he loveth our s. as well as		24:14
even to the salvation of our s.		26:20
thousands of s. to repentance.		26:22
might save some few of their s.		26:26
bless their s. forever.		28:8
many s. down to destruction,		30:47
thou comfort their s. in Christ.		31:32
O Lord, their s. are precious,		31:35
that the word hath swelled your s.,		32:34
pour out your s. in your closets,		34:26
might bring s. unto repentance;		36:24
about the salvation of many s.		37:7
unto the salvation of their s.		37:8
for such shall find rest to their s.		37:34
what becometh of the s. of men		40:7
what becometh of the s. of men		40:9
the state of the s. of the wicked,		40:14
can be the resurrection of the s.		40:17
whether the s. and the bodies of		40:19
the s. and the bodies are reunited,		40:20
their s. were miserable, being		42:11
bring s. unto repentance,		42:31
believing that their s. were		46:39
so doing they should lose their s.;		53:15
I trust that the s. of them who		57:36
pour out our s. in prayer to God,		58:10
he did speak peace to our s.,		58:11
to the church of God, many s.,	He	3:26
And land their s., yea, their		3:30
souls, yea, their immortal s.,		3:30
unto the filling their s. with joy		3:35
unto the salvation of their s.		5:11
there were about three hundred s.		5:49
is seeking to hurl away your s.		7:16
seeketh to destroy the s. of men.		8:28
who hath sought to destroy our s.		13:37
unto the salvation of our s.	3Ne	5:20
of the joy which filled our s.		17:17
thousand and five hundred s.;		17:25
bring the s. of men unto me,		28:9
of them unto Jesus many s.,		28:29
to harrow up the s. of men	Mrm	5:8
bring damnation upon your s.?		8:33
when your s. are racked with		9:3
with the damned s. in hell.		9:4
about twenty and two s.;	Eth	6:16
were twenty and two s.;		6:20
even all, save it were thirty s.,		9:12
an anchor to the s. of men,	Eth	12:4
the s. of all those who partake	Mro	4:3
the s. of all those who drink of it,		5:2
concerning the welfare of their s.		6:5
and rest our s. in the kingdom		9:6
live and bring s. unto thee.	DC	7:2
he might bring s. unto me,		7:4
may lead their s. to destruction.		10:22
their s. down to hell;		10:26
to destroy the s. of men.		10:27
you may bring s. unto me,		15:6
you may bring s. unto me,		16:6
the worth of s. is great in the		18:10
should bring many s. unto me!		18:16
to the s. of all those who		20:77
to the s. of all those who drink		20:79
to be answered upon your s.		41:12
ended, and your s. not saved.		45:2
unto me and your s. shall live,		45:46
shall find rest to their s.		54:10
your riches will canker your s.;		56:16
and for the salvation of s.,		64:3
death and misery of many s.;		87:1
their s. may escape the wrath		88:85
bringeth a snare upon your s.		90:17
in me for the salvation of s.		100:4
ye may possess your s.,		101:38
their s. are precious before thee;		109:43
upon the s. of the children of men,		121:37
that they may bear the s. of men;		132:63
that your s. may be joyful.		136:29
and they were also living s.;	Mses	3:19
were created and became living s.		6:9
the s. that we had won in Haran,	Abr	2:15
these s. that they were good,		3:23
family consisting of eleven s.,	JS	2:4

SOUND

were not under the s. of his voice,	Mos	2:8
of copper, and are perfectly s.		8:10
when the second trump shall s.		26:25
he doth s. these glad tidings	Al	13:22
were men of a s. understanding		17:2
eyes were towards the s.	3Ne	11:5
heaven, from whence the s. came.		11:5
do not s. a trumpet before you,		13:2
when the trump shall s.;	Mrm	9:13
s. a trumpet unto the armies	Eth	14:28
with a s. of rejoicing, crying—	DC	19:37
gospel with the s. of rejoicing.		28:16
gospel with the s. of rejoicing,		29:4
a trump shall s. both long		29:13
archangel, shall s. his trump,		29:26
as with the s. of a trump,		33:2
as with the s. of a trump,		34:6
as with the s. of a trump,		42:6
the trump of God shall s. both		43:18
and by the great s. of a trump,		43:25
an angel shall s. his trump,		45:45
angel shall s. his trumpet.		49:23
the s. must go forth from this		58:64
as with the s. of a trump,		75:4
under the s. of your voice.		80:1
cities with the s. of the gospel,		84:114
angel shall s. his trump,		88:94
And he shall s. his trump both		88:94
another angel shall s. his trump,		88:99
again, another trump shall s.,		88:100
And another trump shall s.,		88:102
And another trump shall s.,		88:103
shall be the s. of his trump,		88:104
they hear the s. of the trump,		88:104
another angel shall s. his trump,		88:105
another angel shall s. his trump,		88:106
first angel again s. his trump		88:108
the second angel s. his trump,		88:109
angel shall s. his trump;		88:110
the trump shall s. for the dead,		109:75
s. of the rushing of great waters,		110:3
as with the s. of a trump,		124:106
with the great s. of a trumpet,	JS	1:37

SOUNDING

SOUNDING
by the s. of the trumpets,	DC	77:12
and the s. of the trumpets of		77:12
s. the trump of God, saying:		88:92
voice of the s. of the trump		88:98

SOURCE
may know to what s. they may	2Ne	25:26
s. from whence they sprang.	JS	2:34

SOUTH
nearly a s. southeast direction,	1Ne	16:13
and in the north, and in the s.,	2Ne	29:11
on the s. of the land of Shilom,	Mos	9:14
yea, on the north and on the s.,		27: 6
the s. of the city of Ammonihah.	Al	8:18
river Sidon in the s. wilderness,		16: 6
of Manti into the s. wilderness,		16: 7
there up into the s. wilderness.		22:31
in the Lamanites on the s.,		22:33
the s. of the land Bountiful;		27:22
was s. of the land of Jershon,		31: 3
bordered upon the wilderness s.,		31: 3
on the s. of the hill Riplah;		43:31
concealed on the s. of the hill,		43:35
was s. of the land Desolation,		46:17
on the north and on the s.—		46:17
were s. of the land of Zarahemla.		50: 7
he also placed armies on the s.,		50:10
it was on the s. by the line of		50:13
to protect the s. and the west		52:15
Lamanites, on the west sea, s.,		53: 8
borders of the land on the s.		53:22
by the wilderness on the s.,		62:34
on the north, nor on the s.,	He	1:31
from the sea s. to the sea north,		3: 8
land s. and in the land north.		6: 9
the land s. was called Lehi		6:10
and Lehi into the land s.		6:10
both in the north and in the s.;		6:12
both in the north and in the s.		6:12
land north and in the land s.,	3Ne	1:17
both which were in the land s.		4: 1
the robbers who were on the s.		4:26
on the north and on the s.,		6: 2
from the s. and from the north;		20:13
escaped into the s. countries,	Mrm	6:15
west, to the north and to the s.	DC	42:63
from the north and from the s.,		44: 1
Go ye into the s. countries.		75: 8
also into the s. country.		75:17
or to the north, or to the s.		75:26
whether to the north or to the s.,		80: 3
at the rebellion of S. Carolina,		87: 1
And let the first lot on the s.		94: 3
the second lot on the s. shall		94:10
the corner s. of the Ozondah		104:39
west, and the north, and the s.,		125: 4
will be in S. Carolina.		130:12
going on still towards the s.;	Abr	2:21
in S. Bainbridge, Chenango	JS	2:58

SOUTHEAST
nearly a south-s. direction,	1Ne	16:13

SOUTHERN
the S. States shall be divided	DC	87: 3
the S. States will call on other		87: 3

SOUTHWARD
from the land of Gideon s.,	Al	17: 1
the land on the s. was called		22:31
land northward and the land s.		22:32
land s. to the land northward,	He	3: 8
Nephites which was in the land s.		4: 8
Nephi who were in the land s.;		5:16
on the northward and on the s.,		11:20
together in the land s.,	3Ne	3:24
northward and on the land s.		6: 2
destruction in the land s.		8:11
by my father into the land s.,	Mrm	1: 6
which led into the land s.		2:29
unto the Lamanites all the land s.		2:29

905

pass which led into the land s.	Mrm	3: 5
had escaped into the country s.		8: 2
serpents, towards the land s.,	Eth	9:31
some which fled into the land s.		9:32
they did go into the land s.,		10:19
they did preserve the land s.		10:21
and they did flee s.,		15:10

SOVEREIGN
or the will of the s.	DC	134: 3

SOW
we did s. seed, and we did reap	2Ne	5:11
If my people shall s. filthiness	Mos	7:30
If my people shall s. filthiness		7:31
like the s. to her wallowing in	3Ne	7: 8
for they s. not, neither do they		13:26
both to plow and to s.,	Eth	10:25
whatsoever ye s., that shall	DC	6:33
if ye s. good ye shall also reap		6:33

SOWED
after thou hast s. thy fields	DC	24: 3

SOWERS
were the s. of the seed;	DC	86: 2

SOWETH
behold he s. the tares;	DC	86: 3

SPACE

traveled for the s. of many hours	1Ne	8: 8
Spirit for the s. of a time		11:19
yea, for the s. of many years,		15:13
traveled for the s. of four days,		16:13
travel for the s. of many days,		16:15
traveled for the s. of many days		16:17
tents for the s. of a time		16:17
traveled for the s. of many days		16:33
tarry for the s. of a time.		16:33
sojourn for the s. of many years,		17: 4
Bountiful for the s. of many days,		17: 7
even for the s. of many days.		17:52
wind for the s. of many days,		18: 9
waters for the s. of three days;		18:13
waters for the s. of four days,		18:15
sailed for the s. of many days		18:23
loosed for the s. of many years;		22:26
for the s. of many generations;	2Ne	1:18
for the s. of many days.		5: 7
for the s. of many days		5: 7
for the s. of three days		25:13
for the s. of many generations,		25:16
nourished for the s. of many days.	Jac	7:15
for the s. of much of the time.	Jar	1:13
for the s. of nine moons.	Om	1:21
for the s. of three years.	Mos	6: 7
peace for the s. of three years,		7: 1
wilderness for the s. of many days,		8: 8
land for the s. of twelve years		9:11
for the s. of twenty and two years.		10: 3
for the s. of twenty and two years.		10: 5
after the s. of two years that		12: 1
for the s. of two years,		19:29
for the s. of two days and two		27:23
there was a s. granted unto man	Al	12:24
for the s. of fourteen years		17: 4
him not for the s. of an hour,		18:14
for the s., of two days and		18:43
for the s. of two days and		19: 5
for the s. of three days and		36:10
a s. betwixt the time of death		40: 6
a s. between the time of death		40: 9
now, concerning this s. of time,		40: 9
there is a s. between death and		40:21
having no s. for repentance;		42: 5
even for the s. of four years did		46:38
even for the s. of four years.		48:20
cease for the s. of many years		48:22
march in so short a s. of time,		56:50
for the s. of many months,		58: 7
for the s. of many years.		62:39
in the s. of not many years.	He	4:26

SPACE 906 SPAKE

in the s. of not many years,	He	6:32	And I also s. unto him, saying:	1Ne	4:34
in the s. of not many years;		7: 6	courage at the words which I s.		4:35
in the s. of not many years,		11:26	my father s. unto her, saying:		5: 4
death, for the s. of three days,		14:20	And she s., saying:		5: 8
for the s. of many hours,		14:21	the Lord s. unto him again, saying		7: 1
for the s. of many hours.		14:26	therefore I s. unto them, saying,		7: 8
earth for the s. of three days.		14:27	and I s. unto them again.		7:18
for the s. of seven years,	3Ne	4: 4	he s. unto us, saying:		8: 2
the s. of twenty and five years;		5: 8	he s. unto me, and bade		8: 6
up for the s. of a long time		6:17	he s. unto them concerning		10: 2
darkness for the s. of three days		8: 3	And he also s. concerning		10: 5
about the s. of three hours;		8:19	And he s. also concerning		10: 7
about the s. of three hours—		8:19	much s. my father concerning		10: 8
last for the s. of three days		8:23	he s. unto my brethren		10:11
land for the s. of many hours;		10: 1	Yea, even my father s. much		10:12
land for the s. of many hours.		10: 2	and also the things which he s.		10:17
for the s. of three days;		26:13	I s. unto him as a man		11:11
for the s. of about four years,	Mrm	1:12	and he s. unto me as a man		11:11
for the s. of four years.	Eth	2:13	the angel s. unto me, saying:		11:19
for the s. of three hours did		2:14	And he s. unto me, saying:		11:23
lasted for the s. of many years,		9:12	the angel s. unto me again,		11:30
land for the s. of two years,		9:15	And he s. unto me again, saying:		11:31
the s. of sixty and two years		9:16	and the angel s. and showed		11:31
the s. of forty and two years		10: 8	the angel s. unto me again,		11:32
after the s. of many years,		10: 9	the angel of the Lord s. unto me		11:35
last for the s. of many years;		10: 9	the angel of the Lord s. unto me		11:36
the s. of forty and two years		10:15	And the angel s. unto me, saying:		12: 8
fought for the s. of many years,		10:32	And the angel s. unto me, saying:		12:16
for the s. of three days.		13:28	even the river of which he s.;		12:16
again for the s. of two years,		13:31	And while the angel s. these words,		12:19
after the s. of two years,		14: 3	the angel s. unto me, saying:		13: 1
for the s. of two years,		14: 7	And the angel s. unto me, saying:		13: 8
for the s. of three days.		14:26	the angel of the Lord s. unto me,		13:34
were for the s. of four years		15:14	And the angel s. unto me, saying:		13:40
for the s. of three hours,		15:27	the angel s. unto me, Nephi,		14: 5
for the s. of five years,	DC	64:21	the angel s. unto me, saying:		14:16
also, for the s. of a season,		71: 2	the angel s. unto me, saying:		14:18
to fill the immensity of s.—		88:12	he truly s. many great things		15: 3
there is no s. in the which		88:37	I s. unto my brethren,		15: 6
in which there is not s.,		88:37	I, Nephi, s. much unto them		15:19
for the s. of half an hour;		88:95	yea, I s. unto them concerning		15:19
for the s. of a thousand years.		88:110	Isaiah, who s. concerning the		15:20
In the short s. of twenty years,		135: 3	And thus I s. unto my brethren.		15:36
for the s. of many hours before	Mses	1:10	of the Lord s. unto my father		16: 9
the s. of many generations.		7: 4	the Lord s. unto me, saying:		17: 8
for the s. of a thousand years		7:64	I, Nephi, s. unto them, saying:		17:23
for the s. of a thousand years;		7:65	an angel, and he s. unto you;		17:45
will go down, for there is s. there,	Abr	3:24	I s. unto them, saying:		17:48
During the s. of time which	JS	2:28	the words of Zenos, which he s.		19:10
			For thus s. the prophet:		19:11
SPACIOUS			Wherefore I s. unto them,		19:24
I beheld a large and s. field.	1Ne	8: 9	words of Moses, which he s.,		22:20
unto a large and s. field,		8:20	this prophet of whom Moses s.		22:21
a great and s. building;		8:26	alos s. many things unto them—	2Ne	1: 1
that great and s. building.		8:31	he s. unto them concerning		1: 2
in a large and s. building,		11:35	he also s. unto them concerning		1: 3
the great and s. building		11:36	And he s. unto them, saying:		4: 9
the large and s. building,		12:18	he s. unto the sons of Ishmael,		4:10
many elegant and s. buildings;	Mos	11: 8	he s. unto Sam, saying:		4:11
he also built him a s. palace,		11: 9	which s. concerning them,		5:19
did build many s. buildings.	Eth	10: 5	which he s. unto me, saying		5:20
			the Lord s. it, and it was done.		5:23
SPAKE			which he s. to the people of		6: 1
and s. unto his children,	1Ne	1:16	which Isaiah s. concerning		6: 5
the Lord s. unto my father,		2: 1	of the angel who s. it unto me.		6: 9
he s. unto Laman, saying:		2: 9	last night the angel s. unto me		10: 3
And he also s. unto Lemuel:		2:10	now, Jacob s. many more things		11: 1
Now this he s. because of		2:11	the Lord s. again unto Ahaz,		17:10
And I s. unto Sam,		2:17	The Lord s. also unto me again,		18: 5
the Lord s. unto me, saying:		2:19	For the Lord s. thus to me		18:11
he s. unto me, saying:		3: 2	Isaiah s. many things which were		25: 1
he s. unto them, saying:		3:29	And as I s. concerning		26:12
I s. unto my brethren, saying:		4: 1	s. unto the people of Nephi,	Jac	2: 1
he truly s. unto the waters of		4: 2	I, Jacob, s. many more things		3:12
of the Lord which he s. unto me		4:14	God also s. them unto prophets		4:13
And he s. unto me concerning		4:22	which he s. unto the house of		5: 1
And I s. unto him as if		4:23	which this prophet Zenos s.,		6: 1
And I also s. unto him that		4:24	and he s. plainly unto them		7:17
And he, supposing that I s. of		4:26	And he s. plainly unto them,		7:18
And he s. unto me many times		4:27	And he s. of hell, and of eternity,		7:18
I s. with him, that if he		4:32	witnessed that he s. these things		7:21
And I s. unto him, even with		4:33	which he s. unto our fathers,	Jar	1: 9

SPAKE

which he s. unto our fathers,	Om	1: 6
It also s. a few words		1:22
Benjamin, of whom Amaleki s..	WM	1: 3
the words which he s. unto him,	Mos	1:10
the words which he s. should be		2: 8
these are the words which he s.		2: 9
s. that which was commanded		2:35
also holy prophets s. unto them		3:15
he s. unto them in this wise,		7:18
he s. many things unto them		8: 1
all the words which he s.		8: 3
he s. with power and authority		13: 6
the time he s. unto his people;		26: 1
and he s. as it were with a		27:11
the words which he s. unto them.		27:12
which the angel s. unto Alma,		27:17
these are the words which he s.	Al	5: 2
not the words which they s.;		9: 3
words which he s. unto Lehi,		9:13
to the words which he s.		10:11
sayest that I s. as though I		11:36
words that Alma s. unto Zeezrom		12: 2
was great, and he s. on this wise:		12: 2
And Alma s. many more words		13:31
the things which they s.,		21: 8
not hear the words which he s.		21:10
which s. of those things to come.		25:16
Zenos alone s. of these things,		33:15
Zenock also s. of these things—		33:15
he s. unto us, as it were the voice		36: 7
the angel s. more things unto me,		36:11
be fulfilled, which he s., saying:		37:24
face to face, and he s. with me,		38: 7
the words which I s. unto thee		45: 2
which he s. unto Lehi, saying:		50:19
father Helaman s. unto them.	He	5: 5
these are the words which he s.:		5: 5
words which king Benjamin s.		5: 9
also the words which Amulek s.		5:10
because he s. plainly unto them		8: 4
which he s. upon the walls of		16: 1
Zenock s. concerning these	3Ne	10:16
and s. unto the people, saying:		11: 9
the Lord s. unto them saying:		11:13
that he s. unto Nephi		11:18
that Jesus s. unto them,		17:19
And he s. unto the multitude,		17:23
and s. unto them as he		18:36
heard not the words which he s.,		18:37
that he s. unto the multitude,		19:16
remember that I s. unto you,		20:11
I am he of whom Moses s.,		20:23
he s. as touching all things		23: 2
all things that he s. have		23: 3
to the words which he s.		23: 3
s. often one to another,		24:16
s. unto his disciples, one by one,		28: 1
they all s., save it were three,		28: 2
as I s. concerning those whom		28:36
though I s. from the dead;	Mrm	9:30
Jared s. again unto his brother,	Eth	1:38
the Lord s. unto me, saying:		12:26
and he s. concerning a		13: 4
he s. also concerning the		13: 5
And the Lord s. unto Ether,		15:33
which he s. unto his disciples,	Mro	2: 1
Now Christ s. these words		2: 3
which he s. concerning faith,		7: 1
he s. these words unto our		7:26
and s. unto him from heaven,	DC	1:17
he who s. unto you, said unto		5: 2
the same that s. unto you from		8:12
who s. as they were inspired		20:26
I am the same which s.,		38: 3
that which I s. by the mouths of		42:39
and s. unto them, saying:		45:16
the parable be fulfilled which I s.		45:56
as I s. concerning my		58:24
The Lord s. unto Enoch		78: 1
the Lord of the vineyard s.		103:21
am he who s. in righteousness,		133:47
words of God, which he s. unto	Mses	1: 1
And God s. unto Moses, saying:	Mses	1: 3
that Moses s. unto the Lord,		1:36
the Lord God s. unto Moses,		1:37
that the Lord s. unto Moses,		2: 1
power, and it was done as I s.;		2: 5
and it was so, even as I s.,		2: 6
and it was so even as I s.		2: 7
and it was so even as I s.		2:11
and it was so, even as I s.		2:30
God, s., and there went up a mist		3: 6
Lord God, s. unto Moses, saying:		4: 1
s. by the mouth of the serpent.)		4: 7
I s. unto my servant Moses,		4:32
And then the angel s., saying:		5: 7
Now this prophecy Adam s.,		6: 8
and s. and prophesied, and called		6:23
and s. before the Lord, saying:		6:31
And the Lord s. unto Enoch,		6:35
the Lord s. with me, and gave me		6:42
The Lord which s. with me,		6:43
Enoch s. forth the words of God,		6:47
our father Adam s. unto the Lord,		6:53
the Lord s. unto Adam, saying:		6:55
and he s. the word of the Lord,		7:13
the Lord s. unto Enoch, and		7:41
the night time when the Lord s.	Abr	3:14
One of them s. unto me, calling	JS	2:17

SPANIARDS

mine having been opened by the S.	JS	2:56

SPANNED

my right hand hath s. the heavens.	1Ne	20:13

SPARE

words, we would s. his life.	1Ne	4:32
no man shall s. his brother.	2Ne	19:19
their eyes shall not s. children.		23:18
and he will s. his people,		30:10
S. it a little longer,	Jac	5:50
Yea, I will s. it a little longer,		5:51
he did s. the righteous then	Om	1: 7
Gideon, s. me, for the Lamanites	Mos	19: 7
Gideon did s. his life.		19: 8
the Lamanites did s. their lives,		19:15
that they would s. them,		23:28
his infinite mercy to s. them;		28: 4
and were we to s. thee	Al	1:13
Lord, have mercy and s. my life,		2:30
I will s. him, and it shall be		19:23
Ammon that he would s. his life.		20:21
If thou wilt s. me I will grant		20:23
he thinketh, then will I s. thee;		20:24
O king, if thou wilt s. our lives,		22: 3
blood, but we will s. your lives,		44: 6
s. the remainder of their lives,		44:19
would s. the people of the city;		47:33
that the Lord will s. you and		60:32
this people repent I will s. them.	He	11:14
who will repent, for them will I s.		13:13
their hand and shall s. not,	3Ne	3: 8
that he would s. them and		4: 8
that they should not s. any		4:13
s. not, lengthen thy cords and		22: 2
and I will s. them as a man		24:17
the Lord did s. them,	Eth	7:26
his kingdom and s. the people—		13:20
that he would s. the people,		15: 4
would s. the lives of the people.		15: 5
and s. the lives of the people.		15:18
God that he will s. thy life,	Mro	9:22
then will I s. the earth but for	DC	29:22
open your mouths and s. not,		33: 9
lift up your voice and s. not,		34:10
Lift up your voices and s. not.		43:20
Father, s. these my brethren		45: 5
I will not s. any that remain		64:24
search diligently and s. not;		84:94
And then if thou wilt s. him,		98:30
for I will not s. them if they		103:14
and there is enough and to s.;		104:17
cry aloud and s. not, with joy		124:101

SPARED

SPARED
those of us that were s.,	Mos	9: 2
of the righteous that ye are s.;	Al	10:23
none other have they s. alive.		56:12
that they should be s. while		57:26
of the righteous, they were s.		62:40
the righteous' sake that it is s.	He	13:14
would our brethren have been s.,	3Ne	8:24
and our children have been s.,		8:25
O all ye that are s. because		9:13
house of Israel whom I have s.,		10: 6
the people who were s. alive		10:10
blood of the saints, who were s.—		10:12
they were s. and were not sunk		10:13
people of Nephi who were s.,		10:18
Lamanites, who had been s.,		10:18
my church, and ye shall be s.	Mrm	3: 2
was the Lord that had s. them,		3: 3
of this people who are s.,		7: 1
if thou art s. and I shall	Mro	9:24
the moneys which can be s.,	DC	63:40

SPARETH
as a man s. his own son that	3Ne	24:17

SPARING
mercies of God in s. their lives,	2Ne	1: 2
s. their lives, and delivering	He	12: 2
s. none, neither old nor young;	Mro	9:19

SPARINGLY
they are to be used s.;	DC	89:12

SPARK
a s. of freedom remaining,	Al	60:27

SPARKS
compass yourselves about with s.,	2Ne	7:11
in the s. which ye have kindled.		7:11

SPEAK
my father did s. unto them	1Ne	2:14
Lemuel did s. many hard words		3:28
manner of language did she s.		5: 8
we did s. unto him the words		7: 4
brother, should s. unto you,		7: 8
the words which I s. unto you,		7:15
constraineth me that I should s.		7:15
I, Nephi, do not s. all the words		8:29
did my father see, and hear, and s.,		9: 1
I must s. somewhat of the things		10: 1
did my father prophesy and s. unto		10:15
giveth authority that I should s.		10:22
and this remnant of whom I s.		13:34
I did s. many words unto my		15:20
they did s. unto me again,		15:21
or doth it s. of the things which		15:31
I, Nephi, did s. much unto my		16:22
did s. many words unto them,		16:39
and to s. with much rudeness,		18: 9
I, Nephi, began to s. unto them		18:10
anyone that should s. for me;		18:17
but I would s. in other words—		19: 7
I s. unto all the house of Israel,		19:19
for I durst not s. further		22:29
And now, Zoram, I s. unto you:	2Ne	1:30
And now, Jacob, I s. unto you:		2: 1
my sons, I s. unto you these things		2:14
And now I s. unto you, Joseph,		3: 1
tongue, that he shall s. much,		3:17
And now, I, Nephi, s. concerning		4: 1
was constrained to s. unto them,		4:14
Nevertheless, I s. unto you again;		6: 3
I would s. unto you concerning		6: 4
desired that I should s. unto you.		6: 4
I s. unto you for your sakes,		6: 4
would s. somewhat concerning		6: 8
should know how to s. a word		7: 4
I s. unto you these things		9: 3
I would s. unto you of holiness;		9:48
I would s. unto you more; but		9:54
now I, Jacob, s. unto you again,		10: 1
s. the word, and it shall not		18:10
if they s. not according to this	2Ne	18:20
they shall s. and say unto thee:		24:10
Nephi, do s. somewhat concerning		25: 1
unto them will I s. particularly,		25: 8
I s. because of the spirit		25:11
we s. concerning the law		25:27
which he shall s. unto you		26: 1
shall s. unto them out of the		26:16
s. as if it were from the dead.		27:13
I s. the same words unto one		29: 8
I s. forth my words according		29: 9
that I cannot s. another;		29: 9
the words which I s. unto them;		29:11
I shall s. unto the Jews		29:12
I shall also s. unto the Nephites		29:12
I shall also s. unto the other		29:12
I shall also s. unto all nations		29:12
brethren, I would s. unto you;		30: 1
be a few words which I must s.		31: 2
I shall s. unto you plainly,		31: 2
then can ye s. with the tongue of		31:13
and can s. with a new tongue,		31:14
ye could s. with the tongue of		32: 2
could ye s. with the tongue of		32: 2
Angels s. by the power of the		32: 3
they s. the words of Christ.		32: 3
it grieveth me that I must s.		32: 8
I s. unto you as the voice of one		33:13
were it not that I must s. unto	Jac	2:22
I, Jacob, would s. unto you that		3: 1
able to s. and the world was,		4: 9
and to s. and man was created,		4: 9
s. of the atonement of Christ,		4:12
on this wise did he s. unto me,		7: 6
that I might s. unto you;		7: 6
I desire to s. unto the people		7:16
heard my father s. concerning	En	1: 3
Behold, I will s. unto you	Om	1:12
And now I would s. somewhat		1:27
now, I s. somewhat concerning	WM	1: 3
and they did s. the word of God		1:17
words which his father should s.	Mos	1:18
which king Benjamin should s.		2: 1
which king Benjamin should s.		2: 6
hear the words which he should s.		2: 7
he began to s. to his people		2: 8
words which I shall s. unto you		2: 9
with the words which I shall s.,		2: 9
while attempting to s. unto you;		2:30
me that I should s. unto you,		2:30
somewhat more to s. unto you;		3: 1
began to s. unto them, saying:		4: 4
words which I shall s. unto you.		4: 4
Ye are permitted to s.		7:11
saw that he was permitted to s.,		7:12
alive, and am permitted to s.;		7:12
will endeavor to s. with boldness;		7:12
the words which he should s.		7:17
they did s. flattering things		11: 7
while they should s. lying and		11:11
Know ye not that I s. the truth?		12:30
Yea, ye know that I s. the truth;		12:30
unto him that he might s.		22: 5
all their children that could s.		24:22
desired that Alma should also s.		25:14
And Alma did s. unto them,		25:15
and s. much flattery to		27: 8
mouth of Alma, that he might s.,		27:22
he stood up and began to s.		27:23
Did he not s. the words of God,	Al	5:11
for I s. in the energy of my soul;		5:43
called to s. after this manner,		5:44
if ye s. against it, it matters not,		5:58
I s. by way of command unto		5:62
I s. by way of invitation,		5:62
the words which he should s.		10:16
and began to s. unto him,		12: 1
And he commanded them to s.;		14:19
Thou mayest s. boldly, and tell		18:20
And Ammon began to s. unto him		18:24
and s. with the trump of God,		29: 1
that I could s. unto all the ends		29: 7
Why do ye s. against all the		30:22

SPEAK 909 SPEAKING

I am dumb, for I cannot s.;	Al	30:52
I will s. unto you concerning		37:21
for he desired to s. with him.		47:10
men to s. unto the Lamanites		48: 1
he did s. peace to our souls,		58:11
unto them that they might s.,	He	5:18
should s. given unto them—		5:18
Therefore they did s. unto the		5:19
began to s. unto them, saying:		5:26
did s. unto them marvelous words		5:33
could s. forth marvelous words.		5:45
yea, many things did Nephi s.		8: 3
and nothing he s. which was		8: 3
began again to s. unto them,		8:10
was constrained to s. more		8:11
do s. the words of the Lord		13: 5
they of whom I s. are they who	3Ne	16: 2
commanded the Father to s.		17: 2
heard Jesus s. unto the Father;		17:16
And no tongue can s., neither		17:17
both saw and heard Jesus s.;		17:17
And tongue cannot s. the words		19:32
that I am he that doth s.		20:39
he must s. also to the Gentiles.		23: 2
they did s. unto their fathers		26:14
they durst not s. unto him the		28: 5
that I should s. concerning you,		30: 1
that I did s. unto my people,	Mrm	2:23
this I s. unto their seed,		5:10
I would s. somewhat unto the		7: 1
I s. unto you, ye remnant of		7: 1
these are the words which I s.:		7: 1
one should s. from the dead.		8:26
I s. unto you as if ye were		8:35
I s. also concerning those		9: 1
again I s. unto you who deny		9: 7
shall s. with new tongues;		9:24
I s. unto you as though I spake		9:30
the words which I shall s.?	Eth	3:11
if it so be that I do not s.,		4:10
would s. somewhat concerning		12: 6
people that they could s. much,		12:23
faith, and did s. in thy name,		12:31
now I s. concerning baptism.	Mro	6: 1
s. one with another concerning		6: 5
did he s. unto the people,		7: 1
now I, Mormon, s. unto you,		7: 2
am permitted to s. unto to you		7: 2
I would s. unto you that are		7: 3
of which I said I would s.;		7:21
I would s. unto you concerning		7:40
I s. unto you concerning that		8: 4
Behold, I s. with boldness,		8:16
I s. it boldly; God hath		8:21
when I s. the word of God		9: 4
now I s. unto all the ends of		10:24
I s. it according to the words		10:26
that every man might s. in the	DC	1:20
And now, again, I s. unto you,		5:23
Did I not s. peace to your mind		6:23
For, behold, it is I that s.;		11:11
I s. unto all who have good		11:27
I s. unto you, and also to all		12: 7
the world, that s. these words,		12: 9
I s. unto you with sharpness		15: 2
I s. unto you with sharpness		16: 2
Oliver Cowdery, I s. unto you,		18: 9
I s. unto you, even as unto		18: 9
and s. the truth in soberness.		18:21
I s. unto you, the Twelve—		18:31
I s. unto you that are chosen		19: 9
s. freely to all; yea, preach,		19:37
Behold, I s. unto you, Oliver,		23: 1
Behold, I s. unto you, Hyrum,		23: 3
I s. a few words unto you,		23: 4
I s. a few words unto you,		23: 5
what thou shalt s. and write,		24: 6
I s. unto you, Emma Smith,		25: 1
the Comforter to s. or teach,		28: 4
to hear, and the dumb to s.,		35: 9
s. in your ears with a voice		38:30
s. and prophesy as seemeth me		42:16
behold, I s. unto the church.		42:18
not s. evil of thy neighbor,	DC	42:27
s. reproachfully of him or her.		42:92
which I shall s. unto you.		43: 1
will s. unto you and prophesy,		45:15
I s. this concerning those		46: 5
to some to s. with tongues;		46:24
I will s. unto my servant		51: 1
I will s. unto you concerning		60: 5
And now I s. of the residue		60:12
that they shall s. as they are		68: 3
whatsoever they shall s. when		68: 4
I who s. even by the voice of		75: 1
who shall s. in your ears		78: 2
tongue of the dumb shall s.;		84:70
neither s. them before the		84:73
but let one s. at a time		88:122
I s. unto you with my voice,		97: 1
Now, I s. unto you concerning		98:23
s. the thoughts that I shall		100: 5
of the twelve shall s. first,		102:12
the councilors shall s. upon it,		102:13
than six be appointed to s.		102:14
the councilors appointed to s.		102:16
every man is to s. according to		102:16
appointed to s. on the case		102:18
ascertain who should s. first,		102:34
their God, shall s. unto them,		103: 7
I s. not concerning those who		105: 7
I s. concerning my churches		105: 8
s. unto them with mine own voice,		110: 8
is that he will s. to them,		113:10
Let the dead s. forth anthems		128:22
and s. often one to another.		133: 6
and he shall s. from Jerusalem,		133:21
cease to s. evil one of another.		136:23
I will s. unto thee concerning this	Mses	1:40
write the things which I shall s.		1:40
write the words which I s.		2: 1
to keep the commandment, I s.		6:42
I s. these things unto you for	JS	1:23
I s. for mine elect's sake;		1:29
so that I could not s.		2:15
of myself, so as to be able to s.,		2:18
and they did in reality s. to me;		2:25

SPEAKEST
Thou s. hard things against us.	1Ne	16: 3
I know that thou s. the truth,	Eth	3:12

SPEAKETH
I spake unto him as a man s.;	1Ne	11:11
he spake unto me as a man s.		11:11
and every mouth s. folly.	2Ne	19:17
for he s. unto men according to		31: 3
when a man s. by the power of		33: 1
and it s. of Jesus,		33: 4
And it s. harshly against sin,		33: 5
for the Spirit s. the truth	Jac	4:13
it s. of things as they really are,		4:13
because he s. flattering words	He	13:28
for I am he who s.	Eth	4: 8
shall know that it is I that s.,		4:10
my power which s. unto thee;	DC	11:11
my voice which s. them unto		18:35
He that s., whose spirit is		52:16
to the voice of him who s.,		81: 1
therefore, as the Lord s.,		85:10

SPEAKING
returned from s. with the Lord,	1Ne	3: 1
he did cease s. unto them.		8:38
father had made an end of s.		10: 2
And now I make an end of s.		14:30
I, Nephi, had made an end of s.		16: 1
will not make him mighty in s.	2Ne	3:17
my father had made an end of s.		4: 3
my father had made an end of s.		4: 8
my father had made an end of s.		4:10
after he had made an end of s.		4:11
mighty in writing, like unto s.		33: 1
I make an end of s. unto you	Jac	2:22
I make an end of s. these words.		3:14
the voice of the Lord s. unto me		7: 5

SPEAKING

the gift of s. with tongues,	Om 1:25
And I make an end of my s.	1:30
made an end of s. the words	Mos 4: 1
having finished s. to the people,	6: 1
made an end of s. to his people,	8: 1
made an end of s. these words	8:19
while s. with the Lord.	13: 5
s. of things to come as though	16: 6
made an end of s. and reading	25:14
had made an end of s. to them,	25:17
after Alma had made an end of s.	Al 6: 1
the gift of s. with tongues,	9:21
man who has been s. unto you	10: 8
when Alma had made an end of s.	12:19
after he had made an end of s.	14: 1
s. many words which were not	19:30
and as he was s. unto them,	21: 5
never s. of their God again	31:23
teaching and s. unto the people	32: 4
those of whom we have been s.,	32: 4
made an end of s. these words,	44:10
shall be heard for their much s.	3Ne 13: 7
I, Mormon, make an end of s.	28:24
I make an end of s. concerning	Mrm 8:13
healing, nor s. with tongues,	9: 7
people of whom I am now s.,	Eth 8:21
as one s. out of the dust?	Mro 10:27
s. unto the church collectively	DC 1:30
for s. my words which I have	15: 5
for s. my words which I have	16: 5
lying, backbiting, nor evil s.;	20:54
S. unto you that you may	29:33
s. to the ears of all that live,	43:21
make an end of s. unto you.	56:20
s. after the manner of the Lord,	63:53
s. after the manner of the Lord—	64:24
S. of the resurrection of the	76:16
privilege of s. for themselves	102:18
s. concerning the church and	105: 2
as the voice was still s., Moses	Mses 1:27
s. unto them, and they saw	5: 4
had withdrawn from s. to me,	Abr 2:12
and heard a voice s. unto him,	JS 2:24
s. all manner of evil against	2:25
him who had been s. to me,	2:43
was a voice s. unto me,	2:49

SPEAKS
which s. concerning the creation	Eth 1: 3

SPEARS
their s. into pruning-hooks—	2Ne 12: 4
took their swords, and their s.,	Al 17: 7

SPECIAL
plates, for the s. purpose that	1Ne 9: 3
Twelve Apostles, or s. witnesses	DC 107:23
Twelve s. witnesses or Apostles	107:26

SPECIFIED
during the time s.,	DC OD

SPEECH
their s. shall be low out of the	2Ne 26:16
their s. shall whisper out of the	26:16
I must use so much boldness of s.	Jac 2: 7
flattery, and much power of s.,	7: 4
exceeding great plainness of s.,	En 1:23
according to our manner of s.	Mrm 9:32
distinctly, not with loud s.	DC 88:129
because of thy s.	112: 5
of Lamech, hearken unto my s.;	Mses 5:47
hate me; for I am slow of s.;	6:31
Enoch continued his s., saying:	6:43
Enoch continued his s., saying:	7: 1

SPEECHES
cease from all your light s.,	DC 88:121
and lay aside all his hard s.;	124:116

SPEED
That say: Let him make s.,	2Ne 15:19

they shall come with s. swiftly;	2Ne 15:26
did s. the march of his army.	Al 56:38
by the s. of their march—	56:51
took our march with s. towards	57:34
follow after us with great s.,	58:19
was with such exceedingly great s.	He 1:19

SPEEDILY
the time cometh s. that Satan	1Ne 22:15
For the time s. shall come that	22:23
And the time cometh s. that	22:24
For I will destroy her s.;	2Ne 23:22
have been destroyed s.;	26:18
God will s. visit the inhabitants	28:16
For the time s. cometh	30:10
his judgments must s. come	Jac 2:14
And the time s. cometh,	3: 4
and the season s. cometh;	5:71
the season, which s. cometh;	5:76
going down s. to destruction.	En 1:23
the fire except they s. repent.	Al 5:56
he returned s. to the land of	8:18
that they must s. repent,	30:57
doth s. drag them down to hell.	30:60
s. unto me of your provisions	60:34
not do this I come unto you s.;	60:35
come unto me s. with a few of	61:15
go s. against those dissenters,	61:17
s. executed according to the law.	62:10
that we may s. come unto thee	3Ne 28: 2
the time s. cometh that ye	Mro 10:27
know that the day s. cometh;	DC 1:35
thou mightest s. come unto me	7: 4
go s. unto the church which is	24: 3
the time s. cometh that great	35:10
Corrill take their journey s.;	52: 7
take up his journey s. to the	56: 5
land of Zion, as s. as can be,	57:14
return s. to the land from	60: 1
take your journey s. for the	60: 5
s. return, proclaiming my word	60:14
such beware and repent s.,	63:15
now s. visit the churches,	63:46
depart s. from that house,	75:20
Yea, Let it be built s., by	97:11
vengeance cometh s. upon	97:22
write s. to Cainhannoch	104:81
they may s. repent and return	109:21
vengeance cometh s. upon	112:24
Far West should be built up s.	115:17
settle up their business s.	117: 1
let him come up hither s.,	117:14
day of my visitation cometh s.,	124:10
be great unless they s. repent,	136:35
speedily repent, yea, very s.	136:35

SPEEDY
a s. destruction cometh unto	2Ne 26:10
then cometh s. destruction,	26:11
so s. was the flight of his people.	Mos 20:12
thine anger with s. destruction.	Al 33:10
s. was the flight of Kishkumen	He 1:10
so s. was their march that it	3Ne 7:13
so swift and s. was the war	Eth 14:22

SPEND
do not s. money for that which	2Ne 9:51
to s. my days in your service,	Mos 2:12
priests s. their time with harlots,	11:14
s. your strength with harlots,	12:29
and rather than s. their days in	Al 24:18
s. the remainder of his days in	62:43
to s. all his time in the labors	DC 41: 9

SPENT
I have s. my strength for naught	1Ne 21: 4
days shall be s. in the service of	2Ne 2: 3
I had s. my days in your service,	Mos 2:16
has s. his days in your service,	2:19
he s. his time in riotous living	11:14
been s. in the grossest iniquity;	Al 26:24

SPHERE 911 SPIRIT

SPHERE
order or s. of creation,	DC	77: 3
independent in that s. in which		93:30
it remaineth in the s. in which	Mses	3: 9

SPIES
had sent my s. out round about	Mos	10: 7
And Alma sent s. to follow	Al	2:21
Moroni sent s. into the		43:23
Moroni placed s. round about,		43:28
he found by his s. which course		43:30
that we kept s. out round about,		56:22
had been informed by their s.,		56:35
did meet the s. of our armies,		57:30
out their s. round about us		58:14
cut off the s. of the Lamanites		58:20

SPILL
s. your blood upon the ground,	Al	44:11

SPILT
their blood has been s. in vain,	Mos	7:24
this their blood was s.	Al	57: 9
of the blood which I have s.,	DC	38: 4

SPIN
the women should s., and toil,	Mos	10: 5
their women did toil and s.,	He	6:13
they toil not, neither do they s.;	3Ne	13:28
toil not, neither do they s.;	DC	84:82

SPINDLES
And within the ball were two s.;	1Ne	16:10
those s. should point the way	Al	37:40

SPIRIT
and also by the s. of prophecy	TPg	
being overcome with the S.	1Ne	1: 7
being thus overcome with the S.,		1: 8
was filled with the S. of the Lord.		1:12
power, being filled with the S.,		2:14
unto me by his Holy S.		2:17
delivered unto them by the S.		3:20
And I was led by the S.,		4: 6
I was constrained by the S. that		4:10
And the S. said unto me again:		4:11
the S. said unto me again:		4:12
I did obey the voice of the S.,		4:18
he was filled with the S.,		5:17
the S. of the Lord ceaseth soon		7:14
the S. of the Lord constraineth me		7:15
I was caught away in the S.		11: 1
And the S. said unto me:		11: 2
And the S. said unto me:		11: 4
the S. cried with a loud voice,		11: 6
the S. said unto me:		11: 8
I said unto the S.:		11: 9
that it was the S. of the Lord;		11:11
she was carried away in the S.,		11:19
had been carried away in the S.		11:19
they were carried away in the S.		11:29
and I beheld the S. of God,		13:12
I beheld the S. of God,		13:13
And I beheld the S. of the Lord,		13:15
while I was carried away in the s.;		14:30
had been carried away in the s.,		15: 1
by the S. of the Lord which was		15:12
I am full of the S. of God,		17:47
so powerful was the S. of God;		17:52
wrought upon by the S. of God,		19:12
behold, I have workings in the s.,		19:20
God, and his S., hath sent me.		20:16
to the s. and not the flesh?		22: 1
by the voice of the S.; for by		22: 2
for by the S. are all things		22: 2
to the workings of the S.	2Ne	1: 6
but it was the S. of the Lord		1:27
for the S. is the same, yesterday,		2: 4
a broken heart and a contrite s.;		2: 7
it again by the power of the S.,		2: 8
to the will of his Holy S.;		2:28
giveth the s. of the devil power		2:29
the latter days, in the s. of power,		3: 5
his heart and the S. of the Lord	2Ne	4:12
And upon the wings of his S.		4:25
broken and my s. is contrite!		4:32
and also the death of the s.		9:10
the s. and the body is restored		9:13
thereof by the s. of judgment		14: 4
and by the s. of burning.		14: 4
And the S. of the Lord shall		21: 2
the s. of wisdom and		21: 2
the s. of counsel and might,		21: 2
the s. of knowledge and of the		21: 2
are filled with the s. of prophecy.		25: 4
according to the s. which is in		25: 4
because of the s. which is in me.		25:11
the S. of the Lord will not always		26:11
when the S. ceaseth to strive with		26:11
as one that hath a familiar s.;		26:16
out upon you the s. of deep sleep.		27: 5
They also that erred in s. shall		27:35
as the S. hath constrained me;		28: 1
the S. stoppeth mine utterance,		32: 7
if ye would hearken unto the S.		32: 8
the evil s. teacheth not a man to		32: 8
their hearts against the Holy S.,		33: 2
he shall be of the s. of the devil.		33: 5
and the s. of much prophecy;	Jac	1: 6
revelations and the s. of prophecy;		4: 6
for the S. speaketh the truth		4:13
I, Jacob, am led on by the S.		4:15
by the workings of the S.		4:15
from my firmness in the S.,		4:18
and quench the Holy S.,		6: 8
poured in his S. into my soul,		7: 8
I was thus struggling in the s.,	En	1:10
communion with the Holy S.,	Jar	1: 4
the workings of the S. of the Lord	WM	1: 7
my immortal s. may join the	Mos	2:28
and ye list to obey the evil s.,		2:32
him who listeth to obey that s.;		2:33
from the S. of the Lord,		2:36
he listeth to obey the evil s.,		2:37
to the enticings of the Holy S.,		3:19
the S. of the Lord came upon them,		4: 3
or who is the evil s. which hath		4:14
has poured out his S. upon you,		4:20
because of the S. of the Lord		5: 2
and the manifestations of his S.,		5: 3
the s. of prophesying,		12:25
the S. of the Lord was upon him;		13: 5
flesh becoming subject to the S.,		15: 5
that he may pour out his S.		18:10
O Lord, pour out thy S. upon		18:12
the S. of the Lord was upon him,		18:13
and may the S. of the Lord be		18:13
rejoicing, being filled with the S.		18:14
they might wax strong in the S.,		18:26
waiting upon the S. of the Lord.		21:34
did pour out his S. upon them,		25:24
Alma was troubled in his s.,		26:10
the s. of Alma was again troubled;		26:13
behold I am born of the S.		27:24
thus did the S. of the Lord work		28: 4
the s. which they listed to obey,	Al	3:26
it be a good s. or a bad one.		3:26
words of the s. of prophecy;		3:27
according to the s. of prophecy;		4:13
the S. of the Lord did not fail		4:15
the s. of revelation and prophecy.		4:20
unto me by the Holy S. of God.		5:46
manifest unto me by his Holy S.;		5:46
and this is the s. of revelation		5:46
according to the s. of prophecy		5:47
manifestation of the S. of God.		5:47
Yea, thus saith the S.:		5:50
I say unto you, that the S. saith:		5:50
And also the S. saith unto me,		5:51
again I say unto you, the S. saith:		5:52
been sanctified by the Holy S.,		5:54
according to the s. of prophecy		6: 8
according to the S. of God which		7: 5
the S. hath not said unto me that		7: 8
behold, the S. hath said this much		7: 9
Now the S. knoweth all things;		7:13

for the S. saith if ye are not	Al	7:14
to the testimony of the Holy S.,		7:16
by the manifestation of the S.		7:17
to the S. which testifieth in me;		7:26
Alma labored much in the s.,		8:10
pour out his S. upon the people		8:10
according to the s. of revelation		8:24
according to the s. and power		8:32
been visited by the S. of God;		9:21
and having the s. of prophecy,		9:21
and the s. of revelation,		9:21
according to the s. of prophecy		10:12
be according to the S. of the Lord,		11:22
is contrary to the S. of the Lord.		11:22
The s. and the body shall be		11:43
the Father, and the Holy S.,		11:44
made known unto us by his S.;		12: 3
according to the s. of prophecy.		12: 7
others would reject the S. of God		13: 4
according to the s. of prophecy		13:26
and thus be led by the Holy S.,		13:28
The S. constraineth me that I		14:11
that he had the s. of prophecy,		16: 5
the Lord did pour out his S. on		16:16
they had the s. of prophecy,		17: 3
and the s. of revelation,		17: 3
and also much labor in the s.		17: 5
a portion of his S. to go with them,		17: 9
the Lord did visit them with his S.,		17:10
Behold, is not this the Great S.		18: 2
he be the Great S. or a man,		18: 3
I know that it is the Great S.;		18: 4
this is the Great S. of whom		18: 4
father, that there was a Great S.		18: 5
they believed in a Great S.		18: 5
know that this is the Great S.,		18:11
being filled with the S. of God,		18:16
Art thou that Great S., who		18:18
thou that there is a Great S.?		18:26
Believest thou that this Great S.,		18:28
called by his Holy S. to teach		18:34
a portion of that S. dwelleth in me,		18:35
being overpowered by the S.		19:13
seeing the S. of the Lord poured		19:14
that Ammon was the Great S.,		19:25
said he was sent by the Great S.;		19:25
Ammon was sent by the Great S.		19:27
and that it was the Great S. that		19:27
this Great S. who had destroyed		19:27
begin to pour out his S. upon them;		19:36
were led by the S. of the Lord,		21:16
led by the S. to the land of Nephi,		22: 1
Behold, the S. of the Lord has		22: 4
concerning the S. of the Lord?		22: 5
Is God that Great S. that		22: 9
Yea, he is that Great S., and he		22:10
the Great S. created all things,		22:11
having this wicked s. rooted out		22:15
of my breast, and receive his S.,		22:15
according to the s. of revelation		23: 6
he has given us a portion of his S.		24: 8
enlightened by the S. of God,		24:30
relying upon the s. of prophecy,		25:16
art possessed with a lying s.,		30:42
ye have put off the S. of God		30:42
will still resist the s. of the truth,		30:46
art holy, and that thou wast a s.,		31:15
a spirit, and that thou art a s.,		31:15
that thou wilt be a s. forever.		31:15
they were filled with the Holy S.		31:36
ye will resist the S. of the Lord.		32:28
that same s. which doth possess		34:34
that same s. will have power to		34:34
subjected to the s. of the devil,		34:35
the S. of the Lord hath withdrawn		34:35
may be in, in s. and in truth;		34:38
I tell you by the s. of prophecy,		37:15
is the S. of God which is in me		38: 6
now the S. of the Lord doth say		39:12
nor portion of the S. of the Lord;		40:13
therefore the s. of the devil did		40:13
the raising of the s. or the soul		40:15
according to the s. of prophecy		43: 2
worship God in s. and in truth,	Al	43:10
according to the s. of revelation		45:10
that he was taken up by the S.,		45:19
also received Alma in the s.,		45:19
having an unconquerable s.,		52:33
in body as well as in s.,		56:16
unto me a true s. of freedom,		60:25
according to the S. of God,		61:15
also the s. of freedom which		61:15
denying the s. of prophecy and	He	4:12
disbelieve in the s. of prophecy		4:23
and in the s. of revelation;		4:23
the S. of the Lord did no more		4:24
the S. of the Lord doth not dwell		4:24
the Holy S. of God did come		5:45
that the S. of the Lord began to		6:35
Lord began to pour out his S.		6:36
with faith, having a contrite s.,		8:15
for he was taken by the S.		10:16
thus he did go forth in the S.,		10:17
will withdraw my S. from them,		13: 8
but the S. of the Lord was with		16: 2
of their unconquerable s.,	3Ne	3: 4
noble s. in the field of battle.		3: 5
that had the s. of revelation		3:19
by the power and S. of God,		7:21
wrought upon by the S. of God,		7:22
a broken heart and a contrite s.		9:20
a broken heart and a contrite s.,		9:20
that hath the s. of contention		11:29
blessed are the poor in s. who		12: 3
a broken heart and a contrite s.		12:19
shall have my S. to be with you.		18: 7
shall have my S. to be with you.		18:11
they were filled with the S.;		20: 9
forsaken and grieved in s.,		22: 6
the S. of the Lord did not abide	Mrm	2:26
to the manifestations of the S.		3:16
these things doth the S. manifest		3:20
the S. of the Lord hath already		5:16
my S. will not always strive	Eth	2:15
behold, is the body of my s.;		3:16
created after the body of my s.;		3:16
appear unto thee to be in the s.		3:16
himself within this man in the s.,		3:17
the manifestations of my S.,		4:11
because of my S. he shall		4:11
broken heart and a contrite s.,		4:15
because of the S. of the Lord		12: 2
the S. of the Lord had ceased		15:19
have his S. to be with them.	Mro	4: 3
have his S. to be with them.		5: 2
a broken heart and a contrite s.,		6: 2
manner of the workings of the S.,		6: 9
the S. of Christ is given to		7:16
and the power of his Holy S.,		8:23
I fear lest the S. hath ceased		8:28
I fear lest the S. of the Lord		9: 4
manifestations of the S. of God		10: 8
to one is given by the S. of God,		10: 9
of knowledge by the same S.;		10:10
gifts of healing by the same S.;		10:11
gifts come by the S. of Christ;		10:17
until my s. and body shall again		10:34
my S. shall not always strive	DC	1:33
and the S. beareth record,		1:39
with the manifestation of my S.;		5:16
even of water and of the S.—		5:16
received instruction of my S.		6:14
enlightened by the S. of truth;		6:15
by the manifestation of my S.		8: 1
this is the s. of revelation;		8: 3
the s. by which Moses brought		8: 3
that S. which leadeth to do good—		11:12
righteously; and this is my S.		11:12
will impart unto you of my S.,		11:13
your peace; appeal unto my S.;		11:18
shall have my S. and my word,		11:21
Deny not the s. of revelation,		11:25
nor the s. of prophecy, for		11:25
by my S. in many instances,		18: 2
are given by my S. unto you,		18:35
power of my S. have spoken it.		18:47

SPIRIT

to suffer both body and s.—	DC 19:18
at the time I withdrew my S.	19:20
walk in the meekness of my S.,	19:23
will pour out my S. upon you,	19:38
received of the S. of Christ	20:37
have his S. to be with them.	20:77
have his S. to with them.	20:79
words, in the s. of meekness.	25: 5
shall be given thee by my S.	25: 7
Continue in the s. of meekness,	25:14
be filled with the s. of Elias;	27: 7
and the sword of my S.,	27:18
which is the power of my S.	29:30
power of my S. created I them;	29:31
not given heed unto my S.,	30: 2
joints and marrow, soul and s.;	33: 1
the power of my S. quickeneth	33:16
nations by the power of my S.;	35:13
and you shall receive my S.,	36: 2
and you shall receive my S.,	39:10
given by the power of the S.	42: 5
go forth in the power of my S.,	42: 6
shall be directed by the S.	42:13
the S. shall be given unto you	42:14
and if ye receive not the S. ye	42:14
and shall not have the S.;	42:23
hands by the power of my S.;	43:15
will pour out my S. upon them	44: 2
the Holy S. for their guide,	45:57
and guided by the Holy S.	46: 2
that which the S. testifies unto	46: 7
given a gift by the S. of God.	46:11
the manifestations of the S.	46:16
is given, by the S. of God,	46:17
that he that asketh in S.	46:28
in Spirit shall receive in S.;	46:28
He that asketh in the S.	46:30
whatsoever you do in the S.;	46:31
give thanks unto God in the S.	46:32
saith the Lord, by the S.,	50:10
To preach my gospel by the S.,	50:14
Comforter, in the S. of truth,	50:17
preach it by the S. of truth	50:17
he receive it by the S. of truth	50:19
the word by the S. of truth	50:21
preached by the S. of truth?	50:21
light, the S. and the power,	50:27
if you behold a s. manifested	50:31
and you receive not that s.,	50:31
he give not unto you that s.,	50:31
unto you, power over that s.;	50:32
shall proclaim against that s.	50:32
last days, by the voice of his S.—	52: 1
prayeth, whose s. is contrite,	52:15
speaketh, whose s. is contrite,	52:16
the reception of the Holy S.	53: 3
and a reception of the Holy S.	55: 1
power to give the Holy S.	55: 3
proved by the S. through him.	57:13
shall be given him of the S.,	58:38
known by the s. unto him.	58:50
broken heart and a contrite s.	59: 8
and the S. beareth record.	59:24
unto him it is given by the S.	61:27
do as the S. of the living God	61:28
and the directions of the S.	62: 8
they shall not have the S.,	63:16
I am holding my S. from the	63:32
enabled to discern by the S.	63:41
counsel, but grieved the S.;	63:55
and by constraint of the S.;	63:64
receive the s. through prayer;	63:64
taught through prayer by the S.	63:65
I, the Lord, withheld my S.	64:16
quickened by the s. of God.	67:11
by the S. of the living God,	68: 1
the manifestations of the S.	70:13
the manifestations of the S.	70:14
that portion of S. and power	71: 1
are appointed by the Holy S.	72:24
even by the voice of my S.,	75: 1
For by my S. will I enlighten	76:10
being in the S. on the sixteenth	DC 76:11
By the power of the S.	76:12
it was given unto us of the S.	76:18
while we were yet in the S.	76:28
Having denied the Holy S.	76:35
and receive the Holy S. by	76:52
by the Holy S. of promise,	76:53
while we were yet in the S.	76:80
they who deny not the Holy S.	76:83
but of the Holy S. through	76:86
while we were yet in the S.	76:113
while we were yet in the S.,	76:115
by the power of the Holy S.,	76:116
and manifestation of the S.,	76:118
the s. of man in the likeness of	77: 2
as also the s. of the beast,	77: 2
are santified by the s. unto	84:33
and whatsoever is light is S.,	84:45
even the S. of Jesus Christ.	84:45
And the S. giveth light to	84:46
and the S. enlighteneth every	84:46
to the voice of the S.	84:46
to the voice of the S.	84:47
solemnity and the s. of prayer,	84:61
my S. shall be in your hearts,	84:88
be strong in the S.,	84:106
even the Holy S. of promise;	88: 3
And the s. and the body are	88:15
who are of a celestial s.	88:28
voice, because my voice is S.;	88:66
voice is Spirit; my S. is truth;	88:66
as the S. shall give utterance	88:137
a tabernacle of the Holy S.	88:137
for the s. manifesteth truth;	91: 1
whoso is enlightened by the S.	91: 5
whoso receiveth not by the S.,	91: 6
the S. of truth, who came into	93: 9
and truth, even the S. of truth,	93:11
that which is S., even the	93:23
Spirit, even the S. of truth;	93:23
is the s. of that wicked one	93:25
The S. of truth is of God.	93:26
I am the S. of truth,	93:26
whose s. receiveth not the light	93:32
For man is s. The elements	93:33
and s. and element, inseparably	93:33
Every s. of man was innocent	93:38
that I may pour out my S.	95: 4
voice, even the voice of my S.,	97: 1
demonstration of my Holy S.	99: 2
heart, in the s. of meekness,	100: 7
by the voice of the S.,	104:36
shall be dictated by my S.;	104:81
servant, by the voice of the S.,	105:36
voice of the S. which is in you,	105:40
by the S. of truth;	107:71
help us by the power of thy S.,	109:79
by the peace and power of my S.,	111: 8
hearken to the voice of my S.	112:22
knowledge by his Holy S.,	121:26
the S. of the Lord is grieved;	121:37
by the influence of that s.	123: 7
be written in the s. of meekness	124: 4
in the s. of meekness,	124:18
shall be moved upon by my S.,	124:88
and he shall receive of my S.,	124:97
even the Holy S. of promise;	124:124
for a s. hath not flesh and bones,	129: 2
the s. of a just man made perfect	129: 6
but is a personage of S.	130:22
and the s. of prophecy,	131: 5
All s. is matter,	131: 7
sealed by the Holy S. of promise,	132: 7
sealed by the Holy S. of promise,	132:18
by the Holy S. of promise,	132:19
sealed by the Holy S. of promise,	132:26
by the power of his S.	133:59
For my S. is sent forth into the	136:33
for his S. hath not altogether	Mses 1:15
discerning it by the s. of God.	1:27
discerned them by the S. of God;	1:28
my s. moved upon the face of	2: 2

SPIRIT

write by the s. of inspiration;	Mses	6: 5
the S. of God descended out of		6:26
Behold my S. is upon you,		6:34
by water, and blood, and the s.,		6:59
of water, and of the S., and be		6:59
by the S. ye are justified, and		6:60
away by the S. of the Lord,		6:64
the S. of God descended upon		6:65
and thus he was born of the S.,		6:65
My S. shall not always strive		8:17
the S. of the Gods was brooding	Abr	4: 2
took his s. (that is, the man's		5: 7
his spirit (that is, the man's s.),		5: 7
the man whose s. they had put		5: 8
a s. of the most bitter	JS	2:23
I also had the s. of prophecy,		2:73
owing to a s. of persecution		2:74

SPIRITS

and with devils and unclean s.;	1 Ne	11:31
the devils and the unclean s.		11:31
our s. must become subject to	2 Ne	9: 8
our s. must have become like unto		9: 9
hell must deliver up its captive s.,		9:12
the s. of men will be restored		9:12
deliver up the s. of the righteous,		9:13
unto them that have familiar s.,		18:19
cast out devils, or the evil s.	Mos	3: 6
their s. uniting with their bodies,	Al	11:45
the s. of all men, as soon as		40:11
yea, the s. of all men, whether		40:11
the s. of those who are righteous		40:12
that the s. of the wicked, yea,		40:13
he cast out devils and unclean s.;	3 Ne	7:19
broken hearts and contrite s.,	Mrm	2:14
of angels and ministering s.;	Mro	10:14
broken hearts and contrite s.,	DC	20:37
the long absence of your s.		45:17
not be seduced by evil s.,		46: 7
to others the discerning of s.		46:23
the s. which have gone abroad		50: 1
there are many s. which are		50: 2
many spirits which are false s.,		50: 2
then received ye s. which ye		50:15
the s. shall be subject unto you.		50:30
shall know the s. in all cases		52:19
whose s. are not contrite,		56:17
and whose s. are contrite,		56:18
they who are the s. of men		76:73
to be ministering s. for them;		76:88
then come the s. of men who		88:100
broken, and their s. contrite,		97: 8
the s. of just men made perfect,		129: 3
the s. that God had created;	Mses	6:36
the s. as were in prison came		7:57
as, also, if there be two s., and	Abr	3:18
yet these two s., notwithstanding		3:18
there are two s., one being		3:19
stood among those that were s.,		3:23

SPIRITUAL

of things both temporal and s.;	1 Ne	15:32
as to the things which are s.,		15:33
according to things which are s.,		22: 1
to things both temporal and s.;		22: 3
by the s. law they perish	2 Ne	2: 5
which is the s. death,		9:12
which s. death is hell;		9:12
all things, both temporal and s.;	Mos	2:41
in need, both s. and temporal;	Al	7:23
becoming s. and immortal,		11:45
second death, which is a s. death;		12:16
death, shall also die a s. death;		12:16
of the temporal but of the s.,		36: 4
so it is with things which are s.		37:43
upon all mankind a s. death		42: 9
reclaimed from this s. death.		42: 9
the first death—that s. death;	He	14:16
things temporal and to things s.		14:16
upon them again a s. death,		14:18
I have spoken, which are s.,	Mro	10:19
all things both s. and temporal—	DC	29:31
First s., secondly temporal,		29:32
first temporal, and secondly s.,	DC	29:32
that all things unto me are s.,		29:34
for my commandments are s.;		29:35
is the last death, which is s.,		29:41
be redeemed from their s. fall,		29:44
natural mind, but with the s.		67:10
to administer s. things,		70:12
faithful who labor in s. things,		72:14
that which is s. being in the		77: 2
likeness of that which is s.;		77: 2
shall rise again, a s. body.		88:27
to administer in s. things,		107: 8
in administering s. things,		107:10
to administer in s. things,		107:12
the keys of all the s. blessings		107:18
the s. authorities of the church;		107:32
upon controversies in s. matters.		107:80
concerning your s. standing,		108: 2
that was not first which is s.,		128:14
and afterward that which is s.		128:14
which is s. Babylon.		133:14
prescribing rules on s. concerns,		134: 6
proscribed in its s. privileges,		134: 9
not my natural, but my s. eyes,	Mses	1:11
was s. in the day that I created it;		3: 9
and things which are s.;		6:63

SPIRITUALLY

both temporally and s.,	1 Ne	14: 7
to be s.-minded is life eternal.	2 Ne	9:39
relief, both s. and temporally,	Mos	4:26
this day he hath s. begotten you;		5: 7
temporally and s. according		18:29
have ye s. been born of God?	Al	5:14
cut off both temporally and s.		42: 7
both temporally and s.;	Mrm	2:15
blessed both s. and temporally,	DC	14:11
them both s. and temporally;		24: 3
wherein he became s. dead,		29:41
of which I have spoken, s., before	Mses	3: 5
s. were they created and made		3: 7

SPIRITUALLY-MINDED: see SPIRITUALLY and MINDED.

SPIT

Yea, they s. upon him,	1 Ne	19: 9
reviled him, and s. upon him,	Al	8:13
And they s. upon him, and cast		14: 7
should they s. upon them,		23: 2
cast out, and mocked, and s. upon,		26:29

SPITTING

not my face from shame and s.	2 Ne	7: 6
upon them, and s. upon them,	Al	14:21

SPOIL

the s. of the poor in your houses.	2 Ne	13:14
the s. of Samaria shall be taken		18: 4
rejoice when they divide the s.		19: 3
give him a charge to take the s.,		20: 6
they shall s. them of the east		21:14
returned rejoicing in their s.	Mos	11:18
divide the s. with the strong;		14:12
the enemy shall come to s. and	DC	101:45
that they may cease to s.,		109:50

SPOILED

their houses shall be s.	2 Ne	23:16
and the level roads were s.,	3 Ne	8:13

SPOILS

works and partake of their s.,	He	6:38

SPOKE

as they s. so shall it come to	DC	29:10
who s. of these things,		29:21

SPOKEN

which had been s. by my father;	1 Ne	2:16
s. by the mouth of all the holy		3:20
after the angel had s. unto us,		3:30
that an angel hath s. unto you;		4: 3

SPOKEN

Now when I had s. these words,	1 Ne	4: 4
s. by the mouth of Jeremiah.		5:13
all things which the Lord hath s.		7:13
when I, Nephi, had s. these words		7:16
after my father had s. all the		8:36
And now, as I have s.		9: 2
this Messiah, of whom he had s.,		10: 5
after my father had s. these		10:11
these things, of which I have s.,		10:16
the tree of which he hath s.?		11: 4
And when I had s. these words,		11: 6
of whom my father had s.;		11:27
of the devil, of which I have s.		14: 7
when the angel had s. these words,		14: 8
which my father had s. unto them.		15: 2
the words which our father hath s.		15: 7
our father hath not s. of our		15:18
awful hell of which I have s.,		15:35
that justice of which I have s.		15:35
knew that I had s. hard things		16: 2
and he hath s. unto you in		17:45
wherefore, he has s. unto you like		17:45
when I had s. these words,		17:48
to the word which he had s.		17:54
of his word which he had s.		18:11
those plates of which I have s.;		19: 2
according to that which I have s.;		19: 5
I have s.; yea, I have called him		20:15
I have not s. in secret;		20:16
that it was declared have I s.;		20:16
these things of which are s. are		22: 6
I have s. these few words unto	2 Ne	2:30
to the words which I have s.		3:25
of which my father hath s.,		4: 1
after my father, Lehi, had s.		4:12
I had s. many things unto them,		4:14
I have s. unto you exceeding		6: 2
I have s. unto you concerning		6: 3
which have been s. by Isaiah		6: 5
That he has s. unto the Jews,		9: 2
this death, of which I have s.,		9:11
And this death of which I have s.,		9:12
for the Lord God hath s. it,		9:16
the Holy One of Israel, has s. it.		9:24
that I have s. hard things		9:40
have s. the words of your Maker.		9:40
the words which I have s.;		9:51
branch of which I have s.		10: 1
unto the Gentiles, for he hath s. it,		10: 9
been s. by the mouth of Isaiah.		25: 1
to the word which he hath s.		25: 3
which were s. unto the Jews		25: 5
to all that which Isaiah hath s.,		25: 6
Messiah s. of by the prophets,		25:18
my brethren, I have s. plainly		25:20
Jesus Christ, of which I have s.,		25:20
wherefore, I have s. plainly unto		25:28
words which I have s. shall stand		25:28
unto the man of whom I have s.,		27:12
my brethren, I have s. unto you,		28: 1
because that I have s. one word		29: 9
of the words which have been s.		30: 1
after the book of which I have s.		30: 3
remember that I have s. unto		31: 4
now after I have s. these words,		32: 4
I have s. unto you concerning	Jac	2:20
according to that which I have s.		5:76
all the words which have been s.		6: 8
many have s. concerning him;		6: 8
have s. concerning this Christ.		7:11
when I, Jacob, had s. these words,		7:15
the prophecies which had been s.	Mos	1: 2
all these things which I have s.,		2:14
the evil spirit, which was s. of		2:32
the prophecies which have been s.		2:34
that has been s. by our fathers		2:35
to that which has been s.,		2:36
for I have s. plainly unto you		2:40
for the Lord hath s. it.		2:41
words which I have s. unto thee.		3:22
I have s. the words which the		3:23
after they had s. these words		4: 3
words which king Benjamin had s.		4: 3
save this which hath been s. of;	Mos	4: 8
was s. by the mouth of the angel.		4:11
evil spirit which hath been s. of		4:14
things which I have s. unto you—		4:26
when king Benjamin had thus s.		5: 1
words which he had s. unto them.		5: 1
words which thou hast s. unto us;		5: 2
the things which our king has s.		5: 4
as has been s. by the angel,		5: 5
Ye have s. the words that I		5: 6
when Abinadi had s. these words		11:26
the words which Abinadi had s.		11:27
he pretendeth the Lord hath s. it.		12:12
because I have s. the word of God		13: 4
after Abinadi had s. these words		13: 5
have they not s. more or less		13:33
after Abinadi had s. these words		16: 1
the words which Abinadi had s.,		17: 2
the words which Abinadi had s.		17: 4
thou hast s. evil concerning me		17: 8
recall the words which I have s.		17: 9
and which had been s. by		18:19
which had been s. by Abinadi.		21:30
which thou hast s. unto them.		26:16
which had been s. of by our fathers;		27:30
it has been s. by our fathers,	Al	5:21
for the Lord God hath s. it!		5:32
I have s. unto you plainly that		5:43
or have s. according to the		5:43
the things which have been s. by		5:44
these things whereof I have s.		5:45
which have been s. by our fathers		5:47
the Holy One hath s. it.		5:52
words which I have s. unto you.		5:61
which had been s. by his fathers,		6: 8
first time that I have s. unto		7: 1
the things which I have s.,		7:17
I have s. these words unto you		7:26
And thus I have s.		7:27
s. unto by the voice of the Lord;		9:21
when I, Alma, had s. these words,		9:31
when Amulek had s. these words		10:12
understand the words which are s.,		10:25
that I have s. against your law;		10:26
I have s. in favor of your law,		10:26
when Amulek had s. these words		10:28
for he hath s. against our law.		10:28
says that he has not s. against it.		10:28
I have s. unto you concerning		11:45
when Alma had s. these words,		12: 7
this mean which Amulek hath s.		12: 8
And Amulek hath s. plainly		12:12
which has been s. of by Amulek,		12:24
which has been s. of by us,		12:24
of the dead, of which has been s.		12:25
judgment of which we have s.,		12:27
this same order which I have s.,		13:14
which they have s. concerning him,		13:26
at the words which had been s.;		14: 6
words which had been s. by Alma		14: 7
when the last had s. unto them		14:25
of whom our fathers have s.		18: 4
these things which thou hast s.		18:33
had been s. by the prophets,		18:36
at the words which he had s.		20:27
had been s. by his s. Lamoni,		20:27
life of which thou hast s.?		22:15
of whose bones we have s.,		22:30
in the place which have been s.;		27:16
to my words, even as I have s.		29:17
had been s. by the prophets,		30: 6
after Alma had s. these words,		33: 1
this fruit of which he had s.,		33: 1
or the word of which he had s.,		33: 1
are not the only ones who have s.		33:18
Behold, he was s. of by Moses;		33:19
after Alma had s. these words		34: 1
the things which have been s.		34: 2
he hath s. somewhat unto you		34: 3
for the Lord God hath s. it.		34: 8
the words which had been s.		35: 4
words which had been s. by Alma		35: 6
of these things of which I have s.,		36:26

SPOKEN — SPOKESMEN

words which I have s. unto you;	Al	37:32	What I the Lord have s., I	DC	1:38
to the words which have been s.		40:15	Lord have spoken, I have s.,		1:38
behold, again it hath been s.,		40:16	of the things of which I have s.		5:28
which is s. of in this manner,		40:17	I have s. unto thee because		6:20
of those of whom has been s.		40:19	been s. by the manifestation of		8: 1
s. by the mouths of the prophets.		40:22	it is I that have s. it;		8:12
restoration of which has been s.		40:24	things of which has been s.—		11:19
restoration of which has been s.;		41: 1	your God, have s. it unto you,		17: 9
been s. concerning restoration,		41:10	Lord and your God, have s. it.		18:33
the words which I have s.,		44:11	the desires of which I have s.;		18:37
all the words which thou hast s.		45: 5	power of my Spirit have s. it.		18:47
of these of whom I have s.;		57:27	punishments of which I have s.,		19:20
of whom I have so highly s.,		58:39	For the Lord God has s. it;		20:16
Gadianton shall be s. hereafter.	He	2:12	And the Lord God has s. it;		20:36
what I have s. had passed		3:17	all things s. by the mouth of		27: 6
Nephi had s. unto them		8: 3	which was s. by mine apostles		29:10
have been s. by our fathers,		8:13	is s. by the mouth of Ezekiel		29:21
words which were s. by this man,		8:13	for the Lord God hath s.;		34:10
words which he hath s. concerning		8:13	and sent forth, even as I have s.		36: 7
when Nephi had s. these words,		9: 1	ye may give even as I have s.		43:16
words which he has s. are true.		9: 2	Millennium, of which I have s.		43:30
the words which Nephi had s.		9: 4	I the Lord had s. these words		45:34
judgments which Nephi had s.		9: 5	these things were s. unto you		46: 1
which they had s. against Nephi,		9:18	Lord God, have s. it;		49: 7
when the Lord had s. these		10:12	let those of whom I have s.		57:14
which had been s. unto him,		10:12	those things even as I have s.		57:14
all the words which thou hast s.		11: 8	I, the Lord, have s. it.		58:12
and have s. unto you the words		14:10	I, the Lord, have s. it,		59:24
thus hath the angel s. unto me;		14:26	concerning whom I have s.,		61:21
hath been s. of by our fathers,		15:11	sacred, and must be s. with care,		63:64
to pass, of which has been s.		16:16	this cause have I s. these things.		64:19
and of earth, as it has been s.,		16:18	The Lord hath s. it.		64:43
which were s. by Samuel,	3Ne	1: 5	the sea of glass s. of by John,		77: 1
those things which had been s.		1: 7	beasts, s. of in the same verse?		77: 2
which I have caused to be s.		1:13	twenty elders, s. of by John?		77: 5
according as they had been s.;		1:15	s. of in the 7th chapter and		77: 8
which was s. of by the prophets,		2: 7	the things s. of in this chapter		77:10
which had been s. by Lachoneus,		3:25	s. by the mouth of his		84: 2
all the holy prophets who had s.;		5: 1	of which I have s.,		84:33
to that which had been s.		5: 2	restoration of all things s.		86:10
had been s. by the prophets.		10:11	all have s. that all may be		88:122
when Jesus had s. these words		11:12	I, the Lord, have s. it.		90:37
the words which I have s.,		11:41	I, the Lord, have s. it.		97: 7
when Jesus had s. these words		12: 1	accuser and accused have s.,		102:19
when Jesus had s. these words		13:25	councilors, who have not s.,		102:20
the words which I have s.		13:25	to fulfil that which thou hast s.		109:23
when Jesus had s. these words		14: 1	s. by the mouths of thy prophets.		109:41
destroy that which hath been s.		15: 7	We know that thou hast s.		109:45
when Jesus had s. these words,		15:11	O Lord, we have s. before thee,		109:60
when Jesus had s. these words		17: 1	s. of by the mouth of Malachi—		110:14
that when Jesus had thus s.,		17: 5	Who is the stem of Jesse s. of		113: 1
that when he had thus s.,		17: 9	What is the rod s. of		113: 3
when Jesus had s. these words		18:17	What is the root of Jesse s. of		113: 5
when Jesus had s. these words,		18:26	s. of by Daniel the prophet.		116: 1
same words which Jesus had s.—		19: 8	for the Lord God hath s. it.		127: 2
the words which Jesus had s.—		19: 8	the books s. of must be		128: 7
when Jesus had s. these words		19:30	the Lord your God hath s. it.		133:74
as many as have s., have		20:24	s. unto Moses in the mount,	Mses	1:42
What have we s. against thee?		24:13	And now they are s. unto you.		1:42
the words which Jesus hath s.		26: 8	things, of which I have s.,		3: 5
multitude of whom hath been s.,		26:14	and I have s. them unto you.		4:32
when he had s. unto them,		28: 4	men these things were not s.,		5:53
when Jesus had s. these words,		28:12	that Lamech had s. the secret		5:53
been s. by the holy prophets.		29: 2	when the Lord had s. with Adam,		6:64
which have been s. are vain,		29: 3	are they of whom I have s.,		7:53
for the Lord hath s. it;	Mrm	8:26	s. of by Daniel the prophet,	JS	1:12
passed, of which I have s.?		9:15	these things I have s. unto you		1:21
been s. by the mouth of Jared.	Eth	1:39	s. of by Daniel the prophet,		1:32
these things which I have s.,		4:11	both good and evil s. of		2:33
it is I that hath s. it.		4:19	plates of which he had s.—		2:42
for the Lord had s. it.		10:28			
word which he had s. unto him,		12:20	**SPOKESMAN**		
of which hath been s.		13:15	and I will make a s. for him.	2Ne	3:17
prophecies which had been s.		13:21	and I will make for him a s.		3:18
the words which Ether had s.		15: 1	the s. of thy loins shall declare it.		3:18
the words which had been s. by		15: 3	a s. unto this people;	DC	100: 9
true which I have s. unto you,	Mro	7:35	a s. unto my servant Joseph.		100: 9
which were s. by the prophets,		8:29	mayest be a s. unto him,		100:11
after I have s. a few words by		10: 2	and be a s. before my face.		124:104
these gifts of which I have s.,		10:19			
be s. upon the housetops,	DC	1: 3	**SPOKESMEN**		
I am God and have s. it;		1:24	let not all be s. at once;	DC	88:122

SPOT

For behold, it was the poorest s.	Jac	5:21
knew that it was a poor s. of ground;		5:22
that this s. of ground was poorer		5:23
I planted in a good s. of ground;		5:25
plant in a good s. of ground;		5:43
cumbered this s. of ground,		5:44
when they had come to the s.,	Al	47:27
that ye become holy, without s.	Mro	10:33
a righteous people, without s.	DC	38:31
a s. for the temple is lying		57: 3
and the s. for the temple,		58:57
who are assembled upon this s.,		61: 2
upon the consecrated s. as I		84:31
had a s. of land, very choice;		101:44
on the building—s. of my house,		118: 5
that is the s. which I have chosen		124:43
I will consecrate that s.		124:44

SPOTLESS

that ye may be found s.	TPg	
many souls s. at his judgment-seat.	2Ne	33: 7
and we would not be found s.	Jac	1:19
garments are cleansed and are s.,	Al	5:24
and keep your garments s.,		7:25
having your garments s. even		7:25
even as their garments are s.,		7:25
we shall not be found s.;		12:14
being pure and s. before God,		13:12
these men are s. before God.		14: 7
that ye may stand s. before me	3Ne	27:20
perhaps ye may be found s.,	Mrm	9: 6
and they shall be s. before me.	DC	61:34
present it unto the Father, s.,		76:107

SPOTTED

are not s. with your blood.	Eth	12:38
the garments s. with the flesh.	DC	36: 6
are not s. with your blood.		135: 5

SPRANG

from Hagar s. many people.	DC	132:34
this descent s. all the Egyptians,	Abr	1:22
from Ham, s. that race which		1:24
source from whence they s.	JS	2:34

SPREAD

the worm is s. under thee,	2Ne	24:11
s. upon the face of the land,	Jar	1: 8
knowledge of the Savior shall s.	Mos	3:20
were s. through the wilderness	Al	22:28
s. forth into all parts of the land,	He	3: 5
that they did multiply and s.,		3: 8
did s. insomuch that they began		3: 8
who s. the works of darkness		6:28
and began to multiply and s.,		11:20
and the church did s. throughout		11:21
s. so much death and carnage	3Ne	2:11
they durst not s. themselves		4: 6
were s. upon all the face of	4Ne	1:23
s. over all the face of the land;		1:46
s. throughout all the face of	Mrm	2: 8
to s. upon the face of the land,	Eth	6:18
he did s. his kingdom upon		7:11
they shall s. over the nation,		8:22
the people had s. again over all		9:26
to s. over all the face of the land.		10: 4
she shall prosper, and s. herself	DC	97:18
have s. lying reports abroad,		109:29
the fame of this house shall s. to		110:10
to s. among all the sons of men.	Mses	5:52

SPREADETH

adversary s. his dominions,	DC	82: 5

SPREADING

an end to the s. of priestcraft	Al	1:16
s. the work of death around you?		60: 7
s. rumors and contentions upon	He	16:22
the s. of this wicked and secret	Eth	9: 6

SPRING

whatsoever tree should s. up	He	3: 9
be prepared in the coming s.	DC	63:39
a mission unto me next s.,		114: 1
next s. let them depart to go		118: 4
decide how many can go next s.;		136: 7
prepare for putting in s. crops.		136: 7
in the S. of 1889,		OD
s. all the kingdoms of the earth	Mses	8: 3
the s. of eighteen hundred and	JS	2:14

SPRINGING

a tree s. up unto everlasting life.	Al	32:41
s. up in you unto everlasting		33:23
s. up unto everlasting life.	DC	63:23
and the blade is s. up and is		86: 4

SPRINGS

their bows having lost their s.,	1Ne	16:21
by the s. of water shall he guide		21:10

SPRINKLE

So shall he s. many nations;	3Ne	20:45

SPRINKLED

their blood have I s. upon	DC	133:51

SPROUTED

also know that it hath s. up,	Al	32:34

SPROUTETH

as the seed swelleth, and s.,	Al	32:30
for behold it swelleth, and s.,		32:30
the seed, and it swelleth and s.,		32:33

SPRUNG

it had s. forth and begun to	Jac	5:17

SPURN

s. at the doings of the Lord,	3Ne	29: 4
if ye shall s. at his doings he		29: 4
need not any longer hiss, not s.,		29: 8

SPURNETH

Wo unto him that s. at the	3Ne	29: 5

SPY

having been sent as a s. among	Mos	9: 1
that I might s. out their forces,		9: 1
to s. out in what part of the city	Al	62:20

SQUIRE

at the house of S. Tarbill,	JS	2:58

ST.: *see SAINT.*

STAB

s. Kishkumen even to the heart,	He	2: 9

STABBED

he s. the king to the heart;	Al	47:24
servants of the king have s. him		47:26
he being s. by his brother by	He	9: 6

STAFF

the stay and the s.,	2Ne	13: 1
the whole s. of bread,		13: 1
and the s. of his shoulder,		19: 4
the s. in their hand is their		20: 5
as if the s. should lift up itself		20:15
shall lift up his s. against thee,		20:24
hath broken the s. of the wicked,		24: 5
of beasts, to be the s. of life,	DC	89:14

STAGGER

shall s. but not with strong drink.	2Ne	27: 4

STAIN

they are cleansed from all s.,	Al	5:21
that he would take away our s.—		24:11
let us s. out swords no more		24:12
if we should s. our swords		24:13

STAINED

your garments s. with blood	Al	5:22

STAINED

they be not s. with the blood of	Al	24:13
not s. our swords in the blood		24:15
and s. all my raiment;	DC	133:51

STAINS

God hath taken away our s.,	Al	24:12
get our s. taken away from us,		24:15

STAKE

and for a s. to Zion.	DC	82:13
the city of the s. of Zion,		94: 1
this s. that I have set for		96: 1
I have established for my s.		104:40
Order of the S. of Zion,		104:48
or in a s. of Zion,		107:74
of this s. which I have planted to		124: 2
also the president of the s. and		124:142
the Lord shall locate a s. of Zion.		136:10

STAKES

thy cords and strengthen thy s.;	3Ne	22: 2
strengthen thy s. and enlarge	Mro	10:31
in Zion, or in any of her s.	DC	68:25
Zion, or in any of her s.		68:26
her s. must be strengthened;		82:14
and they shall be called s.,		101:21
at the s. of Zion,		107:36
the Twelve at the s. of Zion.		107:37
forth to Zion, or to her s.,		109:39
other s. besides this one		109:59
the land of Zion, and upon her s.,		115: 6
places should be appointed for s.		115:18
be an ensample unto all the s.		119: 7
that in Zion, and in her s.,		124:36
different s. scattered abroad;		124:134
the s. which I have appointed,		125: 4
her s. may be strengthened,		133: 9

STALK

that thou shalt be as a s., even	Mos	12:11
even as a dry s. of the field,		12:11

STALL

must be led up as calves of the s.,	1Ne	22:24
and grow up as calves in the s.	3Ne	25: 2

STAND

must be brought to s. before God,	1Ne	15:33
and they s. up together.		20:13
they s. in the presence of him to	2Ne	2:10
Let us s. together.		7: 8
Awake, awake, s. up, O Jerusalem,		8:17
that all might s. before him		9:22
I s. with brightness before him,		9:44
It shall not s., neither shall it		17: 7
speak the word, and it shall not s.;		18:10
which shall s. for an ensign of		21:10
as I have purposed, so shall it s.—		24:24
as long as the earth should s.		25:21
as long as the earth shall s.;		25:22
shall s. as a testimony against you;		25:28
must s. before the throne of God,		28:23
you and I shall s. face to face		33:11
will bring you to s. with shame	Jac	6: 9
and shall s. before him;	En	1:27
and he may s. against them;	WM	1:13
when I shall s. to be judged	Mos	2:27
shall s. as a bright testimony		3:24
that s. in need of your succor;		4:16
s. up before the multitude,		8: 2
he could s. upon the top thereof		11:12
fifty could s. against thousands		11:19
to s. before the bar of God,		16:10
s. as a testimony against you.		17:10
s. as a testimony against you		17:10
those that s. in need of comfort		18: 9
and to s. as witnesses of God		18: 9
fair daughters should s. forth		19:13
ye should s. fast in this liberty		23:13
that ye may s. as witnesses		24:14
come forth and shall s. before me.		26:25
Alma, arise and s. forth, for why		27:13

STAND

men shall s. to be judged of him,	Mos	27:31
that did s. fast in the faith?	Al	1:25
to s. before God to be judged		5:15
shall s. before the bar of God,		5:22
commanded to s. and testify		5:44
whatsoever things ye s. in need,		7:23
from the dead and s. before God,		11:41
shall be brought to s. before God,		11:43
and are brought to s. before God		12: 8
and s. before him in his glory,		12:15
shall s. as a witness against them,		14:11
Will ye s. again and judge this		14:20
should s. forth and testify to		18: 1
to s. by the waters of Sebus		18: 1
and said unto him: S.		22:22
and his brethren should s. forth		22:26
to s. before him to be judged,		24:15
and s. upon the top thereof,		31:14
being interpreted, is the holy s.		31:21
from this s. they did offer up,		31:22
together again to the holy s.,		31:23
that all men shall s. before him,		33:22
to those who s. in need—		34:28
s. in the presence of my God,		36:15
s. as a testimony against you		39: 8
ye s. in need to be nourished by		39:10
and be brought to s. before God,		40:21
and thus they s. or fall;		41: 7
to s. against the Lamanites		43:50
who should s. fast in the faith		45:17
not s. fast in the faith of Christ.		46:27
to s. against Amalickiah and		46:28
armies should s. in readiness,		51:36
we could not s. against them,		56:40
they s. fast in that liberty		58:40
who s. fast in that liberty		61:21
could s. against the Nephites,	He	1:16
that Nephi and Lehi did s. forth		5:26
And he shall s. with fear,		9:30
ye do s. well, as if ye were	3Ne	3: 2
s. against so many brave men		3: 3
at this time s. in their arms,		3: 3
go down and s. in the water,		11:23
and the gates of hell s. open		11:40
arise and s. up upon their feet.		20: 2
who shall s. when he appeareth?		24: 2
and tongues shall s. before God,		26: 4
by the Father, to s. before me,		27:14
I shall s. to judge the world.		27:16
ye may s. spotless before me		27:20
unto me, while the world shall s.		28: 9
s. before the judgment-seat of		28:31
s. boldly before the Lamanites	Mrm	2:23
s. with boldness against them.		2:24
we did s. before them with		2:25
and I did s. as an idle witness		3:16
s. before the judgment-seat of		3:20
s. to be judged of your works,		3:20
s. before the judgment-seat of		3:22
they did s. against the Lamanites		4:20
did s. against them boldly;		5: 6
how can ye s. before the		5:22
s. before the judgment seat of		6:21
to s. before his judgment-seat.		7: 6
s. before the Lamb of God—		9: 2
and all shall s. before his bar,		9:13
who can s. against the works of		9:26
soever ye shall s. in need.		9:27
all this shall s. as a testimony	Eth	5: 4
s. before God at the last day.		5: 6
Who can s. before the army of		14:18
shall last, or the earth shall s.,	Mro	7:36
or they s. against you at the		8:21
as long as the world shall s.,		10:19
may s. blameless before God	DC	4: 2
s. as a witness of these things;		5: 2
s. still until I command thee,		5:34
s. by my servant Joseph,		6:18
S. fast in the work wherewith		9:14
s. as a witness of the things		14: 8
all, that ye may be able to s.		27:15
S., therefore, having your loins		27:16

STAND 919 STARS

and the wicked shall not s.	DC 29:11	the earth upon which thou s.,	Abr 3: 5	
s. at my right hand at the day	29:12	of the earth upon which thou s.,	3: 6	
again I will s. upon it.	38:17	of the earth upon which thou s.	3: 7	
forever, while the earth shall s.,	38:20	order as that upon which thou s.	3: 9	
s. in the office whereunto I	42:10			
Thou shalt s. in the place of	42:53	STANDETH		
disciples shall s. in holy places,	45:32	for there s. one among you	1Ne 10: 8	
wherefore we cannot s.	45:70	The Lord s. up to plead,	2Ne 13:13	
and they shall s. afar off	45:74	and s. to judge the people.	13:13	
s. fast in the office whereunto	54: 2	he s. to judge the world;	Mos 3:10	
Sidney Gilbert s. in the office	57: 6	unto him that s. in need;	4:16	
Edward Partridge s. in the office	57: 7	My soul s. fast in that liberty	Al 61: 9	
the Zion of God shall s.;	58: 7	s. as though they had been the	He 12:15	
Phelps s. in the office to	58:40	whoso s. in this mission	DC 58:17	
s. as a member in the church,	58:60	he s. no longer in the office	63:56	
s. upon the land of Zion,	59: 3	s. condemned before the Lord;	64: 9	
s. to receive an inheritance.	63:31	it s. above the earth upon	Abr 3: 5	
with you, and will s. by you;	68: 6			
church may s. independent	78:14	STANDING		
s. in the office which I have	81: 5	and s. steadfastly in the faith	Mos 4:11	
to s. upon Mount Zion,	84: 2	s. betwixt them and justice;	15: 9	
every man s. in his own office,	84:109	they were on the same s. with	Al 13: 5	
shall the body be able to s.?	84:109	s. as though they had been the	22:19	
s. ye in holy places, and be	87: 8	a place for s., which was	31:13	
the earth upon which you s.	88:10	were as s. in the midst of fire	He 5:23	
and shall not be able to s.	88:89	was s. in the midst of them.	10: 1	
he shall s. forth upon the land	88:110	s. among the people in all the	3Ne 6:20	
must needs s. rebuked before	93:47	s. in the synagogues and in	13: 5	
and s. rebuked before my face;	95: 2	thy s. images out of the midst	21:17	
shall s. against your enemy	98:27	regular members and in good s.,	DC 20:84	
and s. in holy places;	101:22	be men s. in that generation,	45:31	
s. up in behalf of the accused,	102:17	office and s. in the church,	78:12	
the first decision shall s.,	102:22	s. ministers unto the church.	84:111	
assurance wherewith he may s.;	106: 8	shall be found s. in his place,	88:128	
shall not be counted worthy to s.,	107:100	a s. council for the church,	102: 3	
shall not be counted worthy to s.	107:100	right to officiate in their own s.,	107:10	
Thy friends do s. by thee,	121: 9	s. high councils, at the stakes of	107:36	
is left to s. by the wall.	121:15	rest concerning your spiritual s.,	108: 2	
God shall s. by thee forever	122: 4	honorably hold a name and s.	109:24	
we shall be brought to s.,	123: 7	We saw the Lord s. upon	110: 2	
and to s. aghast and pale,	123:10	be a s. law unto them forever,	119: 4	
and then may we s. still,	123:17	be appointed s. presidents or	124:134	
and s. by you,	124:16	be ordained for s. presidents:	124:135	
and s. in the office of his calling,	124:103	is instituted for s. ministers;	124:137	
have addressed them from the s.	127:10	are ordained to be s. ministers	124:137	
small and great, s. before God;	128: 6	be for fellowship and good s.;	134:10	
who can s. when he appeareth?	128:24	s. upon the hills and the high	Mses 6:37	
Lamb shall s. upon Mount Zion,	133:18	s. before the gods of Elkenah,	Fac 1: 4	
s. upon the mount of Olives.	133:20	s. above me in the air.	JS 2:17	
s. in the midst of his people,	133:25	men of high s. would take	2:22	
s. on the right hand of the Lamb,	133:56	my state and s. before him;	2:29	
he shall s. upon Mount Zion,	133:56	at my bedside, s. in the air,	2:30	
And there are many that now s.,	Mses 1:35	same messenger s. over my head,	2:49	
and could not s. in his presence.	6:47	when, s. up, I prophesied	2:73	
while the earth should s.;	7:52			
you shall s. in the holy place;	JS 1:12	STANDS		
s. in our New Testament.	2:40	he s. in the midst of his people.	DC 84:101	
		[mercantile] establishment s.,	104:39	
STANDARD		to suit my purpose as it s.	128:18	
set up my s. to the people;	1Ne 21:22	S. next to Kolob, called	Fac 2: 2	
and set them up for a s.,	22: 6	s. a hill of considerable size	JS 2:51	
and set up my s. to the people;	2Ne 6: 6			
be as when a s.-bearer fainteth.	20:18	STANTON, Daniel		
for a s. unto my people,	29: 2	And also my servant S. and	DC 75:33	
Moroni planted the s. of liberty	Al 46:36			
yielded to the s. of liberty,	51:20	STAR		
he did raise the s. of liberty	62: 4	there shall a new s. arise,	He 14: 5	
thousands did flock unto his s.,	62: 5	also that a new s. did appear,	3Ne 1:21	
to be a s. for my people,	DC 45: 9	as one s. differs from another	DC 76:98	
first lift a s. of peace unto	98:34	differs from another s. in glory,	76:98	
light may be a s. for the nations;	115: 5	unto me: Kolob, which is s.	Abr 3:13	
		or a s. may exist above it;	3:17	
STANDARD-BEARER: see STANDARD and BEARER.		that he made the greater s.;	3:18	
		STARE		
STANDEST		of God did s. them in the face.	He 4:23	
upon which thou s. is holy.	DC 115: 7			
this earth upon which thou s.;	Mses 1:40	STARRY		
the earth upon which thou s.	2: 1	the s. heavens shall tremble.	DC 84:118	
as that upon which thou s.	Abr 3: 3			
unto that whereon thou s.	3: 4	STARS		
than that upon which thou s.	3: 5	that of the s. in the firmament.	1Ne 1:10	

STARS

For the s. of heaven and	2Ne 23:10
my throne above the s. of God;	24:13
and also the moon and the s.;	He 14:20
sun, nor the moon, nor the s.,	3Ne 8:22
the s. shall fall from heaven,	DC 29:14
the s. shall refuse their shining,	34: 9
and the s. fall from heaven.	45:42
as the glory of the s. differs	76:81
as the glory of the s. is one;	76:98
as innumerable as the s. in	76:109
As also the light of the s.,	88: 9
the s. also give their light,	88:45
the s. shall become exceedingly	88:87
or to the sun, moon, or s.—	121:30
the morning s. sing together,	128:23
continue as innumerable as the s.;	132:30
and the s. shall be hurled from	133:49
and the s. also were made	Mses 2:16
other fixed planets or s.,	Fac 2: 5
the s. represented by numbers	2: 5
of the planets, and of the s.,	Abr 1:31
I saw the s., that they were	3: 2
the s. that are set to give light,	3:10
Kokaubeam, which signifies s.,	3:13
the lesser light they set the s.	4:16
the s. shall fall from heaven,	JS 1:33

START

Behold, we did s. to go down to	Al 57:30
While preparing to s.—	JS 2:61

STARTED

on the morrow they s. to go up,	Mos 7: 3
and s. again on our journey	9: 3
s. from the land of Zarahemla	Al 26: 1
whom they had s. to go down	57:28
I s. with the intention of	JS 2:48
and s. with them to the city	2:63

STATE

in a lost and in a fallen s.,	1Ne 10: 6
in that awful s. of blindness,	13:32
the final s. of the soul after	15:31
the final s. of the souls of men	15:35
their s. became a state of	2Ne 2:21
became a s. of probation,	2:21
the same s. in which they were	2:22
in a s. of innocence,	2:23
for awful is his s.!	9:27
from their lost and fallen s.	25:17
on the blessed and happy s. of	Mos 2:41
a s. of never-ending happiness.	2:41
into a s. of misery and endless	3:25
in their own carnal s., even less	4: 2
and your worthless and fallen s.—	4: 5
from their lost and fallen s.	16: 4
remaineth in his fallen s.	16: 5
of their sinful and polluted s.,	25:11
even in their carnal and sinful s.;	26: 4
from their carnal and fallen s.,	27:25
to a s. of righteousness, being	27:25
not in a s. of so much unbelief	Al 7: 6
ye were not in the s. of dilemma	7:18
a s. of endless misery and woe.	9:11
remain in their s. of ignorance;	9:16
mortality to a s. of immortality,	12:12
then will our s. be awful, for then	12:13
in this awful s. we shall not dare	12:14
this mortal to an immortal s.	12:20
life became a probationary s.;	12:24
to prepare for that endless s.	12:24
having no preparatory s.;	12:26
placing themselves in a s. to act,	12:31
or being placed in a s. to act	12:31
and their carnal s. and also the	22:13
thus their s. becomes worse	24:30
awful, sinful, and polluted s.?	26:17
consigned to a s. of endless wo.	28:11
a s. of never-ending happiness.	28:12
this is the final s. of the wicked.	34:35
concerning the s. of the soul	40:11
received into a s. of happiness,	40:12
a s. of rest, a state of peace,	Al 40:12
a s. of peace, where they shall	40:12
the s. of the souls of the wicked,	40:14
and a s. of awful, fearful looking	40:14
thus they remain in this s.,	40:14
that this s. of happiness and	40:15
this s. of misery of the soul,	40:15
a s. of the soul in happiness or	40:21
all men that are in a s. of nature,	41:11
or I would say, in a carnal s.,	41:11
a s. contrary to the nature of	41:11
to take a thing of a natural s.	41:12
place it in an unnatural s.,	41:12
in a s. opposite to its nature?	41:12
be consigned to a s. of misery.	42: 1
this probationary s. became	42:10
a s. for them to prepare;	42:10
it became a preparatory s.	42:10
to reclaim men from this fallen s.,	42:12
of men in this probationary s.,	42:13
state, yea, this preparatory s.;	42:13
the cause of your thoughtless s.	60: 6
in a s. of thoughtless stupor,	60: 7
had fallen into a s. of unbelief	He 4:25
that they were in an awful s.,	6:40
a s. of such awful wickedness,	7: 4
to a s. of endless misery,	12:26
in a s. of many afflictions,	3Ne 2:19
in a s. of awful wickedness.	6:17
of flesh into an immortal s.,	28:15
in this s. they were to remain	28:40
of heaven, knoweth your s.;	Mrm 6:22
a s. of happiness which hath no	7: 7
in your awful s. of wickedness,	Eth 4:15
and awful is the s. of man,	Mro 7:38
immortal, and eternal s.	DC 77: 1
of the S. of Missouri,	84: 3
again, in their infant s.,	93:38
by the people of this S.;	123: 1
both in Missouri and this S.,	127: 1
in its sanctified and immortal s.,	130: 9
the escutcheon of the S. of Illinois,	135: 7
with the broken faith of the S.	135: 7
Windsor county, S. of Vermont	JS 2: 3
left the S. of Vermont, and	2: 3
in the S. of New York,	2: 3
know of my s. and standing	2:29
county, S. of New York.	2:56
county, S. of Pennsylvania;	2:56
in the S. of Pennsylvania.	2:61
county, in the S. of New York,	2:61

STATED

as I have s. in my epistle;	Al 55: 2
As I s. to you in my letter	DC 128: 1
he further s. that the fulness	JS 2:41
as s. by the messenger.	2:52
Professor Anthon s. that the	2:64
He s. to me that having been	2:66

STATEMENT

and a s. of the will of God,	DC 58:50
with a full s. of the testimony	102:26
own s. that he verily believes	128: 4
above s. and records to be true,	128: 4

STATEMENTS

and s. accompanying it.	DC 102:33
and to take s. and affidavits;	123: 4

STATES: *see also* UNITED STATES.

the Southern S. shall be divided	DC 87: 3
divided against the Northern S.,	87: 3
the Southern S. will call on	87: 3
We believe that rulers, s., and	134: 7

STATING

s. the affairs of the people in	Al 56: 1
s. that if I would deliver up	57: 1

STATION

should be honored in his s.,	DC 134: 6

STATIONED

Moroni had s. an army by	Al	49: 2
were s. the strongest army of		56:34
fortified and s. their armies	He	4: 7

STATIONS

according to their several s.,	Al	17:18

STATURE

nevertheless being large in s.,	1Ne	2:16
being a man large in s.,		4:31
the high ones of s. shall be hewn	2Ne	20:33
can add one cubit unto his s.?	3Ne	13:27
being young, was large in s.;	Mrm	2: 1
and Lib was a man of great s.,	Eth	14:10

STATUTES

for they kept the s. and judgments	1Ne	17:22
should remember to observe the s.	2Ne	1:16
keep the judgments, and the s.,		5:10
and I have not kept the s.	Om	1: 2
observe his judgments and his s.,	Mos	6: 6
which is contrary to the s.,	Al	8:17
his commandments and his s.		25:14
of God, and his s.,		31: 9
they do observe to keep his s.,		58:40
yea, he did observe to keep the s.,	He	3:20
they did begin to keep his s.		6:34
and his s. and his judgments		15: 5
with the s. and judgments.	3Ne	25: 4
that my s. and my judgments	DC	119: 6
and your s. and judgments,		124:39
and s. of the Lord our God.		136: 2

STAVES

no purse nor scrip, neither s.,	DC	24:18

STAY

but they do not s. themselves upon	1Ne	20: 2
from Judah, the s. and the staff,	2Ne	13: 1
and the whole s. of water—		13: 1
shall no more again s. upon him		20:20
but shall s. upon the Lord,		20:20
that doeth iniquity, s. yourselves		27: 4
therefore I will s. my hand,	Mos	4:17
rather s. and perish with them.		19:12
will not the Lord s. his hand;	Al	10:23
the king desireth thee to s.		18:13
they would s. in their won land.		61:10
that he could not s. among them,	He	7: 3
they shall not s. their hand	3Ne	3: 8
of the Lord, and none can s. it;	Mrm	8:26
that God will s. his hand in	Mro	9:14
forth and none shall s. them,	DC	1: 5
and what can s. my hand?		38:22
and no power shall s. my hand.		38:33
I will s. my hand in judgment		39:16
will s. mine hand in judgment.		39:18
ye sinners s. and sleep until		43:18
not appointed to s. in this land,		58:46
there any who can s. his hand.		76: 3
that can s. in the region round		105:20
the region round about, let them s.;		105:20
And those that cannot s.,		105:21
What power shall s. the heavens?		121:33
why can't you s. with us?		122: 6
s. herself and partake not of that		132:51
shall no longer s. themselves;		133:26
oath, that he would s. the floods;	Mses	7:51

STAYED

their tongues shall be s. that	DC	29:19
whose hands are not s. from		56:17
it shall not be s. until the Lord		97:23
How long shall thy hand be s.,		121: 2

STEAD

whoso should reign in his s. were	Jac	1:11
graft them in, in the s. thereof;		5: 9
plant this tree in the s. thereof.		5:44
of the tree in the s. thereof.		5:52
his son, reigneth in his s.	Om	1:23
began to reign in his father's s.	Mos	6: 4
his son began to reign in his s.	Mos	10: 6
Noah began to reign in his s.;		11: 1
consecrated new ones in their s.,		11: 5
be another appointed in his s.,		29: 7
he should be appointed in his s.		29: 8
leaving none to reign in his s.,	Al	1: 1
to another, to reign in my s.;		7: 2
and to place another in his s.,		24:20
in the s. of his father;		50:39
appointed to reign in his s.		52: 3
in the s. of his brother Pahoran;	He	1:13
Nephi began to reign in his s.		3:37
appointed by the people in his s.,		6:15
did keep the records in his s.,	3Ne	1: 3
to come up in the s. thereof,		9: 7
and waters came up in the s.	4Ne	1: 9
disciples ordained in their s.;		1:14
his son Amos kept it in his s.,		1:19
Amos kept the record in his s.;		1:21
did keep the record in his s.		1:47
that Kib reigned in his s.;	Eth	7: 3
to reign in the s. of his father.		7:10
build up his kingdom in his s.;		7:19
and Omer reigned in his s.		8: 1
and Akish reigned in his s.		9: 6
to be king to reign in his s.		9:14
that Emer did reign in his s.,		9:15
Coriantum to reign in his s.		9:21
Coriantum to reign in his s.		9:22
and Com reigned in his s.;		9:25
and he did reign in his s.		9:27
and Riplakish reigned in his s.		10: 4
did reign in the s. of his father;		10:13
whom he anointed king in his s.		10:16
and Kish reigned in his s.		10:17
and Lib reigned in his s.		10:18
reigned in the s. of his father.		10:30
and Shiblom reigned in his s.		11: 4
that Moron did reign in his s.;		11:14
Coriantumr in the s. thereof,		14:16
unto them another in his s.	DC	28: 7
another will I plant in his s.		35:18
shall be appointed in his s.		42:10
to appoint another in his s.		43: 4
shall be planted in their s.		64:40
power to preside in his s.		102:11
shall be appointed in his s.		104:77
has a right to officiate in his s.		107:11
others shall be planted in their s.		114: 2
unto the same priesthood in his s.;		124:132
unto this calling in his s.—		124:132
up the flesh in the s. thereof;	Mses	3:21
closed up the flesh in the s.	Abr	5:15

STEADFAST

like unto this valley, firm and s.,	1Ne	2:10
I would that ye should be s. and	Mos	5:15
they were s. and immovable in	Al	1:25
are firm and s. in the faith	He	15: 8
for they were firm, and s.,	3Ne	6:14
would make them sure and s.,	Eth	12: 4
house in meekness, and be s.	DC	31: 9
you remain s. in your minds		84:61
But he that remaineth s. and	JS	1:11

STEADFASTLY

and standing s. in the faith	Mos	4:11
who s. believeth on his name.	Al	5:48
did watch s. for that day	3Ne	1: 8
did look s. towards heaven,		11: 5
did look s. upon him as if		17: 5
and behold they did pray s.,		19:30

STEADFASTNESS

look forward with s. unto Christ,	2Ne	25:24
look forward unto Christ with s.		26: 8
forward with a s. in Christ,		31:20
because of their s. when they	He	15:10
not deceived, but continue in s.,	DC	49:23
if you fall not from your s.		82:24

STEADINESS

because of the s. of the church	Al	1:29

STEADINESS

joy in you, because of your s.	Al	38: 2
observed the s. of thy brother,		39: 1
and their s. in the faith.	He	6: 1

STEADY

to s. the ark of God,	DC	85: 8

STEAL

that they should not s.;	2Ne	26:32
should murder, or plunder, or s.,	Mos	2:13
Thou shalt not s.		13:22
And they durst not s., for fear	Al	1:18
nor to plunder, nor to s.,		23: 3
did s. away the hearts of many;		39: 4
murder, and plunder, and s.,	He	6:23
commit adultery, and s., and kill,		7: 5
murder, and plunder, and s.,		7:21
thieves break through and s.;	3Ne	13:19
do not break through nor s.		13:20
thieves can break through and s.		27:32
Thou shalt not s.; and he that	DC	42:20
And if he or she shall s.,		42:85
Thou shalt not s.;		59: 6

STEALETH

he that s. and will not repent	DC	42:20

STEALING

s. away the hearts of the people;	Mos	27: 9
no wars nor contentions, no s.,		29:14
and the s., and the plundering,		29:36
malice, and revilings, and s.,	Al	16:18
murdering, plundering, lying, s.,	He	4:12

STEALINGS

and their plunderings, and their s.	He	6:21

STEEL

was of the most precious s.	1Ne	4: 9
bow, which was made of fine s.;		16:18
of copper, and of brass, and of s.,	2Ne	5:15
and copper, and brass and s.,	Jar	1: 8
and made swords out of s. for	Eth	7: 9

STEER

whither they should s. the ship,	1Ne	18:13
anything wherewith to s. her;	Mrm	5:18
no light; whither shall we s.?	Eth	2:19

STEM

a rod out of the s. of Jesse,	2Ne	21: 1
Who is the S. of Jesse	DC	113: 1
come of the S. of Jesse?		113: 3

STEP

men should s. forward and use	DC	134: 8

STEPHEN: see BURNETT, Stephen.

STEPS

and did fill the s. of his father.	Eth	9:15
did walk in the s. of his father,		9:23

STEWARD

a s. over his own property,	DC	42:32
faithful, a just, and a wise s.		51:19
at the hand of every s.,		72: 3
to be received as a wise s.		72:17
be accounted as a wise s.		72:26
that is a faithful and wise s.		78:22
a faithful and wise s. in		101:61
as a s. over earthly blessings,		104:13
unfaithful and an unwise s.		104:74
unfaithful and an unwise s.,		104:77
that thou mayest be a wise s.;		136:27
and thou art his s.		136:27

STEWARDS

ordained them to be s. over	DC	70: 3
s. over the literary concerns		72:20
and be accounted as wise s.		72:22
unfaithful, and unjust s.,		101:90
are mine, then ye are s.;		104:56
otherwise ye are no s.		104:56
you to be s. over mine house,		104:57
mine house, even s. indeed.		104:57
are mine, and ye are my s.,		104:86

STEWARDSHIP

stand in the place of thy s.	DC	42:53
either a s. or otherwise, as		42:72
an account of this s. will I		70: 4
requires of every man in his s.,		70: 9
a s. over temporal things.		70:11
those who are appointed to a s.		70:12
to render an account of his s.,		72: 3
render an account of their s.		72: 5
give an account of his s.		72:16
and appoint every man his s.;		104:11
the s. which is appointed		104:12
[the tannery] for his s.,		104:20
And this s. and blessing,		104:22
appointed unto him, for his s.,		104:24
And this shall be their s.		104:30
this is the beginning of the s.		104:32
the s. which I have appointed		104:37
[Newel K. Whitney] for his s.,		104:40
the s. which I have appointed		104:41
the s. which I have appointed		104:44
your s. which I have appointed		104:54
the s. which I have appointed		104:63
need of this to help me in my s.—		104:72
requires to help him in his s.—		104:73
is faithful and wise in his s.,		104:75
remember that his s. will I require		124:14

STEWARDSHIPS

teachers shall have their s.,	DC	42:70
are not faithful in their s.		64:40
forth the accounts of their s.		69: 5
follow, in your several s.—		82:11
the concerns of your s.,		82:17
that you receive in your s.,		104:68

STICK

and out of a straight s., an arrow;	1Ne	16:23
record of the s. of Ephraim;	DC	27: 5

STIFF

They wear s. necks and high	2Ne	28:14
wear s. necks and high heads	Jac	2:13

STIFFEN

will s. their necks against him,	2Ne	10: 5
s. not their necks against me,	DC	112:13

STIFFENED

and s. their necks against the Holy	2Ne	6:10

STIFFNECKED

my people, ye are a s. people;	2Ne	25:28
the Jews were a s. people;	Jac	4:14
a s. and a gainsaying people;		6: 4
the people were a s. people,	En	1:22
for they are not all s.	Jar	1: 4
And as many as are not s.		1: 4
mighty man, and a s. man,	Om	1:28
that his people were a s. people,	Mos	3:14
for they were a s. people,		13:29
a hard-hearted and a s. people.	Al	9: 5
a hard-hearted and a s. people.		9:31
a hard-hearted and a s. people;		15:15
hardened and a more s. people;		20:30
as s. a people as they are;		26:24
thousands of our s. brethren,		37:10
they had been a s. people,	He	4:21
they were a s. people, insomuch		5: 3
ye blind, and ye s. people,		9:21
ye hardened and ye s. people,		13:29
and perverse and s. people,	Mrm	8:33
unbelieving and s. generation—	DC	5: 8

STIFFNECKEDNESS

because of the s. of Laman	1Ne	2:11

STIFFNECKEDNESS 923 STIRRING

STIFFNECKEDNESS (continued)
the ignorance, and the s. of men;	2Ne 32: 7
because of the s. of the people—	WM 1:17
because of s. and unbelief	3Ne 15:18
of the s. of my people which	DC 56: 6

STIFFNESS
and the s. of their necks.	2Ne 25:12
and the s. of their necks;	Jar 1: 3

STILL
and did s. continue to murmur;	1Ne 4: 4
spoken unto you in a s. small voice,	17:45
for they s. wait for the coming of	2Ne 6:13
are righteous shall be righteous s.,	9:16
who are filthy shall be filthy s.;	9:16
but his hand is stretched out s.	15:25
but his hand is stretched out s.	19:12
but his hand is stretched out s.	19:17
but his hand is stretched out s.	19:21
but his hand is stretched out s.	20: 4
that ye ponder s. in your hearts;	32: 8
I did s. raise my voice high	En 1: 4
And ye are s. indebted unto him,	Mos 2:24
that are s. publishing peace!	15:16
they became more s., and durst not	Al 1:33
you and is s. calling after you,	5:37
ye s. persist in the wearing of	5:53
were s. his brethren in the Lord;	17: 2
the Amulonites were s. harder;	21: 3
s. have been racked with hatred	26: 9
will s. resist the spirit of the truth,	30:46
and he will s. deliver me.	36:27
will also s. show forth his power	37:19
ye are s. determined to carry on	54: 5
s. determined to maintain the	57:11
that the Lord will s. deliver us,	60:21
sit s. and behold these things?	60:23
there was s. great contention in	He 3:19
a s. voice of perfect mildness,	5:30
s. carry on the work of darkness,	6:29
they did s. harden their hearts	10:15
And the robbers did s. increase	11:32
unto man that the sun standeth s.;	12:15
did s. remain in wickedness,	13: 1
did s. remain in wickedness,	3Ne 2:10
did s. continue to have those	5: 5
did s. continue, without ceasing,	19:24
there s. continued to be peace	4Ne 1: 4
there was s. peace in the land,	1:20
s. continue to build up churches	1:41
did s. remain in wickedness)	1:47
that is filthy shall be filthy s.;	Mrm 9:14
righteous shall be righteous s.;	9:14
that is happy shall be happy s.;	9:14
is unhappy shall be unhappy s.	9:14
and thou art s. chosen, and art	DC 3:10
stand s. until I command thee,	5:34
he shall be appointed s. to go	56: 9
thus saith the s. small voice,	85: 6
they must remain filthy s.	88:35
who shall remain filthy s.	88:102
be s. and know that I am God.	101:16
and then may we stand s.,	123:17
but he will s. deliver his message.	129: 7
marriages are s. being solemnized	OD
as the voice was s. speaking, Moses	Mses 1:27
thy curtains are stretched out s.;	7:30
going on s. towards the south;	Abr 2:21
of time shall be longer s.;	3: 8
s. I kept myself aloof from all	JS 2: 8
s. there were but few who	2:24
persecution s. followed me,	2:58
however, s. continued,	2:61
We s. continued the work of	2:68

STIMULATE
I did s. them to go to battle	Mos 10:19

STING
and that death should have no s.,	Mos 16: 7
the s. of death is swallowed up	16: 8
the s. of death should be	Al 22:14
is the s. of death swallowed up.	Mrm 7: 5

STINK
and their fish to s. because	2Ne 7: 2
of sweet smell there shall be s.;	13:24
for myself, to me he doth not s.	Al 19: 5
their fish s., and die for thirst.	DC 133:68

STINKETH
that he is dead and that he s.,	Al 19: 5

STIR
to s. them up in the ways of	1Ne 2:24
Laman s. up their hearts to anger.	16:38
to s. them up in remembrance of	2Ne 5:25
shall s. up a scourge for him	20:26
will s. up the Medes against them,	23:17
s. them up to anger against that	28:20
to s. them up in remembrance of	Mos 1:17
to s. them up in remembrance of	6: 3
Laman began to s. up his people	9:13
to s. his people up in rebellion	10: 6
might s. up my people to anger	11:28
cries did s. up the remainder of	21:11
but Amlici did s. up those who	Al 2: 8
to s. them up in remembrance of	4:19
did s. up the people to riotings,	11:20
they did s. up the people against	11:20
to s. up the people in anger	27: 2
who do s. up the Lamanites	27:12
did s. up the Zoramites to anger	35:10
and to s. them up also to anger	35:10
to s. up the Lamanites to anger	43: 8
he did s. up the remainder of	44:16
s. up the Lamanites to anger	46:30
s. up the Lamanites to anger	47: 1
s. up insurrections among you,	60:27
he did s. them up to anger,	He 1:17
to s. up the Lamanites to war	4: 3
Satan did s. up the hearts of	6:21
did s. up the people to anger	8: 7
to s. them up in remembrance of	11: 4
s. them up again in remembrance	11:34
for Satan did s. them up to do	16:22
to s. up the hearts of men with	3Ne 11:30
that s. up the hearts of the	Mrm 4: 5
s. them up to anger against you,	DC 10:32
Satan s. up the hearts	10:63
no small s. and division amongst	JS 2: 5

STIRRED
needs be s. up unto repentance,	2Ne 28:19
they be s. up to anger, and perish;	28:19
the king was s. up in anger	Mos 17:12
began again to be s. up in anger	21: 2
were s. up by the Amalekites	Al 24: 1
to be s. up in remembrance	25: 6
should be s. up to anger;	25: 8
and s. them up to anger,	48: 3
s. up the hearts of the people of	51: 9
s. yourselves more diligently for	60:10
they were s. up again to anger	63:14
had not been s. up to anger,	He 6:17
being s. up to anger by them,	11:24
of Coriantumr were s. up to	Eth 15: 6
the people of Shiz were s. up to	15: 6
men are s. up unto repentance,	DC 18: 6
may not be s. up unto anger.	63:27

STIRRETH
and s. up the children of men	2Ne 9: 9
it s. up the dead for thee,	24: 9
he s. up the hearts of men to	3Ne 11:29
Satan s. them up continually	Mro 9: 3
he s. them up to iniquity against	DC 10:20
Satan s. them up, that he may	10:22
he s. up their hearts to anger	10:24

STIRRING
s. them up continually to keep	En 1:23
s. them up unto repentance.	Jar 1:12
was s. up the people to rebellion	Mos 18:33
in s. them up to anger against	He 4: 4
s. up of the people to do all	3Ne 6:15

STOAL — 924 — STOOD

STOAL, Josiah
gentleman by the name of S.,   JS   2:56
employed in the service of Mr. S.   2:57

STOAL'S
I left Mr. S. and went to   JS   2:58

STOCK
s. for the building of that house,	DC	124:63
for a share of s. in that house,		124:64
any one man for s. in that house.		124:64
over fifteen thousand dollars s.		124:65
under fifty dollars for a share of s.		124:66
pay his s. into their hands		124:67
at the time he receives s.;		124:67
proportion to the amount of s.		124:68
he shall receive s. in that house;		124:68
not receive any s. in that house.		124:68
if any pay s. into their hands		124:69
it shall be for s. in that house,		124:69
he and his heirs shall hold that s.,		124:69
do not sell or convey the s. away		124:69
receive any s. into their hands,		124:70
of that s. to any other purpose,		124:70
portion of that s. anywhere else,		124:71
do not repay fourfold for the s.		124:71
Joseph pay s. into their hands		124:72
over fifteen thousand dollars s.		124:72
let him put s. into that house		124:74
Hyrum put s. into that house		124:77
Galland put s. into that house;		124:78
Marks pay s. into that house,		124:80
Henry G. Sherwood pay s. into		124:81
William Law pay s. into		124:82
Amos Davies pay s. into		124:111
pay s. also into the hands of		124:117
And again verily I say		124:119
let every man who pays s. bear		124:122
unto them for s. in that house.		124:122

STOCKHOLDER
as a s. in this house,	DC	124:67
without the consent of the s.,		124:71

STOLE
if he s. he was also punished;	Al	30:10
and his servant s. forth and		51:33
Teancum s. privily into the tent		51:34

STOLEN
s. the daughters of the Lamanites?	Mos	20:18
s. the daughters of the Lamanites,		21:20
their hearts were not s. away	Al	31:22

STOMACHER
instead of a s., a girding of   2Ne 13:24

STONE
but for a s. of stumbling,	2Ne	18:14
and s. them, and slay them;		26: 3
s. upon which they might build	Jac	4:15
this s. shall become the great,		4:16
a large s. brought unto him	Om	1:20
a s., which shall shine forth in	Al	37:23
and also building walls of s.		48: 8
and they did s. the prophets	3Ne	7:14
ask bread, will give him a s.?		14: 9
he hath written from that s.	DC	28:11
shall not be left one s. upon		45:20
and the s. of Israel.		50:44
as the s. which is cut out of		65: 2
corner s. thereof unto the top		115:12
planted to be a corner-s. of Zion,		124: 2
the corner-s. I have appointed		124:23
the glory of this, the corner-s.		124:60
for the corner-s. of Zion—		124:131
Then the white s. mentioned in		130:10
And a white s. is given to each		130:11
was bdellium and the onyx s.	Mses	3:12
to worship gods of wood or of s.,	Abr	1:11
one s. upon another that shall	JS	1: 3
under a s. of considerable size,		2:51
plates, deposited in a s. box.	JS	2:51
This s. was thick and rounding		2:51
fixed under the edge of the s.,		2:52

STONED
whom they had cast out, and s.,	1Ne	1:20
who had been cast out and s.,	Al	15: 1
and we have been s., and taken		26:29
they s. him to death.		33:17
wast s. for the word's sake;		38: 4
we would not have s. them,	He	13:25
killed the prophets, and s. them,		13:33
had been s. and suffered death	3Ne	7:19
not killed and s. the prophets,		8:25
the prophets and s. them not;		10:12
the prophets, and s. them,	Eth	8:25

STONES
he built an altar of s.,	1Ne	2: 7
arrows and our s. and our slings.		16:15
with a sling and with s.		16:23
I did smite two s. together		17:11
and gathered out the s. thereof,	2Ne	15: 2
but we will build with hewn s.;		19:10
go down to the s. of the pit;		24:19
and with s., and with slings;	Mos	10: 8
by the means of those two s.		28:13
and with s., and with slings,	Al	2:12
and their s., and their slings,		3: 5
sent men to cast s. at them.		14: 7
gold and silver, and precious s.;		17:14
to cast s. at them with his sling;		17:36
he did sling s. amongst them;		17:36
could not hit him with their s.,		17:36
should they cast s. at them,		23: 2
arrows, their s. and their slings;		43:20
and the s. of the Lamanites;		49: 2
fought with s. and with arrows.		49: 2
not cast their s. and their		49: 4
by casting over s. and arrows		49:19
swept off by the s. and arrows		49:22
the s. and the arrows of the		50: 4
cast s. from the top thereof,		50: 5
and would fight with s., and		57:14
mock them. and cast s. at them.	He	13:24
they cast s. at him upon the wall,		16: 2
could not hit him with their s.		16: 2
could not hit him with their s.		16: 6
we cannot hit him with our s.		16: 6
will lay thy s. with fair colors,	3Ne	22:11
all thy borders of pleasant s.		22:12
out of a rock sixteen small s.;	Eth	3: 1
touch these s., O Lord, with		3: 4
and touched the s. one by one		3: 6
two s. will I give unto thee,		3:23
these s. shall magnify to the		3:24
seal up the two s. which he		3:28
s. which the brother of Jared had		6: 2
put forth the s. into the vessels		6: 2
caused s. to shine in darkness,		6: 3
your silver, and your precious s.,	DC	124:26
were two s. in silver bows—	JS	2:35
and these s., fastened to a		2:35
possession and use of these s.		2:35
formed by laying s. together		2:52
two s. crossways of the box,		2:52
on these s. lay the plates		2:52

STONING
s. those whom I did send to   3Ne 9:10

STOOD
came and s. before my father,	1Ne	1:11
came and s. before them,		3:29
and I s. before my brethren,		7:18
and he came and s. before me.		8: 5
they s. as if they knew not		8:14
led to the tree by which I s.		8:19
even to the tree by which I s.;		8:20
led unto the tree by which I s.		8:21
it s. as it were in the air,		8:26
came down and s. before me;		11:14

STOOD

Above it s. the seraphim;	2Ne 16: 2
and behold he s. before me.	Mos 3: 2
and they s. before the king,	7: 8
And they s. forth and	13: 2
went and s. forth in the water,	18:12
to those priests that s. in need,	18:28
went forth and s. before the king,	22: 3
went forth and s. among them,	23:27
s. and testified of their iniquity	26: 9
to shake upon which they s.;	27:11
he s. up and began to speak	27:23
he s. before Alma and pleaded	Al 1:11
whatsoever they s. in need—	1:29
as to those who s. in need.	1:30
who s. in need of their succor,	4:13
s. forth to lay their hands on me;	9: 7
And I s. with boldness to declare	9: 7
that Amulek went and s. forth,	9:34
and s. before Alma and Amulek,	14:14
that the judge s. before them,	14:19
the chief judge s. before them,	14:24
they rose and s. upon their feet.	14:25
s. and scattered the flocks of	17:27
again s. to scatter their flocks;	17:33
and s. to contend with those who	17:34
who s. by the waters of Sebus;	17:34
they s. to scatter the flocks of	17:35
But Ammon s. forth and began	17:36
who had s. before the king	19:15
who had s. at the waters of Sebus	19:21
she arose and s. upon her feet,	19:29
he arose and s. upon his feet.	19:30
But Ammon s. forth and said	20:17
And he s. upon his feet,	22:22
And the king s. forth, and began	22:23
But the king s. forth among	22:25
And I arose and s. up, and	36: 8
again, and I s. upon my feet,	36:23
that the soldier who s. by,	44:13
s. as if they were struck dumb	He 5:25
at him as he s. upon the wall;	16: 2
had s. and fought with boldness,	3Ne 4:14
cleave together again, that it s.;	10:10
and s. in the midst of them;	11: 8
And he arose and s. before him.	11:20
and Jesus s. in the midst;	17:12
and Jesus s. in the midst,	17:13
s. in the midst of the multitude.	19: 4
Jesus came and s. in the midst	19:15
arose up and s. upon their feet.	20: 2
and s. in the midst of them,	27: 2
who s. with open arms to receive	Mrm 6:17
with them as he s. in a cloud,	Eth 2: 5
and s. in a cloud and talked	2:14
I s. before them in the flesh,	DC 45:16
And Adam s. up in the midst of	107:56
s. before us, and said:	110:13
so that Moses s. in the presence	Mses 1:31
and s. upon the place Mahujah,	7: 2
as I s. upon the mount, I beheld	7: 3
s. before my face, and he talked	7: 4
that they fled and s. afar off and	7:14
the giants of the land also, s. afar	7:15
s. on the right hand of God;	7:57
the altar which s. by the hill	Abr 1:10
it s. before the gods of Elkenah,	1:13
angel of his presence s. by me,	1:15
and he s. in the midst of them,	3:23
s. among those that were spirits,	3:23
there s. one among them that	3:24
Personages who s. above me	JS 2:18
he s. up and prophesied many	2:73

STOP

let us put a s. to the shedding of	Mos 20:22
that they should s. their cries;	24:11
and I will s. the Lamanites in	24:23
a s. to the shedding of blood;	Al 34:13
God sent his holy angel to s. us	36: 6
must s. the work of destruction	38: 7
should s. shedding their blood.	43:54
they did s. and withdrew a pace	44: 1

did not s. making preparations	Al 50: 1
to s. their flight into the land	50:33
he did s. and did not go unto his	He 10:12
be a s. put to this work of	11:28
before it was possible to s. them	Mrm 2:16
s. the armies of the Lamanites,	3: 6
should s. beyond the sea in the	Eth 2: 7
ye shall s. the hole, that ye	2:20
thou shalt s. for a season,	DC 5:30
S., and stand still until I	5:34
to s. the Missouri river in its	121:33
not have power to s. my work.	136:17

STOPPED

that your mouths should be s.	Mos 4:20

STOPPETH

the Spirit s. mine utterance,	2Ne 32: 7

STORE

which they had laid up in s.	3Ne 4:18
and silver did they lay up in s.	4Ne 1:46
the same layeth up in s. that	DC 4: 4
have a great work laid up in s.,	38:33
I have kept in s. a blessing	39:15
in this place, and establish a s.,	57: 8
Newel K. Whitney retain his s.,	63:42
or in other words, the s.,	63:42
should sell their s. and their	64:26
man who has got riches in s.—	90:22
now already in s. sufficient,	101:75
I have a mission in s. for	124:102
which is in s. for a time to come.	125: 2

STOREHOUSE

Bring ye all the tithes into the s.,	3Ne 24:10
residue shall be kept in my s.,	DC 42:34
thou shalt give it into my s.,	42:55
let the bishop appoint a s.	51:13
have appointed to keep my s.;	58:24
for the place of the s., and also	58:37
it shall be given into my s.;	70: 7
agent who keepeth the Lord's s.,	70:11
To keep the Lord's s.;	72:10
establishing the affairs of the s.	78: 3
to be cast into the Lord's s.,	82:18
other words upon the Lord's s.,	83: 5
the s. shall be kept by the	83: 6
the s. of the Lord may not be	90:23
Gilbert should sell my s.,	101:96

STORM

there arose a great s.,	1Ne 18:13
and the s. did cease,	18:21
a covert from s. and from rain.	2Ne 14: 6
with a great noise, and with s.,	27: 2
not be beaten down by the s.	Al 26: 6
when the s. cometh they shall be	26: 6
that the s. cannot penetrate	26: 6
mighty s. shall beat upon you,	He 5:12
there arose a great s.,	3Ne 8: 5
the lightnings, and the s.,	8:19
and for a refuge from the s.,	DC 115: 6
small helm in the time of a s.,	123:16
that the s. is fully blown over,	127: 1

STORMS

and fall when the s. descend,	DC 90: 5

STORY

my telling the s. had excited	JS 2:22
the very prevalent s. of my	2:56

STOUT

the s. heart of the king of Assyria,	2Ne 20:12
words have been s. against me,	3Ne 24:13

STOUTNESS

say in the pride and s. of heart:	2Ne 19: 9

STRAIGHT

a s. and narrow path,	1Ne 8:20

STRAIGHT 926 STRENGTH

and make his paths s.;	1Ne 10: 8	s. and pilgrims on the earth;	DC	45:13
out of a s. stick, an arrow;	16:23	a house that s. may come		124:23
thou make my path s. before me!	2Ne 4:33	for the boarding of s.,		124:56
lieth in a s. course before him,	9:41			
are ye in this s. and narrow path	31:18	**STRATAGEM**		
into this s. and narrow path,	31:19	he should defend them by s.;	Al	43:30
and walk in the s. path which	33: 9	he might take again by s. or		52:10
walk in his paths, which are s.;	Al 7: 9	Moroni resolved upon a s. to		54: 3
that ye are making his paths s.	7:19	desirous to bring a s. into effect		56:30
his paths are s., and his course	37:12	resolving by s. to destroy us;		58: 6
a s. course to eternal bliss,	37:44	that by this s. we did take		58:28
a s. course to the promised land.	37:44	did not resolve upon any s.		62:35
did run in a s. course from the	50: 8	Every s. that could be	JS	2:60
march in a s. course after us;	56:37			
in a s. and narrow course across	He 3:29	**STRAYED**		
therefore his paths are s.,	DC 3: 2	For they have s. from mine	DC	1:15
and make his paths s.;	33:10			
of the Lord, make his paths s.	65: 1	**STRAW**		
make s. the way of the Lord	84:28	the lion shall eat s. like the ox.	2Ne	21: 7
and make his paths s.,	133:17	the lion shall eat s. like the ox.		30:13
STRAIGHTNESS		**STREAK**		
the s. of the path,	2Ne 31: 9	the lightnings shall s. forth from	DC	43:22
STRAIGHTWAY		**STREAM**		
s. came forth out of the prison;	Al 14:28	a goodly land, by a pure s.,	DC	97: 9
they s. came forth into the city.	14:28	or to turn it up s.,		121:33
but s. Satan tempted him; and	DC 40: 2			
but s. shut it up again;	76:47	**STREAMS**		
Go ye s. unto the land of	101:56	shall smite it in the seven s.,	2Ne	21:15
get ye s. unto my land;	101:57			
go ye s., and do all things	101:60	**STREET**		
And his servant went s.,	101:62	as the s. to them that went over.	2Ne	8:23
not repay then go s. and tell	136:25			
		STREETS		
STRAIT		they lie at the head of all the s.;	2Ne	8:20
The place is too s. for me;	1Ne 21:20	were torn in the midst of the s.		15:25
and enter in at the s. gate,	Jac 6:11	down like the mire of the s.		20: 6
Enter ye in at the s. gate;	3Ne 14:13	we have taught them in their s.;	Al	26:29
Because s. is the gate, and	14:14	did preach the word in their s.		32: 1
Enter ye in at the s. gate;	27:33	in the synagogues and in the s.,	3Ne	13: 2
for s. is the gate, and narrow is	27:33	and in the corners of the s.,		13: 5
cannot enter in at the s. gate	DC 22: 2			
For s. is the gate, and narrow	132:22	**STRENGTH**		
		received much s. of the Lord,	1Ne	4:31
STRAITEN		s. that I may burst these bands		7:17
did s. them in the wilderness	1Ne 17:41	after I had received s. I spake		15: 6
		that day, will they not receive the s.		15:15
STRAITENED		that my frame has no s.		17:47
the Lord s. them because of	1Ne 17:41	I have spent my s. for naught		21: 4
		and my God shall be my s.		21: 5
STRANGE		my s. slacken, because of mine	2Ne	4:26
wandering in s. roads.	1Ne 8:32	Do not slacken my s. because		4:29
did enter into that s. building.	8:33	him with the s. of my mouth.		7: 8
away into some s. wilderness;	16:38	Put on s., O arm of the Lord;		8: 9
being wanderers in a s. land;	Al 13:23	put on thy s., O Zion;		8:24
lost from its body in a s. land;	26:36	men of s. to mingle strong drink;		15:22
of us, wanderers in a s. land.	26:36	saith: By the s. of my hand		20:13
nevertheless, it is s. to relate,	47:36	for the Lord JEHOVAH is my s.		22: 2
may bring to pass my s. act,	DC 95: 4	with all your might, mind, and s.,		25:29
to pass my act, my s. act,	101:95	hath brought forth much s.;	Jac	5:18
perform my work, my s. work,	101:95	and because of the much s. of		5:18
there is a s. thing in the land;	Mses 6:38	and because of their much s.		5:36
the offering unto these s. gods,	Abr 1: 8	faster than the s. of the roots,		5:48
a s. land which thou knowest	1:16	taking s. unto themselves.		5:48
to bear my name in a s. land	2: 6	the roots thereof may take s.		5:59
how very s. it was that an	JS 2:23	according to the s. of the good		5:65
But s. or not, so it was, and	2:23	and the top may be equal in s.,		5:66
not seem very s. to any one who	2:28	according to the s. thereof.		5:73
		fight with the s. of his own arm,	WM	1:13
STRANGENESS		And in the s. of the Lord		1:14
on the s. of what I had	JS 2:47	with all the might, mind and s.	Mos	2:11
		should run faster than he has s.		4:27
STRANGER		in the s. of the Lord did we go		9:17
and who is a s. unto him,	Mos 5:13	we did go up in the s. of the Lord		10:10
thy s. that is within thy gates;	13:18	the Lord, nor the s. of the Lord,		10:11
and that turn aside the s.,	3Ne 24: 5	they depended upon their own s.		10:11
		people, as to the s. of men.		10:11
STRANGERS		they did boast in their own s.,		11:19
themselves in the children of s.	2Ne 12: 6	and spend your s. with harlots,		12:29
of the fat ones shall s. eat.	15:17	the s. and power of God,		21:30
and the s. shall be joined with	24: 1	limbs might receive their s.—		27:22
also have been s. to God.	Al 26: 9	limbs of Alma received their s.,		27:23

STRENGTH

and was noted for his much s.	Al	1: 2
every man according to his s.		1:26
with the Nephites with great s.,		2:17
give us s. according to our faith		14:26
to flee by the s. of his arm.		17:37
of his expertness and great s.;		18: 3
in the s. of the Lord thou canst		20: 4
upon his feet, receiving his s.		22:22
I do not boast in my own s.,		26:11
as to my s. I am weak;		26:12
in his s. I can do all things;		26:12
even to the exhausting of his s.;		27:17
was not that to exceed their s.		27:19
conquered according to his s.,		30:17
O Lord, wilt thou give me s.,		31:30
unto me that I may have s.,		31:31
them that they may have s.,		31:33
yea, and he also gave them s.,		31:38
limbs did receive their s. again,		36:23
wisdom, nor of your much s.		38:11
go on unto boasting in thy s.		39: 2
all your mind, might, and s.;		39:13
with such exceeding great s.		43:43
forth in the s. of the Lord,		46:20
should have any more s.;		46:30
with the s. of the Nephites,		48: 5
to exceed the s. of the city		49:14
to their pleasure and their s.,		50: 5
did seek to cut off the s. and		50:12
exceed the Lamanites in their s.		51:31
might receive s. to his army.		52:17
whom were fresh and full of s.;		52:31
and also for s. and activity;		53:20
having been prepared in its s.		55:13
and were a great s. to his army.		55:24
in which S. Antipus did rejoice		56:10
a greater s. to his army,		56:18
our receiving provisions and s.		56:29
fought as if with the s. of God;		56:56
fought with such miraculous s.;		56:56
that we might receive more s.		58: 3
wait to receive provisions and s.		58: 4
receiving great s. from day to		58: 5
did not send more s. unto us,		58: 9
give us s. that we might		58:10
number and the s. of our army.		58:14
does not grant us more s.;		58:34
we have not received greater s.		58:34
receiving s. from day to day,		59: 7
sufficient s. and succor for them.		60: 5
if we had united our s. as we		60:16
them in the s. of the Lord,		60:16
and I will leave the s. and		60:25
the s. of our God according		61:17
them in the s. of the Lord,		61:18
their riches, or their s., or their		62:49
with his s. and also with his	He	1:16
their greatest s. was in the		1:24
their boastings in their own s.,		4:13
they were left in their own s.;		4:13
the s. of the Lamanites was		4:26
was as great as their s., even		4:26
Lord will not grant unto you s.,		7:22
show unto the wicked of my s.,		7:23
to depend upon their own s.		16:15
should cry unto the Lord for s.	3Ne	3:12
the s. thereof should be		3:14
in the s. of the Lord they did		4:10
and put on thy s., O Zion;		20:36
the s. of the Lord was not	Mrm	2:26
began to boast in their own s.,		3: 9
did again boast of their s.;		4: 8
mighty as to the s. of their army,	Eth	7: 8
receive great s. to his army.		14: 7
received great s. to his army,		14: 8
all the s. which it was possible		15:14
mighty men as to the s. of men.		15:26
received sufficient s. that they		15:28
I have but the s. of a man,	Mro	9:18
with all your might, mind and s.,		10:32
yet if he boasts in his own s.,	DC	3: 4
your heart, might, and s.,		4: 2
servant Joseph sufficient s.,		9:12
s. and means provided to enable	DC	10: 4
all your might, mind and s.		11:20
all their mights, minds, and s.		20:31
and in this thou shalt have s.		24: 7
labors thou shalt not have s.,		24: 9
whether in weakness or in s.,		24:11
And I will give unto him s.		24:12
have not relied on me for s.		30: 1
all your might, mind, and s.		33: 7
it shall bring forth in its s.		59: 3
all thy might, mind, and s.;		59: 5
and brought forth her s.;		84:101
have set for the s. of Zion		96: 1
all their might, mind, and s.,		98:47
curtains or the s. of Zion.		101:21
take all the s. of mine house,		101:55
who are the s. of mine house,		101:55
unto the s. of my house		103:22
of the s. of my house		103:30
of the s. of my house,		103:34
unto the s. of my house,		105:16
the s. of mine house have not		105:17
gather up the s. of my house,		105:27
Put on thy s., O Zion—		113: 7
to put on her s. is to put on		113: 8
traveling in the greatness of his s.?		133:46
did again receive his natural s.	Mses	1:10
calling upon God, he received s.,		1:20
Moses received s., and called		1:21
yield unto thee her s.		5:37
light had departed, I had no s.;	JS	2:20
I found my s. so exhausted		2:48
my s. entirely failed me,		2:48

STRENGTHEN

he doth nourish them, and s. them,	1Ne	17: 3
And the Lord did s. them,	Mos	23: 2
the Lord did s. them that they		24:15
did s. the hand of the Nephites,	Al	2:18
their cries, and did s. them,		2:28
serve to s. their faith in Christ;		25:16
he did fortify and s. the land		48: 9
number of men to s. his army.		52: 7
and s. the cities round about,		52:10
which will s. us to go against		55:11
supposing that God would s. us,		56: 8
he would s. us and deliver		58:10
together to s. Helaman,		59: 3
also men to s. our armies?		60:19
to s. and fortify our armies,		60:25
See that ye s. Lehi and		61:21
did s. the army of Moroni		62:30
thy cords and s. thy stakes;	3Ne	22: 2
s. thy stakes and enlarge thy	Mro	10:31
and be with and s. them;	DC	20:53
to s. the church continually.		23: 3
and to s. the chruch;		23: 4
and to s. the church;		23: 5
shall s. them and prepare them		31: 8
and s. them by the word of		50:37
to s. the body and to enliven		59:19
and s. the feeble knees.		81: 5
s. your brethren in all your		108: 7
henceforth I will s. him.		132:53

STRENGTHENED

being s. by the hand of the Lord,	Al	2:28
and he was s., insomuch that		2:31
and s. him in the Lord.		15:18
God, who has s. our arms that		44: 5
unto them, to have s. them,		60: 8
s. up the church whithersoever	DC	37: 2
enlarged; her stakes must be s.;		82:14
that her stakes may be s.,		133: 9
me, and I were s. before him.	Mses	1:14

STRENGTHENING

s. the armies of the Nephites,	Al	48: 8
people for the s. of his army.		54: 2
labor in s. the fortifications		55:25

STRENUOUS

most s. exertions were used	JS	2:60

STRETCH   928   STROKES

STRETCH
S. forth thine hand again unto	1 Ne 17:53
S. forth thy hand and prophesy	Mos 12: 2
let us s. forth our hands	Al 14:10
I must not s. forth mine hand;	14:11
and s. forth his hands towards	31:14
let them s. forth the curtains	3 Ne 22: 2
s. forth thy hand;	DC 121: 4
man s. forth his puny arm to	121:33
I can s. forth mine hands and	Mses 7:36
I s. my hand over the sea,	Abr 2: 7

STRETCHED
I s. forth my hand unto my	1 Ne 17:54
that hath s. forth the heavens,	2 Ne 8:13
and walk with s.-forth necks	13:16
he hath s. forth his hand against	15:25
but his hand is s. out still.	15:25
but his hand is s. out still.	19:12
but his hand is s. out still.	19:17
but his hand is s. out still.	19:21
but his hand is s. out still.	20: 4
that is s. out upon all nations.	24:26
And his hand is s. out,	24:27
and I have s. forth mine hand	Jac 5:47
he s. forth his hand and said:	Mos 16: 1
But Amulek s. forth his hand,	Al 10:25
he s. forth his hand unto them	13:21
he s. forth his hand, and	15: 5
he s. forth his hand unto the	19:12
he s. forth his hand to slay	20:20
but he s. forth his hand,	32: 7
and s. it forth unto them,	44:13
and s. forth his hand and cried	He 13: 4
that he s. forth his hand	3 Ne 11: 9
he s. forth his hand unto the	12: 1
the Lord s. forth his hand and	Eth 3: 6
and with a s.-out arm.	DC 103:17
the Lord, s. out the heavens,	104:14
my arm is s. out in the last days,	136:22
and thy curtains are s. out still;	Mses 7:30
misery, and wept and s. forth his arms,	7:41
son (and his hand was s. out),	Abr 3:12

STRETCHED-FORTH: *see* STRETCHED *and* FORTH.

STRETCHED-OUT: *see* STRETCHED *and* OUT.

STRETCHES
and he s. forth his hands	Jac 6: 4

STRETCHING
and the s. out of his wings	2 Ne 18: 8

STREWED
s. upon the face of the land,	Eth 14:22

STRICKEN
my parents being s. in years,	1 Ne 18:17
yet we did esteem him s.,	Mos 14: 4
of my people was he s.	14: 8
Gideon being s. with many years,	Al 1: 9

STRICT
I may be s. in the plain road!	2 Ne 4:32
of the s. commandment	Jac 2: 9
to the s. commands of God,	2:10
of the land were exceedingly s.	Jar 1: 5
yea, even a very s. law;	Mos 13:29
And there was a s. command	27: 3
was a s. law among the people of	Al 1:21
are laid under a s. command	12: 9
s. in observing the ordinances	30: 3
how s. are the commandments	37:13
are s. to remember the Lord	58:40
they did establish very s. laws	3 Ne 7:14
they were s. to observe that	Mro 6: 7
s. were your commandments;	DC 3: 5
s. charges to keep them safe,	JS 2:60

STRICTLY
to observe s. from day to day,	Mos 13:30
s. contrary to the commands	Al 30: 7
this law should be s. observed	62:10
Lamanites did observe s. to keep	He 13: 1

STRICTNESS
of the s. of the word of God,	Jac 2:35
because of the s. of the word,	Al 35:15

STRIFE
babblings, and in envyings and s.;	Al 1:32
yea, there were envyings, and s.,	4: 9
there began to be much s.	He 11:23
they did put an end to their s.	11:23
neither in wrath nor with s.	DC 60:14
entirely lost in a s. of words	JS 2: 6
great were the confusion and s.	2: 8

STRIFES
envyings, and s., and malice.	2 Ne 26:21
and envyings, and s., and malice,	Al 16:18
unto great swelling, envyings, s.,	He 13:22
deceivings, and envyings, and s.,	3 Ne 21:19
and your envyings, and your s.,	30: 2
envyings, nor s., nor tumults,	4 Ne 1:16
shall breathe out wrath and s.	Mrm 8:21
envying, and s., and malice,	8:36
and envyings, and s., and	DC 101: 6

STRIKE
knew not whether to go or to s.	Al 52:36

STRIKETH
which bar s. the wicked with	Jac 6:13

STRIP
by a narrow s. of wilderness,	Al 22:27
s. yourselves of all uncleanness;	Mrm 9:28
s. yourselves from jealousies	DC 67:10

STRIPES
God will beat us with a few s.,	2 Ne 28: 8
and with his s. we are healed.	Mos 14: 5

STRIPLING
his two thousand s. soldiers,	Al 53:22
to my s. Ammonites,	56:57

STRIPPED
Behold, are ye s. of pride?	Al 5:28
among you who is not s. of envy?	5:29
pay that which he owed, or be s.,	11: 2

STRIVE
ceaseth soon to s. with them;	1 Ne 7:14
s. to keep the commandments	17:15
Lord will not always s. with man.	2 Ne 26:11
Spirit ceaseth to s. with man	26:11
s. to strengthen and fortify our	Al 60:25
ceased to s. with their fathers;	Mrm 5:16
will not always s. with man;	Eth 2:15
shall not always s. with man,	DC 1:33
shall not always s. with man,	Mses 8:17

STRIVEN
hath sincerely s. to do thy will.	DC 109:68

STRIVING
cease s. to take away my life.	1 Ne 7:19
s. to repair all the injuries	Mos 27:35
are s. with unwearied diligence	He 15: 6
had ceased s. with them,	Eth 15:19
Spirit hath ceased s. with them;	Mro 8:28
Lord hath ceased s. with them.	9: 4

STROKE
in wrath with a continual s.,	2 Ne 24: 6
brought death almost at every s.	Al 43:37

STROKES
from the s. of the Lamanites,	Al 43:38

STRONG

let us be s. like unto Moses;	1Ne	4: 2
were s., yea, even like unto the men;		17: 2
of weakenss he shall be made s.,	2Ne	3:13
their words will I make s. in		3:21
that they may follow s. drink,		15:11
of strength to mingle s. drink;		15:22
waters of the river, s. and many,		18: 7
spake thus to me with a s. hand,		18:11
them with his s. cords forever.		26:22
shall stagger but not with s. drink.		27: 4
will be made s. unto them;		33: 4
they shall be sufficiently s.	Jac	5:54
roots thereof should be too s.		5:65
had waxed s. in the land.	Jar	1: 5
being a s. and mighty man,	Om	1:28
sixteen of their s. men might	Mos	7: 2
being a s. and mighty man,		7: 3
people should wax s. in the land,		9:11
Yet they were a s. people, as to		10:11
And behold, we are s., we shall not		12:15
shall divide the spoil with the s.;		14:12
they might wax s. in the Spirit,		18:26
and he being a s. man and an		19: 4
wax s. in love towards Mosiah;		29:40
your faith is s. concerning that,	Al	7:17
they having waxed s. in battle,		9:22
people had waxed s. in iniquity		13:17
and bound them with s. cords,		14: 4
thus they were bound with s. cords,		14:22
s. in the knowledge of the truth;		17: 2
of being bound with s. cords.		20:29
and bound with s. cords,		20:30
should wax s. in wickedness		21: 3
taken and bound with s. cords,		26:29
was a large and a s. man;		46: 3
Moroni was a s. and a mighty		48:11
become s., yea, even to exceed		49:14
and they were s. and high.		50: 3
multiply and were s. in the land.		50:18
Nephites were not sufficiently s.		51:23
with such fury with his s. men,		52:36
a s. wall of timbers and earth,		53: 4
it was s., having been prepared		55:13
city with an exceeding s. force.		55:26
not sufficiently s. to meet them;		56:23
they should not be sufficiently s.		56:24
Now we were not sufficiently s.		56:39
And now behold, we were s.,		57: 6
with our s. force, or with a part		57: 8
or with a part of our s. force,		57: 8
they saw that we were not s.,		58:15
their faith is s. in the prophecies		58:40
live and wax s. in your iniquities		60:31
they became exceeding s.,		62: 6
prepare in haste s. cords and		62:21
by the means of their s. cords		62:23
until they were sufficiently s.,		62:42
and to wax exceeding s. again		62:48
they did wax s. and prosper		62:51
their s. armies should maintain	He	1:26
wax exceedingly s. in the land.		6:12
they sent an army of s. men into		11:28
did still increase and wax s.,		11:32
they began to wax s. in iniquity.		11:36
so s. were their holds and their	3Ne	1:27
and began to wax s. in years,		1:29
began to wax s. in wickedness		2: 3
they should be s. with armor,		3:26
not so s. in number as the		7:11
sufficiently s. to contend with		7:12
the people of Nephi did wax s.,	4Ne	1:10
part of the people did wax s.,		1:40
they did wax s. in the land.	Eth	6:18
and Shule waxed s., and		7: 8
they had become exceeding s.,		9:16
whose faith was so exceeding s.,		12:19
I make weak things become s.		12:27
weakness thou shalt be made s.,		12:37
of s. faith and a firm mind	Mro	7:30
become s. in their perversion;		9:19
down the mighty and s. ones,	DC	1:19
they might be made s.,	DC	1:28
purchase wine neither s. drink		27: 3
be ye s. from henceforth;		38:15
show unto you my s. reasoning.		45:10
shall multiply and wax s.,		45:58
hereafter shall be made s.		50:16
my power shall be made s.,		52:17
will to retain a s. hold in		64:21
be made s. in every place;		66: 8
bring forth their s. reasons		71: 8
among you be s. in the Spirit,		84:106
that he may become s. also.		84:106
will send one mighty and s.,		85: 7
her bands are made s.,		88:94
drinketh wine or s. drink		89: 5
s. drinks are not for the belly,		89: 7
man of God, and of s. faith—		90:22
and plead with her s. ones,		90:36
of Zion should be made s.		96: 1
and their bands made s.,		101:66
then shall thy confidence wax s.		121:45
is an iron yoke, it is a s. band;		123: 8
the little one become a s. nation,		133:58
thou shalt be made s.,		135: 5

STRONGER

even s. than the men of Pachus,	Al	62: 6
did wax s. and stronger in	He	3:35
stronger and s. in their humility,		3:35
did wax s. and stronger in		11:37
stronger and s. in their pride,		11:37
is s. than the cords of death.	DC	121:44
has been growing s. and stronger,		123: 7
has been growing stronger and s.,		123: 7
be made s. than many waters;	Mses	1:25

STRONGEST

yea, a body of their s. men,	Al	49:20
the s. holds of the Lamanites		53: 6
the s. army of the Lamanites;		56:34
the possession of the s. hold	He	1:22
upon my feelings the s.,	DC	128: 1

STRONGHOLD

city became an exceeding s.	Al	53: 5
a s. to retain his prisoners.		53: 6
had become an exceeding s.		55:33

STRONGHOLDS

Moroni did prepare s. against	Al	50: 6
all the s. of the Lamanites		50:11
afforded s. for the Lamanites.		51:27
flatter them out of their s.,		52:19
the Lamanites out of their s.		52:21
an attack upon them in their s.		56:21
decoy them away from their s.		58: 1
and attack them in their s.		58: 2
of their retreats and their s.		58: 6
obtained possession of their s.		58:23
of many cities and of many s.	He	1:27
the wilderness, and their s.,	3Ne	4: 1
and throw down all thy s.;		21:15
which s. did cut them off that	Mrm	5: 4

STRONGLY

all of which were s. fortified	Al	51:27
so s. riveted the creeds of	DC	123: 7

STRUCK

s. with wonder and amazement.	Mos	25: 7
and s. with much fear, saying:	Al	2:23
they were s. with great fear,		14:29
he was s. as if he were dead.		22:18
that thou shalt be s. dumb,		30:49
of God, ye shall be s. dumb,		30:49
words, Korihor was s. dumb,		30:50
I was s. with such great fear		36:11
they were s. with terror.		43:53
that were s. with fear;		44:15
and s. with great fear,		58:29
were s. dumb with amazement.	He	5:25
for he was s. with fear.	Eth	3: 6

STRUGGLE

STRUGGLE
an effectual s. to be made.	Mos	7:18
Nevertheless they would s. with	Mrm	2:14
did s. for their lives without		5: 2
be the last s. of my people,		6: 6

STRUGGLED
| after that he had s. for breath, | Eth | 15:31 |

STRUGGLES
| many s. to destroy them, | Al | 27: 1 |

STRUGGLING
| I was thus s. in the spirit, | En | 1:10 |

STRUGGLINGS
many long s. for my brethren,	En	1:11
at the present our s. were vain		1:14
notwithstanding our many s.,	Mos	7:18

STUBBLE
who do wickedly shall be as s.;	1Ne	22:15
those who must be consumed as s.;		22:23
as the fire devoureth the s.,	2Ne	15:24
for they shall be as s.		26: 4
and they shall be as s.,		26: 6
that do wickedly shall be s.;	3Ne	25: 1
that do wickedly shall be as s.;	DC	29: 9
that do wickedly shall be as s.;		64:24
all that do wickedly, shall be s.;		133:64
do wickedly shall burn as s.;	JS	2:37

STUBBORN
| and so s. were the people of | Al | 50:35 |

STUBBORNNESS
baptized without s. of heart,	Al	32:16
of the s. of the Lamanites;		44:17
because of the s. of those		51:14
thus he put an end to the s.		51:21

STUDIED
| ye have s. and taught iniquity | Mos | 13:11 |
| Coriantumr, having s., himself, | Eth | 13:16 |

STUDY
And now all the s. of Ammon	Mos	21:36
they do s. at this time that they	Al	8:17
you must s. it out in your mind;	DC	9: 8
s. my word which hath gone		11:22
s. my word which shall come		11:22
seek learning, even by s. and		88:118
and s. and learn, and become		90:15
seek learning even by s. and		109: 7
they may seek learning even by s.,		109:14

STUDYING
| to the s. of the scriptures, | DC | 26: 1 |

STUMBLE
an exceeding great many do s.,	1Ne	13:29
and after the Gentiles do s.		13:34
be weary nor s. among them.	2Ne	15:26
And many among them shall s.		18:15
hath done it, that they may s.	Jac	4:14
s. because of my overanxiety		4:18
s. because of the placing of	Eth	12:25
and s. and fall when the storms	DC	90: 5

STUMBLED
| s., because of the greatness of | 2Ne | 26:20 |

STUMBLING
the taking away of their s. blocks—	1Ne	14: 1
not place a s. block in my way—	2Ne	4:33
but for a stone of s.,		18:14
of the greatness of their s. block,		26:20
by the s. of the Jews	Jac	4:15
be as s. block before them.	Mos	7:29
was a great s.-block to those	Al	4:10

STUMBLING-BLOCK: *see STUMBLING and BLOCK.*

STUNG
| for they were s. for the murders | Al | 24:25 |

STUPOR
| in a state of thoughtless s., | Al | 60: 7 |
| shall have a s. of thought | DC | 9: 9 |

SUBDUE
s. all things unto myself—	DC	19: 2
s. all enemies under his feet.		76:61
replenish the earth, and s. it,	Mses	2:28
replenish the earth, and s. it,	Abr	4:28

SUBDUED
that thine enemies may be s.;	DC	65: 6
s. all enemies under his feet,		76:106
kingdoms of the world are s.		103: 7

SUBDUES
| s. all enemies under his feet. | DC | 58:22 |

SUBDUING
| s. the hearts of the children of | DC | 96: 5 |

SUBJECT
become s. unto man in the flesh,	2Ne	9: 5
men might become s. unto him.		9: 5
become s. to that angel who fell		9: 8
s. to all manner of infirmities	Mos	2:11
flesh becoming s. to the Spirit,		15: 5
becoming s. even unto death,		15: 7
for he was s. to king Laman,		24: 9
did that he might s. them to him.	Al	2:10
your mind somewhat on this s.		39:17
or to s. them and bring them		43:29
diseases, to which men were s.		46:40
s. their brethren to the yoke of		49: 7
s. yourselves to be governed by		54:18
We would s. ourselves to		61:12
s. ourselves to our enemies,		61:13
but should be s. unto kings.	3Ne	6:30
whoso would not be s. unto taxes	Eth	10: 6
who s. themselves unto him.	Mro	7:17
behold, they are s. unto him,		7:30
shall become s. unto him,		9:26
s. to the will of the devil,	DC	29:40
for all things are s. unto him,		50:27
the spirits shall be s. unto you.		50:30
be s. to the powers that be,		58:22
all things shall be s. unto me.		63:59
become s. to the law of Moses,		74: 3
shall be s. unto the council		104:76
he shall be s. to the council		104:77
let us become s. unto her laws.		105:32
the s. of baptism for the dead,		127:10
from time to time, on that s.,		127:10
s. of the baptism for the dead,		128: 1
s. seems to occupy my mind,		128: 1
was contemplating this very s.		128: 6
summum bonum of the whole s.		128:11
upon some s. or other—		128:18
and behold what is that s.?		128:18
things to say to you on the s.;		128:25
continue the s. another time.		128:25
was praying earnestly on the s.,		130:13
all things are s. unto them.		132:20
the angels are s. unto them.		132:20
case, in relation to this s.,	Fac	1:12
excitement on the s. of religion.	JS	2: 5
with him on the s. of religion,		2:21
believe in being s. to kings,	AoF	12

SUBJECTED
having s. the flesh to the will of	Mos	15: 2
the devil, who hath s. them,		16:11
s. them according to his will.	Al	12:17
s. to the spirit of the devil,		34:35
s. to go against the Nephites.		47: 6
s. them to the yoke of bondage.		49:26

SUBJECTEST
| who controllest and s. the devil, | DC | 121: 4 |

SUBJECTING

SUBJECTING
s. themselves to the devil. — Mos 16: 3
s. themselves to the yoke of — 21:13
s. them to peace and civilization, — Al 51:22
either to the s. the Nephites to — 54:20

SUBJECTION
when we shall no longer be in s. — Mos 7:18
of bringing this people into s. — 7:22
might bring you into s. unto him, — Al 12: 6
that he might bring them into s. — 43: 7
up in s. to the law of Moses, — DC 74: 4

SUBJECTS
people, and became his s. — Mos 22:13
to become s. to the devil? — Al 5:20
become his s. at the last day; — 34:39
they became s. to follow after — 42: 7
information in relation to many s., — DC 128: 1
this most glorious of all s. — 128:17

SUBMISSIVE
a child, s., meek, humble, patient, — Mos 3:19
humble, and be s. and gentle; — Al 7:23
becoming humble, meek, s., — 13:28

SUBMIT
willing to s. to all things which — Mos 3:19
as a child doth s. to his father. — 3:19
and they did s. cheerfully and — 24:15
ye shall s. to the conditions — Al 44:11
intention to s. to those laws, — DC OD

SUBMITTING
s. themselves to be smitten, — Mos 21:13

SUBSCRIBE
I s. myself your servant in — DC 127:12

SUBSCRIPTION
And an epistle and s., to be — DC 58:51

SUBSIST
s. for the space of seven years, — 3Ne 4: 4
no way that they could s. save — 4: 5
labors, wherewith to s. upon; — 6: 3
they might s. upon the water, — Eth 6: 4

SUBSISTENCE
save it were meat for their s., — 3Ne 4:19

SUBSTANCE
as an oak whose s. is in them — 2Ne 16:13
holy seed shall be the s. thereof. — 16:13
and free with your s., — Jac 2:17
administer of your s. unto him — Mos 4:16
nor impart unto him of my s. — 4:17
for all the s. which we have, — 4:19
to impart of the s. that ye have — 4:21
up his petition to you for your s. — 4:22
for withholding your s., — 4:22
for his s. shall perish with him; — 4:23
impart of your s. to the poor, — 4:26
church should impart of their s., — 18:27
they should impart of their s. — 18:28
And they did impart of their s., — Al 1:27
imparting their s. to the poor — 4:13
withholding your s. from them? — 5:55
will give us a portion of their s. — 27:24
afflicted, and impart of your s., — 34:28
a large portion of their s. to — 43:13
ye will give unto him of your s.; — He 13:28
and partners of all our s. — 3Ne 3: 7
and their herds, and all their s., — 3:13
and their grain, and all their s., — 3:22
and their herds and all their s., — 4: 3
and their s. unto the Lord of — 20:19
s. no more common among — 4Ne 1:25
do love money, and your s., — Mrm 8:37
and whose s. is that of an idol, — DC 1:16
impart of your s. unto the poor, — 42:31
not give your s. to the poor, — 56:16
and do not impart of their s., — 105: 3

we have given of our s. — DC 109: 5
our s. that we had gathered, — Abr 2:15

SUBTLE
that thy plan was a very s. plan, — Al 12: 4
being a very s. man to do evil — 47: 4
by the s. craftiness of men, — DC 123:12
now the serpent was more s. — Mses 4: 5

SUBTLETY
people, full of mischief and s., — 2Ne 5:24
plan, as to the s. of the devil, — Al 12: 4

SUCCEED
s. with his armies in obtaining — He 4: 9

SUCCEEDED
they s. with those others in — He 4: 4
they s. in obtaining possession — 4: 5
s. in regaining even the half of — 4:10

SUCCESS
much s. in bringing many to the — Al 17: 4
thus they began to have great s. — 23: 4
the s. which they had had among — 25:17
and I will give unto you s. — 26:27
and hath given me much s., — 29:13
I do not joy in my own s. alone, — 29:14
of the s. of my brethren, — 29:14
when I think of the s. of these — 29:16
here he did not have much s., — 30:21
even until I had much s., — 30:53
my soul, and give unto me s., — 31:32
have s. in bringing them again — 31:34
s. among the poor class of people; — 32: 2
ye may have s. in obtaining — 58:41
s. which Helaman had had, — 59: 1
of the s. of the Lamanites — 59:12
without s. in our undertaking, — JS 2:56

SUCCESSION
in s. to number twelve. — DC 102:12

SUCCESSORS
unto you, and unto your s., — DC 82:20
their regularly appointed s. — 102: 6

SUCCOR
will s. those that stand in need — Mos 4:16
that stand in need of your s.; — 4:16
I will not s. my people in the — 7:29
who stood in need of their s., — Al 4:13
how to s. his people — 7:12
began to lose all hopes of s.; — 57:12
sufficient strength and s. for them. — 60: 5
to s. them who are tempted. — DC 62: 1
s. the weak, lift up the hands — 81: 5

SUCCORED
that ye might have s. them, — Al 60: 8

SUCCORING
s. those who stood in need of — Al 4:13

SUCH
s. as: great and marvelous — 1Ne 1:14
maketh no s. thing known unto us. — 15: 9
if the Lord has s. great power, — 17:51
not be s. as was in her vexation, — 2Ne 19: 1
and s. as are escaped of the house — 20:20
s. as like unto David of old — Jac 1:15
s. things are abominable unto him — 2:21
no man knoweth of s. things; — 7: 7
miracles, s. as healing the sick, — Mos 3: 5
For salvation cometh to none s. — 3:12
causeth s. exceeding great joy — 4:11
s. as feeding the hungry, — 4:26
with s. exceeding great joy. — 5: 4
of unfolding all s. mysteries — 8:19
s. as were lifted up in the pride — 11: 5
upon my people s. great affliction? — 11:27
for the Lord redeemeth none s. — 15:26
For salvation cometh to none s.; — 15:27

SUCH   932   SUCKING

the Lord hath redeemed none s.;	Mos	15:27	s. as the wearing of costly	4Ne 1:24
neither can the Lord redeem s.;		15:27	before them with s. firmness	Mrm 2:25
had caused s. a great destruction		21:20	s. an awful scene of blood and	5: 8
he could interpret s. engravings;		21:28	I know that s. will sorrow for	5:11
had not any s. thing happened		26:10	for the Lord will uphold s. at	8:31
brethren, for I esteem you as s.,		29: 5	wo unto s. for they are in the	8:31
that s. abominations should come		29:24	with s. exceeding faith as thou	Eth 3: 9
of the law, for s. were punished;	Al	1:18	help s. as sought power to	8:16
s. things much be established		2: 3	uphold s. secret combinations,	8:22
s. as imparting their substance to		4:13	for upon s., saith the Lord:	9:20
that s. an one can have a place		5:24	s. things which had been restored	10:12
suppose that s. can have place		5:25	s. an one as never had been	11: 6
s. an one hath not eternal life.		5:28	s. an one as never had been	11: 7
that s. an one is not prepared;		5:29	for God receiveth none s.	Mro 7: 9
s. an one is not found guiltless.		5:29	Wo unto s., for they are in	8:21
Wo unto s. an one, for he is not		5:31	and unto s. baptism availeth	8:22
believe in s. foolish traditions.		8:11	he shall have no s. views,	DC 5:28
God could do s. marvelous works,		9: 5	you shall have no s. feelings,	9: 9
of s. great and marvelous things?		9: 6	s. are not exempt from the	10:28
been s. a highly favored people		9:20	s. shall inherit the kingdom of	10:55
s. great hold upon your hearts?		10:25	strength s. as is not known	24:12
yieldeth to no s. temptations?		11:23	on the land, s. as is required,	26: 1
for on s. the plan of redemption		12:32	a blessing s. as is not known	39:15
a preparatory redemption for s.		13: 3	s. as he shall appoint or has	42:31
for s. as would not harden their		13: 5	s. as shall be sufficient to	42:67
s. things did the people testify		14: 5	receive none s. among you if	42:76
If ye have s. great power why		14:20	unto s. as God shall appoint	46:27
And many s. things did they say		14:21	behold s. shall be reclaimed;	50: 7
And many s. things, yea, all		14:22	But wo unto s., for their reward	58:33
all manner of s. things did they say		14:22	Wo unto s., for mine anger is	60: 2
s. as hunger, thirst and fatigue,		17: 5	there have been s. even from	63: 8
doth send s. great punishments		18: 2	unto s. he showeth no signs,	63:11
that a man has s. great power,		18: 3	Let s. beware and repent	63:15
this man that has s. great power?		18: 8	s. may receive a more exceeding	63:66
had infused s. joy into his soul,		19: 6	let all s. as can obtain places	75:26
there has not been s. great faith		19:10	say unto you, blessed are s.,	97: 2
that thou knowest any s. thing.		21: 8	to preside over s. council for	102:25
unto us s. great glessings?		26: 1	as though no s. decision had	102:27
unto s. it is given to know the		26:22	be sufficient to call s. council.	102:28
unto s. it shall be given to		26:22	is necessary to call s. a council	102:29
it shall be given unto s. to bring		26:22	determine whether any s. case,	102:33
even s. an one as never had been		28: 2	was s. a great high priest.	107: 2
yourselves with s. foolish things?		30:13	s. a one as my servant Joseph shall	124:22
s. things did he say unto them,		30:17	s. are they also that are earthy;	128:14
causes s. joy in their hearts?		30:35	s. are they also that are heavenly.	128:14
to behold s. gross wickedness		31:26	no s. thing as immaterial matter.	131: 7
that s. wickedness and iniquity		31:30	except s. laws are framed and	134: 2
s. wickedness among this people		31:30	s. as will administer the law in	134: 3
s. great fear and amazement		36:11	by the laws of s. governments;	134: 5
them to abhor s. wickedness		37:29	have a right to enact s. laws as	134: 5
for s. shall find rest to their souls.		37:34	rulers and magistrates as s.,	134: 6
not prepared with any s. thing;		43:20	and s. religious opinions do not	134: 7
with s. exceeding great strength		43:43	and regulations of s. societies;	134:10
destroy all s. as should attempt		49:19	provided that s. dealings be for	134:10
for s. contentions to be among		51: 9	where s. laws exist as will protect	134:11
to put an end to s. contentions		51:16	s. interference we believe to be	134:12
upon their rear with s. fury		52:36	that forty or more s. marriages	OD
to receive s. murderers as thou		54: 7	appeared to convey any s. teaching,	OD
behold, we know not s. a being;		54:21	the father of s. as dwell in tents,	Mses 5:45
so be that there is s. a thing,		54:21	s. as handle the harp and organ.	5:45
that he hath done s. a place?		54:22	s. as was had among the	Abr 1:13
with s. miraculous strength;		56:56	s. as was not before sent	JS 1:18
with s. mighty power did they		56:56	in s. an hour as ye think not	1:48
s. as rebellions and dissensions,		61:14	so far as I have s. facts in	2: 1
with s. exceedingly great speed	He	1:19	that I had made s. an attempt,	2:14
s. great power and authority,		5:18	s. an astonishing influence	2:15
a state of s. awful wickedness,		7: 4	had s. marvelous power as	2:16
God gave unto this man s. power,		8:12	were no s. things as visions or	2:21
who had s. great power given		8:13	all s. things had ceased with	2:21
to prophesy s. marvelous things		9: 2	my circumstances in life s. as	2:22
this with s. unweariedness,		10: 5	A disposition to commit s. was	2:28
s. an one as ye never have		14: 5	received s. strict charges to	2:60
s. a being as a Christ shall come;		16:18	of s. of them as had been	2:64
all s. as should come unto them	3Ne	7:25	no s. thing now as ministering	2:65
s. an one as never had been		8: 5		
s. as never had been known in		8: 7	**SUCK**	
of s. is the kingdom of God.		9:22	plenty of s. for their children,	1Ne 17: 2
for s. I have laid down my		9:22	the day that they shall give s.;	He 15: 2
s. things should be done away.		11:30	them that give s. in those days;	JS 1:16
of hell stand open to receive s.		11:40		
unto s. shall ye continue to		18:32	**SUCKING**	
s. as they have not heard.		21:21	can a woman forget her s. child,	1Ne 21:15

SUCKING

And the s. child shall play on the	2Ne 21: 8
And the s. child shall play on the	30:14

SUCKLING

beasts as a child with a s. lamb,	3Ne 28:22

SUCKLINGS

be revealed unto babes and s.	DC 128:18

SUDDEN

lest s. destruction shall come	DC 133:15
were doomed to s. destruction.	JS 2:15

SUDDENLY

I did show them s.	1Ne 20: 3
It shall be at an instant, s.—	2Ne 26:18
shall s. come to his temple,	3Ne 24: 1
I will s. come to my temple.	DC 36: 8
Lord who shall s. come to	133: 2
by a whirlwind, in an instant, s.	Abr 2: 7
I s. discovered that my room	JS 2:44

SUE

until they shall s. for peace.	Al 55: 3
any man will s. thee at the law	3Ne 12:40
I say unto you, s. for peace,	DC 105:38

SUFFER

thou wilt not s. those who come	1Ne 1:14
God will not s. that the Gentiles	13:30
Neither will he s. that	13:31
Neither will the Lord God s. that	13:32
they did s. much for the want of	16:19
but I would not s. them, saying:	17:55
the Lord did s. it that he might	18:11
for I will not s. my name to be	20:11
for he will not s. that the wicked	22:16
lest he shall s. again;	2Ne 1:25
God will not s. that ye shall perish;	4: 7
not s. the laborer in Zion to perish.	26:30
not s. that ye should suppose that	30: 1
and s. his cross and bear the	Jac 1: 8
God will not s. that this people	2:26
And I will not s., saith the Lord	2:32
For the Lord would not s., after	Om 1: 6
he would not s. that the words	1: 6
And lo, he shall s. temptations,	Mos 3: 7
even more than man can s.,	3: 7
ye will not s. your children that	4:14
neither will ye s. that they	4:14
ye will not s. that the beggar	4:16
my substance that he may not s.,	4:17
he will not even s. that he shall	5:14
and how long doth he s. with his	8:20
and I will s. them that they be	11:24
God will not s. that I shall be	13: 3
but s. that he might depart	17: 2
and I will s. even until death,	17:10
s. even the pains of death by fire;	17:15
then ye shall s., as I suffer,	17:18
as I s., the pains of death by fire.	17:18
s., even unto death by fire.	19:20
that they did not s. with hunger.	21:16
ye s. no ravenous wolf to enter	Al 5:60
For he will not s. you that ye	9:19
rather s. that the Lamanites	9:19
the Lord did not s. them that they	9:33
may not s. the second death.	13:30
he doth s. that they may do	14:11
How long shall we s. these great	14:26
they did s. much, both in body	17: 5
s. that my son Lamoni should	20:26
would not s. that Ammon should	21:19
I will not s. that ye shall be	22: 3
would not s. their afflictions	22:34
and would s. even unto death	24:19
that he should s. death by fire.	25: 9
many should s. death by fire,	25:11
not s. themselves to be slain.	26:34
they would s. death in the most	27:29
wilt thou s. that thy servants	31:26
how long wilt thou s. that such	31:30
that I may s. with patience these	31:31
should s. no manner of afflictions,	Al 31:38
s. and die to atone for their s.;	33:22
S. not yourself to be led away	39:11
s. not the devil to lead away your	39:11
not s. that they should be	43:12
not s. yourselves to be slain by	43:46
s. that we shall be destroyed	44: 4
not s. ourselves to take an oath	44: 8
s. that we may depart into	44: 8
Surely God shall not s. that we,	46:18
would s. them to fall in with	47:15
not s. to lay down their lives,	48:24
nor s. the law to be altered;	51: 3
not s. the Lamanites to go	51:25
not s. them that they should	56: 8
that we should not s. more	56: 8
not s. that my little sons should	56:39
will not s. that we should fall;	56:46
s. their whole army, save a few	58:22
s. all manner of afflictions,	60:17
the Lord will not s. that ye	60:31
will not s. that we should perish	60:35
and they did s. whatsoever tree	He 3: 9
people to s. great persecutions,	3:34
should not s. for their murders,	6:21
Why do you s. this man to revile	8: 5
the Lord your God will s. you	9:21
do not s. that this people shall	11: 4
not s. that he should enter into	13: 4
and shall s. many things and shall	13: 6
I will s. them no longer,	13: 8
do that and ye shall not s.;	13:27
suppose that the Lord will s. you?	13:29
how long will ye s. yourselves to be	13:29
shall s. yourselves to come under	14:19
that day that he shall s. death	14:20
the time that he shall s. death,	14:20
they will s. themselves that they	15: 9
that ye s. none of these things	3Ne 12:29
And I will not s. my people,	16:14
I will s. them, yea, I will	16:15
I will s. my people, O house of	16:15
s. them that they may come	18:22
not s. any one knowingly to	18:28
might not s. pain nor sorrow	28:38
not always s. them to take	Mrm 2:13
s. the records which had been	6: 6
how long the Lord will s. that	8: 5
the Lord would not s. them to	8:10
the Lord should s. to bring	8:25
s. the hungry, and the needy,	8:39
will not s. their cries any longer.	8:41
the Lord would not s. that they	Eth 2: 7
and when thou shalt s. for air	2:20
wilt thou s. that we shall cross	2:22
s. not that they shall go forth	3: 3
thou shalt not s. these things	3:21
S. them that they may have a	6:24
the Lord will not s. that the	8:22
s. not that these murderous	8:23
if ye shall s. these things to be.	8:23
that I s. the will of the Lord	15:34
I will not s. that Satan shall	DC 10:14
I will not s. that they shall	10:43
every man must repent or s.,	19: 4
not s. if they would repent;	19:16
repent they must s. even as I;	19:17
to s. both body and spirit—	19:18
lest you s. these punishments	19:20
relief that they shall not s.;	38:35
not s. that ye should part until	61: 8
doomed to s. the wrath of God,	76:33
they who s. the wrath of God	76:104
they who s. the vengeance	76:105
s. the wrath of Almighty God,	76:106
shall not s. that mine house	88:134
shall not s. any unclean thing	94: 8
do not s. any unclean thing	97:15
all they who s. persecution for	101:35
not s. his house to be broken	104:86
by the things which they s.	105: 6
wilt thou s. this people to bear	109:49
O Lord, how long shall they s.	121: 3

SUFFER 934 SUFFICE

and love to have others s., DC 121:13
not s. any pollution to come 124:24
weep, seeing these shall s.? Mses 7:37

SUFFERED
we have s. much affliction, 1Ne 16:35
we had s. many afflictions 17: 6
s. that we should make much fire, 17:12
s. all things, save it were death; 17:20
than to have s. these afflictions. 17:20
these many years we have s. in 17:21
and having s. much grief 18:17
s. much sorrow because of you. 2Ne 1:24
thou hast s. afflictions 2: 1
and shall not be s. to perish, 6:11
we must have s. in ignorance, Mos 1: 3
s. by the hand of the Lord that 2:11
as I have been s. to spend my 2:12
Neither have I s. that ye should be 2:13
nor even have I s. that ye should 2:13
hath s. me that I should speak 2:30
he s. that ye have begged in vain? 4:20
I s. that ye should be preserved 7:11
ye would not have s. that I should 7:13
for they had s. many things; 7:16
they had s. hunger, thirst, and 7:16
the Lord would not have s. that 7:25
s. these many years in the land. 10:18
I have s. myself that I have 17: 9
he fell, having s. death by fire; 17:20
and s. in the like manner; 21:12
they s. much anguish of soul 28: 4
he s. an ignominious death. Al 1:15
whosoever s. himself to be led 3:10
after they had thus s. for many 14:23
he had s. that the Nephite should 19:19
they also had s. hunger, thirst, 20:29
cast into prison s. many things, 21:14
and thus they had s. 21:15
after having s. much loss and 25: 6
the first that s. death by fire 25:11
by fire, according as he had s. 25:11
and we have s. every privation; 26:28
have s. all manner of afflictions, 26:30
they s. themselves to be slain 27: 3
they s. to depart into the 44:15
they were s. to depart into 44:20
s. themselves to have fallen into 53:11
thus they had s. great afflictions 56:16
we had s. great loss. 57:23
have s. exceeding great sufferings; 60: 3
behold, were this all we had s. 60: 4
that we have s. so much loss. 60:28
s. very many exceedingly sore 62:37
pride which ye have s. to enter He 7:26
and s. death by the people. 3Ne 7:19
I have s. the will of the Father 11:11
or no food until he had s. death. Eth 9: 7
the brother of him that s. death, 9: 8
thou hast s. the counsel of thy DC 3:15
the Lord has s. to destroy their 3:18
Redeemer s. death in the flesh; 18:11
he s. the pain of all men, 18:11
God, have s. these things for all, 19:16
He s. temptations but gave no 20:22
I s. it that ye might bear 61: 4
and s. themselves through 76:31
I s. them not to have purse or 84:78
the Lord, have s. you to come 100: 4
have s. the affliction to come 101: 2
which I have s. to be established, 101:77
For I have s. them thus far, 103: 3
which they have s. these things. 109:31
not have s. his house to have JS 1:47

SUFFERETH
they scourge him, and he s. it; 1Ne 19: 9
they smite him, and he s. it. 19: 9
they spit upon him, and he s. it, 19: 9
he s. himself to become subject 2Ne 9: 5
he s. the pains of all men, 9:21

he s. this that the resurrection 2Ne 9:22
s. temptation, and yieldeth not Mos 15: 5
but s. himself to be mocked, 15: 5
nevertheless the Son of God s. Al 7:13
the Lord s. the righteous to 60:13
s. himself to be led into 3Ne 18:25
And charity s. long, and is Mro 7:45
Wherefore, he s. for their sins, Mses 7:39

SUFFERING
his long s. towards the children of 1Ne 19: 9
exhorting with all long-s. Jar 1:11
his patience, and his long-s. Mos 4: 6
and long s. towards you, 4:11
driven back again, s. much loss. 21:11
s. all manner of afflictions, 26:38
and exhorting them with long-s. 27:33
s. much and fearing that they 28: 4
every man s. according to Al 1:33
and s. all manner of afflictions, 4:13
mercy and long-s. towards them? 5: 6
s. pains and afflictions and 7:11
full of patience and long-s.; 7:23
and his long s. towards us, 9:11
of patience, mercy, and long-s., 9:26
full of love and all long-s.; 13:28
yet ye shall be patient in long-s. 17:11
and of his long-s. towards them 26:16
and patience, and long-s., 32:43
thy patience and thy long-s. 38: 3
and his long-s. have full sway 42:30
their own lands, s. great loss. 63:15
and the long-s. of the Lord, Mrm 2:12
the s. of our women and our Mro 9:19
and his mercy and long-s., 9:25
Which s. caused myself, even DC 19:18
meekness and long s., 107:30
and humility, and long-s., 118: 3
Remember thy s. saints, 121: 6
by persuasion, by long-s., 121:41
s. severe persecution at the JS 2:27

SUFFERINGS
The account of their s. 1Ne 1:hd
Their s. and afflictions in the 1:hd
because of their s. and afflictions 16:20
and after all these s. we must 16:35
and s., and death of Christ, Mos 18: 2
Son of God, his s. and death, Al 16:19
their s. and deliverance— 17:hd
their s. with hunger and thirst, 18:37
they were patient in all their s. 20:29
through the death and s. of Christ, 21: 9
but the s. and death of Christ 22:14
we have been patient in our s., 26:28
their s. in the land, their sorrows, 28: 8
have s. exceeding great s.; 60: 3
all their cries, and all their s.— 60:10
testify boldly of his death and s. 3Ne 6:20
concerning the s. of this people. Mro 9: 7
and may his s. and death, 9:25
my anger, and your s. be sore— DC 19:15
the s. and death of him who 45: 4
the s. of those with whom he 76:30
Lord, after the s. of his wrath. 76:38
vision of the s. of the ungodly. 76:49
reap eternal joy for all our s. 109:76
s. and abuses put upon them 123: 1

SUFFERS
to exclaim: The God of nature s. 1Ne 19:12

SUFFICE
what I have said may s. Al 13:20
will s. for the sins of the world. 34:12
And it may s. if I only say 37:12
let it s., that I say that 40:19
a part of them would not s., 3Ne 7:17
this shall s. for thy daily walk, DC 19:32
therefore let this s., and 130:15
this s. for the present, 132:66

SUFFICETH

SUFFICETH
For it s. me to say that	1 Ne	6: 2
which I have written s. me;		14:28
But it s. me to say,	2 Ne	5: 4
And it s. me to say that		5:34
things which I have written s. me.		11: 1
things which I have written s. me,		31: 2
and this s. me.	Jar	1: 2
and it s. me to know that	Al	40: 5
it s. me that I tell you that		56: 5
it s. me to say that Jesus showed	Eth	3:17

SUFFICIENCY
if there is not a s. written	DC	102:23

SUFFICIENT
s. to teach any man the right way;	2 Ne	25:28
that which is s. is written.	Om	1:11
ye who have not and yet have s.,	Mos	4:24
he did not send a s. number,		11:17
a s. army to drive them out	Al	16: 3
s. to take the city of Antiparah		57: 2
more than s. for our own people,		57:15
s. strength and succor for them.		60: 5
with a s. quantity of food,		62:13
that they had not kept s. guards	He	1:18
S. is the day unto the evil	3 Ne	13:34
for I see that your faith is s.		17: 8
not dig pits s. to hold them.		28:20
s. to behold the ways of man.	Mrm	2:18
and my grace is s. for the meek,	Eth	12:26
my grace is s. for all men that		12:27
s. strength that they could wask,		15:28
that have obtained a s. hope by	Mro	7: 3
then is my grace s. for you,		10:32
servant Joseph s. strength,	DC	9:12
for my grace is s. for you,		17: 8
Behold, my grace is s. for you;		18:31
to have a s. time to expound		20:68
is s. for himself and family.		42:32
shall be s. to establish you,		42:67
Behold, this is s. for you,		60:16
even now already in store s.,		101:75
to be s. to call such council.		102:28
I grant unto you a s. time		124:31
after you have had s. time		124:33
It is s. to know, in this case,		128:18
chose out a s. number of		136: 7
s. to excite the public mind	JS	2:22
a character of s. importance		2:23

SUFFICIENTLY
And men are instructed s. that	2 Ne	2: 5
when they shall be s. strong	Jac	5:54
you s. retained in remembrance	Al	5: 6
you s. retained in remembrance		5: 6
ye s. retained in remembrance		5: 6
that ye have been s. humble?		5:27
themselves were s. hardened,		21: 3
do to repent s. before God		24:11
the Nephites were not s. strong		51:23
not s. strong to meet them;		56:23
lest they should not be s. strong		56:24
not s. strong to contend with		56:39
until they were s. strong,		62:42
to build a tower s. high that	He	6:28
to lay siege s. long to have	3 Ne	4:18
become s. strong to contend		7:12
our plates had been s. large	Mrm	9:33
humbled themselves s. before	Eth	9:35
humble himself s. before me;	DC	5:24
he is not s. meek before me.		58:41
until he is s. chastened for		58:60
for ye are not s. humble,		67:10
s. plain to suit my purpose		128:18

SUGGEST
s. for your consideration	DC	123: 1

SUIT
any of you a coat, or a s.,	DC	84:105
sufficiently plain to s. my purpose		128:18

SUITABLE
it shall be s. to your circumstances.	DC	48: 1

SUITING
s. his mercies according to	DC	46:15

SUITS
The changeable s. of apparel,	2 Ne	13:22
to the s. which were brought	Al	11:20

SUM
the s. which he requires to	DC	104:73

SUMMER
even now already s. is nigh.	DC	35:16
think not the s. shall be past,		45: 2
that s. is now nigh at hand;		45:37
harvest is past, the s. is ended,		56:16
this following s.;		115: 9
know that s. is nigh at hand;	JS	1:38

SUMMER'S
I am calm as a s. morning;	DC	135: 4

SUMMUM
the *s. bonum* of the whole subject	DC	128:11

SUN
above that of the s. at noon-day.	1 Ne	1: 9
shall the heat nor the s. smite them;		21:10
the s. shall be darkened in her	2 Ne	23:10
when the heat of the s. cometh	Al	32:38
unto man that the s. standeth still;	He	12:15
earth that moveth and not the s.		12:15
shall know of the rising of the s.		14: 4
the s. shall be darkened and		14:20
at the going down of the s.	3 Ne	1:15
the s. did rise in the morning		1:19
neither the s., nor the moon,		8:22
maketh his s. to rise on the evil		12:45
even as a dew before the s.	Mrm	4:18
the going down of the s.,	Eth	12: 3
as the moon, and fair as the s.,	DC	5:14
come the s. shall be darkened,		29:14
the s. shall be darkened, and		34: 9
the s. shall be darkened,		45:42
whose glory is that of the s.,		76:70
the s. of the firmament is		76:70
the moon differs from the s.		76:71
as the moon differs from the s.		76:78
as the glory of the s. is one,		76:96
As also he in the s.,		88: 7
the s., and the light of the s.,		88: 7
the s. giveth his light by day,		88:45
and the s. shall hide his face,		88:87
may become fair as the s..		105:31
fair as the moon, clear as the s.,		109:73
above the brightness of the s.;		110: 3
the burning rays of the rising s.;		121:11
or to the s., moon, or stars—		121:30
And let the s., moon, and the		128:23
the s. shall hide his face in shame,		133:49
the greater light was the s.,	Mses	2:16
And the s. to rule over the day,		2:18
the god of Shagreel was the s.	Abr	1: 9
this is Shinehah, which is the s.		3:13
the Egyptians to be the S.,	Fac	2: 5
Earth and the S. in their		2: 5
the s. shall be darkened,	JS	1:33
above the brightness of the s.,		2:16

SUNDRY
at s. times, and in divers places	DC	128:21

SUNK
many cities that they were s.;	1 Ne	12: 4
s. deep into my heart.	En	1: 3
and he s. again with joy;	Al	19:13
and the queen also s. down,		19:13
all three had s. to the earth.		19:14
great and notable cities were s.,	3 Ne	8:14
Moroni have I caused to be s.		9: 4

SUNK

of Gilgal have I caused to be s., 3Ne 9: 6
all these have I caused to be s., 9: 8
they were spared and were not s. 10:13
many cities which had been s., 4Ne 1: 9

SUPPER
a s. of the house of the Lord, DC 58: 9
partake of the s. of the Lord, 58:11
prepare ye the s. of the Lamb, 65: 3

SUPPLANTED
be s. by anarchy and terror; DC 134: 6

SUPPLICATE
and did s. him for protection; 3Ne 4:10
to exhort, or to pray, or to s., Mro 6: 9

SUPPLICATING
continued in the s. of his grace, Al 7: 3

SUPPLICATION
prayer and s. for mine own soul; En 1: 4
prayer and s. to God daily, Al 31:10
call on the Lord thy God with s., DC 136:29
and s. to Almighty God for JS 2:29

SUPPLIED
be amply s. and receive DC 42:33

SUPPLIES
and also new s. of provisions. Al 55:34

SUPPLY
we received a s. of provisions, Al 57: 6
to receive a s. of provisions. 57: 8
a new s. of provisions and also 57:17
also a new s. of provisions. 58: 3
appointed to s. the place of those DC 118: 1

SUPPORT
My God hath been my s.; 2Ne 4:20
but the Lord God doth s. me, Mos 2:30
all this did he take to s. himself, 11: 4
labor exceedingly to s. iniquity. 11: 6
with their own hands for their s. 18:24
upon the people for their s.; 18:26
and he did s. his guards out of 19:28
impart to the s. of the widows 21:17
with their own hands for their s. 27: 4
with their own hands for their s., 27: 5
to s. him and give him money. Al 1: 5
with mine own hands for my s., 30:32
to house, begging food for his s. 30:58
the devil will not s. his children 30:60
and cry unto God for all thy s.; 37:36
Nephites was to s. their lands, 43: 9
substance to s. their armies; 43:13
s., and keep, and preserve us, 44: 4
the sacred s. which we owe to 44: 5
that if they would s. him and 46: 5
to s. the cause of freedom, 46:35
preparing to s. their liberty, 48:10
s. and maintain the cause of 50:39
and s. the cause of liberty. 51:17
period of time also a great s.; 53:19
to the s. of the people in the 53:22
the s. of the Lamanite prisoners 54: 2
for the s. of his own people; 54: 2
and provisions arrive for our s., 56:29
being cut off from their s. 57:11
Ammoron had sent to their s. 57:17
for the s. of our people. 58:10
should cut them off from their s. 58:15
from us, which was for our s. 58:41
may s. those parts of our country 60:24
unto them food for their s., 60:25
did build them up and s. them, He 6:38
labor continually for their s.; Eth 10: 6
all save the s. of thy family. DC 19:34
and they shall s. thee; 24: 3
for thy husband shall s. thee 25: 9
of thy properties for their s. 42:30
than is necessary for their s. 42:33

SUPPOSE

that which would be for thy s., DC 42:55
bishop, also, shall receive his s., 42:73
to s. the families of those 75:24
s. of the church for them, 75:26
his stewardship, for his s. 104:20
for his father, for his s.; 104:45
s. the cause of the poor, 124:89
if it must needs be, for their s., 124:122

SUPPORTED
they were s. in their laziness, Mos 11: 6
ought to be s. by the people. Al 1: 3
shall be s. in their trials, 36: 3
And I have been s. under trials 36:27
s. by those who sought power 51: 8
and the Lord has s. them, 58:39
were s. by the hand of a god, 3Ne 3: 2
s. you against all the fiery darts DC 3: 8
are to have their families s. 42:71
s. and urged on and upheld by 123: 7

SUPPORTING
even s. you from one moment to Mos 2:21
in s. the families of those, DC 75:24
s. that principle of freedom 98: 5

SUPPOSE
for I have reason to s. that they, 1Ne 8: 3
do ye s. that they would have been 17:24
do ye s. that the children of 17:33
do ye s. that they were righteous? 17:33
Do ye s. that our fathers would 17:34
ye need not s. that I and my 22:31
needs s. that an angel of God, 2Ne 2:17
ye need not s. that I cannot speak 29: 9
ye need not s. that it contains 29:10
neither need ye s. that I have not 29:10
s. that ye are more righteous than 30: 1
ye need not s. that the Gentiles 30: 1
I s. that ye ponder somewhat in 32: 1
because ye s. that ye are Jac 2:13
do ye s. that God justifieth you 2:14
Do ye not s. that such things 2:21
do ye s. that such an one can Al 5:24
or s. that he is a liar 5:25
ye cannot s. that such can have 5:25
Do you not s. that I know of 5:45
how do ye s. that I know of 5:45
S. ye that we shall believe the 9: 2
they did not s. that salvation came 25:16
Do ye s. that ye can bring the 26:24
Do ye s. that ye can convince 26:24
do ye s. that ye cannot worship 32:10
Do ye s. that ye must not 32:11
do ye not s. that they are more 32:14
that ye should s. that I mean 32:24
if ye s. that ye cannot worship 33: 2
if ye s. that they have taught 33: 2
do not s. that this is all; 34:28
may s. that this is foolishness 37: 6
we do not s. that this first 40:17
Ye cannot s. that this is what 40:17
Do not s., because it has been 41:10
for ye do try to s. that it is 42: 1
What, do ye s. that mercy can 42:25
they did not s. that the armies 43:22
we s. that he has also received 45:19
in him, as we must needs s. 46:41
And we s. that they are now 56:12
you may well s. that this 56:17
as we s., it was their intent 56:37
we should s. ourselves unwise, 57: 2
could ye s. that ye could sit 60:11
Do ye s. that, because so many 60:12
ye need not s. that the righteous 60:13
Or do ye s. that the Lord will 60:21
Do ye s. that God will look 60:23
can you s. that the Lord will 60:32
we s. that they were drowned 63: 8
did s. that he should accomplish He 2: 9
reason to s. hath been given to 5: 8
how long will ye s. that the 13:29
which ye s. to be your right 3Ne 3: 2

SUPPOSE 937 SURELY

to s. that ye can stand against	3Ne 3: 3
they did s. that if they should	4:16
do ye s. that ye can get rid	28:35
ye need not s. that ye can	29: 9
Do ye s. that ye shall dwell	Mrm 9: 3
Do ye s. that ye could be	9: 3
as I s. that the first part of	Eth 1: 3
to s. that God saveth one child	Mro 8:15
you need not s. that you are	DC 11:15
he shall not s. that he can say	24:10
get a little authority, as they s.,	121:39
no one need s. me guilty of	JS 2:28

SUPPOSED
he s. me to be his master, Laban,	1Ne 4:21
for they s. it was Laban,	4:28
she had s. that we had perished	5: 2
s. it to be the land of Zarahemla,	Mos 21:26
for he s. that Alma and Amulek	Al 15: 3
he s. that they had been slain	15: 3
they s. that great was the work	17:13
for they s. that one of their men	17:35
they s. that whatsoever they did	18: 5
for could we have s. when we	26: 1
Who could have s. that our God	26:17
and we s. that our joy would be	26:30
he s. that Amalickiah had	47:21
they s. that it would again	49: 3
leaders of the Lamanites had s.,	49: 6
they s. that they should be	49: 6
they s. that they should easily	49: 7
he had s. that they would be	49:15
We s. that we could overpower	56:23
s. that the Nephites were weary	58:25
Moroni had s. that there	59: 9
he s. that they would easily	59: 9
if ye have s. this ye have	60:11
supposed this ye have s. in vain.	60:11
if ye have s. this ye have	60:12
supposed this ye have s. in vain;	60:12
had s. that the Lamanites	He 1:18
For behold, Moronihah had s. that	1:26
they had s. that the Nephites	3Ne 4: 9
they s. it had been the Gentiles;	15:22
I had s. not to have written	Mro 1: 1
contrary to that which I had s.;	1: 4
I had s. not to have written	1: 4
you have s. that I would	DC 9: 7
which thing I never had s.	Mses 1:10
if they s. me to be deluded	JS 2:28

SUPPOSETH
he that s. that they are not,	2Ne 25: 8
And it s. me that they have	Jac 2: 8
and it s. me that he will witness	WM 1: 2
it s. me that I talk to you	Al 54:11
s. me that thou art a child of hell;	54:11
which maintenance he s. will	61: 8
he that s. that little children	Mro 8:14
he s. that another lieth to	DC 10:28

SUPPOSING
he, s. that I spake of the	1Ne 4:26
s. they know of themselves,	2Ne 9:28
s. them to be priests of Noah	Mos 21:23
will ye persist in s. that ye are	Al 5:54
and s. that this opportunity,	19:17
s. that they were coming to	47: 5
s. that to be the next best place	49:12
s. by their numbers to	52:23
s. that God would strengthen us,	56: 8
s. that they could easily destroy	58:15
s. that they had driven their	58:25
s. that Coriantumr, being a	He 1:16
s. that their greatest strength was	1:24
s. that he would be merciful	Mrm 2:12

SUPRESS
never s. the freedom of the soul.	DC 134: 4

SUPREME
the existence of a S. Being.	Al 11:22
to the s. goodness of God.	12:32

witness that there is a S. Creator.	Al 30:44
the name of the S. Being,	DC 107: 4

SURE
I am s. of the fulfilling of this	2Ne 3:14
I am s. of this things, even as	3:16
even as I am s. of the promise of	3:16
and the only s. foundation,	Jac 4:16
rejected the s. foundation,	4:17
For as s. as thou livest, behold,	Al 19:13
And as s. as the Lord liveth,	23: 6
so s. as many as believed,	23: 6
are ye s. that this is a good seed?	32:31
we were s. our forces were	57: 2
which is a s. foundation,	He 5:12
and your destruction is made s.;	13:32
and your destruction is made s.;	13:38
make them s. and steadfast,	Eth 12: 4
as s. as Christ liveth he spake	Mro 7:26
thus all things shall be made s.,	DC 51: 6
words are s. and shall not fail,	64:31
The more s. word of prophecy	131: 5

SURELY
S. the Lord hath commanded us	1Ne 4:34
s. these things shall be made	15:11
the day must s. come that they	17:43
The Lord God s. shall visit all	19:11
all these things must s. come,	19:12
he s. did show unto the prophets	19:21
s. my judgment is with the Lord,	21: 4
thou shalt s. clothe thee with	21:18
the time s. must come that all	22:19
the Lord will s. prepare a way for	22:20
s. ye shall not be established.	2Ne 17: 9
S. as I have thought, so shall it	24:24
S., your turning of things upside	27:27
that they must s. come to pass.	28: 1
I know must s. come to pass;	31: 1
must s. come to pass.	Jac 6: 1
must s. come to pass—	WM 1: 4
S. he has borne our griefs,	Mos 14: 4
If thou eat thou shalt s. die.	Al 12:23
S., this is more than a man.	18: 2
S. there has not been any servant	18:10
Now I s. know that this is the	18:11
s. this was a sorrowful day;	28: 6
I s. do know that the Lord did	29:11
s., whosoever repenteth shall find	32:13
he s. did deliver them in their	36: 2
just as s. as this director did	37:45
it is he that s. shall come	39:15
S. God shall not suffer that we,	46:18
that the Lord s. should come	He 5:10
will s. come to pass except we	8: 7
s. it is the earth that moveth	12:15
it s. cometh unto this people,	13: 6
who s. shall come into the world,	13: 6
shall s. come except ye repent,	13:10
For behold, he s. must die that	14:15
and as s. as the Lord liveth	15:17
S. he hath blessed the house of	3Ne 5:21
and s. shall he again bring	5:23
And as s. as the Lord liveth,	5:24
all these things shall s. come,	20:46
they shall s. gather together	22:15
s. he spake as touching all	23: 2
when all people must s. stand	28:31
that these things must s. come.	28:33
s. there could not be a happier	4Ne 1:16
things must s. be made known,	Mrm 5: 8
shall not come, for they s. shall,	8:26
S. this thing leadeth into captivity.	Eth 6:23
s. shall you receive a knowledge	DC 8: 1
s. every man must repent or	19: 4
not come to pass but s. must,	29:21
s. these things shall be fulfilled.	35:22
knoweth; but it s. shall come.	39:21
s., men's hearts shall fail them;	88:91
s. Zion is the city of	97:19
s. Zion cannot fall, neither	97:19
Is it not so, s.?	Mses 1:14
eatest thereof thou shalt s. die.	3:17

SURELY 938 SWEARING

not be lost, and s. I will do it;	Mses	4: 1
the woman: Ye shall not s. die;		4:10
eat, if so thou shouldst s. die?		4:17
for thou shalt s. die—for out of it		4:25
if they tell it, they shall s. die;		5:29
s. the flocks of my brother		5:33
S. Zion shall dwell in safety		7:20
eatest thereof, thou shalt s. die.	Abr	5:13

SURETY

Now I know of a s. that the	1Ne	5: 8
and I also know of a s. that the		5: 8
We know of a s. that the Lord		17:55
men shall know of a s.,	2Ne	25: 7
and we can know of their s.	Mos	1: 6
we know of their s. and truth,		5: 2
I know of a s. that my brethren		7:14
that ye may know of their s.		17: 9
know of a s. that I, the Lord		24:14
suppose that I know of their s.?	Al	5:45
How do ye know of their s.?		30:15
then we shall know of a s.;		32:17
cannot know of their s. at first,		32:26
now we will know of a s.	He	9: 2
therefore they shall know of a s.		14: 4
know of a s. and did bear record,	3Ne	11:15
know fo a s. that these things	Eth	5: 3
with s. hope for a better world,		12: 4
shall know of a s. that these	DC	5:12
know fo a s. that they are true,		5:25
may know of a s. my doctrine.		11:16

SURGE

billowing s. conspire against thee;	DC	122: 7

SURPASS

s. all understanding in glory,	DC	76:114

SURPASSES

which s. all understanding;	DC	76:89

SURPLUS

require all their s. property to	DC	119: 1
tithed of their s. properties,		119: 5

SURPRISE

what was my s. when again	JS	2:46

SUPRISED

greatly s. at his behavior;	JS	2:21

SURRENDERED

had s. themselves up unto us,	Al	56:55
s. themselves prisoners of war.		57:14

SURROUND

that his guards should s. Abinadi	Mos	17: 5
s. those men in their camps	Al	47:13
s. the armies of the Lamanites.		55:21
did s. the Lamanites, and did		56:54
s., by night, the city Cumeni,		57: 8

SURROUNDED

s. with numberless concourses of	1Ne	1: 8
were s. by the king's guard,	Mos	7: 7
for the Lamanites had s. them		21: 5
nearly s. by the Lamanites;	Al	22:29
were nearly s. by water,		22:32
s. with numberless concourses		36:22
and s. the men of Amalickiah,		47:14
s. by the armies of Lehonti.		47:14
when they saw that they were s.,		47:15
they were s. by the Nephites,		52:31
s. by the Nephites without,		55:22
might not be s. by our people.		56:37
the left lest they should be s.;		56:40
and ye are s. by security,		60:19
are s. with thousands of those,		60:22
and s. many others, and took		62:25
they were s. on every hand	He	1:31
Behold, we are s. by demons,		13:37
my head, s. by light as before.	JS	2:49

SURVIVE

God grant that he may s. them,	WM	1: 2

SURVIVED

s. the dead of our people,	Mrm	6:11

SUSQUEHANNA

Michael on the banks of the S.,	DC	128:20
between Harmony, S. county,		128:20
on the S. river, declaring		128:20
S. county, State of Pennsylvania;	JS	2:56
going with my wife to S. county,		2:61

SUSTAIN

men are bound to s. and uphold	DC	134: 5
The vote to s. the		OD

SUSTAINED

damages which they have s.,	DC	123: 2

SUSTAINING

obeying, honoring, and s. the law.	AoF	12

SWALLOW

of the earth shall s. them up,	2Ne	26: 5

SWALLOWED

mind s. up in other things	1Ne	15:27
be s. up in the depths of the sea;		18:10
be s. up in the depths of the sea.		18:15
be s. up in the depths of the sea		18:20
and they that s. thee up shall		21:19
they were not s. up in the sea.	2Ne	1: 2
s. up in the will of the Father.	Mos	15: 7
sting of death is s. up in Christ.		16: 8
sting of death should be s. up	Al	22:14
was s. up in the joy of his God,		27:17
death was s. up to them by the		27:28
hearts are s. up in their pride.		31:27
were s. up in the joy of Christ.		31:38
he has s. up the Egyptians in		36:28
Egyptians and s. them up?	He	8:11
is the sting of death s. up.	Mrm	7: 5
s. up in the depths of the sea?	Eth	2:25
the floods came and s. them up.	Mses	7:43

SWARE

that they all s. unto him, by	Eth	8:14
Satan s. unto Cain that he would	Mses	5:30
and s. unto him with an oath,		7:51

SWARMS

carry with them s. of bees,	Eth	2: 3

SWAY

have full s. in your heart;	Al	42:30

SWEAR

who s. by the name of the Lord,	1Ne	20: 1
yet they s. not in truth nor in		20: 1
In that day shall he s., saying:	2Ne	13: 7
he should s. in his wrath	Jac	1: 7
and I s. unto you with an oath	Mos	20:24
behold, I s. in my wrath that	Al	12:35
for I s. unto you, that		36: 1
And behold, I s. unto you,	3Ne	3: 8
I s. unto you with an oath,		3: 8
say unto you, s. not at all;		12:34
shalt thou s. by the head,		12:36
began to s. before the heavens	Mrm	3: 9
And they did s. by the heavens,		3:10
Will ye s. unto me that ye will	Eth	8:13
s. in the name of him who	DC	88:110
those who s. falsely against my		121:18
S. unto me by thy throat, and	Mses	5:29
s. thy brethren by their heads,		5:29

SWEARERS

adulterers, and against false s.,	3Ne	24: 5

SWEARING

s. with an oath that he would	Al	49:27
s. by their everlasting Maker,	He	1:11

SWEAT

SWEAT
By the s. of thy face shalt thou — Mses 4:25
his bread by the s. of his brow, — 5: 1

SWEEP
I will s. it with the besom of — 2Ne 24:23
and thus will I s. away the bad — Jac 5:66
and truth will I cause to s. the — Mses 7:62

SWEEPETH
he s. the earth before him! — Eth 14:18

SWEET
that it was most s., above all that — 1Ne 8:11
food become s., that ye cook it not; — 17:12
their own blood as with s. wine; — 21:26
one being s. and the other bitter. — 2Ne 2:15
their own blood as with s. wine; — 6:18
instead of s. smell there shall be — 13:24
that put bitter for s., and sweet — 15:20
and s. for bitter! — 15:20
is s. above all that is sweet, — Al 32:42
is sweet above all that is s., — 32:42
exquisite and s. as was my joy. — 36:21
they could not know the s.— — DC 29:39
for it shall be s. unto them; — 42:46

SWELL
will begin to s. within your breasts; — Al 32:28
as it beginneth to s. even so — 33:23
heart did s. with thanksgiving — 48:12
but they do s. with great pride, — He 13:22

SWELLED
that the word hath s. your souls, — Al 32:34
his heart s. wide as eternity; — Mses 7:41

SWELLETH
as the seed s., and sprouteth, — Al 32:30
for behold it s., and sprouteth, — 32:30
and it s. and sprouteth, — 32:33

SWELLING
did rise up in great s. words — Al 30:31
when you feel these s. motions, — 32:28
unto boasting, and unto great s., — He 13:22

SWEPT
wherefore, my guilt was s. away. — En 1: 6
has not as yet s. them off — Jar 1: 3
and s. them away out of our lands, — 1: 7
they began to be s. down, — Al 44:18
these attempts they were s. off — 49:22
s. away the band of Gadianton — He 11:10
began to be s. off by them — Mrm 4:18
were s. down and destroyed. — 5: 7
or they should be s. off when — Eth 2: 8
or they shall be s. off when — 2: 9
serve God or shall be s. off; — 2:10
that they are s. off. — 2:10
and s. off the inhabitants — 14:27
and be s. away by the hail, — DC 109:30
may be broken up and s. away as — 109:70
shall be s. from under heaven, — 121:15

SWIFT
Ye are s. to do iniquity — 1Ne 17:45
I will be a s. witness against the — 3Ne 24: 5
so s. and speedy was the war — Eth 14:22
I have in reserve a s. judgment — DC 121:24
And send ye s. messengers, — 124:26

SWIFTER
flight was s. than the Lamanites' — Mrm 5: 7

SWIFTLY
they shall come with speed s.; — 2Ne 15:26
moving s. upon the waters, — DC 61: 3

SWIFTNESS
they rushed forth with much s. — Al 17:32

SWIM
is what I am wont to s. in. — DC 127: 2

SWINE
cast ye your pearls before s., — 3Ne 14: 6
cows, and of sheep, and of s., — Eth 9:18
the pearls to be cast before s. — DC 41: 6
rye for the fowls and for s., — 89:17

SWOLLEN
behold they had s. exceedingly; — 1Ne 18:15
also mine ankles were much s., — 18:15
heart was s. within him with joy; — Al 17:29
his heart was s. within him, — 19:13
many whose hearts had s. in them — 24:24
his heart was s. with sorrow — He 7: 6
their hearts were s. with joy, — 3Ne 4:33

SWORD
many should perish by the s., — 1Ne 1:13
I beheld his s., and I drew it — 4: 9
off his head with his own s. — 4:18
off his head with his own s., — 4:19
the s. girded about my loins. — 4:21
and great slaughters with the s. — 12: 2
made my mouth like a sharp s.; — 21: 2
the s. of their own hands shall fall — 22:13
and ye are visited by s., — 2Ne 1:18
did take the s. of Laban, — 5:14
and the famine and the s.— — 8:19
shall not lift up s. against nation, — 12: 4
Thy men shall fall by the s. — 13:25
the wicked shall fall by the s. — 23:15
slain, thrust through with a s., — 24:19
having wielded the s. of Laban — Jac 1:10
that I fought much with the s. — Om 1: 2
and I, with my own s., have taken — 1:10
and had fallen by the s. from — 1:17
with the s. of Laban. — WM 1:13
and also, the s. of Laban, — Mos 1:16
he drew his s., and swore in his — 19: 4
out of bondage by the s. — 22: 2
and drew his s. and began to — Al 1: 9
therefore he was slain by the s. — 1: 9
to enforce it by the s.; — 1:12
man that slew Gideon by the s., — 2: 1
by the hand of Nehor with the s.; — 2:20
fought with Amlici with the s., — 2:29
that he slew Amlici with the s. — 2:31
had been slain with the s., — 3: 2
by the hand of Nehor with the s. — 6: 7
and by pestilence, and the s. — 10:22
and by pestilence, and by the s.; — 10:23
placed cherubim and a flaming s. — 12:21
smote off their arms with his s.; — 17:37
their arms with the edge of his s., — 17:37
it were their leader with his s.; — 17:38
smitten by the s. of Ammon, — 17:39
with the sling and with the s., — 18:16
been slain with the s. of Ammon, — 19:22
drew his s. and went forth that — 19:22
as he lifted the s. to smite him, — 19:22
who lifted the s. to slay Ammon, — 19:24
slay Ammon with the s. — 20:14
and he drew his s. that he might — 20:16
But Ammon raised his s., and — 20:22
began to slay them with the s. — 24:21
would not flee from the s., — 24:23
act to perishing under the s.— — 24:23
who had fallen under the s., — 24:24
the s. of his justice fall upon us, — 26:19
before they would take the s. — 27:29
minds of the people than the s., — 31: 5
cherubim, and a flaming s. which — 42: 2
cherubim and the flaming s., — 42: 3
forth and delivered up his s. — 44: 8
Moroni returned the s. and — 44:10
Zerahemnah retained his s., — 44:12
but as he raised his s., behold, — 44:12
laid it upon the point of his s., — 44:13
scalp which was upon the s., — 44:15

SWORD — 940 — SYNAGOGUES

never to raise the s. except it	Al	48:14	if we should stain our s.	Al	24:13
bondage, or to perish by the s.,		50:22	and our s. are made bright,		24:15
by the s. to slay them.		50:26	that we have not stained our s.		24:15
who were hewn down by the s.;		51:19	behold, we will hide away our s.,		24:16
down to the earth by the s.,		51:20	they took their s., and all		24:17
the s. of his almighty wrath,		54: 6	his people were armed with s.,		43:18
For Antipus had fallen by the s.,		56:51	only their s. and their cimeters,		43:20
or guard them, s. in hand,		57:15	with their s. and their cimeters,		43:37
not all destroyed by the s.,		57:23	among the Nephites, by their s.		43:38
to fall upon us with the s.,		58:18	otherwise we will retain our s.,		44: 8
kept them from falling by the s.,		58:39	preserved you from our s.		44: 9
thousands have fallen by the s.,		60: 5	did contend with their s. and		44:17
of them from falling by the s.		60: 8	the sharp s. of the Nephites;		44:18
many who have fallen by the s.;		60:12	before the s. of the Nephites;		44:18
murdering our people with the s.,		60:17	with their s. and their slings,		49:20
land who are falling by the s.,		60:22	who would not deliver up their s.		52:39
I do take my s. to defend the		60:28	but we did sleep upon our s.,		57: 9
the s. of justice doth hang over		60:29	our s. should come upon them.		57:33
and smite you with the s.,		60:30	did in a body run upon our s.,		57:33
even if it must be by the s.		60:35	men, and arm them with s.,		60: 2
and take the s. against us.		61:11	taking up their s. against us,		60:16
cut his way through with the s.,	He	1:23	let us resist them with our s.,		61:14
to slay one another with the s.,		10:18	take up their s. in the defence		62: 5
shall be destroyed by the s.;		11: 4	of men, and armed them with s.,	He	1:14
destruction did cease by the s.		11: 5	behold, our s. are taken from us		13:34
pestilence of the s. might cease;		11:14	not lift their s. against them,		15: 9
that the s. of justice hangeth over		13: 5	and made s. out of steel for	Eth	7: 9
save the s. of justice falleth upon		13: 5	he had armed them with s.		7: 9
I will visit them with the s.		13: 9	they slept upon their s.		15:20
the s. of destruction did hang	3Ne	2:19	they slept again upon their s.		15:22
should visit you with the s.		3: 6	slept upon their s. that night,		15:24
shall let fall the s. upon you		3: 8	in their might with their s.		15:24
the s. of my justice shall hang		20:20			
the s. of his justice is in his		29: 4	**SWORE**		
they would struggle with the s.	Mrm	2:14	And they s. in their wrath that,	En	1:14
upon my people with the s.,		6: 9	s. in his wrath that he would	Mos	19: 4
ten more who did fall by the s.,		6:15	therefore they s. vengeance	Al	25: 1
the s. of vengeance hangeth		8:41	s. in his wrath that they	Eth	1:33
the s. of the justice of the	Eth	8:23	he s. in his wrath that he would		15:28
he slew him with his own s.;		9:27	s. that they should not enter	DC	84:24
slain by the s. of those secret		13:18			
tool or his s. upon his shelf,		14: 1	**SWORN**		
hilt of his s. in his right hand,		14: 2	The Lord of Hosts hath s.,	2Ne	24:24
many thousands fell by the s.		14: 4	they had s. in their hearts that	Mos	19:19
should not fall by the s.		14:24	s. with an oath to defend his	Al	48:13
slain by the s. already nearly		15: 2	had s. with an oath to attack		49:17
slay him with his own s.,		15: 5	s. or covenanted to maintain		51: 6
they had all fallen by the s.		15:23	s. to drink the blood of Moroni.		51: 9
or he would perish by the s.		15:28	as I have s. that the waters of	3Ne	22: 9
they fought again with the s.		15:29	so have I s. that I would not		22: 9
they had all fallen by the s.,		15:29	to that which he hath s.		29: 8
had leaned upon his s.,		15:30	s. by all that had been forbidden	Mrm	3:14
Archeantus has fallen by the s.,	Mro	9: 2	he had s. in his wrath unto	Eth	2: 8
his s. is bathed in heaven,	DC	1:13	s. by the oath of the ancients,		9: 5
sharper than a two-edged s.,		6: 2	s. unto him to do all manner		9:10
sharper than a two-edged s.,		11: 2	he had s. to avenge himself		14:24
sharper than a two-edged s.,		12: 2	I have s. in my wrath,	DC	63:33
sharper than a two-edged s.,		14: 2	he hath s. by the power of		97:20
breastplate, the s. of Laban,		17: 1	the Lord hath s. and decreed		98: 2
and the s. of my Spirit,		27:18	I have s., and the decree		101:10
sharper than a two-edged s.,		33: 1	I know thee, and thou hast s.	Mses	7:59
let fall the s. in their behalf,		35:14			
and they will take up the s.,		45:33	**SYCAMORES**		
take his s. against his neighbor		45:68	the s. are cut down,		2Ne 19:10
with the s. and by bloodshed		87: 6			
pestilence, with plague, with s.,		97:26	SYLVESTER: see SMITH, Sylvester.		
the s. of mine indignation		101:10			
thy s. avenge us of our wrongs.		121: 5	**SYNAGOGUE**		
if with a drawn s. thine enemies		122: 6	he departed out of their s.,	Al	21:11
be thrust from thee by the s.,		122: 6	in every s. of the Amalekites,		21:16
cherubim and a flaming s.,	Mses	4:31	up in the center of their s.,		31:13
by famine, s., and pestilence;	JS	2:45	as he taught them in the s.	Mro	7: 1
			and from s. to synagogue,	DC	63:31
SWORDS			and from synagogue to s.,		63:31
manner of it did make many s.,	2Ne	5:14			
beat their s. into plow-shares,		12: 4	**SYNAGOGUES**		
again, they have brought s.,	Mos	8:11	they should depart out of the s.,	2Ne	26:26
with s., and with cimeters, and		9:16	and also in their s., which were	Al	16:13
and with s., and with cimeters,		10: 8	to preach to them in their s.,		21: 4
did arm themselves with s.,	Al	2:12	for they had built s. after the		21: 4
and took their s., and their spears,		17: 7	Aaron entered into one of their s.		21: 5
and our s. have become bright,		24:12	that there should be s. built		21:20
let us stain our s. no more		24:12	nor cast them out of their s.,		23: 2
let us retain our s. that they		24:13	into their temples and their s.		26:29

SYNAGOGUES / TAKE

that the Zoramites had built s.,	Al	31:12
people, entering into their s.,		32: 1
they were cast out of the s.		32: 2
not permitted to enter into their s.		32: 3
they have cast us out of our s.		32: 5
for we are cast out of our s.,		32: 9
God save it be in your s. only?		32:10
well that ye are cast out of your s.,		32:12
ye are cast out of your s.		33: 2
and their temples, and their s.,	He	3: 9
and of s. and their sanctuaries,		3:14
as will hypocrites do in the s.	3Ne	13: 2
standing in the s. and in the		13: 5
not cast him out of your s.,		18:32
every people and in their s.,	DC	66: 7
of the wicked, in their s.,		68: 1

SYRIA
Rezin, king of S., and Pekah	2Ne	17: 1
S. is confederate with Ephraim.		17: 2
the fierce anger of Rezin with S.,		17: 4
Because S., Ephraim, and the son of		17: 5
For the head of S. is Damascus,		17: 8

SYRIANS
The s. before and the Philistines	2Ne	19:12

SYSTEM
that the s. may be kept perfect.	DC	84:110

TABEAL
midst of it, yea, the son of T.	2Ne	17: 6

TABERNACLE
there shall be a t. for a shadow	2Ne	14: 6
and shall dwell in a t. of clay,	Mos	3: 5
of his dwelling in his mortal t.;	Al	7: 8
perform whilst in this t. of clay,	Mro	9: 6
a t. of the Holy Spirit to your	DC	88:137
world and made flesh my t.,		93: 4
elements are the t. of God;		93:35
yea, man is the t. of God,		93:35
covering of my temple, in my t.,		101:23
that he should build a t.,		124:38
for there shall be my t., and it	Mses	7:62

TABLETS
and the t., and the ear-rings;	2Ne	13:20

TABRET
and the viol, the t., and pipe,	2Ne	15:12

TAHHANES
the lot of T. [the tannery]	DC	104:20

TAIL
head and t., branch and rush	2Ne	19:14
that teacheth lies, he is the t.		19:15

TAILS
the two t. of these smoking	2Ne	17: 4

TAKE
They t. the daughters of Ishmael	1Ne	1:hd
They t. their families and depart		1:hd
life, that they might t. it away.		1:20
they seek to t. away thy life.		2: 1
he should t. his family and depart		2: 2
to t. away the life of my father.		2:13
sought to t. away mine own life;		4:11
to t. away their lives also.		4:28
Zoram did t. courage at the words		4:35
that he should t. his family into		7: 1
sons should t. daughters to wife,		7: 1
to t. away the life of my father,		7:14
they sought to t. away my life,		7:16
cease striving to t. away my life.		7:19
t. away the sins of the world.		10:10
he should t. his journey into the		16: 9
and we did t. seed of every kind		16:11
we did t. our tents and depart		16:12
we did t. our bows and our arrows,		16:14
we did again t. our journey,	1Ne	16:33
we did again t. our journey		17: 1
also sought to t. away his life;		17:44
have sought to t. away his life;		17:44
did t. me and bind me with cords,		18:11
to molest them nor to t. away	2Ne	1: 9
t. away from them the lands of		1:11
ye sought to t. away his life;		1:24
I t. away my first blessing.		1:29
they did seek to t. away my life.		5: 2
they did seek to t. away my life.		5: 4
I, Nephi, did t. my family,		5: 6
And we did t. our tents		5: 7
did t. upon them to call themselves		5: 9
Nephi, did t. the sword of Laban,		5:14
they sought to t. away my life.		5:19
Behold, I t. off my garments,		9:44
doth t. away from Jerusalem,		13: 1
a man shall t. hold of his brother		13: 6
the Lord will t. away the bravery		13:18
women shall t. hold of one man,		14: 1
thy name to t. away our reproach.		14: 1
I will t. away the hedge thereof,		15: 5
and t. away the righteousness of		15:23
T. heed, and be quiet;		17: 4
T. thee a great roll,		18: 1
T. counsel together, and it shall		18:10
and to t. away the right from		20: 2
give him a charge to t. the spoil,		20: 6
take the spoil, and to t. the prey,		20: 6
sorrows shall t. hold of them;		23: 8
And the people shall t. them		24: 2
and they shall t. them captives		24: 2
thou shalt t. up this proverb		24: 4
not t. the name of the Lord		26:32
T. these words which are not		27:15
t. the advantage of one because		28: 8
t. away the sins of the world.		31: 4
to t. upon you the name of Christ,		31:13
wherefore, I, Jacob, t. it upon me	Jac	1: 8
but to t. counsel from his hand.		4:10
I t. away many of these young		5: 8
I will t. these young and tender		5: 8
T. thou the branches of the wild		5: 9
T. of the fruit thereof,		5:20
let us t. of the branches of		5:52
I will t. of the branches of		5:54
the roots thereof may t. strength		5:59
my son Enos: T. these plates.		7:27
shall t. from the plates of Nephi;	WM	1: 5
behold, I shall t. these plates,		1: 6
I t. from the plates of Nephi;		1: 9
t. upon you the name of Christ,	Mos	5: 8
t. upon him the name of Christ		5:10
t. heed that ye do not transgress,		5:11
doth a man t. an ass which		5:14
t. the names of all those who		6: 1
t. upon him the image of man,		7:27
and t. upon him flesh and blood,		7:27
t. a journey into the wilderness,		8: 7
and to t. off their flocks,		9:14
this did he t. to support himself,		11: 4
and sought to t. away his life;		11:26
from that time forward to t. him.		11:29
not t. the name of the Lord		13:15
t. upon him the form of man,		13:34
that the priests should t. him		17: 1
surround Abinadi and t. him;		17: 5
were about to t. the priests also		19:21
they might t. those priests		21:20
For they were desirous to t. them		21:21
to t. their women and children,		22: 2
t. upon them the name of Christ,		25:23
Aaron t. upon him the kingdom;		29: 3
to t. upon them the kingdom.		29: 3
will not t. upon him the kingdom.		29: 6
t. up arms against their brethren;	Al	2:10
to t. away the sins of the world,		5:48
he will t. upon him the pains		7:11
And he will t. upon him death,		7:12
will t. upon him their infirmities,		7:12
t. upon him the sins of his people,		7:13

TAKE

I should t. Amulek and go forth	Al	9: 1	and did t. up their swords in	Al 62: 5
suffer them that they should t. me		9:33	whosoever would not t. up arms	62: 9
t. upon him the transgressions		11:40	t. up their weapons of war	62:16
also did t. from them their clothes		14:22	Helaman did t. up him again	62:44
his heart began to t. courage;		15: 4	t. possession of the whole city.	He 1:20
t. one of his daughters to wife.		17:24	to t. this band of robbers and	2:10
they were about to t. his body		19: 1	Helaman sent forth to t. them	2:11
should t. them and slay them.		22:19	forth into the prison to t. them	5:22
that they should t. upon them,		23:16	their hearts did t. courage.	5:24
t. up arms against their brethren;		24: 6	did it t. hold upon the walls of	5:44
to t. them away from our hearts,		24:11	could not t. him to cast him into	10:16
he would t. away our stain—		24:11	I will t. away my word from	13: 8
than t. away from a brother		24:18	and they fear to t. them up lest	15: 9
they would not t. them again,		24:25	T. this fellow and bind him,	16: 6
Let us t. up arms against them,		26:25	therefore t. him and bind him,	16: 6
even to t. the life of their enemy;		26:32	t. up arms against them.	3Ne 2:11
t. up arms against their brethren;		26:34	to t. up arms against those	2:12
refused to t. their arms,		27: 3	to t. possession of the lands,	4: 1
of their fear to t. up arms		27:23	to t. possession of all the lands	4: 1
prevailed upon to t. up arms		27:28	that this siege should t. place.	4:17
before they would t. the sword		27:29	they did t. with them all that	6: 2
t. no thought for its nourishment,		32:38	they should t. their flight into	7:12
fruit thereof, it shall t. root;		32:41	the city of Zarahemla did t. fire.	8: 8
that it may t. root in you,		32:42	wherein ye will t. up your cross,	12:30
t. upon him the transgressions		34: 8	the law and t. away thy coat,	12:40
t. the life of his brother?		34:11	t. heed that ye do not your alms	13: 1
t. upon you the name of Christ;		34:38	t. no thought for your life,	13:25
t. the records which have been		37: 1	why t. ye thought for raiment?	13:28
or hell can t. them from you,		37:16	Therefore t. no thought, saying,	13:31
see that ye t. care of these		37:47	T. therefore no thought for the	13:34
Oh, remember, and t. it upon you,		39: 9	the morrow shall t. thought for	13:34
I command you to t. it upon you		39:10	should t. of the wine of the cup	18: 8
to t. away the sins of the world;		39:15	every man did t. his wife and	19: 1
and t. possession of their house—		40:13	shall be about to t. place—	21: 1
to t. a thing of a natural state		41:12	must t. upon you the name	27: 5
and t. also of the tree of life,		42: 3	shall t. place at the last day;	28:39
mercy could t. not effect except		42:13	ye shall t. the plates of Nephi	Mrm 1: 4
they would not t. up arms,		43:11	t. away his beloved disciples,	1:13
and t. possession of the land;		43:22	we did t. possession of the city,	2: 4
and t. possession of the city,		43:25	them to t. happiness in s.	2:13
course the Lamanites were to t.		43:30	did t. possession of the city	4: 2
to t. an oath unto you,		44: 8	and did t. many prisoners.	4: 2
but t. our weapons of war,		44: 8	might t. possession of the city	4: 7
can cause to t. place among		46: 9	did t. possession of the city	4:13
t. upon us the name of Christ,		46:18	and did t. many prisoners	4:14
t. upon them the name of Christ,		46:21	and did t. up all the records	4:23
to t. them and bring them back,		46:30	did not t. the city at that time.	5: 3
that he should t. his armies,		46:31	that we did again t. to flight,	5: 7
t. possession of the kingdom.		47: 8	and t. them not again,	7: 4
they were sorry to t. up arms		48:23	to t. upon you the name of	8:38
them that they might t. effect,		49: 4	they shall t. up serpents;	9:24
and t. possession of the land		50:29	I t. mine account from the	Eth 1: 2
refused Alma to t. possession		50:38	neither shall ye t. fire with	2:23
and they refused to t. up arms,		51:13	t. upon me flesh and blood;	3: 9
not t. up arms to defend their		51:13	to t. the curse from off the land,	9:16
or they should t. up arms and		51:17	they shall t. no advantage of	12:26
and to t. up arms in defence of		51:20	that thou mightest t. it again	12:33
t. possession of the land		51:30	and t. away their talent, yea,	12:35
might t. again by stratagem or		52:10	that he would t. the kingdom,	15:18
t. possession of their lands		52:13	to t. upon them the name of	Mro 4: 3
and t. again the city of Mulek.		52:19	t. heed, my beloved brethren,	7:14
t. a small number of men and		52:22	I will t. away the things which	DC 5:31
the city, and t. possession of it.		52:24	to t. it away out of your hands,	8: 8
were desirous to t. up arms in		53:13	sought to t. away the things	10: 7
about to t. their weapons of war,		53:14	T. upon you the name of Christ,	18:21
not t. their weapons of war to		53:16	t. upon them the name which is	18:24
as were able to t. up arms,		53:16	shall t. upon them my name;	18:27
therefore let us t. of the wine,		55:11	to t. upon them my name with	18:27
they did t. of the wine freely;		55:13	to t. upon them my name with	18:28
not t. up their weapons of war		56: 6	church t. heed and pray always,	20:33
and t. up their weapons of war		56: 7	who are sanctified t. heed also.	20:34
to t. the city of Antiparah by		57: 2	to t. upon them the name of	20:37
did t. them and their provisions.		57:10	to t. the lead of all meetings.	20:44
we should t. those provisions		57:11	he is to t. the lead of meetings	20:49
which caused them to t. courage;		57:32	he is to t. the lead of meetings	20:56
we did t. courage with our		58:12	may t. a certificate from him	20:64
did t. possession of the city.		58:21	to t. upon them the name of	20:77
did t. possession of the city of		58:28	shall t. the cup also, and say:	20:78
I do t. my sword to defend		60:28	may t. a letter certifying that	20:84
to t. away the judgment-seat		61: 4	you must t. up your cross,	23: 6
and t. the sword against us.		61:11	shalt t. no purse nor scrip,	24:18
will t. possession of the city		61:18	t. upon you my whole armor,	27:15
his heart did t. courage,		62: 1	t. the helmet of salvation,	27:18

TAKE 943 TAKEN

shalt t. thy brother, Hiram Page,	DC 28:11	t. up their inheritance in	DC	125: 4
shalt t. thy journey among	28:14	t. especial care of your family		126: 3
t. vengeance upon the wicked,	29:17	and glories should t. place,		128:18
shall t. hold of the inhabitants	29:18	to t. her and give her unto him		132:44
that you shall t. your journey	30: 5	Abraham to t. Hagar to wife.		132:65
not t. thy brother's garment;	42:54	to t. from them this world's goods,		134:10
Thou shalt t. the things which	42:59	to t. teams, seeds, and farming		136: 7
shalt t. him or her between	42:88	t. the name of the Lord in vain,		136:21
and they will t. up the sword,	45:33	t. many of them from the book	Mses	1:41
not t. his sword against his	45:68	sought Noah to t. away his life;		8:18
to t. the money to provide food	51: 8	endeavored to t. away my life	Abr	1: 7
t. their journey as soon as	52: 3	offer me up and t. away my life,		1:15
John Corrill t. their journey	52: 7	to t. thee away from thy father's		1:16
t. their journey unto the same	52: 8	my son, to t. away thy life.		1:17
Thayre t. their journey also	52:22	I will t. thee, to put upon thee		1:18
Ezra Booth t. their journey,	52:23	against me, to t. away my life.		1:30
Martin Harris t. their journey	52:24	Arise, and t. Lot with thee;		2: 6
Whitlock also t. their journey,	52:25	I have purposed to t. thee away		2: 6
Orson Pratt t. their journey,	52:26	God shall t. in his heart to do		3:17
Carter also t. their journey	52:27	and we will t. of these materials,		3:24
Scott also t. their journey.	52:28	T. heed that no man deceive	JS	1: 5
Coltrin also t. their journey.	52:29	t. anything out of his house;		1:14
Smith also t. their journey.	52:30	return back to t. his clothes;		1:15
Carter also t. their journey.	52:31	t. notice sufficient to excite		2:22
and also t. their journey.	52:32	an attempt to t. them out,		2:53
t. their journey unto one place,	52:33			
t. their journey into the	52:35	**TAKEN**		
t. with them a recommend	52:41	T. FROM THE PLATES OF	T Pg	
T. upon you mine ordination,	53: 3	t. from the Book of Ether	T Pg	
you shall t. your journey with	53: 5	had t. away our property.	1Ne	4:11
t. your journey, and appoint	54: 7	that he was t. by the people;		11:32
thus you shall t. your journey	54: 8	they have t. away from the gospel		13:26
you shall t. your journey with	55: 5	of the Lord have they t. away.		13:26
Joseph Coe also t. his journey	55: 6	things t. away from the book,		13:28
he that will not t. up his cross	56: 2	and precious things were t. away		13:29
he shall t. up his journey	56: 5	have been t. out of the book,		13:29
let him t. heed lest he fall.	58:15	are t. away out of the gospel		13:29
and t. your journey speedily	60: 5	which have been t. away from them;		13:40
t. their journey for Cincinnati;	60: 6	has t. it upon him to be our ruler		16:37
let the residue t. their journey	60: 8	and had t. with us our provisions		18: 8
t. their former company,	61: 9	the prey be t. from the mighty,		21:24
t. their journey in haste that	61: 9	of the mighty shall be t. away,		21:25
t. that which is needful for	61:11	the cursing may be t. from you	2Ne	4: 6
t. that which is not needful	61:12	the prey be t. from the mighty,		6:16
t. their journey in haste—	61:21	of the mighty shall be t. away,		6:17
t. their journey in haste.	61:21	I have t. out of thine hand		8:22
Who willeth to t. even them	63: 3	which he had t. with the tongs		16: 6
even them whom he will t.,	63: 3	and thine iniquity is t. away,		16: 7
I say, let the wicked t. heed,	63: 6	have t. evil counsel against thee,		17: 5
t. righteousness in his hands	63:37	spoil of Samaria shall be t. away		18: 4
t. his journey up unto the land	63:39	broken, and be snared, and be t.		18:15
beware how they t. my name	63:61	that his burden shall be t. away		20:27
should not t. when he please,	64:28	they have t. up their lodging at		20:29
them not, neither t. therefrom.	68:34	from them shall be t. away even		28:30
To t. an account of the elders	72:11	God hath t. away his plainness	Jac	4:14
Smith t. their journey into	75:13	have t. hold of the moisture of		5:18
they shall also t. their journey	75:14	which we have t. of my vineyard,		5:46
they also shall t. their journey	75:15	have t. the lives of many of the	Om	1:10
let them t. their journey also	75:17	t. upon them the name of Christ.	Mos	6: 2
let all those t. their journey,	75:18	and were t., and were bound,		7: 7
to t. the kingdom of our God	76:28	had t. the ruling of the people		10:15
he will t. you up in a cloud,	78:21	be t. captive by our enemies;		12:15
t. ye no thought for the	84:81	He was t. from prison and from		14: 8
let the morrow t. thought for	84:84	t. upon himself their iniquity		15: 9
Neither t. ye thought	84:85	t. by the hand of your enemies,		17:18
this hour t. purse or scrip,	84:86	among those that were t. captive,		19:16
t. the old and cast it unto	84:105	he caused that they should be t.,		21:23
t. with him him that is weak,	84:106	had t. all their gold, and silver,		22:12
t. with you those who are	84:107	t. possession of all these lands,		24: 2
an agent to t. charge and to	84:113	had t. to wife the daughters of		25:12
I will t. care of your flocks,	88:72	have been t. in divers iniquities.		26:11
t. charge of the place which	96: 2	that had been t. in iniquity,		26:34
t. heed that ye see to this	96: 4	was t. by those that were with him,		27:19
to t. away incumbrances that	96: 9	t. by the people of the church,	Al	1:10
t. upon themselves the fruit of	101:45	t. upon them the name of Christ.		1:19
and t. all the strength of	101:55	thou hast fed me and t. me in,		8:26
shall t. of the abundance which	104:18	been t. in thy lying and craftiness,		12: 3
t. up your cross, follow me,	112:14	they are t. captive by the devil,		12:11
Let them t. leave of my saints	118: 5	and t. others captive into the		16: 3
t. them in their own craftiness;	121:12	been t. captive by the Lamanites.		16: 5
to t. statements and affidavits;	123: 4	been t. captive by the Lamanites.		16: 6
let him not t. his family unto	124:83	been t. captive by the Lamanites.		16: 8
Hyrum may t. the office of	124:91	been lost that were t. captive.		16: 8

TAKEN

Having t. leave of their father,	Al	17: 6
they were t. and cast into prison,		20:30
were t. and cast into prison,		21:13
Nephites had t. possession of		22:29
not t. upon them the name of		24: 1
t. away the guilt from our hearts,		24:10
God hath t. away our stains,		24:12
get our stains t. away from us,		24:15
t. and bound with strong cords,		26:29
t. and bound and carried before		30:21
the curse might be t. from him.		30:54
curse should be t. from thee		30:55
curse was not t. off of Korihor;		30:56
t. up arms to defend themselves,		35:14
shall be t. away from you by		37:15
are t. home to that God who		40:11
yea, these are they that are t. out,		41: 7
from whence they were t.—		42: 2
he was t. up by the Spirit,		45:19
of God, and be t. unto himself,		46:24
seed which shall be t. unto God.		46:25
were t. back into the land of		46:33
had t. those who went with him,		47: 1
they had t. from the Nephites.		47:23
were t. and cast into prison,		51:19
had t. by the shedding of blood;		52: 4
they had not t. any cities save		52: 4
those cities which they had t.,		52: 5
Lamanites had t. many prisoners,		52: 8
those whom the Lamanites had t.		52: 8
had been t. out of their hands;		52:10
possess the cities which he had t.,		52:13
were t. and bound, and their		52:39
their weapons of war were t.		52:39
of prisoners who were t.		52:40
had t. an oath that they never		53:11
had t. many women and children,		54: 3
prisoners whom Moroni had t.;		54: 3
whom they have t. prisoners;		55: 3
behold we have t. of their wine		55: 8
glad that ye have thus t. wine		55: 9
whom he had t. prisoners,		55:25
be t. to the city Bountiful;		55:26
the prisoners whom they had t.,		55:27
could not be t. in their snares;		55:31
have t. their weapons of war,		56: 5
the oath which they had t.		56: 8
those cities which they had t.		56:20
those cities which they had t.		56:26
prisoners of war whom we had t.		57: 1
we had t. from the Lamanites.		57:15
should be t. from among the dead,		57:24
t. care of our wounded men,		57:28
had been t. by the Lamanites,		58:31
who have been t. prisoners		58:31
the Lamanites have t. from us,		58:41
the Lamanites had t. from them.		59: 4
had t. possession of the land.		62: 6
and his men were t. prisoners,		62: 8
been t. and cast into prison;		62: 9
after they had t. them,		62:16
having t. many prisoners,		62:30
who had been t. prisoners,		62:30
behold, he was t., and was tried	He	1: 8
were t., and were cast into prison,		1:22
and had t. the capital city which		1:27
the Lamanites who had been t.		1:33
from which I have t. all the		2:14
those parts which he had t.		4:19
t. by an army of the Lamanites		5:21
who had t. this covenant.		6:22
be t. away that ye shall have		7:22
your lands shall be t. from you,		7:28
great cities shall be t. from us,		8: 5
been t. and were cast into prison.		9: 9
that Nephi should be t. and bound		9:19
for he was t. by the Spirit and		10:16
t. upon themselves the name		11:24
our swords are t. from us in the		13:34
their curse was t. from them,	3Ne	2:15
and they had t. their horses,		3:22
was t. and hanged upon a tree,		4:28
had t. all the robbers prisoners,	3Ne	5: 4
record of that which hath t. place		5:15
t. and put to death secretly by		6:23
they were t. and brought up		6:26
and have t. it up again;		9:22
change which had t. place.		11: 1
whither he hath t. them.		17: 4
t. upon them the name of	4Ne	1:20
beloved disciples were t. away	Mrm	1:16
and t. the plates of Nephi,		2:17
until we had again t. possession		2:27
the veil was t. from off the	Eth	3: 6
kingdom was t. away from him.		10:30
Coriantumr had t. all the people		14:15
and their names were t.,	Mro	6: 2
the curse of Adam is t. from		8: 8
have they t. prisoners;		9: 9
shall be t. even the light which	DC	1:33
peace shall be t. from the earth,		1:35
t. away this privilege from you.		9: 5
men have t. them from you.		10: 8
never be t. again from the earth,		13: 1
have t. the Zion of Enoch into		38: 4
cannot be t. from the church,		42:32
revelations until he be t.,		43: 3
if it be t. from him he shall		43: 4
as ye do it not, it shall be t.,		43:10
have t. the Holy Spirit for their		45:57
t. his power on the right hand		49: 6
not be t. and given unto that		51:10
be t. from him, and placed upon		52:37
be t. from him;		58:60
it shall be t. away, even that		60: 3
not be t. from my servant		64: 5
shall be t. and handed over to		72:13
until their husbands are t.;		83: 2
shall not be t. from the earth		84:97
shall never be t. from you,		90: 3
be not t. from you and given		90:26
my gospel until thou be t.		99: 8
hideth the earth, shall be t. off,		101:23
or t. out of the treasury		104:64
or t. out of the treasury,		104:71
t. away out of their minds		104:81
veil was t. from our minds,		110: 1
who was t. to heaven without		110:13
not be t. from him till I come.		112:15
let thy pavilion be t. up;		121: 4
or which he hath t. away,		124:28
Patten I have t. unto myself;		124:130
Brunson I have t. unto myself;		124:132
like a woman that is t. in travail;		136:35
t. down without delay.		OD
t. from man, made I a woman,	Mses	3:22
because she was t. out of man.		3:23
for out of it wast thou t.:		4:25
ground from whence he was t.;		4:29
vengeance shall be t. on him		5:40
time, was t. up into heaven.		7:21
that Zion was t. up into heaven,		7:23
hast t. Zion to thine own bosom,		7:31
the son of Enoch, was not t.,		8: 2
t. unto ourselves the daughters		8:21
they are t. away by a whirlwind,	Abr	2: 7
the rib which the Gods had t.		5:16
because she was t. out of man;		5:17
in the field, the one shall be t.,	JS	1:44
at the mill, the one shall be t.,		1:45
never be t. again from the earth		2:69

TAKETH

He t. three days' journey	1Ne	1:hd
Nephi t. his brethren and		1:hd
the guilty t. the truth to be hard,		16: 2
and t. it again by the power of	2Ne	2: 8
neither that t. her by the hand,		8:18
and as a sheep that no man t. up;		23:14
that t. his name in vain.	Mos	13:15
that t. upon me the sins of		26:23
who t. away the sins of the world,	Al	7:14
whoso t. upon him my name,	3Ne	27: 6
all things before me t. you;	DC	78:20

TAKETH

t. away light and truth,	DC 93:39
priesthood no man t. from him.;	124:130
no man t. his priesthood,	124:132

TAKING

the t. away of their stumbling	1Ne 14: 1
t. upon us the responsibility,	Jac 1:19
t. strength unto themselves.	5:48
have been void, t. none effect.	Al 12:26
t. upon them the high priesthood	13: 8
unto him, t. him by the hand:	15: 6
t. no thought for themselves	31:37
t. possession of many cities,	51:26
had been kept from t. up arms	53:11
t. up their swords against us,	60:16
t. possession of our lands,	60:17
t. possession of many cities and	He 1:27
in t. upon me the sins of the	3Ne 11:11
Which of you by t. thought	13:27
t. all the inhabitants with	Mrm 4:22
T. the shield of faith wherewith	DC 27:17
in t. possession of their own	105:30
qualified for t. accurate minutes;	128: 3
precise in t. the whole proceedings,	128: 3
t. a different view of the	128: 8
in t. the poor, the widows,	136: 8
necessity of t. her elsewhere	JS 2:58

TALE

to relate that t. to their wives	Mos 9: 2
the sad t. of the destruction of	Mrm 8: 3

TALENT

and take away their t.,	Eth 12:35
they hide the t. which I have	DC 60: 2
neither shalt thou bury thy t.	60:13
may improve upon his t.,	82:18

TALENTS

every man may gain other t.,	DC 82:18
you obtain five t. [dollars]	104:69
If it be five t. [dollars],	104:73
or if it be ten t. [dollars],	104:73

TALK

And we t. of Christ,	2Ne 25:26
I, t. to you concerning these	Al 54:11
And now when ye t., ye say:	He 13:25
did t. with them as he stood in	Eth 2: 5
the Lord t. with the brother of	2:14
that she did t. with her father.	8: 9
And of tenents thou shalt not t.,	DC 19:31
T. not of judgments, neither	105:24
very bold doctrine that we t. of—	128: 9

TALKED

he t. with him as he sat in	1Ne 3:11
says that the Lord has t. with him,	16:38
and t. with the brother of Jared;	Eth 2: 4
in a cloud and t. with him.	2:14
hath t. with me face to face,	12:39
t. with the Lord face to face,	DC 17: 1
he t. with him, and the glory	Mses 1: 2
and t. with him face to face.	1:31
and Cain t. with Abel, his brother.	5:32
and he t. with me, even as	7: 4
that Enoch t. with the Lord;	7:20
I, Abraham, t. with the Lord,	Abr 3:11

TALKETH

as a man t. one with another,	Mses 7: 4
as one man t. with another;	Abr 3:11

TALKING

they were in the attitude as if t.	He 5:36

TAME

of Israel, like unto a t. olive-tree,	Jac 5: 3
branches of the t. olive-tree	5:14
have brought forth t. fruit.	5:18
hath brought forth t. fruit,	5:25
them unto a t. olive-tree,	6: 1

TANGIBLE

flesh and bones as t. as man's;	DC 130:22

TANNERY

the lot of Tahhanes [the t.]	DC 104:20

TARBILL

at the house of Squire T.,	JS 2:58

TARES

to gather the t. that they may	DC 38:12
of the wheat and of the t.:	86: 1
behold he soweth the t.;	86: 3
the t. choke the wheat and	86: 3
pluck not up the t. while	86: 6
let the wheat and the t. grow	86: 7
the wheat from among the t.,	86: 7
the t. are bound in bundles,	86: 7
she is the t. of the earth;	88:94
parable of the wheat and the t.,	101:65
t. shall be bound in bundles,	101:66

TARRIED

but had t. at Jerusalem, and had	1Ne 5: 4
my father t. in the wilderness	8: 2
those who t. with their wives	Mos 19:13
also those that had t. with them,	19:19
And having t. in the wilderness,	20: 4
his people who t. in the land	25: 7
Alma t. many days with Amulek	Al 8:27
they t. in the wilderness, or did	37:42
t. with him all that hour,	DC 88:56
father t. in Haran and dwelt	Abr 2: 5

TARRY

he would t. with us from that time	1Ne 4:35
desirous that he should t. with us	4:36
we might t. for the space of a time.	16:33
now he did not t. in the land	He 1:23
ask him to t. a little longer	3Ne 17: 5
it were the three who were to t.,	28:12
were the three who should t.;	4Ne 1:14
of Jesus who did t. with them,	1:30
disciples of Jesus who should t.)	1:37
disciples of Jesus, who did t.	Mrm 8:10
unto his disciples who should t.,	9:22
t. until I come in my glory,	DC 7: 3
If I will that he t. till I come,	7: 4
I say unto you, t. with him,	35:22
of my disciples who shall t.	63:41
unto the disciples that shall t.,	63:45
T. not many days in this place;	66: 6
should go forth and not t.,	75: 3
T. ye, tarry ye in this place,	88:70
t. ye in this place, and call a	88:70
t. ye, and labor diligently,	88:84
therefore I command you to t.,	95: 9
whom I have appointed to t.;	101:55
let them t. for a little season,	105:21
T. in this place,	111: 7
it is my will that you should t.,	111: 8
arise, and come forth, and not t.	117: 2
if they t. it shall not be well	117: 3
my servant Joseph t. at home,	124:102
upon him and not t. with him.	130:23
not been commanded to t.	133: 4
to prepare for those who are to t.	136: 6
T. ye here and keep the tents,	Mses 6:38

TARRYING

of his t. in his own kingdom,	Al 20:12

TARSHISH

and upon all the ships of T.,	2Ne 12:16

TASK

the greatness of the t.,	Jac 2:10
and put t.-masters over them.	Mos 24: 9
and all their t.-masters were in	24:19

TASK-MASTERS: see TASK and MASTERS.

TASKS
laden with t., which were grievous 1Ne 17:25
and put t. upon them, and put Mos 24: 9

TASTE
of the vineyard did t. of the fruit, Jac 5:31
to t. of the exceeding joy of Al 36:24
exceeding joy of which I did t.; 36:24
and it was pleasant to their t., 55:13
for ye shall never t. of death; 3Ne 28: 7
who were never to t. of death, 28:25
be that they must t. of death; 28:37
that they might not t. of death 28:38
they should not t. of death; Eth 12:17
die in me shall not t. of death, DC 42:46
raiment, for t. and for smell, 59:19
they t. the bitter, that they may Mses 6:55

TASTED
above all that I ever before t. 1Ne 8:11
after they had t. of the fruit 8:28
bore the fruit which thy father t., 11: 7
and have t. of his love, Mos 4:11
after ye have t. this light is Al 32:35
and have t. as I have tasted, 36:26
and have tasted as I have t., 36:26
t. and knew of the goodness of Mrm 1:15
in the least degree you have t. DC 19:20

TASTING
to heaven without t. death, DC 110:13

TAUGHT
therefore I was t. somewhat in all 1Ne 1: 1
have testified, and also t. them. 22:31
t. you the words of my father; 2Ne 6: 3
t. them many things concerning 25: 2
that they are t. after the manner of 25: 5
t. my children after the manner of 25: 6
is t. by the precepts of men— 27:25
are t. by the precepts of men. 28:14
which were t. among my people; 33: 1
as I t. them in the temple, Jac 1:17
the things which he had t. them, 7:17
for he t. me in his language, En 1: 1
they t. the people the ways of Jar 1: 7
they should be t. in his language. Om 1:18
t. in the language of Mosiah, 1:18
t. in all the language of his Mos 1: 2
And he also t. them concerning 1: 3
to have t. them to his children, 1: 4
been t. in the language of 1: 4
them when they are t. them, 1: 5
who had t. them to keep the 2: 4
and have t. you that ye should 2:13
that have not been t. concerning 2:34
also have been t. concerning 2:34
and have been t. all these things, 2:36
thou shalt have t. thy people 3:22
which king Benjamin had t. them, 8: 3
been t. in all the language of 9: 1
thus they have t. their children 10:17
which have been t. by our fathers, 12:20
these things ye have not t. them; 12:26
And have ye t. this people that 12:37
ye have studied and t. iniquity 13:11
Have ye t. this people that they 13:25
And he t. them privately, 18: 3
were the things which he had t., 18:19
to be t. among all the people of 24: 4
they t. them that they should 24: 6
after Alma had t. the people 25:17
what he had t. to the people was Al 1:15
having t. the people of Gideon 8: 1
had been t. to believe in the word 14: 8
all the words that thou hast t. 15: 7
which should be t. among them 16:16
were t. that he would appear 16:20
and when they t., they taught 17: 3
they t. with power and authority 17: 3
on the words which they t. 21:12
were t. the records and prophecies 23: 5
into their houses and t. them, 26:29

we have t. them in their streets; Al 26:29
have t. them upon their hills; 26:29
their synagogues and t. them; 26:29
t. to keep the law of Moses 30: 3
he t. me that which I should say. 30:53
And I have t. his words; 30:53
and I t. them because they 30:53
and I t. them, even until I had 30:53
that they have t. you this, 33: 2
t. by us to be the Son of God; 34: 2
these things were t. unto you 34: 2
t. to defend themselves against 48:14
t. never to give an offense, 48:14
t. to keep the commandments 53:21
had been t. by their mothers, 56:47
that their mothers had t. them. 57:21
they had been t. to believe— 57:26
the words which Helaman t. to He 5:13
who taught it unto you by Alma, 5:41
for it had been t. unto them; 3Ne 6:18
have heard the things which I t. 15: 1
children shall be t. of the Lord; 22:13
things which he t. the people. 26: 7
things which he t. the people; 26: 8
And they t., and did minister 26:19
t. to hate the children of God, 4Ne 1:39
t. to hate the children of Nephi 1:39
they were t. to walk humbly Eth 6:17
they were also t. from on high. 6:17
t. his people how great things 6:30
he t. them in the synagogue Mro 7: 1
be t. unto all nations, kindreds, DC 42:58
Ye are not sent forth to be t., 43:15
ye are to be t. from on high. 43:16
that all may be t. to be wise 46:18
that which shall be t. him 49: 4
is t. them by the Comforter 52: 9
t. through prayer by the Spirit. 63:65
this Moses plainly t. to the 84:23
You have not t. your children 93:42
may be t. more perfectly, 105:10
may be t. words of wisdom 109:14
have t., encouraged and urged OD
their children were t. to read and Mses 6: 6
t. his son Enos in the ways of 6:13
t. Enoch in all the ways of God. 6:21
faith was t. unto the children 6:23
father t. me in all the ways of 6:41
father Adam t. these things, 7: 1
that Noah prophesied, and t. the 8:16

TAX
taxed with a t. which is grievous Mos 7:15
he laid a t. of one fifth part of all 11: 3
did t. them with heavy taxes; Eth 10: 5

TAXATION
obtained by the t. of his people. Mos 11:13

TAXED
t. with a tax which is grievous Mos 7:15

TAXES
ye should not be laden with t., Mos 2:14
by the t. which king Noah had 11: 6
did tax them with heavy t.; Eth 10: 5
with the t. he did build many 10: 5
would not be subject unto t. 10: 6
whoso was not able to pay t. 10: 6

TAYLOR, John
Let my servant T., DC 118: 6
Orson Hyde, William Smith, T., 124:129
T. and Willard Richards, two of the 135: 2

TEACH
I, Nephi, did t. my brethren these 1Ne 19:22
And I did t. my people to build 2Ne 5:15
I t. you the consequences of sin. 9:48
and he will t. us of his ways, 12: 3
to t. any man the right way; 25:28
they shall t. with their learning, 28: 4
which shall t. after this manner, 28: 9

TEACH — 947 — TEACHERS

they t. all men that they should	2Ne 33:10
if we did not t. them the word	Jac 1:19
after this manner did they t. them.	Jar 1:11
and t. them to his children,	Mos 1: 4
could t. them to their children,	1: 4
did king Benjamin t. his sons,	1: 8
not t. them all within the walls	2: 7
But ye will t. them to walk in	4:15
will t. them to love one another,	4:15
priests to t. the people,	6: 3
and pretend to t. this people,	12:25
Therefore, what t. ye this people?	12:27
said: We t. the law of Moses.	12:28
If ye t. the law of Moses why do	12:29
said that ye t. the law of Moses.	12:31
if ye t. the law of Moses,	16:14
also t. that it is a shadow of those	16:14
T. them that redemption cometh	16:15
to t. the words of Abinadi—	18: 1
as would hear his word he did t.	18: 3
And he did t. them, and did	18: 7
and to t. them concerning	18:18
that they should t. nothing save	18:19
together to t. the people,	18:25
that they might t. with power	18:26
Thus did Alma t. his people,	23:15
authority to preach or to t.	23:17
the brethren of Amulon t. them	24: 5
they t. them the words of Abinadi;	24: 5
this time forward to t. the people,	27:32
to t. you the commandments of	29:14
he did t. these things so much	Al 1: 5
And he began to t. the people	8: 4
and he began to t. the people	8: 4
to t. these things unto the people.	13: 1
to t. his commandments unto the	13: 6
to t. these things unto this people,	18:34
to t. them the words which	19:31
and he did t. them many things.	21:21
did t. them all things concerning	21:23
to t. the people of Lamoni.	22: 4
and to t. the word of God	23: 4
to t. his word, yea, in wisdom,	29: 8
Why do ye t. this people that	30:22
I do not t. the foolish traditions	30:23
I do not t. this people to bind	30:23
and began to t. them, saying:	34: 1
ye shall t. them to abhor such	37:29
ye shall also t. them that these	37:29
t. them an everlasting hatred	37:32
t. them to humble themselves	37:33
t. them to withstand every	37:33
T. them to never be weary of	37:34
as ye have begun to t. the word	38:10
that ye should continue to t.;	38:10
and t. the word unto this people.	38:15
he did t. them many things	He 5:13
to t. the word of God among all	5:14
upon them to t. us the word;	16:21
the twelve did t. the multitude;	3Ne 19: 6
that they should t. the things	23:14
things which Jesus did truly t.	26: 6
the Lord truly did t. the people,	26:13
he did t. and minister unto the	26:14
to t. as many as did come	26:17
they did t. their children that	4Ne 1:38
that this thing shall ye t.—	Mro 8:10
t. parents that they must repent	8:10
may t. the word of wisdom;	10: 9
may t. the word of knowledge	10:10
And to t., expound, exhort,	DC 20:42
priest's duty is to preach, t.,	20:46
he is only to preach, t.,	20:50
warn, expound, exhort, and t.,	20:59
shalt t. them by the Comforter,	28: 1
the Comforter to speak or t.,	28: 4
t. you the peaceable things of	36: 2
t. one another according to	38:23
t. the principles of my gospel,	42:12
not the Spirit ye shall not t.	42:14
not t. them until ye have	42:57
ye shall t. them unto all men;	42:58
t. them that shall be converted	42:64
to t. those revelations which	DC 43: 7
to t. the children of men the	43:15
was sent forth to t. the truth.	50:14
that t. them not to understand	68:25
also t. their children to pray,	68:28
which shall t. them all things	75:10
which shall t. him the truth	79: 2
to t. them of a judgment which	84:87
t. one another the doctrine of	88:77
T. ye diligently and my grace	88:78
t. one another words of wisdom;	88:118
and to t. them their duty,	107:85
t. them the duties of their office,	107:87
and to t. them according to the	107:89
t. one another words of wisdom;	109: 7
been appointed go and t. this,	136:16
Wherefore t. it unto your children,	Mses 6:57
t. these things freely unto your	6:58
they t. for doctrines the	JS 2:19

TEACHER

a ruler and a t. over thy brethren.	1Ne 2:22
him to be our ruler and our t.,	16:37
should be their ruler and their t.	2Ne 5:19
had been their ruler and their t.,	5:19
and ye look upon me as a t.,	9:48
that I can no longer be your t.,	Mos 2:29
also trust no one to be your t.	23:14
not all be governed by one t.;	25:20
and t. ought to become popular;	Al 1: 3
the t. any better than the learner;	1:26
(or, if he be a t.)	Mro 3: 3
I ordain you to be a t., to	3: 3
elder, priest, t., or deacon is	DC 20:60
Each priest, t., or deacon,	20:64
both elder, priest, t., and also	38:40
the offices of t. and deacon	84:30
Appoint among yourselves a t.,	88:122
appointed to be president, or t.,	88:128
after him, let the t. arise,	88:132
shall salute the president or t.	88:135
t., deacon, and member.	107:10
who are of the office of a t.,	107:62
Wherefore, from deacon to t.,	107:63
and from t. to priest,	107:63

TEACHERS

that they should be priests and t.	2Ne 5:26
and because of false t.,	28:12
been consecrated priests and t.	Jac 1:18
and the priests, and the t.,	Jar 1:11
and false preachers and t.	WM 1:16
appointed just men to be their t.,	Mos 2: 4
all their priests and all their t.;	23:17
appointed t. over his people,	24: 1
t. of the brethren of Amulon	24: 4
priests and t. over every church.	25:19
having their priests and their t.,	25:21
up unto the priests and t.,	26: 7
their priests and t. should labor	27: 5
of God, yea, even one of their t.;	Al 1: 7
Alma had consecrated to be t.,	4: 7
and judges, and priests, and t.,	14:18
and many of their t. and their	14:23
the lawyers, and priests, and t.,	14:27
and consecrated priests and t.	15:13
and consecrating priests and t.	23: 4
revile against the priests and t.,	30:31
and their priests and their t.	35: 5
and t. throughout all the land,	45:22
priests and t. over the churches	45:23
t. were themselves astonished	Hel 3:25
t. shall rise in the pride of	Mrm 8:28
pollutions, ye hypocrites, ye t.,	8:38
church, ordained priests and t.—	Mro 3: 1
did they ordain priests and t.,	3: 4
priests, and t. were baptized;	6: 1
me to ordain priests and t.;	DC 18:32
duty of the elders, priests, t.,	20:38
ordain other elders, priests, t.,	20:39
also ordain other priests, t.,	20:48
neither t. nor deacons have	20:58
send one or more of their t.	20:81

TEACHERS / TELL

TEACHERS
or it may be signed by the t.	DC 20:84
the elders, priests and t. of	42:12
The priests and t. shall have	42:70
deacons and t. should be	84:111
t. to preside over those who	107:62
president over the office of the t.	107:86
preside over twenty-four of the t.,	107:86
president of the t. and his	124:142
the t. of religion of the different	JS 2:12
prophets, pastors, t., evangelists,	AoF 6

TEACHER'S
the t. duty is to watch over	DC 20:53

TEACHES
and he t. unto her the law of	DC 132:64

TEACHETH
the Lord thy God who t. thee	1Ne 20:17
and the prophet that t. lies,	2Ne 19:15
Spirit which t. a man to pray	32: 8
evil spirit t. not a man to pray,	32: 8
t. him that he must not pray.	32: 8
t. the peaceable things of the	DC 39: 6
the Father t. him of the	84:48
or t., to purchase all the lands	101:70

TEACHING
made an end of t. my brethren,	2Ne 1: 1
t. the law of Moses,	Jar 1:11
had made an end of t. his sons,	Mos 1: 9
t. the word of God in all things,	26:38
they had been t. the word of God	Al 17: 4
thus t. the people of Lamoni	22: 1
as Alma was t. and speaking	32: 4
commanded concerning your t.,	DC 42:15
t. them the duties of their office,	107:86
We are not t. polygamy	OD
to convey any such t.	OD
t. school in the neighborhood	JS 2:66

TEACHINGS
inasmuch as they receive thy t.	DC 28: 8
and these shall be their t.,	42:13
receive not the t. of any that	43: 5
There is nothing in my t.	OD

TEAMS
with all the t., wagons, provisions	DC 136: 5
and expert men, to take t., seeds,	136: 7

TEANCUM
by a man whose name was T.,	Al 50:35
T. did slay Morianton and	50:35
that they were met by T.,	51:29
repulsed by T. and his men,	51:31
every man of T. did exceed	51:31
T. and his men did pitch their	51:32
T. and his servant stole forth	51:33
T. stole privily into the tent of	51:34
T. was ready to give them battle	52: 1
T. saw that the Lamanites were	52: 5
T. thought it was not expedient	52: 5
T., by the command of Moroni—	52:15
might assist T. with his men	52:15
T. had received orders to make	52:16
T. made preparations to make	52:17
T. and many of the chief captains	52:19
he caused that T. should take	52:22
the Lamanites had discovered T.,	52:22
did march forth against T.,	52:23
their numbers to overpower T.	52:23
And as T. saw the armies of	52:23
T. was thus leading away the	52:24
return from the pursuit of T.	52:26
the Lamanites did pursue T.	52:27
T., by the orders of Moroni,	53: 3
in the charge of Lehi and T.;	61:15
to send forth unto Lehi and T.,	61:18
that ye strengthen Lehi and T.	61:21
gave Lehi and T. command	62: 3
to the armies of Lehi and T.	62:13
they were met by Lehi and T.;	62:32
Lamanites fled from Lehi and T.;	Al 62:32
T. did encamp with their armies	62:34
the night-time, save it were T.;	62:35
T. in his anger did go forth into	62:36
that they did pursue T.,	62:36
Moroni knew that T. was dead	62:37
the inhabitants of the city T.	Mrm 4: 3
the city T. lay in the borders	4: 3
to come against the city T.	4: 6
did come against the city T.,	4: 7
possession of the city T. also.	4: 7
forward against the city T.,	4:14

TEAR
as a lion, and t. you in pieces,	Mrm 5:24
if they t. thee from the society	DC 122: 6
enemies t. thee from the bosom of	122: 6

TEARETH
he t. up the laws of those who	Mos 29:22
treadeth down and t. in pieces,	3Ne 20:16
treadeth down and t. in pieces,	21:12

TEARS
my wife with her t. and prayers,	1Ne 18:19
and even shed many t. of sorrow.	Mos 25: 9
sorrowful, even unto t.	Al 19:28
the gushing out of many t.,	3Ne 4:33
and beheld they were in t.,	17: 5
did bathe his feet with their t.	17:10
shed t. of joy before the Lord,	Eth 6:12
shed forth their t. as the rain	Mses 7:28

TEASINGS
they wearied him with their t.	Mos 7: 1

TEETH
weep, and wail, and gnash their t.;	Mos 16: 2
gnashing their t. upon them,	Al 14:21
and wailing, and gnashing of t.,	40:13
wailing and gnashing of t.,	DC 19: 5
wailing and gnashing of t.	85: 9
wailing, and gnashing of t.	101:91
where there is gnashing of t.,	124: 8
and gnashing of t. upon	124:52
and wailing, and gnashing of t.	133:73
and wailing, and gnashing of t.,	Mos 1:22
be weeping and gnashing of t.	JS 1:54

TEIL
and shall be eaten, as a t.-tree,	2Ne 16:13

TEIL-TREE: *see TEIL and TREE.*

TELESTIAL
we saw the glory of the t.,	DC 76:81
also the t. receive it of the	76:88
vision, the glory of the t.,	76:89
in all things the glory of the t.,	76:91
the glory of the t. is one,	76:98
in glory in the t. world;	76:98
inhabitants of the t. world,	76:109
or that of a t. kingdom.	88:21
the law of a t. kingdom	88:24
cannot abide a t. glory;	88:24
by a portion of the t. glory	88:31

TELL
declare ye, t. this, utter to the	1Ne 20:20
I will t. you what I will do to	2Ne 15: 5
Go and t. this people—	16: 9
words of Christ will t. you all	32: 3
t. you concerning your thoughts,	Jac 2: 5
and t. you concerning your	2:10
I must t. you the truth	2:11
not that I t. you these things;	4:12
he cannot t. of things to come.	7: 7
I will t. you of the wrestle	En 1: 2
neither do I t. these things that	Mos 2:15
but I t. you these things that ye	2:15
I t. you these things that ye may	2:17
behold, I have things to t. you	3: 1
the things which I shall t. you	3: 2

TELL

the words which I shall t. thee:	Mos	3: 3
I cannot t. you all the things		4:29
But this much I can t. you		4:30
I can assuredly t. thee, O king,		8:13
ye requested that I should t.;		13: 3
because I t. you the truth		13: 7
But this much I t. you,		13:10
and t. the king of these things,		20:19
that he may t. his people that		20:19
Behold, I can t. you—	Al	5:11
and t. me concerning these things;		18:20
also t. me by what power ye slew		18:20
if thou wilt t. me concerning		18:21
if I t. thee by what power I do		18:22
that ye should t. me concerning		22:11
bestowed upon us? Can ye t.?		26: 2
I t. you by the spirit of prophecy,		37:15
I would t. you somewhat		54: 6
I would t. you these things if ye		54: 7
I would t. you concerning that		54: 7
I have somewhat to t. you		56: 2
I t. you that two thousand of		56: 5
t. them to fear not, for God		61:21
that they would t. no man that	He	1:11
may t. you of your iniquities?		7:13
Now t. us, and acknowledge		9:20
thee thy life if thou wilt t. us,		9:20
come and t. this thing unto you;		14: 9
should it t. unto your brethren	3Ne	15:14
I should t. unto them concerning		15:15
that I should t. unto them:		15:16
and I t. it unto you, that ye		15:19
which he should t. unto them.		24: 1
words which he did t. unto them,		24: 1
t. us the name whereby we		27: 3
of the body, they could not t.;		28:15
I will t. you the way whereby	Mro	7:21
tongue cannot t., neither can it		9:19
Behold, I t. you these things,	DC	5:20
now I t. thee these things that		6:15
Yea, I t. thee, that thou mayest		6:16
I t. thee these things as a		6:17
I will t. you in your mind and		8: 2
to t. you by that means,		8: 9
cannot always t. the wicked		10:37
I will t. you that which no		15: 3
I will t. you that which no		16: 3
he saith to thee thou shalt t.		28:10
t. him that those things which		28:11
But now I t. it unto you,		38:14
I t. you these things because		38:30
this, which I t. you before,		58: 5
let me t. you that it is only to		128: 5
and dry lands t. the wonders of		128:23
straightway and t. thy neighbor,		136:25
T. me, I pray thee, why these	Mses	1:30
and t. me concerning this earth,		1:36
if thou t. it thou shalt die;		5:29
the living God, that they t. it not;		5:29
if they t. it, they shall surely die;		5:29
T. us plainly who thou art,		6:40
T. us when shall these things be	JS	1: 4
father and t. him of the vision		2:49

TELLETH

and t. them there is no hell;	2Ne	28:22
as a man t. another in mine	Eth	12:39
t. them that it is no sin to lie	DC	10:25

TELLING

t. him that he was a visionary man;	1Ne	5: 2
t. them the awful consequences	Jac	3:12
t. them that these things ought	Mos	29:36
t. them that there could be no	Al	30:17
t. them that when a man was		30:18
close my epistle by t. you that		54:11
t. them concerning the death	He	10:13
T. them of things which must		16: 5
my t. the story had excited a	JS	2:22
persecute me for t. the truth?		2:25
After t. me these things,		2:36
t. me that Satan would try to		2:46

TELLS

and he t. us these things,	1Ne	16:38

TEMPERAMENT

with my native cheery t.	JS	2:28

TEMPERANCE

faith, virtue, knowledge, t.,	DC	4: 6
and virtue, and knowledge, t.,		107:30

TEMPERATE

being t. in all things;	Al	7:23
diligent and t. in all things.		38:10
Be patient; be sober; be t.;	DC	6:19
charity, being t. in all things,		12: 8

TEMPEST

yea, a great and terrible t.,	1Ne	18:13
the t. began to be exceeding		18:14
by t., by fire, and by smoke,		19:11
both by fire, and by t.,	2Ne	6:15
and with storm, and with t.,		27: 2
the lightning lasted, and the t.,	He	14:27
was also a great and terrible t.;	3Ne	8: 6
because of the t. and the		8:12
and the storm, and the t.,		8:19
O thou afflicted, tossed with t.,		22:11

TEMPESTS

behold, there shall be great t.,	He	14:23
deformed, because of the t.,	3Ne	8:17
and by smoke, and by t.,		10:14
shall be heard of fires, and t.,	Mrm	8:29
the great and terrible t.	Eth	6: 6
lightnings, and by the voice of t.,	DC	43:25
lightnings, and the voice of t.,		88:90

TEMPLE

And I, Nephi, did build a t.;	2Ne	5:16
the manner of the t. of Solomon		5:16
not be built like unto Solomon's t.		5:16
was like unto the t. of Solomon;		5:16
and his train filled the t.		16: 1
as I taught them in the t.,	Jac	1:17
I come up into the t. this day		2: 2
Jacob, get thou up into the t.		2:11
together, to go up to the t.	Mos	1:18
that they might go up to the t.		2: 1
that when they came up to the t.,		2: 5
their tents round about the t.,		2: 6
the door thereof towards the t.,		2: 6
within the walls of the t.,		2: 7
to the t. to hear the words		7:17
work within the walls of the t.,		11:10
he built a tower near the t.;		11:12
the tower which was near the t.		19: 5
which was upon the wall of the t.,	Al	10: 2
this t. it shall be rent in twain,	He	10: 8
round about the t. which was	3Ne	11: 1
shall suddenly come to his t.,		24: 1
I will suddenly come to my t.	DC	36: 8
when I shall come to my t.		42:36
this t. which is in Jerusalem,		45:18
this t. which ye now see shall		45:20
and a spot for the t. is lying		57: 3
and the spot for the t.,		58:57
beginning at the t. lot,		84: 3
place, even the place of the t.,		84: 4
which t. shall be reared in this		84: 4
and whatsoever t. is defiled,		93:35
God shall destroy that t.		93:35
the veil of the covering of my t.,		101:23
Let the work of my t., and		127: 4
put in the archives of my holy t.,		127: 9
let us present in his holy t.,		128:24
shall suddenly come to his t.;		133: 2
in the Holy T. of God	Fac	2: 8
departed from the t.;	JS	1: 2
the buildings of the t.,		1: 2
not be left here, upon this t.,		1: 3
the destruction of the t.,		1: 4

TEMPLES

TEMPLES
for he dwelleth not in unholy t.	Mos	2:37
he doth not dwell in unholy t.;	Al	7:21
to the people in their t., and		16:13
to their houses, and also their t.,		23: 2
have also entered into their t.		26:29
he dwelleth not in unholy t.,		34:36
yea, their cities, and their t.,	He	3: 9
of ships, and their building of t.,		3:14
doth not dwell in unholy t.—		4:24
tabernacle of God, even t.;	DC	93:35
I will not come into unholy t.		97:17
solemnized in our T.		OD

TEMPORAL
after the death of the t. body,	1Ne	15:31
speak of the things which are t.?		15:31
things both t. and spiritual;		15:32
which were done by the t. body		15:32
things both t. and spiritual;		22: 3
things of which are spoken are t.;		22: 6
by the t. law they were cut off;	2Ne	2: 5
I have spoken, which is the t.,		9:11
all things, both t. and spiritual;	Mos	2:41
in need, both spiritual and t.;	Al	7:23
death which is called a t. death;		11:42
loose the bands of this t. death,		11:42
be raised from this t. death.		11:42
in his sins, as to a t. death,		12:16
which is the t. death;		12:24
as to things which were t.,		12:31
not of the t. but of the		36: 4
(now these things were t.)		37:43
be reclaimed from this t. death,		42: 8
spiritual death as well as a t.,		42: 9
things t. and to things spiritual.	He	14:16
which death is a t. death.	Mrm	9:13
in t. labors thou shalt not have	DC	24: 9
all things both spiritual and t.—		29:31
First spiritual, secondly t.,		29:32
first t., and secondly spiritual,		29:32
unto you a law which was t.;		29:34
no t. commandment gave I		29:35
they are not natural nor t.,		29:35
not die as to the t. death,		29:42
arrange their t. concerns,		63:38
stewardship over t. things.		70:11
to administer in t. things;		70:12
in your t. things you shall		70:14
likeness of that which is t.;		77: 2
and that which is t. in the		77: 2
or its t. existence.		77: 6
the t. salvation of all saints		89: 2
in administering all t. things;		107:68
unto the ministering of t. things,		107:71
both things which are t., and	Mses	6:63
be saved with a t. salvation;		7:42

TEMPORALLY
both t. and spiritually,	1Ne	14: 7
relief, both spiritually and t.,	Mos	4:26
both t. and spiritually		18:29
cut off both t. and spiritually	Al	42: 7
both t. and spiritually;	Mrm	2:15
blessed both spiritually and t.,	DC	14:11
them both spiritually and t.;		24: 3

TEMPT
neither will I t. the Lord	2Ne	17:12
What am I that I should t. God	Jac	7:14
thou child of hell, why t. ye me?	Al	11:23
will ye t. your God?		30:44
they that t. God are even	3Ne	24:15
that he could not t. them;		28:39
get thee to t. the Lord thy God,	DC	10:15
get thee to t. the Lord thy God.		10:29
should t. the children of men,		29:39
Satan t. little children,		29:47
have power to t. any man		101:28
that Satan would try to t. me	JS	2:46

TEMPTATION
the provocation in the days of t.	Jac	1: 7
suffereth t., and yieldeth not to	Mos	15: 5
and yieldeth not to the t.,		15: 5
that they might not enter into t.	Al	31:10
led away by the t. of the devil,		34:39
withstand every t. of the devil,		37:33
And lead us not into t., but	3Ne	13:12
always lest ye enter into t.;		18:18
himself to be led into t.		18:25
that ye will yield to no t.,	Mrm	9:28
Be faithful, and yield to no t.	DC	9:13
always, lest they fall into t.;		20:33
lest thou shouldst enter into t.		23: 1
because he yielded unto t.		29:40
always, lest you enter into t.		31:12
that you enter not into t.,		61:39
a t. with which thou hast been		66:10
in all things out of t.,		95: 1
notwithstanding the hour of t.		124:124

TEMPTATIONS
are the t. of the devil,	1Ne	12:17
and the t. of the devil,		12:19
the t. and the fiery darts of		15:24
because of the t. and the sins	2Ne	4:18
why should I give way to t.,		4:27
And lo, he shall suffer t.,	Mos	3: 7
afflictions and t. of every kind;	Al	7:11
righteous yieldeth to no such t.?		11:23
about by the t. of the devil	3Ne	6:17
He suffered t. but gave no	DC	20:22
And after their t.,		112:13
I was left to all kinds of t.;	JS	2:28
led me into divers t., offensive		2:28

TEMPTED
t. above that which ye can bear,	Al	13:28
lest ye be t. by the devil,	3Ne	18:15
Adam, being t. of the devil—	DC	29:36
to pass that the devil t. Adam,		29:40
straightway Satan t. him;		40: 2
how to succor those who are t.		62: 1
may not be t. above that which		64:20
Satan t. me because of my	Mses	5:38

TEMPTETH
and t. them to worship him;	Mses	6:49

TEMPTING
t. them and causing them that	3Ne	2: 3
t. them to seek for power,		6:15
Satan came t. him, saying:	Mses	1:12

TEN
t. acres of vineyard shall yield	2Ne	15:10
prepared with t. thousand men.	Al	56:28
an hundred and t. years had	4Ne	1:18
two hundred and t. years had		1:27
(I being about t. years of age,	Mrm	1: 2
until t. years more had passed		3: 1
t. thousand who were with me,		6:10
the t. thousand of my people		6:11
the t. thousand of my people		6:12
t. thousand of Gidgiddonah		6:13
had fallen with his t. thousand;		6:14
had fallen with his t. thousand;		6:14
had fallen with his t. thousand;		6:14
had fallen with his t. thousand;		6:14
fallen with their t. thousand each.		6:14
there were t. more who did fall		6:15
with their t. thousand each;		6:15
spake concerning the t. virgins.	DC	45:56
or if he obtain t., or twenty,		104:69
or if it be t. talents[dollars],		104:73
Noah was t. years old when he		107:52
the leading of the t. tribes from		110:11
if he have t. virgins given unto		132:62
if one or either of the t. virgins,		132:63
were nine hundred and t. years,	Mos	6:19
the restoration of the T. Tribes;	AoF	10

TEND
again began to t. their flocks,	Mos	10:21
let your words t. to edifying	DC	136:24
to till the land, and to t. flocks,	Mses	5: 3

TENDED

TENDED
shouldst have t. to the ministry	Al	39: 4

TENDENCY
a great t. to lead the people to	Al	31: 5
and their t. to evil among men,	DC	134: 8

TENDER
the t. mercies of the Lord are	1 Ne	1:20
to the multitude of his t. mercies.		8: 8
with all the feeling of a t. parent,		8:37
whose feelings are exceedingly t.	Jac	2: 7
broken the hearts of your t. wives,		2:35
forth young and t. branches,		5: 4
a little, young and t. branches;		5: 6
of these young and t. branches,		5: 8
these young and t. branches,		5: 8
grow up before him as a t. plant,	Mos	14: 2
the multitude of his t. mercies	Eth	6:12
and their leaves are yet t.,	DC	45:37
is springing up and is yet t.—		86: 4
while the blade is yet t.		86: 6
when its branches are yet t.,	JS	1:38
and being of very t. years,		2:28

TENDERNESS
because of their t.,	Jac	2:33
shall be nourished with all t.,	DC	42:43

TENDING
while they were t. their flocks.	Mos	11:16

TENETS
And of t. thou shalt not talk,	DC	19:31
to establish their own t.	JS	2: 9

TENS
or even than his t. of thousands?	1 Ne	4: 1
and t. of thousands of souls	Al	3:26
t. of thousands of the Lamanites		28: 2
yea, and t. of thousands, who		60:22
souls, yea, even t. of thousands.	He	3:26
and by t. of thousands,	3 Ne	3:22
and by t. of thousands.		4:21
up unto the land of Zion, by t.,	DC	103:30
twenties, or by t., or by fives.		104:68
hearts of thousands and t. of		110: 9
put their t. of thousands to flight.		133:58
of fifties, and captains of t.,		136: 3
hundreds, and of fifties, and of t.		136:15

TENT
he pitched his t. in a valley	1 Ne	2: 6
And my father dwelt in a t.		2:15
to the t. of my father.		3: 1
unto the t. of our father.		4:38
had returned to the t. of my father,		5: 7
to the t. of our father.		7: 5
towards the t. of our father.		7:21
unto the t. of our father.		7:22
unto the t. of my father,		7:22
as he dwelt in a t., in the valley		9: 1
as my father dwelt in a t.,		10:16
returned to the t. of my father.		15: 1
as my father dwelt in a t.		16: 6
and went forth to the t. door,		16:10
shall the Arabian pitch t. there;	2 Ne	23:20
every man having his t. with	Mos	2: 6
privily into the t. of the king,	Al	51:34
was dead in his own t.;		52: 1
Enlarge the place of thy t.,	3 Ne	22: 2
and there he pitched his t.,	Eth	9: 3
saying unto the t.-keepers:	Mses	6:38
of Bethel, and pitched my t. there,	Abr	2:20

TENTH
But yet there shall be a t.,	2 Ne	16:13
the commencement of the t. year	Al	8: 3
in the t. year of the reign of		10: 6
one-t. part of all he possessed.		13:15
the twelfth day, in the t. month,		14:23

951

in the t. year of the reign of	Al	14:23
the t. year of the reign of the		15:19
on the t. day of the month,		49: 1
passed away the t. year also:	3 Ne	2:10
this t. year had passed away,	Mrm	3: 4
pay one-t. of all their interest	DC	119: 4
when I was in my t. year,	JS	2: 3

TENT-KEEPERS: *see TENT and KEEPERS.*

TENTS
his family, and provisions, and t.,	1 Ne	2: 4
in the wilderness, with our t.,		3: 9
we did take our t. and depart		16:12
and we did pitch our t. again;		16:13
we did pitch our t. for the space		16:17
I did return to our t.,		16:32
we did pitch our t. again,		16:33
did pitch our t. by the seashore;		17: 6
and did pitch our t.;		18:23
And we did take our t.	2 Ne	5: 7
of many days we did pitch our t.		5: 7
dwelling in t., and wandering	En	1:20
pitched their t. round about,	Mos	2: 5
their t. round about the temple,		2: 6
they might remain in their t.		2: 6
and there they pitched their t.		7: 5
we pitched our t. in the place		9: 4
therefore they took their t.		18:34
and their herds, and their t.,		22: 2
And they pitched their t.,		23: 5
they pitched their t. in a valley,		24:20
his people should pitch their t.	Al	2:20
the Nephites did pitch their t.		2:20
the people of Nephi took their t.,		2:26
the wilderness, and dwelt in t.;		22:28
where they had pitched their t.,		27:25
caused his army to pitch their t.		47: 9
pitch their t. in the borders of		51:32
Amalickiah did pitch his t. in		51:32
pitch our t. by the wilderness		58:13
where we had first pitched our t.		58:17
and they did pitch their t.,		58:25
pitch their t. in the plains of		62:18
land northward did dwell in t..	He	3: 9
did pitch our t. around about	Mrm	6: 4
the sea they pitched their t.;	Eth	2:13
and they dwelt in t., and		2:13
dwelt in t. upon the seashore		2:13
pitched their t. in the valley		14:28
his t. in the valley of Shurr.		14:28
waters they pitched their t.;		15: 8
Shiz also pitched his t. near		15: 8
did pitch their t. in a place		15:10
did pitch their t. by the hill		15:11
pitching their t. by the way.	DC	61:25
the father of such as dwell in t.,	Mses	5:45
Tarry ye here and keep the t.,		6:38
great people which dwelt in t.,		7: 5
of Canaan, which dwelt in t.		7: 6
dwelt in t. as we came on our way;	Abr	2:15

TEOMNER
T. and a small number of men	Al	58:16
by in the midst of Gid and T.,		58:19
Gid and T. did rise up,		58:20
Gid and T. by this means had		58:23

TERAH
but T., my father, yet lived in the	Abr	2: 1

TERMED
he t. to be the word of God,	Al	1: 3
whom he t. to be his brethren.		17:30
admit it may be t. a resurrection,		40:15

TERMINATE
t. in the death and misery of	DC	87: 1

TERMS
made known unto us in plain t.,	Al	13:23

TERRESTRIAL

TERRESTRIAL
again, we saw the t. world,	DC 76:71
these are they who are of the t.,	76:71
Wherefore, they are bodies t.,	76:78
vision which we saw of the t.,	76:80
the ministration of the t.;	76:86
And the t. through the	76:87
thus we saw the glory of the t.	76:91
the glory of the t. is one,	76:97
even that of a t. kingdom,	88:21
abide the law of a t. kingdom	88:23
cannot abide a t. glory.	88:23
by a portion of the t. glory	88:30

TERRIBLE
of the great and t. judgments	1Ne 12: 5
a great and a t. gulf divideth	12:18
yea, a great and t. tempest,	18:13
prey of the t. shall be delivered;	21:25
prey of the t. shall be delivered;	2Ne 6:17
down the haughtiness of the t.	23:11
great and t. shall that day be	26: 3
and the multitude of their t. ones	26:18
the t. one is brought to naught,	27:31
and a t. battle had commenced.	Al 56:49
great and t. was the day that	3Ne 4: 7
great and t. was the appearance	4: 7
and t. was the battle thereof,	4:11
and t. was the slaughter thereof,	4:11
also a great and t. tempest;	8: 6
and there was t. thunder,	8: 6
was a great and t. destruction	8:11
more great and t. destruction	8:12
these great and t. things were	8:19
before this great and t. day,	8:24
before this great and t. day,	8:25
of the people great and t.	8:25
the great and t. tempests	Eth 6: 6
so t. was the destruction among	14:27
and great and t. was that day;	15:17
and t. as an army with banners.	DC 5:14
the inhabitants of Zion are t.;	45:70
he shall be t. unto them,	45:74
fear because of her t. ones.	64:43
glorious, very great, and very t.	97:18
that her banners may be t.	105:31
t. things concerning the wicked,	109:45
and t. as an army with banners;	109:73
t. in the midst of thine enemies	122: 4
When thou doest t. things,	133:43

TERRIBLY
he ariseth to shake t. the earth.	2Ne 12:19
he ariseth to shake t. the earth.	12:21

TERRITORY
the saints in the T. of Iowa?	DC 125: 1
any other place in the T.,	OD

TERROR
shall lop the bough with t.;	2Ne 20:33
upon death with any degree of t.,	Al 27:28
they were struck with t.	43:53
Moroni, when he saw their t.,	43:54
them with death and with t.	He 12: 3
because of the t. of their armies.	3Ne 4: 9
from t. for it shall not come	22:14
every soul was filled with t.	Mrm 6: 8
the t. of the Lord also shall be	DC 45:67
because of the t. of the Lord,	45:75
supplanted by anarchy and t.;	134: 6

TESTAMENT
the New T. be translated,	DC 45:60
with this seal and t.	98: 2
and their t. is in force.	135: 5
the prophecies of the Old T.	JS 2:36
as they stand in our New T.	2:40
John the Baptist in the New T.,	2:72

TESTATORS
The t. are now dead, and	DC 135: 5

TESTIFIED
things which he t. of them;	1Ne 1:19
he truly t. of their wickedness	1:19
he t. that the things which he saw	1:19
a number had t. of these things,	10: 5
and t. that they should be	16: 2
are the only ones that have t.,	22:31
For Joseph truly t., saying:	2Ne 3: 6
Abinadi had t. against them;	Mos 17: 2
t. of their iniquity in abundance.	26: 9
he also t. unto the people that	Al 1: 4
whereof he hath t. are true;	10:10
who t. of the things whereof they	10:12
have I t. against your law?	10:26
had t. so plainly against	14: 3
and also t. that there was	14: 5
had all t. to the things which	18: 2
and t. unto him concerning	19:15
What is that thou hast t.?	21: 5
has t. of the Son of God,	33:17
they all t. unto her that the	47:34
upon us which he has t. unto us;	He 8: 8
we know that he has t. aright	8: 8
have t. concerning those things.	8: 9
been many prophets that have t.	8:19
that same prophet who t. of the	8:20
because he t. of these things.	8:22
Nephi also t. of these things,	8:22
have t. of the coming of Christ,	8:22
all things even as Nephi had t.,	9:14
is because I have t. unto you	9:23
prophets had t. of these things	3Ne 1:18
those who t. of these things;	6:21
those who t. of these things.	6:21
who t. of the things pertaining	6:23
to Christ who t. boldly,	6:23
the prophets who t. of Jesus.	7:10
many have t. of these things	10:15
because they t. of these things.	10:15
t. particularly concerning us,	10:16
Jacob also t. concerning a	10:17
whom the prophets t. shall come	11:10
for they truly t. of me.	15:10
as have spoken, have t. of me.	20:24
which had t. of things to come.	Mrm 3:16
t. that a great curse should come	Eth 11: 6
the plates of which you have t.	DC 5: 1
truly t. of him in all things,	20:26
and are to be t. of in due time.	107:57

TESTIFIES
which the Spirit t. unto you	DC 46: 7

TESTIFIETH
the Holy Spirit, which t. in me.	Al 7:16
to the Spirit which t. in me;	7:26
t. of your sins and iniquities,	He 13:26
he t. that your deeds are evil.	13:26

TESTIFY
they t. that a man must be	1Ne 22:30
shall t. to the truth of the book	2Ne 27:12
I might t. unto you concerning	Jac 2: 6
for they truly t. of Christ.	7:11
and they truly t. of him.	7:19
will these things t. against you?	Al 5:22
not t. that ye are murderers,	5:23
to stand and t. unto this people	5:44
I t. unto you that I do know	5:45
to t. against them concerning	8:25
did boldly t. unto them saying:	9: 7
t. against Alma and Amulek.	14: 5
and t. to all the things which	18: 1
I will t. unto you of myself	34: 8
scriptures t. of these things,	34:30
bring witnesses with him to t.	47:33
does not this t. against them?	47:34
I t. that this is the way.	He 7:29
did not only t. of these things,	8:16
the prophet Zenos did t. boldly;	8:19
they did t. boldly of his death	3Ne 6:20
began to t., boldly, repentance	7:16
Zenos did t. of these things,	10:16
these things which t. of us,	10:17
ye shall t. that ye have seen me,	12: 2
there be that t. of these things.	23: 5
he should t. unto this people,	23: 9

TESTIFY / THAN

TESTIFY

eyes, you shall t. of them,	DC 17: 3
t. that you have seen them,	17: 5
t. they are of me and not of man;	18:34
you can t. that you have heard	18:36
t. before you in all lowliness of	42:74
I may t. unto your Father,	88:75
I sent you out to t. and warn	88:81
to t. of my name and bear	114: 1
murder, and t. against them,	121:23
that he may t. of a truth,	127: 6

TESTIFYING

and t. of the things which	En 1:19
t. that they had reviled against	Al 14: 5
t. unto them there is no God?	30:45
t. boldly of the sins and	3Ne 6:20
t. unto them concerning the	6:20
t. that he [Elijah] should be sent,	DC 110:14
voice, t. against their works;	Mses 6:37

TESTIMONIES

that he has received these t.	DC 42:32
after the many t. which have	76:22
these three t. shall stand	98:27
should bring these t. before	98:35
shalt bring these t. before	98:44
your own lands after these t.,	103:24

TESTIMONY

Bind up the t., seal the law	2Ne 18:16
To the law and to the t.;	18:20
shall stand as a t. against you;	25:28
to bear t. of his word unto	27:13
the t. of two nations is a witness	29: 8
the t. of the two nations shall run	29: 8
a bright t. against this people,	Mos 3:24
And for a t. that the things	8: 9
shall stand as a t. against you.	17:10
as a t. against you at the last day.	17:10
as a t. that ye have entered into	18:13
as a witness and a t. that they	21:35
down in pure t. against them.	Al 4:19
to the t. of the word,	4:20
to the t. of Jesus Christ,	6: 8
this is the t. which is in me.	7:13
to the t. of the Holy Spirit,	7:16
unto you, by the t. of his word,	7:20
believe the t. of one man,	9: 2
a t. of the things which they	17:39
as a t. to our God at the last day,	24:15
as a t. that we have never used	24:16
it being in their view a t. to God,	24:18
a t. that these things are true;	30:41
a t. unto you that they are true;	30:41
the t. of all these thy brethren,	30:44
a t. against you at the last day.	39: 8
because of the t. of the five,	He 9:39
witness and a t. before God,	3Ne 7:25
it shall be a t. unto the Father	18: 7
the t. of three, and this work,	Eth 5: 4
stand as a t. against the world	5: 4
that they may bear t. of him.	Mro 7:31
through the t. of the Jews,	DC 3:16
through the t. of their fathers—	3:17
this t. shall come to the	3:18
And in addition to my t.,	5:11
the t. of three of my servants,	5:11
receive this same t. among	5:14
the t. of three witnesses will I	5:15
their t. shall also go forth	5:18
by the t. which shall be given,	6:31
thinketh to overpower your t.	10:33
your feet against them as a t.,	24:15
to bear t. of the things which	58: 6
the t. might go forth from Zion,	58:13
his people by the t. of the just,	58:18
and bear t. of the truth in	58:47
as a t. against them in the	60:15
the t. which ye have borne is	62: 3
bear t. in every place,	66: 7
a t. of the truth of these	67: 7
t. that cannot be impeached,	68:23
feet as a t. against them.	75:20
this is the t., last of all, which	DC 76:22
this is the t. of the gospel of	76:50
who received the t. of Jesus,	76:51
received not the t. of Jesus	76:74
not valiant in the t. of Jesus;	76:79
neither the t. of Jesus.	76:82
neither the t. of Jesus,	76:101
bearing t. to all the world	84:61
the t. may go from you into	84:62
bear t. of it unto your Father	84:92
or your t. concerning me.	84:94
words, or your t. of me;	84:95
is recorded in the t. of John.	88: 3
up the law and seal up the t.,	88:84
after your t. cometh wrath	88:88
For after your t. cometh	88:89
cometh the t. of earthquakes,	88:89
And also cometh the t. of	88:90
thirteenth chapter of John's t.	88:141
as a t. against thine enemy—	98:39
as a t. before the Lord	98:48
the way for a t. against them.	99: 4
power to be mighty in t.	100:10
with a full statement of the t.	102:26
upon t. as it shall be laid	107:72
power to decide upon t.	107:79
the t. of the covenant,	109:38
of that city receive their t.,	109:39
that city receive not the t. of	109:41
and bind up the t.,	109:46
and their blood come up in t.	109:49
not make a display of thy t.	109:49
to bear t. of thy name;	109:56
chosen to bear t. of my name	112: 1
by the t. of traitors.	122: 3
proclamation, and with your t.,	124: 7
reject my servants and my t.	124: 8
the love which he has to my t.	124:20
they sealed the t. and	133:72
To seal the t. of this book and	135: 1
rejected you and your t.,	136:34
seal his t. with his blood,	136:39
t. of the Father and Son;	Mses 7:27
to bear t. of mine Only Begotten;	7:62
the t. of James to be true—	JS 2:26

THAN

he is mightier t. all the earth,	1Ne 4: 1
then why not mightier t. Laban	4: 1
or even t. his tens of thousands?	4: 1
t. that a nation should dwindle	4:13
and he is mightier t. I,	10: 8
more t. we are able to bear.	16: 1
t. to have suffered these afflictions.	17:20
more choice t. they if they	17:34
there must needs be more t. this,	2Ne 10:21
a man more precious t. fine gold;	23:12
a man t. the golden wedge of	23:12
works of darkness rather t. light,	26:10
that there are more nations t. one?	29: 7
are more righteous t. the Gentiles	30: 1
t. I have hitherto been.	Jac 2: 3
t. that of your brethren	2:13
that ye are better t. they,	2:13
t. the Lamanites, our brethren.	2:35
are more righteous t. you;	3: 5
how much better are you t. they,	3: 7
skins will be whiter t. yours,	3: 8
ground was poorer t. the first.	5:23
faster t. the strength of the	5:48
more t. my fathers have written?	Jar 1: 2
t. were they of the Nephites;	1: 6
myself am more t. a mortal man.	Mos 2:10
am no better t. ye yourselves are;	2:26
even more t. man can suffer,	3: 7
no more deny unto them t. it	3:26
less t. the dust of the earth.	4: 2
run faster t. he has strength.	4:27
t. to pay tribute to the king of	7:15
a seer is greater t. a prophet.	8:15
t. that we should lose our lives;	20:22
more t. there was of men;	21:17
be judged of God t. of man,	29:12

THAN 954 THAN

esteem him more t. any other	Mos 29:40
was no better t. the hearer,	Al 1:26
teacher any better t. the learner;	1:26
far more wealthy t. those who	1:31
ye are better one t. another;	5:54
more importance t. they all—	7: 7
no more authority t. one man	9: 6
the day of judgment t. for you,	9:15
for them in this life t. for you,	9:15
for the Lamanites t. for them.	9:23
more t. one witness who testified	10:12
lovest that lucre more t. him.	11:24
Is there more t. one God?	11:28
righteousness rather t. to perish;	13:10
Surely, this is more t. a man.	18: 2
art more powerful t. all they;	18:21
better that he should fall t. thee,	20:17
of them is mightier t. us all?	22:20
rather t. shed the blood of	24:18
rather t. take away from a	24:18
rather t. spend their days in	24:18
death rather t. commit sin;	24:19
by more t. the number who	24:26
more t. a thousand brought to	24:27
t. though they had never known	24:30
t. even to take the life of their	26:32
more t. to perform the work to	29: 6
more wise t. many of the	30:20
t. that thou shouldst be the	30:47
t. the sword, or anything else,	31: 5
t. they who are compelled to be	32:15
t. he that only believeth,	32:19
t. faith is a perfect knowledge.	32:26
can no more t. desire to believe,	32:27
we are better t. our brethren;	38:14
t. what I said unto thy brother;	39: 1
more t. one time appointed for	40: 8
chose evil works rather t. good;	40:13
t. the Lamanites were,	43: 6
much greater t. the Nephites.	43:21
more t. double the number of	43:51
were more numerous t.	46:29
ferocious t. the Lamanites—	47:36
unto the people t. was Moroni—	48:19
and more t. a thousand of	49:23
t. in the days of Moroni,	50:23
rather t. be smitten down to	51:20
more t. the number of those who	52:40
more t. those who had been slain	52:40
more power t. what he hath got.	55: 2
t. they did upon their lives;	56:47
not any more t. sufficient for	57:15
numerous t. was our army	58: 2
t. that which they have sent.	58:36
t. to retake it from them,	59: 9
stronger t. the men of Pachus,	62: 6
more numerous t. they,	He 4:25
more numerous t. they who	5: 2
to one more t. the other,	7:23
better for the Lamanites t. for	7:23
they are more righteous t. you,	7:24
are less t. the dust of the earth.	12: 7
Behold ye are worse t. they;	13:26
ye choose darkness rather t. light?	13:29
shall see greater things t. these,	14:28
be better for them t. for you	15:14
rather t. that they should visit	3Ne 3: 6
were more numerous t. they,	7:12
he had greater power t. they,	7:18
ye were more righteous t. they,	9:13
declare more or less t. this	11:40
t. that ye should be cast into	12:30
cometh of more t. these is evil.	12:37
Is not the life more t. meat,	13:25
meat, and the body t. raiment?	13:25
ye not much better t. they?	13:26
shall do more or less t. these	18:13
was so marred, more t. any man,	20:44
form more t. the sons of men—	20:44
t. the cunning of the devil.	21:10
t. the children of the married	22: 1
greater t. he had revealed	26:14
t. were the people of God.	4Ne 1:40
was swifter t. the Lamanites'	Mrm 5: 7
know of greater things t. these.	8:12
more t. ye love the poor and	8:37
t. that misery which never dies—	8:38
t. ye would to dwell with	9: 4
be more wise t. we have been.	9:31
none greater t. the nation which	Eth 1:43
Sawest thou more t. this?	3: 9
t. those which were made	4: 4
more blessed t. were they,	10:28
more t. any other man among	14:10
more t. four hundred and	Mro 10: 1
have feared man more t. God.	DC 3: 7
sharper t. a two-edged sword,	6: 2
greater t. the gift of salvation.	6:13
can you have t. from God?	6:23
no more unto you t. unto me.	6:29
t. what he has before done.	7: 5
more t. you have strength and	10: 4
love darkness rather t. light,	10:21
is greater t. the cunning of	10:43
declareth more or less t. this,	10:68
sharper t. a two-edged sword,	11: 2
sharper t. a two-edged sword,	12: 2
sharper t. a two-edged sword,	14: 2
express t. other scriptures,	19: 7
more t. if you should obtain	19:38
love darkness rather t. light,	29:45
more t. on the things of me,	30: 2
sharper t. a two-edged sword,	33: 1
a voice louder t. that which	38:30
more t. is necessary for their	42:33
more t. that which would be for	42:55
but if there are more t. two	42:80
which are more t. is needful	51:13
t. that which the prophets and	52: 9
t. the prophets and apostles,	52:36
t. among the congregations of	61:32
receive more t. is needful for	70: 7
of judgment, t. for that house;	75:22
to sleep longer t. is needful;	88:124
is more or less t. this	93:25
is more or less t. this,	98: 7
is less t. these cometh of evil.	98:10
t. that which I have appointed;	101:20
t. that which I have appointed,	101:20
shall more t. six be appointed	102:14
there are more treasures t. one	111:10
sacred unto me t. his increase.	117:13
is stronger t. the cords of death.	121:44
t. the fierce lion,	122: 4
Art thou greater t. he?	122: 8
shall not receive less t. fifty dollars	124:64
that which is more or less t. this	124:120
not be any sooner t. that time.	130:17
diligence and obedience t. another,	130:19
Jacob did none other things t.	132:37
did none other things t. that	132:37
t. any other man that ever lived	135: 3
be made stronger t. many waters;	Mses 1:25
the serpent was more subtle t.	4: 5
they loved Satan more t. God.	5:13
And Cain loved Satan more t. God.	5:18
they loved Satan more t. God.	5:28
is greater t. I can bear.	5:38
lesser t. that which is to rule the	Abr 3: 5
greater t. that upon which thou	3: 5
t. the reckoning of the time of	3: 7
be more intelligent t. the other,	3:18
is more intelligent t. the other,	3:18
more intelligent t. the other,	3:19
another more intelligent t. they;	3:19
I am more intelligent t. they all.	3:19
were more pretended t. real;	JS 2: 6
t. this did at this time to mine.	2:12
more wisdom t. I then had,	2:12
t. I found myself delivered	2:17
t. I asked the Personages who	2:18
room was lighter t. at noonday,	2:30
t. that of building his kingdom;	2:46
t. the most strenuous exertions	2:60
bitter and severe t. before,	2:60
more so t. any he had before	2:64
t. the Holy Ghost fell upon	2:73

THANK

THANK
what t. they the Jews for the	2Ne	29: 4
ought to t. your heavenly King!	Mos	2:19
I t. my God, my beloved people,	Al	24: 7
I t. my great God that he has		24: 8
I also t. my God, that by		24: 9
And I also t. my God, yea, my		24:10
which holiness, O God, we t. thee;		31:17
we also t. thee that thou hast		31:17
And again we t. thee, O God,		31:18
We t. thee, O God, for we are		31:28
O God, I t. thee that we are		38:14
did t. the Lord their God,		49:28
not to t. the Lord your God	He	13:22
I t. thee that thou hast given	3Ne	19:20
I t. thee that thou hast purified		19:28
he did t. and praise the Lord	Eth	6: 9
Thou shalt t. the Lord thy God	DC	59: 7
even the t.-offering of a child	Abr	1:10

THANKFUL
receive them with t. hearts,	Jac	4: 3
I am very t. before God	Mos	7:12
with a t. heart in all things.	DC	62: 7

THANKFULNESS
who receiveth all things with t.	DC	78:19

THANKING
t. their God that they were	Al	31:22

THANK-OFFERING: *see THANK and OFFERING.*

THANKS
gave t. unto the Lord our God.	1Ne	2: 7
gave t. unto the God of Israel.		5: 9
given t. unto the God of Israel,		5:10
give t. unto the Lord their God;		7:22
and did give t. unto him.		16:32
and give t. unto his holy name	2Ne	9:52
they might give t. to the Lord	Mos	2: 4
do merit any t. from you,		2:19
all the t. and praise which		2:20
and gave t. to God, saying:		8:19
give t. to the Lord their God		18:23
poured out their t. to God		24:21
And they gave t. to God,		24:22
their voices and give t. to God.		25:10
and to give t. in all things.		26:39
always returning t. unto God	Al	7:23
and he gave t. unto God.		8:22
let us give t. to his holy name,		26: 8
I will give t. unto my God		26:37
offered up t. after this manner,		31:23
offer up t. after their manner.		31:23
heart be full of t. unto God;		37:37
t. unto the Lord their God;		45: 1
give t. unto God that he hath	Mrm	9:31
give t. unto God in the Spirit	DC	46:32
and in every thing give t.;		98: 1
T. be to thy name, O Lord God		109: 1

THANKSGIVING
t. and the voice of melody.	2Ne	8: 3
in prayer and t. to God for	Al	19:14
this is my joy, and my great t.;		26:37
and that ye live in t. daily,		34:38
whose heart did swell with t. to		48:12
t. unto the Lord Jesus Christ,	3Ne	10:10
all things with prayer and t.,	DC	46: 7
as ye do these things with t.,		59:15
in t., forever and ever.		88:133
to do this by prayer and t.,		88:137
be used with prudence and t.		89:11
for the use of man with t.;		89:12
a place of t. for all saints,		97:13
with a prayer of praise and t.		136:28

THAT: *see in the APPENDIX.*

THAYRE, Ezra: *see also EZRA.*
and my servant T. take their	DC	52:22

Thomas B. Marsh and T.,	DC	56: 5
my servant T. must repent of		56: 8
And also my servant T. and		75:31

THE: *see in the APPENDIX.*

THEE: *see in the APPENDIX.*

THEFT
that murder, treason, robbery, t.,	DC	134: 8

THEIR: *see in the APPENDIX.*

THEIRS
for t. is the kingdom of heaven.	3Ne	12: 3
for t. is the kingdom of heaven.		12:10
fatness of the earth shall be t.	DC	56:18
Wherefore, all things are t.,		76:59
all are t. and they are		76:59

THEM: *see in the APPENDIX.*

THEMSELVES
should hide t. without the walls.	1Ne	4: 5
And after they had hid t.,		4: 5
did humble t. before the Lord;		13:16
did humble t. before the Lord.		15:20
did humble t. before the Lord;		16: 5
for they had humbled t. because		16:24
did humble t. before the Lord,		16:32
humble t. again before the Lord.		18: 4
wives began to make t. merry,		18: 9
they call t. of the holy city,		20: 2
but they do not stay t. upon the		20: 2
all these gather t. together,		21:18
for they shall war among t.,		22:13
may possess this land unto t.	2Ne	1: 9
act for t. and not to be acted upon,		2:26
to call t. the people of Nephi.		5: 9
do not unite t. to that great and		6:12
supposing they know of t.,		9:28
consider t. fools before God,		9:42
and they please t. in the		12: 6
they have rewarded evil unto t.!		13: 9
they shall fret t., and curse their		18:21
inhabitants of Gebim gather t.		20:31
and they sell t. for naught;		26:10
preach up unto t. their own		26:20
and set t. up for a light unto		26:29
indulge t. somewhat in wicked	Jac	1:15
seek to excuse t. in committing		2:23
the roots, taking strength unto t.		5:48
might gather t. together,	Mos	1:18
people gathered t. together		2: 1
except they humble t. and		3:18
they had viewed t. in their		4: 2
and rest t. from the labors of		7:16
might gather t. together		7:17
they had gathered t. together		7:18
they did shed blood among t.		7:25
glut t. with the labors of our		9:12
feast t. upon the flocks of our		9:12
should gather t. together to		10: 9
should gather t. together that		12:17
subjecting t. to the devil.		16: 3
should gather t. together to		18:25
to assemble t. together.		18:25
were assembling t. together to		18:32
did gather t. together to		20: 1
and to make t. merry.		20: 1
therefore they exerted t.		20:11
deliver t. out of their hands,		21: 5
they gathered t. together again,		21: 7
did humble t. even to the dust,		21:13
subjecting t. to the yoke of		21:13
submitting t. to be smitten,		21:13
humble t. even in the depths of		21:14
for they t. had entered into a		21:31
that time form t. into a church,		21:34
deliver t. out of the hands of		21:36
deliver t. out of bondage;		22: 1
should gather t. together;		22: 1

to deliver t. out of bondage,	Mos	22: 2
to deliver t. out of bondage		22: 2
and gathered t. together in		23:26
delivered t. up into their hands;		23:29
upon t. the name of Nephi,		25:12
they did assemble t. together		25:21
should assemble t. together;		27:22
they did humble t. before him;		29:20
they assembled t. together in		29:39
be no persecution among t.	Al	1:21
And also many withdrew t. from		1:24
did indulge t. in sorceries,		1:32
people assembled t. together		2: 5
they did assemble t. together		2: 6
they gathered t. together,		2: 9
they did arm t. with swords,		2:12
for they had marked t. with red		3: 4
yea, they set the mark upon t.,		3:13
to mark t. in their foreheads;		3:18
they brought upon t. the curse;		3:19
that united t. to the church		4: 5
lifting t. up with their pride,		4:12
while others were abasing t.,		4:13
and they humbled t. and put		5:13
humble t. and do walk after		5:54
and humble t. before God—		6: 3
of assembling t. together		6: 5
gather t. together oft,		6: 6
placing t. in a state to act,		12:31
children, and also concerning t.,		15: 2
began to humble t. before God,		15:17
began to assemble t. together		15:17
had given t. to much prayer,		17: 3
they might provide food for t.		17: 7
they separated t. and departed		17:13
separated t. one from another,		17:17
began to assemble t. together		19:18
began to murmur among t.;		19:19
began to marvel again among t.		19:24
separated t. in the borders of		21: 1
Now the Lamanites of t. were		21: 3
should assemble t. together.		21:20
they may assemble t. together		22: 7
should assemble t. together,		22:22
defend t. against the Lamanites.		24: 5
and prostrated t. before them		24:21
did join t. to the people of God,		25:13
would not suffer t. to be slain		26:34
and they suffered t. to be slain		27: 3
to bind t. down under the		30:23
separated t. from the Nephites		30:59
and called t. Zoramites,		30:59
had gathered t. together in a		31: 3
that they did gather t. together		31:12
had assembled t. together again		31:23
separate t. one from another,		31:37
taking no thought for t. what		31:37
blessed who truly humble t.		32:14
blessed are they who humble t.		32:16
you who would humble t.,		32:25
withdrew t. from the multitude		35: 1
taken up arms to defend t.,		35:14
teach them to humble t. and		37:33
in and of t., therefore,		43: 6
defend t. against the Lamanites.		43:23
gather t. together to battle		43:26
establish a kingdom unto t.		43:29
defend t., and their families,		43:47
who had gathered t. together,		46:31
and armed t., and entered into		46:31
should gather t. together again		47: 1
they had gathered t. together		47: 7
and bowed t. before the king,		47:22
defend t. against their enemies,		48:14
defend t. against their enemies,		48:16
and the people did humble t.		48:20
wars and contentions among t.,		48:20
their peace amongst t.,		48:21
also prepared t. with shields,		49: 6
prepared t. with garments of		49: 6
were they prepared to defend t.		49:20
which were among t.,		50:21
humble t. like unto their brethren,	Al	51:21
of Lehi gathered t. together,		51:24
because of iniquity amongst t.,		53: 9
and intrigue among t.		53: 9
suffered t. to have fallen into		53:11
their weapons of war to defend t.		53:16
they did assemble t. together		53:16
and they called t. Nephites.		53:16
Nephites and t. from bondage.		53:17
their weapons of war and also t.		56:54
had surrendered t. up unto us,		56:55
did the Lamanites deliver t. up		56:56
surrendered t. prisoners of war.		57:14
number of men should secrete t.		58:16
when they had thus secreted t.,		58:17
let t. down into that part of		62:22
did humble t. before God,		62:41
did humble t. exceedingly		62:49
did mingle t. among the people,	He	1:12
no time to assemble t. together		1:24
did yield t. into the hands of		1:32
did join t. unto the church		3:24
t. astonished beyond measure.		3:25
did build up unto t. idols of		6:31
went, and they said among t.,		9: 1
people did gather t. together		9: 7
therefore they said among t.:		9: 8
people did assemble t. together		9:10
that they were divided against t.		10:18
and did humble t. in sackcloth		11: 9
upon t. the name of Lamanites,		11:24
hiding t. that they could not be		11:25
they bring upon t. their own		14:29
they will suffer t. that they be		15: 9
and to contend among t.,		16:17
they became for t., and were led	3Ne	1:29
wronged t. by dissenting away		3:11
did exert t. in their might		3:16
they should gather t. together,		3:22
defend t. against their enemies.		3:22
who did gather t. together in		3:24
gather t. together in the land		3:24
fortify t. against their enemies;		3:25
reserved for t. provisions,		4: 4
durst not spread t. upon the		4: 6
could cause them to yield t. up		4:16
appointed unto t. another leader,		4:17
withdraw t. from the siege,		4:23
who did yield t. up prisoners		4:27
did gather t. together,		6:27
yield t. unto the power of Satan.		7: 5
did gather t. together, and did		7: 9
build up unto t. a kingdom.		7:12
forth and had witnessed for t.,		11:16
sit t. down upon the earth.		18: 2
multitude gathered t. together,		26:16
show t. unto whatsoever man		28:30
to build up churches unto t.	4Ne	1:26
to build up churches unto t.,		1:41
should gather t. together	Mrm	3: 5
avenge t. of the blood of		3: 9
avenge t. of the blood of		3:14
few only who do not lift t. up		8:36
commending t. unto the Lord	Eth	6: 4
they bowed t. down upon		6:12
humble t. before the Lord,		6:12
humbled t. sufficiently before		9:35
clothe t. from their nakedness.		10:24
that humble t. before me;		12:27
they humble t. before me,		12:27
are exceedingly fierce among t.;	Mro	1: 2
they who subject t. unto him.		7:17
showing t. unto them of strong		7:30
humble t. as their little children,		8:10
catch t. in their own snare.	DC	10:26
but build up churches unto t.		10:56
All those who humble t. before		20:37
uniting t. with the church since		20:82
and humble t. before me,		29: 2
they could not be agents unto t.;		29:39
shall assemble t. at the Ohio,		39:15
they t. are the offenders,		42:75

THEMSELVES 957 THEREFORE

they assemble t. together.	DC 44: 2
if not of t., they shall come	49:10
a privilege of organizing t.	51:15
counsel between t. and me.	58:25
wherein they are agents unto t.	58:28
assemble t. together unto	63:24
may render t. approved in	72:22
and suffered t. through the	76:31
having crucified him unto t.	76:35
and purify t. before him;	76:116
of seeing and knowing for t.;	76:117
not boast t. of these things,	84:73
defend t. against other nations;	87: 3
left of the land will marshal t.,	87: 5
cast t. down as a fig that	88:87
heaving t. beyond their bounds.	88:90
avenged t. on all their enemies,	98:37
take upon t. the fruit of my	101:45
they began to say among t.:	101:47
a long time, saying among t.:	101:48
call t. after my name,	101:75
who call t. after my name;	101:97
privilege of speaking for t.	102:18
who call t. after my name	103: 4
of men to be agents unto t.	104:17
That they t. may be prepared,	105:10
warn them to save t. from	109:41
shall humble t. before me,	112:22
may come upon t.	121:13
the children of disobedience t.	121:17
they t. shall be despised by	121:20
the heavens withdraw t.;	121:37
organize t., and appoint one	124:62
as shall be agreed among t.,	124:121
if those who call t. by my name	125: 2
gather t. together unto the	125: 2
whether they t. have attended	128: 8
declaring t. as possessing the keys	128:20
and shall no longer stay t.;	133:26
men are justified in defending t.,	134:11
warn the righteous to save t.	134:12
Let each company provide t. with	136: 5
fig-leaves together and made t.	Mses 4:13
hide t. from the presence of	4:14
they have foresworn t., and,	6:29
they have brought upon t. death;	6:29
they are agents unto t.,	6:56
people of Canaan shall divide t.	7: 7
daughters of thy sons have sold t.;	8:15
the Gods took counsel among t.	Abr 4:26
And the Gods said among t.:	5: 2
(the Gods) counseled among t.	5: 3
that they counseled among t.	5: 3
multitudes united t. to	JS 2: 5

THEN: see in the APPENDIX.

THENCE

from t. throughout all the land.	Al 5: 1
that Alma departed from t.	8: 3
he departed t., and traveled	8: 6
he departed t. and took his	8:13
and from t. they came to the	24: 5
and from t. into the land of	He 5:16
and Lehi did proceed from t.	5:20
shalt by no means come out t.	3Ne 12:26
depart ye, go ye out from t.,	20:41
destroyed, and from t. eastward,	Eth 9: 3
And from t., whosoever I will	DC 38:33
And from t. men shall go	39:15
And let them journey from t.	52: 9
And from t. let my servants,	60: 6
And from t. let them journey	61:32
from t. shall the gospel roll	65: 2
and from t. it was parted,	Mses 3:10
from t. went forth the saying,	7:69
and removed from t. unto a	Abr 2:20
from t. it was parted and	5:10

THENCEFORTH

commandments of God from t.,	Al 7:16
from t. to the city of Gid;	He 5:15
shall be t. good for nothing,	3Ne 12:13
t. good for nothing but to be	3Ne 16:15
you shall from t. preside	DC 90:13
not be idle in her days from t.	90:31
it is t. good for nothing only	101:40
is t. good for nothing but to	103:10
from t. came wars and bloodshed;	Mses 6:15
t. came the saying abroad in the	6:36

THEORY

instructed more perfectly in t.,	DC 88:78
in t., in principle, and in	97:14

THERE: see in the APPENDIX.

THEREABOUTS

I was in my tenth year, or t.	JS 2: 3

THEREAT

many there be who go in t.;	3Ne 14:13
and many there are that go in t.,	DC 132:25

THEREBY

t. they might become men of	Mos 1: 2
that t. they could teach them to	1: 4
diligently, that ye may profit t.;	1: 7
that t. they may be gathered	1:10
that t. they may be distinguished	1:11
that t. they become weak like	1:13
that t. they might be led,	1:16
that t. they might gather	1:18
that t. they might remain in	2: 6
that t. his people might hear	2: 7
that t. I might accuse you;	2:15
that t. they may dwell with God	2:41
that t. whosoever should believe	3:13
that t. salvation might come	4: 6
that t. he might win the prize;	4:27
that t. they might hear and know	6: 3
that t. he might not become	6: 7
that t. they might eat, and	7:16
that t. they might gather	7:17
that t. they might find the	8: 7
that t. I might have weapons	10: 1
t. they might have wherewith	12:19
t. his people might have room	Al 2:34
t. the Lord God might preserve	3: 8
t. they might make him cross his	10:16
that t. the people might know	13: 2
t. the people might look forward	13:16
t. they might drive away many	18: 7
that t. they should have no more	22:33
t. they might be distinguished	23:16
unto us and has made us clean t.	24:15
t. ye may have a remission of	He 14:13
t. men may be brought into	14:15
that t. salvation might come?	3Ne 28:35
that t. they might subsist upon	Eth 6: 4
t. ye may repent of your sins,	8:23
t. others might be partakers of	12: 8
T. showing that he is the same	DC 20:12
that all may be profited t.	46:12
member may be profited t.	46:29
that t. I may save some	64:21
brought under condemnation t.,	90: 5
t. they may be perfected in	90: 8
That t. he may be enabled	90:23
And t. you be hindered in	90:27
and t. ascertain who of	102:12
t. jeopardizing the lives of men;	134:12

THEREFORE

t. I was taught somewhat in all	1Ne 1: 1
t. I make a record of my	1: 1
T., I would that ye should know,	1:18
T. go, my son, and thou shalt	3: 6
t. let us go down to the land	3:16
T. let us go up;	4: 2
T. I did obey the voice of	4:18
t. I did seize upon the	4:31
T., if thou wilt go down	4:34
t. I spake unto them, saying,	7: 8
T. remember, O man,	10:20
T., wo be unto the Gentiles	14: 6

t. they did not look unto	1 Ne 15: 3	T., what teach ye this people?	Mos 12:27
t. I was bidden that I should not	2 Ne 4:25	t., God will not suffer that	13: 3
t. I will lift up my voice unto	4:35	t. I finish my message.	13: 7
t. shall I not be confounded.	7: 7	T. there was a law given them,	13:30
T. have I set my face like a flint,	7: 7	T. will I divide him a portion with	14:12
T., the redeemed of the Lord shall	8:11	t., he bringeth to pass the	15:20
T. hear now this, thou afflicted,	8:21	t., they are the first resurrection.	15:22
T., cheer up your hearts,	10:23	T. ought ye not to tremble?	15:27
T., O Lord, thou hast forsaken	12: 6	t. the Lord redeemeth them not.	16: 2
t., forgive him not.	12: 9	T., he is as though there was no	16: 5
T. the Lord will smite with	13:17	t. the grave hath no victory,	16: 8
T., my people are gone into	15:13	T., if ye teach the law of Moses,	16:14
T., hell hath enlarged herself,	15:14	t. he began to plead with the	17: 2
T., as the fire devoureth the	15:24	T. the king was stirred up in	17:12
T., is the anger of the Lord	15:25	T. on the day that they were	18:32
T., the Lord himself shall give	17:14	t. he sent his army to destroy	18:33
Now t., behold, the Lord bringeth	18: 7	t. they took their tents and their	18:34
T. the Lord shall set up the	19:11	t. he drew his sword, and swore in	19: 4
T. will the Lord cut off from	19:14	T. the Lamanites did spare their	19:15
T. the Lord shall have no joy in	19:17	t. they durst not return to their	20: 3
T. shall the Lord, the Lord of	20:16	T. they sent their armies forth;	20: 7
T., thus saith the Lord God of	20:24	t. he gathered his people	20: 8
T., with joy shall ye draw water	22: 3	t. they exerted themselves and	20:11
T. shall all hands be faint,	23: 7	t., why should ye break the	20:14
T., I will shake the heavens,	23:13	t., in my anger I did cause my	20:15
t. they must go down to hell.	26:10	t. he said: I will search among	20:16
T., I will proceed to do a	27:26	T. he caused a search to be made	20:16
T., thus saith the Lord,	27:33	t., let us put a stop to the shedding	20:22
T., wo be unto him that is at ease	28:24	t. he granted unto them that	21: 6
t., gather it, and lay it up	Jac 5:23	t. king Limhi commanded that	21:17
t. he could read these engravings,	Mos 1: 4	t. they laid wait for them	21:21
t., he thought it expedient that	1: 9	t. he caused that they should be	21:23
T., he had Mosiah brought before	1:10	T. they did not at that time	21:34
T., as they were unfaithful they	1:17	t. let us send a proclamation	22: 2
and t. they were smitten with	1:17	t. they were lost in the	22:16
t. he caused a tower to be	2: 7	t. they gathered together their	23: 1
t. he caused that the words	2: 8	t. I say unto you it is not	23: 7
t., if ye do keep his	2:22	t. ye were bound with the bands	23:12
and t. he hath paid you.	2:24	T. he consecrated all their	23:17
t., of what have ye to boast?	2:24	T. they did watch over their	23:18
T., as I said unto you that	2:27	T. they hushed their fears,	23:28
t., they are just and true.	2:35	t., the king of the Lamanites	24: 1
t. he listeth to obey the evil	2:37	t., the king of the Lamanites	24: 2
t., the Lord has no place in him,	2:37	t. he was called king Laman.	24: 3
T. if that man repenteth not,	2:38	t. he was wroth with him;	24: 9
t. his final doom is to endure	2:39	t. get thee out of this land,	24:23
t. they have drunk damnation to	3:25	t. they took upon themselves the	25:12
T., they have drunk out of the	3:26	T., Alma did go forth into the	25:18
t., mercy could have claim on	3:26	T. they did assemble themselves	25:21
t. I will stay my hand,	4:17	t. it became expedient that	26: 6
t., all things must be done in	4:27	t. Alma was troubled in his	26:10
and t. he said unto them:	5: 6	t. we have brought them before	26:11
t., ye are born of him and	5: 7	t. I deliver them into thy hands	26:12
t., I would that ye should take	5: 8	T. I say unto you, that he that	26:28
t., he findeth himself on the left	5:10	T. I say unto you, Go; and	26:29
t., take heed that ye do not	5:11	t. he led many of the people to do	27: 8
T., I would that ye should be	5:15	t., for this purpose have I come	27:14
t., they wearied him with their	7: 1	t. he was taken by those that were	27:19
t. they wandered many days in	7: 4	T. he took the records which	28:11
T., lift up your heads, and	7:19	t. the king could not confer the	29: 3
t. being deceived by the cunning	7:21	T. king Mosiah sent again among	29: 4
T., who wondereth that they are	7:28	T. I will be your king the	29:11
T. I said unto thee: Canst thou	8:11	T., if it were possible that you	29:13
t. he becometh a great benefit	8:18	T., choose you by the voice of	29:25
T., I contended with my brethren	9: 2	t. this shall ye observe and make	29:26
T. it came to pass, that after	9:11	t. their iniquities are answered	29:31
t. they were desirous to bring	9:12	T. they relinquished their desires	29:38
T. it came to pass that king	9:13	T., it came to pass that they	29:39
t. there began to be wars	9:13	t. they did esteem him, yea,	29:40
t. they began to prepare for war,	10: 6	t. they were obliged to abide by	Al 1: 1
t. they depended upon their own	10:11	t. he was not able to	1: 9
t. he was favored of the Lord,	10:13	t. he was slain by the sword.	1: 9
t. they have an eternal hatred	10:17	T. thou art condemned to die,	1:14
t., we did contend with them,	10:19	t. this people must abide by	1:14
t., I say no more.	10:22	t. he pretended to preach	1:17
t. Noah began to reign in his	11: 1	t. they were liberal to all,	1:30
t. he became a wine-bibber,	11:15	t., there was much peace among	1:33
t., they returned rejoicing in	11:18	T., if it were possible that Amlici	2: 4
t. I will slay him.	11:28	T. the people of the Nephites were	2:12
t. they hardened their hearts	11:29	t. they did prepare to meet	2:12
t., I will visit them in my anger,	12: 1	t. he went up with his people,	2:16
t., this man has lied concerning	12:14	t. the Lord did hear their cries,	2:28
t., ye have perverted the ways	12:26	t. they were cursed;	3: 7
t., ye have not been wise.	12:27	T., whosoever suffered himself to	3:10

THEREFORE

t. it was expedient that the curse	Al	3:18
t. let it be according to the truth.		3:27
t. they were awakened to a		4: 3
t. they were saved.		5:13
T., if a man bringeth forth good		5:41
t., for his wages he receiveth		5:42
t. every tree that bringeth not		5:52
t. I attempt to address you in		7: 1
t. come and be baptized unto		7:14
t., his course is one eternal		7:20
t. I say unto you the time shall		7:21
t. they would not hearken unto		8: 9
t. thou art not the chief judge		8:12
t., lift up thy head and rejoice,		8:15
T., go with me into my house and		8:20
t. the Lord will be merciful		9:16
T., prepare ye the way of the		9:28
t. I knew concerning these		10: 6
t. I went on rebelling against		10: 6
t., if ye will cast out the righteous		10:23
t., a shiblon for half a measure		11:15
t., they did stir up the people to		11:20
t. they did stir up the people		11:20
t., he said unto Amulek:		11:21
t., how can ye be saved, except ye		11:37
T., ye cannot be saved in your		11:37
T. the wicked remain as though		11:41
t., he that will harden his heart,		12:10
t. this life became a		12:24
T. he sent angels to converse		12:29
t. God conversed with men,		12:30
T. God gave unto them		12:32
T., whosoever repenteth, and		12:34
t. your iniquity provoketh him		12:36
t., according to his word, unto		12:36
t. they having chosen good,		13: 3
T. they were called after this		13:11
t. he was called the prince of		13:18
t., of him they have more		13:19
t., we are thus highly favored,		13:23
T. let us stretch forth our hands,		14:10
t. they burn us not.		14:13
t. he began to be scorched with		15: 3
T., after Alma having established		15:17
t. he took Amulek and came over		15:18
T., he that had been appointed		16: 5
t. they went unto him and		16: 5
t. Alma did rejoice exceedingly		17: 2
t. they had the spirit of prophecy,		17: 3
T., this was the cause for which		17:16
T. they separated themselves one		17:17
T. Ammon became a servant to		17:25
T., as Ammon and the servants of		17:27
T., they did as Ammon		17:34
T. they did not fear Ammon, for		17:35
t. t'.ey delighted in the		17:35
t., seeing that they could not hit		17:36
t., we know that he is a friend to		18: 3
t. he was about to return out of		18:12
T. Ammon turned himself unto		18:14
t. he perceived the thoughts of		18:16
t., whatsoever thou desirest which		18:17
t. she sent and desired that he		19: 2
T., if this is the case, I would that		19: 5
T., what the queen desired of him		19: 7
T., he went in to see the king		19: 7
t. bury him not.		19: 8
t., when she saw that all the		19:17
t. she ran forth from house to		19:17
t., Mosiah trusted him unto the		19:23
t. they went their way.		19:32
t. I go to the land of Middoni,		20: 4
t. he was desirous to learn them.		20:27
t. the brethren of Ammon were		20:28
t. they would not hearken unto		20:30
t. they did cause the Lamanites		21: 3
T., as Aaron entered into one of		21: 5
T., when he saw that they would		21:11
t. they departed and came over		21:12
t. they durst not lay their hands		22:20
T. we shall fall before them.		22:20
t. he put forth his hand and		22:22
T. the Lamanites could have no	Al	22:34
t. he sent his proclamation		23: 3
T., we have named all the cities of		23:15
t. the king consulted with Aaron		23:16
t., they did open a		23:18
t., they took up arms against		24: 2
t., in his mercy he doth visit us		24:14
t. we have no reason to doubt		24:26
t. they swore vengeance upon		25: 1
t. they began to disbelieve the		25: 6
t. I will not boast of myself,		26:12
t. have we not great reason to		26:13
T., let us glory, yea, we will		26:16
t. they began again to destroy		27: 2
t., when Ammon and his brethren		27: 4
t. let us go down and rely upon		27: 9
t. get thee out of this land;		27:12
t. they were distinguished by		27:26
t., death was swallowed up to		27:28
T., they would suffer death in		27:29
t. we see that the Lord doth		29: 8
t., a man was punished only		30:11
t. all men were on equal grounds.		30:11
t. ye cannot know that there		30:15
t. every man prospered		30:17
t. if thou shalt deny again,		30:47
t., it shall be unto thee even as		30:55
t. they were all converted again		30:58
t. his heart was exceeding		31: 2
t. Alma thought it was		31: 5
T. he took Ammon, and Aaron,		31: 6
t. they had had the word of God		31: 8
t., for this cause, Alma and his		31:11
T., whosoever desired to worship		31:14
t., give unto us, O Lord, power		31:35
T. they were not permitted to		32: 3
t. they were poor; yea, they were		32: 3
t. they were poor as to things of		32: 3
T. he did say no more to the		32: 7
T., blessed are they who humble		32:16
t. if ye have faith ye hope for		32:21
t. he desireth, in the first place,		32:22
T., if a seed groweth it is good,		32:32
is not good, t. it is cast away.		32:32
t. ye must know that it is good;		32:35
t. ye cannot have the fruit		32:39
t. I will cry unto thee in all		33:11
would not look t. they perished.		33:20
t. there can be nothing which is		34:12
T., it is expedient that there		34:13
t. only unto him that has faith		34:16
T. may God grant unto you,		34:17
T., if ye do not remember to be		34:29
and t., if ye will repent and		34:31
t., the Spirit of the Lord hath		34:35
t. they would not hearken unto		35: 3
t. they found out privily the		35: 5
t. they did not cast them out,		35: 9
T., he caused that his sons should		35:16
t., I beseech of thee that thou		36: 3
t. they do know of these things		36:26
unto me; t. I shall forbear.		37:11
t. they shall be preserved.		37:19
T. I command you, my son		37:20
t. the Lord said, if they did not		37:22
t. they have been destroyed,		37:26
t. I desire that this people		37:28
T. ye shall keep these secret		37:29
t., if they had faith to believe		37:40
t. they had this miracle, and		37:40
T., they tarried in the wilderness,		37:42
t. I command you, my son,		39:12
T., there is a time appointed unto		40: 9
t. the spirit of the devil did		40:13
T., all things shall be restored to		41: 8
t., the way is prepared that		41:11
t., they are in a state contrary		41:14
T., my son, see that you are		41:15
t., the word restoration more fully		42: 6
t., as they were cut off from the		42: 6
T., as the soul could never die,		42: 9

THEREFORE 960 THEREFORE

T., as they had become carnal,	Al 42:10
T., according to justice, the plan	42:13
t. God himself atoneth for the	42:15
T., O my son, whosoever will	42:27
t., in the commencement of	43: 4
t. they made preparations for	43: 4
t., Zerahemnah appointed chief	43: 6
t., if they should fall into the	43:11
t. they gave them lands for their	43:12
t., they were exceedingly afraid of	43:21
t. they departed out of the land	43:22
t. they were prepared against	43:26
t. he thought it no sin that he	43:30
t., he found by his spies which	43:30
T., he divided his army and	43:31
T. for this cause were the Nephites	43:47
T. the armies of Moroni encircled	43:52
T. when Zerahemnah saw the	43:53
t. as the Lord liveth, ye shall	44:11
t. he commanded his people that	44:17
t. they gave thanks unto the	45: 1
t. write the words which I shall	45: 9
t., for this cause we know nothing	45:19
T., Helaman and his brethren	45:22
t. they grew rich in their own	45:24
t. they dissented even from the	46: 7
t., at this time, Moroni prayed	46:16
t., fearing that he should not	46:29
t. he thought to cut off the	46:30
T. Moroni thought it was	46:31
t. he had power according to	46:34
t. he gave Amalickiah the	47: 3
t. he laid the plan in his heart	47: 4
t. he went forward to the	47: 5
t. they fled to Onidah, to the	47: 5
T., when the queen had received	47:33
T. he had accomplished his	48: 3
t. he appointed them to be	48: 5
T. they retreated into the	49:12
t., they marched forward to the	49:13
t. they would march thither to	49:15
t., they brought up their armies.	49:17
t. there began to be a warm	50:26
T., Morianton put it into their	50:29
t. he was angry with one of his	50:30
T. Moroni sent an army, with	50:33
t. Alma had conferred them	50:38
t., he did not hearken to those	51: 3
T., those who were desirous that	51: 4
t. there arose a warm dispute	51: 4
t. Amalickiah did drive them,	51:23
t. I cannot come unto you.	52:11
t. he abandoned his designs	52:17
t., he resolved upon a plan that	52:21
T. he caused that Teancum	52:22
t. Jacob was determined to slay	52:34
t. they did not give way before	52:34
t. all those who had entered into	53:15
t. they did assemble themselves	53:16
t. Moroni resolved upon a	54: 3
T. he wrote an epistle, and sent	54: 4
t. I will close my epistle by	54:11
t. Moroni appointed Laman and	55: 7
t. let us take of the wine,	55:11
t. they took of it more freely;	55:13
t. their chief captains demanded	55:23
T. it sufficeth me that I tell you	56: 5
t. you may well suppose that	56:17
t. we were desirous, if they	56:23
t. Antipus ordered that I	56:30
t. they did not overtake us,	56:38
t. we did camp for the night.	56:38
t. we did continue our march,	56:39
T. what say ye, my sons, will ye	56:44
t. let us go, lest they should	56:46
t. the men of Antipus, being	56:51
t. we sent them to the land	56:57
t. we began to make	57: 3
t., we did take them and their	57:10
t. it became expedient that we	57:11
t. they yielded up the city	57:12
T. it became expedient for us,	57:15
t. we selected a part of our men,	57:16
t. they were driven back to the	Al 57:22
t. we could not decoy them away	58: 1
t. it became expedient that we	58: 3
t. we were grieved and also	58: 9
T. we did pour out our souls in	58:10
t. they began to make	58:15
t. they did follow us into the	58:19
t. they began to retreat into the	58:24
t. they took no thought	58:25
T. he retained all his force to	59:10
t. ye need not suppose that	60:13
t. I would that ye should adhere	60:34
t. he will give unto us of your	60:35
T., my beloved brother, Moroni,	61:14
T., come unto me speedily with	61:15
t. they durst not come out	62:19
t. they did not come to battle	62:19
T., all the prisoners of the	62:29
t. Moroni went forth from the	62:30
t. they did not resolve upon any	62:35
T., Helaman and his brethren	62:45
t. he went forth and built him	63: 5
T. it became expedient for	63:11
t., in this year, they had been	63:13
t. there began to be a serious	He 1: 2
t., they did cause three divisions	1: 4
t., he was about to flatter away	1: 7
t. they were angry, and behold,	1: 9
T., Kishkumen was not known	1:12
T., the king of the Lamanites,	1:16
T. he did stir them up to anger,	1:17
T. Coriantumr did cut down the	1:20
t. he did march forth, giving	1:24
t. Moronihah had caused that	1:26
t. there began to be a	2: 1
t. he became the leader of the	2: 4
T. he did flatter them, and	2: 5
t. Kishkumen sought to destroy	2: 5
t. Kishkumen made known unto	2: 7
t. he caused that his band	2:11
t. they did build houses of	3: 7
t., what I have spoken had	3:17
t. they were not destroyed out of	3:23
t. they did not prosper, but were	4:13
T. they did abandon their design	4:19
t. Moronihah did employ all	4:19
T. the Lord did cease to	4:25
t. they were ripening for	5: 2
T., my sons, I would that ye	5: 7
t. he hath sent his angels to	5:11
and t. they went forth, keeping	5:14
T. they did speak unto the great	5:19
t. they began to set their	6:17
t. they began to commit secret	6:17
t., Nephi had bowed himself	7:10
t., I would that ye should behold,	7:23
t. the Lord will be merciful unto them	7:24
t. I testify that they shall be.	7:29
T. they did cry unto the people,	8: 5
t. our enemies can have no power	8: 6
t. he bagan again to speak	8:10
T. he was constrained to	8:11
t. in this ye have sinned, for	8:24
t. they did quake, and had	9: 5
t. they said among themselves,	9: 8
T. Nephi did declare unto them	10:14
t. they did revile against him,	10:15
t. cry unto the Lord our God	11: 8
t. they did preach unto the	11:23
t. they commenced a war with	11:24
t. they sent an army of strong	11:28
t., for this cause, that men	12:22
T., blessed are they who will	12:23
t. he went and got upon the	13: 4
T., thus saith the Lord:	13: 8
T., there shall be one day and a	14: 4
t. they shall know of a surety that	14: 4
T. repent ye, repent ye, lest	14:19
t., they shall be trodden down	15: 2
t. there are many who do add	15: 6
T., as many as have come to this,	15: 8
T. I say unto you, it shall be	15:14
T., saith the Lord:	15:16

THEREFORE

t. as many as believed on the	He	16: 5	t., whatsoever ye shall do, ye	3Ne	27: 7
t. when they saw that they could		16: 6	t. ye shall call the church in my		27: 7
t. take him and bind him,		16: 6	t. ye shall call whatsoever things		27: 9
t. they can keep us in		16:20	t. if ye call upon the Father,		27: 9
t., your joy and your faith	3Ne	1: 6	t. remember the things that I		27:12
t. in this same year were they		1:25	t., according to the power of		27:15
t. they did commit many murders,		1:27	t. nothing entereth into his		27:19
t., nine years had passed away.		2: 8	T., if ye do these things blessed		27:22
T., all the Lamanites who had		2:12	t. out of the books which shall be		27:26
t. if they should come down		3: 4	T., what manner of men ought ye		27:27
T. I have written this epistle,		3: 5	T., ask, and ye shall receive;		27:29
T. I write unto you, desiring that		3: 6	t., after that ye are seventy and		28: 3
t. he did not hearken to the		3:12	T., more blessed are ye, for ye		28: 7
t., this Gidgiddoni was a great		3:19	t. they could not dig pits		28:20
t. we will prepare ourselves in		3:21	t. I write them not, for they are		28:25
t. as the Lord liveth, if we do		3:21	T., great and marvelous works		28:31
T., there was no chance for the		4: 4	t. he will not receive them at		28:34
t. Giddianhi gave commandment		4: 6	T., that they might not taste of		28:38
t., when the armies of Giddianhi		4:10	T. ye need not suppose that ye		29: 9
t. it was Zemnarihah that did		4:17	t. there were not rich and poor,	4Ne	1: 3
t. he did send out his armies		4:24	t. these cities could not be		1: 9
T. they did forsake all their sins,		5: 3	t. there began to be Lamanites		1:20
T. I have made my record of		5:10	T. they did exercise power and		1:30
T. I do make my record from		5:16	T. the true believers in		1:37
t. they did take with them all		6: 2	T., when ye are about twenty	Mrm	1: 3
t. they had enjoyed peace but		6:16	t. I was visited of the Lord,		1:15
t. they did wilfully rebel against		6:18	t. the people of Nephi appointed		2: 1
T. a complaint came up unto the		6:25	T. it came to pass that in my		2: 2
T. they did combine against		6:29	t. three hundred and twenty		2: 2
t. their tribes became exceeding		7: 4	t. they would not fight, and		2: 3
t. he became a king over this		7:10	t. there was blood and carnage		2: 8
T., Jacob seeing that their		7:12	t. supposing that he would be		2:12
t. he commanded his people that		7:12	t. we had become weak like		2:26
t. having seen angels, and		7:15	t. we did fortify against them		3: 6
T., being grieved for the hardness		7:16	T. I write unto you, Gentiles,		3:17
t. they are not written in this		7:17	t. I write unto you all.		3:20
T., there were ordained to		7:25	t. I did go to the hill Shim,		4:23
t. I did cause them to be burned,		9: 9	t. I write a small abridgment,		5: 9
T., whoso repenteth and cometh		9:22	T., repent ye, and humble		5:24
t. repent, and come unto me		9:22	t. I made this record out of		6: 6
t. there was silence in all the land		10: 2	T. repent, and be baptized in		7: 8
T. for this time I make an end		10:19	t. ye are numbered among the		7:10
T., go forth unto this people,		11:41	T. I will write and hide up		8: 4
t. blessed are ye if ye shall		12: 1	t., he that condemneth, let him		8:17
T. let your light so shine before		12:16	t., he that smiteth shall be		8:19
T. come unto me and be ye		12:20	t. he hath prepared means for		9:34
T., if ye shall come unto me,		12:23	T. I do not write those things	Eth	1: 4
T. those things which were of old		12:46	t. he did not confound the		1:35
T. I would that ye should be		12:48	t. we shall perish.		2:19
T., when ye shall do your alms		13: 2	T. what will ye that I should		2:25
Be not ye t. like unto them,		13: 8	t. touch these stones, O Lord,		3: 4
After this manner t. pray ye:		13: 9	t. ye are brought back into		3:13
if, t., thine eye be single, thy		13:22	t. I show myself unto you.		3:13
If, t., the light that is in thee		13:23	t. it sufficeth me to say that		3:17
T. I say unto you, take no		13:25	t. he saw Jesus; and he did		3:20
T. take no thought, saying, What		13:31	t. the Lord could not withhold		3:26
Take t. no thought for the		13:34	t. I am commanded that I		4: 3
T., all things whatsoever ye		14:12	T., when ye shall receive this		4:17
T., whoso heareth these sayings		14:24	T., repent all ye ends of the		4:18
t., whoso remembereth these		15: 1	t. touch them not in order that		5: 1
t., the law in me is fulfilled,		15: 5	t. when they were encompassed		6: 7
fulfil the law; t. it hath an end.		15: 5	and t. they began to be many.		6:16
t. keep my commandments.		15:10	And t. he said unto them:		6:24
t. I was commanded to say no		15:18	t. he began to reign in the stead		7:10
t. it is because of their iniquity		15:19	t., let my father send for Akish,		8:10
t. I go to show myself unto them.		16: 3	T., behold, it came to pass that		9: 1
T., go ye unto your homes,		17: 3	t. Jared was murdered upon		9: 6
T. blessed are ye if ye shall keep		18:14	t. he shut him up in prison,		9: 7
T. ye must always pray unto		18:19	t. the Lord hath commanded me,		12:22
T., hold up your light that it		18:24	t. on the morrow they did come		15: 8
t. if ye know that a man is		18:29	t. his paths are straight, and	DC	3: 2
T., keep these sayings which I		18:33	t., repent of that which thou hast		3:10
t. they did not bear record;		18:37	T., O ye that embark in the		4: 2
before you, t. search them—		20:11	T., if ye have desires to serve God		4: 3
T., when these works and the		21: 5	t. give heed unto my words.		6: 2
t. they shall not hurt him,		21:10	t., whoso desireth to reap, let		6: 3
T. it shall come to pass that		21:11	T., if you will ask of me you		6: 5
t. it must needs be that he		23: 2	t. thou shalt exercise thy gift,		6:11
T. give heed to my words.		23: 4	T. be diligent; stand by my		6:18
t. it was written according as		23:13	t. treasure up these words in		6:20
t. ye sons of Jacob are not		24: 6	t., if ye sow good ye shall also		6:33
T. I, Mormon, do write the		26:12	T., fear not, little flock; do good;		6:34
T., I would that ye should behold		26:13	t. I will make him as flaming		7: 6

T. this is thy gift; apply unto	DC 8: 4
T., doubt not, for it is the gift of	8: 8
t., whatsoever you shall ask me	8: 9
do nothing; t. ask in faith.	8:10
t., you shall feel that it is right.	9: 8
t., you cannot write that which	9: 9
t. see that you are faithful and	10: 3
T., you have delivered them	10: 9
T. they will not agree, and we	10:18
T. we will destroy him, and also	10:19
t. they will not ask of me.	10:21
t. I say unto you, hold your	10:37
T., you shall translate the	10:41
t., it is wisdom in me that you	10:45
T., whosoever belongeth to my	10:55
T., I will unfold unto them	10:64
t. he is not of my church.	10:68
t. give heed unto my word.	11: 2
t., whoso desireth to reap let	11: 3
T., if you will ask of me you	11: 5
T., treasure up in your heart	11:26
t., give heed unto my word.	12: 2
t., whoso desireth to reap let	12: 3
T., if you will ask of me you	12: 5
t. give heed with your might,	12: 9
t. give heed unto my word.	14: 2
t., whoso desireth to reap let	14: 3
T., if you will ask of me you	14: 5
T. I command you to repent—	19:15
T., having so great witnesses,	20:13
T. let the church take heed and	20:33
Stand, t., having your loins	27:16
t. ye receive these things;	29: 3
t., fear not, but give heed unto	30: 5
T., thrust in your sickle with	31: 5
t., prophesy, and it shall be	34:10
T., be ye strong from henceforth;	38:15
T., the residue shall be kept in	42:34
T., he that lacketh wisdom,	42:68
T., why is it that ye cannot	50:21
Watch, t., that ye may be ready.	50:46
t., he shall not retain the gift,	51: 5
repent, t., of those things	66: 3
T., verily I say unto my servant	75: 6
t., gird up your loins and be	75:22
T., declare the things which ye	80: 4
T., verily I acknowledge him	81: 3
T., what I say unto one I say	82: 5
T., verily I say unto you,	82:11
T., I give unto you this	82:15
T., in the ordinances thereof,	84:20
t., the Lord in his wrath,	84:24
T., he took Moses out of their	84:25
T., as I said concerning the	84:31
t. all that my Father hath	84:38
T., all those who receive the	84:40
T., go ye into all the world;	84:62
T., as I said unto mine apostles	84:64
T., take ye not thought for	84:81
T., let the morrow take thought	84:84
T., let no man among you,	84:86
T., take with you those who	84:107
T., let every man stand in his	84:109
t., as the Lord speaketh, he will	85:10
T., it shall be done unto them	85:12
T., let the wheat and the tares	86: 7
T., thus saith the Lord unto	86: 8
T. your life and the priesthood	86:10
T., blessed are ye if ye continue	86:11
T., it must needs be sanctified	88:18
t. he is not meet for a	88:24
T. he must abide a kingdom	88:24
T., they must remain in his	88:35
T., unto this parable I will	88:61
T., sanctify yourselves that	88:68
T., they are left without excuse,	88:82
T., tarry ye, and labor diligently,	88:84
t., she is ready to be burned.	88:94
T., verily I say unto you,	88:117
T., cease from all your light	88:121
T., he shall be first in the house	88:129
T., thou art blessed from	90: 2
T., let them cease wearying me	90:33
T., whoso readeth it, let him	DC 91: 4
T. it is not needful that it	91: 6
T., in the beginning the Word	93: 8
t., I say unto you, you shall	93:20
t., first set in order thy house.	93:44
t. I command you to tarry,	95: 9
t. I sent them forth to be	95:10
t. you shall walk in darkness.	95:12
T., let it be built after the	95:14
T., let my servant Ahashdah	96: 2
T., take heed that ye see to	96: 4
T. ye shall ordain him unto	96: 9
T., verily, thus saith the Lord,	97:21
t., let Zion rejoice, while all the	97:21
T., he giveth this promise unto	98: 3
T., I, the Lord, justify you,	98: 6
free, t. ye are free;	98: 8
T., be not afraid of your	98:14
T., renounce war and proclaim	98:16
T., follow me, and listen to the	100: 2
T., I, the Lord, have suffered you	100: 4
T., verily I say unto you, lift up	100: 5
T., continue your journey and	100:12
T., let your hearts be comforted;	100:15
T., they must needs be chastened	101: 4
t. by these things they polluted	101: 6
t., the Lord their God is slow	101: 7
T., let your hearts be comforted	101:16
T., care not for the loss, neither	101:37
t., if that salt of the earth lose	101:40
t. they must needs be	101:41
T., get ye straightway unto	101:57
T., I must gather together my	101:65
T., a commandment I give unto	101:67
T., it is not right that any	101:79
Pray ye, t., that their ears	101:92
T., it is my will that my	101:99
T., I will raise up unto my	103:16
T., let not your hearts faint,	103:19
T. let my servant Baurak Ale	103:22
T., if you cannot obtain five	103:32
T., as I said unto you, ask and	103:35
T., inasmuch as some of my	104: 4
T., inasmuch as you are found	104: 8
t., a commandment I give	104:11
T. if any man shall take of the	104:18
t. he shall be reckoned with	104:45
T., you are dissolved as a	104:53
T. write speedily to Cainhannoch	104:81
T., in consequence of the	105: 9
T. it is expedient in me that	105:13
t., let us become subject unto	105:32
T., be faithful; and behold, and lo,	105:41
T., gird up your loins,	106: 5
T., blessed is my servant	106: 7
T., let your soul be at rest	108: 2
T., strengthen your brethren	108: 7
T. we plead before thee	109:32
T., O Lord, deliver thy people	109:46
We t. ask thee to have mercy	109:62
t., lift up your heads and rejoice.	110: 5
T., the keys of this dispensation	110:16
T., it is expedient that you	111: 3
T., be ye as wise as serpents	111:11
t., all thy sins are forgiven thee.	112: 3
Contend thou, t., morning by	112: 5
T., gird up thy loins for the work.	112: 7
T., see to it that ye trouble not	112:27
T., I command you to build a	115: 6
T., if they tarry it shall not be	117: 3
T., will I not make solitary	117: 7
T., come up hither unto the land	117: 9
T., let him contend earnestly	117:13
T., let him come up hither speedily,	117:14
T. let no man despise my servant	117:15
T., hold on thy way,	122: 9
t., fear not what man can do,	122: 9
T. it is an imperative duty that	123: 9
T., that we should waste and	123:13
T., dearly beloved brethren,	123:17
Call ye, t., upon them with	124: 7
Let him, t., hearken to your	124:13
I t. say unto you, I seal upon	124:21

THEREFORE 963 THEREOF

t. let it be a good house,	DC 124:23	many there be that travel t.,	3Ne	27:33
T., verily I say unto you,	124:39	blessed are they who dwell t.,	Eth	13:10
T., for this cause have I	124:51	contained t. that are true,	DC	91: 1
T., let my servant Joseph and	124:59	contained t. that are not true,		91: 2
T., I say unto you concerning	124:74	that he may dwell t.		96: 9
t., let him be remembered for	124:78	and all things t. are mine.		104:14
T., let my servant William put	124:87	may come from afar to lodge t.;		124:23
T., let my servant William	124:101	Lord your God will not dwell t.		124:24
Let him t. abase himself	124:114	for the Most High to dwell t.		124:27
I t. command you to send my	126: 3	For t. are the keys of the		124:34
Let all the saints rejoice, t.,	127: 3	ordinances t. unto my people;		124:40
This, t., is the sealing and	128:14	and his house have place t.,		124:56
Let us, t., as a church and	128:24	that have desires to dwell t.,		125: 4
you may t. detect him.	129: 8	by water, to be immersed t.		128:12
t. let this suffice, and trouble	130:15			
T., prepare thy heart to receive	132: 3	**THEREOF**		
T., if a man marry him a wife	132:15	unto the interpretation t.—	T Pg	
t., they are not bound by any law	132:15	interpretation t. by the gift	T Pg	
T., when they are out of	132:16	destroyed, and the inhabitants t.;	1Ne	1:13
t., they cannot be enlarged,	132:17	in the borders near the mouth t.		2: 8
they cannot, t., inherit my glory;	132:18	drew it forth from the sheath t.;		4: 9
t. shall they be from everlasting	132:20	the hilt t. was of pure gold,		4: 9
Receive ye, t., my law.	132:24	workmanship t. was exceeding		4: 9
Go ye, t., and do the works	132:32	that the blade t. was of the		4: 9
This, t., was fulfilling,	132:34	and partake of the fruit t.;		8:11
Was Abraham, t., under	132:35	that the fruit t. was white,		8:11
t. he hath fallen from his	132:39	as I partook of the fruit t.		8:12
Go, t., and I make way	132:50	I saw the head t. a little way		8:14
Let no one, t., set on my servant	132:60	at the head t. I beheld		8:14
t. is he justified.	132:62	the beauty t. was far beyond,		11: 8
T., it shall be lawful in me,	132:65	the whiteness t. did exceed the		11: 8
t., let this suffice for the present.	132:66	To know the interpretation t.—		11:11
Watch, t., for ye know neither	133:11	the world and the wisdom t.;		11:35
Let them, t., who are among	133:12	the fall t. was exceeding great.		11:36
T., marvel not at these things,	136:37	earth, because of the quaking t.		12: 4
Now, t., hearken, O ye people	136:41	depths t. are the depths of hell.		12:16
I, t., as President of	OD	the brightness t. was like unto the		15:30
t. Moses could endure his	Mses 1: 2	workmanship t. was exceeding		18: 4
T. shall a man leave his father and	3:24	and great was the soreness t.		18:15
T. I, the Lord God, will send him	4:29	of thy bowels like the gravel t.;		20:19
and I in you; t. walk with me.	6:34	workmanship t. was exceeding	2Ne	5:16
T. I give unto you a	6:58	his people and the princes t.;		13:14
T. it is given to abide in you;	6:61	of Jerusalem from the midst t.		14: 4
T. they turned their hearts to the	Abr 1: 7	and gathered out the stones t.,		15: 2
t. they were killed upon this altar,	1:11	I will take away the hedge t.,		15: 5
t. I have come down to visit	1:17	and I will break down the wall t.,		15: 5
t. my father was led away by	1:27	is darkened in the heavens t.		15:30
t. a knowledge of the beginning	1:31	seed shall be the substance t.		16:13
T. I left the land of Ur, of the	2: 4	he shall destroy the sinners t.		23: 9
t. he continued in Haran.	2: 5	constellations t. shall not give		23:10
t. my hand shall be over thee.	2: 8	and destroyed the cities t.,		24:17
t. let thy servant rise up and	2:13	of the world to the ending t.,		27: 7
T., eternity was our covering	2:16	of the world unto the end t.		27:10
T. it shall come to pass, when	2:23	the book and the words t.		27:19
t. see that ye do on this wise:	2:23	and great must be the fall t.		28:18
T. say unto them—I pray thee,	2:25	the main top t. began to perish.	Jac	5: 6
t. the reckoning of its time is not	3: 5	preserve the fruit t. unto myself;		5: 8
t. Kolob is the greatest of all the	3:16	graft them in, in the stead t.;		5: 9
I now, t., have come down unto	3:21	I might preserve the roots t.		5:11
t. we will form an help meet	5:14	that I may lay up fruit t.		5:13
T. shall a man leave his father	5:18	lose this tree and the fruit t.		5:13
When you, t., shall see	JS 1:12	the fruit t. was like unto the		5:17
T., pray ye the Lord that your	1:17	hold of the moisture of the root t.,		5:18
watch, t., for you know not at	1:46	the root t. hath brought forth		5:18
T. be ye also ready, for in such	1:48	the much strength of the root t.		5:18
No sooner, t., did I get	2:18	the tree t. would have perished.		5:18
I was, t., under the necessity of	2:58	which the tree t. hath brought		5:18
t. offered and promised us	2:75	the fruit t. I shall lay up		5:18
		I may lay up of the fruit t.		5:19
THEREFROM		Take of the fruit t.,		5:20
not, neither take t.	DC 68:34	good fruit t. unto mine own self?		5:33
and altogether turneth t.,	84:41	the roots t. profit me nothing		5:35
the Spirit shall obtain benefit t.;	91: 5	and have overrun the roots t.;		5:37
		have overcome the roots t.		5:37
THEREIN		plant this tree in the stead t.		5:44
the flesh and the evil which is t.,	2Ne 2:29	part t. brought forth good fruit,		5:45
Joy and gladness shall be found t.,	8: 3	part t. brought forth wild fruit;		5:45
and they that dwell t. shall die	8: 6	I plucked not the branches t.		5:45
and also made a wine-press t.;	15: 2	trees t. have become corrupted,		5:46
let us make a breach t. for us,	17: 6	to have laid up fruit t. against		5:46
of the book and the things t.	27:12	the branches t. overcome the		5:48
may walk t. and be saved.	Al 41: 8	have overcome the roots t.,		5:48
the Nephites who did enter t.	63: 6	of the tree in the stead t.		5:52

preserve unto myself the roots t.	Jac	5:53	inhabitants t. are consumed	DC	5:19
we will trim up the branches t.;		5:58	pass upon the inhabitants t.,		19: 3
the roots t. may take strength		5:59	corruptibleness to the extent t.		19:38
natural branches and the roots t.,		5:60	to lay the foundation t.,		21: 2
of the good and the size t.;		5:65	great glory, with all the hosts t.,		29:11
ye shall not clear away the bad t.		5:65	take hold of the inhabitants t.,		29:18
the roots t. should be too strong		5:65	the earth, and all the fulness t.,		29:24
and the graft t. shall perish,		5:65	heavens and all the hosts t.,		45: 1
the root and the top t. equal,		5:73	of the earth, in the season t.,		59:18
according to the strength t.		5:73	may partake the fatness t.		61:17
the door t. towards the temple,	Mos	2: 6	rideth upon the face t.,		61:19
they shall reap the chaff t.		7:30	Billings, who has the care t.,		63:39
and the effect t. is poison.		7:30	that dwell upon the face t.,		63:39
the hilts t. have perished,		8:11	inhabitants t. may receive it,		65: 5
blades t. were cankered with rust;		8:11	the Lord in the season t.,		68:33
and a throne in the midst t.,		11: 9	them and the concerns t.,		70: 5
he could stand upon the top t.		11:12	yea, the benefits t.		70: 5
penalty t. being a second death,	Al	12:32	expounding the mysteries t.,		71: 1
were slain by the fall t.		14:27	and rejoice ye inhabitants t.,		76: 1
every soul within the walls t.,		14:28	and the inhabitants t. are		76:24
walls t. had fallen to the earth,		14:29	have been made partakers t.,		76:31
so great was the scent t. that		16:11	And the end t., neither		76:45
was dead, that was the end t.		30:18	neither the place t., nor		76:45
the top t. would only admit one		31:13	who are made partakers t.;		76:46
forth and stand upon the top t.,		31:14	the depth, and the misery t.,		76:48
fruit t. would not be desireable;		32:39	the blessings t. are yours,		78:18
ye cannot have the fruit t.		32:39	in the ordinances t.,		84:20
an eye of faith to the fruit t.,		32:40	without the ordinances t.,		84:21
looking forward to the fruit t.,		32:41	revelations and the printing t.,		84:104
ye shall pluck the fruit t.,		32:42	and the power t. by which it		88: 7
he took a piece t., and wrote		46:12	and the power t. by which it		88: 8
on the end t. his rent coat,		46:13	and the power t. by which		88: 9
could cast stones from the top t.,		50: 5	earth also, and the power t.,		88:10
went and got upon the wall t.,	He	13: 4	and the inhabitants t.—		88:61
works t. I know to be good;	3Ne	3: 9	Every herb in the season t.,		89:11
the strength t. should be		3:14	every fruit in the season t.,		89:11
and terrible was the battle t.,		4:11	sixty-five feet in the width t.		94: 4
and terrible was the slaughter t.,		4:11	thereof and in the length t.,		94: 4
yea, even upon the top t. until		4:28	Lord from the foundation t.,		94: 6
inhabitants t. were drowned.		8: 9	sixty-five feet in the width t.,		94:11
till the buildings t. had fallen		8:14	width thereof and the length t.,		94:11
the inhabitants t. were slain,		8:14	Lord from the foundation t.,		94:12
damage t. was exceeding great,		8:15	And the size t. shall be fifty		95:15
the inhabitants t. who had not		8:20	in length, in the inner court t.		95:15
with fire, and the inhabitants t.		9: 3	report t. shall vex all people;		97:23
inhabitants t. to be drowned.		9: 4	gospel unto the inhabitants t.,		99: 1
earth, and the inhabitants t.,		9: 5	the purpose and the end t.—		101:33
inhabitants t. to be buried up		9: 6	yet laying the foundation t.,		101:47
Onihah and the inhabitants t.,		9: 7	watchmen upon the walls t.		101:53
Mocum and the inhabitants t.,		9: 7	breaking down the hedge t.,		101:54
Jerusalem and the inhabitants t.;		9: 7	and they shall eat the fruit t.		101:101
to come up in the stead t.,		9: 7	and the interpretation t.		109:36
and valleys in the places t.;		9: 8	from the corner stone t.		115:12
inhabitants t. have I buried		9: 8	unto the top t.,		115:12
with fire, and the inhabitants t.,		9:10	my gospel, the fulness t.,		118: 4
were towards the sound t.;		11: 5	swift judgment in the season t.,		121:24
is the day unto the evil t.		13:34	unto the finishing and the end t.,		121:32
the whiteness t. did exceed all		19:25	the world, to the four corners t.,		124: 3
so white as the whiteness t.		19:25	the flower t. which soon falleth,		124: 7
waters came up in the stead t.;	4Ne	1: 9	and the priesthood t.,		124:42
the inhabitants t. began to	Mrm	1:18	glory of this, the corner stone t.;		124:60
the inhabitants t. were not		5: 5	prepared for the inhabitants t.		124:83
he hath written the intent t.		8: 5	as pertaining to the price t.		124:121
the plates t. are of no worth,		8:14	that ye may hold the keys t.,		124:123
the record t. is of great worth;		8:14	the keys t., for helps and		124:143
means for the interpretation t.		9:34	blessing, and the conditions t.,		132: 5
the bottom t. was tight like	Eth	2:17	he that receiveth a fulness t. must		132: 6
the sides t. were tight like		2:17	beheld the world and the ends t.,	Mses	1: 8
the ends t. were peaked;		2:17	beheld also the inhabitants t.,		1:28
the top t. was tight like		2:17	were inhabitants on the face t.		1:29
the length t. was the length		2:17	this earth, and the inhabitants t.,		1:35
the door t., when it was shut,		2:17	this earth, and the inhabitants t.,		1:36
seal up the interpretation t.;		4: 5	pass away, and the heavens t.		1:38
inhabitants t. shall pass away,		4: 9	eatest t. thou shalt surely die.		3:17
prepared, one in each end t.;		6: 2	that should be the name t.		3:19
him who dwell upon the face t.;		13: 2	closed up the flesh in the stead t.;		3:21
the inhabitants t., blessed are		13:11	know that in the day ye eat t.,		4:11
Coriantumr in the stead t.,		14:16	took of the fruit t., and did eat,		4:12
And the scent t. went forth		14:23	of his flock, and of the fat t.		5:20
because of the scent t.		14:23	be in the world, until the end t.;		5:59
according to the power t.;	Mro	7:32	from the foundation t.,		6:30
be one man upon the face t.		7:36	in the world, unto the ends t.		6:30

THEREOF 965 THINE

and the foundation t. is his.	Mses 6:44	taken out of t. hand the cup of	2Ne 8:22
he brought in upon the face t.	6:44	shall be a land of t. inheritance,	10:10
the barrenness t. shall go forth	7: 8	and t. iniquity is taken away,	16: 7
and all the inhabitants t.;	7: 9	t. anger is turned away,	22: 1
heard a voice from the bowels t.,	7:48	for their faith was like unto t.	En 1:18
many of the inhabitants t. died.	8: 4	and this because of t. iniquities.	Mos 12:12
seasons in the revolutions t.;	Abr 3: 4	Amulek, return to t. own house,	Al 10: 7
I could not see the end t.	3:12	this was a plan of t. adversary,	12: 5
in the time that thou eatest t.,	5:13	fall at this time, in t. anger,	20:17
up the flesh in the stead t.;	5:15	bear with patience t. afflictions,	26:27
that should be the name t.	5:20	thou didst visit them in t. anger	33:10
designed by the authors t.	JS 2: 1	and hast not sought t. own life,	He 10: 4
but they deny the power t."	2:19	wilt thou turn away t. anger,	11:11
with the translation t.,	2:64	let t. anger be appeased in the	11:11
administer in the ordinances t.	AoF 5	wilt thou turn away t. anger,	11:12
		wilt thou turn away t. anger,	11:16
THEREON		Because of t. iniquities, thou shalt	12:20
I will have all men that dwell t.	2Ne 10:19	Because of t. iniquities thou shalt	12:21
of the mysteries contained t.	Al 37: 4	not turn away t. anger from us?	13:37
not be permitted to dwell t.	DC 101:99	Agree with t. adversary quickly	3Ne 12:25
say they shall not dwell t.;	101:100	perform unto the Lord t. oaths;	12:33
kingdom they shall dwell t.	101:100	thy neighbor and hate t. enemy;	12:43
my judgments may be kept t.,	119: 6	That t. alms may be in secret;	13: 4
the inhabitants who dwell t.,	130: 9	For t. is the kingdom, and the	13:13
		if, therefore, t. eye be single,	13:22
THERETO		But if t. eye be evil, thy whole	13:23
then shall all things be added t.	DC 11:22	the beam that is in t. own eye?	14: 3
		pull the mote out of t. eye—	14: 4
THEREUNTO		behold, a beam is in t. own eye?	14: 4
things necessary shall be added t.,	DC 106: 3	cast the beam out of t. own eye?	14: 5
are many things pertaining t.	132:58	be lifted up upon t. adversaries,	20:17
		all t. enemies shall be cut off.	20:17
THEREWITH		turn away t. anger from this	Eth 3: 3
itself against him that heweth t.?	2Ne 20:15	not covet t. own property,	DC 19:26
and all that have been seized t.	28:23	thee up out of t. afflictions,	24: 1
rejoicing, lest you be seized t.	DC 50:33	delivered from all t. enemies,	24: 1
		Magnify t. office; and after	24: 3
THESE: see in the APPENDIX.		wherewith to magnify t. office,	24: 9
		Give me t. honor, which is my	29:36
THEY: see in the APPENDIX.		t. heart is now right before me	39: 8
		of the work of t. own hands;	42:40
THICK		are these wounds in t. hands	45:51
were dressed with t. clothing—	Al 43:19	thou shalt offer t. oblations	59:12
very t. garments to cover their	49: 6	to get in debt to t. enemies;	64:27
there was t. darkness upon all	3Ne 8:20	t. enemies may be subdued;	65: 6
T. darkness gathered around me,	JS 2:15	for t. is the honor, power and	65: 6
t. and rounding in the middle	2:51	give him t. instructions;	66: 8
		thou shalt magnify t. office,	66:11
THICKET		I have delivered t. enemy into	98:29
near the water a t. of small trees,	Mos 18: 5	thine enemy into t. hands;	98:29
		t. enemy is in thine hands;	98:31
THICKETS		thine enemy is in t. hands;	98:31
in the t. of the forests,	2Ne 19:18	t. enemy is in thine hands	98:31
cut down the t. of the forests	20:34	thine enemy is in t. hands	98:31
		after t. enemy has come upon	98:39
THIEF		testimony against t. enemy—	98:39
the people as a t. and a robber.	Al 11: 2	as oft as t. enemy repenteth	98:40
as a t. in the night,	DC 45:19	forgive him with all t. heart;	98:45
as a t. in the night—	106: 4	will avenge thee of t. enemy	98:45
shall not overtake you as a t.	106: 5	then t. indignation shall be	98:47
what watch the t. would come,	JS 1:47	to possess t. inheritance;	99: 7
		that it may be done to t. honor	109:10
THIEVES		t. angels have charge over them;	109:22
and t. break through and steal;	3Ne 13:19	that t. anger be kindled against	109:27
where t. do not break through	13:20	wilt send upon them in t. anger,	109:30
t. can break through and steal.	27:32	the places of t. appointment,	109:39
for the t., and the robbers,	Mrm 2:10	to ascend up in t. ears,	109:49
		make bare t. arm, O Lord,	109:51
THIEVING		may t. anger be kindled,	109:52
lying, t., robbing, committing	Al 1:32	and t. indignation fall upon them,	109:52
		upon the face of t. Anointed.	109:53
THIGH		let these, t. anointed ones,	109:80
wounded Coriantumr in his t.,	Eth 13:31	t. alms have come up as a	112: 1
		been some few things in t. heart	112: 2
THINE		and t. eye, yea, thy pure eye,	121: 2
for I have seen t. abominations!	1Ne 1:13	and t. ear be penetrated with	121: 2
Stretch forth t. hand again unto	17:53	before t. heart shall be softened	121: 3
that time t. ear was not opened;	20: 8	let t. eye pierce;	121: 4
Lift up t. eyes round about	21:18	let t. ear be inclined;	121: 4
shall again in t. ears say:	21:20	let t. heart be softened,	121: 4
Then shalt thou say in t. heart;	21:21	Let t. anger be kindled against	121: 5
he shall consecrate t. afflictions	2Ne 2: 2	and, in the fury of t. heart,	121: 5
precious land, for t. inheritance	3: 2	t. adversity and thine afflictions	121: 7

THINE — 966 — THING

t. afflictions shall be but a small	DC 121: 7	
terrible in the midst of t. enemies	122: 4	
if t. enemies fall upon thee;	122: 6	
t. enemies tear thee from the	122: 6	
of thy wife, and of t. offspring,	122: 6	
and t. elder son, although but six	122: 6	
t. enemies prowl around thee like	122: 6	
if fierce winds become t. enemy;	122: 7	
thy name known to t. adversaries,	133:42	
and fear not t. enemies;	136:17	
Fear not t. enemies, for they	136:30	
wherefore give me t. honor.	Mses 4: 1	
and the glory be t. forever.	4: 2	
thy brother Abel into t. hands.	5:29	
Anoint t. eyes with clay, and	6:35	
hast taken Zion to t. own bosom,	7:31	
t. eyes are upon shall perish in	7:38	
the name of t. Only Begotten,	7:50	
in the name of t. Only Begotten;	7:59	
myself, but through t. own grace;	7:59	
didst send t. angel to deliver	Abr 2:13	
facts exist, behold t. eyes see it;	3: 6	
intelligences t. eyes have seen	3:21	

THING

it is a hard t. which I have	1Ne 3: 5	
the t. which he commandeth them.	3: 7	
the t. which the Lord hath	3:15	
commanded us to do this t.;	4:34	
the t. which the Lord hath	5: 8	
forgive them of the t. that they	7:20	
because of the t. which I have	8: 3	
spake my father concerning this t.	10: 8	
no unclean t. can dwell with God;	10:21	
this t. shall be given unto thee	11: 7	
maketh no such t. known unto us.	15: 9	
the t. which our father meaneth	15:13	
What meaneth this t. which our	15:21	
Doth this t. mean the torment	15:31	
there cannot any unclean t. enter	15:34	
the t. which he has commanded	17: 3	
must needs be a good t. for them,	17:25	
there was not any t. done save	17:31	
whatsoever t. we had brought with	18: 6	
they repented of the t. which they	18:20	
judge him to be a t. of naught;	19: 9	
It is a light t. that thou shouldst	21: 6	
been created for a t. of naught,	2Ne 2:12	
this t. must needs destroy the	2:12	
the t. which the Lord shall bring	3:15	
I am sure of this t.	3:16	
and do that t. which is great in	3:24	
is it a small t. for you to weary	17:13	
the Lord hath forbidden this t.;	26:30	
Or shall the t. framed say of him	27:27	
aside the just for a t. of naught.	27:32	
aside the just for a t. of naught	28:16	
must speak concerning this t.	32: 8	
perform any t. unto the Lord	32: 9	
which t. is pleasing unto God;	Jac 2: 7	
that God justifieth you in this t.?	2:14	
which t. was abominable before	2:24	
Now in this t. we do rejoice;	4: 3	
unto myself, I have done this t.	5:11	
in the t. which thou knowest	7:14	
this t. was pleasing unto me,	7:22	
Whatsoever t. ye shall ask in	En 1:15	
have also required of me this t.;	1:18	
of the t. which thou hast done.	Mos 4:22	
return the t. that he borroweth,	4:28	
of any t. in heaven above,	12:36	
whosoever has done this t. shall	20:16	
lay not this t. to their charge.	20:17	
Ammon declined doing this t.,	21:33	
not any such t. happened before	26:10	
there is one t. which is of more	Al 7: 7	
as to this t. I do not know;	7: 8	
the Lord has been verified in this t.,	9:14	
that no unclean t. can inherit the	11:37	
but every t. shall be restored to	11:44	
t. which I was about to explain.	12:22	
suffer that they may do this t.,	14:11	
may do this t. unto them,	14:11	

this is the t. that I desire of thee.	Al	18:22
unto the people the selfsame t.—		19:33
in whatsoever t. he thinketh,		20:24
that thou knowest any such t.		21: 8
the t. which doth trouble me.		22: 5
If thou desirest this t., if thou		22:16
for if a man knoweth a t. he hath		32:18
Now of this t. ye must judge.		32:20
your knowledge is perfect in that t.,		32:34
he rewardeth you no good t.		34:39
the t. which our fathers call a		37:38
I say, is there not a type in this t.?		37:45
away by any vain or foolish t.;		39:11
one t. which I have inquired		40: 3
is the t. which I have inquired		40: 9
this is the t. of which I do know.		40: 9
no unclean t. can inherit the		40:26
far astray because of this t.		41: 1
worried also concerning this t.		41: 1
every t. to its natural frame—		41: 4
to take a t. of a natural state		41:12
I will explain this t. unto thee.		42: 2
not prepared with any such t.;		43:20
Now this was the very t. which		47:15
the t. that Amalichiah desired,		47:16
in whatsoever t. they were		53:20
so be that there is such a t.,		54:21
here is one t. in which we		56: 9
whatsoever t. they could get		57:14
has done this great t. for us.		57:35
unto you this marvelous t.,	He	5:26
if this t. which he has said		9: 2
might know concerning this t.;		9:23
a man that he should do this t.;		9:24
will in this t. seek to destroy me.		9:25
iniquity, which t. is contrary to		13:38
come and tell this t. unto you;		14: 9
in the t. wherewith they have		15: 8
in that t. which they do believe,		15:10
in some great and marvelous t.		16:20
your faith concerning this t.	3Ne	1: 6
Now in this t. they did err,		1:24
Imagining up some vain t. in		2: 2
was a foolish and a vain t.		2: 2
this t. they were disappointed.		4:10
the great t. which he had done		4:31
concerning this t. unto them.		15:18
for this t. which ye have done,		18:10
this is the t. which I will give		21: 2
ye have not written this t.,		23:11
this t. had not been written.		23:12
and dispute because of this t.?		27: 4
no unclean t. can enter into		27:19
ye desired this t. of me;		28: 3
the t. which they desired.		28: 5
ye have desired the t. which		28: 6
the t. which ye have desired		28: 9
because of this great t. which	Mrm	3: 9
unto me the t. which I desired.		6: 3
shall bring this t. to light;		8:16
if they drink and deadly t.		9:24
whatsoever t. persuadeth men	Eth	4:12
for that t. is forbidden you,		5: 1
this t. leadeth into captivity.		6:23
the t. which Shule had done,		7:10
in the t. which I shall desire		8:13
whatsoever t. Akish made known		8:14
to do whatsoever t. he desired.		8:17
by this t. which thou hast said,		12:35
every t. which inviteth and	Mro	7:13
every t. which inviteth to do		7:16
whatsoever t. persuadeth men		7:17
will lay hold upon every good t.,		7:19
can lay hold upon every good t.?		7:20
may lay hold on every good t.		7:21
there cannot come every good t.		7:22
no good t. come unto them.		7:24
did lay hold upon every good t.;		7:25
Whatsoever ye shall ask the		7:26
will cleave unto every good t.;		7:28
whatsoever t. is expedient in me.		7:33
that this t. shall ye teach—		8:10
this t. ought not to be;		8:24

THING 967 THIRD

after they had done this t.,	Mro	9:10
whatsoever t. is good is just		10: 6
the evil gift, nor the unclean t.		10:30
the t. which I have commanded	DC	5:34
my name, as touching one t.,		6:32
forget the t. which is wrong;		9: 9
Do this t. which I have		9:13
his evil design in this t.		10:14
which t. if ye do, and are		14:11
blessed are you for this t.,		15: 5
the t. which will be of the most		15: 6
blessed are you for this t.,		16: 5
the t. which will be of the most		16: 6
because of the t. which you,		18: 1
the t. which I commanded		18: 7
you that are chosen in this t.,		19: 9
to be done away in this t.;		22: 1
a t. which is had in secret		38:13
agreed as touching this one t.,		42: 3
whatsoever t. he needeth to		43:13
the t. which I have commanded		45:72
in this t. my servant Edward		50:39
thou shalt do none other t.,		59:13
that t. in which there was no		64:16
in this t. ye have done wisely,		72: 3
in that t. which you have		78: 2
prepare every needful t.;		88:119
are accounted as a light t.,		90: 5
not suffer any unclean t. to		94: 8
come into it any unclean t.,		94: 9
do not suffer any unclean t.		97:15
declare whatsoever t. ye declare		100: 7
And every corruptible t.,		101:24
prepare every needful t.,		109: 8
to obtain every needful t.;		109:15
no unclean t. shall be permitted to		109:20
they seem but a small t. to me,		127: 2
is no such t. as immaterial matter.		131: 7
this one t. I show unto thee,	Mses	1: 7
which t. I never had supposed.		1:10
of this t. Moses bore record;		1:23
every creeping t. that creepeth		2:26
every living t. that moveth		2:28
What is this t. which thou hast		4:19
This t. is a similitude of the		5: 7
there is a strange t. in the land;		6:38
for no unclean t. can dwell there,		6:57
every t. that creepeth upon	Abr	4:25
every creeping t. that creepeth		4:26
over ever living t. that moveth		4:28
every t. that creepeth upon the		4:30
any earthly t. could be made	JS	2:31
The first t. that I can recollect		2:49
no such t. now as ministering		2:65

THINGS: *see in the APPENDIX.*

THINK		
save it be that I t. it be sacred.	1Ne	19: 6
are learned they t. they are wise,	2Ne	9:28
neither doth his heart t. so;		20: 7
T. of your brethren like unto	Jac	2:17
or that ye should t. that I of	Mos	2:10
not t. himself above another;		23: 7
For they knew not what to t.;		25: 8
can ye t. of being saved when	Al	5:20
when I t. of the success of these		29:16
I t. that it is impossible that ye		34: 2
ye t. that I know of myself—		36: 4
that ye should t. that I know		38: 6
did t. more upon the liberty of		56:47
Can you t. to sit upon your		60: 7
T. not that I am come to	3Ne	12:17
they t. that they shall be heard		13: 7
Why do ye not t. that greater	Mrm	8:38
say and t. in their hearts—	DC	10:16
in an hour when ye t. not		45: 2
in an hour you t. not.		51:20
Let no man t. he is ruler;		58:20
cometh in an hour you t. not.		61:38
t. not of thy property.		66: 6
in an hour when ye t. not of;		124:10

You may t. this order of things	DC	128: 5
in such an hour as ye t. not,	JS	1:48
to make the people t. they were		2: 9
him t. or believe otherwise.		2:24
t. to make me deny what I have		2:25

THINKETH		
he t. that he can build a ship;	1Ne	17:17
he also t. that he can cross		17:17
in whatsoever thing he t.,	Al	20:24
easily provoked, t. no evil.	Mro	7:45
Satan t. to overpower your	DC	10:33
and he t. to hide them.		58:60

THINKING		
t., perhaps, that he may lead us	1Ne	16:38
t. to deliver themselves out of	Mos	22: 2
t. to destroy the work of	DC	10:23
t. I will stay my hand in		39:16

THINKS		
younger brother t. to rule over us;	2Ne	5: 3

THINNER		
and t. towards the edges,	JS	2:51

THIRD		
Nephi, t. Nephi, and so forth,	Jac	1:11
And he shall rise the t. day	Mos	3:10
unto the t. and fourth generations		13:13
they went again even the t. time,		21:12
the thirty and t. year of his reign,		29:46
or a second time, or a t. time,	Al	40: 5
and he sent again the t. time.		47:11
and also the twenty and t. year.		50:24
the t. day of the seventh month.		56:42
in the forty and t. year of	He	3: 1
ending of the forty and t. year.		3: 1
in the fifty and t. year of		3:37
the t. time the voice came.		5:33
thus ended the sixty and t. year.		6: 6
and in the seventy and t. year		11: 2
And in the eighty and t. year		11:36
the ninety and t. year did also	3Ne	1:27
and the twenty and t. year also,		5: 7
of the thirty and t. year;		7:23
the thirty and t. year had		8: 2
again the t. time they did hear		11: 5
the t. time they did understand		11: 6
hundred and sixty and t. year	Mrm	4: 1
in the t. year he did bring him	Eth	13:23
they came again the t. time,		14:29
and rose again the t. day;	DC	20:23
a t. part of the hosts of heaven		29:36
And also unto the t., saying:		88:54
the second also, and the t.,		88:57
sound, which is the t. trump;		88:100
on the t. lot shall my servant		94:13
he shall smite you the t. time,		98:26
the t. and fourth generation.		98:28
the t. and fourth generation.		98:29
the t. and fourth generation.		98:30
the second nor the t. time,		98:35
the t. and fourth generation.		98:37
unto the second and t. time;		98:40
against thee the t. time,		98:43
the t. and fourth generation.		98:46
the t. and fourth generation		103:26
the t. and fourth generation		105:30
unto the t. and fourth generation,		124:50
unto the t. and fourth generation,		124:52
and the morning were the t. day.	Mses	2:13
name of the t. river was Hiddekel;		3:14
day; and it was the t. time.	Abr	4:13
twenty-t. day of December,	JS	2: 3
part of the t. chapter of Malachi;		2:36
also the t. chapter of Acts,		2:40
and twenty-t. verses,		2:40
After this t. visit, he again		2:47
from me for the t. time,		2:47
t., Baptism by immersion for	AoF	4

THIRST

affliction, hunger, t., and fatigue;	1Ne 16:35
of Israel might quench their t.	17:29
They shall not hunger nor t.,	21:10
and they die because of t.	2Ne 7: 2
their multitude dried up with t.	15:13
of body, hunger, t., and fatigue,	Mos 3: 7
suffered hunger, t., and fatigue.	7:16
and water that they might t.;	Al 14:22
such as hunger, t. and fatigue,	17: 5
sufferings with hunger and t.,	18:37
they also had suffered hunger, t.,	20:29
neither should they t.;	31:38
hunger not, neither shall ye t.	32:42
were afflicted with hunger and t.,	37:42
even hunger, t., and fatigue,	60: 3
and t. after righteousness,	3Ne 12: 6
soul shall never hunger nor t.,	20: 8
they t. after blood and revenge	Mro 9: 5
their fish stink, and die for t.	DC 133:68

THIRSTED
And they t. not; 1Ne 20:21

THIRSTETH
every one that t., come ye to the 2Ne 9:50

THIRSTY

unto a t. man which dreameth,	2Ne 27: 3
ferocious and a blood-t. people	En 1:20
austere and a blood t. man	Mos 9: 2
ferocious, and a blood-t. people,	10:12
shall no longer be a t. land.	DC 133:29

THIRTEEN
four priests, and t. members. DC 102: 5

THIRTEENTH

in the t. year of my reign	Mos 9:14
in the t. year there began to	3Ne 2:11
before this t. year had passed	2:13
And thus ended the t. year.	2:16
in the t. chapter of John's	DC 88:141

THIRTIETH

reign in the t. year of his age,	Mos 6: 4
commencement of the t. year	Al 56: 1
in the t. year of the reign	59: 1
thus ended the t. year of	62:11
in the t. year the church was	3Ne 6:14
commencement of the t. year—	6:17
of this, the t. year,	6:17
this same year, yea, the t. year,	7: 1
And thus ended the t. year;	7:13

THIRTY

And t. years had passed away	2Ne 5:28
two hundred and t. and eight	Jar 1:13
the t. and third year of his reign,	Mos 29:46
five hundred and t. and two souls;	Al 2:19
of the t. and first year of the	62:12
thus ended the t. and first year	62:39
in the t. and fifth year of the	62:52
of the t. and sixth year	63: 1
thus ended the t. and sixth year	63: 3
in the t. and seventh year of	63: 4
ended the t. and seventh year.	63: 6
And in the t. and eighth year,	63: 7
ended the t. and eighth year.	63: 9
in the t. and ninth year of	63:10
thus ended the t. and ninth year	63:16
to pass in the t. and first year	3Ne 7:14
the t. and first year did pass	7:21
the t. and second year also.	7:23
of the t. and third year;	7:23
the t. and third year had passed	8: 2
pass in the t. and fourth year,	8: 5
of the t. and fourth year,	10:18
the t. and fourth year passed	4Ne 1: 1
and also the t. and fifth,	1: 1
in the t. and sixth year,	1: 2
the t. and seventh year passed	1: 4
the t. and eighth year pass	1: 6
and also the t. and ninth,	1: 6
two hundred and t. years had	1:34
two hundred and t. and first	1:35
the number of t. thousand.	Mrm 1:11
three hundred and t. years had	2: 9
with an army of t. thousand	2:25
yea, he begat t. and one,	Eth 7: 2
Corihor was t. and two years	7: 4
even all, save it were t. souls,	9:12
t. and two of the people of Shiz,	15:25
eight hundred and t. years	DC 20: 1
eighteen hundred and t.,	21: 3
eight hundred and t.-two—	76:11
t.-four years and four months,	107:44
four hundred and t. years old	107:49
Lamech was t.-two years old	107:51
Joseph Smith was t.-eight in	135: 6
lived one hundred and t. years,	Mses 6:10
were nine hundred and t. years,	6:12
eight hundred and t. years,	6:20
were four hundred and t. years.	8: 1
eight hundred and t.-eight.	JS 2:60

THIRTY-FOUR: see THIRTY and FOUR.

THIRTY-TWO: see THIRTY and TWO.

THIRTY-EIGHT: see THIRTY and EIGHT.

THIS: see in the APPENDIX.

THISTLE
shalt be as the blossoms of a t., Mos 12:12

THISTLES
grapes of thorns, or figs of t.?	3Ne 14:16
Thorns also, and t. shall it	Mses 4:24

THITHER

and they divided hither and t.,	1Ne 4: 2
Sea were divided hither and t.,	17:26
they had been brought t.;	18: 9
and with bows shall men come t.,	2Ne 17:24
there shall not come t. the fear	17:25
Alma resorted t., there being	Mos 18: 5
as many as believed him went t.	18: 6
while he was journeying t.,	Al 8:14
And as I was going t. I found	10: 8
and Lamoni were journeying t.,	20: 8
t. had all the Lamanites fled;	47: 5
they would march t. to battle;	49:15
and they parted hither and t.,	He 8:11
that they divided hither and t.	10: 1
of the earth moveth hither and t.,	12: 8

THOMAS: see also GROVER, THOMAS; and MARSH, THOMAS B.

T., my son, blessed are you	DC 31: 1
unto my servant T.,	56: 5
Lord unto you my servant T.:	112: 1
I say unto you, my servant T.,	112:16
Let my servant T. remain	118: 2

THOMPSON
of my people which are in T., DC 56: 6

THOMPSON, Robert B.
let my servant T. help you to DC 124:12

THORNS

shall come up briers and t.;	2Ne 15: 6
upon all t., and upon all bushes.	17:19
which shall be for briers and t.	17:23
land shall become briers and t.	17:24
thither the fear of briers and t.;	17:25
it shall devour the briers and t.,	19:18
shall devour his t. and his briers	20:17
Do men gather grapes of t.,	3Ne 14:16
T. also, and thistles shall it	Mses 4:24

THOSE: see in the APPENDIX.

THOU: see in the APPENDIX.

THOUGH 969 THOUSAND

THOUGH
t. Israel be not gathered,	1Ne	21: 5
For t. thy people Israel be as	2Ne	20:22
t. thou wast angry with me		22: 1
to come as t. he already was.	Jar	1:11
even as t. he had already come	Mos	3:13
as t. there was no redemption		16: 5
as t. they have already come,		16: 6
as t. it would part asunder.		27:18
as t. he had authority to	Al	11:35
I spake as t. I had authority to		11:36
as t. there had been no		11:41
be as t. there had been no		12:18
lay there as t. they were dead;		19:18
as t. they had been the cause of		22:19
worse than t. they had never		24:30
as t. they were angels sent		27: 4
as light as t. it was mid-day.	3Ne	1:19
as t. I could deliver them	Mrm	5: 1
as t. I spake from the dead;		9:30
away as t. he were dead.	Eth	14:30
are as t. there had been no	Mro	7:38
t. the heavens and the earth pass	DC	1:38
And t. the heaven and the		56:11
t. they are called to lay down		101:35
T. I fear not God, nor regard		101:84
t. they should not be permitted		101:99
as t. no such decision had been		102:27
t. my feelings were deep and	JS	2: 8
t. I attended their several		2: 8
as t. the adversary was aware,		2:20
and t. I was an obscure boy,		2:22
t. they should persecute him unto		2:24
t. I was hated and persecuted		2:25
t. with a little variation from		2:36

THOUGHT
and he t. he saw God sitting	1Ne	1: 8
I also t. that they could not		4:15
he has t. to make himself a king		16:38
as I have t., so shall it come	2Ne	24:24
he t. it expedient that he should	Mos	1: 9
king Benjamin t. it was expedient,		6: 1
they t. it was the people of Limhi.		20: 6
when they t. of their brethren		25: 9
t. of the immediate goodness of		25:10
they t. upon the Lamanites,		25:11
who t. to question them,	Al	10:13
the t. and intent of our hearts?		21: 6
almost as it were, fleeth at the t.		26:20
Alma t. it was expedient that		31: 5
taking no t. for themselves what		31:37
take no t. for its nourishment,		32:38
the very t. of coming into the		36:14
Oh, T. I, that I could be banished		36:15
mind caught hold upon this t.,		36:18
And now, behold, when I t. this,		36:19
therefore he t. it no sin that he		43:30
Moroni t. it was not expedient		46:30
therefore he t. to cut off the		46:30
Moroni t. it was expedient that		46:31
Teancum t. it was not expedient		52: 5
they took no t. concerning the		58:25
they t. it was an angel that had	3Ne	11: 8
take no t. for your life,		13:25
Which of you by taking t. can		13:27
why take ye t. for raiment?		13:28
Therefore take no t., saying,		13:31
therefore no t. for the morrow,		13:34
take t. for the things of itself.		13:34
and that t. upon his name.		24:16
t. to devise a plan whereby she	Eth	8: 8
he be cut off while in the t.,	Mro	8:14
Look unto me in every t.;	DC	6:36
no t. save it was to ask me.		9: 7
you shall have a stupor of t.		9: 9
as may be t. best or decided		42:72
take ye no t. for the morrow,		84:81
let the morrow take t. for the		84:84
Neither take ye t. beforehand		84:85
But if it is t. to be difficult,		102:14
I have t. it expedient and wisdom		127: 1
be t. a character of sufficient	JS	2:23
I have t. since, that I felt		2:24
nor ever before had t. of.		2:74

THOUGHTLESS
the cause of your t. state.	Al	60: 6
thrones in a state of t. stupor,		60: 7

THOUGHTS
I can tell you concerning your t.,	Jac	2: 5
and your t., and your words,	Mos	4:30
the t. and intents of his heart?		5:13
did know the t. of their hearts.		24:12
even the very t. that any soul		28: 3
he perceived their t., and he said	Al	10:17
for behold, he knows all thy t.,		12: 3
thy t. are made known unto us		12: 3
the t. and intents of his heart;		12: 7
and our t. will also condemn us;		12:14
these were the t. of Ammon,		17:30
he perceived the t. of the king.		18:16
Ammon could discern his t.;		18:18
thou the t. of my heart?		18:20
the t. and intents of the heart;		18:32
let thy t. be directed unto the		37:36
their hearts with these t.—		43:48
yea, the t. of their lands,		43:48
told us the t. of our hearts,	He	9:41
I know your t., and ye have	3Ne	28: 6
my t. upon the land which I	Eth	2:15
save God that knowest thy t.	DC	6:16
the t. and intents of the heart.		33: 1
cast away your idle t. and		88:69
t. and intents of their hearts,		88:109
speak the t. that I shall put		100: 5
let virtue garnish thy t.		121:45
in the imagination of his t.		124:99
imagination of the t. of his heart,	Mses	8:22

THOUSAND
where there were a t. vines	2Ne	17:23
thousand vines at a t. silverlings,		17:23
slay three t. and forty-three;	Mos	9:18
twelve t. five hundred thirty	Al	2:19
six t. five hundred sixty		2:19
three t. five hundred souls		4: 5
did slay a t. and five of them;		24:22
more than a t. brought to the		24:27
destruction of many t. lives;		28:10
a t. of the Lamanites were		49:23
four t. of those dissenters who		51:19
two t. of those young men,		53:18
his two t. stripling soldiers,		53:22
two t. of the sons of those		56: 3
two t. of these young men		56: 5
of these two t. young men		56: 9
I did join my two t. sons,		56:10
fathers of those my two t. sons.		56:27
were sent two t. men unto us		56:28
were prepared with ten t. men,		56:28
I did return with my two t.		56:49
I not returned with my two t.		56:50
upon their rear with his two t.,		56:52
of Antipus, and I with my two t.,		56:54
to the number of six t. men,		57: 6
my little band of two t.		57: 6
upwards of two t. of them		57:14
band of two t. and sixty		57:19
those two t. and sixty were		57:20
out of my two t. and sixty,		57:25
a t. of our brethren who were		57:26
to us by an army of two t. men		58: 8
also an army of six t. men		62:12
caused that an army of six t. men,		62:13
four t. who had not been slain.		62:17
five t. and four hundred men,		63: 4
were eight t. of the Lamanites	He	5:19
a great many t. years before		8:18
a great many t. people who were	3Ne	3:24
two t. and five hundred souls;		17:25
exceed the number of thirty t.	Mrm	1:11
an army of forty and four t.		2: 9
with forty and two t.		2: 9
with an army of thirty t.		2:25
against an army of fifty t.		2:25

THOUSAND 970 THREE

my ten t. who were with me,	Mrm 6:10	and many t. fell by the sword.	Eth	14: 4
the ten t. of my people	6:11	money by hundreds, or t.,	DC 104:84	
beheld the ten t. of my people	6:12	Yea the hearts of t.		110: 9
the ten t. of Gidgiddonah	6:13	tens of t. shall greatly rejoice		110: 9
Lamah had fallen with his ten t.;	6:14	shall put their tens of t. to flight.		133:58
Gigal had fallen with his ten t.;	6:14	t. of the Latter-day Saints,		135: 3
Limhah had fallen with his ten t.;	6:14			
Joneam had fallen with his ten t.;	6:14	**THOUSANDTH**		
had fallen with their ten t. each.	6:14	If I were to relate a t. part	JS	2:61
with their ten t. each;	6:15			
one t. eight hundred and	DC 20: 1	**THRASH**		
men on earth a t. years,	29:11	reap and to hoe, and also to t.	Eth	10:25
when the t. years are ended,	29:22	to t. the nations by the power	DC	35:13
one t. eight hundred and	76:11	the Lord shall t. the nations		133:59
during the seven t. years of	77: 6			
things of the first t. years,	77: 7	**THREATEN**		
also of the second t. years,	77: 7	did t. the people of Nephi,	Jar	1:10
in the sixth t. years,	77:10			
one hundred and forty-four t.,	77:11	**THREATENED**		
twelve t. out of every tribe?	77:11	which t. them with destruction,	1Ne	18:20
of the seventh t. years	77:12	were t. with utter destruction	3Ne	2:13
of the seventh t. years—	77:12	been t. with being mobbed,	JS	2:75
until the t. years are ended,	88:101			
of God in the first t. years.	88:108	**THREATENING**		
of God in the second t. years—	88:109	and also of t. the people and	3Ne	3:11
loosed for the space of a t. years.	88:110			
to receive fifteen t. dollars	124:64	**THREATENINGS**		
receive over fifteen t. dollars	124:65	they did breathe out much t.	1Ne	18:17
pay over fifteen t. dollars	124:72	to breathe out t. against the king,	Mos	19: 3
a hundred and forty four t.,	133:18	mighty t. to destroy his church.	Al	26:18
for the space of a t. years the	Mses 7:64	And he breathed out many t.		35: 9
for the space of a t. years;	7:65	my armies for I fear not your t.		54:16
being one t. years according	Abr 3: 4	ye have breathed out many t.		54:19
in Kolob is equal to a t. years	Fac 2: 1	but behold, we fear not your t.		54:19
in Egyptian signifying one t.;	2: 4	and the t. of a robber;	3Ne	3:12
one t. eight hundred and	JS 2: 3	And notwithstanding the t. and		4:12
one t. eight hundred and	2:27	breathing out t. against		5: 5
one t. eight hundred and	2:59			
one t. eight hundred and	2:60	**THREATENS**		
rumor with her t. tongues was	2:61	God t. the people of Nephi	He	7:hd
THOUSANDS		**THREE**		
or even than his tens of t.?	1Ne 4: 1	He taketh t. days' journey	1Ne	1:hd
slain many t. of the Lamanites.	WM 1:14	when he had traveled t. days in		2: 6
against t. of the Lamanites;	Mos 11:19	his wife, and his t. other daughters.		7: 6
showing mercy unto t. of them	13:14	beheld t. generations pass away		12:11
And in one year were t. and	Al 3:26	for the space of t. days;		18:13
and tens of t. of souls sent	3:26	the t. days of darkness,		19:10
t. were brought to the knowledge	23: 5	by the words of t., God hath said,	2Ne	11: 3
yea, t. were brought to believe in	23: 5	and within t. score and five years		17: 8
Behold, t. of them do rejoice,	26: 4	sepulchre for the space of t. days		25:13
how many t. of our brethren	26:13	until t. generations shall have		26: 9
bring t. of souls to repentance,	26:22	save it be that t. witnesses shall		27:12
tens of t. of the Lamanites were	28: 2	t. hundred and twenty years had	Om	1: 5
bodies of many t. are laid low	28:11	that he had t. sons;	Mos	1: 2
many t. are moldering in heaps	28:11	king Benjamin lived t. years		6: 5
many t. are mourning for the	28:11	people for the space of t. years.		6: 7
many t. of others truly mourn for	28:12	peace for the space of t. years,		7: 1
so many t. of the Lamanites of	37: 9	Ammon took t. of his brethren,		7: 6
means of bringing many t. of them,	37:10	that forty and t. of my people		8: 7
t. of our stiffnecked brethren,	37:10	slay t. thousand and forty-three;		9:18
many t. of the Lamanites to	37:19	slay three thousand and forty-t.;		9:18
Lamanites came with their t.;	43: 5	after t. days, having counseled		17: 6
t. of their wicked brethren have	50:22	being sixty and t. years old;		29:46
many t. who had been slain by	51:11	t. thousand five hundred souls	Al	4: 5
yea, t. have fallen by the sword,	60: 5	and traveled t. days' journey on		8: 6
murdering t. of your brethren—	60: 7	is equal to t. shiblons.		11:19
have saved t. of them from	60: 8	had been cast into prison t. days,		14:18
blood of t. shall come upon	60:10	for t. years did the people of		16:12
surrounded with t. of those,	60:22	in the service of the king t. days,		17:26
tens of t., who do also sit in	60:22	all t. had sunk to the earth.		19:14
t. round about in the borders	60:22	the former t. he took with him,		31: 6
t. did flock unto his standard,	62: 5	for the space of t. days and		36:10
were t. who did join themselves	He 3:24	of three days and t. nights		36:10
many souls, yea, even tens of t.	3:26	for t. days and for three nights		36:16
that they did perish by t. in	11: 6	and for t. nights was I racked,		36:16
and did march forth by t.	3Ne 3:22	I was t. days and three nights		38: 8
by thousands and by tens of t.,	3:22	was three days and t. nights in		38: 8
and cutting them off by t. and	4:21	they did cause t. divisions	He	1: 4
by thousands and by tens of t.	4:21	there were about t. hundred souls		5:49
t. who did yield themselves up	4:27	death, for the space of t. days,		14:20
I saw t. of them hewn down	Mrm 2:15	earth for the space of t. days,		14:27
been t. slain on both sides,	4: 9	darkness for the space of t. days	3Ne	8: 3

THREE

about the space of t. hours;	3Ne	8:19
about the space of t. hours—		8:19
did last for the space of t. days		8:23
thus did the t. days pass away.		10: 9
for the space of t. days;		26:13
they all spake, save it were t.,		28: 2
he turned himself unto the t.,		28: 4
save it were the t. who were to		28:12
t. who were caught up into		28:36
it were the t. who should tarry;	4Ne	1:14
were the t. disciples of Jesus		1:37
t. hundred years had passed		1:45
t. hundred and five years had		1:47
t. hundred and twenty years had		1:48
t. hundred and twentieth year		1:48
t. hundred and twenty and	Mrm	2: 2
the t. hundred and twenty and		2: 3
t. hundred and thirty years		2: 9
t. hundred and forty and four		2:15
the t. hundred and forty and		2:16
the t. hundred and forty and		2:22
the t. hundred and forty and		2:28
the t. hundred and fiftieth year		2:28
t. hundred and sixty years		3: 4
the t. hundred and sixty and		3: 7
the t. hundred and sixty and		3: 8
the t. hundred and sixty and		4: 1
the t. hundred and sixty and		4: 7
the t. hundred and sixty and		4:10
the t. hundred and sixty and		4:15
the t. hundred and seventy		4:16
t. hundred seventy and		5: 5
t. hundred and eightieth year		5: 6
t. hundred and eighty and		6: 5
for the space of t. hours did	Eth	2:14
unto t. shall they be shown by		5: 3
in the mouth of t. witnesses		5: 4
and the testimony of t., and		5: 4
t. hundred and forty and four		6:11
whom were twenty and t. sons.		7: 2
the t. disciples obtained a		12:17
for the space of t. days.		13:28
Shiz for the space of t. days.		14:26
for the space of t. hours,		15:27
t. witnesses of the church did	Mro	6: 7
testimony of t. of my servants,	DC	5:11
the testimony of t. witnesses will		5:15
mouth of two or t. witnesses		6:28
where two or t. are gathered		6:32
unto you t. I will give		7: 7
conference once in t. months,		20:61
from t. elders of the church,		72:25
I shall show unto t. of you,		95:14
these t. testimonies shall stand		98:27
and one or t. presidents as the		102: 1
councilors were forty-t.,		102: 5
you may obtain t. hundred.		103:32
if ye cannot obtain t. hundred,		103:33
t. Presiding High Priests,		107:22
and power to the t. presidents		107:24
of a quorum of t. presidents		107:29
blessed by him t. years previous		107:42
t. hundred and sixty-five years,		107:49
T. years previous to the death of		107:53
naming also some t. individuals		128: 3
the mouth of two or t. witnesses		128: 3
declaring the t. witnesses to		128:20
These are t. grand keys whereby		129: 9
there are t. heavens or degrees;		131: 1
two or t. days previous to his		135: 4
t. hundred and sixty-five years	Mses	7:68
as did also his t. sons, Shem, Ham,		8:27
upon this altar t. virgins	Abr	1:11
eight hundred and twenty-t.,	JS	2:27
hundred and twenty-t.—		2:28

THRESHOLD
shall enter upon the t. of the	DC	109:13

THREW
t. down their weapons of war,	Al	24:25
t. down their weapons of war		44:15
t. down their weapons of war		52:38

THRICE
t. they were cast into a furnace	3Ne	28:21
t. have I delivered them out	Mrm	3:13

THRIVE
to grow and t. exceedingly;	Jac	5:73

THROAT
Swear unto me by thy t.,	Mses	5:29

THRONE
God sitting upon his t.,	1Ne	1: 8
Thy t. is high in the heavens,		1:14
the heavens, for it is his t.,		17:39
the Lord sitting upon a t., high	2Ne	16: 1
is no end, upon the t. of David,		19: 7
I will exalt my t. above the stars		24:13
must stand before the t. of God,		28:23
with them before the t. of God.	Jac	3: 8
and a t. in the midst thereof,	Mos	11: 9
God sitting upon his t.,	Al	36:22
by heaven, for it is God's t.;	3Ne	12:34
and also by the t. of God,	Mrm	3:10
and placed him upon his t. in	Eth	7:18
as he sat upon his t., giving		9: 5
Jared was murdered upon his t.,		9: 6
an exceedingly beautiful t.;		10: 6
placed himself upon the t. of		14: 6
him as he sat upon his t.		14: 9
whose t. is high in the heavens,	Mro	9:26
are sanctified before his t.,	DC	76:21
reigns upon his t. forever		76:92
Before whose t. all things bow		76:93
to sit on the t. of his power		76:108
upon the t. forever and ever;		76:110
God who sitteth upon his t.,		88:13
him who sitteth upon the t.		88:40
him who sitteth upon the t.,		88:104
him who sitteth upon the t.,		88:110
him who seeketh the t. of him		88:115
of him who sitteth upon the t.,		88:115
shining seraphs around thy t.,		109:79
him that sitteth upon the t.		124:101
and sitteth upon his t.		132:29
and prepare a t. for you in the		132:49
is the habitation of thy t.,	Mses	7:31
given unto me a right to thy t.,		7:59
nearest unto the t. of God;	Abr	3: 2
is set nigh unto the t. of God,		3: 9
come near unto the t. of God.		3:10
God, sitting upon his t.,	Fac	2: 3
God sitting upon his t.,		2: 7
sitting upon Pharoah's t.,		3: 1

THRONES
it hath raised up from their t.	2Ne	24: 9
you think to sit upon your t.	Al	60: 7
that ye could sit upon your t.,		60:11
while we sit upon our t. and		60:21
All t. and dominions, principalities	DC	121:29
it be ordained of men, by t.,		132:13
inherit t., kingdoms, principalities,		132:19
promises, and sit upon t.,		132:37

THROUGH
fathers came t., out of captivity,	1Ne	4: 2
forward t. the mist of darkness,		8:24
hath gone forth t. the hands of		13:28
t. the fulness of the Gentiles,		15:13
and wade t. much affliction		17: 1
and they passed t. on dry ground.		17:26
he led them t. the deserts;		20:21
in and t. the Holy Messiah;	2Ne	2: 6
save it be t. the merits,		2: 8
eternal life, t. the great mediation		2:27
he hath led me t. mine afflictions		4:20
only in and t. the grace of God		10:24
ye may praise him t. grace divine.		10:25
And he shall pass t. Judah;		18: 8
they shall pass t. it hardly bestead		18:21
T. the wrath of the Lord of Hosts		19:19
that is proud shall be thrust t.;		23:15
are slain, thrust t. with a sword,		24:19

THROUGH

t. the atonement of Christ,	Jac	4:11
of his arm, t. the wilderness,	Om	1:13
except it be t. transgression.	Mos	1:12
led our fathers t. the wilderness,		1:16
even t. faith on his name;		3: 9
except it be t. repentance and		3:12
except it were t. the atonement		3:15
only in and t. the name of Christ,		3:17
t. the atoning blood of Christ,		3:18
a saint t. the atonement of Christ		3:19
only t. repentance and faith on		3:21
salvation, t. the atonement		4: 7
t. the infinite goodness of God,		5: 3
changed t. faith in his name;		5: 7
except it be t. transgression;		5:11
t. the wisdom, and power,		5:15
walk t. the Red Sea on dry ground,		7:19
t. faith, might work mighty		8:18
except it were t. the redemption		13:32
they have eternal life t. Christ,		15:23
in and t. Christ ye can be saved?		16:13
redemption cometh t. Christ		16:15
t. the power, and sufferings,		18: 2
t. the redemption of Christ,		18:13
t. the strength and power of God,		21:30
the back pass, t. the back wall,		22: 6
we will pass t. the secret pass		22: 7
wandering t. much tribulation,		27:28
round about t. all the land,		27:32
save it be t. much contention,		29:21
was continual peace t. the land.		29:43
of priestcraft t. the land;	Al	1:16
t. the blood of him of whom it		5:21
white t. the blood of Christ,		5:27
t. much affliction and sorrow.		7: 5
wading t. much tribulation		8:14
led by him t. the wilderness?		9: 9
repentance, t. faith on his name.		9:27
t. mine Only Begotten Son,		12:33
t. mine Only Begotten Son,		12:34
being in and t. the atonement		13: 5
white t. the blood of the Lamb.		13:11
t. the death and sufferings of		21: 9
foundation of the world, t. Christ,		22:13
t. faith and repentance,		22:14
t. the borders of Manti,		22:27
t. the wilderness on the west,		22:28
t. the preaching of Ammon and		23: 6
t. the merits of his Son.		24:10
bright t. the blood of the Son		24:13
they did retain a hope t. faith,		25:16
t. the power and wisdom of God		26:29
may be light, t. the joy of his Son.		33:23
cometh t. the Son of God,		34: 7
except it be t. the atonement		34: 9
white t. the blood of the Lamb.		34:36
can be saved, only in and t. Christ.		38: 9
of the Lamanites t. the pass,		49:24
t. to the city of Mulek.		52:34
wade t. their afflictions,		53:15
broke t. and fled from us.		53:22
cut his way t. with the sword,	He	1:23
t. the center of the land		1:25
t. the most capital parts of the		1:27
having obtained, t. disguise,		2: 6
and to wade t. much affliction.		3:34
t. the atoning blood of Jesus		5: 9
he saw t. the cloud of darkness		5:36
came t. upon dry ground		8:11
remission of them t. his merits.		14:13
t. the preaching of the		15: 4
t. faith on the Lord Jesus Christ.	3Ne	7:16
repenteth of his sins t. your		11:23
and thieves break t. and steal;		13:19
thieves do not break t. nor steal.		13:20
be converted t. their preaching.		15:22
t. the fulness of the Gentiles,		16: 4
to go t. among them,		16:14
they shall go t. among them,		16:15
in me, t. faith on their words,		19:28
if he goeth t. both treadeth		20:16
out of the Holy Ghost t. me		20:27
if he go t. both treadeth down		21:12

972

THROUGH

thieves can break t. and steal.	3Ne	27:32
bring about, t. his most Beloved,	Mrm	5:14
had gone t. and hewn down all		6:11
t. faith on the name of Jesus		9:37
their brethren t. the Gentiles;	Eth	12:22
white t. the blood of the Lamb;		13:10
remission of sins t. Jesus Christ,	Mro	3: 3
t. the atonement of Christ		7:41
t. his infinite goodness and		8: 3
t. the endurance of faith on		8: 3
t. the shedding of the blood of		10:33
forth triumphant t. the air,		10:34
translate t. the mercy of God,	DC	1:29
t. the testimony of the Jews,		3:16
t. the testimony of their fathers—		3:17
glorified t. faith in his name,		3:20
t. their repentance they might		3:20
shall have my word t. you;		5:10
my words that are given t. you.		5:11
t. the Red Sea on dry ground.		8: 3
t. faith, God ministered unto		20: 6
t. the grace of our Lord and		20:30
t. the grace of our Lord and		20:31
t. the will of God the Father,		21: 1
t. me by the Comforter,		21: 9
t. faith on the name of mine		29:42
world t. mine Only Begotten;		29:46
t. him whom I have appointed		43: 2
this gift except it be t. him;		43: 4
t. him whom I have appointed.		43: 7
of the Father t. Jesus Christ,		50:27
done t. the bishop or the agent,		51:12
Comforter t. the prayer of faith.		52: 9
proved by the Spirit t. him.		57:13
desire it t. the prayer of faith,		58:44
t. faith they shall overcome;		61: 9
over all, and in all, and t. all,		63:59
ye receive the Spirit t. prayer;		63:64
taught t. prayer by the Spirit.		63:65
remain to overcome t. patience,		63:66
t. the means I have appointed,		64: 5
t. the manifestations of the		70:13
sanctified t. the atonement of		74: 7
t. his Only Begotten Son,		76:13
by him, and t. him, and of him,		76:24
t. the power of the devil		76:31
t. the triumph and the glory of		76:39
t. him all might be saved		76:42
t. Jesus the mediator of the		76:69
t. the shedding of his own blood.		76:69
t. the ministration of the		76:86
t. the ministration of the		76:87
t. the power and manifestation		76:118
That t. my providence,		78:14
t. the lineage of his fathers,		84:14
t. the lineage of their fathers;		84:15
every man t. the world,		84:46
which whispereth t. and pierceth		85: 6
t. the lineage of your fathers—		86: 8
remain t. you and your lineage		86:10
t. this priesthood, a savior		86:11
t. Jesus Christ his Son—		88: 5
be in all and t. all things,		88: 6
t. him who enlighteneth your		88:11
that t. the redemption which		88:14
t. him that quickeneth all		88:17
are not sanctified t. the law		88:21
all things, and is t. all things,		88:41
fly t. the midst of heaven,		88:92
flying t. the midst of heaven,		88:103
brother t. the grace of God		88:133
t. you shall the oracles be		90: 4
also t. your administration		90: 7
That t. your administration		90: 9
and t. their administration		90: 9
t. those who are ordained unto		90:11
were made by him, and t. him,		93:10
those who are begotten t. me		93:22
light and truth, t. disobedience,		93:39
t. your diligence, faithfulness,		103:36
the covenant t. covetousness,		104: 4
being broken t. transgression,		104:52
this work t. great tribulation;		109: 5

THROUGH

t. your instrumentality.	DC 111: 2
ordained t. the instrumentality	112: 1
called to pass t. tribulation;	122: 5
wisdom t. the weak things of	124: 1
perils which I am called to pass t.,	127: 2
t. all the travels and tribulations	128:21
arise t. the slave question.	130:13
t. his diligence and obedience	130:19
t. the power of the	131: 5
t. the medium of mine anointed,	132: 7
t. him whom I have anointed	132:18
in time, and t. all eternity;	132:19
of the world, and t. all eternity;	132:49
crying t. the midst of heaven,	133:17
flying t. the midst of heaven,	133:36
t. the providence of God, escaped,	135: 2
t. the blood of mine Only	Mses 6:62
t. faith I am in the bosom of the	7:47
Blessed is he t. whose seed	7:53
myself, but t. thine own grace;	7:59
kingdoms of the earth (t. Noah),	8: 3
father, t. the fathers unto me.	Abr 1: 3
t. thy ministry my name shall	1:19
claim it from Noah, t. Ham,	1:27
I will bless them t. thy name;	2:10
passed from Jershon t. the land	2:18
its light from Kolob t.	Fac 2: 5
receives its power t. the	2: 5
revealing t. the heavens the	2: 7
or t. any neglect of mine,	JS 2:59
t. the Atonement of Christ,	AoF 3

THROUGHOUT

a proclamation t. all this land	Mos 1:10
a proclamation t. all the land,	2: 1
together t. all the land,	2: 1
spread t. every nation, kindred,	3:20
establish churches t. all the land	25:19
sent a proclamation t. the land	27: 2
command t. all the churches	27: 3
they traveled t. all the land	27:35
he sent out t. all the land,	29: 1
to establish peace t. the land,	29:14
an equal chance t. all the land;	29:38
together in bodies t. the land,	29:39
this they did t. all the land.	29:41
t. all the land of Zarahemla,	29:44
together t. all the land	Al 2: 5
and villages t. the land.	5:hd
and from thence t. all the land.	5: 1
church of God t. this land also.	5: 5
people t. all the land of Melek.	8: 4
t. all the borders of the land	8: 5
were baptized t. all the land;	8: 5
the church of God t. the land.	8:23
forth t. all the land of Sidom.	15:11
a cry of war heard t. the land.	16: 1
the word t. all the land.	16:15
became general t. the land,	16:15
been established t. all the land—	16:21
several journeys t. the land.	17:18
a proclamation t. all the land,	22:27
t. the land unto his people,	23: 3
might go forth t. all the land	23: 3
priests and teachers t. the land	23: 4
a proclamation t. all the land,	27:21
heard t. all the land,	28: 4
continual peace t. all the land.	30: 2
published t. all the land,	30:57
gathered together t. all the land	35: 4
should be made t. the church.	45:21
in every city t. all the land	45:22
and teachers t. all the land,	45:22
a proclamation t. all his land,	47: 1
acknowledged king t. all the	47:35
all the cities, t. all the land	50: 1
proclamation t. this part of the	61: 6
church of God, t. all the land.	62:46
children of men t. all the land,	63:12
t. all the regions round about	He 5:50
were wars t. all the land	11: 1
t. the face of all the land,	11:21
a great uproar t. the land;	3Ne 1: 7
contentions t. all the land;	3Ne 2:11
death and carnage t. the land,	2:11
t. all the face of the land,	3:22
spread t. all the face of the land,	Mrm 2: 8
t. all the face of the land.	2: 8
execute a law t. all the land,	Eth 7:25
a fear of Shiz t. all the land;	14:18
a cry went forth t. the land—	14:18
armies, t. all the face of the land.	14:19
t. all their generations,	DC 84:18
t. all their generations.	107:13
famine prevailed t. all the	Abr 1:30

THROW

to t. me into the depths of the	1Ne 17:48
and t. down all thy strongholds;	3Ne 21:15
which do t. greater views upon	DC 10:45
t. down their tower, and scatter	101:57
and t. down the towers of mine	105:16

THROWING

t. the bodies of the Lamanites	Al 2:34
t. up banks of earth round	48: 8
t. down the towers of mine	DC 105:30

THROWN

bank which had been t. up,	Al 49:18
arrows which were t. at them;	49:22
ye now see shall be t. down	DC 45:20
no more to be t. down,	101:75
no more to be t. down.	103:13
they shall be t. down;	103:14
saith the Lord, shall be t. down,	132:13
They shall be t. down, and left	JS 1: 2
that shall not be t. down.	1: 3

THRUST

and t. him out from his presence;	1Ne 3:13
insomuch that he t. us out,	3:25
for he shall be t. down to hell.	2Ne 9:34
for they shall be t. down to hell.	9:36
that is proud shall be t. through;	23:15
slain, t. through with a sword,	24:19
for they shall be t. down to hell!	28:15
are ye, for ye did t. in the sickle	Al 26: 5
t. your hands into my side,	3Ne 11:14
t. their hands into his side,	11:15
let him t. in his sickle with	DC 6: 3
will t. in his sickle and reap,	6: 4
let him t. in his sickle with	11: 3
will t. in his sickle and reap,	11: 4
have t. in their sickle to reap.	11:27
let him t. in his sickle with	12: 3
will t. in his sickle and reap,	12: 4
let him t. in his sickle with	14: 3
will t. in his sickle and reap,	14: 4
And they were t. down,	29:37
t. in your sickle with all your	31: 5
wherefore, t. in your sickles,	33: 7
t. down from the presence of	76:25
who are t. down to hell.	76:84
be t. from thee by the sword,	122: 6

THRUSTETH

he that t. in his sickle with	DC 4: 4

THUMMIM

the means of the Urim and T.,	DC 10: 1
of Laban, the Urim and T.,	17: 1
resides is a great Urim and T.	130: 8
and will be a Urim and T. to	130: 9
will become a Urim and T. to each	130:10
Abraham, had the Urim and T.,	Abr 3: 1
said unto me, by the Urim and T.,	3: 4
what is called the Urim and T.—	JS 2:35
with the Urim and T.;	2:42
the plates, the Urim and T.,	2:52
the plates, the Urim and T.,	2:59
by means of the Urim and T.	2:62

THUNDER

like unto the voice of t.,	1Ne 17:45
with t. and with earthquake,	2Ne 27: 2

THUNDER

as it were with a voice of t.,	Mos 27:11
and his voice was as t., which	27:18
as with the voice of t.,	Al 29: 2
as it were the voice of t.,	36: 7
and his voice was as t.,	38: 7
that it was not a voice of t.,	He 5:30
the t. and the lightning lasted,	14:27
and there was terrible t.,	3Ne 8: 6
and the t. of heaven, and	DC 87: 6
and as the voice of a great t.,	133:22

THUNDERINGS

I heard t., and earthquakes,	1Ne 12: 4
the t. and the lightnings of	19:11
they shall be visited with t.,	2Ne 26: 6
there shall be t. and lightnings	He 14:21
should be t. and lightnings	14:26
and the t. and the lightnings,	3Ne 8:12
and the t., and the lightnings,	8:17
when the t., and the lightnings,	8:19
own voice, and by the voice of t.,	DC 43:25
testimony of the voice of t.,	88:90

THUNDERS

the t. shall utter their voices	DC 43:21

THUS: *see in the APPENDIX.*

THY: *see in the APPENDIX.*

THYSELF

Shake t. from the dust;	2Ne 8:25
loose t. from the bands of thy	8:25
Thou shalt not bow down t. unto	Mos 13:13
even if thou wilt of t. be cast off.	27:16
thou make t. known unto me,	Al 22:18
when thou, of t., knowest that	30:35
thou wilt of t. be destroyed,	36: 9
If thou wilt be destroyed of t.,	36:11
thou shalt not forswear t.,	3Ne 12:33
Shake t. from the dust;	20:37
loose t. from the bands of thy	20:37
Nay; Lord, show t. unto me.	Eth 3:10
thus didst thou manifest t.	12:31
didst show t. unto them in	12:31
destruction of t. and property.	DC 19:33
Release t. from bondage.	19:35
conduct t. wisely before me?	19:41
that t. might be glorified;	45: 4
shalt love thy neighbor as t.	59: 6
keep t. unspotted from	59: 9
as thou hast abased t.	112: 3
thy love be for them as for t.;	112:11
thou mayest choose for t.,	Mses 3:17

TIDINGS

peace, yea, t. of great joy,	1Ne 13:37
the glad t. of great joy.	Mos 3: 3
feet of him that bringeth good t.;	12:21
that bringeth good t. of good;	12:21
have brought good t. of good,	15:14
feet of him that bringeth good t.,	15:18
they did publish good t. of good;	27:37
may have glad t. of great joy;	Al 13:22
glad t. among all his people,	13:22
these glad t. declared unto us	13:23
Alma having receive t. that the	31: 1
to declare glad t. of salvation	39:15
to declare these glad t. unto	39:16
declare these glad t. unto us	39:19
his angels to declare the t. of	He 5:11
sent unto you to declare good t.	5:29
he did bring glad t. to my soul	13: 7
that ye might have glad t.;	13: 7
unto them glad t. of great joy;	16:14
bringing glad t. unto the people	3Ne 1:26
bringeth good t. unto them,	20:40
bringeth good t. unto them	20:40
bearing these t. unto the	DC 1: 8
thou shalt declare glad t.,	19:29
declare glad t. of great joy	31: 3
and declare glad t. unto	62: 5

TIMBERS

this is the gospel, the glad t.,	DC 76:40
glad t. of great joy,	79: 1
exceedingly great and glorious t.,	109:23
bear glad t. unto all the world.	114: 1
glad t. for the dead;	128:19
glad t. of great joy.	128:19
bring glad t. of good things,	128:19
Glad t. from Cumorah!	128:20

TIGHT

that they were exceeding t.,	Eth 2:17
thereof was t. like unto a dish;	2:17
thereof were t. like unto a dish;	2:17
thereof was t. like unto a dish;	2:17
was shut, was t. like unto a dish.	2:17
vessels being t. like unto a dish,	6: 7
t. like unto the ark of Noah;	6: 7

TILL

we did begin to t. the earth,	1Ne 18:24
garden of Eden, to t. the earth.	2Ne 2:19
house to house, t. there can be	15: 8
people of Nephi did t. the land,	En 1:21
of every kind to t. the ground,	Jar 1: 8
that they should t. the earth.	Mos 6: 7
he also, himself, did t. the earth,	6: 7
And we began to t. the ground,	9: 9
that the men should t. the ground,	10: 4
flocks, and t. to their ground.	10:21
and began to t. the ground,	23: 5
and had begun to t. the ground.	23:31
garden of Eden, to t. the ground,	Al 42: 2
t. they should meet Moroni	52:30
t. we go against the Nephites	55:10
t. it should all be fulfilled;	3Ne 1:25
t. they shall come against us;	3:21
t. the buildings thereof had	8:14
t. they had all been brought	17:12
and began to t. the earth.	Eth 6:13
multiply and to t. the earth;	6:18
manner of tools to t. the earth,	10:25
t. the seventy and ninth year	4Ne 1:14
If I will that he tarry t. I come,	DC 7: 4
even t. you come to the reign of	10:41
t. he descends on the earth	49: 6
Return not t. I, the Lord, shall	66: 9
t. we have sealed the servants	77: 9
of his fathers, even t. Noah;	84:14
And from Noah t. Enoch,	84:15
not be taken from him t. I come.	112:15
t. he avenges that blood on the	135: 7
t. thou shalt deliver it to him	136:26
not yet a man to t. the ground;	Mses 3: 5
to t. the ground from whence	4:29
that Adam began to t. the earth,	5: 5
to t. the land and to tend flocks,	5: 3
formed a man to t. the ground.	Abr 5: 5
t. he entirely disappeared,	JS 2:43

TILLER

but Cain was a t. of the ground.	Mses 5:17

TILLEST

When thou t. the ground it	Mses 5:37

TILLING

their flocks, and t. their lands,	Mos 9:14
while t. the land round about,	23:25
labor exceedingly, t. the ground,	Al 62:29

TIMBER

rendered desolate and without t.,	He 3: 3
was desolate, save it were for t.;	3: 6
little t. upon the face of the land,	3: 7
might have t. to build their houses,	3: 9
t. was exceeding scarce in the	3:10

TIMBERS

work t. of curious workmanship.	1Ne 18: 1
I should work the t. of the ship.	18: 1
not work the t. after the manner	18: 2
caused that there should be t.,	Al 50: 2

TIMBERS

works of t. built up to the height	Al	50: 2
upon those works of t. there		50: 3
built upon the t. round about;		50: 3
build a breastwork of t. upon		53: 4
against the breastwork of t.;		53: 4
with a strong wall of t. and earth,		53: 4

TIME

to come forth in due t.		T Pg
at the t. the Lord confounded		T Pg
down unto this present t.	1 Ne	3:20
Never at any t. have I shed		4:10
tarry with us from that t. forth.		4:35
they be dimmed any more by t.		5:19
neither at any t. shall I give it		6: 1
to the own due t. of the Lord,		10: 3
from the t. that my father left		10: 4
in the t. that he should manifest		10:17
for the space of a t.		11:19
beginning of the world until this t.,		12:18
and from this t. henceforth and		12:18
And the t. cometh that he shall		13:42
For the t. cometh, saith the Lamb		14: 7
at the t. they proceeded out of		14:23
at the t. the book proceeded out		14:23
in the own due t. of the Lord,		14:26
for the space of a t.,		16:17
and changed from t. to time,		16:29
and changed from time to t.,		16:29
for the space of a t.		16:33
eastward from that t. forth.		17: 1
which t. we might have enjoyed our		17:21
harden their hearts from t. to		17:42
their hearts from time to t.,		17:42
the t. has come that they have		17:43
heard his voice from t. to time;		17:45
heard his voice from time to t.;		17:45
the Lord did show me from t. to		18: 1
did show me from time to t.		18: 1
out of this t. to meet their God;		18:18
not at the t. when I made them		19: 2
from the t. my father left		19: 8
new things from this t.,		20: 6
from that t. thine ear was		20: 8
from the t. that it was declared		20:16
In an acceptable t. have I heard		21: 8
the t. cometh that after all the		22: 7
the t. cometh speedily that Satan		22:15
the t. soon cometh that the fulness		22:16
for the t. surely must come that		22:19
For the t. speedily shall come that		22:23
And the t. cometh speedily that		22:24
But behold, when the t. cometh	2 Ne	1:10
down with sorrow from t. to time,		1:17
down with sorrow from time to t.,		1:17
from the t. that we left Jerusalem;		1:24
in the fulness of t. he cometh		2: 3
and their t. was lengthened,		2:21
cometh in the fulness of t.,		2:26
by visions in the night-t.		4:23
until the t. they sought to take		5:19
from the t. we left Jerusalem.		5:28
set himself again the second t.		6:14
until the t. comes that they shall		9: 2
led away from t. to time from		10:22
from time to t. from the house of		10:22
things to my people at that t.;		11: 1
in the fulness of his own t.		11: 7
set his hand again the second t.		21:11
and her t. is near to come,		23:22
from the t. that I came out from		25: 4
then, at that t., the day will come		25:16
set his hand again the second t.		25:17
from the t. that my father left		25:19
the own due t. of the Lord,		27:10
them forth in mine own due t.;		27:21
set my hand again the second t.		29: 1
from that t. henceforth and forever		29: 9
For the t. speedily cometh that		30:10
of men no more, for a long t.		30:18
from the t. that Lehi left	Jac	1: 1
And the t. speedily cometh,		3: 4
a long t. passed away,		5:15

TIME

this long t. have I nourished it,	Jac	5:20
I have nourished it this long t.,		5:22
I have nourished it this long t.,		5:23
I have nourished it this long t.,		5:25
a long t. had passed away,		5:29
behold, the t. draweth near,		5:29
this long t. have we nourished		5:31
this t. it hath brought forth		5:32
labor with our might this last t.,		5:62
and this is for the last t.		5:62
once again for the last t.		5:63
once more, for the last t.,		5:64
For behold, this is the last t.		5:71
the t. which will soon come.		5:71
this last t. have we nourished		5:75
for a long t. will I lay up of		5:76
for the last t. have I nourished		5:76
of the fruit, for a long t.,		5:76
when the t. cometh that evil fruit		5:77
set his hand again the second t.		6: 2
is the day, yea, even the last t.,		6: 2
in very word, from t. to time;		7: 5
in very word, from time to t.;		7: 5
that the t. passed away with us,		7:26
the Lamanites in his own due t.	En	1:16
had passed away from the t. that		1:25
for the space of much of the t.	Jar	1:13
at the t. that Zedekiah, king of	Om	1:15
dwelt there from that t. forth.		1:16
the t. that Mosiah discovered them,		1:17
by the sword from t. to time;		1:17
by the sword from time to t.;		1:17
at the t. the Lord confounded		1:22
preserved from this t. henceforth.	WM	1:11
even at this present t.,	Mos	1: 3
even down to this present t.		1: 4
from the t. they left Jerusalem		1: 6
even up to this t., and have not		2:12
I at this t. have caused that		2:27
at this period of t. when I am		2:28
For even at this t., my whole		2:30
even down to the t. our father,		2:34
For behold, the t. cometh,		3: 5
that the t. shall come when		3:20
And behold, when that t. cometh,		3:21
And even at this t., when thou		3:22
at this t. has awakened you		4: 5
And behold, even at this t.,		4:20
from the t. that Lehi left		6: 4
from the t. they left the land of		7: 1
for behold, the t. is at hand,		7:18
we at this t. do pay tribute to		7:22
from the t. that Zeniff went up		8: 2
even until the t. that he himself		8: 2
from the t. that they left the land		8: 5
from the t. they left the land of		9:hd
until the t. that they were		9:hd
against the t. the Lamanites should		10: 1
at the t., they fled out of the		11:13
he spent his t. in riotous living		11:14
priests spend their t. with harlots.		11:14
they drove them back for a t.,		11:18
they sought from that t. forward		11:29
I shall be destroyed at this t.		13: 3
the t. shall come when it shall		13:27
from this t. henceforth and		15:17
the t. shall come that the salvation		15:28
The t. shall come when all shall		16: 1
forth a second t. into the water,		18:15
of Christ, from that t. forward.		18:17
they went again even the third t.,		21:12
even until the t. that Ammon and		21:22
did not at that t. form themselves		21:34
they did prolong the t.;		21:35
listen to my words at this t.,		22: 4
in the night-t. gathered their		24:18
even all the night-t. were they		24:18
from the t. they left the land of		25: 5
from the t. they left the land of		25: 6
until the t. they returned again.		25: 6
little children at the t. he spake		26: 1
be observed from this t. forward.		26:32
Alma began from this t. forward		27:32

TIME 976 TIME

at the t. the angel appeared unto	Mos 27:32
from the t. that they were	28:17
at the t. the Lord confounded	28:17
even from that t. back until	28:17
from the t. that Lehi left	28:20
if the t. comes that the voice of	29:27
then is the t. that the judgments	29:27
then is the t. he will visit you with	29:27
from the t. Lehi left Jerusalem.	29:46
of Nephi, from this t. forward,	Al 1: 1
the first t. that priestcraft has	1:12
at the t. of their coming.	2:13
of Nephi, from that t. forth—	3:11
from this t. henceforth and	3:14
not go up to battle at this t.	3:22
troubled no more for a t.	3:24
continual peace in all that t.	4: 5
if ye were called to die at this t.,	5:27
knoweth not when the t. shall	5:29
the t. is at hand that he must	5:31
the t. is at hand that	5:36
the first t. that I have spoken	7: 1
not have come now at this t.	7: 2
the t. is not far distant that	7: 7
at the t. of his dwelling in his	7: 8
say unto you the t. shall come,	7:21
from this t. forth and forever.	7:27
the t. which thou receivedst thy	8:15
they do study at this t. that they	8:17
earth long before this period of t.,	9:11
at some period of t. they will be	9:17
they shall come in a t. when you	9:18
out of bondage t. after time,	9:22
out of bondage time after t.,	9:22
for the t. is at hand that all men	9:28
they should take me at that t.	9:33
if the t. should come that the	10:19
if the t. should come that this	10:19
and the t. is soon at hand except	10:23
according to the t. which they	11: 1
his wages according to his t.—	11: 3
even as we now are at this t.,	11:43
then is a t. that whosoever dieth	12:16
Then is the t. when their torments	12:17
then is the t. that they shall be	12:17
of the tree of life at that t.,	12:23
a t. to prepare to meet God;	12:24
a t. to prepare for that endless	12:24
they began from that t. forth to	12:30
the t. when the Lord God gave	13: 1
Now is the t. to repent,	13:21
declaring it unto many at this t.	13:24
at the t. of his coming	13:24
for the t. cometh, we know not	13:25
of angels, at the t. of his coming,	13:26
plead for them from that t. forth;	14: 7
he began from that t. forth to	15:12
them at the t. of his coming—	16:16
the t. the angel first appeared	17: 2
dwell among this people for a t.;	17:23
he has come down at this t.	18: 4
previous to the t. of the watering	18: 9
an hour, according to their t.,	18:14
down to the t. that their father,	18:36
the t. that Lehi left Jerusalem	18:38
down to the present t.	18:38
from that t. even until that time	19:11
even until that t. on the morrow	19:11
if thou shouldst fall at this t.,	20:17
from this t. and forever;	20:26
for the first t. out of prison;	21:15
down even to the present t.	23: 5
of Anti-Nephi-Lehi at that t.	25: 1
until the t. that he should be	25:15
from the t. Lehi left Jerusalem;	28: 2
this was a t. that there was a	28: 4
yea, a t. of solemnity, and a	28: 6
a t. of much fasting and prayer.	28: 6
only according to law for our t.	30:33
now is the t. and the day of	34:31
life is the t. for men to	34:32
improve our t. while in this life,	34:33
the t. that ye go out of this life,	34:34

from that t. even until now,	Al 36:24
and captivity from t. to time.	36:28
and captivity from time to t.	36:28
and captivity, from t. to time	36:29
and captivity, from time to t.	36:29
the word at the t. of his coming.	39:16
is not a soul at this t. as	39:17
will be at the t. of his coming?	39:17
as easy at this t. for the Lord	39:19
or as after the t. of his coming?	39:19
there is a t. appointed that all	40: 4
when this t. cometh no one knows;	40: 4
the t. which is appointed.	40: 4
whether there shall be one t.,	40: 5
shall be one time, or a second t.,	40: 5
or a second time, or a third t.	40: 5
that there is a t. appointed that	40: 5
space betwixt the t. of death and	40: 6
and the t. of the resurrection.	40: 6
from this t. of death to the time	40: 7
to the t. appointed for the	40: 7
whether there is more than one t.	40: 8
and t. only is measured unto men.	40: 8
there is a t. appointed unto men	40: 9
space between the t. of death	40: 9
concerning this space of t.,	40: 9
the t. cometh when all shall rise,	40:10
until the t. of their resurrection.	40:14
until the t. which is appointed	40:21
there was a t. granted unto man	42: 4
yea, a probationary t., a time	42: 4
a t. to repent and serve God.	42: 4
against the t. of the coming of	43:26
from the t. that Jesus Christ	45:10
the t. very soon cometh that	45:13
faith from that t. henceforth.	45:17
And therefore, at this t.,	46:16
sent again the second t.,	47:11
and he sent again the third t.	47:11
and he sent again the fourth t.	47:12
with his army in the night-t.,	47:13
Nephi down to the present t.	47:35
at this t. the chief captains of	49: 5
driven back from t. to time,	49:21
driven back from time to t.,	49:21
are verified, even at this t.,	50:19
there never was a happier t.	50:23
of Moroni, yea, even at this t.,	50:23
this was a critical t. for such	51: 9
it was at the same t. that they	51:12
there was no t. for their trials	51:19
circumstances at this t.	53:15
themselves together at this t.,	53:16
became known at this period of t.	53:19
this was done in the night-t.	55:22
in this their t. of affliction.	55:31
they are now at this t. in the	56:12
at the same t. they were met in	56:23
march in so short a space of t.,	56:50
did arrive in t. that we might	57:34
circumstances at this period of t.	58: 5
forth against us from t. to time,	58: 6
forth against us from time to t.,	58: 6
the t. that the Lamanites	58:17
this our march in the night-t.	58:27
are at this period of t. in our	58:31
at the t. we were contending	60:16
Behold it is t., yea, the time	60:29
yea, the t. is now at hand,	60:29
any stratagem in the night-t.,	62:35
they did not return at that t.	62:38
the t. that he murdered Pahoran.	He 1:12
no t. for the Nephites to gather	1:19
no t. to assemble themselves	1:24
that in t. they might have timber	3: 9
at that t. were not known unto	3:23
the third t. the voice came,	5:33
his followers from that t. forth.	6:27
of man even down to this t.	6:29
fathers, even down to this t.;	8:22
at this t., instead of laying up	8:25
even at this t. ye are ripening,	8:26
which at this t. doth await you,	9:22

TIME

thou wilt, even at this t., hearken	He 11:14
And thus in t., yea, even in	11:26
at the very t. when he doth	12: 2
then is the t. that they do	12: 2
this t. henceforth and forever—	12:19
the t. cometh, saith the Lord,	13:14
of this t. which has arrived,	13:24
them, even as they did of old t.	13:24
the t. cometh that he curseth	13:31
a sign at the t. of his coming;	14: 3
the t. that he shall suffer death,	14:20
to the t. that he shall rise again	14:20
at the t. that he shall yield up	14:21
ye know at this t. are solid,	14:21
until the t. shall come which	15:11
at the t. of their coming that they	16: 5
the t. that Lehi left Jerusalem;	3Ne 1: 1
to say that the t. was past for	1: 5
Behold the t. is past, and the	1: 6
for behold, the t. is at hand,	1:13
And behold, the t. is at hand,	1:14
from this t. forth there began	1:22
from the t. when the sign was	2: 7
to reckon their t. from this	2: 8
at this t. stand in their arms,	3: 3
against the t. that the robbers	3:12
at the t. that the robbers should	3:17
in the t. that their enemies	3:25
in the which t. they did hope	4: 4
out his armies in the night-t.,	4:24
this did they do in the night-t.,	4:25
from the t. that Lehi left	5:15
even down until the present t.	5:15
be fulfilled in his own due t.,	5:25
up for the space of a long t.	6:17
in the reckoning of our t.,	8: 2
for the t. that there should be	8: 3
that the t. was greater;	8:19
at the t. of their conversion,	9:20
until the t. of the fulfilling of	10: 7
for this t. I make an end of	10:19
third t. they did hear the voice,	11: 5
third t. they did understand	11: 6
have commanded you at this t.,	12:20
been said by them of old t.,	12:21
lest at any t. he shall get thee,	12:25
it is written by them of old t.,	12:27
things which were of old t.,	12:46
not at any t. hath the Father	15:14
at any t. hath the Father given	15:15
not at any t. hear my voice—	15:23
at any t. manifested myself	16: 2
Behold, my t. is at hand.	17: 1
to speak unto you at this t.	17: 2
at the t. we heard him pray for	17:17
together in mine own due t.	20:29
the t. cometh, when the fulness	20:30
the t. when these things shall	21: 1
according to the t. and the will	23: 4
vine cast her fruit before the t.	24:11
until the t. that he should	26: 3
the second t. that he showed	26:15
began from that t. forth	26:17
concerning these things for a t.	28:24
from that t. forth they did have	4Ne 1:25
from this t. the disciples began	1:44
about the t. that Ammaron	Mrm 1: 2
arms against the t. of battle.	3:11
utterly refuse from this t. forth	4:18
And from this t. forth did the	4:20
had come again the second t.	4:21
they had come the second t.,	5: 3
did not take the city at that t.	5:12
come forth in his own due t.	8:33
the t. cometh at that day when	8:41
the t. soon cometh that he	9:14
then cometh the t. that he that	Eth 1: 3
an account from that t. even to	1: 3
children of men until that t.,	1: 4
days of Adam until that t.;	1:33
at the t. the Lord confounded	1:43
this long t. ye have cried unto	2: 8
that t. henceforth and forever,	
until the t. cometh that I	Eth 3:21
will cause in my own due t.	3:24
show them in mine own due t.	3:27
know that the t. is at hand	4:16
the t. may come that Satan	8:26
which t. Com gained power over	10:32
neither at any t. hath any	12:18
for it had been in a t. of old;	13: 5
in which t. all the people upon	13:31
and they came the second t.,	14:29
were driven again the second t.	14:29
they came again the third t.,	14:29
at the t. of his first appearing;	Mro 2: 3
to speak unto you at this t.	7: 2
from this t. henceforth until	7: 3
will he, so long as t. shall last,	7:36
down unto the t. that ye shall	10: 3
the t. speedily cometh that ye	10:27
knowledge from t. to time.	DC 1:28
knowledge from time to t.	1:28
with you in every t. of trouble.	3: 8
to be poured out from t. to time,	5:19
to be poured out from time to t.,	5:19
shall be verified at this t.	5:20
place where thou art at this t.	6:14
translate at this present t.	9: 3
you feared, and the t. is past,	9:11
lost your gift at the same t.,	10: 2
until the t. which is in my	11:26
at the t. I withdrew my Spirit.	19:20
came in the meridian of t.,	20:26
or from t. to time as said	20:61
time to t. as said conferences	20:61
necessary to be done at the t.	20:62
a certificate from him at the t.,	20:64
a sufficient t. to expound all	20:68
shall appoint from t. to time;	20:82
shall appoint from time to t.;	20:82
your words, in mine own due t.	24:16
yea, even for the last t.;	24:19
wisdom in me in a t. to come.	25: 4
with him at the t. of his going,	25: 6
thy t. shall be given to writing,	25: 8
let your t. be devoted to	26: 1
led at any t. by the Comforter	28: 4
from the t. thou shalt go,	28:15
until the t. thou shalt return,	28:15
at this t. your sins are forgiven	29: 3
never at any t. have I declared	29:29
not at any t. have I given	29:34
no more unto you at this t.	29:50
the t. has come that it is	30: 5
commence from this t. forth to	30: 9
to preach from this t. forth,	31: 4
from them only for a little t.,	31: 6
against the t. when they shall	31: 8
and the last t. that I shall call	33: 3
the t. is soon at hand that I	34: 7
day at the t. of my coming,	34: 8
the t. speedily cometh that great	35:10
forth for the t. of my coming,	35:15
from this t. until the time of	35:15
until the t. of my coming,	35:18
be saved in mine own due t.;	35:25
against the t. that my servant	37: 3
destruction in process of t.,	38:13
in t. ye shall have no king	38:21
which came in the meridian of t.	39: 3
now right before me at this t.;	39: 8
may be pruned for the last t.	39:17
face for the t. of my coming;	39:20
For the t. is at hand; the day	39:21
unto me in t. and in eternity.	39:22
spend all his t. in the labors	41: 9
Until the t. shall come when	42: 9
who have not, from t. to time,	42:33
from time to t., that every man	42:33
unto you in mine own due t.	42:62
my vineyard for the last t.—	43:28
for the last t. shall call upon	43:28
in mine own due t. will I come	43:29
remain for the present t. in	48: 1
let them buy for the present t.	48: 3

TIME 978 TIME

places to live for the present t.	DC 48: 3
in t. ye may be enabled to	48: 4
which t. is nigh at hand—	49: 6
from this t. until the next	52: 2
will hasten the city in its t.,	52:43
made known in a t. to come,	53: 6
be cut off in mine own due t.,	56: 3
natural eyes, for the present t.,	58: 3
the t. has not yet come,	58:44
as soon as t. will permit.	58:52
made known from t. to time,	58:55
made known from time to t.,	58:55
they receive from t. to time.	58:56
they receive from time to t.	58:56
with revelations in their t.—	59: 4
shalt not idle away thy t.,	60:13
have I blessed it, in its t.,	61:17
at hand, and in a t. to come,	63:53
it is not said at any t. that	64:28
must come to pass in their t.	64:32
seen God at any t. in the flesh,	67:11
worthy, in mine own due t.,	67:14
in the due t. of the Lord,	68:14
if at any t. they can prove	68:21
the t. has verily come that it is	71: 1
confounded in mine own due t.	71:10
both in t. and in eternity.	72: 3
in t. is accounted worthy to	72: 4
no more unto you at this t.	73: 6
in the due t. of the Lord,	76:38
What t. are the things spoken	77:10
before the t. of his coming.	77:12
at the t. of the restoration,	77:15
the t. has come, and is now	78: 3
in mine own due t. for the	82:13
at the t. he was eight days old	84:28
against you at the t. I sent you.	84:76
is bound and t. is no longer.	84:100
the t. will come that war will	87: 2
man in his hour, and in his t.,	88:58
in its hour, and in its t.,	88:61
and it shall be in his own t.,	88:68
will hasten my work in its t.	88:73
and fasting from this t. forth.	88:76
the Gentiles for the last t.,	88:84
for their t. is not yet come,	88:85
there shall be t. no longer;	88:110
but let one speak at a t.	88:122
is coming forth for the last t.	90: 2
And from t. to time, as shall	90:14
time to t., as shall be manifested	90:14
rewarded in mine own due t.	90:29
over Zion in mine own due t.	90:32
in due t. receive of his fulness.	93:19
unto you no more at this t.	94:17
my vineyard for the last t.,	95: 4
shall smite you the second t.,	98:25
he shall smite you the third t.,	98:26
the second nor the third t.,	98:35
come upon thee the first t.,	98:39
unto the second and third t.;	98:40
thee and repent not the first t.,	98:41
against thee the second t.,	98:42
against thee the third t.,	98:43
against thee the fourth t.	98:44
and consulted for a long t.,	101:48
seeing this is a t. of peace?	101:48
the t. of harvest is come,	101:64
things be done in their t.,	101:72
and in his fierce anger, in his t.,	101:90
such council for the t. being.	102:25
without measure in mine own t.	103: 2
in t. ye shall possess the goodly	103:20
shall, hereafter, from t. to time	104:58
from time to t. give unto you—	104:58
the t. when I shall dwell with	104:59
deliver them in t. of trouble,	105: 8
of Pharaoh, from t. to time,	105:27
of Pharaoh, from time to t.,	105:27
shall have t. to gather up the	105:27
the t. has come to pass a day of	105:35
And devote his whole t. to this	106: 3
and are to be testified of in due t.	107:57
from henceforth from that t.	DC 108: 6
upon the mountains for a long t.,	109:61
Behold, the t. has fully come,	110:14
whom I will gather out in due t.	111: 2
it shall come to pass in due t.	111: 4
the last days and for the last t.,	112:30
received a dispensation at any t.	112:31
from that t. forth let my people	115:10
let them from that t. forth labor	115:12
unto my servant Joseph, from t.	115:18
servant Joseph, from time to t.,	115:18
in the due t. he shall be made a	117:14
in mine own due t.,	117:16
the t. is now come, that it shall	120: 1
there is a t. appointed for	121:25
A t. to come in the which	121:28
small helm in the t. of a storm,	123:16
the t. of the writing of the same;	124: 4
shall befall them in a t. to come.	124: 5
the set t. has come to favor her.	124: 6
Patten, who is with me at this t.,	124:19
t. to build a house unto me;	124:31
during this t. your baptisms shall	124:31
t. to build a house to me,	124:33
after this t., your baptisms for	124:35
at the t. he receives stock;	124:67
from this t. forth I appoint	124:94
door shall be open to him from t.	124:115
be open to him from time to t.	124:115
over the churches from t. to time;	124:140
over the churches from time to t.;	124:140
of presiding from t. to time;	124:140
of presiding from time to t.;	124:140
which is in store for a t. to come.	125: 2
family from this t., henceforth	126: 3
my debts are canceled in due t.,	127: 1
word of the Lord from t. to time,	127:10
word of the Lord from time to t.,	127:10
for the want of more t.;	127:11
would write to you from t. to time	128: 1
would write to you from time to t.,	128: 1
who can at any t. when called upon	128: 3
of Adam even to the present t.	128:18
Adam down to the present t.,	128:21
continue the subject another t.	128:25
Is not the reckoning of God's t.,	130: 4
reckoning of God's time, angel's t.,	130: 4
angel's time, prophet's t., and	130: 4
man's t., according to the planet	130: 4
to know the t. of the coming of	130:14
not be any sooner than that t.	130:17
as well for t. and for all eternity,	132: 7
one on the earth at a t. on	132: 7
her for t. and for all eternity,	132:18
in t., and through all eternity;	132:19
beginning of creation until this t.;	132:38
unto you all things in due t.	132:45
the t. has come when the voice	133: 7
at the same t., however,	134: 5
persons in the room at the t.;	135: 2
be redeemed in mine own due t.	136:18
during the t. specified, which	OD
present t. who holds the keys	OD
which he spake unto Moses at a t.	Mses 1: 1
from that t. forth, the sons and	5: 3
men began from that t. forth to be	5:13
in process of t. it came to pass	5:19
from this t. forth thou shalt be	5:24
it shall be said in t. to come—	5:25
should come in the meridian of t.,	5:57
shall come in the meridian of t.	6:57
shall come in the meridian of t.	6:62
from that t. forth Enoch began	7: 2
that t. forth there were wars	7:16
Zion, in process of t., was taken	7:21
shall be in the meridian of t.,	7:46
forth for the t. of my coming;	7:62
from the beginning of t., yea,	Abr 1: 3
of the earth to the present t.	1: 3
at this t. it was the custom of the	1: 8
three virgins at one t., who	1:11
which I hold unto this present t.	1:28
according to the t. appointed unto	3: 4

TIME

is the reckoning of the Lord's t.,	Abr	3: 4
the reckoning of its t. is not so		3: 5
of reckoning, and the set t.,		3: 6
the set t. of the earth upon		3: 6
the set t. of the greater light		3: 6
the day and the set t. of the lesser		3: 6
the set t. of the lesser light is		3: 7
is a longer t. as to its reckoning		3: 7
the t. of the earth upon which		3: 7
reckoning of t. shall be longer		3: 8
of the t. of one planet above		3: 9
the reckoning of the Lord's t.;		3: 9
know the set t. of all the stars		3:10
the night t. when the Lord spake		3:14
second t. that they called night		4: 8
day; and it was the third t.		4:13
day; and it was the fourth t.		4:19
day; and it was the fifth t.		4:23
and they numbered the sixth t.		4:31
On the seventh t. we will end our		5: 2
will rest on the seventh t. from		5: 2
concluded upon the seventh t.,		5: 3
the seventh t. they would rest		5: 3
at the t. that they counseled		5: 3
in the t. that thou eatest thereof,		5:13
that it was after the Lord's t.,		5:13
which was after the t. of Kolob;		5:13
to the measurement of t.	Fac	2: 1
according to celestial t.,		2: 1
which celestial t. signifies		2: 1
measuring of the t. of Oliblish,		2: 4
and in its measuring of t.		2: 4
revealed at the present t.		2: 9
own due t. of the Lord.		2:12
to give at the present t.		2:12
of their kingdom until this t.;	JS	1:18
Some t. in the second year		2: 5
at the t. of their conversion,		2: 6
at this t. in my fifteenth year.		2: 7
this t. of great excitement		2: 8
In process of t. my mind		2: 8
this did at this t. to mine.		2:12
It was the first t. in my life		2:14
it seemed to me for a t. as if		2:15
which I cannot write at this t.		2:20
all the t. suffering severe		2:27
During the space of t. which		2:28
between the t. I had the vision		2:28
the t. that they should be		2:42
By this t., so deep were the		2:46
from me for the third t.,		2:47
for a t. was quite unconscious		2:48
the t. for bringing them forth		2:53
until four years from that t.;		2:53
in one year from that t.,		2:53
until the t. should come for		2:53
at each t. I found the same		2:54
During the t. that I was thus		2:57
At length the t. arrived for		2:59
was all the t. employed in		2:61
between the t. I arrived at		2:62
until which t. I had never		2:66
in due t. be conferred on us,		2:72
being mobbed, from t. to time,		2:75
being mobbed, from time to t.,		2:75

TIMELY

By this t. aid was I enabled	JS	2:62

TIMES

And he spake unto me many t.	1Ne	4:27
as well in t. of old as in the time		10:17
as well in these t. as in times		10:19
as in t. of old, and as well		10:19
as well in t. of old as in times		10:19
in times of old as in t. to come;		10:19
shall be alone in his appointed t.	2Ne	24:31
at the t. when they shall come to		25: 7
even as in t. of old,		26:22
they came many t. against us,	Jar	1: 7
infested, by t. or at seasons, by	Mos	18: 4
as witnesses of God at all t.		18: 9
hearkened unto my words many t.	Mos	22: 3
seer, after the manner of old t.		28:16
commandments of God at all t.;	Al	7:23
how many t. he delivered our		9:10
for I was called many t. and I		10: 6
the law at their t. of trials,		10:14
words given unto them many t.		32:23
before God at all t.		38:14
God knoweth all the t. which		40:10
Lord were delivered at all t.,		50:22
men who were true at all t.		53:20
Many t. did the Lamanites		55:29
many t. did they attempt to		55:30
which they attempted many t.;		57: 9
as many t. as they attempted		57: 9
Have ye forgotten the many t.		60:20
in the latter t. the promises of	He	15:12
were in their t. of wickedness)	3Ne	3:19
led them many t. to battle,	Mrm	3:12
and begin as in t. of old,		9:27
said unto him in t. before,	Eth	3:26
many t. buried in the depths		6: 6
many t. you have desired of	DC	15: 4
many t. you have desired of		16: 4
be baptized an hundred t.		22: 2
And at all t., and in all places,		24:12
of the gospel for the last t.;		27:13
and for the fulness of t.,		27:13
or at all t. by the way of		28: 4
must open thy mouth at all t.,		28:16
hast rejected me many t.		39: 9
until the t. of the Gentiles		45:25
the t. of the Gentiles is come		45:28
shall the t. of the Gentiles be		45:30
on all days and at all t.;		59:11
to know the signs of the t.,		68:11
John Whitmer travel many t.		69: 7
until the fulness of t.,		76:106
your minds in t. past have		84:54
often t. it maketh my bones		85: 6
which they move in their t.		88:42
light to each other in their t.		88:44
be used, only in t. of winter,		89:13
only in t. of famine and		89:15
until seventy t. seven.		98:40
until seven t. seventy,		107:96
dispensation of the fulness of t.		112:30
to change the t. and seasons,		121:12
to be revealed in the last t.,		121:27
All the t. of their revolutions,		121:31
all their glories, laws, and set t.,		121:31
despensation of the fulness of t.—		121:31
dispensation of the fulness of t.		124:41
to leave your family as in t. past,		126: 1
recorder to be present at all t.,		128: 3
dispensation of the fulness of t.		128:18
dispensation of the fulness of t.		128:18
dispensation of the fulness of t.!		128:20
at sundry t., and in divers places		128:21
all persons in t. of exigency,		134:11
the Lord's anointed in ancient t.,		135: 3
according to its t. and seasons	Abr	3: 4
thee to know the t. of reckoning,		3: 6
number of the *T. and Seasons.*	Fac	3: 3
My mind at t. was greatly	JS	2: 9
in ancient or former t.;		2:35
to work as at other t.,		2:48

TIMOTHY

dead, whose name was T.,	3Ne	19: 4

TINGLE

the ears of all t. that hear,	DC	43:22

TINKLING

making a t. with their feet—	2Ne	13:16
the bravery of their t. ornaments,		13:18

TIRES

and round t. like the moon;	2Ne	13:18

TITHE

that he may t. his people,	DC	85: 3

TITHED 980 TOGETHER

TITHED
for he that is t. shall not be	DC	64:23
those who have thus been t.		119: 4
t. of their surplus properties,		119: 5

TITHES
to whom Abraham paid t.;	Al	13:15
Abraham paid t. of one-tenth		13:15
In t. and offerings.	3Ne	24: 8
all the t. into the storehouse,		24:10

TITHING
day for the t. of my people;	DC	64:23
by the t. of my people		97:11
this is the t. and the sacrifice		97:12
be the beginning of the t. of		119: 3

TITLE
he called it the t. of liberty)	Al	46:13
whosoever will maintain this t.		46:20
he caused the t. of liberty to		46:36
to hoist the t. of liberty upon		51:20

TITTLE
be all fulfilled, every jot and t.,	Al	34:13
jot or t. should not pass away	3Ne	1:25
one jot nor one t. hath not		12:18

TITUS: *see BILLINGS, Titus.*

TO: *see in the APPENDIX.*

TOBACCO
again, t. is not for the body,	DC	89: 8

TODAY
yesterday, t., and forever.	2Ne	2: 4
yesterday, t., and forever;		27:23
behold there is no God t.,		28: 5
yesterday, t., and forever;		29: 9
Yea, t., if ye will hear his voice,	Jac	6: 6
same yesterday, t., and forever;	Al	31:17
which t. is, and tomorrow is	3Ne	13:30
same yesterday, t., and forever,	Mrm	9: 9
the same t. and tomorrow, and	Mro	10: 7
yesterday, t., and forever.		10:19
God yesterday, t., and forever.	DC	20:12
the same t. as yesterday,		35: 1
voice while it is called t.,		45: 6
t. mine anger is turned away.		61:20
now it is called t. until the		64:23
after t. cometh the burning—		64:24
ye will labor while it is called t.		64:25

TOGETHER
we did gather t. our gold,	1Ne	3:22
had gathered these things t.,		3:23
we had gathered t. all manner of		8: 1
they should be gathered t. again;		10:14
were gathered t. to hear him;		11:28
they were gathered t. to fight		11:34
of the earth was gathered t.;		11:35
Israel hath gathered t. to fight		11:35
multitudes gathered t. to battle,		12: 2
of the earth gathered t.		12:13
gathered t. in multitudes		12:15
they were gathered t. to battle		12:15
gathered t. in multitudes;		12:21
gathered t. upon the waters,		13:17
gathered t. against them to battle.		13:18
did gather t. multitudes		14:13
did gather t. whatsoever things		16:11
I did smite two stones t.		17:11
and they stand up t.		20:13
all these gather themselves t.,		21:18
and they shall be gathered t.		22:12
grow t., unto the confounding	2Ne	3:12
they shall be gathered t. again		6:11
Let us stand t.		7: 8
Take counsel t., and it shall		18:10
and join his enemies t.		19:11
they t. shall be against Judah.		19:21
and the young lion and fatling t.;		21: 6
their young ones shall lie down t.;		21: 7
gather t. the dispersed of	2Ne	21:12
shall spoil them of the east t.;		21:14
kingdoms of nations gathered t.,		23: 4
when the two nations shall run t.		29: 8
of the two nations shall run t. also.		29: 8
the young lion, and the fatling, t.;		30:12
their young ones shall lie down t.;		30:13
thus will I bring them t. again,	Jac	5:68
Gather t. on the morrow,		7:16
the multitude were gathered t.;		7:17
and of Mosiah, did unite t.;	Om	1:19
Benjamin gathered t. his armies,	WM	1:13
thereby they may be gathered t.;	Mos	1:10
might gather themselves t.,		1:18
people gathered themselves t.		2: 1
have assembled yourselves t.,		2: 9
should assemble yourselves t.,		2:27
should assemble yourselves t.		2:28
should assemble yourselves t.,		2:29
might gather themselves t.		7:17
had gathered themselves t.		7:18
should gather themselves t.		10: 9
should gather themselves t.		12:17
the voice t. shall they sing;		12:22
sing t. ye waste places of		12:23
the voice t. shall they sing;		15:29
sing t., ye waste places of		15:30
a goodly number gathered t.		18: 7
all were gathered t. that believed		18: 7
their hearts knit t. in unity		18:21
they should gather themselves t.		18:25
to assemble themselves t.		18:25
were assembling themselves t.		18:32
gather themselves t. to sing,		20: 1
gathered t. to sing and to dance.		20: 2
few of them gathered t. to dance,		20: 5
he gathered his people t.,		20: 8
gathered themselves t. again,		21: 7
the people of Limhi kept t.	Mos	21:18
should gather themselves t.;		22: 1
that they gather t. their flocks		22: 6
should gather their flocks t.;		22:10
they gathered t. their flocks,		23: 1
and gathered themselves t.		23:26
gathered their flocks t.,		24:18
they gathering their flocks t.		24:18
the people should be gathered t.		25: 1
of Nephi were assembled t.,		25: 4
were gathered t. in two bodies.		25: 4
were assembled t. in large bodies,		25:15
themselves t. in different bodies,		25:21
and shalt gather t. my sheep.		26:20
should be gathered t.		27:21
should assemble themselves t.;		27:22
judges should be gathered t.,		29:29
they assembled themselves t.		29:39
people assembled themselves t.	Al	2: 5
they did assemble themselves t.		2: 6
they gathered themselves t.,		2: 9
of assembling themselves t.		6: 5
should gather themselves t. oft.		6: 6
their wives and children t.,		14: 8
came running t. by multitudes		14:29
began to assemble themselves t.		15:17
and we will gather them t.		17:31
and did gather them t. again		17:32
began to assemble themselves t.		19:18
multitude to be gathered t.		19:28
and we do assemble ourselves t.		21: 6
should assemble themselves t.		21:20
they may assemble themselves t.		22: 7
should assemble themselves t.,		22:22
was a multitude gathered t.		22:24
all the people were assembled t.,		24:17
be gathered t. in their place,		26: 6
Let us gather t. this people of		27: 5
they gathered t. all their people,		27:14
did gather t. all their flocks		27:14
gathered themselves t. in a land		31: 3
they did gather themselves t.		31:12
assembled themselves t. again		31:23
of the Zoramites had consulted t.		35: 3
t. throughout all the land		35: 4
his sons should be gathered t.,		35:16

TOGETHER

they gathered t. their armies in	Al	43: 4
gathered t. in the land of		43:15
gather themselves t. to battle		43:26
they were gathered t. in one body		43:51
gathered t. against their brethren.		46: 1
the people came running t. with		46:21
gathered t. all the people who		46:28
had gathered themselves t.,		46:31
they should gather themselves t.		47: 1
they had gathered themselves t.		47: 7
gathered t. so great an army to		47:21
gathered t. a numerous host		48: 3
he was gathering t. soldiers from		51: 9
had gathered t. a wonderfully		51:11
of Lehi gathered themselves t.,		51:24
gathered t. a large number of		52:12
they did assemble themselves t.		53:16
they gathered t. their men and		56:53
cause men to be gathered t.		59: 3
were gathered t. from the city		59: 5
been appointed to gather t. men,		60: 2
Gather t. whatsoever force		61:17
gathered t. whatsoever men		62: 6
all gathered t., insomuch that		62:33
gathered t. an innumerable	He	1:14
and he did gather t. his armies,		1:17
Nephites to gather t. their armies.		1:19
no time to assemble themselves t.		1:24
the people came t. in multitudes		7:11
of people who had gathered t.		7:12
have ye gathered yourselves t.?		7:13
ye have gathered yourselves t.,		7:15
people did gather themselves t.		9: 7
multitude who had gathered t.		9: 8
did assemble themselves t.		9:10
also gathered t. at the burial.		9:11
gather t. their women,	3Ne	3:13
we will gather all our armies t.,		3:21
they should gather themselves t.,		3:22
who did gather themselves t.		3:24
they should gather themselves t.		3:24
did gather themselves t.,		6:27
did gather themselves t.,		7: 9
who were united t. save it were		7:11
earth did cleave t. again,		10:10
were gathered t. in the land		11:hd
a great multitude gathered t.,		11: 1
the voice t. shall they sing,		16:18
Break forth into joy, sing t.,		16:19
And behold, ye shall meet t. oft;		18:22
unto you when ye shall meet t.,		18:22
the multitude was gathered t.,		19: 4
I will gather my people t.		20:18
that I would gather them t.		20:29
the voice t. shall they sing;		20:32
Father gather them t. again,		20:33
Sing t., ye waste places of		20:34
they shall surely build		22:15
shall gather t. against thee		22:15
the earth should be wrapt t.		26: 3
multitude gathered themselves t.,		26:16
the disciples were gathered t.		27: 1
in meeting t. oft both to pray	4Ne	1:12
gathered t. a great number of	Mrm	1:11
might get them t. in one body.		2: 7
should gather themselves t. at		3: 5
the earth shall be rolled t.		5:23
we might gather t. our people		6: 2
the earth shall be rolled t.		9: 2
Go to and gather t. thy flocks,	Eth	1:41
which they had gathered t.,		2: 1
Let us gather t. our people		6:19
the people were gathered t.		6:20
he had gathered t. an army		7: 5
Nimrah gathered t. a small number		9: 9
gathered t. an army of outcasts,		10: 9
began to flock t. in armies,		14:19
armies t. upon the hill Comnor,		14:28
they did gather t. all the people		15:12
t. to the army of Coriantumr;		15:13
gathered t. to the army of Shiz.		15:13
years gathering t. the people,		15:14
when they were all gathered t.,	Eth	15:15
And the church did meet t. oft,	Mro	6: 5
And they did meet t. oft to		6: 6
the islands of the sea, listen t.	DC	1: 1
are gathered t. in my name,		6:32
that the church meet t. often,		20:55
that the church meet t. often		20:75
will gather t. in one all things,		27:13
should assemble t. at the Ohio,		37: 3
ye shall assemble yourselves t.		41: 2
have assembled yourselves t.		42: 1
ye have assembled yourselves t.		42: 3
Thou shalt live t. in love,		42:45
that when ye are assembled t.		43: 8
would I have gathered you t.		43:24
my church should be called t.,		44: 1
they assemble themselves t.		44: 2
and ye elders listen t.,		45: 6
hearken ye t. and let me show		45:11
assemble ye yourselves t. ye		45:64
and shall be assembled t. unto		49:25
his church, and let us reason t.,		50:10
both are edified and rejoice t.		50:22
assemble yourselves t. to rejoice		52:42
have assembled yourselves t.,		57: 1
they shall push the people t.		58:45
assemble yourselves t.;		58:46
And let them journey t.,		61:35
hold a meeting and rejoice t.,		62: 4
the Lord, have brought you t.		62: 6
be preserved and rejoice t.		62: 6
should assemble themselves t.		63:24
have assembled yourselves t.,		67: 1
have assembled yourselves t.,		72: 1
gather t. the tribes of Israel		77: 9
have assembled yourselves t.;		78: 1
who are joined t. in this order;		78: 8
to be bound t. by a bond and		82:11
and with the voice t. sing		84:98
that all may be edified t.,		84:110
the wheat and the tares grow t.		86: 7
have assembled yourselves t.		88: 1
that you assemble yourselves t.,		88:74
and all people shall see it t.		88:93
he may gather t. his armies.		88:111
shall gather t. his armies,		88:112
devil shall gather t. his armies;		88:113
in assembling yourselves t.		89: 5
shall work t. for your good,		90:24
shall work t. for your good,		98: 3
shall work t. for good to them		100:15
should gather t. and stand in		101:22
and all flesh shall see me t.		101:23
Go and gather t. the residue		101:55
they gather t. against you,		101:58
the gathering t. of my saints		101:64
I must gather t. my people,		101:65
gather t. unto the places which		101:67
gather t. all their moneys;		101:72
and gather t. upon them;		101:74
Gather yourselves t. unto the		103:22
have assembled yourselves t.		105: 1
the gathering t. of my saints.		105:15
gather t. for the redemption of		105:16
but carefully gather t., as much		105:24
shall work t. for your good.		105:40
gathering t. upon the land of		115: 6
the gathering t. of my saints,		115: 8
t. with all the precious trees		124:26
let them gather themselves t.		125: 2
and welding t. of dispensations, and		128:18
and the morning stars sing t.,		128:23
gather ye t., O ye people of		133: 4
Listen, ye elders of my church t.,		133:16
and ye elders listen t.;		136:41
be gathered t. unto one place,	Mses	2: 9
the gathering t. of the waters,		2:10
And they sewed fig-leaves t.		4:13
be gathered t. unto one place,	Abr	4: 9
and the gathering t. of the waters,	.	4:10
will the eagles be gathered t.;	JS	1:27
gather t. the remainder of his elect		1:37

TOGETHER

right; or, are they all wrong t.? JS 2:10
was formed by laying stones t. 2:52

TOIL
the women should spin, and t., Mos 10: 5
their women did t. and spin, He 6:13
they t. not, neither do they spin; 3Ne 13:28
they t. not, neither do they spin; DC 84:82
I have seen your labor and t. 126: 2
our work and t. of our hands, Mses 8: 9

TOILED
and our women have t., 1Ne 17:20
t. by night to maintain their Al 56:16

TOILING
t. with their might to fortify Al 56:15

TOKEN
rending their garments in t., Al 46:21
as a t. of peace, which custom 47:23
they do it for a t. of bravery. Mro 9:10
in t. or remembrance of the DC 88:131
in t. or remembrance of the 88:133
saying Amen, in t. of the same. 88:135
his t. unto the treasurer that 104:75

TOLD
t. the things which Laban had 1Ne 3:14
the Lord t. me whither I should 17:10
And it was t. the house of David, 2Ne 17: 2
it hath been t. them concerning 25:10
do the things which I have t. you 31:17
And I t. him the things which Jac 7:27
conditions which I have t. you. Mos 4: 8
who t. them of their wickedness 7:26
he t. his people all the things 8: 1
Ammon t. him that he could not. 8: 6
after having t. all these things 10:19
neither have I t. you that which 13: 3
because I have t. you the truth 13: 6
the men of Gideon t. them of all 19:22
the people t. the men of Gideon 19:23
they t. Gideon what they had 19:24
Limhi t. the king all the things 20:23
he t. them that these things 29:34
t. him all the things concerning Al 18:36
they had t. them things of God, 19:34
Who t. thee that thy brethren 20: 4
No one hath t. me, save it be God; 20: 5
he also t. him all the cause of 20:12
Aaron hath t. me that there is 22:18
servants ran and t. the queen 22:19
Ammon went and t. the king 27:13
went and t. the chief judge 27:20
I have t. you this that ye may 38: 9
t. Moroni all things concerning 50:31
t. them all the things that he 51:35
and t. it unto Jacob, their leader. 52:22
t. him all the things that had 55:15
And he ran and t. Helaman all He 2: 9
and they ran and t. the people 7:11
servants ran and t. the people, 9: 6
they t. them all that they had 9:13
t. us the thoughts of our hearts, 9:41
and also has t. us things; 9:41
that which had not been t. them 3Ne 20:45
that which had not been t. them 21: 8
the things which I have t. you; 23: 4
when Jesus had t. these things 26: 1
the things that I have t. you. 27:12
I have t. you the things which Eth 5: 1
that he t. me in plain humility, 12:39
he truly t. them of all things, 13: 2
as I also t. the people of the DC 5:20
if I have t. you things which 6:24
it has t. you many things; 8: 6
be t. them what they shall do; 38:33
as I have t. you before, 43: 7
desolation which I have t. you 45:21
things which I have t. you 45:23
this I have t. you concerning 45:24
to that which I have t. you. 132:50
and do as I have t. you. 136:17

TONGUES

Who t. thee thou wast naked? Mses 4:17
and t. Enoch all the doings of 7:41
I, Abraham, t. Sarai, my wife, Abr 2:25
he t. me of the works which 3:11
all I have t. you must come JS 1:23
Behold, I have t. you before; 1:24
until all I have t. you shall be 1:34
he t. me, that when I got those 2:42
at what had been t. to me by 2:44
and t. me to go home. 2:48
and t. me to go and do as 2:50
had t. me the plates were 2:50
he t. me that I should come to 2:53

TOLERABLE
it shall be more t. for them Al 9:15
yea, and even more t. for them 9:15
far more t. for the Lamanites 9:23
and it shall be t. for them. DC 45:54
be more t. for the heathen 75:22

TOMORROW
and be merry, for t. we die; 2Ne 28: 7
all these things, for t. we die; 28: 8
and t. is cast into the oven 3Ne 13:30
today and t. and forever Mro 10: 7
t. all the proud and they that DC 64:24

TONGS
which he had taken with the t. 2Ne 16: 6

TONGUE
every nation, kindred, t. and people 1Ne 19:17
Yet I will not loose his t., 2Ne 3:17
given me the t. of the learned 7: 4
destroy the t. of the Egyptian sea; 21:15
nation, kindred, t., and people, 26:13
ye speak with the t. of angels, 31:13
and can speak with a new t., 31:14
even with the t. of angels, 31:14
could speak with the t. of angels? 32: 2
ye speak with the t. of angels 32: 2
to every kindred, nation, and t., Mos 3:13
nation, kindred, t., and people. 3:20
nation, kindred, t., and people. 15:28
nation, kindred, t., and people 16: 1
and every t. confess before him. 27:31
nation, kindred, t., or people; Al 9:20
own nation and t., 29: 8
nation, kindred, t., and people, 37: 4
nation, kindred, t., and people, 45:16
And no t. can speak, neither 3Ne 17:17
And t. cannot speak the words 19:32
every t. that shall rise against 22:17
impossible for the t. to describe, Mrm 4:11
t. cannot tell, neither can it be Mro 9:19
t., or people they may be. DC 10:51
and then shall your t. be loosed; 11:21
is opened, and thy t. loosed; 23: 3
and your t. shall be loosed, 31: 3
every t. shall confess to him 76:110
nation, kindred, t. and people; 77: 8
nation, kindred, t., and people, 77:11
And the t. of the dumb shall 84:70
and every t. shall confess, 88:104
of the gospel in his own t., 90:11
nation, kindred, t., or people, 98:33
if any nation, t., or people 98:34
unto that people, nation, or t.; 98:34
against that nation, t., or people. 98:36
let the t. of the slanderer cease 112: 9
and kindred, and t., and people. 133:37
as to bind my t. so that I JS 2:15

TONGUES
all nations, kindreds, t., and people 1Ne 5:18
all nations, kindreds, t., and people, 11:36
known to all kindreds, t., and people 13:40
all nations, kindreds, t., and people. 14:11
all nations, kindreds, t., and people 22:28
their t. and their doings have 2Ne 13: 8
nations, kindreds, t., and people, 30: 8
in the gift of speaking with t., Om 1:25

TONGUES / TOOK

TONGUES (cont.)

nations, kindreds, t. and people,	Mos	27:25
the gift of speaking with t.,	Al	9:21
and t. shall stand before God,	3Ne	26: 4
he did loose their t., and they		26:14
he loosed their t. that they		26:14
nations, kindreds, t. and people,		28:29
prophecy, or by gifts, or by t.,		29: 6
healing, nor speaking with t.,	Mrm	9: 7
and the interpretation of t.;		9: 7
they shall speak with new t.;		9:24
to another, all kinds of t.;	Mro	10:15
and of divers kinds of t.		10:16
nations, kindreds, t. and people.	DC	7: 3
their t. shall be stayed that		29:19
nations, kindreds, t. and people.		42:58
to some to speak with t.;		46:24
given the interpretation of t.		46:25
nations, kindreds, t., and people;		88:103
with languages, t., and people.		90:15
the gift of t. be poured out		109:36
even cloven t. as of fire,		109:36
among all nations, kindreds, t.,		112: 1
all nations, kindreds, and t.,	JS	2:33
rumor with her thousand t.		2:61
We believe in the gift of t.,	AoF	7
healing, interpretation of t.,		7

TOO

shall even now be t. narrow	1Ne	21:19
The place is t. strait for me;		21:20
yea, even t. great for man;	2Ne	4:25
should be t. strong for the graft,	Jac	5:65
can glory t. much in the Lord?	Al	26:16
say t. much of his great power,		26:16
until it is everlastingly t. late,	He	13:38
might not have t. great sorrow	Mrm	5: 9
avoid the t. frequent repetition	DC	107: 4
and that t. most holy,		132: 7
and one, t., who was doomed to	JS	2:23
this, t., by professors of religion.		2:75

TOOK

and t. nothing with him, save it	1Ne	2: 4
t. our journey in the wilderness,		3: 9
t. Laban by the hair of the head,		4:18
I t. the garments of Laban		4:19
we t. the plates of brass and the		4:38
my father, Lehi, t. the records		5:10
they t. their journey with us		7: 5
I, Nephi, t. one of the daughters		16: 7
my brethren t. of the daughters		16: 7
Zoram t. the eldest daughter of		16: 7
I t. the compass, and it did		18:21
I t. unto me faithful witnesses	2Ne	18: 2
which a man t. and nourished	Jac	5: 3
they t. from the natural tree		5:55
they also t. of the natural trees		5:56
that they also t. others	Om	1:29
and t. their journey again into		1:29
he t. them and put them with	WM	1:10
they also t. of the firstlings of	Mos	2: 3
Ammon t. three of his brethren,		7: 6
he t. the lead of their journey		10:13
and t. the records which were		10:16
they t. him and carried him		12: 9
they t. him and bound him, and		17:13
Alma t. Helam, he being one of		18:12
And again, Alma t. another, and		18:15
they t. their tents and their		18:34
t. them captives and carried them		19:15
and t. them and carried them into		20: 5
they t. him and bound up his		20:13
unless he t. his guards with him,		21:19
t. of their grain, and departed		23: 1
the Lamanites t. possession of		23:29
and t. their journey into the		24:24
therefore they t. upon themselves		25:12
they t. a small number with them		28: 1
And they t. their journey into		28: 9
he t. the records which were		28:11
he t. the plates of brass,		28:20
they t. him; and his name was	Al	1:15
people of Nephi t. their tents,		2:26

TOOK (cont.)

and t. his journey over into the	Al	8: 3
t. his journey towards the city		8:13
t. upon him the high priesthood		13:14
but they t. them and bound them		14: 4
t. them before the chief judge of		14: 4
that they t. Alma and Amulek,		14: 9
he t. Amulek and came over to		15:18
and t. him to his own house,		15:18
they t. their brethren who had		16: 8
t. their swords, and their spears,		17: 7
who were with them, t. courage		17:12
thus they t. their several journeys		17:18
t. him and bound him,		17:20
t. him and carried him in unto		18:43
and t. the queen by the hand,		19:29
she t. the king, Lamoni, by the		19:30
Aaron t. his journey towards		21: 1
they t. up arms against the		24: 2
they t. their swords, and all		24:17
they t. their armies and went		25: 2
t. possession of the land of		27:26
for they t. him, and bound him,		30:20
Therefore he t. Ammon, and		31: 6
the former three he t. with him,		31: 6
and he also t. two of his sons.		31: 6
the eldest of his sons he t. not		31: 7
of those whom he t. with him		31: 7
the chief captain t. the command		43:16
Moroni t. all the command,		43:17
and t. their journey round about		43:22
t. the remaining part of his		43:25
he t. off his scalp and it fell		44:12
t. up the scalp from off the		44:13
he t. the weapons of war from		44:20
the Lord t. Moses unto himself;		45:19
and he t. a piece thereof,		46:12
he t. the pole, which had on		46:13
believers in Christ t. upon them,		46:15
t. those of his people who would		46:29
he t. his army and marched out		46:31
and t. possession of the city.		47:31
Amalickiah t. the same servant		47:34
and t. her unto him to wife;		47:35
they t. their camp, and moved		48: 6
and t. their camp and marched		49:12
came forward and t. an oath		49:13
a contention which t. place		50:25
t. up arms against their		50:26
t. them prisoners, and returned		50:35
a union t. place between them		50:36
t. upon them the name of		51: 6
Amalickiah t. possession of		51:23
t. courage and pursued them		52:24
and t. command of the city		53: 2
and t. their weapons of war		53:18
they t. their weapons of war,		53:19
they t. of it more freely;		55:13
He t. them prisoners of war,		55:24
and t. possession of the city,		55:24
and we t. our march into the		56:39
that the Lamanites t. courage,		56:52
I t. and joined them to my		56:57
t. our march back to the city		56:57
t. our march with speed towards		57:34
we t. our course, after having		58:23
they t. no thought concerning		58:25
Moroni t. a small number of		62: 3
t. his march towards the land of		62: 3
t. their march with a large body		62:14
they t. a large body of men of		62:15
and t. their provisions and their		62:15
others, and t. them prisoners;		62:25
Shiblon t. possession of those		63: 1
they t. their course northward.		63: 6
they also t. much provisions,		63: 7
his heart t. courage insomuch	He	1:22
that Moronihah t. possession of		1:33
t. their flight out of the land,		2:11
t. it upon him to preach the word		5: 4
and he t. their little children,	3Ne	17:21
he t. of the bread and brake		18: 3
t. possession again of the city	Mrm	4: 8
king dwelt, and t. him captive,	Eth	7: 5

TOOK

and he t. Shule, the king,	Eth 7:17
Coriantum t. to wife, in his old	9:24
they t. up a howling and a	15:16
they t. the cup, and said:	Mro 5: 1
they t. upon them the name of	6: 3
t. from the tower of Sherrizah;	9: 7
you t. no thought save it was	DC 9: 7
he t. Moses out of their midst,	84:25
and I t. him to myself.	136:38
t. the man, and put him into	Mses 3:15
I t. one of his ribs and closed up	3:21
she t. of the fruit thereof, and did	4:12
Cain t. one of his brother's	5:28
Lamech t. unto himself two wives;	5:44
and he t. glory unto himself.	8: 3
fair, and they t. them wives,	8:14
I, Abraham, t. Sarai to wife,	Abr 2: 2
Nehor, my brother, t. Milcah	2: 2
and I t. Lot, my brother's son,	2: 4
And I t. Sarai, whom I took to	2:15
Sarai, whom I t. to wife when I	2:15
Gods t. counsel among themselves	4:26
of the ground, and t. his spirit	5: 7
Gods t. the man and put him in	5:11
and they t. one of his ribs,	5:15
came, and t. them all away;	JS 1:43
I t. occasion to give him an	2:21
he t. me, with the rest of his	2:56
For what t. place relative to	2:63
I t. the certificate and put it	2:64
I accordingly t. it out of my	2:65
he t. it and tore it to pieces,	2:65

TOOL

Behold, we lay a t. here and on	He 13:34
if a man should lay his t. or his	Eth 14: 1

TOOLS

make t. to construct the ship	1Ne 17: 9
ore, that I might make t.	17:10
I did make t. of the ore	17:16
making all manner of t.	Jar 1: 8
all manner of t. to till the earth,	Eth 10:25
all manner of t. with which they	10:26

TOOTH

for an eye, and a t. for a tooth;	3Ne 12:38
for an eye, and a tooth for a t.;	12:38

TOP

up into the t. of the mountain,	1Ne 16:30
in the t. of the mountains,	2Ne 12: 2
but behold, the main t. thereof	Jac 5: 6
the root and the t. may be equal	5:66
root and the t. thereof equal,	5:73
he could stand upon the t. thereof	Mos 11:12
upon the t. of the hill Manti,	Al 1:15
the t. thereof would only admit	31:13
and stand upon the t. thereof,	31:14
upon the t. of the mount which	47: 7
upon the t. of these ridges of	50: 2
cast stones from the t. thereof,	50: 5
and came upon the t. of the wall	62:20
let down from the t. of the wall	62:21
and come upon the t. of the wall,	62:22
yea, even upon the t. thereof	3Ne 4:28
from the t. of the hill Cumorah,	Mrm 6:11
the t. thereof was tight like	Eth 2:17
thou shalt make a hole in the t.,	2:20
upon the t. of the mount,	3: 1
again upon the t. of the waters.	6: 7
unto the t. thereof,	DC 115:12
this hill, not far from the t.,	JS 2:51

TOPS

into the t. of the ragged rocks,	2Ne 12:21
shall be read upon the house t.;	27:11
be reavealed upon the house-t.—	Mrm 5: 8

TORCHES

neither candles, neither t.;	3Ne 8:21

TORE

he took it and t. it to pieces,	JS 2:65

TORMENT

thing mean the t. of the body	1Ne 15:31
their t. is as a lake of fire and	2Ne 9:16
brimstone, which is endless t.	9:19
brimstone, which is endless t.;	9:26
brimstone, which is endless t.	28:23
and brimstone is endless t.	Jac 6:10
to endure a never-ending t.	2:39
state of misery and endless t.,	3:25
their t. is as a lake of fire and	3:27
ourselves a never-ending t.,	5: 5
soul was racked with eternal t.;	27:29
soul should indure endless t.	28: 3
from the Nephites to t. them	Al 19:26
I was racked with eternal t.,	36:12
as I was thus racked with t.,	36:17
death, hell, and an endless t.	Mro 8:21
shall be no end to this t.,	DC 19: 6
but it is written *endless t.*	19: 6
quenched, which is their t.—	76:44
the place thereof, nor their t.,	76:45
up his eyes in hell, being in t.	104:18
in t., for the fiery indignation	Mses 7: 1
until that day they shall be in t.;	7:39

TORMENTED

I was t. with the pains of hell;	Al 36:13
father was sorely t. because	Abr 1:30

TORMENTS

their t. shall be as a lake of	Al 12:17

TORN

and their carcasses were t.	2Ne 15:25

TORTURETH

t. them and bindeth them down,	1Ne 13: 5

TORTURING

t. their bodies even unto death;	Mro 9:10

TOSSED

thou afflicted, t. with tempest,	3Ne 22:11
as a vessel is t. about upon	Mrm 5:18
they were t. upon the waves of	Eth 6: 5

TOUCH

command you that ye t. me not,	1Ne 17:48
nor t. me with their fingers,	17:52
T. not the things which are sealed,	2Ne 27:21
that I should not t., save it were	Jac 1: 2
and t. upon them as much as it	1: 4
T. me not, for God shall smite you	Mos 13: 3
and t. not their unclean things;	Al 5:57
put forth their hands to t. him	19:24
t. not that which is unclean;	3Ne 20:41
t. these stones, O Lord, with	Eth 3: 4
therefore t. them not in order	5: 1
and t. not the evil gift, nor	Mro 10:30
will t. the hearts of honest men	DC 135: 7
neither shall ye t. it, lest ye die.	Mses 4: 9
his feet did not t. the floor.	JS 2:30

TOUCHED

Lo, this has t. thy lips;	2Ne 16: 7
as soon as she t. her hand she	Al 19:29
he t. with his hand the disciples	3Ne 18:36
even until he had t. them all,	18:36
unto them as he t. them.	18:36
when Jesus had t. them all,	18:38
he t. every one of them with	28:12
and t. the stones one by one	Eth 3: 6
the Lord t. the eyes of our	DC 76:19

TOUCHING

of my beloved, t. his vineyard.	2Ne 15: 1
as t. all things concerning my	3Ne 23: 2
in my name, as t. one thing,	DC 6:32
be agreed as t. all things	27:18

TOUCHING 985 TOWER

agreed as t. this one thing,	DC	42: 3
are agreed as t. the church,		50: 1
t. the principle and doctrine		132: 1
answer thee as t. this matter.		132: 2
as t. Abraham and his seed,		132:30
as t. the law of the priesthood,		132:58

TOWARD: see also TOWARDS.

went up t. Jerusalem to war	2Ne	17: 1
t. the land of Zarahemla	Al	48: 6
heart shall be softened t. them,	DC	121: 3
moved with compassion t. them?		121: 3
moved with compassion t. us.		121: 4
an increase of love t. him whom		121:43
which goeth t. the east of Assyria.	Mses	3:14
from the way t. the Garden		5: 4

TOWARDS: see also TOWARD.

forth t. the house of Laban.	1Ne	4: 5
forth t. the treasury of Laban,		4:20
t. the land of promise.		5:22
t. the tent of our father.		7:21
t. the head of the river,		8:17
t. those who had come at		8:27
t. that great and spacious building.		8:31
shall be led t. the promised land		17:13
the wind t. the promised land.		18: 8
again t. the promised land.		18:22
-suffering t. the children of men.		19: 9
with their face t. the earth,		21:23
for I know their hatred t. me	2Ne	5:14
with their faces t. the earth,		6: 7
of the Philistines t. the west;		21:14
their fear t. me is taught by		27:25
their hatred t. you is because	Jac	3: 7
arm of mercy is extended t. you		6: 5
with love t. God and all men.	Mos	2: 4
the door thereof t. the temple,		2: 6
and his long-suffering t. the		4: 6
and long-suffering t. you,		4:11
hatred t. the children of Nephi.		10:17
of God and their duty t. him.		13:30
compassion t. the children of men;		15: 9
of mercy were extended t. them;		16:12
of mercy were extended t. them,		16:12
and in love one t. another.		18:21
free will and good desires t. God,		18:28
about t. the land of Shemlon,		19: 6
that they may be pacified t. us;		20:19
the king doth pacify them t. us		20:20
the king was pacified t. his people;		20:24
and were pacified t. them,		20:26
course t. the land of Zarahemla,		22:11
of their hatred t. the Nephites.		28: 2
the arm of mercy t. them that		29:20
did wax strong in love t. Mosiah;		29:40
and their children, t. our city;	Al	2:25
the valley of Gideon t. their city,		2:26
t. the wilderness which was west		2:36
be scornful, one t. another,		4: 8
mercy and long-suffering t. them?		5: 6
of mercy are extended t. them,		5:33
took his journey t. the land		8:13
set my back t. this land forever.		8:24
and his long-suffering t. us,		9:11
and returned t. my house.		10: 8
t. the land of Zarahemla.		17: 1
journey t. the land of Middoni.		20:28
took his journey t. the land		21: 1
they were pacified t. Aaron		22:25
from the east t. the west—		22:27
long-suffering t. the children of		26:16
their love t. their brethren		26:31
their brethren and also t. us.		26:31
of their love t. their brethren.		26:32
distinguished for their zeal t. God,		27:27
towards God, and also t. men;		27:27
arm which he extended t. me.		29:10
forth his hands t. heaven,		31:14
his face immediately t. him,		32: 6
their hatred t. the Nephites,		43: 7
the Lamanites t. their brethren,		43:11
began to flee t. the river Sidon.		43:39

t. the land of Manti;	Al	43:42
t. the land of Ammonihah.		49: 1
marched t. the land of Noah,		49:12
march t. the land Bountiful,		52:15
t. the city of Cumeni;		57:31
speed t. the city Cumeni;		57:34
t. the land of Zarahemla.		58:23
t. the land of Zarahemla,		58:24
way t. the land of Manti.		58:26
great has been your neglect t. us.		60: 5
exceeding great neglect t. them.		60: 9
great neglect t. their brethren,		60:14
t. those who have been slain.		60:14
march t. the land of Gideon.		62: 3
march t. the land of Gideon.		62: 4
t. the land of Nephihah;		62:14
they were marching t. the land,		62:15
march t. the land of Nephihah.		62:18
even t. the city of Bountiful;	He	1:23
back t. the land of Zarahemla.		1:29
went forth t. the judgment-seat		2: 6
went his way t. his own house,		10: 2
goodness and his mercy t. them,		12: 6
their everlasting hatred t. you	3Ne	3: 4
arm of mercy is extended t. you,		9:14
their eyes were t. the sound		11: 5
did look steadfastly t. heaven,		11: 5
their eyes up again t. heaven;		11: 8
filled with compassion t. you.		17: 6
they cast their eyes t. heaven,		17:24
retreat t. the north countries.	Mrm	2: 3
Lamanites marching t. them;		6: 7
waters, t. the promised land;	Eth	6: 5
to blow t. the promised land		6: 8
t. the land southward, which		9:31
lost their love, one t. another;	Mro	9: 5
filled with compassion t. them.	DC	101: 9
Be not partial t. them in love		112:11
be full of charity t. all men,		121:45
void of offense t. God,		135: 4
towards God, and t. all men.		135: 4
Look; and I looked t. the north,	Mses	7: 6
going on still t. the south;	Abr	2:21
and thinner t. the edges,	JS	2:51

TOWER

when they were building a t.	T Pg	
And upon every high t.,	2Ne	12:15
and built a t. in the midst of it,		15: 2
first parents came out from the t.,	Om	1:22
he caused a t. to be erected,		2: 7
to speak to his people from the t.;		2: 8
he built a t. near the temple;		11:12
yea, a very high t., even so high		11:12
he caused a great t. to be built		11:13
and ran and got upon the t.		19: 5
get upon the t. to slay the king,		19: 6
discovered them from the t.,		20: 8
to the building of the great t.,		28:17
to be hoisted upon every t.	Al	46:36
to build a t. sufficiently high	He	6:28
from that t. into this land;		6:28
a t., which was in the garden of		7:10
had bowed himself upon the t.		7:10
which t. was also near unto the		7:10
his soul unto God upon the t.;		7:11
because I have got upon my t.		7:14
that time even to the great t.,	Eth	1: 3
from the t. down until they		1: 5
from the great t., at the time		1:33
took from the t. of Sherrizah;	Mro	9: 7
her salvation and her high t.	DC	97:20
who are found upon the watch-t.,		101:12
about them, and build a t.,		101:45
to be a watchman upon the t.,		101:45
and began to build a t.		101:46
need hath my lord of this t.?		101:47
hath my lord of this t.,		101:48
built the t. also, and set a		101:53
set a watchman upon the t.,		101:53
the watchman upon the t.		101:54
throw down their t., and scatter		101:57

TOWERS

TOWERS
unto the Lamanites from their t.,	Al	48: 1
And he caused t. to be erected		50: 4
to be built upon those t.,		50: 4
the title of liberty upon their t.,		51:20
down the t. of mine enemies	DC	105:16
down the t. of mine enemies		105:30

TOWN
in the t. of Sharon, Windsor	JS	2: 3

TOWNS
both in t. and villages.	Mrm	4:22
their t., and villages, and cities		5: 5

TOWNSHIP
was a resident of Palmyra t.,	JS	2:61

TRACK
neither journey in another's t.	DC	52:33

TRACKS
could no longer follow their t.;	Mos	22:16

TRACT
also every t. lying westward,	DC	57: 4
also every t. bordering by		57: 5

TRADE
began to t. one with another	Mos	24: 7

TRADITION
in the t. of their fathers,	Mos	10:12
believe the t. of their fathers.		26: 1
in the t. of the Lamanites,	Al	3:11
also in the t. of their fathers,		3:11
of the land, according to your t.;		8:11
forgotten the t. of your fathers;		9: 8
Now this was the t. of Lamoni,		18: 5
believe in the t. of our brethren,		31:16
after the t. of their brethren,		31:22
incorrect t. of their fathers;		37: 9
it is the t. of their fathers		60:32
and the t. of their fathers.	He	5:51
iniquity of the t. of their		15: 4
we know that this is a wicked t.,		16:20
faith in the t. of their fathers.	3Ne	1:11
that the t. might be done away,	DC	74: 6
of the t. of their fathers.		93:39

TRADITIONS
also all the t. of our fathers.	En	1:14
because of the t. of their fathers,	Mos	1: 5
mix and believe in incorrect t.	Al	3: 8
do not believe in such foolish t.		8:11
of the t. of their fathers		9:16
of the t. of their fathers;		9:17
of the t. of their fathers,		17: 9
of the t. of their fathers;		17:15
their iniquities and their t.,		19:14
do not believe in these foolish t.		21: 8
and of the t. of their fathers,		21:17
the wicked t. of their fathers,		23: 3
believe in the t. of the Nephites;		23: 5
the t. of our wicked fathers.		24: 7
the t. of their fathers,		25: 6
of the t. of their fathers,		26:24
are foolish t. of your fathers.		30:14
of the t. of your fathers,		30:16
the foolish t. of your fathers,		30:23
the foolish t. of your fathers,		30:27
by their t. and their dreams		30:28
after the silly t. of their fathers,		30:31
foolish t. of our brethren,		31:17
with the t. of the Lamanites;		47:36
unto you concerning their t. or		56: 4
of the t. of their fathers.	He	5:19
abominable t. of their fathers,		15: 7
because of the t. of their fathers,		15:15
who believed in those t.	3Ne	1: 9
heed to the t. of their fathers	DC	74: 4

TRAFFIC
did t. in all manner of traffic.	4Ne	1:46
did traffic in all manner of t.		1:46
sell and t. one with another,	Eth	10:22

TRAIN
and his t. filled the temple	2Ne	16: 1

TRAITOR
that he was not also a t. to	Al	62: 1

TRAITORS
ye are also t. to your country.	Al	60:18
by the testimony of t.	DC	122: 3
by the conspiracy of t. and		135: 7

TRAMPLE
at naught and t. under their feet.	1Ne	19: 7
God of Israel do men t. under		19: 7
trample under their feet; I say, t.		19: 7
t. the Holy One under your feet;	Al	5:53
ye do t. them under your feet.		60:33
and did t. under their feet	He	6:31
they did t. under their feet		6:39
and do t. under their feet the		12: 2
they t. them under their feet,	3Ne	14: 6

TRAMPLED
t. under their feet the laws of	He	4:22
been t. under feet of men,	3Ne	28:35
counsel of thy director to be t.	DC	3:15
And I have t. them in my fury,		133:51

TRAMPLETH
and he t. under his feet the	Mos	29:22

TRANQUILITY
for the public peace and t.	DC	134: 8

TRANSACT
who will t. all business in a	DC	127: 1

TRANSACTION
and the history of the whole t.;	DC	128: 3

TRANSCRIBING
in t. all things which shall be	DC	47: 1

TRANSFIGURATION
unto them like a t. of them,	3Ne	28:15
from the day of their t.,		28:17
when the day of t. shall come;	DC	63:20

TRANSFIGURED
Why have ye t. the holy word	Mrm	8:33
When the earth shall be t.,	DC	63:21
I beheld his face, for I was t.	Mses	1:11

TRANSFORMETH
who t. himself nigh unto an angel	2Ne	9: 9

TRANSGRESS
if ye should t. and go contrary	Mos	2:36
that they t. the laws of God,		4:14
take heed that ye do not t.,		5:11
upon all those who did t. it,	Al	1:32
should t. contrary to the light		9:23
but they are not unto you if ye t.;		9:24
if ye t. the commandments		37:15
t. the commandments of God,		46:21
ye do t. the laws of God,		60:33
if you did not t. them.	DC	3: 5
if he t. another shall be		42:10
And if he shall t. and is		51: 5
wherefore, t. them not, neither		68:34
of the High Priesthood shall t.,		107:82
And when thy people t.,		109:21

TRANSGRESSED
if Adam had not t. he would	2Ne	2:22
I know my guilt; I t. thy law,		9:46
having t. the law of God	Mos	2:33

TRANSGRESSED 987 TRANSLATED

first t. the first commandments	Al	12:31
have t. the commandments	DC	3: 6
and t. the commandment,		29:40

TRANSGRESSES
t. and is not accounted worthy	DC	51: 4

TRANSGRESSETH
and that t. them,	2Ne	9:27
and whosoever t. against me,	Mos	26:29
and t. not the law—	DC	88:25

TRANSGRESSING
in t. against that Holy God,	2Ne	9:39
t., or being overtaken in a fault,	DC	20:80

TRANSGRESSION
of the t. of their parents.	2Ne	2:21
and the fall came by reason of t.;		9: 6
Nephites, should fall into t.,	En	1:13
but should fall into t.,	Jar	1:10
except it be through t.	Mos	1:12
of the Lord should fall into t.,		1:13
of those that have fallen into t.		2:40
have fallen by the t. of Adam,		3:11
except it be through t.,		5:11
this people had not fallen into t.		7:25
my people in the day of their t.;		7:29
that has not fallen into t.,		15:13
save it is the t. of my people.		27:13
upon them because of their t.	Al	3: 6
that if they should fall into t.,		9:23
this people should fall into t.,		10:19
because of t., man had fallen.		22:12
have fallen away into sin and t.,		24:30
of man is because of sin and t.,		28:13
because of the t. of a parent.		30:25
to believe, and falleth into t.?		32:19
except we should fall into t.		44: 4
of God, or fall into t.,		46:21
if we shall fall into t.;		46:22
if we shall fall into t.		46:22
even until they have fallen into t.	He	3:16
had they fallen into this great t.;		4:26
become weak, because of their t.,		4:26
among them after their t.	3Ne	5:12
except they should fall into t.		6: 5
because of t., if thou art not	DC	3: 9
hand, that he will fall into t.;		5:32
by the t. of these holy laws		20:20
my presence, because of his t.,		29:41
In consequence of t.,		52:37
that cannot be broken by t.,		82:11
removal from office for t.,		102: 8
of the church in case of t.		102:32
as ye are cut off for t.,		104: 9
being broken through t.,		104:52
But in case of t., the		104:76
and smitten because of their t.,		109:65
neither charge thee with t.,		121:10
who do charge thee with t.,		121:11
But those who cry t.		121:17
iniquity and t. of my holy laws		124:50
shall commit any sin or t.		132:26
of my t. my eyes are opened,	Mses	5:10
Were it not for our t. we never		5:11
have forgiven thee thy t. in the		6:53
by reason of t. cometh the fall,		6:59
own sins, and not for Adam's t.	AoF	2

TRANSGRESSIONS
for your t. is your mother put	2Ne	7: 1
and my t. are mine;		9:46
their t. will I bring down with	En	1:10
But he was wounded for our t.,	Mos	14: 5
for the t. of my people was he		14: 8
himself their iniquity and their t.,		15: 9
to redeem them from their t.		15:12
that he might blot out their t.	Al	7:13
beginning of their t. in the land.		9:14
they could fall into sins and t.,		9:19
he shall take upon him the t.		11:40
upon him the t. of his people,		34: 8

and thirst, because of their t.	Al	37:42
bring it upon us by our own t.		46:18
thou are not excusable in thy t.;	DC	24: 2
in consequence of their t.;		101: 2
not for the t. of my people,		105: 2
of the t. of my people,		105: 9
forgive the t. of thy people,		109:34
because of their t.,		109:38
require at his hands for his t.,		132:60
believe, and repent of all thy t.,	Mses	6:52

TRANSGRESSOR
called a t. from the womb.	1Ne	20: 8
inquired of me concerning the t.,	Mos	26:19
have been the ways of a t.	Al	26:24
the order shall be found a t.,	DC	104: 5
found a t. and repenteth not		104:10
Until he be found a t.,		104:74
shall be a rebuke unto the t.;		112: 9
and she then becomes the t.;		132:65

TRANSGRESSORS
he was numbered with the t.;	Mos	14:12
and made intercession for the t.		14:12
ye become t.;	DC	82: 4
and if they are not found t.		83: 2
they were found t., therefore		101:41
inasmuch as you are found t.,		104: 8
to sit in judgment upon t.		107:72

TRANSLATE
I said unto thee: Canst thou t.?	Mos	8:11
thou of any one that can t.?		8:12
a man that can t. the records;		8:13
and t. all records that are of		8:13
not in order that ye may t.;	Eth	5: 1
might have power to t.	DC	1:29
thee sight and power to t.,		3:12
have a gift to t. the plates;		5: 4
then thou mayest t. again.		5:30
gift, if you desire of me, to t.,		6:25
may t. and receive knowledge		8:11
did not t. according to that		9: 1
power that you may assist to t.		9: 2
should t. at this present time.		9: 3
when you began to t.,		9: 5
not expedient that you should t.		9:10
had power given unto you to t.		10: 1
provided to enable you to t.		10: 4
which you have pretended to t.		10:13
in asking to t. it over again.		10:15
if God has given him power to t.;		10:16
shall not t. again those words		10:30
that you have pretended to t.,		10:31
t. the engravings which are on		10:41
should t. this first part of the		10:45
to t. the Book of Mormon;		20: 8
that ye should t. any more		37: 1
built, in which to live and t.		41: 7
that ye may now t. it,		45:61
it is expedient to t. again;		73: 3
hasten to t. my scriptures,		93:53
to him he would t. them.	JS	2:65
to t. the Book of Mormon,		2:67

TRANSLATED
should be t. into our language;	Mos	8:12
t. and caused to be written		28:11
he t. them by the means of		28:13
the Lord will that I be t.,	Eth	15:34
thou hast t. a few more pages	DC	5:30
known this you could have t.;		9:10
be written, or which you have t.,		10:10
contrary from that which you t.		10:11
come to that which you have t.,		10:41
And he has t. the book,		17: 6
until the New Testament be t.,		45:60
and it is mostly t. correctly		91: 1
the Apocrypha should be t.		91: 3
needful that it should be t.		91: 6
years old when he was t.		107:49
t. by the gift and power of God,		135: 3
I t. some of them, which	JS	2:62

TRANSLATED 988 TREADING

characters which had been t., JS 2:64
seen t. from the Egyptian. 2:64
those which were not yet t., 2:64
such of them as had been t. 2:64
as far as it is t. correctly; AoF 8

TRANSLATES
power again, or if he t. again, DC 10:17

TRANSLATING
had finished t. these records, Mos 28:17
or that which is not t., DC 11:22
the purpose of t. the book. JS 2:35

TRANSLATION
Holy Ghost, and the gift of t.; Al 9:21
the remainder of the work of t. DC 10: 3
accomplished the work of t. 10:34
yea, the t. of my work; 11:19
to continue the work of t. 73: 4
were doing the work of t., 76:15
the t. of the prophets, 90:13
of the t. of my scriptures, 94:10
and publish the new t. of my 124:89
taking a different view of the t., 128: 8
have rendered a plainer t. 128:18
The above t. is given as Fac 2:12
translated, with t. thereof, JS 2:64
stated that the t. was correct, 2:64
the t. of such of them as 2:64
both the characters and the t." 2:65
still continued the work of t., 2:68
we found mentioned in the t. 2:68
to continue the work of t. 2:75

TRANSLATOR
thou shalt be called a seer, a t., DC 21: 1
to be a seer, a revelator, a t., 107:92
to be a t., a revelator, a seer, 124:125

TRANSMIT
be the duty of said council to t., DC 102:26

TRANSPARENT
and clear, even as t. glass; Eth 3: 1

TRANSPIRE
all things that t. in Zion, DC 85: 1

TRANSPIRED
things which t. before I made 1Ne 19: 2
And there had many things t. 3Ne 5: 8
t. among the children of men Eth 1: 3
which t. from the days of Adam— 1: 4
of the facts, as they have t., JS 2: 1
righteousness, as they have t., 2: 2

TRAPS
for ye are laying t. and snares Al 10:17

TRAVAIL
He shall see the t. of his soul, Mos 14:11
with long-suffering and much t. 27:33
thou that didst not t. with child; 3Ne 22: 1
like a woman that is taken in t.; DC 136:35

TRAVAILED
The earth hath t. and brought DC 84:101

TRAVAILS
all the t. of soul for their people, Mos 29:33

TRAVEL
he did t. in the wilderness 1Ne 2: 5
we did again t. on our journey 7:21
we did t. for the space of many 16:15
and we did t. nearly eastward 17: 1
And we did t. and wade through 17: 1
not the course they should t. Mos 7: 4
we will t. around the land of 22: 8
hunger and thirst, and their t., Al 18:37
they should t. in the wilderness. 37:39

or did not t. a direct course, Al 37:42
t. to an exceeding great distance, He 3: 4
many there be that t. therein, 3Ne 27:33
directions whither they should t. Eth 2: 5
they did t. in the wilderness, 2: 6
John Whitmer t. many times DC 69: 7
the high priests should t., 84:111
also should t. round about 84:112
designed for those who do not t. 107:90
under the responsibility to t. 107:98
t. as their circumstances shall 107:98
they may t. also if they choose, 124:135
nevertheless they may t., 124:137
one is to t. continually, 124:140

TRAVELED
and he t. in the wilderness 1Ne 2: 5
when he had t. three days 2: 6
after I had t. for the space of 8: 8
we t. for the space of four days, 16:13
after we had t. for the space of 16:17
after we had t. for the space 16:33
t. in a land among many waters, Mos 8: 8
and when they had t. all day 24:20
they t. throughout all the land 27:35
and t. three days' journey Al 8: 6
we have t. from house to house, 26:28
t. much in the wilderness 58:23
and t. many days, and came over Eth 9: 3

TRAVELER
from whence no t. can return; 2Ne 1:14
weary t. may find health and DC 124:23
a resting-place for the weary t., 124:60

TRAVELING
t. nearly the same course as 1Ne 16:33
they were t. in the wilderness Mos 23:35
t. round about through all the 27:32
the presiding elders, t. bishops, DC 20:66
of a man t. on the earth. 49:22
t. to preach the gospel in my 84:77
they have warned in their t. 88:71
The t. or located high priests 102:29
or t. high priests abroad, 102:30
the t. high council composed of 102:30
twelve t. councilors are 107:23
a T. Presiding High Council, 107:33
Twelve or the t. high council, 107:34
or to the t. high council. 107:36
duty of the t. high council 107:38
seventy are to be t. ministers, 107:97
over the Twelve t. council; 124:127
for t. elders to bear record of 124:139
wherever the t. high council, 124:139
t. in the greatness of his strength; 133:46

TRAVELS
The course of their t. 1Ne 1:hd
Do they remember the t., 2Ne 29: 4
notwithstanding my many t. Al 30:32
all the t. and tribulations DC 128:21

TREACHEROUSLY
that thou wouldst deal very t., 1Ne 20: 8

TREAD
to t. them down like the mire 2Ne 20: 6
mountains t. him under foot; 24:25
and t. them down, saith the 3Ne 16:14
and shall t. them down, and 16:15
And ye shall t. down the wicked; 25: 3
t. the people of the Nephites Mrm 5: 6
did t. upon them in mine anger, DC 133:51

TREADETH
t. down and teareth in pieces, 3Ne 20:16
t. down and teareth in peices, 21:12
him that t. in the wine-vat. DC 133:48

TREADING
and the t. of lesser cattle. 2Ne 17:25

TREASON
that murder, t., robbery, theft,	DC 134: 8

TREASURE
wherefore, their t. is their God.	2Ne 9:30
their t. shall perish with them	9:30
for yourselves a t. in heaven,	He 5: 8
man hide up a t. in the earth,	12:18
cursed is he, and also the t.,	13:19
For where your t. is, there will	3Ne 13:21
ye shall t. up the things which	Eth 3:21
that he may t. up for his soul	DC 6: 3
t. up these words in thy heart.	6:20
that he may t. up for his soul	11: 3
t. up in your heart until the	11:26
that he may t. up for his soul	12: 3
that he may t. up for his soul	14: 3
t. up wisdom in your bosoms,	38:30
T. these things up in your	43:34
t. up in your minds continually	84:85
much t. in this city for you,	111: 2

TREASURER
a t. appointed to keep the	DC 104:67
man among you say to the t.:	104:72
the t. shall give unto him the	104:73
shall be his token unto the t.	104:75
that the t. shall not withhold.	104:75
the t. shall be subject unto	104:76
in case the t. is found an	104:77

TREASURES
their hearts are upon their t.;	2Ne 9:30
is there any end of their t.;	12: 7
and have robbed their t.,	20:13
up for yourselves t. in heaven,	He 8:25
shall hide up t. in the earth	13:18
shall hide up their t. unto me;	13:19
hide not up their t. unto me;	13:19
none hideth up their t. unto me	13:19
hideth not up his t. unto me,	13:19
that they shall hide up their t.,	13:20
I will hide up their t. when	13:20
cursed be they and also their t.;	13:20
we have hid up our t. and they	13:35
for yourselves t. upon earth,	3Ne 13:19
for yourselves t. in heaven,	13:20
hide up their t. in the earth;	Mrm 1:18
desire to lay up t. for yourself	DC 6:27
you should obtain t. of earth	19:38
He that sendeth up t. unto	63:48
and great t. of knowledge,	89:19
of knowledge, even hidden t.;	89:19
there are more t. than one for	111:10
they shall bring forth their rich t.	133:30

TREASURETH
And whoso t. up my word,	JS 1:37

TREASURY
I went forth unto the t. of	1Ne 4:20
I went forth towards the t. of	4:20
who had the keys of the t.	4:20
should go with me into the t.	4:20
for yourselves a place for a t.,	DC 104:60
one among you to keep the t.,	104:61
shall be a seal upon the t.,	104:62
shall be delivered into the t.;	104:62
things shall be had in the t.,	104:64
taken out of the t. by any one,	104:64
of the sacred things in the t.,	104:65
called the sacred t. of the Lord;	104:66
shall be another t. prepared,	104:67
appointed to keep the t.;	104:67
shall be cast into the t.	104:68
let him cast them into the t.;	104:69
be used, or taken out of the t.,	104:71

TREAT
did t. me with much harshness;	1Ne 18:11

TREATED
t. as though they were angels	Al 27: 4

because you have t. lightly	DC 84:54
he t. my communication not	JS 2:21
and to have t. me kindly,	2:28

TREATY
into a t. with king Zeniff,	Mos 7:21
ruler should make a t. with them;	9: 2
made a t. with the Lamanites	Mrm 2:28

TREE
a t., whose fruit was desirable	1Ne 8:10
the t. of which I was partaking	8:13
led to the t. by which I stood.	8:19
even to the t. by which I stood;	8:20
led unto the t. by which I stood.	8:21
in the path which led to the t.	8:22
partake of the fruit of the t.	8:24
had partaken of the fruit of the t.	8:25
and partook of the fruit of the t.	8:30
compared like unto an olive-t.,	10:12
the natural branches of the olive-t.,	10:14
the t. of which he hath spoken?	11: 4
the t. which bore the fruit which	11: 7
a t.; and it was like unto the	11: 8
unto the t. which my father had	11: 8
after I had seen the t., I said	11: 9
the t. which is precious above all.	11: 9
Knowest thou the meaning of the t.	11:21
living waters, or to the t. of life;	11:25
the t. of life was a representation	11:25
the natural branches of the olive-t.,	15: 7
was compared unto an olive-t.,	15:12
a natural branch of the olive-t.,	15:16
olive tree, into the true olive-t.	15:16
meaneth the t. which he saw?	15:21
a representation of the t. of life.	15:22
our father saw, that led to the t.?	15:23
separated the wicked from the t.	15:28
and also from that t. of life,	15:36
in opposition of the t. of life;	2Ne 2:15
and shall be eaten, as a teil-t.,	16:13
of Israel, like unto a tame olive-t.,	Jac 5: 3
that his olive t. began to decay;	5: 4
that I should lose this t.;	5: 7
the branches from a wild olive-t.,	5: 7
that the root of this t. will perish,	5: 8
the branches of the wild olive-t.	5: 9
the branches of the wild olive-t.	5:10
that I should lose this t.;	5:11
watch the t., and nourish it,	5:12
the natural branches of the t.;	5:13
that I should lose this t.	5:13
branches of the tame olive-t.	5:14
Behold, look here; behold the t.	5:16
looked and beheld the t.	5:17
the branches of the wild t. have	5:18
the t. thereof would have perished.	5:18
the t. thereof hath brought forth;	5:18
the natural branches of the t.	5:19
the natural branches of the t.,	5:20
to plant this t., or this branch of	5:21
tree, or this branch of the t.?	5:21
planted another branch of the t.	5:23
But, behold the t.	5:23
and only a part of the t. hath	5:25
the other part of the t. hath	5:25
have nourished this t. like unto	5:25
the t. whose natural branches had	5:30
all sorts of fruit did cumber the t.	5:30
time have we nourished this t.,	5:31
that I should lose this t.	5:32
What shall we do unto the t.,	5:33
the branches of the wild olive-t.	5:34
The t. profiteth me nothing,	5:35
that part of the t. which brought	5:40
that I might plant this t.	5:44
like unto the wild olive-t.,	5:46
the t. from whence they came;	5:52
pluck from the t. those branches	5:52
the natural branches of the t.	5:52
I do that the t. may not perish,	5:53
the natural branches of the t.	5:54

TREE 990 TREMBLED

take of the branches of this t.,	Jac	5:54
the branches of their mother t.,		5:54
they took from the natural t.		5:55
and grafted into their mother t.		5:56
again into their mother t.,		5:60
the roots of their mother t.,		5:60
the branches of the natural t.		5:67
graft in again into the natural t.;		5:67
the branches of the natural t.		5:68
the natural branches of the t.;		5:68
them unto a tame olive-t.,		6: 1
of the fruit of the t. of life;	Al	5:34
ax is laid at the root of the t.;		5:52
every t. that bringeth not forth		5:52
of the fruit of the t. of life.		5:62
of the fruit of the t. of life,		12:21
of the fruit of the t. of life		12:23
partaken of the t. of life		12:26
a branch of the t. of Israel,		26:36
as the t. beginneth to grow,		32:37
But if ye neglect the t., and take		32:38
and ye will not nourish the t.,		32:39
of the fruit of the t. of life.		32:40
nourish the t. as it beginneth to		32:41
it shall be a t. springing up		32:41
waiting for the t. to bring forth		32:43
And behold, it will become a t.,		33:23
to keep the t. of life—		42: 2
and take also of the t. of life,		42: 3
and partaken of the t. of life,		42: 5
were cut off from the t. of life		42: 6
whatsoever t. should spring up	He	3: 9
was taken and hanged upon a t.,	3Ne	4:28
they did fell the t. to the earth,		4:28
every good t. bringeth forth		14:17
a corrupt t. bringeth forth evil		14:17
A good t. cannot bring forth		14:18
neither a corrupt t. bring forth		14:18
Every t. that bringeth not forth		14:19
thereof was the length of a t.;	Eth	2:17
learn the parable of the fig-t.,	DC	35:16
like as a t. that is smitten by		85: 8
that falleth from off a fig-t.		88:87
every t. that bringeth not forth		97: 7
bring forth as a very fruitful t.		97: 9
life shall be as the age of a t.;		101:30
and bring the box-t., and		124:26
and the fir-t., and		124:26
and the pine-t., together with		124:26
scathe a green t. for the glory of		135: 6
the fruit t. yielding fruit, after	Mses	2:11
the t. yielding fruit, whose seed		2:11
the t. yielding fruit, whose seed		2:12
and every t. in the which shall be		2:29
be the fruit of a t. yielding seed;		2:29
to grow every t., naturally,		3: 9
planted the t. of life also in the		3: 9
t. of knowledge of good and evil.		3: 9
Of every t. of the garden thou		3:16
t. of the knowledge of good and evil,		3:17
not eat of every t. of the garden?		4: 7
But of the fruit of the t. which		4: 9
saw that the t. was good for food,		4:12
t. to be desired to make her wise,		4:12
Hast thou eaten of the t. whereof		4:17
of the fruit of the t. and I did eat.		4:18
hast eaten of the fruit of the t.		4:23
and partake also of the t. of life,		4:28
to keep the way of the t. of life.		4:31
the fruit t. yielding fruit, after his	Abr	4:11
the earth to bring forth the t.		4:12
every t. which shall have fruit		4:29
the fruit of the t. yielding seed		4:29
to grow every t. that is pleasant		5: 9
the t. of life, also, in the midst		5: 9
the t. of knowledge of good and		5: 9
Of every t. of the garden thou mayest		5:12
But of the t. of knowledge of		5:13
learn a parable of the fig-t.—	JS	1:38

TREES

as the t. of the wood are moved	2Ne	17: 2
And the rest of the t. of his forest		20:19
Yea, the fir-t. rejoice at thee,		24: 8

and the very t. obey us,	Jac	4: 6
all the t. of my vineyard		5:42
the t. thereof have become		5:46
all the t. of my vineyard,		5:47
the t. of thy vineyard have		5:48
hew down the t. of the vineyard		5:49
lose the t. of my vineyard.		5:51
grafted in unto the natural t.,		5:55
also took of the natural t.		5:56
not the wild branches from the t.,		5:57
again the t. of the vineyard,		5:58
pluck from the t. those branches		5:58
perhaps, the t. of my vineyard		5:60
and dig about the t.,		5:63
and I lose the t. of my vineyard.		5:65
los the t. of my vineyard;		5:66
the t. had become again the		5:74
the water a thicket of small t.,	Mos	18: 5
Ye look and behold the fig-t.,	DC	45:37
that which climbeth upon the t.		59:16
earth, neither the sea, nor the t.,		77: 9
ax is laid at the root of the t.;		97: 7
land, and plant twelve olive-t.;		101:44
that mine olive-t. may not be		101:45
and planted the olive-t.,		101:46
and broke down the olive t.		101:51
all the precious t. of the earth;		124:26
the t. of the field praise the Lord;		128:23
burn up the dry t. to purify the		135: 6
We may eat of the fruit of the t.	Mses	4: 8
amongst the t. of the garden.		4:14

TREMBLE

did quake and t. exceedingly.	1Ne	1: 6
he began to t., and was about		4:30
he did fear and t. exceedingly,		16:27
are they who need fear, and t.,		22:23
And I exceedingly fear and t.	2Ne	1:25
and the hills did t.,		15:25
man that made the earth to t.,		24:16
Wo unto all those who t.,		28:28
whole frame doth t. exceedingly	Mos	2:30
and you ought to t. before God.		12:30
and fear, and t. before God,		15:26
before God, for ye ought to t.;		15:26
Therefore ought ye not to t.?		15:27
And now, ought ye not to t. and		16:13
and cause it to t. as though it		27:18
and they shall quake, and t.,		27:31
did cause them to quake and t.		28: 3
that they need not fear nor t.,	Al	1: 4
also Zeezrom began to t.		11:46
and seeing that he began to t.		12: 1
Zeezrom began to t. more		12: 7
earth did t. beneath our feet;		36: 7
and the walls did t. again,	He	5:33
And then shall he t., and shall		9:33
the mountains t. and quake.		12: 9
and the earth shall shake and t.;		14:21
and the earth did cease to t.,	3Ne	10: 9
they t. and anger against me;	Mro	9: 4
fear and t., O ye people, for	DC	1: 7
to t. and shake to the center.		10:56
to t. because of pain, and to		19:18
coming, for all nations shall t.		34: 8
Satan shall t. and Zion shall		35:24
shake and the earth shall t.,		43:18
and the earth shall t.,		45:48
they shall stand afar off and t.		45:74
and the earth to t. and to reel		49:23
let the rebellious fear and t.,		63: 6
the nations of the earth shall t.		64:43
the starry heavens shall t.		84:118
and the earth shall t. and reel		88:87
the very devil to t. and palsy.		123:10
hills shall t. at their presence.		133:31
nations shall t. at thy presence—		133:42
And now Satan began to t.,	Mses	1:21

TREMBLED

walls of the prison t. again,	He	5:31
shook again, and the walls t.		5:32
words of God, the people t.,	Mses	6:47
earth t., and the mountains fled,		7:13

TREMBLETH

t. lest he shall fall.   2Ne 28:28
he that t. under my power   DC 52:17

TREMBLING

hear the words of a t. parent,   2Ne 1:14
drunken the dregs of the cup of t.   8:17
out of thine hand the cup of t.,   8:22
with fear and t. before him.   Mrm 9:27

TREMENDOUS

And thus there was a t. battle;   Al 28:2
also there was a t. slaughter   28:3
after the great and t. battle   Mrm 8:2

TRESPASS

should not t. against another,   3Ne 7:14
repenteth of the t. wherewith   DC 98:40
And if he t. against thee and   98:41
And if he t. against thee the   98:42
And if he t. against thee the   98:43
But if he t. against thee the   98:44

TRESPASSED

if any have t., let him not   DC 46:4
he has t. against thee,   98:40
he has t. against thee.   98:44
wherewith they have t.,   98:47
wherewith their fathers have t.,   98:47
wherein she has t. against me;   132:56

TRESPASSES

forgive them their t. against me.   Mos 26:30
also forgive one another your t.;   26:31
forgiveth not his neighbor's t.   26:31
if ye forgive men their t.   3Ne 13:14
if ye forgive not men their t.   13:15
will your Father forgive your t.   13:15
forgiveth not his brother his t.   DC 64:9
forgiven one another your t.,   82:1
restore four-fold for all their t.   98:47
their t. shall never be brought   98:48
forgive my servant Joseph his t.;   132:56
shall she be forgiven her t.,   132:56

TRIAL

have had much t. because of him;   2Ne 5:3
cause of much t. with the church.   Al 1:23
a great t. to those that did   1:25
of Pachus received their t.,   62:9
until after the t. of your faith.   Eth 12:6
thus far for a t. of their faith.   DC 105:19

TRIALS

the t. and troubles of a righteous   Mos 29:33
the law at their times of t.,   Al 10:14
the t. of the crimes of the people   10:14
shall be supported in their t.,   36:3
I have been supported under t.   36:27
shall be delivered out of your t.,   38:5
there was no time for their t.   51:19

TRIBE

every t. did appoint a chief or   3Ne 7:3
every one according to his t.;   7:11
one t. should not trespass   7:14
twelve thousand out of every t.?   DC 77:11
And they also of the t. of Judah,   133:35

TRIBES

shall judge the twelve t. of Israel;   1Ne 12:9
to raise up the t. of Jacob,   21:6
the more part of all the t. have   22:4
other t. of the house of Israel,   2Ne 29:12
the words of the lost t. of Israel;   29:13
the lost t. of Israel shall have the   29:13
one from another into t.,   3Ne 7:2
and thus they became t. and   7:3
became tribes and leaders of t.   7:3
their t. became exceeding great.   7:4
number as the t. of the people,   7:11
with the t. of the people;   7:12
that they were divided into t.,   7:14

other t. of the house of Israel,   3Ne 15:15
the other t. hath the Father   15:20
other t. whom they know not of,   16:4
myself unto the lost t. of Israel,   17:4
even the t. which have been lost,   21:26
all the scattered t. of Israel,   28:29
unto you, twelve t. of Israel,   Mrm 3:18
over the twelve t. of Israel;   DC 77:9
gather together the t. of Israel   77:9
out of all the t. of Israel –   77:11
to gather the t. of Israel;   77:14
ten t. from the land of the north.   110:11
upon the t. of Israel,   133:34
all the t. of the earth mourn;   JS 1:36
the restoration of the Ten T.;   AoF 10

TRIBULATION

days of my t. in the wilderness   2Ne 2:1
born in t., in a wilderness,   Jac 7:26
Nevertheless, after much t.,   Mos 23:10
after wandering through much t.,   27:28
the word of God in much t.,   27:32
much t. and anguish of soul,   Al 8:14
t. and desolation are sent forth   DC 29:8
be patient in t. until I come;   54:10
and he that is faithful in t.,   58:2
shall follow after much t.   58:3
after much t. come the blessings.   58:4
the t. which shall descend upon   78:14
For after much t., as I   103:12
done this work through great t.;   109:5
their temptations, and much t.,   112:13
art called to pass through t.;   122:5
I feel, like Paul, to glory in t.;   127:2
shall be great t. on the Jews,   JS 1:18
after the t. of those days   1:21
after the t. of those days,   1:33
after the t. of those days,   1:36

TRIBULATIONS

by the great t. of his mind   Al 15:3
did administer unto him in his t.,   15:18
t. which the Nephites bore for   53:13
in the Lord as in the t. of   56:2
afflictions and our t. for them,   56:7
and their patience in their t. –   60:26
I have promised after your t.,   DC 103:13
and the t. of your brethren –   103:13
through all the travels and t.   128:21
and great t. shall be among the   Mses 7:61
great t. among the wicked;   7:66

TRIBUNAL

brought before the t. of God   Al 5:18

TRIBUTE

than to pay t. to the king of the   Mos 7:15
do pay t. to the king of the   7:22
they should pay t. to the king of   19:15
paying a t. to the Lamanites   19:22
people should pay t. unto him,   19:26
support his guards out of the t.   19:28
and pay the last t. of wine to   22:7
and he sent the t. of wine to the   22:10

TRIED

ye have t. the experiment,   Al 32:33
t. according to the voice of   He 1:8
should be t., not according to   6:24
to be t. according to the law.   3Ne 6:27
he or she shall be t. before   DC 42:80
shall be t. or condemned   68:22
needs be chastened and t.,   101:4
is t., to sit as a judge   107:76
My people must be t. in all things,   136:31

TRIETH

yea, he t. their patience and   Mos 23:21

TRIFLE

to t. with the words which I shall   Mos 2:9
T. not with sacred things.   DC 6:12
T. not with these things;   8:10
unto these words and t. not,   32:5

TRIM

TRIM
and we will t. up the branches — Jac 5:58

TRIMMED
your lamps t. and burning, — DC 33:17

TRIUMPH
the t. and the glory of the — DC 76:39
thou shalt t. over all thy foes. — 121: 8
shall t. over all my enemies, — 127: 2
and your enemies t. over you. — 136:42

TRIUMPHANT
forth t. through the air, — Mro 10:34

TRODDEN
and it shall be t. down; — 2Ne 15: 5
as a carcass t. under feet. — 24:19
by the beasts and t. under foot. — Mos 12:11
were t. down by the hosts of men. — Al 3: 2
grain, which were t. under foot — 4: 2
he was run upon and t. down, — 30:59
and is t. under foot of men. — 34:29
be t. down and destroyed, — 46:18
at thy feet to be t. under foot. — 46:22
be overpowered, and t. down, — He 4:20
they shall be t. down and shall — 15: 2
that they be t. down and slain — 15: 9
and to be t. under foot of men. — 3Ne 12:13
been t. under feet by them; — 16: 8
be t. under foot of my people, — 16:15
have t. the wine-press alone, — DC 76:107
and t. the wine-press alone, — 88:106
and t. under the feet of men. — 101:40
out and t. under foot of men. — 103:10
be t. down by whom I will; — 104: 5
I have t. the wine press alone, — 133:50

TROUBLE
and behold t., and darkness, — 2Ne 18:22
is the thing which doth t. me. — Al 22: 5
let these things t. you no more, — 42:29
and only let your sins t. you, — 42:29
that t. which shall bring you — 42:29
with you in every time of t. — DC 3: 8
nor t. me any more concerning — 5:29
t. me no more concerning this — 59:22
them in the day of their t. — 101: 7
but, in the day of their t., — 101: 8
will deliver them in time of t., — 105: 8
may not faint in the day of t. — 109:38
t. not yourselves concerning — 112:27
influence shall cast thee into t., — 122: 4
t. me no more on this matter. — 130:15

TROUBLED
Alma was t. in his spirit, — Mos 26:10
the spirit of Alma was again t.; — 26:13
being t. no more for a time — Al 3:24
I have been somewhat t. in mind — 22: 3
t. because of the wickedness — 3Ne 17:14
the people became t. by day — Eth 14:23
unto my disciples, they were t. — DC 45:34
I said unto them: Be not t., — 45:35
with which thou hast been t. — 66:10
Let not your hearts be t. — 98:18
also saw the sea, that it was t., — Mses 7:66
see that ye be not t., for all — JS 1:23

TROUBLES
trials and t. of a righteous king, — Mos 29:33
and their t., and their afflictions, — Al 36: 3
trials and t. of every kind, — 36:27
out of your trials, and your t., — 38: 5
they shall rest from all their t. — 40:12

TROUBLETH
yet because this widow t. me — DC 101:84

TRUE
the record which I make is t.; — 1Ne 1: 3
ye know that this is t.; — 4: 3
the knowledge of the t. Messiah, — 10:14

TRUE

twelve appostles of the Lamb are t. — 1Ne 13:39
which he shall write are just and t.; — 14:23
things which I have written are t. — 14:30
and nourishment from the t. vine? — 15:15
not come unto the t. fold of God? — 15:15
into the t. olive-tree. — 15:16
against the t. and living God. — 17:30
upon the plates of brass are t.; — 22:30
the t. Messiah, their Redeemer — 2Ne 1:10
thou art a t. friend unto my son, — 1:30
shall be restored to the t. church — 9: 2
will give them the t. knowledge of — 10: 2
unto them that my words are t. — 11: 3
them of the t. Messiah, — 25:18
that as these things are t., — 25:20
the words of my Beloved are t. — 31:15
only and t. doctrine of the Father, — 31:21
which thou knowest to be t.? — Jac 7:14
in restoring them to the t. faith. — En 1:14
unto the t. faith in God. — 1:20
that these sayings are t., — Mos 1: 6
also that these records are t. — 1: 6
until now, and they are t.; — 1: 6
therefore, they are just and t. — 2:35
remember that these things are t.; — 2:41
of that which is just and t. — 4:12
things that they had said are t. — 8: 2
this people, for they are t.; — 17: 9
kept the records which are t. — Al 3:12
I say unto you that this is all t. — 5:12
trust in the t. and living God. — 5:13
whereof I have spoken are t. — 5:45
know of myself that they are t.; — 5:46
been spoken by our fathers are t., — 5:47
that which is to come, is t.; — 5:48
do worship the t. and living God, — 7: 6
whereof he hath testified are t.; — 10:10
deny the t. and living God, — 11:25
there is a t. and living God? — 11:26
Yea, there is a t. and living God. — 11:27
these things, and they are t., — 12:37
be grafted into the t. vine, — 16:17
of that which is just and t.; — 18:34
and holy prophets of the t. God. — 20:15
to that which is just and t. — 29: 8
those ancient prophecies are t. — 30:24
ye do not know that they are t. — 30:24
that these things are t.; — 30:41
unto you that they are t.; — 30:41
thou that these things are t.? — 30:41
verily believed that they were t.; — 30:53
which are not seen, which are t. — 32:21
according to that which is t.— — 32:24
behold, if it be a t. seed, or a — 32:28
to prove that these things are t. — 34: 7
myself that these things are t. — 34: 8
the t. and the living God, — 43:10
that this is the t. faith of God; — 44: 4
were all the t. believers of Christ, — 46:14
who were t. believers in Christ — 46:15
men who were t. at all times — 53:20
t. to the cause of our freedom, — 60:16
unto me a t. spirit of freedom, — 60:25
not t. to the cause of freedom. — 62:11
yea, a t. friend to liberty; — 62:37
I know that these things are t. — He 7:29
as a witness that they are t. — 8:24
concerning the chief judge be t., — 9: 2
words which he has spoken are t. — 9: 2
the t. murderer of this judge. — 9:17
words which he had said were t.; — 9:37
the t. murderer of our chief judge. — 9:41
the t. points of doctrine, — 11:23
yea, our great and t. God, — 13:18
be brought to the t. knowledge, — 15:13
and their great and t. shepherd, — 15:13
our own eyes that they are t. — 16:20
a shorter but t. account was — 3Ne 5: 9
to be a just and a t. record; — 5:18
converted unto the t. faith; — 6:14
we know our record to be t., — 8: 1
they know that their record is t. — 17:25
hereafter that this record is t. — 18:37

of the t. points of my doctrine,	3Ne	21: 6	many of my brethren t. penitent,	Al 29:10
to deny the t. church of Christ.	4Ne	1:26	afflictions had t. humbled them	32: 6
did persecute the t. church of		1:29	beheld, who were t. penitent,	32: 7
they were t. believers in Christ;		1:36	who t. humble themselves	32:14
the t. believers in Christ,		1:37	he that t. humbleth himself,	32:15
the t. worshipers of Christ,		1:37	none but the t. penitent are	42:24
none that do know the t. God	Mrm	8:10	t. he was preparing to defend	52: 6
will serve the t. and living God.		9:28	did t. signify unto the people	3Ne 7:21
him, the t. and only God,	Eth	2: 8	t. manifest unto the people	7:22
know that these things are t.;		4:11	he t. did many miracles in the	8: 1
surety that these things are t.		5: 3	he did t. manifest himself unto	10:18
we know the manner to be t.;	Mro	4: 1	for they t. testified of me.	15:10
the case that these things are t.		7:35	he t. gave unto them bread	20: 7
at the last day, that they are t.,		7:35	things which Jesus did t. teach	26: 6
if they are t. has the day of		7:35	Lord t. did teach the people,	26:13
are t. followers of his Son,		7:48	and did t. repent of their sins,	4Ne 1: 1
if these things are not t.,		10: 4	he t. saith that no one shall	Mrm 8:14
thing is good is just and t.;		10: 6	Christ t. had showed himself	Eth 4: 2
that which I have written is t.		10:29	t. saw with their eyes the things	12:19
only t. and living church upon	DC	1:30	he t. told them of all things,	13: 2
for they are t. and faithful,		1:37	they t. repented of all their sins.	Mro 6: 2
record, and the record is t.,		1:39	Christ t. said unto our fathers:	10:23
surety that these things are t.,		5:12	it was t. manifested unto this	DC 20: 5
of a surety that they are t.,		5:25	t. testified of him in all things,	20:26
thou hast been writing are t.		6:17	have t. repented of all their sins,	20:37
the t. points of my doctrine,		10:62	t. manifest by their works	20:37
and your God liveth it it is t.		17: 6	in this ye say t., for so it is;	45:23
which you have written are t.;		18: 2	become t. humble before me	54: 3
you know that they are t.		18: 2	many of whom are t. humble	97: 1
if you know that they are t.,		18: 3	are t. manifest from heaven—	123:13
that the holy scriptures are t.,		20:11	and did it t. and faithfully,	128: 9
the only living and t. God,		20:19	which are t. made out,	128:14
Jesus Christ is just and t.;		20:30	T. I am Mahan, the master of	Mses 5:31
Jesus Christ is just and t.,		20:31	avenged sevenfold, t. Lamech shall	5:48
know that these things are t.		20:35	he t. convenanted with Enoch	8: 2
to unite with the t. church,		23: 7	countenance t. like lightning.	JS 2:32
for they are t. and faithful;		66:11		
ye do not know that they are t.;		67: 7	TRUMP	
bear record that they are t.		67: 8	when the second t. shall sound	Mos 26:25
These sayings are t. and faithful;		68:34	and speak with the t. of God,	Al 29: 1
him who will be t. and faithful.		69: 1	when the t. shall sound;	Mrm 9:13
they are t. and faithful.		71:11	gospel as with the voice of a t.,	DC 24:12
all those who are just and t.		76:53	as with the voice of a t.	29: 4
believe, and know to be t.		80: 4	a t. shall sound both long and	29:13
and that I am the t. light		88:50	archangel, shall sound his t.,	29:26
contained therein that are t.,		91: 1	as with the voice of a t.	30: 9
therein that are not t.,		91: 2	voices as with the sound of a t.,	33: 2
I am the t. light that lighteth		93: 2	voice as with the sound of a t.,	34: 6
in its t. light before the council;		102:16	gospel as with the voice of a t.,	36: 1
be conferred upon us, it is t.;		121:37	voices as with the sound of a t.,	42: 6
let him be faithful and t. in all		124:13	the t. of God shall sound both	43:18
the record they have made is t.		128: 4	and by the great sound of a t.,	43:25
statement and records to be t.,		128: 4	an angel shall sound his t.,	45:45
to know the only wise and t. God,		132:24	voices as with the sound of a t.,	75: 4
and they are t. even as I will;	Mses	4:32	sounding the t. of God, saying:	88:92
that Presbyterianism is not t."	JS	2:20	another angel shall sound his t.,	88:94
had seen a vision, yet it was t.;		2:25	And he shall sound his t.	88:94
testimony of James to be t.—		2:26	of the t. of the angel of God.	88:98
said they were t. characters.		2:64	sound, which is the second t.;	88:99
that they were t. characters,		2:64	again, another t. shall sound,	88:100
the t. meaning and intention of		2:74	sound, which is the third t.;	88:100
We believe in being honest, t.,	AoF	13	And another t. shall sound,	88:102
			sound, which is the fourth t.,	88:102
TRULY			And another t. shall sound,	88:103
he t. testified of their wickedness	1Ne	1:19	sound, which is the fifth t.,	88:103
for he t. spake unto the waters of		4: 2	shall be the sound of his t.,	88:104
and that I was t. that Laban whom		4:26	they hear the sound of the t.,	88:104
she t. had mourned because of us.		5: 1	another angel shall sound his t.,	88:105
he t. spake many great things		15: 3	another angel shall sound his t.,	88:106
he was t. chastened because of		16:25	first angel again sound his t.	88:108
Wherefore, Joseph t. saw our day.	2Ne	3: 5	the second angel sound his t.,	88:109
For Joseph t. testified, saying:		3: 6	seventh angel shall sound his t.;	88:110
Yea, Joseph t. said:		3: 7	the t. shall sound for the dead,	109:75
For behold, he t. prophesied		4: 2	voice as with the sound of a t.,	124:106
it t. had been made manifest	Jac	1: 5		
and Solomon t. had many wives		2:24	TRUMPET	
we t. can command in the name		4: 6	do not sound a t. before you,	3Ne 13: 2
for I t. had seen angels,		7: 5	sound a t. unto the armies of	Eth 14:28
for they t. testify of Christ.		7:11	the angel shall sound his t.	DC 49:23
and they t. testify of him.		7:19	with the great sound of a t.,	JS 1:37
save it be the t. penitent and	Al	27:18		
his brethren was t. great,		27:19	TRUMPETS	
t. mourn for the loss of their		28:12	by the sounding of the t.,	DC 77:12
			and the sounding of the t. of	77:12

TRUST — 994 — TRUTH

TRUST
and I will t. in thee forever.	2Ne	4:34
not put my t. in the arm of flesh;		4:34
putteth his t. in the arm of flesh.		4:34
is he that putteth his t. in man		4:34
and on mine arm shall they t.		8: 5
I will t., and not be afraid;		22: 2
poor of his people shall t. in it.		24:32
is he that putteth his t. in man,		28:31
should put his t. in the Lord,	Mos	4: 6
yet I t. there remaineth an		7:18
rejoice, and put your t. in God,		7:19
of heart, and put your t. in him,		7:33
putting their t. in the Lord;		10:19
did not t. his person without the		21:19
ye t. no man to be a king		23:13
t. no one to be your teacher		23:14
whosoever putteth his t. in him		23:22
them but put their t. in him.		29:20
t. in the true and living God.	Al	5:13
And I t., according to the Spirit		7: 5
I t. that ye are not in a state of		7: 6
I t. that ye are not lifted up		7: 6
I t. that ye have not set your		7: 6
I t. that you do not worship		7: 6
shall put their t. in God		36: 3
and I do put my t. in him,		36:27
t. not those secret plans unto this		37:32
I t. that I shall have great joy		38: 2
as ye shall put your t. in God		38: 5
put their t. in God continually.		57:27
I t. that the souls of them who		57:36
we t. in our God who has given		58:33
we t. God will deliver us,		58:37
that we should put our t. in him,		61:13
those who put their t. in him.	He	12: 1
God in whom they should t.	Mrm	9:20
and putting t. in dead works.	Mro	8:23
I t. in Christ that thou wilt		9:22
I t. that I may see thee soon;		9:24
neither t. in the arm of flesh—	DC	1:19
put your t. in that Spirit which		11:12
Let him t. in me and he shall		84:116
servant William put his t. in me,		124:87

TRUSTED
I know in whom I have t.	2Ne	4:19
O Lord, I have t. in thee,		4:34
Mosiah t. him unto the Lord.	Al	19:23
the man in whom you have t.	DC	10: 6
he may be t. because of the		124:20

TRUSTING
t. in the God and rock of	Jac	7:25
t. in the Lord that they should	Al	17:13
t. in me, reviling not against	DC	19:30

TRUTH
according to the t. which is in the	1Ne	13:24
according to the t. which is in God.		13:25
shall establish the t. of the first,		13:40
according to the t. which is in the		14:26
the wicked, according to the t.;		16: 2
the guilty taketh the t. to be hard,		16: 2
were willing to hearken to the t.,		16: 3
not murmur because of the t.,		16: 3
are, of a t., more particularly		19: 2
yet they swear not in t. nor		20: 1
which ye call anger was the t.,	2Ne	1:26
for he is full of grace and t.		2: 6
according to the t. and holiness		2:10
ye will revile against the t.;		9:40
that the words of t. are hard		9:40
love the t. and are not shaken.		9:40
to the plainness of the t.		9:47
the t. of the coming of Christ;		11: 4
of a t. many houses shall be		15: 9
the Holy One of Israel, in t.		20:20
shall testify to the t. of the book		27:12
angry because of the t. of God!		28:28
to the plainness of the t.;		33: 5
I glory in t.; I glory in		33: 6
Wherefore, I must tell you the t.	Jac	2:11
for the Spirit speaketh the t.		4:13
to the knowledge of the t.;		7:24
the t. which is in Christ.	En	1:26
in the ways of t. and soberness;	Mos	4:15
we know of their surety and t.,		5: 2
Know ye not that I speak the t.?		12:30
Yea, ye know that I speak the t.;		12:30
because I have told you the t.		13: 4
the t. concerning your iniquities.		13: 7
having sealed the t. of his words		17:20
of you to a knowledge of his t.		23:10
to the knowledge of the t.;		27:14
many to the knowledge of the t.,		27:36
convinced of the t. of his words.		29:37
let it be according to the t.	Al	3:27
full of grace, and mercy, and t.		5:48
the t. of the word which had been		6: 8
to declare unto them the t.		9: 6
full of grace, equity, and t.,		9:26
are spoken, according to their t.?		10:25
is full of grace, equity, and t.		13: 9
strong in the knowledge of the t.;		17: 2
many to the knowledge of the t.;		17: 4
to the knowledge of the t.,		17: 9
many to the knowledge of the t.;		21:17
to the knowledge of the t.,		23: 6
to the knowledge of the t.,		23:15
to believe and to know the t.,		24:19
to the knowledge of the t.;		24:27
to the knowledge of the t.?		26:24
save it were to declare the t.,		30:34
convinced of the t. of thy words.		30:43
will still resist the spirit of the t.,		30:46
for this cause I withstood the t.,		30:53
may be in, in spirit and in t.;		34:38
to the knowledge of the t.;		37:19
Behold, he is the word of t. and		38: 9
declare the word with t. and		42:31
preached the word, and the t.,		43: 2
worship God in spirit and in t.,		43:10
were men of t. and soberness,		53:21
to walk in t. and uprightness	He	6:34
behold, ye have rejected the t.,		8:25
to the knowledge of the t.;		15: 6
to the knowledge of the t.,		15: 7
again to the knowledge of the t.—		15:11
the t. come unto the Gentiles,	3Ne	16: 7
know that thou speakest the t.,	Eth	3:12
for thou art a God of t.,		3:12
the life, and the t. of the world.		4:12
iniquity but rejoiceth in the t.,	Mro	7:45
For, if I have learned the t.,		8: 5
manifest the t. of it unto you,		10: 4
may know the t. of all things.		10: 5
t. abideth forever and ever.	DC	1:39
many to the knowledge of the t.,		6:11
enlightened by the Spirit of t.;		6:15
concerning the t. of these things.		6:22
and speak the t. in soberness.		18:21
contains the t. and the word of		19:26
preach, exhort, declare the t.,		19:37
shall be opened to preach the t.		23: 2
your loins girt about with t.,		27:16
will believe and know the t.		31: 2
wise and have received the t.,		45:57
desire to know the t. in part,		49: 2
is not in t. and righteousness		50: 9
was sent forth to teach the t.		50:14
forth to preach the word of t.		50:17
Comforter, in the Spirit of t.,		50:17
he preach it by the Spirit of t.		50:17
that receiveth the word of t.,		50:19
receive it by the Spirit of t.		50:19
the word by the Spirit of t.		50:21
is preached by the spirit of t.?		50:21
that you may know the t.,		50:25
and in the knowledge of the t.		50:40
And ye obey not the t.,		56:15
and bear testimony of the t.		58:47
who is full of grace and t.		66:12
a testimony of the t. of		67: 4

TRUTH

proclaiming the t. according	DC 75: 4
in righteousness and in t.	76: 5
overcome, and to deny the t.	76:31
their hearts away from the t.,	78:10
which shall teach him the t.	79: 2
For the word of the Lord is t.,	84:45
and whatsoever is t. is light,	84:45
and t. is established in her	84:101
grace and t., and peace,	84:102
bowels shall be a fountain of t.,	85: 7
all things, the light of t.;	88: 6
Which t. shineth. This is the	88: 7
wisdom; t. embraceth truth;	88:40
truth embraceth t.; virtue loveth	88:40
voice is Spirit; my Spirit is t.;	88:66
t. abideth and hath no end;	88:66
for the Spirit manifesteth t.;	91: 4
the Spirit of t., who came into	93: 9
the Father, full of grace and t.,	93:11
and truth, even the Spirit of t.,	93:11
is Spirit, even the Spirit of t.;	93:23
And t. is knowledge of things as	93:24
The Spirit of t. is of God.	93:26
I am the Spirit of t.,	93:26
He received a fulness of t.,	93:26
of truth, yea, even of all t.;	93:26
receiveth t. and light, until	93:28
until he is glorified in t.	93:28
Intelligence, or the light of t.,	93:29
All t. is independent in that	93:30
or, in other words, light and t.	93:36
Light and t. forsake that evil	93:37
and taketh away light and t.,	93:39
your children in light and t.	93:40
your children light and t.,	93:42
learn wisdom and to find t.	97: 1
by the Spirit of t.;	107:71
according to t. and righteousness.	107:84
great and glorious tidings, in t.,	109:23
may give way before the t.,	109:56
come to a knowledge of the t.,	109:67
majesty, might, dominion, t.,	109:77
scepter of righteousness and t.;	121:46
only kept from the t. because	123:12
they may come to the light of t.,	124: 9
shall manifest unto him the t.	124:97
that he may testify of a t.,	127: 6
he might make a record of a t.	128: 2
and a voice of t. out of the earth;	128:19
is a witness to the t. of	135: 7
for he is full of grace and t.;	Mses 1: 6
who is full of grace and t.	1:32
which is full of grace and t.	5: 7
who is full of grace and t.,	6:52
the t. of all things; that which	6:61
according to wisdom, mercy, t.,	6:61
which is full of grace and t.,	7:11
t. is the habitation of thy throne;	7:31
and t. will I send forth out of	7:62
righteousness and t. will I cause	7:62
put all inquirers after t.	JS 2: 1
in t. and righteousness, as	2: 2
persecute me for telling the t.?	2:25

TRUTHS

and t. which I have given	DC 52:17
and have received my t.,	66: 1

TRY

will t. the hearts of our brethren,	Al 27:15
t. the virtue of the word of God.	31: 5
that ye might t. the experiment	32:36
that ye may t. the experiment	34: 4
ye do t. to suppose that it is	42: 1
thus they did t. all their liquors.	55:32
t. again if they will serve thee?	He 11:16
have first, to t. their faith,	3Ne 26: 9
I will t. the faith of my people.	26:11
and I will t. you and prove you	DC 98:12
authority to t. men of the right of	134:10
Satan would t. to tempt me	JS 2:46

TUBAL CAIN

And Zillah, she also bare T.,	Mses 5:46
the sister of T. was called Naamah.	5:46

TUBALOTH

whose name was T., who was	He 1:16

TUMBLE

many that did t. to the earth,	1Ne 12: 4
church, shall t. to the dust	22:14
must t. to the earth,	2Ne 28:18
were about to t. to the earth;	He 5:27
it were about to t. to the earth;	5:31
cause prisons to t. to the earth;	Mrm 8:24
the prison to t. to the earth.	Eth 12:13

TUMBLING

I saw mountains t. into pieces;	1Ne 12: 4

TUMULT

the cry and t. were so great	JS 2: 9
of words and t. of opinions,	2:10

TUMULTS

no envyings, nor strifes, nor t.,	4Ne 1:16

TUMULTUOUS

and all manner of t. noises;	1Ne 12: 4
a t. noise of the kingdoms	2Ne 23: 4
it a voice of a great t. noise,	He 5:30
all the t. noises did pass away.	3Ne 10: 9

TURN

they did t. away their anger,	1Ne 16:39
and t. their hearts aside, rejecting	19:13
because they t. their hearts aside,	19:14
they no more t. aside their hearts	19:15
shall t. upon their own heads;	22:13
t. away from your sins;	2Ne 9:45
To t. away the needy from	20: 2
every man t. to his own people,	23:14
and who shall t. it back?	24:27
and t. aside the just for a thing of	27:32
that t. aside the just for a thing	28:16
in vain, and t. him out to perish.	Mos 4:16
But if ye will t. to the Lord with	7:33
and t. to the Lord their God,	11:21
repent and t. unto the Lord	11:23
and t. from our iniquities?	20:21
should t. to be angry and	29: 7
should t. again to his pride	29: 9
and t. to me that I may have	Al 3:14
I should t. again and prophesy	8:25
will not t. my fierce anger away.	8:29
fierce anger he will not t. away,	9:12
neither would they t. aside to the	24:23
and we were about to t. back,	26:27
and thou didst t. them to me.	33: 4
when I did t. to my house thou	33: 6
when I did t. unto my closet,	33: 7
if ye t. away the needy, and	34:28
t. to the Lord with all your mind,	39:13
not t. to the right nor to the left,	56:37
durst not t. to the right nor	56:40
neither would I t. to the right	56:40
that they might t. and look.	He 5:37
them that they did t. and look;	5:37
and did t. unto their own ways,	6:31
and t. their backs upon the poor	6:39
they repent and t. unto him.	7:hd
T. ye, turn ye unto the Lord	7:17
t. ye unto the Lord your God.	7:17
they will repent and t. unto thee.	11: 4
he t. away from us this famine,	11: 8
wilt thou t. away thine anger,	11:11
wilt thou t. away thine anger,	11:12
wilt thou t. away thine anger,	11:16
the Lord did t. away his anger	11:17
and I will t. the hearts of	13: 8
I will t. away mine anger,	13:11
who will repent and t. unto me,	13:11

TURN

not t. away thine anger from us?	He	13:37
would not t. and revile again,	3Ne	6:13
t. to him the other also;		12:39
of thee t. thou not away.		12:42
and t. again and rend you.		14: 6
But if they will not t. unto me,		16:15
and that t. aside the stranger,		24: 5
And he shall t. the heart of the		25: 6
that ye can t. the right hand of		29: 9
T., all ye Gentiles, from your		30: 2
and t. from your evil ways?	Mrm	5:22
unbelieving, t. ye unto the Lord;		9: 6
that he will t. away his anger	Eth	1:36
t. away thine anger from this		3: 3
repent, and t. unto the Lord,		11: 1
shall t. to their fathers.	DC	2: 2
neither doth he t. to the right		3: 2
and it shall t. to their shame		10:23
t. to their own condemnation—		20:15
and they t. their hearts from me		45:29
shall t. unto them for their good.		51:17
Let not your minds t. back;		67:14
seeketh to t. their hearts away		78:10
that it may t. to you for your		82: 9
t. unto your condemnation.		88:65
they shall t. unto the Jews.		90: 9
to t. the hearts of the children		98:16
t. away all wrath and		98:22
and t. to the Lord their God,		98:47
and wilt t. away thy wrath when		109:53
To t. the hearts of the fathers		110:15
or to t. it up stream,		121:33
rejoice and t. away their hearts		124:76
shall t. the heart of the fathers to		128:17
rivers shall t. from their course;	Mses	6:34
If thou wilt t. unto me, and		6:52
T. ye, and get ye upon the mount		7: 2
in their t. were equally zealous	JS	2: 9
children shall t. to their fathers.		2:39

TURNED

shall be t. one against another,	1Ne	22:14
neither t. away back.	2Ne	7: 5
his anger is not t. away,		15:25
his anger is not t. away,		19:12
his anger is not t. away,		19:17
his anger is not t. away,		19:21
his anger is not t. away,		20: 4
thine anger is t. away, and thou		22: 1
shall be t. into a fruitful field;		27:28
t. every one to his own way;	Mos	14: 6
Ammon t. himself unto the king,	Al	18:14
heard this, he t. him about,		32: 6
hast t. thy judgments away		33:11
hast t. away thy judgments		33:13
flaming sword which t. every way,		42: 2
t. them about and began to		43:36
that they t. upon the Lamanites,		43:49
halted and t. upon Helaman.		56:52
Lamanites had t. them about,		56:53
he t. him about, and behold, he	He	5:36
more part of them had t. out of		6:31
the anger of the Lord be t. away		13:39
had t. from their righteousness,	3Ne	7: 8
t. from the Lord their God,		7:14
their mourning was t. into joy,		10:10
multitude were t. upon him,		11: 8
he t. again to the multitude,		14: 1
t. again unto the multitude		18:17
he t. his eyes again upon the		18:26
And he t. from them again,		19:27
he t. himself unto the three,		28: 4
moon shall be t. into blood,	DC	29:14
t. he away from me because of		29:36
the moon be t. into blood;		34: 9
and the moon be t. into blood,		45:42
today mine anger is t. away.		61:20
and many have t. away		63:13
some of whom have t. away		63:14
t. away from your iniquities,		66: 1
indignation shall be t. away;		98:47
be t. out for debts,		117: 5
thy people shall never be t.		122: 3
be t. back into their own place,	DC	133:24
and t. down the leaf upon it:		135: 4
t. every way to keep the way of	Mses	4:31
I t. and went up on the mount,		7: 3
rivers of water were t. out of		7:13
My fathers having t. from their	Abr	1: 5
wholly t. to the god of Elkenah,		1: 6
t. their hearts to the sacrifice		1: 7
they have t. their hearts away		1:17
my father t. again unto his		2: 5
that the famine might be t.		2:17

TURNETH

the people t. not unto him that	2Ne	19:13
and altogether t. therefrom,	DC	84:41

TURNING

your t. of things upside down	2Ne	27:27
t. their backs upon the needy	Al	4:12
in t. your backs upon the poor,		5:55
neither hath he a shadow of t.		7:20
in t. away every one of you	3Ne	20:26
in t. their works upon their own		27:32
t. the hearts of the fathers to	DC	27: 9
by t. out property,		127: 1

TWAIN

with t. he covered his face,	2Ne	16: 2
and with t. he covered his feet,		16: 2
and with t. he did fly.		16: 2
walls of the prison were rent in t.,	Al	14:27
this temple it shall be rent in t.,	He	10: 8
Yea, they shall be rent in t.,		14:22
the rocks were rent in t.,	3Ne	8:18
to go a mile, go with him t.		12:41
for they were rent in t.		28:19
the prisons were rent in t.,	4Ne	1:30
and it shall cleave in t.,	DC	45:48
and they t. shall be one flesh,		49:16

TWELFTH

(and it was on the t. day, in the	Al	14:23
fourth, and so on unto the t.	DC	88:55
fourth, and so on unto the t.		88:57
close of the t. chapter of Ether,		135: 4

TWELVE

he also saw t. others following	1Ne	1:10
I also beheld t. others following		11:29
for thus were the t. called		11:34
against the t. apostles of the Lamb.		11:35
against the t. apostles of the Lamb.		11:36
Holy Ghost fell upon t. others;		12: 7
Behold the t. disciples of the Lamb,		12: 8
rememberest the t. apostles of the		12: 9
shall judge the t. tribes of Israel;		12: 9
the t. ministers of thy seed shall		12: 9
And these t. ministers whom thou		12:10
whom the t. apostles bear record;		13:24
by the hand of the t. apostles		13:26
the prophets and of the t. apostles		13:39
of the t. apostles of the Lamb,		13:40
in the records of the t. apostles		13:41
one of the t. apostles of the		14:20
for the space of t. years	Mos	9:11
been in the wilderness t. days		24:25
t. thousand five hundred thirty	Al	2:19
and authority to baptize, was t.)	3Ne	12: 1
words of these t. whom I have		12: 1
he looked upon the t. whom he		13:25
he said unto those t. whom he		15:11
be separated into t. bodies.		19: 5
the t. did teach the multitude;		19: 6
yea, unto you, t. tribes of Israel,	Mrm	3:18
the t. whom Jesus chose to be		3:18
t. whom Jesus chose in this land;		3:19
the other t. whom Jesus chose		3:19
daughters of Jared were t.,	Eth	6:20
the t. whom he had chosen,	Mro	2: 1
Yea, even t.; and the Twelve	DC	18:27
and the T. shall be my disciples,		18:27
the T. are they who shall desire		18:27
now I speak unto you, the T.—		18:31

TWELVE 997 TWINED

that you shall search out the T.,	DC 18:37
the T. which were with me in	29:12
man among you having t. sons,	38:26
over the t. tribes of Israel;	77: 9
t. thousand out of every tribe?	77:11
and plant t. olive-trees;	101:44
to consist of t. high priests,	102: 1
the duty of the t. councilors	102:12
who of the t. shall speak	102:12
in succession to number t.	102:12
the t. councilors shall consider	102:13
and call upon the t. councilors	102:19
composed of the t. apostles,	102:30
The t. councilors then proceeded	102:34
forty rods long and t. wide,	104:43
The t. traveling councilors are	107:23
are called to be the T. Apostles,	107:23
T. special witnesses or Apostles	107:26
The T. are a	107:33
under the direction of the T.	107:34
The T. being sent out,	107:35
councils of the T. at the stakes	107:37
It is the duty of the T.,	107:39
It is the duty of the T.,	107:58
call other high priests, even t.,	107:79
shall be assisted by t. counselors	107:82
is to preside over t. deacons,	107:85
who belong not unto the T.,	107:98
pray for thy brethren of the T.	112:12
I say unto all the T.: Arise and	112:14
as pertaining to the T.,	112:16
the voice of your brethren, the T.,	112:21
For unto you, the T.,	112:30
even t. including himself,	114: 1
let the T. be organized;	118: 1
over the T. traveling council;	124:127
Which T. hold the keys to	124:128
two of the T.,	135: 2
the direction of the T. Apostles.	136: 3
were nine hundred and t. years,	Mses 6:16

TWENTIES
of Zion, by tens, or by t.,	DC 103:30
hundreds, or by fifties, or by t.,	104:68

TWENTIETH
commencement of the t. year	Al 50: 1
And thus ended the t. year.	50:16
come again in the t. year.	3Ne 4:15
three hundred and t. year	4Ne 1:48

TWENTY
three hundred and t. years had	Om 1: 5
they have brought t.-four plates	Mos 8: 9
for the space of t. and two years.	10: 3
for the space of t. and two years.	10: 5
t. and four of the daughters of	20: 5
concerning those t.-four plates,	Al 37:21
he was only t. and five years old	43:17
of the t. and first year of the	50:17
in the t. and first year of the	50:23
that the t. and second year of	50:24
and also the t. and third year.	50:24
of the t. and fourth year of	50:25
ended the t. and fourth year	50:35
of the t. and fourth year,	50:40
of the t. and fifth year of the	51: 1
the t. and fifth year in peace;	51: 1
in the t. and fifth year of	51:12
endeth the t. and fifth year	51:37
in the t. and sixth year of	52: 1
of the t. and sixth year of	52:14
in the t. and seventh year of	52:15
of the t. and seventh year of	52:18
of the t. and eighth year,	52:19
ended the t. and eighth year	53:23
in the t. and ninth year of	54: 1
ended the t. and ninth year of	55:35
But in the t. and sixth year,	56: 7
in the t. and sixth year,	56: 9
thus ended the t. and sixth year.	56:20
of the t. and seventh year	56:20
ended the t. and eighth year of	57: 5
of the t. and ninth year,	Al 57: 6
this is the t. and ninth year,	58:38
And in the t. and first year	3Ne 4:16
the t. and second year passed	5: 7
and the t. and third year also,	5: 7
and the t. and fourth, and the	5: 7
fourth, and the t. and fifth;	5: 7
t. and five years passed away.	5: 7
the space of t. and five years;	5: 8
lands in the t. and sixth year,	6: 1
the t. and sixth and seventh years	6: 4
away the t. and eighth year,	6: 9
in the t. and ninth year there	6:10
three hundred and t. years had	4Ne 1:48
are about t. and four years old	Mrm 1: 3
hundred and t. and six years	2: 2
hundred and t. and seventh	2: 3
save it were t. and four of us,	6:11
save it were those t. and four	6:15
from the t. and four plates which	Eth 1: 2
number about t. and two souls;	6:16
of Jared were t. and two souls;	6:20
whom were t. and three sons.	7: 2
had reigned t. and four years,	10:30
and t. and seven of the people	15:25
than four hundred and t. years	Mro 10: 1
we came to the t.-ninth verse	DC 76:15
by the four and t. elders,	77: 5
council of t.-four high priests	102: 1
if he obtain ten, or t., or fifty,	104:69
or t., or fifty, or a hundred,	104:73
Enoch was t.-five years old when	107:48
over t.-four of the teachers,	107:86
on the t.-sixth day of April	118: 5
In the short space of t. years,	135: 3
shall be an hundred and t. years;	Mses 8:17
on the t.-third day of December,	JS 2: 3
of eighteen hundred and t.	2:14
until the t.-first of September,	2:27
eight hundred and t.-three,	2:27
hundred and t.-three—	2:28
t.-first of September,	2:29
t.-second and twenty-third	2:40
and t.-third verses, precisely	2:40
from the t.-eighth verse to	2:41
On the t.-second day of	2:59
eight hundred and t.-seven,	2:59

TWENTY-EIGHTH: see TWENTY and EIGHTH.

TWENTY-FIRST: see TWENTY and FIRST.

TWENTY-FIVE: see TWENTY and FIVE.

TWENTY-FOUR: see TWENTY and FOUR.

TWENTY-NINTH: see TWENTY and NINTH.

TWENTY-SECOND: see TWENTY and SECOND.

TWENTY-SEVEN: see TWENTY and SEVEN.

TWENTY-SIXTH: see TWENTY and SIXTH.

TWENTY-THIRD: see TWENTY and THIRD.

TWENTY-THREE: see TWENTY and THREE.

TWICE
was t. the value of a senine.	Al 11: 8
was t. the value of a seon.	11: 9
t. were they cast into a den of	3Ne 28:22

TWINED
and scarlets, and fine-t. linen,	1Ne 13: 7
scarlets, and the fine-t. linen,	13: 8
of silk and fine-t. linen,	Al 1:29
fine silks, and their fine-t. linen,	4: 6
of fine-t. linen and cloth	He 6:13
have silks, and fine t. linen;	Eth 10:24

TWINKLING

TWINKLING
be changed in the t. of an eye	3Ne	28: 8
changed in the t. of an eye,	DC	43:32
changed in the t. of an eye,		63:51
changed in the t. of an eye,		101:31

TWO
t. of the daughters of Ishmael,	1Ne	7: 6
and the t. sons of Ishmael		7: 6
there are save t. churches only;		14:10
within the ball were t. spindles;		16:10
I did smite t. stones together		17:11
now, my father had begat t. sons		18: 7
These t. sons are come unto thee,	2Ne	8:19
Thy sons have fainted, save these t.;		8:20
for the t. tails of these smoking		17: 4
nourish a young cow and t. sheep;		17:21
the testimony of t. nations is a		29: 8
when the t. nations shall run		29: 8
the testimony of the t. nations		29: 8
t. hundred years had passed	Jar	1: 5
t. hundred and thirty and eight		1:13
t. hundred and seventy and six	Om	1: 3
t. hundred and eighty and two		1: 3
and t. years had passed away		1: 3
they had been in prison t. days	Mos	7: 8
t. hundred and seventy-nine of		9:19
the space of twenty and t. years.		10: 3
the space of twenty and t. years.		10: 5
after the space of t. years that		12: 1
about t. hundred and four souls;		18:16
for the space of t. years,		19:29
they had pursued them t. days,		22:16
were gathered together in t. bodies.		25: 4
for the space of t. days and two		27:23
space of two days and t. nights,		27:23
by the means of those t. stones		28:13
fastened into the t. rims of a bow.		28:13
died, being eighty and t. years old,		29:45
five hundred thirty and t. souls;	Al	2:19
five hundred sixty and t. souls.		2:19
was as great as t. senums.		11:11
with her young from t. lions;		14:29
he had t. sons, Lehi and Aha)—		16: 5
now Zoram and his t. sons,		16: 5
for the space of t. days and two		18:43
space of two days and t. nights;		18:43
after t. days and two nights		19: 1
after two days and t. nights		19: 1
for the space of t. days and two		19: 5
space of two days and t. nights;		19: 5
and he also took t. of his sons.		31: 6
and also my t. sons—		31:32
and also the t. sons of Alma		35:14
they did smite in t. many of		43:44
the plains between the t. cities.		52:20
t. thousand of those young men,		53:18
t. thousand stripling soldiers,		53:22
t. thousand of the sons of those		56: 3
t. thousand of these young men		56: 5
of these t. thousand young men		56: 9
did join my t. thousand sons,		56:10
of those my t. thousand sons.		56:27
sent t. thousand men unto us		56:28
did return with my t. thousand		56:49
returned with my t. thousand,		56:50
their rear with his t. thousand,		56:52
and I with my t. thousand,		56:54
my little band of t. thousand.		57: 6
upwards of t. thousand of them		57:14
band of t. thousand and sixty		57:19
those t. thousand and sixty were		57:20
that there were t. hundred,		57:25
out of my t. thousand and sixty,		57:25
by an army of t. thousand men		58: 8
came to pass that he had t. sons.	He	3:21
shall be t. days and a night;		14: 4
No man can serve t. masters;	3Ne	13:24
t. thousand and five hundred		17:25
are seventy and t. years old		28: 3
t. hundred years had passed	4Ne	1:22
this t. hundred and first year		1:24
t. hundred and ten years had		1:27
t. hundred and thirty years	4Ne	1:34
t. hundred and thirty and first		1:35
t. hundred and forty and four		1:40
t. hundred and fifty years pass		1:41
also t. hundred and sixty years.		1:41
the t. parties were Nephites and	Mrm	1: 9
with forty and t. thousand.		2: 9
these t. stones will I give unto	Eth	3:23
should seal up the t. stones		3:28
about twenty and t. souls;		6:16
Jared were twenty and t. souls;		6:20
Corihor was thirty and t. years		7: 4
and there were t. kingdoms,		7:20
land for the space of t. years,		9:15
the space of sixty and t. years		9:16
an hundred and t. years old.		9:24
and forty and t. years old.		9:24
the space of forty and t. years		10: 8
the space of forty and t. years.		10:15
the kingdom forty and t. years;		10:32
again for the space of t. years,		13:31
after the space of t. years,		14: 3
for the space of t. years,		14: 7
nearly t. millions of his people,		15: 2
slain t. millions of mighty men,		15: 2
were fifty and t. of the people of		15:23
thirty and t. of the people of		15:25
sharper than a t.-edged sword,	DC	6: 2
mouth of t. or three witnesses		6:28
where t. or three are gathered		6:32
sharper than a t.-edged sword,		11: 2
sharper than a t.-edged sword,		12: 2
sharper than a t.-edged sword,		14: 2
neither staves, neither t. coats,		24:18
sharper than a t.-edged sword,		33: 1
preaching my gospel, t. by two,		42: 6
gospel, two by t., in my name,		42: 6
t. of the elders, or high priests,		42:31
elders of the church, t. or more,		42:44
before t. elders of the church,		42:80
by t. witnesses of the church,		42:80
but if there are more than t.		42:80
by the mouth of t. witnesses;		42:81
Let them go t. by two,		52:10
Let them go two by t.,		52:10
from St. Louis, t. by two,		60: 8
St. Louis, two by t.,		60: 8
journey together, or t. by two,		61:35
or two by t., as seemeth them		61:35
even altogether, or t. by two,		62: 5
or two by t., as seemeth you		62: 5
eight hundred and thirty-t.—		76:11
understood by the t. witnesses,		77:15
They are t. prophets that are		77:15
obtaining these t. priesthoods		84:33
purse or scrip, neither t. coats.		84:78
These t. houses are not to be		94:16
by t. other presidents,		102:10
t. only of the councilors shall		102:13
are, in the church, t. priesthoods,		107: 1
are t. divisions or grand heads—		107: 6
offices in these t. priesthoods.		107:21
Jared was t. hundred years old		107:47
Lamech was thirty-t. years old		107:51
mouth of t. or three witnesses		128: 3
are t. kinds of beings in heaven,		129: 1
t. shall put their tens of thousands		133:58
t. of the Twelve, were the only		135: 2
of publishing it on t. continents;		135: 3
t. or three days previous to his		135: 4
a president and his t. counselors		136: 3
I, God, made t. great lights;	Mses	2:16
to divide t. and two in the land,		5: 3
to divide two and t. in the land,		5: 3
Lamech took unto himself t. wives;		5:44
one hundred and sixty-t. years,		6:21
nine hundred and sixty-t. years,		6:24
seven hundred and eighty-t. years,		8: 6
one hundred and eighty-t. years,		8: 8
forty-t. years afterward he begat		8:12
Abraham, was sixty and t. years	Abr	2:14
Abraham, these t. facts exist,		3: 6
And where these t. facts exist,		3: 8

TWO 999 UNCHANGEABLE

If t. things exist, and there be	Abr	3:16
if there be t. things, one above the		3:17
if there be t. spirits, and one shall		3:18
these t. spirits, notwithstanding		3:18
These t. facts do exist, that there		3:19
there are t. spirits, one being		3:19
Gods organized the t. great lights,		4:16
t. shall be in the field, the one	JS	1:44
T. shall be grinding at the mill,		1:45
upon me I saw t. Personages,		2:17
that light I saw t. Personages,		2:25
were t. stones in silver bows—		2:35
were laid t. stones crossways		2:52
T. days after the arrival of Mr.		2:67

TWO-EDGED: *see* TWO *and* EDGED.

TYPE
shall be as a t. and a shadow of	Mos	13:10
it being a t. of his order,	Al	13:16
shall be a t. of things to come.		25:10
of Moses was a t. of his coming,		25:15
behold a t. was raised up in the		33:19
is there not a t. in this thing?		37:45
which things there has been a t.	Eth	13: 6

TYPES
many signs, and wonders, and t.,	Mos	3:15
things were t. of things to come.		13:31

TYPICAL
is written of as being t.	DC	76:70

TYPIFYING
are the t. of him.	2Ne	11: 4

TYRANNY
damning hand of murder, t.,	DC	123: 7

TYRANT
did not look upon him as a t.	Mos	29:40

UNABLE
as to render me entirely u.	JS	2:48

UNACQUAINTED
so u. with men and things,	JS	2: 8

UNALTERABLE
Now, the decrees of God are u.;	Al	41: 8
And he sent forth an u. decree,	Mses	7:52

UNANIMOUS
by the u. voice of the council.	DC	102: 3
by the u. voice of the same;		107:27
foregoing motion was u.		OD

UNAVOIDABLY
and knew they must u. come	1Ne	15: 4
that they must u. perish,	Mos	13:28
they must u. remain in bondage		29:19
should u. have been cut off	Al	9:11
all mankind must u. perish;		34: 9
they must u. perish.	He	4:25

UNAWARES
might not come upon us again u.	Mos	10: 2

UNBECOMING
u. every citizen thus protected,	DC	134: 5

UNBELIEF
should dwindle and perish in u.	1Ne	4:13
the dwindling of the Jews in u.		10:11
these shall dwindle in u.		12:22
after they had dwindled in u.		12:23
be destroyed, and dwindle in u.,		13:35
seed shall have dwindled in u.,		15:13
that they shall dwindle in u.	2Ne	1:10
perish in the flesh because of u.,		10: 2
shall have dwindled in u.,		26:15
those who have dwindled in u.		26:15
those who have dwindled in u.	2Ne	26:17
those who have dwindled in u.		26:19
left to mourn because of the u.,		32: 7
their u. and their hatred	Jac	3: 7
would have dwindled in u.	Mos	1: 5
And now because of their u.		26: 3
a state of so much u. as were	Al	7: 6
veil of u. was being cast away		19: 6
ye do not cast it out by your u.,		32:28
rather harden your hearts in u.,		33:21
unto them, shall dwindle in u.		45:10
because they shall dwindle in u.		45:12
the sword, or to dwindle in u.,		50:22
their traditions or their u.,		56: 4
they had fallen into a state of u.	He	4:25
did begin to dwindle in u.,		6:34
there should be no cause for u.		14:28
if they should dwindle in u.		15:11
them who have dwindled in u.		15:15
again have dwindled in u.		15:15
because of their u.		15:17
of their iniquity and their u.	3Ne	1:18
because of stiffneckedness and u.		15:18
of the earth because of their u.,		16: 4
and because of the u. of you,		16: 7
miracles, because of their u.		19:35
seed which shall dwindle in u.		21: 5
dwindle in u. and wickedness,	4Ne	1:34
and they did not dwindle in u.,		1:38
of their wickedness and u.	Mrm	1:14
this because of their u.		5:15
because that they dwindle in u.,		9:20
who have dwindled in u.		9:35
they have all dwindled in u.;	Eth	4: 3
which is hid up because of u.		4:13
come unto you, because of u.		4:14
when ye shall rend that veil of u.		4:15
for it is because of u., and	Mro	7:37
the u. of the children of men.		10:19
it shall be because of u.		10:24
dwindled in u. because of	DC	3:18
who harden their hearts in u.,		20:15
neither your hearts of u.;		38:14
are u. and blindness of heart,		58:15
are perishing in u.		61: 3
have been darkened because of u.,		84:54
Which vanity and u. have		84:55
for their evil hearts of u.,		84:76

UNBELIEVER
should not any u. persecute	Mos	27: 2
should not be united to an u.;	DC	74: 5

UNBELIEVERS
inflicted on the church by the u.	Mos	27: 1
were numbered among the u.		27: 8
persecuted by those who were u.,		27:32
to lead those who were u. on	Al	4:11
was a day set apart by the u.,	3Ne	1: 9
be appointed them among u.,	DC	85: 9
portion among hypocrites, and u.;		101:90

UNBELIEVING
that they might not be u.,	Al	16:17
unto the u. of the Gentiles—	3Ne	16: 8
shall go unto the u. of the Jews;	Mrm	5:14
O then ye u., turn ye unto		9: 6
the u. and rebellious;	DC	1: 8
u. and stiffnecked generation—		5: 8
let the u. hold their lips,		63: 6
that the fearful, and the u.,		63:17
the u. husband is sanctified		74: 1
the u. wife is sanctified by		74: 1
the u. husband was desirous		74: 3

UNCEASINGLY
virtue garnish thy thoughts u.;	DC	121:45

UNCHANGEABLE
and yet be an u. Being?	Mrm	9:19
he is u. from all eternity	Mro	8:18

UNCHANGEABLE 1000 UNDER

UNCHANGEABLE		
to everlasting the same u. God,	DC	20:17
that is fixed, immovable, and u.,		88:133
With promise immutable and u.,		104: 2

UNCHANGING		
u. scepter of righteousness and	DC	121:46

UNCIRCUMCISED		
no more come into thee the u.	2Ne	8:24
Wo unto the u. of heart,		9:33
O ye fools, ye u. of heart,	He	9:21
no more come into thee the u.	3Ne	20:36

UNCLEAN		
then ye are found u. before	1Ne	10:21
and no u. thing can dwell		10:21
and will devils and u. spirits;		11:31
the u. spirits were cast out.		11:31
there cannot any u. thing enter		15:34
the uncircumcised and the u.	2Ne	8:24
because I am a man of u. lips;		16: 5
midst of a people of u. lips;		16: 5
and touch not their u. things;	Al	5:57
filthiness or anything which is u.		7:21
no u. thing can inherit the		11:37
for they are u., and no unclean		40:26
no u. thing can inherit the		40:26
nothing can come which is u.,	He	8:25
he cast out devils and u. spirits;	3Ne	7:19
the uncircumcised and the u.		20:36
touch not that which is u.;		20:41
no u. thing can enter into his		27:19
evil gift, nor the u. things.	Mro	10:30
else were your children u.,	DC	74: 1
Cease to be idle; cease to be u.;		88:124
ye shall not suffer any u. thing		94: 8
shall come into it any u. thing,		94: 9
any u. thing to come into it,		97:15
no u. thing shall be permitted to		109:20
for no u. thing can dwell there,	Mses	6:57

UNCLEANNESS		
of all our guilt, and our u.,	2Ne	9:14
of truth are hard against all u.;		9:40
strip yourselves of all u.;	Mrm	9:28
keep slothfulness and u. far	DC	90:18

UNCONQUERABLE		
and having an u. spirit,	Al	52:33
I, knowing of their u. spirit,	3Ne	3: 4

UNCONSCIOUS		
was quite u. of anything.	JS	2:48

UNDAUNTED		
and sixty were firm and u.	Al	57:20

UNDEFILED		
to be holy, u., according to	DC	94:12
language which was pure and u.	Mses	6: 6

UNDER		
and trample u. their feet.	1Ne	19: 7
do men trample u. their feet;		19: 7
I say, trample u. their feet		19: 7
not this ruin come u. thy hand—	2Ne	13: 6
shall bow down u. the prisoners,		20: 4
and they shall fall u. the slain.		20: 4
u. his glory he shall kindle a		20:16
the worm is spread u. thee,		24:11
as a carcass trodden u. feet.		24:19
mountains tread him u. foot;		24:25
none other name given u. heaven		25:20
way nor name given u. heaven		31:21
u. the reign of the second king,	Jac	1:15
responsibility which I am u.		2: 2
u. the glance of the piercing eye		2:10
were not u. the sound of his voice,	Mos	2: 8
u. this head ye are made free,		5: 8
the beasts and trodden u. foot.		12:11
are in the water u. the earth.		13:12
u. the conditions that they would		19:15
brought himself u. condemnation.		26:31

u. the reign of king Mosiah,	Mos	27:35
and he trampleth u. his feet the		29:22
the disadvantages they labored u.,		29:35
was called u. that head,	Al	3:10
grain, which were trodden u. foot		4: 2
trample the Holy One u. your feet;		5:53
u. a consciousness of his guilt,		12: 1
they are laid u. a strict command		12: 9
and he did reign u. his father.		13:18
u. a consciousness of his own		14: 6
Lamoni was u. the power of God;		19: 6
the people who were u. his reign,		21:20
were a people who were u. him,		21:21
was u. the reign of king Lamoni.		21:22
act of perishing u. the sword—		24:23
who had fallen u. the sword,		24:24
down u. a foolish and a vain hope,		30:13
down u. the foolish ordinances		30:23
and is trodden u. foot of men.		34:29
supported u. trials and troubles		36:27
thy feet to be trodden u. foot,		46:22
do trample them u. your feet.		60:33
be conquered u. the Lamanites.		61: 8
and trampled u. their feet the	He	4:22
and did trample u. their feet		6:31
they did trample u. their feet		6:39
and do trample u. their feet the		12: 2
to come u. condemnation,		14:19
her chickens u. her wings,	3Ne	10: 4
her chickens u. her wings,		10: 5
her chickens u. her wings,		10: 6
to be trodden u. foot of men.		12:13
a candle and put it u. a bushel?		12:15
old time, which were u. the law,		12:46
they trample them u. their feet,		14: 6
been trodden u. feet by them;		16: 8
trodden u. foot of my people,		16:15
ye come not u. condemnation;		18:33
ashes u. the soles of your feet		25: 3
been trampled u. feet of men,		28:35
of the Nephites u. their feet.	Mrm	5: 6
u. a consciousness of your guilt?		9: 3
u. a consciousness of your		9: 4
all other nations u. heaven,	Eth	2:12
above the water or u. the water.		6:10
his people u. Corihor his son,		7: 7
who were u. the reign of Shule		7:19
u. the reign of Emer;		9:16
exceeding rich u. his reign,		10:12
he that is u. no condemnation,	Mro	8:22
them that are u. condemnation		8:24
u. the curse of a broken law.		8:24
be brought u. condemnation;		9: 6
her chickens u. her wings,	DC	10:65
and ordained u. his hand;		20: 3
you are an elder u. his hand,		21:11
and art u. no condemnation.		23: 1
also art u. no condemnation,		23: 3
also art u. no condemnation,		23: 4
also art u. no condemnation,		23: 5
shalt be ordained u. his hand		25: 7
her chickens u. her wings,		29: 2
enemies shall be u. their feet;		35:14
her chickens u. her wings,		43:24
out of every nation u. heaven;		45:69
to put all enemies u. his feet,		49: 6
repent, for all are u. sin,		49: 8
that trembleth u. my power		52:17
all cases u. the whole heavens.		52:19
subdues all enemies u. his feet.		58:22
who are u. this condemnation,		63:62
out of every nation u. heaven.		64:42
ye are u. condemnation if ye		67: 8
u. the hands of the First		68:19
u. the hands of this Presidency,		68:20
u. the hands of the above		68:21
subdue all enemies u. his feet.		76:61
subdued all enemies u. his feet,		76:106
u. the counsel and direction of		78:16
u. the sound of your voice.		80: 1
u. the hand of his father-in-law,		84: 6
u. the hand of Caleb;		84: 7
u. the hand of Elihu;		84: 8

UNDER

Elihu u. the hand of Jeremy;	DC 84: 9
Jeremy u. the hand of Gad;	84:10
Gad u. the hand of Esaias;	84:11
received it u. the hand of God.	84:12
and groaneth u. darkness and	84:49
and u. the bondage of sin.	84:49
are u. the bondage of sin,	84:50
is u. the bondage of sin.	84:51
u. sin and darkness even now.	84:53
whole church u. condemnation.	84:55
remain u. this condemnation	84:57
in the earth, and u. the earth;	88:79
are found u. condemnation;	88:100
and that are u. the earth—	88:104
are brought u. condemnation	90: 5
the light is u. condemnation.	93:32
continued u. this condemnation;	93:41
trodden u. the feet of men.	101:40
world are subdued u. my feet,	103: 7
and trodden u. foot of men.	103:10
not all u. this condemnation;	105: 7
an elder comes u. the priesthood of	107: 7
u. the direction of the presidency,	107:10
u. the direction of the Presidency	107:33
u. the direction of the Twelve	107:34
ordained u. the hand of Adam,	107:47
ordained u. the hand of Adam;	107:48
ordained u. the hand of Adam.	107:50
ordained u. the hand of Seth.	107:51
u. the hand of Methuselah.	107:52
are not u. the responsibility to	107:98
deliverance from u. this yoke;	109:32
from u. heaven;	109:52
u. his feet was a paved work of	110: 2
shall be swept from u. heaven,	121:15
blessings constantly from u. thy	122: 2
u. the most damning hand of	123: 7
groans u. the weight of its iniquity.	123: 7
murdered u. its iron hand;	123: 9
receive u. fifty dollars for a	124:66
nor u. fifty dollars;	124:72
therefore, u. condemnation?	132:35
he was u. a vow, he hath broken	132:43
u. the alter that John saw,	135: 7
u. the direction of the Twelve	136: 3
great waters u. the firmament	Mses 2: 7
Let the waters u. the heaven be	2: 9
which shall be given u. heaven,	6:52
and things which are u. the earth,	6:63
and was laid u. the water, and	6:64
the land it was u. water,	Abr 1:24
which were u. the expanse	4: 7
Let the waters u. the heaven be	4: 9
u. the extreme difficulties caused	JS 2:11
all the persecution u. heaven	2:24
and come u. condemnation.	2:25
u. a stone of considerable size,	2:51
fixed u. the edge of the stone,	2:52
u. the necessity of laboring	2:55
I was, therefore, u. the necessity	2:58
u. the necessity of leaving	2:61
acted u. the direction of Peter,	2:72
u. the hand of this messenger,	2:72
(u. Divine providence),	2:75

UNDERNEATH

to be in a place u. where	DC 128:13

UNDERSTAND

Behold, we cannot u. the words	1Ne 15: 7
and u. with their heart,	2Ne 16:10
for many of my people to u.;	25: 1
do u. the things of the prophets,	25: 5
there is none other people that u.	25: 5
in that day shall they u. them;	25: 8
if ye cannot u. them it will be	32: 4
nor u. great knowledge,	32: 7
they u. not the scriptures,	Jac 2:23
for things that they could not u.	4:14
things which they cannot u.,	4:14
Then ye do not u. them;	7:11
a stiffnecked people, hard to u.	En 1:22
of Mosiah, could u. them.	Om 1:17
that we might read and u. of	Mos 1: 5
and your hearts that ye may u.,	2: 9
children who can u. my words,	2:40
unto you that ye might u.,	2:40
that ye may hear and u. the	4: 4
u. all the words which he spake.	8: 3
to u. the spirit of prophesying,	12:25
For if ye u. these things ye have	12:26
And now, did they u. the law?	13:32
they did not all u. the law;	13:32
I would that ye should u. that	15: 1
rising generation that could not u.	26: 1
could not u. the word of God;	26: 3
Now I would that ye should u.	Al 6: 5
that ye will not u. the words	10:25
Ye do not u.; ye say that	10:26
in plain terms, that we may u.,	13:23
taught you this, ye do not u. them.	33: 2
they will not u. thy mercies	33:16
people would not u. his words	33:17
I would that ye should u. that	37:43
your mind, which ye cannot u.—	42: 1
um that this is done unto us	44: 3
great mystery which we cannot u.,	He 16:21
now, whoso readeth, let him u.;	3Ne 10:14
they did u. the voice which	11: 6
that ye cannot u. all my words	17: 2
that ye may u., and prepare	17: 3
they did u. in their hearts	19:33
I would that ye should u.;	27:31
if so, he does not u. them.	Mrm 9: 8
that we may not u. our words.	Eth 1:34
and do not u. them.	DC 10:63
you that you may naturally u.;	29:33
given unto you that ye may u.,	29:33
together, that ye may u.;	50:10
with you that you may u.	50:12
spirits which ye could not u.,	50:15
that ye cannot u. and know,	50:21
u. one another, and both are	50:22
manifested that you cannot u.,	50:31
and whoso readeth let him u.—	57: 9
to u. the doctrine of repentance,	68:25
whoso readeth, let him u.	71: 5
and u. the things of God—	76:12
they u. not, neither	76:48
What are we to u. by	77: 2
What are we to u. by	77: 4
What are we to u. by	77: 5
We are to u. that these	77: 5
What are we to u. by	77: 6
Wea re to u. that it contains	77: 6
What are we to u. by	77: 7
We are to u. that the first	77: 7
What are we to u. by	77: 8
We are to u. that they are	77: 8
What are we to u. by	77: 9
We are to u. that the angel	77: 9
What are we to u. by	77:11
We are to u. that those	77:11
What are we to u. by	77:12
We are to u. that as God	77:12
What are we to u. by	77:14
We are to u. that it was	77:14
and u. not the things which	78:10
that you may u. my will	82: 8
kingdoms, that ye may u.?	88:46
are expedient for you to u.;	88:78
whoso readeth it, let him u.,	91: 4
u. and know how to worship,	93:19
What are we to u. by	113: 9
We are to u. that the	113:10
not u. his marvelous workings;	121:12
u., wherein I, the Lord, justified	132: 1
and do ye not u. them?	JS 1: 3
whoso readeth let him u.	1:12

UNDERSTANDING

the u. of the children of men,	1Ne 13:29
easy to the u. of all men.	14:23
which did give us u. concerning	16:29
the spirit of wisdom and u.,	2Ne 21: 2
shall make him of quick u.	21: 3

UNDERSTANDING

the u. of their prudent shall be	2Ne	27:26
him that farmed it, he had no u.?		27:27
erred in spirit shall come to u.,		27:35
Lord God giveth light unto the u.;		31: 3
to their language, unto their u.		31: 3
let him prophesy to the u. of men;	Jac	4:13
the u. which God has given me.	WM	1: 9
they might become men of u.;	Mos	1: 2
not applied your hearts to u.;		12:27
for they were men of a sound u.	Al	17: 2
all power, all wisdom, and all u.;		26:35
it beginneth to enlighten my u.,		32:28
u. doth begin to be enlightened,		32:34
he was a man of a perfect u.;		48:11
small unto the u. of men.	Eth	3: 5
that they might come to u.	DC	1:24
the church of Christ to their u.,		20:68
And he that hath no u.,		29:50
may unfold the same to their u.		32: 4
their u. reach to heaven;		76: 9
the u. of the prudent shall		76: 9
telestial, which surpasses all u.;		76:89
which surpass all u.		76:114
the u. of their ministry		97:14
according to the u. which he		102:19
the eyes of our u. were opened.		110: 1
may have an u. of these gods,	Abr	1:14

UNDERSTANDINGLY

setting forth clearly and u.,	DC	84:117

UNDERSTANDINGS

the u. of the children of men;	Mos	8:20
our u. were enlightened,	DC	76:12
touched the eyes of our u.		76:19
light that quickeneth your u.;		88:11
the scriptures laid open to our u.,	JS	2:74

UNDERSTOOD

which were hard to be u., save	1Ne	15: 3
are they to be u. according to		22: 1
Hear ye indeed, but they u. not;	2Ne	16: 9
and u. not that the law of Moses	Mos	3:15
u. not the dealings of the Lord;		10:14
for they u. not that there		13:32
and u. not the words which		27:12
Now they u. not the words	Al	9: 3
many words which were not u.;		19:30
But few u. the meaning of		33:20
there are some that have u. that		40:15
having not u. the scriptures.	3Ne	1:24
they u. not the voice which		11: 3
the voice, and they u. it not.		11: 4
as they u. they cast their eyes		11: 8
they u. not the saying that		15: 2
unbelief they u. not my word;		15:18
And they u. me not, for they		15:22
they u. not that the Gentiles		15:22
they u. me not that I said		15:23
they u. me not that the Gentiles		15:23
Behold, you have not u.,	DC	9: 7
there were that u. me not.		10:59
he is u. of man,		50:12
and u. by the power of the		76:116
to be u. by the two witnesses,		77:15
and ye have not as yet u.		78:17
heaven, as u. by the Egyptians.	Fac	1:11
Then u. his disciples that he	JS	1: 1
u. the same passages of		2:12

UNDERTAKE

but when we u. to cover our sins,	DC	121:37

UNDERTAKEN

was the work which they had u.	Al	17:13
for they had u. to preach the word		17:14
of Mosiah had u. the work,		17:16
the cause in which they had u.—		46:29
he has u. a greater work;	DC	7: 6

UNDERTAKING

without success in our u.,	JS	2:56

UNDERTAKINGS

your elder brothers in your u.;	Al	39:10

UNDONE

Wo is unto me! for I am u.;	2Ne	16: 5

UNEASINESS

to serious reflection and great u.;	JS	2: 8

UNEASY

the Lamanites began to grow u.	Al	56:30
king Laman began to grow u.;	Mos	9:11

UNEQUAL

bring men on to u. grounds.	Al	30: 7

UNFAITHFUL

as they were u. they did not	Mos	1:17
u., and unjust stewards,	DC	101:90
an u. and an unwise steward.		104:74
an u. and an unwise steward,		104:77

UNFEIGNED

and by love u.;	DC	121:41

UNFOLD

I will u. this mystery unto you;	Jac	4:18
or to u. the scriptures beyond	Al	12: 1
Now, I u. unto you a mystery;		40: 3
u. unto them this great mystery;	DC	10:64
that I may u. the same to		32: 4
u. the mysteries of the kingdom;		90:14

UNFOLDED

mysteries of God shall be u. unto	1Ne	10:19
of God may be u. to your view.	Mos	2: 9
he also u. unto them all the		29:35
u. in the eyes of all the people.	Eth	4:16
mysteries of God shall be u.	DC	6: 7
mysteries of God shall be u.		11: 7
the curtain of heaven be u.,		88:95
as a scroll is u. after it is		88:95

UNFOLDING

purpose of u. all such mysteries	Mos	8:19
u. unto them all the trials		29:33
u. unto them all my revelations,	Eth	4: 7

UNFRUITFUL

not be u. in the knowledge of	DC	107:31
the land shall be barren and u.,	Mses	7: 7

UNGODLINESS

and deny yourselves of all u.;	Mro	10:32
ye shall deny yourselves of all u.		10:32

UNGODLY

vision of the sufferings of the u.	DC	76:49
unrighteous and u. deeds,		84:117
cometh speedily upon the u.		97:22
convince all of their u. deeds		99: 5
and upon all the u. among you.		133: 2
to the condemnation of the u.		136:33

UNHAPPY

he that is u. shall be unhappy	Mrm	9:14
that is unhappy shall be u. still.		9:14

UNHOLY

more need have we, being u.,	2Ne	31: 5
for he dwelleth not in u. temples.	Mos	2:37
he doth not dwell in u. temples;	Al	7:21
he dwelleth not in u. temples,		34:36
doth not dwell in u. temples—	He	4:24
wherein they became u.	DC	74: 4
saith that little children are u.;		74: 6
will not come into u. temples.		97:17

UNION

a u. took place between them	Al	50:36
according to the u. required	DC	105: 4
and complete and perfect u.,		128:18

UNITE

UNITE
and do not u. themselves to that	2Ne	6:12
and of Mosiah, did u. together;	Om	1:19
and u. with his people, and thus	Al	50:32
did u. with the voice of the people.	He	1: 6
u. with those bands of robbers,		6:21
did u. with their brethren,	3Ne	2:12
u. with us and become acquainted		3: 7
and u. with the kindreds of those		6:27
to u. with the true church,	DC	23: 7

UNITED
and in one heart, u. in all things,	2Ne	1:21
that u. themselves to the church	Al	4: 5
if we had u. our strength as we		60:16
and u. with us, and gone forth		60:16
ye have u. yourselves unto it,	He	7:25
who had u. with the Nephites	3Ne	2:14
who were u. together save it were		7:11
were u. in the hatred of those		7:11
they were not u. as to their laws,		7:14
u. in mighty prayer and fasting		27: 1
u. unto the church of Christ,		28:23
u. in prayer according to my	DC	29: 6
not be u. to an unbeliever;		74: 5
be u. in the ministry;		75:30
as they u. their hearts and		84: 1
I give unto the u. order,		92: 1
established, to be a u. order,		104: 1
u. consent or voice of the order,		104:21
longer be bound as a u. order		104:47
the U. Order of the Stake of		104:48
the U. Order of the City of		104:48
are dissolved as a u. order		104:53
And are not u. according to		105: 4
multitudes u. themselves to	JS	2: 5
some desire to be u. with them;		2: 8
all u. to persecute me.		2:22

UNITED STATES
on the *magna charta* of the U.,	DC 135: 7

UNITING
their spirits u. with their bodies,	Al	11:45
and u. his forces with those of		62: 6
and u. to the church of God,	He	3:26
u. as many to the church as would	3Ne	28:18
members u. themselves with	DC	20:82

UNITY
together in u. and in love	Mos 18:21

UNJUST
both the just and the u.,	Al	12: 8
in the resurrection of the u.—	DC	76:17
the woman and the u. judge,		101:81
unfaithful, and u. stewards,		101:90
be condemned with the u.;		104: 7
we believe to be unlawful and u.,		134:12

UNKNOWN
their words, offend some u. being,	Al	30:28
all gone astray after an u. God.		30:53
was murdered by an u. hand	He	6:15

UNLAWFUL
wrongs and u. oppressors,	DC 121: 3
from the u. assults and	134:11
interference we believe to be u.	134:12
from all u. proceedings,	JS 2:75

UNLEARNED
who are u. and despised,	DC 35:13

UNLESS
cannot be blessed u. he shall	1Ne	22:10
u. a man shall endure to the end,	2Ne	31:16
u. ye shall repent of your sins	Jac	3: 8
u. he yields to the enticings of	Mos	3:19
u. thou wilt recall all the words		17: 8
u. he took his guards with him,		21:19
and u. they do this, they can		27:26
u. this be the case, they must be		27:27

UNSHAKEN

u. he has arrived unto the	DC	20:71
a fulness u. he keepeth his		93:27
u. it is by the principles of		105: 5
U. this is the case,		107:29
u. he is a literal descendant		107:69
For u. he is a literal descendant		107:70
u. he shall be a believer in the		124:119
u. I was ordained from before		127: 2
u. there is a welding link		128:18
u. their religious opinions		134: 4
u. they speedily repent,		136:35
u. I could get more wisdom	JS	2:12

UNLOCK
to u. the door of the kingdom	DC 112:17

UNLOOSE
latchet I am not worthy to u.	1Ne 10: 8

UNLOOSED
by me, and immediately u. my	Abr 1:15

UNNATURAL
and place it in an u. state,	Al 41:12

UNNOTICED
shall not fall to the ground u.	DC 84:80
shall not fall to the ground u.	84:116

UNPARDONABLE
lest I have committed the u. sin,	Jac	7:19
behold, this is a sin which is u.;	Al	39: 6

UNPREPARED
u. to meet their God.	Al 48:23

UNPROFITABLE
yet ye would be u. servants.	Mos	2:21
found me to be an u. servant,		22: 4

UNPUNISHED
the guilty and the wicked go u.	He 7: 5

UNQUENCHABLE
brimstone, whose flames are u.,	Jac	6:10
which is like an u. fire,	Mos	2:38
brimstone, whose flames are u.,		3:27
be consumed, even an u. fire.	Al	5:52
will kindle a flame of u. fire	Mrm	9: 5
shall go away into u. fire,	DC	43:33
the wicked with u. fire.		63:34
cast them into u. fire.		63:54
may be burned with u. fire.		101:66

UNRIGHTEOUS
unto them that decree u. decrees,	2Ne	20: 1
an u. king doth pervert	Mos	29:23
an u. king to rule over them;		29:35
world of all their u. deeds,	DC	84:87
their u. and ungodly deeds,		84:117
to exercise u. dominion		121:39

UNRIGHTEOUSNESS
save and to cleanse from all u.	Al	7:14
by the u. of your lawyers		10:27
but have pleasure in u.	DC	56:15
Forsake all u.		66:10
that there is no u. in them,		67: 9
to cleanse it from all u.;		76:41
with the mammon of u.		82:22
needs be sanctified from all u.,		88:18
of these quorums is made in u.,		107:32
in any degree of u.,		121:37

UNSEARCHABLE
How u. are the depths of	Jac 4: 8

UNSEEN
being from the u. world	JS 2:16

UNSHAKEN
Christ with u. faith in him,	2Ne 31:19
and our faith becometh u.,	Jac 4: 6

UNSHAKEN

my faith began to be u.	En 1:11
but ask with a firmness u.,	Mrm 9:28

UNSPEAKABLE

filled with that joy which is u.	He 5:44
of them saw and heard u. things,	3Ne 26:18
and saw and heard u. things.	28:13
the u. gift of the Holy Ghost,	DC 121:26

UNSPOTTED

keep thyself u. from the world,	DC 59:9

UNSTEADINESS

also the u. of the hearts of	He 12:1

UNSTOP

u. the hole and receive air.	Eth 2:20
and u. the ears of the deaf;	DC 84:69

UNSTOPPED

and u. the ears of the deaf,	3Ne 26:15

UNSUCCESSFUL

do not know but what ye are u.,	Al 58:35

UNTIL

u. their frames did shake before	1Ne 2:14
u. we have accomplished the thing	3:15
u. we came without the walls of	4:4
even u. they did come forth	8:24
u. they came forth and fell down	8:30
u. this time, and from this time	12:18
u. after they are scattered by	15:17
u. further commandments of the	19:4
u. the time they sought to take	2Ne 5:19
u. the time comes that they shall be	9:2
that continue u. night,	15:11
U. the cities be wasted without	16:11
u. they shall be persuaded to	25:16
u. the law shall be fulfilled.	25:24
u. the law shall be fulfilled	25:30
u. three generations shall have	26:9
u. he bindeth them with his	26:22
u. the own due time of the Lord,	27:10
u. I shall see fit in mine own	27:22
u. he grasps them with his awful	28:22
neither shall it be u. the end of	29:9
u. after he shall manifest himself	32:6
u. the end of the day of probation.	33:9
u. that great day shall come.	33:13
u. the good shall overcome the	Jac 5:66
u. the bad had been cast away	5:74
u. ye shall obtain eternal life.	6:11
u. I shall meet you before the	6:13
u. they came down into the land	Om 1:13
u. the days of king Benjamin.	WM 1:10
u. they have fallen into my hands.	1:11
until they had slain many thousands	1:14
u. they had driven them out of	1:14
time they left Jerusalem u. now,	Mos 1:6
been spoken by our fathers u. now.	2:35
preserved his people even u. now;	7:20
even u. the time that he himself	8:2
u. *the time that they were*	9:hd
u. the greater number of our army	9:2
even u. we had driven them out	9:18
even u. the resurrection of	15:21
and I will suffer even u. death,	17:10
ye may be in, even u. death,	18:9
to serve him u. you are dead	18:13
even u. the time that Ammon	21:22
u. they returned again.	25:5
u. the time they returned again.	25:6
even u. he was laid before his	27:19
back u. the creation of Adam.	28:17
remain in bondage u. now.	29:19
u. the fifth year of the reign of	Al 1:33
u. he slew and drove them back.	2:33
u. they were scattered on the west,	2:37
u. they had reached the wilderness,	2:37
they were faithful u. the end;	5:13
u. they are cleansed from all stain,	5:21
u. they were bound in bands	8:31

UNTIL

kept and preserved u. now;	Al 9:22
been prospered u. they are rich	9:22
even u. the fourth day of this	10:6
u. the reign of the judges,	11:4
u. it is given unto him to know	12:10
of God u. he know them in full.	12:10
u. they know nothing concerning	12:11
the same words, even u. the last;	14:25
u. it did become exceeding sore,	15:3
even u. the fifth day of the	16:1
u. the fourteenth year of the	16:12
and perhaps u. the day I die.	17:23
u. that time on the morrow which	19:11
u. they had all fallen to the earth,	19:16
u. they had arrived in the land	20:30
even u. they came to the land	22:29
u. the time that he should be	25:15
u. we repair unto them the	27:8
shall remain here u. we return;	27:15
of Moses u. it should be fulfilled.	30:3
the reign of the judges u. now,	30:32
even u. I had much success,	30:53
u. I have brought this great curse	30:53
down, even u. he was dead.	30:59
u. they had assembled themselves	31:23
u. ye believe in a manner that	32:27
this fruit even u. ye are filled,	32:42
of your repentance u. the end;	34:33
your repentance even u. death,	34:35
and from that time even u. now,	36:24
u. they should go forth unto	37:4
u. I did cry out unto the Lord	38:8
u. after the coming of Christ.	40:2
u. the time of their resurrection.	40:14
u. the time which is appointed of	40:21
u. the end of his days,	41:6
u. they began to flee towards	43:39
even u. the prophecy is fulfilled;	45:9
u. the people of Nephi shall	45:11
even u. they shall become extinct.	45:14
u. we bring it upon us by our	46:18
u. nearly the end of the	46:37
u. their chief captains were all	49:23
u. they had come to the borders	50:34
slay them even u. it was dark.	51:32
u. Moroni had sent a large number	52:7
u. they came near the city	52:27
u. they had given up their	52:32
u. they had encircled the city of	53:4
u. you are destroyed from off	54:12
u. they shall sue for peace.	55:3
u. it had become an exceeding	55:33
u. I had gone forth with my	56:33
wilderness, even u. it was dark.	56:40
u. we were about to perish for	58:7
u. we have first cleansed our	60:24
u. those who have desires to	60:27
perish u. ye can come unto me.	61:16
u. they were met by Lehi and	62:32
u. they came to the land of	62:32
u. they were sufficiently strong,	62:42
even u. they have fallen into	He 3:16
u. they are no more called the	3:16
u. they had lost possession of	4:13
u. they had regained the one-half	4:16
u. they had gone forth among	5:16
u. ye shall have faith in Christ,	5:41
u. the cloud of darkness was	5:42
u. he dragged the people down to	6:28
u. they had overspread all the	6:38
u. they had come down to believe	6:38
u. he had declared it unto them	10:17
u. they did cover the whole face	11:20
u. it is everlastingly too late,	13:38
u. the time shall come which	15:11
u. ye shall become extinct.	3Ne 3:8
u. they had all gone forth to the	3:22
even u. they had fulfilled the	4:13
the top thereof u. he was dead.	4:28
had hanged him u. he was dead	4:28
even down u. the present time.	5:15
u. the commencement of my	5:16
of the land u. after their death.	6:23

UNTIL

u. they were joined by dissenters,	3Ne	7:12
u. they had gone forth out of		7:13
u. the time of the fulfilling of		10: 7
u. they had all gone forth,		11:15
u. thou hast paid the uttermost		12:26
u. he had touched them all,		18:36
u. the time that he should come		26: 3
u. the elements should melt with		26: 3
u. the night cometh, wherein		27:33
u. all things shall be fulfilled		28: 7
u. the judgment day of Christ;		28:40
u. forty and nine years had	4Ne	1: 6
u. fifty and nine years had		1: 6
u. an hundred and ten years		1:18
u. two hundred and thirty years		1:34
u. the three hundred and		1:48
pursued u. they came even to	Mrm	2:16
u. we had come northward to		2:20
u. we had again taken possession		2:27
u. ten years more had passed		3: 1
u. the three hundred and		4:16
u. they had come again		4:20
u. they were all destroyed.		8: 2
even u. they are no more;		8: 7
u. the wickedness of the people		8:10
u. all his promises shall be		8:22
the children of men u. that time,	Eth	1: 3
days of Adam u. that time;		1: 4
down u. they were destroyed.		1: 5
u. the fulness of iniquity among		2:10
iniquities u. the fulness come,		2:11
will sin u. ye are fully ripe		2:15
u. the time cometh that I		3:21
u. the Lord should show them		3:28
u. after that he should be lifted		4: 1
u. after Christ should show		4: 1
u. the day that they shall repent		4: 6
u. he became exceeding old;		7: 7
u. he had gained the half of		8: 2
u. they shall spread over the		8:22
food u. he had suffered death.		9: 7
even u. he was exceeding old.		9:23
lived u. he was an hundred and		9:24
u. they had devoured them all.		9:34
u. the going down of the sun,		12: 3
u. after the trial of your faith.		12: 6
u. after they had faith in him;		12: 7
not himself u. after their faith.		12:12
the promise u. after their faith;		12:17
miracles u. after their faith;		12:18
u. we shall meet before the		12:38
the end come when the earth		13: 8
u. he came to the plains of		13:28
u. he came to the plains of Agosh		14:15
he smote upon him u. he died;		14:16
fought even u. the night came.		15:21
u. ye shall rest with him in	Mro	7: 3
it was u. the coming of Christ.		7:25
prayer, u. the end shall come,		8:26
u. I shall write unto you,		8:30
u. all things shall become subject		9:26
u. my spirit and body shall		10:34
u. my purpose is fulfilled in this;	DC	5: 4
no other gift u. it is finished.		5: 4
u. the earth is empty, and the		5:19
even u. I command thee again;		5:30
stand still u. I command thee,		5:34
tarry u. I come in my glory,		7: 3
keys of this ministry u. I come.		7: 7
u. you have finished this record,		9: 1
u. he draggeth their souls		10:26
u. you have accomplished the		10:34
u. I shall see fit to make all		10:37
u. you come to that which you		10:41
to preach u. you are called.		11:15
u. you shall have my word,		11:16
u. you shall accomplish it.		11:19
u. you have obtained all which		11:22
u. the time which is in my		11:26
u. the sons of Levi do offer		13: 1
the world u. it is wisdom in me.		19:21
u. after you shall go to the		26: 1
and be faithful u. I come,		27:18
u. I shall appoint unto them	DC	28: 7
place u. after the conference;		28:10
u. the time thou shalt return,		28:15
u. I, the Lord God, should send		29:42
u. they begin to become		29:47
u. I give unto you further		30: 4
u. I command you to go from		30:10
I am with you u. I come—		34:11
u. the time of my coming,		35:18
kingdom is yours u. I come.		35:27
u. ye shall go to the Ohio,		37: 1
u. ye have preached my gospel		37: 2
choose for himself u. I come.		37: 4
u. the judgment of the great		38: 5
U. the time shall come when		42: 9
u. the fulness of my scriptures		42:15
u. ye have received them in		42:57
revelations u. he be taken,		43: 3
and sleep u. I shall call again.		43:18
shall know, u. they come before		43:33
u. all things may be done		44: 6
a city reserved u. a day of		45:12
u. every desolation which I		45:21
u. all shall be fulfilled.		45:23
u. the times of the Gentiles		45:25
coming u. the end of the earth.		45:26
u. they shall see an overflowing		45:31
u. the New Testament be		45:60
u. it is expedient in me,		45:72
u. ye have accomplished the		45:72
u. he makes reconciliation.		46: 4
u. he is called to further duties.		47: 1
nor shall they know u. he comes.		49: 7
and brighter u. the perfect day.		50:24
u. he transgresses and is not		51: 4
u. I, the Lord, shall provide		51:16
u. the next conference,		52: 2
u. I prepare a place for you.		54: 9
patient in tribulation u. I come;		54:10
u. he reigns whose right is is to		58:22
anything u. he is commanded,		58:29
u. he is sufficiently chastened		58:60
u. they return to the churches		60: 8
u. you were chastened for		61: 8
u. they arrive at Cincinnati;		61:30
u. they return to their homes,		61:35
u. I shall command them.		63:39
grow up u. they become old;		63:51
And u. that hour there will be		63:54
u. the coming of the Son of		64:23
u. the residue of the church,		64:26
u. it has filled the whole earth.		65: 2
in patience u. ye are perfected.		67:13
u. it shall be made known		71: 2
round about, u. conference;		73: 1
round about u. conference,		73: 4
of translation u. it be finished.		73: 4
elders u. further knowledge,		73: 5
the devil u. the last resurrection,		76:85
u. the Lord, even Christ the		76:85
u. the fulness of times, when		76:106
and so on u. the seventh.		77: 7
u. the day of redemption.		78:12
u. the day of redemption.		82:21
u. their husbands are taken;		83: 2
u. they are of age.		83: 4
u. an house shall be built unto		84: 5
u. John, whom God raised		84:27
u. they repent and remember		84:57
u. I have completed my work,		84:97
U. all shall know me, who		84:98
u. the harvest is fully ripe;		86: 7
u. the restoration of all things		86:10
u. the consumption decreed		87: 6
u. the day of the Lord come;		87: 8
u. his hour was finished,		88:60
u. the mouth of the Lord shall		88:85
be clean, u. the Lord comes.		88:86
u. the thousand years are		88:101
again, u. the end of the earth.		88:101
u. that great and last day,		88:1Q2
u. the seventh angel shall sound		88:110
ye may not faint, u. I come.		88:126

UNTIL 1006 UPPER

u. the mouth of the Lord	DC	90:20
u. the mouth of the Lord		90:21
chasten her u. she overcomes		90:36
u. he received a fulness;		93:13
u. he is glorified in truth and		93:28
not to be built u. I give unto		94:16
u. I shall give unto him other		97: 4
be stayed u. the Lord come;		97:23
u. they had avenged themselves		98:37
u. seventy times seven.		98:40
u. he repent and reward thee		98:44
u. your children are provided		99: 6
my gospel u. thou be taken.		99: 8
U. the day cometh when there		101:21
shall not die u. he is old;		101:30
u. the kingdoms of the world		103: 7
u. they have obtained companies		103:30
u. they have obtained to the		103:30
u. you have obtained a		103:34
salvation of men u. I come—		104: 1
u. the day of redemption.		104: 9
U. he be found a transgressor,		104:74
u. I shall send means unto		104:80
u. you shall load enough to		104:84
u. they learn obedience,		105: 6
u. mine elders are endowed		105:11
u. it is wisdom in me that		105:23
u. the army of Israel becomes		105:26
u. my servant Baurak Ale		105:27
u. the borders of Zion are		107:74
u. seven times seventy,		107:96
Wait patiently u. the		108: 4
And u. this be accomplished,		109:40
Be faithful u. I come,		112:34
labor diligently u. it shall be		115:12
u. there shall not anything remain		115:12
since the world was u. now;		121:26
if thou livest u. thou art		130:15
from the beginning of creation u.		132:38
u. we shall meet before the		135: 5
u. thou shalt return unto the	Mses	4:25
no man, u. I command you,		4:32
be in the world, u. the end thereof;		5:59
and u. that day they shall be in		7:39
chains of darkness u. the judgment		7:57
u. thou come nigh unto Kolob,	Abr	3: 9
u. thou come near unto the		3:10
from the evening u. morning		4: 5
the morning u. the evening		4: 5
it was from evening u. morning		4: 8
it was from morning u. evening		4: 8
the evening u. the morning		4:13
the morning u. the evening		4:13
they had ordered u. they obeyed.		4:18
it was from evening u. morning		4:19
it was from morning u. evening		4:19
it was from evening u. morning		4:23
it was from morning u. evening		4:23
it was from evening u. morning		4:31
it was from morning u. evening		4:31
by the prophets, u. ye shall say:	JS	1: 1
of their kingdom u. this time;		1:18
u. all I have told you shall		1:34
u. the day that Noah entered		1:42
knew not u. the flood came,		1:43
gradually u. it fell upon me.		2:16
as I was u. further directed.		2:26
u. the twenty-first of September,		2:27
u. the room was lighter than		2:30
u. the room was again left dark,		2:43
u. four years from that time;		2:53
u. the time should come for		2:53
u. he, the messenger, should		2:59
u. I had accomplished by them		2:60
in his charge u. this day,		2:60
u. which time I had never		2:66
u. the sons of Levi do offer		2:69

UNTO: *see in the APPENDIX.*

UNTOWARD		
from this u. generation,	DC	36: 6
from this u. generation,		109:41
UNUSUAL		
an u. excitement on the subject	JS	2: 5
UNVEIL		
he will u. his face unto you,	DC	88:68
when thou shalt u. the heavens,		109:74
shall u. the face of my covering,		124: 8
UNVEILED		
the face of the Lord shall be u.;	DC	88:95
UNWEARIED		
are striving with u. diligence	He	15: 6
UNWEARYINGNESS		
hast with u. declared the word,	He	10: 4
thou hast done this with such u.,		10: 5
UNWISE		
we should suppose ourselves u.,	Al	57: 2
unfaithful and an u. steward.	DC	104:74
unfaithful and an u. steward,		104:77
UNWORTHILY		
of my flesh and blood u.,	3Ne	18:28
drinketh my flesh and blood u.		18:29
that ye are not baptized u.,	Mrm	9:29
of the sacrament of Christ u.;		9:29
UNWORTHINESS		
rather say: O Lord, forgive my u.,	Al	38:14
acknowledge your u. before God		38:14
been forbidden because of u.	4Ne	1:27
UNWORTHY		
towards you, u. creatures,	Mos	4:11
considering himself an u. servant.		21:33
for I am u. to glory of myself.		23:11
that a man is u. to eat and	3Ne	18:29
that we are u. before thee;	Eth	3: 2
found u. of this salutation	DC	88:134

UP: *see in the APPENDIX.*

UPBRAID		
him liberally and u. him not.	DC	42:68
give liberally, and not u.,	JS	2:13
UPBRAIDED		
be u. for their evil hearts	DC	84:76
and obtain, and not be u.	JS	2:26
UPBRAIDETH		
men liberally, and u. not;	JS	2:11
UPHELD		
and he was u. by his band,	He	2: 3
u. by the confidence, faith,	DC	107:22
u. by the influence of that spirit		123: 7
u. by the voice of the people		134: 3
UPHOLD		
the Lord will u. such at the last	Mrm	8:31
u. such secret combinations,	Eth	8:22
of Satan that do u. his work.	DC	10: 5
u. him before me by the prayer		43:12
with one consent I will u. him.		93:51
men ye should observe to u.;		98:10
u. the respective governments		134: 5
UPLIFTED		
u. hands unto the Most High.	DC	88:120
and, with u. hands to heaven,		88:132
with u. hands to heaven,		88:135
u. hands unto the Most High—		109: 9
hands, u. to the Most High;		109:19

UPON: *see in the APPENDIX.*

UPPER		
end of the conduit of the u. pool	2Ne	17: 3
in the middle on the u. side,	JS	2:51

UPRIGHT

UPRIGHT
honest and u. in all things;	Al 27:27
but he that is u. in heart.	DC 61:16

UPRIGHTLY
ye might walk u. before God,	1Ne 16: 3
they did walk u. before God,	Mos 18:29
walking u. before God,	Al 1: 1
to walk u. before God.	45:24
and to walk u. before him.	53:21
he did walk u. before God;	63: 2
and walk more u. before me,	DC 5:21
walk u. before me and sin not.	18:31
walking u. before me,	46: 7
to walk u. before the Lord.	68:28
if ye walk u. and remember	90:24
for good to them that walk u.,	100:15
who walk u. before thee,	109: 1

UPRIGHTNESS
with perfect u. before God.	Al 50:37
in truth and u. before him.	He 6:34

UPROAR
great u. throughout the land;	3Ne 1: 7

UPSIDE
your turning of things u. down	2Ne 27:27

UPWARD
and their God, and look u.	2Ne 18:21

UPWARDS
did slay u. of two thousand	Al 57:14

UR
in the land of U., of Chaldea.	Abr 1:20
to wax sore in the land of U.,	2: 1
father, yet lived in the land of u.,	2: 1
Therefore I left the land of U.,	2: 4
I took to wife when I was in U.,	2:15
unto me, in u. of the Chaldeans;	3: 1

URGE
did u. them with great energy	Mrm 2:23

URGED
supported and u. on and	DC 123: 7
taught, encouraged and u.	OD

URIAH
witnesses to record, U. the Priest,	2Ne 18: 2
in the case of U. and his wife;	DC 132:39

URIM
means of the U. and Thummim,	DC 10: 1
the U. and Thummim, which	17: 1
is a great U. and Thummim.	130: 8
will be a U. and Thummim to	130: 9
will become a U. and Thummim	130:10
I, Abraham, had the U. and	Abr 3: 1
Lord said unto me, by the U.	3: 4
called the U. and Thummim—	JS 2:35
with the U. and Thummim,	2:42
plates, the U. and Thummim,	2:52
plates, the U. and Thummim,	2:59
means of the U. and Thummim	2:62

US: *see in the APPENDIX.*

USE
which were for the u. of men.	1Ne 18:25
that I must u. so much boldness	Jac 2: 7
he could u. much flattery,	7: 4
and they did u. much sharpness	WM 1:17
his arm that he could not u. it.	Al 20:20
never would u. weapons again for	24:18
they durst not make u. of that	30:28
neither had I the u. of my limbs.	36:10
U. boldness, but not	38:12
able to u. a weapon of war,	55:17
do not make u. of the means	60:21
did u. every means in their power	He 6:20
for them who despitefully u. you	3Ne 12:44
u. not vain repetitions,	13: 7
and when I u. no sharpness	Mro 9: 4
is ordained for the u. of man	DC 49:19
the benefit and the u. of man,	59:18
its time, for the u. of my saints,	61:17
who u. the name of the Lord,	63:62
of the Lord, and u. it in vain,	63:62
make u. of it for their benefit,	84:103
nature, and u. of man—	89:10
have ordained for the u. of man	89:12
is ordained for the u. of man	89:14
God made for the u. of man	89:15
and make u. of the stewardship	104:63
u. their ability in bringing	134: 8
Let every man u. all his influence	136:10
to u. my influence with the	OD
I prepared for the u. of man;	Mses 3: 9
and u. of these stones were	JS 2:35
if I would u. all my endeavors	2:59

USED
Ye say that he hath u. sharpness;	2Ne 1:26
that we have never u. them,	Al 24:16
u. for the shedding of man's blood,	24:17
they have u. great flattery,	61: 4
this end were they made to be u.,	DC 59:20
u. by the Revelator, John,	77: 2
be u. with judgment and skill.	89: 8
these to be u. with prudence	89:11
they are to be u. sparingly;	89:12
that they should not be u.,	89:13
u. or taken out of the treasury	104:64
shall not any part of it be u.,	104:71
u. language which appeared	OD
u. all the powers of both reason	JS 2: 9
exertions were u. to get them	2:60

USEFUL
were u. for the food of man.	Eth 9:18
of which were u. unto man,	9:19
and barley for all u. animals,	DC 89:17

USHER
is now beginning to u. in,	DC 128:18

USHERING
in the u. in of the dispensation of	DC 128:18

USUAL
as u., went to the necessary	JS 2:48
gone as u. at the end of	2:59

USURP
to u. power and authority over	Al 30:23
might u. great power over them,	43: 8
who have desires to u. power	60:27

USURPED
having u. the power and authority	Al 25: 5
u. the power and authority of	He 7: 4

UTAH
effect that the U. Commission,	DC OD
have been contracted in U.	OD
Salt Lake City, U., October	OD

UTENSILS
take teams, seeds, and farming u.,	DC 136: 7

UTMOST
stand still, with the u. assurance,	DC 123:17

UTTER
that they durst not u. against him;	1Ne 2:14
unto their u. destruction,	14: 3
u. to the end of the earth;	20:20
be visited with u. destruction;	Al 9:18
the u. destruction of this people.	10:18
now be visited with u. destruction;	10:22
even to your u. destruction.	54: 9

UTTER — VALIANTLY

UTTER

overthrow and u. destruction.	Al	58: 9
even to your u. destruction.		60:29
to their u. destruction except	He	7:hd
to behold your u. destruction;		13:10
threatened with u. destruction	3Ne	2:13
visit you with u. destruction.		3: 4
their tongues that they could u.		26:14
and u. marvelous things;		26:16
the things which they did u. were		26:16
them that they should u.;		28:14
that they could u. the things		28:14
to their u. destruction;	Eth	11:20
or their u. destruction;	Mro	9:22
they shall not u. against me;	DC	29:19
the Lord shall u. his voice out		43:18
thunders shall u. their voices from		43:21
u. forth their voices unto all		43:22
the Lord shall u. his voice out		43:23
the Lord shall u. his voice,		45:49
I, the Lord, u. my voice,		63: 5
are not lawful for man to u.;		76:115
desolation and u. abolishment		84:114
whose mouth shall u. words,		85: 7
he shall u. his voice out of Zion,		133:21

UTTERANCE

which opened his mouth to u.	2Ne	1:27
the Holy Ghost, which giveth u.		28: 4
the Spirit stoppeth mine u.,		32: 7
stopped that ye could not find u.,	Mos	4:20
that ye shall no more have u.	Al	30:49
that he could not have u.,		30:50
Holy Ghost, which giveth u.,	DC	14: 8
as the Spirit shall give u. in all		88:137
as I shall give him u.;		93:51
be filled, and I will give thee u.,	Mses	6:32

UTTERED

words which cannot be u. by man;	He	5:33
neither can they be u. by man.	3Ne	19:34

UTTERLY

u. destroy the mixture of thy	1Ne	13:30
thy seed shall not u. be destroyed.	2Ne	3: 3
thou shalt not u. be destroyed;		4: 9
our seed shall not u. be destroyed,		9:53
the idols he shall u. abolish.		12:18
and the land be u. desolate;		16:11
shall u. destroy the tongue of		21:15
that the Gentiles are u. destroyed.		30: 1
I will u. destroy them from	Mos	12: 8
or he will u. destroy you from	Al	9:12
that ye shall u. be destroyed		9:24
band of robbers was u. destroyed	He	6:37
when thou shalt be u. destroyed		7:24
I will not u. destroy them, but I		15:16
my will, I will u. destroy them,		15:17
u. refuse from this time forth	Mrm	3:11
I u. refused to go up against		3:16
the Lord would u. destroy them	Eth	11:12
whole earth was u. wasted	DC	2: 3
u. destroyed by the brightness		5:19
I will not u. cast them off;	DC 101: 9
that they shall be u. destroyed;	Mses	7: 7
u. refused to hearken to my	Abr	1: 5
u. destroyed them, and smote		1:20
whole earth would be u. wasted	JS	2:39

UTTERMOST

that is in the u. part of Egypt,	2Ne	17:18
behold, to their u. astonishment,	Al	49: 8
thou hast paid the u. senine.	3Ne	12:26
the u. parts of the earth—	DC	58:64
upon themselves to the very u.;		121:13

UZZIAH

In the year that king U. died,	2Ne	16: 1
the son of U., king of Judah,		17: 1

VACANCY

whenever any v. shall occur	DC 102: 8

VAGABOND

a v. shalt thou be in the earth.	Mses	5:37
I shall be a fugitive and a v. in		5:39

VAIN

is v. imaginations and the pride of	1Ne	12:18
Then I said, I have labored in v.,		21: 4
my strength for naught and in v.;		21: 4
name of the Lord their God in v.;	2Ne	26:32
and v. and foolish doctrines,		28: 9
but it all was v., for they	Jac	7:24
our strugglings were v. in	En	1:14
But our labors were v.;		1:20
up his petition to you in v.,	Mos	4:16
that ye have begged in v.?		4:20
strugglings, which have been in b.;		7:18
their blood has been spilt in v.,		7:24
by the v. and flattering words of		11: 7
lying and v. words to his people.		11:11
and he has prophesied in c.		12:14
name of the Lord thy God in v.;		13:15
that taketh his name in v.		13:15
having searched in v. for the		19: 1
turn again to his pride and v. things		29: 9
loved the v. things of the world,	Al	1:16
upon the v. things of the world,		4: 8
up in the v. things of the world,		5:37
upon the v. things of the world,		5:53
and the v. things of the world;		7: 6
in v. to seek their destruction,		27: 1
under a foolish and a v. hope,		30:13
with the v. things of the world.		31:27
behold, your prayer is v., and		34:28
away by any v. or foolish thing;		39:11
nor the v. things of this world;		39:14
having pursued after them in v.;		47:30
with his army, but it was in v.,		47:32
who were pursuing them in v.,		52:24
concerning these things in v.;		54:11
this ye have supposed in v.		60:11
this ye have supposed in v.;		60:12
and the v. things of v.?		60:32
and the v. things of this world,	He	7:21
O how foolish, and how v.,		12: 4
upon the v. things of the world!		12: 4
and in v. shall ye cry, for your		13:32
hearts, which were foolish and v.;		16:22
concerning this thing hath been v.	3Ne	1: 6
that their faith had not been v.		1: 8
Imagining up some v. thing		2: 2
was a foolish and v. thing.		2: 2
so foolish and v. as to suppose		3: 3
and the v. things of the world.		6:15
ye pray, use not v. repetitions,		13: 7
It is v. to serve God, and what		24:14
which have been spoken are v.,		29: 3
v. like unto their brethren,	4Ne	1:43
But behold this my joy was v.,	Mrm	2:13
this people, but it was in v.;		3: 3
but it was all in v., for so great		5: 6
of unbelief, and all is v.	Mro	7:37
If so, his faith and hope is v.,		7:44
of the Lord, and use it in v.,	DC	63:62
mine, or else your faith is v.,		104:55
gratify our pride, our v. ambition,		121:37
take the name of the Lord in v.,		136:21

VAINNESS

O the v., and the frailties,	2Ne	9:28

VALE

us beyond this v. of sorrow	Al	37:45

VALIANT

the inhabitants like a v. man;	2Ne	20:13
were exceedingly v. for courage,	Al	53:20
blood of so many of our v. men:		56:13
not v. in the testimony of Jesus;	DC	76:79

VALIANTLY

to fight v. for their freedom	Al	51:21
they had fought v. by day		56:16

VALIANTLY   1009   VENGEANCE

had fought v. for his country,   Al   62:37
have endured v. for the gospel   DC 121:29

VALID
then it is not v. neither of force   DC 132:18

VALIDITY
decisions of the same power or v.   107:27

VALLEY
he pitched his tent in a v.   1Ne   2: 6
the v. was in the borders near   2: 8
mightest be like unto this v.,   2:10
unto them in the v. of Lemuel,   2:14
in a tent, in the v. of Lemuel,   9: 1
in a tent, in the v. of Lemuel.   10:16
in the v. which he called Lemuel.   16: 6
my soul linger in the v. of sorrow,   2Ne   4:26
walk in the path of the low v.,   4:32
they pitched their tents in a v.,   Mos 24:20
and they called the v. Alma   24:20
in the v. of Alma they poured   24:21
will stop the Lamanites in this v.   24:23
that they departed out of the c.,   24:24
their tents in the v. of Gideon,   Al   2:20
v. being called after that Gideon   2:20
in this v. the Nephites did   2:20
departed out of the v. of Gideon   2:26
river Sidon, into the v. of Gideon,   6: 7
in the v. that was called Gideon,   6: 7
established in the v. of Gideon,   6: 8
the v. which was near the bank of   43:27
brought a part over into the v.,   43:31
he concealed in the west v.,   43:32
and came into the v., and began   43:35
met the Lamanites in the v.,   43:41
together in one body in the v.,   43:51
to pitch their tents in the v.   47: 9
in the v. on the east of the   49:16
smooth, yea, even like unto a v.   He 12:10
laid low, like unto a v.,   14:23
into the v. which is northward.   Eth   1:42
the v. which was northward,   2: 1
the name of the v. was Nimrod,   2: 1
down into the v. of Nimrod   2: 4
did meet in the v. of Gilgal;   13:27
back again to the v. of Gilgal.   13:29
battle again in the v. of Gilgal,   13:30
tents in the v. of Corihor;   14:28
his tents in the v. of Shurr.   14:28
the v. of Shurr was near the   14:28
into the v. of Adam-ondi-Ahman,   DC 107:53
I beheld in the v. of Shum,   Mses 7: 5

VALLEYS
rest all of them in the desolate v.,   2Ne 17:19
v. which shall become mountains,   He 14:23
made hills and v. in the places   3Ne   9: 8
and for the v. to be exalted,   DC 49:23
and the v. to be exalted,   109:74
and all ye v. cry aloud;   128:23
and the v. shall not be found.   133:22

VALUE
their silver, according to their v.   Al 11: 4
was twice the v. of a senine.   11: 8
was twice the v. of a seon.   11: 9
was the v. of them all.   11:10
is the v. of the lesser numbers   11:14
the v. of an endless happiness   Mrm 8:38
receive the real v. of moneys,   DC 124:70

VALUED
shall be v. even as a garment in   Mos 12: 3

VANISH
for the heavens shall v. away   2Ne   8: 6
must perish and v. away;   Jac   4: 2

VANISHED
all things must have v. away.   2Ne   2:13

VANITIES
again in the v. of the world;   DC 20: 5

VANITY
that draw iniquity with cords of v.,   2Ne 15:18
Which v. and unbelief have   DC 84:55
the v. of his heart,   106: 7

VAPOR
I saw the v. of darkness,   1Ne 12: 5
by smoke, and v. of darkness,   19:11
fire, and v. of smoke must come;   22:18
could feel the v. of darkness;   3Ne   8:20
overpowered by the v. of smoke   10:13

VAPORS
and v. of smoke in foreign lands;   Mrm 8:29
and fire, and v. of smoke.   DC 45:41

VARIABLENESS
and in him there is no v.   Mrm 9: 9

VARIANCE
were at v. one with another   DC 101:50

VARIATION
with a little v. from the way   JS   2:36
first visit, without the least v.;   2:45

VARIOUS
the v. events in relation to   JS   2: 2

VARY
he never doth v. from that   Mos   2:22
neither doth he v. from that   Al   7:20
yourselves a god who doth v.,   Mrm   9:10
v. from the assistance which   Eth   8:14
neither doth he v. from that   DC   3: 2

VARYING
nothing v. from the words   3Ne 19: 8

VAST
slain a v. number of our men,   Al 56:10

VAT
him that treadeth in the wine-v.   DC 133:48

VEIL
the dark v. of unbelief was being   Al 19: 6
the v. was taken from off the   Eth   3: 6
from beholding within the v.;   3:19
be kept from within the v.;   3:20
ye shall rend that v. of unbelief   4:15
not be kept from within the v.,   12:19
longer be kept without the v.   12:21
the v. of darkness shall soon be   DC 38: 8
the v. shall be rent and you shall   67:10
when the v. of the covering of   101:23
v. was taken from our minds,   110: 1
a v. of darkness shall cover the   Mses 7:61

VEILED
it v. the whole face of the earth   Mses 7:26
and the heavens were v.;   7:56

VEILS
fine linen, and hoods, and the v.   2Ne 13:23

VENGEANCE
Thus God executeth v. upon   Mos 17:19
blood would come upon us for v.   Al   1:13
for v. to come upon thee;   20:18
swore v. upon the Nephites;   25: 1
unto the Lord their God for v.   37:30
come upon your heads for v.;   60:10
I will execute v. and fury   3Ne 21:21
V. is mine, and I will repay;   Mrm   3:15
and v. is mine also, and I will   8:20
for v. upon your heads?   8:40
sword of v. hangeth over you;   8:41
the ground for v. upon them   Eth   8:22

VENGEANCE — VERY

VENGEANCE (cont.)
from the dust for v. upon it,	Eth	8:24
incur the v. of a just God	DC	3: 4
will take v. upon the wicked,		29:17
suffer the v. of eternal fire.		76:105
the day of v. and burning,		85: 3
v. cometh speedily upon the		97:22
with plague, with sword, with v.,		97:26
that enemy shall escape my v.,		98:28
v. shall no more come upon		98:48
v. cometh speedily upon the		112:24
for this was the day of v.		133:51
Whosoever slayeth thee, v. shall	Mses	5:40
in the days of wickedness and v.		7:46
in the days of wickedness and v.,		7:60

VENTURE
he did v. to lead them forth from	He	4:16
not upbraid, I might v.	JS	2:13

VERIFIED
the word of the Lord was v.,	Jar	1: 9
that the words should not be v.,	Om	1: 6
the word of the Lord has been v.	Al	9:14
now behold, these words were v.,		25:12
had also v. his word unto them		25:17
behold that his words are v.,		50:19
these promises have been v. to		50:21
my word shall be v. at this	DC	5:20
as it hath hitherto been v.		5:20

VERILY: see in the APPENDIX.

VERMONT
Windsor county, State of V. . . .	JS	2: 3
left the State of V., and moved		2: 3

VERSE
to the twenty-ninth v. of the	DC	76:15
4th chapter, and 6th v. of		77: 1
spoken of in the same v.?		77: 2
in the 7th chapter and 1st v.		77: 8
7th chapter and 2nd v.?		77: 9
first v. of the 11th chapter of		113: 3
the 10th v. of the 11th chapter?		113: 5
in Isaiah, 52d chapter, 1st v.,		113: 7
from the bands of her neck; 2d v.?		113: 9
Father and the Son, in that v.,		130: 3
first chapter and fifth v.,	JS	2:11
quoting the first v. as it reads		2:36
he quoted the fifth v. thus:		2:38
quoted the next v. differently:		2:39
twenty-eighth v. to the last.		2:41

VERSES
and second v. of Ezra.	DC	85:12
v. of the 11th chapter of Isaiah.		113: 1
See the 6th, 7th, and 8th v.		113:10
last chapter, v. 5th and 6th:		128:17
and twenty-third v.,	JS	2:40

VERY
and also in power, in v. deed,	1Ne	14: 1
and the v. points of his doctrine,		15:14
for the v. cause that he shall		15:17
cutteth them to the v. center.		16: 2
Yea, even the v. God of Israel		19: 7
thou wouldst deal v. treacherously,		20: 8
a vineyard in a v. fruitful hill.	2Ne	15: 1
For yet a v. little while,		20:25
that Jesus is the v. Christ,		26:12
that it is yet a v. little while		27:28
appeareth v. abominable unto me,	Jac	2: 5
and the v. trees obey us,		4: 6
speaking unto me in v. word,		7: 5
he must v. soon go the way of	Mos	1: 9
I am v. thankful before God		7:12
a knowledge of this v. people		8:12
For this v. cause has king Laman,		10:18
yea, a v. high tower, even so high		11:12
yea, even a v. strict law;		13:29
the v. Eternal Father of heaven		15: 4
who is the v. Eternal Father.		16:15
a v. beautiful and pleasant land,		23: 4
yea, a v. cunning people,		24: 7
people began to be v. numerous,	Mos	27: 6
a v. wicked and an idolatrous man.		27: 8
the v. thoughts that any soul		28: 3
they were the v. vilest of sinners.		28: 4
and to wear v. costly apparel.	Al	1: 6
he being a v. cunning man,		2: 1
they began to be v. powerful;		2: 2
began to wear v. costly apparel.		4: 6
began to be v. sorrowful;		4:15
shall v. soon shine forth among		5:50
to see a v. near kindred,		10: 7
of God the v. Eternal Father?		11:38
he is the v. Eternal Father of		11:39
thy plan was a v. subtle plan,		12: 4
v. low with a burning fever;		15: 5
they were a v. indolent people,		17:15
to be a v. industrious people;		23:18
even in the v. act of perishing		24:23
the Lord in v. many instances;		31:11
being a v. wicked man, sent		35: 8
the v. thought of coming into the		36:14
by v. small means the Lord doth		37: 7
this is the v. cause for which ye		44: 2
I perceive that v. people,		45:10
the time v. soon cometh that		45:13
one v. wicked man can cause		46: 9
were v. frequent in the land—		46:40
a v. subtle man to do evil		47: 4
this was the v. thing which		47:15
the v. powers of hell would have		48:17
v. thick garments to cover their		49: 6
many of which were v. severe.		49:24
they were all of them v. young)		56:46
a v. serious matter to determine		57:16
suffered v. many exceedingly		62:37
which are particular and v. large,	He	3:13
did pierce even to the v. soul—		5:30
the v. day that he has delivered		7:20
he himself was the v. murderer,		9:38
the v. time when he doth prosper		12: 2
rock, even to the v. center.		12:12
began to be v. sorrowful,	3Ne	1: 7
they did establish v. strict laws		7:14
did pierce them to the v. soul,		11: 3
and extolled and be v. high.		20:43
was the v. Christ and the	Mrm	3:21
the very Christ and the v. God.		3:21
the wearing of v. fine apparel,		8:36
the v. things which the brother	Eth	4: 4
be made manifest in v. deed.		4:16
for this v. purpose are these	DC	3:19
be given thee in the v. moment		24: 6
give unto thee in the v. hour		24:18
is in force from this v. hour		84:75
be given you in the v. hour		84:85
against me a v. grievous sin,		95: 3
have sinned a v. grievous sin,		95: 6
sinned a v. grievous sin;		95:10
which was v. grievous unto me,		95:10
as a v. fruitful tree which is		97: 9
herself and become v. glorious,		97:18
become very glorious, v. great,		97:18
very great, and v. terrible.		97:18
be given you in the v. your,		100: 6
hour, yea, in the v. moment,		100: 6
had a spot of land, v. choice;		101:44
this v. choice piece of land,		101:44
they became v. slothful,		101:50
raised up unto this v. purpose,		101:80
this is a v. sore and grievous sin		101:98
hearken from this v. hour		103: 5
enemies from this v. hour.		103: 6
a v. sore and grievous curse.		104: 4
you power from this v. hour,		104:10
the earth, my v. handiwork;		104:14
unto you from this v. hour;		104:63
round about be v. faithful,		105:23
army of Israel becomes v. great.		105:26
let my army become v. great,		105:31
kingdom of Zion is in v. deed		105:32
to the v. uttermost;		121:13
if the v. jaws of hell shall gape		122: 7
the v. mainspring of all corruption,		123: 7

VERY — VINE

VERY (cont.)
they are the v. handcuffs, and	DC 123: 8
hands of the v. devil to tremble	123:10
a v. large ship is benefited	123:16
benefited v. much by a very small	123:16
by a v. small helm in the time of	123:16
give him, in the v. hour, what he	124:97
v. difficult for one recorder to be	128: 3
let him be v. particular and	128: 3
order of things to be v. particular;	128: 5
was contemplating this v. subject	128: 6
to some to be a v. bold doctrine	128: 9
praying v. earnestly to know	130:14
speedily repent, yea, v. speedily.	136:35
which I had made were v. good;	Mses 2:31
And Cain was v. wroth, and his	5:21
for the famine became v. grievous.	Abr 2:21
is a v. fair woman to look upon;	2:22
stars, that they were v. great,	3: 2
they shall be v. obedient.	4:31
they shall deceive the v. elect,	JS 1:22
at the v. moment when I was	2:16
a v. early period of my life,	2:20
who was v. active in the before	2:21
how v. strange it was that an	2:23
and being of v. tender years,	2:28
this will not seem v. strange to	2:28
not so v. bright as immediately	2:32
related the v. same things	2:45
circumstances were v. limited,	2:55
the v. prevalent story of my	2:56
were v. much opposed to our	2:58
being v. poor, and the persecution	2:61
become v. friendly to me,	2:75

VESSEL
virgin, a precious and chosen v.,	Al 7:10
inward v. shall be cleansed first,	60:23
the outer v. be cleansed also.	60:23
have first cleansed our inward v.,	60:24
as a v. is tossed about upon	Mrm 5:18
and they did also prepare a v.,	Eth 2: 2

VESSELS
that bear the v. of the Lord.	3Ne 20:41
prepared the v. for my people,	Eth 2:22
ye may have light in your v.?	2:23
the number of the v. which	3: 1
shine forth unto us in the v.	3: 4
into the v. which were prepared,	6: 2
they did give light unto the v.	6: 2
Aboard of their v. or barges,	6: 4
v. being tight like unto a dish,	6: 7
unto the chosen v. of the Lord,	Mro 7:31
that bear the v. of the Lord.	DC 38:42
For they are v. of wrath,	76:33
that bear the v. of the Lord.	133: 5

VEX
us go up against Judah and v. it,	2Ne 17: 6
and Judah shall not v. Ephraim.	21:13
and shall v. the Gentiles with	DC 87: 5
thereof shall v. all people;	97:23
and in his fury v. the nation;	101:89

VEXATION
not be such as was in her v.,	2Ne 19: 1
vex the Gentiles with a sore v.	DC 87: 5

VICTIMS
and become v. to their hatred.	Mos 1:14
v. to their awful brutality.	Mro 9:17

VICTORIOUS
Nephites began again to be v.,	Al 55:28

VICTORY
now, because of this great v. they	Mos 11:19
having gained the v. over death;	15: 8
that the grave should have no v.,	16: 7
therefore the grave hath no v.,	16: 8
having got the v. over the devil,	Al 16:21
that the grave shall have no v.,	22:14
by the v. of Christ over it.	Al 27:28
notwithstanding their great v.	46: 7
Moroni had thus gained a v. over	53: 6
to whom we owe this great v.;	57:22
given us v. over those lands,	58:33
gained the v. over the grave;	Mrm 7: 5
will send forth Judgment unto v.	DC 52:11
All v. and glory is brought to	103:36
behold, I will give you the v.	104:82
and on, on to the v.!	128:22

VIENNA: see JAQUES, Vienna.

VIEW
and many were lost from his v.,	1Ne 8:32
he v. me with his all-searching eye;	2Ne 9:44
is none other which shall v. it,	27:13
in Christ, and v. his death,	Jac 1: 8
of God may be unfolded to your v.	Mos 2: 9
to an awful v. of their own guild	3:25
and v. this mortal body raised	Al 5:15
it being in their v. a testimony to	24:18
and v. these things as they are;	DC 5:13
a v. of the things which he	5:24
shall have a v. of the plates,	17: 1
you shall obtain a v. of them,	17: 2
a different v. of the translation,	128: 8
have no other object in v.	JS 2:46

VIEWED
they had v. themselves in their	Mos 4: 2

VIEWING
v. the things which should come	Eth 13:13
v. the destructions which came	13:14

VIEWS
whose v. have been glorious,	2Ne 1:24
have great v. of that which is to	Mos 5: 3
for their hope and v. of Christ	Al 27:28
he shall have no such v.,	DC 5:28
I will grant unto him no v. of	5:28
greater v. upon my gospel;	10:45
I have had a few additional v.	128: 2

VIGOR
and pursued them with v.	Al 52:24
pursuing them with great v.	56:52
arouse them somewhat to v.,	Mrm 2:24

VILEST
they were the very v. of sinners.	Mos 28: 4

VILLAGE
came over to a v. which was	Al 21:11
house to house, and from v. to	DC 75:18
house, and from village to v.,	75:18
whatsoever v. or city ye enter,	84:93
v. or city that rejecteth you,	84:94
v. or city that rejecteth you,	84:95
to house, from v. to village,	99: 1
from village to v., and from	99: 1
to the v. of Manchester,	JS 2:51

VILLAGES
building large cities and v. in	Mos 27: 6
cities and v. throughout the land.	Al 5:hd
and their cities, and their v.,	8: 7
yea, even all their small v.,	8: 7
and all their v. and all their cities.	23:14
both in towns and v.	Mrm 4:22
their towns, and v., and cities	5: 5
great and notable cities and v.,	DC 84:117

VINE
and nourishment from the true v.?	1Ne 15:15
planted it with the choicest v.,	2Ne 15: 2
branch be grafted into the true v.,	Al 16:17
neither shall your v. cast her	3Ne 24:11
drink of the fruit of the v.	DC 27: 5
pure wine of the grape of the v.,	89: 6
as also the fruit of the v.;	89:16

VINES

VINES
where there were a thousand v.	2Ne 17:23

VINEYARD
for ye have eaten up the v.	2Ne 13:14
my beloved, touching his v.	15: 1
my well-beloved hath a v.	15: 1
betwixt me and my v.	15: 3
have been done more to my v.	15: 4
tell you what I will do to my v—	15: 5
For the v. of the Lord of Hosts	15: 7
ten acres of v. shall yield	15:10
took and nourished in his v.;	Jac 5: 3
the master of the v. went forth,	5: 4
the master of the v. saw it,	5: 7
behold, saith the Lord of the v.,	5: 8
not cumber the ground of my v.	5: 9
servant of the Lord of the v.	5:10
the word of the Lord of the v.,	5:10
And the Lord of the v. caused	5:11
in the nethermost part of my v.,	5:13
the Lord of the v. went his way,	5:14
in the nethermost parts of the v.,	5:14
the Lord of the v. said unto	5:15
Come, let us go down into the v.,	5:15
that we may labor in the v.	5:15
the Lord of the v., and also	5:16
went down into the v. to labor.	5:16
the Lord of the v. looked	5:17
the Lord of the v. said unto	5:19
to the nethermost part of the v.,	5:19
spot in all the land of the v.	5:21
the Lord of the v. said unto	5:22
the Lord of the v. said unto	5:23
the Lord of the v. said again	5:24
the Lord of the v. said unto	5:26
the Lord of the v. and the	5:28
the servant of the Lord of the v.	5:28
did nourish all the fruit of the v.	5:28
the Lord of the v. said unto	5:29
Come, let us go down into the v.,	5:29
we may labor again in the v.	5:29
the Lord of the v. and the	5:30
servant went down into the v.;	5:30
the Lord of the v. did taste	5:31
the Lord of the v. said:	5:31
the Lord of the v. said unto	5:33
the Lord of the v. said unto	5:35
the Lord of the v. said unto	5:38
the nethermost parts of the v.,	5:38
the nethermost parts of the v.	5:39
the Lord of the v. wept,	5:41
could I have done more for my v.?	5:41
that all the fruit of the v.,	5:42
and now all the trees of my v.	5:42
other parts of the land of my v.	5:43
which we have taken of my v.,	5:46
could I have done more in my v.?	5:47
hew down all the trees of my v.,	5:47
is it that has corrupted my v.?	5:47
Is it not the loftiness of thy v.—	5:48
the trees of thy v. have become	5:48
the Lord of the v. said unto	5:49
hew down the trees of the v.	5:49
not cumber the ground of my v.,	5:49
could I have done more for my v.?	5:49
said unto the Lord of the v.:	5:50
I should lose the trees of my v.	5:51
in the nethermost parts of my v.,	5:52
glory in the fruit of thy v.	5:54
the Lord of the v. said unto	5:57
nourish again the trees of the v.	5:58
the trees of my v. may bring forth	5:60
joy again in the fruit of my v.,	5:60
with our might in the v.,	5:61
last time that I shall prune my v.	5:62
and I lose the trees of my v.	5:65
I should lose the trees of my v.;	5:66
cumber not the ground of my v.;	5:66
I sweep away the bad out of my v.	5:66
out of all the land of my v.;	5:69
only this once will I prune my v.	5:69
the Lord of the v. sent his	Jac 5:70
the Lord of the v. said unto	5:71
Go to, and labor in the v.,	5:71
last time that I shall nourish my v.;	5:71
the Lord of the v. labored also	5:72
the Lord of the v. in all things.	5:72
the natural fruit again in the v.;	5:73
of the Lord of the v.	5:74
had been cast away out of the v.,	5:74
the Lord of the v. had preserved	5:74
the Lord of the v. saw that his	5:75
that his v. was no more corrupt,	5:75
last time have we nourished my v.;	5:75
in laboring with me in my v.,	5:75
my v. has become corrupted	5:75
because of the fruit of my v.	5:75
will I lay up of the fruit of my v.	5:76
last time have I nourished my v.,	5:76
shall again come into my v.,	5:77
my v. will I cause to be burned	5:77
to nourish and prune his v.;	6: 2
have labored diligently in his v.;	6: 3
unto us in all parts of our v.	Al 13:23
all those who labor in my v.	DC 21: 9
art called to prune my v.	24:19
shall call laborers into my v.	33: 3
my v. has become corrupted	33: 4
art called to labor in my v.,	39:13
call faithful laborers into my v.,	39:17
labor ye, labor ye in my v.	43:28
and let them labor in the v.;	50:38
according to your labor in my v.	53: 6
Wherefore, labor ye in my v.	71: 4
in this part of the Lord's v.	72: 2
the church in this part of my v.	72: 5
of me in this part of my v.	72: 5
church in this part of the v.,	72: 9
the church in this part of the v.;	72:10
every elder in this part of the v.	72:16
the bishop in this part of the v.—	72:16
or bishop in this part of the v.,	72:17
the church in this part of the v.	72:19
gospel, and to prune my v.	75: 2
elders continue in the v.	88:85
prune my v. for the last time,	95: 4
Go ye unto my v., even	101:44
themselves the fruit of my v.	101:45
nobleman, the lord of the v.,	101:52
after ye had planted the v.,	101:53
tower, and watched for my v.,	101:53
saved my v. from the hands of	101:54
the lord of the v. said unto	101:55
unto the land of my v.,	101:56
vineyard, and redeem my v.;	101:56
whom the Lord of the v. spake	103:21
while he is laboring in my v.,	104:20
labor in the v. of necessity	107:96
to purify the v. of corruption.	135: 6

VINEYARDS
v. round about in the land;	Mos 11:15
to labor in the v. of the Lord;	Al 28:14
or for gardens, or for v.;	DC 59:17
they shall plant v., and they	101:101

VINSON: see KNIGHT, Vinson.

VIOL
And the harp, and the v.,	2Ne 15:12

VIOLENCE
lay their hands upon you by v.,	DC 24:16
and it was filled with v.	Mses 8:28
for the earth is filled with v.,	8:30
the priests laid v. upon me,	Abr 1:12

VIOLS
the noise of thy v. is not heard;	2Ne 24:11

VIPERS
v. shall not excape the damnation	DC 121:23

VIRGIN

I beheld a v., and she was — 1Ne 11:13
A v., most beautiful and fair — 11:15
the v. whom thou seest is — 11:18
the v. again, bearing a child — 11:20
Behold, a v. shall conceive, — 2Ne 17:14
she being a v., a precious and — Al 7:10
if any man espouse a v., — DC 132:61

VIRGINS

and fair above all other v. — 1Ne 11:15
spake concerning the ten v. — DC 45:56
be foolish v. among the wise; — 63:54
and they are v., — 132:61
if he have ten v. given unto him — 132:62
But if one or either of the ten v., — 132:63
offered upon this altar three v. — Abr 1:11
These v. were offered up because — 1:11
me also, as they did those v. — 1:12

VIRTUE

try the v. of the word of God. — Al 31: 5
things, which is chastity and v.— — Mro 9: 9
faith, v., knowledge, temperance, — DC 4: 6
in the paths of v. before me, — 25: 2
by the v. of the blood which I — 38: 4
and practise v. and holiness — 38:24
must practise v. and holiness — 46:33
by v. of the decree concerning — 68:21
v. loveth virtue; light cleaveth — 88:40
virtue loveth v.; light cleaveth — 88:40
in faith, and v., and knowledge, — 107:30
by virtue of the priesthood, — 121:41
let v. garnish thy thoughts — 121:45
are of no efficacy, v., or force — 132: 7
by v. of his position — OD
offered up because of their v.; — Abr 1:11

VIRTUOUS

and the noble, and the v., — DC 122: 2
who are v. and pure before me; — 132:52
true, chaste, benevolent, v., — AoF 13
If there is anything v., lovely, — 13

VISAGE

his v. was so marred, more than — 3Ne 20:44

VISIBLE

were not v. to the natural eye; — Mses 6:36
of it was v. above the ground, — JS 2:51

VISION

he was carried away in a v., — 1Ne 1: 8
seen the things of God in a v. — 5: 4
in other words, I have seen a v. — 8: 2
all the words of his dream or v., — 8:36
these things which he saw in v., — 8:36
the things which he saw in a v., — 10:17
I have seen a v., in which — 2Ne 1: 4
be as a dream of a night v.; — 27: 3
man whom an angel said in a v.: — Al 8:20
a remarkable v. of her father— — 19:16
we conversed in the heavenly v. — DC 76:14
that we should write the v.; — 76:28
we saw a v. of the sufferings — 76:30
show it by v. unto many, — 76:47
Write the v., for lo, this is — 76:49
this is the end of the v. of the — 76:49
the end of the v. which we saw — 76:80
thus we saw, in the heavenly v., — 76:89
the end of the v. which we saw, — 76:113
And it is according to the v. — 107:93
After this v. closed, — 110:11
After this v. had closed, — 110:13
another great and glorious v. — 110:13
by the sea east, I beheld a v.; — Mses 6:42
with the v. of the Almighty, — Abr 1:15
few days after I had this v., — JS 2:21
of the v. which I had had. — 2:21
a fact that I had beheld a v. — 2:24
the account of the v. he had — 2:24
not destroy the reality of his v. — 2:24
He had seen a v., he knew he — 2:24
saying that I had seen a v., — JS 2:25
I have actually seen a v.; — 2:25
For I had seen a v.; I knew — 2:25
to affirm that I had seen a v. — 2:27
between the time I had the v. — 2:28
the v. was opened to my mind — 2:42
my father and tell him of the v. — 2:49
to the distinctness of the v. — 2:50
to assert that I had seen a v., — 2:58

VISIONARY

because he was a v. man, — 1Ne 2:11
that he was a v. man; — 5: 2
I know that I am a v. man; — 5: 4

VISIONS

things which he saw in v. — 1Ne 1:16
hath given me knowledge by v. — 2Ne 4:23
and their whims and their v. — Al 30:28
there were no such things as v. — JS 2:21
tongues, prophecy, revelation, v., — AoF 7

VISIT

and behold he did v. me, — 1Ne 2:16
God surely shall v. all the — 19:11
will speedily v. the inhabitants of — 2Ne 28:16
I shall v. them with a sore curse — Jac 2:33
I will v. thy brethren according — En 1:10
I will v. thy brethren according — 1:10
Wherefore the Lord did v. them — Om 1: 7
I will v. them in mine anger — Mos 11:20
I will v. them in my anger, — 12: 1
in my fierce anger will I v. them — 12: 1
do v. my people in their afflictions. — 24:14
Lord did v. them and prosper them, — 27: 7
will v. you with great destruction — 29:27
will v. this people in mine anger; — Al 8:29
yea, he will v. you in his anger, — 9:12
his angel to v. many of his people, — 9:25
Lord did v. them with his Spirit, — 17:10
in his mercy he doth v. us by his — 24:14
thou didst v. them in thine anger — 33:10
and v. not the sick and afflicted, — 34:28
v. us with assurances that he — 58:11
it shall fall upon you and v. you — 60:29
he will v. them in his anger, — He 7:hd
did v. many parts of the land, — 11:33
he doth v. them with death — 12: 3
I will v. them with the sword — 13: 9
I will v. them in my fierce anger, — 13:10
shall v. your destruction. — 13:10
v. you with utter destruction. — 3Ne 3: 4
should v. you with the sword — 3: 6
he will v. him with fire and — 11:35
And in that day will I v. them, — 27:32
I v. with the manifestations of — Eth 4:11
the Lord did v. them in the — 14:25
I v. with the manifestation of — DC 5:16
And v. the house of each member, — 20:47
And v. the house of each member, — 20:51
ye must v. the poor and the — 44: 6
now speedily v. the churches, — 63:46
the second hour I will v. you — 88:53
the third, saying: I will v. you; — 88:54
he might v. the second also, — 88:57
I will v. her according to all — 97:26
Adam shall come to v. — 116: 1
that I may v. them in the day — 124: 8
I will v. and soften their hearts, — 124: 9
commandments I will v. upon — 124:50
I have come down to v. them, — Abr 1:17
which he had done at his first v., — JS 2:45
After this third v., he again — 2:47

VISITATION

what will ye do in the day of v., — 2Ne 20: 3
believe in the day of your v.— — Mrm 9: 2
the v. of the Holy Ghost, — Mro 8:26
in the day of v. and of wrath — DC 56: 1
lamentation in the day of v., — 56:16
may visit them in the day of v., — 124: 8
day of my v. cometh speedily, — 124:10

VISITATIONS

VISITATIONS
and great v. among them; — 2Ne 1:12

VISITED
after I have v. the remnant — 1Ne 13:34
after I have v. them in judgment, — 13:34
and ye are v. by sword, — 2Ne 1:18
hath v. men in so much mercy, — 4:26
they shall be v. with thunderings, — 26:6
shall be v. of the Lord of Hosts, — 27:2
as he has hitherto v. this land. — Mos 29:27
be v. with utter destruction; — Al 9:18
been v. by the Spirit of God; — 9:21
now be v. with utter destruction; — 10:22
ye shall soon be v. with death, — 54:10
also v. with much destruction. — He 11:30
Having been v. by angels and — 3Ne 7:15
been v. by the power and Spirit — 7:21
they shall be v. with fire and — 12:2
therefore I was v. of the Lord, — Mrm 1:15
which Zacharias he (Elias) v. — DC 27:7
in prison, whom the Son v., — 76:73
it shall be v. with blessings — 132:48
the place again when I v. it. — JS 2:42
The messenger who v. us on this — 2:72

VISITING
unto the v. of the remnant — 1Ne 13:33
v. the sick and administering to — Mos 4:26
v. the iniquities of my people. — 11:22
v. the iniquities of the fathers — 13:13

VITAL
the more v. parts of the body, — Al 43:38
the more v. parts of the body — 43:38

VIVID
by the v. shaft of lightning. — DC 85:8
fierce and v. lightning also, — 87:6

VIZ.
v., apostles, prophets, pastors, — AoF 6

VOCALLY
pray v. as well as in thy heart; — DC 19:28
to pray v. and in secret and — 20:47
to pray v. and in secret and — 20:51
must pray v. before the world — 23:6
always, v. and in thy heart, — 81:3
made the attempt to pray v. — JS 2:14

VOCATIONS
pursue my common v. in life — JS 2:27

VOICE
I did obey the v. of the Spirit, — 1Ne 4:18
I commanded him in the v. of Laban, — 4:20
did say unto them with a loud v. — 8:15
the Spirit cried with a loud v., — 11:6
the v. of the Lord spake unto my — 16:9
the v. of the Lord came unto my — 16:25
the v. of the Lord said unto him: — 16:26
even the v. of the Lord came — 16:39
chastened by the v. of the Lord — 16:39
the v. of the Lord came unto me, — 17:7
heard his v. from time to time; — 17:45
unto you in a still small v., — 17:45
like unto the v. of thunder, — 17:45
the v. of the Lord came unto my — 18:5
not to the v. of his counsels. — 19:7
some with his v., because of — 19:11
with a v. of singing declare ye, — 20:20
prophet by the v. of the Spirit; — 22:2
hearken unto the v. of Nephi — 2Ne 1:28
my voice have I sent up on high; — 4:24
I will lift up my v. unto thee; — 4:35
my v. shall forever ascend up — 4:35
that obeyeth the v. of his servant, — 7:10
thanksgiving and the v. of melody. — 8:3
if they will hearken unto his v.; — 9:21
moved at the v. of him that cried, — 16:4
Also I heard the v. of the Lord, — 16:8
Lift up the v., O daughter of — 20:30

exalt the v. unto them, — 2Ne 23:2
their v. shall be as one that hath — 26:16
And also, the v. of the Son came — 31:12
thus came the v. of the Son unto — 31:14
I heard a v. from the Father, — 31:15
as the v. of one crying from the — 33:13
Yea, today, if ye will hear his v., — Jac 6:6
I had heard the v. of the Lord — 7:5
I did still raise my v. high — En 1:4
there came a v. unto me, — 1:5
the v. of the Lord came into — 1:10
hearken unto the v. of the Lord — Om 1:12
hearken unto the v. of the Lord; — 1:13
were not under the sound of his v., — Mos 2:8
they all cried aloud with one v., — 4:2
they all cried with one v., saying: — 5:2
the v. by which ye shall be called, — 5:12
a king by the v. of the people. — 7:9
Thy watchmen shall lift up the v.; — 12:22
with the v. together shall they — 12:22
thy watchmen shall lift up their v.; — 15:29
with the v. together shall they — 15:29
hearken unto the v. of the Lord; — 16:2
might have the v. of the people — 22:1
the v. of the Lord came to them — 24:13
the v. of the Lord came unto — 24:16
the v. of the Lord came to him, — 26:14
will hear my v. shall be my sheep; — 26:21
that he that will not hear my v., — 26:28
as it were with a v. of thunder, — 27:11
doth not my v. shake the earth? — 27:15
and his v. was as thunder, — 27:18
the v. of the people came, saying: — 29:2
by the v. of this people, judges, — 29:25
that the v. of the people desireth — 29:26
business by the v. of the people. — 29:26
that the v. of the people doth — 29:27
to the v. of the people. — 29:29
by the v. of the people. — Al 2:3
should gain the v. of the people, — 2:4
the v. of the people came against — 2:7
to the v. of the people, — 4:16
that ye hear the v. of the Lord, — 5:16
ye will not hearken unto his v.! — 5:37
the v. of the good shepherd, — 5:38
the v. of the good shepherd, — 5:41
for he hearkeneth unto his v., — 5:41
crieth unto me with a mighty v., — 5:51
the v. of the good shepherd, — 5:57
if you will hearken unto his v. — 5:60
spoken unto by the v. of the Lord; — 9:21
this is the v. of the angel, — 9:29
I obeyed the v. of the angel, — 10:8
the v. of this people should — 10:19
people, by the v. of his angels: — 10:20
cry, by the v. of his angels that: — 10:21
and cried with a mighty v., saying: — 13:21
Yea, and the v. of the Lord, by — 13:22
and cried with a loud v., saying: — 19:29
And the v. of the Lord came to — 20:2
desiring the v. of the people — 27:21
that the v. of the people came, — 27:22
with a v. to shake the earth, — 29:1
as with the v. of thunder, — 29:2
and cry with a loud v., saying: — 31:14
And he lifted up his v. to heaven, — 31:26
as it were the v. of thunder, — 36:7
behold, the v. said unto me: — 36:8
and his v. was as thunder, — 38:7
cried with one v. unto the Lord — 43:49
saying unto them with a loud v.; — 44:13
and crying with a loud v., saying: — 46:19
and the v. of the people, — 46:34
settled by the v. of the people. — 51:7
the v. of the people came in favor — 51:7
with the v. of the people, — 51:15
according to the v. of the people. — 51:16
appointed by the v. of the people — He 1:5
unite with the v. of the people. — 1:6
according to the v. of the people, — 1:8
according to the v. of the people, — 1:13
by the v. of the people. — 2:2
established by the v. of the people, — 5:2

VOICE 1015 VOICE

a v. as if it were above the cloud	He	5:29
when they heard this v., and beheld		5:30
that it was not a v. of thunder,		5:30
a v. of a great tumultuous noise,		5:30
a still v. of perfect mildness,		5:30
the mildness of the v.,		5:31
behold the v. came again, saying:		5:32
again the third time the v. came,		5:33
must repent, and cry unto the v.,		5:41
all did begin to cry unto the v.		5:42
there came a v. unto them		5:46
unto them, yea, a pleasant v.,		5:46
behold from whence the v. came;		5:48
the v. of the good shepherd;		7:18
a v. came unto him saying:		10: 3
at his v. do the hills and		12: 9
by the power of his v. they are		12:10
by the power of his v. doth		12:11
Yea, by the power of his v., do		12:12
hearken unto the v. of the Lord		12:23
behold, the v. of the Lord came		13: 3
hand and cried with a loud v.,		13: 4
the v. of the Lord came unto	3Ne	1:12
began to shout with a loud v.,		4: 9
and did cry with a loud v.,		4:28
rejoice and cry again with one v.,		4:30
who had given his v. against		7:10
and also the v. of the Lord,		7:15
there was a v. heard among all		9: 1
came a v. again unto the people,		10: 3
a v. as if it came out of heaven;		11: 3
for they understood not the v.		11: 3
and it was not a harsh v.,		11: 3
neither was it a loud v.;		11: 3
a small v. it did pierce them		11: 3
that again they heard the v.,		11: 4
third time they did hear the v.,		11: 5
time they did understand the v.		11: 6
bring, and they shall hear my v.;		15:17
bring, and they shall hear my v.;		15:21
I said they shall hear my v.;		15:23
not at any time hear my v.—		15:23
ye have both heard my v., and		15:24
have not as yet heard my v.;		16: 2
and that they shall hear my v.,		16: 3
me, and hearken unto my v.,		16:15
watchmen shall lift up the v.;		16:18
the v. together shall they sing,		16:18
they did cry out with one v.,		20: 9
their watchmen lift up their v.,		20:32
the v. together shall they sing;		20:32
the v. of the Lord came unto me	Mrm	3:14
not unto the v. of the Lord,	Eth	11: 7
saith the v. of him who dwells	DC	1: 1
the v. of the Lord is unto all		1: 2
the v. of warning shall be unto		1: 4
the v. of the Lord is unto the		1:11
will not hear the v. of the Lord,		1:14
neither the v. of his servants,		1:14
whether by mine own v. or by		1:38
or by the v. of my servants,		1:38
it is my v. which speaketh them		18:35
that you have heard my v.,		18:36
the truth, even with a loud v.,		19:37
the Holy Ghost, the v. of God,		20:35
as with the v. of a trump,		24:12
unto the v. of the Lord your		25: 1
that this is my v. unto all.		25:16
Listen to the v. of Jesus Christ,		27: 1
the conference by the v. of it,		28:10
Listen to the v. of Jesus Christ,		29: 1
many as will hearken to my v.		29: 2
as with the v. of a trump.		29: 4
for mine elect hear my v.		29: 7
as with the v. of a trump.		30: 9
to the v. of the Lord your God,		33: 1
in me, and hearken unto my v.		33: 6
To lift up your v. as with the		34: 6
lift up your v. and spare not,		34:10
the v. of the Lord your God,		35: 1
For they will hear my v.,		35:21
as with the v. of a trump;		36: 1
shall declare it with a loud v.,		36: 3
that will not hear my v., but	DC	38: 6
hear my v. and follow me,		38:22
a v. louder than that which		38:30
by the v. of the church;		38:34
your preaching be the warning v.,		38:41
listen to the v. of him who is		39: 1
if thou wilt hearken to my v.,		39:10
forth, crying with a loud v.,		39:19
by the v. of the church,		41: 9
shall utter his v. out of heaven; the		43:18
do lift up my v. and call upon		43:21
the Lord shall utter his v.		43:23
of angels, and by mine own v.,		43:25
and by the v. of thunderings,		43:25
and by the v. of lightnings,		43:25
and by the v. of tempests,		43:25
and by the v. of earthquakes,		43:25
and by the v. of famines and		43:25
and by the v. of judgment,		43:25
by the v. of mercy all the day		43:25
by the v. of glory and honor and		43:25
I say, hearken unto my v.,		45: 2
and hear my v. while it is		45: 6
the Lord shall utter his v.,		45:49
also lift up his v. in meetings,		47: 2
to the v. of the living God;		50: 1
against that spirit with a loud v.		50:32
that you shall hear my v. and		50:45
worthy by the v. of the church,		51: 4
by the v. of the church.		51:12
by the v. of his Spirit—		52: 1
by the v. of the church,		58:49
let them lift up their v.		60: 7
the v. of him who has all power,		61: 1
I, the Lord, utter my v.,		63: 5
and lift a warning v. unto		63:37
a v. as of one sent down from		65: 1
yea, whose v. is unto men		65: 1
Yea, a v. crying—		65: 3
shall be the v. of the Lord,		68: 4
any man lift his v. against you		71:10
listen to the v. of the Lord,		72: 1
and the v. of the conference.		72: 7
by the v. of the conference,		73: 2
even by the v. of my Spirit,		75: 1
hear the v. of the Son of Man,		76:16
we heard the v. bearing record		76:23
thus came the v. of the Lord		76:30
the v. out of the heavens bore		76:40
And we heard the v. saying:		76:49
heard the v. of the Lord		76:110
under the sound of your v.		80: 1
Listen to the v. of him who		81: 1
by mine own v. out of the		84:42
to the v. of the Spirit.		84:46
to the v. of the Spriit.		84:47
whoso receiveth not my v.		84:52
is not acquainted with my v.,		84:52
my words, which are my v.,		84:60
and shall lift up their v.,		84:98
with the v. together sing this		84:98
of the gospel, with a loud v.,		84:114
thus saith the still small v.,		85: 6
the v. of one crying in the		88:66
my v., because my voice is		88:66
voice, because my v. is Spirit;		88:66
of the v. of thunderings,		88:90
and the v. of lightnings,		88:90
and the v. of tempests,		88:90
the v. of the waves of the sea		88:90
crying with a loud v.,		88:92
by the v. of the sounding of		88:98
my name, and obeyeth my v.,		93: 1
there came a v. out of heaven		93:15
I speak unto you with my v.,		97: 1
even by the v. of my Spirit,		97: 1
the v. of the Lord their God;		101: 7
willing to hearken to my v.		101:75
by the v. of the council;		102: 3
unanimous v. of the council.		102: 3
by the v. of a general council		102: 8
by the v. of the church.		102: 9
Rigdon shall lift up his v. in		103:29

VOICE   1016   VOW

consent or v. of the order,	DC 104:21	he heard a v. from heaven,	Mses 6:27
him by the v. of the Spirit,	104:36	cried with a loud v., testifying	6:37
and by the v. of the order.	104:36	our father Adam by his own v.,	6:51
the v. of the council direct.	104:53	And hearken unto my v.,	6:52
only by the v. of the order,	104:64	he heard a v. out of heaven,	6:66
only by the v. and common	104:71	there came a v. out of heaven,	7: 2
the v. and common consent of	104:72	he heard a loud v. saying:	7:25
council and v. of the order.	104:76	he heard a v. from the bowels	7:48
council and v. of the order,	104:77	And he heard a loud v.;	7:56
servant, by the v. of the Spirit,	105:36	they will not hearken to my v.	8:15
to the v. of the Spirit which	105:40	refused to hearken to my v.;	Abr 1: 5
lift up his v. and warn the	106: 2	and hearkened not unto my v.,	1: 7
by the unanimous v. of the same;	107:27	I lifted up my v. unto the Lord	1:15
because you have obeyed my v.	108: 1	his v. was unto me: Abraham,	1:16
and resist no more my v.	108: 2	when they hearken to my v.	2: 6
have heard thy v.,	109:57	the sea, and it obeys my v.;	2: 7
his v. was as the sound of	110: 3	do well to hearken unto thy v.,	2:13
even the v. of Jehova, saying:	110: 3	saw a light, and heard a v.;	JS 2:24
speak unto them with mine own v.,	110: 8	and heard a v. speaking unto him,	2:24
let thy warning v. go forth;	112: 5	who would not hear his v.	2:40
Thy v. shall be a rebuke unto	112: 9	was a v. speaking unto me,	2:49
v. of your brethren, the Twelve,	112:21		
hearken to the v. of my Spirit.	112:22	VOICES	
by mine own v. unto them,	120: 1	lifted up their v. against him,	Mos 17:12
thy v. shall be more terrible	122: 4	did not raise their v. to the Lord	24:12
people will hearken unto my v.,	124:45	lifted their v. in the praises of	24:22
and unto the v. of my servants	124:45	did raise their v. and give thanks	25:10
if they will not hearken to my v.,	124:46	to cast in their v. concerning who	29:39
nor unto the v. of these men	124:46	to cast in their v. concerning	Al 2: 6
lift up his v. long and loud,	124:75	be governed by their own v.—	10:19
everlasting gospel with a loud v.,	124:88	those who had sent in their v.	51: 3
let him not withhold his v.	124:100	or lifting their v. to some being	He 5:36
and he shall lift up his v.	124:104	ye are called to lift up your v.	DC 33: 2
let him lift up his v. as	124:106	lifting up your v. as with the	42: 6
if he will hearken unto my v.,	124:110	as ye shall lift up your v. by	42:16
Robert D. Foster will obey my v.,	124:115	Lift up your v. and spare not.	43:20
A v. of gladness!	128:19	thunders shall utter their v.	43:21
A v. of mercy from heaven;	128:19	utter forth their v. unto all	43:22
a v. of truth out of the earth;	128:19	men shall lift up their v. and	45:32
a v. of gladness for the living	128:19	declare my word with loud v.,	60: 7
A v. of the Lord in the wilderness	128:20	they shall lift up their v. unto	61:31
The v. of Michael	128:20	Lifting up your v. as with	75: 4
The v. of Peter, James, and John	128:20	and lifted their v. on high.	84: 1
the v. of God in the chamber of	128:21	lift up your v. unto this	100: 5
the v. of Michael, the archangel;	128:21	may mingle our v. with those	109:79
the v. of Gabriel, and of Raphael,	128:21		
how glorious is the v. we hear	128:23	VOID	
This a v. declared to me,	130:13	the word would have been v.,	Al 12:23
I heard a v. repeat the following:	130:14	word of God would have been v.,	12:26
and ye shall obey my v.;	132:53	word of God would have been v.,	42: 5
by mine own v.,	132:59	even so it has become v.	DC 54: 4
by the v. of him that sent me,	132:59	I have a conscience v. of offense	135: 4
when the v. of the Lord is unto you:	133: 7	earth was without form, and v.;	Mses 2: 2
the v. of the Lord unto all people:	133: 9	so my words cannot return v.,	4:30
and hear the v. of the Lord;	133:16		
he shall utter his v. out of Zion,	133:21	VOLUME	
v. shall be heard among all people;	133:21	of me in the v. of the book.	DC 99: 5
And it shall be a v. as the	133:22		
as the v. of many waters,	133:22	VOLUMES	
as the v. of a great thunder,	133:22	of them, it would fill up v.	JS 2:61
their prophets shall hear his v.,	133:26		
go forth, saying with a loud v.:	133:38	VOMIT	
And his v. shall be heard:	133:50	like the dog to his v., or like	3Ne 7: 8
hearken not to the v. of the Lord	133:63		
for ye obeyed not my v. when	133:71	VOTE	
and upheld by the v. of the people	134: 3	by v. of the church to which	DC 20:63
mine own v. out of the heavens,	136:37	without the v. of that church;	20:65
Satan cried with a loud v.,	Mses 1:19	that a v. may be called.	20:66
that Satan cried with a loud v.,	1:22	sanction the same by their v.	102:19
and he heard a v., saying:	1:25	The v. to sustain the	OD
as the v. was still speaking,	1:27		
would not hearken unto my v.	4: 4	VOTED	
they heard the v. of the Lord	4:14	who v. in the name and for	DC 102: 5
I heard thy v. in the garden,	4:16	V.: that the high council	102: 6
hearkened unto the v. of thy wife,	4:23	V.: that whenever any vacancy	102: 8
they heard the v. of the Lord	5: 4		
hearkened unto the v. of the Lord.	5:17	VOUCHING	
any more to the v. of the Lord,	5:26	v. and covenanting with God,	Al 24:18
The v. of thy brother's blood	5:35		
Hear my v., ye wives of Lamech,	5:47	VOW	
would not hearken unto his v.,	5:57	and he was under a v.,	DC 132:43
by his own v., and by the gift	5:58	he hath broken his v. and hath	132:43
hearkened unto the v. of God,	6: 1	and hath not broken her v.,	132:44

VOWED
v. to thee, O Mighty God of	DC 109:68
and have v. to no other man,	132:61

VOWS
thy v. shall be offered up in	DC 59:11
henceforth in observing your v.,	108: 3
bonds, obligations, oaths, v.,	132: 7

VULTURES
and the v. of the air,	Mos 12: 2
and also the v. of the air;	Al 2:38

WADE
and w. through much affliction	1Ne 17: 1
w. through their afflictions,	Al 53:15
to w. through much affliction.	He 3:34

WADING
after w. through much affliction	Al 7: 5
w. through much tribulation	8:14

WAGE
w. a war which shall be eternal,	Al 54:20
had caused him to w. a war	55: 1
it was our desire to w. a battle	57: 7

WAGED
ye have w. against my people,	Al 54: 5
thy brother hath w. against them,	54: 5
this war hath been w. to avenge	54:24

WAGES
his w. an everlasting punishment,	Mos 2:33
man receiveth w. of him whom	Al 3:27
must receive his w. of him;	5:42
for his w. he receiveth death,	5:42
receive w. according to the time	11: 1
his w. according to his time—	11: 3
w. according to their employ,	11:20
oppress the hireling in his w.,	3Ne 24: 5
to his works shall his w. be;	Mrm 8:19
they receive their w. of whom	DC 29:45
have a just recompense of w.	124:121
w. be as shall be agreed	124:121
bear his proportion of their w.,	124:122

WAGONS
with all the teams, w., provisions,	DC 136: 5

WAIL
weep, and w. and gnash their teeth;	Mos 16: 2
same have cause to w. and mourn.	Al 5:36

WAILING
there shall be weeping, and w.,	Al 40:13
and the w. of the people who	3Ne 10:10
w. and gnashing of teeth,	DC 19: 5
and w. among the hosts of men;	29:15
are w. and gnashing of teeth.	85: 9
and w., and gnashing of teeth.	101:91
and indignation, w., and anguish,	124:52
and w., and gnashing of teeth.	133:73
and w., and gnashing of teeth;	Mses 1:22

WAIT
not be ashamed that w. for me.	1Ne 21:23
not be ashamed that w. for me.	2Ne 6: 7
the Lord are they who w. for him;	6:13
for they still w. for the coming of	6:13
The isles shall w. upon me,	8: 5
And I will w. upon the Lord,	18:17
laid w. for them in the fields	Mos 20: 8
therefore they laid w. for them.	21:21
only w. to hear the joyful news	Al 13:25
to w. for the coming of Moroni,	52:17
expedient that we should w.,	58: 3
we did w. to receive provisions	58: 3
that we did w. in these difficult	58: 7
I w. for assistance from you;	60:30
lay w. to destroy Helaman also;	He 2: 3
but we will w. till they shall	3Ne 3:21
you must w. yet a little while,	DC 5:17

the lying in w. to destroy thee,	DC 5:32
that lie in w. to destroy thee	5:33
Deceive and lie in w. to catch,	10:25
W. a little longer, until you shall	11:16
should w. for a little season	105: 9
should w. for a little season,	105:13
W. patiently until the	108: 4
whereby they lie in w. to deceive,	123:12

WAITERS
of the king's principal w.,	Fac 3: 5

WAITETH
for him that w. for thee.	DC 133:45

WAITING
fall upon them from their w. places,	Mos 20: 9
w. upon the Spirit of the Lord.	21:34
w. for the tree to bring forth fruit	Al 32:43
w. the great command to reap	DC 38:12
ready and w. to be sent forth	86: 5
W. patiently on the Lord,	98: 2

WAKEFIELD, Joseph
Let my servant W., in whom	DC 50:37
let my servants W. and Solomon	52:35

WAKETH
he w. morning by morning.	2Ne 7: 4
He w. mine ear to hear as the	7: 4

WALK
ye might w. uprightly before God,	1Ne 16: 3
w. in the paths of righteousness.	16: 5
that I may w. in the path of the	2Ne 4:32
w. in hte light of your fire	7:11
and we will w. in his paths;	12: 3
let us w. in the light of the Lord;	12: 5
and w. with stretched forth necks	13:16
not w. in the way of this people,	18:11
and w. in the straight path	33: 9
causing the lame to w., the blind	Mos 3: 5
to w. in the ways of truth and	4:15
ye may w. guiltless before God—	4:26
did w. in the ways of the Lord,	6: 6
should w. through the Red Sea on	7:19
not w. in the ways of his father.	11: 1
but he would w. after the desires of	11: 2
did w. uprightly before God,	18:29
did w. in the ways of the Lord,	29:43
do w. after the holy order of God,	Al 5:54
and w. in his paths, which are	7: 9
he cannot w. in crooked paths;	7:20
ye may w. blameless before him,	7:22
w. after the holy order of God,	7:22
upon his feet, and began to w.;	15:11
did w. in the ways of the Lord,	25:14
may w. therein and be saved.	41: 8
to w. uprightly before God.	45:24
and to w. uprightly before him.	53:21
he did w. uprightly before God;	63: 2
w. after the ways of his father,	He 3:20
did w. in the ways of his father.	3:37
to w. in truth and uprightness	6:34
slow to w. in wisdon's paths!	12: 5
W. after the pride of your own	13:27
w. after the pride of your eyes,	13:27
do w. circumspectly before God,	15: 5
and cause the lame to w.,	4Ne 1: 5
did not w. any more after the	1:12
w. after the commandments	1:12
ye do w. in the pride of your	Mrm 8:36
to w. humbly before the Lord;	Eth 6:17
did w. humbly before the Lord,	6:30
did w. in the steps of his father,	9:23
did w. in the ways of the Lord;	10: 2
strength that they could w.,	15:28
because of your peaceable w.	Mro 7: 4
God doth not w. in crooked	DC 3: 2
w. more uprightly before me,	5:21
yea, to do justly, to w. humbly,	11:12
must w. uprightly before me	18:31
w. in the meekness of my Spirit,	19:23

WALK 1018 WAR

WALK
this shall suffice for thy daily w.,	DC	19:32
by a godly w. and conversation,		20:69
w. in the paths of virtue before		25: 2
to speak, and the lame to w.		35: 9
w. uprightly before the Lord.		68:28
w. in all the commandments		88:133
and shall w. and not faint.		89:20
if ye w. uprightly and		90:24
you shall w. in darkness.		95:12
to them that w. uprightly,		100:15
who w. uprightly before thee,		109: 1
will w. in all the ordinances of		136: 4
and I in you; therefore w. with	Mses	6:34

WALKED
The people that w. in darkness	2Ne	19: 2
Have ye w., keeping yourselves	Al	5:27
w. mournfully before the Lord of	3Ne	24:14
the Lord, and he w. with him,	DC	107:49
w. with God three hundred and		107:49
w. in holiness before the Lord.	Mses	5:26
heard him; for he w. with God.		6:39
and all his people w. with God,		7:69
and he w. with God, as did		8:27

WALKETH
that w. in darkness	2Ne	7:10
every man w. in his own way,	DC	1:16
trees and w. upon the earth;		59:16

WALKING
w. and mincing as they go,	2Ne	13:16
w. with a clear conscience before	Mos	2:27
a man of God, w. in his ways		23:14
w. circumspectly before God,		26:37
w. in all diligence, teaching the		26:38
w. uprightly before God,	Al	1: 1
part w. more circumspectly	He	16:10
w. in holiness before the Lord.	DC	20:69
w. in all holiness before me;		21: 4
w. uprightly before me,		46: 7
w. in obedience to the		89:18
w. in darkness at noon-day.		95: 6
as they were w. in the garden,	Mses	4:14

WALL
and upon every fenced w.;	2Ne	12:15
I will break down the w. thereof,		15: 5
back pass, through the back w.,	Mos	22: 6
was upon the w. of the temple,	Al	10: 2
a strong w. of timbers and earth,		53: 4
a w. which they had caused		53: 5
were within the w. of the city,		55:20
and came upon the top of the w.		62:20
let down from the top of the w.		62:21
into the inner part of the w.		62:21
and come upon the top of the w.,		62:22
did smite him against the w.,	He	1:21
and got upon the w. thereof,		13: 4
cast stones at him upon the w.,		16: 2
at him as he stood upon the w.;		16: 2
cast himself down from the w.,		16: 7
is left to stand by the w.	DC	121:15

WALLOWING
the sow to her w. in the mire.	3Ne	7: 8

WALLS
without the w. of Jerusalem.	1Ne	4: 4
hide themselves without the w.		4: 5
brethren, who were without the w.		4:24
brethren, who were without the w.		4:27
thy w. are continually before me.		21:16
all within the w. of the temple,	Mos	2: 7
to come near the w. of the city,		7:10
and to repair the w. of the city,		9: 8
the w. of the city of Lehi-Nephi,		9: 8
within the w. of the temple,		11:10
without the w. of the city,		21:19
and the w. of the prison were rent	Al	14:27
every soul within the w. thereof,		14:28
and the w. thereof had fallen to		14:29
and also building w. of stone		48: 8

WALL (cont.)
approach near the w. of the city.	Al	50: 5
by casting up w. round about		52: 6
parts which were within the w.		55:20
all within the w. of the city.		62:23
of Moroni were within the w.,		62:24
down over the w. of the city.		62:36
even to the w. of the city.	He	1:21
the w. of the prison did shake		5:27
the w. of the prison trembled		5:31
shook again, and the w. trembled.		5:32
and the w. did tremble again,		5:33
hold upon the w. of the prison;		5:44
come upon the w. of this city,		14:11
he spake upon the w. of the city.		16: 1
watchmen upon the w. thereof	DC	101:53
down the w. of mine enemies;		101:57
trouble, and into bars and w.,		122: 4
and as watchmen upon her w.		124:61

WANDER
they shall w. in the flesh,	1Ne	19:14
even forty days did they w.	Mos	7: 4
their hearts to w. far from thee,	Al	31:17
I w. whithersoever I can for	Mro	1: 3
to w. whithersoever they can for		9:16

WANDERED
they w. off and were lost.	1Ne	8:23
we have w. much in the wilderness,		16:35
we have w. in the wilderness for		17:20
w. many days in the wildnerness,	Mos	7: 4
when they had w. forty days		7: 5

WANDERERS
w., cast out from Jerusalem,	Jac	7:26
being w. in a strange land;	Al	13:23
of us, w. in a strange land.		26:36

WANDERING
from his view, w. in strange roads.	1Ne	8:32
w. about in the wilderness	En	1:20
many days' w. in the wilderness	Mos	9: 4
after w. through much tribulation,		27:28

WANT
did suffer much for the w. of food.	1Ne	16:19
were in sickness, or in much w.;	Mos	27: 5
to perish for the w. of food.	Al	58: 7
wilderness, for the w. of food;	3Ne	4: 3
because of the w. of food,		4:24
for the w. of more time;	DC	127:11
I w. you to remember that		128: 6

WANTED
their labors even now are w.	DC	61:32

WANTON
stretched-forth necks and w. eyes,	2Ne	13:16

WANTS
temporally, according to their w.	Mos	4:26
to their needs and their w.		18:29
unto them according to their w.	Al	35: 9
receive according to his w.	DC	42:33
and his w. and needs.		51: 3
to the w. of this people.		51: 8
for the w. of this people,		51:13
unto himself for his own w.,		51:14
and for the w. of his family,		51:14
for their necessities and their w.,		70: 7
to administer to their w.,		72:11
to his w. and his needs,		82:17
inasmuch as his w. are just—		82:17
to administer to their w.		84:112

WAR
for they shall w. among themselves,	1Ne	22:13
nation which shall w. against thee,		22:14
shall they learn w. any more.	2Ne	12: 4
mighty man, and the man of w.		13: 2
and thy mighty in the w.		13:25
Jerusalem to w. against it,		17: 1
the ground, and weapons of w.	Jar	1: 8

WAR 　　　　　　　　　　　　　　　　　　1019 　　　　　　　　　　　　　　　　　WARN

javelin, and all preparations for w.	Jar	1: 8	concerning these prisoners of w.;	Al	57:16
of serious w. and bloodshed.	Om	1: 3	manage the affairs of this w.		60: 1
I saw much w. and contention		1:10	weapons of w. of every kind,		60: 2
a serious w. and much bloodshed		1:24	had it not been for the w. which		60:16
should be weapons of w. made	Mos	10: 1	power to conduct the w. in that		61:15
again to w. against my people.		10: 1	and their weapons of w.		62:15
they began to prepare for w.,		10: 6	more take up their weapons of w.		62:16
even all their preparations for w.		20: 8	cause of this great and lasting w.		62:35
up to w. against my people?		20:14	of so much w. and bloodshed,		62:35
come up to w. against thy people.		20:15	exceeding great length of the w.		62:41
send his armies against them to w.		29:23	exceeding great length of the w.;		62:41
And also an account of a w.	Al	1:hd	down with a numerous army to w.		63:15
all manner of weapons of w.,		2:12	to w. against the Nephites;	He	4: 3
all manner of weapons of w.		2:14	were all that year preparing for w.		4: 4
them to w. against their brethren,		2:14	lay down their weapons of w.,		5:51
to make w. with the Nephites.		2:15	this w. did last all that year;		11: 2
not slain by the weapons of w.,		3: 1	they commenced a w. with		11:24
was a cry of w. heard throughout		16: 1	have buried their weapons of w.,		15: 9
did not come again to w. against		16:12	destruction because of this w.,	3Ne	2:13
yea, all their weapons of w.;		23:13	the w. between the robbers and		2:17
to make preparations for w.		24: 4	weapons of w. of every kind,		3:26
make any preparations for w.;		24: 6	not go to w. one with another;		7:14
or they buried the weapons of w.,		24:19	there began to be a w. between	Mrm	1: 8
made preparations for w.,		24:20	this w. was between the Nephites,		1: 8
threw down their weapons of w.,		24:25	the w. began to be among them		1:10
also bury their weapons of w.,		25:14	there began to be a w. again		2: 1
have buried their weapons of w.		26:32	all manner of weapons of w.		6: 9
Lamanites who had gone to w.		27: 1	lay down your weapons of w.,		7: 4
to make preparations for w.		35:11	are at w. one with another;		8: 8
thus commenced a w. betwixt the		35:13	knoweth the end of the w.		8: 8
they made preparations for w.;		43: 4	a w. between the sons of Akish	Eth	9:12
all manner of weapons of w.		43:18	to be w. again in the land,		10: 8
ye deliver up your weapons of w.		44: 6	the w. became exceeding sore,		10: 9
come not again to w. against us.		44: 6	w. against the king of the land,		10:15
here are our weapons of w.;		44: 8	all manner of weapons of w.		10:27
but take our weapons of w.		44: 8	exceeding great w. in all the land.		11: 4
sword and the weapons of w.,		44:10	be a great w. among the people,		13:15
return again against us to w.		44:11	in all the arts of w. and all the		13:16
deliver up your weapons of w.		44:14	there began to be a w. upon all		13:25
threw down their weapons of w.		44:15	and lasting had been the w.,		14:21
never would come to w. again		44:19	so swift and speedy was the w.		14:22
And he took the weapons of w.		44:20	armed with weapons of w.,		15:15
to flee, or to prepare for w.,		48:15	clothed after the manner of w.		15:15
manner of preparation for w.		49: 9	not be at w. one with another.	DC	45:69
stop making preparations for w.,		50: 1	he maketh w. with the saints of		76:29
preparing for w. with all diligence;		51: 9	those with whom he made w.		76:30
they did lift their weapons of w.		51:18	w. will be poured out upon all		87: 2
regulations to prepare for w.		51:22	w. shall be poured out upon all		87: 3
strength and in their skill of w.,		51:31	and disciplined for w.		87: 4
as if making preparations for w.;		52: 6	renounce w. and proclaim peace,		98:16
he kept thus preparing for w.		52: 7	proclaim w. against them,		98:34
captains held a council of w.—		52:19	In the midst of this w. of words	JS	2:10
not yield up their weapons of w.		52:25			
had given up their weapons of w.		52:32	**WARD**		
delivered up their weapons of w.;		52:36	appointed in each w. of the city,	DC	128: 3
bring forth your weapons of w.		52:37			
threw down their weapons of w.		52:38	**WARFARE**		
their weapons of w. were taken		52:39	having warred a good w.,	Al	1: 1
his men in preparing for w.,		53: 7	as in the tribulations of our w.;		56: 2
about to take their weapons of w.,		53:14	concerning our w. in this part		56: 2
not take their weapons of w. to		53:16			
took their weapons of w. to		53:18	**WARM**		
for they took their weapons of w.,		53:19	there began to be a w. contention	Al	50:26
concerning this w. which ye		54: 5	arose a w. dispute concerning		51: 4
and shall be at w. no more.		54:18	w. hearts and friendly hands.	DC	121: 9
my food for my men of w.;		54:20			
wage a w. which shall be eternal,		54:20	**WARMLY**		
this w. hath been waged to avenge		54:24	contend w. with their adversaries,	Al	1:22
had caused him to wage a w.		55: 1			
his men with weapons of w.;		55:16	**WARN**		
weapons of w. unto the prisoners,		55:16	the Lord did w. me, that I,	2Ne	5: 5
able to use a weapon of w.,		55:17	w. them to flee, or to prepare	Al	48:15
demanded their weapons of w.,		55:23	They are, however, to w.,	DC	20:59
He took them prisoners of w.,		55:24	to w. sinners to repentance,		63:57
have taken their weapons of w.,		56: 5	w. the people of those cities		84:114
not take up their weapons of w.		56: 6	out to testify and w. the people,		88:81
take up their weapons of w. in		56: 7	been warned to w. his neighbor.		88:81
deliver up their weapons of w.		56:54	that ye w. him in my name,		98:28
themselves as prisoners of w.		56:54	his voice and w. the people,		106: 2
themselves up as prisoners of w.		56:56	w. them to save themselves from		109:41
deliver up those prisoners of w.		57: 1	w. the inhabitants of the earth		124:106
themselves prisoners of w.		57:14	w. the righteous to save themselves		134:12

WARNED 1020 WAST

WARNED
he being w. of the Lord that he	Om	1:12
they being w. of their iniquities	Mos	16:12
having been w. of the Lord		23: 1
the Lord w. Omer in a dream	Eth	9: 3
they have w. in their traveling	DC	88:71
every man who hath been w.		88:81
in the last days, I have w. you,		89: 4

WARNING
the Lord had been in w. us	2Ne	1: 3
w. them against fornication	Jac	3:12
the voice of w. shall be unto	DC	1: 4
your preaching be the w. voice,		38:41
and lift a w. voice unto the		63:37
For this is a day of w.,		63:58
ponder the w. in their hearts		88:71
let thy w. voice go forth;		112: 5

WARNINGS
were those who believed in the w.	2Ne	5: 6

WARNS
The Lord w. Lehi to depart	1Ne	1:hd
The Lord w. Nephi to depart	2Ne	1:hd

WARRED
having w. a good warfare,	Al	1: 1

WARREN: see also COWDERY, Warren A.
servant W. bowed to my scepter,	DC	106: 6
blessed is my servant W.,		106: 7

WARRIOR
For every battle of the w.	2Ne	19: 5

WARRIORS
his men, for they were great w.;	Al	51:31
mine house, which are my w.,	DC	101:55
of my house, even my w.,		105:16

WARS
w. and contentions of my people;	1Ne	9: 4
w. and contentions of my people.		9: 4
w., and rumors of wars,		12: 2
rumors of w., and great slaughters		12: 2
the manner of w. and contentions		12: 3
w. and rumors of wars among them		12:21
rumors of w. among them;		12:21
and in w. and rumors of wars		12:21
in wars and rumors of w. I saw		12:21
there were w. and rumors of wars		14:15
rumors of w. among all the		14:15
to be w. and rumors of wars		14:16
rumors of w. among all the		14:16
account of the w. and contentions		19: 4
had already had w. and contentions	2Ne	5:34
But, behold, they shall have w.		25:12
shall have wars, and rumors of w.;		25:12
shall be great w. and contentions		26: 2
their w., and their contentions,	Jac	3:13
delighted in w. and bloodshed,		7:24
caused w. and contentions;		7:26
preaching and prophesying of w.,	En	1:23
saw w. between the Nephites and		1:24
after the manner of w.,	Jar	1:13
records of our w. are engraven,		1:14
many and serious contentions,	Om	1:17
w. and contentions in the land.	Mos	9:13
would cause w. and contentions		29: 7
should be no w. nor contentions,		29:14
and all the w., and contentions,		29:36
the w. and contentions among	Al	1:hd
all these w. and contentions were		3:25
w. in the land of Zarahemla;		4: 1
been no w. nor contentions for		16: 1
of the w. and contentions among		28: 9
w. between the Nephites and		28: 9
account shall be given of their w.		35:13
for the w., and the bloodsheds,		35:15
return to an account of the w.		43: 3
and the government of their w.		43:17
and their w. and dissensions,		45:hd
shall they see w. and pestilences,		45:11
because of their w. with the	Al	45:21
free from w. and contentions		48:20
their w. never did cease for the		48:22
brought upon them their w.		50:21
was thus breaking down the w.		51:22
they had had w. and bloodsheds,		62:39
for because of so many w. and		62:44
Their w. and contentions,	He	1:hd
and their w. and contentions,		3:14
and disturbances, and w., and		3:17
the w. and contentions began to		3:22
anger, to w. nor to bloodshed;		6:17
were w. throughout all the land		11: 1
not declare w. against them;		12: 2
began to be w. and contentions	3Ne	2:11
were no w. as yet among them;		7: 5
shall also be heard of w.,	Mrm	8:30
heard of wars, rumors of w.		8:30
no more w. in the days of Shule;	Eth	7:27
there began to be w. and		11: 7
and the w. ceased not;		13:22
their w. are exceedingly fierce	Mro	1: 2
hear of w. in far countries,	DC	38:29
be great w. in far countries,		38:29
that day shall be heard of w.	DC	45:26
of wars and rumors of w.,		45:26
Ye hear of w. in foreign lands;		45:63
hear of w. in your own lands.		45:63
decreed w. upon the face of		63:33
concerning the w. that will		87: 1
the w. and the perplexities of		88:79
thenceforth came w. and	Mses	6:15
w. and bloodshed among them;		7:16
and you also shall hear of w.,	JS	1:23
hear of wars, and rumors of w.;		1:23
And they shall hear of w.		1:28
hear of wars, and rumors of w.		1:28

WARSAW
unto the inhabitants of W.,	DC	124:88

WAS: see in the APPENDIX.

WASH
anoint thy head, and w. thy face;	3Ne	13:17
baptized, and w. away your sins,	DC	39:10
w. thy feet, as a testimony		60:15
w. them, and thou shalt see.	Mses	6:35

WASHED
shall have w. away the filth	2Ne	14: 4
except his garments are w. white;	Al	5:21
that ye may be w. from your sins,		7:14
their garments were w. white		13:11
w. bright through the blood of		24:13
w. their garments in my blood,	3Ne	27:19
w. in the blood of the Lamb;	Eth	13:11
be w. and cleansed from all	DC	76:52

WASHING
ordinance of the w. of feet,	DC	88:139
ordinance of the w. of feet		88:139
the ordinance of w. feet is to		88:140
but for the w. of your bodies.		89: 7

WASHINGS
how shall your w. be acceptable	DC	124:37
your anointings, and your w.,		124:39

WAST
and w. called a transgressor	1Ne	20: 8
thou w. born in the wilderness of	2Ne	3: 1
though thou w. angry with me		22: 1
wherein thou w. made to serve.		24: 3
art holy, and that thou w. a spirit,	Al	31:15
thou w. merciful when I prayed		33: 4
thou w. merciful unto me when I		33: 5
and w. angry with mine enemies,		33:10
I know that thou w. in bonds;		38: 4
I also know that thou w. stoned		38: 4
wherewith thou w. entrusted.		39: 4
thou w. refused, saith thy God.	3Ne	22: 6
thou w. chosen to do the work	DC	3: 9
thou w. called and chosen to		24: 1

WAST 1021 WATER

WAST (cont.)

Behold thou w. sent forth,	DC	35: 4
in whom thou w. well pleased;		45: 4
Who told thee thou w. naked?	Mses	4:17
for out of it w. thou taken:		4:25
for dust thou w., and unto dust		4:25
thou w. also before the world.		5:24
thou w. chosen before thou	Abr	3:23
chosen before thou w. born.		3:23

WASTE

I was in a dark and dreary w.	1Ne	8: 7
and they that made thee w. shall		21:17
For thy w. and thy desolate places,		21:19
and my flesh w. away,	2Ne	4:26
he will comfort all her w. places;		8: 3
our flesh must w. away and die;		9: 4
And I will lay it w.;		15: 6
the w. places of the fat ones		15:17
ye w. places of Jerusalem;	Mos	12:23
ye w. places of Jerusalem;		15:30
to build up their w. places,	He	11:20
and did lay w. so many cities,	3Ne	2:11
ye w. places of Jerusalem;		16:19
ye w. places of Jerusalem;		20:34
build up the w. places of Zion—	DC	101:18
and establish her w. places,		101:75
build up the w. places of Zion.		103:11
and lay w. mine enemies;		105:15
w. and wear out our lives		123:13

WASTED

Until the cities be w. without	2Ne	16:11
the garners, that they are not w.	Al	26: 5
be utterly w. at his coming.	DC	2: 3
that they may be w. away,		109:52
whole earth would be utterly w.	JS	2:39

WASTER

have created the w. to destroy.	3Ne	22:16

WASTETH

that w. the days of his probation,	2Ne	9:27
that w. flesh and hath no need.	DC	49:21

WATCH

and all that w. for iniquity	2Ne	27:31
w. the tree, and nourish it,	Jac	5:12
that if ye do not w. yourselves,	Mos	4:30
sent his servants to w. them.		18:32
should w. the land round about,		21:20
they did w. over their people,		23:18
put guards over them to w. them,		24:11
to w. the camp of the Amlicites	Al	2:22
to w. the camp of the Amlicites.		2:22
sheep doth not w. over them,		5:59
to preside and w. over the church.		6: 1
and w. and pray continually,		13:28
to w. the flocks of Lamoni,		17:25
he may w. over you in your sleep;		37:37
wilderness to w. their camp;		43:23
to w. the movements of the		56:22
w. the camp of the Lamanites.		57:30
Coriantumr did cut down the w.	He	1:20
they did w. steadfastly for that	3Ne	1: 8
guards round about to w. them,		3:14
ye must w. and pray always,		18:15
ye must w. and pray always		18:18
baptize, and w. over the church;	DC	20:42
to w. over the church always,		20:53
Wherefore, w. over him that		35:19
be your king and w. over you.		38:21
ordain to w. over the church		46:27
W., therefore, that ye may be		50:46
the elders w. over the churches,		52:39
W., for the adversary spreadeth		82: 5
to w. over the church,		84:111
are found upon the w.-tower,		101:12
W. therefore, for ye know		133:11
w., therefore, for you know not	JS	1:46
in what w. the thief would come,		1:47

WATCHED

they laid and w. them;	Mos	20: 4
she w. over the bed of her husband,	Al	19:11
they that have w. for iniquity	DC	45:50
tower, and w. for my vineyard,		101:53
the Gods w. those things which	Abr	4:18
he would have w., and would	JS	1:47

WATCHES

and he that w. not for me	DC	45:44

WATCHFUL

be w. unto prayer continually,	Al	34:39
continually w. unto prayer,	Mro	6: 4
that ye shall be w. and careful,	DC	42:76
and be w. and be sober,		61:38

WATCHING

w. and praying continually,	Al	15:17

WATCHMAN

to be a w. upon the tower,	DC	101:45
set a w. upon the tower,		101:53
the w. upon the tower would		101:54

WATCHMEN

Thy w. shall lift up the voice;	Mos	12:22
thy w. shall lift up their voice;		15:29
Thy w. shall lift up the voice;	3Ne	16:18
their w. lift up their voice,		20:32
And set w. round about	DC	101:45
a hedge round about, and set w.		101:46
set w. upon the walls thereof—		101:53
their tower, and scatter their w.		101:57
enemies, scattered their w.;		105:16
and scattering their w.		105:30
and as w. upon her walls.		124:61

WATCH-TOWER: see WATCH and TOWER.

WATER

by the side of a river of w.	1Ne	2: 6
I beheld a river of w.;		8:13
the other side of the river of w.,		8:26
said he should baptize with w.;		10: 9
baptize the Messiah with w.		10: 9
baptized the Messiah with w.,		10:10
the fountain of filthy w.		12:16
What meaneth the river of w.		15:26
the w. which my father saw		15:27
not the filthiness of the w.		15:27
the rock, and there came forth w.,		17:29
say unto this w., be thou earth,		17:50
even by the springs of w. shall		21:10
and the whole stay of w.—	2Ne	13: 1
w. out of the wells of salvation.		22: 3
for the bittern, and pools of w.;		24:23
and the w. should come forth;		25:20
have need to be baptized by w.		31: 5
to be baptized, yea, even by w.!		31: 5
in being baptized by w.?		31: 6
after he was baptized with w.		31: 8
and your Savior down into the w.,		31:13
by the baptism of w.,		31:14
is repentance and baptism by w.;		31:17
mine eyes w. my pillow by night,		33: 3
are in the w. under the earth.	Mos	13:12
in Mormon a fountain of pure w.,		18: 5
being near the w. a thicket of		18: 5
went and stood forth in the w.,		18:12
and Helam were buried in the w.;		18:14
came forth out of the w. rejoicing,		18:14
forth a second time into the w.,		18:15
not bury himself again in the w.		18:15
pleasant land, a land of pure w.		23: 4
into the w. and did baptize;		25:18
and w. that they might thirst;	Al	14:22
their flocks to the place of w.,		17:26
which was called the w. of Sebus,		17:26
hither, that they may have w.—		17:26
their flocks to this place of w.,		17:27
had been with their flocks to w.,		17:27
them back unto the place of w.,		17:31
together again to the place of w.		17:32
their flocks at the place of w.;		18: 6
were nearly surrounded by w.,		22:32

WATER   1022   WATERS

covered with large bodies of w.,	Al	50:29
they came to large bodies of w.,	He	3: 4
who were not baptized with w.	3Ne	7:24
should be baptized with w.,		7:25
go down and stand in the w.,		11:23
shall ye immerse them in the w.,		11:26
come forth again out of the w.		11:26
they may baptize you with w.;		12: 1
that ye are baptized with w.,		12: 1
that Nephi went down into the w.		19:11
And he came up out of the w.		19:12
and had come up out of the w.,		19:13
are baptized, first with w.,	Mrm	7:10
and they were light upon the w.,	Eth	2:16
lightness of a fowl upon the w.		2:16
would hold w. like unto a dish;		2:17
that the w. come in upon thee,		2:20
cross this great w. in darkness?		2:22
they might subsist upon the w.,		6: 4
no w. that could hurt them,		6: 7
whether it was above the w. or		6:10
above the water or under the w.		6:10
and four days upon the w.		6:11
cannot bring forth good w.;	Mro	7:11
fountain bring forth bitter w.;		7:11
no w., save a little, do they		9: 8
even of w. and of the Spirit—	DC	5:16
shall go down into the w. with		20:73
immerse him or her in the w.,		20:74
come forth again out of the w.		20:74
yea, be baptized even by w.,		33:11
baptize by w. unto repentance,		35: 5
that thou shalt baptize by w.,		35: 6
repentance and baptism by w.		39: 6
Go forth baptizing with w.		39:20
many as ye shall baptize with w.,		39:23
go forth baptizing with w.,		42: 7
congregation, baptizing by w.,		52:10
hast been baptized by w.,		55: 1
whether they go by w. or		61:22
be in him a well of living w.,		63:23
buried in the w. in his name,		76:51
and is baptized by w. for the		84:64
not baptized in w. in my name,		84:74
cleanse your feet even with w.,		84:92
even with water, pure w.,		84:92
deep w. is what I am wont to		127: 2
The ordinance of baptism by w.,		128:12
to be immersed in the w. and		128:12
and come forth out of the w.		128:12
come forth pools of living w.;		133:29
moved upon the face of the w.;	Mses	2: 2
firmament in the midst of the w.,		2: 6
in the w., neither in the air;		3: 5
go out of Eden to w. the garden;		3:10
and be baptized even in w.,		6:52
repent and be baptized in w.?		6:53
were born into the world by w.,		6:59
of w., and of the Spirit,		6:59
the w. ye keep the commandment;		6:60
was carried down into the w.,		6:64
and was laid under the w.,		6:64
was brought forth out of the w.		6:64
the rivers of w. were turned out of		7:13
the land it was under w.,	Abr	1:24
out of Eden to w. the garden,		5:10
our coming up out of the w.	JS	2:73

WATERED
returned and they w. their flocks	Al	17:39
w. the whole face of the ground.	Mses	3: 6
w. the whole face of the ground.	Abr	5: 6

WATERING
were w. and feeding their flocks,	Mos	9:14
the time of the w. of their flocks,	Al	18: 9

WATER'S
went down unto the w. edge,	3Ne	19:10
of the hands by the w. side.	DC	52:10

WATERS
They come to the large w.	1Ne	1:hd
They cross the large w.		1:hd
the w. of the river emptied		2: 9
he truly spake unto the w.		4: 2
in the w. of the Red Sea.		4: 2
to the fountain of living w.,		11:25
which w. are a representation		11:25
I looked and beheld many w.;		13:10
of my brethren by the many w.;		13:12
he went forth upon the many w.,		13:12
of captivity, upon the many w.		13:13
gathered together upon the w.,		13:17
even across the many w.		13:29
and she sat upon many w.;		14:11
whore who sat upon many w.;		14:12
being interpreted, is many w.		17: 5
carry thy people across these w.		17: 8
that he can cross these great w.		17:17
w. of the Red Sea were divided		17:26
we were driven back upon the w.		18:13
had been driven back upon the w		18:15
come forth out of the w. of Judah,		20: 1
or out of the w. of baptism,		20: 1
the w. to flow out of the rock		20:21
rock also and the w. gushed out.		20:21
their rebellions upon the w.,	2Ne	1: 2
upon the w. of the great deep.		4:20
because the w. are dried up,		7: 2
the w. of the great deep;		8:10
that thirsteth, come ye to the w.;		9:50
people refuseth the w. of Shiloah		18: 6
upon them the w. of the river,		18: 7
as the w. cover the sea.		21: 9
as the w. cover the sea.		30:15
of the Lord across the great w.,	Om	1:16
in a land among many w.,	Mos	8: 8
also wroth with him upon the w.		10:14
here are the w. of Mormon		18: 8
baptized in the w. of Mormon,		18:16
yea, by the w. of Mormon,		18:30
that was near the w. of Mormon;		18:30
of Mormon, the w. of Mormon,		18:30
brethren in the w. of Mormon,		25:18
baptized in the w. of Mormon.		26:15
been slain into the w. of Sidon,	Al	2:34
were cast into the w. of Sidon;		3: 3
were baptized in the w. of Sidon		4: 4
brethren in the w. of Mormon.		5: 3
bread and the w. of life freely;		5:34
by going into the w. of baptism.		7:15
who stood by the w. of Sebus;		17:34
to stand by the w. of Sebus to		18: 7
scattered at the w. of Sebus.		19:20
who had stood at the w. of Sebus		19:21
their brethren at the w. of Sebus,		19:21
partake of the w. of life freely;		42:27
by Lehi into the w. of Sidon,		43:40
they crossed the w. of Sidon.		43:40
fled even to the w. of Sidon.		43:50
their dead into the w. of Sidon,		44:22
upon the w. of the Red Sea	He	8:11
the w. closed upon the armies of		8:11
unto the w. of the great deep—		12:16
w. have I caused to come up in	3Ne	9: 7
this, the w. of Noah unto me,		22: 9
that the w. of Noah should		22: 9
and w. came up in the stead	4Ne	1: 9
Zarahemla, by the w. of Sidon.	Mrm	1:10
and it was in a land of many w.,		6: 4
with them the fish of the w.	Eth	2: 2
which they did cross many w.,		2: 6
cross the great w. in darkness.		6: 3
blow upon the face of the w.,		6: 5
encompassed about by many w.		6: 7
forth again upon the top of the w.		6: 7
while they were upon the w.;		6: 8
after the w. had receded from		13: 2
to the w. of Ripliancum,		15: 8
when they came to these w.		15: 8

WATERS 1023 WAY

partake of the w. of life freely.	DC 10:66	did w. stronger and stronger in	He	3:35
be moving swiftly upon the w.,	61: 3	and w. exceedingly strong in		6:12
are many dangers upon the w.,	61: 4	did still increase and w. strong,		11:32
many destructions upon the w.;	61: 5	began to w. strong in iniquity.		11:36
and especially upon these w.	61: 5	did w. stronger and stronger in		11:37
you shall not perish by the w.	61: 6	and began to w. strong in years,	3Ne	1:29
the beginning blessed the w.;	61:14	to w. strong in wickedness and		2: 3
servant John, I cursed the w.	61:14	to prosper and to w. great;		6: 4
flesh shall be safe upon the w.	61:15	people of Nephi did w. strong,	4Ne	1:10
to the land of Zion upon the w.,	61:16	part of the people did w. strong,		1:40
brethren concerning these w.,	61:18	they did w. strong in the land.	Eth	6:18
come not again upon the w.,	61:23	prosper exceedingly and w. great.		7:19
they shall not come upon the w.	61:23	the love of men shall w. cold,	DC	45:27
given power to command the w.,	61:27	shall multiply and w. strong,		45:58
upon the land or upon the w.,	61:28	shall thy confidence w. strong		121:45
who sitteth upon many w.,	88:94	famine to w. sore in the land	Abr	2: 1
sound of the rushing of great w.,	110: 3	the love of many shall w. cold;	JS	1:10
depart to go over the great w.,	118: 4	the love of many shall w. cold;		1:30
How long can rolling w. remain	121:33			
voice as the voice of many w.,	133:22	**WAXED**		
and the fountains of w.—	133:39	Lord which was in him, he w. old.	2Ne	4:12
which causeth the w. to boil.	133:41	have I w. bold in mighty prayer		4:24
be made stronger than many w.;	Mses 1:25	and it grew, and w. old,	Jac	5: 3
divide the w. from the waters;	2: 6	had w. strong in the land.	Jar	1: 5
divide the waters from the w.;	2: 6	he w. old, and he saw that he must	Mos	1: 9
firmament and divided the w.,	2: 7	and w. great in the land.		2: 2
great w. under the firmament	2: 7	they having w. strong in battle,	Al	9:22
from the w. which were above the	2: 7	people had w. strong in iniquity		13:17
Let the w. under the heaven be	2: 9	w. strong in the knowledge of		17: 2
the gathering together of the w.,	2:10	Shule w. strong, and became	Eth	7: 8
the w. bring forth abundantly	2:20	for their hearts have w. hard,	Mses	6:27
the w. brought forth abundantly,	2:21			
and fill the w. in the sea;	2:22	**WAXETH**		
brooding upon the face of the w.	Abr 4: 2	which w. old and shall perish	DC	1:16
an expanse in the midst of the w.,	4: 6			
and it shall divide the w. from the	4: 6	**WAY**		
divide the waters from the w.	4: 6	Written by w. of commandment,	T Pg	
it divided the w. which were under	4: 7	in due time by w. of the Gentile—	T Pg	
from the w. which were above	4: 7	he shall prepare a w. for they	1Ne	3: 7
Let the w. under the heaven be	4: 9	the head thereof a little way off;		8:14
the gathering together of the w.,	4:10	in the path did lose their w.,		8:23
waters, pronounced they, great w.;	4:10	they did press their w. forward		8:30
prepare the w. to bring forth	4:20	other multitudes feeling their w.		8:31
prepared the w. that they might	4:21	he prepareth a w. to accomplish		9: 6
w. were to bring forth abundantly	4:21	to prepare the w. of the Lord—		10: 7
and fill the w. in the seas	4:22	Prepare ye the w. of the Lord,		10: 8
the waters in the seas or great w.;	4:22	the w. is prepared for all men		10:18
		should prepare the w. before him.		11:27
WATERY		commence, in preparing the w.		14:17
with sorrow into a w. grave.	1Ne 18:18	shall come by w. of the Gentiles,		15:17
		and the one pointed the w.		16:10
WAVES		slaying food by the w., with our		16:15
righteousness as the w. of the sea.	1Ne 20:18	I will prepare the w. before you,		17:13
Lord thy God, whose w. roared;	2Ne 8:15	a w. that they might be healed;		17:41
mountains, or the w. of the sea.	Jac 4: 6	of the simpleness of the w.,		17:41
is tossed about upon the w.,	Mrm 5:18	plates by w. of commandment,		19: 3
the mountain w. shall dash	Eth 2:24	he shall make his w. prosperous.		20:15
you against the w. of the sea,	2:25	by the w. thou shouldst go,		20:17
tossed upon the w. of the sea	6: 5	I will make all my mountains a w.,		21:11
mountain w. which broke upon	6: 6	surely prepare a w. for his people,		22:20
the voice of the w. of the sea	DC 88:90	and I go the w. of all the earth.	2Ne	1:14
with the wind and the w.	123:16	the w. is prepared from the fall		2: 4
		brought up in the w. ye should go		4: 5
WAVING		should I give w. to temptations,		4:27
w. the rent part of his garment	Al 46:19	thou make a w. for mine escape		4:33
		place a stumbling block in my w.—		4:33
WAX		wouldst clear my w. before me,		4:33
they shall w. old as a garment,	2Ne 7: 9	and hedge not up my w.,		4:33
earth shall w. old like a garment;	8: 6	a w. for the ransomed to pass		8:10
neither shall his face now w. pale.	27:33	who prepareth a w. for our escape		9:10
people begin to w. in iniquity;	Jac 2:23	because of the w. of deliverance		9:11
should w. strong in the land,	Mos 9:11	the w. for man is narrow,		9:41
they might w. strong in the Spirit,	18:26	and there is none other w. save		9:41
one with another and w. great,	24: 7	choose the w. of everlasting death		10:23
w. strong in love towards Mosiah;	29:40	or the w. of eternal life.		10:23
of the church began to w. proud,	Al 4: 6	and destroy the w. of thy paths.		13:12
w. more gross in their iniquities.	8:28	not walk in the w. of this people,		18:11
should w. strong in wickedness	21: 3	afflict by the w. of the Red Sea		19: 1
of the people began to w. hard,	35:15	to teach any man the right w.;		25:28
and w. strong in your iniquities	60:31	the right w. is to believe in Christ		25:28
and to w. exceeding strong again	62:48	the right w. is to believe in Christ,		25:29
they did w. strong and prosper	62:51	they have all gone out of the w.;		28:11

WAY 1024 WAY

pervert the right w. of the Lord,	2 Ne 28:15
that if ye entered in by the w.	31:18
this is the w.; and there is none	31:21
and there is none other w. nor	31:21
after ye have entered in by the w.	32: 1
that if ye will enter in by the w.,	32: 5
go thy w.; watch the tree,	Jac 5:12
of the vineyard went his w.,	5:14
that we may prepare the w.,	5:61
ye prepare the w. for them,	5:64
in the w. which is narrow,	6:11
they pervert the right w. of God,	7: 7
of Moses which is the right w.;	7: 7
soon go the w. of all the earth;	Mos 1: 9
nor any other w. nor means	3:17
turned every one to his own w.;	14: 6
there was no w. that they could	21: 5
they could find no w. to deliver	22: 2
if they would show them the w.	23:36
after Alma had shown them the w.	23:37
he led their w. in the wilderness.	24:20
say unto thee, Alma, go thy w.,	27:16
perverting the w. of the Lord,	29: 7
gone the w. of all the earth,	Al 1: 1
no w. that he might reclaim them	4:19
I speak by w. of command	5:62
I speak by w. of invitation,	5:62
in the w. of his righteousness.	7: 4
and prepare the w. of the Lord,	7: 9
and the w. that I know that ye	7:17
he entered the city by another w.,	8:18
by the w. which is on the south of	8:18
prepare ye the w. of the Lord,	9:28
therefore they went their w.	19:32
Lord has called him another w.;	22: 4
holy angel to stop us by the w.	36: 6
point the w. they should go,	37:40
because of the easiness of the w.;	37:46
The w. is prepared, and if we will	37:46
there is no other w. or means	38: 9
therefore, the w. is prepared that	41: 8
sword which turned every w.,	42: 2
And now, my son, go thy w.,	42:31
if ye will go your w. and come	44: 6
giving w. to indolence, and all	47:36
by any other w. save by the	49:18
to enter the fort by any other w.,	49:19
by stratagem or some other w.	52:10
cut his w. through to the city	52:34
not give w. before the Lamanites.	52:34
to give w. before the Lamanites.	56:51
to give w. before the Lamanites,	57:20
no w. that we could lead them	58: 1
back the same w. which they	58:24
march forward by another w.	58:26
by the w. of condemnation;	60: 2
had gone the w. of all the earth.	62:37
and gone the w. of all the earth;	He 1: 2
and cut his w. through with the	1:23
could not retreat either w.,	1:31
out of the land, by a secret w.,	2:11
much by the w. of shipping.	3:10
there is no other w. nor means	5: 9
out of the w. of righteousness,	6:31
shall go on in this your w. of sin?	9:21
Nephi went his w. towards his	10: 2
and prepare the w. of the Lord.	14: 9
no w. that they could subsist save	3 Ne 4: 5
fall into their hands by the w.;	4:13
cut of their retreat,	4:24
armies in the w. of their retreat.	4:24
Go thy w. unto thy brother,	12:24
while thou art in the w. with him,	12:25
is the gate, and broad is the w.,	14:13
the gate, and narrow is the w.,	14:14
and the multitude gave w. till	17:12
and went a little w. off from	19:19
went a little w. off and bowed	19:27
he went again a little w. off	19:31
to prepare the w. whereby they	21:27
in preparing the w. whereby	21:28
shall prepare the w. before me,	24: 1
and narrow is the w. that leads	27:33
and broad the w. which leads	3 Ne 27:33
and depart from the right w.,	Mrm 9:20
must prepare the w. of the Lord	Eth 9:28
which did perish by the w.;	9:32
they should hedge up the w.	9:33
of them which fell by the w.,	9:34
prepared a w. that thereby others	12: 8
prepared a more excellent w.;	12:11
a w. for their everlasting	14:25
to keep them in the right w.,	Mro 6: 4
and the w. to judge is as plain,	7:15
show unto you the w. to judge;	7:16
the w. whereby ye may lay hold	7:21
to prepare the w. among the	7:31
the Lord God prepareth the w.	7:32
old women do faint by the w.	9:16
a few words by w. of exhortation	10: 2
every man walketh in his own w.,	DC 1:16
by the w. of commandment;	18: 9
by w. of commandment to	20:37
go thy w. and sin no more.	24: 2
by the w. of commandment unto	28: 4
write by w. of commandment,	28: 5
not by w. of commandment.	28: 8
Go your w. whithersoever I	31:11
prepare ye the w. of the Lord,	33:10
preparing the w. of the Lord	34: 6
to prepare the w. before me,	35: 4
preparing the w. before my face	39:20
south, by letter or some other w.	44: 1
to prepare the w. before me.	45: 9
Spirit of truth or some other w.?	50:17
if it be by some other w. it is	50:18
Spirit of truth or some other w.?	50:19
If it be some other w. it is not	50:20
same place by the w. of Detroit.	52: 8
preaching the word by the w.,	52: 9
thus let them preach by the w.	52:10
preaching the word by the w.	52:22
preaching the word by the w.	52:23
and preach by the w. unto this	52:25
journey, and preach by the w.,	52:26
same land, and preach by the w.	52:27
by w. of baptism in the name	55: 2
Let them preach by the w.,	58:47
except he bear record by the w.,	58:59
preaching the gospel by the w.,	58:63
return it by the w. of the agent;	60:11
a w. for the journeying and	61:24
and behold, this is the w.	61:24
pitching their tents by the w.	61:25
the w. for the saints of the camp	61:29
not by the w. of commandment,	63:22
Prepare ye the w. of the Lord,	65: 1
Prepare ye the w. of the Lord,	65: 3
by the w. of commandment	70: 1
the w. for the commandments	71: 4
the preparing of the w. before	77:12
the w. whither he shall go;	79: 2
all have gone out of the w.	82: 6
straight the w. of the Lord	84:28
and go on your w. rejoicing.	84:105
and to prepare the w.,	84:107
this is the w. that mine	84:108
own time, and in his own w.,	88:68
a w. for their deliverance in	95: 1
in the secret places by the w.	99: 4
proper w. for their salvation—	101:63
this w. they may establish Zion.	101:74
needs be done in mine own w.;	104:16
this is the w. that I, the Lord,	104:16
in this w. you may find favor	105:26
may give w. before the truth,	109:56
combine to hedge up the w.;	122: 7
Therefore, hold on thy w.,	122: 9
shall send them to prepare a w.	124:139
is the only w. he can appear—	129: 6
narrow the w. that leadeth unto	132:22
wide the w. that leadeth to the	132:25
I make a w. for your escape,	132:50
Prepare ye the w. of the Lord,	133:17
Go thy w. and do as I have	136:17
which turned every w. to keep	Mses 4:31

WAY / WEAPON

WAY
to keep the w. of the tree of life.	Mses	4:31
the w. toward the Garden		5: 4
corrupted its w. upon the earth.		8:29
came forth in the w. to the land	Abr	2:15
in tents as we came on our w.;		2:15
from Haran by the w. of Jershon,		2:16
the w. it reads in our Bibles.	JS	2:36

WAYNE
Ontario (now W.) county,	JS	2: 3
Palmyra township, W. county,		2:61

WAYS
up in the w. of remembrance.	1Ne	2:24
pervert the right w. of the Lord,		13:27
concerning the w. of the Lord;		16:29
They shall feed in the w.,		21: 9
perverted the right w. of the Lord,		22:14
for his w. are righteousness	2Ne	1:19
but the w. of mine enemy.		4:33
and he will teach us of his w.,		12: 3
astray, every one to his wicked w.		12: 5
unto my God: Thy w. are just.		26: 7
man should find out all his w.	Jac	4: 8
And no man knoweth of his w.		4: 8
the people the w. of the Lord;	Jar	1: 7
the w. of truth and soberness;	Mos	4:15
there are divers w. and means,		4:29
did walk in the w. of the Lord,		6: 6
but I will hedge up their w.		7:29
not walk in the w. of his father.		11: 1
perverting the w. of the Lord!		12:26
perverted the w. of the Lord,		12:26
and goes on in the w. of sin		16: 5
a man of God, walking in his w.		23:14
pervert the w. of all righteousness.		29:23
did walk in the w. of the Lord,		29:43
known the w. of righteousness	Al	5:37
much of the w. of the Lord,		10: 5
pervert the w. of the righteous,		10:18
they departed and went their w.,		14:20
insomuch that they fled many w.		17:27
the Lord worketh in many w.		24:27
did walk in the w. of the Lord,		25:14
whose w. have been the ways of		26:24
the w. of a transgressor from the		26:24
perverting the w. of the Lord?		30:22
perverteth the w. of the Lord;		30:60
perverting the w. of the Lord,		31: 1
did pervert the w. of the Lord		31:11
many of the error of their w.,		37: 8
walk after the w. of his father,	He	3:20
did walk in the w. of his father.		3:37
and did turn unto their own w.,		6:31
to question him in divers w.		9:19
and thither and went their w.,		10: 1
they did not mend their w.		11:36
all manner of w. to destroy him;		13:26
Gentiles, from your wicked w.;	3Ne	30: 2
to behold the w. of man.	Mrm	2:18
repent and turn from your evil w.?		5:22
from the w. of the Lord!		6:17
did walk in the w. of the Lord;	Eth	10: 2
divers w. that he did manifest	Mro	7:24
pervert the w. of the Lord		8:16
different w. that these gifts are		10: 8
them of the error of their w.	DC	6:11
go your w. and sin no more;		6:35
seek to counsel in your own w.		56:14
the Spirit to know all his w.;		61:27
he repent and mend his w.		75:29
wisdom, marvelous are his w.,		76: 2
go your w. and sin no more;		82: 7
their sins, and their wicked w.,		98:20
remembereth thee in thy w.		133:44
his son Enos in the w. of God;	Mses	6:13
taught Enoch in all the w. of God.		6:21
taught me in all the w. of God.		6:41

WAYSIDE
cleansing your feet by the w.	DC	24:15

WE: *see the APPENDIX.*

WEAK
that all my joints are w.,	1Ne	19:20
Art thou also become w. as we?	2Ne	24:10
w. like unto their brethren;	Mos	1:13
yea, and he became w., even that		27:19
as to my strength I am w.;	Al	26:12
had hitherto been a w. place,		49:14
saw that they had become w.,	He	4:24
yea, thus had they become w.,		4:26
I perceive that ye are w.,	3Ne	17: 2
we had become w. like unto	Mrm	2:26
make w. things become strong	Eth	12:27
army which is with me is w.;	Mro	9:17
The w. things of the world	DC	1:19
might be proclaimed by the w.		1:23
upon the w. things of the world,		35:13
he that is w. among you		50:16
succor the w., lift up the hands		81: 5
take with him him that is w.,		84:106
(for verily your faith is w.),		86: 6
to the capacity of the w.		89: 3
the w. things of the earth.		124: 1
To prepare the w. for		133:58
the w. shall confound the wise,		133:58
by the w. things of the earth		133:59

WEAKEN
which did w. the nations!	2Ne	24:12

WEAKER
upon the w. part of the people.	Al	43:24

WEAKEST
the w. parts of their cities;	Al	48: 5
in their w. fortifications he did		48: 9
been the w. part of the land,		49:15
and the w. of all saints,	DC	89: 3

WEAKNESS
because of the w. which is in	1Ne	19: 6
out of w. he shall be made strong,	2Ne	3:13
the w. of their words will I make		3:21
words which I have written in w.		33: 4
things, notwithstanding my w.		33:11
the Lord God showeth us our w.	Jac	4: 7
come upon us in this our w.	Al	56:19
notwithstanding the w. of our		58:37
knowing of their w. because of	3Ne	4:24
because of his w. before thee;	Eth	3: 2
because of our w. in writing;		12:23
when we write we behold our w.,		12:25
take no advantage of your w.;		12:26
I will show unto them their w.		12:27
I give unto men w. that they		12:27
show unto the Gentiles their w.		12:28
not charity, because of our w.,		12:35
because thou hast seen thy w.		12:37
because of my w. in writing.		12:40
unto my servants in their w.,	DC	1:24
whether in w. or in strength,		24:11
and in w. have I blessed him;		35:17
will be merciful unto your w.		38:14
who knoweth the w. of man		62: 1
and because thou hast seen thy w.,		135: 5
and displayed the w. of youth,	JS	2:28
for my w. and imperfections:		2:29

WEALTH
w. pertaining to gold and silver	DC 111: 4

WEALTHY
became a large and w. people.	Mos	27: 7
prosper and become far more w.	Al	1:31

WEANED
the w. child shall put his hand	2Ne	21: 8
the w. child shall put his hand		30:14

WEAPON
were able to use a w. of war,	Al	55:17
No w. that is formed against	3Ne	22:17
there is no w. that is formed	DC	71: 9
no w. formed against them		109:25

WEAPONS 1026 WEIGHTY

WEAPONS
and the w. of his indignation,	2Ne	23: 5
the ground, and w. of war—	Jar	1: 8
and with all manner of w.	Mos	9:16
there should be w. of war made		10: 1
I might have w. for my people		10: 1
with all manner of w. of war,	Al	2:12
with all manner of w. of war		2:14
were not slain by the w. of war,		3: 1
down the w. of their rebellion,		23: 7
down the w. of their rebellion,		23:13
yea, all their w. of war;		23:13
all the w. which were used for		24:17
they never would use w. again		24:18
they buried their w. of peace,		24:19
buried the w. of war,		24:19
they threw down their w. of war,		24:25
did also bury their w. of war,		25:14
they have buried their w. of war		26:32
and all manner of w. of war.		43:18
ye deliver up your w. of war		44: 6
Behold, here are our w. of war;		44: 8
but take our w. of war, and		44: 8
the sword and the w. of war,		44:10
will deliver up your w. of war		44:14
threw down their w. of war at		44:15
he took the w. of war from the		44:20
as they did lift their w. of war		51:18
not yield up their w. of war.		52:25
had given up their w. of war.		52:32
delivered up their w. of war.		52:36
will bring forth your w. of war		52:37
threw down their w. of war at		52:38
their w. of war were taken from		52:39
about to take their w. of war,		53:14
would not take their w. of war		53:16
took their w. of war to defend		53:18
for they took their w. of war,		53:19
people shall lay down their w.		54:18
had prepared his men with w.		55:16
and cast in w. of war unto the		55:16
demanded their w. of war,		55:23
have taken their w. of war,		56: 5
would not take up their w. of war		56: 6
their w. of war in our defence.		56: 7
to deliver up their w. of war		56:54
and all manner of w. of war		60: 2
provisions and their w. of war.		62:15
no more take up their w. of war		62:16
did lay down their w. of war,	He	5:51
have buried their w. of war,		15: 9
they should make w. of war	3Ne	3:26
with all manner of w. of war.	Mrm	6: 9
must lay down your w. of war,		7: 4
make all manner of w. of war.	Eth	10:27
being armed with w. of war,		15:15
lay down their w. of bloodshed,	DC	109:66

WEAR
and w. our own apparel;	2Ne	14: 1
They w. stiff necks and high heads;		28:14
and w. stiff necks and high heads	Jac	2:13
and to w. very costly apparel,	Al	1: 6
they did not w. costly apparel,		1:27
began to w. very costly apparel.		4: 6
w. the garments of the laborer.	DC	42:42
waste and w. out our lives in		123:13

WEARIED
they w. him with their teasings.	Mos	7: 1
were w. because of their march,	Al	52:28
Lamanites were w. because of		52:31

WEARINESS
because of their w., which was	Al	56:51

WEARING
and strife; w. costly apparel;	Al	1:32
in the w. of costly apparel and		5:53
as the w. of costly apparel,	4Ne	1:24
unto the w. of very fine apparel,	Mrm	8:36

WEARY
in the spirit, which doth w. me	1Ne	19:20
When ye are w. he waketh	2Ne	7: 4
none shall be w. nor stumble		15:26
a small thing for you to w. men,		17:13
but will ye w. my God also?		17:13
to never be w. of good works,	Al	37:34
wine with you for we are w.		55: 9
We are w., therefore let us take		55:11
The army of Antipus being w.,		56:50
were w. because of their march;		58:25
w. because of the greatness of		62:35
Nephi had become w. because of	He	5: 4
w. because of his much fighting	3Ne	4:14
And while they were yet w.,	Mrm	4: 2
when it was night they were w.,	Eth	15:16
be not w. in well-doing,	DC	64:33
shall not be w. in mind,		84:80
early, that ye may not be w.;		88:124
And shall run and not be w.,		89:20
continual coming she w. me.		101:84
w. traveler may find health and		124:23
resting-place for the w. traveler,		124:60
I am pained, I am w., because	Mses	7:48

WEARYING
let them cease w. me concerning	DC	90:33

WEDGE
than the golden w. of Ophir.	2Ne	23:12

WEEK
there was one day in every w. that	Mos	18:25
together on one day of the w.,	Al	31:12
worship God only once in a w.?		32:11

WEEKS
Sidney Gilbert, after a few w.,	DC	64:18
in their days, in their w.,		88:44

WEEP
why should my heart w.	2Ne	4:26
shall have cause to howl, and w.,	Mos	16: 2
they began to w. exceedingly,	Al	17:28
and then shall ye w. and howl	He	13:32
they began to w. and howl again	3Ne	10: 8
w. for the loss of them that die,	DC	42:45
then shall they w. because of		45:53
and ye solid rocks w. for joy!		128:23
How is it that the heavens w.,	Mses	7:28
How is it that thou canst w.,		7:29
how is it thou canst w.?		7:31
whole heavens shall w. over them,		7:37
should not the heavens w.		7:37
for this shall the heavens w.,		7:40

WEEPING
there shall be w., and wailing,	Al	40:13
and w. among all the people	3Ne	8:23
and the mourning, and the w.,		10:10
w., wailing and gnashing of	DC	19: 5
his w. for Zion I have seen,		21: 8
there shall be w. and wailing		29:15
where there is w., and wailing,		101:91
a day of desolation, of w.,		112:24
outer darkness, where there is w.,		133:73
cried with a loud voice, with w.,	Mses	1:22
shall be w. and gnashing of teeth.	JS	1:54

WEIGH
to w. thee down unto death;	Mro	9:25

WEIGHED
My heart hath been w. down	2Ne	1:17
but I this day am w. down	Jac	2: 3
being w. down with sorrow,	Al	8:14
was thus w. down with sorrow,		8:14

WEIGHT
and eternal w. of glory,	DC	63:66
under the w. of its iniquits.		123: 7
and an eternal w. of glory.		132:16

WEIGHTY
neglect the more w. matters?	DC	117: 8

WELDING

WELDING
unless there is a w. link	DC 128:18
and w. together of dispensations,	128:18

WELFARE
and your own eternal w.	2Ne 1:25
the everlasting w. of your souls.	2:30
desirous for the w. of your souls.	6: 3
they seek not the w. of Zion.	26:29
may be for the w. of thy soul.	32: 9
in all his days for their w.—	Jac 1:10
for the w. of your souls	2: 3
desire for the w. of my brethren,	En 1: 9
anguish for the w. of their souls.	Mos 25:11
in behalf of the w. of the souls of	Al 6: 6
him continually for your w.,	34:27
w. of those who are around you.	34:27
the w. and safety of his people.	48:12
rejoiced because of the w.,	59: 1
had for the w. of this people;	60: 9
for the w. and the freedom of	60:10
freedom and w. of my country.	60:36
w. and happiness of his people;	He 12: 2
feeling for your w., because of	3Ne 3: 5
the w. of the ancient and long	Mrm 8:15
concerning the w. of their souls.	Mro 6: 5

WELL
as w. in times of old as in the	1Ne 10:17
as w. in these times as in times	10:19
and as w. in times of old as in	10:19
as w. as in the records of the	13:41
it shall be w. with them?	14: 5
as w. as your brethren from whom	19:24
righteous that it is w. with them;	2Ne 13:10
instead of w. set hair, baldness;	13:24
I sing to my w.-beloved a song	15: 1
My w.-beloved hath a	15: 1
and it w. nigh consumeth me	26: 7
and it shall be w. with us.	28: 7
All is w. in Zion; yea, Zion	28:21
yea, Zion prospereth, all is w.—	28:21
unto them that crieth: All is w.!	28:25
be w. for you to have a king.	Mos 23: 8
Yea, w. did Mosiah say, who was	Al 10:19
Yea, w. did he say that is the time	10:19
w. doth the Lord judge of our	10:20
w. doth he cry unto this people,	10:20
w. doth he cry, by the voice of	10:21
provocation as w. as the first,	12:36
the last death, as w. as the first.	12:36
as w. as he loveth our children;	24:14
as w. as unto future generations.	24:14
it is w. that ye are cast out of	32:12
as w. as unto their children?	39:18
as w. as the righteous in	40:14
the wicked as w. as the righteous,	40:19
death as w. as a temporal,	42: 9
Nephites as w. as the Lamanites.	48: 2
he hath made us as w. as you.	54:21
as w. in the Lord as in the	56: 2
depressed in body as w. as in	56:16
you may w. suppose that this	56:17
of your faith in my W. Beloved,	He 5:47
he knoweth as w. all things which	8: 8
as w. as among the Nephites,	11: 6
you, and he saith that all is w.,	13:28
as w. as unto them who shall be	16:18
as w. as in the land of Jerusalem?	16:19
ye do stand w., as if ye were	3Ne 11: 7
Son, in whom I am w. pleased,	Mrm 7:10
it shall be w. with you in the	Mro 7:47
last day, it shall be w. with him.	8:29
as w. as the words of our Savior	DC 1:30
which I, the Lord, am w. pleased,	19:28
vocally as w. as in thy heart;	19:28
the world as w. as in secret,	19:28
in public as w. as in private.	20:11
as w. as in generations of old;	20:27
As w. as those who should	23: 6
the world as w. as in secret,	38:10
with whom I am w. pleased;	45: 4
in whom thou wast w. pleased;	
in whom I am w. pleased,	DC 50:37
in whom I am w. pleased,	51: 3
of wine on the lees w. refined,	58: 8
house of the Lord, w. prepared,	58: 9
am not w. pleased with him,	58:41
with some I am not w.,	60: 2
people who are w. nigh ripened	61:31
with whom I am w. pleased,	61:35
is angry he is not w. pleased;	63:11
be in him a w. of living water,	63:23
be not weary in w.-doing,	64:33
I, the Lord, am not w. pleased	68:31
and have done w. inasmuch as	70:17
whom the Lord was w. pleased.	84: 3
as w. as the lesser priesthood,	85:11
I am not w. pleased with many	90:35
I am not w. pleased with my	90:35
I, the Lord, am w. pleased that	97: 3
I, the Lord, am not w. pleased	98:19
Joseph, your families are w.;	100: 1
I, the Lord, was not w. pleased.	112: 2
of Jesse as w. as of Ephraim,	113: 4
of Jesse, as w. as of Joseph,	113: 6
it shall not be w. with them.	117: 3
And then, if thou endure it w.,	121: 8
As w. might man stretch forth his	121:33
as w. as real property;	123: 2
w. pleased with your offering	124: 1
I am w. pleased with him,	124:12
as w. as my servant Joseph;	124:94
it shall be w. with him.	124:110
and it shall be w. with him	124:118
as w. as in the city of Nashville,	125: 4
Dear and w.-beloved brother,	126: 1
as w. as many other things.	127:10
who is w. qualified for taking	128: 3
as w. for the dead as for the living.	128:11
as w. for time and for all eternity,	132: 7
If thou doest w., thou shalt be	Mses 5:23
if thou doest not w., sin lieth	5:23
I will do w. to hearken unto thy	Abr 2:13
may be w. with me for thy sake,	2:25
"Never mind, all is w.—"	JS 2:20
I am w. enough off."	2:20

WELL-BELOVED: see WELL and BELOVED.

WELL-DOING: see WELL and DOING.

WELL-NIGH: see WELL and NIGH.

WELLS
water out of the w. of salvation.	2Ne 22: 3

WELTON, Micah B.
And also my servant W. and	DC 75:36

WENT
as he w. forth prayed unto	1Ne 1: 5
w. forth upon the face of the	1:11
he w. forth among the people,	1:18
w. in unto the house of Laban,	3:11
we w. down to the land of our	3:22
we w. up again unto the house	3:23
we w. in unto Laban, and desired	3:24
w. forth towards the house of Laban.	4: 5
I w. forth, and as I came near	4: 7
I w. forth unto the treasury of	4:20
as I w. forth towards the treasury	4:20
as I w. forth unto my brethren,	4:27
w. up unto the house of Ishmael,	7: 4
And the Lamb of God w. forth	11:27
he w. forth ministering unto	11:28
and they w. forth in multitudes	12:20
he w. forth upon the many waters,	13:12
they w. forth out of captivity,	13:13
and w. forth to the tent door,	16:10
as I, Nephi, w. forth to slay food,	16:18
and w. up into the mountain,	17: 7
we w. forth upon the land,	18:23
they w. forth out of my mouth,	20: 3
w. and made these plates upon	2Ne 5:31
as the street to them that w. over.	8:23

WENT 1028 WENT

w. up toward Jerusalem to war	2Ne	17: 1
And I w. unto the prophetess;		18: 3
master of the vineyard w. forth,	Jac	5: 4
of the vineyard w. his way,		5:14
w. down into the vineyard		5:16
they w. forth whither the master		5:20
w. down into the vineyard;		5:30
they w. down into the nethermost		5:39
and the servant w. and did as		5:70
I w. to hunt beasts in the forests;	En	1: 3
I, Enos, w. about among the		1:19
who w. up into the wilderness to	Om	1:27
they w. up into the wilderness.		1:28
brother, who also w. with them;		1:30
Mosiah w. and did as his father	Mos	1:18
concerning the people who w. up		7: 1
w. down into the land of Nephi.		7: 6
he w. forth and bowed himself		7:12
Zeniff w. up out of the land		8: 2
I w. again with four of my men		9: 5
And I w. in unto the king, and he		9: 6
I and my people w. into the land		9: 7
and he w. forth among them,		11:20
and w. about privately among the		18: 1
many as believed him w. thither		18: 6
w. and stood forth in the water,		18:12
and w. forth a second time into		18:15
w. forth to the place of Mormon;		18:16
king himself w. before his people;		20: 7
they w. up to the land of Nephi		20: 7
he w. forth and said unto the king:		20:17
and w. forth without arms to		20:25
w. forth against the Lamanites		21: 7
and they w. again to battle, but		21:11
they w. again even the third time,		21:12
and the people that w. with him,		21:30
Gideon w. forth and stood before		22: 3
and they w. round about the land		22:11
Alma w. forth and stood among		23:27
Alma and his brethren w. forth		23:29
remainder of them w. to the land		23:38
he w. from one body to another,		25:15
he w. and inquired of the Lord		26:13
Alma w. and judged those that		26:34
king Mosiah w. and inquired of		28: 6
w. forth preaching false doctrines;	Al	1:16
he w. up with his people,		2:16
they who w. out with their men		2:22
they w. up and slew many of		3:23
and w. over upon the east of the		6: 7
Alma w. and began to declare		6: 8
Alma w. forth, and also Amulek,		8:30
they w. forth and began to preach		8:32
that Amulek w. stood forth,		9:34
I w. on rebelling against God,		10: 6
the people w. forth and witnessed		14: 5
they departed and w. their ways,		14:20
lawyers w. in unto the prison		14:23
they all w. forth and smote them,		14:25
they w. immediately, obeying the		15: 5
w. in unto the house unto Zeezrom;		15: 5
the knowledge of this w. forth		15:11
therefore they w. unto him and		16: 5
And Alma and Amulek w. forth		16:13
and w. up to the land of Nephi		17:hd
and w. forth among them,		17:17
And Ammon w. to the land of		17:19
that they w. in search of the flocks,		17:32
he w. forth and stood to contend		17:34
and then w. in unto the king,		17:39
he w. in unto the king,		18:12
and w. in unto the queen,		19: 3
he w. in to see the king		19: 7
drew his sword and w. forth		19:22
she w. and took the queen by		19:29
w. forth and began to rebuke them,		19:31
therefore they w. their way.		19:32
w. forth again to declare the word,		21:15
And they w. forth whithersoever		21:16
he w. in unto him into the king's		22: 2
w. forth from city to city,		23: 4
they w. out to meet them,		24:21
and w. over into the borders of		25: 2
we w. forth even in wrath,	Al	26:18
Ammon w. and inquired of		27:11
Ammon w. and told the king		27:13
w. and told the chief judge		27:20
w. down into the land of		27:26
this man w. over to the land of		30:19
yea, he w. on to blaspheme.		30:30
w. about from house to house		30:56
as he w. forth among the people,		30:59
as he w. forth amongst them,		30:59
those who w. with him among		31: 7
w. into the land to preach the		31:11
For I w. about with the sons		36: 6
not rest, and he also w. forth.		43: 1
messengers w. and delivered the		43:24
the saying w. abroad in the church		45:19
Helaman w. forth among the		45:20
w. forth to establish the church		45:22
he w. forth among the people,		46:19
he w. forth, and also sent forth		46:28
they w. out of the world rejoicing.		46:39
had taken those who w. with him,		47: 1
and w. up in the land of Nephi		47: 1
he w. forward to the place		47: 5
he w. up into the mount, nearly		47:12
they w. and bowed themselves		47:22
and w. in unto the queen,		47:34
And thus they w. forth, and the		48:20
and they w. forth and drove all		50: 7
And thus he w. on, taking		51:26
stole forth and w. out by night,		51:33
w. into the camp of Amalickiah;		51:33
And Moroni w. to the city of		53: 2
Laman w. to the guards who		55: 8
Moroni and Pahoran w. down		62: 7
and w. forth against the city,		62: 7
Moroni w. forth in the darkness		62:20
Moroni w. forth from the land		62:30
And he w. forth with a cord,		62:36
and his brethren w. forth, and		62:45
he w. forth and built him an		63: 5
were many people who w. forth		63: 9
he w. unto those that sent him,	He	1:11
w. forth towards the judgment-seat		2: 6
w. forth unto the land northward		3: 3
the people who w. forth became		3: 7
who w. up from the Nephites		4: 4
and therefore they w. forth,		5:14
they w. forth into the prison to		5:22
w. into the land northward,		6: 6
even there were five who w.,		9: 1
among themselves, as they w.:		9: 1
they w. and did, even according		9:37
and thither and w. their ways,		10: 1
Nephi w. his way towards his own		10: 2
dissenters that w. forth unto them.		11:25
w. and got upon the wall thereof,		13: 4
w. forth and sought for Nephi;		16: 1
that they w. away unto Nephi		16: 3
w. forth unto him to be baptized,		16: 5
they w. forth to lay their hands		16: 7
whither he w., no man knoweth;	3Ne	1: 3
he w. out and bowed himself		1:11
Nephi w. forth among the		1:23
w. forth among them in that		7:16
they w. no man knoweth,		8:16
that the multitude w. forth,		11:15
And Nephi arose and w. forth,		11:19
they w. forth and stood in the		19: 4
w. down unto the water's edge,		19:10
Nephi w. down into the water		19:11
w. a little way off from them		19:19
w. a little way off and bowed		19:27
he w. again a little way off		19:31
w. forth doing mighty miracles	4Ne	1:30
the armies of the Nephites w. up	Mrm	4: 4
w. forth in their own might,		4: 8
w. down into the valley which	Eth	2: 1
w. forth unto the mount,		3: 1
w. forth upon the face of the		6:13
they w. down to their graves.		6:21
w. over and dwelt in the land		7: 4
w. forth and gave battle unto		10: 9

WENT — 1029 — WHATSOEVER

WENT

w. to battle against the king,	Eth	10:32
and by night he w. forth		13:13
w. against him with his armies		13:27
there w. a fear of Shiz		14:18
a cry w. forth throughout the		14:18
And the scent thereof w. forth		14:23
they w. again to battle'		15:19
And he w. forth, and beheld		15:33
w. unto the first in the first	DC	88:56
the servants of the nobleman w.		101:46
his servant w. straightway,		101:62
When Joseph w. to Carthage		135: 1
there w. up a mist from the earth,	Mses	3: 6
Adam and his wife w. to hide		4:14
words w. forth out of the mouth		5:15
And Cain w. into the field,		5:32
Enoch w. forth in the land,		6:37
I turned and w. up on the mount;		7: 3
w. upon the land which came		7:14
w. forth a curse upon all people		7:15
w. forth the saying, ZION IS		7:69
they w. down at the beginning,	Abr	4: 1
the Gods w. down to organize man		4:27
there w. up a mist from the earth,		5: 6
And Jesus w. out, and departed	JS	1: 2
w. upon the Mount of Olives.		1: 4
in some degree, I w. home.		2:20
w. to the necessary labors of		2:48
and w. to the place where the		2:50
I w. at the end of each year,		2:54
After I w. to live with him,		2:56
so we w. and were married at		2:58
Stoal's, and w. to my father's,		2:58
"I w. to the city of New York,		2:64
and w. to Dr. Mitchell, who		2:65
he w. to board for a season at		2:66
w. into the woods to pray and		2:68
we w. and were baptized.		2:71

WEPT

that the Lord of the vineyard w.,	Jac	5:41
Now they w. because of the fear	Al	17:29
he had said these words, he w.,	3Ne	17:21
he had done this he w. again;		17:22
for the heavens w. over him	DC	76:26
residue of the people, and he w.;	Mses	7:28
w. and stretched forth his arms,		7:41
of soul, and w. over his brethren,		7:44
heard the earth mourn, he w.,		7:49
again Enoch w. and cried unto		7:58

WERE: see in the APPENDIX.

WERT

thy command as if thou w. God.	Mses	1:25

WEST

from the north and from the w.;	1Ne	21:12
of the Philistines towards the w.;	2Ne	21:14
both in the east and in the w.,		29:11
on the east and on the w.,	Mos	27: 6
on the w. of the river Sidon,	Al	2:34
the w. side of the river Sidon.		2:34
which was w. and north,		2:36
they were scattered on the w.,		2:37
on the w. of the river Sidon,		8: 3
on the w. by the borders of		8: 3
on the east and on the w.,		22:27
the sea east even to the sea w.,		22:27
from the east towards the w.—		22:27
through the wilderness on the w.,		22:28
w. of the land of Zarahemla,		22:28
on the w. in the land of Nephi,		22:28
Sidon, from the east to the w.,		22:29
from the east to the w. sea;		22:32
from the east unto the w. sea,		22:33
on the w. of the river Sidon		43:27
he concealed in the w. valley,		43:32
on the w. of the river Sidon,		43:32
on the w. of the river Sidon,		43:53
course from the east sea to the w.		50: 8
and also on the w., fortifying		50:11
from the w. sea, running by the		50:11
sea, on the w. and on the east.		50:34
borders of the land by the w. sea;	Al	52:11
on the borders by the w. sea.		52:12
and the w. borders of the land,		52:15
on the w. of the city Mulek;		52:22
on the w. sea, south, while in		53: 8
on the south by the w. sea.		53:22
of the city, yea, even on the w.,		62:22
launched it forth into the w. sea,		63: 5
nor on the east, nor on the w.,	He	1:31
from the sea w. to the sea east.		3: 8
the w. sea, even unto the east;		4: 7
from the sea w. to the sea east.		11:20
earth from the w. to the east,	3Ne	1:17
in from the east and from the w.,		20:13
the borders w. by the seashore.	Mrm	2: 6
after you shall go to the w.	DC	26: 1
forth to the east and to the w.,		42:63
be converted to flee to the w.,		42:64
forth from the east unto the w.,		43:22
from the east and from the w.,		44: 1
whether to the east or to the w.,		75:26
south, to the east or to the w.,		80: 3
Let the city, Far W., be a holy		115: 7
Far W. should be built up speedily		115:17
my people in the city of Far W.,		117:10
my saints in the city of Far W.,		118: 5
come from the east, and the w.,		125: 4
in their journeyings to the W.,		136: 1
Bethel on the w., and Hai on the	Abr	2:20
and shineth even unto the w.,	JS	1:26
On the w. side of this hill,		2:51

WESTERN

ye forth into the w. countries,	DC	45:64
journey unto the w. countries,		75:15
the w. boundaries of the State		84: 3

WESTWARD

go forth into the regions w.;	DC	42: 8
your journey into the regions w.,		54: 8
a spot for the temple is lying w.,		57: 3
and also every tract lying w.,		57: 4

WHALE

as a w. in the midst of the sea;	Eth	2:24
neither w. that could mar them;		6:10

WHALES

created great w., and every living	Mses	2:21
they might bring forth great w.,	Abr	4:21

WHAT: see in the APPENDIX.

WHATEVER

them be of w. name they would.	Jac	1:11
into w. parts it had not been	He	3: 5
w. church business is necessary	DC	20:62
that w. persons among you,		42:74
and w. ye do according to		64:29
W. principle of intelligence		130:18
new and everlasting covenant w.,		132:26
w. was done in this matter		OD

WHATSOEVER

w. things we should carry into	1Ne	16:11
w. thing we had brought with us,		18: 6
w. he shall say unto you.		22:20
w. things were possible for us,	2Ne	5: 7
But w. things we write upon	Jac	4: 2
W. thing ye shall ask in faith,	En	1:15
or w. place of our inheritance.	Jar	1: 7
write the things w. I write,	Om	1: 4
grant unto you w. ye ask	Mos	4:21
things w. he commanded him.		6: 6
w. is good cometh from God,	Al	1:29
w. is evil cometh from the devil.		5:40
that w. I shall say unto you,		5:40
for w. things ye stand in need,		5:48
for w. things ye do receive.		7:23
that w. they did was right;		7:23
w. thou desirest which is right,		18: 5
w. thou desirest I will give unto		18:17
w. thou desirest of me I will		18:21
		18:21

WHATSOEVER 1030 WHENCE

unto thee w. thou wilt ask,	Al	20:23
desires in w. thing he thinketh,		20:24
in w. place they were in,		21:22
in w. place they should be,		23: 1
w. land they may be in;		26:37
and w. a man did was no crime.		30:17
in w. circumstances they might.		32:25
and w. is light, is good, because		32:35
in w. place may be in,		34:38
things w. ye must do with them)		37:16
in w. thing they were entrusted.		53:20
or w. thing they could get into		57:14
in w. parts they should come		60: 2
w. evil we cannot resist with		61:14
Gather together w. force ye		61:17
in w. place he did enter,		62: 4
gained w. force he could in all		62: 4
w. men he could in all his march,		62: 6
suffer w. tree should spring up	He	3: 9
go into w. part of the land		6: 7
in w. difficult circumstances		6:21
that w. wickedness his brother		6:22
w. ye shall seal on earth shall be		10: 7
w. ye shall loose on earth shall be		10: 7
w. things should come into his		13: 3
w. things the Lord put into		13: 4
do w. your heart desireth—		13:27
things w. did belong unto them.	3Ne	6: 1
do w. iniquity he desired they		6:17
w. cometh of more than these is		12:37
all things w. ye would that		14:12
w. ye shall ask the Father in		18:20
things w. he shall say unto you.		20:23
w. ye shall do, ye shall do it in		27: 7
shall call w. things ye do call,		27: 9
w. things ye shall ask the Father		27:28
w. man it seemeth them good.		28:30
w. lands we had passed by,	Mrm	5: 5
w. he shall ask the Father in		9:21
w. things transpired among	Eth	1: 3
w. nation shall possess it shall		2: 9
w. nation shall possess it shall		2:12
can do w. thou wilt for the		3: 4
w. thing persuadeth men to do		4:12
w. beast or animal or fowl that		6: 4
w. thing Akish made known		8:14
to do w. thing he desired.		8:17
w. nation shall uphold such secret		8:22
w. thing persuadeth men to do	Mro	7:17
W. thing ye shall ask the Father		7:26
do w. thing is expedient in he.		7:33
w. thing is good is just and true;		10: 6
in w. difficult circumstances	DC	6:18
w. ye sow, that shall ye also		6:33
w. things you shall ask in faith,		8: 1
w. you shall ask me to tell you		8: 9
be free unto all of w. nation,		10:51
all things w. you desire of me,		11:14
w. shall be entrusted to his care.		12: 8
And in w. place ye shall enter,		24:15
revealed unto them, w. I will,		25: 9
all things w. ye ask of me,		27:18
all things w. you shalt teach		28: 1
W. ye shall ask in faith, being		29: 6
all things w. I have created		29:30
and w. thing he needeth in		43:13
Christ, w. you do in the Spirit;		46:31
w. blessing ye are blessed with.		46:32
w. you will in the name of Jesus		50:29
w. things the disciples may need		57: 8
obtain w. he can obtain in		57:12
in w. place I shall appoint		57:13
And w. they shall speak when		68: 4
in w. circumstances I, the		70:16
in w. land they shall be		72:23
And in w. house ye enter,		75:19
And in w. house ye enter,		75:20
and w. is truth is light,		84:45
and w. is light is Spirit, even		84:45
unto w. place ye cannot go		84:62
in w. village or city ye enter,		84:93
W. ye ask the Father in my		88:64
And w. is more or less than this		93:25

and w. temple is defiled,	DC	93:35
things w. I shall command you.		94:10
things w. I shall command you,		94:12
w. I have commanded her.		97:25
w. I have commanded her,		97:26
things w. I command them.		98: 4
w. is more or less than this,		98: 7
w. is less than these cometh of		98:10
them and will do w. I list,		98:21
things w. I have said unto them.		98:21
to do w. I command you,		98:22
declare w. thing ye declare		100: 7
unto all things w. ye shall say.		100: 8
w. any man shall ask, it shall		101:27
w. I have commanded you;		101:60
w. his lord commanded him:		101:62
w. he shall appoint unto them		105:22
predicted w. should befall		107:56
w. city thy servants shall enter,		109:39
w. city thy servants shall enter,		109:41
in w. place ye shall proclaim		112:19
w. remaineth, let it remain		117: 5
are faithful in all things w.		124:55
that w. he shall bind on earth		124:93
w. he shall loose on earth		124:93
w. you bind on earth,		127: 7
w. you loose on earth,		127: 7
w. you bind on earth		128: 8
w. you loose on earth		128: 8
w. you record on earth		128: 8
w. you do not record on earth		128: 8
w. those men did in authority,		128: 9
w. thou shalt bind on earth		128:10
w. thou shalt loose on earth		128:10
things of name, w. they may be,		132:13
For w. things remain are by me;		132:14
and w. things are not by me shall		132:14
in all things w. my servant		132:19
w. he received, by revelation		132:29
w. you seal on earth		132:46
w. you bind on earth		132:46
that w. you give on earth,		132:48
receive all things w. I, the Lord		132:65
commanded that w. Adam called	Mses	3:19
w. ye shall ask, it shall be given		6:52
see if they will do all things w.	Abr	3:25
and w. Adam called every living		5:20

WHEAT

with seeds of corn, and of w.,	Mos	9: 9
that he may sift you as w.	3Ne	18:18
of the w. and of the tares:	DC	86: 1
the tares choke the w. and		86: 3
lest you destroy the w. also.		86: 6
let the w. and the tares grow		86: 7
the w. from among the tares,		86: 7
after the gathering of the w.,		86: 7
Nevertheless, w. for man, and		89:17
of the w. and the tares,		101:65
that the w. may be secured in		101:65

WHEELER: see BALDWIN, Wheeler.

WHEELS

and their w. like a whirlwind,	2Ne	15:28

WHEN: see in the APPENDIX.

WHENCE

to behold from w. it came;	1Ne	8:14
from w. no traveler can return;	2Ne	1:14
at Jerusalem, from w. we came,		6: 8
the rock from w. ye are hewn,		8: 1
of the pit from w. ye are digged.		8: 1
at Jerusalem, from w. we came;		9: 5
from w. there is no deliverance.		28:22
from w. they must go into the place		28:23
I mean them from w. I came.		33: 1
into the tree from w. they came;	Jac	5:52
from w. they can no more return;	Mos	3:25
from w. these records came;		8:12
from w. they were taken—	Al	42: 2
behold from w. the voice came;	He	5:48

WHENCE 1031 WHEREBY

WHENCE

From w. cometh this blood?	He	9:32
w. they have been dispersed;	3Ne	5:26
heaven, from w. the sound came.		11: 5
fire, from w. there is no return.		27:11
w. they can no more return,		27:17
from w. their blessings come.	Mrm	5:10
from w. Lehi should come—	Eth	13: 5
the land from w. they came:	DC	60: 1
the land from w. you came.		60: 5
churches from w. they came.		60: 8
from w. they have fallen;		113:10
the ground from w. he was taken;	Mses	4:29
art, and from w. thou comest?		6:40
source from w. they sprang.	JS	2:34

WHENEVER

w. it shall be expedient.	DC	47: 2
w. any vacancy shall occur by		102: 8
W. a high council of the church		102:12
W. this council convenes to act		102:13
w. the Lord has given a dispensation		128: 9

WHERE

these, w. have they been?	1Ne	21:21
W. is the bill of your mother's	2Ne	7: 1
And w. is the fury of the oppressor?		8:13
w. there is no law given there is		9:25
w. there is no punishment		9:25
w. there is no condemnation the		9:25
w. there were a thousand vines		17:23
and w. will ye leave your glory?		20: 3
land w. Mosiah discovered them;	Om	1:16
place w. our brethren were slain,	Mos	9: 4
w. he did hide himself in the		18: 5
w. the daughters of the Lamanites		20: 1
the same place w. the first army	Al	3:20
w. Alma and Amulek were bound		14:23
w. the Son of God should come;		16:20
W. is this man that has such great		18: 8
heavens a place w. God dwells		18:30
w. they could be admitted.		21:16
w. they had pitched their tents,		27:25
w. they shall rest from all their		40:12
w. a part of the army of Moroni		43:34
w. there were dissensions,		46:28
unto the place w. she sat;		47:34
w. the Lamanites do guard my		55: 3
that same place w. we had first		58:17
in that part w. he was,		59: 2
w. the Lamanites did not camp		62:22
w. nothing doth corrupt,	He	8:25
w. nothing can come which is		8:25
W. are the five who were sent to		9:12
w. moth and rust doth corrupt,	3Ne	13:19
w. neither moth nor rust doth		13:20
w. thieves do not break through		13:20
For w. your treasure is, there		13:21
in the place w. Jesus should		19: 3
w. there had been cities burned.	4Ne	1: 7
leave in the place w. they are;	Mrm	1: 4
w. Ammaron had deposited the		2:17
w. there never had man been.	Eth	2: 5
of Moron w. the king dwelt,		7: 5
of Moron, w. the king dwelt,		7: 6
w. the Nephites were destroyed,		9: 3
place w. the sea divides the land.		10:20
w. all men shall know that my		12:38
w. my father Mormon did hide		15:11
come to the place w. thou art	DC	6:14
w. two or three are gathered		6:32
w. there is a regularly organized		20:65
w. there is no branch of the		20:66
from the church w. they reside,		20:84
church w. they are not known,		20:84
where I am you cannot come.		25:15
that w. I am ye shall be also.		27:18
w. the city Zion shall be built,		28: 9
for w. I am they cannot come,		29:29
w. the New Jerusalem shall be		42:62
w. it has not been proclaimed.		66: 5
w. their worm dieth not,		76:44
w. God and Christ are the judge		76:68
w. God, even the Father, reigns		76:92
but w. God and Christ dwell	DC	76:112
w. my Father and I am.		84:74
be had w. it may be found on		85: 4
w. are wailing and gnashing of		85: 9
upon the place w. he now lives;		90:20
remain w. he now resides		90:21
and w. my Father and I am,		98:18
w. there is weeping, and		101:91
the place w. he now resides,		104:20
and lot w. he now resides,		104:39
W. is their God?		105: 8
w. he shall be set apart		107:74
in a case w. a President of the		107:76
w. thou sittest enthroned,		109:77
the place w. it is my will that		111: 8
in all places w. my servant Joseph,		112:17
place w. Adam shall come		116: 1
or the land w. Adam dwelt,		117: 8
w. art thou?		121: 1
And w. is the pavilion that		121: 1
they know not w. to find it—		123:12
w. there is gnashing of teeth,		124: 8
w. shall be the safety of my people,		124:10
w. you have contemplated		124:43
w. the poisonous serpent cannot		124:99
w. the living are wont to assemble,		128:13
w. all things for their glory are		130: 7
The place w. god resides is a		130: 8
w. I am ye shall be also.		132:23
w. there is weeping, and wailing,		133:73
w. personal abuse is inflicted or		134:11
w. such laws exist as will protect		134:11
w. immediate appeal cannot be		134:11
w. all men shall know that		135: 5
w. the Lord shall locate a stake		136:10
w. is thy glory, that I should	Mses	1:13
or else w. is thy glory, for it is		1:15
w. I, the Lord God, created much		3:11
said unto him: W. goest thou?		4:15
W. is Abel, thy brother?		5:34
the place w. God resides,	Fac	2: 2
w. these two facts exist, there	Abr	3: 8
was in the place w. we lived	JS	2: 5
w. I had previously designed to		2:15
w. the plates were deposited,		2:42
out of the field w. we were,		2:48
w. the messenger had told me		2:50
place w. they were deposited,		2:59
the place w. he found them.		2:64
w. my father resided,		2:66
how, w., or what they may.	AoF	11

WHEREAS

W. other officers of the church,	DC	107:98

WHEREBY

power w. they could accomplish	1Ne	5: 8
means w. they can accomplish		17: 3
w. man can be saved	2Ne	25:20
w. man can be saved		31:21
means w. salvation can come	Mos	3:17
means w. salvation cometh.		4: 8
conditions w. man can be saved		4: 8
things w. ye may commit sin;		4:29
knowledge, w. we do rejoice		5: 4
head w. ye can be made free.		5: 8
name given w. salvation cometh;		5: 8
the cause w. ye were so bold		7:10
a gift from God, w. he could		21:28
w. he might guard himself	Al	2:21
or means w. man can be saved,		38: 9
means w. man can be saved,	He	5: 9
no power w. I may know		8:12
w. they may come unto me,	3Ne	21:27
w. his people may be gathered		21:28
the name w. we shall call this		27: 3
w. he hath gained the vistory	Mrm	7: 5
w. man must be raised to stand		7: 6
w. he that is found guiltless		7: 7
a plan w. she could redeem	Eth	8: 8
W. hath my father so much		8: 9
the way w. ye may lay hold	Mro	7:21
w. thou mayest accomplish the	DC	5:34

WHEREBY / WHETHER

strength, w. it is made up?	DC	9:12
given w. man can be saved;		18:23
w. you may accomplish the		78:13
w. ye may know how to act		96: 1
w. they lie in wait to deceive,		123:12
w. they may receive stock for		124:63
keys w. he may ask and receive,		124:95
w. ye are sealed up unto the day		124:124
keys w. you may know whether		129: 9
w. all things pertaining to		130: 9
w. things pertaining to		130:10
w. to shed innocent blood,		132:19
w. to shed innocent blood,		132:19
w. one religious society is fostered		134: 9
w. salvation shall come unto the	Mses	6:52

WHEREFORE: *see in the APPENDIX.*

WHEREIN

for w. is he to be accounted of?	2Ne	12:22
w. thou wast made to serve.		24: 3
w. the Lamb of God did fulfil		31: 6
w. there can be no labor	Al	34:33
w. ye will take up your cross,	3Ne	12:30
ye say: W. shall we return?		24: 7
W. have we robbed thee?		24: 8
cometh, w. no man can work.		27:33
ministry, w. thou hast called us,		28: 2
is w. all men are redeemed,	Mrm	9:13
w. he became subject to the	DC	29:40
w. he became spiritually dead,		29:41
w. they are agents unto		58:28
Christ, w. they became unholy.		74: 4
w. we know them;		123:13
w. ye are not able to build a		124:30
w. the ordinance of baptizing		124:33
w. you receive conversations,		124:39
w. they receive the real value		124:70
w. it is granted that whatsoever		128: 8
w. I, the Lord, justified		132: 1
w. they shed innocent blood,		132:26
w. ye shed innocent blood,		132:27
w. he glorifieth himself.		132:31
w. I restore all things,		132:45
w. she has trespassed against me;		132:56
the earth, w. I grant life,	Mses	2:30
w. he became Master Mahan,		5:49
w. the sins of the parents cannot		6:54
w. my wisdom excelleth them all,	Abr	3:21

WHEREOF

w. he hath commanded me	Mos	2:27
w. they shall be judged,		3:24
things w. I have spoken are true.	Al	5:45
the things w. he hath testified		10:10
the things w. they were accused,		10:12
the things w. he had appointed		12:28
Hast thou eaten of the tree w. I	Mses	4:17

WHEREON

a foundation w. if men build	He	5:12
the place w. it shall be built.	DC	124:42
w. is a new name written,		130:11
unto that w. thou standest.	Abr	3: 4
an earth w. these may dwell;		3:24

WHERESOEVER

part of the land w. they dwelt,	Al	23:14
gospel w. I shall send you,	DC	108: 6
w. the carcass is, there will the	JS	1:27

WHEREUNTO

w. you have been called;	DC	30: 2
w. I have appointed him.		42:10
office w. I have appointed you.		54: 2
the calling w. I have called you,		88:80
right w. I should be ordained	Abr	1: 2

WHEREVER

w. you can be heard, until I	DC	30:10
w. the traveling high council,		124:139

WHEREWITH

w. the Lord had commanded us.	1Ne	5:20
bellows w. to blow the fire,		17:11
might have w. to blow the fire,		17:11
he has w. that he can look,	Mos	8:13
might have w. to accuse him;		12:19
w. God has commanded me;		13: 4
w. ye have been made free,		23:13
w. they have been brought into	Al	5:54
ministry w. thou wast entrusted.		39: 4
w. God has made them free;		58:40
w. God hath made them free.		61:21
w. they have been made free.	He	15: 8
covenant w. he hath covenanted	3Ne	5:25
w. to subsist upon;		6: 3
w. shall the earth be salted?		12:13
anything w. to steer her;	Mrm	5:18
w. I have commanded you;	DC	5:22
the work w. I have called you,		9:14
w. you have been entrusted;		10: 7
w. to magnify thine office,		24: 9
w. ye shall be able to quench		27:17
office w. I have appointed		38:23
w. I commanded you,		42: 3
w. I have commanded him;		43:13
w. the enemy seeketh to destroy		44: 5
as they have w. to pay;		72:11
he who hath not w. to pay,		72:13
preparation w. I prepare you,		78:13
w. he has been ordained,		79: 1
the calling w. you are called,		81: 1
w. to give them inheritances.		83: 5
liberty w. ye are made free;		88:86
covenant w. ye have covenanted		90:24
w. I design to prepare mine		95: 4
w. you have been afflicted		98: 3
w. he has trespassed against		98:40
w. he has trespassed against		98:44
w. they have trespassed,		98:47
w. their fathers have trespassed,		98:47
w. they have been afflicted,		101: 2
assurance w. he may stand;		106: 8

WHEREWITHAL

or, w. shall we be clothed?	3Ne	13:31
or w. ye shall be clothed.	DC	84:81

WHETHER

w. they be good, or whether they	Mos	3:24
they be good, or w. they be evil.		3:24
w. they be good or whether they		16:10
they be good or w. they be evil—		16:10
w. out of the church or in the	Al	1:30
w. it were for or against Amlici,		2: 5
w. they were good or whether		3:26
or w. they were bad,		3:26
w. it be a good spirit or a bad		3:26
w. they be good or whether		11:44
or w. they be evil.		11:44
w. to do evil or to do good—		12:31
to know w. the Lord would that		16: 5
W. he be the Great Spirit or a		18: 3
w. they will that ye shall come		27:15
w. it be unto death or unto life;		29: 4
w. they be unto salvation or unto		29: 4
w. he desireth good or evil,		29: 5
w. they should believe in one		33: 1
w. the word be in the Son of God,		34: 5
or w. there shall be no Christ.		34: 5
w. there shall be one time, or		40: 5
w. there is more than one time		40: 8
all men, w. they be good or evil,		40:11
w. the souls and the bodies of		40:19
w. it be at his resurrection or		40:21
judges, w. to do good or do evil.		41: 7
knew not w. to go or to strike.		52:36
w. they were overtaken by		56:43
w. they should not fall into the		59:11
w. it should be just in us to go		61:19
w. among the Nephites or the	He	6: 7
w. it were among the Lamanites		6: 8

WHETHER 1033 WHILE

WHETHER

w. this man be a prophet and	He	9: 2
the chief judge w. he was dead?		9:12
their works, w. they be good or	3Ne	26: 4
be good or w. they be evil—		26: 4
their works, w. they be good or		27:14
be good or w. they be evil—		27:14
w. they were in the body or out		28:15
w. they were mortal or immortal,		28:17
knew not w. they were cleansed		28:36
works, w. they be good or evil;	Mrm	3:20
And w. they will slay me,		8: 3
w. they be upon the face of the		8:10
w. he will drive us out of	Eth	1:38
w. it was above the water or		6:10
W. the Lord will that I be		15:34
led them w. to preach, or to	Mro	6: 9
w. by mine own voice or by	DC	1:38
w. in weakness or in strength,		24:11
in strength, w. in bonds or free;		24:11
operations, w. they be of God,		46:16
endure, w. in life or in death,		50: 5
w. in life or in death;		58: 2
w. for food or for raiment,		59:17
w. they go by water or by land;		61:22
w. upon the land or upon		61:28
w. in life or in death.		61:39
w. it be little or much,		63:40
w. to the east or to the west,		75:26
theirs, w. life or death,		76:59
w. to the north or to the south,		80: 3
water, w. in heat or in cold,		84:92
w. in the ground or above the		89:16
w. you will abide in my covenant,		98:14
asked w. they accepted their		102: 4
w. they would act in that office		102: 4
w. it is a difficult one or not;		102:13
w. it is necessary to call such		102:29
determine w. any such case.		102:33
w. there be one God or many		121:28
w. it be good or bad.		127: 2
w. they themselves have attended		128: 8
w. any administration is from God.		129: 9
decide w. this coming referred to		130:16
or w. I should die and thus see		130:16
w. it be ordained or men,		132:13

WHICH: *see in the APPENDIX.*

WHILE

w. we journeyed in the wilderness	1Ne	5: 6
w. my father tarried in the		8: 2
w. the angel spake these words,		12:19
w. I was carried away in the		14:30
w. we did live upon raw meat		17: 2
w. we did sojourn in the wilderness.		17: 3
that they might repent w. in the	2Ne	2:21
them w. they are in the flesh,		10:15
them w. they are in the flesh—		10:17
For yet a very little w.,		20:25
that it is yet a very little w.		27:28
w. the children of Israel were	Jac	1: 7
w. his arm of mercy is extended		6: 5
w. I was thus struggling in	En	1:10
w. attempting to speak unto you;	Mos	2:30
also wronged w. crossing the sea;		10:12
wronged w. in the land of their		10:13
w. they should speak lying and		11:11
w. they were tending their flocks.		11:16
w. in the mount of Sinai,		13: 5
w. speaking with the Lord.		13: 5
w. the arms of mercy were		16:12
w. they were in the land of Helam,		23:25
w. tilling the land round about,		23:25
even w. you are in bondage;		24:14
w. he was going about to destroy		27:10
w. others were abasing themselves,	Al	4:13
w. he was journeying thither,		8:14
w. Alma was thus weighed down		8:14
w. this Alma hath dwelt at my		10:10
w. others would reject the Spirit		13: 4
w., if it had not been for this they		13: 4
themselves w. in the wilderness.		17: 7
w. defending the flocks of the king.	Al	19:21
w. they were thus contending,		19:28
w. the bodies of many thousands		28:11
W. many thousands of others		28:12
w. they are puffed up, even to		31:27
unto thee, w. others shall perish.		31:28
w. he that exercises no faith unto		34:16
improve our time w. in this life,		34:33
w. I was harrowed up by the		36:17
W. on the other hand, there was		43:38
w. the remainder of the seed of		46:24
w. Amalickiah had thus been		48: 7
w., on the other hand, there was		49:23
w. Moroni was thus breaking		51:22
w. he had commanded those		52:13
overpower them w. they were		52:17
w. Tenacum was thus leading		52:24
w. he marched with the		52:26
w. they should preform their		53: 1
to guard them w. at their labor;		53: 5
w. in the absence of Moroni		53: 8
w. the Lamanites were in a		55:16
w. there was a thousand of our		57:26
w. Moroni was thus making		59: 5
w. it might have otherwise been		60: 5
w. your enemies are spreading		60: 7
w. they are murdering thousands		60: 7
w. we sit upon our thrones and		60:21
w. ye are surrounded with		60:22
w. there are thousands round		60:22
w. ye sit still and behold these		60:23
w. your iniquity is for the cause		60:32
son, w. in the judgment-seat;	He	6:19
w. the Lamanites began to grow		6:34
converted w. they were in prison.		9:39
w. the Lamanites did ovserve		13: 1
w. the thunder and the lightening		14:27
w. others would receive railing	3Ne	6:13
w. they were thus conversing		11: 3
w. thou art in the way with him,		12:25
w. ye are in prison can ye pay		12:26
w. they were gone for bread and		18: 2
w. they were overshadowed		18:39
w. the angels were ministering		19:15
pain w. ye shall dwell in the flesh,		28: 9
w. the world shall stand.		28: 9
And w. they were yet weary,	Mrm	4: 2
light w. we shall cross the sea.	Eth	3: 4
w. they were upon the waters;		6: 8
w. he was yet in captivity.		7: 7
be cut off w. in the thought,	Mro	8:14
you must wait yet a little w.,	DC	5:17
and reap w. the day lasts,		6: 3
and reap w. the day lasts,		11: 3
and reap w. the day lasts,		12: 3
and reap w. the day lasts,		14: 3
to Lehi w. in the wilderness,		17: 1
your God, w. I speak unto you,		25: 1
w. there is no one to be a scribe		25: 6
forever, w. the earth shall stand,		38:20
my voice w. it is called today,		45: 6
w. journeying unto their homes;		61:23
have appointed, w. he liveth,		64: 5
ye will labor w. it is called today.		64:25
for their benefit w. they remain,		70:15
w. we were doing the work of		76:15
w. we meditated upon these		76:19
w. we were yet in the Spirit,		76:28
w. we were yet in the Spirit.		76:80
w. we were yet in the Spirit.		76:113
w. we were yet in the Spirit,		76:115
of the Spirit, w. in the flesh,		76:118
his rest w. in the wilderness,		84:24
w. he was yet in his childhood,		84:28
yet a little w. and ye shall see		84:119
quake w. it maketh manifest,		85: 6
w. his bowels shall be a fountain		85: 7
W. that man, who was called of		85: 8
w. the Lord is beginning to		86: 6
w. the blade is yet tender		86: 6
call upon me w. I am near—		88:62
w. they hear the sound of		88:104

WHILE

w. thou art in the world, neither	DC 90: 3
w. all the wicked shall mourn.	97:21
And w. they were yet laying the	101:47
And w. they were at variance	101:50
enemy w. he was yet afar off;	101:54
W. the tares shall be bound in	101:66
And he would not for a w.,	101:84
w. he is laboring in my	104:20
w. you are saying unto me	105:25
W. the pure in heart, and the wise,	122: 2
and safety w. he shall contemplate	124:23
w. I was praying earnestly	130:13
w. protected in their inherent and	134: 5
w. they were in the field, Cain	Mses 5:32
w. we go yonder to behold the	6:38
w. the earth should stand;	7:52
W. I was laboring under the	JS 2:11
w. they were persecuting me,	2:25
W. I was thus in the act of	2:30
W. he was conversing with me	2:42
w. I was yet employed in the	2:57
W. preparing to start —	2:61
w. there the family related to	2:66
W. we were thus employed,	2:68

WHILST

w. all around us are elected to be	Al 31:17
w. thousands of their wicked	50:22
w. in this tabernacle of clay,	Mro 9: 6
w. the inhabitants on either side	DC 61: 3

WHIMS

and their dreams and their w.	Al 30:28

WHIRLWIND

and their wheels like a w.,	2Ne 15:28
reap the chaff thereof in the w.;	Mos 7:30
winds, yea, his shafts in the w.,	He 5:12
who were carried away in the w.;	3Ne 8:16
were not carried away in the w.;	10:13
shall come upon them as a w.,	DC 63: 6
upon the ungodly as the w.;	97:22
as a w. it shall come upon	112:24
they are taken away by a w.,	Abr 2: 7

WHIRLWINDS

and w. shall carry them away,	2Ne 26: 5
they be harrowed up by the w.;	Al 26: 6
of the tempest and the w.	3Ne 8:12
and by tempests, and by w.,	10:14

WHISPER

that he may w. concerning them,	2Ne 26:16
speech shall w. out of the dust.	26:16
mildness, as if it had been a w.,	He 5:30
pleasant voice, as if it were a w.,	5:46

WHISPERETH

and thus he w. in their ears,	2Ne 28:22
for thus it w. me, according	WM 1: 7
which w. through and pierceth	DC 85: 6

WHIT

yea, even every w.;	1Ne 4:19
every w. pointing to that great	Al 34:14
I say unto you, Nay; not one w.	42:25
not a w. behind him as to things	He 11:19
to pass, yea, all things, every w.,	3Ne 1:20
it must be fulfilled in every w.;	1:25
save he were cleansed every w.	8: 1
were fulfilled thus far, every w.;	Eth 15: 3
become corrupted every w.;	DC 33: 4

WHITE

he was dressed in a w. robe;	1Ne 8: 5
the fruit thereof was w.,	8:11
she was exceedingly fair and w.	11:13
garments are made w. in his blood.	12:10
and their garments were w.	12:11
made w. in the blood of the Lamb,	12:11
they were w. and exceeding fair	13:15
he was dressed in a w. robe.	14:19
they were w. and exceeding fair	2Ne 5:21
black and w., bond and free,	26:33
be a w. and delightsome people.	30: 6
except his garments are washed w.;	Al 5:21
and are spotless, pure and w.?	5:24
w. through the blood of Christ,	5:27
their garments were washed w.	13:11
having their garments made w.,	13:12
is w. above all that is white,	32:42
is white above all that is w.,	32:42
made w. through the blood of	34:36
w. like unto the Nephites;	3Ne 2:15
he was clothed in a w. robe;	11: 8
not make one hair black or w.;	12:36
as w. as the countenance and	19:25
so w. as the whiteness thereof.	19:25
behold they were w., even as	19:30
found spotless, pure, fair, and w.,	Mrm 9: 6
and they were w. and clear,	Eth 3: 1
they whose garments are w.	13:10
field is w. already to harvest;	DC 4: 4
field is w. already to harvest;	6: 3
field is w. already to harvest;	11: 3
field is w. already to harvest;	12: 3
field is w. already to harvest;	14: 3
whose garments were pure and w.	20: 6
is w. already to be burned.	31: 4
field is w. already to harvest;	33: 3
field is w. already to harvest;	33: 7
the hair of his head was w. like	110: 3
Then the w. stone mentioned in	130:10
And a w. stone is given to each	130:11
exceedingly w. and brilliant.	JS 2:31
was his robe exceedingly w.,	2:32

WHITENESS

white, to exceed all the w.	1Ne 8:11
the w. thereof did exceed	11: 8
exceed the w. of the driven snow.	11: 8
the w. thereof did exceed all the	3Ne 19:25
did exceed all the w., yea, even	19:25
so white as the w. thereof.	19:25
and white above all other w.;	DC 20: 6
loose robe of most exquisite w.	JS 2:31
a w. beyond anything earthly	2:31

WHITER

their skins will be w. than yours,	Jac 3: 8

WHITHER

knew not w. they should go.	1Ne 8:14
the way w. we should go	16:10
W. shall I go to obtain food?	16:23
w. shall I go that I may find	17: 9
Lord told me w. I should go	17:10
knew not w. they should steer	18:13
it did work w. I desired it.	18:21
w. they are none of us knoweth,	22: 4
w. the master had hid the	Jac 5:20
then it matters not w. I go,	Mos 13: 9
they knew not w. they had fled.	21:31
W. art thou going with this	Al 20:10
unto him w. he was going,	20:11
w. the Nephites had driven them.	22:29
have a country w. they might flee,	22:34
would know w. they had gone.	43:22
w. the armies of the Nephites	43:23
w. they should go to defend themselves	48:16
and w. she did go we know not.	63: 8
w. he went, no man knoweth;	3Ne 1: 3
w. they went no man knoweth,	8:16
w. I have been to minister.	16: 1
knoweth w. he hath taken them.	17: 4
and w. I go it mattereth not.	Mrm 8: 4
have not friends nor w. to go;	8: 5
cry unto him w. we shall go.	Eth 1:38
directions w. they should travel.	2: 5
is no light; w. shall we steer?	2:19
the place w. he would keep it,	14: 1
quarter of the land w. he fled.	14:15
shall do and w. you shall go.	DC 31:11
w. they shall go.	75:27
and the way w. he shall go;	79: 2

WHITHERSOEVER

and I will graft them w. I will;	Jac	5: 8
and I will graft them w. I will.		5: 8
part of my vineyard, w. I will,		5:13
which I planted w. I would		5:54
went forth w. they were led	Al	21:16
w. the enemy listeth to carry		26: 6
w. thou goest let it be in the Lord;		37:36
did also go w. they would,	He	6: 8
w. he desired to carry them,	3Ne	6:17
they should go w. they would;	Eth	7:25
wherefore, I wander w. I can	Mro	1: 3
to wander w. they can for food;		9:16
Oliver Cowdery, w. I will.	DC	25: 6
Go your way w. I will,		31:11
the church w. it is found,		37: 2
I will lead them w. I will,		38:33
w. I, the Lord, shall send them.		70:16
w. my servant Joseph Smith,		103:40
w. they shall send you, go ye,		112:19
any nation w. ye shall send them—		112:21

WHITLOCK, Harvey

servants David Whitmer and W.	DC	52:25

WHITMER

in the chamber of old Father W.	DC	128:21

WHITMER, David: *see also DAVID.*

speak unto you, and also unto W.,	DC	18: 9
Cowdery, and also unto W.,		18:37
servants W. and Harvey Whitlock		52:25

WHITMER, John: *see also JOHN.*

my servant, W., should go	DC	69: 2
let my servant W. travel		69: 7
and also unto my servant W.,		70: 1

WHITMER, Peter, Jun.: *see also PETER.*

Oliver Cowdery and W.,	DC	32: 2

WHITNEY, Newel K.

let my servant W. retain	DC	63:42
W. and Sidney Gilbert,		64:26
my servant W. is the man		72: 8
let my servant Ahashdah [W.]		78: 9
Adam and Ahashdah [W.]		82:11
bishop, W., also should travel		84:112
My servant W. also, a bishop		93:50
let my servant Ahashdah [W.]		96: 2
let my servant Ahashdah [W.]		104:39
unto my servant Ahashdah [W.]		104:40
unto my servant Ahashdah [W.]		104:41
also unto my servant W.,		117: 1
Let my servant W. be ashamed		117:11

WHO: *see in the APPENDIX.*

WHOEVER

w. he blesses shall be blessed,	DC	124:93
w. he curses shall be cursed;		124:93

WHOLE

and his w. heart was filled,	1Ne	1:15
the w. staff of bread,	2Ne	13: 1
and the w. stay of water—		13: 1
the w. earth is full of his glory.		16: 3
Lord hath performed his w. work		20:12
to destroy the w. land.		23: 5
The w. earth is at rest,		24: 7
is purposed upon the w. earth;		24:26
Rejoice not thou, w. Palestina,		24:29
thou, w. Palestina, art dissolved;		24:31
and strength, and your w. soul;		25:29
thy faith hath made thee w.	En	1: 8
pour out my w. soul unto God		1: 9
and offer your w. souls as an	Om	1:26
and the faculty of his w. soul,	WM	1:18
which your w. soul has power to	Mos	2:20
serve him with all your w. souls		2:21
my w. frame doth tremble		2:30
making in the w., about four		6: 4
poured out his w. soul to God,		26:14
making in the w., five hundred	Mos	29:46
thus the w. becoming spiritual	Al	11:45
his w. household were converted		22:23
this is the w. meaning of the law,		34:14
is exposed to the w. law of the		34:16
and the w. earth did tremble		36: 7
and it shook the w. earth.		38: 7
second leader over the w. army.		47:13
pass by us with their w. army,		56:24
the w. army of the Lamanites		56:52
also the foes of our w. army,		57:25
was astonishing to our w. army,		57:26
suffer their w. army, save a few		58:22
they had driven their w. army		58:25
did march forth with his w. army	He	1:20
take possession of the w. city.		1:20
to cover the face of the w. earth		3: 8
and the w. earth was smitten,		11: 6
the w. face of the land was filled		11:18
did cover the w. face of the land,		11:20
defy the w. armies of the Nephites,		11:32
voice doth the w. earth shake;		12:11
upon the face of the w. earth,		14:22
cover the face of the w. earth		14:27
upon the face of the w. earth	3Ne	1:17
it did shake the w. earth as if		8: 6
the w. face of the land was		8:12
great quaking of the w. earth;		8:12
the w. earth became deformed,		8:17
upon the face of the w. earth,		8:18
the inhabitants of the w. earth		9: 2
the wickedness of the w. earth,		9: 9
the eyes of the w. multitude		11: 8
the w. multitude fell to the earth;		11:12
and the God of the w. earth,		11:14
thy w. body shall be full of light.		13:22
w. body shall be full of darkness.		13:23
all the people of the w. earth,		16:10
healed and they who were w.,		17:10
unto the Lord of the w. earth.		20:19
the God of the w. earth shall he		22: 5
robbed me, even this w. nation.		24: 9
The w. face of the land had	Mrm	1: 7
upon the face of the w. land,		1:13
in the w., three hundred and		3: 4
the w. human family of Adam;		3:20
the w. face of this land is one		8: 8
And the w. face of the land	Eth	10:21
upon the face of the w. earth		13:17
that the w. face of the land was		14:21
the w. need no physician,	Mro	8: 8
wherefore, little children are w.,		8: 8
upon the face of the w. earth,	DC	1:30
the w. earth would be utterly		2: 3
all the names of the w. church		20:82
that the w. earth may not be		27: 9
take upon you my w. armor,		27:15
to judge the w. house of Israel,		29:12
your w. labor shall be in Zion,		30:11
and the w. earth shall be in		45:26
all cases under the w. heavens.		52:19
even the Lord of the w. earth.		55: 1
this w. region of country,		58:52
this w. company of mine elders		61: 3
until it has filled the w. earth.		65: 2
property of the w. church—		82:18
for the sake of the w. world.		84:48
And the w. world lieth in sin,		84:49
w. world groaneth under sin		84:53
brought the w. church under		84:55
your w. bodies shall be filled		88:67
smite the w. earth with a curse,		98:17
even this w. Ozondah		104:41
And devote his w. time to this		106: 3
is to preside over the w. church,		107:91
and fill the w. earth;		109:72
lest the w. earth is to be smitten with		110:15
without mixture upon the w. earth.		115: 6
present the w. concatenation of		123: 5
the w. nation may be left without		123: 6
w. earth groans under the weight		123: 7
the oracles for the w. church.		124:126
in taking the w. proceedings,		128: 3

WHOLE 1036 WHOSE

the history of the w. transaction;	DC 128: 3
and grand secret of the w. matter,	128:11
summum bonum of the w. subject	128:11
a w. and complete and perfect	128:18
watered the w. face of the ground.	Mses 3: 6
it compasseth the w. land of	3:11
compasseth the w. land of Ethiopia.	3:13
they are w. from the foundation	6:54
veiled the w. face of the earth	7:26
w. heavens shall weep over them,	7:37
watered the w. face of the ground.	Abr 5: 6
west, and covereth the w. earth,	JS 1:26
the w. district of country	2: 5
but his w. person was glorious	2:32
the w. earth would be utterly	2:39
occupied the w. of that night.	2:47
rehearsed the w. matter to him.	2:50

WHOLESOME
all w. herbs God hath ordained	DC 89:10

WHOLLY
relying w. upon the merits of	2Ne 31:19
w. to the high priesthood	Al 4:20
w. confined to the judgment-seat,	7: 1
it shall be w. dedicated unto	DC 94: 7
this house shall be w. dedicated	94:12
w. turned to the god of Elkenah,	Abr 1: 6

WHOM: *see in the APPENDIX.*

WHOMSOEVER
w. ye receive shall believe in	Mos 26:22
and w. shall be called thy seed,	Al 3:17
w. of the Amalickiahites that	46:35
w. the other elders shall	DC 20:82
on w. you shall lay your hands,	55: 3
meek, and upon all w. I will,	97: 2
And w. ye curse, I will curse,	103:25
w. you bless I will bless,	132:47
w. you curse I will curse,	132:47
w. you give any one on earth,	132:48

WHORE
she is the w. of all the earth.	1Ne 14:10
beheld the w. of all the earth,	14:11
and abominations of the w.	14:12
the wickedness of the great w.	14:12
abominable church, which is the w.	22:13
that great w., who hath perverted	22:14
who are the w. of all the earth;	2Ne 10:16
the w. of all the earth,	28:18
which is the w. of all the earth,	DC 29:21
church, the apostate, the w.,	86: 3

WHOREDOMS
Wo unto them who commit w.,	2Ne 9:36
that they should not commit w.;	26:32
and abominations, and w.,	28:14
and all those who commit w.,	28:15
themselves in committing w.,	Jac 2:23
And w. are an abomination	2:28
for they shall not commit w.,	2:33
and there should not be w.	3: 5
Yea, and they did commit w.	Mos 11: 2
in their idolatry, and in their w.,	11: 6
their wickedness, and their w.;	11:20
Why do ye commit w. and spend	12:29
and the committing of w.,	29:36
thieving, robbing, committing w.,	Al 1:32
and also men, to commit w.	30:18
their idolatry, their w., and	50:21
manner of abominations and w.,	He 3:14
and steal, and commit w. and	6:23
their abominations, and their w.,	3Ne 5: 3
murders, and priestcrafts, and w.,	16:10
strifes, and priestcrafts, and w.,	21:19
and deceivings, and of your w.,	30: 2
nor strifes, nor tumults, nor w.,	4Ne 1:16
lying, and deceivings, and w.,	Mrm 8:31
manner of wickedness and w.	Eth 8:16
did afflict the people with his w.	10: 7
because of his many w.;	10:11

WHOREMONGER
and the w., and the sorcerer,	DC 63:17

WHOREMONGERS
and adulterers, and w., and	DC 76:103

WHOSE
a tree, w. fruit was desirable	1Ne 8:10
w. shoe's latchet I am not worthy	10: 8
an olive-tree, whose branches should	10:12
church, w. formation thou hast seen.	13:32
w. foundation is the devil.	14: 9
w. foundation is the devil,	14:17
of life, w. fruit is most precious	15:36
parent, w. limbs ye must soon lay	2Ne 1:14
brother, w. views have been	1:24
people in w. heart I have written	8: 7
Lord thy God, w. waves roared;	8:15
w. flame ascendeth up forever	9:16
w. breath is in his nostrils;	12:22
W. arrows shall be sharp,	15:28
as an oak w. substance is in	16:13
and w. graven images did excel	20:10
many of w. feelings are	Jac 2: 7
the tree w. natural branches had	5:30
this last, w. branch hath withered	5:43
branches w. fruit is most bitter,	5:52
w. flames are unquenchable,	6:10
w. smoke ascendeth up forever	6:10
w. name was Sherin.	7: 1
fire, w. flame ascendeth up forever	Mos 2:38
w. flames are unquenchable,	3:27
w. smoke ascendeth up forever	3:27
among them w. name was Abinadi;	11:20
are they w. sins he has borne;	15:12
among them w. name was Alma,	17: 2
among them w. name was Gideon,	19: 4
taken captive, w. name was Limhi.	19:16
people w. bones they had found;	21:27
w. garments are cleansed and are	Al 5:24
them w. name was Zeezrom.	10:31
w. flame ascendeth up forever	12:17
women, w. name was Abish,	19:16
w. brother had been slain	19:22
w. name is Antiomno, is a friend	20: 4
of w. bones we have spoken,	22:30
w. hearts had swollen in them	24:24
w. arms were lifted to slay them.	24:25
w. hearts delight in the shedding	26:24
w. days have been spent in the	26:24
w. ways have been the ways of	26:24
w. name was Korihor,	30:12
by a man w. name was Zoram—	30:59
led by a man w. name was Lehi,	43:35
Joseph, w. coat was rent by	46:23
w. name was Lehonti, that he	47:10
a man w. soul did joy in the	48:11
a man w. heart did swell with	48:12
a man w. name was Morianton,	50:28
a man w. name was Tenacum,	50:35
their leader, w. name was Jacob,	52:20
found one, w. name was Laman;	55: 5
son, w. name was Moronihah;	62:43
man w. name was Coriantumr;	He 1:15
w. name was Tubaloth, who was	1:16
a man w. name was Cezoram.	5: 1
band, w. author is Gadianton and	8:28
mountains, w. height is great.	14:23
w. name was Zemnarihah;	3Ne 4:17
dead, w. name was Timothy,	19: 4
his son, w. name was Jonas,	19: 4
those w. flight was swifter than	Mrm 5: 7
those w. flight did not exceed	5: 7
w. days were exceeding many.	Eth 7: 1
was one w. name was Noah.	7:14
eldest son, w. name was Shez,	10: 3
w. faith was so exceeding strong,	12:19
they w. garments are white	13:10
of Shared, w. name was Gilead,	14: 8
w. delight is in so much	Mro 9:13
w. throne is high in the heavens,	9:26
and w. eyes are upon all men;	DC 1: 1
w. image is in the likeness of	1:16

WHOSE 1037 WHOSOEVER

w. substance is that of an idol,	DC 1:16	w. believeth in me believeth in	3Ne 11:35
the will of him w. I am,	19: 2	w. buildeth upon this buildeth	11:39
w. countenance was as lightning,	20: 6	w. shall declare more or less	11:40
and w. garments were pure and	20: 6	w. shall marry her who is	12:32
w. word is quick and powerful.	27: 1	w. heareth these sayings of mine	14:24
w. arm of mercy hath atoned	29: 1	w. remembereth these sayings of	15: 1
w. word is quick and powerful,	33: 1	w. among you shall do more or	18:13
w. course is one eternal round,	35: 1	w. eateth and drinketh my flesh	18:29
of old, w. name was Peter:	49:11	w. taketh upon him my name,	27: 6
prayeth, w. spirit is contrite,	52:15	w. repenteth and is baptized in	27:16
speaketh, w. spirit is contrite,	52:16	w. receiveth not the words of	28:34
w. language is meek and	52:16	And w. receiveth this record,	Mrm 8:12
w. hearts are not broken,	56:17	and w. shall bring it to light,	8:14
w. spirits are not contrite,	56:17	that w. believeth in Christ,	9:21
w. bellies are not satisfied,	56:17	and w. findeth them, the same	Eth 1: 4
w. hands are not stayed from	56:17	that w. should possess this land	2: 8
w. eyes are full of greediness,	56:17	that w. should vary from the	8:14
in heart, w. hearts are broken,	56:18	w. should divulge whatsoever	8:14
and w. spirits are contrite,	56:18	w. buildeth it up seeketh to	8:25
he reigns w. right it is to reign,	58:22	w. should possess the land	9:20
w. feet stand upon the land of	59: 3	that w. should attempt to pass	9:33
w. sins are now forgiven you,	61: 2	w. would not be subject unto	10: 6
w. anger is kindled against	61:31	w. was not able to pay taxes	10: 6
w. anger is kindled against	63: 2	w. refused to labor he did cause	10: 6
whose going forth is unto the ends	65: 1	w. believeth in God might with	12: 4
yea, w. voice is unto men	65: 1	and w. was found to commit	Mro 6: 7
w. prayers I have heard,	67: 1	w. is found possessed of it	7:47
heard, and w. hearts I know,	67: 1	therefore, w. desireth to reap,	DC 6: 3
w. desires have come up before	67: 1	w. desireth to reap let him	11: 3
w. mission is appointed unto	68: 2	w. desireth to reap let him	12: 3
into w. hands the Father has	76:55	w. desireth to reap let him	14: 3
w. names are written in heaven,	76:68	w. having knowledge, have I	29:49
they w. bodies are celestial,	76:70	w. having faith you shall confirm	33:15
w. glory is that of the sun,	76:70	w. shall ask it in my name in	35: 9
w. glory the sun of the	76:70	w. doeth this shall receive the	49:14
w. glory differs from that of	76:71	w. forbiddeth to marry is not	49:15
Before w. throne all things bow	76:93	w. forbiddeth to abstain from	49:18
in w. hand is given all power.	84:28	And w. is found a faithful,	51:19
Lord's house, w. sons are ye;	84:32	w. readeth let him understand—	57: 9
w. mouth shall utter words,	85: 7	w. standeth in this mission	58:17
the saints w. names are found,	85: 7	w. readeth, let him understand	71: 5
w. names are not found written	85:11	For w. is faithful unto the	84:33
in w. hearts the enemy,	86: 3	But w. breaketh this covenant	84:41
in w. bosom it is decreed that	88:17	For w. cometh not unto me is	84:51
every man w. spirit receiveth	93:32	And w. receiveth not my voice	84:52
w. offering I have accepted,	96: 6	And w. receiveth you, there I	84:88
w. prayers I have heard,	96: 6	W. receiveth you receiveth	84:89
in w. name alone salvation can be	109: 4	Therefore, w. readeth it, let	91: 4
w. husbands and fathers have been	123: 9	w. is enlightened by the Spirit	91: 5
from w. loins ye are, namely,	132:30	w. receiveth not by the Spirit,	91: 6
w. seed should be in itself upon	Mses 2:11	And w. layeth down his life in	98:13
w. seed should be in itself, after	2:12	And w. rejecteth you shall be	99: 4
w. name was Mahijah, and said	6:40	w. layeth down his life for my	103:27
through w. seed Messiah shall	7:53	w. is not willing to lay down	103:28
planet w. reckoning of time shall	Abr 3: 8	w. cometh in at the gate and	Mses 7:53
w. seed in itself yieldeth its own	4:11	w. readeth let him understand	JS 1:12
w. seed could only bring forth the	4:12	And w. treasureth up my word,	1:37
w. spirit they had put into the	5: 8		
w. name is given in the	Fac 3: 2	**WHOSOEVER**	
(w. name, previous to her	JS 2: 4	w. should believe that Christ	Mos 3:13
w. brightness and glory defy all	2:17	w. doeth this the same hath great	4:18
		w. among you borroweth of his	4:28
WHOSESOEVER		w. doeth this shall be found at	5: 9
w. sins you remit on earth	DC 132:46	w. shall not take upon him the	5:10
w. sins you retain on earth	132:46	w. is commanded to look in	8:13
		w. has heard the words of the	15:11
WHOSO		w. was baptized by the power	18:17
and w. shall publish peace,	1Ne 13:37	w. has done this thing shall	20:16
w. repenteth not must perish.	14: 5	w. putteth his trust in him	23:22
w. belongeth not to the church of	14:10	w. should be found calling upon	24:11
w. would hearken unto the word of	15:24	w. were desirous to take upon	25:23
w. shall lay his hands upon me	17:48	w. is baptized shall be baptized	26:22
And w. knocketh, to him will	2Ne 9:42	w. transgresseth against me,	26:29
that w. of my people shall see	11: 8	w. will not repent of his sins	26:32
for w. doeth them shall perish.	26:32	w. repented of their sins and did	26:35
And w. should reign in his stead	Jac 1:11	w. has these things is called seer,	28:16
w. shall hide up treasures in the	He 13:18	w. has committed iniquity, him	29:15
w. cometh unto me with a broken	3Ne 9:20	w. doth not obey his laws	29:23
w. repenteth and cometh unto	9:22	w. doth rebel against him he	29:23
w. readeth, let him understand;	10:14	w. did not belong to the church	Al 1:19
w. repenteth of his sins	11:23	w. did mingle his seed with	3: 9
w. believeth in me, and is	22:33	w. suffered himself to be led	3:10
And w. believeth not in me, and	11:34	w. would not believe in the	3:11

WHOSOEVER 1038 WICKED

w. bringeth forth not good fruit,	Al 5:36	Yea, w. should I give way to	2Ne	4:27
w. doeth not the works of	5:36	W. am I angry because of mine		4:27
w. denieth this is a liar and a	5:39	w. do ye ponder these things in		32: 1
w. bringeth forth evil works,	5:41	w. not able to command the earth,	Jac	4: 9
w. doeth this must receive his	5:42	w. not speak of the atonement		4:12
w. did not belong to the church	6: 2	for w. will ye die?		6: 6
w. did belong to the church that	6: 3	law of Moses w. do ye not keep it?	Mos	12:29
w. doeth this, and keepeth the	7:16	W. do ye set your hearts upon		12:29
w. dieth in his sins,	12:16	W. do ye commit whoredoms and		12:29
w. repenteth, and hardeneth not	12:34	w. should ye break the oath		20:14
w. will harden his heart and will	12:35	for w. persecutest thou the church		27:13
w. believed or had been taught to	14: 8	w. hath Satan got such great hold	Al	10:25
w. were desirous to be baptized.	15:13	W. will ye yield yourselves unto		10:25
all w. would believe on his name.	22:13	thou child of hell, w. tempt ye me?		11:23
w. desired to worship must	31:14	W. do ye not answer the words of		14:19
w. repenteth shall find mercy;	32:13	w. do ye not deliver yourselves?		14:20
w. would look upon it might live.	33:19	W. did ye not come to the feast		20: 9
w. shall put their trust in God	36: 3	W. do not angels appear unto us?		21: 5
w. murdereth against the light	39: 6	w. he has not come up out of		22: 3
that w. will may walk therein	41: 8	W. commandest thou that we		22:20
w. will come may come and	42:27	w. did he not consign us to an		26:19
w. will not come the same is not	42:27	w. did he not let the sword of		26:19
w. should worship God in spirit	43:10	w. should I desire more than to		29: 6
But w. remaineth, and is not	45:14	W. should I desire that I were an		29: 7
w. will maintain this title upon	46:20	w. do ye yoke yourselves with		30:13
W. loved the king, let him go	47:27	W. do ye look for a Christ?		30:13
all men w. would hearken unto	48:19	W. do ye go about perverting the		30:22
and w. did not doubt,	57:26	W. do ye teach this people that		30:22
w. would not take up arms in	62: 9	W. do ye speak against all the		30:22
w. was found denying their	62:10	w. sayest thou that we preach		30:35
w. will may lay hold upon the	He 3:29	w. these things should be known		39:17
w. of those who belonged to	6:24	the cause w. they did not send		58: 9
w. shall believe on the Son of	14: 8	w. we have not received greater		58:34
w. repenteth the same is not	14:18	But w. should I say much		60:18
w. repenteth not is hewn down	14:18	w. have ye gathered yourselves	He	7:13
w. will believe might be saved,	14:29	W. will ye die?		7:17
w. will not believe, a righteous	14:29	W. has he forsaken you?		7:17
w. perisheth, perisheth unto	14:30	W. do ye not seize upon this man		8: 1
w. doeth iniquity, doeth it unto	14:30	W. seest thou this man,		8: 2
w. will come, him will I receive;	3Ne 9:14	W. do you suffer this man to revile		8: 5
w. shall kill shall be in danger	12:21	w. should ye dispute among		8:12
w. is angry with his brother	12:22	w. not the Son of God come,		8:20
w. shall say to his brother, Raca,	12:22	w. will he not show himself unto		16:18
w. shall say, Thou fool, shall be	12:22	w. will he not show himself in this		16:19
w. looketh on a woman, to lust	12:28	w. take ye thought for raiment?	3Ne	13:28
w. shall put away his wife,	12:31	w. beholdest thou the mote that		14: 3
w. shall put away his wife,	12:32	w. is it that the people should		27: 4
w. shall smite thee on thy right	12:39	w. have ye built up churches	Mrm	8:33
w. shall compel thee to go	12:41	W. have ye transfigured the		8:33
w. breaketh this commandment	18:25	w. have ye polluted the holy		8:38
w. will not believe in my words,	21:11	W. are ye ashamed to take upon		8:38
w. will not repent and come unto	21:20	W. do ye not think that greater		8:38
w. shall gather together against	22:15	W. do ye adorn yourselves		8:39
w. will hearken unto my words	23: 5	w. do ye build up your secret		8:40
w. shall believe in my name,	Mrm 9:25	w. has God ceased to be a god		9:19
w. believeth on my words,	DC 5:16	the reason w. he ceaseth to do		9:20
w. will thrust in his sickle and	6: 4	Arise, w. hast thou fallen?	Eth	3: 7
w. should believe in this gospel	10:50	w. is it that ye cannot	DC	50:21
w. belongeth to my church	10:55	servants, and said unto them, W.!		101:52
w. repenteth and cometh unto	10:67	W. the first is called the		107: 2
W. declareth more or less than	10:68	W. it is called the lesser		107:14
behold, w. is of my church,	10:69	And w. are they not chosen?		121:34
w. will thrust in his sickle and	11: 4	w. can't you stay with us?		122: 6
w. will thrust in his sickle and	12: 4	W. are they then baptized for		128:16
w. will thrust in his sickle and	14: 4	And w. did she do it?		132:34
w. shall lay their hands upon	24:16	pray thee, w. these things are so,	Mses	1:30
w. shall go to law with thee	24:17	W. dost thou offer sacrifices		5: 6
w. I will shall go forth among	38:33	unto Cain: W. art thou wroth?		5:22
And w. among you are sick,	42:43	W. is thy countenance fallen?		5:22
w. loveth and maketh a lie,	63:17	W. is it that I have found favor		6:31
and w. loves and makes a lie.	76:103	w. counsel ye yourselves, and deny		6:43
W. receiveth my word	112:20	W. is it that men must repent		6:53
w. receiveth me,	112:20	else w. should the powers of	JS	2:20
w. ye shall send in my name,	112:21	W. the opposition and persecution		2:20
W. slayeth thee, vengeance shall	Mses 5:40	W. persecute me for telling the		2:25
		w. does the world think to		2:25
WHY		the reason w. I had received		2:60
W. do ye smite your younger	1Ne 3:29	w. it was that the messenger		2:60
he can slay fifty; then w. not us?	3:31			
then w. not mightier than Laban	4: 1	WICKED		
O, then, w. is it, that ye can be	17:46	the Lord slayeth the w. to bring	1Ne	4:13
w. should my heart weep	2Ne 4:26	separated the w. from the tree		15:28
And w. should I yield to sin,	4:27	was prepared for the w.		15:29

WICKED

divide the w. from the righteous?	1Ne 15:30
w. are rejected from the righteous,	15:36
spoken hard things against the w.,	16: 2
destroyeth the nations of the w.	17:37
and the w. he destroyeth,	17:38
that they have become w.,	17:43
had spoken concerning the w.	18:11
a man, into the hands of w. men,	19:10
saith the Lord, unto the w.	20:22
will not suffer that the w. shall	22:16
the more w. part of the world;	2Ne 10: 3
astray, every one to his w. ways.	12: 5
O ye w. ones, enter into the	12:10
Wo unto the w., for they shall	13:11
Who justify the w. for reward,	15:23
of his lips shall he slay the w.	21: 4
and the w. for their iniquity;	23:11
every one that is joined to the w.	23:15
but the w. shall perish.	23:22
hath broken the staff of the w.,	24: 5
shall that day be unto the w.,	26: 3
of his lips shall he slay the w.	30: 9
and the w. will he destroy;	30:10
he must destroy the w. by fire.	30:10
somewhat in w. practices,	Jac 1:15
striketh the w. with awful dread	6:13
to the words of this w. man.	7:23
I of myself am a w. man,	Om 1: 2
more w. part of the Nephites	1: 5
a w. and an adulterous people,	Mos 1:13
he made his grave with the w.,	14: 9
then shall the w. be cast out,	16: 2
a very w. and an idolatrous man.	27: 8
one w. king cause to be committed,	29:17
being a w. man, would deprive	Al 2: 4
come ye out from the w.,	5:57
the names of the w. shall not	5:57
The names of the w. shall not	5:57
O ye w. and perverse generation,	9: 8
O ye w. and perverse generation,	10:17
O ye w. and perverse generation,	10:25
the w. remain as though there	11:41
both the w. and the righteous;	11:44
w. spirit rooted out of my breast,	22:15
the w. traditions of their fathers,	23: 3
traditions of our w. fathers.	24: 7
not a w. man slain among them;	24:27
were a w. and a perverse people;	31:24
this is the final state of the w.	34:35
being a very w. man, sent	35: 8
again after those w. harlots.	39:11
the spirits of the w., yea, who	40:13
the state of the souls of the w.,	40:14
the w. as well as the righteous,	40:19
awful death cometh upon the w.;	40:26
w. and murderous disposition	43: 6
one very w. man can cause to	46: 9
more wild, w. and ferocious	47:36
thousands of their w. brethren	50:22
and to bring the w. to justice	50:39
judgment may come upon the w.;	60:13
called the Nephites, become w.,	He 3:16
is prepared to engulf the w.—	3:29
they had become a w. people,	4:22
w. even like unto the Lamanites.	4:22
and impenitent and grossly w.,	6: 2
to grow exceedingly w. again.	6:16
more w. part of the Lamanites.	6:18
they had become exceedingly w.;	6:31
among the more w. part of them,	6:37
at the more w. part of them,	6:38
letting the guilty and the w. go	7: 5
I will not show unto the w. of	7:23
the more w. parts of the land.	11: 6
the destruction of those w. men	11:11
O ye w. and ye perverse	13:29
the w. and abominable traditions	15: 7
know that this is a w. tradition,	16:20
w. and abominable robbers.	3Ne 3:11
did put an end to all those w.,	5: 6
people had nearly all become w.;	7: 7
became a king over this w. band;	7:10
between the righteous and the w.,	24:18
And ye shall tread down the w.;	3Ne 25: 3
ye Gentiles, from your w. ways;	30: 2
the more w. part of the people	4Ne 1:40
the w. part of the people began	1:42
w. one like unto another.	1:45
of God will overtake the w.;	Mrm 4: 5
it is by the w. that the wicked	4: 5
wicked that the w. are punished;	4: 5
it is the w. that stir up the	4: 5
fills the breasts of all the w.,	6: 7
O ye w. and perverse and	8:33
abominable and w. above all,	Eth 8:18
of this w. and secret society	9: 6
of their w. combinations;	11: 7
that which was w. in his days.	11:11
which was w. before the Lord.	11:14
society and w. abominations.	11:22
be poured out upon the w.	DC 1: 9
into the hands of a w. man,	3:12
into the hands of a w. man,	10: 1
I said that he is a w. man,	10: 7
w. men have taken them from	10: 8
tell the w. from the righteous,	10:37
all the fiery darts of the w.;	27:17
are sent forth upon the w.	29: 8
and the w. shall not stand.	29:11
take vengeance upon the w.,	29:17
the w. on my left hand will I	29:27
shall be pronounced upon the w.,	29:41
destructions await the w.	34: 9
the w. have I kept in chains of	38: 5
will I cause the w. to be kept,	38: 6
And go ye out from among the w.	38:42
lest ye be found among the w.	43:19
And the w. shall go away into	43:33
among the w., men shall lift	45:32
the w. will not come unto it,	45:67
come to pass among the w.,	45:68
it shall be said among the w.:	45:70
the congregations of the w.	60: 8
the congregations of the w.;	60:13
the congregations of the w.,	60:14
the congregations of the w.	61:30
the congregations of the w.	61:32
the congregations of the w.,	61:33
the congregations of the w.	62: 5
anger is kindled against the w.	63: 2
I say, let the w. take heed,	63: 6
the Lord, am angry with the w.;	63:32
and the w. shall slay the wicked,	63:33
and the wicked shall slay the w.,	63:33
and consume the w. with	63:34
shall come upon the w.	63:37
of the righteous and the w.;	63:54
angels to pluck out the w.	63:54
will not overthrow the w.,	64:21
in the congregations of the w.,	68: 1
the righteous from the w.,	84:53
blood of this w. generation;	88:75
abomination which awaits the w.,	88:85
and from all your w. doings.	88:121
is the spirit of that w. one	93:25
And that w. one cometh and	93:39
and that w. one hath power,	93:42
lest that w. one have power	93:49
while all the w. shall mourn.	97:21
and all their w. works.	97:24
when the w. rule the people	98: 9
their sins, and their w. ways,	98:20
cut off those w., unfaithful,	101:90
between the righteous and the w.,	101:95
he shall, with the w., lift up	104:18
things concerning the w.,	109:45
from the calamity of the w.;	109:46
and afflicted by w. men;	109:48
mercy, O Lord, upon the w. mob,	109:50
conspiracy of traitors and w.	135: 7
and the w. might be condemned.	136:39
curse, and was angry with the w.,	Mses 5:56
but upon the residue of the w.	7:43
great tribulations among the w.;	7:66
which should come upon the w.	7:66
or the destruction of the w.,	JS 1: 4

WICKED   1040   WICKEDNESS

or the destruction of the w.;	JS	1:31	because of the w. of the people,	Al 59:11
thus cometh the end of the w.,		1:55	because of the w. of the people,	59:12
			killed it is because of their w.?	60:12
WICKEDLY			were it not for the w. which	60:15
if ye have sought to do w.	1Ne	10:21	this because of the great w. of	60:17
all the proud and they who do w.		22:15	we will resist w. even unto	61:10
who are proud, and that do w.,	2Ne	26: 4	of many people of their w.,	62:45
the hearts of no more to do w.;	Al	39:13	*the w. and abominations of*	He 1:hd
unto destruction, which do w.,		45:16	that no one should know his q.	2: 3
hearts of many people to do w.;		46:10	their w., and their murders,	3:14
proud, yea, and all that do w.,	3Ne	25: 1	their w. and their abomination	4:11
yea, and all those that do w.	DC	10:56	because of this their great w.,	4:13
the proud and they that do w.		29: 9	a state of unbelief and awful w.;	4:25
the proud and they that do w.		64:24	were convinced of the w. of	5:19
that do w., shall be stubble;		133:64	w. his brother should do	6:22
and all that do w. shall burn	JS	2:37	whoredoms and all manner of w.,	6:23
			reveal unto the world of their w.	6:24
WICKEDNESS			according to the laws of their w.,	6:24
for he truly testified of their w.	1Ne	1:19	and their plans of awful w.,	6:30
because of the w. of the people.		3:17	grow in w. and abominations,	6:34
sorrowful, because of their w.,		7:20	because of the w. and the	6:35
upon all those who will work w.		14: 4	*they repent of their w.*	7:hd
were few, because of the w.		14:12	in a state of such awful w.,	7: 4
were small, because of the w.		14:12	of this the w. of my brethren.	7: 9
because of the great w. of the		15: 4	for the w. of the people.	7:11
if they should die in their w.		15:33	of your w. and abominations!	7:27
because of the w. of the pastors		21: 1	and your fornication and w.,	8:26
neither w., neither holiness	2Ne	2:11	that I did know of the w. and	9:23
For w. burneth as the fire;		19:18	of the w. of the people of	10: 3
w. and abominations of the people.		27: 8	to the w. of this people.	10: 6
and because of pride, and w.,		28:14	work of destruction and w.	11: 2
the earth shall repent of their w.		28:17	in their pride, and in their w.;	11:37
because of the unbelief, and the w.,		32: 7	Nephites did still remain in w.,	13: 1
concerning the w. of your hearts.	Jac	2: 6	in wickedness, yea, in great w.,	13: 1
and tell you concerning your w.		2:10	of the w. and abominations	13:14
the w. and abominations of their		2:31	for the w. and abominations	13:15
commit any manner of w.,	Mos	2:13	of the w. and abominations	13:16
shall be his anguish for the w. and		3: 7	their w. and their abominations.	13:17
who told them of their w. and		7:26	remaining in their pride and w.,	16:10
whoredoms and all manner of w.		11: 2	saw this w. of his people,	3Ne 1:10
the w. of their king and priests.		11:19	the w. of thei rising generation.	1:30
their abominations and their w.,		11:20	strong in w. and abominations;	2: 3
delighting in all manner of w.		24: 7	should do great w. in the land.	2: 3
his w. and his abominations,		29:18	the people did still remain in w.,	2:10
also the w. and abominations of		29:18	the w. of the people of Nephi,	2:18
after the manner of his own w.;		29:23	your w. in retaining from them	3:10
murdering, and all manner of w.;	Al	1:32	(save it were in their times of w.)	3:19
commit any w. if it were known;		1:33	the which there was so much w.,	5: 6
except they repent of their w.		3:14	they were in a state of awful w.	6:17
sent upon them because of their w.		4: 3	their w. and abominations;	7:15
were sorely grieved for the w.		4: 7	hide their w. and abominations	9: 7
and the w. of the church was		4:10	hide their w. and abominations	9: 8
Alma saw the w. of the church,		4:11	because of their sins and their w.,	9: 9
the w. and the crimes of the people.		4:16	all the w. of the whole earth,	9: 9
remembrance of all your w.,		5:18	because of their w. in casting	9:10
ye are guilty of all manner of w.?		5:23	unto them concerning their w.	9:10
all ye that will persist in your w.,		5:56	that their w. and abominations	9:11
that did not repent of their w.		6: 3	their w. and their abominations.	9:12
because of the w. of the people		8:14	I am troubled because of the w.	17:14
that if ye persist in your w. that		9:18	they that work w. are set up;	24:15
God, in the w. of my heart,		10: 6	all your w. and abominations,	30: 2
all manner of disturbances and w.,		11:20	they did receive all manner of w.,	4Ne 1:20
they were full of all manner of w.;		13:17	did dwindle in unbelief and w.,	1:34
so plainly against their w.,		14: 3	the w. and abomination of their	1:39
his mind on account of his w.,		15: 3	people did still remain in w.)	1:47
by the w. of these men.		17:28	But w. did prevail upon the face	Mrm 1:13
they should wax strong in w.		21: 3	because of their w. and unbelief.	1:14
to commit any manner of w.	Al	23: 3	make a full account of all the w.	2:18
many murders and their awful w.		27:23	their w. and abominations,	2:18
for all this w. they were punished.		30:10	scene of w. and abominations	2:18
to lift up their heads in their w.,		30:10	wo is me because of their w.;	2:19
convinced of the w. of Korihor;		30:58	with sorrow because of their w.,	2:19
to behold such gross w. among		31:26	because of their w. and their	2:27
such w. and iniquity shall be		31:30	because of their w. and	3:11
such w. among this people doth		31:30	notwithstanding their w. I had	3:12
their plunderings, and all their w.		37:21	persisted in their w. continually.	4:10
and their w. and abominations.		37:23	never had been so great w.	4:12
only their w. and their murders		37:29	because of the w. of this people.	5: 9
abhor such w. and abominations		37:29	w. will not bring them forth	5:12
destroyed on account of their w.		37:29	the w. of the people was so great	8:10
w. never was happiness.		41:10	remain in your awful state of w.,	Eth 4:15
and we also see the great w.		46: 9	the w. and idolatry of the people	7:23
(being inspired by his w. and		50:35	to commit all manner of w.	8:16

WICKEDNESS

the people, by the hand of w.;	Eth	9: 4
to be an exceeding great w.		9:26
forsake their murders and w.		11: 1
they should repent of their w.		11: 6
judgment in w. all his days;		11:14
by their secret plans of w.,		13:15
all manner of w. upon all the		13:26
their w. and abominations had		14:25
awful is the w. to suppose	Mro	8:15
it is awful w. to deny the pure		8:19
and hide their sins, and w., and		9:15
knowest the w. of this people;		9:20
their w. doth exceed that of		9:20
because of the w. of the people;	DC	6:26
that which was sacred, unto w.		10: 9
full of w. and abominations;		10:21
w. shall not be upon the earth;		29: 9
because of the w. of the world,		29:17
lest the w. of men reveal		38:30
these things unto you by their w.,		38:30
they found it not because of w.		45:12
no idolatry nor w. practised.		52:39
that you might not perish in w.;		61: 8
anger is kindled against their w.,		61:31
are also growing up in w.;		68:31
to scourge them for their w.		84:96
the midst of persecution and w.		99: 1
That no combination of w.		109:26
from the midst of w.,		133:14
because of w. it is not had	Mses	1:23
Mahan, and he gloried in his w.		5:31
great w. as among his brethren.		7:36
and looked upon their w.,		7:41
the days of w. and vengence.		7:46
because of the w. of my children.		7:48
the days of w. and vengeance,		7:60
w. of men had become great		8:22

WIDE

for w. is the gate, and broad is	3Ne	14:13
but w. is the gate, and broad the		27:33
the w. expanse of eternity,	DC	38: 1
forty rods long and twelve w.,		104:43
open the mouth w. after thee,		122: 7
Broad is the gate, and w. the		132:25
his heart swelled w. as eternity;	Mses	7:41

WIDELY

have been w. published,	DC	OD

WIDOW

the w. mourning for her husband,	Mos	21: 9
the w. and the fatherless,	3Ne	24: 5
there was a w. in that city,	DC	101:83
because this w. troubleth me		101:84
that the cries of the w. and the		136: 8

WIDOWHOOD

reproach of thy w. any more.	3Ne	22: 4

WIDOWS

mercy on their fatherless and w.;	2Ne	19:17
that w. may be their prey,		20: 2
a great many w. in the land,	Mos	21:10
impart to the support of the w.		21:17
w. mourning for their husbands,	Al	28: 5
cause that w. should mourn	Mrm	8:40
many w. and their daughters	Mro	9:16
and w. and orphans shall be	DC	83: 6
but to the w. and fatherless,		123: 9
in taking the poor, the w.,		136: 8

WIDTH

the end, the w., the height,	DC	76:48
by sixty-five feet in the w.		94: 4
by sixty-five feet in the w.		94:11
and five feet in w.,		95:15

WIELDED

having w. the sword of Laban	Jac	1:10

WIFE

An account of Lehi and his w.	1Ne	1:hd
the daughters of Ishmael to w.	1Ne	1:hd
sons should take daughters to w.,		7: 1
their father, Ishmael, and his w.,		7: 6
of the daughters of Ishmael to w.;		16: 7
of the daughters of Ishmael to w.;		16: 7
eldest daughter of Ishmael to w.		16: 7
and also my w. with her tears		18:19
you have save it be one w.;	Jac	2:27
should have save it were one w.,		3: 5
family, consisting of his w., and	Mos	2: 5
shalt not covet thy neighbor's w.,		13:24
had taken to w. the daughters of		25:12
rake one of his daughters to w.	Al	17:24
and carried him in unto his w.,		18:43
and his w., and his sons, and		18:43
and took her unto him to w.;		47:35
man and his w. and his children,		54:11
whosoever shall put away his w.,	3Ne	12:31
whosoever shall put away his w.,		12:32
every man did take his w. and		19: 1
the children of the married w.,		22: 1
in spirit, and a w. of youth		22: 6
that he will desire me to w.;	Eth	8:10
shall give unto him me to w.,		8:10
that he desired her to w.		8:11
Give her unto me to w.		8:11
unto Akish his daughter to w.		9: 4
his w. died, being an hundred		9:24
Coriantum took to w., in his old		9:24
not covet thy neighbor's w.;	DC	19:25
love thy w. with all thy heart,		42:22
that he should have one w.,		49:16
is sanctified by the w.,		74: 1
the unbelieving w. is sanctified		74: 1
Have mercy, O Lord, upon his w.		109:69
tear thee from the bosom of thy w.;		122: 6
man marry him a w. in the world,		132:15
if a man marry a w., and make a		132:18
if a man marry a w. by my word,		132:19
if a man marry a w. according to		132:26
gave Hagar to Abraham to w.		132:34
in the case of Uriah and his w.;		132:39
if a man receiveth a w. in the		132:41
handmaid, Emma Smith, your w.,		132:51
if any man have a w.,		132:64
Abraham to take Hagar to w.		132:65
and shall cleave unto his w.;	Mses	3:24
both naked, the man and his w.,		3:25
and Adam and his w. went to hide		4:14
unto the voice of thy w., and		4:23
Adam called his w. name Eve,		4:26
Unto Adam, and also unto his w.,		4:27
also, his w., did labor with him.		5: 1
Adam knew his w., and she		5: 2
Adam and Eve, his w., called		5: 4
Eve, his w., heard all these		5:11
Adam and Eve, his w., ceased not		5:16
Adam knew Eve, his w., and she		5:16
Adam and his w. mourned before		5:27
of his brother's daughters to w.,		5:28
and with his w. and many of his		5:41
And Cain knew his w., and the		5:42
Adam knew his w. again, and she		6: 2
I, Abraham, took Sarai to w.,	Abr	2: 2
my brother, took Milcah to w..		2: 2
my brother's son, and his w.,		2: 4
and his wife, and Sarai my w.;		2: 4
Whom I took to w. when I was		2:15
Sarai, thy w. is a very fair woman		2:22
they will say—She is his w.;		2:23
I, Abraham, told Sarai, my w.,		2:25
and shall cleave unto his w.,		5:18
both naked, the man and his w.,		5:19
it was there I first saw my w.	JS	2:57
and going with my w.		2:61

WIFE'S

my w. father's family were	JS	2:58
at the house of my w. father,		2:62
of my w. father's family		2:75

WIGHT, Lyman: see also LYMAN.

let my servant W. and my	DC	52: 7

WIGHT

And let my servant W. beware,	DC 52:12
Pratt and my servant W. should	103:30
Let my servant W. journey	103:38
it is my will that my servant W.	124:18
and my servant W.,	124:62
and my servant W.,	124:70

WILD

to be devoured by w. beasts.	1Ne 7:16
I did slay w. beasts, insomuch	16:31
much fruit and also w. honey;	17: 5
and the goat and the w. goat,	18:25
and all manner of w. animals,	18:25
as a w. bull in a net,	2Ne 8:20
and it brought forth w. grapes.	15: 2
it brought forth w. grapes.	15: 4
But w. beasts of the desert shall	23:21
And the w. beasts of the islands	23:22
the branches from a w. olive-tree,	Jac 5: 7
the branches of the w. olive-tree,	5: 9
the branches of the w. olive-tree.	5:10
the w. olive branches had been	5:17
the branches of the w. tree	5:18
the w. branches have brought forth	5:18
hath brought forth w. fruit;	5:25
the w. branches had been grafted	5:30
the branches of the w. olive-tree	5:34
from the w. branches, good fruit.	5:36
the w. branches have grown and	5:37
the w. branches have overcome the	5:37
the w. fruit of the last had	5:40
part thereof brought forth w. fruit;	5:45
like unto the w. olive-tree,	5:46
tree which had become w.,	5:55
trees, which also had become w.	5:55
trees which had become w.,	5:56
pluck not the w. branches from	5:57
the w. branches began to be	5:73
they became w., and ferocious,	En 1:20
and goats, and w. goats,	1:21
they are as a w. flock which fleeth	Mos 8:21
They were a w., and ferocious,	10:12
the dogs, yea, and the w. beasts,	12: 2
as a w. flock is driven by wild	17:17
driven by w. and ferocious beasts.	17:17
times or at seasons, by w. beasts.	18: 4
by w. and ravenous beasts.	Al 2:37
mangled by dogs and w. beasts	16:10
to a w. and a hardened and a	17:14
with all manner of w. animals	22:31
driven and slain by w. beasts;	25:12
more w., wicked and ferocious	47:36
wicked, and w., and ferocious,	He 3:16
meat for dogs and w. beasts.	7:19
there were no w. beasts nor game	3Ne 4: 2
the w. game became scarce in	4:20
cast into a den of w. beasts;	28:22
cast them into dens of w. beasts,	4Ne 1:33
they did play with the w. beasts	1:33
w. beasts nor poisonous serpents,	Mrm 8:24
their flesh like unto w. beasts,	Mro 9:10
all w. animals that run or creep	DC 89:14
their w. and savage condition	109:65
a w. man hath come among us.	Mses 6:38

WILDERNESS

three days' journey into the w.	1Ne 1:hd
and depart into the w.	1:hd
and afflictions in the w.	1:hd
and depart into the w.	2: 2
he departed into the w.	2: 4
and departed into the w.	2: 4
he traveled in the w.	2: 5
he did travel in the w.	2: 5
traveled three days in the w.,	2: 6
to perish in the w.	2:11
down hither into the w.	3: 4
took our journey in the w.,	3: 9
unto my father in the w.	3:14
unto our father in the w.	3:15
that we fled into the w.,	3:27
he spake unto me in the w.,	4:14
go down in the w. with us.	4:33

WILDERNESS

if thou wilt go down into the w.	1Ne 4:34
he would go down into the w.	4:35
our flight into the w.,	4:36
and departed into the w.,	4:38
we had come down into the w.	5: 1
we had perished in the w.;	5: 2
and we perish in the w.	5: 2
again unto us in the w.	5: 5
while we journeyed in the w.	5: 6
my husband to flee into the w.;	5: 8
as we journeyed in the w.	5:22
take his family into the w.	7: 1
and his family into the w.	7: 2
go forth into the w.	7: 3
with us down into the w.	7: 5
as we journeyed in the w.,	7: 6
they might leave me in the w.	7:16
while my father tarried in the w.	8: 2
in my dream, a dark and dreary w.	8: 4
should go forth and cry in the w.:	10: 8
take his journey into the w.	16: 9
we should go into the w.	16:10
things we should carry into the w.,	16:11
that we might carry into the w.	16:11
and depart into the w.	16:12
and go forth into the w.	16:14
again to our families in the w.,	16:14
we did go forth again in the w.,	16:14
in the most fertile parts of the w.,	16:14
in the more fertile parts of the w.	16:16
sufferings and afflictions in the w.;	16:20
of their afflictions in the w.;	16:35
we have wandered much in the w.,	16:35
we must perish in the w.	16:35
lead us away into some strange w.;	16:38
take our journey in the w.;	17: 1
through much affliction in the w.,	17: 1
did bear children in the w.	17: 1
did live upon raw meat in the w.,	17: 2
while we did sojourn in the w.	17: 3
even eight years in the w.	17: 4
as we journeyed in the w.,	17:12
also be your light in the w.;	17:13
and we have wandered in the w.	17:20
they have borne children in the w.	17:20
we have suffered in the w.,	17:21
were fed with manna in the w.	17:28
he did straiten them in the w.	17:41
he should depart into the w.;	17:44
fruits and meat from the w.,	18: 6
had begat two sons in the w.;	18: 7
as we journeyed in the w.	18:25
our journeyings in the w.,	19: 1
all our proceedings in the w.	19: 2
were preserved in the w.	19:10
Nephi to depart into the w.	2Ne 1:hd
His journeyings in the w.,	1:hd
perished with hunger in the w.;	1:24
days of my tribulation in the w.	2: 1
Jacob, my firstborn in the w.,	2: 2
If not so, my first-born in the w.,	2:11
born in the w. of mine afflictions?	3: 1
out of the w. of mine afflictions,	3: 3
through mine afflictions in the w.;	4:20
from them and flee into the w.,	5: 5
and did journey in the w.	5: 7
seek in the w. for beasts of prey.	5:24
I make their rivers a w.	7: 2
he will make her w. like Eden,	8: 3
And made the world as a w.,	24:17
children of Israel were in the w.	Jac 1: 7
unto Abraham in the w.	4: 5
born in tribulation, in a w.,	7:26
and wandering about in the w.	En 1:20
the land with him, into the w.—	Om 1:12
out of the land into the w.,	1:13
of his arm, through the w.,	1:13
And they journeyed in the w.,	1:16
who went up into the w. to	1:27
they went up into the w.	1:28
were all slain, save fifty, in the w.,	1:28
their journey again into the w.	1:29
led our fathers through the w.,	Mos 1:16

WILDERNESS   1043   WILDERNESS

course they should travel in the w.	Mos	7: 4
wandered many days in the w.,		7: 4
they might not perish in the w.;		7:19
should take a journey into the w.,		8: 7
And they were lost in the w. for		8: 8
with my brethren in the w.,		9: 2
our army was destroyed in the w.;		9: 2
again on our journey into the w.		9: 3
many days' wandering in the w.		9: 4
my people should be hid in the w.;		10: 9
that they were wronged in the w. by		10:12
the lead of their journey in the w.		10:13
because he departed into the w.		10:16
and departed into the w.		18:34
and they did flee into the w.,		19: 9
sent men into the w. secretly,		19:18
they met the people in the w.,		19:18
fled from them farther into the w.		19:23
they might not depart into the w.;		19:28
And having tarried in the w.,		20: 4
and carried them into the w.;		20: 5
Lamanites they carried into the w.		20: 5
And are they not in the w.?		20:18
priests that had fled into the w.,		20:23
priests that fled into the w.,		21:20
and they were lost in the w.		21:25
brethren, who had fled into the w.		21:34
their tents, and depart into the w.;		22: 2
drive them into the w. by night.		22: 6
flocks, and our herds into the w.;		22: 8
did depart by night into the w.		22:11
about the land of Shilom in the w.,		22:11
provisions with them, into the w.;		22:12
after being many days in the w.		22:13
they sent an army into the w.		22:15
therefore they were lost in the w.		22:16
who were driven into the w. by		23:hd
grain, and departed into the w.		23: 1
eight days' journey into the w.		23: 3
lost in the w. for many days.		23:30
they were traveling in the w.		23:35
his people departed into the w.;		24:20
because he led their way in the w.		24:20
and took their journey into the w.		24:24
been in the w. twelve days		24:25
who came with him into the w.		25: 2
they took their journey into the w.		28: 9
the w. which was west and north,	Al	2:36
until they had reached the w.		2:37
that part of the w. which was		2:37
died in the w. of their wounds,		2:38
hands of the Lamanites in the w.;		5: 5
west by the borders of the w.		8: 3
land which was by the w. side.		8: 5
were all led by him through the w.?		9: 9
had come in upon the w. side,		16: 2
taken others captive into the w.		16: 3
carried away captive into the w.		16: 4
that they should go into the w.		16: 5
the river Sidon in the south w.,		16: 6
of Manti into the south w.,		16: 7
scattered and driven into the w.;		16: 8
by dogs and wild beasts of the w.		16:10
for themselves while in the w.		17: 7
thus they departed into the w.		17: 8
journeyed many days in the w.,		17: 9
of their fathers in the w.,		18:37
by a narrow strip of w.,		22:27
the w. which was on the north		22:27
of the Lamanites lived in the w.,		22:28
through the w. on the west,		22:28
of the land bordering on the w.,		22:29
round about on the w. side;		22:29
there up into the south w.		22:31
it being the w. which is filled		22:31
of Nephi, and the w. round about.		22:34
having fled into the east w.,		25: 5
of them converted in the w.		25: 6
began to be contention in the w.;		25: 8
and they fled into the east w.		25: 8
we came into the w. not with		26:26
the w. which divided the land of		27:14
also Alma with him, into the w.,		27:25
their brethren into the w.	Al	28: 1
also bordered upon the w. south,		31: 3
w. was full of the Lamanites.		31: 3
even when I was in the w.;		33: 4
a type was raised up in the w.,		33:19
secret places, and in your w.		34:26
they should travel in the w.		37:39
Therefore, they tarried in the w.,		37:42
land of Antionum in the w.,		43:22
journey round about in the w.,		43:22
as they had departed into the w.		43:23
Moroni sent spies into the w. to		43:23
marching round about in the w.,		43:24
west of the river Sidon in the w.		43:27
that we may depart into the w.;		44: 8
suffered to depart into the w.		44:15
suffered to depart into the w.		44:20
and marched out into the w.,		46:31
course of Amalickiah in the w.		46:31
and marched forth into the w.,		46:32
had fled with him into the w.;		47: 1
and fled into the w., and came		47:29
land of Zarahemla in the w.		48: 6
they retreated into the w.,		49:12
were all slain they fled into the w.		49:25
should go forth into the east w.;		50: 7
who were in the east w.		50: 7
the Lamanites out of the east w.,		50: 9
should go forth into the east w.,		50: 9
of the Lamanites in the east w.,		50:11
by night, marched in the w.,		52:22
we took our march into the w.		56:39
flee all that day into the w.,		56:40
pitch our tents by the w. side,		58:13
the w. which was near the city,		58:14
should secrete himself in the w.,		58:16
secrete themselves also in the w.		58:16
should retreat into the w.		58:18
they did follow us into the w.;		58:19
only, to be led away into the w.		58:22
having traveled much in the w.		58:23
to retreat into the w. again,		58:24
that they did flee into the w.		58:29
borders by the w. on the south,		62:34
borders by the w. on the east.		62:34
by a secret way, into the w.;	He	2:11
up the brazen serpent in the w.,		8:14
into the w. and secret places,		11:25
an army of strong men into the w.		11:28
obliged to return out of the w.		11:31
the mountains and the w.		11:31
away others captive into the w.,		11:33
should come down out of the w.	3Ne	3:17
the mountains and into the w.,		3:20
out of the mountains, and the w.,		4: 1
robbers save it were in the w.		4: 2
not exist save it were in the w.,		4: 3
as far as the borders of the w.,		4:13
to the borders of the w.,		4:13
meat they did obtain in the w.;		4:19
game became scarce in the w.—		4:20
they should go forth into the w.,	Eth	2: 5
that they did travel in the w.,		2: 6
stop beyond the sea in the w.,		2: 7
we have been in the w.;		3: 3
the land southward for a w.,		10:21
pursue him to the w. of Akish.		14: 3
unto him in the w. of Akish;		14: 4
did lay siege to the w.;		14: 5
march forth out of the w. by night,		14: 5
dwelt with his army in the w.		14: 7
fled again to the w. of Akish.		14:14
of my church out of the w.—	DC	5:14
given to Lehi while in the w.,		17: 1
the w. among the Lamanites.		32: 2
and called forth out of the w.		33: 5
from Jerusalem in the w.		33: 8
Jacob shall flourish in the w.		49:24
the children of Israel in the w.		84:23
into his rest while in the w.,		84:24
drive the church into the w.		86: 3
of one crying in the w.—		88:66
in the w., because you cannot		88:66

WILDERNESS

WILDERNESS
called upon Cainan in the w.	DC 107:45
out of the w. of darkness,	109:73
bear it with them in the w.,	124:38
A voice of the Lord in the w. of	128:20
in the w. between Harmony,	128:20
I make the rivers a w.;	133:68
the lions was heard out of the w.;	Mses 7:13

WILES
the snares and the w. of the devil,	He 3:29

WILFORD: see WOODRUFF, Wilford.

WILFULLY
have w. rebelled against God,	Mos 15:26
they did w. rebel against God.	3Ne 6:18
they did w. rebel against	4Ne 1:38
w. rebelled against their God;	Mrm 1:16

WILFULNESS
of the w. of their hearts,	Mro 9:23

WILL: see in the APPENDIX.

WILLARD: see RICHARDS, Willard.

WILLETH
the Lord w. that the disciples	DC 58:52
Who w. to take even them	63: 3
and w. to abide in sin,	88:35

WILLIAM: see also CARTER, William; HUNTINGTON, William; LAW, William; MARKS, William; M'LELLIN, William E.; PHELPS, William W.; and SMITH, William.
Lord unto you, my servant W.,	DC 55: 1
I say unto you, my servant W.,	66: 3
servant W. put his trust in me,	124:87
Let my servant W. go and proclaim	124:88
let my servant W. be appointed,	124:91
let my servant W. cry aloud and	124:101
mission in store for my servant W.,	124:102
myself, Samuel Harrison, W.,	JS 2: 4

WILLIAMS, Frederick G.
servant W. should sell his farm,	DC 64:21
unto you my servant W.;	81: 1
brethren, Sidney Rigdon and W.,	90: 6
counselor and scribe, even W.	90:19
my servant Shederlaomach [W.]	92: 1
my servant Shederlaomach [W.]	92: 2
say unto you, my servant W.,	93:41
Joseph Smith, Jun., and W.	93:52
Sidney Rigdon and W. were	102: 3
journey with my servant W.	103:39
let my servant Shederlaomach [W.]	104:27
my servants Shederlaomach [W.]	104:29

WILLIAMS, Samuel
give unto you John A. Hicks, W.,	DC 124:137

WILLING
were w. to hearken to the truth,	1Ne 16: 3
w. to keep the commandments	2Ne 31:10
w. to take upon you the name	31:13
w. to keep my commandments,	31:14
w. to submit to all things which	Mos 3:19
are w. to enter into a covenant	5: 5
w. to bear one another's burdens,	18: 8
Yea, and are w. to mourn with	18: 9
that they were w. to serve God	21:35
who are w. to bear my name;	26:18
w. to take upon them the kingdom.	29: 3
ye are w. to repent of your sins	Al 7:15
w. with all diligence to keep the	3Ne 6:14
ye are w. to do that which	18:10
w. to take upon them the name	Mro 4: 3
I the Lord am w. to make these	DC 1:34
are w. to take upon them the	20:37
are w. to take upon them the	20:77
I, the Lord, am w., if any	62: 7
the heart and w. mind;	64:34

WILT

the w. and obedient shall eat the	DC 64:34
are w. to open their hearts.	75:25
which they are w. to receive,	88:32
they were not w. to enjoy that	88:32
Lord, am w. to show mercy;	97: 6
are w. to observe their covenants	97: 8
are w. to be guided in a right	101:63
w. to hearken to my voice.	101:75
not w. to lay down his life for	103:28
are w. to bring upon others,	121:13
w. that I should be allowed to	JS 2:75

WILLINGNESS
a w. to answer for his own	Mos 29:38
and w. to believe in his words.	He 6:36

WILLS
according to their own carnal w.	Mos 16:12
to act according to their w.	Al 12:31
unto men according to their w.,	29: 4
rule and do according to their w.,	He 7: 5
do according to their own w.—	7: 5
God w. that it shall be done	Mrm 8:15

WILSON, Calves
Dodds, and unto my servant W.,	DC 75:15

WILSON, Dunbar
Newel Knight, David Dort, W.—	DC 124:132

WILT
thou w. not suffer those who come	1Ne 1:14
Therefore, if thou w. go down into	4:34
w. thou deliver me from the hands	7:17
O Lord, w. thou redeem my soul?	2Ne 4:31
W. thou deliver me out of the hands	4:31
w. thou make me that I may	4:31
Lord, w. thou not shut the gates	4:32
w. thou encircle me around in the	4:33
w. thou make a way for mine	4:33
w. thou make my path straight	4:33
w. thou not place a stumbling	4:33
Yet thou w. deny it, because thou	Jac 7:14
unless thou w. recall all the words	Mos 17: 8
if thou w. of thyself be cast off.	27:16
thou w. be a blessing unto me	Al 8:20
if thou w. deny the existence of	11:22
What w. thou that I should do	18:14
if thou w. tell me concerning	18:21
W. thou hearken unto my words,	18:22
except thou w. grant unto me that	20:22
If thou w. spare me I will grant	20:23
unto thee whatsoever thou w. ask,	20:23
If thou w. grant that my brethren	20:24
O king, if thou w. spare our lives,	22: 3
if thou w. bow down before God,	22:16
if thou w. repent of all thy sins,	22:16
w. thou make thyself known unto	22:18
If thou w. show me a sign,	30:43
that thou w. be a spirit forever.	31:15
O Lord, w. thou suffer that	31:26
how long w. thou suffer that such	31:30
Lord, w. thou give me strength,	31:30
w. thou comfort my soul in	31:31
w. thou grant unto me that I	31:31
Lord, w. thou comfort my soul,	31:32
even all these w. thou comfort,	31:32
w. thou comfort their souls in	31:32
W. thou grant unto them that	31:33
w. thou grant unto us that we	31:34
If thou w. show unto us a sign	32:17
of men, and thou w. hear them.	33: 8
that thou w. hear my words	36: 3
thou w. of thy self be destroyed,	36: 9
thou w. be destroyed of thyself,	36:11
thee thy life if thou w. tell us,	He 9:20
w. thou turn away thine anger,	11:11
w. thou turn away thing anger,	11:12
Lord, w. thou hearken unto me,	11:13
and I know that thou w., even	11:14
w. thou turn away thing anger,	11:16
how w. thou say to thy brother:	3Ne 14: 4
thou w. give the Holy Ghost	19:21

WILT — WINGS

WILT (continued)

w. thou suffer that we shall	Eth	2:22
can do whatsoever thou w. for		3:4
that thou w. prove them,		12:35
in Christ that thou w. be saved;	Mro	9:22
thou art not aware thou w. fall.	DC	3:9
And if thou w. inquire,		6:11
If thou w. do good, yea, and		6:13
if thou w. desire of me in faith,		11:10
if thou w. slight these counsels,		19:33
if thou w. hearken to my voice,		39:10
thou w. remember the poor,		42:30
thou w. do the greatest good		81:4
w. promote the glory of him		81:4
And then if thou w. spare him,		98:30
thou w. smite them;		109:28
thou w. fight for thy people		109:28
judgments which thou w. send		109:30
thou w. pour out thy judgments,		109:45
how long w. thou suffer this		109:49
and w. turn away thy wrath		109:53
If thou w. turn unto me, and	Mses	6:52
w. thou not have compassion		7:49
W. thou not bless the children		7:49
w. have mercy upon Noah and		7:50
W. thou not come again upon the		7:59
I ask thee if thou w. not come		7:59

WIMPLES

and the mantles, and the w.,	2Ne	13:22

WIN

that thereby he might w. the prize;	Mos	4:27
that I may w. the hearts of	Al	17:29

WIND

were driven forth before the w.	1Ne	18:8
been driven forth before the w.		18:9
the wood are moved with the w.	2Ne	17:2
and with his mighty w. he shall		21:15
they shall reap the east w.,	Mos	7:31
also be smitten with the east w.;		12:6
if the w. bloweth, it is driven		12:12
sift you as chaff before the w.	Al	37:15
about as chaff before the w.	Mrm	5:16
as chaff is driven before the w.,		5:18
should be a furious w. blow	Eth	6:5
waves of the sea before the w.		6:5
caused by the fierceness of the w.		6:6
the w. did never cease to blow		6:8
were driven forth before the w.		6:8
as with a rushing mighty w.,	DC	109:37
kept workways with the w. and		123:16
cause the w. and the fire to be my	Abr	2:7

WINDOW

Joseph leaped from the w.	DC	135:1

WINDOWS

I will make thy w. of agates,	3Ne	22:12
not open you the w. of heaven,		24:10
For behold, ye cannot have w.,	Eth	2:23
	1Ne	18:21

WINDS

the w. did cease, and the storm	1Ne	18:21
they be driven with fierce w.	Al	26:6
shall send forth his mighty w.,	He	5:12
come and the w. beat upon them.	3Ne	11:40
floods came, and the w. blew,		14:25
floods came, and the w. blew,		14:27
floods come, and the w. blow,		18:13
the w. have gone forth out of my	Eth	2:24
the w. which have gone forth,		2:25
descend, and the w. blow,	DC	90:5
if fierce w. become thine enemy;		122:7
from the four w., from one end		133:7
of his elect from the four w.,	JS	1:37

WINDSOR

the town of Sharon, W. county,	JS	2:3

WINE

for he was drunken with w.	1Ne	4:7
their own blood as with sweet w.;		21:26
their own blood as with sweet w.;	2Ne	6:18
and drunken, and not with w.:	2Ne	8:21
but w. and milk without money		9:50
and also made a w. press therein;		15:2
until night, and w. inflame them!		15:11
viol, the tabret, and pipe, and w.		15:12
Wo unto the mighty to drink w.,		15:22
shall be drunken but not with w.,		27:4
and he built w.-presses,	Mos	11:15
and made w. in abundance;		11:15
therefore he became a w.-biber,		11:15
tribute of w. to the Lamanites,		22:7
tribute of w. to the Lamanites;		22:10
more w., as a present unto them;		22:10
they did drink freely of the w.		22:10
behold we have taken of their w.	Al	55:8
Give us of your w., that we may		55:9
glad that ye have thus taken w.		55:9
Let us keep of our w. till we go		55:10
more desirous to drink of the w.;		55:10
therefore let us take of the w.,		55:11
shall receive w. for our rations,		55:11
they did take of the w. freely;		55:13
attempt to administer of their w.		55:30
would not partake of their w.,		55:31
for if their w. would poison a		55:32
bring forth some bread and w.	3Ne	18:1
they were gone for bread and w.,		18:2
had come with bread and w.,		18:3
should take of the w. of the cup		18:8
he also gave them w. to drink,		20:5
had been no bread, neither w.,		20:6
bread to eat, and also w. to drink.		20:7
and he that drinketh of this w.		20:8
a man who is drunken with w.:	Eth	15:22
of administering the w.—	Mro	5:1
to bless and sanctify this w. to		5:2
to partake of bread and w.,		6:6
to administer bread and w.—	DC	20:40
to partake of bread and w. in		20:75
of administering the w.—		20:78
to bless and sanctify this w.		20:79
you shall not purchase w.		27:3
drink of the w. of the wrath of		35:11
of fat things, of w. on the lees		58:8
trodden the w.-press alone,		76:107
the s.-press of the fierceness		76:107
of the w. of the wrath of her		88:94
of the w. of the wrath of her		88:105
trodden the w.-press alone,		88:106
the w.-press of the fierceness of		88:106
partaking of bread and w.,		88:141
drinketh w. or strong drink		89:5
And, behold, this should be w.,		89:6
Pure w. of the grape of the vine,		89:6
him that treadeth in the w.-vat.		133:48
I have trodden the w.-press alone,		133:50

WINE-BIBBER: see WINE and BIBBER.

WINE-PRESS: see WINE and PRESS.

WINE-PRESSES: see WINE and PRESSES.

WINE-VAT: see WINE and VAT.

WING

there was none that moved the w.,	2Ne	20:14

WINGED

and every w. fowl after his kind;	Mses	2:21
every w. fowl after their kind.	Abr	4:21

WINGS

And upon the w. of his Spirit	2Ne	4:25
seraphim; each one had six w.;		16:2
and the stretching out of his w.		18:8
the dead, with healing in his w.;		25:13
her chickens under her w.,	3Ne	10:4
her chickens under her w.,		10:5
her chickens under her w.,		10:6
arise with healing in his w.;		25:2
her chickens under her w.,	DC	10:65
her chickens under her w.,		29:2
her chickens under her w.,		43:24

WINGS   1046   WISE

understand by the eyes and w.,	DC	77: 4
their w. are a representation		77: 4
The earth rolls upon her w.,		88:45
as they roll upon their w.		88:45
will bear him up as on eagles' w.;		124:18
his thoughts as upon eagles' w.		124:99

WINTER

be used, only in times of w.,	DC	89:13
your flight be not in the w.	JS	1:17

WISDOM

behold, it is w. in God that	1Ne	3:19
it was w. in the Lord that		5:22
the world and the w. thereof;		11:35
it is w. that this land should be	2Ne	1: 8
must needs destroy the w. of God		2:12
in the w. of him who knoweth all		2:24
which are expedient in my w.		3:19
O the w. of God, his mercy and		9: 8
wherefore, their w. is foolishness		9:28
of their learning, and their w.,		9:42
by my w. I have done these things;		20:13
the spirit of w. and understanding,		21: 2
unto themselves their own w.		26:20
until I shall see fit in mine own w.		27:22
for the w. of their wise		27:26
my counsel, for they shall learn w.;		28:30
that he counseleth in w.,	Jac	4:10
these things that ye may learn w.;	Mos	2:17
his matchless power, and his w.,		4: 6
believe that he has all w.,		4: 9
all these things are done in w.		4:27
through the w., and power,		5:15
for they will not seek w., neither		8:20
as to the w. of the world,		24: 7
as to the w. of the world,	Al	2: 1
thus the Nephites in their w.,		22:33
this was w. in the Nephites—		22:34
own strength, nor in my own w.;		26:11
through the power and w. of God		26:29
for he hath all power, all w.,		26:35
to teach his word, yea, in w.,		29: 8
the Lord doth counsel in w.,		29: 8
unto us, O Lord, power and w.		31:35
and that ye may learn w.;		32:12
necessary that ye should learn w.;		32:12
it has hitherto been w. in God		37: 8
counsel in w. over all his works,		37:12
and learn w. in thy youth;		37:35
told you this that ye may learn w.,		38: 9
do not boast in your own w.,		38:11
and to be praised for their w.		38:13
in thy strength and thy w.		39: 2
because of the w. of the Nephites		49: 5
this was w. in Moroni;		49:15
and also with his great w.,	He	1:16
in the day of my w. they shall		15:16
strength and upon their own w.,		16:15
it is w. in the Father that they	3Ne	21: 4
my w. is greater than the		21:10
it was w. in him that they		26: 2
when the Lord seeth fit in his w.		28:29
the Lord shall see fit, in his w.,		29: 1
when he shall see fit, in his w.,	Mrm	5:13
it shall be w. in God.	Eth	5: 1
it is w. in God that these things		8:23
if it be w. in God that ye	Mro	10: 3
he may teach the word of w.;		10: 9
inasmuch as they sought w.	DC	1:26
and boasted in his own w.		3:13
Seek not for riches but for w.,		6: 7
my son, for it is w. in me,		9: 3
it is w. in me that I have dealt		9: 6
But behold, here is w.,		10:34
and because I show unto you w.,		10:34
Here is w., show it not unto		10:35
which, in my w. I would bring		10:40
that my w. is greater than		10:43
it is w. in me that you should		10:45
Seek not for riches but for w.;		11: 7
my w. that you shall go forth.		11:26
the world until it is w. in me.	DC	19:21
is w. in me in a time to come.		25: 4
Behold, this is w. in me;		27: 5
way of commandment, but by w.;		28: 5
Behold, here is w., and let		37: 4
treasure up w. in your bosoms,		38:30
Therefore, he that lacketh w.—		42:68
show unto you even my w.—		45:11
the w. of him whom ye say		45:11
Spirit of God, the word of w.		46:17
and attend to the words of w.		50: 1
fruits of praise and w.,		52:17
if you will receive w. here		57: 3
will receive wisdom here is w.		57: 3
it is w. that the land should		57: 4
Behold, this is w., that they		57: 5
and as w. shall direct.		57: 6
behold here is w., and whoso		57: 9
behold here is w.—		57:12
Behold, here is w.		58:23
It is w. in me that my servant		58:35
it is w. also that there should		58:37
Behold, here is w.		58:53
let him do according to w.		63:44
this is not w. until the residue		64:26
It is not w. in me that he		69: 1
Now, behold this is w.;		71: 5
Great is his w., marvelous		76: 2
And their w. shall be great,		76: 9
w. of the wise shall perish,		76: 9
in your ears the words of w.,		78: 2
here is w. also in me for your		82:16
I say unto you, and this is w.,		82:22
w. receiveth wisdom; truth		88:40
wisdom receiveth w.; truth		88:40
teach one another words of w.;		88:118
the best books words of w.;		88:118
A Word of W., for the benefit		89: 1
revelation and the word of w.,		89: 2
this word of w. by revelation—		89: 4
And shall find w. and great		89:19
Now here is w., and the mind		95:13
I say unto you, here is w.,		96: 1
into lots, according to w..		96: 3
it is w. and expedient in me,		96: 6
to learn w. and to find truth.		97: 1
and observe the words of w.		98:20
here is w. concerning the		101:41
show unto you w. in me		101:63
It is w. in me; therefore,		104:11
until it is w. in me that they		105:23
Behold, here is w.;		107:92
teach one another words of w.;		109: 7
of the best books of w.;		109: 7
be taught words of w. out of		109:14
It is w. in my servant		114: 1
that I might show forth my w.		124: 1
have thought it expedient and w.		127: 1
him that is ignorant learn w. by		136:32
is w. and it remaineth in me.	Mses	1:31
hath all power according to w.,		6:61
and with the blessings of w.,	Abr	1:26
wherein my w. excelleth them all,		3:21
in all w. and prudence, over		3:21
If any of you lack w.,	JS	2:11
person needed w. from God,		2:12
unless I could get more w.		2:12
if he gave w. to them that		2:13
wisdom to them that lacked w.,		2:13
lacked w. might ask of God,		2:26
But by the w. of God, they		2:60

WISDOM'S

in you to guide you in w. paths	Mos	2:36
how slow to walk in w. paths!	He	12: 5

WISE

make these plates for a w. purpose	1Ne	9: 5
and also for other w. purposes,		19: 3
are learned they think they are w.,	2Ne	9:28
and the w., and the learned,		9:42
But the things of the w. and the		9:43

WISE — WITHHELD

WISE

Wo unto the w. in their own eyes	2Ne	15:21
wisdom of their w. and learned		27:26
O the w. and the learned,		28:15
O be w.; what can I say more?	Jac	6:12
on this w. did he speak unto me,		7: 6
And I do this for a w. purpose;	WM	1: 7
he spake unto them in this w.,	Mos	7:18
therefore, ye have not been w.		12:27
to be a cunning and a w. people,		24: 7
Now I say unto you let us be w.		29: 8
now let us be w. and look forward		29:10
will appoint w. men to be judges,		29:11
of their all-w. Creator,		29:19
yea, a w. man as to the wisdom	Al	2: 1
And he selected a w. man who was		4:16
and our w. lawyers whom we		10:24
and he spake on this w.:		12: 2
Ammon being w., yet harmless,		18:22
they were more w. than many of		30:20
confound the w. and the learned.		32:23
for it is for a w. purpose that		37: 2
instances doth confound the w.		37: 6
the Lord doth confound the w.		37: 7
are preserved for a w. purpose,		37:12
for a w. purpose in him,		37:14
things for a w. purpose in him,		37:18
to grow uneasy on this w.		56:30
did appear unto men, w. men,	He	16:14
on this w. did he show himself	3Ne	11:hd
On this w. shall ye baptize;		11:22
on this w. shall ye baptize them—		11:23
I will liken him unto a w. man,		14:24
Be w. in the days of your	Mrm	9:28
be more w. than we have been.		9:31
on this w. do I give the account.	Eth	1: 6
on this w. did he write unto	Mro	8: 1
for a w. purpose in me,	DC	5: 9
on this w., the devil has sought		10:12
For they that are w. and have		45:57
that all may be taught to be w.		46:18
a just, and a w. steward		51:19
learned, the w. and the noble;		58:10
slothful and not a w. servant;		58:26
this for a w. purpose in me.		61:35
be foolish virgins among the w.;		63:54
that is the most w. among you;		67: 6
For he who is faithful and w.		72: 4
be received as a w. steward		72:17
be accounted as w. stewards.		72:22
accounted as a w. steward.		72:26
wisdom of the w. shall perish,		76: 9
is a faithful and w. steward		78:22
w. men should be sought for		98:10
good men and w. men ye should		98:10
a faithful and w. steward		101:61
men be appointed, even w. men,		101:73
of w. men whom I raised up		101:80
That w. men and rulers may		101:94
the churches send up w. men		103:23
of Zion, only on this w.—		104:47
unto them, only on this w.,		104:53
and w. in his stewardship,		104:75
And to have sent w. men,		105:28
be ye as w. as serpents and		111:11
While the pure in heart, and the w.,		122: 2
hid from the w. and prudent,		128:18
to know the only w. and true God,		132:24
the weak shall confound the w.,		133:58
and many other w. documents and		135: 3
thou mayest be a w. steward;		136:27
tree to be desired to make her w.,	Mses	4:12
see that ye do on this w.:	Abr	2:23
is a faithful and w. servant,	JS	1:49

WISELY

conduct thyself w. before me?	DC	19:41
in this thing ye have done w.,		72: 3
judged his people w. and justly	Abr	1:26

WISH

I w. from the inmost part of my	Al	13:27
could have the w. of mine heart,		29: 1
a man, and do sin in my w.;		29: 3

did curse God and w. to die.	Mrm	2:14
w. to know my will concerning	DC	124:73
the will and w. of their masters,		134:12

WISHES

up according to their w.	3Ne	4:16

WIST

and w. not what to say.	He	9:30
and w. not what it meant,	3Ne	11: 8

WITCHCTAFT

the w. which was in the land.	Mrm	2:10

WITCHCRAFTS

cut off w. out of thy land,	3Ne	21:16
sorceries, and w., and magics;	Mrm	1:19

WITH: *see in the APPENDIX.*

WITHAL

given to every man to profit w.	DC	46:16

WITHDRAW

that ye do w. yourselves from	Mos	2:36
repent and w. your armies into	Al	54: 6
w. your murderous purposes,		54: 7
except you w. your purposes,		54: 9
shall come upon you except ye w.,		54:10
save he will w. his purpose,		55: 2
to w. a pace from them,		55:21
Spirit of the Lord began to w.	He	6:35
I will w. my Spirit from them,		13: 8
the people of Zemnarihah to w.	3Ne	4:22
w. themselves from the siege,		4:23
the heavens w. themselves;	DC	121:37
w. from them their fellowship.		134:10

WITHDRAWN

of the Lord hath w. from you,	Al	34:35
yea, it had w. from them	He	4:24
when it is w., Amen to the	DC	121:37
hath not altogether w. from me,	Mses	1:15
Lord had w. from speaking to	Abr	2:12
w. his face from me, I said in my		2:12

WITHDREW

And also many w. themselves	Al	1:24
w. themselves from the multitude		35: 1
stop and w. a pace from them.		44: 1
Zerahemnah w. from before		44:12
the Lamanites w. their design,	Mrm	1:12
and w. from among the people.	Eth	11:13
at the time I w. my Spirit.	DC	19:20
then he w. from the first that		88:57
the presence of God w. from	Mses	1: 9

WITHER

shall w. even as a dried reed;	1Ne	17:48
lest they should w. before me,		17:52
they shall not w. before thee,		17:53
they did not w. before me;		17:54
which are beginning to w. away,	Jac	5: 7

WITHERED

the branch had w. away and died.	Jac	5:40
whose branch hath w. away,		5:43
good branch that it hath w. away		5:45
or leprous, or that are w., or	3Ne	17: 7
for I should have w. and died	Mses	1:11

WITHERS

because it hath no root it w. away,	Al	32:38

WITHHELD

ye have w. your provisions from	Al	60: 9
they have w. our provisions,		61: 4
things be w. from them	3Ne	26:10
he w. them not from his sight,	Eth	3:25
w. the power of the Holy Ghost	Mro	7:36
for they are w. from thee and	DC	25: 4
and I. the Lord, w. my Spirit.		64:16

WITHHELD 1048 WITHOUT

of the Spirit shall be w.	DC 70:14
which nothing shall be w.,	121:28

WITHHOLD
neither should they w. their labor	1Ne 17:49
they did w. food from them	Al 14:22
could not w. anything from him,	Eth 3:26
not w. anything from his sight;	12:21
that the treasurer shall not w.	DC 104:75
let him not w. his voice.	124:100
and the moon shall w. its light,	133:49
And the Lord could not w.;	Mses 7:51

WITHHOLDING
for w. your substance, which doth	Mos 4:22
w. your substance from them?	Al 5:55
w. their food from the hungry,	He 4:12
w. their clothing from the naked,	4:12

WITHIN
w. the ball were two spindles;	1Ne 16:10
w. three score and five years shall	2Ne 17: 8
all w. the walls of the temple,	Mos 2: 7
is contained w. these plates,	8:19
w. the walls of the temple,	11:10
thy stranger that is w. thy gates;	13:18
were w. the borders of the land.	19: 6
w. yourselves, that ye have been	Al 5:27
every soul w. the walls thereof,	14:28
his heart was swollen w. him	17:29
his heart was swollen w. him,	19:13
will begin to swell w. your breasts;	32:28
begin to say w. yourselves—	32:28
this thought, I cried w. my heart:	36:18
w. a wall which they had caused	53: 5
Nephites who were w. the wall	55:20
parts which were w. the walls.	55:20
that their prisoners were armed w.	55:22
were all within the walls of the city.	62:23
of Moroni were w. the walls,	62:24
swollen with sorrow w. his breast;	He 7: 6
Jesus groaned w. himself,	3Ne 17:14
heart did begin to rejoice w. me,	Mrm 2:12
kept from beholding w. the veil;	Eth 3:19
not be kept from w. the veil,	3:20
not be kept from w. the veil,	12:19
your bosom shall burn w. you;	DC 9: 8
afterward he said w. himself:	101:84

WITHOUT
came w. the walls of Jerusalem.	1Ne 4: 4
should hide themselves w. the walls.	4: 5
brethren, who were w. the walls.	4:24
brethren, who were w. the walls.	4:27
we did return w. food to our	16:19
bear their journeyings w. murmurings.	17: 2
w. money and without price.	2Ne 9:50
without money and w. price.	9:50
great and fair cities w. inhabitant.	15: 9
and opened her mouth w. measure;	15:14
cities be wasted w. inhabitant,	16:11
and the houses w. man,	16:11
w. me they shall bow down under	20: 4
w. money and without price.	26:25
without money and w. price.	26:25
which is one God, w. end.	31:21
was with my guards w. the gate?	Mos 7:10
to meet my people, w. arms,	20:24
and went forth w. arms to meet	20:25
that they were w. arms,	20:26
his person w. the walls of the city,	21:19
been w. the gates of the city	21:23
of God to pray w. ceasing,	26:39
who live w. God in the world,	27:31
w. money and without price.	Al 1:20
without money and w. price.	1:20
w. beginning of days or end of	13: 7
is w. beginning of end—	13: 8
w. beginning of days or end of	13: 9
w. any respect of persons,	16:14
thus w. meeting any resistance,	24:22
prayeth continually w. ceasing—	26:22
w. being compelled to be humble;	32:16
baptized w. stubbornness of heart,	Al 32:16
w. being brought to know the	32:16
I have labored w. ceasing,	36:24
things are not w. a shadow;	37:43
they are w. God in the world,	41:11
surrounded by the Nephites w.,	55:22
Manti w. the shedding of blood.	58:28
Nephihah w. the loss of one soul;	62:26
that he fell dead w. a groan.	He 2: 9
rendered desolate and w. timber,	3: 5
into prison many days w. food,	5:22
w. the shedding of blood,	3Ne 3:10
continue, w. ceasing, to pray	19:24
pray steadfastly, w. ceasing,	19:30
shall be redeemed w. money.	20:38
nevertheless, it was w. faith,	Mrm 3:12
But behold, I was w. hope,	5: 2
w. calling upon that Being who	5: 2
they are w. Christ and God in	5:16
upon the waves, w. sail or anchor,	5:18
w. anything wherewith to steer	5:18
no longer be kept w. the veil.	Eth 12:21
w. faith there cannot be any hope.	Mro 7:42
children have died w. baptism!	8:12
could not be saved w. baptism,	8:13
all they that are w. the law.	8:22
that are w. civilization—	9:11
They are w. order and without	9:18
are without order and w. mercy.	9:18
that they are w. principle,	9:20
that ye become holy, w. spot.	10:33
upon the wicked w. measure—	DC 1: 9
w. faith you can do nothing;	8:10
canst thou read this w. rejoicing	19:39
infinite and eternal, w. end.	20:28
w. the vote of that church;	20:65
w. faith shall not anything be	35:11
people, w. spot and blameless—	38:31
grow up w. sin unto salvation.	45:58
he may sell goods w. fraud,	57: 8
voices, w. wrath or doubting,	60: 7
w. faith no man pleaseth God;	63:11
w. this there remaineth	63:64
occasion against him w. cause;	64: 6
cut out of the mountain w. hands	65: 2
might remain w. circumcision;	74: 6
these are they who died w. law;	76:72
cannot come, worlds w. end.	76:112
who is w. beginning of days or	78:16
is w. beginning of days or	84:17
w. the ordinances thereof,	84:21
w. this no man can see the	84:22
for w. the feet how shall the	84:109
they are left w. excuse,	88:82
to be poured out w. measure	101:11
all men may be left w. excuse;	101:93
w. seven of the above-named	102: 6
the council w. an assistant;	102:11
pour out my wrath w. measure	103: 2
independently, w. counselors,	107:76
pour out thy judgments, w. measure;	109:45
which thou hast set up w. hands,	109:72
to heaven w. tasting death,	110:13
as serpents and yet w. sin;	111:11
shall be poured out w. mixture	115: 6
greatly enlarge the soul w. hypocrisy,	121:42
without hypocrisy, and w. guile—	121:42
w. compulsory means it shall	121:46
whole nation may be left w. excuse	123: 6
they may be left also w. excuse—	124: 7
George Miller is w. guile;	124:20
w. the consent of the stockholder,	124:71
and be w. guile, and he shall	124:97
as they pursue me w. a cause,	127: 1
die w. a knowledge of the gospel.	128: 5
they w. us cannot be made perfect—	128:15
we w. our dead be made perfect.	128:15
w. them cannot be made perfect;	128:18
they w. us be made perfect.	128:18
perfect w. those who have died	128:18
w. being able to decide whether	130:16
singly, w. exaltation, in their	132:17
w. condemnation on earth and in	132:48

WITHOUT 1049 WIVES

WITHOUT
as w. them peace and harmony	DC	134: 6
w. even a hole in his robe.		135: 2
was w. my knowledge.		OD
taken down w. delay.		OD
w. beginning of days or end of	Mses	1: 3
not all, for my works are w. end,		1: 4
worlds w. number have I created;		1:33
earth we w. form, and void;		2: 2
who was w. beginning of days or		6:67
they are w. affection, and they		7:33
first visit, w. the least variation;	JS	2:45
w. success in our undertaking,		2:56
of translation w. interruption;		2:75

WITHSTAND
did w. them in all their questions,	Mos	12:19
was not able to w. his blows,	Al	1: 9
can ye w. these sayings;		5:53
for he did w. their blows by		17:37
to w. every temptation of the		37:33
to w. against the Lamanites,		43:13
to w. against your enemies.	He	7:22
be able to w. the evil day,	DC	27:15
who am I that I can w. God,	JS	2:25

WITHSTOOD
wherefore, we w. the Lamanites	Jar	1: 7
boldly, and w. all their questions,	Mos	12:19
he w. them and said unto them:		13: 2
but the man w. him,	Al	1: 7
because Gideon w. him with		1: 9
said this, and w. all his words,		8:13
But Ammon w. his blows,		20:20
for this cause I w. the truth,		30:53
we could have w. our enemies		60:15
I w. him with forty and two	Mrm	2: 9

WITNESS
of heaven, and him shall ye w.;	1Ne	11: 7
the God of Israel did w. that	2Ne	9:44
countenance doth w. against them,		13: 9
a w. unto you that I am God,		29: 8
will w. the entire destruction of	WM	1: 2
Thou shalt not bear false w.	Mos	13:23
as a w. before him that ye		18:10
desirous to be baptized as a w.		21:35
might w. what the Lord had done		27:21
and w. it unto him this day	Al	7:15
more than one w. who testified of		10:12
they might find w. against them,		10:13
make appear or w. against them.		10:13
they might w. the destruction		14: 9
How can we w. this awful scene?		14:10
shall stand as a w. against them,		14:11
I have had no w. save thy word,		19: 9
and we can w. of their sincerity,		26:31
w. that there is a supreme		30:44
and bear false w. against your	He	7:21
as a w. that they are true.		8:24
yea, even for a w. unto you,		9:23
we cannot w. with our own eyes		16:20
seen angels, and being eye-w.,	3Ne	7:15
eye-w. to their quick return		7:15
people saw it, and did w. of it,		7:20
a w. and a testimony before God,		7:25
these sayings, and did w. of it.		10: 1
did hear, and did w. of it, saying:		10: 3
this doth w. unto the Father		18:10
may w. unto the Father that ye		18:11
and the multitude did w. it,		19:14
I will be a swift w. against the		24: 5
and I did stand as an idle w.	Mrm	3:16
other w. besides him whom they		3:21
ye receive no w. until after the	Eth	12: 6
w. unto thee, O God, the	Mor	4: 3
they may w. unto thee, O God, the		5: 2
to w. the return of his people		9:22
has desired a w. at my hand,	DC	5: 1
stand as a w. of these things;		5: 2
the man that desires the w.—		5:23
receive a w. from my hand,		5:32
things as a w. unto thee—		6:17
if you desire a further w.,		6:22
What greater w. can you have	DC	6:23
behold, you have received a w.;		6:24
have you not received a w.?		6:24
stand as a w. of the things of		14: 8
heard and bear w. to the words		20:16
w. before the church that they		20:37
and w. unto thee, O God,		20:77
may w. unto thee, O God,		20:79
he continue to be a faithful w.		106: 8
be eye-w. of your baptisms;		127: 6
recorder, who should be eye-w.,		128: 2
is a w. to the truth of the		135: 7
have left a w. of my name?		136:40
for a w. unto all nations,	JS	1:31

WITNESSED
and after ye have w. him	1Ne	11: 7
and w. unto the Father that ye are	2Ne	31:14
w. that he spake these things as	Jac	7:21
have w. almost all the destruction	WM	1: 1
went forth and w. against them—	Al	14: 5
know of yourselves, for ye have w.	He	15: 7
forth and had w. for themselves,	3Ne	11:16
the Father, and ye all have w.		18:24
w. unto the church that they	Mro	6: 2

WITNESSES
God sendeth more w.,	2Ne	11: 3
I took unto me faithful w.		18: 2
be that three w. shall behold it,		27:12
as many w. as seemeth him good		27:14
the w. which I have promised unto		27:22
the Holy Ghost, which w. of		31:18
and having all these w.	Jac	4: 6
we are not w. alone in these		4:13
ye yourselves are w. this day,	Mos	2:14
And ye all are w. this day,		7:21
and to stand as w. of God		18: 9
stand as w. for me hereafter,		24:14
were many w. against them;		26: 9
ye deny against all these w.?	Al	30:45
ye have received so many w.,		34:30
as ye have had so many w.,		34:33
should bring w. with him		47:33
which w. unto them of me and	3Ne	16: 6
in the mouth of three w. shall	Eth	5: 4
three w. of the church did	Mro	6: 7
the testimony of three w. will I	DC	5:15
the mouth of two or three w.		6:28
Therefore, having so great w.,		20:13
and especial w. of my name,		27:12
by two w. of the church,		42:80
more than two w. it is better.		42:80
by the mouth of two w.;		42:81
be understood by the two w.,		77:15
special w. of the name of		107:23
especial w. unto the Gentiles		107:25
special w. or Apostles		107:26
in the mouth of two or three w.		128: 3
and all the attending w.,		128: 4
declaring the three w. to bear		128:20

WITNESSETH
and w. unto the Father that he	2Ne	31: 7

WITNESSING
w. unto the Father that ye are	2Ne	31:13

WIVES
the sons of Ishmael and our w.	1Ne	16:27
down into the ship, with our w.		18: 6
sons of Ishmael and also their w.		18: 9
be spoiled and their w. ravished.	2Ne	23:16
desiring many w. and concubines,	Jac	1:15
before your w. and your children,		2: 7
had many w. and concubines,		2:24
the hearts of your tender w.,		2:35
their husbands love their w.,		3: 7
their w. love their husbands;		3: 7
their w. love their children;		3: 7
to relate that tale to their w.	Mos	9: 2
he had many w. and concubines.		11: 2
and his w. and his concubines;		11: 4

WIVES / WO

and their w. and their concubines;	Mos	11: 4
with his w. and his concubines;		11:14
leave their w. and their children,		19:11
left their w. and their children		19:12
with their w. and their children		19:13
if their w. and their children were		19:19
to their w. and their children;		19:22
their w. and their children were		19:24
to their w. and their children.		20: 3
their w., and for their children;		20:11
and their w., and their children.		23:28
and he also sent forth their w.,		23:33
destroy them, because of their w.		23:34
and also brought with them the w.		23:38
and their w. and their children,	Al	2:25
our w., and our children be slain.		2:25
and their w., and their children.		3: 1
their w. and children together,		14: 8
unto their w. and children,		15: 2
defend themselves, their w.,		35:14
and their houses, and their w.,		43: 9
their w. and their children,		43:45
support which we owe to our w.		44: 5
our w., and our children—		46:12
liberty, their lands, their w.,		48:10
that their w. and their children		48:24
for their w. and their children.		56:28
and our w., and our children,		58:12
with their w. and their children,		63: 4
your w. and your children may	3Ne	18:21
Lamanites and fight for their w.,	Mrm	2:23
with their w. and their children,		6: 7
and mothers, ye husbands and w.,		6:19
he did have many w. and	Eth	10: 5
and of his w. and children.		14: 2
also their w. and their children.		15: 2
their w. and their children—		15:15
ourselves, to our w. and children,	DC	123: 7
to our own w. and children,		123: 9
many w. and concubines—		132: 1
David also received many w. and		132:38
David's w. and concubines were		132:39
houses and lands, w. and children,		132:55
Lamech took unto himself two w.;	Mses	5:44
And Lamech said unto his w.,		5:47
ye w. of Lamech, hearken unto		5:47
spoken the secret unto his w.,		5:53
fair, and they took them w.,		8:14
our w. bear unto us children,		8:21

WIZARDS

unto w. that peep and mutter—	2Ne	18:19

WO

W., wo, unto Jerusalem,	1Ne	1:13
Wo, w., unto Jerusalem,		1:13
w. be unto the Gentiles if		14: 6
But w. unto him that has the law	2Ne	9:27
But w. unto the rich, who are rich		9:30
And w. unto the dear that will not		9:31
W. unto the blind that will not		9:32
W. unto the uncircumcised of heart		9:33
W. unto the liar, for he shall be		9:34
W. unto the murderer who		9:35
W. unto them who commit		9:36
W. unto those that worship idols,		9:37
W. unto all those who die in their		9:38
W. unto their souls, for they have		13: 9
W. unto the wicked, for they shall		13:11
W. unto them that join house		15: 8
W. unto them that rise up early		15:11
W. unto them that draw iniquity		15:18
W. unto them that call evil good,		15:20
W. unto the wise in their own eyes		15:21
W. unto the mighty to drink wine,		15:22
W. is unto me! for I am undone;		16: 5
W. unto them that decree		20: 1
w. unto them that fight against		25:14
w. be unto him that rejecteth		27:14
w. unto them that seek deep to		27:27
w., wo, wo be unto them,		28:15
wo, w., wo be unto them,		28:15

wo, wo, w. be unto them,	2Ne	28:15
W. unto them that turn aside the		28:16
w. be unto him that is at ease		28:24
W. be unto him that crieth:		28:25
w. be unto him that hearkeneth		28:26
Yea, w. be unto him that saith:		28:27
w. unto all those who tremble,		28:28
W. be unto him that shall say:		28:29
W. be unto the Gentiles, saith		28:32
But, w. , wo., unto you that are	Jac	3: 3
w., unto you that are not pure		3: 3
there is a w. pronounced upon him	Mos	2:33
But w., wo unto him who knoweth		3:12
w. unto him who knoweth that he		3:12
w. be unto that man, for his		4:23
W. be unto this people, for I have		11:20
Yea, w. be unto this generation!		12: 2
w. be unto you for perverting the		12:26
W. unto such an one, for he is not	Al	5:31
even w. unto all ye workers of		5:32
redemption from everlasting w.		26:36
to a state of endless w.		28:11
If so, w. shall come upon you;		33:22
the gulf of misery and endless w.,	He	5:12
everlasting misery and endless w.?		7:16
for this cause w. shall come unto		7:22
w. be unto you because of that		7:25
w. shall come unto you because		7:26
w. be unto you because of		7:27
And w. unto him to whom he shall		12:22
w. unto him that repenteth not.		13:11
Yea, w. unto this great city of		13:12
yea, w. unto this great city, for I		13:12
yea, w. be unto this great city,		13:14
w. be unto the city of Gideon,		13:15
w. be unto all the cities which		13:16
w. unto this people, because of		13:24
and w. unto them which are with		15: 2
w. unto this people who are		15: 3
W., wo, unto this people;	3Ne	9: 2
Wo, w., wo unto this people;		9: 2
Wo, wo, w. unto this people;		9: 2
w. unto the inhabitants of the		9: 2
But w., saith the Father unto		16: 8
w. unto him whom the Father		18:33
w. be unto the Gentiles except		21:14
w. be unto him that will not		28:34
W. unto him that spurneth at the		29: 5
w. unto him that shall deny the		29: 5
w. unto him that shall deny the		29: 6
w. unto him that shall say at that		29: 7
And w. is me because of their	Mrm	2:19
But w. unto such for they are in		8:31
w. be unto it, because of the	Eth	8:24
w. be unto the children of men,	Mro	7:37
W. be unto them that shall pervert		8:16
W. unto such, for they are in		8:21
W. unto this people.		9:15
w. be unto the children of men		10:25
w. unto them who shall do		10:26
w. be unto him that lieth to	DC	10:28
w. unto him that denieth these		11:25
and w., wo, wo, is their doom.		38: 6
and wo, w., wo, is their doom.		38: 6
and wo, wo, w., is their doom.		38: 6
w. unto them, for their death		42:47
w. be unto man that sheddeth		49:21
w. unto them that are deceivers		50: 6
w. unto them who are cut off		50: 8
w. to him by whom this offense		54: 5
W. unto you rich men,		56:16
W. unto you poor men,		56:17
w. unto such, for their reward		58:33
W. unto such, for mine anger		60: 2
w. unto all those who come not		84:42
and w. unto that house, or that		84:94
W., I say again, unto that house,		84:95
W. unto them; because		121:19
W. unto all those that discomfort		121:23
W., wo be unto the inhabitants	Mses	7:25
Wo, w. be unto the inhabitants		7:25
W., wo is me, the mother of men;		7:48

WO

Wo, w. is me, the mother of men; Mses 7:48
And w. unto them that are JS 1:16

WOE

the eternal gulf of misery and w. 2Ne 1:13
a state of endless misery and w. Al 9:11
w. shall come unto the DC 5: 5
made partakers of misery and w. Mses 6:48

WOES

w. shall go forth, weeping, DC 19: 5

WOLF

w. also shall dwell with the lamb, 2Ne 21: 6
shall the w. dwell with the lamb; 30:12
And behold, if a w. enter his flock Al 5:59
ye suffer no ravenous w. to enter 5:60

WOLVES

that the w. enter not and devour Al 5:59
inwardly they are ravening w. 3Ne 14:15
enemies prowl around thee like w. DC 122: 6

WOMAN

can a w. forget her suckling child, 1Ne 21:15
I say unto thee, w., there has not Al 19:10
his hand unto the w., and said: 19:12
come forth, and be born of a w., 19:13
the w. servant who had caused 19:28
there was not a w. nor a child 54: 3
whosoever looketh on a w., 3Ne 12:28
as a w. forsaken and grieved 22: 6
that looketh upon a w. to lust DC 42:23
if any man or w. shall commit 42:80
And if a man or w. shall rob, 42:84
cometh not in the form of a w., 49:22
on a w. to lust after her, 63:16
the parable of the w. and 101:81
if her husband be with another w., 132:43
like a w. that is taken in travail; 136:35
taken from man, made I a w., Mses 3:22
she shall be called w. because 3:23
And he said unto the w.: 4: 7
And the w. said unto the serpent: 4: 8
And the serpent said unto the w.: 4:10
when the w. saw that the tree 4:12
the man said: The w. thou gavest 4:18
the Lord God, said unto the w.: 4:19
the w. said: The serpent 4:19
enmity between thee and the w., 4:21
Unto the w., I, the Lord God, 4:22
being first discovered by a w., Abr 1:23
When this w. discovered the land 1:24
is a very fair w. to look upon; 2:22
from man, formed they a w., 5:16
now she shall be called W., because 5:17

WOMB

called a transgressor from the w. 1Ne 20: 8
Lord hath called me from the w.; 21: 1
lord—that formed me from the w. 21: 5
compassion on the son of her w.? 21:15
no pity on the fruit of the w.; 2Ne 23:18
Ghost from his mother's w. DC 84:27

WOMEN

and our w. did bear children 1Ne 17: 1
our w. did give plenty of suck 17: 2
and our w. have toiled, being 17:20
both men, w., and children, 2Ne 9:21
and w. rule over them. 13:12
seven w. shall take hold of one man 14: 1
delight in the chastity of w. Jac 2:28
the w. should spin, and toil, Mos 10: 5
the w. and children of my people 10: 9
with their w. and their children. 19: 9
with the beauty of their w. 19:14
there was a great number of w., 21:17
to take their w. and children, 22: 1
with our w. and our children, 22: 8
all their men and all their w. 24:22
that all mankind, yea, men and w., 27:25

many w. and children had been Al 3: 2
of Ishmael, and Ishmaelitish w. 3: 7
your w. and your children, 7:27
he hath blessed me, and my w., 10:11
pains of the w. and children who 14:10
were one of the Lamanitish w., 19:16
yea, leading away many w., 30:18
yea, not only men but w. also. 32:23
and also delivering their w. and 53: 7
taken many w. and children, 54: 3
will arm my w. and my children, 54:12
even to their w., and all those 55:17
have carried with them many w. 58:30
and our w. and our children are 58:31
yea, our w. and our children, 60:17
and also many w. and children; 63: 6
both men, w., and children, He 1:27
Behold their w. did toil and spin, 6:13
yea, and more especially their w. 11:33
your w. shall have great cause to 15: 2
and their w. and their children, 3Ne 2:12
should gather together their w., 3:13
consist of men, w., and children. 17:25
prisoners both w. and children, Mrm 4:14
had sacrificed their w. and 4:15
their w. and their children were 4:21
light unto men, w., and children, Eth 6: 3
slay both w. and children, 14:17
of both men, w., and children 14:22
the loss of men, w. and children 14:31
men, w. and children being armed 15:15
were men, w., and children. Mro 9: 7
of those w. and children 9: 8
feed the w. upon the flesh of 9: 8
many old w. do faint by the 9:16
and the suffering of our w. and 9:19
and not only men, but w., DC 18:42
concerning w. and children, 83: 1
W. have claim on their husbands 83: 2
God, called the first of all w., Mses 4:26
unto these strange gods, men, w., Abr 1: 8

WON

w. the hearts of the people, Eth 9:10
the souls that we had w. in Haran, Abr 2:15

WONDER

do a marvelous work and a w. 2Ne 25:17
stay yourselves and w., 27: 4
a marvelous work and a w., 27:26
and my words fill you with w. Mos 13: 8
struck with w. and amazement. 25: 7
ye shall be amazed, and w., He 14: 7
at a sign or a w. from heaven, 3Ne 2: 1
for ye shall w. and perish. Mrm 9:26
O then despise not, and w. not, 9:27

WONDERED

w. what he would concerning 3Ne 15: 2
same he greatly marveled and w. Mses 1: 8

WONDERETH

who w. that they are in bondage, Mos 7:28

WONDERFUL

and his name shall be called, W. 2Ne 19: 6
w. contentions one with another. Al 2: 5
thy name done many w. works? 3Ne 14:22
make known his w. works DC 65: 4
they shall do many w. works: 84:66

WONDERFULLY

together a w. great army, Al 51:11

WONDERING

and w. one with another, 3Ne 11: 1

WONDERS

rejecting signs and w., 1Ne 19:13
faith, to work mighty w., 2Ne 3:24
for signs and for w. in Israel 18:18
mighty miracles, signs, and w., 26:13

WONDERS — WORD

WONDERS (cont.)

And many signs, and w.,	Mos 3:15
and all their signs and their w.	37:27
many signs and w. in heaven.	He 14: 6
these w. should come to pass	14:28
they shall see all these signs and w.	15: 3
the people, showing signs and w.,	16: 4
given unto the people, and w.;	16:13
and the w. which were wrought	16:23
and w. which they had seen;	3Ne 1:22
forget those signs and w. which	2: 1
be any more signs or w. given;	2: 3
show miracles, signs, and w.,	DC 35: 8
they shall see signs and w.,	45:40
have sought after signs and w.	63:12
even the w. of eternity shall	76: 8
tell the w. of your Eternal King!	128:23
shall show great signs and w.,	JS 1:22

WONT

is what I am w. to swim in.	DC 127: 2
where the living are w. to assemble,	128:13

WOOD

did make out of w. a bow,	1Ne 16:23
and to work in all manner of w.,	2Ne 5:15
as the trees of the w. are moved	17: 2
lift up itself as if it were no w.!	20:15
and in fine workmanship of w.,	Jar 1: 8
with fine work of w.,	Mos 11: 8
all of which was of fine w.	11: 9
of fine w., and of copper, and of	11:10
cities, both of w. and of cement.	He 3:11
fine and exceedingly dry w..	3Ne 8:21
to worship gods of w. or of stone,	Abr 1:11

WOODRUFF, Wilford

and also my servant W.,	DC 118: 6
John Taylor, John E. Page, W.,	124:129
and W. organize a company.	136:13
W. president of the church	OD
recognizing W. as the president	OD

WOODS

Let the w. and all the trees of the	DC 128:23
I retired to the w. to make the	JS 2:14
went into the w. to pray and	2:68

WOOL

the worm shall eat them like w.	2Ne 8: 8

WORD

obedient unto the w. of the Lord,	1Ne 2: 3
hearkened unto the w. of the Lord?	7: 9
the w. of the Lord shall be fulfilled	7:13
fulfilling of the w. of the Lord,	10:13
the w. of God, which led to the	11:25
the w. of the justice of the	12:18
according to the w. of the angel;	12:19
manifest himself unto them in w.,	14: 1
according to the w. of the angel.	14:27
that it was the w. of God;	15:24
would hearken unto the w. of God,	15:24
give heed unto the w. of the Lord;	15:25
give heed to the w. of God	15:25
themselves because of my w.;	16:24
ye know that by his w. the waters	17:26
Moses, by his w. according to the	17:29
according to his w. he did destroy	17:31
according to his w. he did lead	17:31
according to his w. he did do all	17:31
done save it were by his w.	17:31
had rejected every w. of God,	17:35
by the power of his almighty w.	17:46
by his w. he can cause the	17:46
according to the w. which he had	17:54
according to the w. of the Lord,	18: 4
unto the fulfilling of his w.	18:11
and become a hiss and a by-w.,	19:14
and he will fulfill his w.	20:14
sharpness of the power of the w.	2Ne 1:26
give power to bring forth my w.	3:11
to the bringing forth my w. only,	3:11
to the convincing them of my w.,	3:11
much good, both in w. and in	2Ne 3:24
unto them, according to his w.;	4:14
the w. of the Lord was fulfilled	5:20
how to speak a w. in season	7: 4
and it is his eternal w.,	9:16
I will establish my w.	11: 3
The w. that Isaiah, the son of	12: 1
the w. of the Lord from Jerusalem.	12: 3
despised the w. of the Holy One	15:24
the w. of the Lord said unto me:	18: 1
speak the w., and it shall not	18:10
speak not according to this w.,	18:20
The Lord sent his w. unto Jacob	19: 8
according to the w. which he	25: 3
and also the w. of the angel	25:19
to bear testimony of his w. unto	27:13
will he establish his w.;	27:14
him that rejecteth the w. of God!	27:14
make a man an offender for a w.,	27:32
We have received the w. of God,	28:29
need no more of the w. of God,	28:29
and I bring forth my w. unto	29: 7
that ye shall receive more of my w.?	29: 8
because that I have spoken one w.	29: 9
my w. also shall be gathered	29:14
unto them that fight against my w.	29:14
into the water, according to his w.,	31:13
save it were by the w. of Christ	31:19
feasting upon the w. of Christ,	31:20
even as plain as w. can be.	32: 7
not teach the w. of God	Jac 1:19
declare unto you the w. of God.	2: 2
unto the w. of the Lord,	2: 4
to hear the pleasing w. of God,	2: 8
yea, the w. which healeth	2: 8
upon the pleasing w. of God.	2: 9
the plainness of the w. of God.	2:11
thus came the w. unto me,	2:11
declare the w. which I shall	2:11
this is the w. which I declare	2:12
unto the w. of his commands,	2:16
But the w. of God burthens me	2:23
hearken to the w. of the Lord:	2:27
strictness of the w. of God,	2:35
receive the pleasing w. of God,	3: 2
unto you, which is the w. of God,	3: 9
my brethren, hearken unto my w.;	3:11
much unto my people in w.,	4: 1
by the power of his w. man came	4: 9
created by the power of his w.	4: 9
nourished it according to his w.	5: 5
the w. of the Lord of the vineyard,	5:10
by the good w. of God	6: 7
and deny the good w. of Christ,	6: 8
speaking unto me in very w.,	7: 5
and declare the w. according to	En 1:26
the w. of the Lord was verified,	Jar 1: 9
according to the w. of God,	1:10
did prick their hearts with the w.,	1:12
continually by the w. of God;	Om 1:13
according to the w. of God,	WM 1:11
they did speak the w. of God	1:17
heart against the w. of the Lord	Mos 11:29
I have spoken the w. of God	13: 4
release him, for he feared his w.;	17:11
as would have his w. he did teach.	18: 3
together that believed on his w..	18: 7
to hear the w. of the Lord	18:32
that the w. of the Lord might be	21: 4
could they all hear the w. of God	25:20
every priest preaching the w.	25:21
not understand the w. of God;	26: 3
according to the w. of the Lord.	26:34
the w. of God in all things,	26:38
every one by the w. of God,	26:39
and preaching the w. of God	27:32
they might impart the w. of God	28: 1
the Lamanites to preach the w.	28: 6
the w. among the Lamanites;	28: 9
yea, even a written w. sent he	29: 4
he termed to be the w. of God,	Al 1: 3
to those who believed on his w.,	1: 7
was contrary to the w. of God;	1:15

WORD

they did impart the w. of God,	Al 1:20	land to preach the w. unto them.	Al	31:11
labor to impart the w. of God	1:26	began to preach the w. of God		32: 1
labors to hear the w. of God.	1:26	did preach the w. in their streets.		32: 1
imparted unto them the w. of God	1:26	in a preparation to hear the w.		32: 6
Thus the w. of God is fulfilled,	3:14	themselves because of the w.?		32:14
he might preach the w. of God	4:19	that believeth in the w. of God,		32:16
pull down, by the w. of God,	4:19	being brought to know the w.,		32:16
of God, to the testimony of the w.,	4:20	believe, yea, even on his w.		32:22
began to deliver the w. of God	5: 1	he imparteth his w. by angels		32:23
bondage by the power of his w.;	5: 5	will compare the w. unto a seed.		32:28
by the light of the everlasting w.;	5: 7	of that the w. is good, for it		32:28
he preached the w. unto your	5:13	the w. hath swelled your souls,		32:34
the w. of God may be fulfilled,	5:57	if ye will not nourish the w.,		32:40
the w. of God must be fulfilled.	5:58	But if ye will nourish the w.,		32:41
the w. of God was liberal unto	6: 5	with the w. in nourishing it,		32:42
together to hear the w. of God.	6: 5	the w. of which he ahd spoken,		33: 1
to declare the w. of God unto	6: 8	plant this w. in your hearts,		33:23
revelation of the truth of the w.	6: 8	to plant the w. in your hearts,		34: 4
which are according to his w.	7: 8	the w. be in the Son of God,		34: 5
that the w. might be fulfilled	7:11	the w. is in Christ unto salvation.		34: 6
by the testimony of his w.,	7:20	the w. unto the Zoramites,		35: 2
which ye have given unto my w.	7:26	were angry because of the w.,		35: 3
he began to preach the w. of God	8: 8	having been to declare the w.,		35:15
called to preach the w. of God	8:24	of sent to declare the w.,		35:15
And the w. came to Alam,	8:29	of the strictness of the w.,		35:15
the w. of the Lord has been verified	9:14	the w. which he has imparted		36:26
will be brought to believe in his w.,	9:17	Now this is according to his w.		36:30
hardened against the w. of God,	9:30	that the w. of God might be		37:24
impossible for him to deny his w.	11:34	the w. of God has been fulfilled:		37:26
for l cannot deny his w.,	11:37	give heed to the w. of Christ,		37:44
the portion of his w. which he	12: 9	this people and declare the w.,		37:47
the lesser portion of the w.;	12:10	Behold, he is the w. of truth		38: 9
the greater portion of the w.,	12:10	as ye have begun to teach the w.		38:10
the lesser portion of the w. until	12:11	and teach the w. unto this people.		38:15
hardened our hearts against the w.,	12:13	of their children to hear the w.		39:16
according to the w. of God;	12:22	the meaning of the w. restoration		41:12
and the w. would have been void,	12:23	the meaning of the w. restoration		41:13
the w. of God would have been	12:26	the w. restoration more fully		41:15
yea, according to his w. in the	12:36	according to the w. of God,		42: 5
therefore, according to his w.,	12:36	also the w. of God would have		42: 5
is prepared according to his w.	12:37	preach the w. unto this people.		42:31
children of men to receive his w.	13:24	declare the w. with truth and		42:31
taught to believe in the w. of God	14: 8	to declare the w. unto them.		43: 1
for the w. of God, he being	15:16	preached the w., and the truth,		43: 2
they did impart the w. of God,	16:14	the w. of the Lord came unto		43:24
to preach the w. throughout	16:15	of the sacred w. of God,		44: 5
their hearts to receive the w.	16:16	to declare the w. unto them.		45:20
not be hardened against the w.,	16:17	the w. of God should be declared		45:21
might receive the w. with joy,	16:17	they did preach the w. of God,		48:19
the w. of God being preached	16:21	they gave unto the w. of God,		49:30
the kingdom for the w. of God,	17:hd	by the power and w. of God;		53:10
they might know the w. of God.	17: 2	perform every w. of command		57:21
had been teaching the w. of God	17: 4	to the fulfilling of his w.		60:16
to preach the w. of God unto	17: 8	should adhere to the w. of God,		60:34
brethren, and establish my w.;	17:11	see that ye fulfil the w. of God.		60:35
declare unto them the w. of God.	17:12	unto the people the w. of God;		62:44
to preach the w. of God to a	17:14	and did declare the w. of God		62:45
to the w. and power of God	17:17	bless them, according to his w.		62:51
having imparted the w. of God	17:18	may lay hold upon the w. of God,	He	3:29
have had no witness save thy w.,	19: 9	to preach the w. of God all		5: 4
word, and the w. of our servants;	19: 9	to teach the w. of God among all		5:14
preaching the w. unto them;	21:11	they did reject the w. of God		6: 2
contended with many about the w.	21:11	they did preach the w. of God		6:37
did preach the w. unto many,	21:12	and did preach the w. of God		7: 2
went forth again to declare the w.,	21:15	declared the w., which I have		10: 4
preaching the w. of God in every	21:16	thee mighty in w. and in deed,		10: 5
and they gave heed unto his w.,	21:23	unto thee according to thy w.,		10: 5
should preach the w. unto them.	22:26	unto them the w. of the Lord		10:12
forth preaching the w. of God,	23: 1	unto them the w. of the Lord,		10:14
go forth and preach the w.	23: 3	had declared unto them the w.,		10:15
the w. of God might have no	23: 3	declaring the w. of God,		10:17
and to teach the w. of God	23: 4	according to his w. the earth		12:15
he imparted his w. unto us	24:15	will take away my w. from them,		13: 8
also verified his w. unto them	25:17	unto you the w. of the Lord,		13:26
because of the power of his w.	26:13	that the w. of the Lord came		13:36
to teach his w., yea, in wisdom,	29: 8	as many as believed on his w.		16: 1
to preach the w. unto this people,	29:13	upon them to teach us the w.;		16:21
to declare the w. of God unto	30:32	did appear, according to the w.	3Ne	1:21
none, save it be your w. only.	30:40	the w. came unto them that it		1:25
as the preaching of the w. had a	31: 5	with great anxiety for the w.–		3: 3
try the virtue of the w. of God.	31: 5	the w. of God to be preached		5: 4
to preach unto them the w.	31: 7	declare his w. among his people,		5:13
w. of God preached unto them.	31: 8	them according to his w.		5:22

WORD

they understood not my w.;	3Ne	15:18	
hiss and a by-w. among them		16: 9	
this is the w. which he hath		27:18	
the earth with the w. of God,		28:20	
according to the w. of Jesus.		28:23	
Gentiles according to his w.,		29: 1	
according to the w. of Christ!		29: 7	
and to hear the w. of the Lord.	4Ne	1:12	
by the power of the w. of God,		1:30	
to kill Jesus, according to his w.		1:31	
to the w. of Ammaron,	Mrm	2:17	
according to the w. of God;		8:16	
by the power of his w. did they		8:24	
because of the power of his w.		8:24	
transfigured the holy w. of God,		8:33	
by his w. the heaven and the		9:17	
by the power of his w. man was		9:17	
by the power of his w. have		9:17	
according to the w. of the Lord	Eth	1:33	
against the w. of the Lord,		4: 8	
at my w. the earth shall shake;		4: 9	
power of God and also his w.,		5: 4	
because of his w. which he		12:20	
which w. he had obtained by		12:20	
mighty in w. by faith,		12:23	
the w. of the Lord came to		13:20	
the w. of the Lord which came		14:24	
by the good w. of God,	Mro	6: 4	
For I remember the w. of		7: 5	
every w. which proceeded forth		7:25	
to the w. of his command,		7:30	
by declaring the w. of Christ		7:31	
the w. of the Lord came to me		8: 7	
the w. of God unto me;		8: 9	
when I speak the w. of God		9: 4	
may teach the w. of wisdom;		10: 9	
teach the w. of knowledge by		10:10	
his w. shall hiss forth from		10:28	
my w. shall not pass away,	DC	1:38	
shall have my w. through you;		5:10	
will I send forth of my w.		5:15	
my w. shall be verified at this		5:20	
give heed unto my w., which		6: 2	
shall every w. be established.		6:28	
give heed to my w., which is		11: 2	
therefore give heed unto my w.		11: 2	
until you shall have my w.,		11:16	
Seek not to declare my w.,		11:21	
but first seek to obtain my w.,		11:21	
shall have my Spirit and my w.,		11:21	
study my w. which hath gone		11:22	
study my w. which shall come		11:22	
give heed to my w., which is		12: 2	
therefore, give heed unto my w.		12: 2	
give heed to my w., which is		14: 2	
therefore give heed unto my w.		14: 2	
you must rely upon my w.,		17: 1	
the truth and the w. of God—		19:26	
Which is my w. to the Gentile,		19:27	
For his w. ye shall receive,		21: 5	
whose w. is quick and powerful.		27: 1	
my w. which I reveal unto you,		27:18	
created by the w. of my power,		29:30	
a little time, and declare my w.,		31: 6	
whose w. is quick and powerful,		33: 1	
but I cannot deny my w.		39:16	
that he would obey my w.		40: 1	
received the w. with gladness,		40: 2	
caused him to reject the w.		40: 2	
together to agree upon my w.;		41: 2	
my w. like unto angels of God.		42: 6	
every w. shall be established		42:80	
of God, the w. of wisdom.		46:17	
is given the w. of knowledge,		46:18	
Hearken unto my w.,		49: 1	
to preach the w. of truth		50:17	
that receiveth the w. of truth,		50:19	
receiveth the w. by the Spirit		50:21	
by the w. of exhortation;		50:37	
preaching the w. by the way,		52: 9	
preaching the w. by the way		52:22	
preaching the w. by the way		52:23	
declare the w. in the regions		52:39	
of sins, according to my w.,		53: 3	

WORD'S

and give ear to my w.,	DC	58: 1
declare my w. with loud voices,		60: 7
two by two, and preach the w.,		60: 8
and hast proclaimed by w.,		60:14
proclaiming my w. among		60:14
and declare the w. among the		61:33
and hear the w. of the Lord		63: 1
hear the w. of him whose anger		63: 2
declare both by w. and by		63:37
shall be the w. of the Lord,		68: 4
This is the w. of the Lord unto		68: 7
and hear the w. of the Lord		70: 1
The w. of the Lord, in addition		72: 9
to the w. of the Lord your God,		81: 1
the w. of the Lord concerning		84: 2
this is the w. of the Lord,		84: 4
every w. that proceedeth forth		84:44
For the w. of the Lord is truth,		84:45
beginning to bring forth the w.,		86: 4
A W. of Wisdom, for the benefit		89: 1
and the w. of wisdom,		89: 2
unto you this w. of wisdom		89: 4
they may receive the w.,		90: 9
the w. may go forth unto		90: 9
in the beginning the W. was,		93: 8
for he was the W., even the		93: 8
purpose of bringing forth my w.		96: 4
that my w. should go forth		96: 5
assist in bringing forth my w.		96: 8
every w. which proceedeth forth		98:11
have power to declare my w.		99: 2
unto you a w. concerning Zion.		100:13
my w. must needs be fulfilled		101:64
go out and proclaim thy w.		109:38
But thy w. must be fulfilled.		109:44
shalt send forth my w. unto		112: 4
by thy w. many high ones shall		112: 8
by thy w. many low ones shall		112: 8
that they may receive my w.		112:19
Whosoever receiveth my w.		112:20
abide in my w., and hearken to		112:22
Zion, to publish my w.		118: 2
your labor in sending my w. to		124:16
contemplate the w. of the Lord;		124:23
new translation of my holy w.		124:89
send my w. to every creature.		124:128
send my w. abroad,		126: 3
I give unto you a w. in relation to		127: 5
I will write the w. of the Lord		127:10
every w. may be established.		128: 3
and in one sense the w.,		128:14
The new name is the key w.		130:11
The more sure w. of prophecy		131: 5
but by me or by my w.,		132:12
are not by me or by my w.,		132:13
not by me nor by my w.,		132:15
is not by me or by my w.		132:18
neither by my w.;		132:18
if a man marry a wife by my w.,		132:19
marry a wife according to my w.,		132:26
and commandment by my w.,		132:29
unto you according to my w.		132:40
in my name and by my w.,		132:46
my w. and according to my law,		132:48
to my law and by my w.,		132:59
unto him according to my w.;		132:65
and hear the w. of the Lord		133: 1
The W. and Will of the Lord		136: 1
by the w. of my power, have	Mses	1:32
have passed away by the w. of		1:35
this I did by the w. of my power,		2: 5
made even according to my w.		2:16
and made according to my w.		3: 7
and he spake the w. of the Lord,		7:13
so powerful was the w. of Enoch,		7:13
the Hebrew w. Shaumahyeem.	Fac	1:12
to the Hebrew w. Raukeeyang,		2: 4
And whoso treasureth up my w.,	JS	1:37
the Bible to be the w. of God	AoF	8
of Mormon to be the w. of God.		8

WORD'S

wast stoned for the w. sake;	Al	38: 4
he may be for the w. sake.	DC	6:18

WORDS

WORDS		
or in other w., I Nephi wrote	1 Ne	1:hd
according to the w. of the		2:13
all the w. which had been spoken		2:16
that he believed in my w.		2:17
would not hearken unto my w.;		2:18
when my father had heard these w.		3: 8
rejected the w. of the prophets.		3:18
the w. which have been spoken		3:20
hearkened unto the w. of Laman.		3:28
did speak many hard w. unto us,		3:28
Now when I had spoken these w.,		4: 4
when I, Nephi, had heard these w.,		4:14
remembered the w. of the Lord		4:14
if he would hearken unto my w.,		4:32
if he would hearken unto our w.,		4:32
courage at the w. which I spake.		4:35
unto him the w. of the Lord.		7: 4
remember the w. which I speak		7:15
when I, Nephi, had spoken these w.		7:16
when I had said these w.,		7:18
or, in other w., I have seen a		8: 2
speak all the w. of my father.		8:29
These are the w. of my father:		8:34
spoken all the w. of his dream		8:36
that they would hearken to his w.,		8:37
unto the fulfilling of all his w.		9: 6
of speaking the w. of his dream,		10: 2
or, in other w., a savior of the		10: 4
my father had spoken these w.		10:11
heard all the w. of my father,		10:17
believe all the w. of my father.		11: 5
And when I had spoken these w.,		11: 6
And after he had said these w.,		11:24
while the angel spake these w.,		12:19
according to the w. which shall		13:41
the w. of the Lamb shall be made		13:41
when the angel had spoken these w.,		14: 8
w. which our father hath spoken		15: 7
unto them the w. of Isaiah,		15:20
speak many w. unto my brethren,		15:20
and did speak many w. unto them,		16:39
we would hearken unto his w.;		17:22
hearkened unto the w. of the Lord?		17:23
that ye could not feel his w.;		17:45
when I had spoken these w.,		17:48
but I would speak in other w.—		19: 7
according to the w. of the angel,		19: 8
according to the w. of the angel,		19:10
according to the w. of Zenock,		19:10
according to the w. of Neum,		19:10
according to the w. of Zenos,		19:10
according to the w. of the		19:16
Hear ye the w. of the prophet,		19:24
hear ye the w. of the prophet,		19:24
fulfilling of the words of Moses,		22:20
according to the w. of the		22:23
that ye would hearken unto my w.	2Ne	1:12
the w. of a trembling parent,		1:14
and be faithful unto his w.,		2:28
spoken these few w. unto you		2:30
according to the w. of the		2:30
the w. which he shall write		3:19
be the w. which are expedient		3:19
to the simpleness of their w.		3:20
their w. shall proceed forth out		3:21
and the weakness of their w. will		3:21
hearken unto the w. of the book,		3:23
hearken unto the w. of thy brother,		3:25
according to the w. which I		3:25
the w. of thy dying father.		3:25
ye should give ear unto my w.		4: 3
afflicted more because of his w.		5: 3
write upon these plates all the w.		5: 4
they did hearken unto my w.		5: 6
the w. of the Lord had been		5:19
will not hearken unto thy w.		5:20
and hearken unto my w.,		5:25
The w. of Jacob, the brother		6: 1
taught you the w. of my father;		6: 3
I will read you the w. of Isaiah.		6: 4
And they are the w. which my		6: 4
now, the w. which I shall read		6: 5
And now these are the w.:	2Ne	6: 6
somewhat concerning these w.		6: 8
according to the w. of the angel		6: 9
according to the w. of the		6:14
I have put my w. in thy mouth,		8:16
For he executeth all his w.,		9:17
brethren, give ear to my w.		9:40
spoken the w. of your Maker.		9:40
the w. of truth are hard against		9:40
brethren, remember my w.		9:44
remember the w. which I have		9:51
remember the w. of your God:		9:52
unto you the remainder of my w.		9:54
them forever, that hear my w.		10:14
write more of the w. of Isaiah,		11: 2
for my soul delighteth in his w.		11: 2
will liken his w. unto my people,		11: 2
I will send their w. forth unto		11: 3
unto them that my w. are true.		11: 3
Wherefore, by the w. of three,		11: 3
and he proveth all his w.		11: 3
write some of the w. of Isaiah,		11: 8
of my people shall see these w.		11: 8
Now these are the w., and ye may		11: 8
concerning the w. which I have		25: 1
and give ear unto my w.;		25: 4
the w. of Isaiah are not plain		25: 4
soul delighteth in the w. of Isaiah,		25: 5
confine the w. unto mine own		25: 8
he shall bring forth his w. unto		25:18
which w. shall judge them at		25:18
according to the w. of the		25:19
according to the w. of the		25:19
to the w. which are written.		25:22
the w. which I have spoken		25:28
the w. which he shall speak unto		26: 1
unto the w. of the prophets,		26: 8
the w. of the righteous shall be		26:15
unto you the w. of a book,		27: 6
w. of them which have slumbered.		27: 6
shall deliver the w. of the book,		27: 9
w. of those who have slumbered		27: 9
deliver these w. unto another;		27: 9
But the w. which are sealed he		27:10
w. of the book which were sealed		27:11
w. of the faithful should speak		27:13
bring forth the w. of the book;		27:14
these w. which are not sealed		27:15
the book and the w. thereof		27:19
wherefore thou shalt read the w.		27:20
when thou hast read the w. which		27:22
that I may preserve the w.		27:22
unto him that shall read the w.		27:24
the deaf hear the w. of the book,		27:29
advantage of one because of his w.,		28: 8
the w. of your seed should		29: 2
my w. shall hiss forth unto		29: 2
because my w. shall hiss forth—		29: 3
the same w. unto one nation like		29: 8
I speak forth my w. according		29: 9
that it contains all my w.;		29:10
shall write the w. which I speak		29:11
shall have the w. of the Nephites,		29:13
shall have the w. of the Jews;		29:13
have the w. of the lost tribes		29:13
shall have the w. of the Nephites		29:13
of the w. which have been spoken		30: 1
believe the w. which are written;		30: 3
a few of the w. of my brother		31: 1
a few w. which I must speak		31: 2
the w. of my Beloved are true		31:15
they speak the w. of Christ.		32: 3
feast upon the w. of Christ;		32: 3
the w. of Christ will tell you all		32: 3
now after I have spoken these w.,		32: 4
And the w. which I have written		33: 4
at the w. which I have written		33: 5
hearken unto these w. and believe		33:10
and if ye believe not in these w.		33:10
ye will believe in these w.,		33:10
for they are the w. of Christ,		33:10
if they are not the w. of Christ,		33:11
that they are his w.,		33:11

WORDS

and respect the w. of the Jews,	2Ne	33:14
and also my w., and the		33:14
the w. which shall proceed forth		33:14
for these w. shall condemn you		33:14
The w. of his preaching	Jac	1:hd
A few w. concerning the		1:hd
Jacob, gave unto them these w.		1:17
The w. which Jacob, the brother		2: 1
make an end of speaking these w.		3:14
cannot write but a little of my w.,		4: 1
engraving our w. upon plates)		4: 1
can write a few w. upon plates,		4: 2
to engraven these w. upon plates,		4: 3
they despised the w. of plainness,		4:14
the w. of the prophet Zenos,		5: 1
and hear the w. of me, a prophet		5: 2
nourish it, according to my w.		5:12
of you in w. of soberness		6: 5
Behold, will ye reject these w.?		6: 8
ye reject the w. of the prophets;		6: 8
all the w. which have been spoken		6: 8
I did confound him in all his w.		7: 8
when I, Jacob, had spoken these w.,		7:15
when he had spoken these w.		7:20
to the w. of this wicked man.		7:23
of my brethren may read my w.		7:27
the w. which I had often heard	En	1: 3
when I had heard these w.		1: 9
after I, Enos, had spoken these w.,		1:11
behold, I, Jarom, write a few w.	Jar	1: 1
the w. should not be verified,	Om	1: 6
a few w. concerning his fathers.		1:22
THE W. OF MORMON	WM	1:hd
also written of the w. of Nephi.		1: 3
these are the w. shich he spake	Mos	1:10
w. which his father should speak		1:18
the w. which king Benjamin		2: 1
the w. which king Benjamin		2: 6
the w. which he should speak		2: 7
they could not all hear his w.		2: 8
that the w. which he spake		2: 8
they might also receive his w.		2: 8
these are the w. which he spake		2: 9
you that can hear my w. which		2: 9
to trifle with the w. which I shall		2: 9
who can understand my w.,		2:40
the w. which I shall tell thee;		3: 3
the w. which I have spoken		3:22
the w. which the Lord God hath		3:23
the w. which had been delivered		4: 1
after they had spoken these w.		4: 3
the w. which king Benjamin had		4: 3
the remainder of my w. which		4: 4
and your thoughts, and your w.,		4:30
if they believed the w. which		5: 1
Uea, we believe all the w. which		5: 2
the w. which king Benjamin		5: 6
have spoken the w. that I desired;		5: 6
had heard the w. of Ammon,		7:14
the w. which he should speak		7:17
they would not hearken unto his w.;		7:25
or in other w., he said that		7:27
the last w. which king Benjamin		8: 3
all the w. which he spake		8: 3
and end of speaking these w.		8:19
by the vain and flattering w. of		11: 7
lying and vain w. to his people.		11:11
when Abinadi had spoken these w.		11:26
the w. which Abinadi had spoken		11:27
hearts against the w. of Abinadi,		11:29
their hearts against my w.;		12: 1
did confound them in all their w.		12:19
meaneth the w. which are written,		12:20
the king had heard these w.,		13: 1
after Abinadi had spoken these w.		13: 5
and he continued his w., saying:		13: 6
my w. fill you with wonder and		13: 8
had heard the w. of the prophets,		15:11
who have hearkened unto their w.,		15:11
that have believed in their w.,		15:22
after Abinadi had spoken these w.		16: 1
the w. which Abinadi had spoken,		17: 2
the w. which Abinadi had spoken.		17: 4
all the w. which thou hast spoken	Mos	17: 8
not recall the w. which I have		17: 9
and I will not recall my w.,		17:10
when Abinadi had said these w.,		17:20
the truth of his w. by his death.		17:20
began to teach the w. of Abinadi—		18: 1
And many did believe his w.		18: 3
went thither to hear his w.		18: 6
to hear the w. of Alma.		18: 7
the people had heard these w.,		18:11
And when he had said these w.,		18:13
after Alma had said these w.,		18:14
the w. of Abinadi fulfilled,		20:21
hearken unto the w. of the Lord,		20:21
the w. which had been spoken by		21:30
hitherto hearkened unto my w.		22: 3
hitherto listened to my w.		22: 4
listen to my w. at this time,		22: 4
unto the w. of Gideon.		22: 9
they teach them the w. of Abinadi;		24: 5
believed the w. of Abinadi		24: 9
of their belief on the w. of Alma.		25:18
the w. of king Benjamin,		26: 1
many with their flattering w.,		26: 6
the w. alone of my servant Abinadi.		26:15
the w. alone which thou hast		26:16
when Alma had heard these w.		26:33
And he was a man of many w.,		27: 8
the w. which he spake unto them.		27:12
the last w. which the angel spake		27:17
for many shall believe on their w.,		28: 7
were the w. that were written,		29: 4
convinced of the truth of his w.		29:37
that many did believe on his w.,	Al	1: 5
him with the w. of God.		1: 7
him with the w. of God		1: 9
afflict them with all manner of w.,		1:20
when Alma had said these w.		2:31
the w. which he said to Nephi:		3:14
they were fulfilling the w. of God		3:18
the w. of the spirit of prophecy;		3:27
The w. which Alma, the High Priest		5:hd
these are the w. which he spake		5: 2
my father Alma believe in the w.		5:11
Did he not speak the w. of God,		5:11
the w. which have been spoken by		5:47
w. which I have spoken unto you.		5:61
The w. of Alma which he delivered		7:hd
unto you by the w. of my mouth,		7: 1
I have spoken these w. unto you		7:26
hearken unto the w. of Alma.		8: 9
said this, and withstood all his w.,		8:13
declare the w. of God unto them;		8:30
The w. of Alma, and also the		9:hd
and also the w. of Amulek,		9:hd
Now they understood not the w.		9: 3
We will not believe thy w. if		9: 4
the w. which he spake unto Lehi,		9:13
when I, Alma, had spoken these w.,		9:31
And now the w. of Amulek are		9:34
a part of his w. are written in		9:34
the w. which Amulek preached		10: 1
to the w. which he spake.		10:11
when Amulek had spoken these w.		10:12
they might catch them in their w.,		10:13
they might make him cross his w.,		10:16
the w. which he should speak.		10:16
that ye will not understand the w.		10:25
when Amulek had spoken these w.		10:28
when Amulek had finished these w.		11:46
thus ended the w. of Amulek,		11:46
the w. of Amulek had silenced		12: 1
to establish the w. of Amulek,		12: 1
w. that Alma spake unto Zeezrom		12: 2
when Alma had spoken these w.,		12: 7
For our w. will condemn us,		12:14
made an end of speaking these w.,		12:19
or in other w., being without		13: 7
when Alma had said these w.		13:21
that the w. of our fathers may be		13:26
ye would hearken unto my w.,		13:27
And Alma spake many more w.		13:31
of them did believe on his w.,		14: 1

of the plainness of his w.	Al	14: 2
the w. which had been spoken;		14: 6
among the people by his lying w.;		14: 6
the w. which had been spoken		14: 7
questioned them about many w.;		14:18
not answer the w. of this people?		14:19
this people according to your w.		14:24
smote them, saying the same w.,		14:25
they believed in the w. of Alma.		15: 1
all the w. that thou hast taught.		15: 7
Yea, I believe according to thy w.		15: 9
And when Alma had said these w.,		15:11
as many as would hear their w.,		16:14
yea, by the power of their w.		17: 4
lead them to believe in my w.		17:29
he flattered them by his w.,		17:31
when the king heard these w.,		18: 4
when the king had heard these w.,		18:18
Wilt thou hearken unto my w.,		18:22
Yea, I will believe all thy w.		18:23
when Ammon had said these w.,		18:36
that the king believed all his w.		18:40
according to the w. of Ammon;		19:12
Now, when he had said these w.,		19:13
w. which were not understood;		19:30
the w. which he had heard from		19:31
as many as heard his w. believed,		19:31
them who would not hear his w.;		19:32
many that did believe in their w.;		19:35
when his father had heard these w.,		20:16
when Ammon had said these w.		20:19
when Ammon had said these w.,		20:25
the w. which he had spoken,		20:27
the w. which had been spoken		20:27
would not hearken unto their w.,		20:30
not hear the w. which he spake.		21:10
that they would not hear his w.,		21:11
on the w. which they taught.		21:12
the w. of thy brother Ammon;		22: 3
things, and I will believe thy w.		22:11
that the king would believe his w.,		22:12
when Aaron had said these w.,		22:17
when the king had said these w.,		22:18
these are the w. which he said		24: 7
in remembrance of the w.		25: 6
the w. of Abinadi were brought		25: 9
behold, these w. were verified,		25:12
these are the w. of Ammon to		26: 1
when Ammon had said these w.,		26:10
the w. which the Lord had said		27:13
be done according to my w.,		29:17
brought down according to thy w.		30:23
did not do according to their w.,		30:28
not make any reply to his w.;		30:29
great swelling w. before Alma,		30:31
convinced of the truth of thy w.		30:43
thy lying and by thy flattering w.;		30:47
struck dumb, according to my w.;		30:49
when Alma had said these w.,		30:50
according to the w. of Alma.		30:50
And I have taught his w.;		30:53
believed in the w. of Korihor		30:57
when Alma had said these w.,		31:36
or rather, in other w., blessed is		32:16
do have w. given unto them		32:23
even so it is with my w.		32:26
to an experiment upon my w.,		32:27
give place for a portion of my w.		32:27
after Alma had spoken these w.,		33: 1
would not understand his w.		33:17
after Alma had spoken these w.		34: 1
called upon the w. of Zenos,		34: 7
also upon the w. of Zenock;		34: 7
had made an end of these w.,		35: 1
the w. which had been preached		35: 3
would not hearken unto the w.		35: 3
the w. which had been spoken.		35: 4
in favor of the w. which had		35: 6
Ammon did not fear their w.;		35: 9
My son, give ear to my w.;		36: 1
wilt hear my w. and learn of me;		36: 3
for when I heard the w.—		36:11
and their w. brought them unto		37: 9
to the fulfilling of all his w.	Al	37:16
diligent in fulfilling all my w.,		37:20
the w. which I have spoken		37:32
shall the w. of Christ, if we		37:45
My son, give ear to my w.,		38: 1
give somuch heed unto my w.		39: 2
they would not believe in my w.		39:11
or, I would say, in other w.,		40: 2
the w. which have been spoken.		40:15
in other w., their resurrection		40:19
unto you even according to my w.		42:31
an end of speaking these w.,		44:10
I cannot recall the w. which		44:11
when Moroni had said these w.,		44:12
when they heard these w. and		44:15
Believest thou the w. which I		45: 2
I believe all the w. which thou		45: 5
write the w. which I shall say.		45: 9
And these are the w.:		45:10
when Alma had said these w.		45:17
heed to the w. of Helaman		45:23
would not give heed to their w.,		45:24
hearken to the w. of Helaman		46: 1
flattering w. of Amalickiah,		46: 7
a man of many flattering w.,		46:10
when Moroni had said these w.,		46:19
Moroni had proclaimed these w.,		46:21
or, in other w., if they should		46:21
remember the w. of Jacob,		46:24
when Moroni had said these w.		46:28
when they heard these w.,		47:28
in other w., if they were		48:15
would hearken unto their w.		48:19
themselves because of their w.,		48:20
to the fulfilling of all his w.		50:19
behold that his w. are verified,		50:19
hearken to the w. of Morianton		50:32
wickedness and his flattering w.)		50:35
Lamanites had heard these w.,		52:38
these are the w. which he wrote		54: 4
these are the w. which he wrote,		54:15
unto him according to my w.;		55: 3
when Moroni had said these w.,		55: 5
the Lamanites heard these w.		55: 9
these are the w. which he wrote,		56: 2
unto me the w. of their mothers,		56:48
I did remember the w. which		57:21
these are the w. which Gid said		57:30
had heard these w. of Gid,		57:36
these are the w. which he wrote,		60: 1
are the w. which he received;		61: 1
do send these w. unto Moroni,		61: 2
we cannot resist with our w.,		61:14
exceeding expert in many w.,	He	2: 4
to the w. of those dissenters.		4: 3
and also the w. of Mosiah;		4:21
w. which their father Helaman		5: 5
these are the w. which he spake:		5: 5
declare unto the people these w.		5: 6
w. which king Banjamin spake		5: 9
the w. which Amulek spake unto		5:10
the w. which Helaman taught		5:13
And they did remember his w.;		5:14
when they had said these w.,		5:27
did speak unto them marvelous w.		5:33
could speak forth marvelous w.		5:45
secret signs, and their secret w.;		6:22
willingness to believe in his w.		6:36
And they did reject all his w.,		7: 3
unto the w. of the Lord—		7: 7
their sins, and hearken unto my w.		7:23
that when Nephi had said these w.,		8: 1
behold, ye not only deny my w.,		8:13
the w. which have been spoken		8:13
the w. which were spoken by this		8:13
w. which he hath spoken		8:13
according to the w. of Jeremiah.		8:20
when Nephi had spoken these w.,		9: 1
other w. which he has spoken		9: 2
the w. which Nephi had spoken		9: 4
garden of Nephi, and heard his w.,		9:11
according to the w. of Nephi.		9:15
the w. which they had spoken		9:18

w. which he had said were true;	He 9:37	great and marvelous were the w.	3Ne 19:34
according to the w. he did deny	9:37	w. of Isaiah should be fulfilled—	20:11
also according to the w. he did	9:37	will not believe in my w.,	21:11
believed on the w. of Nephi;	9:39	repent and hearken unto my w.,	21:22
had spoken these w. unto Nephi,	10:12	for great are the w. of Isaiah.	23: 1
hearken unto the w. of the Lord.	10:13	to the w. which he spake.	23: 3
would not hearken unto his w.;	10:15	Therefore give heed to my w.;	23: 4
would not hearken unto his w.;	10:18	will hearken unto my w. and	23: 5
according to the w. of Nephi.	11: 5	when Jesus had said these w.	23: 6
to remember the w. of Nephi.	11: 7	prophesy according to thy w.,	23:10
lest all the w. which thou hast	11: 8	write the w. which the Father	24: 1
the w. which had been desired.	11: 9	the w. which he did tell unto	24: 1
may be done according to my w.,	11:13	Your w. have been stout	24:13
thou didst hearken unto my w.	11:14	the w. which Jesus hath spoken.	26: 8
at this time, hearken unto my w.,	11:14	the w. which he hath given,	27:18
bless them according to thy w.	11:16	lieth not, but fulfilleth all his w.	27:18
unto the w. of the evil one,	12: 4	when Jesus had said these w.,	28: 1
fulfilling the w. which say:	12:26	when Jesus had spoken these w.,	28:12
do speak the w. of the Lord	13: 5	according to the w. of Christ,	28:33
city, and hearken unto my w.;	13:21	hearken unto the w. of Jesus,	28:34
unto the w. which the Lord saith;	13:21	receiveth not the w. of Jesus	28:34
hearkened unto the w. of him	13:21	the w. of those whom he hath	28:34
speaketh flattering w. unto you,	13:28	know that the w. of the Lord,	29: 2
that ye would hear my w.!	13:39	the w. which have been spoken	29: 3
the w. which the Lord hath	14:10	hear the w. of Jesus Christ,	30: 1
And ye shall hear my w.,	14:11	of all the w. of Abinadi,	Mrm 1:19
who heard the w. of Samuel,	16: 1	to the w. of Ammaron.	2:17
not believe in the w. of Samuel	16: 2	And my w. did arouse them	2:24
more who did believe on his w.,	16: 3	according to the w. of the Lord,	4:12
as believed on the w. of Samuel	16: 5	God may give unto them my w.;	7: 1
not believe in the w. of samuel;	16: 6	these are the w. which I speak:	7: 1
the w. of the prophets began to	16:13	him will I confirm all my w.,	9:25
down to be servants to their w.,	16:21	unto the w. of the Lord.	9:27
past for the w. te be fulfilled,	3Ne 1: 5	know that ye shall hear my w.	9:30
the w. of Samuel are not	1: 6	we may not understand our w.	Eth 1:34
the w. which came unto Nephi	1:15	of Jared had said these w.,	3: 6
believed the w. of the prophets,	1:16	Believest thou the w. which I	3:11
in the w. of the prophets	1:16	when he had said these w.,	3:13
to the w. of the prophets.	1:20	the Lord had said these w.,	3:25
to the w. of the prophecy of	1:26	he that believeth not my w.	4:10
lyings and their flattering w.,	1:29	that will not believe my w.	4:12
were the w. which were written,	3: 1	have written the w. which were	5: 1
in other w., yield yourselves up	3: 7	because of his cunning w.,	8: 2
marvelous were the w. and	3:16	not the w. of the prophets,	9:29
to the w. of Lachoneus.	3:16	not hearken unto their w.;	11:13
did fear the w. which had been	3:25	reject all the w. of the prophets,	11:22
w. of all the holy prophets who	5: 1	our w. powerful and great,	12:25
to the w. of the prophets;	5: 2	because of the placing of our w.;	12:25
in other w., the resurrection of	6:20	Gentiles shall mock at our w.	12:25
that they could disbelieve his w.,	7:18	Moroni, having heard these w.,	12:29
the people had heard these w.,	10: 8	rejected all the w. of Ether;	13: 2
when Jesus had spoken these w.	11:12	the w. which Ether had spoken	15: 1
of his sins through your w.	11:23	teh w. which had been spoken by	15: 3
the w. which ye shall say,	11:24	the w. of the Lord had all been	15:33
the w. which I have spoken,	11:41	the last w. which are written by	15:34
spoken these w. unto Nephi,	12: 1	The w. of Christ, which he	Mro 2: 1
heed unto the w. of these twelve	12: 1	Christ spake these w. unto	2: 3
who shall believe in your w.	12: 2	a few of the w. of my father	7: 1
who shall believe in your w.,	12: 2	spake these w. unto our fathers,	7:26
when Jesus had spoken these w.	13:25	according to the w. of Christ,	7:38
Remember the w. which I have	13:25	Listen to the w. of Christ, your	8: 8
when Jesus had spoken these w.	14: 1	as the w. of our Savior himself.	8:29
when Jesus had said these w.	15: 2	a few w. by way of exhortation	10: 2
when Jesus had spoken these w.,	15:11	according to the w. of Christ;	10:26
the w. of the prophet Isaiah	16:17	I not declare my w. unto you,	10:27
when Jesus had spoken these w.	17: 1	w. of the prophets and apostles,	DC 1:14
ye cannot understand all my w.	17: 2	of God, and despise his w.—	3: 7
when he had said these w.,	17:15	will not hearken unto my w.;	5: 5
And when he had said these w.,	17:21	go forth and deliver my w.	5: 6
that when he said these w.,	18: 8	if they will not believe my w.,	5: 7
when Jesus had spoken these w.	18:17	they shall go forth with my w.	5:11
when Jesus had spoken these w.,	18:26	whosoever believeth on my w.,	5:16
heard not the w. which he spake,	18:37	are the w. which he shall say.	5:26
w. which Jesus had spoken—	19: 8	therefore give heed unto my w.	6: 2
w. which Jesus had spoken—	19: 8	the w. or the work which thou	6:17
that shall believe in their w.	19:21	therefore treasure up these w.	6:20
who shall believe on their w.,	19:23	if they reject my w., and this	6:29
they did not multiply many w.,	19:24	But if they reject not my w.,	6:31
shall believe on their w.,	19:28	remember these w., and keep	8: 5
in me, through faith on their w.,	19:28	the w. which you have caused to	10:10
when Jesus had spoken these w.	19:30	they have altered the w.,	10:11
speak the w. which he prayed,	19:32	they have caught you in the w.	10:13
by man the w. which he prayed.	19:32	in other w., if he bringeth	10:17
hearts the w. which he prayed.	19:33		

bringeth forth the same w.,	DC	10:17
say that he has lied in his w.,		10:18
they have altered these w.,		10:29
those w. which have gone forth		10:30
in lying against those w.		10:31
should bring forth the same w.		10:31
they will not believe my w.		10:32
those who have altered my w.		10:42
remember the w. of him who		10:70
I give these w. unto thee.		11:11
the world, that speak these w.,		12: 9
listen to the w. of Jesus Christ,		15: 1
my w. which I have given you		15: 5
listen to the w. of Jesus Christ,		16: 1
my w. which I have given unto		16: 5
I give unto you these w.:		18: 1
to the w. which are written.		18:30
These w. are not of men nor		18:34
my voice, and know my w.		18:36
of me, and listen to my w.;		19:23
the w. of the glorious Majesty		20:16
in the w. of the holy prophets,		20:26
shalt give heed unto all his w.		21: 4
and they shall believe on his w.,		21: 9
unto you, Oliver, a few w.		23: 1
unto you, Hyrun, a few w.;		23: 3
a few w. unto you, Samuel;		23: 4
a few w. unto you, Joseph;		23: 5
Joseph Knight, by these w.,		23: 6
smite them according to your w.,		24:16
afflictions, with consoling w.,		25: 5
the w. have gone forth out of		29:30
give heed unto the w. and		30: 5
These w. are not of man nor of		31:13
shall give heed unto these w.		32: 5
the holy prophets to prove his w.,		35:23
These w. are given unto you,		41:12
or in other w., unto me—		42:37
or in other w., the keys of		42:69
or in other w., if they shall		42:74
give ear to the w. which I shall		43: 1
tingle that hear, saying these w.—		43:22
hear the w. of that God who		43:23
the w. of the Lord your God.		43:27
Hearken ye to these w.		43:34
I the Lord had spoken these w.		45:34
given to believe on their w.,		46:14
attend to the w. of wisdom		50: 1
now hearing these w. of mine		50:36
these w. shall not pass away,		56:11
in other w., him that counseleth		58:20
in other w., that thy joy may		59:13
or in other w., rejoicing and		59:14
in other w., they shall not come		61:23
or in other w., the store,		63:42
and not a day of many w.		63:58
and my w. are sure and shall		64:31
A few w. in addition to my		72:24
your ears the w. of wisdom,		78: 2
in other w., the city of Enoch		78: 4
Or, in other w., let my servant		78: 9
these are the w. of Alpha and		81: 7
in other w., I give unto you		82: 9
in other w., you are to have		82:17
in other w. upon the Lord's		83: 5
heed to the w. of eternal life.		84:43
you who now hear my w.,		84:60
who believeth on your w.,		84:64
who believe not on your w.,		84:74
continually the w. of life,		84:85
that rejecteth you, or your w.,		84:94
that rejecteth you, or your w.,		84:95
whose mouth shall utter w.,		85: 7
shall utter words, eternal w.;		85: 7
one another w. of wisdom;		88:118
the best books w. of wisdom;		88:118
in other w., those who are called		88:127
in the house may hear his w.		88:129
or brethren with these w.:		88:132
in other w., light and truth.		93:36
in other w., I will call you		93:45
or, in other w., Alphus;		95:17
or, in other w., Omegus;		95:17
and observe the w. of wisdom	DC	98:20
in other w., all mine Israel,		101:12
to observe all the w. which		103: 7
not to observe all my w.,		103: 8
and with feigned w.,		104: 4
in other w., shall break the		104: 5
for the proclaiming of my w.,		104:26
covetousness and feigned w.—		104:52
to shinelah [print] my w.,		104:58
Or in other w., if any man		104:69
not hearkened unto my w.		105:17
have hearkened unto my w.,		105:18
Or, in other w., the		107:66
teach one another w. of wisdom;		109: 7
of the best books w. of wisdom,		109: 7
may be taught w. of wisdom		109:14
Now these w., O Lord,		109:60
my holy w. which I give unto		124:46
I wrote a few w. of revelation		128: 2
in other w., taking a different		128: 8
let your w. tend to edifying		136:24
are faithful in keeping all my w.		136:37
The w. of God, which he spake	Mses	1: 1
are without end, and also my w.,		1: 4
when Moses had said these w.,		1:12
when Moses had said these w.,		1:19
to my works, neither to my w.		1:38
shall esteem my w. as naught		1:41
(These w. were spoken unto		1:42
write the w. which I speak.		2: 1
so my w. cannot return void,		4:30
these are the w. which I spake		4:32
w. went forth out of the mouth		5:15
he may not reject his w.		5:16
when Enoch had heard these w.,		6:31
wherefore all thy w. will I justify;		6:34
I speak forth these w.		6:42
Enoch spake forth the w. of God,		6:47
enjoy the w. of eternal life in this		6:59
they hearkened not unto his w.;		8:20
hearkened not unto the w. of Noah.		8:21
and give heed unto my w.;		8:23
also the grand Key-w. of the	Fac	2: 3
in other w., the governing		2: 5
the grand Key-w. of the		2: 7
the Lord spake these w. unto me:	Abr	3:14
that ye may declare all these w.		3:15
my w. shall not pass away,	JS	1:35
entirely lost in a strife of w.		2: 6
In the midst of this war of w.		2:10

WORK

I do not write it in this w.	1Ne	6: 1
all those who will w. wickedness		14: 4
will w. a great and a marvelous		14: 7
a great and a marvelous w.		14: 7
a w. which shall be everlasting,		14: 7
the w. of the Father shall		14:17
did w. according to the faith		16:28
canst not accomplish so great a w.		17:19
of the Lord to do that great w.;		17:26
we did w. timbers of curious		18: 1
manner I should w. the timbers		18: 1
did not w. the timbers after the		18: 2
of the Lord, did cease to w.		18:12
it did w. whither I desired it.		18:21
and my w. with my God.		21: 4
will proceed to do a marvelous w.		22: 8
that he shall do a w.	2Ne	3: 7
that he shall do none other w.,		3: 8
save the w. which I shall command		3: 8
for he shall do my w.		3: 8
when my w. shall commence		3:13
faith, to w. mighty wonders,		3:24
and to w. in all manner of wood,		5:15
worship the w. of their own hands,		12: 8
regard not the w. of the Lord,		15:12
hasten his w., that we may see it;		15:19
Lord hath performed his whole w.		20:12
do a marvelous w. and a wonder		25:17
and I am able to do mine own w.;		27:20
I am able to do mine own w.		27:21
I w. not among the children of		27:23

WORK 1060 WORK

proceed to do a marvelous w.	2Ne 27:26	I have performed the w. which	Eth	2:18
a marvelous w. and a wonder,	27:26	w. of the Father has commenced		4:17
the w. say of him that made it,	27:27	shall assist to bring forth this w.;		5: 2
children, the w. of my hands,	27:34	testimony of three, and this w.,		5: 4
the Redeemer hath done his w.,	28: 5	the w., yea, even the work of		8:23
of miracles; he hath done his w.	28: 6	the w. of destruction come upon		8:23
proceed to do a marvelous w.	29: 1	he did obtain all his fine w.,		10: 7
for my w. is not yet finished;	29: 9	did w. in all manner of ore,		10:23
Lord God shall commence his w.	30: 8	did w. all manner of fine work.		10:23
there is no w. of darkness save	30:17	did work all manner of fine w.		10:23
this manner doth the Lord God w.	31: 3	did w. all manner of cloth,		10:24
might w. mighty miracles;	Mos 8:18	which they did w. their beasts.		10:26
should spin, and toil, and w.,	10: 5	did w. all manner of work of		10:27
and w. all manner of fine linen,	10: 5	or w. of exceedingly curious		10:27
them with fine w. of wood,	11: 8	this manner doth the devil w.,	Mro	7:17
that his workmen should w. all	11:10	do the w. of the covenants of		7:31
work all manner of fine w.	11:10	his ministry, and to his holy w.		8: 2
shalt thou labor, and do all thy w.;	13:17	he may w. mighty miracles;		10:12
thou shalt not do any w., thou, nor	13:18	w. by the power and gifts of God.		10:25
do this w. with holiness of heart.	18:12	every man according to his w.,	DC	1:10
Spirit of the Lord w. upon them,	28: 4	it is not the w. of God that is		3: 3
doth the Lord w. with his power	29:20	frustrated, but the w. of men;		3: 3
he had finished his w. at Melek	Al 8: 6	chosen to do the w. of the Lord,		3: 9
to repent and w. righteousness	13:10	and art again called to the w.;		3:10
behold, our w. is not finished;	14:13	my w. shall go forth,		3:16
who had been chosen for the w.,	16:15	a marvelous w. is about to		4: 1
the w. which they had undertaken.	17:13	ye are called to the w.		4: 3
had undertaken the w.,	17:16	qualify him for the w.		4: 5
the w. of the Lord did commence	19:36	A great and marvelous w. is		6: 1
God to bring about this great w.	26: 3	assist to bring forth my w.,		6: 9
he doth w. righteousness forever.	26: 8	the w. which thou hast been		6:17
doing this great and marvelous w.	26:15	perform with soberness the w.		6:35
saw this w. of destruction	27: 4	a greater w. yet among men		7: 5
saw this great w. of destruction,	27: 4	he has undertaken a greater w.;		7: 5
perform the w. to which I have	29: 6	for it is the w. of God.		8: 8
every man according to his w.	32:20	the w. which you are called to		9: 4
let this desire w. in you, even	32:27	the w. wherewith I have called		9:14
should w. out your salvation	34:37	of the w. of translation		10: 3
the Lord God doth w. by means	37: 7	Satan that do uphold his w.		10: 5
people began to w. in darkness,	37:22	that he may destroy this w.;		10:12
yea, w. secret murders and	37:22	destroy him, and also the w.;		10:19
any man w. after the manner of	37:39	to destroy the w. of God;		10:23
it did w. for them according to	37:40	hearts to anger against this w.		10:24
must stop the w. of destruction	38: 7	the w. may not come forth in		10:33
it should destroy the w. of justice.	42:13	the w. of translation.		10:34
the w. of justice could not be	42:13	that they shall destroy my w.;		10:43
the w. of death commenced	43:37	and send forth in this w.		10:45
did carry on the w. of death	43:38	all the remainder of this w.		10:46
that the w. of death should cease	44:20	A great and marvelous w. is		11: 1
are spreading the w. of death	60: 7	assist to bring forth my w.,		11: 9
carry on the secret w. of murder	He 2: 4	the translation of my w.;		11:19
cannot be contained in this w.	3:14	this is your w., to keep my		11:20
the w. of the Lord did prosper	3:26	A great and marvelous w. is		12: 1
did commence the w. of death;	4: 5	forth and establish this w.		12: 7
who did w. all kinds of ore and	6:11	no one can assist in this w.		12: 8
still carry on the w. of darkness,	6:29	A great and marvelous w. is		14: 1
carry on this w. of destruction	11: 2	the children of men in this w.		17: 4
the w. of destruction did cease	11: 5	And by your hands I will w. a		18:44
this w. of destruction did also	11: 6	I will work a marvelous w.		18:44
should be a stop put to this w. of	11:28	might w. upon the hearts of		19: 7
w. some great mystery which we	16:21	and call them to his holy w.		20:11
from me, ye that w. iniquity.	3Ne 14:23	come to a knowledge of this w.		20:13
that the w. of the Father hath	21: 7	in faith, and w. righteousness,		20:14
shall the Father w. a work,	21: 9	is the beginning of my w.;		29:32
shall the Father work a w.,	21: 9	which is the last of my w.—		29:32
be a great and a marvelous w.	21: 9	because of your faith in my w.		31: 9
the w. of the Father commence	21:26	prepared thee for a greater w.		35: 3
the w. of the Father commence	21:26	shall be a great w. in the land,		35: 7
the w. shall commence among	21:27	a great w. laid up in store,		38:33
then shall the w. commence,	21:28	And this shall be their w.,		38:36
forth an instrument for his w.;	22:16	prepared thee for a greater w.		39:11
they that w. wickedness are set	24:15	of the w. of thine own hands;		42:40
cometh, wherein no man can w.	27:33	needeth to accomplish the w.		43:13
marvelous w. wrought by them,	28:32	ye may accomplish this w.		45:72
manner of miracles did they w.	4Ne 1: 5	shall be ordained unto this w.,		49: 4
nothing did they w. miracles save	1: 5	I will cut my w. short in		52:11
the w. of miracles and of	Mrm 1:13	to do the w. of printing,		55: 4
when the w. shall commence,	3:17	your inheritance to do this w.		55: 5
against the w. of the Lord,	8:21	This is not the w. of the Lord,		58:33
will destroy the w. of the Lord,	8:21	let the w. of the gathering be		58:56
and w. out your own salvation	9:27	accomplish the residue of the w.		58:58
Go to w. and build, after the	Eth 2:16	the foundation of a great w.		64:33
brother of Jared did go to w.,	2:16	to continue the w. of translation		73: 4

WORK 1061 WORKS

doing the w. of translation,	DC 76:15	Lord God w. not in darkness	2Ne 26:23
shall have finished his w.	76:85	he w. in me to do according to	WM 1: 7
shall have perfected his w.;	76:106	the Lord w. in many ways to	Al 24:27
in the w. of the ministry	77: 5	Lord no longer w. by revelation,	3Ne 29: 6
seventh day he finished his w.,	77:12	the Lord w. not in secret	Eth 8:19
and finishing of his w.,	77:12	he w. by power, according to	Mro 10: 7
until I have completed my w.,	84:97	same God who w. all in all;	10: 8
I will hasten my w. in its time.	88:73	rejoiceth and w. righteousness,	DC 133:44
all things shall w. together for	90:24		
for you, to bring to pass my w.,	90:26	**WORKING**	
commence a w. of laying out	94: 1	w. mighty miracles, signs, and	2Ne 26:13
for the w. of the presidency,	94: 3	amongst men, w. mighty miracles,	Mos 3: 5
for the w. of the ministry of	94: 3		15: 6
for the w. of the presidency.	94: 7	after w. many mighty miracles	Al 23: 6
for the w. of the printing of	94:10	the power of God w. miracles	30:42
for the w. of the printing,	94:12	w. devices that he may destroy	He 3: 7
the w. which I have appointed	94:15	expert in the w. of cement;	16: 4
to the w. of the ministry	97:13	w. miracles among the people,	DC 46:21
w. together for your good,	98: 3	is given the w. of miracles;	
all things shall w. together for	100:15		
for the w. of the gathering of	101:20	**WORKINGS**	
That the w. of the gathering	101:64	I have w. in the spirit,	1Ne 19:20
according as his w. shall be;	101:65	according to the w. of the Spirit	2Ne 1: 6
and perform my w.,	101:95	by the w. of the Spirit	Jac 4:15
my work, my strange w.,	101:95	according to the w. of the Spirit	WM 1: 7
all things shall w. together for	105:40	manner of the w. of the Spirit,	Mro 6: 9
we have done this w. through	109: 5	understand his marvelous w.;	DC 121:12
may know that this is thy w.,	109:23		
and do thy w.	109:33	**WORKMANSHIP**	
that thy w. may be cut short	109:59	w. thereof was exceeding fine,	1Ne 4: 9
unto thee, the w. of our hands,	109:78	a round ball of curious w.;	16:10
was a paved w. of pure gold,	110: 2	did work timbers of curious w.	18: 1
have a great w. for thee to do,	112: 6	w. thereof was exceeding fine;	18: 4
gird up thy loins for the w.	112: 7	the w. thereof was exceeding fine.	2Ne 5:16
every man according as his w.	112:34	or the w. of his hands	Jac 4: 9
let there be a beginning of this w.,	115: 9	and in fine w. of wood,	Jar 1: 8
foundation, and a preparatory w.,	115: 9	the manner of so curious a w.	Al 37:39
seen the w. which he hath done,	124:17	all manner of fine w. he did	Eth 10: 7
That when he shall finish his w.	124:19	work of exceedingly curious w.	10:27
to do a w. unto my name,	124:49	for it is the w. of mine hand.	DC 29:25
all they have to perform that w.,	124:49	the w. of the hands of us,	109: 4
from performing that w.,	124:49	show thee the w. of mine hands;	Mses 1: 4
to require that w. no more	124:49	are the w. of mine own hands,	7:32
of those who hindered my w.,	124:50	among all the w. of mine	7:36
been commanded to do a w.	124:53	even all the w. of mine hands;	7:37
love him for the w. he hath done,	124:78	and all the w. of mine hands.	7:40
to accomplish the w. that	124:79		
for the w. of the ministry and	124:143	**WORKMEN**	
Let the w. of my temple,	127: 4	caused that his w. should work	Mos 11:10
herein is the w. of my Father	132:63	and there were also curious w.,	He 6:11
not have power to stop my w.	136:17	let there be w. sent forth	DC 58:54
to bring forth my w.:	136:37		
And I have a w. for thee, Moses,	Mses 1: 6	**WORKS**	
this is my w. and my glory	1:39	Great and marvelous are thy w.,	1Ne 1:14
day I, God, ended my w., and	3: 2	a way to accomplish all his w.	9: 6
the seventh day from all my w.,	3: 2	they must be judged of their w.,	15:32
rested from all my w. which	3: 3	even the w. which were done by	15:32
comfort us concerning our w. and	8: 9	God, to be judged of their w.;	15:33
seventh time we will end our w.,	Abr 5: 2	if their w. have been filthiness	15:33
from all our w. which we have	5: 2	and marvelous w. of the Lord	2Ne 1:10
God had a w. for me to do;	JS 2:33	his great and marvelous w.,	4:17
in attempting to w. as at other	2:48	of secret w. of darkness.	9: 9
by day's w. and otherwise,	2:55	men shall be judged of their w.,	9:44
to w. for nearly a month,	2:56	the secret w. of darkness,	10:15
continued the w. of translation,	2:68	for their w. were works of	25: 2
continue the w. of translation	2:75	works were w. of darkness.	25: 2
		and choose w. of darkness	26:10
WORKED		murder, and w. of darkness;	26:22
miracles were w. by small means	Al 37:41	And their w. are in the dark;	27:27
		that I know all their w.	27:27
WORKERS		and their w. shall be in the dark.	28: 9
wo unto all ye w. of iniquity;	Al 5:32	be judged according to their w.,	28:23
O ye w. of iniquity;	5:37	every man according to their w.,	29:11
upon all those w. of darkness,	37:28	marvelous are the w. of the Lord.	Jac 4: 8
come upon these w. of darkness	37:30	and in great mercy, over all his w.	4:10
unto those w. of darkness and	37:31	every man according to his w.,	Mos 3:24
		always abounding in good w.,	5:15
WORKEST		marvelous are the w. of the Lord,	8:20
thou w. unto the children of	Eth 12:29	of him according to their w.	16:10
thou w. after men have faith.	12:30	rewards according to their w.,	Al 3:26
		your w. have been the works of	5:16
WORKETH		have been the w. of righteousness	5:16
he w. many things by his cunning	1Ne 16:38	our w. have been righteous works	5:17
		righteous w. upon the face of the	5:17

bring forth w. of righteousness,	Al	5:35	shall deny the Christ and his w.!	3Ne 29: 5
not the w. of righteousness,		5:36	great and marvelous w. wrought	4Ne 1: 5
a man bringeth forth good w.		5:41	judged according to your w.	Mrm 3:18
whosoever bringeth forth evil w.,		5:41	stand to be judged of your w.,	3:20
being dead unto all good w.		5:42	judged according to your w.;	6:21
they do bring forth w. which are		5:54	w. which were wrought by	7: 9
will always abound in good w.		7:24	according to his w. shall his	8:19
to your faith and good w.,		7:27	and the w. of darkness.	8:27
God could do such marvelous w.,		9: 5	the marvelous w. of God?	9:16
men shall reap a reward of their w.,		9:28	against the w. of the Lord?	9:26
to bring forth w. which are		9:30	will despise the w. of the Lord?	9:26
be judged according to their w.		11:41	despisers of the w. of the Lord,	9:26
to be judged according to their w.,		11:44	many great w. which the Lord	Eth 3:18
be judged according to their w.?		12: 8	always abounding in good w.,	12: 4
to be judged according to our w.		12:12	by their w. ye shall know them;	Mro 7: 5
yea, all our w. will condemn us;		12:14	for if their w. be good,	7: 5
that he is just in all his w.,		12:15	and putting trust in dead w.	8:23
repentance and their holy w.		12:30	The w., and the designs, and	DC 3: 1
the w. of justice could not be		12:32	power to do many mighty w.,	3: 4
their exceeding faith and good w.;		13: 3	hands, and do marvelous w.;	8: 8
and all the w. of the Lord		18:39	to light their marvelous w.,	10:61
do many mighty w. in his name;		19: 4	by their desires and their w.	18:38
and bringeth forth good w.,		26:22	destroying of Satan and his w.	19: 3
according to their w.		33:22	every man according to his w.	19: 3
counsel in wisdom over all his w.,		37:12	truly manifest by their w.	20:37
and the w. of darkness,		37:21	w. and faith agreeable to the	20:69
of darkness, and their secret w.,		37:21	of my blessings upon his w.	21: 8
the secret w. of those people		37:21	neither by your dead w.	22: 2
the w. of their brethren,		37:23	it is because of your dead w.	22: 3
brethren, yea, their secret w.,		37:23	myself my w. have no end,	29:33
works, their w. of darkness,		37:23	looked upon thee and thy w.	35: 3
unto light all their secret w.		37:25	I have looked upon thy w.	39: 7
to never be weary of good w.,		37:34	they may know your w.	45:72
show unto them marvelous w.		37:41	their w. shall follow them;	59: 2
those marvelous w. ceased,		37:41	doeth the w. of righteousness	59:23
chose evil w. rather than good;		40:13	come by faith, unto mighty w.,	63:11
be judged according to their w.		40:21	their w. shall follow them in	63:15
fruits of their labors or their w.,		40:26	and his w. shall follow him,	63:48
be judged according to their w.;		41: 3	make known his wonderful w.	65: 4
if their w. were good in this life,		41: 3	saves all the w. of his hands,	76:43
And if their w. are evil they		41: 4	be judged according to their w.,	76:111
the w. of justice would be		42:22	according to his own w.,	76:111
be judged according to their w.,		42:23	are the w. of the Lord,	76:114
and fall into the w. of darkness,		45:12	mysteries, and the w. of God;	77: 6
yea, w. of timbers built up to		50: 2	shall do many wonderful w.;	84:66
that upon those w. of timbers		50: 3	repent of their former evil w.,	84:76
overlooked those w. of pickets,		50: 4	of life, their faith, and w.;	85: 2
which his w. did bring forth		50:12	and the mighty w. of God in	88:108
them ye may remember their w.;	He	5: 6	and the mighty w. of God in	88:109
when ye remember their w. ye		5: 6	the w. of him were plainly	93: 5
who spread the w. of darkness		6:28	their w. shall be made known.	97: 6
carry on his w. of darkness		6:30	and all their wicked w.	97:24
come down to believe in their w.		6:38	according to all her w.,	97:26
their secret w. of darkness;		8: 4	him according to his w.	98:31
their secret w. of darkness,		10: 3	the enemy destroyed their w.,	101:51
and in deed, in faith and in w.;		10: 5	w. meet for my kingdom	101:100
unto repentance and good w.,		12:24	of faith nor of mighty w.,	105:24
for grace, according to their w.		12:24	w. may be brought to naught,	109:30
had the mighty w. been shown		15:15	eyes see and know all their w.,	121:24
mighty w. which I have done		15:17	according as his w. shall be.	121:25
w. cannot come to pass,		16:16	by your own w., bring cursings,	124:48
acquainted with our secret w.,	3Ne	3: 7	and shall continue their w.	124:86
w. thereof I know to be good;		3: 9	the w. which I have appointed	127: 4
that they may see your good w.		12:16	and your w. be redoubled,	127: 4
name done many wonderful w.?		14:22	*according to their w.*	128: 6
when these w. and the works		21: 5	according to their w.;	128: 7
the w. which shall be wrought		21: 5	contained the record of their w.,	128: 7
worship the w. of thy hands;		21:17	according to their own w.,	128: 8
God, to be judged of their w.,		26: 4	law is the continuation of the w.	132:31
Father show forth his own w.		27:10	and do the w. of Abraham;	132:32
is built upon the w. of men,		27:11	has sealed his mission and his w.	135: 3
or upon the w. of the devil,		27:11	for my w. are without end,	Mses 1: 4
joy in their w. for a season,		27:11	no man can behold all my w.,	1: 5
For their w. do follow them,		27:12	and there is no end to my w.,	1:38
it is because of their w. that		27:12	and their w. were in the dark,	5:51
me, to be judged of their w.,		27:14	and their w. were abominations,	5:52
be judged according to their w.		27:15	thus the w. of darkness began	5:55
the w. which ye have seen me do		27:21	death, because of secret w.,	6:15
Write the w. of this people,		27:24	testifying against their w.;	6:37
by them shall their w. be known		27:25	he told me of the w. which	Abr 3:11
even in turning their w. upon		27:32	w. which my hands have made,	3:21
marvelous w. shall be wrought		28:31	they would rest from all their w.	5: 3
all the marvelous w. of Christ,		28:33		

WORKWAYS

kept w. with the wind — DC 123:16

WORLD

also the redemption of the w.	1Ne	1:19
since the w. began, even down		3:20
an account of the creation of the w.,		5:11
which are pleasing unto the w.		6: 5
unto those who are not of the w.		6: 5
field, as if it had been a w.		8:20
in other words, a Savior of the w.		10: 4
or this Redeemer of the w.		10: 5
should take away the sins of the w.		10:10
men from the foundation of the w.,		10:18
and beheld the Redeemer of the w.,		11:27
God was judged of the w.;		11:32
and slain for the sins of the w.		11:33
the w. and the wisdom thereof;		11:35
building was the pride of the w.;		11:36
from the beginning of the w.		12:18
And also for the praise of the w.		13: 9
and the Savior of the w.;		13:40
concerning the end of the w.		14:22
the w., because of their iniquity,		19: 9
popular in the eyes of the w.,		22:23
flesh and the things of the w.,		22:23
from the creation of the w.;	2Ne	1:10
might leave this w. with gladness		1:21
written, from the creation of the w.		6: 3
have endured the crosses of the w.		9:18
from the foundation of the w.,		9:18
And he cometh into the w. that		9:21
rich as to the things of the w.		9:30
are the more wicked part of the w.;		10: 3
from the beginning of the w.,		11: 4
And I will punish the w. for evil,		23:11
And made the w. as a wilderness,		24:17
fill the face of the w. with cities.		24:21
it be for the benefit of the w.;		26:24
for he loveth the w.,		26:24
up for a light unto the w.,		26:29
may get gain and praise of the w.;		26:29
from the beginning of the w.		27: 7
from the foundation of the w.		27:10
be hid from the eyes of the w.,		27:12
because of the glory of the w.		27:16
I will show unto the w. that		27:23
I will judge the w., every man		29:11
take away the sins of the w.		31: 4
and bear the shame of the w.;	Jac	1: 8
able to speak and the w. was,		4: 9
resurrection and the w. to come?		4:12
the w. shall be burned with fire.		6: 3
in it above that of the w.	En	1:26
he standeth to judge the w.;	Mos	3:10
from the foundation of the w.		4: 6
from the foundation of the w. for		4: 7
even unto the end of the w.		4: 7
pertaining to the things of this w.		4:23
ever since the w. began—		13:33
prophets ever since the w. began?		15:13
from the foundation of the w.		15:19
their sins ever since the w. began,		15:26
if Christ had not come into the w.,		16: 6
is the light and the life of the w.;		16: 9
from the foundation of the w.		18:13
people, as to the wisdom of the w.,		24: 7
taketh upon me the sins of the w.;		26:23
who live without God in the w.,		27:31
loved the vain things of the w.,	Al	1:16
as to the wisdom of the w.,		2: 1
of souls sent to the eternal w.,		3:26
upon the vain things of the w.,		4: 8
up in the vain things of the w.,		5:37
to take away the sins of the w.,		5:48
upon the vain things of the w.,		5:53
and the vain things of the w.;		7: 6
taketh away the sins of the w.,		7:14
have been ever since the w. began,		7:25
And he shall come into the w.		11:40
from the foundation of the w.		12:25
from the foundation of the w.;		12:30
from the foundation of the w.		13: 3
from the foundation of the w.;	Al	13: 5
from the foundation of the w.		13: 7
began at the creation of the w.,		18:36
from the foundation of the w.,		18:39
from the foundation of the w.,		22:13
upon the mercies of the w.—		26:28
the mercies of the w. alone		26:28
rejoice as we, since the w. began;		26:35
be slain for the sins of the w.—		30:26
with the vain things of the w.		31:27
poor as to things of the w.;		32: 3
poverty as to the things of the w.		32: 4
atone for the sins of the w.;		34: 8
will suffice for the sins of the w.		34:12
your body in that eternal w.		34:34
to atone for the sins of the w.		36:17
is the life and the light of the w.		38: 9
nor the vain things of this w.;		39:14
to take away the sins of the w.		39:15
they are without God in the w.,		41:11
atoneth for the sins of the w.,		42:15
from the foundations of the w.		42:26
they went out of the w. rejoicing.		46:39
of their brethren out of this w.		48:23
this world into an eternal w.,		48:23
and the vain things of the w.?		60:32
I seek not for honor of the w.,		60:36
that he cometh to redeem the w.	He	5: 9
from the foundation of the w.		5:47
so long with the riches of the w.		6:17
should reveal unto the w. of		6:24
should not go forth unto the w.,		6:25
should not be known unto the w.		6:27
get gain and glory of the w.,		7: 5
and the vain things of this w.,		7:21
upon the vain things of the w.!		12: 4
who surely shall come into the w.,		13: 6
the morrow come I into the w.,	3Ne	1:13
show unto the w. that I will		1:13
from the foundation of the w.,		1:14
Christ should come into the w.		2: 7
and the vain things of the w.		6:15
the light and the life of the w.		9:18
have come unto the w. to bring		9:21
bring redemption unto the w.,		9:21
to save the w. from sin.		9:21
testified shall come into the w.		11:10
the light and the life of the w.;		11:11
upon me the sins of the w.,		11:11
slain for the sins of the w.		11:14
that it may shine unto the w.		18:24
even so shall ye do unto the w.;		18:25
have chosen them out of the w.		19:20
I pray not for the w., but for		19:29
thou hast given me out of the w.,		19:29
who was before the w. began.		26: 5
I came into the w. to do the		27:13
I shall stand to judge the w.		27:16
written shall the w. be judged.		27:26
save it be for the sins of the w.;		28: 9
while the w. shall stand.		28: 9
for they are hid from the w.		28:25
save it were for the sins of the w.		28:38
and of the fine things of the w.	4Ne	1:24
to sorrow for the sins of the w.		1:44
manifest unto the w. the things	Mrm	3:16
without Christ and God in the w.;		5:16
the redemption of the w.,		7: 7
because of the praise of the w.?		8:38
Go ye into all the w., and		9:22
concerning the creation of the w.,	Eth	1: 3
from the foundation of the w.		3:14
to go forth unto the w.,		3:21
should not come unto the w.		4: 1
the life, and the truth of the w.		4:12
from the foundation of the w.;		4:14
from the foundation of the w.		4:15
from the foundation of the w.		4:19
as a testimony against the w.		5: 4
and upon the glory of the w.		8: 7
surety hope for a better w.,		12: 4
show unto the w. that faith is		12: 6
showed himself not unto the w.		12: 7

WORLD

has shown himself unto the w.,	Eth 12: 8	from this place into all the w.,	DC 58:64
that thou hast loved the w.,	12:33	thyself unspotted from the w.,	59: 9
down of thy life for the w.,	12:33	reward, even peace in this w.,	59:23
and all the cunning of the w.,	13:16	eternal life in the w. to come.	59:23
I came into the w. not to call	Mro 8: 8	have advantage of the w.,	63:27
from the foundation of the w.;	8:12	endureth shall overcome the w.	63:47
as long as the w. shall stand,	10:19	receive an inheritance in this w.,	63:48
is in the likeness of the w.,	DC 1:16	a reward in the w. to come.	63:48
these things unto the w.;	1:18	preached the apostles unto the w.	63:52
The weak things of the w. shall	1:19	ye should overcome the w.;	64: 2
Lord, even the Savior of the w.;	1:20	Redeemer, the Savior of the w.,	66: 1
simple unto the ends of the w.,	1:23	Go ye into all the w., preach	68: 8
upon Idumea, of the w.	1:36	church, neither unto the w.;	70: 6
a Savior has come unto the w.,	3:16	proclaim unto the w. in the	71: 2
that we may get glory of the w.	10:19	the church, and unto the w.,	72:14
show it not unto the w. until	10:34	needs be sent unto the w.	75:24
show it not unto the w.—	10:35	proclaim the gospel unto the w.	75:24
I said, show it not unto the w.,	10:35	not fail to go into the w.,	75:26
all things known unto the w.	10:37	beginning before the w. was,	76:13
is the life and light of the w.,	10:70	is no forgiveness in this w.	76:34
the life and the light of the w.,	11:28	nor in the w. to come—	76:34
the light and the life of the w.,	12: 9	That he came into the w.	76:41
the w. is ripening in iniquity;	18: 6	Jesus, to be crucified for the w.,	76:41
called to go into all the w.	18:28	and to bear the sins of the w.,	76:41
you must preach unto the w.,	18:41	and to sanctify the w., and to	76:41
the end, the Redeemer of the w.	19: 1	we saw the terrestrial w.,	76:71
his works at the end of the w.	19: 3	his fulness in the eternal w.,	76:86
not these things unto the w.	19:21	in glory in the telestial w.;	76:98
before the w. as well as in	19:28	inhabitants of the telestial w.,	76:109
again in the vanities of the w.;	20: 5	his prescence in the w. of glory.	76:118
declared unto the w. by them—	20:10	God made the w. in six days,	77:12
Proving to the w. that the holy	20:11	you a place in the celestial w.,	78: 7
them shall the w. be judged,	20:13	beneath the celestial w.;	78:14
men for the sins of the w.,	21: 9	Go ye, go ye into the w.	80: 1
the church, and before the w.,	21:12	forgiveness of sins in this w.	84:41
church, and also before the w.,	23: 2	world, nor in the w. to come.	84:41
called to preach before the w.	23: 4	man that cometh into the w.;	84:46
pray vocally before the w.	23: 6	every man through the w.,	84:46
bearing my name before the w.,	24:10	for the sake of the whole w.	84:48
from thee and from the w.,	25: 4	And the whole w. lieth in sin,	84:49
lay aside the things of this w.,	25:10	whole w. groaneth under sin	84:53
holy prophets since the w. began,	27: 6	testimony to all the w. of	84:61
hath given me out of the w.	27:14	go ye into all the w.;	84:62
ye are chosen out of the w.	29: 4	all the w. unto every creature.	84:62
of the wickedness of the w.,	29:17	speak them before the w.;	84:73
from the foundation of the w.	29:46	this very hour upon all the w.,	84:75
the church, and before the w.,	30: 4	send you out to prove the w.,	84:79
the church, but not unto the w.,	31:10	and the kingdoms of the w.,	84:82
The light and the life of the w.,	34: 2	send you out to reprove the w.	84:87
Who so loved the w. that he gave	34: 3	reproving the w. in	84:117
crucified for the sins of the w.,	35: 2	the field was the w.,	86: 2
upon the weak things of the w.,	35:13	have been hid from the w.	86: 9
from the foundation of the w.,	35:18	prophets since the w. began.	86:10
before the w. was made;	38: 1	even them of the celestial w.	88: 2
spake, and the w. was made,	38: 3	both in this w. and in the	88:85
The light and the life of the w.;	39: 2	world and in the w. to come.	88:85
pride and the cares of the w.	39: 9	while thou art in the w.,	90: 3
the cares of the w. caused	40: 2	neither in the w. to come;	90: 3
living God, the Savior of the w.;	42: 1	man that cometh into the w.;	93: 2
have forgiveness in this w.,	42:18	because I was in the w. and	93: 4
this would, nor in the w. to come,	42:18	I was in the w. and received	93: 5
unto the w. it is not given to	42:65	beginning, before the w. was;	93: 7
and that not before the w.	42:89	and the Redeemer of the w.;	93: 9
Christ, the Savior of the w.	43:34	truth, who came into the w.,	93: 9
light and the life of the w.—	45: 7	the w. was made by him,	93: 9
everlasting covenant into the w.,	45: 9	not be confounded in this w.,	93:52
to be a light to the w.,	45: 9	world, nor in the w. to come.	93:52
that the end of the w. cometh;	45:22	after the manner of the w.,	95:13
from going abroad unto the w.	45:72	live after the manner of the w.;	95:13
which are held before the w.	46: 3	in this w. your joy is not full,	101:36
crucified for the sins of the w.,	46:13	kingdoms of the w. are subdued	103: 7
Only Begotten Son into the w.	49: 5	the kingdoms of the w. shall	103: 8
for the redemption of the w.,	49: 5	set to be a light unto the w.,	103: 9
before the w. was made.	49:17	the kingdoms of this w. may be	105:32
wherefore the w. lieth in sin.	49:20	overtaketh the w. as a thief	106: 4
in the earth, deceiving the w.	50: 2	in all ages of the w.,	107: 8
same are overcome of the w.	50: 8	name of Christ in all the w.—	107:23
and I have overcome the w.,	50:41	the Gentiles and in all the w.—	107:25
cricified for the sins of the w.,	53: 2	who do not travel into all the w.	107:90
that you shall forsake the w.	53: 2	lying reports abroad, over the w.,	109:29
cricified for the sins of the w.—	54: 1	and then go ye into all the w.,	112:28
the w. receive his writings—	57:12	bear glad tidings unto all the w.	114: 1
he seeketh the praise of the w.	58:39	scattered abroad in all the w.;	115: 3

WORLD — WORSHIP

not been revealed since the w. was	DC 121:26
before this w. was,	121:32
upon the things of this w.,	121:35
not only publish to all the w.,	123:6
and filled the w. with confusion,	123:7
be made to all the kings of the w.,	124:3
confessing me before the w.;	124:18
before the foundation of the w.,	124:33
hid from before the w. was.	124:38
before the foundation of the w.,	124:41
record of my name in all the w.,	124:139
before the foundation of the w.	127:2
the prince of this w. cometh,	127:11
before the foundation of the w.,	128:5
before the foundation of the w.,	128:8
in all ages of the w.,	128:9
from the foundation of the w.,	128:18
ordained, before the w. was,	128:22
advantage in the w. to come.	130:19
before the foundations of this w.,	130:20
before the foundation of the w.	132:5
before the w. was?	132:11
And everything that is in the w.,	132:13
man marry him a wife in the w.,	132:15
with her so long as he is in the w.	132:15
and when they are out of the w.;	132:15
when they are out of the w.	132:15
when they are out of the w.	132:16
when they are out of the w.,	132:18
when they are out of the w.	132:18
when they are out of the w.;	132:19
ye receive me not in the w.	132:22
But if ye receive me in the w.,	132:23
shall not be forgiven in the w.	132:27
in the world nor out of the w.,	132:27
before the w. was.	132:28
so long as they were in the w.;	132:30
out of the w. they should continue;	132:30
both in the w. and out of the world	132:30
both in the world and out of the w.	132:30
not inherit them out of the w.,	132:39
even unto the end of the w.,	132:49
an hundredfold in this w.,	132:55
before the foundation of the w.,	132:63
who shall come down upon the w.	133:2
For since the beginning of the w.	133:45
commanded to be dept from the w.	133:60
from the corruption of the w.;	134:12
the salvation of men in this w.,	135:3
for the salvation of a ruined w.;	135:6
that all the w. cannot impeach;	135:7
my Spirit is sent forth into the w.	136:33
for thou art in the w., and now I	Mses 1:7
beheld the w. upon which he	1:8
beheld the w. and the ends	1:8
he sought to destroy the w.	4:6
for thou wast also before the w.	5:24
before the foundation of the w.	5:57
that it should be in the w.,	5:59
shall be in the end of the w. also.	6:7
forth in the beginning of the w.,	6:30
it shall be sent forth in the w.,	6:30
I am God; I made the w.,	6:51
from the foundation of the w.	6:54
were born into the w. by water,	6:59
the words of eternal life in this w.,	6:59
and eternal life in the w. to come,	6:59
I will show unto thee the w. for	7:4
from the foundation of the w.;	7:47
even unto the end of the w.;	7:67
be revealed unto the w.;	Fac 2:8
If the w. can find out these	2:11
were organized before the w. was;	Abr 3:22
and of the end of the w.,	JS 1:4
which is the end of the w.?	1:4
shall be preached in all the w.,	1:31
and its progress in the w.—	2:1
actual being from the unseen w.,	2:16
boy of no consequence in the w.,	2:22
all the w. could not make him	2:24
why does the w. think to make	2:25
sectarian w. was concerned—	2:26

WORLDLY

my father's w. circumstances	JS 2:55

WORLDS

the w. are and were created,	DC 76:24
before the w. were made.	76:39
cannot come, w. without end.	76:112
The w. were made by him;	93:10
eternal lives in the eternal w.	132:55
their exaltation in the eternal w.,	132:63
w. without number have I	Mses 1:33
many w. that have passed away	1:35

WORLD'S

you servants for the w. sake,	DC 93:46
to take from them this w. goods,	134:10

WORM

the w. shall eat them like wool.	2Ne 8:8
the w. is spread under thee,	24:11
where their w. dieth not,	76:44

WORMS

and the w. cover thee.	2Ne 24:11
a prey to the w. of the flesh.	Eth 14:22

WORN

that I should have w. these bands.	Mos 7:13
their skins were w. exceedingly	Al 20:29

WORRIED

I perceive that thy mind is w.	Al 40:1
thy mind has been w. also	41:1
I was somewhat w. concerning	61:19

WORRY

more which doth w. your mind,	Al 42:1

WORSE

w. than though they had never	Al 24:30
Behold ye are w. than they;	He 13:26

WORSHIP

fall down at his feet and w. him.	1Ne 11:24
and were about to w. me, but	17:55
w. the Lord thy God,	17:55
they did w. the Lord,	18:1
princes also shall w.,	21:7
Yea, wo unto those that w. idols.	2Ne 9:37
that they shall w. me, saith God.	10:19
w. the work of their own hands,	12:8
he hath made for himself to w.,	12:20
and w. the Father in his name,	25:16
and w. him with all your might,	25:29
or out of the houses of w.?	26:26
we w. the Father in his name.	Jac 4:5
into the w. of a being which	7:7
and to w. the Lord their God,	Mos 18:25
I trust that you do not w. idols,	Al 7:6
ye do w. the true and living God,	7:6
to w. God before the altar,	15:17
many of whom did w. idols,	17:15
ourselves together to w. God.	21:6
themselves together to w. him.	22:7
from one house of w. to another,	23:4
they did w. after a manner which	31:12
whosoever desired to w. must	31:14
into their synagogues to w. God,	32:3
have no place to w. our God;	32:5
that we cannot w. our God.	32:9
suppose that ye cannot w. God	32:10
not w. God only once in a week?	32:11
that ye could not w. your God	33:2
suppose that ye cannot w. God,	33:2
said concerning prayer or w.?	33:3
even to the dust, do w. him.	34:38
w. God according to their desires.	43:9
w. God in spirit and in truth,	43:10
their rites of w. and their church.	43:45
religion, and by our rites of w.,	44:5
they did w. God with exceeding	45:1
to w. the Lord their God,	50:39

WORSHIP 1066 WOUNDS

of their church and of their w.,	3Ne 2:12	that they are w. of it,	DC 20:69
feet of Jesus, and did w. him.	11:17	the laborer is w. of his hire.	31: 5
down at his feet, and did w. him;	17:10	given to them that are not w.,	41: 6
or your places of w.,	18:32	accounted of God w. to receive.	50:34
shalt no more w. the works of	21:17	and is not accounted w. by	51: 4
had built for the place of w.	Mro 7: 1	is not accounted w. to belong	51: 5
and w. the Father in my name.	DC 18:40	and when ye are w., in mine	67:14
being whom they should w.	20:19	be high priests who are w.,	68:15
and w. the Father in his name,	20:29	and found w. and anointed,	68:20
and building houses of w.,	42:35	the same is w. of his hire,	70:12
who w. him forever and ever.	76:21	accounted w. to inherit the	72: 4
understand and know how to w.,	93:19	the laborer is w. of his hire.	84:79
and know what you w.,	93:19	to those that are not w.—	90:26
and w. me according to mine	101:22	that you may be found w.	98:14
those who shall w. in this house	109:14	covenant ye are not w. of me.	98:15
establish the people that shall w.,	109:24	consider w. and capable to act	102: 7
that they may w. me.	115: 8	let those be chosen that are w.	105:35
for the w. of my people.	124:84	for the laborer is w. of his hire.	106: 3
And w. him that made heaven,	133:39	shall not be counted w. to stand.	107:100
interfere in prescribing rules of w.	134: 4	shall not be counted w. to stand.	107:100
concerns, for faith and w.,	134: 6	that we may be found w.,	109:11
Moses, son of man, w. me.	Mses 1:12	shall not be found w. to abide	119: 5
thy glory, that I should w. thee?	1:13	w. of all acceptation,	124:23
W. God, for him only shalt thou	1:15	shall be w. of all acceptation.	128:24
mine Only Begotten, and w. me.	1:17	who are w. of a far more,	132:16
the Only Begotten, w. me.	1:19	not bear chastisement is not w.	136:31
for this one God only will I w.,	1:20		
they should w. the Lord their	5: 5	WOULD: *see in the APPENDIX.*	
and temptest them to w. him;	6:49		
would not bow down to w. gods	Abr 1:11	WOULDST	
to w. the god of Elkenah,	1:17	thou w. deal very treacherously,	1Ne 20: 8
let them w. how, where, or	AoF 11	thou w. clear my way before me,	2Ne 4:33
		that thou w. listen to my words	Mos 22: 4
WORSHIPPED		perhaps thou w. lose thy soul.	Al 20:18
and w. the Father in his name,	Jac 4: 5	thou w. again lead away the	30:55
		we will that thou w. tell us the	3Ne 27: 3
WORSHIPPERS		thou w. not have come to the	DC 6:14
and the true w. of Christ,	4Ne 1:37	that thou w. rend the heavens,	133:40
		that thou w. come down,	133:40
WORSHIPPING			
have the liberty of w. the Lord	Al 21:22	WOUND	
throne, w. God, and the Lamb,	DC 76:21	and w. their delicate minds.	Jac 2: 9
w. of the gods of the heathen,	Abr 1: 5	having received a w. has fallen	Mos 20:13
privilege of w. Almighty God	AoF 11	himself being afflicted with a w.	Al 3:22
WORTH		WOUNDED	
even of great w. unto us,	1Ne 5:21	cut Rahab, and w. the dragon?	2Ne 8: 9
things which are not of w. unto	6: 6	word which healeth the w. soul.	Jac 2: 8
of great w. unto the Gentiles.	13:23	of those who are already w.,	2: 9
some men esteem to be of great w.,	19: 7	and those who have not been w.,	2: 9
shall be of w. unto our seed;	22: 8	he was w. for our transgressions,	Mos 14: 5
also be of w. unto the Gentiles;	22: 9	been w. and left upon the ground,	20:13
shall be of great w. unto them,	2Ne 3: 7	with their dead and w. bodies.	Al 49:22
money for that which is of no w.,	9:51	were about fifty who were w.,	49:24
are of w. unto the children of men,	25: 8	Moroni was w. and Jacob was	52:35
shall be of great w. unto them	25: 8	that my men who had been w.	57:24
great w. unto the children of men,	28: 2	thus taken care of our w. men,	57:28
and say that is of no w.!	28:16	sword, yea w. and bleeding?	60:22
and I esteem it as of great w.,	33: 3	and I fell w. in the midst;	Mrm 6:10
of no w. but to be hewn down	Jac 5:46	And Shared w. Coriantumr	Eth 13:31
onties, which are of great w.,	Al 11:25	upon his arm that he was w.;	14:12
do cast out. (it being of no w.)	34:29	Coriantumr was w. again,	15: 9
the plates thereof are of no w.,	Mrm 8:14	I was w. in the house of	DC 45:52
the record thereof is of great w.;	8:14	was w. in a savage manner	135: 2
be of w. unto my brethren,	Mro 1: 4		
be of the most w. unto you.	DC 15: 4	WOUNDING	
will be of the most w. unto you	15: 6	I have slain a man to my w.,	Mses 5:47
be of the most w. unto you.	16: 4		
will be of the most w. unto you	16: 6	WOUNDS	
the w. of souls is great in the	18:10	to enlarge the w. of those who	Jac 2: 9
		consoling and healing their w.;	2: 9
WORTHINESS		hearts died, pierced with deep w.	2:35
unto me, not of any w. of myself.	Al 36: 5	took him and bound up his w.,	Mos 20:13
see that ye do all things in w.,	Mrm 9:29	dide in the wilderness of their w.,	Al 2:38
		inflict the w. of death in your	44: 7
WORTHLESS		their w. were upon their legs,	49:24
and your w. and fallen state—	Mos 4: 5	that their w. should be dressed.	57:24
		who had not received many w.	57:25
WORTHY		they have received many w.;	58:40
latchet I am not w. to unloose.	1Ne 10: 8	he gave him many deep w.;	Eth 14:30
and thou art w. of death.	Mos 17: 1	had recovered of his w.,	15: 1
they are w. to be called sons)	Al 56:10	the w. which pierced my side,	DC 6:37
meet that they were w. of it.	Mro 6: 1	What are these w. in thine	45:51

WOUNDS

These w. are the wounds with	DC 45:52
w. with which I was wounded	45:52

WRAPT

should be w. together as a scroll,	3Ne 26: 3

WRATH

the w. of God is upon the seed	1Ne 13:11
the w. of God, that it was upon	13:14
that the w. of God was upon	13:18
the w. of God was poured out	14:15
the w. of God is upon the	14:16
the w. of God is poured out	14:17
the fulness of the w. of God	17:35
the fulness of the w. of God	22:16
the fulness of his w. must come,	22:17
the fulness of his w. upon you,	2Ne 1:17
Through the w. of the Lord	19:19
and against the people of my w.	20: 6
both with w. and fierce anger,	23: 9
in the w. of the Lord of Hosts,	23:13
He who smote the people in w.	24: 6
he should swear in his w.	Jac 1: 7
And they swore in their w. that,	En 1:14
out of the cup of the w. of God,	Mos 3:26
out of the cup of the w. of God.	5: 5
which brought down the w. of God	7:28
swore in his w. that he would	19: 4
to bring down the w. of God	Al 10:18
I swear in my w. that he shall not	12:35
he sendeth down his w. upon you	12:36
to pull down his w. upon us	12:37
not bring down his w. upon you,	13:30
shall exercise upon them in his w.	14:11
Behold, we went forth even in w.,	26:18
be cast by thy w. down to hell;	31:17
of the w. of God upon them;	40:14
the sword of his almighty w.,	54: 6
pull down the w. of that God	54: 9
w. against the day of judgment.	He 8:25
In a little w. I hid my face	3Ne 22: 8
he that shall breathe out w.	Mrm 8:21
swore in his w. that they	Eth 1:33
he had sworn in his w. unto	2: 8
fulness of his w. should come	2: 8
the fullness of his w. shall come	2: 9
the fulness of his w. cometh	2: 9
the fulness of the w. of God	2:11
pour out the fulness of my w.	9:20
in the fulness of his w.,	14:25
he swore in his w. that he	15:28
the w. of God shall be poured	DC 1: 9
by my w., and by mine anger,	19:15
of the w. of her fornication.	35:11
of the w. of mine indignation	43:26
and of w. upon the nations.	56: 1
against none is his w. kindled,	59:21
without w. or doubting,	60: 7
neither in w. not with strife.	60:14
for the day of w. shall come	63: 6
only in w. unto their	63:11
I have sworn in my w.,	63:33
For they are vessels of w.,	76:33
to suffer the w. of God,	76:33
after the sufferings of his w.	76:38
suffer the w. of God on earth.	76:104
suffer the w. of Almighty God,	76:106
of the w. of Almighty God.	76:107
therefore, the Lord in his w.,	84:24
which the Lord in his w. caused	84:27
earth be made to feel the w.,	87: 6
may escape the w. of God,	88:85
after your testimony cometh w.	88:88
of the w. of her fornication,	88:94
of the w. of her fornication;	88:105
of the w. of Almighty God.	88:106
away all w. and indignation	98:22
and in the day of w. I will	101: 9
I will pour out my w. without	103: 2
you cannot escape my w. in	104: 8
art about to send, in thy w.,	109:38
and wilt turn away thy w.	109:53
a day of w., a day of burning,	112:24
w. when it shall be poured out	DC 115: 6
bring cursings, w., indignation,	124:48
I will answer judgment, w.,	124:52
to flee the w. to come.	124:106
as the envy and w. of man	127: 2
the w. of God to be poured out	Mses 7: 1

WREST

if ye will w. them it shall be to	Al 13:20
for they do w. the scriptures	DC 10:63

WRESTED

some have w. the scriptures,	Al 41: 1

WRESTLE

the w. which I had before God,	En 1: 2

WRESTLING

w. with God in mighty prayer,	Al 8:10

WRETCHED

and marvelous works my heart	2Ne 4:17

WRIST

the bands which were upon my w.,	1Ne 18:15
arms, also, a little above the w.;	JS 2:31

WRIT

do contain that which is holy w.	Al 37: 5

WRITE

I do not w. it in this work.	1Ne 6: 1
may w. of the things of God.	6: 3
unto the world I do not w.,	6: 5
which I do not w. in this book;	10:15
they shall w. many things which	13:35
w. the remainder of these things;	14:21
he shall also w. concerning	14:22
the things which he shall w. are	14:23
this apostle of the Lamb shall w.	14:24
see hereafter thou shalt not w.;	14:25
Lamb of God that he should w. them.	14:25
am forbidden that I should w. the	14:28
so much that we cannot w. them	17: 6
not w. anything upon plates save	19: 6
the fruit of thy loins shall w.;	2Ne 3:12
of the loins of Judah shall w.;	3:12
But I will w. unto him my law,	3:17
that he shall w. the writing	3:18
And the words which he shall w.	3:19
these I w. the things of my soul,	4:15
bidden that I should not w. them.	4:25
I do not w. upon these plates all	5: 4
w. more of the words of Isaiah,	11: 2
I w. some of the words of Isaiah	11: 8
and w. in it with a man's pen,	18: 1
and that w. grievousness which	20: 1
that a child may w. them.	20:19
I w. unto my people unto,	25: 3
hereafter these things which I w.,	25: 3
and I do not w. them.	25: 6
things which I w. shall be kept	25:21
For we labor diligently to w.,	25:23
we w. according to our prophecies,	25:26
They shall w. the things which	26:17
shall w. the words which I speak	29:11
the Jews and they shall w. it;	29:12
the Nephites and they shall w. it;	29:12
led away, and they shall w. it;	29:12
of the earth and they shall w. it.	29:12
I cannot w. but a few things,	31: 1
can I w. but a few of the words of	31: 1
Nephi, cannot w. all the things	33: 1
commanded of him to w. these	33:11
that I should w. upon these plates	Jac 1: 2
I cannot w. but a little of my	4: 1
things which we w. upon plates	4: 1
But whatsoever things we w. upon	4: 2
can w. a few w. upon plates,	4: 2
And after this manner do I w.	En 1:23
behold, I, Jarom, w. a few words	Jar 1: 1
must needs be that I w. a little;	1: 2
but I shall not w. the things of	1: 2

WRITE / WRITTEN

For what could I w. more than	Jar	1: 2	W. the vision, for lo, this is the	DC	76:49
And I, Jarom, do not w. more,		1:14	Lord commanded us to w.		76:80
that I should w. somewhat upon	Om	1: 1	we were commanded to w.		76:113
w. the things whatsoever I write,		1: 4	commanded us we should not w.		76:115
write the things whatsoever I w.,		1: 4	ye shall w. this commandment,		90:32
w. what few things I write,		1: 9	w. speedily to Cainhannoch		104:81
write what few things I w.,		1: 9	w. according to that which		104:81
he may w. somewhat concerning	WM	1: 2	help you to w. this proclamation,		124:12
I cannot w. the hundredth part		1: 5	I will w. the word of the Lord		127:10
did w. all the words which Abinadi	Mos	17: 4	I would w. to you		128: 1
that they might w. one to another.		24: 6	thou shalt w. the things which	Mses	1:40
did king Mosiah w. unto them,		29:33	from the book which thou shalt w.,		1:41
w. the words which I shall say.	Al	45: 9	w. the words which I speak.		2: 1
I w. this eipstle unto you,	3Ne	3: 2	to w. by the spirit of inspiration;		6: 5
Therefore I w. unto you,		3: 6	were taught to read and w.,		6: 6
I w. this epistle unto you,		3:10	shall endeavor to w. some of these	Abr	1:31
language, we are not able to w.		5:18	induced to w. this history,	JS	2: 1
that ye shall w. these sayings		16: 4	which I cannot w. at this time.		2:20
these sayings which ye shall w.		16: 4	and he began to w. for me.		2:67
w. the things which I have told		23: 4			
I would that ye should w.,		23: 6	**WRITETH**		
w. the words which the Father		24: 1	w. them for the learning and	2Ne	4:15
I was about to w. them,		26:11			
I, Mormon, do w. the things		26:12	**WRITING**		
proceed to w. the things which		26:12	these plates which I am w.;	1Ne	6: 1
should not any man w. them.		26:16	But, to be short in w.,		8:30
W. the things which ye have seen		27:23	written upon them a new w.,		16:29
W. the works of this people,		27:24	give judgment unto him in w.	2Ne	3:17
I was about to w. the names		28:25	shall write the w. of the fruit of		3:18
therefore I w. them not, for		28:25	mighty in w., like unto speaking;		33: 1
commandeth me that I should w.,		30: 1	And I make an end of my w.	Jac	7:27
I w. unto you, Gentiles, and	Mrm	3:17	which w. has been small;		7:27
I w. unto all the ends of		3:18	the w. which was upon the wall	Al	10: 2
I w. also unto the remnant of		3:19	that all might see the w. which		46:19
therefore I w. unto you all.		3:20	give her a w. of divorcment.	3Ne	12:31
for this cause I w. unto you,		3:20	because of our weakness in w.;	Eth	12:23
or for man to w. a perfect		4:11	hast not made us mighty in w.;		12:23
I w. a small abridgment,		5: 9	hast not made us mighty in w.		12:24
I have but few things to w.,		8: 1	because of my weakness in w.		12:40
w. the sad tale of the destruction		8: 3	people of whom I have been w.		13: 1
I will w. and hide up the		8: 4	which thou hast been w. are true.	DC	6:17
I would w. it also if I had		8: 5	w. the things which shall be		24: 5
Behold, I cannot w. them.		8:23	thy time shall be given to w.,		25: 8
I do not w. those things which	Eth	1: 4	give unto him a w. that		51: 4
ye shall w. them and shall seal		3:22	of selecting and w. books		55: 4
shall w. them in a language		3:22	his w. is not acceptable unto		63:56
the things which ye shall w.		3:23	that he shall continue in w.		69: 3
the language which ye shall w.		3:24	Preaching and expounding, w.,		69: 8
these things which ye shall w.		3:24	and are w., and by whom,		123: 5
W. these things and seal them		3:27	at the time of the w. of		124: 4
w. the things which he had seen;		4: 1	Contains w. that cannot be	Fac	2: 8
hath commanded me to w. them;		4: 5			
not w. the manner of their oaths		8:20	**WRITINGS**		
commanded to w. these things		8:26	according to the w. of the kings,	Jar	1:14
that we could w. but little,		12:24	you delivered up those w.	DC	10: 1
even that we cannot w. them;		12:25	you have delivered the w.		10: 8
when we w. we behold our		12:25	it was said in those w. that		10:39
And I was about to w. more,		13:13	if he would receive his w.—		57:12
I w. a few more things,	Mro	1: 4	it be the holy and sacred w.,		104:68
but I w. a few more things,		1: 4			
I, Moroni, w. a few of the words		7: 1	**WRITTEN**		
on this wise did he w. unto me,		8: 1	An Account w. by	T Pg	
I will w. unto you again if I go		8:27	W. to the Lamanites,	T Pg	
until I shall w. unto you,		8:30	W. by way of commandment	T Pg	
I w. unto you again that ye may		9: 1	W. and sealed up, and	T Pg	
I w. somewhat of that which		9: 1	things which my father hath w.,	1Ne	1:16
now I w. somewhat concerning		9: 7	for he hath w. many things		1:16
w. somewhat a few things, if		9:24	he also hath w. many things		1:16
w. somewhat as seemeth me		10: 1	cannot be w. upon these plates,		6: 3
and I w. unto my brethren,		10: 1	cannot be w. upon these plates.		9: 1
did commence again to w. for	DC	9: 1	I have w. as many of them as		10:15
is to w. for my servant Joseph.		9: 4	in them shall be w. my gospel,		13:36
cannot w. that which is sacred		9: 9	behold they are w. in the book		14:23
to w. the Book of Mormon,		24: 1	the things which were w. were plain		14:23
what thou shalt speak and w.,		24: 6	and they have w. them;		14:26
w. by way of commandment,		28: 5	the things which I have w.		14:28
w. them not by way of		28: 8	I have w. but a small part		14:28
that thou shalt w. for him;		35:20	things which I saw are not w.,		14:30
And inasmuch as ye do not w.,		35:23	things which I have w. are true.		14:30
w. and keep a regular history,		47: 1	behold the things which are w.		16:26
w. and keep a regular history,		47: 4	things which we w. upon the ball,		16:27
w. a description of the land		58:50	there was also w. upon them		16:29
that we should w. the vision;		76:28	w. and changed from time to time,		16:29

WRITTEN

should be w. upon these plates;	1Ne 19: 3
the things which were w. should	19: 3
w. these things unto my people,	19:18
are w. upon the plates of brass.	19:21
were w. in the book of Moses;	19:23
was w. by the prophet Isaiah;	19:23
w. unto all the house of Israel,	19:24
this manner has the prophet w.	19:24
been w. upon the plates of brass	22:30
according to that which is w.,	2Ne 2:17
be w. by the fruit of thy loins	3:12
w. by the fruit of the loins of	3:12
are w. upon the plates of brass.	4: 2
are w. upon mine other plates;	4:14
are w. upon mine other plates.	4:14
according to that which is w.	5:12
concerning all things which are w.,	6: 3
they of whom the prophet has w.;	6:12
the prophet has w. these things.	6:12
in whose heart I have w. my law,	8: 7
these things have I caused to be w.,	11: 1
things which I have w. sufficeth me.	11: 1
that is w. among the living	14: 3
the words which I have w.,	25: 1
for their good have I w. them.	25: 8
to the words which are w.	25:22
words of the righteous shall be w.,	26:15
w. and sealed up in a book,	26:17
The things which shall be w. out	28: 2
I have not caused more to be w.	29:10
out of the books which shall be w.	29:11
according to that which is w.	29:11
and be w. unto the Gentiles,	30: 3
believe the words which are w.;	30: 3
things which I have w. sufficeth me,	31: 2
many things away which are w.	33: 2
But I, Nephi, have w. what I	33: 3
have written what I have w.,	33: 3
which I have w. in weakness	33: 4
at the words which I have w.	33: 5
which were w. concerning David,	Jac 2:23
cannot be w. upon these plates;	3:13
are w. upon the larger plates,	3:13
for this intent have we w. these	4: 4
none of the prophets have w.,	7:11
that I have w. according to	7:26
as these things are w. for	Jar 1: 2
more than my fathers have w.?	1: 2
which they caused to be w.	1:14
save that which has been w.,	Om 1:11
that which is sufficient is w.	1:11
they are w., but not in these	1:18
concerning that which I have w.;	WM 1: 3
there are great things w. upon them,	1:11
to the word of God which is w.	1:11
which are not w. in this book	Mos 1: 8
words which he spake should be w.	2: 8
he spake and caused to be w.,	2: 9
name w. always in your hearts,	5:12
of them have I w. in this book,	8: 1
meaneth the words which are w.,	12:20
they are not w. in your hearts;	13:11
translated and caused to be w.	28:11
this account shall be w. hereafter;	28:19
which are w. in this account.	28:19
yea, even a w. word sent he	29: 4
the words that were w., saying:	29: 4
shall be w. in the book of Lehi,	Al 5:58
And thus it is w.. Amen.	6: 8
many things which cannot be w.,	8: 1
words of Amulek are not all w.,	9:34
of his words are w. in this book.	9:34
which was w. by the finger of God.	10: 2
or this is all that I have w.	11:46
which are not w. in this book.	13:31
have been w. by them of old?	33:12
not w. that Zenos alone spake	33:15
of God as they are w.	37:20
which was w. upon the plates of	44:24
he had w. upon the rent part,	46:19
I have w. unto you somewhat	54: 5
he hath w. unto the king of the	61: 8
were w. and sent forth among	63:12

the account which I have w.	He 2:14
how that it is said, and also w.,	5: 6
it may be said of you, and also w.,	5: 7
it has been said and w. of them.	5: 7
many things which are not w.,	5:13
also many things which are w.	5:13
Nephi speak which cannot be w.;	8: 3
more things which cannot be w.	14: 1
the holy prophets, which are w.,	15: 7
were the words which were w.,	3Ne 3: 1
I have w. this epistle,	3: 5
cannot all be w. in this book;	5: 8
and all of them cannot be w.,	7:17
they are not w. in this book.	7:17
w. upon the plates of brass	10:17
whom it was w. by the prophets,	11:15
and it is also w. before you,	12:21
it is w. by them of old time,	12:27
It hath been w., that whosoever	12:31
And again it is w., thou shalt	12:33
it is w., an eye for an eye, and	12:38
And behold it is w. also, that	12:43
which he prayed cannot be w.,	17:15
can there be w. by any man,	17:17
neither can be w. by man the	19:32
he prayed that they cannot be w.,	19:34
behold they are w., ye have	20:11
brought to pass that which is w.:	20:36
that which is w. come to pass:	22: 1
that ye have not w. this thing,	23:11
that this thing had not been w.	23:12
commanded that it should be w.;	23:13
w. according as he commanded.	23:13
in one, which they had w.,	23:14
after they were w. he expounded	24: 1
book of remembrance was w.	24:16
cannot be w. in this book	26: 6
And these things have I w.,	26: 8
I have w. them to the intent	26: 8
which are not lawful to be w.	26:18
shall be, even as hath been w.,	27:24
of the books which have been w.,	27:25
written, and which shall be w.,	27:25
all things are w. by the Father;	27:26
of the books which shall be w.	27:26
also w. in the book of Nephi,	4Ne 1:21
these things are w. unto the	Mrm 5:12
they are w. after this manner,	5:12
this is w. for the intent that ye	7: 9
he hath w. the intent thereof.	8: 5
them who have w. before him;	9:31
we have w. this record according	9:32
we should have w. in Hebrew;	9:33
if we could have w. in Hebrew,	9:33
the things which we have w.,	9:34
these things are w. that we may	9:35
the things which we have w.	Eth 2:12
of these things which are w.	3:17
I have w. upon these plates the	4: 4
write them; and I have w. them.	4: 5
to be w. by my servant John	4:16
have w. the words which were	5: 1
And only a few have I w.,	12:40
prophets and apostles have w.,	12:41
hundredth part I have not w.)	15:33
words which are w. by Ether	15:34
supposed not to have w. more,	Mro 1: 1
not to have w. any more;	1: 4
Mormon, w. to me, Moroni;	8: 1
it was w. unto me soon after	8: 1
intent I have w. this epistle.	8: 6
cannot tell, neither can it be w.	9:19
which I have w. grieve thee,	9:25
which were w. by this man,	10:27
that which I have w. is true.	10:29
which was w. by the prophets—	DC 1:18
which you have caused to be w.,	10:10
translated and caused to be w.	10:11
those things that you have w.,	10:38
the things which you have w.	18: 2
upon the things which are w.;	18: 3
are all things w. concerning	18: 4
according to that which is w.;	18:29

that which is w. before you;	DC 18:30	**WROTE**	
to the words which are w.	18:30	*I, Nephi, w. this record.*	1Ne 1:hd
it is not w. that there	19: 6	And the prophecies which he w.,	2Ne 4: 2
but it is w. *endless torment.*	19: 6	I saw the last which he w.,	Om 1: 9
Again, it is w. *eternal damnation;*	19: 7	that he w. it with his own hand;	1: 9
as it is w. in those scriptures	20:21	he w. it in the day that he	1: 9
according to that which is w.	24:14	he w. them down that he might	Mos 26:33
which he hath w. from that stone	28:11	his hand and w. unto Korihor,	Al 30:51
And, as it is w.—	29: 6	Korihor put forth his hand and w.,	30:52
me to do according as it is w.	29:50	a piece thereof, and w. upon it—	46:12
give heed to that which is w.,	32: 4	Therefore he w. an epistle,	54: 4
those things which are w.,	46: 2	which he w. unto Ammoron,	54: 4
prophets and apostles have w.,	52: 9	w. another epistle unto Moroni,	54:15
as it was w. by the prophets	66: 2	these are the words which he w.,	54:15
signs following, even as it is w.	68:10	these are the words which he w.,	56: 2
knowledge, even as it is w.	73: 5	he w. again to the governor of	60: 1
as it is w., they are gods,	76:58	these are the words which he w.,	60: 1
whose names are w. in heaven,	76:68	since I w., I have inquired of	3Ne 28:37
sun of the firmament is w. of	76:70	I, Mormon, w. an epistle unto	Mrm 6: 2
are w. in the 9th chapter of	77:13	He that w. this record was	Eth 1: 6
Elias, who, as it is w., must come	77:14	that the things which he w.	12:24
to that which I have w.—	84:57	he w. an epistle unto Shiz,	15: 4
w. in the book of the law	85: 5	w. an epistle unto Coriantumr,	15: 5
w. in the book of remembrance	85: 9	w. again an epistle unto Shiz,	15:18
w. in the book of the law,	85:11	the apostle w. unto the church,	DC 74: 5
as it is w. of me in the volume	99: 5	I w. a few words of revelation	128: 2
according to the form above w.	102:13	contained in the letter which I w.	128: 7
if there is not a sufficiency w.	102:23		
to the former pattern w.,	102:27	**WROTH**	
all w. in the book of Enoch,	107:57	these words, they were yet w.,	1Ne 4: 4
Let it be w. in the spirit of	124: 4	behold, they were exceeding w.,	7:16
which were w. in the books,	128: 6	his brethren were w. with him	Mos 10:14
which were w. in the books,	128: 9	they were also w. with him upon	10:14
whereon is a new name w.,	130:11	And again, they were w. with him	10:15
w. in the Lamb's Book of Life,	132:19	and again they were w. with him	10:16
it was w.: Thou shalt not kill.	132:36	them they were w. with him,	11:26
having his Father's name w. on	133:18	unto the people, he was also w.;	11:27
was w. by the prophet Moses,	133:63	But the king was more w.,	17: 3
w. by the prophet Malachi,	133:64	therefore he was w. with him;	24: 9
of remembrance we have w.	Mses 6:46	of God he was w. with Gideon,	Al 1: 9
as w. above the hand.	Fac 3: 4	the people were w. with me	9:31
of whom it is w. by the prophets,	JS 1: 1	Zerahemna was exceeding w.,	44:16
be fulfilled that which is w.,	1:44	behold, they were exceeding w.,	46: 2
deposited, w. upon gold plates,	2:34	the leader of those who were w.	46: 3
		and those people who were w.	46: 4
WRONG		the king was w. because of their	47: 3
should do w. in the sight of God.	Mos 26:13	Amalickiah pretended to be w.,	47:27
which is right to that which is w.;	Al 7:20	Yea, he was exceedingly w.,	49:27
with fear lest he had done w.	18: 5	were so w. with the chief judge,	51:13
and that w. which ye have done.	39:13	he was exceeding w. because of	51:14
behold they were not in the w.	50:27	yea, he was exceeding w.;	51:14
fathers did w. their brethren,	54:17	was exceeding w.; therefore, he	He 1: 7
of those that had received no w.,	3Ne 3:11	I would not be w. with thee.	3Ne 22: 9
that he has done which are w.,	DC 5:28	And Cain was very w., and his	Mses 5:21
to forget the thing which is w.;	9: 9	unto Cain: Why art thou w.?	5:22
who was right and who was w.	JS 2: 8	Cain was w., and listened not	5:26
or, are they all w. together?	2:10	I was w. also; for his offering	5:38
of them for they were all w.;	2:19		
something to be w. with me,	2:48	**WROUGHT**	
		came down and w. upon the man;	1Ne 13:12
WRONGED		that it w. upon other Gentiles;	13:13
they were w. in the wilderness	Mos 10:12	and has w. so many miracles	17:51
also w. while crossing the sea;	10:12	that it had w. upon them.	17:52
they were w. while in the land of	10:13	be w. upon my the Spirit of God,	19:12
were they had w. themselves	3Ne 3:11	should the mighty miracles be w.	2Ne 10: 4
		w. upon by the hand of the Lord,	28: 6
WRONGFULLY		w. upon by the power of God	En 1:26
see that ye do not judge w.;	Mro 7:18	has w. a mighty change in us,	Mos 5: 2
and counsel w. to your hurt,	DC 64:20	a mighty change w. in his heart.	Al 5:12
		change was also w. in their hearts,	5:13
WRONGS		that he had w. upon the old king	20:24
been waged to avenge their w.,	Al 54:24	miracles we have w. in this land,	26:12
freedom, and to avenge our w.	61: 6	miracles w. by the power of God,	37:40
the w. which they had done.	He 5:17	and the wonders which were w.	He 16:23
many w. which ye have done	3Ne 3: 4	signs and greater miracles w.	3Ne 1: 4
do this, I will avenge their w.	3:10	that it was w. by men and by	2: 2
avenging the w. of those that	3:11	w. upon by the Spirit of God,	7:22
law, and redress us of our w.	DC 105:25	the works which shall be w.	21: 5
the w. of thy people and	121: 2	works shall be w. by them,	28:31
how long shall they suffer these w.	121: 3	a great and marvelous work w.	28:32
thy sword avenge us of our w.	121: 5	change w. upon their bodies,	28:37
redress of all w. and grievances,	134:11	change w. upon their bodies,	28:38

WROUGHT 1071 YEAR

change w. upon them,	3Ne	28:39
no miracle w. by Jesus Christ;		29: 7
w. by the disciples of Jesus,	4Ne	1: 5
there were mighty miracles w.		1:13
many miracles which were w.		1:29
the power of the evil one was w.	Mrm	1:19
were w. by the power of God		7: 9
things that God hath w. marvelous		9:16
his word have miracles been w.?		9:17
were many mighty miracles w.		9:18
if there were miracles w. then,		9:19
did cause to be w. in prison.	Eth	10: 7
that w. the change upon the		12:14
w. so great a miracle among		12:15
even all they who w. miracles		12:16
miracles w. them by faith,		12:16
hath any w. miracles until after		12:18
were w. upon and cleansed by	Mro	6: 4
by faith that miracles are w.;		7:37
w. out this perfect atonement	DC	76:69

WRUNG

of the cup of trembling w. out —	2Ne	8:17

YE: *see in the APPENDIX.*

YEA: *see in the APPENDIX.*

YEAR

the commencement of the first y.	1Ne	1: 4
and in that same y. there came		1: 4
In the y. that hing Uzziah died,	2Ne	16: 1
In the y. that king Ahaz died		24:28
in the thirtieth y. of his age,	Mos	6: 4
in the thirteenth y. of my reign		9:14
of the Lamanites from y. to year.		19:15
of the Lamanites from year to y.		19:15
the thirty and third y. of his reign,		29:46
first y. of the reign of the judges	Al	1: 1
the first y. of the reign of Alma		1: 2
second y. of the reign of Alma,		1:23
fifth y. of the reign of the judges.		1:33
of the fifth y. of their reign		2: 1
fifth y. of the reign of the judges.		3:25
And in one y. were thousands and		3:26
fifth y. of the reign of the judges.		3:27
sixth y. of the reign of the judges		4: 1
in the seventh y. of the reign of		4: 5
thus endeth the seventh y. of		4: 5
in the eighth y. of the reign of		4: 6
in this eighth y. of the reign of		4: 9
thus ended the eighth y. of the		4:10
commencement of the ninth y.,		4:11
the ninth y. of the reign of		4:20
ended the ninth y. of the reign of		8: 2
the tenth y. of the reign of the		8: 3
in the tenth y. of the reign of		10: 6
in the tenth y. of the reign of		14:23
ended the tenth y. of the reign of		15:19
in the eleventh y. of the reign of		16: 1
in the eleventh y., there was a cry		16: 1
ended the eleventh y. of the judges,		16: 9
the fourteenth y. of the reign of		16:12
the fourteenth y. of the reign of		16:21
in the first y. of the judges;		17: 6
the king died in that selfsame y.		24: 4
thus endeth the fifteenth y.		28: 7
and the fifteenth y. of the reign		28: 9
from the first y. to the fifteenth		28:10
(and it was in the sixteenth y.		30: 2
in all the sixteenth y. of the reign		30: 4
in the seventeenth y. of the reign		30: 5
latter end of the seventeenth y.,		30: 6
thus ended the seventeenth y.		35:12
in the eighteenth y. of the reign		35:13
in the eighteenth y. of the reign		43: 3
of the eighteenth y.		43: 4
thus ended the eighteenth y. of		44:24
in the nineteenth y. of the reign		45: 2
of the nineteenth y. of the reign		45:20
the end of the nineteenth y. of		46:37
at some seasons of the y. were		46:40
latter end of the nineteenth y.		48: 2
latter end of the nineteenth y.,		48:21
month of the nineteenth y.,	Al	49: 1
thus ended the nineteenth y.		49:29
of the twentieth y. of the		50: 1
they also began in that same y.		50:15
thus ended the twentieth y.		50:16
of the twenty and first y. of		50:17
in the twenty and first y. of the		50:23
the twenty and second y. of the		50:24
and also the twenty and third y.		50:24
of the twenty and fourth y. of		50:25
ended the twenty and fourth y.		50:35
in the same y. that the people		50:37
of the twenty and fourth y.;		50:40
of the twenty and fifth y. of		51: 1
the twenty and fifth y. in peace;		51: 1
in the twenty and fifth y. of		51:12
endeth the twenty and fifth y.		51:37
in the twenty and sixth y. of		52: 1
of the twenty and sixth y. of		52:14
in the twenty and seventh y. of		52:15
of the twenty and seventh y.		52:18
of the twenty and eighth y.,		52:19
with the Lamanites in that y.,		53: 7
ended the twenty and eighth y.		53:23
in the twenty and ninth y. of		54: 1
ended the twenty and ninth y. of		55:35
of the thirtieth y. of the reign		56: 1
But in the twenty and sixth y.,		56: 7
in the twenty and sixth y.,		56: 9
ended the twenty and sixth y.		56:20
of the twenty and seventh y.		56:20
in the second month of this y.,		56:27
ended the twenty and eighth y.		57: 5
of the twenty and ninth y.,		57: 6
this is the twenty and ninth y.,		58:38
in the thirtieth y. of the		59: 1
thus ended the thirtieth y. of		62:11
of the thirty and first y. of the		62:12
ended the thirty and first y. of		62:39
in the thirty and fifth y. of		62:52
of the thirty and sixth y. of		63: 1
ended the thirty and sixth y. of		63: 3
in the thirty and seventh y. of		63: 4
ended the thirty and seventh y.		63: 6
And in the thirty and eighth y.,		63: 7
in this y. there were many people		63: 9
ended the thirty and eighth y.		63: 9
in the thirty and ninth y. of		63:10
in this y., they had been		63:13
also in this y. that there were		63:14
also in this same y. they came		63:15
ended the thirty and ninth y. of		63:16
y. of the reign of the judges over	He	1: 1
y. of the reign of the judges;		1:13
y. of the reign of the judges,		1:14
y. of the reign of the judges.		1:34
y. of the reign of the judges,		2: 1
y. of the reign of the judges over		2:12
y. of the reign of the judges,		3: 1
ending of the forty and third y.		3: 1
in the forty and fourth y.;		3: 2
in the forty and fifth y.		3: 2
y. of the reign of the judges		3:18
even in the forty and seventh y.,		3:19
also in the forty and eighth y.		3:19
y. of the reign of the judges over		3:22
y. of the reign of the judges,		3:23
in this same y. there was		3:24
in this y. there was continual		3:31
of the forty and ninth y.;		3:32
y. of the reign of the judges.		3:32
y. of the reign of the judges		3:33
the fifty and second y. ended in		3:36
y. of the reign of the judges,		3:37
in the fifty and fourth y. there		4: 1
y. of the reign of the judges		4: 4
all that y. preparing for war.		4: 4
in the fifty and seventh y. they		4: 5
y. of the reign of the judges,		4: 5
y. of the reign of the judges,		4: 9
y. of the reign of the judges.		4:10
y. of the reign of the judges,		4:17
y. of the reign of the judges,		4:18
in this same y., behold, Nephi		5: 1

YEAR / YEARNED

y. of the reign of the judges	He	6: 1	away the twenty and eighth y.,	3Ne	6: 9
ended the sixty and third y.		6: 6	in the twenty and ninth y.		6:10
sixty and fourth y. did pass away		6:13	in the thirtieth y. the church		6:14
in the sixty and fifth y. they		6:14	of the thirtieth y —		6:17
away the sixty and fifth y.		6:14	of this, the thirtieth y.,		6:17
y. of the reign of the judges,		6:15	did govern the people that y.		6:19
in the same y., that his son,		6:15	in this same y., yea, the		7: 1
thus ended the sixty and sixth y.		6:15	same year, yea, the thirtieth y.,		7: 1
of the sixty and seventh y.		6:16	And thus ended the thirtieth y.;		7:13
y. of the reign of the judges over		6:32	in the thirty and first y. that		7:14
in the sixty and eighth y. also,		6:33	wmong them in that same y.,		7:16
y. of the reign of the judges over		6:41	the thirty and first y. did pass		7:21
y. of the reign of the judges over		7: 1	the thirty and second y. also.		7:23
y. of the reign of the judges over		10:19	of the thirty and third y.;		7:23
y. of the reign of the judges		11: 1	in the commencement of this y.		7:26
And this war did last all that y.;		11: 2	more part of the y. did pass		7:26
in the seventy and third y. it		11: 2	the thirty and third y. had		8: 2
in this y. Nephi did cry unto		11: 3	in the thirty and fourth y.,		8: 5
in the seventy and fourth y.		11: 5	of the thirty and fourth y.,		10:18
in the seventy and fifth y.		11: 6	and fourth y. passed away,	4Ne	1: 1
in the seventy and sixth y.		11:17	in the thirty and sixth y.,		1: 2
seventy and sixth y. did end		11:21	the thirty and seventh y. passed		1: 4
seventy and seventh y. began		11:21	thirty and eighth y. pass away,		1: 6
ended the seventy and seventh y.		11:21	seventy and first y. passed away,		1:14
peace in the seventy and eighth y.,		11:22	also the seventy and second y.,		1:14
in the seventy and ninth y.		11:23	till the seventy and ninth y.		1:14
to their strife in that same y.		11:23	this two hundred and first y.		1:24
y. of the reign of the judges over		11:24	from y. to year, even until		1:34
in that same y. they were driven		11:29	from year to y., even until		1:34
y. of the reign of the judges over		11:29	in this y., yea, in the two		1:35
of the eighty and first y. they did		11:30	hundred and thirty and first y.,		1:35
to pass that thus ended this y.		11:32	in this y. there arose a people		1:36
y. of the reign of the judges.		11:35	three hundred and twentieth y.		1:48
in the eighty and second y. they		11:36	in this y. there began to be	Mrm	1: 8
And in the eighty and third y.		11:36	they did have in this same y.		1:11
And in the eighty and fourth y.		11:36	in that same y. there began		2: 1
in the eighty and fifth y. they		11:37	in my sixteenth y. I did go		2: 2
thus ended the eighty and fifth y.		11:38	and twenty and seventh y.		2: 3
pass in the eighty and sixth y.,		13: 1	hundred and forty and fifth y.		2:16
in this y. there was one Samuel,		13: 2	in this y. the people of Nephi		2:20
y. of the reign of the judges over		16: 9	hundred and forty and sixth y.		2:22
y. of the reign of the judges,		16:10	hundred and forty and ninth y.		2:28
y. of the reign of the judges.		16:11	three hundred and fiftieth y.		2:28
y. of the reign of the judges.		16:12	this tenth y. had passed away,		3: 4
y. of the reign of the judges,		16:13	hundred and sixty and first y.		3: 7
thus in this y. the scriptures		16:14	in that y. we did beat them,		3: 7
y. of the reign of the judges over		16:24	hundred and sixty and second y.		3: 8
the first y. of the reign of	3Ne	1:hd	hundred and sixty and third y.		4: 1
ninety and first y. had passed		1: 1	hundred and sixty and fourth y.		4: 7
in the y. that Lachoneus was		1: 1	hundred and sixty and sixth y.		4:10
of the ninety and second y.,		1: 4	and sixty and seventh y.,		4:15
this same y. were they brought		1:25	and seventy and fifth y.		4:16
the ninety and second y. did		1:26	in this y. they did come down		4:17
the ninety and third y. did also		1:27	three hundred and eightieth y.		5: 6
in the ninety and fourth y. they		1:28	in that same y. in which he was	Eth	13:15
the ninety and fifth y. also,		2: 1	in the first y. that Ether dwelt		13:18
away the ninety and sixth y.;		2: 4	in the second y. the word of the		13:20
also the ninety and seventh y.;		2: 4	in the third y. he did bring		13:23
also the ninety and eighth y.;		2: 4	in the fourth y., did beat Shared,		13:24
also the ninety and ninth y.;		2: 4	that in the first y. of Lib,		14:11
passed away the tenth y. also;		2:10	the y. of your Lord eighteen	DC	21: 3
eleventh y. also passed away in		2:10	in the y. of our Lord one		76:11
in the thirteenth y. there began		2:11	these are one y. with God,		88:44
before this thirteenth y. had		2:13	the acceptable y. of the Lord,		93:51
thus ended the thirteenth y.		2:16	in the fortieth y. of his age;		107:45
of the fourteenth y.,		2:17	And in one y. from this day		115:11
thus ended the fourteenth y.		2:18	the y. of my redeemed is come;		133:52
in the fifteenth y. they did		2:18	or during the past y.,		OD
thus ended the fifteenth y.,		2:19	being now the eighth y. since	JS	2: 2
in the sixteenth y. from the		3: 1	I was born in the y. of our		2: 3
to pass in the seventeenth y.,		3:22	when I was in my tenth y.,		2: 3
in the latter end of the y.,		3:22	in the 27th y. of his age),		2: 4
latter end of the eighteenth y.		4: 1	the second y. after our removal		2: 5
the eighteenth y. did pass away.		4: 4	at this time in my fifteenth y.		2: 7
in the nineteenth y. Giddianhi		4: 5	and the year eighteen hundred		2:28
in this y. they should go up		4: 6	in one y. from that time,		2:53
nineteenth y. did pass away,		4:15	I went at the end of each y.,		2:54
come again in the twentieth y.		4:15	In the y. 1824 my father's		2:56
in the twenty and first y. they		4:16	as usual at the end of another y.		2:59
the twenty and second y. passed		5: 7			
the twenty and third y. also,		5: 7	YEARNED		
in the twenty and sixth y.,		6: 1	bowels y.: and all eternity shook.	Mses	7:41

YEARS

YEARS

six hundred y. from the time that	1 Ne	10: 4
yea, for the space of many y.,		15:13
sojourn for the space of many y.,		17: 4
even eight y. in the wilderness.		17: 4
wilderness for these many y.;		17:20
these many y. we have suffered		17:21
my parents being stricken in y.,		18:17
in six hundred y. from the time		19: 8
loosed for the space of many y.;		22:26
And thirty y. had passed away	2 Ne	5:28
say that forty y. had passed away,		5:34
within three score and five y.		17: 8
cometh in six hundred y.		25:19
fifty and five y. had passed	Jac	1: 1
many hundred y. before his		4: 4
after some y. had passed away,		7: 1
come many hundred y. hence.		7: 7
And many y. pass away before	En	1: 8
hundred and seventy and nine y.		1:25
two hundred y. had passed away,	Jar	1: 5
hundred and thirty and eight y.		1:13
and six y. had passed away,	Om	1: 3
and two y. had passed away,		1: 3
and twenty y. had passed away,		1: 5
it is many hundred y. after	WM	1: 2
four hundred and seventy-six y.	Mos	6: 4
And king Benjamin lived three y.		6: 5
people for the space of three y.		6: 7
peace for the space of three y.,		7: 1
land for the space of twelve y.		9:11
land of our fathers for many y.,		10: 3
for the space of twenty and two y.		10: 3
for the space of twenty and two y.		10: 5
we have suffered these many y.		10:18
that after the space of two y.		12: 1
for the space of two y.,		19:29
being eighty and two y. old;		29:45
being sixty and three y. old;		29:46
five hundred and nine y. from		29:46
being stricken with many y.,	Al	1: 9
beginning of days or end of y.,		13: 7
beginning of days or end of y.,		13: 9
for a certain number of y.,		16: 1
of Ammonihah for many y.		16:11
thus for three y. did the people		16:12
for the space of fourteen y.		17: 4
unto the Lord for many y.,		19:16
was only twenty and five y. old		43:17
four hundred y. from the time		45:10
for the space of four y. did		46:38
even for the space of four y.		48:20
cease for the space of many y.		48:22
for the space of many y.		62:39
y. of the reign of the judges.	He	4: 8
in the space of not many y.		4:26
in the space of not many y.,		6:32
in the space of not many y.		7: 6
a great many thousand y. before		8:18
had some y. before gone over		11:24
in the space of not many y.,		11:26
four hundred y. pass not away		13: 5
And four hundred y. shall not		13: 9
for five y. more cometh,		14: 2
it was six hundred y. from the	3 Ne	1: 1
of these things for many y.,		1:18
and began to wax strong in y.,		1:29
an hundred y. had passed away		2: 5
six hundred and nine y. had		2: 6
nine y. had passed away from		2: 7
nine y. had passed away.		2: 8
subsist for the space of seven y.,		4: 4
twenty and five y. passed away.		5: 7
the space of twenty and five y.;		5: 8
twenty and sixth and seventh y.		6: 4
enjoyed peace but a few y.		6:16
six y. had not passed away		7: 8
days of old, and as in former y.		24: 4
are seventy and two y. old		28: 3
until forty and nine y. had	4 Ne	1: 6
until fifty and nine y. had		1: 6
hundred y. had passed away,		1:14
an hundred and ten y. had		1:18
he kept it eighty and four y.,		1:20
hundred and ninety and four y.		1:21
two hundred y. had passed		1:22
two hundred and ten y. had		1:27
two hundred and thirty y. had		1:34
hundred and forty and four y.		1:40
two hundred and fifty y. pass		1:41
also two hundred and sixty y.		1:41
three hundred y. had passed		1:45
three hundred and five y.		1:47
three hundred and twenty y.		1:48
(I being about ten y. of age,	Mrm	1: 2
about twenty and four y. old		1: 3
that I, being eleven y. old,		1: 6
for the space of about four y.,		1:12
I, being fifteen y. of age and		1:15
and twenty and six y. had		2: 2
three hundred and thirty y.		2: 9
hundred and forty and four y.		2:15
ten y. more had passed away.		3: 1
three hundred and sixty years		3: 4
hundred and seventy and nine y.		5: 5
hundred and eighty and four y.		6: 5
four hundred y. have passed		8: 6
seashore for the space of four y.	Eth	2:13
to pass at the end of four y.		2:14
for these many y. we have		3: 3
was thirty and two y. old		7: 4
for the space of many y.,		9:12
land for the space of two y.,		9:15
the space of sixty and two y.		9:16
he lived four y., and he saw		9:22
an hundred and two y. old.		9:24
and forty and two y. old.		9:24
he reigned forty and nine y.,		9:25
the space of forty and two y.		10: 8
after the space of many y.,		10: 9
last for the space of many y.;		10: 9
and he did reign eight y.,		10:13
the space of forty and two y.		10:15
that Lib did live many y.,		10:29
reigned twenty and four y.,		10:30
he served many y. in captivity,		10:30
the kingdom forty and two y.;		10:32
fought for the space of many y.,		10:32
of the kingdom for many y.		11:15
again for the space of two y.,		13:31
after the space of two y.,		14: 3
for the space of two y.,		14: 7
were for the space of four y.		15:14
only a few y. have passed away,	Mro	9:12
four hundred and twenty y.		10: 1
at the y. of accountability.	DC	18:42
eight hundred and thirty y.		20: 1
unto the y. of accountability		20:71
men on earth a thousand y.,		29:11
when the thousand y. are ended,		29:22
not many y. hence ye shall		45:63
act upon this land as for y.,		51:17
not yet come, for many y.,		58:44
Kirtland, for the space of five y.,		64:21
the hands, when eight y. old,		68:25
their sins when eight y. old,		68:27
the same, and his y. never fail.		76: 4
during the seven thousand y.		77: 6
things of the first thousand y.,		77: 7
also of the second thousand y.,		77: 7
in the sixth thousand y.,		77:10
of the seventh thousand y.		77:12
of the seventh thousand y.—		77:12
beginning of days or end of y.		84:17
in their months, in their y.—		88:44
the thousand y. are ended,		88:101
of God in the first thousand y.		88:108
in the second thousand y.—		88:109
for the space of a thousand y.		88:110
And after a few y., if thou		99: 7
and not many y. hence they		105:15
at the age of sixty-nine y.,		107:42
three y. previous to his		107:42
one hundred and thirty-four y.		107:44

YEARS　　　　　1074　　　　　YET

He was eighty-seven y. old	DC 107:45	y. nevertheless, I knew that it	1Ne 11:11
four hundred and ninety-six y.	107:46	y. they swear not in truth nor	20: 1
Jared was two hundred y. old	107:47	y. shall I be glorious in the	21: 5
Enoch was twenty-five y. old	107:48	y. will I not forget thee,	21:15
three hundred and sixty-five y.,	107:49	I durst not speak further as y.	22:29
four hundred and thirty y. old	107:49	kept as y. from the knowledge of	2Ne 1: 8
Methuselah was one hundred y.	107:50	Y. I will not loose his tongue,	3:17
Lamech was thirty-two y. old	107:51	But y. there shall be a tenth,	16:13
Noah was ten y. old when	107:52	y. a remnant of them shall	20:22
Three y. previous to the death	107:53	For y. a very little while,	20:25
And not many y. hence,	121:15	As y. shall he remain at Nob	20:32
appointed days, months, and y.,	121:31	and will y. choose Israel,	24: 1
of their days, months, and y.,	121:31	Y. thou shalt be brought down to	24:15
although but six y. of age,	122: 6	y. we keep the law because of	25:25
thy y. shall not be numbered less;	122: 9	y. the words of the righteous	26:15
until thou art eighty-five y. old,	130:15	that it is y. a very little while	27:28
In the short space of twenty y.,	135: 3	for my work is not y. finished;	29: 9
Hyrum Smith was forty-four y. old	135: 6	For behold, as y., ye have been	Jac 2: 4
beginning of days or end of y.;	Mses 1: 3	beholded that they are y. good.	5:34
seasons, and for days, and for y.;	2:14	are y. alive; wherefore,	5:54
lived one hundred and thirty y.,	6:10	I may y. have glory in the fruit	5:54
eight hundred y., and he begat	6:11	Y. thou wilt deny it, because	7:14
were nine hundred and thirty y.,	6:12	wherefore, they became as y.,	7:25
lived one hundred and five y.,	6:13	has not as y. swept them off	Jar 1: 3
eight hundred and seven y.,	6:14	y. I have been chosen by this	Mos 2:11
nine hundred and twelve y.,	6:16	Y., my brethren, I have not done	2:15
And Enos lived ninety y., and	6:17	and y. has been in the service of	2:19
eight hundred and fifteen y.,	6:18	y. ye would be unprofitable	2:21
were nine hundred and five y.,	6:18	y. ye were created of the dust	2:25
And Cainan lived seventy y.,	6:19	Y. the Lord God saw that his	3:14
eight hundred and forty y.,	6:19	y. they hardened their hearts,	3:15
were nine hundred and ten y.,	6:19	and y. ye put up no petition,	4:22
And Mahalaleel lived sixty-five y.,	6:20	have not and y. have sufficient,	4:24
eight jundred and thirty y.,	6:20	God this day that I am y. alive,	7:12
eight hundred and ninety-five y.,	6:20	land of Zarahemla are y. alive.	7:14
one hundred and sixty-two y.,	6:21	y. I trust there remaineth an	7:18
he begat Enoch, eight hundred y.,	6:21	y. they were diligent,	8: 8
nine hundred and sixty-two y.,	6:24	y. a man may have great power	8:16
And Enoch lived sixty-five y.,	6:25	And y., I being over-zealous to	9: 3
beginning of days or end of y.,	6:67	Yet. they were a strong people, as	10:11
for the space of a thousand y.	7:64	y. they shall leave a record behind	12: 8
for the space of a thousand y.:	7:65	and y. desire to know of me what	12:25
three hundred and sixty-five y.	7:68	keep the law of Moses as y.;	13:27
four hundred and thirty y.	8: 1	y. we did esteem him stricken,	14: 4
one hundred and eighty-seven y.,	8: 5	y. he opened not his mouth;	14: 7
seven hundred and seventy-two y.,	8: 6	Y. it pleased the Lord to bruise	14:10
nine hundred and sixty-nine y.,	8: 7	and y. they would not depart	16:12
one hundred and eighty-two y.,	8: 8	and y. they would not repent.	16:12
five hundred and ninety-five y.,	8:10	y. they were not half so numerous	20:11
hundred and seventy-seven y.,	8:11	y. he was not dead, having been	20:12
was four hundred and fifty y.	8:12	y. the Lord did not see fit to	21:15
forty-two y. afterward he begat	8:12	Y. Ammon and his brethren were	21:29
when he was five hundred y.	8:12	y. he exercised authority over	24: 9
be an hundred and twenty y.;	8:17	y. they were neat and comely.	Al 1:27
is equal to a thousand y.	Fac 2: 1	y. I would not know;	10: 6
was sixty and two y. old when	Abr 2:14	y. it would not be by flood,	10:22
one thousand y. according to the	3: 4	y. he saith that the Son of God	11:35
of days, and of months, and of y.	3: 5	they y. remained a hard-hearted	15:15
seasons, and for days, and for y.;	4:14	y. ye shall be patient in	17:11
In about four y. after my	JS 2: 3	y. they sought to obtain these	17:14
fourteen and fifteen y. of age,	2:22	Ammon being wise, y. harmless,	18:22
little over fourteen y. of age,	2:23	keep the law of Moses as y.,	25:15
and being of very tender y.,	2:28	y. they rejoice and exult in the	28:12
until four y. from that time;	2:53	And y. do ye go about, leading	30:45
		And y. will ye deny against all	30:45
YES		y. their hearts are swallowed up	31:27
I answer, y. but there	DC 130: 5	y. they cry unto thee and say—	31:28
be said to the slaughter? Y.,	135: 4	not y. fully made known unto me;	37:11
		my son, the resurrection is not y.	40: 3
YESTERDAY		y. we do not desire to slay you.	44: 1
the same y. to-day, and forever;	1Ne 10:18	fought, y. they did not fear death;	56:47
y., today, and forever.	2Ne 2: 4	y. it did harm them not, neither	He 5:44
y., today, and forever;	27:23	that the law was not y. fulfilled,	3Ne 1:25
y., today, and forever;	29: 9	were no wars as y. among them;	7: 5
the same y., today, and forever;	Al 31:17	y. they were united in the	7:11
God is the same y., today,	Mrm 9: 9	nor y. for your body, what ye	13:25
same y., today, and forever,	Mro 10:19	y. your heavenly Father feedeth	13:26
that he is the same God y.,	DC 20:12	y. I say unto you, that even	13:29
same today as y., and forever.	35: 1	have not as y. heard my voice;	16: 2
Lord, was angry with you y.,	61:20	before it was y. dark, that the	19: 2
		Y. I will heal him, for I will show	21:10
YET		Y. ye have robbed me.	24: 8
these words, they were y. wroth,	1Ne 4: 4	Y. ye say: What have we	24:13

YET — YIELD — YOKETH

YET

y. they did deny the more parts	4Ne 1:27
And while they were y. weary,	Mrm 4: 2
y. the Nephites repented not of	4:10
were present, and y. ye are not.	8:35
y. suffer the hungry, and the	8:39
Has the end come y.?	9:15
y. be an unchangeable Being?	9:19
while he was y. in captivity.	Eth 7: 7
and y. he avenge them not.	8:22
but I have not as y. perished;	Mro 1: 1
may know that I am y. alive;	9: 1
the hour is not y., but is nigh	DC 1:35
y. if he boasts in his own	3: 4
Y. you should have been faithful;	3: 8
you must wait y. a little while,	5:17
for ye are not y. ordained—	5:17
a greater work y. among men	7: 5
art not as y. called to preach	23: 4
y. men will harden their hearts	45:33
and their leaves are y. tender,	45:37
professing and y. be not of God.	46:27
place is not y. to be revealed;	48: 5
the hour is not y., but is nigh	58: 4
the time has not y. come,	58:44
not as y. gone up unto the land	62: 2
your mission is not y. full.	62: 2
fulness ye have not y. received.	63:21
And behold, this is not y.,	63:35
the store, y. for a little season.	63:42
up unto the land of Zion as y.;	66: 6
nor y. entered into the heart	76:10
while we were y. in the Spirit,	76:28
while we were y. in the Spirit,	76:80
while we were y. in the Spirit	76:113
while we were y. in the Spirit,	76:115
ye have not as y. understood	78:17
even y. the kingdom is yours,	82:24
y. they may remain upon	83: 3
while he was y. in his childhood,	84:28
y. a little while and ye shall	84:119
springing up and is y. tender—	86: 4
while the blade is y. tender	86: 6
for their time is not y. come;	88:85
hath power, as y., over you,	93:42
Y. I will own them, and they	101: 3
y. shall they partake of all	101:35
were y. laying the foundation	101:47
enemy while he was y. afar off;	101:54
y. because this widow troubleth	101:84
as serpents and y. without sin;	111:11
Thou art not y. as Job;	121:10
For there are many y. on the earth	123:12
y. they are ordained ot be	124:137
y. they shall come forth in the	132:26
y. my arm was not shortened	133:67
IT SHALL Y. BE SAID OF ME—	135: 4
for ye are not y. pure;	136:37
ye can not y. bear my glory;	136:37
not y. a man to till the ground;	Mses 3: 5
was not y. flesh upon the earth,	3: 5
y. thou art there, and thy bosom	7:30
y. his days shall be an hundred	8:17
father, y. lived in the land of Ur,	Abr 2: 1
than the other, y. these two spirits,	3:18
as y. the Gods had not appointed	5:13
to pass; but the end is not y.	JS 1:23
y. my words shall not pass,	1:35
When its branches are y. tender,	1:38
the end of the earth is not y.,	1:55
y. when the converts began to	2: 6
never as y. made the attempt	2:14
y. men of high standing would	2:22
y. he knew, and would know to	2:24
seen a vision, y. it was true;	2:25
the day had not y. come when	2:40
that this was not y. fulfilled,	2:41
obtained was not y. fulfilled—	2:42
them forth had not y. arrived,	2:53
y. employed in the service of	2:57
which were not y. translated,	2:64
He will y. reveal many great and	AoF 9

YIELD

And why should I y. to sin,	2Ne 4:27
of vineyard shall y. one bath;	15:10
of a homer shall y. an ephah.	15:10
because they y. unto the devil	26:10
about to y. up this mortal frame	Mos 2:26
Why will ye y. yourselves unto	Al 10:25
not y. up their weapons of war.	52:25
the Lamanites did y. themselves	He 1:32
did y. up unto the Nephites	5:52
and did not y. forth grain in	11: 6
that he shall y. up the ghost	14:21
shall y. up many of their dead;	14:25
we will y. ourselves unto them,	16:21
would y. up unto this my people,	3Ne 3: 6
y. yourselves up unto us, and	3: 7
to y. themselves up according	4:16
did y. themselves up prisoners	4:27
y. themselves unto the power of	7: 5
that ye will y. to not temptation,	Mrm 9:28
y. to the persuasions of man	DC 5:21
and y. to no temptation.	9:13
it shall not henceforth y. unto	Mses 5:37

YIELDED

having y. up into his hands	Mos 7:21
he y. up the land that we might	9:10
when you have y. yourselves to	Al 5:20
y. to the standard of liberty,	51:20
y. up the city unto our hands;	57:12
Moroni y. up the command of	62:43
and he y. up the judgment-seat,	He 5: 4
because he y. unto temptation.	DC 29:40

YIELDETH

the God of Jacob, y. himself,	1Ne 19:10
and y. not to the temptation,	Mos 15: 5
that the righteous y. to no such	Al 11:23
that which y. fruit, whether	DC 89:16
that y. much precious fruit.	97: 9
whose seed in itself y. its own	Abr 4:11

YIELDING

the awfulness of y. to	2Ne 9:39
their y. their hearts unto God.	He 3:35
bring forth grass, the herb y. seed,	Mses 2:11
the fruit tree y. fruit, after his	2:11
the tree y. fruit, whose seed	2:11
every herb y. seed after his kind,	2:12
y. fruit, whose seed should be in	2:12
be the fruit of a tree y. seed;	2:29
forth grass, the herb y. seed;	Abr 4:11
fruit tree y. fruit, after his kind,	4:11
y. seed after his kind;	4:12

YIELDS

unless he y. to the enticings of	Mos 3:19
tree from its own seed, y. fruit,	4:12
the fruit of the tree y. seed	4:29

YOKE

yoketh them with a y. of iron,	1Ne 13: 5
hast broken the y. of his burden,	2Ne 19: 4
and his y. from off thy neck,	20:27
and the y. shall be destroyed	20:27
shall his y. depart from off them,	24:25
themselves to the y. of bondage,	Mos 21:13
why do ye y. yourselves with	Al 30:13
who do y. them according to	30:28
any one to the y. of bondage.	44: 2
brethren to the y. of bondage,	49: 7
them to the y. of bondage.	49:26
ourselves to the y. of bondage	61:12
deliverance from under this y.;	DC 109:32
break off, O Lord, this y. of	109:47
y. of bondage may begin to be	109:63
an iron y., it is a strong band;	123: 8

YOKETH

y. them with a yoke of iron,	1Ne 13: 5

YONDER

YONDER
we go y. to behold the seer, — Mses 6:38

YORK
bishop go unto the city of New Y.,	DC 84:114
speedily to Cainhannoch [New Y.]	104:81
county, State of New Y.,	JS 2: 3
Ontario county, New Y.,	2:51
county, State of New Y.,	2:56
Chenango county, New Y.	2:58
in the State of New Y.,	2:61
with them to the city of New Y.	2:63
"I went to the city of New Y.,	2:64

YOU: *see in the APPENDIX.*

YOUNG: *see also YOUNG, Brigham; and YOUNG, Joseph.*
I, Nephi, being exceeding y.,	1Ne 2:16
with people, both old and y.,	8:27
and Joseph also, being y.,	18:19
They shall roar like y. lions;	2Ne 15:29
a man shall nourish a y. cow	17:21
have no joy in their y. men,	19:17
the y. lion and fatling together;	21: 6
y. ones shall lie down together;	21: 7
also dash the y. men to pieces,	23:18
y. lion, and the fatling, together;	30:12
y. ones shall lie down together;	30:13
forth y. and tender branches,	Jac 5: 4
a little, y. and tender branches;	5: 6
of these y. and tender branches,	5: 8
these y. and tender branches,	5: 8
both old and y., the first and the	5:63
all ye old men, and also ye y. men,	Mos 2:40
all my y. men that were able	10: 9
And he was a y. man, and he	17: 2
both old and y., both bond and	Al 1:30
both old and y., both bond and	5:49
both old and y., both bond and	11:44
even as a goat fleeth with her y.	14:29
two thousand of those y. men,	53:18
And they were all y. men,	53:20
two thousand of these y. men	56: 5
of these two thousand y. men	56: 9
they were all of them very y.)	56:46
I numbered those y. men who	56:55
they are y., and their minds are	57:27
their y. men and their daughters	3Ne 2:16
as a y. lion among the flocks	20:16
as a y. lion among the flocks	21:12
And notwithstanding I being y.,	Mrm 2: 1
wife, in his old age, a y. maid,	Eth 9:24
sparing none, neither old nor y.;	Mro 9:19
to repent, both old and y.,	DC 43:20
are my warriors, my y. men,	101:55
y. men and the middle aged—	103:22
even my warriors, my y. men,	105:16
for a person y. as I was,	JS 2: 8
how the y. man found out that	2:64

YOUNG, Brigham: *see also BRIGHAM.*
unto you my servant Y.	DC 124:127
well-beloved brother, Y.,	126: 1

YOUNG, Joseph
unto you Y., Josiah — DC 124:138

YOUNGER
unto us, their y. brothers,	1Ne 3:28
Why do ye smite your y. brother	3:29
that I, your y. brother, should	7: 8
yea, even thy y. brother;	17:55
was called Jacob and the y. Joseph.	18: 7
We will not that our y. brother	18:10
Our y. brother thinks to rule	2Ne 5: 3
Jacob and Joseph, my y. brethren,	5: 6

YOUNGEST
from the eldest down to the y.,	Mos 2: 5
unto the y., the name of Lehi.	He 3:21

YOUR: *see in the APPENDIX.*

YOURS
skins will be whiter than y.,	Jac 3: 8
the kingdom is y. until I come.	DC 35:27
Behold, the kingdom is y.,	38: 9
not, for the kingdom is y.,	38:15
the fulness of the earth is y.	59:16
blessings of the kingdom are y.	61:37
Behold, the kingdom is y.	62: 9
The kingdom is y. and the	78:18
the blessings thereof are y.,	78:18
the riches of eternity are y.	78:18
even yet the kingdom is y.,	82:24
gold and silver shall be y.	111: 4
This promise is y. also,	132:31

YOURSELF
cross y. in all these things;	Al 39: 9
and cross y. in these things.	39: 9
Suffer not y. to be led away by	39:11
Do not endeavor to excuse y.	42:30
the plates of Nephi unto y.,	Mrm 1: 4
up treasures for y. in heaven—	DC 6:27
that you have contradicted y.	10:31
you are left to inquire for y.	30: 3
to deliver y. from bondage,	104:84

YOURSELVES
and liken them unto y.,	1Ne 19:24
All ye, assemble y.,	20:14
that sit in darkness: Show y.	21: 9
ye y. know that it ever has	2Ne 6: 3
your iniquities have ye sold y.,	7: 1
compass y. about with sparks,	7:11
that ye are free to act for y.—	10:23
reconcile y. to the will of God,	10:24
Associate y., O ye people,	18: 9
gird y., and ye shall be brokin	18: 9
gird y., and ye shall be broken	18: 9
stay y. and wonder,	27: 4
ye y. know that I have	Jac 2: 3
of your brethren like unto y.,	2:17
shake y. that ye may awake from	3:11
loose y. from the pains of hell	3:11
ye y. know that he counseleth	4:10
have assembled y. together,	Mos 2: 9
But I am like as y., subject to	2:11
ye y. are witnesses this day.	2:14
now I ask, can ye say aught of y.?	2:25
king, am no better than ye y. are;	2:26
ye should assemble y. together,	2:27
ye should assemble y. together	2:28
ye should assemble y. together	2:29
withdraw y. from the Spirit of the	2:36
and humble y. before God;	4:10
humble y. even in the depths of	4:11
ye y. will succor those that	4:16
that if ye do not watch y.,	4:30
can you imagine to y. that ye	Al 5:16
ye imagine to y. that ye can lie	5:17
can ye imagine y. brought	5:18
yielded y. to become subjects	5:20
keeping y. blameless before God?	5:27
within y., that ye have been	5:27
ye had humbled y. before God,	7: 3
Why will ye yield y. unto him	10:25
ye should humble y. before God,	13:13
humble y. even as the people in	13:14
would humble y. before the Lord,	13:28
and asked: what say ye for y.?	14:15
why do ye not deliver y.?	14:20
deliver y. from these bands, and	14:24
yoke y. with such foolish things?	30:13
ye may glut y. with the labors	30:27
been compelled to humble y.;	32:25
ye will begin to say within y.—	32:28
humble y., and continue in prayer	34:19
humble y. even to the dust,	34:38
shall not suffer y. to be slain	43:46
subject y. to be governed by	54:18
ye y. know that ye have been	60: 2
stirred u. more diligently for	60:10
ye y. are seeking for authority.	60:18

YOURSELVES 1077 ZARAHEMLA

except ye do bestir y. in the	Al	60:29	Keep y. from evil to take	DC	136:21
up for y. a treasure in heaven,	He	5: 8	why counsel ye y., and deny	Mses	6:43
Behold, why have ye gathered y.		7:13			
ye have gathered y. together,		7:15	**YOUTH**		
and ye have united y. unto it,		7:25	hast beheld in thy y. his glory;	2Ne	2: 4
should ye dispute among y.,		8:12	behold, thou art in thy y.,	Al	36: 3
up for y. treasures in heaven,		8:25	and learn wisdom in thy y.;		37:35
ye are heaping up for y. wrath		8:25	yea, learn in thy y. to keep the		37:35
suffer y. to be led by foolish		13:29	commenced in your y. to look to		38: 2
ye shall suffer y. to come under		14:19	for behold, thou art in thy y.,		39:10
ye are permitted to act for y.;		14:30	shalt forget the shame of thy y.,	3Ne	22: 4
And behold, ye do know of y.,		15: 7	the reproach of thy y.,		22: 4
ye know of y. are firm and		15: 8	grieved in spirit, and a wife of y.,		22: 6
ye can see of y. that they never		15:15	displayed the weakness of y.,	JS	2:28
yield y. up unto us, and unite	3Ne	3: 7	any one who recollects my y.,		2:28
should deny y. of these things,		12:30			
up for y. treasures upon earth,		13:19	**YOUWARD**		
up for y. treasures in heaven,		13:20	given unto him, and also to y.,	DC	112:15
Ye have sold y. for naught,		20:38			
repent ye, and humble y.	Mrm	5:24	**ZACHARIAS**		
ye built up churches unto y.		8:33	And also John the son of Z.,	DC	27: 7
sell y. for that which will		8:38	which Z. he (Elias) visited		27: 7
Why do ye adorn y. with		8:39			
imagined up unto y. a god who		9:10	**ZARAHEMLA**		
imagined up unto y. a god who		9:10	was made king over the land of Z.;	Om	1:12
imagined up unto y. a god who		9:15	which is called the land of Z.		1:13
strip y. of all uncleanness;		9:28	who were called the people of Z.		1:14
and deny y. of all ungodliness;	Mro	10:32	rejoicing among the people of Z.;		1:14
shall deny y. of all ungodliness		10:32	also Z. did rejoice exceedingly,		1:14
Save y. from this untoward	DC	36: 6	the people of Z. came out from		1:15
Save y. be ye clean that		38:42	Z. gave a genealogy of his		1:18
ye shall assemble y. together		41: 2	the people of Z., and of Mosiah,		1:19
have assembled y. together		42: 1	discovered by the people of Z.;		1:21
have assembled y. together		42: 3	them out of the land of Z.		1:24
bind y. to act in all holiness		43: 9	again to the land of Z.		1:28
sanctify y. before me;		43:11	contention in all the land of Z.,	Mos	1: 1
Sanctify y. and ye shall be		43:16	all this people, or the people of Z.,		1:10
Prepare y. for the great day		43:20	who were in the land of Z.		1:18
obtain power to organize y.		44: 4	peace in the land of Z.,		2: 4
assemble ye y. together ye		45:64	the time they left the land of Z.;		7: 1
shall answer this question y.;		50:16	and a descendant of Z.;		7: 3
ye shall assemble y. together		52:42	who came up out of the land of Z.		7: 9
have assembled y. tofether,		57: 1	and am a descendant of Z.,		7:13
assemble y. together;		58:46	come up out of the land of Z.		7:13
have humbled y. before me,		61:37	who were in the land of Z.		7:14
Assemble y. upon the land of		62: 4	who were in the land of Z.		8: 1
call y. the people of the Lord,		63: 1	that they left the land of Z.,		8: 5
have assembled y. together,		67: 1	they might find the land of Z.,		8: 7
strip y. from jealousies and		67:10	and found not the land of Z.		8: 8
and humble y. before me,		67:10	people who are in the land of Z.		8:14
have assembled y. together,		72: 1	*the time they left the land of Z.*		9:hd
have assembled y. together;		78: 1	were spared, to the land of Z.,		9: 2
you must prepare y. by		78: 7	had come from the land of Z.,		21:24
organize y. by a bond or		78:11	to search for the land of Z.,		21:25
ye bind y. by this covenant,		82:15	supposed it to be the land of Z.,		21:26
make unto y. friends with		82:22	course towards the land of Z.,		22:11
to beware concerning y.,		84:43	they arrived in the land of Z.,		22:13
go away from him alone by y.,		84:92	they arrived in the land of Z.;		24:25
you y. are not able to fill.		84:107	as there were of the people of Z.,		25: 2
have assembled y. together		88: 1	of Nephi and of the people of Z.		25: 3
sanctify y. that your minds		88:68	and also all the people of Z.,		25: 4
you assemble y. together,		88:74	the time they left the land of Z.		25: 5
together, and organize y.,		88:74	the time they left the land of Z.		25: 6
yourselves, and prepare y.,		88:74	people of Z. were numbered with		25:13
yourselves, and sanctify y.;		88:74	throughout all the land of Z.;		25:19
entangle not y. in sin, but		88:86	churches in the land of Z.		25:23
Organize y.; prepare every		88:119	throughout all the land of Z.,		27:35
Appoint among y. a teacher,		88:122	throughout all the land of Z.,		29:44
clothe y. with the bond of		88:125	which ran by the land of Z.,	Al	2:15
in assembling y. together		89: 5	of Minon, above the land of Z.,		2:24
Gather y. together unto the		103:22	city, which was the city of Z.		2:26
that ye shall organize y. and		104:11	which was fought in the land of Z.,		3:20
commanded you to organize y.,		104:58	nor wars in the land of Z.;		4: 1
shall prepare for y. a place for		104:60	first in the land of Z. and from		5: 1
shall humble y. before me,		104:79	was established in the city of Z.,		5: 2
have assembled y. together		105: 1	was established in the land of Z.,		6: 1
Organize y.; prepare every		109: 8	of the church in the city of Z.		6: 4
Concern not y. about your debts,		111: 5	which was in the city of Z.,		6: 7
Concern not y. about Zion,		111: 6	that our brethren were in at Z.		7: 3
Exalt not y.; rebel not against		112:15	had for the brethren at Z.,		7: 5
trouble not y. concerning		112:27	before done in the land of Z.,		8: 1
that you may prove y. unto me		124:55	returned to his own house at Z.		8: 1
Judge ye for y.		127: 2	and came over to the land of Z.,		15:18
O my people; sanctify y.;		133: 4	much peace in the land of Z.,		16: 1
Prepare y. for the great day		133:10	towards the land of Z.		17: 1
			departed out of the land of Z.,		17: 7

ZARAHEMLA

was divided from the land of Z.	Al	22:27
on the north by the land of Z.,		22:27
on the west of the land of Z.,		22:28
discovered by the people of Z.,		22:30
land of Nephi and the land of Z		22:32
the borders of the land of Z.,		25: 2
we started from the land of Z.		26: 1
come up out of the land of Z.,		26: 9
our brethren in the land of Z.,		26:23
let us go down ot the land of Z.		27: 5
of Nephi from the land of Z.,		27:14
will go forth into the land of Z.,		27:15
back to the land of Z.;		27:20
round about the land of Z.		28: 1
came a man into the land of Z.,		30: 6
sent him to the land of Z.,		30:29
which was east of the land of Z.,		31: 3
he did leave in the church in Z.;		31: 6
returned to the land of Z.		35:14
departed out of the land Z.,		45:18
taken back into the land of Z.		46:33
came over into the land of Z.		47:29
forth toward the land of Z.		48: 6
were south of the land of Z.		50: 7
who were in the land of Z.		50: 9
between the land of Z. and the		50:11
to come down to the land of Z.		51:11
departed out of the land of Z.,		52:12
down into the land of Z.		53:10
brought down into the land of Z.;		53:12
down against the city of Z.;		56:25
unto us from the land of Z.		56:28
them to the land of Z.,		56:57
our army, from the land of Z.		57: 6
our prisoners to the land of Z.		57:11
in hand, down to the land of Z.;		57:15
them down to the land of Z.;		57:16
to go down to the land of Z.		57:16
go down to the land of Z. with.		57:28
to go down to the land of Z.		57:30
strength from the land of Z.		58: 3
strength from the land of Z.		58: 4
wilderness towards the land of Z.		58:23
marching towards the land of Z.,		58:24
sent this epistle to the land of Z.,		59: 4
to Pahoran, in the city of Z.,		60: 1
even in the land of Z.,		60:30
of the land, or the city, of Z.;		61: 8
to maintain the city of Z.,		61: 8
possession of the city of Z.,		61:18
freemen out of the land of Z.,		62: 6
their armies into the land of Z.,		62: 7
restored peace to the land of Z.,		62:11
body of men in the land of Z.		62:14
he returned to the city of Z.;		62:42
departed out of the land of Z.		63: 4
and he was a descendant of Z.;	He	1:15
march down to the land of Z.		1:17
sufficient guards in the land of Z.		1:18
to attack that great city Z.		1:18
in possession of the city of Z.,		1:22
not tarry in the land of Z.,		1:23
city which was the city of Z.,		1:27
back towards the land of Z.		1:29
took possession of the city of Z.		1:33
departed out of the land of Z.,		3: 3
rejoicing in the land of Z.		3:31
possession of the land of Z.;		4: 5
from thence into the land of Z.,		5:16
who were in the land of Z.		5:19
down into the land of Z.		6: 4
returned to the land of Z. from		7: 1
which was in the city of Z.;		7:10
came into the land of Z., and		13: 2
wo unto this great city of Z.;		13:12
departed out of the land of Z.,	3Ne	1: 2
not return to the land of Z.,		2: 9
appointed was the land of Z.		3:23
came up unto the land of Z.,		6:25
the city of Z. did take fire.		8: 8
been burned in that great city Z.		8:24
great city Z. have I burned		9: 3
even that great city Z. did they	4Ne	1: 8
even to the land of Z.	Mrm	1: 6
among them in the borders of Z.,		1:10
was called by the Nephites Z.	Eth	9:31
let the name of Z. be named	DC	125: 3

ZEAL

The z. of the Lord of Hosts	2Ne	19: 7
also distinguished for their z.	Al	27:27
and the great z. manifested by	JS	2: 6

ZEALOUS

he being over-z. to inherit	Mos	7:21
I being over-z. to inherit the		9: 3
and they were z. for keeping	Al	21:23
were a z. and beloved people,		27:30
equally z. in endeavoring to	JS	2: 9

ZEALOUSLY

z. striving to repair all the	Mos	27:35

ZEBDEE: see COLTRIN, Zebdee.

ZEBULIN

he lightly afflicted the land of Z.,	2Ne	19: 1

ZECHARIAH

and Z. the son of Jeberechiah.	2Ne	18: 2

ZEDEKIAH

the reign of Z., king of Judah,	1Ne	1: 4
the reign of Z., king of Judah;		5:12
commencement of the reign of Z.;		5:13
Z., king of Judah, was carried	Om	1:15
which was after the son of Z.,	He	6:10
that the sons of Z. were not slain,		8:21
that the seed of Z. are with us,		8:21
first year of the reign of Z.,	3Ne	1:hd
Jonas, and Z., and Isaiah—		19: 4

ZEEZROM

among them whose name was Z.	Al	10:31
this Z. began to question Amulek,		11:21
Zeezrom was a man who was expert in		11:21
And Z. said unto him:		11:22
And Z. said unto him:		11:26
Now Z. said: Is there		11:28
Now Z. said unto him again:		11:30
And Z. said again:		11:32
And Z. said again:		11:34
Now Z. said unto the people:		11:35
Now Z. saith unto him:		11:38
and also Z. began to tremble.		11:46
words of Amulek had silenced Z.,		12: 1
words that Alma spake unto Z.		12: 2
Now Z.. seeing that thou hast		12: 3
Z. began to tremble more		12: 7
Z. began to inquire of them		12: 8
plainness of his words unto Z.;		14: 2
Z. was astonished at the words		14: 6
And also Z. lay sick at Sidom,		15: 3
went in unto the house unto Z.;		15: 5
Z. leaped upon his feet, and		15:11
Alma baptized Z. unto the Lord;		15:12
and also Amulek and Z., who		31: 6
Omner, and also Amulek and Z.		31:32
city of Manti, and the city of Z.,		56:14
which Amulek spake unto Z.,	He	5:10
by Alma, and Amulek, and Z.;		5:41

ZEMNARIHAH

leader, whose name was Z.,	3Ne	4:17
it was Z. that did cause that		4:17
the desire of the people of Z. to		4:22
Z. did give command unto his		4:23
their leader, Z., was taken		4:28

ZENEPHI

army of Z. has carried away,	Mro	9:16

ZENIFF

Noah, who was the son of Z.,	Mos	7: 9
brethren, whom Z. brought up		7:13
that Z., who was made king over		7:21

ZENIFF

entered into a treaty with king Z.,	Mos	7:21
from the time that Z. went up		8: 2
THE RECORD OF Z.—		9:hd
I, Z., having been taught in all		9: 1
And now I, Z., after having told		10:19
Z. conferred the kingdom upon		11: 1
caused to be read, the records of Z.		25: 5
the records of the people of Z.,		25: 5

ZENOCK

according to the words of Z.,	1Ne	19:10
but Z. also spake of these things.—	Al	33:15
and also upon the words of Z.;		34: 7
behold, also Z., and also Ezias,	He	8:20
Z. spake concerning these things,	3Ne	10:16

ZENOS

according to the words of Z.,	1Ne	19:10
come, saith the prophet Z.		19:12
to the words of the prophet Z.,		19:16
the words of the prophet Z.,	Jac	5: 1
which this prophet Z. spake,		6: 1
read what Z., the prophet of old,	Al	33: 3
ye must believe what Z. said;		33:13
Z. alone spake of these things,		33:15
has called upon the words of Z.,		34: 7
the prophet Z. did testify boldly;	He	8:19
and also by the prophet Z.,		15:11
the prophet Z. did testify of	3Ne	10:16

ZERA: *see* PULSIPHER, Zera.

ZERAHEMNAH

a man by the name of Z. was	Al	43: 5
Z. appointed chief captains over		43: 6
the army of Z. was not		43:20
by Z., who was their chief captain,		43:44
when Z. saw the men of Lehi on		43:53
And Moroni said unto Z.:		44: 1
Behold, Z., that we do not desire		44: 1
Z., I command you, in the name		44: 5
when Z. had heard these sayings		44: 8
when Z. had made an end of		44:10
which he had received, unto Z.,		44:10
Z. retained his sword, and he		44:12
he also smote Z. that he took off		44:12
Z. withdrew from before them		44:12
who smote off the scalp of Z.,		44:13
that Z. was exceeding wroth,		44:16
Z., when he saw that they were all		44:19

ZERAM

were called Z., and Amnor, and	Al	2:22

ZERIN

said unto the mountain Z.,	Eth	12:30

ZIBA: *see* PETERSON, Ziba.

ZIFF

and a fifth part of their z.,	Mos	11: 3
of brass, and of z., and of copper;		11: 8

ZILLAH

and the name of the other, Z.	Mses	5:44
And Z., she also bare Tubal Cain,		5:46
said unto his wives, Adah and Z.,		5:47

ZINC

and with brass, and with z.,	DC	124:27

ZION

shall seek to bring forth my Z.	1Ne	13:37
But, behold, Z. hath said:		21:14
all that fight against Z. shall be		22:14
they who fight against Z. shall be		22:19
repent and fight not against Z.,	2Ne	6:12
they that fight against z. and the		6:13
For the Lord shall comfort Z.,		8: 3
and come with singing unto Z.;		8:11
and say unto Z.:		8:16
put on thy strength, O Z.;		8:24
O captive daughter of Z.		8:25
And he that fighteth against Z.	2Ne	10:13
he that fighteth against Z.,		10:16
out of Z. shall go forth the law,		12: 3
the daughters of Z. are haughty,		13:16
the head of the daughters of Z.,		13:17
they that are left in Z.		14: 3
the filth of the daughters of Z.,		14: 4
every dwelling-place of mount Z.,		14: 5
the glory of Z. shall be a defence.		14: 5
which dwelleth in Mount Z.		18:18
his whole work upon Mount Z.		20:12
O my people that dwellest in Z.,		20:24
the mount of the daughter of Z.,		20:32
and shout, thou inhabitant of Z.;		22: 6
That the Lord hath founded Z.,		24:32
they seek not the welfare of Z.		26:29
suffer he in Z. to perish.		26:30
But the laborer in Z. shall labor		26:31
laborer in Zion shall labor for Z.;		26:31
the nations that fight against Z.,		27: 3
be that fight against Mount Z.		27: 3
they will say: All is well in Z.;		28:21
yea, Z. prospereth, all is well —		28:21
be unto him that is at ease in Z.!		28:24
saith unto Z., Thy God reigneth;	Mos	12:21
when the Lord shall bring again Z.;		12:22
said unto Z.: Thy God reigneth!		15:14
when the Lord shall bring again Z.		15:29
the Lord shall bring again Z.	3Ne	16:18
and put on thy strength, O Z.;		20:36
neck, O captive daughter of Z.		20:37
salvation; that saith unto Z.:		20:40
again among them my Z.;		21: 1
garments, O daughter of Z.;	Mro	10:31
and establish the cause of Z.;	DC	6: 6
and establish the cause of Z.		11: 6
and establish the cause of Z.		12: 6
forth and establish my Z.		14: 6
to move the cause of Z. in		21: 7
his weeping for Z. I have seen,		21: 8
devote all thy service in Z.;		24: 7
receive an inheritance in Z.		25: 2
the city Z. shall be built,		28: 9
your whole labor shall be in Z.,		30:11
Z. shall rejoice upon the hills		35:24
taken the Z. of Enoch into mine		38: 4
church, and to bring forth Z.,		39:13
and it shall be called Z.		45:67
flee unto Z. for safety.		45:68
go up to battle against Z.,		45:70
inhabitants of Z. are terrible;		45:70
and shall come to Z., singing		45:71
Z. shall flourish upon the hills		49:25
and the place for the city of Z.		57: 2
be planted in the land of Z.,		57:14
the Z. of God shall stand;		58: 7
might go forth from Z.,		58:13
moneys to purchase lands in Z.		58:49
a description of the land of Z.,		58:50
stand upon the land of Z.,		59: 3
come up unto the land of Z.,		60:14
able to go up to the land of Z.		61:16
and go up unto the land of Z.;		61:24
gone up unto the land of Z.,		62: 2
yourselves upon the land of Z.;		62: 4
together unto the land of Z.,		63:24
Behold, the land of Z.—		63:25
the land of Z. shall not be		63:29
assembled upon the land of Z.;		63:36
journey up unto the land of Z.,		63:39
be sent up unto the land of Z.,		63:40
go up unto the land of Z.,		63:41
sent up unto the land of Z.		63:43
treasures unto the land of Z.		63:48
to his agency in the land of Z.;		64:18
open heart up to the land of Z.;		64:22
shall go up unto the land of Z.		64:26
inheritance in the land of Z.		64:30
eat the good of the land of Z.,		64:34
cut off out of the land of Z.,		64:35
the inhabitants of Z. shall judge		64:38
judge all things pertaining to Z.		64:38
unto you that Z. shall flourish,		64:41

up unto the land of Z. as yet;	DC 66: 6	build up the waste places of Z.	DC 103:11
and push many people to Z.	66:11	restoration to the land of Z.,	103:13
as parents have children in Z.,	68:25	the redemption of Z. must needs	103:15
law unto the inhabitants of Z.,	68:26	shall the redemption of Z. be.	103:18
the inhabitants of Z. shall	68:29	together unto the land of Z.,	103:22
the inhabitants of Z. also shall	68:30	consecrated to be the land of Z.,	103:24
with the inhabitants of Z.,	68:31	and redemption of Z.	103:29
sayings unto the land of Z.	68:32	to go up unto the land of Z.,	103:30
shall carry unto the land of Z.,	69: 1	not go up unto the land of Z.	103:34
stewardships to the land of Z.;	69: 5	up with you unto the land of Z.	103:34
the land of Z. shall be a seat	69: 6	establish the children of Z. upon	103:35
shall grow up on the land of Z.,	69: 8	I give unto you concerning Z.,	104:47
hearken, O ye inhabitants of Z.,	70: 1	order to your brethren of Z.,	104:47
unto the inhabitants of Z.,	70: 8	United Order of the Stake of Z.,	104:48
over unto the bishop in Z.	72: 6	United Order of the City of Z.	104:48
over to the bishop of Z.,	72:13	cannot be built up unless it	105: 5
the debt unto the bishop in Z.;	72:14	we will not go up unto Z.,	105: 8
every man that cometh up to Z.	72:15	for the redemption of Z.—	105: 9
things before the bishop in Z.	72:15	for the redemption of Z.	105:13
vineyard, unto the bishop in Z.,	72:17	to fight the battles of Z.;	105:14
accepted of the bishop of Z.	72:18	kingdom of Z. is in very deed	105:32
Holy Spirit to go up unto Z.,	72:24	I have given concerning Z.	105:34
privileged to go up unto Z.—	72:24	all things pertaining to Z.	105:37
shall go up unto the land of Z.,	72:26	high councils, at the stakes of Z.,	107:36
who are come unto Mount Z.,	76:66	The high council in Z. form	107:37
this place and in the land of Z.—	78: 3	the Twelve at the stakes of Z.	107:37
the saints which are in Z.;	78: 9	church of Christ in the land of Z.,	107:59
Lord God, the Holy One of Z.,	78:15	judge among the inhabitants of Z.,	107:74
both in the land of Z. and in	82:12	or in a stake of Z.,	107:74
Most High, and for a stake to Z.	82:13	until the borders of Z. are enlarged	107:74
For Z. must increase in beauty,	82:14	bishops or judges in Z.	107:74
Z. must arise and put on her	82:14	that they may come forth to Z.,	109:39
to stand upon Mount Z.,	84: 2	which thou didst appoint a Z	109:51
Mount Z. in the Lord's house,	84:32	appoint unto Z. other stakes	109:59
upon the children of Z.,	84:56	for the benefit of Z.,	111: 2
out upon the children of Z.	84:58	for the benefit of Z.,	111: 2
your brethren in Z. for their	84:76	Concern not yourselves about Z.,	111: 6
Lord hath brought again Z.;	84:99	Let thy habitation be known in Z.,	112: 6
brought down Z. from above.	84:100	Put on thy strength, O Z.—	113: 7
brought up Z. from beneath.	84:100	to bring again Z.,	113: 8
send it up unto the bishop in Z.,	84:104	she, Z., has a right to by lineage;	113: 8
thereof, and for establishing Z.	84:104	Z. loosing herself from the bands	113: 9
all things that transpire in Z.,	85: 1	high council of my church in Z.,	115: 3
and also the saints in Z.—	89: 1	together upon the land of Z.,	115: 6
ministry for the salvation of Z.,	90: 8	the land of my people, even Z.	117: 9
and go up unto the land of Z.;	90:28	speedily, unto the land of Z.;	117:14
go up unto the land of Z.	90:30	for a season in the land of Z.,	118: 2
say unto your brethren in Z.,	90:32	of the bishop of my church in Z.,	119: 1
also to preside over Z. in mine	90:32	laying of the foundation of Z.	119: 2
brethren in Z. begin to repent,	90:34	who gather unto the land of Z.	119: 5
the Lord, will contend with Z.,	90:36	sanctify the land of Z.	119: 6
all this for the salvation of Z.	93:53	it shall not be a land of Z.	119: 6
of the city of the stake of Z.,	94: 1	unto all the stakes of Z.	119: 7
I have set for the strength of Z.	96: 1	planted to be a corner-stone of Z.,	124: 2
brethren in the land of Z.,	97: 1	heed to the light and glory of Z.,	124: 6
concerning the school in Z.,	97: 3	exaltation or lifting up of Z.	124: 9
there should be a school in Z.,	97: 3	the house of the daughters of Z.	124:11
the school in the land of Z.	97: 4	continue in preaching for Z.,	124:18
school, and of the church in Z.	97: 5	I have appointed for Z.	124:23
built unto me in the land of Z.,	97:10	For it is ordained that in Z.,	124:36
unto me for the salvation of Z.—	97:12	revelations and foundation of Z.,	124:39
if Z. do these things she shall	97:18	may contemplate the glory of Z.,	124:60
Surely Z. is the city of our	97:19	called to lay the foundation of Z.;	124:118
surely Z. cannot fall, neither	97:19	for the corner-stone of Z.—	124:131
saith the Lord, let Z. rejoice,	97:21	unto Z.: Behold, thy God reigneth!	128:19
Zion rejoice, for this is Z.—	97:21	upon the land of Z.,	133: 4
therefore, let Z. rejoice, while	97:21	Go ye forth unto the land of Z.,	133: 9
Z. shall escape if she observe	97:25	that Z. may go forth unto the	133: 9
kindly unto the bishop of Z.	99: 6	among the Gentiles flee unto Z.	133:12
unto you a word concerning Z.	100:13	shall stand upon Mount Z.,	133:18
Z. shall be redeemed, although	100:13	and upon the land of Z.	133:20
be comforted concerning Z.;	101:16	he shall utter his voice out of Z.,	133:21
Z. shall not be moved out of	101:17	land of Z. shall be turned back	133:24
up the waste places of Z.—	101:18	crowned with glory, even in Z.,	133:32
curtains or the strength of Z.	101:21	he shall stand upon Mount Z.,	133:56
concerning the children of Z.	101:41	the Lord shall locate a stake of Z.	136:10
concerning the redemption of Z.	101:43	Z. shall be redeemed in	136:18
appointed to be the land of Z.,	101:70	even the glory of Z.;	136:31
this way they may establish Z.	101:74	the Lord called his people Z.,	Mses 7:18
an abundance, to redeem Z.,	101:75	the City of Holiness, even Z.	7:19
shall I liken the children of Z.?	101:81	Z. shall dwell in safety forever.	7:20
will I liken the children of Z.	101:85	Z. have I blessed, but the residue	7:20
scattered on the land of Z.;	103: 1	Z., in process of time, was taken	7:21

ZION

after that Z. was taken up into	Mses	7:23
by the powers of heaven into Z.		7:27
taken Z. to thine own bosom,		7:31
and behold, Z. is with me.		7:47
I am Messiah, the King of Zion,		7:53
be called Z., a New Jerusalem.		7:62
mine abode, and it shall be Z.,		7:64
all the days of Z., in the days		7:68
and he dwelt in the midst of Z.;		7:69
Z. was not, for God received it		7:69
forth the saying, Z. IS FLED;		7:69
that Z. will be built upon this	AoF	10

ZOMBRE

my servant Z. [John Johnson]	DC	96: 6
my servant Z. [John Johnson]		104:24
my servant Z. [John Johnson]		104:34

ZORAM

Z. did take courage at the words	1Ne	4:35
Z. was the name of the servant;		4:35
Z. had made an oath unto us,		4:37
Z. took the eldest daughter		16: 7
And now, Z., I speak unto you:	2Ne	1:30
and also Z. and his family,		5: 6
(and his name was Z., and he	Al	16: 5
now Z. and his two sons, knowing		16: 5
Z. and his sons crossed over the		16: 7
by a man whose name was Z.—		30:59
that Z., who was their leader,		31: 1
and a descendant of Z.,		54:23

ZORAMITE

behold, Jacob, who was a Z.,	Al	52:20
their leader, being also a Z., and		52:33

ZORAMITES

Josephites, Z., Lamanites,	Jac	1:13
and called themselves Z., being	Al	30:59
the Z. were perverting the ways		31: 1
of the Z. from the Nephites.		31: 2
the Z. had gathered themselves		31: 3
that the Z. would enter into a		31: 4
went with him among the Z.,		31: 7
the Z. were dissenters from		31: 8
the Z. had built synagogues,		31:12
preached the word unto the Z.,		35: 2
the more popular part of the Z.		35: 3
the people of the Z. were angry		35: 8
and the chief ruler of the Z.,		35: 8
did receive all the poor of the Z.		35: 9
this did stir up the Z. to anger		35:10
thus the Z. and the Lamanites		35:11
and the armies of the Z.;		35:13
many of the Z. to repentance;		35:14
among the people of the Z.		38: 3
Do not pray as the Z. do,		38:13
among the people of the Z.		39: 2
iniquity ye brought upon the Z.;		39:11
that the Z. became Lamanites;		43: 4
which is the land of the Z.;		43: 5
they were all Amalekites and Z.		43: 6
who were Amalekites and Z.,		43:13
were the Z. and the Amalekites;		43:20
they were inspired by the Z.		43:44
appoint chief captains of the Z.,		48: 5
led away by some who were Z.,	3Ne	1:29
Jacobites, and Josephites, and Z.	4Ne	1:36
Jacobites, and Josephites, and Z.		1:37
and the Josephites and the Z.;	Mrm	1: 8
and the Josephites, and the Z.,	DC	3:17

1976 SUPPLEMENT

TO AN

EXHAUSTIVE CONCORDANCE

OF THE

BOOK OF MORMON

DOCTRINE AND COVENANTS

AND

PEARL OF GREAT PRICE

Compiled by
R. GARY SHAPIRO

Hawkes Publishing Inc.
3775 South 500 West
(P.O. Box 15711)
Salt Lake City, Utah 84115
Phone (801) 262-5555

ABBREVIATIONS

JS-V . . . . Joseph Smith–Vision
JFS-V . . . . Joseph F. Smith–Vision

Copyright 1977
Hawkes Publishing Inc.
All Rights Reserved

Typesetting by R. Gary Shapiro

Lithographed in the United States of America
PUBLISHERS PRESS
Salt Lake City, Utah

1976 SUPPLEMENT
TO
AN EXHAUSTIVE CONCORDANCE

A: *see in the APPENDIX.*

ABEL
A., the first martyr, was there   JFS-V 40

ABOUT
the Savior spent a. three years in   JFS-V 25

ABRAHAM
I saw Father Adam and A.;   JS-V   5
A., the father of the faithful;   JFS-V 41

ABROAD
the primitive saints scattered a.   JFS-V   5

ABSENCE
long a. of their spirits from   JFS-V 50

ACCEPTABLE
declare the a. day of the Lord   JFS-V 31

ACCORDING
judge all men a. to their works,   JS-V   9
a. to the desire of their hearts.   9
judged a. to men in the flesh,   JFS-V 10
live a. to God in the spirit."   10
judged a. to men in the flesh,   34
live a. to God in the spirit.   34
a reward a. to their works,   59

ACCOUNTABILITY
arrive at the years of a.   JS-V   10

ACKNOWLEDGED
bowed the knee and a. the Son   JFS-V 23

ADAM
I saw Father A. and Abraham;   JS-V   5
Father A., the Ancient of Days   JFS-V 38
express image of his father, A.   40

ADVENT
awaiting the a. of the Son of God   JFS-V 16

AFTER
preached a. the crucifixion of   JFS-V   5
come forth, a. his resurrection   51
a. they have paid the penalty of   59

AGAIN
united never a. to be divided,   JFS-V 17
come forth a. in the resurrection   43
never a. to be destroyed nor   44

AGES
who had lived through the a.   JFS-V 39

ALL: *see in the APPENDIX.*

ALSO: *see in the APPENDIX.*

ALVIN
my brother A.,   JS-V   5

AMEN
even so. A.   JFS-V 60

AMONG
a. the ungodly and the unrepentant JFS-V 20

a. the righteous there was peace;   JFS-V 22
in his ministry a. the Jews   25
ministry a. those who were dead   27
the necessary labor a. them   28
went not in person a. the wicked   29
a. the righteous, he organized   30
was made known a. the dead   35
A. the great and mighty ones   38
who dwelt a. the Nephites   49
a. the noble and great ones   55
a. those who are in darkness   57

AN: *see in the APPENDIX.*

ANCIENT
warnings of the a. prophets   JFS-V 21
Father Adam, the A. of Days   38

AND: *see in the APPENDIX.*

ANOINTED
Redeemer was a. to bind up the   JFS-V 42

APOSTLE
the writings of the a. Peter,   JFS-V   5

APPEARANCE
a. of being paved with gold.   JS-V   4

APPEARED
the Son of God a., declaring   JFS-V 18

APPOINTED
a. messengers, clothed with power   JFS-V 30

ARE: *see in the APPENDIX.*

ARK
while the a. was a preparing,   JFS-V   9

ARRIVE
a. at the years of accountability   JS-V   10

AS: *see in the APPENDIX.*

ASIA
and other parts of A., where the   JFS-V   5

ASSEMBLED
They were a. awaiting the advent   JFS-V 16
were a. in this vast congregation   38

ASSEMBLY
mingled in the vast a. and waited   JFS-V 49

AT: *see in the APPENDIX.*

ATONEMENT
That through his a., and by   JFS-V   4

ATONING
the great a. sacrifice that was made   JFS-V   2

AUTHORITY
truth, in great power and a.   JFS-V 26
clothed with power and a.,   30

AWAITING
a. the advent of the Son of God   JFS-V 16

BANDS 2 CHILDREN

BANDS
redemption from the b. of death. JFS-V 16

BAPTISM
vicarious b. for the remission of JFS-V 33

BAPTIZED
b. for the remission of sins. JS-V 6

BE: *see in the APPENDIX.*

BEAR
revealed to me, and I b. record, JFS-V 60

BEAUTIFUL
saw the b. streets of that kingdom JS-V 4

BEAUTY
the transcendent b. of the gate JS-V 2

BECAUSE
rejoicing together b. the day of JFS-V 15
b. of their rebellion and 37

BEEN: *see in the APPENDIX.*

BEFORE
b. the Lord had set his hand JS-V 6
die b. they arrive at the years of 10
more than I had ever been b., JFS-V 6
b. the ushering in of the great and 46
Even b. they were born, 56

BEGINNING
chosen in the b. to be rulers JFS-V 55

BEGOTTEN
his Only B. Son, Jesus Christ. JFS-V 14
the sacrifice of the Only B. Son 57

BEHELD
b. the celestial kingdom of God, JS-V 1
b. that all the children who die 10
b. that they were filled with joy JFS-V 15
I b. that the faithful elders 57

BEHOLD
b. his presence, nor look upon JFS-V 21
But b., from among the righteous, 30

BEING
appearance of b. paved with gold. JS-V 4
b. put to death in the flesh, JFS-V 7

BETWEEN
time intervening b. the crucifixion JFS-V 27

BIBLE
I opened the B. and read JFS-V 6

BIND
to b. up the broken-hearted JFS-V 42

BLAZING
Also the b. throne of God, JS-V 3

BLESSING
through the b. of our Lord and JFS-V 60

BLESSINGS
and be partakers of all b. which JFS-V 52

BODIES
spirits from their b. as a JFS-V 50

BODY
in the b. or out I cannot tell. JS-V 1
the spirit and the b. to be united JFS-V 17

BONDAGE
spirits from their bodies as a b. JFS-V 50
and under the b. of sin 57

BONE
its perfect frame, b. to his bone, JFS-V 17
its perfect frame, bone to his b., 17

BONES
in vision the great valley of dry b., JFS-V 43

BORN
Even before they were b., JFS-V 56

BOTH
of the dead, b. small and great. JFS-V 11
the dead, b. small and great, 35

BOUND
to the captives who were b., JFS-V 31
of the prison to them that were b., 42

BOWED
b. the knee and acknowledged JFS-V 23

BRIEF
limited to the b. time intervening JFS-V 27

BRIGHAM: *see YOUNG, Brigham.*

BRING
that he might b. us to God, JFS-V 7

BROTHER
my b. Alvin, JS-V 5
his b. Seth, one of the mighty JFS-V 40

BROKEN
to bind up the b.-hearted, JFS-V 42

BROKEN-HEARTED: *see BROKEN and HEARTED.*

BUILDING
Including the b. of the temples JFS-V 54

BUT: *see in the APPENDIX.*

BY: *see in the APPENDIX.*

CALL
and c. them unto repentance; JFS-V 25

CAME: *see in the APPENDIX.*

CANNOT
in the body or out I c. tell. JS-V 1

CAPPADOCIA
throughout Pontus, Galatia, C. JFS-V 5

CAPTIVES
declaring liberty to the c. who JFS-V 18
proclaim liberty to the c. who 31
proclaim liberty to the c., 42

CARRY
c. the light of the gospel to them JFS-V 30
c. the message of redemption 37

CAUSE
for this c. was the gospel preached JFS-V 10

CELESTIAL
I beheld the c. kingdom of God, JS-V 1
heirs of the c. kingdom of God; 7
saved in the c. kingdom of heaven. 10

CHAINS
deliverance from the c. of death, JFS-V 18
from death and the c. of hell. 23

CHAPTERS
read the third and fourth c. of JFS-V 6

CHILDREN
that all c. who die before JS-V 10

CHILDREN

was to plant in the hearts of the c.	JFS-V	47
the sealing of the c. to their		48

CHOICE
c. spirits who were reserved	JFS-V	53

CHOSEN
And the c. messengers went forth	JFS-V	31
c. in the beginning to be rulers		55

CHRIST
For C. also hath once suffered	JFS-V	7
Only Begotten Son, Jesus C.		14
Our Lord and Savior, Jesus C.,		60

CHURCH
to be rulers in the C. of God,	JFS-V	55

CIRCLING
like unto c. flames of fire;	JS-V	2

CLEAN
transgressions, and are washed c.,	JFS-V	59

CLOTHED
c. with power and authority,	JFS-V	30
were to be c. upon with flesh,		43

COME: *see in the APPENDIX.*

COMING
in the c. of the Redeemer into	JFS-V	3
testified of the c. of Elijah—		46
and utterly wasted at his c.		48
testified of the c. of the Son		49

COMMISSIONED
c. them to go forth and carry	JFS-V	30

COMPANY
innumerable c. of the spirits of	JFS-V	12

CONDITIONS
sins on c. of repentance.	JFS-V	19

CONGREGATION
in this vast c. of the righteous	JFS-V	38

CONTINUE
And c. thenceforth their labor as	JFS-V	52
c. their labors in the preaching		57

CONVERSED
vast multitude waited and c.,	JFS-V	18

COULD
unto whom he c. not go	JFS-V	37

COUNTENANCES
Their c. shone, and the radiance	JFS-V	24

CROSS
of the Son of God upon the c.	JFS-V	35

CROWNED
there to be c. with immortality	JFS-V	51

CRUCIFIXION
preached after the c. of the Lord.	JFS-V	5
time intervening between the c.		27

CURSE
whole earth be smitten with a c.	JFS-V	48

DANIEL
D., who foresaw and foretold	JFS-V	44

DARKNESS
Where these were, d. reigned,	JFS-V	22
gospel to them that were in d.,		30
among those who are in d.		57

DAUGHTERS
with many of her faithful d.	JFS-V	39

DISOBEDIENT

DAY
the d. of their deliverance was at	JFS-V	15
the acceptable d. of the Lord		31
great and dreadful d. of the Lord—		46
of the great latter-d. work,		53

DAYS
God waited in the d. of Noah,	JFS-V	9
God waited in the d. of Noah—		28
Father Adam, the Ancient of D.		38
the kingdom of God in the latter d.,		44

DEAD
preached also to them that are d.,	JFS-V	10
and I saw the hosts of the d..		11
among those who were d.		27
was the gospel preached to the d.		30
it was made known among the d.,		35
of redemption unto all the d.,		37
again in the resurrection of the d.,		43
for the redemption of the d.,		48
For the d. had looked upon		50
after his resurrection from the d.,		51
for the redemption of the d.,		54
world of the spirits of the d.		57
d. who repent will be redeemed,		58
vision of the redemption of the d.		60

DEATH
being put to d. in the flesh,	JFS-V	7
redemption from the bands of d.		16
deliverance from the chains of d.,		18
Redeemer and Deliverer from d.		23

DECLARE
to d. their redemption from	JFS-V	16
d. the acceptable day of the Lord		31

DECLARED
Isaiah, who d. by prophecy	JFS-V	42

DECLARING
d. liberty to the captives who had	JFS-V	18
d. that he should come before		46

DEFILED
d. themselves while in the flesh,	JFS-V	20

DEPART
when they d. from mortal life,	JFS-V	57

DEPARTED
seeing that he had d. this life	JS-V	6
All these had d. the mortal life,	JFS-V	14

DELIVERANCE
the day of their d. was at hand.	JFS-V	15
rejoicing in the hour of their d.		18
and waited for their d.,		49

DELIVERER
Redeemer and D. from death.	JFS-V	23

DESIRE
to the d. of their hearts.	JS-V	9

DESTROYED
never again to be d. nor given	JFS-V	44

DID: *see in the APPENDIX.*

DIE
shall d. henceforth without a	JS-V	8
all children who d. before they		10

DIED
who have d. without a knowledge	JS-V	7
preached to those who had e.	JFS-V	32

DISOBEDIENT
"Which sometime were d.,	JFS-V	9
who sometime were d.,		28
among the wicked and the d.		29

DISPENSATION

DISPENSATION
in the d. of the fulness of times, JFS-V 48
that the faithful elders of this d., 57

DIVIDED
be united never again to be d., JFS-V 17

DOCTRINE
the d. of the resurrection and JFS-V 19

DONE
great work to be d. in the temples JFS-V 48

DREADFUL
great and d. day of the Lord— JFS-V 46

DRY
the great valley of d. bones, JFS-V 43

DUE
in the d. time of the Lord JFS-V 56

DURING
d. his sojourn in the world of JFS-V 36

DUST
Their sleeping d. was to be JFS-V 17

DWELT
even the prophets who d. among JFS-V 49

EARTH
whole e. be smitten with a curse JFS-V 48

EIGHT
e. souls were saved by water." JFS-V 9

EIGHTEEN
year nineteen hundred and e., JFS-V 1

ELDERS
the faithful e. of this dispensation, JFS-V 57

ELIAS
E., who was with Moses on the JFS-V 45

ELIJAH
testified of the coming of E.— JFS-V 46
E. was to plant in the hearts of 47

ENDEAVORING
e. to teach them the everlasting JFS-V 25

ENGAGED
While I was thus e., my mind JFS-V 5

ENTER
heirs of that kingdom will e., JS-V 2
to e. into his Father's kingdom, JFS-V 51

EPISTLE
chapters of the first e. of Peter, JFS-V 6

ESTABLISHMENT
the e. of the kingdom of God JFS-V 44

ETERNAL
with immortality and e. life, JFS-V 51

EVE
And our glorious Mother E., JFS-V 39

EVEN: *see in the APPENDIX.*

EVER
impressed, more than I had e. been JFS-V 6

EVERLASTING
preached to them the e. gospel, JFS-V 19
to teach them the e. gospel 25

EXPRESS
in the e. image of his father, JFS-V 40

4

FORCES

EYES
the e. of my understanding were JFS-V 11
wondered, my e. were opened, 29

EZEKIEL
E., who was shown in vision the JFS-V 43

FACE
his presence, nor look upon his f. JFS-V 21

FAITH
These were taught f. in God, JFS-V 33

FAITHFUL
f. in the testimony of Jesus JFS-V 12
to the captives who had been f.; 18
the unrighteous as well as the f., 35
instructing and preparing the f. 36
with many of her f. daughters 39
Abraham, the father of the f.; 41
f. elders of this dispensation, 57

FALL
redemption of mankind from the f., JFS-V 19

FATHER
was seated the F. and the Son. JS-V 3
I saw F. Adam and Abraham; 5
and my f. and my mother; 5
love made manifest by the F. JFS-V 3
through the grace of God the F. 14
F. Adam, the Ancient of Days 38
the Ancient of Days and f. of all, 38
express image of his f., Adam. 40
Abraham, the f. of the faithful; 41
and my f., Hyrum Smith, 53

FATHER'S
to enter into his F. kingdom, JFS-V 51

FATHERS
the promises made to their f., JFS-V 47

FEW
Wherein f., that is, eight souls JFS-V 9
there were but f. who hearkened 26

FILLED
they were f. with joy and JFS-V 15

FIRM
f. in the hope of a glorious JFS-V 14

FIRE
was like unto circling flames of f.; JS-V 2

FIRST
chapters in the f. epistle of Peter, JFS-V 6
Abel, the f. martyr, was there, 40
received their f. lessons in the 56

FLAMES
was like unto circling f. of fire; JS-V 2

FLESH
being put to death in the f., JFS-V 7
judged according to men in the f., 10
the sinews and the f. upon them, 17
defiled themselves while in the f., 20
judged according to men in the f., 34
had testified of him in the f.; 36
were to be clothed upon with f., 43

FLOOD
Noah, who gave warning of the f.; JFS-V 41

FOLLOWING
with the f. passages: JFS-V 6

FOR: *see in the APPENDIX.*

FORCES
he organized his f. and appointed JFS-V 30

FORESAW

FORESAW
Daniel, who f. and foretold — JFS-V 44

FORESHADOWING
F. the great work to be done in — JFS-V 48

FORETOLD
Daniel, who foresaw and f. — JFS-V 44

FORTH
commissioned them to go f. and — JFS-V 30
the chosen messengers went f. to — 31
come f. again in the resurrection — 43
and gave them power to come f., — 51
who were reserved to come f. in — 53
were prepared to come f., in — 56

FOUNDATIONS
to take part in laying the f. — JFS-V 53

FOURTH
read the third and f. chapters of — JFS-V 6

FRAME
to be restored unto its perfect f., — JFS-V 17

FROM: *see in the APPENDIX.*

FULNESS
they might receive a f. of joy. — JFS-V 17
dispensation of the f. of times, — 48
to come forth in the f. of times — 53

GALATIA
abroad throughout Pontus, G. — JFS-V 5

GATE
g. through which the heirs of — JS-V 2

GATHER
hand to g. Israel the second time, — JS-V 6

GATHERED
And there were g. together — JFS-V 12

GAVE
Noah, who g. warning of the — JFS-V 41
and g. them power to come forth, — 51

GHOST
gift of the Holy G. by the laying on — JFS-V 33

GIFT
the g. of the Holy Ghost by the — JFS-V 33

GIVEN
destroyed nor g. to other people; — JFS-V 44

GIVER
Moses, the great law-g. of Israel; — JFS-V 41

GLADNESS
they were filled with joy and g., — JFS-V 15

GLORIOUS
in the hope of a g. resurrection, — JFS-V 14
And our g. Mother Eve, — 39

GLORY
kingdom of God, and the g. — JS-V 1

GO
But unto the wicked he did not g., — JFS-V 20
commissioned them to g. forth — 30
whom he could not g. personally, — 37

GOD
beheld the celestial kingdom of G., — JS-V 1
Also the blazing throne of G., — 3
heirs of the celestial kingdom of G.; — 7
that was made by the Son of G., — JFS-V 2
that he might bring us to G., — 7
the long-suffering of G. waited — 9

HEAR

the long-suffering of G. waited — JFS-V 9
live according to G. in the spirit." — 10
great sacrifice of the Son of G., — 13
the grace of G. the Father and — 14
the advent of the Son of G. into — 16
the Son of G. appeared, declaring — 18
acknowledged the Son of G. as — 23
said that the Son of G. preached — 28
the long-suffering of G. waited — 28
These were taught faith in G., — 33
live according to G. in the spirit. — 34
the sacrifice of the Son of G. — 35
worshiped the true and living G. — 39
kingdom of G. in the latter days, — 44
of the coming of the Son of G., — 49
to be rulers in the Church of G. — 55
of the Only Begotten Son of G., — 57
ordinances of the house of G.; — 58

GOLD
appearance of being paved with g. — JS-V 4

GOSPEL
without a knowledge of this g., — JS-V 7
to the principles of the g., — JFS-V 4
where the g. had been — 5
for this cause was the g. preached — 10
to them the everlasting g., — 19
to teach them the everlasting g. — 25
and carry the light of the g. to — 30
was the g. preached to the dead. — 30
of their sins and receive the g. — 31
Thus was the g. preached — 32
And all other principles of the g. — 34
labors in the preaching of the g. — 57

GRACE
through the g. of God the Father — JFS-V 14

GREAT
upon the g. atoning sacrifice — JFS-V 2
And the g. and wonderful love — 3
of the dead, both small and g. — 11
in the similitude of the g. sacrifice — 13
truth, in g. power and authority, — 26
the dead, both small and g., — 35
Among the g. and mighty ones — 38
Shem, the g. high priest; — 41
Moses, the g. law-giver of Israel; — 41
the g. valley of dry bones, — 43
g. and dreadful day of the Lord— — 46
g. work to be done in the temples — 48
of the g. latter-day work, — 53
among the noble and g. ones — 55
g. world of the spirits of the dead. — 57

GREATLY
as I read I was g. impressed, — JFS-V 6

HAD: *see in the APPENDIX.*

HAND
had set his h. to gather Israel — JS-V 6
day of their deliverance was at h. — JFS-V 15

HANDS
and received salvation at his h. — JFS-V 26
Holy Ghost by the laying on of h., — 33

HAS: *see in the APPENDIX.*

HATH: *see in the APPENDIX.*

HAVE: *see in the APPENDIX.*

HAVING
h. rejected the prophets. — JFS-V 32

HE: *see in the APPENDIX.*

HEAR
might also h. his words. — JFS-V 37

HEARKENED
but few who h. to his voice — JFS-V 26

HEARTED
to bind up the broken-h., — JFS-V 42

HEARTS
have received it with all their h., — JS-V 8
according to the desire of their h. — 9
to plant in the h. of the children — JFS-V 47

HEAVEN
in the celestial kingdom of h. — JS-V 10

HEAVENS
The h. were opened upon us, — JS-V 1

HEIRS
h. of that kingdom will enter, — JS-V 2
be h. of the celestial kingdom — 7
shall be h. of that kingdom, — 8
for they are h. of salvation. — JFS-V 59

HELD
blessings which were h. in reserve — JFS-V 52

HELL
from death and the chains of h. — JFS-V 23

HENCEFORTH
die h. without a knowledge of it, — JS-V 8

HER
many of h. faithful daughters — JFS-V 39

HIGH
Shem, the great h. priest; — JFS-V 41

HIM: *see in the APPENDIX.*

HIS: *see in the APPENDIX.*

HOLY
sang praises unto his h. name — JFS-V 24
the gift of the H. Ghost by the — 33

HOPE
the h. of a glorious resurrection, — JFS-V 14

HOSTS
And I saw the h. of the dead, — JFS-V 11

HOUR
the h. of their deliverance from — JFS-V 18

HOUSE
and those of the h. of Israel, — JFS-V 25
ordinances of the h. of God, — 58

HOW
h. it was that he had obtained — JS-V 6
and h. it was possible for him to — JFS-V 28

HUNDRED
year nineteen h. and eighteen, — JFS-V 1

HYRUM: *see SMITH, Hyrum.*

I: *see in the APPENDIX.*

IF: *see in the APPENDIX.*

IMAGE
express i. of his father, Adam. — JFS-V 40

IMMORTALITY
crowned with i. and eternal life, — JFS-V 51

IMPRESSED
and as I read I was greatly i., — JFS-V 6

IN: *see in the APPENDIX.*

INCLUDING
I. the building of the temples — JFS-V 54

INDIVIDUAL
i. sins on conditions of repentance. — JFS-V 19

INHERITANCE
obtained an i. in that kingdom, — JS-V 6

INNUMERABLE
an i. company of the spirits of — JFS-V 12

INTERVENING
time i. between the crucifixion — JFS-V 27

INTO: *see in the APPENDIX.*

INSTRUCTING
i. and preparing the faithful — JFS-V 36

IS: *see in the APPENDIX.*

ISAAC
I., Jacob, and Moses — JFS-V 41

ISAIAH
I., who declared by prophecy — JFS-V 42

ISRAEL
had set his hand to gather I. — JS-V 6
and those of the house of I., — JFS-V 25
Moses, the great law-giver of I.; — 41

IT: *see in the APPENDIX.*

ITS
be restored to i. perfect frame, — JFS-V 17

JACOB
Isaac, J., and Moses — JFS-V 41

JESUS
faithful in the testimony of J. — JFS-V 12
his Only Begotten Son, J. Christ — 14
our Lord and Savior, J. Christ, — 60

JEWS
in his ministry among the J. — JFS-V 25

JOHN: *see TAYLOR, John.*

JOSEPH: *see SMITH, Joseph.*

JOY
were filled with j. and gladness, — JFS-V 15
they might receive a fulness of j. — 17

JUDGE
For I, the Lord, will j. all men — JS-V 9

JUDGED
j. according to men in the flesh, — JFS-V 10
j. according to men in the flesh, — 34

JUST
the j. for the unjust, — JFS-V 7
company fo the spirits of the j., — 12

KINGDOM
I beheld the celestial k. of God, — JS-V 1
the heirs of that k. will enter, — 2
the beautiful streets of that k., — 4
obtained an inheritance in that k., — 6
shall be heirs of the celestial k. — 7
shall be heirs of that k.; — 8
are saved in the celestial k. — 10
establishment of the k. of God — JFS-V 44
to enter into his Father's k., — 51

KNEE
bowed the k. and acknowledged — JFS-V 23

KNOW

KNOW
that were necessary for them to k.   JFS-V   34
I k. that this record is true,   60

KNOWLEDGE
All who have died without a k.   JS-V   7
shall die henceforth without a k.   8
died in their sins, without a k. of   JFS-V   32

KNOWN
so it was made k. among the dead,   JFS-V   35
made k. that our Redeemer   36

LABOR
and perform the necessary l.   JFS-V   28
And continue thenceforth their l.   52
to l. in his vineyard for the   56

LABORS
their l. in the preaching of   JFS-V   57

LATTER
the kingdom of God in the l. days,   JFS-V   44
of the great l.-day work,   53

LATTER-DAY: *see LATTER and DAY.*

LATTER-DAYS: *see LATTER and DAYS.*

LAW
Moses, the great l.-giver of Israel;   JFS-V   41

LAW-GIVER: *see LAW and GIVER.*

LAYING
Holy Ghost by the l. on of hands,   JFS-V   33
take part in l. the foundations of   53

LESSONS
first l. in the world of spirits   JFS-V   56

LEST
l. the whole earth be smitten   JFS-V   48

LIBERTY
declaring l. to the captives who   JFS-V   18
proclaim l. to the captives who   31
to proclaim l. to the captives,   42

LIFE
that he had departed this l. before   JS-V   6
these had departed the mortal l.,   JFS-V   14
with immortality and eternal l.,   51
when they departed from mortal l.,   57

LIGHT
carry the l. of the gospel to them   JFS-V   30

LIKE
was l. unto circling flames of fire;   JS-V   2

LIMITED
l. to the brief time intervening   JFS-V   27

LIVE
l. according to God in the spirit."   JFS-V   10
l. according to God in the spirit.   34

LIVED
while they l. in mortality;   JFS-V   12
her faithful daughters who had l.   39

LIVING
worshiped the true and l. God.   JFS-V   39
resurrection of the dead, l. souls;   43

LONG
Alvin, that has l. since slept;   JS-V   5
the l.-suffering of God waited   JFS-V   9
the l.-suffering of God waited   28
l. absence of their spirits from   50

MIGHT

LONG-SUFFERING: *see LONG and SUFFERING.*

LOOK
his presence, nor l. upon his face.   JFS-V   21

LOOKED
For the dead l. upon the   JFS-V   50

LORD
before the L. had set his hand   JS-V   6
Thus came the voice of the L.   7
For I, the L., will judge all men   9
after the crucifixion of the L.—   JFS-V   5
the Spirit of the L. rested upon me   11
presence of the L. rested upon them,   24
I perceived that the L. went not   29
the acceptable day of the L.   31
and dreadful day of the L.—   46
to be done in the temples of the L.   48
These the L. taught, and gave them   51
as had been promised by the L.,   52
forth in the due time of the L.   56
through the blessings of our L.   60

LOVE
And the great and wonderful l.   JFS-V   3
in reserve for them that l. him,   52

MADE
atoning sacrifice that was m. by   JFS-V   2
love m. manifest by the Father   3
so it was m. known among the dead,   35
m. known that our Redeemer   36
promises m. to their fathers.   47

MALACHI
M., the prophet who testified   JFS-V   46

MANIFEST
love made m. by the Father   JFS-V   3

MANKIND
gospel, m. might be saved.   JFS-V   4
redemption of m. from the fall,   19

MANY
with m. of her faithful daughters   JFS-V   39
All these and m. more, even   49
they, with m. others received   56

MARTYR
Abel, the first m., was there,   JFS-V   40

MARVELED
And m. how it was that he   JS-V   6
I m., for I understood that   JFS-V   25

ME: *see in the APPENDIX.*

MEN
For I, the Lord, will judge all m.   JS-V   9
judged according to m. in the   JFS-V   10
even to all the spirits of m.;   30
judged according to m. in the   34
the salvation of the souls of m.   56

MESSAGE
might carry the m. of redemption   JFS-V   37

MESSENGERS
his forces and appointed m.,   JFS-V   30
And the chosen m. went forth   31

MIGHT
mankind m. be saved.   JFS-V   4
that he m. bring us to God,   7
m. be judged according to men   10
they m. receive a fulness of joy.   17
m. be judged according to men   34
That they m. carry the message   37
m. also hear his words.   37

MIGHTY

MIGHTY
notwithstanding his m. works, JFS-V 26
Among the great and m. ones 38
Seth, one of the m. ones, 40

MIND
my m. reverted to the writings of JFS-V 5

MINGLED
m. in the vast assembly JFS-V 49

MINISTRATION
through the m. of his servants JFS-V 37

MINISTRY
spent about three years in his m. JFS-V 25
m. among those who were dead 27

MIRACLES
his mighty works and m., JFS-V 26

MORE
impressed, m. than I had ever been JFS-V 6
All these and many m., 49

MOREOVER
M., Ezekiel, who was shown JFS-V 43

MORONI
Elijah—of whom also M. spake JFS-V 46

MORTAL
All these had departed the m. life JFS-V 14
when they depart from m. life, 57

MORTALITY
while they lived in m., JFS-V 12

MOSES
M., the great law-giver of Israel; JFS-V 41
Elias, who was with M. on the 45

MOTHER
and my father and my m.; JS-V 5
And our glorious M. Eve, JFS-V 39

MOUNT
on the M. of Transfiguration; JFS-V 45

MULTITUDE
While this vast m. waited JFS-V 18

MY: *see in the APPENDIX.*

NAME
tribulation in their Redeemer's n. JFS-V 13
sang praises unto his holy n. 24

NECESSARY
perform the n. labor among JFS-V 28
principles of the gospel that were n. 34

NEITHER
N. did the rebellious who rejected JFS-V 21

NEPHITES
prophets who dwelt among the N. JFS-V 49

NEVER
united n. again to be divided, JFS-V 17
n. again to be destroyed 44

NINETEEN
the year n. hundred and eighteen JFS-V 1

NOAH
of God waited in the days of N., JFS-V 9
of God waited in the days of N.— 28
N., who gave warning of the flood; 41

NOBLE
among the n. and great ones JFS-V 55

NOR
presence, n. look upon his face. JFS-V 21
destroyed n. given to other people; 44

NOT: *see in the APPENDIX.*

NOTWITHSTANDING
And yet, n. his mighty works, JS-V 26

OBEDIENCE
o. to the principles of the gospel, JFS-V 4
through o. to the ordinances of 58

OBSERVED
I o. that they were also among JFS-V 55

OBTAINED
o. an inheritance in that kingdom, JS-V 6

OCTOBER
On the third of O., in the year JFS-V 1

OF: *see in the APPENDIX.*

OFFERED
o. sacrifice in the similitude of JFS-V 13

ON: *see in the APPENDIX.*

ONCE
"For Christ also hath o. suffered JFS-V 7
o. the long-suffering of God 9
o. the long-suffering of God 28

ONE: *see in the APPENDIX.*

ONES
Among the great and mighty o. JFS-V 38
Seth, one of the mighty o., 40
among the noble and great o. who 55

ONLY
his O. Begotten Son, Jesus Christ. JFS-V 14
sacrifice of the O. Begotten Son 57

OPENED
The heavens were o. upon us, JS-V 1
I o. the Bible and read the third JFS-V 6
eyes of my understanding were o., 11
as I wondered, my eyes were o., 29

OPENING
the o. of the prison to them that JFS-V 42

OR: *see in the APPENDIX.*

ORDER
know in o. to qualify themselves JFS-V 34

ORDINANCES
the performances of o. therein JFS-V 54
o. of the house of God, 58

ORGANIZED
he o. his forces and appointed JFS-V 30

OTHER
Capadocia, and o. parts of Asia, JFS-V 5
And all o. principles of the gospel 34
destroyed nor given to o. people; 44
and o. choice spirits who were 53

OTHERS
they, with many o. received JFS-V 56

OUR: *see in the APPENDIX.*

OUT: *see in the APPENDIX.*

OVER
pondering o. the scriptures; JFS-V 1
As I pondered o. these things 11

PAID after they have p. the penalty	JFS-V	59	**PREACH** how it was possible for him to p.	JFS-V	28
PARENTS sealing of the children to their p.,	JFS-V	48	**PREACHED** where the gospel had been p.	JFS-V	5
PART take p. in laying the foundations	JFS-V	53	"By which also he went and p. for this cause was the gospel p. p. to them the everlasting gospel,		8 10 19
PARTAKERS and be p. of all blessings	JFS-V	52	said that the Son of God p. unto was the gospel p. to the dead. gospel p. to those who had died		28 30 32
PARTS Capadocia, and other p. of Asia,	JFS-V	5	**PREACHING** continue their labors in the p. of	JFS-V	57
PASSAGES with the following p.:	JFS-V	6	**PREPARED** p. to come forth in the due time	JFS-V	56
PAVED appearance of being p. with gold.	JS-V	4	**PREPARING** Noah, while the ark was a p., instructing and p. the faithful	JFS-V	9 36
PEACE among the righteous there was p.;	JFS-V	22	**PRESENCE** behold his p., nor look upon his	JFS-V	21
PENALTY And after they have paid the p.	JFS-V	59	radiance from the p. of the Lord and rejoiced in his p., and		24 26
PEOPLE be destroyed nor given to other p.;	JFS-V	44	**PRIEST** Shem, the great high p.;	JFS-V	41
PERMITTED if they had been p. to tarry,	JS-V	7	**PRIMITIVE** to the p. saints scattered abroad	JFS-V	5
PERCEIVED I p. that the Lord went not	JFS-V	29	**PRINCIPLES** Obedience to the p. of the gospel, And all other p. of the gospel	JFS-V	4 34
PERFECT to be restored unto its p. frame,	JFS-V	17	**PRISON** preached unto the spirits in p.;	JFS-V	8
PERFORM p. the necessary labor among	JFS-V	28	preached unto the spirits in p., opening of the p. to them that		28 42
PERFORMANCE temples and the p. of ordinances	JFS-V	54	**PROCLAIM** p. liberty to the captives who to p. liberty to the captives,	JFS-V	31 42
PERSON the Lord went not in p. among	JFS-V	29	**PROCLAMATION** of the truth, in great power	JFS-V	26
PERSONALLY unto whom he could not go p.,	JFS-V	37	**PROMISED** as had been p. by the Lord,	JFS-V	52
PETER the writings of the apostle P., chapters of the first epistle of P.,	JFS-V	5 6	**PROMISES** the p. made to their fathers,	JFS-V	47
saved by water." (1P. 3:18-20.) in the spirit." (1P. 4: 6.) I wondered at the words of P.—		9 10 28	**PROPHECY** Isaiah, who declared by p.	JFS-V	42
PLACE were gathered together in one p.	JFS-V	12	**PROPHET** Malachi, the p. who testified spake to the p. Joseph Smith,	JFS-V	46 46
PLANT to p. in the heart of the children	JFS-V	47	p. Elijah was to plant in the hearts p. Joseph Smith, and my father,		47 53
PONDERED As I p. over these things which	JFS-V	11	**PROPHETS** the warnings of the ancient p. having rejected the p.	JFS-V	21 32
PONDERING in my room p. over the scriptures;	JFS-V	1	the faithful spirits of the p. p. who dwelt among the Nephites		36 49
PONTUS scattered abroad throughout P.,	JFS-V	5	**PUT** being p. to death in the flesh,	JFS-V	7
POSSIBLE how it was p. for him to preach	JFS-V	28	**QUALIFY** know in order to q. themselves	JFS-V	34
POWER truth, in great p. and authority, clothed with p. and authority,	JFS-V	26 30	**QUICKENED** but q. by the Spirit: and my understanding q.,	JFS-V	7 29
and gave them p. to come forth,		51	**RADIANCE** r. from the presence of the Lord	JFS-V	24
PRAISES sang p. unto his holy name.	JFS-V	24			

RAISED

RAISED
his voice was not r.;   JFS-V   20

READ
I opened the Bible and r.   JFS-V   6
as I r. I was greatly impressed,   6

REBELLION
because of their r. and   JFS-V   37

REBELLIOUS
Neither did the r. who rejected   JFS-V   21

RECEIVE
they might r. a fulness of joy.   JFS-V   17
and r. the gospel.   31
shall r. a reward according to   59

RECEIVED
who would have r. it if they had   JS-V   7
who would have r. it with all   8
and r. salvation at his hands.   JFS-V   26
r. their first lessons in the   56

RECORD
revealed to me, and I bear r.,   JFS-V   60
and I know that this r. is true,   60

REDEEMED
The dead who repent will be r.,   JFS-V   58

REDEEMER
coming of the R. into the world;   JFS-V   3
as their R. and Deliverer   23
that our R. spent his time during   36
R. was anointed to bind up   42

REDEEMER'S
tribulation in their R. name.   JFS-V   13

REDEMPTION
for the r. of the world;   JFS-V   2
r. from the bands of death.   16
r. of mankind from the fall,   19
the saints rejoiced in their r.,   23
that r. had been wrought   35
might carry the message of r.   37
for the r. of the dead,   48
for the r. of the dead,   54
gospel of repentance and r.,   57
vision of the r. of the dead   60

REFLECTING
r. upon the great atoning   JFS-V   2

REIGNED
Where these were, darkness r.,   JFS-V   22

REJECTED
rebellious who r. the testimonies   JFS-V   21
disobedient who had r. the truth,   29
having r. the prophets.   32

REJOICED
saints r. in their redemption,   JFS-V   23
and r. in his presence,   26

REJOICING
r. together because the day of   JFS-V   15
r. in the hour of their deliverance   18

REMISSION
baptized for the r. of sins.   JS-V   6
baptism for the r. of sins,   JFS-V   33

REPENT
even unto all who would r.   JFS-V   31
The dead who r. will be redeemed,   58

REPENTANCE
individual sins on conditions of r.   JFS-V   19
and call them unto r.;   25

SAW

taught faith in God, r. from sins,   JFS-V   33
gospel of r. and redemption,   57

RESERVE
blessings which were held in r.   JFS-V   52

RESERVED
other choice spirits were r.   JFS-V   53

RESTED
Spirit of the Lord r. upon me,   JFS-V   11
presence of the Lord r. upon them,   24

RESTORED
Their sleeping dust was to be r.   JFS-V   17

RESURRECTION
firm in the hope of a glorious r.,   JFS-V   14
the doctrine of the r. and   19
the crucifixion and his r.;   27
to come forth again in the r.   43
after his r. from the dead,   51

REVEALED
the redemption of the dead r.   JFS-V   60

REVERTED
my mind r. to the writings of   JFS-V   5

REWARD
a r. according to their works,   JFS-V   59

RIGHTEOUS
among the r. there was peace;   JFS-V   22
from among the r., he organized   30
in this vast congregation of the r.   38

ROOM
I sat in my r. pondering over the   JFS-V   1

RULERS
to be r. in the Church of God.   JFS-V   55

SACRIFICE
upon the great atoning s.   JFS-V   2
offered s. in the similitude of   13
the great s. of the Son of God,   13
the s. of the Son of God   35
s. of the Only Begotten Son   57

SAID
s. that the Son of God preached   JFS-V   28

SAINTS
the primitive s. scattered abroad   JFS-V   5
s. rejoiced in their redemption,   23

SALVATION
and received s. at his hands.   JFS-V   26
for the s. of the sould of men.   56
for they are heirs of s.   59

SANG
s. praises unto his holy name.   JFS-V   24

SAT
I s. in my room pondering over   JFS-V   1

SAVED
are s. in the celestial kingdom   JS-V   10
the gospel, mankind might be s.   JFS-V   4
eight souls were s. by water."   9

SAVIOR
S. spent about three years in his   JFS-V   25
the blessings of our Lord and S.,   60

SAW
I s. the transcendent beauty of   JS-V   2
I s. the beautiful streets of   4
I s. Father Adam and Abraham;   5
and I s. the hosts of the dead   JFS-V   11

SAYING
the voice of the Lord unto me, s.: JS-V 7

SCATTERED
to the primitive saints s. abroad JFS-V 5

SCRIPTURES
pondering over the s.; JFS-V 1

SEALING
s. of the children to their JFS-V 48

SEATED
was s. the Father and the Son. JS-V 3

SECOND
to gather Israel the s. time, JS-V 6

SEEING
s. that he had departed this life JS-V 6

SET
the Lord had s. his hand to JS-V 6

SERVANTS
through the ministration of his s. JFS-V 37

SETH
S., one of the mighty ones,] JFS-V 40

SHALL: *see in the APPENDIX.*

SHEM
S., the great high priest; JFS-V 41

SHONE
Their countenances s., JFS-V 24

SHORT
labor among them in so s. a time. JFS-V 28

SHOULD: *see in the APPENIDX.*

SHOWN
Ezekiel, who was s. in vision JFS-V 43

SIMILITUDE
the s. of the great sacrifice of JFS-V 13

SIN
faith in God, repentance from s., JFS-V 33
under the bondage of s. 57

SINCE
Alvin, that has long s. slept; JS-V 5

SINEWS
the s. and the flesh upon them, JFS-V 17

SINS
baptized for the remission of s. JS-V 6
also hath once suffered for s. JFS-V 7
from individual s. on conditions 19
all who would repent of their s. 31
to those who had died in their s., 32
baptism for the remission of s., 33

SLEEPING
Their s. dust was to be restored JFS-V 17

SLEPT
Alvin, that has long since s.; JS-V 5

SMALL
of the dead, both s. and great. JFS-V 11
the dead, both s. and great; 35

SMITH, Hyrum
and my father, S., Brigham JFS-V 53

SMITH, Joseph
spake to the Prophet S., JFS-V 46
Prophet S., and my father 53

SMITTEN
whole earth be s. with a curse JFS-V 48

SO: *see in the APPENDIX.*

SOJOURN
Spent his time during his s. JFS-V 36

SOMETIME
"Which s. were disobedient, JFS-V 9
who s. were disobedient, 28

SON
was seated the Father and the S. JS-V 3
that was made by the S. of God, JFS-V 2
manifest by the Father and the S. 3
great sacrifice of the S. of God, 13
Only Begotten S., Jesus Christ. 14
the advent of the S. of God into 16
the S. of God appeared, declaring 18
the S. of God as their Redeemer 23
S. of God preached unto the spirits 28
sacrifice of the S. of God upon 35
of the coming of the S. of God, 49
sacrifice of the Only Begotten S. 57

SOULS
Wherein few, that is, eight s. JFS-V 9
resurrection of the dead, living s.; 43
the salvation of the s. of men, 56

SPAKE
Elijah—of whom also Moroni s. JFS-V 46

SPENT
the Savior s. about three years in JFS-V 25
our Redeemer s. his time during 36

SPIRIT
but quickened by the S.: JFS-V 7
but live according to men in the s." 10
S. of the Lord rested upon me, 11
Son of God into the s. world, 16
the s. and the body to be united 17
live according to God in the s. 34
were also in the s. world. 54

SPIRITS
preached unto the s. in prison; JFS-V 8
company of the s. of the just, 12
preached unto the s. in prison, 28
for him to preach to those s. 28
even to all the s. of men; 30
his sojourn in the world of s., 36
the faithful s. of the prophets who 36
absence of their s. from their 50
choice s. who were reserved 53
first lessons in the world of s. 56
world of the s. of the dead. 57

STREETS
I saw the beautiful s. of that JS-V 4

SUFFERED
Christ also hath once s. for sins, JFS-V 7
and had s. tribulation in their 13

SUFFERING
when once the long-s. of God JFS-V 9
when once the long-s. of God 28

TAKE
t. part in laying the foundations JFS-V 53

TARRY
if they had been permitted to t., JS-V 7

TAUGHT
These were t. faith in God, JFS-V 33
These the Lord t., and gave 51

TAYLOR, John
T., Wilford Woodruff, and other JFS-V 53

TEACH 12 UTTERLY

TEACH
t. them the everlasting gospel — JFS-V 25
had rejected the truth, to t. them; — 29

TELL
in the body or out I cannot t. — JS-V 1

TEMPLES
great work to be done in the t. — JFS-V 48
Including the building of the t. — 54

TESTIFIED
prophets who had t. of him — JFS-V 36
Malachi, the prophet who t. — 46
t. of the coming of the Son of — 49

TESTIMONIES
rebellious who rejected the t. — JFS-V 21

TESTIMONY
faithful in the t. of Jesus — JFS-V 12

THAN
impressed, more t. I had ever been — JFS-V 6

THAT: *see in the APPENDIX.*

THE: *see in the APPENDIX.*

THEE: *see in the APPENDIX.*

THEIR: *see in the APPENDIX.*

THEM: *see in the APPENDIX.*

THEMSELVES
defiled t. while in the flesh, — JFS-V 20
know in order to qualify t. — 34

THENCEFORTH
continue t. their labor — JFS-V 52

THERE: *see in the APPENDIX.*

THEREOF
of God, and the glory t., — JS-V 1

THEREIN
the performance of ordinances t. — JFS-V 54

THESE: *see in the APPENDIX.*

THEY: *see in the APPENDIX.*

THINGS: *see in the APPENDIX.*

THIRD
On the t. of October, in the year — JFS-V 1
read the t. and fourth chapters — 6

THIS: *see in the APPENDIX.*

THOSE: *see in the APPENDIX.*

THREE
Savior spent about t. years in — JFS-V 25

THRONE
Also the blazing t. of God, — JS-V 3

THROUGH
the gate t. which the heirs of — JS-V 2
That t. his atonement, and by — JFS-V 4
t. the grace of God the Father — 14
t. the sacrifice of the Son — 35
t. the ministration of his servants — 37
who had lived t. the ages — 39
t. the sacrifice of the Only — 57
t. obedience to the ordinances — 58
t. the blessing of our Lord — 60

THROUGHOUT
t. Pontus, Galatia, Capadocia — JFS-V 5

THUS: *see in the APPENDIX.*

TIME
to gather Israel the second t. — JS-V 6
was limited to the brief t. — JFS-V 27
labor among them in so short a t. — 28
our Redeemer spent his t. — 36
in the due t. of the Lord — 56

TIMES
dispensation of the fulness of t., — JFS-V 48
come forth in the fulness of t. — 53

TO: *see in the APPENDIX.*

TOGETHER
gathered t. in one place — JFS-V 12
and were rejoicing t. — 15

TRANSCENDENT
I saw the t. beauty of the gate — JS-V 2

TRANSFIGURATION
with Moses on the Mount of T.; — JFS-V 45

TRANSGRESSION
a knowledge of the truth, or in t., — JFS-V 32
because of their rebellion and t., — 37

TRANSGRESSIONS
paid the penalty of their t., — JFS-V 59

TRIBULATION
t. in their Redeemer's name. — JFS-V 13

TRUE
worshiped the t. and living God. — JFS-V 39
I know that this record is t., — 60

TRUTH
and proclamation of the t., — JFS-V 26
who had rejected the t., — 29
without a knowledge of the t., — 32

UNDER
and u. the bondage of sin — JFS-V 57

UNDERSTANDING
the eyes of my u. were opened, — JFS-V 11
and my u. quickened — 29

UNDERSTOOD
I u. that the Savior spent about — JFS-V 25

UNGODLY
the u. and unrepentant who — JFS-V 20

UNITED
the spirit and the body to be u. — JFS-V 17

UNJUST
the just for the u., — JFS-V 7

UNREPENTANT
among the ungodly and u. — JFS-V 20

UNRIGHTEOUS
the u. as well as the faithful, — JFS-V 35

UNTO: *see in the APPENDIX.*

UP: *see in the APPENDIX.*

UPON: *see in the APPENDIX.*

US: *see in the APPENDIX.*

USHERING
u. in of the great and dreadful day — JFS-V 46

UTTERLY
and u. wasted at his coming. — JFS-V 48

VALLEY

VALLEY
the great v. of dry bones, — JFS-V 43

VAST
While this v. multitude waited — JFS-V 18
v. congregation of the righteous — 38
mingled in the v. assembly — 49

VICARIOUS
baptism for the remission of — JFS-V 33

VINEYARD
labor in his v. for the salvation — JFS-V 56

VISION
Ezekiel, who was shown in v. — JFS-V 43
v. of the redemption of the dead — 60

VOICE
Thus came the v. of the Lord — JS-V 7
his v. was not raised; — JFS-V 20
few who hearkened to his f., — 26

WAITED
the long-suffering of God w. — JFS-V 9
While this vast multitude w. — 18
the long-suffering of God w. — 28
w. for their deliverance, — 49

WAS: *see in the APPENDIX.*

WARNING
Noah, who gave w. of the flood; — JFS-V 41

WARNINGS
rejected the testimonies and w. — JFS-V 21

WASHED
w. clean, shall receive a reward — JFS-V 59

WASTED
and utterly w. at his coming. — JFS-V 48

WATER
eight souls were saved by w." — JFS-V 9

WELL
unrighteous as w. as the faithful, — FS-V 35

WENT
"By which also he w. and preached — JFS-V 8
the Lord w. not in person among — 29
the chosen messengers w. forth to — 31

WERE: *see in the APPENDIX.*

WHEN: *see in the APPENDIX.*

WHERE
w. the gospel had been preached — JFS-V 5
W. these were, darkness reigned, — 22

WHEREIN
w. few, that is, eight souls — JFS-V 9
w. he said that the Son of God — 28

WHEREON
w. was seated the Father and — JS-V 3

WHETHER
w. in the body or out I cannot — JS-V 1

WHICH: *see in the APPENDIX.*

WHILE
W. I was thus engaged, — JFS-V 5
w. the ark was a preapring, — 9
w. they lived in mortality; — 12
W. this vast multitude waited — 18
defiled themselves w. in the flesh, — 20

WHO: *see in the APPENDIX.*

WHOLE
w. earth be smitten with a curse — JFS-V 48

WHOM: *see in the APPENDIX.*

WICKED
But unto the w. he did not go, — JFS-V 20
went nto in person among the w. — 29

WILFORD: *see WOODRUFF, Wilford.*

WILL: *see in the APPENDIX.*

WITH: *see in the APPENDIX.*

WITHOUT
died w. a knowledge of this gospel, — JS-V 7
die henceforth w. a knowledge — 8
a knowledge of the truth, — JFS-V 32

WONDERED
And I w. at the words of Peter— — JFS-V 28
as I w., my eyes were opened, — 29

WONDERFUL
great and w. love made manifest — JFS-V 3

WOODRUFF, Wilford
W., and other choice spirits who — JFS-V 53

WORDS
I wondered at the w. of Peter— — JFS-V 28
might also hear his w. — 37

WORK
great w. to be done in the temples — JFS-V 48
of the great latter-day w. — 53

WORKS
judge all men according to their s., — JS-V 9
notwithstanding his mighty w., — JFS-V 26
a reward according to their w., — 59

WORLD
for the redemption of the w., — JFS-V 2
of the Redeemer into the w.; — 3
the Son of God into the spirit w., — 16
his sojourn in the s. of spirits, — 36
were also in the spirit w. — 54
first lessons in the w. of spirits. — 56
great w. of the spirits of the dead. — 57

WORSHIPPED
w. the true and living God. — JFS-V 39

WOULD: *see in the APPENDIX.*

WRITINGS
the w. of the apostle Peter, — JFS-V 5

WRITTEN
these things that are w., — JFS-V 11

WROUGHT
w. through the sacrifice of — JFS-V 35

YEAR
y. nineteen hundred and eighteen — JFS-V 1

YEARS
arrive at the y. of accountability — JS-V 10
the Savior spent about three y. — JFS-V 25

YET
y.; notwithstanding his mighty — JFS-V 26

YOUNG, Brigham
Y., John Taylor, Wilford Woodruff, — JFS-V 53